The
Middle East
and
North Africa
1995

The Middle East and North Africa 1995

FORTY-FIRST EDITION

EUROPA PUBLICATIONS LIMITED

Forty-first Edition 1995

© **Europa Publications Limited 1994**
18 Bedford Square, London, WC1B 3JN, England

Australia and New Zealand
James Bennett (Collaroy) Pty Ltd, 4 Collaroy Street,
Collaroy, NSW 2097, Australia

Japan
Maruzen Co Ltd, POB 5050, Tokyo International 100–31

British Library Cataloguing in Publication Data
The Middle East and North Africa—1995
1. Africa, North—Periodicals
961'. 048'05   DT160
ISBN 0-946653-99-2
ISSN 0076-8502

Library of Congress Catalog Card Number 48–3250

Printed in England by
Staples Printers Rochester Limited,
Rochester, Kent.
Bound by
Hartnolls Ltd
Bodmin, Cornwall.

FOREWORD

The forty-first edition of THE MIDDLE EAST AND NORTH AFRICA includes one new essay which examines the causes of the current crisis in Algeria, where many observers now regard civil war as inevitable if not already under way. This is a reminder—if any were needed after a year in which Yemen has experienced civil war and Iraq has threatened further confrontation in the Gulf—of the region's undiminished capacity for conflict despite the achievement of progress in the Middle East peace process. In any case, it is debatable whether anything like the foundations of a durable, not to mention a just, peace have been laid by Israel and the PLO. Those Palestinian groups which reject the Declaration of Principles remain as implacably hostile to Israel as they ever were, and not all of them will be appeased or incapacitated by the eventual conclusion of a peace agreement between Israel and Syria. Unless the PLO can rapidly bring about economic gains that far outweigh the perceived injustices of the peace agreement with Israel, then there will be no future shortage of recruits to Palestinian movements far less amenable to compromise; and no real stability in the West Bank and Gaza.

As usual, all statistical and directory material in the new edition has been extensively revised and expanded. A calendar of political events provides a convenient reference guide to the year's main developments in the countries covered in this volume.

The Editor would once again like to thank all the contributors for their articles and advice, and the various governmental and other organizations which have returned questionnaires and provided statistical information.

October 1994

ACKNOWLEDGEMENTS

The editors gratefully acknowledge the interest and co-operation of all the contributors to this volume, and of numerous national statistical and information offices, and government departments, as well as embassies in London and throughout the region, whose kind assistance in updating the material contained in THE MIDDLE EAST AND NORTH AFRICA is greatly appreciated.

We are particularly indebted to the Food and Agriculture Organization of the United Nations for permission to reproduce statistics from its various publications, most notably the *Production Yearbook 1992*; to the International Institute for Strategic Studies, 23 Tavistock Street, London, WC2E 7NQ, for the use of defence statistics from *The Military Balance 1994–95*; and to the Israeli Embassy, London, for the use of two maps illustrating the disengagement agreements between Israel and Egypt (1974) and Israel and Syria.

Our thanks also go to the following for particular assistance: Bank Markazi Islamic Republic of Iran; Middle East Economic Digest; Saudi Arabian Monetary Agency, Riyadh; Suez Canal Authority, Ismailia; United Nations Relief and Works Agency for Palestine Refugees in the Near East.

EXPLANATORY NOTE ON THE DIRECTORY SECTION

The Directory section of each chapter is arranged under the following headings, where they apply:

THE CONSTITUTION

THE GOVERNMENT
   HEAD OF STATE
   CABINET/COUNCIL OF MINISTERS
   MINISTRIES
   POLITICAL BUREAU OF PARTY

LEGISLATURE

POLITICAL ORGANIZATIONS

DIPLOMATIC REPRESENTATION

JUDICIAL SYSTEM

RELIGION

THE PRESS

PUBLISHERS

RADIO AND TELEVISION

FINANCE
   CENTRAL BANK
   STATE BANKS
   DEVELOPMENT BANKS
   COMMERCIAL BANKS
   FOREIGN BANKS
   STOCK EXCHANGE
   INSURANCE

TRADE AND INDUSTRY
   PUBLIC CORPORATIONS
   CHAMBERS OF COMMERCE AND INDUSTRY
   COMMERCIAL AND INDUSTRIAL ORGANIZATIONS
   EMPLOYERS' ORGANIZATIONS
   TRADE UNIONS
   CO-OPERATIVES
   PETROLEUM
   MAJOR INDUSTRIAL COMPANIES

TRANSPORT
   RAILWAYS
   ROADS
   SHIPPING
   CIVIL AVIATION

TOURISM

DEFENCE

EDUCATION

CONTENTS

List of Maps   *page* xi

Abbreviations   xiii

Transcription of Arabic Names   xvii

Calendar of Events October 1993–October 1994   xix

PART ONE
General Survey

Algeria: The Failure of Dialogue   GEORGE JOFFÉ   3

The Religions of the Middle East and North Africa   14
    Islam   R. B. SERJEANT   14
    Christianity   20
    Judaism   21
    Other Communities   21

The Arab-Israeli Confrontation 1967–94
PAUL COSSALI (based on an original article by
MICHAEL ADAMS, with subsequent additions by
DAVID GILMOUR, PAUL HARPER and STEVEN SHERMAN)   23

The Jerusalem Issue   PAUL COSSALI (based on an
original article by MICHAEL ADAMS, with
subsequent additions by DAVID GILMOUR, PAUL
HARPER and STEVEN SHERMAN)   72

Documents on Palestine   79

Palestine Organizations   109

Oil in the Middle East and North Africa
PETER BILD   119
    Oil Statistics   155
    Principal Oil Groups Producing or Refining
      in the Gulf   158

Natural Gas in the Middle East
and North Africa   CHRIS CRAGG   161

Water Resources in the Middle East
and North Africa   CHRIS CRAGG   162

Islamic Banking and Finance
RODNEY WILSON   166

The Suez Canal   171

Calendars, Time Reckoning, and Weights and
Measures   174

Research Institutes   177

Select Bibliography   184
    Books on the Middle East   184
    Books on North Africa   189
    Periodicals   191

PART TWO
Regional Organizations

The United Nations in the Middle East and
North Africa   197

Members, Contributions, Year of Admission   197

Permanent Missions to the United Nations   197

General Assembly Committees Concerned
with the Middle East   *page* 197

Economic Commission for Africa—ECA   198

Economic and Social Commission for
Western Asia—ESCWA   201

United Nations Development Programme
—UNDP   202

United Nations High Commissioner
for Refugees—UNHCR   204

United Nations Peace-keeping Operations   205

United Nations Relief and Works
Agency for Palestine Refugees
in the Near East—UNRWA   207

Food and Agriculture Organization—FAO   208

International Bank for Reconstruction and
Development—IBRD and International
Development Association—IDA (World Bank)   210

International Finance Corporation—IFC   212

Multilateral Investment Guarantee Agency (MIGA)   213

International Fund for Agricultural
Development—IFAD   213

International Monetary Fund—IMF   214

United Nations Educational, Scientific and
Cultural Organization—UNESCO   216

World Health Organization—WHO   218

Other UN Organizations active in the
Middle East and North Africa   220

United Nations Information Centres   221

Arab Fund for Economic and Social
Development—AFESD   222

The Arab League (see League of
Arab States)

Arab Monetary Fund   223

Co-operation Council for the Arab States
of the Gulf   224

Council of Arab Economic Unity   227

The European Union   228

Islamic Development Bank   230

League of Arab States   232

Organization of Arab Petroleum Exporting
Countries—OAPEC   237

Organization of the Islamic Conference—OIC   238

Organization of the Petroleum Exporting
Countries—OPEC   240

OPEC Fund for International Development   243

Other Regional Organizations   245

Index of Regional Organizations   248

PART THREE
Country Surveys

See page vii for explanatory note on the
Directory Section of each country.

ALGERIA

Physical and Social Geography   253

CONTENTS

History   (revised for this edition by RICHARD I. LAWLESS)   *page* 254

Economy   (revised for this edition by RICHARD I. LAWLESS)   277

Statistical Survey   291

Directory   297

Bibliography   306

BAHRAIN

Geography   307

History   (revised for this edition by RICHARD I. LAWLESS)   307

Economy   P. T. H. UNWIN
(revised for this edition by RICHARD I. LAWLESS)   309

Statistical Survey   314

Directory   315

Bibliography   320

CYPRUS

Physical and Social Geography   W. B. FISHER   321

History   (revised for this edition by ALAN J. DAY)   321

Economy   (revised for this edition by ALAN J. DAY)   333

Statistical Survey   338

Directory   340

Bibliography   353

EGYPT

Physical and Social Geography   W. B. FISHER   354

History   (revised for this edition by RICHARD I. LAWLESS)   356

Economy   (revised for this edition by ALAN J. DAY)   373

Statistical Survey   388

Directory   393

Bibliography   405

IRAN

Physical and Social Geography   W. B. FISHER   407

History   (revised for this edition by JON LUNN)   408

Economy   (revised for this edition by RICHARD I. LAWLESS)   424

Statistical Survey   448

Directory   454

Bibliography   461

IRAQ

Physical and Social Geography   W. B. FISHER   464

History   465

Economy   (revised for this edition by ALAN J. DAY)   482

Statistical Survey   496

Directory   500

Bibliography   508

ISRAEL

Physical and Social Geography   W. B. FISHER   510

History   TOM LITTLE
(with subsequent revisions by the Editor)   511

Economy   530

Statistical Survey   540

Directory   545

Bibliography   *page* 558

Israeli-Occupied Territories   561

JORDAN

Physical and Social Geography   W. B. FISHER   565

History   (revised for this edition by RICHARD I. LAWLESS)   566

Economy   (revised for this edition by ALAN J. DAY)   581

Statistical Survey   593

Directory   596

Bibliography   603

KUWAIT

Physical and Social Geography   604

History   (revised for this edition by JON LUNN)   604

Economy   P. T. H. UNWIN   611

Statistical Survey   620

Directory   624

Bibliography   631

LEBANON

Physical and Social Geography   W. B. FISHER   632

History   633

Economy   (revised for this edition by ALAN GEORGE)   654

Statistical Survey   665

Directory   669

Bibliography   679

LIBYA

Physical and Social Geography   W. B. FISHER   680

History   (Revised for this edition by RICHARD I. LAWLESS)   681

Economy   (revised for this edition by ALAN J. DAY)   696

Statistical Survey   708

Directory   712

Bibliography   717

MOROCCO

Physical and Social Geography   718

History   (revised for this edition by RICHARD I. LAWLESS)   719

Economy   DAVID SEDDON
(revised for this edition by RICHARD I. LAWLESS)   733

Statistical Survey   744

Directory   749

Bibliography   757

OMAN

Geography   758

History   758

Economy   761

Statistical Survey   767

Directory   771

Bibliography   776

QATAR

Geography   777

History   777

Economy   P. T. H. UNWIN
(revised for this edition by ALAN J. DAY)   779

Statistical Survey   784

Directory   785

CONTENTS

Bibliography   *page* 788

SAUDI ARABIA

Physical and Social Geography of the
    Arabian Peninsula   789

History   (revised for this edition by JON LUNN)   790

Economy   (revised for this edition by ALAN J. DAY) 797

Statistical Survey   809

Directory   813

Bibliography   822

SPANISH NORTH AFRICA

Ceuta   823

Melilla   823

Bibliography   829

SYRIA

Physical and Social Geography   W. B. FISHER   830

History   831

Economy   (revised for this edition by ALAN J. DAY) 848

Statistical Survey   857

Directory   861

Bibliography   867

TUNISIA

Physical and Social Geography   D. R. HARRIS   869

History   (revised for this edition by
    RICHARD I. LAWLESS)   870

Economy   (revised for this edition by ALAN J. DAY) 885

Statistical Survey   894

Directory   900

Bibliography   *page* 906

TURKEY

Physical and Social Geography   W. B. FISHER   907

History   (revised for this edition by JON LUNN)   908

Economy   DAVID SEDDON
    (revised for this edition by ERGIN YILDIZOGLU and
    RONNIE MARGULIES)   925

Statistical Survey   932

Directory   937

Bibliography   950

UNITED ARAB EMIRATES

Geography   952

History   952

Economy   P. T. H. UNWIN
    (revised for this edition by ALAN J. DAY)   955

Statistical Survey   966

Directory   971

Bibliography   979

YEMEN

Geography   980

History   ROBIN BIDWELL
    (revised for this edition by JON LUNN)   981

Economy   ALAN J. DAY   996

Statistical Survey   1009

Directory   1016

Bibliography   1021

List of Maps

Territories occupied by Israel   *page* 88

Disengagement Agreement of 18 January 1974,
    between Israel and Egypt   90

Disengagement Agreement of 30 May 1974,
    between Israel and Syria   90

Cyprus, showing border of 'Turkish
    Republic of Northern Cyprus'   337

Israeli-occupied areas and Palestinian
    semi-autonomous areas   574

xi

ABBREVIATIONS

AAHO	Afro-Asian Housing Organization
AAPSO	Afro-Asian People's Solidarity Organization
Acad.	Academy
AD	Algerian Dinars
ADC	Aide-de-camp
ADCO	Abu Dhabi Company for Onshore Oil Operations
ADMA-OPCO	Abu Dhabi Marine Areas Operating Company
Admin.	Administrative, Administration, Administrator
Admin.-Gen	Administrator-General
ADMA	Abu Dhabi Marine Areas
ADOCO	Abu Dhabi Oil Company
ADPC	Abu Dhabi Petroleum Company
AfDB	African Development Bank
Afs	Afghanis
Agric.	Agriculture
a.i.	ad interim
AIWO	Agudath Israel World Organization
ALF	Arab Liberation Front
ALN	Armée de Libération Nationale (National Liberation Army of Algeria)
AMINOIL	American Independent Oil Company
AMOSEAS	American Overseas Petroleum Ltd
AOC	Arabian Oil Company
AOF	Afrique Occidentale Française (French West Africa)
Apdo	Apartado (Post Box)
API	American Petroleum Institute
approx.	approximately
apptd	appointed
Aramco	Arabian-American Oil Company
ARE	Arab Republic of Egypt
AŞ	Anonim Şirketi
Ass.	Assembly
Asscn	Association
Assoc.	Associate
Asst	Assistant
ATAS	Anatolian Refinery Company
ATUC	African Trade Union Confederation
AUA	Austrian Airlines
auth.	authorized
AUXERAP	Société Auxiliaire de la Régie du Pétrole
Ave	Avenue
Avda	Avenida
BADEA	Banque Arabe de Développement Economique en Afrique (Arab Bank for Economic Development in Africa)
BAPCO	The Bahrain Petroleum Company Ltd
b/d	barrels per day
BD	Bahrain Dinars
Bd	Board
Bde	Brigade
Bldg	Building
Blvd	Boulevard
BP	Boîte Postale (Post Box)
BP	British Petroleum Company PLC
BPC	Basrah Petroleum Company
br.(s)	branch(es)
Brig.	Brigadier
BST	British Standard Time
BUSHCO	Bushehr Petroleum Company
C	Centigrade
c.	circa
CAFRAD	Centre Africain de Formation et de Recherches Administratives pour le Développement
CAMEL	Compagnie Algérienne du Méthane Liquide
cap.	capital
Capt.	Captain
CARE	Co-operative for American Relief Everywhere
Cdre	Commodore
cen.	central
CENTO	Central Treaty Organization
CEO	Chief Executive Officer
CEP	Compagnie d'Exploration Pétrolière
CEPT	Conférence Européenne des Administrations des Postes et des Télécommunications
cf.	confer (compare)
CFP	Compagnie Française des Pétroles
Chair.	Chairman
Cie	Compagnie (Company)
c.i.f.	cost, insurance and freight
C-in-C	Commander-in-Chief
circ.	circulation
cm	centimetre(s)
cnr	corner
c/o	care of
Co	Company
Col	Colonel
Comm.	Commission
Commdr	Commander
Commdt	Commandant
Commr	Commissioner
Conf.	Conference
Confed.	Confederation
Cons.-Gen.	Consul-General
COO	Chief Operating Officer
COPE	Compagnie Orientale des Pétroles
COPEFA	Compagnie des Pétroles France-Afrique
Corpn	Corporation
CPA	Compagnie des Pétroles d'Algérie
CREPS	Compagnie de Recherches et d'Exploration de Pétrole du Sahara
CRNA	National Council of the Algerian Revolution
CRUA	Revolutionary Council for Unity and Action (now FLN)
Cttee	Committee
cu	cubic
cwt	hundredweight
Del.	Delegate, Delegation
Dep.	Deputy
dep.	deposits
Dept	Department
Devt	Development
DFLP	Democratic Front for the Liberation of Palestine
Dir	Director
Div.	Division
DPA	Deutsche Presse-Agentur
DPC	Dubai Petroleum Company
Dr	Doctor
DUP	Democratic Unionist Party (Sudan)
dwt	dead weight tons
E	East, Eastern
EC	European Community
ECOSOC	Economic and Social Council (UN)
ECU	European Currency Unit(s)
Ed.(s)	Editor(s)
edn	edition
EFTA	European Free Trade Association
e.g.	exempli gratia (for example)
EOKA	National Organization of the Struggle for Freedom of Cyprus
ERAP	Entreprise des Recherches et d'Activités Pétrolières
est.	established; estimate(d)
excl.	excluding
Exec.	Executive
f.	founded
FAO	Food and Agriculture Organization
FCM	Federation of Muslim Councillors
Fed.	Federal, Federation
FFS	Socialist Forces Front
FIDES	Fonds d'Investissement pour le Développement Economique et Sociale de la France d'Outre-Mer
FLN	Front de Libération Nationale (National Liberation Front)

xiii

ABBREVIATIONS

FLOSY	Front for the Liberation of Occupied South Yemen		LINOCO	Libyan National Oil Corporation
Flt	Flight		Lt	Lieutenant
FM	Frequency Modulation		Ltd	Limited
fmr(ly)	former(ly)			
f.o.b.	free on board		m	metre(s)
Fr.	Franc		m.	million
ft	foot (feet)		Maj.	Major
			Man.	Manager, Managing
GATT	General Agreements on Tariffs and Trade		MB	Bachelor of Medicine
GCC	Gulf Co-operation Council		MD	Doctor of Medicine
GDA	Gas Distribution Administration		mem.(s)	member(s)
GDP	gross domestic product		MEOC	Middle East Oil Company
Gen.	General		Mfg	Manufacturing
GHQ	General Headquarters		Mgr	Monseigneur, Monsignor
GMT	Greenwich Mean Time		Mil.	Military
GNP	gross national product		mm	millimetre(s)
Gov.	Governor		MNA	Mouvement National Algérien (Algerian National Movement)
Govt	Government		MP	Member of Parliament
GPC	General People's Congress (Libya)		MRP	Mouvement Républicain Populaire
GPRA	Gouvernement Provisoire de la République Algérienne (Provisional Government of the Republic of Algeria)		MSS	Manuscripts
			Mt	Mount
			MTA	Mineral Research and Exploration Institute of Turkey
grt	gross registered ton(s)		MTLD	Mouvement au Triomphe des Libertés Démocratiques (Movement for the Triumph of Democratic Liberties in Algeria)
GUPCO	Gulf of Suez Petroleum Company			
GW	gigawatt(s)			
GWh	gigawatt hour(s)		MW	megawatt(s); medium wave
			MWh	megawatt hour(s)
ha	hectare(s)			
HE	His (or Her) Excellency, His Eminence		N	North, Northern
HIM	His Imperial Majesty		n.a.	not available
hl	hectolitre(s)		Nat.	National
HM	His (or Her) Majesty		NATO	North Atlantic Treaty Organization
Hon.	Honorary; Honourable		NDRC	National Defence Research Council
HQ	Headquarters		NECCCRW	Near East Christian Council Committee for Refugee Work
HRH	His (or Her) Royal Highness		n.e.s.	not elsewhere specified
IAEA	International Atomic Energy Authority		NGLs	natural gas liquids
IATA	International Air Transport Association		n.i.e.	not included elsewhere
ibid	ibidem (from the same source)		NIOC	National Iranian Oil Company
IBRD	International Bank for Reconstruction and Development		NLF	National Liberation Front (People's Democratic Republic of Yemen)
ICAO	International Civil Aviation Organization		no.	number
ICATU	International Conference of Arab Trade Unions		nr	near
			nrt	net registered ton(s)
ICFTU-AFRO	International Confederation of Free Trade Unions—African Regional Organization		NUP	National Unionist Party (Sudan)
ICOO	Iraqi Company for Oil Operations		OAPEC	Organization of Arab Petroleum Exporting Countries
IDA	International Development Association			
i.e.	id est (that is to say)		OAS	Secret Army Organization (Algeria)
IFC	International Finance Corporation		OAU	Organization of African Unity
IISS	International Institute of Strategic Studies		OCAM	Organisation Commune Africaine, Malgache et Mauricienne
ILO	International Labour Organisation			
IMF	International Monetary Fund		OCRA	Clandestine Organization of the Algerian Revolution
IMINOCO	Iranian Marine International Oil Company			
in	inch(es)		OECD	Organization for Economic Co-operation and Development
Inc	Incorporated			
incl.	include, including		OPEC	Organization of the Petroleum Exporting Countries
Ind.	Independent			
INOC	Iraq National Oil Company		ORP	Organisation de la Résistance Populaire (Organization of Popular Resistance in Algeria)
Insp.	Inspector			
Inst.	Institute; Institution			
Int.	International		Org.(s)	Organization(s)
IOP	Iranian Oil Participants		oz	ounce(s)
IPAC	Iran-Pan American Oil Company			
IPC	Iraq Petroleum Company		p.a.	per annum
Is	Islands		Parl.	Parliament(ary)
ITU	International Telecommunications Union		PDFLP	Popular Democratic Front for the Liberation of Palestine
ISIC	International Standard Industrial Classification			
			PDO	Petroleum Development Oman
Jr	Junior		PDP	People's Democratic Party (Sudan)
Jt	Joint		PDR	People's Democratic Republic
			Perm.	Permanent
kg	kilogramme(s)		Perm. Rep.	Permanent Representative
KFAED	Kuwait Fund for Arab Economic Development		PFLO	Popular Front for the Liberation of Oman
km	kilometre(s)		PFLP	Popular Front for the Liberation of Palestine
KNPC	Kuwait National Petroleum Company		PhD	Doctor of Philosophy
KOC	Kuwait Oil Company		PLA	Palestine Liberation Army
KPC	Kuwait Petroleum Corporation		PLC	Public Limited Company
KSPC	Kuwait Spanish Petroleum Company		PLO	Palestine Liberation Organization
kV	kilovolt(s)		POB	Post Office Box
kW	kilowatt(s)		Pres.	President
kWh	kilowatt hour(s)		Prof.	Professor
			Propr	Proprietor
lb	pound(s)		PSD	Parti Socialiste Destourien (Tunisia)
Legis.	Legislative		PPA	Parti des Peuples Algériens (Party of the

ABBREVIATIONS

	Algerian People)
Pty	Proprietary
p.u.	paid up
publ.(s)	publication(s)
Publr	Publisher
QGPC	Qatar General Petroleum Company
QPC	Qatar Petroleum Company
RCC	Revolutionary Command Council (Iraq, Libya)
RCD	Regional Co-operation for Development
Rd	Road
RDA	Rassemblement Démocratique Africain
regd	registered
Rep.	Representative
Repub.	Republic
res	reserves
retd	retired
Rev.	Reverend
ro-ro	roll-on roll-off
RPP	Republican People's Party
S	South, Southern
SDF	Sudan Defence Force
SDR(s)	special drawing right(s)
Sec.	Secretary
Secr.	Secretariat
SEHR	Société d'Exploitation des Hydrocarbures de Hassi R'Mel
SIRIP	Société Irano-Italienne des Pétroles
SITC	Standard International Trade Classification
SNPA	Société Nationale des Pétroles d'Aquitaine
SNREPAL	Société Nationale de Recherche et d'Exploitation des Pétroles en Algérie
Soc.	Society; Société
SOFIRAN	Société Française des Pétroles d'Iran
SONATRACH	Société Nationale pour la Recherche, la Production, la Transformation et la Commercialisation des Hydrocarbures
SpA	Società per Azioni (Limited Company)
sq	square (in measurements)
Sq.	Square
Sr	Senior
St	Saint; Street
Stn	Station
subs.	subscribed
Supt	Superintendent
TAL	Trans-Alpine Line
Tapline	Trans-Arabian Pipeline Company
TAŞ	Türk Anonim Şirketi
TASS	Telegrafnoye Agentstvo Sovietskogo Soyuza
TPAO	Turkish Petroleum Corporation
Treas.	Treasurer
trans.	translated; translation
TRAPES	Société de Transport de Pétrole de l'Est Saharien
TRAPSA	Compagnie de Transport par Pipe-line au

	Sahara
TV	Television
TW	terawatt(s)
TWh	terawatt hour(s)
UA	Unit(s) of Account
UAE	United Arab Emirates
UAR	United Arab Republic
UBAF	Union des Banques Arabes et Françaises
UDMA	Union Démocratique du Manifeste Algérien (Democratic Union of the Algerian Manifesto)
UGTA	Union Générale des Travailleurs Algériens (Algerian General Workers' Union)
UHF	Ultra High Frequency
UK	United Kingdom
UN	United Nations
UNCTAD	United Nations Conference on Trade and Development
UNDOF	United Nations Disengagement Observer Force
UNDP	United Nations Development Programme
UNEA	Union Nationale des Etudiants Algériens (National Union of Algerian Students)
UNEF	United Nations Emergency Force
UNEP	United Nations Environment Programme
UNESCO	United Nations Educational, Scientific and Cultural Organization
UNFICYP	United Nations Peace-keeping Force in Cyprus
UNFP	Union Nationale des forces Populaires (National Union of Popular Forces in Morocco)
UNFPA	United Nations Population Fund
UNICEF	United Nations Children's Fund
UNIDO	United Nations Industrial Development Organization
UNIFIL	United Nations Interim Force in Lebanon
Univ.	University
UNMEM	United Nations Middle East Mission
UNRWA	United Nations Relief and Works Agency for Palestine Refugees in the Near East
UNTSO	United Nations Truce Supervision Organization
UPAF	Union Postale Africaine (African Postal Union)
UP	University Press
UPI	United Press International
USA (US)	United States of America (United States)
USIS	United States Information Services
USSR	Union of Soviet Socialist Republics
UTA	Union de Transports Aériens
VHF	Very High Frequency
vol.(s)	volume(s)
VSO	Voluntary Service Overseas Limited
W	West, Western
WEPCO	Western Desert Petroleum Company
WFTU	World Federation of Trade Unions
WHO	World Health Organization
yr	year

TRANSCRIPTION OF ARABIC NAMES

The Arabic language is used over a vast area. Though the written language and the script are standard throughout the Middle East, the spoken language and also the pronunciation of the written signs show wide variation from place to place. This is reflected, and even exaggerated, in the different transcriptions in use in different countries. The same words, names and even letters will be pronounced differently by an Egyptian, a Lebanese, or an Iraqi—they will be heard and transcribed differently by an Englishman, a Frenchman, or an Italian. There are several more or less scientific systems of transliteration in use, sponsored by learned societies and Middle Eastern governments, most of them requiring diacritical marks to indicate Arabic letters for which there are no Latin equivalents.

Arabic names occurring in the historical and geographical sections of this book have been rendered in the system most commonly used by British and American Orientalists, but with the omission of the diacritical signs. For the convenience of the reader, these are explained and annotated below. The system used is a transliteration—i.e. it is based on the writing, which is standard throughout the Arab world, and not on the pronunciation, which varies from place to place. In a few cases consistency has been sacrificed in order to avoid replacing a familiar and accepted form by another which, although more accurate, would be unrecognizable.

Consonants

d   represents two Arabic letters. The second, or emphatic d, is transliterated ḍ. It may also be represented, for some dialects, by dh and by z, e.g. Qāḍī, qadhi, qazi.

dh   in literary Arabic and some dialects pronounced like English th in this. In many dialects pronounced z or d.

gh   A strongly guttural g—sometimes written g, e.g. Baghdād, Bagdad.

h   represents two Arabic letters. The second, more guttural h, is transliterated ḥ, e.g. Husain, Husein.

j   as English j in John, also represented by dj and g. In Egypt this letter is pronounced as a hard g, and may be thus transcribed (with u before e and i), e.g. Najib, Nadjib, Nagib, Naguib, Neguib.

kh   as ch in Scottish loch, also sometimes represented by ch and h, e.g. Khalīl, Chalil, Halil.

q   A guttural k, pronounced farther back in the throat. Also transcribed ḳ, k, and, for some dialects, g, e.g. Waqf, Waḳf, Wakf, wagf.

s   represents two Arabic letters. The second, emphatic s, is transliterated ṣ. It may also be represented by ç, e.g. Sāliḥ, Saleh, Çaleh.

sh   as in English ship. The French transcription ch is found in Algeria, Lebanon, Morocco, Syria and Tunisia, e.g. Shaikh, Sheikh, Cheikh.

t   represents two Arabic letters. The second, emphatic t, is transliterated ṭ.

th   in literary Arabic and some dialects pronounced as English th in through. In many dialects pronounced t or s, e.g. Thābit, Tabit, Sabit.

w   as in English, but often represented by ou or v, e.g. Wādā, Vadi, Oued.

z   represents two Arabic letters. The second, or emphatic z, is transliterated ẓ. It may also be represented, for some dialects, by dh or d, e.g. Ḥāfiẓ, Hafidh, Hafid.

'   A glottal stop, as in Cockney 'li'l bo'ls'. May also represent the sound transliterated ', a deep guttural with no English equivalent.

Vowels

The Arabic script only indicates three short vowels, three long vowels, and two diphthongs, as follows:

a   as in English hat, and often rendered e, e.g. balad, beled, emir, amire; with emphatics or gutturals usually pronounced as u in but, e.g. Khalīfa, Baghdād.

i   as in English bit. Sometimes rendered e, e.g. jihād, jehād.

u   as in English good. Often pronounced and written o, e.g. Muhammad, Mohammad.

In some Arabic dialects, particularly those of North Africa, unaccented short vowels are often omitted altogether, and long vowels shortened, e.g. Oued for Wādī, bled for balad, etc.

ā   Long a, variously pronounced as in sand, dart and hall.

ī   As ee in feet. In early books often rendered ee.

ū   As oo in boot. The French transcription ou is often met with in English books, e.g. Maḥmūd, Mahmood, Mahmoud.

ai   Pronounced in classical Arabic as English i in hide, in colloquial Arabic as a in take. Variously transcribed as ai, ay, ei, ey and ê, e.g. sheikh, shaikh, shaykh, etc.

aw   Pronounced in classical Arabic as English ow in town, in colloquial Arabic as in grow. Variously rendered aw, ew, au, ô, av, ev, e.g. Tawfīq, Taufiq, Tevfik, etc.

Sun- and Moon-Letters

In Arabic pronunciation, when the word to which the definite article, al, is attached begins with one of certain letters called 'Sun-letters', the l of the article changes to the initial letter in question, e.g. al-shamsu (the sun) is pronounced ash-shamsu; al-rajulu (the man) is pronounced ar-rajulu. Accordingly, in this book, where the article is attached to a word beginning with a Sun-letter, it has been rendered phonetically.

There are 14 Sun-letters in the Arabic alphabet, which are transcribed as: d, dh, n, r, s, sh, t, th, z, zh (d, s, t and z, and their emphatic forms, ḍ, ṣ, ṭ and ẓ, are not differentiated in this book). The remaining 15 letters in the Arabic alphabet are known as 'Moon-letters'.

TURKISH ORTHOGRAPHY AND PRONUNCIATION

Turkish has been written in Roman characters since 1928. The following pronunciations are invariable:

c   hard j, as in majority, jam.

ç   ch, as in church.

g   hard g, as in go, big.

ğ   not voiced, or pronounced y; Ereğli is pronounced erayly.

ı   short vowel, as the second vowel of 'centre', or French 'le'.

i   i sound of Iran, bitter (NOT as in bite, might).

o   o, as in hot, boss.

ö   i sound of 'birth', or French 'oeuvre'.

u   as in do, too, German 'um'.

ü   as in burette, German 'Hütte'.

xvii

CALENDAR OF EVENTS IN THE MIDDLE EAST AND NORTH AFRICA, OCTOBER 1993–OCTOBER 1994

1993

OCTOBER

5 Elections held to Kuwaiti National Assembly.

8 Reorganization of Libyan governmental secretariats.

17 New Kuwaiti Council of Ministers appointed.

21 Seventh round of bilateral negotiations between Israeli and Arab delegations commenced in Washington, DC.

22 Rafik Hariri appointed Prime Minister of Lebanon.

31 New Lebanese Government announced.

NOVEMBER

8 Elections held to Jordanian House of Representatives.

8–9 GCC member states agreed to increase security co-operation and develop Peninsular Shield Force.

11 UN Security Council approved more stringent economic sanctions against Libya.
New, non-partisan Moroccan Government appointed.

24 Imad Akel, a commander of Qassem (the military wing of Hamas), shot dead by Israeli forces.

26 Iraq accepted long-term international monitoring of its defence industries in accordance with UN Security Council Resolution 715.

28 Turkish Cabinet reshuffled.

DECEMBER

1–2 Turkey and Iran signed security co-operation agreement.

10 Hanan Ashrawi resigned as spokeswoman of Palestinian delegation to the Middle East peace talks.

13 Date by which Israeli forces should have begun to withdraw from the Gaza Strip and the Jericho area under the terms of the Declaration of Principles on Palestinian Self-Rule.

20–22 GCC summit meeting held in Riyadh.

29 Inauguration of Saudi Arabian Consultative Council took place.

30 Israel and the Vatican signed an agreement on mutual recognition.

31 New coalition government formed in Turkish Republic of Northern Cyprus.

1994

JANUARY

5 Omani Council of Ministers reshuffled.

9–10 Ministers of Foreign Affairs of the Damascus Declaration signatories met in Damascus.

16 US President Bill Clinton met President Assad of Syria to discuss Middle East peace process.

18 Main Yemeni political parties signed Document of Pledge and Agreement.

22–29 Libyan General People's Congress convened. Approved new appointments to the General People's Committee.
Twelfth round of bilateral negotiations in Middle East peace process commenced in Washington, DC.

27 Gen. Lamine Zérroual appointed President of Algeria.

FEBRUARY

1 Assassination attempt on President Rafsanjani of Iran.

5 Ministers of Foreign Affairs of Iran, Syria and Turkey met in Istanbul for talks on Iraqi Kurdistan.

6 Israeli Minister of Health resigned.

8 New Turkish Minister of Economic Co-ordination appointed.

14 and 22 New appointments to Iranian Council of Ministers.

19 UAE Minister of Petroleum and Mineral Resources resigned.

20 Application of Islamic law in UAE extended.
Yemeni President and Vice-President signed Document of Pledge and Agreement.

25 Muslim worshippers murdered in mosque in Hebron.
PLO withdrew from Middle East peace negotiations.

27 Jordan, Syria and Lebanon withdrew from Middle East peace process.

MARCH

3 Jordan and the Vatican established diplomatic relations.

13 Kach and Kahane Chai political parties proscribed by the Israeli Government.

18 UN Security Council adopted a resolution condemning the Hebron massacre.

19 Political dialogue began in Algeria.

20 Presidential and legislative elections held in Tunisia.

23 Lebanese Forces proscribed.

APRIL

2–3 Union of the Arab Maghreb summit meeting held in Tunis.

8 UN economic sanctions against Libya extended for a further 120 days.

11 Mokdad Sifi appointed Prime Minister of Algeria.
Egyptian emergency laws extended for three years.

12–13 Military committee of the GCC met for the first time in Dubai.

13 New Kuwaiti Council of Ministers appointed.

15 New Algerian Council of Ministers appointed.

27 Fighting erupted between rival northern and southern Yemeni army units.

28 Polisario Front agreed to observe UN Security Council Resolution 907.

29 Israel and the PLO signed economic agreement.

MAY

4 Israel and the PLO signed agreement providing for Palestinian Self-Rule in the Gaza Strip and Jericho.

8 Lebanese Prime Minister Hariri withdrew from his official duties.

13 Israeli armed forces completed their withdrawal from the Gaza Strip.

National Transition Council appointed in Algeria.

21 Formation of breakaway Democratic Republic of Yemen announced.

23 270 pilgrims trampled to death on *Hajj* in Mecca.

Coalition Government formed in Yemen.

25 New Moroccan Prime Minister appointed.

26–28 Newly-appointed Palestine National Authority met for first time in Tunis.

29 Ahmad Hussein Khudayer replaced as Iraqi Prime Minister by President Saddam Hussain.

31 Report by UN Secretary-General claimed that Turkish Cypriot recalcitrance impeded the conclusion of a peace agreement between Greek and Turkish Cypriots.

JUNE

1 UN Security Council urged immediate cease-fire in civil war in Yemen.

Israeli forces launched major attack on Hezbollah training camp in Lebanon.

8 Jordanian Cabinet reshuffled.

14 Destruction of Iraq's chemical weapons completed.

Changes to Omani Consultative Council announced.

15 Israel and the Vatican established full diplomatic relations.

16 Turkish Democracy Party proscribed.

25 Egyptian National Dialogue General Congress opened in Cairo.

26 Palestine National Authority met in Gaza for the first time.

JULY

1 PLO leader Arafat arrived in the Gaza Strip.

18 Bomb attack on a Jewish community building in Buenos Aires, Argentina, killed 100 people.

19 Moroccan Cabinet reorganized.

25 Israel and Jordan signed a joint declaration formally ending the state of war between them.

AUGUST

3 New Egyptian Minister of Supply and Internal Trade appointed.

5 US Secretary of State began four-day visit to Middle East.

21 and 24 Talks held between Algerian President and opposition leaders.

24 Elections to Syrian People's Assembly took place.

SEPTEMBER

1 Morocco announced decision to open a liaison office in Tel-Aviv, Israel.

2 Lebanese Cabinet reshuffled.

5–13 UN population conference held in Cairo.

7 Palestine National Authority signed loan agreement with World Bank.

13 Algerian FIS leaders transferred from prison to house arrest.

20 Talks between Algerian government representatives and FIS leaders began.

30 GCC ended secondary and tertiary trade boycott of Israel.

OCTOBER

1 President Saleh of Yemen re-elected.

6 Iraqi armed forces advanced south towards Iraq-Kuwait border.

New Yemeni Council of Ministers announced.

12 Iraqi troops began to withdraw from Kuwaiti border area.

26 Israel and Jordan signed comprehensive peace treaty.

PART ONE
General Survey

ALGERIA: THE FAILURE OF DIALOGUE

GEORGE JOFFÉ

At the start of 1994, the appointment of a new president in Algeria—Lamine Zeroual—seemed to presage a solution to the prolonged crisis into which the country had been plunged by the army-backed *coup d'état* in January 1992. The coup had originally been launched to cut short the legislative electoral process which had begun the previous month and which seemed certain to bring Algeria's powerful Islamist movement, the Front Islamique du Salut (FIS) to power. Two years later, as the term of office of the temporary collegiate body, the Haut Conseil d'Etat (HSC), created in the aftermath of the coup, came to an end, the crisis of political legitimacy which the coup had been intended to solve was still no nearer a solution. Indeed, the failure had been in large measure due to confusion within government over the way in which the crisis was to be resolved.

The new president was, however, expected to provide a new dynamism for a policy of dialogue and, thereby, for a lasting solution to the crisis. His advent to power was accompanied by an agreement with the IMF on economic restructuring and the offer of a US$1,100m.—IMF standby credit (comprising a SDR500m.—standby loan and a SDR300m.—compensatory and contingent financing facility); a further agreement with Algeria's official creditors for the rescheduling of 60% of the country's $26,000m. medium- and long-term foreign debt; and a final arrangement with commercial creditors for similar adjustments to the repayment of commercial debt. A year later, however, despite the release of the FIS leadership and the beginning of a political dialogue, the Algerian political process was still threatened by political violence. The slow progress was a measure of the seriousness, complexity and chronic nature of the crisis that Algeria faces for it is, in reality, rooted in the origins of the independent Algerian state.

Antecedents to the crisis

The current crisis in Algeria stems from two, intertwined sources: the political legacy of the war of independence between 1954 and 1962 and the economic failure that developed during the 1980s but which had its origins in the policy choices made during the Boumédienne regime.

The economic dimension

Algeria, at independence in 1962, suffered from an economy which had been prostrated by the damage done to it by the eight year-long war fought by the Front de Libération National (FLN) against the French army. Apart from limited investment provided under the 1958 Plan Constantine, little had been done to transform Algeria away from its dependent colonial economic status. The situation was worsened by the fact that, not only did the new state possess virtually no properly trained and qualified personnel capable of operating a complex modern economy, but also almost every member of the European managerial work-force, which itself was an integral part of the one million-strong colonial population of Algeria, left the country within six months of independence. By September 1962, only 250,000 Europeans remained. Within a year of independence being granted on 5 July 1962, only 30,000 Europeans remained in the country.

The new government's response was, not surprisingly given its paucity of resources, confused. Although the Tripoli Programme, adopted by the FLN in May 1962, fore-shadowed wide-ranging agrarian reform and state control of much of the economy, the lack of personnel reduced these objectives largely to rhetoric. Indeed, as unemployment soared towards 70% of the work-force, much of the economy was spontaneously taken over by those workers who remained, thus forming what was to become a unique experiment in *autogestion*—worker's self-management. Only later was this brought under central government control. In addition, the Ben Bella regime, which had seized power in July and August 1962, with the help of the Algerian Armée

Nationale Populaire (ANP) under Houari Boumédienne, was distracted from economic issues by ongoing problems of political control, including a major rebellion in Kabylia led by Hoceine Ait Ahmed in 1964.

The inevitable result was Ben Bella's removal from power in July 1965 by his erstwhile military colleague, Houari Boumédienne. The Boumédienne regime, which remained in charge of Algeria until President Boumédienne's death in December 1978, soon opted for a centralized socialist economic system. Some 70% of the economy came under state control and, with the development of Algeria's hydrocarbon resources—the oil industry was nationalized in 1971—a conscious decision was made to rebuild the economy by concentrating on infrastructure and industrial development. The primary objective was, as President Boumédienne himself explained, to liberate 'the economy from all foreign hegemonies' and to build up 'a genuinely national economy'. This was to be done by building up the industrial sector through the development of heavy industry first of all, while the petroleum sector generated the necessary foreign exchange. This policy of 'industrializing industries'—as it was christened by its creator, Gérard de Stanne de Bernis, necessarily implied the relative neglect of the agricultural sector and was also based on the assumption that surplus labour would be mopped up by labour migration to Europe, mainly to France. From the Algerian population at large which had suffered throughout the war, the regime demanded that it delay its expectations of improvements in living conditions until the basic restructuring and modernization of the economy had occurred.

The popular revolutionary consensus which had made this demand acceptable had begun to break down by the time of President Boumédienne's unexpected death in 1978. It had also become clear that state control of the economy had introduced massive inefficiencies into the 70 major state industries that had been created, while social and economic conditions, particularly in housing and consumer supply, had stagnated—if not worsened, as was the case with urban water supply. Houari Boumédienne's successor, Chadli Ben Djedid, came to power, therefore, on a wave of popular anticipation of radical change—in living conditions, at least, if not in the political sphere as well. President Ben Djedid did indeed introduce policies ostensibly designed to respond to the worsening economic situation in which the country found itself. The 70 state industries were broken up into around 350 autonomous units to improve efficiency and a greater emphasis was placed on the production of consumer goods. The private sector was also slowly allowed a greater role, a development which immediately began to undermine the egalitarian assumptions of the original Algerian revolution and of the Boumédienne era. Towards the end of the 1980s a plan to privatize these industries was also put forward by placing them in the control of a series of state holding companies—the *entreprises publiques economiques* (EPEs)—whose shares would eventually be made available for public purchase.

The agricultural sector—which had been subjected to an unsuccessful agrarian reform process after 1971—was also liberalized in order to stimulate food production for, by the 1980s, Algeria was importing up to 65% of the food it consumed. Unfortunately, this initiative turned out to be a passport to massive enrichment to the enterprising rather than a means of significantly stimulating domestic food production. It created a class which Algerians came to call the *milliardaires de légumes* (vegetable millionaires) who controlled food supply in fresh vegetables. At the same time, living conditions deteriorated as the housing crisis worsened—it was estimated that up to 250,000 new housing units were needed annually to cope with the effects of an exploding demography and urban drift, a target far beyond the capacity of the construction industry—and measures to improve, *inter alia*, urban water supply and public transport took time to have effect. Indeed, the most visible sign of change was the emergence of a new and conspicuous class of increasingly wealthy entrepreneurs. By the middle of the 1980s the country was rumbling with barely suppressed discontent.

It was at this point that Algeria's international economic position suddenly deteriorated. Algeria, like other oil producers, had suffered from declines in foreign exchange earnings as oil prices steadily declined from the heights reached during the Islamic revolution in Iran in 1979–80. The consequences for Algeria were, however, particularly acute since the country had also deliberately incurred heavy foreign debt as part of the process of financing major industrial projects, particularly in connection with the oil and natural gas sectors. From $1,300m. in 1971, total foreign debt rose to $6,100m. five years later, to $15,700m. in 1978, to $22,900m. in 1986 and to a staggering $28,600m. in 1991. Debt service ratios showed similar, frightening rates of growth: from 26.18% in 1980 to 52.86% in 1987 and 75.55% in 1988, before showing a slight decline to 62.08% in 1991.

The government's assumption had always been that, first, oil revenues and, second, growing revenues from industrial exports would easily allow such sums to be serviced. The reality was that, in a world of declining oil prices and stagnant economic growth, Algeria's debt servicing could only be met by ever more severe import compression. Although Algeria could have had recourse to IMF help, this was generally unattractive to government because of the demands for economic restructuring that would have been an obligatory condition. Similarly, the Algerian Government rejected debt rescheduling on the grounds that this would weaken the country's high credit rating in international financial markets. This massive burden of debt, of course, immediately affected the population through declines in consumer goods supply because of the import compression involved.

The second adverse economic indicator, which only strengthened the difficulties created by foreign debt was the sudden decline in oil prices in 1986. Only about a quarter of Algeria's hydrocarbon receipts actually come from exports of crude, the balance being generated by refined petroleum products, natural gas and liquefied petroleum gas exports. However, crude sales are denominated in US dollars and, in 1986, the dollar underwent a spontaneous 40% devaluation while crude oil prices fell suddenly by about the same amount. The cause of the price collapse was an unexpected Saudi decision unilaterally to increase its output and exports, rather than to maintain its role within OPEC as the 'swing producer'. The combined effect of both events was that Algeria's receipts from crude sales dropped in real terms by 80% and its overall hydrocarbon export receipts fell by 20%.

There were similar, albeit smaller falls in earnings from condensate and refined product exports, so that hydrocarbon revenues dropped from $12,970m. in 1985 to $7,633m. the following year and continued to be depressed for the remainder of the decade. In the context of the savage restrictions on imports already in force because of the effect of foreign debt, these cuts were extremely damaging and further worsened the import picture.

Within months, domestic unrest in Constantine, where there were serious riots sparked off by student protests, indicated the likely consequences of these developments. Their full effect, however, was to be delayed by two years, until October 1988 when country-wide rioting exploded. The link between these events and the worsening economic situation in which Algeria found itself because of developments in world energy markets is undeniable. It was worsened by the popular perception inside Algeria that the adverse consequences of international price movements were not shared equally throughout the population at large and that corruption had become an endemic social and political problem. In short, alongside the economic failure now facing the country, there was a growing sense of a political crisis as well.

The political crisis

The success of the FLN in the war of independence was predicated on its ability both to monopolize the Algerian political scene (all competitors were simply eliminated if they could not be co-opted) and to embody the core aspirations of Algerians themselves. These were encapsulated in the concept of popular Algerian sovereignty, the sense that the colonial experience had forged an Algerian nation and that nation was now forcing its independence out of the colonizing power, France. Until the Tripoli Charter, the FLN had little to offer by way of detailed social and economic programmes and its political programme consisted of its own continued mastery of the political arena after the struggle for independence was over, as the embodiment of the collective Algerian aspiration to achieve true nationhood and statehood. This was, in essence, the motivation of what has since come to be called the 'historic FLN'.

It is 'historic' in the sense that, shortly after independence, it lost the core role it had anticipated for itself. Between July and September 1962, the leadership of the Gouvernement provisoire de la République Algérienne (GPRA), the government-in-exile which had been set up by the FLN in the early years of the struggle in 1958, deliberately allied itself with the FLN guerrilla leaderships of several of the *wilayat*, the administrative divisions of Algeria created by the movement for the semi-autonomous guerrilla groups which had borne the brunt of the fighting with the French army. The most important of such alliances was forged with *wilaya 4* around Algiers. The GPRA had been forced to make these explicit alliances with elements within the FLN—thereby undermining the normative unity of the movement as a whole—because Ahmad Ben Bella, one of the founding *chefs historiques* of the FLN who had been in a French prison for most of the war, had deliberately allied himself with the ANP, led by Houari Boumédienne, in a bid to unseat the GPRA and replace it by his own supporters in the *bureau politique*. The ANP itself had been confined by the French army's very effective border defences to Tunisia and Morocco throughout the war, but had captured control of Constantine and Annaba when hostilities ended, thus providing a power base for an alternative FLN leadership. In September 1962, after a brief but brisk resistance, Ben Bella and the ANP took control of Algiers and secured the election of a constituent assembly from which their rivals were excluded.

With the disappearance of the GPRA, the FLN dramatically and abruptly ceased to be the guiding hand for the new state. Instead it was transformed into a servant of those who had replaced it. It became the single political party inside the independent Algerian state, it is true, but it was subservient to government and a vehicle for articulating government policy to the population, rather than the forum in which policy was discussed and decided and which, in its ideology, incarnated the essence of the revolutionary ideal. It had, in short, lost its historic role. As time went by, the FLN as a political party became ever more discredited and, despite periodic attempts to revive it, never gained the popular credibility it had enjoyed before Ben Bella's *coup d'état*.

Although the Ben Bella regime was unable to recapture the sense of popular legitimacy that the FLN had acquired during the war and, partly for that reason, was pushed aside in 1965, its successor, under the austere figure of Houari Boumédienne, did achieve such a status. It acted as a rallying point for the expression of aspirations and objectives of Algerians collectively and, in turn, was respected and accepted by large parts of the population. It did not succeed, however, in welding a genuine nation from the different elements within the population and several groups, particularly the Berbers and activist religious elements, always stood somewhat apart from it and were often marginalized in consequence. Some of the elements which it created, such as the growing number of young people educated in Arabic as a result of the Arabization campaign, were also adversely affected. Nevertheless, the period from 1964 to 1978 saw the rapid construction and consolidation of Algeria as a neutralist, socialist and modern state.

At the same time, however, the political foundations of this edifice were, perhaps, rather weaker than they appeared to be at the time. For a long time there was no formal constitution for the state, for the original 1962 constitution was suspended in 1965 and a new constitution was only introduced by 1976. Secondly, although the FLN existed as a single political party, it was only one of the mechanisms which mediated between the administration and the population. It did, however, represent the political continuity between the original revolution which it had organized and dominated and the state to which that revolution had given birth and which it was now obliged to serve, thus providing the state and the regime with political continuity, credibility and legitimacy. Thirdly, the state was now effectively controlled by the presidency, to which all other institutions were subordinate, thus providing a coherence to policy formulation and execution. And finally, the ultimate guarantor of the state and an active participant in its operation was the Algerian army leadership, from which the president himself came—and the ANP had, after all, claimed to be the true embodiment of the revolution in 1962, thus offering the state an alternative mode of legitimization.

The causes of discontent

The socio-political consensus created by the Boumédienne regime began to waver, however, towards its end. In part, this was an inevitable consequence of the process of modernization, as urban drift expanded, rural social structures declined and urban populations grew massively, while the state inevitably failed to keep pace with the demands made upon it. Under the subsequent Chadli Ben Djedid regime, also effectively a creation of the army, the consensus was completely lost, partly because of continuation of the authoritarian political structures created by its predecessor and partly because of the consequences of the liberalizing economic reforms it introduced.

Several specific factors were also responsible for this decline in active popular support, however. First and foremost was the growing weariness of the population with the constant sacrifices it was forced to bear and a growing sense, as the generation which had actually fought the war was replaced by new and expanding generations which had not experienced colonialism, that the time had come for the period of sacrifices to come to an end. Rhetoric, in short, could not substitute for real material benefits indefinitely. The Boumédienne regime realized this and, two years before the president's death, tried to revive the social consensus by drawing up the *Charte Nationale*, a document which was submitted to quite unprecedented public debate and which was to point the way forward for Algeria as it entered its third decade of independence. At the same time, a new constitution was introduced and presidential elections were held, so that President Boumédienne could formally claim a popular mandate. The Chadli Ben Djedid regime tried to revive its popular support base by a similar technique in the mid-1980s, but by then popular cynicism had increased markedly and the device failed.

Secondly, the very changes wrought in Algerian society by economic and social development began to tear the fabric of social consensus. One of the consequences of the rapid programme of development undertaken by the Boumédienne regime was the creation of a new technocratic class. This was primarily occupied with operating the institutions, both political and economic, of the state. However, as time passed and individual opportunities became ever more circumscribed by the dominant nature of the regime, so members of this class began to seek ideological and practical alternatives within the not insignificant private sector of the Algerian economy. Around 30% of the economy remained in private hands and, ideologically, educated Algerian youth began to abandon its belief in the austere socialism of the Boumédienne era, turning instead towards the lure of the free market.

The role of Islam

Thirdly, allied to this growing sense of disillusion with Algeria's economic—and, by logical extension, political—option, there was also an active and increasing alienation from the political paradigm chosen by the regime. In part, this arose because the regime tried to square the political circle which it had created for itself, partly because of the legacy it inherited from the FLN during the war. While proclaiming itself to be socialist, it also denied that it was Marxist. Instead it argued that its socialism was 'Islamic', so that the Islamic traditions of Algerian society could be used to legitimize the regime. This did not, however, mean that Algeria was or was to become an Islamic state. In practice, the Boumédienne regime, whatever the religious proclivities of its members, was determined to control religious expression in Algeria as part of its general control over the population at large. Islam had always been an important strand within the FLN, stemming from the activism of Sheikh Abdulhamid bin Badis who, in the 1930s, had created the *Association des Ulemas algériens*, and, when the FLN was formed, its objective was defined as '. . . the restoration of the sovereign, democratic and social Algerian state within the framework of Islamic principles'. Independent Algeria, however, transformed the *ulema* effectively into civil servants and strictly controlled their activities—something, incidentally, that every other state in the Islamic world also tried to do.

The *ulema's* tradition of independent opposition to colonialism, however, made this unacceptable to them and, as early as 1964, some *ulema* tried to found an Islamic organization independent of the state, the *al-Qiyam* (values) movement. It was suppressed in 1970, but its major figures—Malek Bennabi, Sheikh Abdellatif Soltani and Sheikh Ahmed Sahnoun—continued to be the focus of informal Islamist currents in Algerian society that began to grow stronger towards the end of the 1970s and were expressed through the semi-clandestine *Ahl ad-Dawa'a* movement. Its supporters resented their exclusion from the political process and disapproved of the socialist content of much of the state's ideology. Its ideas were encapsulated in an attack on the Boumédienne regime, published by Sheikh Soltani in 1974. This set down many of the themes—opposition to socialism and Marxism, concern over the degradation of public morality, anger over perceptions of official antagonism towards Islam—that were later to become an integral part of the ideological platform of the Islamist movement.

By this time, the movement, which operated outside the formal political arena in semi-clandestinity, had been reinforced by other currents. In addition to the *salajiyyist* Islamic reformism which had characterized Bin Badis and his successors, Islamists in Algeria had acquired two other sources of ideological support. One formed part of the mainstream of sunni radicalism that derived from the *Jkhwan Muslimin* in Egypt and elsewhere. This incorporated the ideas of Sayyid Qutb and his Pakistani counterpart, Mawlana Maududi, and defined the structure of the state and the society it had created as *Jahiliyya* calling for its replacement by a state based on *tawhid* the 'oneness of God' and the unity of *din* (faith) and *dinya* (society) and, by extension, *dawla* (the state) as well.

The other element came from a specifically Algerian experience and owed much to the work of Malek Bennabi. It was primarily composed of the growing numbers of young people who had been educated in Arabic, not in French, and were marginalized as a result within Algerian society. Many of those involved had been educated by Egyptian teachers who had themselves been influenced by the *Ikhwan Muslimin* and, as a result, an elision occurred between the fact of Arabic as the official means of communication within the future Algerian state and Islam as its means of cultural articulation. Such individuals found in Bennabi justification for their rejection of the Algerian state as it existed which, despite its claims to be 'Islamic', was, in reality, based on a modernist concept of nationalism derived originally from the European experience. For this group, it was the failure of the Algerian state to realize its Islamic credentials which lay at the failure of development, the state's betrayal of the ideals of the Algerian revolution and their own exclusion from the political and economic process. During the 1980s, the leadership of this group was captured by Dr Abbasi Madani who was active within the Islamic movement in the University of Algiers.

Under the Chadli Ben Djedid regime, the Islamist movement re-emerged with renewed confidence. Indeed, the strength of the Islamist revival was demonstrated in 1984, when Sheikh Soltani died and, within hours of his death despite a news blackout, 25,000 mourners were thronging the streets around his home in the Algiers suburb of Hussain Dey. The regime was not unaware of what was happening and responded by trying to co-opt Islamist sentiment, appointing sympathetic ministers for Islamic affairs and encouraging the building of mosques. Indeed, this was to become one of the major means by which support for Islam was to spread. Under Algerian law, a mosque did not fall under official control until it was completed. As a result, many of the new mosques were never completed and, because they were uncontrolled, acted as powerful centres for Islamist propaganda. By the early 1980s there were 2,000 unofficial mosques and by 1990 it was estimated that, of the 10,000 mosques in Algeria, 8,000 fell outside official control.

The most obvious arena of confrontation with the regime and with other elements of Algerian society was in higher education. This began in the wake of riots in Kabylia in April 1980 which were initially a protest against the regime's marginalization of the country's Berber community yet became the vehicle for nationwide protests over official policies towards national culture and political liberalization, particularly the official attempt to create an Arabo-Islamic destiny for the country. In the wake of the riots, Berberophone and Arabophone students, the latter also active Islamists, frequently clashed, thus highlighting another aspect of the complex tensions that were developing throughout Algerian society. After 1982, the regime severely punished all such incidents and they came to an end. The spread of Islamist support did not, however.

A much more serious incident occurred in August 1985, although its significance for the Islamist movement overall was not to be very great. This was the creation of an armed clandestine Islamist group which targeted the Algerian state itself. It was led by a veteran of the FLN in the war of independence, Mohamed Bouyali, and based itself in the *maquis*. Its effect at the time on the Islamist movement was, however, marginal and it was finally wiped out in January 1987 when Mohamed Bouyali himself was killed near to his headquarters in Larba in the foothills of the Atlas behind Algiers. Its significance was that it was organized by an FLN veteran, thus underlining the loss in credibility that the FLN had suffered, and that its members were quite prepared to use violence as the only means of effecting change. This was a pattern that was to be repeated after the army-backed coup which prevented the FIS coming to power in January 1992.

The hizb fransa

The issue of Arabization highlighted another growing contradiction within society and state. This was that the colonial legacy in cultural and linguistic terms, combined with the process of modernization, had reinforced the Francophone nature of Algeria, despite the sufferings of the war and the popular nationalism of the historic FLN. The creation of a technocratic élite intended to operate the apparatus of a modern state and largely trained abroad formed one component of this development. Another was the burgeoning private sector which expanded significantly during the 1980s and which depended increasingly on its links with Europe, particularly France. A third element was formed from Algerians who had been involved in the colonial administration and military forces before rallying to the FLN. In short, despite the brutal war of liberation against France, which had cost, according to Algerian sources, around one million persons, and the ideology of the new state which emphasized its neutralist and nationalist destiny, the process of economic and social development during independence inexorably reinforced neo-colonial cultural and economic links.

France, of course, did everything it could to reinforce such links and, under the latter period of the Chadli regime, when governments became preoccupied with economic modernization through liberalization and the operations of the free market, also attempted to strengthen its political ties. This modernist, francophone component of Algerian society, not a conscious movement but nonetheless a powerful tendency pulling against both the nationalist and Islamist strains within the population, was to play a potent role after 1988. In Algerian eyes it has acquired a coherent identity, even a personality, of its own and has been christened with the generic name of the *hizb fransa*—the 'party of France'.

By the end of the 1980s, public opinion had assimilated another group into the *hizb fransa*, a group which had developed in the shadow of the economic reforms and liberalization programme undertaken by the Chadli Ben Djedid regime. It consisted of the shadowy pattern of corruption that had flourished in the atmosphere created by the reforms and most Algerians, by the 1990s, had come to see it as their own version of the mafia. It was seen as being intimately associated with the administration and, behind the administration, with the army. For the army had, as a result of the growing popular disillusion with the Chadli Ben Djedid regime, also lost much of its popular esteem as the guarantor of the Algerian revolution and the Algerian state. The process culminated in the riots of October 1988, when the army incurred intense popular anger by the way in which it subdued the rioters. Official sources admitted to 159 killed, whilst well-informed unofficial sources claimed that many more people were involved. The army tacitly acknowledged its loss of status by withdrawing from participation in formal political activities in 1989.

The aftermath of the 1988 riots

The riots of October 1988 were to be the culmination of the crisis of confidence in the independent state of Algeria. They were also to mark the open reappearance of the Islamist movement into the mainstream of political life. The riots were initiated by a series of strikes, particularly at the vehicle assembly plant in Rouiba, just outside Algiers. There were, at the time, suspicions that the situation had been engineered by left-wing elements within the FLN and from the banned communist party movement which had considerable influence within the trade union federation, the Union Générale des Travailleurs Algériens (UGTA), to bring pressure to bear on government to moderate its espousal of the extreme liberalization policies which had been introduced in December 1987. Whatever the cause, the riots rapidly became a vehicle for expressing the intense frustration and alienation of a predominantly youthful population against a regime which appeared to have abandoned them.

The Islamist movement was not responsible for initiating the riots. It did, however, become a prominent target of the subsequent repression. Furthermore, it was the only organized and coherent voice to articulate the frustration expressed by the rioters. Thus, in the political debris left by the riots, it soon became clear that the Islamist movement, however loosely organized it may have been, had become a significant voice in its own right on the formal political scene. Another feature which also became clear was that the FLN was irredeemably associated in the popular mind with the regime and had, in consequence, lost all credibility as the embodiment of the original principles of the Algerian revolution or as the representative of popular aspiration. What this was to mean became evident over the five months following the riots.

The Chadli Ben Djedid regime responded to the riots by reaffirming its commitment to radical economic reform and by distancing itself from the FLN. The presidency was separated from the Government which was then made answerable to the country's legislative assembly, the Assemblée Populaire Nationale elected in February 1987 which, in turn, was given greater powers. The media were also liberalized, although the state retained ultimate control over their activities. Finally, a further reform at the start of 1989 allowed political associations to emerge and a formal law instituting a plural political process was passed by the Assembly in July 1989. Political parties were required, however, to ensure that their platforms were not overtly religious or regionalist, in an attempt to control the growth of Islamist and Berberist movements.

The new laws concerning political parties not only drastically reduced the formal role of the FLN, although it continued to be the formal party of government, but also provided the door through which the FIS could enter the political arena. Indeed, the new party was formally registered—by Abbassi Madani and the imam of the mosque in Bab el-Oued, Ali Bel Hadj, who had sprung to national prominence through his fiery *khotbas* (sermons) in the wake of the riots—on 1 March 1989. There are grounds for suspecting that the Algerian presidency encouraged its creation, for the FIS's platform clearly contravened the party law yet it was registered by the authorities without demur. It seemed as if the Chadli Ben Djedid regime intended to use the FIS against the FLN, to break the power of the old single political party and to allow the presidency to develop a novel and crucial political role as arbiter between the new range of political parties.

In addition to the FIS, some 30 other parties were to appear, including at least three other Islamist parties: the Harakat an-Nahda al-Islamiyya (The Islamic Renaissance Movement), popularly known as the Hizb Nahda and founded by Shaykh Abdallah Djaballah; the Harakat li'l-Mojtama' Islami (The Islamic Society Movement), popularly known as Hamas and founded by Sheikh Mahfoud Nahnah; and the Rabitah ad-Daw'a al-Islamiyya (The League of the Islamic Call), created by the veteran Sheikh Ahmed Sahnoun, which did not operate as a conventional political party but rather as a religious association. Few of the other parties were significant; those that were included the veteran Front des Forces Socialistes (FFS), founded by the former *chef historique* of the Algerian revolution, Hoceine Ait Ahmed and with a strong presence in Kabylia, and the newly created Rassemblement pour la Culture et la Démocratie (RCD), created by the old Kabyli Berber activist, Said Sadi. The only other party of note was Ahmad Ben Bella's Mouvement pour la Démocratie Algérienne.

The dual electoral process and the coup

The Government also announced that municipal elections would take place in 1990 and legislative elections the following year. It was clear that these elections would take place in a quite different context from their predecessors. Not only was there to be a range of political choices but also the army was now no longer a formal part of the political process, while the FLN would become merely one party amongst others. It seemed as if Algeria had managed the seemingly impossible by rapidly transforming a rigidly controlled political system into one of the freest in the Arab world. Unfortunately, the future was not to prove to be so rosy, mainly because of the regime's determination to distance itself from the FLN and to use the FIS to achieve this end.

In reality, it was not so much a question of the regime distancing itself from the FLN as such, but rather of isolating those figures within the FLN which were opposed to its policies. One of the surprising features of the slogans which accompanied the riots had been the fact that, although the FLN itself might have been discredited as a political movement, the Boumédienne era and the values attached to it were not. Indeed, it could be argued that it had really been the Chadli Ben Djedid regime which had been the major target of the rioters and that the FLN was contaminated by association with it. In effect, it was the regime itself which, in the wake of riots, threw the blame for them on the FLN, in an attempt to divert popular anger. Even more tellingly, the regime did not abandon its economic liberalization programme after the riots, despite the fact that it had been responsible for much of the popular anger; indeed, it accelerated the programme in the name of the FLN from which the Government was still drawn.

The key to this strange pattern of behaviour—which was reinforced by senior government figures, including the president himself and his prime minister, Mouloud Hamrouche, warning of the growing popularity of the FIS and of the threat this offered to the role of the FLN in the future pluralist democracy being created in Algeria—lies within the internal structures of the FLN itself. For the riots had meant that, after them, all of the policies of the Chadli Ben Djedid regime were open to intense questioning within the FLN itself by those opposed to the regime and its policies. In November 1989, an extraordinary party congress brought back into power a series of figures from the Boumédienne era, untainted by the compromises and corruption of the previous decade. It also brought back other figures who had even stood aside from the Boumédienne era as well. Thus the Chadli regime stood accused by the personalities it had marginalized within the FLN but who represented the essence of the 'historic FLN' which had been progressively sidelined for the previous decade at least. As a result, in associating the FLN as closely as possible with economic policies that were intensely unpopular and talking up the electoral danger that the Islamist movement represented, the Chadli regime sought an electoral situation in which the FLN would be neutralized by the success of the FIS and in which the presidency would be able to dominate both as the sole arbiter of power.

The one mistake the regime made, however, was to underestimate the very widespread popular support, particularly amongst the urban poor, that the new Islamist movement, now a legalized political party, actually enjoyed. The result was that, in the municipal elections which took place in June 1990, the FIS won a crushing victory, completely humiliating the FLN in the process. The FIS won control of 856 of the 1,541 communes in the country and of 31 of the 48 provincial assemblies with 55% of the vote (4,331,472 votes). The FLN, in contrast, won control of only 487 communes and 14 provincial assemblies with 32% of the vote. Most of the other political parties, except for the RCD—which won control of 87 municipalities—boycotted the elections.

Surprisingly, in view of unexpectedly complete FIS success, the regime allowed the same thing to happen 18 months later! It was not simply a question of popular support for the FIS itself, as a detailed examination of the electoral statistics shows. It has been argued that this second success occurred largely because the nationalist wing of the FLN, having been humiliated by the regime in the municipal elections, stood aside in December 1991 when the legislative elections took place, thus ensuring an even greater FLN humiliation and the collapse of the regime's strategy for creating itself as the executive cornerstone of the new political system.

Yet, even if this is the case—and there is strong circumstantial evidence to suggest that it is—a further question arises. Why did the army, which, despite its withdrawal from a formal political role in 1989, was still the guarantor of the constitution, not intervene earlier? In fact it did, for in June 1991, just after successful FIS demonstrations against a new electoral law produced by the Hamrouche Government which loaded the electoral dice against it, the army suddenly moved against the FIS-controlled communes and arrested the two paramount FIS leaders, Abbassi Madani and Ali Bel Hadj. However, once this had occurred, and once the president had been obliged to dismiss his prime minister who had been closely identified with the liberal economic reform programme, the army went no further, not even demanding the banning of the FIS as a movement which had transgressed the electoral law.

This is a mystery which has never been properly explained, for the army then waited a further six months before it decisively moved against the regime and forced a change. And there is evidence to show that it was prepared to go further in June 1991, for there were persistent and well-informed rumours in Algiers that an army-backed regime was to be created with the president being replaced by the sole remaining significant *chef historique* Mohamed Boudiaf, who, after participating in the 1964 rebellion in

Kabylia, had gone into exile in Morocco. The answer appears to be that the army leadership was persuaded that the FIS victory in 1990 would not be repeated and that the president's strategy would work successfully. It did, however, insist that two leading members of the military hierarchy, Khalid Nezzar and Larbi Belkhair, should enter the Government in the defence and interior portfolios respectively. An alternative explanation is that the army leadership also wanted to demonstrate to foreign opinion that the Chadli regime was not capable of controlling the political situation and that, as a result, it had to be removed. In other words, the period between June 1991 and January 1992 was meant to demonstrate the vital necessity of what actually occurred—an army-backed coup to ensure the integrity of the state against the threat of an Islamist take-over caused by the incompetence of the regime.

As suggested above, there is also evidence to show that the FLN leadership opposed to the Chadli regime—those who embodied both the legacy of the Boumédienne era and of the 'historic FLN'—stood aside from the legislative electoral process after their humiliation in the municipal elections. Indeed, there is no other way in which the staggering drop in the FLN vote by 633,851 votes—from 17.49% of the electorate in June 1990 to 12.17% in December 1991—can be explained. The FIS did not pick up these voters, for its own level of electoral support dropped by over one million votes between the two elections, while the percentage of the electorate which voted for it fell from 55 to 47.5. Nor does the fact that other political parties participated alter this picture because, on the Islamist side, Hamas and Nahda only garnered just over 500,000 votes, while, as far as the secular parties—the FFS and the MDA—were concerned, they only won 647,000 votes between them, the majority of these coming from constituencies which had boycotted the previous elections. Finally, the number of spoiled ballot papers rose from just under 400,000 to over one million between the two electoral cycles.

Furthermore, the FIS's surprisingly complete victory in the first round of the legislative elections in December 1991—it won 188 of the 232 seats won outright and was well-placed to capture the majority of the remaining 198 seats on the second round of voting—was based on the positive votes of only 24.59% of the electorate (compared with 33.72% in June 1990). Thus the final result would not have reflected the political balance inside Algeria as a whole, especially since only 58.2% of the electorate actually turned out to vote (compared with around 65% in June 1990). In addition, around 900,000 persons were disenfranchised because their voting registration papers were never delivered, a further one million were estimated to have been prevented from voting by FIS election officials—control of the voting stations was in municipal hands—and the results in 145 seats were contested on the grounds of electoral fraud. In short, the legislative electoral process was profoundly unsatisfactory, although it certainly demonstrated the point that the army apparently wanted to make. The coup which followed was, therefore, inevitable because, as far as the army was concerned, the Chadli Ben Djedid regime had been shown to be demonstrably incompetent at being able to control the genie it had itself unleashed.

The FIS

The FIS was not, however, merely a creation of the Chadli Ben Djedid regime. It was a genuinely popular mass movement which captured support both from convinced Islamists and from the vast mass of the urban and, to a lesser extent, rural poor who felt that official Algeria had simply forgotten them. It was able to do this because it embodied both the Islamist tradition which had become an active, even if clandestine, element of the Algerian political scene by the end of the 1980s and the ideological mainstream of the Algerian revolution which had been part of the legacy of the 'historic FLN' and had reappeared during the Boumédienne era but which had been so singularly lacking from the Chadli Ben Djedid regime. In addition, its paramount leader, Abbassi Madani, embodied both traditions, having been one of the original members of the FLN who launched the

revolution on 1 November 1954 and having been prominent in the Islamist movement throughout the 1980s.

The new party clearly espoused the typical demands of the Algerian Islamist movement from the time of Bin Badis onwards: the championing of cultural authenticity in the sense of organizing public life in accordance with Algerian social and cultural tradition, itself profoundly conditioned by Islam; the control of public morality (hisba); and the condemnation of corruption in government and its replacement by *shura* and *shari'a* law. Its platform also included additional elements, however: the tacit acceptance of the policy of economic liberalism put forward by the Chadli Ben Djedid regime, as opposed to socialism; and a determination to create an Islamic state in Algeria, as opposed to the single party rule of the FLN or the concept of a multi-party democracy. Most importantly in terms of its electoral appeal, however, it also espoused, indeed, incorporated into its own programme, the essential concepts of Algerian nationalism: opposition to France and French influence in Algeria; anti-imperialism and pan-Arabism (as it demonstrated during the Iraqi invasion of Kuwait when the movement unequivocally supported Iraq against the multinational coalition). Finally, it also explicitly contrasted the 'historic FLN' with the FLN's behaviour after 1962, to the detriment of the latter. In effect, it portrayed itself as the legitimate inheritor of the principles and objectives of the originale historic FLN'—a vitally important point in its search for popular support, for the memory of the war for independence is still vivid amongst all social groups in Algeria.

In addition to these new elements in its ideological platform which distinguished it from the mainstream Islamist movements, the FIS also acted in ways which underlined the distinctions. Its political programme, published in April 1990, emphasized the political content over the purely Islamist aspects. Indeed, two-thirds of the platform was concerned with political considerations and that portion which dealt with Islam, unlike the political portion, was bland and predictable. The FIS's political rhetoric was also always highly intolerant, particularly towards the FLN and, surprisingly enough, towards other elements of the Islamist movement which were not associated with it. There was clearly no intention to share power, once it was achieved, even with those who could be construed to be the FIS's ideological companions. The intolerance was also directed against any hint of government or army intervention in the political process and, finally, rejected any idea of preserving democracy once it came to power. The FIS objective, in public statements at least, was an Islamic state. Yet, it was also clear that the paramount leader of the FIS, Abbassi Madani, was quite prepared to moderate the FIS message towards government and the democratic system, at least, in his own public statements. In effect, the primary objective of the FIS was to replace the FLN as the embodiment of the true principles of the Algerian revolution, to capture the popular mandate and to become the accepted partner to the presidency in power.

Seen in this light, then, the FIS was a rather different animal from a straightforward Islamist party. It was, in reality, an evolution from within the Algerian political tradition, in which an Islamist rhetoric had become the preferred mode of expression. This is not to suggest, however, that its Islamist objectives were not real, they certainly were—the movement was, after all, pledged to replace popular sovereignty by divine sovereignty as the basis of governmental legitimacy—but they formed only part of a much more complex political agenda. Indeed, when the organizational make-up of the movement is considered, this aspect of the movement becomes even clearer.

By the time of the municipal elections in June 1990, the FIS had created a five-level national organization. At the national level was the *Bureau Executif National* or *Majlis ash-Shura* to which were linked five commissions responsible for organization, education, social affairs, planning and information. This structure was replicated at the provincial (*wilaya*) level and at the communal (*communes*) level. Within each *commune*, a number of mosques were grouped together to form the fourth level and, around each mosque, were gathered a number of neighbourhoods (*quartiers*). In each neighbourhood was the fifth organizational level, the *comité de quartier*. Authority was delegated down the chain of command and, at its apex, above the *Majlis ash-Shura* stood the paramount leadership—Abbassi Madani and Ali Bel Hadj, with Abbassi Madani as the senior figure. When both leaders were arrested in June 1991, Abbassi Madani selected his own successor: Abdelkader Harchani, a former petroleum engineer.

Despite this tight organizational structure, the actual make-up of the FIS was far more heterogeneous, for it brought together a series of different groups in a political coalition. Its political programme was, therefore, also designed to bridge the gaps between the groups and, once the organizational structure collapsed, as it did after the movement was banned in 1992, neither the political programme nor the cohesion of the FIS survived for long in clandestinity. The three components, each of which contained its own extremists and moderates, were:-

(1) One important component was clearly derived from the *salafiyyist* traditions of Bin Badis and his supporters. This included the paramount leadership, as far as their Islamist credentials were concerned, as well as the first leader of the FIS in clandestinity, Mohammed Said.

(2) The second component was made up by *Djeza'ara Group* (the Islamic Association for Civilisation Development) which represented a group of Islamic nationalists, seeking an Islamic solution for Algeria alone, not for the Islamic world as a whole as was the case with the *Salafiyyists*. A leading representative of this group was the second paramount leader of the FIS, Abdelkader Harchani.

(3) The third strand comprised the so-called *Afghanists*, Algerian Islamists who had served with the *Mujahidin* in Afghanistan during the war against the Soviet Union there. It also included personalities such as Abdelwahab Mughni, the successor imam of the As-Sunna mosque in Bab al-Oued after Ali Bel Hadj, the original imam, had been arrested. Significantly, he had also been a close associate of Mustapha Bouyali and had spent four-and-a-half years in prison as a result. This group was predisposed to violent resistance to established authority and lies at the origins of the *Groupe Islamique Armé* (GIA), which has been responsible for many of the more provocative assassinations since 1992.

This, then, was the movement which formed the major challenge to the tradition of government in Algeria up to January 1992 and the movement which the Chadli Ben Djedid regime attempted to co-opt in order to force the FLN out of its paramount position after the October 1988 riots. The regime, of course, miscalculated by underestimating the very wide degree of genuine popular support which the FIS enjoyed. It, in turn, was therefore elbowed aside by the Algerian army when it proved incapable of controlling the situation it had unleashed. The stage was thus set for a far more difficult confrontation: that between a new army-backed regime and an Islamist movement which, although beheaded, nonetheless was able to spring up, hydra-like, and threaten the very survival of the state which the FLN had originally created.

The aftermath of the coup

The army did not move immediately against President Chadli Ben Djedid in the wake of the first round of the legislative elections on 26 December 1991. Several incidents precipitated its intervention, however. Firstly, the other Islamist parties—Hamas, Nahda and Umma—declared for the FIS in the second round, thus removing themselves from the contest. Secondly, the secular parties which had not obtained any seats (the FFS had won 25 seats, mainly in Kabylia, while the FLN had won 15 and independent candidates had won a further three seats) did not, as expected, declare for the FLN, thus making sure that its vote would be split in the second round. Thirdly, and most

importantly, Chadli Ben Djedid stated that he would continue to act as president—he had resigned from the FLN the previous July to maintain his posture as being above party politics—even if the FIS won an outright majority of the seats, in an arrangement which he described, with a fateful echo of French politics in the mid-1980s, as 'cohabitation'.

The FIS, however, made it clear that it did not agree, for it now realized that its absolute majority would allow it to act independently of the other political parties and that it no longer needed to collaborate with the presidency. In consequence, it called for immediate presidential elections—not due under the constitution until December 1993—and the appointment of Abbassi Madani as premier. It was clear that, if the elections went ahead, the FIS might well win two-thirds of the seats in the Assembly. If there were then presidential elections, the FIS would undoubtedly win them. Then, since the constitution provided for constitutional change to be initiated by the president and to be approved by a two-thirds majority of the Assembly, the FIS would be able to make whatever constitutional changes it wished. And its spokesmen had made it plain that the movement sought an Islamic state and an end to multi-party democracy! Of course, if Chadli Ben Djedid remained in office despite a FIS victory, then this programme would be delayed, so the FIS offered to accept his continuation in office, provided that the Minister of Defence, General Khalid Nezzar, and the Minister of the Interior, General Larbi Belkhair, were dismissed. Unfortunately, both were leading members of the army high command and the army was determined not to be sidelined in what it construed to be a critical moment, given its constitutional obligation to 'safeguard national independence and sovereignty' and its responsibility before constitutional amendment in 1989 to protect the constitution as well. It also had support from the middle ranks of the officer corps, as a result of a petition condemning the FIS signed by 181 officers of the rank of colonel.

As a result, the president was forced to prorogue the National Assembly on 4 January 1992 and on 11 January 1992, just five days before the second round of the elections was due, Chadli Ben Djedid resigned his office as a result of massive army pressure. Because the National Assembly had already been prorogued, the normal provision for a forty-five day period in which presidential power would be held by the president of the Assembly before new presidential elections would be held did not apply. Instead, the High Security Council, as provided for in the Algerian Constitution to advise an incumbent president on security matters and consisting of the defence and interior ministers, together with a third military figure, the army chief-of-staff, General Abdelmalek Guennaizia, and the premier, Sid Ahmed Ghozali, the justice minister, Hamdan Ben Khelil, and the foreign minister, Lakhdar Brahimi, was called upon to replace it in this function, although this was not the purpose defined for the Council in the Constitution—a fact which led many Algerian politicians to accuse it of acting unconstitutionally. The Council, in turn, appointed a collegiate presidency, the High State Council (HSC) to act for the remainder of the original presidential term. The HSC was made up of Khalid Nezzar, by now identified as the real military power behind the presidency; Ali Kafi, the powerful head of the Organization of Mujahidin (veterans of the war of independence); Ali Haroun, the minister for human rights; Sheikh Tejini Haddam, the rector of the Paris mosque; and, most important of all, Mohamed Boudiaf, now returned from Morocco, as chairman. Thus, the army plan of June 1991 was finally completed. The membership of the HSC had clearly been chosen in an attempt to persuade Algerians of its impartiality. Unfortunately, not one political party accepted that it was constitutionally sound and, for the vast mass of the population, the interruption of the electoral process was clear evidence of the heavy hand of the army, however well-concealed it was by constitutional niceties.

The reality of power was soon demonstrated as violence flared a week later and the authorities accused the FIS leadership of attempting to suborn the loyalty of the armed forces. During February the FIS came under ever greater official pressure, with its members being arrested, its mosques occupied and its offices closed. On 9 February a state of emergency was announced and, within one week, at least 6,000 persons were being held in detention camps in the Sahara. By the middle of the month, amidst pleas for dialogue, the FIS announced that at least 150 people had already died in clashes with the military—figures which were disputed by the authorities who, at the end of March announced that there had been 103 deaths, 31 of them amongst the security forces, and that 9,000 people were now being held, including the FIS paramount leader, Abdelkader Harchani. This was of little interest to the FIS because, by that time, the movement had been banned after a court judgement authorizing such government action had been issued on 4 March 1992.

The assassination of Mohamed Boudiaf

The inclusion of Mohamed Boudiaf within the HSC was clearly an attempt by the new army-backed regime—in which Khalid Nezzar and Larbi Belkhair were the dominant figures—to create a sense of legitimacy for itself despite the unorthodox and unconstitutional way it had come to power. Boudiaf was one of the few remaining public figures from the 'historic FLN' period who, furthermore, was not contaminated by the compromises and concessions forced upon Algeria's revolutionary heritage by the past three decades of independence. His departure into exile after the abortive 1964 rebellion led by Hoceine Ait Ahmed and his refusal to compromise with subsequent regimes meant that he could still be seen to embody the original principles and aspirations of the revolution. Although 75% of the modern Algerian population knew little of him, having been born after the war, he still retained a massive reputation.

There is little doubt that Boudiaf knew the dangers of the course upon which he had embarked. He was aware of the antagonism towards the HSC because of the interrupted elections and he certainly appreciated the catastrophic economic situation facing the country. According to the premier's report on the economy in late February 1992, 1.5m. people were unemployed, industry was operating at half its capacity because of the shortage of spare parts and essential imported inputs and Algeria had to import $2,000m.-worth of food annually. The massive foreign debt continued to grow and debt servicing absorbed ever greater proportions of the country's foreign exchange earning, with the debt service ratio reaching 78% in 1992, when debt servicing cost $7,000m., and a projected 82% the following year. Even though $1,500m.-worth of debt was 'reprofiled' in 1992, it was clear that rescheduling would eventually become inevitable, although the Government still tried to resist this. However, IMF aid would be inevitable and, as a precursor to this, consumer subsidies, which on foodstuffs alone had cost Algeria $2,400m. in 1991, were reduced dramatically in March, with the result that there were massive price rises for foodstuffs which doubled in some cases. Remaining subsidies were removed in July, a saving said to total $500m. in a full year.

Boudiaf rejected the aspirations of the FIS which he condemned as being a distortion of Islam. As a pious Muslim himself, however, he did not wish to exclude Islamists from the political process, provided that they observed the political pluralism which the HSC under his leadership wished to recreate. He publicly promised that the electoral process would be renewed, once the situation had calmed down. In these objectives he enjoyed the support of the HSC. However, other aspects of his agenda occasioned considerable alarm. Boudiaf accepted that one of the major problems in achieving political credibility lay in the fact that the Chadli Ben Djedid regime was widely perceived to have been corrupt. During the electoral campaign, a former prime minister, Abdulhamid Brahimi, created a massive stir in public opinion when he publicly claimed that up to $26,000m. had been embezzled from the state during its period of office. Despite attempts to prevent Mohamed Boudiaf from addressing this issue, he ensured that at least one senior army officer, Mustafa Beloucif, was put on trial for embezzlement.

Boudiaf, in short, refused to accept the role planned for him by the army leadership: that of figurehead whose reputation would legitimize the HSC and the regime. Nor was he satisfied with the cosmetic measures taken by the regime to create a sense of popular participation, so he created a 60-member National Consultative Council in April 1992. When the political parties stood aloof from this initiative, he also decided to appeal above their heads and that of the regime for popular support by creating a new mass political movement, the *Rassemblement Patriotique National* despite their protests. He also authorized the release of up to 2,000 detainees, as a measure of conciliation. On the other hand, at the same time the military authorities continued with their policy of suppression which provoked the growing clandestine Islamist opposition to threaten *jihad*. By May, up to 400 people had died. The following month, Abbassi Madani and Ali Bel Hadj were tried before a military court in Blida, to be sentenced several weeks later to long prison terms—relatively lenient sentences in view of the fact that the military had clearly wanted them to be executed, a fact that suggested that eventual negotiations with them had not been ruled out.

There was little doubt that the independent policy line that Mohamed Boudiaf was creating was profoundly worrying for the army, particularly his emphasis on rooting out corruption. It threatened the remnants of the old regime now out of power, reaching even as high as the former president himself. It threatened those still in power who had an investment in the existing system. In short it threatened all those who had gained personal advantage from their positions, a shadowy but widespread group which had earned the sobriquet of the mafia in popular parlance. It was a group which was also linked in the popular mind with that other shadowy but real element of the Algerian power structure, the *hizb fransa*. Leading elements of the regime, including much of the army high command, persons such as Khalid Nezzar and Larbi Belkhair, were believed to maintain close links to France and were therefore seen as being part of the *hizb fransa*. Boudiaf's attempt to create the same type of popular consensus as had existed under the original FLN was deeply repugnant to many of them.

As a result, when Boudiaf was assassinated in Annaba on 29 June 1992, popular suspicion immediately fell on the mafia and its associate, the *hizb fransa*. Although one of the guard detail was almost immediately arrested for the offence and was later claimed to have been acting alone on behalf of the FIS, virtually nobody, including Boudiaf's family, believed the official account. Instead he was seen as a martyr to the corrupt interests of the mafia within the ruling group, with Larbi Belkhair, as interior minister, being held directly liable for the crime in the popular mind. For many, his death marked the end of all possibility of a genuine resolution of the crisis before violence became the rule. Not even his replacement by Ali Kafi as chairman of the HSC, with concomitant changes in the Government, where Sid Ahmed Ghozali was replaced by the former minister for energy and heavy industry under the Boumédienne regime, Belaid Abdessalam, restored public confidence. The vacant place on the HSC was filled by a former ambassador, Rehda Malek and, as a sop to public opinion, Larbi Belkhair retired from active political life, although his influence behind the scenes continued to be felt.

The Belaid Abdessalam interregnum

In many respects, the army's choice of Belaid Abdessalam was astute, for he was drawn from the same mould as Mohamed Boudiaf. He had also been an early member of the FLN and had been active in Algerian political life even earlier, as a member of the Messalist movement. Unlike Boudiaf, however, he had remained in Algeria, coming to prominence under the Boumédienne regime but being pushed into the background under its successor. He had opposed the liberalization policies of the radical technocrats under Miloud Hamrouche and represented precisely that aspect of the FLN which the president had tried to outmanoeuvre by building up the FIS. He was certainly not tainted by association with the corruption of Algerian public life and retained popular respect for his political and intellectual toughness which was associated with the Boumédienne era. He also enjoyed extended powers, for the HSC abandoned the practice of Mohamed Boudiaf of taking the leading role in government, allowing this to devolve back to the premier.

On coming into power, he also made it clear that he would not continue the policies of previous governments. Liberalization was to be put on hold, although the new premier did not intend to abandon the general tilt towards free market economics. He did intend to correct economic distortions, however, before allowing the reform programme to continue. His general approach was to be far more *dirigiste* and nationalist, with the economy being placed, in his own words, 'on a war footing'. The old policy of avoiding debt rescheduling was to be continued and Belaid Abdessalam also made it clear that he would not accept further devaluation of the currency which had already dropped by two-thirds in value against the dollar since 1989. This put him on an immediate collision course with the IMF which was determined that reform of the economy should proceed apace, whatever the social consequences. On the other hand, the new premier was determined to press ahead with the established policy of inviting in foreign investment, particularly in the oil sector where commitments of $4,200m. had already been made. Typically, however, Belaid Abdessalam warned that the maximum level of foreign holdings would be 49% of total equity, thus preserving Algerian economic sovereignty. At the same time, he made it clear that the new maximum limits outside the oil sector, where foreigners could control up to 63% of total equity, would remain unchanged.

In terms of the domestic security situation, Belaid Abdessalam also initiated a new policy based on an attempt to stamp out the growing violence. It had by now become clear that several different organizations were involved in the casual killings that had come to punctuate Algerian daily life.

(1) Some were certainly being carried out by the clandestine 'Afghaniste' cells which had been reluctantly part of the FIS but which had never really accepted its objective of political power through an open mass movement. They were particularly strong around the Algiers region. In the summer of 1993 these eventually linked together into the *Groupe Islamique Armé* (GIA) and developed a power base within the eastern suburbs of the capital and amongst the impoverished peasantry of the Algerois—the plains stretching south from Algiers down towards Medea and Blida. The original GIA then linked up with two other groups around Sidi Bel Abbès in the west and Jijel on the edge of Petite Kabylie to the east. It was founded by Abdelkader Layada, who fled to Morocco but who was eventually repatriated to Algeria. He was succeeded by Mourad Si Ahmed, better known by his nickname of Djafaar al-Afghani, who was killed with nine of his lieutenants in a shoot-out with the police in Algiers in February 1993. He was, in turn, replaced by Ahmed Abu Abdallah. There were rumours that these killings were carried out by the security services at moments when the GIA seemed likely to escape from their control (see below) and ally with the MIA.

(2) At the same time, a wider and better organized armed and clandestine movement directly linked to the FIS and derived from the old Bouyali group developed, the *Mouvement Islamique Armé* (MIA). It was led by Abdelkader Chebouti and Said Mekhloufi, the former originally a close associate of Mustafa Bouyali and the latter an army officer who had deserted. Unlike their counterparts on the GIA, the leadership of the MIA has so far avoided the regime's success in eliminating its leading members. The movement became particularly strong in the Oranais, the area stretching eastwards from the western city of Oran, and in the hinterland behind Kabylia. It was, however, present throughout the country except in the immediate hinterland of the capital. Strikingly, there was little clandestine resistance in Kabylia itself.

(3) There was evidence, however, that many of the more spectacular assassinations were linked to the macabre activities of the security services, particularly those linked with military security which was popularly assumed to have links with the shadowy mafia. Military security was also believed to have penetrated the GIA (see above) and to have been able to manipulate the movement sufficiently for some of its terrorist actions to have served regime, rather than Islamist, ends.

(4) Many other killings were simply the settling of old scores as law and order progressively broke down. They often involved local groups who, apart from revenge, were often more interested in crime and used an Islamist rhetoric to disguise their objectives.

One of the major problems for the regime was that the forces available to the state to contain the intensifying terrorism were very limited. Half of the 120,000-strong army was made up of conscripts who were not considered reliable for security operations, particularly after several spectacularly successful guerrilla operations against them. Otherwise there were only 80,000 paramilitary units, including the police, the gendarmerie, the anti-riot squads and the sinister special units who rapidly became known as the *ninja* because of their black uniforms.

Nonetheless, in October 1992, a new security policy was announced under which, after a three-month amnesty period, new and more draconian security laws would be introduced, together with special military courts. It replaced an earlier proposal to shut down the Saharan detention camps and indicated a hardening of the security line in the wake of the bombing of Algiers airport in August 1992. It reflected the strength of '*la toute sécuritaire*' within the army and the administration; the concept that terrorism had to be rooted out at all costs and that no compromise could be made with the FIS or its violent offshoots. This policy enjoyed a degree of popular support—from urban communities, the technocratic élite and the francophone community and women's groups, as well as much of the Berber population who had been labelled as 'non-Muslim' by certain FIS spokesmen. However, the vast impoverished urban poor and the peasantry were increasingly cajoled and coerced into the Islamist camp. And, against that background of mass support, the regime could do little except use crude techniques of mass repression which dramatically increased popular resentment—and support for the FIS. Belaid Abdessalam, who certainly realized that simple repression would fail and that some kind of dialogue was essential, had little option but to agree with the demand for improved security before any kind of negotiation could be opened. Nonetheless, within the year, he was warning of the impossibility of excluding Islam from the eventual political settlement, even if it were not to be articulated by the FIS or its violent offshoots. Indeed, this was always his ultimate political programme.

The underlying problem for the army-backed regime was that its policy approach was trapped in a major contradiction. On the one hand, it sought to persuade Algerians that it was seeking to recreate the political aura of the 'historic FLN' and the Boumédienne era as a means of rallying popular support for its policies of a controlled return to democracy and of economic revival. In this connection, personalities such as Mohamed Boudiaf and Belaid Abdessalam played a crucial role in providing the sense of revolutionary legitimacy and continuity. On the other hand, it sought to crush and delegitimize its opposition through repression which was increasingly general in its effects and thus vitiated its own efforts to seek popular acceptance. Indeed, whenever there was a choice between dialogue or repression, it seemed that repression was the preferred option for the state. Thus, the attempts by both Boudiaf and Belaid Abdessalam to recreate consensus around the old values of the Algerian revolution were rendered irrelevant by the demands of the security apparatus.

Behind this was a further and more profound contradiction within the army leadership and its civilian supporters. This reflected the opposed views of those who wished to exterminate the Islamist influence in Algeria, or rather wished to discipline it to fit into an agenda dominated by the regime—the '*eradicateurs*'—and those who recognized that this was not possible and that dialogue and compromise were the only means by which the political crisis could be resolved—the '*conciliateurs*'.

(1) The hardliners tended to be supported by the secularist urban middle class which, in turn, tended to be part of the francophone Algerian community—and thus distrusted by the bulk of the population which was Arabophone and thus favourably predisposed towards the FIS's objectives. Outside the army, the formal political support for this hardline tendency was very limited—the Algerian trade union movement, the smaller of the two Berberist parties, the RCD, and the communists of the *Ettihadi* movement. An unwanted source of support, of course, came from the mafia and the *hizb fransa* both of which could and would not accept the Islamist agenda or any compromise with it.

(2) The moderates who sought compromise had little formal support within the army. They did, however, have the support of all the major political parties which had long since recognized that compromise was essential. The FIS, particularly its violent offshoots which now dominated the political scene inside Algeria, however, saw little need to compromise with them. The moderates, therefore, had little concrete to offer by way of new and viable policies against the dangerous simplicities of the hardliners.

In fact, the FIS itself was undergoing a profound transformation. Once it had been banned and dismantled by the regime in early 1992, the original movement had neither an organization, nor, indeed, a role. The armed clandestine opposition movements inside Algeria seized its original role of opposing the state, with even the MIA acting with a degree of autonomy. The FIS itself was confined increasingly into the role of becoming an exile support group to these movements, in an eerie echo of what had happened to the FLN during the Algerian war of independence. Thus, the FIS spokesmen abroad—Anouar Haddam in the USA, Rabih Kebir in Germany and Mustafa Krouach in France—increasingly tried to influence Western public opinion, rather than to control the activities of the movement inside Algeria. The paramount influence of Abbassi Madani and Ali Bel Hadj continued to shadow the movement, but the longer they remained outside the formal political arena, the more their potential for undertaking the eventual negotiations diminished.

The other major foreign influence, which had a profound effect on the policies of the regime, was France. French links with Algeria since the war of independence had been complex and tortuous and, during the Chadli Ben Djedid regime had grown closer. The Francophone component of Algeria had cultural and, often, socio-political links with France and, as the economic liberalization programme progressed, intensifying professional links as well. Indeed, this growing French influence within Algeria had been one of the major criticisms levelled by the FIS against the regime. After the coup, despite official French anger at the interruption of the democratic process, support for the Francophone Algerian community continued. Much of the official anger in Paris about the coup was really directed against the fact that one of the apparent objectives of the coup organizers was to recreate precisely that sense of popular sovereignty and consensus that was seen in France as inimical to French interests and redolent of the attitudes of the Boumédienne era. The socialist government in France, therefore, was able to refuse the financial aid Algeria requested until the democratic system was restored as a means of undermining the recreation of the revolutionary ideal. The socialist government in France thus became, wittingly or unwittingly (and there was evidence of close collaboration between the French and

Algerian security services) an ally of the '*eradicateurs*' in Algeria. Despite its public stance in favour of dialogue and the restitution of the democratic process, in reality its dislike of the Boudiaf and Abdessalam options forced it to support the hardline Francophone elements in the regime.

It was only with the legislative elections in France in March 1993 and the appearance of a conservative government there that this contradiction disappeared. Now France openly called for the suppression of the clandestine Islamist movements and offered financial support to the embattled regime while encouraging the removal of Belaid Abdessalam from power as well. The new French interior minister, Charles Pasqua, in response to the kidnapping of several members of the French embassy in Algiers—who were later released unharmed—clamped down on FIS fund-raising activities in France, in a show of strength over the influence of Islamic fundamentalism in Europe, while open support was given to the regime's increasingly harsh policies of repression. It was only at the beginning of 1994 that France reluctantly accepted the need for dialogue between government and Islamists if the crisis in Algeria were ever to be satisfactorily solved. Even here, this was predicated on the construction of a Francophone consensus within Algeria which would protect French interests while satisfying the FIS's desire to participate in the formal political process. One of the major influences in producing this slight change of heart was that the USA, as part of its new policy towards political Islam—the USA had no fundamental objection to Islamic governments and was quite prepared to enjoy normal relations with them; it would not, however, countenance violence or terrorism within the political process—now began gently to pressure the Algerian Government to expand its efforts at finding a negotiated solution to the crisis.

It was quite clear, once the new Government had come to power in Algeria, that the Belaid Abdessalam Government only had a limited future. Abdessalam did not enjoy French support and French hostility only increased the strength of the '*eradicateurs*' within the regime who were in any case opposed to him. In early July 1993, in a move which presaged an increase in their influence within the regime, Khalid Nezzar gave up the defence portfolio on the grounds of illness. However, he, together with Larbi Belkhair, retained control of the crucial levers of power. His replacement was a man who, on the face of it, appeared to strengthen the hand of the moderates. Lamine Zeroual had been an army general who had left the service in a dispute with the president in 1989 about the future organization of the armed forces. He had then served briefly as a diplomat before retiring. His return to the political arena brought back someone with no connections with the Francophone community or with France, someone who, furthermore, had impeccable revolutionary credentials, having joined the FLN in 1957. He therefore seemed like an admirable foil for the premier. However, a price was paid for his appointment, in that five days later, the army chief-of-staff, Abdelmalek Guennaizia, was replaced. His replacement, Mohamed Lamari, had been in charge of the security operation and was a noted hardliner who was said to have originally been close to Larbi Belkhair. He was, in turn, replaced by another hardliner, Mohamed Mediene. Thus the position of the equally hardline interior minister, Selim Saadi, was significantly bolstered and the potential role of the new defence minister was undercut.

Indeed, by then the writing was on the wall for Belaid Abdessalam. His economic policies were not working and the security situation was deteriorating. The activities of the GIA in the capital were constantly intensifying with open attacks, first, on the security services, then on civil servants (in order to render the country ungovernable) and finally on Francophone intellectuals, a process dubbed '*intellocide*' by the French press and apparently intended by the GIA to underline the fact that there would be no room for the *hizb fransa* in the new Islamist Algeria it wished to create. Finally, the GIA warned foreigners to leave Algeria or face attack. Five weeks after Lamine Zeroual joined the Cabinet, Belaid Abdessalam resigned. The day after his resignation, a former premier and leader of the Movement for Justice and Democracy, Kasdi Merbah, was killed, apparently by the GIA, although popular opinion was quick to see the hand of the military security service behind his assassination. With his death, one of the last of the major voices urging negotiation and reconciliation was removed from the scene.

Zeroual comes to power

Belaid Abdessalam's replacement as premier was Redha Malek, a self-proclaimed modernist, who was quite prepared to support the hardline approach to security. His real function, however, was to renegotiate a standby agreement with the IMF as a preliminary step to rescheduling Algeria's massive $26,000m. foreign debt. This was achieved on 8 April 1994, and one day later the Algerian dinar underwent a massive devaluation—by 40.17%, according to the Banque d'Algérie, but by only 26.8% according to IMF sources. The day after Redha Malek resigned, to be replaced by a technocrat, Mokdad Sifti, whose real role was to carry out the policies of Algeria's new president, Lamine Zeroual.

The arrival of Lamine Zeroual to power marked the latest stage in the regime's search for a solution to the seemingly intractable crisis which now faces Algeria. It arose from the fact that the collegiate presidency, the HSC, had a term of office which expired at the end of December 1993. At the start of the year, the head of the HSC had promised that there would be a referendum on the future course for Algeria before the body's term of office came to an end, but, in the event, this proposal was quietly forgotten, as was another for a further interim three-year collegiate presidency. Instead, the HSC proposed a constitutional conference for January 1994 and unilaterally prolonged its own life by one month. The conference proposal also came to nothing, for virtually all the political parties boycotted it, including the FLN and the FFS, both of which rejected the idea because the FIS could not participate.

By this time it was evident that a single strong hand would be needed to restore coherence to government policy. Violence had escalated, despite the intensified security policy, and the regime was even more discredited than ever in the popular mind. Tensions between the secularist middle class and the remainder of the population had worsened. Government control of security had declined, with many rural areas being apparently quite outside governmental control and control elsewhere often being tenuous. The FIS's hold over the clandestine resistance movements had weakened, too, and the GIA and the MIA were at loggerheads. Indeed, in December 1993, 66 MIA militants had been killed by the GIA as a warning to the MIA leadership not to contemplate a negotiated solution. The GIA was determined, in fact, to pre-empt the Islamist movement's options and to force a violent solution to the crisis. The MIA, with the backing of the FIS leadership, whether in prison or abroad, was not prepared to submit and maintained its own policy of selective terror to force the Government to the negotiating table.

Indeed, it was by now obvious to everyone, even the hardliners, that some sort of negotiation would have to take place. The problem was to create a regime which could do this without giving the impression that it was capitulating to the FIS. It was in this context that the State Security Council, after considering other possibilities, such as the former foreign minister under President Boumédienne, Ahmed Boutaflika—the preferred option of the *hizb fransa*—or a former foreign minister under Chadli Ben Djedid, Taleb Ibrahimi, turned to Lamine Zeroual. After ensuring his military support base, Zeroual accepted the presidency on 1 February 1994 and immediately set about the process of constructing an administration and seeking opportunities for dialogue, as he signalled to all Algerians in his first speech as president.

In the event, constructing the administration proved to be the easier of the two issues. The removal of Redha Malek from the premiership, and with him Selim Saadi, was the first step. Then, in May President Zeroual reconstructed the army command, removing Francophone officers from their posts and replacing them with his own supporters, particu-

larly in the Blida, Oran and Constantine military regions. At the same time, he left the hardliners—Generals Lamari, Mediene and Touati (an aide to the ailing Khalid Nezzar who still retained overall control of the army)—in charge of security operations and bolstered them by appointing a former security head, Mohamed Betchine, as his personal adviser. It was clear that the new president was not going to imperil security, or, indeed, his own position *vis-à-vis* the hardliners, as part of his initiatives on dialogue.

Indeed, it could be argued that the hardliners continued to exert their stranglehold on the regime despite the widespread perception that there was an urgent need for dialogue between the Government and the FIS to begin. In fact, President Zeroual's moves towards dialogue turned out to be extremely cautious. Despite rumours during Ramadan in 1994 that Abbassi Madani and Ali Bel Hadj would become the president's partners in dialogue, they remained in Blida prison. Instead, two high-ranking FIS members, Aldi Djeddi and Abdelkader Boukhamkham, were released from prison with the specific mandate to investigate the possibilities for dialogue. It soon became clear that the FIS's preconditions for dialogue could not be met by government and, by mid-1994, the whole process seemed to have stalled and the president's initiative was slipping away.

By the beginning of July, the Islamist resistance movements—particularly the GIA—had also concluded that the dialogue process was not going to advance. Instead, the lull in killings and assassinations was abruptly shattered by a new wave of killings of foreigners, culminating in the disappearance of two Arab ambassadors (from Yemen and Oman) who were travelling together in the same car at Khemis al-Khechni. By now official statistics admitted that around 4,000 people had died since the beginning of the crisis—unofficial statistics suggest that the true figure was nearer 8,000—including more than 30 journalists and intellectuals and 47 foreigners. The regime continued to insist that the situation was improving, despite all the evidence, but popular enthusiasm for dialogue also began to ebb away. It was difficult to avoid the conclusion that President Zeroual, despite his personal standing and proclaimed belief in dialogue, had been defeated by the internal contradictions of the regime and the growing intransigence of the Islamist movements in Algeria.

It remained to be seen whether the president could eventually remove the remaining elements of the *hizb fransa* and the hardliners from the administration and continute an effective dialogue with the FIS leadership; and whether that leadership could control the violence. Yet, without dialogue, the future seemed extremely bleak. Indeed, it seemed that civil war could hardly be avoided in which the regime would face an intolerant and unforgiving Islamist resistance movement, whilst regional movements would develop in Kabylia and elsewhere. In essence, then, the fundamental assumption behind the Algerian state, that of popular national sovereignty, would have been torn up, to be replaced by a series of differing views of what Algeria should be which could only be reconciled by violence. Yet, for dialogue to succeed, the president is going to have to accept the FIS as negotiating partners on terms that it, too, can accept. That might restore a situation in which a pluralist democratic process could begin again, this time carefully controlled by the regime with FIS support. It is more likely, however, to produce an Islamist regime backed by the army which will not be notable for its tolerance. But time is short, for the FIS is ever less able to control what is happening inside Algeria. The outlook, in short, is grim, whatever option the president chooses.

Bibliography

Roberts, Hugh. *'From radical mission to equivocal ambition: the expansion and manipulation of Algerian Islamism 1979–1992'*, in Marty, M.E., Scot-Aplby, R. (Eds) *Accounting for Fundamentalism*. Chicago, Fundamentalism Project Volume IV

Roberts, Hugh. *Algeria between eradicators and conciliators*. MERIP Report, July–August 1994

THE RELIGIONS OF THE MIDDLE EAST AND NORTH AFRICA

Islam

R. B. SERJEANT

Islam is a major world religion and the faith predominating throughout the Middle East (with the exception of Israel) and North Africa. There are substantial Christian minorities in some countries (e.g. Lebanon) and communities of oriental Jews and other faiths, for centuries integrated with the Muslim majority. Islam is not only a highly developed religious system, but also an established and distinctive culture embracing every aspect of human activity from theology, philosophy and literature to the visual arts and even the individual's routine daily conduct. Its characteristic intellectual manifestation, therefore, is in the field of Islamic law, the *Shari'a*. Though in origin a Semitic Arabian faith, Islam was also the inheritor of the legacy of classical Greek and Roman civilization and, in its major phase of intellectual, social and cultural development after its emergence from its Arabian womb, it was affected by Christian, Jewish and Persian civilization. In turn, Greek scientific and philosophical writings—in the form of direct translations into Arabic or as a principal element in the books of Arab scholars—began to enter medieval Europe in Latin renderings about the early 12th century from the brilliant intellectual circles of Islamic Spain, and formed a potent factor in the little Renaissance of western Europe.

Islamic civilization had, by about the 18th century, clearly lost its initiative to the ascendant West and has not since regained it. Today, however, certain oil-rich Arab states, notably Saudi Arabia and Kuwait, have entered in a large way into the world of international finance and mercantilism, including the provision of Islamic banking services for which there has been an increase in demand over the last two decades.

HISTORY

The founder of the religion of Islam was the Prophet Muhammad b. 'Abdullah, born about AD 570, a member of the noble house of Hashim, belonging to the 'Abd Manaf clan, itself a part of the Quraish tribal confederation of Mecca. 'Abd Manaf may be described as semi-priestly since they had the privilege of certain functions during the annual pilgrimage to the Meccan Ka'ba, a cube-shaped temple set in the sacred enclave (*haram*). Quraish controlled this enclave which was maintained inviolate from war or killing, and they had established a pre-eminence and loose hegemony even, over many Arabian tribes which they had induced to enter a trading alliance extending over the main Arabian land routes, north and south, east and west. With the powerful Quraish leaders in Mecca, temple guardians, chiefs, merchant adventurers, Muhammad clashed, when, aged about 40, he began to proclaim the worship of one God, Allah, as against their multiplicity of gods. These Quraish leaders were contemptuous of his mission.

While his uncle Abu Talib, head of the house of Hashim, lived, he protected Muhammad from physical harm, but after his death Muhammad sought protection from tribes outside Mecca. However, even after asking to remain quietly without preaching, they would not accept him and Thaqif of Taif drove him roughly away. Ultimately pilgrims of the Aws and Khazraj tribes of Yathrib (Medina), some 200 miles north of Mecca, agreed to protect him there, undertaking to associate no other god with Allah and accepting certain moral stipulations. Muhammad left Mecca with his Companion Abu Bakr in the year 622—this is the year of the *hijra* or hegira.

Arriving in Yathrib, Muhammad formed a federation or community (*umma*) of Aws and Khazraj, known as the 'Supporters' (*Ansar*), followed by their Jewish client tribes, and the 'Emigrants' (*Muhajirun*), i.e. his refugee Quraish adherents, with himself as the ultimate arbiter of the *umma* as a whole, though there remained a local opposition covertly antagonistic to him, the *Munafiqun*, rendered as 'Hypocrites'. Two internal issues had now to be fought by Muhammad—the enforcement of his position as theocratic head of the federation, and the acquisition of revenue to maintain his position; externally he took an aggressive attitude to the Meccan Quraish.

In Yathrib his disposal of the Jewish tribes who made common cause with the 'Hypocrites' improved his financial position. The Meccan Quraish he overcame more by skilful political manoeuvre than through the occasional armed clashes with them, and in year 8 he entered Mecca without fighting. Previously he had declared Yathrib a sacred enclave (*haram*), renaming it Medina, the City (of the Prophet)—the two cities known as al-Haraman have become the holy land of Islam. Muhammad was conciliatory to his defeated Quraish kinsmen, and after his success against Taif, south of Mecca, deputations came from the Arabian tribes to make terms with the new prophet—the heritor of the influence of the Meccan Quraish.

Early Islam

The two main tenets of Islam are embodied in the formula of the creed, 'There is no god but Allah and Muhammad is the Apostle of God'. Unitarianism (*tawhid*), as opposed to polytheism (*shirk*) or making partners with God, is Islam's basic principle, coupled with Muhammad's authority conferred on him by God. Muhammad made little change to the ancient Arabian religion—he abolished idolatry but confirmed the pilgrimage to the Ka'ba; the Koran, the sacred Book in Arabic revealed to Muhammad for his people, lays down certain social and moral rules. Among these are the condemnation of usury or interest (*riba*) on loans and the prohibition of wine (*khamr*)—both ordinances have always been difficult to enforce. On the whole the little change involved seems to have made it easy for Arabia to accept Islam. While there is incontrovertible evidence of Muhammad's contact with Judaism, and even with Christianity, and the Koran contains versions of narrative known to the sacred books of these faiths, yet these are used to point purely Arabian morals. The limited social law laid down by the Koran is supplemented by a body of law and precept derived from the *Hadith* or Tradition of Muhammad's practice (*Sunna*) at Medina, and welded into the Islamic system, mainly in its second and third centuries.

Subsequent History

Immediately after Muhammad's death in 632, Abu Bakr, delegated by him to lead the prayer during his last indisposition, became his successor or Caliph. Some Medinan 'Supporters' had attempted a breakaway from Quraish overlordship but Abu Bakr adroitly persuaded them to accept himself to follow Muhammad. Office in Arabia, generally speaking, is hereditary within a family group, though elective within that group, and Abu Bakr's action had taken no account of the claims of 'Ali, the Prophet's cousin and son-in-law. The house of Hashim to which Muhammad and 'Ali belonged was plainly aggrieved that a member of a minor Quraish clan, not of the 'house' (Bait) of their ancestor, Qusaiy, the holder of religious offices in Mecca, which he bequeathed to his descendants, should have snatched supreme power. Muhammad's Arabian coalition also showed tendencies to disintegrate, the tribes particularly objecting to paying taxes to Medina, but Abu Bakr's firm line held it together. The expansionist thrusts beyond Arabia during his Caliphate, continuing under his successor 'Umar and for part of the reign of the third Caliph, 'Uthman, diverted tribal energies to profitable warfare in Mesopotamia, Palestine-Syria, Egypt and Persia. Muslim armies were eventually to conquer North Africa, much of Spain, parts of France, and even besiege Rome, while in the east they later penetrated to Central Asia and India.

During 'Uthman's tenure of office the tide of conquest temporarily slackened and the turbulent tribes, now settled in southern Iraq and Egypt, began to dispute the Caliph's disposal of booty and revenue, maintaining that he unduly favoured members of his own house. A delegation of tribal malcontents from Egypt murdered 'Uthman in the holy city of Medina, and in the resultant confusion 'Ali, Muhammad's cousin, was elected Caliph with the support of the tribesmen responsible for murdering 'Uthman. This raised grave constitutional problems for the young Muslim state, and is regarded as the origin of the first and greatest schism in Islam.

If legitimist arguments were the sole consideration 'Ali's claims to succession seem the best, but he had previously lost it to 'Uthman—whose father belonged to the Umaiya clan which had opposed Muhammad, but whose mother was of Hashim. 'Uthman naturally appointed Umaiya men loyal to him to commands in the Empire, notably Mu'awiya as governor of Syria—the son of the very Abu Sufyan who headed Quraish opposition to Muhammad at Mecca, though later reconciled to him. Mu'awiya demanded 'Uthman's murderers be brought to justice in accordance with the law, but 'Ali, unable to cope with the murderers, his supporters, was driven by events to take up arms against Mu'awiya. When they clashed at Siffin, in Syria, 'Ali was forced, against his better judgement, to submit to the arbitration of the Koran and Sunna, thus automatically losing the position of supreme arbiter, inherited by the Caliphs from Muhammad. Although history is silent as to what the arbiters actually judged upon, it was most likely as to whether 'Ali had broken the law established by Muhammad, and that he was held to have sheltered unprovoked murderers. The arbiters deposed him from the Caliphial office, though historians allege trickery entered into their action.

'Ali shortly after was murdered by one of a group of his former supporters which had come out against the arbitration it had first urged upon him. This group, the Khawarij, is commonly held to be the forerunner of the Ibadis of Oman and elsewhere. Mu'awiya became Caliph and founder of the Umaiyad dynasty with its capital at Damascus. The ambitions of the Hashim house were not, however, allayed, and when Umaiyad troops slew 'Ali's son Husain at Karbala' in south Iraq they created the greatest Shi'a martyr (see Religious Groupings, p. 17).

The house of Hashim also included the descendants of 'Abbas the Prophet's uncle, a relative, in Arabian eyes, as close as 'Ali to him, but 'Abbas had opposed Muhammad till late in the day. The 'Abbasids made common cause with the 'Ali-id Shi'a against the Umaiyads, but were evidently abler in the political field. In the Umaiyad empire the Arabian tribes formed a kind of military élite but were constantly at factious war with one another. The Hashimites rode to power on the back of a rebellion against the Umaiyads which broke out in Khurasan in east Persia, but it was the 'Abbasid branch of Hashim which assumed the Caliphate and ruled from the capital they founded at Baghdad.

The 'Abbasid Caliphate endured up to the destruction of Baghdad in 1258 by the devastating Mongol invaders of the eastern empire, but the Caliphs had long been mere puppets in the hands of Turkish and other mercenaries, and the unwieldy empire had fragmented into independent states which rose and fell, though they mostly conceded nominal allegiance to the 'Abbasid Caliphs.

The Mongol Ilkhanid sovereigns, now turned Muslim, were in turn displaced by the conquests of Tamerlane at the end of the 14th century. In fact the Islamic empire had largely been taken over by Turkic soldiery. The Mameluke or Slave rulers of medieval Egypt who followed the Aiyubid (Kurdish) dynasty of Salah ud-Din (Saladin) were mainly Turks or Circassians. It was they who checked the Mongol advance at 'Ain Jalut in Palestine (1260). The Ottoman Turks cap-tured Constantinople in 1453, and took Egypt from the Mamelukes in 1516, following this up by occupying the Hijaz where the Ashraf, descendants of the Prophet, ruled in Mecca and Medina, under first Mameluke then Turkish suzerainty. In 1533 the Turks took Baghdad and Iraq became part of the Ottoman Empire. The Ottoman Sultans assumed the title of Caliph—though in Islamic constitutional theory it is not easy to justify this. The Ottoman Caliphs endured till the Caliphate was abolished by Mustafa Kemal in 1924. The Turks have always been characterized by their adherence to Sunni orthodoxy.

Throughout history the 'Ali-ids have constantly asserted their right to be the Imams or leaders of the Muslim community—this in the religious and political senses, since Islam is fundamentally theocratic. The Shi'a, or followers of 'Ali and his descendants, were in constant rebellion against the 'Abbasids and came to form a distinct schismatic group of legitimist sects—at one time the Fatimid Shi'a rulers of Egypt were near to conquering the main part of the Islamic world. The main Shi'a sects today are the Ithna'asharis, the Isma'ilis, and the near-orthodox Zaidis of Yemen. The Safavids who conquered Persia at the beginning of the 16th century brought it finally into the Shi'a fold. Sunni Hashimite dynasties flourish today in Jordan and Morocco as they did until fairly recently in Iraq and Libya, and the Shi'a Zaidi ruler of Yemen was only displaced in 1962. The main difference between Sunnis and Shi'a is over the Imamate, i.e. the temporal and spiritual leadership of Islam, for Sunnis, while they respect the Prophet's house, do not consider the Imam must be a member of it—the Shi'a insist on an Imam of the descendants of 'Ali and Fatima his wife, the Prophet's daughter.

It has been too readily assumed that, during the later Middle Ages and long Turkish domination, the Islamic Middle East was completely stagnant. The shift in economic patterns after the New World was discovered, and the Cape route to India, coupled with widening Western intellectual horizons and the development of science and technology did push European culture far ahead of the Muslim Middle East. It was confronted by a vigorous and hostile Christianity intent on proselytizing in its very homelands. Muslims had to face the challenge of the ideas and attitudes of Christian missionaries. Muslim thinkers like Muhammad 'Abduh (1849–1905) of Egypt and his school asserted that Islam had become heavily overlaid with false notions—hence its decline; like earlier reformers they were convinced that present difficulties could be solved by reversion to an (idealized) pure, primitive Islam. Sometimes, in effect, this meant reinterpreting religious literature to suit attitudes and ideas of modern times—as for instance when they saw the virtual prohibition of polygamy in the restrictions which hedge it about. Since the earlier modern days political leaders like Mustafa Kemal of Turkey have often taken drastic measures, secularizing the state itself even up to the sensitive field of education, and accusing the more conservative forms of Islam of blocking progress. In recent years the Islamic Middle East has had regimes ranging from the strong supporters of traditional Islam—like Saudi Arabia and Libya—to the anti-religious Marxist group which controlled Aden (the People's Democratic Republic of Yemen until 1990). In Libya, nevertheless, Colonel Qaddafi has published *The Green Book*, embodying his personal solution, very socialist in tone, of problems of democracy and economics. Theocratic Shi'a Iran has a distinctive character of its own.

ISLAMIC LAW

Orthodox Sunni Islam finds its main expression in *Shari'a* law which it regards with great veneration. The Sunnis have crystallized into four 'schools' (*madhhab*) or 'rites', all of which are recognized as valid. Although in practice the adherents of one school can sometimes be at loggerheads with another, in modern times it is claimed that the law of any one of the rites can be applied to a case. The schools, named after their founders, are the Hanbali, regarded as the strictest, with adherents mainly in Saudi Arabia; the Shafi'is, the widest in extent with adherents in Egypt, Palestine-Syria, South Arabia and the Far East; the moderate Hanafi school which was the official rite of the Ottoman Turkish empire and to which most Muslims in the Indian sub-continent belong; and the Malikis of the North African states, Nigeria and Sudan. The Shi'ite sects have developed their own law, and give prominence to *ijtihad*, the forming of independent judgement, whereas the Sunnis are more bound by *taqlid* or following ancient models. However, as the law of Sunnis, the moderate Shi'a and the Ibadis is basically derived from the same sources, the differences are generally more of emphasis than principle.

The completely Islamic state as the theorists envisage it, run in conformity with the rules of the *Shari'a*, has probably never been achieved, and people's practice is often at variance with some or other requirements of *Shari'a*. The imprint of Islam is nevertheless unmistakably evident, in one way or another, on every country in this volume.

Civil Courts

In modern states of the Islamic world there exists, side by side with the *Shari'a* court (judging cases on personal status, marriage, divorce, etc.), the secular court which has a wide jurisdiction (based on Western codes of law) in civil and criminal matters. This court is competent to give judgment irrespective of the creed or race of the defendant.

Islamic Law as Applying to Minorities

In cases of minorities (Christian or Jewish) residing as a community in Muslim countries, spiritual councils are established where judgment is passed according to the law of the community, in matters concerning personal status, under the jurisdiction of the recognized head of that community.

Tribal Courts

In steppe and mountain areas of some countries a proportion of the population maintain tribal courts which administer law and justice in accordance with ancient custom and tribal procedure. Among tribes these courts are often more popular than *Shari'a* courts, because justice is swifter. Conciliation (*sulh*) is generally their objective. There is, nonetheless, constant pressure to eliminate customary practices where they are unequivocally seen to be contrary to Islamic principles.

Awqaf

In Muslim countries the law governing *awqaf* (singular, *waqf*) (called in North Africa *habous* (*hubus*)) is the law applied to religious and charitable endowments, trust and settlements. This important Islamic institution is administered in most Muslim countries by a special ministry of *awqaf*. *Awqaf*, or endowments, are pious bequests made by Muslims for the upkeep of religious institutions, public benefits, etc. Family *awqaf* provide an income partly for religious purposes and partly for the original donor's family.

SUFIS

In common with other religions where simple observance of a code of law and morals proves spiritually unsatisfying, some Muslims have turned to mysticism. From early times Islamic mystics existed, known as Sufis, allegedly from their wearing a woollen garment. They seek complete identification with the Supreme Being and annihilation of the self—the existence of which latter they call polytheism (*shirk*). The learned doctors of Islam often think ill of the Sufis, and indeed rogues and wandering mendicants found Sufism a convenient means of livelihood. Certain Sufi groups allowed themselves dispensations and as stimulants even used hashish and opium which are not sanctioned by the Islamic moral code. The Sufis became organized in what are loosely called brotherhoods (*turuq*; singular, *tariqa*), and have to a large extent been incorporated into the structure of orthodox Islamic society. Some *turuq* induce ecstatic states by their performance of the *dhikr*, meaning, literally, the mentioning (of Allah). Today there is much disapproval of the more extravagant manifestations of the Sufis and in some places these have been banned entirely.

BELIEF AND PRACTICE

'Islam' means the act of submitting or resigning oneself to God, and a Muslim is one who resigns or submits himself to God. Muslims disapprove of the term 'Muhammadan' for the faith of Islam, since they worship Allah, and Muhammad is only the Apostle of Allah whose duty it was to convey revelation, though he is regarded as the 'Best of Mankind'. He is the Seal (*Khatam*) of the prophets, i.e. the ultimate Prophet in a long series in which both Moses and Jesus figure. They are revered, but, like Muhammad the Prophet, they are not worshipped.

Nearly all Muslims agree on acceptance of six articles of the faith of Islam: (i) Belief in God; (ii) in His angels; (iii) in His revealed books; (iv) in His Apostles; (v) in the Resurrection and Day of Judgement; and (vi) in His predestination of good and evil.

Faith includes works, and certain practices are obligatory on the believing Muslim. These are five in number:

1. The recital of the creed (*Shahada*)—'There is no god but God (Allah) and Muhammad is the Apostle of God.' This formula is embodied in the call to prayer made by the *muezzin* (announcer) from the minaret of the mosque before each of the five daily prayers.

2. The performance of the Prayer (*Salat*) at the five appointed canonical times—in the early dawn before the sun has risen above the horizon, in the early afternoon when the sun has begun to decline, later when the sun is about midway in its course towards setting, immediately after sunset, in the evening between the disappearance of the red glow in the west and bedtime. In prayer Muslims face towards the Ka'ba in Mecca. They unroll prayer mats and pray in a mosque (place of prostration), at home, or wherever they may be, bowing and prostrating themselves before God and reciting set verses in Arabic from the Koran. On Fridays it is obligatory for men to attend congregational Prayer in the central mosque of the quarter in which one lives—women do not normally attend. On this occasion formal prayers are preceded by a sermon.

3. The payment of the legal alms (*Zakat*). In early times this contribution was collected by officials of the Islamic state, and devoted to the relief of the poor, debtors, aid to travellers and other charitable and state purposes and it often became, in effect, a purely secular tax on crops. Nowadays the fulfilment of this religious obligation is left to the conscience of the individual believer. The *zakat* given at the breaking of the fast at the end of Ramadan, for example, is a voluntary gift of provisions.

4. The 30 days of the fast in the month of Ramadan, the ninth month in the lunar year. As the lunar calendar is shorter by 11 days than the solar calendar, Ramadan moves from the hottest to the coldest seasons of the solar year. It is observed as a fast from dawn to sunset each day by all adults in normal health, during which time no food or drink may be taken. The sick, pregnant women, travellers and children are exempt; some states exempt students, soldiers and factory workers. The fast ends with one of the two major Muslim festivals, 'Id al-Fitr.

5. The pilgrimage (*Hajj*) to Mecca. Every Muslim is obliged, circumstances permitting, to perform this at least once in his lifetime, and when accomplished he may assume the title, *Hajji*. Well over two million pilgrims go each year to Mecca, but the holy cities of Mecca and Medina are prohibited to non-Muslims.

Before entering the sacred area around Mecca by the seventh day of Dhu'l-Hijja, the twelfth month of the Muslim year, pilgrims must don the *ihram*, consisting of two unseamed lengths of white cloth, indicating that they are entering a state of consecration and casting off what is ritually impure. The pilgrims circumambulate the Ka'ba seven times, endeavouring to kiss the sacred Black Stone. Later they run seven times between the near-by twin hills of Safa and Marwah (now covered in by an immense hall), thus recalling Hagar's desperate search for water for her child Ishmael (from whom the Arabs claim descent). On the eighth day of the month the pilgrims leave the city for Mina, a small town six miles to the east. Then before sunrise of the next day all make for the plain below Mount 'Arafat some 12 miles east of Mecca where they pass the day in prayers and recitation until sunset. This point is the climax of the pilgrimage when the whole gathering returns, first to Muzdalifah where it spends the night, then to Mina where pilgrims stone the devil represented by three heaps of stones (*jamra*). The devil is said to have appeared to Abraham here and to have been driven away by Abraham throwing stones at him. This day, the 10th of Dhu'l-Hijja, is 'Id al-Adha, the Feast of the Sacrifices, and the pilgrims sacrifice an animal, usually a sheep, and have their heads shaved by one of the barbers at Mina. They return to Mecca that evening. For some years past the enormous and ever-increasing numbers of pilgrims arriving by air especially has presented the Saudi authorities, guardians of the Holy Places, with major problems of organization, supply, health and public order. In 1988, following the tragic events of July 1987, when 402 people, including 275 Iranian pilgrims, lost their lives in clashes between the Iranians and Saudi security forces, and in order to reduce overcrowding, the Saudi Government imposed national quotas for the numbers of pilgrims performing the *Hajj*.

The Holy War (*Jihad*) against the infidel was the means whereby Arab Muslim rule made its immense expansion in the first centuries of Islam, but despite pressures to do so, it has never been elevated to form a sixth Pillar of Islam. Today some theologians interpret *jihad* in a less literal sense as the combating of evil, but it is significant that the Afghan guerrillas, who resisted the Soviet presence in their country, called themselves *mujahidin*, i.e. those who wage the *jihad* against the enemies of Islam.

The Koran (*Qur'an*, 'recital', 'reading') is for Muslims the very Word of God. The Koran consists of 114 chapters (*surah*) of uneven length, the longest coming first after the brief opening chapter called *al-Fatiha*. (The Koran is about as long as the New Testament). *Al-Fatiha* (The Opener) commences (as does every chapter) with the words, '*Bismillahi 'l-Rahmani 'l-Rahim*', 'In the name of God, the Compassionate, the Merciful', and forms part of the ritual five prayers (*salat*). Other special verses and chapters are also used on a variety of occasions, and, of course, Muslim children are taught to recite by heart a portion of the Koran or, preferably, the whole of it. The Koran has been the subject of vast written commentaries, but translation into other languages is not much approved by Muslims, though interlinear translations (a line of Koran underneath which is a line of translation) are used, and a number of modern translations into English and most other languages exist. The earlier (Meccan) chapters of the Koran speak of the unity of God and his wonders, of the Day of Judgement and Paradise, while the Medinan chapters tend to be occupied more with social legislation for marriage, divorce, personal and communal behaviour. The definitive redaction of the Koran was ordered by the Caliph 'Uthman (644–56).

HOLY PLACES

Mecca: Hijaz province of Saudi Arabia. Mecca is centred around the Ka'ba, the most venerated building in Islam, traditionally held to have been founded by Abraham, recognized by Islam also as a Prophet. It stands in the centre of the vast courtyard of the Great Mosque and has the form of a cube; its construction is of local grey stone and its walls are draped with a black curtain embroidered with a strip of writing containing verses from the Koran. In the eastern corner is set the famous Black Stone. The enlarging of the Great Mosque commenced under the second Caliph 'Umar. Both the Ka'ba and Great Mosque have undergone many renovations, notably since 1952. Mecca is the centre of the annual pilgrimage from all Muslim countries.

Al-Medina (*The City*, i.e. of the Prophet): Hijaz province of Saudi Arabia. Medina, formerly called Yathrib, was created as a sacred enclave (*haram*) by Muhammad who died there in the year 11 of the *hijra* and was buried in the Mosque of the Prophet. Close to his tomb are those of his companions and successors, Abu Bakr and 'Umar, and a little further away that of his daughter Fatima. Frequently damaged,

restored and enlarged, the mosque building was extensively renovated by the Saudi Government in 1955.

Jerusalem (Arabic *al-Quds* or *Bait al-Maqdis, The Hallowed/Consecrated*): Jordan (currently annexed by Israel). Jerusalem is Islam's next most holy city after al-Haraman (Mecca and Medina), not only because it is associated with so many pre-Islamic prophets, but because Muhammad himself is popularly held to have made the 'Night Journey' there. Jerusalem contains the magnificent Islamic shrine, the Dome of the Rock (688–91), built by the Caliph 'Abd al-Malik, and the famous al-Masjid al-Aqsa, severely damaged by arson a few years ago.

Hebron (Habrun): Israeli-occupied Jordan. The Mosque of Abraham, called al-Khalil, the 'Friend of God', is built over the tomb of Abraham, the Cave of Machpelah; it also contains the tombs of Sarah, Isaac, Rebecca, Jacob, and Leah. The shrine is revered by Muslims and Jews, and is also important to Christians.

Qairawan: Tunisia. The city is regarded as a holy place for Muslims, seven pilgrimages to the Great Mosque of Sidi 'Uqbah b. Nafi' (an early Muslim general who founded Qairawan as a base for the Muslim invaders of North Africa) being considered the equivalent of one pilgrimage to Mecca.

Muley Idris: Morocco. The shrine at the burial-place of the founder of the Idrisid dynasty in the year 687, at Walili, near Fez.

Every Middle Eastern country has a multitude of shrines and saints' tombs held in veneration, except Wahhabi states which consider saint cults to be polytheism (*shirk*). In Turkey, however, the policy of secularization led to Aya Sofya Mosque (St Sophia) being turned into a museum.

The following shrines are associated with the Shi'a or Legitimist sects of Islam.

Mashhad (Meshed): Iran. The city is famous for the shrine of Imam 'Ali ar-Rida/Riza, the eighth Imam of the Ithna'ashari group, which attracts some hundred thousand pilgrims each year. The shrine is surrounded by buildings with religious or historical associations.

Qom: Iran. A Shi'a centre, it is venerated as having the tomb of Fatima, the sister of Imam ar-Rida/Riza, and those of hundreds of saints and kings including Imams 'Ali b. Ja'far and Ibrahim, Shah Safi and Shah 'Abbas II. Following the Iranian Revolution it became the centre favoured by Ayatollah Khomeini.

Najaf: Iraq. Mashhad 'Ali, reputed to be constructed over the place where 'Ali b. Abi Talib, fourth Caliph, the cousin and son-in-law of Muhammad, is buried, is a most venerated Shi'a shrine drawing many pilgrims.

Karbala': Iraq. The shrine of Husain b. 'Ali where, at Mashhad Husain, he was slain with most of his family, is today more venerated by the Shi'a than the Mashhad 'Ali. 'Ashoura Day (10th Muharram) when Husain was killed is commemorated by passion plays (*ta'ziya*) and religious processions when the drama of his death is re-enacted with extravagant expressions of emotion.

Baghdad: Iraq. The Kazimain/Kadhimain Mosque is a celebrated Shi'a shrine containing the tomb of Musa al-Kazim/Kadhim, the seventh Imam of the Ithna'asharis.

RELIGIOUS GROUPINGS

Sunnis

The great majority, probably over 80% of Muslims, are Sunni, followers of the *Sunna*, i.e. the way, course, rule or manner of conduct of Prophet Muhammad; they are generally called 'Orthodox'. The Sunnis recognize the first four Caliphs (Abu Bakr, 'Umar, 'Uthman, 'Ali) as Rashidun, i.e. following the right course. They base their *Sunna* upon the Koran and 'Six Books' of Traditions, and are organized in four Orthodox schools or rites (*madhhab*), all of equal standing within the Orthodox fold. Many Muslims today prefer to avoid identification with any single school and simply call themselves Muslim or Sunni.

Wahhabis

The adherents of 'Wahhabism' strongly disapprove of this title by which they are known outside their own group, for they call themselves Muwahhidun or Unitarians. In fact they belong to the strict Hanbali school following its noted exponent, the 13th/14th century Syrian reformer Ibn Taimiyah. The founder of 'Wahhabism', Muhammad b. 'Abd al-Wahhab of Arabian Najd (1703–87), sought to return to the pristine purity of early Islam freed from all accretions and what he regarded as innovations contrary to its true spirit, such as saint worship, lax sexual practices, and superstition. His doctrine was accepted by the chief Muhammad b. Sa'ud of Dar'iya (near ar-Riyadh). Ibn Sa'ud and his son 'Abd al-'Aziz—who proved a capable general—conquered much of Arabia. Medina fell in 1804 and Mecca in 1806 to Sa'ud son of 'Abd al-'Aziz, but after his death in 1814 the Wahhabis were gradually broken by the armies of the Pasha of Egypt, Muhammad 'Ali acting nominally on behalf of the Ottoman Sultan of Turkey. After varying fortunes in the 19th century the Wahhabis emerged as an Arabian power in the opening years of the 20th century. By the close of 1925 they held the Holy Cities and Jeddah and are today the strongest power in the Arabian Peninsula. Though Wahhabism remains the strictest of the Orthodox groups, Saudi Arabia has made some accommodation to modern times.

The Turuq or Religious Orders

In many Middle Eastern countries the religious orders (*turuq*) have important political-cum-religious roles in society. There are the widely spread Qadiriya who with Tijaniya are found in North Africa, the Khatmiya in Sudan, the Rifa'iya in Egypt and Syria, to pick out a few at random. The West has no organizations exactly equivalent to these Sufi orders into which an individual has to be initiated, and in which, by dint of ascetic exercises and study, he may attain degrees of mystical enlightenment—this can also bring moral influence over his fellow men. The Orders may be Sunni or Shi'a; some few Orders are even so unconventional as to be hardly Islamic at all. Although Sufism is essentially uninterested in worldly politics, the *turuq* have, nonetheless, at times been drawn into the political arena. It was the Orthodox reformist Sanusi Order that played the most significant role in our time. The Grand Sanusi, Muhammad b. 'Ali, born at Mustaghanem in Algeria of a Sharif family, founded the first *zawiya* or lodge of the Sanusis in 1837. The Sanusi *tariqa* is distinguished for its exacting standards of personal morality. The Sanusis set up a network of lodges in Cyrenaica (Libya) and put up strong resistance to Italian colonization. The Grand Sanusi was recognized as King Idris of Libya in 1951, but lost his throne in the military revolt led by Colonel Qaddafi in 1969.

The Muslim Brothers (al-Ikhwan al-Muslimun)

Founded in Egypt by Hasan al-Banna in 1928, the career of the Muslim Brothers in Middle East political history has been active and often violent. Westernizing influences and intellectual emancipation in Egypt he regarded as weakening Islam, itself in decline since the ideal age of the first four Caliphs. So, the movement has a rigidity and intolerant attitude towards Christians and Jews, but this may even extend to other Muslim groups. Al-Banna was a member of a *tariqa* and the Brothers (*Ikhwan*) were initially organized along *tariqa* lines with a graded membership. This membership is not restricted to particular social classes but finds support especially among Azhar students, particularly those graduates of the Azhar who hold teaching and minor religious office. By 1939 the Brothers were one of the most important political groups in Egypt.

In 1944 a 'secret apparatus' was formed, rationalized as for the *jihad* in defence of Islam but used to defend the movement against the government. The *Ikhwan* became involved in acts of terrorism and murder, but in 1949 al-Banna himself was murdered by the political police. At first the *Ikhwan* supported the Egyptian revolution but, falling out with the republican government, attempted the assassination of Nasser in 1954 following which he put down the society with a stern hand. The society opened branches in other Arab states—one of their emissaries was implicated in the 1948 Revolution in Yemen—and the movement flourishes in these states.

Ideologically the *Ikhwan* seeks a return to Islam and the *Shari'a*; it accepts all orthodox Islamic groups but it is anti-Qadiyani and Bahá'í. In Egypt it provided certain welfare projects and it has been active in publishing its views. A section of 'Muslim Sisters' was set up in 1933.

Shi'a

The Legitimist Shi'a pay allegiance to 'Ali as mentioned above. 'Ali's posterity, which must number at least hundreds of thousands scattered all over the Muslim world, are customarily called Sharifs if they trace descent to his son al-Hasan, and Saiyids if descended from al-Husain, but while the Sharifs and Saiyids, the religious aristocracy of Islam, traditionally are accorded certain privileges in Islamic society, not all are Shi'a, many being Sunnis. By the ninth century many strange sects and even pagan beliefs had become associated with the original Shi'a or Party of 'Ali, but these extremist sects called *ghulat* have mostly vanished except for a few, often practising a sort of quietism or dissimulation (*taqiyya*) for fear of persecution. All Shi'a accord 'Ali an exalted position, the extreme (and heretical) Shi'a at one time even according him a sort of divinity. Shi'ite Islam does not in the main differ on fundamental issues from the Sunni Orthodox since they draw from the same ultimate sources, but Shi'a *mujtahids* have, certainly in theory, greater freedom to alter the application of law since they are regarded as spokesmen of the Hidden Imam.

The Ithna'asharis (Twelvers)

The largest Shi'a school or rite is the Ithna'ashariya or Twelvers, acknowledging a succession of 12 Imams. From 1502 Shi'ism became the established school in Iran under the Safavid ruler Sultan Shah Isma'il who claimed descent from Musa al-Kazim (see below). There are also Ithna'ashariya in southern Iraq, al-Hasa, Bahrain and the Indian subcontinent.

The last Shi'a Imam, Muhammad al-Mahdi, disappeared in 878, but the Ithna'asharis believe he is still alive and will re-appear in the last days before the Day of Judgement as the Mahdi (Guided One)—a sort of Messiah—who will rule personally by divine right.

The 12 Imams recognized by the Twelver, Ithna'ashari Shi'a are:

(1) 'Ali b. Abi Talib, cousin and son-in-law of the Prophet Muhammad.
(2) Al-Hasan, son of 'Ali.
(3) Al-Husain, second son of 'Ali.
(4) 'Ali Zain al-'Abidin, son of Husain.
(5) Muhammad al-Baqir, son of 'Ali Zain al-'Abidin.
(6) Ja'far as-Sadiq, son of Muhammad al-Baqir.
(7) Musa al-Kazim, son of Ja'far as-Sadiq.
(8) 'Ali ar-Rida, son of Musa al-Kazim.
(9) Muhammad at-Taqi, son of 'Ali ar-Rida.
(10) 'Ali an-Naqi, son of Muhammad at-Taqi.
(11) Al-Hasan az-Zaki, son of 'Ali an-Naqi, al-'Askari.
(12) Muhammad al-Mahdi, son of al-Hasan b. 'Ali, al-'Askari, known as al-Hujja, the Proof.

Isma'ilis

This group of the Shi'a does not recognize Musa al-Kazim as seventh Imam, but holds that the last Imam visible on earth was Isma'il, the other son of Ja'far as-Sadiq. For this reason they are also called the Sab'iya or Seveners. There is, however, much disagreement among the Seveners as to whether they recognized Isma'il himself as seventh Imam, or one of his several sons, and the Fatimids of Egypt (10th–12th centuries) in fact recognized a son of Isma'il's son Muhammad. Schismatic off-shoots from the Fatimid-Isma'ili group are the Druzes, the Musta'lians first settled in Yemen but now with their main centre in Bombay—where the Daudi section, under the chief 'missionary' (Da'i al-Du'a), is known as Bohoras, but who are properly called the Fatimi Taiyibi Da'wa, and the Nizari Isma'ilis of whom the Aga Khan is the spiritual head. These sects have a secret literature embodying their esoteric philosophies. Both groups are very active and a large Isma'ili Institute, sponsored by the Agha Khan, was opened in London in 1985. Small groups of Isma'ilis are to be found in north-west Syria, Iran, Afghanistan, East Africa and Zanzibar, and larger numbers in India and Pakistan.

'Alawis (Nusairis)

The 'Alawis believe Muhammad was a mere forerunner of 'Ali and that the latter was an incarnation of Allah. This Shi'i extremist sect established in the ninth century has also adopted practices of both Christian and pagan origin. Most of its members today live in north-west Syria.

Druze

The Druze are heretics, an offshoot of the Fatimid Isma'ilis (see above), established in Lebanon and Syria. Their name (Duruz) derives from ad-Darazi, a missionary of Persian origin who brought about the conversion of these Syrian mountaineers to the belief of the divine origin of the Fatimid Caliph al-Hakim. The origins of this sect and its subsequent expansion are still obscure. Hamza b. 'Ali, a Persian contemporary of ad-Darazi, is the author of several of the religious treatises of the Druze. This community acknowledges one God and believes that he has on many occasions become incarnate in man. His last appearance was in the person of the Fatimid Caliph al-Hakim (disappeared 1020). The Druze have played a distinctive role in the political and social life of their country and are renowned for their independence of character. They have engaged ardently in the *jihad* (holy war) against the Israeli invaders of Lebanon and their Christian allies. Druze morale is reinforced by the inspiration of the Islamic revolution in Shi'ite Iran.

Zaidis

The Zaidis are a liberal and moderate sect of the Shi'a, close enough to the Sunnis to call themselves the 'Fifth School' (*al-madhhab al-khamis*). Their name is derived from a grandson of al-Husain b. 'Ali' called Zaid b. 'Ali' whom they recognize as fifth Imam. They reject religious dissimulation (*taqiyya*) and are extremely warlike. Zaidism is the dominant school of Islam in Yemen, its main centres being San'a and Dhamar, but Shafi'is form roughly half the population.

Ibadis

The Ibadis are commonly held to have their origins in the Khawarij who dissociated themselves from 'Ali b. Abi Talib when he accepted arbitration in his quarrel with Mu'awiya, but this is open to question. They broke off early from the main stream of Islam and are usually regarded as heretics though with little justification. Groups of the sect, which has often suffered persecution, are found in Oman where Ibadism is the state religion, Zanzibar, Libya and Algeria, mainly in the Mzab.

THE ISLAMIC REVIVAL

In a number of Muslim countries revivalist or reactionary Islamic movements are taking place. Islam makes no essential distinction between religion and politics so this affects not only the whole Muslim community but also those of other faiths residing in an Islamic state. In one sense it may be said that there is a common basis to the revival in all the Islamic states in that people believe that a reversion to an idealized Islamic community, or the substitution of the principles embodied in *Shari'a* law for the practice of a secular state, will resolve current problems and tensions. Each country, however, seems to differ as to what it expects the Islamic revival to react against. Since imported ideologies like socialism, communism, etc., have not solved political, social and economic problems besetting the Islamic world, in the popular return to the indigenous cultural heritage, Islam has tended to become the ideology of political opposition to existing political establishments and to be regarded as the means to link current development with the traditions of the past.

Saudi Arabia, the heartland of Islam, has always maintained a strict formal adherence to traditional Islam. The late King Faisal, though tactfully curbing the extreme tendencies of Saudi Arabia's Mutawwa' 'clergy', initiated and financed a policy of promoting Islam to counter President Nasser's alignment with socialist propaganda to subvert monarchic regimes elsewhere. King Faisal's initiative took the form of subsidizing the building of mosques in Muslim countries (and, later, also in Europe and other parts of the world), the publication of Islamic books and religious tracts, and the founding or support of such institutions as the Islamic Council of Europe. Links were made with groups like the Muslim Brothers, the well-established inter-state Islamic society which Nasser tried to crush, and which has been ruthlessly suppressed by the Syrian Government, notwithstanding recent shows of toleration by the authorities.

In general the concept of a 'permissive society' as promoted by certain Western elements, is rejected with distaste by all Muslim countries. Saudi Arabia's financial and moral strength has enabled it to take practical steps to pressure other Islamic states to conform, sometimes if they fear only to be out of line, to such Islamic prescriptions as the prohibition of liquor. Even in Egypt alcoholic beverages are not served at public occasions or in public places. On the other hand banks and insurance companies which depend on taking interest on loans, seem to be regarded as earning profit (*ribh*), which is lawful to a Muslim, not taking usury (*riba*), which is unlawful. Since the recent wide revivalist trend that has reasserted itself in Islamic countries, the ethics of banking have troubled the conscience of certain Muslim states and experiments have been made with Islamic banks which, formally at least, avoid interest. A change-over to an Islamic banking system began in Iran in 1984. Colonel Qaddafi has also been making highly original experiments in the monetary field which he would regard as Islamic. To the West certain Islamic laws are repugnant, such as amputation of a hand for persistent theft, but the benefit in Saudi Arabia in compelling a high standard of honesty is undeniable—the penalty is probably not frequently inflicted. Its reintroduction in Sudan as part of a return to strict *Shari'a* practice was not welcomed by many of the educated. Former President Nimeri was compelled to withdraw from the strict application of *Shari'a* law before his deposition in April 1985, although officially it has remained in force ever since then. In February 1991 a decree was enacted whereby a new penal code based on *Shari'a* law, would be applied everywhere in Sudan, from March 1991, except in the southern states of Bahr al-Ghazal, Upper Nile and Equatoria. In Algeria the revival of conservative Islam was manifest in June 1990 with the success in the local elections in the main cities of the Front Islamique du Salut (FIS). In May and June 1991 demonstrations and riots in Algiers by supporters of the FIS led to the dismissal of the Algerian Government by President Chadli, the postponement of the general election (which had been scheduled for 27 June) and the deployment of the army to restore order.

In Iran the motivation of Islamic reaction, as was symbolized by the Ayatollah (a high religious office) Khomeini, is in part that of the conservative, even chauvinistic, provinces against a secular monarch who introduced foreigners bringing with them Western manners distasteful to Islamic society. This found expression in the destruction of bars, cinemas, etc., the banning of music on the radio, and the attempt, by imposing the veil, to reverse the tide of female emancipation. Persecution of the Bahá'ís put the clock back to the late 19th century. In 1982, all courts established prior to the Islamic Revolution of 1979 were abolished, and all laws not conforming with Islam were revoked. Although interest-free banking is being introduced there are difficulties in applying Islamic law to economic policy as there seems to be fundamental disagreement on how to apply it. In practice, too, *Shari'a* penalties are not easy to enforce.

In Iran Khomeini aimed to return to the ideal 'Islamic' state as conceived of by the Shi'a mullahs. The emphasis on the concept that the *ulema* (mullahs) have had trusteeship over the entire community deputed to them by the invisible Imam, has led to rule by them of a theocratic type, but Khomeini maintained that they must share in the Islamic ideology as interpreted by his group. Khomeini considered Islam's contemporary state as decadent and deviating from Islamic principles. He was critical of other Muslim governments, in part, as they were affected by Western influences, and his dictum, 'we should try hard to export our revolution to the world', though he considered this 'revolution' a spiritual, not a nationalistic one, had an aggressive ring to it. The actions and practice of the new state have often been of an extremity rejected by Muslims and non-Muslims alike. Yet if on the one hand some Muslim countries criticized the Khomeini regime for actions difficult to reconcile with the spirit of Islam, on the other there has been a widespread sentiment of sympathy among ordinary Muslims for the 'Islamic' government of Iran in its opposition to the 'Great Satan' USA, supporter of Israel, etc.

As the very existence of Pakistan lies in the conception of a 'pure' Islamic community opposed to heathen Hindustan, this, coupled with its internal troubles, has encouraged the retreat into a more rigid Islamic state.

The Turkey of Mustafa Kemal Atatürk aimed at a complete separation of religion and state—in this secular state women were accorded equal rights with men. It is now clear that secularization did not penetrate deeply into the urban and particularly the rural population. After the Second World War resentment of financial hardships against the Government was fanned by religious leaders, and ever increasing religious freedom has had to be conceded within the secular state. Many women have, illegally, resumed the veil. The upper classes tend to favour a secular state, but religious feeling combined with chauvinism are behind the popular revival of Islam.

In no way was the interdependence of religion and politics in Islam better illustrated than in the condemnation of Israel by 40 Islamic states, over the question of Jerusalem, a city sacred to Muslims from which the Prophet made his celebrated Night Ascent to Heaven. Intensity of feeling over the Palestine issue varies in degree from one Islamic country to another and is often far overshadowed by local issues, but it remains everywhere a major obstacle to East-West understanding. Israel's invasion of Lebanon in 1982 and the horrific massacre perpetrated by a Christian Lebanese group at the Sabra and Chatila Palestinian refugee camps in Beirut, apparently with Israeli connivance, and the Israeli suppression of the Palestinian *intifada* (uprising) in the Occupied Territories, have added new bitterness to an already tense situation, persuading the Islamic world at large of the West's underlying hostility. To many Muslims the attempt by President Saddam Hussain to link Iraq's occupation of Kuwait in August 1990 with the Israeli occupation of Arab territories was justifiable. The vigour with which Western governments reacted against the Iraqi occupation, having effectively condoned the Israeli occupations for so long, appeared to them to be blatant hyprocrisy.

Arabs and Iranians frequently complain of the 'bad press' and distortion of their religion and politics in the West through ignorance or deliberate bias. Unfortunately, this has been compounded by the offence to Muslims caused by Salman Rushdie's novel *The Satanic Verses*, and by Western, and specifically American, actions against Iraq after the Gulf War. Muslims contrast the latter with the West's failure to halt Serbian aggression against the Bosnian Muslims.

A Muslim writer recently distinguished between 'Westernization' and 'modernization', describing the latter as broadly acceptable, except to a reactionary minority. If the distinction between the two is a little blurred, the idea has some validity. In general, however, the Islamic revival among ordinary Muslims is bound up with factors, simple conservatism apart, varying from country to country and class to class, and it may oppose either governments run on a secular basis, or those claiming to be 'Islamic'.

Christianity

DEVELOPMENT IN THE MIDDLE EAST

Christianity was adopted as the official religion of the Roman empire in AD 313, and the Christian Church came to be based on the four leading cities, Rome, Constantinople (capital from AD 330), Alexandria and Antioch. From the divergent development of the four ecclesiastical provinces there soon emerged four separate churches: the Roman Catholic or Latin Church (from Rome), the Greek Orthodox Church (from Constantinople), the Syrian or Jacobite Church (from Antioch) and the Coptic Church (from Alexandria).

Later divisions resulted in the emergence of the Armenian (Gregorian) Church, which was founded in the fourth century, and the Nestorian Church, which grew up in the fifth century in Syria, Mesopotamia and Iran, following the teaching of Nestorius of Cilicia (d. 431). From the seventh century onwards followers of St Maron began to establish themselves in northern Lebanon, laying the foundations of the Maronite Church.

Subsequently the Uniate Churches were brought into existence by the renunciation by formerly independent churches of doctrines regarded as heretical by the Roman Church and by the acknowledgement of Papal supremacy. These churches—the Armenian Catholic, the Chaldean (Nestorian) Catholic, Greek Catholic, the Coptic Catholic, the Syrian Catholic and the Maronite Church did, however, retain their Oriental customs and rites. The independent churches continued in existence alongside the Uniate Churches with the exception of the Maronites, who reverted to Rome.

HOLY PLACES

Bethlehem: Israeli-occupied Jordan. The traditional birthplace of Jesus is enclosed in the Basilica of the Nativity, revered also by Muslims. Christmas is celebrated here by the Roman and Eastern Rite Churches on 25 December, by the Greek Orthodox, Coptic and Syrian Orthodox Churches on 6 and 7 January, by the Ethiopian Church on 8 January, and by the Armenian Church on 19 January. The tomb of Rachel, important to the three faiths, is just outside the town.

Jerusalem: Jordan (but annexed by Israel). The most holy city of Christianity has been a centre for pilgrims since the Middle Ages. It is the seat of the patriarchates of the Roman, Greek Orthodox and Armenian Churches, who share the custodianship of the Church of the Holy Sepulchre and who each own land and buildings in the neighbouring area.

The Church of the Holy Sepulchre stands on the hill of Golgotha in the higher north-western part of the Old City. In the central chamber of the church is the Byzantine Rotunda built by 12th century crusaders, which shelters the small shrine of the traditional site of the tomb. Here the different patriarchates exercise their rights in turn. Close by is the Rock of Calvary, revered as the site of the Crucifixion.

Most pilgrims devoutly follow the Way of the Cross leading from the Roman Praetorium through several streets of the Old City to the Holy Sepulchre. Franciscan monks, commemorating the journey to the Crucifixion, follow the course of this traditional route each Friday; on Good Friday this procession marks a climax of the Easter celebrations of the Roman Church.

Outside the Old City stands the Mount of Olives, the scene of Jesus' Ascension. At the foot of its hill is the Garden of Gethsemane which is associated with the vigil on the eve of the Crucifixion. The Cenaculum or traditional room of the Last Supper is situated on Mount Zion in Israel.

Nazareth: Israel. This town, closely associated with the childhood of Jesus, has been a Christian centre since the fourth century AD. The huge, domed Church of the Annunciation has recently been built on the site of numerous earlier churches to protect the underground Grotto of the Annunciation. Nearby the Church of St Joseph marks the traditional site of Joseph's workshop.

Galilee: Israel. Many of the places by this lake are associated with the life of Jesus: Cana, scene of the miracle of water and wine, which is celebrated by an annual pilgrimage on the second Sunday after Epiphany; the Mount of Beatitudes; Tabgha, scene of the multiplication of the loaves and fish; and Capurneum, scene of the healing of the Centurion's servant.

Mount Tabor: Israel. The traditional site of the Transfiguration, which has drawn pilgrims since the fourth century, is commemorated by a Franciscan Monastery and a Greek Basilica, where the annual Festival of the Transfiguration is held.

Jericho: Palestinian autonomous enclave. The scene of the baptism of Jesus; nearby is the Greek Monastery of St John the Baptist.

Nablus (*Samaria*): Israeli-occupied Jordan. This old town contains Jacob's Well, associated with Jesus, and the Tomb of Joseph.

Qubaibah (*Emmaus*): Israeli-occupied Jordan. It was near this town that two of the Disciples encountered Jesus after the Resurrection.

'Azariyyah (*Bethany*): Israeli-occupied Jordan. A town frequented by Jesus, the home of Mary and Martha, and the scene of the Raising of Lazarus.

Mount Carmel: Haifa, Israel. The Cave of Elijah draws many pilgrims, including Muslims and Druzes, who celebrate the Feast of Mar Elias on 20 July.

Ein Kerem: Israel. Traditional birthplace of John the Baptist, to whom a Franciscan church is dedicated; nearby is the church of the Visitation.

Ephesus: Turkey. The city, formerly a great centre of pagan worship, where Paul founded the first of the seven Asian Churches. The recently restored Basilica, built by Justinian, is dedicated to John the Evangelist, who legend claims died here; a fourth-century church on Aladag Mountain commemorating Mary's last years spent here now draws an annual pilgrimage in August.

Judaism

There are two main Jewish communities, the Ashkenazim and the Sephardim, the former from east, central and northern Europe, the latter from Spain, the Balkans, the Middle East and North Africa. The majority of immigrants into Israel were from the Ashkenazim, and their influence predominates there, though the Hebrew language follows Sephardim usage. There is no doctrinal difference between the two communities, but they observe distinct rituals.

HOLY PLACES

Wailing Wall: Jerusalem. This last remnant of the western part of the wall surrounding the courtyard of Herod's Temple, finally destroyed by the Romans in AD 70, is visited by devout Jews, particularly on the Fast Day of the ninth of Av, to grieve at the destruction of the First and Second Temples which had once stood on the same site.

Mount Zion: Israel. A hill south-west of the Old City of Jerusalem, venerated particularly for the tomb of David, acknowledged by Muslims as Abi Dawud (the Jebuzite hill on which David founded his Holy City is now known as Mount Ophel, and is in Jordan, just to the east of the modern Mount Zion). Not far from the foot of the hill are the rock-cut tombs of the family of King Herod.

Cave of Machpelah: Hebron, Israeli-occupied Jordan. The grotto, over which was built a mosque, contains the tombs of Abraham and Sarah, Isaac and Rebecca, Jacob and Leah.

Bethlehem: Israeli-occupied Jordan. The traditional tomb of Rachel is in a small shrine outside the town, venerated also by Muslims and Christians.

Mount Carmel: Israel. The mountain is associated with Elijah, whose Cave in Haifa draws many pilgrims. (See Christianity section.)

Safad: Israel. Centre of the medieval Cabbalist movement, this city contains several synagogues from the 16th century

associated with these scholars, and many important tombs, notably that of Rabbi Isaac Louria.

Meiron: Israel. The town contains the tombs of Shimon bar Yohai, reputed founder in the second century of the medieval Cabbalist movement, and his son Eleazer. A yearly Hassidic pilgrimage is held to the tomb to celebrate Lag Ba'Omer with a night of traditional singing and dancing in which Muslims also participate.

Tiberias: Israel. An ancient city containing the tombs of Moses Maimonides and Rabbi Meir Baal Harness. Famous as an historical centre of Cabbalist scholarship, it is with Jerusalem, Safad and Hebron, one of the four sacred cities of Judaism, and once accommodated a university and the Sanhedrin.

Other Communities

ZOROASTRIANS

Zoroastrianism developed from the teaching of Zoroaster, or Zarathustra, who lived in Iran some time between 700 and 550 BC. Later adopted as the official religion of the Persian empire, Zoroastrianism remained predominant in Iran until the rise of Islam. Many adherents were forced by persecution to emigrate, and the main centre of the faith is now Bombay, where they are known as Parsees. Technically a monotheistic faith, Zoroastrianism retained some elements of polytheism. It later became associated with fire-worship.

Yazd: Iran. This city was the ancient centre of the Zoroastrian religion, and was later used as a retreat during the Arab conquest. It contains five fire temples and still remains a centre for this faith, of which some 35,000 adherents live in Iran.

BAHÁ'ÍS

Bahá'ísm developed in the mid-19th century from Babism. The Bab, or Gateway (to Truth), Saiyid Ali Muhammad of Shiraz (1821–1850), was opposed to the corrupt Shi'a clergy in the Iran of his day and was executed in 1850. His remains were later taken to Haifa and buried in a mausoleum on the slopes of Mount Carmel. Mirza Husain Ali Bahá'ullah ('Splendour of Allah', 1817–1892), a follower of Babism, experienced a spiritual revelation while in prison and, in 1863, declared himself to be 'he whom Allah shall manifest' as predicted by the Bab. A member of the Persian nobility, he devoted his life to preaching against the corruption endemic in Persian society and as a result spent many years in exile. He died at Acre in Palestine in 1892 and is buried in a shrine adjacent to the mansion in which the Bab died, at Bahji, some miles north of Acre on the road to Beirut.

It was in the will and testament of Abdul Bahá, the eldest son and successor of Bahá'ullah that after his death (in 1921) the head of the Bahá'í faith would be Shoghi Effendi known as the Guardian of the Bahá'í faith ('Guardian of Allah's Command') and that he would be the 'President' of the Universal House of Justice which would be elected in due course. In fact Shoghi Effendi died in London in November 1957 after 36 years as Guardian but the Universal House of Justice was not elected from the Bahá'í world until 1963. The presidency was never assumed and there is no possibility of a second Guardian being appointed.

In 1846 the Babis declared their secession from Islam, and the Bahá'ís claim independence from all other faiths. They believe that the basic principles of the great religions of the world are in complete harmony and that their aims and functions are complementary. Other tenets include belief in the brotherhood of man, the opposition to racial and colour discrimination, the equality of the sexes, progress towards world peace, monogamy, chastity and the encouragement of family life. Bahá'ísm has no priesthood and discourages asceticism, monasticism and mystic pantheism. Most of Bahá'ísm's Middle Eastern adherents live in Iran and—on a temporary basis—Israel, but since the Islamic Revolution those in Iran have suffered from severe official persecution. More than 1m. Bahá'ís live in India and in fact there are now Bahá'ís in every country of the world with 172 national administrative bodies.

Haifa: Israel. Shrine and gardens of the Bab on Mount Carmel, world centre of the Bahá'í faith. Pilgrims visit the Bahá'í holy places in Haifa and in and around Acre. The Pilgrimage lasts for nine days and the pilgrimage period extends over the whole year with the exception of the months of August and September.

SAMARITANS

Mount Gerazim: Jordan. The mountain is sacred to this small sect, who celebrate Passover here. The Samaritan High Priest lives at Nablus.

THE ARAB-ISRAELI CONFRONTATION 1967–94

Updated for this edition by PAUL COSSALI

Based on an original article by MICHAEL ADAMS, with subsequent additions by DAVID GILMOUR, PAUL HARPER and STEVEN SHERMAN

Israel's decisive victory over the Arab states in the Six Day War of 1967 raised hopes that at last it would be possible to reach a definitive settlement of the 19-year-old Arab-Israeli conflict. Instead it soon became apparent that the conflict had merely been complicated by the occupation of further Arab territory, the displacement of still more refugees and the aggravation of the sense of grievance felt by the Palestinians and now shared more widely than ever in the rest of the Arab world.

Once a cease-fire was in operation in June 1967, the UN Security Council's next step was to pass a resolution (No. 237, of 14 June 1967), calling on Israel to facilitate the return of the new refugees who had fled (and were still fleeing) from the areas occupied by Israel during the war. The resolution also called on Israel to ensure the safety, welfare and security of the inhabitants of the 'Occupied Areas'.

An emergency meeting of the UN General Assembly reiterated on 4 July the Security Council's call for the return of the refugees and on the same day it declared 'invalid' the Israeli annexation of the Arab sector of Jerusalem; but the Assembly failed to produce an agreed resolution for a settlement.

The deadlock became total when an Arab summit conference, held in Khartoum between 29 August and 3 September 1967, confirmed earlier decisions not to negotiate directly with Israel, not to accord it recognition and not to sign a peace treaty. The Israeli Government, for its part, announced its refusal to undertake any but direct negotiations; if no such negotiations developed, Israeli forces would maintain their occupation of the Arab territories conquered during the war.

RESOLUTION 242

In late 1967 the UN Security Council considered a number of draft resolutions which failed to gain approval, either because (according to supporters of the Arabs) they condoned the acquisition or occupation of territory by military force, or because (according to supporters of Israel) they contained no adequate guarantee of Israel's security. Finally, on 22 November 1967, the Security Council unanimously adopted Resolution 242 (see Documents on Palestine, p. 86), which was to be the basis of all peace initiatives during the next five years and which remains an important element in attempts to resolve the Palestinian question. By emphasizing the illegitimacy of the acquisition of territory by war, the resolution satisfied the demand of the Arabs and their supporter, the USSR, for an Israeli withdrawal. At the same time, by being less than categorical about the extent of that withdrawal, it was acceptable to the Israelis and their supporter, the USA. All the subsequent arguments which developed centred on the question of whether the Israelis, in return for a definitive peace treaty, should have the right to retain parts of the Arab territories occupied during the war.

PALESTINIAN RESISTANCE

In the immediate aftermath of the fighting, despite the Israeli Prime Minister's declaration on the eve of the war that Israel had no intention of annexing 'even one foot of Arab territory', the Israeli Knesset had legislated the 'reunification' of Jerusalem,* which in fact amounted to the annexation of the Arab sector of the city. This appeared to confirm Arab allegations of Israeli expansionism, and greatly encouraged the rise of a Palestinian resistance movement,

already stimulated by the impotence of the Arab governments and the humiliation which the war had brought on the Arab world. When the Israelis began, as early as September 1967, to establish Jewish settlements in the Occupied Territories†, support for the resistance movement became widespread in the Arab world. It was reinforced when the Israelis, after agreeing to allow the return of refugees (who were still streaming eastward), closed the border again after only 14,000 out of the 150,000 who had filed applications with the Red Cross had been allowed to re-enter Palestine.

The situation, then, was deteriorating even before Dr Gunnar Jarring, whom the Secretary-General had appointed as his Special Representative in accordance with Resolution 242, went to the Middle East at the end of 1967. During the first half of 1968 there were increasingly frequent breaches of the cease-fire along the Suez Canal (which remained blocked to traffic), while Palestinian guerrilla raids led to heavy Israeli reprisals in the Jordan valley. In July 1968, guerrillas of the Popular Front for the Liberation of Palestine (PFLP) carried out the first hijack operation in the Middle East, diverting an Israeli airliner to Algiers.

PHANTOMS FOR ISRAEL

Israel, while not rejecting Resolution 242, said it could not be a substitute for specific agreements between the parties. When the UN General Assembly met in late 1968, Israel put forward a nine-point plan for a Middle East settlement which made no mention of withdrawal, but rather of 'a boundary settlement compatible with the security of Israel and the honour of the Arab states'. This produced no response from the Arab governments, which were shocked when President Johnson, at the height of the US election campaign, announced that the USA was considering the sale of *Phantom* aircraft to Israel. A month later Richard Nixon was elected as President Johnson's successor. The sale of 50 *Phantoms* to Israel was confirmed at the end of December and marked an important stage in the escalation of the arms race in the Middle East.

The day after the sale of the *Phantoms* was announced, Israeli commandos raided Beirut airport, in reprisal for an Arab guerrilla attack on an Israeli airliner in Athens, and destroyed 13 aircraft. This incident brought Lebanon directly into the Arab-Israeli confrontation. After the Security Council had unanimously condemned Israel for the raid, the Soviet Government took up an earlier French proposal for talks between the USSR, the USA, the United Kingdom and France to obtain agreement between the major powers over the implementation of Resolution 242.

At the beginning of February 1969, President Nasser of Egypt declared his willingness to enter into direct negotiations once Israeli forces had withdrawn from Arab territory. Mr Eshkol, the Prime Minister of Israel, stated his readiness to meet President Nasser and declared that Israel was prepared to be flexible about all the Occupied Territories except Jerusalem and the Golan Heights (captured from Syria in 1967). But, as the year wore on, spasmodic fighting continued along both the Suez Canal and the Jordan fronts, until in July 1969 President Nasser publicly gave up hope of a peaceful settlement, forecasting that a long 'war of attrition' would be necessary to dislodge Israel from the Occupied Territories.

---

* For a discussion of the Jerusalem issue, *see* p. 72.

† Between September 1967 and June 1993 168 of these settlements were established by the Israelis in the occupied areas of the West Bank of the Jordan, the Gaza Strip and the Golan Heights in south-west Syria.

THE ROGERS PLAN

The four-power talks were suspended while Soviet and US representatives met separately. There was optimism when it appeared likely that a formula had been found for 'Rhodes-style' negotiations (after the talks conducted in Rhodes which led to the armistice agreements between Israel and the Arab states in 1949), but an Israeli suggestion that this would amount to direct negotiations prompted the Arabs to reject the formula. Instead the US Secretary of State, William Rogers, produced on 9 December 1969 a set of proposals which came to be known as the Rogers Plan. This was an attempt to steer a middle course between the Arab view, that the Security Council resolution should be implemented *in toto* and did not call for negotiation, and the Israeli preference for direct negotiations which would decide where the new borders should be drawn. The most important aspect of the plan was that it made clear the US view that there should only be minor modifications of the pre-June 1967 boundaries. This ensured Israeli hostility to the plan, since, despite the insistence of the Israeli Minister of Foreign Affairs, Abba Eban, that 'everything is negotiable', it had now become clear that his Cabinet colleagues were deeply divided on this crucial question.

In January 1970 Israel initiated a series of bombing raids (using the new US Phantom aircraft) on targets inside Egypt. General Dayan, Israel's Minister of Defence, announced at the beginning of February that the Israeli bombing attacks had three aims: to force the Egyptians to respect the cease-fire along the Suez Canal front, to prevent Egyptian preparations for a new war and to weaken the Egyptian regime. In practice, the raids had three results: they strengthened Egyptian support for President Nasser, they damaged Israel's image in the outside world and they drew the USSR into providing further assistance to Egypt.

International concern over these developments led to a renewal of diplomatic efforts. Israel's requests for more *Phantoms* in early 1970 were not granted and it appeared that the immediate US objectives were to renew the cease-fire and to extract from the Israeli Government an undertaking to withdraw from the greater part of the Occupied Territories as part of an overall peace settlement. Israel made no public commitment to withdrawal, but its response in private was sufficiently encouraging for Mr Rogers to relaunch his proposals, with the backing of the four major powers. In a speech on 23 July 1970 President Nasser announced Egypt's acceptance of the US proposal for a renewal of the cease-fire, followed by negotiations through Dr Jarring for the implementation of Resolution 242. A week later, the Israeli Government, after receiving assurances on the future supply of arms from the USA, also agreed to the US proposal, with the provisos that Israel would never return to the pre-war boundaries and that none of its troops would be withdrawn from the cease-fire lines until a binding peace agreement had been signed.

The renewed cease-fire along the Suez Canal front came into operation on the night of 7/8 August. It was to last 90 days, during which the two sides were to engage in indirect negotiations through Dr Jarring. However, after a single meeting with Dr Jarring in New York, the Israeli representative was recalled and the Israeli Government protested that the cease-fire had been violated by the movement of Soviet missiles behind the Egyptian lines. Negotiations had not been renewed when a serious crisis in Jordan distracted the attention of all the parties concerned.

KING HUSSEIN AND THE PALESTINE GUERRILLAS

On 6 September 1970, Palestinian guerrillas of the PFLP hijacked two airliners and diverted them to a desert airfield near Zerqa, in Jordan. A third airliner was taken to Cairo and destroyed there. Three days later a fourth aircraft was hijacked and joined the two in Jordan, where the guerrillas demanded the release of a substantial number of Palestinians held prisoner in Israel, in exchange for some 300 hostages.

This episode proved the last straw for the Jordanian Government. During the previous two years, as the strength of the guerrilla movement increased, it had faced a dilemma.

By allowing the guerrillas freedom of movement in Jordan, it had invited (and would continue to invite) retaliation from Israel in the form of ground and air raids which had depopulated the East Bank of the Jordan and caused severe casualties. If, however, the Government tried to control or suppress the activities of the guerrillas, it faced the possibility of civil war in Jordan.

The Palestine resistance movement, whose declared objective was the reconstitution in Palestine of a democratic state open to Jews and Arabs alike, opposed the idea of a political settlement with Israel implying the recognition and perpetuation of a Zionist state. King Hussein had accepted the Rogers Plan and was thus committed to the principle of a political settlement. So long as this was not in prospect, it had been possible for the King and the guerrillas to pursue their diverse objectives without coming into open conflict, but as soon as such a settlement became a serious possibility the uneasy coexistence between them was threatened. On several occasions in 1969 and 1970 the Jordanian Government and the guerrillas had come close to a confrontation, and after the renewal of the cease-fire in August 1970 and the acceptance by the Jordanian Government of the Rogers Plan, a clash became inevitable.

On 16 September King Hussein appointed a military government in Jordan which the next day set about the liquidation of the resistance movement. After 10 days of heavy fighting in Amman, mediation efforts by other Arab governments, and in particular by President Nasser, brought about a truce, which was signed in Cairo on 27 September 1970. On the following day President Nasser suffered a heart attack and died almost immediately.

PRESIDENT SADAT AND THE CEASE-FIRE

There was both surprise and relief when the new President of Egypt, Anwar Sadat, showed himself willing to take up the search for a settlement. He agreed to renew the cease-fire for 90 days and, after intensive consultations between Israeli and US leaders and the extension of American credits worth $500m., Israel agreed to return to the Jarring talks. As the cease-fire was expiring on 5 February 1971, President Sadat once more agreed to renew it, for 30 days, proposing that Israel should begin to withdraw its forces from the east bank of the canal, which Egypt would then be able to clear for navigation.

On 8 February Dr Jarring wrote to the Governments of Israel and Egypt, expressing his optimism about the desire of both parties for a settlement and inviting each of them to give firm commitments which would resolve the central deadlock. Israel, he suggested, should agree on certain stated conditions (providing guarantees for security and freedom of navigation) to withdraw to the international boundary between Egypt and the Palestine of the British Mandate. Egypt should give a parallel undertaking to conclude a peace agreement explicitly ending the state of belligerence and recognizing Israel's right to exist in peace and security. In other words, both parties were asked formally to accept the principal obligations imposed on them by Resolution 242.

The Egyptian reply gave the undertaking called for by Dr Jarring, provided that Israel did the same and agreed to withdraw its forces to the international border. Israel's reply stated firmly that, while it would be prepared to withdraw its forces to 'secure, recognized and agreed boundaries to be established in the peace agreement', it would in no circumstances withdraw to the pre-June 1967 lines. This embarrassed the US Government, which had first withheld and then granted military and economic assistance to Israel, in the attempt to persuade the Israeli Government to accept only 'minor rectifications' of the armistice lines. The USA made one further attempt when William Rogers urged Israel to accept international guarantees in place of territorial gains, adding that security did not 'necessarily require additions of territory' and that in the US view 'the 1967 boundary should be the boundary between Israel and Egypt'.

PROPOSAL FOR A 'PARTIAL SETTLEMENT'

The US Government took up instead President Sadat's suggestion of an Israeli withdrawal for some distance into

Sinai to allow the reopening of the Suez Canal. But the new proposal for a partial settlement quickly became bogged down in arguments over the extent of the Israeli withdrawal and whether it should be seen as the first step to complete withdrawal. The arguments continued through most of 1971 until the proposal was finally dropped by the USA in November.

In December the UN General Assembly, in a resolution reaffirming the 'inadmissibility of the acquisition of territory by war' and calling for an Israeli withdrawal, also urged Israel to 'respond favourably' to the proposals made by Dr Jarring in February. Only seven states, including Israel, voted against the resolution and the USA, which had always voted in support of Israel on territorial questions, abstained, reflecting its view that Israel should withdraw from almost all of the Occupied Territories. The year ended with President Sadat in a dangerously weakened position. He had taken considerable risks in pursuit of a political settlement and had promised the Egyptian people that 1971 would be the 'year of decision'. He blamed the lack of progress on American 'political manoeuvring', and when 1972 (a US election year) began with the US Government promising Israel a further 42 *Phantom* and 90 *Skyhawk* aircraft, it seemed unlikely that a fresh US suggestion of indirect talks between Israel and Egypt in New York would come to anything.

In February 1972 the Israelis launched a large-scale incursion into Lebanon, stating that its aim was the elimination of guerrilla bases near Israel's northern border. In June a further Israeli raid on Lebanon was condemned by the Security Council after more than 70 civilians had been killed or wounded.

In July 1972 President Sadat unexpectedly called for the withdrawal from Egypt of the Soviet advisers engaged in the reorganization of Egypt's defence system. This was interpreted as a final appeal to the US Government to bring pressure to bear on Israel to accept a settlement involving an Israeli withdrawal from Sinai.

In Europe, however, a reappraisal of Middle Eastern policy was taking place. This found expression in the annual Middle East debate in the General Assembly of the UN, when all the members of the European Community (EC), except Denmark, followed the lead of the UK (which entered the Community on 1 January 1973) and France in voting for a resolution strongly critical of Israel. (The USA again abstained.)

TERROR AND COUNTER-TERROR IN THE MIDDLE EAST

The cease-fire along the Suez Canal was maintained, but along the northern borders of Israel and Israeli-held territory there was a renewal of violence in the second half of 1972, accompanied by a mounting series of terrorist attacks by both Israelis and Palestinians in various parts of the world. In mid-1972, a number of Palestinian leaders were killed or seriously injured by explosive devices sent to them in Beirut. In September, during the Olympic Games in Munich, Palestinian guerrillas captured Israeli athletes and held them hostage in an attempt to obtain the release of Palestinians held captive in Israel. West German police, after promising the Palestinians safe conduct out of Germany, opened fire on them at Munich airport, whereupon the guerrillas killed the hostages and were themselves either killed or captured.

The Munich attack was followed by heavy Israeli ground and air raids into Lebanon, which the Israeli Government held responsible for the activities of guerrillas whose bases (since their expulsion from Jordan in 1970 and 1971) were in the refugee camps of Beirut and elsewhere in Lebanon. Letter bombs were subsequently posted to Israeli representatives in various countries and representatives of the Palestine Liberation Organization (PLO) were attacked in Rome, Stockholm, Paris and Nicosia.

At the beginning of 1973 Mr Hafez Ismail (President Sadat's political adviser), King Hussein of Jordan and Mrs Golda Meir (the Israeli Prime Minister) visited Washington for talks with President Nixon. However, the frail hopes aroused by this were dashed when an Israeli attack on guerrilla installations in a refugee camp in northern Lebanon was followed within 24 hours by the shooting down by Israeli fighters of a Libyan airliner which had strayed over occupied Sinai. The two incidents provoked an unprecedented wave of criticism of Israel on the eve of Mrs Meir's arrival in Washington.

STALEMATE

In the autumn of 1973, the Arab-Israeli conflict appeared to be further than ever from solution. Israel, confident that its military supremacy over the Arabs had increased, remained in control of all the territories it had occupied in 1967 and had established in these territories some 50 civilian and paramilitary settlements. The Egyptian and Jordanian Governments—though not yet the Syrian—had long since modified their earlier refusal to negotiate a settlement and had indicated their willingness to recognize the State of Israel; but they still refused to envisage a peace settlement which did not provide for the return of all the Occupied Territories. The UN, despite the passage every year of resolutions calling for an Israeli withdrawal, found all its efforts to devise a settlement blocked by Israel's refusal to relinquish its 1967 conquests.

More than ever, the key to the situation rested in the hands of the USA, which found itself isolated in support of Israel while becoming increasingly dependent on Arab oil. The USA's allies, for whom dependence on Arab oil was already a fact, were increasingly impatient with the US Government's Middle East policy, which seemed to be aimed at maintaining Israel's overall supremacy without seeking any concessions from the Israeli Government over the Occupied Territories. The isolation of the USA was emphasized in the Security Council in the summer of 1973, when it vetoed a resolution put forward by eight non-aligned members, which was strongly critical of Israel's continued occupation of Arab territory. All the other Council members except China, which abstained, voted affirmatively.

RENEWAL OF THE WAR

The attack which was launched on two fronts by the Egyptian and Syrian forces on 6 October 1973 took everyone by surprise. Unusual activity behind the lines had been observed by Israeli and US intelligence agencies west of the Suez Canal and east of the cease-fire line on the Golan Heights; but the Israelis were convinced that the Egyptian army was incapable of the elaborate operation required to cross the canal and breach the chain of Israeli fortifications, known as the Bar-Lev line, on the east bank. This element of surprise won for the Egyptian and Syrian forces a substantial initial advantage on both fronts. This was enhanced by the fact that 6 October was Yom Kippur, the Day of Atonement in the Jewish calendar, when all public services were suspended, making it unusually difficult for the Israelis to rapidly mobilize their forces. By midnight on the first day of the war, 400 Egyptian tanks had crossed the canal, the Bar-Lev line had been outflanked and a massive Syrian tank attack beyond the Golan Heights had only been stemmed by a masterly rearguard action by greatly outnumbered Israeli armour, aided by air strikes.

During the next three weeks (despite a UN cease-fire on 22 October), the Syrians were driven back beyond the old cease-fire line and counter-attacking Israeli forces effected a westward crossing of the Suez Canal. At the end of the war, the military advantage lay with the Israelis, who had occupied a further area of Syrian territory and were threatening Damascus, while their units west of the canal had isolated an Egyptian army in Suez. However, largely as a result of the intervention of the Arab oil-producing states, the political objectives of the Arabs had been achieved and the whole context of the confrontation decisively altered.

By making unexpectedly efficient use of new weapons the Arab armies demonstrated that since 1967 they had significantly narrowed the military technological gap between themselves and Israel. They had exposed the fallacy on which Israeli strategy had been based since the Six Day War: that the control of wide buffer zones (the territories occupied since 1967), together with the military supremacy of which it felt assured, rendered Israel immune to Arab attack. This assumption had encouraged the Israeli leaders to disregard the mounting pressure of world opinion calling for an Israeli withdrawal as the essential condition of a negotiated settlement with the Arabs.

THE OIL WEAPON

Soon after the outbreak of the war, there were calls within the Arab world to deny Middle East oil to the supporters of Israel. In October a meeting in Kuwait of representatives of the Arab oil producers resulted in an agreement to reduce output, while Abu Dhabi took the lead in halting the export of oil to the USA. In adopting and then intensifying these measures, the Arab oil-producing states displayed unexpected unity. This had an evident effect on the governments of Western Europe, conscious of their dependence on the free flow of oil from the Middle East. On 6 November the nine member states of the EC endorsed a statement calling for an Israeli withdrawal from the territories occupied in 1967 and asserting that, while all states in the Middle East should enjoy the right to secure boundaries, the legitimate rights of the Palestinians should be taken into account in any settlement (see Documents on Palestine, p. 87). Israel accused the Europeans of giving in to Arab 'blackmail', but for several years the Europeans had been dissociating themselves from US policy and registering their growing impatience with Israel's intransigence.

AMERICAN INITIATIVE

The USA, which alone possessed the influence that could induce Israel to withdraw—and which now found itself inconvenienced much more by the oil embargo than it had anticipated—accepted its responsibility to bring about a settlement. The US Secretary of State, Dr Kissinger, now embarked on a dramatic series of visits to Middle Eastern capitals, out of which resulted disengagement agreements between Egypt and Israel (signed on 18 January 1974) and between Syria and Israel (signed on 30 May 1974). In the middle of June 1974 President Nixon, whose domestic position had become dangerously insecure after the Watergate scandal, embarked on a triumphant tour of the Middle East, forecasting a new era of co-operation between the USA and the Arab world, while reassuring Israel of continuing US support. This US initiative was generally well received, except by some Israelis who foresaw mounting pressure on Israel to make concessions inconsistent with its security, and by the extreme wing of the Palestinian resistance movement, which engaged in a series of terrorist attacks on targets in northern Israel in an effort to frustrate a settlement which did not guarantee Palestine's total liberation. Otherwise, President Nixon's visit revealed a strong desire on the part of the Arab governments to restore friendly relations with the USA. Diplomatic relations between Washington and Damascus were re-established and the embargo on the export of Arab oil to the USA was lifted.

CHANGE IN THE BALANCE OF POWER

This reconciliation was one of the most striking results of the October war; it was a reminder of the greatly increased influence of the Arab states so long as they continued to act in concert. Conversely, Israel's international position had been much weakened by the failure of its pre-war policies and by the revelation of the extent to which the rest of the world was dependent on Arab goodwill. The Government headed by Golda Meir was widely blamed both for provoking the October war by its policy of 'creeping annexation' and for being caught unawares when the war came. After winning a narrow victory in a general election at the end of 1973, Mrs Meir finally abandoned the attempt to rebuild her coalition in April 1974. She was succeeded as leader of the Labour Party and Prime Minister by Gen. Yitzhak Rabin, who had been chief of staff at the time of the 1967 war and later Israeli Ambassador in Washington. In the Arab world, the effect of the war was to strengthen the position of the regimes in Cairo and Damascus and to

give new authority to King Faisal of Saudi Arabia, whose control of the greatest share of the oil reserves of the Middle East made him a dominant figure in Arab politics. The fact that the disengagement agreements involved small but significant Israeli withdrawals from Arab territory gave satisfaction throughout the Arab world, but the central problem of the future of the Palestinians remained unsolved. The difficulty of finding a solution acceptable both to Israel and to the PLO (which the Arab governments, meeting in Algiers in November 1973, had recognized as 'the sole legitimate representative of the Palestinian people') posed a continuing threat to the stability of the disengagement agreements of 1974.

Despite the new unity of the Arab world, the movement towards a settlement in the Middle East lost momentum during the second half of 1974 and a further outbreak of war seemed imminent at times. The disengagement agreements were honoured and UN forces were inserted between the combatants in Sinai and on the Golan front, but Syria and Israel exchanged mutual recriminations over the ill-treatment of prisoners and the destruction of the Syrian town of Quneitra by the Israelis on the eve of their withdrawal.

While the optimism generated by the disengagement agreements gave way to stalemate between the Arab governments and Israel, the Palestinians' central role in the conflict was strikingly endorsed. On 21 September 1974, the UN General Assembly voted to include 'the Palestine Question' on its agenda for the first time since the establishment of the State of Israel in 1948. (Only four Governments opposed this decision: Israel, the USA, the Dominican Republic and Bolivia.) On 14 October the General Assembly invited the PLO to take part in the debate and a month later the Chairman of the PLO, Yasser Arafat, outlined to the Assembly the PLO's design for a 'democratic, secular state' in Palestine in which Jews and Arabs would coexist on terms of equality, specifying that 'all Jews now living in Palestine who choose to live with us there in peace and without discrimination' were included in this design. At the end of October a meeting of Arab Heads of State in Rabat confirmed that the PLO was the 'sole legitimate representative of the Palestinian people', with the right to speak for the Palestinians at any future Middle East peace talks and to establish an independent national authority in any part of Palestine liberated from Israeli occupation.

These decisions greatly strengthened the hand of the Palestinians and the PLO. However, they also deepened the impasse over a settlement because the Israeli Government refused to have any dealings with the PLO, dismissing it as a terrorist organization. The PLO's position was also complicated by internal divisions over the objective which the organization should pursue. Although Yasser Arafat at the UN had spoken only of the PLO's goal of a unitary Palestine (which would mean the elimination of the State of Israel), he was under pressure from the Arab governments to accept the limited objective of a Palestinian state on the West Bank and the Gaza Strip, which could only be envisaged in the context of the recognition of Israel within its pre-1967 borders. A majority within the PLO appeared at the end of 1974 to be moving towards acceptance of this formula, but the minority rejected any thought of compromising the long-term goal of the total liberation of Palestine. This 'rejectionist front', with the backing of the Governments of Iraq and Libya, made it difficult for the PLO openly to align itself with those Arab governments (notably Egypt) which were prepared to exchange recognition of Israel for withdrawal from the territories occupied in 1967, including Arab Jerusalem, and the creation of a Palestinian state on the West Bank.

This was in effect the pattern for a settlement which had been envisaged in the Security Council's Resolution 242 and which had provided the basis for all the international initiatives undertaken between 1967 and 1973. These initiatives had failed because Israel, before October 1973, had felt confident of its ability to retain control of at least substantial parts of the Occupied Territories. The October war, by undermining this confidence, had highlighted Israel's dependence on US support; moreover, the initial efforts of

Dr Kissinger immediately after the war had encouraged the Arabs to believe that US influence would at last be used to promote a settlement based on Israel's withdrawal.

ARAB IMPATIENCE

The Arab-US reconciliation, in which President Sadat had taken the lead and to which he totally committed himself during 1974, had failed by the end of the year to produce any results beyond the initial disengagement agreements. Apart from the tiny areas of territory conceded by Israel under those agreements, the Israeli occupation was maintained in Sinai, the Golan Heights (including the plateau up to the outskirts of Quneitra), the West Bank (including the Old City of Jerusalem) and the Gaza Strip, with no relaxation of the ban on political activity by the Arab population and other repressive measures. None of the Jewish settlements, of which about 50 had been established in the Occupied Territories before October 1973, had been given up; indeed the Israeli Government, under pressure from the right-wing opposition and the religious parties in the Knesset, continued to announce plans to extend Jewish settlement.

These developments caused growing impatience in the Arab world. When Dr Kissinger returned to the Middle East in March in an attempt to further the process of disengagement between Israel and Egypt, it was widely assumed that he had obtained prior assurances from both sides. However, after two weeks of intensive 'shuttle diplomacy' he had to admit failure when Israel refused to withdraw from the Mitla and Giddi passes in Sinai and from the oilfield at Abu Rudeis, without an explicit assurance of future non-aggression from President Sadat. The latter was clearly unrealistic, since it would have confirmed Arab suspicions that Egypt was prepared to abandon its allies for a separate peace with Israel. There was therefore little surprise when the US Secretary of State (and later President Ford) blamed Israeli obstinacy for the breakdown of the negotiations and announced that the USA would embark on a 'reassessment' of its Middle East policy. This was held to mean that Israel's latest request for increased military and economic aid from the USA would not be granted until Israel showed a more conciliatory attitude.

The breakdown of Dr Kissinger's mission coincided with the assassination in Riyadh of King Faisal of Saudi Arabia, whose prestige and authority had been greatly increased by his support for the Arab war effort during and after the October war. In May the Syrian Government unexpectedly agreed to renew for a further six months the mandate of the UN force separating the two sides on the Golan front, and on 5 June the Egyptian Government reopened the Suez Canal, eight years to the day after the outbreak of the war which had led to its closure in 1967.

FURTHER DISENGAGEMENT IN SINAI

On 21 August Dr Kissinger flew to Israel to promote a second disengagement agreement between Israel and Egypt. After two weeks of intensive negotiations Dr Kissinger persuaded Israel and Egypt to accept an agreement which was signed in Geneva on 4 September 1975 (see Documents on Palestine, p. 90). The new agreement provided for an Israeli withdrawal from the strategic Mitla and Giddi passes and the return to Egypt of the Abu Rudeis oilfields, on which Israel had depended for some 50% of its oil supplies since 1967. As in the first disengagement agreement, a UN buffer zone was established separating the Egyptian and Israeli forces. The most important new element was the provision for five electronic listening posts in this zone, of which one was to be manned by Egyptians, one by Israelis and the other three by a team of 200 US civilians who would monitor troop movements both east and west of the passes. Both sides undertook to respect the cease-fire and to resolve the conflict between them by peaceful means. Non-military cargoes in ships sailing to or from Israel were to be allowed through the Suez Canal and the agreement was to remain in force 'until superseded by a new agreement'.

The conclusion of this second agreement was considered a triumph for US diplomacy and it had significant effects on Egypt's relations with its Arab allies. Only Saudi Arabia, Sudan and (with reservations) Kuwait expressed approval of the agreement, which was criticized—most vehemently by the Syrians and the PLO—as a surrender to US and Israeli interests. The united Arab front visible during the October war was now seriously disrupted.

The agreement marked a further stage in the US-Egyptian *rapprochement* and the estrangement between Egypt and its former ally, the USSR. In October 1975 President Sadat made an official visit to Washington, while his repeated criticisms of the USSR led to a steady deterioration of relations culminating in Egypt's abrogation of the Soviet-Egyptian Treaty of Friendship in March 1976.

Syria now assumed the leadership of the Arab cause. President Assad found his position in the Arab world greatly strengthened and even succeeded in restoring close relations with King Hussein of Jordan, establishing a joint Syrian-Jordanian Command Council. In October 1975 he visited Moscow for talks with President Podgorny and other leaders and gained a promise of further arms supplies to counter the deliveries reaching Israel from the USA. At the end of November Syria's already considerable prestige as the most consistent defender of the rights of the Palestinians was enhanced when President Assad agreed to renew the mandate of the UN Disengagement Observer Force (UNDOF) on the Golan Heights, extracting in return a promise that the Security Council would hold a special debate on the Palestine question in January with the PLO taking part.

PLO'S STANDING ENHANCED

This debate further strengthened the international position of the PLO. In November 1975 the UN General Assembly had adopted three resolutions concerning Palestine. The first had established a 20-nation committee to work out plans for the implementation of the Palestinian right 'to self-determination and national independence', the second invited the PLO to take part in all future UN debates on the Middle East, and the third denounced Zionism as 'a form of racism and racial discrimination'. (The last of these provoked an international storm of criticism in which the importance of the other two resolutions was widely overlooked.) A month later a US veto saved Israel from censure by the Security Council for a series of air raids on targets in Lebanon in which 75 people were killed. When the Security Council debated the Palestine question in January 1976, the USA again used the veto to prevent the adoption of a resolution affirming the Palestinians' right to establish a state of their own and calling for an Israeli withdrawal from all the territories occupied since June 1967.

In January 1976 Western press reports suggested that US officials were in secret contact with Palestinian representatives, and the impression that a major change in US policy was in the offing was reinforced in March when the UN Security Council debated the question of Israeli policies in the Occupied Territories. Although the USA again exercised the veto to defeat a resolution on Israel's behalf, its delegate strongly condemned Israel's establishment of 'illegal' settlements in Jerusalem and other occupied areas.

Israel's persistence in establishing these settlements was a major factor in provoking serious rioting all over the occupied West Bank and in Gaza during mid-1976. The riots had a decisive effect on the outcome of municipal elections organized by the Israeli occupation authorities in the West Bank in April. Instead of producing, as the Israelis had hoped, 'moderate' Palestinian leaders who would accept a measure of autonomy under continuing Israeli occupation, the elections demonstrated the strength of Palestinian nationalism and widespread support for the PLO.

CIVIL WAR IN LEBANON

The disunity in the Arab camp was highlighted by events in Lebanon, where armed clashes between Palestinian guerrillas and Christian militiamen in April 1975 led to a civil war which threatened to destroy the Lebanese state and almost provoked another Arab-Israeli confrontation. Attempts at mediation by the Arab League and by French and American emissaries failed to reconcile the warring parties, which, in turn, were supported by rival Arab interests. In January 1976, after nine months of heavy fighting, in which Palestinian guerrillas were drawn into a leftist alliance against the defenders of the conservative Christian establishment, the Syrian Government employed Syrian-based units of the Palestine Liberation Army to impose a cease-fire which was to be followed by a reform of the Lebanese political system. However, the cease-fire broke down in March, when Christian extremists, supporting President Franjiya, prevaricated over the implementation of the reform programme and the Druze leader of the leftist alliance tried to force the President's resignation.

Faced with a victory for the leftists and their Palestinian allies, which might provoke an Israeli military intervention in southern Lebanon, Syria used its influence to restrain the leftists, sending Syrian troops across the border at the end of May 1976, with tacit US approval. At the same time President Assad renewed the mandate of the UN force on the Golan front for a further six months.

In late 1976 the obstacles which had prevented any movement towards an Arab-Israeli settlement were removed. After repeated failures on the part of the Arab League to play an effective mediating role in Lebanon, determined efforts by the Saudi Arabian and Kuwaiti Governments brought about a restricted Arab summit meeting in Riyadh in October, at which the leaders of Egypt, Syria, Lebanon and the PLO agreed to the terms of a cease-fire. These were confirmed at a further meeting in Cairo on 26 October, and provided for the creation of a substantial Arab peace-keeping force which within a month had halted the savage fighting in Beirut, reopened the Beirut-Damascus road and occupied the main towns in the north and south of the country.

NEW ADMINISTRATION IN WASHINGTON

In the USA the President-elect, Jimmy Carter, had indicated his intention to take early action over the Middle East. Once more the Israelis found themselves under pressure both from the Arabs and from the USA. On 11 November 1976, the USA approved a unanimous 'consensus statement' by the Security Council which 'strongly deplored' Israel's actions in establishing settlements in the Occupied Territories and attempting to alter the demographic balance in Jerusalem. On 19 November the US Ambassador to Israel, speaking to the annual convention of B'nai B'rith in Jerusalem, said that 'unless Israel's professed willingness to return occupied territory is seen as more than mere rhetoric, the vicious circle of mutual mistrust cannot be broken'. On 24 November the USA joined 117 other nations in voting in the UN General Assembly (against the opposition of Israel and Costa Rica) to deplore Israel's refusal to allow the return of the Palestinian refugees who had left their homes in 1967.

On the occupied West Bank intermittent unrest continued throughout 1976. Demonstrations in Nablus, Ramallah and the Old City of Jerusalem in May and June were subdued by the Israeli security forces with exceptional violence. In October there were serious riots in Hebron over the respective rights of Jews and Arabs to pray in the mosque built over the Tombs of the Patriarchs. Israel's occupation policy was again condemned by the UN General Assembly on 20 December, following the publication of a report by the UN Special Committee for the Investigation of Israeli Practices in the Occupied Territories. The UN Human Rights Commission expressed 'grave concern' over the deteriorating situation in the Occupied Territories, and unanimously called on the Government of Israel to adhere to the terms of the Fourth Geneva Convention in its treatment of civilians.

Conscious of the growing tension in the Middle East and of the steadily increasing dependence of the Western world on Arab oil, the new US Administration moved swiftly to revive the Arab-Israeli peace process. In February President Carter dispatched his Secretary of State, Cyrus Vance, on a tour of the Middle East and invited Israeli and Arab leaders to visit him in Washington. During an interim period and as the prelude to a final peace agreement, the US President indicated that arrangements might be made to extend Israel's defence capability beyond its eventual legal frontiers. A week later President Carter stated, unexpectedly,

that the final element in an Arab-Israeli settlement should be the creation of a 'homeland' for the dispossessed Palestinians.

ISRAELI GOVERNMENT RESIGNS

The renewed emphasis on the Palestinian aspect of the problem was unwelcome to the Israelis. The governing coalition was already under considerable internal pressure as a result of the difficult economic situation and the failure to devise any constructive policy for achieving peace with the Arabs; in addition, it had been undermined by a series of scandals involving leading figures in the Labour Party, which had dominated every government since the creation of the state. The most crucial issue facing the Government concerned the Occupied Territories and in particular the extent to which it should allow—or could control—Jewish settlement on the West Bank. The right-wing Likud coalition opposed any withdrawal from the West Bank, and Mr Rabin's Cabinet was divided on the issue; following a dispute with one of his coalition partners, Mr Rabin announced the Government's resignation. A general election was fixed for 17 May 1977.

ARAB GOVERNMENTS AND THE PLO

Once they had achieved a reconciliation between themselves and put an end to the war in Lebanon in late 1976, the Arab governments enlisted the help of the new US Administration in working towards a peace settlement with Israel. Their common position was that the Geneva conference should be reconvened, with the Palestinians participating, and that an overall settlement should be negotiated on the basis of an Israeli withdrawal to the 1967 borders and the establishment of a Palestinian state on the West Bank and the Gaza Strip. However, the PLO refused to renounce its objective of a unitary, 'secular, democratic state' in the whole of Palestine (which would replace the existing State of Israel), although PLO spokesmen did indicate their willingness to establish a state 'on any part of Palestine' from which the Israelis would withdraw.

Since the Israelis refused either to entertain the idea of an independent Palestinian state or to negotiate under any circumstances with the PLO (whether or not the PLO agreed to recognize the State of Israel), no accommodation appeared possible unless the US Government brought pressure to bear on Israel. This the Carter Administration was reluctant to do in the run-up to the Israeli general election, although there were indications that the USA was in contact with the PLO in an effort to persuade the Palestinians to modify their attitude.

RIGHT-WING VICTORY IN ISRAEL

The prospects for a negotiated Arab-Israeli settlement received a severe setback in May, when the elections in Israel resulted in an unexpected victory for the right-wing Likud grouping. The elections were fought mainly on domestic issues and the defeat of the ruling Labour Party was widely attributed to discontent over the economy and the series of scandals involving senior figures in the former administration. Likud, led by Menachem Begin (who, pre-1948, had been the leader of the terrorist organization, Irgun Zvai Leumi), was committed to maintaining Israeli rule over the whole of the occupied West Bank, on the grounds that it constituted part of Israel's divinely-ordained inheritance.

Faced with this challenge, President Carter invited the new Prime Minister of Israel to Washington and took steps to restate his own view of the prerequisites for a peace settlement in the Middle East and to obtain the acceptance of these by the USA's allies in Europe. A statement published at the end of June by the State Department reaffirmed US adherence to Security Council Resolution 242, stressing that a settlement had to involve Israeli withdrawal 'on all three fronts of the Middle East—that is, Sinai, Golan, West Bank and Gaza—and reiterating President Carter's belief in 'the need for a homeland for the Palestinians, whose exact nature should be negotiated between the parties'.

The theme of a Palestinian 'homeland' was taken up at a meeting of the heads of government of the EC in London. In a declaration published on 29 June 1977, the leaders of the nine members restated 'their view that a peace settlement should be based on Security Council Resolutions 242 and 338', adding that a solution to the Middle East conflict would be possible 'only if the legitimate right of the Palestinian people to give expression to its national identity is translated into fact, which would take into account the need for a homeland for the Palestinians'. The Declaration also said that representatives of 'the Palestinian people' must be included in peace negotiations.

When Mr Begin arrived in Washington in July 1977, he achieved an unexpected success with the US public, but it was clear that no serious attempt had been made in the talks between the two leaders to examine the basic conditions for a peace settlement. The US Administration was now intent on securing Palestinian participation in any peace negotiations, to which the Israeli Government was strenuously opposed. When the Secretary of State, Cyrus Vance, in the course of a tour of Middle Eastern capitals in August, was told by the Saudi Arabian Government that the PLO would accept Resolution 242 if it were amended to include provision for Palestinian self-determination, there was a moment of optimism in which Mr Carter spoke of the possibility that acceptance by the PLO of Resolution 242 might open the way to PLO participation in a reconvened Geneva peace conference. But Mr Vance's visit ended discouragingly in Israel, where Mr Begin's Government refused categorically to negotiate under any circumstances with the PLO or to consider the idea of a Palestinian 'homeland'. In any case, the PLO, sceptical about the terms of the proposed bargain, finally refused to amend its stand over Resolution 242 without firm assurances that it would receive in return something more substantial.

Within days of Mr Vance's departure, Israel announced that social services in the fields of education, health and welfare were to be extended to the Arab population of the West Bank and the Gaza Strip, which was widely interpreted as a step towards the annexation of these areas. This, and the decision to authorize three new Jewish settlements on the West Bank, caused an immediate hardening of the PLO attitude and complicated still further the task of the USA in bringing the Israelis and the Arabs—including, if possible, the Palestinians—to the negotiating table.

When the Israeli Foreign Minister, Moshe Dayan, went to Washington in September 1977, he took with him draft proposals for a territorial settlement which envisaged the maintenance of the Israeli occupation throughout the West Bank and the Gaza Strip. These proposals expressed the continuing resolve of Mr Begin's Government not to agree to any step which could lead to the creation of an independent Palestinian state. The USA, by contrast, was apprehensive that anything which appeared to extinguish all hope of that ill-defined Palestinian 'homeland', would not merely ensure the continuation of Palestinian resistance but would also alienate those Arab governments on whose goodwill the USA was increasingly dependent.

Towards the end of September there was a fresh outbreak of fighting in southern Lebanon, with Israeli troops openly intervening across the border in support of right-wing forces and against the Palestinians. This prompted a US initiative, reluctantly accepted by the Israeli Government, to include Palestinian representatives in a joint Arab delegation to the peace conference in Geneva. Moshe Dayan emphasized that this did not mean that Israel was ready to abandon its attitude towards the PLO or its rejection of a Palestinian state. A joint Soviet-US statement published on 1 October 1977 called for a Middle East settlement that would ensure 'the legitimate rights of the Palestinians'. The use for the first time of this phrase by the US Government alarmed Israel and was taken by the Arabs as an indication that President Carter was prepared for the confrontation that had long been threatening with the Israeli Government and its powerful supporters in the USA. The prospect raised by the joint statement, however, that the two superpowers were prepared to collaborate again made a renewal of the Geneva Conference more likely and encouraged diplomatic activity, with even the PLO expressing its qualified acceptance of the Soviet-US statement as the basis for a reconvened peace conference.

PRESIDENT SADAT'S VISIT TO JERUSALEM

On 9 November, in the course of a speech to the Egyptian Parliament in which he expressed impatience with the endless debates over procedural questions, President Sadat said that he would be willing to go to Jerusalem and to the Knesset itself to negotiate with Israel. Despite widely expressed scepticism, the suggestion was immediately taken up by the Israeli Prime Minister and pursued through intermediaries in the US embassies in Cairo, Beirut and Jerusalem. Resisting a rising tide of Arab disapproval, and despite the last-minute resignation of his Minister of Foreign Affairs, President Sadat flew to Jerusalem on 19 November 1977, and the next day made a dramatic appeal for peace in the Knesset and before the television cameras of the world.

This unexpected initiative was greeted with enthusiasm in the West, where it was regarded as a constructive break with the sterile attitudes of the past, and with incredulous delight by Israel, which glimpsed the prospect of an end to its dangerous isolation. Among the Arabs, however, while there were scattered expressions of approval and optimism, the general reaction of furious resentment left the Arab world in a state of unparalleled disunity, making it harder than ever to achieve a common platform on which to negotiate with Israel.

Nor did the euphoria which surrounded President Sadat in Jerusalem long survive his return to Cairo. It soon became apparent that his Israeli hosts had assumed—like his Arab critics—that President Sadat had despaired of achieving an overall settlement and had set himself the more limited objective of an Egyptian-Israeli peace treaty. The Israeli leaders were ready to withdraw from almost all Egyptian territory but they were not prepared to meet Mr Sadat's other demands for a complete withdrawal from all Arab territory occupied in 1967 and recognition of the Palestinian right to self-determination.

Serious negotiations were postponed until 25 December 1977, when Mr Begin flew to Ismailia for a summit meeting with President Sadat, at which the Israeli Prime Minister produced a set of proposals for the future of Sinai, the West Bank and the Gaza Strip. On the crucial question of the future of the Palestinians, Mr Begin offered only a limited form of self-rule for the population of the West Bank and the Gaza Strip, with Israel remaining in control of 'security and public order'. This was criticized in the Arab world as being merely a formula for the maintenance of the Israeli occupation.

President Sadat's position was made more difficult by a statement from President Carter apparently approving the Begin proposal for Palestinian 'self-rule'. When Mr Carter, in an evident attempt to repair the damage, altered the schedule of a foreign tour in order to meet Mr Sadat at Aswan, he took the opportunity to reiterate the need to recognize 'the legitimate rights of the Palestinian people' and to enable the Palestinians 'to participate in the determination of their own future'. Elsewhere in the Arab world, however, cynicism about an overall Arab-Israeli settlement was deepened by mistrust of Sadat's motives and by the apparent inconsistency of US policy.

The Ismailia summit meeting produced a commitment to bilateral talks on political and military questions affecting a settlement. The military talks opened in Cairo on 11 January and were at once complicated by a dispute over Israeli settlements in Sinai, which had been criticized as illegal by the International Commission of Jurists. This criticism was echoed by President Carter a week later and when the political talks opened in Jerusalem on 16 January they were interrupted after only 24 hours when President Sadat recalled the Egyptian delegation, saying that in view of Israel's insistence on retaining the settlements he saw no hope of reaching agreement.

ISRAELI INVASION OF SOUTH LEBANON

A visit by Mr Begin to Washington in March 1978 was delayed for a week after a terrorist raid near Tel-Aviv by Palestinian guerrillas operating from south Lebanon, in which 36 Israelis were killed. Israel mounted a major attack across the border into southern Lebanon, initially to wipe out Palestinian guerrilla bases and establish a security belt along the Lebanese side of the frontier. After the USA hurriedly introduced a resolution in the UN Security Council calling for an Israeli withdrawal to be supervised by a UN force, the Israelis advanced further, and by the time a cease-fire finally came into effect on 20 March their forces were in occupation of the whole of south Lebanon as far as the Litani river, with the exception of the port of Tyre.

The Israeli invasion, which was accompanied by heavy and indiscriminate land, sea and air bombardments, provoked world-wide denunciation, especially as it became clear that an estimated 1,000 Lebanese civilians had been killed, in addition to some 200 guerrillas, and more than 200,000 refugees had been driven from their homes. When Mr Begin finally met President Carter on 20 March, the differences between them over the basic prerequisites of a Middle East peace settlement led to a confrontation which was barely masked by diplomatic protocol. Mr Begin returned from Washington to face a threat to his leadership in Israel, where there was dissension within the Cabinet.

There was friction over the role of the UN Interim Force in Lebanon (UNIFIL), whose mandate was to supervise the withdrawal of the Israeli army from southern Lebanon and to restore the authority of the Lebanese Government. The Israelis carried out a partial withdrawal at the end of April but insisted that they would maintain an armed presence in Lebanon until the UN force could ensure the security of northern Israel against attacks by Palestinian guerrillas. The PLO, which was determined not to relinquish its last area of operations, promised to co-operate with UNIFIL.

In May 1978 Mr Begin again visited Washington, where President Carter assured him that 'we will never waver in our absolute commitment to Israel's security'. However, two weeks later the US Senate authorized the sale of advanced fighter aircraft to Saudi Arabia. This decision clearly reflected US impatience with Mr Begin's stand on peace negotiations, and the importance the USA attached to retaining the friendship of Saudi Arabia, the leading oil producer in the Middle East.

When the Israelis withdrew the last of their forces from south Lebanon on 13 June, they refused to hand over their positions to UNIFIL but left them in the hands of Lebanese Christian militia units which had been collaborating with the Israelis against the Lebanese Government. This contributed to a crisis in Beirut at the beginning of July, when the Syrian-dominated Arab peace-keeping force attempted to impose its authority on the right-wing Christian militias.

The US Government, alarmed at the prospect of renewed Israeli intervention and of the final breakdown of the peace initiative launched by President Sadat in November 1977, exerted its influence to restrain both sides in Lebanon and persuaded the Israeli and Egyptian governments to send their ministers of foreign affairs to a meeting in the United Kingdom, which took place at Leeds Castle on 18 July. When this meeting failed to narrow the gap between the two sides, President Sadat announced that he would not engage in further negotiations with Israel unless the Israeli Government changed its position. Faced with a deteriorating situation, President Carter took the unexpected step of inviting the Egyptian and Israeli leaders to meet him in a final attempt to break the deadlock at Camp David at the beginning of September 1978.

CAMP DAVID SUMMIT AND REACTIONS

The Camp David meeting, which lasted for 12 days and appeared more than once to be on the point of breaking down, ended on 17 September when President Carter made a triumphant appearance on television to announce that Mr Begin and President Sadat had signed two documents which together provided a framework for peace in the Middle East (see Documents on Palestine, p. 91). One of these dealt with the bilateral problems between Egypt and Israel, which the two leaders undertook to resolve by concluding within three months a peace treaty providing for an Israeli withdrawal from Sinai and the establishment of normal relations between the two countries. The other dealt with the wider question of the future of the West Bank and Gaza and provided for the election of a self-governing Palestinian authority to replace the existing Israeli military Government; once the authority was in being, there should be a transitional period of not more than five years, during which the inhabitants of the West Bank and Gaza would exercise autonomy; and finally, 'as soon as possible, but not later than the third year after the beginning of the transitional period', there should be negotiations to determine the final status of the West Bank and Gaza and to conclude a peace treaty between Israel and Jordan.

The Camp David agreements were greeted with a mixed reception by the participants. President Carter's own standing was greatly enhanced in the USA, where it was felt that his daring personal diplomacy had forced the Israeli and Egyptian leaders to make concessions. In Israel the agreements were greeted with more cautious approval, in the belief that Mr Begin had realized Israel's long-standing ambition to conclude a separate peace with Egypt without making any substantive concessions over Israel's right to maintain control of the West Bank and Gaza. In the Arab world, however, the agreements were regarded as proof that President Sadat had abandoned the Palestinians and his Arab allies. Even the Government of Saudi Arabia commented that the Camp David agreements constituted 'an unacceptable formula for a definitive peace', while the resignation of the Egyptian Minister of Foreign Affairs (who was at Camp David with President Sadat) showed that not even Egyptian opinion was whole-heartedly in favour of the Camp David formula.

The controversy within the Arab world centred on whether or not the agreements offered any real promise of eventual self-determination for the Palestinians. The advocates of the Camp David 'framework for peace' argued that if the Palestinians co-operated in the arrangements for a transitional period of self-rule they would set in motion a process which would be irreversible; that the end result of this process would be an independent Palestinian state; and that, if the Palestinians refused to co-operate, they would provide Israel with an excuse to perpetuate its occupation of the West Bank and Gaza. Critics argued that it was futile for Egypt to negotiate on behalf of the Palestinians over an issue on which the Palestinians themselves had not been consulted; that the arrangements for Palestinian autonomy outlined at Camp David were so imprecise as to be useless; that in any case Israel would hold a power of veto over their implementation and over the eventual future of the West Bank; and that Israel had no intention of ending its occupation or of allowing any development which might lead to Palestinian independence.

The last of these arguments was given greater credence in the immediate aftermath of the Camp David meeting by the actions of Mr Begin. As soon as he was back in Israel, he declared emphatically in the Knesset that Israel would not allow 'under any conditions or in any circumstances' the establishment of an independent Palestinian state, and that Israel would continue to create new settlements on the West Bank and would expect to maintain an armed presence there even after the end of the five-year transitional period.

ARAB OPPOSITION HARDENS

In the circumstances it was not surprising that the US Secretary of State, Mr Vance, whom President Carter despatched to the Middle East to enlist Arab support for the Camp David agreements, met with a frosty reception. The Governments of Jordan (whose co-operation would be necessary if the provisions for the West Bank were to be put into effect) and of Saudi Arabia (whose influence was important in shaping Arab opinion) both expressed serious reservations, while the more radical Arab governments, led by Syria acting in co-operation with the PLO, declared their rejection of the agreements.

So strong were the feelings aroused in the Arab world that they led to a reconciliation between the rival Baathist Governments of Iraq and Syria, and to a summit conference of all the Arab states (apart from Egypt) in Baghdad at the beginning of November 1978 to consider means of preventing the implementation of the Camp David agreements. After a fiery debate in which various proposals were aired for isolating Egypt and denying it economic aid, the Arab leaders agreed, at the insistence of Saudi Arabia, to delay implementation until Egypt should actually sign a peace treaty with Israel.

In this way the door was left open for President Sadat to reconsider a policy which would leave him totally dependent on the support of the USA. Further decisions by the Israelis to press ahead with their settlements in the West Bank led President Sadat to press for a revision of the Camp David agreements in order to link the provisions concerning the future of the West Bank more closely to those for a bilateral peace treaty between Egypt and Israel. In addition, President Sadat demanded that a specific timetable be adopted for the introduction of autonomy in the West Bank. This brought the peace-making process once again to a standstill, and the target date of 18 December (by which the two sides had agreed at Camp David to sign a peace treaty) passed with the outstanding issues unresolved.

REVOLUTION IN IRAN

The disintegration of the Shah's regime in Iran at the end of 1978 had important repercussions throughout the Middle East. The suspension of oil exports from Iran, as a result of a strike in the oilfields, threatened an international energy crisis and cut off the most important source of Israel's oil supplies. It also became clear, even before the Shah went into exile on 15 January 1979, that whatever government might succeed him would give strong backing to the Palestinians.

These developments gave added urgency to the US desire to achieve at least a partial Arab-Israeli settlement, but hardened the attitudes of all the possible participants. Israel insisted on an Egyptian undertaking in the draft peace treaty to guarantee them access to oil from Sinai after their evacuation of the peninsula. For President Sadat it became more necessary than ever to obtain some concession over the West Bank. Without such a concession it was less likely that Saudi Arabia or Jordan—let alone the other Arab states—would moderate their opposition to the Camp David peace formula.

PRESIDENT CARTER VISITS THE MIDDLE EAST

When a further ministerial meeting in Washington between Egypt and Israel failed to remove the remaining obstacles to an agreement, President Carter flew to the Middle East on 7 March 1979 in a final effort to persuade Egypt and Israel to sign the long-deferred peace treaty. Mr Carter returned to Washington to announce that 'we have now defined the major components of a peace treaty'; but before the treaty could be signed there were further acrimonious arguments about Israeli settlements on the West Bank, while opposition to the peace treaty on the part of even the most moderate Arab governments emphasized the isolation of Egypt.

ARAB BOYCOTT OF EGYPT

The attitude of Saudi Arabia was crucial, and the euphoria in the USA over the signing of the peace treaty—which finally took place in Washington on 26 March (see Documents on Palestine, p. 92)—was dispelled when Saudi Arabia made plain its opposition by attending a meeting of the Arab League in Baghdad at which a decision was taken to impose a political and economic boycott against Egypt. Arab ambassadors were recalled from Cairo, economic aid to Egypt was suspended and it was announced that the headquarters of the Arab League would be transferred from Cairo to Tunis. In agreeing to these measures and in subsequently breaking off diplomatic relations with Egypt, the Government of Saudi Arabia in effect chose to maintain solidarity with the rest of the Arab world at the expense of an open breach with the USA.

Arab opposition to the peace treaty focused on its failure to make any clear provision for Palestinian self-determination. President Sadat maintained that the treaty was the first step towards a comprehensive settlement which would restore Palestinian rights; but to the other Arabs it appeared to be a separate peace between Egypt and Israel which would restore Sinai to Egypt but would leave Israel in control of the rest of the Occupied Territories. That this was also the view of the Israeli Government seemed to be confirmed when Mr Begin, in a broadcast on Israel's Independence Day, reiterated that no border would ever again be drawn through 'the land of Israel' and that 'we shall never withdraw from the Golan Heights'.

THE AUTONOMY TALKS

Soon after the signing of the Egyptian-Israeli peace treaty the two countries began negotiations on the question of autonomy for the Palestinians in the Occupied Territories. The principal issue on which the two sides differed was the establishment of Israeli settlements in the Occupied Territories, which the Israeli Prime Minister, Mr Begin, insisted were in no way contrary to the Camp David Accords. When the Israeli Minister in Charge of Settlements, Ariel Sharon, announced plans at the end of May to build new settlements on the West Bank and in the Gaza Strip, the Egyptian Prime Minister, Mustapha Khalil, warned Israel that this would jeopardize the peace process. Shortly afterwards, on 12 June, the second round of talks broke up with the two sides unable to agree on even the first principles of the autonomy plan.

On 4 September President Sadat went to Haifa to begin new talks with Mr Begin and announced that he was 'determined to spread the umbrella of peace to include the Palestinian people'. Bilateral agreements were made on the issues of border patrols, oil sales from Egypt to Israel, and the return of the Santa Caterina monastery to the Egyptians, but no progress was registered on the autonomy question. The two countries drifted still further apart a week later when the Israeli Government withdrew its ban on the purchase by Israeli citizens of Arab land in the Occupied Territories, an action immediately condemned by the US Government.

ISRAEL'S INTERNAL DISPUTES

In Israel, although the opposition movement, Peace Now, organized demonstrations against the establishment of more settlements in the Occupied Territories, a parliamentary committee in July 1979 approved plans to build 13 during the next 12 months. However, the Israeli Supreme Court ruled that the Elon Moreh settlement near Nablus was illegal. The ruling denied that the settlement served a necessary military function and ordered the expropriated land to be restored to its Arab owners. At the end of October an extremist nationalist party, Tehiya, was founded, its principal objective being the construction of Jewish settlements throughout the West Bank.

PALESTINIAN DIPLOMATIC GAINS

In mid-1979 there was speculation that the USA was making overtures to the PLO in order to bring it into the peace process. Although this was repeatedly denied by President Carter, the US Ambassador at the UN, Andrew Young, met the PLO observer, Zehdi Labib Terzi, in September. After strong protests from the Israelis, Young resigned, declaring that the USA's refusal to talk to the PLO was ridiculous.

Meanwhile, the PLO was making significant diplomatic headway in western Europe. In July Yasser Arafat had talks with Chancellor Kreisky of Austria and in September he was officially received by King Juan Carlos of Spain and his Prime Minister, Adolfo Suárez. At the UN General Assembly meeting later in the month, the Irish Minister of Foreign Affairs, Michael O'Kennedy, speaking on behalf of the EC, voiced strong criticism of current Israeli policy and mentioned, for the first time, the role of the PLO. In the same debate the British Foreign Secretary, Lord Carrington, called for an end to Israel's policy of settlement in the Occupied Territories and for a reversal of the decision to allow Israeli citizens to buy land there. In November the PLO was accorded 'political recognition' by the Italian Government and at the same time Arafat was received by the President and Prime Minister of Portugal. In addition, the PLO's spokesman on foreign affairs, Farouk Kaddoumi, held talks with the foreign ministers of Belgium, Italy and Greece.

UNREST IN THE WEST BANK

While Egypt and Israel made little progress on the autonomy question, the Palestinian population of the West Bank grew increasingly restless and frustrated. In February 1980 a new crisis arose when the Israeli Cabinet decided in principle to allow Jews to settle in the town of Hebron. This action was widely condemned in Israel and abroad and led to increased tension throughout the West Bank. Riots and demonstrations took place in a number of towns and in April a group of Jewish extremists mounted attacks in Ramallah. On 1 May a Palestinian youth was shot dead by an Israeli officer in Anabta, and the following day PLO guerrillas struck in Hebron and killed six Jewish settlers. The Israeli authorities reacted by blowing up a number of houses near the scene of the ambush and deporting the mayors of Hebron and Halhul and the Qadi (religious leader) of Hebron.

NO PROGRESS TOWARDS REAL PEACE

The seizure of US embassy officials in Iran and the Soviet invasion of Afghanistan at the end of 1979 diverted international attention from the Arab-Israeli conflict and the USA concentrated its attention on the recovery of the hostages in Teheran. On 1 March, however, the UN Security Council unanimously adopted a resolution (465—see Documents on Palestine, p. 94) calling upon Israel to 'dismantle the existing settlements' and 'to cease, on an urgent basis, the establishment, construction and planning' of new ones. Two days later President Carter astonished the international community by retracting the affirmative US vote and announcing that it had been a mistake. The US vote, he said, had been 'approved with the understanding that all references to Jerusalem would be deleted', and he added: 'While our opposition to the establishment of the Israeli settlements is long-standing and well-known . . . the call for dismantling was neither proper nor practical.' This retraction was widely seen as a surrender to the Zionist lobby by a US president needing votes in an election year.

As the autonomy negotiations showed little sign of progress, the EC sought new ways to break the deadlock. One idea was the suggestion that Resolution 242 should be amended to include a reference to the right of self-determination for the Palestinians. In February, during a visit to Bahrain, the Irish Minister of Foreign Affairs recognized the PLO and called for the establishment of a Palestinian state. In the course of an important tour of the Middle East in the following month, President Giscard d'Estaing of France supported the principle of self-determination for the Palestinians and spoke of the need to include the PLO in peace negotiations. In April the PLO's diplomatic success in Europe continued when Chancellor Kreisky of Austria officially recognized the PLO as the representative of the Palestinian people.

The USA made it clear that it disapproved of European attempts to intervene in the peace process. In March President Carter, under attack from the other presidential candidates for his inept handling of the Security Council vote, decided to make yet another attempt to mediate between Israel and Egypt. Although the two countries had exchanged ambassadors and some successes had been achieved on bilateral relations, their positions on the autonomy issue were as far apart as ever. Determined to make some progress before 26 May (the target date for the completion of the autonomy talks), Carter invited President Sadat and Mr Begin to visit him separately in Washington during April. Nothing was achieved and at the beginning of May President

Sadat announced that Egypt was suspending the negotiations indefinitely.

THE EUROPEAN INITIATIVE

Despite the opposition of Israel, Egypt and the USA, the EC countries finally produced their Middle East statement at a meeting in Venice on 13 June (see Documents on Palestine, p. 95). After criticism from the new US Secretary of State, Edmund Muskie, and a warning from President Carter that the USA would not hesitate to use its veto in the Security Council, the EC abandoned any attempt to introduce a resolution on Palestinian rights at the UN. However, they did go further than ever before in their support of Palestinian aspirations.

In the Venice statement, the EC declared, for the first time collectively, that the Palestinian people must be allowed 'to exercise fully its right to self-determination', and called for the PLO 'to be associated with the negotiations'. It also repeated its condemnations of Israeli settlements and any attempt to change the status of Jerusalem. Finally the EC announced its intention of consulting all the parties concerned, in order to determine the form of a European initiative.

EGYPTIAN-ISRAELI RELATIONS

The negotiations over Palestinian autonomy, which President Sadat had postponed in May, were reopened in Washington in July. However, the parties remained as far apart as ever, and it appears that President Sadat decided to resume the talks only in order to increase the chances of President Carter's re-election in the forthcoming American elections.

Meanwhile the so-called 'normalization' of relations between Egypt and Israel was moving forward at a slow pace. Although both countries had established embassies in each other's capitals and there were regular air-flights between the two, other agreements were taking a long time to implement.

WEST BANK NATIONALISM

Only a month after the mayors of Hebron and Halhul had been deported by the Israeli authorities, Jewish extremists placed bombs in the cars of three other West Bank mayors. Two of them were severely injured, including Bassam Shaka, the Mayor of Nablus, who lost both his legs. The attacks revealed the existence of a militant underground movement among Jewish settlers in the West Bank, which, in the ensuing weeks, issued death threats to Arabs and moderate Israelis, including Knesset members and prominent journalists. Tension increased as leading Palestinians, including Mayor Shaka, accused the Israeli Government of having links with the extremists. The Government's failure to investigate the crime properly, and the allegation that the head of the Shin Bet (Israel's internal security and intelligence service) had resigned because Mr Begin had refused to allow him to carry out an investigation of members of Gush Emunim (the main West Bank settlement organization), added substance to these suspicions.

PARTY RIVALRY IN ISRAEL

Opinion polls in Israel had long been predicting a disastrous defeat for Mr Begin's Government at the next general election, which had to be held before November 1981. Likud's unpopularity stemmed largely from its failure to solve the country's economic problems but during the early months of 1981 attention in Israel and abroad was focused on the parties' conflicting policies towards the Occupied Territories.

For electoral and other reasons, the Labour Party refused to define its policy towards the West Bank but it emphasized that it did not plan to annex the area. The Labour leader, Shimon Peres, seemed to favour the so-called 'Jordanian option', involving the return of the populated areas to Jordan but the retention of the Jordan Valley and various blocks of settlements. Although King Hussein of Jordan repeatedly declared that no such option existed and that he was not empowered to speak for the Palestinians, Labour politicians continued to think in terms of a partition of the West Bank.

The Likud Government was determined to make it impossible to implement this policy. In the months before the election, which was to be held in June 1981, the Likud coalition decided to launch a vast new settlement programme which an incoming Labour government would be unable to dismantle.

THE EUROPEAN ROLE

As a consequence of the Venice Declaration, Mr Gaston Thorn, the President-elect of the EC Commission, was sent in August on a fact-finding tour of the Middle East. He visited eight Arab countries and Israel, where he had an acrimonious meeting with Mr Begin, who claimed that the European initiative was a recipe for 'the eventual destruction of Israel'. Mr Thorn received greater encouragement in the Arab countries, particularly Jordan, Kuwait and Saudi Arabia, and in Beirut he met the PLO chairman, Yasser Arafat.

The outbreak of the war between Iran and Iraq in September 1980 and the campaign for the US presidency temporarily halted European peace initiatives but at a summit meeting in Luxembourg in December the EC heads of government discussed a secret document putting forward a number of possible solutions to the Arab-Israeli conflict. The Dutch Minister of Foreign Affairs, Christopher van der Klaauw, was asked to discuss these proposals with the parties involved, and in March 1981 he visited Syria, Jordan and Iraq.

REAGAN IN THE WHITE HOUSE

The election of Ronald Reagan as President of the USA was greeted enthusiastically in Israel but caused dismay in the Arab world. During the campaign Mr Reagan had made pro-Israeli statements that seemed excessive even for a US presidential candidate and his early appointments reflected the influence of his team of Zionist advisers. Nearly all of the Reagan appointees shared the feelings of the new Secretary of State, Alexander Haig, and the National Security Adviser, Richard Allen, who judged the Arab-Israeli conflict not on its merits but in terms of the East-West confrontation. The gloom in the Arab world was increased by Dr Henry Kissinger's return to the Middle East on an unofficial visit in January 1981, where he contemptuously dismissed the European initiative, and by the new President's apparent ignorance of the issues. In an interview soon after taking office, Mr Reagan declared that the Israeli settlements were 'not illegal', thereby contradicting what had long been official US policy.

The US Administration soon made it clear that it regarded the European initiative as a hindrance to its own efforts in the Middle East. The USA's main preoccupation was not with the Palestinian question, but with the threat which it believed the USSR posed to the oil-rich Gulf. To counter this threat, the USA created a rapid deployment force able to intervene where necessary in the Gulf area. Although the Gulf Arabs denied the existence of a Soviet threat and declared their opposition to such a force, the USA went ahead with its plans to establish bases in Oman, Somalia and Kenya. In April Mr Haig visited Egypt, Israel, Jordan and Saudi Arabia, intent on convincing the conservative Arab regimes of the Soviet threat. Both Jordan and Saudi Arabia, two of the USA's closest allies in the Arab world, showed themselves to be highly sceptical about the Reagan Administration's new priorities, while Syria, the PLO and other forces in the region were even more critical of US policies.

THE LEBANESE ERUPTION

At the beginning of March 1981 the Syrian and Lebanese Governments agreed to send regular units of the Lebanese army to join UNIFIL forces in southern Lebanon. This move was opposed by the Israeli-backed Lebanese rebel leader, Maj. Sa'ad Haddad, whose troops subsequently opened fire on UNIFIL positions. It was in response to this action and to attempts by the Phalangist Christian militia to strengthen its positions around the Lebanese town of Zahle that Syrian troops of the Arab Deterrent Force moved against the Maronite Christian positions in central Lebanon.

In early April Lebanon saw its most serious fighting since the end of the civil war in 1976. The battles around Zahle were followed by fighting in Beirut and Baalbek and in the south between Haddad's forces and the Palestinians. After a truce during the week before Easter, Israel launched a series of attacks against the south. Renewed fighting broke out between the Syrians and the Phalangists on 27 April and the following day the Israeli air force shot down two Syrian helicopters. In response to this attack Syria deployed a number of SAM-6 anti-aircraft missiles to defend its positions in the Beka'a valley.

THE SYRIAN MISSILE CRISIS

Although the Syrian missiles were stationed deep inside Lebanon far from the Israeli border and fulfilled a defensive function, Mr Begin demanded their withdrawal because they limited Israel's ability to fly over its northern neighbour. Subsequently, he admitted that he had planned to destroy the missile site but had been persuaded by the USA to wait while they tried to defuse the crisis.

Philip Habib, the US Special Envoy to the Middle East, made a series of visits to Jerusalem and Damascus during May in an attempt to work out a compromise formula to persuade Saudi Arabia to encourage the Syrians to modify their position. Instead, Saudi Arabia opened a round of inter-Arab negotiations aimed at reaching agreement on the main points of a comprehensive Lebanese settlement, which would then make it easier to solve the crisis caused by the missiles. The settlement envisaged was to be based on the conclusions of the Beiteddine conference of 1978 with provisions for the future relations between the Lebanese factions, between Syria and Lebanon, and between the Palestinians and the Lebanese Government. Meanwhile, inter-Arab relations, which had deteriorated since the beginning of the Iran-Iraq War, improved, and at a meeting of Arab Ministers of Foreign Affairs, in Tunis on 23 May, Syria received the almost unanimous backing of the Arab world.

Hopes that Syria might accept a formula offered by the USA were frustrated by a new wave of Israeli attacks on Lebanon and by the further demands of Mr Begin, who insisted on the removal of anti-aircraft missiles inside Lebanon, and a Syrian promise not to fire at Israeli aircraft while they were 'patrolling' Lebanon. In June Mr Begin warned that, if the USA failed to arrange the withdrawal of the missiles through diplomacy, Israel would remove them by force.

ISRAEL ATTACKS IRAQ

On 7 June, with the Syrian missile crisis still unresolved, the Israelis bombed and destroyed the Iraqi nuclear plant near Baghdad. Mr Begin immediately claimed that the attack was justified on the grounds of self-defence, as Iraq would soon have had the capacity to produce nuclear bombs. However, the International Atomic Energy Agency (IAEA) in Vienna, which had recently inspected the plant, said that Iraq would not have had the means to make nuclear weapons for many years, a view supported by the Congressional research service in Washington. The IAEA pointed out that Iraq, unlike Israel, was a signatory of the Nuclear Non-Proliferation Treaty and that it had co-operated with the agency over safeguards.

The raid was criticized by governments all over the world, while in the UN Security Council, the United Kingdom and France demanded a 'firm resolution' condemning Israel. Even the Israeli opposition leader, Shimon Peres, accused Mr Begin of 'acting out of electoral considerations which ignore the national interest'. President Reagan responded by suspending the delivery of four F-16 aircraft to Israel until the US Congress had decided whether or not Israel had violated an agreement whereby US weapons were sold on condition they were not used in 'an act of aggression against any other state'. Nevertheless, the President made it clear where his sympathies lay when he stated that Israel had 'reason for concern' about Iraq's nuclear capacity.

BEGIN RETAINS POWER

The Israeli general elections, which took place on 30 June 1981, were the most violent in the country's history. The campaign was characterized by the Prime Minister's demagogic performances in front of huge crowds and by the physical attacks of his Likud supporters against members and property of the opposition Labour Party. Mr Begin's aggressive foreign policy obscured his Government's failures in tackling domestic problems and, in the elections, the Labour Party failed to gain the predicted huge victory. The results showed the two main parties to be evenly balanced, but it was soon clear that the Prime Minister would remain in power if he could persuade the various religious parties to join him in a coalition. This he achieved and a new Cabinet emerged, more homogeneous and hard-line than its predecessor. The most significant appointment was that of Ariel Sharon, one of Israel's leading 'hawks', to the defence ministry.

Ten days after the elections, Israel launched a series of air strikes against Palestinian targets in southern Lebanon. Guerrillas belonging to the PLO retaliated with rocket and artillery attacks against settlements in Galilee and Israel responded with further air strikes and with raids by seaborne commandos. This time the targets included urban areas and in one strike against Beirut on 17 July more than 150 people were killed and 600 wounded. The international community was shocked by the action and the USA reacted by suspending the delivery of F-16 aircraft to Israel and by making intensive attempts to bring about a cease-fire. While President Reagan's special envoy, Philip Habib, was trying to persuade Israel to accept a truce, Saudi Arabia was putting similar pressure on the Palestinians. A cease-fire finally came into effect on 24 July.

THE DEATH OF SADAT

In August 1981 President Sadat visited Washington for the first time since the election of President Reagan. Although the USA did not accept his suggestion that it should negotiate with the PLO, the visit was considered to be a diplomatic success. Yet, for all his popularity in the West, Sadat faced major problems inside Egypt.

During the summer there had been serious clashes between Copts and Muslim fundamentalists, and at the beginning of September some 1,700 people were arrested, a number of newspapers closed down and several foreign journalists expelled. Among those arrested were a large number of the President's political opponents who were neither Copts nor Muslim fundamentalists, which suggested that Sadat was using the religious clashes as a pretext to purge the opposition. A month after the arrests, however, President Sadat was assassinated by Muslim extremists at a military parade in Cairo. The large Western attendance at his funeral, which included three former US Presidents, was in stark contrast to the lack of grief shown on the streets of the capital and indicated how much Sadat's popularity in his own country had declined as a result of his pro-Western stance on foreign policy.

EUROPE AND THE FAHD PLAN

The major diplomatic initiative of the second half of 1981 came from Saudi Arabia. The so-called 'Fahd Plan' was put forward by Crown Prince Fahd (see Documents on Palestine, p. 95). Although the USA reacted cautiously to the plan, European Ministers of Foreign Affairs called it 'extremely positive' and particularly welcomed Point Seven which, by guaranteeing 'the right of all states in the region to live in peace', indicated that Saudi Arabia was prepared to recognize Israel in return for a complete withdrawal from the Occupied Territories and the establishment of an independent Palestinian state.

Although Mr Begin described the Fahd Plan as a recipe for the destruction of Israel, the Europeans were quick to note its similarities to their own Venice Declaration of June

1980. By the end of the year, however, both plans had been virtually abandoned. Europe's initiative was wrecked when the French Minister of Foreign Affairs, Claude Cheysson, dissociated his Government from it during a visit to Israel and the Saudi plan collapsed at the end of November. Since its publication in August no member of the Arab League, apart from Libya, had rejected the Fahd Plan outright and even the PLO chairman, Yasser Arafat, had expressed approval. The Saudi delegation went to the Fez summit confident, therefore, that it could win broad support for its proposals. However, a number of Arab states, led by Syria, were opposed to the plan, not so much for its content as for its timing. At Fez the opposition hardened and, rather than allow it to degenerate into a lengthy public quarrel, King Hassan of Morocco closed the meeting after only a few hours.

THE GOLAN ANNEXATION

In December 1981, while international attention was concentrated on the crisis in Poland, the Israeli Government decided to annex the Syrian Golan Heights. Overruling the more cautious minority in his Cabinet, on 14 December Mr Begin pushed through the Knesset a bill which extended Israeli laws, jurisdiction and administration to the territory Israel had occupied since 1967. The UN Security Council unanimously condemned the action and gave Israel two weeks to rescind its decision. When the Israeli Government refused to comply, the Security Council reconvened at the beginning of January 1982 in order to study what measures should be taken against Israel. Syria advocated a resolution calling for mandatory sanctions under Chapter Seven of the UN Charter but, in a bid to attract wider international support, Jordan introduced a milder resolution calling merely for voluntary sanctions against Israel. Even this was too strong for the USA, which vetoed it, although at the same time stressing its opposition to the annexation.

THE USA WITHOUT A POLICY

After more than a year in office, the Reagan Administration, which had been lukewarm to the Fahd Plan and hostile to the European initiative, had still not made any proposals of its own. While ostensibly working towards a resumption of the autonomy talks between Egypt and Israel, and hoping that the Israeli withdrawal from Sinai in April 1982 would take place smoothly, the Administration's main concern remained the so-called 'Soviet threat'. It was primarily for strategic reasons that the USA made its two most important moves in the autumn of 1981: the sale of sophisticated radar aircraft (AWACS) to Saudi Arabia, which was passed by Congress after strong opposition from the Zionist lobby in October, and the signing of a 'memorandum of understanding' on defence co-operation with Israel on 30 November. However, this last agreement was suspended by the USA a fortnight later to show its disapproval of Israel's annexation of the Golan Heights; Begin reacted by verbally attacking the USA and repudiating the memorandum altogether.

ISRAEL WITHDRAWS FROM SINAI

Although President Mubarak of Egypt indicated soon after he succeeded Sadat that he wanted to improve his country's relations with the rest of the Arab world, it was clear that his immediate goal was the return of the last third of Sinai, which Israel was due to hand back in April 1982. Consequently, he was anxious not to do anything which might offer Israel a pretext to continue the occupation. Within Israel there was much apprehension over the evacuation of Sinai and fears that it might lead to violence within the Jewish population.

In March, after months of hesitation, the Government finally ordered the army to move into the Yamit area and evict illegal settlers who had recently entered it. The withdrawal took place as scheduled on 25 April, and, in order not to antagonize Israel, Egypt took over the key points of Rafah and Sharm esh-Sheikh with as little pomp as possible.

THE WEST BANK REVOLTS

For several months Israel had been trying to create an 'alternative' leadership among the inhabitants of the West Bank which would collaborate in imposing some form of limited autonomy on the Palestinians. With financial aid and military protection from Israel, a small number of 'village leagues' were established in a move to counter the radical nationalism of the urban leadership. Although the attempt was largely unsuccessful, it did provoke several of the West Bank's more radical mayors into refusing to collaborate with the Israeli administration. In response, on 18 March, the occupation authorities dismissed the Mayor of al-Bireh, Ibrahim Tawil, as well as the town's council.

The dismissals caused a three-day strike in East Jerusalem and the rest of the West Bank, which was later extended as a result of the harsh manner in which the Israeli army dealt with Palestinian demonstrators. Rioting took place in most West Bank towns and spread to the Gaza Strip. A week after the action taken against the al-Bireh town council, Israel issued summary dismissal orders against the Mayor of Ramallah, Karim Khalaf, and the Mayor of Nablus, Bassam Shaka. These dismissals provoked two weeks of the worst rioting the West Bank had yet seen, in which several Palestinians were killed.

ISRAEL'S INVASION OF LEBANON

The cease-fire on the Israel-Lebanon border, which had been arranged by the US Special Envoy Philip Habib in July 1981, held for less than a year. In May 1982 the Israeli air force struck at Palestinian positions inside Lebanon and PLO guerrillas retaliated by shelling Galilee. On 4 June, anti-PLO Arab gunmen shot and wounded the Israeli Ambassador to London, Shlomo Argov, and Israeli aircraft bombed targets in southern Lebanon and west Beirut. The PLO's subsequent bombardment of northern Israel—which did not result in the death of a single Israeli—was the official pretext for an invasion the Israelis entitled 'Operation Peace for Galilee'. However, as General Sharon later admitted, he had been planning the operation since becoming Minister of Defence in July 1981 and he had even visited Beirut secretly in January 1982 to prepare for it.

On 6 June the Israeli army, numbering some 30,000, brushed aside the UN forces in southern Lebanon and attacked Palestinian positions around Beaufort Castle and along the coast road to Tyre. While Israel's air force, backed up by the navy, bombed Beirut and other towns, infantry units were landed along the Lebanese coast. The Israelis captured Nabatiyah, Tyre, Sidon and Damour after massive bombardments which caused severe damage and thousands of civilian casualties. By 10 June Israeli troops had reached positions overlooking Beirut.

Syria, which had kept some 30,000 troops in Lebanon since its intervention in 1976, tried to avoid being drawn into the war but on the fourth day of the invasion its forces clashed with the advancing Israelis. Although the battles on the ground never became as serious as in the 1973 war, Syria committed its air force against the Israelis and suffered a heavy defeat. On 11 June, under diplomatic pressure from the USA, Israel agreed to a cease-fire with Syria. However, fighting continued between Palestinian guerrillas and Israeli forces. During the siege of Beirut Sharon announced that the PLO should be expelled from the country and, if possible, destroyed altogether. As for Lebanon, Sharon's intention was to clear the Syrian troops out of Beirut and the centre of the country and to install a client regime based on the right-wing Phalangist Party.

THE SIEGE OF BEIRUT

The siege of Lebanon's capital began a week after the invasion and lasted almost two months. It was bombed almost continuously from land, sea and air from 13 June to 12 August. When the siege had ended two Lebanese newspapers, quoting government sources, calculated that since the beginning of the invasion 18,000 people had been killed and 30,000 wounded. About 85% of the casualties were civilians.

Israel's terms for raising the siege were that PLO forces in Beirut, numbering some 9,000 combatants, should surrender or leave the country, along with those Syrian troops still in the city, otherwise the Israeli army would force its way into Beirut and forcibly expel them. While US officials tried to negotiate an agreement with the PLO, the Israeli armed forces continued to bombard the city. They also cut off water and electricity supplies to west Beirut and prevented food and medical supplies from reaching its beleaguered population. Finally the PLO agreed to leave and on 21 August its guerrillas began their evacuation. By the end of the month the last Palestinian units had left the city that had been their headquarters since the Jordanian civil war 12 years earlier. Israel had achieved one of its principal objectives. A second goal was attained almost immediately when, on 23 August, the Lebanese National Assembly was persuaded to choose the right-wing, pro-Israeli, Phalangist commander, Bachir Gemayel, as the new President of Lebanon.

THE SABRA/CHATILA MASSACRE

The agreement governing the evacuation of the PLO from Beirut provided for the deployment of a multinational force to supervise the Palestinian withdrawal and to protect the inhabitants of Muslim west Beirut. On 25 August this force, composed of US, French and Italian soldiers, disembarked at Beirut. Only two weeks later, they began to withdraw, a fortnight earlier than provided for in the agreement.

On 14 September the President-elect, Bachir Gemayel, was killed by a bomb explosion at the Phalangist Party headquarters and a few hours later, in contravention of the evacuation agreement, the Israeli army moved into west Beirut. The day after the assassination Israeli officers held a meeting with local Phalangist commanders in which they agreed to help a force of Phalangist militiamen to 'clean up' the Palestinian refugee camps of Sabra and Chatila. On the evening of 16 September the Phalangists entered the camps and began the massacre which was to end in the death of perhaps 2,000 refugees. Although it has since been established that Israeli officers knew the massacre was taking place that same evening, they allowed the Phalangists to remain inside the camps until 18 September and even gave logistical support and provided flares.

The outrage which the atrocity caused throughout the world eventually forced the Israeli Prime Minister to order an inquiry. In its report published in February 1983, the Israeli Commission of Inquiry criticized a number of leading Israelis including Begin, Sharon, the Minister of Foreign Affairs, Shamir, as well as high-ranking officers, such as the Chief of Staff, Eitan. Sharon was considered principally responsible for planning the operation. He resigned as Minister of Defence but Begin allowed him to remain in the Cabinet as a Minister without portfolio.

TWO PEACE PLANS

On 1 September 1982 President Reagan announced a new plan to settle the Arab-Israeli conflict (see Documents on Palestine, p. 96). It was widely considered to be the work of the new Secretary of State, George Shultz, and it represented a significant change in US policy. While the Camp David Accords had been ambiguous about the future of the territories occupied by Israel since 1967, the Reagan Plan envisaged their restoration to the Arabs. Nevertheless, at the same time the USA reaffirmed its opposition to the creation of a Palestinian state and proposed 'self-government in association with Jordan'.

The Reagan Plan was rejected by the Israeli Government, which immediately embarked on a new and more intensive programme of building settlements on the West Bank. A week after the announcement of the Reagan Plan, the Arab states, meeting in Fez, countered with their own proposals (see Documents on Palestine, p. 96), which were almost identical to the Fahd Plan of the year before and called for the creation of a Palestinian state in the Occupied Territories. Point Seven of the proposals, which called on 'the United Nations Security Council to provide guarantees for peace between all states of the region . . .', implicitly recognized Israel's right to exist.

At the end of October King Hassan of Morocco led a delegation of Arab Ministers of Foreign Affairs to Washington to explain their proposals to President Reagan. Although the US and Arab plans both envisaged the restoration of Arab rule over the Occupied Territories, they disagreed over the issue of which Arabs would govern them. The crucial figure in the US strategy was King Hussein of Jordan, who visited Washington in December. Hussein was prepared to negotiate with the USA on the basis of the Reagan Plan only if he received a mandate to do so from the Palestinians. In January 1983 the King held talks with the PLO leader Yasser Arafat, aimed at establishing a joint Jordanian-Palestinian position and the following month the Palestine National Council (PNC) debated the matter in Algiers.

Although it was clear that Arafat and the Palestinian moderates were anxious to give Hussein the mandate he needed, there was strong opposition from some sections of the PNC, particularly from those groups backed by Syria. The PNC duly endorsed the Fez proposals and criticized the Reagan Plan without rejecting it outright. Although Arafat failed to achieve his objectives, discussions between Jordan and the PLO continued until King Hussein brought them to an end in April.

AMERICAN DIPLOMATIC EFFORTS

On 24 April 1983 the US Secretary of State George Shultz left for the Middle East, shortly after a bomb attack, apparently committed by an unknown Shi'ite group, had destroyed the US Embassy in Beirut and left a large number of dead, including 17 US citizens. After a series of consultations with Arab and Israeli leaders, Shultz was able to persuade the Lebanese and Israeli Governments to sign an agreement on 17 May providing for the withdrawal of Israeli troops from Lebanon. Although Israel did not manage to achieve some of the ambitious security demands it had been making earlier, the agreement did provide for the establishment of joint Israeli-Lebanese patrols operating inside the Lebanese border.

The Israeli Government had made clear at the time that any agreement to withdraw its troops from southern Lebanon was conditional on a commitment by Syria simultaneously to withdraw its army from the Beka'a valley. The Syrian Government, however, which had recently entered into a closer alliance with the USSR, quickly denounced an agreement that seemed to benefit only the USA and its allies, Israel and the Lebanese Government of Amin Gemayel (the brother of the late President-elect). Negotiations had neglected consideration of an Israeli withdrawal from the Syrian Golan Heights and the Occupied Territories of Palestine and President Assad, therefore, adopted an intransigent attitude. As an indication of Syrian policy, Assad supported a revolt by Palestinian dissidents inside Fatah (the Palestine National Liberation Movement) who were opposed to their leader Yasser Arafat's moderate, diplomatic approach. With the help of the Syrian army, the Fatah rebels under their extremist commander, Abu Musa, captured Palestinian loyalist positions in the Beka'a valley and in June Assad expelled Arafat from Syria.

The Israeli Government, meanwhile, was refusing to pull its army out of Lebanon without a simultaneous withdrawal by the Syrians—yet it was reluctant to leave its troops in occupation of so much Lebanese territory because of the toll being taken on them in attacks by Lebanese and Palestinian guerrillas. In Israel, demonstrations were held to demand the immediate withdrawal of Israeli troops. A year after the invasion the Government admitted that 500 soldiers had been killed in Lebanon and people began to question whether the war's objectives could justify such losses. It was in this atmosphere that the Israeli Government began to discuss proposals for a limited withdrawal to the Awali river north of Sidon.

THE ISRAELI WITHDRAWAL FROM BEIRUT

Growing factional violence in Lebanon during the summer of 1983 underlined the impracticability of both Israel's and the USA's plans for that country. A principal aim of Israel's invasion, the establishment of a strong central government closely allied to Israel, had clearly been abandoned when on 20 July the Israeli Cabinet decided, unilaterally, to pull back its forces behind the more easily defensible line of the Awali river. Simultaneously, a visit to Washington by President Gemayel left the US Administration with few illusions that the 17 May Lebanon/Israel agreement, which it had brokered, would ever be ratified, far less implemented. The sense of failure provoked the replacement of Philip Habib as special Middle East envoy by Robert McFarlane, and the announcement by Menachem Begin, on 28 August, of his intention to resign as Prime Minister. The situation in Lebanon deteriorated further (on 23 July the Druze leader Walid Joumblatt had announced the formation of a pro-Syrian coalition, the National Salvation Front, in opposition to the Gemayel government). Any hope that without external support Gemayel's authority could be extended beyond the capital itself was dashed following Israel's sudden withdrawal to the Awali on 4 September, which precipitated a war between the Druze and the right-wing Christian forces. With Syrian logistical support, the Druze quickly gained the upper hand; their advance was checked only at Souk el-Gharb, a strategic mountain town overlooking Beirut, at which point the USA took the decision to intervene directly in the conflict with shelling by its offshore fleet of Druze and Syrian-controlled territory.

AMERICAN INVOLVEMENT

The growing US involvement in the Lebanese conflict, with the concomitant danger of superpower confrontation, alarmed not just the USA's European partners in the MNF but all levels of opinion in the USA itself, which was for the first time paying the price in American lives for its Middle East policy. The longer-term worry was that such involvement would destroy US credibility as the broker of a wider settlement of the Arab-Israeli conflict. On 26 July masked gunmen killed 3 Palestinian students and wounded 38 others in an attack on Hebron University. Then, on 2 August the US vetoed a UN Security Council resolution declaring the West Bank settlements illegal and condemning the violence against Palestinian civilians. Although, on 27 August, President Reagan declared the establishment of new Israeli settlements in the Occupied Territories to be 'an obstacle to peace', two days later the USA boycotted the UN International Conference on the Palestinian Question in Geneva, which was attended by 137 states, including its NATO allies in Europe.

BEGIN'S RESIGNATION

Any hopes that the resignation of Menachem Begin as Prime Minister on 30 August heralded a change in Israeli policies were banished when the Herut Party chose the even more hardline Minister of Foreign Affairs, Itzhak Shamir, to be his successor as leader of the party. Shamir, a veteran of the Jewish underground group, Lehi, allegedly gave the order for the assassination of UN mediator Count Folke Bernadotte in 1948, and had opposed the Camp David accords. Begin withheld his formal resignation until 15 September, giving Shamir time to form a viable Likud coalition. Sure of a narrow majority in the Knesset, Shamir was asked to form a government on 21 September.

THE INFLUENCE OF SYRIA

If Lebanon was the key to progress towards a wider settlement, it appeared to many observers that President Reagan believed that the civil war there could be settled in President Gemayel's favour through the exercise of US military might. This was despite efforts in the US Congress to invoke the 1973 War Powers Act requiring presidential consultations with Congress if US forces abroad faced 'imminent hostilities'. The impossibility of a force of 1,600 Marines with naval support sustaining the authority of Gemayel's Government, whose pleas to Israel for help against the Druze offensive had been dismissed, became increasingly clear in the aftermath of the fragile cease-fire agreed on 25 September through Saudi Arabian mediation. The terms of the cease-fire provided for a dialogue of national reconciliation with Syrian participation, in recognition of Syria's effective power of veto over decisions relating to the future of Lebanon.

There were signs too that Syria was seeking to extend its control over another key area of the Middle East conflict. On 29 July Yasser Arafat declared that Syrian and Libyan troops were involved in continuing clashes between pro- and anti-Arafat Palestinian factions in the Beka'a valley. Prolonged meetings of the PLO's Executive Committee and Central Council in Tunis in early August were unable to heal the rift in Palestinian ranks. Arafat managed to retain the loyalty, or at least the neutrality, of the more radical groupings such as the People's Front for the Liberation of Palestine (PFLP), led by George Habash, and the Democratic Front for the Liberation of Palestine (DFLP), led by Naif Hawatmeh, but was obliged in return to submit to the Central Council's denunciation of the Reagan Plan, something which the last PNC meeting had carefully avoided. The remaining pro-Arafat forces in Syrian-controlled northern Lebanon were steadily losing ground, and Arafat seemed to have decided to make his last stand with them when in mid-September he returned to the loyalist stronghold in the northern Lebanese port of Tripoli. This soon came under siege from Syrian and Palestinian forces.

With Syria dominating events in Lebanon and with the pro-Syrian Fatah dissidents led by Abu Musa apparently poised to inherit Arafat's leadership of the PLO, it seemed that any solution of the crisis must be acceptable in Damascus. The US Administration was forced belatedly to recognize Syria's influence and negotiations were initiated by special envoy Robert McFarlane through the Saudi Arabian Ambassador to the USA, Prince Bandar ibn Sultan. Much to the consternation of its European allies, however, the USA appeared unwilling to alter its perception of the conflict in Lebanon in terms of a Soviet threat to its interests in the region, a view in which it was encouraged by Syria's acquisition of Soviet long-range SS-21 missiles in early October. There was, equally, no hint of US readiness to put pressure on Israel over the issues necessary for Syrian acceptance of a peace settlement: Israeli withdrawal from southern Lebanon and, crucially, the inclusion of the Syrian Golan Heights, annexed by Israel in 1981, in any talks aimed at a wider settlement. Israel in turn applied its own leverage, threatening to close the bridges over the Awali river, now Lebanon's *de facto* line of partition. President Reagan's domestic position improved somewhat on 30 September 1983 with a Senate vote approving the deployment of US forces in Beirut for a further 18 months, but the precarious position of these forces made their withdrawal imperative before the 1984 presidential election campaign began in earnest.

SUICIDE BOMBINGS IN LEBANON

All the Reagan Administration's calculations were overturned on 23 October when simultaneous suicide bomb attacks destroyed the headquarters of the US and French contingents of the MNF in Beirut, killing 241 Marines and 58 French soldiers. Two extremist Shi'ite groups thought to have had links with a detachment of Iranian revolutionary guards stationed in Baalbek in eastern Lebanon claimed responsibility for the attacks. Responsibility for the attacks, initially ascribed by the USA to Iran, was widened to include Syria and the USSR, all of whom vigorously denied any involvement. Although President Reagan was quick to reaffirm America's commitment to keeping the Marines in Lebanon—a determination echoed at a meeting of the Ministers of Foreign Affairs of all four countries contributing to the MNF in Paris on 27 October—domestic opposition to his Middle East policy inevitably increased. In the case of the attack on the French forces, there was reason to believe it was linked with France's support for Iraq in the Iran-Iraq War; in the case of the USA the Marines' deaths could not

help but be attributed to its decision to intervene, as it appeared, directly on the side of Lebanon's Christian President against the largely Muslim opposition, and to the antipathy which US support for Israel had provoked among the Arabs at large. Israel's distancing itself from the US involvement in Lebanon, as reaction to the bombings set in, was evidence of its sensitivity to the charge that by invading Lebanon it had set in motion the chain of events leading to the disaster. US resentment was evinced by the rejection of Israel's offer to help in treating the victims of the attack. Ten days before the Beirut attacks Israel had leaked secret US plans to arm and equip a Jordanian military force for possible intervention in a Gulf crisis. The leak led to the Senate Appropriations Committee vetoing the idea on 2 November and was a grave setback to the US-Jordanian dialogue, which was focused on King Hussein's willingness to revive talks with the Palestinians on the basis of the Reagan Plan.

The USA moved closer to Israel after a bomb attack on Israel's military headquarters in Tyre which killed 60 people, including 32 Palestinians and Lebanese held captive there. Israeli planes immediately bombed Palestinian and Druze positions in the Chouf, and a 72-hour blockade of the occupied south was imposed. The USA seemed to be convinced by the Israeli Minister of Defence, Moshe Arens, that US setbacks in Lebanon were due to lack of co-ordination with Israeli forces there and it decided on a policy of 'strategic co-operation' with Israel. Syria, which Israel publicly held ultimately responsible for the Tyre attack, warned of 'aggressive US and Israeli intentions' and ordered a general mobilization of its forces on 7 November.

THE LEBANESE NATIONAL RECONCILIATION CONFERENCE

Despite the relative success of the national reconciliation conference, which was convened in Geneva at the beginning of November, in actually getting the protagonists, including the Syrian Minister of Foreign Affairs, Abd al-Halim Khaddam, to participate, Lebanon's internal strife persisted. The demand by the Syrians and their allies in the National Salvation Front for the abrogation of the 17 May agreement with Israel had met with a compromise whereby President Gemayel was to seek a substitute arrangement for securing Israeli withdrawal with the USA. The new US strategy (which coincided with the appointment on 3 November of a new special envoy for the Middle East, Donald Rumsfeld) of ever closer identification of its interests with those of Israel dictated the joint US-Israeli refusal to reconsider the unratified accord. President Gemayel's Christian constituency still had sufficient faith in US support and in the possibility of further Israeli military intervention on its side to resist changes to its constitutional privileges, and internal reconciliation made no progress. That US and Israeli strategies were coinciding more and more was shown by a massive increase in US military aid to Israel and in Lebanon by further Israeli air raids on Syrian-controlled territory and a direct US-Syrian clash on 4 December in which two US planes were shot down.

ARAFAT'S DEPARTURE FROM TRIPOLI

The prestige which Syrian President Assad won in the Arab world by his policy of confrontation with the USA was enhanced by Arab dismay at the US-Israeli accord. President Mubarak of Egypt, the USA's closest ally in the Arab world, described it as catastrophic and King Hussein of Jordan as a reward for Israeli intransigence. President Assad's apparent propaganda success in defying the USA was partly vitiated, however, by the bloody assault against forces loyal to Yasser Arafat in Tripoli, which by the end of November had claimed at least 500 lives. His evident determination to prevent Yasser Arafat from leaving the country alive was conditioned by the knowledge that, freed from the influence of hardline dissidents backed by Syria, the PLO Chairman would be in a position to try to forge a joint Jordanian-Palestinian alliance based on the Reagan Plan, a move repeatedly advocated by King Hussein. Although the PLO dissidents had initially attracted considerable sympathy, their collaboration with Syria against the loyalists swung opinion behind Arafat, especially in the Occupied Territories, and the struggle was increasingly seen as one for PLO independence from external control. Arafat's standing was enhanced on 24 November when six Israeli prisoners held by his forces in Tripoli were exchanged for 4,800 Palestinians and Lebanese imprisoned by Israel in southern Lebanon. Support for Arafat from many quarters, including the USSR, but especially from the Arab Gulf states, helped to secure a Saudi-Syrian-sponsored agreement to end the fighting on 24 November, according to which Arafat and his supporters were to withdraw from Lebanon within two weeks. The UN Security Council agreed on 4 December to grant the ships evacuating Arafat's 4,000 supporters the protection of the UN flag, but naval attacks on Tripoli by Israel and its refusal to guarantee the evacuation fleet safe passage delayed its departure until 20 December.

ISRAEL'S DOMESTIC PROBLEMS

Whether through US pressure, the status of the UN flag, or fear of a post-Arafat PLO, Israel was deterred from grasping the opportunity finally to dispose of the Palestinian leader. Nevertheless, bombing raids continued against what were termed terrorist bases in Syrian-controlled Lebanon, inflicting heavy civilian casualties. Losses were mounting from almost daily guerrilla attacks on Israeli forces in occupied southern Lebanon, where the overwhelmingly Shi'ite population had built up an increasingly effective military resistance movement. In addition, Israelis had to endure an economic crisis and record rates of inflation, which threatened the new Government of Itzhak Shamir. Huge debts had brought the country to the verge of bankruptcy and induced the new Minister of Finance, Yigal Cohen-Orgad, to devalue the shekel, drastically cut subsidies on basic commodities and draw up an austerity package which included cuts in the hitherto sacred areas of defence and settlement. This, in turn, further endangered the ruling coalition's narrow majority in the Knesset, as the religious parties threatened to withdraw their support if the rapid colonization of the Occupied Territories was not sustained.

ARAFAT'S DIPLOMATIC INITIATIVES

On leaving Tripoli Arafat went to Egypt for a meeting with President Mubarak, becoming the first Arab leader of importance to set foot there since the signing of the Camp David accords. However, Egypt's continued commitment to the treaty was emphasized immediately after the meeting by the visit of a senior Egyptian official to Israel, the first of its kind since the 1982 invasion of Lebanon. Nevertheless, Arafat's visit was followed by the signing of an Egyptian-Jordanian trade protocol, a visit to Cairo by the Saudi Prince Talal ibn Abd al-Aziz, and, on 19 January, by the decision of the Organization of the Islamic Conference to readmit Egypt to its ranks. The *de facto* ending of the Arab boycott of Egypt could, it was felt, provide the bridge for possible Arab-Israeli negotiations and the emergence of a moderate Arab alignment between Egypt, Jordan, the PLO and possibly Iraq. Syria, Libya and the PLO's left-wing factions vehemently denounced the *rapprochement* with Egypt and the burgeoning Jordan-PLO relationship. Although the Israeli Prime Minister, Itzhak Shamir, also denounced the Arafat-Mubarak meeting as a 'severe blow to the peace process', the US Administration welcomed it as a boost for the Reagan Plan.

In a move which was interpreted as preparing the constitutional ground for a joint Palestinian-Jordanian initiative, King Hussein decided on 5 January to reconvene the Jordanian Parliament (its representation theoretically divided between the East and the (occupied) West Banks of the Jordan), which had been suspended since 1974, (when the Rabat Arab summit accorded the PLO the status of sole representative of the Palestinian people), and had not actually sat since 1967.

DISQUIET AT THE USA'S ROLE IN LEBANON

The Reagan Administration in the USA refused to acknowledge the untenability of the position of US forces in Lebanon, despite warnings from Marine commanders in Beirut, mounting dissent on Capitol Hill, and public disquiet among the USA's European partners in the MNF, who in January announced partial withdrawals of their contingents. The difference between US and European perceptions of the Arab-Israeli conflict was illustrated on 11 January when the British Foreign Secretary, Sir Geoffrey Howe, called for a radical change in Israeli policies and urged Israel to negotiate with the PLO. The influence of the 1984 US presidential election campaign was already evident in dissuading the Reagan Administration from responding to the Arab peace initiative. A formal request from Egypt that 160 members of the PNC from the Occupied Territories be allowed to attend a proposed session of the Jordanian Parliament, aimed at securing a mandate for Arafat's progress towards a joint position with Jordan, was rejected by Israel, with no sign of US opposition.

THE MULTINATIONAL FORCE'S WITHDRAWAL FROM BEIRUT

Meanwhile US naval bombardments of anti-Gemayel forces in the hills overlooking Beirut were followed by renewed attacks on the Marine contingent. At the beginning of February more than 200 people died in three days of continuous heavy fighting, the Lebanese Government resigned, and the Lebanese army disintegrated along sectarian lines. Druze militiamen from the mountains linked up with their Shi'ite allies in the southern suburbs of Beirut on 15 February. The USA still refused to consider the one thing that might have halted the onslaught against Gemayel—the abrogation of the 17 May agreement—but it had clearly lost all control of events. Despite public avowals of support for the Gemayel government and promises to keep US forces in the country, the decision had already been taken to 'redeploy' the Marines even before President Reagan announced their withdrawal on 7 February. The next day the United Kingdom announced and completed the withdrawal of its token contribution to the MNF, followed by the Italian force on 20 February. The last US Marines were evacuated from Beirut on 26 February, to be followed by the French in March, leaving the western sector of the city, as in the days before the Israeli invasion, under the control of Muslim and left-wing militias. On 5 March, bowing to Syrian influence, President Gemayel abrogated the 17 May Lebanon-Israel agreement in return for guarantees of internal security from President Assad.

THE CONSEQUENCES OF ISRAEL'S INVASION

The failure of Israel's 1982 invasion was now laid bare. Far from securing a 'client regime' in Beirut, it had brought about the defeat of Israel's Christian allies, who had been forced to retreat into their traditional enclaves in east Beirut and around Jounieh. Abandoned by the USA, and with little prospect of further military support from Israel, there seemed little alternative to cantonization or a power-sharing deal with the Muslim majority. Meanwhile, the enormous cost of the Lebanese campaign in lives and resources appeared to have endangered Israel's security, not enhanced it. The death of the pro-Israeli militia commander, Maj. Sa'ad Haddad, on 15 January, further reduced Israel's hopes of creating a security zone along the Lebanese side of its northern border, and despite the setbacks suffered by the PLO in Lebanon, armed attacks against Israelis in Israel continued. In addition, the growth and increasing sophistication of a Jewish anti-Arab terrorist underground was both embarrassing the Government and threatening a backlash throughout the Arab and Muslim world. The Karp report, drawn up by a Ministry of Justice commission in May 1982, but suppressed until 8 February 1984, was a litany of the Government's failures to curb Jewish terrorism against Arab civilians. At the end of April Israeli security services finally acted, arresting over 30 people suspected of planting bombs on Arab buses. By that time the defection of the small Tami party from the ruling Likud coalition had led to the defeat of the Government in a vote to dissolve the Knesset and hold early elections, which were subsequently scheduled for 23 July.

ARAB-ISRAELI CONFLICT 1984–85

The lengthy trial of members of the Jewish terrorist underground, arrested in April 1984, distracted attention from the election campaign, especially after it became known that some of the suspects, who consisted principally of Gush Emunim settlers but also included two army officers, had confessed to the 1980 assassination attempts on three Palestinian mayors in the West Bank and the previous year's attack on the Islamic college in Hebron. Their stated aim was to force a mass exodus of Palestinians from the Occupied Territories. The Government's own attitude toward the underground movement was called into question by a statement by the Cabinet minister Yuval Ne'eman, of the Tehiya party, who cited the bombing of the Palestinian mayors as having 'effectively paralysed the leading agitators' in the West Bank.

Abroad, Lebanon remained a cause for concern. On 4 April, a new commander, ex-Lebanese Army Col Antoine Lahad, was installed at the head of the militia in southern Lebanon, formerly led by Maj. Haddad, which the Israelis had reinforced and renamed the 'South Lebanon Army' (SLA). Israel's strategy was to remain in occupation of southern Lebanon until the SLA was capable of maintaining control there. However, neither Israel nor its surrogate force seemed capable of preventing a growing number of guerrilla attacks against the occupying army.

LEBANON'S GOVERNMENT OF NATIONAL RECONCILIATION

In Beirut, the new Government of national unity installed at the end of April 1984 had resolved to secure Israel's complete and unconditional withdrawal. Comprising a delicate balance of Christians and Muslims achieved after a year's painstaking mediation on the part of Syria, the new Lebanese Cabinet's inclusion of Shi'ite leader Nabih Berri was an indication both of the rising influence of the Shi'ites and of how far the balance of power had shifted in favour of Lebanon's non-Christian communities (though Amin Gemayel retained the presidency). Berri, leader of the Shi'ite Amal movement, which was spearheading the resistance to Israel in the south, joined the Government on the condition that he be made Minister for the south, and his appointment signalled the first test of President Gemayel's pledge of 'support for the national resistance' given at the reconvened national reconciliation conference in Lausanne, Switzerland, in March. The new Prime Minister, Rashid Karami, a Sunni Muslim, confirmed the Government's intentions on 3 June by calling for the removal of Israel's 'liaison office' at Dbayye, in the Christian enclave north of Beirut. Israel's Likud Government was adamant that it would not leave southern Lebanon in the hands of a Syrian-influenced government in Beirut. The USA was unwilling to mediate between Lebanon and Israel to secure a withdrawal, even assuming that its participation would have been countenanced by Syria. On 10 June, during a tour of the Middle East, the UN Secretary-General, Javier Pérez de Cuéllar, quashed Israeli hopes that UN forces could act as a buffer north of Israel's lines, on the ground that this would reinforce Lebanon's *de facto* partition. Israel, in turn, rejected the suggestion that UNIFIL could police Israel's northern border and ensure its security after an Israeli withdrawal. By the second anniversary of the invasion, the war in Lebanon had cost almost 600 Israeli lives, with 3,049 wounded—more than the total number of military and civilian casualties in the Six Day War of 1967.

ISRAEL'S INCONCLUSIVE GENERAL ELECTION

In his election manifesto, Shimon Peres, who had been unanimously re-adopted on 12 April as leader of the opposition Labour Party, pledged to bring Israel's troops home within 'three to six' months of gaining power, and this appeared to be a crucial factor in his party's favour. However, the immediate concern of the Israeli voter as the election approached was the economy. With inflation reaching 15% a month, a balance-of-payments deficit of

$5,000m., foreign debt of $23,000m. and a chronic shortage of foreign currency reserves, Israel was on the verge of bankruptcy; the occupation of Lebanon alone was costing the country an estimated $1m. a day.

At the election on 23 July, the major party groupings, Likud and the Labour Alignment, each secured just over one-third of the Knesset's 120 seats. The balance of power lay once again with the minority parties, which won the remaining 35 seats. The result confirmed the trend towards polarization in Israeli politics: the extreme right-wing Tehiya party increased its representation from three to five seats, and was joined on the far right by two members of the religious-nationalist Morasha party, which drew its support from the Gush Emunim movement, and by Rabbi Meir Kahane of the Kach party, who had campaigned on an openly racist platform. At the other political pole, Reserve General Matti Peled and Muhammad Mv'ari were elected as representatives of a newly formed Arab-Jewish coalition, the Progressive List for Peace, which called for dialogue with the PLO and the establishment of an independent Palestinian state in the Occupied Territories. The deadlock was resolved when Labour leader Shimon Peres was entrusted with forming the new Government after the factions in the political centre, Yahad and the National Religious Party, agreed to lend their support to Labour on condition that Peres formed a 'national unity' government with Likud. On 30 August Labour and Likud agreed to such an arrangement, with Peres as Prime Minister and Shamir as Minister of Foreign Affairs, their posts to be exchanged every two years. On 13 September the Knesset approved a bi-partisan Cabinet, completing the political rehabilitation of Ariel Sharon, who was appointed Minister of Industry and Trade.

SYRIAN INFLUENCE IN LEBANON

In Lebanon, Syria was exercising unprecedented control over the Government in Beirut. On 18 June President Assad succeeded in sponsoring a Christian-Muslim power-sharing agreement, which included the implementation of a balanced security plan throughout Beirut, where local militias were to be disbanded and the port and airport re-opened. The plan was executed on 4 July, the army taking over positions in the city from the militias, including the hitherto intransigent Lebanese Forces (LF), the military wing of the Christian Phalangist Party), within hours. However, despite Syria's efforts, plans to extend the Lebanese army's deployment throughout the rest of the country made no headway, and renewed sectarian clashes threatened to reverse the progress that had been made, exposing Syria's inability to control its Druze and Shi'ite allies. Israel showed its determination to thwart Syria's designs in Lebanon by a series of air raids on Druze- and Syrian-controlled areas and, on 10 September, by sending an armoured column north of its lines on the Awali River into the Kharroub region to support Christian militias under attack from the Druze.

MOVES TOWARDS AN ISRAELI WITHDRAWAL FROM LEBANON

Under the new Government in Israel came the first public admission, by the Minister of Defence, Itzhak Rabin, that Israel had lost the political struggle for Lebanon; the hitherto rigid insistence on a simultaneous withdrawal of Syrian troops from the country was abandoned, and the Minister of Foreign Affairs, Shamir, said that Israel wanted the USA to mediate with Syria on a procedure for Israeli withdrawal. The US Assistant Secretary of State for Near East Affairs, Richard Murphy, visited Lebanon, Syria and Israel in September, holding two rounds of talks with President Assad in Damascus, the first such US-Syrian contact and the first display of active US diplomacy in the region since the withdrawal of US forces from Beirut in February. Murphy followed in the footsteps of the UN Assistant Secretary-General, Brian Urquhart, who returned assured by all parties of their desire for UNIFIL to play a larger part in any settlement. However, Israel insisted that, though a withdrawal of forces need not be simultaneous, it should not be unilateral. Nevertheless, talks began under UN auspices on 8 November, at UNIFIL's headquarters in the Israeli-Lebanese border town of Naqoura, between military delegations from Israel and Lebanon, within the framework of the 1949 Armistice Commission.

DIPLOMATIC INITIATIVES ON PALESTINE

The new Israeli Government had also to contend with the nascent Arab 'peace alliance' between Yasser Arafat's wing of the PLO, Jordan and Egypt. Egypt's credibility in the Arab world and non-aligned movement was strengthened by its decision to restore full diplomatic relations with the USSR. However, it was King Hussein of Jordan's surprise decision on 25 September to restore diplomatic ties with Cairo, which first raised the possibility of talks between the new Israeli Government and a joint Jordanian-PLO delegation supported by Egypt. Yasser Arafat was preoccupied by a long and difficult struggle to win the agreement of the various PLO factions to convene the PNC, which Arafat hoped would supply the Palestinian consensus for a joint peace strategy with Jordan. Amid signs of a thaw in relations between Syria and Arafat's mainstream PLO, and after mediation efforts by the USSR, the People's Democratic Republic of Yemen and Algeria, leaders of Fatah and the quadripartite Damascus-based Democratic Alliance, including the Popular Front for the Liberation of Palestine (PFLP) and the Democratic Front for the Liberation of Palestine (DFLP), met in Algiers on 18 April. Subsequently it was declared that the PFLP and DFLP had dropped their opposition both to Arafat's leadership and to the dialogue with Jordan. Syria, however, remained opposed to any Damascus-based group attending a PNC meeting, and warned that those who did attend would not be allowed to return to Syria. The stalemate was finally broken on 14 October at a meeting in Tunis of the PLO Executive Committee, Fatah's Central Council and about 80 representatives of other Palestinian organizations, at which it was declared that the PNC must be convened before the end of November, and that 'the minority must accept the decision of the majority'. The 17th session of the PNC was duly scheduled for 22 November in Amman. On 9 October, President Mubarak visited the Jordanian capital, where a joint Egyptian-Jordanian strategy on Palestine was announced. Israel welcomed the new Egyptian-Jordanian relationship as helpful to peace, but Egypt, while welcoming the inauguration of Shimon Peres as Israel's Prime Minister, made it clear that its primary commitment was to the Arab world, and that it stood by its conditions for normalizing the frosty relations between them that had prevailed since Israel's invasion of Lebanon: namely, the initiation of steps to gain the confidence of the Palestinians living in areas under Israeli occupation, and talks on the disputed border strip of Taba on the Red Sea, which Israel continued to occupy after vacating Sinai in 1982. For his part, King Hussein dismissed speculation that a US-sponsored peace initiative along the lines of Camp David was in prospect when, on 10 October, he denounced Israeli Prime Minister Peres' call for direct negotiations between Jordan and Israel, explicitly excluding Palestinian involvement, as 'subterfuge and deception'.

REAGAN IS RETURNED TO THE WHITE HOUSE

In the USA the Administration concentrated on advancing the US-Israel strategic relationship. An unprecedented military exchange agreement between the countries' air forces was announced in early September, and, during a visit to Israel in mid-October by the US Defense Secretary, Caspar Weinberger, details were released of the transfer of hitherto restricted US technology crucial to the development of Israel's *Lavi* fighter aircraft. To help Israel cope with its economic crisis the US also consented to transfer the whole of its $1,200m. annual civilian aid grant immediately, rather than in instalments.

As far as the Arab world was concerned, the US Administration appeared to be retreating into a defensive posture, as evinced by the 'anti-terrorist' legislation drafted by the State Department in April. It was indisputable that the Reagan Administration had attracted an unprecedented degree of hostility in the Middle East. Threats of violence

against and kidnappings of US citizens led on 28 May to the recall of Marines to protect the US Embassy in Beirut. Nevertheless, on 20 September a suicide bomb attack, responsibility for which was claimed by the Shi'ite Islamic Jihad (Holy War) organization, killed more than 20 people and accelerated the steady exodus of American diplomats, journalists and relief workers from Lebanon. Although, as a result of the intervention in Lebanon, more US citizens had been killed in international conflict than at any time since the Viet Nam war, seemingly no blame was attached to President Reagan, who was re-elected by a massive majority on 5 November.

FAILURE OF TALKS ON ISRAELI WITHDRAWAL

At the talks in Naqoura on Israel's withdrawal from Lebanon, Lebanon's demands included an unconditional Israeli withdrawal, the abolition of the SLA and $10,000m. in war reparations. Israel responded by threatening to withdraw unilaterally, without making provision for local security. The talks remained deadlocked, with Syria evidently refusing to give Israel any assurance of its security once its forces had withdrawn. The pressure was, nevertheless, increasing on Israel to withdraw. Guerrilla attacks on the Israeli army, the Israeli Defence Force (IDF), continued during the negotiations, and both the troops and the Israeli public were becoming increasingly frustrated at the high casualty toll. On 8 January 1985 Israel announced its withdrawal from the Naqoura talks; a week later, the Israel Cabinet approved a three-phase unilateral withdrawal from Lebanon, which, Prime Minister Peres pledged, would be completed by July. Israel remained committed to intervening in Lebanon if it perceived a threat to its security, and to aiding 'friendly' militias and maintaining a security zone patrolled by the SLA on the Lebanese side of the border.

JORDANIAN-PALESTINIAN PARTNERSHIP

Matters elsewhere looked more promising in the wake of Arafat's success at the PNC meeting in Amman in late November 1984. Although the PFLP and DFLP did not attend, they undertook not to approve the formation of an alternative organization, and the PLO succeeded in demonstrating its independence from Syria. In his address to the PNC, King Hussein laid down the guidelines for a new Arab approach to the peace process, consisting of a joint Jordanian-PLO initiative, based on UN Resolution 242 and the right of the Palestinian people to self-determination, in accordance with the principle of an exchange of territory for peace with Israel. The PNC, however, reiterated its rejection of Resolution 242, which refers to the Palestinians only as refugees, implicitly denying their right to self-determination and recognizing the State of Israel. Israel, which had always prohibited Palestinians living in areas under its occupation from attending the PNC, ignored King Hussein's proposals, nor did it respond to a statement by the Egyptian Minister of State for Foreign Affairs, Boutros Ghali, expressing Egypt's willingness to back a new initiative in which Jordan and a delegation of West Bank and Gaza Palestinians would enter peace talks with Israel under a mandate from the PLO. In this, however, Egypt was not supported by either Jordan or the Palestinians, who made it clear that the PLO should be a full partner in any future peace negotiations. PLO-Jordanian relations were strengthened by a series of meetings between King Hussein and Yasser Arafat, culminating on 11 February in the signing in Amman of a PLO-Jordanian accord, which provided for Palestinian self-determination within the framework of a Jordanian-Palestinian confederation and for peace negotiations between all parties to the conflict, including the PLO, and the five permanent members of the UN Security Council. Israel promptly rejected the agreement.

The Amman agreement, which drew strong opposition from Syria and Arafat's PLO opponents, and was clearly a source of contention among the PLO Executive Committee itself, illustrated the urgency with which King Hussein and Yasser Arafat viewed the need to salvage the Occupied Territories for a future Palestinian homeland before Jewish settlement established a *de facto* extension of Israel. Despite pledges from the new Israeli Government to raise the quality of life for the Palestinians in the Occupied Territories, violence against the Arab population there persisted. Nor did the Labour component of the Government of national unity seem able or willing to halt the continued seizure of Palestinian land for Israeli settlement. On 10 February, a study by the US-financed West Bank Data Project found that, as of 1 January 1985, there were 42,500 Israeli settlers living on the occupied West Bank, double the figure of just two years earlier.

ISRAEL'S ECONOMIC CRISIS

The decision to spend more on colonizing the Occupied Territories drew protests from Israelis alarmed by soaring inflation and, for the first time in the country's history, widespread unemployment. A wages and prices freeze agreed on 2 November 1984 between the Government and trades unions and employers temporarily checked the rise in inflation, but did not tackle the deep-rooted crisis in the economy. The Israeli shekel, having fallen to less than one five-hundredth of its 1977 value, was replaced for most practical purposes by the dollar. An Israeli economic delegation went to Washington at the end of December to request $4,100m. in aid in 1986, an increase of $1,500m. on the 1985 total approved by the US Congress just three months previously. Initially, the US Government insisted that any increase in aid should be conditional on the introduction of more rigorous measures to tackle the crisis. On 17 January, Israel and the USA finalized a free-trade agreement, and on 30 January President Reagan agreed to increase US military aid to Israel by $400m. to $1,800m. for the 1986 fiscal year. The same day, the Administration bowed to pressure from the pro-Israel lobby and delivered what appeared to be a deliberate snub to Saudi Arabia, its most important Arab ally. Less than two weeks before King Fahd was to pay a state visit to Washington, it was announced that the sale of 40 F-15 fighter bombers to Saudi Arabia had been postponed pending a review of US arms sales to the Middle East. King Fahd's appeal to the USA to revive the peace process was made in Washington on the same day, 11 February, that Yasser Arafat and King Hussein signed the Amman agreement but the USA continued to insist that the PLO explicitly accept UN Resolution 242 before admitting it to negotiations. The Arab initiative was complicated shortly afterwards when President Mubarak of Egypt launched proposals for direct talks between Israel and a Jordanian-Palestinian delegation, following preliminary discussions between the latter and the USA, a suggestion which clearly went beyond anything envisaged by King Hussein and Yasser Arafat. Mubarak's move, which drew sharp opposition from Syria and many Palestinians, as well as from the USSR, was cautiously welcomed by Israeli Prime Minister Peres, who said on 25 February that Israel would be willing to meet such a delegation provided it did not contain PLO members.

ISRAEL'S BLOODY WITHDRAWAL FROM LEBANON

The first phase of Israel's withdrawal plan, the evacuation of the western seaboard from the Awali to the Litani, was accomplished peacefully in February 1985. Almost immediately, however, Shi'ite guerrillas stepped up their attacks. Israel launched a policy of 'Iron Fist' reprisal against villages suspected of harbouring guerrillas, storming scores of townships, killing and wounding their inhabitants, blowing up houses and taking away hundreds of men to prison camps. The IDF clashed with UNIFIL forces protesting against the destruction of Shi'ite homes, and on 12 March, the USA vetoed a UN Security Council resolution, proposed by Lebanon, which condemned Israel's behaviour in southern Lebanon.

Israel's reprisal tactics rebounded on it: UN figures showed that in the first month in which the 'Iron Fist' policy operated, attacks on the IDF in Lebanon actually doubled. On 17 March, Israeli Prime Minister Peres announced that the withdrawal was to be speeded up and completed in 8–10 weeks. In late March elements of the LF, determined to salvage what they could from the retreat and the increas-

ingly pro-Syrian policies pursued by the Gemayel Government, staged a revolt. Fighting in the capital and in the south between the Lebanese army and the Christian rebels soon degenerated into a general conflict between Christians and Muslims, which was accompanied by a fresh Israeli onslaught against Shi'ite villages in the occupied southern area. Israeli-Shi'ite antagonism was exacerbated by the news that, in contravention of the Geneva Convention, Israel had secretly transferred more than 1,000 Lebanese Shi'ite detainees to Israel, where the army chief of staff, General Moshe Levi, said they would remain imprisoned until 'the security situation improved'. The second phase of Israel's withdrawal (from the central and eastern sectors of southern Lebanon) was completed during April, as the sectarian fighting north of its lines intensified. Druze and Muslim militias took control of the main Sidon-Beirut highway on 28 April, overrunning many Christian villages whose inhabitants fled in their thousands towards the new Israeli lines. Israel, which at the beginning of May began fortifying its international border with Lebanon, made it clear that it would not intervene again to help the beleaguered Christians.

THE SUPPRESSION OF THE PLO IN BEIRUT

Meanwhile, in Beirut, Syria's two main militia allies in Lebanon, the Druze and the Shi'ite Amal, unleashed a violent putsch against the Sunni Murabitoun militia. The Sunni Prime Minister, Rashid Karami, resigned in protest on 17 April but was persuaded to remain in office. Significantly, the Murabitoun were the only force in Lebanon still supportive of Yasser Arafat's PLO. The determination of Syria and its Lebanese allies to prevent the resurgence of pro-Arafat Palestinian forces in Lebanon after the Israeli withdrawal, was ruthlessly demonstrated when troops of the Shi'ite Amal movement attacked the Palestinian refugee camps in Beirut on 20 May. The savagery of the assault, which claimed hundreds of Palestinian lives, led the hitherto pro-Syrian Palestinian factions in the camps to join forces with pro-Arafat fighters. As the third anniversary of Israel's invasion approached it appeared that a *pax Syriana* could be established in Lebanon after the Israelis had withdrawn if Syria could control its Lebanese allies and prevent the country dividing along sectarian lines into religious cantons.

ISRAEL'S CONTINUED REFUSAL TO NEGOTIATE WITH THE PALESTINIANS

On the wider front, the refusal of Israel and the USA to deal directly with the PLO remained the single greatest obstacle to all negotiations, including those on the basis of 'territory for peace' involving Israel, the Palestinians, Jordan and Egypt, proposed by King Hussein and President Mubarak. However, on 5 April the US Administration finally took a more active role, with visits to the Middle East by Assistant Secretary of State Richard Murphy and Secretary of State George Shultz. Neither Murphy nor Shultz, who toured the Middle East in April and May respectively, succeeded in resolving the central issue of Palestinian representation at peace talks, despite reports that, while in Jordan, the US Secretary of State had been presented with a list of Palestinians who were not PLO members for possible inclusion in a joint Jordanian-Palestinian delegation. Shultz was denied the economic pressure, which he could have brought to bear on Israel over the issue of Palestinian representation, when the US Administration finally decided to recommend to Congress, shortly before he left Washington, that Israel receive the additional $1,500m. in emergency aid which it had requested. Israel's position hardened on 12 May when it announced that members of the PNC were also unacceptable as negotiating partners.

On 20 May three Israeli prisoners of war who had been held since the invasion of Lebanon by the hardline PFLP General Command, led by Ahmad Jibril, were exchanged for 1,150 Palestinians detained in Israel. The release of the Palestinian prisoners, some of them convicted terrorists, sparked a political storm in Israel, generating intense pressure on the Government to release Jews convicted of, or awaiting trial for, terrorist offences against Arabs.

THE ARAB-ISRAELI CONFRONTATION 1985–86

In an attempt to lend momentum to the peace initiative launched by the Jordan-PLO agreement, King Hussein went to Washington at the end of May to establish some form of international framework for his proposals. Radical quarters of the Arab world had already accused Jordan of seeking a separate deal with Israel, and King Hussein was clearly anxious to avoid the ostracism suffered by Egypt as a result of the Camp David treaty, preferring an international conference co-sponsored by both superpowers. By far the greatest obstacle to talks remained the issue of Palestinian representation. It was not until July that the PLO submitted to Jordan a list of names of 22 leading Palestinians for inclusion in a joint Jordanian-Palestinian delegation to meet US officials prior to the opening of wider negotiations involving Israel. Israel rejected the list (with two exceptions), calling for 'authentic Palestinian representatives' from the Occupied Territories, who had no direct links with the PLO.

ISRAEL COMPLETES ITS WITHDRAWAL

Israel announced the completion of its withdrawal from Lebanon on 10 June, but its retention of an 8–10 km wide 'security zone' along the border inside Lebanon, policed by the Israeli-sponsored SLA and supported by smaller numbers of Israeli troops, proved a constant source of friction with UNIFIL, to the north.

Syria succeeded in sponsoring a cease-fire of sorts on 31 May in the battle for control of the Palestinian refugee camps in Beirut, after Shi'ite Amal militiamen had failed to subdue stubborn Palestinian resistance, but there was no foreseeable end to the sectarian violence. The rise of Lebanon's Shi'ite factions in particular (supported by Iran in certain cases), with their associated underground guerrilla groups, compounded the descent into anarchy, which extreme Islamic and anti-Western groups began increasingly to exploit. On 11 June a Jordanian airliner with 65 passengers on board was diverted by Shi'ites to Beirut, where the hostages were later released and the plane destroyed. Less than 48 hours later a US TWA airliner carrying 153 passengers including 43 US citizens was also hijacked, and flown between Beirut and Algiers (where 100 hostages were released) before landing for the third time in Beirut on 16 June. The USA responded with a build-up of naval forces off Lebanon, but the dispersal of the hostages in Shi'ite-controlled west Beirut precluded any US attempt to free them by force, putting pressure instead on Israel to accede to the hijackers' demands and release over 700 Lebanese Shi'ites being held in Israel. The intervention of President Assad of Syria resulted in the US hostages being freed unharmed (with the exception of one who had been killed when the plane was first seized) on 30 June. In return Israel released its Shi'ite prisoners in stages to avoid the impression of a surrender to terrorism. For the USA, the TWA hijacking was instrumental in diverting attention from a Middle East peace settlement to the immediate problem of combating terrorism.

Further Arab-Israeli violence on the occupied West Bank also threatened the prospects for negotiations. After the killing of two Israeli teachers, and of an occupation official, reprisal actions by Jewish settler groups were accompanied by additional security measures, including curfews, the closure of universities and newspapers, and detention without trial. Palestinians were also deported (a total of 26 in 1985)—a practice which Israel had discontinued in 1980 after widespread international criticism. The result was an escalation of violence by Arabs and Jews throughout August and September, at the end of which regular army troops were sent into occupied areas. The harassment of Palestinians by both the Israeli army and settler vigilantes was widespread, and there were signs that the Israeli coalition Government's right-wing Likud component was exploiting the unrest to sabotage the prospect of talks with a joint Jordanian-Palestinian delegation. Blaming PLO 'command centres' in Jordan for co-ordinating Palestinian resistance in the Occupied Territories, the Likud leader and Minister of Foreign Affairs Itzhak Shamir urged that Israel suspend diplomatic contacts so long as the PLO was allowed to maintain 'forward headquarters' on Jordanian soil. The future of the proposed talks was already in serious doubt after the failure of US Assistant Secretary of State Richard Murphy to meet members of a Jordanian-Palestinian delegation during his tour of the Middle East in mid-August.

Jordan was increasingly fearful of isolation within the Arab world, a fear heightened by the refusal of the Arab summit held in Casablanca on 7 August to endorse the aims of the Jordanian-Palestinian accord. This fear was somewhat allayed by the US decision, prior to King Hussein's visit to Washington on 30 September, to submit to Congress a $1,900m. arms deal with Jordan despite intense opposition to it from the Zionist lobby. Moreover, although US opposition to a meeting with PLO or PLO-associated Palestinians was as firm as ever, Jordanian hopes of progress were boosted in late September when the British Prime Minister Margaret Thatcher, following her visits to Amman and Cairo, invited a Palestinian-Jordanian delegation (including two members of the PLO Executive Committee) to London for talks with the British Foreign Secretary, Sir Geoffrey Howe. Nevertheless, King Hussein was clearly insuring against the initiative's failure when, before leaving for the USA, he sanctioned the initial approaches in a *rapprochement* between Jordan and its main opponent in the Arab world, Syria.

ESCALATION OF VIOLENCE

On 1 October 1985, three days after King Hussein had arrived in the USA to address the UN General Assembly with an appeal for Arab-Israeli peace, Israeli jets bombed the PLO's headquarters in Tunis, killing 75 people, in retaliation for the killing of three Israelis by the PLO's élite Force 17 in Cyprus. The Israeli raid was condemned by the UN and by European leaders, but support for it from the White House as a 'legitimate response' to terrorism was a serious blow to US-Arab relations and to the USA's credibility as a peace-broker. Despite Jordanian and PLO pledges of continued commitment to the peace process, Arab anger over the affair clearly led to increased violence in the Israeli-occupied territories. Also on 7 October, four Palestinians succeeded in hijacking an Italian cruise liner, the *Achille Lauro*, with over 400 passengers and crew on board. The action was condemned by the PLO, which swiftly persuaded the hijackers to surrender themselves to the Egyptian authorities, but not before one passenger, an elderly American Jew, had been murdered. Egypt had agreed with the PLO that the hijackers would be flown to PLO headquarters in Tunis to stand trial, but the Egyptian airliner carrying them was intercepted *en route* by US fighter-planes and forced to land at a NATO base in Sicily. The US plan to take the hijackers, who were accompanied by the alleged mastermind of the operation, the leader of the Palestine Liberation Front, Muhammad Abu al-Abbas, to the USA for trial was thwarted by the Italians, who prevented the Americans from taking custody of the Palestinians and subsequently allowed Abu al-Abbas to leave the country on the grounds that he had not been actively involved in the hijack.

The political repercussions of the *Achille Lauro* affair set back the prospect of peace talks. In US and Israeli eyes, it further justified the exclusion of the PLO from the peace process for as long as it was involved in terrorism. On 21 October Jordan signed a three-point agreement with Syria which included a pledge not to seek a separate peace with Israel and was seen as a clear move away from the peace process based on Jordan's collaboration with Yasser Arafat, towards whom Syria and the Damascus-based PLO factions remained hostile.

With the peace process deadlocked, attention focused on the summit meeting between President Reagan and Mr Gorbachev on 19 November in Geneva. There was speculation that a new approach based on US-Soviet co-operation might result, but the summit meeting passed with no sign of any agreement on the Middle East, and the prospect of an international conference began to recede. One reason was the PLO's continued refusal to accede to the USA's precondition that it accept UN Resolution 242, renounce terrorism and recognize Israel. Jordanian impatience with the PLO mounted, as the reconciliation between King Hussein and President Assad of Syria proceeded apace; on 10 November King Hussein issued a statement accepting responsibility for the long period of poor relations with Syria and pledging an end to the activities of anti-Syrian elements based in Jordan. Syria did not conceal its view that the *rapprochement*, which continued with a meeting in Damascus between King Hussein and President Assad on 30–31 December, foreshadowed the end of the Jordan–PLO agreement. Yasser Arafat, despite warm support from Egypt during a visit to Cairo in mid-November, in the course of which the PLO leader renounced terrorist violence outside the Occupied Territories and against civilians, was becoming increasingly isolated. His position and the credibility of the PLO as a participant in peace talks was not improved by simultaneous terrorist attacks by Palestinians at Rome and Vienna airports on 27 December which killed 19 people (including five US citizens) and injured more than 100. Yet in the aftermath of the atrocities the US Administration, and the Government of Israel, whose El Al airline facilities had been the target of the attacks, for the first time made a distinction between the PLO, led by Arafat, and the dissident PLO splinter group (the Fatah Revolutionary Council), led by Abu Nidal, which was widely held to be responsible for the attacks. US and Israeli anger, and the threat of military retaliation, was directed almost exclusively toward Abu Nidal's alleged sponsor and protector, Libya, despite the more prominent links between the Abu Nidal group and Syria. The US Sixth Fleet was deployed off the Libyan coast, and on 7 January a package of anti-Libyan political and economic sanctions was announced by President Reagan, though European Governments refused to participate in them.

JORDAN RENOUNCES ITS AGREEMENT WITH THE PLO

The first few weeks of 1986 made it clear that the Jordan-PLO peace initiative had no chance of making progress. A 12-day session of talks in January between King Hussein and Yasser Arafat, who came to Amman to reply to 'final' US terms for Palestinian participation in peace negotiations, collapsed without agreement. Although these terms represented a concession on the long-established US-Israeli position in that they entailed an invitation to the PLO to attend an international peace conference in return for the organization's acceptance of Resolution 242, this the PLO refused to do, unless the USA first recognized the Palestinian right to self-determination. No sooner had the Jordanian-Palestinian talks ended than the US Administration notified King Hussein that it was postponing indefinitely its request to Congress to sell advanced weaponry to Jordan, a sale which President Reagan had earlier said was 'essential to create the conditions for a lasting Middle East peace'. The Jordanian–PLO peace initiative was formally dissolved on 19 February, when King Hussein announced the end of political collaboration with the PLO leadership, strongly hinting that he would now seek a new partner in peace moves in the form of alternative representatives of the Palestinians. The principal reason given by King Hussein for the breakdown was the PLO's preoccupation with Palestinian self-determination at the expense of the 'liberation of the land' and its refusal to accept Resolution 242. The immediate effect was to raise Arafat's standing among the considerable body of Palestinians who had suspected him of giving up the Palestinians' 'last card', by acknowledging Resolution 242, with its implicit recognition of Israel, in return for vague US promises of participation in peace talks. King Hussein's chances of finding alternative Palestinian representatives, who would have the backing of the majority of Palestinians and the Arab world at large, seemed negligible.

Israel's reaction to the collapse of the Jordan-PLO initiative was one of relief at avoiding a US-PLO dialogue and with it the threat of a split in the Government between the Labour bloc and the Likud faction, which was militantly opposed to any form of territorial concession. The fragile Israeli coalition Government had already been seriously threatened by the issue of Taba, the tiny coastal enclave claimed by both Egypt and Israel and outwardly the principal cause of the discord between the two, which had begun with the 1982 Israeli invasion of Lebanon. Prime Minister Peres, keen to improve relations with Egypt, was in favour of acceding to Egypt's demand to submit the issue to international arbitration, a course bitterly opposed by Likud leader Itzhak Shamir, a veteran critic of the Camp David treaty. Israel's overtures to Egypt were, however, undermined by its bombing of Tunis on 1 October, which President Mubarak denounced as a 'fatal blow' to peace; five days later seven Israeli tourists, including four children, were murdered by an Egyptian policeman in Sinai. Israeli-Egyptian contacts resumed in December, and on 14 January Peres succeeded in obtaining the Likud's approval to submit the Taba issue to arbitration. In return Egypt agreed to a series of measures to improve bilateral relations, including the return of Egypt's Ambassador to Tel Aviv. However, the expected improvement quickly became bogged down in low-level talks and Peres' hopes of a summit meeting with President Mubarak were not realized.

US-ISRAELI TIES

During his visit to Washington in early April the Israeli Prime Minister, Shimon Peres, proposed that the USA should support a 'Marshall Plan' (such as was employed to assist European recovery after World War II) for the Middle East— a $20,000m.–$30,000m. development fund, primarily designed to help Arab states affected by the sharp drop in the price of oil. The proposal was welcomed by US officials as worthy of serious consideration, despite the unlikelihood that Arab states would co-operate in any plan involving Israel, while the latter was in occupation of Arab territory. The positive US response to Peres' proposals underlined the strength of the US-Israeli alliance, despite two developments which were outwardly damaging to the relationship. First, on 24 November 1985 a US naval intelligence officer, Jonathan Pollard, was arrested by the FBI and charged with supplying classified documents to Israel. Then, in April 1986 a licensed Israeli arms dealer, retired Gen. Avraham Baram, was indicted in the USA for his part in a conspiracy to smuggle $2,500m. worth of advanced US weaponry, including tanks, missiles and fighter planes, to Iran. The indictment listed, among the items in the attempted sale, $800m. worth of arms that had been delivered to Israel as part of the US military aid programme.

On 17 January the USA invoked its veto in the UN Security Council to prevent the adoption of a resolution deploring Israel's behaviour in southern Lebanon, where the presence of Israeli troops remained a source of conflict. On 30 January the USA vetoed a draft resolution, which had won the support of all Council members with the exception of Thailand, condemning Israel's actions over Islamic holy places in Jerusalem, where religious extremists had provoked Palestinian rioting by attempting to establish a Jewish foothold in the compound of the al-Aqsa Mosque (see article on The Jerusalem Issue, p. 72).

Shimon Peres was keen to gain credit for some progress in Arab-Israeli relations before surrendering power to Itzhak Shamir under the terms of their power-sharing agreement. With Egypt proving unco-operative, and King Hussein ignoring repeated Israeli appeals to proceed to peace talks independently of the PLO, in February Peres resorted to the idea of 'imposing' a limited autonomy on the Palestinian inhabitants of the Occupied Territories. As with similar attempts in the past, the 'unilateral autonomy' plan quickly foundered in the face of Palestinian opposition that united pro-Jordanian and pro-PLO leaders in the West Bank, who refused to countenance anything short of an end to Israeli occupation.

The dashing of peace prospects was followed by rising tension between Israel and Syria, which had been re-equipped militarily by the USSR to the point where its forces threatened Israel's long-standing military supremacy. On 19 November the Israeli air force had shot down two Syrian MiG fighters, reportedly in Syrian airspace. In response, Syria deployed SAM missiles in eastern Lebanon, a move denounced by Israel as a threat to its reconnaissance flights over that country. Its own threat to destroy the missile sites provoked a crisis which could have escalated into armed conflict, and which was only defused by US mediation. The underlying tension between the two countries remained and President Assad of Syria made a defiant speech reasserting Syria's determination to recover the Golan Heights 'annexed' to Israel in 1981. In turn, Israeli military analysts began to discuss the possibility of a preemptive Israeli attack to prevent Syria achieving military parity with Israel. In mid-April the Syrian Government accused Israel of responsibility for a series of terrorist bomb attacks inside Syria, which claimed many lives, while Israel charged Syria with sponsoring Arab terrorism in Europe.

THE USA CLASHES WITH LIBYA

US mediation in the Middle East was effectively ruled out by the Reagan Administration's preoccupation with combating terrorism, at the expense of tackling the fundamental causes of regional violence and instability. This narrowly focused policy led to a military exchange between the USA and Libya, whose alleged sponsorship of international terrorism was apparently regarded by US policy-makers as the root cause of Middle East tension. On 24 March, after SAM-5 missiles had been fired at US aircraft, aircraft from the US Sixth Fleet in the Mediterranean sank four Libyan patrol vessels in the Gulf of Sirte and destroyed shore-based missile and radar facilities near the town of Sirte. The pretext for the incident was a US challenge to Libya's claim that the entire Gulf constituted Libyan territorial waters. Two weeks later a bomb exploded at a nightclub in West Berlin frequented by US servicemen, killing two people and injuring more than 200, in what the US Administration claimed was a Libyan-sponsored attack. In response US planes, including US air force bombers based in the United Kingdom, carried out air raids on Tripoli and Benghazi, which resulted in many civilian casualties, including members of Qaddafi's own family. The confrontation destroyed what little credibility the USA still had as a potential mediator in the Middle East conflict and many feared that, far from discouraging terrorism, the US action would encourage it.

THE VANUNU AFFAIR

The international media focused on Israel's nuclear weapons capability with the arrival in London, in October 1986, of Mordechai Vanunu, a former employee at the so-called 'textile factory' at Dimona in the Negev Desert in southern Israel. Vanunu claimed that he had worked as a technician at Dimona and that Israel had succeeded in developing thermonuclear weapons, and was stockpiling them there. The true nature of the Dimona plant had long been common knowledge in the West, in spite of official Israeli denials, yet the Israeli Government's first reaction to Vanunu's 'defection' was to prohibit Israeli papers from reporting the affair. Subsequently, Vanunu was lured to Rome by a female agent of Mossad, the Israeli external security service, which then kidnapped him and took him back to Israel to stand trial for treason.

SUPPORT FOR AN INTERNATIONAL PEACE CONFERENCE

Hopes of a revival in the peace process had been rekindled on 12 September when the Israeli Prime Minister, Shimon Peres, only a month before the scheduled handover of power to coalition partner Itzhak Shamir, met President Mubarak of Egypt in Alexandria. In a two-day summit, staged with the US and Israeli media very much in mind, the two leaders agreed, in principle, on the formation of a preparatory committee for an international conference to discuss the Arab-Israeli conflict. Such a conference, they agreed, should include the five permanent members of the UN Security Council, but the thorny issue of Arab, and particularly Palestinian, representation was left untouched. Support for an international conference grew to include King Hussein and the Ministers of Foreign Affairs of the EC; the fact that

clear backing, at least in principle, for such a conference had also been forthcoming from the USSR and the PLO, was a sign of both the range of possible delegates envisaged by the various parties concerned, and of how far the project was from becoming a reality. For the two main protagonists, Israel and the PLO, were no nearer the required goal of mutual recognition than they had ever been.

SHAMIR ASSUMES THE PREMIERSHIP OF ISRAEL

In Israel, the major obstacle to an international conference was the assumption of power, on 16 October, of Likud leader Itzhak Shamir, in accordance with the rotation agreement of September 1984 between the two main parties. Shamir unequivocally opposed such a conference. Shimon Peres, however, who assumed the Minister of Foreign Affairs' portfolio, made it quite clear that he had no intention of relinquishing the conference idea. Peres continued to promote the idea of an international conference, causing great embarrassment to Shamir. Indeed, Peres went to Egypt on 22 February to meet President Mubarak, and both leaders made repeated visits to Washington to secure the support of the US Administration. The coalition Government repeatedly teetered on the brink of disintegration, but Shimon Peres failed to secure the necessary support in the Knesset for his Labour bloc to carry a motion of 'no confidence' in the Government, which would have precipitated a general election. From Peres' point of view, however, the danger inherent in forcing a general election was that it might leave Likud in a position to form a coalition government which excluded Labour.

THE 'IRANGATE' SCANDAL

Having already seen its standing in the region plummet after a series of foreign-policy miscalculations, the final blow to the USA's credibility in Arab eyes came with the revelation, in November 1986, in the Lebanese magazine *Ash-Shira'*, of secret arms deals between Iran and the USA. The progressively more damaging disclosures which followed the publication of the article seriously damaged President Reagan's domestic popularity. It transpired that the arms contracts were brokered by Israeli arms merchants acting with the backing of the Israeli intelligence services and Government. From the perspective of links between Israel and Iran, the deal was not very unusual, Israel having been a major source of arms for Iran since the 1950s. On the other hand, the active part played by the USA, through its National Security Agency and with the clear knowledge and connivance of both President Reagan and many of his senior aides, was a stark contradiction of the USA's stated policy of not negotiating with regimes it held responsible for international terrorism. Israel originally convinced the USA of the desirability of the arms sales by claiming that they would help to bring about the release of a number of Western hostages held by Iranian-backed groups in Lebanon. An additional incentive was that the profits from the transaction could be used to circumvent US Congressional restrictions on aiding the Contra guerillas who were waging, by their own admission, a campaign of terror against the legitimate, but socialist, Government of Nicaragua.

The USA's traditional allies in the Arab world were dismayed by this further demonstration of the way in which supporters of Israel seemed to be able to sway US foreign policy so easily, even against the USA's own stated interests. Israel's success in persuading the USA to sell to Iran the very weapons systems that it had only recently refused to sell to Jordan, a staunch ally, made the Arab states' sense of betrayal even more acute.

THE POLLARD SPY CASE

At the beginning of March 1987, after a presidential commission had strongly criticized both President Reagan and Israel for their parts in the 'Irangate' affair, more pressure was brought to bear on the Israeli–US relationship in the aftermath of the trial of Jonathan Pollard, a US citizen, and his wife. The couple were arrested in November 1985 and charged with spying for Israel. Although their conviction was widely expected, the severe sentences, announced on 4 March, were received with surprise. Jonathan Pollard was sentenced to life imprisonment, in spite of the expectation that, having spied for an ally of the USA, he would be treated more leniently. Pollard was a committed Zionist who was recruited as a spy during a visit to Israel. His work in US naval intelligence gave him access to vast quantities of classified information. Of particular interest to Israel was material concerning the defence facilities of the USA's allies in the Middle East and North Africa, including, it is believed, data which enabled the Israelis to carry out the bombing of the PLO headquarters in Tunis in October 1985. These revelations caused both astonishment and disillusionment in the pro-US Arab states. Although the deep-rooted and far-reaching nature of Israel's alliance with the USA had long been understood, and the support enjoyed by Israel in the US legislature and in successive administrations widely acknowledged, few of the Arab states were aware to what extent Israel had also succeeded in penetrating the upper echelons of the US intelligence establishment.

DEVELOPMENTS IN THE OCCUPIED TERRITORIES

In the Occupied Territories the cycle of repression and protest continued. The appointment by the Israeli military authorities of Arab mayors in three West Bank towns was interpreted as part of a policy to isolate the PLO in the territories by fostering a more moderate Palestinian constituency and an alternative, 'acceptable', Palestinian leadership, and coincided with Jordanian efforts to the same end. These included the announcement in August of a five-year development plan for the West Bank and the Gaza Strip involving projected expenditure of US $1,300m. This apparent coincidence of interests resulted in the arrest and deportation of Akram Haniya, editor of the Jerusalem daily newspaper, *Ash-Sha'ab*. This action was regarded as a sop to Jordanian wishes—Haniya's hostility to Israel was no more threatening than that of any other newspaper editor in the Occupied Territories, but his aversion to King Hussein's plans in the West Bank clearly rankled with the Jordanian authorities. This episode was the prelude to a series of demonstrations by Palestinians and arrests by the military authorities, interspersed with acts of violence against Palestinian communities by Israeli settlers. December began with a number of clashes between the Israeli army and Palestinian demonstrators, the worst occurring at Bir Zeit University, where two students were shot dead. The subsequent closure of Bir Zeit, as well as an-Najah University in Nablus, brought no reduction in the level of Palestinian protests or in the consequent level of Israeli reprisals.

THE 'WAR OF THE CAMPS' SPREADS IN LEBANON

Lebanon continued to stumble from crisis to crisis in the second half of 1986. With sporadic fighting in the south between Israel's proxy SLA and the various Lebanese, mainly Shi'ite, forces opposing it, elements of the Maronite Lebanese Forces (LF) militia, opposed to President Gemayel, attempted a coup in east Beirut, which would have succeeded, but for the intervention of the Lebanese army. The failure of the coup was a blow to Syria's plans for a reconciliation of the many opposing forces in the country, for the Maronite forces loyal to President Gemayel remained the major stumbling block to a Syrian-brokered peace plan. In the south violent clashes flared up between Amal and PLO forces in and around Tyre and Sidon. Paralleled by the so-called 'war of the camps' in south Beirut, these clashes, which ushered in a prolonged period of conflict between the two forces, were a clear indication of the extent to which armed Palestinians from various PLO factions had re-established themselves in Lebanon, particularly in the Palestinian refugee camps. To the Syrians, this PLO revival, particularly in the number of fighters loyal to the leader of Fatah, Yasser Arafat, was another challenge to their hegemony over the country and to their bid to create an alternative PLO, independent of Arafat. Amal, as Syria's closest ally in Lebanon,

was the only Lebanese militia involved in this conflict, and Damascus relied on its ability to crush the resurgence of Palestinian military strength. Another source of concern for Syria was that pro- and anti-Arafat fighters made common cause in the defence of the camps, and their shared resentment of the Syrian role in suppressing the PLO threatened to cause a reconciliation. By December, with over 500 dead, there was no sign of any respite in the fighting in Tyre, Sidon and Beirut. The refugee camps at the core of the conflict were besieged, with essential supplies from outside effectively cut off.

THE WAVE OF ABDUCTIONS IN LEBANON

It was not until January 1987, however, that the Western news media turned its attention back to Lebanon, with the return to Beirut on 12 January of the Archbishop of Canterbury's special envoy, Terry Waite. The purpose of Waite's mission, against which he was strongly warned by both the British Ambassador and the Archbishop, was to negotiate the release of the 20 remaining Western hostages being held in Beirut. The kidnapping of foreigners had begun in Beirut in early 1984, and by the time of Waite's second visit more than 60 abductions had taken place, several of the hostages having been killed by their captors. No reliable figures are available for the numbers of Lebanese who had been kidnapped, many never to be seen again, since the civil war began. Waite himself disappeared on 21 January 1987 and remained in captivity until the end of 1991. Shi'a Muslims in the pay of Iran were believed to be responsible for his kidnapping.

Waite's disappearance, which was followed three days later by that of three US lecturers from the Beirut University College, provoked a strong response from the USA, whose Sixth Fleet was increasing its strength off the Lebanese coast. This deployment was backed up by calls for Westerners remaining in west Beirut to leave, as well as by strong criticism of the Iranian Government, which many held to be ultimately responsible for the kidnappings. Significantly, however, the group which held the three lecturers called itself 'Islamic Jihad for the Liberation of Palestine', and made its hostages' safe return dependent on Israel's release of 400 Arab prisoners. Whatever the true identity and motivation of the kidnappers, they drew attention to Israel's role in the Lebanese crisis, to the complexity of the problems affecting the Middle East, and the need to address the fundamental problem of Palestine, as a precondition of a wider settlement.

Israel's involvement in Lebanon was by no means confined to the security zone that it had established to the north of its northern border, policed by the SLA with support from Israeli troops. Israeli air raids on Palestinian targets around Tyre and Sidon continued, and were usually claimed to be retaliation for mortar and *katyusha* rocket attacks from south Lebanon into Galilee. On 2 January 1987 the Israelis intercepted a passenger ferry bound for the Maronite port of Jounieh from Larnaca, in Cyprus, accusing the LF of allowing PLO fighters to use the ferry to reach Lebanon and the Palestinian camps. This was neither the first time the Israelis had held up a Cyprus–Lebanon ferry, nor the first evidence of clandestine collaboration between Fatah and the Maronites loyal to President Gemayel. The Maronite leadership, presumably seeing little immediate prospect of relief from its traditional ally, Israel, sought instead to strengthen anti-Syrian forces in west Beirut.

SYRIAN TROOPS ASSERT THEIR AUTHORITY IN BEIRUT

Throughout January 1987, however, it became clear, as the 'war of the camps' continued, that the pro-Syrian nexus of Muslim forces in west Beirut was about to crumble. The Druze militia, the Sunni-dominated PSP militia and the Shi'ite-dominated Hezbollah and Lebanese Communist Party militias, had never shared Amal's enthusiasm for fighting the Palestinians. On several occasions the PSP had sent supplies into the camps and actively supported the besieged Palestinians. As a result, in February, open fighting broke out in Shi'ite areas between Amal and the Communists, supported by the PSP. Amal suffered a heavy defeat and this, coupled with increasingly heavy casualties sustained in the siege of Chatila and Bourj el-Barajneh, threatened Syria's position of influence in west Beirut, raising the prospect of an alliance of PLO and leftist forces in control of the city. With Western media attention arousing widespread international sympathy for the plight of the besieged Palestinians, President Assad of Syria decided to act. On 22 February some 4,000 Syrian troops occupied west Beirut, put an end to the clashes between the rival militias and lifted the siege of the Palestinian camps in Beirut, though Syrian influence failed permanently to relieve those in the south of Lebanon, and Syrian troops stopped short of precipitating a confrontation with Hezbollah by entering the Shi'a-dominated southern suburbs of Beirut.

PLO REUNIFICATION

The 'war of the camps' in Beirut resulted in another serious blow to President Assad's regional plans. Faced with Amal's onslaught and besieged in poorly fortified refugee camps, the disparate factions of the PLO had no choice but to unite on the ground in order to protect the Palestinian population whose defence was their ultimate *raison d'être* in Lebanon. After months of mediation by Algeria, Libya and, perhaps most significantly, the USSR, factions representing the majority of the PLO were finally brought together in March 1987. The principal rebel groups, the Democratic Front for the Liberation of Palestine (DFLP), the Palestine Communist Party (PCP), the two wings of the Palestine Liberation Front and the largest left-wing group, the Popular Front for the Liberation of Palestine (PFLP), agreed to attend a session of the PNC, after agreement on key issues had been reached with Yasser Arafat. The PLO's reunification at the 18th session of the PNC in Algiers from 20–25 April appeared to signal an end to the post–1982 alignments within the movement. Resolutions adopted by the PNC confirmed the agreements between the factions made prior to the session. Under the agreements, Arafat undertook to abrogate the Amman accord between Jordan and the PLO and to downgrade co-operation with Egypt until that country formally rejected the Camp David agreements with Israel (the PFLP had initially demanded the immediate severing of links with Egypt); while the left-wing factions (principally the PFLP and the DFLP) endorsed Arafat's continued leadership of the movement, effectively emasculating the Syrian-backed Palestine National Salvation Front, based in Damascus.

The reunification caused genuine celebration among the Palestinians under Israeli rule, whose attempts at resistance had been severely limited by years of factional wrangling. It alienated the Arab front-line states, Jordan, Egypt and Syria, each of whom saw their future ability to manipulate the PLO seriously undermined. The Israeli leadership was evidently dismayed at the PNC's failure to relapse into internal division but, with the PLO thus isolated from the most important Arab states, Peres was able to predict a decline in its relevance to a solution of the Middle East conflict. Indeed, as far as the much-vaunted idea of a Middle East peace conference was concerned, the reunification of the PLO, which urged the rejection of the USA's terms for negotiation, specifically Resolution 242, if taken in isolation, underlined the problem of accommodating the PLO at such a conference. However, the PNC explicitly supported the idea of a conference, with the PLO as the sole representative of the Palestinians, a suggestion which remained unacceptable to Israel.

POLITICAL DEADLOCK IN ISRAEL

Frustration at Palestinian unity was reinforced by the bitter deadlock within Israeli politics. The Labour-Likud coalition Government of national unity had only managed to survive thus far because each party feared the consequences of fresh elections. Despite indications of a significant lead for Labour in opinion polls in early 1987, the party was unable to rally enough support in the divided Knesset to be sure of winning a vote to dissolve Parliament and force new elections. With the political parties divided on the fundamental issue of peace moves, polarization within Israeli society

over the same issue was increasing. While Labour supporters became more and more frustrated with Prime Minister Shamir's dogged refusal in mid-1987 even to contemplate the possibility of an international conference, the Right grew increasingly contemptuous of what it saw as pandering to the Arabs with talk of land for peace. The Labour leader Shimon Peres' visit to Washington in May confirmed the isolation of his Likud rival in the international arena. Peres' opinion of the form which a peace conference should take was given strong backing by US Secretary of State George Shultz, who, however, was unwilling to bring pressure to bear on the Israeli Prime Minister to take a more flexible line.

September 1987 brought a direct attack on the PLO's status in the USA. Bowing to Congressional pressure the US State Department arrogated to itself the right to close the PLO's observer mission at the UN, in New York, and the Palestine Information Office in Washington, in spite of objections from US human rights groups protesting against what they believed to be a denial of freedom of speech. The move came as a surprise to US allies in Europe, who saw it as counterproductive to a proposed peace conference. With increased diplomatic activity by the USSR, which led to an improvement in Soviet relations with Israel, the proposed international conference was beginning to gather momentum again. The crucial obstacle remained the position of Shamir's Likud party, which remained doggedly opposed to any form of conference conducted on the basis of an exchange of land for peace, and had not even conceded the notion of a conference with superpower or UN Security Council participation, whatever the terms of negotiation. With George Shultz's visit to Moscow in October expected to cover the Middle East, it was widely hoped that he might bring some pressure to bear on Shamir during a brief visit to Israel. In the event, however, his views failed to make any impression on Shamir. Besides, the USA's Middle East preoccupations were, at this time, focused on developments in the Iran-Iraq War, with the Arab-Israeli conflict of secondary importance.

ARAB PRIORITIES

Such preoccupations were also troubling the Arab states themselves. The Arab League summit meeting in Amman, in November, had been convened primarily to consider the Iran–Iraq War, and the Palestine issue had been shuffled well down the agenda. Faced with the deepening involvement of Saudi Arabia and Kuwait in the war, it was hoped that the Amman summit would unite the Arab nations against Iran. In fact the summit was the first such gathering not to give the Palestine issue priority. Although the PLO's status as sole Palestinian representative was upheld, in spite of Syrian efforts to undermine it, it was only entrusted with joint responsibility, with Jordan and Syria, for drafting the meeting's Palestine resolution. With peace moves baulked and the Israelis seemingly entrenched in the Occupied Territories, there appeared to be little to distract Arab attention from Iran's perceived belligerence.

THE PALESTINIAN UPRISING

The events of the second week of December 1987 in the Gaza Strip and the West Bank took everybody by surprise. Thirteen Palestinian civilians were killed, 50 wounded and hundreds arrested in the most serious and sustained clashes between Palestinian youths and the Israeli army for many years. These clashes proved to be the beginning of what has become known as the *intifada* (uprising), a mass Palestinian demonstration against Israeli rule, which surprised none more than the Palestinians themselves by lasting into the 1990s. A number of factors clearly played a part in creating the conditions that led to a revolt on such a scale.

Ten days of serious clashes took place in Gaza in October, in which seven supporters of a resistance group new to the Occupied Territories, calling itself 'Islamic Jihad', were killed by the security forces. The very emergence of a radical fundamentalist group in Palestine was significant in itself; three of those killed had escaped from prison and returned to lead attacks on the Israelis and thereby greatly enhanced their popularity. As a result of this, the demonstrations which followed their deaths were particularly ferocious, but the Israelis were able eventually to restore order in the Strip. Indeed, the level of repression in the Occupied Territories was at its highest level for many years: a large number of Palestinians had been 'administratively' detained (i.e. without trial) during 1987, and deportations, house demolitions, and other repressive measures were beginning to sap the Palestinians' collective patience. The Amman summit itself was, doubtless, another factor in driving the Palestinians to revolt. At the time it was being held, widespread demonstrations were taking place in the Occupied Territories to protest at Arafat's cold reception in the Jordanian capital. The heavy-handed Israeli response provoked further clashes.

The spark that actually lit the *intifada* torch, however, appears to have been a traffic accident. On 8 December an Israeli army lorry crashed into a car queuing at the roadblock on the Gaza Strip's northern frontier, crushing four Palestinians to death. Few people believed it was an accident, and the Gaza Strip erupted in violent demonstrations. Quickly spreading to Nablus, the West Bank's largest town, the scale of the uprising caught the Israelis quite unprepared. Their panic-response—shooting on sight, harassing Muslim worshippers, attacking hospital patients and staff—was probably crucial in establishing and then maintaining the uprising's momentum. By the end of 1987, 28 Palestinians had been killed, the great majority in the Gaza Strip.

INTERNATIONAL REACTION TO THE INTIFADA

By mid-January 1988 it had become clear that what was under way in the Occupied Territories was a mass popular revolt. The Israelis had adopted a series of severely repressive measures (including curfews and travel bans), none of which had brought the recalcitrant Palestinians to heel. One of the uprising's most notable achievements in its earlier stages was to attract international press, particularly television, coverage which was unprecedentedly hostile to Israel. Western TV viewers were shown footage of Israeli troops firing live bullets and tear gas at Palestinian demonstrators; most spectacularly on 15 January, when the security forces invaded the precincts of the al-Aqsa mosque in Jerusalem, and attacked worshippers. Israel's attempts to restrict press access to areas of unrest merely provoked media fury, attracting further criticism from the Western press, which previously had generally been sympathetic towards Israel. Other Israeli countermeasures included the imposition of a curfew in towns, villages and refugee camps, which caused serious absenteeism of Palestinian workers from their jobs in Israel (an estimated 120,000 Palestinians from the Occupied Territories worked in Israel), adding economic hardship to Israel's difficulties. But the most disturbing aspect of the *intifada*, from Israel's viewpoint, was the emergence, as early as January 1988, of an underground leadership (the Unified National Leadership of the Uprising (UNLU)). The UNLU was composed of representatives of the various PLO factions and co-ordinated strikes and demonstrations. It issued regular, serialized communiqués which detailed day-to-day protest activities.

Lacking a coherent strategy in response to the uprising, the Israelis attempted various ways of undermining it. Apart from shooting at demonstrators (46 had been shot dead by 15 January), mass arrests and other collective punishments, nine Palestinians were served with deportation orders on 3 January (in the face of international opposition), and a concerted campaign against the Palestinian press was launched, including the arrest and detention of many journalists, the closure of newspapers and press bureaux, and the imposition of stricter than usual military censorship.

Faced with mounting international censure over the high Palestinian casualty toll, the Israeli Minister of Defence, Itzhak Rabin, issued new instructions to his troops in the Territories at the end of January. Firing live ammunition at demonstrators was to be superseded by the widespread use of CS tear gas and indiscriminate, pre-emptive, beatings. The spate of savage assaults by club-wielding Israeli soldiers on unarmed and often infirm Palestinians (not necessarily demonstrators—the stone-throwers could usually run

away) recorded by television cameras were merely the tip of the iceberg in a campaign that lasted three weeks.

Israel's reputation was suffering particular damage in the USA, most significantly among the American Jewish community, its staunchest and most crucial source of support. Shocked by extensive TV coverage of violent scenes, American Jewish leaders began to voice the community's discontent to their Israeli counterparts and to the US Government. The Reagan Administration was further spurred to action by the visit of President Mubarak of Egypt to Washington at the end of January. Mubarak emphasized the need for the US to re-engage itself in the peace process. As a result, the USA prepared for a foreign policy initiative in an area from which it would normally have remained aloof at the start of an election year. Special envoy Philip Habib was dispatched to Amman to seek King Hussein's views on 30 January.

The Arabs too were by now taking notice of the *intifada*. An extraordinary meeting of Arab Ministers of Foreign Affairs in Tunis, in January, effectively reversed the previous deprioritization of the Palestine question, putting it back at the top of the Arab world's agenda. Such was the response to the uprising in the Occupied Territories that a special fund was set up, under PLO supervision, to which member states of the Arab League were to be obliged to contribute to 'ensure the continuation of the uprising'. EC Commissioner Claude Cheysson publicly condemned Israel's actions as 'shameful' and called for its 'evacuation' of the Occupied Territories. The incoming chairman of the EC Council of Ministers, the West German Minister of Foreign Affairs, Hans Dietrich Genscher, caused further embarrassment to Israel by stating his intention to make the Middle East the priority of his foreign policy during his six-month 'presidency'. He made clear, with full EC backing, his intention to seek a role for Europe in pushing forward plans for an international peace conference under UN auspices.

THE SHULTZ PLAN

Herr Genscher's initiative (which led him to undertake visits to various regional capitals during his 'presidency') was, however, overshadowed by that of his US counterpart, Secretary of State George Shultz. Shultz made his first visit of the year to the Middle East on 25 February, impelled not so much by an overriding desire to settle the region's problems as equitably as possible (his record in office contained no previous diplomatic successes of any note, relating to the Arab-Israeli conflict), as by pressure from within the USA, particularly the Jewish community, to do something to relieve the pressure on Israel which the *intifada* had brought about. His plan was outlined by the US Under-Secretary of State for Near Eastern and South Asian Affairs, Richard Murphy, on a preliminary visit to the region between 5 and 11 February. The plan proposed: a six-month period of negotiations, beginning on 1 May 1988, on the basis of UN Security Council resolutions 242 and 338, between Israel and a joint Jordanian-Palestinian delegation, to determine a form of interim autonomy for the Occupied Territories, which would last for three years pending a permanent negotiated settlement; the provision in the interim agreement for an Israeli military withdrawal from the West Bank, and for municipal elections of Palestinian officials to be held during 1989; and negotiations on a final settlement, to be started by the end of 1988; both sets of negotiations to run concurrently with an international conference, involving the five permanent members of the UN Security Council and all other parties to the conflict, proceeding on the basis of UN Security Council Resolutions 242 and 338, but having no power to impose a settlement or veto any agreement reached in the separate Israeli-Jordanian-Palestinian negotiations. (See Documents on Palestine, p. 97.) The plan was fatally flawed. Some form of interim arrangement would clearly be a requirement of any peace plan, but the absence of PLO representation and the 'toothless' nature of the international conference would not endear Shultz's proposals to Arab governments and the Israeli obstacle was well known. The time-scale for the plan's operation was an indication of the importance Washington attached to the peace process. However, another fundamental obstacle to the plan's acceptance was the Reagan Administration's lack of credibility in the Arab world. In the Arab view, the USA had done little or nothing in recent years to bring pressure to bear on Israel to reconsider its stance on peace negotiations—was it prepared to act differently now?

When Shultz visited the Middle East at the end of February to consult regional leaders, Israel's response to his plan, or, rather, the divided response of its two main leaders, was all too predictable: general endorsement, after some initial reservations, from Shimon Peres; outright rejection, after initial, hesitant interest, from Itzhak Shamir. For Shamir, the US plan had 'no prospect of implementation'; if Shultz pushed too hard for its implementation, Shamir believed, the Israeli Government would fall, and, given the new political climate engendered by the Palestinian uprising, Likud would win the ensuing election outright. Egypt and Syria stopped short of an outright rejection of the plan but Syria, in particular, gave no cause to suggest that it would in any way support its implementation. Jordan pronounced itself sceptical that Israel would relinquish control over the Territories and reiterated its opposition to 'partial or interim solutions', though it welcomed the USA's acceptance on 1 March of the concept of the Palestinians' 'legitimate rights'. The UNLU interpreted the Shultz plan as an attempt to abort the uprising and halt the political momentum it was generating world-wide in favour of Palestinian national rights. The PLO rejected the plan outright, as it made no provision for the creation of a Palestinian state and did not recognize the PLO's right to be involved in the peace negotiations. So, when Shultz returned to the USA, following another visit to the region at the beginning of March, it was with virtually nothing to show for his peace initiative. In his absence US TV cameras had continued to record Israel's repressive measures to put down the uprising and the climate of sympathy for the Palestinians had not faded.

THE INTIFADA CONTINUES

In the Territories themselves, there had been no slackening in the intensity of the *intifada*. A total of 76 Palestinians had been shot dead by the end of February; others were beaten to death or killed by exposure to CS tear gas. Fifteen were victims of the gas (over 80 aborted pregnancies were also attributed to the exposure of the mothers to the gas) following its use in confined spaces (narrow alleyways or even inside people's homes), in contravention of the manufacturer's recommendations. (The chemical was sold, and is used elsewhere, as a means of crowd dispersal in open areas. At the beginning of May the manufacturers eventually agreed to ban its sale to Israel.) Meanwhile, arrests, beatings, press restrictions, deportations, prolonged curfews, the forced opening of shops (closed according to strike instructions issued by the Palestinian underground leadership), and the closure of schools and colleges, all continued to be employed by the Israelis to contain the uprising.

NEW LEADERSHIP IN THE OCCUPIED TERRITORIES

In response, the Palestinians used a surprise weapon: unity. After its apparently spontaneous beginnings, it became clear to the Israeli authorities that the uprising was being carefully orchestrated. The degree of cohesion and co-ordination this gave to the various components of Palestinian society was unprecedented in its recent history. The solidarity engendered among Palestinians was the key factor in making the uprising viable on a prolonged basis. With clear support from Palestinians and Arabs inside pre-1967 Israel, and from many groups and individuals on the left of Israeli politics, the uprising had already made an indelible mark on Israeli society by March 1988.

Palestinian politics were also greatly affected. That the uprising was a spontaneous expression of popular frustration with Israel's rule and of the solidarity between Palestinian Christians and Moslems against Israel's oppression, was undeniable, but it marked a new departure in that the PLO leadership outside the Occupied Territories

was not instrumental in organizing and sustaining it. After initial reports of differences between the PLO in Tunis and the underground leadership in the Territories, a working relationship between the two was quickly established, principally to ensure the passage of funds from outside into the Territories, but also to co-ordinate, as far as possible, the political strategy of the PLO as a whole. (The new leadership in the Territories was unequivocal in its allegiance to the PLO.)

At the end of March, the Israelis intensified their crackdown on the rebellion. Telephone links between the Occupied Territories and the outside world were severed; restrictions were placed on movement between districts within the Territories, and between the Territories and Israel and Jordan; a twenty-four hour curfew was imposed on the entire Gaza Strip for three successive days. The restrictions, which were primarily intended to prevent a massive Palestinian demonstration planned for Land Day on 30 March (commemorating the killing in 1976 of six Israeli Arabs, demonstrating against Israeli land seizures), also included the suspension of fuel supplies and severe restrictions on press and media access. The arrest and detention without trial of suspected ringleaders was also stepped up. However, these measures only hardened Palestinian resolve. Local committees organized the distribution of food, fuel and other resources (as they also supervised strikes and the closure of shops, which the Israelis attempted to keep open by force, to preserve an appearance of normality), as well as taking responsibility for security after a mass resignation of Palestinian policemen, who had been threatened with reprisals for co-operating with the occupying power. Solidarity between Palestinian communities on both sides of the pre-1967 frontier was, if anything, strengthened.

With battle-lines thus, uncompromisingly, drawn, George Shultz returned to the Middle East in mid-April. To the surprise of no one, he achieved nothing, his efforts obstructed by Shamir's obstinacy, and hamstrung by his own unwillingness to bring pressure to bear on the Israeli Prime Minister. Despite a loss of interest in the Western media, engendered chiefly by the restrictions Israel had imposed on reporting in the Occupied Territories, the *intifada* continued. Shootings, beatings, tear-gassing and other less 'telegenic' acts of violence remained the Israelis' most visible means of combating the uprising. In addition, universities and schools were closed for four months, from April until the end of July; petrol supplies were periodically suspended; there were weeks of continuous night-time curfew throughout the Gaza Strip, and thousands of Palestinians were detained, many without trial, for six months, under martial law. By the end of July more than 290 Palestinians had been killed in the uprising and 28 deported. Fundamental changes had taken place in Palestinian society since the *intifada* began; old class divisions had begun to break down, as the West Bank's urban élite found itself as dependent on home-produced food as the poorest peasant families. In such a climate, Israeli repression alone could not break the popular will to continue the uprising, which was now a central fact in the life of every Palestinian in the Occupied Territories, and a rallying point for Palestinians throughout the diaspora.

THE ASSASSINATION OF 'ABU JIHAD'

On 16 April 1988, in Tunis, an Israeli assassination squad murdered Khalil al-Wazir (alias 'Abu Jihad'), Yasser Arafat's deputy as commander of the Palestine Liberation Army. In the wave of ensuing demonstrations in the Occupied Territories, 16 Palestinians were killed in a single day. The assassination prompted a *rapprochement* between Arafat and President Assad, who had been at odds since 'Abu Musa', a Fatah dissident, led a Syrian-backed revolt in Lebanon against Arafat's leadership of the PLO in 1983. On 25 April 1988 Arafat and President Assad met in Damascus, where 'Abu Jihad' was buried, to discuss their differences. It was Arafat's first visit to Syria since his expulsion in June 1983. However, any prospect of a further improvement in relations was nullified by the renewal, in May 1988, of attempts by Syrian-backed PLO guerrillas, led by 'Abu

Musa', to drive Arafat loyalists out of the Palestinian refugee camps in Beirut.

At the beginning of June 1988 an extraordinary summit meeting of the Arab League was held in Algiers to discuss the *intifada* and Middle East peace moves. The final communiqué of the summit, endorsed by all 21 League members, effectively rejected the Shultz plan by demanding PLO participation in the proposed international peace conference and insisting on the Palestinians' right to self-determination and the establishment of an independent Palestinian state in the Occupied Territories (i.e. the principles of the 1982 Fez plan). The summit hailed the 'heroic' Palestinian uprising and pledged all necessary assistance (including an unspecified amount of financial aid) to sustain it.

JORDAN SEVERS TIES WITH THE WEST BANK

On 28 July 1988 Jordan cancelled a $1,300m. five-year development plan for the Occupied Territories, which had been launched in November 1986 but had failed to attract sufficient foreign funds. Then, two days later, King Hussein severed Jordan's 'administrative and legal links' with the West Bank, dissolving the House of Representatives (the lower house of the Jordanian National Assembly), where West Bank Palestinians occupied 30 of the 60 seats. The King explained that his actions were taken in accordance with the wishes of the PLO and the Arab League, as expressed in the resolutions of the Rabat summit of 1974, which recognized the PLO as the sole legitimate representative of the Palestinian people and which advocated the establishment of an independent Palestinian state in the West Bank, and in the peace plan proposed at the Fez summit of 1982. Commentators were quick to point out that King Hussein stopped short of actually repealing the annexation of the West Bank, which would have constituted a formal and irrevocable abrogation of Jordan's 38-year old ties with the region, while the dissolution of the House of Representatives would have little effect, as the Jordanian legislature had exerted little practical influence over affairs in the West Bank since the Israeli occupation in 1967.

King Hussein's decision to reduce Jordan's links with the West Bank was interpreted as partly a response to the Palestinian *intifada*, which had encouraged support amongst Palestinians for an independent Palestinian state, and partly as an attempt to persuade the PLO to accept responsibility for the Palestinian people and the peace process. It was suggested, however, that King Hussein considered the PLO constitutionally incapable of making the concessions necessary to the progress towards peace, and that the necessity of involving Jordan in any settlement would inevitably become apparent. In the short term, however, the effect of Jordan's actions was to strengthen the position of the Likud bloc (which had always ridiculed the Labour party's support for a Jordanian-Palestinian federation in the West Bank) in the period preceding the Israeli general election in November 1988. They also isolated the USA, whose peace initiatives, because they would not countenance negotiations involving the PLO, depended on Jordan's acting as interlocutor and forming part of a delegation representative of the Palestinians in any future peace talks.

To the PLO, King Hussein's move represented a considerable challenge. The Occupied Territories, with the exception of East Jerusalem, were now claimed *de jure* by no state as part of its sovereign territory, providing the PLO with an historic opportunity to assert sovereignty over a specific area. The PLO immediately began to make preparations for the issues of a provisional government and Palestinian statehood to be included on the agenda at the next session of the Palestine National Council in the autumn of 1988. In the Occupied Territories themselves, Jordan's severing of its ties with the West Bank was widely applauded. Communiqué No. 24 of the UNLU described the move as the *intifada's* 'greatest accomplishment'.

With Jordan's disengagement leaving the PLO the exclusive voice of Palestinian national aspirations, Yasser Arafat began to seek diplomatic support for a 'two-state' solution to the Arab-Israeli conflict. Addressing the European Parliament in Strasbourg on 12 September 1988, he sought the EC's active endorsement for the PLO's strategy. In his speech, he made a number of new concessions, stating that the PLO was ready to negotiate with Israel at an international peace conference on the basis of the UN Security Council's Resolutions 242 and 338, and to seek 'reciprocal recognition', whereby, in return for Israeli recognition of an independent Palestinian state, the PLO would accept Israel's right to security. Arafat also repeated his declaration, made in Cairo in 1985, which eschewed armed action outside the Occupied Territories. Armed struggle within the Territories remained, Arafat said, a justifiable option for the Palestinians, although firearms were only used in isolated instances.

POPULAR COMMITTEES OUTLAWED

However, the general tactic of demonstrations and stone-throwing continued unabated, as did the Israelis' counter-measures. Widespread demonstrations in Gaza on 14 August 1988 led to the imposition of a curfew throughout the Strip, and the protests spread to the West Bank during the following week. Here the two most immediate grievances were the deaths, by shooting, of two Palestinian political prisoners, and the deportation orders served on 25 activists on 17 August. The deportation orders provoked a spontaneous appeal for a three-day general strike in Nablus, Ramallah and Bethlehem. A military order (issued on the same day), outlawing the 'popular committees' (*lijan ash-sha'biya*), was of more far-reaching significance. Membership of the committees was declared to be an imprisonable offence, thus providing Israel with 'a more convenient legal means to deal with the institutionalization of the uprising', according to the Israeli Minister of Defence, Itzhak Rabin. The popular committees had been established at a very early stage of the uprising to organize day-to-day activities, such as the distribution of food and other supplies, agriculture, medical care, education and security. When the committees were forced underground, it became more difficult both for them to function and for the authorities to monitor and suppress their activities. The Israeli intelligence services therefore increased their efforts to infiltrate Palestinian organizations, while the Palestinians, in turn, intensified their campaign of exposing, and often executing, people known to have collaborated with the Israelis.

THE EFFECT OF THE INTIFADA ON PLO POLICY

Mass popular participation in 'grass-roots' organizations in the West Bank and Gaza had a major impact on PLO policy. The growth of the popular committees and the gradual, although partial, abrogation by Israeli state institutions of their role in the Territories encouraged Palestinian intellectuals to formulate ideas for the establishment of a provisional government for an independent Palestinian state. Despite the occupation, many national institutions had been established over the years, and, with the widening participation in the management of Palestinian society that was brought about by the *intifada*, they suggested the model for the structure of such a government. From a series of meetings of the Executive Committee of the PLO in August and September 1988, there emerged two basic proposals for debate at the meeting of the PNC in Algiers in November. The first was for the declaration of an independent state in the West Bank and Gaza, and advocated the establishment of a provisional government. The second recommended that the Occupied Territories be placed under the trusteeship of the UN, pending a settlement of the conflict.

DECLARATION OF PALESTINIAN INDEPENDENCE

The 19th session of the PNC, held in Algeria on 12–15 November 1988, brought together all the major factions of the PLO, including those based in Damascus. As expected, the PNC unilaterally declared the establishment of the independent State of Palestine, with its capital at Jerusalem. The UN General Assembly's Resolution 181 (see Documents on Palestine, p. 86) had provided the principle for Palestinian statehood in 1947, proposing the partition of Palestine into two states with defined borders. However, the Declaration of Independence left open the question of the new state's territory. The state was declared to be established, 'relying on the authority bestowed by international legitimacy as embodied in the resolutions of the United Nations since 1947', no mention being made of the specific details of any particular resolution, other than the principle of partition (and, thereby, a Palestinian state) in Resolution 181.

The UN General Assembly's Resolution 181 stipulated specific borders for two states in Palestine, while the UN Security Council's Resolution 242 of 1967 urged Israel to withdraw from territories occupied in the 1967 war. The borders that had been established by the 1948–49 Armistice Agreements between Israel, Egypt, Jordan, Lebanon and Syria, since they were 'dictated exclusively by military and not political considerations', gave Israel no technical right, under international law, to territories other than those designated by Resolution 181, which it had occupied in the hostilities of 1947–48. According to a strict interpretation of the international legal status of the former British mandated territory of Palestine, the declaration of an independent Palestinian state could have made reference to a specific territory, and many delegates representing the Occupied Territories at the PNC's 19th session urged such a move, and the creation of a provisional government. In the run-up to the meeting, however, there had been considerable disagreement within the PLO regarding the composition of such a government, and it was decided to refer the matter back to the Executive Committee for further consideration. The Executive Committee, it was decided, would function as an *ad hoc* government.

ACCEPTANCE OF RESOLUTION 242

Another source of controversy was the question of the UN Security Council's Resolution 242. For many years, the USA, supported by Israel, had demanded that the PLO should accept its provisions. However, since this Resolution sought 'respect for the sovereignty, territorial integrity and political independence of every state in the area', such a concession would amount to recognition of the State of Israel. As the Fez Arab summit proposal of 1982, endorsed by the PLO, explicitly recognized Israel's existence, the PLO had already effectively recognized Israel. It had, furthermore, repeatedly stated its acceptance of all the pertinent UN resolutions. At the 19th session of the PNC in Algiers, Arafat and others within Fatah wanted to accept Resolution 242 'in isolation', in order to appease the USA and to spur it into action. However, left-wing factions within the wider Palestinian movement, as well as many Fatah cadres, forced the leadership to adopt a compromise formula: the PLO's acceptance of Resolution 242 was, in conjunction with Palestinian rights of self-determination and to international legality on the basis of UN resolutions, to provide the basis of an international peace conference. In a press conference at the end of the PNC session, Arafat was explicit: he sought acceptance of UN Security Council Resolution 242 as a mandate 'to actively pursue peace', and challenged the USA to respond to the PLO's overtures.

RESPONSES TO THE DECLARATION OF INDEPENDENCE

By the time that the 19th session of the PNC took place, the Israeli general election had resulted in a narrow victory (but not a clear parliamentary majority) for Itzhak Shamir's Likud Party, while, in the USA, a Republican President had again been returned to power and the Democrats retained control of Congress. Shamir dismissed the results of the 19th PNC as 'tactical moves devoid of any importance'. The response of the outgoing US Administration was more damaging. Invited to address the UN General Assembly in New York in December 1988, Yasser Arafat and his aides had to obtain visas to enter the USA. On the personal instructions of the US Secretary of State, George Shultz, the visas were denied. Elsewhere in the world, however, the PNC's declaration of independence encountered more favourable responses. By the time that Shultz had banned Arafat from entering the USA, more than 60 states,

including two permanent members of the UN Security Council (China and the USSR), had recognized the State of Palestine. Although the 12 members of the EC had not recognized the new state, they welcomed the decisions of the 19th PNC as a 'positive step forward', and continued, with the backing of the USSR, to support the PLO's appeal for the convening of an international peace conference.

ARAFAT ADDRESSES THE UN GENERAL ASSEMBLY

Arafat eventually addressed the UN General Assembly on 13 December 1988, the meeting having been relocated to Geneva, where he made a number of historic concessions. Inviting the 'leaders of Israel' to join him in reaching a peace agreement, Arafat presented the General Assembly with a three-point programme, the main proposals of which were that the UN Secretary-General should establish a preparatory committee for an international peace conference; that the Occupied Territories should be brought under the temporary supervision of UN forces, who would oversee Israel's withdrawal; and that there should be a comprehensive settlement, among the parties concerned, including Israel, at an international peace conference to be held on the basis of UN Security Council Resolutions 242 and 338. In his address, Arafat explicitly recognized Israel and rejected 'terrorism', as the USA had demanded.

Prime Minister Shamir of Israel, however, dismissed Arafat's address as a 'public relations exercise'. Its impact on the attitude of the USA towards the PLO was, nevertheless, alarming enough to persuade Shamir to disregard most of his party's differences with the Israeli Labour Party and to establish a new coalition government of national unity.

US RECOGNITION OF THE PLO

Although he found his Government almost completely isolated (in particular among its European allies) over its decision to ban Arafat from entering the USA, Shultz still refused to acknowledge that Arafat had conceded anything previously demanded of him by the USA. Following Arafat's address in Geneva, it required hours of intense Swedish diplomacy to detail the concessions asked of the PLO in words which the USA would find unambiguous. Even then, it took pressure from the incoming Administration of President-elect George Bush to convince Shultz. On 16 December 1988 the US Ambassador to Tunisia, Robert Pelletreau, held talks lasting 90 minutes with two representatives of the PLO. The USA had finally recognized the PLO. At the meeting, it was agreed that the dialogue should be maintained, and a second session of talks was planned for 20 January 1989. The PLO thus achieved its most important diplomatic breakthrough, although it did not necessarily expect any concrete advances in the peace process to follow quickly.

THE FIRST YEAR OF THE INTIFADA

In the Occupied Territories, the outcome of the 19th session of the PNC was greeted with widespread jubilation, and the declaration of independence was regarded as the greatest achievement of the *intifada*. The opening of a dialogue between the PLO and the USA was also widely perceived as a victory for the uprising, although many in the Occupied Territories feared that Arafat had conceded too much in return for too few guarantees. By the end of 1988, with more than 300 Palestinians shot dead and another 100 killed by other means in the first year of the uprising, a widespread pessimism had developed among the population of the Territories.

Apart from momentary lulls, there was no relaxation of the uprising. Palestinian protestors were still able to surprise the Israeli authorities by means of an underground network. Furthermore, despite the emergence of an autonomous Islamic fundamentalist group in Gaza (the Islamic Resistance Movement, allied to the Muslim Brotherhood and known by its Arab acronym, Hamas), both the UNLU and the people at large had managed to maintain unity of action and purpose. Israel's only real resort remained brute force.

The use of pre-emptive beatings to suppress the uprising, espoused by Israel's Minister of Defence, Itzhak Rabin, in the spring of 1988, gave way to the more widespread use of plastic and rubber bullets, many of which also contained lead, and which, contrary to official guidelines, were often discharged at very close range. On 18 December violent demonstrations erupted in Nablus after troops opened fire on a funeral procession, killing two people. The Israelis reacted severely and a further eight Palestinians were killed, and a curfew was imposed on the city for six consecutive days. By 16 January 1989 a total of 31 Palestinians had been killed, and more than 1,000 wounded, in confrontations with troops, as the indiscriminate firing of 'non-lethal' ammunition into crowds of demonstrators became commonplace. A further alarming development was the emergence of Israeli 'death-squads' which sought out, and attempted to liquidate, leaders of the uprising.

ISRAEL'S DIPLOMATIC INITIATIVE

Meanwhile, there were signs that Israel was preparing to announce a diplomatic initiative. Pressure from the USA and Europe, from both governments and Jewish communities, for Israel to redeem its image, together with condemnations of the high casualties, led to rumours that Prime Minister Shamir intended to reveal the initiative when he made his first visit to Washington since the election of President Bush.

However, even after the dialogue between the USA and the PLO had begun, and most Arab states had expressed support for Arafat's strategy, Shamir could still say, in January 1989, that 'nothing has changed' and that the 'Arab intention is the same: the destruction of Israel'. It was surprising, therefore, to learn that discussions had been taking place between Israeli officials and a prominent Jerusalem Palestinian, Faisal Husseini, the head of the Arab Studies Centre in Jerusalem, since the beginning of 1989. Despite this diplomatic initiative, there was no sign of an end to Israel's use of brutal methods to suppress the uprising. Indeed, discussions of Israeli concessions caused further problems for Palestinian communities in the form of attacks by Israeli settlers in the West Bank and Gaza. The death of a West Bank settler in February 1989 provoked a series of revenge attacks on the town of Qalqiliya and a raid on the village of Burin, near Nablus. It was alleged in the Knesset that a well-armed settlers' militia was operating in the West Bank. Further serious disturbances occurred in Rafah and Nablus at the end of February.

THE USSR ENDORSES THE PLO'S PROPOSALS

Diplomatic initiatives from the USA were slow to develop. A tour of the Middle East by the Soviet Minister of Foreign Affairs, Eduard Shevardnadze, in February 1989 emphasized the USA's inactivity, as he demonstrated, by his talks in Syria, Jordan, Egypt, Iran and Iraq, that the USSR was the only superpower able to talk freely to all parties to the Middle East conflict. With the exception of Israel's Likud Party, all concerned agreed with Shevardnadze's proposal for the convening of an international peace conference.

THE USA CLARIFIES ITS POSITION

Despite a visit to Washington by the Israeli Minister of Foreign Affairs, Moshe Arens, in early March 1989, it became clear, when the dialogue between the USA and the PLO resumed, that the USA now accepted that the PLO was the only negotiating partner qualified to represent the Palestinians. However, several serious points of contention remained, in particular the purpose of the dialogue itself, which the PLO regarded as a prelude to wider negotiations and, eventually, an international peace conference. The USA rejected this notion.

During Arens' visit to Washington, the US Government hinted that Israel might eventually have to negotiate with the PLO, and pressure on Israel to formulate peace plans intensified. By the time that Prime Minister Shamir met President Bush in Washington on 6 April 1989, the details of his peace plan were widely known. Based largely on the proposals that Minister of Defence Rabin had presented, the plan offered 'free and democratic' elections in the Occupied Territories in return for the ending of the *intifada*. The elections, according to Shamir's plan, would produce a delegation to conduct negotiations with Israel for a permanent settlement. The USA gave its cautious approval to the plan, while Palestinians, both inside and outside the Territories, sought more specific details and attached a number of conditions to their acceptance of it. Israeli right-wing parties condemned the proposals and demanded a firmer suppression of the *intifada*.

THE VIOLENCE ESCALATES

April 1989 was one of the *intifada's* bloodiest months, with the death toll since the outbreak of the uprising exceeding 500. The worst atrocity of the uprising to date occurred on 7 April at the village of Nahalin, near Bethlehem. Members of the Israeli border police entered the village early in the morning and attacked people leaving a mosque, killing five and injuring more than 50. Violence in Gaza on 22–23 April left a further two people dead and 87 injured.

In Gaza, following demonstrations during the Islamic festival of Id al-Fitr, three Palestinians were shot dead, and more than 400 wounded, as troops fired 'plastic' bullets and canisters of CS tear gas into crowds. On 8 May the territory was sealed off, with border crossings closed and telephone connections severed. An indefinite curfew was imposed, which continued until the end of the month, when the Israelis began to issue identity cards to all Gazans with a record of political activity, effectively denying them entry into Israel.

PALESTINIANS' RESPONSE TO ISRAEL'S PLAN FOR PEACE

These tougher measures were in accordance with Minister of Defence Rabin's warning, issued on 15 May 1989, when he threatened Palestinians with greater repression if they did not accept the Israeli Government's peace proposals. However, the leadership of the *intifada* and of the PLO in Tunis remained adamant that certain conditions must be satisfied before the plans could be accepted, although they did not reject the proposals outright. Full details of the Israeli peace plan were disclosed after its approval by the Knesset on 14 May. The plan was similar to the Camp David proposals in many respects. Its failure to clarify either who would be eligible to be a candidate or to vote in the proposed elections or the status of the residents of East Jerusalem; its reiteration of Israel's opposition to the creation of a Palestinian state and its proviso that no change in the status of the Territories could take place without the consent of the Israeli Government, all fell short of what was acceptable not only to the Palestinians and the USSR, but also to the EC states. However, the plan made too many concessions for right-wing opinion in Israel, and its announcement provoked threats by settlers to establish their own independent state on the West Bank if Israel ever agreed to relinquish the territory.

PRESSURE ON ISRAEL INCREASES

In early May 1989 Yasser Arafat was invited by President Mitterrand of France to make an official visit to Paris. The visit was a great success, especially after Arafat declared that the Palestinian National Charter had been superseded by the resolutions of the Algiers session of the PNC in November 1988. Israel was sufficiently disturbed by the success of Arafat's visit to Paris for Prime Minister Shamir to begin a European tour two weeks later, fearing, perhaps, that the PLO's publicity exercise might be repeated in other European capitals.

The USA was also beginning to give the Israeli Government cause for alarm. Shamir's visit to Washington had coincided with that of Egypt's President Mubarak, to whom President Bush had confided that the US Government shared Egypt's aim of ending Israel's occupation of the West Bank and Gaza. A warning by the USA that the time had come for Israel to renounce the idea of maintaining its control over the Territories, and the USA's description of the vision of a Greater Israel as 'unrealistic', caused further anxiety.

The USA seemed to be gradually distancing itself from the policy of almost unquestioned support for Israel, which had characterized President Reagan's term of office. In July 1989, however, in order to appease critics of Israel's peace initiative within the Likud, Shamir agreed to a resolution which added four principles to the original plan. These clarified four areas of the initiative which had deliberately been left ambiguous to avoid alienating the USA and the PLO from the outset. They stipulated that residents of East Jerusalem would not be permitted to participate in the proposed elections in the West Bank and in Gaza; that violent attacks by Palestinians must cease before elections could be held in the Occupied Territories; that Jewish settlement should continue in the Territories and that foreign sovereignty should not be conceded in any part of Israel; and that the establishment of a Palestinian state west of the River Jordan was out of the question, as were negotiations with the PLO. In response the leadership of Israel's Labour Party recommended that the Party should withdraw from the coalition Government. At the end of July, however, it was reported that the Israeli Cabinet had voted in favour of endorsing the peace plan in its original form.

The *intifada* continued unabated throughout the summer of 1989. On 19 June the deportation of a further eight Palestinians was ordered, giving rise to more street protests, and in August the newly appointed commander of Israeli forces in the West Bank, Itzhak Mordechai, issued an order permitting troops to open fire on Palestinians who wore face masks during demonstrations. An increase in raids on Palestinian villages by the Israeli Defence Force (IDF), together with the deliberate targeting of organizers of the popular committees, contributed to a rising casualty toll.

In Gaza, meanwhile, a fierce battle of wills developed between the local population and the Israeli authorities over the introduction of new identity cards. The Israelis stipulated that possession of a new, computer-readable, magnetic identity card was necessary for all those travelling outside of the Gaza Strip. However, such cards would only be issued to those Palestinians who acquired security clearance and who could prove they were up-to-date with payment of taxes. As the majority of Gazans earned their living inside Israel, the Israeli authorities hoped that economic pressure would force them to accept the new identity cards. The popular committees responded by urging a boycott of the new identity cards, which were confiscated as soon as they were issued. By mid-July so few Gazans were reporting for work in Israel that employers pressurized the IDF into allowing some Gazans to leave the Gaza Strip without identity cards. However, fearing the financial hardships of a prolonged boycott, the UNLU eventually abandoned it.

Acts of communal resistance persisted in the West Bank. In Beit Sahour, a small Christian town near Bethlehem, residents had observed a total boycott of tax payments ever since the UNLU had first called for payments to the civil administration to be withheld. A six-week campaign to break the boycott was launched by the Israelis in 1989. It began with arrests, the imposition of lengthy curfews and the cutting of electricity and telephone lines, and ended with the blockading of the town and the confiscation of property in lieu of payment.

Despite the defiance in Beit Sahour and the struggle against the new identity cards in Gaza, there were signs that a combination of exhaustion and frustration at the lack of political return was fostering extremism. At the end of June 1989, a US aid worker was the victim of an unprecedented kidnapping in Gaza and two weeks later 14 people died when a young Palestinian seized control of an Israeli bus in which they were travelling and sent it crashing down a ravine.

MUBARAK'S ATTEMPT TO RESTART THE PEACE PROCESS

In mid-September President Mubarak attempted to restart the peace process by asking the Israeli Government to clarify 10 points concerning the procedure and substance of Prime Minister Shamir's peace plan. Mubarak sought commitment to the principle of exchanging land for peace and the partici-

pation of the residents of East Jerusalem in the plan's proposed election. At the same time, Mubarak offered to convene an early meeting of Israeli and Palestinian delegations to discuss the details of the election. The US Government had been privy to Mubarak's proposals since mid-July, but had cautioned against making them public in the hope that the Israeli Government would be able to sustain what was, after all, its own peace initiative. The fact that the US President George Bush had now permitted Mubarak to announce an initiative of his own revealed the US Government's ebbing faith in the Israeli Government.

The reaction of the Israeli Government to Mubarak's initiative was divided. The Labour leader Shimon Peres voiced his support, while Prime Minister Shamir stated his opposition and spoke of the need 'to fight off grave threats'. No formal rejection was sent to Cairo, but the Israeli Prime Minister was clearly irritated by the Egyptian Government's attempt to usurp his peace initiative. Both Mubarak and the US Secretary of State, James Baker, anxious not to further alienate the Israeli Prime Minister, insisted that the Egyptian proposal was merely a supplement to Shamir's plan, not a replacement. By mid-October, however, it was clear the USA was failing to persuade Likud to embrace the revised peace proposals. Prime Minister Shamir and the Israeli Minister of Foreign Affairs, Moshe Arens, did not regard Mubarak's 10 points as a basis for negotiations, nor would they agree to talks with a Palestinian delegation which had any connection whatsoever with the PLO. In a final attempt to keep the peace initiative alive, US Secretary of State James Baker put forward five proposals (the 'Baker plan') which aimed to remove Israeli objections. Essentially, Baker proposed that acceptance of Mubarak's 10 points should not be a precondition for participation in the Cairo talks and that the composition of the Palestinian delegation should be decided by the Governments of Israel, the USA and Egypt.

PLO'S FORMAL RESPONSE TO THE 'SHAMIR PLAN'

The 'Shamir plan' and the subsequent attempts to modify it aroused little enthusiasm in Palestinians or the PLO, who were convinced that Shamir had only conceived his peace initiative as a concession to the USA, and in order to pressurize the Palestinians. Moreover, the PLO believed that Mubarak's clarifications of the 'Shamir plan' still fell short of its own minimum negotiating position. At a meeting of the PLO's central council in Baghdad in October, the PLO stated that the negotiating team should be selected by the PLO and should comprise Palestinians from both inside the Occupied Territories and the Palestinian diaspora; and that the dialogue should be attended by the five permanent members of the UN Security Council and should constitute the preliminary stage in the convening of an international peace conference.

Although the gulf between the 'Baker plan' and the PLO's response appeared to be unbridgeable, the PLO was not keen to be seen to officially abandon a peace initiative which was being promoted by the USA. Privately, however, PLO officials complained that the USA was ignoring the need for the PLO to play a role in the peace process while, at the same time, seeking its support for the same process. All the more galling was the USA's insistence that its endorsement of the peace process should be private rather than public so as not to deter Israel.

EXECUTION OF COLLABORATORS

Within the Occupied Territories opposition to the Baker proposals was widespread and was expressed in the underground communiqués of the UNLU. However, during the latter half of 1989 another issue drew the attention of the international media. The execution of Palestinians suspected of collaborating with the Israeli security forces had been accepted as necessary by most Palestinians, especially after it emerged that the Israelis had organized 'hit squads' of their own. During the second half of 1989, however, there was a dramatic increase in the killing of collaborators. Palestinian leaders began to fear that unless the killing was checked it might legitimize the use of violence to resolve factional disputes; they also recognized that the death of Palestinians at the hands of other Palestinians was a public relations disaster.

By the beginning of October 1989 the UNLU was urging the popular committees to show maximum restraint in their dealings with suspected collaborators. The activities of vigilante groups, such as the Red Eagles and the Black Panthers, were ultimately halted by the Israelis. However the widespread mourning and disturbances following the deaths of their members demonstrated to the UNLU and to the PLO that as the *intifada* approached the end of its second year, the political stalemate inside the Territories and the diplomatic impasse outside was strengthening the hand of radicals.

DIVISIONS WITHIN THE ISRAELI GOVERNMENT

There were few signs from Israel that the 'Baker plan' was improving the prospect of an Israeli-Palestinian dialogue in Cairo. Shimon Peres had signalled Labour's readiness to talk to a Palestinian delegation composed of deportees living outside the Occupied Territories as well as pro-PLO personalities from within the Territories. For Shamir, this was tantamount to talking to the PLO itself and he warned that Israel would boycott any talks with a delegation endorsed by the PLO. Moreover, in what amounted to a significant retreat from the terms of the original 'Shamir plan', the Israeli leadership demanded a guarantee that at any future meeting discussion would be confined to electoral procedure and would not address the question of a final settlement. In a visit to Washington in November Prime Minister Shamir failed to gain assurances on these questions, but did not face any real pressure from the US Government. In a private meeting with Shamir, President Bush reportedly criticized Israel's handling of the *intifada*, while Secretary of State James Baker called for Israel to show greater flexibility towards the peace process. Shortly before Shamir's visit, however, the USA had once again vetoed a UN Security Council resolution criticizing Israeli policy in the West Bank and in Gaza, and at the end of the visit Shamir was confident enough to declare that 'tensions had been relieved' by his trip.

In a letter to President Bush PLO chairman Yasser Arafat stated that Israeli intransigence was convincing Palestinians that Israel was not serious in its quest for peace and 'creating an atmosphere that rouses the radicals against the moderates'. The USA did not reply to the letter and, in a further rebuff, announced that it would cut funds to the UN's Food and Agriculture Organization if it co-operated with the PLO over agricultural development in the Occupied Territories.

Divisions in the Israeli Cabinet intensified in 1990. After returning from a visit to Cairo at the end of January, Shimon Peres announced that he had the support of the Labour Minister of Defence, Itzhak Rabin, for breaking up the Government if there was no progress on the issue of the Israeli-Palestinian dialogue. Shamir also faced pressure from right-wing elements within the Likud. At a meeting of Likud's central committee on 7 February 1990, the Minister of Trade, Ariel Sharon, the populist leader of the 'rejectionists', announced his resignation from the Cabinet. Sharon's resignation was ostensibly prompted by disagreement with Shamir over the 'Baker plan', but in reality it amounted to a thinly veiled bid for the party leadership. While Shamir managed to retain the support of the majority of Likud members within the Knesset, the attempted *putsch* weakened his authority. It was followed, a few days later, by the decision of Itzhak Modai to withdraw his Liberal faction from Likud. On 21 February, with Shamir barely recovered from the dissent in his own ranks, Peres announced that he would give him two weeks to respond positively to the 'Baker plan' before withdrawing the Labour Party from the coalition. Moreover, the USA declared that further dilatory tactics by Israel might lead it to abandon the Middle East peace process altogether.

COLLAPSE OF THE COALITION

On 10 March 1990 Labour ministers walked out of a cabinet meeting after Shamir had refused to allow a vote on a proposal regarding the Cairo talks. Three days later, after Labour had stated its intention to vote with the opposition in favour of a no-confidence motion against the Government, Shamir dismissed Peres from the Cabinet. The remaining Labour ministers immediately submitted their own resignations. In the ensuing no-confidence debate, the small religious party, Shas, abstained, causing the collapse of the coalition. Israel's President Herzog granted Peres two weeks to form a Labour-led administration. Meanwhile Shamir would continue as 'caretaker' Prime Minister.

PROGRESS OF THE INTIFADA

The publication on 21 February of the US State Department's Country Reports on human rights indicated that despite the lower profile of the Palestinian *intifada* in 1989, its second year had been as bloody and intense as its first. The US report claimed that 304 Palestinians had been killed by Israeli soldiers and settlers in the year under review, while a further 128 suspected Palestinian collaborators had been killed by other Palestinians and 13 Israelis had died in *intifada* incidents. Up to 20,000 Palestinians had been wounded, 26 deported and 164 homes demolished or partially sealed. At the beginning of 1990 9,138 Palestinians, more than 2% of the adult male population, were being held in jail, more than 1,200 without charge or trial. The Palestinian universities remained closed throughout 1989 and the schools for many months.

Throughout 1989 the UNLU coalition had maintained an operational unity, although factional tension was increasing. Disputes concerned the PLO's pursuit of a diplomatic solution to the Middle East conflict and the short-term tactics of the *intifada*. In general, the PCP was prepared to give qualified support to Fatah, and sought to maintain the momentum of the *intifada*. The traditionally radical PFLP put the least faith in talks and moderation, and, unlike the PCP, favoured the steady escalation of strikes, street confrontations and civil disobedience. The DFLP occupied a position between that of the PCP and that of the PFLP. In the first quarter of 1990 disagreements between DFLP 'hardliners', led by Naif Hawatmeh, and a more pragmatic faction led by Yasser Abed Rabbo, caused a serious rift in the party.

Relations within the Occupied Territories between the nationalists of the UNLU and the fundamentalist grouping Hamas remained strained, although in some areas a *modus vivendi* was achieved. Gaza remained the stronghold of Hamas and of the more militant Islamic Jihad organization. The latter enjoyed a revival in 1989, having been weakened by arrests and deportations in 1988. It remained strongly opposed to the PLO's diplomacy.

EMIGRATION OF SOVIET JEWS TO ISRAEL

Following the USSR's relaxation of restrictions on Jewish emigration in 1989, a reported upsurge of anti-semitism in the Russian Republic and Washington's decision to reduce the number of visas it issued to Soviet Jews, 1990 offered the prospect of a huge increase in the emigration of Soviet Jews to Israel. Prime Minister Shamir claimed that up to 1m. Soviet emigrants might settle in Israel. More realistic estimates put the number at 150,000, but, whatever the figure, an influx of immigrants was regarded as a fillip for the Israeli right. Increased immigration helped counter the demographic argument used by those Israelis who favoured a withdrawal from the Occupied Territories and argued for increased 'colonization' of the West Bank and Gaza. Shamir commented on 14 January, 'We will need a lot of room to absorb everyone and every immigrant will go where he wants . . . for a big immigration we will need a big and strong state'.

In Arab capitals and in the Occupied Territories the prospect of mass Jewish emigration to Israel, together with Shamir's statement, caused grave concern. King Hussein expressed a fear that the settlement of Jewish immigrants in the West Bank would presage the 'transfer' of the indigenous population to the East Bank, thus transforming the Hashemite Kingdom into a Palestinian state. Similar concern was expressed by the Arab League, which decided to send a high-level delegation to the superpowers and to the EC in order to discuss ways of reducing the flow of emigrants to Israel. Yasser Arafat conceded the right of Israel to accept Jewish refugees, but stated the PLO's opposition to the use of immigrants to perpetuate the occupation of the West Bank and Gaza. Within the Occupied Territories the UNLU urged the convening of an Arab summit meeting to debate the issue.

There was no clear evidence that Israel's Ministry of Immigrant Absorption was directing Soviet Jews to settle in the West Bank and in Gaza and only a small number were said to be considering making a home there. However, Israeli officials stated repeatedly that they would not discourage the new immigrants from settling in Judea, Samaria and Gaza. Many of the new arrivals were already being directed to housing in occupied East Jerusalem. This caused considerable anger in the USA, from which Israel had requested an extra $400m. to facilitate the absorption of Jewish immigrants, at a time when Israeli intransigence over the peace process was straining US-Israeli relations. In a noticeable departure from the policy of the Reagan Administrations, President Bush stated his Administration's strong opposition not only to the settlement of Jews in the West Bank and in Gaza, but also in East Jerusalem. This pronouncement on what Israel regarded as its 'undivided and eternal' capital would certainly have provoked an acrimonious confrontation, had it not been for the collapse of the Likud-Labour coalition in March. A few weeks earlier, the leader of the Republican Party in the US Senate, Robert Dole, had attacked another 'sacred cow' of US-Israeli relations by suggesting that the USA's aid programme to eastern Europe should be financed by a 5% cut in aid to the five principal recipients of US aid, of which Israel was the major beneficiary.

LABOUR'S FAILURE TO FORM A NEW GOVERNMENT

By mid-April Peres' attempts to form a new government had failed, despite the Labour leader's determination to persuade the orthodox religious parties to lend their support to a new, Labour-dominated coalition. As the chance to form a new government passed back to Shamir, the Minister of Defence in the former Government, Itzhak Rabin, was reported to be considering challenging Shimon Peres for the leadership of the Labour Party. Meanwhile, both Peres' and Shamir's unseemly attempts to gain the support of the religious parties with lavish offers of cash and cabinet posts had prompted widespread disaffection among Israelis. On 7 April 100,000 people gathered in Tel Aviv to call for an end to such political 'horsetrading' and for the reform of the country's electoral system.

FURTHER ESCALATION OF VIOLENCE

Soviet immigration, and the continuing controversy over Israeli settlement policy, was continuing to raise tension in the Occupied Territories. On 9 March violent protests against the settlement of Soviet Jews in East Jerusalem led to the killing of two young Palestinians. One month later attempts by a nationalist-religious group to settle in the Christian quarter of Jerusalem's Old City provoked violent confrontations with Israel's security forces. Palestinian anger was deepened by revelations that the Israeli Government had funded the settlers' fraudulent purchase of a building belonging to the Greek Orthodox Church.

By May 1990 the situation in the Occupied Territories was extremely volatile. On 20 May a uniformed Israeli approached a group of Palestinians congregating at a roadside labour market in Rishon le Zion. After checking their identity cards, he opened fire with an automatic rifle, killing eight of them and wounding 10 more. Demonstrations erupted and attempts at suppression by the army were ignored. By the end of that week more than 20 Palestinians had been killed and, for only the second time since December 1987, the *intifada* spilled over into Arab-populated regions inside Israel.

Following international criticism of Israel's response to the demonstrations, the US Government stated that it would consider an Arab-sponsored move to send UN observers to the Occupied Territories. At a specially convened session of the UN Security Council in Geneva Yasser Arafat accused Israel of attempted 'genocide' in the Occupied Territories. While no agreement was reached to send the UN observers to the Territories, Israel was now arguably more isolated than at any other time in its 42-year history. Further, and more predictable pressure came from the Arab summit meeting held in Baghdad at the end of May 1990 to discuss Soviet Jewish immigration to Israel and western hostility to Iraq's reported attempts to develop a nuclear capability. A bellicose Saddam Hussain reiterated his threat to unleash a chemical attack on Israel if the Israelis attacked Iraqi nuclear sites. The Jordanian delegation suggested that Israel was trying to engineer a war with Jordan as a means of expelling the Palestinian population from the West Bank. The USA was also criticized for its support of Israel and a pledge was made to honour a two-year-old promise of the Arab states to 'fund the *intifada*' at a rate of US $40m. per month.

NEW COALITION FORMED

The new Israeli coalition Government (an alliance of the Likud and small, right-wing religious groupings formed in early June 1990) was regarded as the least conciliatory in recent Israeli history, and unlikely to further the peace process. Rather, its very survival was dependent on its ability to appease those within the Knesset who sought to prevent any future dialogue between Israelis and Palestinians. A further setback to the peace process was the decision of the USA on 20 June to suspend its dialogue with the PLO after the PLO had failed satisfactorily to condemn an abortive attempt by the PLF (led by Muhammad Abbas—'Abu Abbas', a member of the PLO's Executive Committee) to land guerrillas on Israel's Mediterranean coast in May. At the same time, in a formal letter to Prime Minister Shamir, President Bush questioned the commitment of the new Israeli Government to the revival of the Middle East peace process. The first talks between representatives of the USA and the new Israeli Government were held in late July 1990.

IRAQ INVADES KUWAIT

Iraq's invasion of Kuwait in August 1990 was not regarded with the same sense of outrage in the Arab world as it was in the West. Although few Arabs condoned Iraq's occupation of Kuwait, there were many who admired the Iraqi President, Saddam Hussain. At a time of considerable disillusion with Western attitudes towards the emigration of Soviet Jews to Israel, and with the US Administration's decision to terminate its dialogue with the PLO, the militant rhetoric of the Iraqi leader and his promises to use Iraq's formidable military strength to confront Israeli expansionism had been favourably received by the Arab masses. Kuwait, on the other hand, was resented both for its prosperity and for its pro-Western outlook. As Arab Heads of State tried unsuccessfully to mediate between Iraq and Kuwait, two developments attracted popular support for Iraq. The first was Saddam Hussain's attempt to link Iraq's withdrawal from Kuwait to that of Israel from the Occupied Territories. The second was the decision of the USA to dispatch a large military force to the Gulf region in order, initially, to defend Saudi Arabia. What had begun as an act of aggression by one Arab state against another was now perceived by many Arabs as a confrontation between the forces of Arab nationalism and Western imperialism.

Many Palestinians, in particular, shared this perception. That the USA should act so swiftly to deter territorial conquest in Kuwait when it had effectively sustained such conquest in the areas occupied by Israel since 1967 was taken by Palestinians as proof of the West's hypocrisy and hostility to their cause. Saddam Hussain was swiftly championed as a saviour in the style of Nasser. By mid-August large pro-Iraqi demonstrations were taking place throughout the Occupied Territories and Jordan, and in the countries of the Maghreb.

THE POSITION OF THE PLO

The position of the PLO was far from clear at the outset of the new crisis in the Gulf. Privately, its leadership was said to be dismayed by the Iraqi invasion of Kuwait because it deflected attention from the *intifada* and created further divisions in the Arab world. However, the PLO's wish to broker an Arab solution to the crisis, together with its traditionally close ties to Iraq, made it reluctant to condemn the invasion. At the chaotic Arab summit meeting convened in Cairo on 10 August 1990 the PLO condemned Iraq's annexation of Kuwait, but abstained in the vote on whether to deploy a pan-Arab military force in Saudi Arabia. Furthermore, the PLO joined Jordan, Yemen, Tunisia and Algeria in denouncing the proposed deployment of US armed forces in the Gulf region.

On 19 August the PLO confirmed its opposition to the invasion of Kuwait in its first official statement on the crisis in the Gulf. Together with Libya and Jordan, it continued to attempt to act as a mediator, but with the US success in building an anti-Iraq coalition rapidly polarizing the Arab states, there was no sign of the consensus that was needed to make their proposals feasible. Instead, the concept of linkage of the Gulf conflict with the Palestinian question, popular support for Iraq and distrust of the USA all dictated that the PLO should align itself with Iraq. At the end of August 1990 Yasser Arafat issued a joint statement with the Iraqi leader in Baghdad, proclaiming that the Palestinians and the Iraqis were united in a common struggle against Israeli occupation and US military intervention in the Gulf. The political risks of such a firm alliance with Iraq were immense, but PLO officials argued that, given the mood of their constituency, they had no other option. Inside the Occupied Territories a special UNLU communiqué condemned the deployment of the US-led multinational force in Saudi Arabia and elsewhere in the Gulf region. It also upheld the rights of peoples to self-determination, but noticeably refrained from demanding Iraq's withdrawal from Kuwait.

The PLO's partisanship earned it the opprobrium of the West and alienated its principal financial supporters, Saudi Arabia and the Gulf states. Jordan, Yemen and Sudan, whose Governments were most hostile to Western military involvement in the Middle East, similarly had to endure the full weight of US and conservative Arab displeasure. Jordan, traditionally pro-Western and in the process of democratization, was subjected to particular criticism for having allowed a meeting of Arab nationalist and left-wing political parties to take place in Amman in mid-November 1990.

ISRAEL AS BENEFICIARY

Israel was one of the principal beneficiaries of the events which followed the invasion of Kuwait. It had until recently been internationally isolated for its procrastination over the peace process and the repression in the Occupied Territories; the Gulf crisis offered it the prospect of rehabilitation. Israeli leaders lost no time in restating their old claim that it was the lack of democracy in the Arab world, not Israel's occupation of Arab territory, which was the principal cause of instability in the region. The PLO's stance on the Iraqi invasion, they argued, conclusively validated their refusal to negotiate with it. Equally, the vociferous support in the West Bank and Gaza for Saddam Hussain confirmed Israel's wisdom in treading the path of diplomacy with caution, and maintaining its opposition to a Palestinian state.

Moreover, in President Bush's attempt to persuade Arab and majority Muslim states to participate in 'Operation Desert Shield', the codename for the deployment of the multinational force in Saudi Arabia, Israel also saw scope for political gain. The Israeli Prime Minister, Itzhak Shamir, understood that Israeli military action against Iraq, like its attack in 1981 on Iraq's nuclear reactor, would be disastrous for the USA: it would spell the end of Arab involvement in the multinational force, a political if not a military prerequisite for its success, and would also threaten a wider conflagration in the Middle East. Israel hinted that its restraint would be conditional upon its receiving certain guarantees from the USA: of increased military and economic aid, and of an easing of pressure with regard to the peace process. Israel's Minister of Defence, Moshe Arens, also made it clear that, from an Israeli point of view, the only acceptable conclusion to the crisis would be one that included the dismantling of the Iraqi military machine.

THE PRICE OF ISRAEL'S SUPPORT FOR THE USA

Just as the USA had to pay for Israel's passivity, so it had to offer inducements for Arab governments to participate in the multinational force. The Gulf states, potentially vulnerable to further Iraqi aggression, needed little persuasion to do so. Egypt, Syria and Morocco were also in favour of deploying armed forces in Saudi Arabia, the Governments of Syria and Egypt being deeply mistrustful of Baathist Iraq. However, it was the prospect of economic aid and of influence in any post-crisis settlement which ultimately persuaded them to dispatch troops to fight alongside Americans against fellow Arabs. President Assad of Syria, a longstanding radical and hence the most unlikely of the coalition partners, certainly expected the crisis to be followed by moves to end the Israeli occupation of Arab, including Syrian, territory. President Mubarak of Egypt, who was anxious to see his country reinstated as the *primus inter pares* of the Arab world, aired the same concerns in discussions with his US and European counterparts.

The burden of conflicting expectations from Israel and the Arab states placed the USA in a delicate position. President Bush and the US Secretary of State, James Baker, had to avoid any linkage of the crisis in the Gulf with the Arab–Israeli conflict since this would effectively reward Saddam Hussain and displease Israel. At the same time they had to reassure the Arab world. Speaking in September 1990, President Bush agreed that sooner rather than later the Arab-Israeli conflict had to be resolved. Nevertheless he dismissed the possibility of an international conference on the issue in the near future. The EC states were more sensitive to Arab charges of hypocrisy over tackling the problems of the Middle East and hence to an implicit linkage of the occupation of Kuwait with other outstanding issues. During an emergency debate on the Gulf crisis in the British Parliament at the end of August 1990, members of all political parties spoke of the urgent need for a swift conclusion of the crisis, to be followed by the resolution of the Palestine problem. In an address to the UN General Assembly on 24 August, President Mitterrand of France proposed a timetable for the settlement of all the Middle East's problems. This would begin with an Iraqi declaration of intention to withdraw from Kuwait, but would also include direct dialogue between the concerned parties on the issues of Palestine, Lebanon and Israel's security. Moreover, at a meeting of EC Ministers of Foreign Affairs in Paris in mid-September, the President of the EC Commission, Jacques Delors, warned Israel that once the Gulf crisis was over it would have to accept 'the legitimate rights of the Palestinians'. In addition, the Italian Minister of Foreign Affairs, Gianni de Michelis, who was acting as chairman of EC foreign policy meetings, informed his Israeli counterpart, the newly-appointed David Levy, that the Palestinians had a right to their own state.

EVENTS IN THE OCCUPIED TERRITORIES

Meanwhile, the Palestinian *intifada* continued, albeit with less intensity. Exhaustion, and the adoption of new tactics by Israel's Ministry of Defence, contributed to the decrease in activity. Israel's Minister of Defence, Moshe Arens, believed that intensive policing of population centres was largely counter-productive. Instead, he instructed the IDF to reduce its presence in the towns and villages of the West Bank and Gaza, and to redeploy troops on highways and at major road intersections. Fewer clashes and fewer Palestinian casualties resulted, but arrests and collective punishments continued. Palestinians were encouraged by Saddam Hussain's rhetoric, but the economic repercussions of the Gulf crisis were very damaging. Many Palestinian families relied on remittances from relatives working in Kuwait, and the loss of this income at a time when the population was already suffering economically, caused severe hardship. Factionalism was another source of concern for the Palestinian leadership. In September 1990 fierce disputes in Gaza and some towns of the West Bank, between the nationalists of Fatah and the fundamentalists of Hamas, led to ugly street brawls and at least one death. Divisions within the DFLP also resulted in a *de facto* split, prompting a struggle for the control of its various front organizations, such as trade unions, women's committees and press offices.

Yet even while international attention was firmly fixed on the huge military deployment in the Gulf, events in the Occupied Territories continued to remind the world of the unresolved issue of Palestine. On 8 October 1990 at least 17 Palestinians were shot dead in the Old City of Jerusalem when a large crowd, protesting at an attempt by an extremist Israeli group to lay the symbolic cornerstone of the Third Temple on the Temple Mount, was indiscriminately fired on by Israeli security forces. News of the killings at Islam's third holiest shrine immediately precipitated a wave of protests which claimed a further three lives and left many injured. It was the bloodiest day yet of the *intifada*. Palestinian leaders in the Occupied Territories responded to the killings with an emotional appeal to the UN Security Council: 'We do not understand how oil in the Gulf can be more highly prized by you than Palestinian blood . . .' they wrote; 'we do not understand how the Security Council can ignore our pleas for protection when it is prepared to send troops to the Gulf region'. Moreover, the UNLU issued its most uncompromising communiqué so far, calling for a week of mourning and declaring that 'every soldier setting foot on the land of Palestine is a fair target to be liquidated'. Anxious to avoid charges of hypocrisy at such a sensitive time in Arab-US relations, the USA submitted a draft resolution to the UN Security Council condemning the Temple Mount killings. It also supported the decision of the UN Secretary General to dispatch an investigative mission to Jerusalem. Although this fell short of the PLO's demand for UN protection for the population of the Occupied Territories, the USA's censure of Israel at the UN Security Council was significant for being the first vote of its kind for eight years. Predictably, Israel denounced the UN vote, and its decision to send a fact-finding mission to the Occupied Territories, as interference in its internal affairs. It declared that the UN representatives would only be admitted as 'tourists'. In an interview with the Israeli daily newspaper, *Ma'ariv*, Prime Minister Shamir castigated both President Bush and Secretary of State Baker for 'messing with Israel'. What they failed to understand, opined Shamir, 'is that Israel is Washington's only reliable ally'. The Arab League's own deliberations in Tunis on the Temple Mount killings ended in acrimony and confirmed the rift provoked by the Gulf crisis. A resolution which condemned the killings, but was also sharply critical of US bias towards Israel, was defeated by 11 votes to 10. In what was effectively a vote on the US military presence in the Gulf, only Morocco, facing mounting domestic criticism for having agreed to participate in the multinational force, confounded expectations by voting with the anti-US faction.

The killings of 8 October were followed by a spate of attacks by Palestinians on Israeli civilians and soldiers. The worst incidents occurred on 21 October, when three people were stabbed to death by a lone Palestinian in West Jerusalem, and at the beginning of December, when a series of attacks in Tel Aviv claimed four lives and left several people injured. A number of Palestinians died in anti-Arab protests following the stabbings, and also in the violence precipitated by the assassination, in New York, of Rabbi Meir Kahane, the leader of the neo-fascist Kach movement. Nearly all the attacks by Palestinians were the work of individuals acting on their own initiative, although Hamas did claim responsibility for some of the murders in Tel Aviv, and Islamic Jihad gave its wholehearted support to a 'revolution of knives'. The PLO factions were more ambivalent in their attitude towards the stabbings: Faisal Husseini denied that the stabbing of Israeli civilians had been sanctioned by the leadership of the *intifada*; the UNLU spoke only of the need

to employ 'all forms of resistance'; and graffiti praising the use of knives was signed by both Fatah and the PFLP. Shortly after the incident on 21 October, the Israeli Ministry of Defence ordered all Palestinians from the Occupied Territories working in Israel to return to their homes. The borders were sealed for four days, after which the Minister of Defence, Moshe Arens, declared an intention to reduce the number of Palestinians working inside the 'Green Line' and to bar altogether those with a record of activism. The announcement was welcomed by some Palestinians as a further step towards redefining the 'Green Line'.

UN SECURITY COUNCIL RESOLUTION 678

The passing of UN Security Council Resolution No. 678 on 29 November 1990, which effectively authorized the use of military force against Iraq if it had not withdrawn from Kuwait by 15 January 1991, considerably increased tension in the region. In Israel the authorities completed the distribution of gas masks to the civilian population and issued instructions on civil defence against attacks with chemical weapons. Only belatedly did they decide to provide masks to limited areas of the West Bank. Iraq and Israel continued to exchange threats, while Jordanians and Palestinians expressed fears that Israel might use the pretext of military conflict in the Gulf to drive Palestinians from the West Bank into Jordan. Palestinian support for Saddam Hussain remained high during the weeks preceding the UN deadline for Iraq's withdrawal from Kuwait, while the PLO's relations with the USA's Arab allies continued to deteriorate. The leader of the PLF, 'Abu Abbas', warned that his organization would strike against Western targets if hostilities erupted. In mid-December Israel's Prime Minister travelled to Washington for his first meeting with the US President in more than a year. The proximity of the deadline set by UN Resolution 678 ensured that the encounter was cordial, despite a strong undercurrent of mutual distrust. Shamir sought and received assurances that the Gulf crisis would not be resolved at Israel's expense. However, no promises were made on the question of aid for the settlement of the 200,000 Soviet Jews who had emigrated to Israel during 1990, or on the sale of arms by the USA to Arab participants in the multinational force.

There was a resurgence of the *intifada* at the beginning of 1991. Seven Palestinians were killed in protests linked to the anniversary, on 1 January 1991, of the founding of Yasser Arafat's Fatah organization. On 6 January Saddam Hussain declared that the impending military conflict would be a 'battle for the sake of Palestine'. After the failure of meetings in Geneva on 9 January between the Iraqi Minister of Foreign Affairs, Tariq Aziz, and the US Secretary of State, war was generally accepted as inevitable.

IRAQ ATTACKS ISRAEL

On 19 January 1991, less than three days after the multinational force had begun a massive aerial bombardment of Iraq, Iraq launched an attack on Israel, employing adapted *Scud* missiles against Tel Aviv and Haifa. The missiles were fitted with conventional, rather than chemical warheads, and although damage to buildings was considerable, casualties were light. Further attacks with *Scud* missiles on the nights of 20 and 22 January provoked panic, but resulted in only two deaths. The attacks drew immediate demands for retaliation from some senior Israeli military figures and politicians, but both the USA and the European members of the multinational force vigorously urged Israel to exercise restraint. Their concerns were obvious: while Arab states in the force had indicated that they would not be opposed to Israel taking appropriate and proportionate defensive action against an Iraqi attack, Syria and Egypt had made it quite clear that they could not remain aligned against Iraq if Israel were to attack it. Furthermore, Jordan had warned Israel that it would be forced to respond if there was any violation of its airspace. The US Administration backed its calls for restraint with an urgent airlift of *Patriot* anti-missile batteries to Tel Aviv, and undertook to make the destruction of Iraq's mobile missile launchers a military priority. To be courted so attentively by the West after such a long period of soured relations was an agreeable novelty for Israel, and not one it had much incentive to jeopardize. Given the intensity of the bombing of Iraq, Israel's leaders were aware that any Israeli contribution to the campaign would be militarily insignificant as well as potentially catastrophic in political terms. Moreover, the Israeli Government knew that as long as the casualties from the *Scud* attacks remained minimal and chemical warheads were not employed, domestic pressure for retaliation would be containable. Shamir consequently assured the USA that there would be no unilateral retaliation by Israel. Immediate benefits were reaped from the policy of restraint: the USA indicated that it would provide funding for the development of Israel's anti-ballistic missile project, hitherto in some financial difficulty, while Germany promised up to US $1,000m. in military and economic aid. However, just as important for Israel's leaders was the wave of international sympathy for Israel which the Iraqi attacks provoked.

THE CONSEQUENCES OF IRAQ'S DEFEAT FOR THE PLO

Palestinians of the West Bank and Gaza endured a strict curfew for most of the duration of the war in the Gulf. The UNLU and Hamas instructed their supporters not to clash with the Israeli army during the curfew in order to avoid reprisals. Nevertheless, a number of people were shot and killed for curfew violations. The economic impact of the curfew was severe. According to Palestinian economists, losses to the local economy ranged from $150m.–$200m., equivalent to approximately 8% of the GDP of the Occupied Territories.

The decisive defeat of Iraq by the multinational force in February 1991 left the PLO demoralized and in its most vulnerable state for several years. As expected, the Gulf Co-operation Council (GCC) countries cut their funding to the PLO, thereby raising the prospect of financial crisis. It was also made clear in the USA and the Gulf that the best chance of improving relations lay in a change in the PLO leadership. Overtures were made by Saudi Arabia and other GCC member states to anti-Arafat Palestinian groups based in Damascus, but, given the political radicalism and the small following of these factions, it was difficult to imagine what Saudi Arabia hoped to achieve. Within the PLO itself there were a number of senior figures, for the most part identified with the conservative wing of Fatah, who had voiced criticism of the organization's support for Iraq and who could have formed the nucleus of a leadership acceptable to both Saudi Arabia and the USA. Yet the fact that the PLO had enjoyed overwhelming support among Palestinians for its stance on the Gulf crisis proved an important antidote to US and Arab hostility. The EC adopted a more pragmatic approach towards the PLO. At the conclusion of hostilities with Iraq it agreed to 'freeze' contacts at ministerial level. By the end of April 1991, however, the French Minister of Foreign Affairs, Roland Dumas, had met Yasser Arafat in Tripoli.

BAKER VISITS THE MIDDLE EAST

The Israeli Government drew comfort from the PLO's isolation, but was wary of the political pressures that might accompany the post-war search for a resolution of the Arab–Israeli conflict. As expected, US Secretary of State Baker undertook several tours of the Middle East in the weeks following the end of the war. He hoped to persuade Israel and the Arab states which had participated in the multinational force to move towards mutual recognition, and to win support for a regional peace conference, to be sponsored by the USA and the USSR. It soon became clear, however, that these propositions were not acceptable to either side. Although the Israeli Minister of Foreign Affairs, David Levy, indicated that Israel would give its approval to such a regional conference if it led directly to bilateral talks, and conceded that issues like the status of the Golan Heights could be negotiated, these were not views shared by Shamir and most of his colleagues within the Likud. Rebuking Levy, Shamir stated his opposition to Soviet involvement in the Middle East peace process. He also opposed negotiating the future of the Golan Heights or making goodwill gestures to the Palestinian population of the West Bank and Gaza, as urged by Baker, as long as the *intifada* continued. After the US Secretary of State had held talks with leading pro-PLO figures in East Jerusalem, Shamir warned that Israel did not consider any of them to be suitable partners for negotiation.

Israel's Arab neighbours expressed their own reservations about Baker's proposals. After lengthy talks with Baker in Damascus, Syrian officials reaffirmed that Syria would only attend a peace conference held under UN sponsorship and based on the implementation of UN Security Council Resolutions 242 and 338. Jordan and the PLO indicated that they were in full agreement with Syria. The PLO also voiced its suspicions that the concept of a regional conference had been promoted with the intention of normalizing Arab-Israeli relations and of avoiding the issue of Palestinian national rights. The PLO was relieved by the reluctance of the GCC states to open a dialogue with Israel. At the end of May 1991 PLO representatives made a rare visit to Damascus in order to discuss their common position with Syria on the peace process. Syrian officials also urged the PLO to readmit pro-Syrian Palestinian groups, including Fatah rebels from the 1983 revolt and the PFLP-GC, into the Organization.

Baker was reluctant to apportion blame for the lack of progress in his peace mission. However, the continued settlement of Soviet Jewish immigrants in the Occupied Territories angered the US Secretary of State enough for him to testify: 'I don't think there is any bigger obstacle to peace than the settlement activity that not only continues unabated but at an enhanced pace'. Further US pressure on Israel, regarded by much of the international community as essential if the opportunity for a peace agreement in the Middle East was not to be missed, did not materialize. Continued US arms supplies to Israel and the Gulf states, together with promises that the USA would guarantee Israel's regional military superiority, appeared to contradict President Bush's stated goal of working towards disarmament in the region, and heightened Arab cynicism about the US President's much-vaunted 'new world order'.

WORSENING CONDITIONS IN THE OCCUPIED TERRITORIES

There was little optimism in the Occupied Territories following the defeat of Iraq. After the lifting of the curfew many Palestinians discovered that they had lost their jobs in Israel to Soviet immigrants. Another series of knife attacks, including the killing of four women at a bus stop in Jerusalem in March 1991, prompted the Israeli authorities to impose further travel and employment restrictions. Only Palestinians with the requisite permits were allowed to enter Israel, including East Jerusalem. Those Palestinians fortunate enough to be issued with work permits had to be transported in buses to and from work by their employers. Those found working without permits faced fines or imprisonment. The result was soaring unemployment in the West Bank and in Gaza and the effective division of the West Bank into northern and southern zones. Concerns over the economic situation and continued Israeli settlement were raised in meetings with the US Secretary of State. There was debate within the Occupied Territories as to whether these meetings were appropriate, and the Palestinians who did meet Baker only did so after they had received the formal authorization of the PLO. Nevertheless, the US Administration's refusal to hold direct talks with the PLO led the organization's Communist and PFLP affiliates to boycott the meetings.

Adding to Palestinian gloom was uncertainty over the direction of the *intifada*. The killing and intimidation of Palestinians by other Palestinians, increasing criminal activity and further outbreaks of violence between followers of Hamas and the PLO factions were causing much public alarm. Several articles appeared in the Arab press in the first half of 1991, urging an end to the killing of suspected collaborators and a complete reappraisal of *intifada* tactics. Palestinian activists subsequently announced that strikes and demonstrations would be scaled down, and efforts made to control the masked fugitives responsible for most of the *intifada's* excesses. The use of firearms against military targets was widely predicted. Calls were made for greater democracy within the PLO, including elections to the PNC. Senior Communist Party officials also challenged the Palestinian leadership over its uncritical support for Iraq during the Gulf War and for having unrealistically raised Palestinian expectations of an Iraqi victory.

THE SYRIAN-LEBANESE TREATY

In May 1991 the Syrian and Lebanese Presidents signed a treaty of 'fraternity, co-operation and friendship', confirming Syria's dominant role in the affairs of its neighbour. Israel condemned the treaty as tantamount to a Syrian takeover of Lebanon and as a threat to its security. On 3 June the Israeli airforce launched its heaviest raids on Lebanon since 1982. At least 20 people were killed and many injured in a series of attacks on Palestinian and Lebanese militia targets in the south of the country.

NEGOTIATIONS WITH SYRIA

Meanwhile PLO forces grouped around the Lebanese port of Sidon fell victim to the Lebanese Government's plan to disarm the country's militias and deploy the Lebanese army nationally. The attempts of PLO leaders to persuade the Lebanese Government that their forces should be exempt from the disarmament process, or at least that the process should be delayed until the rights of the country's Palestinian population had been formally safeguarded, were ignored. At the beginning of July, in a brief but bloody battle, units of the Lebanese army expelled PLO fighters from positions above Sidon. The defeated Palestinians withdrew to the refugee camps and were subsequently forced to give an undertaking to surrender their heavy weaponry. The circumstances surrounding the PLO's loss of its sole military stronghold in Lebanon fuelled speculation that Syria, deprived of its Soviet sponsor, had reached an understanding with the USA whereby the latter would tolerate Syria's control over Lebanese affairs in return for President Assad's backing for the Bush Administration's Middle East peace plans. Palestinians expressed suspicions that Damascus and the USA had been conspiring to ensure that the PLO remained militarily weakened and diplomatically isolated.

The extent to which the end of the cold war had pushed Syria to revise its foreign policy was underlined in dramatic fashion in mid-July. During US Secretary of State James Baker's fifth peace mission to the Middle East, it was announced that President Assad had acceded to US and Israeli conditions for the convening of a Middle East peace conference. Abandoning his long-held insistence that any conference on the Arab-Israeli dispute should have the coercive weight of the UN behind it, Assad gave his consent to a more symbolic gathering. Although based on UN Resolutions 242 and 338, this would only feature the UN in the role of an observer and would pave the way for direct negotiations between Israel and its Arab adversaries. Assad agreed to a joint Soviet-US chairing of the proposed conference with EC observers also present.

TOWARDS A PEACE CONFERENCE

The Syrian *volte face* was swiftly followed by Jordanian, Egyptian and Lebanese acceptance of the USA's proposals. Baker also received the backing of the G7 nations meeting in London, United Kingdom, and, more significantly, of Saudi Arabia. Saudi Arabia also gave its support to an Egyptian proposal that the Arab states should end their trade boycott of Israel in return for a freeze on new settlements in the Occupied Territories, a gambit that Israel declined. Indeed, despite a *de facto* Arab capitulation to Shamir's conditions, the Israeli Government's attitude to the progress engineered by Baker was far from generous. The Israeli Cabinet endorsed Shamir's acceptance of the Baker conference proposals, but with the proviso that Israel hold a veto over the composition of any Palestinian negotiating team. Even this, however, failed to satisfy three

right-wing members of the Cabinet, including Ariel Sharon, who voted against Israel's acceptance of the Baker formula. Moreover, in a pointed snub to both Arab states and the USA, which were hoping for a goodwill gesture from Israel in return for Arab flexibility, a new West Bank settlement was inaugurated less than two days after the cabinet meeting.

At the heart of Palestinian uncertainty over the proposed conference lay the issues of representation and settlement. It was accepted that the PLO would not participate officially and that Palestinians might have to be represented as part of a joint team with Jordan, but the threat of an Israeli veto of a Palestinian delegation that included East Jerusalem residents, led those Palestinians who had met with Baker to warn that they might not get popular backing for their attendance. They also demanded that the USA should apply pressure on Israel to halt settlement during negotiations, and that a letter of assurance be drafted on such issues as the USA's interpretation of UN resolutions and its commitment to mandatory international arbitration in the event of a deadlock in negotiations. Some PLO factions, notably the PFLP and the DFLP faction loyal to Naif Hawatmeh, rejected Palestinian participation outright. The PFLP issued a communiqué within the Occupied Territories calling the conference 'a conspiracy aimed at bypassing the PLO and Palestinian rights'. The fundamentalists of Hamas were even more forthright in their opposition, condemning the Baker proposals as a 'conference for selling land' and threatening any would-be participants. However, the two leading Palestinian participants in the Baker talks, Faisal Husseini and Hanan Ashrawi, made it clear that it would be the PLO which ultimately decided whether the Palestinians were represented at the conference.

It was clearly dangerous for the PLO to exclude itself from a process that might offer an opportunity to end the occupation of the West Bank and Gaza. However, the PLO was concerned that by giving approval to the peace conference it might be abdicating its role as the Palestinians' sole representative. There was also the sobering realization that the Organization could no longer rely on the support of Arab states for its own negotiating positions and that there was a real danger that a normalization of Arab-Israeli relations could be achieved without addressing the fundamentals of the Palestinian problem. Initiatives by the PLO, supported by Jordan, to organize a meeting with Arab front-line states in order to co-ordinate negotiating positions in the run-up to the conference, were rejected by Egypt and Syria.

At the end of August the PLO held a meeting in London, United Kingdom, attended by a number of Palestinian personalities from the Occupied Territories, to set guidelines for the letter of assurances from the USA that would facilitate Palestinian participation in the planned conference. The letter that Baker did finally present to Hanan Ashrawi in Amman did not fulfil all the Palestinian criteria for attending the conference, not least because Baker refused to contradict assurances he had already given to Israel. Arafat described the letter as 'a positive step, but one which fell short', referring to the fact that while Baker had clarified the US interpretations of the relevant UN resolutions and the status of East Jerusalem, which agreed with that of the Arabs, there was no mention of the USA's commitment to Palestinian self-determination nor any proposals for a resolution of the Jerusalem issue. Nor was there any suggestion that Baker would demand a freeze on settlements in the Occupied Territories or allow the PLO to formally nominate the Palestinian delegation. Arafat left it to the PNC meeting in September to debate the question of Palestinian involvement in the peace conference. The Council's resolutions reiterated Palestinian commitment to the principle of autonomy, but such was the pressure on the PLO—from the USA and the Arab states—to support the US proposals that by the end of September 1991 it was clear that the Palestinians would be sending representatives, albeit on terms that were far from satisfactory. Jordan, with which the Palestinians were now certain to form a joint delegation, had assured the PLO leader that it would fight for Palestinian objectives, but had also stressed that it would attend the conference whether these were achieved or not. Moreover, the failure in the Soviet Union of the attempted coup, which had been welcomed by some prominent Palestinians, removed any hopes that the USSR would counteract US authority in the Middle East.

SUSPENSION OF LOAN GUARANTEES

Israel, meanwhile, was engaged in its own battle of wills with the Bush Administration. The Likud Government had sought US $10,000m. in loan guarantees from the USA in order to help the settlement of immigrants from the USSR. However, in the run-up to the peace conference the combination of Bush's displeasure at the continuing settlement, and a desire not to offend Arab sensibilities, led the US President to ask Israel for a four-month delay in its formal submission for the loan guarantees. Bush also warned that if the loan request was approved by the US Congress, he would impose his veto. Shamir accepted the challenge and set Israel's formidable lobbying machine in motion. However, opinion polls in the USA suggested that an overwhelming majority of the public supported the Government's position and this was reflected in Congressional support for the President's stance. It was the first time since the Suez crisis that a US administration had made aid conditional on Israeli policy.

THE MADRID CONFERENCE

The peace conference, to be held in Madrid on 30 October 1991 (see Documents on Palestine, p. 100), was preceded by a series of inter-Arab meetings. Denied the Arab summit he had originally proposed, Arafat was nevertheless invited to talks in Cairo, Amman and Damascus—his first visit to the Syrian capital for eight years—where he was assured that there would be no Arab concessions until the question of territory was resolved. Faced with Israel's insistence that residents of East Jerusalem be barred from the Palestinian negotiating team, the PLO offered a compromise whereby the Palestinian delegation should include an advisory body made up largely of East Jerusalem residents. The USA supported this proposal, recognizing the advisers as an official part of the Palestinian delegation. Dr Haider Abdel Shafei, veteran chief of the Gaza Red Crescent Society, was named head of the negotiating team and Hanan Ashrawi was to be chief spokesperson. Faisal Husseini was in overall charge of the delegation which included supporters of Fatah, the Abed Rabbo faction of the DFLP, and the PCP as well as several independents. Shamir decided to head Israel's team himself, intimating that he did not trust the Minister of Foreign Affairs, David Levy, with such an important mission.

As Israel had never before attended a peace conference with its Arab neighbours, including the Palestinians, the Madrid conference generated intense media interest. In spite of the precedent, however, no real progress was made. During the three-day plenary session the Israeli delegation offered no prospect of an Israeli withdrawal from the Occupied Territories, while Arab Ministers of Foreign Affairs and Palestinians stated that there could be no peace without territorial compromise. Exchanges between Syria and Israel were particularly hostile and rapidly degenerated into mutual invective. Predictably their first round of bilateral talks, which followed the plenary sessions, ended in early deadlock, Syria's Minister of Foreign Affairs left Madrid repeating that Syria would not attend the proposed multilateral negotiations on regional issues until Israel committed itself to territorial concessions. Israel's talks with the other Arab delegations were more cordial but scarcely more productive. On the two principal issues of discussion, a venue and an agenda for the second round of talks, there was no agreement. Israeli officials demanded that the negotiations be held in the Middle East to emphasize the regional rather than the international nature of the process, and, for the opposite reason, the Arab states and the Palestinians insisted on a European venue. Only the Palestinian delegation had cause for satisfaction after the Madrid conference. It had won an early procedural victory by gaining the same (45 minute) period in which to make its represen-

tations as the other Arab delegations, and enjoyed public relations successes with eloquent and dignified articulations of the Palestinian case. Madrid was also significant for the Palestinian acceptance that self-determination should follow a period of autonomy in the Occupied Territories. However, the presence in Madrid of a high-level PLO delegation left little doubt that the Palestinian team was in close contact with the PLO.

The impression that the Palestinians had successfully exploited the opportunities afforded by the Madrid conference was reflected in several peace marches in the Occupied Territories. Some were tolerated by the Israeli army, but others ended in confrontation; a 15-year-old from Hebron became the thousandth casualty of the *intifada* when he was shot dead during a demonstration in support of the conference. However, the strong support for a general strike called by Hamas and the Popular and Democratic Fronts to protest against the conference underlined the strength of the radical opinion opposed to Palestinian participation in the peace talks. Meanwhile in southern Lebanon there were Israeli and SLA air strikes and artillery bombardments of Shi'ite and Palestinian positions, ostensibly in revenge for successful Palestinian and Hezbollah ambushes.

THE WASHINGTON CONFERENCE

The failure of the Arabs and Israelis to agree a venue or agenda for the next session of bilateral talks prompted James Baker to issue invitations for negotiations in Washington on 4 December 1991. A set of US guidelines suggesting how each delegation might conduct its negotiations was included with the invitations. However, while these efforts to maintain momentum in the peace process were largely welcomed by the Arab side, they were coolly received in Israel. Shamir announced that the Israeli delegation would not be going to Washington until five days after the scheduled opening of the talks. US disappointment was contrasted with satisfaction from Israeli government hardliners who applauded the 'revolt against American compulsion' and called on Shamir to take further steps to disrupt the peace process.

Israel's decision was interpreted in the Occupied Territories, as in the rest of the Arab world, as evidence of Shamir's contempt for the peace process. On the West Bank and in Gaza, it became increasingly difficult to convince the growing number of sceptics that there was any value in pursuing negotiations with an intransigent Israel. A decision by the USA to refuse US visas to several senior PLO figures who had played a covert role in Madrid further eroded Palestinian goodwill. Yasser Arafat tried to mobilize Arab support for a delayed attendance at the talks in solidarity with the PLO, but he was informed that the Arabs in general and the Palestinians in particular could not afford to be seen to disrupt the peace process. In the end the Palestinian delegation registered its disapproval by delaying its flight to Washington by 12 hours.

Israel's absence from the first days of the talks meant that the Arab delegations had to sit opposite empty chairs in the conference rooms. When the Israeli delegation did arrive, they immediately tried to undermine the Palestinian status as a delegation in their own right in Madrid by refusing to negotiate on Palestinian issues with a team that did not come under Jordanian auspices. As a result most of the time allocated for Israeli-Palestinian and Israeli-Jordanian talks was spent on procedural issues. The questions of a freeze on settlements in the Occupied Territories, interpretations of UN Resolutions and the nature of interim autonomy in the Occupied Territories were barely discussed. Israeli talks with Syrian and Lebanese delegations also achieved very little. Israel's refusal to accept that Resolution 242 called on it to withdraw from occupied Arab territories continued to infuriate the Syrians. Lebanese-Israeli talks were less disorderly but threatened to founder on the Lebanese insistence that Resolution 425, calling for an Israeli withdrawal from Lebanese territory, was non-negotiable, and Israeli demands that it had to be discussed as part of the peace process. As the deadlock increased, the Arab delegation signalled that there was need of some form of US intervention. However, Baker had indicated that the USA would be adopting a 'hands-off' approach, commenting that the USA could not want peace more than the concerned parties themselves. For the Arabs this was tantamount to a surrender to Israeli obstructionism. 'If the Americans want us to talk to Israel without them . . . well, we have done', commented one Arab delegate, 'Without US intervention, however, they should have known success would be a long shot'. In New York, meanwhile, the UN General Assembly voted overwhelmingly to repeal its 1975 Resolution equating Zionism with racism. Several Arab states refused to participate in the vote.

EVENTS IN THE OCCUPIED TERRITORIES

Palestinian frustration was exacerbated by the accelerated settlement drive in the Occupied Territories. Indeed 1991 had been the most vigorous year for the building of settlements in nearly 25 years of occupation. Under the supervision of the Ministry of Housing, work had begun on 13,500 housing units in the Occupied Territories, excluding East Jerusalem, a 65% increase over all the units established in the previous 23 years. It was also reported that 13% of immigrants from the former USSR were being settled on occupied Arab lands, boosting the Israeli population in the territories to over 200,000. While the Washington talks were in progress a leaked report revealed that government approval had been given for a massive programme of Jewish colonization of Arab neighbourhoods in East Jerusalem. This was confirmed in mid-December, when a combined force of settlers and Israeli police took over several houses in the Silwan district of the city, evicting Palestinian families in the process. 'The Israelis are destroying the ground under our feet', commented Faisal Husseini on the effects of the settlement policy on his efforts to build support for the peace process. Israel's decision in early January 1992 to deport a further 12 Palestinians (reportedly in retaliation for the killing of a Jewish settler in Gaza) and to establish a settlers' Civil Guard in the West Bank and in Gaza, was further evidence that the Shamir Government was trying to provoke the Palestinians to withdraw from the peace talks, or, at least, to widen the rift between opponents and supporters of negotiation.

Clashes between Fatah and Hamas activists in Gaza and the West Bank became increasingly common as the *intifada* entered its fifth year. Despite appeals from PLO figures and community leaders for an end to the killing of collaborators, suspected informers were still stabbed and shot almost daily. In the refugee camps of Gaza and the nationalist strongholds of the West Bank the knives and axes once carried in ceremonial fashion by masked activists were being replaced by pistols and automatic rifles. As predicted, there was an increase in armed attacks on settlers and soldiers at the beginning of 1992. In the most serious incident, in mid-February, three soldiers were bludgeoned to death in a raid on an army camp just inside the Green Line. Meanwhile, Israel's Ministry of Defence relied more heavily on the activities of undercover units to combat the *intifada*. An upsurge in what witnesses described as summary executions of Palestinian activists led journalists and human rights organizations to accuse Israel of operating Latin American style death squads in the Occupied Territories.

Following the deportation orders in January, the Palestinians decided to postpone the sending of a delegation to the next round of bilateral talks in Washington. The other Arab delegations subsequently agreed to follow the Palestinian lead. The deportations also seemed to draw a more conciliatory line from the Bush Administration; visas, which had been refused to PLO members the previous month, were now granted. When the negotiations began on 16 January, Israel dropped its earlier objections to separate Palestinian representation, but refused to address the principal items on the Arab agenda, namely the interpretation of Resolution 242, borders, and settlements. The Palestinian delegation was told that the issue of settlements had no bearing on the autonomy details and could only be discussed when the final status of the territories had been decided. Arab frustration was compounded by the premature departure of the Israeli delegation. Israel's steadfast avoidance and obstruction of substantive negotiations created profound disillusion in Palestinian ranks; many believed that it was only to avoid alienating the USA while the question of loan guarantees was in the balance that Israel remained at the conference table. It was also recognized that US President Bush was unlikely to pressurize Israel into breaking the deadlock with an election due in November.

TALKS IN MOSCOW

The prospect of a negotiated settlement receded further in January when the far-right Moledet and Tehiya parties resigned from the Israeli Government in protest at discussion of Palestinian autonomy in the Occupied Territories. This left the Shamir Government without a majority in the Knesset and made an early election inevitable. Nevertheless, multilateral regional talks opened in Moscow at the end of January. With inter-Arab relations still strained in the wake of the 1991 Gulf War, it came as little surprise that they failed to agree on a coherent policy. Eleven states attended, a sufficient number for Israel to claim a diplomatic breakthrough, while Syria and Lebanon stuck to their earlier promise to observe a boycott of regional talks until progress had been made in the bilateral negotiations. The PLO, concerned at Arab disarray but determined to use the multilateral session to highlight the issue of Palestinian representation, sent a delegation composed of personalities from the West Bank and Gaza, Jerusalem and the diaspora. While conceding that representatives from the diaspora and Jerusalem could be included in some of the working groups that the conference was to establish—on the refugee problem for example—the USA only issued invitations to the plenary session to Palestinian delegates from Gaza and the West Bank. Believing that they had already made too many concessions, especially on the issue of representation, the Palestinian delegation refused to attend the talks. US Secretary of State Baker voiced his disappointment at the Palestinian decision and promised that diaspora Palestinians could be included in two of the five working groups scheduled to meet in the spring. The Palestinians had demanded free representation on all five, but could take some solace in the fact that their fears of Israeli and Arab participants taking steps towards normalizing relations were unfounded.

ESCALATION OF HOSTILITIES IN LEBANON

On 16 February the leader of the Lebanese Hezbollah, Sheikh Abbas Moussawi, was killed in an Israeli helicopter attack on his motorcade in southern Lebanon. Moussawi's wife, child and several bodyguards also died. Many observers were puzzled by the assassination; for all its anti-Israeli rhetoric Hezbollah had never launched attacks against targets inside Israel, nor had there been a noticeable increase in raids on the IDF or its SLA allies in the Israeli security zone prior to the killing. One SLA spokesman even described Hezbollah as 'militarily insignificant'. Moreover, the killing halted negotiations to exchange Lebanese and Palestinian prisoners in return for news of Israeli servicemen missing in Lebanon. It also provoked an escalation of warfare in the south. Hezbollah rocket attacks on northern Israel were followed by heavy Israeli shelling of Shi'ite villages. Syria eventually persuaded Hezbollah to halt its salvoes, which led the organization to search for other means of retaliation. On 9 March Israel's chief security officer in Ankara was assassinated, and on 17 March a massive car-bomb wrecked the Israeli Embassy in Buenos Aires, Argentina, leaving 30 dead. Responsibility for both attacks was claimed by 'Islamic Jihad'.

The situation in Lebanon deepened the pessimism surrounding the peace process. The Israeli delegation arrived in Washington for the fourth round of bilateral talks in an unforgiving mood. At the end of February James Baker had finally ended speculation over Israel's request for $10,000m. in loan guarantees. He told Congress that they would not be granted unless there was a halt to new settlement activity in the Occupied Territories, a condition that Shamir had already rejected.

BILATERAL TALKS IN WASHINGTON

Negotiations over the form of Palestinian autonomy within the Occupied Territories confirmed the extent of the gulf between Israel and Arab/Palestinian aspirations. The Israeli delegates outlined a proposal which would maintain Israeli control over land, and guarantee the right of unlimited settlement and full responsibility for public order. There was no mention of elections with the implication that the limited administrative powers devolved to the Palestinians would be executed by official appointees. This contrasted with the Palestinian plan for a Palestinian interim self-governing authority along with the election of a legislative assembly, a halt to all settlement, a transfer of judicial and administrative power and the phased withdrawal of Israeli forces leading to Palestinian self-determination throughout the Occupied Territories. A US State Department spokesman described both positions as 'maximalist', but went on to criticize the Palestinians for trying to pre-empt the negotiations by declaring sovereignty as their goal. Although this criticism reflected the USA's longstanding opposition to a Palestinian nation, it was interpreted as an attempt to counterbalance the refusal to grant Israel's loan guarantees. Israel's outright rejection of territorial compromises left negotiations with Syria and Jordan in stalemate. Trying to negotiate with Israel, said a Syrian spokeswoman, was 'an exercise in futility'.

REACTIONS IN THE OCCUPIED TERRITORIES AND ISRAEL

Within the Occupied Territories there was further opposition to continued Palestinian involvement in the peace process. The PCP, renamed the Palestinian People's Party (PPP), had initially supported the Washington talks, but withdrew its backing during the fourth round after the Palestinian delegation had agreed to negotiate on the issue of autonomy without having secured Israel's prior agreement to a settlement freeze. Yet more evidence of public opinion turning against the talks came in the elections to the Ramallah Chamber of Commerce in early March. Hamas supporters won a clear majority of seats despite the fact that Ramallah had a sizeable Christian majority and had long been considered as the stronghold of liberal, secular nationalism.

Party manoeuvring and infighting were also in evidence in Israel in the run-up to the general election. In February Shimon Peres was deposed as the leader of the Labour Party by his more hawkish, but equally veteran colleague, Itzhak Rabin. Rabin's reputation as a hardliner on defence and security was widely regarded as a boost to the Labour Party's battle to win voters from Likud. Their fortunes were further enhanced by rifts within the Likud ranks. In a speech broadcast live on Israeli TV, the Minister of Foreign Affairs, David Levy, angered by what he claimed was a plot against his supporters during internal party elections, accused Likud of being 'racist'. Although he was dissuaded from resigning, Levy's vitriolic attack on his own party undoubtedly contributed to steady Labour gains in the opinion polls. Meanwhile three parties of the centre-left, the Citizen Rights Movement, Shinui and Mapam, decided to merge their lists to form a new electoral bloc, Meretz.

The fifth round of the bilateral talks were held in Washington at the end of April, but were largely overshadowed by the Israeli election campaign. As predicted, the Israeli delegation arrived in Washington with a plan for phased municipal elections in the West Bank and in Gaza. The Palestinian delegation offered to consider the proposal, but reiterated its commitment to a nationally-elected legislative assembly. Hanan Ashrawi later described municipal elections as 'a dead-end'. There was also a suspicion among Palestinians that the Israeli offer was a Likud public relations exercise designed to win the moderate vote. Interestingly, those Palestinian factions which had raised the strongest objections to the autonomy negotiations—Hamas, the PFLP and DFLP—argued that municipal elections were a better option precisely because they did not commit Palestinians to the autonomy plan. Following its gains in the Ramallah Chamber of Commerce election, Hamas also viewed municipal elections as a welcome test of strength against a divided nationalist bloc. However, in elections to the Nablus Chamber of Commerce in mid-May, the nationalist bloc, standing as the National Muslim Coalition, won nine of the 12 seats contested.

There was an increase of violence associated with the *intifada* in the weeks leading up to the election. Four Palestinians were shot dead and 80 injured in Rafah on 7 April and several were killed in armed clashes during May. There was also a rise in the death-toll during demonstrations. The killing of an Israeli girl in a Tel-Aviv suburb at the end of May by a lone Palestinian was the catalyst for several nights of anti-Arab rioting and a government decision to further restrict the movement of Gazans into Israel; unemployment rates in some parts of the Gaza Strip were reported to exceed 50%. The stabbing of an Israeli settler in Gaza shortly afterwards was followed by widescale destruction of Palestinian crops and property.

In mid-June 1992 members of the Palestinian negotiating team travelled to Amman for a televised meeting with Yasser Arafat. Israeli government ministers condemned the meeting and demanded the arrest of the participants on their return. The USA made clear its firm opposition to such measures, leaving Israel's Minister of Police to make the somewhat lame threat of calling in the Palestinians concerned for questioning.

ELECTION VICTORY FOR LABOUR

A combination of public discontent over the economy, the state of relations with the USA, the plight of Russian immigrants and the lack of progress in the peace process, made Labour gains in the Israeli elections on 23 June inevitable. However, the extent of the Labour majority over the Likud, 44 seats to 32, exceeded most expectations. Meretz became the third largest party in the new Knesset with 12 seats, while the right-wing Tzomet Party, headed by the fiercely anti-clerical Rafael Eitan, made an unexpectedly strong showing and won eight seats. The right-wing Tehiya Party failed to win any seats. There was a slight drop in support for the orthodox religious parties and the Arab-dominated lists.

As expected, Meretz entered into partnership with Labour. The inclusion of the Sephardi Orthodox party, Shas, gave Rabin an overall majority, but an attempt to increase his majority and broaden his constituency by recruiting Tzomet into the coalition came to nothing. Former Labour leader Shimon Peres was appointed Minister of Foreign Affairs in the new Government, while Prime Minister Rabin retained the defence portfolio.

INITIAL REACTIONS TO RABIN

The USA and the EC, in the belief that only a Labour victory could keep the peace process alive, warmly welcomed the outcome of the election. The defeat of Shamir and the Likud was also greeted with relief in the Arab capitals where the attitude towards the new Israeli Government was one of official caution and unofficial optimism. The reaction of Palestinians was more equivocal. Those who had supported the peace negotiations saw Rabin's election as a positive development. But left-wing and Islamic factions feared that a Labour government would pave the way for an agreement on the autonomy proposals they so bitterly opposed. Relations between Fatah and Hamas supporters in particular grew more volatile following the election and, in July, the Occupied Territories witnessed the worst round of internecine fighting in many years. Several people had been killed and scores injured in gun battles and street confrontations before an uneasy truce was brokered.

Rabin's initial comments on the peace process did little to reassure Palestinians. He stated that he would be willing to travel to any Arab capital to pursue peace negotiations, but stopped short of instituting the settlement freeze the Palestinians had demanded. He promised a halt to the building of 'non-political' settlements, but insisted that all existing contracts would be honoured. This was positive enough for Egypt's President Mubarak to issue an invitation to Rabin to visit Cairo—the first visit by an Israeli Prime

Minister for six years—and for the USA to intimate that it might release at least part of the $10,000m. in loan guarantees that Israel had requested. In mid-July James Baker began another round of 'shuttle' diplomacy in the Middle East in an effort to reactivate the peace process. In the wake of the Baker mission, Arab leaders, including the PLO, met in Damascus with Palestinians from the Occupied Territories in order to co-ordinate policy before a possible renewal of bilateral talks.

In mid-August Rabin travelled to the USA for a visit intended to restore US-Israeli relations to their traditional amicability after the frostiness of the Bush-Shamir years. The Israeli Prime Minister left Washington with pledges of further military aid and assurances of Israel's enhanced strategic importance to the USA in the post-cold war era. For his part, Rabin promised that the coming round of bilateral talks would achieve progress on substantive issues.

OPTIMISM AND DISAPPOINTMENT

Rabin's optimistic approach to the peace process was not shared by the Palestinians. There was disappointment that the new Israeli Government had refrained from implementing a complete freeze on settlement in the Occupied Territories, and dismay at the USA's readiness to grant the $10,000m. in loan guarantees without such a policy change. Moreover, the goodwill measures that the Labour Government had announced prior to the resumption of negotiations—the rescinding of deportation orders against 11 Palestinians, the release of a small number of political prisoners and the reopening of some of the roads sealed during the *intifada*—were considered to be little more than political cosmetics. Government spokesmen in Jordan and Syria also expressed concern at the repercussions that the rapidly improved US-Israeli relations would have on the USA's supposed impartiality as cosponsor of the peace process.

Despite Arab reservations, Israel's continued intimations that there was a real prospect of a breakthrough in the stalled peace process ensured that the mood before the sixth round of bilateral talks began in Washington was more sanguine than for some time. Delegates spoke of a 'positive new tone' and a constructive informality that previous encounters had lacked. However, by the end of the fourth week, the longest round of bilateral talks to date, the Arab parties described the negotiations as deadlocked. Syria's chief negotiator accused Rabin's Government of exhibiting 'exactly the same attitude and policy as Shamir'. His comments were provoked by Israel's insistence that Syria should commit itself to a full, normal peace with Israel before the issue of withdrawal from the Golan Heights could be discussed. The Palestinian delegation expressed similar frustration with its Israeli counterpart on the land for peace issue. While the Palestinians insisted that the entire peace process—including discussions on Palestinian autonomy—should be guided by Resolution 242, the Israelis argued that UN resolutions were only applicable to negotiations on the ultimate status of occupied Arab land. Hanan Ashrawi, the chief Palestinian spokesperson, told journalists that Israel was still adhering to the notion of 'autonomy for the people but not the land'.

PEACE TALKS FOUNDER

The failure of the sixth round to produce tangible results strengthened the hand of Palestinian groups opposed to the peace process. Meeting in Damascus in mid-September, 10 Palestinian organizations, four from within the PLO and six from outside, signed a memorandum urging a withdrawal from the Madrid process. A strike called by the 10 factions was widely observed in the Occupied Territories and caused clashes between Fatah and Hamas supporters. However, while pressure from the rejectionist group narrowed Arafat's field of manoeuvre and reflected the substantial opposition to further Palestinian involvement in the Washington talks, other developments encouraged the Palestinians to remain engaged. Israel's Minister of Justice announced his intention to repeal legislation outlawing contact between Israelis and Palestinians and the PLO, and

economic controls were eased in order to allow a less restricted flow of capital to the Occupied Territories. One of the quietest periods in the *intifada* finally came to an end in mid-October when a hunger strike called by Palestinian prisoners in Israeli jails prompted a series of violent protests in the Occupied Territories and a sharp rise in Palestinian deaths and injuries.

A meeting of the PLO's Central Committee was called by Arafat in October in order to obtain official approval for Palestinian participation in the seventh round of peace talks in Washington. Arafat achieved a minor victory in persuading the PFLP and DFLP to attend the meeting, although both factions refused to vote on the issue of participation and were bitter critics of the Palestinian negotiating position. Their opposition was intensified by reports that Israel was considering an exchange of land in return for peace with Syria. At a meeting of Arab foreign ministers in Amman, Jordan, in mid-October Syria refused to give assurances to its Jordanian and Palestinian colleagues that it would not conclude a separate Israeli-Syrian peace treaty, arguing that progress in the Israeli-Palestinian talks could take years. An angry Arafat cancelled a scheduled visit to Damascus.

The Israeli delegation travelled to Washington for the seventh round of bilateral talks buoyed by the USA's formal approval of the release of $10,000m. in loan guarantees, and with an apparent willingness to discuss 'withdrawal in the Golan' with its Syrian counterpart. However, the proximity of the US presidential election and an expected change to an unambiguously pro-Israeli administration ensured that the negotiations would be cautious. The Israeli-Lebanese dialogue was given a particular poignancy by artillery duels between the IDF and Hezbollah fighters that were prompted by the deaths of five Israeli soldiers in a land-mine explosion. Israel used the pretext of the fighting to try to persuade Lebanon to agree to the establishment of a joint military commission in the south of the country. Lebanon interpreted the offer as a ploy to legitimize Israel's occupation of the south and insisted that there could be no peace without a full Israeli withdrawal. After the Israeli delegation accused its Lebanese counterpart of 'abdicating responsibility to terrorists' and warned that they 'could make normal life impossible' for Lebanon, the Lebanese delegation walked out of the talks. The Israeli-Palestinian dialogue again foundered on disagreement over the applicability of UN resolutions to the interim negotiations on Palestinian autonomy in the Occupied Territories. Deadlock was only averted by Palestinian consent to a series of 'informal' talks on the substance of interim Palestinian autonomy. The Palestinian delegation was at pains to stress the exploratory nature of the talks for fear of being seen to give assent to discussions on the technicalities of autonomy before the broader political principles governing interim and final phase negotiations had been established. Israel's talks with Syria also disappointed. The Israeli delegation had come to Washington prepared to discuss territorial compromise in the Golan, but it rapidly became obvious that it would only commit itself to discussing a limited withdrawal. Talks with Syria were further soured by Israel's repeating of its earlier call that Syria should not hold out for a comprehensive resolution of Arab-Israeli disputes but should 'stand on its own'. Only in the talks between Israel and Jordan was there a modicum of success, with both parties agreeing on a provisional agenda for the next round of talks.

CLINTON ADMINISTRATION TAKES OVER IN USA

The seventh round of bilateral talks coincided with Bill Clinton's victory in the 1992 US presidential election. The outgoing Bush Administration was eager to bequeath a viable Middle East peace process to the new administration and dutifully called for a resumption of talks in December. Not surprisingly, however, there was little enthusiasm for a further round of negotiations before the formal inauguration of the new US President. The Palestinians, under mounting pressure from a sceptical constituency to protest at the lack of progress in and general media indifference to the peace process, were the most reluctant to attend.

However, with the Arab states committed to returning to Washington, the Palestinians were left to register their unhappiness by sending a delegation of only four to deal with Israel's controversial proposals for Palestinian 'interim self-government'. The draft model for Palestinian autonomy envisaged a stratified system of authority in the Occupied Territories (excluding east Jerusalem); Israeli jurisdiction would be maintained over Israeli settlements, public lands would come under joint Palestinian-Israeli jurisdiction, and an Israeli-supervised Palestinian authority (whose composition and competence were to be negotiated) would govern private Palestinian lands and municipalities. While the Palestinian delegation was not in a position to reject the Israeli proposals outright, it argued that they would lead to the creation of a Palestinian Bantustan.

The inconclusive eighth round of Washington talks coincided with the fifth anniversary of the *intifada*. The character of the Palestinian uprising had changed considerably since its beginnings in Gaza. The popular committees that had served as the *intifada's* original dynamo had long since fallen victim to Israeli repression and factional infighting. The UNLU itself existed largely in name only and its bi-weekly communiqués no longer set the tone or tenor of resistance. Instead the activities of small armed groups had come to be viewed as the principal focus of the uprising. Many of these owed only nominal allegiance to identifiable political factions and some of their more dubious activities, especially the settling of political scores in the guise of eliminating collaborators, had led to heated debate and calls for the young gunmen to be reined in. However, with scant prospect of a breakthrough in the Washington talks, there was undeniable political capital to be made out of successful armed attacks against Israeli targets. Hamas, as self-appointed inheritor of the radical Palestinian mantle and an uncompromising opponent of the peace process, was the best placed, politically and militarily, to exploit the armed option. Bolstered by generous financial backing from Iran (which reportedly paid a bonus for every Israeli soldier killed), Hamas fighters embarked on a spectacular series of military operations. During two weeks in December four Israeli soldiers were killed in Hamas ambushes in Gaza and Hebron, and another was kidnapped inside Israel and later murdered (the IDF lost a further soldier to an Islamic Jihad gunman near Jenin in the same week).

DEPORTATION OF ALLEGED ISLAMIC ACTIVISTS

Rabin promised radical steps to counter the Islamic movement's military successes. On 16 and 17 December 1,600 alleged Hamas and Islamic Jihad activists were detained by the Israeli security forces. Some 413 of those arrested were subsequently transported to the Lebanese border and, with the approval of Israel's Supreme Court, expelled through Israel's security zone into south Lebanon. The Lebanese Government refused to accept the deportees, a stance which the Arab world unanimously applauded, leaving the displaced Palestinians to establish a makeshift refugee camp on a barren mountainside wedged between the IDF and Lebanese army front lines. Although Rabin explained that the deportees would be eligible to return to their homes after a two-year period, the mass expulsions elicited a chorus of international condemnation. The UN Security Council, affirming the inadmissibility of deportations under the Fourth Geneva Convention, unanimously passed Resolution 799 demanding the immediate safe return of the expelled Palestinians. UN Secretary-General Boutros Boutros-Ghali also warned Israel that he might ask the Security Council to take further measures if it did not comply with the UN Resolution. In the Occupied Territories, and particularly in Gaza, where the majority of the deportees originated, Rabin's action provoked another surge of violent street protests—six demonstrators were killed in Khan Yunis on 21 December alone.

The mainstream PLO appeared to benefit from the political and diplomatic repercussions of the deportations. Firstly, it was believed that the PLO would be able to extract significant concessions from Israel and the USA before sanctioning a Palestinian return to the negotiating table;

secondly, in the opinion of some observers, Rabin's demonization of Hamas was effectively paving the way for a future Israeli-PLO dialogue; and thirdly the December events provided Yasser Arafat with an opportunity to manage his troublesome opposition. In reluctant admission of the PLO Chairman's stewardship of the Palestinian cause in times of crisis, Hamas and the Damascus-based rejectionists accepted invitations to a series of talks in Tunis. Although no real concessions were made by either side, with Arafat ignoring calls for a Palestinian withdrawal from the peace process, Hamas representatives agreed to work towards ending sectarian conflict and to co-ordinate activities with Fatah inside and outside the Occupied Territories. Hamas later signalled a significant revision of its maximalist position of settling for nothing less than an Islamic state in all of historical Palestine, by dropping objections to an independent state in part of Palestine.

US ATTEMPTS TO SAVE PEACE PROCESS

The deportations were a clear embarrassment for the new Clinton Administration. With the PLO and the Arab states urging the imposition of sanctions on Israel for non-compliance with Resolution 799, Clinton and his Secretary of State, Warren Christopher, persuaded Israel to take steps to defuse international unease over the expulsions. The Rabin Government subsequently announced that the expulsions had been an 'exceptional' measure and that the Palestinians would be allowed to return home before the end of 1993. It added that 101 of the deportees would be allowed back to the Occupied Territories immediately (this was rejected by the deportees' spokesman). Armed with the Israeli concessions, the USA embarked on a vigorous diplomatic campaign to persuade the six Third World members of the UN Security Council to abandon their support for sanctions against Israel. The USA argued that Israel had moved towards compliance with resolution 799 and that the imposition of sanctions would irreparably damage the fragile peace process. Madeleine Albright, the new US Ambassador to the UN, also warned that the USA would veto any move to impose sanctions. By 12 February 1993 the USA's heavy-handed diplomacy had borne fruit. The President of the UN Security Council issued a statement to the effect that there was to be no further debate on Resolution 799. He called on all parties 'to reinvigorate the Middle East peace process'. The UN decision caused glee in the Rabin Government, but confirmed the deep-seated Arab and Palestinian belief that Israel was immune to international law.

CHRISTOPHER TOURS MIDDLE EAST

In mid-February Warren Christopher made a tour of the Middle East with the primary intention of enticing the Palestinians and the front-line Arab states to resume talks in Washington. Syria and Lebanon were the easiest targets, since they had already indicated that they were prepared to separate the deportation issue from the peace process. However, Syria's President Assad went some way towards allaying Palestinian fears by stressing, in his talks with Christopher, that a separate Syrian-Israeli peace was impossible without a resolution of the Palestinian issue. Jordan proved to be less amenable to Christopher's urgings. It had said that it would not accept an invitation to Washington as long as the deportation issue was outstanding. This was not repeated by King Hussein in his talks with Christopher, but the Jordanian monarch left the US Secretary of State in no doubt that it would be almost impossible for a Jordanian delegation to attend the next round of talks if the Palestinians did not do so. It was clear, therefore, that the success or failure of the Christopher mission depended on the outcome of his meetings with the Palestinian peace team in Jerusalem. Initial reports suggested that progress had been made, and a six-point plan, designed to address Palestinian grievances, was agreed by the two sides. The outcome was a further letter of US assurances to the Palestinians. The Administration reiterated its commitment to Resolutions 242 and 338, stated its willingness to participate as a full partner in the peace talks, expressed opposition to deportation and settlement and affirmed its readiness to stand by assurances given by the previous Administration with regard to the peace process (most crucially the acknowledgement that East Jerusalem was occupied territory). Christopher also told the Palestinians that Israel would not resort to deportations in the future. However, while the Secretary of State flew back to the USA, the Palestinians waited in vain for a positive Israeli response to the six points and a statement of principle on deportations. Instead, the Israeli media announced that the Palestinians would be attending the ninth round of talks on 20 April. Angered by subsequent US inaction and complaining bitterly that it was being taken for granted, the PLO ordered the Palestinian delegates to refuse an invitation to the talks. 'If Israel cannot comply with the six points,' commented one PLO official, 'then we cannot participate in the next round'.

PALESTINIANS UNWILLINGLY RETURN TO TALKS

The PLO's refusal to accept an invitation to the talks led to a series of inconclusive inter-Arab meetings and the postponement, at the end of March, of any decision on whether to attend until further talks had been held with the US Administration. Privately the Palestinians had by now resigned themselves to the resumption of negotiations before the return of the deportees, but they insisted that they could not resume talks without major Israeli concessions on the issue of the deportations. The USA and Egypt's President Mubarak subsequently urged Rabin to adopt some confidence-building measures to smooth the way for Arab participation. The result was a declaration by Rabin that mass deportation was not government policy and a promise to allow the return of a small number of Palestinians expelled since 1967. In a departure from the Israeli Government's previously-held policy of refusing to allow Palestinians from East Jerusalem to participate in the negotiations, Rabin also announced that it no longer objected to Faisal Husseini becoming the official leader of the Palestinian delegation. This last point was regarded by some Palestinians, not least by Husseini himself, as an important gain and a sufficient concession for the Palestinian delegation to attend talks in Washington. However, for the majority of Palestinians, including delegation leader Haider Abdel Shafei, who had given an undertaking in his native Gaza that there would be no return to the talks while the deportees languished on a Lebanese hillside, Israel's concessions and the USA's promise to play a full and active role in the talks still fell short of the minimum required to enable them to return to Washington.

RENEWED VIOLENCE IN THE WEST BANK AND GAZA

Public opinion in the Occupied Territories remained firmly opposed to a retreat from commitments made to the deportees and had hardened as repression escalated in the West Bank and Gaza. Since the deportations there had been a dramatic increase in violent incidents in Gaza and the West Bank, with Palestinian deaths and injuries equalling those of the *intifada's* bloodiest months. Child deaths had reached alarmingly high levels, as had summary executions of Palestinian fugitives by Israeli undercover units. Scores of homes were also being destroyed as the IDF adopted the controversial new tactic of targeting houses suspected of harbouring wanted Palestinians with rocket fire. Yet the militarization of occupation policy failed, as had mass expulsions, to halt anti-Israeli violence. Instead, the frequency of attacks and demonstrations in the Gaza Strip led some Israeli military figures to conclude that Gaza had been 'lost'. Each Israeli casualty drew appeals for stiffer policies to be applied in the Territories. Following the killing of two secondary school students in Jerusalem in March, Rabin ordered the closure of the Occupied Territories. Such a measure had been employed many times during the *intifada* but this time, Rabin stated, the West Bank and Gaza would be sealed for an indefinite period. Tens of thousands of Palestinians lost their livelihoods as a result. Pressure from Israeli employers eventually persuaded the government to issue work permits for a few thousand Palestinians, but

this still left many areas of Gaza and the West Bank in the grip of an economic catastrophe.

Against this background the PLO faced unenviable choices. Domestic animosity to the Middle East peace process was counterbalanced by pressure from the USA, the EC and Arab states for the PLO to resume talks. Syria paid official lip-service to Resolution 799, but it was eager to capitalize on its improving relations with the USA and sensed that there might be some movement on the Golan issue. Saudi Arabia also made it clear to the cash-starved PLO that restored relations and future funding would be contingent on Palestinian attendance at the ninth round of bilateral talks. Despite huge misgivings and against a chorus of protest from the Occupied Territories, Arafat finally consented to Palestinian participation in the ninth round, stating that 'We go to the negotiations because if we do not have a place on the political map we will not have a place on the geographical map either'. Another member of the PLO's old guard, Faruq Kaddoumi, called attendance 'the lesser of two evils'. The Palestinian peace delegates, who remained strongly opposed to Palestinian attendance at the talks, had to be ordered back to Washington. Hamas called the PLO's decision an act of 'treason' and severed contact with the Organization. A protest strike called by opposition factions shut down the Occupied Territories and precipitated a further round of bloody demonstrations.

Palestinian disarray immediately before the ninth round of bilateral talks fuelled Israeli intransigence. No promises were given on the return of the deportees, Rabin still refused to acknowledge that the West Bank and Gaza were 'Occupied Territories', in accordance with UN Security Council Resolution 242, and, despite the inclusion of Faisal Husseini in the Palestinian delegation, its Israeli counterpart continued to insist that East Jerusalem was not on the agenda. When, during the last days of negotiations, the USA submitted a draft proposal of principles in an attempt to break the deadlock and honour its earlier promise of playing a more active role in the negotiations, the Palestinian delegates complained that it was almost a carbon copy of Israeli positions. Further evidence of the USA's tilt towards Israel came in Assistant Secretary of State Edward Djerejian's testimony to a US Congress foreign affairs sub-committee on the Middle East in which he voiced no objections to the use of the unfrozen $10,000m. in loan guarantees to finance 'natural growth' of existing settlements in the Occupied Territories. A disgruntled Haider Abdel Shafei concluded at the end of the ninth round of bilateral talks that nothing had been accomplished. He said that the delegation would not return for further talks unless the PLO Chairman convened a session of either the PNC or the PLO's Central Council to assess the situation. This brought a sharp rejoinder from Faisal Husseini who said that the decision on whether to attend further talks rested with the PLO leadership. Rifts within Palestinian ranks grew wider with the resignation of the PNC's veteran speaker in protest at the direction of the peace process. 'Tragedies are befalling the Palestinian people', he said in his resignation address, 'and I do not want to be blamed for it'. There was little progress in the other bilateral talks. A claim by Israel's Minister of Foreign Affairs, Shimon Peres, that the Jordanian and Israeli delegations were on the brink of agreement was angrily denied by Jordan.

SOMBRE MOOD AT TENTH ROUND OPENING

The tenth round of bilateral negotiations opened in mid-June in quiet, almost ritualistic fashion and without Arab preconditions or expectations. Several Palestinian delegates, including Abdel Shafei, did not attend the talks but refrained from announcing an official boycott. The sense of Palestinian demoralization was deepened by comments made by the PLO Chairman to an Israeli newspaper to the effect that if Israel agreed to withdraw from Gaza and parts of the West Bank it would be proof of its implementation of Resolution 242. Arafat's statement was cited as evidence of the PLO leadership's abandonment of principle and absence of policy and led to calls for a complete re-evaluation of the Palestinian negotiating strategy. In a thinly-veiled attack on the PLO leader, Abdel Shafei also pleaded for democratization of the Organization. There was no progress in Washington to provide relief for the beleaguered Chairman. US efforts to produce a joint Israeli-Palestinian declaration of principles eventually led to the issuing of a draft proposal designed to constitute the new terms of reference for the peace talks. For the Palestinians the US document was an unacceptable departure from the assurances upon which their participation in the peace process was premised; firstly, because the USA insinuated that both Israel and the Palestinians had claims to sovereignty over the West Bank and Gaza; and secondly, because the issue of East Jerusalem was excluded from negotiations on interim self-government arrangements. The US proposals, Palestinian leaders agreed, were not even suitable as a starting point. Speculation that there might be progress between Israel and Syria was scotched after Rabin, under pressure from right-wing Jewish settlers, rejected a Syrian offer of a 'total' peace in exchange for a 'total' withdrawal from the Golan Heights.

At the end of July, following the killing of seven Israeli soldiers in south Lebanon by Hezbollah fighters, the IDF launched its severest bombardment of Lebanese territory since 1982. More than 55 villages were heavily damaged, 130 people, mainly civilians, were killed and 300,000 Lebanese fled north during the week-long assault. Hezbollah responded by firing salvoes of *Katyusha* rockets into northern Israel. These reportedly caused little damage and few casualties. Prime Minister Rabin code-named the IDF's action 'Operation Accountability' and stated that its purpose was to create a refugee crisis in Lebanon and thus pressurize Lebanon and Syria into taking action against Hezbollah. The deliberate targeting of civilians provoked harsh international condemnation. The UN Secretary-General, Dr Boutros Boutros-Ghali, declared it 'deplorable that any government would consciously adopt policies that would lead to the creation of a new flow of refugees and displaced persons', sentiments that were echoed by Arab states and the European Union. Fears that the fighting would deal a fatal blow to the faltering peace process prompted Syria and the USA to mediate an end to the hostilities and to arrange what was termed an 'understanding' between Israel and Hezbollah whereby the IDF would refrain from attacking civilian targets as long as Hezbollah fighters confined their military operations to Lebanese territory. Israel declared its attack on south Lebanon a success, but it quickly became evident that Hezbollah had not been entirely subdued by the IDF. Less than three weeks after the Israeli bombardment, nine Israeli soldiers were killed in two ambushes carried out by Hezbollah fighters in Israel's security zone. Significantly, Israeli reprisals were confined to limited air strikes on Hezbollah bases in the Beka'a valley.

THE OSLO ACCORDS

Throughout the summer the political and financial crisis within the PLO deepened. Two prominent members of the PLO Executive Committee resigned before the beginning of the 11th round of bilateral talks in protest at Arafat's negotiating strategy; the resignation of Faisal Husseini, Saeb Erakat and Hanan Ashrawi from the Palestinian delegation was only averted by the PLO's acceptance of their demands for greater democratization of the decision-making process. Rumours of corruption and mismanagement of the Organization's finances caused further erosion of support for Arafat's leadership, as did the growing chorus of dissent from the Damascus-based Palestinian groups, independents and erstwhile Fatah supporters. With the prospect of the PLO's disintegration seeming ever more likely, a dramatic development at the end of August injected sudden energy into the peace process and promised to shift Arab-Israeli relations onto a more positive footing. It emerged that Israel and the PLO had been engaged in secret negotiations in the Norwegian capital, Oslo, and had reached agreement on mutual recognition and a plan for staged Palestinian autonomy in the West Bank and the Gaza Strip. The precise details of the autonomy agreement were purposefully vague, but according to initial press reports the key components

of the 'Oslo Accords' were said to include an early withdrawal of Israeli forces from Gaza and the Jericho area; the redeployment of Israeli troops in other areas of the West Bank; the gradual transfer of power from the Civil Administration to a Palestinian authority; the creation of a Palestinian police force; and the election of a Palestinian Council. Permanent status negotiations were to begin within two years of the Israeli withdrawal from Gaza and Jericho, be concluded within five years and would address such issues as Jerusalem, borders, settlement, co-operation, security and refugees. The reaction of the Arab world to the nascent PLO-Israeli agreement was decidedly mixed, not least amongst Palestinians themselves. Arafat managed to secure majority support for the Accords from the Fatah Central Committee, but failed to persuade three of the movement's co-founders, Farouk Kaddoumi and Khalid and Hani Hassan, to give their backing. Hamas and the Damascus-based Palestinian groups denounced the agreement as a betrayal, an interpretation that was shared by the majority of Palestinian refugees in Lebanon who staged protest marches and decked their camps with the black flags of mourning. The prominent Palestinian writer, Edward Said, scorned the agreement for transforming the PLO from a national liberation movement to a municipal council. Within the Occupied Territories, many ordinary Palestinians, no doubt swayed by the attrition of the *intifada* years, expressed guarded approval of the plan. Nevertheless there was widespread concern among activists of all persuasions that the agreement represented a capitulation to Israeli demands and a dangerous journey into the unknown. Crucially, however, there was a strong consensus against the use of violence to settle inter-Palestinian differences. Gaining the support of the Arab world was as important for Arafat as winning over his domestic constituency and to this end the PLO Chairman embarked on a hurried tour of regional capitals at the beginning of September. President Mubarak predictably gave full support to the agreement, while Egyptian officials let it be known that Cairo had played a seminal role in securing the two sides' agreement. King Hussein of Jordan initially displayed considerable pique at the failure of the PLO to consult him over the details of its talks in Oslo, and the Jordanian press expressed official disquiet at a 'separate' Israeli-Palestinian peace. However, given the USA's endorsement of the Oslo Accords and Jordan's traditional, if cautious, advocacy of Israeli-Arab peace, it came as little surprise that Jordan soon expressed support for the PLO Chairman. On 4 September King Hussein told a press conference that the Oslo Accords were 'part of a process leading to the implementation of (Security Council Resolution) 242 . . . so I will emphasize our full support.' A day later the foreign ministers of the Gulf Co-operation Council (GCC) member states gave their qualified support to what was described as 'a first step towards the liberation of all occupied land, including Jerusalem.' President Assad of Syria proved to be far less amenable to the new developments. At various times during the peace process Syria had been accused of negotiating a separate peace deal with Israel regarding the Golan Heights. Revelations that the PLO was on the verge of concluding its own agreement with Israel prompted the government-controlled media in Syria to issue lengthy commentaries denouncing disunity within Arab ranks. During six hours of talks in Damascus, Arafat failed to persuade the Syrian President to endorse the Oslo Accords. Assad stressed that he believed the PLO's action had made the achievement of an Israeli withdrawal from the Golan Heights and southern Lebanon more difficult. These fears were shared by the Lebanese Prime Minister, Rafik Hariri, who was even more outspoken in his objections to the Israel-PLO deal. Addressing concerns that the Accords effectively froze the position of Palestinian refugees in Lebanon, he announced that 'under no circumstances whatsoever' would Palestinians be allowed to settle permanently in Lebanon.

The Israeli Cabinet unanimously approved the Oslo Accords on 30 August and early opinion polls suggested that there was a significant majority in the country in favour of the agreement. As government officials were quick to explain, there was little in the substance of the Oslo Accords to cause alarm in Israel. Withdrawal from the chaos of the Gaza Strip was broadly popular and dialogue with the PLO had become far more acceptable to the national psyche since the growth of Islamic fundamentalism. For the more hawkish and sceptical sectors of the Israeli population there was solace in the fact that, under the terms of the agreement, security for the West Bank and Gaza would remain an Israeli responsibility, and that the short-term future of Israeli settlements was assured. Agreement with the Palestinians also offered the prospect of an end to the Arab economic boycott of Israel and of normalized relations with the Arab world. The Likud opposition was largely unimpressed by Labour's arguments, however. It accused Prime Minister Rabin and Minister of Foreign Affairs Peres of laying the cornerstone of a Palestinian state and stated that if the Likud came to power it would refuse to honour the agreement. Representatives of the settler movement and of the extreme right-wing vowed to resort to civil disobedience in order to prevent the implementation of the Accords.

The official signing of the Israeli-PLO Declaration of Principles took place on 13 September 1993 on the White House lawn in Washington. In front of 3,000 international guests Israeli Prime Minister Rabin declared: 'We the soldiers who have returned from the battle stained with blood, we who have fought against you the Palestinians, we say to you today in a loud and clear voice: "Enough blood and tears! Enough!"'. For his part, Yasser Arafat pleaded for 'courage and determination to continue the course of building coexistence and peace between us', and added, 'Our people do not consider the exercising of our right to self-determination could violate the rights of their neighbours or infringe on their security.' Significantly, however, it was the Israeli Minister of Foreign Affairs, Shimon Peres, and the PLO spokesman on foreign policy, Mahmud Abbas, who actually signed the Declaration documents. The ceremony was concluded by an embarrassed, but highly symbolic handshake between Arafat and Rabin. Support for the Oslo Accords had grown steadily in the Occupied Territories in the two weeks since the PLO-Israeli agreement had been made public and the day of the signing was marked by massive celebrations throughout the West Bank and the Gaza Strip. Detecting the shift, and fearful of its marginalization, Hamas revealed once again its pragmatic streak. While stressing its continued opposition to the Accords, it acknowledged that a new reality had been created which it would be foolish for it to ignore. It also agreed with Fatah that their respective demonstrations in favour of and in opposition to the Accords should be allowed to pass without interference. Contrary to the fears of Palestinians there were few reports of clashes between the two sides. Nevertheless, on the eve of the Washington ceremony Hamas sent a warning signal to the PLO and Israel when its gunmen ambushed and killed three Israeli soldiers on the edge of Gaza city; while in Beirut eight people were killed when units of the Lebanese Army fired on a Hezbollah demonstration protesting against the PLO-Israeli agreement.

There were immediate and positive results from the signing of the Declaration of Principles for both Israel and the PLO. On 14 September Israeli Prime Minister Rabin was hosted in Morocco by King Hassan, in the first official visit by an Israeli Prime Minister to any Arab country other than Egypt. On the same day in Washington, Israeli and Jordanian representatives signed an agreement on an agenda for forthcoming negotiations between the two states. A number of issues of concern to Jordan were covered, including the return of Jordanian territory (adjoining the Dead Sea) occupied by Israel since the late 1960s; the fate of Palestinian refugees in Jordan; water rights; and a number of security issues. Jordan also committed itself not to threaten Israel by force and to work towards the removal of weapons of mass destruction from the Middle East. Meanwhile, Yasser Arafat was being feted by the media networks in the USA and enjoying the sort of rehabilitation in the eyes of the US public that would have been unthinkable only a few months previously. There was a developing awareness among all the parties who wished to see the peace process maintain its momentum that future progress depended on the ability of Arafat to demonstrate to his own constituency that the benefits of the deal outweighed its obvious shortcomings. Particularly important, PLO officials stressed, was the immediate commitment of the international community to the kind of substantial aid package that would be needed to revitalize the economy and to improve social conditions in the Occupied Territories. The Clinton Administration responded to these pleas by organizing a donors' conference in Washington that secured promises of $23,000m. in emergency aid for the West Bank and Gaza over the following five years; the EU and the USA pledged $600m. and $500m. respectively.

PLO LEADERSHIP CRISIS

Securing promises of substantial financial aid was an important fillip for the PLO Chairman in managing the scepticism with which the Oslo Accords were still regarded within PLO circles. In mid-October the PLO's Central Council met in Tunis to debate the Accords. The boycotting of the meeting by the Popular and Democratic Fronts (for the Liberation of Palestine) and the other opposition groups ensured that the ratification of the Accords was passed by a bigger majority (63 votes to 8 with 11 abstentions) than might have been expected. Yet, despite the margin of the victory, the Central Council session and subsequent meetings in Tunis were not the triumph that Arafat loyalists claimed. Delegates complained that there was little substantive discussion of the Accords and no attempt to map out a coherent negotiating strategy in the forthcoming talks with Israel over their implementation. Moreover, Arafat's autocratic handling of the meetings revived fears that the PLO Chairman lacked the requisite political skills to resist Israeli pressure to make further concessions, or for that matter to transform the Palestinian struggle from one of national liberation to one of nation building. Haider Abdel Shafei, the erstwhile chief Palestinian negotiator in the peace process, signalled his own lack of faith in the ability and motives of the PLO leadership by announcing his resignation from his post. The lack of confidence in the political leadership extended to the Damascus-based opposition, in particular to the PFLP and DFLP, which were widely criticized for boycotting the Tunis meetings and for their preference for sloganeering rather than establishing an alternative programme to the autonomy proposals. It also appeared increasingly obvious that the secular opposition was being outflanked and outmanoeuvred by Hamas. After the rejectionist PLO factions had announced their intentions to boycott a proposed Palestinian reconciliation conference in the Yemeni capital, San'a, Hamas informed Arafat that it would be attending. Behind the Islamic movement's contradictory pronouncements on its intended relationship with the new Palestinian authority (in contrast to the Popular and Democratic Fronts which insisted that they would have no dealings with the new autonomous Palestinian institutions) many observers claimed to detect a bid by Hamas to posit itself as the only credible opposition to the Arafat wing of the PLO.

Israeli-Palestinian negotiations on the implementation of the first stages of the Declaration of Principles began in Cairo and the Red Sea resort of Taba on 13 October. It quickly emerged during the first round of talks that there were several potentially serious obstacles to be overcome. Firstly, the Israeli and Palestinian delegations had widely differing definitions of what constituted the geographical area referred to as Jericho. According to the chief Palestinian negotiator, Nabil Sha'ath, Jericho referred to the old British Mandate Administrative Area comprising some 390 sq km and currently encompassing a number of Israeli settlements, as well as Arab villages. According to his Israeli counterpart, Gen. Amnon Shahak, the area in question was Jericho limited to its present municipal boundaries of a mere 25 sq km. More emotively, the two sides failed to agree on a timetable for the release of the estimated 11,000 Palestinian political prisoners in Israeli jails. For the Palestinian side a comprehensive release of Palestinian prisoners was crucial to the maintenance of any degree of popular support for the autonomy plan. However, its request that Israel should draw up a timetable for release bore little fruit. Six hundred and seventeen prisoners were released on 25 October as a confidence-building measure. However, the majority of these were Fatah loyalists, leading one of the Palestinian negotiators to remark that they were 'trying to make peace between Palestinians and Israelis, not between Israel and a faction of the PLO'. Israel responded by saying that it would wait until the Palestinian police force was in place before releasing the majority of the detainees. Shortly afterwards it bowed to right-wing pressure and ended nearly all releases. The moratorium provoked one prominent Palestinian, Ziyad Abu Zayad, to tender his resignation from the negotiating team. The issue of border security proved just as intractable. From Israel's point of view this was its most sensitive domestic concern and, as such, the one area of the autonomy negotiations where it was least likely to compromise. On 1 November the Israeli delegation submitted proposals on security and the withdrawal of troops from the self-governing enclaves of Gaza and Jericho. These envisaged not so much the withdrawal of troops from Gaza as their redeployment in buffer zones around the Gaza Strip's Jewish settlements. They also proposed the retention of 20 checkpoints along the 1967 border to ensure the security of soldiers and settlers, and Israeli control over crossing points into and out of the autonomous enclaves. The Israeli proposals were condemned as unacceptable by Sha'ath, who withdrew the Palestinian delegation from the negotiations; it only returned after the Israeli delegation agreed to revise its plans for the redeployment of the IDF in Gaza. Palestinian critics of the autonomy proposals commented that this early dispute over security went to the core of their dissatisfaction with the Declaration of Principles, namely its studied refusal to address the status of Jewish settlements. 'If Israelis and Palestinians can't agree that the settlements are illegal entities on our land,' commented one Gazan economist, 'then we are saying that in the Occupied Teritories there are *de facto* two separate entities and that these are somehow equivalent. They are both legal or legitimate presences'. An inescapable corollary of this failure to define the status of the settlements was implicit acceptance of the long-held Israeli view that the West Bank and Gaza were not so much occupied territories as disputed ones.

Hopes that the signing of the Declaration of Principles would lead to a reduction in violent incidents in Gaza and the West Bank were also frustrated. In Gaza the impending transfer of power to a PLO authority gave rise to a secret feud within Fatah that claimed the lives of three top figures in the Organization, including that of As'ad Saftawi, a co-founder of the Fatah movement and its leading activist in Gaza. At the same time the IDF maintained its policy of pursuing wanted activists, killing and arresting gunmen of all political factions, including those identified as Fatah loyalists. Protests from the Palestinian negotiators that the targeting of activists was a violation of the spirit of the newly signed Accords failed to end the operations of Israeli undercover units. The killing of Hamas's senior military leader in Gaza in November gave rise to a massive increase in confrontations which were reignited two weeks later when a leading Fatah hawk, Ahmad Abu Rish, was shot dead by an Israeli undercover unit in Khan Yunis. Only a few days before his killing Abu Rish had received a much publicized amnesty from the Israeli authorities for obeying an Arafat directive and surrendering his weapon. His colleagues subsequently announced that they would resume their military operations unless Israel stopped pursuing wanted activists. Hamas, which was the principal target of the IDF's operations in Gaza, had never shown any sign of scaling down its attacks on Israeli targets. Despite the deaths and arrests of scores of its activists it continued to demonstrate that it was by far the most effective Palestinian military force in the Occupied Territories. Seemingly impervious to penetration by the Israeli security services, it was able to inflict regular casualties on both soldiers and settlers. Indeed, the killing of Jewish settlers by Palestinian gunmen

during the autumn of 1993 produced fierce right-wing reprisals that escalated with every passing incident. Arguably more opposed to their Government's deal with the PLO than the Islamists of Hamas, the settlers' desire to avenge attacks on their own community became intertwined with a desire to derail the negotiation process. Such was the scale of the assaults on Palestinian targets that Israeli newspapers started to refer to a 'Jewish *intifada*'. Right-wing spokesmen hinted darkly that as long as the twin provocations of Palestinian violence and government talks with the PLO existed, there was every likelihood of the re-emergence of the kind of settler underground that had operated during the late 1970s and early 1980s. At a nationalist rally in Jerusalem, settlers were urged to 'rise up against this government of iniquity, against the evil ruling over us', and were told that 'these are not days of peace but of war'. The warnings proved to be prophetic. In mid-December, after two settlers were killed in an attack by Hamas fighters near Hebron, Israeli gunmen shot dead three young Palestinian workers in retaliation.

The cycle of violence made the prospect of an agreement on withdrawal from Gaza and Jericho by the 13 December deadline (as set down in the Declaration of Principles) increasingly unlikely. The main obstacles remained security and the size of the Jericho enclave. At a joint press conference in Cairo on 12 December, the Israeli and Palestinian negotiators announced their failure to meet the deadline. Rabin complained that the PLO Chairman 'lacked the inner strength' to reach an agreement, while the Israeli Chief of Staff, Gen. Ehud Barak, complained that it was unlikely that the IDF would hand over Gaza to the Palestinians as long as the PLO seemed unable to halt the violence there. Unlike Rabin, who appeared unperturbed by the delay and made a point of stating that the timetable laid out in the Declaration of Principles was not a rigid one, the PLO Chairman was visibly upset. And not without good reason. Failure to meet the deadline had further undermined dwindling support for the peace process — in the student council elections at Bir Zeit University, long regarded as a good indicator of Palestinian public opinion, Fatah had lost control of the student body to a coalition of rejectionist groups — and was an undoubted setback for the beleaguered Chairman. While he did receive grudging recognition for his refusal to accept Israel's proposals for the redeployment of the IDF to protect Jewish settlements in the Gaza Strip, this was small comfort when compared with the renewed chorus of criticism of the style and substance of his leadership. Calls for a clearer negotiating strategy and the democratization of the PLO were too loud to be ignored and compelled the PLO leader to accept demands for a dialogue with the nationalist opposition. Yet for some Fatah elements in Gaza patience with the PLO leadership had clearly run out. At the end of December three senior Fatah members resigned their posts in protest at the 'cronyism and favouritism' that had characterized political advancement in the Occupied Territories. They were articulating a concern of many Palestinians from within the Occupied Territories: that local cadres belonging to the *intifada* generation of activists were being marginalized by the imposition of political appointees from outside the Occupied Territories, and by 'salon spokesmen', with little experience of activism, from within. These were not new criticisms, but such a public airing of them at such a sensitive time pointed to an ever deepening crisis within the Fatah movement. The PLO Chairman also had to contend with a crisis in the Organization's relationship with Jordan. While the PLO and Israel had been struggling to overcome their differences on the autonomy accords, Israel and Jordan had been making swift progress in their own talks in Washington. The claim, by an Israeli minister, that everything with Jordan 'is tied up and signed' hardly pleased the PLO leader. There was also strong annoyance with Jordan for signing a memorandum with Israel that allowed the opening of branches of Jordanian banks in the Occupied Territories during the interim period. According to the PLO, Jordan should have waited to sign an agreement with the new Palestinian authority, and by not doing so it had undermined Palestinian attempts to secure practical acknowledgement of Palestinian sovereignty. As a result, Arafat refused to sign an agreement that would have allowed Jordan's Central Bank to regulate monetary policies in the Occupied Territories during the interim period. The deadlock was finally broken in mid-January after a strong attack by the Jordanian monarch on the PLO's delaying tactics finally persuaded Arafat to dispatch Farouk Kaddoumi to Amman to sign an economic agreement. This allowed for the reopening of 20 branches of Jordanian banks closed in 1967 and confirmed the use of the Jordanian dinar in the Occupied Territories. The banks would be supervised by the Central Bank of Jordan until a Palestinian Central Bank was established. Syria, meanwhile, continued to smart at the perfidy of the Oslo Accords and at Jordan's apparently fruitful negotiations with Israel. King Hussein assured the Syrian leader that Jordan would not sign a separate deal with Israel, despite pressure to do so from Rabin and President Clinton of the USA. Nevertheless the feeling in Damascus remained one of perceived betrayal and injured pride, Syria regarding itself as the standard-bearer of Arab unity while all around the Arab world drifted into unprincipled accommodation with Israel. The USA's concern that Syrian isolation threatened to unbalance the peace process led to a summit meeting between the US and Syrian Presidents in Geneva, Switzerland, in January 1994. Assad stressed to Clinton that Syria could not consider a separate peace deal with Israel, and that he would not entertain a normalization of relations with Israel until Israel had committed itself to full withdrawal from the Golan Heights. Assad did, however, confirm that peace with Israel was Syria's goal and intimated that, in return for an Israeli withdrawal from south Lebanon, the Syrian army would disarm Hezbollah. Fearing that the Clinton-Assad summit meeting was a dangerous step towards the rehabilitation of the Syrian President and a prelude to US pressure on Israel to make concessions over the Golan Heights, representatives of the Jewish settler movement delivered a letter of protest to the US Embassy in Tel-Aviv stating that any US interference would be harmful to the peace process. Despite claims that 90% of Israelis were opposed to withdrawal from the Golan Heights, a radio opinion poll revealed that nearly half of the 12,000 Israeli settlers there had considered moving back to the pre-1967 borders of Israel. Several of the more dovish members of the Israeli Cabinet, including the Deputy Minister of Foreign Affairs, Yosi Beilin, used the occasion of the Clinton-Assad meeting to concede that, given the proper security guarantees, Israel would have to withdraw from the Golan Heights. Rabin distanced himself from such remarks, preferring to allude to withdrawal in the Golan Heights rather than from the Golan Heights. Interestingly, however, the Israeli Prime Minister hinted at greater Israeli flexibility with the assessment that the 'extent of the withdrawal will be as the extent of the peace'.

Yasser Arafat and the Israeli Minister of Foreign Affairs, Shimon Peres, met in Davos, Switzerland, in January for talks aimed at resolving the differences that were preventing the signing of an agreement on implementation of the Gaza-Jericho component of the Declaration of Principles. Sufficient progress was made for a resumption of talks in Cairo, Egypt, on 6 February. After three days of intense discussion it was announced that agreement had been reached on most of the issues that had been dividing the two sides. On the question of the control of border crossings between the autonomous zones and neighbouring states, it was agreed that Israel would maintain military control and have a veto over Palestinian visitors. The latter would be allowed to stay in Gaza and Jericho for a maximum period of four months only and would have to apply to the Israeli authorities for any extension of that time. The Palestinian presence at the borders was to be limited to flags, entry stamps, guards and immigration officials, although Israel acknowledged that the searching of Palestinian visitors would be largely a Palestinian responsibility. It was also agreed that the territory of Gaza would be divided into three zones; Israeli settlements and the Egyptian border area, which were to remain under Israeli control; a second area, encompassing the perimeter of the Israeli settlements

and access roads, to be jointly patrolled; and the rest of the Gaza Strip, which was to be transferred to the new Palestinian authority. There was no resolution of the dispute over the precise size of the Jericho enclave, but Palestinian officials maintained that the 'size of Jericho will not be a problem in itself'. The agreement reached in Cairo was widely regarded as Palestinian capitulation to Israel's conception of what shape the interim autonomy period should take. In Damascus the 10 Palestinian rejectionist factions, grouped under the umbrella of the newly formed Alliance of Palestinian Forces (APF), condemned the new security arrangements and insisted that they would refuse to co-operate with the PLO or take part in elections scheduled for July 1994. The APF announced the formation of a new central council to rival that of the PLO and pledged an escalation of the *intifada*. The decision of the Palestinian rejectionists, together with continued Fatah infighting, was further evidence of the painful process of disintegration and realignment that was steadily transforming the face of Palestinian politics. In Gaza, which continued to be affected by both inter-Palestinian violence and Israeli-Palestinian clashes, there were reports that huge numbers of arms were being stockpiled for the purpose of settling political differences once the Israeli forces withdrew. The visibility and availability of weapons led to allegations that the IDF was encouraging future disorder in Gaza by ignoring the organized gun-running to the Strip.

THE HEBRON MASSACRE

The peace process suffered a dramatic setback on 25 February 1994 when Baruch Goldstein, an American-born adherent of the extremist Kach movement and resident of Kiryat Arba, carried out an armed attack on Palestinian worshippers in the Ibrahim Mosque in the centre of Hebron. Goldstein entered the mosque during early morning Ramadan prayers and sprayed the congregation with a hail of automatic gunfire. Twenty-nine people died before worshippers managed to overpower and kill their attacker. Palestinian fury at the massacre was heightened by reports that Israeli soldiers on duty at the mosque had contributed to the casualty toll by failing to intercept Goldstein and by barring the doors of the mosque to fleeing worshippers. As news of the massacre spread violent protests erupted throughout the Occupied Territories and among Arab communities inside Israel; a further 33 Palestinians were killed in the eight days following the massacre despite widespread curfews and massive troop deployment. The massacre and its bloody aftermath was roundly denounced in the Arab world. The Jordanian, Syrian and Lebanese Governments declared the suspension of their participation in the peace process. The Rabin Government responded to the events in Hebron by announcing its intention to set up a commission of enquiry and ordering the detention of a handful of known settler extremists. A ban was also declared on the Kach organization and its offshoot, Kahane Lives. These measures failed to mollify Palestinians, who asserted that only the disarming of settlers and the dismantling of the settlements could guarantee Palestinian security in the Occupied Territories. PLO spokesmen called for a revision of the Declaration of Principles to allow immediate discussion of the future of Israeli settlements and for the dispatch of an international protection force to the Occupied Territories, a suggestion that was endorsed by Arab states and the UN Secretary-General, but dismissed as 'neither particularly helpful or useful' by the USA. Several prominent PLO figures stated publicly that the removal of 400 or so militant settlers from the heart of Hebron was the *sine qua non* of the PLO's decision to restart talks with Israel. Both Hamas and Islamic Jihad vowed to take revenge for the Hebron massacre, a predictable response, but one that only added to the burden of pressure on the PLO leader. The massacre placed Arafat in a delicate position. Although it was believed that Hebron would allow the PLO Chairman to exact concessions from Israel in return for an early end to the Organization's suspension of participation in the autonomy negotiations, it was unlikely that Rabin would entertain the PLO's demands for immediate action against core settler interests. The Labour

Government had little ideological affinity with hardline settlers. However, Rabin recognized that they were valuable bargaining chips and that it would be a mistake to cash them in before the final status negotiations. Moreover, it was clear to Arafat that the best hope to bolster his own standing and to regain support for the peace process lay in demonstrating the benefits of the Oslo Accords by securing an early Israeli withdrawal from Gaza and Jericho. Any residual willingness of the PLO Chairman to hold out for Israeli concessions was also undermined by Syrian and Jordanian assurances to the USA that their withdrawal from the peace talks with Israel was only temporary. The somewhat surprising stance of the Syrian Government was explained by its Minister of Foreign Affairs as a response to the PLO's 'isolationist' approach and its refusal to co-ordinate its position with the front-line Arab states. But it was also clear that the USA had lobbied hard in Damascus for a Syrian return to the negotiation table, primarily as a means of putting pressure on the PLO to end its boycott of the talks. The USA similarly promised Jordan that it would lift the naval blockade of the Jordanian port of Aqaba (in place since the Iraqi invasion of Kuwait) as a reward for Amman's early resumption of talks with Israel. In the mean time, the USA maintained its pro-Israel diplomacy at the UN. US Ambassador Albright effectively delayed a vote on Resolution 904, which condemned the Hebron massacre and urged protection for Palestinians in the Occupied Territories, because the USA objected to the inclusion of paragraphs describing Jerusalem and the territories seized in 1967 as 'occupied Palestinian territory'. Resolution 904 was finally adopted by the Security Council on 10 March 1994, with the USA abstaining on two of its preambular paragraphs referring to occupied Palestinian territory. Albright justified the USA's abstentions on the ground that it did not wish to prejudice the course of the final status negotiations agreed upon in the Declaration of Principles. Nevertheless, Nasir el-Kidwa, the Palestinian observer at the UN, remarked that the USA's decision marked a disturbing departure from early US assurances that it regarded all of the 1967 territories as occupied. There was further Palestinian disappointment with Resolution 904's demand for their protection in the Occupied Territories. Instead of a UN armed force, as favoured by the PLO, the UN Security Council — again acting under US pressure — voted for a temporary observer force to be dispatched to Hebron. It was agreed that the force would not be under the control of the UN and that its mode of operations would be decided through negotiation between Israel and the PLO within the framework of the Declaration of Principles. Israel eventually agreed to the presence of 160 lightly armed, mainly Norwegian, observers operating under ultimate Israeli control. Their rather limited remit was 'to monitor Palestinian safety' and to aid the return of Hebron to 'normal life'.

By the beginning of April 1994 the PLO had agreed to resume negotiations with Israel despite the failure to secure the reassurances on settlements that PLO leaders had initially demanded. Its decision was perceived negatively by many Palestinians in the Occupied Territories, where dwindling goodwill towards the Oslo process was undergoing further erosion as a result of IDF security operations. Several people were killed in Hebron and a number of houses were destroyed by rocket fire in an army attempt to flush out Hamas gunmen. At the end of March six members of a pro-Arafat Fatah security team were shot dead in an ambush in Gaza. The latter incident forced an apology by the IDF and underlined a belief shared by many in the Israeli political establishment that urgent steps would have to be taken to reinforce Arafat's position and guarantee the viability of the peace process. The return of 47 Palestinian deportees, most of them senior PLO figures, was widely welcomed in the Occupied Territories. More importantly, the IDF began to redeploy its forces in response to news from Egypt that an agreement had been reached on the final issues dividing Israel and the PLO over the implementation of autonomy in the Gaza Strip and Jericho. However, even as the Oslo Accords were on the verge of being translated into reality, there came a deadly reminder of the fragility of that process.

On 6 April 1994 a car bomb in the Israeli town of Afula killed seven Israelis and maimed scores of others, many of them schoolchildren. A week later five more people were killed in a similar outrage in Hadera. Hamas claimed responsibility for both attacks and claimed that they were in response to the Hebron massacre. Some 300 Islamic activists were rounded up after the bombings and the Occupied Territories were sealed off. The Hamas spokesman in Amman said his Organization would halt attacks on civilians in return for an end to the Israeli offensive. He also promised that Hamas would support a peace agreement with Israel in return for an Israeli withdrawal from all of the Palestinian territory occupied in 1967. The Hamas offer received no official reply from Israel except an appeal to Jordan to close down Hamas's offices on its territory. Israel was also highly critical of an agreement reached in Gaza between Hamas and Fatah that had been precipitated by an outbreak of armed clashes between the two factions. Both sides agreed to a month-long moratorium on the killing of collaborators and 'an end to violence in Palestinian society'. Commenting on Israel's criticism of its talks with Hamas, a Fatah spokesman rejoined that Fatah's dealings with Hamas to secure order in the Gaza Strip would be on the PLO's terms and not Rabin's. He added that 'Our decision to co-operate with Hamas is an internal Palestinian issue and does not concern any other side. Fatah and Hamas are in the same boat and we will not allow anyone to sink it.'

AUTONOMY IN GAZA AND JERICHO

Against a backdrop of weary anticipation and lawless confusion in Gaza, Israeli and Palestinian officials met in Cairo on 4 May for a signing ceremony to seal the successful conclusion of eight months of troubled talks on the implementation of an autonomy agreement for Gaza and Jericho. Yet, in ironic accordance with the problems that had bedevilled the negotiations from the start, the dignified proceedings turned to high farce when Arafat refused to sign one of the documents pertaining to the size of the Jericho enclave. A highly embarrassing moment for the assembled dignitaries and the Egyptian President was eventually resolved by a hasty adjournment and an agreement that Arafat would annotate the offending document with a comment to the effect that it was awaiting final agreement. On returning to Israel an outraged Rabin insinuated that the problems at the Cairo ceremony were symptomatic of the PLO Chairman's inability to provide leadership. Arafat was also reproached by members of the PLO Executive Committee for having failed to discuss the agreement about to be concluded with Israel at a meeting held just a few days before the Cairo signing. Many PLO executive members stayed away from Cairo in protest at Arafat's autocracy, while within the Occupied Territories deepening reservations over the style of Arafat's leadership and the substance of the agreement reached with Israel meant that the PLO Chairman experienced great difficulty in trying to persuade political figures to take seats on the 24-member Palestinian Authority Council, the body designed to oversee the implementation of the autonomy agreement. Nevertheless, the signing of the agreement in Cairo resulted in rapid change in Gaza and Jericho. The IDF hastened its withdrawal from centres of Palestinian population, and on 10 May the first contingent of the Palestinian police force arrived in Gaza. A further 400 arrived in Jericho a few days later. Israel had also announced the imminent release of 5,000 Palestinian detainees. On 13 May and 17 May, in Jericho and Gaza respectively, the IDF handed over its positions to the commanders of the Palestinian forces in simple ceremonies. The Chief of Palestinian Police Forces told crowds in Gaza that they were witnessing 'a historic day for the Palestinian people, the first step on the way to independence.' The following day, in the early hours of the morning, Israel evacuated its last position in Gaza city. Bitter memories of the occupation meant that even at this final hour there would be no dignity in the Israeli withdrawal. The departing troops left under a cloud of tear-gas and a shower of rocks and bottles, while tens of Palestinian gunmen joined members of the Palestinian police force in a deafening salute to the beginning of a somewhat different reality.

Finalization of the agreement on autonomy for Gaza and Jericho was met with scorn in Syria, where Arafat was widely perceived as having allowed the Palestinian national movement to be humiliated by Israel. Syria refused an invitation to attend the Cairo ceremony and the state-controlled media commented that, 'There can be no middle way. There can be no compromise over land and peace. Comprehensive peace in the Middle East depends on the return of all occupied land.' Syria's unwavering commitment to these principles was regarded by the USA as the principal obstacle to achieving a wider Middle East settlement. The US Secretary of State Warren Christopher was dispatched to the Middle East at the end of April and again in May in an attempt to reconcile the Syrian and Israeli positions. His mission proved largely fruitless. Rabin stated that he would entertain no greater compromise than a promise to dismantle some of the settlements on the Golan Heights and to make a phased withdrawal, over a number of years, from some areas of the Heights. This was unacceptable to President Assad, who insisted that a peace agreement had to be preceded by a total Israeli withdrawal from occupied Syrian territory accomplished within a one- to two-year period. Plans for a further visit by the US Secretary of State in June were abandoned after Rabin confirmed that negotiations with Syria were totally deadlocked and Syria reiterated that there was little purpose in further dialogue until Israel made a public pledge that its withdrawal from the Golan Heights would be total. Controversial Israeli military operations in Lebanon during May and June made it even less likely that Syria would soften its stance. On 22 May Mustafa ad-Dirani, a leader of the radical Iranian-backed Faithful Resistance Organization, was kidnapped by Israeli forces from the Beka'a valley. The raid, reminiscent of the abduction of Sheikh Obeid in 1989, was justified on the ground that ad-Dirani had information about the missing Israeli navigator, Ron Arad, who had been shot down over Lebanon in 1986. Ten days after ad-Dirani had been seized, Israeli aircraft were once again in action over Lebanon, attacking a Hezbollah training camp in the Beka'a valley and killing, according to Israeli sources, 36 Hezbollah fighters and wounding more than one hundred. The attack was of questionable political value and it was regarded as an indication of a shift to the right in the governing Israeli Labour party.

In Gaza and Jericho there was widespread jubilation at the departure of Israeli troops and an end to the curfews and restrictions that had been part of daily existence during the years of the *intifada*. Israel's own relief at being rid of the security problem of Gaza was marred, only two days after the withdrawal, when two Israeli soldiers were shot dead by Islamic Jihad gunmen near the Erez border crossing to Israel. Significantly, the IDF did not pursue the gunmen into Palestinian-controlled territory, and while the PLO assured Israel that it would try to curb such actions, it insisted that the disarming of Palestinian groups could only take place within the framework of broad factional agreement. Nevertheless, the agreed joint patrols by Israeli and Palestinian security forces along the demarcation lines of authority in Gaza and Jericho appeared to function in a spirit of comparative harmony. A far greater worry for Palestinians than any security co-ordination with Israel, and one that was only briefly masked by the general euphoria, was the financial and administrative chaos in Gaza. The difficulty Arafat was experiencing in recruiting appointees to the new Palestinian Autonomy Council — to be composed of 15 personalities from inside the Occupied Territories and nine from the Palestinian diaspora — resulted in the 3,000-strong police force operating in a judicial and legal vacuum. This situation was aggravated by the absence of properly constituted structures to co-ordinate and implement administrative change. The extent of the financial crisis was epitomized by the fact that the new police force was having to subsist on munitions donated by the local population. High unemployment levels made matters worse. Israel had placed a limit of 23,000 on the number of Gazan workers it

was prepared to allow into Israel and had sealed its border completely in response to the killings at the Erez checkpoint. Under pressure from Israeli farmers, Rabin had also reneged on an earlier decision to allow the importation of Gazan agricultural produce into Israel. Further trouble loomed for the nascent Palestinian authority in Gaza with the prospect of having to pay the estimated 7,000 employees of the previous Israeli Civilian Administration. With little prospect of revenue from tax collection from a population for whom tax avoidance had been seen until now as a patriotic as well as a personal imperative, there were desperate pleas from the PLO for international aid. Palestinian economists had estimated that Palestinian self-rule would require an annual budget of $240m., with a maximum of $127m. likely to be raised in tax revenues. First year start-up costs were likely to be in the region of $600m., leaving a huge budgetary deficit. Although $2,300m. had been promised to the Palestinians at the international donors' conference held in Washington in October 1993, the international community was reluctant to disburse funds until the Palestinians had established proper accounting procedures and clear project proposals. The PLO rejoined that without immediate funds to set up a basic administrative structure — which the donors were reluctant to subsidize — it would be impossible to meet the international requirements. Arafat expressed his personal fury at the implications of corruption and mismanagement and stated that he would not visit the autonomous regions to take charge of the transition until pledges of aid were forthcoming. The Israeli media appeared to take delight in the discomfort of the PLO leader and cited the financial wrangling as further evidence of his unredeemable political shortcomings. However, for once, Arafat's brinkmanship appeared to pay off. In a series of tense meetings in Paris, France, in June the donor countries agreed to the immediate release of $42m. in aid, with at least one-quarter of this sum going to fund the setting up of the Palestinian administration — without the *quid pro quo* of detailed accounting. They also agreed to take measures to make up the shortfall to meet the expected 1994 deficit. There were also positive developments in the West Bank and Gaza. By the end of June most of the 24 places on the Autonomy Council had been filled, mostly by Arafat loyalists, but also by several quasi-independents and members of Fida, the faction of the DFLP led by Abed Rabbo. In Gaza the Palestinian police force had won an assurance from Hamas that the killing of collaborators would stop. And in Damascus the ageing leader of the PFLP, George Habash, marked a considerable softening of his organization's position on the new Palestinian authority by instructing his supporters 'not to take a negative stance towards the institutions that offer services during the interim phase.'

ARAFAT VISITS GAZA

The easing of the PLO's financial worries, coupled with criticism of the PLO Chairman's apparent hesitation in taking control of the Palestinian self-rule areas, was answered with a commitment by Arafat to make his long-awaited visit to the newly autonomous enclaves. On 1 July 1994, with little advance warning, the PLO leader crossed from Egypt into Gaza to step foot on Palestinian soil for the first time in 25 years. His reception was more muted than might have been expected for a returning leader who had for so many years been an international symbol of the Palestinian cause. Yet large crowds did gather both in Gaza city and in Jabalia refugee camp, birthplace of the *intifada*, to hear Arafat's address. There was little of note in either speech beyond the repeated pleas for Palestinian unity — directed principally at the Islamic opposition — and an acknowledgement that there was little popular enthusiasm for the Oslo Accords. Arafat reassured his audience that the Gaza and Jericho enclaves were the stepping-stones to an independent Palestinian state with Jerusalem as its capital. Similar sentiments were voiced two days later in Jericho. When the PLO Chairman ended his four-day visit to meet with Rabin and Peres in Paris, France, his aides announced that he would soon be returning 'for good' and that Gaza, rather than Jericho, would be the home of the new Palestinian administration. Arafat's visit had raised more questions than it had answered. Despite the affection extended to him, Arafat's performances failed to convince anybody that he possessed the requisite political skills to tackle the shortcomings of the autonomy accords or to build on their openings. The presence of the PLO Chairman in Gaza and Jericho had as much symbolic resonance on the boulevards of Tel-Aviv as in the alley-ways of Gaza. The return of a personality who for more than two decades had been demonized by politicians and the media alike, was seized on by the Israeli right wing as a focus to rally opposition to the Oslo Accords. A demonstration in Jerusalem organized by the nationalist right to protest at Arafat's visit ended as something of an own goal for the Likud when some 10,000 demonstrators left the main rally and ran amok in East Jerusalem. Scenes of settlers and their supporters not only attacking Palestinians and their property, but also fighting running battles with the Israeli security forces, were a severe embarrassment for the struggling Likud leader, Binyamin Netanyahu. Rabin lambasted the settlers as the Israeli equivalent of Hamas, while the Likud quietly reflected that they had lost an opportunity to garner the moderate support needed to obstruct the PLO-Israeli agreement. Rabin's own fortunes were fortified in July with news that the orthodox Shas party would be rejoining the Labour coalition, as would Ye'ud, a splinter group from the right-wing Tzomet Party. There was no such comfort for Arafat. Shortly after returning to Gaza, the PLO leader became embroiled in the most serious incident of the Strip's two-month-old autonomy. In the early morning of 17 July a clash occurred at the Erez checkpoint between Palestinian labourers and units of the IDF trying to check that they possessed the correct documentation for entry into Israel. Pent-up frustrations at the slowness of the process led to a full-scale riot, with the Palestinian workers burning down an Israeli bus depot and Israeli soldiers attempting to restore order with live ammunition. There then followed a prolonged gun battle between members of the Palestinian police force and soldiers of the IDF. Two Palestinians were killed in the clash and 75 were injured; 18 Israeli soldiers also suffered gun-shot wounds. The mutual recriminations that followed failed to obscure the underlying tensions that had given the incident an air of inevitability. Firstly, rather than easing the process by which Palestinian workers gained employment in Israel, the advent of autonomy had merely added to it a further tier of administrative bureaucracy. Secondly, the Erez violence confirmed the fears of Palestinians that the security arrangements agreed in Cairo had created a kind of Gaza gulag. Finally, the entire autonomy process appeared to be doomed to failure unless something could be done to address the perilous state of the Gazan economy. 'What happened in Gaza today,' the Palestinian Minister of Justice, Furaih Abu Middain, commented 'was a battle for a loaf of bread.' The Israeli decision to seal off the Strip in response to the violence was condemned as incendiary by Palestinian sources and cast a further shadow over impending negotiations on the implementation of the next phase of the autonomy accords.

ISRAELI-JORDANIAN RELATIONS IMPROVE

The depressed mood that characterized Israeli-Palestinian relations was thrown into sharp relief by dramatic progress in Israel's bilateral talks with Jordan. On 9 July King Hussein announced to the Jordanian National Assembly that he was prepared to meet the Israeli Prime Minister, and on 18 July Jordanian and Israeli negotiators sat at a table straddling the Israel-Jordan border to take part in the first bilateral talks to be held in the Middle East itself. The decision of the Jordanian monarch to make such a highly symbolic concession to Israel was widely interpreted as an exercise in pragmatic self-interest. Anxious to maintain the momentum for a comprehensive peace settlement in the Middle East, the USA had offered appealing incentives to King Hussein to move Israeli-Jordanian relations to the centre of the peace process. Not least among these was US President Clinton's promise that his Government would work towards the waiving of Jordan's $900m. debt to the USA, provide military assistance to Jordan and seek to persuade Saudi Arabia and the Gulf States to end their economic and political boycott of the Hashemite regime. An announcement by Shimon Peres in mid-July acknowledging the Golan Heights to be Syrian territory was seen as Israel's contribution to the wider US plan of muting Syrian criticism of Jordan's effective *coup de grâce* to the dying beast of Arab unity. That Jordan refrained from signing a full peace treaty with Israel did not disguise the fact that the normalization of Israeli-Jordanian relations was close. In Washington on 25 July King Hussein and Itzhak Rabin formally ended the state of belligerency between their two nations in a ceremony that underlined not only the understanding that had been a feature of Israeli-Jordanian relations for many years, but also the personal warmth that existed between King Hussein and Rabin, a quality that was visibly absent from relations between the Israeli Prime Minister and the PLO Chairman. With the exception of the extreme right-wing fringe of Israeli politics, the country met the formal end of the state of war with Jordan with general acclaim, and a feeling that the key issues of contention with Jordan, the sharing of water resources and the return of a small area of Jordanian territory seized by Israel in the late 1960s, could be easily resolved. Jordan's citizens were less sanguine. Fundamentalist and left-wing groups were critical of the *rapprochement*, while the majority of the population saw the overtures to Israel as the inevitable price that had to be paid if Jordan was to solve the problem it had created for itself in the aftermath of Iraq's invasion of Kuwait in 1990. Palestinian reaction, in contrast, was sharply critical. There were strong suspicions that Israel, the USA and Jordan were engaged in a concerted effort to isolate the PLO and prepare for a reassertion of Hashemite control over the West Bank, leaving the PLO Chairman as 'mayor of Gaza.' There was particular concern at the inclusion in the document signed by King Hussein and Itzhak Rabin in Washington of a paragraph acknowledging Jordan's 'special role' as guardian of the Muslim holy sites in Jerusalem. Assurances from King Hussein that there was no contradiction between Jordan reaching an understanding over guardianship of religious sites in East Jerusalem and Palestinian political sovereignty, failed to convince the PLO leadership. On 20 July the PLO retaliated against Jordan's perceived treachery by banning the sale and distribution of the pro-Jordanian daily, *An-Nahar*, in the autonomous enclaves. Arafat reportedly justified the decision on the ground that he could not 'tolerate any undermining of Palestinian national interest in the name of press freedom.' The irony of a Palestinian authority restricting Palestinian freedom of speech was not lost on anyone, least of all Israel. The Arab world responded to both the Israeli-Jordanian agreement and the PLO's quarrel with Jordan with a large measure of indifference, damning evidence, if such was still needed, that the Arab world could not muster sufficient enthusiasm even to pay lip-service to the notion of Arab solidarity. Of the region's principal powers, only Syria condemned Jordan's agreement with Israel, in a statement that was made much easier by an earlier refutation, by Rabin, of Shimon Peres' comment that Israel regarded the Golan Heights as Syrian territory.

THE JERUSALEM ISSUE
Updated for this edition by PAUL COSSALI

Based on an original article by Michael Adams, with subsequent additions by David Gilmour, Paul Harper
and Steven Sherman

The Arab sector of Jerusalem, including the old walled city, was captured during the June War in 1967 by Israeli forces, which went on to occupy all the Jordanian territory lying west of the River Jordan. Theoretically, there was no difference in status between Jerusalem and the rest of the West Bank; both were occupied territory. In practice, Israel immediately removed the walls and barriers dividing the western (Israeli) and eastern (Arab) sectors of the city and at the end of June 1967 the Knesset passed legislation incorporating the Arab sector into a reunited Jerusalem under Israeli sovereignty. At the same time the boundaries of the municipal area of Jerusalem were greatly extended, reaching to near Bethlehem in the south and incorporating Kalandia airport (close to Ramallah) in the north.

Faced with Israel's effective annexation of the Arab sector, the UN General Assembly on 4 July 1967, ruled, by 99 votes to none, that the annexation was invalid and called on Israel not to take any measures to alter the status of the city. Ten days later the Assembly adopted a second resolution 'reiterating' the earlier one and 'deploring' Israel's failure to implement it.

Before the first of these resolutions was passed, the Israeli authorities had embarked on a series of structural alterations and demolitions in the Old City of Jerusalem, which aroused strong Arab protests and whose continuation was to lead to considerable international controversy. In clearing the area in front of the Western (Wailing) Wall, they expropriated 50 Arab families at very short notice and demolished their houses, while in the Jewish Quarter they dispossessed a further 200 Arab families. In all, and before the end of June 1967, some 4,000 Arabs in Jerusalem had lost their homes. In some cases, but not all, they were provided with alternative accommodation.

In November 1967 the UN Security Council passed its unanimous Resolution 242 setting out the basis for an overall settlement between Israel and its Arab neighbours. However, it was not until May 1968 that the Security Council passed its first resolution dealing specifically with the Jerusalem issue.

The resolution (No. 252 of 21 May 1968) deplored Israel's failure to comply with the two General Assembly resolutions of 4 and 14 July 1967, confirmed that any measures taken by Israel to alter the status of Jerusalem were invalid and called on Israel to rescind all such measures and to refrain from similar action in the future. The effect was only to increase the haste with which Israel set about changing the face of the city. Bulldozers had been at work on Mount Scopus since February, and soon the first of the new housing estates began to take shape beside the Nablus Road leading northwards out of Jerusalem. In the absence of any progress towards a peace settlement, it became clear that the Israeli Government intended to forestall, by establishing a physical presence in the Arab sector of Jerusalem, any future attempt to challenge its sovereignty over the whole of the municipal area.

Meeting again to consider the question in July 1969, the Security Council adopted, this time by a unanimous vote (in the previous year the USA had abstained from voting on the Jerusalem resolution), an even stronger resolution (No. 267 of 3 July 1969). Reaffirming its earlier stand and deploring 'the failure of Israel to show any regard' for the previous resolutions both of the General Assembly and of the Security Council, the Council 'censured in the strongest terms' all measures taken by Israel to change the status of Jerusalem, confirmed that all such measures were 'invalid' and again called on Israel to desist from taking any further action of a similar kind. Israel formally rejected the resolution and the Israeli Minister of Information stated in Jerus-

alem that it could not influence the 'facts' which had been intentionally created by Israel 'after due consideration of the political danger involved'.

The situation in Jerusalem itself was further aggravated in August 1969 by a disastrous fire in the al-Aqsa mosque, which at first sight appeared to confirm the fears of the Arabs for the safety of the Islamic and Christian shrines in the Old City. Israel investigations showed that the fire had been caused by a deranged Australian religious fanatic who was later brought to trial; but from that moment the concern of Muslim communities throughout the world reinforced the Arab sense of grievance at the loss of the Holy City.

In the following year Christian concern also began to make itself felt, especially after the publication of an Israeli 'master plan' for the future of Jerusalem. This plan envisaged the doubling of the Jewish population of the city by 1980 and an eventual total population of 900,000. An international conference of town planners, convoked by the Israeli municipal authorities at the end of 1970 to consider the plan, was almost unanimous in condemning its aesthetic implications. Early in 1971 a dispute also developed between the UN and the Israeli Government over the intention, announced in the master plan, to build another housing estate in the neighbourhood of Government House, the headquarters in Jerusalem of the UN. In March 1971 articles in the official Vatican newspaper *L'Osservatore Romano* and in the English Catholic weekly *The Tablet* revealed the strength of Catholic feeling over developments in the Holy City, and these feelings were strengthened when it became known that in the same month Israel had destroyed an Arab village on the hill of Nebi Samwil, north-west of Jerusalem, in preparation for the building on Arab land of yet another housing estate for immigrant Jews.

Israeli opinion was divided over the future of Jerusalem. Only a small minority of Israelis were in favour of relinquishing Israeli sovereignty over the Arab sector of the city, if negotiations for an overall settlement of the Arab-Israeli conflict should ever materialize. In the absence of any sign of such negotiations, the issue remained a hypothetical one and the Israeli Government made no secret of its determination to establish a hold on Jerusalem which would prove unbreakable. A further resolution by the Security Council (No. 298 of 25 September 1971—see Documents on Palestine, p. 87) was rejected by Israel as brusquely as the previous ones, and even the provision in the resolution that the Secretary-General, 'using such instrumentalities as he may choose', should report to the Council within 60 days on the implementation of the resolution, failed to achieve any result since the Secretary-General eventually had to report that he had been unable to execute his mission, for lack of co-operation from the Israeli authorities.

On purely aesthetic grounds, however, many Israelis were disturbed by the physical changes overtaking Jerusalem. Within five years of the June War of 1967 the construction of large housing estates had transformed the appearance of Mount Scopus, where the Old City (and the whole of the Arab sector) was dominated by a row of apartment blocks breaking the historic skyline. There were acute disagreements between the Mayor of Jerusalem and the ministers of housing and of tourism over some of the implications of this building programme, but continuing uncertainty over the prospects for a political settlement with the Arabs gave encouragement to the 'activists' in Israel, and the creation of 'facts' continued, in Jerusalem as in the rest of the Occupied Territories, throughout 1972 and most of 1973.

Anxiety over the future of Jerusalem and resentment at Israel's treatment both of the Arab population and of the physical fabric of the city played a part in provoking the

Arab decision to resort to war in October 1973. In particular, these feelings influenced King Faisal to throw Saudi Arabia's weight behind the attempt to enforce Israel's withdrawal from the Occupied Territories, including Arab Jerusalem. Henceforth, the restoration of Arab sovereignty over the Old City became one of the principal conditions demanded by the Arabs for a comprehensive peace settlement with Israel.

Immediately after the October war political and economic conditions in Israel combined to slow down for a time the work of demolition and construction by which the face of the city is being transformed. In the course of 1974, however, the same general pattern as before was maintained, resulting in the steady eviction from the Old City of Arabs, whose houses were demolished and replaced by dwellings for Jewish immigrants. Between 1967 and 1977, 6,300 Arab residents of Jerusalem were evicted in this way from their homes in the Old City. Protests from the international community, stimulated by anxiety over the continuing exodus from Jerusalem of Christian Arabs, became more frequent but achieved only publicity.

Similar protests over excavations being conducted by the Israeli authorities in the vicinity of Islamic and Christian holy places in the Old City of Jerusalem brought to a head criticisms which had been voiced for more than five years within UNESCO. Recalling that urgent appeals previously addressed to the Israeli Government to suspend these excavations had been ignored, the Executive Board of UNESCO, in June 1974, voted 'to condemn the persistent violation by Israel of the resolutions and decisions adopted by the General Conference and the Executive Board'. In its turn the General Conference of UNESCO, meeting in November 1974, condemned Israel's attitude as 'contradictory to the aims of the Organization as laid down in its Constitution' and resolved to withhold assistance in the fields of education, science and culture until Israel agreed to respect previous conference resolutions in the matter.

The attitude previously expressed by both the Security Council and the General Assembly of the UN was reaffirmed in subsequent years despite the failure to obtain the compliance of the Government of Israel with existing resolutions. In a unanimous 'consensus statement' adopted on 11 November 1976, the Security Council 'strongly deplored' Israel's actions in the Occupied Territories, including Jerusalem; required Israel once more to 'desist forthwith from any action which tends to alter the status of Jerusalem'; and called on Israel to comply with the terms of the Geneva Convention on the Protection of Civilians in Wartime.

Jerusalem once again became a controversial issue in May 1980, when the ultra-nationalist Israeli Knesset (Parliament) member, Mrs Geula Cohen, tabled a bill in the Knesset with the object of confirming Jerusalem as Israel's indivisible capital. Despite strong protests from the Egyptian Government, which made it clear that it would not resume the peace negotiations on Palestinian autonomy (see The Arab-Israeli Confrontation 1967–94, p. 31) unless the bill was rejected, it was placed before a Knesset committee. Egypt was further antagonized when, on 23 June, the Israeli Prime Minister, Mr Begin, announced that he was moving his offices to the Arab sector of Jerusalem.

At a time when the USA was desperately trying to produce some compromise on the Jerusalem issue which would enable Israel and Egypt to resume the negotiations, the Knesset's legal committee voted in favour of giving a first reading of the bill confirming the annexed status of the Arab sector of Jerusalem. As the originator of the bill told *The Times* of London on 30 June: 'This Bill is designed to ensure that there will never be any compromise over the sovereignty of Jerusalem'.

Nevertheless, a debate taking place in the UN Security Council on the same day made it clear that this view would not be accepted by the international community. In a vote of 14 to none, with only the USA abstaining, the Security Council passed a resolution denying Israel the right either to change the status of Jerusalem or to declare the city to be its capital.

The action of the Security Council was followed by an emergency resolution in the UN General Assembly on 29 July 1980, which called upon Israel to withdraw completely and unconditionally from all territories occupied in 1967, including Jerusalem. The resolution (ES-7/2) was passed by 112 votes to 7, with 24 abstentions. The following day Israel enacted its 'basic law' proclaiming Jerusalem as its 'eternal capital'.

The Arab reaction to this law was swift and on 6 August Saudi Arabia and Iraq, the Middle East's two largest oil exporters, announced that they would break off economic and diplomatic relations with any country which recognized Jerusalem as Israel's capital. A fortnight later the Security Council adopted Resolution 478, which declared Israel's enactment of the 'basic law' to be a violation of international law and urged 'those states that have established diplomatic missions in Jerusalem to withdraw such missions from the Holy City'. The resolution was passed by 14 votes to none, with the USA abstaining. In his speech during the debate the US Secretary of State, Edmund Muskie, berated the council for passing a 'series of unbalanced and unrealistic resolutions on Middle East issues'.

Shortly afterwards those Latin American countries with embassies in Jerusalem announced that they would be moving them to Tel-Aviv. They were Venezuela, Uruguay, Chile, Ecuador, El Salvador, Costa Rica, Haiti, Panama, Colombia and Bolivia. The only European country which retained its Ambassador in Jerusalem, the Netherlands, also decided to move to Tel-Aviv.

Jerusalem continued to figure prominently in international efforts to promote an overall settlement of the Arab-Israeli conflict: the European Community's (EC) Venice Declaration of 13 June 1980 (see Documents on Palestine, p. 95) rejected any unilateral actions designed to change the status of the city, and proposals adopted by the Fez Arab summit and a plan put forward by the Soviet President, Leonid Brezhnev, in September 1982 both called for Israeli withdrawal from the eastern sector of the city and its inclusion in a future Palestinian state. The initiative of President Reagan, also announced in September 1982, confined itself to declaring that the city must remain undivided and its final status be negotiable. Every indication remained, however, that Israel was not deterred from its resolve to ensure in advance the city's ultimate status by pursuing an accelerated programme of 'Judaization'. To the south and east of the Old City, plans to complete the encirclement of the Arab population with high-rise, high-density housing complexes proceeded apace with the Neve Yaacov South, Gilo and Ma'aleh Edomin schemes, which, between them, were planned to comprise 26,000 apartments. Over 10,000 dunums of land (1,000 dunums = 1 sq km) were seized for these schemes, virtually all of it expropriated from private Arab owners. In July 1981 the Knesset reaffirmed the designation of the whole of Jerusalem as Israel's 'eternal capital'.

The undiminished sensitivity to the issue of Arabs and the whole Islamic world was demonstrated following an indiscriminate gun attack on worshippers at the Dome of the Rock mosque by an Israeli soldier on 11 April 1982, in which two Arabs were killed and more than 30 wounded. The day of protest called for by the Organization of the Islamic Conference was observed throughout the Islamic world, while a UN Security Council draft resolution condemning the attack and deploring 'any act or encouragement of destruction or penetration of the holy places, religious buildings and sites in Jerusalem' was vetoed by the USA, though otherwise gaining unanimous approval. The threat posed by Jewish religious extremists increased throughout 1983 with the emergence of an underground group calling itself 'Terror against Terror', which claimed responsibility for a series of bomb attacks on Islamic and Christian sites around Jerusalem, which fortunately resulted in few casualties and no deaths. This campaign culminated in January 1984 in an attempt to smuggle explosives into the al-Aqsa mosque, which was foiled at the last moment by security guards. The implications of the plot were particularly horrendous, not just because the attack had been timed to coincide with the congregation of thousands for Friday services on the following day but also because of evidence that the motivation of the group responsible, which was in possession of standard Israeli army-issue weapons, was to advance the reconstruction of the Jewish Temple by ridding the Temple Mount area of its 'encumbrance' of Islamic holy sites.

The twofold physical threat to Jerusalem posed by Israeli settlement and Jewish religious fanaticism was overshadowed by another to the city's legal status, when it became clear that a number of countries, including, most importantly, the USA, were prepared to signal their acceptance of Israel's claim to the city as its sovereign capital by transferring their embassies from Tel-Aviv to Jerusalem. Discussion of such a move on the part of the USA began in Washington in February 1984 and the proposal rapidly gained momentum, winning the sponsorship of over 180 members of the House of Representatives and some 37 senators. The Reagan Administration did not, however, lend its support to the move, and the Secretary of State, George Shultz, wrote to the Senate Foreign Relations Committee, calling the proposed legislation 'damaging to the cause of peace' and contrary to the US position on Jerusalem of refusing 'to recognize unilateral acts by any party'. Such opposition was felt to spring more from fear of the anti-US backlash, which relocating the embassy would provoke throughout the Islamic world, than from respect for successive UN resolutions stating East Jerusalem to be occupied territory, or for the Hague Convention of 1907 and the Geneva Civilians Convention of 1949, which held that purported annexations of territory occupied in war were a violation of international law (as treaties of the USA, both these conventions are parts of 'the Supreme Law of the Land' under Article VI of the US Constitution, and for the US Government to assent to or condone Israel's violation of them would be unconstitutional).

The extreme importance attached to the issue in Arab and Islamic quarters was illustrated again when, on 21 March, El Salvador followed Costa Rica's decision of 1982 to relocate its embassy in Jerusalem, a move which, it had been led to believe, would result in the pro-Israel lobby in Congress helping to clear the way for US military assistance programmes for El Salvador. A meeting of the Organization of the Islamic Conference in Fez in April, which spoke of the obligation to make Jerusalem an international, independent city open to all peoples and faiths, passed a resolution to the effect that member states should sever all diplomatic, economic and cultural relations with any country that moved its embassy to Jerusalem. Egypt made a similar declaration and duly severed diplomatic ties with El Salvador and Costa Rica on 22 April.

The US Administration remained firmly opposed to relocating its embassy in Israel in Jerusalem in the foreseeable future. US officials rejected as 'ridiculous' and potentially dangerous a formal statement issued on 4 April by leaders of the American Jewish Congress asserting that the status of the US Consulate in Jerusalem was 'intolerable' and undermined US interests in the Middle East. For its part, the Israeli Government stood by its claim that Jerusalem was Israel's 'eternal' capital, rejecting outright a call by the Pope on 25 April for an internationally guaranteed status for Jerusalem in the interests of Christianity, Islam and Judaism.

Israeli settlement projects in the city proceeded apace in 1984 and 1985, with many thousands of new apartments being built and occupied within the boundary of annexed East Jerusalem. Just outside the municipal line, in the occupied West Bank, there was also rapid construction of the satellite towns of Efrat, south of Bethlehem, Ma'aleh Edomin to the east, and Givat Zeev to the north, which between them were designed to provide housing for over 50,000 Israelis. The completion of these new towns filled the last remaining gaps in the ring of settlements enclosing East Jerusalem as part of Israel's Metropolitan Plan, which aimed to achieve a Jewish majority of 120,000 over the Arab population in the Greater Jerusalem area by 1986.

The focus of the conflict over Jerusalem soon shifted back to the competing claims of possession of Jews and Muslims within the Old City. The increasing numbers of Jews settling in the Muslim Quarter, which before 1980 had housed no Jews at all, threatened to introduce strife into an area where relations between the two communities had long been exemplary. Cases of Jewish settlers intimidating Arab residents in order to establish proprietorial rights, and of Jewish-occupied buildings being illegally extended, greatly alarmed the Muslim population, who feared that the inroads could be the start of a campaign to expel the Old City's inhabitants. The new settlers, who, by mid-1985, numbered some 200 among the Muslim Quarter's 20,000 Arabs, were nearly all religious-nationalist extremists, openly dedicated to rebuilding the Jewish Temple on the site of the Muslim sanctuary and mosques, the Haram ash-Sharif. Traditionally, the controversy over the Temple Mount issue had been minimized by Jewish religious rulings forbidding Jews even to enter the area, but the encroachment by Jewish zealots on Muslim areas bordering on the shrine was a sign that this precept was now being challenged. In the Old City alone, seven *yeshivas* (Jewish religious colleges) had been set up expressly to study the issue of the Temple and how Jews could, once again, pray there.

In January 1986, members of the Israeli Knesset Interior Committee asked permission to visit the compound of al-Aqsa mosque on the Temple Mount, ostensibly to ensure that restoration work being undertaken by the Islamic authorities was not detrimental to the ancient remains of the Jewish Temple. Although it was known that the Knesset committee was acting at the instigation of Jewish extremists, who had been attempting to establish a foothold in the mosque compound by conducting prayers there, the Islamic Awqaf department, entrusted with safeguarding the shrine, nevertheless gave permission for members of the committee to visit certain unused chambers beneath the al-Aqsa structure known to Jews as Solomon's Stables. On 7 January the Israeli parliamentarians arrived at the site accompanied by television crews and a number of religious and nationalist extremists, including the leader of the 'Temple Mount Faithful', a Jewish group dedicated to rebuilding the Temple in place of the al-Aqsa mosque. Islamic officials decided that the Israeli delegation intended a political demonstration of Jewish claims to the site rather than an inspection of restoration work, and refused it entry, whereupon members of the group, led by Knesset member Geula Cohen, of the extreme right-wing Tehiya Party, tried to force their way through. Calls for help were broadcast from the minarets of the Old City's mosques, and alarmed Muslims rushed to the site. The ensuing riot was controlled only by police escorting the Israeli group away and firing tear gas into the crowd. A week later, despite an inspection of the site in the interim by the leader of the Knesset, Shlomo Hillel, and the Mayor of Jerusalem, Teddy Kollek, who testified that no structural changes had been made, the extremist group returned to the compound and attempted to pray inside it. More Arab rioting followed, which was broken up by police using tear gas.

The al-Aqsa riots were seized upon by Israeli nationalists as a vehicle for publicizing Jewish claims to the site, and there were signs that the Temple Mount was increasingly becoming a nationalist, as well as a religious issue in Israeli politics, in that it was a means of asserting Israeli sovereignty over what was internationally considered to be occupied territory. On 30 January the UN Security Council drafted a resolution strongly condemning Israel's 'provocative acts', which 'violated the sanctity of the sanctuary of the Haram ash-Sharif in Jerusalem' and constituted 'a serious obstruction to achieving a comprehensive, just and lasting peace in the Middle East'. The resolution, otherwise supported by all the Security Council members except Thailand, which abstained, was vetoed by the USA. Although the US Administration maintained its official position that East Jerusalem was occupied territory and that the ultimate status of the city should be determined through negotiation, it was clearly embarrassed by the resolution's reiteration of the UN's rejection of Israeli claims to sovereignty over the entire city. Despite the intense anger and alarm which was generated throughout the Arab and Muslim world by the perceived threat to Islam's third holiest shrine, Israel's Chief Rabbi, Mordechai Eliahu, shortly afterwards proposed the construction of a synagogue next to the mosques on Temple Mount. The proposed synagogue would be 'higher and more elevated' than the mosques of al-Aqsa and the Dome of the Rock, which would remain only 'to commemorate the Destruction' and the day when the Temple would be rebuilt.

There was a marked increase in tension in the Old City in the autumn of 1986, with acts of intimidation against Palestinians by religious zealots, as well as attacks against Israeli security personnel by Palestinians, occurring with greater frequency. The tension climaxed in November after the stabbing of a *yeshiva* student (one of a group of religious nationalists which had resorted to the violent intimidation of neighbouring Palestinian families in an effort to force them to abandon their homes in the Aqabat al-Khaldi quarter). The subsequent backlash from Israeli extremists shocked even Israeli officials. For several days they pursued a campaign of burning and looting Palestinian homes and shops, and assaulting individual Palestinians throughout the Old City. In the days following the violence, vigilante groups were set up to warn and protect the community against the Israeli extremists.

While the level of violence diminished in the early part of 1987, the attitude of the Palestinian population in East Jerusalem continued to harden. Calls for protest action that were formerly heeded elsewhere in the Occupied Territories but only to a very limited extent in Jerusalem, began to win more active support. On Land Day in 1987, almost every shop in East Jerusalem closed in observance of the annual commemorative strike, marking a departure from previous years when few shopkeepers had been prepared to lose a day's takings, and a change in the political climate which prefigured confrontation on an increasing scale.

The sharpened nationalist consciousness of Palestinians in East Jerusalem progressively involved them in an extension of the running conflict between the people of the Occupied Territories and the Israeli authorities, which began in December 1987. Clashes in Jerusalem grew more frequent in 1987, and the Palestinian *intifada* (uprising), although it began in Gaza and spread to the West Bank, took root in Jerusalem as firmly as anywhere else. The city's historical status has made it a centre of Palestinian resistance, particularly for the Unified National Leadership of the Uprising (UNLU), whose organizational work has largely been conducted there. Israeli repression has been a little less in evidence in Jerusalem than elsewhere in the Occupied Territories, but arrests, beatings, deportations, curfews and other measures have all been employed there as well.

The city's central importance to the international community was underlined at the summit meeting of the Arab League in Amman in November 1987. Jerusalem was cited as a 'symbol of peace' and as the 'embodiment of the historic ties between the Muslim and Christian faiths'. This was in a little-noticed passage of the official communiqué at the end of the summit in which King Hussein, rather than the PLO, was mandated to undertake contacts with the Vatican on the Jerusalem issue.

Being an election year in the USA, there were bound to be outpourings on the subject of Jerusalem from presidential candidates during 1988. Calls for the relocation of the US Embassy from Tel-Aviv to Jerusalem were frequently made as a ploy to gain Jewish support. All the candidates for the Democratic Party presidential nomination, with the exception of Jesse Jackson, promised to support such a relocation, if elected. Among the most ardent supporters of this move was Michael Dukakis who, having received the nomination of the Democratic Party in July 1988, was the favourite to succeed Ronald Reagan in the White House. As the November party conventions approached, there was a real fear in the Arab world of the election of a US President who would endorse the relocation of the US Embassy, conferring implicit US recognition of Israel's annexation of East Jerus-

alem. Such recognition had hitherto been withheld even by the Reagan Administration—probably the most overtly pro-Israeli US Government since 1948. By the time George Bush had overtaken his Democratic rival in the polls, however, the danger of such a move had faded.

The peace proposals first put forward by the Israeli Government in April 1989 (see The Arab-Israeli Confrontation 1967–94, p. 51), while incorporating elections in the Occupied Territories, made no mention of the eligibility or otherwise of Palestinians in East Jerusalem to vote or stand as candidates in such elections. This question was repeatedly raised by those seeking to obtain more concessions from Israel in order to make the proposals more acceptable to Palestinians, but Israel's agreeing to allow the participation of residents of East Jerusalem would clearly have contradicted its formal annexation of the city in 1967.

At the 19th session of the Palestine National Council (PNC) in Algiers in November 1988, Jerusalem was named the capital of the newly declared independent state of Palestine, and in July 1989 was recognized as such by more than 60 countries.

Disagreements over the status of East Jerusalem and its residents continued to frustrate the progress of the various peace proposals put forward during 1989. The US Secretary of State James Baker's preference for 'constructive ambiguity'—keeping the peace agenda deliberately vague in order not to snare progress on controversial issues—was sorely tested by the Israeli right's insistence that Palestinians from East Jerusalem be barred from prospective elections for the Occupied Territories. Moreover, after President Mubarak of Egypt had suggested that pre-election talks between an Israeli and a Palestinian delegation should be convened in Cairo, Israel's Prime Minister Shamir stated the opposition of the Likud to the inclusion of East Jerusalemites in the talks. Attempts by James Baker and Israel's Labour Party to coax Shamir into accepting a compromise formula, whereby Palestinians who had East Jerusalem identity papers but who lived in the West Bank would be allowed to participate in the talks, were unsuccessful. Indeed, in what was widely interpreted as a move to emphasize his opposition to such a compromise, Shamir was said to have ordered the arrest in February 1990 of Faisal Husseini, a leading pro-PLO personality and East Jerusalem resident. The charge brought against Husseini—that he had supplied funds for the purchase of uniforms by the Palestine Popular Army—was as transparently ridiculous as his arrest was politically motivated. An international outcry forced Husseini's quick release and at a press conference he subsequently alleged that his arrest had been meant to discredit him in view of his association with the proposed Cairo talks.

There was little doubt that Shamir's refusal to compromise on the issue of East Jerusalem stemmed as much from tactical as from ideological imperatives. Endless debate over the details of Palestinian representation seemed the least damaging way for Israel to stifle the peace process. However, such delaying tactics risked frustrating the USA to such an extent that it would be compelled, against Secretary of State James Baker's wishes, to state its position on East Jerusalem. However, it was not the stalled peace process which finally led the US Administration to reveal its hand, but, rather, the issue of Soviet Jewish emigration to Israel. Angry that 10% of the new Jewish immigrants from the USSR were being settled in East Jerusalem, Bush unequivocally equated East Jerusalem with occupied territory during a telephone conversation with Prime Minister Shamir on 10 February 1990. One week later he commented that US foreign policy was opposed to any new settlements in either the West Bank or East Jerusalem.

While President Bush's comment marked a radical departure from the strong pro-Israeli sentiments of the Reagan Administration, there were few signs that the Senate was about to abandon its traditional support for Israel. In March 1990 the Democrat-dominated chamber voted perfunctorily but overwhelmingly to recognise Jerusalem as the capital of Israel. Interestingly, the leader of the Republican minority in the Senate, Robert Dole, who had originally supported the

Jerusalem resolution, but who was increasingly regarded as a stalking horse for a less slavish US foreign policy towards Israel, admitted that he had 'made a mistake' in voting for the resolution.

In 1989, as in 1988, the Palestinian *intifada* was waged with less ferocity in Jerusalem than in other cities in the West Bank and Gaza. Owing to the city's high profile and its importance to Israel's tourist industry, the Israelis were wary of employing the same kind of lethal force there as they did in Nablus or Gaza. The tactics of the security forces in Jerusalem were noticeably different from those employed elsewhere in the Occupied Territories. Whenever tension was high or a nationalist anniversary approached Israel was prepared to swamp Arab Jerusalem with huge numbers of police and border guards. Nevertheless, clashes between demonstrators and the security forces in and around the city claimed a number of lives during 1989. There were also frequent confrontations between Palestinians living in the eastern suburbs of Jerusalem and Israelis from the settlement of Ma'aleh Edomin. At the end of 1989 Israeli riot police violently dispersed a legal peace rally held by Palestinians, Israelis and Europeans in the eastern half of the city. Many people, including several foreigners, suffered injury.

The influx of Soviet Jews into Israel at the beginning of 1990 was regarded with dismay by Palestinians living in Jerusalem. The settlement of the new immigrants on Jewish housing estates, built on confiscated Arab lands in the eastern half of the city, produced an upsurge in street confrontations during the early part of the year. At Easter a force of 120 Jewish religious nationalists forcibly occupied the St John's Hospice in the Christian quarter of the Old City, claiming they had purchased the building from an Armenian tenant for the sum of US $1.8m., most of which had been supplied by the Israeli Government. The owner of the building, the Greek Orthodox Church, disputed the legality of the purchase and mounted an international campaign to have the 'settlers' removed. Anger among local Palestinian Christians was especially strong, not only because of the provocative timing of the action, but also because it was the first attempt by Israeli right-wingers to settle in the Christian quarter of Jerusalem. Demonstrations outside the Hospice by Greek Orthodox and Muslim clergy quickly developed into violent confrontations. The occupation of the Hospice was also condemned by the Israeli left and Jerusalem's Labour mayor, Teddy Kollek, who reportedly threatened to resign unless the 'settlers' were evicted from the Hospice. While the Israeli courts eventually decided that most of the 'settlers' should leave the Hospice, 20 were given permission to remain until the ownership of the building was conclusively established.

The bloodiest incident yet of the Palestinian *intifada* occurred in Jerusalem on 8 October 1990, when members of the 'Temple Mount Faithful' (see above) made one of their periodic and highly conspicuous attempts to lay the symbolic cornerstone of the Third Temple at the al-Aqsa mosque. Both the Israeli police and the Palestinian population had been forewarned and prepared accordingly. The police refused the members of the 'Temple Mount Faithful' permission to enter the mosque compound, while Palestinians gathered at the site to defend it against the intruders. A full-scale riot rapidly developed. The paramilitary Border Guard opened fire indiscriminately on the crowds inside the compound and on medical staff called to treat casualties. By the time the violence had ceased, 17 Palestinians had been shot dead and many more had been injured. International condemnation, expressed in a unanimous UN Security Council resolution (supported by the USA), followed swiftly. However, a proposal to send a fact-finding mission to Jerusalem was rejected by the Israeli Government as interference in Israel's internal affairs. A commission of inquiry set up by the Israeli Government and chaired by an ex-General and former chief of Mossad known for his right-wing views, predictably absolved the security forces of responsibility for the bloodshed. In the months following the killings there was a spate of 'revenge' stabbings in West Jerusalem that claimed several Israeli lives and led to further anti-Arab violence. Many Palestinians employed in the West Bank

either gave up their jobs or were forced to leave by gangs of right-wing vigilantes. Not since the early days of the occupation had the city appeared so divided.

The defeat of Iraq in the Gulf War in February 1991 by the multinational force led to a renewal of efforts to settle the Arab-Israeli conflict. The Israeli Government showed no signs of willingness to compromise on any of the substantive issues, arguably adopting its most intransigent stance on the issue of Jerusalem. Prime Minister Shamir took the opportunity of Jerusalem Day, the anniversary of the annexation of the city, to tell an audience of Soviet immigrants that 'Jerusalem has never been subject to negotiation. United Jerusalem is the capital of Israel'. This position was forcibly underlined by an ambitious programme of building for settlement in and around East Jerusalem, a policy that continued to exasperate both US President Bush and the US Secretary of State, James Baker. Furthermore, the confiscation of Arab property in the Muslim quarter of the Old City continued.

The dispute over the status of East Jerusalem and its Palestinian inhabitants initially threatened to obstruct the Arab-Israeli peace talks that began in Madrid in October 1991. Israel had made it clear to the USA that it regarded the participation in the talks of Palestinian residents of East Jerusalem as unacceptable because this would represent an implicit challenge to Israel's claim that the city was not occupied territory. Such a condition was unacceptable to the Palestinians, not only because it would have established the principle of an Israeli veto over Palestinian representation, but also because it would have made it even more difficult for the Palestinians to force the issue of Jerusalem onto the agenda. US Secretary of State James Baker assured the Palestinians that the USA did consider East Jerusalem to be occupied territory, but he cautioned that the Palestinians could not afford to be seen to be wrecking the peace talks by their inflexible attitude over representation. Similar warnings came from Egypt and Jordan and resulted in a compromise, supported by the USA and, somewhat reluctantly, by the PLO, whereby the official members of the Palestinian-Jordanian negotiating team would be accompanied by an advisory team composed primarily of East Jerusalem residents. At the Madrid conference and subsequent rounds of bilateral talks in Washington it became clear that the principal function of the advisory body was to co-ordinate negotiation tactics and positions with the PLO. In the course of the talks the meetings between East Jerusalem Palestinians and PLO representatives became more overt and there was pressure from the Israeli establishment to charge the offending Palestinians under anti-terrorism legislation which forbade such contact. But, although Faisal Husseini and Hanan Ashrawi were questioned by the police, US opposition restrained any further action.

The Palestinian delegation tried unsuccessfully to raise the subject of Jerusalem during various rounds of the peace process. James Baker's attitude towards the Arab-Israeli talks was that their continuation depended upon avoiding the more intractable problems until progress had been made in less controversial areas. As progress under the Shamir premiership was agonizingly slow, Jerusalem did not come onto the negotiation agenda.

In 1991 Israel began its most aggressive settlement building programme in the Occupied Territories since 1967. The settlement drive was concentrated in the West Bank and in Gaza, but included considerable building activity in and around Arab Jerusalem. A disturbing development for Palestinians were attempts to extend colonization to parts of the city hitherto regarded as exempt from them. In July 1991 security guards acting for a department of the Ministry of Housing took possession of a house in the Arab suburb of Sheikh Jarrah under orders from the Custodian of Absentee Property. Since the owners lived in the West Bank, the seizure set an ominous precedent by classifying West Bank residents as 'absentees'. On the eve of the Madrid conference, Jewish settlers occupied seven houses in the Silwan district outside the Old City walls, evicting a number of families in the process. Court action forced them to leave six of the houses, but the settlers returned in December, assured by Israel's Attorney General that he found nothing wrong with the settlers' titles to 20 houses in the district. These titles were based on the assertion that the properties had been owned by Jews in the 1930s. The Arab owners gained a temporary injunction for the eviction of some of the settlers, but the settlers appealed against this, guaranteeing a lengthy round of legal battles before ownership could be established. Jerusalem's Labour Mayor, Teddy Kollek, joined Palestinian leaders in condemning the settlers and their sponsors. The Government, he said, was sacrificing calm in the city 'on the altar of ideology'. Controversy over the Silwan incident was heightened by the leaking of a Ministry of Housing blueprint for extensive land expropriation in the Arab suburbs of the city.

The election of a Labour-led Government in Israel in July 1992 brought little hope that Jerusalem would be included on the agenda of the peace process. Although the new Government seemed sure to refrain from the ideological excesses of the Likud when it came to settlement in traditional Arab areas of East Jerusalem, Prime Minister Itzhak Rabin repeated that Israeli sovereignty over the whole of Jerusalem would remain non-negotiable if the peace talks were revived. His promise was borne out by Israel's continued refusal, during the sixth and subsequent rounds of the Middle East peace process, to discuss the issue of Jerusalem in negotiations on the period of interim self-rule for Palestinians in the Occupied Territories. Rabin's position received the unspoken support of the Bush Administration when the latter declared that the USA would not deduct from the $10,000m. in loan guarantees recently released to Israel sums that were spent on financing settlement construction in East Jerusalem. This appeared to be a clear retreat from earlier assurances given to the Palestinian peace delegation on the US position regarding Jerusalem and was fundamental in strengthening Palestinian opposition to the peace process.

The election of Bill Clinton as President of the USA in late 1992 was greeted with some trepidation by the PLO. Both Clinton and his Vice-President, Al Gore, were regarded as committed Zionists. During the presidential campaign Gore had voiced his support for the transfer of the US Embassy to Jerusalem. Although such a step was highly unlikely, given sensitivities surrounding the peace process, Palestinians believed that the new US Administration would be reluctant to pressurize Israel into allowing Jerusalem onto the agenda of the bilateral negotiations. Attempts by Palestinian negotiators to extract from the USA a statement of principle regarding East Jerusalem produced conflicting signals. When US Secretary of State Warren Christopher visited East Jerusalem in the wake of the deportation affair (see The Arab-Israeli Confrontation 1967–94, p. 63) to try to establish grounds for a restart of the peace process, he reassured members of the Palestinian delegation that President Clinton was committed to assurances on Jerusalem made by his predecessor—namely that it was considered to be occupied territory. However, during the ninth and tenth rounds of bilateral talks in Washington in the spring and early summer of 1993, US negotiators supported Israel in its insistence that Jerusalem would not be discussed until final status negotiations took place some years hence. By the summer of 1993 the conflict over Jerusalem at the Washington talks was threatening to make progress on any other issue an impossibility.

Palestinians feared that the Rabin Government was adopting the same approach to negotiations on Jerusalem as the Shamir Government had towards the Occupied Territories as a whole, i.e. avoiding discussion of fundamental issues at the negotiating table while creating 'facts' on the ground. There was increasing evidence to support this view. In March 1993 Rabin sealed off the West Bank and Gaza from Israel proper, including annexed East Jerusalem, following the killing of two young Israelis by a Palestinian in West Jerusalem. As the cultural, political, geographical and economic capital of the Occupied Territories, the isolation of Jerusalem from the West Bank was extremely disruptive to Palestinian populations on both sides of the divide (it was

possible for West Bank and Gaza residents to get permits to visit Jerusalem but these were reportedly very difficult to obtain). Most worrying from the Palestinian point of view were the political implications of the new measure. There was a widespread conviction that the closure heralded an attempt to cantonize the Occupied Territories and bring about the permanent separation of East Jerusalem from the West Bank. In June it was also revealed that, for the first time since 1967, there were more Israelis than Palestinians living in East Jerusalem.

The Declaration of Principles agreed in Oslo and signed by Yasser Arafat and Itzhak Rabin in September 1993 stipulated that issues relating to Jerusalem would be left until final status negotiations took place. Given the polarized positions of Palestinians and Israel on the future of the city, it was hardly surprising that discussion of Jerusalem would not take place during the interim negotiations. Palestinians were far less comfortable with this than their Israeli counterparts. A highly visible and ambitious programme of settlement and road building in and around the occupied east side of the city appeared as irrefutable confirmation that Israel was transforming East Jerusalem into a ghetto cut off from its West Bank hinterland. The rapid physical transformation suggested that by the time Jerusalem came on to the negotiation agenda, the proposed capital of a future Palestinian state would be dwarfed by a ring of Jewish suburbs and a major ring road. The deposition of the long-standing, moderate Labour mayor, Teddy Kollek, in municipal elections in late 1993, and his replacement by the Likud candidate, Ehud Olmert, implied that this process of encirclement would be hastened. Kollek had tried to avoid a Likud victory in the municipal polls by appealing to Palestinians in East Jerusalem to vote. Significantly, however, the city's Arab population observed its customary boycott of Israeli elections: only 6% of Jerusalem's Palestinians exercised their voting rights.

Palestinians attempted to use the political space conferred by the legalization of the PLO to push their own claim to sovereignty over East Jerusalem. Orient House, once home to the Arab Studies centre, became the semi-official headquarters of the PLO in the Occupied Territories and there were moves to establish similar quasi-governmental offices in the city. This largely symbolic attempt to create the 'fact' of a Palestinian 'capital' was viewed with suspicion by the Israeli Government and the new Likud administration in the city. Indeed, public pronouncements by Israeli leaders about Jerusalem continued to be united by the common thread of a refusal to countenance any compromise on Israeli sovereignty. While the Israeli position was clear to the PLO, it was dismayed at what appeared to be a shift in the USA's policy towards Jerusalem. During the 1992 presidential campaign there had been unconfirmed rumours that Bill Clinton and his strongly pro-Zionist running mate, Al Gore, had promised Jewish leaders that they would revise US policy on the status of Jerusalem by excluding reference to Jerusalem as occupied territory — a formulation that the USA had accepted in UN resolutions since 1971. However, during a UN Security Council vote on a resolution (No. 904) condemning the massacre of worshippers in Hebron, the USA abstained on a preambulary clause defining Jerusalem as occupied Palestinian territory and stated that if the definition had been in an operative paragraph they would have voted against it. The US Ambassador to the UN defended this apparent shift in policy by saying that Israel and the Palestinians had agreed, under the Declaration of Principles, to negotiate the city's final status and the Clinton administration did not wish to prejudice the outcome of those negotiations.

The conclusion of the first stage of the Declaration of Principles, with the redeployment of Israeli troops in Gaza and Jericho, once again focused attention on Jerusalem. The PLO Chairman was criticized in Israel when he appealed for a 'jihad' to free Jerusalem. Although Arafat later attempted a clarification by insisting that he meant a peaceful crusade, his comment was acknowledged to be a public relations disaster. Israeli leaders responded to Arafat's gaffe with an offensive of their own. The Jerusalem municipality announced its intention to begin the process of demolishing an estimated 2,000 Arab dwellings in East Jerusalem that had been built without licences. Rabin, meanwhile, instructed his Government's legal experts to explore the possibility of drawing up legislation that would forestall the PLO's plans to develop its institutional base in East Jerusalem. A confidential Cabinet report leaked to the Israeli press in July detailed plans to reinforce Israeli control of Jerusalem during the approach to the 1996 talks on the status of the city. It proposed the adoption of measures to stop the 'illegal' ingress of outsiders — presumably Arabs — to the city and the creation of job opportunities for Arabs outside the city boundaries. The inescapable conclusion was that the Israeli Government was trying to engineer a further change in the demographic balance, not just by settling Jews in the eastern half of the city, but also by trying to exclude its non-Jewish population.

Palestinian despondency over the developing battle for Jerusalem deepened with Israel's agreement, on 25 July, with Jordan to formally end the state of war that had existed between the two countries. One of the articles in the Israeli-Jordanian agreement acknowledged the special role of Jordan as guarding Muslim sites in Jerusalem. Responding to Palestinian objections to the implications of such an agreement, King Hussein stated that 'religious and political sovereignty over the holy city were two separate issues'. Further comments from Jordanian officials, that the motivation for the controversial clause was a desire to save the holy sites from Israeli control before the final status negotiations, failed to allay Palestinian fears that Jordan was being used by Israel to undermine Palestinian claims to sovereignty over East Jerusalem. Although the PLO had until this point declined to challenge Jordan's custodianship of the Muslim holy sites, King Hussein's agreement with Israel revived speculation that the Palestinians would work towards the creation of a Palestinian *waqf* (religious endowment fund) department to replace the existing Jordanian one. A furious Arafat insisted that only Palestinians could decide the fate of East Jerusalem and called a meeting of the Arab League to discuss the Jerusalem clause. There were also reports that King Hassan of Morocco had been asked to mediate between King Hussein and Arafat. Commentaries in the Arab press were generally critical of the Jordanian monarch's agreement with Israel on Jerusalem. Israel, meanwhile, appeared to take particular delight at the disarray. Speaking in Washington, Rabin commented, 'It wouldn't bother me at all if there is a little friction between Jordanians and Palestinians over Jerusalem.'

DOCUMENTS ON PALESTINE

DECLARATION OF FIRST WORLD ZIONIST CONGRESS

*The Congress, convened in Basle by Dr Theodor Herzl in August 1897, adopted the following programme.**

The aim of Zionism is to create for the Jewish people a home in Palestine secured by public law.

The Congress contemplates the following means to the attainment of this end:

1. The promotion on suitable lines, of the settlement of Palestine by Jewish agriculturists, artisans and tradesmen.

2. The organization and binding together of the whole of Jewry by means of appropriate institutions, local and general, in accordance with the laws of each country.

3. The strengthening of Jewish sentiment and national consciousness.

4. Preparatory steps towards obtaining government consent as are necessary, for the attainment of the aim of Zionism.

McMAHON CORRESPONDENCE†

Ten letters passed between Sir Henry McMahon, British High Commissioner in Cairo, and Sherif Husain of Mecca from July 1915 to March 1916. Husain offered Arab help in the war against the Turks if Britain would support the principle of an independent Arab state. The most important letter is that of 24 October 1915, from McMahon to Husain:

... I regret that you should have received from my last letter the impression that I regarded the question of limits and boundaries with coldness and hesitation; such was not the case, but it appeared to me that the time had not yet come when that question could be discussed in a conclusive manner.

I have realized, however, from your last letter that you regard this question as one of vital and urgent importance. I have, therefore, lost no time in informing the Government of Great Britain of the contents of your letter, and it is with great pleasure that I communicate to you on their behalf the following statement, which I am confident you will receive with satisfaction:

The two districts of Mersina and Alexandretta and portions of Syria lying to the west of the districts of Damascus, Homs, Hama and Aleppo cannot be said to be purely Arab, and should be excluded from the limits demanded.

With the above modification, and without prejudice to our existing treaties with Arab chiefs, we accept those limits.

As for those regions lying within those frontiers wherein Great Britain is free to act without detriment to the interest of her ally, France, I am empowered in the name of the Government of Great Britain to give the following assurances and make the following reply to your letter:

(1) Subject to the above modifications, Great Britain is prepared to recognize and support the independence of the Arabs in all the regions within the limits demanded by the Sherif of Mecca.

(2) Great Britain will guarantee the Holy Places against all external aggression and will recognize their inviolability.

(3) When the situation admits, Great Britain will give to the Arabs her advice and will assist them to establish what may appear to be the most suitable forms of government in those various territories.

(4) On the other hand, it is understood that the Arabs have decided to seek the advice and guidance of Great Britain only, and that such European advisers and officials as may be required for the formation of a sound form of administration will be British.

(5) With regard to the *vilayets* of Baghdad and Basra, the Arabs will recognize that the established position and interests of Great Britain necessitate special administrative arrangements in order to secure these territories from foreign aggression, to promote the welfare of the local populations and to safeguard our mutual economic interests.

I am convinced that this declaration will assure you beyond all possible doubt of the sympathy of Great Britain towards the aspirations of her friends the Arabs and will result in a firm and lasting alliance, the immediate results of which will be the expulsion of the Turks from the Arab countries and the freeing of the Arab peoples from the Turkish yoke, which for so many years has pressed heavily upon them. ...

ANGLO-FRANCO-RUSSIAN AGREEMENT (SYKES—PICOT AGREEMENT)

April-May 1916

The allocation of portions of the Ottoman empire by the three powers was decided between them in an exchange of diplomatic notes. The Anglo-French agreement‡ dealing with Arab territories became known to Sherif Husain only after publication by the new Bolshevik government of Russia in 1917:

1. That France and Great Britain are prepared to recognize and protect an independent Arab State or a Confederation of Arab States in the areas (A) and (B) marked on the annexed map, under suzerainty of an Arab Chief. That in area (A) France, and in area (B) Great Britain shall have priority of right of enterprises and local loans. France in area (A) and Great Britain in area (B) shall alone supply foreign advisers or officials on the request of the Arab State or the Confederation of Arab States.

2. France in the Blue area and Great Britain in the Red area shall be at liberty to establish direct or indirect administration or control as they may desire or as they may deem fit to establish after agreement with the Arab State or Confederation of Arab States.

3. In the Brown area there shall be established an international administration of which the form will be decided upon after consultation with Russia, and after subsequent agreement with the other Allies and the representatives of the Sherif of Mecca.

4. That Great Britain be accorded

   (*a*) The ports of Haifa and Acre;

   (*b*) Guarantee of a given supply of water from the Tigris and the Euphrates in area (A) for area (B).

His Majesty's Government, on their part, undertake that they will at no time enter into negotiations for the cession of Cyprus to any third Power without the previous consent of the French Government.

5. Alexandretta shall be a free port as regards the trade of the British Empire and there shall be no discrimination in treatment with regard to port dues or the extension of special privileges affecting British shipping and commerce; there shall be freedom of transit for British goods through Alexandretta and over railways through the Blue area, whether such goods are going to or coming from the Red area, area (A) or area (B); and there shall be no differentiation in treatment, direct or indirect, at the expense of British goods on any railway or of British goods and shipping in any port serving the areas in question.

---

* Text supplied by courtesy of Josef Fraenkel.
† British White Paper, Cmd. 5957, 1939.

‡ E. L. Woodward and Rohan Butler (Eds). *Documents on British Foreign Policy 1919–1939*. First Series, Vol. IV, 1919. London, HMSO, 1952.

Haifa shall be a free port as regards the trade of France, her colonies and protectorates, and there shall be no differentiation in treatment or privilege with regard to port dues against French shipping and commerce. There shall be freedom of transit through Haifa and over British railways through the Brown area, whether such goods are coming from or going to the Blue area, area (A) or area (B), and there shall be no differentiation in treatment, direct or indirect, at the expense of French goods on any railway or of French goods and shipping in any port serving the areas in question.

6. In area (A), the Baghdad Railway shall not be extended southwards beyond Mosul, and in area (B), it shall not be extended northwards beyond Samarra, until a railway connecting Baghdad with Aleppo along the basin of the Euphrates will have been completed, and then only with the concurrence of the two Governments.

7. Great Britain shall have the right to build, administer and be the sole owner of the railway connecting Haifa with area (B). She shall have, in addition, the right in perpetuity and at all times of carrying troops on that line. It is understood by both Governments that this railway is intended to facilitate communication between Baghdad and Haifa, and it is further understood that, in the event of technical difficulties and expenditure incurred in the maintenance of this line in the Brown area rendering the execution of the project impracticable, the French Government will be prepared to consider plans for enabling the line in question to traverse the polygon formed by Banias-Umm Qais-Salkhad-Tall 'Osda-Mismieh before reaching area (B).

Clause 8 referred to customs tariffs.

9. It is understood that the French Government will at no time initiate any negotiations for the cession of their rights and will not cede their prospective rights in the Blue area to any third Power other than the Arab State or Confederation of Arab States, without the previous consent of His Majesty's Government who, on their part, give the French Government a similar undertaking in respect of the Red area.

10. The British and French Governments shall agree to abstain from acquiring and to withhold their consent to a third Power acquiring territorial possessions in the Arabian Peninsula; nor shall they consent to the construction by a third Power of a naval base in the islands on the eastern seaboard of the Red Sea. This, however, will not prevent such rectification of the Aden boundary as might be found necessary in view of the recent Turkish attack.

11. The negotiations with the Arabs concerning the frontiers of the Arab State or Confederation of Arab States shall be pursued through the same channel as heretofore in the name of the two Powers.

12. It is understood, moreover, that measures for controlling the importation of arms into the Arab territory will be considered by the two Governments.

BALFOUR DECLARATION
2 November 1917

Balfour was British Foreign Secretary, Rothschild the British Zionist leader.

Dear Lord Rothschild,

I have much pleasure in conveying to you on behalf of His Majesty's Government the following declaration of sympathy with Jewish Zionist aspirations, which has been submitted to and approved by the Cabinet.

'His Majesty's Government view with favour the establishment in Palestine of a national home for the Jewish people, and will use their best endeavours to facilitate the achievement of this object, it being clearly understood that nothing shall be done which may prejudice the civil and religious rights of existing non-Jewish communities in Palestine, or the rights and political status enjoyed by Jews in any other country.'

I should be grateful if you would bring this declaration to the knowledge of the Zionist Federation.

Yours sincerely,
Arthur James Balfour.

HOGARTH MESSAGE*
4 January 1918

The following is the text of a message which Commander D. G. Hogarth, CMG, RNVR, of the Arab Bureau in Cairo, was instructed on 4 January 1918 to deliver to King Husain of the Hijaz at Jeddah:

1. The *Entente* Powers are determined that the Arab race shall be given full opportunity of once again forming a nation in the world. This can only be achieved by the Arabs themselves uniting, and Great Britain and her Allies will pursue a policy with this ultimate unity in view.

2. So far as Palestine is concerned, we are determined that no people shall be subject to another, but—

(a) In view of the fact that there are in Palestine shrines, Wakfs and Holy places, sacred in some cases to Moslems alone, to Jews alone, to Christians alone, and in others to two or all three, and inasmuch as these places are of interest to vast masses of people outside Palestine and Arabia, there must be a special régime to deal with these places approved of by the world.

(b) As regards the Mosque of Omar, it shall be considered as a Moslem concern alone, and shall not be subjected directly or indirectly to any non-Moslem authority.

3. Since the Jewish opinion of the world is in favour of a return of Jews to Palestine, and inasmuch as this opinion must remain a constant factor, and, further, as His Majesty's Government view with favour the realization of this aspiration, His Majesty's Government are determined that in so far as is compatible with the freedom of the existing population, both economic and political, no obstacle should be put in the way of the realization of this ideal.

In this connection the friendship of world Jewry to the Arab cause is equivalent to support in all States where Jews have political influence. The leaders of the movement are determined to bring about the success of Zionism by friendship and co-operation with the Arabs, and such an offer is not one to be lightly thrown aside.

ANGLO-FRENCH DECLARATION†
7 November 1918

The object aimed at by France and Great Britain in prosecuting in the East the war let loose by the ambition of Germany is the complete and definite emancipation of the peoples so long oppressed by the Turks and the establishment of national Governments and Administrations deriving their authority from the initiative and free choice of the indigenous populations.

In order to carry out these intentions France and Great Britain are at one in encouraging and assisting the establishments of indigenous Governments and Administrations in Syria and Mesopotamia, now liberated by the Allies, and in the territories the liberation of which they are engaged in securing and recognizing these as soon as they are actually established.

Far from wishing to impose on the populations of these regions any particular institutions they are only concerned to ensure by their support and by adequate assistance the regular working of Governments and Administrations freely chosen by the populations themselves. To secure impartial and equal justice for all, to facilitate the economic development of the country by inspiring and encouraging local initiative, to favour the diffusion of education, to put an end to dissensions that have too long been taken advantage of by Turkish policy which the two Allied Governments uphold in the liberated territories.

---

* British White Paper, Cmd. 5964, 1939.

† Report of a Committee set up to consider Certain Correspondence between Sir Henry McMahon and the Sherif of Mecca in 1915 and 1916, 16 March 1939 (British White Paper, Cmd. 5974).

RECOMMENDATIONS OF
THE KING—CRANE COMMISSION‡
28 August 1919

The Commission was set up by President Wilson of the USA to determine which power should receive the Mandate for Palestine. The following are extracts from their recommendations on Syria:

1. We recommend, as most important of all, and in strict harmony with our Instructions, that whatever foreign administration (whether of one or more Powers) is brought into Syria, should come in, not at all as a colonising Power in the old sense of that term, but as a Mandatory under the League of Nations with the clear consciousness that 'the well-being and development' of the Syrian people form for it a 'sacred trust'.

2. We recommend, in the second place, that the unity of Syria be preserved, in accordance with the earnest petition of the great majority of the people of Syria.

3. We recommend, in the third place, that Syria be placed under one mandatory Power, as the natural way to secure real and efficient unity.

4. We recommend, in the fourth place, that Amir Faisal be made the head of the new united Syrian State.

5. We recommend, in the fifth place, serious modification of the extreme Zionist programme for Palestine of unlimited immigration of Jews, looking finally to making Palestine distinctly a Jewish State.

(1) The Commissioners began their study of Zionism with minds predisposed in its favor, but the actual facts in Palestine, coupled with the force of the general principles proclaimed by the Allies and accepted by the Syrians have driven them to the recommendation here made.

(2) The Commission was abundantly supplied with literature on the Zionist program by the Zionist Commission to Palestine; heard in conferences much concerning the Zionist colonies and their claims; and personally saw something of what had been accomplished. They found much to approve in the aspirations and plans of the Zionists, and had warm appreciation for the devotion of many of the colonists, and for their success, by modern methods in overcoming great, natural obstacles.

(3) The Commission recognised also that definite encouragement had been given to the Zionists by the Allies in Mr Balfour's often-quoted statement, in its approval by other representatives of the Allies. If, however, the strict terms of the Balfour Statement are adhered to—favoring 'the establishment in Palestine of a national home for the Jewish people', 'it being clearly understood that nothing shall be done which may prejudice the civil and religious rights of existing non-Jewish communities in Palestine'—it can hardly be doubted that the extreme Zionist program must be greatly modified. For 'a national home for the Jewish people' is not equivalent to making Palestine into a Jewish State; nor can the erection of such a Jewish State be accomplished without the gravest trespass upon the 'civil and religious rights of existing non-Jewish communities in Palestine'. The fact came out repeatedly in the Commission's conference with Jewish representatives, that the Zionists looked forward to a practically complete dispossession of the present non-Jewish inhabitants of Palestine, by various forms of purchase.

In his address of 4 July 1918, President Wilson laid down the following principle as one of the four great 'ends for which the associated peoples of the world were fighting': 'The settlement of every question, whether of territory, of sovereignty, of economic arrangement, or of political relationship upon the basis of the free acceptance of that settlement by the people immediately concerned, and not upon the basis of the material interest or advantage of any other nation or people which may desire a different settlement for the sake of its own exterior influence or mastery.' If that principle is to rule, and so the wishes of Palestine's population are to be

decisive as to what is to be done with Palestine, then it is to be remembered that the non-Jewish population of Palestine—nearly nine-tenths of the whole—are emphatically against the entire Zionist program. The tables show that there was no one thing upon which the population of Palestine were more agreed than upon this. To subject a people so minded to unlimited Jewish immigration, and to steady financial and social pressure to surrender the land, would be a gross violation of the principle just quoted, and of the people's rights, though it kept within the forms of law.

It is to be noted also that the feeling against the Zionist program is not confined to Palestine, but shared very generally by the people throughout Syria, as our conferences clearly showed. More then 72%—1,350 in all—of all the petitions in the whole of Syria were directed against the Zionist program. Only two requests—those for a united Syria and for independence—had a larger support. This general feeling was duly voiced by the General Syrian Congress in the seventh, eighth and tenth resolutions of their statement.

The Peace Conference should not shut its eyes to the fact that the anti-Zionist feeling in Palestine and Syria is intense and not lightly to be flouted. No British officer, consulted by the Commissioners, believed that the Zionist program could be carried out except by force of arms. The officers generally thought that a force of not less than 50,000 soldiers would be required even to initiate the program. That of itself is evidence of a strong sense of the injustice of the Zionist program, on the part of the non-Jewish populations of Palestine and Syria. Decisions requiring armies to carry out are sometimes necessary, but they are surely not gratuitously to be taken in the interests of serious injustice. For the initial claim, often submitted by Zionist representatives, that they have a 'right' to Palestine, based on an occupation of 2,000 years ago, can hardly be seriously considered.

There is a further consideration that cannot justly be ignored, if the world is to look forward to Palestine becoming a definitely Jewish State, however gradually that may take place. That consideration grows out of the fact that Palestine is the Holy Land for Jews, Christians, and Moslems alike. Millions of Christians and Moslems all over the world are quite as much concerned as the Jews with conditions in Palestine, especially with those conditions which touch upon religious feelings and rights. The relations in these matters in Palestine are most delicate and difficult. With the best possible intentions, it may be doubted whether the Jews could possibly seem to either Christians or Moslems proper guardians of the holy places, or custodians of the Holy Land as a whole.

The reason is this: The places which are most sacred to Christians—those having to do with Jesus—and which are also sacred to Moslems, are not only not sacred to Jews, but abhorrent to them. It is simply impossible, under those circumstances, for Moslems and Christians to feel satisfied to have these places in Jewish hands, or under the custody of Jews. There are still other places about which Moslems must have the same feeling. In fact, from this point of view, the Moslems, just because the sacred places of all three religions are sacred to them, have made very naturally much more satisfactory custodians of the holy places than the Jews could be. It must be believed that the precise meaning in this respect of the complete Jewish occupation of Palestine has not been fully sensed by those who urge the extreme Zionist program. For it would intensify, with a certainty like fate, the anti-Jewish feeling both in Palestine and in all other portions of the world which look to Palestine as the Holy Land.

In view of all these considerations, and with a deep sense of sympathy for the Jewish cause, the Commissioners feel bound to recommend that only a greatly reduced Zionist program be attempted by the Peace Conference, and even that, only very gradually initiated. This would have to mean that Jewish immigration should be definitely limited, and that the project for making Palestine distinctly a Jewish commonwealth should be given up.

There would then be no reason why Palestine could not be included in a united Syrian State, just as other portions of the country, the holy places being cared for by an international and inter-religious commission, somewhat as at present, under the oversight and approval of the Mandatory and of the

---

‡ US Department of State. *Papers Relating to the Foreign Relations of the United States. The Paris Peace Conference 1919.* Vol. XII. Washington, 1947.

League of Nations. The Jews, of course, would have representation upon this commission.

ARTICLE 22 OF THE
COVENANT OF THE LEAGUE OF NATIONS

1. To those colonies and territories which as a consequence of the late War have ceased to be under the sovereignty of the States which formerly governed them and which are inhabited by peoples not yet able to stand by themselves under the strenuous conditions of the modern world, there should be applied the principle that the well-being and development of such peoples form a sacred trust of civilization and that securities for the performance of this trust should be embodied in this Covenant.

2. The best method of giving practical effect to this principle is that the tutelage of such peoples should be entrusted to advanced nations who by reason of their resources, their experience or their geographical position can best undertake this responsibility, and who are willing to accept it, and that this tutelage should be exercised by them as Mandatories on behalf of the League.

3. The character of the Mandate must differ according to the stage of the development of the people, the geographical situation of the territory, its economic conditions and other similar circumstances.

4. Certain communities formerly belonging to the Turkish Empire have reached a stage of development where their existence as independent nations can be provisionally recognized subject to the rendering of administrative advice and assistance by a Mandatory until such time as they are able to stand alone. The wishes of these communities must be a principal consideration in the selection of the Mandatory.

7. In every case of Mandate, the Mandatory shall render to the Council an annual report in reference to the territory committed to its charge.

8. The degree of authority, control, or administration to be exercised by the Mandatory shall, if not previously agreed upon by the Members of the League, be explicitly defined in each case by the Council.

9. A permanent Commission shall be constituted to receive and examine the annual reports of the Mandatories and to advise the Council on all matters relating to the observance of the Mandates.

MANDATE FOR PALESTINE*
24 July 1922

The Council of the League of Nations:

Whereas the Principal Allied Powers have agreed, for the purpose of giving effect to the provisions of Article 22 of the Covenant of the League of Nations to entrust to a Mandatory selected by the said Powers the administration of the territory of Palestine, which formerly belonged to the Turkish Empire, within such boundaries as may be fixed by them; and

Whereas the Principal Allied Powers have also agreed that the Mandatory should be responsible for putting into effect the declaration originally made on 2 November 1917 by the Government of His Britannic Majesty, and adopted by the said Powers, in favour of the establishment in Palestine of a National Home for the Jewish people, it being clearly understood that nothing should be done which might prejudice the civil and religious rights of existing non-Jewish communities in Palestine, or the rights and political status enjoyed by Jews in any other country; and

Whereas recognition has thereby been given to the historical connection of the Jewish people with Palestine and to the grounds for reconstituting their National Home in that country; and

Whereas the Principal Allied Powers have selected His Britannic Majesty as the Mandatory for Palestine; and

Whereas the Mandate in respect of Palestine has been formulated in the following terms and submitted to the Council of the League for approval; and

---

* British White Paper, Cmd. 1785.

Whereas His Britannic Majesty has accepted the Mandate in respect of Palestine and undertaken to exercise it on behalf of the League of Nations in conformity with the following provisions; and

Whereas by the afore-mentioned Article 22 (paragraph 8), it is provided that the degree of authority, control or administration to be exercised by the Mandatory, not having been previously agreed upon by the Members of the League, shall be explicitly defined by the Council of the League of Nations;

Confirming the said Mandate, defines its terms as follows:

ARTICLE 1. The Mandatory shall have full powers of legislation and of administration, save as they may be limited by the terms of this Mandate.

ARTICLE 2. The Mandatory shall be responsible for placing the country under such political, administrative and economic conditions as will secure the establishment of the Jewish National Home, as laid down in the preamble, and the development of self-governing institutions, and also for safeguarding the civil and religious rights of all the inhabitants of Palestine, irrespective of race and religion.

ARTICLE 3. The Mandatory shall, so far as circumstances permit, encourage local autonomy.

ARTICLE 4. An appropriate Jewish Agency shall be recognized as a public body for the purpose of advising and co-operating with the Administration of Palestine in such economic, social and other matters as may affect the establishment of the Jewish National Home and the interests of the Jewish population in Palestine, and, subject always to the control of the Administration, to assist and take part in the development of the country.

The Zionist organization, so long as its organization and constitution are in the opinion of the Mandatory appropriate, shall be recognized as such agency. It shall take steps in consultation with His Britannic Majesty's Government to secure the co-operation of all Jews who are willing to assist in the establishment of the Jewish National Home.

ARTICLE 5. The Mandatory shall be responsible for seeing that no Palestine territory shall be ceded or leased to, or in any way placed under the control of, the Government of any foreign Power.

ARTICLE 6. The Administration of Palestine, while ensuring that the rights and position of other sections of the population are not prejudiced, shall facilitate Jewish immigration under suitable conditions and shall encourage, in co-operation with the Jewish Agency referred to in Article 4, close settlement by Jews on the land, including State lands and waste lands not required for public purposes.

ARTICLE 7. The Administration of Palestine shall be responsible for enacting a nationality law. There shall be included in this law provisions framed so as to facilitate the acquisition of Palestinian citizenship by Jews who take up their permanent residence in Palestine.

ARTICLE 13. All responsibility in connection with the Holy Places and religious buildings or sites in Palestine, including that of preserving existing rights and of securing free access to the Holy Places, religious buildings and sites and the free exercise of worship, while ensuring the requirements of public order and decorum, is assumed by the Mandatory, who shall be responsible solely to the League of Nations in all matters connected herewith, provided that nothing in this Article shall prevent the Mandatory from entering into such arrangements as he may deem reasonable with the Administration for the purpose of carrying the provisions of this Article into effect; and provided also that nothing in this Mandate shall be construed as conferring upon the Mandatory authority to interfere with the fabric of the management of purely Moslem sacred shrines, the immunities of which are guaranteed.

ARTICLE 14. A special Commission shall be appointed by the Mandatory to study, define and determine the rights and claims in connection with the Holy Places and the rights and claims relating to the different religious communities in Palestine. The method of nomination, the composition and the functions of this Commission shall be submitted to the Council of the League for its approval, and the Commission shall not be appointed or enter upon its functions without the approval of the Council.

ARTICLE 28. In the event of the termination of the Mandate hereby conferred upon the Mandatory, the Council of the League of Nations shall make such arrangements as may be deemed necessary for safe-guarding in perpetuity, under guarantee of the League, the rights secured by Articles 13 and 14, and shall use its influence for securing, under the guarantee of the League, that the Government of Palestine will fully honour the financial obligations legitimately incurred by the Administration of Palestine during the period of the Mandate, including the rights of public servants to pensions or gratuities.

CHURCHILL MEMORANDUM*
3 June 1922

The Secretary of State for the Colonies has given renewed consideration to the existing political situation in Palestine, with a very earnest desire to arrive at a settlement of the outstanding questions which have given rise to uncertainty and unrest among certain sections of the population. After consultation with the High Commissioner for Palestine the following statement has been drawn up. It summarizes the essential parts of the correspondence that has already taken place between the Secretary of State and a Delegation from the Moslem Christian Society of Palestine, which has been for some time in England, and it states the further conclusions which have since been reached.

The tension which has prevailed from time to time in Palestine is mainly due to apprehensions, which are entertained both by sections of the Arab and by sections of the Jewish population. These apprehensions, so far as the Arabs are concerned, are partly based upon exaggerated interpretations of the meaning of the Declaration favouring the establishment of a Jewish National Home in Palestine, made on behalf of His Majesty's Government on 2 November 1917. Unauthorized statements have been made to the effect that the purpose in view is to create a wholly Jewish Palestine. Phrases have been used such as that Palestine is to become 'as Jewish as England is English.' His Majesty's Government regard any such expectation as impracticable and have no such aim in view. Nor have they at any time contemplated, as appears to be feared by the Arab Delegation, the disappearance or the subordination of the Arabic population, language or culture in Palestine. They would draw attention to the fact that the terms of the Declaration referred to do not contemplate that Palestine as a whole should be converted into a Jewish National Home, but that such a Home should be founded *in Palestine*. In this connection it has been observed with satisfaction that at the meeting of the Zionist Congress, the supreme governing body of the Zionist Organization, held at Carlsbad in September 1921, a resolution was passed expressing as the official statement of Zionist aims 'the determination of the Jewish people to live with the Arab people on terms of unity and mutual respect, and together with them to make the common home into a flourishing community, the upbuilding of which may assure to each of its peoples an undisturbed national development.'

It is also necessary to point out that the Zionist Commission in Palestine, now termed the Palestine Zionist Executive, has not desired to possess, and does not possess, any share in the general administration of the country. Nor does the special position assigned to the Zionist Organization in Article IV of the Draft Mandate for Palestine imply any such functions. That special position relates to the measures to be taken in Palestine affecting the Jewish population, and contemplates that the Organization may assist in the general development of the country, but does not entitle it to share in any degree in its Government.

Further, it is contemplated that the status of all citizens of Palestine in the eyes of the law shall be Palestinian, and it has never been intended that they, or any section of them, should possess any other juridical status.

So far as the Jewish population of Palestine are concerned, it appears that some among them are apprehensive that His Majesty's Government may depart from the policy embodied in the Declaration of 1917. It is necessary, therefore, once more to affirm that these fears are unfounded, and that the Declaration, re-affirmed by the Conference of the Principal Allied Powers at San Remo and again in the Treaty of Sèvres, is not susceptible of change.

During the last two or three generations the Jews have recreated in Palestine a community, now numbering 80,000, of whom about one-fourth are farmers or workers upon the land. This community has its own political organs; an elected assembly for the direction of its domestic concerns; elected councils in the towns; and an organization for the control of its schools. It has its elected Chief Rabbinate and Rabbinical Council for the direction of its religious affairs. Its business is conducted in Hebrew as a vernacular language, and a Hebrew Press serves its needs. It has its distinctive intellectual life and displays considerable economic activity. This community, then, with its town and country population, its political, religious and social organizations, its own language, its own customs, its own life, has in fact 'national' characteristics. When it is asked what is meant by the development of the Jewish National Home in Palestine, it may be answered that it is not the imposition of a Jewish nationality upon the inhabitants of Palestine as a whole, but the further development of the existing Jewish community, with the assistance of Jews in other parts of the world, in order that it may become a centre in which the Jewish people as a whole may take, on grounds of religion and race, an interest and a pride. But in order that this community should have the best prospect of free development and provide a full opportunity for the Jewish people to display its capacities, it is essential that it should know that it is in Palestine as of right and not on sufferance. That is the reason why it is necessary that the existence of a Jewish National Home in Palestine should be internationally guaranteed, and that it should be formally recognized to rest upon ancient historic connection.

This, then, is the interpretation which His Majesty's Government place upon Declaration of 1917, and, so understood, the Secretary of State is of opinion that it does not contain or imply anything which need cause either alarm to the Arab population of Palestine or disappointment to the Jews.

For the fulfilment of this policy it is necessary that the Jewish community in Palestine should be able to increase its numbers by immigration. This immigration cannot be so great in volume as to exceed whatever may be the economic capacity of the country at the time to absorb new arrivals. It is essential to ensure that the immigrants should not be a burden upon the people of Palestine as a whole, and that they should not deprive any section of the present population of their employment. Hitherto the immigration has fulfilled these conditions. The number of immigrants since the British occupation has been about 25,000. . . .

REPORT OF PALESTINE ROYAL COMMISSION PEEL COMMISSION*
July 1937

The Commission under Lord Peel was appointed in 1936. The following are extracts from recommendations made in Ch. XXII:

Having reached the conclusion that there is no possibility of solving the Palestine problem under the existing Mandate (or even under a scheme of cantonization), the Commission recommend the termination of the present Mandate on the basis of Partition and put forward a definite scheme which they consider to be practicable, honourable and just. The scheme is as follows:

The Mandate for Palestine should terminate and be replaced by a Treaty System in accordance with the precedent set in Iraq and Syria.

Under Treaties to be negotiated by the Mandatory with the Government of Transjordan and representatives of the Arabs

---

* Palestine, Correspondence with the Palestine Arab Delegation and the Zionist Organization (British White Paper, Cmd. 1700), pp. 17–21.

* *Palestine Royal Commission: Report*, 1937 (British Blue Book, Cmd. 5479).

of Palestine on the one hand, and with the Zionist Organization on the other, it would be declared that two sovereign independent States would shortly be established—(1) an Arab State consisting of Transjordan united with that part of Palestine allotted to the Arabs, (2) a Jewish State consisting of that part of Palestine allotted to the Jews. The Mandatory would undertake to support any requests for admission to the League of Nations made by the Governments of the Arab and Jewish States. The Treaties would include strict guarantees for the protection of minorities. Military Conventions would be attached to the Treaties.

A new Mandate should be instituted to execute the trust of maintaining the sanctity of Jerusalem and Bethlehem and ensuring free and safe access to them for all the world. An enclave should be demarcated to which this Mandate should apply, extending from a point north of Jerusalem to a point south of Bethlehem, and access to the sea should be provided by a corridor extending from Jerusalem to Jaffa. The policy of the Balfour Declaration would not apply to the Mandated Area.

The Jewish State should pay a subvention to the Arab State. A Finance Commission should be appointed to advise as to its amount and as to the division of the public debt of Palestine and other financial questions.

In view of the backwardness of Transjordan, Parliament should be asked to make a grant of £2,000,000 to the Arab State.

WHITE PAPER†
May 1939

The main recommendations are extracted below:

10. . . . His Majesty's Government make the following declaration of their intentions regarding the future government of Palestine:

(i) The objective of His Majesty's Government is the establishment within ten years of an independent Palestine State in such treaty relations with the United Kingdom as will provide satisfactorily for the commercial and strategic requirements of both countries in the future. This proposal for the establishment of the independent State would involve consultation with the Council of the League of Nations with a view to the termination of the Mandate.

(ii) The independent State should be one in which Arabs and Jews share in government in such a way as to ensure that the essential interests of each community are safeguarded.

(iii) The establishment of the independent State will be preceded by a transitional period throughout which His Majesty's Government will retain responsibility for the government of the country. During the transitional period the people of Palestine will be given an increasing part in the government of their country. Both sections of the population will have an opportunity to participate in the machinery of government, and the process will be carried on whether or not they both avail themselves of it.

(iv) As soon as peace and order have been sufficiently restored in Palestine steps will be taken to carry out this policy of giving the people of Palestine an increasing part in the government of their country, the objective being to place Palestinians in charge of all the Departments of Government, with the assistance of British advisers and subject to the control of the High Commissioner. With this object in view His Majesty's Government will be prepared immediately to arrange that Palestinians shall be placed in charge of certain Departments, with British advisers. The Palestinian heads of Departments will sit on the Executive Council, which advises the High Commissioner. Arab and Jewish representatives will be invited to serve as heads of Departments approximately in proportion to their respective populations. The number of Palestinians in charge of Departments will be increased as circumstances permit until all heads of Departments are Palestinians, exercising the administrative and advisory functions which

are at present performed by British officials. When that stage is reached consideration will be given to the question of converting the Executive Council into a Council of Ministers with a consequential change in the status and functions of the Palestinian heads of Departments.

(v) His Majesty's Government make no proposals at this stage regarding the establishment of an elective legislature. Nevertheless they would regard this as an appropriate constitutional development, and, should public opinion in Palestine hereafter show itself in favour of such a development, they will be prepared, provided that local conditions permit, to establish the necessary machinery.

(vi) At the end of five years from the restoration of peace and order, an appropriate body representative of the people of Palestine and of His Majesty's Government will be set up to review the working of the constitutional arrangements during the transitional period and to consider and make recommendations regarding the Constitution of the independent Palestine State.

(vii) His Majesty's Government will require to be satisfied that in the treaty contemplated by sub-paragraph (i) or in the Constitution contemplated by sub-paragraph (vi) adequate provision has been made for:

(a) the security of, and freedom of access to, the Holy Places, and the protection of the interests and property of the various religious bodies;

(b) the protection of the different communities in Palestine in accordance with the obligations of His Majesty's Government to both Arabs and Jews and for the special position in Palestine of the Jewish National Home;

(c) such requirements to meet the strategic situation as may be regarded as necessary by His Majesty's Government in the light of the circumstances then existing.

His Majesty's Government will also require to be satisfied that the interests of certain foreign countries in Palestine, for the preservation of which they are present responsible, are adequately safeguarded.

(viii) His Majesty's Government will do everything in their power to create conditions which will enable the independent Palestine State to come into being within ten years. If, at the end of ten years, it appears to His Majesty's Government that, contrary to their hope, circumstances require the postponement of the establishment of the independent State, they will consult with representatives of the people of Palestine, the Council of the League of Nations and the neighbouring Arab States before deciding on such a postponement. If His Majesty's Government come to the conclusion that postponement is unavoidable, they will invite the co-operation of these parties in framing plans for the future with a view to achieving the desired objective at the earliest possible date.

14. . . . they believe that they will be acting consistently with their Mandatory obligations to both Arabs and Jews, and in the manner best calculated to serve the interests of the whole people of Palestine by adopting the following proposals regarding immigration:

(i) Jewish immigration during the next five years will be at a rate which, if economic absorptive capacity permits, will bring the Jewish population up to approximately one-third of the total population of the country. Taking into account the expected natural increase of the Arab and Jewish populations, and the number of illegal Jewish immigrants now in the country, this would allow of the admission, as from the beginning of April this year, of some 75,000 immigrants over the next five years. These immigrants would, subject to the criterion of economic absorptive capacity, be admitted as follows:

(a) For each of the next five years a quota of 10,000 Jewish immigrants will be allowed, on the understanding that a shortage in any one year may be added to the quotas for subsequent years, within the five-year period, if economic absorptive capacity permits.

† British White Paper, Cmd. 6019.

(*b*) In addition, as a contribution towards the solution of the Jewish refugee problem, 25,000 refugees will be admitted as soon as the High Commissioner is satisfied that adequate provision for their maintenance is ensured, special consideration being given to refugee children and dependants.

(ii) The existing machinery for ascertaining economic absorptive capacity will be retained, and the High Commissioner will have the ultimate responsibility for deciding the limits of economic capacity. Before each periodic decision is taken, Jewish and Arab representatives will be consulted.

(iii) After the period of five years no further Jewish immigration will be permitted unless the Arabs of Palestine are prepared to acquiesce in it.

(iv) His Majesty's Government are determined to check illegal immigration, and further preventive measures are being adopted. The numbers of any Jewish illegal immigrants who, despite these measures, may succeed in coming into the country and cannot be deported will be deducted from the yearly quotas.

15. His Majesty's Government are satisfied that, when the immigration over five years which is now contemplated has taken place they will not be justified in facilitating, nor will they be under any obligation to facilitate, the further development of the Jewish National Home by immigration regardless of the wishes of the Arab population.

16. The Administration of Palestine is required, under Article 6 of the Mandate, 'while ensuring that the rights and position of other sections of the population are not prejudiced,' to encourage 'close settlement by Jews on the land,' and no restriction has been imposed hitherto on the transfer of land from Arabs to Jews. The Reports of several expert Commissions have indicated that, owing to the natural growth of the Arab population and the steady sale in recent years of Arab land to Jews, there is now in certain areas no room for further transfers of Arab land, whilst in some other areas such transfers of land must be restricted if Arab cultivators are to maintain their existing standard of life and a considerable landless Arab population is not soon to be created. In these circumstances, the High Commissioner will be given general powers to prohibit and regulate transfers of land. These powers will date from the publication of this statement of Policy and the High Commissioner will retain them throughout the transitional period.

17. The policy of the Government will be directed towards the development of the land and the improvement, where possible, of methods of cultivation. In the light of such development it will be open to the High Commissioner, should he be satisfied that the 'rights and position' of the Arab population will be duly preserved, to review and modify any orders passed relating to the prohibition or restriction of the transfer of land.

BILTMORE PROGRAMME*
11 May 1942

The following programme was approved by a Zionist Conference held in the Biltmore Hotel, New York City:

1. American Zionists assembled in this Extraordinary Conference reaffirm their unequivocal devotion to the cause of democratic freedom and international justice to which the people of the United States, allied with the other United Nations, have dedicated themselves, and give expression to their faith in the ultimate victory of humanity and justice over lawlessness and brute force.

2. This Conference offers a message of hope and encouragement to their fellow Jews in the Ghettos and concentration camps of Hitler-dominated Europe and prays that their hour of liberation may not be far distant.

3. The Conference sends its warmest greetings to the Jewish Agency Executive in Jerusalem, to the Va'ad Leumi, and to the whole Yishuv in Palestine, and expresses its profound

---

* Text supplied by courtesy of Josef Fraenkel.

admiration for their steadfastness and achievements in the face of peril and great difficulties. . . .

4. In our generation, and in particular in the course of the past twenty years, the Jewish people have awakened and transformed their ancient homeland; from 50,000 at the end of the last war their numbers have increased to more than 500,000. They have made the waste places to bear fruit and the desert to blossom. Their pioneering achievements in agriculture and in industry, embodying new patterns of co-operative endeavour, have written a notable page in the history of colonization.

5. In the new values thus created, their Arab neighbours in Palestine have shared. The Jewish people in its own work of national redemption welcomes the economic, agricultural and national development of the Arab peoples and states. The Conference reaffirms the stand previously adopted at Congresses of the World Zionist Organization, expressing the readiness and the desire of the Jewish people for full co-operation with their Arab neighbours.

6. The Conference calls for the fulfilment of the original purpose of the Balfour Declaration and the Mandate which '*recognizing the historical connexion of the Jewish people with Palestine*' was to afford them the opportunity, as stated by President Wilson, to found there a Jewish Commonwealth.

The Conference affirms its unalterable rejection of the White Paper of May 1939 and denies its moral or legal validity. The White Paper seeks to limit, and in fact to nullify Jewish rights to immigration and settlement in Palestine, and, as stated by Mr Winston Churchill in the House of Commons in May 1939, constitutes 'a breach and repudiation of the Balfour Declaration'. The policy of the White Paper is cruel and indefensible in its denial of sanctuary to Jews fleeing from Nazi persecution; and at a time when Palestine has become a focal point in the war front of the United Nations, and Palestine Jewry must provide all available manpower for farm and factory and camp, it is in direct conflict with the interests of the allied war effort.

7. In the struggle against the forces of aggression and tyranny, of which Jews were the earliest victims, and which now menace the Jewish National Home, recognition must be given to the right of the Jews of Palestine to play their full part in the war effort and in the defence of their country, through a Jewish military force fighting under its own flag and under the high command of the United Nations.

8. The Conference declares that the new world order that will follow victory cannot be established on foundations of peace, justice and equality, unless the problem of Jewish homelessness is finally solved.

The Conference urges that the gates of Palestine be opened; that the Jewish Agency be vested with control of immigration into Palestine and with the necessary authority for upbuilding the country, including the development of its unoccupied and uncultivated lands; and that Palestine be established as a Jewish Commonwealth integrated in the structure of the new democratic world.

Then and only then will the age old wrong to the Jewish people be righted.

UN GENERAL ASSEMBLY RESOLUTION ON THE FUTURE GOVERNMENT OF PALESTINE (PARTITION RESOLUTION)
29 November 1947

The General Assembly,

Having met in special session at the request of the mandatory Power to constitute and instruct a special committee to prepare for the consideration of the question of the future government of Palestine at the second regular session;

Having constituted a Special Committee and instructed it to investigate all questions and issues relevant to the problem of Palestine, and to prepare proposals for the solution of the problem, and

Having received and examined the report of the Special Committee (document A/364) including a number of unanimous recommendations and a plan of partition with economic union approved by the majority of the Special Committee,

Considers that the present situation in Palestine is one which is likely to impair the general welfare and friendly relations among nations;

Takes note of the declaration by the mandatory Power that it plans to complete its evacuation of Palestine by 1 August 1948;

Recommends to the United Kingdom, as the mandatory Power for Palestine, and to all other Members of the United Nations the adoption and implementation, with regard to the future government of Palestine, of the Plan of Partition with Economic Union set out below;

Requests that

(a) The Security Council take the necessary measures as provided for in the plan for its implementation;

(b) The Security Council consider, if circumstances during the transitional period require such consideration, whether the situation in Palestine constitutes a threat to the peace. If it decides that such a threat exists, and in order to maintain international peace and security, the Security Council should supplement the authorization of the General Assembly by taking measures, under Articles 39 and 41 of the Charter, to empower the United Nations Commission, as provided in this resolution, to exercise in Palestine the functions which are assigned to it by this resolution;

(c) The Security Council determine as a threat to the peace, breach of the peace or act of aggression, in accordance with Article 39 of the Charter, any attempt to alter by force the settlement envisaged by this resolution;

(d) The Trusteeship Council be informed of the responsibilities envisaged for it in this plan;

Calls upon the inhabitants of Palestine to take such steps as may be necessary on their part to put this plan into effect;

Appeals to all Governments and all peoples to refrain from taking any action which might hamper or delay the carrying out of these recommendations . . .

Official Records of the second session of the General Assembly, Resolutions, p. 131.

UN GENERAL ASSEMBLY RESOLUTION
194 (III)
11 December 1948

The resolution's terms have been reaffirmed every year since 1948.

11. . . . the refugees wishing to return to their homes and live at peace with their neighbours should be permitted to do so at the earliest practicable date, and that compensation should be paid for the property of those choosing not to return and for the loss of or damage to property which, under principles of international law or in equity, should be made good by the Governments or authorities responsible;

Official Records of the third session of the General Assembly, Part I, Resolutions, p. 21.

UN GENERAL ASSEMBLY RESOLUTION ON THE
INTERNATIONALIZATION OF JERUSALEM
9 December 1949

The General Assembly,

Having regard to its resolution 181 (II) of 29 November 1947 and 194 (III) of 11 December 1948,

Having studied the reports of the United Nations Conciliation Commission for Palestine set up under the latter resolution,

I. *Decides*

In relation to Jerusalem,

Believing that the principles underlying its previous resolutions concerning this matter, and in particular its resolution of 29 November 1947, represent a just and equitable settlement of the question,

1. To restate, therefore, its intention that Jerusalem should be placed under a permanent international regime, which should envisage appropriate guarantees for the protection of the Holy Places, both within and outside Jerusalem, and to

confirm specifically the following provisions of General Assembly resolution 181 (II): (1) The City of Jerusalem shall be established as a *corpus separatum* under a special international regime and shall be administered by the United Nations; (2) The Trusteeship Council shall be designated to discharge the responsibilities of the Administering Authority . . .; and (3) The City of Jerusalem shall include the present municipality of Jerusalem plus the surrounding villages and towns, the most eastern of which shall be Abu Dis; the most southern, Bethlehem; the most western, Ein Karim (including also the built-up area of Motsa); and the most northern, Shu'fat, as indicated on the attached sketchmap; . . . [*map not reproduced: Ed.*]

Official Records of the fourth session of the General Assembly, Resolutions, p. 25.

TEXT OF UN SECURITY COUNCIL
RESOLUTION 242
22 November 1967

The Security Council,

Expressing its continued concern with the grave situation in the Middle East,

Emphasizing the inadmissibility of the acquisition of territory by war and the need to work for a just and lasting peace in which every state in the area can live in security,

Emphasizing further that all Member States in their acceptance of the Charter of the United Nations have undertaken a commitment to act in accordance with Article 2 of the Charter

1. *Affirms* that the fulfilment of Charter principles requires the establishment of a just and lasting peace in the Middle East which should include the application of both the following principles:

(i) Withdrawal of Israel armed forces from territories occupied in the recent conflict;

(ii) Termination of all claims or states of belligerency and respect for the acknowledgement of the sovereignty, territorial integrity and political independence of every State in the area and their right to live in peace within secure and recognized boundaries free from threats or acts of force.

2. *Affirms further* the necessity

(a) For guaranteeing freedom of navigation through international waterways in the area;

(b) For achieving a just settlement of the refugee problem;

(c) For guaranteeing the territorial inviolability and political independence of every State in the area, through measures including the establishment of demilitarized zones;

3. *Requests* the Secretary-General to designate a Special Representative to proceed to the Middle East to establish and maintain contacts with the States concerned in order to promote agreement and assist efforts to achieve a peaceful and accepted settlement in accordance with the provisions and principles in this resolution;

4. *Requests* the Secretary-General to report to the Security Council on the progress of the efforts of the Special Representative as soon as possible.

Source: UN Document S/RES/242 (1967).

UN SECURITY COUNCIL RESOLUTION ON JERUSALEM
25 September 1971

The resolution, No. 298 (1971), was passed nem. con., *with the abstention of Syria.*

The Security Council,

Recalling its resolutions 252 (1968) of 21 May 1968, and 267 (1969) of 3 July 1969, and the earlier General Assembly resolution 2253 (ES-V) and 2254 (ES-V) of 4 and 14 July 1967, concerning measures and actions by Israel designed to change the status of the Israeli-occupied section of Jerusalem,

Having considered the letter of the Permanent Representative of Jordan on this situation in Jerusalem and the reports of the Secretary-General, and having heard the statements of the parties concerned in the question,

Recalling the principle that acquisition of territory by military conquest is inadmissible,

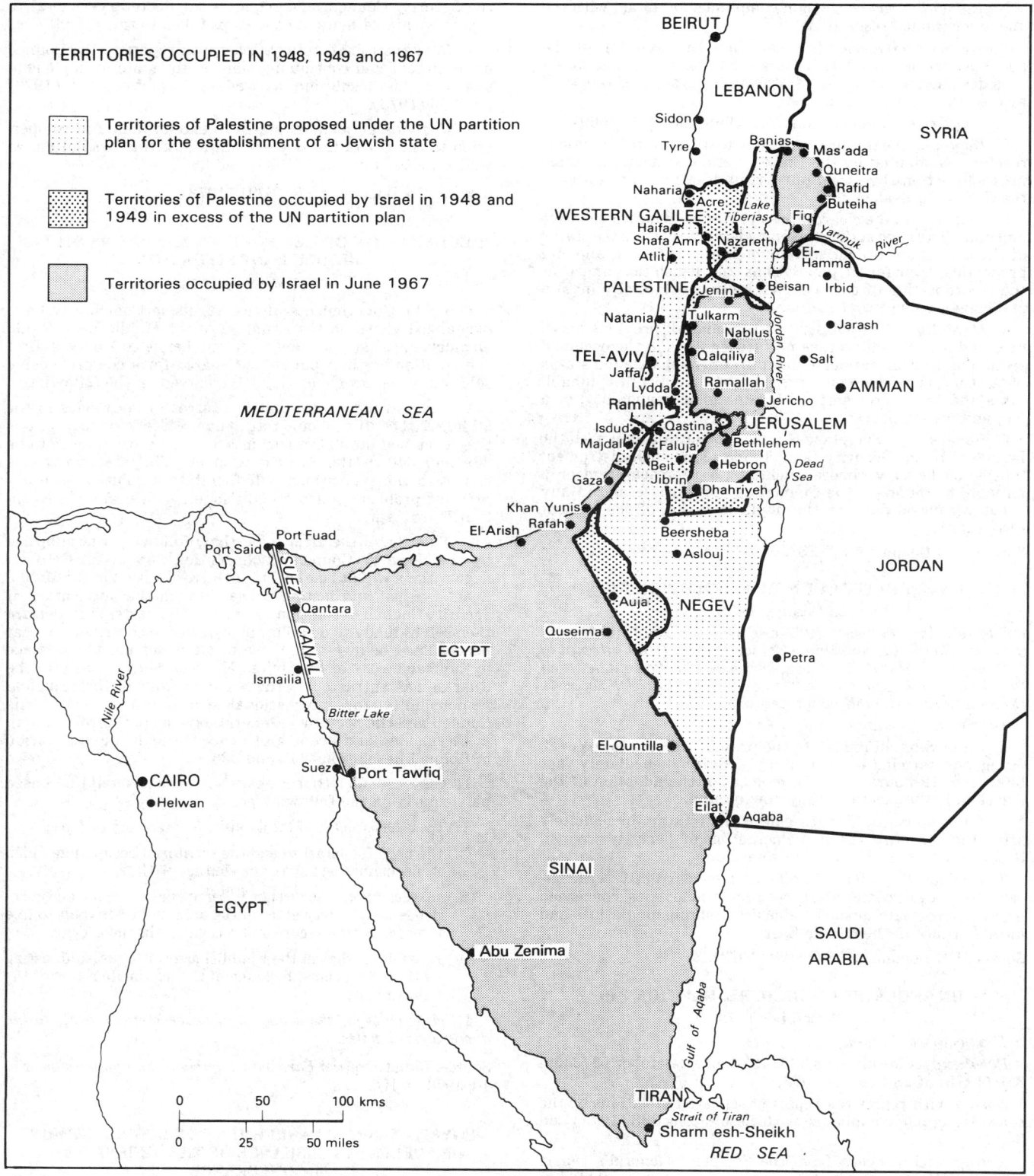

TERRITORIES OCCUPIED IN 1948, 1949 and 1967

Territories of Palestine proposed under the UN partition plan for the establishment of a Jewish state

Territories of Palestine occupied by Israel in 1948 and 1949 in excess of the UN partition plan

Territories occupied by Israel in June 1967

Territories occupied by Israel. See also map on page 89.

Noting with concern the non-compliance by Israel with the above-mentioned resolutions,

Noting with concern also that since the adoption of the above-mentioned resolutions Israel has taken further measures designed to change the status and character of the occupied section of Jerusalem.

1. *Reaffirms* its resolutions 252 (1968) and 267 (1969);

2. *Deplores* the failure of Israel to respect the previous resolutions adopted by the United Nations concerning measures and actions by Israel purporting to affect the status of the City of Jerusalem;

3. *Confirms* in the clearest possible terms that all legislative and administrative actions taken by Israel to change the status of the City of Jerusalem, including expropriation of land and properties, transfer of populations and legislation aimed at the incorporation of the occupied section, are totally invalid and cannot change that status;

4. *Urgently calls upon* Israel to rescind all previous measures and actions and to take no further steps in the occupied section of Jerusalem which may purport to change the status of the City, or which would prejudice the rights of the inhabitants and the interests of the international community, or a just and lasting peace;

5. *Requests* the Secretary-General, in consultation with the President of the Security Council and using such instrumentalities as he may choose, including a representative or a mission, to report to the Council as appropriate and in any event within 60 days on the implementation of the present resolution.

Source: UN Document S/RES/298 (1971).

UN SECURITY COUNCIL RESOLUTION 338
22 October 1973

UN Resolutions between 1967 and October 1973 reaffirmed Security Council Resolution 242 (see above). In an attempt to end the fourth Middle East war, which had broken out between the Arabs and Israel on 6 October 1973, the UN Security Council passed the following Resolution:

The Security Council,

1. *Calls upon* all parties to the present fighting to cease all firing and terminate all military activity immediately, not later than 12 hours after the moment of the adoption of the decision, in the positions they now occupy;

2. *Calls upon* the parties concerned to start immediately after the ceasefire the implementation of Security Council Resolution 242 (1967) in all of its parts;

3. *Decides that,* immediately and concurrently with the ceasefire negotiations start between the parties concerned under appropriate auspices aimed at establishing a just and durable peace in the Middle East.

Source: UN Document PR/73/29 (1973).

UN SECURITY COUNCIL RESOLUTION 340
25 October 1973

The Security Council,

Recalling its Resolutions 338 (1973) of 22 October 1973 and 339 (1973) of 23 October 1973,

Noting with regret the reported repeated violations of the ceasefire in non-compliance with Resolutions 338 (1973) and 339 (1973),

Noting with concern from the Secretary-General's report that the UN military observers have not yet been enabled to place themselves on both sides of the ceasefire line,

1. *Demands* that an immediate and complete ceasefire be observed and that the parties withdraw to the positions occupied by them at 16.50 hours GMT on 22 October 1973;

2. *Requests* the Secretary-General as an immediate step to increase the number of UN military observers on both sides;

3. *Decides* to set up immediately under its authority a UN emergency force to be composed of personnel drawn from member states of the UN, except the permanent members of

the Security Council, and requests the Secretary-General to report within 24 hours on the steps taken to this effect.

4. *Requests* the Secretary-General to report to the Council on an urgent and continuing basis on the state of implementation of this Resolution, as well as Resolutions 338 (1973) and 339 (1973);

5. *Requests* all member states to extend their full co-operation to the UN in the implementation of this Resolution, as well as Resolutions 338 (1973) and 339 (1973).

Source: UN Document PR/73/31 (1973).

DECLARATION OF EEC FOREIGN MINISTERS ON THE MIDDLE EAST SITUATION
6 November 1973

The Nine Governments of the European Community have exchanged views on the situation in the Middle East. While emphasizing that the views set out below are only a first contribution on their part to the search for a comprehensive solution to the problem, they have agreed on the following:

1. They strongly urge that the forces of both sides in the Middle East conflict should return immediately to the positions they occupied on 22 October in accordance with Resolutions 339 and 340 of the Security Council. They believe that a return to these positions will facilitate a solution to other pressing problems concerning prisoners of war and the Egyptian Third Army.

2. They have the firm hope that, following the adoption by the Security Council of Resolution 338 of 22 October, negotiations will at last begin for the restoration in the Middle East of a just and lasting peace through the application of Security Council Resolution 242 in all of its parts. They declare themselves ready to do all in their power to contribute to that peace. They believe that those negotiations must take place in the framework of the United Nations. They recall that the Charter has entrusted to the Security Council the principal responsibility for international peace and security. The Council and the Secretary-General have a special role to play in the making and keeping of peace through the application of Council Resolutions 242 and 338.

3. They consider that a peace agreement should be based particularly on the following points:

(i) the inadmissibility of the acquisition of territory by force;

(ii) the need for Israel to end the territorial occupation which it has maintained since the conflict of 1967;

(iii) respect for the sovereignty, territorial integrity and independence of every state in the area and their right to live in peace within secure and recognized boundaries;

(iv) recognition that in the establishment of a just and lasting peace account must be taken of the legitimate rights of the Palestinians.

Article 4 calls for the despatch of peace-keeping forces to the demilitarized zones.

Source: *Bulletin of the European Communities Commission*, No. 10, 1973, p. 106.

EGYPTIAN-ISRAELI AGREEMENT ON DISENGAGEMENT OF FORCES IN PURSUANCE OF THE GENEVA PEACE CONFERENCE

(signed by the Egyptian and Israeli Chiefs of Staff, 18 January 1974)

This agreement was superseded by the second Egyptian-Israeli Disengagement Agreement signed in September 1975 (see p. 90 below) and then by the Peace Treaty between Egypt and Israel signed on 26 March 1979 (see p. 92 below). A map showing the boundaries of the first agreement is reproduced in this edition (p. 89) and the terms can be found in the 1975–76 edition of The Middle East and North Africa.

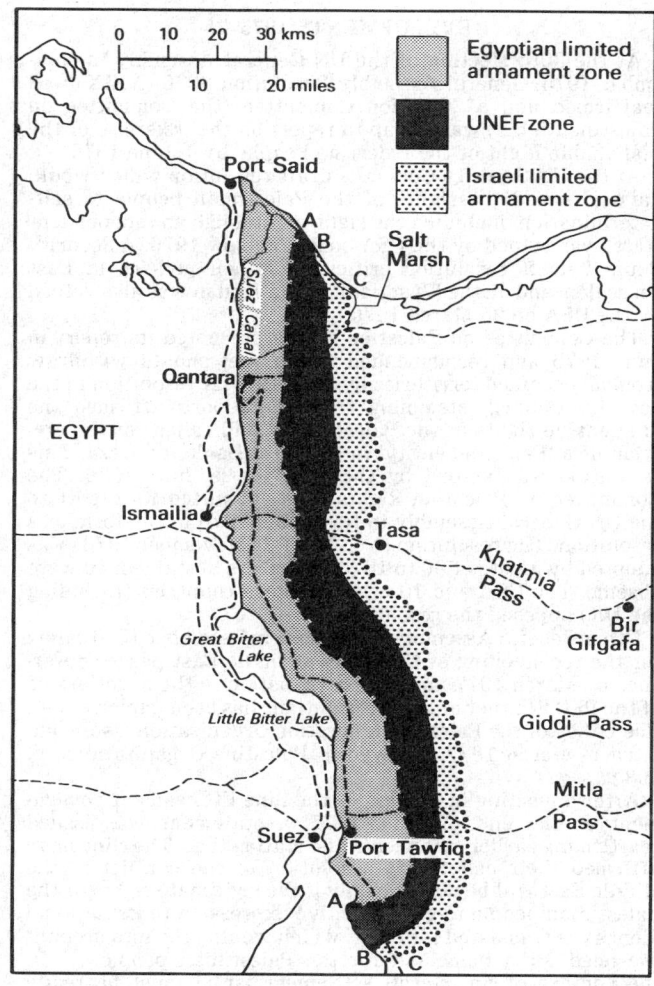

Disengagement Agreement of 18 January 1974 between Israel and Egypt.

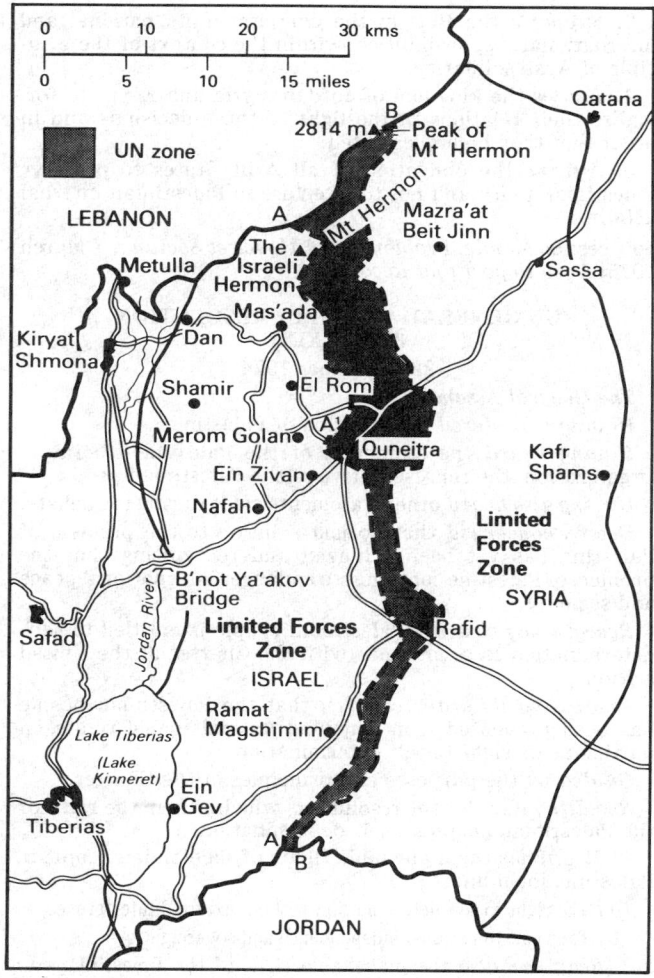

Disengagement Agreement of 30 May 1974 between Israel and Syria.

DISENGAGEMENT AGREEMENT BETWEEN SYRIAN AND ISRAELI FORCES
AND
PROTOCOL TO AGREEMENT ON UNITED NATIONS DISENGAGEMENT OBSERVER FORCE (UNDOF)
(signed in Geneva, Friday 31 May 1974)

(Annex A)

A. Israel and Syria will scrupulously observe the cease-fire on land, sea and air and will refrain from all military actions against each other, from time of signing this document in implementation of the United Nations Security Council Resolution 338 dated 22 October 1973.

B. The military forces of Israel and Syria will be separated in accordance with the following principles:

1. All Israeli military forces will be west of a line designated line A on the map attached hereto (reproduced below), except in Quneitra (Kuneitra) area, where they will be west of a line A-1.

2. All territory east of line A will be under Syrian administration and Syrian civilians will return to this territory.

3. The area between line A and the line designated as line B on the attached map will be an area of separation. In this area will be stationed UNDOF established in accordance with the accompanying Protocol.

4. All Syrian military forces will be east of a line designated as line B on the attached map.

5. There will be two equal areas of limitation in armament and forces, one west of line A and one east of line B as agreed upon.

C. In the area between line A and line A-1 on the attached map there shall be no military forces.

D. *Paragraph D deals with practical details of signing and implementation.*

E. Provisions of paragraphs A, B and C shall be inspected by personnel of the United Nations comprising UNDOF under the Agreement.

F. *Paragraphs F and G deal with repatriation of prisoners and return of bodies of dead soldiers.*

H. This Agreement is not a peace agreement. It is a step towards a just and durable peace on the basis of the Security Council Resolution 338 dated 22 October 1973.

A. *Protocol to the Disengagement Agreement outlined the functions of the United Nations Disengagement Observer Force (UNDOF).*

RESOLUTION OF CONFERENCE OF ARAB HEADS OF STATE
Rabat, 28 October 1974

The Conference of the Arab Heads of State:

1. *Affirms* the right of the Palestinian people to return to their homeland and to self-determination.

2. *Affirms* the right of the Palestinian people to establish an independent national authority, under the leadership of the PLO in its capacity as the sole legitimate representative of the Palestine people, over all liberated territory. The Arab States are pledged to uphold this authority, when it is established, in all spheres and at all levels.

3. *Supports* the PLO in the exercise of its national and international responsibilities, within the context of the principle of Arab solidarity.

4. *Invites* the kingdom of Jordan, Syria and Egypt to formalize their relations in the light of these decisions and in order that they be implemented.

5. *Affirms* the obligation of all Arab States to preserve Palestinian unity and not to interfere in Palestinian internal affairs.

Sources: *Le Monde: Problèmes Politiques et Sociaux*, 7 March 1975; *Arab Report and Record.*

UN GENERAL ASSEMBLY RESOLUTION 3236 (XXIX)
22 November 1974

The General Assembly,

Having considered the question of Palestine,

Having heard the statement of the Palestine Liberation Organization, the representative of the Palestinian people,

Having also heard other statements made during the debate,

Deeply concerned that no just solution to the problem of Palestine has yet been achieved and recognizing that the problem of Palestine continues to endanger international peace and security,

Recognizing that the Palestinian people is entitled to self-determination in accordance with the Charter of the United Nations,

Expressing its grave concern that the Palestinian people has been prevented from enjoying its inalienable rights, in particular its right to self-determination,

Guided by the purposes and principles of the Charter,

Recalling its relevant resolutions which affirm the right of the Palestinian people to self-determination,

1. *Reaffirms* the inalienable rights of Palestinian people in Palestine, including:

(*a*) The right to self-determination without external interference;

(*b*) The right to national independence and sovereignty;

2. *Reaffirms also* the inalienable right of the Palestinians to return to their homes and property from which they have been displaced and uprooted, and calls for their return;

3. *Emphasizes* that full respect for and the realization of these inalienable rights of the Palestinian people are indispensable for the solution of the question of Palestine;

4. *Recognizes* that the Palestinian people is a principal party in the establishment of a just and durable peace in the Middle East;

5. *Further Recognizes* the right of the Palestinian people to regain its rights by all means in accordance with the purposes and principles of the Charter of the United Nations;

6. *Appeals* to all States and international organizations to extend their support to the Palestinian people in its struggle to restore its rights, in accordance with the Charter;

7. *Requests* the Secretary-General to establish contacts with the Palestinian Liberation Organization on all matters concerning the question of Palestine;

8. *Requests* the Secretary-General to report to the General Assembly at its thirtieth session on the implementation of the present resolution;

9. *Decides* to include the item 'Question of Palestine' in the provisional agenda of its thirtieth session.

Source: UN Document BR/74/55 (1974).

SECOND INTERIM PEACE AGREEMENT BETWEEN EGYPT AND ISRAEL
(signed 4 September 1975)

This agreement was superseded by the Peace Treaty between Egypt and Israel signed on 26 March 1979 (see p. 92 below). A map showing the boundaries of the Second Interim Peace Agreement is reproduced in the 1979–80 edition (p. 74) and the terms can be found in the 1978–79 edition of The Middle East and North Africa *(p. 70).*

DEVELOPMENTS 1975–78

At the 30th Meeting of the UN General Assembly in November 1975, General Assembly Resolution 3236 (XXIX) was reaffirmed and a 20-nation Committee (the Committee on Palestine Rights) was set up to report on the 'Exercise of the Inalienable Right of the Palestine People' by 1 June 1976.

At the UN Security Council a draft resolution which would have affirmed the rights of the Palestinian people to self-determination, including the right to establish an independent state, was vetoed by the USA on 26 January 1976. A Security Council draft resolution criticizing Israeli policies in East Jerusalem and on the West Bank of the Jordan was also vetoed by the USA on 25 March 1976.

The Committee on Palestine Rights presented its report in June 1976 and recommended that Israel should withdraw from all occupied territories by June 1977. A resolution in the Security Council, stemming from the report, affirmed the 'inalienable rights of the Palestinians' and called for the creation of a 'Palestine entity' in the West Bank and Gaza. This resolution was vetoed by the USA on 29 June 1976. The Committee on Palestine Rights then submitted its report to the UN General Assembly in November 1976 in the form of a resolution. The resolution (No. 20, of 24 November 1976) was adopted by a vote of 90 to 16 (30 members abstained; 10 were absent). The USA and 10 other Western countries (including the UK) opposed the resolution.

Other General Assembly resolutions in December 1976 called for the reconvening of the Geneva Middle East peace conference by March 1977 and the participation in the negotiations of the PLO. Neither of these resolutions has been implemented. The policy of the Palestine Liberation Organization, as formulated in March 1977, is given in Palestine Organizations, p. 108 *et seq.*

After a meeting in London of the nine EC heads of government at the end of June 1977, a statement was issued reaffirming earlier statements and stating that 'The Nine have affirmed their belief that a solution to the conflict in the Middle East will be possible only if the legitimate rights of the Palestinian people to give effective expression to its national identity is translated into fact, which would take into account the need for a homeland for the Palestinian people.... In the context of an overall settlement Israel must be ready to recognize the legitimate rights of the Palestinian people; equally, the Arab side must be ready to recognize the right of Israel to live in peace within secure and recognized boundaries'.

A UN General Assembly Resolution of 25 November 1977 (32/30) 'called anew' for the early convening of the Geneva Middle East peace conference.

A further UN General Assembly Resolution (33/29 of 7 December 1978) repeated the call for the convening of the Geneva Middle East peace conference. The main focus of attention, however, had now moved away from the UN. President Sadat of Egypt visited Jerusalem in November 1977, and after protracted negotiations, President Sadat and Menachem Begin first of all signed two agreements at Camp David in the USA under the auspices of the US President, Jimmy Carter, and subsequently signed a Peace Treaty in Washington on 26 March 1979. The Arab League Council, angry at Egypt's unilateral action, met in Baghdad on 27 March and passed a series of resolutions aimed at isolating Egypt from the Arab world.

CAMP DAVID: THE FRAMEWORK OF PEACE IN THE MIDDLE EAST

Muhammad Anwar as-Sadat, President of the Arab Republic of Egypt, and Menachem Begin, Prime Minister of Israel, met with President Carter of the USA at Camp David from 5 September to 17 September 1978, and agreed on the following framework for peace in the Middle East. They invited other parties to the Arab-Israeli conflict to adhere to it.

Preamble:

The search for peace in the Middle East must be guided by the following:

The agreed basis for a peaceful settlement of the conflict between Israel and its neighbours is UN Security Council Resolution 242 in all its parts.

The historic initiative by President Sadat in visiting Jerusalem and the reception accorded to him by the Parliament, Government and people of Israel, and the reciprocal visit of Prime Minister Begin to Ismailia, the peace proposals made by both leaders, as well as the warm reception of these missions by the peoples of both countries, have created an unprecedented opportunity for peace which must not be lost if this generation and future generations are to be spared the tragedies of war.

The provisions of the Charter of the UN and the other accepted norms of international law and legitimacy now provide accepted standards for the conduct of relations between all states.

To achieve a relationship of peace, in the spirit of article 2 of the UN Charter, future negotiations between Israel and any neighbour prepared to negotiate peace and security with it, are necessary for the purpose of carrying out all the provisions and principles of Resolutions 242 and 338.

Peace requires respect for the sovereignty, territorial integrity and political independence of every state in the area and their right to live in peace within secure and recognized boundaries free from threats or acts of force. Progress toward that goal can accelerate movement towards a new era of reconciliation in the Middle East marked by co-operation in promoting economic development, in maintaining stability and in assuring security. . . .

Framework

Taking these factors into account, the parties are determined to reach a just, comprehensive and durable settlement of the Middle East conflict through the conclusion of peace treaties based on Security Council Resolutions 242 and 338 in all their parts. Their purpose is to achieve peace and good neighbourly relations. They recognize that, for peace to endure, it must involve all those who have been most deeply affected by the conflict. They therefore agree that this framework as appropriate is intended by them to constitute a basis for peace not only between Egypt and Israel but also between Israel and each of its other neighbours which is prepared to negotiate peace with Israel on this basis. With that objective in mind, they have agreed to proceed as follows:

A. West Bank and Gaza

1. Egypt, Israel, Jordan and the representatives of the Palestinian people should participate in negotiations on the resolution of the Palestinian problem in all its aspects to achieve that objective, negotiations relating to the West Bank and Gaza should proceed in three stages.

(A) Egypt and Israel agree that, in order to ensure a peaceful and orderly transfer of authority, and taking into account the security concerns of all the parties, there should be transitional arrangements for the West Bank and Gaza for a period not exceeding five years. In order to provide full autonomy to the inhabitants, under these arrangements the Israeli military government and its civilian administration will be withdrawn as soon as a self-governing authority has been freely elected by the inhabitants of these areas to replace the existing military government.

To negotiate the details of transitional arrangement, the Government of Jordan will be invited to join the negotiations on the basis of this framework. These new arrangements should give due consideration to both the principle of self-government by the inhabitants of these territories and to the legitimate security concerns of the parties involved.

(B) Egypt, Israel and Jordan will agree on the modalities for establishing the elected self-governing authority in the West Bank and Gaza. The delegations of Egypt and Jordan may include Palestinians from the West Bank and Gaza or other Palestinians as mutually agreed. The parties will negotiate an agreement which will define the powers and responsibilities of the self-governing authority to be exercised in the West Bank and Gaza. A withdrawal of Israeli armed forces will take place and there will be a redeployment of the remaining Israeli forces into specified security locations.

The negotiations shall be based on all the provisions and principles of UN Security Council Resolution 242. The negotiations will resolve, among other matters, the location of the boundaries and the nature of the security arrangements. The solution from the negotiations must also recognize the legitimate rights of the Palestinian people and their just requirements. In this way, the Palestinians will participate in the determination of their own future through:

(i) The negotiations among Egypt, Israel, Jordan and the representatives of the inhabitants of the West Bank and Gaza to agree on the final status of the West Bank and Gaza and other outstanding issues by the end of the transitional period.

(ii) Submitting their agreement to a vote by the elected representatives of the inhabitants of the West Bank and Gaza.

(iii) Providing for the elected representatives of the inhabitants of the West Bank and Gaza to decide how they shall govern themselves consistent with the provisions of their agreement.

(iv) Participating as stated above in the work of the committee negotiating the peace treaty between Israel and Jordan.

The agreement will also include arrangements for assuring internal and external security and public order. A strong local police force will be established, which may include Jordanian citizens. In addition, Israeli and Jordanian forces will participate in joint patrols and in the manning of control posts to assure the security of the borders.

(C) When the self-governing authority (administrative council) in the West Bank and Gaza is established and inaugurated, the transitional period of five years will begin. As soon as possible, but not later than the third year after the beginning of the transitional period, negotiations will take place to determine the final status of the West Bank and Gaza and its relationship with its neighbours, and to conclude a peace treaty between Israel and Jordan by the end of the transitional period. These negotiations will be conducted among Egypt, Israel, Jordan and the elected representatives of the inhabitants of the West Bank and Gaza.

Two separate but related committees will be convened; one committee, consisting of representatives of the four parties which will negotiate and agree on the final status of the West Bank and Gaza, and its relationship with its neighbours, and the second committee, consisting of representatives of Israel and representatives of Jordan to be joined by the elected representatives of the inhabitants of the West Bank and Gaza, to negotiate the peace treaty between Israel and Jordan, taking into account the agreement reached on the final status of the West Bank and Gaza.

2. All necessary measures will be taken and provisions made to assure the security of Israel and its neighbours during the transitional period and beyond. To assist in providing such security, a strong local police force will be constituted by the self-governing authority. It will be composed of inhabitants of the West Bank and Gaza. The police will maintain continuing liaison on internal security matters with the designated Israeli, Jordanian and Egyptian officers.

3. During the transitional period, the representatives of Egypt, Israel, Jordan and the self-governing authority will constitute a continuing committee to decide by agreement on the modalities of admission of persons displaced from the West Bank and Gaza in 1967, together with necessary measures to prevent disruption and disorder. Other matters of common concern may also be dealt with by this committee.

4. Egypt and Israel will work with each other and with other interested parties to establish agreed procedures for a prompt, just and permanent implementation of the resolution of the refugee problem.

B. Egypt-Israel

1. Egypt and Israel undertake not to resort to the threat or the use of force to settle disputes. Any disputes shall be settled

by peaceful means in accordance with the provisions of article 33 of the Charter of the UN.

2. In order to achieve peace between them, the parties agree to negotiate in good faith with a goal of concluding within three months from the signing of this framework a peace treaty between them, while inviting the other parties to the conflict to proceed simultaneously to negotiate and conclude similar peace treaties with a view to achieving a comprehensive peace in the area. The framework for the conclusion of a peace treaty between Egypt and Israel will govern the peace negotiations between them. The parties will agree on the modalities and the timetable for the implementation of their obligations under the treaty.

Associated principles

1. Egypt and Israel state that the principles and provisions described below should apply to peace treaties between Israel and each of its neighbours—Egypt, Jordan, Syria and Lebanon.

2. Signatories shall establish among themselves relationships normal to states at peace with one another. To this end, they should undertake to abide by all the provisions of the Charter of the UN. Steps to be taken in this respect include:

(a) Full recognition.

(b) Abolishing economic boycotts.

(c) Guaranteeing that under their jurisdiction the citizens of the other parties shall enjoy the protection of the due process of law.

3. Signatories should explore possibilities for economic development in the context of final peace treaties, with the objective of contributing to the atmosphere of peace, co-operation, and friendship which is their common goal.

4. Claims commissions may be established for the mutual settlement of all financial claims.

5. The United States shall be invited to participate in the talks on matters related to the modalities of the implementation of the agreements and working out the time-table for the carrying out of the obligation of the parties.

6. The UN Security Council shall be requested to endorse the peace treaties and ensure that their provisions shall not be violated. The permanent members of the Security Council shall be requested to underwrite the peace treaties and ensure respect for their provisions. They shall also be requested to conform their policies and actions with the undertakings contained in this framework.

The second agreement signed at Camp David was a framework for the conclusion of a peace treaty between Egypt and Israel. The actual Treaty was signed on 26 March 1979, and is reproduced below.

THE PEACE TREATY BETWEEN EGYPT AND ISRAEL SIGNED IN WASHINGTON ON 26 MARCH 1979

The Government of the Arab Republic of Egypt and the Government of the State of Israel:

Preamble

Convinced of the urgent necessity of the establishment of a just, comprehensive and lasting peace in the Middle East in accordance with Security Council Resolutions 242 and 338:

Reaffirming their adherence to the 'Framework for Peace in the Middle East agreed at Camp David', dated 17 September 1978:

Noting that the aforementioned framework as appropriate is intended to constitute a basis for peace not only between Egypt and Israel but also between Israel and each of the other Arab neighbours which is prepared to negotiate peace with it on this basis:

Desiring to bring to an end the state of war between them and to establish a peace in which every state in the area can live in security:

Convinced that the conclusion of a treaty of peace between Egypt and Israel is an important step in the search for comprehensive peace in the area and for the attainment of the settlement of the Arab-Israeli conflict in all its aspects:

Inviting the other Arab parties to this dispute to join the peace process with Israel guided by and based on the principles of the aforementioned framework:

Desiring as well to develop friendly relations and co-operation between themselves in accordance with the UN Charter and the principles of international law governing international relations in times of peace:

Agree to the following provisions in the free exercise of their sovereignty, in order to implement the 'framework for the conclusion of a peace treaty between Egypt and Israel'.

Article I

1. The state of war between the parties will be terminated and peace will be established between them upon the exchange of instruments of ratification of this treaty.

2. Israel will withdraw all its armed forces and civilians from the Sinai behind the international boundary between Egypt and Mandated Palestine, as provided in the annexed protocol (annexed), and Egypt will resume the exercise of its full sovereignty over the Sinai.

3. Upon completion of the interim withdrawal provided for in Annex 1, the parties will establish normal and friendly relations, in accordance with Article II (3).

Article II

The permanent boundary between Egypt and Israel is the recognized international boundary between Egypt and the former Mandated Territory of Palestine, as shown on the map at Annex 2, without prejudice to the issue of the status of the Gaza Strip. The parties recognize this boundary as inviolable. Each will respect the territorial integrity of the other, including their territorial waters and airspace.

Article III

1. The parties will apply between them the provisions of the Charter of the UN and the principles of international law governing relations among states in times of peace.

In particular:

A. They recognize and will respect each other's sovereignty, territorial integrity and political independence.

B. They recognize and will respect each other's right to live in peace within their secure and recognized boundaries.

C. They will refrain from the threat of use of force, directly or indirectly, against each other and will settle all disputes between them by peaceful means.

2. Each party undertakes to ensure that acts or threats of belligerency, hostility, or violence do not originate from and are not committed from within its territory, or by any forces subject to its control or by any other forces stationed on its territory, against the population, citizens or property of the other party. Each party also undertakes to refrain from organizing, instigating, inciting, assisting or participating in acts or threats of belligerency, hostility, subversion or violence against the other party, anywhere, and undertakes to ensure that perpetrators of such acts are brought to justice.

3. The parties agree that the normal relationship established between them will include full recognition, diplomatic, economic and cultural relations, termination of economic boycotts and discriminatory barriers to the free movement of people and goods, and will guarantee the mutual enjoyment by citizens of the due process of law. The process by which they undertake to achieve such a relationship parallel to the implementation of other provisions of this treaty is set out in the annexed protocol (Annex 3).

Article IV

1. In order to provide maximum security for both parties on the basis of reciprocity, agreed security arrangements will be established including limited force zones in Egyptian and Israeli territory, and UN forces and observers, described in detail as to nature and timing in Annex 1, and other security arrangements the parties may agree upon.

2. The parties agree to the stationing of UN personnel in areas described in Annex 1, the parties agree not to request

withdrawal of the UN personnel and that these personnel will not be removed unless such removal is approved by the Security Council of the UN, with the affirmative vote of the five members, unless the parties otherwise agree.

3. A joint commission will be established to facilitate the implementation of the treaty, as provided for in Annex 1.

4. The security arrangements provided for in paragraphs 1 and 2 of this article may at the request of either party be reviewed and amended by mutual agreement of the parties.

Article V

Article V deals with rights of passage of shipping through the Suez Canal, the Strait of Tiran and the Gulf of Aqaba.

Article VI

1. This treaty does not affect and shall not be interpreted as affecting in any way the rights and obligations of the parties under the Charter of the UN.

2. The parties undertake to fulfil in good faith their obligations under this treaty, without regard to action or inaction of any other party and independently of any instrument external to this treaty.

3. They further undertake to take all the necessary measures for the application in their relations of the provisions of the multilateral conventions to which they are parties. Including the submission of appropriate notification to the Secretary-General of the UN and other depositories of such conventions.

4. The parties undertake not to enter into any obligation in conflict with this treaty.

5. Subject to Article 103 of the UN Charter, in the event of a conflict between the obligations of the parties under the present treaty and any of their other obligations, the obligations under this treaty will be binding and implemented.

Article VII

1. Disputes arising out of the application or interpretation of this treaty shall be resolved by negotiations.

2. Any such disputes which cannot be settled by negotiations shall be resolved by conciliation or submitted to arbitration.

Article VIII

The parties agree to establish a claims commission for the mutual settlement of all financial claims.

Article IX

1. This treaty shall enter into force upon exchange of instruments of ratification.

2. This treaty supersedes the agreement between Egypt and Israel of September 1975.

3. All protocols, annexes, and maps attached to this treaty shall be regarded as an integral part hereof.

4. The treaty shall be communicated to the Secretary-General of the UN for registration in accordance with the provisions of Article 102 of the Charter of the UN.

Annex 1—military and withdrawal arrangements:

Israel will complete withdrawal of all its armed forces and civilians from Sinai within three years of the date of exchange of instruments of ratification of the treaty. The withdrawal will be accomplished in two phases, the first, within nine months, to a line east of Al Arish and Ras Muhammad; the second to behind the international boundary. During the three-year period, Egypt and Israel will maintain a specified military presence in four delineated security zones (see map), and the UN will continue its observation and supervisory functions. Egypt will exercise full sovereignty over evacuated territories in Sinai upon Israeli withdrawal. A joint commission will supervise the withdrawal, and security arrangements can be reviewed when either side asks but any change must be by mutual agreement.

Annex 2—maps.

Annex 3—normalization of relations:

Ambassadors will be exchanged upon completion of the interim withdrawal. All discriminatory barriers and economic boycotts will be lifted and, not later than six months after the completion of the interim withdrawal, negotiations for a trade and commerce agreement will begin. Free movement of each other's nationals and transport will be allowed and both sides agree to promote 'good neighbourly relations'. Egypt will use the airfields left by Israel near Al Arish, Rafah, Ras an-Naqb and Sharm ash-Shaikh, only for civilian aircraft. Road, rail, postal, telephone, wireless and other forms of communications will be opened between the two countries on completion of interim withdrawal.

Exchange of letters

Negotiations on the West Bank and Gaza—Negotiations on autonomy for the West Bank and Gaza will begin within one month of the exchange of the instruments of ratification. Jordan will be invited to participate and the Egyptian and Jordanian delegations may include Palestinians from the West Bank and Gaza, or other Palestinians as mutually agreed. If Jordan decides not to take part, the negotiations will be held by Egypt and Israel. The objective of the negotiations is the establishment of a self-governing authority in the West Bank and Gaza 'in order to provide full autonomy to the inhabitants'.

Egypt and Israel hope to complete negotiations within one year so that elections can be held as soon as possible. The self-governing authority elected will be inaugurated within one month of the elections at which point the five year transitional period will begin. The Israeli military Government and its civilian administration will be withdrawn, Israeli armed forces withdrawn and the remaining forces redeployed 'into specified security locations'.

MAIN POINTS OF THE RESOLUTIONS PASSED BY THE ARAB LEAGUE COUNCIL IN BAGHDAD ON 27 MARCH 1979

—To withdraw the ambassadors of the Arab states from Egypt immediately.

—To recommend the severance of political and diplomatic relations with the Egyptian Government. The Arab governments will adopt the necessary measures to apply this recommendation within a maximum period of one month from the date of the issue of this decision, in accordance with the constitutional measures in force in each country.

—To consider the suspension of the Egyptian Government's membership in the Arab League as operative from the date of the Egyptian Government's signing of the peace treaty with the Zionist enemy. This means depriving it of all rights resulting from that membership.

—To make the city of Tunis, capital of the Tunisian Republic, the temporary headquarters of the Arab League, its general secretariat, the competent ministerial councils and the permanent technical committees, as of the date of signing of the treaty between the Egyptian Government and the Zionist enemy. This shall be communicated to all international and regional organizations and bodies. They will also be informed that dealings with the Arab League will be conducted with its secretariat in its new temporary headquarters.

—To condemn the policy that the United States is practising regarding its role in concluding the Camp David agreements and the Egyptian-Israeli treaty.

The Arab League Council, at the level of Arab Foreign and Economy Ministers, has also decided the following:

—To halt all bank loans, deposits, guarantees or facilities, as well as all financial or technical contributions and aid by Arab Governments or their establishments to the Egyptian Government and its establishments as of the treaty-signing date.

—To ban the extension of economic aid by the Arab funds, banks and financial establishments within the framework of the Arab League and the joint Arab co-operation to the Egyptian Government and its establishments.

—The Arab governments and institutions shall refrain from purchasing the bonds, shares, postal orders and public credit loans that are issued by the Egyptian Government and its financial foundations.

—Following the suspension of the Egyptian Government's membership in the Arab League, its membership will also be suspended from the institutions, funds and organisations deriving from the Arab League.

—In view of the fact that the ill-omened Egyptian-Israeli treaty and its appendices have demonstrated Egypt's commitment to sell oil to Israel, the Arab states shall refrain from providing Egypt with oil and its derivatives.

—Trade exchanges with the Egyptian state and with private establishments that deal with the Zionist enemy shall be prohibited.

Source: *MEED Arab Report*, 11 April 1979, p. 9.

UN SECURITY COUNCIL RESOLUTION ON ISRAELI SETTLEMENTS
1 March 1980

The resolution, No. 465, was adopted unanimously by the 15 members of the Council. The USA repudiated its vote in favour of the resolution on 3 March 1980 (see below).

The Security Council, taking note of the reports of the Commission of the Security Council established under resolution 446 (1979) to examine the situation relating to the settlements in the Arab territories occupied since 1967, including Jerusalem, contained in documents S/13450 and S/13679,

—Taking note also of letters from the permanent representative of Jordan (S/13801) and the permanent representative of Morocco, Chairman of the Islamic Group (S/13802),

—Strongly deploring the refusal by Israel to co-operate with the Commission and regretting its formal rejection of resolutions 446 (1979) and 452 (1979),

—Affirming once more that the fourth Geneva Convention relative to the protection of civilian persons in time of war of 12 August 1949 is applicable to the Arab territories occupied by Israel since 1967, including Jerusalem,

—Deploring the decision of the Government of Israel to officially support Israeli settlement in the Palestinian and other Arab territories occupied since 1967,

—Deeply concerned over the practices of the Israeli authorities in implementing that settlement policy in the occupied Arab territories, including Jerusalem, and its consequences for the local Arab and Palestinian population,

—Taking into account the need to consider measures for the impartial protection of private and public land and property, and water resources,

—Bearing in mind the specific status of Jerusalem and, in particular, the need for protection and preservation of the unique spiritual and religious dimension of the holy places in the city,

—Drawing attention to the grave consequences which the settlement policy is bound to have on any attempt to reach a comprehensive, just and lasting peace in the Middle East,

—Recalling pertinent Security Council resolutions, specifically resolutions 237 (1967) of 14 June 1967, 252 (1968) of 21 May 1968, 267 (1969) of 3 July 1969, 271 (1969) of 15 September 1969 and 298 (1971) of 25 September 1971, as well as the consensus statement made by the President of the Security Council on 11 November 1976,

—Having invited Mr Fahd Qawasmah, Mayor of Al-Khalil (Hebron), in the occupied territories, to supply it with information pursuant to rule 39 of provisional rules of procedure,

1. Commends the work done by the Commission in preparing the report contained in document S/13679,

2. Accepts the conclusions and recommendations contained in the above-mentioned report of the Commission,

3. Calls upon all parties, particularly the Government of Israel, to co-operate with the Commission,

4. Strongly deplores the decision of Israel to prohibit the free travel of Mayor Fahd Qawasmah in order to appear before

the Security Council, and requests Israel to permit his free travel to the United Nations headquarters for that purpose,

5. Determines that all measures taken by Israel to change the physical character, demographic composition, institutional structure or status of the Palestinian and other Arab territories occupied since 1967, including Jerusalem, or any part thereof, have no legal validity and that Israel's policy and practices of settling parts of its population and new immigrants in those territories constitute a flagrant violation of the Fourth Geneva Convention relative to the protection of civilian persons in time of war and also constitute a serious obstruction to achieving a comprehensive, just and lasting peace in the Middle East,

6. Strongly deplores the continuation and persistence of Israel in pursuing those policies and practices and calls upon the Government and people of Israel to rescind those measures, to dismantle the existing settlements and in particular to cease, on an urgent basis, the establishment, construction and planning of settlements in the Arab territories occupied since 1967, including Jerusalem,

7. Calls upon all states not to provide Israel with any assistance to be used specifically in connection with settlements in the occupied territories,

8. Requests the Commission to continue to examine the situation relating to settlements in the Arab territories occupied since 1967 including Jerusalem, to investigate the reported serious depletion of natural resources, particularly the water resources, with a view of ensuring the protection of those important natural resources of the territories under occupation, and to keep under close scrutiny the implementation of the present resolution,

9. Requests the Commission to report to the Security Council before 1 September 1980, and decides to convene at the earliest possible date thereafter in order to consider the report and the full implementation of the present resolution.

PRESIDENT CARTER'S STATEMENT REPUDIATING US VOTE IN SUPPORT OF UN SECURITY COUNCIL RESOLUTION 465
3 March 1980

I want to make it clear that the vote of the US in the Security Council of the UN does not represent a change in our position regarding the Israeli settlements in the occupied areas nor regarding the status of Jerusalem.

While our opposition to the establishment of the Israeli settlements is long-standing and well-known, we made strenuous efforts to eliminate the language with reference to the dismantling of settlements in the resolution. This call for dismantling was neither proper nor practical. We believe that the future disposition of the existing settlements must be determined during the current autonomy negotiations.

As to Jerusalem, we strongly believe that Jerusalem should be undivided with free access to the holy places for all faiths, and that its status should be determined in the negotiations for a comprehensive peace settlement.

The US vote in the UN was approved with the understanding that all references to Jerusalem would be deleted. The failure to communicate this clearly resulted in a vote in favour of the resolution rather than abstention.

EEC STATEMENT ON THE MIDDLE EAST
Issued in Venice, 13 June 1980

1. The heads of state and government and the ministers of foreign affairs held a comprehensive exchange of views on all aspects of the present situation in the Middle East, including the state of negotiations resulting from the agreements signed between Egypt and Israel in March 1979. They agreed that growing tensions affecting this region constitute a serious danger and render a comprehensive solution to the Israeli-Arab conflict more necessary and pressing than ever.

2. The nine member-states of the European Community consider that the traditional ties and common interests which link Europe to the Middle East oblige them to play a special role and now require them to work in a more concrete way towards peace.

3. In this regard, the nine countries of the Community base themselves on Security Council resolutions 242 and 338 and the positions which they have expressed on several occasions, notably in their declarations of 29 June 1977, 19 September 1978, 26 March and 18 June 1979, as well as the speech made on their behalf on 25 September 1979, by the Irish Minister of Foreign Affairs at the thirty-fourth United Nations General Assembly.

4. On the bases thus set out, the time has come to promote the recognition and implementation of the two principles universally accepted by the international community: the right to existence and to security of all the states in the region, including Israel, and justice for all the peoples which implies the recognition of the legitimate rights of the Palestinian people.

5. All of the countries in the area are entitled to live in peace within secure, recognized and guaranteed borders. The necessary guarantees for a peace settlement should be provided by the United Nations by a decision of the Security Council and, if necessary, on the basis of other mutually agreed procedures. The Nine declared that they are prepared to participate within the framework of a comprehensive settlement in a system of concrete and binding international guarantees, including (guarantees) on the ground.

6. A just solution must finally be found to the Palestinian problem, which is not simply one of refugees. The Palestinian people, which is conscious of existing as such, must be placed in a position, by an appropriate process defined within the framework of the comprehensive peace settlement, to exercise fully its right to self-determination.

7. The achievement of these objectives requires the involvement and support of all the parties concerned in the peace settlement which the Nine are endeavouring to promote in keeping with the principles formulated in the declaration referred to above. These principles apply to all the parties concerned, and thus the Palestinian people, and to the PLO, which will have to be associated with the negotiations.

8. The Nine recognize the special importance of the role played by the question of Jerusalem for all the parties concerned. The Nine stress that they will not accept any unilateral initiative designed to change the status of Jerusalem and that any agreement on the city's status should guarantee freedom of access for everyone to the holy places.

9. The Nine stress the need for Israel to put an end to the territorial occupation which it has maintained since the conflict of 1967, as it has done for part of Sinai. They are deeply convinced that the Israeli settlements constitute a serious obstacle to the peace process in the Middle East. The Nine consider that these settlements, as well as modifications in population and property in the occupied Arab territories, are illegal under international law.

10. Concerned as they are to put an end to violence, the Nine consider that only the renunciation of force or the threatened use of force by all the parties can create a climate of confidence in the area, and constitute a basic element for a comprehensive settlement of the conflict in the Middle East.

11. The Nine have decided to make the necessary contacts with all the parties concerned. The objective of these contacts would be to ascertain the position of the various parties with respect to the principles set out in this declaration and in the light of the result of this consultation process to determine the form which such an initiative on their part could take.

Subsequent UN Resolutions (General Assembly Resolutions ES-7/2, 29 July 1980; Security Council Resolution 478, 20 August 1980; General Assembly Resolutions 35-169 and 35-207 of 15 and 16 December 1980, etc.) have reaffirmed earlier resolutions and condemned the Israeli 'Jerusalem Bill' of July 1980, which stated explicitly that Jerusalem should be for ever the undivided Israeli capital and seat of government, parliament and judiciary. A UN General Assembly Resolution of 6 February 1982, condemned Israel's annexation of the Golan Heights. UN Resolutions in June 1982 condemned the Israeli invasion of Lebanon, and called for the withdrawal of Israeli forces.

THE FAHD PLAN

In August 1981 Crown Prince Fahd of Saudi Arabia launched an 8-point peace plan for the Middle East. During the remainder of 1981 some Arab States showed their support, but failure to agree on the 'Fahd Plan' caused the break-up of the Fez Arab Summit in November only a few hours after it had opened. The plan is as follows:

1. Israel to withdraw from all Arab territory occupied in 1967, including Arab Jerusalem.

2. Israeli settlements built on Arab land after 1967 to be dismantled.

3. A guarantee of freedom of worship for all religions in holy places.

4. An affirmation of the right of the Palestinian Arab people to return to their homes, and compensation for those who do not wish to return.

5. The West Bank and Gaza Strip to have a transitional period under the auspices of the United Nations for a period not exceeding several months.

6. An independent Palestinian state should be set up with Jerusalem as its capital.

7. All states in the region should be able to live in peace.

8. The UN or member-states of the UN to guarantee carrying-out of these principles.

THE REAGAN PLAN

After the Israeli invasion of Lebanon in June 1982, and the consequent evacuation of the PLO from Beirut, the US Government made strenuous efforts to continue the Camp David peace process and find a permanent solution that would ensure peace in the Middle East. On 1 September 1982 President Reagan outlined the following proposals in a broadcast to the nation from Burbank, California:

'. . . First, as outlined in the Camp David accords, there must be a period of time during which the Palestinian inhabitants of the West Bank and Gaza will have full autonomy over their own affairs. Due consideration must be given to the principle of self-government by the inhabitants of the territories and to the legitimate security concerns of the parties involved.

The purpose of the 5-year period of transition, which would begin after free elections for a self-governing Palestinian authority, is to prove to the Palestinians that they can run their own affairs and that such Palestinian autonomy poses no threat to Israel's security.

The United States will not support the use of any additional land for the purpose of settlements during the transition period. Indeed, the immediate adoption of a settlement freeze by Israel, more than any other action, could create the confidence needed for wider participation in these talks. Further settlement activity is in no way necessary for the security of Israel and only diminishes the confidence of the Arabs that a final outcome can be freely and fairly negotiated.

I want to make the American position well understood: The purpose of this transition period is the peaceful and orderly transfer of authority from Israel to the Palestinian inhabitants of the West Bank and Gaza. At the same time, such a transfer must not interfere with Israel's security requirements.

Beyond the transition period, as we look to the future of the West Bank and Gaza, it is clear to me that peace cannot be achieved by the formation of an independent Palestinian state in those territories. Nor is it achievable on the basis of Israeli sovereignty or permanent control over the West Bank and Gaza.

So the United States will not support the establishment of an independent Palestinian state in the West Bank and Gaza, and we will not support annexation or permanent control by Israel.

There is, however, another way to peace. The final status of these lands must, of course, be reached through the give-and-take of negotiations. But it is the firm view of the United States that self-government by the Palestinians of the West Bank and Gaza in association with Jordan offers the best chance for a durable, just and lasting peace.

We base our approach squarely on the principle that the Arab-Israeli conflict should be resolved through negotiations involving an exchange of territory for peace. This exchange is enshrined in UN Security Council Resolution 242, which is, in turn, incorporated in all its parts in the Camp David agreements. UN Resolution 242 remains wholly valid as the foundation stone of America's Middle East peace effort.

It is the United States' position that—in return for peace—the withdrawal provision of Resolution 242 applies to all fronts, including the West Bank and Gaza.

When the border is negotiated between Jordan and Israel, our view on the extent to which Israel should be asked to give up territory will be heavily affected by the extent of true peace and normalization and the security arrangements offered in return.

Finally, we remain convinced that Jerusalem must remain undivided, but its final status should be decided through negotiations.

In the course of the negotiations to come, the United States will support positions that seem to us fair and reasonable compromises and likely to promote a sound agreement. We will also put forward our own detailed proposals when we believe they can be helpful. And, make no mistake, the United States will oppose any proposal—from any party and at any point in the negotiating process—that threatens the security of Israel. America's commitment to the security of Israel is ironclad. And, I might add, so is mine.'

FEZ SUMMIT PEACE PROPOSAL

A further Fez Arab Summit was held in September 1982, and produced a set of peace proposals. The following excerpts are from the official English-language text of the final declaration on 9 September 1982, and are reproduced from American Arab Affairs, No 2:

I. The Israeli-Arab conflict:

The summit adopted the following principles:

1. The withdrawal of Israel from all Arab territories occupied in 1967 including Arab Al Qods (East Jerusalem).

2. The dismantling of settlements established by Israel on the Arab territories after 1967.

3. The guarantee of freedom of worship and practice of religious rites for all religions in the holy shrine.

4. The reaffirmation of the Palestinian people's right to self-determination and the exercise of its imprescriptible and inalienable national rights under the leadership of the Palestine Liberation Organization (PLO), its sole and legitimate representative, and the indemnification of all those who do not desire to return.

5. Placing the West Bank and Gaza Strip under the control of the United Nations for a transitory period not exceeding a few months.

6. The establishment of an independent Palestinian state with Al Qods as its capital.

7. The Security Council guarantees peace among all states of the region including the independent Palestinian state.

8. The Security Council guarantees the respect of these principles.

II. The Israeli aggression against Lebanon:

The summit was informed of the Lebanese Government's decision to put an end to the mission of the Arab deterrent forces in Lebanon. To this effect, the Lebanese and Syrian governments will start negotiations on measures to be taken in the light of the Israeli withdrawal from Lebanon.

JOINT JORDAN–PLO PEACE PROPOSALS

After a series of negotiations which began in January 1984, establishing a platform for joint action, King Hussein of Jordan and Yasser Arafat, Chairman of the PLO, announced their proposals for a Middle East peace settlement in Amman, on 23 February 1985. The failure of these proposals to further the peace process was acknowledged by King Hussein on 19 February 1986, when he abandoned Jordan's political collaboration with the PLO. The PLO did not formally abrogate the Amman agreement until the 18th session of the PNC in Algiers in April 1987. The following is the entire text of the

joint agreement in an English-language version distributed by the Jordanian Government.

A PLAN OF JOINT ACTION

Proceeding from the spirit of the Fez summit resolutions approved by the Arab states and from UN resolutions on the Palestinian question, in accordance with international legitimacy, and proceeding from a common understanding on the building of a special relationship between the Jordanian and Palestinian peoples, the Government of the Hashemite Kingdom of Jordan and the Palestine Liberation Organization have agreed to work together with a view to a just and peaceful settlement of the Middle East crisis and to the termination of the occupation by Israel of the occupied Arab territories, including Jerusalem, on the basis of the following principles:

1. The return of all territories occupied in 1967 in exchange for a comprehensive peace, as stipulated in the resolutions of the United Nations and its Security Council.

2. The right of the Palestinian people to self-determination: in this respect the Palestinians will exercise their inalienable right to self-determination within the context of the formation of the proposed confederated states of Jordan and Palestine.

3. The solution of the Palestinian refugee problem in accordance with United Nations resolutions.

4. The solution of all aspects of the Palestinian question.

5. On this basis, negotiations should be undertaken under the auspices of an international conference to be attended by the five permanent members of the United Nations Security Council and all parties to the conflict, including the Palestine Liberation Organization, which is the sole legitimate representative of the Palestinian people, in the form of a joint delegation (a joint Jordanian–Palestinian delegation).

THE SHULTZ PLAN

At the beginning of February 1988 the Government of the USA announced a new plan for the resolution of the Palestine issue, which came to be known as the 'Shultz Plan', after the US Secretary of State, George Shultz. The presentation of the plan followed more than a year of diplomatic activity during which the idea of an international peace conference under the auspices of the UN, which had been agreed in principle by Shimon Peres, the Israeli Minister of Foreign Affairs, and King Hussein of Jordan, had won increasing support. The main provisions of the plan, as they were subsequently clarified, were for a six-month period of negotiations between Israel and a joint Jordanian/Palestinian delegation, to determine the details of a transitional autonomy arrangement for the West Bank and the Gaza Strip, which would last for three years; during the transitional period a permanent settlement would be negotiated by the Israeli and Jordanian/Palestinian delegations; both sets of negotiations would run concurrently with and, if necessary, with reference to, an international peace conference, involving the five permanent members of the UN Security Council and all the interested parties (including the Palestinians in a joint Jordanian/Palestinian delegation), which, like the separate Israeli-Jordanian/Palestinian negotiations, would be conducted on the basis of all the participants' acceptance of UN Security Council resolutions 242 and 338, but would have no power to impose a settlement.

On 6 March 1988, the Israeli newspaper, Yedioth Aharonoth, published a photocopy of a letter from George Shultz to the Israeli Prime Minister, Itzhak Shamir, containing details of his peace proposals. The contents of the letter, identical versions of which were believed to have been delivered to the governments of Egypt, Jordan and Syria, were as follows:

Dear Mr. Prime Minister,

I set forth below the statement of understandings which I am convinced is necessary to achieve the prompt opening of negotiations on a comprehensive peace. This statement of understandings emerges from discussions held with you and other regional leaders. I look forward to the letter of reply of the government of Israel in confirmation of this statement.

The agreed objective is a comprehensive peace providing for the security of all the States in the region and for the legitimate rights of the Palestinian people.

Negotiations will start on an early date certain between Israel and each of its neighbors which is willing to do so. Those negotiations could begin by May 1, 1988. Each of these negotiations will be based on United Nations Security Council Resolutions 242 and 338, in all their parts. The parties to each bilateral negotiation will determine the procedure and agenda of their negotiation. All participants in the negotiations must state their willingness to negotiate with one another.

As concerns negotiations between the Israeli delegation and Jordanian-Palestinian delegation, negotiations will begin on arrangements for a transitional period, with the objective of completing them within six months. Seven months after transitional negotiations begin, final status negotiations will begin, with the objective of completing them within one year. These negotiations will be based on all the provisions and principles of the United Nations Security Council Resolution 242. Final status talks will start before the transitional period begins. The transitional period will begin three months after the conclusion of the transitional agreement and will last for three years. The United States will participate in both negotiations and will promote their rapid conclusion. In particular, the United States will submit a draft agreement for the parties' consideration at the outset of the negotiations on transitional arrangements.

Two weeks before the opening of negotiations, an international conference will be held. The Secretary-General of the United Nations will be asked to issue invitations to the parties involved in the Arab-Israeli conflict and the five permanent members of the United Nations Security Council. All participants in the conference must accept United Nations Security Council Resolutions 242 and 338, and renounce violence and terrorism. The parties to each bilateral negotiations may refer reports on the status of their negotiations to the conference, in a manner to be agreed. The conference will not be able to impose solutions or veto agreements reached.

Palestinian representation will be within the Jordanian-Palestinian delegation. The Palestinian issue will be addressed in the negotiations between the Jordanian-Palestinian and Israeli delegations. Negotiations between the Israeli delegation and the Jordanian-Palestinian delegation will proceed independently of any other negotiations.

This statement of understandings is an integral whole. The United States understands that your acceptance is dependent on the implementation of each element in good faith.

Sincerely yours,
George P. Shultz.

DECLARATION OF PALESTINIAN INDEPENDENCE

In November 1988, the 19th session of the Palestine National Council (PNC) culminated in the declaration 'in the name of God and the Palestinian Arab people' of the independent State of Palestine, with the Holy City of Jerusalem as its capital. The opportunity for the PLO to assert sovereignty over a specific area arose through the decision of King Hussein of Jordan, in July 1988, to sever Jordan's 'administrative and legal links' with the West Bank. The Declaration of Independence cited United Nations General Assembly Resolution 181 of 1947, which partitioned Palestine into two states, one Arab and one Jewish, as providing the legal basis for the right of the Palestinian Arab people to national sovereignty and independence. At the end of the session, the PNC issued a political statement. Details of the Declaration of Independence, and of the political statement, set out below, are taken from an unofficial English-language translation of the proceedings, distributed by the PLO.

'The National Council proclaims, in the name of God and the Palestinian Arab people, the establishment of the State of Palestine on our Palestinian land, with the Holy City of Jerusalem as its capital.

The State of Palestine is the state of Palestinians wherever they may be. In it they shall develop their national and cultural identity and enjoy full equality in rights. Their religious and political beliefs and their human dignity shall be safeguarded under a democratic parliamentary system of government built

on the freedom of opinion; and on the freedom to form parties; and on the protection of the rights of the minority by the majority and respect of the decisions of the majority by the minority; and on social justice and equal rights, free of ethnic, religious, racial or sexual discrimination; and on a constitution that guarantees the rule of law and the independence of the judiciary; and on the basis of total allegiance to the centuries-old spiritual and civilizational Palestinian heritage of religious tolerance and coexistence.

The State of Palestine is an Arab state, an integral part of the Arab nation and of that nation's heritage, its civilization and its aspiration to attain its goals of liberation, development, democracy and unity. Affirming its commitment to the Charter of the League of Arab states and its insistence on the reinforcement of joint Arab action, the State of Palestine calls on the people of its nation to assist in the completion of its birth by mobilizing their resources and augmenting their efforts to end the Israeli occupation.

The State of Palestine declares its commitment to the principles and objectives of the United Nations, and to the Universal Declaration of Human Rights, and to the principles and policy of non-alignment.

The State of Palestine, declaring itself a peace-loving state committed to the principles of peaceful coexistence, shall strive with all states and peoples to attain a permanent peace built on justice and respect of rights, in which humanity's constructive talents can prosper, and creative competition can flourish, and fear of tomorrow can be abolished, for tomorrow brings nothing but security for the just and those who regain their sense of justice.

As it struggles to establish peace in the land of love and peace, the State of Palestine exhorts the United Nations to take upon itself a special responsibility for the Palestinian Arab people and their homeland; and exhorts the peace-loving, freedom-cherishing peoples and states of the world to help it attain its objectives and put an end to the tragedy its people are suffering by providing them with security and endeavouring to end the Israeli occupation of the Palestinian territories.

The State of Palestine declares its belief in the settlement of international and regional disputes by peaceful means in accordance with the Charter and resolutions of the United Nations; and its rejection of threats of force or violence or terrorism and the use of these against its territorial integrity and political independence or the territorial integrity of any other state, without prejudice to its natural right to defend its territory and independence.

The Palestine National Council resolves:

First: On the escalation and continuity of the *intifada*

A. To provide all the means and capabilities needed to escalate our people's *intifada* in various ways and on various levels to guarantee its continuation and intensification.

B. To support the popular institutions and organizations in the occupied Palestinian territories.

C. To bolster and develop the Popular Committees and other specialized popular and trade union bodies, including the attack group and the popular army, with a view to expanding their role and increasing their effectiveness.

D. To consolidate the national unity that emerged and developed during the *intifada*.

E. To intensify efforts on the international level for the release of the detainees, the repatriation of the deportees, and the termination of the organized, official acts of repression and terrorism against our children, our women, our men, and our institutions.

F. To call on the United Nations to place the occupied Palestinian land under international supervision for the protection of our people and the termination of the Israeli occupation.

G. To call on the Palestinian people outside our homeland to intensify and increase their support, and to expand the family-assistance program.

H. To call on the Arab nation, its people, forces, institutions and governments, to increase their political, material and informational support of the *intifada*.

I. To call on all free and honorable people worldwide to stand by our people, our revolution, our *intifada* against the Israeli occupation, the repression, and the organized, fascist official terrorism to which the occupation forces and the armed fanatic settlers are subjecting our people, our universities, our institutions, our national economy, and our Islamic and Christian holy places.

Second: In the political field

Proceeding from the above, the Palestine National Council, being responsible to the Palestinian people, their national rights and their desire for peace as expressed in the Declaration of Independence issued on November 15, 1988; and in response to the humanitarian quest for international entente, nuclear disarmament and the settlement of regional conflicts by peaceful means, affirms the determination of the Palestine Liberation Organization to arrive at a political settlement of the Arab-Israeli conflict and its core, the Palestinian issue, in the framework of the UN Charter, the principles and rules of international legitimacy, the edicts of international law, the resolutions of the United Nations, the latest of which are Security Council Resolutions 605, 607 and 608, and the resolutions of the Arab summits, in a manner that assures the Palestinian Arab people's right to repatriation, self-determination and the establishment of their independent state on their national soil, and that institutes arrangements for the security and peace of all states in the region.

Towards the achievement of this, the Palestine National Council affirms:

1. The necessity of convening an international conference on the issue of the Middle East and its core, the Palestinian issue, under the auspices of the United Nations and with the participation of the permanent members of the Security Council and all parties to the conflict in the region, including, on an equal footing, the Palestine Liberation Organization, the sole legitimate representative of the Palestinian people; on the understanding that the international conference will be held on the basis of Security Council Resolutions 242 and 338 and the safeguarding of the legitimate national rights of the Palestinian people, foremost among which is the right to self-determination, in accordance with the principles and provisions of the UN Charter as they pertain to the right of peoples to self-determination, and the inadmissibility of the acquisition of others' territory by force or military conquest, and in accordance with the UN resolutions relating to the Palestinian issue.

2. The withdrawal of Israel from all the Palestinian and Arab territories it occupied in 1967, including Arab Jerusalem.

3. The annulment of all expropriation and annexation measures and the removal of the settlements established by Israel in the Palestinian and Arab territories since 1967.

4. Endeavouring to place the occupied Palestinian territories, including Arab Jerusalem, under the supervision of the United Nations for a limited period, to protect our people, to create an atmosphere conducive to the success of the proceedings of the international conference toward the attainment of a comprehensive political settlement and the achievement of peace and security for all on the basis of mutual consent, and to enable the Palestinian state to exercise its effective authority in these territories.

5. The settlement of the issue of the Palestinian refugees in accordance with the pertinent United Nations resolutions.

6. Guaranteeing the freedom of worship and the right to engage in religious rites for all faiths in the holy place in Palestine.

7. The Security Council shall draw up and guarantee arrangements for the security of all states concerned and for peace between them, including the Palestinian state.

The Palestine National Council confirms its past resolutions that the relationship between the fraternal Jordanian and Palestinian peoples is a privileged one and that the future relationship between the states of Jordan and Palestine will be built on confederal foundations, on the basis of the two fraternal peoples' free and voluntary choice, in consolidation of the historic ties that bind them and the vital interests they hold in common.

The National Council also renews its commitment to the United Nations resolutions that affirm the right of peoples to resist foreign occupation, imperialism and racial discrimination, and their right to fight for their independence; and it once more announces its rejection of terrorism in all its forms, including state terrorism, emphasizing its commitment to the resolutions it adopted in the past on this subject, and to the resolutions of the Arab summit in Algiers in 1988, and to UN Resolutions 42/159 of 1967 and 61/40 of 1985, and to what was stated in this regard in the Cairo Declaration of 7/11/85.

Third: In the Arab and international fields

The Palestine National Council emphasizes the importance of the unity of Lebanon in its territory, its people and its institutions, and stands firmly against the attempts to partition the land and disintegrate the fraternal people of Lebanon. It further emphasizes the importance of the joint Arab effort to participate in a settlement of the Lebanese crisis that helps crystallize and implement solutions that preserve Lebanese unity. The Council also stresses the importance of consecrating the right of the Palestinians in Lebanon to engage in political and informational activity and to enjoy security and protection; and of working against all the forms of conspiracy and aggression that target them and their right to work and live; and of the need to secure the conditions that assure them the ability to defend themselves and provide them with security and protection.

The Palestine National Council affirms its solidarity with the Lebanese nationalist Islamic forces in their struggle against the Israeli occupation and its agents in the Lebanese South; expresses its pride in the allied struggle of the Lebanese and Palestinian peoples against the aggression and toward the termination of the Israeli occupation of parts of the South; and underscores the importance of bolstering this kinship between our people and the fraternal, combative people of Lebanon.

And on this occasion, the Council addresses a reverent salute to the long-suffering people of our camps in Lebanon and its South, who are enduring the aggression, massacres, murder, starvation, air raids, bombardments and sieges perpetrated against the Palestinian camps and Lebanese villages by the Israeli army, air force and navy, aided and abetted by hireling forces in the region; and it rejects the resettlement conspiracy, for the Palestinians' homeland is Palestine.

The Council emphasizes the importance of the Iraq–Iran cease-fire resolution toward the establishment of a permanent peace settlement between the two countries and in the Gulf Region; and calls for an intensification of the efforts being exerted to ensure the success of the negotiations toward the establishment of peace on stable and firm foundations; affirming, on this occasion, the price of the Palestinian Arab people and the Arab nation as a whole in the steadfastness and triumphs of fraternal Iraq as it defended the eastern gate of the Arab nation.

The National Council also expresses its deep pride in the stand taken by the peoples of our Arab nation in support of our Palestinian Arab people and of the Palestine Liberation Organization and of our people's *intifada* in the occupied homeland; and emphasizes the importance of fortifying the bonds of combat among the forces, parties and organizations of the Arab national liberation movement, in defense of the right of the Arab nation and its peoples to liberation, progress, democracy and unity. The Council calls for the adoption of all measures needed to reinforce the unity of struggle among all members of the Arab national liberation movement.

The Palestine National Council, as it hails the Arab states and thanks them for their support of our people's struggle, calls on them to honour the commitments they approved at the summit conference in Algiers in support of the Palestinian people and their blessed *intifada*. The Council, in issuing this appeal, expresses its great confidence that the leaders of the Arab nation will remain, as we have known them, a bulwark of support for Palestine and its people.

The Palestine National Council reiterates the desire of the Palestine Liberation Organization for Arab solidarity as the framework within which the Arab nation and its states can organize themselves to confront Israel's aggression and American support of that aggression, and within which Arab prestige can be enhanced and the Arab role strengthened to the point of influencing international policies to the benefit of Arab rights and causes.

The Palestine National Council expresses its deep gratitude to all the states and international forces and organizations that support the national rights of the Palestinians; affirms its desire to strengthen the bonds of friendship and co-operation with the Soviet Union, the People's (Republic of) China, the other socialist countries, the non-aligned states, the Islamic states, the African states, the Latin American states and the other friendly states; and notes with satisfaction the signs of positive evolution in the positions of some West European states and Japan in the direction of support for the rights of the Palestinian people, applauds this development, and urges intensified efforts to increase it.

The National Council affirms the fraternal solidarity of the Palestinian people and the Palestine Liberation Organization with the struggle of the peoples of Asia, Africa and Latin America for their liberation and the reinforcement of their independence; and condemns all American attempts to threaten the independence of the states of Central America and interfere in their affairs.

The Palestine National Council expresses the support of the Palestine Liberation Organization for the national liberation movements in South Africa and Namibia . . . .

The Council notes with considerable concern the growth of the Israeli forces of fascism and extremism and the escalation of their open calls for the implementation of the policy of annihilation and individual and collective expulsion of our people from their homeland, and calls for intensified efforts in all areas to confront this fascist peril. The Council at the same time expresses its appreciation of the role and courage of the Israeli peace forces as they resist and expose the forces of fascism, racism and aggression, support our people's struggle and their valiant *intifada* and back our people's right to self-determination and the establishment of an independent state. The Council confirms its past resolutions regarding the reinforcement and development of relations with these democratic forces.

The Palestine National Council also addresses itself to the American people, calling on them all to strive to put an end to the American policy that denies the Palestinian people's national rights, including their sacred right to self-determination, and urging them to work toward the adoption of policies that conform to the Declaration of Human Rights and the international conventions and resolutions and serve the quest for peace in the Middle East and security for all its peoples, including the Palestinian people.

The Council charges the Executive Committee with the task of completing the formation of the Committee for the Perpetuation of the Memory of the Martyr-Symbol Abu Jihad, which shall initiate its work immediately upon the adjournment of the Council.

The Council sends its greetings to the United Nations Committee on the Exercise of the Inalienable Rights of the Palestinian People, and to the fraternal and friendly international and non-governmental institutions and organizations, and to the journalists and media that have stood and still stand by our people's struggle and *intifada*.

The National Council expresses deep pain at the continued detention of hundreds of combatants from among our people in a number of Arab countries, strongly condemns their continued detention, and calls upon those countries to put an end to these abnormal conditions and release those fighters to play their role in the struggle.

In conclusion, the Palestine National Council affirms its complete confidence that the justice of the Palestinian cause and of the demands for which the Palestinian people are struggling will continue to draw increasing support from honorable and free people around the world; and also affirms its complete confidence in victory on the road to Jerusalem, the capital of our independent Palestinian state.'

THE ISRAELI PEACE INITIATIVE

In May 1989 the Government of Israel approved a four-point peace initiative for a resolution of the Middle East conflict, the

details of which had first been announced during a meeting between US President George Bush and Israeli Prime Minister, Itzhak Shamir, in Washington on 6 April. Based largely on peace proposals made by Israeli Defence Minister, Itzhak Rabin, in January 1989, the new plan followed increased international diplomatic pressure on Israel to respond to the uprising in the Occupied Territories with constructive action to end the conflict. The main proposals of the Israeli initiative were that elections should be held in the West Bank and Gaza Strip in order to facilitate the formation of a delegation of appropriate interlocutors (i.e. non-PLO representatives) to take part in negotiations on a transitional settlement, when a self-ruling authority might be established. The transitional period would serve as a test of co-operation and coexistence and would be followed by negotiations on a final agreement in which Israel would be prepared to discuss any option presented; that Israel, Egypt and the USA should reconfirm their commitment to the Camp David Agreements of 1979; that the USA and Egypt should seek to persuade Arab countries to desist from hostility towards Israel; and that an international effort should be made to solve the 'humanitarian issue' of the inhabitants of refugee camps in Judaea, Samaria and the Gaza Strip. In July 1989 four amendments to the Israeli peace initiative were approved by the central committee of the Likud. These stipulated that residents of East Jerusalem would not be allowed to take part in the proposed elections in the West Bank and Gaza; that violent attacks by Palestinians must cease before elections could be held in the Occupied Territories; that Jewish settlement should continue in the Territories and that foreign sovereignty should not be conceded in any part of Israel; and that the establishment of a Palestinian state west of the River Jordan was out of the question, as were negotiations with the PLO. At the end of July, however, the Israeli Cabinet once again endorsed the peace initiative in its original form.*

In September 1989 President Mubarak of Egypt sought ten assurances from the Israeli Government with regard to its peace initiative: (i) a commitment to accept the results of the elections proposed by the peace initiative; (ii) the vigilance of international observers at the elections; (iii) the granting of immunity to all elected representatives; (iv) the withdrawal of the Israel Defence Force from the balloting area; (v) a commitment by the Israeli Government to begin talks on the final status of the Occupied Territories on a specific date within three to five years; (vi) an end to Jewish settlement activities in the Occupied Territories; (vii) a ban on election propaganda; (viii) a ban on the entry of Israelis into the Occupied Territories on the day of the proposed elections; (ix) permission for residents of East Jerusalem to participate in the elections; (x) a commitment by the Israeli Government to the principle of exchanging land for peace. Mubarak also offered to host talks between Palestinian and Israeli delegations prior to the holding of the elections, but a proposal by the Labour component of the Israeli Government to accept his invitation was rejected by Israel's 'inner' Cabinet in October 1989. In the same month the US Secretary of State, James Baker, put forward a series of unofficial proposals which aimed to give new impetus to the Israeli peace initiative and the subsequent clarification proposed by President Mubarak. On the basis of its understanding that a dialogue between Israeli and Palestinian delegations would take place, the USA, through the 'Baker plan', sought assurances that Egypt could not and would not substitute itself for the Palestinians in any future negotiations, and that both Israel and the Palestinians would take part in any future dialogue on the basis of the 'Shamir plan'.

THE 1991 MIDDLE EAST PEACE CONFERENCE

On 30 October 1991 the first, symbolic session of a Middle East peace conference, sponsored by the USA and the USSR and attended by Israeli, Syrian, Egyptian, Lebanese and Palestinian/Jordanian delegations, commenced in Madrid, Spain. The text of the invitation sent to the participants by the US and Soviet Presidents is reproduced from Al-Hayat, London

After extensive consultations with Arab states, Israel and the Palestinians, the US and the Soviet Union believe that an historic opportunity exists to advance the prospects for genuine peace throughout the region. The US and the Soviet Union are prepared to assist the parties to achieve a just, lasting and comprehensive peace settlement, through direct negotiations along two tracks, between Israel and the Palestinians, based on UN Security Council resolutions 242 and 338. The objective of this process is real peace.

Towards that end, the president of the US and the president of the USSR invite you to a peace conference, which their countries will co-sponsor, followed immediately by direct negotiations. The conference will be convened in Madrid on 30 October 1991.

President Bush and President Gorbachev request your acceptance of this invitation no later than 6.00pm Washington time, 23 October 1991, in order to ensure proper organisation and preparation of the conference.

Direct bilateral negotiations will begin four days after the opening of the conference. Those parties who wish to attend multilateral negotiations will convene two weeks after the opening of the conference to organise those negotiations. The co-sponsors believe that those negotiations should focus on regionwide issues such as arms control and regional security, water, refugee issues, environment, economic development, and other subjects of mutual interest.

The co-sponsors will chair the conference which will be held at ministerial level. Governments to be invited include Israel, Syria, Lebanon and Jordan. Palestinians will be invited and attend as part of a joint Jordanian-Palestinian delegation. Egypt will be invited to the conference as a participant. The EC will be a participant in the conference alongside the US and Soviet Union and will be represented by its presidency. The GCC will be invited to send its secretary-general to the conference as an observer, and GCC member states will be invited to participate in organising the negotiations on multilateral issues. The UN will be invited to send an observer, representing the secretary-general.

DECLARATION OF PRINCIPLES ON PALESTINIAN SELF-RULE

13 September 1993

The Government of the State of Israel and the Palestinian team (in the Jordanian-Palestinian delegation to the Middle East Peace Conference) (the 'Palestinian Delegation') representing the Palestinian people, agree that it is time to put an end to decades of confrontation and conflict, recognize their mutual legitimate and political rights, and strive to live in peaceful coexistence and mutual dignity and security and achieve a just, lasting and comprehensive peace settlement and historic reconciliation through the agreed political process.

Accordingly, the two sides agree to the following principles:

Article I

Aim of the negotiations

The aim of the Israeli-Palestinian negotiations within the current Middle East peace process is, among other things, to establish a Palestinian Interim Self-Government Authority, the elected Council, (the 'Council') for the Palestinian people in the West Bank and the Gaza Strip, for a transitional period not exceeding five years, leading to a permanent settlement based on Security Council Resolutions 242 and 338.

It is understood that the interim arrangements are an integral part of the overall peace process and that final status negotiations will lead to the implementation of Security Council Resolutions 242 and 338.

Article II

Framework for the interim period

The agreed framework for the interim period is set forth in the Declaration of Principles.

Article III

Elections

1. In order that the Palestinian people in the West Bank and Gaza Strip may govern themselves according to democratic principles, direct, free and general political elections will be held for the Council under agreed supervision and international observation, while the Palestinian police will ensure public order.

2. An agreement will be concluded on the exact mode and conditions of the elections in accordance with the protocol attached as Annex I, with the goal of holding the elections not later than nine months after the entry into force of this Declaration of Principles.

3. These elections will constitute a significant interim preparatory step toward the realization of the legitimate rights of the Palestinian people and their just requirments.

Article IV

Jurisdiction of the Council will cover West Bank and Gaza Strip territory, except for issues that will be negotiated in the permanent status negotiations. The two sides view the West Bank and the Gaza Strip as a single territorial unit, whose integrity will be preserved during the interim period.

Article V

Transitional period and permanent status negotiations

1. The five-year transitional period will begin upon the withdrawal from the Gaza Strip and Jericho area.

2. Permanent status negotiations will commence as soon as possible, but not later than the beginning of the third year of the interim period, between the Government of Israel and the Palestinian people representatives.

3. It is understood that these negotiations shall cover remaining issues, including Jerusalem, refugees, settlements, security arrangements, borders, relations and co-operation with other neighbours, and other issues of common interest.

4. The two parties agree that the outcome of the permanent status negotiations should not be prejudiced or pre-empted by agreements reached for the interim period.

Article VI

Preparatory transfer of powers and responsibilities

1. Upon the entry into force of this Declaration of Principles and the withdrawal from the Gaza Strip and Jericho area, a transfer of authority from the Israeli military government and its Civil Administration to the authorized Palestinians for this task, as detailed herein, will commence. This transfer of authority will be of preparatory nature until the inauguration of the Council.

2. Immediately after the entry into force of this Declaration of Principles and the withdrawal from the Gaza Strip and Jericho area, with the view to promoting economic development in the West Bank and Gaza Strip, authority will be transferred to the Palestinians in the following spheres: education and culture, health, social welfare, direct taxation, and tourism. The Palestinian side will commence in building the Palestinian police force, as agreed upon. Pending the inauguration of the Council, the two parties may negotiate the transfer of additional powers and responsibilities as agreed upon.

Article VII

Interim agreement

1. The Israeli and Palestinian delegations will negotiate an agreement on the interim period (the 'Interim Agreement').

2. The Interim Agreement shall specify, among other things, the structure of the Council, the number of its members, and the transfer of powers and responsibilities from the Israeli military government and its Civil Administration to the Council. The Interim Agreement shall also specify the Council's executive authority, legislative authority in accordance with Article IX below, and the independent Palestinian judicial organs.

3. The Interim Agreement shall include arrangements, to be implemented upon the inauguration of the Council, for the assumption by the Council of all of the powers and responsibilities transferred previously in accordance with Article VI above.

4. In order to enable the Council to promote economic growth, upon its inauguration, the Council will establish, among other things, a Palestinian Electricity Authority, a

Gaza Sea Port Authority, a Palestinian Development Bank, a Palestinian Export Promotion Board, a Palestinian Environmental Authority, a Palestinian Land Authority and a Palestinian Water Administration Authority, and any other authorities agreed upon, in accordance with the Interim Agreement that will specify their powers and responsibilities.

5. After the inauguration of the Council, the Civil Administration will be dissolved, and the Israeli military government will be withdrawn.

Article VIII
Public order and security

In order to guarantee public order and internal security for the Palestinians of the West Bank and the Gaza Strip, the Council will establish a strong police force, while Israel will continue to carry the responsibility for defending against external threats, as well as the responsibility for overall security of the Israelis to protect their internal security and public order.

Article IX
Laws and military orders

1. The Council will be empowered to legislate, in accordance with the Interim Agreement, within all authorities transferred to it.

2. Both parties will review jointly laws and military orders presently in force in remaining spheres.

Article X
Joint Israeli-Palestinian liaison committee

In order to provide for a smooth implementation of this Declaration of Principles and any subsequent agreements pertaining to the interim period, upon the entry into force of this Declaration of Principles, a Joint Israeli-Palestinian Liaison Committee will be established in order to deal with issues requiring co-ordination, other issues of common interest, and disputes.

Article XI
Israeli-Palestinian co-operation in economic fields

Recognizing the mutual benefit of co-operation in promoting the development of the West Bank, the Gaza Strip and Israel, upon the entry into force of this Declaration of Principles, an Israeli-Palestinian Economic Co-operation Committee will be established in order to develop and implement in a co-operative manner the programmes identified in the protocols attached as Annex III and Annex IV.

Article XII
Liaison and co-operation with Jordan and Egypt

The two parties will invite the Governments of Jordan and Egypt to participate in establishing further liaison and co-operation arrangements between the Government of Israel and the Palestinian representatives, on one hand, and the Governments of Jordan and Egypt, on the other hand, to promote co-operation between them. These arrangements will include the constitution of a Continuing Committee that will decide by agreement on the modalities of the admission of persons displaced from the West Bank and Gaza Strip in 1967, together with necessary measures to prevent disruption and disorder. Other matters of common concern will be dealt with by this Committee.

Article XIII
Redeployment of Israeli forces

1. After the entry into force of this Declaration of Principles, and not later than the eve of elections for the Council, a redeployment of Israeli military forces in the West Bank and the Gaza Strip will take place, in addition to withdrawal of Israeli forces carried out in accordance with Article XIV.

2. In redeploying its military forces, Israel will be guided by the principle that its military forces should be redeployed outside the populated areas.

3. Further redeployments to specified locations will be gradually implemented commensurate with the assumption of

responsibility for public order and internal security by the Palestinian police force pursuant to Article VIII above.

Article XIV
Israeli withdrawal from the Gaza Strip and Jericho area

Israel will withdraw from the Gaza Strip and Jericho area, as detailed in the protocol attached as Annex II.

Article XV
Resolution of disputes

1. Disputes arising out of the application or interpretation of this Declaration of Principles, or any subsequent agreements pertaining to the interim period, shall be resolved by negotiations through the Joint Liaison Committee to be established pursuant to Article X above.

2. Disputes which cannot be settled by negotiations may be resolved by a mechanism of conciliation to be agreed upon by the parties.

3. The parties may agree to submit to arbitration disputes relating to the interim period, which cannot be settled through conciliation. To this end, upon the agreement of both parties, the parties will establish an Arbitration Committee.

Article XVI
Israel-Palestinian co-operation concerning regional programs

Both parties view the multilateral working groups as an appropriate instrument for promoting a 'Marshall Plan,' the regional programs and other programs, including special programs for the West Bank and Gaza Strip, as indicated in the protocol atttached as Annex IV.

Article XVII
Miscellaneous provisions

1. This Declaration of Principles will enter into force one month after its signing.

2. All protocols annexed to this Declaration of Principles and Agreed Minutes pertaining thereto shall be regarded as an integral part hereof.

Annex 1—protocol on the mode and conditions of elections

1. Palestinians of Jerusalem who live there will have the right to participate in the election process, according to an agreement between the two sides.

2. In addition, the election agreement should cover, among other things, the following issues:

   a. the system of elections,

   b. the mode of the agreed supervision and international observation and their personal composition, and

   c. rules and regulations regarding election campaign, including agreed arrangements for the organizing of mass media, and the possibility of licensing a broadcasting and TV station.

3. The future status of displaced Palestinians who were registered on 4th June 1967 will not be prejudiced because they are unable to participate in the election process due to practical reasons.

Annex 2—protocol on withdrawal of Israeli forces from the Gaza Strip and Jericho Area

1. The two sides will conclude and sign within two months from the date of entry into force of this Declaration of Principles, an agreement on the withdrawal of Israeli military forces from the Gaza Strip and Jericho area. This agreement will include comprehensive arrangements to apply in the Gaza Strip and the Jericho area subsequent to the Israeli withdrawal.

2. Israel will implement an accelerated and scheduled withdrawal of Israeli military forces from the Gaza Strip and Jericho area, beginning immediately with the signing of the agreement on the Gaza Strip and Jericho area and to be completed within a period not exceeding four months after the signing of this agreement.

3. The above agreement will include, among other things:

   a. Arrangements for a smooth and peaceful transfer of authority from the Israeli military government and its Civil Administration to the Palestinian representatives.

b. structure, powers and responsibilities of the Palestinian authority in these areas, except, external security, settlements, Israelis, foreign relations, and other subjects mutually agreed upon.

c. Arrangements for assumption of internal security and public order by the Palestinian police force consisting of police officers recruited locally and from abroad (holding Jordanian passports and Palestinian documents issued by Egypt). Those who will participate in the Palestinian police force coming from abroad should be trained as police and police officers.

d. A temporary international or foreign presence, as agreed upon.

e. Establishment of a joint Palestinian-Israeli co-ordination and co-operation committee for mutual security purposes.

f. An economic development and stablization program, including the establishment of an Emergency Fund, to encourage foreign investment, and financial and economic support. Both sides will co-ordinate and co-operate jointly and unilaterally with regional and international parties to support these aims.

g. Arrangements for a safe passage for persons and transportation between the Gaza Strip and Jericho area.

4. The above agreement will include arrangements for co-ordination between both parties regarding passages:

a. Gaza–Egypt; and

b. Jericho–Jordan.

5. The offices responsible for carrying out the powers and responsibilities of the Palestinian authority under this Annex II and Article VI of the Declaration of Principles will be located in the Gaza Strip and in the Jericho area pending the inauguration of the Council.

6. Other than these agreed arrangements, the status of the Gaza Strip and Jericho area will continue to be an integral part of the West Bank and Gaza Strip, and will not be changed in the interim period.

PROTOCOL ON ISRAELI-PALESTINIAN CO-OPERATION IN ECONOMIC AND DEVELOPMENT PROGRAMS

The two sides agree to establish an Israeli-Palestinian Continuing Committee for Economic Co-operation, focusing, among other things, on the following:

1. Co-operation in the field of water, including a Water Development Program prepared by experts from both sides, which will also specify the mode of co-operation in the management of water resources in the West Bank and Gaza Strip, and will include proposals for studies and plans on water rights of each party, as well as on the equitable utilization of joint water resources for implementation in and beyond the interim period.

2. Co-operation in the field of electricity, including an Electricity Development Program, which will also specify the mode of co-operation for the production, maintenance, purchase and sale of electricity resources.

3. Co-operation in the field of energy, including an Energy Development Program, which will provide for the exploitation of oil and gas for industrial purposes, particularly in the Gaza Strip and in the Negev, and will encourage further joint exploitation of other energy resources. This Program may also provide for the construction of a Petrochemical industrial complex in the Gaza Strip and the construction of oil and gas pipelines.

4. Co-operation in the field of finance, including a Financial Development and Action Program for the encouragement of international investment in the West Bank and the Gaza Strip, and in Israel, as well as the establishment of a Palestinian Development Bank.

5. Co-operation in the fields of transport and communications, including a Program, which will define guidelines for the establishment of a Gaza Sea Port Area, and will provide for the establishing of transport and communications lines to and from the West Bank and the Gaza Strip to Israel and to

other countries. In addition, this Program will provide for carrying out the necessary construction of roads, railways, communications lines, etc.

6. Co-operation in the field of trade, including studies, and Trade Promotion Programs, which will encourage local, regional and inter-regional trade, as well as a feasiblity study of creating free trade zones in the Gaza Strip and in Israel, mutual access to these zones, and co-operation in other areas related to trade and commerce.

7. Co-operation in the field of industry, including industrial Development Programs, which will provide for the establishment of joint Israeli-Palestinian Research and Development Centers, will promote Palestinian-Israeli joint ventures, and provide guidelines for co-operation in the textile, food, pharmaceutical, electronics, diamonds, computer and science-based industries.

8. A program for co-operation in, and regulation of, labour relations and co-operation in social welfare issues.

9. A Human Resources Development and Co-operation Plan, providing for joint Israeli-Palestinian workshops and seminars, and for the establishment of joint vocational training centres, research institutes and data banks.

10. An Environmental Protection Plan, providing for joint and/or co-ordinated measures in this sphere.

11. A program for developing co-ordination and co-operation in the field of communication and media.

12. Any other programs of mutual interest.

PROTOCOL ON ISRAELI-PALESTINIAN CO-OPERATION CONCERNING REGIONAL DEVELOPMENT PROGRAMS

1. The two sides will co-operate in the context of the multilateral peace efforts in promoting a Development Program for the region, including the West Bank and the Gaza Strip, to be initiated by the G-7. The parties will request the G-7 to seek the participation in this program of other interested states, such as members of the Organization for Economic Co-operation and Development, regional Arab states and institutions, as well as members of the private sector.

2. The Development Program will consist of two elements:

a) an Economic Development Program for the West Bank and the Gaza Strip;

b) a Regional Economic Development Program

A. The Economic Development Program for the West Bank and the Gaza Strip will consist of the following elements:

(1) A Social Rehabilitation Program, including a Housing and Construction Program.

(2) A Small and Medium Business Development Plan.

(3) An Infrastructure Development Program (water, electricity, transportation and communications, etc.)

(4) A Human Resources Plan.

(5) Other programs.

B. The Regional Economic Development Program may consist of the following elements:

(1) The establishment of a Middle East Development Fund, as a first step, and a Middle East Development Bank, as a second step.

(2) The development of a joint Israeli-Palestinian-Jordanian Plan for co-ordinated exploitation of the Dead Sea area.

(3) The Mediterranean Sea (Gaza)—Dead Sea Canal.

(4) Regional Desalinization and other water development projects.

(5) A regional plan for agricultural development, including a co-ordinated regional effort for the prevention of desertification.

(6) Interconnection of electricity grids.

(7) Regional co-operation for the transfer, distribution and industrial exploitation of gas, oil and other energy resources.

(8) A regional Tourism, Transportation and Telecommunications Development Plan.

(9) Regional co-operation in other spheres.

3. The two sides will encourage the multilateral working groups, and will co-ordinate towards its success. The two parties will encourage international activities, as well as pre-feasibility and feasibility studies, within the various multilateral working groups.

AGREED MINUTES TO THE DECLARATION OF PRINCIPLES ON INTERIM SELF-GOVERNMENT ARRANGEMENTS

A. General Understandings and Agreements

Any powers and responsibilites transferred to the Palestinians pursuant to the Declaration of Principles prior to the inauguration of the Council will be subject to the same principles pertaining to Article IV, as set out in these Agreed Minutes below.

B. Specific Understandings and Agreements

Article IV

It is understood that:

1. Jurisdiction of the Council will cover West Bank and Gaza Strip territory, except for issues that will be negotiated in the permanent status negotiations: Jerusalem, settlements, military locations and Israelis.

2. The Council's jurisdiction will apply with regard to the agreed powers, responsibilities, spheres and authorities transferred to it.

Article VI (2)

It is agreed that the transfer of authority will be as follows:

(1) The Palestinian side will inform the Israeli side of the names of the authorized Palestinians who will assume the powers, authorities and responsibilities that will be transferred to the Palestinians according to the Declaration of Principles in the following fields: education and culture, health, social welfare, direct taxation, tourism, and any other authorities agreed upon.

(2) It is understood that the rights and obligations of these offices will not be affected.

(3) Each of the spheres described above will continue to enjoy existing budgetary allocations in accordance with arrangements to be mutually agreed upon. These arrangements also will provide for the necessary adjustments required in order to take into account the taxes collected by the direct taxation office.

(4) Upon the execution of the Declaration of Principles, the Israeli and Palestinian delegations will immediately commence negotiations on a detailed plan for the transfer of authority on the above offices in accordance with the above understandings.

Article VII (2)

The Interim Agreement will also include arrangements for co-ordination and co-operation.

Article VII (5)

The withdrawal of the military government will not prevent Israel from exercising the powers and responsibilities not transferred to the Council.

Article VIII

It is understood that the Interim Agreement will include arrangements for co-operation and co-ordination between the two parties in this regard. It is also agreed that the transfer of powers and responsibilities to the Palestinian police will be accomplished in a phased manner, as agreed in the Interim Agreement.

Article X

It is agreed that, upon the entry into force of the Declaration of Principles, the Israeli and Palestinian delegations will exchange the names of the individuals designated by them as members of the Joint Israeli-Palestinian Liaison Committee.

It is further agreed that each side will have an equal number of members in the Joint Committee. The Joint Committee will reach decisions by agreement. The Joint Committee may add other technicians and experts, as necessary. The Joint Committee will decide on the frequency and place or places of its meetings.

Annex II

It is understood that, subsequent to the Israeli withdrawal, Israel will continue to be responsible for external security, and for internal security and public order of settlements and Israelis. Israeli military forces and civilians may continue to use roads freely within the Gaza Strip and the Jericho area.

Article XVI

Israeli-Palestinian Co-operation Concerning Regional Programs

Both parties view the multilateral working groups as an appropriate instrument for promoting a 'Marshall Plan,' the regional programs and other programs, including special programs for the West Bank and Gaza Strip, as indicated in the protocol attached as Annex IV.

Article XVII

Miscellaneous Provisions

1. This Declaration of Principles will enter into force one month after its signing.

2. All protocols annexed to this Declaration of Principles and Agreed Minutes pertaining thereto shall be regarded as an integral part hereof.

THE CAIRO AGREEMENT ON THE GAZA STRIP AND JERICHO
4 May 1994

The Government of the State of Israel and the Palestine Liberation Organization (hereinafter 'the PLO'), the representative of the Palestinian people;

Preamble

Within the framework of the Middle East peace process initiated at Madrid in October 1991;

Reaffirming their determination to live in peaceful co-existence, mutual dignity and security, while recognizing their mutual legitimate and political rights;

Reaffirming their desire to achieve a just, lasting and comprehensive peace settlement through the agreed political process;

Reaffirming their adherence to the mutual recognition and commitments expressed in the letters dated September 9, 1993, signed by and exchanged between the Prime Minister of Israel and the Chairman of the PLO;

Reaffirming their understanding that the interim self-government arrangements, including the arrangements to apply in the Gaza Strip and the Jericho Area contained in this Agreement, are an integral part of the whole peace process and that the negotiations on the permanent status will lead to the implementation of Security Council Resolutions 242 and 338;

Desirous of putting into effect the Declaration of Principles on Interim Self-Government Arrangements signed at Washington, D.C. on September 13, 1993, and the agreed minutes thereto (hereinafter 'The Declaration of Principles'), and in particular the protocol on withdrawal of Israeli forces from the Gaza Strip and the Jericho Area:

Hereby agree to the following arrangements regarding the Gaza Strip and the Jericho Area:

Article I
Definitions

For the purpose of this Agreement:

    a. The Gaza Strip and the Jericho Area are delineated on Map Nos. 1 and 2 attached to this Agreeement (*Maps not reproduced: Ed.*);

    b. 'The settlements' means the Gush Katif and Erez settlement areas, as well as the other settlements in the Gaza Strip, as shown on attached Map No. 1;

    c. 'The military installation area' means the Israeli military installation area along the Egyptian border in the Gaza

Strip, as shown on Map No. 1; and

d. The term 'Israelis' shall also include Israeli statutory agencies and corporations registered in Israel.

Article II
Scheduled withdrawal of Israeli military forces

1. Israel shall implement an accelerated and scheduled withdrawal of Israeli military forces from the Gaza Strip and from the Jericho Area to begin immediately with the signing of this Agreement. Israel shall complete such withdrawal within three weeks from this date.

2. Subject to the arrangements included in the Protocol concerning withdrawal of Israeli military forces and security arrangements attached as Annex I, the Israeli withdrawal shall include evacuating all military bases and other fixed installations to be handed over to the Palestinian Police, to be established pursuant to Article IX below (hereinafter 'the Palestinian Police').

3. In order to carry out Israel's responsibility for external security and for internal security and public order of settlements and Israelis, Israel shall, concurrently with the withdrawal, redeploy its remaining military forces to the settlements and the military installation area, in accordance with the provisions of this Agreement. Subject to the provisions of this Agreement, this redeployment shall constitute full implementation of Article XIII of the Declaration of Principles with regard to the Gaza Strip and the Jericho Area only.

4. For the purposes of this Agreement, 'Israeli military forces' may include Israeli police and other Israeli security forces.

5. Israelis, including Israeli military forces, may continue to use roads freely within the Gaza Strip and the Jericho Area. Palestinians may use public roads crossing the settlements freely, as provided for in Annex I.

6. The Palestinian Police shall be deployed and shall assume responsibility for public order and internal security of Palestinians in accordance with this Agreement and Annex I.

Article III
Transfer of authority

1. Israel shall transfer authority as specified in this Agreement from the Israeli military government and its Civil Administration to the Palestinian Authority, hereby established, in accordance with Article V of this Agreement, except for the authority that Israel shall continue to excercise as specified in this Agreement.

2. As regards the transfer and assumption of authority in civil spheres, powers and responsibilities shall be transferred and assumed as set out in the Protocol concerning civil affairs attached as Annex II.

3. Arrangements for a smooth and peaceful transfer of the agreed powers and responsibilities are set out in Annex II.

4. Upon the completion of the Israeli withdrawal and the transfer of powers and responsibilities as detailed in Paragraphs 1 and 2 above and in Annex II, the Civil Administration in the Gaza Strip and the Jericho Area will be dissolved and the Israeli military government will be withdrawn. The withdrawal of the military government shall not prevent it from continuing to excercise the powers and responsibilities specified in this Agreement.

5. A joint Civil Affairs Co-ordination and Co-operation Committee (hereinafter 'the CAC') and two joint regional civil affairs subcommittees for the Gaza Strip and the Jericho Area respectively shall be established in order to provide for co-ordination and co-operation in civil affairs between the Palestinian Authority and Israel, as detailed in Annex II.

6. The offices of the Palestinian Authority shall be located in the Gaza Strip and the Jericho Area pending the inauguration of the council to be elected pursuant to the Declaration of Principles.

Article IV
Structure and composition of the Palestinian Authority

1. The Palestinian Authority will consist of one body of 24 members which shall carry out and be responsible for all the legislative and executive powers and responsibilities transferred to it under this Agreement, in accordance with this article, and shall be responsible for the excercise of judicial functions in accordance with Article VI, subparagraph 1.b of this Agreement.

2. The Palestinian Authority shall administer the departments transferred to it and may establish, within its jurisdiction, other departments and subordinate administrative units as necessary for the fulfilment of its responsibilities. It shall determine its own internal procedures.

3. The PLO shall inform the Government of Israel of the names of the members of the Palestinian Authority and any change of members. Changes in the membership of the Palestinian Authority will take effect upon an exchange of letters between the PLO and the Government of Israel.

4. Each member of the Palestinian Authority shall enter into office upon undertaking to act in accordance with this Agreement.

Article V
Jurisdiction

1. The authority of the Palestinian Authority encompasses all matters that fall within its territorial, functional and personal jurisdiction, as follows:

a. The territorial jurisdiction covers the Gaza Strip and the Jericho Area territory, as defined in Article I, except for settlements and the military installation area.

Territorial jurisdiction shall include land, subsoil and territorial waters, in accordance with the provisions of this Agreement.

b. The functional jurisdiction encompasses all powers and responsibilities as specified in this Agreement. This jurisdiction does not include foreign relations, internal security and public order of settlements and the military installation area and Israelis, and external security.

c. The personal jurisdiction extends to all persons within the territorial jurisdiction referred to above, except for Israelis, unless otherwise provided in this Agreement.

2. The Palestinian Authority has, within its authority, legislative, executive and judicial powers and responsibilities, as provided for in this Agreement.

3.a. Israel has authority over the settlements, the military installation area, Israelis, external security, internal security and public order of settlements, the military installation area and Israelis, and those agreed powers and responsibilities specified in this Agreement.

b. Israel shall exercise its authority through its military government, which for that end, shall continue to have the necessary legislative, judicial and executive powers and responsibilities, in accordance with international law. This provision shall not derogate from Israel's applicable legislation over Israelis in personam.

4. The exercise of authority with regard to the electromagnetic sphere and airspace shall be in accordance with the provisions of this Agreement.

5. The provisions of this article are subject to the specific legal arrangements detailed in the Protocol concerning legal matters attached as Annex III. Israel and the Palestinian Authority may negotiate further legal arrangements.

6. Israel and the Palestinian Authority shall co-operate on matters of legal assistance in criminal and civil matters through the legal subcommittee of the CAC.

Article VI
Powers and responsibilities of the Palestinian Authority

1. Subject to the provisions of this Agreement, the Palestinian Authority, within its jurisdiction:

a. has legislative powers as set out in Article VII of this Agreement, as well as executive powers;

b. will administer justice through an independent judiciary:

c. will have, inter alia, power to formulate policies, supervise their implementation, employ staff, establish departments, authorities and institutions, sue and be sued and conclude contracts; and

d. will have, inter alia, the power to keep and administer registers and records of the population, and issue certificates, licenses and documents.

2.a. In accordance with the Declaration of Principles, the Palestinian Authority will not have powers and responsibilities in the sphere of foreign relations, which sphere includes the establishment abroad of embassies, consulates or other types of foreign missions and posts or permitting their establishment in the Gaza Strip or the Jericho Area, the appointment of or admission of diplomatic and consular staff, and the exercise of diplomatic functions.

b. Notwithstanding the provisions of this paragraph, the PLO may conduct negotiations and sign agreements with states or international organizations for the benefit of the Palestinian Authority in the following cases only:

(1) Economic agreements, as specifically provided in Annex IV of this Agreement;

(2) Agreements with donor countries for the purpose of implementing arrangements for the provision of assistance to the Palestinian Authority;

(3) Agreements for the purpose of implementing the regional development plans detailed in Annex IV of the Declaration of Principles or in agreements entered into in the framework of the multilateral negotiations; and

(4) Cultural, scientific and education agreements.

c. Dealings between the Palestinian Authority and representatives of foreign states and international organizations, as well as the establishment in the Gaza Strip and the Jericho Area of representative offices other than those described in subparagraph 2.a, above, for the purpose of implementing the agreements referred to in subparagraph 2.b above, shall not be considered foreign relations.

Article VII

Legislative powers of the Palestinian Authority

1. The Palestinian Authority will have the power, within its jurisdiction, to promulgate legislation, including basic laws, laws, regulations and other legislative acts.

2. Legislation promulgated by the Palestinian Authority shall be consistent with the provisions of this Agreement.

3. Legislation promulgated by the Palestinian Authority shall be communicated to a legislation subcommittee to be established by the CAC (hereinafter 'the Legislation Subcommittee'). During a period of 30 days from the communication of the legislation, Israel may request that the Legislation Subcommittee decide whether such legislation exceeds the jurisdiction of the Palestinian Authority or is otherwise inconsistent with the provisions of this Agreement.

4. Upon receipt of the Israeli request, the Legislation Subcommittee shall decide, as an initial matter, on the entry into force of the legislation pending its decision on the merits of the matter.

5. If the Legislation Subcommittee is unable to reach a decision with regard to the entry into force of the legislation within 15 days, this issue will be referred to a Board of Review. This Board of Review shall be comprised of two judges, retired judges or senior jurists (hereinafter 'Judges'), one from each side, to be appointed from a compiled list of three judges proposed by each.

6. Legislation referred to the Board of Review shall enter into force only if the Board of Review decides that it does not deal with a security issue which falls under Israel's responsibility, that it does not seriously threaten other significant Israeli interests protected by this Agreement and that the entry into force of the legislation could not cause irreparable damage or harm.

7. The Legislation Subcommitte shall attempt to reach a decision on the merits of the matter within 30 days from the date of the Israeli request. If this subcommittee is unable to reach such a decision within this period of 30 days, the matter shall be referred to the joint Israeli-Palestinian Liaison Committee referred to in Article XV below (hereinafter 'the Liaison Committee'). This Liaison Committee will deal with the matter immediately and will attempt to settle it within 30 days.

8. Where the legislation has not entered into force pursuant to paragraphs 5 or 7 above, this situation shall be maintained pending the decision of the Liaison Committee on the merits of the matter, unless it has decided otherwise.

9. Laws and military orders in effect in the Gaza Strip or the Jericho Area prior to the signing of this Agreement shall remain in force, unless amended or abrogated in accordance with this Agreement.

Article VIII

Arrangements for security and public order

1. In order to guarantee public order and internal security for the Palestinians of the Gaza Strip and the Jericho Area, the Palestinian Authority shall establish a strong police force, as set out in Article IX below. Israel shall continue to carry the responsibility for defence against external threats, including the responsibility for protecting the Egyptian border and the Jordanian line, and for defence against external threats from the sea and from the air, as well as the responsibility for overall security of Israelis and settlements, for the purpose of safeguarding their internal security and public order, and will have all the powers to take the steps necessary to meet this responsibility.

2. Agreed security arrangements and co-ordination mechanisms are specified in Annex I.

3. A Joint Co-ordination and Co-operation committee for mutual security purposes (hereinafter 'the JSC'), as well as three joint district co-ordination and co-operation offices for the Gaza District, the Khan Younis District and the Jericho District respectively (hereinafter 'the DCOS') are hereby established as provided for in Annex I.

4. The security arrangements provided for in this Agreement and in Annex I may be reviewed at the requests of either party and may be amended by mutual agreement of the parties. Specific review arrangements are included in Annex I.

Article IX

The Palestinian Directorate of Police Force

1. The Palestinian Authority shall establish a strong police force, the Palestinian Directorate of Police Force (hereinafter 'the Palestinian Police'). The duties, functions, structure, deployment and composition of the Palestinian Police, together with provisions regarding its equipment and operation, are set out in Annex I, Article III. Rules of conduct governing the activities of the Palestinian Police are set out in Annex I, Article VIII.

2. Except for the Palestinian Police referred to in this article and the Israeli military forces, no other armed forces shall be established or operate in the Gaza Strip or the Jericho Area.

3. Except for the arms, ammunition and equipment of the Palestinian Police described in Annex I, Article III, and those of the Israeli military forces, no organization or individual in the Gaza Strip and the Jericho Area shall manufacture, sell, acquire, possess, import or otherwise introduce into the Gaza Strip or the Jericho Area any firearms, ammunition, weapons, explosives, gunpowder or any related equipment, unless otherwise provided for in Annex I.

Article X

Passages

Arrangements for co-ordination between Israel and the Palestinian Authority regarding the Gaza-Egypt and Jericho-Jordan passages, as well as any other agreed international crossings, are set out in Annex 1.

Article XI

Safe passage between the Gaza Strip and the Jericho Area

Arrangements for safe passage of persons and transportation between the Gaza Strip and the Jericho Area are set out in Annex I, Article IX.

Article XII

Relations between Israel and the Palestinian Authority

1. Israel and the Palestinian Authority shall seek to foster mutual understanding and tolerance and shall accordingly abstain from incitement, including hostile propaganda, against each other and, without derogating from the principle of freedom of expression, shall take legal measures to prevent such incitement by any organizations, groups or individuals within their jurisdiction.

2. Without derogating from the other provisions of this agreement, Israel and the Palestinian Authority shall co-operate in combating criminal activity which may affect both sides, including

offences related to trafficking in illegal drugs and psychotropic substances, smuggling, and offences against property, including offences related to vehicles.

Article XIII
Economic relations

The economic relations between the two sides are set out in the Protocol on Economic Relations signed in Paris on April 29, 1994 and the appendixes thereto, certified copies of which are attached as Annex IV, and will be governed by the relevant provisions of this agreement and its annexes.

Article XIV
Human rights and the rule of law

Israel and the Palestinian Authority shall exercise their powers and responsibilities pursuant to this Agreement with due regard to internationally-accepted norms and principles of human rights and the rule of law.

Article XV
The Joint Israeli-Palestinian Liaison Committee

1. The Liaison Committee established pursuant to Article X of the Declaration of Principles shall ensure the smooth implementation of this Agreement. It shall deal with issues requiring co-ordination, other issues of common interest and disputes.

2. The Liaison Committee shall be composed of an equal number of members from each party. It may add other technicians and experts as necessary.

3. The Liaison Committee shall adopt its rules of procedure, including the frequency and place or places of its meetings.

4. The Liaison Committee shall reach its decision by agreement.

Article XVI
Liaison and Co-operation with Jordan and Egypt

1. Pursuant to Article XII of the Declaration of Principles, the two parties shall invite the governments of Jordan and Egypt to participate in establishing further Liaison and Co-operation Arrangements between the Government of Israel and the Palestinian Representatives on the one hand, and the governments of Jordan and Egypt on the other hand, to promote co-operation between them. These arrangements shall include the constitution of a Continuing Committee.

2. The Continuing Committee shall decide by agreement on the modalities of admission of persons displaced from the West Bank and the Gaza Strip in 1967, together with necessary measures to prevent disruption and disorder.

3. The Continuing Committee shall deal with other matters of common concern.

Article XVII
Settlement of differences and disputes

Any difference relating to the application of this agreement shall be referred to the appropriate co-ordination and co-operation mechanism established under this agreement. The provisions of Article XV of the Declaration of Principles shall apply to any such difference which is not settled through the appropriate co-ordination and co-operation mechanism, namely:

1. Disputes arising out of the application or interpretation of this agreement or any subsequent agreements pertaining to the interim period shall be settled by negotiations through the Liaison Committee.

2. Disputes which cannot be settled by negotiations may be settled by a mechanism of conciliation to be agreed between the parties.

3. The parties may agree to submit to arbitration disputes relating to the interim period, which cannot be settled through conciliation. To this end, upon the agreement of both parties, the parties will establish an arbitration committee.

Article XVIII
Prevention of hostile acts

Both sides shall take all measures necessary in order to prevent acts of terrorism, crime and hostilities directed against each other, against individuals falling under the other's authority and against

their property, and shall take legal measures against offenders. In addition, the Palestinian side shall take all measures necessary to prevent such hostile acts directed against the settlements, the infrastructure serving them and the military installation area, and the Israeli side shall take all measures necessary to prevent such hostile acts emanating from the settlements and directed against Palestinians.

Article XIX
Missing persons

The Palestinian Authority shall co-operate with Israel by providing all necessary assistance in the conduct of searches by Israel within the Gaza Strip and the Jericho Area for missing Israelis, as well as by providing information about missing Israelis. Israel shall co-operate with the Palestinian Authority in searching for, and providing necessary information about, missing Palestinians.

Article XX
Confidence-building measures

With a view to creating a positive and supportive public atmosphere to accompany the implementation of this agreement, and to establish a solid basis of mutual trust and good faith, both parties agree to carry out confidence-building measures as detailed herewith:

1. Upon the signing of this agreement, Israel will release, or turn over, to the Palestinian Authority within a period of 5 weeks, about 5,000 Palestinian detainees and prisoners, residents of the West Bank and the Gaza Strip. Those released will be free to return to their homes anywhere in the West Bank or the Gaza Strip. Prisoners turned over to the Palestinian Authority shall be obliged to remain in the Gaza Strip or the Jericho Area for the remainder of their sentence.

2. After the signing of this Agreement, the two parties shall continue to negotiate the release of additional Palestinian prisoners and detainees, building on agreed principles.

3. The implementation of the above measures will be subject to the fulfilment of the procedures determined by Israeli law for the release and transfer of detainees and prisoners.

4. With the assumption of Palestinian Authority, the Palestinian side commits itself to solving the problem of those Palestinians who were in contact with the Israeli authorities. Until an agreed solution is found, the Palestinian side undertakes not to prosecute these Palestinians or to harm them in any way.

5. Palestinians from abroad whose entry into the Gaza Strip and the Jericho Area is approved pursuant to this agreement, and to whom the provisions of this article are applicable, will not be prosecuted for offences committed prior to September 13, 1993.

Article XXI
Temporary international presence

1. The parties agree to a temporary international or foreign presence in the Gaza Strip and the Jericho Area (hereinafter 'the TIP'), in accordance with the provisions of this article.

2. The TIP shall consist of 400 qualified personnel, including observers, instructors and other experts, from 5 or 6 of the donor countries.

3. The two parties shall request the donor countries to establish a special fund to provide finance for the TIP.

4. The TIP will function for a period of 6 months. The TIP may extend this period, or change the scope of its operation, with the agreement of the two parties.

5. The TIP shall be stationed and operative within the following cities and villages: Gaza, Khan Younis, Rafah, Deir al-Balah, Jabalya, Absan, Beit Hanun and Jericho.

6. Israel and the Palestinian Authority shall agree on a special protocol to implement this article, with the goal of concluding negotiations with the donor countries contributing personnel within two months.

Article XXII
Rights, liabilities and obligations

1.a. The transfer of all powers and responsibilities to the Palestinian Authority, as detailed in Annex II, includes all related rights, liabilities and obligations arising with regard to acts or omissions which occurred prior to the transfer. Israel will cease to bear any financial responsibility regarding such acts or omissions and the Palestinian Authority will bear all financial responsibility for these and for its own functioning.

b. Any financial claim made in this regard against Israel will be referred to the Palestinian Authority.

c. Israel shall provide the Palestinian Authority with the information it has regarding pending and anticipated claims brought before any court or tribunal against Israel in this regard.

d. Where legal proceedings are brought in respect of such a claim, Israel will notify the Palestinian Authority and enable it to participate in defending the claim and raise any arguments on its behalf.

e. In the event that an award is made against Israel by any court or tribunal in respect of such a claim, the Palestinian Authority shall reimburse Israel the full amount of the award.

f. Without prejudice to the above, where a court or tribunal hearing such a claim finds that liability rests solely with an employee or agent who acted beyond the scope of the powers assigned to him or her, unlawfully of with willful malfeasance, the Palestinian Authority shall not bear financial responsibility.

2. The transfer of authority in itself shall not affect rights, liabilities and obligations of any person or legal entity, in existence at the date of signing of this Agreement.

Article XXIII
Final clauses

1. This Agreement shall enter into force on the date of its signing.

2. The arrangements established by this Agreement shall remain in force until and to the extent superseded by the Interim Agreement referred to in the Declaration of Principles or any other Agreement between the parties.

3. The five-year Interim Period referred to in the Declaration of Principles commences on the date of the signing of this Agreement.

4. The parties agree that, as long as this Agreement is in force, the security fence erected by Israel around the Gaza Strip shall remain in place and that the line demarcated by the fence, as shown on attached Map No. 1, shall be authoritative only for the purpose of this Agreement.

5. Nothing in this Agreement shall prejudice or pre-empt the outcome of the negotiations on the Interim Agreement or on the Permanent Status to be conducted pursuant to the Declaration of Principles. Neither party shall be deemed, by virtue of having entered into this Agreement, to have renounced or waived any of its existing rights, claims or positions.

6. The two parties view the West Bank and the Gaza Strip as a single territorial unit, the integrity of which will be preserved during the Interim Period.

7. The Gaza Strip and the Jericho Area shall continue to be an integral part of the West Bank and the Gaza Strip, and their status shall not be changed for the period of this Agreement. Nothing in this Agreement shall be considered to change this status.

8. The preamble to this Agreement, and all Annexes, Appendices and Maps attached hereto, shall constitute an integral part hereof.

PALESTINE ORGANIZATIONS*
PALESTINE LIBERATION ORGANIZATION (PLO)
Hammam ash-Shaat, Tunis, Tunisia

The Palestine Liberation Organization was founded in 1964 at the first Arab summit meeting, and the Palestine Liberation Army was established in the same year. The supreme organ of the PLO is the Palestine National Council (PNC—see below), while the Palestine Executive Committee, consisting of 14 members, deals with the day-to-day business. Fatah (the Palestine National Liberation Movement) joined the PNC in 1968, and all the guerrilla organizations joined the Council in 1969. The Palestine Executive Committee controls the following departments, and a member of the Executive Committee is at the head of each department:

(i) Military Department, which includes Palestine Liberation Army.

(ii) Cultural Department.

(iii) Education Department.

(iv) Political Department.

(v) Administrative Affairs Department.

(vi) Social Affairs (includes Palestine Red Crescent).

(vii) Occupied Homeland Affairs Department.

(viii) Information and National Guidance Department.

(ix) Popular Organizations Department (Trade Unions, Students, Workers, Women, etc.).

(x) Labour Department.

(xi) Economic Affairs Department.

(xii) Repatriates' Affairs Department.

(xiii) Pan-Arab and International Relations Department.

(xiv) Palestine National Fund.

(xv) Supreme Council for Culture, Heritage and Information.

The PLO is funded by annual contributions from Arab countries and aid from other friendly countries, and by an annual tax of between 3% and 6% which is levied on the income of every Palestinian. At the Arab summit in Baghdad in 1978, Arab countries pledged $300m. per year to the PLO from 1979–89.

The PLO has offices and representatives in every Arab country and in many non-Arab states. In 1985 Spain became the first Western European country to grant full diplomatic status to a PLO representative. The Rabat Arab summit, in October 1974, affirmed the right of the Palestinian people to establish an independent national authority, under the leadership of the PLO in its capacity as the sole legitimate representative of the Palestine people, over all liberated territory (see Documents on Palestine, p. 89). In November 1974 Yasser Arafat addressed the UN General Assembly, and on 22 November 1974, the UN General Assembly passed a resolution acknowledging and reaffirming the PLO position (see Documents on Palestine, p. 90). On the same day the PLO was granted permanent observer status at the General Assembly of the UN and at international conferences sponsored by the UN. A PLO delegation was present at the Conference of the Inter-Parliamentary Union in London in September 1975, and also at the 30th Session of the UN General Assembly in November 1975. The PLO became a full member of the Arab League in September 1976.

The PLO condemned the Second Interim Egyptian-Israeli Disengagement Agreement as seriously weakening the united Arab effort to achieve the liberation of territories occupied by Israeli armed forces. In response Egypt closed the 'Voice of Palestine' radio operating from Cairo. The general policy of the PLO was to remain aloof from the Lebanese civil war of 1975 and 1976, but after 1976 it became increasingly

involved, particularly after the Syrian intervention. Although many guerrilla units suffered heavy losses the PLO did not moderate its official policy, and when an enlarged PNC met in Cairo in March 1977, no changes were made in the Palestine National Charter (see below), and a 15-point political programme (see below) was adopted which set out in a forthright fashion the aims and principles of the PLO. The PLO condemned the Camp David agreements of September 1978 (see p. 90) and the Peace Treaty between Egypt and Israel of March 1979 (see p. 92).

The PLO experienced a major upheaval after the Israeli invasion of Lebanon in June 1982. Israeli forces surrounded West Beirut, trapping thousands of Palestinian fighters. In late August Philip Habib, President Reagan's special Middle East envoy, secured an agreement which brought about the dispersal of the PLO fighters from Beirut. Over 12,000 PLO fighters subsequently left Lebanon. PLO Headquarters were established in Tunis, Tunisia, and fighters were dispersed to Algeria, Iraq, Jordan, Sudan, Syria, the Yemen Arab Republic (YAR) and the People's Democratic Republic of Yemen (PDRY). More than half the fighters were dispersed to Syria. The PLO's military infrastructure, the basis of the 'armed struggle', which had been built up in Lebanon, was destroyed; its fighters were scattered throughout the Middle East and the base from which to launch attacks on Israel was lost.

The PLO interest in a final Middle East peace settlement, with provision for a Palestinian state, remained as vital as ever, and at the 16th Session of the PNC, held in Algiers in February 1983, the PLO declared its 'refusal to consider the (Reagan) plan (see Documents on Palestine, p. 96) as a sound basis for a just and permanent settlement to the Palestinian question and the Arab-Zionist conflict'. The PNC considered the Fez plan (see Documents on Palestine, p. 96) 'as the minimum for Arab political action'. Yasser Arafat, however, continued discussions with King Hussein of Jordan, thus feeding speculation that the PLO might be considering a Palestinian state in association with Jordan (an essential ingredient of the Reagan plan), but when these talks were broken off in April further progress on reaching a negotiated solution appeared to have come to a halt. By May, some of the fighters who had been dispersed from Beirut in the previous year had returned to northern Lebanon.

A revolt against Arafat's leadership then broke out in the Beka'a valley in Lebanon. This was led by 'Abu Musa' and 'Abu Salih' (members of the Fatah Central Committee) and stemmed from dissatisfaction with Arafat's pursuit of a course of diplomatic compromise and apparent betrayal of the commitment to 'armed struggle'. Arafat was expelled from Syria in June and he subsequently accused Syria and Libya of orchestrating the revolt in order to gain control of the PLO, and in this belief he had the sympathy of the majority of the Palestinian diaspora. In September Arafat joined his supporters who were besieged by Syrian forces and Fatah rebels in their last Lebanese stronghold, the port of Tripoli, in northern Lebanon, and the surrounding Palestinian refugee camps of Baddawi and Nahr el-Bared. Heavy fighting was finally brought to an end on 24 November with an agreement, formulated by Saudi Arabia and Syria, requiring Arafat's departure from Lebanon within two weeks and the subsequent peaceful settlement of differences. Despite Israeli refusals to guarantee his safe passage, Arafat and 4,000 loyalists finally left Tripoli in Greek ships under the protection of the UN flag on 20 December, variously destined for Algeria, Tunisia and the YAR. (The military headquarters of Fatah were relocated in San'a (YAR)—though they were subsequently moved to Tunis.) Arafat immediately recommenced the diplomatic round in search of international support, which he had begun during the rebellion, with visits to President Mubarak of Egypt (which were condemned by most PLO groups) and to King

---
* For those organizations formed as part of the implementation of the Declaration of Principles on Palestinian Self-Rule, see Israeli-Occupied Territories appended to the chapter on Israel.

Hussein of Jordan (the first of a series of talks between them in 1984). The latter visit, in January, combined with the reconvening of the Jordanian House of Representatives earlier in the month, raised the possibility of a revival of the Reagan plan, despite the fact that the Fatah Central Committee had followed the PNC in rejecting the plan and the proposal of Jordan as an alternative Palestinian homeland, insisting on the creation of a separate and independent state of Palestine in the West Bank and Gaza.

The Fatah Central Committee expelled 10 of the leading dissidents from the movement in November 1983, including 'Abu Salih', 'Abu Musa' and Samih Abu Quwayq. Shortly afterwards the Fatah rebels and the leaders of the Popular Front for the Liberation of Palestine—General Command (PFLP-GC), the Palestine Popular Struggle Front (PPSF) and Saiqa announced the formation of an anti-Arafat Palestine National Alliance. Another alignment of Palestinian organizations, the Palestine Democratic Alliance, was also formed at this time. Comprising the pflp, the democratic front for the Liberation of Palestine (DFLP), the Palestine Liberation Front (PLF—the wing of the party led by Muhammad 'Abu' Abbas) and the Palestine Communist Party, the Democratic Alliance stood between Arafat's wing of Fatah and the pro-Syrian National Alliance. It did not call for the replacement of Arafat as PLO Chairman (though it would have preferred him to wield less power) but rejected links with Egypt and any approach to the question of a Palestine state based on the principle of an exchange of territory for peace with Israel, which is enshrined in the UN Security Council Resolution 242. Arafat and the Democratic Alliance met in Aden in June to clear the way for a meeting of the PNC. The Democratic Alliance confirmed Arafat's leadership of the PLO in return for pledges that the powers and status of the chairman would be amended to reduce his freedom of action and render him more accountable to the movement as a whole. Talks between Arafat's Fatah and the groups opposed to him took place in Algiers and Aden between April and July 1984. In their turn, as if accepting that the movement could no longer be united around Arafat, the Fatah Central Committee, though it expressed only surprise at his talks in Egypt and condemned the Syrian-Libyan 'plot' against the PLO, made it plain that it wished to move towards a collective style of leadership.

The PNC was initially scheduled to meet in Algiers in September but various disagreements caused these plans to be discarded. Arafat continued his talks with King Hussein of Jordan and in August the two leaders agreed the principle of a confederation comprising Jordan and a future sovereign Palestinian state. King Hussein offered Amman as the venue for the 17th session of the PNC. Syria was strongly opposed to this and the Speaker of the PNC, Khaled Fahoum, in a statement from Damascus, refused formally to invite the PNC to meet in Amman. The PLO Executive Committee also failed to approve Amman as the venue for the PNC. Arafat proceeded to muster the two-thirds majority of the surviving 379 PNC members necessary to achieve a quorum, replacing dissident members of Fatah with his own loyalists. The 17th session of the PNC accordingly convened in Amman on 22 November, without the members of the pro-Syrian Palestine National Alliance (including the newly-formed al-Intifada, or 'Uprising' group, led by 'Abu Musa'), who boycotted the session, protesting that the PNC should not meet until Arafat had been replaced as chairman; and without some 180 PNC members living in the West Bank whom the Israelis would not allow to travel. Arafat's intention was to win PNC approval for his diplomatic initiatives and, simply by succeeding in convening the PNC, to demonstrate the independence of the PLO from external, specifically Syrian, influence. King Hussein delivered the inaugural address to the PNC and called for a joint Jordanian-Palestinian peace initiative based on UN Security Council Resolution 242 and negotiated within the framework of an international conference involving all the interested parties and the members of the UN Security Council. (Resolution 242 had traditionally been anathema to the PLO as it refers only to a Palestinian refugee problem, implicitly excluding consideration of a Palestinian state and the right of the Palestinian people to self-determination.) The PNC gave a guarded welcome to King Hussein's proposals, neither accepting nor rejecting Resolution 242 as the point of departure for peace talks, and delegated the PLO Executive Committee to examine them.

In a dramatic gesture designed to demonstrate his value to the movement, Arafat tendered his resignation as chairman of the PLO and then, to popular acclaim, was publicly seen to withdraw it. The PNC voted to expel from its ranks Ahmad Jibril, leader of the PFLP-GC, who had participated in Abu Musa's revolt against Arafat's leadership in Lebanon. Khaled Fahoum, the absent Speaker of the PNC, was not re-elected and Sheikh Abd al-Hamid as-Sayeh, a former Jordanian Cabinet minister, was appointed in his place. Yasser Arafat did not obtain the clear mandate he had sought, enabling him to continue his diplomatic initiatives without referral to a collective PLO decision-making process, but his position was more secure than had seemed possible only weeks before.

On 23 February 1985, in Amman, Jordan, King Hussein and Arafat announced the terms of a joint Jordanian-Palestinian agreement on the framework for a peace settlement in the Middle East, which the two sides had finalized on 11 February. The Jordanian Government denied that the basis of this agreement was solely UN Resolution 242, though the published text of the accord gave land in exchange for peace (see Documents on Palestine, p. 96), a central tenet of that resolution, as its first principle. Taher Hikmat, the Jordanian Minister of Culture, averred that Resolution 242 was only one of a number of UN resolutions and other documents on which the principles of the agreement had been based. In fact, the PLO Executive Committee, in approving the terms of the accord (providing that they received full Arab support) on 20 February, stressed that the joint position stemmed from a rejection of Camp David, the Reagan plan and Resolution 242. According to King Hussein, Arafat subsequently accepted Resolution 242 as the basis of future peace negotiations. Arafat, however, was at pains to make a distinction between accepting the clause in the resolution referring to the right of all states in the dispute to live in peace within recognized boundaries, and conceding Israel's right to exist. Arguments over the precise meaning of the agreement persisted and the PLO adopted a new position on the status of the Palestinian representation at future peace negotiations, which, it said, should be within a united Arab, not merely a Jordanian-Palestinian, delegation. There was also the question of the composition of the Palestinian element in an Arab (or other) delegation. Israel steadfastly refused to negotiate with members of the PLO but, given the PLO's accepted standing among the Arab states as the sole legitimate representative of the Palestinian people, it was unlikely that the PLO and the Arab community would endorse a delegation that excluded the PLO.

In March 1985 President Mubarak of Egypt called for talks in Cairo between Israel, Egypt, the USA and a joint Jordanian-Palestinian delegation. This proposal was immediately rejected by the PLO Executive Committee as a deviation from its recently announced accord with Jordan.

Also in March, Khaled Fahoum, the former Speaker of the PNC, announced the formation in Damascus, under Syrian auspices, of a Palestinian National Salvation Front, comprising the members of the Palestine National Alliance, one half of the old PLF, led by Talaat Yaqoub (the original group having split into pro- and anti-Arafat factions), and the PFLP (led by George Habash, who had previously refused publicly to oppose Arafat's leadership of the PLO), as a radical alternative to Arafat's wing of the PLO.

To prevent Arafat from establishing a new power-base in Lebanon, Syria, through its proxy, the Shi'ite Amal militia, attempted to wipe out the PLO guerrilla force loyal to the PLO Chairman which had grown up again in the Palestinian refugee camps of Bourj el-Barajneh, Sabra and Chatila in Beirut. Fighting began in May but, having failed to subdue PLO resistance, Syria drafted a cease-fire agreement which was signed by Amal and the pro-Syrian Palestinians (who had made common cause with Arafat loyalists when the camps were attacked) on 17 June. Skirmishing continued sporadically around the camps and in May 1986, almost exactly one year after fighting first broke out, Amal and the largely Shi'ite sixth brigade of the Lebanese army launched another concerted effort to dislodge the Palestinians. Fighting was briefly halted by a cease-fire, which was agreed by Lebanese Muslim leaders under Syrian auspices in June.

In the months following the announcement of the Jordan/PLO peace initiative, hopes for its progress focused on attempts to put together a joint Jordanian/Palestinian delegation which would be acceptable to Israel and the USA as a participant in peace talks. King Hussein proposed the names of seven Palestinians for US consideration from a list of 22 given to him by the PLO. However, Israel rejected the seven in July, though it subsequently stated that two names on the list met its requirement for 'authentic Palestinian representatives' from the Occupied Territories who were not members of the PLO. The USA, for its part was committed not to hold negotiations with the PLO until it renounced the use of terrorism, recognized the right of Israel to exist and, effectively, accepted UN Security Council Resolution 242.

King Hussein and Yasser Arafat continued to seek Arab support for their initiative but an extraordinary meeting of Arab states in Casablanca in August 1986 (which was boycotted by opponents of the Amman accord, notably Syria and Libya) merely noted its existence and reaffirmed Arab allegiance to the Fez plan of September 1982.

In September, in an attempt to revive the stalled peace process, the British Government offered to hold talks with a joint Jordanian/Palestinian delegation in London in October. The delegation included two members of the PNC's Executive Committee, Muhammad Milhem and Bishop Ilya Khuri, but the meeting was cancelled at the last minute when they refused to sign a document renouncing violence and specifically recognizing Israel's right to exist within its pre-1967 boundaries.

A series of terrorist attacks by Palestinian organizations between September and December 1985 were a further setback to the progress of the Jordan/PLO peace initiative. On 1 October, after three Israelis had been murdered in Cyprus by members of the PLO's élite Force 17, Israel bombed the PLO's headquarters in Tunis. In October an Italian cruise ship, *Achille Lauro*, was hijacked in the eastern Mediterranean by members of the PLF (the 'Abu Abbas' faction) loyal to Yasser Arafat, and an elderly Jewish American passenger was killed. Arafat was under pressure from King Hussein and from President Mubarak of Egypt to renounce the use of violence. He responded to their appeals in November by reiterating a PLO decision of 1974 to confine military operations to the Occupied Territories and Israel. Later that month an Egyptian airliner was hijacked to Malta and in December 17 people were killed when terrorists, believed to belong to the Damascus-based, anti-Arafat, Fatah Revolutionary Council, led by 'Abu Nidal', attacked passengers at the desks of El Al (the Israeli state airline) in Rome and Vienna airports. Whether these incidents were the work of Arafat loyalists or of PLO rebels acting at Syrian or Libyan instigation, their effect was to undermine still further the PLO's credibility as a potential partner in peace negotiations and to frustrate King Hussein in his goal of an international peace conference.

King Hussein had already taken steps towards a *rapprochement* with Syria (preparing the ground for another approach to the Palestinian question) and the demise of his joint initiative with Yasser Arafat had been forecast for some time when, on 19 February 1986, he publicly severed political links with the PLO 'until such time as their word becomes their bond, characterized by commitment, credibility and constancy'. Above all he was referring to Arafat's persistent equivocation regarding acceptance of UN Security Council Resolutions 242 and 338. In January, without Israel's knowledge, the USA (Israel having agreed with King Hussein on the need for an international peace conference) had undertaken to invite the PLO to such a conference (not merely preliminary talks) provided it publicly accepted Resolutions 242 and 338 as the basis for negotiation. This Arafat refused to do without an acknowledgement by the USA of the Palestinians' right to self-determination.

Following King Hussein's announcement, Arafat was ordered to close his main offices in Jordan by 1 April, though he refused to recognize that the Jordan/PLO accord was moribund. The activities of PLO members in the country were henceforth to be restricted to an even greater extent than before, and a number of Fatah officers loyal to Arafat were expelled, including the deputy commander of the Fatah forces, Khalil al-Wazir (*nom de guerre*, 'Abu Jihad'). King Hussein called for the PLO either to change its policies or its leadership and the Jordanian Government tried further to dissociate itself from and to discredit Arafat by allegedly encouraging support among Palestinians for Col Atallah Atallah (alias 'Abu Za'im'), a member of the mainstream Fatah group, who advocated a 'corrective movement' within the PLO. After the breakdown of the Amman accord he was highly critical of Yasser Arafat, challenging him to convoke the General Congress of Fatah (for the first time since 1980) to answer charges of military, financial and organizational mismanagement. Colonel Atallah (who was head of PLO intelligence until 1982) was accordingly expelled from Fatah with six of his supporters, and in April, the PLO's Supreme Military Council dismissed him from his position as Assistant Chief of Staff of the PLA and rescinded his membership of the PNC. On 7 July Jordan ordered the closure of the 25 Fatah offices in Amman. However, Col Atallah's proposals failed to win sufficient support and his 'corrective movement' gradually died out.

The efforts of the Shi'ite Amal militia, sanctioned by Syria, to suppress the revival of the PLO in Lebanon, spread from Beirut to Palestinian communities in the south of the country in October 1986. Amal, which had already surrounded the refugee camps in Beirut, laid siege to Palestinian camps near Tyre (Rashidiyah) and Sidon (Ain al-Hilweh and Miyeh Miyeh), and by the beginning of 1987 the inhabitants, unable to obtain food or medical supplies from outside, faced starvation and the spread of disease, in addition to the danger from the fighting. A major catastrophe was only averted by the deployment of some 7,000 Syrian troops in Beirut in February, which allowed the passage of supplies into the camps, and by the temporary lifting of the siege of southern camps at Syria's request (see chapter on Lebanon, History). The fact that both pro- and anti-Arafat guerrillas made common cause in the defence of the camps against an agent of Syria, was a significant factor in creating an atmosphere conducive to the reconciliation of the opposing PLO factions which subsequently took place.

In March and April 1987 Soviet, Algerian and Libyan mediation succeeded in bringing together most PLO factions for a series of meetings designed to reunify the divided movement. Agreements reached in Tunis and Tripoli, embodying concessions made by Yasser Arafat to the views of dissident groups within the PLO (in particular the abrogation of the Jordan-PLO accord of February 1985—the *sine qua non* of PFLP participation in a meeting of the PNC), enabled the 18th session of the PNC to be convened in Algiers on 20 April. The two largest groups in the Syrian-backed Palestine National Salvation Front (PNSF), the PFLP and the DFLP, the Palestine Communist Party and the two wings of the divided PLF attended the session, effectively extinguishing the PNSF's claim to be a credible alternative to the Arafat-led PLO. The Fatah Revolutionary Council, led by 'Abu Nidal', the smaller elements in the PNSF (the PFLP-GC, Saiqa, the Popular Struggle Front) and the rebel Fatah group of 'Abu Musa' did not attend but the absentees represented less than 20% of the PLO's total membership. The PNC elected a 15-member Executive Committee, including representatives of factions which had boycotted the 17th session in 1984, and Yasser Arafat was re-elected as chairman. However, the creation of a new executive body, with responsibility for day-to-day decisions, was consistent with the former rebels' requirement for a move towards collective leadership and a diminution of the power of the chairman. The resolutions approved by the PNC followed closely the terms of the agreements negotiated by Fatah and other PLO factions prior to the session. The principal resolutions concerned: the formal abrogation of the Jordan-PLO accord of February 1985; support for an international peace conference under UN auspices, attended by the permanent members of the UN Security Council and all the parties to the Middle East conflict on equal terms, including the PLO (possibly as part of a unified Arab delegation), to be conducted on the basis of all relevant UN and Arab summit resolutions; the reappraisal of links with Egypt, with reference to previous PNC and Arab summit resolutions, making future relations conditional on Egypt's abrogation of the Camp David agreements with Israel (this represented a compromise between Arafat and George Habash of the PFLP, who, at the pre-session talks, had demanded the immediate severance of all links with Egypt); and the need for improved relations with Syria.

After the conclusion of the PNC session President Mubarak responded to the resolution on the links between the PLO and Egypt by closing all the PLO's offices in Egypt, while President Assad of Syria affirmed his support for the diminished PNSF (which comprised Saiqa, the Popular Struggle Front, the PFLP-GC and the rebel Fatah group al-Intifada). The PLO's offices in Egypt were allowed to reopen in November. In the same month, at an extraordinary meeting of the Arab League to discuss the Iran–Iraq War, Yasser Arafat and King Hussein of Jordan agreed to resume efforts to co-ordinate their strategy for peace in the Middle East.

The progressive restriction of PLO activities in Tunisia by the Tunisian Government, which was interpreted as an attempt to dissociate Tunisia from Palestinian terrorist operations and to pre-empt the identification of subversive elements within Tunisia with the Palestinian cause, led Yasser Arafat to transfer the PLO's military headquarters to Baghdad, Iraq, in October 1987. The PLO presence in Tunis was reduced to a minimal diplomatic and administrative level.

A Syrian-supervised cease-fire at the besieged Palestinian refugee camps in Beirut (negotiated by representatives of Syria, Amal and the pro-Syrian PNSF) took effect in April 1987, and supplies were allowed to enter Chatila and Bourj el-Barajneh. However, the siege of these camps was, effectively, still in force. In Sidon, meanwhile, outside effective Syrian jurisdiction, renewed fighting broke out between Amal and members of the PLO loyal to Yasser Arafat, and Rashidiyah camp, near Tyre, remained under siege. It was not until September that Amal and the Arafat wing of the PLO reached a comprehensive cease-fire agreement, purportedly ending the 'war of the camps', in which more than 2,500 people had died. The agreement provided for the permanent lifting of the siege of the Beirut, Tyre and Sidon camps, in return for the withdrawal of PLO fighters from strategic positions around the Ain al-Hilweh camp, on the eastern outskirts of Sidon, which they had captured from Amal in October 1986. However, neither measure was implemented, and in October differences over the withdrawal of some 5,000–8,000 PLO guerrillas led to renewed fighting around the disputed positions to the east of Sidon. In January 1988, avowedly as a gesture of support to the Palestinian uprising in the Israeli-occupied territories (see below), Nabih Berri, the leader of Amal, announced the lifting of the siege of the Palestinian refugee camps in Beirut and southern Lebanon. Syrian troops replaced Amal fighters and soldiers from the largely Shi'ite Sixth Brigade of the Lebanese army in positions around Bourj el-Barajneh and Chatila, and the 14-month siege of Rashidiyah camp, near Tyre, was lifted. However, Arafat loyalists refused to withdraw from their positions overlooking Ain al-Hilweh camp, near Sidon.

The frequency of anti-Israeli demonstrations and violent incidents in the Occupied Territories increased during 1987, in particular following the reunification of the PLO in Algiers in April. However, the authorities were not prepared for the wave of violent demonstrations and strikes against Israeli rule, the worst since Israel occupied the West Bank and the Gaza Strip in 1967, that began on 8 December 1987. The PLO was not slow to exploit the unrest, or *intifida* (uprising), as it came to be known, for propaganda advantage, although it appeared that the disturbances began more as a spontaneous expression of accumulated frustration at the constraints imposed by Israeli rule than as a politically motivated and co-ordinated demonstration.

In June 1988 an extraordinary meeting of the Arab League was convened in Algiers to discuss the Palestinian *intifida* in the Occupied Territories and the Palestine question in general. The meeting hailed the 'heroic' uprising and pledged the support of the League for its continuance, including an unspecified amount of financial aid (believed to total some $43m. per month). The meeting's final communiqué endorsed the Palestinian claim to independent statehood and PLO participation (on an equal footing with the other participants) in an inter-

national peace conference, which would proceed on the basis of the principles of the Fez plan. This constituted a rejection of the peace proposals presented by US Secretary of State George Shultz in February, which referred only to Palestinian 'legitimate rights', ruled out an independent Palestinian state, and envisaged the participation of Palestinians in a peace conference in a joint delegation with Jordan, excluding the PLO. (For later developments, see chapter on Jordan.)

In autumn 1987 the US Congress, to the embarrassment of the US Government, adopted an anti-terrorist law denying the PLO the right to maintain offices in the USA. The following March the US State Department ordered the closure of the PLO observer mission at the UN and the Palestine information office in Washington. The General Assembly of the UN condemned the order relating to the observer mission and referred the issue to the International Court of Justice in the Hague, to determine whether the USA was bound to submit the case to compulsory arbitration, as laid down in the 1947 agreement between the UN and the USA, establishing the headquarters of the UN in New York. According to that agreement, it is not within the competence of the host country, the USA, to close a recognized mission to the UN.

On 16 April 1988 Khalil al-Wazir (alias 'Abu Jihad'), Yasser Arafat's deputy as commander of the Palestine Liberation Army, was assassinated in Tunis by agents of the Israeli external security service, Mossad.

After two months of fighting in Beirut, between pro-Arafat PLO guerrillas and the Syrian-backed rebel Fatah faction led by 'Abu Musa', Arafat loyalists were driven out of the Chatila refugee camp on 27 June, and out of Bourj el-Barajneh, Fatah's last stronghold in Beirut, on 9 July, destroying the prospect of an improvement in relations between Arafat and President Assad of Syria.

In July 1988 King Hussein of Jordan severed Jordan's 'administrative and legal links' with the West Bank, presenting the PLO with the historic opportunity to assert sovereignty over a specific area, since Jordan's move meant that the Occupied Territories were no longer claimed *de jure* by any state as part of its sovereign territory (see The Arab-Israeli Confrontation 1967–93, p. 49). While a PLO delegation, visiting Jordan in mid-August, complained that the PLO had not been consulted prior to Jordan's action, it nevertheless expressed its conviction that the action had been taken in order to further the Palestinian cause. In Egypt on 15 August, the delegation announced that a provisional Palestinian government-in-exile would be formed at a forthcoming extraordinary meeting of the PNC, which was to be held to discuss the PLO's response to Jordan's decision.

Addressing the European Parliament in Strasbourg on 13 September, Yasser Arafat stated publicly, for the first time, that the PLO was prepared to negotiate with Israel at an international peace conference held on the basis of UN Security Council Resolutions 242 and 338, and to accept Israel's right to security in return for Israel's recognition of an independent Palestinian state and the legitimate rights of the Palestinian people.

At the 19th session of the PNC, held on 12–15 November in Algiers, and attended by all the major components of the PLO, the PNC unilaterally declared the establishment of the independent State of Palestine, with its capital at Jerusalem, on the basis of UN General Assembly Resolution 181 of 1947 (see Documents on Palestine, p. 85). The Declaration of Independence left open the question of Palestinian territorial claims, although a strict interpretation of the international legal status of the former British Mandate Territory of Palestine would have permitted reference to a specific area. While the PNC announced its intention to form a provisional government-in-exile, disagreement within the PLO regarding its composition caused the question to be referred back to the PLO's Executive Committee. A political statement released by the PNC at the end of the session called for an international conference on the Middle East, under UN supervision, to be convened on the basis of UN Security Council Resolutions 242 and 338, and of a guarantee of the legitimate national rights of the Palestinian people. While Arafat and others within Fatah wished to adopt Resolution 242 in isolation in order to satisfy the demands of the USA, other factions within the

PLO forced the leadership to adopt a compromise formula, whereby the PNC accepted Resolution 242 in conjunction with recognition of Palestinian rights to self-determination and to legality on the basis of the relevant UN resolutions. A majority vote in favour of the incorporation of the compromise formula into the political statement issued by the PNC at the end of the session, was denounced by the PPSF, the PFLP-GC, the Fatah Revolutionary Council, the Palestine Revolutionary Council and the Islamic Jihad Movement.

The newly-declared Palestinian state received immediate recognition from all the Arab states (except Syria), from countries belonging to the Non-Aligned Movement and from China. The USSR recognized the Declaration of Independence, but not the state itself. By mid-1989 more than 90 countries had recognized either the state itself or the Declaration of Independence.

The PLO's qualified acceptance of Resolution 242 effectively challenged the USA to respond. In late November, however, the US State Department, on the personal instructions of US Secretary of State, George Shultz, refused to grant a US entry visa to Yasser Arafat, who had been invited to address the UN General Assembly in New York. On 28 November the General Assembly voted to reconvene the meeting to Geneva.

In his address to the General Assembly on 13–15 December, Arafat presented a three-point programme, calling on the UN Secretary-General to establish a preparatory committee for an international peace conference; for the temporary supervision of the Occupied Territories by UN forces, which would oversee Israel's withdrawal; and for the convening of a peace conference, to be held on the basis of UN Security Council Resolutions 242 and 338. In his address Arafat also explicitly rejected terrorism. The meeting of the General Assembly concluded on 15 December with the adoption of two resolutions, one calling for the convening of an international peace conference on the Middle East 'with the participation of all parties to the conflict, including the PLO, on an equal footing'; and one changing the name of the PLO observer mission at the UN to the Palestine observer mission.

The PLO had now made all the concessions which the USA had previously demanded of it. On 16 December a meeting took place between the US Ambassador in Tunis, Robert Pelletreau, and PLO officials, the USA emphasizing that its willingness to begin a dialogue with the PLO did not imply its recognition of the Palestinian state. On 22 March a second session of talks took place, during which the two sides reportedly disagreed over the issue of preparations for an international conference on the Middle East, the urgency of which the USA was believed to have questioned (although it did not argue against the convening of such a conference in principle), and the question of military attacks against Israel.

A meeting of the PLO's Central Council on 31 March–1 April unanimously confirmed an earlier decision of the PLO's Executive Council to nominate Yasser Arafat as President of the State of Palestine.

In May 1989 Yasser Arafat paid an official visit to France, during which he declared the Palestinian National Charter (see p. 115) to have been superseded by the PNC's qualified acceptance of UN Security Council Resolution 242 in November 1988. At a press conference at the end of his visit to France he refused to clarify his statement, or to indicate whether he intended to have the Charter modified. The description of the Charter as 'null and void' was denounced by George Habash, Secretary-General of the PFLP, on 11 May, when he described the Charter as a rallying point for the Palestinian people which could not be altered by any one individual.

On 6 April, during a meeting with President Bush of the USA, Prime Minister Shamir of Israel announced details of a four-point peace initiative for the Middle East (see Documents on Palestine, p. 99), which proposed the holding of elections in the West Bank and Gaza Strip, leading to the formation of a non-PLO delegation to take part in negotiations on an 'interim settlement'. The initial reaction of the PLO was to condemn the Israeli peace proposals for ignoring the central issue of Palestinian political rights. However, it subsequently responded with peace proposals of its own, presented in a formal memorandum to US representatives in Tunis, which insisted that the proposed elections should be linked to an overall settlement involving the exchange of land for peace and the convening of an international peace conference. A third round of talks between representatives of the USA and the PLO took place on 8 June and concluded without tangible results. According to Yasser Abd Rabbuh, head of the PLO delegation, the PLO had underlined the position (endorsed at the Arab summit meeting in Casablanca in late May) that elections could only take place after Israel's withdrawal from the Occupied Territories, and under international supervision.

In May 1989, by a majority vote, members of the WHO approved a resolution postponing for one year the consideration of an application for membership by the PLO. The USA had warned that it would immediately withhold its financial contributions to any international organization which admitted Palestine as a full member. According to the USA, the Palestinian application for membership risked complicating the dialogue between the USA and the PLO. In the same month, the PLO applied for full membership of UNESCO.

At the fifth congress of Fatah, held in Tunis on 3–9 August 1989, the moderate, 'two state solution' to the Arab-Israeli conflict was overwhelmingly approved. At the same time, however, the congress called for the intensification of the struggle to end the Israeli occupation of Palestine. On 14 August the US Ambassador to Tunisia, Robert Pelletreau, held talks with a PLO delegation in an attempt to persuade the PLO to modify its opposition to the Israeli peace initiative. The position of the PLO remained that it would only agree to the elections proposed under the Israeli initiative after Israeli forces had withdrawn from the Occupied Territories, and as a preliminary step towards the declaration of an independent Palestinian state.

On 15 September 1989 President Mubarak of Egypt attempted to give impetus to the Israeli peace initiative by seeking the clarification of its provisions by the Israeli Government (for full details see Documents on Palestine, p. 99). The Palestinian response to the 'Mubarak plan' was mixed. While Arafat welcomed its proposal of an unconditional dialogue between Israelis and Palestinians, Sawt al-Quds, the unofficial radio station run by the PFLP-GC, described it as merely an improved version of the Israeli initiative. However, the progress of the peace process was halted on 5–6 October 1989 when Israel's 12-member inner Cabinet voted to reject a proposal by the Labour Party to accept Mubarak's invitation to attend preliminary talks with a Palestinian delegation in Cairo. Israel's Likud remained resolutely opposed to the participation of the PLO in the peace process. Five unofficial proposals by the US Secretary of State, James Baker (the 'Baker plan'—see Documents on Palestine, p. 99), put forward on 10 October 1989, were received with caution by the Israeli Government, which sought assurances that the PLO would remain excluded from the peace process. On 16 October the PLO's Central Council rejected the 'Baker plan', calling for the PLO's role in the peace process to be more clearly defined.

Both the Israeli Government and the PLO subsequently modified their positions regarding the 'Baker plan'. On 5 November 1989 Israel's inner Cabinet announced its conditional acceptance of Baker's five informal proposals, although it continued to insist that the PLO remain excluded from any future negotiations. On 3–5 November the PLO's Executive Committee met in Cairo, where it reportedly reaffirmed that any meeting between Palestinian and Israeli delegations should take place as a preliminary step towards an international peace conference on the Middle East, and that the PLO should have the right to nominate its own delegation.

The peace process remained deadlocked throughout the first half of 1990, with none of the parties to it prepared to modify the stance it had already adopted. In May, in a move which expressed its frustration at what it perceived as the Israeli Government's intransigence, the USA announced its readiness to consider the placing of an international observer force in the Occupied Territories. This idea had always been resolutely opposed by Israeli governments, which considered it to be interference in Israel's internal affairs. Addressing an emergency session of the UN Security Council in Geneva on 25 May, Arafat called for UN observers and international emergency forces to be deployed in the Occupied Territories and also urged the UN to implement sanctions against Israel. On 31 May, however, the USA vetoed a proposal by the Security Council to send international observers to the Occupied Territories to examine ways of protecting the Palestinian population.

On 20 June 1990 the US Administration formally terminated its dialogue with the PLO on the grounds that it had failed to renounce terrorism. The decision to do so was taken in the wake of an abortive seaborne guerrilla attack on Israel at the beginning of June 1990. The US Government had pressed the PLO to condemn the attack, which had been carried out by the PLF, a faction of the PLO not directly under Arafat's control. However, a PLO statement condemning all attacks on civilians was judged to be insufficiently specific by the USA. Following the cessation of dialogue between the USA and the PLO, some Palestinian groups urged the PLO to abandon the policy of moderation set out at the 19th session of the PNC, and to resume the armed struggle.

The support of the PLO leadership for Iraq and Saddam Hussein for the duration of the crisis in the Gulf, which began with Iraq's invasion of Kuwait in August 1990, was widely regarded as nothing short of disastrous. Not only did it alienate the Organization's principal financial backers, the Arab Gulf states, but it also led, following Iraqi attacks with *Scud* missiles on Israel, to a transfer of international sympathy from the Palestinian cause to Israel.

In the aftermath of hostilities between Iraq and the multinational force, US diplomacy focused on the Arab-Israeli confrontation with renewed vigour. In late March 1991 the Israeli Prime Minister, Itzhak Shamir, indicated that Israel was prepared to take steps to reduce tension in the Middle East, and reaffirmed his commitment to the peace initiative which he had proposed in May 1989. In late April, immediately prior to a visit to Damascus by the US Secretary of State, James Baker, Syria set out a series of conditions for a peace settlement with Israel. These included the withdrawal of Israel from the Occupied Territories; the safeguarding of Palestinian national rights; and a prominent role for the UN in any future peace conference. The Israeli Government had already made it clear that it regarded these conditions as unacceptable.

In May 1991 the principal obstacle to progress in the peace process appeared to be the opposed positions of the Israeli and Syrian Governments. Syria remained adamant that talks with Israel should take place within the framework of an international conference, with the full partcipation of the UN, and that afterwards such a conference should reconvene at regular intervals. Israel remained opposed both to the participation of the UN and to the reconvening of the conference after an initial session had been held. The USA, for its part, excluded the possibility of holding a peace conference without Syrian participation. In mid-July, however, a significant advance was achieved, when Syria agreed to take part in direct negotiations with Israel on the basis of UN resolutions 242 and 338. In early August the Israeli Government agreed to participate in a Middle East peace conference, under the auspices of the USA and the USSR, and attended by all parties to the Arab-Israeli conflict. (For details of the conference proceedings, see the Arab-Israeli Confrontation 1967–93, pp. 59–71, and chapters on those countries participating in the conference.)

In September 1993, following a series of secret negotiations, the PLO and Israel agreed formally to recognize each other and signed a Declaration of Principles on Palestinian Self-Rule in the Occupied Territories (for details of the Declaration of Principle, see Documents on Palestine, p. 100). This was followed by the signing, in May 1994, of an agreement that provided—in accordance with the Declaration of Principles—for Palestinian autonomy in the Gaza Strip and the Jericho area. The agreement set out the arrangements for the withdrawal of Israeli armed forces from Gaza and Jericho and for the deployment there of a Palestinian police force. The Israeli army was to retain control of security in Israeli settlements in the Gaza Strip and Israel would remain responsible for movements in and out of the Gaza Strip and the Jericho area. Israel's military administration was to be superseded by an appointed Palestine National Authority (PNA, see section on Occupied Territories appended to the chapter on Israel)—

except in the spheres of external security and foreign affairs. The PNA would assume jurisdiction over the whole of the Gaza Strip and Jericho with the exception of Israeli settlements there. The PLO took formal control of the Israeli Civil Administration's 38 departments in the Gaza Strip and Jericho on 17 May 1994. Israeli armed forces had withdrawn from the Jericho area by 13 May and from the Gaza Strip by 18 May. On 26–28 May a newly appointed but incomplete PNA held its first meeting in Tunis, Tunisia, where it approved a political programme and distributed portfolios. The PNA held its first meeting in Gaza on 26 June.

Chairman: 1964–67   Ahmad Shukairi.

1967–68   Yahya Hammouda.

1968–   Yasser Arafat.

Head of PLO Observer Mission at UN: Zehdi Labib Terzi; 115 East 65th St, New York, NY 10021; tel. (212) 288-8500.

By July 1991 the following states had recognized the independent State of Palestine, and more than 70 states had accorded Palestinian representatives full diplomatic status.

Afghanistan, Albania, Algeria, Angola, Austria, Bahrain, Bangladesh, Benin, Bhutan, Botswana, Brunei, Bulgaria, Burkina Faso, Burundi, Cambodia, Cameroon, Cape Verde, Central African Republic, Chad, China, Comoros, Congo, Cuba, Cyprus, Czechoslovakia, Djibouti, Egypt, Equatorial Guinea, Ethiopia, Gabon, Gambia, Germany, Ghana, Guinea, Guinea Bissau, Hungary, India, Indonesia, Iran, Iraq, Jordan, Korea (Dem. People's Rep.), Kuwait, Laos, Lebanon, Libya, Madagascar, Malaysia, Maldives, Mali, Malta, Mauritania, Mauritius, Mongolia, Morocco, Mozambique, Nepal, Nicaragua, Niger, Nigeria, Oman, Pakistan, Philippines, Poland, Qatar, Romania, Rwanda, Saõ Tomé e Príncipe, Saudi Arabia, Senegal, Seychelles, Sierra Leone, Somalia, Sri Lanka, Sudan, Swaziland, Tanzania, Togo, Tunisia, Turkey, Uganda, USSR, United Arab Emirates, Vanuatu, Vietnam, Yemen, Yugoslavia, Zaire, Zambia, Zimbabwe.

The following states, while they did not recognize the State of Palestine, allowed the PLO to maintain a regional office: Belgium, Brazil, France, Greece, Italy, Japan, the Netherlands, Portugal, Spain, Sweden, Switzerland, UK.

PALESTINE NATIONAL COUNCIL

It had 426 members in April 1987 and formerly met once a year. Cairo was the usual venue until the Egyptian *rapprochement* with Israel that gave rise to the Camp David agreements of 1978, and the Egyptian-Israeli Peace Treaty of 1979 (see Documents on Palestine pp. 90–94). As well as the guerrilla organizations, the other PLO bodies, trade and student unions, etc. are represented. The Council also includes Palestinian representatives from Jordan, the West Bank, the Gulf States and other countries. At the 14th session in Damascus in January 1979 a unity plan to reconcile the various elements in the PLO was adopted, but the PFLP did not rejoin the Executive Committee. The 15th PNC session was held in Damascus in April 1981 and voted to increase the number of members by between 30 and 40. The 16th PNC session was held in Algiers in February 1983. The 17th PNC session was held in Amman, Jordan, in November 1984, when it was decided to move the headquarters of the PNC from Damascus to Amman. At the 18th session of the PNC, held in Algiers in April 1987, a total of 21 new members, including, for the first time, members of the Palestine Communist Party, were admitted. At the 19th session of the PNC, held in Algiers in November 1988, the unilateral declaration of the independent State of Palestine was announced. At the 20th session of the PNC, held in Algiers in September 1991, a new Executive Committee of 18 members was elected.

Speaker: Salim Zaanoun ('Abu Adib').

Secretary-General: Jamal as-Surani.

CENTRAL COUNCIL

It is elected by the PNC; consists of the members of the Executive Committee, and other members, with a total possible membership of 107; acts as a steering group when the PNC is not in session.

EXECUTIVE COMMITTEE
(elected September 1991)

This is elected by the PNC and is responsible for the running of the PLO between meetings of the Central Council. In September 1974 the PFLP withdrew from the Executive Committee and Central Council of the PLO because it rejected PLO policies which recognized the existence of Israel. This 'rejectionist front' was later joined by the PFLP—General Command, the Arab Liberation Front and the Front for the Popular Palestinian Struggle, and in practice their members ceased to serve on the Executive Committee and Central Council, although they remained members of the PNC. At the March 1977 meeting of the PNC only the PFLP continued to boycott the work of the Executive Committee. At the 16th PNC session in Algiers in February 1983, the Executive Committee was re-elected, but was reduced from 15 to 14 members by the resignation of Dr Salah ad-Dabbagh (then Chairman of the Palestine National Fund) on health grounds. At the 17th PNC session in Amman in November 1984, it was decided to move the headquarters of the Secretariat of the Executive Committee from Damascus to Tunis. Only 11 of the 14 seats on the Executive Committee were filled at the 17th PNC session owing to a boycott of the proceedings by some factions. Fahd al-Qawasmeh, who was elected to the Executive Committee at the 17th PNC session, was assassinated in December 1984. At the 18th PNC session, in Algiers, in April 1987, the membership of the Executive Committee was increased to 15, including members of factions who had boycotted the previous session. At the 20th session of the PNC, held in September 1991, a new Executive Committee of 18 members was elected. By mid-October 1993 seven members of the Executive Committee elected in September 1991 (Mahmoud Ismail, Ali Is'hak, Abd ar-Rahim Mallouh, Abdullah Hourani, Tayseer Khaled, Mahmoud Darwish, Shafik al-Hout) had resigned in protest at the Declaration of Principles on Palestinian Self-Rule signed by the PLO and Israel in September 1993.

Chairman: YASSER ARAFAT (also known as 'ABU AMMAR'—Fatah—Head of Military Dept).

Members: FAROUK KADDOUMI (also known as 'ABU LUTF'—Fatah—Head of Political Dept), MAHMOUD ABBAS (also known as 'ABU MAZIN'—Fatah—Head of Pan-Arab and Int. Relations Dept), Archbishop ILYA KHURI (independent), JAWID AL-GHUSAYN (independent), JAMAL AS-SURANI (independent—Sec. and Head of Administrative Affairs Dept), YASSER ABD AR-RABBUH (DFLP—Head of Information Dept), SULAYMAN AN-NAJJAB (Palestine People's Party—Head of Social Affairs Dept), SAMIR GHOUSHA (PSF), YASSER AMR (independent), MUHAMMAD ZOHDI AN-NASHASHIBI (independent).

PALESTINE LIBERATION ARMY (PLA)

The PLA was founded in 1964 and numbers 16,000 men, mainly infantry, currently dispersed in countries throughout the Middle East; the commando wing (Popular Liberation Forces) was formed in 1968 but had only a short existence. An élite force called Force 17 (originally designed to be Yasser Arafat's personal bodyguard) was allegedly enlarged in 1985 to carry out operations in Israel.

Commander-in-Chief: YASSER ARAFAT.

Military Commander: (vacant).

PALESTINE NATIONAL FUND

The Fund is financed by a contribution of between 3% and 6% from the income of every Palestinian and also aid from Arab and friendly countries. The Fund's headquarters were moved from Damascus to Amman at the 17th PNC session in November 1984 and from Amman to Abu Dhabi, after the Government of the UAE gave its permission, in February 1987. In August 1989, following an improvement in the PLO's relations with Jordan, the Fund's headquarters were transferred back to Amman. The Fund administers assets estimated in the Western press at $5,000m.

Chairman: JAWID AL-GHUSAYN.

Director: DARWISH ABYAD.

PALESTINE PLANNING CENTRE

Director: MUNIR SHAFIQ.

PALESTINE RED CRESCENT

Palestine Hospital, 64 Sharia ath-Thawra, Heliopolis, Cairo.

President: Dr FATHI ARAFAT; f. 1969; operated 7 hospitals, several emergency centres and clinics and 150 ambulances until Israeli invasion of Lebanon in June 1982. In early 1983 the Red Crescent was still functioning in areas of Lebanon under Syrian and Lebanese control, but not in areas under Israeli control.

PALESTINE MARTYRS' WORKS SOCIETY (SAMED)

Previously in Beirut, but reopened in Damascus, 1983, and subsequently transferred to Tunis; runs workshops making blankets, tents, uniforms, civilian clothes, toys, furniture, etc.

President: 'ABU ALA'.

PRESS AND RADIO

Filastin ath-Thawra (Palestine Revolution): normally published in Beirut, but resumed publication from Cyprus, November 1982; weekly newspaper of the Palestine Liberation Organization.

Al-Hadaf: organ of the Popular Front for the Liberation of Palestine; weekly.

Al-Haria (Liberation): organ of the Democratic Front for the Liberation of Palestine.

Shu'un Filastiniya (Palestine Affairs): Palestine Research Centre, POB 5614, 92 Gr. Afxentiou St, Nicosia, Cyprus; tel. 461140; telex 4706; monthly.

Sawt Filastin (Voice of Palestine): official radio station of Palestine Liberation Organization; broadcasts from Baghdad and Algiers, and also from San'a and Aden.

Sawt al-Quds (Voice of Jerusalem): unofficial radio station run by the Popular Front for the Liberation of Palestine—General Command; broadcasts from Damascus.

Wikalat Anbaa' Filastiniya (WAFA) (Palestine News Agency): formerly in Beirut, but resumed activities in Cyprus and Tunis, November 1982; official PLO news agency; Editor ZIAD ABD AL-FATTAH.

CENTRAL COUNCIL OF THE PALESTINE RESISTANCE MOVEMENT

It was created early in 1970 and represents all the guerrilla groups. The most important guerrilla organizations are:

Fatah (The Palestine National Liberation Movement): f. 1957; the largest single Palestinian movement, embraces a coalition of varying views from conservative to radical; leader YASSER ARAFAT; Sec.-Gen. FAROUK KADDOUMI; Central Cttee elected by Fatah's 530-member Congress, 31 May 1980): YASSER ARAFAT ('ABU AMMAR'), SALAH KHALAF ('ABU IYAD'), FAROUK KADDOUMI ('ABU LUTF' also Sec. of Central Cttee), MAHMOUD ABBAS ('ABU MAZIN'), KHALID AL-HASSAN ('ABU AS-SAID'), HAYIL ABD AL-HAMID ('ABU AL-HAWL'), MUHAMMAD GHUNAIM ('ABU MAHIR'), SALIM AZ-ZA'NUN ('ABU AL-ADIB'), RAFIQ AN-NATSHAH ('ABU SHAKIR'), HANI AL-HASAN. (Nimr Salih ('Abu Salih'), Samih Abu Quwayq ('Qadri'), Said Musa Muragha ('Abu Musa') and seven others were expelled from Fatah in Nov. 1983 for their part in the revolt against Yasser Arafat.)

Al-Asifah (Fatah Forces): Commdr YASSER ARAFAT.

Popular Front for the Liberation of Palestine (PFLP): f. 1967; Marxist-Leninist; leader Dr GEORGE HABASH; publ. Democratic Palestine (monthly, in English), Box 12144, Damascus, Syria.

Democratic Front for the Liberation of Palestine (DFLP): split from PFLP in 1969; based in Damascus, Syria; Marxist; leader NAIF HAWATMEH.

Arab Liberation Front (ALF): f. 1969; Iraqi-backed; leader MAHMOUD ISMAIL.

Palestine Popular Struggle Front (PPSF): f. 1967; Sec.-Gen. SAMIR GHOUSHA.

Palestine People's Party: formerly Palestine Communist Party, admitted to PNC at its 18th session, Algiers, April 1987; Sec.-Gen. SULEIMAN NAJJAB.

Palestine Liberation Front (PLF): split from PFLP—GC in April 1977; the PLF split into two factions at the end of 1983, both of which retained the name PLF; one faction (leader 'ABU ABBAS') based in Tunis and Baghdad and remaining nominally loyal to Yasser Arafat; the other faction belonging to the anti-Arafat National Salvation Front and having offices in Damascus, Syria, and Libya. A third group derived from the PLF was reported to have been formed by its Central Cttee Secretary, ABD AL-FATTAH GHANIM, in June 1986. At the 18th session of the PNC, a programme for the unification of the PLF was announced, with Talaat Yaqoub (died November 1988) named as secretary-general and 'Abu Abbas' appointed to the PLO Executive Committee, while unification talks were held. The merging of the two factions was announced in June 1987 with 'Abu Abbas' becoming Deputy Secretary-General.

The anti-Arafat **National Salvation Front** includes the following organizations:

Popular Front for the Liberation of Palestine-General Command (PFLP-GC): split from PFLP; based in Damascus; pro-Syrian; leader AHMAD JIBRIL.

Saiqa (Vanguard of the Popular Liberation War): f. 1967; Syrian-backed; leader ISSAM AL-QADI.

Palestine Revolutionary Communist Party: based in Damascus; Sec.-Gen. ARBI AWAD.

Alliance of Palestinian Forces: f. January 1994; 10 members representing the PFLP, the DFLP, the PLF, the PPSF, the Palestine Revolutionary Communist Party and the PFLP–GC; opposes the Declaration of Principles on Palestinian Self-Rule signed by Israel and the PLO (Fatah) in September 1993.

The **Fatah Revolutionary Council**, headed by SABRI KHALIL AL-BANNA, alias 'ABU NIDAL', split from Fatah in 1973. Its headquarters were formerly in Baghdad, Iraq, but the office was closed down and its staff expelled from the country by the Iraqi authorities in November 1983 and a new base was established in Damascus, Syria, in December 1983. 'Abu Nidal' was readmitted to Iraq in 1984, having fled Syria. With 'ABU MUSA' (whose rebel Fatah group is called **Al-Intifada**, or 'Uprising'), 'Abu Nidal' formed a joint rebel Fatah command in February 1985, and both had offices in Damascus until June 1987, when those of 'Abu Nidal' were closed by the Syrian Government. In 1989 the Fatah Revolutionary Council was reported to have disintegrated, and in June 1990 forces loyal to Abu Nidal surrendered to Fatah forces at the Rashidiyeh Palestinian refugee camp near Tyre, northern Lebanon.

The Islamic fundamentalist organizations *'Islamic Jihad'* (Gen.-Sec. FATHI SHQAQI) and the *'Islamic Resistance Movement'* (Hamas) are also active in the Occupied Territories, where they began to play an increasingly prominent role in the *intifada* during 1989. Like the organizations represented in the Alliance of Palestinian Forces they are strongly opposed to the Declaration of Principles on Palestinian Self-Rule.

THE PALESTINIAN NATIONAL CHARTER
(Palestine Liberation Organization)*

1. Palestine is the homeland of the Palestinian Arab people; it is an indivisible part of the Arab homeland, and the Palestinian people are an integral part of the Arab nation.

2. Palestine, with the boundaries it had during the British mandate, is an indivisible territorial unit.

3. The Palestinian Arab people possess the legal right to their homeland and have the right to determine their destiny after achieving the liberation of their country in accordance with their wishes and entirely of their own accord and will.

4. The Palestinian identity is a genuine, essential and inherent characteristic; it is transmitted from parents to children. The Zionist occupation and the dispersal of the Palestinian Arab people, through the disasters which befell them, do not make them lose their Palestinian identity and their membership of the Palestinian community, nor do they negate them.

5. The Palestinians are those Arab nationals who, until 1947, normally resided in Palestine regardless of whether

they were evicted from it or have stayed there. Anyone born, after that date, of a Palestinian father—whether inside Palestine or outside it—is also a Palestinian.

6. The Jews who had normally resided in Palestine until the beginning of the Zionist invasion will be considered Palestinians.

7. That there is a Palestinian community and that it has material, spiritual and historical connection with Palestine are indisputable facts. It is a national duty to bring up individual Palestinians in an Arab revolutionary manner. All means of information and education must be adopted in order to acquaint the Palestinian with his country in the most profound manner, both spiritual and material, that is possible. He must be prepared for the armed struggle and ready to sacrifice his wealth and his life in order to win back his homeland and bring about its liberation.

8. The phase in their history, through which the Palestinian people are now living, is that of national struggle for the liberation of Palestine. Thus the conflicts among the Palestinian national forces are secondary, and should be ended for the sake of the basic conflict that exists between the forces of Zionism and of imperialism on the one hand, and the Palestinian Arab people on the other. On this basis the Palestinian masses, regardless of whether they are residing in the national homeland or in diaspora, constitute—both their organizations and the individuals—one national front working for the retrieval of Palestine and its liberation through armed struggle.

9. Armed struggle is the only way to liberate Palestine . . . .

10. Commando action constitutes the nucleus of the Palestinian popular liberation war. This requires its escalation, comprehensiveness and the mobilization of all the Palestinian popular and educational efforts and their organization and involvement in the armed Palestinian revolution. It also requires the achieving of unity for the national struggle among the different groupings of the Palestinian people, and between the Palestinian people and the Arab masses so as to secure the continuation of the revolution, its escalation and victory.

11. The Palestinians will have three mottoes: national unity, national mobilization and liberation.

12. The Palestinian people believe in Arab unity. In order to contribute their share towards the attainment of that objective, however, they must, at the present stage of their struggle, safeguard their Palestinian identity and develop their consciousness of that identity, and oppose any plan that may dissolve or impair it.

13. Arab unity and the liberation of Palestine are two complementary objectives, the attainment of either of which facilitates the attainment of the other. Thus, Arab unity leads to the liberation of Palestine; the liberation of Palestine leads to Arab unity; and work towards the realization of one objective proceeds side by side with work towards the realization of the other.

14. The destiny of the Arab nation, and indeed Arab existence itself, depends upon the destiny of the Palestine cause. From this interdependence springs the Arab nation's pursuit of, and striving for, the liberation of Palestine. The people of Palestine play the role of the vanguard in the realization of this sacred national goal.

15. The liberation of Palestine, from an Arab viewpoint, is a national duty and it attempts to repel the Zionist and imperialist aggression against the Arab homeland, and aims at the elimination of Zionism in Palestine. Absolute responsibility for this falls upon the Arab nation—peoples and governments—with the Arab people of Palestine in the vanguard. Accordingly the Arab nation must mobilize all its military, human, moral and spiritual capabilities to participate actively with the Palestinian people in the liberation of Palestine. It must, particularly in the phase of the armed Palestinian revolution, offer and furnish the Palestinian people with all possible help, and material and human support, and make available to them the means and opportunities that will enable them to continue to carry out their leading role in the armed revolution, until they liberate their homeland.

---

* Decisions of the National Congress of the Palestine Liberation Organization held in Cairo 1–17 July 1968.

16. The liberation of Palestine, from a spiritual point of view, will provide the Holy Land with an atmosphere of safety and tranquillity, which in turn will safeguard the country's religious sanctuaries and guarantee freedom of worship and of visit to all, without discrimination of race, colour, language, or religion. Accordingly, the people of Palestine look to all spiritual forces in the world for support.

17. The liberation of Palestine, from a human point of view, will restore to the Palestinian individual his dignity, pride and freedom. Accordingly the Palestinian Arab people look forward to the support of all those who believe in the dignity of man and his freedom in the world.

18. The liberation of Palestine, from an international point of view, is a defensive action necessitated by the demands of self-defence. Accordingly, the Palestinian people, desirous as they are of the friendship of all people, look to freedom-loving, justice-loving and peace-loving states for support in order to restore their legitimate rights in Palestine, to re-establish peace and security in the country, and to enable its people to exercise national sovereignty and freedom.

19. The partition of Palestine in 1947 and the establishment of the state of Israel are entirely illegal, regardless of the passage of time, because they were contrary to the will of the Palestinian people and to their natural right in their homeland, and inconsistent with the principles embodied in the Charter of the United Nations, particularly the right to self-determination.

20. The Balfour Declaration, the mandate for Palestine and everything that has been based upon them, are deemed null and void. Claims of historical or religious ties of Jews with Palestine are incompatible with the facts of history and the true conception of what constitutes statehood. Judaism, being a religion, is not an independent nationality. Nor do Jews constitute a single nation with an identity of its own; they are citizens of the states to which they belong.

21. The Palestinian Arab people, expressing themselves by the armed Palestinian revolution, reject all solutions which are substitutes for the total liberation of Palestine and reject all proposals aiming at the liquidation of the Palestinian problem, or its internationalization.

22. Zionism is a political movement organically associated with international imperialism and antagonistic to all action for liberation and to progressive movements in the world. It is racist and fanatic in its nature, aggressive, expansionist and colonial in its aims, and fascist in its methods. Israel is the instrument of the Zionist movement, and a geographical base for world imperialism placed strategically in the midst of the Arab homeland to combat the hopes of the Arab nation for liberation, unity and progress. Israel is a constant source of threat vis-à-vis peace in the Middle East and the whole world. Since the liberation of Palestine will destroy the Zionist and imperialist presence and will contribute to the establishment of peace in the Middle East, the Palestinian people look for the support of all the progressive and peaceful forces and urge them all, irrespective of their affiliations and beliefs, to offer the Palestinian people all aid and support in their just struggle for the liberation of their homeland.

23. The demands of security and peace, as well as the demands of right and justice, require all states to consider Zionism an illegitimate movement, to outlaw its existence, and to ban its operations, in order that friendly relations among peoples may be preserved, and the loyalty of citizens to their respective homelands safeguarded.

24. The Palestinian people believe in the principles of justice, freedom, sovereignty, self-determination, human dignity, and in the right of all peoples to exercise them.

25. For the realization of the goals of this Charter and its principles, the Palestine Liberation Organization will perform its role in the liberation of Palestine in accordance with the Constitution of this Organization.

26. The Palestine Liberation Organization, representative of the Palestinian revolutionary forces, is responsible for the Palestinian Arab people's movement in its struggle—to retrieve its homeland, liberate and return to it and exercise the right to self-determination in it—in all military, political

and financial fields and also for whatever may be required by the Palestine case on the inter-Arab and international levels.

27. The Palestine Liberation Organization shall co-operate with all Arab states, each according to its potentialities; and will adopt a neutral policy among them in the light of the requirements of the war of liberation; and on this basis it shall not interfere in the internal affairs of any Arab state.

28. The Palestinian Arab people assert the genuineness and independence of their national revolution and reject all forms of intervention, trusteeship and subordination.

29. The Palestinian people possess the fundamental and genuine legal right to liberate and retrieve their homeland. The Palestinian people determine their attitude towards all states and forces on the basis of the stands they adopt vis-à-vis the Palestinian case and the extent of the support they offer to the Palestinian revolution to fulfil the aims of the Palestinian people.

30. Fighters and carriers of arms in the war of liberation are the nucleus of the popular army which will be the protective force for the gains of the Palestinian Arab people.

31. The Organization shall have a flag, an oath of allegiance and an anthem. All this shall be decided upon in accordance with a special regulation.

32. Regulations, which shall be known as the Constitution of the Palestine Liberation Organization, shall be annexed to this Charter. It shall lay down the manner in which the Organization, and its organs and institutions, shall be constituted; the respective competence of each; and the requirements of its obligations under the Charter.

33. This Charter shall not be amended save by (vote of) a majority of two-thirds of the total membership of the National Council of the Palestine Liberation Organization (taken) at a special session convened for that purpose.

15-POINT POLITICAL PROGRAMME

(adopted by the Palestine National Council, 20 March 1977 and reaffirmed by the PLO Central Council, 25 August 1977)

Proceeding from the Palestine national charter and the previous national councils' resolutions; considering the decisions and political gains achieved by the PLO at the Arab and international levels during the period following the 12th session of the PNC; after studying and debating the latest developments in the Palestine issue; and stressing support for the Palestinian national struggle in the Arab and international forums, the PNC affirms the following:

1. The PNC affirms that the Palestine issue is the essence and the root of the Arab-Zionist conflict. Security Council Resolution 242 (see Documents on Palestine, p. 86) ignores the Palestinian people and their firm rights. The PNC therefore confirms its rejection of this Resolution, and rejects negotiations at the Arab and international levels based on this Resolution.

2. The PNC affirms the stand of the PLO in its determination to continue the armed struggle, and its concomitant forms of political and mass struggle, to achieve our inalienable national rights.

3. The PNC affirms that the struggle, in all its military, political and popular forms, in the occupied territory constitutes the central link in its programme of struggle. On this basis, the PLO will strive to escalate the armed struggle in the occupied territory, to escalate all other concomitant forms of struggle, and to give all kinds of moral support to the masses of our people in the occupied territory in order to escalate the struggle and to strengthen their steadfastness to defeat and liquidate the occupation.

4. The PNC affirms the PLO's stand which rejects all types of American capitulationist settlement and all liquidationist projects. The Council affirms the determination of the PLO to abort any settlement achieved at the expense of the firm national rights of our people. The PNC calls upon the Arab nation to shoulder its Pan-Arab responsibilities and to pool all its energies to confront these imperialist and Zionist plans.

5. The Palestine National Council stresses the importance and necessity of national units, both political and military,

among all the contingents of the Palestine Revolution within the framework of the PLO, because this is one of the basic conditions for victory. For this reason, it is necessary to co-ordinate national units at all levels and in all spheres on the basis of commitment to all these resolutions, and to draw up programmes which will ensure the implementation of this.

6. The Palestine National Council affirms the right of the Palestine Revolution to be present on the soil of fraternal Lebanon within the framework of the Cairo agreement and its appendices, concluded between the PLO and the Lebanese authorities. The Council also affirms adherence to the implementation of the Cairo agreement in letter and in spirit, including the preservation of the position of the Revolution and the security of the camps. The Palestine National Council refuses to accept any interpretation of this agreement by one side only. Meanwhile, it affirms its eagerness for the maintenance of the sovereignty and security of Lebanon.

7. The Palestine National Council greets the heroic fraternal Lebanese people and affirms the eagerness of the PLO for the maintenance of the territorial integrity of Lebanon, the unity of its people and its security, independence, sovereignty and Arabism. The Palestine National Council affirms its pride in the support rendered by this heroic fraternal people to the PLO, which is struggling for our people to regain their national rights to their homeland and their right to return to this homeland. The PNC strongly affirms the need to deepen and consolidate cohesion between all Lebanese nationalist forces and the Palestine Revolution.

8. The Council affirms the need to strengthen the Arab front participating in the Palestine Revolution, and to deepen cohesion with all forces participating in it in all Arab countries, as well as to escalate the joint Arab struggle and to further strengthen the Palestine Revolution in order to contend with the imperialist and Zionist designs.

9. The Palestine National Council has decided to consolidate Arab struggle and solidarity on the basis of struggle against imperialism and Zionism, to work for the liberation of all the occupied Arab areas, and to adhere to the support for the Palestine Revolution in order to regain the constant national rights of the Palestinian Arab people without any conciliation or recognition.

10. The Palestine National Council affirms the right of the PLO to exercise its struggle responsibilities at the Pan-Arab level and through any Arab land in the interest of liberating the occupied areas.

11. The Palestine National Council has decided to continue the struggle to regain the national rights of our people, in particular their rights of return, self-determination and establishing an independent national state on their national soil.

12. The Palestine National Council affirms the significance of co-operation and solidarity with socialist, non-aligned, Islamic and African countries, and with all the national liberation movements in the world.

13. The Palestine National Council hails the stands and struggles of all the democratic countries and forces against Zionism in its capacity as one form of racism, as well as against its aggressive practices.

14. The Palestine National Council affirms the significance of establishing relations and co-ordinating with the progressive and democratic Jewish forces inside and outside the occupied homeland, since these forces are struggling against Zionism as a doctrine and in practice. The Palestine National Council calls on all states and forces who love freedom, justice and peace in the world to end all forms of assistance to and co-operation with the racist Zionist regime, and to end contacts with it and its instruments.

15. Taking into consideration the important achievements in the Arab and international arenas since the conclusion of the PNC's 12th session, the PNC, which has reviewed the political report submitted by the PLO, has decided the following:

A. The Council confirms its wish for the PLO's right to participate independently and on an equal footing in all the conferences and international forums concerned with the Palestine issue and the Arab-Zionist conflict, with a view to achieving our inalienable national rights as approved by the United Nations General Assembly in 1974, namely in Resolution 3236 (see Documents on Palestine, p. 90).

B. The Council declares that any settlement or agreement affecting the rights of our Palestinian people made in the absence of this people will be completely null and void.

Long live the Palestine Revolution. Long live Palestinian unity among the Revolution's contingents. Glory and immortality to our innocent martyrs. This Revolution will continue until victory.

RECOMMENDATIONS OF THE MILITARY COMMITTEE OF THE PALESTINE NATIONAL COUNCIL
(approved by the Council, 20 March 1977)

1. Unification of the fighting forces of all the Palestinian revolutionary contingents, including the Palestinian armed struggle, the militia forces and the Palestine Liberation Army, in a united force to be named the army and the armed forces of the Palestine revolution that will be the military arm of the PLO.

2. The army and the armed forces of the Palestine revolution are to be composed of the following: (a) regular forces, to be named the Palestinian National Liberation Army, which will comprise all regular forces; (b) irregular forces; (c) the militia forces, including the youth and cubs organizations.

3. The Chairman of the PLO Executive Committee is the supreme commander of the army and the armed forces of the Palestine revolution; at the same time he will hold the position of general commander until someone is appointed to fill this post.

4. A supreme military council will be established under the leadership of the supreme commander, to include the military commanders of the organizations, the general commanders of the organizations, the general commander and commanders of the three forces—the regular, irregular and militia forces. This council will pass the rules and regulations that are necessary to organize the army and the armed forces, appointing the commanders, establishing the military units and laying down the plans, programme and budgets to guarantee the unification, the strengthening and development of the army and the armed forces.

5. The Palestine National Fund will undertake the task of meeting the financial needs of this army, in light of the regulations to be promulgated by the supreme military council. The organizations will pay in their commitments to the National Fund during the transitional period until financial unification is achieved.

6. All Palestinian military personnel who are not drafted into the army and the armed forces are to be considered members of the reserve, and the leadership retains the right to call them up for duty when it is deemed necessary.

7. National service is compulsory for all Palestinians in the Arab world. This will be carried out by co-ordinating with the Arab host countries, so that Palestinians serve in the Palestinian army and the armed forces.

8. Reconsideration of the military agreements that were reached between the PLO and the Arab countries in which Palestinian Liberation Army units are stationed, in order to reach new agreements that will enable the PLO's political leadership to control and command this army.

9. Confirmation of the need to step up the armed struggle in the occupied territories and to demand of the Arab confrontation states that they open their fronts for the Palestinian revolutionary forces to work against the Zionist enemy and guarantee the revolutionary forces the right to stay and operate in these countries.

10. Emphasizing of the right reserved for the Palestine struggle to retain all of its weapons in Lebanon, and its absolute right to defend the camps of our people.

11. That the Chairman of the PLO Executive Council, the general commander of the army and the armed forces of the Palestine revolution, be asked to carry out these resolutions, and that he be assisted by the supreme military council, on condition that this be done as soon as possible.

SUBSEQUENT PROGRAMME

On 18 January 1979, the Palestine National Council adopted a 'National Unity' Political and Organizational Programme which reaffirmed past policy, condemned the Camp David accords and proposed a reorganization of the PLO departments. The PLO continued to oppose the Camp David agreements in 1980, and also strongly opposed the Israeli policy of Jewish settlements on the West Bank (see Arab-Israeli Confrontation pp. 30–31).

The 16th session of the PNC, meeting in Algiers in February 1983, made no changes in the PLO Charter. It rejected the Reagan plan (see p. 95) and stated that the Fez plan was the minimum acceptable to the PLO. The 17th session of the PNC, meeting in Amman in November 1984, delegated the PLO Executive Committee to examine King Hussein's proposals for a joint Jordanian-Palestinian position on a Middle East peace settlement. The formal establishment of the joint negotiating platform was endorsed by the PLO Executive Committee in February 1985, on the condition that it received full Arab support.

The 18th session of the PNC, in Algiers in April 1987, formally abrogated the Jordanian-Palestinian peace agreement and reaffirmed the PLO's 'adherence to the Arab summit resolutions on the Palestine question, particularly the 1974 Rabat summit and consideration of the Arab peace plan, which was approved by the 1982 Fez summit and confirmed by the extraordinary Casablanca summit as a framework for Arab action on the international level to achieve a solution to the Palestine question and to regain the occupied Arab territories'. It also supported 'the convening of an international conference within the framework of the UN and under its auspices to be attended by the permanent member-states of the UN Security Council and the parties to the conflict in the region, including the PLO, on equal footing with the other parties'.

At the 19th session of the PNC, in Algiers in November 1988, the independent State of Palestine was unilaterally declared. At the end of the session the PNC issued a political statement, calling for the convening of an international conference on the Middle East, under the auspices of the UN and with the participation of the permanent members of the UN Security Council and all parties to the conflict in the region, on an equal footing, to be held on the basis of UN Security Council Resolutions 242 and 338 and the safeguarding of the legitimate national rights of the Palestinian people (see Documents on Palestine pp. 86–88).

OIL IN THE MIDDLE EAST AND NORTH AFRICA

PETER BILD

Updated for this edition by the Editor

INTRODUCTION

At the time of writing, in early July 1994, oil prices were strengthening in response to OPEC's decision, taken at a meeting of member states' oil ministers in mid-June, to freeze production at 24.52m. b/d for the remainder of 1994 and to cancel its regular September meeting. Another cause of firmer prices was growth in US demand, which was reported to have risen by some 1m. b/d since the beginning of 1994. Also, it appeared likely, owing to constraints on production in certain countries, that OPEC would be able to observe the production ceiling more easily than it had others in the past.

OPEC's decision consolidated a recovery in the price of world crude petroleum, which had risen by some 25% between the end of March and mid-May 1994. Factors involved in the recovery had included an upward revision in the forecast demand for crude petroleum in 1994 by the International Energy Agency (IEA); and a slight reduction, in April, in OPEC's total production of crude.

This recovery was in contrast to the trend that had prevailed for most of the previous 12 months. Indeed, OPEC's decision, in March 1994, to maintain production at 24.52m. b/d for the remainder of the year had led to fears of a collapse in the world price of oil and to speculation that OPEC might take emergency measures if prices fell any closer to $10 per barrel in the spring and summer. OPEC's inability to reduce surplus supplies to the market had been determined, in part, by Kuwait's unwillingness to accept a pro-rata cut in production, although all other OPEC states had indicated their readiness to act to reduce combined crude oil production by up to 10% for the second and third quarters of 1994. In 1993 OPEC production reportedly rose by 2.9% to an average of just under 25m. b/d, while world oil prices declined by some 30%. In December prices fell to their lowest level for five years as a consequence of OPEC's failure, in late November, to modify the production ceiling of 24.52m. b/d first fixed in September. This had initially provoked a positive reaction from the market, but prices subsequently fell owing to weak demand and doubts whether the OPEC member states would adhere to their individual quotas.

For many observers, oil and money in the Middle East and North Africa mean the same thing. Inseparable they may be, but they are not the whole story. For all but the technical expert, it is the activities of governments, as represented by their politicians, civil servants and oil market experts, which constitute the history of oil. During the 1950s and 1960s, as the Middle East and North Africa came to dominate world supplies, this history was relatively simple: world demand for oil grew steadily and rapidly on the basis of low prices and rapid economic growth in the industrialized world. Although governments tried increasingly to become involved and to take more direct control of their economic destinies, it was the major international oil companies (the so-called 'seven sisters'), in concert with the governments of Europe and the USA, that played the key role. These companies assessed demand for oil products and balanced it internally with supplies that they both owned and controlled. The first 'oil shock' in 1973 changed the situation in two important ways. The quadrupling of prices, together with the embargoes and reductions in production imposed by Arab governments, focused the attention of Western governments on oil. The cost of oil imports became a major element in international monetary affairs, creating massive but unequal balance-of-payments deficits in the West. It also gave rise to fears that the 'petrodollars' of the newly-rich Middle Easterners would exacerbate monetary upheavals and vastly increase already existing inflationary pressures. The International Energy Agency (IEA), essentially a rich oil consumers' club, was set up in an atmosphere of hostility and confrontation. More significantly for the oil-producing states of the Middle East and North Africa today, the IEA caused the fragmentation of the hitherto integrated operations of the international oil companies, forcing governments with little experience in handling major international economic forces to deal with the consequences of their decisions on prices. The disintegration of the oil industry, as governments took control of production, coincided with huge, unprecedented reversals in the previously growing role of oil as the industrialized world's chief source of energy. High prices, combined with the widespread belief that 'rapacious' Middle Eastern governments would again hold the Western world to ransom, by raising prices *ad infinitum* or by cutting off supplies or both, provoked a new wave of exploration and development which brought oil on to world markets just as demand was dropping most steeply in the early 1980s. The spiralling price increases in 1979–81 (the second 'oil shock'), and the initially determined effort by OPEC members to keep them at a peak of almost ten times their level of only ten years previously led inevitably to the third 'oil shock' of 1986, when prices and revenues in real inflation-adjusted terms declined to well below their pre-1973 levels.

From a dominant position in 1973 when OPEC supplied 65% of the oil produced outside the centrally-planned economies, its share had declined to only 40% by 1985, the year in which OPEC finally abandoned its attempt to maintain oil prices at unrealistic levels. For the Middle East and North Africa, the loss in market share was even more drastic and was concentrated in the short period of six years from 1979 to 1985. From a peak of nearly 24m. b/d in 1979, the eight OPEC members in the Middle East and North Africa were forced by falling demand and the availability of new supplies to reduce production by almost one-half to 13m. b/d in 1985. At that level of production, control over world oil prices became ever more difficult to maintain.

Today's problems stem largely from that time and were exacerbated by Iraq's ill-fated Kuwaiti adventure. The peoples of the Middle East and North Africa, naturally, but unwisely, regarded their enormously enhanced revenues as the pattern for the future, spending and over-spending their annual revenues on gigantic domestic infrastructural and industrial development projects. Adapting to the loss of up to 80% of national income in the space of four or five years would have been a major trauma even if the governments in question had had the discipline and foresight to treat their 1980/81 income levels as the temporary boon they turned out to be. However, governments and whole nations had borrowed and invested in the belief that these income levels would be sustained into the future.

On a day-to-day level, it was the unwillingness of major oil companies to buy what they regarded as over-priced oil that forced OPEC members to wage an ultimately self-defeating price war, and it became politically convenient to blame the 'conspiracies' of Western companies and governments for the oil states' inability to sell as much crude as they had hoped, and at a price which they themselves had determined. While it is still true that relationships with the major international oil companies are the everyday reality for government officials charged with marketing crude oil, these relationships are a symptom rather than the cause of long-term developments. The time is past when the oil companies could be grouped together by the oil exporters as 'the enemy'. The reality that oil-exporting governments now recognize to a greater or lesser extent is that the market is impartial. They are also aware that the regulation of oil supplies is the only way they can influence the market. This, in turn, means that their relationships amongst themselves determine oil prices in the short-to medium-term. The 'enemy', if there is one, is within.

At the same time, in describing the geopolitics of the oil industry, it is easy to overlook the complexity of the everyday operations that take place out of sight of the general public. Producing, separating, treating, piping, storing, shipping, refining, marketing and distributing the oil are each major and complex industries in their own right, with their own economic rules and political logic. Equally, it is important to remember that it is the oil producers' resources which provide the framework for the operations of the oil industry.

Whilst it is true that the distribution of oil resources is the most important factor in determining the ultimate winners and losers in the 'oil game', the skill with which these resources are managed, the financial and political strengths and weaknesses of the countries involved are what makes the industry fascinating and crucial to all those who depend on oil. These strengths and weaknesses significantly augment or diminish the intrinsic value of naturally distributed resources. Nowhere in the world is this more true than in the Middle East and North Africa.

Oil is not the only thing that Middle Eastern and North African countries have in common. They have been linked (and sometimes divided) by permutations of religion, language, ethnic similarities, by conquest from within and without, and by the social and political legacy these conquerors have left behind. The unremitting thirst of the industrialized countries and their oil companies for the huge, though still unquantified, reserves of oil and gas is only the latest in a long line of 'Acts of God' and 'Acts of Man' to impinge on the countries of the Middle East and North Africa. With all they have in common, it would be natural to expect them to act in harmony, to imagine that oil producers would always think the same way about the important decisions and developments that confront them all in promoting and operating their oil industries, which are their major source of money and wealth. It is all the more puzzling, then, that so many major divisions should occur regarding policy. But those who are prepared to step back from their own political concerns in Europe and the USA and, simultaneously, to look more closely at the realities of the Middle Eastern and North African countries should not really be surprised by this. Common interests in Europe, which led to the establishment of the EC, sprang from the ravages of two hugely destructive wars in this century, but these same common interests have not prevented major policy disputes within the EC.

The diplomatic history that preceded the founding of OPEC in 1960 is an instructive pointer to the problems of today. It took the intervention of far-sighted statesmen from Venezuela to overcome the political and personal rivalries endemic to the Middle East to create OPEC in the first place, and for more than a decade after its establishment, even some of its more ardent admirers would have admitted, based on its apparent achievements, that it might as well never have been created. Today, in OPEC's 32nd year, all of its members, particularly the Middle Eastern and North African countries, can point to impressive achievements and economic developments in which they have all shared. Likewise, they share many of the social and political problems that accompany economic upheavals. However, neither massive increases in monetary reserves, nor the subsequent devastating reduction in national income have been sufficient to overcome the obstacles to a common policy that all OPEC members recognize as being desirable. Within OPEC, the 'awkwardness' of the Arab countries, especially those in the Gulf, is a constant complaint of representatives of other countries. However, although they portray themselves as the victims of the Arab countries, their problem, in trying to reach agreements on oil prices or production, results from their own disunity rather than the unity of the Middle Eastern and North African countries.

The recent vicissitudes of the oil markets illustrate the need to look for the detailed national differences which lie beyond superficial similarities in the geological, social, political, economic and religious structures of the Middle Eastern and North African countries in order to understand their actions in the international arena.

As they entered the 1990s, the oil exporters of the Middle East and North Africa looked forward to healthier demand for their oil. 1988 and 1989 were eventful years, bringing both achievements and setbacks. They were years in which some longstanding problems were solved, but in which new problems also arose. Iraq agreed to abide by a production allocation equal to that of its erstwhile enemy Iran. However, the relief experienced by all oil exporters at the agreement of all 13 OPEC members to restrict output and observe a price target of $18 per barrel was shattered in the spring of 1989 when Kuwait declined to accept its quota within an overall production ceiling of 19.5m. b/d. Again, the stumbling block was a disagreement over policy objectives within the Middle Eastern and North African countries, rather than any clash between them and their counterparts in Asia, South America and West Africa. As prices began to weaken during the summer of 1989, after peaking at a level close to OPEC's official price target, many exporters felt they had almost exhausted all possibilities in their search for policies that all could accept.

It is worth recalling the geological, financial and political situations of the principal oil producers, which will continue to shape their attitudes on the fundamental questions facing oil exporters: what price should they aim to achieve in the short-, medium- and long-term, and to what extent are they prepared to achieve their objectives by reducing production? After the 'boom and bust' cycle of the period 1973–1986, producers are aware that the demand for oil is 'price elastic'. Sudden price increases do reduce the demand for oil, high prices do stimulate exploration, development and the production of new oil which competes with and replaces OPEC supplies. There were many economists and political leaders in the Middle East and North Africa who believed that oil's importance to the industrial economies was so great that it was immune to the conventional laws of supply and demand. Even though these laws are no longer in dispute, oil producers still respond to them in different ways.

For producers with relatively small remaining reserves, the long-term demand for and price of oil is of relatively little concern. Algeria, for example, can reasonably argue that it is not concerned that high oil prices may lead to exploitation of alternative sources of energy and/or alternative supplies of oil in twenty or thirty years' time. The same is true for Dubai and Qatar whose wealth depends on obtaining the highest possible price for their exports while resources last. On the other hand, Saudi Arabia, Kuwait, Iran, Iraq and Abu Dhabi, with a minimum of 100 years of oil reserves, regard excessively high prices as likely to deprive them of any source of revenue in the years ahead.

For all their cultural affinities, the perceived objectives of countries in the same reserves category differ in accordance with their domestic political systems.

The ability of those countries which possess high reserves of oil to accept lower prices at the expense of immediate income varies according to their financial strength and political stability. Kuwait's careful investment of its oil revenues over many years created an investment income comparable with its national income for oil exports. Saudi Arabia's decision in 1973 to build a modern physical infrastructure across its huge territory, its need to raise an enormously expensive army to defend its long borders with troublesome neighbours, and the financial needs of its ruling family have left it vulnerable to unexpected reductions in oil income. During the Iran–Iraq War, Iraq, which received massive financial support from Saudi Arabia and Kuwait, regarded lower prices as beneficial since they deprived Iran of the means to replace military equipment. Following the cease-fire declared in July 1988 both Iran and Iraq pursued a high-price policy in order to finance the rebuilding of their shattered economies. In Iran the ascendancy of more pragmatic politicians has modified this policy such that reasonably high prices, together with the development of alternatives to crude petroleum, are now the main aim. Iraq's adventure in Kuwait, which was ostensibly motivated by Kuwait's persistent flouting of its OPEC quota, has left its economy in a state of collapse. Kuwait, having followed a path dictated almost entirely by self-interest, could have expected some retaliation from its less fortunate OPEC partners. The invasion by Iraq and its vicious policy of destruction went far beyond the avowed aim of bringing a recalcitrant OPEC partner back in to line, giving the lie to assertions of regional solidarity.

OWNERSHIP OF THE INDUSTRY AND SUPPLY CONTRACTS

Concessions

Until the end of 1972 the bulk of the Middle East's and North Africa's output was produced under the traditional concession agreements. The first of the concessions was granted in 1901 in Iran by Muzzaffareddin Shah to William Knox D'Arcy, in return for £20,000 in cash and the promise of a further £20,000 in shares. Oil was finally discovered in 1908 at Masjid-i-Sulaiman, and just before the beginning of the First World War, the Anglo-Persian Oil Company, which had been formed to take over the concession, began exports through the port of Abadan. (APOC was renamed the Anglo-Iranian Oil Company in 1935 and British Petroleum in 1954.)

During the 1920s and 1930s further concessions were granted in Iraq and in the states of the Arabian Peninsula—and in every case the concessionaire companies were made up chiefly by members of the seven major oil companies which have dominated the world oil business throughout this century. In approximate order of size these were: Standard Oil of New Jersey (which changed its name to Exxon in 1972 and markets its products in Europe under the name Esso), the Royal Dutch/Shell group, Texaco, Standard Oil of California (known as Socal and marketed as Chevron), Mobil, Gulf and British Petroleum. The only other company to participate in the early days was Compagnie Française des Pétroles (CFP—marketing as Total but known as Total-CFP since 1985), which is considerably smaller than the big seven, but is often regarded as an eighth major company because of the world-wide spread of its operations.

At first these companies held exclusive rights for drilling, production, sales, the ownership at the wellhead of all oil produced, and immunity from taxes and customs dues. The governments' receipts, apart from an initial downpayment and a rental, came either as a share of profits (which is how Iran's income was worked out until 1933, when Iran negotiated a fixed royalty plus share of company dividends formula) or as a fixed royalty of four gold shillings a ton (22 cents per barrel).

In view of the vast amounts of oil discovered during the 1930s and 1940s, and the extremely low cost of production, the Middle Eastern governments by the later 1940s no longer felt that the companies had been as generous as they had originally believed, and all aspects of the concessions came under attack. The main complaints, apart from criticism of the financial terms, were that the concessions were too large in area and their duration too long, that they were run almost entirely by foreign nationals, that the companies had appropriated for themselves a quasi-colonial authority, and that the host governments had no control over the amount of drilling carried out nor the volume of exports. The strength of the producers' feelings was only reinforced when Kuwait in 1948 and Saudi Arabia in 1949 granted concessions in their respective halves of the Neutral Zone (otherwise known as the Partitioned Zone) to independent US companies, Aminoil and Getty, on conditions which were very much more favourable than those obtained earlier from the Kuwait Oil Company (BP and Gulf) and Aramco (Exxon, Socal, Texaco and Mobil).

The major change in the financial terms of the concessions which followed did not, however, stem from events in the Middle East, but from Venezuela, where, after the first free elections in the country's history, the Acción Democrática party in November 1948 passed an income tax law giving the government 50% of the companies' profits. A year later Venezuela sent a delegation to the Gulf to explain the advantages of the new legislation, and the companies, realizing that such a revolutionary change could not be confined to one country, and that they would be able to deduct tax payments made abroad from tax paid in their home countries, promptly offered the same deal to the Middle Eastern governments. Under the new system, introduced in Saudi Arabia at the end of 1950 and in Iraq and Kuwait a few months later, the companies' 'profits', arrived at by deducting the production cost per barrel from the posted price, were divided equally between the companies and the governments. Assuming that no special discounts off the posted price were given, this arrangement increased the producers' revenue per barrel from 22 cents to about 80 cents.

The only country not to receive the 50-50 profit split at this time was Iran. Despite various revisions in concession terms during the inter-war years, relations between Anglo-Iranian and the Government were bedevilled not only by financial disputes, but also by the Iranian population's view of the company as the symbol of their country's subjugation to foreign influence and of Britain's colonial power—which had involved Iran being invaded in 1941 (so that the allies could secure a supply route to the Soviet armies in the Caucasus) and Reza Shah's deportation. In 1949, Anglo-Iranian and the Government resolved their differences in a Supplemental Agreement which gave Iran royalty and profit-sharing terms as good as those concluded in the Arab states 18 months later. But the Iranian National Assembly was dissatisfied with the deal, and during the following months, Dr Muhammad Mussadiq, an extreme nationalist demagogue and chairman of the Assembly's Oil Committee, managed to discredit the agreement totally. In December 1950, the Government, which had hoped that it would be able to solve the issue peacefully by negotiating minor revisions, was forced to renounce the agreement altogether. Anglo-Iranian immediately suggested further talks leading to a 50-50 settlement, while Mussadiq in February 1951 suggested nationalization, and, with Iran slipping into a state of internal chaos, the Shah on 1 May was forced to give his assent to the nationalization bill and appoint Mussadiq as Prime Minister.

Over the next two years, Mussadiq refused all compromise solutions offered to him, Iranian oil exports, embargoed by all the companies, rapidly ceased, and the economy collapsed. In July 1953, having tried to dismiss Mussadiq, the Shah was forced to flee to Rome; but within a few days, Mussadiq was overthrown by a coup, and the Shah returned. In subsequent negotiations, the principle of nationalization was recognized, but the National Iranian Oil Company (NIOC) was forced to grant a lease (which was a concession in all but name) incorporating the 50–50 profit split to Iranian Oil Participants (known as 'The Consortium') made up of BP, Shell, CFP (known as Total-CFP since 1985) and the five US majors—who were later obliged by the US Government to give a 5% shareholding to a group of US independents.

The Mussadiq débâcle provided a reminder of the strength of the majors and although in 1961 the revolutionary Government of General Kassem expropriated more than 99.5% of the concession held by the Iraq Petroleum Company group (BP, Shell, CFP, Exxon, Mobil and Gulbenkian), on the grounds that this area was not being exploited by the companies, no Middle Eastern government again nationalized an important productive operation until 1971—when Algeria seized a majority share of the local operations of CFP and the French State company, ERAP.

Partnerships, contracts and production sharing

Although, at the time, the nationalization of AIOC was a disaster for Iran, the dispute marked the end of the period in which Middle Eastern governments gave 75- or 95-year concessions, covering their whole country, to a single group. New concessions signed in the Arabian Peninsula states during the later 1950s and 1960s had a duration of 35 to 45 years, covered much smaller areas, and contained relatively tough terms, with bigger signature bonuses and provisions for the rapid relinquishment of acreage. Even in Libya, where the financial terms of the concessions let at the end of the 1950s were considerably more generous than those applying in the Gulf, the available acreage was divided among more than 10 different groups.

From 1957 the concession concept began to be replaced by new arrangements giving the state a degree of direct participation, and placing heavier financial burdens and greater risks on the companies. The first of the new arrangements was the partnership of Société Irano-Italienne des Pétroles (SIRIP) between the NIOC and the Italian state concern ENI. ENI's subsidiary, AGIP, agreed to bear the whole exploration cost (only to be repaid half if oil was found), and undertook to spend not less than $22m. on exploration. It was arranged that half of any oil produced would be owned by NIOC and sold by AGIP on Iran's behalf, while half would be owned by the Italian company and taxed at the normal 50% rate—giving the government a 75-25 profit split, and valuable experience.

One year later Iran substantially improved its terms when it formed IPAC, a partnership with Amoco (a subsidiary of Standard Oil of Indiana). During the early 1960s and early 1970s, it signed further partnerships containing cash bonuses, production bonuses, minimum exploration guarantees and minimum development expenditure guarantees. Eventually four of the partnerships struck oil.

With certain variations Iran's example was followed in the allocation of new acreage by Saudi Arabia and Kuwait in the Neutral Zone, where in 1957, a few months after the formation of SIRIP, the two countries obtained a stake of 10% each when offshore acreage was let to a group of Japanese companies. Other countries that copied Iran were Kuwait, in leasing some of its own territory to Hispanoil (in an unsuccessful partnership with the Kuwaiti national oil company which was later abandoned), Egypt, and Algeria, which has applied partnerships to all areas let since 1973. In Qatar, Abu Dhabi, Tunisia and Kuwait (with its offshore areas granted to Shell), the governments have concluded carried interest arrangements, where acreage has been let originally as a concession, with the proviso that the state has the right to negotiate a shareholding once oil is discovered. In few cases have these ventures been successful, so the carried interest charges have seldom come into operation. In all countries, the tax terms have been adjusted to reflect current OPEC rates.

In 1966 Iran introduced the still more radical idea of service contracts, relinquishing Consortium acreage to a French group, SOFIRAN. Like the foreign companies in partnership arrangements, SOFIRAN agreed to bear the whole cost of exploration; but if oil was struck it was to be refunded completely, and NIOC was also to provide all development capital. NIOC was to be the sole owner of all oil produced, while the foreign contractor was to act as a broker for the national company on a commission of 2% of the realized price, being paid by the guaranteed purchase of between 35% and 45% of production at cost plus 2%. Of the difference between this sum and the realized price 50% was to be payable as income tax—though when oil was brought on stream the financial terms were to be adjusted.

After 1966 Iran signed a further seven service contracts, the last (in 1974) allowing the foreign companies to purchase about half of production at discounts of up to 5%. But only SOFIRAN brought oil on stream. Iraq signed three service contracts, which it later cancelled. One of these, involving ERAP, brought the Buzurgan, Abu Ghrab and Fuka fields on stream. None of the other Middle Eastern or North African states has concluded service contracts (service contractors should not be confused with ordinary foreign drilling contractors, such as Santa Fé and the South Eastern Drilling Company—SEDCO, which are employed on a straight fee basis by almost all oil companies and oil producing governments).

Not dissimilar to service contracts are 'production-sharing' arrangements, of a type pioneered by Indonesia. Production sharing arrangements have been concluded by Egypt (which invited Western companies to bid for new acreage in 1973, following a period in which oil exploration had been given over to the USSR), and by Libya in 1974. In the mid-1970s Syria signed a number of production-sharing agreements, allowing Western companies into the country for the first time since 1964. There are considerable variations in this type of agreement, but in most cases the foreign company is compensated for its share of expenditure in cash or kind, or by favourable tax terms, while production is divided in a ratio of between 75:25 and 85:15 in favour of the state.

After the Islamic Revolution in Iran, the new Government decided to end its four successful production partnerships— SIRIP, IPAC (with Amoco), LAPCO (with Arco, Murphy, Sun and Unocal) and IMINOCO (with AGIP, Phillips and the Indian Oil and Natural Gas Commission). The Government took over the foreign partners' shareholdings and in August 1980

announced that, in future, their operations were to be run by a new Continental Shelf Oil Company. This was to be supervised by a specially created directorate in the Ministry of Oil.

The drive for participation, and Algerian takeovers

In the 1960s producer governments sought participation in existing concessions. This idea was originally put by Saudi Arabia to Aramco in 1964, and in 1968 it was given formal voice in OPEC's Declaratory Statement of Petroleum Policy. Apart from being satisfactory on nationalist grounds, and giving the producers a more direct say in such matters as the relinquishment of acreage, the employment of nationals, production rates and investment in new capacity, the governments felt that participation would later enable them to mount their own crude oil sales operations, or expand their national companies downstream into tankering, refining and marketing. The producers, however, did not feel strong enough to press their claim until after the appearance of a seller's market and their success in the Teheran price negotiations of February 1971; and so it was not until OPEC's Twenty-fifth Conference in Vienna in July 1971 that the members decided to call the companies to formal talks on participation.

By this time a precedent had already been set by Algeria. For political reasons Algeria had nationalized its US concessionaires and Shell in 1967, without causing itself economic harm. This left the French companies, CFP and ERAP, which were responsible for most of the country's production, and were in a special position under the 1965 Franco-Algerian Evian Agreement. Hopes of a satisfactory relationship under this agreement were not fulfilled, and in 1969, under the terms of the agreement, Algeria opened negotiations for higher prices. The talks were inconclusive, and in July 1970 Algeria increased its prices unilaterally. After further fruitless discussions, it seized 51% of the two French companies on 24 February 1971. France sponsored a highly effective boycott, but in June CFP settled its differences with the Government— Algeria agreeing to pay $60m. compensation, while CFP paid $40m. in backpayments and accepted a higher price. Five months later ERAP also came to terms, agreeing that compensation and backpayments should cancel each other out and entering into a minority partnership with Sonatrach in the Hassi Messaoud South field. In 1975 CFP agreed to extend its partnership with Sonatrach for a further five years, but ERAP allowed its agreement to lapse at the end of the year.

The takeover of CFP and ERAP was not directly related to the formal OPEC participation demand, being very much a Franco-Algerian affair, but it increased the confidence of the other producers when they began negotiations with the companies in Geneva in January 1972. The countries concerned in these negotiations were just the five Arab producers in the Gulf (Venezuela and Indonesia having already achieved a degree of participation or close involvement in the running of their oil industries, and Iran, Libya and Nigeria having made it clear that they would pursue their own negotiations), and in practice the talks were conducted by Sheikh Ahmad Zaki Yamani of Saudi Arabia, representing the producers, and Aramco, representing the companies. Yamani's initial demand was for an immediate 25% share rising to 51%, with compensation to be at net book value, and that part of the government share of production sold back to the companies should be priced between the posted price and the tax paid cost (government revenue plus production cost). The companies' counterproposal, offering 50-50 joint ventures on new acreage, showed how big the gap between the two sides was at this point. In March, however, the companies agreed in principle to surrender 20% of their operations, and in October, by which time Iraq, having nationalized IPC five months earlier, was no longer concerned in the negotiations, an outline agreement was reached in New York.

The General Agreement of 1972

The details of the General Agreement on Participation were finalized in December 1972, and ratified by Saudi Arabia, Qatar and Abu Dhabi at the turn of the year. Under the Agreement the producers took an immediate 25% stake in the concessionaire companies. The earliest date for majority participation laid down was 1 January 1982, with the initial shareholding rising by 5% in 1978, 1979, 1980 and 1981 and by 6% in 1982. This timetable was designed to make for a smooth transition and to enable all the companies to adjust their supply arrangements over the following decade.

The need to ease company problems also accounted for the complex arrangements for pricing and disposing of the states' 25% share of production. The 75% companies' entitlement, which became known as 'equity crude', remained subject to the provisions of the Teheran Agreement of February 1971, but the balance belonging to the producing states was divided into three categories, each priced in a different way. A small proportion of production (only 10% of the states' share or 2.5% of total output in 1973) the governments undertook to sell on the open market for whatever price they could get. The other two categories of crude were 'bridging crude' and 'phase-in crude', both priced at above the normal tax paid cost and both set to decline in volume as the states' direct sales were to increase. Within nine months of the General Agreement taking effect, however, the Gulf producers decided that both bridging and phase-in crude should be treated on the same basis, and priced at 93% of the posting—this being the price Saudi Arabia had obtained in the sale of its own 2.5% crude entitlement in May.

For compensation under the General Agreement the criterion adopted was 'updated book value' which took account of the cost of replacement of the companies' assets. This was a compromise between the producers' demand for compensation to be on a net book value basis (i.e. after depreciation) and the companies' efforts to obtain a formula which would repay them for some of the value of the proven reserves discovered in their concessions. In the event, the system adopted involved Saudi Arabia paying Aramco $500m., Abu Dhabi paying $162m. in almost equal parts to Abu Dhabi Marine Areas and the Abu Dhabi Petroleum Company, and Qatar paying $28m. to the Qatar Petroleum Company and $43m. to Shell.

Iraqi nationalization

Iraq ceased to have any involvement in the participation negotiations in 1972, when it nationalized the Iraq Petroleum Company. For 20 years relations between the government and the company had been poor. In the later 1950s, a dispute had arisen over the fact that IPC and its sisters, the Basra Petroleum Company in the south and the Mosul Petroleum Company in the north, had developed only a very minor part of their 160,000-square-mile concession. Combined with disagreements over the group's accounting procedures, this led to Law 80 of 1961 expropriating more than 99.5% of the group's acreage. The companies never accepted the expropriation and, although attempts were made to settle this and many other outstanding differences over the next 10 years, the two parties were forced to accept a position of stalemate, in which Iraqi production expanded very slowly.

In June 1971, as part of the agreement on Iraqi Mediterranean crude prices which followed the Teheran pact in February, the IPC group undertook to increase production, but in the following spring, the company found itself obliged to cut the throughput of its pipeline from Kirkuk to the Mediterranean terminals of Banias (Syria) and Tripoli (Lebanon). In a period of low Gulf/Europe freight rates, the high prices negotiated for all Mediterranean crudes in the previous years made it uneconomic for its owners to run the pipe at more than half capacity. The Iraqi Government claimed that the cut-back was politically motivated, and presented IPC with alternatives: either the company was to restore Kirkuk production to normal levels and hand the extra production over to the government, or it was to surrender the field entirely and concentrate production on BPC's acreage in the south. This conflict was exacerbated by IPC's threats of legal action to prevent the sale of the Iraq National Oil Company's crude from North Rumaila (in expropriated BPC acreage), and by a number of old issues, including an Iraqi claim for royalty backpayments dating from 1964, which IPC had refused to pay until it received the compensation it was claiming for the acreage expropriated in 1971. On 31 May IPC presented its answers to the Iraqi ultimatum. These did not satisfy the government, and on the next day, IPC was nationalized. The affiliates, BPC and MPC, were not immediately affected.

In mid-July negotiations commenced, with Nadim Pachachi, then Secretary-General of OPEC, and M. Jean Duroc-Danner of CFP acting as mediators. IPC promptly announced that it would not pursue legal action against buyers of Kirkuk crude while mediation efforts were in progress, and Iraq was able to sell substantial amounts of oil—including a deal in February 1973 under which CFP agreed to take 23.75% of Kirkuk's output (equivalent to the company's stake in IPC) over 10 years. On 28 February 1973, IPC and the government finally reached agreement. IPC accepted the expropriations of 1961 and the nationalization of the Kirkuk producing area, and at the same time handed over MPC and paid the government $141m. of outstanding royalty backpayments. In return it was promised 15m. tons of oil in two batches in 1973 and 1974, and was given some assurance of the long-term security of its investment and growth of output from BPC's southern fields, where it agreed to more than double production from 640,000 b/d in 1972 to 1,626,000 b/d in 1976.

In the event, it was only seven months before BPC suffered the seizure, during the October war, of the holdings of Exxon and Mobil, and 60% of Shell's share (a proportion relating to the Dutch-registered part of the group) as a political gesture against the USA's and the Netherlands' association with Israel. Later the 5% share of the Participations and Explorations Corporations (owned by the Gulbenkian family) was seized on the grounds that the company was registered in Portugal, which was pursuing racist policies in Africa. Thereafter the government watched the progress of the takeover negotiations in Saudi Arabia and Kuwait, and a few days after a final agreement had been signed in Kuwait, it nationalized the remaining Western-owned share in BPC. It then held negotiations with the BPC partners over compensation and supply arrangements.

Iranian Sales and Purchase Agreement

Although it was clear from the beginning of the Saudi Arabian-Aramco negotiations in January 1972 that Iran was not interested in the type of participation envisaged by the Gulf states, the Shah did not decide exactly what Iran would demand instead until early 1973. On 23 January the Shah gave the Consortium an ultimatum: Iran would not extend its lease, and the companies could either continue under existing arrangements until the expiry of their lease in 1979 and then become ordinary buyers under contract, or they could negotiate an entirely new agency agreement immediately. The Consortium opted for the latter plan, and, under the Iranian Sales and Purchase Agreement signed in Teheran in May, NIOC took formal control of the management of the Consortium's entire production operation and the Abadan refinery. The agreement laid down that NIOC would provide 60% of the capital for expanding production and that the companies would contribute 40% of the funds needed in the first five years (then expected to be the period of greatest expansion) in return for a 22 cents discount on their liftings.

Under the Sales and Purchase Agreement, though NIOC became owner/manager, the Consortium members established a service company, the Oil Service Company of Iran (OSCO), to carry out operations on NIOC's behalf for an initial period of five years, which could be renewed. NIOC undertook to raise total installed production capacity to 8m. b/d by October 1976. It was agreed that the national company would be entitled to take the oil needed for internal consumption and a 'stated quantity' for export, which was to rise from 200,000 b/d in 1973 to 1.5m. b/d in 1981, and therefore, except in certain cases of *force majeure*, would remain in the same proportion to total crude available for export as 1.5m. b/d represented to oil available for export in 1981. The balance of crude production went to the Consortium members, which were guaranteed security of supply for 20 years.

Libya asserts 51% control

Only weeks after OPEC had made its formal call for participation in July 1971, Libya, ever anxious to be first among the producers in militancy and to upstage any participation agreement negotiated by Saudi Arabia, announced that it would be interested in nothing less than an immediate 51% share. Four months later, at the beginning of December 1971,

Libya nationalized outright BP's half-share of the Sarir field, but this was a purely political gesture (against alleged British connivance in the Iranian invasion of the Tumbs Islands some 24 hours before Britain's withdrawal from the Gulf)—and for the next year the Libyan Government made no move while it awaited the outcome of the participation negotiations in the Gulf.

Talks on Libya's demand for majority control began in early 1973, with the government adopting its usual policy of negotiating on a company by company basis; but they made no progress. In June Libya nationalized outright the American independent Nelson Bunker Hunt. This company had been BP's 50% partner in the Sarir field, and the government had chosen it for its first negotiations because it had no other source of oil outside the USA and seemed therefore to be especially vulnerable. Bunker Hunt, however, resisted hard. Being a private company it did not have shareholders to worry about and it was confident in the Libyan operators' secret agreement, under which the companies had promised to meet the supply commitments of any one of their number whose concession was expropriated. Colonel Qaddafi, the Libyan leader, correctly characterized the Bunker Hunt seizure as 'a warning to the companies to respond to the demands of the Libyan Arab Republic'. From circumstantial evidence it seems that Libya fully decided on nationalizing Bunker Hunt when it concluded that it would have no difficulty in selling the oil to markets apart from the Eastern bloc. This followed the judgment of a local court in Sicily which dismissed a suit brought by BP against the importers and refiners of its expropriated Sarir oil.

Following its nationalization of Bunker Hunt, the Libyan Government proceeded in August to seize 51% of Occidental's operations. Faced with the threat of having the rest of its assets seized and being deprived of its most vital source of oil outside the USA, Occidental announced its 'acquiescence' in the measure. For the other companies the significance of this 'acquiescence' lay in the fiscal terms. The companies had in fact been prepared to offer Libya a nominal 51% on the condition that the financial results gave parity with those deriving from the participation agreements with the Gulf producers and Nigeria—but this was not so in the terms settled with Occidental. Compensation was agreed on at book value, rather than the updated book value formula used in the Gulf, and the buy-back price was set above the posting, rather than between the posting and the tax paid cost.

Five days after the Occidental seizure, three independent companies in the Oasis group, Continental, Marathon and Amerada Hess, accepted a majority takeover on similar terms, though Shell, the only major in Oasis, did not comply. Then in September the government announced 51% take-overs of all the other significant producing groups. Gelsenberg, a German concern in partnership with Mobil, and W. R. Grace, a small shareholder in the Esso Sirte venture, agreed to Libya's terms; but Atlantic Richfield (another partner in Esso Sirte) and the majors, Mobil, Esso (which held a concession on its own as well as the biggest share in Esso Sirte) and the Texaco-Socal company, Amoseas, joined Shell in resisting any sort of arrangement which might have undermined their participation agreements in the Gulf.

In February 1974 Libya seized all of the remaining assets of Texaco, Socal and Atlantic Richfield; and in the following month, Shell too was nationalized. Finally Mobil, in March, and Esso, in April, accepted the 51% seizure of the previous September.

Exxon and Mobil eventually withdrew from their concessions on their own initiative in November 1981 and April 1982. Exxon's liftings had stopped in the summer of 1981 and Mobil's liftings by the time of its withdrawal had fallen to only 10,000 b/d. Some months after its withdrawal Exxon negotiated an agreement with the Libyan Government whereby it received compensation for the assets of its two former concessionaires—Esso Sirte and Esso Standard Libya—at about 70% of net book value. The Libyans established the Sirte Oil Company, wholly owned by the National Oil Corporation, to run both operations formerly managed by Exxon. The W. R. Grace interest in the Sirte concession was unaffected.

Gulf states achieve 60% participation

The General Agreement on Participation concluded at the end of 1972 had satisfied the Kuwaiti Government, and had been signed by the Minister of Finance and Oil, Abd ar-Rahman Atiqi, at the beginning of January 1973; but the Kuwait National Assembly refused its approval. The determination of a handful of radicals opposed to the measure was fortified by Iraq's success in settling its dispute with IPC in February and by the signature of Iran's Sale and Purchase Agreement in May; and by the summer of 1973 it was clear that the government would not, as it had originally hoped, be able to rally sufficient support to get the General Agreement accepted. On 13 June, the Ruler formally requested a revision of the accord, and during the autumn, when Libya announced its series of 51% takeovers, the other Gulf producers followed Kuwait's example. In November Sheikh Ahmad Zaki Yamani announced that Saudi Arabia would not accept a simple majority holding, and it was made clear early in 1974 that the Saudi Government would be negotiating a complete takeover of Aramco's operations.

Negotiations between the Kuwait Government and the Kuwait Oil Company shareholders, BP and Gulf, during the winter, resulted at the end of January in the state gaining a holding of 60%, which, after several months of further wrangling in the national assembly, was ratified on 14 May 1974. The new agreement was made valid from 1 January, meaning that the companies had conceded the principle of retroactivity on which they had held so firm in the past, and was to last for six years—though the government reserved the right to call fresh negotiations at any point before the end of 1974. The compensation formula agreed was net book value (giving KOC $112m.), rather than updated book value, but there was no settlement of buy-back terms, with the volume and price of oil being left for more hard bargaining over the summer. In fact Kuwait did not conclude a buy-back deal with BP and Gulf until after it had rejected all bids put in for its 60% crude share at an auction in July. For the third quarter of the year, the government then sold rather over 55% of its entitlement to the two companies at 94.8% of the posted price; and for the last quarter, BP and Gulf bought two-thirds of the state's crude at 93% of the posting.

Three months before the ratification of the Kuwaiti participation agreement, Qatar concluded a similar accord with its concessionaires (the Qatar Petroleum Company and Shell) in February, and in April it settled buy-back arrangements for the following six months. These involved the two companies purchasing 60% of the state entitlement (about 36% of total output) at 93% of the posted price—the same level as that agreed in September 1973 in the original modification of the terms of the General Agreement. Then in June, after the Kuwait ratification, Saudi Arabia concluded an 'interim' 60% participation agreement with Aramco though no details emerged about the buy-back arrangements. Finally, in September, Abu Dhabi negotiated a 60% share in the Abu Dhabi Petroleum Company and Abu Dhabi Marine Areas, backdated to the beginning of the year.

Aramco take-over negotiations

Although Saudi Arabia had decided to ask for more than a simple majority stake in Aramco in November 1973, it was not until early 1974 (shortly before the government took 60% of Aramco as an interim measure in June) that it became clear that the government sought a complete take-over. This was to be linked to sales and contracting arrangements similar to those agreed between Iran and the Consortium in May 1973. Within weeks the government and Aramco were reported to be close to clinching the deal, but over the next six years changing circumstances in the Middle East, in Saudi Arabia and in the world oil market continually postponed the conclusion of an agreement.

There was an initial breakthrough in November 1974 when Aramco conceded the principle of a complete take-over, and during the following 18 months in successive rounds of negotiations general agreement was reached on all major practical issues. Indeed the two sides said as much in an announcement made after talks in Panama City, Florida, in March 1976. It was reported at this time that compensation was to be a little more than $1,500m. for 75% of Aramco's assets (which had expanded considerably since 1973) at net book value. In due course part of this sum was transferred to the Aramco partners, bringing the compensation they had received for their assets up to the 60% level. It was also reported from Florida that the companies would continue to take the bulk of Saudi production; that they would be paid a fee of 15 cents a barrel for production operations plus six cents a barrel for new reserves discovered; and that they would continue to put up part of the risk capital in exploration—only being refunded in the event of success.

During the four years that followed the announcement in Florida there were further rounds of negotiations, but an almost complete lack of news as to the substance of the talks. It was known that there were problems over the fees that Aramco would be paid: the four Aramco partners feared that under some of the formulae put forward their fees would not be big enough to cover their share of investment. On one occasion the companies were known to be objecting to a formula under which their fee would come out of a 75 cents per barrel margin allowed after deducting operating costs and payments to the government. This margin was supposed to cover exploration and the expansion of production capacity as well as the companies' fees.

Other problems centred on the companies' crude oil entitlements. The original understanding of 1976 and 1977 was that the Aramco partners should take up to 7.3m. barrels a day. But early in 1979 when Saudi Arabia's output was raised from the normal 8.5m. b/d to 9.5m. b/d in an attempt to stabilize the market in the aftermath of the Iranian Revolution, the companies' entitlement was increased for a short time to 8.1m. b/d. In 1980 this figure was cut to 7.2m. b/d, at which level it was maintained through the early part of 1981. For short periods during the three years from 1977 to 1980 the government cut Aramco's entitlement to below 7m. b/d—for different reasons on each occasion.

The Aramco partners always argued against short-term cuts in their entitlements, and in the longer term they were worried about their entitlements undergoing a progressive, permanent reduction. This seemed likely to be caused mainly by Saudi Arabia developing its own crude oil sales. It had long been Saudi policy to sell more oil directly to Third World countries and to the national oil companies of the industrial powers, rather than selling it through the integrated chains of the majors. (From just 190,000 b/d in 1973, Petromin's own sales by early 1981 had risen to some 2m. b/d.) It was also clear that the amounts of crude available to Aramco would gradually be reduced further by three other developments. These were the rise in domestic consumption, supplies to new export refineries, and allocations of 'incentive crude' being promised to foreign companies agreeing to invest in refineries and petrochemical plants in Saudi Arabia. An example of the volumes of crude involved in these deals—in this case applying to an Aramco partner—was provided by Mobil's commitment to invest in a petrochemical plant and a refinery at Yanbu. Over 15 years, beginning at the time of the project's start-up, Mobil is to receive 1,400m. barrels of oil, an average of 225,000 b/d. Although Exxon, Socal and Texaco were all involved in their own projects with the Saudi Government—albeit on a smaller scale than Mobil—most of the companies which concluded such deals in 1979 and 1980 were not Aramco partners. (In 1981 the Saudi Government announced that incentive crude would only be given to companies that had already signed agreements to participate in Saudi industrial projects. It was thought that the economics of Arabian industrialization had improved sufficiently since 1979 for prospective future partners not to need special incentives.)

In the background there was the further possibility of the Aramco partners' supplies being reduced by the government cutting production for internal or external political reasons— or because supplies from other producers had increased. A cutback was also thought likely to follow the government achieving its aim of stabilizing prices.

In 1980 the Aramco partners reckoned that if the Saudi Government were to return production to its 'normal' 8.5m. b/d 'ceiling', they would be lucky to receive 5m. b/d. (In practice, when Saudi production was reduced to 8.5m. b/d in

November 1981, it was thought that the Aramco partners were getting 5.4m. b/d. This compared with some 6.5m.–7.0m. b/d when the government was running production at 9m. or 10m. b/d, or more.) A cutback in overall production to 5m. b/d, as advocated by the Saudi conservationists, would leave the Aramco partners with virtually no oil.

Both of the issues in dispute—the companies' fee and their crude entitlements—were apparently resolved early in 1980. In April the Saudi Government transferred to the companies the final instalment of compensation for their assets— $1,500m., in respect of the 40% share in Aramco retained by the companies since the second participation accord was reached in 1974. At the same time the government completed its takeover of the Ras Tanura refinery and natural gas liquids facilities, which had been excluded from the 60% participation deal and for several years after 1974 had remained 100% Aramco owned. The government then announced in April 1981 that it was taking 50% of Tapline, in which the Aramco partners each had the same shares as they had in Aramco itself. Exports via Tapline had been suspended for economic reasons in February 1975 and the pipeline had been used only sporadically since.

Exactly what commitments the government had given the companies on crude oil entitlements were not revealed. However, it was known that as of 1980 the Aramco partners were receiving a fee of 27 cents per barrel produced—though again there was no announcement of the details of the formula on which the fee was based. Nor was there any announcement on the form of the new state oil corporation which would hold the government's production assets; only the Ras Tanura refinery had been handed over to the existing state oil company, Petromin. Likewise nothing official was said about what arrangements were to be made by the Aramco partners to form a service company to run the industry on behalf of the new state corporation.

In practice, while the negotiations with Aramco were in progress the oil industry in Saudi Arabia was run as if the government had total control—in other words the government made decisions but the day to day operations were managed by Aramco. The process of participation had involved the government's acquisition of the company's assets in Saudi Arabia and its decision-making powers over exploration, the development of production capacity and the volume and allocation of output. Technically Aramco remained (and remains) a wholly US-owned and US-registered company. Before the completion of the takeover it was part owner of the Saudi production operation; after the signing of the takeover agreement it was assumed in 1981 that its status would change to that of owner of a service company. For practical purposes within Saudi Arabia Aramco was seen both before and after the complete takeover as a giant foreign contractor and contract manager working for the government.

Take-over in Kuwait

Over a year before Aramco and the Saudi Government reached even the general agreement in Panama City on the major issues of the take-over, the initiative in the movement towards complete ownership of oil-producing operations in the Arabian Peninsula had been taken up by Kuwait, which announced on 5 March 1975 that as of that date it had taken over all assets of the Kuwait Oil Company and would be beginning negotiations to settle the terms with BP and Gulf retroactively. The Kuwaitis made it clear that they wanted a continuing relationship with the KOC owners, but that they felt quite capable of running the production operations themselves. Since geological and topographical conditions made Kuwaiti oil extremely cheap and easy to produce, and as the state had been fairly thoroughly explored and did not require large-scale new exploration or development work, the continued presence of the major companies was very much less necessary for Kuwait than it was for Saudi Arabia and Abu Dhabi, where there were large potentially oil-bearing areas still to be opened up. For this reason it was felt at the time of the announcement that Kuwait might have decided on a complete take-over after consultation with the other Gulf producers—wanting to use Kuwait's negotiations to gauge what conditions the major companies might be prepared to accept.

Successive rounds of negotiations, however, stuck on the problems of compensation, the service fee and credit terms, but at the beginning of December 1975 an agreement was announced. This involved: compensation of $66m.; a discount on the 93% of postings third party selling price of 15 cents per barrel reflecting BP's and Gulf's continuing provision of technical services and technical personnel, the large size of their purchases and their undertakings to buy Kuwait's bunker fuel and use Kuwaiti tankers; and commitments by BP to take an average of 450,000 b/d between 1 January 1976 and 1 April 1980 and by Gulf to take 500,000 b/d over the same period. The two companies received an option on a further 400,000 b/d. All of these quantities were subject to the normal plus or minus 12.5% variations.

Since the completion of the takeover the special relationship between Gulf and BP and the Kuwaiti oil industry has been reduced virtually to nothing. As Kuwait has successfully Arabized many of the technical jobs in oil production and launched its own direct expatriate recruitment programmes to fill those jobs for which it has been unable to find experienced Arab personnel, the numbers seconded by BP and Gulf have fallen to a nominal level. The two companies' purchases of Kuwaiti crude were greatly reduced when their supply contracts were renegotiated in early 1980. Gulf took only 75,000 b/d at the official government selling price (GSP) under a two-and-a-half-year contract, while BP took 75,000 b/d at the GSP plus a further 75,000 b/d for one year (to 1 April 1981) at a premium price. When these contracts were negotiated the original 15 cents discount of 1975 was eliminated.

Beginning in early 1981, the main traditional customers for Kuwaiti crude, Gulf, BP and Shell (which had bought much of Gulf's entitlement in the old concession days), began further to reduce their purchases of Kuwaiti crude. Shell and BP opted out of their contracts altogether in November 1981, and Gulf in January 1982 cut its liftings to just 35,000 b/d.

Take-overs in the Lower Gulf

The take-over in Kuwait in 1975 opened the way for other producers to take 100% of their former concessionaires. Within days of the announcement in December 1975 Iraq nationalized the Basra Petroleum Company, and in February 1976 Kuwait began negotiations for the take-over of Aminoil in its half of the Neutral Zone (while stating that it did not intend to change the status of the Arabian Oil Company's operation offshore). Negotiations did not go well and in September 1977 Kuwait nationalized the company. For a few months a Kuwaiti Wafra Oil Company was established to run operations, until in April 1978 it was decided that KOC should take over the production operation and KNPC the Mina Abdullah refinery, which had processed Aminoil's entire output.

Starting in June 1976 Qatar negotiated the complete take-over of its two concessionaires, signing broadly similar agreements with QPC in September that year and, after a somewhat tougher series of talks, with Shell in February 1977. Compensation was calculated on the basis of net book value, involving the payment of $14m. for Shell's remaining assets and $18m. for QPC's; both companies established new contracting subsidiaries (Dukan Oil Services and Qatar Shell Service Company) to second personnel to run the industry for the state oil corporation; and both companies accepted a fee of 15 cents per barrel of oil produced. This fee, which compared with the Kuwaiti terms of a 15 cents per barrel discount on just that part of production sold back to BP and Gulf, reflected the much bigger oil company presence retained in Qatar. (These fees, although invariably referred to as being 15 cents, were in fact tied to the official government selling prices, which meant that by mid-1980 the fee had risen to 42 cents.) Furthermore it was agreed that Shell should be paid an unspecified lump sum bonus as a condition of its undertaking further exploration (for gas) for QGPC on a contracting basis.

The five-year operating agreements between the Qatar Government, the QPC group and Shell expired at the end of 1981 and early 1982. Dukan Oil Services and the Qatar Shell Service Company continued their work without interruption. It was assumed that the government would renegotiate the onshore contract with just one of QPC's shareholders—probably BP.

In Bahrain the government announced the take-over of the production operations of BAPCO in April 1978, the arrangement being backdated to the beginning of January. The Sitra refinery was left in the hands of BAPCO (owned by Caltex—50-50 Texaco and Socal) until May 1980, when the government took a stake of 60%.

In Abu Dhabi, meanwhile, the government made it clear that it felt that its big potential for further discoveries and the technical problems involved in its offshore production made it very much in the state's interest for the companies to retain an equity participation and that the 60–40 agreement would be maintained. (Details of the main companies operating in Abu Dhabi are given in the company lists at the end of this chapter.) Payment for the companies' services in Abu Dhabi came out of the margin between the GSP and the lower price, known as the tax paid cost, at which the companies got the 40% of their supplies represented by their equity stakes. (See prices section below.) In 1978 the companies' margin of their 40% crude entitlement worked out at 65 cents per barrel. With the oil price rises of 1979/80 this figure rose to $1.60, which the Abu Dhabi Government felt was excessive. It was therefore agreed in 1980 that the margin would be reduced to $1, which averaged over the full amount of production worked out at 40 cents per barrel.

The policy of retaining the concessionaire as a partner also applied in Oman. There were several reasons for this: the small size of the country's oil industry, its shortage of financial resources, the complexity of Oman's oil fields and the Sultanate's acute lack of trained manpower, which made the government reluctant to undertake any inessential commitments. In practice, the foreign company 'presence' in Oman was considerably bigger than in Abu Dhabi. Shell not only provided virtually all of the staff and did the purchasing of equipment, it also seemed to take many of the management decisions.

The end of the Iranian Consortium

In the true tradition of agreements of its type in the Middle East, it was not long before most of the Iranian Sales and Purchase Agreement became out of date. Whereas at one stage in 1973 the Shah had suggested that Iran's reserves might turn out to be more than 100,000m. barrels, in 1975 and 1976 it came to be realized quite suddenly that this was grossly over-optimistic. To add anything to the country's recoverable reserves beyond 65,000m. barrels, or even to recover that volume of oil, the Iranians realized that they would have to invest huge sums in a gas reinjection secondary recovery system.

At the end of 1975 the Consortium ceased contributing the 40% of development capital which it was supposed to invest under the Agreement, and in return NIOC reduced the Consortium's 22 cents per barrel discount to take account of interest accruing on the capital which NIOC saw itself as investing on the Consortium's behalf. Unsuccessful talks on a revision of the Agreement were held in late 1975 and early 1976. However, it was not until the beginning of 1978, after two years in which NIOC-Consortium relations had been further complicated by occasional big falls in Iranian production and by NIOC periodically lifting more than its share, that the two sides sat down to work out a complete replacement for the Agreement. After several rounds of difficult talks the negotiations were made irrelevant by the Iranian Revolution of February 1979.

The disturbances of the autumn that preceded the Revolution had disrupted production (which normally ran at just below 6m. b/d) and in January and February 1979 exports stopped altogether. Production ran at only 235,000 b/d, not even enough to meet domestic demand of 700,000 b/d. At the end of February, soon after the Ayatollah Khomeini had appointed his government, the NIOC Chairman, Hassan Nazih, announced that Iran was to have nothing to do with the Consortium ever again. It was reckoned that if Iran ran production at about two-thirds of its previous level, closing the more complex production areas and halting the development of its gas reinjection system, NIOC could carry out its work with minimal foreign assistance.

On 5 March exports started again, with production rising rapidly to over 4m. b/d, though this level was trimmed back by the beginning of May. It slowly emerged that government policy was not to allow production to exceed 4m. b/d, leaving about 3.3m. b/d for export. Later it was made known that the optimal production level was considered to be 3m. b/d, a figure which was still being quoted occasionally when the Iran-Iraq War broke out in the autumn of 1980. In practice during most of 1980 Iranian production ran at a level far below 3m. b/d.

Early sales contracts after the Revolution were with former direct customers of NIOC and the Consortium and former Consortium members, though by mid-May 1979 NIOC was talking to a number of entirely new companies. In total the Consortium members, who had been lifting 3.3m. b/d before the Revolution, got 1.1m. b/d, of which BP took 450,000 b/d and Shell 235,000 b/d. Up to 1.9m. b/d was allocated for about 50 other companies—some 30 of which had signed by mid-May—including among the biggest buyers old NIOC and Consortium customers such as Japan, Ashland, Petrofina (of Belgium), Amerada Hess and Marathon. All buyers soon found their contracts subject to volume reductions, which NIOC made in order to have more crude available for new customers. As contracts came up for renewal the trend away from traditional customers continued. For a long period in late 1979 and 1980 the major companies stopped liftings entirely—partly because the premiums being charged by Iran were too high and partly because it was the policy of the companies (acting under pressure from the US Government) not to take Iranian oil while the American diplomats in Teheran were held hostage. A further disruptive element was introduced by the outbreak of the Iran-Iraq War in the autumn of 1980, which temporarily brought production to a standstill.

THE DEVELOPMENT OF PRICES

The 1940s and 1950s

In the years before the introduction of the 50–50 profit split in 1950 and 1951, when most producers received their revenues on the basis of the fixed royalty arrangements (22 cents per barrel) the development of prices was of only academic interest to the Middle Eastern governments. For all of the 1930s, and the first half of the 1940s, the pricing formula applied was the 'US Gulf Plus' system, which was worked out by the chairmen of Shell, Standard of New Jersey and Anglo-Persian when they drew up their famous cartel agreement at Achnacarry House in 1928. The US Gulf Plus system laid down that the price of oil in every export centre throughout the world should be the same as that obtaining in the Gulf of Mexico, but that the price at the point of delivery should be made up of the Gulf of Mexico price plus the cost of freight to that point from the Gulf of Mexico. It made no difference to the buyer where the oil actually came from. If a buyer in Bombay, for example, placed an order with a cartel company, the oil would probably be supplied from Persia, but he would still be charged the same freight cost as if the oil had been brought from the USA—and the saving, known as 'phantom freight', would go to the cartel company. This system could also work in reverse. A shipment of Persian oil to London, which was nearer to the US than to the Middle East, would still be priced at the Gulf of Mexico price plus freight from the Gulf of Mexico to London—leading to the company accepting an element of 'freight absorption'. The explanation for this peculiar system lay in the fact that the major companies, as a group, had their biggest and most valuable investments in the USA, and therefore had an interest in maintaining the biggest possible market for US oil.

Given that all of the other major companies and most of the larger US independents joined the cartel, the US Gulf Plus system operated successfully until near the end of the Second World War, when the British Government objected to paying phantom freight for bunker fuel supplied to the navy in the Indian Ocean, and forced the companies to institute a Persian Gulf base. Under the new system, crudes f.o.b. the Persian Gulf were given the same price as similar crudes f.o.b. the Gulf of Mexico, and at the point of delivery only real freight was levied on top. This resulted in crude oils from the two producing areas finding their natural markets (which met in the Mediterranean near Italy)—though if Middle East oil was landed in north-west Europe, the company would, of course, still have to bear an element of freight absorption if its oil was to be competitive.

It was not long, however, before the Persian Gulf Base system itself began to come under attack from the governments of the importing countries. Immediately after the war, the USA changed from being a big net exporter to being a small net importer (a position it maintained for the next 25 years), and as soon as domestic price controls were removed in 1946, prices in the Gulf of Mexico rose quickly. Persian Gulf prices followed automatically, and because the production cost of Middle Eastern oil was very much lower than that of Texan oil, the companies made enormous profits. Despite the freight disadvantage they were able to import Middle Eastern oil into the US and undercut domestic oil as far inland as the mid-West. In 1948 the companies, influenced in part by criticism from the US Government, lowered their Persian Gulf prices so that the delivered prices of Middle Eastern and Texan oil equalized at London; and in 1949 the US Government forced a further cut in the Persian Gulf so that the delivered prices of Texan and Middle Eastern oil were made to equalize at New York. This reduction, of course, affected only the profits of the companies in their sales to third parties, and made no difference to the profits down their integrated chain of affiliates.

The large profits made by the companies in this period were a major factor behind the Middle Eastern governments' demands in the late 1940s for better financial terms—demands which were met in 1950 and 1951 by the introduction of the 50-50 profit split (see 'Concessions' above). The new financial terms (which increased government revenues on Saudi Arabian Light from some $0.22 per barrel to about $0.80—depending on the fluctuations of prices in Texas) served to make the producers price-conscious. In retrospect they did not fail to notice that the price adjustments of the later 1940s had been to their disadvantage.

The producers also noticed soon after the introduction of 50-50 that the profit split was not quite as even as it seemed, because the companies were always able to press them into giving discounts and the marketing allowance (which was hardly justified when almost all production was sold to affiliates of the operator or to major companies under long-term contracts). In fact, Abdullah Tariki, the radical Saudi Arabian Minister of Oil during the 1950s, calculated soon after 50-50 came into force that the effective split of profits was 32-68 in favour of the companies.

Worse still, in the early 1950s, the price discrepancies between Texan, Venezuelan and Gulf crudes continued to expand, destroying the principle of the three crudes equalizing at New York. This ushered in a new era in which the price of Gulf crudes was to be determined by the supply and demand situation in Europe rather than in America—which directly or indirectly had been the basis for all quotations for Gulf crudes since 1929. The growing availability of production capacity in the Middle East, and increasing competition in the European market, led the companies to start giving their own discounts on the posted price for sales to third parties. It was at this stage that posted (or tax reference) prices and f.o.b. (or market) prices in the Gulf began to part company. Given that the 50-50 profit split was still worked out on the basis of the posting, this meant that the producer government's effective share of profits began to climb back towards the 50% it was always supposed to have been.

Then in 1957, after the closure of the Suez Canal, all prices went up—and although in the Middle East the increase was smaller than in Texas or Venezuela, the new price of $2.12 represented the highest posting for Saudi Arabian Light since 1948. These levels were maintained until February 1959, when there was a general reduction, in which Gulf crudes fell by more than the others. Two months later, the Venezuelan price was lowered again, and in August 1960, the Gulf price was reduced without any parallel reduction being made elsewhere. Thus the discrepancy between Arabian Light and Texan crude had expanded from zero in 1948 (when both crudes were priced at $2.68) to $1.20 in 1960—when Texan crude stood at $3.00 and the Saudi Arabian Light posting at $1.80.

From the point of view of the governments in the Middle Eastern capitals and Caracas, the price cuts of 1959 and 1960 (about which they were never consulted) were very damaging—affecting the size of their budgets and their development prospects. In April 1959, at the first Arab Petroleum Congress in Cairo (to which Iranian and Venezuelan representatives were invited as observers), the oil ministers of Saudi Arabia and Venezuela, Abdullah Tariki and Perez Alfonso, sponsored the formation of the Oil Consultation Commission. Then in September 1960, a month after the further reduction of Middle Eastern prices, the ministers of Iran, Iraq, Saudi Arabia, Kuwait and Venezuela met again in an atmosphere of crisis in Baghdad. The Oil Consultation Commission was already defunct, having met opposition from Iran and Iraq who objected to the inclusion of Egypt, and the ministers decided to create a permanent and stronger institution. The body that emerged was OPEC—the Organization of Petroleum Exporting Countries.

Since OPEC's formation, the original five members have been joined by Qatar in 1961, Libya and Indonesia in 1962, Abu Dhabi in 1967, Algeria in 1969, Nigeria in 1971, Ecuador in 1973 and Gabon—as an associate member in 1973 and a full member in 1975. The membership of Abu Dhabi was transferred to the United Arab Emirates (UAE) in 1974. In late 1992 Ecuador announced its decision to exchange full for associate membership of the Organization.

OPEC in the 1960s

At first the major companies ignored OPEC. In accordance with a resolution passed at the Organization's fourth conference in June 1962, the members addressed protests to the companies against the price cuts of August 1960, and demanded that prices be restored to their previous level. But the companies refused to enter into any collective negotiations, and in their individual replies they argued that the development of prices did not depend on their own will, but was determined by economic factors over which they had no control.

OPEC realized that the only way to restore posted prices would be to force up market prices, and this the producers decided would best be done by limiting the annual growth in their output. So over two years (from mid-1965 to mid-1967) the members worked out a joint production programme. In both years they overestimated the overall growth in demand for their oil, and at the same time certain members, notably Libya and Saudi Arabia, and, to a lesser extent, Iran, made no effort to keep within their quotas. The obvious conclusion was that in a period when prices were low enough to cause a tight budgeting condition in some states, those countries which were either new exporters and/or had big oil reserves and expensive development programmes, would not be willing to make a temporary sacrifice and await an improvement in the unit price of their oil, but would be tempted to increase revenues by maximizing the volume of their output.

However, OPEC did manage to increase its members' effective share of profits during the 1960s. First in 1963 the companies accepted a cut in the marketing allowance (which they were able to deduct as an expense before making the profit split) from some $0.01–$0.02, depending on arrangements in different states, to a uniform half-cent through the Gulf. Secondly, and more important, the Organization negotiated two agreements on the expensing of royalties. These agreements the Middle Eastern members saw as removing an anomaly in their fiscal arrangements, and as bringing their taxes into line with the system prevailing in Venezuela. Although the producers' revenues since 1950 had nominally been made up of a royalty of 12.5% of the posted price (as payment for the oil itself) and income tax (representing the 50% tax on the profits from the sale of this oil), payments made under the heading of royalties had always been totally deducted from tax. The producers, referring to the normal internationally accepted arrangements, under which the royalty payer was entitled to deduct the royalty only from his gross income when computing his tax liability, wanted royalties to be treated as an expense in their own countries also—and in 1964 this was what was agreed. As part of a package deal the companies received various further discounts on the posted price in respect of 'royalty expensing'

and 'gravity differential'. These discounts were to be reduced each year—this process being accelerated by a second agreement in 1968, which arranged for the complete disappearance of the royalty expensing discount in 1972 and of the gravity allowance in 1975. Under the new system the companies deducted their production cost, the 12.5% royalty, and the applicable allowances and discounts from the posted price, then split the remainder 50-50, and then added the royalty on the government's share. For Arabian Light, the royalty expensing agreements and the reduction of the marketing allowance increased government take from $0.84 at the end of 1960 to about $0.90 in 1968.

The independents in Libya

It was not, however, OPEC's achievements in improving its members' share of profits that were to be of the greatest long-term significance for the oil industry in the 1960s. In 1957, oil had been found in Libya. Unlike the governments in the Gulf, Libya had not awarded all its acreage to a single group, and as the discoveries were brought on stream in the early 1960s, it became clear that some of the largest fields lay in concessions held by independent US companies. These companies had originally ventured out of the USA in the late 1940s with the intention of finding new supplies for their marketing operations at home, but when the US Government imposed import controls in 1959, they were forced either to launch themselves downstream in Europe, as Occidental (marketing as VIP or Oxy) and Continental (marketing as Conoco or Jet) did, or to sell their crude to others, as Marathon and Amerada Hess did.

Libya proved to be an ideal source of crude for such operations. Its oil yielded a high proportion of high value products such as gasoline and heating oils, and had a low sulphur content. The country's position gave its crude a big freight advantage over Gulf crudes (an advantage only enhanced by the closure of the Suez Canal in 1967), concession terms were uniquely generous, and for the first half of the decade the profit split was made not on posted prices, but on the much lower realized prices. In the mid-1960s these advantages were reduced when Libya seized the occasion of the first royalty expensing agreement as an opportunity to renegotiate its profit split on the basis of postings. The majors in Libya, who did not favour the independents having access to crude on terms so much more generous than those applying to their own production in the Gulf, agreed to Libya's request in 1965, but the independents only gave in in 1966, after a bitter struggle in which the government threatened to stop exports or nationalize their assets. Even with these new terms, Libyan crude was very competitive with Gulf crudes in Europe, because its posted prices, while higher than those in the Gulf, only partially reflected its freight advantage.

Given the relatively low price, Libyan production expanded extremely fast—from 20,000 b/d in 1962 to 3.3m. b/d in 1970—and throughout the decade prices in Europe fell. The majors' response to the independents' sales and marketing operations was to seek economies of scale in building ever larger tankers, refineries and storage and distribution facilities; but because larger units become most attractive when operated at near full capacity, this led the majors themselves to look for the highest possible market share, and led to an acceleration of price cutting. Although this process was most apparent at the downstream end of the industry, there was also an erosion of market prices in the Gulf, and because the existence of OPEC prevented a lowering of postings, the majors' margins were squeezed. The net earnings per barrel on the seven majors' eastern hemisphere operations dropped from $0.60 in 1958 to $0.33 in 1970, while the effective profit split in the Gulf climbed to about 70–30 in favour of the governments.

Teheran and Tripoli Agreements

In 1970 the marginal surpluses which had been so strong a feature of the previous decade suddenly disappeared. A combination of higher than expected demand as the Western economies entered a period of upturn, a shortage of tankers and a growing tightness of European refinery capacity, led to an unusually tight supply situation, which left the oil industry with very little flexibility to deal with any disruption which might occur in the Middle East.

These conditions coincided with a series of negotiations in Libya, where in January the new revolutionary regime of Colonel Qaddafi had started pursuing a claim, originally formulated by King Idris' government in 1969, for higher prices which would reflect the true freight advantage enjoyed by Libyan crude since the closure of the Suez Canal, and would incorporate a premium for the oil's high quality. During the early months of 1970, the government took a notably moderate stance, but negotiations made rather slow progress, and although it seemed that they might still be brought to a satisfactory conclusion, by the beginning of the summer the government's position had hardened. In part the regime's determination stemmed from an agreement in the spring to co-ordinate its efforts with Algeria, which was engaged in similar negotiations with its French concessionaires, but at the same time, Libya could see that its bargaining position as a short-haul supplier was being considerably strengthened by events in the tanker market. The economic upturn in Europe was resulting in a rapid rise in demand for industrial fuel oils of the type derived from the heavier Gulf crudes, and this additional pull on long-haul supplies increased the demand for tanker charters. The strain was only made worse by the loss of several of the new class of mammoth tankers in mysterious explosions early in the year; and in May the situation deteriorated further when a Syrian bulldozer broke Tapline, running from Saudi Arabia to the Mediterranean port of Sidon, and deprived the industry of 480,000 b/d of short-haul crude.

In the same month, Libya ordered Occidental, a particularly vulnerable independent which derived nearly a third of its earnings from its Libyan concession, to reduce its production. Whether this decision was made for conservation reasons, or because the government realized what chaos a further reduction in the supply of short-haul crude would cause, remains unclear—but, either way, Libya soon appreciated the value of production cuts as a lever in their price negotiations, and they quickly imposed further reductions on Occidental and on the other companies. By September, the industry had lost about 1m. b/d of Libyan production, and freight rates soared as extra supplies had to be brought in from the Gulf. One by one the companies surrendered—led, naturally, by Occidental and followed by the other independents in the Oasis group. The majors held out a bit longer, but finally Texaco and Socal broke ranks, and then Esso, Mobil and, eventually, Shell gave in too. The Libyans achieved a price rise of $0.30, rising to $0.40 over the next five years, and their tax rate rose from 50% to amounts varying from 54% to 58% in payment for what the government claimed should have been higher prices since 1965.

Although in theory these changes were made only to reflect the freight and quality advantages of Libyan crudes, the majors realized that they would be bound to result in higher prices in the Gulf, and they promptly decided to pay the Gulf producers a higher tax rate of 55% and an extra $0.09 on heavier crudes (which although normally regarded as of lower quality, were in particularly high demand in 1970). Then in December 1970, at OPEC's 21st Conference, in Caracas, the members decided that the Gulf countries should press for further price increases.

The oil industry, with the support of the consumer governments, formed itself into the united front combining majors, independents and European national companies. When talks with the producers' representatives began in Teheran in January 1971, the companies agreed in principle to a price revision, but insisted that negotiations should cover all OPEC states, so as to avoid the leapfrogging of the past few months. The companies were forced to concede this point and a parallel series of negotiations was begun in Libya. During the second half of January the gap between the Gulf producers and the companies gradually narrowed, but on 2 February the talks collapsed. OPEC then held an extraordinary conference, and all members resolved to legislate a price increase if the companies did not respond to their minimum demands by 15 February. But none of the parties wanted a confrontation, and one day before the OPEC deadline, the companies gave in.

The producers were given: an immediate $0.33 basic increase, $0.02 for freight disparities, half a cent for every degree API by which any crude fell below 40° API, the elimination of all remaining discounts and allowances, and provision for prices to increase by 2.5% and $0.05 on 1 June 1971, and 1 January 1973, 1974 and 1975. This took 34° API Saudi Arabian Light from $1.80 to $2.18. In return, the companies were guaranteed that there would be no further claims until after 31 December 1975, no more leapfrogging if the Mediterranean producers concluded better terms, and no embargoes.

Later, in March, negotiations were resumed in Libya, and on 2 April an agreement was signed giving Libya $0.90, a uniform 55% tax rate, and provision for annual price increases of 2.5% and $0.07. Subsequent negotiations secured similar terms for Iraqi and Saudi crude arriving at Mediterranean terminals through the IPC pipe and Tapline.

The price explosion

It was hoped that the Teheran and Tripoli Agreements would give a full five years of price stability—but it was only months before they came under strain. In August 1971, President Nixon's decision to float the dollar (leading to a formal devaluation in December) produced OPEC claims for compensation—though in a notably moderate tone. The claim was settled on 20 January 1972, when the companies agreed in Geneva to an immediate price rise of 8.49% in the Gulf; and later, in May, after rather tougher negotiations, the same was agreed for Libya.

In February 1973 the dollar was devalued a second time by 10% and under the terms of the Geneva Agreement prices were duly raised by 5.8% on 1 April. The OPEC states were disappointed by the time the adjustment mechanism took to operate, and by the small size of their compensation, and, after a further series of discussions with the companies, on 1 June a second dollar compensation agreement was signed in Geneva. The producers obtained an 11.9% increase (which included the 5.8% increase in April plus compensation for the further slide in the dollar's parity during May) and it was agreed that prices would in future be adjusted monthly according to a weighted average movement of 11 major currencies against the dollar. This formula resulted in further rises in August and September and a reduction in October.

The companies presented the Geneva agreements as supplementary to the Teheran Agreement—although they both involved a significant rise in revenues, and could equally be characterized as a breach of the five-year price programme. Similarly, the participation arrangement negotiated in 1972 meant a significant increment in government receipts and a modification of the fiscal structure; and a still more drastic alteration came in September 1973 when Saudi Arabia agreed with Aramco that both categories of buy-back crude should be priced at 93% of postings—this being the price obtained by the Saudis in May at the first auction of their own direct crude entitlement.

In the summer of 1973, there were, however, much more fundamental forces undermining the Teheran Agreement. As production in the USA began to fall after 1970, the world's biggest consumer began to look to the eastern hemisphere not only to make up for its declining domestic output, but also for an annual increment in supplies that was nearly as big as the annual increase demanded by the whole of Western Europe. US imports from the Arab countries and Iran grew from 0.6m. b/d in 1971, to 1.0m. b/d in 1972, and to 1.7m. b/d in 1973. It was in 1973 that US demand became really noticeable in the Middle East, and prices on the open market began to rise accordingly.

The OPEC states profited from this situation in as much as they received bids close to postings for the small amounts of crude they were selling on the market themselves; but, with the fiscal terms applied to the bulk of their production still tied to modified 1971 prices, they were for the most part excluded from sharing in the boom, and the main benefit went to the companies. The producers calculated that the effective profit split had changed from about 80-20 in their favour at the time of the Teheran Agreement to about 64-36, and they suggested that the companies were making excessive profits, and that the whole set of prices negotiated two years earlier had become obsolete. These arguments were backed up by the producers pointing out that the small annual increments agreed at Teheran were not keeping up with the rate of world inflation.

At the OPEC conference in Vienna on 15 and 16 September the members agreed to call the companies to negotiations in the following month, and to seek a sizeable lump increase in posted prices to bring them sufficiently above market realizations to permit them to resume their function as a realistic tax reference, while establishing a mechanism whereby the desired differential between posted and realized prices could be maintained in future. The six Gulf members of the Organization began meetings with a company delegation in Vienna on 8 October, two days after the beginning of the Arab-Israeli October war, but the two sides' positions were far apart. The producers demanded an increase of some 70% and the companies offered only 20%. At the end of the week, the companies requested a fortnight's adjournment. The producers immediately held a meeting of their own, and decided to hold a conference in Kuwait four days later on 16 October 'to decide on a course of collective action to determine the true value of the oil they produced'.

When the producers met again, they quickly abandoned the idea of holding any further consultations with the companies, and raised their posted prices by 70%. For the Arabian light 'marker' crude, the posting rose from $3.01 to $5.12, while government take went up by a slightly larger proportion from $1.77 to $3.05. Subsequently, Libya raised its price by 94% from $4.60 to $8.92, thereby widening further the differential between Gulf and Mediterranean crudes. The new prices were designed to be 40% above the market price for any given crude as determined by the direct sales of governments to third parties, and OPEC announced that the movement of prices would in future be determined for each quarter by actual market realizations. Both the size of the October increase and the fact that it was made unilaterally were unprecedented, and signalled the final complete transfer of control over the price system, which until 1971 had been in the hands of the companies, into the hands of the producers—after a transitional three-and-a-half-year period of negotiated prices.

The price increase of 16 October was an important milestone in oil politics, but immediately, for the world economy, the meeting of Arab producers in Kuwait on the following day was far more cataclysmic. Gathering under the aegis of the Organization of Arab Petroleum Exporting Countries (OAPEC), they decided to use the 'oil weapon' in support of Egypt and Syria in their war with Israel. With Iraq opting out, the other nine members of OAPEC decided upon a policy of 5% cumulative monthly cuts in production from the levels of September—to continue until the political objective of Israeli withdrawal from the territories occupied in 1967 and the 'restoration of the rights of the Palestinians' had been achieved. The meeting was far from being an occasion of complete unanimity, and the decision on 5% cuts was taken with a degree of hesitancy on the part of some members and amounted to something of a compromise. But once the cuts had started, they escalated rapidly. Within days all of the Arab producers (including Iraq) placed embargoes on the USA and the Netherlands and reduced their production by equivalent additional amounts, while Saudi Arabia and Kuwait also incorporated the 5% reduction scheduled for November in their initial cutback. Irritated by the lack of response from the West, the Arab producers then decided at a further meeting in Kuwait on 4 November to reduce output across the board by 25% of the September level, and gave notice of a further 5% cut in December. But in practice, the cutback again turned out to be rather larger than it appeared to be on paper, and by the middle of November output in the two biggest Arab producers, Saudi Arabia and Kuwait, was down by between 30% and 40%.

With winter setting in, the Arab cuts had a dramatic effect on the market. Cargoes of Algerian and Nigerian short-haul crude fetched as much as $16 a barrel, and in December the National Iranian Oil Company, in an auction of its crude entitlement under the Sales and Purchase Agreement, sold oil at the staggering price of $17.40. In these conditions, the OPEC Economic Commission's search for a market price on

which to base the quarterly revision of postings became impossible, and the views of company representatives, who suggested in November in a brief exchange in Vienna that no changes should be made until the market had become more stable, were discounted. When the Gulf producers met in Teheran on 22 December, the new price level set was an arbitrary one dictated largely by the Shah of Iran, who suggested a price of $14, while Sheikh Ahmad Zaki Yamani, the Saudi Oil Minister, argued for a price of about $7.50—though he did not, perhaps, put his plea for restraint as strongly as King Faisal would have wished. The other ministers gave Sheikh Yamani little backing, although they resented the way in which the Shah took control of the meeting, and it was eventually decided that the posted price should be increased by nearly 130% from $5.12 to $11.65—taking the government revenue from $3.05 to $7.00. The Libyan price rise which followed was rather more modest in percentage terms—from $8.92 to $15.76.

1974—changing the tax system

The OPEC conference at Geneva on 17–19 January 1974, revealed the full extent of Saudi Arabia's opposition to the price increase announced in the previous month—although in the conference chamber itself, Sheikh Yamani did not raise a formal objection. As it was, members endorsed the new prices while deciding on a three-month freeze. This was extended for a further quarter, after a rather tougher argument, at the next meeting in March.

Coinciding with the OPEC conference in March, was another review by the Arab states of their embargo policy. In effect the cuts had come to an end in December, when they announced that they would not be imposing a further 5% reduction in January, and reclassified most of the EC and Japan as 'favoured nations' for which they were prepared to run production as normal. But it was not until their meeting in March, by which time Dr Kissinger had arranged the Egyptian-Israeli disengagement, that they lifted the embargo on the USA (with Libya and Iraq temporarily dissenting) and only in July was the embargo on the Netherlands lifted. The resumption of normal exports to the USA was accompanied by a decision to restore output to September 1973 levels, and Saudi Arabia, with an eye on the coming price battle within OPEC, which it saw would not be settled without reference to actual market realizations, let it be known that it would raise its output somewhat above September levels.

Inevitably, market prices weakened over the following months. After the failure of several participation crude auctions and price cuts of up to $3 by non-Gulf producers, in August, in the biggest single sale of 1974, the Kuwaitis failed to sell any of their 60% of production at the 97% of postings demanded. For the third quarter of the year they subsequently sold rather over 55% of the oil on offer to BP and Gulf at 94.8% of postings.

As Saudi Arabia had hoped in March, the excess of supply assumed a critical importance in the struggle within OPEC over pricing policy. In June Sheikh Yamani indicated the size of the reduction sought when he formally proposed that the marker crude posting should be lowered by $2.50. But when OPEC held its third meeting of the year at Quito in June, the other members argued for formulas which would have raised the cost of oil to the consumers by as much as $1.50. Saudi Arabia again threatened a unilateral lowering of prices, and a cheap auction of its participation crude entitlement, and the result was a stalemate in which it was decided (with Saudi Arabia dissenting) to increase the royalty rate on the companies' 40% crude entitlement (known as equity oil) from 12.5% to 14.5%.

Although within OPEC in the summer of 1974 a major battle was being fought over the level of postings, there was at the same time a considerable (and unopposed) increase in government take (and therefore in the cost of oil to the consumers) as a result of the 60% participation agreements, concluded in the middle of the year but backdated to the beginning of 1974. In that the states' participation crude was either sold back to the companies at a level well above the governments' take on equity crude, or was sold on the open market at roughly similar prices, the average government revenue over their whole production was increased, even though on participation crude the governments had to bear the production cost themselves. In 1973, under the 25% regime, the overall effect of participation was fairly small—increasing average government revenues by about $0.10 in the first nine months of the year and by $0.15/20 from September, when the 93% of postings buy-back price came into force. But in mid-1974, under the 60% participation regime, the weighted average revenue worked out, in theory, at some $2 above the government revenue on equity crude (which after the December 1973 increases was about $7.00). In practice, however, there were considerable variations between the different producers in the amount by which the weighted average revenue exceeded the take on equity crude, and in every case, the actual weighted average was lower than it appeared to be in theory. A relatively small factor in determining the variations between the states was the different percentages of postings (93% or 94.8%) charged to the companies for buy-back crude. Much more important was that, following the failure of their auctions (or, in Saudi Arabia's case, in the event of their not holding an auction), the governments kept part of their crude entitlement in the ground, and thus lowered the proportion of participation crude in their overall output, and reduced their weighted average revenues. In Kuwait, for instance, during the third quarter of the year, the ratio of the two types of crude was 65% equity and 35% participation.

One of the consequences of this dual pricing system was that the companies got their crude on average at a price well below that demanded by governments for their direct sales. The OPEC states realized that the companies' own sales of this relatively cheap crude to third parties were not only undercutting state prices and causing the failure of the auctions, but were also giving the companies large windfall profits. It was these problems that the producers tackled during the latter part of 1974. When OPEC held its fourth meeting of the year in Vienna on 12 and 13 September the members decided on a further increase in the royalty rate on equity crude to 16.67%, and an increase in the tax rate on equity crude from 55% to 65.65%. Saudi Arabia argued that these tax increases should have been accompanied by a cut in postings, and again declined to implement the changes. It was only in the following month that Saudi Arabia, increasingly irritated by the companies' profits, decided to call on Aramco for back-payments to cover the Quito and Vienna tax adjustments.

In November Saudi Arabia took a more decisive step. A Saudi delegation held a meeting with the Qatar and Abu Dhabi oil ministers in Abu Dhabi and agreed with effect from the beginning of the month to raise the royalty rate on equity crude to 20% and the tax rate to 85%. At the same time $0.40 was cut from postings. This was meant to further narrow the gap between the weighted average cost of crude to the companies and the prices demanded at state sales—as well as reducing the impact of the changes on the consumers.

When OPEC met in Vienna for its fifth and final conference of 1974, on 13 and 14 December, the other members endorsed the new arrangements, and decided that from 1 January 1975 (the date to which it was assumed the final takeover of Aramco would be backdated) all of the Gulf states would apply the new weighted average cost to all of their production exported by their concessionaire companies, and that the new price levels should be frozen for nine months. The distinction between equity and participation crude, and the possibility of variations in the weighted average cost being caused by alterations in the ratio between the two crudes, therefore ceased to exist—even though the notion of a 40:60 split was still used to work out the new cost, known afterwards as the 'acquisition price'. The new single price system involved a big jump in government revenue, not only because it was based in part on the higher tax and royalty rates agreed at Abu Dhabi but also because it was based on a 40:60 equity-participation crude ratio which in practice had not existed before. The government revenue on the 'market' crude rose to $10.13, and the acquisition price for the companies to $10.25, reflecting the notional 'marker' production cost of $0.12. The gap between the acquisition price and the 93% of postings,

$10.46, which remained the official sale price, was narrowed to $0.21.

Over the following years the acquisition price applied only in countries where the companies retained a 40% equity stake—which soon meant just Abu Dhabi and Saudi Arabia, among the bigger producers. In Kuwait and Qatar the former concessionaires got their crude at the government selling price (93% of postings) less a discount. This gave the companies a smaller margin than in Abu Dhabi and Saudi Arabia, which reflected the fact that in Kuwait and Qatar the companies were no longer investing capital. In Iran, where until the end of 1975 the companies continued to invest capital, the discount off the state selling price was bigger. In practice it was the state selling prices, in all countries, that became henceforth the important prices for OPEC.

Differentials—1975-78

December 1974 marked the end of the oil price explosion; in the space of 15 months government revenues and the cost of oil to the consumer had multiplied almost exactly five times. From then until 1 January 1979 there were only two OPEC price rises. One was agreed in Vienna in September 1975, when the state selling price was raised by 10%, and the other in Doha, in December 1976, when the majority of OPEC members raised their prices by a further 10%—causing a split with Saudi Arabia and the UAE.

During much of the four-year period 1975-78, demand was rather weak. There was something of a revival in the market in 1976, but in late 1977 and most of 1978 there was a serious glut caused by the new Mexican fields, Alaska and the North Sea, which had a significant impact on the world market at the same time. In these conditions OPEC members' attention became focused mainly on differentials —the different margins between crudes of different qualities in different locations. This problem was an important theme (sometimes the only theme) in at least half a dozen OPEC meetings: at Vienna in September and December 1975, Geneva in April 1976, Bali in May 1976, Stockholm in July 1977 and Caracas in December 1977.

Although ministers reached a flexible understanding on differential adjustments at the Bali meeting in May 1976, and periodically referred the matter to special committees (at Geneva in April 1976 and Stockholm in July 1977), the Organization could not agree on any comprehensive new system. Adjustments were made unilaterally, sometimes in accordance with guidelines laid down by one of the committees, but more often they took place when a state experienced a particularly embarrassing fall in demand, or when a price rise (in October 1975 or January 1977) produced an opportunity for producers to adjust their own crudes by implementing a fractionally bigger or smaller rise than that announced of the marker crude.

Apart from the differentials issue, OPEC meetings in 1975-78 were marked by quite frequent battles over price rises. Iraq and Libya were always numbered amongst the 'hawks' (often with Iran, Algeria and Nigeria), and Saudi Arabia generally stood as the single 'dove'—though sometimes it had the support of the UAE, Qatar and occasionally Kuwait. Although Saudi Arabia was forced to compromise in September 1975 and before Stockholm in July 1977, it succeeded in preventing rises at Bali, at Caracas in December 1977 and at Geneva in June 1978.

Other recurrent issues were production programming (the artificial limiting of output so as to influence the state of the market) and the protection of oil prices against the dollar's fluctuations. Saudi Arabia invariably rejected the idea of production programming, or even to discuss its own output, on which any programme would have hinged. On the matter of dollar compensation mechanisms, which was an issue in early 1975 (at Vienna and Libreville) and late 1977/early 1978, Saudi Arabia was less adamant, but still doubtful of the value of any of the formulas proposed.

OPEC split and reconciliation—
December 1976–December 1977

The major event in OPEC—and the major confrontation over prices—in 1975-78 occurred at Doha in December 1976. Saudi

Arabia, with the support of the UAE, refused to countenance the increases demanded by other OPEC members, ranging upwards from 10%, though it emerged later that had compromise been possible it would have been prepared to accept 7%. The outcome was that Saudi Arabia and the UAE opted for an immediate 5% increase for the whole of 1977, while the other members decided on 10% for the first six months of the year with an additional 5% to take effect on 1 July.

In part the Saudi policy at Doha stemmed from a hard-headed realization that the health of the OPEC economies is linked to that of the Western economies, and that inflation caused by oil price rises rebounds on the OPEC members; but at the same time there is no doubt that Saudi Arabia felt a genuine sense of responsibility for the West's economic well-being.

After the Doha meeting Saudi Arabia announced that it was raising its production ceiling from 8.5m. b/d to 10m. b/d, and immediately there were big drops in the production of some of the other states. Yet there was no increase in Saudi production at the beginning of the year; indeed output in January and February fell from the record levels of late 1976 (9.2m. b/d in December) to only 8.2m. b/d and 8.7m. b/d respectively. During the next four months, however, production rose, reaching over 10m. b/d at one point. There was some mystery surrounding the reasons for this performance. On one hand, it was suggested that the initial drop in output was caused either by the inevitable time-lag that would elapse before Saudi Arabia could sign up new customers or by Saudi Arabia realizing that the expansion of production might be more effective as a threat than as a *fait accompli*. On the other hand, there was evidence that Saudi Arabia had tried from the start to raise production to 10m. b/d but had been frustrated partly by bad weather preventing tankers loading, and partly by the realization that although it had rather more than 10m. b/d of capacity installed in hardware terms and was planning to expand this to some 12m. b/d by the end of the year, it did not have the personnel and management systems needed to maintain output at these levels.

Throughout the early months of 1977 attempts were made to heal the rift in OPEC. At quite an early stage it became clear that the 11 upper-tier countries would agree to a compromise involving Saudi Arabia and the UAE raising their prices by 5% in July and the rest at the same time forgoing their own scheduled 5% increase, but it was not until sometime in June that it emerged that Saudi Arabia would accept this formula. Some two weeks before the OPEC conference at Stockholm on 12 July, which it had been agreed should not be held unless a solution had been reached in advance, the two sides made their compromise public. The Stockholm meeting itself concentrated on the issue of differentials. At the later meeting in Caracas in December 1977 prices remained frozen, not because of a consensus, but because Saudi Arabia managed to assemble behind it Iran, Kuwait, the UAE and Qatar.

The second oil crisis—1979

Despite the oil glut of most of 1978, relations between OPEC members improved from the middle of the year. On 6 and 7 May the ministers held an informal exchange of ideas on long-term strategy in Taif, Saudi Arabia. The relaxed atmosphere, free of the pressures of decision-making, was enhanced by the steps that Saudi Arabia was taking to cut its output. Late in 1977 it had reimposed its 8.5m. b/d ceiling, and in early 1978 it had decided to limit liftings of Arabian Light to not more than 65% of total liftings (compared with 72%–80% in 1975–77). The market, however, was unable to absorb the extra amounts of heavy crude that this ratio implied at prevailing production rates, so for the first nine months of the year Saudi output fell sharply.

The broad drift of the ministers' discussions at Taif assumed that the glut would begin to come to an end in later 1978 or 1979, that there would then be a period of balance in the market—how long a period depending on the consumers' growth rates and their success or failure at developing alternatives and conserving energy—and that at some point in the 1980s the world would return to conditions of shortage. In these circumstances it was felt that the market itself would look after oil prices and that OPEC might possibly orient itself

to using its increased bargaining power for bringing about the new international economic order which had failed to emerge from the North-South dialogue in Paris. To study these questions the meeting established another ministerial committee composed of Saudi Arabia, Iran, Iraq, Kuwait, Venezuela (the five founder-members) and Algeria.

The turn-round in the market came much sooner than expected. At the end of October 1978 the strikes in Iran which were paralysing the Shah's regime began to affect oil production. During the next two months Iranian production varied between its norm of about 5.8m. b/d and 1.2m. b/d, but at the end of December it fell to 235,000 b/d (insufficient to meet domestic demand), at which point it remained until March 1979.

Up to the end of the year the companies made up the shortfall by increasing liftings elsewhere; Saudi output in December ran at a record 10m. b/d—it being permissible for Aramco to exceed the 8.5m. b/d limit for a month or so as long as it kept within it over the whole year. The Iranian crisis had no effect on the spot market. Nor did the crisis add much impetus to the OPEC meeting at Abu Dhabi on 16 and 17 December, when it was decided to raise prices for 1979 by 10% in quarterly instalments. These would bring the marker crude selling price from $12.70 in December 1978 to $14.54 in October 1979—a rise of 14.5% over nine months, but an average increase for the year 1979 of 10%. What was remarkable was the storm of protest with which the rise was greeted by Western governments, which seemed to ignore the fact that the rise was extremely modest and followed a long period of price stability.

In the month that followed the OPEC meeting, spot market prices began to climb at a rate which was to destroy the price programme agreed at Abu Dhabi and, by mid-May, to cause the Western world to talk of a 'second oil crisis'. With Iranian exports halted the international oil industry was short of some 5m. b/d, which was only partially made up by Saudi Arabia raising its production ceiling from 8.5m. b/d to 9.5m. b/d and by smaller increases in Kuwait, Iraq and other producer countries. By the middle of February, at which point OPEC announced an extraordinary meeting to be held in Geneva at the end of March, spot prices for light Gulf crudes had risen to $21 and higher, involving premiums of above $7.50.

In February Abu Dhabi, Qatar, Libya, Kuwait, Iraq, Oman and the USSR (for its Western customers) imposed surcharges on their crudes of between 68 cents and $1.41 per barrel.

On 5 March Iran resumed oil exports, building up over the next two months to a production level of some 4m. b/d (which meant exports of 1.5m.–2.0m. b/d less than before the Revolution). This caused the spot premiums to fall from their end-February peak of $23, but the market pressure for a rise was still impossible for Saudi Arabia to resist when OPEC met at Geneva on 26 and 27 March. All producers agreed to bring forward their scheduled 1979 last quarter increase to the second quarter (raising the marker to $14.55), and it was decided that producers could impose any additional surcharges they deemed 'justifiable in the light of their own circumstances'. Saudi Arabia added no premiums to its Light, Medium and Heavy crudes, but $1.14 to its high quality Berri crude. All of the other Gulf producers increased the surcharges they had imposed in February (on top of the new price levels), while the African producers raised their selling prices to the $17.50–$18.50 range.

In the middle of April it became known that Saudi Arabia was not maintaining its extra 1m. b/d of output in the second quarter, partly because it argued that the resumption of Iranian exports made this unnecessary, and partly, it was thought, to show its displeasure with the USA over the Egypt–Israel peace treaty. Shortly after this the effects of the Iranian stoppage began finally to feed through to the market, as oil companies cut back their deliveries. These developments set off in May another jump in the spot market price for light crudes, taking the price above the end-February level and then on to extraordinary levels in the region of $33 per barrel in mid-May. Nobody in the industry was surprised when the surge in the spot market was followed by two further rounds of leapfrogging increases—both led by Iran.

To try to lessen the pressure for higher prices, Saudi Arabia announced before the OPEC meeting in Geneva on 26 and 28 June 1979 that it was considering raising its output again. At the meeting the other members demanded further increases, which, if Saudi Arabia had co-operated, would have raised the marker crude to at least $20. Saudi Arabia, concerned at the recessionary influences that the oil price increases were having on the Western economies, sought to stabilize the price at a lower level of $17–$18. In the end OPEC reached an amicable compromise in which Saudi Arabia raised its marker price to $18 while the other members were allowed to impose surcharges up to $23.50. This figure was adopted for some of their crudes by Algeria, Libya, Nigeria and Venezuela. Soon after the meeting the Saudis announced that they were raising production for the third quarter of 1979 by 1m. b/d to 9.5m. b/d.

It was not until September 1979 that Nigeria broke the $23.50 ceiling by imposing a further premium on the price of its crude—and so triggered yet another round of increases.

Saudi attempts to reunify prices—
December 1979–September 1980

Saudi Arabia made a major attempt to restore order to the situation in December 1979, when it raised its crude prices by $6 per barrel, taking Arabian Light from $18 to $24. In doing this Saudi Arabia obviously hoped to set the stage for the unification of prices at the OPEC meeting in Caracas later in the month, but in the event, the Caracas meeting broke up in disarray. During January 1980 most OPEC members announced further increases backdated to the beginning of the year. Saudi Arabia felt that there would be no point in allowing their prices to fall further out of line with other members and so raised its own crudes by $2 per barrel. For the future they were encouraged by a softening of the spot market, caused by the downturn in economic activity in the industrialized world. Other producers, however, were not deterred from asking for even larger premiums and bonuses over and above their official prices on new crude sales contracts.

Saudi Arabia made another attempt to rationalize the price structure in May 1980, raising its prices by a further $2, taking Arabian Light to $28, effective from 1 April. This initiative, like its predecessor, failed. Within a week or so all other OPEC members—except Iran, which had already increased its second quarter prices—had matched the Saudi increase. When OPEC met at Algiers in early June the best that could be managed was an agreement to accept a two-tier price system. A theoretical marker price was set at $32 per barrel and on this basis producers of light crudes were allowed to charge differentials of up to $5. This established a new ceiling for OPEC prices of $37 but, in the following weeks, the price charged for Arabian Light stayed at $28. When the other producers realized that no changes would come from Saudi Arabia, they gradually raised their prices in line with the new accord. The African producers put their best crudes at the $37 limit.

During the summer the market moved steadily in Saudi Arabia's favour. The Kingdom's production had stayed at 9.5m. b/d since the middle of 1979. At the same time the oil companies had continued to pay high prices, with premiums, for other producers' crude in spite of the over-supply that had begun to be obvious in the winter of 1979/80. By mid-1980 stocks in the industrialized world had risen to unprecedented levels, to the extent that the oil companies' storage facilities were simply unable to accommodate further crude. By September spot market prices for African crudes had fallen to some $5 below official levels, and OPEC production had dropped 1.5m. b/d below the 28.5m. b/d recorded early in the year.

It was against this background that OPEC held two meetings in Vienna in September 1980—a regular oil ministers' meeting and a tri-ministerial meeting of oil, finance and foreign ministers. The latter group was convened to discuss the Organization's 'long-term strategy'. This involved a formula for future price increases, a wide-ranging programme of aid to the Third World, a revived North-South dialogue between the industrial powers and the developing countries, and a further bilateral dialogue between OPEC and the industrialized countries—all subjects which the Organization had begun to study at the meeting held in Taif in May 1978. Given the state of the market, the Saudi delegation in Vienna was able to make what seemed to be real progress towards a reunification of prices and agreement on a proper system of differentials. It was agreed that the actual Arabian Light price should be raised $2 to $30 per barrel and that this should be regarded as the official marker price. It was accepted that other OPEC crudes, aligned on the theoretical $32 marker, should not be reduced but would remain frozen until the next OPEC conference in December.

Saudi Arabia argued strongly at the Vienna meeting that any price for Arabian Light of over $30 would be too high to serve as a starting point for the Organization's long-term price formula, which members were hoping to implement at the beginning of 1981. Noting that conservation and diversification measures in the industrialized world were at last beginning to bite, Saudi Arabia was concerned that anything over $30 as the starting point for escalation might permanently damage the world economy and cause an undesirably large drop in demand for OPEC crude. Arguing against Saudi Arabia, the more militant OPEC members refused to accept the $30 starting point because it would have involved a reduction of their existing prices. The eventual compromise, lobbied most strongly by Kuwait, was based on the idea that if the majority of members agreed to freeze their prices, the escalation formula would quite quickly bring the Saudi price up to their desired $32 starting point—possibly as soon as the end of the first quarter of 1981.

There remained the question of the details of the price formula. The 'draft plan' presented by the working group presided over by Sheikh Yamani envisaged quarterly price adjustments based on three indices: the exchange rates of the main industrial currencies, inflation in the industrial countries' consumer prices and export prices, and a GNP index reflecting the real rate of growth of the 10 biggest industrial countries. The purpose of the last index was to bring the price of OPEC oil gradually up to the price of the 'alternatives'— oil from tar sands, shales and coal. The plan also provided for the co-ordinated adjustment of production upwards and downwards to preserve the price structure in the face of serious glut or shortage, and for moderate one-off price increases in time of acute shortage.

Most of the OPEC members backed the draft plan and were broadly in sympathy with the Saudi stand. The dissenters were Algeria, Iran and Libya, which rejected the use of inflation and growth indices from the industrial nations in constructing the price escalation formula. They argued instead for an index based on the much higher growth rates of the OPEC members and on the inflation of OPEC's imports of industrial goods. As the tri-ministerial meeting proceeded there were indications that Algeria would be prepared to compromise with the majority—in which case it was thought that any further resistance by Libya or Iran would have little practical significance. This left only the issue of differentials. Here disagreements revolved around the Gulf producers' opinion that the $7 difference between African crudes and the new marker price of $30 were $4–$4.50 too high. As with the differences over the structure of the long-term price formula there was some cautious optimism that the issue of differentials could be solved if there was the political will to do so.

Iran-Iraq War: renewed price discord

All optimism was destroyed at the end of September by the outbreak of the Iran-Iraq War, which soon led to the abandonment of the OPEC summit meeting. The two countries' attacks on each others' loading terminals and refineries led to a complete halt in exports and the removal of 4m. b/d from the international market. Iraq asked other producers to increase their output to compensate for the loss. In October the oil ministers of the four Arabian OPEC members met in Taif, Saudi Arabia, and agreed on a programme of increases, though given the 2m.–2.5m. b/d surplus that had existed in the market before the war the amounts involved were modest. In all, the Arabian producers' output was raised by only some 1m. b/d of which some 700,000–800,000 b/d came from Saudi Arabia.

This involved a new Saudi production level of 10.2m.–10.3m. b/d. The extra Saudi crude was sold to state-owned oil companies of industrialized and developing countries at a $2 premium over the official Arabian Light price of $30. The production increases were not big enough to prevent a gradual rise in spot market prices. In November the Rotterdam price for Arabian Light rose to $40, and by the end of the month there were a few examples of Arabian Light and African oils being traded for between $42 and $43.

It was against this background that OPEC met again in Bali, Indonesia, in December 1980. In view of the renewed discord and the more buoyant state of the market, the more moderate OPEC members were pleased to achieve even a minimal degree of pricing order. The conference took a series of decisions very similar to those taken at the Algiers conference in June 1980. Saudi Arabia agreed to raise the price of Arabian Light by $2 to $32, and the conference as a whole set a theoretical marker crude price of $36—this being intended as the basis for increases in the prices of other crudes. A differentials limit of $5 was set, making an OPEC ceiling price of $41. Somewhat to the oil industry's surprise, in early January 1981 Kuwait, Qatar and Iraq raised their prices by $4 aligning them either side of the theoretical marker price of $36. Abu Dhabi raised its price for Murban crude by just $3 to $36.56. The African producers moved the prices of their light crudes to the $40–$41 range.

1981—Price reunification

During December 1980 both Iran and Iraq began exporting crude again. From the time lifting began both producers offered substantial discounts, nominally to offset the extra insurance premiums that tanker owners were obliged to pay for sailing their ships into a war zone. In response to the renewal of exports by the two countries, Abu Dhabi had promptly stopped its output of 80,000 b/d of war-relief crude, but Saudi Arabia maintained its output at 10.3m. b/d. This meant that the Kingdom was accounting for 43% of total OPEC output—a figure which it had never attained in the 1970s and which gave it unprecedented power within OPEC. Certainly in 1980 Saudi Arabia seemed much better equipped to dictate price levels to the other members of OPEC than it had been during the previous confrontation of 1977. In the circumstances it was inevitable that Iran's and Iraq's return to the market would lead to a general erosion of prices. In April and May several companies, including Atlantic Richfield in Nigeria, 'walked away' from their contracts. Qatar dropped its $6.50 premium.

As it approached the next OPEC conference, scheduled for 25 May 1981 in Geneva, Saudi Arabia felt confident of being able to persuade its fellow members, without too much difficulty, to accept a price 'freeze' for the rest of the year. Sheikh Yamani made it known before the meeting that the Kingdom would like the 'freeze' to be extended through 1982, to give the Western economies 'time to breathe and recover'. Saudi Arabia also wanted to move towards a unified price structure and revive the long-term strategy plan. This had been the subject of informal discussions which it had held with Kuwait, Nigeria, Algeria, Venezuela and Indonesia at a secret meeting in Geneva in February.

At the OPEC conference no progress was made towards reunification. A mooted compromise, which would have involved Saudi Arabia increasing its price by $2 to $34 and the other members lowering their theoretical marker price to the same figure proved unacceptable to the militants. Instead all members agreed to 'freeze' the theoretical marker price at $36 and the maximum OPEC price at $41 until the end of the year.

Most of the members at the conference—the exceptions being Saudi Arabia, Iran and Iraq—also agreed to cut their output by 10% in an attempt to reduce the surplus on world markets. This was important as the first occasion since the 1960s that OPEC had taken a decision on production levels. However, it was announced that the basis for the 10% cut was to be the output levels obtaining at the beginning of the year and, as most producers' output was running at well below these levels in May 1981, the actual reductions that resulted from the decision were not very large.

There was another abortive attempt to reunify prices at $34 when OPEC held a consultative meeting in Geneva in August. Events in the period immediately after the meeting, however, influenced OPEC attitudes. Saudi Arabia in September reduced its production to 9m.–9.5m. b/d as a gesture of goodwill, while Nigeria, Indonesia, Gabon and Iraq all found that to maintain acceptable production levels they had unilaterally to cut their prices.

At the end of October, when OPEC gathered for its third Geneva meeting of 1981, the members were at least able to agree on reunification. As had been suggested at earlier meetings, the point of reunification was $34—a figure which involved Saudi Arabia increasing its price by $2 and the other members of OPEC cutting their prices by $1–$2. Saudi Arabia agreed to underpin the new price structure by restoring its production level to the traditional ceiling of 8.5m. b/d. Various loose ends concerning differentials were tied up at a meeting in Abu Dhabi in December. On this occasion there was a general lowering of the prices of both light and heavy crudes, to be effective from the beginning of 1982, which cut the average cost of OPEC crudes to consumers by some 50 cents per barrel.

OPEC's first production programme

Only weeks after the reunified price structure and the new, more realistic differentials had come into effect OPEC found itself facing the worst crisis in its history. The continuing recession in the industrialized countries and a run-down of stocks at a rate believed to be 4m. b/d cut demand for OPEC oil in February to just 20.5m. b/d. This compared with a forecast of 23m. b/d made before the new year. In response to the pressure of the market Iran in February made three price cuts totalling $4; North Sea prices were reduced by similar amounts to around $31 per barrel. The spot market price for Arabian Light fell to $28.50—$5.50 below the government selling price.

Slightly to the surprise of many outside the Organization, OPEC met the challenge fairly effectively. On 6 March 1982 Saudi Arabia made a further cut in its production to 7.5m. b/d. On the same day informal discussion by some of the OPEC ministers, attending an Arab conference in Doha, resulted in a tentative agreement that the production of OPEC as a whole should be limited to 18.5m. b/d, and that a full, extraordinary meeting of the Organization should be called two weeks later in Vienna.

The extraordinary meeting, on 19 and 20 March 1982, started badly. Individual members produced a series of inflated figures for what they regarded as their minimum acceptable production quotas. The total of all quotas initially demanded came to 21.9m. b/d, and Sheikh Yamani warned that if the OPEC nations were not serious in their defence of the $34 marker price, and allowed the market to degenerate into a free for all, Saudi Arabia would have no alternative but to go it alone, which would entail a whole barrage of competitive measures—reduction of the Arabian Light price to $24 per barrel, an increase in output to 10m. or 11m. b/d, and extensive sales of Saudi crude on the spot market. This glimpse of the abyss concentrated the minds of the other members wonderfully and caused them to agree on a realistic set of quotas involving an 18m. b/d ceiling. This was slightly below the ceiling which had been mentioned at Doha and some 1m. b/d below average first quarter production levels. The decision was accompanied by a further lowering of light crude prices in Africa and the Gulf, the establishment of a ministerial 'watchdog' committee to monitor the market and the implementation of the quotas, and an agreement that the 18m. b/d ceiling should be reviewed at the next ordinary conference in Quito in May.

The quotas agreed at the Vienna meeting, in millions of b/d, were as follows: Iraq 1.2, Iran 1.2, Saudi Arabia 7.5, Kuwait 0.65, Neutral Zone 0.3, UAE 1.0, Qatar 0.3, Nigeria 1.3, Libya 0.75, Algeria 0.65, Venezuela 1.5, Indonesia 1.3, Ecuador 0.2, Gabon 0.15. Immediately after the meeting Sheikh Yamani announced yet another cut in the Saudi production ceiling to 7m. b/d in April—0.5m. b/d below its quota level.

For three months following the Vienna meeting the OPEC production programme seemed to be working and prices on the spot market responded reassuringly by closing to official selling rates. At the next ordinary conference held in Quito on 20 and 21 May ministers expressed satisfaction with the success of the quota system. They decided to review the 17.5m. b/d ceiling later in the summer and there was some hope that it might be raised. By mid-June, however, it was clear that the limit on collective output had been exceeded. In that month production averaged nearly 18m. b/d despite the fact that Saudi Arabia's output was running well below its self-imposed ceiling at about 6m. b/d and Iraq, unable to export from the Gulf, was fulfilling little more than two-thirds of its quota. At the time the production programme was adopted Iran's attitude had seemed ambivalent and its participation doubtful. In the event it steadily increased its production from April onwards, stimulating exports through the offer of discounts of up to $3 and more below the officially agreed OPEC level. Its output had reached about 2.5m. b/d by July. Muhammad Gharazi, Iranian Minister of Oil, stated that the objective was 3m. b/d. Libya was estimated to be producing at a rate of 1.2m. b/d and in contracts had agreed to prices $2 below the official level. Because of their non-observance of the pact Venezuela declared that it would not be bound by the agreement. By the time the ministers gathered in Vienna for an extraordinary conference planned two months earlier the production programme was disintegrating. Chances of it being salvaged were not improved by Saudi Arabia's demand that the differential for the premium North African crudes should be increased from $1.50 to at least $3. This reflected the dissatisfaction of Saudi Arabia and the other Arab producers of the Gulf over the way in which their output was falling.

The fact that the extraordinary ministerial conference held on 9 and 10 July was suspended—rather than ended without any agreement—indicated the extent of its failure. Apart from a common commitment to the $34 reference price and recognition of the need to restrain production within a 17.5m. b/d ceiling, Iran, Libya and Algeria insisted that Saudi Arabia should further cut its production to accommodate other producers, in particular Iran. Saudi Arabia's response was that it still refused to discuss its level of output with other members and that it had already made substantial sacrifices. At a time when Libya and, to a lesser extent, Algeria were offering discounts in various forms off existing official prices, the Kingdom's insistence on widening differentials seemed a somewhat irrelevant, as well as disruptive, preoccupation. Above all, though, the belligerence of Iran, which had just previously taken the Gulf conflict into Iraq's territory, poisoned the atmosphere. Ministers dispersed comforted only by the strong expectation that demand for OPEC oil would revive in the second half of the year.

The willingness and ability of oil companies, banking on a price reduction, to run down stocks came as a surprise. OPEC production of about 18m. b/d in the third quarter and 19m. b/d in the fourth was too high to maintain the $34 reference price and Arabian producers grew restive. Meeting within the context of the Gulf Co-operation Council (GCC) made up of Saudi Arabia, Kuwait, the UAE, Qatar, Oman and Bahrain, they issued a thinly disguised threat of price cuts and increases in production by themselves if other exporters continued 'in their misguided actions'. The warning was evidently aimed at Britain, Norway and Mexico as well as OPEC recalcitrants.

OPEC's next biannual ministerial conference in Vienna from 18–20 December could do no more than agree that the $34 reference price should be defended and that collective output should be no more than 18.5m. b/d in 1983. Little progress was made on the allocation of production quotas, the elimination of discounting, and the correction of differentials. The lack of realism was clear from the fact that the initial quota nominations by individual members amounted to 23.4m. b/d. The possibility of the Gulf producers acting independently recurred but they decided against such a course.

A gathering in Bahrain on 23 January 1983 of oil ministers of the GCC, who were joined by their counterparts from Iraq, Indonesia, and Nigeria, paved the way for a full ministerial consultative meeting in Geneva on 23 and 24 January. Once again members failed to agree upon a concerted strategy in the face of a growing threat, although members moved a little closer to adoption of a new system of quotas. Once again the consultations were plagued by the issue of differentials and pressure from the Arab producers of the Gulf to obtain an accord on their increase. The central question, though, related to the $34 reference price. Saudi Arabia and its allies were clearly in favour of a cut to $30 per barrel.

The chief delegates of OPEC eventually reconvened in formal session in London on 6 March, though negotiations had been conducted continuously since mid-January. The common interest of producers looked imperilled in mid-February as, first, the British National Oil Corporation (BNOC) proposed to its customers a reduction in the top North Sea rate (in competition with the premium North African crudes) from $33.50 to $30.50 per barrel, and, then, a day later, Nigeria slashed its official selling rate from $35.50 to $30 in a bid to boost exports. Far from rising significantly there had been no recovery in demand for OPEC oil. On the contrary, destocking surged to a rate generally estimated at more than 4.5m. b/d during the first quarter of 1983, while members' output of oil and NGLs dropped to about 15.5m. b/d. The underlying desperation was, perhaps, best articulated by the Venezuelan Minister of Energy and Mines, who said on the third day of the conference: 'If we don't reach agreement this week we will meet in two months and be discussing $25 as a price'. The prospect of a general price collapse drew out reserves of endurance, as well as patience, from the delegates. The essential parts of the package finalized on 14 March were: a 15% cut in the reference price from $34 to $29 per barrel; a new production programme under a ceiling on collective output of 17.5m. b/d; and differentials on the bases set in March 1982.

Iran expressed strong reservations about the price cut, despite having previously given the biggest discounts to customers. It did so on principle and also, it seemed, as a ploy to secure a dispensation for acceptance by other members of a price for its own crudes below the OPEC structure. This was granted to take account of the higher insurance premiums and freight costs in respect of oil shipments from the Kharg Island terminal which had been the subject of periodic, if ineffective, Iraqi attacks in the continuing Gulf conflict. No limit was set but other members did not object to the announced $1.20 discount which more or less reflected the extra costs involved in shipping Iranian crude in March 1983.

The part of the agreement covering production caused the most trouble. Members appreciated from the outset the particular problems of Iran and Iraq—it was recognized that the latter could not fulfil its quota, but there was an understanding that Saudi Arabia and Kuwait would make up some of the difference. Three members caused particular difficulties as far as quotas were concerned. Saudi Arabia began by insisting on 6m. b/d for itself but, in the end, implicitly assented to produce no more than 5m. b/d without waiving its principle of refusing to participate in a production-sharing programme. The UAE held out to a late stage for 1.5m. b/d but ultimately agreed to an allocation of 1.1m. b/d. Venezuela, which demanded no less than 1.8m. b/d, settled in the end for 1.6725m. b/d. The quotas agreed, in millions of b/d, were as follows: Algeria 0.725, Ecuador 0.2, Gabon 0.15, Indonesia 1.3, Iran 2.4, Iraq 1.2, Kuwait 1.05, Libya 1.1, Nigeria 1.3, Qatar 0.3, UAE 1.1, Venezuela 1.6725, Saudi Arabia 5.0.

Where differentials were concerned, Nigeria posed one of the biggest problems confronting efforts to complete a satisfactory package, since it was politically impossible for the government of President Shagari, with an election looming, to revise upwards the price of Bonny Light in line with the $30.50 per barrel set by BNOC. The greatest danger to any new defence of a basic, albeit, lower price was a price-cutting war between Nigeria and the North Sea producers. The industry generally viewed the top Nigerian variety as being underpriced in comparison with its North Sea competitors. Algeria and Libya agreed to set the rate for their premium crudes at $30.50. In doing so they put themselves at a slight disadvantage. It was calculated that, if production limits were observed, each of the three would enjoy a fair share. In the mean time, the question of what constituted the right differential for premium grades and the Arabian Light reference price, in a constantly shifting market, remained unresolved.

OPEC's struggle to maintain stability

After the conclusion of their prices and production pact, the OPEC producers, the world's marginal suppliers of energy, not only had to face lower per-barrel revenues but also a depressed level of output at least until the summer of 1983 in order to maintain the value of their petroleum, the source of their livelihood.

Two months after the conclusion of the agreement there was optimism that the line could be held. Crucial, in this respect, was the fact that an official selling rate for North Sea oil compatible with OPEC's price structure was proposed by the BNOC and, after initial misgivings, accepted by the industry as a whole. Anything less than the $30 per barrel set for the Brent blend would have prompted retaliation from Nigeria and almost certainly set off a price-cutting war. The UK Government, with its ideological adherence to the principle of 'free-market forces', strenuously sought to avoid any impression that it had colluded with OPEC, but stressed its intention of doing nothing to destabilize market forces. Norway, as usual, aligned itself with Britain. The collaboration of Mexico, which had also been on the lower price tier, had previously been obtained by OPEC. Having emerged as the main single threat to the new price structure, the USSR raised its official selling rates closer to those of OPEC and trimmed back supplies after prices on the spot market rose in April 1983, as if finally alerted to the common danger facing all producers.

At the outset the new price structure together with the system of production controls looked fragile. By early summer, however, confidence had grown that the market was stabilizing and that the goal of balancing supply with demand could be achieved at the cost of short-term sacrifice. Iran and Libya had evidently overcome early resistance from customers to their new official price levels. There was a consensus that demand for OPEC oil would rise at least to between 18m. and 20m. b/d in the last quarter from a level of only about 14.5m. b/d in the first quarter, depending on the rate of restocking and economic recovery. Thus, it was imperative that OPEC as a whole and its members individually should keep their nerve and discipline.

At first sight it was ironical that Britain, with exports of only about 600,000 b/d, should have assumed such a pivotal position in this crucial period. In fact, the importance attached to it, while essentially arising from the crucial relationship between North Sea and Nigerian prices, highlighted OPEC's loss of control over the world's oil market as a result of declining demand and competition from non-member producers.

After an initial period of uncertainty over OPEC's revised production-sharing agreement and doubts about its ability to maintain sufficient discipline, the market had strengthened considerably by the time that the Organization met for its next ministerial conference in Helsinki on 18 July. During the April–June (1983) quarter OPEC production of crude oil fell to about 16.7m. b/d as members made something like a concerted effort to discipline output and observe official prices. For that quarter Indonesia, Nigeria and the UAE exceeded their quotas by between 70,000 b/d and 100,000 b/d. However, there were no significant breaches of quota allocations as Saudi Arabia bore the brunt of slack demand during this period. Moreover, after Iran and Libya had withstood pressure from customers to concede discounts, price levels were successfully maintained.

With demand for OPEC oil clearly starting to grow it was hoped that economic recovery and an increase in the demand for oil might make it possible to raise the limit on output. As it was, however, OPEC output surged well above the ceiling to pass 19m. b/d, an average rate which was maintained until the end of the year. Indonesia was obviously in breach of its quota of 1.3m. b/d with a rate of more than 1.4m. b/d during the second half of 1983. Iranian production probably ran at a rate 100,000 b/d or so above its 2.4m. b/d allocation. Kuwait also exceeded its quota of 1.05m. b/d with actual production of 1.2m. b/d or more. But, again, it was Saudi Arabia, the acknowledged 'swing producer' within OPEC (i.e. meeting any

increase in demand for OPEC crude above the 17.5m. b/d ceiling or absorbing any drop below it), which was mainly responsible for the increase. At an estimated average of 5.87m. b/d its output during the July–December period was substantially higher than the 5m. b/d accorded it by other members of OPEC in the general understanding relating to the production-sharing programme of March 1983. This extra production would have accounted for about 60% of all OPEC output in excess of the 17.5m. b/d ceiling during the second half of 1983. Saudi Arabia had not, in fact, agreed to any limitation on its production, and at the end of the protracted London meeting in March 1983 it did no more than commit itself to being the Organization's 'swing producer'. The surge in its exports in the second half of 1983 coincided with the start of operations by NORBEC, a marketing company established to supplement the work of the state hydrocarbons corporation Petromin. When OPEC's market-monitoring committee called upon Saudi Arabia late in October 1983 to account for its high rate of output Riyadh's bland response was that the Kingdom could not perform its role as 'swing producer' if other members did not observe their quotas and price commitments. The Saudi statement also pointed to the oil being produced on behalf of Iraq (250,000 b/d from the Neutral Zone, shared with Kuwait, and 60,000 b/d from Saudi Arabia) to compensate it for the constraints on its exports imposed by the Iran–Iraq War, and to crude oil produced for storage rather than immediate sale so that, it was claimed, seasonal demand for natural gas could be met. There was some confusion, too, as to why Saudi Arabia was chartering a large number of supertankers and placing a considerable volume of crude in them. Initially, it was suggested that the oil was being stored because of the temporary shut-down of two offshore fields, Zuluf and Marjan, while they were being incorporated into the Kingdom's Master Gas System. Saudi Arabia sought to give the impression that the stockpile was not related to the possibility of a supply crisis resulting from the closure of the Strait of Hormuz or any other disruption of oil traffic. The cumulative total built up in floating storage by the end of 1983—just over 20m. barrels—was not sufficient to account for Saudi output over and above 5m. b/d.

The breakdown in OPEC discipline was seriously destabilizing the market again by the end of 1983 and when OPEC delegates met for a full ministerial conference in Geneva on 6 December the need to restore confidence in the market had become urgent.

The onus was on OPEC and the world was sceptical of its ability to defend the $29 per barrel reference price and the price structure relating to it. Even if there had been any scope for raising the ceiling the exercise would have been dangerous in the absence of an agreed mechanism for adjusting quotas and with the existence of conflicting quota claims. The UAE believed that it should have priority, with an increase in its allocation from 1.1m. b/d to 1.5m. b/d, if the ceiling was to be raised.

As early as July 1983 at the Helsinki meeting, Iran had given notice that it would demand a bigger quota at the Geneva conference and prior to it specified the increase being sought as 800,000 b/d in addition to the 2.4m. b/d accorded it under the London agreement of March 1983. Iraq, meanwhile, had voiced its claim for an increase from 1.2m. b/d to 1.8m. b/d. In any dispute over increased production the pleas of populous, debt-ridden Nigeria and Indonesia, two of the weakest links in the OPEC chain, could not be ignored. As it was, over-production had pre-empted the possibility of lifting the ceiling and there was a strong argument for lowering it with percentage cuts in individual quotas. At the Geneva conference OPEC had little choice but to reaffirm the production ceiling and allocations agreed in London. Iran did press its claim for a bigger allocation at Saudi Arabia's expense, though not to the point of threatening a rupture. The Kingdom also came under fire from other members but Sheikh Ahmad Zaki Yamani, its Minister of Oil, did no more than promise privately that Saudi output would be restricted to a maximum of 5m. b/d without making it clear whether the pledge included oil produced on behalf of Iraq. Iran struck a discordant note by proposing that the $34 reference price should be restored because the $5 cut had not in any way stimulated demand but finally relented when other members agreed that a committee should be established to discuss the question.

OPEC and the world price structure looked very vulnerable to a further decline in prices on the spot market, and a chain reaction of price cuts by non-members eventually forcing Nigeria and perhaps others to give way. The UK again found itself in the pivotal position as it had in the spring of 1983 because of the close relationship between North Sea and North African crudes. The subsequent recommendation of the BNOC for unchanged prices in the first quarter of 1984, citing OPEC's production agreement as 'a sound basis for stability in the market', was couched in terms indicative of a general change of attitude on the part of the UK Government. It had watched the crisis early in 1983 with impassivity and little appreciation of the dangers involved. By the end of the year the implications for state revenue and the country's balance of payments were fully appreciated and reckoned to be more serious than any lapse in respect for free-market forces. At the same time the companies responsible for the greater part of production in the UK sector of the North Sea had come to appreciate that their interests lay in market stability and maintenance of the price structure. In the event BNOC obtained overwhelming acceptance for its proposal, with only two of its customers phasing out their contract options.

OPEC succeeded in pulling through the critical spring months without any serious price cutting, despite a fall in demand for members' crude. Output in the first quarter was estimated by the IEA to have averaged 17.8m. b/d. Saudi production, at about 5m. b/d, came more or less within the limit recognized by other OPEC members. Nigeria's production surged ahead to about 1.46m. b/d over the three months. Subsequently, output was reined in and Nigeria pledged not to seek a quota increase until the ministerial conference in July. The other main offender was Indonesia whose production averaged something like 1.5m. b/d. It, like Qatar, evidently resorted to giving some disguised discounts.

OPEC's collective output exceeded the 17.5m. b/d limit by a clear margin over the 12-month period following conclusion of the pact on production and prices but no precise figures were available. Indeed, the failure of member countries to report accurately made more difficult the job of the Organization's market monitoring committee, which was to supervise adherence to quotas. The IEA calculated average OPEC production from the beginning of April 1983 to the end of March 1984 at 18.1m. b/d (not including NGLs). That compared with an estimate of 17.67m. b/d for the production year 1982/83, when the average was depressed to a low point of less than 15.5m. b/d in the fourth quarter of the year (January–March). Members were not helped by the continued rundown of inventories, but early in 1984 severe winter weather in North America boosted demand. An unexpected bonus was the miners' strike in the UK which began in the spring of 1984, initially creating an extra demand for fuel oil of 200,000–300,000 b/d, and of as much as 600,000 b/d before the industrial dispute came to an end a year later. In the early part of 1984 there was also an unexplained fall in Soviet supplies. Rising tension in the Gulf also helped to sustain the market and to support prices in the early part of the year. The potential danger to oil traffic passing through the Strait of Hormuz had become apparent in the summer of 1983 when it became known that France was to provide Iraq with *Super Etendard* aircraft, capable of delivering the *Exocet* missiles already in its possession. These could be used to hit tankers loading at Kharg Island, Iran's main oil terminal, though it seemed they were not sufficiently effective to cause much damage there. In September 1983 Ayatollah Khomeini himself had said 'I warn oil states of the region, and the other countries which use oil in one way or the other, that the Government of Iran, exerting its utmost power, will oppose this aggression and is determined to block the Strait of Hormuz, thus obstructing the passage of a single drop of petroleum'. The danger became far more real as Iraq began to step up its attacks, with a fair measure of success, from February 1984 onwards, although Iran soon proved that it could maintain exports at something approaching its quota entitlement by offering the inducement of discounts and later by ferrying an increasing proportion of its output to Sirri Island in small tankers for onward shipment.

OPEC's production-monitoring scheme

The increase in oil demand, which became evident in the last quarter of 1983 following a decline totalling 20.5% from 1980 to 1984 in the industrialized world, as defined by membership of the Organization for Economic Co-operation and Development (OECD), was maintained in 1984 when it rose by 2.3% compared with the previous year, according to the calculations of the IEA. However, the rate of growth declined progressively during the year from 6.1% in the first quarter, to 3.4% in the second and third quarters and to 2.6% in the fourth. Disappointingly for OPEC, despite the general recovery of demand for oil throughout the OECD, it did not keep pace with economic growth in the industrialized world and the ratio of oil consumption to the Gross Domestic Product (GDP) of the OECD as a whole continued to fall as a result of further energy conservation and switching to coal, gas and electricity. Moreover, OPEC's share of the market in 1984 fell for the sixth year in succession. Its output of crude at about 17.2m. b/d, plus 1.3m. b/d of NGLs or condensates, was marginally up on 1983 but accounted for only 40.2% of estimated supplies to the world outside the Communist world compared with 41.2% in 1983, according to IEA estimates. Total non-OPEC supplies in 1984 rose from 26.1m. b/d to 27m. b/d.

Over 1984 as a whole OPEC's output of crude oil was just under 17.5m. b/d, marginally less than in the previous year, according to the most authoritative estimates. The IEA calculated OPEC output at 17.2m. b/d, or exactly the same rate as in 1983, not including condensates and NGLs, production of which, the agency calculated, had risen from 1.2m. b/d to 1.3m. b/d. The well-informed Petroleum Intelligence Weekly (PIW) put the OPEC rate for 1984 at 17.49m. b/d, including condensates, which would have amounted to 450,000 b/d–500,000 b/d. The Royal Dutch/Shell group figures gave a total for 1984 of 18.57m. b/d compared with 18.5m. in 1983, including all condensates and NGLs.

In 1984 there were some significant changes in the national shares of total OPEC output. That of Saudi Arabia, including its 50% entitlement of almost exactly 200,000 b/d from the Neutral Zone shared with Kuwait, fell by about 8% to 4.64m. b/d, and Iran's by nearly 10% to 2.18m. b/d, according to PIW calculations. By contrast, Iraq's production rose by about 20% to about 1.2m. b/d, its full OPEC quota, as throughput via the pipeline to Ceyhan, the terminal on Turkey's south-east coast, rose to a capacity of 1m. b/d, with the remainder accounted for by domestic consumption and some 50,000 b/d of petroleum products transported by road to Aqaba, Jordan, for onward shipment. When the volume in excess of 300,000 b/d of 'war relief' crude produced on its behalf by Saudi Arabia and Kuwait (technically taking the latter above its quota) was taken into account, though, Iraq could be considered to have been the biggest violator of the prices and production pact. Nigeria was 100,000 b/d above its 1.3m. b/d allocation. Proportionately, Qatar was the biggest offender, with average output for the year running at no less than 400,000 b/d compared with a quota of 300,000 b/d. At about 250,000 b/d, Ecuador was 25% above its 200,000 b/d quota.

Rising consumption, which was evident in the winter of 1983/84 led OPEC to hope that it might be possible to raise the ceiling on output to as much as 19m. b/d for the last quarter of the year. The expectation was that, by then, demand for OPEC crude might amount to as much as 20m. b/d depending on the extent to which stocks were drawn down. In the mean time OPEC struggled for the third summer in succession, to maintain its price structure and the related, all-important credibility in terms of the observance of production and pricing discipline. In the spring of 1984 the market had revived to the extent that spot rates for Brent blend, the North Sea reference crude, marginally exceeded its official selling rate of $30 per barrel at the end of April. It was strengthened by fears of serious disruption of supplies from the Gulf resulting from a continuation of Iraq's attacks on tankers lifting oil at Iran's Kharg Island terminal and from the possibility of serious Iranian retaliation following attacks on Kuwaiti and Saudi vessels in May.

International anxiety reached its highest point in mid-May, when the Saudi super-tanker *Yanbu Pride* was set ablaze by rocket fire from an Iranian aircraft only 30 miles from the Saudi coast. That was enough to send the price of Brent, now established as the all-important market indicator, soaring to $30.70 per barrel on the spot market. Orders for Saudi oil pumped through the Trans-Arabian pipeline (Tapline) rose from less than one-third of its 1.85m. b/d capacity, prior to the *Yanbu Pride* incident, to 1.5m. b/d in June. Iran had already threatened to prevent oil supplies leaving the Gulf via the Strait of Hormuz, through which a little over 20% (7m. b/d–8m. b/d) of supplies required by the non-Communist world were passing, if Iraqi military action prevented its own oil export industry from operating.

An increase in the use of the Tapline facility apart, it was reckoned that, in the event of the termination of supplies from the Gulf, other OPEC members would be able to provide 3.7m. b/d from idle capacity, while more than 500,000 b/d might be available from non-OPEC producers. In theory that would leave a shortfall in supply of up to 3m. b/d. The situation was potentially serious for Arab producers of the Gulf, as well as consumers, in view of the fact that a 2.5m. b/d shortfall over a period of a few months in 1970 sent spot rates soaring and led to the eventual doubling of official selling rates by the end of 1980 to the high point from which the subsequent deterioration in OPEC's fortunes began.

In the summer of 1984 there was no panic comparable to that experienced in 1979 and the concern over supplies proved to be short-lived. On the one hand, it was realized that Iran probably had not the capability to block the Strait of Hormuz by military means for more than a very brief period, if at all. Moreover, stocks were still at a high level, despite a steady rundown of company inventories since mid-1982. The stated readiness of the Reagan Administration to release oil from the US Strategic Petroleum Reserve of non-commercial stocks, then accounting for 80% or 400m. barrels, helped suppress any adverse speculation. In addition, there was the reassurance of the 55m.–60m. barrels which had been placed in floating storage by Saudi Arabia during the previous summer. Saudi Arabia had denied that the action was related to the possibility of the Strait of Hormuz being closed, but in the late summer of 1983 it did much to weaken the market, though little of the stored oil was released on to the market.

The oil market concluded that the situation was not as serious as first feared. The average spot rate for Brent fell below the official selling price in the last week of May. Having suffered a temporary reduction in oil liftings from Kharg Island, Iran moved rapidly to rectify the situation, offering discounts in the range of $2.50–$3.00 per barrel below the preferential rate relative to other Gulf crudes accorded it under the production and prices pact concluded by OPEC in March 1983. Exports quickly recovered to a level of 2.1m. b/d–2.2m. b/d, within its quota, with about another 700,000 b/d being used for domestic refining. It became evident that Qatar was far more flagrantly flouting the pact as its output rose above 400,000 b/d, stimulated by the offer of a discount of $1 or so below official selling prices.

A far more serious threat to the structure of the OPEC prices and production programme came from Nigeria, as it pressed for a rise in its quota to ease its grave financial and foreign exchange problems. There was the danger that Nigeria might go its own way, cutting its prices as it did in February 1983, which precipitated the OPEC crisis meeting in the following month and the traumatic $5 per barrel price reduction across the board. That was the main issue facing OPEC's 11–12 July ordinary mid-summer ministerial conference in Vienna, following a month which saw a steady decline in prices on the spot market. The unsatisfactory compromise reached at the conference was that Nigeria should be allowed an extra 100,000 b/d of output for August and 150,000 b/d for September with Saudi Arabia reducing its share to accommodate the increment. Yet, even at this stage there was optimism that there would be an appreciable rise in demand for OPEC oil in the latter half of the year.

OPEC's hopes were confounded. With available supplies greatly exceeding demand and, for the most part, selling at a discount on official prices, the market continued to sag. Saudi

oil output surged to 5.5m. b/d in July and the OPEC total to over 18m. b/d. Largely as a result of these two factors the spot rate for Brent plummeted to $26.85–$26.95 at the end of the month. The crisis was such that Mr Alick Buchanan-Smith, British Minister of State for Energy, took the unprecedented step—given the UK's *laissez-faire* policy towards the oil industry—of writing to the eight largest operators in the North Sea urging them not to bring pressure on the BNOC to cut prices over the coming weeks. This, and subsequent clarification that Saudi output had been running at no more than 4.5m. b/d and that OPEC's output as a whole was more or less within its ceiling, did much to stabilize the market for a while.

It was becoming apparent that the growth in overall demand was slowing down, and OPEC crude output fell below 17m. b/d, with Saudi Arabia fulfilling its role as the 'swing producer', with its production falling below 4m. b/d, so that it seemed in September as if the market might be gaining some equilibrium. But with non-OPEC sources of supply progressively increasing, Nigeria raising its rate to 1.6m. b/d in October, and only a modest build-up of inventories, spot-market realizations began to sag again.

Even so, it was without any warning that OPEC found itself faced with a full-scale crisis in October, the market being thrown into panic with the news that Norway had offered its customers secret discounts on a month-by-month basis amounting to $1.35 per barrel off its Statjford crude for October and $1.05 for November. Already under some pressure from some customers (rather than the big suppliers) BNOC followed suit, cutting the rate for its Brent blend to $28.65 per barrel. Nigeria reacted predictably, leap-frogging the North Sea producers with a cut of $2 per barrel on its lighter varieties of crude and setting a price for Bonny Light (with which, in the spring of 1983, BNOC had managed to align Brent), to $28 per barrel, thereby threatening a vicious downward price spiral. Brent plummeted towards $26 per barrel on the spot market.

OPEC had no choice but to resist the downward trend set in motion by the North Sea producers and its recalcitrant member, Nigeria—any cut in per barrel revenues was not going to be off-set by higher demand in the foreseeable future. Its response in consultations held in Geneva between six ministers on 22 October and the subsequent full extraordinary ministerial conference held from 29 to 31 October, was impressive. With remarkable speed, given the contortions which had been involved in apportioning output allocations in 1982 and 1983, it was decided to lower the ceiling on collective production to 16m. b/d (from the 17.5m. b/d set in spring 1982), and a new system of quotas was agreed upon. The limit was intended to be a temporary one, of unspecified duration, which would be lifted when the supply situation tightened up and spot-market prices came into line with official selling rates. Proportionately, Kuwait (14.3%), the UAE (13.6%), Saudi Arabia (an implied 12.9%, tacitly accepting the anticipated shortfall from Nigeria and a proportion of the cuts for Venezuela, Ecuador and Indonesia) and Libya (10.0%) agreed to the largest reductions in their output. In conformity with its traditional policy of refusing to allow its own output policy to be determined within the context of OPEC, Saudi Arabia made no formal commitment. The understanding was that it would not allow its rate to pass 4.353m. b/d, compared with 5m. b/d under the March 1983 pact. Nigeria's quota was left unchanged at 1.3m. b/d but it made it clear that it considered its entitlement to be no less than the 1.45m. b/d it was granted in September, and refused to rescind its $2 per barrel price cut bringing its prices back into line with those of other members. The Saudi and Kuwaiti chief delegates were confident that spot-market rates would come back into line with official selling rates before the end of the year and persuade Nigeria to conform. The new quotas (in millions of b/d, with the previous quotas in brackets) were as follows: Algeria 0.663 (0.725); Ecuador 0.183 (0.200); Gabon 0.137 (0.150); Indonesia 1.189 (1.300); Iran 2.300 (2.400); Iraq 1.200 (1.200); Kuwait 0.900 (1.050); Libya 0.990 (1.100); Nigeria 1.300 (1.300); Qatar 0.280 (0.300); Saudi Arabia 4.353 (5.000); UAE 0.950 (1.100); Venezuela 1.555 (1.675); total 16.0 (17.5).

No progress was made on the increasingly critical issue of OPEC's price differentials. By the late summer of 1984 it had become apparent that the defence of OPEC's crumbling price structure required a radical revision. Since they were last adjusted early in 1983, perhaps insufficiently for a system which had basically remained intact since 1979, rates had fallen glaringly out of line with market realities. In particular, the problem of a wide disparity between the prices of lighter crudes and those of the cheaper, heavier grades had become much too wide. This had been caused by the expansion of up-grading capacity in refineries world-wide to convert high gravity, sulphurous oil into premium products. The difficulties of the light producers were compounded by Saudi Arabia's decision to change the proportions of its export contract 'mix' from a blend of 20% Arabian Light, 20% Arabian Heavy and 60% Arabian Light, to 35%, 25% and 40% respectively. In the long term the switch was made in order to gear Saudi output to the level of its reserves, but the immediate purpose seemed, to producers dependent on lighter varieties, to be to ensure demand for the Kingdom's crude because it effectively lowered the price of the Kingdom's average barrel in the composite package from $28.08 to $27.55.

OPEC's October conference did no more than appoint a three-man committee, comprising a chairman, Sheikh Yamani of Saudi Arabia, and the chief delegates of the UAE and Libya, to deal with the problem of differentials. The consensus in the oil industry was that the gap between heavy and light crudes should be closed by no less than $1.50 per barrel to bring a measure of greater stability to the market. The conference which was held in Geneva in two sessions in December only marginally closed the gap of $4.50 between the $26 per barrel official selling price for Arabian Heavy and the $30.50 charged, notionally, for the premium varieties of Algeria and Libya. Algeria and Nigeria pressed for a reduction in the differential of as much as $2, to be achieved mainly by an increase in the price of the heavy crudes. Saudi Arabia adamantly opposed anything but a small increase in their rates and there was general reluctance in principle and some fierce opposition in practice to paring back the $29 per barrel price set in March 1983 for the Arabian Light reference or 'marker' crude, because such a cut would constitute a reduction in the price conceded in the face of market pressures. The interim decision, from which Algeria and Nigeria dissociated themselves, was for a 50 cents increase in the price of Arabian Heavy, and a 25 cents increase for Arabian Medium, with a reduction of 25 cents for the ultra-light Gulf crudes. This, in effect, was a 75 cents reduction in the differential, setting Abu Dhabi's Murban crude, the Gulf's top variety, at $29.31 per barrel. It left the premium North African grades of Algeria and Libya theoretically where they were before, while Nigeria, in practice, showed no sign of realigning its rates with the rest of OPEC. The price of an average barrel in Saudi Arabia's export package rose by 22 cents.

In the event a much more coherent system was evolved at the extraordinary ministerial conference held in Geneva from 28–30 January 1985. Ten members in all overcame the psychological barrier relating to Arabian Light (which had been OPEC's reference crude since 1973) by bringing its price down by $1 to $28 per barrel. The differential *vis-à-vis* the ultra light Gulf crudes was reduced to a maximum of 15 cents for Murban and Arabian Medium was switched back to its old level of $27.40 per barrel. It was agreed that Nigeria, because of its special problems in relation to the North Sea and its dire financial state, could keep Bonny Light at $28.65, the price which BNOC was still paying to its suppliers while suffering mounting losses in its sales of participation crude to third parties. It was calculated that the reduction in the average weighted OPEC price was 29 cents per barrel but that of the Saudi Arabian 'mix' was cut by 47 cents to $27.33.

Algeria, Libya and Iran dissociated themselves from the agreement, though this did not make much difference to its potential ability to stabilize the market. The greater part of Algeria's exports were in the form of refined products sold at spot-market-related prices. A large proportion of sales by Libya were accounted for by barter deals involving discounts which it was offering more directly to customers, anyway, in its efforts to maintain shipments and fulfil its quota. The

fact that the official selling price of Algeria's Sahara blend remained at $30.50 per barrel and Libya's Brega blend at $30.40 was, therefore, somewhat notional. Despite its opposition to the majority agreement, however, Iran quickly adjusted its prices in line with those of the other producers. It set them for liftings from Sirri Island, to which it was transporting an increasing volume of oil for onward transhipment, owing to buyers' inhibitions about lifting from the more vulnerable terminal at Kharg Island.

Another OPEC Monitoring Scheme

OPEC had, meanwhile, taken a major step towards enforcing more effectively the pact on production, pricing and sales. It was agreed at the 19–21 December 1984 conference session to establish a supervisory body, called the Ministerial Executive Council (MEC), under the chairmanship of Sheikh Yamani with the chief delegates of Venezuela, Nigeria, Indonesia and the UAE as the other participants. The far-reaching plan involved acquiescence by the 13 member states in an intrusion into their affairs and sovereignty unprecedented in the history of international organizations. The resolution empowered the council to employ independent auditors whom member states agreed to allow 'to check on member countries' petroleum sales, tanker nominations, shipments, pricing, quantities etc.' and 'to check the books, invoices, or any other documents that are deemed necessary by the firm in the fulfilment of its tasks'. Moreover, the brief of the council covered petroleum products and condensates as well as oil. Petroleum sales were also defined as covering barter deals, processing agreements, inter-governmental agreements, exchange and direct sales, equity oil, and all marketing arrangements—under most of which oil was disposed of at below official selling rates. The Dutch firm of auditors, KHG-Klynveld-Kraayenhof, was appointed before the end of January 1985. Although its role had been subsumed, OPEC's Market-Monitoring Committee continued.

In the second half of 1984 OPEC's output responded, despite varying degrees of indiscipline by nearly all members, to the slow-down in the short-lived growth in world demand and an actual decline in the preceding three months. The IEA calculated that collective production ran at 16.7m. b/d during the July–December period, well below the old ceiling. Not only was OPEC faced with increased supplies and greater price responsiveness to market pressures from its competitors but also by a large run-down of inventories in anticipation of cuts in official selling rates by the Organization. During the first quarter of 1985, with only a minimal build-up of 100,000 b/d by governments, the industrial stocks in the OECD area fell by no less than 2m. b/d.

In February 1985 the market strengthened, as a result of lower OPEC output and a measure of confidence arising from the revised differentials system and the new production-policing measures. Important short-term factors were a period of freezing weather in North America and Europe, together with a sudden shortfall in the availability of Soviet crude. The end of the UK miners' strike, however, removed 400,000 b/d–500,000 b/d in demand and, with a slump in demand forecast for the spring, OPEC needed support from other producers in its battle to hold the line. At the Geneva meeting in December 1984, Malaysia, Brunei and Egypt had encouragingly agreed to token cuts to show solidarity with OPEC, while Mexico repeated its commitment not to increase exports. On the critical North Sea front, however, hopes that the UK would try to hold Brent at $28.65 per barrel, with the aim of maintaining revenue and the value of sterling, were soon dashed.

In mid-March the British Government announced its decision to phase out the state-owned BNOC by July. The BNOC had, hitherto, purchased 51% of output from the UK sector and disposed of the critical volume (amounting to 700,000 b/d–800,000 b/d by 1985) which was not bought back by the larger companies with integrated operations and downstream (refining and marketing) interests. The implied threat of the abandonment of any form of structured-term pricing was soon realized as BNOC informed sellers that it would relate its prices to the spot market during its three-month period of phasing out. The announcement further depressed the market, which fell sharply at the end of April.

OPEC's prices and production discipline was still slack. Output in the first quarter of 1985 was reckoned by the IEA to have averaged 16.2m. b/d, just above the ceiling, having risen from 15.3m. b/d in January to 16.4m. b/d in February and fallen to 16.2m. b/d in March. There was evidence, though, that it was edging towards 16.5m. b/d by the end of April. Nigeria had not responded to the North Sea price cuts but its output, boosted by a series of new barter deals, was reckoned to be running at 1.7m. b/d. Four other members—Libya, Indonesia, the UAE and Ecuador—were exceeding their quotas, collectively by 400,000 b/d–450,000 b/d. Only the production below quota in Saudi Arabia and Iran was keeping production in check. Co-operation with the MEC had been reasonable. Nigeria refused access to the auditors until April, while Algeria refused to let them examine its production of condensates. The Council had made much slower progress than had been hoped: it was close to full monitoring of OPEC output, yet far from exposing the scale of price discounting.

OPEC was faced with the harsh fact that the $5 per barrel price cut of March 1983 had not stimulated any increase in demand for its members' own oil. The growth in consumption world-wide, such as it had been, had only benefited non-members whose own investment in exploration and development had been given a big boost by the scale of the second 1979–81 price escalation. Conservation and the substitution of oil by other sources of energy had established themselves, for the foreseeable future, as enduring features of the economic life of the industrialized world. The extent of the damage was reflected in the fall in OPEC output from a high point of over 31m. b/d in 1979 to about 18.5m. b/d (including NGLs) in 1984, a drop of 40%. In the same period OPEC's share of the market fell from 60% to 40%. New sources of energy emerged over the five years, contributing to the market the equivalent of about 20m. b/d of oil half of which was in the form of non-OPEC petroleum supplies.

In terms of financial resources, Saudi Arabia was best equipped to deal with the crisis. Kuwait, with its large investment income, was also well placed. The UAE and Qatar, though not without some painful belt-tightening, also looked capable of balancing budgets and payments. Overall, the Gulf producers, including Iran and Iraq with their export potential restricted by the war between them, had borne the brunt of the cuts in output over the years, with only 50% of capacity being utilized in 1985 compared with 65% of other members'. As far as the poorer members were concerned, though, the four producers of the area hitherto regarded as perpetually in surplus—Saudi Arabia, Kuwait, the UAE and Qatar—still enjoyed too great a share of the much-diminished cake, especially Saudi Arabia, with an effective quota over three times that conceded to Nigeria which had a population perhaps 15 times as large. This remained a cause of underlying tension. So, too, did the ideological commitment of Algeria and Iran to maintaining, officially, the highest possible price whatever they or other members did in practice (i.e. discounting).

Yet it was understood that no one would benefit by boosting oil exports by lowering prices, since the loss of per barrel revenues would generally cancel out any gain in sales volume and could risk a free-fall or even a collapse of prices. For OPEC, the main compensation had been the strength of the US dollar, the currency in which all oil prices are set. Owing to the remorseless rise in the value of the dollar from the end of 1982 to the beginning of 1985, western European countries, on average, were paying 13% more for their oil in local currency terms, with a roughly similar increase for Japan. At the same time, however, the appreciation of the dollar, alone, could have been responsible for reducing demand by 2m. b/d.

During the summer of 1985 it became increasingly clear that, on the one hand, OPEC would not be able to raise the 16m. b/d production ceiling, and that, on the other, several members could not live comfortably with their quotas under the pact agreed in 1984. The breakdown of even the pretence to a firm commitment to production discipline was brought about by Iraq's determination not to observe any restrictions on its oil exports, and by growing Saudi impatience over production quota violations by other members and the fall in

its output level as a result of its strict adherence to official selling rates. (By mid-1985 it was the only member of OPEC respecting them fully.)

The erosion of the official price structure worsened despite the efforts of the MEC to eliminate abuses. When the MEC met in Taif, Saudi Arabia, in early June 1985, it was apparent that the auditors, Klynveld-Kraayenhof, were encountering obstacles from nearly all member states. At this point, however, respect for the ceiling was not the main problem. In the first half of 1985 collective OPEC output had been slightly above the ceiling, at 16.2m. b/d but in the second had dropped to around 15m. b/d, when Saudi Arabia's production averaged just under 3m. b/d, compared with the maximum of 4.35m. b/d conceded under the revised 1984 production and prices pact. It had become clear that control of production was not, in itself, enough to strengthen the market, and drastic action on the issue of price was imperative. So-called 'net-back' deals, whereby prices for crude oil are related to current realizations for petroleum products on a spot-market basis, less agreed transportation and refining costs, assumed greater significance during 1985, having the effect of depressing prices further by locking them into a downward spiral of spot rates for products.

When OPEC met again in Vienna from 5–7 July, spot prices had fallen to a level $2–$3 per barrel below official selling rates, as output continued to stagnate. The need to restore a measure of credibility to official OPEC rates was more urgent than ever, and this meant resisting the drift towards market prices. Kuwait suggested that the ceiling should be adjusted on a seasonal basis, with a 7% reduction for the third quarter and a 7% increase for the fourth. For various reasons, five members opposed the Kuwaiti plan. In particular, Iraq gave notice that it not only wanted a bigger allocation but intended to pump to the full 500,000-b/d capacity of its new export outlet across Saudi Arabia via the new pipeline link which was scheduled for completion in August 1985. For the rest of OPEC and the oil market as a whole an important factor was the assertion by Saudi Arabia that it no longer considered itself to be the 'swing producer', and that it regarded the 4.35m. b/d conceded to it by the other members of OPEC, under the production-sharing pact of October 1984, as a 'fixed quota'.

At a subsequent consultative meeting in Vienna OPEC members agreed that they should cease direct discounting and phase out more involved price-cutting methods such as 'net-back' arrangements and counter-trade deals. The supervisory MEC was charged with contacting the governments of member states with a view to opening discussions on how this could be achieved.

At the next of OPEC's two annual ordinary conferences, in Geneva from 22–25 July, the majority of members agreed to a drop of 50 cents in the price of heavy Gulf crudes and to one of 20 cents in the prices of medium varieties, thus widening the differential between the former and ultra-light, North African crudes from $2.40 to $3 per barrel. The change reduced the weighted average official price for all OPEC crudes from $27.96 to $27.82 per barrel. Predictably, Algeria, Iran and Libya dissociated themselves from the majority decision, as they had done in the previous January, when a majority of 10 agreed to a lowering of the price for Arabian Light, then the essential reference for all other crudes, from $29 to $28 per barrel. It was doubtful whether the adjustment in price differentials would appreciably affect liftings of Saudi oil in the absence of a (totally unexpected) surge in demand. The triple alliance of Algeria, Iran and Libya, although they were dogged in their refusal to countenance any price cuts, were no respecters of the official rates. At this point, 70%–75% of OPEC exports were reckoned to be selling at rates conforming to the official structure but abuses were rapidly becoming more widespread.

Saudi Arabia's patience, meanwhile, was exhausted. The Kingdom's average output during the second quarter of 1985, including 50% of production from the Neutral Zone with Kuwait, ran at an average rate of something less than 3m. b/d, rather than the 3.8m. b/d that it could have expected on a *pro rata* basis under the quota system; and in May the rate of output fell to its lowest level for 20 years. The level of production officially regarded as necessary to cover the requirements of the 1984/85 budget was 3.85m. b/d, or the equivalent of $55,400m. at an average price of $27–$28 per barrel. By the time of the July 1985 meeting of OPEC, Saudi oil production was little more than 2m. b/d and, taking into account domestic consumption of about 800,000 b/d, sufficient to generate foreign exchange earnings from oil of only $11,000m.–$12,000m. As it was, the Saudi Government's revenue had fallen from a peak of $108,800m. in 1981/82 to $47,400m. in 1984/85, and it was becoming alarmed at the decline in economic activity, which was still very heavily dependent on state spending. The decision had almost certainly been made that the time had come for Saudi Arabia to cease making sacrifices on behalf of the other members of OPEC.

Saudi Arabia's decision to renounce the role of 'swing producer' and its determination to enjoy the maximum entitlement of 4.35m. b/d allowed it under the OPEC output sharing agreement became fully apparent in September. Saudi Arabia abandoned its previously strict adherence to official selling prices with three deals on a net-back basis with Exxon, Texaco and Mobil, involving 800,000 b/d. Almost simultaneously the Kingdom persuaded the UK to accept payment for 132 military aircraft, from early 1986 onwards, in the form of crude oil, following the precedent set in the summer of 1984 with Boeing and Rolls-Royce in respect of 747 'Jumbo' jets wanted by the Saudi Ministry of Defence. The far more significant development in Saudi policy, the reversion to net-back deals, remained officially unacknowledged. King Fahd stressed the Kingdom's continued belief in the need for discipline among OPEC members and for the observance of common accords. Nevertheless, he continued, the principle of free trade was crucial, and 'nobody should blame anyone else for breaking the rules in pursuit of his own interests if he believes he is compelled to do so'.

Saudi Arabia's categorical insistence on its full portion of OPEC's diminishing share of the oil market was, in itself, enough to ensure the failure of the next OPEC meeting, in Vienna, on 3–4 October, which, it was hoped, would agree upon a revised system of quotas satisfying those members claiming larger allocations. It was clear that increases would have to be at Saudi Arabia's expense. As it was, the ministerial conference had no choice but to reaffirm the ceiling on collective output of 16m. b/d, with the economic experts' optimum estimate of demand for OPEC crude amounting to only 15.6m. b/d, despite the onset of winter. The meeting foreshadowed the abandonment of any real effort to control production, despite the fact that discipline over output had become imperative if prices were to be maintained. Quota increments were requested by Ecuador, Iraq, Qatar and Gabon. Iran responded to the Iraqi demand by pledging to produce two barrels for each one produced by its enemy. The UAE warned that it, also, wanted a bigger quota. The issue was deferred until the next ordinary conference, which was scheduled for the end of 1985. The inescapable, though unvoiced conclusion, was that it was impossible to agree on any distribution of quotas under such a low ceiling. At this point, Sheikh Yamani spoke of the need for serious discussions with non-member producers if a collapse of the market was to be avoided.

In the event, prices held up surprisingly well until the end of November, when Arabian Light, at $27.95 per barrel, was close to its official selling rate of $28 and premium North African crudes were being quoted at over $30 per barrel. One reason for this short-lived resilience was seasonal demand and a build-up of stocks, which rose at a rate of 500,000 b/d during the fourth quarter of 1985 in the industrialized countries belonging to the OECD. Secondly, non-OPEC supplies did not rise. A third factor was the intensified campaign by Iraq to blockade Iran's oil exports, which was signalled by the low-level air raid on the Kharg Island oil terminal on 15 August, the first such attack since June 1984.

Analysts had been puzzled by Iraq's apparent unwillingness to make telling raids on the prime economic target and its concentration instead on the tankers shuttling oil to Sirri Island. It was not clear whether this restraint arose from simple military or logistical factors, or from the persuasions of Iraq's major aid donors in the Gulf area, Saudi Arabia and

Kuwait, which were anxious to prevent an escalation of the conflict which might involve them. The raid on Kharg Island temporarily reduced output from the terminal to only about one-half of the maximum export level of 1.6m. b/d, which was possible under Iran's 2.3m. b/d production quota. An increased number of Iraqi attacks from the air during the following months, aimed mainly at oil tanker traffic rather than the Kharg Island terminal, failed to have such a disruptive effect. The intensified campaign temporarily stabilized the spot market and forced Iran to consider various projects for reducing its dependence on Kharg Island. In practice, Iraq's failure to press home a potentially decisive advantage and Iran's resilience, enabled the latter to maintain the level of its exports, giving an output in the final quarter of the year of about 18.3m. b/d.

During the October–December quarter, OPEC output averaged rather more than 17.5m. b/d, far in excess of the optimum demand which had been estimated by the Organization's experts prior to the Vienna meeting in October. Saudi Arabia fulfilled its quota as progressively it offered all its customers oil priced on a net-back basis. With the commissioning of its new pipeline facility Iraq was able to achieve a production rate of about 1.7m. b/d. Nigeria, whose output rose from 1.3m. b/d to 1.7m. b/d, was responsible for most of the remainder of the rise in collective output. Demand was greater than OPEC's experts had forecast but actual supplies were in excess of requirements. According to a subsequent estimate by the IEA, the surplus during the final quarter of 1985 was about 1m. b/d. Moreover, by the end of the year the surge in Gulf production had led to a substantial increase in stocks afloat which had yet to reach the market.

OPEC'S 'fair' market share policy

OPEC met again in Geneva on 7 December in a mood of growing desperation. Early in November, Sheikh Yamani had warned of the possibility of a 'price war', yet the decision of the Organization at the three-day meeting, 'to secure and defend a fair share of the world oil market', came as a surprise, and had enormous implications for prices. The 16m. b/d ceiling remained notionally in force and so, too, did official selling rates. In practice, the majority had abandoned them both in preference for a strategy aimed at forcing other producers to collaborate with OPEC in maintaining prices and to concede to them a part of their market share.

By the end of January 1986 the price of the North Sea Brent blend had fallen to $18.80 per barrel on the spot market. In the period from November 1985 to March 1986, prices on the spot market for widely traded crudes plummeted by between 60% and 75%, to their lowest level, in real terms, since 1973. Iran, Algeria and Libya had publicly dissociated themselves from the new policy, urging, instead, a reduction in OPEC output, in order to restore prices to former levels. The strategy being pursued by the majority, albeit with misgivings in some quarters, was very much the invention of Saudi Arabia, Kuwait and the UAE—three states with financial reserves large enough to cushion them against the effects of a period of drastically reduced per-barrel revenues. Others had no such safety net.

Nine days of arduous debate at the ministerial conference held in Geneva from 16–24 March failed to produce an agreement on what the level of OPEC production should be and how it should be shared. Iran, Algeria and Libya demanded a cut in production to 14m. b/d for the second quarter of 1986, but Saudi Arabia insisted that any such reduction would be contrary to the policy of regaining market share, and that there would be no possibility of members observing such a ceiling if they were unable to respect one of 16m. b/d or to agree on how to distribute output under the higher limit. The only agreement to be reached was with a group of non-member producers (Mexico, Egypt, Oman, Malaysia and Angola), who signed a memorandum of understanding on co-operation and committed themselves, in principle, to curbing their own output, with the implicit proviso that OPEC first establish a workable system of quotas.

The conference was adjourned and reconvened in Geneva on 15 April. After several days of tense discussion, the deadlock remained unbroken, but a clear majority of 10 had emerged in favour of maintaining the strategy of recovering a 'fair' market share. They agreed that an OPEC production rate of 16.3m. b/d in the third quarter of 1986 and 17.3m. b/d in the fourth, giving an average of 16.7m. b/d for 1986 as a whole, would be compatible with the aim of restoring market stability. Adamant that the prime objective should be the restoration of prices to $28 per barrel by the end of the year, Iran, Algeria and Libya dissociated themselves from the majority view, declaring that OPEC output should be limited to 14m. b/d, 14.5m. b/d and 16.8m. b/d for the second, third and fourth quarters, respectively.

There were practical reasons why these three countries should propose a policy of production restraint. Despite its promise to produce two barrels of oil for every extra Iraqi barrel, the intensification of Iraqi attacks on Iranian oil installations and on tanker traffic during the spring prevented Iran from producing much more than its quota allowed. Algeria was committed to respecting its quota, and Libya, meanwhile, looked as if it would face some marketing difficulties after the withdrawal of the five US companies (Occidental, Continental, Amerada Hess, Marathon and W. R. Grace) involved in exploration and production operations there, following the USA's identification of Libya as a promoter of international terrorism and its punitive air raids on Tripoli and Benghazi in April.

The critical question of quotas remained unresolved, and was deferred to the next ordinary ministerial conference in July. Following the marathon Geneva conference sessions, OPEC showed no sign of asserting any discipline. Collective OPEC output rose to about 17.5m. b/d in April, to about 18m. b/d in May and to more than 19m. b/d in the first two weeks of June, with Iran and Libya registering substantial increases in their production. So, too, did Saudi Arabia, which offered customers discounts ranging from 50 cents to $1.10 per barrel in order to maintain the level of liftings. Other producers, who had exceeded their quotas under the defunct 16m. b/d ceiling, continued to produce at these levels.

Saudi Arabia, Kuwait and the UAE seemed to want to inflict as much damage as possible on high-cost producers, in a bid to bring about the collaboration of the UK and Norway in OPEC's market-stabilization policy. By mid-1986, after six months of its application, they could derive some satisfaction from the fact that the strategy had had some tangible effect. Firstly, it was calculated that 800,000 b/d–900,000 b/d of capacity, mainly in the USA and Canada, had been closed down as a result of lower prices. Secondly, apart from the willingness, in principle, of five non-member exporters to co-operate with OPEC, the new Labour government in Norway, alarmed by the fall in state revenue and confronted by an economic crisis, suggested that it might be prepared to restrict the growth in the country's output provided that OPEC achieved a realistic system of production control. The British Government, however, remained dogged in its refusal to contemplate any intervention. Also, though at a considerable cost in pricing terms, OPEC had recovered some of its market share. According to the estimates of the IEA, OPEC's output of crude in the first half of 1986 was about 17.3m. b/d, a rise, which an increase in consumption of nearly 3% in the industrialized world, represented by members of the OECD, during the same period, helped to accommodate.

On 25 June OPEC oil ministers met on the Yugoslavian island of Brioni in another attempt to agree upon production levels and quotas. No progress was made towards agreement on a new quota system, although there was general agreement that the free-for-all should end. The demands of individual states totalled 20m.–21m. b/d, compared with IEA forecasts of demand for OPEC oil of 17.7m. b/d and 18.4m. b/d in the third and fourth quarters, respectively. Iran, Algeria and Libya continued to insist that the median price should be raised to $28 per barrel (OPEC's ultimate aim, officially) as soon as possible. It was recognised that the big surplus of supply overhanging the market, which had resulted from the June surge in OPEC production (19m. b/d—nearly 2m. b/d more than actual demand), would have an immediate, depressive effect on prices. Within a fortnight they had plummeted below $10 per barrel, the Brent blend falling to a nadir of $8.60. Early in July, Saudi Arabia's output soared to 5.7m. b/d, as it built up stocks in floating storage, in a move seem-

ingly aimed at asserting more fully the Kingdom's influence over the market and OPEC, and collective production remained in excess of 18.5m. b/d well into July.

The reintroduction of quotas

The next OPEC meeting in Geneva on 28 July proved to be a turning point. It began with further talk about voluntary production cutbacks. By the fifth day of the conference the deadlock with Iraq, inevitably, proved to be an obstacle, with its refusal to join any production pact unless it was given parity with Iran. The impasse was surprisingly broken by Gholamreza Aqazadeh, Iran's Minister of Oil. He secretly proposed to Sheikh Ahmad Zaki Yamani, Saudi Arabia's Minister of Oil, that all members should return to the old quota system, under a ceiling of 16m. b/d (which had been determined in October 1984, and which had remained in force until the end of 1985), except for Iraq, which would be free to go its own way. In effect, the proposal set a limit for the 12 members, excluding Iraq, of 14.8m. b/d. Opposition from the UAE and Ecuador, which both demanded a larger share, had still to be overcome. Kuwait insisted that any evidence of quota violations by even one member would release the others from any obligation. As commitments had already been made to buyers, the proposal, if approved, could not take effect until September. Moreover, at the insistence of Saudi Arabia, Kuwait, the UAE and Ecuador, the resolution adopted on 5 August stressed that 'this agreement is temporary and does not constitute a basis for any fair distribution of national quotas in any future negotiations thereon nor does it bear any prejudice on OPEC's appropriate and rightful production'. This qualification was enough to ensure that the next conference, in October, to decide on a definitive and permanent allocation of shares, would be a lengthy affair. Under the two-month interim pact the quotas (in millions of b/d) were as follows: Algeria 0.663, Ecuador 0.183, Gabon 0.137, Indonesia 1.189, Iran 2.300, Kuwait 0.999, Libya 0.999, Nigeria 1.300, Qatar 0.280, Saudi Arabia 4.353, UAE 0.950 and Venezuela 1.555; giving an OPEC total of nearly 17.1m. b/d during September and October, after taking into account estimated Iraqi production and 'war-relief crude' produced on its behalf from the Neutral Zone by Saudi Arabia and Kuwait, and assuming that the other 12 countries observed their quotas.

When the interim pact came into force the price of the UK's Brent blend had climbed to $14.45 per barrel. A significant boost to OPEC's attempts to stabilize the market was given by Norway, when the government there announced cuts in exports amounting to about 10% for November and December. Oman had previously showed solidarity with OPEC with a cut in output of 50,000 b/d and there was support for the interim agreement from some non-OPEC countries, including Mexico and Malaysia. The main threat to market stability came from within OPEC's own ranks, most seriously from the UAE. Dubai refused to contemplate any reduction in its output of about 380,000 b/d; while Abu Dhabi only trimmed its rate during September to 900,000 b/d, so that UAE production during that month was nearly 350,000 b/d above its quota. Ecuador and Gabon also exceeded their entitlements. Venezuela and Libya sold oil from stocks over and above their quotas which, they were to argue, related to production rather than exports. By the end of September Brent was selling at around $14 per barrel, having risen at one point to $16.

OPEC met again on 6 October with little scope for raising the production ceiling to satisfy the demands of some members for larger quotas. The majority were in favour of extending the two-month interim agreement until the end of the year. This was ruled out by Sheikh Yamani, who said a redistribution of quotas was 'absolutely essential'. The other matter to be settled was the GCC's insistence on the establishment of prices in a $17–$19 per barrel range. Some members, while not rejecting the objective, believed it better to concentrate on production control. The meeting proved to be the longest and most exhausting OPEC had ever held. Kuwait complicated and prolonged it by claiming a larger share of whatever production total was arrived at. In the past, it maintained, and especially at the time of the 1983 production pact, it had made bigger 'sacrifices' than any other member in accepting a lower share of the total production (5.6% under the existing formula). Kuwait wanted greater recognition for its substantial oil reserves, output capacity and historic production rate, in the form of a larger quota. There ensued lengthy discussions and argument over the proper criteria for determining the allocation of quotas. The deadlock was finally broken by a Saudi statement on 18 October that the Kingdom was willing, on two conditions, to adhere to its quota of 4.353m. b/d until the end of the year, 'in order to ease the obstacles facing' all members. The first condition was that minor upward adjustments in production should not total more than 200,000 b/d. The second was that 'the per barrel price should be set at not less than $18 and that everyone should adhere to this price'.

On 22 October agreement was reached on a complex formula under which a higher production ceiling for OPEC members (excluding Iraq) of 14.961m. b/d was set for November and one of 15.039m. b/d for December. The starting point for the calculation of quotas was the 16m. b/d ceiling set in Geneva in October 1984 (less the 1.2m. b/d then accorded Iraq). A 161,000 b/d overall increment was shared by the participating members in November. Kuwait was conceded the entire 78,000 b/d increase for December when the total was distributed thus (in millions of b/d): Algeria 0.669, Ecuador 0.221, Gabon 0.160, Indonesia 1.193, Iran 2.137, Kuwait 0.999, Libya 0.999, Nigeria 1.304, Qatar 0.300, Saudi Arabia 4.353, the UAE 0.950 and Venezuela 1.574.

On 31 October, King Fahd of Saudi Arabia dismissed Sheikh Yamani, who had been his Minister of Oil since March 1962. It is possible that he was a scapegoat for the financial consequences of OPEC's policy of recovering market share, regardless of the effect on prices. The ostensible reason for his dismissal, however, was his opposition to the King's demand for the immediate restoration of a fixed price of $18 or possibly $20 per barrel, and for a higher production quota for Saudi Arabia. Hisham Nazer, the Minister of Planning, and a known favourite of King Fahd, was appointed Acting Minister of Oil.

At Hisham Nazer's request, an emergency meeting of OPEC's pricing committee was convened in Quito, Ecuador, on 14 November. It urged 'a prompt return to the system of fixing officially the prices for OPEC, as the appropriate means to restore to the Organization its capacity for controlling the price structure and maintaining the necessary stability in the world oil market. The committee also recommended that a reference price of $18 should not be fixed solely on the basis of 34° API Arabian Light (which Saudi Arabia, as it had previously made known, did not want to be the 'marker' crude) but on a 'basket' of seven crudes—Arabian Light, Dubai (UAE), Minas (Indonesia), Bonny Light (Nigeria), Saharan Blend (Algeria), Tia Juana Light (Venezuela) and Isthmus (Mexico).

During November the market strengthened with Britain's Brent crude, which commanded a premium of some 60 US cents over the chosen OPEC basket, averaging $14.40 per barrel, compared with $13.70 in October. OPEC output in November averaged about 16.5m. b/d. With the exception of the UAE, the output of the other 11 members party to the latest production pact was within their collective quota.

OPEC met in Geneva on 11 December, for its sixth conference of 1986, a year in which members suffered a drastic decline in oil revenue. All members were in favour of the $18 per barrel price target set by King Fahd but the majority were convinced that a reduction in the ceiling of 5%–10% would be necessary to achieve it. Iraq rejected a Saudi proposal that it should be given a quota of 1.466m. b/d. Final agreement was delayed by the Iranian demand that Iraq's expulsion from OPEC should be considered, and that a resolution should be adopted giving Iraq two months in which to reverse its decision not to participate in production agreements. Both measures were successfully opposed by the Arab members. The Arab producers opposed any censure of Iraq.

The result of the conference was an accord amongst the 12 on a 4.7% reduction in the limit on collective production from 15.039m. b/d in December, to 14.334m. b/d for the first half of 1987. A theoretical quota of 1.466m. b/d was allocated to Iraq, giving a notional ceiling for OPEC as a whole of 15.8m. b/d. It was agreed that fixed prices should be imposed from 1 February. Differential prices were fixed for the 17 most

important crudes, apart from those in the basket, varying from $18.87 per barrel for Algeria's ultra-light Zarzaitine, to $16.67 for Kuwait's Export.

OPEC's new ceiling once again took into account certain factors which were becoming almost traditional: Iraq's refusal to participate in any production pact; the UAE's consistent violation of its quota; and the fact that, because of the Gulf conflict, Kuwait and Saudi Arabia refused to treat oil from the Neutral Zone produced on Iraq's behalf as contributing to their own output.

The cost of the 'price war'

Collective OPEC production in 1986, including NGLs, was 19.3m. b/d, compared with total consumption (outside the centrally planned economies of the Communist world) of 46.6m. b/d and supplies of 47.5m. b/d, according to IEA calculations. The discrepancy between consumption and supplies of 900,000 b/d was accounted for by the build-up of stocks largely caused by OPEC overproduction. Nevertheless, in terms of supply, OPEC increased its market share to 40.6%, compared with 37.7% in the previous year, thereby reversing the steady decline since 1979, when it was 61.7%. Non-OPEC supplies in 1986 were reckoned to be the same as in 1985, at 28.2m. b/d, with a 300,000 b/d decline in output by OECD member states, compensated for by a 300,000 b/d increase in net Communist (in practice Soviet) exports. Overall consumption rose by 1m. b/d, which could be partly attributed to lower oil prices, and a switch from other fuels as a result, rather than to economic growth. These somewhat bald statistics did not in any way highlight the one success of the 'price war' that could be identified. The damage to the high-cost US industry became apparent when US production figures were published. They showed that output had declined by 8.5% from 9.12m. b/d in 1985 to 8.34m. b/d in 1986. OPEC tended to claim sole responsibility for this decline. In May 1987 Peter Holmes, Chairman of Shell Transport and Trading Company, suggested that the price collapse of 1986 might have accounted for losses of 'perhaps as much as 500,000 b/d', but he added that exploration activity in the USA had declined 'catastrophically'.

The reason for the effective abandonment of OPEC's 'fair' market share strategy at the meeting on Brioni in June 1986, despite the fact that its two leading proponents (Saudi Arabia and Kuwait) were still cushioned by substantial, if diminishing, financial reserves, was that it was proving too costly. Prior to the Brioni meeting OPEC experts had estimated the overall annual loss of revenue by the 13 members at $50,000m.–$60,000m. Despite a strengthening of prices in the second half of 1986 actual losses were probably much greater. For instance, the Royal Dutch/Shell group later estimated that the value of collective OPEC oil exports fell from $133,000m. in 1985 to $75,000m. in 1986, despite the fact that output was up by about 12%, and exports, in volume terms, by about 16%.

OPEC's efforts to control prices and production during 1987

OPEC's performance under the new agreement of December 1986 was sufficiently impressive to boost the price of Brent to $17.55 per barrel at the end of March 1987, compared with an average of $16.20 during February. Before the OPEC conference in Vienna in June, however, collective output rose to 17.3m. b/d, significantly in excess of demand, and there were signs of growing indiscipline. The UAE and Qatar, in particular, flagrantly exceeded their quotas. The prospect of 500,000 b/d of extra Iraqi pipeline capacity becoming available in September (in fact, the new Kirkuk-Ceyhan (Turkey) pipeline became operational in July 1987) overshadowed the future.

At least, however, when OPEC met again in Vienna, from 25–27 June (its first meeting of the year), prices on the spot market were more or less in line with official selling rates. This was very much to the satisfaction of Saudi Arabia and Kuwait, whose policy had largely been oriented to making oil competitive with other fuels and, thereby, to ensuring a future demand for their abundant reserves. The so-called 'price hawks' (Iran, Algeria and Libya) were not so happy with the outcome because of their anxiety to see the $28 per barrel level (which had effectively been abandoned in December 1986) restored as soon as possible and production levels kept at 15.8m. b/d. The result of the Vienna conference was an agreement on raising the limit on OPEC output by 800,000 b/d to 16.6m. b/d for the rest of the year. (Iraq, once again, refused to participate in the agreement.) The higher ceiling, incorporating an overall rise of about 5%, gave new quotas (including a notional figure for Iraq) as follows (in millions of b/d, with the previous quotas in brackets): Algeria 0.667 (0.635); Ecuador 0.221 (0.210); Gabon 0.159 (0.152); Indonesia 1.190 (1.133); Iran 2.369 (2.255); Iraq 1.540 (1.466); Kuwait 0.996 (0.948); Libya 0.996 (0.948); Nigeria 1.301 (1.238); Qatar 0.299 (0.285); Saudi Arabia 4.343 (4.133); the UAE 0.948 (0.902); Venezuela 1.571 (1.495); total 16.600 (15.800). A committee, composed of the oil ministers of Indonesia, Nigeria and Venezuela, was asked to visit member countries 'in order to motivate them to comply with the terms of the agreement'—meaning, in effect, persuading or cajoling quota violators to stop exceeding their entitlements. In practice, of course, no one expected collective output to be contained within a 16.6m. b/d ceiling. The level was calculated to be significantly lower than actual demand to make allowance for Iraq's likely output and quota violations by other members.

In mid-1987 OPEC was able to derive some comfort from the marked reduction in stocks, which had been built up to an inordinately high level by members' overproduction in the autumn and summer of 1986. It appeared, too, as if prices on the spot market would continue to be buoyed up by tension in the Gulf arising from the prospect of a military confrontation between the USA and Iran. The US Administration insisted on proceeding, in the face of Congressional opposition, with its plan to protect Kuwaiti oil tankers reregistered under the American flag, in defence of the principle of freedom of shipping in international waters. In July it was reported that Iran, in what appeared to be a very ominous move, had finally begun to deploy Chinese-supplied *Silkworm* surface-to-sea missiles, with a range of 50 miles (80 km), in the vicinity of the Strait of Hormuz. It was also increasing its mine-laying operations around Kuwaiti coastal waters. Closure of the Strait of Hormuz would cut off supplies of more than one-third of OPEC output at its mid-1987 level, a shortfall which other members would be more than happy to make up.

Whilst a confrontation between the USA and Iran remained a matter of speculation, the Gulf conflict had made surprisingly little difference to the oil market, notwithstanding the sustained aggravation prompting Kuwait to seek assistance from the USSR, which chartered three supertankers to it, and then the USA.

In the face of repeated Iraqi air attacks (which were suspended for three weeks from 17 May when an Iraqi *Mirage* F-1 fighter plane mistakenly fired an *Exocet* missile at the *USS Stark*, killing 37 US sailors) Iran had managed to restore exports to the level of its OPEC quota by the spring of 1987. During 1986 Iraqi air raids had limited Iran's exports to little more than 1m. b/d. It was after Iraqi raids on the Iranian transhipment terminal at Sirri Island in August 1986 had reduced Iran's exports to 500,000 b/d (compared with 1.6m. b/d before) that Iran had begun its campaign of attacks against oil traffic to and from Kuwait. Kuwait was supporting Iraq financially in its war with Iran and selling oil on its behalf. What was probably a critical point in relation to the involvement of the superpowers in the Gulf and in prompting Kuwait's initial approach to the USA and the USSR came early in February 1987, when Lloyds of London announced that it was putting Kuwait on a par with Iraq and Iran with regard to insurance rates, charging a war premium of 3.75% of hull value on vessels using Kuwaiti ports, compared with 0.25% previously.

Iran criticized the Soviet decision to charter tankers to Kuwait (one of which struck a mine near the coast of Kuwait on 17 May—the same day as the *USS Stark* incident). On 29 April the Commander of the Iranian Navy warned that 'if there is any disruption in the movement of our ships and our imports and exports, this waterway would not be left open to any country. Subsequently, the Iranian Prime Minister proclaimed: 'everyone should know that we do not hesitate to make America's military presence in the region the target of

our crushing blows'. The Iranian threat to close the Strait of Hormuz, first made in the autumn of 1983, when it became known that Iraq was to receive *Exocet* missiles, was once again being taken seriously. As the US Navy prepared to escort the reregistered Kuwaiti vessels in mid-July, any repercussions on the oil market and producers of the region from the heightened tension and looming confrontation in the Gulf were largely imponderable. There was general confidence that official selling rates of around $18 per barrel could be maintained, though it was realized that any serious development in the Gulf could send spot-market prices soaring, even if only briefly. The dangers of an Iranian-American confrontation were heightened on 24 July when the 400,000-dwt Ultra-Large Crude Carrier *Bridgeton*, one of the reflagged vessels, hit a mine near Farsi Island, when travelling in the first convoy to be escorted by the US Navy. Apparently undeterred by the prospect of conflict with the USA, Iran threatened to strike Kuwaiti onshore and offshore oil facilities with surface-to-surface missiles, if it continued to support Iraq in the Gulf conflict. Tension remained at a high level as the crude carrier *Texaco Caribbean* struck a mine in the Gulf of Oman off the coast of Fujairah on 10 August and another was discovered off Farsi Island, halting the progress of the second US-escorted convoy. Britain and France announced that they were reinforcing their naval forces in the region with minesweepers. Italy dispatched naval units, including minesweepers, which the Netherlands and Belgium also decided to send.

Nevertheless, with the escorting operation quickly established, the Iranian leadership made it clear that it wished to avoid a direct clash. As tension was defused, oil prices fell (prompting the OPEC committee meetings in September). Ironically, Iran enjoyed a period of just over six weeks, during which its oil exports were totally unimpeded by the Iraqi Air Force. On 20 July the UN Security Council adopted Resolution No. 598, urging an immediate cease-fire and the withdrawal of forces to recognized pre-war international boundaries, and a negotiated end to all hostilities. Iraq accepted the resolution, and halted attacks against Iran's oil traffic and economic targets. It evidently did so under diplomatic pressure from the USA to the effect that the chances of a settlement could only be jeopardized by attacks on shipping. Iran's response to the resolution was ambivalent. It avoided outright rejection, not least because such a reaction could only encourage US-led moves towards international sanctions. Teheran insisted that the first priority was for an international tribunal to identify the original aggressor in the conflict. The USSR and China were both reluctant to support Western diplomatic efforts to impose an arms embargo against Iran, because of their concern about long-term relations with the Islamic Republic, which, they argued, should be given more time to comply with Resolution 598. Faced with what seemed to be Iranian temporizing, Iraqi patience wore thin. On 29 August it resumed attacks on vessels bound to and from Iranian ports within its declared maritime exclusion zone. There followed an unprecedented series of attacks, in which 17 vessels were damaged in a period of six days from 29 August to 3 September—eight by Iraq and seven by Iran. Iraq also resumed attacks on Iranian economic targets. As a result, Lloyds raised the war-risk premiums on the hulls of all vessels plying the waters of the Gulf by 50%.

The first direct clash in the Gulf itself between the USA and Iran came on 21 September when two US Navy helicopters attacked the Iranian vessel *Iran Ajr*, as it was laying mines in international waters. During September there was an intensification and a shift in direction as well. Of the 15 assaults mounted in September, 11 were on Saudi-directed traffic. Iraq stepped up its raids on Iranian oil traffic and in the most devastating attack yet, on 7 October, struck five chartered shuttle and storage tankers at the Larak Island export transhipment terminal, including the 256,263-dwt Cypriot-registered storage tanker *Shining Star*, and the 564,739-dwt *Seawise Giant*, the largest vessel in the world, both of which had to be written off as total losses. Iran came under more pressure as the US Navy sank three Iranian speedboats on the following day, alleging that they had fired on a US observation helicopter. On 15 October Iran fired two Chinese-manufactured *Silkworm* missiles from the Faw Peninsula, which it had occupied early in 1986, at the Liberian-registered, but US-owned, 275,932-dwt *Sungari* as it was waiting to load oil at Kuwait's Mina Ahmadi terminal. On the next day the US-flagged 81,283-dwt product carrier *Sea Island City*, was struck by a similar projectile off Kuwait's Shuaiba terminal. The US Navy's 'measured and appropriate response' was to destroy the two offshore oil platforms on the Rostam and Rakhsh oilfield, which it claimed were being used as bases from which to track and launch attacks against shipping. According to Iran, Rostam had been producing 20,000 b/d–25,000 b/d, and Rakhsh was being repaired having been bombed by Iraqi aircraft a year earlier. Iran retaliated on 22 October by firing another *Silkworm* missile at Kuwait's deep-water terminal at Sea Island. In practice Kuwait's capacity to export was not seriously affected—the main terminal at al-Ahmadi was out of range of the *Silkworm*.

Neither the USA nor Iran showed any inclination further to escalate hostilities. Iran's speedboat attacks increased but care was taken not to interfere with shipping escorted by US, west European or Soviet vessels. At the same time, Iraq intensified its raids on Iranian oil traffic with attacks taking an unprecedented toll during December. Over the year as a whole, the number of attacks increased by more than 50%. In 1987 there were 163 compared with 107 in 1986, 47 in 1985 and 71 in 1984, according to a report to the US Senate's Committee on Foreign Relations. Of the total, 76 were carried out by Iraq and 87 by Iran—a reversal of previous proportions.

The summit meeting of the Arab League held in Amman, Jordan, in November 1987, condemned Iran for its occupation of Iraqi territory, its negative attitude towards peace efforts, and the Mecca disturbances but refrained from recommending the severance of economic and diplomatic relations with Iran.

Iraqi military pressure on Iran's oil exports was the main factor cutting the volume of its actual production from something like 2.8m. b/d in August to 2m. b/d, or less, in October (when domestic consumption totalled an estimated 600,000 b/d). Another factor was the overwhelming vote in the US Congress banning imports of Iranian oil, which had reached 260,000 b/d in the January–August period. In August, France, in the midst of its diplomatic dispute with Iran, had taken a similar measure. The devastating raid on the Larak terminal was a particularly severe set-back. Early in November Lloyds List of London estimated that Iraqi air strikes had reduced the fleet of chartered tankers shuttling oil between Kharg and Larak island from 26 to 20, and the number actually owned by the Iranian National Tanker Company (INTC) from 12 to nine. The INTC was successful, however, in chartering six ultra large and very large crude carriers to ship oil from the Larak area for storage outside the war zone.

In the face of these difficulties Iran showed a resilience and flexibility in its selling arrangements which could only serve to undermine oil prices. Buyers were offered crude on a c.i.f., rather than an f.o.b., basis, delivered from floating storage near the major marketing areas. It offered Japanese customers discounts, which were the equivalent of $1 per barrel, based on spot-market rates for Oman and Dubai crude, in its attempts to sell an increasing volume of 'distress cargoes'. By mid-November it was estimated that there were as many as 20m. barrels of unsold Iranian crude in storage, mainly at Rotterdam, and another 14m. barrels at sea. The market was becoming awash with excess supplies from other producers, too. By December OPEC production was running at about 19m. b/d. The growing surplus had an inevitable impact on price levels. They slid ominously during November when the spot rate for the Brent blend fell to $17.37 in mid-month and was consistently below $18 throughout the month. As OPEC prepared for its end-of-year ministerial conference, it was clear that the price structure was coming under grave strain, largely as a result of the accumulated stresses of the Gulf conflict.

The meeting started amidst considerable despondency and scepticism as to what OPEC could and should do to stop the downward drift of prices from the $18 per barrel target, which had been set over a year before. Only six months before the issue had been whether OPEC could or should raise the reference price to a level higher than $18 per barrel. In general terms, the prospects for a successful meeting were blighted by deteriorating relations between Iran and Saudi Arabia,

which would almost certainly make impossible the kind of compromises reached in August and December 1986, as well as June 1987. On the question of production OPEC was still divided between the 'hawks', seeking a lowering of the ceiling, and the Arab producers of the Gulf, who expressed confidence that demand could accommodate a higher limit. The OPEC Secretariat's assessment of future oil requirements was the most optimistic, with demand for members' crude in the second half of 1988 (assuming no change in the level of stocks) calculated at 18.4m. b/d. The minority on the Economic Commission Board (essentially the Arab states of the Gulf) estimated the requirement at 18.2m. b/d (assuming no change in stocks), while the majority put it at 17.6m. b/d (after a stock reduction of 300,000 b/d). The most pessimistic of the forecasts was almost identical to that of the IEA and closely in line with those of most major oil companies. True to form, Iran, at the outset, called for an increase in the reference price of at least $2.70 ($2.18 to compensate for the fall in the value of the dollar and 52 cents for inflation). The ritualistic demand received little sympathy from even the traditional 'price hawks' who fully appreciated that the burning priority was production restraint. On this front also Iran created initial turmoil and a fall in spot-market prices by threatening to opt out of any production pact that was agreed. That raised the possibility of only 11 of the 13 members subscribing to an agreement or, more intriguingly, of Iraq becoming party to an agreement while Iran excluded itself. In the run-up to the meeting Iraq had repeated its offer to participate in a production pact if it were given quota-parity with Iran, (i.e. a quota of 2.369m. b/d, compared with its notional quota of 1.54m. b/d). Such an arrangement would have set a more realistic upper limit on collective production of 15.89m. b/d; increasing the possibility that a market price of above $18 per barrel could be achieved if all members honoured their commitments. Moreover, as Iraq's sustained attacks on its enemy's oil exports effectively limited Iran's production to 2.37m. b/d, an arrangement under which Iraq produced as much as Iran would actually have significantly lowered Iraq's output which, Baghdad had boasted, had reached no less than 2.83m. b/d in November, with the advantage of new pipeline capacity. As it was, Iraq's sincerity was never put to the test—Iran, once again, rejected outright the concept of parity. There was also vehement opposition from Venezuela which was not prepared to see any diminution of its percentage share. The only possible outcome of the meeting was a 'roll-over' (continuation) of the output sharing accord concluded in the previous June. Despite Iranian reluctance, the accord was renewed and the existing quotas of the 12 remained in force. The only difference was that any pretence about Iraq having a notional allocation was abandoned. The five-member ministerial committee on price monitoring was again empowered to call an extraordinary conference to restore stability if 'there was any significant change in market prices'.

At the December meeting OPEC seriously addressed the problem of over-production, to the extent that it rehired KHG-Klynveld-Kraayenhof, the Dutch auditing firm, to monitor members' production and exports. It had originally been appointed to undertake this task at the end of 1984, when its efforts were obstructed by several countries. At its second attempt, it was assured of better collaboration and it was agreed that the auditors would send teams to all member states simultaneously, to preclude prevarication. The UAE inevitably found itself cast in the role of principal quota violator. In the late summer its output had risen to a peak estimated at 1.9m. b/d (compared with a quota of 948,000 b/d), 1.5m. b/d accounted for by Abu Dhabi and 400,000 b/d by Dubai (which was beyond the purview of OPEC, anyway, because of the peculiar nature of the federation). UAE output subsequently fell to 1.6m.–1.7m. b/d in November and December. After the December meeting, Abu Dhabi felt sufficiently chastened to order its operating companies to cut back by about 350,000 b/d, which effectively reduced the UAE's output to 900,000 b/d for a while. Sheikh Ali al-Khalifa as-Sabah, Kuwait's Minister of Oil, acknowledged that his country had been producing at a rate of 100,000–150,000 b/d above its quota. He attributed the excess to Iranian attacks against its oil tankers and the need to build up inventories outside the Gulf, as well as to its frustration with quota breaches by other members. Only after the meeting did it emerge that Saudi Arabia and Kuwait had agreed to resume supplies of 'war-relief crude' to Iraq at the full rate of 310,000 b/d.

According to revised calculations by the IEA, OPEC production had run at 18.9m. b/d during the last quarter of 1987. In the first half of 1988, it was clear, the price levels would not only depend on greater production discipline but also on the rate at which stocks were drawn down. The assumption was that they could come under heavy pressure in the second quarter of the year. Overall, however, there was optimism that demand for OPEC crude would rise in 1988. For instance, the Kuwaiti Minister of Oil predicted that over the year as a whole demand would be between 18.5m. b/d and 19m. b/d.

OPEC reaffirmed official selling prices based on the $18 reference level, but it was, in reality, on the verge of abandoning any real pretence or effort at maintaining them. The emphasis had switched decisively towards concentration on output control which, if effectively applied, would keep prices around $18 per barrel. Some producers—Iran, Iraq and Qatar—were already negotiating rates with their customers which were wholly and unashamedly market-related. A proportion of UAE output was priced in the same way, apart from the preferential treatment given to its equity partners. At their annual summit in Riyadh, on 26–29 December, the Heads of State of the GCC (Saudi Arabia, Kuwait, the UAE, Oman, Bahrain and Qatar) called on all OPEC members to abide by official prices. The ring of hollow hypocrisy about the appeal was confirmed shortly afterwards when it emerged that Saudi Arabia had been offering preferential prices to its four old US partners in the Aramco operation (Exxon, Mobil, Texaco, and Chevron) since the late summer. It conceded similar terms, based on spot rates for Dubai and Oman crude, to smaller US customers, and Japanese companies were demanding similar terms. By the end of March, Saudi Arabia was offering the market-related price formula to all contract volumes of 100,000 b/d. Other Gulf producers had no choice but to sell to US customers on a 'delivered' basis, linked to prices of Alaskan crude. From the beginning of January they met dogged resistance from Japanese customers, who were well cushioned by stocks, and were forced to give ground. By the spring, even Indonesia was selling to the Japanese at $1.56 below official prices. The respected Dr Fadhil ash-Shalabi, OPEC's Acting Secretary-General since 1982, publicly recognized in mid-March that the Organization was fighting a losing battle in trying to maintain official prices. He told the Arab Energy Conference in Baghdad that OPEC should revert to a system under which prices were allowed to fluctuate within a specified target range, using market-related formulae to sell quotas. The production ceiling would be lowered when rates fell within the agreed margin and raised when they exceeded it.

1988—no progress on prices or production

During January OPEC output dropped to about 17m. b/d. At the end of the month the spot rate for Brent blend had fallen to $16.25 per barrel, compared with $17.95 at the beginning. By the end of February Brent had dropped to only $14.77, despite the fact that collective production had averaged only 17.4m. b/d, with an estimated 500,000 b/d of Saudi Arabia's shipments and 300,000 b/d of Iran's in onshore storage overseas or in tankers. Throughout March the market remained weak, with the spot rate for North Sea crude dropping to a low point of $13.80 per barrel early in the month but recovering to $15.79 by its close. Over the first quarter, OPEC crude production averaged a modest 17.5m. b/d (well within the 15.06m. b/d ceiling after taking into account Iraq and oil production from the Neutral Zone sold on Iraq's behalf), as commercial stocks in the industrial world were drawn down at the rate of 1.9m. b/d, according to IEA calculations. After a hiatus at the turn of the year, when Syria attempted, unsuccessfully, to initiate a dialogue between Iran and the conservative Arab regimes of the Gulf, Iraq resumed attacks on Iranian oil and economic targets, while Iran retaliated against shipping on the Arab side of the Gulf. The new wave of attacks did not compare in intensity with the hostilities in the

October–December period and, during the first quarter of 1988, the Gulf conflict was largely irrelevant to the oil market and, certainly, no salvation for prices. Indeed, it was indicative of the easing of tension that, early in February, Lloyds committee for rating war risk reduced premiums for oil and gas cargoes to and from Kuwait, Saudi Arabia, Bahrain and the UAE from 0.75% of hull value to 0.45%, and for other merchandise from 0.45% to 0.375%. The rate for all shipments to the Iranian port of Bandar Abbas was cut from 0.45% to 0.375%.

Despite a very 'significant change in market prices' in the early part of the year, it was not until 19 April that OPEC's price-monitoring committee met in Vienna. It did so mainly in response to an initiative by a group of non-member producers, Angola, the People's Republic of China, Egypt, Malaysia, Mexico and Oman. Mexico had indicated that the group would be prepared to cut its exports by 5% (equivalent to 183,000 b/d—including exports by Colombia, which took part in the group's preliminary discussions but which was not represented in the approach to OPEC) in return for a comparable reduction by OPEC. Mexico's Secretary of State for Energy, Mines and State Industries emphasized that collaboration would have to be 'a long-term endeavour', the 'beginning of a new stage of co-operation'. Prior to the meeting of the committee Saudi Arabia did little to disguise its lack of enthusiasm for any such collaboration. Nevertheless, King Fahd took the opportunity to reaffirm his country's commitment to a price of $18 per barrel and at the same time attributed the weakness of prices in the market to discounts offered by other members, while denying that Saudi Arabia was offering any itself. Of the countries represented on the committee, Nigeria and Indonesia were reluctant to call a full ministerial emergency meeting in advance of the biannual ordinary conference, which was scheduled for June. Venezuela and Algeria, however, were strongly in favour of one. They were supported by Iran, which, though not represented on the committee, sent Hossain Ardebili, its Deputy Minister of Oil. His intervention was probably crucial. Surprisingly, Hisham Nazer, Saudi Arabia's Minister of Oil, consented to a full consultative meeting (which would automatically become an extraordinary conference if any decision was taken) and a joint session with the non-OPEC ('NOPEC', as it was dubbed by the media) group immediately after it. Agreement was only reached after an intensive exchange between Arturo Hernandez Grisanti, Venezuela's Minister of Energy and Mines, and Hisham Nazer. Mr Hernandez accused Saudi Arabia of secretly aiming at a price of $15 per barrel, and was sharply critical of the price discounts that the Kingdom was known to be giving. Their confrontation was to set the scene for one of the most bitter OPEC conferences ever at the end of April. Before, it was convened, however, the chances for a reasonably amicable compromise were badly impaired by a further deterioration in relations between Saudi Arabia and Iran leading to the former severing diplomatic links on 26 April.

On the eve of the OPEC consultative conference, which began on 28 April, the proposal by six 'NOPEC' countries for a joint output reduction initiative with OPEC, received a polite but non-committal response from an OPEC ministerial committee. The 'NOPEC' delegation departed, leaving a senior Omani official to liaise with them on the outcome of the OPEC meeting. This, probably, was a tactical mistake, because it relieved OPEC members of any immediate pressure to reach a decision. The likelihood of an accord between the two groups was not great. Most OPEC members had been thinking in terms of matching barrel-for-barrel cuts, rather than of a reduction on the basis of a common percentage of total exports. (Saudi Arabia and Kuwait were known to have grave reservations about any lowering of the disrespected 15.06m. b/d ceiling.) On the second day of the conference, Algeria proposed that OPEC should respond to the 'NOPEC' proposal with an offer of a 300,000 b/d reduction (i.e. about 2.5% of current collective OPEC exports, compared with the 5% sought by the 'NOPEC' group), as a compromise. It was supported by seven other members leaving the Arab producers of the Gulf in a minority. Saudi Arabia produced a counter-proposal, to the effect that OPEC should match the non-members on a 183,000 b/d barrel-for-barrel basis but that the cut should be divided into 12 equal parts amongst the 12 members of the current production agreement. Hisham Nazer, the Saudi Oil Minister, defended the principle of equal distribution, according to which small producers like Gabon and Ecuador would have had to accept a disproportionately large reduction in their output, by saying that they should be made aware of what cutting back really meant. The proposal elicited more astonishment than support. The division of opinion over the 'NOPEC' offer remained, and the most that could be decided before the meeting ended on 2 May was to maintain contact with the group, with the aim of establishing the basis for long-term collaboration.

Prices dropped sharply in the aftermath of the meeting, with the Brent blend falling by 50 cents per barrel. At the same time OPEC was confronted with new, and potentially divisive issues relating to definitions of production. They were raised by Sheikh Ali al-Khalifa, the Kuwaiti chief delegate, largely as a result of the difficulties encountered by the Dutch auditing firm which had been re-engaged at the conference in December 1988. The most contentious issue concerned the definition of condensates, also known as NGL's, or gas which liquefies at the surface after being treated. KHG-Klynveld-Kraayenhof's study of the records of various member countries showed that, over the years, some of them had reclassified crude as condensates, production of which had been covered by none of OPEC's accords on output sharing. In retrospect, their exclusion was generally regarded as a mistake within OPEC but not one which could be rectified in the foreseeable future.

On the question of the reclassification of crude as condensates, Sheikh Ali al-Khalifa's attack was mostly directed at Venezuela. According to official figures published by the state oil corporation, Petróleos de Venezuela, Venezuela's output of condensates had increased from 17,000 b/d in 1982, to 142,000 b/d in 1987. Moreover, it was planned to increase to 190,000 b/d in 1988. Production of condensates by other members like Indonesia and Nigeria had also risen significantly. The auditors said in their report that Venezuela had defined condensates as NGLs with the American Petroleum Institute (API) gravity of 40.2° and above—an assertion which the Venezuelan delegation rejected. For their part, the auditors proposed defining condensates as all 'natural gas liquids and hydrocarbons with an API of 47° or higher, obtained from lease separators and field facilities when these are measured separately from crude oil'. Sheikh Ali al-Khalifa pointed out that a number of important crude streams produced by member states were lighter than 40.20° API gravity, and that such a definition could put as much as 2m. b/d of OPEC supply outside the ambit of the production sharing system. Evidence was also produced that some members were excluding from their quotas so-called 'own use' oil, which was accounted for by industrial operations including refining. Sheikh Ali al-Khalifa calculated that, if such crude was excluded from quotas, it could add another 500,000 b/d–700,000 b/d to overall production. A special committee of experts was charged with drawing up a report on the problem of definition prior to the next OPEC ordinary ministerial conference in June.

OPEC's crude output was reckoned to have risen above 18.5m. b/d in May, compared with the modest 17.5m. b/d in the second quarter. From 11 to 16 May Iraq launched a punishing series of raids on Iran's Larak Island transhipment centre, hitting seven vessels, including the *Seawise Giant*, which was severely damaged again. But the raids did nothing to prevent the passage of the large volume of Iranian crude on the water in transit. Abu Dhabi apparently trimmed its allowable production by about 150,000 b/d in mid-May. In practice, however, making allowance for Iraq and production from the Neutral Zone, OPEC's rate of output was still some 500,000 b/d above the stipulated ceiling. In the circumstances a decision to roll-over the current agreement on quotas seemed to be a foregone conclusion. The pact seemed less tenable than ever, however, after Dr Mana bin Said al-Oteiba, the UAE Minister of Petroleum, walked out of the OPEC conference in Vienna on the second evening and flew to Rabat, Morocco, apparently to see his Head of State and the Ruler of Abu Dhabi, President Zaid. There he publicly repudiated the federation's quota of 948,000 b/d, saying that it could no longer accept so little. In a sense, his statement merely formalized the UAE's

consistent violation of its allocation, which it had exceeded by 50% or more. Whilst disagreeing on forecasts for demand in the second half of 1988, Saudi Arabia and Kuwait threatened to flood the market with more than 1m. b/d of oil equivalent (in the form of condensates), unless the Organization agreed in December on precise technical definitions to distinguish between condensates and crude. Prior to the conference, at the experts' meeting, Venezuela had made a vigorous effort to convince other members that condensates could only be defined by certain reservoir characteristics and that neither specific gravity nor oil gas ratios should be the criteria. The majority seemed to believe that 'user oil' should be included in production. As long as members' behaviour was consistent, that question seemed relatively easy to solve. However, it looked as though the dispute over condensates would continue to be a far more contentious issue. After the conference, Sheikh Ali al-Khalifa said that any definition of what constituted condensates would have to be easily applicable and one which auditors could easily understand—suggesting that it would have to be fairly arbitrary in terms of its prescribed gravity. There was general recognition that the problem of Iraq's exclusion from the production-sharing system had to be dealt with but no progress was made towards solving it. Also, Saudi Arabia and Kuwait remained adamant that the 310,000 b/d, mostly from the Neutral Zone, which they were 'lending' to Iraq was (Iraq's) part of its quota, to be repaid at some future date, and that production from the territory as a whole was outside the pact.

In July, in the wake of the June conference, prices fell to around $14 per barrel, and, with stocks high, looked as though they would weaken further in the third quarter. Having failed to make positive progress towards (or even achieved a consensus in favour of) a collaborative production programme with the 'NOPEC' group, which might have stabilized prices, OPEC's $18 target seemed something of a chimera in mid-1988.

The acceptance, in July, by Iraq and Iran of UN cease-fire terms opened up new prospects for OPEC to take a firmer grip on oil supply. Iraq's freedom, for many years, to produce oil unconstrained by quota had been a major irritant to other oil exporters, in that it provided a precedent for over-production. However, the prospects of peace also changed other policy attitudes among Iraq's neighbours, suggesting that there was now a possibility of a lasting OPEC accord and of meetings which would resolutely tackle the other issues which previous agreements had avoided. Iraq's self-exemption from quota curbs was not, however, the only obstacle to a production agreement to support prices.

Saudi Arabia, the world's largest oil exporter, whose support was crucial to the success of any agreement to regulate supply, had previously tended to temporize when other governments suggested that OPEC ministers should meet to suggest ways of reversing the price slide to an extraordinary conference of the whole group. Saudi Arabia disapproved of such meetings which tended, unfairly, in the view of its officials, to place the onus for restoring price stability on Saudi Arabia. The Saudi view was that it was the over-production of other countries, mainly in the Arab Gulf, that was causing price weakness. Meetings of ministers simply focused international attention on Saudi Arabia's political weakness by highlighting its inability to persuade its smaller neighbours to observe OPEC discipline. Saudi Arabia's fear was that it would be asked, in effect, to sacrifice production to other exporters, both inside and outside the Middle East, in order to support prices. Its refusal to do so was based on its experience, in mid-1985, of being forced to cut its production to less than half of its official quota level while other producers continued to ignore quotas. However, as the cease-fire became a reality in July, Saudi Arabia reversed its opposition to an emergency meeting of OPEC's five-minister Pricing Committee, the group charged with convening the 13-nation conference if market prices were deviating too far from the official target. If Saudi Arabia, unlike other exporters, had been prepared to allow prices to slide rather than be put on a political spot, its ability to make up per barrel revenue losses with large scale over-production was an option not open to many oil exporters. The threat of 'flooding' oil markets, with gains in volume compensating for price losses, was one that Saudi Arabia had used before, notably in 1986, and is a constant factor in oil politics.

With Saudi Arabia's agreement, five oil ministers met in Lausanne on 3 August. They were realistic enough to recognize there was little they could do until Iran and Iraq had begun to tackle directly the question of prisoners of war and the other outstanding issues which divided them. It was agreed that the Secretary General of OPEC, the former Indonesian Minister of Oil, Dr Subroto, should try to act as an intermediary in an attempt to either persuade Iraq to relinquish its arbitrary demand for quota parity with Iran; or to press Iran to accept Iraq's claims in the interests of achieving a 13-nation agreement. The Lausanne session, despite the scepticism of market operators and some ministers, was ultimately to prove important in setting a politically realistic agenda for the 'reconstruction' of OPEC.

Saudi Arabian and Kuwaiti political and financial support for Iraq's war-effort also raised new difficulties for the oil-exporting countries. Iraq argued that the war with Iran had been fought not only for the sake of Iraq itself, but had also been important in maintaining the political, social and religious status quo in the face of Iran's destabilizing Islamic fundamentalism. If Iraq had failed to overcome or, at least, contain Iran, how long would it have been before Iran came to dominate the conservative Sheikhdoms of the Gulf? Along with direct financial support, Saudi Arabia and Kuwait agreed to 'lend' Iraq up to 330,000 b/d of oil exports from the shared Neutral Zone. In one respect, this was in response to justified Iraqi claims that it had lost longstanding and loyal crude oil customers when Iran destroyed its Gulf export facility at Fao in 1981. Saudi Arabia and Kuwait had prevailed upon other OPEC members to change the way quota production was defined and measured in such a way that crude oil exports 'loaned' to another country were attributed to the 'production' of the recipient. In this way, Saudi Arabia and Kuwait, which had already made the largest sacrifices, in both volume and percentage terms, to support falling oil prices, were able to produce their Neutral-Zone contribution to Iraq outside of their own allocations. Other OPEC members felt, with some justice, that their sales were being correspondingly reduced to balance finite demand, making them involuntary financial and political supporters of Iraq in its war with Iran. That situation was uncomfortable enough while Iraq was itself constrained by a quota. But in 1986, when OPEC reversed its market-share policy and reimposed quotas, Iraq refused to accept the quota allotted to it. This meant that the Neutral-Zone production of Saudi Arabia and Kuwait was now being attributed to no OPEC member at all. Iran, Algeria and Libya, the traditional supporters of high prices and lower OPEC production, were outraged and gained the support of traditional moderates in accusing Kuwait and Saudi Arabia of adding to the market glut at a time when Iraq was not only producing more than its official quota, but even more than it was claiming as its rightful share.

This issue was also recognized in Lausanne as an important impediment to an overall production agreement. However, the five-minister Pricing Committee also demonstrated again that the Iran-Iraq conflict, together with the related Neutral Zone issue, was not the only regional problem impeding oil-exporter unity. The longstanding issue of over-production by the UAE dominated the discussions at the Lausanne meeting. It had fallen to Dr Subroto to visit the President of the UAE, Sheikh Zayed, on behalf of OPEC, to seek assurances that the UAE would abide by the quota agreement which its Minister of Oil, Dr Mana Otaiba, had signed only weeks earlier. Market operators were as sceptical in public, as illustrated by a sharp drop in prices the day after the ministers had met, as other ministers were in private about the assurances that the UAE would always 'endeavour' to act in the best interests of OPEC as a whole. This lay oddly with the UAE's claim that its quota should be 1.5m. b/d, or more than 50% higher than that assigned by the rest of the group. While both Dr Subroto and the President of OPEC, the Nigerian Minister of Oil, Rilwanu Lukman, had to pretend to believe that the UAE would, in future, curtail output to the agreed level, the contradiction

between its claim for a 1.5m. b/d quota and its assurances of co-operation, damaged market confidence.

The failure of the UAE to adhere to its quota was a mystery to many observers, since the UAE had one of the highest per capita oil incomes in the world. The origins of this failure lay in the fluctuating and uncertain relationship between Abu Dhabi and Dubai, the two leading Sheikhdoms in the federation, and in Dubai's refusal to accept federal (i.e. Abu Dhabi's) control over its oil policies and revenues. Dubai's adoption of an independent pricing policy had enabled it to maintain production at close to its 400,000 b/d capacity; Abu Dhabi had been put in the position of 'UAE swing producer'. This meant, in effect, that Abu Dhabi would have had to cut its production to the low level of 500,000 b/d, or less, in order to maintain the federation's output at its officially agreed level. This would have posed severe technical problems for its oilfield operators, which could have been overcome, had it not been for the financial contribution that Abu Dhabi was committed to making to the federal budget. With the relationship between individual rulers always uneasy, Abu Dhabi had in effect refused to cut its production to a level less than double that of Dubai, and, often, it had produced significantly more than that. The fault, as far as OPEC and its attempts to regulate production were concerned, lay with the decision to convert Abu Dhabi's 1967 membership to cover the whole of the UAE. The simple fact was that the Abu Dhabi and federal ministries had virtually no influence on Dubai's oil policy, making any quota for the UAE applicable only in theory. Whatever the historical background, the intra-emirate rivalry also provided a convenient excuse for Abu Dhabi to increase its revenue through bigger sales.

As prices continued to slide towards $10 a barrel (and below for some heavier Middle Eastern crude oils) ministers and Heads of State were in regular contact. However, with Iran and Iraq still unable to agree on quotas, as well as on territorial and other war-related issues, OPEC's Middle Eastern members increasingly took matters into their own hands and started to push up their production to compensate for lower prices, which were therefore subjected to further pressure. The UAE, Kuwait and lastly Saudi Arabia increased their exports, especially to the USA where Iraq had significantly increased its sales.

On 25 September the same five oil ministers who had met in Lausanne met in Madrid. Their decision to reconstitute OPEC's Long-Term Strategy Committee led to the addition to OPEC's steering group of three crucial Middle Eastern oil exporters: Iran, Iraq and Kuwait. Their statement, that a review of objectives and strategies in the context of current circumstances, '*especially concerning the price of oil and the production mechanism to support it*' was necessary, was a clear warning to all oil exporters that OPEC would either have to tackle outstanding issues, or give up all attempts to control prices and production. The meeting of the wider group was seen as a necessary precursor to a full OPEC conference which would end the isolation of Iraq. Meanwhile, throughout October, Saudi Arabia, the UAE and Kuwait continued to boost output, as did other exporters, until the group was producing at levels as high as or even higher than they were at the peak of the 1986 price war. Saudi Arabia was demonstrating its unwillingness to carry the burden of price support at a time when other exporters were ignoring their obligations and showing that it could, unlike most other exporters, compensate in full, by higher sales, for any loss in revenue caused by lower prices.

With OPEC's 8-minister Pricing and Long-Term Strategy Committees due to meet again in Madrid on 20 October, the Arab Gulf countries grouped in the GCC (which included non-OPEC states) made their position clear when their oil ministers broke with their normal practice of steering clear of OPEC disputes. They issued a communiqué, in which they stated that their participation in a new production agreement for 1989 would be conditional on the 12 countries returning to and adhering to the agreed quotas which had been ignored since June, with the exception of Iraq, which would be given parity with Iran at 2.369m. b/d. The second, enlarged Madrid session on 20–22 October failed to overcome Iranian resistance to quota parity with Iraq, while Iraq remained adamant that it would accept nothing less than that. By the end of October, OPEC production had soared to over 22m. b/d, far in excess of what most analysts believed the market could absorb. The Gulf Arab states increased their production markedly and made it clear that they would not adhere to their official quotas unless there was total discipline. However, although prices were weak, they did not fall to the $5 per barrel level that some feared. The Madrid session was adjourned, rather than abandoned, until mid-November, when the full OPEC conference was due to assemble in Vienna. This reinforced the hope in the commercial oil industry that OPEC would, under pressure, find a solution. The result was that crude oil looked 'cheap' and was bought on that basis. More significantly, consumer demand for oil was increasing.

When the Long-Term Strategy Committee reassembled in Vienna on 17 November, there were signs that Iran had adopted a more flexible approach. A crucial consideration, both for Iran and for the other Middle Eastern countries which were anxious to reach an agreement, was the knowledge that Iraq had already commenced major pipeline expansion schemes across Saudi Arabia into the Red Sea and was repairing its Gulf export facilities which had been destroyed in the War. Unless Iraq agreed to adhere to its quota, it would be in the position to supply all of the likely increase in world demand for OPEC crude oil over the coming year and was likely to supply it anyway, if growth in demand declined, at the expense of other exporters' market share. The choice appeared to be simple: Iraq's demand for a quota of about 2.5m. b/d would have to be met, or Iraq would undermine the market for all other exporters with production of around 4m. b/d within the coming year. It required ten days of tortuous negotiations to overcome the political problems that such a deal gave rise to within the faction-riven Iranian Government, and even so political sensitivities prevailed over economic sense in the agreement that was finally concluded. In resisting Iraq's demand for quota parity, Iran justified its stance by arguing that it would not relinquish its market share and insisted on retaining the same percentage of total allocations which it had been granted prior to 1986, when Iraq had last officially accepted an OPEC quota. Iranian delegates invited other OPEC members, notably Iraq's supporters in the Middle East, to sacrifice market share to Iraq if they so wished. The ploy was a subtle one. In the distribution that resulted, Iran's quota was 125,000 b/d higher than it would have been under the distribution proposed by the GCC. Iraq was granted the same amount while the other 11 members of OPEC sacrificed pro-rata 250,000 b/d out of the 18.5m. b/d ceiling agreed for the first half of 1989. Iran's Minister of Oil, Gholamreza Aqazadeh, who had sworn he would never sign an accord giving Iraq quota parity, flew home to consult his government colleagues, leaving a deputy to sign the OPEC resolution. Even then, the agreement almost collapsed at the eleventh hour when the Saudi Arabian Minister of Oil, Hisham Nazer, insisted that a 'floor price' of $15 should be incorporated into the agreement. Suspicions, unfounded in 1988, but deriving from the price collapse of 1986, that Saudi Arabia actually wanted a lower price, led to opposition to this move, which Saudi Arabia believed would boost the market, even though it was unclear which producers would join Saudi Arabia in curtailing supplies if prices threatened to fall through the agreed 'floor-level'.

Very high production in November and December, after the OPEC agreement had been signed, but before the new 18.5m. b/d ceiling took effect, underlined that most exporters intended to abide by the letter of the agreement. Saudi Arabia increased production to 6m. b/d, the UAE produced more than double its allocation of 948,000 b/d and Kuwait, too, showed that it could easily produce and export up to 2m. b/d. In the final weeks of 1988, production reached 23m. b/d, 4.5m. above the ceiling agreed for the first six months of 1989, and 6m.–7m. b/d in excess of the ceiling then officially still in force. It was feared that the rush to export ahead of the 1 January deadline would place huge stock in the hands of consumers, which they would draw upon in early 1989 in order to subject prices and sales to further pressure.

An 'audit' of each member's production, internal consumption and exports was agreed to buttress the agreement for the first six months of 1989, to be conducted once a month by officials from each of the 13 OPEC member states. However, it quickly became evident, as members claimed each month to have hit production and export targets almost to the barrel, that information was regarded as a tool to justify national policy stances, and not as the means of regulating the market which some had hoped for. The UAE, whose long-standing over-production was well-known, declined to supply monthly data and sent no representatives to the agreed monthly meetings of experts. Its production did, however, decline sharply from the 23m. b/d peak of December. This fact, rather than continued 'cheating', became the focus of market attention. As it became clear that the demand for oil had surged ahead in late 1988 and was continuing to do so, oil prices strengthened to a level close to and, in some cases, above the official $18 per barrel target price.

In the first three months of 1989, OPEC and world oil markets received a morale booster from the activities of a loose collection of other exporters, in which Oman, a member of the GCC of Arab exporters, played a prominent role. Since 1986, Saudi Arabia and Kuwait had led an OPEC campaign for non-member oil-exporting countries to share the burden of market stabilization, and to curtail their growing, capacity-level production. Since 1983, the growing production and exports of non-OPEC members had been perceived as a major threat to price stability, with the pricing and production policy of the UK viewed as a major problem. With its high profile in world markets due to its transparent pricing, North Sea oil had posed a particular problem for Nigeria, one of OPEC's poorest members, with whose crude exports British and Norwegian supplies competed directly both in terms of quality and location. Attempts at political persuasion failed and the price war of 1986 was regarded as a means of forcing the British Government to abandon its inflexible stance with regard to oil production levels. However, the British Government refused to do so, despite the huge loss of government revenues and the damaging impact on the UK's balance of payments. However, Mexico agreed to reduce its exports by 5% and Norway reduced its planned increases by limiting output to 92.5% of its rising capacity. A meeting between non-OPEC ministers and the OPEC conference had failed in 1986, at the height of the crisis, to produce anything more than positive words. By 1988, when OPEC had managed to boost prices somewhat through its own efforts, an offer by non-OPEC ministers to reduce their exports by 5%, if OPEC members did likewise, was rebuffed by Saudi Arabia and Kuwait, since they felt that they had already reduced their production sufficiently.

On 27 January, representatives of 13 non-OPEC oil exporters met with counterparts from six OPEC nations to indicate their willingness to support OPEC's efforts to stabilize prices. Saudi Arabia insisted that OPEC, by setting a ceiling of 18.5m. b/d for the first-half of 1989, had taken an important first step which should be matched by the non-members. Like many analysts, Saudi Arabian officials were sceptical about reports that demand for oil was rising rapidly, and they were deeply concerned about the possibility that prices would decline drastically in the traditionally weak April–June quarter. After a second meeting in London in late February, the non-OPEC governments announced that they would reduce exports by 5% (or freeze them at 5% below planned levels) for the April–June period at least. Although Mexico had initially played a major role in organizing the non-OPEC group, it was two countries from the Middle East and North Africa region, albeit with very different structures, that now played a major political role. Oman convened and chaired the first session, while the second was hosted by Egypt.

Market confidence that OPEC had solved the problems of its troublesome Middle Eastern and North African members was shaken when its eight-minister Price-Monitoring Committee met in late March, ostensibly to review how closely the membership had adhered to the agreement signed in November. Kuwait dramatically announced its intention of seeking a higher market-share for itself, the UAE and for the three smallest exporters, Gabon, Ecuador and Qatar. However, prices remained steady during April as supplies were reduced and demand continued to rise. In May, however, markets began to react to the disputes that were dividing traditional allies, and weaker prices led to a long, tense OPEC conference in early June.

When oil ministers reassembled on 1 June 1989, many were unable to believe that Kuwait would insist on a quota increase larger than the 5%–8% increase in the OPEC total which was under discussion for the second-half of the year. However, they failed to take account of Kuwait's situation in early 1989, which was unique within OPEC. In percentage terms, it had made greater production sacrifices during the 1980s than any other OPEC member, despite having less financial interest than others in maintaining prices at a high level. Days of negotiations between Kuwait and the other OPEC members failed to reach an accommodation. Other governments' fear of the domestic political consequences of acceding to Kuwait's demands proved stronger, ultimately, than their desire to reach a compromise between Kuwait's claim for a quota of 1.35m. b/d and the 1.12m. which it would have been allocated under a straight pro-rata distribution of the 20m. b/d ceiling which a majority thought reasonable to stabilize prices. Leaving no room for doubt about his intentions, Kuwait's Minister of Oil, Sheikh Ali Khalifa as-Sabah, proposed an amendment to the final OPEC resolution, exempting Kuwait from the agreed production quotas. To take account of the additional volume of Kuwaiti production, which was now regarded as inevitable (it had already been overproducing in May and June by some 800,000 b/d–900,000 b/d), the production ceiling was raised by only 1m. b/d to 19.5m. b/d, correspondingly reducing the extra volumes to which other members were entitled.

The 1990s is crucial decade for all oil exporters, especially for those with large reserves who are mainly in the Middle East and North Africa. Kuwait and Saudi Arabia have attempted to reduce their dependence on buyers of crude oil, beginning with the acquisition, in the 1970s, of control over their natural oil resources by buying into the downstream oil industry in Europe and the USA. While the reintegration of the oil industry is seen by many observers as inevitable and a force for stability, the restoration of direct ownership links between Middle Eastern producers and the refiners and distributors of oil products in the consuming countries may act as a counterweight to OPEC and the attempts to co-ordinate oil interests in the Middle East and North Africa. In September 1989, a meeting of OPEC's Long-Term Strategy Committee was due to attempt to solve the perennial problems of quota distribution, oil prices and the likely impact on oil producers of the growing 'environmentalist' movement in western consumer countries. In the event, the Long-Term Strategy Committee convened in Geneva from 23–27 September and, the eight permanent members being joined by ministers from all other OPEC adherents, a full-scale quota and pricing meeting took place. An interim report on long-term strategy talked airily about co-operation within OPEC, with non-OPEC producers and with consumers, but the meeting subsequently lapsed into the familiar pattern of proposal, counter-proposal, objection and final agreement on quotas. None of the participants appeared to be convinced that they would be adhered to. Iran called for a redistribution of quotas, to favour Kuwait, the UAE, Ecuador and Gabon, within a ceiling of 21.5m. b/d. However, the call was rejected because of Libya's demand for parity with Kuwait, and the UAE's insistence on an even larger quota than Iran had proposed. The old *pro-rata* formula was revived, within a new ceiling of 20.5m. b/d, just 1m. b/d lower than the level set previously. Kuwait duly rejected its quota of 1.149m. b/d for the final quarter of 1989.

At the next full OPEC meeting, held from 25–28 November 1989, quotas were redistributed, with Kuwait being allocated 6.82% of total output compared with 5.61% previously. The production ceiling was raised to 22m. b/d, although most members regarded this as insignificant since the *de facto* level of production was already 24m. b/d. Iran, Algeria and Indonesia all relinquished quota shares in Kuwait's favour even though, given the parlous state of their economies, they were themselves probably more suitable candidates for increases. However, with Saudi Arabia refusing to make any concessions, someone had to give way to bring some semblance of peace. The immediate result was that the UAE, seeing how

a rich member like Kuwait could achieve its aims by totally ignoring the needs of poorer members, felt obliged to follow suit. So the November 1989 agreement left the overall situation much as before, with Kuwait adhering to its quota, but the UAE producing 100% more than it had been allocated. Overall output continued to run at nearly 24m. b/d, apart from a dip in January 1990, when over-production was limited to 830,000 b/d.

The hyperbole surrounding the new agreement had an unforeseen side-effect: the price of crude petroleum started to rise and by January 1990 it had reached its highest level for two years. To some extent this was prompted by optimistic demand estimates issued by OPEC, and by a closer adherence by members to their quotas. However, between January–May 1990, prices fell steadily, with discounting and 'new formula' pricing rife. The one thing that could have stabilised matters—adherence to quotas—was forgotten.

To a large extent, the first quarter of 1990 may go down in history as a period of lost opportunity for OPEC. World demand for oil rose slowly at a time when several non-OPEC producers were experiencing difficulties. The continued fall in US production, the problems facing the UK and Mexico and the inability of Soviet infrastructure to maintain oil-production levels all combined to open a sizeable gap in the market which OPEC producers could have filled. The rapid change of regime in virtually all Eastern European countries reinforced this trend. However, disputes between Middle Eastern producers once more resulted in over-production and prices slumped. Moreover, despite professing concern over environmental issues, OPEC did not appear to have realized that the industrialized part of the world was becoming serious about eliminating the more noxious aspects of fossil-fuel use. The fact that the price of many oil products in consuming countries does not decline in line with declines in the price of crude petroleum also seemed to have gone unnoticed.

With the market behaving unpredictably, the meeting of the Ministerial Monitoring Committee, held on 16–17 March, took no action, hoping that the situation would become clearer before the next full OPEC meeting on 25 May. In the event, prices continued to decline, and over-production continued to such an extent that, immediately before a further meeting of the Monitoring Committee, on 2 May, increasing numbers of tankers were being chartered to serve as floating storage in a glutted market. The next full OPEC meeting was thus postponed, first until June and then until late July.

At the meeting of the Monitoring Committee held on 2 May it was agreed to reduce production by 1.445m. b/d from an average level of 23.5m. b/d. This measure brought production to just within the previously agreed ceiling and had little more than a cosmetic effect on the market. Prices strengthened for a day or two, then resumed their steady downward slide. And while producers all willingly agreed to cut back their production, some weeks later the overall cut was only around half that which had been agreed.

The full OPEC meeting which began on 25 July 1990 took place in an atmosphere of increasing tension caused by Iraq's threats of military action against countries which failed to observe production quotas. Iraq had accused both the UAE and Kuwait of flouting their quotas and claimed, with reference to a long-standing territorial dispute, that Kuwait had violated the Iraqi border in order to steal Iraqi oil. At the meeting Iraq sought to raise OPEC's minimum reference price to $25 per barrel, but in the event the ministerial council adopted a new price of $21 per barrel—which it hoped to achieve by the end of 1990—and fixed a new production ceiling of 22.5m. b/d for the remainder of 1990. Quotas for individual countries remained unchanged, except that of the UAE which was raised to 1.5m. b/d. The immediate effect of Iraq's invasion—and subsequent annexation—of Kuwait at the beginning of August, and of the economic sanctions imposed on Iraq by the UN in response to it, was the loss of about 8% of world oil production. By late August prices had risen to about $30 per barrel and OPEC members were divided over whether to increase production to compensate for the loss of supplies from Iraq and Kuwait.

Within a matter of weeks, however, many OPEC members had decided that it was in everybody's best interest to make good the 4.5m. b/d loss to the market. Saudi Arabia in particular pledged massive support for the reversal of Iraq's action, inviting foreign military assistance to defend its borders. It also raised its petroleum production considerably, partly to pay for such assistance and partly as a *quid pro quo*. Other OPEC members, mindful that non-OPEC sources might be used to make good the loss of Iraqi and Kuwaiti supplies, followed suit. Such non-OPEC action was not, in fact, immediately forthcoming, the option of marketing oil from the US Strategic Petroleum Reserve being withheld until the situation clarified. Similarly, the IEA declared that it would hold back its reserves until shortages were confirmed. Some non-OPEC producers raised their production, while planned closures for maintenance in areas such as the North Sea were postponed until the market stabilized.

The *de facto* raising of production by a number of OPEC member states duly became *de jure* on 29 August 1990, when 10 OPEC ministers of oil met in Vienna and agreed to compensate for 3.0–3.5m. b/d of lost production. By this time the price of crude petroleum had risen to $32 per barrel. A further meeting took place on 12 December 1990 and it was agreed to continue with the suspension of quotas until the Iraqi-Kuwaiti conflict was resolved. Once it was resolved, it was decided that quotas would be brought back into force, with the target price of $21 per barrel being retained.

The next meeting of OPEC, on 12 March 1991, confirmed that whatever decisions OPEC took, the market remained the dominant force. Oil producers had by this time increased output to such an extent that, even as the loss of Iraqi and Kuwaiti production continued, prices had plummeted and storage capacity had become scarce. Pledges that the strategic reserves of consuming countries might be brought into use had acted as a spur. Saudi Arabian production peaked at more than 9m. b/d, while the UAE had raised its output to more than 2.5m. b/d.

With supplies abundant and demand moving from winter to summer levels, prices fell by about 50% from their peak of $32 per barrel. Saudi Arabia reduced production and by April 1991 the market had become more balanced, with prices having recovered to around $4 below the OPEC target price of $21 per barrel. The situation was more or less as it had been before Iraq's invasion of Kuwait. It was decided at the OPEC meeting on 12 March 1991 to reduce production by about 5%, from 23.4m. b/d to 22.298m. b/d. However, individual OPEC members had already taken account of falling demand and the true level of OPEC production was little above the newly targeted level. The cut was thus more apparent than real and had no effect on prices.

However, by formalizing new quotas the OPEC meeting of 12 March 1991 did allow most producers to maintain output at a level close to their production capacity. A further meeting was held on 4 June 1991 at which it was agreed to maintain the *status quo*. The quotas which had been set in March were to remain in force until September 1991, when a further meeting would decide whether any adjustments needed to be made. Ironically, Iraq's invasion of Kuwait, which had aimed to prevent the latter's persistent flouting of its OPEC quota, had had the effect of stabilizing the market, balancing supply with demand; but neither Iraq nor Kuwait were any longer in a position to take advantage of the new equilibrium.

The meeting of OPEC held on 24–26 September 1991 set a new production ceiling of 23.6m. b/d. In fact, OPEC production had averaged 23.636m. b/d during the first half of 1991, far above the production ceiling that had been agreed in March 1991; while in the second half of that year it had averaged 24.741m. b/d. Clearly, OPEC members were seeking to maximize their production regardless of their quota allocations, and prices remained far below the OPEC target price of $21 per barrel.

Kuwait recommenced production of oil in June 1991, increasing it gradually from 70,000 b/d to 550,000 b/d by the end of the year. It was clear that if Kuwait continued to restore capacity at this rate, then other OPEC producers would have to reduce theirs in order to accommodate it. At an interim meeting of OPEC held on 27 November 1991, it was agreed to reappraise the level of production within the Organization in February 1992. Meanwhile, however, the market began to

dictate production levels. The situation was further complicated by a steep decline in production by the former Soviet republics, although this was offset by the continued economic recession in many consuming countries. As a result total demand for oil declined by 1.1% and it became clear that, without a voluntary reduction in production, the market would enforce a collapse in prices.

Before the OPEC meeting of February 1992 took place, nine of the 13 OPEC member states announced reductions in production totalling 400,000 b/d. Consequently there was little dissent when, at the meeting on 15 February, a new production quota of 22.982m. b/d was set. The new ceiling was opposed only by Saudi Arabia, whose official policy was now to seek quotas in accordance with production capacity.

In February 1992 Iraq was granted a production quota which, at 505,000 b/d, was sufficient to satisfy domestic demand. Kuwait was granted a quota of 812,000 b/d, although at the time it was unclear whether it would be able to achieve this level of production. Individual OPEC member states continued to abide by, or ignore, their production quotas as it suited them, but overall OPEC production remained more or less in line with the production ceiling as a result of market forces.

At the OPEC meeting held on 22 May 1992 ministers agreed, with some reservations, to maintain the production ceiling at 22.982m. b/d, although Kuwait was allowed to produce more than its previous quota of 812,000 b/d in order to compensate for production lost during the Iraqi occupation. Finally, the market met the wishes of almost all the OPEC member states. Increasing demand for oil for storage, for example, allowed Saudi Arabia, which had requested a higher quota, to continue to produce above the level of its formal quota. Iran had sought a reduction in the production ceiling in order to raise prices, and in fact increased demand raised spot market prices to close to the OPEC target price of $21 per barrel. However, the market remained exposed to factors that were beyond OPEC's control. Production by Russia and the UK, for instance, had begun to increase, while oil from recently-discovered fields in, for example, Colombia, increased the pressure on the cartel.

Spot prices continued to firm in the immediate aftermath of the OPEC meeting of 22 May 1992, and in late June reached their highest level for seven months. Factors influencing the market included the failure, on 22 June, of the UN and Iraq to reach any agreement on the resumption of Iraqi petroleum exports, and forecast higher demand for OPEC petroleum in the USA in the summer months. On the whole prices remained firm during July, August and the early weeks of September. By mid-September, however, when the Ministerial Monitoring Committee met in Geneva, concern was being expressed at the margin by which spot prices were failing to reach the target price of $21 per barrel, especially since market conditions were considered to be fundamentally favourable. By this time OPEC production was substantially in excess of the previously agreed level. Saudi Arabia, for instance, was reported to be producing, on average, 8.3m. b/d, compared with its allocation of 7.887m. b/d. Iranian production was also significantly above allocated level.

It was widely agreed that the statement issued at the conclusion of the Ministerial Monitoring Committee meeting contained no measures that were likely to raise prices to the target level. The statement indicated that OPEC's market share in the fourth quarter of 1992 should be 24.2m. b/d in order to achieve the target price, and reaffirmed OPEC's earlier decision to allow for additional, unspecified Kuwaiti production. However, some analysts and OPEC ministers argued that the agreement would boost prices to the target level. Taking into account Kuwaiti production of 200,000 b/d, OPEC production was likely to be more than 24.4m. b/d during the final quarter of 1992. However, winter demand for OPEC oil was estimated at 25m. b/d–25.5m. b/d. Also at the September meeting Ecuador confirmed its withdrawal from OPEC with effect from November 1992, after which time it would enjoy 'associate status' of the Organization only.

As demand for OPEC crude oil rose, total production averaged some 24.75m. b/d in September. By early October demand had risen to such an extent that the Secretary-General of OPEC, Dr Subroto, dismissed the idea of reimposing quotas at the next OPEC meeting in November. Prices were reportedly sustained by forward winter demand and by continued political tension in the Middle East. However, as seasonal demand for petroleum began to reach its peak in early October, prices remained below the level that had been expected.

At the OPEC meeting held in November 1992 in Vienna measures were taken that were designed to remove some 400,000 b/d of OPEC crude from the market in December. These included the establishment of a total OPEC production level of slightly less than 24.6m. b/d for the first quarter of 1993; and the establishment of new production allocations for OPEC member states to take effect from 1 December 1992. It was also agreed to allow Kuwait to continue to produce more than its allocated level of crude.

By mid-December a feared collapse in the price of petroleum appeared to have been averted. By early January 1993, however, prices had fallen to almost the lowest levels recorded in 1992 as a result of weak demand and production that remained in excess of the levels agreed in Vienna the previous November. Indeed, it was reported that production by the 12 OPEC member states and Ecuador in December 1992 had averaged 25.27m. b/d, its highest level since 1980. During the remainder of January, with stock levels remaining high, prices continued to weaken and towards the end of the month the Saudi Arabian Minister of Oil suggested that member states should reduce their collective production by 1m. b/d in order to check the decline in prices, which had fallen from $21 per barrel to $17 per barrel over the previous four months.

At the next full OPEC meeting, held in Vienna in February, it was agreed to make pro rata reductions in production that would effectively remove almost 1.5m. b/d from the market. The reductions, which pertained to the second quarter of 1993, were to take effect from 1 March. However, OPEC's declared commitment to maintaining a production ceiling of 23.58m. b/d met with the strongest scepticism from most observers, who believed that the new agreement would only begin to support prices in mid-March when it would be clear whether or not it was being observed. It appeared that attention would be closely focused on Kuwaiti production in the second quarter. Kuwait had agreed, reluctantly, to reduce its output to 1.6m. b/d, but warned that the slightest non-observance by other OPEC member states would immediately cause it to produce at a claimed capacity level of 2.1m. b/d. Kuwait had reportedly only agreed to reduce its second-quarter production in exchange for a third-quarter allocation equal to that of other countries with similar production capacity, historical market share and quota. Above all, the agreement indicated that the pressures relieved by the loss of Kuwaiti production in the 1990/91 crisis in the Gulf now applied to the market once again.

By late February the price of crude petroleum had reached a three-month peak since it appeared that OPEC's biggest producers would observe the agreement of 16 February. Prices did, in fact, remain firm during March, even though it appeared that production had averaged between 24m. b/d–24.3m. b/d. This compared with estimated production of 25.35m. b/d in February and the reduction was greater than most observers had expected it to be. However, there was concern that Iran was continuing to produce above its allocated level and that such over-production might cause Kuwait to flout its own allocated level of 1.6m. b/d. Observers also expressed fears that OPEC's efforts to support prices would be cancelled out if the industry failed to build up its stocks during the second quarter of 1993. At an unofficial meeting in Muscat, Oman, in mid-April the oil ministers of the OPEC member states determined to adhere more closely to the production levels allocated in February. OPEC's own estimate of total production in March was 23.8m. b/d, some 290,000 b/d in excess of the agreed ceiling.

At the beginning of May 1993 the market was reported to be broadly in balance and prices were steady though below the levels OPEC producers had hoped to achieve. According to one analyst OPEC production had averaged 24.32m. b/d in April, with Saudi Arabia and Iran allegedly the main over-producers. Later in the month the CGES forecast that demand for OPEC oil would reach 25.3m. b/d in the third quarter of 1993. Fears were expressed that individual OPEC member states might be tempted to increase their production in pursuit of increased sales and greater revenue. The CGES suggested that additional demand for OPEC petroleum could be allocated on a pro rata basis, using the production agreement of February as a guide; or that extra demand could be shared according to each member state's sustainable capacity.

The spot price of a representative selection of OPEC crudes was reported to have averaged $18.20 per barrel in May, almost 1.5% lower than in April and March. Production in May was reportedly 230,000 b/d lower than in April, but, at an estimated 24.1m. b/d, still higher than OPEC's second-quarter output ceiling of 23.58m. b/d. Prices weakened during the approach to OPEC's next full ministerial meeting in June, in Geneva, not least because there was little confidence that the meeting would conclude a credible production agreement.

During June 1993 oil prices remained below the targeted level of $21 per barrel that OPEC had sought to achieve through the reintroduction—in all but name—of the quota system it had abandoned during the 1990/91 crisis in the Gulf, in the form of production allocations agreed by the member states. The problem, as far as the market was concerned, was that nobody involved in the industry believed that the member states would be able to summon sufficient discipline to observe the production ceiling of 23.58m. b/d introduced in February 1993 and extended, in June, to the third quarter of 1993. In its forecast of price trends for the year to June 1994 the Centre for Global Energy Studies (CGES, London) considered three possible developments, each based on the assumption that the supply of OPEC oil would continue to exceed demand for it: that OPEC would respond to demand by raising its production to 24.9m. b/d, in which case prices would remain below $19 per barrel; that OPEC would be able to hold production at or below 24.5m. b/d, in which case the CGES forecast that the average price for OPEC crude petroleum would reach $20.10 in the period April–June 1994; or, if OPEC were unable to exercise sufficient discipline and production rose to 25.2m. b/d in the third quarter of 1993, that the average price of OPEC crude would remain at or below $18.10 per barrel in October–December 1993, falling to $17.90 in April–June 1994.

The market had every reason to suspect that the OPEC member states would fail to observe their declared production target. Kuwait had begun to claim, with increasing insistence, an allocation that fully reflected its restored production capacity. At the OPEC ministerial meeting held in Geneva on 8–10 June 1993 Kuwait requested an official allocation of 2.16m. b/d for the third quarter of 1993, claiming that it had effectively been promised an increase in its allocation to 2m. b/d at the OPEC meeting in Vienna in February 1993. Saudi Arabia gave no indication of any willingness to renounce what it considered to be its right to one-third of total OPEC production, and Iran remained keen to maximize revenues by maximizing its production. The prospect of the removal of the UN's economic sanctions on Iraq remained distant, although Iraq had claimed, one year earlier, to have fully repaired all war damage to its oil production facilities and to have boosted its capacity. The vexed and potentially disruptive issue of quota parity between Iran and Iraq could thus be dismissed for the time being, and producing countries could concentrate on optimistic predictions of the increasing dependence of the large industrial countries on oil over the coming twenty years. Indeed, it had been argued that lower prices for oil since 1985 had acted in the interest of OPEC—and other—producers by discouraging research, investment in and development of alternative energy sources; and by making North American and North Sea fields less competitive, enabling OPEC to regain most of the markets it had lost after 1979.

Oil Statistics
(compiled by the Editor)

CRUDE OIL PRODUCTION[1] (million barrels per day)

	1991	1992	1993
Middle East OPEC:			
Saudi Arabia	8.645	8.895	8.695
Kuwait	0.180	1.070	1.950
Neutral Zone[2]	0.100	0.325	n.a.
Iran	3.260	3.455	3.620
Iraq	0.235	0.480	0.455
UAE—Abu Dhabi	2.130	2.050	2.035
UAE—Dubai	0.465	0.440	0.440
Qatar	0.440	0.485	0.500
North Africa OPEC:			
Libya	1.510	1.520	1.420
Algeria	1.310	1.325	1.320
Other OPEC:			
Venezuela	2.490	2.500	2.565
Nigeria	1.895	1.850	1.910
Indonesia	1.670	1.580	1.530
Ecuador	0.320	0.345	0.365
Gabon	0.300	0.295	0.295
Other Middle East and North Africa:			
Oman	0.725	0.725	0.780
Bahrain	0.055	0.055	0.055
Syria	0.465	0.475	0.570
Egypt	0.910	0.920	0.945
Tunisia	0.145	0.145	0.150
Turkey	0.085	0.085	0.085
Yemen	0.225	0.185	0.220
Other producers:			
USA	9.075	8.870	8.565
Canada	1.980	2.060	2.180
Mexico	3.135	3.125	3.135
Trinidad and Tobago	0.150	0.145	0.150
Colombia	0.425	0.440	0.465
Argentina	0.490	0.555	0.585
Brazil	0.655	0.660	0.670
Brunei	0.160	0.180	0.175
India	0.640	0.580	0.560
Malaysia	0.655	0.665	0.650
Australasia	0.600	0.585	0.550
United Kingdom	1.895	1.955	2.085
Norway	1.905	2.175	2.340
Ex-USSR	10.430	9.055	7.975
China, People's Rep.	2.815	2.850	2.900
Other Non-OECD	0.285	0.260	0.260
World total	64.490	64.910	65.075
OPEC total	24.530	25.945	26.695
Middle East and North Africa total	20.885	22.655	23.240

[1] Includes shale oil, oil sands and natural gas liquids.
[2] Shared equally between Saudi Arabia and Kuwait.
Source: Mainly *BP Statistical Review of World Energy*, June 1994.

Conversion factors based on world average crude oil gravity:
1 long ton = 7.42 barrels
1 short ton = 6.63 barrels
1 metric ton = 7.30 barrels
1 barrel = 35 imperial gallons
1 barrel = 42 US gallons
To convert metric tons per year into b/d divide by 50.0
To convert long tons per year into b/d divide by 49.2

**PROVEN PUBLISHED WORLD OIL RESERVES AS AT
1 JANUARY 1994** ('000 million barrels)

	Reserves	Years of production* at 1993 levels		Reserves	Years of production* at 1993 levels
Middle East and North Africa			**Other leading producers**		
Saudi Arabia	261.2	83.7	Other OPEC		
Kuwait	96.5	†	Venezuela	63.3	68.90
Neutral Zone	n.a.	n.a.	Nigeria	17.9	25.8
Iran	92.9	70.4	Indonesia	5.8	10.8
Iraq	100.0	†	Ecuador	2.0	15.1
UAE—Abu Dhabi	92.2	†	Gabon	0.7	6.9
UAE—Dubai	5.9	40.7	**Total OPEC**	772.1	79.6
UAE—Sharjah	1.5	56	Rest of World:		
Qatar	3.7	20.8	USA	31.2	9.9
Oman	4.7	16.5	Canada	7.4	8.9
Bahrain	0.07	5	Mexico	50.9	46.4
Syria	1.7	8.2	United Kingdom	4.6	6.1
Algeria	9.2	21.2	Norway	9.3	10.6
Libya	22.8	44.2	USSR	57.0	19.7
Egypt	6.3	18.5	Other Eastern Europe	2.2	23.4
Tunisia	1.7	43.5	China, People's Repub.	24.0	21.9
Yemen	4.0	51.7	**World total**	1,009.0	43.1
Middle East and North Africa total	704.4	75.0			

* Including crude oil, shale oil, oil sands and natural gas liquids.   † More than 100.

Sources: *Oil and Gas Journal*, 28 December 1993, *BP Statistical Review of World Energy*, June 1994.

Note: Reserve figures are subject to wide margins of error, and there are considerable differences between sources—including oil companies and governments. Proven reserves do not denote 'total oil in place', but only that proportion of the oil in a field that drilling has shown for certain to be there and to be recoverable with current technology and at present prices. Normally recoverable reserves amount to about a third of the oil in place. Because the potential of fields is continually being reassessed in the light of production experience and because the production characteristics of a field can (and often do) change as it gets older, proven reserves figures may sometimes be revised upwards or downwards by quite dramatic amounts without any new discoveries being made. Price rises tend inevitably to increase reserves figures by making small fields or more complex recovery techniques economic.

The only exception to the proven commercially recoverable reserves formula used in this table applies to the USSR figure. The Soviet figures reported by *Oil and Gas Journal* are 'explored reserves', which include proved, probable and some possible reserves.

OILFIELDS IN THE MIDDLE EAST WITH RESERVES OF MORE THAN 5,000 MILLION BARRELS

		Year of discovery	Age of principal reservoirs	Estimated reserves ('000 million barrels)
Ghawar	Saudi Arabia	1948	Jurassic	83
Burgan	Kuwait	1948	Cretaceous	72
Safaniyah-Khafji	Saudi Arabia (Neutral Zone)	1951	Cretaceous	30
Rumaila	Iraq	1953	Cretaceous	20
Ahwaz	Iran	1958	Oligocene, Miocene, Cretaceous	17.5
Kirkuk	Iraq	1927	Oligocene-Eocene, Cretaceous	16
Marun	Iran	1964	Oligocene-Miocene	16
Gach Saran	Iran	1928	Oligocene-Miocene, Cretaceous	15.5
Agha Jari	Iran	1938	Oligocene-Miocene, Cretaceous	14
Abqaiq	Saudi Arabia	1940	Jurassic	12.5
Berri	Saudi Arabia	1964	Jurassic	12
Zakum	Abu Dhabi	1964	Cretaceous	12
Manifah	Saudi Arabia	1957	Cretaceous	11
Fereidoon-Marjan	Iran/Saudi Arabia	1966	Cretaceous	10
Bu Hasa	Abu Dhabi	1962	Cretaceous	9
Qatif	Saudi Arabia	1945	Jurassic	9
Khurais	Saudi Arabia	1957	Jurassic	8.5
Zuluf	Saudi Arabia	1965	Cretaceous	8.5
Raudhatain	Kuwait	1955	Cretaceous	7.7
Shayban	Saudi Arabia	1968	Cretaceous	7
Abu Safah	Saudi Arabia/Bahrain	1963	Jurassic	6.6
Asab	Abu Dhabi	1965	Cretaceous	6
Bab	Abu Dhabi	1954	Cretaceous	6
Umm Shaif	Abu Dhabi	1958	Jurassic	5

Source: *Oilfields of the World*, E.N. Tiratsoo (Scientific Press Ltd).

GOVERNMENT OIL REVENUES OF OPEC MEMBER COUNTRIES IN THE MIDDLE EAST AND NORTH AFRICA*
(million US dollars)

	1980	1981	1982	1983	1984	1985	1986	1987	1988	1989	1990	1991
Iran	13,286	12,053	19,233	19,255	12,255	13,115	7,183	10,515	8,170	14,000	15,240	19,300
Saudi Arabia‡	105,813	116,183	75,534	42,809	34,243	24,180	16,975	19,271	20,500	16,000	40,700	47,900
Kuwait‡	17,678	13,790	8,827	9,736	10,740	9,817	6,378	7,520	6,295	9,250	5,800	1,100
Iraq	26,296	10,422	10,096	7,816	9,354	10,685	6,905	11,416	10,952	12,000	8,000	1,600
UAE	19,558	18,815	15,337	12,235	12,978	11,842	7,453	8,665	7,352	10,438	21,100	14,000
Qatar	5,406	5,350	4,108	3,110	4,386	3,068	1,720	1,829	1,709	1,800	2,000	2,200
Libya	21,378	15,254	12,769	11,909	10,631	9,962	5,787	6,011	5,169	5,000	9,000	8,800
Algeria	12,647	12,985	10,770	9,467	9,189	9,170	4,819	6,057	4,988	3,800	12,300	10,300

* Figures include income from refined products and natural gas liquids, except Saudi Arabian figures which exclude natural gas liquids. Figures for Algeria from 1990 include revenue from sales of natural gas.
‡ Including an equal share of revenue from Neutral Zone sales.
Sources: OPEC, to 1988; government and oil industry estimates from 1989.

Principal Oil Groups Producing or Refining in the Gulf

This list accounts for well over 90% of oil exploring, producing and refining operations in the Middle East, but it is not a complete list. There are a large number of small operators either exploring or producing oil in minor quantities. Further details of the national take-overs of the Gulf oil industry are given in the text which precedes the oil statistics.

NATIONAL IRANIAN OIL COMPANY

The National Iranian Oil Company (NIOC) is responsible for all oil operations in Iran. At the end of February 1979 it was announced that the company was taking over entirely the role of producing and marketing oil in the area of 'the Consortium'. The Consortium, officially Iranian Oil Participants, had originally been formed as a lessee following the settlement of the 1951–53 Mussadiq crisis in which the Anglo-Iranian Oil Company (BP) had been nationalized. Its members were BP with 40%; Shell 14%; Exxon, Mobil, Socal, Texaco and Gulf with 7% each; CFP (known as Total-CFP since 1985) 6%; and a group of US independents with 5% between them. In 1973 this group surrendered administration of the oilfields to NIOC, but remained as privileged buyers of Iranian crude. To help run the industry the Consortium members founded two service companies, wholly owned by themselves. These were the Oil Service Company of Iran (OSCO) which operated the fields for NIOC in Iran, and Iranian Oil Services (IROS) which was London based and had the job of procuring equipment, organizing the training of Iranians and recruiting some of the non-Iranian staff of OSCO. (Most of OSCO's expatriate staff were seconded by the company's shareholders.) The OSCO operation accounted for about 90% of Iranian crude production, and OSCO shareholders took over half of the crude produced—the rest being marketed by NIOC. Well before the whole operation was terminated by the Revolution in 1979, the financial and crude oil lifting terms of the agreement of 1973 were mainly inoperative following the failure of successive rounds of re-negotiations.

After the Revolution NIOC crude sales moved away from members of the Consortium. OSCO was suspended. Its expatriate employees left Iran and its Iranian employees were transferred to NIOC. IROS, however, continued to work for NIOC. Intermittent discussions were held in 1979 and 1980 between the company's shareholders and the Iranians on NIOC's taking over IROS, and these resulted in early 1981 in IROS being replaced by Kala Limited. The new company, whose name means *supplies*, is wholly owned by NIOC and has taken some of IROS's employees onto its payroll.

Before it took over operations in the Consortium area NIOC had for some years itself operated a small oil field at Naft-i-Shah. Beginning in 1959 it has also entered a number of partnerships and service contracts with foreign companies (see main text for details)—five of which were producing oil (mostly from offshore fields) at the time of the Revolution. In 1979 NIOC terminated these agreements by taking over the foreign shareholdings. In August 1980 it was announced that a new company, the Continental Shelf Oil Company, was to be formed to operate the fields formerly run by the partnerships. The company was to be supervised by a directorate in the oil ministry.

NIOC owns all of Iran's refineries and the internal distribution business (before the Revolution Iran was consuming some 700,000 b/d). It also owns a tanker fleet and before the Revolution had a number of overseas investments in refineries. Most of these investments have now been sold or abandoned.

Apart from Kala, NIOC has a number of longer established subsidiaries. The National Iranian Tanker Company transports a significant and growing share of the country's oil exports. The National Iranian Drilling Company was established in 1979 to co-ordinate all activity in this sphere. The Iranian Offshore Oil Company (IOOC) was created in 1980 to manage all offshore operations in the Gulf.

IRAQ NATIONAL OIL COMPANY

In an attempt to improve efficiency and productivity within the oil industry, the Iraq National Oil Company (INOC), hitherto responsible for all exploration, production, pipeline operations and crude oil marketing, was merged with the Ministry of Oil in May 1987. Some of its functions were transferred to newly created ministerial departments, and others to companies created to replace the state organizations formerly under INOC's control, which were abolished by the merger decree. The Northern Petroleum Organization, in charge of the Kirkuk and Mosul fields, became the Northern Petroleum Company (also incorporating the former Central Petroleum Organization), and the Southern Petroleum Organization, in charge of the Basra fields, became the Southern Petroleum Company, and both are now responsible to the Ministry of Oil.

Until the nationalization measures of the early 1970s Iraq's production and exports were run entirely by the Iraq Petroleum Company (operating around Kirkuk) and its affiliates, The Basra Petroleum Company and the Mosul Petroleum Company. These companies (together with the Qatar Petroleum Company and the Abu Dhabi Petroleum Company) were known collectively as IPC. They were owned by a consortium of BP, Shell, CFP (known as Total-CFP since 1985) and an Exxon-Mobil partnership, with 23.75% each, and the Participations and Explorations Corporation (Gulbenkian) with 5%.

KUWAIT PETROLEUM CORPORATION

The Kuwait Petroleum Corporation (KPC) was formed in 1980 as part of a rationalization of the structure of the Kuwaiti oil industry. It took over the existing state oil companies, which had inherited different parts of the former concessionaires' operations, and assigned them specialist roles as producers, refiners etc. The companies that now form the operating arms of KPC are as follows:

Kuwait Oil Company (KOC): runs oil and gas production both in Kuwait itself and in the Kuwait part of the onshore Neutral (or Partitioned) Zone. Before the take-overs of the 1970s Kuwaiti production was run by a BP-Gulf partnership, also known as KOC. Production in the northern half of the Neutral Zone was run by an independent US group, Aminoil.

Kuwait National Petroleum Company (KNPC): runs liquefied petroleum gases processing, domestic products marketing and Kuwait's three refineries. Before the take-overs and subsequent rationalization of the Kuwaiti oil industry, KNPC was the 'national oil company', concerned with internal products distribution, the Shuaiba refinery and several investments in oil operations abroad.

Petrochemicals Industries Company: main operation at present is Kuwait Chemical Fertiliser Company's plant at Shuaiba. Runs various minor plants and will run new petrochemical plants planned in Kuwait.

Kuwait Oil Tankers Company (KOTC): crude oil and products shipping. KOTC was formerly a public company, in which the government held a large minority stake.

Kuwait Petroleum International (KPI): the London-based affiliate established in 1983 to run KPC's refining and marketing operations in Europe and anywhere else where the corporation might expand.

Kuwait Foreign Exploration Company: KPC's affiliate for overseas hydrocarbons exploration and development had a direct stake in licences in seven countries by 1985 and had assumed the role of operator in two Tunisian concessions as well as one in Bahrain. The rest of its interests were held through its 60% share in the International Energy Development Corporation (IEDC) which has a 25% share in Chevron's oil discovery in Sudan. In March 1985 it bought out the remaining shareholders (Volvo Energi, Apicorp, and Sogenor of Switzerland) of the Geneva-based IEDC.

Santa Fe International Corporation: formerly US-owned, was bought by KPC in 1982. It had four divisions: oil and gas exploration (controlling production of 23,000 b/d of oil and 60m. cu ft per day of natural gas); drilling contracting; engineering (C. F. Braun); and petrochemicals. It holds a share in a significant gas discovery in Chinese waters south of Hainan island, and has acquired a 21% share in the North Sea Miller field.

KPC also owns 70% of the Kuwait International Petroleum Investments Company.

Already a well-integrated oil company at home, KPC moved 'downstream' overseas early in 1983, when it purchased Gulf Oil's Benelux and Scandinavian assets, including two refineries, at Rotterdam, in the Netherlands, and Skaelskor, Denmark, four lube plants, 17 terminals, a half-share of a storage and distribution system in Sweden, and 1,500 service stations. By the end of the year, the five distribution networks provided a secure outlet for 175,000 b/d of Kuwaiti crude. At the beginning of 1984 KPC took over Gulf Oil's Italian interests, including a 75% share of the Bertonico refinery near Sarni (Mobil owns the other 25%), which was moth-balled in 1982, and 1,500 service stations, as well as several aviation fuelling outlets. KPC is unlikely to reactivate the Italian refinery and will continue supplying the market with products processed in Kuwait.

Early in 1988, KPI put the capacity of its refining and retailing operations outside Kuwait at 250,000 b/d. It was generally satisfied with its market share in Western Europe but still wished to expand its operations in Italy and the Netherlands. It was KPI's aim to double the capacity of its captive 'downstream' sales outlets world-wide, to 500,000 b/d, giving priority to expansion in the Far East, South-East Asia and the USA.

SAUDI ARAMCO

Aramco (the Arabian-American Oil Co) dates back to 1936 when Standard Oil of California invited Texaco to take a one-half share in the Saudi Arabian concession, which had originally been granted in 1932. Exxon (Standard Oil of New Jersey) and Mobil subsequently took a share in the operation in 1947. In November 1988, after negotiations which had continued for some years (see below), Aramco was finally acquired by the state and renamed the Saudi Arabian Oil Company (Saudi Aramco). Saudi Aramco is responsible for all exploration and production on shore and off shore in the Eastern Province of Saudi Arabia. It accounts for all Saudi production except that coming from the Neutral Zone, where Getty operates on shore and the Japanese Arabian Oil Company off shore. In the mid-1970s Aramco was given charge of the construction of the government's gas-gathering system, a pipeline for NGLs across the Kingdom to Yanbu and the unification of the Eastern Province electricity grid. In 1987 the Saudi Government began to plan a complete restructuring of its oil industry, with the aim of creating a national petroleum corporation, whose foundation was to be the extensive Aramco operations, which had been built up over the preceding five decades.

Until the beginning of the participation process in the early 1970s, Aramco was Saudi Arabia's concessionaire. The company was formed by Socal, Texaco and Exxon, with 30% each, and Mobil with 10%. Despite the assumption of 60% majority control in 1974, the partners continued to run the operation, on behalf of the Saudi Government, much as they had done before, enjoying privileged lifting rights and paying a proportionate cost of the expenses. Under a five-year agreement which expired in 1983, they were allowed up to 7.7m. b/d of production, and in the period of the prices split within OPEC from the start of that year until the autumn of 1981, when Saudi rates were lower and its output high, they derived a considerable advantage. The impending complete take-over of Aramco by the state was announced in 1980. While most of the expatriate staff remained and at senior level the company continued to be run predominantly by them, the US partners established a separate concern called Stemco to provide technical expertise for both exploration and production. In return for it they were understood to have received a discount, amounting, in the first half of 1984, to 25 cents for each barrel lifted but also undertook to finance a proportion of the costs of exploration under an undisclosed incentive system. With the reunification of OPEC prices the advantage disappeared and there was believed to have been some concern on the part of the government about the declining volume of oil purchased by the partners and dissatisfaction on the part of the companies at their exploration obligations.

Aramco's first Saudi president was appointed in 1983 but the chairman remained a US citizen until 1987, and the company continued to be registered in Delaware, New Jersey. The long delay before the formal take-over in November 1988 was attributable to a wish to reconstruct the petroleum industry around Aramco.

When in 1983 the government sought to boost exports it looked to Aramco, rather than Petromin, the entity originally established as a state oil corporation, which had been given responsibility for certain contract sales. Early in 1988 Petromin's well-established marketing operation in Dhahran was strengthened with the opening of branches in New York, Houston and Tokyo. Together they constituted the embryo of a new marketing affiliate which was to be one part of the reorganized industry. The plan began to take shape in 1989 with the creation of the Supreme Petroleum Council, which is chaired by King Fahd. Petromin was superseded by the Saudi Arabian Marketing and Refining Company (SAMAREC), a single agency with responsibility for all Saudi Arabian oil refineries and the marketing of oil products. Petrolube had been set up in February 1988 to run the lubricating oil blending plants in Jeddah, Riyadh and Jubail. It was decided in principle that another, Petroref, would operate the Kingdom's three domestic refineries and also, probably, market the state's share of output from the export refineries. Also under consideration were companies to undertake joint ventures in the development of the petrochemicals and minerals industries. It was expected that the new integrated entity would maintain Aramco's technical and managerial assistance contracts with Exxon, Mobil, Socal and Texaco.

In June 1988, Aramco Services Co (a Houston-based subsidiary) signed a letter of intent with Texaco, on behalf of the Saudi Government, providing for the acquisition of a 50% interest in the US company's refining and marketing assets in 23 states on or near the eastern coast of the USA, as well as the District of Columbia. Altogether, the $800m.-purchase appeared to ensure exports of at least 600,000 b/d. Included in the deal were three refineries at Delaware, New Jersey, Convent, Louisiana and Port Arthur, Texas, with a total crude capacity of 715,000 b/d and catalytic cracking capacity of 240,000 b/d. Also included were 49 terminals, nearly 1,450 owned and leased service stations and a branded distributor network of 10,000 petrol stations. It was announced that Saudi Refining Inc., a wholly owned, Delaware-registered, subsidiary of Aramco Services Co, would represent Aramco interests in the operation.

SAUDI ARABIAN MARKETING AND REFINING COMPANY (SAMAREC)

Petromin (the General Petroleum and Minerals Organization) was established in 1982 as the State Petroleum Corporation and a vehicle for industrialization. It was made responsible for exploration not assigned to Aramco but none of the concessions leased by it in the 1960s resulted in discoveries. Petromin built up the Kingdom's domestic refining operations and internal distribution network. It also took charge of processing and of foreign sales of natural gas liquids, which became available when the gas-gathering system constructed by Aramco came on stream. After 1974, when state participation came into effect, Petromin handled certain of the state's long-term contract sales but did not have the expertise to sell crude on a short-term basis in the kind of weakening and volatile market which was a recurring phenomenon from 1982 onwards. It did, however, become fully involved in the export of products when it was vested with the ownership of the Ras Tanura refinery in 1980. Petromin also became the Saudi partner in the Kingdom's joint-venture, export-oriented refineries. In the restructuring of the industry Petromin was superseded in January 1989 by a new organization, the Saudi Arabian Marketing and Refining Company (SAMAREC), responsible for all Saudi Arabian refineries and the marketing of oil products.

QATAR GENERAL PETROLEUM CORPORATION

QGPC owns all production, refining and distribution operations in Qatar, and holds the Qatar Government's shares in the Qatar Fertiliser Company, the Qatar Gas Company and the Qatar Petrochemicals Company. It also holds the government's shares in oil industry ventures outside Qatar and pan-Arab oil operations, such as the Arab Shipbuilding and Repairs Yard in Bahrain.

Before the take-overs of the 1970s Qatar's territory and offshore areas were divided between two concessionaires: off shore was Shell Qatar, operating three relatively small fields (Idd ash-Shargi, Maydan Mahzam and Bul Hanine), and on shore was the Qatar Petroleum Company, owned by the IPC shareholders. (See INOC notes above.) QPC operated the large Dukhan field. After the take-overs of 1976 and 1977 the two production operations were vested in the state-owned Qatar Petroleum Producing Authority (Onshore Operations) and the Qatar Petroleum Producing Authority (Offshore Operations). Both of these operations were incorporated into the Qatar General Petroleum Corporation in 1980, becoming the corporation's oil production divisions. Personnel for the onshore operation is provided by the Dukhan Service Company, owned by the IPC shareholders, and for the offshore operation by the Qatar Shell Service Company, owned by Shell.

ABU DHABI COMPANY FOR ONSHORE OIL OPERATIONS (ADCO)

Before 'participation' the Abu Dhabi onshore oil operation was owned by the Abu Dhabi Petroleum Company (ADPC)—an IPC company (see Iraq notes above). This company had been given a concession covering all onshore areas and territorial waters for 75 years from 1939 to 2014, though, subsequently, large areas had been relinquished. In 1973 the government took a 25% share in the operation, and in 1974 negotiated a 60% participation. No attempt is being made to complete the take-over. In 1978 the owners of ADPC (which remains a London-registered company) established a locally incorporated operating company, the Abu Dhabi Company for Onshore Oil Operations (ADCO). In the new company the state oil corporation, the Abu Dhabi National Oil Company (ADNOC) has a stake of 60%. ADCO accounts for all of Abu Dhabi's onshore oil production—though there are other foreign groups exploring on shore on a partnership or carried interest basis. Local refining operations are owned by ADNOC.

ABU DHABI MARINE AREAS OPERATING COMPANY—(ADMA-OPCO)

In 1953 Abu Dhabi's offshore concession was awarded to Abu Dhabi Marine Areas, a company owned by BP (two-thirds) and CFP (known as Total-CFP since 1985) (one-third). The concession was to run to 2018 and covered areas of the continental shelf beyond the state's three-mile limit. In December 1972 BP sold part of its stake to a large group of Japanese industrial companies which formed the Japan Oil Development Company. In 1973 the government took a 25% stake, and in 1974 negotiated a 60% participation. No attempt has been made since to complete the take-over.

Early in 1979 all the shareholders established a locally incorporated operating company (ADMA-OPCO) in which the shareholdings are: Abu Dhabi National Oil Company (ADNOC) 60%, BP 14.67%, Total-CFP 13.33% and Japan Oil Development Company (JODCO) 12%. This company operates the Umm Shaif field and the lower strata of the Zakum field, which together account for most of Abu Dhabi's offshore production. Technical staff for the operation are provided

mainly by BP, which also manages the procurement of equipment and owns the BP Project Group in Abu Dhabi. The Project Group acts as the project arm of ADMA-OPCO.

ZAKUM DEVELOPMENT COMPANY (ZADCO)

The Zakum Development Company has been formed to develop the upper strata of the giant Zakum field. The company is registered in Abu Dhabi and is purely an operating company, with its shares held 50:50 by ADNOC and CFP (known as Total-CFP since 1985). In practice, development work is carried out entirely by Total-CFP.

The Zakum development itself, however, is owned 88% by ADNOC and 12% by the Japan Oil Development Co, JODCO. These are the companies that pay for the development work and will own the oil produced. The ADNOC-JODCO partnership does not have a name and is not incorporated in Abu Dhabi. The partnership came about through CFP and BP, both shareholders in ADMA-OPCO, declining to participate in the development of Upper Zakum and having their shares taken by ADNOC.

Upper Zakum came on stream in the spring of 1983. A production capacity of 500,000 b/d is planned—equivalent to the combined output of Umm Shaif and Lower Zakum. There were doubts, however, as to when it might reach its full potential because of the high cost of development and uncertain demand projections. In 1985 it was still very much regarded as an investment for the future.

DUBAI PETROLEUM COMPANY (DPC) GROUP

In July 1976 Dubai announced that it had negotiated a 100% take-over of the DPC group, though the terms of the take-overs were very different from those applying anywhere else in the Middle East. Ownership of the DPC group's offshore concession, originally granted in 1952 for 60 years to BP and CFP (now known as Total-CFP) as Dubai Marine Areas, had changed on a number of occasions before July 1976, but the government had not previously taken a 25% or 60% holding. Under the terms of the July agreement DPC itself (Conoco) remained as operator, and the DPC group continued to market Dubai's oil, take the risks, make the investment and bear the costs. The group was, however, paid back by the state all of its previous investment, and was in future to be able to depreciate new investments over three years instead of ten, giving the government ownership of the oil-producing assets. DPC accounts for all of Dubai's production.

Ownership

Dubai Petroleum Company (Continental) [Operator]	30%
Dubai Marine Areas (50:50 Hispanoil and Total-CFP)	50%
Deutsche Texaco	10%
Sun Oil	5%
Wintershall	5%

PETROLEUM DEVELOPMENT OMAN (PDO)

Originally a concession of 75 years from 1937, expiring 2012. Onshore areas, originally covering northern provinces, now including Dhofar. Government took a 25% share in 1973, and increased this to 60% in 1974. PDO accounts for all of Oman's oil production, though other foreign groups are exploring.

Ownership

Oman Government	60%
Shell	34%
Total-Compagnie Française des Pétroles	4%
Participations and Explorations Corpn (Gulbenkian)	2%

NATURAL GAS IN THE MIDDLE EAST AND NORTH AFRICA

CHRIS CRAGG

The Middle East now accounts for more than 30% of the world's proven reserves of natural gas. With the addition of Algeria, Libya, Tunisia and Egypt, the figure rises to 34%. This amounts to 48,505,000m. cu m, according to a 1992 survey, but even this figure should be regarded as conservative. The eastern part of the region lies in a trend that most geologists now believe contains the bulk of Eurasia's hydro-carbons. This runs from the Yamal peninsular in Russian Siberia to the Caspian Sea, across the 'fertile crescent' into Saudi Arabia, and across the Red Sea towards Sudan. Proven reserves in the region, second only to those of Russia, have more than quadrupled since 1970. Indeed, since the mid-1980s they have risen by more than two-thirds, the additional amount alone sufficient for almost 8 years' of global gross consumption. These reserves would enable Iran to maintain production at its 1991 level for 635 years, Qatar for 494 years and Abu Dhabi for 250 years. At current levels of production, proven reserves in the Middle East could last until 2242, and proven reserves underestimate potential reserves, sometimes by as much as a factor of two.

In 1992 there was a substantial increase in this reserve figure, amounting to 5,133,000m. cu m, although owing to increased consumption the reserves-to-production ratio fell marginally. The Iranian South Pars field was substantially upgraded and is now one of the largest offshore gas reservoirs in the world. However, many countries, especially those on the shores of the Persian (Arabian) Gulf, have sufficient proven reserves to meet any short-term requirements and have simply not tried to discover more gas. Where this is not so, notably in Syria, Egypt, Yemen and, to a lesser extent, Algeria, the search has continued successfully. In general, however, more attention has been paid to the expansion of domestic, western and eastern European and Japanese markets, but by mid-1992 certain geopolitical changes had begun to change the situation.

In spite of huge reserves, natural gas has until very recently been an under-utilized resource in much of the Middle East and North Africa. In contrast to oil, it was difficult to export, requiring either large pipeline systems or very expensive conversion into liquefied natural gas (LNG). Since in terms of volume, oil has a far greater thermal content than gas, gas produced far less reward than oil for a given capital expenditure. Local markets were generally dominated by oil burning, or did not exist. As a result, oil companies looking for oil and finding gas, shut in the gas and went elsewhere. Where gas was found with oil—'associated' gas—the oil was used and the gas flared. In 1973, Saudia Arabia was flaring as much as 86% of its gross production and its flare stacks were visible to the early astronauts. Some countries, notably Algeria, Libya and Abu Dhabi did export by liquefying the gas for European, American or Japanese consumption. Yet this was a formidable technical undertaking, requiring liquefaction plants to cool the gas to −165°C, each costing as much as $2,000m., and special ships costing over $100m. Constructed in the late 1970s, these plants came into operation at an inopportune moment, since between 1979 and 1982 world gas consumption actually fell. In the USA, there was a huge surplus of domestic-ally-produced gas, while in Europe, large volumes of Soviet gas from Siberia reached the market. Only the Japanese, with no resources of their own, remained faithful to their supplier in Abu Dhabi. Much of the extremely expensive Algerian LNG capacity became idle after a series of disputes with US distributors.

Many countries, however, perhaps motivated by this experience, began to realize the value of what was being flared. As a substitute for oil, gas could be burnt in power stations, desalination plants, and wherever heat was required. This, in an era of high oil prices, would free crude for export. As a result, the flaring of 'associated' gas was gradually cut, a process which, in the case of Saudi Arabia, required a major offshore and onshore gathering grid. By 1991 flaring in that country had been reduced to only 6% of total—greatly increased—production. Compared with 1983, when Saudi Arabia used some 4,000m. cu m of natural gas and flared 26,900m. cu m, in 1991 it used 32,000m. cu m and flared only 4,400m. cu m. Iran, too, had realized the waste involved in flaring gas and had begun to use gas-reinjection techniques in order to assist the recovery of oil. In 1991, having increased its production of natural gas by 97% since 1983, Iran reinjected into the ground more gas than it had actually been using a decade earlier. In the Middle East and North Africa generally, however, flaring remained high, involving 52,420m. cu m in 1991—an amount almost double Norway's marketed pro-duction—compared with 43,840m. cu m in 1980. A sudden increase in 1991 was largely due to the tragedy of Kuwait, where the Iraqi invasion and subsequent war flared 96% of total production in that year. Over the same period, gross production in the region had increased by 110%. A greater achievement was to have found a commercial use for the gas. In 1991 the Middle East and North Africa used or exported some 179,760m. cu m of natural gas, more than double the level of consumption seven years earlier. Iran, Abu Dhabi, Saudi Arabia, Bahrain, Oman, Egypt, Libya and Qatar have all doubled domestic consumption of natural gas since the mid-1980s, water desalination plants, power-stations and even town distribution grids having been constructed near where the gas used to be flared. Equally, the development of the petrochemical and metal industries has increasingly utilized gas rather than oil. By 1991 the Middle East and North Africa had more gas-fired power-stations than both Western Europe and North America Combined.

Natural gas is also a major petrochemical feedstock. With environmental awareness growing, the region has quickly realized the value of gas for production of methanol and, from it, MTBE. With the search now on for cleaner fuels, methanol itself may one day become an important vehicle fuel and it requires a gas feedstock. In 1991, however, MTBE was in short supply as a gasoline octane enhancer, since lead was being phased out. Since 1986 the region's MTBE capacity has quadrupled and is expected to double again by 1994. Saudi Arabia's output alone will soon amount to 1,700,000 tons annually, equivalent to more than 50% of Western European capacity in 1990. Looking further ahead, it seems likely that Shell's pioneering project in Malaysia, to produce diesel fuel directly from gas, will be transferred to the region with the most abundant resources.

The increase in demand for natural gas has not only occurred in the countries that produce it. By 1991 the countries of the Middle East and North Africa were exporting 44,430m. cu m of natural gas, compared with only 2,300m. cu m a decade earlier. In 1990 Algeria, which had found it difficult to export natural gas in the early 1980s, received orders from Italy, Germany, Yugoslavia, Spain and France and had fully to utilize its previously idle LNG capacity. In addition, the capacity of the Transmediterranean pipeline to Italy via Libya had tripled between 1984 and 1991 and the construction of two new pipelines was planned. To the west, Spain and Morocco had agreed to begin constructing another pipeline to Spain, passing beneath the Strait of Gibraltar, in mid-1992. Algerian exports of natural gas had risen to 33,900m. cu m by 1991, compared with about 17,000m. cu m annually in the mid-1980s, and a further increase appeared likely. Spain alone was expected to be importing 10,000m. cu m of Algerian natural gas by 1996. Indeed, by 1992 European dependency on Algerian supplies had begun to cause alarm owing to political unrest in that country. Yet, with its rapidly increasing, youthful population, no Algerian government would be able to afford to reduce its exports. By the late 1990s SONATRACH, the Algerian state oil company, will almost certainly dominate the entire European market, with its gas able to reach southern France via either Italy or Spain. In 1992 Portugal was added to the list.

Algeria is not alone in having come to regard exports of natural gas as a major source of revenue. In the Persian (Arabian) Gulf Abu Dhabi has long been a major supplier of LNG to Japan and plans to expand its production capacity by one-third, beginning in 1994. Qatar, which has huge offshore reserves—including 4,400,000m. cu m in a single field—has spent US $2,200m. on constructing a LNG plant. (The whole project, including the construction of offshore platforms and ships to transport the LNG, will cost several times that amount.) This project, which was first conceived in the 1970s, will come into operation in 1997 and may eventually supply more than 6,000m. cu m of natural gas to Japanese electricity producers. In 1992 Oman announced similar plans to develop its LNG production capacity, in a deal with Shell, with the aim of exporting some 6,000m. cu m to Japan by 1999.

Iran plans to develop its South Pars field. The country has been interested in exporting natural gas since the fall of the Shah as its proven reserves are greater than those of North America, South America and Europe combined. In fact, its proven resources are second only to those of the former USSR, and this after very little detailed exploration. Iranian domestic demand, while it is growing rapidly, uses only a tiny fraction of potential production. The problem for Iran has been transporting the gas. In 1991 a joint Pakistani-Iranian team completed a feasibility study on the construction of a trunk line from Iran to Pakistan. It is possible that Iran will be selling natural gas eastwards, perhaps even to India, by 2000. (Qatar, too, regards India as a market for its gas, foreseeing a submarine pipeline to its west coast.)

The question of constructing pipelines in the opposite direction is much more complex politically, but Iran's ambitions have been boosted by the collapse of the USSR. The USSR achieved its export links with western Europe with a system that took very little account of the real investment costs of the very long Siberian pipelines. These pipelines and the reserves that filled them were in poor condition, but the construction of new capacity was likely to be extremely expensive. The collapse of the communist system freed Eastern European countries and the republics of the former USSR to seek alternative suppliers of fuel. The implications of this geopolitical shift in the international gas business have yet to be fully understood. None the less, Iran now has two options for expanding its sales of natural gas in Europe. It can either conclude agreements with Turkey, or it can enter Eastern Europe through the Ukraine. Iran's search for markets to the west received a significant boost in mid-1992, when a World Bank study of Eastern Europe's gas supplies concluded that Iran was potentially the cheapest source to meet demand in the early part of the 21st century.

If Iran appears likely to become a major exporter of natural gas in the 21st century, then the underlying reason is the increasing importance of gas to the global economy. By 1992 world consumption of natural gas had risen by 3.9% compared with 1990 to 1,781.0m. tons of oil equivalent. Such a growth rate had been more or less constant for 10 years by 1992. The market for natural gas, in terms of energy equivalence, is about half the size of that for crude oil. Gas has a number of advantages over oil in an era of environmental concern. In contrast to coal or oil, gas produces less carbon dioxide on combustion and generally contains less sulphur. Any carbon tax thus discriminates against gas rather less than it does against rival fuels. In addition, the use of gas for generating electricity has greatly increased and will continue to increase because the fuel can be used in combined-cycle turbines. Such turbines generate power with a 50% rate of efficiency, compared with the 34% generally achieved by standard, single-cycle oil- or coal-fired power stations. The International

Energy Agency (IEA) has forecast that the consumption of gas for power generation alone will increase from 32,000m. cu m in 1989 to at least 81,000m. cu m by 2000. By mid-1992 Algeria had received orders for 25,000m. cu m of natural gas for post-2000 delivery. Furthermore the UN Climate Change Convention, signed in Rio de Janeiro, Brazil, in mid-1992 urges members of the OECD and other states to stabilize their emissions of carbon dioxide. Apart from nuclear energy, gas is the fuel best suited to this process. By the late 1990s projects now under way in the region will guarantee a doubling of gas exports. Abu Dhabi, one of the original LNG exporters, will double its production capacity. Algeria alone will be exporting an additional 27,000m. cu m after 1995. With more than 12,000m. cu m from Arabian Gulf countries, export output will double in the next decade. The only threat to this relatively new source of revenue to the region is likely to be internal consumption, which has been rising at a rate of 6% a year, if the impact of the invasion of Kuwait is ignored. The impact that this event and the Gulf War had on Iraqi supplies was considerable, since Iraqi gas is primarily associated with oil. Consequently, as Iraqi export sales of petroleum have been reduced, Iraq has lost its source of domestic gas supply. This has led to the necessity to produce crude oil and then return it back into the ground, simply to sustain the gas supply.

It is thus virtually certain that the role of Middle Eastern gas in world trade will grow, increasing exporters' revenues. However, the role of natural gas in many of the less fortunate Middle Eastern states should not be forgotten. Compared with Iran's resources, Jordan's reserves of 15,000m. cu m are minute, but gas from the al-Lisheh region now supplies 15% of Jordan's electricity, saving a considerable amount of foreign exchange. In Syria, where Shell has been remarkably successful at finding local supplies where none were previously believed to be, new reserves have rapidly been put to use for the production of electricity. In Egypt, in the western desert, offshore of Alexandria and in the Red Sea, small fields have all yielded quantities that would probably not have been developed in the Gulf region. These are now used to supply industry and an incipient Cairo gas distribution system. Since the mid-1980s pipeline development has doubled Egyptian consumption, but diligent exploration has discovered sufficient natural gas to produce a healthy reserves-to-production ratio of 44 years. In the 1970s few believed that any such resource existed in Egypt.

The importance of natural gas to the future of the Middle East and North Africa has thus increased enormously since the early 1970s. A new appreciation of the fuel as clean-burning has created potential demand that will be a major element in the region's development over the next 20 years. In recognition of this, a new spirit of co-operation has developed. Unlike crude oil, the production of which is controlled by OPEC and thus dominated by the politics of oil pricing and the Organization's internal disputes, gas diplomacy is largely free of past east-west recriminations. The development of reserves, pipelines, liquefaction units and power plants in the region is being aided by Western multinational companies—Shell, Total, Agip, Elf and others—in a way that no longer applies in the oil business. Even Algeria, where the gas industry was formerly dominated by its state company, requested inward investment in early 1992. Japanese trading groups, such as Mitsui and Mitsubishi, have also established a foothold in the industry. Gas remains a capital-intensive business and external assistance is required in both the financial and technical spheres. Yet, in contrast to oil, the development of gas resources and their exploitation seems to have an internationally binding effect. Gas supply is a central element in the Gulf Co-operation Council's plans for economic development. Iran trades with its northern neighbours. Trade in natural gas with Europe has made a major contribution to Algeria's economic development, and one which has been mutually beneficial. Despite their apparent vulnerability to civil commotion, the long gas pipelines that are beginning to spread across the region and on into Europe have become links that the beneficiaries are reluctant to break.

GAS: RESERVES, PRODUCTION AND TRADE
(b.c.m. = billion ('000 million) cu metres; LNG = liquefied natural gas)

Country	Reserves 1 Jan. 1992 (b.c.m.)	Production 1991 Gross —Including Gas Flared or Reinjected (b.c.m.)	Gas Flared 1991 (b.c.m.)*	Gas Reinjected to maintain Oil Field Pressure 1991 (b.c.m.)*	Exports of Gas by Pipeline or as LNG 1991 (b.c.m.)	Consumption— Methane 1991 (b.c.m.)
Saudi Arabia	5,170	64.7	13.10	4.4	nil	32.00
Kuwait	1,500	16.0	15.5	nil	nil	0.50
Iran	19,800	57.5	11.0	18.4	2.5	23.50
Iraq	3,100	1.89	0.7	nil	nil	1.10
Abu Dhabi	5,335	23.3	0.2	2.00	3.45 LNG to Japan	15.15
Qatar	6,428	10.13	nil	nil	nil	9.30
Libya	1,309	15.6		4.9	nil LNG	5.17
Algeria	3,626	126.27	4.5	60.48	nil both	20.86
Nigeria	3,400	29.8	22.65	2.40	nil	4.75
Gabon	11	2.69	1.92	0.57	nil	0.10
Indonesia	2,950	65.57	5.06	10.43	29.71	19.12
Venezuela	3,530	44.19	3.30	14.5	nil	23.59
Ecuador	110	0.67	0.52	0.05	nil	0.10
USA	4,650	610.62	3.74	68.16	3.32 to Canada	68.53
Canada	2,719	146.37	2.70	13.2	47.36 to USA	68.53
Mexico	2,009	37.55	1.07	nil	nil	28.21
UK	540	65.18	2.4	5.02	nil	61.92
Norway	2,353	41.71	0.36	12.61	24.65	2.32
Netherlands	1,950	82.41	nil	nil	38.64	45.73
France	35	4.85	nil	nil	nil	34.11
Italy	350	17.40	nil	nil	nil	51.44
W. Germany	200	17.35	nil	nil	1.11 to France, Austria and Switzerland	69.95
Japan	35	2.07	nil	nil	nil	52.71
Asia and Australasia	12,484	191.75	11.48	13.18	51.47	166.43
Ex-USSR	55,000	832.63	12.0	nil	107.20	705.83
World total	142,004	2,598.53	124.76	237.42	321.65	2,119.19
OPEC total	53,316	465.26	82.12	118.95	74.14	162.28
OPEC % World total	37.5	17.9	66	50.1	23.0	7.65

* Source: Cedigaz, Paris, France.

Notes: Figures in the Reserves column are for gas recoverable with present technology and at present prices. Figures for reserves of gas—like reserves of oil—may be subject to wide margins of error.

Definitions: Natural gas may be found on its own ('unassociated' gas) or with oil ('associated' gas). 'Associated' gas exists partly as a gas cap above the oil and partly dissolved in oil—it is the presence of gas under pressure in new oil fields which drives the oil to the surface. 'Associated' gas is unavoidably produced with oil and may be flared, reinjected or used as fuel.

Natural gas is a mixture of numerous hydrocarbons and varying amounts of inert gases, including nitrogen, carbon dioxide and sulphur compounds. (Gas containing large quantities of sulphur is know as *sour* gas; gas without sulphur is *sweet* gas.) By far the biggest component of all natural gas by volume (at least 75%) is methane, CH_4. Other components are ethane—C_2H_6, propane—C_3H_8, and butane—C_4H_{10}. All of these hydrocarbons are gases at normal temperatures and pressures. Suspended in the gas are various heavier hydrocarbons, pentane (C_5H_{12}), octane etc., which are liquids at normal temperatures and pressures. Gas with a relatively high proportion of propane, butane and the heavier hydrocarbons is known as *wet* gas. 'Associated' natural gas tends to be wetter than 'unassociated' gas.

Methane is the normal pipeline natural gas used for domestic and industrial purposes. It liquefies at very low temperatures (−160°C) and very high pressures, and in this condition is known as *liquefied natural gas,* LNG.

Ethane is either kept with methane and used as a fuel, or is separated and used as a feedstock for petrochemicals production. Ethane is not traded on its own internationally.

Propane and butane are used as cylinder gases for a large number of industrial and domestic purposes—camping gas and cigarette lighter gas is either propane or butane. The two gases liquefy at higher temperatures and lower pressures than methane.

In their liquid state they are known as *liquefied petroleum gases*—LPGs.

Pentane and other heavier liquids are used for a variety of purposes, including the spiking of heavy crude oils and as petrochemical feedstocks. These hydrocarbons, liquid at normal temperatures and pressures, are known as *natural gasolines* or *condensate.*

Together, liquefied petroleum gases and natural gasolines are referred to as *natural gas liquids*—NGLs.

NATURAL GAS CONSUMPTION
(millions of metric tons of oil equivalent*)

	1991	1992	1993
USA	494.1	507.3	523.8
Canada	56.7	60.2	62.5
North America Total	550.8	567.5	586.4
Belgium/Luxembourg	9.0	9.0	9.5
Netherlands	34.2	33.2	33.8
France	27.5	28.3	29.2
Germany	56.6†	56.7†	59.6†
UK	53.0	52.5	60.5
Western Europe Total	244.7	245.0	260.1
Middle East	68.8	75.5	81.6
Latin America	74.0	73.9	79.4
Africa	32.7	34.2	35.5
S. and S.E. Asia	60	65.5	
Japan	49.2	50.4	50.7
Former USSR	599.0	559.8	531.9
China, People's Republic	13.4	13.6	14.2
Eastern Europe	659.0	612.1	587.2
World Total	1,772.6	1,759.3	1,787.1

* One metric ton of oil equivalent = 1,120 cu m of gas.
† After unification. Earlier figures refer to W. Germany only.

WATER RESOURCES IN THE MIDDLE EAST AND NORTH AFRICA

CHRIS CRAGG

Water in the Middle East and North Africa, as the present Secretary-General of the United Nations, Dr Boutros Boutros-Ghali, has observed, may soon become a more precious resource than oil. The control of this fundamental resource has been regarded as the underlying cause of wars in the past, and as the potential cause of future conflicts. For example, some observers have suggested that rumours of Jordanian and Syrian plans to divert the head-waters of the River Jordan were the principal cause of the 1967 war between Israel and the Arab states. Others believe that Israel's systematic exploitation of the water resources of the Golan Heights and the West Bank has been the main reason for its reluctance to consider a peace agreement based on the exchange of land for peace, and that the control of the flow of the River Litani is the real reason for Israel's continued occupation of southern Lebanon.

It is not only in the context of the Arab-Israeli confrontation that the issue of water resources is a potential cause of further conflict. In October 1991 Egypt warned that it was prepared to use force, if necessary, to protect the head-waters of the Nile for reasons of national security. The warning was aimed at Ethiopia, which controls 85% of the Nile's higher flow, and at Sudan, through which the Nile passes. Elsewhere, Syria has in the past threatened to attack dam facilities in Turkey, while its own use of water from the River Euphrates has been a source of dispute with Iraq. Speculation about the long-term consequences of water consumption has led some ecologists to fear that the depletion of ground water in the Middle East and North Africa may in the future prove to be catastrophic. Libya's enormous 'Great Man-made River' project (GMR) has aroused such fears because the source of the ancient water—trapped beneath the Eastern Desert—that it utilizes is unknown and therefore unrenewable. Similarly, Saudi Arabia is also exploiting 'fossil' reserves of water which are believed to have come from the mountains of Yemen.

Whether the control of water resources from the Rivers Jordan and Yarmuk really was the decisive factor causing the 1967 Arab-Israeli conflict is open to doubt. Certainly there were other, more immediate causes. However, the issue of water resources does undoubtedly cloud regional relations and is a prominent feature of diplomatic rhetoric. Most governments in the Middle East and North Africa are aware that the problem of increasing the availability of water for agriculture, industry and to meet the needs of growing populations cannot be solved without a variety of bilateral and international agreements. However, the basis for such agreements in international law is singularly vague and unhelpful. The accepted practice is to prohibit appreciable harm caused by deprivation of water rights and pollution. Each riparian state also has the right to an equal and reasonable share of water resources. Yet, for obvious reasons, states have different perceptions of what constitutes an equal and reasonable share, while concepts of harmful practice also vary. In addition, only one major international institution—the World Bank—attempts actively to invoke these principles with any significant effect.

Mutual suspicion between Middle Eastern and North African states—especially between Israel and its neighbours—has led some to observe that the issue of water resources is caught in a vicious circle. There can be no basic agreement on an equitable distribution of water resources until a formal Middle Eastern peace settlement has been concluded; but no such settlement can be concluded until an agreement on the equitable distribution of water resources has been reached. However, the problem of water resources may eventually become so great as to make an international solution inevitable. Indeed, numerous water-sharing projects have already been proposed with the aim of achieving greater regional stability. The technical possi-

bilities are considerable, but they cannot be developed without co-operation over distribution. In Jordan a governmental scheme at el-Muwaqqar effectively turns an annual precipitation rate of 150 millilitres into one of 300 millilitres through the simple expedient of using half of the available land as additional catchment for the other half. Since a precipitation rate of 150 millilitres is insufficient for agriculture, the result is that half of the land in the project can become fertile where none was fertile before. The experiment could serve as a paradigm for the region as a whole, since some areas, notably eastern Turkey, have average rainfall in excess of 2,500 millilitres, while others have virtually none at all.

Yet not all of the regional problems connected with water concern transborder river flows. Just as in other arid regions, and even in the United Kingdom and France, aquifers increase in salinity as they are used and take longer to fill after periods of drought than they do to deplete. Intensive agriculture increases nitrate concentrations, although the greatest threat to water resources is caused by ever increasing irrigation. Industrial consumption is also growing. Dams prevent the flow of silt, which is often of primary importance in the productivity of land. The best example of this is that of the Aswan High Dam, which has combined with other, smaller dams to reduce the land area of the Nile delta, where coastal retreat is now sometimes as high as 200 m annually. Some have suggested that this process, combined with global warming and rising sea levels could cause Egypt to lose as much as 19% of its habitable land area by 2050.

Egypt's position in relation to the Nile is part of one of the three major water-related regional disputes that are discussed in more detail below. However, it must be emphasized that increased use of water, whether for generating power, irrigation, industry or simply for drinking, is a function of modernity. Much is often made of the estimate that the average Israeli uses at least three times as much water as the average West Bank Palestinian. Yet, while this may be regarded as a fundamental inequity in the use of resources, few would argue that Israel should reduce the level of its water consumption to that of its neighbours. The level of domestic water consumption in Israel is due not only to the country's competence in the area of water engineering, but also to its population's enjoyment of a near OECD-level lifestyle. The Palestinian population, forced by necessity to collect roof-top rain-water, and forbidden to drill wells without permission, aspires to use more, not less, water. Nor is the issue the simple one of comparing the consumption of two peoples in terms of household use alone. If Israelis ceased to wash, the difference between their own consumption and that of the Palestinian population would not be greatly reduced. Agriculture accounts for some 75% of Israel's water consumption.

In Libya itself the US $25,000m. GMR project that uses 'fossil' water left from prehistoric times has not given rise to environmental concerns. International observers have cast doubt on the feasibility of the project ever since it was first proposed in 1983, not least because of its close association with the Libyan leader, Col Qaddafi. International objections to the GMR have been based on the uncertainty regarding the quantity of the buried resource, and on the probability that the reservoir being tapped lies beneath Sudan, Chad and Egypt as well as Libya. The first phase of the GMR to tap the subterranean reservoirs of the south-eastern desert, linking Sirte and Benghazi, was completed in September 1991 and has the potential to benefit agriculture enormously. The second phase of the project, GMR 2, will link Tripoli to similar underground reservoirs in the Western Desert, while the third phase—GMR 3—will link the first two pipelines, creating a comprehensive grid. With a claimed daily delivery potential of 2m.–4m. cu m, sustainable for 400 years, some of the water from the GMR will enter the aquifers of the Mediterranean coastline and be used again. These aquifers, in common with many on the southern littoral—and in Israel—are increasing in salinity. The GMR is thus not only a major feat of engineering by the South Korean Dong Ah Industrial Construction Company, but also a necessity for Libya's continued economic growth.

Those who object to the tapping of 'fossil' water resources probably have a firmer basis for their objections in relation to Saudi Arabia than to Libya. Saudi Arabia's policy of agricultural self-sufficiency is causing the extremely rapid depletion of aquifers. One estimate suggests that the current annual rate of consumption of 6,000m. cu m will cause the total depletion of ground water within 30 years. In Yemen the water-table is believed to be falling, creating the need for ever deeper drilling in order to sustain supplies. As always in water-table ecology, the evidence is at best vague. None the less, Saudi Arabia's fifth Five-Year Development Plan outlines a serious effort to conserve water resources and makes available some 22,200m. Saudi riyals for the construction of five new desalination plants between 1991 and 1995. There is also evidence to suggest that many in Saudi Arabian government circles would prefer to see more distance between those who devise water policy and those concerned with agriculture.

Environmental objections to the way in which water is used in the Middle East and North Africa are thus opposed to far more powerful forces than simple wastefulness and apparent indifference towards the future. Compared to most nationals of OECD member states, most Arabs have a considerably more developed sense of the value of water, for obvious reasons. The narrow green strips that are maintained in the cities of the southern Persian (Arabian) Gulf are a much more carefully considered luxury than the golf-courses of Europe, since they use water purified at desalination plants at a cost of more than $1 per cu m. Israel's decision in January 1991 to reduce supplies of water to farmers by 60% owing to drought was hardly popular, but it was better understood than the hosepipe bans occasionally imposed in northern Europe, where the technology of water supply remains obscure, by and large, to the general public. In the wider context of, for example, the danger of large dams, Iran's decision to expand its hydropower capacity from 1,968 MW in 1990 to 6,620 MW by 1998 has provoked concern. From Iran's point of view, however, this increase in capacity will stabilize the role of hydropower in the generation of electricity, so fast is domestic demand rising. Above all, before taking too pessimistic a view of the region's problems—for environmental and political reasons, it must be remembered that water projects bring technical control and value to the resource. The region has a long tradition of hydrology. The Aswan dam is heir to the water control systems of the Pharaohs; and if disputes over water resources in the fertile crescent threaten to provoke conflict, this is hardly new. What is new is the size of the populations which the Middle East and North Africa now has to sustain.

Egypt and the Nile

Egypt provides a good example of the pressure placed on water resources by rapidly increasing populations. A census carried out in 1991 estimated that Egypt's population had reached 57m., just three million short of the projection made in 1975 for the year 2000. In 1975 the census estimated the population at only 37m. To supply all the domestic, industrial and agricultural demands of its rapidly rising population, Egypt has only one major source of supply: the Nile. As measured at Aswan, the normal flow of the river is 84,000m. cu m per year, giving a rough total per capita availability of 1,470 cu m annually. However, although the population is increasing, the water flow is not. The rate of population growth therefore means that annual per capital availability of water declines by around 30 cu m–40 cu m each year. By 2000 it will almost certainly have fallen to 1,200 cu m per year, 50% lower than in 1975.

The growth of the Egyptian population would thus be causing problems even if the Nile itself was an entirely reliable source of water and did not flow across any national boundaries. However, it is not reliable in its flow and its waters are shared by nine often unstable riparian states. The problem of water flow has been exacerbated during the past five years by the drought in Ethiopia. In 1988, an especially difficult year, Egypt was forced to adopt an emergency programme of power-station construction. In effect it had to choose between keeping the turbines at the Aswan High Dam running in order to supply Cairo with electricity, and reducing the flow of irrigation water to farmers. The drought in Ethiopia had other effects, not least that of confirming Ethiopia's view that it has significant rights to the waters of the Blue Nile for irrigation purposes. While the six nations that control the White Nile are all members of a governmental committee—UNDUGU—formed to co-ordinate water policies, Kenya and Ethiopia, which are responsible for 85% of the flow of the Blue Nile, have refused to join.

So far, despite persistent rumours to the contrary in the late 1980s, Ethiopia has been both too poor and too afflicted with civil unrest to implement a major dam construction programme. In 1990 Egypt blocked a loan to Ethiopia from the African Development Bank for fear that it might be used for this purpose. However, Ethiopia can argue with some justice that it has as much need of irrigation water and electricity as Egypt. Much the same applies to Tanzania, Uganda, Kenya, Rwanda and Zaire, where poverty and civil unrest have also prevented the construction of dams that might benefit the Nile's water flow. In Sudan a scheme to drain the Sudd marshes by building a 360 km-long canal, which would have saved some 2,000m. cu m of water each year from evaporation, was halted in 1987. Much of the work was complete, but persistent unrest in the southern part of Sudan, the kidnapping of foreign engineers and the murder of workers forced the project to stop. The marshland north of Juba was effectively the main base for Sudan's Christian or animist African opposition. Draining it was thus part of an internal security plan to be imposed by the Muslim north.

Turkey and the head-waters of the Tigris and the Euphrates

Turkey's decision in the 1960s to develop south-eastern Anatolia gave rise to a second major regional crisis in hydropolitics. A scheme, known as 'GAP', on which work commenced in 1984, combines 18 major irrigation and hydropower projects. When completed it will encompass 20 dams and 17 hydropower plants, and it will control enough water to irrigate 1.7m. hectares of land. Its centre-piece is the Ataturk dam on the Euphrates, which was completed in 1990. This will hold behind it some 48,000m. cu m of water, some of which will be diverted to new areas by the Sanliurfa tunnels. While the Ataturk dam is the most publicized of all these projects, Turkey has also completed the Keban dam and a filling dam north of it on the Euphrates at Karakaya, and plans to construct two more large dams on the Tigris. The project has the potential to electrify large parts of undeveloped Turkey and also to turn Anatolia into a major food-producing area. All the major problems connected with it are downstream and in Syria and Iraq.

About 90% of the waters of the Euphrates and the Tigris is raised in Anatolia. To complicate matters, many of the tributaries of the Tigris flow from Iran into Iraq. Estimates vary, but the water flow in the Euphrates as it crosses into Syria is put at 30,000m. cu m per year. Together with some additional water from Syria, it then flows into Iraq at the estimated annual rate of 20,000m.–25,000m. cu m. At least some of this water comes from evaporation at the At-Thawra dam in Syria, which itself has an annual capacity of 11,000m. cu m. In Iraq the Qadisiya dam also has a substantial lake. Not the least of the problems associated with the Ataturk dam is that water levels in Syria have been so low that some hydroelectric plants have regularly stopped functioning, substantially reducing the supply of power to Damascus. To put the GAP scheme in perspective, estimates of the loss of water from the rivers through evaporation and irrigation have been put as high as 14,000m. cu m per year.

With the transfer of water resources taking place on this scale, neither Syria nor Iraq have been pleased by Turkey's plans. At an early stage of the project the USSR—the main source of engineering technology for Turkey—established a technical committee to organize talks between the three countries. Since 1980 the committee has met many times but has so far failed to reach any long-term agreement. At the heart of the issue is a fundamentally different perception of water rights. Turkey effectively asserts its sovereign rights over water arising from its own territory. By contrast, Iraq adheres to a historically-based notion of 'acquired rights', suggesting that established patterns of use are paramount. Syria does not adhere to the notion of 'acquired rights'—if it did the two Arab states could form a united front against Turkey—because it has designs on more water from the Euphrates, especially for new dams at Al-Baath and Techrine. Nevertheless Syria frequently complains to Turkey about the Ataturk project, while the Iraqi Government often blames Syria as much as it blames Turkey.

The search for a compromise did achieve some results in 1987 when Turkey agreed—unilaterally and without further consultation—not to allow the water flow into Syria to fall below 500 cu m per second. Problems developed in 1990, however, when Turkey cut the flow of water completely for a month in order to help fill the Ataturk reservoir. Both Iraq and Syria complained vociferously, but, as Turkey pointed out, additional flow had been allowed prior to the cut in supply to allow the filling of winter storage facilities. Turkey has subsequently maintained that it did allow some 1,000 cu m per second to flow, considerably more than the level it had previously guaranteed. In response Syria has asserted that the guaranteed level is far lower than historical levels and that Syria has been suffering from a severe drought and thus needs more water from the Euphrates, not less.

How the dispute will be solved, if at all, remains uncertain. One potential solution is the so-called 'peace pipeline', which is examined below. Yet both Syria and Iraq remain extremely vulnerable to water shortages as a result of Turkey's actions. Indeed, during the war between Iraq and the multinational force in early 1991 it was seriously suggested that Turkey might try to reduce the flow of water from the Tigris to Iraq in order to increase pressure on Saddam Hussain's regime. After the war, with much of its complex pumping and sewage disposal plant destroyed, Iraq had a major water supply problem. If Turkey continues with its plans to dam the Tigris as well as the Euphrates, and if Iran dams various tributaries, then this problem may become much more serious. Yet Iraq itself has used the diversion of water from the Tigris into Lake Tharthar as a political instrument. The process is now steadily draining the area inhabited by the Marsh Arabs, thereby making it easier for the Iraqi regime to control this area.

Israel and its neighbours

The conflict over water between Israel and its neighbours has a long history. Even at the time of the British Mandate for Palestine the process of Jewish immigration into Palestine was regarded by many Arabs as a potential threat to water supplies. After 1949 Israel began to develop both aquifers and the available resources of the River Jordan. Water from the River Jordan was fundamental to the State of Israel's continued existence. 'Making the desert bloom' with intensive agriculture was part of Israel's self-image and a powerful element in the fascination that Israel exercised on the Western imagination. Through its superior engineering skills Israel was perceived as utilizing land left fallow through Arab inefficiency. Between 1948 and 1980 the area of cultivated land in Israel rose from 400,000 acres to 1.1m. acres, of which at least one-half was irrigated.

Israel's use of water from Lake Tiberias gave rise to the first attempt to conclude an agreement on the use of water resources with Jordan, Lebanon and Syria. From the Golan Heights, Syria had shelled Israel's pumping facilities as early as 1953. In response to this action US President Eisenhower established a commission of inquiry which was charged with the complex task of working out how a fair distribution of water resources could be achieved. With the exception of about 30% of the water that it receives from the Tanninim coastal aquifer, Israel's water comes from the River Jordan. This rises with the River Hasbani in Lebanon and the basin of the River Yarmuk in Jordan and Syria. Unfortunately, both Jordan and Syria rely on the same upstream area. The

commission of inquiry established by President Eisenhower concluded that an equitable distribution of water resources would give Israel 394m. cu m annually, Jordan 774m. and Syria 45m. It proposed the construction of a high dam on the River Yarmuk, with two canals: the East Ghor canal along the eastern side of the Jordan valley and another along the West Bank. Predictably, all of the interested parties complained about the amount of water allocated to them under the commission's proposals and Israel simply refused to recognize any commission on which Arab delegates had any control over the allocation of its water resources. The dam on the River Yarmuk was never built, although Syria and Jordan still have plans to build such a dam, the water flow through which remains a cause of dispute between them. By 1960 Arab states had begun to discuss diverting the flow of the Rivers Hasbani and Baniyas away from Israel. However, irrigation schemes that subsequently attempted to do this were bombed by Israel. By 1964 Israel had gained total control of Lake Tiberias by damming its southern end. Israel proceeded to construct the National Water Carrier, a pipeline which took 320m. cu m of water per year from Lake Tiberias to Rosh Ha'Ayin near Tel-Aviv. Extensions were added to the pipeline to transport water to the Negev Desert. In December 1964 the al-Fatah movement of the PLO attempted to blow up the pipeline. Syrian military action against the pipeline subsequently intensified and full-scale war finally erupted in 1967.

Israel's victory in the 1967 war left it in a much stronger position. Its control of the Golan Heights prevented further Syrian military action against the upper tributaries of the River Jordan and the vital reservoir on Lake Tiberias. It also gained control over the head-waters of River Baniyas. The worst blow to Jordan was the loss of the West Bank from which Israel now takes most of its aquifer water. Restrictions forbidding West Bank Arabs from drilling any new wells are primarily designed to prevent any further depletion of these aquifers. To exacerbate Jordan and Syria's problems over water resources, after the 1967 war more refugees fled to the east than to the west, and Jordan lost most of the fertile area around Jericho.

If the events of 1967 placed Israel in a position of greater security *vis-à-vis* water supplies, they did nothing to lessen controversy over the resource. Israeli actions in the Occupied Territories, where new Israeli settlements are allowed to seek new supplies of water while existing villages are not, have confirmed Arabs in the view that any accommodation over the issue of water is unlikely. It has also been claimed that Israeli expansion into Lebanon and its continued control of the southern Lebanese buffer zone were motivated by the search for further supplies of water. Rumours persist that Israel has plans to divert the flow of the River Litani towards its own territory. In response Israel has claimed that water is actually flowing from Israel into Lebanon, with Lake Tiberias being used as a source of supply for some allied southern Lebanese villages. The fact that at the time of the Israeli invasion of Lebanon in 1982 the River Litani was dry has been cited as proof that Israel harboured no designs on the river. However, it is well known that most of the region's rivers fall to low levels from time to time and later recover.

Not the least of the problems associated with any future exchange of land for peace in order to resolve the Arab-Israeli conflict is that any such exchange involving land on the West Bank or the Golan Heights would effectively require Israel to surrender control of most of its water supplies. At the heart of the issue is the question of whether Israel can afford to put any of its supplies at risk, especially in the light of large-scale immigration of Jews from the former USSR. Since water statistics are state secrets in Israel, it is difficult to answer this question with any certainty. Prior to the winter of 1992 Israel acknowledged that it was becoming progressively more difficult to obtain supplies. Underground aquifers were increasing in salinity and in 1991 a substantial reduction was made in the amount of water supplied to agriculture. In the winter of 1992, however, snowfall was the heaviest for 25 years and flood water from Lake Tiberias had to be released down the River Jordan. This has greatly alleviated the water supply problem for the present.

Annual per capita consumption of water in Israel—excluding that used for agricultural purposes—is estimated at about 100 cu m, and total consumption at some 430m. cu m. When water used for agriculture is added the total amounts to some 1,600m. cu m. Consequently Israel regards the issue of increased immigration as irrelevant to problems concerning water supplies. Rather, it regards water for agriculture as the crux of the problem. Indeed, it has been suggested that Israel's existing supplies of water could support a population as large as 16m., but that this would require the virtual elimination of agricultural irrigation schemes. In January 1991 Israel's State Comptroller criticized the practice of selling water to farmers at less than cost price and revealed that Israel's perceived water deficit amounted to about one full year's consumption. At the same time fears were expressed that Lake Tiberias was becoming increasingly saline. Israel now has an emergency plan to recycle four-fifths of its urban waste water for agricultural purposes by 2000. At present one-third is recycled in this way.

While the winter of 1992 alleviated the immediate salinity problem, the political and environmental issues concerning water remain unresolved. One of the ironies of the situation is that the quantities of water involved in this most intractable of disputes are small by comparison with the Nile and the Euphrates. Israel has even suggested that Egypt might supply water to the Gaza Strip since the volume required would be less than the statistical error involved in the calculation of the flow of the Nile. (The Gaza Strip has been particularly badly affected by the problem of salinity in its aquifers, and by inequity of consumption.) Since 1989 Israel has been involved in discussions with Turkey on a plan to ship as much as 400m. cu m per year of water by tanker to Israel—some 26% of Israel's total annual requirement. Such discussions have also prompted serious consideration of a Middle Eastern network of pipelines, the so-called 'Peace Water' project.

Water for peace?

The 'Peace Water' project, which has been studied in depth by the US engineering company, Brown and Root, would utilize water from the Turkish Rivers Ceyhan and Seyhan to fill two trunklines. Both would initially flow through Syria and part near Homs, with the western spur then continuing through Jordan and terminating near Jeddah, and with a possible spur line running to Israel. The eastern spur would give access to Iraqi waters and then run south to Oman via the United Arab Emirates. Costed at US $21,000m., the network of pipelines would deliver 6,000m. cu m of clear water annually, using about one-quarter of the water flow of the two Turkish rivers. However, Syria and other Arab states have refused to attend a water conference to discuss Turkey's proposals. Syria regards the plan as a plot to divert attention from the issue of the Ataturk dam, and within Turkey itself some have suggested that adequate supplies are not available for export and that the cost of the pipeline scheme has been grossly underestimated.

None the less, proposals such as Turkey's may represent the only possible solution to the various conflicts over water in the Middle East and North Africa. They at least grasp the essential truth that if water resources are potentially a *casus belli*, they could also form the foundation of a more secure peace by promoting mutual dependency. It should be noted that Jordan and Israel have held unpublicized meetings on water through the UN since the 1980s simply because the issue is too important to be left to mutual rivalry. Most estimates suggest that water consumption in Israel and Jordan will rise to almost double its present level by 2010, so a stable external supply is likely to be the *sine qua non* of any future peace settlement.

ISLAMIC BANKING AND FINANCE

RODNEY WILSON

The development of modern commercial banking has been relatively slow in the Middle East and, even today, most people do not use banks. To some extent this reflects the historical underdevelopment of the region as, for ordinary people, the monetarization of transactions has been a relatively recent phenomenon. In other Third World societies there were no moral objections to the replacement of barter with cash and credit transactions. Due to the Islamic code of ethics, however, there has been popular resistance to modern financial developments in many parts of the Muslim world, including the Middle East. Saudi Arabia, for example, did not issue its own notes until the 1960s, as before then gold and silver coins were the major instruments for transactions. Although most people no longer regard paper money as being un-Islamic, the use of cheques, commercial bank credit and other banking instruments are viewed with suspicion by many devout Muslims.

Arab-owned commercial banks were only founded in the Middle East in the 1920s, the first being Banque Misr of Egypt and the Arab Bank, a Palestinian institution. Most financial activity up until then was handled by foreign banks, and even banks such as the Ottoman Bank or the National Bank of Egypt were foreign-owned. As these banks were largely involved in trade finance or arranging government loans, they were not dealing directly with ordinary local Muslims. In any case, trade was often in the hands of non-Muslims; the Egyptian cotton trade, for example, being largely handled by foreigners resident in Alexandria. Hence, banks were regarded as institutions serving infidels, and not organizations with which the devout Muslim should get involved. This attitude has persisted, and despite the development of indigenous commercial banking, it tends to be only the more Westernized elements in Muslim societies which use modern banking services.

Principles of Islamic Finance

Perhaps the most widely known tenet of Islamic finance in the West is the prohibition of *riba*. What constitutes *riba* has long been the subject of debate amongst Islamic scholars. Some believe that *riba* refers to usury, whereas others believe that all interest is *riba*. Certainly, one Muslim objection to interest payments is on the grounds of equity. It is the poor and needy who are often forced to borrow, whereas the rich have surplus funds to save. Interest thus penalizes the poor and benefits the rich. To the devout Muslim this is anathema, as it results in hardship, and increasing social polarization. Such practices could not be tolerated in a community of believers.

A further objection to interest is that it corrupts the recipient. It is viewed as an unearned income, a reward without productive effort. Interest can be a deterrent to honest toil, as it may be tempting to rely on unearned income rather than working for a wage or salary. Western neo-classical economics sees interest as a reward for waiting or deferring consumption until a future time. The Protestant ethic which underlies Western capitalism regarded saving as virtuous. Time is treated as a type of commodity by Western economists, which has a price. There is believed to be a trade-off between earnings and leisure, and wages are a reward for foregoing leisure. Muslim scholars reject such notions. The just wage reflects the workers' contribution to society, not the time spent working. Time itself is valueless. Hence there can be no justification in a reward for time.

To the devout Muslim abstinence needs no material reward. The earth's bounty is to be used, but Allah demands certain sacrifices, such as fasting during the month of Ramadan. The rewards for such abstinence are spiritual, and the introduction of monetary incentives would only undermine the spiritual value of such practices. Furthermore, an incentive for saving may result in underconsumption, and a lack of effective demand in the economy. Hoarding is viewed as socially undesirable in Muslim societies, as it can result in unemployment and idle capacity. In this sense Muslim ideals are consistent with Keynesian views on economic management. Currency must circulate, and the accumulation of the means of exchange for its own sake is seen as undesirable. In the view of Muslim economists, capitalism does not achieve the right balance. Too much power is vested in the suppliers of capital; and the loanable fund market is distorted. A market system is viewed as natural, it is capitalism that is unnatural.

Application of Islamic Ideals

Although there is little disagreement over the principles of Islamic finance, the interpretation of the prohibition of *riba* in practice has been subject to much greater controversy. Should the prohibition apply to all interest, or does it merely mean that interest rates should be constrained at moderate levels? Are interest charges for business loans permissible, as the borrowers are seeking to use their credit to generate profits? Are fixed interest loans preferable to those subject to interest rate variations, as at least the borrower knows the exact charges in advance, and there is no element of uncertainty? Finally under inflationary conditions, should interest rewards be allowed to compensate savers for the depreciation of the value of their savings? A prohibition of nominal interest to compensate for inflation would penalize lenders, and subsidize borrowers. It could be argued that the prohibition of *riba* applies to real interest, not nominal interest, as with inflation, a ban on the latter may result in negative real interest.

Most Islamic states in practice have tried to restrain nominal interest rates. As inflation results in social strains in any Muslim community, and also poses moral dilemmas, the control of price increases has been an important economic priority for Muslim governments. In the Middle East inflation has been a major worry in Turkey and Sudan, and a cause of concern in Iran, Egypt and Jordan. The consequences of inflation for nominal interest rates appalled the majority of devout Muslims. Double-figure nominal interest rates have become all too prevalent in these countries, and even when action against price rises has succeeded problems can remain. As there are some lags in adjustment, it is possible to have high real rates, especially as inflation starts to fall.

Some states such as Saudi Arabia have a prohibition on all interest payments and receipts under their Islamic laws. Service charges are permitted, however, on bank loans, and in practice, as they are calculated on a percentage basis, they resemble interest in many respects. The service charges are fixed, however, and hence borrowers are not subject to the uncertainty over the future costs of debt servicing which arises when interest rates vary. In Saudi Arabia most bank deposits are in current accounts which earn no income, but even deposits in savings accounts only earn a modest fixed return, not an interest receipt. There was no question of raising these returns when interest rates on dollar deposits in Bahrain and elsewhere rose to very high levels in the early 1980s, even though the Saudi Arabian monetary system was disrupted as a result of the exodus of capital. It was widely felt that it was better to suffer such disruptions, than to compromise Islamic principles.

Modern Islamic Banking

In Islamic states where commercial banks are free to charge and receive interest, many Muslim businessmen felt obliged to participate in *riba* transactions, even though they felt a moral guilt in doing so. To overcome this dilemma of conscience specifically Islamic banks were founded which could compete with conventional commercial banks but which adhered to Islamic principles. The movement was started in Pakistan in the 1950s, but soon spread to the Arab World, with the opening of the Mitr Ghams Savings Bank in Egypt in 1963, which later was superseded by the Nasser Social Bank. The impact of these institutions was modest, as the major state-owned banks continued to account for most of the banking business in Egypt. Nevertheless, the Nasser Social Bank attracted deposits from an influential group of pious farmer landlords, and backed some significant agro-industrial ventures.

It was, however, the devout Muslim merchants of the Gulf who were largely responsible for the rapid expansion of Islamic banking during the last two decades. These conservative merchants were reluctant to use the services of conventional commercial banks yet, with the rapid business expansion in the Gulf following the oil price rises of 1973–74, some type of financial intermediation was clearly needed. Institutions such as the Dubai Islamic Bank (founded 1975), the Kuwait Finance House (1977), and the Bahrain Islamic Bank (1979) were established to serve such clients, while at the same time avoiding *riba* transactions. There was some government encouragement, with the states taking a minority shareholding in each of the institutions, but most of the finance came from the merchants themselves, especially in the case of the Dubai Islamic Bank which is 80% privately owned.

The Islamic banks in the Gulf account for around 10% of total bank deposits. Although their role in Gulf finance is modest, the banks' market penetration is considered a success, given that they represent a new type of institution adopting innovative financial techniques. Although there have been setbacks, notably as a result of dealings in precious metals, the track record of the Islamic banks has been favourable so far, and the returns to investors have been competitive with those offered by more conventional banks. As most deposits are of modest amounts, the total number of depositors is higher than their share of total deposits indicates. Many customers maintain accounts with both the new Islamic banks and conventional commercial banks. In this sense the Islamic banks complement rather than replace conventional banks. Nevertheless, the ultimate objective for the Islamic banks is to provide a comprehensive range of banking services as a complete alternative to *riba* finance.

In terms of domestic market penetration, the Kuwait Finance House has been the most successful Islamic bank, accounting for almost one-fifth of total bank deposits in Kuwait. Its activities are more diverse than those of the commercial banks in Kuwait, as it is heavily involved in construction finance and housing loans, in addition to trade and commerce. The extent of its involvement in real estate means that, in many respects, it resembles a building society. Islamic services are provided in a modern fashion, with computerized accounts, fully automatic telling facilities and even Islamic credit cards. During Iraq's occupation of Kuwait in August 1990–February 1991, the Kuwait Finance House refused to remain open for business, unlike other Kuwaiti banks. Following the country's liberation, the Kuwait Finance House reopened, having gained much respect by its refusal to collaborate with the Iraqis in any way.

In Saudi Arabia there has been considerable support for Islamic banking, even though the Kingdom had no specifically Islamic banks until recently. As all banks in Saudi Arabia are supposed to operate according to Islamic principles, the Saudi Arabian Monetary Agency saw no need to license a specially designated Islamic bank. Indeed it was thought that granting such a licence would place the commercial banks in an invidious position. Hence the only Islamic financial institution in the Kingdom was the Jeddah-based Islamic Development Bank, but it is a development assistance agency, and not a bank which deals with the general public. Its principal aim is to provide *riba*-free finance for Islamic countries, especially those with low per caput income levels.

Money-lenders as Islamic Banks

Most Saudi citizens do not maintain accounts with the commercial banks in the Kingdom. Instead they resort to money-lenders and money-changers for their financial requirements. Some of these informal bankers offer a wide range of financial services, including the exchange of currency, the handling of overseas remittances, deposit facilities and loans. Interest is not earned on loans, which are often in kind rather than cash. For example, if a client needs some item of equipment, the money-lender will usually purchase it on behalf of the client, and then either collect instalments from the client, or else enter a leasing arrangement. In either case the payments over a period will exceed the initial cost of the item, the difference representing the money-lender's profit.

One Saudi Arabian money-lending and money-changing family, the ar-Rajhis, have grown to become the third largest commercial financial institution in the Kingdom, after the National Commercial and the Riyadh banks. Their assets exceed $5,000m., and all of the business has been built up on the basis of *riba*-free transactions. In 1983 there were pressures on the ar-Rajhis to register as a commercial bank, as, unlike the other banks, they did not hold reserves with the Saudi Arabian Monetary Agency and were completely unregulated. Rather than register as a conventional commercial bank, the ar-Rajhis decided to seek Islamic banking status, as they claimed their business methods conformed to Koranic principles in any case.

There was some hesitation on the part of the Saudi Arabian Monetary Agency, given the implications for the other banks and the problems in acting as a lender of the last resort for this type of financial institution. In the end, however, the Saudi Arabian Monetary Agency decided to license the ar-Rajhis officially in 1985 as deposit-takers and exchange-dealers, largely in order to help safeguard the stability of the domestic financial system. In 1988 the ar-Rajhis decided to increase their capital base by becoming a public company and sold one-half of their shares outside the family. Although the Monetary Agency is not obliged to act as lender of the last resort with respect to institutions such as the ar-Rajhis, it is widely believed that it would if the need arose. It is only the unregistered money-changers who refuse to submit properly audited annual accounts that lie outside the Monetary Agency's protective net. With the registration of the money-lenders as Islamic banks, the Monetary Agency has conceded that Islamic financial principles can be interpreted in different ways. Plurality exists as both the conventional commercial banks and the money-lenders claim to conform with Islamic principles, even though their methods of operation differ considerably.

Islamic Banks in International Markets

Prince Muhammad al-Faisal as-Saud of Saudi Arabia is one of the leading activists in the Islamic banking movement. Although he has not established a domestic banking operation within Saudi Arabia, he was the prime instigator of the Faisal Islamic Banks of Egypt and Sudan, both of which were founded in 1977. Both banks received some local deposits, but much of their funds for lending came from Saudi Arabia. Hence in this sense the institutions represented a vehicle for the intra-regional recycling of petroleum revenue to less affluent Muslim states. Prince Muhammad al-Faisal as-Saud, however, decided that it would be desirable to have an Islamic banking presence in Western financial markets. It was felt necessary to provide some mechanism whereby investors from Saudi Arabia and elsewhere in the Gulf could participate in Western markets on the basis of *riba*-free transactions. Consequently Dar al-Maal al-Islami, the House of Islamic Funds, was founded in Geneva in 1981, with a paid-up capital of $316m.

Despite some initial teething problems, and losses during the 1983/84 financial year, Dar al-Maal al-Islami seems to have established a sound base, and is widening its lending and investment activities. There seems to be little problem in attracting deposits, though the 1983/84 losses deterred some investors, but the major difficulty has been to identify *riba*-free projects to back profitably in Western markets. There is no objection to dealing with institutions which participate in *riba* transactions, however, as long as the Islamic institution is not directly involved, though in the longer term it is hoped to avoid such dealings. In practice, Dar al-Maal al-Islami functions as a kind of investment company, deploying most of its funds in equity markets and in property, though it also holds short-term assets in the form of cash and commodities. It is the appropriate choice of liquid financial instruments which has caused greatest difficulty, as Islamic institutions cannot hold government bills or bonds which yield interest.

There is little doubt that the number of Islamic financial institutions represented in Western financial markets will continue to increase. The ar-Rajhis maintain an office in London, not only for exchange dealings, but also to provide investment services for their clients from Saudi Arabia. Another Jeddah-based group, the al-Barakas, was also represented in London. This group is primarily an investment company, but as its paid-up capital is $1,500m., and with their substantial deposit base, the al-Barakas are a significant force in Islamic finance. In 1989 it opened a branch in Birmingham, United Kingdom. However, confidence in its UK operations was undermined by the collapse of the Bank of Credit and Commerce International (BCCI) in 1991. In 1993 it decided to close its UK branches, but depositors were fully compensated. Like Dar al-Maal al-Islami, the al-Baraka group maintains an offshore banking unit in Bahrain, and it has also opened branches in Sudan, while further branches are planned in Turkey, Egypt, Tunisia and Malaysia. It seems likely that there will be increasing competition between the al-Baraka group, the ar-Rajhis and Dar al-Maal al-Islami in the years ahead, although at present there seems to be no shortage of deposits for all these institutions.

Constraints in Secular Societies

Problems inevitably arise when Islamic financial institutions operate in a non-Islamic environment. As the Islamic banks do not hold Western government securities as part of their liquid assets, they cannot be registered in Western Europe or the USA as fully-fledged commercial banks. Commodity holdings are not recognized as liquid assets, and the maintenance of a large proportion of non-earning cash reserves would substantially reduce the banks' returns on their assets. One possible solution in the West is to act as a kind of building society, lending to Muslims for house purchases. This approach has been adopted by First Path Financial Services of Michigan and Ontario, the leading Islamic retail financial institution in North America.

The Bank of England has been reluctant even to register the Islamic banks as licensed deposit-takers, and those operating in the United Kingdom are regarded as investment companies rather than so-called 'secondary' banks. Islamic banks, of course, do not want to be regarded as secondary in any case, but the lack of banking status has drawbacks. Islamic institutions cannot solicit for deposits from Muslim investors who reside in the United Kingdom, nor can they carry out normal banking operations in London, as they have to resort to conventional *riba* banks for the clearance of cheques and banker's drafts. The Islamic financial institutions in London are mainly engaged in trade finance. This largely involves Euro-Arab trade, with finance provided for both European exporters and Arab importers. Clients of British banks exporting to the Islamic world are often referred to Islamic institutions in London. One new development has been for Western commercial banks to offer Islamic financial services to their Muslim clients. The Union Bank of Switzerland, for example, offers an Islamic investment fund, while the British merchant bank, Kleinwort Benson, has marketed an Islamic unit trust in the Gulf. The Australia and New Zealand banking group, ANZ, also maintains an Islamic Finance Department in London, partly for business with Pakistan and Malaysia. The Saudi International Bank in London offers Islamic trade finance and is also offering Islamic portfolio management services for clients of substantial means. The United Bank of Kuwait has opened a specialized Islamic Investment Banking Unit in London. It is now the leading provider of such services in Europe.

Indebtedness and the Shari'a Law

With the slump in oil revenues since 1983, and the intensified depression caused by the oil price falls of 1986, an increasing number of commercial bank loans in the Gulf are no longer performing. Though the financial situation is now improving, many bad debts remain. Many borrowers argue that they should not be liable for interest payments when they fall into debt. The *Shari'a* courts have usually sided with the debtors rather than with the banks, and in Saudi Arabia there is some doubt if even service charges can be legally enforced.

In the United Arab Emirates the courts have ruled that simple interest is permissible, but that borrowers are not liable for compound interest payments. As the *Shari'a* law does not follow case precedent, there is much confusion about the situation. Commercial banks operating in the Gulf are increasingly reluctant to take debtors to court, and many are trying to reach out-of-court settlements by granting payment moratoriums. Rolling over credits is regarded as preferable to writing down the value of bank assets.

In order to avoid problems of this kind in the future the commercial banks in Saudi Arabia are now offering Islamic finance. Some, including the Kingdom's largest bank, the National Commercial, have opened separate branches for women, a move favoured by some Islamic theologians, who advocate the sexual segregation of finance in accordance with Islamic inheritance laws. This is partly in response to clients' wishes, but also because, in the event of repayments' failure, restitution can be more easily sought through the courts. Trade credit is granted through resale and leasing arrangements, and the profit-sharing principle covers medium- and long-term finance. It seems likely that an increasing proportion of commercial banking business in the Gulf will be Islamized, even though it requires much more work by the banks. The emphasis switches from mere risks' appraisal, to the fuller evaluation of returns which is necessary with Islamic finance.

Islamization of Banking

In post-revolutionary Iran a major policy objective has been the Islamization of the nation's institutions. In an Islamic society it is felt that all institutions should operate in accordance with Islamic principles, including banks and financial institutions. Merely permitting Islamic banks to operate alongside Westernized commercial banks is unsatisfactory. In a society of believers there is no place for *riba* financial institutions, indeed the workings of commercial banks are an affront to the faithful. Instead, to ensure conformity with Koranic ideas and the spirit of Shi'ism, the Teheran authorities have Islamized the entire banking system which precludes the operation of commercial banks using principles of Western finance.

Iranian commentators have repeatedly attacked the Arab Islamic banking movement as a camouflage for capitalism. Merely using the word 'Islamic' does not change the nature of the banks themselves. The expression 'Islamic banking' is itself a contradiction in terms according to these critics. The word 'bank' comes from the Italian 'banco', meaning 'table', as in the past money-changers from Lombardy used to place money on a table. Such practices are inappropriate in Islamic financial transactions, which are based on trust. The word of a devout Muslim is believed, and he has no need to produce proof of his worth. This explains why even some Arab Islamic institutions are called houses rather than banks, the Kuwait Finance House and Dar al-Maal al-Islami (literally, Islamic House of Funds) being notable examples.

Merely providing interest-free transactions, though a welcome development, is insufficient, according to Iranian critics. Islamic financial institutions cannot be limited liability companies as obligations between Muslims who enter transactions must be absolute. There can be no escape from personal liability, and institutions can have no personality of their own in any case.

Implementation of Islamic Financial Law

Iran's new Islamic financial laws were passed by the Majlis (Islamic Consultative Assembly) in February 1984. They provided for the Islamization of all Iran's financial institutions by 22 March 1985, although the implementation of the new regulations took four years to complete. Interest has been phased out of the system, and the banks now offer either interest-free current and savings deposits, or long-term investment deposits. With current account deposits customers can use chequing facilities, but only those with savings deposits are given preferential treatment with respect to loan applications. Incentives are also offered on savings deposits, including the possibility of a funded pilgrimage to Mecca. Those with long-term investment deposits cannot withdraw their funds without several months notice, but they are entitled to share in the bank's profits, in accordance with the Islamic *mudaraba* (speculation) system. Borrowers are encouraged to enter into partnership arrangements with the banks, under which they share any profits which arise as a result of the investments which the bank has financed. The partnership arrangement may be only in respect of one project which the bank backs, or it may be with the business as a whole. In the case of a limited partnership the profits shared are only those which arise from the specific project for which funds have been obtained. Under a full partnership arrangement all profits are shared. Machinery purchases are often financed by the bank purchasing the item required on behalf of the client, who repays by instalments. In this case the ownership is transferred on payment of the first instalment. An alternative arrangement is leasing conditioned to purchase, whereby the ownership is only transferred when the final instalment is paid.

Under the Islamic banking laws banks may also finance trade through forward purchases on a client's behalf. There is a distinction drawn between such purchases and futures trading, which is regarded as speculative, and therefore prohibited. Under a forward purchase the bank pays for the commodity being traded on behalf of the import agent or wholesaler, who will repay the bank when he resells the merchandise to the retailer or final customer. The Arab Islamic banks have similar resale contracts, the time period for this type of credit typically being 90 or 180 days.

Employee Attitudes

In practice, in Iran, there has been some opposition to the new laws from existing bankers, and many bank employees are less than enthusiastic about the new systems. To facilitate implementation the banks have been reorganized into three groups, Melat, Melli and Tejarat. A Council of Money and Credit Regulation has been established to supervise the banking system, the Council consisting of representatives from the banks themselves, independent financial experts, and religious advisors, two of whom are mullahs. The Central Bank retains its executive role, but the Council is responsible for bank policy, and the implementation of the new code. In 1994 it was announced that foreign banks could operate in Iran again, and not be confined solely to maintaining representative offices. It remains to be seen how they will be regulated under the Islamic banking laws.

The Arab Islamic financial institutions have had fewer personnel problems. All of the staff recruited by the Islamic banks are practising Muslims, apart from some employees in Europe. Many are experienced bankers, who took salary cuts to join the new institutions, because they wished to work in an Islamic environment, and refrain from participation in *riba* transactions. Their attitude is extremely positive, and they are genuinely seeking to make Islamic principles work. The bank employees view their jobs as part of their religious devotion and there is little doubt that in many respects a voluntary system of Islamic banking is preferable to compulsion.

Monetary Policy Issues

Islamic financial principles are not only applicable to banking activity, but also to government finance and management of the economy at the national level. The prohibition of *riba* precludes the use of interest-rate changes as an instrument of monetary policy. Islamic economists believe it is unfair to penalize borrowers by raising interest rates merely for the sake of demand management, when the problems which resulted in such an action were not the fault of individual borrowers. Hence, even in Muslim economies where interest is permitted, it is felt desirable to keep rates stable, and preferably at low levels. Other instruments of monetary policy can be used, including control of the money supply, and the regulation of bank lending through reserve requirements and special deposits. Indeed a strict monetary policy is thought to be essential in order to keep inflation under control. High and unpredictable rates of price increase result in social strains and uncertainty which can undermine the cohesion of Islamic societies.

Many Islamic economists urge balanced budgets, as, if government expenditure exceeds tax receipts, borrowing becomes necessary. If resort is made to bill or bond issues this implies the government is dependent on *riba* finance, an undesirable state of affairs for any government in the Islamic world. In Saudi Arabia the authorities have attempted to avoid interest by issuing government securities at a discount below their redeemable value. The difference represents the return to purchasers of the securities. Islamic fundamentalists object to this practice, however, as the yield on the securities resembles interest. Indeed the price at which this type of Saudi Government security has been traded has been influenced by interest-rate developments in Western markets. This is a result of the openness of the Kingdom's economy, and the ease with which foreign assets can be substituted for domestic assets.

Fiscal Policy Constraints

The public sector borrowing requirement can of course be controlled through fiscal policy, by restraining government expenditure or increasing taxation. The governments of many of the poorer Islamic states find great difficulty in restraining expenditure, especially on items such as food subsidies, given the pressing social needs. Many face a dilemma, as the reduction of the food subsidies results in inflationary pressures, which cause Islamic critics to assert that they are penalizing the poor, and are acting contrarily to the spirit of Islamic brotherhood. On the other hand if the subsidies are maintained, the governments are forced to borrow, not only from their own citizens, but also from Western infidels, or non-believers. In neither case can the governments satisfy their critics. It is this kind of dilemma which confronts the Government of President Mubarak in Egypt, and to which there seems to be no solution.

In many of the poorer Islamic states the tax base is extremely restricted, as most of the population do not earn enough to pay income tax, and purchase taxes on basic commodities would penalize the needy. Import duties usually constitute the major source of government revenue, except in the oil-exporting states. Islamic law provides for *zakat*, a type of wealth tax, which is on the statutes of all Muslim countries. This is levied annually on both businesses and individuals at a rate of 2.5% of their total net value. *Zakat* is a unique tax, as contributions are entirely voluntary, but most believers pay, as it is regarded as one of the five central obligations of the Islamic faith.

In some countries such as Saudi Arabia, *zakat* collection is encouraged, and the funds are collected by a special ministry, which uses the revenue for social purposes. *Zakat* has to be administered separately from other tax revenue, and cannot be used for general government spending, even on development projects. For this reason some governments have done little to encourage *zakat*. In Iran under the Shah many of the bazaar merchants paid *zakat*, but not to the secular Teheran authorities. Instead they paid *zakat* to local relief agencies organized by the mullahs through the local mosques. Most of the revenue was used to help poor rural immigrants to the cities who had difficulty in finding employment and who often lived in appalling conditions. Since the revolution the Islamic Government has taken over the administration of the tax, and there has been much debate about whether it should be made compulsory given the great social problems inherited from the Shah's regime.

There has also been some debate amongst Islamic economists about whether the level of *zakat* should be varied in the interests of demand management. Hence, the rate could be increased to control inflationary pressures, or reduced in a slump to stimulate demand. This type of Keynesian application has been rejected by the majority of Islamic economists, as it could penalize beneficiaries, and might only confuse payers concerning the true nature of *zakat*. This and other issues in Islamic monetary and fiscal policy remain to be resolved.

It is clear that the application of Islamic ideas at the grassroots is much more advanced than at a higher level. Much of the initiative in the modern Islamic movement has come from individuals rather than governments. The experience of the Islamic banks suggests that there is much popular support for the application of Islamic principles to finance. It

MAJOR ISLAMIC BANKS

Institution	Country	Date of foundation	Paid-up capital (million US $)
Bahrain Islamic Bank	Bahrain	1979	19.0
Bahrain Islamic Investment Company	Bahrain	1981	15.0
Bank Islam Malaysia	Malaysia	1983	206.0
Al-Baraka Group	Saudi Arabia	1982	183.0
Beit Ettamouil Saudi Tounsi	Tunisia	1984	50.0
Dar al-Maal al-Islami	Switzerland	1981	316.0
Dubai Islamic Bank	UAE	1975	62.0
Faisal Islamic Bank of Egypt	Egypt	1977	109.0
Faisal Islamic Bank of Sudan	Sudan	1977	30.0
Faisal Islamic Bank of Turkey	Turkey	1985	6.0
International Islamic Bank	Bangladesh	1983	19.0
Islamic Development Bank	Saudi Arabia	1975	2,000.0
Jordan Islamic Bank for Finance & Investment	Jordan	1978	18.0
Kuwait Finance House	Kuwait	1977	175.0
Kuwait Finance House (Turkey)	Turkey	1983	20.0
Nasser Social Bank	Egypt	1972	29.0
Qatar Islamic Bank	Qatar	1983	53.0
Ar-Rajhi Company for Currency Exchange & Commerce	Saudi Arabia	1985	812.0
Saudi-Philippine Islamic Development Bank	Saudi Arabia	1982	5.0
Tadamon Islamic Bank	Sudan	1983	9.0

* Authorized capital.

remains to be seen whether the governments of Muslim countries will respond to this constituency and initiate serious consideration in the Organization of the Islamic Conference and other forums as to how their economies can be managed in accordance with the tenets of Islam.

Prospects for the Future

The prospects for Islamic finance were dealt several blows in the late 1980s, most notably the collapse in 1988 of the Egyptian Islamic investment house, Ar-Rayan, which was widely publicized. The Central Bank refused to intervene, thousands of small investors lost their savings and although Egypt's Islamic banks were not directly involved, confidence in the whole sector was shaken. This had implications well beyond Egypt, as did the difficulties of the Jordan Islamic Bank, which were caused by the effect on the Jordanian economy of the crisis in the Gulf in 1990/91.

Despite these reversals, the outlook for Islamic banking for the mid-1990s and beyond is encouraging. The existing Islamic financial institutions are now well-established and Islamic financial instruments are now widely recognized as a viable alternative to *riba* finance. Investors in the Ar-Rayan company were eventually compensated by an anonymous Gulf source and confidence among depositors with Islamic banks in Egypt was restored. The four principal state-owned commercial banks in Egypt now offer Islamic banking facilities to their clients. These facilities have proved to be very successful, attracting 10% of total deposits in the Egyptian banking system within one year of their introduction. Islamic laws were enacted in Pakistan following the demise of the Bhutto Government in 1977, and, despite some internal opposition, in Sudan.

Most importantly, the political hand of Saudi Arabia and the other Gulf states has been strengthened considerably as a result of the Gulf conflict in 1990/91. Although these states face short-term economic problems in the aftermath of the conflict, their long-term economic outlook is good. They are certain to exercise more influence in the Middle East and the Islamic world now that the challenge from secularist Iraq has been resisted, and this will result in more emphasis being placed on the importance of Muslim values, of which Islamic finance is only one manifestation.

SELECT BIBLIOGRAPHY

Abdeen, Adnan M., and Shook, Dale N. *The Saudi Financial System in the Context of Western and Islamic Finance*. Chichester, John Wiley, 1984.

Ali, Muazzam, (Ed.). *Islamic Banks and Strategies of Economic Development*. London, New Century Publishers, 1982.

Beaugé, Gilbert, (Ed.). *Les Capitaux de l'Islam*. Paris, Presses du CNRS, 1990.

Chapra, M. Umer. *Islam and the Economic Challenge*. Islamic Foundation, Leicester, 1992.

Homoud, Sami H. *Islamic Banking*. Arabian Information, London, 1985.

Kazarian, Elias. *Islamic Banking in Egypt*. Lund Economic Studies, 1991.

Mallat, Chibli, (Ed.). *Islamic Law and Finance*. London, Graham and Trotman, 1988.

Mannan, Muhammad Abd al-. *Islamic Economics: Theory and Practice*. Hodder and Stoughton, Sevenoaks, 1986.

Mayer, Ann Elizabeth. 'Islamic Banking and Credit Policies in the Sadat Era: The Social Origins of Islamic Banking'. *Arab Law Quarterly*. Vol. 1, part 1, 1985.

Naqvi, Syed Nawab Haider. *Islam, Economics and Society*. London, Kegan Paul International, 1994.

Nomani, Farhad and Rahnema, Ali. *Islamic Economic Systems*. London, Zed Books, 1994.

Piccinelli, Gian Maria, (Ed.). *Banche Islamiche in Contesto Non-Islamico*. Rome, Instituto per l'Oriente, 1994.

Rodinson, Maxime. *Islam and Capitalism*. Harmondsworth, Penguin Books, 1979.

Sadeq, Abul Hasan M., (Ed.). *Financing Economic Development: Islamic and Mainstream Approaches*. Longman Malaysia, 1992.

Siddiqi, Muhammad, N. *Banking Without Interest*. The Islamic Foundation, Leicester, 1983.

Wilson, Rodney J. A. *Banking and Finance in the Arab Middle East*. London, Macmillan, 1983.

Islamic Business: Theory and Practice. Economist Intelligence Unit, Special Report No. 221, London, 1985.

'Islamic Banking—the Jordanian Experience'. *Arab Law Quarterly*. Vol. 3, part 1.

Islamic Financial Markets. London, Routledge, 1990.

THE SUEZ CANAL

The Suez Canal joins the Mediterranean and Red Seas between Port Said and Suez, in Egypt. It was closed during the Arab-Israeli war of June 1967 and was not reopened until 5 June 1975. Between June 1967 and October 1973 the Canal formed the demarcation line between Egypt and the Israeli-occupied Sinai peninsula. After 13 months spent clearing the Canal of obstacles, it was reopened by President Sadat on 5 June 1975. Transit rates were fixed at a level which represented an increase of more than 90% on the rates before the closure in June 1967. Rates were then only marginally altered until January 1981, when a new tariff scale came into force, meaning average rises of between 22% and 25%, but with discounts for larger tankers.

PRINCIPAL FACTS

Length: 195 km including approach fairways.
Maximum Depth: 20 m.
Maximum Width: 350 m.
Minimum Width: 286 m.
Maximum Draught: 53 ft (16.15 m).
Transit Time: Average transit time is 15 hours.
Numerical Capacity: 76 ships per day.

ORGANIZATION

Suez Canal Authority (*Hay'at Canal as-Suess):* Irshad Bldg, Ismailia, Egypt; tel. (064) 394100; telex 63238; fax (064) 320784; Cairo Office: 6 Sharia Lazoghli, Garden City, Cairo; f. 1956; Chair. MUHAMMAD EZZAT ADEL. The Suez Canal Authority manages the Canal on behalf of the Government of Egypt.

CHRONOLOGY

1854 Ferdinand de Lesseps granted building concession.
1859 Excavation began.
1869 Canal opened.
1875 Ismail Pasha of Egypt sold his shares in the French Suez Canal Company (44% of total) to the British Government for nearly £4m.
1888 Convention of Constantinople declared Canal open to vessels of all nations.
1956 President Nasser of Egypt nationalized Canal. Canal closed following invasion of Egypt.
1957 Canal reopened under the control of the Egyptian Suez Canal Authority (April).
1959 World Bank lends the Authority US $56.5m.
1961 UN surcharge of 3% on transit dues, levied in 1958 to pay for clearing the Canal, was lifted (March).
1964 Loan of £E9.8m. granted by Kuwait Fund for Arab Development for dredging and widening operations. Permissible draught increased to 38 ft (11.6 m).
1965 Transit rates increased 1% (July).
1966 Transit rates increased 1% (July).
1967 Canal closed (June) during war with Israel.
1975 Canal reopened (June).
1979 First transit of Israeli ship (April).
1980 Maximum permissible draught raised to 53 ft (16.15 m) (December).

1981 The Suez Canal Vessel Traffic Management System (SCVTMS) inaugurated (October).
1984 Transit rates increased by average of 5% (January).
1985 Transit rates increased by average of 5% (January).
1986 Transit rates increased by average of 3.4% (January).
1987 Transit rates increased by average of 5.6% (January).
1988 The cease-fire in the Iran–Iraq War led to increased Canal traffic. December figures for ships and tonnage were the highest monthly figures since the reopening of the Canal in 1975.
1990 Transit rates increased by average of 5% (January).
1991 Transit rates increased by 4% for dry bulk carriers and 6% for other ships.

IMPROVEMENT SCHEMES

In the years following the opening of the Canal the depth of the channel was 26.2 ft (8 m) and its breadth at the bottom 72.2 ft (22 m), with a wet cross-sectional area of 3,272 sq ft (304 sq m). The average gross tonnage of transiting vessels was then 1,794 tons and the highest authorized draught was 24.6 ft (7.5 m). Navigation speed was 6.21 miles (10 km) per hour.

Nasser Project

Seven programmes of improvement were executed between 1876 and 1954. The eighth programme had started before nationalization, was modified thereafter to achieve better results and is now called the Nasser project. Under this scheme the Canal was widened and deepened to take large tankers. New navigational aids and dockyard facilities were built and tug and salvage services improved. A research centre has been founded at Ismailia.

Under the first stage, finished in 1961, the Canal was widened and deepened to take vessels of 37 ft (11.3 m) draught. Under the second stage, finished in 1964, the Canal was widened and deepened to take vessels of 38 ft (11.6 m) draught. The installation of two salvage stations and a system of direct radio between vessels and the traffic control station at Ismailia were finished during 1962.

Suez Area Redevelopment

After the war of October 1973 Egypt announced a plan to reopen the Suez Canal and generally develop the Canal area. The Canal was reopened in June 1975 with a permissible draught of 33 ft (10.1 m), increased to 38 ft (11.6 m) in July 1975. A £558m. Japanese-aided widening and deepening scheme raised the maximum permissible draught to 53 ft (16.15 m) in December 1980, enabling the passage of vessels of 150,000 tons (fully laden), 260,000 tons (partly-loaded) and 370,000 tons (unloaded). The 36-km Port Said bypass was opened on 16 December 1980, and the extension operations enabled a maximum of 80 ships per day to transit the Canal instead of the former 65. Other bypasses were constructed at Timsah and Deversoir. The Ahmad Hamdi Tunnel is the first to traverse the Canal, and it went into service on 1 October 1980. However, a $1,000m. second-phase development project to deepen the Canal to accept vessels with a draught of up to 68 ft (20.7 m) was shelved in 1984. In July 1989 a contract was signed for a feasibility study on widening and deepening the canal to accommodate ultra-super tankers (second stage of canal development project).

Statistics

SUEZ CANAL TRAFFIC

Year	Ships		Merchandise ('000 tons)		Number of Passengers	Total Transit Receipts (US $'000)
	Number	Displacement ('000 net tons)	Northbound	Southbound		
1966	21,250	274,250	194,168	47,725	299,557	210,000
1984	21,361	371,039	154,237	109,491	18,176	961,000
1985	19,991	352,579	151,901	105,695	n.a.	925,000
1986	18,403	366,076	165,048	97,404	n.a.	1,117,000
1987	17,541	347,038	152,951	103,984	10,933	1,223,000
1988	18,190	356,913	140,401	119,093	n.a.	n.a.
1989	17,628	373,429	150,348	115,471	n.a.	n.a.
1990	17,664	410,322	155,045	116,836	n.a.	n.a.
1991	18,326	426,449	153,220	119,322	n.a.	n.a.
1992	16,629	369,779	152,522	122,505	n.a.	n.a.
1993	17,317	396,550	149,027	147,887	n.a.	m.a.

NORTHBOUND GOODS TRAFFIC ('000 tons)

	1991	1992	1993
Cereals	1,484	1,706	2,106
Oil seeds	2,228	1,516	1,741
Ores and metals	7,946	7,467	8,649
Petroleum products . .	70,535	71,283	60,502
Textile fibres (raw) . .	122	130	118
Others	70,905	70,420	75,911
Total	153,220	152,522	149,027

SOUTHBOUND GOODS TRAFFIC ('000 tons)

	1991	1992	1993
Cement	1,726	2,670	3,838
Cereals	12,929	11,949	6,868
Coal and coke	654	347	550
Fabricated metals . . .	13,111	17,244	39,408
Fertilizers	15,329	17,835	12,039
Petroleum products . . .	14,342	11,987	15,540
Railway materials . . .	75	41	21
Salt	—	1	2
Wood pulp and paper . .	72	241	341
Others	61,084	60,190	69,280
Total	119,322	122,505	147,887

DISTRIBUTION OF NORTHBOUND PETROLEUM AND PRODUCTS ('000 tons)

Unloading Country	1991	1992	1993
Egypt	323	398	46
France	7,683	5,009	2,616
Italy	18,066	17,490	11,834
Morocco	2,585	4,601	4,608
Netherlands	3,290	2,595	2,258
Romania	1,486	645	393
Spain	3,694	3,165	2,251
Turkey	12,931	13,927	17,174
USA	4,694	5,570	5,034
Others	15,783	17,883	14,288
Total	70,535	71,283	60,502

FLAG DISTRIBUTION OF NET TONNAGE ('000 tons)

	1991		1992		1993	
	Tankers	All Vessels	Tankers	All Vessels	Tankers	All Vessels
Bahamas	11,364	18,936	4,946	12,890	7,498	15,440
China, People's Republic	105	10,620	213	9,279	82	8,115
Cyprus	5,573	16,561	3,634	14,127	3,154	16,428
Denmark	4,090	13,232	2,092	10,391	2,947	11,195
France	3,969	9,421	2,324	6,572	2,178	6,579
Germany, Federal Republic . . .	353	12,550	692	12,028	410	11,884
Greece	17,277	27,796	17,755	28,746	22,352	33,030
India	1,085	7,819	915	5,152	1,136	4,606
Italy	2,464	7,210	3,413	7,540	3,631	7,813
Japan	236	9,675	204	9,269	435	10,128
Kuwait	2,491	2,499	2,404	2,965	5,785	6,402
Liberia	33,188	49,917	21,248	41,029	25,238	46,793
Netherlands	420	4,428	472	6,040	439	6,861
Norway	21,556	28,341	14,671	21,121	13,919	20,251
Panama	8,166	38,200	8,509	38,391	9,292	40,159
Poland	75	2,941	150	1,921	—	1,599
Romania	1,858	3,508	126	1,234	251	1,535
Russia	3,163	21,633	1,377	19,712	1,960	13,204
Saudi Arabia	680	5,110	399	3,468	549	3,299
Singapore	1,510	7,893	880	7,807	1,203	9,760
Spain	3,527	3,843	2,046	2,399	329	687
Sweden	1,556	5,088	246	4,269	1,391	4,409
United Kingdom	7,808	19,938	3,966	17,239	5,476	18,062
USA	2,793	22,108	1,738	6,273	1,741	6,506
Yugoslavia	—	3,559	—	262	—	—
Others	21,502	73,623	23,734	79,655	26,483	91,805
Total	156,809	426,449	118,154	369,779	137,879	396,550

DISTRIBUTION OF NET TONNAGE BY TYPE OF VESSEL
('000 tons)

	1991	1992	1993
Tanker	156,809	118,154	137,879
Bulk carrier	57,454	55,885	65,698
Combined carrier . . .	13,542	15,959	10,982
General cargo	35,937	30,971	31,044
Container	87,630	93,152	100,913
Lash	3,890	2,724	2,353
Ro/Ro	20,715	12,537	9,635
Car carrier	35,160	34,290	31,250
Passenger	462	519	799
Warship	11,566	1,666	1,934
Others	3,284	3,922	4,063
Total	426,449	369,779	396,550

CALENDARS, TIME RECKONING, AND WEIGHTS AND MEASURES

The Islamic Calendar

The Islamic era dates from 16 July 622, which was the beginning of the Arab year in which the *Hijra* ('flight' or migration) of the prophet Muhammad (the founder of Islam), from Mecca to Medina (in modern Saudi Arabia), took place. The Islamic or *Hijri* Calendar is lunar, each year having 354 or 355 days, the extra day being intercalated 11 times every 30 years. Accordingly, the beginning of the *Hijri* year occurs earlier in the Gregorian Calendar by a few days each year. Dates are reckoned in terms of the *anno Hegirae* (ah) or year of the Hegira (*Hijra*). The Islamic year 1415 AH began on 10 June 1994.

The year is divided into the following months:

1. Muharram	30 days	7. Rajab	30 days
2. Safar	29 ,,	8. Shaaban	29 ,,
3. Rabia I	30 ,,	9. Ramadan	30 ,,
4. Rabia II	29 ,,	10. Shawwal	29 ,,
5. Jumada I	30 ,,	11. Dhu'l-Qa'da	30 ,,
6. Jumada II	29 ,,	12. Dhu'l-Hijja	29 or 30 days

The *Hijri* Calendar is used for religious purposes throughout the Islamic world and is the official calendar in Saudi Arabia. In most Arab countries it is used in conjunction with the Gregorian Calendar for official purposes, but in Turkey and Egypt the Gregorian Calendar has replaced it.

PRINCIPAL ISLAMIC FESTIVALS

New Year: 1st Muharram. The first 10 days of the year are regarded as holy, especially the 10th.

Ashoura: 10th Muharram. Celebrates the first meeting of Adam and Eve after leaving Paradise, also the ending of the Flood and the death of Husain, grandson of the prophet Muhammad. The feast is celebrated with fairs and processions.

Mouloud or **Yum an-Nabi** (Birth of Muhammad): 12th Rabia I.

Leilat al-Meiraj (Ascension of Muhammad): 27th Rajab.

Ramadan (Month of Fasting).

Id al-Fitr or **Id as-Saghir** or **Küçük Bayram** (The Small Feast): Three days beginning 1st Shawwal. This celebration follows the constraint of the Ramadan fast.

Id al-Adha or **Id al-Kabir** or **Büyük Bayram** (The Great Feast, Feast of the Sacrifice): Four days beginning on 10th Dhu'l-Hijja. The principal Islamic festival, commemorating Abraham's sacrifice and coinciding with the pilgrimage to Mecca. Celebrated by the sacrifice of a sheep, by feasting and by donations to the poor.

Islamic Year	1414		1415		1416	
New Year	21 June	1993	10 June	1994	31 May	1995
Ashoura	30 June	1993	19 June	1994	9 June	1995
Mouloud	30 Aug.	1993	19 Aug.	1994	9 Aug.	1995
Leilat al-Meiraj . . .	10 Jan.	1994	30 Dec.	1994	20 Dec.	1995
Ramadan begins . . .	12 Feb.	1994	1 Feb.	1995	22 Jan.	1996
Id al-Fitr	14 March	1994	3 March	1995	21 Feb.	1996
Id al-Adha	21 May	1994	10 May	1995	29 April	1996

Note: Local determinations may vary by one day from those given here.

The Iranian Calendar

The Iranian Calendar, introduced in 1925, was based on the Islamic Calendar, adapted to the solar year. Iranian New Year (*Now Ruz*) occurs at the vernal equinox, which usually falls on 21 March in the Gregorian Calendar. In Iran it was decided to base the calendar on the coronation of Cyrus the Great, in place of the *Hijra*, from 1976, and the year beginning 21 March 1976 became 2535. During 1978, however, it was decided to revert to the former system of dating. The year 1373 began on 21 March 1994.

The Iranian year is divided into the following months:

1. Favardine	31 days	7. Mehr	30 days
2. Ordibehecht	31 ,,	8. Aban	30 ,,
3. Khordad	31 ,,	9. Azar	30 ,,
4. Tir	31 ,,	10. Dey	30 ,,
5. Mordad	31 ,,	11. Bahman	30 ,,
6. Chariver	31 ,,	12. Esfand	29 or 30 days

The Iranian Calendar is used for all purposes in Iran and Afghanistan, except the determining of Islamic religious festivals, for which the lunar Islamic Calendar is used.

The Hebrew Calendar

The Hebrew Calendar is solar with respect to the year but lunar with respect to the months. The normal year has 353–355 days in 12 lunar months, but seven times in each 19 years an extra month of 30 days (*Adar II*) is intercalated after the normal month of Adar to adjust the calendar to the solar year. New Year (*Rosh Hashanah*) usually falls in September of the Gregorian calendar, but the day varies considerably. The year 5754 began on 16 September 1993, and 5755 begins on 6 September 1994.

The months are as follows:

1. Tishri	30 days	7. Nisan	30 days
2. Marcheshvan	29 or 30 days	8. Iyyar	29 ,,
3. Kislev	29 or 30 ,,	9. Sivan	30 ,,
4. Tebeth	29 days	10. Tammuz	29 ,,
5. Shebat	30 ,,	11. Ab	30 ,,
6. Adar	29 ,,	12. Ellul	29 ,,
(Adar II)	30 ,,		

The Hebrew Calendar is used to determine the dates of Jewish religious festivals only. The civil year begins with the month Tishri, while the ecclesiastical year commences on the first day of Nisan.

Standard Time

The table shows zones of standard time, relative to Greenwich Mean Time (GMT). Many of the individual countries adopt daylight saving time at certain times of year.

Traditional Arabic time is still widely used by the local population in Saudi Arabia except in most of the Eastern Province. This system is based on the local time of sunset when timepieces are all set to 12.

GMT	One hour ahead	Two hours ahead	Three hours ahead	Three and one-half hours ahead	Four hours ahead	Four and one-half hours ahead

Algeria
Morocco
Spanish North
    Africa
	Tunisia	Cyprus
		Egypt
		Israel
		Jordan
		Lebanon
		Libya
		Sudan
		Syria
		Turkey
			Bahrain
			Iraq
			Kuwait
			Yemen
				Iran	Oman
					Qatar
					United Arab
					    Emirates
						Afghanistan

Note: Saudi Arabia uses solar time.

Weights and Measures

Principal weights and units of measurement in common use as alternatives to the metric and imperial systems.

WEIGHT

Unit	Country	Metric equivalent	Imperial equivalent
Charak	Afghanistan	1.764 kg	3.89 lb
Hogga	Iraq	1.27 kg	2.8 lb
Kharwar	Afghanistan	564.528 kg	1,246.2 lb
Khord	Afghanistan	110.28 grams	3.89 oz
Maund	Yemen Saudi Arabia	} 37.29 kg	82.28 lb
Qintar (Kantar) or Buhar	Cyprus Egypt and Sudan	228.614 kg 44.928 kg	504 lb 99.05 lb
Ratl or Rotl	Saudi Arabia Egypt	} 0.449 kg	0.99 lb
Seer	Afghanistan	7.058 kg	15.58 lb
Uqqa or Oke	Cyprus Egypt	1.27 kg 1.245 kg	2.8 lb 2.751 lb
Yeni Okka	Turkey	1 kg	2.205 lb

LENGTH

Unit	Country	Metric equivalent	Imperial equivalent
Busa	Saudi Arabia Sudan	} 2.54 cm	1 in
Dirraa, Dra or Pic	Cyprus	60.96 cm	2 ft
Gereh-gaz-sha	Afghanistan	6.6 cm	2.6 in
Kadam or Qadam	Sudan	30.48 cm	1 ft

CAPACITY

Unit	Country	Metric equivalent	Imperial equivalent
Ardabb or Ardeb	Saudi Arabia Sudan Egypt	} 198.024 litres	45.36 gallons
Kadah	Sudan Egypt Cyprus	} 2.063 litres 36.368 litres	3.63 pints 8 gallons
Keila	Sudan Egypt	} 16.502 litres	3.63 gallons
Ratel	Sudan	0.568 litre	1 pint

AREA

Unit	Country	Metric equivalent	Imperial equivalent
Donum or Dunum	Cyprus	1,335.8 sq m	0.33 acre
	Iraq	2,500 sq m	0.62 acre
	Israel	} 1,000 sq m	0.2471 acre
	Jordan		
	Syria	} 919.04 sq m	0.2272 acre
	Turkey		
Feddan	Saudi Arabia		
	Sudan	} 4,201 sq m	1.038 acres
	Egypt		
Yeni Donum	Turkey	10,000 sq m (1 ha)	2.471 acres

Metric to Imperial Conversions

Metric units	Imperial units	To convert metric into imperial units multiply by:	To convert imperial into metric units multiply by:
Weight:			
Gram	Ounce (Avoirdupois)	0.035274	28.3495
Kilogram (kg)	Pound (lb)	2.204622	0.453592
Metric ton ('000 kg)	Short ton (2,000 lb)	1.102311	0.907185
	Long ton (2,240 lb)	0.984207	1.016047
	(The short ton is in general use in the USA, while the long ton is normally used in Britain and the Commonwealth.)		
Length			
Centimetre (cm)	Inch (in)	0.3937008	2.54
Metre (m)	Yard (=3 feet)	1.09361	0.9144
Kilometre (km)	Mile	0.62137	1.609344
Volume			
Cubic metre (cu m)	Cubic foot	35.315	0.0283
	Cubic yard	1.30795	0.764555
Capacity			
Litre	Gallon (=8 pints)	0.219969	4.54609
	Gallon (US)	0.264172	3.78541
Area			
Square metre (sq m)	Square yard	1.19599	0.836127
Hectare (ha)	Acre	2.47105	0.404686
Square kilometre (sq km)	Square mile	0.386102	2.589988

RESEARCH INSTITUTES

ASSOCIATIONS AND INSTITUTES STUDYING THE MIDDLE EAST AND NORTH AFRICA

(See also Regional Organizations—Education)

AFGHANISTAN

Anjumani Tarikh (Historical Society): Kabul; f. 1931; to study and promote international knowledge of the history of Afghanistan; Head AHMAD ALI MOTAMEDI; publs *Aryana* (quarterly, in Pashtu and Dari) and *Afghanistan* (English and French, quarterly).

The Asia Foundation: POB 257, Kabul; f. 1955; assists local institutions and organizations concerned with education and socio-economic development; Representative JOEL W. SCARBOROUGH.

British Institute of Afghan Studies: POB 3052, Kabul; f. 1972; supports research relating to history, antiquities, archaeology, languages, literature, art, culture, customs and natural history of Afghanistan; Dir R. H. PINDER WILSON; publs *Annual Report, Afghan Studies* (annually).

ALGERIA

Institut d'Etudes Arabes: Université d'Alger, 2 rue Didouche Mourad, Algiers.

Institut d'Etudes Orientales: Université d'Alger, 2 rue Didouche Mourad, Algiers; publ. *Annales*.

ARGENTINA

Instituto de Filosofía, Sección de Estudios Interdisciplinarios de Asia y Africa: Universidad de Buenos Aires, 25 de Mayo 221, 4° piso, 1002 Buenos Aires; tel. (1) 334-7512; fax (1) 432-2292; f. 1982; multidisciplinary seminars and lectures; Dir Prof. MARÍA ELENA VELA; publs *Temas de Africa y Asia* (2 a year).

ARMENIA

Institute of Oriental Studies of the Academy of Sciences of Armenia: Pr. Marshal Bagranyan 24G, 375019, Yerevan 19, Armenia; tel. (8852) 583382; f. 1971; Dir G. K. SARKISYAN.

AUSTRALIA AND NEW ZEALAND

Australasian Middle East Studies Association: POB 64, Footscray 3011, Australia; Department of Semitic Studies, University of Sydney, N.S.W. 2006; tel. (2) 692-2190; Pres. Dr A. SHBOUL; Past Pres. NEIL TRUSCOTT; publ. *Conference Proceedings*.

Programme in Middle East Studies: University of Western Australia, Nedlands, Western Australia 6009; tel. (9) 380-2926; telex 92992; fax (9) 380-1035; f. 1975 to promote, encourage and facilitate teaching, research and the dissemination of information on the Middle East; Dir Prof. R. GABBAY.

AUSTRIA

Afro-Asiatisches Institut in Wien: A-1090 Vienna, Türkenstrasse 3; tel. (1) 3105145; f. 1959; seminars, scholarship programmes and other cultural exchange between African and Asian students in Vienna; Gen. Sec. Dr NICOLAI WOCHINZ; Pres. Bishop FLORIAN KUNTNER.

Institut für Orientalistik der Universität Wien: A-1010 Vienna, Universitätsstrasse 7/V; tel. 2593; fax (1) 4020533; f. 1886; library of 26,200 vols; Dir Prof. Dr HANS E. HIRSCH; publs *Wiener Zeitschrift für die Kunde des Morgenlandes* (annually), *Turkologischer Anzeiger* (annually), *Archiv für Orientforschung* (annually).

AZERBAIJAN

Institute of Peoples of the Near and Middle East of the Academy of Azerbaijan: Pr. Narimanova 31, Baku 370143, Azerbaijan; f. 1958; Dir ZIYA MUSA BUNIYATOV.

BELGIUM

Centre pour l'Etude des Problèmes du Monde Musulman Contemporain: 44 ave Jeanne, 1050 Brussels; f. 1957; publs *Correspondance d'Orient-Etudes* and collections *Correspondance d'Orient* and *Le monde musulman contemporain—Initiations.*

Departement Oriëntalistiek: Faculteit van de Letteren en Wijsbegeerte, Katholieke Universiteit te Leuven, Blijde Inkomststraat 21, B—3000 Leuven; tel. (16) 28-50-80; f. 1936; Pres. Prof. U. VERMEULEN; 25 mems; publs *Orientalia Lovaniensia Analecta, Orientalia Lovaniensia Periodica, Bibliothèque du Muséon* (1929–68), *Orientalia et Biblica Lovaniensia* (1957–68), *Inforient, Inforient-Reeks.*

Fondation Egyptologique Reine Elisabeth: Parc du Cinquantenaire, 10, B1040 Brussels; tel. (2) 7417364; f. 1923 to encourage Egyptian studies; 1,450 mems; library of 90,000 vols; Pres. Comte D'ARSCHOT; Dirs M. J. BINGEN and H. DE MEULENAERE; publs *Chronique d'Egypte, Bibliotheca Aegyptiaca, Papyrologica Bruxellensia, Bibliographie Papyrologique sur fiches, Monumenta Aegyptiaca, Rites égyptiens, Papyri Bruxellenses Graecae, Monographies Reine Elisabeth.*

CZECH REPUBLIC

Oriental Institute: 11837 Prague 1, Lázeňská 4; f. 1922; tel. (2) 533051; fax (2) 533184; Head of Inst. S. PANTŮČEK; publs *Archív Orientální* (quarterly), *Nový Orient* (monthly).

CYPRUS

PLO Research Centre: 16 Artemidos St, Strovolos, POB 5614, Nicosia; tel. (2) 429396; telex 4706; fax (2) 312104; fmrly in Beirut, Lebanon; f. 1965; studies Palestine question; Dir SABRI JIRYIS; publs *Shu'un Filastiniya* (Palestine Affairs, monthly) and various books and pamphlets on aspects of the Palestine problem.

DENMARK

Center for Mellemøst-Studier (Centre for Contemporary Middle East Studies): University of Odense, Campusvej 55, 5230 Odense M; tel. 66158600; fax 65931158; f. 1983; national centre for interdisciplinary research in cultures and societies of the contemporary Middle East; 9-member research team; library of 3,000 vols and 90 periodicals; Dir Prof. SØREN MØRCH; publs *Mellemøst Information* (monthly in Danish) and a monographical series (semiannually).

Orientalsk Samfund (Orientalist Association): Institute of Oriental Philology, Njalsgade 80, 2300 Copenhagen S; tel. 542211; f. 1915 to undertake the study and further the understanding of Oriental cultures and civilizations; 50 mems; Pres. Prof. SØREN EGEROD; Sec. Prof. J. P. ASMUSSEN; publ. *Acta Orientalia* (annually).

EGYPT

Academy of the Arabic Language: 15 Aziz Abaza St, Zamalek, Cairo; tel. (2) 340-5931; f. 1932; Pres. Dr IBRAHIM MADKOUR; Vice-Pres. Dr MAHDI ALLAM; Sec.-Gen. Dr AHMED SHAWKY DIEF; library of 40,000 vols and periodicals; publs *Review* (2 a year), books on reviving Arabic heritage, council and conference proceedings, biographies of members of Academy, lexicons and directories of scientific and technical terms.

American Research Center in Egypt Inc: 2 Midan Qasr ad-Dubarah, Cairo; tel. (2) 354-8239; telex 23227; fax (2) 355-3052; and The Kevorkian Center, New York University, 50 Washington Square South, New York, NY 10012, tel. (212) 998-8890; f. 1948 by American universities to promote research by US and Canadian scholars in all phases of Egyptian civilization, including archaeology, art history, humanities and social sciences; grants and fellowships available; 32 institutional mems and 1,250 individual mems; Pres. JANET JOHNSON; Vice-Pres. CHARLES D. SMITH; Cairo Dir MARK M. EASTON; New York Dir TERENCE WALZ; publs *Journal* (annually), *Newsletter* (quarterly).

Deutsches Archäologisches Institut (German Institute of Archaeology): 31 Abu El Feda, Zamalek, Cairo; tel. (2) 340-1460; fax (2) 342-0770; Dir Prof. Dr RAINER STADELMANN.

Institut Dominicain d'Etudes Orientales: Priory of the Dominican Fathers, 1 Sharia Masna at-Tarabish, B.P. 18 Abbasiyah, 11381 Cairo; tel. (2) 825509; fax (2) 282-0682; f. 1953; Dir Père REGIS MORELON; publ. *Mélanges* (annually).

Institut d'Egypte: 13 Sharia Sheikh Rihane, Cairo; f. 1798; studies literary, artistic and scientific questions relating to Egypt and neighbouring countries; Pres. Dr SULAIMAN HAZIEN; Sec. Gen. P. GHALIOUNGU; publs *Bulletin* (annually), *Mémoires* (irregular).

Institut Français d'Archéologie Orientale: 37 rue ech-Cheikh Aly Yousuf, BP Kasr el-Eini 11562, Cairo; tel. (2) 354-8245; fax (2) 354-4635; f. 1880; excavations, research and publications; library of 60,000 vols; Dir Prof. NICOLAS GRIMAL; publs *Bulletin de l'Institut Français d'Archéologie Orientale, Annales Islamologiques*, etc.

Netherlands Institute for Archaeology and Arabic Studies: 1 Sharia Dr Mahmoud Azmi, Zamalek, POB 50, Cairo; tel. (2) 340-0076; fax (2) 340-4376; f. 1971; Dir Dr F. LEEMHUIS; publs in the field of Arabic and Coptic Studies.

Société Archéologique d'Alexandrie: POB 815, 6 Mahmoud Mokhtar St, 21111 Alexandria; tel. and fax (3) 482-0650; f. 1893; 248 mems; Pres. A. M. SADEK; Vice-Pres. YOUSSEF EL-GHERIANI; Treas. K. EL-ADM; publs *Bulletins, Mémoires, Monuments de l'Egypte Gréco-Romaine, Cahiers, Publications Spéciales, Archaeological and Historical Studies*.

Société Egyptienne d'Economie Politique, de Statistique et de Législation: 16 rue Ramses, BP 732, Cairo; f. 1909; 1,550 mems; Pres. Dr GAMAL EL-OTEIFI; Sec.-Gen. Dr MAHMOUD HAFEZ GHANEM; Tech.-Secs Dr FATHI EL-MASSAFAWI and Dr SAKR AHMAD SAKR; publ. *Revue* (quarterly in Arabic, French and English).

Society for Coptic Archaeology: 222 ave Ramses, Cairo; tel. (2) 824252; f. 1934; 170 mems; library of 14,450 vols; Pres. WASSIF BOUTROS GHALI; Sec.-Gen. Dr A. KHATER; Treas. AMIN F. ABD EN-NOUR; publs *Bulletin* (annually), *Fouilles, Bibliothèque d'Art et d'Archéologie, Textes et Documents*, etc.

FINLAND

Suomen Itämainen Seura (Finnish Oriental Society): c/o Department of Asian and African Studies, POB 13 (Meritullink 1B), SF-00014 University of Helsinki; fax (0) 1912094; f. 1917; 160 mems; Pres. Prof. HEIKKI PALVA; Sec. Prof. T. HARVIAINEN; publ. *Studia Orientalia*.

FRANCE

Centre d'Etudes de l'Orient Contemporain: 13 rue de Santeuil, 75231 Paris Cedex 05; tel. (1) 45-87-41-65; f. 1943; collaborates with *la Documentation française* and runs course on contemporary Arab world; 5-mem. collaboration with *Maghreb-Machrek*; Dir P. BALTA.

Centre des Hautes Etudes sur l'Afrique et l'Asie Modernes: 13 rue du Four, 75006 Paris; tel. (1) 44-41-38-80; (1) 40-50-03-58; f. 1936; Dir PH. DECRAENE; publs *L'Afrique et l'Asie Modernes* (quarterly), *Les Publications du CHEAM* (irregular), Lettre d'Information (2 a year) *Notes Africaines, Caraïbes et Asiatiques* (irregular).

Fondation Nationale des Sciences Politiques: 27 rue Saint-Guillaume, 75337 Paris; fax (1) 44-10-84-50; f. 1945; Administrator M. LANCELOT; Centre d'Etudes et de Recherches Internationales, Dir J. F. LEGUIL-BAYART; Arab world section has research team of 5 mems; publs include *Maghreb-Machrek* (quarterly).

Institut d'Etudes palestiniennes: Paris; publ. *Revue d'Etudes palestiniennes* (quarterly).

Institut d'Etudes Arabes et Islamiques: Université de la Sorbonne Nouvelle (Paris III), 13 rue de Santeuil, 75231 Paris Cedex 05; tel. (1) 45-87-41-39; Dir ALI MÉRAD.

Institut d'Etudes Iraniennes: Université de la Sorbonne Nouvelle (Paris III), 13 rue de Santeuil, 75231 Paris Cedex 05; tel. (1) 45-87-40-69; fax (1) 45-87-41-70; f. 1947; Dir RICHARD YANN; publs *Travaux, Studia Iranica* (journal), *Abstracta Iranica* (annual bibliography).

Institut d'Etudes Sémitiques: Institut d'Etudes Sémitiques, 11 place Marcelin-Berthelot, 75231 Paris Cedex 05; tel. (1) 44-27-10-51; fax (1) 44-27-11-09; f. 1930; Pres. A. GUILLAUMONT; publ. *Semitica*.

Institut d'Etudes Turques: Unité de Recherche Associée du Centre Nationale de la Recherche Scientifique, Université de la Sorbonne Nouvelle (Paris III), 13 rue de Santeuil, 75231 Paris Cedex 05; tel. (1) 45-87-40-73; fax (1) 45-87-41-61; f. 1967; Dir RÉMY DOR; research team has 18 mems; publs *Collection Turcica, Turcica* (annual review).

Institut du Monde Arabe: 1 rue des Fossés Saint-Bernard, 75936 Paris Cedex 05; tel. (1) 40-51-38-38; telex 203832; fax (1) 43-54-76-45; f. 1980; Pres. EDGARD PISANI.

Institut National des Langues et Civilisations Orientales: 2 rue de Lille, 75343 Paris Cedex 07; tel. (1) 49-26-42-00; fax (1) 49-26-42-99; f. 1795; faculties of languages and civilizations of West Asia and Africa; the Far East, India and Oceania; Eastern Europe; North and Central America; library of 430,000 vols and 7,000 periodicals; c. 9,000 students, 300 teachers and lecturers; Pres. A. BOURGEY; Vice-Pres. M. FOURNIÉ; Sec. Gen. S. SANGALLI; High International Studies (DHEI), Department of International Business (CPEI), Automatic Languages Treatment (TAL); publs *Livret de l'Etudiant* (annually), various Oriental studies.

Institut de Papyrologie: Université de Paris-Sorbonne, 1 rue Victor-Cousin, 75005 Paris; tel. (1) 40-46-26-45; Dir ALAIN BLANCHARD.

Société Asiatique: 3 rue Mazarine, 75006 Paris; tel. (1) 44-41-43-14; fax (1) 44-41-43-16; f. 1822; 700 mems; library of 100,000 vols; Pres. ANDRÉ CAQUOT; Vice-Pres C. CAILLAT, L. BAZIN; Secs J. L. BACQUE-GRAMMONT, P. B. LAFONT, C. ROBIN; publs *Journal Asiatique* (quarterly), *Cahiers de la Société Asiatique*.

UFR Langues, Sociétés, Cultures Etrangères (LSCE)—UFR 5—: 2 rue de la Liberté, 93526 St Denis Cedex 02; Dir MIREILLE AZZOUG; Département d'Etudes hébraïques; tel. (1) 48216364 (ext. 1253); Dir EPHRAÏM RIVELINE; Département d'Etudes arabes; tel. (1) 48216364 (ext. 1249); Dir JACQUELINE CHABBI.

GEORGIA

Institute of Oriental Studies of the Academy of Sciences of Georgia: Ul. G. Tsereteli 3, 380062 Tbilisi, Georgia; tel. (8832) 233885; Dir T. V. GAMKRELIDZE.

GERMANY

Altorientalisches Seminar der Freien Universität Berlin: D-14195 Berlin, Bitterstr. 8–12; tel. (30) 838-3347; fax (30) 831-4252; f. 1950.

Deutsche Arbeitsgemeinschaft Vorderer Orient (DAVO): 20148 Hamburg, Mittelweg 150; tel. (40) 441481; fax (40) 418214; consists of German research orgs into politics, economics and society of the Middle East; 36 mem. insts; Sec. Prof. Dr UDO STEINBACH.

Deutsche Morgenländische Gesellschaft: D-69120 Heidelberg, Im Neuenheimer Feld 330; tel. (6221) 562900; fax (6221) 564998; Sec. MANFRED HAKE; f. 1845; publs *Zeitschrift* (two a year), *Abhandlungen für die Kunde des Morgenlandes, Bibliotheca Islamica, Wörterbuch der Klassischen Arabischen Sprache, Beiruter Texte und Studien, Verzeichnis der orientalischen Handschriften in Deutschland*, etc.

Deutsches Orient-Institut: 20148 Hamburg, Mittelweg 150; tel. (40) 441481; fax (40) 441484; f. 1960 from the Nah- und Mittelostverein e.V.; since 1965 has been affil. to Deutsches Übersee-Institut; devoted to research in politics, science and economics of Near and Middle East and provides a fortnightly press cutting service on the Middle East; Dir Prof. Dr UDO STEINBACH; publs *Nahost Jahrbuch* (annually), *Orient* (quarterly), *Mitteilungen* (irregular), *Schriften* (irregular).

Internationale Gesellschaft für Orientforschung: Orientalisches Seminar, J. W. Goethe-Universität, Postfach 11-1932,

D-60054, Frankfurt/Main 11; f. 1948; 400 mems; Pres. Prof. R. SELLHEIM; publ. *Oriens* (annually).

Nah- und Mittelost Verein e.V. (German Near and Middle East Association): D20148 Hamburg, Mittelweg 151; tel. (040) 440251; telex 212253; fax (040) 418214; f. 1934; 600 mems; Chair. Dr ROLF E. BREUER; Gen.-Sec. Dr OTTO PLASSMANN.

Seminar für Orientalische Sprachen: Adenauerallee 102, D-53113 Bonn 7; tel. and fax (228) 73-84-15; f. 1959 (1887 Berlin); University of Bonn, Near East Department; Dir Prof. Dr W. SCHMUCKER.

INDIA

Asiatic Society of Bombay: Town Hall, Bombay 400 023; tel. 286-0956; f. 1804; 2,171 mems; to investigate and encourage Sciences, Arts and Literature in relation to Asia; maintains Central Library of the State of Maharashtra; 219,370 vols (626,720 in Cen. Library); 2,357 MSS and 10,443 old coins; Pres. Dr D. R. SARDESAI; Hon. Sec. VIMAL SHAH; in 1973 the society established the Dr P. V. Kane Research Inst. to promote, encourage and facilitate research in Oriental studies; publs annual *Journal*, reports, critical annotated texts of rare Sanskrit and Pali MSS.

Indian Institute of Islamic Studies: Panchkuin Rd, New Delhi 110 001 and Tughlaqabad, New Delhi, 110 062; tel. 643-9685; f. 1963; library of 50,000 vols and 2,400 MSS; Pres. HAKIM ABD AL-HAMID; Dir S. A. ALI; publs *Studies in Islam* (quarterly), *Islamic and Comparative Law Quarterly*, *Bulletin of Comparative Religion* (quarterly), *Newsletter* (quarterly).

Iran League: Navsari Bldg (2nd floor), Dr Dadabhoy Navroji Rd, Fort, Bombay 400 001; f. 1922; 300 mems; Pres. Sir JAMSETJEE JEEJEEBHOY, Bart; Sec. FALI S. MASTER; publs *The Iran League Quarterly Newsletter* and translations and commentaries in modern Persian of Avesta texts.

IRAN

The Asia Institute: University of Shiraz; Dir Dr Y. M. NAWABI; publs *Bulletin, Monographs.*

British Institute of Persian Studies: Kucheh Alvand, Khiaban Dr Ali Shariati, Gholhak, POB 11365-6844, Teheran; f. 1961; cultural institute, with emphasis on history and archaeology; 850 individual mems; Hon. Sec. Dr R. HILLENBRAND; publ. *Iran* (annually).

IRAQ

British School of Archaeology in Iraq: 31–34 Gordon Sq., London, WC1H OPY; tel. (071) 733-8912; British Archaeological Expedition to Iraq, 34/3/609 Mansour, Baghdad; Dir Dr R. J. MATTHEWS.

Deutsches Archäologisches Institut: Hay al-Maarife 821/63, POB 2105, Alwiya, Baghdad; tel. 543-1353.

Instituto Hispano-Arabe de Cultura: Hurriya Sq, Hay Babil 925/25/80, POB 2256, Alwiyah; tel. 776-6045; f. 1958; Dir JUAN M. CASADO RAMOS.

Iraq Academy: Waziriyah, Baghdad; f. 1947 to maintain the Arabic language to undertake research into Arabic history, Islamic heritage and the history of Iraq, and to encourage research in the modern arts and sciences; Pres. Dr SALEH A. AL-ALI; Sec.-Gen. Dr NOORI H. AL-QISSI; publ. *Bulletin of the Iraq Academy* (2 a year).

ISRAEL

The Academy of the Hebrew Language: POB 3449, Jerusalem 91034; tel. (02) 632242; fax (02) 617065; f. 1953; study and development of the Hebrew language and compilation of a historical dictionary; Pres. Prof. J. BLAU; publs *Zikhronot, Leshonenu* (quarterly), *Leshonenu La'am*, monographs and dictionaries.

Arab Studies Society: POB 20479, Jerusalem; tel. (02) 281012; f. 1980 to promote Arabic culture in general and Palestinian thought and culture in particular; library of more than 5,000 vols on Palestine and the Middle East; Dir FAISAL HUSSEINI; publs more than 40 books on culture and history of Palestine.

W. F. Albright Institute of Archaeological Research in Jerusalem: 26 Salah ed-Din, POB 19096, Jerusalem; tel. (2) 282131; fax (2) 894424; f. 1900 by American Schools of Oriental Research; research in Syro-Palestinian archaeology, Biblical studies, Near Eastern languages; sponsors excavations; Pres. MAX MILLER; Dir S. GITIN.

The Ben-Zvi Institute for the Study of Jewish Communities in the East: POB 7504, Abravanel St, Jerusalem 91076; tel. (02) 639204; fax (02) 638310; f. 1948; sponsors research in the history and culture of Jewish communities in the East; library of MSS and printed books; Chair. Prof. MICHEL ABITBOL; publs *Sefunot, Pe'amim* (quarterly), and monographs.

British School of Archaeology in Jerusalem: POB 19283, Jerusalem; tel. (02) 828101; fax (02) 323844; f. 1920; archaeological research and excavation; hostel and library; Chair. P. G. DE COURCY IRELAND; Dir R. P. HARPER; publ. *Levant.*

Couvent Saint Etienne des Pères Dominicains, Ecole Biblique et Archéologique Française: POB 19053, Jerusalem 91190; tel. (02) 894468; fax (02) 282567; f. 1890; research, Biblical and Oriental studies, exploration and excavation in Palestine and Jordan; Dir Dr ANTHONY WARD; library of 110,000 vols; publs *Revue Biblique, Etudes Bibliques, Cahiers annexes de la Bible de Jérusalem, Cahiers de la Revue Biblique, Bible de Jérusalem.*

Moshe Dayan Centre for Middle Eastern and African Studies/Shiloah Institute: Tel-Aviv University, Ramat Aviv, Tel-Aviv 69978; tel. (03) 640-9646; telex 342171; fax (03) 641-5802; f. 1959; Head Prof. Dr ASHER SUSSER; publs *Middle East Contemporary Survey* (annually), *Current Contents of Periodicals on the Middle East* (bi-monthly), also monographs, teaching aids, studies and occasional papers and computerized database on the Middle East.

Historical Society of Israel: POB 4179, Jerusalem 9041; tel. (02) 637171; fax (02) 662135; f. 1925 to promote the study of Jewish history and general history; 1,000 mems; Chair. Prof. YOSEF KAPLAN; Gen. Sec. ZVI YEKUTIEL; publ. *Zion* (quarterly).

Institute of Asian and African Studies: Hebrew University, Mount Scopus, Jerusalem 91905; tel. (02) 883516; telex 26458; fax (02) 322545; f. 1926; studies of medieval and modern languages, culture and history of Middle East, Asia and Africa; Chair. Prof. ARYEY LEVIN; publs *Max Schloessinger Memorial Series, Jerusalem Studies in Arabic and Islam*, translation series.

Institute of Holy Land Studies: POB 1276 Mt Zion, Jerusalem 91012; tel. (02) 718628; fax (02) 732717; f. 1959; Christian study centre, grad. and undergrad. in the history, languages, religions and cultures of Israel in the Middle Eastern Context; Pres. Dr SIDNEY DEWAAL.

Israel Exploration Society: 5 Avida St, POB 7041, Jerusalem 91070; tel. (02) 257991; fax (02) 247772; f. 1913; excavations and historical research, congresses and lectures; 4,000 mems; Chair. Prof. A. BIRAN; Hon. Pres. Prof. B. MAZAR; Hon. Sec. J. AVIRAM; publs *Eretz Israel* (Hebrew annual, with English summaries), *Qadmoniot* (Hebrew quarterly), *Israel Exploration Journal* (English quarterly), various books on archaeology (in Hebrew and English).

Israel Oriental Society: The Hebrew University, Jerusalem 91905; tel. (02) 883633; f. 1949; lectures and symposia to study all aspects of contemporary Middle Eastern, Asian and African affairs; Pres. TEDDY KOLLEK; publs *Hamizrah Hehadash* (Hebrew (with English summary) annual), *Oriental Notes and Studies* (1951–71), *Asian and African Studies* (3 a year).

Orientalisches Institut der Görres-Gesellschaft: Schmidt-Schule, POB 19424, Jerusalem; historical and archaeological studies.

Pontifical Biblical Institute: 3 Paul Emile Botta St, POB 497, Jerusalem 91004; tel. (02) 252843; fax (02) 241203; f. 1927; study of Biblical languages and Biblical archaeology, history, topography; in conjunction with Hebrew University of Jerusalem; seminar for post-graduate students, student tours; Dir Rev. CARLOS SOLTERO.

The Harry S. Truman Research Institute for the Advancement of Peace: Hebrew University, Mount Scopus, Jerusalem 91905; tel. (02) 882300; telex 26458; fax (02) 828076; f. 1966;

conducts and sponsors social science and historical research, organizes conferences on Third-World and non-Western countries, with special emphasis on the Middle East; Dir Prof. MOSHE MA'OZ; publs works on the Middle East, Africa, Asia and Latin America.

Wilfrid Israel House for Oriental Art and Studies: Kibbutz Hazorea, Post Hazorea 30060; tel. (04) 899566; telex 471418; f. 1947; opened 1951 in memory of late Wilfrid Israel; a cultural centre for reference, study and art exhbns; houses Wilfrid Israel collection of Near and Far Eastern art and cultural materials; local archaeological exhibits from neolithic to Byzantine times; science and art library; Dir G. MAANIT; Sec. and Curator for Far and Middle Eastern Art Dr U. R. BAER; Curator for Archaeology E. MEIRHOF.

ITALY

Istituto di Studi del Vicino Oriente: Dipartimento di Scienze Storiche, Archeologiche ed Antropologiche dell'Antichità, Sezione Vicino Oriente, Università degli Studi di Roma 'La Sapienza', P.le Aldo Moro, 5-00100 Rome; Dir Prof. PAOLO MATTHIAE.

Istituto Italiano per il Medio ed Estremo Oriente (ISMEO): Palazzo Brancaccio, via Merulana 248, Rome; tel. (6) 4874273; telex 624163; fax (6) 487-3138; f. 1933; Pres. Prof. GHERARDO GNOLI; publs *East and West* (quarterly), *Rome Oriental Series, Nuovo Ramusio, Archaeological Reports and Memoirs, Restorations.*

Istituto Italo-Africano: via Ulisse Aldrovandi 16, Rome; tel. (6) 321-6712; telex 620386; fax (6) 322-5348; f. 1906; Pres. Prof. TULLIA CARETTONI; Dir-Gen. Amb. Dott. PASQUALE ANTONIO BALDOCCI.

Istituto per le relazioni tra l'Italia e i paesi dell'Africa, America Latina e Medio Oriente: via del Tritone 62B, 00187 Rome; tel. (6) 679-2321; fax (2) 679-7849; f. 1971; publ. *Politica Internazionale* (quarterly Italian edition).

JAPAN

Ajia Keizai Kenkyusho (Institute of Developing Economies): 42 Ichigaya-Hommura-cho, Shinjuku-ku, Tokyo 162; tel. (3) 353-4231; telex 32473; fax (3) 226-8475; f. 1958; 263 mems; Chair. YŌHEIM MIMURA; Pres. YOSHITOSHI MUNAKATA; library of 264,462 vols; publs *Ajia Keizai* (Japanese, monthly), *The Developing Economies* (English, quarterly), occasional papers in English.

Chuto Chosakai (Middle East Institute of Japan): 15 Mori Bldg, 8–10 Toranomon 2-chome, Minato-ku, Tokyo; tel. (3) 3591-0958; fax (3) 3591-0957; f. 1960; Chair. WASUKE MIYAKE; publs *Chuto Kenkyu* (Journal of Middle Eastern Studies—monthly), *Chuto Nenkan* (Yearbook of Middle East and North Africa), *Newsletter.*

Nippon Oriento Gakkai (Society for Near Eastern Studies in Japan): Tokyo Tenrikyokan. 9, 1-chome, Kanda Nishiki-cho, Chiyoda-ku, Tokyo 101; tel. (3) 3291-7519; f. 1954; about 910 mems; Pres. Dr NAMIO EGAMI; publs *Oriento* (Japanese, 2 a year), *Orient* (European languages annual).

LEBANON

Arab Institute for Research and Publishing: Carlton Tower Bldg, Saqiat el-Janzeer, 3rd Floor, POB 11-5460, Beirut; telex 40067; Gen. Man. MAHER KAYALI; works in Arabic and English.

Centre d'Etudes et de Recherches sur le Moyen-Orient contemporain (CERMOC): rue de Damas, BP 2691, Beirut; tel. (1) 640694; fax (1) 644857; POB 830413, Zahran, Amman, Jordan; Ambassade de France au Liban, Ministère des Relations Extérieures, 37 Quai d'Orsay, 75007 Paris, France; f. 1977; 4 research fellows and 9 contractual researchers; university research and documentation institution; library specializes in human and social sciences concerning the Middle East; Dir JEAN HANNOYER; publs 27 books on contemporary Middle East.

Centre de Documentation Economique sur le Proche-Orient Arabe: Fawlté des Sciences Economiques, Université Saint-Joseph, BP 175-208, Beirut; tel. (1) 200625; f. 1971; economic documentation on the Arab countries of the Middle East; Man. MARCELLE NASSAR.

Centre for Economic, Financial and Social Research and Documentation SAL: Gefinor Centre, Bloc B 500–502 Clemenceau St, POB 11-6068, Beirut; f. 1958; Chair. Dr CHAFIC AKHRAS; Dir-Gen. Dr SABBAH AL-HAJ.

Institut Français d'Archéologie du Proche Orient: rue de Damas, BP 11-1424, Beirut; Jordanian Section: BP 5348, Amman, Jordan; tel. (6) 611872; fax (6) 643840; Syrian Section: BP 3694, Damascus, Syria; tel. 3338727; f. 1946; library of 45,000 vols (Bibliothèque Henri Seyrig); Dir F. VILLENEUVE; publs *Syria, Revue d'Art et d'Archéologie* (annually), *Bibliothèque Archéologique et Historique.*

Institute for Palestine Studies, Publishing and Research Organization: POB 11-7164, Nsouli-Verdun St, Beirut; tel. and fax (1) 868387; telex 23317; 3501 M St, NW, POB 25301, Washington, DC 20007, USA; tel. (202) 342-3990; telex 71082-21166; fax (202) 3423927; 13 Hera St, POB 5658, Nicosia, Cyprus; tel. (2) 456165; fax (2) 456324; f. 1963; independent non-profit Arab research organization; to promote better understanding of the Palestine problem and the Arab-Israeli conflict; library of 30,000 vols, microfilm collection, private papers and archives; Hon. Chair. Dr CONSTANTINE ZURAYK; Chair. Dr HISHAM NASHABE; Exec. Sec. Prof. WALID KHALIDI; publs *Journal of Palestine Studies, Révue d'études palestiniennes* and documentary series, reprints, research papers, etc.

Islamic Institute for Information and Development: POB 4823, Ramel az-Zarif, Independence St, Saradar Bldg, Beirut; tel. (1) 221480; telex 43409; f. by *al-Liwa* newspaper to promote Islamic thought and literature.

THE NETHERLANDS

Assyriologisch Instituut der Rijksuniversiteit: Rijksuniversiteit Leiden, POB 9515, 2300 RA Leiden; tel. (71) 272033; fax (71) 272615; Dir Prof. Dr K. R. VEENHOF; publs *Altbabylonische Briefe in Umschrift und Übersetzung* (12 vols, continuing series), *Collection, Liagre Böhl Collection* (c. 3,000 cuneiform tablets) published in conjunction with the Netherlands Institute for the Near East, Leiden.

Netherlands Council for Trade Promotion (Middle East Institute): Bezuidenhoutseweg 181, POB 10, 2501 CA The Hague; tel. (70) 3441544; telex 32306; fax (070) 385-3531; f. 1949; publ. *Bulletin* (Press Digest, for mems only).

Netherlands Institute for the Near East (*Nederlands Instituut voor het Nabije Oosten*): Witte Singel 25, POB 9515, 2300 RA Leiden; tel. (71) 272036; fax (71) 272038; Dir Dr J. DE ROOS; library of c. 30,000 vols and 600 periodicals; publs *Anatolica, Studia Francisci Scholten Memoriae dicata, Scholae de Buck, Publications de l'Institut historique et archéologique néerlandais de Stamboul, Bibliotheca Orientalis, Tabulae de Liagre Böhl, Studia de Liagre Böhl, Egyptologische Uitgaven* (monographs, 8th vol. in production), *Achaemenid History* (monographs, 8th volume in production).

PAKISTAN

Institute of Islamic Culture: 2 Club Rd, Lahore 3; tel. (42) 363127; f. 1950; Dir MUHAMMAD SOHAIL UMAR; Sec. MALIK FAIZ BAKHSH; publs *Al-Ma'arif* (quarterly), *Jamal* (annually) and about 200 publications on Islamic subjects in English and Urdu.

Islamic Research Institute: International Islamic University, POB 1035, Islamabad 44000; tel. (51) 850751; telex 54068; f. 1960; conducts research in Islamic studies; Dir-Gen. Dr ZAFAR ISHAQ ANSARI; publs *Ad-Dirasat al-Islamiyah* (Arabic, quarterly), *Islamic Studies* (English, quarterly), *Fikr O-Nazar* (Urdu, quarterly).

POLAND

Polskie Towarzystwo Orientalistyczne (Polish Oriental Society): Zarząd Główny, ul. Śniadeckich 8, 00-656 Warsaw; tel. (2) 6282471; f. 1922; 200 mems; Pres. STANISŁAW KAŁUŻYŃSKI, JERZY HAUZIŃSKI, ALEKSANDER DUBIŃSKI; Sec. LESZEK CYRZYK; publ. *Przegląd Orientalistyczny* (quarterly).

Zakład Archeologii Śródziemnomorskiej (Research Centre for Mediterranean Archaeology): Pałac Kultury i Nauki, Room 2105, 00-901 Warsaw; tel. (22) 200211 (Ext.

20-64); telex 817633; fax (22) 207651; f. 1956; 18 mems; Research Institute of Academy of Sciences; documentation and publication of Polish excavations in the Middle East and antiquities in Polish museums; Prof KAROL MYŚLIWIEC, Prof. ZSOLT KISS; publs *Etudes et Travaux du Centre d'Archéologie Méditerranéenne, Palmyre, Nubia, Faras, Deir el-Bahari, Nea Paphos, Alexandrie, Corpus Vasorum Antiquorum, Corpus Signorum Imperii Romani.*

PORTUGAL

Instituto de Estudos Árabes e Islâmicos: Faculdade de Letras, Cidade Universitária, 1699 Lisbon; tel. (1) 7965162; fax (1) 7960063; f. 1966; library; 5 teachers; specializes in Arabic and Islamic studies; Dir A. DIAS FARINHA.

RUSSIA

Institute of Oriental Studies, Russian Academy of Sciences: 12 Rozhdestvenka St, Moscow; tel. (095) 924-5150; telex 412157; fax (095) 975-2396; f. 1818; attached to Dept of History; Acad. Sec. IVAN KOVALCHENKO; Dir MIKHAIL KAPITZA; Russian and English journals.

SAUDI ARABIA

Arab Urban Development Institute: POB 6892, Riyadh 11452; tel. (1) 441-8100; telex 403566; fax (1) 441-8235; f. 1980; affiliated to the Arab Towns Organization; provides training, research, consultancy and documentation services to Arab cities and municipalities and members of ATO for improving the Arab city and preserving its original character and Islamic cultural heritage; Dir-Gen. Dr M. A. AL-HAMMAD; library of 65,000 vols and 675 periodicals; publs books and research papers.

King Faisal Centre for Research and Islamic Studies: Riyadh; to advance research and studies into Islamic civilization; provides grants for research and organizes symposia, lectures and workshops on Islamic subjects.

SLOVAKIA

Institute of Asian and African Studies: Slovak Academy of Sciences, Klemensova 19, 813 64 Bratislava; tel. and fax (7) 326326; f. 1960; 14 mems; Dir Institute Dr V. KRUPA; publ. *Asian and African Studies* (2 a year).

SPAIN

Asociación Española de Orientalistas: Universidad Autónoma, Edificio Rectorado, Canto Blanco, 28049 Madrid; tel. (1) 397-4112; f. 1965; publs *Boletín* (annually), etc.

Egyptian Institute of Islamic Studies: Francisco de Asis Méndez Casariego 1, Madrid 2; tel. (1) 563-9468; affiliated to Ministry of Higher Education, Cairo; f. 1950; Dir Dr AHMAD ALI MORSI; publs *Magazine of the Egyptian Institute* and other educational books.

Instituto de Filología: Duque de Medinaceli 6, 28014 Madrid; tel. (1) 585-4866; fax (1) 585-4878; f. 1985 as a result of the amalgamation of four existing institutes (the Benito Arias Montano, Miguel Asin, Miguel de Cervantes and Antonio de Nebrija); six depts: Departamento de Estudios Arabes (four members), Departamento de Filologia Biblica y de Oriente Antiguo (eight members), Departamento de Estudios Hebraicos (four members); Dir TERESA ORTEGA MONASTERIO; Sec. JULIO CÉSAR SUILS; publs *Sefarad* (review of Hebrew, Sephardic and Ancient Studies, 2 a year), *Alqantara* (review of Arab Studies, 2 a year) and books.

SWEDEN

Nordiska Afrikainstitutet (Scandinavian Institute of African Studies): POB 1703, S-75147, Uppsala; tel. (18) 15-54-80; telex 8195077; fax (18) 69-56-29; research and documentation centre, organizes seminars and publishes wide range of books and pamphlets in Swedish and English; library of 39,000 vols; Dir L. WOHLGEMUTH; publs *Seminar Proceedings, Research Reports, Discussion Papers, Africana, Annual Report.*

SWITZERLAND

Centre d'Etude du Proche-Orient Ancien: Université de Genève, 3 place de l'Université, 1211 Geneva 4; tel. (22) 705-7307; telex 423801; Dir ALBERT DE PURY; Sec. IVANKA URIO.

Schweizerische Asiengesellschaft: Ostasiatisches Seminar der Universität Zürich, Zürichbergstr. 4, 8032 Zürich; tel. (1) 257-3181; fax (1) 2615687; f. 1939; 220 mems; Pres. Prof. Dr R. GASSMANN; publs *Asiatische Studien/Etudes Asiatiques* (4 a year), *Schweizer Asiatische Studien* (Monographien und Studienhefte).

SYRIA

Institut Français d'Etudes Arabes: BP 344, Damascus; tel. (11) 330214; telex 412272; fax (11) 3327887; f. 1922; library of 45,000 vols, 900 periodicals; Dir JACQUES LANGHADE; 20 scholars; publs *Bulletin d'Etudes Orientales* (annually, 46 vols published), monographs, translations and Arabic texts (145 vols published).

Near East Foundation: BP 427, Damascus.

TAJIKISTAN

Institute of Oriental Studies of Tajikistan: Ul. Parvin 8, Dushanbe, Tajikistan; tel. (3772) 243010; Dir AKBAR TURSONOV.

TUNISIA

Institut des Belles Lettres Arabes: 12 rue Jamâa el-Haoua, 1008 Tunis BM; tel. (1) 560133; f. 1930; cultural centre; Dir E. RENAUD; publs *IBLA* (2 a year) and special studies.

TURKEY

British Institute of Archaeology at Ankara: Tahran Caddesi 24, Kavaklidere, 06700 Ankara; tel. (4) 427-5487; fax (4) 4280159; f. 1948; archaeological research and excavation; Dir Dr DONALD EASTON; publs *Anatolian Studies* (annually), *Occasional Publications.*

Centri di Studi Italiani in Turchia: Ataç Sokak 22, Yenişehir, Ankara; tel. (4) 314026; Dir Prof. GIANCLAUDIO MACCHIARELLA; Mesrutiyet Caddesi 161, Istanbul; tel. 144-9848; Dir Prof. ADELIA RISPOLI.

Deutsches Archäologisches Institut: Gümüşsuyu/Ayazpaşa Camii SK. 48, TR-80090, Istanbul; tel. (1) 244-0714; fax (1) 252-3491; f. 1929; Dir Prof. Dr-Ing. W. KOENIGS; publs *Istanbuler Mitteilungen* (annually), *Istanbuler Forschungen, Beihefte zu Istanbuler Mitteilungen.*

Institut Français d'Etudes Anatoliennes: Palais de France, PK 54, Beyoğlu, 80072 Istanbul; tel. (1) 244-3327; fax (1) 2528091; f. 1930; 10 scientific mems; library of c. 15,000 vols; Dir JACQUES THOBIE; publs *Collection IFEA, Collection Varia Turcica, Collection Varia Anatolica, Anatolica Antiqua, Anatolica Moderna.*

Netherlands Historical Archaeological Institute: Istiklâl Caddesi 393, Beyoğlu, Istanbul; tel. (1) 293-9283; fax (1) 251-3846; f. 1958; library of 12,000 vols; Dir Dr H. E. LAGRO; publs *Publications de l'Institut Historique et Archéologique Néerlandais de Stamboul, Anatolica.*

Österreichisches Kulturinstitut Istanbul: Köybaşi Cad. 46, 80870 Yeniköy, Istanbul; tel. (1) 236-1581; fax (1) 258-0222; Dir Consul Dr ERWIN LUCIUS.

Türk Dil Kurumu (Turkish Language Institute): 217 Atatürk Bulevar, 06680 Ankara; tel. (4) 126-8124; fax (4) 128-5288; f. 1932; 40 mems; library of 28,000 vols; Pres. Prof. Dr HASAN EREN; Vice-Pres. Prof. Dr HIMMET UMUNÇ; publs *Türk Dili* (monthly), *Türk Dili Araştırmaları Yilliği-Belleten* (annually).

Türk Kültürünü Araştırma Enstitüsü (Institute for the Study of Turkish Culture): 17 Sokak No. 38, Bahçelievler, Ankara; tel. (4) 0312-2133100; f. 1961; scholarly research into all aspects of Turkish culture; Dir Prof. Dr SÜKRÜ ELÇIN; publs *Türk Kültürü* (monthly), *Cultura Turcica* (annually), *Türk Kültürü Araştırmaları* (annually).

Türk Tarih Kurumu (Turkish Historical Society): Kizilay Sok. 1, 06100 Ankara; tel. (4) 3102368; telex 42214; fax (4) 3101698; f. 1931; 40 mems; library of 210,000 vols; Pres. Prof.

YAŞAR YÜCEL; Gen. Dir ULUĞ IĞDEMİR; publs *Belleten* (3 a year), *Belgeler* (annually), *Höyük* (annually).

Türkiyat Araştırma Merkezi (Turkish Research Centre): University of Istanbul, Bayezid, Istanbul; tel. (1) 522-3626; f. 1924; research into Turkish language, literature, history and culture; library of 55,000 vols; Dir Dr ALI ALPARSLAN.

UNITED KINGDOM

Arab Research Centre: 76/78 Notting Hill Gate, London, W11 3HS; tel. (071) 221-2425; fax (071) 221-5899; f. 1979; research into problems and issues concerning the Arab world; library of 27,000 vols; commissions writing of special papers; holds international symposia; Chair. ABD AL-MAJID FARID; Man. ALIA ARNALL; publs. *The Arab Researcher* (English and Arabic, quarterly).

Centre for Arab Gulf Studies: University of Exeter, Old Library Bldg, Prince of Wales Rd, Exeter, EX4 4JZ; tel. (0392) 264041; telex 42894; fax (0392) 264023; f. 1978 to promote knowledge and understanding of the Arab Gulf; Dir B. R. PRIDHAM.

Centre for Lebanese Studies: 59 Observatory St, Oxford, OX2 6EP; tel. (0865) 58465; fax (0865) 514317; Dir NADIM SHEHADI; Research Associate Dr FIDAH NASRALLAH.

Centre for Middle Eastern and Islamic Studies: University of Durham, South End House, South Rd, Durham, DH1 3TG; tel. (091) 374-2822; telex 537351; fax (091) 374-2830; f. 1962; responsible for teaching undergraduate and postgraduate courses in Arabic, Middle Eastern and Islamic studies; organizes seminars, lectures and conferences; documentation unit f. 1970 to monitor economic, social and political devts in the region with some 200,000 documents; publication programme of research monographs and bibliographies; Chair. Prof. T. C. NIBLOCK.

Centre of Middle Eastern Studies: Faculty of Oriental Studies, Sidgwick Ave, Cambridge CB3 9DA; tel. (0223) 335103; fax (0223) 335110; Dir Prof M. C. LYONS; publ. *Arabian Studies* (annually).

Council for the Advancement of Arab-British Understanding (CAABU): The Arab-British Centre, 21 Collingham Rd, London, SW5 0NU; tel. (071) 373-8414; fax (071) 835-2088; f. 1967; Dir BERNARD MILLS.

Egypt Exploration Society: 3 Doughty Mews, London, WC1N 2PG; tel. (071) 242-1880; fax (071) 404 6118; f. 1882; library of 4,500 vols; Sec. PATRICIA A. SPENCER; publs *Bulletin of the Egypt Exploration Society, Excavation Memoirs, Archaeological Survey, Graeco-Roman Memoirs, Journal of Egyptian Archaeology, Texts from Excavations, Bulletin of Egyptian Archaeology,* etc.

Islamic Cultural Centre (and London Central Mosque): 146 Park Rd, London, NW8 7RG; tel. (071) 724-3363; f. 1944 to provide information and guidance on Islam and Islamic culture and to provide facilities for Muslims residing in Great Britain; library of 10,000 vols in Arabic, English, Urdu and Persian; Dir-Gen. Dr A. A. MUGHRAM-AL-GHAMDI.

Maghreb Studies Association: c/o The Executive Secretary, M. BEN-MADANI, 45 Burton St, London, WC1H 9AL; tel. (071) 388-1840; f. 1981; independent; to promote the study of and interest in the Maghreb; organizes lectures and conferences; issues occasional publications and co-operates with the periodical *The Maghreb Review* (q.v.); Chair. Prof. HÉDI BOURAOUI.

Middle East Association: Bury House, 33 Bury St, London, SW1Y 6AX; tel. (071) 839-2137; fax (071) 839-6121; f. 1961; an asscn for firms actively promoting UK trade with 20 Arab countries, plus Afghanistan, Ethiopia, Eritrea, Iran and Turkey; 300 mems; Dir-Gen. JOHN GRUNDON; Sec. R. BROWN.

Middle East Centre: St Antony's College, 68 Woodstock Rd, Oxford, OX2 6JF; tel. (0865) 59651; fax (0865) 311475; f. 1958; Dir Dr DEREK HOPWOOD; library of 30,000 vols and archive of private papers and photographs; publs St Antony's Middle East monographs.

Muslim Institute for Research and Planning: 6 Endsleigh St, London, WC1H 0DS; tel. (071) 388-2581; telex 912881; fax (071) 383-5006; f. 1974; research and teaching programmes,

academic and current affairs seminars, library of 6,000 vols; 800 mems; Dir Dr KALIM SIDDIQUI; publ. *Crescent International* (2 a month), *Issues in the Islamic Movement* (annually). Supplies publications of the Muslim Parliament of Great Britain.

Oxford Centre for Islamic Studies: St Cross College, Oxford OX1 3TU; tel. (0865) 725077; telex 83147; fax (0865) 248942; f. 1985; Dir Dr FARHAN A. NIZAMI; Reg. Dr DAVID G. BROWNING; publs *Journal of Islamic Studies* (2 a year).

Palestine Exploration Fund: 2 Hinde Mews, Marylebone Lane, London, W1M 5RR; tel. (071) 935-5379; f. 1865; 900 subscribers; Pres. The Archbishop of Canterbury; Exec. Sec. Dr R. L. CHAPMAN, III; Hon. Sec. Mrs Y. HODSON; publ. *Palestine Exploration Quarterly.*

Royal Asiatic Society of Great Britain and Ireland: 60 Queen's Gardens, London, W2 3AF; tel. (071) 724-4741; f. 1823 for the study of the history, sociology, institutions, customs, languages and art of Asia; approx. 900 mems; approx. 700 subscribing libraries; library of 100,000 vols and 1,500 MSS; branches in various Asian cities; Pres. Dr D. W. MACDOWALL; Sec. Miss L. COLLINS; publs *Journal* and monographs.

Royal Society for Asian Affairs: 2 Belgrave Square, London, SW1; tel. (071) 235-5122; f. 1901; 1,100 mems with past or present knowledge of the Middle East, Central Asia or the Far East; library of about 7,000 vols; Pres. Lord DENMAN; Chair. Sir MICHAEL WILFORD; Sec. Miss M. FITZSIMONS; publ. *Journal* (3 a year).

Saudi-British Society, The: 21 Collingham Rd, London, SW5 0NU; tel. (071) 373-8414; fax (071) 835-2088; non-political; Chair. Lord DENMAN; Sec. ANTHONY LEE.

School of African and Asian Studies: University of Sussex, Falmer, Brighton, Sussex, BN1 9QN; tel. (0273) 606755; fax (0273) 623572; Dean Dr D. ROBINSON.

School of Oriental and African Studies, University of London: Thornhaugh St, London, WC1H 0XG; tel. (071) 637-2388; telex 262433; fax (071) 436-3844; f. 1916; library of over 750,000 vols and 2,750 MSS; Dir M. D. MCWILLIAM.

UNITED STATES OF AMERICA

America-Mideast Educational & Training Services, Inc (AMIDEAST): 1100 17th St, NW, Washington, DC 20036; tel. (202) 785-0022; telex 440160; fax (202) 822-6563; f. 1951; a private, non-profit organization promoting understanding and co-operation between Americans and the people of the Middle East and North Africa through programmes of education, development and information; offices in Washington DC, and Bahrain, Egypt, Jordan, Kuwait, Lebanon, Morocco, Tunisia, Yemen, the Israeli-occupied Territories and Syria; Pres. ROBERT S. DILLON; publs on education in the Middle East, *Advising Quarterly, AMIDEAST News* (quarterly), *Introduction to the Arab World* (educational videotape), and *Arab World Almanac* (three times per year).

American Oriental Society: 329 Sterling Memorial Library, Box 1603A, Yale Station, New Haven, Conn 06520; tel. (203) 747-4760; f. 1842; 1,350 mems; library of 23,500 vols; Sec. JONATHAN RODGERS; publs *Journal* (quarterly), monograph series, essay series and offprint series.

American Schools of Oriental Research: 3301 N. Charles St, Baltimore, MD 21218; tel. (410) 516-3498; f. 1900; approx. 2,000 mems; support activities of independent archaeological institutions abroad: The Albright Institute of Archaeological Research, Jerusalem, Israel, the American Center of Oriental Research in Amman, Jordan, and the Cyprus American Archaeological Research Institute in Nicosia, Cyprus; Pres. ERIC M. MEYERS; publs *Newsletter* (quarterly), *Biblical Archaeologist* (quarterly), *Bulletin* (quarterly), *Journal of Cuneiform Studies* (quarterly), *Annual.*

Center for Contemporary Arab Studies: Georgetown University, Washington, DC 20057-1052; tel. (202) 687-5793; fax (202) 687-7001; f. 1975; Dir Dr BARBARA R. F. STOWASSER; Academic Dir Dr JUDITH TUCKER; publs on social, economic, political, cultural and development aspects of Arab World; publ. newsletter (four a year).

Center for Middle Eastern Studies: University of Chicago, 5828 S. University Ave, Chicago, Ill 60637; tel. (312) 702-

8297; fax (312) 702-2587; f. 1965; research into medieval and modern cultures of the Middle East from Morocco to Pakistan; Dir RASHID I. KHALIDI; Assoc. Dir RALPH AUSTEN.

Center for Middle Eastern Studies: Harvard University, 1737 Cambridge St, Cambridge, Mass 02138; tel. (617) 495-4055; fax (617) 496-8584; research on Middle Eastern subjects and Islamic studies; Dir Prof. WILLIAM A. GRAHAM; Publs *Middle East Monograph Series, Harvard Middle Eastern and Islamic Review.*

Center for Middle Eastern Studies: The University of Texas at Austin, Tex 78712; tel. (512) 471-3881; telex 91087-41305; fax (512) 471-7834; f. 1960; linguistic, humanistic and social studies of Middle East languages and cultures; Dir Dr ROBERT K. HOLZ; publs a book series on 19th and 20th century Middle East and translations of contemporary fiction and memoirs.

Center for Middle Eastern and North African Studies: University of Michigan, 144 Lane Hall, Ann Arbor, Mich 48109-1290; tel. (313) 764-0350; telex 4320815; fax (313) 764-8523; f. 1961; research into the ancient, medieval and modern cultures of the Near East and North Africa, Near Eastern languages and literature; library includes 290,470 vols on Middle East and North Africa; Dir Dr JUAN R. I. COLE.

Gustave E. von Grunebaum Center for Near Eastern Studies: University of California, Los Angeles, 405 Hilgard Ave, Los Angeles, Calif 90024; tel. (310) 825-1181; telex 3716012; fax (310) 206-2406; f. 1957; social sciences, culture and language studies of the Near East since the rise of Islam; a growing programme of Ancient Near Eastern Studies; library of over 100,000 vols and outstanding MSS collection in Arabic, Armenian, Hebrew, Persian and Turkish; Dir Dr GEORGES SABAGH; Assoc. Dir Dr RICHARD G. HOVANNISIAN.

Hairenik Association, Inc: Boston, Mass; f. 1899; Man. Editor Dr KEVORK DONOYAN; publs *Armenian Review, The Armenian Weekly, Hairenik Daily;* circ. 8,000.

Hoover Institution on War, Revolution and Peace: Stanford University, Stanford, Calif 94305-6010; tel. (415) 723-2050; telex 3722871; fax (415) 723-1687; f. 1919; library of 1.7 million vols and 4,000 archives on 20th-century history includes important collection of 125,000 vols and 150 archives on Middle East and North Africa; Dir J. RAISIAN; Middle East Dep. Curator E. A. JAJKO; publs about 20 books each year.

The Iran Foundation, Inc: New York; project assistance relating to the advancement of health and education in Iran and other culturally related areas.

Institute for Mediterranean Affairs: 428 East 83rd St, New York, NY 10028; tel. (212) 988-1725; established under charter of the University of the State of New York to evolve a better understanding of the historical background and contemporary political and socio-economic problems of the nations and regions that border on the Mediterranean Sea, with special reference to the Middle East and North Africa; 350 mems; Pres. Ambassador SEYMOUR M. FINGER; Dir SAMUEL MERLIN.

Joint Committee on the Near and Middle East: c/o Social Science Research Council, 605 Third Ave, New York, NY 10158; tel. (212) 661-0280; fax (212) 370-7896; the Committee administers (for pre-dissertation students who are citizens or permanent residents of the USA; for doctoral dissertation researchers who are either citizens or permanent residents of the USA, or for foreign students enrolled full-time in doctoral programmes in the USA) a programme of grants for research by individual scholars in the social sciences and humanities.

Middle East Center: University of Utah, Salt Lake City, Utah 84112; tel. (801) 581-6181; telex 3789459; fax (801) 581-6183; f. 1960; co-ordinates programme in Middle East languages and area studies in 12 academic departments; BA, MA and PhD in Middle East Studies with area of concentration in Arabic, Hebrew, Persian, Turkish, anthropology, history and political science; annual summer programme for Utah educators in the Middle East, research and exchange agreements with several universities; pre-doctoral and teaching fellowships in Middle Eastern languages; library of 150,000 vols; Acting Dir Dr LOIS A. GIFFEN.

Middle East Institute: 1761 N St, NW, Washington, DC 20036; tel. (202) 785-1141; f. 1946; exists to develop and maintain facilities for research, publication and dissemination of information, with a view to developing in the United States a more

thorough understanding of the countries of the Middle East; the Institute holds an annual conference on Middle East affairs, seminars on business in the Middle East and a continuing series of language classes, colloquia and lectures; it also conducts Islamic affairs programmes, maintains a research centre and administers grant programmes in the US through its Outreach Fund; Keiser Library 25,000 vols; 1,200 mems; Pres. Hon. ROBERT V. KEELEY; Vice-Pres. Hon. PAUL J. HARE; publs *Middle East Journal* (quarterly) and occasional books.

Middle East Institute: Columbia University, 1113 International Affairs Bldg, New York, NY 10027; f. 1954; a graduate training programme on the modern Middle East for students seeking professional careers as regional specialists, research into problems of economics, government, law, and international relations of the Middle East countries, and their languages and history; library of more than 150,000 vols in Middle East vernaculars and equally rich in Western languages including Russian; Dir RICHARD W. BULLIET.

Middle East Studies Association of North America: University of Arizona, 1232 N. Cherry Ave, Tucson, AZ, 85721; tel. (602) 621-5850; fax (602) 321-7752; f. 1966 to promote high standards of scholarship and instruction in Middle East studies, to facilitate communication among scholars through meetings and publications, and to foster co-operation among persons and organizations concerned with the scholarly study of the Middle East since the rise of Islam; 2,400 mems; Pres. (1993) JOHN O. VOLL; Exec. Dir ANNE H. BETTERIDGE; publs *International Journal of Middle East Studies* (quarterly), *Bulletin* (2 a year), *Newsletter* (4 a year), edited works and collections on the Middle East, etc.

Middle East Studies Center: Portland State Univ., POB 751, Portland, Ore 97207; tel. (503) 725-4074; fax (503) 725-4882; f. 1959; Middle East language and area studies, emphasizing Arabic and Hebrew languages; area classes in history, political science, geography, anthropology and sociology; extensive outreach activities; Dir GRANT M. FARR.

Near East Foundation: 342 Madison Ave, Suite 1030, New York, NY 10173-0020; tel. (212) 867-0064; telex 226000; fax (212) 867-0169; f. 1930; provides technical and financial assistance in support of locally-organized projects in agriculture and rural/community development in the Middle East and Africa; Chair. DAVID S. DODGE; Pres. RICHARD C. ROBARTS; publs *Annual Report.*

Near Eastern Languages and Cultures, Department of: Indiana University, Bloomington, Ind 47405; tel. (812) 855-4323; fax (812) 855-7500; courses in Arabic, Persian and Hebrew languages and literature, women's studies, history, civilization and religions of the region. Turkish available through the Department of Central Eurasian Studies; Chair. FEDWA MALTI-DOUGLAS.

Oriental Institute: 1155 East 58th St, Chicago, Ill 60637; tel. (312) 702-9514; telex 687-1133; fax (312) 702-9853; f. 1919; principally concerned with cultures and languages of the ancient Near East; extensive museum; affiliated to the University of Chicago; Dir WILLIAM M. SUMNER.

Program in Near Eastern Studies: Princeton University, Jones Hall, Princeton, NJ 08544; tel. (609) 258-4272; fax (609) 258-1242; f. 1947; research in all aspects of the modern Near East and North Africa; library of 340,000 vols; Dir HEATH W. LOWRY; publs *Princeton Studies on the Near East* (irregular), *Princeton Near East Papers* (irregular).

Semitic Museum: Harvard University, 6 Divinity Ave, Cambridge, Mass 02138; tel. (617) 495-4631; fax (617) 496-8904; f. 1889; sponsors exploration and research in Western Asia; contains collection of exhibits from ancient Near East; research collections open by appointment, museum open to general public; Dir LAWRENCE E. STAGER.

VATICAN CITY

Pontificium Institutum Orientale (Pontifical Oriental Institute): 7 Piazza Santa Maria Maggiore, 00185-Rome; tel. (6) 446-5589; fax (6) 446-5576; f. 1917; library of 146,000 vols; Rector Rev. CLARENCE GALLAGHER; Sec. Rev. JAKOV KULIČ; publs *Orientalia Christiana Periodica, Orientalia Christiana Analecta, Concilium Florentinum (Documenta et Scriptores), Anaphorae Syriacae, Kanonika.*

SELECT BIBLIOGRAPHY

Books on the Middle East

See also bibliographies at end of relevant chapters in Part Three.

Abdel Malek, A. *La pensée politique arabe contemporaine.* Paris, Editions du Seuil, 1970.

Abed, George T. (Ed.). *The Palestinian Economy: Studies in Development under Prolonged Occupation.* London, Routledge, 1988.

The Economic Viability of a Palestinian State. Washington, Institute for Palestine State, 1990.

Abir, Mordechai. *Oil, Power and Politics: Conflict in Arabia, The Red Sea and The Gulf.* London, Frank Cass, 1974.

Abu Jaber, Kamel S. *The Arab Baath Socialist Party.* New York, Syracuse University Press, 1966.

Abu-Lughod, Ibrahim (Ed.). *The Transformation of Palestine: Essays on the Development of the Arab-Israeli Conflict.* Evanston, Ill, Northwestern University Press, 1971.

Aburish, Said. *Cry Palestine: Inside the West Bank.* London, Bloomsbury, 1991.

Acharya, Amitar. *US Military Strategy in the Gulf.* London, Routledge, 1989.

Adams, Michael and Mayhew, Christopher. *Publish it Not . . . the Middle East Cover-up.* London, Longman, 1975.

Ahmed, Akbar S. *Discovering Islam: making Sense of Muslim History and Society.* London, Routledge, 1989.

Ajami, Fouad. *The Arab Predicament.* Cambridge University Press, 1981.

Alderson, A. D. *The Structure of the Ottoman Dynasty.* New York, Oxford University Press, 1956.

al-Algosaibi, Ghazi. *The Gulf crisis—an attempt to understand.* London, Kegan Paul International, 1993.

Allen, Richard. *Imperialism and Nationalism in the Fertile Crescent: Sources and Prospects of the Arab-Israeli Conflict.* London, Oxford University Press, 1975.

Anderson, Jack, and Boyd, James. *Oil: The Real Story Behind the World Energy Crisis.* London, Sidgwick and Jackson, 1984.

Arberry, A. J. (Ed.). *Religion in the Middle East*—Volume I, *Judaism and Christianity*, Volume II, *Islam and General Summary.* Cambridge University Press, 1969.

Ashtor, E. *A Social and Economic History of the Near East in the Middle Ages.* London, Collins, 1976.

Askari, Hossein, and Cummings, John Thomas. *Middle East Economies in the 1970s.* New York, Praeger, 1976.

Astor, David, and Yorke, Valerie. *Peace in the Middle East: Superpowers and Security Guarantees.* Transworld Publishers—Corgi Books, 1978.

Atiyah, Edward. *The Arabs.* Baltimore, 1955.

Atlas of the Arab World and the Middle East. London, Macmillan, 1960.

Ayoob, M. (Ed.). *The Middle East in World Politics.* London, Croom Helm, 1981.

Azzam, Salem (Ed.). *Islam and Contemporary Society: Islamic Council of Europe.* London, Longman, 1982.

Baer, Gabriel. *Population and Society in the Arab East.* London, Routledge, 1964.

Bailey, Sydney. *Four Arab-Israeli wars and the Peace Process.* London, Macmillan, 1990.

Barkey, Henri. *The Politics of Economic Reform in the Middle East.* London, Macmillan, 1993.

Barnaby, Frank. *The Invisible Bomb: The Nuclear Arms Race in the Middle East.* London, I. B. Taurus, 1989.

Baster, James. *The Introduction of Western Economic Institutions into the Middle East.* Royal Institute of International Affairs and Oxford University Press, 1960.

Behbehani, Hashim S. H. *China's Foreign Policy in the Arab World 1955–75.* Henley-on-Thames, Kegan Paul International, 1982.

Bell, J. Bowyer. *The Long War, Israel and the Arabs since 1946.* Englewood Cliffs, NJ, 1969.

Bennis, Phyllis, and Moushabeck, Michael (Eds). *Beyond the Storm: A Gulf Crisis Reader.* Edinburgh, Canongate Press, 1992.

Berberoglu, Berch (Ed.). *Power and Stability in the Middle East.* London, Zed Books, 1989.

Berque, Jacques. *L'Islam au défi.* Paris, Gallimard, 1980.

Berque, Jacques and Charnay, J.-P. *Normes et valeurs dans l'Islam contemporaine.* Paris, Payot, 1966.

Bethell, Nicholas. *The Palestine Triangle.* London, André Deutsch, 1979.

Bethmann, Erich W. *A Selected Basic Bibliography on the Middle East.* Washington, DC, American Friends of the Middle East, 1964.

Bidwell's Guides to Government Ministers, Vol. II, *The Arab World 1900–1972.* Compiled and edited by Robin Bidwell. London, Frank Cass, 1973.

Binder, Leonard. *The Ideological Revolution in the Middle East.* New York, 1964.

Blake, Gerald H., and Drysdale, Alasdair. *The Middle East and North Africa: A Political Geography.* Oxford University Press, 1985.

Boulares, Habib. *Islam: the Fear and the Hope.* London, Zed Books, 1991.

Boyd, Douglas A. *Broadcasting in the Arab World: A Survey of Radio and Television in the Middle East.* Philadelphia, Temple University Press, 1982.

Brenchley, Frank. *Britain and the Middle East: an economic history, 1945–1987.* London, Lester Crook Academic Publishing, 1989.

Breslauer, George W. (Ed.). *Soviet Strategy in the Middle East.* London, Routledge, 1989.

Brittain, Victoria (Ed.). *The Gulf Between Us: The Gulf War and Beyond.* London, Virago, 1991.

Brockelmann, C. *History of the Islamic Peoples.* New York and London, 1947–48.

Brown, Malcolm. *The Letters of T.E. Lawrence.* Oxford University Press, 1991.

Bull, General Odd. *War and Peace in the Middle East: the Experience and Views of a UN Observer.* London, Leo Cooper, 1976.

Bullard, Sir R. *Britain and the Middle East from the earliest times in 1952.* London, 1952.

Bulloch, John. *The Making of a War: The Middle East from 1967–1973.* London, Longman, 1974.

Bulloch, John, and Morris, Harvey. *The Gulf War.* London, Methuen, 1990.

Burke, Edmond. *Struggle for Survival in the Modern Middle East.* London, I. B. Tavris, 1994.

Burrows, Bernard. *Footnotes in the Sand: the Gulf in Transition.* London, Michael Russell, 1991.

Butt, Gerald. *A Rock and a Hard Place: origins of Arab-Western conflict in the Middle East.* London, Harper Collins, 1994.

Calabrese, John. *China's changing relations with the Middle East.* London, Pinter, 1990.

Carré, Olivier. *L'Idéologie palestinienne de résistance.* Paris, Armand Colin, 1972.

Mystique et Politique. Paris, Presses de la Fondation nationale des sciences politiques and Editions du Cerf, 1984.

Carrère d'Encausse, Hélène. *La politique soviétique au Moyen-Orient, 1955–1975.* Paris, Presses de la Fondation Nationale des Sciences Politiques, 1976.

Cattan, Henry. *Palestine and International Law: The Legal Aspects of the Arab-Israeli Conflict.* London, Longman, 1973.

Jerusalem. London, Croom Helm, 1981.

Cattan, J. *Evolution of Oil Concessions in the Middle East and North Africa.* New York, Oceana, Dobbs Ferry, 1967.

Chaliand, Gérard. *People Without a Country: The Kurds and Kurdistan.* London, Zed Press, 1980.

Chevallier, Dominique, Guellouz, Azzedine and Miquel, André. *Les arabes, l'islam et l'europe.* Paris, Flammarion, 1991.

Chomsky, Noam. *Peace in the Middle East?: Reflections on Justice and Nationhood.* London, Collins, 1976.

The Fateful Triangle: The United States, Israel and the Palestinians. London, Pluto Press, 1983.

Pirates and Emperors: International Terrorism in the Real World. New York, Claremont Publications.

Choveiri, Youssef M. *Arab History and the Nation-State: A Study in Modern Arab Historiography 1820–1980.* London, Routledge, 1980.

Clarke, John I., and Fisher, W. B. (Ed.). *Populations of the Middle East and North Africa.* University of London Press, 1972.

Cobban, Helena. *The Palestinian Liberation Organization: People, Power and Politics.* Cambridge University Press, 1984.

Cohen, Michael J. *Palestine: Retreat from the Mandate.* London, Elek Books, 1978.

Conrad, Lawrence J. (Ed.). *The Formation and Perception of the Modern Arab World, Studies by Marwan R. Buheiry.* Princeton, The Darwin Press, 1989.

Cook, M. A. (Ed.). *Studies in the Economic History of the Middle East.* Oxford University Press, 1970.

Cooley, John K. *Green March, Black September: The Story of the Palestinian Arabs.* London, Frank Cass, 1973.

Payback: America's Long War in the Middle East. London, Brassey's UK, 1992.

Coon, C. S. *Caravan: the Story of the Middle East.* New York, 1951, and London, 1952.

The Impact of the West on Social Institutions. New York, 1952.

Corbin, Henry. *History of Islamic Philosophy.* London, Kegan Paul International, 1992.

Cordesman, Anthony. *Weapons of mass destruction in the Middle East.* London, Brasseys, 1991.

Corm, Georges. *Fragmentation of the Middle East: the last thirty years.* London, Unwin Hyman, 1988.

Costello, V. F. *Urbanisation in the Middle East.* Cambridge University Press, 1977.

Crone, Patricia. *Meccan Trade and the Rise of Islam.* Oxford, Basil Blackwell, 1987.

Cudsi, Alexander, and Dessouki, Ali E. Hillal (Eds). *Islam and Power.* London, Croom Helm, 1981.

Cunningham, Michael. *Hostages to Fortune—The Future of Western Interests in the Arabian Gulf.* Oxford, Brassey's Defence Publishers Ltd, 1988.

Curtiss, Richard H. *Stealth PACs: how Israel's American lobby took control of US-Middle East policy.* Washington, American Educational Trust, 1990.

Daniel, Norman. *Islam and the West.* Edinburgh University Press, revised edition 1963.

Islam, Europe and Empire. Edinburgh University Press, 1964.

Decobert, Christian. *Le mendiant et le combattant: l'institution de l'islam.* Paris, Editions du Sevil, 1991.

De la Billière, Peter. *Storm Command: a personal account of the Gulf War.* London, Harper Collins, 1992.

De Vore, Ronald M. (Ed.). *The Arab-Israeli Conflict: A Historical, Political, Social and Military Bibliography.* Oxford, Clio Press, 1977.

Dimbleby, Jonathan, and McCullin, Donald. *The Palestinians.* London, Quartet, 1970.

Dupuy, Trevor N. *Elusive Victory: The Arab-Israeli Wars 1947–1974.* London, MacDonald and Jane's, 1979.

Easterman, Daniel. *New Jerusalems—reflections on Islam, fundamentalism and the Rushdie affair.* London, Grafton Books, 1992.

Efrat, Moshe, and Bercovitch, Jacob. *Superpowers and Client States in the Middle East: The Imbalance of Influence.* London, Routledge, 1991.

Ehtashami, Anoushiravan, and Nonneman, Gerd. *War and Peace in the Gulf: Domestic Politics and Regional Relations into the 1990s.* Reading, Ithaca Press, 1991.

Enayat, Hamid. *Modern Islamic Political Thought: The Response of the Shi'i and Sunni Muslims to the Twentieth Century.* London, Macmillan, 1982.

Encyclopaedia of Islam, The. 4 vols and supplement. Leiden, 1913–38.

Esposito, John L. (Ed.). *Voices of Resurgent Islam.* New York, Oxford University Press, 1983.

The Islamic Threat, Myth or Reality? New York, Oxford University Press Inc., 1992.

Ettinghausen, Richard. Books and Periodicals in Western Languages dealing with the Near and Middle East. Washington, Middle East Institute, 1952.

Fahmy, Mansour. *La condition de la femme en islam.* Paris, Editions Allia, 1991.

Field, Henry. *Bibliography on Southwestern Asia: VII, A Seventh Compilation.* University of Miami, 1962.

Field, Michael. *$100,000,000 a Day—Inside the World of Middle East Money.* London, Sidgwick and Jackson, 1975.

Fisher, S. N. *Social Forces in the Middle East.* Ithaca, NY, Cornell University Press, 3rd edition, 1977.

The Middle East: A History. New York, Alfred Knopf, revised edition, 1978.

Fisher, W. B. *The Middle East—a Physical, Social and Regional Geography.* London, 7th edition, 1978.

Frangi, Abdallah. *The PLO and Palestine.* London, Zed Press, 1984.

Freedman, Robert O. *Soviet Policy toward the Middle East since 1970.* New York, Praeger, 3rd edition, 1983.

Friedman, Thomas. *From Beirut to Jerusalem.* New York, Farrar, Straus and Giroux, 1989.

Frye, R. N. (Ed.). *The Near East and the Great Powers.* Cambridge, Mass, Harvard University Press, 1951; London, New York and Toronto, Oxford University Press, 1952.

Gibb, H. A. R. *Mohammedanism.* London, 1949.

Modern Trends in Islam. Chicago, 1947.

Studies on the Civilisation of Islam. London, 1962.

Gibb, H. A. R., and Bowen, Harold. *Islamic Society and the West.* London, 2 vols, 1950, 1957.

Gilbert, Martin. *The Arab-Israeli Conflict: Its History in Maps.* London, Weidenfeld and Nicolson, 1974.

Gilmour, David. *The Dispossessed: The Ordeal of the Palestinians 1917–80.* London, Sidgwick & Jackson, 1980.

Gilsenan, Michael. *Recognizing Islam.* London, Croom Helm, 1983.

Gittings, John (Ed.). *Beyond the Gulf War: The Middle East and the New World Order.* London, Catholic Institute for International Relations, 1991.

Glassé, Cyril. *The Concise Encyclopedia of Islam.* London, Stacey International, 1989.

Glubb, Lt-Gen. Sir John. *A Short History of the Arab Peoples.* London, Hodder and Stoughton, 1969.

Golan, Galia. *The Soviet Union and the Middle East Crisis.* Cambridge University Press, 1977.

Gomaa, Ahmed M. *The Foundation of the League of Arab States.* London, Longman, 1977.

Gowers, Andrew, and Walter, Tony. *Behind the Myth: Yasir Arafat and the Palestinian revolution.* London, W.H. Allen, 1990.

Graz, Liesl. *The Turbulent Gulf.* London, I.B. Tauris, 1990.

Gresh, Alain, and Vidal, Dominique. *A–Z of the Middle East.* London, Zed Books, 1991.

Grundwald, K., and Ronall, J. O. *Industrialisation in the Middle East.* New York, Council for Middle East Affairs, 1960.

Grunebaum, Gustave E. von (Ed.). *Unity and Variety in Muslim Civilisation.* Chicago, 1955.

Islam: Essays on the Nature and Growth of a Cultural Tradition. London, Routledge and Kegan Paul, 1961.

Modern Islam: the Search for Cultural Identity. London, 1962.

Halpern, Manfred. *The Politics of Social Change in the Middle East and North Africa.* New York, Princeton University Press, 1963.

Hardy, Roger. *Arabia after the Storm: internal stability of the Gulf Arab states.* London, Royal Institute of International Affairs, 1992.

Harris, Lillian Craig. *China Considers the Middle East.* London, I. B. Tavris, 1994.

Hart, Alan. *Arafat—Terrorist or Peacemaker?* London, Sidgwick and Jackson, 1984.

Hartshorn, J. E. *Oil Companies and Governments.* London, Faber, 1962.

Hassan bin Talal, Crown Prince of Jordan. *A Study on Jerusalem.* London, Longman, 1980.

Hatem, M. Abdel-Kader. *Information and the Arab Cause.* London, Longman, 1974.

Hayes, J. R. (Ed.). *The Genius of Arab Civilisation.* London, Phaidon, 1976.

Hazard, *Atlas of Islamic History.* Oxford University Press, 1951.

Heikal, Mohammed. *Illusions of Triumph: An Arab View of the Gulf War.* London, Harper Collins, 1992.

Hershlag, Z. Y. *Introduction to the Modern Economic History of the Middle East.* Leiden, E. J. Brill, 1964.

Herzog, Maj.-Gen. Chaim. *The War of Atonement.* London, Weidenfeld and Nicolson, 1975.

The Arab-Israeli Wars. London, Arms and Armour Press, 1982.

Hewedy, Amin. *Militarisation and Security in the Middle East.* London, Pinter, 1989.

Higgins, Rosalyn. *United Nations Peacekeeping 1946–67: Documents and Commentary*, Volume I, *The Middle East.* Oxford University Press, 1969.

Hiro, Dilip. *Inside the Middle East.* London, Routledge and Kegan Paul, 1981.

Islamic Fundamentalism. London, Paladin, 1988.

The Longest War. London, Grafton Books, 1990.

Hirst David. *Oil and Public Opinion in the Middle East.* New York, Praeger, 1966.

The Gun and the Olive Branch: the Roots of Violence in the Middle East. London, Faber, 1977.

Hirszowicz, Lukasz. *The Third Reich and the Arab East.* London, Routledge and Kegan Paul, 1966.

A Short History of the Near East. New York, 1966.

Makers of Arab History. London, Macmillan, 1968.

Islam. A Way of Life. London, Oxford University Press, 1971.

Hoare, Ian and Tayar, Graham (Eds). *The Arabs. A handbook on the politics and economics of the contemporary Arab world.* London, BBC Publications, 1971.

Hodgkin, E. C. *The Arabs.* Modern World Series, Oxford University Press, 1966.

Holt, P. M. *Studies in the History of the Near East.* London, Cass, 1973.

Holt, P. M., Lambton, A. K. S., and Lewis, B. (Eds.). *The Cambridge History of Islam.* Vol. I, *The Central Islamic Lands.* Cambridge University Press, 1970; Vol. II, *The Further Islamic Lands, Islamic Society and Civilization.* Cambridge University Press, 1971.

Hopwood, Derek (Ed.). *Studies in Arab History.* London, Macmillan, 1990.

Hourani, A. H. *Minorities in the Arab World.* London, 1947.

A Vision of History. Beirut, 1961.

Arabic Thought in the Liberal Age 1798–1939. Oxford University Press, 1962.

Europe and the Middle East. London, Macmillan, 1980.

The Emergence of the Modern Middle East. London, Macmillan, 1981.

A History of the Arab Peoples. London, Faber and Faber, 1991.

Islam in European Thought. Cambridge University Press, 1991.

Hoveyda, Fereydoun. *Que veulent les arabes?* Paris, Editions First, 1991.

Hudson, Michael C. *Arab Politics: The Search for Legitimacy.* New Haven and London, Yale University Press, 1977/78.

Hurewitz, J. C. *Unity and Disunity in the Middle East.* New York, Carnegie Endowment for International Peace, 1952.

Middle East Dilemmas. New York, 1953.

Diplomacy in the Near and Middle East. Vol. I, *1535–1914;* Vol. II, *1914–56.* Van Nostrand, 1956.

Soviet-American Rivalry in the Middle East (Ed.). London, Pall Mall Press, and New York, Praeger, 1969.

Middle East Politics: The Military Dimension. London, Pall Mall Press, 1969.

Al-Husari, Khaldun S. *Three Reformers; A Study in Modern Arab Political Thought.* Beirut, Khayats, 1966.

Hussein, Mahmoud. *Les Arabes au présent.* Paris, Seuil, 1974.

Ibrahim, Saad Eddin. *The New Arab Social Order: A Study of the Social Impact of Oil Wealth.* Boulder, Colorado, Westview Press, 1982.

International Institute for Strategic Studies. *Sources of Conflict in the Middle East.* London, Adelphi Papers, International Institute for Strategic Studies, 1966.

Domestic Politics and Regional Security: Jordan, Syria and Israel. London, Gower, International Institute for Strategic Studies, 1989.

Ionides, Michael. *Divide and Lose: the Arab Revolt 1955–58.* London, Bles, 1960.

Irwin, I. J. *Islam in the Modern National State.* Cambridge University Press, 1965.

Isaak, David T., and Fesharaki, F. *OPEC, the Gulf and the World Petroleum Market.* London, Croom Helm, 1983.

Issawi, Charles. *An Economic History of the Middle East and North Africa.* London, Methuen, 1982.

Issawi, Charles, and Yeganeh, Mohammed. *The Economics of Middle Eastern Oil.* London, Faber, 1963.

Izzard, Molly. *The Gulf.* London, John Murray, 1979.

Janin, R. *Les églises orientales et les rites orientaux.* Paris, 1926.

Jansen, G. H. *Non-Alignment and the Afro-Asian States.* New York, Praeger, 1966.

Militant Islam. London, Pan Books, 1979.

Johnson, Nels. *Islam and the Politics of Meaning in Palestinian Nationalism.* Henley-on-Thames, Kegan Paul International, 1983.

Jones, David. *The Arab World.* New York, Hilary House, 1967.

Karpat, Kemal H. *Political and Social Thought in the Contemporary Middle East.* London, Pall Mall Press, 1968.

Katz, Mark N. *Russia and Arabia: Soviet Foreign Policy toward the Arabian Peninsula.* Baltimore and London, Johns Hopkins University Press, 1986.

Keay, John. *The Arabs: A Living History*. London, Harvill, 1983.

Kedourie, Elie. *England and the Middle East*. London, 1956.

The Chatham House Version and other Middle-Eastern Studies. London, Weidenfeld and Nicolson, 1970.

Arabic Political Memoirs and Other Studies. London, Frank Cass, 1974.

In the Anglo-Arab Labyrinth. 1976.

Islam in the Modern World and Other Studies. London, Mansell, 1980.

Towards a Modern Iran. 1980.

Kelly, J. B. *Eastern Arabian Frontiers*. London, Faber, 1963.

Arabia, the Gulf and the West: A Critical View of the Arabs and their Oil Policy. London, Weidenfeld and Nicolson, 1980.

Kerr, Malcolm. *The Arab Cold War 1958-1964*. Oxford University Press, 1965.

Khadouri, M. *Political Trends in the Arab World*. Baltimore, Johns Hopkins Press, 1970.

Khadouri, M., and Lievesny, H. J. (Eds). *Law in the Middle East*, Vol. I, Washington, 1955.

Khalil, Muhammad. *The Arab States and the Arab League* (historical documents). Beirut, Khayat's.

Khouri, Fred J. *The Arab-Israeli Dilemma*. Syracuse/New York, 1968.

Khuri, Fuad I. *Imams and Emirs: state, religion and sects in Islam*. London, Saqi Books, 1990.

Tents and Pyramids. London, Saqi Books, 1992.

Kingsbury, R. C., and Pounds, N. J. G. *An Atlas of Middle Eastern Affairs*. New York, 1963.

Kirk, George E. *The Middle East in the War*. London, 1953.

A Short History of the Middle East: from the Rise of Islam to Modern Times. New York, 1955.

Contemporary Arab Politics. London, Methuen, 1961.

Kreyenbroek, Philip G., and Sperl, Stefan (Eds). *The Kurds: a contemporary overview*. London, Routledge, 1992.

Kreutz, Andrej. *Vatican Policy on the Palestinian—Israeli Conflict: the struggle for the Holy Land*. London, Greenwood Press, 1990.

Kumar, Ravinder. *India and the Persian Gulf Region*. London, 1965.

Kurzman, Dan. *Genesis 1948: The First Arab/Israeli War*. London, Vallentine, Mitchell, 1972.

Kutschera, Chris. *Le mouvement national kurde*. Paris, Flammarion, 1979.

Laffin, John. *Holy War: Islam Fights*. London, Grafton Books, 1988.

Lall, Arthur. *The UN and the Middle East Crisis*. New York/London, 1968.

Lapidus, Ira M. *A History of Islamic Societies*. Cambridge University Press, 1989.

Laqueur, W. Z. *Communism and Nationalism in the Middle East*. London and New York, 1957.

A History of Zionism. London, Weidenfeld and Nicolson, 1972.

The Struggle for the Middle East: The Soviet Union and the Middle East 1958-68. London, Routledge and Kegan Paul, 1969.

Confrontation: The Middle-East War and World Politics. London, Wildwood, 1974.

(Ed.) *The Middle East in Transition*. London, Routledge and Kegan Paul, 1958.

(Ed.) *The Israel-Arab Reader*. New York/Toronto/London, 1969.

Lawrence, T. E. *The Seven Pillars of Wisdom*. London, 1935.

Lieden, Karl. (Ed.). *The conflict of traditionalism and modernism in the Muslim Middle East*. Austin, Texas. 1969.

Lenczowski, George. *The Middle East in World Affairs*. Ithaca, N.Y., Cornell University Press, 1956.

Oil and State in the Middle East. Cornell University Press, 1960.

Lewis, B. *The Arabs in History*. London, 1950 and 1954.

The Middle East and the West. London, 1964.

Race and Colour in Islam. London, 1971.

Islam in History. London, 1973.

Islam to 1453. London, 1974.

Lippman, Thomas W. *Understanding Islam: An Introduction to the Moslem World*. New York, New American Library, 1982.

Lloyd, Selwyn. *Suez 1956: A Personal Account*. London, Jonathan Cape, 1978.

Longrigg, S. H. *Oil in the Middle East*. London, 1954, 3rd edition, London 1968.

The Middle East: a Social Geography. London, 2nd revised edition, 1970.

Louis, William Roger. *The British Empire in the Middle East 1945–51*. Oxford University Press, 1984.

Maalouf, Amin. *The Crusades Through Arab Eyes*. Al-Saqi Books, 1984.

Mabro, Judy (Ed.). *Veiled Half-Truths: Western Travellers' Perceptions of Middle Eastern Women*. London, I. B. Tauris, 1992.

McCarthy, Justin. *The Population of Palestine*. New York, Columbia University Press, 1991.

Macdonald, Robert W. *The League of Arab States*. Princeton, Princeton University Press, 1965.

McDowall, David. *The Kurds: a nation denied*. London, Minority Rights Group, 1992.

Europe and the Arabs: discord and symbiosis. London, Royal Institute of International Affairs, 1992.

Mannin, Ethel. *A Lance for the Arabs*. London, 1973.

Mansfield, Peter. *The Ottoman Empire and Its Successors*. London, Macmillan, 1973.

(Ed.). *The Middle East: A Political and Economic Survey*. London, Oxford University Press, 5th edition, 1980.

The Arabs. London, Allen Lane, 1976.

Maull, Hanns, and Pick, Otto (Eds). *The Gulf War*. London, Pinter Publishers, 1989.

Mendelsohn, Everett. *A Compassionate Peace: a future for Israel, Palestine and the Middle East*. New York, The Noonday Press, 1989.

Michaelis, Alfred. *Wirtschaftliche Entwicklungsprobleme des Mittleren Ostens*. Kiel, 1960.

Mikdashi, Zuhayr. *The Community of Oil Exporting Countries*. London, George Allen and Unwin, 1972.

Miquel, André. *Islam et sa civilisation*. Paris, 1968.

Momen, Moojan. *An Introduction to Shi'i Islam*. London, Yale University Press, 1985.

Monroe, Elizabeth. *Britain's Moment in the Middle East 1914–71*. London, Chatto and Windus, new edition 1981.

Moore, John Morton. *The Arab-Israeli Conflict*. 3 vols. Princeton, Readings and Documents, 1976.

Mortimer, Edward. *Faith and Power: The Politics of Islam*. London, Faber, 1982.

Morzellec, Joëlle Le. *La question de Jérusalem devant l'Organisation des Nations Unies*. Brussels, Emile Bruylant, S.A., 1979.

Mosley, Leonard. *Power Play: The Tumultuous World of Middle East Oil 1890–1973*. London, Weidenfeld and Nicolson, 1973.

Munson, Henry Jr. *Islam and Revolution in the Middle East*. New Haven and London, Yale University Press, 1988.

Nasr, Seyyed Hossein. *Science and Civilization in Islam*. Harvard, 1968.

Nevakivi, Jukka. *Britain, France and the Arab Middle East 1914–20*. Athlone Press, University of London, 1969.

Niblock, Tim, and Murphy, Emma. *Economic and Political Liberalism in the Middle East*. London, British Academic Press, 1993.

Nonneman, Gerd. *Development, Administration and Aid in the Middle East*. London, Routledge, 1988.

(Ed.) *The Middle East and Europe*. London, Federal Trust, 1992.

Nutting, Anthony. *The Arabs*. London, Hollis and Carter, 1965.

No End of a Lesson, The Story of Suez. London, Constable, 1967.

Nydell, Margaret K. *Understanding Arabs: A Guide for Westerners*. Yarmouth, Maine, Intercultural Press, 1992.

O'Ballance, Edgar. *The Third Arab-Israeli War*. London, Faber and Faber, 1972.

The Gulf War. London, Brassey's Defence Publishers, 1990.

Odell, Peter. *Oil and World Power*. London, Penguin, 1983.

Owen, Roger. *The Middle East in the World Economy 1800–1914*. London, Methuen, 1972.

State, Power and Politics in the making of the Modern Middle East. London, Routledge, 1992.

Oxford Regional Economic Atlas. *The Middle East and North Africa*. Oxford University Press, 1960.

Palmer, Alan. *The Decline and Fall of the Ottoman Empire*. London, John Murray, 1992.

Palumbo, Michael. *The Palestinian Catastrophe*. London, Faber, 1987.

Pantelides, Veronica S. *Arab Education 1956–1978: A Bibliography*. London, Mansell, 1982.

Pearson, J. D. (Ed.). *Index Islamicus*. Cambridge, 1967.

Pennar, Jaan. *The USSR and the Arabs: The Ideological Dimension*. London, Hurst, 1973.

Piscatori, James P. (Ed.). *Islam in the Political Process*. Cambridge University Press, 1983.

Playfair, Ian S. O. *The Mediterranean and the Middle East*. London, History of the Second World War, HMSO, 1966.

Poliak, A. N. *Feudalism in Egypt, Syria, Palestine and the Lebanon, 1250–1900*. London, Luzac, for the Royal Asiatic Society, 1939.

Polk, W. R. *The United States and the Arab World*. Harvard University Press, 1965, revised edition 1970.

(Ed. with Chambers, R. L.) *Beginnings of Modernization in the Middle East: the Nineteenth Century*. University of Chicago Press, 1969.

The Elusive Peace: The Middle East in the Twentieth Century. London, Frank Cass, 1980.

Porath, Y. *The Emergence of the Palestinian Arab National Movement 1918–1929*. London, Frank Cass, 1974.

Qubain, Fahim I. *Education and Science in the Arab World*. Baltimore, Johns Hopkins Press, 1967.

Raufer, Xavier. *Atlas Mondial de l'Islam Activiste*. Paris, Editions de la Table Ronde, 1991.

Ridgeway, James (Ed.). *The March to War*. New York, Four Walls Eight Windows, 1991.

Rikhye, Maj.-Gen. I. J. *The Sinai Blunder*. London, Frank Cass, 1980.

Rivlin, B., and Szyliowicz, J. S. (Eds) *The Contemporary Middle East—Tradition and Innovation*. New York, Random House, 1965.

Roberts, D. S. *Islam: A Concise Introduction*. New York, Harper and Row, 1982.

Robinson, Francis. *Atlas of the Islamic World since 1500*. London, Phaidon, 1983.

Rodinson, Maxime. *Islam and Capitalism*. France, 1965, England, 1974.

Muhammad. London, Penguin, 1974.

La fascination de l'Islam. Paris, Maspero, 1980.

The Arabs. London, Croom Helm, 1981.

Israel and the Arabs. London, Penguin, 1982.

Europe and the Mystique of Islam. London, I. B. Tauris, 1989.

Ro'i, Ya'acov. *The Limits of Power: Soviet Policy in the Middle East*. London, Croom Helm, 1978.

Ronart, Stephan and Nandy. *Concise Encyclopaedia of Arabic Civilization*. Amsterdam, 1966.

Rondot, Pierre. *The Destiny of the Middle East*. London, Chatto & Windus, 1960.

L'Islam. Paris, Prismes, 1965.

Rouhani, Fuad. *A History of OPEC*. London, Pall Mall Press, 1972.

Rubin, Barry M. *The Arab and the Palestine Conflict*. New York, Syracuse University Press, 1981.

Ruthven, Malise. *Islam in the World*. Harmondsworth, Penguin, 1984.

A Satanic Affair: Salman Rushdie and the Rage of Islam. London, Chatto and Windus, 1990.

Sachar, Howard M. *Europe Leaves the Middle East 1936–1954*. London, Allen Lane, 1973.

Said, Edward W. *The Question of Palestine*. London, Routledge, 1979.

Covering Islam. London, Routledge, 1982.

Sardar, Ziauddin (Ed.). *Science and Technology in the Middle East*. Harlow, Longman, 1982.

Sauvaget, J. *Introduction à l'histoire de l'orient musulman*. Paris, 1943. 2nd edition re-cast by C. Cahen, University of California Press, 1965.

Savory, R. M. *Introduction to Islamic Civilization*. Cambridge University Press, 1976.

Sayigh, Fatallah. *Le Désert et la Gloire*. Paris, Editions Gallimard, 1993.

Sayigh, Yusif, A. *The Determinants of Arab Economic Development*. London, Croom Helm, 1977.

The Economies of the Arab World. London, Croom Helm, 1978.

Arab Oil Policies in the 1970s. London, Croom Helm, 1983.

Elusive Development: From Dependence to Self-Reliance in the Arab Region. London, Routledge, 1991.

Schimmel, Annemarie. *Islam: An Introduction*. State University of New York Press, 1992.

Seale, Patrick. *Abu Nidal: A Gun for Hire*. London, Hutchinson, 1992.

Searight, Sarah. *The British in the Middle East*. London, Weidenfeld and Nicolson, 1969.

Shaban, M. A. *The Abbasid Revolution*. Cambridge University Press, 1970.

Islamic History AD 600–750 (AH 132) A New Interpretation. Cambridge University Press, 1971.

Shadid, Muhammad K. *The United States and the Palestinians*. London, Croom Helm, 1981.

Sharabi, H. B. *Governments and Politics of the Middle East in the Twentieth Century*. New York, Van Nostrand, 1962.

Nationalism and Revolution in the Arab World. New York, Van Nostrand, 1966.

Palestine and Israel: The Lethal Dilemma. New York, Pegasus Press, 1969.

Sid-Ahmed, Muhammad. *After the Guns Fell Silent*. London, Croom Helm, 1976.

Sivan, Emmanuel. *Radical Islam: Medieval Theology and Modern Politics*. Yale University Press, 1991.

Smith, W. Cantwell. *Islam and Modern History*. Toronto, 1957.

Sourdel, Dominique. *Medieval Islam*. London, Routledge and Kegan Paul, 1984.

Southern, R. W. *Western Views of Islam in the Middle Ages*. Oxford, 1957.

Stark, Freya. *Dust in the Lion's Paw*. London and New York, 1961.

Stevens, Georgina G. (Ed.). *The United States and the Middle East*. Englewood Cliffs, NJ, Prentice-Hall, 1964.

Stewart, Desmond. *The Middle East: Temple of Janus*. London, Hamish Hamilton, 1972.

Stocking, G. W. *Middle East Oil. A Study in Political and Economic Controversy*. Nashville, Vanderbilt University Press, 1979.

Sumner, B. H. *Tsardom and Imperialism in the Far East and Middle East.* London, Oxford University Press, 1940.

Talbot Rice, David. *Islamic Art.* London, Thames and Hudson, 1991.

Taylor, Alan R. *The Arab Balance of Power.* New York, Syracuse University Press, 1982.

Thayer, P. W. (Ed.). *Tensions in the Middle East.* Baltimore, 1958.

Thomas, L. V., and Frye, R. N. *The United States and Turkey and Iran.* Cambridge, Massachusetts, 1951.

Tillman, Seth P. *The United States in the Middle East.* Hemel Hempstead, Indiana University Press, 1982.

Trevelyan, Humphrey (Lord). *The Middle East in Revolution.* London, Macmillan, 1970.

Trimingham, J. Spencer. *The Sufi Orders in Islam.* Oxford, Clarendon Press, 1971.

Tschirgi, Dan. *The American Search for Mideast Peace.* New York, Praeger, 1989.

Tugendhat, C. *Oil: The Biggest Business.* London, Eyre and Spottiswoode, 1968.

Vassilier, Alexei. *Russian Policy in the Middle East: from messianism to pragmatism.* Reading, Ithaca Press, 1993.

Vatikiotis, P. J. *Conflict in the Middle East.* London, George Allen and Unwin, 1971.

Islam and the State. London, Routledge, 1991.

Viorst, Milton. *Reaching for the Olive Branch: UNRWA and peace in the Middle East.* Washington, Middle East Institute, 1989.

Wadsman, P., and Teissedre, R.-F. *Nos politiciens face au conflict israélo arabe.* Paris, 1969.

Waines, David. *The Unholy War.* Wilmette, Medina Press, 1971.

Walker, Christopher J. *Armenia: The Survival of a Nation.* London, Croom Helm, 1980.

Warriner, Doreen. *Land and Poverty in the Middle East.* London, 1948.

Land Reform and Development in the Middle East: Study of Egypt, Syria and Iraq. London, 1962.

Watt, W. Montgomery. *Muhammad at Mecca.* Oxford, Clarendon Press, 1953.

Muhammad at Medina. Oxford, Clarendon Press, 1956.

Muhammad, Prophet and Statesman. Oxford University Press, 1961.

Muslim Intellectual—Al Ghazari. Edinburgh University Press, 1962.

Islamic Philosophy and Theology. Edinburgh University Press, 1963.

Islamic Political Thought: The Basic Concepts. Edinburgh University Press, 1968.

What is Islam? London, Longman, 2nd edition 1979.

Wilson, Rodney. *Trade and Investment in the Middle East.* Macmillan Press, 1977.

Woolfson, Marion. *Prophets in Babylon: Jews in the Arab World.* London, Faber, 1980.

Wright, Clifford A. *Facts and Fables: the Arab Israeli conflict.* London, Kegan Paul International, 1989.

Yale, William, *The Near East.* Ann Arbor, University of Michigan Press, 1968.

Yapp, M. E. *The Near East since the First World War.* London, Longman, 1991.

Yergin, Daniel. *The Prize: the Epic Quest for Oil, Money and Power.* New York, Simon and Schuster, 1990.

Zahlan, Rosemarie Said. *The Making of the Modern Gulf States.* London, Unwin Hyman Ltd, 1989.

Zeine, Z. N. *The Struggle for Arab Independence.* Beirut, 1960.

Zouilaï, Kaddour. *Des voiles et des serrures: de la fermeture en islam.* Paris, L'Harmattan, 1991.

Books on North Africa

See also bibliographies at end of relevant chapters in Part Three.

Abun-Nasr, Jamil M. *A History of the Maghreb.* Cambridge University Press, 1972.

Allal El-Fassi. *The Independence Movements in Arab North Africa.* trans. H. Z. Nuseibeh. Washington, DC, 1954.

Amin, Samir. *L'Economie du Maghreb.* 2 vols Paris, Editions du Minuit, 1966.

The Maghreb in the Modern World. London, Penguin Books, 1971.

Balta, Paul. *Le Grand Maghreb.* Paris, Editions La Découverte, 1990.

Balta, Paul, and Rulleau, Claudine. *L'Algérie des algériens.* Paris, Editions Ouvrières, 1982.

Barbour, Neville, (Ed.) *A Survey of North West Africa (The Maghreb).* Royal Insitute of International Affairs, Oxford University Press, 1959.

Berque, Jacques. *Le Maghreb entre deux guerres.* 2nd edition, Paris, Editions du Seuil, 1967.

Bonnefous, Marc. *Le Maghreb: repères et rappels.* Editions du Centre des Hautes Etudes sur l'Afrique et l'Asie modernes de Paris, 1991.

Brace, R. M. *Morocco, Algeria, Tunisia.* Englewood Cliffs, N.J., Prentice-Hall, 1964.

Brown, Leon Carl (Ed.). *State and Society in Independent North Africa.* Washington, Middle East Institute, 1966.

Burgat, Francois. *The Islamic Movement in North Africa.* University of Texas, 1993.

Capot-Rey, R. *Le Sahara français.* Paris, 1953.

Centre d'Etudes des Relations Internationales. *Le Maghreb et la communauté economique européenne.* Paris, Editions FNSP, 1965.

Centre de Recherches sur l'Afrique Méditerranéenne d'Aix en Provence. *L'Annuaire de l'Afrique du Nord.* Paris, Centre Nationale de la recherche scientifique, annually.

Charbonneau, J. (Ed.). *Le Sahara français.* Paris, Cahiers Charles de Foucauld, No. 38, 1955.

Damis, John. *Conflict in Northwest Africa: The Western Sahara Dispute.* Stanford University, California, Hoover Institute Press, 1983.

Duclos, J., Leca, J., and Duvignaud, J. *Les nationalismes maghrébins.* Paris, Centre d'Etudes des Relations Internationales, 1966.

Economic Commission for Africa. *Main Problems of Economic Co-operation in North Africa.* Tangier, 1966.

Furlonge, Sir Geoffrey. *The Lands of Barbary.* London, Murray, 1966.

Gallagher, C. F. *The US and North Africa.* Cambridge, Massachusetts, 1964.

Gardi, René. *Sahara, Monographie einer grossen Wüste.* Berne, Kummerley and Frey, 1967.

Gautier, E. F. *Le Passé de l'Afrique du Nord.* Paris, 1937.

Germidis, Dimitri, with the help of Delapierre, Michel. *Le Maghreb, la France at l'enjeu technologique.* Paris, Editions Cujas, 1976.

Gordon, D. C. *North Africa's French Legacy 1954–62.* Harvard, 1962.

Hahn, Lorna. *North Africa: from Nationalism to Nationhood.* Washington, 1960.

Hermassi, Elbaki. *Leadership and National Development in North Africa.* University of California Press, 1973.

Heseltine, N. *From Libyan Sands to Chad.* Leiden, 1960.

Joffe, E. G. H. (Ed.). *North Africa: Nation, State and Region.* London, Routledge/University of London, 1993.

Julien, Ch.-A. *Histoire de l'Afrique du nord.* 2nd edition, 2 vols, Paris 1951–52.

L'Afrique du nord en marche. Paris, 1953.

History of North Africa: From the Arab Conquest to 1830.

Revised by R. Le Tourneau. Ed. C. C. Stewart. London, Routledge and Kegan Paul, 1970.

Khaldoun, Ibn. *History of the Berbers*. Translated into French by Slane. 4 vols, Algiers, 1852–56.

Knapp, Wilfrid. *North West Africa: A Political and Economic Survey*. Oxford University Press, 3rd edition, 1977.

Le Tourneau, Roger. *Evolution politique de l'Afrique du nord musulmane*. Paris, 1962.

Liska, G. *The Greater Maghreb: From Independence to Unity?* Washington, DC, Center of Foreign Policy Research, 1963.

Marçais, G. *La Berberie musulmane et l'Orient au moyen age*. Paris, 1946.

Moore, C. H. *Politics in North Africa*. Boston, Little, Brown, 1970.

Mortimer, Edward. *France and the Africans, 1944–1960*. London, Faber, 1969.

Muzikár, Joseph. *Les perspectives de l'intégration des pays maghrébins et leur attitude vis-à-vis du marché commun*. Nancy, 1968.

Nickerson, Jane S. *Short History of North Africa*. New York, 1961.

Parrinder, Geoffrey. *Religion in Africa*. London, Pall Mall Press, 1970.

Polk, William R. (Ed.). *Developmental Revolution: North Africa, Middle East, South Asia*. Washington, DC, Middle East Institute, 1963.

Raven, Susan. *Rome in Africa*. London, Evans Brothers, 1970.

Robana, Abderrahma. *The Prospects for an Economic Community in North Africa*. London, Pall Mall, 1973.

Sahli, Mohamed Cherif. *Décoloniser l'histoire; introduction à l'histoire du Maghreb*. Paris, Maspero, 1965.

Schramm, Josef. *Die Westsahara*. Freilassing, Paunonia-Verlag, 1969.

Steel, R. (Ed.). *North Africa*. New York, Wilson, 1967.

Toynbee, Sir Arnold. *Between Niger and Nile*. Oxford University Press, 1965.

Trimingham, J. S. *The influence of Islam upon Africa*. London, Longmans, and Beirut, Libraire du Liban, 1968.

Tutsch, Hans E. *Nordafrika in Gärung*. Frankfurt, 1961.

From Ankara to Marrakesh. New York, 1962.

UNESCO. *Arid Zone Research*, Vol. XIX: *Nomades et Nomadisme au Sahara*. UNESCO, 1963.

Warren, Cline and Santmyer, C. *Agriculture of Northern Africa*. Washington, US Department of Agriculture, 1965.

Zartman, I. W. *Government and Politics in North Africa*. New York, 1964.

(Ed.) *Man, State and Society in the Contemporary Maghreb*. London, Pall Mall, 1973.

SELECT BIBLIOGRAPHY (PERIODICALS)

Al-Abhath. Published by American University of Beirut, Beirut, Lebanon; telex 20801; fax (1) 4781995; f. 1948; Editor Ramzi Baalbaki; English and Arabic; annual on Middle East studies.

Acta Orientalia. East Asian Institute, University of Copenhagen, Njalsgade 80, 2300 Copenhagen S, Denmark; tel. (31) 54-22-11; f. 1922; publ. by the East Asian Institute under auspices of the Oriental Societies of Denmark, Finland, Norway, and Sweden; history, language, archaeology and religions of the Near and Far East; Editor Prof. Søren Egerod; annually.

Acta Orientalia Academiae Scientiarum Hungaricae. H-1363 Budapest, POB 24, Hungary; f. 1950; text in English, French, German or Russian; Editor A. Sárközi; 3 a year.

Africa Contemporary Record. Africana Publishing Co, Holmes & Meier Publishers Inc, IUB Building, 30 Irving Place, New York, NY 10003, USA; tel. (212) 254-4100; fax (212) 254-4104; annual surveys, special essays and indices.

Africa Quarterly. Indian Council for Cultural Relations, Azad Bhavan, Indraprastha Estate, New Delhi 110002, India; tel. 3319309; telex 3161860; fax 3712639; f. 1961; Editor T. G. Ramamurthi; circ. 700.

Africa Review. Walden Publishing, 2 Market St, Saffron Walden, Essex CB10 1HZ, England; tel. (0799) 521150; fax (0799) 524805; political and economic analysis; Editor Howard Hill; annually.

Africa Research Bulletins. Africa Research Ltd, 1A Summerland St, Exeter, EX1 2AF, Devon, England; tel. (0392) 215655; f. 1964; monthly bulletins on (*a*) political and (*b*) economic subjects.

L'Afrique et l'Asie modernes. 13 rue du Four, 75006 Paris, France; tel. (1) 43-26-96-90; f. 1948; political, economic and social review; quarterly.

Alam Attijarat (The World of Business). Johnston International Publishing Corpn (New York), Beirut, Lebanon; Arabic; business; Editor Nadim Makdisi; 10 a year.

Anatolian Studies. BIAA, 31–34 Gordon Square, London, WC14 OP4, England; tel. and fax (071) 388 2361; f. 1949; annual of the British Institute of Archaeology at Ankara; Editor Prof. O. R. Gurney.

Anatolica. Netherlands Historical Archaeological Institute at Istanbul, Istiklâl Caddesi 393, Istanbul-Beyoğlu, Turkey; tel. 2939283; fax 2513846; f. 1967; Editors B. Flemming, C. Nijland, J. J. Roodenberg, J. de Roos, D. J. W. Meijer, M. Özdoğan; annually.

Annales archéologiques Arabes Syriennes. Direction Générale des Antiquités et des Musées, University St, Damascus, Syria; tel. 2214854; telex 412491; f. 1951; archaeological and historical review; Dir-Gen. Dr Sultan Moheisen; annually.

Annuaire de l'Afrique du Nord. Edited by the Institut de recherches et d'études sur le Monde Arabe et Musulman, 3 blvd Pasteur, 13100 Aix-en-Provence; tel. 42-21-59-88; telex 13100; fax 42-21-52-75; published by the Centre National de la Recherche Scientifique, 15 quai Anatole France, 757000 Paris, France; Editor Jean-Claude Santucci; f. 1962; yearbook contains special studies on current affairs, report on a collective programme of social sciences research on North Africa, chronologies, chronicles, documentation and bibliographies.

Annual Survey of African Law. Rex Collings Ltd, 'Chaceside', Coronation Rd, South Ascot, Berks, SL5 9LB, England; tel. (0344) 872453; fax (0344) 872858.

The Arab Economist. Centre for Economic, Financial and Social Research and Documentation SAL, Gefinor Tower, Clemenceau St, Bloc B-POB 11-6068, Beirut, Lebanon; f. 1969; Chair. Dr Chafic Akhras; monthly; circ. 7,300.

Arab Oil and Gas. The Arab Petroleum Research Centre, 7 avenue Ingres, 75016 Paris, France; tel. (1) 45-24-33-10; telex 642963; fax (1) 45-20-16-85; f. 1971; petroleum and gas; English, French and Arabic; Editor Dr Nicolas Sarkis; 2 a month.

Arab Oil and Gas Directory. The Arab Petroleum Research Centre, 7 avenue Ingres, 75016 Paris, France; tel. (1) 45-24-33-10; telex 642963; fax (1) 45-20-16-85; f. 1974; annually.

Arab Political Documents. publ. American University of Beirut, Beirut, Lebanon; f. 1963; Editor Yousuf Khoury; Arabic; compiles important political documents of the year in various Arab countries; annually.

Arab Studies Quarterly. Association of Arab-American University Graduates, Inc. (AAUG), POB 408, Normal, IL 61761-0408, USA; tel. (309) 452-6588; fax (309) 452-8335; f. 1976; Editor Jamal R. Nassar.

Arabia: The Islamic World Review. Crown House, Crown Lane, East Burnham, Bucks, SL2 3SG, England; tel. (02814) 5177; telex 847031; monthly.

Arabica. c/o Université de la Sorbonne Nouvelle, 13 rue de Santeuil, 75231 Paris Cedex 05, France; tel. (1) 45-87-41-39; Dir Mohammed Arkoun; 3 a year.

Aramtek Mideast Review. Aramtek Corporation, 122 East 42nd Street, Suite 3703, New York, NY 10017, USA; f. 1976; business news and features; USA Editor-in-Chief M. Handal; Man. Editor B. F. Ottaviani.

Archiv für Orientforschung. c/o Institut für Orientalistik der Universität Wien, Universitätsstrasse 7/V, A-1010 Vienna I, Austria; tel. (0222) 40103-2596; fax (0222) 4020533; f. 1923; Editors Hans Hirsch, Hermann Hunger; annually.

Armenian Review. The Armenian Review Inc., 80 Bigelow Ave, Watertown, MA 02172, USA; tel. (617) 926-4037; f. 1948; Editor Mr Tatul Sonentz; quarterly.

Asian Affairs. Royal Society for Asian Affairs, 2 Belgrave Square, London, SW1, England; tel. (071) 235-5122; fax (071) 259 6771; f. 1901; 3 a year.

Asian and African Studies. Israel Oriental Society, The Gustav Heinemann Institute of Middle Eastern Studies, Haifa University, Mount Carmel, Haifa 31999, Israel; tel. (04) 240654; fax (04) 342104; f. 1965; Editors Gabriel R. Warburg, Gad G. Gilbar; 3 a year.

L'Asie nouvelle. 94 rue St Lazare, 75442 Paris Cédex 09, France; tel. (1) 45-26-67-01; weekly and special issues; Dir André Roux.

Belleten. Türk Tarih Kurumu, Kizilay Sokak no. 1, 06100 Ankara, Turkey; tel. 3102368; telex 42214; fax 3101698; f. 1937; history and archaeology of Turkey; Editor Prof. Dr Yasar Yucel; 3 a year.

The Bibliography of the Middle East. Publisher L. Farès, BP 2712, Damascus, Syria; annually.

Bibliotheca Orientalis. Published by Netherlands Institute for the Near East, Witte Singel 25, POB 9515, 2300 RA, Leiden, Netherlands; tel. (071) 272036; fax (071) 272038; f. 1943; edited by J. de Roos, D. J. W. Meijer, H. J. A. de Meulenaere, M. J. Mulder, C. Nijland, J. J. Roodenberg, M. Stol; 3 double issues a year.

British Society for Middle Eastern Studies Journal. Administrative Office, Dept of Politics, University of Exeter, Exeter EX4 4RJ; tel. (0392) 263165; f. 1974 (as *British Society of Middle Eastern Studies Bulletin*); Editor Dr P. G. Starkey, Centre for Middle Eastern Studies, University of Durham, South Road, Durham, DH1 3TG; tel. (091) 374 3035; fax (091) 374 2830; 2 a year.

Bulletin d'études orientales. Institut français d'études arabes, BP 344, Damascus, Syria; tel. (11) 330214; telex 412272; fax (11) 247887; f. 1922; annually (40 vols published).

Bulletin of the School of Oriental and African Studies. School of Oriental and African Studies, University of London, Thornhaugh Street, Russell Sq., London, WC1H 0XG, England; tel. (071) 637-2388; fax (071) 436-3844; 3 a year.

Bulletin of Sudanese Studies. POB 321, Khartoum; Arabic; published by The Institute of African and Asian Studies, University of Khartoum, Sudan; tel. 75820; telex 22133; f. 1968; Editor Abdullahi ali Ibrahim; 2 a year.

Les Cahiers de l'Orient. 80 rue Saint Dominique, 75007 Paris, France; published by CERPO (Centre of Near East Studies); review of Islamic and Arab affairs; quarterly.

Les Cahiers de Tunisie. Publ. by Faculté des sciences humaines et sociales de Tunis, 94 blvd de 9 Avril 1938, Tunis, 1007 Tunisia; tel. 260858; f. 1953; research in humanities; Dir Hédi Cherif; Editor-in-Chief Hassan Annabi; every six months.

Chuto Kenkyu (Journal of Middle Eastern Studies). The Middle East Institute of Japan, 15 Mori Bldg, 8-10 Toranomon 2-chome, Minato-ku, Tokyo, Japan; f. 1960; Editor Wasuke Miyake; monthly.

Le Commerce du Levant. Centre Azzam, Jdeidé-Metn, BP 90-1397, Beirut, Lebanon; tel. 899005; telex 40085; weekly.

Comunitá Mediterranea. Lungotevere Flaminio 34, Rome, Italy; law and political science relating to Mediterranean countries; Pres. E. Bussi.

Crescent International. 300 Steelcase Rd West, Unit 8, Markham, Ontario, Canada L3R 2W2; tel. (905) 474-9292; fax (905) 474-9293; f. 1980; deals with Islamic movement throughout the world; 2 a month.

Deutsche Morgenländische Gesellschaft; Zeitschrift. Seminar für Arabistik, Prinzenstr. 21, D-37073 Göttingen, Germany; tel. (0551) 394398; f. 1847; covers the history, languages and literature of the Orient; Editor Prof. Dr Tilman Nagel; 2 a year.

Developing Economies. Institute of Developing Economies, 42 Ichigaya Hommura-cho, Shinjuku-ku, Tokyo 162, Japan; tel. (03) 3353-4231; telex 32473; fax (03) 3226-8475; f. 1962; English; quarterly.

L'Economiste Arabe. Centre d'études et de documentation économiques, financières et sociales, SAL, BP 6068, Beirut, Lebanon; Pres. Dr Chafic Akhras, Dir-Gen. Dr Sabbah al-Haj; monthly.

Europe Outremer. 178 quai L. Blériot, 75016 Paris, France; tel. (1) 46-47-78-44; f. 1923; economic and political material on French-speaking states of Africa; monthly.

France-Pays Arabes. 14 rue Augereau, 75007 Paris, France; tel. (1) 4555-27-52; fax 4551-27-26; f. 1968; politics, economics and culture of the Arab world; Dir Lucien Bitterlin; monthly.

Grand Maghreb. BP 45, 38402 Saint-Martin-d'Hères, France; monthly.

Hamizrah Hehadash. Israel Oriental Society. The Hebrew University, Jerusalem, Israel; f. 1949; Hebrew with English summary; Middle Eastern, Asian and African affairs; Editor Jacob Landau.

Hesperis-Tamuda. Faculté des Lettres et des Sciences Humaines, Université Muhammad V, BP 1040, Rabat, Morocco; tel. (212) 777-1989; fax (212) 777-2068; f. 1921; history, anthropology, civilization of Maghreb and Western Islam, special reference to bibliography; Chief Editor B. Boutaleb.

Huna London (BBC Arabic Radio Times). BBC Arabic Service, POB 76, Bush House, Strand, London, WC2B 4PH, England; tel. (071) 257-2983; telex 264057; fax (071) 836-2264; f. 1960; circ. throughout the Arab world; Editor Mustapha Karkouti; Advertising Reps: Mongoose Communications; monthly.

Ibla. Institut des belles lettres arabes, 12 rue Jamâa el-Haoua, 1008 Tunis BM, Tunisia; tel. 560133; f. 1937; 2 a year.

Indo-Iranian Journal. Kluwer Academic Publishers, POB 17, 3300 AA Dordrecht, Netherlands; tel. (78) 334911; telex 29245; f. 1957; Editors H. W. Bodewitz, J. W. de Jong and M. Witzel; quarterly.

Indo-Iranica. Iran Society, 12 Dr M. Ishaque Road, Calcutta 700016, India; tel. 29-9899; f. 1946; promotion of Persian studies and Indo-Iranian cultural relations; Gen. Sec. and Man. Editor M. A. Majid; quarterly.

International Crude Oil and Product Prices. Middle East Petroleum and Economic Publications (Cyprus), POB 4940, Nicosia, Cyprus; tel. (02) 445431; telex 2198; fax (02) 474988; f. 1971 (in Beirut); review and analysis of oil price trends in world markets; Publisher Basim W. Itayim; 2 a year.

International Journal of Middle East Studies. Cambridge University Press, The Edinburgh Bldg, Shaftesbury Road, Cambridge, CB2 2RU, England; tel. (0223) 312393; telex 817256; fax (0223) 315052; Journal of the Middle East Studies Association of North America and the British Society for Middle Eastern Studies; first issue Jan. 1970; Editor Dr Leila Fawaz; 4 a year.

Iraq. British School of Archaeology in Iraq, 31–34 Gordon Square, London, WC1H 0PY, England; f. 1932; annually.

Der Islam. D-20148 Hamburg 13, Rothenbaumchaussee 36, Germany; tel. (040) 4123-3180; fax (040) 4123-5674; 2 a year.

Islamic and Comparative Law Review. Dept of Law, Hamdard University, Tughlaqabad, New Delhi 110062, India; tel. (011) 6439685; f. 1981; Founder-Editor Tahir Mahmood; two a year.

Islamic Quarterly. The Islamic Cultural Centre, 146 Park Road, London, NW8 7RG, England; tel (071) 724-3363; f. 1954; Editor Dr A. A. Mughram; quarterly.

Israel and Palestine. POB 44, 75462 Paris Cedex 10, France; tel. (1) 42-46-82-47; fax (1) 42-46-51-77; f. 1971; Editor Maxim Ghilan; International Secretariat of the International Jewish Peace Union (IJPU); monthly.

Izvestia Rossiiskoi Akademii Nauk-Seriya Literatury i Yazyka. Russian Academy of Sciences, Moscow, Russia; tel. 290-17-09; f. 1852; 2 a month.

Jeune Afrique. Groupe Jeune Afrique, 51 ave des Ternes, Paris 17e, France; tel. (1) 47-66-52-42; telex 280674; f. 1960; Publisher Bechir ben Yahmed; weekly.

Journal of the American Oriental Society. American Oriental Society, 329 Sterling Memorial Library, Box 1603A, Yale Station, New Haven, Conn 06520, USA; tel. (313) 747-4760; f. 1842; Ancient Near East, Inner Asia, South and Southeast Asia, Islamic Near East, and Far East; quarterly.

Journal Asiatique. Journal de la société asiatique, 3 rue Mazarine, 75006 Paris, France; f. 1822; Dir D. Matringe; covers all phases of Oriental research; quarterly.

Journal of Indian Philosophy. Kluwer Academic Publishers, POB 17, 3300 AA Dordrecht, Netherlands; tel. (78) 334911; telex 29245; f. 1970; Editor Bimal K. Matilal; quarterly.

Journal of the Institute of Muslim Minority Affairs. 46 Goodge St, London, W1P 1FJ, England; tel. (071) 636-6740; telex 296182; fax (071) 255-1473; f. 1976; Man. Editor Dr Saleha Mahmood; 2 a year.

Journal of Near Eastern Studies. Oriental Institute, University of Chicago, 1155 East 58th Street, Chicago, Ill 60637, USA; tel (312) 702-9540; telex 687-1133; fax (312) 702-9853; devoted to the Ancient and Medieval Near and Middle East, archaeology, languages, history, Islam; Editor R. Biggs.

Journal of Palestine Studies. POB 25697, Georgetown Station, Washington, DC 20007, USA; tel. (202) 342-3990; fax (202) 342-3927; f. 1971; publ. by the University of California Press for the Inst. for Palestine Studies, Washington, DC and Kuwait Univ.; Palestinian affairs and the Arab-Israeli conflict; Editor Hisham Sharabi; Assoc. Editor Philip Mattar; circ. 4,600; quarterly.

Maghreb-Machrek-Monde-Arabe. Direction de la Documentation, Secrétariat général du gouvernement, La documentation française, 29–31 quai Voltaire, 75344 Paris Cedex 07, France; tel. (1) 40-15-71-00; telex 204826; fax (1) 40-15-72-30; f. 1964; published with the assistance of the Fondation nationale des Sciences politiques and the Centre d'étude de l'Orient contemporain (University of Paris III); quarterly.

The Maghreb Review. 45 Burton St, London WC1H 9AL, England; tel. (071) 388-1840; f. 1976; North African and Islamic studies from AD 600 to the present; Editor Muhammad ben Madani; quarterly.

Maghreb-Sélection. IC Publications, 10 rue Vineuse, 75116 Paris, France; tel. (1) 44-30-81-00; fax (1) 44-30-81-11; f. 1979; economic information about North Africa; weekly.

Marchés Arabes. IC Publications, 10 rue Vineuse, 75116 Paris, France; tel. (1) 44-30-81-00; fax (1) 44-30-81-11; f. 1978; economic information about the Middle East; fortnightly.

Marchés Tropicaux et Mediterranéens. 190 blvd Haussmann, 75008 Paris, France; tel. 45-63-11-55; telex 641544; f. 1945; economics; Editor Serge Marpaud; weekly.

MEN Weekly. Middle East News Agency, Hoda Sharawi St, Cairo, Egypt; f. 1962; weekly news bulletin.

Le Message de l'Islam. BP 14155, 3899 Teheran, Iran; theoretical review of Iranian Islam; monthly.

The Middle East. 7 Coldbath Sq., London, EC1R 4LQ, England; tel. (071) 713-7711; telex 8811757; fax (071) 713-7970; f. 1974; political, economic and cultural; Editor Graham Benton; Publisher Ahmad Afif ben Yedder; circ. 12,000; monthly.

Middle East Business Intelligence. 717 D St, NW, Suite 300, Washington, DC 20004, USA; tel. (202) 628-6900; telex 440462; fax (202) 628-6618; Publisher William C. Hearn; 2 a month.

Middle East Contemporary Survey. Westview Press, 5500 Central Ave, Boulder, CO 80301, USA; tel. (303) 444-3541; telex 239479; fax (303) 449-3356; 36 Lonsdale Rd, Oxford, OX2 7EW, England; tel. (0865) 53032; fax (0865) 511489; annual record of political developments, country surveys, special essays, maps, tables, notes, indices.

Middle East Economic Digest. MEED Ltd, 21 John Street, London, WC1N 2BP, England; tel. (071) 404-5513; telex 27165; f. 1957; weekly report on economic, business and political developments; Publ. Dir Dante Mencacci; Editor-in-Chief Edmund O'Sullivan.

Middle East Economic Survey. Middle East Petroleum and Economic Publications (Cyprus), POB 4940, Nicosia, Cyprus; tel. (02) 445431; telex 2198; fax (02) 474988; f. 1957 (in Beirut); weekly review and analysis of petroleum, finance and banking, and political developments; Publisher Basim W. Itayim; Editor Ian Seymour.

Middle East Executive Reports. 717 D Street, NW, Suite 300, Washington, DC 20004, USA; tel. (202) 628-6900; telex 440462; fax (202) 628-6618; legal and business guide to the Middle East; monthly.

Middle East International. 21 Collingham Road, London, SW5 0NU, England; tel. (071) 373-5228; telex 8953551; fax (071) 370-5956; f. 1971; fortnightly; political and economic developments, book reviews; Editor Michael Wall.

The Middle East Journal. Middle East Institute, 1761 N Street, NW, Washington, DC 20036, USA; tel. (202) 785-0191; fax (202) 331-8861; journal in English devoted to the study of the modern Near East; f. 1947; Editor Eric Hooglund; circ. 4,000; quarterly.

Middle East Monitor. Business Monitor International Ltd, 56–60 St John St, London EC1M 4DT, England; tel. (071) 608-3646; fax (071) 608-3620; monthly; economic and political brief; Editor John Roberts.

Middle East Perspective. New York, USA; monthly newsletter on Eastern Mediterranean and North African affairs; Editor Dr Alfred Lilienthal.

Middle East Policy. Middle East Policy Council, 1730 M Street, NW, Suite 512, Washington, DC 20036, USA; tel. (202) 296-6767; telex 440506; fax (202) 296-5791; policy analysis; quarterly; Editor Anne Joyce.

Middle East Report. Room 518, 475 Riverside Drive, New York, NY 10115, USA; tel. (212) 870-3281; f. 1971; Publisher James Paul; Editor Joe Stork; circ. 6,000; every 2 months.

Middle East Review. Walden Publishing Ltd, 2 Market St, Saffron Walden, Essex, CB10 1HZ, England; tel. (0799) 521150; telex 817197; fax (0799) 524805; political and economic analysis; Editor Howard Hill; annually.

Middle East Studies Association Bulletin. 200 LCI, Catholic University of America, Washington DC 20064, USA; tel. (202) 319-5999; fax (202) 319-6267; Editor Jon Anderson; 2 a year.

Middle Eastern Studies. Frank Cass & Co Ltd, Newbury House, 890–900 Eastern Ave, Newbury Park, Ilford, Essex IG2 7HH; tel. (081) 599-8866; fax (081) 599 0984; f. 1964; Editor Sylvie Kedourie; 4 a year.

Mideast Report. 60 East 42nd Street, Suite 1433, New York, NY 10017, USA; political analysis, oil and finance and business intelligence.

The Muslim World. 77 Sherman Street, Hartford, Conn 06105, USA; tel. (203) 232-4451; f. 1911; Islamic studies in general and Muslim-Christian relations in past and present; Editors Willem A. Bijlefeld, Wadi' Z. Haddad and David A. Kerr; quarterly.

The Muslim World League Journal. Press and Publications Department, Muslim World League, POB 537, Mecca al-Mukarramah, Saudi Arabia; tel. (02) 5362995; Chief Editor Sayyid Hasan Mutahar; monthly in English.

Near East Report. 440 First St, NW, Suite 607, Washington, DC 20001, USA; tel. (202) 639-5268; fax (202) 347-4916; f. 1957; analyses US policy in the Middle East; Editor Raphael Danziger; circ. 55,000; weekly.

New Outlook. 9 Gordon St, Tel Aviv 63458, Israel; tel. (03) 236496; fax (03) 232492; f. 1957; Israeli and Middle Eastern Affairs; dedicated to Jewish-Arab rapprochement; Editor-in-Chief Chaim Shur; circ. 10,000; monthly.

Oil and Gas Journal. Penn Well Publishing Co, 1421 S. Sheridan, Tulsa, Oklahoma 74101, USA; tel. (918) 835-3161; fax (918) 832-9295; f. 1902; petroleum industry and business weekly; Editor John L. Kennedy; circ. 42,000.

Orient. German Orient Institute, 2 Hamburg 13, Mittelweg 150, Federal Republic of Germany; tel. (040) 441481; fax (040) 441484; f. 1960; current affairs articles in German and English; documents, book reviews and bibliographies; Editor Prof. Dr Udo Steinbach; quarterly.

Oriente Moderno. Istituto per l'Oriente C.A. Nallino, via A. Caroncini 19, 00197 Rome, Italy; tel. (06) 8084106; f. 1921; articles, book reviews.

Palestine Affairs. POB 1691, Beirut, Lebanon; studies of Palestine problem; f. 1971; monthly in Arabic; Editor Bilal El-Hassan.

Persica. Netherlands-Iranian Society; c/o NINO, Witte Singel 24, POB 9515, 2300 RA Leiden, Netherlands; tel. (071) 272019; f. 1963; Editors E. During Caspers, J. de Bruijn, R. Hillenbrand, K. Kremer and C. Nijland; every 2 years.

Petroleum Economist. POB 105, Export House, 25/31 Ironmonger Row, London, EC1V 3PN, England; tel. (071) 251-3501; fax (071) 253-1224; f. 1934; monthly, in English and Japanese editions; Editor Ian Bourne; English circ. 5,500.

Petroleum Times Price Report. Whitehall Press Ltd, Earl House, Maidstone, Kent, ME14 1PE, England; tel. (0622) 59841; telex 965204; 2 a month.

Politica Internazionale. Via del Tritone 62B, 00187 Rome, Italy; tel. (06) 6792321; fax (06) 6797849; published by Istituto per le relazioni tra Italia e i Paesi dell' Africa, America Latina e Medio Oriente; Italian edition (quarterly).

Pour la Palestine. BP 184, 75160 Paris Cedex 04, France; tel. (1) 48-57-68-55; fax (1) 49-88-96-88; f. 1979; quarterly.

Revue d'assyriologie et d'archéologie orientale. Presses universitaires de France, 12 rue Jean-de-Beauvais, 75005 Paris, France; f. 1923; Dirs Paul Garelli, Pierre Amiet; 2 a year.

Revue des études islamiques. Librairie Orientaliste Paul Geuthner SA, 12 rue Vavin, 75006 Paris, France; f. 1927; Editors J. D. Sourdel and J. Sourdel-Thomine.

Revue d'études Palestiniennes. Published by l'Institut des études palestiniennes, POB 11-7164, Beirut, Lebanon; distributed by Les Editions de Minuit, 7 rue Bernard Palissy, 75006 Paris, France; tel. (1) 42-22-54-78; f. 1981; Chief Editor Elias Sanbar; quarterly.

Rivista Degli Studi Orientali. Dipartimento di Studi Orientali, Facoltà di Lettere, Università Degli Studi, 'La Sapienza', Rome, Italy; tel. (06) 49913562; fax (06) 4451209; Publisher Giovanni Bardi; quarterly.

Rocznik Orientalistyczny. Instytut Orientalistyczny, Uniwersytet Warszawski, Warszawa 64, Poland; f. 1915; Editor-in-Chief Edward Tryjarski; Sec. Janusz Danecki; 2 a year.

Royal Asiatic Society of Great Britain and Ireland Journal. 60 Queen's Gardens, London W2 3AF, England; tel. (071) 724-

4742; f. 1823; covers all aspects of Oriental research; Pres. Prof. A. D. H. Bivar; Editor Dr D. O. Morgan; 3 a year.

Studia Islamica, G. P. Maisonneuve et Larose, 15 rue Victor-Cousin, 75005 Paris, France; tel. (1) 44-41-49-30; fax (1) 43-25-77-41; f. 1953; Editors A. L. Udovitch and A. M. Turki; 2 a year.

Studies in Islam. Indian Institute of Islamic Studies, Panchkuin Road, New Delhi 110001, India; f. 1964; quarterly.

Sudanow. POB 2651, Khartoum, Sudan; tel. (0249) 77915; telex 22418; f. 1976; political, economic and cultural; Editor-in-Chief Ahmed Kamal ed-Din; circ. 7,000; monthly.

Sumer. State Antiquities and Heritage Organization, Karkh, Salihiya, Jamal abd an-Nasr St, Baghdad, Iraq; tel. 537-6121; f. 1945; archaeological and historical; Chair. Editorial Bd Dr M. Said; annually.

At-Tijara al-Arabiya al-Inkleezya (World Arab Trade). Sahara Publications, 91 King Street, London, W6 9HW, England; tel. (081) 741-4921; telex 926493; f. 1947; Arabic; 6 a year.

Turcica. Published by Université des sciences humaines, Strasbourg, and Association pour le développement des études turques, EHESS, 54 blvd Raspail, 75006 Paris, France; tel. (1) 49-54-23-01; fax (1) 49-54-26-72; f. 1971; all aspects of Turkish and Turkic culture; annually; Editors Prof. Gilles Veinstein and Paul Dumont.

Türk Kültürü Araştırmaları. T. K. Araştırma Enstitüsü, 17 Sokak No. 38 Bahçelievler, Ankara, Turkey; tel. (0312) 213-13-00; f. 1964; scholarly articles in Turkish; Editor Dr Şükrü Elçin; 1 a year.

Turkologischer Anzeiger (Turkology Annual). Oriental Institute of the University of Vienna; A-1010 Vienna I, Universitätsstrasse 7/V, Austria; tel. (1) 40103-2593; fax (1) 4020533; annually.

Al-Urdun al-jadid (New Jordan). POB 4856, Nicosia, Cyprus; Arabic; quarterly.

Vostok (*Orient*). Russian Academy of Sciences, ul. Spiridonovka 30/1, Moscow, Russia: tel. 290-05-31; f. 1955; Afro-Asian Societies past and present; Editor-in-Chief Dr L. Alayev; 6 a year.

The Washington Report on Middle East Affairs. POB 53062, Washington, DC 20009, USA; tel. (202) 939-6050; fax (202) 265-4574; f. 1982; monthly.

Die Welt des Islams. Published by E. J. Brill, postbus 9000, 2300 PA, Leiden, Netherlands; tel. (071) 312624; telex 39296; fax (071) 228735579; Orientalisches Seminar der Universität, Regina-Pacis-Weg 7, 53113 Bonn 1, Federal Republic of Germany; tel. (0228) 737462; fax (0228) 735601; f. 1913; contains articles in German, English and French on the contemporary Muslim world with special reference to literature; Editors Prof. Dr S. Wild (University of Bonn), Prof. Dr W. Ende (University of Freiburg), Prof. Dr K. Kreiser (University of Bamberg).

Wiener Zeitschrift für die Kunde des Morgenlandes. Oriental Institute of the University of Vienna, A-1010 Vienna I, Universitätsstrasse 7/V, Austria; tel. (1) 40103-2599; fax (1) 4020533; f. 1887; Editors O. Prof. Dr Arne A. Ambros, O. Prof. Dr Hans Hirsch, O. Prof. Dr Markus Köhbach; annually.

PART TWO
Regional Organizations

THE UNITED NATIONS IN THE MIDDLE EAST AND NORTH AFRICA

Address: United Nations Plaza, New York, NY 10017, USA.

Telephone: (212) 963-1234; **fax:** (212) 758-2718.

The United Nations (UN) was founded on 24 October 1945. The organization aims to maintain international peace and security and to develop international co-operation in economic, social, cultural and humanitarian problems. The principal organs of the UN are the General Assembly, the Security Council, the Economic and Social Council (ECOSOC), the International Court of Justice and the Secretariat. The General Assembly, which meets for three months each year, comprises representatives of all UN member states. The Security Council investigates disputes between member countries, and may recommend ways and means of peaceful settlement: it comprises five permanent members (the People's Republic of China, France, Russia, the United Kingdom and the USA) and 10 other members elected by the General Assembly for a two-year period. The Economic and Social Council comprises representatives of 54 member states, elected by the General Assembly for a three-year period: it promotes co-operation on economic, social, cultural and humanitarian matters, acting as a central policy-making body and co-ordinating the activities of the UN's specialized agencies. The International Court of Justice comprises 15 judges of different nationalities, elected for nine-year terms by the General Assembly and the Security Council: it adjudicates in legal disputes between UN member states.

Secretary-General of the United Nations: Dr BOUTROS BOUTROS-GHALI (Egypt) (1992–96).

MEMBER STATES IN THE MIDDLE EAST AND NORTH AFRICA

(with assessments for percentage contributions to UN budget for 1992–94, and year of admission)

Algeria	0.16	1962
Bahrain	0.03	1971
Cyprus	0.02	1960
Egypt	0.07	1945
Iran	0.77	1945
Iraq	0.13	1945
Israel	0.23	1949
Jordan	0.01	1955
Kuwait	0.25	1963
Lebanon	0.01	1945
Libya	0.24	1955
Morocco	0.03	1956
Oman	0.03	1971
Qatar	0.05	1971
Saudi Arabia	0.96	1945
Syria	0.04	1945
Tunisia	0.03	1956
Turkey	0.27	1945
United Arab Emirates	0.21	1971
Yemen	0.01	1947/67*

* The Yemen Arab Republic became a member of the UN in 1947, and the People's Democratic Republic of Yemen was admitted in 1967. The two countries formed the Republic of Yemen in 1990.

PERMANENT MISSIONS TO THE UNITED NATIONS
(with Permanent Representatives—August 1993)

Algeria: 15 East 47th St, New York, NY 10017; tel. (212) 750-1960; fax (212) 759-9538; RAMLANE LAMAMRA.

Bahrain: 2 United Nations Plaza, 25th Floor, New York, NY 10017; tel. (212) 223-6200; fax (212) 319-0687; Chargé d'affaires SAEED MOHAMED AL-FAIHANI.

Cyprus: 13 East 40th St, New York, NY 10016; tel. (212) 481-6023; fax (212) 685-7316; ALECOS H. SHAMBOS.

Egypt: 36 East 67th St, New York, NY 10021; tel. (212) 879-6300; fax (212) 794-3874; Dr NABIL A. ELARABY.

Iran: 622 Third Ave, 34th Floor, New York, NY 10017; tel. (212) 687-2020; fax (212) 867-7086; Dr KAMAL KHARRAZI.

Iraq: 14 East 79th St, New York, NY 10021; tel. (212) 737-4434; fax (212) 772-1794; NIZAR HAMDOON.

Israel: 800 Second Ave, New York, NY 10017; tel. (212) 351-5200; fax (212) 697-6272; GAAD YAACOBI.

Jordan: 866 United Nations Plaza, Room 550–552, New York, NY 10017; tel. (212) 752-0135; fax (212) 826-0830; ADNAN S. ABU ODEH.

Kuwait: 321 East 44th St, New York, NY 10017; tel. (212) 973-4300; fax (212) 370-1733; MUHAMMAD A. ABULHASAN.

Lebanon: 866 United Nations Plaza, Room 531–533, New York, NY 10017; tel. (212) 355-5460; fax (212) 838-2819; Dr SAMIR MOUBARAK.

Libya: 309–315 East 48th St, New York, NY 10017; tel. (212) 752-5775; fax (212) 593-4787; MOHAMED A. AZWAI.

Morocco: 767 Third Ave, 30th Floor, New York, NY 10017; tel. (212) 421-1580; fax (212) 980-1512; AHMED SNOUSSI.

Oman: 866 United Nations Plaza, Suite 540, New York, NY 10017; tel. (212) 355-3505; fax (212) 644-0070; SALIM BIN MUHAMMAD AL-KHUSSAIBY.

Qatar: 747 Third Ave, 22nd Floor, New York, NY 10017; tel. (212) 486-9335; fax (212) 758-4952; Dr HASSAN ALI HUSSAIN AL-NI'MAH.

Saudi Arabia: 405 Lexington Ave, 56th Floor, New York, NY 10017; tel. (212) 697-4830; fax (212) 983-4895; (vacant).

Syria: 820 Second Ave, 10th Floor, New York, NY 10017; tel. (212) 661-1313; fax (212) 983-4439; (vacant).

Tunisia: 31 Beekman Place, New York, NY 10022; tel. (212) 751-7503; fax (212) 751-0569; SLAHEDDINE ABDELLAH.

Turkey: 821 United Nations Plaza, 10th Floor, New York, NY 10017; tel. (212) 949-0150; fax (212) 949-0086; INAL BATU.

United Arab Emirates: 747 Third Ave, 36th Floor, New York, NY 10017; tel. (212) 371-0480; fax (212) 371-4923; MOHAMMAD JASIM SAMHAN.

Yemen: 866 United Nations Plaza, Room 435, New York, NY 10017; tel. (212) 355-1730; fax (212) 750-9613; ABDALLA SALEH AL-ASHTAL.

Observers

Asian-African Legal Consultative Committee: 404 East 66th St, Apt 12C, New York, NY 10021; tel. (212) 734-7608; K. BHAGWAT-SINGH.

Economic Co-operation Organization: c/o Permanent Mission of Pakistan to the UN, Pakistan House, 8 East 65th St, New York, NY 10021; tel. (212) 879-8600; fax (212) 744-7348.

International Committee of the Red Cross: 801 Second Ave, 18th Floor, New York, NY 10017; tel. (212) 599-6021; fax (212) 599-6009; PETER KÜNG.

League of Arab States: 747 Third Ave, 35th Floor, New York, NY 10017; tel. (212) 838-8700; fax (212) 355-3909; MAHMOUD ABOUL-NASR.

Organization of the Islamic Conference: 130 East 40th St, 5th Floor, New York, NY 10016; tel. (212) 883-0140; fax (212) 883-0143; (vacant).

Palestine: 115 East 65th St, New York, NY 10021; tel. (212) 288-8500; fax (212) 517-2377; Dr NASSER AL-KIDWA.

GENERAL ASSEMBLY COMMITTEES CONCERNED WITH THE MIDDLE EAST

Committee on the Exercise of the Inalienable Rights of the Palestinian People: f. 1975; 23 members, elected by the General Assembly.

Special Committee on Peace-keeping Operations: f. 1965; 33 members.

Economic Commission for Africa—ECA

Address: Africa Hall, POB 3005, Addis Ababa, Ethiopia.
Telephone: (1) 517200; **telex:** 21029; **fax:** (1) 514416.
The UN Economic Commission for Africa was founded in 1958 by a resolution of ECOSOC to initiate and take part in measures for facilitating Africa's economic development.

MEMBERS*

Algeria	Ethiopia	Niger
Angola	Gabon	Nigeria
Benin	The Gambia	Rwanda
Botswana	Ghana	São Tomé and
Burkina Faso	Guinea	Príncipe
Burundi	Guinea-Bissau	Senegal
Cameroon	Kenya	Seychelles
Cape Verde	Lesotho	Sierra Leone
Central African	Liberia	Somalia
Republic	Libya	Sudan
Chad	Madagascar	Swaziland
Comoros	Malawi	Tanzania
Congo	Mali	Togo
Côte d'Ivoire	Mauritania	Tunisia
Djibouti	Mauritius	Uganda
Egypt	Morocco	Zaire
Equatorial Guinea	Mozambique	Zambia
Eritrea	Namibia	Zimbabwe

* South Africa's membership was suspended in 1965; however, following its readmission to the UN General Assembly in June 1994 South Africa was expected to reassume its membership of ECA.

Organization

(June 1994)

COMMISSION

The Commission may only act with the agreement of the government of the country concerned. It is also empowered to make recommendations on any matter within its competence directly to the government of the member or associate member concerned, to governments admitted in a consultative capacity, and to the UN Specialized Agencies. The Commission is required to submit for prior consideration by ECOSOC any of its proposals for actions that would be likely to have important effects on the international economy.

CONFERENCE OF MINISTERS

The Conference, which meets annually, is attended by ministers responsible for economic or financial affairs, planning and development of governments of member states, and is the main deliberative body of the Commission. A Technical Preparatory Committee of the Whole, representing all member states, was established in 1979 to deal with matters submitted for the consideration of the Conference.

The Commission's responsibility to promote concerted action for the economic and social development of Africa is vested primarily in the Conference, which considers matters of general policy and the priorities to be assigned to the Commission's programmes, considers inter-African and international economic policy, and makes recommendations to member states in connection with such matters. It reviews the course of programmes being implemented in the preceding year and examines and approves the programmes proposed for the next.

OTHER POLICY-MAKING BODIES

Conference of African Ministers of Economic Planning and Development.
Conference of African Ministers of Finance.
Conference of African Ministers of Industry.
Conference of African Ministers of Social Affairs.
Conference of African Ministers of Trade.
Conference of African Ministers of Transport, Communications and Planning.
Conference of Ministers of Finance.
Conference of Ministers Responsible for Human Resources Planning, Development and Utilization.
Councils of Ministers of the MULPOCs (see below).

SECRETARIAT

The Secretariat provides the services necessary for the meeting of the Conference of Ministers and the meetings of the Commission's subsidiary bodies, carries out the resolutions and implements the programmes adopted there.

The headquarters of the Secretariat is in Addis Ababa, Ethiopia. It comprises an Executive Direction and Management office and 10 Divisions.

Executive Direction and Management:
African Training and Research Centre for Women
Economic Co-operation Office
Information Service
Office of the Secretary of the Commission
Pan-African Documentation and Information Service (PADIS)
Policy and Programme Co-ordination
Technical Assistance Co-ordination and Operations Office

Divisions:
Administration and Conference Services
Industry and Human Settlements
Joint ECA/FAO Food and Agriculture
Natural Resources
Population
Public Administration, Human Resources and Social Development
Socio-Economic Research and Planning
Statistics
Trade and Development Finance
Transport, Communications and Tourism

Executive Secretary: LAYASHI YAKER (Algeria).

Subsidiary Bodies

Conference of Ministers of African Least-Developed Countries.
Follow-up Committee on Industrialization in Africa.
Intergovernmental Committee of Experts of African Least-Developed Countries.
Intergovernmental Committee of Experts for Science and Technology Development.
Intergovernmental Regional Committee on Human Settlements and Environment.
Joint Conference of African Planners, Statisticians and Demographers.

Regional Operational Centres

Multinational Programming and Operational Centres (MULPOC) act as 'field agents' for the implementation of regional development programmes. The Centres are located in Yaoundé, Cameroon (serving central Africa), Gisenyi, Rwanda (Great Lakes Community), Lusaka, Zambia (east and southern Africa), Niamey, Niger (west Africa) and Tangier, Morocco (north Africa). Each centre holds regular ministerial meetings.

African Institute for Economic Development and Planning: POB 3186, Addis Ababa, Ethiopia; tel. (1) 22577; Dir JEGGAN C. SENGHOR.

Activities

The Commission's activities are designed to encourage sustainable socio-economic development in Africa and to increase economic co-operation among African countries and between Africa and other parts of the world. The Secretariat is guided in its efforts by major regional strategies including the Abuja Treaty establishing the African Economic Community signed under the aegis of the Organization of African Unity and the UN New Agenda for the Development for Africa covering the period 1991–2000.

AGRICULTURE

During 1991–92 ECA's activities in the agricultural sector were intended to achieve three principal objectives: the alleviation of poverty, the attainment of food self-sufficiency and the promotion of food security. To these ends ECA provided support in the areas of development of livestock; inter-state co-operation; reduction or prevention of food losses; monitoring and evaluation of agricultural and rural development projects; conservation, expansion and rational utilization of natural resources, particularly land and forests; and preparation of related technical publications or reports.

ENERGY

In 1991–92 the ECA, under its Energy Programme, provided assistance to member states in the development of indigenous energy resources and the formulation of energy policies to extricate member states from continued energy crises. Studies were carried out on strengthening the institutional arrangements for management in the energy sector in Zambia and Zimbabwe; on increasing the efficiency in the utilization of energy in Burundi, Rwanda and Zaire; on maximizing revenue from petroleum operations; and on new and renewable sources of energy and the technologies needed to harness them. The ECA's Secretariat supports the African Regional Centre for Solar Energy (Bujumbura, Burundi). Together with the World Bank, the ECA organized a training workshop on energy policy and the environment for senior African officials involved in energy planning and management.

ENVIRONMENT AND DEVELOPMENT

During 1991–92 reports were compiled on the development, implementation and sound management of environmental programmes at national, sub-regional and regional levels. ECA members adopted a common African position for the UN Conference on Environment and Development, held in June 1992.

INDUSTRY

Following the failure to implement many of the proposals under the UN Industrial Development Decade for Africa (IDDA, 1980–90) and the UN Programme of Action for African Economic Recovery and Development (1986–90), a second IDDA was adopted by the Conference of African Ministers of Industry in July 1991. The main objectives of the second IDDA include the consolidation and rehabilitation of existing industries, the expansion of new investments, and the promotion of small-scale industries and technological capabilities. Various technical publications were to be produced, including a directory of project profiles in the field of entrepreneurship in small-scale industries.

ECA is organizing a global conference for the promotion of investment in Africa, scheduled to be held in November 1994.

INFORMATION

The Pan-African Documentation and Information Service (PADIS) was established in 1980. The main objectives of PADIS are: to provide access to numerical and other information on African social, economic, scientific and technological development issues; to assist African countries in their efforts to develop national information handling capabilities through advisory services and training; to establish a data communication network to facilitate the timely use of information on development; and to design sound technical specifications, norms and standards to minimize technical barriers in the exchange of information.

INTERNATIONAL TRADE AND FINANCE

ECA assists African countries in expanding trade among themselves and with other regions of the world and in promoting financial and monetary co-operation. ECA attempts to ensure that African countries should participate effectively in current international negotiations. To this end, assistance has been provided to member states in negotiations under UNCTAD and GATT; in the annual conferences of the IMF and the World Bank; in negotiations with the EC; and in meetings related to economic co-operation among developing countries. Studies have been prepared on problems and prospects likely to arise for the African region from the implementation of the Common Fund for Commodities and the Generalized System of Trade Preferences (both supervised by UNCTAD); the impacts of exchange-rate fluctuations on the economies of African countries; and on long-term implications of different debt arrangements for African economies. ECA assists individual member states by undertaking studies on domestic trade, expansion of inter-African trade, transnational corporations, integration of women in trade and development, and strengthening the capacities of state-trading organizations. ECA promotes co-operation between developing countries, and the expansion of African trade with overseas countries.

The expansion of trade within Africa is constrained by the low level of industrial production, and by the strong emphasis on commodity trade. ECA encourages the diversification of production and the expansion of domestic trade structures, within regional economic groupings. ECA helps to organize regional and 'All-Africa' trade fairs.

In early 1992 ECA, in co-ordination with the OAU and the African Development Bank (q.v.), embarked on a series of meetings with western governments and financial institutions in an attempt to persuade them to cancel, partially or completely, debts owed by African countries, and to encourage them to invest in the region.

NATURAL RESOURCES

The Fourth Regional Conference on the Development and Utilization of Mineral Resources in Africa, held in March 1991, adopted an action plan that included the formulation of national mineral exploitation policies; and the promotion of the gemstone industry, small-scale mining and the iron and steel industry. ECA continues to provide support to the Southern African Mineral Resources Development Centre in Dar-es-Salaam, Tanzania, and the Central African Mineral Development Centre in Brazzaville, Congo, which provide advisory and laboratory services to their respective member states.

ECA sponsors the two leading institutions in the field of cartography and remote-sensing. The Regional Centre for Services in Surveying, Mapping and Remote-Sensing is based in Nairobi, Kenya; it is currently establishing a satellite receiving station for processing remotely-sensed data for use by member states. The Regional Centre for Training in Aerospace Surveys, base in Ile Ife, Nigeria, provides training in cartography and remote-sensing. The Eighth Regional Cartographic Conference for Africa was scheduled to be held in early 1993.

ECA assists member states in the assessment and use of water resources and the development of river and lake basins common to more than one country. The annual information bulletin on water resources in Africa, *Maji*, disseminates technical information to African governments, and inter-governmental and non-governmental organizations. In the field of marine affairs, ECA provides advisory services to member states on the opportunities and challenges provided by the UN Convention on the Law of the Sea. A guide to African policy-makers and negotiators on legal arrangements for joint ventures among developed and developing countries for the exploration and exploitation of non-living resources of the sea was published in 1991.

POLICY AND PROGRAMME CO-ORDINATION

Policy and programme co-ordination is one of the tasks of the Executive Direction and Management office. The office provides guidance in the formulation of policies towards the achievement of Africa's development objectives to the policy-making organs of the UN and OAU. It contributes to the work of the General Assembly and other specialized agencies by providing an African perspective in the preparation of development strategies.

POPULATION

ECA assists its member states in (i) population data collection and data processing, which is carried out by the Statistics Division of the Commission (q.v.); (ii) analysis of demographic data obtained from censuses or surveys: this assistance is given by the Population Division; (iii) training demographers at the Regional Institute for Population Studies (RIPS) in Accra (Ghana) and at the Institut de formation et de recherche démographiques (IFORD) in Yaoundé (Cameroon); (iv) formulation of population policies and integrating population variables in development planning, through advisory missions and through the organization of national seminars on population and development; and (v) dissemination of information through its *Newsletter, Demographic Handbook for Africa,* the *African Population Studies* series and other publications. The Sixth Joint Conference of African Planners, Statisticians and Demographers was held in 1990; the Third African Population Conference was held in Dakar, Senegal, in December 1992, in order to prepare for the International Conference on Population and Development in September 1994.

PUBLIC ADMINISTRATION, HUMAN RESOURCES AND SOCIAL DEVELOPMENT

The Division aims to assist governments, public corporations, universities and the private sector in improving their financial management; strengthening policy-making and analytical capacities; adopting measures to redress skill shortages; enhance human resources development and utilization; and promote social development through programmes focusing on youth, people with disabilities and the elderly. The Division conducts training workshops, seminars and conferences at national, sub-regional and regional levels for ministers, public administrators, senior policy-makers as well as for private and non-governmental organizations.

SCIENCE AND TECHNOLOGY

The Commission's activities in the field of science and technology focus on three areas: the development of policies and institutions; the training and effective utilization of the work-force; and the promotion of regional and inter-regional co-operation. In 1991–92 ECA's Secretariat completed a review of science and technology policy institutions; provided advisory services to a number of countries on strengthening their science and technology structures; and provided technical support to the African Regional Centre for Technology and the African Regional Organization for Standardization.

SOCIO-ECONOMIC RESEARCH AND PLANNING

Monitoring economic and social trends in the African region and studying the development problems concerning it are among the fundamental tasks of the Commission. Every year the Commission publishes the *Survey of Economic and Social Conditions in Africa* and the *Economic Report on Africa*.

The Commission gives assistance to governments in general economic analysis, in fiscal, financial and monetary issues and in planning. The ECA's work on economic planning has been recently broadened, in order to give more emphasis to macro-economic management in a mixed economy approach: a project is being undertaken to develop short-term forecasting and policy models to support economic management. The Commission has also started a major study on the informal sector in African countries. Special assistance is given to least-developed, land-locked and island countries which have a much lower income level than other countries and which are faced with heavier constraints than others. Studies are also undertaken to assist longer-term planning.

The Conference of African Planners, Statisticians and Demographers is held every two years and provides an opportunity for African governments to exchange views and experiences, and to keep abreast of new policy approaches.

In 1989 ECA published a report entitled *African Alternative Framework to Structural Adjustment Programmes for Socio-Economic Recovery and Transformation*, which argued that programmes of strict economic reform, as imposed by the International Monetary Fund and the World Bank, had not resulted in sustained economic growth in Africa over the past decade. In July 1991 ECA proposed a series of measures which countries might adopt, in a more flexible approach to long-term development. These proposals were subsequently published under the title *Selected Policy Instruments* and included multiple exchange rates (as opposed to generalized currency devaluation), differential interest rates and subsidies to agricultural producers.

STATISTICS

The Statistics Division of ECA, which comprises two sections (Statistical Development and Economic Statistics) promotes the development and co-ordination of national statistical services in the region and the improvement and comparability of statistical data. It prepares documents to assist in the improvement of statistical methodology and undertakes the collection, evaluation and dissemination of statistical information. A plan of action for statistical development in Africa in the 1990s has been drawn up and a Co-ordinating Committee on African Statistical Development (CASD) has been established. ECA's work in the field of statistics has been concentrated in five main areas: the African Household Survey Capability Programme, which aims to assist in the collection and analysis of demographic, social and economic data on households; the Statistical Training Programme for Africa, which aims to make the region self-sufficient in statistical personnel at all levels; the Technical Support Services, which provides technical advisory services for population censuses, demographic surveys and civil registration; the National Accounts Capability Programme, which aims at improving economic statistics generally by building up a capability in each country for the collection, processing and analysis of economic data; and the ECA-Regional Statistical Data Base, part of PADIS (see above), which provides on-line statistical information to users.

TRANSPORT AND COMMUNICATIONS

The ECA was appointed lead agency for the second United Nations Transport and Communications Decade in Africa (UNTACDA II), comprising the period 1991–2000. The principal aim of UNTACDA II is the establishment of an efficient integrated transport and communications system in Africa, to facilitate national and international traffic. The specific objectives of the programme include: (i) the removal of physical and non-physical barriers to intra-African trade and travel, and improvement in the road transport sector; (ii) improvement in the efficiency and financial viability of railways; (iii) development of Africa's shipping capacity and improvement in the performance of Africa's ports; (iv) development of integrated transport systems for each lake and river basin; (v) improvement of integration of all modes of transport in order to carry cargo in one chain of transport smoothly; (vi) integration of African airlines, and restructuring of civil aviation and airport management authorities; (vii) improvement in the quality and availability of transport in urban areas; (viii) development of integrated regional telecommunications networks; (ix) development of broadcasting services, with the aim of supporting socio-economic development; and (x) expansion of Africa's postal network.

In May 1991 the Conference of African Ministers of Transport, Communications and Planning approved a programme which comprised 669 projects, of which 478 were in the transport and 191 were in the telecommunications sector. The projects were submitted by 43 African countries, four sub-regional organizations and eight specialized institutions.

BUDGET

ECA's proposed programme budget for the two years 1992–93 was US $143.9m.

PUBLICATIONS

ECA Annual Report.

Africa Index (3 a year).

African Compendium on Environmental Statistics (irregular).

African Directory of Demographers (irregular).

African Population Newsletter (2 a year).

African Population Studies Series (irregular).

African Socio-Economic Indicators (annually).

African Statistical Yearbook.

African Trade Bulletin (2 a year).

Bulletin of ECA-sponsored Institutions (irregular).

Demographic Handbook for Africa (irregular).

Devindex Africa (quarterly).

Directory of African Statisticians (every 2 years).

ECA Environment Newsletter (3 a year).

Flash on Trade Opportunities (quarterly).

Focus on African Industry (2 a year).

Foreign Trade Statistics for Africa series.
   Direction of Trade (quarterly).
   Summary Table (annually).

Maji Water Resources Bulletin (annually).

PADIS Newsletter (quarterly).

Report of the Executive Secretary (every 2 years).

Rural Progress (2 a year).

Statistical Newsletter (2 a year).

Survey on Economic and Social Conditions in Africa (annually).

Economic and Social Commission for Western Asia—ESCWA

Address: PO Box 927115, Amman, Jordan.
Telephone: (6) 606847; **telex:** 216917; **fax:** (6) 694981.
The UN Economic Commission for Western Asia was established in 1974 by a resolution of the UN Economic and Social Council (ECOSOC), to provide facilities of a wider scope for those countries previously served by the UN Economic and Social Office in Beirut (UNESOB). The name 'Economic and Social Commission for Western Asia' (ESCWA) was adopted in 1985.

MEMBERS

Bahrain	Palestine
Egypt	Qatar
Iraq	Saudi Arabia
Jordan	Syria
Kuwait	United Arab Emirates
Lebanon	Yemen
Oman	

Organization

(August 1994)

COMMISSION

The sessions of the Commission (held every two years) are attended by representatives of member states and bodies, of UN bodies and specialized agencies, of regional and intergovernmental organizations, and of other states attending as observers.

SECRETARIAT

In 1982 the Commission established its permanent headquarters in Baghdad, Iraq. In 1991 temporary headquarters were established in Amman, Jordan, where the secretariat subsequently remained.

Divisions:
  Administration
  Development Planning
  General Economic Analysis
  Human Settlements and Environment
  Joint ESCWA/FAO Agriculture
  Joint ESCWA/UNIDO Industry
  Natural Resources, Science and Technology
  Social Development and Population
  Statistics
  Transport and Communications
Executive Secretary: Dr SABAH BAKJAJ (Syria).

Activities

ESCWA undertakes or sponsors studies of economic and social issues of the region, collects and disseminates information, and provides advisory services.

Much of ESCWA's work is carried out in co-operation with other UN bodies. It conducts industrial studies for individual countries in conjunction with UNIDO. It co-operates with FAO in regional planning, food security and management of agricultural resources. UNDP supports ESCWA's work on household surveys in western Asia and the Arab Planning Institute in Kuwait. Work is also undertaken with UNFPA and UNIFEM in population and women's programmes, with ILO in statistical surveys on labour, with UNCTAD in development planning and maritime transport training, with UNEP in integrating environmental considerations (particularly control of desertification) into development programmes, and with OIC on issues concerning natural resources and trade and industry.

The programme of work and priorities comprises studies of various technical and socio-economic problems, particularly those demanding inter-country and sub-regional co-operation. The main areas are:

development planning (particularly in the least-developed countries in the region);

food and agriculture;

human settlement (particularly housing finance and city management);

industrial development (appraisal of potential and co-ordination of policies);

international trade (identification of intra-regional trade and integration opportunities);

labour, management and employment (making the best use of available manpower and development of required skills);

natural resources (energy planning, minerals and water development);

science and technology (problems of dependence on imported technology and training of manpower);

social development (welfare, participation in development, and training and planning);

statistics (improvement of procedures and adopting uniform standards);

transnational corporations.

transport and communications (multinational shipping enterprises, railway networks, and road construction and maintenance);

In June 1992 an international symposium on 'gas development and market prospects', organized by ESCWA, was held in Damascus, Syria.

BUDGET

ESCWA's share of the UN budget for the two years 1994–95 was US $51m.

PUBLICATIONS

All publications are annual, unless otherwise indicated.
Agriculture and Development in Western Asia.
External Trade Bulletin.
Industrial Development/Development of Selected Industrial Branches.
National Accounts Studies.
Population Bulletin (2 a year).
Prices and Financial Statistics in the ESCWA Region.
Review of Monetary and Banking Policy in the ESCWA Region.
Socio-economic Data Sheet.
Statistical Abstract.
Survey and Assessment of Energy-Related Activities and Developments in the ESCWA Region.
Survey of Economic and Social Developments in the ESCWA Region.
Transport Bulletin.

United Nations Development Programme—UNDP

Address: One United Nations Plaza, New York, NY 10017, USA.
Telephone: (212) 906-5000; **fax:** (212) 826-2057.

The Programme was established in 1965 by the UN General Assembly to help the developing countries increase the wealth-producing capabilities of their natural and human resources.

Organization

(August 1994)

UNDP is responsible to the UN General Assembly, to which it reports through the UN Economic and Social Council.

EXECUTIVE BOARD

In January 1994 the Governing Council of UNDP and the UN Population Fund (UNFPA, of which UNDP is the governing body) was replaced by an Executive Board, as agreed by the UN General Assembly. The Board is responsible for providing intergovernmental support to and supervision of the activities of UNDP and UNFPA. It comprises 36 members: eight from Africa, seven from Asia, four from eastern Europe, five from Latin America and the Caribbean and 12 from western Europe and other countries.
President: MOHAMMAD HAMID ANSARI (India).

SECRETARIAT

Administrator: JAMES GUSTAVE ('GUS') SPETH (USA).

REGIONAL BUREAUX

Headed by assistant administrators, the regional bureaux share the responsibility for implementing the programme with the Administrator's office. Within certain limitations, large-scale projects may be approved and funding allocated by the Administrator, and smaller-scale projects by the Resident Representatives, based in 132 countries.

The four regional bureaux, all at the Secretariat in New York, cover: Africa; Asia and the Pacific; the Arab states; and Latin America and the Caribbean; there are also Divisions for Europe and the former USSR, and for Global and Interregional Programmes.
Assistant Administrator and Director of the Regional Bureau for Arab States and European Programmes: ALI AHMED ATTIGA.

FIELD OFFICES

In almost every country receiving UNDP assistance there is a Country Office, headed by the UNDP Resident Representative, who advises the Government on formulating the country programme, sees that field activities are carried out, and acts as the leader of the UN team of experts working in the country. Resident Representatives are normally designated as co-ordinators for all UN operational development activities; the field offices function as the primary presence of the UN in most developing countries.

OFFICES OF UNDP REPRESENTATIVES IN THE MIDDLE EAST AND NORTH AFRICA

Algeria: 19 ave Chahid el-Quali, Mustapha Sayed, BP 823, Algiers 16000; tel. (2) 74-50-87; telex 66144; fax (2) 74-50-81.
Bahrain: Bldg 1083 Rd No 4225, Juffair 342, POB 26814, Manama; tel. 729569; fax 729922.
Cyprus: 115 Prodromos St, Strovolos, POB 5605, Nicosia; tel. (2) 303194; fax (2) 366125.
Egypt: World Trade Centre Bldg, 4th Floor, 1191 Corniche El-Nil St, Boulak, POB 982, Cairo; tel. (2) 768517; telex 92034; fax (2) 779145.
Iran: United Nations Bldg, 185 Ghaem Magham Farahani Ave, POB 15875-4557, Teheran 15868; tel. (21) 8862816; telex 212397; fax (21) 5048864.
Iraq: Bldg No. 153, 102 Abi Nawas St, POB 12048 (Alwiyah), Baghdad; tel. (1) 886-0164; telex 212271; fax (1) 886-2523.
Jordan: Hirbawi Bldg, 'Obadah Ibn Al-Samet St, POB 35286, Amman; tel. (6) 668171; telex 21654; fax (6) 676582.
Kuwait: St No. 7, Block No. 12, Villa No. 145, Jabriya, POB 2993 Safat; tel. 5325967; fax 5325879.
Lebanon: POB 11–3216 Unifil House, Capt. Ali Ahmed Bldg, Bir Hassan (near Kuwaiti embassy), Beirut; tel. (1) 822146; fax (1) 603461.
Libya: 67–71 Turkiya St, POB 358, Tripoli; tel. (21) 36297; telex 20582; fax (21) 30856.

Morocco: Immeuble de l'ONU, Angle ave Moulay Hassan et rue Assafi, Rabat; tel. (7) 709811; fax (7) 701566.
Qatar: Fariq Bin Omran (near English Speaking School and Doha Players' Theatre), Box 3233, Doha; tel. 863260; fax 861552.
Saudi Arabia: King Faysel St (Olaya St), POB 558, Riyadh 11421; tel. (1) 465-1031; fax (1) 465-2087.
Syria: Abou Roumaneh 28, al-Jala'a St, POB 2317, Damascus; tel. (11) 3339532; fax (11) 3327764.
Tunisia: 61 blvd Bab Benat, BP 863, 1006 Tunis; tel. (1) 264-011; fax (1) 560-094.
Turkey: 197 Atatürk Bulvari, 06680 Kavaklidere, PK 407, Ankara; tel. (312) 4268113; fax (312) 4261372.
United Arab Emirates: Sheikh Khalifa bin Shakhbout St, West 17/1 Villa no. 41, POB 3490, Abu Dhabi; tel. (2) 655300; fax (2) 650818.
Yemen: Al-Khorashi Bldg, opposite Awqaf Housing Complex, Shar'a Siteen, POB 551, San'a; tel. (1) 215455; fax (1) 263067.

Activities

As the world's largest source of grant technical assistance in developing countries, UNDP works with more than 150 governments and 40 international agencies for faster economic growth and better standards of living throughout the world. Agriculture (including forestry and fisheries) is a major component of UNDP activities, accounting for about 15% of field programme expenditure in 1993. Most of the work is undertaken in the field by the various United Nations agencies, or by the government of the country concerned.

Assistance is mostly non-monetary, comprising the provision of experts' services, consultancies, equipment, and fellowships for advanced study abroad. In 1993 nearly one-half of spending on projects was for the services of experts, 19% was for sub-contracts, 15% for equipment, 9% for training, and the remainder was for other costs, such as maintenance of equipment. Most UNDP projects incorporate training for local workers. Developing countries themselves provide 50% or more of the total project costs in terms of personnel, facilities, equipment and supplies.

UNDP concentrates on building national capacity in six specific areas (as defined by the Governing Council in 1990): eradication of poverty through 'grass-roots' participation in development; environmental protection; management development (under the Management Development Programme); technical co-operation among developing countries; transfer of technology; and the promotion of women in development (under the Division for Women and Development).

Countries receiving UNDP assistance are allocated an indicative planning figure (IPF) for a five-year period. The IPF represents the approximate total value of funding that a country can expect to receive, based on a formula taking per caput gross national product (GNP), population size and other criteria into account. In partnership with UNDP's Country Offices, governments calculate their technical assistance requirements on the basis of this formula. Activities involving several countries in a region also receive a share of UNDP funding and activities covering more than one region are developed by UNDP's Division for Global and Interregional Projects, in consultation with the relevant national and regional institutions. These activities include the promotion of international agricultural research, the improvement of drinking water supply and sanitation, and addressing the economic consequences of HIV/AIDS, while promoting measures to prevent its spread.

From 1990 UNDP published an annual *Human Development Report* and adopted an overall approach to its work, described as 'sustainable human development'. The objective of this approach was to put the focus of UNDP's work on people and to measure the effectiveness of programmes by their capacity to promote individual well-being and choice (in terms of health, education and purchasing power). UNDP also introduced the Human Development Index, which ranked countries in terms of human development, using three key indicators: life expectancy, adult literacy and basic income required for a decent standard of living.

In 1991 the Global Environment Facility, which is managed jointly by UNDP, the World Bank and the UN Environment Programme became operational. The GEF supports projects in developing countries aimed at protecting the environment, where UNDP is responsible for technical assistance and training. UNDP administers the Small Grants Programme of the GEF, which finances non-governmental and community initiatives. Also in 1991

UNDP established a panel of experts, the Environmental and Natural Resources Group, which was to monitor the environmental implications of the Programme's work; and the Sustainable Development Network (SDN) designed to facilitate the exchange of information on environmental protection between developing countries. At the UN Conference on Environment and Development (UNCED), held in Rio de Janeiro, Brazil, in June 1992, UNDP initiated 'Capacity 21', a programme to support developing countries in preparing and implementing sustainable development policies.

During 1993, UNDP made available the services of 28,409 experts world-wide, of whom 20,244 were national experts, and awarded 14,785 fellowships for nationals of developing countries to study abroad. In 1993 UNDP expenditure on projects in the Arab states (which excludes Iran) amounted to US $72m., or about 7% of total projects expenditure.

In February 1991 a UNDP 'Gulf Task Force' was formed to provide volunteers for relief work among refugees, following the outbreak of war against Iraq. In late 1991 UNDP convened an international conference to formulate recovery plans for those countries which suffered social, economic or environmental damage as a result of the war. In March 1992 UNDP and the Office of the UN Disaster Relief Co-ordinator (UNDRO) co-ordinated the relief programme to assist the victims of an earthquake in Turkey. In early 1992 the establishment of the Centre for Environment and Development in the Arab Region and Europe, based in Cairo, Egypt, was announced. The Centre was to initiate and co-ordinate regional environmental projects. During 1993 UNDP continued to provide assistance to Palestinians in the West Bank and Gaza Strip. In August UNDP announced it would participate in a project, with UNICEF and UNRWA, to encourage cultural and sporting activities for young people in the Occupied Territories. Following the Israeli-Palestinian peace accord, signed in September, UNDP's Programme of Assistance to the Palestinian People, which was set up in 1980, formulated 38 projects to develop infrastructure and income-generating activities in the area. In October two new fruit and vegetable processing plants, which were financed and built with UNDP support, were completed. Other projects supported by UNDP included the following: in Yemen, a campaign to combat a locust infestation (UNDP provided aircraft for the widespread spraying of pesticides); in Lebanon, assistance to some 350,000 displaced persons who had fled hostilities in late July; in Morocco, a programme to involve local populations in watershed planning and management; and in Kuwait, restructuring of the public administration system.

In February 1994 a new regional programme for the period 1994–96 was approved by a UNDP intergovernmental meeting of Arab States, that was convened in Yemen. The programme was to include three new initiatives: incorporating human development issues into the region's development planning and resource allocation; an economic integration and trade initiative to improve the capacity for intra-regional trade; and promoting sustainable energy through public awareness programmes and the introduction of energy-saving techniques.

FINANCE

UNDP and its various funds and programmes (see below) are financed by the voluntary contributions of members of the United Nations and the Programme's participating agencies. Voluntary contributions pledged for 1993 amounted to US $1,426m. (of which $376m. was cost-sharing by recipient governments. In 1993 total project expenditure amounted to $1,017m.

In UNDP's 1992–96 programme cycle 87% of funds is reserved for countries with per caput GNP of US $750 or less, and 58% of the resources available is devoted to 45 of the world's poorest developing countries. In June 1993 UNDP's Governing Council approved a revised budget of $609.6m. for the two years 1992–93, and a budget of $628.4m. for 1994–95.

PUBLICATIONS

Annual Report.

Human Development Report (annually).

Update (every 2 weeks).

Feedback (monthly).

Choices (quarterly).

Co-operation South (quarterly).

Source (quarterly).

Associated Funds and Programmes

UNDP is the central funding, planning and co-ordinating body for technical co-operation within the UN. Associated programmes,

financed separately by means of voluntary contributions, provide specific services through the UNDP network. Contributions to UNDP-administered funds in 1993 totalled US $69.2m. Expenditure on projects carried out under the aegis of these funds and programmes amounted to $173.4m. in 1993, of which 11.5% was for Arab states.

UNITED NATIONS CAPITAL DEVELOPMENT FUND—UNCDF

The Fund was established in 1966 and became fully operational in 1974. It assists developing countries by supplementing existing sources of capital assistance by means of grants and loans on concessionary terms. Rapid assistance is available to governments for small-scale projects directly and immediately benefiting the low-income groups who have not benefited from earlier development efforts. Assistance may be given to any of the member states of the UN system, and is not necessarily limited to specific projects. The Fund is mainly used for the benefit of the least-developed countries. In 1992 UNCDF approved $50m. in new projects, and approved almost $30m. in 1993.

Examples of projects financed by UNCDF include: creation of 'revolving funds' for village co-operatives to obtain supplies of seeds and fertilizers; credit for low-cost housing or small businesses; provision of facilities for irrigation, drinking-water and food storage; construction of roads, schools and health centres; and reafforestation of land.

Executive-Secretary: JULES FRIPPIAT (Belgium).

UNITED NATIONS DEVELOPMENT FUND FOR WOMEN—UNIFEM

UNIFEM (formerly the Voluntary Fund for the UN Decade for Women) became an associated fund of UNDP in 1985. Its purpose is to involve women in development and to support innovative activities benefiting, in particular, women on low incomes, e.g. credit funds, small-scale group enterprises to raise incomes, and training in labour-saving and fuel-conserving technologies. UNIFEM funded a special advisor representing women's interest at the UN Conference on Environment and Development held in June 1992. Pledges for 1992 amounted to US $10.5m.

Director: NOELEEN HEYZER.

UNITED NATIONS FUND FOR SCIENCE AND TECHNOLOGY FOR DEVELOPMENT—UNFSTD

UNFSTD was established in 1982 to help developing countries make use of the latest advances in science and technology. Advisory services and the exchange of information are its principal activities, including a 'Transfer of Knowledge through Expatriate Nationals' programme, whereby expatriates volunteer to return to their countries of origin for short-term consultancy assignments. By the end of 1993 more than 4,000 professionals had undertaken such assignments in 39 developing countries. A Technology Rights Bank enables small businesses in developing countries to acquire technical expertise from their counterparts in Europe and North America. In 1992 a pilot 'Technology Incubator Scheme', whereby small and medium-sized businesses share office services, marketing assistance and access to new capital, was implemented in 15 countries. In 1993 a programme for the repair and maintenance of scientific equipment was extended from Africa into Asia.

Director: SHIGEAKI TOMITA (Japan).

UNITED NATIONS REVOLVING FUND FOR NATURAL RESOURCES EXPLORATION—UNRFNRE

UNRFNRE was established in 1973 to provide risk capital to finance exploration for natural resources (particularly minerals) in developing countries and, when discoveries are made, to help to attract investment. The revolving character of the Fund, which distinguishes it from most other UN technical co-operation programmes, lies in the undertaking of contributing governments to make replenishment contributions to the Fund when the projects it finances lead to commercial production. Since its inception UNRFNRE has made 11 significant mineral discoveries in 33 projects it has financed and executed. Contributions pledged to the Fund amounted to US $3.3m. in 1992.

Director: SHIGEAKI TOMITA (Japan).

UNITED NATIONS SUDANO-SAHELIAN OFFICE—UNSO

Established in 1973, UNSO assists 23 countries across the Sudano-Sahelian belt of Africa in combating drought and desertification. In 1992 UNSO approved 14 new projects concerned with the sustainable management of natural resources. Ongoing activities included the provision of tree seedlings, and land rehabilitation. Special emphasis is given to strengthening the environmental planning and management capacities of national institutions.

UNSO has drafted a desertification strategy for UNDP, and is supporting negotiations for an international convention on desertification.

UN Sahelian Regional Office: 14 ave Dimdolobsom, BP 366, Ouagadougou, Burkina Faso; tel. 30-63-35; telex 5262; fax 31-05-81.

Director: PETER BRANNER.

UNITED NATIONS VOLUNTEERS—UNV

The United Nations Volunteers is an important source of middle-level skills for the UN development system, supplied at modest cost, particularly in the least-developed countries. Volunteers expand the scope of UNDP project activities by supplementing the work of international and host country experts and by extending the influence of projects to local community levels. UNV also supports technical co-operation within and among the developing countries by encouraging volunteers from the countries themselves and by forming regional exchange teams made up of such volunteers. In 1993 UNV was involved in areas such as peace-building, elections, human rights and community-based environmental programmes, in addition to development activities. The largest single deployment of volunteers in the programme's history, amounting to some 671, served in Cambodia in 1993 to assist in the preparations for democratic elections.

In 1993 3,563 volunteers from both developed and developing nations served in 134 countries.

Executive Co-ordinator: BRENDA MCSWEENEY.

United Nations High Commissioner for Refugees—UNHCR

Address: CP 2500, 1211 Geneva 2 dépôt, Switzerland.
Telephone: (22) 7398111; **telex:** 415740; **fax:** (22) 7319546.

The Office of the High Commissioner was established in 1951 to provide international protection for refugees and to seek durable solutions to their problems.

Organization

(September 1994)

HIGH COMMISSIONER

The High Commissioner is elected by the United Nations General Assembly on the nomination of the Secretary-General, and is responsible to the General Assembly and to the UN Economic and Social Council (ECOSOC).

High Commissioner: SADAKO OGATA (Japan).
Deputy High Commissioner: GERALD WALZER (Austria).

EXECUTIVE COMMITTEE

The Executive Committee of the High Commissioner's Programme, established by ECOSOC, gives the High Commissioner policy directives in respect of material assistance programmes and advice in the field of international protection. It meets once a year in Geneva. It includes representatives of 46 states, both members and non-members of the UN.

ADMINISTRATION

Headquarters includes the High Commissioner's Office, the Division of International Protection, and five Regional Bureaux (Africa; Asia and Oceania; Europe; the Americas; South-West Asia, the Middle East and North Africa). In 1993 the High Commissioner had some 193 field offices.

Director of Regional Bureau for Asia and Oceania: WERNER BLATTER.

Offices in the Far East and Australasia: 9 Terrigal Crescent, O'Malley, ACT 2606, Australia; tel. (6) 290-1355; telex 61741; fax (6) 290-1315; Shin Aoyama Bldg, Nishikan, 19th Floor, 1-1-1, Minami Aoyama, Minato-ku, Tokyo 107, Japan; tel. (3) 3475-1615; telex 34181.

Activities

The competence of the High Commissioner extends to any person who, owing to well-founded fear of being persecuted for reasons of race, religion, nationality or political opinion, is outside the country of his or her nationality and is unable or, owing to such fear or for reasons other than personal convenience, remains unwilling to accept the protection of that country; or who, not having a nationality and being outside the country of former habitual residence, is unable or, owing to such fear or for reasons other than personal convenience, is unwilling to return to it. Refugees meeting these criteria are entitled to the protection of the Office of the High Commissioner irrespective of their geographical location. Refugees who are assisted by other United Nations agencies, or who have the same rights or obligations as nationals of their country of residence, are outside the mandate of UNHCR.

INTERNATIONAL PROTECTION

As laid down in the Statute of the Office, one of the two primary functions of UNHCR is to extend international protection to refugees. In the exercise of this function UNHCR seeks to ensure that refugees and asylum-seekers are protected against *refoulement* (forcible return), that they receive asylum, and that they are treated according to internationally recognized standards of treatment. UNHCR pursues these objectives by a variety of means which include promoting the conclusion and ratification by states of international conventions for the protection of refugees, particularly the 1951 UN Convention relating to the Status of Refugees, extended by a Protocol adopted in 1967. The Convention defines the rights and duties of refugees and contains provisions dealing with a variety of matters which affect their day-to-day lives. By mid-1994 127 states had acceded to either the Convention or the Protocol, or both.

Palestine refugees in the region are under the care of UNRWA (q.v.).

MATERIAL ASSISTANCE TO REFUGEES

Emergency relief is provided to refugees when food supplies, medical aid or other forms of assistance are required on a large scale at short notice. Other members of the UN system, as well as inter-governmental and non-governmental organizations, co-operate closely with UNHCR in this field.

Even in the more stable refugee situations, UNHCR is often called upon to provide material assistance beyond the initial emergency phase, while permanent solutions are being sought. This assistance can take various forms, including the provision of food, shelter, medical care and essential supplies. Also covered in many instances are basic services, including education and counselling. Whenever possible, measures of this kind are accompanied by efforts to encourage maximum levels of self-reliance among the refugee population.

As far as possible, assistance is geared towards the identification and implementation of durable solutions to refugee problems—this being the second statutory responsibility of UNHCR. Such solutions generally take one of three forms: voluntary repatriation, local integration and resettlement. Where voluntary repatriation is feasible, the Office assists refugees to overcome obstacles preventing their return to their country of origin. This may be done through negotiations with governments involved, or by providing funds either for the physical movement of refugees or for the rehabilitation of returnees once back in their own country.

When voluntary repatriation is not feasible, efforts are made to assist refugees to integrate locally and to become self-supporting in their countries of asylum. In cases where resettlement through emigration is the only viable solution to a refugee problem, UNHCR negotiates with governments in an endeavour to obtain resettlement opportunities, to encourage liberalization of admission criteria and to draw up special immigration schemes.

From 1974 onwards UNHCR acted as co-ordinator of the UN Humanitarian Programme of Assistance for Cyprus, assisting some 250,000 displaced persons on the island. An estimated $9.5m. was allocated to Cyprus for 1988.

UNHCR continues to co-ordinate humanitarian assistance for Sahrawis in camps in the Tindouf area of Algeria; there were 165,000 Sahrawis registered as refugees in Algeria in December 1993, of whom about one-half were being assisted by UNHCR.

From 1979, as a result of civil strife in Afghanistan, there was a massive movement of refugees from that country into Pakistan and Iran creating the world's largest refugee population of approximately 4.5m. people. In 1988 UNHCR allocated $60.8m. of assistance for refugees in Pakistan and $22.4m. to help those in Iran. Following the signing in April 1988 of an agreement on the withdrawal of Soviet troops from Afghanistan, and on the voluntary repatriation of refugees, UNHCR agreed to provide assistance in the repatriation programme (in co-operation with the office of the UN Co-ordinator for Humanitarian and Economic Assistance to Afghanistan), both in ensuring the rights of the returning population and in providing material assistance such as transport, immunization, and supplies of food and other essentials.

In April 1992, following the establishment of a new government in Afghanistan, refugees began to return in substantial numbers (hitherto only a small number had returned). By March 1993 it was estimated that 2m. Afghans had returned to their country—some 200,000 from Iran and 1.8m. from Pakistan, mostly without assistance. In June 1992 the UN Secretary-General appealed for US $180m. in aid for Afghanistan, of which $52.8m. was to be allocated to UNHCR's programme to assist the returnees. UNHCR was responsible for providing returnees with a repatriation allowance, but a poor response to the UN's appeal for international aid resulted in UNHCR's assistance being reduced to a minimum. In March 1994 renewed fighting caused a further large-scale movement of displaced persons, for which UNHCR estimated it needed $6m. to finance emergency relief operations.

In March–May 1991, following the war against Iraq by a multinational force, and the subsequent Iraqi suppression of resistance in Kurdish areas in the north of the country, there was massive movement of mainly Kurdish refugees into Iran and Turkey. In April the UN appealed for US $400m. in humanitarian assistance for the region of the Persian (Arabian) Gulf, of which $239m. was to be allocated to UNHCR for refugees in Turkey and Iran. UNHCR was designated the principal UN agency to deal with the crisis. By mid-May there were some 1.4m. refugees from Iraq in Iran, and some 500,000 in Turkey. In late May the refugees began to return to Iraq in huge numbers and UNHCR assisted in their repatriation, establishing relief stations along their routes from Iran and Turkey. UNHCR provided winter shelter for those refugees encamped in northern Iraq. Following the war to liberate Kuwait UNHCR gave protection and assistance to Iraqis, Bidoons (stateless people) and Palestinians who were forced to leave that country.

At the end of December 1993 Iran was hosting approximately 2.5m. refugees, of whom 1.85m. were from Afghanistan and 645,000 were Iraqis.

In June 1992 people fleeing the civil war and famine in Somalia began arriving in Yemen in large numbers. UNHCR set up camps to accommodate the refugees, providing them with shelter, food, water and sanitation. By December 1993 UNHCR estimated there were still over 50,000 Somali refugees in Yemen.

FINANCE

UNHCR administrative expenditure is financed under the United Nations regular budget, under which it was allocated US $20.5m. for 1993. General Programmes of material assistance are financed from voluntary contributions made by governments, and also from non-governmental sources. In addition, UNHCR undertakes a number of Special Programmes, as requested by the UN General Assembly, the Secretary-General of the UN or a member state, to assist returnees and, in some cases, displaced persons. Total contributions in 1993 were estimated to amount to more than $1,000m.

UNHCR Expenditure (US $'000)

Source	1992	1993	1994*
UN Regular Budget . .	21.2	20.5	21.0
Voluntary funds:			
General Programmes .	382.1	392.4	418.5
Special Programmes .	689.3	914.6	399.2
Total	1,092.6	1,327.7	838.7

*Projected figures.

In 1993 UNHCR expenditure for South-West Asia, North Africa and the Middle East (including Mauritania and Pakistan) amounted to US $115.4m. (about 9% of total expenditure world-wide).

PUBLICATIONS

Refugees (quarterly, in English, French, German, Italian, Japanese and Spanish).

UNHCR Handbook for Emergencies.

Refugee Abstracts.

United Nations Peace-keeping Operations

Address: Department of Peace-keeping Operations, Room S-3727-B, United Nations, New York, NY 10017, USA.

Telephone: (212) 963-5055; **telex:** 420544; **fax:** (212) 963-4879.

United Nations peace-keeping operations have been conceived as instruments of conflict control. Each operation has been established with a specific mandate. The UN has used these operations in various conflicts, with the consent of the parties involved, to maintain peaceful conditions, without prejudice to the positions or claims of parties, in order to facilitate the search for political settlements through peaceful means such as mediation and the good offices of the Secretary-General. United Nations peace-keeping operations fall into two categories: peace-keeping forces and observer missions.

Peace-keeping forces are composed of contingents of lightly-armed troops, made available by member states. These forces assist in preventing the recurrence of fighting, restoring and maintaining peace, and promoting a return to normal conditions. To this end, peace-keeping forces are authorized as necessary to undertake negotiations, persuasion, observation and fact-finding. They run patrols and interpose physically between the opposing parties. Peace-keeping forces are permitted to use their weapons only in self-defence.

Military observer missions are composed of officers (usually unarmed), who are made available, on the Secretary-General's request, by member states. A mission's function is to observe and report to the Secretary-General (who in turn informs the UN Security Council) on the maintenance of a cease-fire, to investigate violations and to do what it can to improve the situation.

Peace-keeping forces and observer missions must at all times maintain complete impartiality and avoid any action that might affect the claims or positions of the parties.

The UN's peace-keeping forces and observer missions are financed in most cases by assessed contributions from member states of the organization. These operations have suffered increasingly from underfunding, with member states delaying payment. At 31 January 1994 outstanding assessed contributions to the peace-keeping budget amounted to US $1,100m.

UNITED NATIONS TRUCE SUPERVISION ORGANIZATION—UNTSO

Headquarters: Government House, Jerusalem.

Officer-in-Charge: Col. JOSEPH BUJOLD (Canada).

UNTSO was established initially to supervise the truce called by the UN Security Council in Palestine in May 1948 and has assisted in the application of the 1949 Armistice Agreements. Its activities have evolved over the years, in response to developments in the Middle East and in accordance with the relevant resolutions of the Security Council.

UNTSO observers assist the UN peace-keeping forces in the Middle East (see below), UNIFIL and UNDOF. UNTSO maintains a presence in Egypt, organized as Observer Group Egypt which has its headquarters at Ismailia, in the area of the Suez canal, and conducts patrols and operates outposts in the Sinai region. There is also a small detachment of observers in Beirut, Lebanon and liaison offices in Amman, Jordan and Gaza. UNTSO observers have been available at short notice to form the nucleus of other peace-keeping operations.

The authorized strength of UNTSO at 30 April 1994 was 220 military observers from 19 countries. UNTSO expenditures are covered by the regular budget of the United Nations. The annual cost of the operation is approximately US $30m.

UNITED NATIONS DISENGAGEMENT OBSERVER FORCE—UNDOF

Headquarters: Damascus, Syria.

Commander: Maj.-Gen. ROMAN MISZTAL (Poland).

UNDOF was established for an initial period of six months by a UN Security Council resolution in May 1974, following the signature in Geneva of a disengagement agreement between Syrian and Israeli forces. The mandate has since been extended by successive resolutions. The initial task of the Force was to take over territory evacuated in stages by the Israeli troops, in accordance with the disengagement agreement, to hand over territory to Syrian troops, and to establish an area of separation on the Golan Heights.

UNDOF continues to monitor the area of separation; it carries out inspections of the areas of limited armaments and forces; uses its best efforts to maintain the ceasefire; and undertakes activities of a humanitarian nature, such as arranging the transfer of prisoners and war-dead between Syria and Israel. The Force operates exclusively on Syrian territory.

At 30 April 1994 the Force comprised 1,035 troops from Austria, Canada, Finland and Poland, assisted by the military observers of UNTSO's Observer Group Golan. Further UNTSO military observers assist UNDOF in the performance of its tasks, as required. The annual cost to the United Nations of the operation is approximately US $35m.

UNITED NATIONS INTERIM FORCE IN LEBANON—UNIFIL

Headquarters: Naqoura, Lebanon.

Commander: Maj.-Gen. TROND FURUHOVDE (Norway).

UNIFIL was established by a UN Security Council resolution in March 1978. The mandate of the force is to confirm the withdrawal of Israeli forces from southern Lebanon, to restore international peace and security, and to assist the Government of Lebanon in ensuring the return of its effective authority in the area. UNIFIL has also extended humanitarian assistance to the population of the area, particularly since the second Israeli invasion of Lebanon in 1982. By mid-1993 UNIFIL had been unable to fulfil its mandate, with Israel continuing to occupy an area of southern Lebanon. In April 1992, however, in accordance with its mandate, UNIFIL completed the transfer of part of its zone of operations to the control of the Lebanese army. UNIFIL maintains checkpoints and observation posts, which are designed to monitor movement on the principal roads and to deter hostilities. UNIFIL provides civilians with food, water, medical supplies, fuel and escorts to farmers. UNIFIL medical centres and mobile teams provide care to an average 2,800 civilian patients each month, and a field dental programme has been established.

At 30 April 1994 the Force comprised 5,313 troops from nine countries. A group of 59 UNTSO military observers (the Observer Group, Lebanon), and some 540 international and local civilian staff assist UNIFIL in the performance of its tasks.

The annual cost to the United Nations of the operation is approximately US $138m. Owing to the failure of some states to pay their assessed contributions, UNIFIL had an accumulated financial shortfall of $216m. at the end of April 1994.

UNITED NATIONS IRAQ-KUWAIT OBSERVATION MISSION—UNIKOM

Headquarters: Umm Qasr, Kuwait.

Commander: Maj.-Gen. KRISHNA NARAYAN SINGH THAPA (Nepal).

UNIKOM was established by a UN Security Council resolution (initially for a six-month period) in April 1991, to monitor a 200-km demilitarized zone along the border between Iraq and Kuwait. The task of the mission was to deter violations of the border, to monitor the Khawr 'Abd Allah waterway between Iraq and Kuwait, and to prevent military activity within the zone. UNIKOM provides technical support to other UN operations in the area, particularly the Iraq–Kuwait Boundary Demarcation Commission, and has assisted with the relocation of Iraqi citizens from Kuwait, which was completed in February 1994. In early February 1993 the Security Council adopted a resolution to strengthen UNIKOM, following incursions into Kuwaiti territory by Iraq, and replace the unarmed observer mission by a military force. At 30 April 1994 UNIKOM comprised 896 troops from Argentina, Austria, Bangladesh and Denmark, in addition to 251 observers from 33 countries.

The annual cost to the United Nations of the reinforced Mission is approximately US $70m. With effect from 1 November 1993 two-thirds of the total cost were to be paid by the Government of Kuwait.

UNITED NATIONS MISSION FOR THE REFERENDUM IN WESTERN SAHARA— MINURSO

Headquarters: Laayoune, Western Sahara.

Special Representative of the UN Secretary-General: SAHABZADA YAQUB KHAN (Pakistan).

Commander: Brig.-Gen. ANDRÉ VAN BAELEN (Belgium).

In April 1991 the UN Security Council endorsed the establishment of MINURSO to monitor a cease-fire and a referendum on self-determination in the disputed territory of Western Sahara (claimed by Morocco). The task of the mission was to verify a cease-fire (which came into effect in September 1991), to secure the release of all Western Saharan political prisoners, to implement a programme of repatriation of Western Saharan refugees (in co-ordination with UNHCR), and to organize a referendum on the future of the territory. The referendum, originally envisaged for January 1992 was, however, postponed indefinitely. In 1992–93 the Secretary-General's Special Representative organized negotiations between the Frente Popular para la Liberación de Saguia el Hamra y Rio de Oro (Frente Polisario) and the Moroccan Government, who were in serious disagreement regarding criteria for eligibility to vote in the referendum. In early June 1993 the UN Secretary-General proposed a compromise solution on voter eligibility based on the results of the 1974 census. An Identification Commission was established in April 1993 to begin the process of voter registration. In November preliminary application forms were distributed and registration offices were opened within the territory and in a few locations outside the territory inhabited by Sahrawis. The failure to achieve an agreement between the Moroccan Government and the Frente Polisario delayed the registration process, however, and in March 1994 the Security Council decided that the Identification Commission should proceed with its work and the UN continued its efforts to obtain the co-operation of the two parties based on the Secretary-General's compromise proposal. The Council resolved to consider the future of MINURSO if the referendum had not been conducted by the end of 1994. In mid-1994 the referendum was scheduled to be held on 14 February 1995.

The Mission has headquarters in the north and south of the territory, and there is a liaison office in Tindouf, Algeria, in order to maintain contact with Polisario (which is based in Algeria) and the Algerian Government.

At 30 April 1994 MINURSO comprised 224 military observers, 97 military support personnel, 26 police officers and 179 international and local civilian staff. The annual cost to the United Nations of the Mission is approximately US $40m. At the end of April 1994 $20m. remained to be paid to MINURSO's account.

UNITED NATIONS PEACE-KEEPING FORCE IN CYPRUS—UNFICYP

Headquarters: Nicosia, Cyprus.

Special Representative of the UN Secretary-General: JOE CLARK (Canada).

Commander: Maj.-Gen. MICHAEL FINBARR MINEHANE (Ireland).

UNFICYP was established in March 1964 by a UN Security Council resolution (for a three-month period, subsequently extended) to prevent a recurrence of fighting between the Greek and Turkish Cypriot communities, and to contribute to the maintenance of law and order and a return to normal conditions. The Force controls a 180-km buffer zone, established (following the Turkish intervention in 1974) between the cease-fire lines of the Turkish forces and the Cyprus National Guard. The Force also performs humanitarian functions, such as facilitating the supply of electricity and water across the cease-fire lines, and providing emergency medical services.

In September 1992 the troop-providing countries announced that they were to reduce substantially the number of troops in UNFICYP, as a result of lack of financing, as well as a more pressing need for military personnel in other peace-keeping operations. This entailed a gradual reduction in UNFICYP personnel from 2,078 in November 1992 to 1,235 personnel at 30 April 1994. In June 1993 the Security Council approved a resolution that the costs of the Force not covered by voluntary contributions be treated as expenses of the United Nations to be financed by assessed contributions from member states. The annual cost to the United Nations of maintaining the Force is estimated at US $47m. By May 1994 the account for voluntary contributions to finance the Force prior to June 1993 had an accumulated deficit of $194m.

United Nations Relief and Works Agency for Palestine Refugees in the Near East—UNRWA

Addresses: Vienna International Centre, POB 700, 1400 Vienna, Austria;
Bayader Wadi Seer, POB 484, Amman, Jordan.

Telephone (Vienna): (1) 211-31-4530; **telex:** 135310; **fax:** (1) 23-72-83.

Telephone (Amman): (6) 826171; **telex:** 21170; **fax:** (6) 826179.

UNRWA began operations in 1950 to provide relief, health, education and welfare services for Palestine refugees in the Near East.

Organization

(August 1994)

UNRWA employs an international staff of about 180 and more than 20,000 local staff, mainly Palestine refugees. The Commissioner-General is appointed by the UN General Assembly, is the head of all UNRWA operations and is assisted by an Advisory Commission consisting of representatives of the governments of:

Belgium	Jordan	Turkey
Egypt	Lebanon	United Kingdom
France	Syria	USA
Japan		

Commissioner-General: ILTER TÜRKMEN (Turkey).

Co-ordinator of Headquarters Branch (Jordan): ELE J. SAAF.

FIELD OFFICES

Each field office is headed by a director and has departments responsible for education, health and relief and social services programmes, finance, administration, supply and transport, legal affairs and public information.

Gaza: POB 61, Gaza; tel. (7) 822660; telex 25461; fax (7) 821765.

Jordan: Al Zubeidi Bldg, Shmeisani, POB 484, Amman; tel. (6) 607194; telex 23402; fax (6) 685476.

Lebanon: POB 947, Beirut; tel. (1) 832811; telex 1502564; fax (2124) 781686.

Syria: POB 4313, Damascus; tel. (11) 3327514; telex 412006; fax (11) 3327513.

West Bank: Sheik Jarrah Qtr, POB 19149, Jerusalem; tel. (2) 890400; telex 26194; fax (2) 322714.

LIAISON OFFICES

Egypt: 2 Dar-el-Shifa St, Garden City, POB 277, Cairo; tel. (2) 354-8502; telex 94035; fax (2) 354-8504.

United States: Room DC 2-0550, United Nations, New York, NY 10017; tel. (212) 963-2255; telex 422311; fax (212) 935-7899.

Activities

SERVICES FOR PALESTINE REFUGEES

Since 1950 UNRWA has provided relief, health and education services for the needy among the Palestine refugees in Lebanon, Syria, Jordan, the West Bank and the Gaza Strip. For UNRWA's purposes, a Palestine refugee is one whose normal residence was in Palestine for a minimum of two years before the 1948 conflict and who, as a result of the Arab–Israeli hostilities, lost his or her home and means of livelihood. To be eligible for assistance, a refugee must reside in one of the five areas in which UNRWA operates and be in need. A refugee's children and grandchildren who fulfil certain criteria are also eligible for UNRWA assistance. At December 1993 UNRWA was providing essential services to 2,913,237 refugees. Of these an estimated 972,418 (approximately 33%) were living in 59 camps serviced by the Agency, while the remaining refugees had settled in the towns and villages already existing.

UNRWA's three principal areas of activity are education; health services; and relief and social services. More than 81% of the Agency's 1994/95 budget is devoted to these three operational programmes.

Education (under the technical supervision of UNESCO) accounts for 47% of UNRWA's 1994–95 budget. In the 1993/94 school year there were 398,648 pupils in 641 UNRWA schools (77 schools in Lebanon, 109 in Syria, 201 in Jordan, 100 on the West Bank and 154 in the Gaza Strip), and 12,158 staff. At 80% of the schools, morning and afternoon shifts are held in order to accommodate more pupils. UNRWA also operates eight vocational and teacher-training centres with 5,646 places. UNRWA awarded 795 scholarships for study at Arab universities in 1993/94. Technical co-operation for the Agency's education programme is provided by UNESCO.

Health services account for some 21% of UNRWA's 1994–95 budget. At December 1993 there were 120 health units, 105 diabetes clinics, 68 dental clinics and 108 family planning clinics. Nearly 6m. visits by patients were made to UNRWA medical units during 1993. UNRWA also operates a supplementary feeding programme, mainly for children, to combat malnutrition. Technical assistance for the health programme is provided by WHO.

Relief and social services account for over 13% of UNRWA's budget for 1994–95. These services comprise the distribution of food rations, the provision of emergency shelter and the organization of welfare programmes for about 167,000 of the poorest refugees (at December 1993 5.7% of the total registered refugee population was classified as eligible to receive special hardship assistance). UNRWA's social services programme operates 71 women's centres, serving more than 5,000 women, and 18 community-based rehabilitation centres for disabled people.

In order to encourage Palestinian self-reliance the Agency issues grants to ailing businesses and loans to families who qualify as special hardship cases. Between 1983 and early 1993 608 such grants and loans were made. In 1991 UNRWA launched an income generation programme, which was designed to combat rising unemployment, particularly in the occupied territories. By 31 January 1994 203 loans with a total estimated value of US $3.1m. had been issued to new and existing Palestinian-owned enterprises.

AID TO DISPLACED PERSONS

After the renewal of Arab–Israeli hostilities in the Middle East in June 1967, hundreds of thousands of people fled from the fighting and from Israeli-occupied areas to east Jordan, Syria and Egypt. UNRWA provided emergency relief for displaced refugees and was additionally empowered by a UN General Assembly resolution to provide 'humanitarian assistance, as far as practicable, on an emergency basis and as a temporary measure' for those persons other than Palestine refugees who were newly displaced and in urgent need. In practice, UNRWA lacked the funds to aid the other displaced persons and the main burden of supporting them devolved on the Arab governments concerned. The Agency, as requested by the Government of Jordan in 1967 and on that Government's behalf, distributes rations to displaced persons in Jordan who are not registered refugees of 1948.

RECENT EMERGENCIES

Since 1982 UNRWA has run a specially-funded operation in Lebanon aimed at assisting refugees displaced by the continued civil conflict. In late 1986 and early 1987 fighting caused much destruction to Palestinian housing and UNRWA facilities in Lebanon and an emergency relief operation was mounted.

Following the start of the Palestinian *intifada* (uprising) in December 1987 UNRWA faced increasing problems in the Israeli-occupied territories of the West Bank and the Gaza Strip. Schools in the West Bank were closed for extended periods in 1988–89, and UNRWA services in both territories were frequently interrupted as curfews were imposed on camps. Since the start of the *intifada* UNRWA has provided expanded medical aid and relief in the West Bank and Gaza Strip.

In January 1991 (following the outbreak of war between Iraq and a multinational force whose aim was to enforce the withdrawal of Iraqi forces from Kuwait) the Israeli authorities imposed a curfew on Palestinians in the Israeli-occupied territories, and in February UNRWA began an emergency programme of food distribution to Palestinians who had thereby been prevented from earning a living. Following the Gulf War, Jordan absorbed over 300,000 people fleeing Kuwait and other Gulf countries. Many of these people are eligible for UNRWA services.

In September 1992 an UNRWA mission was sent to Kuwait, following allegations of abuses of human rights perpetrated by the Kuwaiti authorities against Palestinian refugees living there. The mission was, however, limited to assessing the number of Palestinians from the Gaza Strip in Kuwait, who had been unable to obtain asylum in Jordan, since Jordan did not recognize Gazan identity documents.

Following the signing of the Declaration of Principles by the Palestine Liberation Organization and the Israeli Government in September 1993, UNRWA initiated a Peace Implementation Programme (PIP) to improve services and infrastructure for Palestinian refugees. By April 1994 UNRWA had identified projects totalling US $165m., of which $100m. was to be spent in the Gaza Strip and West Bank, and $65m. on projects to improve facilities and services for refugees in Jordan, Lebanon and Syria. By April pledged funds for the Programme amounted to more than $81m. and work had begun on the most urgent projects, including the improvement of shelters and education facilities.

FINANCE

For the most part, UNRWA's income is composed of voluntary contributions, almost entirely from governments and the European Union, the remainder being provided by non-governmental organizations, business corporations and private sources.

As of January 1992 UNRWA adopted a biennial budgetary cycle. The budget for 1994–95 amounted to US $632.3m., of which $552.8m. was to be in cash and $79.5m. in kind. At the start of

1994 UNRWA had a financial deficit of more than $21m., with some essential services under threat.

STATISTICS
Refugees Registered with UNRWA (20 April 1994)

Jordan	1,176,208
Gaza Strip	336,669
West Bank	324,250
Lebanon	497,958
Syria	635,099
Total	**2,970,184**

PUBLICATIONS
Annual Report of the Commissioner-General of UNRWA.
Palestine Refugees Today—the UNRWA Newsletter (2 a year).
UNRWA—An Investment in People (every 2 years).
UNRWA News (fortnightly).
UNRWA Accounts Summary (annually).
Catalogues of publications and audio-visual materials.

Food and Agriculture Organization—FAO

Address: Viale delle Terme di Caracalla, 00100 Rome, Italy.
Telephone: (6) 52251; **telex:** 625852; **fax:** (6) 5225-5155.
FAO, the first specialized agency of the UN to be founded after World War II, was established in Quebec, Canada, in October 1945. The Organization combats malnutrition and hunger and serves as a co-ordinating agency for development programmes in the whole range of food and agriculture, including forestry and fisheries. It helps developing countries to promote educational and training facilities and institution-building.

Organization
(August 1994)

CONFERENCE

The governing body is the FAO Conference of member nations. It meets every two years, formulates policy, determines the Organization's programme and budget on a biennial basis, and elects new members. It also elects the Director-General of the Secretariat and the independent chairman of the Council. Every second year, FAO also holds conferences in each of its five regions (designated the Near East, Asia and the Pacific, Africa, Latin America and the Caribbean, and Europe).

COUNCIL

The FAO Council is composed of representatives of 49 member nations, elected by the Conference for staggered three-year terms. It is the interim governing body of FAO between sessions of the Conference. The most important standing Committees of the Council are: the Finance and Programme Committees, the Committee on Commodity Problems, the Committee on Fisheries, the Committee on Agriculture and the Committee on Forestry.

SECRETARIAT

The total number of staff at FAO headquarters in December 1992 was 3,147, while staff in field, regional and country offices numbered 2,717; there were also 66 associate experts at headquarters and 206 in field, regional and country offices. Work is supervised by the following Departments: Administration and Finance; General Affairs and Information; Economic and Social Policy; Agriculture; Forestry; Fisheries; and Development.
Director-General: JACQUES DIOUF (Senegal).

REGIONAL OFFICE

Regional Office for the Near East: 11 el-Eslah el-Zerai St, POB 2223, Dokki, Giza, Cairo, Egypt; tel. (2) 702229; telex 21055; fax (2) 3495981; Regional Rep. ATIF Y. BUKHARI.

Activities

FAO aims to raise levels of nutrition and standards of living, by improving the production and distribution of food and other

commodities derived from farms, fisheries and forests. Under FAO's medium-term plan for 1992–97 its work covers five basic areas: advising governments on policy and planning; training and technical assistance; promotion of sustainable development; enhancing the economic status of women; and promotion of economic and technical co-operation between developing countries. In June 1994 FAO emphasized the following two programmes which were to be a priority: the promotion of increased and sustainable food production in 78 low-income food deficit countries; the creation of an emergency prevention system for a rapid response to transboundary animal and plant pests and diseases.

AGRICULTURE

FAO's Field Programme provides training and technical assistance to enable small farmers to increase crop production, by a number of methods, including improved seeds and fertilizer use, soil conservation and reforestation, better water resource management, upgrading storage facilities, and improvements in processing and marketing. Governments are advised on the conservation of genetic resources, on improving the supply of seeds, and on crop protection: animal and plant gene banks are maintained.

Examples of FAO crop improvement activities under way in the region during the 1980s (usually in the form of technical assistance in conjunction with UNDP, financed by donor governments or international organizations) included the improvement of wine and grape production in Tunisia; quality testing for cotton in Egypt; and a seed production and certification project in Sudan; there were also regional projects for the improvement of olive oil and date production. The Seed Exchange and Information Centre, based in Rome, helps to locate and distribute seed samples for trial and evaluation in developing countries. In 1992 20,000 samples were dispatched to more than 100 developing countries.

Plant protection, weed control and animal health programmes form an important part of FAO's work as farming methods become more intensive, and pests more resistant to control methods. In 1985 the FAO Conference approved an International Code of Conduct on the Distribution and Use of Pesticides, and in 1989 adopted an additional clause concerning 'Prior Informed Consent', whereby international shipments of newly banned or restricted pesticides should not proceed without the agreement of importing countries. Under the clause FAO aims to inform governments about the hazards of toxic chemicals and to encourage them to take proper measures to curb trade in highly toxic agrochemicals, while keeping the pesticides industry informed of control actions. In accordance with its efforts to reduce over-reliance on pesticides and to encourage the use of biological control methods and natural predators to avert pests, FAO is expanding its Integrated Pest Management (IPM), which began in Asia in 1988, by introducing IPM principles into Africa and the Near East. FAO's Joint Division with the International Atomic Energy Agency (IAEA), tests controlled-release formulas of pesticides and herbicides that can limit the amount of agrochemicals needed to protect crops. The Joint FAO-IAEA Division is engaged in exploring biotechnologies and in developing non-toxic fertilizers (especially those that are locally available) and improved strains of food crops (especially from indigenous varieties). In animal production and health, the Joint

Division has developed progesterone-measuring and disease-diagnostic kits, thousands of which are delivered to developing countries every year. In December 1990–October 1991 FAO undertook a campaign to eradicate an infestation of screw-worm in Libya (discovered in 1989) using the 'sterile insect technique'. By late 1991 the screw-worm's successful eradication was announced, signalling that a potentially catastrophic spread of the insect to the rest of Africa, the Middle East and southern Europe had been averted. In 1986 FAO set up the Emergency Centre for Locust Operations (ECLO) to counter the threat to much of Africa posed by enormous numbers of five separate species of grasshoppers and locusts. ECLO was reactivated in September 1992, following outbreaks of the 'migratory locust' in Madagascar and in countries on either side of the Red Sea, to act as co-ordinator for efforts to combat the pest. In January 1994 FAO issued an appeal for international assitance to protect against the reappearance of locust infestation in north-west Africa and requested funds totalling US \$4.5m. to maintain surveillance in that region.

FAO's work on soil conservation includes erosion control and the reclamation of degraded land. The fertilizer programme demonstrates to farmers and government officials the benefits of fertilizers, including locally available organic wastes. FAO also assists in developing water resources and irrigation.

During 1987 a three-year regional project was under way in Algeria, Iraq, Jordan, Morocco, Syria and Tunisia, to increase livestock production and improve the quality of life in pastoral communities.

FISHERIES

FAO's Fisheries Department consists of a multi-disciplinary body of experts who are involved in every aspect of fisheries development from coastal surveys, improved production, processing and storage, to the compilation of statistics, development of computer databases, improvement of fishing gear, institution building and training. In the early 1990s FAO fisheries initiatives included an investigation of the use of selected fishing gear to reduce the incidental catch of non-target fish species, support for aquaculture, the protection and restocking of endangered species, and programmes aimed at supporting women in the fisheries communities of developing countries.

FORESTRY

In collaboration with UNDP, the World Bank and the World Resources Unit, FAO has devised the Tropical Forestry Action Programme (TFAP). The Programme aims to improve the lives of rural people, increase food production, intensify forestry activities and set up interdisciplinary national and regional programmes that both safeguard the forest and make rational use of its resources. Another primary concern of the Forestry Department is the critical fuel wood situation in many developing countries. In 1991 FAO estimated that by 2000 more than one-half of the population of the developing world will face fuel wood shortages and will be caught in a cycle of deforestation, fuel wood scarcity, poverty and malnutrition.

PROCESSING AND MARKETING

An estimated 20% of all food harvested is lost before it can be consumed. FAO helps reduce immediate post-harvest losses, with the introduction of improved processing methods and storage systems. It also advises on the distribution and marketing of agricultural produce and on the selection and preparation of foods for optimum nutrition. Processing and marketing activities form part of wider rural development projects.

ENVIRONMENT

In April 1991 a Conference on Agriculture and the Environment was held in the Netherlands, organized jointly by FAO and the Netherlands Government. The alleviation of poverty was identified as being a major prerequisite for sustainable agricultural production. At the UN Conference on Environment and Development, held in Rio de Janeiro in June 1992, FAO played a leading role in drafting several sections, notably the chapters on sustainable mountain development, sustainable agriculture and rural development and oceans and marine resources, all of which have long been integral parts of FAO programmes.

NUTRITION

In December 1992 an International Conference on Nutrition was held in Rome, administered jointly by FAO and WHO. The Conference approved a World Declaration on nutrition and a Plan of Action, with the aim of eliminating hunger and reducing levels of malnutrition by incorporating nutritional objectives into national development policies and governmental programmes.

FOOD SECURITY

FAO's food security policy aims to encourage the production of adequate food supplies, to maximize stability in the flow of supplies, and to ensure access on the part of those who need them. The Food Security Assistance Scheme, established in 1976, aims to help developing countries in strengthening their food security by setting up food reserves and by developing national and regional early warning systems. The Global Information and Early Warning System (GIEWS) monitors the world food situation and identifies countries threatened by shortages to guide potential donors. An environmental monitoring system, ARTEMIS (Africa Real-Time Environmental Monitoring using Imaging Satellites), installed in 1988, processes data from orbiting and stationary satellites to provide continuous monitoring of rainfall and vegetation conditions across Africa, the Near East and south-west Asia.

FAO INVESTMENT CENTRE

The Investment Centre was established in 1964 to help countries prepare viable investment projects that would attract external financing. By the end of 1992 it had assisted 916 investment projects, which were expected to generate US \$46,900m. of agricultural investment in more than 100 countries. Each year the centre undertakes about 200 missions under its own responsibility, and participates in about 50 missions led by co-operating financial institutions.

EMERGENCY RELIEF

The Office for Special Relief Operations (OSRO) was established in 1973, in response to the disastrous drought in the Sahel in that year. In 1975 the office was expanded to handle such emergencies globally. As well as providing emergency aid, OSRO aims to rehabilitate agricultural production following disasters. Jointly with the United Nations, FAO is responsible for the World Food Programme (q.v.) which provides emergency food supplies, and food aid in support of development projects.

INFORMATION AND RESEARCH

FAO issues regular statistical reports, commodity studies, and technical manuals in local languages (see list of publications below).

General and specialized computer data-bases co-ordinated by FAO contain information on every area of food and agriculture; the Current Agricultural Research Information System (CARIS), for example, enables over 70 countries to exchange information on current research. The International Information System for Agricultural Sciences and Technology (AGRIS) is a co-operative system whereby participating countries (of which there are over 135) give notice of the publication of all literature on agricultural science and technology and may drawn on information provided by other countries. By March 1993 AGRIS had a data-base comprising 1,920,000 titles. Other systems provide information on commodities (ICS), fisheries (ASFIS, GLOBEFISH and FISHDAB), fish-marketing (INFOSAMAK—serving the Middle East only) forest resources (FORIS) and plant genetics (PGRIS). In 1993 FAO awarded priority to its computerized network of Geographic Information Systems (GIS) which assess land and water resources with information on regional climate and population. FAO's Research and Technology Development Division helps to co-ordinate members' research. In mid-1993 FAO sponsored the establishment by 10 countries, including Egypt, Iraq, Syria and Turkey, of an Inter-Regional Co-operative Research Network on Buffalo.

FAO REGIONAL COMMISSIONS

Commission for Controlling the Desert Locust in the Near East: f. 1965 to carry out all possible measures to control plagues of the desert locust within the region and to reduce crop damage. Mems: 13 states.

Commission for Controlling the Desert Locust in North-West Africa: f. 1971 to promote research on control of the desert locust. Mems: 4 states.

General Fisheries Council for the Mediterranean—GFCM: f. 1952 to develop aquatic resources, to encourage and co-ordinate research in the fishing and allied industries, to assemble and publish information, and to recommend the standardization of scientific equipment, techniques and nomenclature. Mems: 19 states.

Near East Forestry Commission: f. 1953 to advise on formulation of forest policy and review and co-ordinate its implementation throughout the region; to exchange information and advise on technical problems. Mems: 20 states.

Near East Regional Commission on Agriculture: f. 1983 to conduct periodic reviews of agricultural problems in the region; to promote policies and regional and national programmes for improving production of crops and livestock; to expand agricultural services and research; to promote the transfer of technology and regional technical co-operation; and to provide guidance on training and manpower development. Mems: 15 states.

Near East Regional Economic and Social Policy Commission: f. 1983 to review developments relating to food, agriculture and food security; to recommend policies on agrarian reform and rural development; to review and exchange information on food and nutrition policies and on agricultural planning; and to compile statistics. Mems: 15 states.

Regional Commission on Land and Water Use in the Near East: f. 1967 to review the current situation with regard to land and water use in the region; to identify the main problems concerning the development of land and water resources which require research and study and to consider other related matters. Mems: 21 states.

FINANCE

FAO's Regular Programme, which is financed by contributions from the member governments, covers the cost of FAO's Secretariat, its Technical Co-operation Programme (TCP) and part of the cost of several special action programmes. The working budget proposed for the two years 1994–95 amounted to US $752m. Much of FAO's Field Programme of technical assistance is funded from extra-budgetary sources. The single largest contributor is the United Nations Development Programme (UNDP), which in 1992 accounted for $136.2m., or 40%, of Field Programme expenditure. Equally important are the trust funds that come mainly from donor countries and international financing institutions. In 1992 they totalled $164.3m., or 49% of Field Programme expenditure. FAO's contribution under the TCP was some $36.1m.

WORLD FOOD PROGRAMME—WFP

Address: Via Cristoforo Colombo 426, 00145 Rome, Italy.

Telephone: (6) 522821; **telex:** 626675; **fax:** (6) 5127400.

WFP is a joint UN-FAO effort to stimulate economic and social development through food aid and to provide emergency relief. It became operational in 1963.

WFP provides food aid to low income, food deficit countries to support economic and social development projects. The food is supplied, for example, as an incentive in development self-help schemes, as part wages in labour-intensive projects of many kinds, particularly in the rural economy, but also in the industrial field, and in support of institutional feeding schemes where the emphasis is mainly on enabling the beneficiaries to have an adequate and balanced diet. One of the criteria for WFP aid to projects is that the recipient country can continue them after the aid has ceased. Priority is given to vulnerable groups such as pregnant women and children. Some WFP projects are intended to alleviate the effects of structural adjustment programmes (particularly programmes which involve reductions in public expenditure and in subsidies for basic foods).

Examples of development projects in the region being supported by WFP in the late 1980s were: reclamation of desert land for agriculture in Egypt (for which WFP provided food aid worth US $48m. in 1980–89); stabilization of sand-dunes and prevention of erosion in Tunisia; road-building, construction of schools, land reclamation and fisheries co-operatives in the People's Democratic Republic of Yemen; and centres for training in crafts for women in Syria.

In the early 1990s there was a substantial shift in the balance between emergency and development assistance provided by WFP, owing to the growing needs of victims of drought and other natural disasters, refugees and displaced persons. WFP provides food supplies mainly from the International Emergency Food Reserve, which it manages. In mid-1991 WFP provided emergency food aid to Iraqi Kurds in Iran who fled Iraq in March–May, in the aftermath of Iraq's defeat by a multinational force. In the latter half of 1991, WFP distributed food to vulnerable people in Iraq, mostly Iraqi Kurds who had returned from Iran and Turkey. In 1992 WFP provided food assistance to Palestinians in the occupied territories of the West Bank and Gaza Strip, where people were suffering great hardship as a result of a severe winter, Israeli-imposed curfews and travel restrictions, and a substantial reduction in aid from Arab countries in the Persian (Arabian) Gulf. Some 1,286 metric tons of food commodities were supplied to hospitals and other institutions, and to Palestinian welfare organizations. In early August 1993 the UN Secretary-General asked FAO and WFP to send immediate food assistance to southern Lebanon to facilitate the return of some 350,000 people displaced by Israeli bombing.

WFP Executive Director: CATHERINE A. BERTINI (USA).

FAO PUBLICATIONS

FAO Annual Review.
Quarterly Bulletin of Statistics.
Food Outlook (monthly).
Production Yearbook.
Yearbook of Fishery Statistics.
Yearbook of Forest Products.
Trade Yearbook.
Fertilizer Yearbook.
Commodity Review and Outlook (annually).
Animal Health Yearbook.
The State of Food and Agriculture (annually).
Technical Co-operation Among Developing Countries Newsletter.
Plant Protection Bulletin.
Ceres (every 2 months).
Unasylva (quarterly).
Environment and Energy Bulletin.
Commodity reviews; studies; manuals.

International Bank for Reconstruction and Development—IBRD, and International Development Association—IDA (World Bank)

Address: 1818 H St, NW, Washington, DC 20433, USA.

Telephone: (202) 477-1234; **telex:** 248423; **fax:** (202) 477-6391.

The IBRD was established on 27 December 1945. Initially it was concerned with post-war reconstruction in Europe; since then its aim has been to assist the economic development of member nations by making loans where private capital is not available on reasonable terms to finance productive investments. Loans are made either direct to governments, or to private enterprises with the guarantee of their governments. The IBRD has three affiliates, the International Development Association (IDA), the International Finance Corporation (IFC, q.v.) and the Multilateral Investment Guarantee Agency (MIGA, q.v.). The 'World Bank', as it is commonly known, comprises the IBRD and IDA. Only members of the International Monetary Fund (IMF, q.v.) may be considered for membership in the Bank. Subscriptions to the capital stock of the Bank are based on each member's quota in the IMF, which is designed to reflect the country's relative economic strength. Voting rights are related to shareholdings.

Organization
(August 1994)

Officers and staff of the IBRD serve concurrently as officers and staff in the International Development Association (IDA). The World Bank has offices in New York, Paris, London and Tokyo; regional missions in Nairobi (for eastern Africa), Abidjan (for western Africa), Bangkok and Riga, Latvia; and resident missions in 56 countries.

BOARD OF GOVERNORS

The Board of Governors consists of one Governor appointed by each member nation. Typically, a Governor is the country's finance minister, central bank governor, or a minister or an official of comparable rank. The Board normally meets once a year.

EXECUTIVE DIRECTORS

The general operations of the World Bank are conducted by a Board of 24 Executive Directors. Five Directors are appointed by the five members having the largest number of shares of capital stock, and the rest are elected by the Governors representing the other members. The President of the Bank is Chairman of the Board.

OFFICERS

President and Chairman of Executive Directors: LEWIS PRESTON, (USA).

Vice-President, Middle East and North Africa Region: CAIO KOCH-WESER.

Activities

FINANCIAL OPERATIONS

The World Bank has traditionally financed capital infrastructure projects (e.g. in communications and energy). In the early 1990s the World Bank's primary objectives were the achievement of sustainable economic growth and the reduction of poverty in developing countries, and the protection of the environment. In the context of stimulating economic growth the bank promotes both private-sector development and human resource development. The bank's efforts to reduce poverty comprise two main elements: the compiling of country-specific assessments and the formulation of country-specific strategies to ensure that the bank's own projects support and complement the programmes of the country concerned.

IBRD loans are usually for a period of 20 years or less. Loans are made to governments, or must be guaranteed by the government concerned. IDA assistance is aimed at the poorer developing countries, numbering more than 40 (i.e. those with a gross national product—GNP—per head of less than US $765 in 1991 dollars). Under IDA lending conditions, credits can be extended to countries whose balance of payments could not sustain the burden of repayment required for IBRD loans. Terms are more favourable than those provided by the IBRD; credits are for a period of 40 or 50 years, with a 'grace' period of 10 years, and no interest charges.

The IBRD's capital is derived from members' subscriptions to capital shares, the calculation of which is based on their quotas in the International Monetary Fund. In April 1988 the Board of Governors approved an increase of about 80% in the IBRD's authorized capital, to US $171,000m. At 30 June 1993 the total subscribed capital of the IBRD was $165,589m., of which the paid-in portion was 6.5%; the remainder is subject to call if required. Most of the IBRD's lendable funds come from its borrowing in world capital markets, and also from its retained earnings and the flow of repayments on its loans. Bank loans carry a variable interest rate, rather than a rate fixed at the time of borrowing.

IDA's total resources, consisting of members' subscriptions and supplementary resources (additional subscriptions and contributions) amounted to US $80,886m. at 30 June 1993. Resources are replenished periodically by contributions from the more affluent member countries. In December 1989 a ninth replenishment, amounting to $15,500m. was approved for the period July 1990–June 1993, and in December 1992 34 donor countries agreed on a tenth replenishment of SDR 13,000m. (see IMF for explanation of SDR), roughly equivalent to US $18,000m.

During the year ending 30 June 1993 US $1,880m., or about 8% of World Bank assistance approved, was for the Middle East and North Africa: of the total, $124m. was in the form of IDA credits and the rest in IBRD loans.

In 1987 the World Bank undertook to strengthen its work in alleviating poverty, and to attempt to mitigate the social effects of economic adjustment programmes. It subsequently increased its focus on operations which promote productive employment and give the poor greater access to health care, education and physical infrastructure; in particular, emphasis was placed on operations designed to improve conditions for women. Improvements in food security were also to be given greater support. From 1987 the World Bank accorded greater importance to the protection of the environment and in 1989/90 systematic 'screening' of all new projects was introduced, in order to assess their environmental impact. The World Bank administers the Global Environment Facility (GEF), which was established in 1990 in conjunction with UNDP and UNEP. GEF, which became operational in 1991 for an initial three-year period, to provide grants to developing countries for measures that protect the environment. In March 1994 87 countries participating in the Facility agreed to restructure and replenish the GEF for a further three-year period from mid-1994. Funds amounting to US $2,000m. were to be made available by 26 donor countries which would enable the GEF to act as the financial mechanism for the conventions on climate changes and biological diversity that were signed at the UN Conference on Environment and Development in June 1992.

TECHNICAL ASSISTANCE

The provision of technical assistance to member countries is a major component of Bank activities. The economic, sector and project analysis undertaken by the Bank in the normal course of its operations is the vehicle for considerable technical assistance. In addition, project loans and credits may include funds designated specifically for feasibility studies, resource surveys, management or planning advice, and training. Technical assistance (usually reimbursable) is also extended to countries that do not need Bank financial support e.g. for training and transfer of technology.

In 1992 the Bank established an Institutional Development Fund (IDF), a US $25m. grant facility, which became operational on 1 July. During its first year, the IDF provided 57 grants for institutional development in 46 countries, at a total cost of $16.3m.

ECONOMIC RESEARCH AND STUDIES

The World Bank's research, carried out by its own research staff, is intended to provide a source of policy advice to members, and to encourage the development of indigenous research. The principal areas of research in 1992/93 included: alleviation of poverty; human resource development; the environment and natural resources; macroeconomic issues and management (including structural adjustment, debt, trade, finance, reform of the public sector and development of the private sector); and infrastructure and urban development. The Bank chairs the Consultative Group for International Agricultural Research (CGIAR), which was formed in 1971 to raise financial support for research on improving crops and animal production in developing countries. CGIAR supports 18 research centres.

CO-OPERATION WITH OTHER ORGANIZATIONS

The World Bank co-operates closely with other UN bodies through consultations, meetings, and joint activities; co-operation with UNDP and WHO, in their programmes to improve health, nutrition and sanitation, is especially important. It collaborates with the IMF in implementing economic adjustment programmes in developing countries. The Bank holds regular consultations with the European Community and OECD on development issues, and the Bank-NGO Committee provides an annual forum for discussion with non-governmental organizations (NGOs). The Bank chairs meetings of donor governments and organizations for the co-ordination of aid to particular countries. The Bank also conducts co-financing and aid co-ordination projects with official aid agencies, export credit agencies and commercial banks.

PUBLICATIONS

World Bank Catalog of Publications.

World Bank News (weekly).

World Bank Annual Report.

World Development Report (annually).

The World Bank and the Environment (annually).

Global Economic Prospects and Developing Countries (annually).

World Bank Economic Review (3 a year).

World Bank Research Observer (2 a year).

Research News (quarterly).

World Bank Atlas (annually).

Abstracts of Current Studies: The World Bank Research Program (annually).

Annual Review of Project Performance Results.

Staff Working Papers.

World Tables (annually).

WORLD BANK OPERATIONS IN THE MIDDLE EAST AND NORTH AFRICA

IBRD Loans Approved, July 1992–June 1993 (US $ million)

Country	Purpose	Amount
Algeria. . .	Basic and secondary education	40.0
	Housing completion and sector development	200.0
Egypt (Guarantor)	Tourism infrastructure and environment management	130.0
Iran . . .	Primary health care and family planning	141.4
	Irrigation	157.0
Iran (Guarantor)	Power sector efficiency	165.0
Jordan . . .	Health management	20.0
	Transport	35.0
Lebanon . .	Emergency reconstruction and rehabilitation	175.0
Morocco . .	Municipal finance	4.0
	Land development for low-income families	66.0
	Large-scale irrigation	215.0
Morocco (Guarantor) . .	Land development for low-income families	64.0*
	Municipal finance	100.0
	Telecommunications restructuring	100.0
Tunisia . .	Forestry development	69.0
	Municipal investment	75.0

* Three loans.
Note: Joint IBRD/IDA operations are counted only once, as IBRD operations.

IDA Credits Approved, July 1992–June 1993 (US $ million)

Country	Purpose	Amount
Egypt . . .	Matruh resource management	22.0
	Basic education	55.5
Yemen . . .	Family health	26.6
	Basic education	19.7

Source: *World Bank Annual Report 1993.*

International Finance Corporation—IFC

Address: 1850 I St, NW, Washington, DC 20433, USA.
Telephone: (202) 473-7711; **telex:** 248423; **fax:** (202) 676-0365.
IFC was founded in 1956 as an affiliate of the World Bank to encourage the growth of productive private enterprise in its member countries, particularly in the less-developed areas.

Organization

(August 1994)

IFC is a separate legal entity in the World Bank Group. Executive Directors of the World Bank also serve as Directors of IFC. The President of the World Bank is, ex officio, Chairman of the IFC Board of Directors, which has appointed him President of IFC. Subject to his overall supervision, the day-to-day operations of IFC are conducted by its staff under the direction of the Executive Vice-President.

PRINCIPAL OFFICERS

President: LEWIS PRESTON (USA).
Executive Vice-President: JANNIK LINDBAEK (Norway).

REGIONAL MISSIONS

Regional Mission in the Middle East: 5 El Falah St, Mohandessin, Giza, Egypt; tel. (2) 347-3739; telex 93110; fax (2) 347-3738; Dir JOHN H. STEWART.

Regional Mission in North Africa: 30 ave des FAR, Casablanca, Morocco; tel. (2) 312888; telex 22606; fax (2) 315181; Dir PIERRE M. SALA.

Activities

The IFC's activities are guided by three major principles:
(i) The catalytic principle. IFC should seek above all to be a catalyst in helping private investors and markets to make good investments.
(ii) The business principle. IFC should function like a business in partnership with the private sector and take the same com-mercial risks, so that its funds, although backed by public sources, are transferred under market disciplines.
(iii) The principle of the special contribution. IFC should partici-pate in an investment only when it makes a special contribution that supplements or complements the role of market operators.

From 1989/90 onwards, IFC adopted a 'rolling' three-year plan-ning process, with annual updating of objectives for the next three years. Emphasis was placed on closer co-operation with the World Bank, particularly in the following areas: development of the financial sector in member countries; privatization of public enter-prises; encouraging private investment; and conducting research and policy studies. IFC's agenda for the 1990s, as discussed by the Board of Directors in 1990/91, was to involve an expansion of its direct resource mobilization operations and the creation of other mobilizing activities. In June 1991 the Board of Directors approved an increase in authorized capital, by US $1,000m., to $2,300m. This was expected to allow IFC to expand its project-financing at a rate of 11%–12% annually through the 1990s.

At 30 June 1993 IFC's paid-in capital was US $1,423m. The World Bank is the principal source of borrowed funds, but IFC also borrows from private capital markets.

In the financial year ending 30 June 1993 total investments approved amounted to US $3,936m. for 185 projects, compared with $3,226m. for 167 projects in the previous year. Of the total approved, $2,133m. was for IFC's own account, while $1,803m. was used in loan syndications and underwriting of securities issues and investment funds. About 22% of financing was for countries with a per caput annual income of less than $400.

During the year ending 30 June 1993 IFC approved 20 projects for six countries in the Middle East and north Africa. Projects supported by IFC in the region included the following: in Egypt, tourism and investment in the country's first privatized bank; in Jordan, pharmaceutical production; in Lebanon, ceramics industry and lines of credit to five commercial banks; in Morocco, tourism and a privatization investment fund; and in Tunisia, petroleum exploitation.

The Foreign Investment Advisory Service (FIAS) is operated jointly by IFC and MIGA (q.v.), and provides advice to govern-ments on attracting foreign investment. During 1993 FIAS reviewed the investment environment in Algeria and the United Arab Emirates, advised the Moroccan Government on a revision of the country's investment codes, and made preliminary rec-ommendations for an investment promotion strategy in Jordan.

FIAS also began a study, in Egypt, of ways to facilitate linkages between foreign and local companies. In the same year, IFC also provided technical assistance in the financial, economic and industrial sectors to Algeria, Egypt and Iran and Jordan in the form of advice, studies and technical analyses.

Multilateral Investment Guarantee Agency—MIGA

Address: 1818 H Street, NW, Washington, DC 20433, USA.
Telephone: (202) 477-1234; **telex:** 248423; **fax:** (202) 477-6391.
MIGA was founded in 1988 as an affiliate of the World Bank, to encourage the flow of investments for productive purposes among its member countries, especially developing countries, through the mitigation of non-commercial barriers to investment (especially political risk).

Organization

(August 1994)

MIGA is legally and financially separate from the World Bank. It is supervised by a Board of Directors.
President: LEWIS PRESTON (USA).
Executive Vice-President: AKIRA IIDA (Japan).

Activities

The convention establishing MIGA took effect in April 1988. Authorized capital was US $1,082m. By mid-1993 subscribed capital amounted to $948m.

MIGA's purpose is to guarantee eligible investments against losses resulting from non-commercial risks, under four main categories:
    transfer risk resulting from host government restrictions on currency conversion and transfer;
    risk of loss resulting from legislative or administrative actions of the host government;
    repudiation by the host government of contracts with investors in cases in which the investor has no access to a competent forum;
    the risk of armed conflict and civil unrest.

Before guaranteeing any investment MIGA must ensure that it is commercially viable, contributes to the development process and will not be harmful to the environment. During the year to June 1993 MIGA issued 27 investment insurance contracts. Approximately US $1,900m. worth of direct investment was involved, and the contracts had a combined maximum coverage of $374m. Guarantees were issued for investment projects in Turkey and Saudi Arabia.

MIGA also provides policy and advisory services to promote foreign investment in developing countries. Jointly with IFC, MIGA operates the Foreign Investment Advisory Service (FIAS), which advises governments on their legislation and policies relating to foreign investment.

International Fund for Agricultural Development—IFAD

Address: Via del Serafico 107, 00142 Rome, Italy.
Telephone: (6) 54591; **telex:** 620330; **fax:** (6) 5043463.
Following a decision by the 1974 UN World Food Conference, IFAD was established in 1976 to fund rural development programmes specifically aimed at the poorest of the world's people. It began operations in December 1977.

Organization

(August 1994)

GOVERNING COUNCIL

Each member state is represented in the Governing Council by a Governor and an Alternate. There are three categories of members: industrialized countries (OECD members) forming Category I; petroleum-exporting developing countries (OPEC members) forming Category II; and recipient developing countries (Category III). Categories I and II *shall* contribute to the resources of the Fund while Category III *may* do so.

EXECUTIVE BOARD

The Board consists of 18 members and 17 alternates, elected by the Governing Council, one-third by each category of membership. Members serve for three years. The Executive Board is responsible for the conduct and general operation of IFAD and approves loans and grants for projects; it holds three regular sessions a year.

The total number of votes in the Governing Council and the Executive Board is 1,800, distributed equally between the three categories of membership. Thus two-thirds of the votes lie with the developing countries (Categories II and III) which will therefore have a major influence on the investment decisions of the Fund. At the same time two-thirds of the votes are held by donor countries (Categories I and II).
President and Chairman of Executive Board: FAWZI HAMAD AL-SULTAN (Kuwait).
Vice-President: DONALD S. BROWN.

Activities

The Fund's objective is to mobilize additional resources to be made available on concessional terms for agricultural development in developing member states. IFAD provides financing primarily for projects and programmes specifically designed to introduce, expand or improve food production systems and to strengthen related policies and institutions within the framework of national priorities and strategies. In allocating resources IFAD is guided by: the need to increase food production in the poorest food-deficit countries; the potential for increasing food production in other developing countries; and the importance of improving the nutritional level of the poorest people in developing countries and the conditions of their lives. All projects focus on those who often do not benefit from other development programmes: small farmers, artisanal fishermen, nomadic pastoralists, women, and the rural landless.

IFAD is empowered to make both grants and loans. Under its Agreement, grants are limited to 12.5% of the resources committed in any one financial year. There are three kinds of loan: highly concessional loans, which carry no interest but have an annual service charge of 1% and a maturity period of 50 years, including a grace period of 10 years; intermediate term loans, which have an annual interest rate of 4% and a maturity period of 20 years, including a grace period of five years; and ordinary term loans, which have an interest rate of 8% and a maturity period of 15–18 years, including a grace period of three years. To avoid duplication of work, the administration of loans, for the purposes of disbursements and supervision of project implementation, is entrusted to competent international financial institutions, with the Fund retaining an active interest.

IFAD's development projects usually include a number of components, such as infrastructure (e.g. improvement of water supplies, small-scale irrigation and road construction); input supply (e.g. improved seeds, fertilizers and pesticides); institutional support (e.g. research, training and extension services); and producer incentives (e.g. pricing and marketing improvements). IFAD also attempts to enable the landless to acquire income-generating assets: by increasing the provision of credit for the rural poor, it seeks to free them from dependence on the unorganized and exploitative capital market and to generate productive activities.

From the late 1980s, increased emphasis was given to environmental conservation, in an effort to alleviate poverty that results from the deterioration of natural resources. In addition to promoting small-scale irrigation (which has proved more economically and ecologically viable than large-scale systems), projects include low-cost anti-erosion measures, land improvement, soil conservation, agro-forestry system, improved management of arid range-land, and safe biological control of pests.

In addition to its regular efforts to identify projects and programmes, IFAD organizes special programming missions to certain selected countries to undertake a comprehensive review of the constraints affecting IFAD-type projects among the rural poor, and to help countries to design strategies for the removal of these constraints. Based on the recommendations of these missions, a number of projects have been identified or prepared. In general, these projects tend to focus on institutional improvements at the national and local level to direct inputs and services to small farmers and the landless rural poor.

In 1992 the following loans were approved for projects in the Middle East and North Africa: in Egypt, assistance to smallholders in farming reclaimed land (US $25.0); in Iran, assisting poor smallholders, particularly women, in increasing agricultural production, and thereby their incomes ($20.1); in Lebanon, rehabilitation of livestock production among smallholders ($10.0); and in Syria, rendering cultivable rocky land ($18.0). In addition, IFAD extended a grant of $75,000 to a foundation in Jordan, whose aim is to assist women in agricultural activities.

FINANCE

IFAD is financed by contributions from OECD and OPEC member states. IFAD's proposed administrative budget for 1993 was US $61.2m. Agreed funds for loans and grants to be allocated during the year amounted to $425m.

PUBLICATION

Annual Report.

International Monetary Fund—IMF

Address: 700 19th St, NW, Washington, DC 20431, USA.
Telephone: (202) 623-7430; **telex:** 440040; **fax:** (202) 623-6772.
The IMF was established at the same time as the World Bank in December 1945.

Organization

(August 1994)

BOARD OF GOVERNORS

The highest authority of the Fund is exercised by the Board of Governors, on which each member country is represented by a Governor and an Alternate Governor. The Board normally meets annually, and an Interim Committee meets twice a year. The voting power of each country is related to its quota in the Fund.

BOARD OF EXECUTIVE DIRECTORS

The 24-member Board of Executive Directors is responsible for the day-to-day operations of the Fund. The USA, the United Kingdom, Germany, France, Japan and Saudi Arabia each appoint one Executive Director, while 16 of the remainder are appointed by groups of member countries sharing similar interests; there is also one Executive Director each from the People's Republic of China, Russia and Saudi Arabia.

OFFICERS

Managing Director: MICHEL CAMDESSUS (France).
Deputy Managing Directors: RICHARD D. ERB (USA), (from 1 September 1994) STANLEY FISCHER (USA); ALASSANE D. OUTTARA (Côte d'Ivoire); PRABHAKAR R. NARVEKAR (India).
Director, Middle Eastern Department: PAUL CHABRIER.

Activities

The purposes of the IMF, as set out in the Articles of Agreement, are:

(i) To promote international monetary co-operation through a permanent institution which provides the machinery for consultation and collaboration on monetary problems.

(ii) To facilitate the expansion and balanced growth of international trade, and to contribute thereby to the promotion and maintenance of high levels of employment and real income and to the development of members' productive resources.

(iii) To promote exchange stability, to maintain orderly exchange arrangements among members, and to avoid competitive exchange depreciation.

(iv) To assist in the establishment of a multilateral system of payments in respect of current transactions between members and in the elimination of foreign exchange restrictions which hamper the growth of trade.

(v) To give confidence to members by making the general resources of the Fund temporarily available to them, under adequate safeguards, thus providing them with the opportunity to correct maladjustments in their balance of payments, without resorting to measures destructive of national or international prosperity.

(vi) In accordance with the above, to shorten the duration of and lessen the degree of disequilibrium in the international balances of payments of members.

In joining the Fund, each country agrees to co-operate with the above objectives, and the Fund monitors members' compliance by holding an annual consultation with each country, in order to survey the country's exchange rate policies and determine its need for assistance.

RESOURCES

Members' subscriptions form the basic resource of the IMF. They are supplemented by borrowing. Under the General Arrangements to Borrow (GAB), established in 1962, the 'Group of Ten' industrialized nations (Belgium, Canada, France, Germany, Italy, Japan, the Netherlands, Sweden, the United Kingdom and the USA) and Switzerland (which became a member of the IMF in 1992, but which had been a full participant in the GAB from 1984) undertake to lend the Fund up to SDR 17,000m. (increased from SDR 6,400m. in December 1983) in their own currencies, so as to help meet the balance-of-payments requirements of any member of the group, or to meet requests to the Fund from countries with balance-of-payments problems that could threaten the stability of the international monetary system. In July 1983 the Fund entered into an agreement with Saudi Arabia, in association with the GAB, making available SDR 1,500m., and other borrowing arrangements were completed in 1984 with the BIS, the Saudi Arabian Monetary Agency, Belgium and Japan, making available a further SDR 6,000m.

DRAWING ARRANGEMENTS

Exchange transactions within the Fund take the form of members' purchases (i.e. drawings) from the Fund of the currencies of other members for the equivalent amounts of their own currencies. Fund resources are available to eligible members on an essentially short-term and revolving basis to provide members with temporary assistance to contribute to the solution of their payments problems. Before making a purchase, a member must show that its balance of payments or reserve position make the purchase necessary. Apart from this requirement, reserve tranche purchases (i.e. purchases that do not bring the Fund's holdings of the member's currency to a level above its quota) are permitted unconditionally.

With further purchases, however, the Fund's policy of 'conditionality' means that a member requesting assistance must agree to adjust its economic policies, as stipulated by the IMF. All requests other than for use of the reserve tranche are examined by the Executive Board to determine whether the proposed use would be consistent with the Fund's policies, and a member must discuss its proposed adjustment programme (including fiscal, monetary, exchange and trade policies) with IMF staff. Purchases outside the reserve tranche are made in four credit tranches, each equivalent to 25% of the member's quota; a member must reverse the transaction by repurchasing its own currency (with SDRs or currencies specified by the Fund) within a specified time. A credit tranche purchase is usually made under a 'stand-by arrangement' with the Fund, or under the extended Fund facility. A stand-by arrangement is normally of one or two years' duration, and the amount is made available in instalments, subject to the member's observance of 'performance criteria'; repurchases must be made within three-and-a-quarter to five years. An extended arrangement is normally of three years' duration, and the member must submit detailed economic programmes and progress reports for each year; repurchases must be made within four-and-a-half to 10 years. A member whose payments imbalance is large in relation to its quota may make use of temporary facilities established by the Fund using borrowed resources, namely the 'enlarged access policy' established in 1981, which helps to finance stand-by and extended arrangements for such a member, up to a limit of between 90% and 110% of the member's quota annually.

During the year ending 30 April 1993, Jordan purchased SDR 33.3m. from the fund; in September 1993 Egypt made an arrangement to purchase SDR 400.0m., although at 30 April 1994 the amount remained undrawn.

In addition, there are special-purpose arrangements, all of which are subject to the member's co-operation with the Fund to find an appropriate solution to its difficulties. The buffer stock financing facility (established in 1969) enables members to pay their contributions to the buffer stocks which are intended to stabilize primary commodity markets. Members may draw up to 45% of their quota for this purpose. In August 1988 the Fund established the compensatory and contingency financing facility (CCFF), which replaced and expanded the former compensatory financing facility, established in 1963. The CCFF provides compensation to members whose export earnings are reduced owing to circumstances beyond their control, or who are affected by excess costs of cereal imports. Contingency financing is provided to help members maintain their efforts at economic adjustment even when affected by a sharp increase in interest rates or other externally-derived difficulties. In April 1992 the IMF disbursed SDR 178.6m. to Israel under the CCFF.

The structural adjustment facility (SAF, established in 1986) supports medium-term macroeconomic adjustment and structural reforms in low-income developing countries on concessionary terms. SAF loans carry an interest rate of 0.5%, repayable within 10 years, including a five-and-a-half year grace period, and the recipient must agree to a three-year structural adjustment programme to restore sustainable economic growth.

The enhanced structural adjustment facility (ESAF, established in 1987) provides assistance on a similar basis to the SAF except that maximum access is set at 250% (350% in exceptional circumstances) of the member's quota (compared with 70% under the SAF). By 30 April 1993 total commitments approved under SAF and ESAF arrangements amounted to SDR 4,600m., while total disbursements amounted to SDR 3,700m. From April 1992 11 additional countries were eligible to borrow from the ESAF, including Egypt.

In December 1993 the Executive board approved a new ESAF to replace the facility which had been due to expire in November. The commitment period of the existing ESAF was extended and its successor became operational in February 1994, to ensure continuity of lending. The terms and conditions of the new facility remain the same as those of the original ESAF, but the list of countries eligible for assistance was enlarged by six, to 78. By mid-April 43 IMF member countries had committed funds to the renewed ESAF amounting to SDR 1,373m. in subsidies and SDR 4,501.4m. in loan contributions.

TECHNICAL ASSISTANCE

Technical assistance is provided by special missions or resident representatives who advise members on every aspect of economic management. The Central Banking Department and the Fiscal Affairs Department are particularly involved in technical assistance. The IMF Institute, founded in 1964, trains officials from member countries in financial analysis and policy, balance-of-payments methodology and public finance: it also gives assistance to national and regional training centres.

MEMBERSHIP AND QUOTAS IN THE MIDDLE EAST AND NORTH AFRICA (million SDR)*

Country	October 1993
Algeria	914.4
Bahrain	82.8
Cyprus	100.0
Egypt	678.4
Iran	1,078.5
Iraq†	(864.8) 504.0
Israel	666.2
Jordan	121.7
Kuwait	995.2
Lebanon†	(146.0) 78.7
Libya	817.6
Morocco	427.7
Oman	119.4
Qatar	190.5
Saudi Arabia	5,130.6
Syria	209.9
Tunisia	206.0
Turkey	642.0
United Arab Emirates	392.1
Yemen	176.5

* The Special Drawing Right (SDR) was introduced in 1970 as a substitute for gold in international payments, and is intended eventually to become the principal reserve asset in the international monetary system. Its value (which was US $1.44837 at 30 June 1994 and averaged $1.39633 in 1993) is based on the currencies of the five largest exporting countries. Each member is assigned a quota related to its national income, monetary reserves, trade balance and other economic indicators; the quota approximately determines a member's voting power and the amount of foreign exchange it may purchase from the Fund. A member's subscription is equal to its quota. Under the Ninth General Review of quotas, which was completed in June 1990, an increase of 50% in total quotas (from SDR 90,000m. to SDR 135,200m.) was authorized. The increase entered into effect in November 1992; with additional contributions from countries that joined the IMF subsequent to June 1990, by October 1993 total quotas amounted to SDR 144,606.2m.

† As of 13 October 1993, these members had not yet paid for their quota increases under the Ninth General Review. The quotas listed are those determined under the Eighth General Review, and the figures in parenthese are the proposed Ninth Review quotas.

PUBLICATIONS

Annual Report.

Balance of Payments Statistics (monthly, with yearbook).

Direction of Trade Statistics (monthly, with yearbook).

Government Finance Statistics Yearbook.

International Financial Statistics (monthly, with yearbook).

Staff Studies for the World Economic Outlook (annually).

Finance and Development (quarterly, issued jointly with the World Bank).

IMF Survey (2 a month).

World Economic Outlook (2 a year).

Export Credits: Development and Prospects (annually).

International Capital Markets (annually).

Primary Commodities: Market Developments and Outlook (annually).

Occasional papers, books and pamphlets, publications brochure.

United Nations Educational, Scientific and Cultural Organization—UNESCO

Address: 7 place de Fontenoy, 75352 Paris, France.
Telephone: (1) 45-68-10-00; **telex:** 204461; **fax:** (1) 45-67-16-90.
UNESCO was established in 1946 'for the purpose of advancing, through the educational, scientific and cultural relations of the peoples of the world, the objectives of international peace and the common welfare of mankind'.

Organization

(August 1994)

GENERAL CONFERENCE

The supreme governing body of the Organization, the Conference meets in ordinary session once in two years and is composed of representatives of the member states.

EXECUTIVE BOARD

The Board, comprising 50 members, prepares the programme to be submitted to the Conference and supervises its execution; it meets twice or sometimes three times a year.

SECRETARIAT

Director-General: FEDERICO MAYOR ZARAGOZA (Spain).
Director of the Executive Office: DANIEL JANICOT (France).

REGIONAL OFFICES

Regional Centre for Functional Literacy in Rural Areas: Sirs-el-Layan, Menoufia, Egypt; tel. (48) 351202; fax (48) 351201.
Regional Office for Education in the Arab States: POB 2270, Amman, Jordan; tel. (6) 604653; telex 24304; fax (6) 682183; f. 1972.
Regional Office for Science and Technology in the Arab States—ROSTAS: 8 Abdel Rahman Fahmy St, Cairo, Garden City, Egypt; tel. (2) 3541455; fax (2) 3545296; Dir Dr ADNAN SHIHAB-ELDIN.

An office in Tunis co-ordinates relations with the League of Arab States and other regional organizations.

Activities in the Middle East and North Africa

UNESCO's activities, which take three main forms as outlined below, are funded through a regular budget provided by member states and also through other sources, particularly UNDP. UNESCO co-operates with many other UN agencies and international non-governmental organizations.

International Intellectual Co-operation: UNESCO assists the interchange of experience, knowledge and ideas through a world network of specialists. Apart from the work of its professional staff, UNESCO co-operates regularly with the national associations and international federations of scientists, artists, writers and educators, some of which it helped to establish. UNESCO convenes conferences and meetings, and co-ordinates international scientific efforts; it helps to standardize procedures of documentation and provides clearing house services; it offers fellowships; and it publishes a wide range of specialized works, including source books and works of reference. UNESCO promotes various international agreements, including the International Copyright Convention and the World Cultural and Natural Heritage Convention, which member states are invited to accept.

Operational Assistance: UNESCO has established missions which advise governments, particularly in the developing member countries, in the planning of projects; and it appoints experts to assist in carrying them out. The projects are concerned with the teaching of functional literacy to workers in development undertakings; teacher training; establishing of libraries and documentation centres; provision of training for journalists, radio, television and film workers; improvement of scientific and technical education; training of planners in cultural development; and the international exchange of persons and information.

Promotion of Peace: UNESCO organizes various research efforts on racial problems, and is particularly concerned with prevention of discrimination in education, and improving access for women to education. It also promotes studies and research on conflicts and peace, violence and obstacles to disarmament, and the role of international law and organizations in building peace. It is stressed that human rights, peace and disarmament cannot be dealt with separately, as the observance of human rights is a prerequisite to peace and vice versa.

In November 1992 UNESCO announced the establishment of a 21-member panel, composed mainly of academics and writers with experience in government, to draw up guidelines for the agency's activities in the coming decade.

EDUCATION

UNESCO's most important activities, as stipulated in its programme for 1990–95, are in the sphere of education, particularly the spread of literacy, adult education, teacher-training, and the encouragement of universal primary education, partly through assistance for the construction of primary schools. It places special emphasis on the attainment of education by women and people with disabilities, and on literacy as an integral part of rural development. Each year UNESCO sends expert missions to member states on request to advise on all matters concerning education, and provides fellowships and travel grants. In these forms of assistance priority is given to the rural regions of developing member countries. The International Institute for Educational Planning and the International Bureau of Education carry out training, research and the exchange of information on aspects of education.

UNESCO was given responsibility for organizing International Literacy Year (1990), the principal aims of which were to increase action by governments to eliminate illiteracy among women and disadvantaged groups; and to increase public awareness of the extent and implications of illiteracy.

In March 1990 UNESCO, with other UN agencies, sponsored the World Conference on Education for All.

In the Middle East and North Africa, the Regional Centre for Functional Literacy in Rural Areas sends out mobile teams of experts and organizes courses and seminars for specialists in literacy and adult education. UNESCO co-operates with UNRWA (q.v.) to provide schooling for Palestinian refugee children. UNESCO has also undertaken a number of projects financed by other bodies, for example literacy campaigns in the Yemen Arab Republic and the People's Democratic Republic of Yemen (financed by AGFUND); building low-cost schools (financed by AFESD); development of industries for the production of educational materials (also financed by AFESD); and a regional programme in population education (financed by UNFPA).

NATURAL SCIENCES AND TECHNOLOGY

At the international level, UNESCO has established various forms of intergovernmental co-operation concerned with the environmental sciences and research on natural resources. Examples of these are the Man and Biosphere Programme (MAB) which by late 1992 had undertaken over 1,000 projects in 100 countries involving local people in solving practical problems of environmental resource management in diverse bioclimatic and geographical situations around the world; the International Geological Correlation Programme (IGCP), run jointly with the International Union of Geological Sciences; the International Hydrological Programme (IHP), dealing with the scientific aspects of water resources assessment and management; and the Intergovernmental Oceanographic Commission (IOC), which promotes scientific investigation into the nature and resources of the oceans through the concerted action of its member states. In mid-1991 the IOC initiated a programme to co-ordinate research into the effects on the marine environment of the massive oil spillages and oil-well fires (which produced huge amounts of toxic smoke) which occurred in the Persian (Arabian) Gulf region during the war between Iraq and a multinational force in January–February. The bulk of the research was to be undertaken by scientists in the countries affected, with the IOC facilitating the exchange of information between the participants. The programme was to have both short-term dimensions (to aid immediate decision-making) and long-term dimensions (to ensure the optimum response to similar disasters in the future). The Intergovernmental Informatics Programme encourages co-operation between developed and developing countries in computer sciences.

At the regional and sub-regional level, UNESCO develops co-operative scientific and technological research programmes through organization and support of scientific meetings and contacts with research institutions, and the establishment or strengthening of co-operative networks. In February 1994 UNESCO launched the International Fund for the Technological Development of Africa, which was to be jointly managed by UNESCO and the African scientific community.

At the national level, UNESCO assists member states, upon request, in policy-making and planning in the field of science and technology generally, and by organizing training and research programmes in basic sciences, engineering sciences and environmental sciences, particularly work relevant to development, such as projects concerning the use of small-scale energy sources for rural and dispersed populations. It assists the teaching of the natural sciences in universities in the developing countries, through grants for the production of low-cost laboratory equipment and teaching materials, and training courses for university teachers and laboratory technicians.

The Regional Office for Science and Technology (ROSTAS) organizes courses and studies on the teaching of basic science, computer science, hydrology, oceanography, geophysics, soil biology, geomorphology and seismology. It provides regional seminars, training courses and consultancy missions. As part of its programmes in arid zone research, UNESCO has helped to establish research institutes in Iraq and Saudi Arabia, and has given financial aid to Egypt's Desert Research Institute.

UNESCO has been actively involved in the establishment of several engineering institutes in the region, in Syria, Saudi Arabia, Iraq, Lebanon, Libya and Morocco; with the support of the governments concerned, these institutes have developed into yimportant university engineering faculties. In 1982 a regional network of engineering education institutions was established, to encourage co-operation in training and research and the exchange of information.

SOCIAL SCIENCES

UNESCO's activities in the field of the social and human sciences aim to promote teaching and research in these disciplines and to encourage their application to a number of issues prioritized by the Organization including education, development, urbanization, population, youth, human rights, democracy and peace. The social sciences constitute a link between UNESCO's two main functions: international intellectual co-operation leading to reflection on major problems, and action to solve these problems. For example, studies are conducted to elucidate the complex relations between demographic changes and socio-cultural transformation on a global scale, and the ways in which societies react to climatic and environmental change. Co-operation with the United Nations Population Fund (UNFPA) has led to a technical assistance programme which benefits developing countries in the areas of population education and communication.

UNESCO's social and human sciences programme gives high priority to the problems of young people who are the first victims of unemployment, economic and social inequalities and the widening gap between developing and industrialized countries. Under the project 'Youth Shaping the Future', an International Youth Clearing House and Information Service was to be established in order to increase and consolidate the information available on the situation of young people in society, and to heighten awareness of their needs, aspirations and potential among public and private decision-makers. UNESCO's programme also focuses on the educational and cultural dimensions of physical education and sport and their capacity to maintain and improve health. An activity specifically aimed at young people is education designed to prevent the spread of AIDS.

The programme helps countries in defining national strategies for the development of human resources and in strengthening research and training capabilities in order better to anticipate social, economic and cultural changes and their impact on development. The social and human sciences programme also focuses on the promotion and protection of human rights and democracy through education, information and documentation and research, particularly those rights related to UNESCO's areas of competence, i.e. education, science, culture and communication. The struggle against all forms of discrimination is a central part of the programme. It disseminates scientific information aimed at combating racial prejudice, works to improve the status of women and their access to education, and promotes equality between men and women.

CULTURE

UNESCO's cultural heritage programme is in three parts: activities designed to foster the world-wide application of three international conventions that aim to protect and conserve cultural property; international safeguarding campaigns to help member states to conserve and restore monuments and sites (in 1992 there were 24 such campaigns in progress); and the training of museum managers and conservationists and promotion of public awareness of the cultural heritage.

UNESCO encourages the translation and publication of literary works, publishes albums of art, and produces records, audiovisual programmes and travelling art exhibitions. It supports the development of book publishing and distribution and the training of editors and managers in publishing. UNESCO is active in preparing and encouraging the enforcement of international legislation on copyright. A 10-year programme for the collection and safeguarding of humanity's non-material heritage (oral traditions, music, dance, medicine etc.) began in 1988.

UNESCO's World Heritage Programme, launched in 1978, aims to protect historic sites and natural landmarks of outstanding universal significance, in accordance with the 1972 UNESCO Convention Concerning the Protection of the World Cultural and Natural Heritage, by providing financial aid for restoration, technical assistance, training and management planning. UNESCO is assisting in the exploration of prehistoric sites in Libya, and in the preservation of sites and monuments in other countries, for example Carthage and Al-Qairawan in Tunisia, Fez in Morocco, Tyre in Lebanon and the Casbah of Algiers in Algeria. UNESCO has assisted Iraq in the establishment of a regional training centre for the conservation of cultural property in the Arab countries. As part of its World Decade of Cultural Development, which began in 1990, UNESCO undertook a project to reconstruct the ancient library in Alexandria, Egypt.

In December 1992 UNESCO established the World Commission on Culture and Development to strengthen links between culture and development and to prepare a report on the issue.

COMMUNICATION

UNESCO has provided expert services, fellowships and equipment for the development of national press agencies, radio and television organizations and film production, particularly in Algeria, Jordan, Kuwait and Libya. It helped to establish the Arab States Broadcasting Union in 1966, and collaborates with member states in the setting-up of communications satellites. Under the International Programme for the Development of Communications, launched in 1981, UNESCO supports a scheme for planning and exchange of information in the field of communications, and a regional training centre is also envisaged.

FINANCE

UNESCO's Regular Programme budget for the two years 1992–93 was $444.7m., with extra-budgetary resources estimated at $274.9m.

PUBLICATIONS

(mostly in English, French and Spanish editions; Arabic, Chinese and Russian versions are also available in many cases)

UNESCO Statistical Yearbook.

UNESCO Courier (monthly, in 36 languages).

UNESCO Sources (monthly).

Copyright Bulletin (quarterly).

Museum (quarterly).

Impact of Science on Society (quarterly).

International Social Science Journal (quarterly).

Nature and Resources (quarterly review of the Man and Biosphere programme, the International Hydrological Programme and the International Geological Correlation Programme).

Prospects (quarterly review on educational planning).

Books, statistics, scientific maps and atlases.

World Health Organization—WHO

Address: ave Appia, 1211 Geneva 27, Switzerland.
Telephone: (22) 7912111; **telex:** 415416; **fax:** (22) 7910746.
WHO was established in 1948 as the central agency directing international health work. Of its many activities, the most important single aspect is technical co-operation with national health administrations, particularly in the developing countries.

Organization

(August 1994)

WORLD HEALTH ASSEMBLY

The Assembly meets annually in Geneva; it is responsible for policy making, and the biennial programme and budget; it appoints the Director-General, admits new members and reviews budget contributions.

EXECUTIVE BOARD

The Board is composed of 31 health experts designated by, but not representing, their governments; they serve for three years, and the World Health Assembly elects 10 or 11 member states each year to the Board. It meets at least twice a year to review the Director-General's programme, which it forwards to the Assembly with any recommendations that seem necessary. It advises on questions referred to it by the Assembly and is responsible for putting into effect the decisions and policies of the Assembly. It is also empowered to take emergency measures in case of epidemics or disasters.

SECRETARIAT

Director-General: Dr HIROSHI NAKAJIMA (Japan).
Assistant Directors-General: Dr HU CHING-LI (People's Republic of China), Dr JEAN-PAUL JARDEL (France), Dr RALPH H. HENDERSON (USA), Dr NIKOLAI P. NAPALKOV (Russia), DENIS G. AITKEN (UK), Dr FERNANDO ANTEZANA ARANIBAR (Bolivia).
Regional Office for Africa: POB 6, Brazzaville, Congo; tel. 83-91-11; telex 5217; fax 83-94-00; Dir Prof. GOTTLIEB LOBE MONEKOSSO.
Regional Office for the Eastern Mediterranean: POB 1517, Alexandria 21511, Egypt; tel. (3) 4830090; telex 54028; fax (3) 4838916; Dir Dr HUSSEIN ABD AR-RAZZAQ GEZAIRY.

Activities

WHO's objective is stated in the constitution as 'the attainment by all peoples of the highest possible level of health'.

It acts as the central authority directing international health work, and establishes relations with professional groups and government health authorities on that basis.

It supports, on request from member states, programmes to prevent and control health problems, control and eradicate disease, train health workers best suited to local needs and strengthen national health systems. Aid is provided in emergencies and natural disasters.

A global programme of collaborative research and exchange of scientific information is carried out in co-operation with about 900 leading national institutions. Particular stress is laid on the widespread communicable diseases of the tropics, and the countries directly concerned are assisted in developing their research capabilities.

It keeps diseases and other health problems under constant surveillance, formulates health regulations for international travel, and sets standards for the quality control of drugs, vaccines and other substances affecting health.

It collects and disseminates health data and carries out statistical analyses and comparative studies in such diseases as cancer, heart disease and mental illness.

It promotes improved environmental conditions, including housing, sanitation and working conditions. All available information on effects on human health of the pollutants in the environment is critically reviewed and published.

Co-operation among scientists and professional groups is encouraged, and the organization may propose international conventions and agreements. It assists in developing an informed public opinion on matters of health.

The WHO Regional Office for the Eastern Mediterranean works principally in the preparation of national and regional strategies for the achievement of Health For All by the Year 2000 in the Eastern Mediterranean region, in accordance with the Global Strategy adopted by the World Health Assembly in May 1981. Primary health care (PHC) is seen as the key to 'Health For All', with the following as minimum requirements:

Safe water in the home or within 15 minutes' walking distance, and adequate sanitary facilities in the home or immediate vicinity;

Immunization against diphtheria, pertussis, tetanus, poliomyelitis, measles and tuberculosis;

Local health care, including availability of at least 20 essential drugs, within one hour's travel;

Trained personnel to attend childbirth, and to care for pregnant mothers and children up to at least one year old.

The development of health manpower is given high priority in the region. Educational development and support forms a prominent feature of the Regional Office's work. It awards fellowships in health-related subjects. The Regional Arabic Programme issues training manuals and working guidelines.

DISEASE PREVENTION AND CONTROL

One of WHO's major achievements was the eradication of smallpox, which, following a massive international campaign of vaccination and surveillance, begun in 1958 and intensified in 1967, was declared to have been achieved in 1977. In 1988 the World Health Assembly declared its commitment to the similar eradication of poliomyelitis by the year 2000; and in 1990 the Assembly resolved to eliminate iodine deficiency disorders (causing mental handicap) by 2000.

The objective of providing immunization for all children by 1990 was adopted by the World Health Assembly in 1977. Six diseases (measles, whooping cough, tetanus, poliomyelitis, tuberculosis and diphtheria) that killed or maimed some 10m. children annually became the target of the Expanded Programme on Immunization (EPI) in which WHO, UNICEF and many other organizations collaborated. In 1990 more than 100m. children in the developing world under the age of one had been successfully vaccinated against the targeted diseases. This achieved the EPI's objective of a rate of vaccination of 80%, which compared with a rate of vaccination of 20% in 1980. Some 74 governments and more than 400 voluntary organizations were involved in the Programme. The achievement of the 80% target meant that the lives of about 3m. children were being saved every year. In September 1991 WHO launched the Children's Vaccine Initiative (CVI), jointly sponsored by the Rockefeller Foundation, UNDP, UNICEF, and the World Bank, which aims to facilitate the development and provision of children's vaccines. The CVI has as its ultimate goal the development of a single oral immunization shortly after birth that will protect against all major childhood diseases.

WHO's Division of Diarrhoeal and Acute Respiratory Disease Control encourages national programmes aimed at reducing childhood deaths as a result of diarrhoea, particularly through the use of oral rehydration therapy, and preventive measures. The Division is also seeking to reduce deaths from pneumonia in infants through the use of a simple case-management strategy involving the recognition of danger signs and treatment with an appropriate antibiotic. In keeping with the priority given by WHO to integrated disease control, an integrated approach to management to the sick child is being developed by the Division in collaboration with other relevant WHO programmes and with UNICEF.

The Division of Integrated Control of Tropical Diseases provides member states with technical support to assist in the implementation of disease control. The programme focuses on six major groups of tropical diseases: malaria, leprosy, schistosomiasis and other trematode (fluke) infections, filariasis (onchocerciasis and the lymphatic filariases), leishmaniasis, African and American trupanosomiasis and dracunculiasis (Guinea worm disease). The Division formulates control strategies for global, regional or subregional application. Direct technical support is given to the design of realistic sustainable control programmes and to the integration of such programmes in the health services and the social and economic sectors of member countries. WHO's special programme for research and training in tropical diseases, sponsored jointly by WHO, UNDP and the World Bank, was established in 1975, and comprises a world-wide network of about 4,000 scientists working on the development of vaccines, new drugs, diagnostic kits, non-chemical insecticides and epidemiology and social and economic research on the target diseases. The programme aims to strengthen research institutions in developing countries, and to encourage participation by scientists from the countries most affected by tropical diseases. A Ministerial Conference on Malaria, organized by WHO in October 1992 adopted a global strategy specifying requirements for effective control of the disease, which kills about 2.5m. people every year.

WHO's Global Programme on AIDS (Acquired Immunodeficiency Syndrome) began in 1987 with the aim of preventing transmission of the human immunodeficiency virus (HIV), which causes AIDS, caring for people with HIV or AIDS, and co-ordinating national and international efforts against AIDS. At July 1994 WHO estimated the total number of cases of AIDS to be 4m. (compared with 2.5m. in July 1993), and the number of adults infected with HIV to be 16m. A further 1m. children were estimated to be infected with HIV. WHO supports national AIDS control plans, which (in the absence of a vaccine) stress education and information as vital in stopping the spread of HIV. Programmes also include funds for training health personnel; improving facilities for testing and protecting blood supplies; epidemiological surveillance; and establishing or expanding laboratory facilities for diagnosing AIDS and treatment facilities for AIDS patients. WHO's Global Programme on AIDS was to receive US $180m. for the period 1994–95, the largest amount allocated to a single programme within WHO. The Global Commission on AIDS, comprising biomedical and social scientists and other experts, is the advisory body to the WHO's Global Programme on AIDS. In January 1994 WHO approved the establishment of a UN co-sponsored Programme on HIV/AIDS, which WHO was to administer.

WHO's Programme for the Promotion of Environmental Health undertakes a wide range of initiatives to tackle the increasing threats to health and well-being from a changing environment, especially in relation to air pollution, control of monitoring of water quality, sanitation, protection against radiation, management of hazardous waste, chemical safety and housing hygiene. The major part of WHO's technical co-operation in environmental health in developing countries is concerned with community water supply and sanitation. The Programme also gives prominence to the assessment of health risks from chemical, physical and biological agents. To contribute to the solution of environmental health problems associated with the rapid urbanization of cities in the developing world, the Programme was promoting globally in the early 1990s the Healthy City approach that had been initiated in Europe.

WHO's Tobacco or Health Programme aims to reduce the use of tobacco, which is estimated to be responsible for more than 3m. deaths annually. The Programme aims to educate tobacco-users and to prevent young people from adopting the habit.

'Inter-Health', a programme to combat non-communicable chronic diseases (such as those arising from an unhealthy diet) was initiated in 1990, with the particular aim of preventing an increase in the incidence of such diseases, and their related lifestyle determinants, in developing countries.

MATERNAL HEALTH

WHO's Safe Motherhood Initiative supports a programme of action for women's health and the reduction of maternal mortality (estimated to claim 500,000 victims annually).

FOOD AND NUTRITION

With FAO and UNICEF, WHO operates a programme of surveillance of food and nutrition and supports those countries with high levels of malnutrition. The Regional Office has initiated a programme of nutritional research in some countries of the region, aimed at improving the nutrition of infants and young children affected by an unsuitable choice of foods and the lack of hygienic practices. In May 1981 the International Code of Marketing of Breastmilk Substitutes was adopted by the World Heath Assembly, aiming to provide safe and adequate nutrition for infants by promoting breast-feeding and by ensuring the proper use of breastmilk substitutes, when necessary, with controls on production, storage and advertising. WHO operates a data bank on breast-feeding and its effects, and, with UNICEF, initiated a programme for promoting breast-feeding in the 1990s.

In December 1992 an International Conference on Nutrition, co-sponsored by FAO and WHO, was held in Rome. It was attended by ministers of agriculture and health from over 150 countries and adopted a World Declaration on Nutrition and a Plan of Action designed to make the fight against malnutrition a development priority. Following the Conference WHO identified 81 countries that required immediate support in drawing up their national plans of action on nutrition.

DRUGS

The WHO Action Programme on Essential Drugs aims to prevent the inappropriate and excessive prescription of drugs. The Programme maintains and regularly revises a Model List of Essential Drugs, comprising nearly 270 substances that will treat most health problems of a given population, and should be available in adequate quantities at all times. WHO's Division of Drug Policies and Management provides information on international standards for the manufacture of pharmaceutical products in international trade, and advises national health agencies on the safety and efficacy of drugs. WHO is also active in monitoring drug abuse and in developing effective approaches to the management of health problems resulting from drug abuse.

WHO's programme on traditional medicine encourages the incorporation of traditional health practices that have been evaluated as safe and effective into primary health care systems.

EMERGENCY RELIEF

Through its Emergency Relief Operations, WHO acts as the 'health arm' of disaster relief undertaken by the UN system. It works in close co-operation with UNHCR, UNDP, the UN's Department of Humanitarian Affairs/UNDRO and UNICEF. Its emergency preparedness activities include co-ordination, policy making and planning, awareness-building, technical advice, training, publication of standards and guidelines, and research on emergency preparedness issues. Its emergency relief activities include an emergency response fund, emergency drugs and supplies, stockpiles and technical emergency assessment missions. The goal of WHO Emergency Relief Operations is to build the capacity of disaster-vulnerable member states to reduce the adverse heatlh consequences of disasters.

Following the Iraqi invasion of Kuwait in August 1990, WHO provided emergency assistance for those fleeing from Kuwait into neighbouring countries. In March 1991, after the end of the armed conflict between Iraq and a multinational force authorized by the UN, WHO announced plans to provide immediate emergency assistance and longer-term aid for rehabilitation in both Kuwait and Iraq. WHO also provided emergency medical supplies for refugees from Iraq who had fled to Turkey and Iran.

WHO assists UNRWA (q.v.) in providing healthcare to Palestinians living in the Occupied Territories. In October 1993, following a peace accord reached by Israel and Palestine in September, WHO launched an appeal for US $10m. to finance a technical assistance programme that was to implement the transfer of health services to a Palestinian self-governing authority, and provide for primary health care projects in the Occupied Territories. In May 1994 the World Health Assembly adopted a resolution to support the programme and to allocate the necessary funds to meet the urgent health needs of the Palestinian people.

FINANCE

WHO's regular budget is provided by assessment of member states and associate members. An additional fund for specific projects is provided by voluntary contributions from members and other sources. Funds are received from the UN Development Programme and from UNFPA for population programmes. A budget of $734.9m. was approved for 1992–93. Extra-budgetary funds were expected to amount to $926.6m. during this period. For the period 1994–95 the regular working budget was to amount to US $822.1m., while extra-budgetary contributions were expected to total nearly $1,000m.

PUBLICATIONS

Full catalogue of publications supplied free on request.

World Health (6 a year in English, French, Russian and Spanish; quarterly in Arabic and Farsi).

Environmental Health Criteria.

Bulletin of WHO (6 a year).

Weekly Epidemiological Record.

World Health Statistics Quarterly.

World Health Statistics Annual.

International Digest of Health Legislation (quarterly).

Reports on the World Health Situation (approximately every 6 years).

World Health Forum (quarterly, in Arabic, Chinese, English, French, Russian and Spanish).

WHO Drug Information (quarterly).

Other UN Organizations active in the Middle East and North Africa

OFFICE OF THE UNITED NATIONS DISASTER RELIEF CO-ORDINATOR—UNDRO

Address: Dept of Humanitarian Affairs, Palais des Nations, 1211 Geneva 10, Switzerland.

Telephone: (22) 9171234; **telex:** 414242; **fax:** (22) 9170023.

UNDRO was established in 1972 to mobilize and co-ordinate international emergency relief to disaster-stricken areas, and to co-operate in promoting disaster preparedness and prevention. In 1992 UNDRO became part of the newly-established United Nations Department of Humanitarian Affairs.

UNITED NATIONS CENTRE FOR HUMAN SETTLEMENTS—UNCHS (Habitat)

Address: POB 30030, Nairobi, Kenya.

Telephone: (2) 520600; **telex:** 22996; **fax:** (2) 226473.

The Centre was established in 1978 to service the inter-governmental Commission on Human Settlements, and to serve as a focus for human settlements activities in the UN system.

UNITED NATIONS CHILDREN'S FUND—UNICEF

Address: 3 United Nations Plaza, New York, NY 10017, USA.

Telephone: (212) 326-7000; **telex:** 7607848; **fax:** (212) 888-7465.

UNICEF was established in 1946 by the UN General Assembly as the UN International Children's Emergency Fund, to meet the emergency needs of children in post-war Europe and China. In 1950 its mandate was changed to emphasize programmes giving long-term benefits to children everywhere, particularly those in developing countries who are in the greatest need.

Regional Office for the Middle East and North Africa: POB 811721, Amman, Jordan.

UNITED NATIONS CONFERENCE ON TRADE AND DEVELOPMENT—UNCTAD

Address: Palais des Nations, 1211 Geneva 10, Switzerland.

Telephone: (22) 9071234; **telex:** 412962; **fax:** (22) 9070057.

UNCTAD was established in 1964. Its role is to promote international trade, particularly that of developing countries, with a view to accelerating economic development. It is the principal instrument of the UN General Assembly for deliberation and negotiation in the field of international trade and related issues of international economic co-operation, including commodity agreements.

UNITED NATIONS ENVIRONMENT PROGRAMME—UNEP

Address: POB 30552, Nairobi, Kenya.

Telephone: (2) 230800; **telex:** 22068; **fax:** (2) 226890.

UNEP was established in 1972 to encourage international co-operation in matters relating to the human environment.

UNITED NATIONS POPULATION FUND—UNFPA

Address: 220 East 42nd St, New York, NY 10017, USA.

Telephone: (212) 297-5000; **telex:** 422031; **fax:** (212) 370-0201.

Created in 1967 as the Trust Fund for Population Activities, the UN Fund for Population Activities (UNFPA) was established as a Fund of the UN General Assembly in 1972 and was made a subsidiary organ of the UN General Assembly in 1979, with the UNDP Governing Council designated as its governing body. In 1987 UNFPA's name was changed to the United Nations Population Fund (retaining the same acronym).

UN Specialized Agencies

GENERAL AGREEMENT ON TARIFFS AND TRADE—GATT

Address: Centre William Rappard, 154 rue de Lausanne, 1211 Geneva 21, Switzerland.

Telephone: (22) 7395007; **telex:** 412324; **fax:** (22) 7395458.

GATT was established in 1948 as a multilateral treaty aiming to liberalize world trade and place it on a secure basis. Contracting parties conduct negotiations on specific trade problems affecting individual commodities or countries, and also major multilateral trade negotiations.

INTERNATIONAL ATOMIC ENERGY AGENCY—IAEA

Address: Wagramerstrasse 5, POB 100, 1400 Vienna, Austria.

Telephone: (1) 2360; **telex:** 1-12645; **fax:** (1) 234564.

The Agency was founded in 1957 with the aim of enlarging the contribution of atomic energy to peace, health and prosperity throughout the world, through technical co-operation (assisting research on and practical application of atomic energy for peaceful uses) and safeguards (ensuring that materials and services provided by the Agency are not used for any military purpose).

INTERNATIONAL CIVIL AVIATION ORGANIZATION—ICAO

Address: 1000 ouest, rue Sherbrooke, Montréal, PQ H3A 2R2, Canada.

Telephone: (514) 285-8219; **telex:** 05-24513; **fax:** (514) 288-4772.

ICAO was founded in 1974 to develop the techniques of international air navigation and to help in the planning and improvement of international air transport. It is based on the Convention on International Civil Aviation, signed in Chicago, 1944.

Regional Office for the Middle East: 9 Shagaret el-Dorr, Zamalek, Cairo, Egypt.

INTERNATIONAL LABOUR ORGANISATION—ILO

Address: 4 route des Morillons, 1211 Geneva 22, Switzerland.

Telephone: (22) 7996111; **telex:** 415647; **fax:** (22) 7988685.

ILO was founded in 1919 to work for social justice as a basis for lasting peace. It carries out this mandate by promoting decent living standards, satisfactory conditions of work and pay and adequate employment opportunities. Methods of action include the creation of international labour standards; the provision of technical co-operation services; and research and publications on social and labour matters.

Regional Office for Africa: 01 BP 3960, Abidjan 01, Côte d'Ivoire.

Regional Office for Arab States: 4 route des Morillons, 1211 Geneva 22, Switzerland.

INTERNATIONAL MARITIME ORGANIZATION—IMO

Address: 4 Albert Embankment, London, SE1 7SR, England.

Telephone: (171) 735-7611; **telex:** 23588; **fax:** (171) 587-3210.

The Inter-Governmental Maritime Consultative Organization (IMCO) began operations in 1959, as a specialized agency of the UN to facilitate co-operation among governments on technical matters affecting international shipping. Its main aims are to improve the safety of international shipping, and to prevent pollution caused by ships. IMCO became IMO in 1982.

INTERNATIONAL TELECOMMUNICATION UNION—ITU

Address: Place des Nations, 1211 Geneva 20, Switzerland.

Telephone: (22) 7305111; **telex:** 421000; **fax:** (22) 7337256.

Founded in 1865, ITU became a specialized agency of the UN in 1947. It acts to encourage world co-operation in the use of telecommunication, to promote technical development and to harmonize national policies in the field.

UNITED NATIONS INDUSTRIAL DEVELOPMENT ORGANIZATION—UNIDO

Address: POB 300, 1400 Vienna, Austria.

Telephone: (1) 211310; **telex:** 135612; **fax:** (1) 232156.

UNIDO began operations in 1967, following a resolution of the UN General Assembly, to assist in the industrialization of the developing countries through direct assistance and mobilization of national and international resources.

UNIVERSAL POSTAL UNION—UPU

Address: Case postale, 3000 Berne 15, Switzerland.

Telephone: (31) 3503111; **telex:** 912761; **fax:** (31) 3503110.

The General Postal Union was founded by the Treaty of Berne (1874), begining operations in July 1875. Three years later its name was changed to the Universal Postal Union. In 1948 UPU became a specialized agency of the UN. It aims to develop and unify the international postal service, to study problems and to provide training.

WORLD INTELLECTUAL PROPERTY ORGANIZATION— WIPO

Address: 34 chemin des Colombettes, 1211 Geneva 20, Switzerland.

Telephone: (22) 7309111; **telex:** 22376; **fax:** (22) 7335428.

WIPO was established in 1970. It became a specialized agency of the UN in 1974. WIPO aims to promote the protection of intellectual property (e.g. industrial and technical patents and literary copyrights) throughout the world through co-operation among states and, where appropriate, with other international organizations. It also centralizes the administration of the Unions which deal with legal and technical aspects of intellectual property. Each Union is founded on a multilateral treaty.

WORLD METEOROLOGICAL ORGANIZATION—WMO

Address: 41 ave Giuseppe Motta, CP 2300, 1211 Geneva 2, Switzerland.

Telephone: (22) 7308111; **telex:** 23260; **fax:** (22) 7342326.

WMO started its activities in 1951, aiming to improve the exchange of weather information and its applications.

United Nations Information Centres

Algeria: BP 823, 19 ave Chahid el-Ouali, Mustapha Sayed, Algiers; tel. (2) 744902; telex (936) 66144; fax (2) 745082.

Bahrain: POB 26004, House 131, Rd 2803, Block 328, Segaya, Manama; tel. 231046; telex 9011; fax 270749 (also covers Qatar and the United Arab Emirates).

Egypt: POB 982, World Trade Centre, 1191 Corniche El Nile, Cairo; tel. (2) 769-595; fax (2) 769-393 (also covers Saudi Arabia and Yemen).

Iran: POB 15875-4557, Ghaem Magham Farahani Ave 185, Teheran 15868; tel. (21) 8862812; telex 212397; fax (21) 5048864.

Jordan: POB 927115, 28 Abdul Hamid Sharaf St, Shmeisani, Amman; tel. (6) 694351; telex 21691; fax (6) 694980 (also covers Iraq).

Lebanon: POB 4656, Apt No 1, Fakhoury Bldg, Montée Bain Militaire, Ardati St, Beirut; tel. (6) 867700 (also covers Jordan, Kuwait and Syria).

Libya: POB 286, Muzzafar al-Aftas St, Hay el-Andalous, Tripoli; tel. (21) 77885; telex 20733; fax (21) 77343.

Morocco: BP 601, Angle Charia Moulay Ibnouzaid et Zankat Roundanat No. 6, Rabat; tel. (7) 68633; telex 32947; fax (7) 68377.

Tunisia: BP 863, 61 blvd Bab-Benat, 1035 Tunis; tel. (1) 260203; telex 13777; fax (1) 568811.

Turkey: PK 407, 197 Atatürk Bul., Ankara; tel. (312) 4265485; telex 821-43684; fax (312) 4261372.

ARAB FUND FOR ECONOMIC AND SOCIAL DEVELOPMENT—AFESD

Address: POB 21923, Safat, 13080 Kuwait.
Telephone: 2451580; **telex:** 22153; **fax:** 2416758.
Established in 1968 by the Economic Council of the Arab League, the Fund began its operations in 1973. It participates in the financing of economic and social development projects in the Arab states.

MEMBERSHIP

Twenty countries and the Palestine Liberation Organization (see table of subscriptions below).

Organization

(October 1994)

BOARD OF GOVERNORS

The Board of Governors consists of a Governor and an Alternate Governor appointed by each member of the Fund. The Board of Governors is considered as the General Assembly of the Fund, and has all powers.

BOARD OF DIRECTORS

The Board of Directors is composed of eight Directors elected by the Board of Governors from among Arab citizens of recognized experience and competence. They are elected for a renewable term of two years.

The Board of Directors is charged with all the activities of the Fund and exercises the powers delegated to it by the Board of Governors.

Director-General and Chairman of the Board of Directors: ABDLATIF YOUSUF AL-HAMAD.

FINANCIAL STRUCTURE

In 1982 the authorized capital was increased from 400m. Kuwaiti dinars (KD) to KD 800m., divided into 80,000 shares having a value of KD 10,000 each. At the end of 1991 subscribed capital was KD 694.8m., and paid-up capital was KD 663.04m.

SUBSCRIPTIONS (KD million, December 1991)*

Algeria	. . .	64.78
Bahrain	. . .	2.16
Djibouti	. . .	0.02
Egypt	. . .	40.50
Iraq	. . .	63.52
Jordan	. . .	17.30
Kuwait	. . .	169.70
Lebanon	. . .	2.00
Libya	. . .	59.85
Mauritania	. . .	0.82
Morocco	. . .	16.00
Oman	. . .	17.28
Palestine Liberation Organization	. . .	1.10
Qatar	. . .	6.75
Saudi Arabia	. . .	159.07
Somalia	. . .	0.21
Sudan	. . .	11.06
Syria	. . .	24.00
Tunisia	. . .	6.16
United Arab Emirates	. .	28.00
Yemen	. . .	4.25
Total	. . .	**694.80**

* 100 Kuwaiti dinars = US $351.62 (December 1991).

Activities

The Fund participates in the financing of economic and social development projects in the Arab states and countries by:

1. Financing economic projects of an investment character by means of loans granted on easy terms to governments, and to public or private organizations and institutions, giving preference to economic projects of interest specifically to Arab peoples, and to joint Arab projects.

2. Encouraging, directly or indirectly, the investment of public and private capital in such a manner as to ensure the development and growth of the Arab economy.

3. Providing technical expertise and assistance in the various fields of economic development.

The Fund co-operates with other Arab organizations such as the Arab Monetary Fund, the League of Arab States and OAPEC in preparing regional studies and conferences, and acts as the secretariat of the Co-ordination Group of Arab National and Regional Development Institutions.

By the end of 1991 the Fund had made 262 loans for projects in 17 countries, since the beginning of its operations. The total value of these loans was KD 1,498m. Disbursements amounted to KD 710m. by the end of 1991.

During 1991 the Fund approved 11 loans totalling KD 171.45m. for projects in eight Arab countries (see table below). The energy sector received some 61% of total commitments.

The total number of technical assistance grants provided by the end of 1991 was 299, with a value of KD 34.33m. During 1991 eight new grants were approved, totalling KD 3.34m., of which the largest proportion (61%) was for training and institutional support.

LOANS BY SECTOR, 1991

Sector	Amount (KD million)	%
Agriculture, livestock and fisheries . .	7.20	4.2
Industry and mining	22.70	13.2
Transport and communications . . .	11.00	6.4
Water and sewerage	5.5	3.2
Energy	104.05	60.7
Other	21.00	12.3
Total	**171.45**	**100.0**

LOANS BY COUNTRY, 1991

Country	Project	Amount (KD million)
Algeria	Electricity	21.00
Bahrain	Roads	11.00
	Medical Centre	21.00
Egypt	Electricity	36.25
	Factory rehabilitation	10.50
	Social development	14.40
Jordan	Industrial development	5.00
Lebanon	Electricity	22.00
Oman	Natural gas	7.00
Syria	Water	5.50
Tunisia	Electricity	17.80
Total		**171.45**

ARAB MONETARY FUND

Address: POB 2818, Abu Dhabi, United Arab Emirates.
Telephone: 215000; **telex:** 22989; **fax:** (9712) 326454.
The Agreement establishing the Arab Monetary Fund was approved by the Economic Council of Arab States in Rabat, Morocco, in April 1976 and entered into force on 2 February 1977.

MEMBERS

Algeria	Oman
Bahrain	Palestine
Egypt	Qatar
Iraq*	Saudi Arabia
Jordan	Somalia*
Kuwait	Sudan*
Lebanon	Syria
Libya	Tunisia
Mauritania	United Arab Emirates
Morocco	Yemen

* From July 1993 loans to Iraq, Somalia and Sudan were suspended as a result of their failure to repay debts to the Fund totalling US $603m. By December 1993 the arrears amounted to $628m.

Organization

(August 1994)

BOARD OF GOVERNORS

The Board of Governors is the highest authority of the Arab Monetary Fund. It formulates policies on Arab economic integration and liberalization of trade among member states. With certain exceptions, it may delegate to the Board of Executive Directors some of its powers. The Board of Governors is composed of a governor and a deputy governor appointed by each member state for a term of five years. It meets at least once a year; meetings may also be convened at the request of half the members, or of members holding half of the total voting power.

BOARD OF EXECUTIVE DIRECTORS

The Board of Executive Directors exercises all powers vested in it by the Board of Governors and may delegate to the Director-General such powers as it deems fit. It is composed of the Director-General and eight non-resident directors elected by the Board of Governors. Each director holds office for three years and may be re-elected.

DIRECTOR-GENERAL

The Director-General of the Fund is appointed by the Board of Governors for a renewable five-year term, and serves as Chairman of the Board of Executive Directors.

The Director-General supervises a Committee on Loans and a Committee on Investments to make recommendations on loan and investment policies to the Board of Executive Directors, and is required to submit an Annual Report to the Board of Governors.

Director-General and Chairman of the Board of Executive Directors: Dr JASSIM AL-MANNAI.

FINANCE

The Arab Accounting Dinar (AAD) is a unit of account equivalent to 3 IMF Special Drawing Rights. (The average value of the SDR in 1993 was US $1.373560.)

Each member paid, in convertible currencies, 5% of the value of its shares at the time of its ratification of the Agreement and another 20% when the Agreement entered into force. In addition, each member paid 2% of the value of its shares in its national currency regardless of whether it is convertible. The second 25% of the capital was to be subscribed by the end of September 1979, bringing the total paid-up capital in convertible currencies to AAD 131.5m. (SDR 394.5m.). An increase in requests for loans led to a resolution by the Board of Governors in April 1981, giving members the option of paying the balance of their subscribed capital. This payment became obligatory in July 1981, when total approved loans exceeded 50% of the already paid-up capital in convertible currencies. In April 1983 the authorized capital of the Fund was increased from AAD 288m. to AAD 600m. The new capital stock comprised 12,000 shares, each having the value of AAD 50,000. At the end of 1993 total paid-up capital was AAD 326m.

CAPITAL SUBSCRIPTIONS
(million Arab Accounting Dinars, 31 December 1993)

Member	Authorized capital	Paid-up capital	Votes
Algeria	60.00	42.40	923
Bahrain	9.00	5.00	175
Egypt	60.00	32.00	715
Iraq	60.00	42.40	923
Jordan	11.00	5.40	183
Kuwait	60.00	32.00	715
Lebanon	13.00	5.00	175
Libya	30.00	13.44	344
Mauritania	9.00	5.00	175
Morocco	35.00	15.00	375
Oman	9.00	5.00	175
Palestine	4.00	2.16	118
Qatar	24.00	10.00	275
Saudi Arabia	90.00	48.40	1,043
Somalia	9.00	4.00	155
Sudan	25.00	10.00	275
Syria	20.00	7.20	219
Tunisia	15.00	7.00	215
United Arab Emirates	36.00	19.20	459
Yemen	21.00	15.40	408
Total	**600.00**	**326.00**	**8,095**

Activities

The creation of the Arab Monetary Fund was seen as a step towards the goal of Arab economic integration. It assists member states in balance of payments difficulties, and also has a broad range of aims.

The Articles of Agreement define the Fund's aims as follows:

(*a*) to correct disequilibria in the balance of payments of member states;

(*b*) to promote the stability of exchange rates among Arab currencies, to render them mutually convertible, and to eliminate restrictions on current payments between member states;

(*c*) to establish policies and modes of monetary co-operation to accelerate Arab economic integration and economic development in the member states;

(*d*) to tender advice on the investment of member states' financial resources in foreign markets, whenever called upon to do so;

(*e*) to promote the development of Arab financial markets;

(*f*) to promote the use of the Arab dinar as a unit of account and to pave the way for the creation of a unified Arab currency;

(*g*) to co-ordinate the positions of member states in dealing with international monetary and economic problems; and

(*h*) to provide a mechanism for the settlement of current payments between member states in order to promote trade among them.

The Arab Monetary Fund functions both as a fund and a bank. It is empowered:

(*a*) to provide short- and medium-term loans to finance balance of payments deficits of member states;

(*b*) to issue guarantees to member states to strengthen their borrowing capabilities;

(*c*) to act as intermediary in the issuance of loans in Arab and international markets for the account of member states and under their guarantees;

(*d*) to co-ordinate the monetary policies of member states;

(*e*) to manage any funds placed under its charge by member states;

(*f*) to hold periodic consultations with member states on their economic conditions; and

(*g*) to provide technical assistance to banking and monetary institutions in member states.

Loans are intended to finance an overall balance of payments deficit and a member may draw up to 75% of its paid-up subscription, in convertible currencies, for this purpose unconditionally (automatic loans). A member may, however, obtain loans in excess of this limit, subject to agreement with the Fund on a programme aimed at reducing its balance of payments deficit (ordinary and extended loans, equivalent to 175% and 225% of its quota respectively). From 1981 a country receiving no extended loans was entitled to a loan under the Inter-Arab Trade Facility (discontinued in 1989) of up to 100% of its quota. In addition, a member has the right to borrow up to 100% of its paid-up capital in order to cope with an unexpected deficit in its balance of payments resulting from a decrease in its exports of goods and services or a large increase in its imports of agricultural products following a poor harvest (compensatory loans). Over the period 1978–93, 91 loans were extended to 12 member countries.

Automatic and compensatory loans are repayable within three years, while ordinary and extended loans are repayable within five and seven years respectively. Loans are granted at concessionary and uniform rates of interest which increase with the length of the period of the loan.

At the end of 1993 total approved loans amounted to AAD 583.4m., of which AAD 572.0m. had been disbursed and AAD 420.9m. repaid.

In 1988 the Fund's executive directors agreed to modify their policy on lending, placing an emphasis on the correction of economic imbalances in recipient countries. In that year the Fund approved 14 loans totalling AAD 121.0m. During 1989 the Fund made six loans amounting to AAD 73.4m. During 1990 the Fund approved two loans amounting to AAD 15.7m., but in 1991 no new loans were approved. In 1992 the Fund approved two loans amounting to AAD 18.5m, and in 1993 approved one loan of AAD 3.25m.

In March 1989 Arab financial institutions agreed to establish an Arab Trade Financing Program (ATFP), to increase inter-Arab trade in goods and services (excluding petroleum) (see below).

The Fund also provides technical assistance to its member countries. Such assistance is furnished through either the provision of experts to the country concerned or in the form of specialized training of officials of member countries. In view of the increased importance of this type of assistance, the Fund established, in 1988, the Economic Policy Institute (EPI) which offers regular training courses and specialized seminars for middle-level and senior staff, respectively, of financial and monetary institutions of the Arab countries.

TRADE PROMOTION

Arab Trade Financing Program (ATFP): POB 26799, Abu Dhabi, United Arab Emirates; tel. 316999; telex 24166; fax 316793; f. 1989 to develop and liberalize trade between Arab countries, and to enhance the competitive ability of Arab exporters; operates by extending lines of credit to national agencies (designated by Arab governments) for exports and imports. The Arab Monetary Fund provided 50% of the ATFP's capital of US $500m., and participation was also invited from private and official Arab financial institutions and joint Arab/foreign institutions. Chief Exec. Dr JASSIM AL-MANNAI.

PUBLICATIONS

Annual Report.

Arab Countries: Economic Indicators (annually).

Cross Exchange Rates of Arab Currencies (annually).

Foreign Trade of Arab Countries (annually).

Joint Arab Economic Report (annually).

Money and Credit in Arab Countries.

National Accounts of Arab Countries (annually).

Balance of Payments and Public Debt of Arab Countries (annually).

AMF Publications Catalog (annually).

Reports on commodity structure (by value and quantity) of member countries' imports from and exports to other Arab countries.

LOANS APPROVED, 1993

Borrower	Type of loan	Amount (AAD million)
Mauritania	Extended	3.25
Total		3.25

LOANS APPROVED, 1978–93

Type of loan	Number of loans	Amount (AAD '000)
Automatic	51	241,260
Ordinary	9	89,080
Compensatory	9	67,365
Extended	11	120,915
Inter-Arab Trade Facility (cancelled in 1989)	11	64,730
Total	91	583,350

CO-OPERATION COUNCIL FOR THE ARAB STATES OF THE GULF

Address: POB 7153, Riyadh 11462, Saudi Arabia.

Telephone: (1) 482-7777; **telex:** 403635; **fax:** (1) 482-9089.

More generally known as the Gulf Co-operation Council (GCC), the organization was established on 25 May 1981 by six Arab states.

MEMBERS

Bahrain	Oman	Saudi Arabia
Kuwait	Qatar	United Arab Emirates

Organization

(August 1994)

SUPREME COUNCIL

The Supreme Council is the highest authority of the GCC, comprises the heads of member states and meets annually in ordinary session, and in emergency session if demanded by two or more members. The Presidency of the Council is undertaken by each state in turn, in alphabetical order. The Supreme Council draws up the overall policy of the organization; it discusses recommendations and laws presented to it by the Ministerial Council and the Secretariat General in preparation for endorsement. The GCC's charter provides for the creation of a commission for the settlement of disputes between member states, to be attached to and appointed by the Supreme Council.

MINISTERIAL COUNCIL

The Ministerial Council consists of the foreign ministers of member states, meeting every three months, and in emergency session if demanded by two or more members. It prepares for the meetings of the Supreme Council, and draws up policies, recommendations, studies and projects aimed at developing co-operation and co-ordination among member states in various spheres.

SECRETARIAT GENERAL

The Secretariat assists member states in implementing recommendations by the Supreme and Ministerial Councils, and prepares reports and studies, budgets and accounts. The Secretary-General is appointed by the Supreme Council for a renewable three-year term. The Assistant Secretary-Generals are appointed by the Ministerial Council upon the recommendation of the Secretary-General. All member states contribute in equal proportions towards the budget of the Secretariat.

Secretary-General: Sheikh FAHIM AL-QASSIMI (Qatar).

Assistant Secretary-General for Political Affairs: SAIF BIN HASHIL AL-MASKERY (Oman).

Assistant Secretary-General for Economic Affairs: Dr ABDULLAH AL-KUWAIZ (Saudi Arabia).

Activities

The GCC was set up following a series of meetings of foreign ministers of the states concerned, culminating in an agreement on the basic details of its charter on 10 March 1981. The Charter was signed by the six heads of state on 25 May. It describes the organization as providing 'the means for realizing co-ordination, integration and co-operation' in all economic, social and cultural affairs. A series of ministerial meetings subsequently began to put the proposals into effect.

ECONOMIC CO-OPERATION

In November 1982 GCC ministers drew up a 'unified economic agreement' covering freedom of movement of people and capital, the abolition of customs duties, technical co-operation, harmonization of banking regulations and financial and monetary co-ordination. At the same time GCC heads of state approved the formation of a Gulf Investment Corporation, with capital of US $2,100m., to be based in Kuwait (see below). Customs duties on domestic products of the Gulf states were abolished in March 1983, and new regulations allowing free movement of workers and vehicles between member states were also introduced. In 1985 unified patent legislation was discussed, to deal with the increasing problem of counterfeit goods in the region. A common minimum customs levy (of between 4% and 20%) on foreign imports was imposed in 1986. In May 1992 GCC trade ministers announced the objective of establishing a GCC common market by 2000. In September GCC ministers reached agreement on the application of a unified system of tariffs by March 1993. At a meeting of the Supreme Council, held in December 1992, however, it was decided to mandate GCC officials to formulate a plan for the introduction of common external tariffs, to be presented to the Council in December 1993. Only the tax on tobacco products was to be standardized from March 1993, at a rate of 50%. In April 1994 ministers of finance agreed to pursue a gradual approach to unifying tariffs, which was to be achieved according to a schedule over two to three years.

In February 1987 the governors of the member states' central banks agreed in principle to co-ordinate their rates of exchange, and this was approved by the Supreme Council in November. It was subsequently agreed to link the Gulf currencies to a 'basket' of other currencies. In October 1990, following the Iraqi invasion of Kuwait, GCC Governments agreed to provide support for regional banks affected by the crisis. In July 1991 GCC central bank governors agreed to co-operate on reducing the risks involved in banking in GCC countries, following the collapse of the Bank of Credit and Commerce International (BCCI) of which the an-Nahyan family (the ruling family in Abu Dhabi, United Arab Emirates) was the majority shareholder. The GCC central bank governors agreed in April 1993 to establish a joint banking supervisory committee, in order to set out rules for GCC banks operating in other member states. They also decided to allow Kuwait's currency to become part of the GCC monetary system that was set up following Iraq's invasion of Kuwait in order to defend the Gulf currencies.

TRADE

In 1982 a ministerial committee was formed to co-ordinate trade development in the region. A feasibility study was commissioned on the establishment of strategic food reserves for the member states, and the joint purchase of rice was undertaken. In November 1986 the Supreme Council approved a measure whereby citizens of GCC member states were enabled to undertake certain retail trade activities in any other member state, with effect from 1 March 1987. The ministerial committee in charge of trade also forms the board of directors of the GCC Standards and Metrology Organization, which approves minimum standards for goods produced in or imported to the region: by mid-1988 99 Gulf standards had been approved. A joint trade exhibition is held annually.

INDUSTRY

In 1985, following a series of meetings of the GCC ministers of industry, the Supreme Council endorsed a common industrial strategy for the GCC states. It approved regulations stipulating that priority should be given to imports of GCC industrial products, and permitting GCC investors to obtain loans from GCC industrial development banks. In November 1986 resolutions were adopted on the protection of industrial products, and on the co-ordination of industrial projects, in order to avoid duplication. A number of studies of investment opportunities, and feasibility studies for joint industrial projects, were undertaken in the late 1980s.

AGRICULTURE

A unified agricultural policy for GCC countries was endorsed by the Supreme Council in November 1985. Between 1983 and 1987

ministers also approved proposals for harmonizing legislation relating to water conservation, veterinary vaccines, insecticides, fertilizers, fisheries and seeds. Studies on the establishment of two joint veterinary laboratories (for diagnosis of virus diseases and for production of vaccines), and on agricultural and veterinary quarantine, have also been undertaken. In 1987 two private Saudi Arabian companies were designated as official GCC producers of seed and poultry.

TRANSPORT AND COMMUNICATIONS

During 1985 feasibility studies were undertaken on new rail and road links between member states, and on the establishment of a joint coastal transport company. In December it was announced that implementation of a scheme to build a 1,700-km railway to link all the member states and Iraq (and thereby the European railway network) had been postponed, owing to its high cost (estimated at US $4,000m.). In January 1986 ministers agreed to establish a joint telecommunications network. In November 1993 ministers agreed to request assistance from the International Telecommunications Union on the integration of the region's telecommunications networks, which was approved in 1986. The telecommunications systems were to be integrated through underwater fibre-optic cables and a regional satellite-based mobile telephone network, which was to be fully operational by late 1994.

ENERGY

In 1982 a ministerial committee was established to co-ordinate hydrocarbons policies and prices. Sub-committees were also formed to exchange information on marketing and prices; to discuss the development of the hydrocarbons refining industry; to examine domestic energy consumption and subsidies; to co-ordinate training by national petroleum companies; and to co-ordinate exploration for minerals. In 1982 ministers also adopted a petroleum security plan to safeguard individual members against a halt in their production, to form a stockpile of petroleum products, and to organize a boycott of any non-member country when appropriate. In December 1987 the Supreme Council adopted a plan whereby a member state whose petroleum production was disrupted could 'borrow' petroleum from other members, in order to fulfil its export obligations.

In late 1992 GCC ministers were examining proposals, based on a feasibility study, to integrate the electricity networks of the six member countries. In the first stage of the plan the networks of Saudi Arabia, Bahrain, Kuwait and Qatar would be integrated; those of the United Arab Emirates and Oman would be interconnected and finally linked to the others in the second stage, to be completed by 2003.

REGIONAL SECURITY

Although no mention of defence or security was made in the original charter, the summit meeting which ratified the charter also issued a statement rejecting any foreign military presence in the region. The Supreme Council meeting in November 1981 agreed to include defence co-operation in the activities of the organization: as a result, defence ministers met in January 1982 to discuss a common security policy, including a joint air defence system and standardization of weapons. In November 1984 member states agreed to form the Peninsula Shield Force for rapid deployment against external aggression, comprising units from the armed forces of each country under a central command to be based in Saudi Arabia.

In October 1987 (following an Iranian missile attack on Kuwait, which supported Iraq in its war against Iran) GCC ministers of foreign affairs issued a statement declaring that aggression against one member state was regarded as aggression against them all. In December the Supreme Council studied a report by ministers of defence on protecting vessels and coastal installations against Iranian attacks, and approved a joint pact on regional co-operation in matters of security. In early August 1990, following the Iraqi invasion of Kuwait, the Ministerial Council issued a statement describing the invasion as a violation of sovereignty, and demanding the withdrawal of Iraqi troops from Kuwait. GCC ministers of defence met towards the end of August and put on alert the Peninsula Shield Force to counter any attempted invasion of Saudi Arabia by Iraq. In December, the GCC Supreme Council meeting, held in Qatar, issued a communiqué demanding that Iraq should withdraw completely from Kuwait or be faced with the prospect of war.

During the crisis and the ensuing war between Iraq and a multinational force which took place in January and February 1991, the GCC developed closer links with Egypt and Syria, which, together with Saudi Arabia, played the most active role among the Arab countries in the anti-Iraqi alliance. In March the six GCC nations, Egypt and Syria formulated the 'Declaration of Damascus', which announced plans to establish a regional peace-keeping force. The Declaration also urged the abolition of all weapons of mass destruction in the area, and recommended the resolution of the Palestinian question by an international conference. In June 1991 Egypt and Syria, whose troops were to have formed the largest proportion of the peace-keeping force, announced their withdrawal from the project, reportedly as a result of disagreements with the GCC concerning the composition of the proposed force and the remuneration involved. A meeting of ministers of foreign affairs of the eight countries took place in July, but agreed only to provide mutual military assistance when necessary, thus apparently abandoning the establishment of a joint force. Subsequently, GCC countries appeared more concerned to conclude individual security agreements with the USA, with Kuwait (still the most vulnerable of the GCC states) eager for a US, rather than Egyptian or Syrian, military presence. In June 1992 the GCC member states indicated that they had not completely abandoned the Declaration of Damascus, when they consented in principle to the convening of a summit conference on the pact, proposed by the Egyptian President. A meeting of the signatories of the Damascus Declaration, convened in September, adopted a joint statement on regional questions, including the Middle East peace process and the UAE's dispute with Iran (see below), but rejected an Egyptian proposal to establish a series of rapid deployment forces which could be called upon to defend the interests of any of the eight countries. A meeting of GCC ministers of defence in November agreed to maintain the Peninsula Shield Force. In November 1993 GCC ministers of defence approved a proposal to expand the force from 8,000 to 17,000 troops and incorporate air and naval units. Ministers also agreed to strengthen the defence of the region by developing joint surveillance and early warning systems. A GCC military committee was established, and convened in April 1994, to discuss the implementation of the proposals.

In early September 1992 a meeting of the Ministerial Council endorsed the imposition by the USA, the United Kingdom, France and Russia of an air exclusion zone over southern Iraq in late August, which was designed to protect the population of that part of the country from attacks by the Iraqi armed forces. At the same meeting the GCC expressed opposition to Iran's 'continued occupation' of islands claimed by the United Arab Emirates (UAE): namely Abu Musa and the Greater and Lesser Tumb islands. The Supreme Council, which met in December, reiterated the GCC's demand that Iran should withdraw from the three islands in the Persian (Arabian) Gulf claimed by the UAE. Iran responded by stating that the GCC would have to take the islands by force. In April 1993, however, Iran removed its restrictions on the movement of people to the island of Abu Musa, a development welcomed by the GCC states. In December the Supreme Council urged Iran to respond to the UAE request to conduct direct negotiations on the sovereignty of the islands.

In late September 1992 a rift within the GCC was caused by an incident on the disputed border between Saudi Arabia and Qatar, in which two Qatari soldiers and one Saudi civilian were killed. Qatar's threat to boycott a meeting of the Supreme Council in December was allayed at the last minute as a result of mediation efforts by the Egyptian President. At the meeting, which was held in UAE, Qatar and Saudi Arabia agreed to establish a joint commission to demarcate the disputed border by 1994. However, by mid-1994 no progress had been made to establish the commission.

In July 1994 ministers of foreign affairs of the eight signatories of the Damascus Declaration met to discuss a united policy in response to civil war in Yemen. Seven of the countries issued a communique stating their condemnation of the continued fighting and demanding a cease-fire. Qatar did not give its support to the document, which failed to award recognition to a separate southern Yemen state.

EXTERNAL RELATIONS

In 1984 and 1985 representatives of the GCC and the European Community discussed access to European markets by GCC petro-chemical products (with reference to tariffs that were imposed on GCC petrochemicals by the EC in June 1984). In June 1988 an agreement was signed by GCC and EC ministers on economic co-operation (with effect from January 1990): the EC agreed to assist the GCC states in developing their agriculture and industry. A Joint Co-operation Council was established under the agreement, which was to comprise EC and GCC ministers, and which met annually from 1990. In October 1989 the Commission of the EC proposed to EC member governments that Community tariffs on imports of petrochemicals from the GCC should be phased out over a period of 12–16 years. In March 1990, at the first meeting of the Joint Co-operation Council, GCC and EC ministers of foreign affairs undertook to hold negotiations on a free-trade agreement. Discussions began in October, although any final accord would require the GCC to adopt a unified structure of customs duties. In early 1992 the agreement was jeopardized by the GCC's opposition to the EC's proposed tax on fossil fuels (in order to reduce pollution) which would have raised the price of a barrel of petroleum by US $10 by 2000, although in May EC member states failed to agree on the 'carbon tax'.With the new US administration proposing a similar energy tax, in March 1993 GCC oil ministers threatened to restrict the supply of petroleum (the GCC countries control almost one-half of the world's petroleum reserves) in retaliation. By mid-1994 the European Union (as the restructured EC was now known) had still not reached agreement on the tax.

The second joint EC/GCC industrial conference was held in Doha, Qatar, in October 1992. In the early 1990s countries in the Far East overtook European countries and the USA as the GCC states' leading trading partners, with the largest amount of trade being conducted with Japan and China (followed by the USA and Germany).

In April 1991, in the wake of the Gulf War, the GCC announced that a development fund was to be created, with the intention of creating greater political and economic stability in the region. This fund, which would be financed by the GCC states, would assist mainly Egypt and Syria, as a reward for their active military part in the Gulf War and their major role in the security force envisaged by the Declaration of Damascus. The GCC made it clear that those countries and organizations which had supported Iraq during its occupation of Kuwait would not be beneficiaries of the new fund. Jordan, Yemen and the PLO, which had received millions of dollars in aid from the GCC countries in 1990, would not be assisted by the Council in the near future. The establishment of the Arab Development Fund (as it became known) was formally approved by GCC ministers of finance and foreign affairs in late December 1991. The Fund was to be administered by the Saudi Arabian Monetary Agency. A starting capital of US $10,000m. was originally envisaged for the Fund, although by mid-1992 only $6,500m. had been pledged, with reports that the project had been scaled down. In May 1993 ministers of finance from the GCC states, Egypt and Syria, meeting in Qatar, failed to agree on the level of contributions to the Fund.

INVESTMENT CORPORATION

Gulf Investment Corporation (GIC): Joint Banking Center, Kuwait Real Estate Bldg, POB 3402, Safat 13035, Kuwait; tel. 2431911; telex 44002; fax 2448894; f. 1983 by the six member states of the GCC, each contributing US $350m. of the total capital of $2,100m.; paid-up capital $540m. (Dec. 1989), total assets $7,565m. (1992); investment chiefly in the Gulf region, financing industrial projects (including pharmaceuticals, chemicals, steel wire, aircraft engineering, aluminium, dairy produce and chicken-breeding). By the end of 1988, 120 proposed projects had been reviewed, and 11 (with equity participation by the Corporation amounting to $45m.) had been approved. GIC provides merchant banking and financial advisory services, and in 1992 was appointed to advise the Kuwaiti Government on a programme of privatization. In 1993 GIC expanded its investment banking, financial services and capital markets sectors, and was expected to develop these further in 1994. Chair. MUHAMMAD ABALKHALI (Saudi Arabia); Chief Exec. Dr KHALED AL-FAYEZ. Publ. *The GIC Gazetteer* (annually).

COUNCIL OF ARAB ECONOMIC UNITY

Address: PO Box (1) Mohammed Fareed, Cairo, Egypt.
Telephone: (2) 755321; **fax:** (2) 754090.
The first meeting of the Council was held in 1964.

MEMBERS

Egypt	Palestine Liberation
Iraq	Organization
Jordan	Somalia
Kuwait	Sudan
Libya	Syria
Mauritania	United Arab Emirates
	Yemen

Organization

(August 1994)

COUNCIL

The Council consists of representatives of member states, usually ministers of economy, finance and trade. It meets twice a year; meetings are chaired by the representative of each country for one year.

GENERAL SECRETARIAT

Entrusted with the implementation of the Council's decisions and with proposing work plans, including efforts to encourage participation by member states in the Arab Economic Unity Agreement. The Secretariat also compiles statistics, conducts research and publishes studies on Arab economic problems and on the effects of major world economic trends.

Secretary-General: HASAN IBRAHIM.

Assistant Secretary-General: MAHMOUD KHALIL EL-GAZZAR.

COMMITTEES

There are seven standing committees: preparatory, follow-up and Arab Common Market development; Permanent Delegates; budget; economic planning; fiscal and monetary matters; customs and trade planning and co-ordination; statistics. There are also seven 'ad hoc' committees, including meetings of experts on tariffs, trade promotion and trade legislation.

Activities

A five-year work plan for the General Secretariat in 1986–90 was approved in December 1985. As in the previous five-year plan, it included the co-ordination of measures leading to a customs union subject to a unified administration; market and commodity studies; unification of statistical terminology and methods of data collection; studies for the formation of new joint Arab companies and federations; formulation of specific programmes for agricultural and industrial co-ordination and for improving road and railway networks.

ARAB COMMON MARKET

Members: Egypt, Iraq, Jordan, Libya, Mauritania, Syria and Yemen.

Based on a resolution passed by the Council in August 1964; its implementation is supervised by the Council and does not constitute a separate organization. Customs duties and other taxes on trade between the member countries were eliminated in annual stages, the process being completed in 1971. The second stage was to be the adoption of a full customs union, and ultimately all restrictions on trade between the member countries, including quotas, and restrictions on residence, employment and transport, were to be abolished. In practice, however, the trading of national products has not been freed from all monetary, quantitative and administrative restrictions.

Between 1978 and 1989, the following measures were undertaken by the Council for the development of the Arab Common Market:

Introduction of flexible membership conditions for the least developed Arab states (Mauritania, Somalia, Sudan and Yemen).

Approval in principle of a fund to compensate the least developed countries for financial losses incurred as a result of joining the Arab Common Market.

Approval of legal, technical and administrative preparations for unification of tariffs levied on products imported from non-member countries.

Formation of a committee of ministerial deputies to deal with problems in the application of market rulings and to promote the organization's activities.

Adoption of unified customs legislation and of an integrated programme aimed at enhancing trade between member states and expanding members' productive capacity.

MULTILATERAL AGREEMENTS

The Council has initiated the following multilateral agreements aimed at achieving economic unity:

Agreement on Basic Levels of Social Insurance.

Agreement on Reciprocity in Social Insurance Systems.

Agreement on Labour Mobility.

Agreement on Organization of Transit Trade.

Agreement on Avoidance of Double Taxation and Elimination of Tax Evasion.

Agreement on Co-operation in Collection of Taxes.

Agreement on Capital Investment and Mobility.

Agreement on Settlement of Investment Disputes between Host Arab Countries and Citizens of Other Countries.

JOINT VENTURES

A number of multilateral organizations in industry and agriculture have been formed on the principle that faster development and economies of scale may be achieved by combining the efforts of member states. In industries that are new to the member countries, Arab Joint Companies are formed, while existing industries are co-ordinated by the setting up of Arab Specialized Unions. The unions are for closer co-operation on problems of production and marketing, and to help companies deal as a group in international markets. The companies are intended to be self-supporting on a purely commercial basis; they may issue shares to citizens of the participating countries. The joint ventures are:

Arab Joint Companies (cap.=capital; figures in Kuwaiti dinars unless otherwise stated):

Arab Company for Drug Industries and Medical Appliances: POB 925161, Amman, Jordan; cap. 60m.

Arab Company for Industrial Investment: POB 2154, Baghdad, Iraq; cap. 150m.

Arab Company for Livestock Development: POB 5305, Damascus, Syria; tel. 666037; telex 11376; cap. 60m.

Arab Mining Company: POB 20198, Amman, Jordan; telex 21169; cap. 120m.

Specialized Arab Unions and Federations:

Arab Co-operative Federation: POB 57640, Baghdad, Iraq; telex 2685.

Arab Federation of Chemical Fertilizers Producers: POB 23696, Kuwait.

Arab Federation of Engineering Industries: POB 509, Baghdad, Iraq; tel. 776-1101; telex 2724.

Arab Federation of Leather Industries: POB 2188, Damascus, Syria.

Arab Federation of Paper Industries: POB 5456, Baghdad, Iraq.

Arab Federation of Shipping Industries: POB 1161, Baghdad, Iraq.

Arab Federation of Textile Industries: POB 620, Damascus, Syria.

Arab Federation of Travel Agents: POB 7090, Amman, Jordan.

Arab Seaports Federation: Basrah, Iraq.

Arab Sugar Federation: POB 195, Khartoum, Sudan.

Arab Union for Cement and Building Materials: POB 9015, Damascus, Syria; tel. (11) 6665070; telex 412602; fax (11) 6621525.

Arab Union of Fish Producers: POB 15064, Baghdad, Iraq; tel. 551-1261.

Arab Union of Food Industries: POB 13025, Baghdad, Iraq.

Arab Union of Land Transport: POB 926324, Amman, Jordan.

Arab Union of Pharmaceutical Manufacturers and Medical Appliance Manufacturers: POB 1124, Amman, Jordan; tel. 665320; telex 21528.

Arab Union of Railways: POB 6599, Aleppo, Syria; tel. 220302; telex 331009.

General Arab Insurance Federation: POB 611, Cairo, Egypt; telex 93141; fax 762310.

PUBLICATIONS

Annual Bibliography.

Annual Bulletin for Arab Countries' Foreign Trade Statistics.

Annual Bulletin for Official Exchange Rates of Arab Currencies.

Arab Economic Unity Bulletin (2 a year).

Demographic Yearbook for Arab Countries.

Economic Report of the General Secretary (2 a year).

Guide to Studies prepared by Secretariat.

Progress Report (2 a year).

Statistical Yearbook for Arab Countries.

Yearbook for Intra-Arab Trade Statistics.

Yearbook of National Accounts for Arab Countries.

THE EUROPEAN UNION

The Mediterranean Policy of the European Union*

The European Community's scheme to negotiate a series of parallel trade and co-operation agreements encompassing almost all of the non-member states on the coast of the Mediterranean, known as the global policy for the Mediterranean, was formulated in 1972. Association agreements, intended to lead to customs union or the eventual full accession of the country concerned, had been signed with Greece in 1962, Turkey in 1964, and Malta in 1971, and a fourth agreement was signed with Cyprus in 1972. Simple trade agreements with Spain, Portugal and Yugoslavia were all effective by September 1973. (Greece became a member of the Community in 1981, and Portugal and Spain did so in 1986). During the 1970s a series of agreements, covering trade and economic co-operation were concluded, with the Arab Mediterranean countries and Israel.

The trade and co-operation agreements all had a similar structure, and had much in common with the main provisions of the Association agreements. Special organizations (Association or Co-operation Councils, comprising representatives of the Community and of the respective countries) were instituted to supervise the implementation of the agreements for each country.

All agreements established free access to EC markets for most industrial products, either soon or immediately. Access for agricultural products was facilitated, although some tariffs remained. For refined petroleum, cotton and phosphate fertilizers the EC imposed quotas for a transitional period on some of the Mediterranean countries. The principle of reciprocity (the granting of preferences in return) was not applied immediately in all of the co-operation agreements; in the Association agreements, and some others, there were provisions for its introduction in the medium- or long-term future, should the economic progress of the Mediterranean country concerned warrant this. In the event of a disturbance in a particular sector, or of economic decline in a particular region, the contracting party concerned was entitled to take protective action.

Many of the agreements were accompanied by financial protocols stating the amount of each category of aid which the Mediterranean country would receive. Financial aid takes the form of direct grants, as well as loans from the European Investment Bank (EIB).

A review carried out by the Commission of the European Communities in 1982 concluded that the policy was far from achieving its aim of creating a free-trade zone encompassing the EC and most of its southern neighbours. Agricultural items which the Mediterranean countries all wished to export to the Community, such as citrus fruits, olive oil and wine, were in surplus in the Community already. In addition, instead of providing a market for industrial products from its Mediterranean neighbours, the Community had been obliged to protect its own producers against competitive imports, particularly of textiles, footwear and processed food-stuffs.

In 1982 the Commission formulated an integrated plan for the development of its own Mediterranean regions and recommended the adoption of a new policy towards the non-Community countries of the Mediterranean. This would include greater co-operation in helping to diversify agriculture, so as to avoid surpluses and reduce the countries' dependence on imported food. The Commission also called for a return to the original principle of free access to the Community market for industrial goods from its Mediterranean neighbours, together with more efficient negotiating machinery to take action when problems arise.

In 1985 the Commission negotiated modifications in agreements with non-member Mediterranean countries to ensure that their exports of agricultural produce to the EC would not be adversely affected by the accession of Portugal and Spain to the Community at the beginning of 1986.

In December 1990, as part of the EC's new policy on the Mediterranean of providing greater financial assistance, the European Council approved ECU 2,075m. in loans and grants for the Maghreb and Mashreq countries and Israel, over the five-year period from November 1991. This amount was to include support for structural adjustment programmes, undertaken in conjunction with the IMF and the World Bank, and in particular to compensate for the adverse social effects of adjustment programmes. Particular emphasis was also to be placed on increasing production of food, promoting investment, the development of small and medium-sized businesses, and protection of the environment. In July 1991 an additional ECU 60m. was granted to the Palestinians in the Occupied Territories who had been adversely affected by the Gulf War in January–February. In 1992 the EC spent ECU 17m. on aid to the Occupied Territories, in addition to funds channelled through UNRWA (q.v.). In September 1993, following the signing of an Israeli-PLO peace agreement, the EC committed ECU 33m. in immediate humanitarian assitance for the provision of housing, education and the development of small businesses in Jericho and the Gaza Strip. In addition, a five-year assistance programme for the period 1994–98 was proposed, which was to consist of ECU 500m. in grants and loans to improve the economic and social infrastructure in the Occupied Territories. The programme was to promote the Commission's declared commitment to support regional co-operation and development in order to consolidate the peace process. In May 1994 the Commission awarded ECU 10m. to support the establishment of a Palestinian police force in the Occupied Territories.

In 1992 the EC began implementing a new Mediterranean policy, the basis of which was to be a consistent political approach for the development of the region. From 1 January 1993 the majority of agricultural exports from Mediterranean non-Community countries were granted exemption from customs duties. The new policy incorporated initiatives, additional to financial protocols concluded with each country, to strengthen EC-Mediterranean financial co-operation. In 1993 ECU 52.6m. was committed for operations concerning the environment, research and co-operation programmes. In addition, the EIB granted loans totalling ECU 220m., mostly for the energy, telecommunications and environment sectors.

Co-operation Agreements

THE MAGHREB COUNTRIES

Countries: Algeria, Morocco, Tunisia.

Signature: April 1976.

Date of coming into force: (trade provisions only) July 1976; full agreement signed January 1979.

Legal basis: Article 238 of the Treaty of Rome.

Under the agreement, industrial products were granted immediate duty free entry to the EC, while customs preferences were awarded for certain agricultural products. Restrictive quotas were, however, subsequently imposed on textile exports from the Maghreb, in order to protect the EC's domestic industry.

Conditions for migrant workers from the Maghreb countries were slightly improved under the agreement. One innovation was

---

* The European Union was formally established on 1 November 1993 under the Treaty on European Union; prior to this it was known as the European Community (EC).

the right to accumulate pension rights and other social benefits from periods of residence in different EC countries; another was the right to continue to draw pensions and other allowances after returning to the country of origin.

Economic and technical co-operation is included in the agreement. Financial assistance approved for 1987–91 amounted to ECU 239m. for Algeria, ECU 324m. for Morocco and ECU 224m. for Tunisia. In January 1992 the European Parliament blocked ECU 438m. of grants and loans to Morocco for 1991–96 (under the fourth financial protocol with that country) in protest at Morocco's activities in Western Sahara, and made Algeria's aid of ECU 350m. conditional on progress towards democracy. Financial assistance of ECU 284m. was approved for Tunisia for 1991–96. In October 1992 the European Parliament released the financial aid to Morocco.

In 1987 Morocco applied to join the EC but its application was rejected on the grounds that it is not a European country. In 1988 the EC reached an agreement with Morocco concerning fishing rights for the Spanish and Portuguese fleets in Moroccan waters (formerly subject to bilateral treaties).

In June 1992 the EC approved a proposal to conclude new bilateral agreements with the Maghreb countries. The new agreements were to have four main components: political dialogue; economic, technical and cultural co-operation; financial co-operation; and the eventual establishment of a free trade area. Preliminary negotiations for the conclusion of a new agreement with Morocco commenced in December 1993.

THE MASHREQ COUNTRIES

Countries: Egypt, Jordan, Lebanon, Syria.

Signature: (Egypt, Jordan, Syria) January 1977; (Lebanon) April 1977.

Date of coming into force: (trade provisions) July 1977; (financial protocols) March 1977; the financial protocol with Lebanon was signed later in 1977; full agreement signed in September 1978 after ratification.

Legal basis: Egypt, Jordan, Syria: Article 113 of the Treaty of Rome; Lebanon: Article 238.

Under the agreement, industrial products were granted tariff reductions of 80% until July 1977, and afterwards exempted from tariffs by the EC. Quantitative restrictions were removed as from January 1977. A wide range of tariff reductions were also granted for agricultural produce, varying between products from 30% to 80%.

In order to further economic and technical development in the Mashreq countries the EC approved a total of ECU 449m. for Egypt, ECU 100m. for Jordan and ECU 73m. for Lebanon to cover the period 1987–91. In November 1986 the EC imposed limited sanctions against Syria, in response to Syria's alleged involvement in international terrorism, and the disbursement of aid was not resumed until September 1987. Negotiations on assistance for Syria for 1987–91 (totalling ECU 146m.) were not concluded until late 1990.

Following the Iraqi invasion of Kuwait in August 1990, additional financial aid was provided to Egypt and Jordan, which, together with Turkey, were the two countries most directly affected by the regional crisis. Assistance approved in December for the three countries amounted to ECU 500m., and an additional ECU 58m. in emergency aid was approved for the repatriation of refugees living in Egypt and Jordan. For 1991–96 assistance approved amounted to ECU 568m. for Egypt, ECU 126m. for Jordan, ECU 69m. for Lebanon and ECU 126m. for Syria.

ISRAEL

Signature: May 1975.

Date of coming into force: (trade provisions) July 1975; (financial protocol) February 1977.

Legal basis: Article 113 of the Treaty of Rome.

In industrial sectors, according to the agreement, tariffs and related obstacles to free trade were to be removed on both sides. This was to be achieved for Israel's exports to the EC by July 1977, for 60% of EC exports to Israel by 1980 and for the remaining 40% by 1985. In 1980 Israel was authorized to defer by two years certain tariff provisions applicable to industrial products.

As regards agriculture, the EC reduced its tariffs substantially for products accounting for 85% of Israel's exports to the EC; these included products which the community had traditionally imported from Israel, for example some vegetables and fruit juices.

An additional protocol on industrial, technical and financial co-operation was signed in February 1977. Assistance for the period 1987–91, amounting to ECU 63m., was approved by the Community in early 1987. In 1988, however, the European Parliament delayed a vote on the aid protocol, together with two other protocols that were intended to modify the co-operation agree-

ment, following the accession to the Community of Portugal and Spain. The Parliament criticized Israel's response to unrest in the Occupied Territories of the West Bank and the Gaza Strip, and also Israel's initial refusal to permit independent exports of Palestinian agricultural produce to Europe. The three protocols were not ratified by the Parliament until October 1988.

In July 1991 additional aid of ECU 187.5m. was granted to Israel to alleviate the effects of the Gulf War that had followed Iraq's invasion of Kuwait. For 1991–96 loans to Israel amounting to ECU 82m. were approved.

In December 1993 the European Council authorized the Commission to commence negotiations for a new association agreement with Israel to replace that of 1975. The agreement was to boost trade, liberalize contract procurement and include the provision of EU support for co-operation projects, in accordance with the EU's objective of achieving a balanced approach to economic development in the whole region.

YEMEN ARAB REPUBLIC

Signature: October 1984.

Date of coming into force: January 1985.

The non-preferential agreement was to run for an initial period of five years, covering commercial, economic and development co-operation. In May 1989 the EC decided to intensify and diversify its co-operation with the Yemen Arab Republic. In June 1992 the European Council agreed to extend the original co-operation agreement to include the whole of the new Republic of Yemen (formed by the unification of the Yemen Arab Republic with the People's Democratic Republic of Yemen in 1990). In February 1993 the Joint EC-Yemen Committee met to discuss issues concerning trade, and economic and development co-operation.

CO-OPERATION COUNCIL FOR THE ARAB STATES OF THE GULF

Countries: Bahrain, Kuwait, Oman, Qatar, Saudi Arabia, United Arab Emirates.

Signature: June 1988.

Date of coming into force: January 1990.

In March 1983 it was agreed that the Commission and the Co-operation Council for the Arab States of the Gulf (GCC, q.v.) should undertake a programme of technical co-operation in statistics, customs matters, information and energy. During 1984–86 discussions were held on trade, and in particular on access to European markets for the GCC's refined petroleum products, after tariffs were imposed by the EC in 1984 on certain petrochemicals from the region. Following the signature of the co-operation agreement, further negotiations were held on the liberalization of trade, and a meeting on industrial co-operation was held in February 1990. Negotiations on a full free-trade pact began in October, but it was expected that any agreement would involve transition periods of some 12 years for the reduction of European tariffs on 'sensitive products' (i.e. petrochemicals). In 1992–93 the agreement was jeopardized as a result of the GCC's opposition to an EC proposal to introduce a supplementary tax on petroleum, in order to reduce the use of pollutant-releasing fossil fuels as well as the failure of the GCC to adopt a unified tariff structure. (See p. 226). In May 1994 the two parties held further discussions, but agreed that conclusion of the agreement was not imminent given the persisting obstacles.

IRAN

In April 1992 the EC held talks with Iran aimed at eventually concluding a co-operation agreement with that country.

Association Agreements

CYPRUS

Signature: 1972.

Date of coming into force: June 1973.

Legal basis: Article 238 of the Treaty of Rome.

Immediate tariff reductions were made by the EC of 70% in the industrial sector, 40% for citrus fruit and 100% for carob beans. From July 1977 onwards the EC granted duty-free entry to industrial goods from Cyprus, limited by tariff quotas in respect of man-made textiles and some garments. Since 1978 specific tariff reductions have been granted on fruit and vegetables.

Tariffs on imports into Cyprus from the EC were generally reduced in annual stages, except in certain sectors, where the competition was felt to be harmful. Since 1978 Cyprus has been applying 35% tariff reductions on most Community products.

In December 1987 the European Council adopted two protocols, one adapting the Association Agreement in the light of the accession of Portugal and Spain to the Community, and the other providing for the establishment of a full customs union, to be completed in two phases.

In June 1990 a third financial protocol entered into force, providing ECU 62m. for Cyprus in 1989–93.

In July 1990 Cyprus made a formal application to join the EC. In June 1993 the European Commission approved the eligibility of Cyprus to join the Community, but stated that it would consider the application only when significant progress had been achieved in the UN-sponsored negotiations concerning the island. In the event of a breakdown in the talks, Cyprus' position would be reviewed in January 1995. In June 1994 EU heads of state urged the Commission to conclude negotiations on the renewal of the financial protocol to enable Cyprus to proceed towards integration with the EU.

TURKEY

Signature: September 1963.

Date of coming into force: December 1964.

Legal basis: Article 238 of the Treaty of Rome.

The preparatory phase lasted from 1964 to 1973, during which preferences were given on agricultural products accounting for 40% of Turkey's exports to the EC: unmanufactured tobacco, dried raisins and figs, and nuts.

The transitional phase began in 1973, aiming to introduce a customs union by gradual stages over 12 to 22 years, depending on the product. The EC granted immediate duty and quota free access for industrial products, but placed restrictions on refined petroleum products and three textile products. The fourth financial protocol to the Association Agreement was to make available ECU 600m. for the period 1981–86 but, following the 1980 coup in Turkey, EC aid was suspended. A ministerial meeting was held in September 1986 to reactivate the Association Agreement. In April an agreement was reached determining levels of clothing imports from Turkey for 1986–88.

In April 1987 Turkey submitted a formal application for full membership of the EC. In 1989, however, the Commission stated that formal negotiations on Turkish membership could not take place until 1993, and that it would first be necessary for Turkey to restructure its economy, improve its observance of human rights, and harmonize its relations with Greece. The Commission undertook, however, to increase the EC's financial assistance for Turkey. In 1990 and 1991 additional assistance was provided for Turkey, as one of the countries directly affected by the crisis that followed the Iraqi invasion of Kuwait in August 1990. In April 1991 emergency aid (ECU 37m.) was also approved for Kurdish refugees who had fled from Iraq to Turkey.

In February 1992 the EC approved a co-operation agreement with Turkey on medical and health research. In June 1992 the European Council agreed that relations with Turkey should be upgraded and in November a framework programme was adopted for the conclusion of a customs union. Discussions on the issue were pursued in 1993–94, and the Turkish Government undertook domestic economic reforms, to ensure that the customs union enters into effect on 1 January 1995. By mid-1994, however, there was no prospect of Turkey's application to join the Community being accepted in the near future, with Turkey's position on Cyprus and its human rights record remaining substantive obstacles.

Euro-Arab Dialogue

The 'Euro-Arab Dialogue' was begun in 1973, initially to provide a forum for discussion of economic issues: the principal organ was a General Committee, and about 30 working groups were set up to discuss specific issues and prepare projects, such as the creation of a Euro-Arab Centre for the Transfer of Technology. After the Egypt-Israel peace agreement in 1979 all activity was suspended at the request of the Arab League. In November 1980 Community representatives held a meeting with an Arab League delegation, chaired by the PLO, to arrange for the resumption of the Dialogue at every level, but the first-ever Euro-Arab meeting of ministers of foreign affairs, planned for July 1981, did not take place. Work on drawing up codes for investment protection and conditions of contract continued during 1982, however, and in April 1983 joint seminars were held on European and Arab cultures and on Arab trade with the EC.

In December 1989 a meeting of ministers of foreign affairs of Arab and EC countries agreed to reactivate the Dialogue, entrusting political discussions to an annual ministerial meeting, and economic, technical, social and cultural matters to the General Committee of the Dialogue. However, meetings were suspended as a result of Iraq's invasion of Kuwait in August 1990; senior officials from the EC and Arab countries agreed in April 1992 to resume the Dialogue.

In 1992 the EC was involved in the Middle East peace negotiations, and participated in and chaired working groups on specific issues that formed part of the process.

ISLAMIC DEVELOPMENT BANK

Address: POB 5925, Jeddah 21432, Saudi Arabia.

Telephone: (2) 6361400; **telex:** 601137; **fax:** (2) 6366871.

An international financial institution established following a conference of finance ministers of member countries of the Organization of the Islamic Conference (q.v.), held in Jeddah in December 1973. Its aim is to encourage the economic development and social progress of member countries and of Muslim communities in non-member countries, in accordance with the principles of the Islamic Shari'a (sacred law). The Bank formally opened in October 1975.

MEMBERS

There are 46 members (see table of subscriptions below). Turkmenistan was admitted as a member in June 1992, and Azerbaijan in July.

Organization

(June 1994)

BOARD OF GOVERNORS

Each member country is represented by a governor, usually its Finance Minister, and an alternate. The Board of Governors is the supreme authority of the Bank, and meets annually.

BOARD OF EXECUTIVE DIRECTORS

The Board consists of 11 members, five of whom are appointed by the five largest subscribers to the capital stock of the Bank; the remaining six are elected by Governors representing the other subscribers. Members of the Board of Executive Directors are elected for three-year terms. The Board is responsible for the direction of the general operations of the Bank.

President of the Bank and Chairman of the Board of Executive Directors: OSSAMA JAAFAR FAQIH (Saudi Arabia).

Bank Secretary: Dr MOHAMED BEN SEDDIQ.

FINANCIAL STRUCTURE

In July 1992 the Board of Governors decided to increase the authorized capital of the Bank from 2,028.74m. to 6,000m. Islamic Dinars (to be divided into 600,000 shares, having a value of 10,000 Islamic Dinars each). The Islamic Dinar (ID) is the Bank's unit of account and is equivalent to the value of one Special Drawing Right of the IMF (SDR 1 = US \$1.40360 at 30 June 1993).

In July 1992 subscribed capital was raised from ID 2,028.74m. to ID 4,000m.; in the Islamic year 1413 (1 July 1992–20 June 1993) paid-up capital and reserves amounted to ID 2,293.5m.

Activities

The Bank adheres to the Islamic principle forbidding usury, and does not grant loans or credits for interest. Instead, its methods of financing are: provision of interest-free loans (with a service fee), mainly for infrastructural projects which are expected to have a marked impact on long-term socio-economic development; provision of technical assistance (e.g. for feasibility studies); equity participation in industrial and agricultural projects; leasing operations, involving the leasing of equipment such as ships, and instalment sale financing; and profit-sharing operations. Funds not immediately needed for projects are used for foreign trade financing for importing commodities to be used in development (i.e. raw materials and intermediate industrial goods, rather than consumer goods); priority is given to the import of goods from other member countries (see table). A longer-term trade financing scheme was introduced in 1987/88. In addition, the Special Assistance Account provides emergency aid and other assistance, with particular emphasis on education in Islamic communities in non-member countries.

SUBSCRIPTIONS (million Islamic Dinars, as at 30 June 1993)

Afghanistan	5.00	Maldives	2.50
Algeria	124.32	Mali	4.92
Azerbaijan	2.50	Mauritania	4.92
Bahrain	7.00	Morocco	24.81
Bangladesh	49.29	Niger	12.41
Benin	4.92	Oman	13.78
Brunei	12.41	Pakistan	124.26
Burkina Faso	12.41	Palestine	
Cameroon	12.41	Liberation	
Chad	4.92	Organization	9.85
Comoros	2.50	Qatar	49.23
Djibouti	2.50	Saudi Arabia	997.17
Egypt	49.23	Senegal	12.42
Gabon	14.77	Sierra Leone	2.50
The Gambia	2.50	Somalia	2.50
Guinea	12.41	Sudan	19.69
Guinea-Bissau	2.50	Syria	5.00
Indonesia	124.26	Tunisia	9.85
Iran	349.97	Turkey	315.47
Iraq	13.05	Uganda	12.41
Jordan	19.89	United Arab	
Kuwait	496.64	Emirates	283.03
Lebanon	2.50	Yemen	24.81
Libya	315.30	**Total**	**3,654.29**
Malaysia	79.56		

Operations approved, Islamic year 1413 (1 July 1992–20 June 1993)

Type of operation	Number of operations	Total amount (million Islamic Dinars)
Ordinary operations	50	236.10
Loan	15	74.72
Equity	8	20.92
Leasing	2	14.80
Lines of finance	2	8.60
Instalment sales	12	110.47
Technical assistance	11	6.58
Project financing	39	229.52
Foreign trade financing	82	411.43
Operations financed from the Special Assistance Account	23	11.37
Total	**155**	**658.90**

Project financing and technical assistance by sector, 1 July 1992–20 June 1993

Sector	Amount (million Islamic Dinars)	%
Agriculture and agro-industry	52.62	22.3
Industry and mining	38.32	16.2
Transport and communications	39.86	16.9
Utilities	51.88	22.0
Social services	23.60	10.0
Other	29.81	12.6
Total	**236.10**	**100.0**

By 20 June 1993 the Bank had approved a total of ID 2,408.81m. for project financing and technical assistance, a total of ID 7,008.25m. for foreign trade financing, and ID 346.41 for special assistance operations. During the Islamic year 1413, from 1 July 1992 to 20 June 1993, the Bank approved a total of ID 658.90m. for 155 operations, compared with ID 713.01m. for 158 operations in the previous year. Of financing approved in the year to 20 June 1993, about 62% was for foreign trade financing.

The Bank approved 15 interest-free loans in the year ending 20 June 1993, amounting to ID 74.72m. (compared with 13 loans, totalling ID 63.75m., in the previous year). These loans supported the following projects: rural electrification and road construction in Bangladesh; an agricultural college in Benin; land development in Chad and Guinea; a general hospital in Indonesia; telecommunications in Lebanon; the International Islamic University in Malaysia; livestock development in Mali; agricultural development in Mauritania; a technical institute and village support in Pakistan; construction of dykes in Senegal; road construction in Sudan; and sewerage in Tunisia.

The Bank approved 11 technical assistance operations for 7 countries in the form of grants during the year, amounting to ID 6.58m.

Twenty member countries are among the world's least-developed countries (as designated by the United Nations). During the year 63% of loan financing was directed to these countries.

Import trade financing approved during the year amounted to ID 380.54 for 68 operations in 12 member countries: of this amount 29.7% was for imports of intermediate industrial goods, 26.6% for crude petroleum, 10.6% for cotton, 9.7% for vegetable oil and 7.5% for fertilizers.

Under the Bank's Special Assistance Account, 23 operations were approved during the year, amounting to ID 11.37m., providing assistance primarily in the education and health sectors; 15 of the operations were for Muslim communities in non-member countries. The Bank's scholarships programme sponsored 420 students from 27 countries during the year to 20 June 1993. The Bank also undertakes the distribution of meat sacrificed by Muslim pilgrims: during the year to July 1991 meat from 410,566 head of sheep, 2,262 head of cows and 8,912 head of camel was distributed to the needy in 23 member countries.

Disbursements during the year ending 20 June 1993 totalled ID 386.65m. (compared with ID 410.96m. in the previous year). Of this total ID 96.79m. was for project financing and technical assistance, and ID 273.30m. was for foreign trade financing, while ID 16.56m. was provided for special operations.

In January 1990 the Bank launched its Unit Investment Fund in order to mobilize additional resources. The initial issue of the Fund was US $100m., with a minimum subscription of $100,000. By 20 June 1993 18 institutions, mainly in GCC countries, had subscribed to the Fund. The Fund finances mainly private-sector industrial projects in middle-income countries; by 20 June 1993 a total of US $171.81m. had been approved in financing for 18 projects in nine countries.

RESEARCH AND TRAINING INSTITUTE

Islamic Research and Training Institute: POB 9201, Jeddah 21413, Saudi Arabia; tel. (2) 6361400; telex 601137; fax (2) 6378927; f. 1982 for research enabling economic, financial and banking activities to conform to Islamic law, and to provide training for staff involved in development activities in the Bank's member countries. During the Islamic year 1 July 1992–20 June 1993 the Institute conducted 12 research studies on economic, financial and general development issues relevant to the Bank's member states. The Institute also organized seminars and workshops, and held training courses aimed at furthering the expertise of government and financial officials in Islamic developing countries. Dir Dr ABDELHAMID EL-GHAZALI.

PUBLICATION

Annual Report.

LEAGUE OF ARAB STATES

Address: Arab League Bldg, Tahrir Square, Cairo, Egypt.
Telephone: (2) 5750511; **telex:** 92111; **fax:** (2) 5775626.

The League of Arab States (more generally known as the Arab League) is a voluntary association of sovereign Arab states, designed to strengthen the close ties linking them and to co-ordinate their policies and activities and direct them towards the common good of all the Arab countries. It was founded in March 1945 (see Pact of the League, p. 235).

MEMBERS

Algeria	Lebanon	Somalia
Bahrain	Libya	Sudan
Comoros‡	Mauritania	Syria
Djibouti	Morocco	Tunisia
Egypt*	Oman	United Arab
Iraq	Palestine†	Emirates
Jordan	Qatar	Yemen
Kuwait	Saudi Arabia	

* In March 1979 Egypt's membership of the Arab League was suspended; subsequently, the headquarters of the League was moved to Tunis until Egypt's readmission in May 1989.
† Palestine is considered an independent state, as explained in the Charter Annex on Palestine, and therefore a full member of the League.
‡ The Comoros was admitted to the League in September 1993.

Organization

(August 1994)

COUNCIL

The supreme organ of the Arab League, the Council consists of representatives of the member states, each of which has one vote, and a representative for Palestine. Unanimous decisions of the Council shall be binding upon all member states of the League; majority decisions shall be binding only on those states which have accepted them.

The Council may, if necessary, hold an extraordinary session at the request of two member states. Invitations to all sessions are extended by the Secretary-General. The ordinary sessions are presided over by representatives of the member states in turn.

Fourteen committees are attached to the Council:

Arab Women's Committee.

Committee of Arab Experts on Co-operation.

Communications Committee: supervises land, sea and air communications, together with weather forecasts and postal matters.

Conference of Liaison Officers: complemented by the Economic Council since 1953; co-ordinates trade activities among commercial attachés of various Arab embassies abroad.

Cultural Committee: in charge of following up the activities of the Cultural Department and the cultural affairs within the scope of the secretariat; co-ordinates the activities of the general secretariat and the various cultural bodies in member states.

Health Committee: for co-operation in health affairs.

Human Rights Committee: studies subjects concerning human rights, particularly violations by Israel; collaborates with the Information and Cultural Committees.

Information Committee: studies information projects, suggests plans and carries out the policies decided by the Council of Information Ministers.

Legal Committee: an extension of the Nationality and Passports Committee abolished in 1947; studies and legally formulates draft agreements, bills, regulations and official documents.

Organization of Youth Welfare.

Permanent Committee for Administrative and Financial Affairs.

Permanent Committee for Meteorology.

Political Committee: studies political questions and reports to the Council meetings concerned with them. All member states are members of the Committee. It represents the Council in dealing with critical political matters when the Council is meeting. Usually composed of the foreign ministers.

Social Committee: supports co-operation in such matters as family and child welfare.

The Arab League maintains a permanent office at the United Nations in New York, and has observer status at the UN General Assembly.

GENERAL SECRETARIAT

The administrative and financial offices of the League. The Secretariat carries out the decisions of the Council, and provides financial and administrative services for the personnel of the League. Administrative departments comprise: Arab Affairs, Economic Affairs, International Affairs, Palestine Affairs, Legal Affairs, Military Affairs, Social and Cultural Affairs, Information, and Administrative and Financial Affairs; in addition, there are units for internal auditing, and for the development of working methods.

The Secretary-General is appointed by the League Council by a two-thirds majority of the member states, for a five-year term. He appoints the assistant Secretaries-General and principal officials, with the approval of the Council. He has the rank of ambassador, and the assistant Secretaries-General have the rank of ministers plenipotentiary.

Secretary-General: Dr AHMAD ESMAT ABD AL-MEGUID (Egypt).

Assistant Secretaries-General:

Arab Affairs: (vacant).

Economic Affairs: ABDUL RAHMAN AL-SOUHAIBANI (Saudi Arabia).

Head of Arab League Centre, Tunis: MONJI AL-FAQIH (Tunisia).

Head of Secretary-General's Office: AHMAD IBRAHIM ADEL (Egypt).

Information Affairs: DAWO ALI SIWEDAN (Libya).

Internal Auditing: Dr ALI ABDELKARIM (Yemen).

International Affairs: ADNAN OMRAN (Syria).

Military Affairs: MUHAMMED SAID BEN HASSAN EL-BERQDAR (Syria).

Palestine Affairs: SAID KAMAL (Palestine).

Social and Cultural Affairs: AHMED QADRI (Egypt).

DEFENCE AND ECONOMIC CO-OPERATION

Groups established under the Treaty of Joint Defence and Economic Co-operation, concluded in 1950 to complement the Charter of the League.

Arab Unified Military Command: f. 1964 to co-ordinate military policies for the liberation of Palestine.

Economic Council: to compare and co-ordinate the economic policies of the member states; the Council is composed of ministers of economic affairs or their deputies. Decisions are taken by majority vote. The first meeting was held in 1953.

Joint Defence Council: supervises implementation of those aspects of the treaty concerned with common defence. Composed of foreign and defence ministers; decisions by a two-thirds majority vote of members are binding on all.

Permanent Military Commission: established 1950; composed of representatives of army general staffs; main purpose: to draw up plans of joint defence for submission to the Joint Defence Council.

ARAB DETERRENT FORCE

Created in June 1976 by the Arab League Council to supervise successive attempts to cease hostilities in Lebanon, and afterwards to maintain the peace. The mandate of the Force has been successively renewed. The Arab League Summit Conference in October 1976 agreed that costs were to be paid in the following percentage contributions: Saudi Arabia and Kuwait 20% each, the United Arab Emirates 15%, Qatar 10% and other Arab states 35%.

OTHER INSTITUTIONS OF THE LEAGUE

Other bodies established by resolutions adopted by the Council of the League:

Administrative Tribunal of the Arab League: f. 1964; began operations 1966.

Arab Fund for Technical Assistance to African Countries: 37 ave Khereddine Pacha, Tunis, Tunisia; tel. (1) 890 100; telex 13242; f. 1975 to provide technical assistance for development projects by providing African and Arab experts, grants for scholarships and training, and finance for technical studies. Exec. Sec. HASSAN ABADI (Egypt).

Special Bureau for Boycotting Israel: POB 437, Damascus, Syria; f. 1951 to prevent trade between Arab countries and Israel, and to enforce a boycott by Arab countries of companies outside the region that conduct trade with Israel. Commr-Gen. ZUHEIR AQUIL (Syria).

SPECIALIZED AGENCIES

All member states of the Arab League are also members of the Specialized Agencies, which constitute an integral part of the Arab League. (See also chapters on the Arab Fund for Economic and Social Development, the Council of Arab Economic Unity and the Organization of Arab Petroleum Exporting Countries, and the small entry on the Arab Monetary Fund.)

Arab Administrative Development Organization: POB 17159, Amman, Jordan; tel. (6) 696904; telex 21594; fax (6) 681018; f. 1961 (as Arab Organization of Administrative Sciences), although became operational in 1969, to improve Arab administrative systems, develop Arab administrative organizations and enhance the capabilities of Arab civil servants, through training, consultancy, research and documentation; includes Arab Network of Administrative Information. Dir-Gen. Dr AHMAD SAKR ASHOUR. Publs *Arab Journal of Administration* (quarterly), *Management Newsletter* (quarterly), research series, training manuals.

Arab Atomic Energy Agency (AAEA): El-Manzah 5, POB 402, 1004 Tunis, Tunisia; telex 14896; fax (1) 766010; f. 1988 to co-ordinate research into the peaceful uses of atomic energy. Dir-Gen. Dr MAHMOUD FOUAD BARAKAT (Egypt).

Arab Bank for Economic Development in Africa (Banque arabe pour le développement économique en Afrique—BADEA): Sayed Abdar-Rahman el-Mahdi Ave, POB 2640, Khartoum, Sudan; tel. (11) 73646; telex 22248; f. 1973 by Arab League; provides loans and grants to sub-Saharan African countries to finance development projects; paid-up capital US $1,045.8m. (Dec. 1991). By March 1994 loans and grants approved since funding activities began in 1975 totalled US $1,432m. Subscribing countries: all countries of Arab League, except Djibouti, Somalia and Yemen; recipient countries: all countries of Organization of African Unity (q.v.), except those belonging to the Arab League. Chair. AHMAD ABDALLAH AL-AKEIL (Saudi Arabia); Dir.-Gen. AHMAD AL-HARTI AL-OUARDI (Morocco). Publs *Annual Report, Co-operation for Development*, Studies on Afro-Arab co-operation.

Arab Centre for the Study of Arid Zones and Dry Lands (ACSAD): POB 2440, Damascus, Syria; tel. (11) 755713; telex 412697; f. 1971 to conduct regional research and development programmes related to water and soil resources, plant and animal production, agro-meteorology, and socio-economic studies of arid zones. The Centre holds conferences and training courses and encourages the exchange of information by Arab scientists. Dir-Gen. Dr MUHAMMAD EL-KHASH.

Arab Industrial Development and Mining Organization: POB 3156, Al-Sa'adoun, Baghdad, Iraq; tel. (1) 7184655; telex 2823; fax (1) 7184658; f. 1990 by merger.

Arab Labour Organization: POB 814, Cairo, Egypt; established in 1965 for co-operation between member states in labour problems; unification of labour legislation and general conditions of work wherever possible; research; technical assistance; social insurance; training, etc.; the organization has a tripartite structure: governments, employers and workers. Dir-Gen. BAKR MAHMOUD RASOUL (Iraq). Publs *ALO Bulletin* (monthly), *Arab Labour Review* (quarterly), *Legislative Bulletin* (quarterly).

Arab League Educational, Cultural and Scientific Organization—ALECSO: BP 1120, ave Mohamed V, Tunis, Tunisia; tel. (1) 784-466; telex 13825; fax (1) 784-965; f. 1970 to promote and co-ordinate educational, cultural and scientific activities in the Arab region. Regional units: Arab Centre for Arabization, Translation, Authorship, and Publication—Damascus, Syria; Institute of Arab Manuscript—Cairo, Egypt; Institute of Arab Research and Studies—Cairo, Egypt; Khartoum Institute for Arabic Language—Khartoum, Sudan; and the Arabization Co-ordination Bureau—Rabat, Morocco. Dir-Gen. MOHAMED ALMILI IBRAHIMI (Algeria). Publs *Arab Journal of Language Studies, Arab Journal of Educational Research, Arab Journal of Culture, Arab Journal of Science, Arab Bulletin of Publications, Statistical Yearbook, Journal of the Institute of Arab Manuscripts, Arab Magazine for Information Science.*

Arab Maritime Transport Academy, Alexandria: POB 1029, Alexandria, Egypt; tel. (3) 5602366; telex 54160; fax (3) 5602144; f. 1989 by merger; 130 teaching staff. Dir-Gen. Dr GAMAL EL-DIN MOUKHTAR. Publs *Maritime Technology* (every 2 months), *News Bulletin, Bulletin of Maritime Transport Information Analysis* (monthly), *Current Awareness Bulletin* (monthly), *Journal of the Arab Maritime Transport Academy* (2 a year).

Arab Organization for Agricultural Development: POB 474, Khartoum, Sudan; tel. (11) 452176; telex 22554; fax (11) 451402; f. 1970 to contribute to co-operation in agricultural activities, and in the development of natural and human resources for agriculture; compiles data, conducts studies, training and food security

programmes; has regional offices in eight countries; includes Arab Forestry and Pastures Institute, Syria. Dir-Gen. Dr YAHIA BAKOUR (Syria). Publs *Agriculture and Development in the Arab World* (quarterly), *Statistics* (annually), monthly newsletter.

Arab Organization for Social Defence against Crime: POB 1341, Rabat, Morocco; tel. (7) 22207; telex 32914; f. 1960; aims to promote co-operation among Arab states in preventing crime, and to formulate unified criminal legislation based on Islamic principles; includes Arab Bureau for the Prevention of Crime. Sec.-Gen. MOHAMMED AL-SHADADI. Publs *AOSD Information Bulletin* (quarterly), *Arab Review of Social Defence* (twice a year).

Arab Postal Union: c/o Arab League secretariat; f. 1952; aims to establish stricter postal relations between the Arab countries than those laid down by the Universal Postal Union, and to pursue the development and modernization of postal services in member countries. Publs *APU Bulletin* (monthly), *APU Review* (quarterly), *APU News* (annually).

Arab Satellite Communication Organization—ARABSAT: POB 1038, Riyadh, Saudi Arabia; tel. (1) 464-6666; telex 401400; manages the ARABSAT project, under which the first two satellites were launched in 1985, for the improvement of telephone, telex, data transmission and radio and television in Arab countries; a third satellite was launched in February 1992 with a 10-year operational life, and two more satellites were under construction in early 1993. Dir-Gen. SAAD IBN ABD AL-AZIZ AL-BADNA (Saudi Arabia).

Arab States Broadcasting Union—ASBU: POB 65, 17 rue el-Mensoura, el-Mensah 4, Tunis 1014, Tunisia; tel. (1) 238044; telex 13398; fax (1) 766551; f. 1969 to promote Arab fraternity, co-ordinate and study broadcasting subjects, to exchange expertise and technical co-operation in broadcasting; conducts training and audience research. Mems: 21 Arab radio and TV stations and seven foreign associates. Sec.-Gen. RAOUF BASTI. Publ. *ASBU Review* (2 a year).

Arab Telecommunications Union: POB 2397, Baghdad, Iraq; tel. (1) 776901; telex 212007; f. 1953 to co-ordinate and develop telecommunications between member countries; to exchange technical aid and encourage research; promotes establishment of new cable telecommunications networks in the region. Sec.-Gen. ABD AL-JAFFAR HASSAN KHALAF IBRAHIM AL-ANI. Publs *Arab Telecommunications Union Journal* (twice a year), *Economic and Technical Studies.*

Council of Arab Ministers of the Interior: POB 490, Hashad, Tunis, Tunisia; tel. (1) 237320; telex 14887; fax (1) 767822; f. 1982 to reinforce internal security and combat crime; Sec.-Gen. AHMED BIN MOHAMED AL-SALIM (Saudi Arabia).

Inter-Arab Investment Guarantee Corporation: POB 23568, Safat 13096, Kuwait; tel. 2404740; telex 22562–46312; fax 2405406; operating from its office in Riyadh, Saudi Arabia; f. 1975; insures Arab investors for non-commercial risks, and export credits for commercial and non-commercial risks; authorized capital 25m. Kuwaiti dinars (Dec. 1991). Mems: 22 Arab governments. Dir-Gen. MAMOUN I. HASSAN. Publ. *News Bulletin* (monthly), *Arab Investment Climate Report* (annually).

External Relations

ARAB LEAGUE OFFICES AND INFORMATION CENTRES ABROAD

Established by the Arab League to co-ordinate work at all levels among Arab embassies abroad.

Austria: Grimmelshausengasse 12, 1030 Vienna.

Belgium: 106 ave Franklin D. Roosevelt, 1050 Brussels.

Brazil: Shis-Qi 15, Conj. 7, Casa 23, 71600 Brasília, DF.

China, People's Republic: Beijing.

Ethiopia: POB 5768, Addis Ababa.

France: 114 blvd Malesherbes, 75017 Paris.

Germany: Friedrich Wilhelm Str. 2A, 5300 Bonn 1.

Greece: Martious St, Filothei, Athens.

India: A-137, Neeti Bagh, New Delhi 110 049.

Italy: Piazzale delle Belle Arti 6, 00196 Rome.

Japan: 1-1-12 Moto Asabu, Minato-ku, Tokyo 106.

Russia: 28 Koniouch Kovskaya, Moscow.

Spain: Paseo de la Castellana 180, 6°, Madrid 16.

Switzerland: 9 rue du Valais, 1202 Geneva.

United Kingdom: 52 Green St, London W1Y 3RH.

USA: 1100 17th St, NW, Suite 602, Washington, DC 20036; 747 Third Ave, New York, NY 10017 (UN Office).

Record of Events

1945 Pact of the Arab League signed, March.

1946 Cultural Treaty signed.

1950 Joint Defence and Economic Co-operation Treaty.

1952 Agreements on extradition, writs and letters of request, nationality of Arabs outside their country of origin.

1953 Formation of Economic Council.
Convention on the privileges and immunities of the League.

1954 Nationality Agreement.

1956 Agreement on the adoption of a Common Tariff Nomenclature.
Sudan joined League.

1961 Kuwait joined League.
Syrian Arab Republic rejoined League as independent member.

1962 Arab Economic Unity Agreement.

1964 First Summit Conference of Arab kings and presidents, Cairo, January.
First meeting of Economic Unity Council, June. Arab Common Market approved by Arab Economic Unity Council, August.
Second Summit Conference welcomed establishment of Palestine Liberation Organization (PLO), September.

1965 Arab Common Market established, January.

1969 Fifth Summit Conference, Rabat. Call for mobilization of all Arab nations against Israel.

1971 Bahrain, Qatar and Oman admitted to League, September.

1973 Mauritania admitted to League, December.

1974 Somalia admitted to League, February.

1977 Djibouti admitted to membership, September.
Tripoli Declaration, December. Decision of Algeria, Iraq, Libya and Yemen PDR to boycott League meetings in Egypt in response to President Sadat's visit to Israel.

1978 69th meeting of Arab League Council in Cairo, March, boycotted by 'rejectionist' states.

1979 Council meeting in Baghdad, March: resolved to withdraw Arab ambassadors from Egypt; to recommend severance of political and diplomatic relations with Egypt; to suspend Egypt's membership of the League on the date of the signing of the peace treaty with Israel; to make the city of Tunis the temporary headquarters of the League; to condemn US policy regarding its role in concluding the Camp David agreements and the peace treaty; to halt all bank loans, deposits, guarantees or facilities, as well as all financial or technical contributions and aid to Egypt; to prohibit trade exchanges with the Egyptian state and with private establishments dealing with Israel.

1980 The Summit Conference in November approved a wider 'Strategy for Joint Arab Economic Action', covering pan-Arab development planning up to the year 2000.

1981 In March the Council of Ministers set up a conciliation mission to try to improve relations between Morocco and Mauritania. In November the 12th Summit Conference, held in Fez, Morocco, was suspended after a few hours, following disagreement over a Saudi Arabian proposal known as the Fahd Plan, which included not only the Arab demands on behalf of the Palestinians, as approved by the UN General Assembly, but also an implied *de facto* recognition of Israel.

1982 Twelfth Summit Conference reconvened, Fez, September: adopted a peace plan, similar to the Fahd Plan mentioned above. The plan demanded Israel's withdrawal from territories occupied in 1967, and removal of Israeli settlements in these areas; freedom of worship for all religions in the sacred places; the right of the Palestinian people to self-determination, under the leadership of the PLO; temporary UN supervision for the West Bank and the Gaza Strip; the creation of an independent Palestinian state, with Jerusalem as its capital; and a guarantee of peace for all the states of the region by the UN Security Council.

1983 The summit meeting due to be held in November was postponed owing to members' differences of opinion concerning Syria's opposition to Yasser Arafat's chairmanship of the PLO, and Syrian support of Iran in the war against Iraq.

1984 In March an emergency meeting established an Arab League committee to encourage international efforts to bring about a negotiated settlement of the Iran–Iraq war. In May ministers of foreign affairs adopted a resolution urging Iran to stop attacking non-belligerent ships and installations in the Gulf region: similar attacks by Iraq were not mentioned.

1985 In August an emergency Summit Conference was boycotted by Algeria, Lebanon, Libya, Syria and the People's Demo-

cratic Republic of Yemen, while of the other 16 members only nine were represented by their heads of state. The conference reaffirmed its support for the peace plan adopted in 1982 (see above), but was non-committal on proposals made by Jordan and the PLO, envisaging eventual talks with Israel on Palestinian rights. Two commissions were set up to mediate in disagreements between Arab states (between Jordan and Syria, Iraq and Syria, Iraq and Libya, and Libya and the PLO).

1986 In July King Hassan of Morocco announced that he was resigning as chairman of the next League Summit Conference, after criticism by several Arab leaders of his meeting with the Israeli Prime Minister earlier that month. A ministerial meeting, held in October, condemned any attempt at direct negotiation with Israel, and reiterated that an international conference convened by the United Nations would be the only acceptable means of bringing about a peaceful settlement in the Middle East. In December a special ministerial committee was created to attempt to stop the fighting for control of the Palestinian refugee camps in Lebanon between Palestinian guerrillas and the Shi'ite Amal militia.

1987 In August the Council agreed on a resolution condemning Iran for persisting in its hostilities against Iraq and for making threats against the Gulf states. An extraordinary Summit Conference was held in November, mainly to discuss the war between Iran and Iraq. Contrary to expectations, the participants (including President Assad of Syria) unanimously agreed on a statement expressing support for Iraq in its defence of its legitimate rights, and criticizing Iran for its procrastination in accepting the UN Security Council Resolution No. 598 of July 1987, which had recommended a cease-fire in the Iran-Iraq war and negotiations on a settlement of the conflict. The meeting also stated that the resumption of diplomatic relations with Egypt was a matter to be decided by individual states.

1988 In June a Summit Conference agreed to provide finance for the PLO to continue the Palestinian uprising in Israeli-occupied territories. It reiterated the Arab League's demand for the convening of an international conference, attended by the PLO, to seek to bring about a peaceful settlement in the Middle East (thereby implicitly rejecting recent proposals by the US Government for a conference that would exclude the PLO).

1989 In January (responding to the deteriorating political situation in Lebanon) an Arab League mediation group, comprising six ministers of foreign affairs, began discussions with the two rival Lebanese governments on the possibility of a political settlement in Lebanon. In April the League issued a provisional peace plan, which would involve a cease-fire in Lebanon, supervised by a force of Arab military observers. At a Summit Conference, held in May, Egypt was readmitted to the League. The Summit Conference expressed support for the chairman of the PLO, Yasser Arafat, in his recent peace proposals made before the UN General Assembly, and reiterated the League's support for proposals that an international conference should be convened to discuss the rights of Palestinians: in so doing, it accepted UN Security Council Resolutions 242 and 338 on a peaceful settlement in the Middle East and thus gave tacit recognition to the State of Israel. The meeting also supported Arafat in rejecting Israeli proposals for elections in the Israeli-occupied territories of the West Bank and the Gaza Strip. A new mediation committee, comprising the heads of state of Algeria, Morocco and Saudi Arabia, was established, with a six-month mandate to negotiate a cease-fire in Lebanon, and to reconvene the Lebanese legislature with the aim of holding a presidential election and restoring constitutional government in Lebanon. In September the principal factions in Lebanon agreed to observe a cease-fire, and the surviving members of the Lebanese legislature (originally elected in 1972) met at Taif, in Saudi Arabia, in October, and approved the League's proposed 'charter of national reconciliation' (see chapter on Lebanon).

1990 In May a Summit Conference, held in Baghdad, Iraq (which was boycotted by Syria and Lebanon), condemned the recent increase in the emigration of Jews from the USSR to Israel, and strongly criticized the US Government's support for Israel. The meeting also criticized recent efforts by Western governments to prevent the development of advanced weapons technology in Iraq. In August an emergency Summit Conference was held to discuss the invasion and annexation of Kuwait by Iraq. Twelve members (Bahrain, Djibouti, Egypt, Kuwait, Lebanon, Morocco, Oman, Qatar, Saudi Arabia, Somalia, Syria and the United Arab Emirates) approved a resolution condemning Iraq's action, and demanding the withdrawal of Iraqi forces from Kuwait and the reinstatement of the Government. The 12 states expressed support for the Saudi Arabian Government's invitation to the USA to send forces to defend Saudi Arabia; they also agreed to impose economic sanctions on Iraq, and to provide troops for an Arab defensive force in Saudi Arabia. The remaining member states, however, condemned the presence of foreign troops in Saudi Arabia, and their ministers of foreign affairs refused to attend a meeting, held at the end of August, to discuss possible solutions to the crisis. The dissenting countries also rejected the decision, taken earlier in the year, to return the League's headquarters from Tunis to Cairo. In September the Secretary-General of the League, Chedli Klibi, resigned, reportedly after incurring criticism by moderate Arab leaders, and the League's representative at the UN, Clovis Maksoud, also resigned, deploring both the Iraqi invasion and the Western military presence in Saudi Arabia. The official transfer of the League's headquarters to Cairo took place on 31 October. In November King Hassan of Morocco urged the convening of an Arab Summit Conference, in an attempt to find an 'Arab solution' to Iraq's annexation of Kuwait. However, the divisions in the Arab world over the issue meant that conditions for such a meeting could not be agreed. Saudi Arabia was prepared to attend only after an Iraqi withdrawal from Kuwait, while Iraq itself demanded that the conference should address the Palestinian question.

1991   The first meeting of the Arab League since August 1990 took place at the end of March, attended by representatives of all 21 member nations, including Iraq. Discussion of the recently-ended war against Iraq was avoided, in an attempt to re-establish the unity of the League. In May the Egyptian Minister of Foreign Affairs, Dr Ahmad Esmat Abd al-Meguid, was unanimously elected Secretary-General of the League, a decision seen as returning to Egypt the pre-eminence that it had enjoyed before 1979. At the meeting of the Council in September, deep divisions between member states, resulting from Iraq's invasion of Kuwait, remained, particularly between Iraq and Kuwait, and Egypt and Jordan. Nevertheless, it was agreed that a committee should be formed to co-ordinate Arab positions in preparation for the US-sponsored peace talks between Arab countries and Israel (which began in late October). (In the event, an *ad hoc* meeting, attended by Egypt, Jordan, Syria, the PLO, Saudi Arabia—representing the Gulf Co-operation Council, and Morocco—representing the Union of the Arab Maghreb, was held in late October, prior to the start of the talks.) In the context of the peace process, a modification of the Arab boycott of companies dealing with Israel was discussed. In early December the League expressed solidarity with Libya, which was under international pressure to extradite two Libyan government agents who were suspected of involvement in the explosion which destroyed a US passenger aircraft over Lockerbie, United Kingdom, in December 1988.

1992   In mid-February the League, together with other regional organizations, participated in a conference, hosted by the UN in New York, designed to bring about a cease-fire in Somalia. The League was subsequently involved in mediation efforts between the warring factions in the Somali capital, Mogadishu. In late March the League appointed a committee to seek to resolve the disputes between Libya and the USA, the United Kingdom and France over the Lockerbie explosion and the explosion which destroyed a French passenger aircraft over the Sahara (in Niger) in September 1989; and proposed a compromise solution, whereby Libya would surrender the alleged terrorists to the League, which would, in turn, deliver the suspects to either the USA or the United Kingdom, under UN supervision. However, Libya's initial readiness to comply with the plan gave way to renewed refusal to extradite its nationals. The League condemned the UN's decision, at the end of March, to impose sanctions against Libya, and appealed for a negotiated solution. In mid-September the League's Council issued a condemnation of Iran's alleged occupation of three islands in the Persian (Arabian) Gulf that were claimed by the United Arab Emirates, and decided to refer the issue to the United Nations.

1993   In early January a meeting of the Council of Interior Ministers discussed internal security, terrorism and crime. In the same month ministers of foreign affairs of the League appealed to the UN to impose sanctions on Israel if it failed to comply with a UN resolution demanding the return of Palestinians who had been deported by Israeli forces into Lebanon in December 1992. In mid-April the Council approved the creation of a committee to consider the political and security aspects of water supply in Arab coun-

tries. In the same month the League pledged its commitment to the Middle East peace talks, but warned that Israel's continued refusal to repatriate the Palestinians who were stranded in Lebanon remained a major obstacle to the process. The Arab League sent an official observer to the independence referendum in Eritrea, held on 23–25 April. In September the Council admitted the Comoros as the 22nd member of the League. Following the signing of the Israeli-PLO peace accord in September the Council convened in emergency session, at which it approved the agreement, despite opposition from some members, notably Syria. In November it was announced that the League's boycott of commercial activity with Israel was to be maintained.

1994   In January the US Secretary of Commerce met with the League's Secretary-General in an attempt to negotiate an end to the secondary and tertiary boycott against Israel, by which member states refuse to trade with international companies which have investments in Israel.

PUBLICATIONS

Information Bulletin (Arabic and English, daily).

Sh'oun Arabiyya (Journal of Arab Affairs, quarterly).

Bulletins of treaties and agreements concluded among the member states.

Bonn Office: *Arabische Korrespondenz* (fortnightly).

Brasília Office: *Oriente Arabe* (monthly).

Geneva Office: *Le Monde Arabe* (monthly), and *Nouvelles du Monde Arabe* (weekly).

London Office: *The Arab* (monthly).

New Delhi Office: *Al Arab* (monthly).

New York Office: *Arab World* (monthly), and *News and Views*.

Paris Office: *Actualités Arabes* (fortnightly).

Rome Office: *Rassegna del Mondo Arabo* (monthly).

The Pact of the League of Arab States

(22 March 1945)

Article 1. The League of Arab States is composed of the independent Arab States which have signed this Pact.

Any independent Arab state has the right to become a member of the League. If it desires to do so, it shall submit a request which will be deposited with the Permanent Secretariat-General and submitted to the Council at the first meeting held after submission of the request.

Article 2. The League has as its purpose the strengthening of the relations between the member states; the co-ordination of their policies in order to achieve co-operation between them and to safeguard their independence and sovereignty; and a general concern with the affairs and interests of the Arab countries. It has also as its purpose the close co-operation of the member states, with due regard to the organization and circumstances of each state, on the following matters:

(*a*) Economic and financial affairs, including commercial relations, customs, currency, and questions of agriculture and industry.

(*b*) Communications: this includes railways, roads, aviation, navigation, telegraphs and posts.

(*c*) Cultural affairs.

(*d*) Nationality, passports, visas, execution of judgments, and extradition of criminals.

(*e*) Social affairs.

(*f*) Health problems.

Article 3. The League shall possess a Council composed of the representatives of the member states of the League; each state shall have a single vote, irrespective of the number of its representatives.

It shall be the task of the Council to achieve the realization of the objectives of the League and to supervise the execution of agreements which the member states have concluded on the questions enumerated in the preceding article, or on any other questions.

It likewise shall be the Council's task to decide upon the means by which the League is to co-operate with the international bodies to be created in the future in order to guarantee security and peace and regulate economic and social relations.

Article 4. For each of the questions listed in Article 2 there shall be set up a special committee in which the member states of the

League shall be represented. These committees shall be charged with the task of laying down the principles and extent of co-operation. Such principles shall be formulated as draft agreements, to be presented to the Council for examination preparatory to their submission to the aforesaid states.

Representatives of the other Arab countries may take part in the work of the aforesaid committees. The Council shall determine the conditions under which these representatives may be permitted to participate and the rules governing such representation.

Article 5. Any resort to force in order to resolve disputes arising between two or more member states of the League is prohibited. If there should rise among them a difference which does not concern a state's independence, sovereignty, or territorial integrity, and if the parties to the dispute have recourse to the Council for the settlement of this difference, the decision of the Council shall then be enforceable and obligatory.

In such a case, the states between whom the difference has arisen shall not participate in the deliberations and decisions of the Council.

The Council shall mediate in all differences which threaten to lead to war between two member states, or a member state and a third state, with a view to bringing about their reconciliation.

Decisions of arbitration and mediation shall be taken by majority vote.

Article 6. In case of aggression or threat of aggression by one state against a member state, the state which has been attacked or threatened with aggression may demand the immediate convocation of the Council.

The Council shall by unanimous decision determine the measures necessary to repulse the aggression. If the aggressor is a member state, its vote shall not be counted in determining unanimity.

If, as a result of the attack, the government of the state attacked finds itself unable to communicate with the Council, that state's representative in the Council shall have the right to request the convocation of the Council for the purpose indicated in the foregoing paragraph. In the event that this representative is unable to communicate with the Council, any member state of the League shall have the right to request the convocation of the Council.

Article 7. Unanimous decisions of the Council shall be binding upon all member states of the League; majority decisions shall be binding only upon those states which have accepted them.

In either case the decisions of the Council shall be enforced in each member state according to its respective basic laws.

Article 8. Each member state shall respect the systems of government established in the other member states and regard them as exclusive concerns of those states. Each shall pledge to abstain from any action calculated to change established systems of government.

Article 9. States of the League which desire to establish closer co-operation and stronger bonds than are provided by this Pact may conclude agreements to that end.

Treaties and agreements already concluded or to be concluded in the future between a member state and another state shall not be binding or restrictive upon other members.

Article 10. The permanent seat of the League of Arab States is established in Cairo. The Council may, however, assemble at any other place it may designate.

Article 11. The Council of the League shall convene in ordinary session twice a year, in March and in September. It shall convene in extraordinary session upon the request of two member states of the League whenever the need arises.

Article 12. The League shall have a permanent Secretariat-General which shall consist of a Secretary-General, Assistant Secretaries, and an appropriate number of officials.

The Council of the League shall appoint the Secretary-General by a majority of two-thirds of the states of the League. The Secretary-General, with the approval of the Council, shall appoint the Assistant Secretaries and the principal officials of the League.

The Council of the League shall establish an administrative regulation for the functions of the Secretariat-General and matters relating to the Staff.

The Secretary-General shall have the rank of Ambassador and the Assistant Secretaries that of Ministers Plenipotentiary.

Article 13. The Secretary-General shall prepare the draft of the budget of the League and shall submit it to the Council for approval before the beginning of each fiscal year.

The Council shall fix the share of the expenses to be borne by each state of the League. This share may be reconsidered if necessary.

Article 14. (confers diplomatic immunity on officials).

Article 15. The first meeting of the Council shall be convened at the invitation of the head of the Egyptian Government. Thereafter it shall be convened at the invitation of the Secretary-General.

The representatives of the member states of the League shall alternately assume the presidency of the Council at each of its ordinary sessions.

Article 16. Except in cases specifically indicated in this Pact, a majority vote of the Council shall be sufficient to make enforceable decisions on the following matters:

(*a*) Matters relating to personnel.

(*b*) Adoption of the budget of the League.

(*c*) Establishment of the administrative regulations for the Council, the Committees, and the Secretariat-General.

(*d*) Decisions to adjourn the sessions.

Article 17. Each member state of the League shall deposit with the Secretariat-General one copy of every treaty or agreement concluded or to be concluded in the future between itself and another member state of the League or a third state.

Article 18. (deals with withdrawal).

Article 19. (deals with amendment).

Article 20. (deals with ratification).

ANNEX REGARDING PALESTINE

Since the termination of the last great war, the rule of the Ottoman Empire over the Arab countries, among them Palestine, which has become detached from that Empire, has come to an end. She has come to be autonomous, not subordinate to any other state.

The Treaty of Lausanne proclaimed that her future was to be settled by the parties concerned.

However, even though she was as yet unable to control her own affairs, the Covenant of the League (of Nations) in 1919 made provision for a regime based upon recognition of her independence.

Her international existence and independence in the legal sense cannot, therefore, be questioned, any more than could the independence of the Arab countries.

Although the outward manifestations of this independence have remained obscured for reasons beyond her control, this should not be allowed to interfere with her participation in the work of the Council of the League.

The states signatory to the Pact of the Arab League are therefore of the opinion that, considering the special circumstances of Palestine and until that country can effectively exercise its independence, the Council of the League should take charge of the selection of an Arab representative from Palestine to take part in its work.

ANNEX REGARDING CO-OPERATION WITH COUNTRIES WHICH ARE NOT MEMBERS OF THE COUNCIL OF THE LEAGUE

Whereas the member states of the League will have to deal in the Council as well as in the committees with matters which will benefit and affect the Arab world at large;

And whereas the Council has to take into account the aspirations of the Arab countries which are not members of the Council and has to work toward their realization;

Now therefore, it particularly behoves the states signatory to the Pact of the Arab League to enjoin the Council of the League, when considering the admission of those countries to participation in the committees referred to in the Pact, that it should do its utmost to co-operate with them, and furthermore, that it should spare no effort to learn their needs and understand their aspirations and hopes; and that it should work thenceforth for their best interests and the safeguarding of the future with all the political means at its disposal.

ORGANIZATION OF ARAB PETROLEUM EXPORTING COUNTRIES—OAPEC

Address: POB 108, Majlis ash-Sha'ab, 11516 Cairo, Egypt; (from 30 June 1994) POB 20501, Safat 13066, Kuwait.

Telephone: 3542660; (from 30 June 1994) 5340713; **telex:** 21158; **fax:** 3542601; (from 30 June 1994) 5340694.

OAPEC was established in 1968 to safeguard the interests of members and to determine ways and means for their co-operation in various forms of economic activity in the petroleum industry. In 1992 member states accounted for 25.2% of total world petroleum production.

MEMBERS*

Algeria	Kuwait	Syria
Bahrain	Libya	United Arab Emirates
Egypt	Qatar	
Iraq	Saudi Arabia	

* Egypt's membership was suspended in April 1979, but restored in May 1989. Tunisia ceased to be a member from 1 January 1987.

Organization

(August 1994)

MINISTERIAL COUNCIL

The Council consists normally of the ministers of petroleum of the member states, and forms the supreme authority of the Organization, responsible for drawing up its general policy, directing its activities and laying down its governing rules. It meets twice yearly, and may hold extraordinary sessions. Chairmanship is on an annual rotation basis.

EXECUTIVE BUREAU

Assists the Council to direct the management of the Organization, approves staff regulations, reviews the budget, and refers it to the Council, considers matters relating to the Organization's agreements and activities and draws up the agenda for the Council. The Bureau comprises one senior official from each member state. Chairmanship is by rotation. The Bureau convenes twice a year before meetings of the Ministerial Council.

SECRETARIAT

Secretary-General: ABDUL AZIZ AL-TURKI (Saudi Arabia).

Besides the Office of the Secretary-General, there are four departments: Finance and Administrative Affairs, Information and Library, Technical Affairs and Economics Departments. The last two form the Arab Centre for Energy Studies (which was established in 1983).

JUDICIAL TRIBUNAL

The Tribunal comprises seven judges from Arab countries. Its task is to settle differences in interpretation and application of the OAPEC Agreement, arising between members and also between OAPEC and its affiliates; disputes among member countries on petroleum activities falling within OAPEC's jurisdiction and not under the sovereignty of member countries; and disputes that the Ministerial Council decides to submit to the Tribunal.

President: FARIS ALWAGAYAN.

Registrar: RIAD DAOUDI.

Activities

OAPEC co-ordinates different aspects of the Arab petroleum industry through the joint undertakings described below. It co-operates with the League of Arab States and other Arab organizations, and attempts to link petroleum research institutes in the Arab states. It organizes or participates in conferences and seminars, many of which are held in co-operation with non-Arab organizations; examples include the Fifth Arab Conference on Mineral Resources and the Fourth Arab Energy Conference (1988), seminars on the Arab refining industry in the 1990s, on the hydrocarbon-producing potential of deep geological formations in the Arab countries and techniques for exploring them, and on the utilization of natural gas in the Arab world (all in 1989), and an OAPEC/EC seminar on energy markets integration in Arab and European countries (1990).

OAPEC provides training in technical matters and in documentation and information. The General Secretariat also conducts technical and feasibility studies and carries out market reviews. It provides information through a library, data base and the publications listed below.

OAPEC's budget for 1991 was about US $4.5m., compared with $4.2m. for 1989.

The invasion of Kuwait by Iraq in August 1990, and the subsequent international embargo on petroleum exports from Iraq and Kuwait, severely disrupted OAPEC's activities. In December the OAPEC Council decided to establish its temporary headquarters in Cairo while Kuwait was under occupation. The Council decided to reschedule overdue payments by Iraq and Syria over a 15-year period, and to postpone the Fifth Arab Energy Conference from mid-1992 to mid-1994.

JOINTLY SPONSORED UNDERTAKINGS

Arab Maritime Petroleum Transport Company—AMPTC: POB 143, el-Giza 1211, Egypt (temporary address—normally in Kuwait); tel. 629411; telex 23362; fax 3496457; f. 1973 to undertake transport of crude petroleum, gas, refined products and petro-chemicals, and thus to increase Arab participation in the tanker transport industry; capital (authorized and subscribed) $500m. Chair. IBRAHIM T. ABURKHES; Man.-Dir SULEIMAN AL-BASSAM.

Arab Petroleum Investments Corporation—APICORP: POB 448, Dhahran Airport 31932, Saudi Arabia; tel. 864-7400; telex 870068; fax 8945076; f. 1975 to finance investments in petroleum and petrochemicals projects and related industries in the Arab world and in developing countries, with priority being given to Arab joint ventures. Projects financed include gas liquefaction plants, petrochemicals, tankers, oil refineries, pipelines, exploration, detergents, fertilizers and process control instrumentation. Authorized capital: US $1,200m.; subscribed capital: $400m. Shareholders: Kuwait, Saudi Arabia and United Arab Emirates (17% each), Libya (15%), Iraq and Qatar (10% each), Algeria (5%), Bahrain, Egypt and Syria (3% each). Chair. ABDELLAH A. AL-ZAID; Gen.-Man. Dr NUREDDIN FARRAG.

Arab Petroleum Services Company—APSC: POB 12925, Tripoli, Libya; tel. 45861; telex 20405; f. 1977 to provide petroleum services through the establishment of companies specializing in various activities, and to train specialized personnel. Authorized capital: 100m. Libyan dinars; subscribed capital: 15m. Libyan dinars. Chair. AYYAD AD-DALY; Gen.-Man. ISMAIL AL-KORAITLI.

    Arab Drilling and Workover Company: POB 680, Tripoli, Libya; f. 1980 as a subsidiary of APSC; subscribed capital: 12m. Libyan dinars; Gen. Man. MUHAMMAD AHMAD ATTIGA.

    Arab Geophysical Exploration Services Company: POB 12925, Tripoli, Libya; tel. 38700; telex 20405; f. 1985.

    Arab Well Logging Company: POB 6225, Baghdad, Iraq; tel. 5411125; telex 213688; f. 1983; provides well-logging services and data interpretation.

Arab Petroleum Training Institute: POB 6037, Al-Tajeyat, Baghdad, Iraq; f. 1979; tel. 5234100; telex 212728; Dir HAZIM B. ASAD (acting).

Arab Shipbuilding and Repair Yard Company—ASRY: POB 50110, Manama, Bahrain; tel. 671111; telex 8455; fax 670236; f. 1974 to undertake repairs and servicing of vessels; operates a dry dock in Bahrain; two floating docks purchased in 1991. Capital (authorized and subscribed) $340m. Chair. Sheikh DAIJ BIN KHALIFA AL-KHALIFA; Gen. Man. HANS G. FRISK.

PUBLICATIONS

Energy Resources Monitor (quarterly, Arabic).

OAPEC Monthly Bulletin (Arabic and English editions).

Oil and Arab Cooperation (quarterly, Arabic).

Secretary-General's Annual Report (Arabic and English editions).

Papers, studies, conference proceedings.

ORGANIZATION OF THE ISLAMIC CONFERENCE—OIC

Address: Kilo 6, Mecca Rd, POB 178, Jeddah 21411, Saudi Arabia.
Telephone: (2) 680-0800; **telex:** 601366; **fax:** (2) 687-3568.

The Organization was formally established in May 1971, when its Secretariat became operational, following a summit meeting of Muslim heads of state at Rabat, Morocco, in September 1969, and the Islamic Foreign Ministers' Conference in Jeddah in March 1970, and in Karachi, Pakistan, in December 1970.

MEMBERS

Afghanistan	Indonesia	Qatar
Albania	Iran	Saudi Arabia
Algeria	Iraq	Senegal
Azerbaijan	Jordan	Sierra Leone
Bahrain	Kuwait	Somalia
Bangladesh	Kyrgyzstan	Sudan
Benin	Lebanon	Syria
Brunei	Libya	Tajikistan
Burkina Faso	Malaysia	Tunisia
Cameroon	Maldives	Turkey
Chad	Mali	Turkmenistan
The Comoros	Mauritania	Uganda
Djibouti	Morocco	United Arab
Egypt	Niger	Emirates
Gabon	Nigeria	Yemen
The Gambia	Oman	Zanzibar
Guinea	Pakistan	
Guinea-Bissau	Palestine	

Note: Observer status has been granted to the Muslim community of the 'Turkish Federated State of Cyprus' (which declared independence as the 'Turkish Republic of Northern Cyprus' in November 1983). Mozambique also has observer status. Azerbaijan was admitted as a member in 1991, Turkmenistan in June 1992, and Albania, Kyrgyzstan, Tajikistan and Zanzibar (which forms part of Tanzania) were granted membership of the Conference in December 1992.

Organization

(August 1994)

SUMMIT CONFERENCES

The supreme body of the Organization is the Conference of Heads of State, which met in 1969 at Rabat, Morocco, in 1974 at Lahore, Pakistan, and in January 1981 at Mecca, Saudi Arabia, when it was decided that summit conferences would be held every three years in future. Fifth Conference: Kuwait, January 1987; sixth Conference: Dakar, Senegal, December 1991. The next Conference was to be held in Saudi Arabia.

CONFERENCE OF MINISTERS OF FOREIGN AFFAIRS

Conferences take place annually, to consider the means for implementing the general policy of the Organization, although they may also be convened for extraordinary sessions.

SECRETARIAT

The executive organ of the Organization, headed by a Secretary-General (who is elected by the Conference of Ministers of Foreign Affairs for a non-renewable four-year term) and four Assistant Secretaries-General (similarly appointed).

Secretary-General: Dr HAMID ALGABID (Niger).

At the summit conference in January 1981 it was decided that an International Islamic Court of Justice should be established to adjudicate in disputes between Muslim countries. Experts met in January 1983 to draw up a constitution for the court, but by 1994 it was not yet in operation.

SPECIALIZED COMMITTEES

Al-Quds Committee: f. 1975 to implement the resolutions of the Islamic Conference on the status of Jerusalem (Al-Quds); it meets at the level of foreign ministers; Chair. King HASSAN II of Morocco.

Standing Committee for Economic and Commercial Co-operation (COMCEC): f. 1981; Chair. SÜLEYMAN DEMIREL (Pres. of Turkey).

Standing Committee for Information and Cultural Affairs (COMIAC): f. 1981; Chair. ABDOU DIOUF (Pres. of Senegal).

Standing Committee for Scientific and Technological Co-operation (COMSTECH): f. 1981; Chair. FAROOQ A. LEGHARI (Pres. of Pakistan).

Islamic Commission for Economic, Cultural and Social Affairs: f. 1976.

Permanent Finance Committee.

Other committees comprise the Committee for Southern Africa, the Committee of Islamic Solidarity with the Peoples of the Sahel, the Six-Member Committee on the Situation of Muslims in the Philippines, the Six-Member Committee on Palestine, the ad-hoc Committee on Afghanistan, and the OIC contact group on Bosnia and Herzegovina.

Activities

The Organization's aims, as proclaimed in the Charter that was adopted in 1972, are:

(i) To promote Islamic solidarity among member states;

(ii) To consolidate co-operation among member states in the economic, social, cultural, scientific and other vital fields, and to arrange consultations among member states belonging to international organizations;

(iii) To endeavour to eliminate racial segregation and discrimination and to eradicate colonialism in all its forms;

(iv) To take necessary measures to support international peace and security founded on justice;

(v) To co-ordinate all efforts for the safeguard of the Holy Places and support of the struggle of the people of Palestine, and help them to regain their rights and liberate their land;

(vi) To strengthen the struggle of all Muslim people with a view to safeguarding their dignity, independence and national rights; and

(vii) To create a suitable atmosphere for the promotion of co-operation and understanding among member states and other countries.

The first summit conference of Islamic leaders (representing 24 states) took place in 1969 following the burning of the Al Aqsa Mosque in Jerusalem. At this conference it was decided that Islamic governments should 'consult together with a view to promoting close co-operation and mutual assistance in the economic, scientific, cultural and spiritual fields, inspired by the immortal teachings of Islam'. Thereafter the foreign ministers of the countries concerned met annually, and adopted the Charter of the Organization of the Islamic Conference in 1972.

At the second Islamic summit conference (Lahore, Pakistan, 1974), the Islamic Solidarity Fund was established, together with a committee of representatives which later evolved into the Islamic Commission for Economic, Cultural and Social Affairs. Subsequently, numerous other subsidiary bodies have been set up (see below).

ECONOMIC CO-OPERATION

A general agreement for economic, technical and commercial co-operation came into force in 1981, providing for the establishment of joint investment projects and trade co-ordination. This was followed by an agreement on promotion, protection and guarantee of investments among member states. A plan of action to strengthen economic co-operation was adopted at the third Islamic summit conference in 1981, aiming to promote collective self-reliance and the development of joint ventures in all sectors. In May 1993 the OIC committee for economic and commercial co-operation, meeting in Istanbul, agreed to review and update the 1981 plan of action.

A meeting of ministers of industry was held in February 1982, and agreed to promote industrial co-operation, including joint ventures in agricultural machinery, engineering and other basic industries.

In December 1988 it was announced that a committee of experts, established by the OIC, was to draw up a 10-year programme of assistance to developing countries (mainly in Africa) in science and technology.

CULTURAL CO-OPERATION

The Organization supports education in Muslim communities throughout the world, and, through the Islamic Solidarity Fund, has helped to establish Islamic universities in Niger, Uganda, Bangladesh and Malaysia. It organizes seminars on various aspects of Islam, and encourages dialogue with the other monotheistic religions. Support is given to publications on Islam both in Muslim and Western countries.

In March 1989 the Conference of Ministers of Foreign Affairs denounced as an apostate the author of the controversial novel *The Satanic Verses* (Salman Rushdie), demanded the withdrawal of the book from circulation, and urged member states to boycott publishing houses that refused to comply.

HUMANITARIAN ASSISTANCE

Assistance is given to Muslim communities affected by wars and natural disasters, in co-operation with UN organizations, particularly UNHCR. The countries of the Sahel region (Burkina Faso, Cape Verde, Chad, The Gambia, Guinea, Guinea-Bissau, Mali, Mauritania, Niger and Senegal) receive particular attention as victims of drought. In April 1993 member states pledged US $80m. in emergency assistance for Muslims affected by the war in Bosnia and Herzegovina.

POLITICAL CO-OPERATION

The Organization is also active at a political level. From the beginning it called for vacation of Arab territories by Israel, recognition of the rights of Palestinians and of the Palestine Liberation Organization as their sole legitimate representative, and the restoration of Jerusalem to Arab rule. The 1981 summit conference called for a *jihad* (holy war—though not necessarily in a military sense) 'for the liberation of Jerusalem and the occupied territories'; this was to include an Islamic economic boycott of Israel.

In January 1980 an extraordinary conference of ministers of foreign affairs demanded the immediate and unconditional withdrawal of Soviet troops from Afghanistan and suspended Afghanistan's membership of the organization. The conference adopted a resolution condemning armed aggression against Somalia and denouncing the presence of military forces of the USSR and some of its allies in the Horn of Africa.

In 1982 Islamic ministers of foreign affairs decided to establish Islamic offices for boycotting Israel and for military co-operation with the Palestine Liberation Organization. The 1984 summit conference agreed to reinstate Egypt (suspended following the peace treaty signed with Israel in 1979) as a member of the Organization, although the resolution was opposed by seven states.

The fifth summit conference, held in January 1987, discussed the continuing Iran–Iraq war, and agreed that the Islamic Peace Committee should attempt to prevent the sale of military equipment to the parties in the conflict. The conference also discussed the conflicts in Chad and Lebanon, and requested the holding of a United Nations conference to define international terrorism, as opposed to legitimate fighting for freedom. The conference also approved proposals for joint development of modern technology, and for improving scientific and technical skills in the less-developed Islamic countries.

In March 1989 ministers of foreign affairs agreed to readmit Afghanistan, as represented by the 'interim government' formed by the *mujahidin* ('holy warriors'), following the withdrawal of Soviet troops from Afghanistan.

In August 1990 a majority of ministers of foreign affairs condemned Iraq's recent invasion of Kuwait, and demanded the withdrawal of Iraqi forces. In August 1991 the Conference of Ministers of Foreign Affairs obstructed Iraq's attempt to propose a resolution demanding the repeal of economic sanctions against the country. The sixth summit conference, held in Senegal in December 1991, reflected the divisions in the Arab world that resulted from Iraq's invasion of Kuwait and the ensuing war. Twelve heads of state did not attend, sending representatives, reportedly to register protest at the presence of Jordan and the PLO at the conference, both of which had given support to Iraq. Disagreement also arose between the PLO and the majority of other OIC member states when it was proposed to cease the OIC's support for the PLO's *jihad* in the Arab territories occupied by Israel. The proposal, which was adopted, represented an attempt to further the Middle East peace negotiations currently being sponsored by the USA.

In late August 1992 the UN General Assembly approved a non-binding resolution, introduced by the OIC, that requested the UN Security Council to take increased action, including the use of force, in order to defend the non-Serbian population of Bosnia and Herzegovina (some 43% of Bosnians being Muslims) from Serbian aggression, and to restore its 'territorial integrity'. The OIC Conference of Ministers of Foreign Affairs, which was held in Jeddah, Saudi Arabia, in early December, demanded anew that the UN Security Council take all necessary measures against Serbia and Montenegro, including military intervention, in accordance with Article 42 of the UN Charter, in order to protect the Bosnian Muslims. In early February 1993 the OIC appealed to the Security Council to remove the embargo on armaments to Bosnia and

Herzegovina with regard to the Bosnian Muslims, to allow them to defend themselves from the Bosnian Serbs, who were far better armed. At the Conference of Ministers of Foreign Affairs, held in Karachi, Pakistan, in late April 1993, a co-ordination group on action to help the Bosnian Muslims was created, composed of representatives from Egypt, Iran, Malaysia, Saudi Arabia, Senegal and Turkey.

A report by an OIC fact-finding mission investigating allegations of repression of the largely Muslim population of the Indian state of Jammu and Kashmir by the Indian armed forces was presented to the 1993 Conference. The Conference urged member states to take the necessary measures to persuade India to cease the 'massive human rights violations' in Jammu and Kashmir and to allow the Indian Kashmiris to 'exercise their inalienable right to self-determination'. A second OIC fact-finding mission was to be dispatched to Kashmir. The Conference also condemned the destruction of a historic mosque in India by extremist Hindus; 'Israeli acts of terrorism, suppression, killing and deportation', directed at Palestinians; and Armenian offensive action against Azerbaijan.

A special ministerial meeting on Bosnia and Herzegovina was held in mid-July 1993, at which seven OIC countries committed themselves to sending troops to serve in the UN Protection Force in the former Yugoslavia (UNPROFOR), to assist the United Nations in providing adequate protection and relief to the victims of war in Bosnia and Herzegovina. More than 17,000 troops were to be made available, with the OIC demanding that member states should be represented at the highest level in UNPROFOR's command structure. (The UN subsequently decided that 5,000 troops from three Islamic countries—Malaysia, Pakistan and Tunisia—should be dispatched to Bosnia and Herzegovina before the end of the year.) The meeting also decided to dispatch immediately a ministerial mission to persuade influential governments to support the OIC's demands for the removal of the arms embargo on Bosnian Muslims and athe convening of a restructured international conference to bring about a political solution to the conflict.

SUBSIDIARY ORGANS

Al-Quds Fund: c/o OIC, Kilo 6, Mecca Rd, POB 178, Jeddah 21411, Saudi Arabia; f. 1976 to support the struggle of the Palestinian people in Jerusalem.

International Commission for the Preservation of Islamic Cultural Heritage: POB 24, 80692 Beşiktaş, Istanbul, Turkey; tel. (212) 2605988; telex 26484; fax (212) 2584365; f. 1982. Chair. Prince Faisal bin Fahd bin Abdul Aziz (Saudi Arabia).

Islamic Centre for the Development of Trade: Complexe Commerciale des Habous, ave des FAR, BP 13545, Casablanca, Morocco; tel. (2) 314974; telex 46296; fax (2) 310110; f. 1983 to encourage regular commercial contacts, harmonize policies and promote investments among OIC members. Dir Badre Eddine Allali. Publs *Tijaris: International and Inter-Islamic Trade Magazine, Inter-Islamic Trade Report* (annual).

Islamic Centre for Technical and Vocational Training and Research: KB Bazar, Joydebpur, Gazipur Dist., Dhaka, Bangladesh; tel. (2) 892366; telex 642739; fax (2) 892396; f. 1981 to provide skilled technicians and instructors in mechanical, electrical, electronic and chemical technology, and to conduct research; capacity of 65 staff and 650 students. Dir Prof. A. M. Patwari. Publs News Bulletin (quarterly), reports, human resources development series.

Islamic Foundation for Science, Technology and Development—IFSTAD: POB 9833, Jeddah 21423, Saudi Arabia; tel. (2) 632-2273; telex 604081; fax (2) 632-2274; f. 1981 to promote co-operation in science and technology within the Islamic world. Dir-Gen. Dr Arafat R. Altamemi.

Islamic Jurisprudence Academy: Jeddah, Saudi Arabia; f. 1982. Sec.-Gen. Sheikh Mohamed Habib Belkhojah.

Islamic Solidarity Fund: c/o OIC Secretariat, POB 178, Jeddah, Saudi Arabia; f. 1974 to meet the needs of Islamic communities by providing emergency aid and the wherewithal to build mosques, Islamic centres, hospitals, schools and universities. Chair. Sheikh Nasir Abdullah bin Hamdan; Exec. Dir Abdullah Hersi.

Research Centre for Islamic History, Art and Culture: POB 24, Beşiktaş 80692, Istanbul, Turkey; tel. (212) 2605988; telex 26484; fax (212) 2584365; f. 1979; library of 40,000 vols. Dir-Gen. Prof. Dr Ekmeleddin İhsanoğlu. Publ. *Newsletter* (3 a year).

Statistical, Economic and Social Research and Training Centre for the Islamic Countries: Attar Sok. 4, GOP, Ankara, Turkey; tel. (4) 1286105; telex 43163; f. 1978. Dir Dr Şadi Cindoruk.

SPECIALIZED INSTITUTIONS

International Islamic News Agency (IINA): King Khalid Palace, Madinah Rd, POB 5054, Jeddah, Saudi Arabia; tel. (2) 665-8561; telex 601090; fax (2) 665-9358; f. 1972. Dir-Gen. Abdulwahab Kashif.

Islamic Development Bank: POB 5925, Jeddah 21432, Saudi Arabia; tel. (2) 6361400; telex 601137; fax (2) 6366871; f. 1975; promotes the economic and social development of OIC member countries and Muslim communities in non-member countries; provides assistance in the form of loans and grants for technical aid, in accordance with the principles of the Islamic Shari'a (sacred law). Pres. and Chair. OSSAMA JAAFAR FAQIH (Saudi Arabia).

Islamic Educational, Scientific and Cultural Organization (ISESCO)' BP 755, 16 bis Charia Omar Ben Khattab, Agdal, Rabat, Morocco; tel. (7) 772433; telex 32645; fax (7) 777425; f. 1982. Dir-Gen. Dr ABDULAZIZ BIN OTHMAN AL-TWAIJRI. Publs *ISESCO Bulletin* (quarterly), *Islam Today* (2 a year), *ISESCO Triennial*.

Islamic States Broadcasting Organization (ISBO): POB 6351, Jeddah 21442, Saudi Arabia; tel. (2) 6721121. Sec.-Gen. HUSSEIN AL-ASKARY.

OTHER INSTITUTIONS

Islamic Research and Training Institute: POB 9201, Jeddah 21413, Saudi Arabia; tel. (2) 636-1400; telex 601137; fax (2) 637-8927; f. 1982 for research enabling economic, financial and banking activities to conform to Islamic law, and to provide training for staff involved in development activities in member countries.

AFFILIATED INSTITUTIONS

International Association of Islamic Banks: 47 Aruba St, Heliopolis Houria'a, POB 2828, Cairo, Egypt; mems: 28 banks and other financial institutions in 11 Islamic countries. Sec.-Gen. SAMIR A. SHEIKH.

Islamic Cement Association: Posta Kutsu 2, 06582 Bankanhiklar, Ankara, Turkey; f. 1984; aims to encourage co-operation in the production of cement.

Islamic Chamber of Commerce, Industry and Commodity Exchange: POB 3831, Karachi, Pakistan; tel. (21) 530535; telex 25533; fax (21) 532656; f. 1979 to promote trade and industry among member states; comprises national chambers or federations of chambers of commerce and industry. Sec.-Gen. AGEEL AHMAD AL-JASSIM.

Islamic Committee for the International Crescent: Benghazi, Libya; f. 1979 to attempt to alleviate the suffering caused by natural disasters and war. Sec.-Gen. Dr AHMAD ABDALLAH CHERIF.

Islamic Shipowners'Association: POB 14900, Jeddah 21434, Saudi Arabia; tel. (2) 6653379; telex 607303; fax (2) 6604920; f. 1981 to promote co-operation among maritime companies in Islamic countries. Sec.-Gen. ABDULLATIF A. SULTAN.

Organization of Islamic Capitals and Cities: POB 13621, Jeddah 21414, Saudi Arabia; tel. (2) 6657516; telex 606562; fax (2) 6657516; f. 1978 to develop co-operation among the Islamic capitals and to preserve their character and heritage. Sec.-Gen. ABDULQADIR HAMZAK KOSHAK.

Sports Federation of Islamic Solidarity: POB 5844, Riyadh, Saudi Arabia; telex 404760; fax (1) 4013216; f. 1981. Sec.-Gen. Dr SALEH GAZDAR.

ORGANIZATION OF THE PETROLEUM EXPORTING COUNTRIES—OPEC

Address: Obere Donaustrasse 93, 1020 Vienna, Austria.

Telephone: (1) 21-11-20; **telex:** 134474; **fax:** (1) 26-43-20.

OPEC was established in 1960 to link countries whose main source of export earnings is petroleum; it aims to unify and co-ordinate members' petroleum policies and to safeguard their interests generally. The OPEC Fund for International Development is described on p. 243.

OPEC's share of world petroleum production was 38% in 1993 (compared with 45% in 1980 and a peak of 55.5% in 1973). It is estimated that OPEC members possess 77% of the world's known reserves of crude petroleum, of which 66% is in the Middle East. In 1991 OPEC members possessed about 39.8% of known reserves of natural gas.

MEMBERS*

Algeria	Iraq†	Qatar
Gabon	Kuwait	Saudi Arabia
Indonesia	Libya	United Arab Emirates
Iran	Nigeria	Venezuela

* Ecuador left OPEC in November 1992 (see below).

† In August 1990, following its invasion of Kuwait, Iraq's petroleum exports were halted by a UN embargo. In August 1991 the UN permitted Iraq to sell petroleum worth up to US \$1,600m., the revenue from which would be used for the humanitarian needs of Iraq's population. Iraq, however, refused to comply with the terms set by the UN, and by mid-1994 had not recommenced the export of its petroleum.

Organization

(August 1994)

CONFERENCE

The Conference is the supreme authority of the Organization, responsible for the formulation of its general policy. It consists of representatives of member countries, who examine reports and recommendations submitted by the Board of Governors. It approves the appointment of Governors from each country and elects the Chairman of the Board of Governors. It works on the unanimity principle, and meets at least twice a year.

President: ABDULLAH BIN HAMAD AL-ATTIYAH (Qatar).

BOARD OF GOVERNORS

The Board directs the management of the Organization; it implements resolutions of the Conference and draws up an annual budget. It consists of one governor for each member country, and meets at least twice a year.

MINISTERIAL MONITORING COMMITTEE

The Committee (f. 1988) is responsible for monitoring price evolution and ensuring the stability of the world petroleum market. As such, it is charged with the preparation of long-term strategies, including the allocation of quotas to be presented to the Conference. The Committee consists of all 13 national representatives, and is normally convened four times a year.

ECONOMIC COMMISSION

A specialized body operating within the framework of the Secretariat, with a view to assisting the Organization in promoting stability in international prices for petroleum at equitable levels; consists of a board, national representatives and a commission staff; meets at least twice a year.

SECRETARIAT

Secretary-General: (acting) ABDALLAH SLEM EL-BADRI (Libya).

Deputy Secretary-General: Dr RAMZI SALMAN (Iraq).

Research Division: comprises three departments:

Data Services Department: Computer Section maintains and expands information services to support the research activities of the Secretariat and those of member countries. Statistics Section collects, collates and analyses statistical information from both primary and secondary sources.

Economics and Finance Department: Analyses economic and financial issues of significant interest; in particular those related to international financial and monetary matters, and to the international petroleum industry.

Energy Studies Department: Conducts a continuous programme for research in energy and related matters; monitors, forecasts and analyses developments in the energy and petrochemical industries; and evaluates hydrocarbons and products and their non-energy uses.

Division Director: Dr SHOKRI M. GHANEM.

Personnel and Administration Department: Responsible for all organization methods, provision of administrative services for all meetings, personnel matters, budgets accounting and internal control; **Head:** ABBAS N. AFSHAR.

OPECNA and Information Department: Formed in 1990 by the merging of the former Public Information Department and the OPEC News Agency (OPECNA, f. 1980). Responsible for a central public relations programme; production and distribution of publications, films, slides and tapes; and communication of OPEC objectives and decisions to the world at large; **Head:** Dr MOHAMED AL-SAHLAWI.

Legal Office: Undertakes special and other in-house legal studies and reports to ascertain where the best interests of the Organization and member countries lie; **Head:** AHMED ABDULAZIZ.

Office of the Secretary-General: Provides the Secretary-General with executive assistance in maintaining contacts with governments, organizations and delegations, in matters of protocol and in the preparation for and co-ordination of meetings; **Head:** Dr NAFRIZAL SIKUMBANG.

Record of Events

1960 The first OPEC Conference was held in Baghdad in September, attended by representatives from Iran, Iraq, Kuwait, Saudi Arabia and Venezuela.

1961 Second Conference, Caracas, January. Qatar was admitted to membership; a Board of Governors was formed and statutes agreed.

1962 Fourth Conference, Geneva, April and June. Protests were addressed to petroleum companies against price cuts introduced in August 1960. Indonesia and Libya were admitted to membership.

1965 In July the Conference reached agreement on a two-year joint production programme, implemented from 1965 to 1967, to limit annual growth in output to secure adequate prices.

1967 Abu Dhabi was admitted to membership.

1968 Fifteenth Conference (extraordinary), Beirut, January. OPEC accepted an offer of elimination of discounts submitted by petroleum companies following negotiations in November 1967.

1969 Algeria was admitted to membership.

1970 Twenty-first Conference, Caracas, December. Tax on income of petroleum companies was raised to 55%.

1971 A five-year agreement was concluded in February between the six producing countries in the Gulf and 23 international petroleum companies (Teheran Agreement). Twenty-fourth Conference, Vienna, July. Nigeria was admitted to membership.

1972 In January petroleum companies agreed to adjust petroleum revenues of the largest producers after changes in currency exchange rates (Geneva Agreement).

1973 OPEC and petroleum companies concluded an agreement whereby posted prices of crude petroleum were raised by 11.9% and a mechanism was installed to make monthly adjustments to prices in future (Second Geneva Agreement). Negotiations with petroleum companies on revision of the Teheran Agreement collapsed in October, and the Gulf states unilaterally declared 70% increases in posted prices, from US $3.01 to $5.11 per barrel. Thirty-sixth Conference, Teheran, December. The posted price was to increase by nearly 130%, from US $5.11 to $11.65 per barrel, from 1 January 1974. Ecuador was admitted to full membership and Gabon became an associate member.

1974 As a result of Saudi opposition to the December price increase, prices were held at current level for first quarter (and subsequently for the remainder of 1974). Abu Dhabi's membership was transferred to the United Arab Emirates. A meeting in June increased royalties charged to petroleum companies from 12.5% to 14.5% in all member states except Saudi Arabia. A meeting in September increased governmental take by about 3.5% through further increases in royalties on equity crude to 16.67% and in taxes to 65.65%, except in Saudi Arabia.

1975 OPEC's first summit conference was held in Algiers in March. Gabon was admitted to full membership. A ministerial meeting in September agreed to raise prices by 10% for the period until June 1976.

1976 The OPEC Special Fund for International Development was created in May. In December, a general 15% rise in basic prices was proposed and supported by 11 member states. This was to take place in two stages: a 10% rise as of 1 January 1977, and a further 5% rise as of 1 July 1977. However, Saudi Arabia and the United Arab Emirates decided to raise their prices by 5% only.

1977 Following an earlier waiver by nine members of the 5% second stage of the price increase agreed at Doha, Saudi Arabia and the United Arab Emirates announced in July

that they would both raise their prices by 5%. As a result, a single level of prices throughout the organization was restored. Because of continued disagreements between the 'moderates', led by Saudi Arabia and Iran, and the 'radicals', led by Algeria, Libya and Iraq, the year's second Conference at Caracas, December, was unable to settle on an increase in prices.

1978 At the fifty-first Conference, held in June, it was agreed that price levels should remain stable until the end of the year. A committee of experts, chaired by Kuwait, met in July to consider ways of compensating for the effects of the depreciation of the US dollar. In December 1978 it was decided to raise prices by instalments of 5%, 3.8%, 2.3% and 2.7%. These would bring a rise of 14.5% over nine months, but an average increase of 10% for 1979.

1979 At an extraordinary meeting in Geneva at the end of March members decided to raise prices by 9%. In June the Conference agreed minimum and maximum prices which seemed likely to add between 15% and 20% to import bills of consumer countries.
The December Conference recommended replenishment of the OPEC Fund and agreed in principle to convert the Fund into a development agency with its own legal personality.

1980 In June the Conference decided to set the price for a marker crude at US $32 per barrel, and that the value differentials which could be added above this ceiling (on account of quality and geographical location) should not exceed $5 per barrel.
The planned OPEC summit meeting in Baghdad in November was postponed indefinitely because of the Iran–Iraq war, but the scheduled price-fixing meeting of petroleum ministers went ahead in Bali in December, with both Iranians and Iraqis present. A ceiling price of US $41 per barrel was fixed for premium crudes.

1981 In May attempts to achieve price reunification were made, but Saudi Arabia refused to increase its US $32 per barrel price unless the higher prices charged by other countries were lowered. Most of the other OPEC countries agreed to cut production by 10% so as to reduce the surplus. An emergency meeting in Geneva in August again failed to unify prices, although Saudi Arabia agreed to reduce production by 1m. barrels per day, with the level of output to be reviewed monthly. In October OPEC countries agreed to increase the Saudi marker price by 6% to US $34 per barrel, with a ceiling price of $38 per barrel. Saudi Arabia also announced that it would keep its production below 8.5m.b/d.

1982 The continuing world glut of petroleum forced prices below the official mark of $34 per barrel in some producer countries. In March an emergency meeting of petroleum ministers was held in Vienna and agreed (for the first time in OPEC's history) to defend the Organization's price structure by imposing an overall production ceiling of 18m. b/d, effectively 17.5m. b/d with Saudi Arabia's separate announcement of a cut to 7m. b/d in its own production. In December the Conference agreed to limit OPEC production to 18.5m. b/d in 1983 (representing about one-third of total world production) but postponed the allocation of national quotas pending consultations among the respective governments.

1983 In January an emergency meeting of petroleum ministers, fearing a collapse in world petroleum prices, decided to reduce the production ceiling to 17.5m. b/d (itself several million b/d above actual current output) but failed to agree on individual production quotas or on adjustments to the differentials in prices charged for the high-quality crude petroleum produced by Algeria, Libya and Nigeria compared with that produced by the Gulf States.
In February Nigeria cut its prices to US $30 per barrel, following a collapse in its production. To avoid a 'price war' OPEC set the official price of marker crude at $29 per barrel, and agreed to maintain existing differentials among the various OPEC crudes at the level agreed on in March 1982, with the temporary exception that the differentials for Nigerian crudes should be $1 more than the price of the marker crude. It also agreed to maintain the production ceiling of 17.5m. b/d and allocated quotas for each member country except Saudi Arabia, which was to act as a 'swing producer' to supply the balancing quantities to meet market requirements. The official marker price and production ceiling were maintained throughout the year, although actual production by members was believed to be in excess of 18m. b/d at the end of the year.

1984 The production ceiling of 17.5m. b/d and the official price of US $29 per barrel were maintained until October, when the production ceiling was lowered to 16m. b/d. In December price differentials for light (more expensive) and heavy (cheaper) crudes were slightly altered in an attempt to counteract price-cutting by non-OPEC producers, particularly Norway and the United Kingdom.

1985 In January members (except Algeria, Iran and Libya) effectively abandoned the marker price system: the price of Arabian light crude (the former marker price) was lowered to US $28 per barrel, and price differentials between the cheapest and most expensive grades were cut from $4 to $2.40; this system was also adopted by Iran in February. During the year production in excess of quotas by OPEC members, unofficial discounts and barter deals by members, and price cuts by non-members (such as Mexico, which had hitherto kept its prices in line with those of OPEC) contributed to a weakening of the market. Saudi Arabia indicated that it was not prepared to continue cutting its own output, to make up for others' increases, in an attempt to support world prices.

1986 During the first half of the year prices dropped to below US $10 per barrel. In April ministers from 10 member states agreed to set OPEC production at 16.7m. b/d for the third quarter of 1986 and at 17.3m. b/d for the fourth quarter. Algeria, Iran and Libya dissented, arguing that production should be reduced to 14.5m. b/d and 16.8m. b/d respectively for those periods, in order to restore prices. Discussions were also held with non-member countries (Angola, Egypt, Malaysia, Mexico and Oman), which agreed to co-operate in limiting production, but the United Kingdom refused to reduce its petroleum production levels. In August all members, with the exception of Iraq (which demanded to be allowed the same quota as Iran and, when this was denied it, refused to be a party to the agreement), agreed upon a return to production quotas, with the aim of cutting production to 14.8m. b/d (about 16.8m. b/d including Iraq's production) for the ensuing two months. This measure resulted in an increase in prices to about $15 per barrel, which was extended until the end of the year. In December members (with the exception of Iraq) agreed to return to a fixed pricing system at a level of $18 per barrel as the OPEC reference price, with effect from 1 February 1987. OPEC's total production for the first and second quarters of 1987 was not to exceed 15.8m. b/d.

1987 In June, with prices having stabilized, the Conference decided that production during the third and fourth quarters of the year should be limited to 16.6m. b/d (including Iraq's production). It established a committee of three heads of delegations to visit member countries, to motivate them to comply with the agreement, while another group of five heads of delegations undertook to seek the co-operation of non-member producers. During the third and fourth quarters, however, total production was reported to be at least 1m. b/d above the agreed level. In December ministers decided to extend the existing agreement for the first half of 1988, although Iraq, once more, refused to participate.

1988 By March petroleum prices had fallen below US $15 per barrel. In April non-OPEC producers offered to reduce the volume of their petroleum exports by 5% if OPEC members would do the same. Saudi Arabia, however, refused to accept further reductions in production, saying that existing quotas should first be more strictly enforced. In June the previous production limit (15.06m. b/d, excluding Iraq's production) was again renewed for six months, in the hope that increasing demand would be sufficient to raise prices. By October, however, petroleum prices were below $12 per barrel. OPEC members (excluding Iraq) were estimated to be producing about 21m. b/d. In November a new agreement was reached, limiting total production (including that of Iraq) to 18.5m. b/d, with effect from 1 January 1989. Iran and Iraq finally agreed to accept identical quotas.

1989 In June (when prices had returned to about $18 per barrel) ministers agreed to increase the production limit to 19.5m. b/d for the second half of 1989. However, Kuwait and the United Arab Emirates indicated that they would not feel bound to observe this limit. In September the production limit was again increased, to 20.5m. b/d, and in November the limit for the first half of 1990 was increased to 22m. b/d.

1990 In May those members that had been exceeding their quotas declared that they would reduce their production to the agreed limit, in response to a decline in prices of some 25% since the beginning of the year. By late June, however, it was reported that total production had decreased by only 400,000 b/d, and prices remained at about US$14 per barrel.

In July Iraq threatened to take military action against Kuwait unless it reduced its petroleum production. In the same month OPEC members agreed to raise prices to $21 per barrel, and to limit output to 22.5m. b/d. In August, however, Iraq invaded Kuwait, and petroleum exports by the two countries (estimated to have a combined production capacity of 5m. b/d) were halted by an international embargo. Petroleum prices immediately increased to exceed $25 per barrel. Later in the month an informal consultative meeting of OPEC ministers placed the July agreement in abeyance, and permitted a temporary increase in production of petroleum, of between 3m. and 3.5m. b/d (mostly by Saudi Arabia, the United Arab Emirates and Venezuela). In September and October prices fluctuated in response to political developments in the Gulf region, reaching a point in excess of $40 per barrel in early October, but falling to about $25 per barrel by the end of the month. In October OPEC officials urged the industrialized countries to release their stocks of petroleum, in order to prevent further price increases. In December a meeting of OPEC members voted to maintain the high levels of production and to reinstate the quotas that had been agreed in July, once the Gulf crisis was over. During the period August 1990–February 1991 Saudi Arabia increased its petroleum output from 5.4m. to 8.5m. b/d. Seven of the other OPEC states also produced in excess of their agreed quotas. It was estimated that OPEC producers' revenues from petroleum sales rose by 40% in 1990, owing to increased prices and panic buying by consumer countries.

1991 In the first quarter OPEC members were producing about 23m. b/d, and the average price of petroleum was US $19 per barrel, the lowest since the Gulf crisis began. In the second quarter the price dropped further to an average of $17.5 per barrel. This was, however, a smaller decline than OPEC had feared would occur after the end of hostilities against Iraq. In an attempt to reach the target of a minimum reference price of $21 per barrel, ministers agreed in March to reduce production from 23m. b/d to 22.3m. b/d, although Saudi Arabia refused to return to its pre-August 1990 quota of 5.4m. b/d. In June ministers decided to maintain the ceiling of 22.3m. b/d into the third quarter of the year. A further reduction in the members' output was not thought to be necessary, even though most of them were producing at almost maximum capacity, since Iraq and Kuwait were still unable to export their petroleum. In July OPEC ministers met representatives of 10 consumer countries and nine international organizations to discuss petroleum market co-operation. In September it was agreed that OPEC members' production for the last quarter of 1991 should be raised to 23.65m. b/d in anticipation of increased demand from the industrialized countries, with uncertainty surrounding petroleum supplies from the USSR. In November the OPEC Conference decided to maintain the increased production ceiling during the first quarter of 1992. From early November, however, the price of petroleum declined sharply, with demand less than anticipated as a result of continuing world recession and a mild winter in the northern hemisphere.

1992 At a meeting of ministers in February there was disagreement between those member states which desired a substantial reduction of the production ceiling and Saudi Arabia, which was determined to maintain high output (which had remained at about 8.5m. b/d since early 1991). Agreement was reached on a production ceiling of 22.98m. b/d for the second quarter of 1992, and quotas were reintroduced for the first time since the start of the Gulf crisis. The agreement, was, however, subsequently repudiated by both Saudi Arabia, which stated that it would not abide by its allocated quota of 7.9m. b/d, and Iran, unhappy that the production ceiling had not been set lower. In May, the average price of petroleum having risen from US $16 per barrel in March to $18 per barrel in mid-April, it was agreed to continue the production restriction of 22.98m. b/d during the third quarter of 1992, despite pressure from Saudi Arabia to increase the ceiling to 24m. b/d. In addition, Kuwait, which was resuming production in the wake of the extensive damage inflicted on its oil-wells by Iraq during the Gulf War, was granted a special dispensation to produce without a fixed quota. During the first half of 1992 member states' petroleum output consistently exceeded agreed levels, with Saudi Arabia and Iran (despite its stance on reducing production) the principal over-producers. In April the OPEC Secretariat organized and hosted a conference on the environment; at the UN Conference on Environment and Development in June OPEC's Secretary-General expressed its member countries' strong objections to the tax on fossil fuels (designed to reduce pollution) proposed by the EC. In September negotiations between OPEC ministers in Geneva were complicated by Iran's alleged annexation of Abu Musa and two other islands in the territorial waters of the United Arab Emirates. However, agreement was reached on a production ceiling of 24.2m. b/d for the final quarter of 1992, in an attempt to raise the price of crude petroleum to the OPEC target of $21 per barrel. At a ministerial meeting in late November Ecuador formally resigned from OPEC, citing the high membership fee ($2m. per year) and OPEC's refusal to increase Ecuador's quota as reasons for doing so. Ecuador was the first country ever to leave the Organization. At the meeting, agreement was reached on a production ceiling of 24.58m. b/d for the first quarter of 1993 (24.46m. b/d, excluding Ecuador).

1993 In mid-February a quota was set for Kuwait for the first time since the onset of the Gulf crisis. Kuwait agreed to a quota of 1.6m. b/d (400,000 less than current output) from 1 March, on the understanding that it would be substantially increased in the third quarter of the year. The quota for overall production from 1 March was set at 23.58m. b/d. If adhered to, this new ceiling was to reduce total OPEC production by around 1.5m. b/d, since current output amounted to about 25m. b/d. A monitoring sub-committee was established, comprising the energy ministers of Libya and Qatar and OPEC's Secretary-General, to ensure compliance with quotas. In mid-April OPEC held a joint meeting with ministers of the Independent Petroleum Exporting Countries, which focused on proposals by the USA and EC to introduce increased taxes on petroleum. The meeting issued a communiqué claiming that such a 'carbon tax' would destabilize the petroleum market. It was agreed to establish a joint working group to co-ordinate strategies to deal with the effects of the tax, if introduced, and to co-operate in other ways. Output in March, while still not within the agreed limit, was substantially reduced, at 24–24.4m. b/d. Iran, Kuwait and Nigeria were reported to be exceeding their quotas by the largest margin, with Iran producing about 450,000 b/d in excess of its agreed ceiling. Ministers meeting in June decided to 'roll over' the overall quota of 23.58m. b/d into the third quarter of the year. However, Kuwait rejected its new allocation of 1.76m. b/d, demanding a quota of at least 2m. In mid-July discussions between Iraq and the UN on the possible supervised sale of Iraqi petroleum worth $1,600m. depressed petroleum prices to below $16 per barrel. An emergency meeting was called for late July, but was postponed as a result of a dispute between Iran and Saudi Arabia, with Iran declaring that Saudi Arabia's quota should be reduced to 5.3m. b/d and Saudi Arabia holding Iran solely responsible for excesses in production and the consequent low petroleum prices. The three-member compliance sub-committee, meeting with the OPEC President in August, urged member states to adhere to their production quotas (which were exceeded by a total of 1m. b/d in July). At the end of

September an extraordinary meeting of the Conference was convened in Geneva. Members agreed on a raised production ceiling of 24.52m. b/d, to be effective for six months from 1 October. Kuwait accepted a quota of 2m. b/d, which brought the country back into the production ceiling mechanism. Iran agreed on an allocation of 3.6m. b/d, while Saudi Arabia consented to freeze production at current levels. The accord was intended effectively to lower production by ensuring that countries did not exceed their quotas, and thus boost petroleum prices which remained persistently low. In November the Conference, meeting in Vienna, rejected any further reduction in production. Prices subsequently fell below the $14 level, partly owing to a decision by Iraq to allow the UN to monitor its weapons programme—a move that would consequently lead to a lifting of the UN embargo on Iraqi petroleum exports, and reached a low point of $12.87 per barrel.

1994 Prices remained depressed during the first quarter of the year. In March, at the 12th meeting of the ministerial monitoring committee, held in Geneva, members opted to maintain the output quotas, agreed in September 1993, until the end of the year, and urged non-OPEC producers to freeze their production levels. (Iraq failed to endorse the agreement, since it only recognizes the production agreement adopted in July 1990). At the meeting Saudi Arabia resisted a proposal from Iran and Nigeria, both countries severely affected by reduced petroleum revenue, to reduce production by 1m. b/d in order to boost prices. In June the Conference, convened in Vienna, endorsed the decision to maintain the existing production ceiling, and stated that there would be no further meeting of the Conference until November, in an attempt to emphasize that the production agreement would remain in effect until the end of 1994. Ministers acknowledged that there had been a gradual increase in petroleum prices in the second quarter of the year, with an average basket price of $15.60 per barrel for that period. At mid-1994 it was estimated that members were exceeding the production ceiling by some 260,000 b/d, of which 150,000 was Iraqi output.

FINANCE

Total expenditure in 1993 amounted to 204.0m. Austrian schillings. The budget for 1994 was 234.2m. schillings.

PUBLICATIONS

Annual Report.

Facts and Figures.

OPEC Annual Statistical Bulletin.

OPEC Bulletin (10 a year).

OPEC at a Glance.

OPEC Information.

OPEC Official Resolutions and Press Releases.

OPEC Review (quarterly).

OPEC FUND FOR INTERNATIONAL DEVELOPMENT

Address: POB 995, 1011 Vienna, Austria.

Telephone: (1) 51-56-40; **telex:** 131734; **fax:** (1) 513-92-38.
The Fund was established by OPEC member countries in 1976.

MEMBERS

Member countries of OPEC (q.v.).

Organization

(August 1994)

ADMINISTRATION

The Fund is administered by a Ministerial Council and a Governing Board. Each member country is represented on the Council by its minister of finance. The Board consists of one representative and one alternate for each member country.

Chairman, Ministerial Council: AGUS TARMIDZI (Indonesia).

Chairman, Governing Board: OSAMAH FAQUIH (Saudi Arabia).

Director-General of the Fund: Dr YESUFU SEYYID ABDULAI (Nigeria).

FINANCIAL STRUCTURE

The resources of the Fund, whose unit of account is the US dollar, consist of contributions by OPEC member countries, and income received from operations or otherwise accruing to the Fund.

The initial endowment of the Fund amounted to US $800m. Its resources have been replenished three times, and have been further increased by the profits accruing to seven OPEC member countries through the sales of gold held by the International Monetary Fund. The pledged contributions to the OPEC Fund amounted to US $3,435m. at the end of 1993, and paid-in contributions totalled $2,790m.

Activities

The OPEC Fund for International Development is a multilateral agency for financial co-operation and assistance. Its objective is to reinforce financial co-operation between OPEC member countries and other developing countries through the provision of financial support to the latter on appropriate terms, to assist them in their economic and social development. The Fund was conceived as a collective financial facility which would consolidate the assistance extended by its member countries; its resources are additional to those already made available through other bilateral and multilateral aid agencies of OPEC members. It is empowered to:

(*a*) Provide concessional loans for balance-of-payments support;

(*b*) Provide concessional loans for the implementation of development projects and programmes;

(*c*) Make contributions and/or provide loans to eligible international agencies; and

(*d*) Finance technical assistance and research through grants.

The eligible beneficiaries of the Fund's assistance are the governments of developing countries other than OPEC member countries, and international development agencies whose beneficiaries are developing countries. The Fund gives priority to the countries with the lowest income.

The Fund may undertake technical, economic and financial appraisal of a project submitted to it, or entrust such an appraisal to an appropriate international development agency, the executing national agency of a member country, or any other qualified agency. Most projects financed by the Fund have been co-financed by other development finance agencies. In each such case, one of the co-financing agencies may be appointed to administer the Fund's loan in association with its own. This practice has enabled the Fund to extend its lending activities to 90 countries over a short period of time and in a simple way, with the aim of avoiding duplication and complications. As its experience grew, the Fund increasingly resorted to parallel, rather than joint financing, taking up separate project components to be financed according to its rules and policies. In addition, it started to finance some projects completely on its own. These trends necessitated the issuance in 1982 of guidelines for the procurement of goods and services under the Fund's loans, allowing for a margin of preference for goods and services of local origin or originating in other developing countries: the general principle of competitive bidding is, however, followed by the Fund. The loans are not tied to procurement from Fund member countries or from any other countries. The margin of preference for goods and services obtainable in developing countries is allowed on the request of the borrower and within defined limits. Fund assistance in the form of programme loans has a broader coverage than project lending. Programme loans are used to stimulate an economic sector or subsector, and assist recipient countries in obtaining inputs, equipment and spare parts.

The Fund's eleventh lending programme, covering a two-year period effective from 1 January 1994, was approved in June 1993. Besides extending loans for project and programme financing and balance of payments support, the Fund also undertakes other operations, including grants in support of technical assistance and other activities (mainly research), and financial contributions to other international institutions.

By the end of December 1993 the number of loans extended by the Fund was 609, totalling US $2,966m., of which 68.4% was for project financing, 24.4% was for balance-of-payments support and 7.1% was for programme financing.

Direct loans are supplemented by grants to support technical assistance, food aid and research. By the end of December 1993, 354 grants, amounting to $223.3m., had been extended, including $83.6m. to the Common Fund for Commodities (established by UNCTAD), and a special contribution of $20m. to the International Fund for Agricultural Development (IFAD). In addition, the Fund had contributed $971.9m. to other international institutions by the end of 1993, comprising OPEC members' contributions to the resources of IFAD, and irrevocable transfers in the name of its members to the IMF Trust Fund. By the end of 1993 some 74% of total commitments had been disbursed.

During the year ending 31 December 1993 the Fund's total commitments amounted to US $146.6m. (compared with $125.7m. in 1992 and $181.5m. in 1991). These commitments consisted of 24 project loans amounting to US $119.2m. and four programme loans amounting to $25.6. The largest proportion of project loans (29%) was for the health sector, which financed the construction of a general hospital in Albania, the improvement of health care centres in Bolivia, the construction of a public health laboratory in Burkina Faso, the construction of two general hospitals in Lebanon, and the rehabilitation of a medical centre in Tanzania. Transportation received 21% to finance road improvement projects in Burkina Faso, Lesotho, Peru and Yemen and to upgrade the airports in Laos, while 16% was for water supply and sewerage projects in Burkina Faso, Cape Verde, Chad, Guinea, the Maldives and Niger. The education sector received 13% to construct and equip education facilities in Comoros and Guatemala, and to establish an advanced research institute for engineering science and technology in Pakistan, and 13% was allocated for an energy project in Bangladesh under the country's fourth rural electrification programme. The agriculture sector received 9% for projects in Burundi, Mali, Mauritania and Mozambique. The four programme loans were made to Mali, Grenada, Nicaragua and Senegal. The Fund also extended 21 grants totalling $1.81m., of which $1.64m. was for technical assistance activities and $165,000 was for research.

PUBLICATIONS

Annual Report (in Arabic, English, French and Spanish).
OPEC Aid and OPEC Aid Institutions—A Profile (annually).
OPEC Fund Newsletter (3 a year).
Occasional books and papers.

OPEC FUND COMMITMENTS AND DISBURSEMENTS, 1993
(US $ million).

	Commitments	Disbursements
Lending operations:	144.77	62.08
Project financing	119.17	54.76
Balance of payments support	—	0.5
Programme financing	25.60	6.82
Grant Programme	1.81	1.96
Technical assistance	1.64	1.81
Research and other activities	0.17	0.08
Emergency aid	—	0.06
Total	146.58	64.04

Project loans approved in 1993 (US $ million)

Region and country	Loans approved
Africa	48.87
Burkina Faso	12.45
Burundi	2.52
Cape Verde	1.50
Chad	2.41
Comoros	2.25
Guinea	2.44
Lesotho	1.00
Mali	3.50
Mauritania	3.00
Mozambique	2.00
Niger	5.80
Tanzania	10.00
Asia	50.80
Bangladesh	15.30
Lao P.D.R.	8.00
Lebanon	10.00
Maldives	3.00
Pakistan	8.50
Yemen	6.00
Europe	5.00
Albania	5.00
Latin America and the Caribbean	14.50
Bolivia	5.00
Guatemala	4.50
Peru	5.00
Total	119.17

OTHER REGIONAL ORGANIZATIONS

These organizations are arranged under the following sub-headings:

Agriculture	International Relations	Science and Technology
Development and Economic Co-operation	Law	Trade and Industry
Education, Arts and Sport	Medicine and Health	Transport
Finance and Economics	Planning and Administration	
Industrial Relations	Religion and Welfare	

(See also lists of subsidiary bodies in the chapters on the main regional organizations, e.g. Council of Arab Economic Unity, League of Arab States, OIC, etc.; and the list of Research Institutes, p. 177.)

AGRICULTURE

Arab Authority for Agricultural Investment and Development—AAAID: POB 2102, Khartoum, Sudan; tel. 73752; telex 23017; fax 72600; f. 1976 to accelerate agricultural development in the Arab world and to ensure food security; acts principally by equity participation in agricultural projects, in Iraq, Sudan and Tunisia; authorized capital US $542m., paid-in capital $345m. (Dec. 1987). Mems: Algeria, Egypt, Iraq, Jordan, Kuwait, Mauritania, Morocco, Oman, Qatar, Saudi Arabia, Somalia, Sudan, Syria, Tunisia, United Arab Emirates. Pres. Dr HUSAIN YOUSUF AL-ANI.

DEVELOPMENT AND ECONOMIC CO-OPERATION

Afro-Asian Housing Organization—AAHO: POB 5623, 28 Ramses Ave, Cairo, Egypt; f. 1965 to promote co-operation between African and Asian countries in housing, reconstruction, physical planning and related matters. Mems: 18 countries. Sec.-Gen. HASSAN M. HASSAN (Egypt).

Afro-Asian Rural Reconstruction Organization—AARRO: Plot No. 2, State Guest House Complex (Near Chanakyapuri Telephone Exchange), Chanakyapuri, New Delhi 110021, India; tel. (11) 600475; telex 72326; fax (11) 672045; f. 1962 to act as catalyst for co-operative restructuring of rural life in Africa and Asia; to explore collectively opportunities for co-ordination of efforts for promoting welfare and eradicating hunger, thirst, disease, illiteracy and poverty amongst the rural people; and to assist the formation of organizations of farmers and other rural people. Activities include collaborative research on development issues; training; assistance in forming organizations of farmers and other rural people; the exchange of information; international conferences and seminars; and awarding 100 individual training fellowships at nine institutes in Egypt, India, Japan, the Republic of Korea and Taiwan. Mems: 11 African, 12 Asian and one African associate. Sec.-Gen. AHMED ABDELWAHED KHALIL. Publs *Rural Reconstruction* (two a year), *AARRO Newsletter* (four a year), conference and committee reports.

Arab Co-operation Council: Amman, Jordan; f. 1989 to promote economic co-operation between member states, including free movement of workers, joint projects in transport, communications and agriculture, and eventual integration of trade and monetary policies. Mems: Egypt, Iraq, Jordan, Yemen. Sec.-Gen. HELMI NAMAR (Egypt).

Arab Gulf Programme for the United Nations Development Organizations—AGFUND: POB 18371, Riyadh 11415, Saudi Arabia; tel. (1) 4416240; telex 404071; fax (1) 4412963; f. 1981 to provide grants (not exceeding 50% of project costs) for projects in mother and child care undertaken by the United Nations and by Arab non-governmental organizations and to co-ordinate assistance by the nations of the Gulf; between 1981 and January 1993 AGFUND committed a total of over US $179m. for the benefit of 116 countries. Mems: Bahrain, Iraq, Kuwait, Oman, Qatar, Saudi Arabia, United Arab Emirates. Pres. HRH Prince BIN ABDUL AZIZ AS-SAUD.

Economic Co-operation Organization—ECO: 5 Hejab Ave, Blvd Keshavarz, POB 14155-6176, Teheran, Iran; tel. (21) 658045; telex 213774; fax (21) 658046; f. 1985 (as successor to Regional Co-operation for Development, f. 1964); a tripartite arrangement aiming at closer economic, technical and cultural co-operation; members aim to co-operate in certain industrial projects, trade, tourism, transport (including the building of road and rail links), communications and cultural affairs. A joint postal organization (the South and West Asia Postal Union) was established in 1988, and a joint Chamber of Commerce and Industry in 1990; the summit meeting of February 1992 agreed on the establishment of an ECO investment and development bank and a preferential tariff arrangement. A meeting of heads of state in Istanbul in July 1993 agreed that the ECO bank should be set up in Istanbul itself, that a joint shipping company and airline should be established in Iran, and that an ECO insurance company should be based in Pakistan. 1994 summit: Pakistan. Mems: Azerbaijan, Afghanistan, Turkish Republic of Northern Cyprus, Iran, Kazakhstan, Kyrgyzstan, Pakistan, Tajikistan, Turkey, Turkmenistan, Uzbekistan. Sec.-Gen. ALI REZA SALARI (Iran).

Economic Research Forum for the Arab Countries, Iran and Turkey: Cairo, Egypt; f. 1993 to conduct in-depth economic research, compile an economic database for the region, and provide training; Dir HEBA HANDOUSSA (Egypt).

Third World Forum: 39 Dokki St, POB 43, Orman, Cairo, Egypt; f. 1973 to link social scientists and others from the developing countries, to discuss alternative development policies and encourage research. Regional offices in Egypt, Mexico, Senegal and Sri Lanka. Mems: individuals in 52 countries. Chair. ISMAIL-SABRI ABDALLA.

Union of the Arab Maghreb (Union du Maghreb arabe—UMA): 26–27 rue Okba Agdal, Rabat, Morocco; tel. (7) 772668; telex 36488; fax (7) 772693; f. 1989; aims to encourage joint ventures and to create a single market; structure comprises a council of heads of state (meeting twice a year), a council of ministers of foreign affairs, a consultative council of 20 delegates from each country, a UMA court, and several specialized ministerial commissions. Chairmanship rotates every six months between heads of state. By late 1993 joint projects that had been approved or were under consideration included: creation of a free trade zone; establishment of the Maghreb Investment and Foreign Trade Bank to fund joint agricultural and industrial projects; free movement of citizens within the region; joint transport undertakings, including railway improvements; formation of a Maghreb union of textile and leather industries; and the creation of a customs union by 1995, and of a 'North African Common Market' by the end of the century. The UMA represents member countries' interests in negotiations with the EU, Arab and African regional organizations, as well as other international organizations. In November 1992 member countries agreed to take joint action to combat the rise in Islamic extremism in the Maghreb, but in February 1993 a meeting of ministers of foreign affairs agreed to a 'pause' in the work of the organization, with none of the 15 conventions signed since the UMA's inception having been implemented, as a result of economic differences. In April 1994, the Supreme Council, meeting in Tunis, agreed to establish a Maghrebian Agency for Youth Tourism, and a Maghrebian Union of Sport. Mems: Algeria, Libya, Mauritania, Morocco, Tunisia. Sec.-Gen. MOHAMED AMAMOU (Tunisia).

EDUCATION, ARTS AND SPORT

Afro-Asian Writers' Association: 'Al Ahram' Bldg, Al-Gala'a St, Cairo, Egypt; tel (2) 5747011; telex 20185; fax (2) 5747023; f. 1958. Mems: writers' orgs in 50 countries. Sec.-Gen. LOTFI EL-KHOLY. Publs *Lotus Magazine of Afro-Asian Writings* (quarterly in English, French and Arabic), *Afro-Asian Literature Series* (in English, French and Arabic).

Alliance israélite universelle: 45 rue La Bruyère, 75425 Paris Cedex 09, France; tel. (1) 42-80-35-00; fax (1) 48-74-51-33; f. 1860 to work for the emancipation and moral progress of the Jews; maintains 41 schools in the Mediterranean area and Canada; library of 120,000 vols. Mems: 8,000 in 14 countries. Pres. ADY STEG; Dir JACQUES LÉVY (France). Publs *Cahiers de l'Alliance Israélite Universelle* (2 a year), *The Alliance Review, Les Nouveaux Cahiers* (quarterly).

Arab Bureau of Education for the Gulf States: POB 3908, Riyadh 11481, Saudi Arabia; tel. (1) 4774644; telex 401441; fax (1) 4783165; f. 1975; aims at co-ordination, integration and, wherever possible, unification of member states' efforts in education, culture and science. Specialized organs: Gulf Arab States' Educational Research Center (POB 25566, Safat, Kuwait), Council of Higher Education, Arabian Gulf University (opened in Bahrain in 1982). Mems: Governments of Bahrain, Kuwait, Oman, Qatar, Saudi

Arabia and the United Arab Emirates. Dir-Gen. Dr ALI M. AL-TOWAGRY.

Arab Sports Confederation: POB 62997, Riyadh, Saudi Arabia; tel. (1) 4829427; telex 403099; fax (1) 4823196; f. 1976 to encourage regional co-operation in sport. Mems: 20 national Olympic Committees, 34 Arab sports federations. Pres. Prince FAISAL BIN FAHD BIN ABD AL-AZIZ; Sec.-Gen. OTHMAN M. AL-SAAD.

Association of Arab Historians: POB 4085, Baghdad, Iraq; tel. (1) 443 88 68; f. 1974. Mems: historians in 22 countries of the region. Sec.-Gen. Prof. MUSTAFA AN-NAJJAR. Publ. *Arab Historian*.

Association of Arab Universities: POB 401, Jubeyha, Amman, Jordan; tel. (6) 845131; telex 23855; fax (6) 832994; f. 1964. A scientific conference is held every 3 years. Mems: 103 universities in 20 countries and territories. Sec.-Gen. Dr EHAB ISMAIL. Publ. *AARU Bulletin* (annually).

European Union of Arabic and Islamic Scholars (Union européenne d'Arabisants et d'Islamisants—UEAI): c/o Institut für Orientalistik, Liebiggasse 6, 1010 Vienna, Austria; tel. (1) 40103-2593; f. 1962 to organize Congresses of Arabic and Islamic Studies; 1994 Congress: St Petersburg, Russia. Mems: about 220 in 19 countries. Pres. Dr JOHN MATTOCK (UK); Sec.-Gen. Dr ARNE A. AMBROS (Austria).

International Institute for Adult Literacy Methods: POB 13145-654, Teheran, Iran; tel. (21) 6408879; fax (21) 6404272; f. 1968 by UNESCO and the Government of Iran; collects, analyzes and distributes information concerning the methods, media and techniques used in literacy programmes; maintains documentation service and library on literacy; arranges seminars. Dir MOHAMMED REZA HAMIDIZADE. Publs *Selection of Adult Education Issues* (monthly), *Adult Education and Development* (quarterly), *New Library Holdings* (quarterly).

International Union for Oriental and Asian Studies: Institute of Turcology, University of Cyprus, POB 537, Nicosia, Cyprus; fax (2) 366198; f. 1951 by the 22nd International Congress of Orientalists under the auspices of UNESCO, to promote contacts between orientalists throughout the world, and to organize congresses, research and publications. Mems: in 24 countries. Sec.-Gen. Prof. GEORG HAZAI. Publs *Philologiae Turcicae Fundamenta, Materialien zum Sumerischen Lexikon, Sanskrit Dictionary, Corpus Inscriptionum Iranicarum, Linguistic Atlas of Iran, Matériels des parlers iraniens, Turcology Annual, Bibliographie egyptologique*.

FINANCE

Arab Society of Certified Accountants: POB 55, Mohammed Farid 11518, Cairo, Egypt; tel. (2) 3462951; fax (2) 3445729; f. 1987 as a professional body to supervise qualifications for Arab accountants and to maintain standards. Mems: 225. Pres. TALAL ABU GHAZALEH (Jordan). Publs *Certified Public Accountant* (monthly), *ASCA Information Guide, International Accountancy Standards, International Audit Standards, Abu-Ghazaleh Dictionary of Accountancy*.

International Association of Islamic Banks: Baroom Centre, 11th Floor, POB 9707, Jeddah 21423, Saudi Arabia; tel. (2) 6516900; telex 607351; fax (2) 651552; f. 1977 to link Islamic banks, which do not deal at interest but work on the principle of participation: activities include training and research. Mems: 28 banks and financial institutions in 11 countries. Sec.-Gen. SAMIRA SHAIKH.

Union of Arab Banks (UAB): POB 2416, Beirut, Lebanon; tel. (1) 802968; fax (1) 867925; f. 1972; aims to foster co-operation between Arab banks and to increase their efficiency; prepares feasibility studies for projects; 1992 Conference: Casablanca, Morocco.

Union of Arab Stock Exchanges: POB 8802, Amman, Jordan; tel. (6) 663170; telex 21711; fax (6) 686830; f. 1982 to develop capital markets in the Arab world; Chair. MUHAMMAD HASSAN FAG EL-NOUR; Sec.-Gen. SAFIQ AL-RUKEIBI (Kuwait).

INDUSTRIAL RELATIONS

Arab Federation of Petroleum, Mining and Chemicals Workers: POB 5339, Tripoli, Libya; tel. (21) 608501; fax (21) 608989; f. 1961 to establish proper industrial relations policies and procedures for the guidance of all affiliated unions; promotes establishment of trade unions in the relevant industries in countries where they do not exist. Publs *Arab Petroleum* (monthly, in English, Arabic and French editions), specialized publications and statistics.

Arab Federation of Textile Workers: Al Fardaus St, POB 620, Damascus, Syria; tel. (11) 335592. Mems: eight organizations. Sec.-Gen. DAHER ABOU KHLEIF.

Arab Federation of Transport Workers: BP 643, blvd Ousama 2, Tripoli, Libya; tel. (21) 116200; telex 411011; f. 1966. Mems: 32 unions in 13 countries. Sec.-Gen. BACHIR AL-CHARIF.

International Confederation of Arab Trade Unions—ICATU: POB 3225, Samat at-Tahir, Damascus, Syria; tel. (11) 459544; telex 411319; f. 1956. Holds General Congress every four years. Mems: trade unions in 18 countries, and 12 affiliate international federations. Sec.-Gen. AHMAD JALLOUD. Publ. *Al-Amal al-Arab* (monthly).

INTERNATIONAL RELATIONS

Afro-Asian Peoples' Solidarity Organization—AAPSO: 89 Abd al-Aziz as-Saoud St, 11459-61 Manial el-Roda, Cairo, Egypt; tel. (2) 3636081; telex 92627; fax (2) 3637361; f. 1957 as the Organization for Afro-Asian Peoples' Solidarity; acts as a permanent liaison body between the peoples of Africa and Asia and aims to ensure their sovereignty, peace, disarmament and their economic, social and cultural development; sixth Congress held in 1984 (the first since 1972). Mems: 82 national committees and 10 European associates. Pres. Dr MORAD GHALEB; Sec.-Gen. NOURI ABD EL-RAZZAK (Iraq). Publ. *Development and Socio-Economic Progress* (quarterly).

Parliamentary Association for Euro-Arab Co-operation: 21 Rue de la Tourelle, 1040 Brussels, Belgium; tel. (2) 231-13-00; telex 25542; fax (2) 231-06-46; f. 1974 as an association of more than 650 parliamentarians of all parties from the national parliaments of 18 of the Council of Europe countries and from the European Parliament, to promote friendship and co-operation between Europe and the Arab world; Executive Committee (which has at least two members per country) holds annual meeting with Arab Parliamentary Union: the Euro-Arab Parliamentary Dialogue; works for the progress of the Euro-Arab Dialogue and a settlement in the Middle East which takes into account the national rights of the Palestinian people. Joint Chair. JACQUES ROGER-MACHART (France), RUI AMARAL (Portugal); Sec.-Gen. JEAN-MICHEL DUMONT (Belgium).

LAW

Arab Organization for Human Rights: 17 Midan Aswan, Giza 12311, Cairo, Egypt; tel. (2) 3466582; fax (2) 3448166; f. 1983 to defend fundamental freedoms of citizens of the Arab states; assists political prisoners and their families; has consultative status with UN Economic and Social Council. General Assembly convened every three years; 1993: Cairo, Egypt. Mems in 16 regional and 14 other countries. Sec.-Gen. MUHAMMAD FAYEK. Publs *Newsletter* (monthly), *Annual Report*.

Asian-African Legal Consultative Committee: 27 Ring Road, Lajpat Nagar-IV, New Delhi 110024, India; tel. 6414265; fax 6451344; f. 1956 to consider legal problems referred to it by member countries and to serve as a forum for Asian-African co-operation in international law and economic relations; provides background material for conferences, prepares standard/model contract forms suited to the needs of the region; promotes arbitration as a means of settling international commercial disputes; trains officers of member states. Mems: 44 states. Pres. ABUBAKER MAYANJA (Uganda); Sec.-Gen. FRANK X. NJENGA (Kenya).

Union of Arab Jurists: POB 6026, al-Mansour, Baghdad, Iraq; tel. (1) 5376377; telex 212661; fax (1) 5375238; f. 1975 to safeguard the Arab legislative and judicial heritage; to facilitate contacts between Arab lawyers; to encourage the study of Islamic jurisprudence; and to defend human rights. Mems: national jurists associations in 15 countries. Sec.-Gen. Dr ALI AL-NEJEDI. Publs *Al-Hukuki al-Arabi* (Arab Jurist), documents and studies.

MEDICINE AND HEALTH

International Federation of Red Cross and Red Crescent Societies: 17 Chemin des Crêts, Petit-Saconnex, Case Postale 372, 1211 Geneva 19, Switzerland; tel. (22) 7304222; telex 412133; fax (22) 7330395; f. 1919 to prevent and alleviate human suffering and to promote humanitarian activities by national Red Cross and Red Crescent societies; conducts relief operations for refugees and victims of disasters, co-ordinates relief supplies and assists in disaster prevention; Sec.-Gen. GEORGE WEBER; Treas.-Gen. BENGT BERGMAN (Sweden). Publs *Annual Review, Red Cross Red Crescent* (quarterly), *Weekly News, World Disasters Report*.

Middle East Neurosurgical Society: Neurosurgical Department, American University Medical Centre, POB 113-6044, Beirut, Lebanon; tel. (1) 353486; telex 20801; f. 1958 to promote clinical advances and scientific research and to spread knowledge of neurosurgery and related fields among all members of the medical profession in the Middle East. Mems in 17 countries. Pres. Dr FUAD S. HADDAD; Sec. Dr GEDEM MOHASSEB.

PLANNING AND ADMINISTRATION

African Training and Research Centre in Administration for Development (Centre africain de formation et de recherche administratives pour le développement—CAFRAD): Pavillon International, BP 310, Tangier, Morocco; tel. 36430; telex 33664;

f. 1964 by agreement between Morocco and UNESCO; undertakes research into administrative problems in Africa, documentation of results, provision of a consultation service for governments and organizations; holds frequent seminars; library of 20,000 vols. Mems: 27 African states. Pres. Aziz Hasbi; Dir-Gen. Mamadou Thiam. Publs *Cahiers Africains d'Administration Publique* (2 a year), *African Administrative Studies* (2 a year), *Documents and Studies, Répertoire des Consultants, CAFRAD News* (3 a year in English, French and Arabic).

Arab Towns Organization: PO Box 4954, Safat 13050, Kuwait; tel. 2435540; telex 46390; fax 2448653; f. 1967 to help Arab towns in solving problems, preserving the natural environment and cultural heritage; runs a fund to provide concessional loans for needy members, and an Institute for Urban Development (AUDI) based in Riyadh, Saudi Arabia; offers awards for preservation of Arab architecture; provides training courses for officials of Arab municipalities and holds seminars on urban development and other relevant subjects. Mems: 380 towns. Dir-Gen. Wassel Mansour; Sec.-Gen. Abd al-Aziz Y. al-Adsani. Publ. *Al-Madinah Al-Arabiyah* (every 2 months).

Centre for Social Science Research and Documentation for the Arab Region: Zamalek PO, Cairo, Egypt; tel. (2) 3472099; fax (2) 3470019; f. 1978 to encourage co-operation between regional research bodies; Mems: Egypt, Iraq, Kuwait, Saudi Arabia, Tunisia; Dir-Gen. Dr Ahmad M. Khalifa. Publs *Newsletter* (3 a year), *Arab Comnet* (3 a year).

International Planned Parenthood Federation: Regional Bureau for the Arab World, Regent's College, Inner Circle, Regent's Park, London, NW1 4NS; tel. (71) 486-0741; telex 919573; fax (71) 487-7950; office in Tunis; aims to advance education in family planning, to promote the use of family planning services through local voluntary associations, and to organize the training of service delivery providers. Member associations in Afghanistan, Algeria, Bahrain, Egypt, Iraq, Jordan, Lebanon, Mauritania, Morocco, Palestine Liberation Organization, Somalia, Sudan, Syria, Tunisia, Yemen. Sec.-Gen. Dr Halfdan Mahler; Regional Dir Dr Hamouda Hanafi.

RELIGION AND WELFARE

Bahá'í International Community: Bahá'í World Centre, POB 155, 31 001 Haifa, Israel; tel. (4) 510344; telex 46626; fax (4) 358522; f. 1844 in Persia to promote the unity of mankind and world peace through the teachings of the Bahá'í religion, which include the equality of men and women and the elimination of all forms of prejudice; maintains schools for children and adults worldwide, and maintains educational and cultural radio stations in the Americas; there are 30 Bahá'í Publishing Trusts in countries throughout the world. Governing body: The Universal House of Justice, consisting of nine members elected by 172 National Spiritual Assemblies. Mems: in 120,046 centres worldwide. The Association for Bahá'í Studies (Ottawa, Canada) has affiliates in 20 countries. Deputy Secs-Gen. Albert Lincoln (USA), Murray R. Smith (New Zealand). Publs *The Bahá'í World* (annually), *La Pensée Bahá'ie* (quarterly), *World Order* (quarterly), *Opinioni Bahá'i* (quarterly), *One Country* (quarterly), *Herald of the South* (quarterly), *Bahá'í Briefe* (two a year).

Middle East Council of Churches: rue Makhoul, DEEB bldg, POB 5376, Beirut, Lebanon; tel. (1) 344894; telex 22662; f. 1974. Mems: 26 churches. Pres. Patriarch Ignatius Zakkai Iwas, Patriarch Ignatius IV, Rt Rev. Samir Kafity, Archbishop Yousuf el-Khoury; Gen. Sec. Gabriel Habib. Publs *MECC News Report* (monthly), *Al Montada News Bulletin* (quarterly, in Arabic), *Courrier oecuménique du moyen-Orient* (quarterly), *MECC Perspectives* (3 a year).

Muslim World League (Rabitat al-Alam al-Islami): Mecca al-Mukarramah, POB 537-538, Mecca, Saudi Arabia; tel. 5422733; telex 54009; fax 5436619; London office: 46 Goodge St, London W1, England; tel. (71) 636-7568; telex 296182; f. 1962; aims to advance Islamic unity and solidarity, and to promote world peace and respect for human rights; provides financial assistance for Islamic education, medical care and relief work; has 26 offices throughout the world. Sec.-Gen. Mohammed bin Nasir al-Oboody. Publs *Majalla al-Rabita* (monthly, Arabic), *Akhbar al-Alam al Islami* (weekly, Arabic), *Muslim World League Journal* (monthly, English), *Dawat al-Haq* (monthly, Arabic), *The Call of the Truth* (monthly, English), *Muslim World News* (weekly, English).

World Jewish Congress (Congrès Juif Mondial): 501 Madison Ave, New York, NY 10022, USA; tel. (212) 755-5770; telex 236129; fax (212) 755-5883; f. 1936 as a voluntary association of representative Jewish communities and organizations throughout the world, aiming to foster the unity of the Jewish people and to ensure the continuity and development of its religious, spiritual, cultural and social heritage. Mems: Jewish communities in 70 countries. Pres. Edgar M. Bronfman; Sec.-Gen. Israel Singer. Publs *WJC Report* (New York), *Gesher* (Hebrew quarterly, Jerusalem), *Batfutstot* (Jerusalem), *Boletin Informativo OJI* (fortnightly, Buenos Aires), *Christian Jewish Relations* (quarterly, London).

SCIENCE AND TECHNOLOGY

Federation of Arab Engineers: POB 6117, Baghdad, Iraq; tel. (1) 7762366; telex 212761; f. 1963 as Arab Engineering Union; a regional body of the World Federation of Engineering Organizations; co-operates with the Arab League, UNESCO and the other regional engineering federations. Holds a Pan-Arab conference on engineering studies every three years and annual symposia and seminars in different Arab countries. Mems: engineering asscns in 15 Arab countries; Sec.-Gen. Dr H. J. al-Khashali.

Federation of Arab Scientific Research Councils: POB 13027, Baghdad, Iraq; tel. (1) 5381090; telex 212466; f. 1976 to encourage co-operation in scientific research, to promote the establishment of new institutions and plan joint regional research projects. Mems: national science bodies, Governments of 14 countries. Sec.-Gen. Prof. Taha al-Nueimi. Publs *Journal of Arab Scientific Research, Federation News*. Reports from conferences, seminars and workshops.

TRADE AND INDUSTRY

Arab Iron and Steel Union—AISU: BP 4, Chéraga, Algiers, Algeria; tel. (2) 37-27-05; telex 71158; fax (2) 37-19-75; f. 1972 to develop commercial and technical aspects of Arab steel production by helping member associations to commercialize their production in Arab markets, guaranteeing them high quality materials and intermediary products, informing them of recent developments in the industry and organizing training sessions. Mems: 73 companies in 13 Arab countries. Gen.-Sec. Muhammad Laid Lachgar. Publs *Arab Steel Review* (monthly).

General Union of Chambers of Commerce, Industry and Agriculture for Arab Countries: POB 11-2837, Beirut, Lebanon; tel. (1) 814269; telex 20347; fax (1) 806840; f. 1951 to foster Arab economic collaboration, to increase and improve production and to facilitate the exchange of technical information in Arab countries. Mems: chambers of commerce, industry and agriculture in 21 countries. Gen.-Sec. Burhan Dajani. Publ. *Economic Studies* (in Arabic).

Gulf Organization for Industrial Consulting—GOIC: POB 5114, Doha, Qatar; tel. 831234; telex 4619; fax 831465; f. 1976 by seven Gulf Arab states to co-ordinate industrial development and encourage joint regional projects; undertakes feasibility studies, market diagnosis, assistance in policy-making, legal consultancies, project promotion and technical training. Mems: Bahrain, Kuwait, Oman, Qatar, Saudi Arabia, United Arab Emirates. Sec.-Gen. Dr Abdulrahman A. al-Jaafary. Publs *GOIC Monthly Bulletin* (Arabic and English), *Al Ta' Awon al-Sinaie* (quarterly, in Arabic and English), *Annual Report*.

International Olive Oil Council: Príncipe de Vergara 154, Madrid 28002, Spain; tel. (1) 5630071; telex 48197; fax (1) 5631263; f. 1959 to administer the International Agreement on Olive Oil and Table Olives, the objectives of which are as follows: to promote international co-operation in connection with problems of the world economy for olive products; to prevent the occurrence of any unfair competition in the world olive products trade; to encourage the production and consumption of, and international trade in, olive products, and to reduce the disadvantages due to fluctuations of supplies on the market. Mems: of the 1986 Agreement (Fourth Agreement), as amended and extended, 1993: seven mainly producing members, one mainly importing member, and the EC. Dir Fausto Luchetti. Publs *Information Sheet* (fortnightly, French and Spanish), *OLIVAE* (5 a year, in English, French, Italian and Spanish), *National Policies for Olive Products* (annually), economic and technical studies, etc.

TRANSPORT

Arab Air Carriers' Organization—AACO: POB 930039, Amman, Jordan; tel. (6) 683381; telex 24375; fax (6) 683383; f. 1965 to co-ordinate and promote co-operation in the activities of Arab airline companies. Mems: 13 Arab air carriers. Pres. Muftah Eddlew (Libya); Sec.-Gen. Adli Dajani; Dir-Gen. Amer Sharif. Publs monthly statistical bulletins and research documents on aviation in the Arab world.

Arab Union of Railways: POB 6599, Aleppo, Syria; tel. (21) 220302; telex 331009; f. 1979 to stimulate and co-ordinate the development of Arab railways, particularly regional and international railway links. Mems: railways of Algeria, Egypt, Iraq, Jordan, Lebanon, Libya, Morocco, Palestine, Syria and Tunisia. Fifth symposium: Cairo, Egypt, 1991. Chair. Tahar Azaiez; Sec.-Gen. Mourhaf Sabouni. Publs *As-Sikak al-Arabiye* (Arab Railways, quarterly), *Statistics of Arab Railways* (annually), glossary of railway terms in Arabic, French, English and German.

INDEX OF REGIONAL ORGANIZATIONS

(main references only)

A

African Regional Centre for Solar Energy, 199
— — — — Technology, 200
— — Organization for Standardization, 200
— Training and Research Centre in Administration for Development, 246
Afro-Asian Housing Organization, 245
— Peoples' Solidarity Organization, 246
— Rural Reconstruction Organization, 245
— Writers' Association, 245
AGFUND, 245
Alliance israélite universelle, 245
Al-Quds Committee, 238
Arab Administrative Development Organization, 233
— Air Carriers' Organization, 247
— Atomic Energy Agency, 233
— Authority for Agricultural Investment and Development, 245
— Bank for Economic Development in Africa, 233
— Bureau of Education for the Gulf States, 245
— Centre for the Study of Arid Zones and Dry Lands, 233
— Co-operation Council, 245
— Co-operative Federation, 227
— Federation of Chemical Fertilizers Producers, 227
— — — Engineering Industries, 227
— — — Leather Industries, 227
— — — Paper Industries, 227
— — — Petroleum, Mining and Chemicals Workers, 246
— — — Shipping Industries, 227
— — — Textile Industries, 227
— — — Textile Workers, 246
— — — Transport Workers, 246
— — — Travel Agents, 227
— Fund for Economic and Social Development—AFESD, 222
— — — Technical Assistance to African Countries, 232
— Gulf Programme for the United Nations Development Organizations, 245
— Industrial Development and Mining Organization, 233
— Iron and Steel Union, 247
— Labour Organization, 233
— League, 232
— — Educational, Cultural and Scientific Organization—ALECSO, 233
— Maritime Petroleum Transport Company, 237
— — Transport Academy, 233
— Monetary Fund, 223
— Organization for Agricultural Development, 233
— — — Human Rights, 246
— — — Social Defence against Crime, 233
— Petroleum Investments Corporation, 237
— — Services Company, 237
— — Training Institute, 237
— Postal Union, 233
— Satellite Communication Organization, 233
— Seaports Federation, 227
— Shipbuilding and Repair Yard Company, 237
— Society of Certified Accountants, 246
— Sports Confederation, 246
— States Broadcasting Union, 233
— Sugar Federation, 227
— Telecommunications Union, 233
— Towns Organization, 247
— Union for Cement and Building Materials, 227
— — of Fish Producers, 227
— — — Food Industries, 227
— — — Land Transport, 227
— — — Pharmaceutical Manufacturers, 228
— — — Railways, 228
Asian-African Legal Consultative Committee, 246
Association of Arab Historians, 246
— — — Universities, 246

B

Bahá'í International Community, 247

C

Centre africain de formation et de recherches administratives pour le développement—CAFRAD, 246

— for Social Science Research and Documentation for the Arab Region, 247
Commission for Controlling the Desert Locust in the Near East (FAO), 209
— — — — — — in North-West Africa (FAO), 209
Consultative Group for International Agricultural Research, 211
Co-operation Council for the Arab States of the Gulf, 224
Council of Arab Economic Unity, 227
— — — Ministers of the Interior, 233

E

Economic Co-operation Organization—ECO, 245
— Research Forum for the Arab Countries, Iran and Turkey, 245
Euro-Arab Dialogue, 230
European Union, 228
— — of Arabic and Islamic Scholars, 246

F

Federation of Arab Engineers, 247
— — — Scientific Research Councils, 247
Food and Agriculture Organization—FAO, 208
Foreign Investment Advisory Service—FIAS, 212

G

General Agreement on Tariffs and Trade—GATT, 220
— Arab Insurance Federation, 228
— Fisheries Council for the Mediterranean (FAO), 209
— Union of Chambers of Commerce, Industry and Agriculture for Arab Countries, 247
Global Environment Facility, 202, 211
Gulf Co-operation Council, 224
— Investment Corporation, 226
— Organization for Industrial Consulting, 247

I

Inter-Arab Investment Guarantee Corporation, 233
International Association of Islamic Banks, 240
— Atomic Energy Agency, 220
— Bank for Reconstruction and Development—IBRD, 210
— Civil Aviation Organization—ICAO, 220
— Commission for the Preservation of Islamic Cultural Heritage, 239
— Confederation of Arab Trade Unions, 246
— Development Association—IDA, 210
— Federation of Red Cross and Red Crescent Societies, 246
— Finance Corporation—IFC, 212
— Fund for Agricultural Development—IFAD, 213
— Institute for Adult Literacy Methods, 246
— Islamic News Agency, 239
— Labour Organisation—ILO, 220
— Maritime Organization—IMO, 220
— Monetary Fund—IMF, 214
— Olive Oil Council, 247
— Planned Parenthood Federation, 247
— Telecommunication Union—ITU, 220
— Union for Oriental and Asian Studies, 246
Islamic Cement Association, 240
— Centre for the Development of Trade, 239
— — — Technical and Vocational Training and Research, 239
— Chamber of Commerce, Industry and Commodity Exchange, 240
— Commission for Economic, Cultural and Social Affairs, 238
— Committee for the International Crescent, 240
— Conference, 238
— Court of Justice, 238
— Development Bank, 230
— Educational, Scientific and Cultural Organization, 240
— Foundation for Science, Technology and Development, 239
— Jurisprudence Academy, 239
— Research and Training Institute, 231
— Shipowners' Association, 240
— Solidarity Fund, 239
— States Broadcasting Organization, 240

L

League of Arab States, 232

M

Middle East Council of Churches, 247
— — Neurosurgical Society, 246
Multilateral Investment Guarantee Agency, 213
Muslim World League, 247

N

Near East Forestry Commission (FAO), 209
— — Regional Commission on Agriculture (FAO), 209
— — Regional Economic and Social Policy Commission (FAO), 210

O

Office of the UN Disaster Relief Co-ordinator—UNDRO, 220
OPEC Fund for International Development, 243
Organization of Arab Petroleum Exporting Countries—OAPEC, 237
— — Islamic Capitals and Cities, 240
— — the Islamic Conference—OIC, 238
— — — Petroleum Exporting Countries—OPEC, 240

P

Pan-African Documentation and Information Service—PADIS, 199
Parliamentary Association for Euro-Arab Co-operation, 246

R

Regional Centre for Functional Literacy in Rural Areas, (UNESCO), 216
— Commission on Land and Water Use in the Near East, 210
— Office for Education in the Arab States (UNESCO), 216
— — — Science and Technology in the Arab States (UNESCO), 216
Research Centre for Islamic History, Art and Culture, 239

S

Special Bureau for Boycotting Israel, 232
Sports Federation of Islamic Solidarity, 240
Statistical, Economic and Social Research and Training Centre for the Islamic Countries, 239

T

Third World Forum, 245

U

Union du Maghreb arabe, 245
— of Arab Banks, 246
— — Arab Jurists, 245
— — — Stock Exchanges, 246
— — the Arab Maghreb, 246
United Nations, 197
— — Capital Development Fund—UNCDF, 203
— — Centre for Human Settlements—UNCHS, 220
— — Children's Fund—UNICEF, 220
— — Conference on Trade and Development—UNCTAD, 220
— — Development Fund for Women—UNIFEM, 203
— — — Programme—UNDP, 202
— — Disengagement Observer Force—UNDOF, 205
— — Economic Commission for Africa—ECA, 198
— — — and Social Commission for Western Asia—ESCWA, 201
— — Educational, Scientific and Cultural Organization—UNESCO, 216
— — Environment Programme—UNEP, 220
— — Fund for Science and Technology for Development—UNFSTD, 203
— — High Commissioner for Refugees—UNHCR, 204
— — Industrial Development Organization—UNIDO, 220
— — Information Centres, 221
— — Interim Force in Lebanon—UNIFIL, 206
— — Iraq-Kuwait Observation Mission—UNIKOM, 206
— — Mission for the Referendum in Western Sahara—MINURSO, 206
— — Peace-keeping Force in Cyprus—UNFICYP, 206
— — — Operations, 205
— — Population Fund, 220
— — Relief and Works Agency for Palestine Refugees in the Near East—UNRWA, 207
— — Revolving Fund for Natural Resources Exploration—UNRFNRE, 203
— — Sudano-Sahelian Office, 203
— — Truce Supervision Organization—UNTSO, 205
— — Volunteers, 204
Universal Postal Union—UPU, 220

W

World Bank, 210
— Food Programme, 210
— Health Organization—WHO, 218
— Intellectual Property Organization—WIPO, 221
— Jewish Congress, 247
— Meteorological Organization—WMO, 221

PART THREE
Country Surveys

ALGERIA

Physical and Social Geography

Algeria is the largest of the three countries in north-west Africa that comprise the Maghreb, as the region of mountains, valleys and plateaux that lies between the sea and the Sahara desert is known. It is situated between Morocco and Tunisia, with a Mediterranean coastline of nearly 1,000 km and a total area of some 2,381,741 sq km, over four-fifths of which lies south of the Maghreb proper and within the western Sahara. Its extent, both from north to south and west to east, exceeds 2,000 km. The Arabic name for the country, el-Djezaïr (the Islands), is said to derive from the rocky islands along the coastline.

According to the census of April 1987, the population of Algeria was 23,038,942. The total increased to 26,581,000 (official estimate) at 1 January 1993. The great majority of the inhabitants reside in the northern part of the country, particularly along the Mediterranean coast where both the capital, Algiers or el-Djezaïr (population, not including suburbs, 1,483,000 in April 1987), and the second largest town, Oran or Ouahran (590,000), are located. Many settlements reverted to their Arabic names in 1981 (for the principal changes, see Statistical Survey, p. 291). The population is almost wholly Muslim, of whom a majority speak Arabic and the remainder Berber, the language of the original inhabitants of the Maghreb. Most educated Algerians, however, speak French.

PHYSICAL FEATURES

The major contrast in the physical geography of Algeria is between the mountainous, relatively humid terrain of the north, which forms part of the Atlas mountain system, and the vast expanse of desert to the south, which is part of the Saharan tableland. The Atlas Mountains extend from southwest to north-east across the whole of the Maghreb. Structurally they resemble the 'Alpine' mountain chains of Europe north of the Mediterranean and, like them, they came into existence during the Tertiary era. They are still unstable and liable to severe earthquakes, such as those which devastated el-Asnam in 1954 and 1980. The mountains consist of rocks, now uplifted, folded and fractured, that once accumulated beneath an ancestral Mediterranean sea. Limestone and sandstone are particularly extensive and they often present a barren appearance in areas where the topsoil and vegetation is thin or absent altogether.

In Algeria the Atlas mountain system is made up of three broad zones running parallel to the coast: the Tell Atlas, the High Plateaux and the Saharan Atlas. In the north, and separated from the Mediterranean only by a narrow and discontinuous coastal plain, is the complex series of mountains and valleys that comprise the Tell Atlas. Here individual ranges, plateaux and massifs vary in height from about 500 m to 2,500 m above sea-level and are frequently separated from one another by deep valleys and gorges which divide the country into self-contained topographic and economic units. Most distinctive of these are the massifs of the Great and Little Kabyle between Algiers and the Tunisian frontier, which have acted as mountain retreats where Berber ways of village life persist.

South of the Tell Atlas lies a zone of featureless plains known as the High Plateaux of the Shotts. To the west, near the Moroccan frontier, they form a broad, monotonous expanse of level terrain about 160 km across and more than 1,000 m above sea-level. They gradually narrow and fall in height eastward to end in the Hodna basin, a huge enclosed depression, the bottom of which is only 420 m above sea-level. The surface of the plateaux consists of alluvial debris from erosion of the mountains to north and south. The plateaux owe their name to the presence of several vast basins of internal drainage, known as shotts, the largest of which is the Hodna basin. During rainy periods water accumulates in the shotts to form extensive shallow lakes which give way, as the water is absorbed and evaporated, to saline mud flats and swamps.

The southern margin of the High Plateaux is marked by a series of mountain chains and massifs that form the Saharan Atlas. They are more broken than the Tell Atlas and present no serious barrier to communication between the High Plateaux and the Sahara. From west to east the chief mountain chains are the Ksour, Amour, Ouled Naïl, Ziban and Aurès. The latter is the most impressive massif in the whole Algerian Atlas system and includes the highest peak: Djebel Chelia, 2,328 m (7,638 ft). The relief of the Aurès is very bold, with narrow gorges cut between sheer cliffs surmounted by steep bare slopes, and to the east and north of the Hodna basin its ridges merge with the southernmost folds of the Tell Atlas. North-eastern Algeria forms, therefore, a compact block of high relief in which the two Atlas mountain systems cease to be clearly separated. Within it there are a number of high plains studded with salt flats but their size is insignificant compared with the enormous shotts to the west.

CLIMATE AND VEGETATION

The climate of northernmost Algeria, including the narrow coastal plain and the Tell Atlas southward to the margin of the High Plateaux, is of 'Mediterranean' type with warm, wet winters and hot, dry summers. Rainfall varies from over 1,000 mm annually on some coastal mountains to less than 130 mm in sheltered, lee situations, and occurs mostly during the winter. Complete drought lasts for three to four months during the summer and at this time, too, the notorious sirocco occurs. It is a scorching, dry and dusty southerly wind blowing from the Sahara, and is known locally as the Chehili. It blows on 40 or more days a year over the High Plateaux but nearer the coast this is reduced to about 20 days. When the sirocco arrives, shade temperatures often rise rapidly to more than 40°C (104°F), while vegetation and crops, unable to withstand the intensity of evaporation, may die within a few hours. As a result of low and uneven rainfall combined with high rates of evaporation, the rivers of the Tell tend to be short and to suffer large seasonal variations in flow. Many dry out completely during the summer and are full only for brief periods following heavy winter rains. The longest perennially flowing river is the Oued Chélif, which rises in the High Plateaux and crosses the Tell to reach the Mediterranean Sea east of Oran.

Along the northern margin of the High Plateaux 'Mediterranean' conditions give way to a semi-arid or steppe climate in which summer drought lasts from five to six months and winters are colder and drier. Rainfall is reduced to between 200 mm and 400 mm annually and tends to occur in spring and autumn rather than in winter. It is, moreover, variable from year to year, and under these conditions the cultivation of cereal crops without irrigation becomes unreliable. South of the Saharan Atlas annual rainfall decreases to below 200 mm and any regular cultivation without irrigation becomes impossible. There are no permanent rivers south of the Tell Atlas and any surface run-off following rain is carried by temporary watercourses towards local depressions, such as the shotts.

The soils and vegetation of northern Algeria reflect the climatic contrast between the humid Tell and the semi-arid lands farther south, but they have also suffered widely from the destructive effects of over-cultivation, over-grazing and deforestation. In the higher, wetter and more isolated parts of the Tell Atlas relatively thick soils support forests of Aleppo pine, cork-oak and evergreen oak, while the lower, drier, and more accessible slopes tend to be bare or covered only with thin soils and a scrub growth of thuya, juniper and various drought-resistant shrubs. Only a few remnants survive of the once extensive forests of Atlas cedar which have been exploited for timber and fuel since classical times. They are found chiefly above 1,500 m in the eastern Tell Atlas. South of the Tell there is very little woodland except in the higher and wetter parts of the Saharan Atlas. The surface of the High Plateaux is bare or covered only with scattered bushes and clumps of esparto and other coarse grasses.

SAHARAN ALGERIA

South of the Saharan Atlas, Algeria extends for over 1,500 km into the heart of the desert. Structurally, this huge area consists of a resistant platform of geologically ancient rocks against which the Atlas Mountains were folded. Over most of the area relief is slight, with occasional plateaux, such as those of Eglab, Tademaït and Tassili-n-Ajjer, rising above vast spreads of gravel, such as the Tanezrouft plain, and huge sand accumulations, such as the Great Western and Eastern Ergs. In the south-east, however, the great massif of Ahaggar rises to a height of 2,918 m (9,573 ft). Here, erosion of volcanic and crystalline rocks has produced a lunar landscape of extreme ruggedness. Southward from the Ahaggar the massifs of Adrar des Iforas and Aïr extend across the Algerian frontier into the neighbouring countries of Mali and Niger.

The climate of Saharan Algeria is characterized by extremes of temperature, wind and aridity. Daily temperature ranges reach 32°C and maximum shade temperatures of over 55°C have been recorded. Sometimes very high temperatures are associated with violent dust storms. Mean average rainfall, although extremely irregular, is everywhere less than 130 mm, and in some of the central parts of the desert it falls to less than 10 mm. These rigorous conditions are reflected in the extreme sparseness of the vegetation and in a division of the population into settled cultivators, who occupy oases dependent on permanent supplies of underground water, and nomadic pastoralists who make use of temporary pastures which appear after rain.

History

Revised for this edition by RICHARD I. LAWLESS.

EARLY HISTORY

The Berber people have comprised the majority of the population of this part of Africa since the earliest times. From 208 to 148 BC Numidia occupied most of present-day Algeria north of the Sahara. After the destruction of Carthage in 146 BC, Numidia, greatly reduced in extent, was transformed into a Roman vassal-state, while the rest of the area formed a loose confederacy of tribes, which maintained their independence by frequent revolt. After a brief period of Vandal dominance, Roman rule was restored in the provinces of Africa (modern Tunisia) and Numidia, and parts of the coast. Elsewhere, the Berber confederacies, centred in the Aurès and the Kabyle, maintained their independence.

The rise of Islam in Arabia was soon followed by its penetration of North Africa, the first Arab raids taking place about the middle of the seventh century. Qairawan (in present-day Tunisia) was founded by the Arabs in 670 as a base; the other towns remained under Byzantine control, and the Berber tribes set up a state centred on the eastern Maghreb. Increasing Arab immigration towards the end of the seventh century finally overcame Berber and Byzantine resistance, the Berbers gradually converted to Islam, and the whole of the area was incorporated into the Ummayad Empire. In 756 the Berbers freed themselves from the control of the recently established Abbasid Caliphate, and for the next three centuries power was disputed between various Arab dynasties and Berber tribes. After the invasion in *c.* 1050 of the Banu Hilal, a confederation of nomadic Arab tribes dislodged from Egypt, a period of anarchy ensued, but the Berber dynasty of the Almoravids, from Morocco, temporarily restored order in the area of modern Algiers and Oran. In *c.* 1147 the Almoravids were succeeded by the Almohads, who unified the whole of the Maghreb and Muslim Spain, bringing cultural and economic prosperity to North Africa. From the middle of the 13th century, however, the region entered a period of decline, both economic, and in terms of its political influence, which persisted for more than two centuries.

In the closing years of the 15th century, the Spanish monarchy carried its crusade against Muslim power to North Africa, the fragmented political state of that area offering little resistance. On the death of Ferdinand of Castile in 1516, the Algerines sought the assistance of the Turkish corsair Aruj, who took possession of Algiers and several other towns and proclaimed himself Sultan. In 1518 he was succeeded by his brother Khayr ad-Din (Barbarossa), who placed all his territories under the nominal protection of the Ottoman Sultan. This decisive act may be said to mark the emergence of Algiers as a political entity. After numerous efforts to re-establish their position, the Spanish finally withdrew in 1541 and Algeria was left for three centuries to the Muslims. Power in Algiers lay in the hands of the dey and there was a rapid succession of deys, often due to assassinations. Each dey established his relationship with the Sultan by sending him tribute. Real power in Algiers was held by two bodies—the janissary corps and the guild of corsair captains. The Regency of Algiers reached its peak in the 17th century, the profitable trade of piracy bringing great wealth. Despite Turkish attempts to control the interior, several Berber tribes most distant from Algiers retained their independence. During the 18th century the growth of European seapower in the Mediterranean brought a period of decline to the littoral, while in the interior a period of relative economic prosperity ensued.

THE FRENCH CONQUEST

On 5 July 1830 Algiers fell to a French expedition, and the dey and most of the Turkish officials were sent into exile. The pretext for intervention was an insult offered by the dey to the French consul in 1827: the real cause was the pressing need of Polignac, the chief minister under Charles X, to secure some credit for his administration in the eyes of the French public and to provide employment for the Napoleonic veterans. However, the Polignac administration was unable to reap the fruits of its triumph before the Bourbon dynasty and its government were overthrown by revolution. Polignac's plan to hand over the rest of the country, and the decision on its future, to a European congress was abandoned. In Algeria the absence of any central authority increased the prestige of the tribal chiefs. Several years later, in 1834, the further conquest and annexation of Algeria was decided upon, and a governor-general was appointed.

Over the next quarter of a century, France pursued its conquest of Algeria, despite bitter opposition. Constantine, the last Turkish stronghold, was captured in 1837, and by 1841 French rule had been consolidated in most of the ports and their immediate environs. By 1844 most of the eastern part of Algeria was under French control, but in the west the conquerors were faced with the formidable Abd al-Kadir, who claimed descent from the Prophet Muhammad. A skilful diplomat and military commander, he at first concluded treaties with the French, which consolidated his position as leader of the Berber confederacies in the west. In 1839, however, he declared war on France, achieving widespread unity between Berbers and Arabs against the invaders. He held out until 1847, when he was finally defeated by Gen. Bugeaud, the real architect of French rule in Algeria. During the late 1840s and 1850s, the tribes on the edge of the Sahara were pacified, while the conquest was effectively completed by the submission of the hitherto independent Berber confederacies of the Kabyle in 1857. Further rebellions were to occur, however, throughout the 19th century.

Meanwhile, a policy of colonization, with widespread confiscation of land and its transference to settler groups, had been adopted. Bugeaud had at first encouraged colonization in the coastal plains; after 1848 the influx of colonists was much increased, especially following the annexation of Alsace-Lorraine by Germany in 1871. A further stimulus to colonization was provided by the widespread confiscation of lands after the unsuccessful rebellion of 1871. By that time the French settlers had become the dominant power in Algeria, owning much of the best land and initiating extensive agricultural development.

After the Muslim revolt of 1871, the situation was regularized by the new French administration under Thiers. A civil administration with the status of a French *département* was set up for much of Algeria, while the amount of territory under military rule steadily declined. From 1871 to 1900 there was considerable economic development in Algeria and increasing European immigration, especially from Italy. A feature of this period was the growth of large-scale agricultural and industrial enterprises, which further concentrated power in the hands of the leaders of the settler groups. In 1900 Algeria secured administrative and financial autonomy, to be exercised through the so-called 'Financial Delegations', composed of two-thirds European and one-third Muslim members, which were empowered to fix the annual budget and to raise loans for further economic development.

Within 70 years the Muslim people of Algeria had been reduced from relative prosperity to economic, social and cultural inferiority. Three million inhabitants had died, tribes had been disbanded and the traditional economy altered during the prolonged 'civilizing' campaigns. In particular, the production of wine for export had replaced the growing of cereals for domestic consumption. By contrast the settlers enjoyed a high level of prosperity in the years before the First World War.

BIRTH OF NATIONALISM

The spirit of nationalism was spreading throughout the Middle East, however, and it emerged among the Algerian Muslims after the First World War. Nationalist aspirations began to be voiced not only by Algerian veterans of the war in Europe but also by Algerians who had gone to France to study or work. In 1924 one of these students, Messali Hadj, in collaboration with the French Communist Party, founded in Paris the first Algerian nationalist newspaper; the link with the Communists was, however, severed in 1927. Messali Hadj and his movement were forced into hiding by the French Government, but reappeared in 1933 to sponsor a congress on the future of Algeria, which demanded full independence, the recall of French troops, the establishment of a revolutionary government, large-scale reforms in land ownership and the nationalization of industrial enterprises.

More moderate doctrines were advanced in the post-war years by an influential body of French-educated Muslims, formalized in 1930 as the Federation of Muslim Councillors. Under the leadership of Ferhat Abbas, this group called for integration with France on a basis of complete equality. The victory of the Popular Front in the French elections of 1936 gave rise to the hope that at least some of these aspirations might be peaceably achieved. The Blum-Viollet Plan, which would have granted full rights of citizenship to an increasing number of Algerian Muslims, was, however, dropped by the French Government in the face of fierce opposition from the French settlers and the Algerian civil service.

The years immediately prior to the Second World War were characterized by growing nationalist discontent, in which Messali Hadj played a significant part with the formation of the Party of the Algerian People (PPA). The outbreak of war in 1939 suspended the nationalists' activities, but the war greatly strengthened their position. Although the Vichy administration in Algeria, strongly supported by the French settlers, was antipathetic to nationalist sentiment, the Allied landings in North Africa in 1942 provided an opportunity for the Algerian nationalists to put forward constitutional demands. On 22 December 1942 a group headed by Ferhat Abbas presented to the French authorities and the Allied military command a memorandum demanding the post-war establishment of an Algerian constituent assembly, to be elected by universal suffrage. However, no demand was made for Algerian independence outside the French framework.

These proposals, to which the French authorities remained unresponsive, were followed early in 1943 by the 'Manifesto of the Algerian People', which demanded immediate reforms, including the introduction of Arabic as an official language and the end of colonization. Further proposals, submitted in May, envisaged the post-war creation of an Algerian state with a constitution to be determined by a constituent assembly, and looked forward to an eventual North African Union, comprising Tunisia, Algeria and Morocco. The newly-established Free French administration in Algiers categorically rejected the Manifesto and the subsequent proposals.

Confronted by growing Muslim discontent, and following a visit to Algiers by Gen. Charles de Gaulle, a new statute for Algeria came into effect in March 1944. It was an attempt at compromise which satisfied neither the Algerian nationalists nor the European settlers. Membership of the French electoral college was opened to 60,000 Muslims, but there were still 450,000 European voters, and in the event only 32,000 Muslims accepted inscription. The Muslim share of the seats in the *communes mixtes* was restricted to 40%. All further discussion of Algeria's future relationship with France was ruled out.

Shortly afterwards, Ferhat Abbas founded the Friends of the Manifesto of Freedom (AML), which aimed to found an autonomous Algerian republic linked federally with France. The new movement was based mainly on the support of middle-class Muslims. The AML also gained a certain following among the masses, who comprised the main support of the PPA during 1944 and 1945.

FRENCH INTRANSIGENCE

All possibility of a gradually negotiated settlement was destroyed by blunders of post-war French policy and the opposition of the French settlers to any concessions to Muslim aspirations. The riots in Sétif in May 1945 were ruthlessly suppressed; estimates of the number of Muslims killed varied from 8,000 to 40,000. This suppression, the subsequent arrest of Ferhat Abbas and the dissolution of the AML convinced many of the nationalist leaders that force was the only means of gaining their objective.

Nevertheless, attempts to reach a compromise continued for some time. In March 1946 Ferhat Abbas, released under an amnesty, launched the Democratic Union of the Algerian Manifesto (UDMA), with a programme providing for the creation of an autonomous, secular Algerian state within the French Union. Colonists were invited to join, but few did so. Despite successes in elections to the French Assembly, the UDMA failed to achieve its objectives. It withdrew from the Assembly in September 1946 and refused to participate in the next elections. The breach was filled by the more radical Movement for the Triumph of Democratic Liberties (MTLD), formed by Messali Hadj at the end of the war, which demanded the creation of a sovereign constituent assembly and the withdrawal of French troops.

In another attempt at compromise, the French Government introduced a new Constitution, which became law on 20 September 1947. This granted French citizenship, and therefore the vote, to all Algerian citizens, both men and women, and recognized Arabic as equal in status to French. The proposed new Algerian Assembly, however, was to be divided into two colleges, each of 60 members, one to represent the 1.5m. Europeans, the other the 9m. Muslims. Other provisions excluded any legislation contrary to the interest of the colonists.

The new Constitution was never brought fully into operation. Following MTLD successes in the municipal elections of October 1947, the elections to the Algerian Assembly were openly interfered with, many candidates being arrested, election meetings forbidden and polling stations improperly operated. As a result only a quarter of the members returned to the second college in April 1948 belonged to the MTLD or the UDMA; the remainder, known as the 'Beni Oui Oui', were nominally independent, but easy to manipulate. Such methods continued to be employed in local and national elections during the next six years, as well as in the Algerian elections to the French National Assembly in June 1951. Some of the improvements that the 1947 Constitution envisaged were never put into effect. The aim was to destroy, or at least render harmless, opposition to French rule; the result was to compel the main forces of nationalism to operate clandestinely.

As early as 1947 several of the younger members of the MTLD had formed the 'Secret Organization' (OS), which collected arms and money and built up a network of cells throughout Algeria in preparation for armed insurrection and the establishment of a revolutionary government. Two years later the OS felt itself strong enough to launch a terrorist attack in Oran. The movement was subsequently discovered and most of its leaders were arrested. A nucleus survived, however, in the Kabyle region, ever a stronghold for dissident groups, and the organizer of the attack, Ben Bella, escaped in 1952 to Cairo.

A decisive split was opening in the ranks of the MTLD, and the veteran Messali Hadj, who now embraced nebulous doctrines of Pan-Arabism, was gradually losing control of the party organization to more activist members. In March 1954 nine former members of the OS formed the Revolutionary Council for Unity and Action (CRUA) to prepare for an immediate revolt against French rule.

WAR OF INDEPENDENCE

Plans for the insurrection were worked out at a series of CRUA meetings in Switzerland between March and October 1954. Algeria was divided into six *wilaya* (administrative districts) and a military commander appointed for each. When the revolt was launched on 1 November the CRUA changed its name to the National Liberation Front (Front de Libération Nationale—FLN), its armed forces being known as the National Liberation Army (Armée de Libération Nationale— ALN). Starting from the Aurès, the revolt had spread by early 1955 to the Constantine area, the Kabyle and the Moroccan frontier west of Oran. By the end of 1956 the ALN was active throughout the settled areas of Algeria.

Ferhat Abbas and Ahmad Francis, of the more moderate UDMA, and the religious leaders of the *ulema* (Muslim scholar/lawyers) joined the FLN in April 1956, making it representative of all shades of Algerian nationalist feeling apart from Messali Hadj's Algerian National Movement (MNA). In August a secret congress of the FLN, held at Soummam in the Kabyle, formed a central committee and the National Council of the Algerian Revolution; drew up a socialist programme for the future Algerian republic; and approved plans for a terrorist offensive in Algiers.

Between September 1956 and June 1957 bomb explosions engineered by the FLN caused great loss of life. This terrorism was halted only by severe French repression of the Muslim population, including the use of torture and internment. Guerrilla activities continued but electrified barriers were erected along the Tunisian and Moroccan borders and ALN bands attempting to cross into Algeria suffered heavy losses.

In June 1957 the new Bourgès-Manoury administration in France introduced legislation to link Algeria indissolubly with France, but the measure was not approved. Following the Soummam conference, a joint Moroccan-Tunisian plan had been announced for the establishment of a North African federation linked with France. FLN leaders began negotiations in Morocco in October 1957. However, Ben Bella and his companions were kidnapped *en route* from Morocco to Tunisia, when the French pilot of their aircraft landed at Algiers. The French authorities could hardly ignore this *fait accompli*, and the hijacked leaders were arrested and interned in France.

Neither the internment of FLN leaders nor the bombing by French aircraft, in February 1958, of the Tunisian border village of Sakhiet Sidi Youssif, in which 79 villagers were killed, had any effect on the FLN's capacity to continue fighting, and the failure of these desperate measures only made the possibility of French negotiations with the FLN more likely. This, in turn, provoked a violent reaction from the Europeans in Algeria (only about one-half of whom were of French origin).

In May 1958 the colonists rebelled and installed committees of public safety in the major Algerian towns. Supported by the army and exploiting the widespread fear of civil war, the colonists prompted the overthrow of the discredited Fourth French Republic and Gen. de Gaulle's return to power, in the belief that he would further their aim of complete integration of Algeria with France. Although de Gaulle intensified military action against the FLN, this was only at the cost of increased terrorism in Algiers and of growing tension on the Tunisian and Moroccan borders. The FLN responded in August 1958 by establishing in Tunis the Provisional Government of the Algerian Republic (GPRA), headed by Ferhat Abbas, and including Ben Bella and the other leaders who had been interned in France. De Gaulle was already beginning to recognize the strength of Algerian nationalism and was moving cautiously towards accepting FLN demands.

NEGOTIATIONS AND THE COLONISTS' LAST STAND

Initially de Gaulle's public statements on Algeria were vague. When he did make an unequivocal pronouncement in September 1959, which upheld the right of Algerians to determine their own future, the colonists reacted swiftly. In January 1960 they rebelled again, this time against de Gaulle, and erected barricades in Algiers. However, without the support of the army the insurrection collapsed within nine days. Provisional talks between French and FLN delegates took place in secret near Paris in the summer of 1960 but were inconclusive.

In November de Gaulle announced that a referendum was to be held on the organization of government in Algeria, pending self-determination, and in December he visited Algeria to prepare the way. In the referendum the electorate was asked to approve a draft law providing for self-determination and immediate reforms to give Algerians the opportunity to participate in government. There were mass abstentions from voting in Algeria, however, and in February 1961 new French approaches to the FLN were made through the President of Tunisia. Secret talks led to direct negotiations between French and FLN representatives at Evian, on the Franco-Swiss border. These began in May but foundered in August over the question of the Sahara and because of the French attack on Bizerta.

Europeans in Algeria and sections of the French army had meanwhile formed the Secret Army Organization (OAS) to resist a negotiated settlement and the transfer of power from European hands. On 22 April 1961 four generals, Challe, Zeller, Jouhaud and Salan, organized the seizure of Algiers, but this attempt at an army coup proved abortive, most regular officers remaining loyal to de Gaulle. Offensive operations against the Algerian rebels, which had been suspended when the Evian talks began, were resumed by the French Government, and fighting continued, although on a reduced scale. At the same time, the OAS began its campaign of indiscriminate terrorism against native Algerians. The Mayor of Evian had already been killed by an OAS bomb, and attacks were now also mounted in Paris.

Secret contacts between the French Government and the FLN were re-established in October. Negotiations were resumed in December 1961 and January 1962 in Geneva and Rome, the five members of the GPRA interned in France taking part through a representative of the King of Morocco. Meetings at ministerial level were held in strict secrecy in Paris in February and the final stage of the negotiations was concluded at Evian on 18 March with the signing of a cease-fire agreement and a declaration of future policy. The declaration provided for the establishment of an independent Algerian state after a transitional period, and for the safeguarding of individual rights and liberties. Other declarations issued the following day dealt with the rights of French citizens in Algeria and with future Franco-Algerian co-operation. In the military sphere, France was to retain the naval base at Mers el-Kebir for 15 years and the nuclear testing site in the Sahara, together with various landing rights, for five years.

In accordance with the Evian agreements, a provisional Government was formed on 28 March 1962, with Abderrahman Farès as President and an executive composed of FLN members, other Muslims and Europeans. The USSR, the East European and many African and Asian countries quickly gave *de jure* recognition to the GPRA.

The signing of the Evian agreements was the signal for a final desperate stand by the OAS. A National Council of French Resistance in Algeria was formed, with General Salan as commander-in-chief, and OAS commando units attempted by attacks on the Muslim population and the destruction of public buildings to provoke a general breach of the cease-fire. After the failure of the OAS to establish an 'insurrectional zone' in the Orléansville (El-Asnam) area and the capture of General Salan on 20 April, and with a renewal of FLN terrorist activity and reprisals, increasing numbers of Europeans began to leave Algeria for France. Secret negotiations by OAS leaders with the FLN, aimed at securing guarantees for the European population, revealed a split in the OAS, which heralded the virtual end of European terrorist activity. By the end of June more than half of the European population of Algeria had left.

The final steps towards Algerian independence were now taken. In a referendum on 1 July, 91% of the electorate voted for independence, which was proclaimed by Gen. de Gaulle on 3 July 1962.

THE INDEPENDENT STATE

The achievement of power by the FLN revealed serious tensions within the government, while the problems facing the new state after eight years of civil war were formidable.

The dominant position in the GPRA of the 'centralist' group, headed by Ben Khedda and consisting of former members of the MTLD, was threatened by the release in March 1962 of the five GPRA members who had been detained in France— Ben Bella, Muhammad Khider, Muhammad Boudiaf, Ait Ahmad and Rabah Bitat. Boudiaf and Ait Ahmad rallied temporarily to the support of Ben Khedda, while the others formed yet another opposition faction besides that of Ferhat Abbas, who had been dropped from the GPRA leadership in 1961.

The ALN leadership was also split. The commanders of the main armed forces in Tunisia and Morocco were opposed to the politicians of the GPRA, and the commanders of the internal guerrilla groups were opposed to all external and military factions.

Serious differences had emerged when the National Council of the Algerian Revolution (CRNA) met in Tripoli in May 1962 to consider policies for the new state. A commission headed by Ben Bella produced a programme which included large-scale agrarian reform, involving expropriation and the establishment of peasant co-operatives and state farms; a state monopoly of external trade; and a foreign policy aimed towards Maghreb unity, neutrality and anti-colonialism, especially in Africa. Despite the opposition of Ben Khedda's group, the Tripoli programme became the official FLN policy.

After independence, the GPRA Cabinet, with the exception of Ben Bella, flew to Algiers, where they installed themselves alongside the official Provisional Executive. Ben Khedda attempted to reassert control over the ALN by dismissing the Commander-in-Chief, Col Boumedienne. Ben Bella, however, flew to Morocco to join Boumedienne, and on 11 July they crossed into Algeria and established headquarters in Tlemcen. Here Ben Bella established the Political Bureau as the chief executive organ of the FLN and a rival to the GPRA. After negotiations, he was joined by some of the GPRA leaders, leaving Ben Khedda isolated in Algiers, with Boudiaf and Ait Ahmad in opposition.

Several of the *wilaya* leaders, however, felt that, having provided the internal resistance, they represented the true current of the revolution, and they were opposed to the Political Bureau and Boumedienne. While ALN forces loyal to the Bureau occupied Constantine and Bône (Annaba) in the east on 25 July, Algiers remained in the hands of the leadership of *wilaya* IV, who refused the Bureau entry. When Boumedi-

enne's forces marched on Algiers from Oran at the beginning of September there were serious clashes with *wilaya* IV troops. Total civil war was averted, however, partly because of mass demonstrations against the fighting which were organized by the Algerian General Workers' Union (UGTA).

The struggle for power had gone against Ben Khedda. Before the elections were held on 20 September 1962, a third of the 180 candidates on the single list drawn up in August had been purged, including Ben Khedda himself, and replaced with lesser-known figures. Although the elections failed to arouse much public enthusiasm, some 99% of the electorate were declared to have voted in favour of the proposed powers of the Constituent Assembly. The functions of the GPRA were transferred to the Assembly when it met on 25 September, and Ferhat Abbas was elected its President. The Algerian Republic was proclaimed, and on the following day Ben Bella was elected Prime Minister. He subsequently appointed a cabinet comprising his personal associates and former ALN officers.

BEN BELLA IN POWER

The new Government immediately acted to consolidate its position. Messali Hadj's PPA (formerly the MNA), the Algerian Communist Party, and Boudiaf's Party of the Socialist Revolution were all banned in November; the *wilaya* system was abolished the following month, and, apart from the UGTA, all organizations affiliated to the FLN were brought firmly under control.

The economic plight of the country was severe. Some 90% (1m.) of the Europeans, representing virtually all the entrepreneurs, technicians, administrators, teachers, doctors and skilled workers, had left the country. Factories, farms and shops had closed, leaving 70% of the population unemployed. Public buildings and records had been destroyed by the OAS. At the end of the war, in which more than 1m. people had died, there had been 2m. in internment camps and 500,000 refugees in Tunisia and Morocco. In December 1962 an austerity plan was drawn up. Large loans and technical assistance from France, plus other emergency foreign aid, enabled the Government to remain in power.

By packing the first UGTA congress with FLN militants and unemployed, the FLN managed in January 1963 to gain control of the UGTA executive, which had been opposed to the dictatorial nature of the new Government. The decrees of March legalized the workers' committees which, aided by the UGTA, had taken over the operation of many of the abandoned European estates in mid-1962; the remaining estates were nationalized in 1963. The system of workers' management, known as *autogestion*, under which the workers elected their own management board to work alongside a state-appointed director, became the basis of 'Algerian socialism'.

In April 1963 Ben Bella assumed the post of Secretary-General of the FLN. In August he secured the adoption by the Assembly of a draft constitution providing for a presidential regime, with the FLN as the sole political party. The new Constitution was approved in a referendum and on 13 September Ben Bella was elected President for a period of five years, assuming the title of Commander-in-Chief of the armed forces as well as becoming Head of State and head of government. These moves towards dictatorial government aroused opposition. Ferhat Abbas, the leading proponent of a more liberal policy, resigned from the presidency of the Assembly and was subsequently expelled from the FLN. In the Kabyle, where discontent was accentuated by Berber regionalism, revolts had to be suppressed in 1963 and 1964.

BOUMEDIENNE TAKES OVER

On 19 June 1965 Ben Bella was deposed and arrested in a swift and bloodless military *coup d'état*, led by the Minister of Defence, Col Houari Boumedienne, whose army had brought Ben Bella to power in 1962. In view of Algeria's economic plight and Ben Bella's dictatorial tendencies, many administrators and politicians did not oppose the coup. Moreover, Ben Bella's elimination of most of the traditional leaders, his repeated attacks on the UGTA and his failure to turn the FLN into a representative party left him without organized support when the army turned against him. Bereft of its leader, the

FLN accepted the coup, and the UGTA, while expressing no real support for Boumedienne, did not oppose it.

Supreme political authority in Algeria passed to the Council of the Revolution, consisting mostly of military figures and presided over by Col Boumedienne. Under the Council's authority a new government of 20 members was formed on 10 July, with Boumedienne as Prime Minister and Minister of Defence. Nine members of the Government, which included technocrats and members of the radical wing of the FLN, had held office under Ben Bella. To ensure a satisfactory relationship between the Government and the FLN, a five-man party secretariat under Cherif Belkacem was set up on 17 July.

The aims of the new regime, as described by Boumedienne, were to remedy the abuses of personal power associated with Ben Bella, to end internal divisions, and to create an 'authentic socialist society' based on a sound economy. In international relations a policy of non-alignment was to be pursued and support for people struggling for freedom was to continue.

Apart from preparations for elections to the Communal People's Assemblies, the regime made no attempt to secure a popular mandate, and the Algerian National Assembly remained in abeyance. New penal and civil legal codes were promulgated in 1966, the judiciary was 'Algerianized' and tribunals to try 'economic crimes', with powers to impose the death penalty, were created in July. New conditions of service and training schemes for public employees were introduced, with the aim of improving the standard of administration. In accordance with its socialist policies, the regime increased state participation during 1966 in concerns previously left to private enterprise, particularly in the mining and insurance sectors. A National Bank of Algeria, specializing in short-term credit for the nationalized sector of the economy, was inaugurated in July.

Industrial activity continued at a low level and the country remained heavily dependent on foreign aid for industrial development. A new investment code, designed to attract both domestic and foreign capital and promulgated in September, contained assurances of indemnification in the event of nationalization.

CAUTION IN FOREIGN POLICY

The relationship with France, Algeria's main customer and the source of substantial assistance, remained of paramount importance. In 1966 agreements were signed which provided for French technical and educational assistance for 20 years, cancelled Algeria's pre-independence debts and reduced indebtedness to France to 400m. dinars. France was disturbed by the growing Soviet influence in Algeria. Soviet advisers played a leading role in the development of mining and industry, and the Algerian army received training and equipment from the USSR. However, French fears that the Soviet navy might be allowed to use the Mers el-Kebir base, handed over by France in January 1968, proved groundless. The French cultural influence remained: there were still French teachers, although the teaching of Arabic was extended in the schools; large numbers of Algerians worked in France; there was a preference for such French consumer goods as were still imported; and France continued to give assistance, including training and equipment, to Algeria's armed forces.

Algerian involvement in the six-day war in June 1967 was minimal. When the cease-fire came, however, there were demonstrations against Nasser's 'treason' and also against the USSR for lack of support for the Arab countries. At the Khartoum conference Algerian delegates advocated a people's war, and detachments of Algerian troops were maintained in the Suez Canal area until August 1970.

A highly critical, often openly hostile, attitude to the USA was maintained, and diplomatic relations were severed in 1967. Nevertheless, US petroleum technology was welcomed, as was investment in Algeria's oil industry; a contract to sell liquefied natural gas (LNG) to the USA was signed in 1969.

In Africa the Boumedienne Government took a consistently anti-colonial line, severing relations with the United Kingdom over Rhodesia in 1965 (but restoring them in 1968), and providing training and facilities for the liberation movements of southern Africa, as well as for the Eritrean Liberation

Front and the National Liberation Front of Chad. A determined effort was made to improve relations with neighbouring countries in the Maghreb. In January 1969 President Boumedienne made his first official visit to Morocco, where he conferred with King Hassan, and in the following June frontier posts were reopened for the first time since 1963. In May 1970 the Algerian and Moroccan Governments signed an agreement to settle a long-standing border dispute and to co-operate on the question of the Spanish presence in North Africa. In June 1972 the two leaders signed two further agreements: one demarcating the Algerian–Moroccan border (ratified by Algeria in May 1973, but not by Morocco until 1989), the other providing for joint exploitation of the Gara-Djebilet mines in the border regions. An agreement with Mauritania was signed in December 1969, and a friendship treaty with Tunisia, agreeing on common borders, in January 1970. While Algeria welcomed the Libyan revolution in 1969, the subsequent orientation of the Libyan leaders towards Egypt and Sudan, rather than the Maghreb, was not conducive to close relations between the two regimes.

INTERNAL OPPOSITION OVERCOME

Opposition came from certain left-wing ministers, such as Ali Yahia and Abd al-Aziz Zerdani, the UGTA, students, and sections of the army, notably the former *wilaya* leaders. They feared the imposition of a technocratic and centralized socialism, different from the syndicalist concepts embodied in *autogestion*, and felt that collegial rule was being supplanted by the dictatorship of the coterie round Boumedienne. An armed uprising in the Mitidja, launched in December 1967, was suppressed. Various members of the UGTA and of the Boumedienne administration were arrested. Boumedienne announced a series of selective dismissals in the FLN and the army, and appointed well-known supporters to vacant ministerial offices.

Opposition to Boumedienne, however, was by no means crushed. FLN attempts in February 1968 to impose a new loyal student committee at Algiers University provoked a strike by students and teachers, and there were numerous reports of guerrilla activity in the Aurès and the Kabyle. The Organization of Popular Resistance (ORP) appeared to be active both in these areas and among students. An attempt to assassinate Boumedienne was made on 25 April in Algiers, but he escaped with minor injuries.

The second stage of the reform of governmental institutions (the first being the 1967 communal elections) was put into operation in May 1969, when elections were held for the 15 *wilaya* (administrative districts) and 72% of the electorate voted for candidates on a single FLN list. In June 1970, following the celebration of his first five years in power, Boumedienne undertook an extensive tour of western Algeria, and when Cabinet changes were made in July, his key colleagues retained their places, a fact which emphasized the regime's stability. On the anniversary of the revolution in November 1970 he pardoned about 100 political prisoners. The release of these former enemies was seen as indicative of the weakness of opposition to Boumedienne.

RELATIONS WITH FRANCE

The consolidation of President Boumedienne's position at home enabled him to adopt a more militant attitude towards France. He could afford to demand more for Algerian oil, and the resultant dispute over the price to be paid by the French oil companies culminated in the decision to nationalize them.

The two companies concerned, the Compagnie Française des Pétroles (CFP) and the Entreprise de Recherches et d'Activités Pétrolières (ERAP), were responsible for some two-thirds of Algeria's total production. In February 1971, following unproductive discussions with the French Government, Boumedienne announced the acquisition by the Algerian Government of a 51% holding in CFP and ERAP and the complete nationalization of the companies' gas and pipeline interests.

The French Government regarded this move as a breach of the 1965 agreement but could only ask for fair compensation. The subsequent Algerian offer was found unacceptable and in April 1971 France discontinued negotiations. It was announced that many French technicians and teachers were to leave Algeria, and attacks were made on some of the 700,000 Algerians in France. The French Government imposed a boycott against Algerian oil and tried to persuade other major consumers to do the same. Talks between the two French companies and SONATRACH, the Algerian state oil concern, were resumed, however, and agreements were reached in June and September under which the role of CFP and ERAP became that of minority partners of the Algerian state in return for guaranteed oil supplies. After approval by the two Governments a final agreement, which also provided for compensation and reduced back claims of taxes, was signed on 15 December.

In April 1975 Valéry Giscard d'Estaing became the first French President to visit Algeria since independence. However, the goodwill that was generated by the visit quickly dissipated. French economic policies were resented by the Boumedienne Government, as they maintained an imbalance in trade between the two countries, and French support for, and provision of large quantites of arms to, Morocco, Algeria's potential enemy, during the Western Sahara dispute (see below) were regarded as a betrayal.

PALESTINE AND WESTERN SAHARA

The Boumedienne Government's stand on the Palestine question remained uncompromisingly militant. Algeria accepted neither the 1967 UN resolution nor the cease-fire. When a further cease-fire was agreed in August 1970, Algerian troops were withdrawn from the Suez Canal. Radio stations of Palestine liberation movements expelled from Cairo in July 1970 were allowed to broadcast from Algiers and relations with Jordan were broken off in June 1971 after the final destruction of Palestinian guerrilla bases in Jordan by King Hussein's forces. During the October War in 1973 Algeria was active on the diplomatic front, encouraging African countries to sever relations with Israel. It participated fully with other Arab oil-producing states in reducing production and boycotting countries regarded as hostile to the Arab cause. Relations with Jordan were restored after the dispatch of Jordanian troops to the Syrian front, but Algeria continued to support the Palestinians against any Jordanian territorial claims. In December 1977 Algeria was one of the signatories of the Declaration of Tripoli, opposing President Sadat's attempts to negotiate with Israel, and in 1978 Algeria severed diplomatic relations with Egypt.

Despite the Government's policy towards Palestine and its support of almost any exiled foreign opposition group, Algeria was prepared to co-operate in the economic field with any state willing to do so. Fears that Algeria might fall under Soviet dominance proved groundless, although the USSR was a major source of military equipment. Despite disagreements with the USA over Viet Nam and the Palestinian question, full diplomatic relations were restored at the end of 1974 and trade between the two countries increased dramatically—by the end of 1977 the USA had replaced France as Algeria's leading trade partner.

From early 1975 a major confrontation developed with Morocco over the future of the Spanish Sahara. Algeria opposed Morocco's claim to the territory, advocating the founding of an independent Saharan state after decolonization. In May 1975, at the International Court of Justice, Algeria called for genuine self-determination for the Saharans and denied any self-interest in the matter. When, in November 1975, Spain agreed to hand over the territory to Morocco and Mauritania, Boumedienne protested vehemently and promised full support for the Polisario Front, the Saharan liberation movement. As Moroccan troops moved into the territory, now known as Western Sahara, Algeria mobilized part of its armed forces, and in January and February 1976 there were heavy clashes between units of the two armies in the territory, far from the Algerian border. In March Algeria recognized the Sahrawi Arab Democratic Republic (SADR), proclaimed by the Polisario Front. Both Morocco and Mauritania subsequently severed diplomatic relations with Algeria. The prospect of a full-scale war in Western Sahara quickly receded, especially as there was little enthusiasm for war among the Algerian population, but the Government continued to provide support and refuge for displaced persons and Polisario troops. Morocco

and Mauritania refused to recognize the Polisario Front and interpreted all armed incursions into Western Sahara as Algerian attacks against their national territory. French bombing raids on Polisario troops, beginning in December 1977, were strongly condemned by Algeria, although the French Government declared that its intervention was solely for the protection of French citizens working in the area.

HOME AFFAIRS

By 1971 Boumedienne's Government felt secure enough to initiate a more active social policy. In that year a programme of agrarian reform, known as the Agrarian Revolution, was initiated. The reform was to proceed in three phases: the reallocation of state-owned and foreign land, the redistribution of private estates, and the transformation of the lives of the pastoral nomads. At the same time, the Government resolved to develop workers' control in industry and to reanimate the FLN as a radical force. Elected workers' councils slowly spread through nationalized industries, but the reorganization of the FLN was a failure prompting the resignation of Kaid Ahmad, the party leader, in 1972. The initiative in promoting the Agrarian Revolution passed to a student *volontariat*. Boumedienne's determination to build a socialist society was resisted by conservative elements of the population, especially after the redistribution of private estates and the nationalization of food distribution. Conflict erupted in May 1975 when there were clashes at Algiers University between students, supporting the Agrarian Revolution, and others, who wished to give priority to Arabization.

The personal authority of Boumedienne increased in the 1970s. Following the death of Ahmad Medeghri and Belkacem's dismissal from the Cabinet in 1974, Bouteflika was the only figure of comparable stature in the Government. Encouraged by the success of local and provincial elections since 1967 and 1969 respectively, Boumedienne announced in June 1975 that elections for a National Assembly and a President were to be held, and that a national charter would be drafted to provide the state with a new Constitution.

Boumedienne's decision to consolidate the regime and his personal power provoked a resurgence of opposition, including the circulation, in March 1976, of a manifesto signed by, among others, Ferhat Abbas and Ben Youssef ben Khedda, both former presidents of the Algerian government-in-exile during the war of liberation. The manifesto criticized Boumedienne for his totalitarian rule and his fostering of a personality cult. The signatories were reportedly placed under house arrest. Boumedienne rejected these criticisms of his rule as the work of bourgeois reactionaries, and declared that the revolution could not now be reversed.

In April 1976 the Algerian press began publication of the national charter, which, after public discussion, received the approval of 98.5% of the voters in a referendum in June. The essence of the charter was the irreversible commitment of Algeria to socialism, albeit a socialism specifically adapted to Third World conditions. The dominant role of the FLN was reasserted, but, as a concession to the conservatives, Islam was recognized as the state religion. In the following November a new Constitution, embodying the principles of the charter, was also approved by referendum, and in December Boumedienne was elected unopposed as President, with 99% of votes cast. To complete the new formal structure of power, a National Assembly of 261 members was elected in February 1977 from among 783 candidates selected by a committee of the FLN. Next, further steps were taken to strengthen and enlarge the FLN, in order to make it the guiding political force envisaged in the national charter. FLN officials were installed alongside local administrative officials to form the basis of a full party apparatus at all levels, and the mass organizations affiliated to the FLN (the unions of workers, peasants, war veterans, women and youth) held a series of congresses which was to culminate in a national FLN Congress (the first since 1964) in early 1979.

THE DEATH OF BOUMEDIENNE

Following a short illness, President Boumedienne died on 27 December 1978. During his illness there was speculation as to his successor, particularly since he had nominated neither a

Vice-President nor a Prime Minister and was himself Minister of Defence (a post which had included, from 1977 onwards, direct supervision of the police and secret service) and Chief of Staff of the armed forces. For the time being, government was assumed by the Council of the Revolution, which by now consisted of only eight members, apart from Boumedienne. Although it had been given no official status in the 1976 Constitution, the Council declared that it would maintain continuity and protect existing institutions, and succeeded in bringing about a smooth transfer of power.

After Boumedienne's death, Rabah Bitat, the President of the National Assembly, was automatically sworn in as Head of State for a 45-day period. At the end of January 1979 the delayed FLN Congress was held. It now had the double task of revitalizing the party and of choosing a presidential candidate. New statutes on party structure were adopted, whereby a Central Committee of between 120 and 160 members and between 30 and 40 advisory members, meeting at least once every six months, was to be elected by Congress and form the highest policy-making body not only of the party but of the country as a whole. The Committee was to select a party secretary-general who would automatically become the FLN's (and therefore the only) presidential candidate. A political bureau of between 17 and 21 members, nominated by the Secretary-General, would be elected by the Central Committee and be responsible to it. These structures superseded the Council of the Revolution, which was formally disbanded on 27 January.

CHADLI IN POWER

It was expected that the presidential candidate would be a member of the former Council, and the most likely choice appeared to be either Abd al-Aziz Bouteflika, the Minister for Foreign Affairs, or Muhammad Salah Yahiaoui, the administrative head of the FLN. The eventual choice, Col Ben Djedid Chadli, the commander of the Oran military district, was regarded as a compromise between the two. He was inaugurated as President on 9 February 1979, after his candidature had been approved by 94% of the electorate. He declared that he would uphold the policies of Boumedienne, the 'irreversible option' of socialism and 'national independence' in both political and economic spheres. It soon became clear that Chadli did not intend to monopolize power to the extent that Boumedienne had. For the first time since independence, a Prime Minister was named: Col Muhammad ben Ahmad Abd al-Ghani, who also kept his post as Minister of the Interior until January 1980. This nomination preceded the constitutional changes that were adopted by the National Assembly in June 1979, which made the appointment of a Prime Minister obligatory, and also reduced the President's term of office from six to five years, to coincide with five-yearly party congresses.

Within the first few months of his presidency, Chadli showed signs of breaking away from Boumedienne's doctrinaire policies. A new Government was formed, and Bouteflika was removed from the post of Minister of Foreign Affairs, which he had held for 15 years. Some of Boumedienne's political opponents were released from prison and it was announced that the former President, Ben Bella, had been freed, although it later transpired that he had merely been placed under a less stringent form of house arrest; he was finally freed from restrictions in October 1980. Exit visas for Algerians, compulsory since 1967, were abolished; income tax was reduced and restrictions on owning property eased. In September, however, a 'clean-up' campaign was mounted in Algiers and other cities. It was initially intended to improve the appearance of the streets in preparation for the 25th anniversary of the revolution, but was expanded to include the arrest and imprisonment of hundreds of 'social parasites' and a campaign against inefficiency and corruption. During 1980 and 1981 this campaign was extended to the highest levels of state organizations, and numerous senior officials were arrested and tried by the Cour des Comptes for financial mismanagement.

A meeting of the FLN Central Committee in December 1979 resulted in some important decisions concerning economic and social development. It announced that Algeria would reduce its dependence on foreign financial and technical assistance, diversify its economic partners, and reduce its petroleum and gas exports in order to conserve these resources. The massive industrialization programme was to be scaled down and the large state companies reorganized into smaller units. Details of these changes were given in a new five-year plan adopted in June 1980. The emphasis of government policy was to shift from heavy industry to social areas, such as health, education and infrastructure, and raising agricultural production. The private sector was to be considerably liberalized.

FOREIGN POLICY UNDER CHADLI

During Chadli's presidency, Algerian foreign policy became more pragmatic and less determined by ideological considerations. Boumedienne's aim to present Algeria as one of the leaders of the Third World was abandoned. Chadli also abandoned his predecessor's policy of distracting attention from problems at home by stridency abroad, in favour of concentration on domestic matters, especially the need for development. He sought good relations with states of every political ideology and made friends with conservatives without alienating radicals. Algeria therefore became highly regarded as a mediator, and in October 1987 the country was elected to the UN Security Council for a two-year term beginning on 1 January 1988.

Relations with other Arab states

Algeria under Chadli had no aspirations to leadership of the Arab world and contented itself with being a loyal member of the team. It worked for Arab unity and made attempts to mediate in disputes. The prestige that Chadli had gained was shown by his selection, together with Kings Hassan and Fahd, to form a committee to pursue the decisions of the Casablanca Arab summit meeting.

Diplomatic relations were restored with Egypt after a nine-year break in November 1988, and three months later Dr Esmat Abd al-Meguid became the first Egyptian minister to visit Algiers for 11 years. Algeria remained a staunch supporter of the Palestinian cause, and in June 1988 Chadli convened a special summit meeting to rally support for the *intifada* and provided a venue for the declaration of Palestinian statehood. Algeria strongly opposed the settlement of Soviet Jews in the West Bank region of Jordan, but Chadli declined to attend the Baghdad Arab summit meeting in person in May 1990 on the grounds that, without the participation of Syria, the meeting would be pointless.

Algeria, despite suspicions that it was covertly supporting its local Islamic fundamentalists, enjoyed friendly relations with the conservative Arab monarchies and co-operated with them in financial matters. Algeria also developed friendly diplomatic and commercial ties with Iran.

Relations with the superpowers

Whereas former President Boumedienne had restored diplomatic links with the USA while maintaining relations at a commercial level, Chadli sought to improve relations, with the aims of gaining higher levels of US investment and of promoting regional stability. Thus, Algeria played an important part in the negotiations over US hostages being detained in Iran, leading to their release in January 1981. However, relations with the USA became strained shortly afterwards when the US Government announced its decision to sell tanks to Algeria's then hostile neighbour, Morocco, and refused to agree to Algerian demands that the price of liquefied natural gas (LNG—a major Algerian export) should be increased to a level of parity with the price of petroleum (see Economy).

By 1985 relations with the USA had improved, and in April the two countries held a summit meeting in Washington. This marked the first official visit to the USA by an Algerian Head of State since independence. As a result of his visit, Chadli was successful in having Algeria removed from the list of countries that the US Government had declared 'ineligible' to purchase US military equipment. In order to balance this *rapprochement* with the USA, Chadli made an official visit to Moscow in March 1986. In October 1987 the USA expressed alarm when it was revealed that Algeria had agreed, in principle, to establish a political union with Libya. This agreement directly contravened the US policy of 'isolating' that country, and, after diplomatic pressure from the USA (in addition to opposition from within the Algerian Government), Chadli postponed the announcement of a treaty of political union with Libya.

Relations with France

After Chadli took office as President, relations with France began to improve. In September 1980 Algeria and France signed an agreement whereby the French Government provided incentives for the repatriation of some 800,000 Algerian workers and their dependants living in France, while Algeria released French bank assets which had been frozen since independence. With the election of a socialist government in France in 1981, relations became more cordial. Gaston Defferre, the French Minister of the Interior, visited Algeria to discuss the problem of illegal immigration, and, shortly afterwards, President Mitterrand made an official visit. In February 1982 a dispute over the price of Algerian gas exports to France was settled, and in December Chadli made the first official visit to France by an Algerian Head of State since independence.

After the election of a right-wing French Government in 1986, co-operation between France and Algeria increased. In September the French Prime Minister, Jacques Chirac, visited Algiers to discuss bilateral trade and foreign policy, although the positive aspects of his visit were vitiated by the announcement of proposals to introduce visa requirements for visitors from non-EC countries to France, following a series of bombings in Paris. In October Algeria retaliated by introducing similar requirements for French visitors to Algeria. In the same month, however, France expelled 13 members of the Algerian Democratic Movement (MDA—founded by Ben Bella in 1984) and banned the MDA newspaper, *Al-Badil*, after Algerian security forces co-operated with France over the Paris bombings. In April 1987 the Algerian Government agreed to release the assets of former French settlers, which had been frozen since independence, and subsequently allowed former French property-owners to sell their land in Algeria to the Algerian state, and French workers in Algeria to transfer their income to France. In return, the French Government agreed to provide financial assistance to Algeria for three years.

Relations deteriorated, however, during the riots in Algiers in October 1988, as Algerian state-controlled newspapers accused the French media of exaggerating the unrest, and the Algerian Government criticized the French Minister of Co-operation for objecting to the severe measures taken against the rioters. However, in March 1989, during a visit to Algeria, President Mitterrand of France demonstrated his firm support for Chadli and his reforms. In June the Association for Franco-Algerian Friendship was founded, with the aim of strengthening links between the two countries.

The crisis in the Gulf which developed as a result of Iraq's invasion of Kuwait in August 1990 caused Presidents Mitterrand and Chadli to work together closely to avert war. However, after hostilities between Iraq and the multinational force had begun, there was popular indignation in Algeria against France. In December 1990 relations between Algeria and France were subjected to further strain after Algeria issued a decree which made Arabic the country's official language, and which appeared to penalize the official use of French. In response, the French Minister Delegate responsible for Francophone Countries appealed to Algerians to apply pressure on their Government to permit the continued official use of the French language. By May 1991 the tension appeared to have eased: France and Algeria concluded four oil agreements and French oil companies were granted two new concessions in the Sahara.

Co-operation with Spain

Until 1986 Algeria's relations with Spain had been cool, owing to Algerian suspicion of Spain's pro-Moroccan position in the Western Sahara conflict. In October 1986 the Spanish Government claimed that 'Txomin', the leader of the military wing of ETA (the Basque separatist movement), and a number of ETA supporters were living in Algeria, with the tacit approval of the Algerian Government. Algeria hastily denied any involvement with ETA and assured Spain that it would not allow the ETA members to engage in 'terrorist' activities. In December the Spanish deputy Prime Minister visited Algeria and was reported to have met representatives of the Polisario Front. In the following month, Spain announced that it would incorporate Algeria into its programme of overseas military co-operation. The death of 'Txomin' in a road accident outside Algiers in February 1987 increased Spanish suspicions of the Algerian Government's stance on ETA. However, the tension was resolved by a pact, signed by the two countries in August, which allowed an Algerian security official to be stationed in Spain to monitor the activities of Algerian dissidents, in exchange for closer supervision of members of ETA in Algeria. In December an MDA activist was arrested by the Spanish authorities and expelled to Algeria. In April and May 1989 16 ETA members were expelled from Algeria, following the collapse of peace talks with the Spanish Government and a resumption of ETA violence in Spain. In December a Spanish company, Cepsa, signed a gas exploration and production agreement with the Algerian state monopoly SONATRACH. The reconciliation with Morocco removed political obstacles to the construction of a gas pipeline between Algeria and Spain. It was anticipated that Spain and Italy would play a large part in financing the gas pipeline across Morocco to the Spanish region of Andalusia.

In December 1990 the Algerian Minister of Foreign Affairs, Sid-Ahmad Ghozali, visited Madrid, where he voiced support for a Spanish proposal that North African visitors to Spain should require visas. In February 1991 the Spanish Minister of Foreign Affairs visited Algiers, where he praised Algeria's efforts to introduce democracy and its pursuit of a peaceful solution to the conflict in the Gulf.

Relations with other EC countries

There was an obvious need to regulate relations between the EC and North Africa prior to the introduction of changes in the community, due to take effect at the end of 1992. During the second half of 1990, when President Chadli was Chairman of the Union of the Arab Maghreb (UAM), Algeria played a leading role in negotiations with the EC. The establishment of a 'Western Mediterranean Organization' provided an official forum for discussions.

In April 1991 the Algerian Minister of Foreign Affairs, Sid-Ahmad Ghozali, visited Brussels. Among other business, he presented the EC with an Algerian application for a loan of US $900m. However, the United Kingdom and Germany stated that even a loan of $560m. would be too high, and any decision on the application was postponed until September 1991. The European Parliament, meanwhile, recommended that a loan of $550m., raised on financial markets, should be guaranteed. In the event, a loan of $450m. was granted to Algeria.

Bilaterally, relations with Italy are of considerable importance to Algeria. In November 1989 Presidents Chadli and Cossiga inaugurated a joint venture between Algeria and the Fiat motor company to produce some 30,000 vehicles annually. In the previous month the Italian Minister of Foreign Affairs, Gianni De Michelis, had visited Algiers to discuss increasing Italian investment in Algerian projects and the extension of the gas pipeline between Algeria and Italy. During 1990 it was decided to double the length of the pipeline, and its possible extension into Central Europe—where Czechoslovakia had expressed an interest in importing Algerian gas—was discussed. In November De Michelis made a further visit to Algiers and trade agreements between Algeria and Italy were concluded. In January 1991 Italy granted Algeria a 'credit package' of $7,200m. on terms so generous that the subsequent controversy in Italy led to the resignation of a senior treasury official. However, De Michelis emphasized the need to support Algerian democracy, and the first tranche of the loan was released in June. De Michelis revisited Algiers in September 1991, in order to promote further bilateral projects between Algeria and Italy, and to discuss Algeria's links with the EC.

Algeria and the 1990–91 Gulf crisis

Algeria condemned both the invasion of Kuwait by Iraq in August 1990, and the subsequent deployment of US and other

Western armed forces in the Arabian peninsula. The Algerian Minister of Foreign Affairs, Sid-Ahmad Ghozali, advocated an 'Arab solution' to the conflict in the Persian (Arabian) Gulf region and deplored the UN's imposition of economic sanctions on Iraq. At the August 1990 summit meeting of Arab leaders, held in Cairo, President Chadli abstained in a vote to decide whether to deploy Arab forces alongside Western forces in Saudi Arabia. The Islamic fundamentalist Front Islamique du Salut (FIS), which received financial assistance from Saudi Arabia, initially supported the military operation to defend that country. However, public opinion favoured the stance of the secular political parties, such as the Parti Social-Démocrate (PSD), which attempted to undermine the economic sanctions imposed on Iraq by sending supplies there. At the end of August 1990 the FIS advocated a popular uprising against the 'corrupt' rulers of Iraq, Kuwait and Saudi Arabia.

President Chadli, both in a personal capacity and as Chairman of the UAM, made strenuous efforts to avert war in the Gulf region. In December 1990 he embarked on an extensive tour of the Middle East, but he denied that he was trying to arrange a summit meeting or that he had any particular plans to mediate in the conflict.

In mid-January 1991, as military hostilities in the Gulf began to appear inevitable, the FIS organized large demonstrations in support of Iraq. Its leaders visited Baghdad and, on their return to Algeria, appealed for volunteers to oppose the multinational force. The British and US Governments advised their citizens to leave the country. After the bombing campaign by the multinational force had begun, FIS leaders urged worldwide attacks on US and Jewish interests. At the conclusion of the hostilities between Iraq and the multinational force, the Algerian Minister of Foreign Affairs commended the resistance mounted by the Iraqi forces.

Moves towards Maghrebin unity

Although Algeria continued to support the Polisario Front in the Western Sahara conflict, Chadli did not share Boumedienne's zeal to be regarded as a fighter against injustice or his animosity towards Morocco. He was more interested in creating a 'Great Arab Maghreb', which would unify the five Maghrebin states politically and economically. In order to achieve this long-term goal, Chadli was prepared to display a greater flexibility than his predecessor with regard to Algeria's relations with Morocco and the Polisario Front.

Algeria's relations with other Maghrebin states improved considerably in the early 1980s. In 1979 Algeria assisted in negotiations with Mauritania over the withdrawal of its claim to Western Sahara. Mauritania signed a peace treaty in August, and Algeria resumed diplomatic relations. However, owing to the deadlock in Western Sahara, Algeria's relations with Morocco remained unfriendly until 1983. In February of that year, as the culmination of a series of secret negotiations held since the death of Boumedienne, President Chadli and King Hassan of Morocco held a summit meeting on the Moroccan-Algerian border. The meeting focused on the normalization of relations and the construction of the Great Arab Maghreb. The meeting succeeded in reducing some of the mistrust between the two countries, and, a few months later, restrictions on movements across the frontier were withdrawn.

In March 1983 Algeria and Tunisia signed the Maghreb Fraternity and Co-operation Treaty, which provided a framework for the creation of the Great Arab Maghreb. Unlike previous agreements made in the region, this treaty was not directed against neighbouring countries but was explicitly open to them to sign if they accepted the terms. At the same time, Algeria signed another treaty which delineated its borders with Tunisia, thus settling a 20-year old disagreement between the two countries. In April a tripartite meeting was held between representatives from Algeria, Morocco and Tunisia, at which the normalization of Moroccan-Algerian relations and the construction of the Great Arab Maghreb were discussed. It was agreed that further conferences would be held on Maghrebin unity, which Libya and Mauritania would be particularly welcome to attend. In December Mauritania signed the Maghreb Fraternity and Co-operation Treaty, and in April 1985, after three years of negotiations, it signed a border agreement with Algeria.

In the mid-1980s, however, Maghrebin unity became an increasingly remote ideal, owing to the deterioration of relations between the five nations. Algeria's relations with Libya became strained after Libya signed the Treaty of Oujda with Morocco in August 1984 and expelled Tunisian workers in 1985. Meanwhile, the *rapprochement* with Morocco was hindered by Algeria's continuing support of the Polisario Front, and in July 1985 the Moroccan Minister of the Interior accused Algeria of training 'Moroccan terrorists' for operations against his government. After Morocco had completed the construction of a new defensive wall on the borders of Western Sahara and Mauritania in April 1987, the Algerian Government expressed its concern that Mauritania might become involved in fighting between Moroccan troops and the Polisario Front.

In May 1987, however, President Chadli met King Hassan on the Moroccan-Algerian border, under the auspices of King Fahd of Saudi Arabia. After the meeting, the two leaders issued a joint communiqué, which stated that consultations to resolve differences between the two countries would continue. Later in the month, the Algerian Government released 150 Moroccan soldiers, in exchange for 102 Algerian prisoners being held in Morocco.

Meanwhile, relations with Libya improved, following Chadli's meetings with the Libyan Secretary for Foreign Liaison, Dr Ali Abd as-Salim Treiki, in November 1985, and with Col Qaddafi in January 1986. Both Libya and Algeria reiterated their commitment to Maghreb unity and deplored the conflict over Western Sahara, demanding self-determination for the Sahrawi people. Following the US attack on Libya in April, Algeria unsuccessfully appealed for the convening of an emergency meeting of Arab nations. In an attempt to consolidate its good relations with Algeria, Libya advocated a union with Algeria in March and June. A year later, in June 1987, a proposal for political union between Libya and Algeria was submitted to Chadli by Col Qaddafi's deputy, Maj. Abd as-Salam Jalloud, during his visit to Algiers. After the visit, however, Algeria suggested that the Maghreb Fraternity and Co-operation Treaty already provided a framework for a new Algerian-Libyan relationship.

Towards the end of 1987 and during the early months of 1988, the process of achieving Maghrebin unity gathered momentum. In November 1987 Chadli received the Moroccan Minister of Foreign Affairs, and they discussed means of accelerating the development of the Great Arab Maghreb and of resolving the Western Sahara conflict. Maghreb unity also formed the agenda of a meeting between the Algerian, Mauritanian and Tunisian Ministers of Foreign Affairs in December, when hopes were again expressed that Libya might sign the Maghreb Fraternity and Co-operation Treaty. The restoration of diplomatic relations between Tunisia and Libya in the same month was viewed as a triumph of Algerian diplomacy. In January 1988, during a meeting in Tunis, Chadli and the new Tunisian President, Zine al-Abidine ben Ali, issued directives to intensify bilateral co-operation, demanded a just resolution of the Western Sahara conflict, and pledged to work for regional stability and to hasten the creation of the Great Arab Maghreb. Chadli then visited Col Qaddafi, in an apparent attempt to persuade him to sign the Maghreb Fraternity and Co-operation Treaty, possibly in March, on the fifth anniversary of its inception. At a tripartite meeting in Tunis in February, Chadli, President Ben Ali of Tunisia and Col Qaddafi of Libya all expressed their determination to encourage co-operation between Maghreb countries and to work towards the creation of the Great Arab Maghreb.

In the hope that Libya would sign the Maghreb Fraternity and Co-operation Treaty (and with a view to the subsequent creation of a four-nation Great Arab Maghreb), Chadli aimed to isolate Morocco and thus force it to reach a settlement in the Western Sahara conflict. This would be a prelude to the eventual establishment of a complete five-nation Great Arab Maghreb. Faced with the collapse of this strategy (owing to Libya's failure to sign the treaty in March), and wishing to present a unified Maghreb front and to increase the number of 'moderate' Arab countries represented at the special Arab League summit which he had convened for June (see above), Chadli decided to seek the restoration of diplomatic relations with Morocco. In early May the Secretary-General of the FLN and Algerian deputy leader, Muhammad Cherif Messaadia, went to Rabat to invite King Hassan of Morocco to the Arab League summit in Algiers. A few days later, King Hassan dispatched two senior advisers to Algiers for further discussions, and on 16 May the two countries announced the re-establishment of diplomatic relations at ambassadorial level. The Moroccan-Algerian border was subsequently opened in early June, before the Arab League summit. It was reported that Algeria had offered to restore diplomatic relations if King Hassan agreed to attend the Arab League summit, and had withdrawn its insistence that Morocco should hold direct talks with the Polisario Front. At the summit King Hassan abandoned his former claim to Tindouf, and it became clear that Chadli was preparing to abandon the Western Sahara.

The creation of the Great Arab Maghreb became a reality in June 1988, when the first meeting of the five Heads of State of the Maghrebin countries was held in Algiers, following the conclusion of the Arab League summit. The five leaders issued a joint communiqué, which announced the creation of a Maghreb commission, comprising a delegation from each of the five countries, whose responsibility was to focus on the establishment of a semi-legislative, semi-consultative council to align legislation in the region, and to prepare joint economic projects. At the end of June, Algeria and Libya agreed to hold referendums on a proposed union of the two countries. Unlike the proposals issued by Col Qaddafi in 1987 (which envisaged total merger), this revised proposal aimed merely to establish a federation between the two countries. President Chadli later announced that the Algerian referendum on the union would be held in 1989. In July 1988 Algeria and Morocco signed a co-operation agreement, and the two countries announced plans to harmonize their railway, postal and telecommunications systems. Later that month, the Maghreb commission met in Algiers and announced the creation of five working groups to examine areas of regional integration, each to be chaired by a representative of a member country.

At the end of August, Morocco and the Polisario Front accepted a UN peace plan to settle the Western Sahara conflict. During the negotiations, it became apparent that Algeria's restoration of diplomatic relations with Morocco had forced Polisario, which was heavily dependent on Algerian support, to make concessions. (For a more detailed account of the Western Sahara conflict and moves towards its resolution, see the chapter on Morocco.)

On 17 February 1989 the treaty creating the Union of the Arab Maghreb (UAM) was signed in Marrakesh, Morocco, by the leaders of Algeria, Libya, Mauritania, Morocco and Tunisia. Modelled on the EC, the UAM was formed principally to enable its members to negotiate with that body when it declared a single European market at the end of 1992. It was also intended to encourage trade and economic co-operation by allowing freedom of movement across frontiers. The treaty created a policy-making council of Heads of State, to meet every six months under an annually rotating chairman, and other administrative bodies, including a court, comprising 10 members, to consider disputes between member states. In June 1989 the five nations formed a joint Parliament, and a defence clause prohibited aggression between the states.

In the second half of 1989 and the first half of 1990 Algeria seemed too preoccupied with domestic affairs and the overwhelming need to sell its hydrocarbons abroad and attract foreign investment to have much time to devote to affairs in the Maghreb. Although in no way obstructive, it did not show the leadership that its strength and central position should have enabled it to extend and left much of the administration to Tunisia. At the same time, as was evident at the Tunis summit meeting in January 1990, its partners looked rather askance at its tolerance of an avowedly Islamic fundamentalist political party (the FIS) and at the pace of its liberal reforms. In May Algeria hosted a meeting at which the UAM Ministers of Transport approved a draft agreement to create a joint airline and to expand rail links to provide a continuous track from Tobruk to Nouakchott.

Chadli earned the gratitude of Col Qaddafi in August 1989 by mediating an acceptable settlement of the dispute between Chad and Libya over the Aozou strip and also by attempting

to calm the USA's apprehension about Libya's so-called 'mustard-gas factory' at Rabta. Relations with Morocco were complicated by deadlock in Western Sahara: Chadli continued to urge King Hassan to hold direct talks with the Polisario Front. Moroccan co-operation was vital for perhaps the most important of all Algeria's development projects, the gas pipeline to Western Europe, which the Minister of Energy, Sadok Boussena, wished to see in place by the mid-1990s. In February 1990 the Ministers of the Interior of the two countries signed agreements to co-operate in facilitating the movement of people and goods and in combating drug-smuggling. It was agreed to promote co-operation between provincial and municipal authorities in the border regions.

In July 1990 the chairmanship of the UAM passed to Algeria. On 22 July, at the third meeting of the UAM Heads of State, President Chadli outlined proposals to unify tariffs by 1992 and to create a full customs union by 1995. Six agreements were signed. These provided for: exchanges of agricultural products; the creation of a joint airline, to operate initially alongside the national carriers; measures to stop the spread of agricultural diseases; measures to encourage and guarantee investment; the ending of double taxation; and the freedom of movement for goods and people. The meeting also expressed support for a strengthening of links with the EC, fearing that the rise of the new democracies in Eastern Europe would divert the Community's attention from North Africa. No agreement was reached on the choice of a Secretary-General for the UAM, nor on the location of its headquarters. The meeting issued a declaration of support for the Palestinian *intifada* and condemned the mass emigration of Soviet Jews to Israel. In private the Heads of State were believed to have discussed the threat being presented by Islamic fundamentalism, in the light of recent elections in Algeria and Tunisia.

Initially the five members of the UAM reacted separately to the Iraqi occupation of Kuwait. At the summit meeting of Arab leaders in Cairo in August 1990, Morocco voted in favour of a resolution demanding Iraq's withdrawal from Kuwait. Libya and Mauritania voted against the resolution, while Algeria abstained. Tunisia did not attend the meeting. Before the end of August, however, Algeria had convened a meeting of the Ministers of Foreign Affairs of the UAM member states, and thereafter they presented a more unified stance with regard to the conflict in the Gulf region. President Chadli acted as spokesman for the UAM, invoking the principle of 'international legitimacy' and rejecting the use of force to resolve inter-Arab disputes. In October 1990 the Algerian Minister of Foreign Affairs, Sid-Ahmad Ghozali, led a UAM delegation to a conference, in Rome, of the Western Mediterranean members of the EC and Malta. The conference issued a declaration which urged the convening of a Middle East security conference, to be attended by Israel and the PLO. It also established working groups to create a multilateral Mediterranean financial institute and data bank; to pursue self-sufficiency in food and combat desertification in North Africa; and to seek relief from international debts and regulate the flow of North African emigrants to southern Europe. In November 1990 the UAM Ministers of Foreign Affairs met again in Algiers to co-ordinate their countries' positions regarding future negotiations with the EC. In December 1990, after he had already visited nine countries in an attempt to avert war in the Gulf, President Chadli met King Hassan of Morocco. In addition to discussing the conflict in the Gulf, the two leaders concluded economic agreements.

After the beginning of hostilities between Iraq and the multinational force in January 1991, the five UAM states urged the convening of a special session of the UN Security Council. The permanent members of the Security Council rejected this appeal, even though an Algerian envoy had travelled to Beijing to enlist Chinese support. In March 1991 the chairmanship of the UAM passed from Algeria to Libya. It was generally recognized that, during Algeria's chairmanship, genuine progress towards unity had been made, and that the UAM had shown itself to be uniquely qualified to mediate between Arab states.

CHANGES WITHIN THE FLN

During 1980 a general streamlining of the FLN took place, and the President's control over it was strengthened. In June, at an extraordinary congress of nearly 4,000 delegates, important changes in the party structure were initiated. The Political Bureau was now to consist of between seven and 11 members (having previously numbered between 17 and 21), and was to meet monthly instead of weekly. The President, as Secretary-General of the FLN, was empowered to select the members of the Political Bureau rather than merely to 'propose' them, although the choice would still be subject to the Central Committee's approval; he was also given freedom to make other changes in the party which he considered necessary. All this reinforced the President's position, and reduced the role of the Political Bureau to that of an advisory body. Chadli immediately reduced its numbers to the new statutory minimum of seven. The Prime Minister, Col Abd al-Ghani, and several other ministers were dropped from the Bureau, although it still represented a wide range of opinion. In addition, the number of FLN committees was reduced from 12 to five (dealing with general organizations, external relations, internal party discipline, economic and social affairs, and information and culture). Changes were also made in the wider membership of the FLN. The congress agreed that all officials of the UGTA and the other mass organizations should have to be members of the FLN. In this way members of 'unofficial' parties, such as the Communist Parti d'Avant-Garde Socialiste (PAGS), would be excluded from official positions.

Further changes were made to the composition of the FLN's Political Bureau in July 1981, when its membership was increased to 10. Col Abd al-Ghani was reappointed, but Yahiaoui and Bouteflika, Chadli's rivals for the presidency in 1979, were removed, although they retained their membership of the Central Committee. In the following December Bouteflika was dismissed from the FLN Central Committee, as were three other senior members who had held important portfolios under Boumedienne. Legislative elections were held on 5 March 1982, when 72.65% of the electorate voted for FLN candidates. The National Assembly's membership was increased to 281, of whom 55 were permanent members of the FLN.

At the fifth congress of the FLN, held in December 1983, Chadli was re-elected to the post of Secretary-General of the party, and became the sole candidate for the presidential elections, held on 12 January 1984. His candidature was endorsed by 95.4% of the electorate, and he was returned to office for another five years. Ten days after his re-election, President Chadli effected a major government reshuffle, and appointed a new Prime Minister, Abd al-Hamid Brahimi, formerly Minister of Planning.

MOVES TOWARDS LIBERALIZATION

Following public consultations and debate initiated by Chadli in February 1985, a new national charter was adopted at a special congress of the FLN, held in December. The charter's programme encouraged private enterprise and proposed a balance between socialism and Islam as the state ideology. In a referendum held in January 1986, in which 95.92% of the eligible population took part, 98.37% of the votes were cast in favour of the adoption of the new charter. In February Chadli implemented a series of cabinet reshuffles, although none of these affected the essential ministries of the Interior, Foreign Affairs or Energy, probably because of Chadli's wish to maintain party unity at a time when Algeria was confronted by falling oil prices.

At a general election for the National Assembly on 26 February 1987, a record 87.9% of the electorate voted for FLN candidates. The number of seats in the Assembly was increased to 295, owing to demographic changes. The newly-elected National Assembly comprised a larger number of younger, liberal deputies who were more likely to support Chadli's policy of liberalization.

In June 1987, in response to an increase in social unrest, a new Minister of the Interior was appointed and changes were made in the military hierarchy. In July, as part of its liberalization policy, the Government introduced legislation which permitted the formation of local organizations without prior consent from the authorities except where these were deemed to threaten Algeria's security or the policies of the revised national charter. 'National' organizations continued to require government approval. Even this relatively moderate measure aroused misgivings among 'conservative' deputies in the National Assembly, who feared that it might lead to the creation of alternative political organizations.

Meanwhile, Chadli accelerated the implementation of his policy to restructure and liberalize the economy. In July 1987 the National Assembly began to consider proposals that aimed to remove various state controls from agricultural co-operatives and public enterprises, in contrast to the collectivization of the 1970s, which was being increasingly criticized as inefficient. In accordance with this forthcoming legislation, during an extensive cabinet reshuffle in November, Chadli abolished the Ministry of Planning, which had previously supervised every aspect of Algeria's economy. The remaining functions of the ministry were assumed by a national Council of Planning, directly accountable to the Prime Minister, Brahimi. Chadli also took the opportunity to create a new Ministry of Education and Training, in response to the growth in demand for employment and educational opportunities for young people—an issue that had been brought to the Government's attention by a student boycott at the beginning of the month.

However, the implementation of the new economic legislation, scheduled for 1988, was hindered by Algeria's complex bureaucratic procedures. In December 1987 Chadli announced a series of reforms intended to improve the efficiency of the country's administrative structures. Two measures to take immediate effect were the abolition of certain documents hitherto required by every citizen for each administrative procedure, and the instant application of legal decisions. In the short term, the Government was to introduce a single identity card, with a multiplicity of uses, and to appoint a national mediator to facilitate relations between the public and civil servants. In the medium term, measures were to be introduced in order to effect a complete reorganization of the administrative structure.

In February 1988, in preparation for the sixth FLN congress, Chadli appointed a national commission to evaluate Algeria's second Five-Year Development Plan, taking into consideration the effects of the international economic crisis on the Algerian economy, and to assist with the drafting of an appropriate plan for the 1990s. Later in February, Chadli announced several government changes whereby 'technocrat' ministers were appointed to preside over the more problematic sectors of the economy. Thus, Col Kasdi Merbah, the Minister of Agriculture and a former Minister of Heavy Industry, assumed the health portfolio, with responsibility for a sector which was viewed as being high-spending and inefficient, while the agricultural portfolio was assumed by the former Minister of Hydraulics, Forestry and Fishing, Muhammad Rouighi.

INTERNAL UNREST

In 1979 the Government encountered criticism from students, who boycotted classes to protest at the slow implementation of the policy of replacing French with Arabic. The students' demands were partly met by measures intended to accelerate the process of 'Arabization' in education, and 600 Arabic-speaking trainee magistrates were appointed. In May 1980 the FLN Central Committee announced that a central co-ordinating body was to be established to encourage the use of Arabic, and that official newspapers should be printed in Arabic only. By the following year, many settlements had reverted to their Arabic names.

Protests against the suppression of the Berber language and culture continued in the early 1980s. These generally centred on the Kabyle, a region regarded for many years as having dangerously separatist intentions. Although some concessions were made (including the creation of chairs in Berber languages at the universities of Tizi-Ouzou and Algiers and the provision of Berber radio programmes), President Chadli made it clear that he viewed the Berber demands as a threat to national unity. In 1981 a 'cultural charter' was proposed, which made provisions for the Berber culture as part of Algeria's national heritage. However, the charter received little approval; the discussions were accompanied by outbreaks of violence and had to be abandoned. Later, in September, the tension in the Kabyle was alleviated by the announcement that departments of popular literature and dialect were to be opened in Algiers, Constantine, Oran and Annaba (although not in Tizi-Ouzou).

Throughout 1985 there was increased activity among opposition groups. In June Adbennoun Ali-Yahia, the president of the unauthorized Algerian League of Human Rights (ALHR), was arrested for forming an illegal organization, and was imprisoned for 11 months. In July and August further members of the ALHR and the Association of the Sons of Chouhada, another unauthorized organization, were arrested. Clashes broke out in November at Tizi-Ouzou between public order forces and members of the Association of the Sons of Chouhada who were protesting against the arrests of fellow members during the summer. Following the theft of weapons and ammunition from an army barracks at Soumaa in August, several Islamic fundamentalists were arrested. In December 19 of Ben Bella's alleged supporters were imprisoned on charges of threatening state security.

In November 1986 four people were reportedly killed and 186 people arrested during three days of rioting at Constantine, which followed student protests against poor living conditions and inadequate tuition. In other parts of Algeria students and secondary school pupils held demonstrations against government attempts to reform the *baccalauréat* examination. Amid criticism, the 186 detainees were swiftly brought to trial and given severe sentences, ranging from two to eight years' imprisonment. Following the riots, the Chief of Staff of the army, Gen. Mustafa ben Loucif, was discharged from his duties, and lost his deputy membership of the FLN. The ALHR became affiliated to the International League for Human Rights (ILHR) in December, but the leaders of the ALHR were later arrested and exiled to southern Algeria.

In 1987 the Government issued amnesties as part of its liberalization policy. In March 22 people were released from internal exile, including the leaders of the ALHR, and a branch of Amnesty International was established in Algeria. The Algerian League for the Defence of Human Rights (ALDHR) was formed with government authorization in April, as a rival to the illegal ALHR. Following discussions between the Government and the ALDHR, the authorities released 186 people, imprisoned after the Constantine riots, and six members of the ALHR and two members of the Association of the Sons of Chouhada, imprisoned in 1985.

Nevertheless, the authorities continued to act vigorously against any signs of organized opposition which they considered to constitute a threat to the state. In January 1987 security forces shot dead Mustafa Bouiali, the leader, and three other members of the Islamic fundamentalist group responsible for the theft of weapons at Souma in 1985, who had been in hiding for 18 months. In June 12 people received prison sentences ranging from two to 10 years for distributing subversive literature and receiving funds from abroad, particularly from Libya and Ben Bella's ADF. The authorities also banned the leaders of the ALHR from leaving the country to attend a meeting of the ILHR. At the end of a trial in July, involving 202 defendants accused of involvement in the activities of Bouiali's Islamic fundamentalist group, four people received death sentences for plotting against the state, murder, armed attacks and robbery. Other defendants received sentences ranging from life to one year's imprisonment, while 15 people were acquitted. However, during a series of amnesties to commemorate the 25th anniversary of Algerian independence in August, the four death sentences were commuted to life imprisonment, and life sentences were reduced to 20 years in detention.

THE OCTOBER 1988 RIOTS

Boumedienne had insisted upon rigid state socialism controlled by an increasingly ponderous and corrupt bureaucracy and after his death his appointees fought to maintain their grip upon the state and the economy. The FLN had, however, abandoned any pretence to ideology or purpose beyond that of staying in power. In December 1987 Chadli felt secure enough to introduce limited liberalization, giving more freedom to private enterprise and allowing managers in the public sector to make some decisions without reference to the bureaucracy. In June 1988 he went a step further and reorganized the public sector by creating state-sponsored Trust Companies (Fonds de Participation) to which managers were to be accountable. The private sector was also allowed some access to foreign exchange. This economic restructuring was not extended to the political sphere, where the FLN continued to exercise complete control. In his speeches Chadli urged reform but seemed unable or unwilling to implement it.

Algeria had amassed a debt of some $24,000m. and found the annual interest of $6,000m. an almost impossible burden, owing to the depressed price of oil and gas which brought in 97% of the country's foreign exchange. The Government, for reasons of prestige and its unwillingness to accept the intervention of the World Bank, refused to reschedule the debt and instead reduced imports, 70% of which were foodstuffs. These became extremely scarce and expensive. The exposure of the economy to market forces while trying to service the huge debt precipitated an economic crisis. The increasing hardship and the sense of inequality produced a wave of strikes from July onwards.

On the evening of 4 October 1988 as many as 5,000 youths destroyed shops selling luxury goods, and on the following day widespread looting occurred. Government buildings in Algiers were also targets for attack. On 6 October a state of emergency was declared, and a curfew imposed on Algiers. The army, equipped with tanks, was deployed ruthlessly to suppress the disturbances, making no attempt to avoid civilian casualties. Special military courts were also established to punish the rioters. On 10 October Chadli, who had hitherto remained silent, promised to present a programme of reforms for debate when the violence, which had spread to Oran, Annaba and other towns, subsided. On 12 October the tanks were withdrawn. Officials stated that 159 people had been killed during the disturbances, but unofficial estimates indicated at least 500 deaths, while more than 3,500 had been arrested, some of whom were reported to have been tortured. The rioters, some of whom had expressed support for Ben Bella (the first President of the Republic), had called themselves the Movement for Algerian Renewal. They were not Islamic fundamentalists, although fundamentalists did later participate in the disturbances; nor were they Berbers, who had their own grievances. On 15 October schools reopened; on the following day 500 minors, who had been detained, were freed, and the special courts were suspended. Stocks of food were released from warehouses to be sold, often at less than half the previous prices.

CONSTITUTIONAL REFORM

Young people were at the forefront of this uprising against the FLN. Half of the Algerian people in their early twenties were unemployed, and there was widespread anger at the move towards an élitist education system. Little hostility was shown towards Chadli himself; observers noted that the young people recognized his attempts to introduce reforms, despite the opposition of uncompromising elements within the FLN. Chadli exploited this sentiment by attempting to overcome vested interests and achieve reform. On 25 October 1988 he proposed that the identification of the state with the FLN be ended by allowing non-party candidates to contest elections. Furthermore, the Prime Minister would no longer be responsible to the President, who would stand above party politics, but to the National Assembly. To show that these measures would not be merely superficial, five days later Chadli dismissed his official FLN deputy, Mohammad Cherif Messaadia (a resolute opponent of reform, widely regarded as the most unpopular politician in the country), replacing him with the more liberal Abd al-Hamid Mehiri, who had been the Algerian Ambassador to France and Morocco. At the same time the chief of internal security was also replaced. On 3 November the proposed reforms were approved in a referendum by 92.27% of votes cast by 83.1% of those eligible to vote.

On 7 November 1988 Chadli dismissed the Prime Minister, Abd al-Hamid Brahimi, replacing him by Col Kasdi Merbah, who had been chief of police under Boumedienne but had become a liberal Minister of Agriculture, allowing peasants to operate farms without state control, and a reforming Minister of Health. He had more charisma and independence than his predecessor and declared that he would form a cabinet of men of 'integrity, competence and efficiency' answerable to the National Assembly. Merbah announced proposals which laid emphasis on helping the young people, incorporating plans for an increase in expenditure on education, a building programme, wage rises from January 1989, a reduction in the duration of military service and a rise in taxes for the wealthy. Merbah's programme of reforms was submitted to the Assembly and, for the first time ever, the ensuing debate was broadcast live on television. The fact that 21 members of the National Assembly dared to vote against the programme was an even greater departure from precedent.

At the end of November 1988, a special two-day congress of the FLN accepted further reforms. Chadli was endorsed as the sole candidate for the presidency but he divorced himself from the party by relinquishing his post of Secretary-General to Abd al-Hamid Mehiri. It was decided that the FLN should revert to its former role as a forum for competing views, instead of the monolith that it had become under Boumedienne. It was agreed that independent candidates could contest elections, but the formation of other parties was forbidden, in order to exclude the Islamic fundamentalists. In early December Chadli instituted a reorganization of the army, replacing six military commanders. The army, which had played an important role in Algerian politics since independence, had been widely criticized by intellectuals and human rights activists for its violent suppression of the October riots. On 22 December Chadli was elected President for a third term of office, receiving 81% of the votes cast.

In early February 1989 a new draft Constitution was published. It completed the separation of the state from the FLN and permitted the 'creation of associations of a political nature', with certain restrictions. The 'irreversible commitment to socialism' of the previous Constitution was abandoned, while the army was entrusted with the sole task of defending the country and not of 'participating in the building of socialism'. The new Constitution emphasized individual and collective rights rather than those of 'the People' as a whole. Public-sector workers were given the right to strike. Executive, legislative and judicial functions were separated and no longer controlled by the party, but supervised by a Constitutional Council. The new draft was regarded as a complete break with the past, shifting Algeria from the socialist into the Western capitalist group of nations, and it was approved in a referendum on 23 February by 73.4% of votes cast by 79% of the total electorate.

In early March 1989 another significant reform of the political system was implemented. Senior army officers asked to be relieved of their duties as members of the FLN Central Committee, claiming that the army should be concerned exclusively with the defence of 'the superior interests of the nation and the free choice of the people', although it would remain in the background to act as an arbiter if necessary. After the turbulence of the past year, Chadli's task was to maintain control of the process of reform, but the Algerian people took advantage of a loosening of control and started to react against the inadequacy of their living conditions. In April there were demonstrations against sharp rises in food prices, and in May there were strikes and riots in protest against the slow pace of reform and the corrupt practices of local officials. The construction of only about one-third of 90,000 projected dwellings, and the allocation of those through favouritism, led to an outbreak of violence in Souk Ahras in May. Army units were dispatched to the area to control the unrest, but housing conditions also caused the blocking of roads and the seizure of the town hall in Didouche Mourad in September. Another town hall was seized by municipal workers who had remained unpaid for three months. In October more than 1,000 people, deprived of drinking water for several days, rioted in Sidi Aissa. Later in the month, after an earthquake had devastated Nador, roads were blocked as a protest against the slowness of government relief.

In early June 1989 Merbah denied that there had been a breakdown in security, but said that the worst of the crisis, that of the economy, lay ahead. The FLN Central Committee convened a few days later, and pledged to expedite reforms,

but it declared that the party should preserve its leadership role in all spheres of political and economic activity. The IMF granted an unprecedented stand-by credit to Algeria, but urged the adoption of wide-ranging reforms.

TOWARDS MULTI-PARTY ELECTIONS

On 2 July 1989 the National People's Assembly approved a new law on associations, revoking the ban on the formation of political parties (introduced in November 1988). New parties were obliged to be licensed by the Ministry of the Interior, and were not to be externally financed or based exclusively on religious, professional or regional interest. On the same day, the Assembly adopted legislation reducing the role of the state in controlling the economy, thus increasing its exposure to market forces. Later in the same month, the Assembly adopted a new electoral law permitting opposition political parties to contest future elections and to occupy seats in the Assembly. Elections to the Assembly were to be held every five years, with one round of voting, after which the winning list of candidates in each multi-member constituency would take all the seats. For local and municipal elections the new electoral law stipulated that any party obtaining at least 50% of the votes in a multi-member constituency should take all the seats. If no party received 50% of the votes, the party with the largest share was to take one-half of the seats, while the remainder were to be divided proportionately among all the other parties that obtained more than 10% of the total vote. Other legislation, also adopted in July 1989, allowed greater investment in the economy by foreign companies and ended the state monopoly of the press while, controversially, leaving the principal newspapers under the control of the FLN.

In September 1989 President Chadli dismissed the Prime Minister, Col Kasdi Merbah, whom he regarded as insufficiently committed to the process of reform. Merbah was replaced by Mouloud Hamrouche (hitherto a senior official in the presidential office), who immediately declared his determination to end the identification of the party (i.e. the FLN) with the state, and to transform the country by means of dialogue with other political parties, trade unions and the public. In his new Council of Ministers Hamrouche retained only eight of his predecessor's appointees, replacing FLN officials and retired military officers with progressive politicians. Hamrouche abolished the Ministry of Information, which he regarded as incompatible with democracy. His programme, incorporating proposals for defending living standards while 'freeing public and private industry from all forms of obstacles', anti-inflation measures, educational reform, the introduction of free wage-bargaining and the encouragement of investment, was approved by 281 votes to 33 in the National People's Assembly, and endorsed by President Chadli, who declared the process of reform to be irreversible.

In response to a complaint by newly-licensed political parties that they had insufficient time to prepare, local and municipal elections, which had been scheduled to take place in December 1989, were postponed until June 1990. President Chadli welcomed the formation of parties representing all shades of opinion, and by early 1990 more than 20 parties had been formally registered. They included the PSD; the communist PAGS; the FIS; the Berber Rassemblement pour la Culture et la Démocratie (RCD); the Front des Forces Socialistes (FFS), originally founded in 1963; and the strongly Islamic Mouvement pour la Démocratie en Algérie (MDA).

At the end of November 1989 some 5,000 members of the FLN attended an extraordinary party congress, at which the anxiety of many of them at the sudden onset of political pluralism was apparent. Many of the speeches made at the conference expressed regret for the passing of the certainties of the days of Boumedienne, a large number of whose former lieutenants were elected to a new, enlarged central committee. It also revealed that many party members had strong Islamic sentiments. However, President Chadli and his Council of Ministers had not been marginalized in their enthusiastic espousal of political reform: the majority of a new politburo, elected at the end of December, were likewise in favour of change.

The amendments to the Constitution of February 1989 gave public-sector workers the right to strike and they took such advantage of this provision that the number of strikes rose by 25% in the following 12 months, averaging 250 per month. In early 1990 students demonstrated against police brutality. Hundreds of thousands of women demonstrated in favour of the traditional Islamic role of women, after thousands of others had demonstrated against any reversion to such a role. There were reports of assaults on women wearing Western-style clothes, while an estimated 10,000 people in Oran demonstrated in support of the closure of brothels and of establishments selling alcohol. About 50,000 Berbers demonstrated in support of demands for an increase in the teaching of the Berber language.

Meanwhile, the Minister of the Economy, Ghazi Hidouci, expressed pessimism about the country's economic situation, indicating the difficulties of reform and urging all public-sector managers to increase their efforts. In order to stimulate the economy, he announced the ending of the distinction between the public and private sectors—both were now open for investment. In March 1990 a new joint-venture law was announced, foreign banks were permitted to open branches and a powerful new Conseil de Monnaie et de Crédit was created to regulate the inflow and repatriation of capital.

Following a meeting of its central committee in March, the FLN declared itself united. President Chadli even hinted that elections to the National People's Assembly might be brought forward from 1992, as the FIS demanded, and that he might consider 'coexisting' as President with an opposition government. However, the FLN was adversely affected by a statement from the former Prime Minister, Abd al-Hamid Brahimi, in which he alleged that government officials had received $26,000m. ($2,000m. more than the entire national debt) in bribes during the previous 10 years. The situation was hardly alleviated by Prime Minister Hamrouche's objection that the sum could not possibly have exceeded $2,000m. The FLN was further damaged by the allegation of a former government minister, Abubakr Belkaid, that mismanagement of gas development in the 1980s had cost the country $40,000m. in lost revenues; and by the demand of the FLN-affiliated trade union, the Union Générale des Travailleurs Algériens (UGTA), for the abrogation of the law that permitted the establishment of rival unions. Meanwhile, rank-and-file members of the UGTA demonstrated against their leaders, accusing them of corruption, inactivity and subservience to the FLN.

On 19 March 1990 the National People's Assembly approved amendments to the electoral law that had been introduced in July 1989. Under the amended law, a party gaining 50% or more of the votes in a multi-member constituency would no longer take all of the seats, which were to be divided proportionally instead. If no party gained a majority, the party gaining the most votes was to take one-half of the seats. Parties would need to gain only 7% of the total votes cast to achieve representation, rather than 10% as previously. The amendments to the electoral law were regarded as having been introduced to counter the perceived strength of the FIS in the approach to the municipal and local elections. The demands of opposition parties for a further postponement of the elections, so that they would have more time to prepare, were rejected, even though it was apparent that only the FLN and the FIS would be able to present candidates in all of Algeria's 48 *wilayat*. Even the FLN appeared unlikely to be able to contest all 1,539 council seats because in some localities conflicting elements within the party had been unable to agree on a candidate.

On 20 April 1990 thousands of FIS supporters demonstrated in Algiers, demanding that the National People's Assembly should be dissolved within three months and that *Shari'a* (Islamic) law should be introduced. Out of concern that the strength of the FIS constituted a threat to democracy, the RCD organized a pro-democracy demonstration on 10 May, in which tens of thousands were estimated to have participated. The election campaign began officially on 21 May. On the day that it ended, 4 June, the FIS rallied more than 100,000 of its supporters, in front of whom its leader, Abbasi Madani, warned the Algerian army not to attempt a military coup.

At the local elections, held on 12 June 1990, the FIS received some 55% of the total votes cast and obtained a majority of seats in 853 municipalities and 32 *wilayat*, while the FLN,

which obtained about 32% of the votes, retained control of 487 municipalities and 14 *wilayat*. Independent candidates won 11.7% of the votes in the municipal elections, the RCD 2.1% and the Parti National pour la Solidarité et le Développement (PNSD) 1.6%. In the elections to the *wilayat* the RCD gained control in 87 localities, and the PNSD in two.

While the success of the FIS was, to some extent, vitiated by a high rate of abstention—estimated at between 35% and 40%—and by a boycott of the elections by two main opposition parties, the MDA and the FFS—on the grounds that the Government should have held elections to the National People's Assembly first—the scale of the victory that the FIS had achieved was remarkable, even unique, in the Arab world. Some Western observers claimed that it was the first occasion on which any Arab country had been allowed freely to express itself in a multi-party election. It was certainly the first time that an Islamic fundamentalist party had won a majority of the votes on such an election, and this achievement was particularly remarkable in Algeria, which had been widely regarded as one of the most secular, westernized countries in the Arab world.

THE AFTERMATH OF THE MUNICIPAL ELECTIONS OF 12 JUNE 1990

Following its successes in the municipal elections of June 1990, the FIS demanded the dissolution of the National People's Assembly, to be followed by a general election contested by all political parties. At the same time, the FIS denied any aspiration to establish an Iranian-style Islamic republic in Algeria, and that it wished to oust President Chadli. The leader of the FIS, Abbasi Madani, issued a warning to the army not to attempt to rob the party of its victory. Another senior figure in the FIS, Ali Belhadj, claimed that democracy was not an Islamic concept and demanded the introduction of *Shari'a* law in Algeria. From exile, the leader of the MDA, Ben Bella, claimed that the results of the municipal elections were 'an undeniable step forward'. Meanwhile, the Arab world pondered the significance of an overwhelming victory for Islamic fundamentalists in a free election in one of the most westernized Arab states. Tunisia and Morocco were especially alarmed. Some observers, however, thought that Chadli had deliberately given the FIS an opportunity to exercise limited local power so that it could discredit itself through dogmatism and inefficiency and destroy its chances of success in elections to the National People's Assembly.

It was uncertain, indeed, whether the inexperienced administrators of the FIS could implement large, expensive projects to provide housing and jobs and thus make Islamic municipal socialism succeed. There was no reduction in unemployment, and riots erupted in protest at the allegedly unfair distribution of food. Workers went on strike to protest against shortages of food. In November 1990 some 5,000 FIS mayors and councillors marched on the presidential palace to demonstrate against 'politically-motivated' obstruction by government officials.

In the immediate aftermath of its poor performance in the municipal elections, the FLN denounced the use of religion for political ends and sought the co-operation of other political parties to safeguard democracy. The Prime Minister, Mouloud Hamrouche, rejected demands for his resignation and for the dissolution of the National People's Assembly, and promised that the process of reform would continue. However, by early July 1990 it was clear that the FLN was too divided to implement further reforms. Hamrouche and four other government ministers, including the Minister of Foreign Affairs, Sid-Ahmad Ghozali, and the Minister of the Economy, Ghazi Hidouci, resigned from the politburo of the FLN in order to concentrate on affairs of state, distancing themselves from the party, which, Hamrouche believed, should renew itself free of governmental responsibilities. They were replaced in the politburo by young, university-educated professional men, rather than by veterans of the war of independence against France. One such veteran, Ben Khedda, founded a moderate Islamic party, El-Oumma (The Community), with the aim of gradually introducing *Shari'a* law into Algeria, without coercion. Another, Lakhdar Bentobbal, became honorary president of a new National Democratic Conference, in which the RCD, the PAGS and the PSD agreed to collaborate to contest the forthcoming elections to the National People's Assembly. At the end of July, in a reshuffle of the Council of Ministers, President Chadli appointed Maj.-Gen. Khaled Nezzar, hitherto the Chief of Staff of the armed forces, as Minister of Defence. It was the first time since Boumedienne's seizure of power that the office had not been held by the President. In the same month, Chadli announced that elections to the National People's Assembly, which were not due to take place until 1992, would be held during the first four months of 1991. While the President declared that he was confident that Algeria's political parties would 'respect the rules of democracy', the newly-appointed Minister of Defence warned that the army might intervene in the event of unrest. Thousands of political prisoners, most of whom had been incarcerated after the riots of October 1988, were released.

Iraq's invasion of Kuwait in August 1990 had less effect on Algerian domestic politics than it did on those of neighbouring countries, since there was virtually unanimous opposition to the intervention of non-Arab forces in an inter-Arab dispute. The leader of the MDA, Ben Bella, returned to Algeria in September 1990 to a less enthusiastic welcome than had been anticipated. There was no response to his demands for the Government to resign, for the creation of a 'united front', for a reduction in the number of opposition political parties and for unreserved support for Iraq. The Government continued to implement its programme of economic reforms, which included plans to establish a stock market; to 'liberalize' imports; and to make the Algerian dinar fully convertible. It claimed that a market economy, in which state enterprises would be fully autonomous, would be in place within months. The economic reform programme created further, more serious divisions within the FLN. One of the party's founders, the President of the National People's Assembly, Rabah Bitat, resigned, accusing Prime Minister Hamrouche of dismantling the public sector. The former Prime Minister, Abd al-Hamid Brahimi, also resigned from the FLN, complaining of a lack of democracy within the party.

In December 1990 the National People's Assembly passed a vote of confidence in favour of Prime Minister Hamrouche, the first such vote for 20 years. At the end of the month the Assembly approved a law stipulating that, after 1997, Arabic would become Algeria's official language and that the use of the French and Berber languages by private companies and by political parties would thereafter be subject to heavy fines. The new law was regarded as an attack on Algeria's Western-educated élite and the Berber people. In response, some 500,000 people demonstrated in Algiers against religious and political intolerance. The FIS regarded the adoption of the 'Arabization' law as a political triumph, but it no longer enjoyed a monopoly on 'Islamic activism'. There were now two new political parties which aimed to recruit people who were dissatisfied with the intolerance of the FIS and those who saw no incompatibility between Islam and liberal economics. Sheikh Abdullah Djaballah founded the Islamic Renaissance Movement (Nahdah), while Sheikh Mahfoud Nahnah founded Hamas. The FIS, which was also losing support to Ben Bella's MDA, claimed that these new parties had been sponsored by the Government. The FIS itself appeared to be suffering from divisions between Madani and Belhadj. While the latter urged his supporters to prepare to give military support to Iraq, Madani argued that military training should be restricted to the army and that the FIS should achieve power through electoral means.

By early 1991 rising prices and unemployment were widely perceived to be the result of Hamrouche's economic policies. Opponents of the Government accused it of allowing the country to be controlled by the IMF. On 12 and 13 March the UGTA organized a general strike, the first since independence, which was claimed to be 90% effective. In response, Prime Minister Hamrouche announced a wide-ranging programme to improve economic efficiency and to satisfy the demands of the trades unions: child benefits, which had remained frozen for 29 years, were increased by 300% and it was announced that more than $1,500m. (14.5% of the national budget) was to be spent on subsidizing essential commodities in the current financial year.

At the beginning of April 1991 the Government announced that elections to the National People's Assembly would be held on 27 June and, at the same time, proposed some major revisions of the country's electoral law. In constituencies where no candidate achieved an absolute majority in the first round of voting, second ballots were to be allowed. Campaigning in mosques and proxy voting were to be restricted. The number of constituencies was increased from 290 to 542. The FIS regarded all these changes to the electoral law as a deliberate ploy to reduce its chances of victory in the forthcoming elections. It also demanded that a presidential election should be held at the same time as elections to the National People's Assembly.

It appeared that some 40 political parties, including the first 'Green Party' in the Arab world, would contest the elections. However, the PAGS stated that there was insufficient time to prepare for the elections and declined to present candidates. Hamrouche, meanwhile, sought allies among the secular opposition parties and among moderate Muslims, letting it be known that, even in the event of an outright victory by the FLN, he would incorporate opposition leaders into the Government in the interest of national unity. Some 80% of the FLN's deputies in the National People's Assembly were omitted from the party's new lists of candidates.

The leaders of Algeria's Islamic political parties conferred and agreed not to oppose each other's candidates, and that the FIS should provide two-thirds of the Islamic candidates in the elections. However, Madani subsequently renounced this agreement and decided to campaign for changes to the electoral law, while the other Islamic parties attempted to avoid confrontation. When the electoral campaign commenced in May 1991, the founder of El-Oumma, Ben Khedda, announced that his party would not present any candidates, in order to avoid further division among Muslims. Hamas, on the other hand, presented 366 candidates, and the MDA 367. Altogether 5,000 candidates were nominated.

On 23 May 1991 Abbasi Madani appealed for an indefinite general strike in protest at the new electoral law, and demanded President Chadli's resignation. In response to these exhortations, about 40,000 people demonstrated on the streets of Algiers, and violence erupted when the police used tear-gas to disperse the crowds. President Chadli warned that it might be necessary to use force to maintain public order so that the elections could be held. On 4 June the police opened fire on militant Islamic activists, allegedly killing at least five of them, while some 700 people who had taken part in demonstrations were admitted to hospital, suffering from the effects of tear-gas. Other observers estimated that as many as 50 people had died in unrest around the country. On 5 June, after further violent incidents had occurred, President Chadli declared a 'state of siege' and suspended the elections indefinitely. Tanks were deployed on the streets of Algiers, and a curfew was imposed. The army was authorized to ban strikes and 'subversive' literature, and to search buildings and control the distribution of food. In response to the intervention of the army, Madani announced that the FIS had reached an agreement with the Government and, claiming victory, abandoned the general strike.

The agreement between the FIS and the Government seemed to involve the removal of Mouloud Hamrouche, whose resignation had been announced earlier on 5 June 1991, and his replacement, as Prime Minister, by the Minister of Foreign Affairs, Sid-Ahmad Ghozali, who was a practising Muslim and a liberal. Ghozali promised that a presidential election and elections to the National People's Assembly would be held before the end of 1991. On 18 June, after having consulted opposition parties, Ghozali announced his Council of Ministers, which Madani welcomed for its political neutrality. It included two women, 21 newcomers to politics and the first Arab Minister for Human Rights. The new Minister of the Interior, Abd al-Latif Rahal, was a former diplomat with no known political links. Gen. Nezzar retained the defence portfolio, and the army, rather than the Government, remained responsible for security, although its presence on the streets was quickly reduced. Ghozali proposed an ambitious programme of reforms, which included the establishment of a Ministry of Small Business. The National People's Assembly approved the programme by a large majority. On 28 June President Chadli announced his resignation from the FLN, in order to demonstrate the end of one-party rule, and Ben Bella declared that he would contest the forthcoming presidential election.

Tension nevertheless remained high, and there were further outbreaks of violence as the army began to remove FIS symbols which had replaced national insignia on municipal buildings. Caches of weapons were found, and later in June more than 40 people were killed, and over 350 wounded, in violent unrest. Belhadj seemed to be provoking the security forces, demanding their exclusion from parts of Algiers. On the night of 26–27 June 1991 tanks were redeployed on the streets of Algiers, and on 28 June, in his Friday sermon, Madani threatened to declare a *jihad* (holy war) if they were not withdrawn. On 30 June Madani, Belhadj and some 2,500 of their supporters (8,000, according to opponents of the Government) were arrested, and more weapons were seized. There were clashes in several places, ranging from Mostaganem in the west to Guelma on the Tunisian frontier, and in Djelfa on the edge of the Sahara, in which perhaps another 15 people were killed, but by mid-July the army had begun to reduce its presence on the streets and more than half of those arrested had been provisionally released.

Despite pressure from the army, Chadli refused to proscribe the FIS, but on 30 June–2 July 1991 military personnel occupied its headquarters, so paralysing the party's communication network throughout the country. The Prime Minister announced that Madani and Belhadj would stand trial for 'fomenting, organizing, launching and leading an armed conspiracy against the security of the state', accusing them of seeking to establish a dictatorship. At the same time, he stated that general and presidential elections would be held as soon as possible and announced a series of economic liberalization measures to combat 'poverty and misery' and to attract foreign investment. Muhammad Said, the acting leader of the FIS, was arrested while giving a news conference on 7 July, and there were signs of divisions within the party when moderates informed the Prime Minister that they wished to operate within the law. Fewer than 5% of the FIS' supporters responded to an appeal for a political strike, but a delegate conference re-elected Madani as leader of the FIS, and Belhadj as deputy leader.

In July 1991 Ghozali reorganized his Council of Ministers, distancing it still further from the FLN by dismissing the Minister of Justice, Ali Benflis, who had complained of the excessive power of the army. President Chadli severed his own formal connections with the party, and for the rest of the year maintained a low profile while Ghozali took the lead, declaring his readiness to meet representatives of the 51 political parties which by now existed, and to amend the electoral law. At a meeting between the Prime Minister and the political parties—boycotted by the FLN, the FIS, the PAGS and some others—no agreement on electoral reform was reached in three days of discussions, but Ghozali said that it might still be possible to hold elections by the end of November. The meeting was adjourned for three weeks, during which the FLN elected a new politburo, which included the former Prime Minister, Hamrouche, and eight parties, including the MDA and Hamas, presented a joint plan to reduce the number of deputies in the National Assembly and to redraw constituency boundaries. When the meeting was reconvened, Prime Minister Ghozali agreed to these changes in the electoral law. Regarding an election as imminent, the FLN-dominated Assembly rejected a government proposal to reduce food subsidies, thus imperilling negotiations with the IMF. The Assembly also complained that there would be insufficient time to consider new electoral laws, and criticized individual ministers. On 29 September the 'state of siege', declared on 5 June, was repealed. At the same time, Abd al-Qadr Hachani, the last prominent member of the Madani wing of the FIS, was arrested. The Minister of Human Rights stated that there were 357 political detainees awaiting trial in civilian prisons, and 99 held by the armed forces. A national conference of FIS representatives, held on 3 October, declared its aim to establish an Islamic state and its support for the FIS' imprisoned leaders.

On 13 October 1991 the National People's Assembly approved amendments to the electoral law, establishing the number of single-member parliamentary constituencies at 430. (Changes to the electoral law that were adopted in April 1991 had never been implemented.) Other amendments concerned independent candidates, who would in future need to obtain only 300 (rather than 500) supporters of the candidacy; and the minimum age of parliamentary candidates, which was lowered from 35 to 28 years. On 15 October President Chadli announced that the first round of voting in the general election would take place on 26 December, and that a second round of voting would be held on 16 January 1992 in constituencies where there had been no outright winner in the first round. On 16 October Prime Minister Ghozali reshuffled his Council of Ministers, taking charge of the economy portfolio himself, and appointing Maj.-Gen. Larbi Belkheir as Minister of the Interior and Local Authorities, with responsibility for supervising the forthcoming elections.

THE GENERAL ELECTION OF DECEMBER 1991

In October an estimated 60,000 people took part in an anti-FLN march, organized by the RCD, and between 100,000 and 300,000 supporters of the FIS demonstrated for the establishment of an Islamic state without the formality of an election. The FIS threatened to boycott the election unless its leaders were released, but the threat was withdrawn and the party subsequently campaigned on extreme free-market policies, stating that it would end subsidies and state monopolies and allow the dinar to 'float' on foreign exchange markets. Prime Minister Ghozali admitted that the Algerian people were tired of 30 years of FLN rule and that 'the people don't trust us any more. We have lied to them too much'.

The 430 seats in the National People's Assembly were contested by 5,712 candidates representing 49 political parties and more than 1,000 independents. It was forecast that the FIS would obtain more than one-third of the votes (its leaders predicted at least 70%), and the FLN rather less, with the remaining one-third shared among the other parties. In the first round of voting in the general election, in which some 59% of the electorate participated, the FIS took an unassailable lead, winning 188 seats outright, although it had obtained just 3.2m. votes (1.5m. fewer than in the municipal elections) from an electorate of 13.3m. The FFS, led by Aït Ahmad, gained 25 seats, the FLN was humiliated with only 15 seats (although it won about half as many votes as the FIS), and independent candidates gained three seats. The FLN complained of intimidation and malpractice in 340 constituencies in which officials of FIS-controlled municipalities had distributed the voting slips. A second round of voting was required in 199 seats and the FIS needed to win only 20 to gain an absolute majority in the Assembly. Nahdah, Hamas and the El-Oumma instructed their supporters to vote for the FIS against the FLN in the second round. The secular parties failed to declare their support for the FLN: Ghozali described them as ostriches. President Chadli, faced with the choice of cancelling the elections or allowing them to proceed, indicated his willingness to 'cohabit' with an FIS government, but the FIS excluded the possibility of any sharing of power and demanded the appointment of Madani as Prime Minister and the holding of a presidential election. There were demonstrations urging the defence of democracy against an Iranian-style regime, and reports that mass emigration of intellectuals and women would follow an FIS victory.

THE MILITARY TAKE-OVER

On 4 January 1992 the National People's Assembly was dissolved by presidential decree. On 11 January, five days before the second round of the election was due to be held, President Chadli, apparently under intense pressure from military leaders, resigned in order 'to safeguard the interests of the country'. He had failed to persuade either the unemployed to desert the FIS and trust him to implement reforms or the armed forces to accept the inevitable result of the election. According to the Constitution, the President of the National People's Assembly, Abd al-Aziz Belkhadem, should have replaced Chadli on an interim basis for 45 days while a presidential election was held, but, as the Assembly had been dissolved, his status was uncertain. On 12 January the High Security Council, which comprised the Prime Minister, three senior generals and the Ministers of Justice and Foreign Affairs, appointed Abd al-Malek Benhabiles, the Chairman of the Constitutional Council, as acting Head of State (he was apparently unwilling to accept the position on a permanent basis), announced a 'state of exception' and cancelled the second round of the elections. Only a few tanks appeared on the streets, and for two days the FIS leaders remained silent.

On 14 January 1992 a five-member High Council of State (HCS) was appointed to operate as a collegiate presidency until the expiry of Chadli's term of office in December 1993. The leading figure in the Council was clearly Maj.-Gen. Nezzar, the Minister of Defence, but its Chairman was Muhammad Boudiaf, one of the leaders of the War of Independence, who had been in exile in Morocco since quarrelling with Ben Bella in 1964. Although Boudiaf was untainted by the corruption of the old regime, his return was greeted without enthusiasm by the 75% of the population born after he had left the country. The other members of the HCS were the Minister of Human Rights, Ali Haroun, Sheikh Tejini Haddam, the Rector of the Paris Mosque, and Ali Kafi, the long-serving President of the National Organization of Mujahiddin (War Veterans), a member of the FLN establishment. Ghozali, although he remained Prime Minister, was not included. The constitutional legality of the Council was challenged by all the political parties, including the FLN. Both Boudiaf and Ghozali promised that elections would be held within two years.

On the first Friday after the resignation of Chadli, police turned worshippers away from mosques, but, amid claims that there had been 500 arrests, Hachani appealed to his followers not to give the authorities any excuse to massacre them in the streets. He gathered the 188 FIS deputies who had been elected in December 1991 as a 'shadow' Assembly, which demanded a return to legality. The HCS announced that it planned to introduce new rules for political parties and began a desperate pursuit of foreign aid to alleviate the country's economic difficulties.

Violence broke out on 19 January 1992, when a soldier was killed, and two gendarmes wounded, in a machine-gun attack on a police post 20 km from the capital, and later there were clashes at other checkpoints. The HCS started to move against the municipalities, newspapers and mosques controlled by the FIS, banned political speeches and assemblies and rearrested Hachani on a charge of inciting soldiers to desert. The remaining leaders again appealed for dialogue with the HCS, as the police fired on crowds gathering for prayer and hunted dissident prayer-leaders.

On 3 February 1992 the security forces took control of the FIS offices and those of the Islamic Labour Union, arresting a further 122 people, including moderates with whom it might have been possible to negotiate. In running battles in Batna, 14 people were killed as the army fired on demonstrators, and within three days the national total of those killed in clashes with the army exceeded 50. Tejini Haddam withdrew from the HCS, which, on the evening of 9 February, declared a 12-month state of emergency. The Minister of the Interior was empowered to open detention centres in the Sahara (which, within one week, were holding 6,000 people), to order house searches, to ban marches, to close public places, to dissolve local authorities and to order trial by military courts. On the following day Boudiaf, justifying these measures in the name of democracy, announced an economic programme which included plans for the provision of jobs and housing, improved supplies of food and medicines and a campaign against corruption. Opponents of the new regime retaliated by killing eight policemen, two of them inside a mosque. University students rioted, but the FIS abandoned a protest march when confronted by a huge deployment of troops. There were explosions and street battles. Three men who were rumoured to be members of Hezbollah, operating on the fringe of the FIS, were sentenced to death for murder, and in Batna 82 activists were sentenced to up to 20 years' imprisonment. The FIS, which claimed that 150 people had been killed and 30,000 detained since 'the junta' took over, and feared formal dissolution, made another appeal for talks. The FLN, meanwhile, showed signs of moderating its opposition to the new regime.

On 22 February 1992 Ghozali again reorganized his Council of Ministers. Gen. Nezzar and the Minister of the Interior, Gen. Belkheir, retained their places, but several portfolios were eliminated, in favour of 'super-ministries'. An interesting newcomer was Saeed Guechi (a founder member of the FIS who had left the party in June), who became Minister of Professional Training and Employment, while two other new ministers came from Islamic backgrounds. Ghozali announced that Algeria had obtained a loan of nearly $1,500m. from a consortium of 240 banks to refinance the foreign debt. He produced a 100-page action plan to address the country's economic problems: Algeria, which had once exported food, now had to import $2,000m.-worth per year; Algerian industry was operating at about one-half of full capacity because of lack of materials and spare parts; and about 1.5m. people were unemployed. The economy, Ghozali admitted, was in a disastrous state.

On 4 March 1992, at the request of Belkheir, a court ruled that the Government was entitled to dissolve the FIS for 'pursuing by subversive means goals that endanger public order'. Boudiaf promised radical reform, but this could not be introduced hastily. Further discontent followed increases in the price of food that the state radio described as 'breathtaking'; the cost of some items more than doubled in the first days of Ramadan (early March). It was estimated that about 14m. people (out of a population of slightly more than 25m.) were living in conditions of poverty. Bombs were found, local 'incidents' occurred daily, and the universities were closed. Arrests impaired local administration, as the FIS had controlled 32 regional and 853 local authorities, more than 400 of which were dissolved at the end of March. Belkheir announced the official number of dead since January as 103, of whom 31 had been members of the security forces, and estimated the number of arrests at 9,000. Amnesty International expressed concern at cases of torture. The FIS threatened that violence would not stop until a general election was held. The trials of Madani, Belhadj and Hachani were postponed until 27 June, but Muhammad Said was sentenced to 10 years' imprisonment *in absentia*.

THE ASSASSINATION OF BOUDIAF

The constitutional position of Boudiaf was anomalous. Widely respected as a man of integrity but apparently appointed as a figurehead by a junta which had seized power, he began to give indications that he had ideas of his own.

In April 1992 the HCS announced the creation of a National Human Rights Monitoring Centre, under the presidency of Abd ar-Razzek Barra, to replace the former Ministry of Human Rights; its 26 members were to report directly to Boudiaf. A 60-member National Consultative Council (NCC) was also appointed. Under the chairmanship of Redha Malek, it was to meet in the building of the former National People's Assembly and included women, journalists and intellectuals, but failed to find favour with opposition parties. A reference to combating corruption in Boudiaf's first speech was censored, but in April he again showed his serious intentions when Maj.-Gen. Mustafa Beloucif, a former senior defence ministry official who had been mentioned as a possible Head of State, was charged before a military tribunal with the theft of millions of dinars. The HCS also ordered the FIS to surrender its headquarters and other buildings, as well as its newspapers, to the Government. After the loss of an appeal against the dissolution of the party, elements within the FIS advocated armed rebellion. Amid mounting violence, military courts in Ouargla and Blida condemned 16 FIS members to death.

At the beginning of June 1992, after dismissing an appeal by Mouloud Hamrouche for the formation of a national government, Boudiaf attempted to address the people directly, disregarding politicians, by appealing for the establishment of a National Patriotic Rally, with committees in every village and workplace, to prepare the way for a genuine multi-party democracy. Ait Ahmad and other opposition leaders denounced the proposal as a ruse to dragoon the masses into participation. Boudiaf also promised a constitutional review, the dissolution of the FLN and a presidential election. Moreover, he ordered the release of more than 2,000 FIS detainees, although operations against several hundred Islamic radicals in the mountains threatened to provoke civil war, with 700 people, including some 100 police personnel, having been killed in four months. Gen. Nezzar promised 'implacable war', and there were accusations of a 'shoot-to-kill' policy against suspected opponents of the regime. Dissidents threatened to launch a *jihad* and to kill 1,000 policemen and magistrats from the end of June. On 27 June Abbasi Madani and Ali Belhadj were brought before a military court in Blida, accused of aggression and conspiracy against the state. Defence lawyers withdrew from the court, and the trial had to be adjourned until 12 July. Further unrest was expected as a result of a decree which removed subsidies from all basic commodities apart from bread, milk and semolina, while even the prices of these items rose by at least 50%.

On 29 June 1992, while opening a cultural centre in Annaba, Boudiaf was assassinated. Although the event was televised, it was by no means clear whether the assassination was the action of a lone killer or part of a conspiracy. The HCS declared seven days of mourning and cancelled planned celebrations to commemorate the 30th anniversary of independence on 5 July. It also ordered a commission of inquiry into the assassination, which was to announce its findings by the end of July. Islamic extremists applauded the killing but did not claim credit for it, and Boudiaf's widow stated that she did not believe them to have been responsible. Although the assassin had been seized on the spot, the motive for the killing remained a mystery. In December the commission's report was made available to the media with 76 of its 111 pages missing. The conclusion was that the killer had not acted alone but on behalf of an unspecified organization that was increasingly identified with the FLN. One of the demands of those taking part in a demonstration on 22 March 1993, the first permitted for over a year, was for the truth about the murder of Boudiaf to be published. One year later his alleged assassin had still not been brought to trial, while all of those arrested at the same time had been released.

'WAR AGAINST THE ALGERIAN PEOPLE'

The shock of the assassination of Boudiaf did not reduce the violence which had begun within days of the military take-over. Documents found in Oran showed that the police were a particular target of the militants. Senior officers were ambushed with their drivers and sometimes their families. By the end of December some estimates (no official totals have been published) put the number of security men killed since the imposition of the state of emergency at nearly 200, an average of more than four a week: the number of members of the so-called Mouvement Islamique Armé (MIA) who were killed in action seems to have been higher.

Whereas in the towns the MIA operated in small groups, in the mountainous countryside and on the borders of the Sahara they operated at considerable strength, co-ordinated by means of a clandestine radio station and fax machines. An FIS leaflet advocated a campaign of 'sabotage and fire', and power cables were destroyed and government buildings attacked. Some of the guerrillas who took part in these attacks were known to have fought as *Mujahidin* in Afghanistan and others were believed to have received training in Hezbollah camps in Lebanon. In June the Government denied that there had been mass desertions from the army, but admitted that a small number of soldiers had taken refuge in the mountains, where they were hunted by helicopters.

Forts and police stations were ransacked for arms, and the Government was particularly worried about disaffection in the armed forces as it became obvious that military supporters of the MIA remained at their posts to participate in the attacks. In December 79 officers, privates and civilians were charged before a military court in Béchar with attempting subversion in the barracks of Oran and Sidi-Bel-Abbès, and in January 1993 19 of them were sentenced to death. The military court at Béchar, to which foreign observers were not admitted, sentenced a further seven soldiers to death in February. The death toll increased in March when sympathisers let a party of guerrillas into the fort at Boughzoul, where they murdered 18 soldiers; after a hunt lasting a week, the alleged killers were caught and 23 of them killed.

The authorities had already shown themselves sensitive to press coverage of such incidents when, in January, they closed the newspaper *El Watan* and arrested six journalists for 'premature reporting' of the murder of five gendarmes at Laghouat. They stated that security news could only be reported with the 'stamp of the competent services'. Since the announcement of an enabling decree in August, 10 newspapers had already been closed down.

The activities of the MIA were not, however, directed solely against state employees. There were also deliberate attempts to damage the economy by deterring potential foreign investors. The most notorious of these was a bomb attack at Algiers airport on 26 August 1992, in which nine people died and 120 were wounded. The Government denounced the attack as 'War against the Algerian People', promising to respond with 'draconian security'. On the same day, bombs were exploded near airline offices in Algiers and others, later, in Constantine. In September there were more bomb attacks at airline offices, and on the eve of the independence celebration a bomb was found near its centre-piece, the Martyrs' Memorial. The British and US Governments advised their nationals against visiting Algeria, and later the US Embassy sent home the children of its staff. In October two men, an acknowledged leader of the FIS who had headed the office staff of Abbasi Madani and been elected as a deputy for Algiers in December 1991 and an *Air Algérie* pilot, were arrested in connection with the bombing at Algiers airport and in May 1993 54 defendants (26 *in absentia*) went on trial. For a time their lawyers boycotted the court but eventually 38 were condemned to death, bringing the number of death sentences pronounced since the beginning of the state of emergency to about 80.

Before the bomb explosion at Algiers airport, the HCS had offered to close the Saharan detention camps, from which 5,000 of the original 8,000 detainees had already been released before October. Instead, new security laws now came into force. In order to try 'terrorism and subversion', which were very loosely defined, three special courts, from which there was no right of appeal, were set up. Membership of a terrorist organization could be punished by a sentence of up to 20 years' imprisonment, as could selling a firearm. Printing or copying a subversive document could result in a five-year sentence, as could identifying the judges or other officials of the special courts. The age of penal responsibility was lowered from 18 to 16. Reduced sentences were offered to those who surrendered during the following two months, and about 100 took advantage of this partial amnesty.

The number of arrests increased. There were 460 in one fortnight in October 1992 and 60 during a single day in November. Prime Minister Abd es-Salam, who had replaced Ghozali and appointed a new Council of Ministers in July, declared 'total war' on terrorism and stated that the time had come for the state to go on the offensive. A new offence of justifying terrorism was created, punishable by a minimum of five years' imprisonment. Amnesty International was to report a dramatic increase in the use of torture in subsequent months.

On 3 December 1992 new measures were introduced, including the dissolution of local authorities still controlled by the FIS and the appointment of administrators chosen by the Government. Similarly, mosques were forced to accept government-appointed preachers or risk closure. A curfew was imposed in Algiers and the six surrounding districts, where 60% of the entire population of the country lived. In January 1993 three state security courts were established with authority to impose harsh sentences including the death penalty. Later that month the first two Islamic terrorists were executed. Both of them were soldiers, and there was speculation about the extent of support for the Islamic cause within the lower ranks of the Algerian military. According to one report between 500 and 800 junior and non-commissioned officers deserted in the early part of the year. More executions followed, including that of Hocine Abderramane, a close associate of Abbasi Madani, the imprisoned FIS leader. In February the HCS renewed indefinitely the state of emergency which gave the security forces wide-ranging powers of arrest and detention. In May the curfew was extended to 10 further provinces. In April 1993 the HCS announced that since December 1992 211 terrorists had been killed 3,800 arrested and a further 1,100 were being pursued. By the middle of the year some 400 Islamic militants had been killed and another 150 sentenced to death. Yet despite an intense assault by the authorities on militant Islam, the violence continued to escalate. Terrorists targeted not just members of the security forces, but prominent public figures, local government officials, members of the judiciary, intellectuals, journalists, foreign nationals and ordinary civilians. The exiled FIS leadership continued to advocate armed struggle and the elimination of the junta in power and those who influenced it.

In February 1993 the Minister of Defence Maj.-Gen. Nezzar narrowly escaped death when a car bomb exploded, and in March the former Minister of Education, Djilali Liabes, and two members of the Conseil Consultatif National, were killed by gunmen. On 21 August, in one of the most brutal of the attacks, former Prime Minister Kasdi Merbah, his son, brother, driver and one of his bodyguards were assassinated. The Groupe Islamique Armé (GIA), a more radical rival of the MIA, claimed responsibility for the killing but an FIS statement denied any role in the assassination. Merbah had many enemies inside and outside the ruling establishment and there was intense speculation about the true identity of his assassins. Between March and June 1993 six leading intellectuals were murdered, including the well-known writer Tahar Djaout. Others were forced into hiding fearing for their lives. In August Omar Belhouchet criticized the authorities for their failure to protect intellectuals and to stop 'this descent into madness'. There were reports that Islamic militants were increasingly attacking economic targets such as the transport system, gas pipelines and factories, and carrying out arson attacks against schools. According to some observers, terrorist operations intensified from the beginning of August. At the end of September Islamic militants began to target foreign nationals. Two French surveyors kidnapped by an armed gang near Tiaret, one of the strongholds of the GIA, were found dead in late September. The FIS again denied responsibility for these killings. The kidnapping of three French consular officials in early October was reported to have provoked an exodus of some 3,000 foreign residents, including about 2,000 French nationals. The three officials were later released. On 27 October the EU and its member states issued a statement calling on the Algerian authorities to take every possible measure to secure the safety of their nationals. The GIA claimed responsibility for the deaths of several foreign nationals, and warned all foreigners to leave the country by 30 November. By the end of December at least 24 foreigners had been killed and both France and the USA began withdrawing their nationals. Terrorist attacks on foreigners further undermined Algeria's efforts to attract foreign investment, especially in the important energy sector, where international oil companies withdrew staff and delayed exploration programmes. In September the German Government had refused to extradite Rabah Kebir, the main spokesman for the FIS in Europe, and Ossama Madani, son of the imprisoned FIS leader, who had both been sentenced to death *in absentia* for their part in the bomb attack on Algiers airport in August 1992. In a statement on 19 December Rabah Kebir denied that the FIS was responsible for the attacks on foreigners, and declared that all those responsible for the killings in Algeria should be prosecuted.

The mass arrests and other repressive policies had seriously disrupted command structures within the FIS and new hierarchies emerged and attempted to gain control of the Islamic resistance within Algeria. Organizations such as the MIA of Abdelkader Chebouti and the GIA, well established in the Mitidja behind Algiers, and at Tiaret and Sidi-Bel-Abbès in the west of the country, recruited their guerrillas from the ranks of FIS militants but their leaders were unable to impose supreme authority on the armed opposition movement. In an attempt to overcome the disruption of the FIS caused by the arrest of its leaders, and to improve co-ordination between FIS militants in exile and those inside Algeria, in September 1993 a reorganization of the FIS leadership in exile was announced. The new executive was believed to include Rabah Kebir, Ossama Madani, Khareddin Kheraban, Anwar Haddam and Boujenaa Bounoua, representing different factions of the movement. Rabah Kebir, having escaped house arrest and

taken refuge in Germany, had served for some time as official spokesman for the FIS outside Algeria, but his role had been questioned by some FIS members. This new unified leadership was reported to have ordered an intensification of military operations in Algeria, but also to have demanded direct negotiations with the HCS. On 18 October Abbasi Madani, serving a 12 year prison sentence, was reported to be in a critical condition in hospital, after suffering a heart attack. On 28 December Abderrazak Radjam, a spokesman for the banned FIS, called for unity in the Islamic movement and urged Islamic militants to continue their jihad against the Algerian authorities.

Strict controls made it difficult to gauge the attitude of the ordinary population, but on 22 May 1993 demonstrations were officially sanctioned in Algiers, Oran and Constantine. In the capital a crowd, estimated by the organizers at 1.5m. and by others at 100,000, demanded, in what was regarded as a genuine expression of opinion, that there should be no negotiation with terrorists. Over 500 councillors, members of the secularist RCD, resigned in protest at rumours that an amnesty would be granted to Islamic terrorists. A statement by FFS officials that the HCS was using Islamic fundamentalism as a pretext to prolong its hold on power was dismissed. At the beginning of June the HCS urged a 'general mobilization against terrorism', but later in the month Abd es-Salam stated that he favoured dialogue with militants if they were not tainted with 'the cancer of terrorism': the 3m. Algerians who had voted for the FIS were not enemies, but citizens who had voted in good faith.

POLITICS AFTER BOUDIAF

There was speculation that Maj.-Gen. Nezzar would succeed Boudiaf as Chairman of the HCS, but he was not in good health and was apparently unwilling to make too obvious the military's control of the state. After conferring with party leaders (including Ben Bella, Aït Ahmad, Mehiri of the FLN and Sheikh Nahnah of Hamas), another member of the HCS, Ali Kafi, was nominated for the chairmanship on 2 July 1992. An experienced diplomat, Kafi was regarded as a figure-head, a man who enjoyed good relations with the army and who was a political foe of Chadli and Hamrouche. He pledged adherence to Boudiaf's programme, but showed no signs of carrying it out. The Chairman of the NCC, Redha Malek, also became a member of the HCS. One of the first actions of the new regime was to promote five senior officers to the rank of general.

Ghozali resigned on 8 July in order to enable Kafi to appoint his own Prime Minister. He was succeeded by Belaid Abd es-Salam, who, for nearly 20 years after independence, had directed Algeria's oil and industrial policy. On 19 July, after 12 days of consultations, Abd es-Salam appointed a new Council of Ministers. Seven of Ghozali's ministers retained their posts, but Gen. Belkheir, whose management of the aftermath of the Boudiaf assassination had been much criticized, was replaced as Minister of the Interior by Muhammad Hardi, a former Secretary-General of the Ministry of Information, who was believed to have close links with the security services. There were few other significant changes, with Maj.-Gen. Nezzar retaining the defence portfolio and Lakhdar Brahimi that of foreign affairs. Many of the new appointees were unknown technocrats, some of whom had previously served under Abd es-Salam. In October a reshuffle brought in three women and the first private businessman to serve in an Algerian Council of Ministers. In February 1993, in a more significant reshuffle, the professional diplomat Lakhdar Brahimi was replaced by Redha Malek—who had previously been engaged in negotiations with the non-Islamic opposition—as Minister of Foreign Affairs. He was said to have been given charge of the ministry as a friend of the new US Secretary of State and because Abd es-Salam wished to exert more control over foreign affairs. After a year in office, the Prime Minister was unpopular, accused of being authoritarian and of seeking a return to the rigidities of the Boumedienne era: his long-term position was considered to be insecure.

The trial of Madani, Belhadj and other FIS leaders was held in July 1992, although the defendants boycotted the proceedings in protest at the exclusion of foreign observers.

After two former Prime Ministers, Hamrouche and Ghozali, had testified, the court rejected the prosecution's demand for life imprisonment and pronounced sentences of 12 years' imprisonment instead. The verdict was greeted with immediate protest demonstrations and henceforward all government hints of readiness to negotiate with the FIS were met with the demand that the prisoners first be released.

The struggle to maintain itself in the face of armed resistance and the parlous state of the economy gave the HCS little opportunity to concentrate on other major problems—ending corruption and securing popular support. Many feared the influence of a corrupt 'mafia' of past and present officials. In November the Minister of Justice, Abd el-Hamed Mahi-Bahi, suspended several senior officials, including the Prosecutor-General; the President of the court of Mostaghanem, who was Chairman of the Judges' Syndicate; and other officials who had been appointed under the Chadli regime. There were rumours that he had been obstructed in his attempt to investigate official embezzlement as well as the murder of Boudiaf. The dismissed officials were also said to have helped the military against the FIS, and a fortnight later, despite the reported support of Kafi and Abd es-Salam, Mahi-Bahi was dismissed and the suspended officials reinstated. However, in December 10 special magistrates were appointed to tackle corruption and in February 1993 Gen. Beloucif was sentenced to 15 years' imprisonment and confiscation of property for the theft of $6.4m.

In his first public statement Abd es-Salam had refused to set a deadline for new elections, citing the need to revise the electoral rolls and to devise a procedure to eliminate the possibility of another victory for the FIS. Nothing more was heard of Boudiaf's project of a National Patriotic Rally. Kafi, in his first public address, stated that he was aiming for a democratic system based on consensus, and in a speech on the anniversary of the beginning of the War of Independence he promised to rebuild a modern, efficient state based on social justice. He blamed mismanagement in the Chadli era, referred to in the official press as 'the black decade', for poverty and inflation. At about the same time Abd es-Salam said that there was no possibility of elections taking place until the economy had recovered, and that such a recovery would take at least three years. On the anniversary of the take-over by the military Kafi promised that a new Constitution would be drafted after consultation with groups not pledged to violence and that it would be pluralist and allow genuinely democratic elections. There would be a referendum on the balance of power between the President and the Government. Regarded as a further pretext for postponing elections, this proposal was greeted with scepticism as the largest political party, the FIS, was still banned and the second largest, the FFS, refused to have any contact with the regime, accusing the HCS of using instability as an excuse for retaining absolute power. The moderate Islamic Hamas hesitated, advocating involvement of the less extreme members of the FIS, while the Berber RCD refused to commit itself. In March 1993, however, talks got off to a hesitant start, with Kafi meeting representatives of the War Veterans, of whom he was still President, and representatives of the FLN. A presidential communiqué stated that the talks had focused on enlarging and strengthening the NCC, on possible formulae for a 'transition' period, on the amendment of the Constitution to establish a better balance between the authorities and on the rationalization of institutions. On 9 May Kafi promised a referendum before the end of the year on how a return to democracy should be managed and, after briefing from Ali Haroun and Redha Malek, the Algerian press forecast that this would take place in October. At the same time it forecast the reduction of the HCS to three members (a President and two Vice-Presidents), an enlargement of the NCC from 60 to 300 members and an increase of its powers. Later in June the HCS announced that it would dissolve itself in December 1993, as originally proposed, and that there would follow a period of not more than three years by the end of which modern democracy with a free market economy would have been created. Detailed proposals on how this was to be brought about would be discussed at a future national conference.

In July Maj.-Gen. Khaled Nezzar, who had been reported to be suffering from poor health for some time, was replaced as Minister of Defence by Gen. Lamine Zérroual, although Nezzar remained a member of the HCS, and Gen. Muhammad Lamari, who since September 1992 had been responsible for organizing anti-terrorist units, was appointed Chief of Staff. These changes were preceded by a series of promotions of officers close to the HCS leadership including Muhammad Ghenim, Secretary General of the Ministry of Defence, Muhammad Mediene, the security chief, Mohamed Touati and Abdelmajid Taghit, councillors at the Ministry of Defence and Ahmed Gaid, military commander of the Oran region, all promoted to Major-General.

On 21 August the HCS appointed the Minister of Foreign Affairs, Redha Malek, as Prime Minister in place of Belaid Abd es-Salam. Malek remained a member of the HCS. There had been speculation about the departure of Abd es-Salam since July and both the French and the US Governments, it was reported, had favoured the appointment of Malek. It was not until 4 September that the new Prime Minister announced his Government, and the delay was thought to reflect the deep divisions within the ruling establishment. Unlike his two predecessors, who had both assumed simultaneous responsibility for the economy portfolio, Malek, a former career diplomat, had no experience of economic affairs. He appointed Mourad Benachenhou, a former Algerian representative at the World Bank, as Minister of the Economy, signalling a return to the reform programme. During a speech as his Government was inaugurated, Malek declared 'We will go to a free market economy with pragmatism, taking into account the particular needs of our society' (see Economy). He also made it clear that he would maintain a hard line against Islamic militancy. The Minister of Defence and Chief of Staff appointed in July retained their posts, and a senior army officer, Col. Sélim Saadi, a former regional military commander who had held a number of ministerial posts in the early 1980s, was appointed as Minister of the Interior. It was thought that the military had instigated the replacement of the outgoing Minister of the Interior, Muhammad Hardi, a civilian, by a senior army officer, and that Saadi's appointment followed consultations with the senior officer corps over government policy on security. His appointment accelerated the reorganization of the security forces and the creation of a unified command between the military and police forces in order to combat Islamic violence. A diplomat, Muhammad Salah Dembri, was appointed Minister of Foreign Affairs, and Ahmed Benbitour was promoted to Minister of Energy. Twelve ministers remained from the Abd es-Salam Government, including Mokdad Sifi, the Minister of Equipment, and Tahar Allan, Minister of Posts and Telecommunications. Despite strong denials in Algiers, there were rumours of contacts between the HCS and exiled leaders of the FIS through intermediaries such as former President Ahmed Ben Bella, who was reported to have met Rabah Kebir and Anwar Haddam in Spain in late September.

GENERAL ZÉRROUAL BECOMES HEAD OF STATE

The mandate of the HCS was scheduled to expire on 31 December 1993, and in October the formation of an eight-member National Dialogue Commission (NDC) was announced, which was to organize a gradual transition to an elected government. Three generals were appointed to the commission, Muhammad Touati, a councillor at the Ministry of Defence, Maj.-Gen. Tayeb Derradji, Inspector Gen. of land forces, and Gen. Ahmed Senhadji, Director-General of military infrastructure, bringing the military openly into the political process for the first time. But little progress was made by the NDC in its negotiations with opposition parties about the creation of a transitional regime. Leading opposition figures such as Hocine Ait Ahmed of the FFS and Ahmed Ben Bella of the MDA withdrew from the negotiations, and both military and political leaders in the ruling establishment remained divided about overtures to the banned FIS. On 19 December the HCS issued a statement indicating that it would not disband itself until a new presidential body had been inaugurated. It proposed to hold a national dialogue conference on 25 and 26 January 1994 to choose a new collective leadership. The NDC recommended that FIS members who renounced violence and criminal activities should be allowed to participate, although the proscription of the party itself would remain in force. This approach appeared to have the support of some senior officers, while others, such as the Chief of Staff, Maj.-Gen. Muhammad Lamari, were firmly opposed to it. Some politicians also rejected negotiation with the FIS, including Said Saadi of the RCD, who some observers expected to play a leading role in the conference. In response to the HCS statement, Rabah Kebir declared that there could only be dialogue if all political prisoners were released and the decrees imposing a state of emergency were revoked. The imprisoned leader, Ali Belhadj, had ordered that the FIS should have no contacts with the military-backed regime.

A draft document circulated by the HCS to parties before the national dialogue conference recommended a three-man presidency to replace the HCS and rule during a transitional period from 1994-96. The document also suggested the creation of a new Consultative Assembly of some 180 members, who would be appointed rather than elected, and referred to the need to 'widen the dialogue' during the transition period. On 19 January 1994 the Government announced the release of almost 800 political prisoners held in two Saharan detention camps. In a statement to *Radio France Internationale* on 20 January, exiled FIS leader, Rabah Kebir, welcomed the release of the detainees but stated that it was not enough and demanded the release of all political prisoners, beginning with the FIS leadership.

In the event none of the main political parties, with the exception of the moderate Islamic party, Hamas, participated in the national dialogue conference in late January. Efforts to persuade a few FIS members to participate failed and even the FLN and the RCD boycotted the meetings. There were threats of violence from the GIA against anyone participating in the conference. The two-day meeting, which it had been hoped, would end the violence, was an abject failure. Exiled FIS leader, Rabah Kebir, described the event as 'a serious defeat' for the military-backed regime. Faced with a boycott by the leading political parties, the HCS had turned to Abdelaziz Bouteflika, Boumedienne's Minister of Foreign Affairs, as their first choice for the new Head of State, hoping that an internationally-known leader would command widespread support in the country. Bouteflika, however, declined the offer and is reported to have returned to Europe before the conference ended. A conflicting source, however, suggested that Bouteflika's candidature was contested—he had many enemies within the ruling establishment—and then rejected, representing a major defeat for the Nezzar, Belkheir, Gheziel and Mediene faction, which had nominated him. Subsequently the HCS named the Minister of Defence, Gen. Lamine Zérroual, as Head of State and he was inaugurated on 31 January. The idea of a collective leadership with two vice-presidents was abandoned. An eight-man Higher Security Committee, mainly composed of senior army officers, is believed to have played an important part in Zérroual's selection. There was speculation that the Higher Security Committee would remain in existence to 'advise' on security matters. The NDC endorsed plans for a three-year transitional period leading to presidential elections and the appointment of a 180-member Transitional National Council to promote political consensus.

On his appointment as Head of State, Zérroual retained the defence portfolio and the Cabinet under Redha Malek remained unchanged. In his first public statements the new President called for 'serious dialogue' to find a solution to the country's crisis and emphasized that the role of the army was to build 'national consensus'. In early February he declared that Algeria's problems could not be overcome only by addressing security issues, but that solutions had to be found to the country's economic and political difficulties. In response to General Zérroual's appointment, the FIS leadership issued statements which called on militants to limit their targets to members of the security forces rather than foreign nationals and Algerian civilians. Youcef Khatib, President of the NDC, admitted that it had contacts with FIS members inside the country and that these took place with the approval of the imprisoned leadership. The release at the end of February of Ali Djeddi and Abdelkader Boukhamkham, who represent the second tier in the FIS leadership below Madani, Belhadj and

Hachani, was interpreted as an attempt to conciliate the FIS. But the FIS reaction remained contradictory. On 1 March it was declared that Djeddi and Boukhamkham had been released 'against their will'. Earlier in the year Anwar Haddam, one of the exiled leaders of the FIS based in the USA, described the radical GIA as 'the principal armed branch of the FIS'. In the past the FIS had tried to avoid overt support for the violent attacks perpetrated by armed Islamic groups. At the end of March, Mihoub Mihoubi, the presidential spokesman, told the official Algérie Presse Service that Zérroual had met imprisoned Islamic leaders and obtained their assurance that the campaign of violence would end. According to the FIS, Zérroual had initiated contact with their movement at the end of 1993 before he became Head of State.

In March there were rumours of divisions within the military over Zérroual's efforts to establish dialogue with the Islamic opposition. After reports that dialogue with the FIS could endanger the unity of the armed forces and that a growing number of army officers were unhappy with Zérroual's overtures to the Islamic opposition, Gen. Lamari, the Chief of Staff, felt it necessary to issue a statement on 19 March reaffirming the army's confidence in Zérroual and 'his delicate mission'. It was also reported that Lamari had been given new powers confirming his position as number two in the new regime. In addition, *Asharq al-Awsat* reported that a number of senior officers believed to have opposed Lamari's appointment as Minister of Defence in January had been removed from their posts.

On 11 April Redha Malek resigned and Zérroual appointed Mokdad Sifi, the Minister of Equipment, as Prime Minister. Malek was known to be opposed to any compromise with the Islamic militants. He resigned the day after the Government had finally agreed a new accord with the IMF opening the way for a debt rescheduling, a move that was certain to provoke new tensions within the ruling establishment. The appointment of Sifi, a civil servant and technocrat, as Prime Minister, was interpreted by some observers as a move by Gen. Zérroual to increase his own direct involvement in government. Sifi stated that his priorities would be the consolidation of state institutions, respect for the national and international commitments of the state and the promotion of 'national unity'. When he announced his new Government on 15 April only 12 ministers retained their portfolios and the majority of those appointed were technocrats or senior civil servants. Changes included the departure of Sélim Saadi, a hard-line opponent of the Islamic militants and a close associate of Redha Malek, from the Ministry of the Interior and the return of Sassi Lamouri to the highly sensitive Ministry of Religious Affairs. Saadi's replacement as Minister of the Interior was Abderrahmane Meziane Cherif, a former Governor of Algiers. Three ministers with responsibility for implementing the government's difficult economic programme demanded by the IMF accord, were Ahmed Benbitour, who was moved from industry and energy to become Minister of the Economy, Mourad Benachenhou, transferred to head the new Ministry of Industrial Restructuring and Participation, and Amar Mekhloufi, appointed Minister of Industry and Energy.

In May, in what was seen as an initiative of the President to strengthen his authority, Zérroual effected some major changes to senior posts in the military. Maj.-Gen. Khalifa Rahim was replaced as land commander by Maj.-Gen. Ahmed Gaid, believed to be a close associate of Zérroual. A new head of the air force was appointed and there were changes to five out of the six *wilayat* or regional commanders. In the same month Zérroual inaugurated the Conseil National de Transition (CNT) an interim legislature of 200 appointed members, which was supposed to provide a forum for debate until legislative elections were held. Abdelkader Ben Salah was subsequently elected President of the CNT. Of the main political parties, only the 'moderate' Islamic party, Hamas, agreed to participate and was allocated five seats. Most of the 21 parties that agreed to take part were virtually unknown. Some 22 seats were set aside for the major parties, a gesture which seemed unlikely to encourage their participation in the new body which became the target of ridicule in the media.

Also in May, in a move to promote dialogue with the Islamic militants and with other opposition groups, Zérroual appointed a group of six 'independent national figures'. They included former President Ahmed Ben Bella, Colonel Tahar Zbiri, the leader of a failed coup against Boumedienne in 1967, Colonel Muhammad Yahiaoui, a contender for the presidency after the death of Boumedienne, Haji Ben Alla, the former Speaker of the National Assembly, and two well-known socialists from the Boumedienne period, Muhammad Said Mazouzi and Ahmed Mahsas. The group was reported to have made contact with the two FIS leaders released in March, Ali Djeddi and Abdelkader Boukhamkham, but little progress appeared to have been made.

In August 1994 members of the FLN, PRA, MDA, Nahdah and Hamas participated in national dialogue with the Government; the FFS, Ettahaddi and the RCD boycotted the meetings. A further meeting held on 5 September focused on two letters sent to the President by Abbasi Madani, which, according to Zérroual, offered a 'truce'. In the letters Madani called for the rehabilitation of the FIS, the lifting of the state of emergency, and a general amnesty before negotiations could take place. In mid-September Madani and Belhadj were released from prison and placed under house arrest; three other leading Islamist militants were also freed. On 19 September the Secretary of State for National Solidarity and the Family, Leila Aslaoui, resigned in protest at their release. The FIS, however, did not join the next round of national dialogue on 20 September as Madani argued that the FIS would first have to consult with its local leadership. There was speculation that the mainstream FIS leadership would be unwilling to negotiate anything less than an FIS Government and doubts that it could actually deliver an effective cease-fire given the rivalry between the two main elements of the guerrilla resistance, the GIA and MIA. Demonstrations in Algiers against political violence in March and May did not attract more than 50,000 people, and a march organized by the RCD on 29 June was disrupted by two explosions which injured some 60 people. A general strike was staged on 21 September in the Kabyle as Berber activists protested at the prospect of national talks with Islamic fundamentalists, and demanded the official recognition of the Berber language. The Berber RCD urged a boycott of the start of the school year because the Berber language was not included in the syllabus, and announced that it was to set up vigilante groups.

THE DIRTY WAR

Despite the talk about dialogue, the first months of Zérroual's presidency were marked by escalating violence in which the barbarous acts reported recalled the worst days of the struggle for independence. Certain towns such as Blida, Médéa, Tiaret and Chlef and entire neighbourhoods in some of the cities were virtually controlled by Islamic militants. Islamic attacks on government officials, judges, politicians, intellectuals, journalists, and teachers continued while the murder of more foreign nationals led several countries to advise their citizens to leave. In early February Muhammad Touali, a member of the former communist Ettahadi party was killed, and in May Laïd Grine, a founder member of the Rassemblement Arabe-Islamique, a small moderate Islamic party, was murdered by unidentified assassins. A new underground group emerged in February, the Force Islamique du Djihad Armé (FIDA) and claimed responsibility for the death of a French bookshop owner in February, and in March that of Ahmad Asselah, the director of the Institut National des Beaux Arts. Between March and May nine foreign nationals were killed, including a French nun and priest. At the end of March, Alain Juppé, the French Minister of Foreign Affairs, advised all French citizens whose presence was not essential to leave the country because of the deteriorating security situation. The USA, the United Kingdom and Spain had already advised their nationals to leave. At the end of March the French Ministry of Foreign Affairs announced that it was closing all French schools and cultural centres, except for the Lycée Decartes at Staoueli outside Algiers. Claude Pierre, the head of the French community in Algeria, stated that the closures marked 'the end of a French presence in Algeria'. Japan also advised its nationals in Algiers to leave and cancelled all visits by Japanese busi-

nessmen to the capital. Attacks by armed Islamic groups on the security forces included an assault on the high security Tazoult prison near Batna in March, which resulted in the release of more than 1,000 political prisoners. There were reports in the French press that armed Islamic groups had become heavily involved in drug trafficking, the proceeds of which helped to finance much of their activities. Youth associations expressed concern at the increasing use of hard drugs, such as cocaine, by young Algerians in some cities.

The security forces intensified their campaign against the armed Islamic groups and resorted to air attacks, using napalm, punitive raids, torture and psychological warfare in their efforts to eradicate the militants. According to figures compiled by Agence France Presse, more than 600 alleged terrorists were killed between mid-March and mid-May, an indication of the scale of operations mounted by the security forces during the first half of 1994. At the end of February the security forces claimed a major success when they killed Djafar al-Afghani, the leader of the radical GIA. The GIA's *majlis ash-shura* or leadership council, immediately declared Abu-Abdallah Ahmad to be the group's new leader, condemned all negotiations with the regime and warned the authorities that it would intensify the fight against them. In January the US human rights organization, Middle East Watch, condemned both the military-backed regime and the Islamic militants for human rights abuses. Their report claimed that, during 1993, Algeria had carried out the highest number of judicial executions for politically motivated offences of any Arab state except Iraq.

In July 1994 the Ambassadors of Oman and Yemen in Algiers were kidnapped by members of the GIA but were subsequently released unharmed. In September the GIA claimed responsibility for the deaths of most of the 60 foreign nationals since September 1993, and official estimates indicated that 10,000 people had been killed since February 1992. A communiqué issued by the GIA on 15 September 1994 threatened reprisals if the FIS entered into dialogue with the Government; the following day 16 civilians were found decapitated, allegedly by fundamentalist groups. In mid-September two journalists were killed and a popular Berber singer, Lounes Matoub, was kidnapped by the GIA. The GIA claimed responsibility for the killing of one of Algeria's most popular singers, Cheb Hasni, in late September, signalling the opening of a new front in the GIA's battle with secular society. Matoub Lounes was released on 10 October with a message from the GIA seeking Berber support in opposing national dialogue.

FOREIGN RELATIONS AFTER THE 1992 COUP

The resignation of President Chadli and the blocking by the military of any advance towards a parliamentary system had no adverse effect on Algeria's international relations. In those Arab countries that had their own problems with Islamic fundamentalists it was generally welcomed. Soon after the coup the Minister of Foreign Affairs, Lakhdar Brahimi, visited the Arabian (Persian) Gulf to explain the motives behind it and to draw attention to his country's economic plight. Later Maj.-Gen. Nezzar went there to discuss co-operation on security matters. At a meeting of Arab Ministers of the Interior in Tunis in January 1993, Algeria, Egypt and Tunisia attempted to convince the other participants that terrorism resulting from extremism was a common concern. Egypt also took steps to ensure that Algeria was fully supportive of Washington peace initiatives. Only with Sudan did relations become strained as Algeria accused it of providing training for at least 500 Islamic guerrillas: the Algerian ambassador was recalled from Khartoum in December 1992. In late August 1994 the Heads of State of Algeria and Sudan met for the first time since the incident, marking the resumption of Sudanese-Algerian relations.

Iran had previously warned that force should not be used against the FIS, and declared the postponement of the second round of voting in the general election to be illegal. Prime Minister Ghozali claimed that he had evidence that Iran had given financial support to the FIS and that it had otherwise interfered in Algeria's internal affairs. Iran denied this but maintained its criticism of the Algerian Government, which continued to accuse it of financing terrorists. As a protest,

Algiers reduced its embassy staff in Teheran in November 1992 and severed relations completely in March 1993.

Algeria's North African neighbours did not disguise their relief that a possible fundamentalist take-over had been averted. Tunisia was one of the first countries to welcome the return to Algeria of Muhammad Boudiaf and frequent exchanges of visits and a ministerial declaration in April 1992 showed how closely the two Governments were co-operating.

Relations with Morocco fluctuated. Under Boudiaf, who had long been resident in that country, Algeria reduced still further its support for the Polisario Front, and collaborated in security matters, sending Gen. Belkheir to Marrakesh in March. Subsequently, however, relations deteriorated to the extent that, in January 1993, King Hassan stated that it would have been better if the FIS had been allowed to take power in Algeria. There were angry press exchanges and localized disputes over traffic temporarily closed the frontier. Later in the month, however, a long-overdue exchange of ambassadors took place and it was announced that work would start on the gas pipeline across Morocco to Spain, which was of prime economic importance to both countries. Border posts were reopened and aid to the Polisario Front, which had initially increased under Abd es-Salam, appeared to have been reduced again. In June 1993 the Minister of the Interior, Muhammad Hardi, said that he hoped that even long-standing frontier problems would be solved before the end of 1993. On 26 August 1994 Morocco imposed entry visas on Algerian nationals following the killing of two Spanish tourists in a Moroccan hotel which Moroccan authorities blamed on Algerian extremists. Algeria reciprocated on 27 August, imposing entry visas on Moroccan nationals and temporarily closing the Algerian land border with Morocco. In mid-September tensions between the two countries eased slightly when Algeria announced the appointment of an ambassador extraordinary to Morocco.

The instability of the region paralysed the UAM despite efforts by the Mauritanian and Tunisian Prime Ministers to revitalize it. Kafi's first visit abroad was to Nouakchott, Mauritania, for the UAM November summit which King Hassan of Morocco did not attend. In May 1992 Boudiaf informed a Libyan envoy that Algeria, while deploring Western coercion of Libya over the Lockerbie affair (see chapter on Libya), was not prepared to risk flouting the economic sanctions that the UN had imposed.

Gen. Zérroual attended the sixth UAM summit in Tunis in early April 1994, at which Algeria assumed the UAM presidency for the next twelve months. At the meeting Zérroual expressed Algeria's commitment to working towards Maghreb unity and his country's solidarity with the 'the sufferings of the fraternal Libyan people as a result of the continuation of the blockade'. Several new accords to promote regional co-operation were signed but the threat from militant Islam and the effect of UN sanctions on Libya suggested that, as in the past, little real progress would be made. Talks with President Ben Ali of Tunisia after the UAM meeting focused mainly on security issues.

The need for foreign investment dominated Algeria's relations with the developed world and brought some useful dividends. In October 1992 a 20-year contract to supply gas was signed with Italy, following the signing of one with Spain. Japan made two loans to SONATRACH and in February it signed a contract to develop Saharan gas. Contracts were also signed with Portugal, Belgium and the USA and diplomatic relations established with Croatia, a possible customer for gas carried via the pipeline across Italy, for which the EC provided credits. In January British Petroleum had obtained a concession to prospect for gas in 6,000 sq km of the Tellian-Atlas and the company appeared to be making Algeria its principal base in the area. Fear of offending a western government muted Algerian criticism of Germany's failure to extradite the FIS leader, Rabah Kebir.

Despite rumours that France, worried about the possibility of a fundamentalist Algeria, had prior knowledge of the military coup, and that it had even promised asylum to its leaders should it fail, the French Government disapproved of the subsequent harsh repression and did not wish to be identified too closely with an anti-Islamic Government. It was not until January 1993 that a senior figure, Roland Dumas, French Minister of Foreign Affairs, went to Algiers, where he admitted that there had been a widening gap between the two countries. However, he had 'very friendly and useful' talks with Kafi and, declaring that France wished to participate in the modernization of Algeria, he announced that it would grant commercial credits of 5,500m. francs. On 22 June, after a visit to Paris by Redha Malek in the course of which he met both the French President and the Prime Minister, the French Government pledged to help Algeria to combat 'terrorism'.

After the right-wing Government of Edouard Balladur took office in early 1993, France became Algeria's leading supporter in the West and lent its political and economic backing to the military regime in its struggle to eradicate the Islamic underground and manage its severe economic problems, notably the burden of the country's large external debt. The French police continued to prosecute FIS cells in France which were accused of providing funds and weapons for the Islamic underground in Algeria. Following the killing of five French embassy employees by suspected Muslim guerrillas at an embasssy housing compound in Algiers in August 1994, 26 Algerian Muslim fundamentalists were interned in northern France, most of whom were expelled to Burkina Faso. In September the French Embassy in Algiers confirmed the closure of its visa section, announcing that entry visas would only be issued in exceptional cases. There was speculation, however, that the Clinton administration in the USA was adjusting its policy towards Algeria and that, in order to avoid the mistakes made in Iran, it was preparing for a possible Islamic regime to assume power there in the future. Giving evidence to the House of Representatives' Foreign Affairs Committee, the acting Secretary of State for Near Eastern Affairs, Mark Parris, argued that the regime in Algeria had to find ways of bringing 'disaffected elements of the populace' into a process that would put the country on a new democratic course. He admitted that US officials had held talks with exiled FIS officials and maintained that the FIS was not responsible for terrorist acts perpetrated by the GIA and other militant groups; some of these groups were competing with the FIS for power. In June President Clinton confirmed that there had been low-level contacts between US officials and the FIS in the USA and Germany and stated that his administration was not opposed to some form of power sharing between the Zérroual regime and 'dissident groups who are not involved in terrorism'.

The unstable state of the Sahara had implications for Algeria. In September 1992 a group of 53 armed dissidents from Niger was rounded up and later 3,500 illegal immigrants were returned to that country. In November some bandits from Mali were arrested and in December an agreement was signed with the Malian Government to return an estimated 25,000 refugees in an operation financed by the International Fund for Agricultural Development.

Economy

Revised for this edition by RICHARD I. LAWLESS

Algeria covers an area of 2,381,741 sq km (919,595 sq miles), of which a large part is desert. At the census of February 1977 the population (excluding Algerians abroad) was 16,948,000. At the census of April 1987 the population had reached 23,038,942, in addition to about 1m. Algerians living abroad (mainly in France). In early 1993 the population was estimated at 26.6m. and, according to projections by the Office National des Statistiques, will have risen to 32.5m. by the year 2000. About 51% of the population reside in rural areas, but some 100,000 peasants migrate every year to the towns in search of work. Between 1967 and 1977 about 1.7m. people moved from the countryside to the towns. The largest towns are Algiers or el-Djezaïr, the capital (estimated population 2.6m. in 1987, including suburbs), Oran or Ouahran (590,000, excluding suburbs) and Constantine or Qacentina (438,000, excluding suburbs). According to UN estimates the population was increasing at an annual rate of 2.72%, and the birth rate was 35.5 per 1,000, between 1985 and 1990. The Office National des Statistiques, however, has stated that the birth rate in 1991 was 3.01%, with some 773,000 births recorded in that year. About 60% of the population are less than 19 years of age. In an effort to reduce the flow of peasants to the towns, the Government introduced a series of measures to stimulate the rural economy. According to government figures, the urban population increased by 4.8% annually in the period 1977–87. For administrative purposes, the country is divided into *wilayat* (departments). In December 1983, 17 new *wilayat* were created, bringing the total to 48.

Algeria has varied natural resources. In the coastal region are fertile plains and valleys, where profitable returns are made from cereals, wine, olives and fruit. However, the remainder of the country supports little agriculture, though in the mountains grazing and forestry produce a small income, and dates are cultivated in the oases of the Sahara. Mineral resources, in particular petroleum and natural gas, are abundant and dominate Algeria's export trade.

GOVERNMENT STRATEGY

After independence in 1962, Algerian governments sought to promote economic growth as a foundation for a future socialist society. They acquired either a complete or a controlling interest in most foreign-owned companies. In 1966 the Government nationalized foreign-owned mines, land which had been abandoned by Europeans at independence, and insurance companies. In 1971 it assumed control of the hydrocarbon sector.

The need to increase the production and distribution of consumer goods persuaded the Chadli Government to initiate a policy of gradual economic liberalization. Heavy industries remained under the control of state-owned enterprises, while the private sector was allowed to participate in the consumer-oriented light industries. About one-half of private light industrial firms were in the textile and leather sectors. From 1981, in an attempt to increase productivity and efficiency, more than 90 of Algeria's giant state corporations were reorganized into some 300 more specialized units, many with decentralized management away from Algiers. In March 1982 the Government published a new investment code, intended to encourage private savings and business in non-strategic fields such as shops, bars, restaurants, hotels, housing, small handicrafts and some light industry. In April a new law on private joint ventures included tax concessions for foreign partners. In the same year, some import procedures were simplified to facilitate urgent projects. The regulations for the repatriation of profits were clarified in 1984, but foreign companies were reluctant to commit themselves to the terms of the offer. Following the enactment of new legislation in December 1987, state-controlled enterprises were allowed to adopt their own annual plans, to determine the prices of their products and to invest their profits freely. These newly autonomous companies were termed *entreprises publiques économiques* (EPEs), and it was originally intended that all state-controlled

enterprises would acquire that status by the end of 1989. In fact, by mid-1989 three-quarters of the state-controlled enterprises had become EPEs. The capital and shares of the EPEs, previously held by the state, were transferred to eight state holding companies, called *fonds de participation*, which were established in mid-1988. Each *fonds de participation* was responsible for enterprises in a particular sector, previously controlled by a ministry (agriculture, food and fishing; mining; hydrocarbons and hydraulics; equipment; construction; chemicals, petrochemicals and pharmaceuticals; electronics, telecommunications and computers; textiles, leather, shoes and furniture; service industries), but the *fonds* could hold shares in any EPE. The *fonds* were to be administered by state appointees, chosen for their expertise but otherwise independent of the Government. The 1987 legislation also encouraged private ventures, by enabling commercial banks to allocate credit to projects according to their economic viability, rather than their social value. The 1988 budget contained measures to encourage the development of international joint ventures by exempting them from profit taxes and other taxes, according to the amount of business that they conducted in foreign currency. The EPEs were encouraged to develop their export markets by legislation introduced in April 1988, which enabled them to retain 10%, rather than 4%, of their foreign currency earnings, for export investment purposes. In July the Government introduced new proposals which aimed to make it easier for Algerian companies to gain access to foreign markets. In an effort to encourage productive investment and larger-scale development projects, the Government introduced a series of incentives, including access to convertible currency through bank accounts for investors in productive sectors. Fresh controls on exploitative practices in the private sector were also announced. In 1990 the Assemblée Nationale Populaire (ANP) approved clauses in a supplementary finance act allowing international manufacturers and traders the opportunity to sell imported goods on the domestic market. This act allowed concessionaires—or agents—and wholesalers to import for resale, hitherto a state monopoly. The main aim of these amendments was to channel money from the black market into the local banks. Companies setting up operations benefited equally from tax incentives, especially for reinvestment. It was hoped that the new tax laws would stimulate economic activity in a market restricted by shortages. Prices, however, continued to be monitored as distributors were obliged to present dossiers showing the exact amount they paid for imports, and the real exchange rate, in order to enable accurate profit margins to be calculated.

In November 1991 a senior official of the *Confédération Générale des Entrepreneurs Algériens* criticized the policy of allowing international companies into the local market with concessionaire status. He argued that concessions granted to foreign companies eliminated the private sector from activities in which it could be active through national production, added nothing to the country's wealth and failed to solve the problem of shortages. The local private sector which created employment was being penalized and there were no guarantees that the concessionaires would actually fulfil their commitments to invest in production units. In December 1991 two decades of state monopoly in the hydrocarbons and minerals sector were reversed when the ANP adopted new legislation permitting foreign investment in the energy and mining sectors. In April 1992 the Minister of Mines and Industry announced that foreign companies would be allowed to participate in the industrial sector on similar terms to those being offered in oil and gas. The pharmaceutical, detergent and cement industries were cited for early privatization. Shares were to be sold in state companies, and efforts to be made to secure export markets through association with foreign companies. As part of the reform of the public sector, a new bankruptcy law was to be introduced which threatened the future of many public-sector firms. Of 189 public companies identified for reform, only 25 were financially sound. The Minister of the Treasury stated that some AD 48,300m. ($2,137m.) would be allocated to cancel or reschedule the debts of the 165 loss-making companies and the treasury would also take responsibility for over AD 25,600m. ($1,133m.) of public-sector debt owed to local banks. A new holding company was to be formed to manage building and public works companies which formed part of the holdings of the *fonds de participation construction*. The new *fonds de participation* were to be created to manage textiles and leather companies as part of a restructuring of the *fonds de participation industries diverses*. In May 1992 officials argued that the *fonds de participation* should become holding companies which accepted the principle of bankruptcy and were allowed to transfer shares outside the existing *fonds de participation* structure. The scale of the planned privatiz- ation of public companies became clear in early May, when it was announced that local private and foreign investors would be allowed to buy into the majority of state companies, the only exceptions being those classified as strategic, including the state steel company, the Entreprise Nationale de Sid- érurgie, the state power corporation, SONELGAZ, and agroin- dustrial companies. In June 1992 it was reported that the Government had presented plans to the High Council of State (HCS) for new legislation and revisions of existing business laws to open the way for privatization, domestic and foreign investment by individuals in public companies and the com- plete decentralization of agriculture.

After taking office as Prime Minister and Minister of the Economy in July 1992, Belaid Abd es-Salam, the architect during the 1970s of much of Algeria's nationalization, expressed strong reservations about the economic reforms pursued by his predecessor. In particular, he dismissed pri- vatization as a means to revive public-sector industries. In April 1993, following talks with the *Union Générale des Tra- vailleurs Algériens* (UGTA), the Government announced that the restructuring of loss-making public companies was to be reversed. It was reported that the new measures included abolishing the system of holding companies and the dissolution of the *fonds de participation*. Public companies were to be regrouped on the basis of efficiency and economic viability and reintegrated into the major state companies. The first conglomerate to be enlarged would be SONATRACH (see p. 281), into which all companies directly or indirectly involved in the hydrocarbons sector would be progressively integrated. The debts of loss-making companies would become the responsibility of their conglomerate, and plans for bank- ruptcies and the rationalization of state companies were aban- doned. The main reason given for these policy changes was the protection of jobs. They also allowed the state to reassert its control over the economy. Several key laws, including new commerce, investment and share-ownership laws, were delayed while the new Prime Minster reviewed policy. In August a joint committee comprising members of the Govern- ment and of the *Union Générale des Travailleurs Algériens* (UGTA) considered the state of 1,800 public companies and agreed that funds should be made available to 831 of these, saving 140,000 jobs. Their study concluded that a further 57 companies, employing 5,000 workers, could not be saved. Of the companies in the public sector only 147 did not require reform or special measures.

In August 1993 one of the first acts of the new Government headed by Redha Malek was to approve the long-awaited investment code intended to stimulate investment outside the hydrocarbons sector. The new code granted protection to investors as well as a range of incentives including reduced import duties, and exemption from value-added tax and cor- poration tax. A new agency, the *Agence de Promotion de Soutien et de Suivi des Investissements* (APSI), established to accelerate investment applications, commenced operations in November and was promoted by the Government as an important element in its return to a more liberal economic policy. The APSI replaced the *Conseil de la Monnaie et de Crédit* as the national investment agency. Following his appointment as Minister of the Economy, Mourad Benachenou stated that the process of economic reform would continue, but that it had to be gradual and adapted to the Algerian context. In April 1994, following a further reorganization of

the Government, Mokdad Sifi became Prime Minister, and Benachenou was transferred to the new Ministry of Industrial Restructuring and Participation. It was reported that this ministry was to oversee the restructuring of state companies in order to meet targets set by the IMF for reducing Algeria's budget deficit. In the same month, Michel Camdessus, the Managing Director of the IMF, emphasized that the proposed IMF reform programme for Algeria would permit the faster development of the private sector.

The Government's strategy for development traditionally involved a high degree of austerity, with heavy restrictions placed on the import of luxury and consumer goods. The first Four-Year Plan, covering the period 1970–73, emphasized the establishment of a capital-intensive sector, involving the hydrocarbons, iron and steel, chemical and engineering indus- tries, and an annual growth rate of 9.7% was achieved. The second Plan, for 1974–77, aimed to establish a sound industrial base and also put emphasis on better agricultural methods, housing, health, job-creation and training. A high level of investment (40% of GDP) was maintained, and the Government aimed to achieve an average annual growth rate of 10%. Total expenditure, originally projected at AD 52,000m., was later increased to AD 110,000m., on the basis of increased income, due to higher oil prices. The country's GDP grew by an average annual rate of 6%–6.5% in the 1970s, reaching AD 120,825m. in 1979.

The 1980–84 Five-Year Plan forecast total investment of AD 400,600m., almost four times that for 1974–77. The pro- jected GDP growth rate was 8.2%. Target growth rates of 12.3% for manufacturing and 12.9% for other industries reflected a determination to overcome severe shortages of consumer goods and to make full use of existing productive capacity. Per caput GDP was expected to reach about AD 7,500 by 1984.

In the event, investment spending in the 1980–84 period totalled AD 345,000m., according to government estimates. GDP, measured at constant prices, increased at an average rate of only 4.5% per year, considerably below target. However, the restructuring of public-sector companies and the new policy of encouraging the Algerian private sector were put into effect. Total private-sector investment during the term of the Plan was estimated at AD 3,400m., creating some 20,000 jobs.

The 1985–89 Development Plan, which required total invest- ment of AD 550,000m., was approved in late 1984. It reflected the Government's new priorities for development, shifting investment away from industry and into agriculture and irri- gation projects. Industry was to receive 32% of the total investment, compared with 38% in the previous Five-Year Plan. Agriculture and hydraulics were to receive 14% of investment, compared with 11% in 1980–84. About 30% of total investment spending in the Plan was allocated to the social infrastructure, with projects for the development of housing, education, health and transport receiving particular emphasis. The targeting of these sectors reflected the need to satisfy the requirements of a rapidly expanding population, and to compensate for the imbalances of previous plans. More than one-half of the credits in the new Plan were to be allocated to the completion of existing projects. During the period of the Plan, GDP in the agricultural sector was expected to grow by 5% annually: by 4% in hydrocarbons and the processing industry, by 9% in public works and by 6.6% in mining.

The diversification of government revenue away from dependence on sales of crude petroleum to include refined products, natural gas and condensates—each contributing about one-quarter of total revenue by 1983—insured Algeria against the falls in OPEC-sponsored prices and quotas. During the term of the 1985–89 Development Plan the Government aimed to increase non-hydrocarbon exports, particularly those of agricultural produce, other minerals and manufactured goods, which in 1984 accounted for only about 2% of total exports. In December 1985 a further slump in oil prices gave added urgency to the promotion of non-hydrocarbon exports. By 1988, however, revenue from the export of non-hydro- carbons had reached only AD 2,500m., just over 50% of the target figure. Meanwhile, the erosion of government income in 1986, as a result of the collapse in oil prices, had prevented the achievement of the investment targets of the 1985–89 Plan. In October 1988 economic reforms were introduced. More than 70 state-controlled companies became EPEs (see above), including banks, insurance companies, industrial, commercial and service companies.

The principal aim of the 1990–94 Development Plan was to liberalize the economy, allowing companies to become more independent of the state and encouraging more foreign investment in Algeria. It was planned that more companies would become EPEs and about 40 committees would be set up, each responsible for a sector of the economy, to produce medium-term strategies. In order to reduce the debt-service ratio, the aggressive marketing of hydrocarbons would be pursued in combination with the promotion of non-hydrocarbon industries and agriculture. However, it was clear that the success of the Algerian economy would continue to depend heavily upon the price of oil and on political stability. Soon after his appointment as Prime Minister in June 1991, Sid-Ahmad Ghozali highlighted the economic difficulties facing the country. He informed the ANP that in 1990 real GDP fell by 2.4% and living standards by 8%. According to official figures, inflation rose from 9.9% in 1990 to 16.5% in 1991. The average use of industrial capacity was only 62% in 1990 and fell even lower in the first half of 1991. After months of political crisis, Ghozali announced the outline of a recovery programme in February 1992. Official data accompanying the programme revealed that the economic crisis was more serious than many observers had believed. Reflecting the radical devaluation of the dinar, GDP had declined, in dollar terms, by 26.9% in 1991. GDP per head had declined from $2,752 in 1987 to $1,607 in 1991. Production in 1991 was only 8% higher than in 1984 even though agricultural GDP and hydrocarbons output had risen substantially. Industrial output, in contrast, had fallen by 5.5% between 1987 and 1991. Consumer prices were rising by about 28% a year. The debt-service ratio had risen from 35% in 1985 to 72.7% in 1991. Unemployment stood at 21% in 1991. Ghozali's recovery programme gave priority to key sectors of the economy, such as agriculture, public works and construction, which were targeted in a carefully structured import programme. Priority was also to be given to purchases of pharmaceuticals, essential consumer goods, food and spare parts. Ambitious plans were announced to develop small- and medium-sized companies and to restructure public companies. While the programme envisaged a strong public sector at the centre of the economy, Ghozali favoured the private management of tourism, agriculture and trade. Financing the programme depended on the availability of international credit and success in attracting international oil companies to invest in the hydrocarbons sector.

On 22 July 1992, addressing the nation for the first time since becoming Prime Minister, Belaid Abd es-Salam declared that Algeria had deviated from the principles of the revolution over the previous decade, and expressed strong reservations about Ghozali's economic reforms. He warned that a period of austerity lay ahead, stating that he intended to cut imports to the bare minimum and close some factories, if necessary, in order to service the $25,000m.-foreign debt. He rejected debt rescheduling, devaluation and further trade liberalization. In September 1992 the Government imposed controls on imports, indicating that preference would be given in foreign exchange allocations to basic foods, spare parts and construction materials. The new Prime Minister wanted to cut imports and limit demand, rather than use the exchange rate and other free-market mechanisms favoured by previous governments and the IMF. On 20 September the Government published its economic programme, which was to be presented to the IMF and other leading donors in negotiations about new credits. Its key elements were import controls, the taxation of wealthier Algerians, and investment incentives. In contrast to previous policies of opening up the economy, the programme envisaged a ban on imports that competed with locally produced goods. In November 1992 the Government suspended indefinitely imports of luxury goods in order to conserve foreign exchange. According to official statistics, the trade surplus had fallen to AD 15,545m. ($703m.) in July–September 1992, compared with AD 23,575m. ($1,067m.) for the comparable period in 1991. Hydrocarbon earnings had fallen from AD 68,412m.

($3,096m.) in the second quarter of 1992 to AD 58,457m. ($2,645m.) in the third quarter, as a result of lower oil prices and changes in dollar exchange rates. Unemployment stood at 1.27m. in early 1993, 21% of the working population. In a strategy statement in March 1993 Abd es-Salam stated that devaluation had to be halted in order to save jobs and to avoid the threat of hyperinflation. The Government's priority was to deal with inflation and tackle social issues, rather than to pursue reform policies which resulted in the loss of jobs and triggered price increases.

In August 1993 the decision of the High Council of State (HCS) to dismiss Abd es-Salem and to appoint Redha Malek resulted in a further change of economic policy. Mourad Benachenou, formerly the Algerian representative at the World Bank and an advocate of debt rescheduling, was appointed Minister of the Economy in the new Government. It became clear that important decisions on economic policy would only be taken when the HCS, the Government and a majority of the conflicting pressure groups could agree on the correct strategy to be adopted. In the mean time the deteriorating security situation severely reduced the number of policy options. The growing number of attacks on foreign residents by Islamic militants prompted international companies to withdraw their staff, further undermining the Government's efforts to attract foreign investment.

In December talks recommenced with the IMF concerning a new loan to be linked to an economic stabilization programme, and government statements indicated a return to a more liberal economic policy. Officials stated that there were plans to ease import controls and to dissolve the committee established under the previous Government to allocate hard currency. Negotiations with the IMF ended without agreement but resumed in January 1994. The economic situation was exacerbated by the depressed price of petroleum on world markets. In January 1994 Algeria ceased repayment of most of its medium- to long-term debt insured by European export credit agencies, including payments to its largest creditors. Talks on a standby loan from the IMF continued and, although the Government was still advocating bilateral rescheduling, most creditors were convinced that a 'Paris Club' of creditor governments rescheduling had become inevitable.

In March 1994 Algeria further reduced its forecast of export revenues for that year. A spokesman for SONATRACH stated that exports would earn only $8,000m. rather than the $9,000m. previously forecast. In the same month Benachenou stated that rescheduling had become inevitable, and in April it was announced that Algeria had formally applied to the 'Paris Club' to reschedule debts of some $13,500m., more than half of its total debt. According to the Banque d'Algérie, rescheduling would reduce debt repayments by $4,000m. in 1994 and by $5,000m. in 1995. In the same month the Managing Director of the IMF, Michel Camdessus, announced a standby package for Algeria and requested donor agencies to provide substantial new loans over the next year. The package of rescheduling and refinancing was intended to stabilize the economy sufficiently to produce sustained growth in the second half of the 1990s. Over the next twelve months the IMF was to provide a $500m.-standby loan and a $300m.-compensatory and contingency financing facility. The agreement committed Algeria to a number of reforms, including a 40% devaluation and a sharp increase in interest rates which had already been implemented at the beginning of April. With the agreement in place it was anticipated that loans from the EU, the World Bank and Japan would be forthcoming.

It was not clear whether the resignation of Redha Malek as Prime Minister was connected with the acceptance of the IMF package. In a reshuffle of the Council of Ministers which followed the appointment of Mokdad Sifi as Prime Minister in April, Benachenou became Minister of Industrial Restructuring and Participation, with responsibility for managing the reform of the public sector as required by the new IMF programme. Analysts predicted that the programme would be extremely difficult to implement, and there were serious doubts that it would provide the solution to the country's economic problems or increase popular support for the regime.

AGRICULTURE

Agriculture is still an important sector of the Algerian economy, employing 23.3% of the country's labour force in 1992 and accounting for 13% of GDP in 1990. More than 90% of the land consists of arid plateaux, mountains or desert, supporting herds of sheep, goats or camels. Only the northern coastal strip, 100 km–200 km wide, is suitable for arable farming. There are about 7.6m. ha of cultivable land, representing less than one ha per rural inhabitant. Forests cover about 4.4m. ha. Most of the Sahara is devoted to semi-desert pasturage. The most valuable crop is the grape harvest, and wheat, barley and oats, grown for local consumption, cover a large area. Other crops include maize, sorghum, millet, rye, rice, citrus fruit, olives, figs and dates, and tobacco.

Scarcity of food is an acute problem in Algeria. In 1969 the country was 73% self-sufficient in food. However, by 1986 it was importing 75% of its food requirements, and by 1990 produced only 25% of its domestic cereal requirements. In 1991 food and live animals comprised about 24% of total imports. The recovery programme announced by the Government in February 1992 drew attention to a dangerous level of dependence on strategic products such as cereals, animal feed and milk and stated that efforts to raise agricultural production were central to economic policy. In March 1994 it was announced that spending on food imports would be reduced to $1,493m. in 1994 from $1,940m. in 1993. Foodstuffs had accounted for 75% of the $2,600m. allocated for importing consumer goods in 1993.

AGRICULTURAL REFORM

By October 1963 state-owned farm land accounted for 2.7m. ha, roughly one-half of the cultivable land in Algeria. In May 1966 all remaining unoccupied property which had been evacuated by settlers was finally taken over by the state. These expropriated lands were turned into state farms run by workers' committees.

In July 1971 President Boumedienne announced an agrarian reform programme which provided for the break-up of large, Algerian-owned farms and their redistribution to families of landless peasants, or *fellahin*, who would be organized in co-operatives. A census begun in September 1972 showed that a quarter of cultivable land was in the hands of 16,500 large landowners who represented only 3% of the total number of farmers. In 1973 the reform programme entered its second phase, that of redistributing over 650,000 ha of private land to 60,000 *fellahin*. Those receiving land were to be granted permanent use of it, on condition that they belonged to one of the new co-operatives. Through these they were to be given state loans and assistance in the form of seed, fertilizers and equipment. By early 1979, 22,000 absentee landowners had been obliged either to cultivate their land or to cede it to peasant farmers, and more than 6,000 agricultural co-operatives of various kinds had been established.

Following Boumedienne's death, there was a gradual change of priorities and the private sector was given new freedom to produce and market agricultural goods. The Chadli Government encouraged private, small-scale farmers by supplying equipment, loans and assistance. At the same time, investment in the agricultural infrastructure, particularly the construction of dams, was increased in an attempt to reduce the need for food imports. Moreover, to discourage rural drift (particularly among young people), farmers' earnings were more closely related to those of their industrial counterparts.

A new Banque de l'Agriculture et do Développement Rural (BADR) was established in 1982, expressly to serve the rural sector, whether socialist, state-owned or private. One of the BADR's first projects was a lending programme which aimed to make Algeria self-sufficient in eggs and poultry. In the same year, the Government relaxed price controls, allowing farmers to sell directly to markets or to private vendors and across *wilaya* boundaries. After 1983, farmers who brought desert land under cultivation automatically received a title to own the land. In 1987, in an attempt to increase efficiency and improve motivation, the Government introduced major reforms, whereby the *fellahin* were allowed to form autonomous collectives, comprising at least three members, and to lease land units, formed from the subdivision of the existing

3,347 co-operatives. The *fellahin* were to be allowed to transfer or trade their leases after five years, to control their own operations, to work directly with the banks and to make a profit. The state, as owner of the land, was to restrict its role to the provision of aid and to mediation in disputes over land division. By October 1987 the reforms were being implemented in 41 *wilayat*. By the end of 1988, 3,000 state farms were controlled by private entrepreneurs. Meanwhile, subsidies on staple foods were drastically reduced. In January 1989 the Banque Nationale de Paris agreed to channel an agroindustrial loan of nearly $750m. for 1989 through the BADR. In 1990 the Government announced plans to encourage agricultural producers to form a new type of co-operative which would market goods directly, thereby promoting price competition between the co-operatives. A public fund to protect farmers against climatic and other disasters became operational in May 1990. The fund guaranteed loans and other credits to small farmers affected by natural disasters. In the same month the Government released $107m. to support farmers affected by drought. State subsidies for agriculture totalled $1,000m. in 1990. In June 1992 the Government announced that its plans for new legislation included a decree to allow farmland remaining under state control to be transferred to private hands. In January 1994 it was reported that the EU was preparing a grant of ECU 30m. ($33.3m.) to finance imports in the agricultural sector. It was anticipated that the funds would be distributed in the form of loans to local operators through the BADR.

CROPS

Wines have been one of Algeria's principal agricultural exports since the time of the French. However, Algeria's annual output of wine declined from 8m. hl in the early 1970s to around 3m. hl by the end of the decade. The Government planned to maintain production at the latter level for the rest of the century, while developing the production of better-quality wines, which are more easily marketable in the EU. In the early 1980s annual production fell to less than 2m. hl, before recovering to 2.2m. hl in 1985. In 1989 Algeria produced only about 1m. hl of wine.

Production of cereals, grown principally in the Constantine, Annaba, Sétif and Tiaret areas, fluctuates considerably, largely as a result of drought, and grains have to be imported, particularly from Canada, France and the USA. Wheat and barley are the most important cereals. Yields are very low, at 26 cwt–32 cwt of wheat per ha, compared with average US yields of 70 cwt. In September 1993 it became apparent that drought had ravaged the 1993 harvest. Total production of cereals was estimated to have been reduced to approximately 2m. tons from 3.2m. tons in 1992.

Olives are grown mainly in the western coastal belt and in the Kabylie. Production fluctuates because of the two-year flowering cycle of the olive. Production of olives totalled an estimated 130,000 tons in 1992. The citrus crop, grown in the coastal districts, totals between 270,000 and 290,000 tons per year. Production of potatoes was estimated at 900,000 tons in 1990. About 200,000 tons of dried onions are produced annually. Algeria is the world's fifth largest producer of dates, the crop averaging 200,000 tons per year, some 80% of which are consumed locally. About 4,000 tons of tobacco are produced each year.

LIVESTOCK, FORESTRY AND FISHING

Sheep, goats and cattle are raised, but great improvements are needed in stock-raising methods, grassland, control of disease and water supply if the increasing demand for meat is to be satisfied. The cost of increasing milk production is prohibitive, and a high level of imports is likely to continue. By 1990 60% of milk requirements were imported. However, there has been a notable success in increasing production of white meat, in which the country was self-sufficient by 1984. About 1m. eggs, or one-half of total consumption, are imported annually. In September 1992 there were about 1.4m. head of cattle, 18.6m. sheep and 2.5m. goats (according to FAO estimates). Private farmers produce 90% of local meat.

The area covered by forests declined rapidly between 1970 and 1990 in spite of the Government's plans to reafforest

364,000 ha during the 1985–89 Plan period. In 1975 work began to grow a 'green wall' of pines and cypresses 20 km. wide, planted along 1,500 km. on the northern edge of the Sahara from the Moroccan to the Tunisian frontier in order to arrest steady northward desertification. The project, which encountered numerous problems, also involved the construction of roads, reservoirs and plantations of fruit trees and vegetables.

The Government believes that Algeria is not exploiting its fishing potential and has attempted to increase the annual catch. The total catch in 1991 amounted to some 80,000 tons.

METALLIC MINERALS

Algeria has rich deposits of iron ore, phosphates, lead, zinc and antimony. Mining is controlled by the state enterprises that were created in 1983 by the restructuring of the former monopoly, SONAREM. A new mining law, passed by the ANP in December 1991, allowed local private sector and foreign investment in the mining sector, which had been nationalized in 1966. The aim was to increase exploration and reverse declining production. Under the terms of the new law, foreign companies could form joint ventures and benefit from tax concessions. The *Office de Recherche Géologique et Minière* (ORGM) was created to co-ordinate the various enterprises, state and private, involved in this sector. In September 1993 the Government authorized the allocation of mineral research permits to local companies and included for the first time enterprises from outside the mining sector.

Iron ore is mined at Beni-Saf, Zaccar, Timezrit and near the eastern frontier at Ouenza and Bou Khadra. The average grade of ore is between 50% and 60%. Production has fluctuated greatly since independence, reaching 2.06m. metric tons (metal content) in 1974, falling to 897,000 tons in 1981, and recovering to 1,589,000 tons in 1990. The deposits at Ouenza represent 75% of total production. Important deposits were found in 1975 at Djebel Bouari in Batna *wilaya*. Italy is the biggest customer, followed by the United Kingdom. Production of bituminous coal, mined at Colomb Béhar-Kenadza and Ksiksou, declined steadily from 153,000 tons in 1958 to about 5,000 tons in 1978. Production was estimated at between 7,000 and 15,000 tons per year during 1981–90.

The main deposits of lead and zinc ores are at el-Abed, on the Algerian-Moroccan frontier, and at the Kherzet Youcef mine, in the Sétif region. Total zinc output (metal content) declined from 12,200 tons in 1988 to 8,000 tons in 1990, and deposits could be exhausted by the late 1990s. Production of lead in 1991 was estimated at 1,900 tons (metal content).

Exploitation of large phosphate deposits at Djebel-Onk, 340 km from Annaba, began in 1960, and Algeria now mines about 1m. tons of phosphate rock each year. About one-half of the total is exported, mainly to France and Spain. Exports of phosphates earned AD 240m. ($27m.) in 1990.

Other mineral resources include tungsten, manganese, mercury, copper and salt. In early 1992 it was reported that a group of public companies led by the *Enterprise Nationale des Métaux Non-Ferreux* (ENOF) had begun preliminary work to develop the Tirek and Amessmessa gold deposits in the Hoggar region. Reserves were estimated at 150m. tons. Annual production of 56 tons is envisaged initially with production due to start in 1995. Black Hole Technologies of the USA signed an agreement in 1992 to provide research data and feasibility studies for the project. Marble production at Bendjerah in Guelma amounted to 3,500 cu m in 1990.

ENERGY RESOURCES

Production of crude petroleum in the Algerian Sahara began, on a commercial scale, in 1958. The principal producing areas were at Hassi Messaoud, in central Algeria, and round Edjeleh-Zarzaitine in the Polignac Basin, near the Libyan frontier. Algeria's production of crude petroleum increased from 1.2m. metric tons in 1959 to 26m. tons per year in 1964 and 1965, with output limited by the capacity of the two pipelines to the coast, one from the eastern fields through Tunisia to La Skhirra, and the other from Hassi Messaoud to Béjaia on the Algerian coast. The Government established a state-controlled company, the *Société Nationale pour la Recherche, la Production, le Transport, la Transformation et la Commercialis-*

ation des Hydrocarbures (SONATRACH), to be responsible for the construction of a third pipeline from Hassi Messaoud to Arzew on the coast. This pipeline came into operation in early 1966. In that year Algeria's production of crude petroleum was increased by substantial quantities from oilfields at Gassi Touil, Rhourde el-Baguel and Rhourde Nouss. Subsequent discoveries of petroleum were made at Nezla, Hoaud Berkaoui, Ouargla, Mesdar, el-Borma, Hassi Keskessa, Guellala, Tin Fouyé and el-Maharis. There were about 50 oilfields in operation in early 1989. Export pipelines link the oilfields to Algiers, to supply the refinery at el-Harrach, and to Skikda. Increased production of condensates and liquefied petroleum gas (LPG) prompted the construction of special pipelines to Arzew.

Petroleum production reached a peak of almost 1.2m. barrels per day (b/d) in 1978, but subsequently declined, more or less steadily. The Government restricted output in order to prolong the life of the oilfields and, after 1983, to conform to the production quotas set by OPEC. Production of other hydrocarbons, particularly gas, liquefied natural gas (LNG), condensates and refined products, assumed greater importance as a source of government revenues. By 1986 production of crude petroleum had fallen to an average of 670,000 b/d, mainly from the Hassi Messaoud oilfield. In 1992 Algeria produced 1,325,000 b/d. In February 1993 SONATRACH reported that it had been producing 780,000 b/d during the past three months. In May 1993 analysts reported that crude oil production that month was 770,000 b/d compared with Algeria's production allocation of 730,000 b/d. Crude and petroleum product exports were estimated to have exceeded 1.2m. b/d in that month. Algeria produces a light crude, with a low sulphur content, which is attractive to foreign refiners. Proven reserves of petroleum at the end of 1992 were assessed at 9,200m. barrels, sufficient for about another 21 years' production at 1992 levels. About 72% of Algeria's exports of crude petroleum go to Western Europe, and another 17% to North America.

Algeria had a total refining capacity of 464,000 b/d in January 1988, and by February 1989 capacity had risen to more than 470,000 b/d. The Government has complete control of the Algiers refinery (capacity 58,000 b/d) and of the domestic distribution network. The expansion of a small refinery at Hassi Messaoud was completed in 1979, and it has a capacity of about 23,000 b/d. There are other refineries at Arzew (built by a Japanese consortium and completed in June 1973; capacity 60,000 b/d) and Skikda (built by Snamprogetti of Italy and completed in March 1980; capacity 323,000 b/d). Production of refined petroleum products in 1989 was about 20m. tons.

In 1984 Algeria's consumption of petroleum rose by 8%, to 150,000 b/d. This reflected disturbing growth in total energy consumption, which was estimated at more than 18m. tons of petroleum equivalent. Power consumption rose by 10% in 1983, to 8,926m. kWh. Domestic fuel prices had been very low by international standards until March 1994, when the Government doubled the retail price of diesel fuel and petrol.

At the beginning of 1989 the Government announced its intention to increase the efficiency of the energy sector through new exploration and the introduction of a market-related price structure; also, exports of value-added products, such as condensate and LPG, were to be increased at the expense of those of crude oil. In May 1991 Total of France and SONATRACH signed an agreement to develop condensate and LPG reserves in the Hamra field, 250 km from Hassi Messaoud. Most of the production costs were to be provided by Total and its investments will be amortized from output over a period of 14–17 years. Production was scheduled to begin in 1994 and the field will supply Total with 10m. tons of condensate and 6m. tons of LPG over this period. It forms the first element in SONATRACH's plans to develop LPG and condensate resources in the Hassi R'Mel Sud area.

In 1991 the Government established a new organization to monitor energy strategy and projects. Its duties were to include approving oil-exploration concessions. Its members initially comprised the Minister for Industry and Mines, the Ministers of Commerce and Economic Affairs, the heads of

SONATRACH and SONELGAZ and the Governor of the Central Bank.

When petroleum production began to decline, after 1978, natural gas became Algeria's most valuable export. In 1989 SONATRACH provided 30.9% of France's total gas purchases, and was providing about 70% of Spain's gas requirement in February 1989. Algeria aims to expand its gas exports, especially to the European market. On 1 January 1992 Algeria's published proven gas reserves, mostly unassociated with the oil fields, totalled 3,626,000m. cu m. Most of the gas is in the Hassi R'Mel region, 400 km south of Algiers. The field was discovered in 1956, and is still considered to be one of the largest in the world. Unassociated gas is also found near In Amenas, Alrar, Gassi Touil, Rhourde Nouss, Tin Fouyé and In Salah. The Government has invested heavily in the development of these gas fields. Pipelines have been laid to the coast, to supply local gas distribution systems, and LNG has been exported since 1965. In 1991 Algeria's production of natural gas totalled 126,270m. cu m: about 4,500m. cu m were flared and 60,480m. cu m were reinjected. In August 1993 it was reported that SONATRACH had set an annual combined export target of 60,000m. cu m of piped gas and LNG by the year 2000, compared with LNG exports of 32,890m. cu m in 1992 and sales of piped gas of 15,690m. cu m. The increased capacity is to be achieved by expanding the facilities at Skikda and Annaba, doubling capacity through the Transmed pipeline and building the Maghreb-Europe pipeline to Spain.

Before 1962 Algeria exported relatively small amounts of LNG from the Camel liquefaction plant at Arzew. The second phase of Algeria's gas development, beginning in the early 1970s, when the Government approved a plan to export 70,000m. cu m per year by the year 2000. The major clients that were secured during this period included the USA's Distrigas, Trunkline and El Paso, Belgium's Distrigaz, Enagas of Spain, and SNAM of Italy. Exports of LNG to the United Kingdom continued, and new contracts were signed with Gaz de France. The price of the gas to be delivered under the contracts was calculated according to the value of equivalent amounts of refined petroleum products (on a calorific basis).

In 1978, there was a shift to a more aggressive pricing policy. The Government argued that the old pricing terms did not fully compensate Algeria for the massive investments in LNG facilities and transportation that it had made. The central feature of the change in Algerian gas policy was the demand that natural gas prices be linked to the then rapidly rising price of crude petroleum.

The change in policy was strongly opposed by Algeria's customers, but the Government was able to persuade several clients to accept the new terms, using various economic and political sanctions. The first customer to capitulate was Belgium's Distrigaz, which signed a 20-year accord for purchases of LNG, starting in 1982. Distrigas of Boston, USA, agreed to the new indexing system in July 1982, followed by Trunkline the following August. However, the contract with El Paso, for much larger quantities of gas, was not renegotiated. A crucial victory for SONATRACH came in November 1981, when President Mitterrand of France visited Algiers and agreed, mainly for political reasons, that France would pay the higher LNG prices that Algeria demanded. With contracts for deliveries totalling 9,150m. cu m per year, the implications for Gaz de France were serious, but the French Government decided to pay an annual subsidy to the company. Meanwhile, French companies were to benefit from large contracts in Algeria's housing, transport and agricultural sectors, as a result of the accords that followed the agreement on gas prices. Strong political pressure was then put on Italy to agree to the higher prices, and an accord was finally reached in April 1983.

Owing to SONATRACH's insistence on higher prices, Algeria lost several customers—El Paso in the USA, British Methane (after 1981) and Trunkline, which suspended purchases at the end of 1983. Other countries, such as the Federal Republic of Germany and Austria, considered buying Algerian gas, but then obtained cheaper supplies from the USSR and Norway. SONATRACH therefore became more flexible on the link between crude oil and gas prices in order to win new customers, while insisting on the existing index with current buyers. The price clause in the contracts with Gaz de France,

SNAM and Belgium's Distrigaz became due for renegotiation during 1985–86. The French and Belgian companies demanded a change in the crude oil index, but SNAM finally signed a new accord in September 1986, which acceded to SONATRACH's demands on prices, while allowing the Italian company some flexibility on volume. In 1991 a gas export agreement was signed with Italy's state energy group, Ente Nazionale Idorcarburi (ENI). The accord envisaged that ENI's subsidiary, SNAM, would increase purchases by almost 60%, to a total of 530,000m. cu m of natural gas over the next 25 years. In April 1987 the US Panhandle Eastern Corporation, the parent company of Trunkline, agreed to resume shipments of Algerian LNG in late 1988. The price of deliveries was to be based on a flexible formula which would preserve SONATRACH's interests, while taking account of developments in the international market. In late 1987 Distrigas of Boston, USA, resumed shipments at the spot market price, after reaching a short-term agreement with SONATRACH in November. Distrigas had gone into liquidation under the US federal bankruptcy code in 1985, when its previous long-term contract with SONATRACH had proved to be too expensive. In February 1988 SONATRACH and Distrigas signed a 15-year contract, for the supply of LNG, whereby gas would be sold at 'market-responsive' prices. According to the terms of the contract, Distrigas was to pay for shipping and regasification, after which the gas would be sold at market prices and the profits divided on a ratio of 63:37 basis in SONATRACH's favour. In early 1988 SONATRACH reached similar long-term agreements with DEP of Greece and Botas of Turkey. Meanwhile, the signing of an agreement with Ruhrgas of the Federal Republic of Germany over purchases of LNG, discussed in late 1987, was delayed until SONATRACH's dispute with Gaz de France and Distrigaz of Belgium had been resolved, in January 1989. A compromise price of slightly less than $2.30 per British Thermal Unit (btu) was agreed, to be applied retrospectively from January 1987 to 1990. The dispute with Belgium ended in June 1989, when it was decided that Distrigaz would pay $2.3 per btu, and would purchase 4,500m. cu m per year of LNG.

In October 1992 Ente Nazionale per l'Energia Elettrica (ENEL) of Italy signed a 20-year supply contract with SONATRACH, starting in the last quarter of 1994, to lift 4,000m. cu m of gas annually through the enlarged Transmed pipeline and 1,000m. cu m–2,000m. cu m of LNG. The agreement helped to diversify gas exports and to strengthen Algeria's position in the Italian market. In January 1992 it was reported that Gaz de France had signed a series of new agreements with SONATRACH to extend its three gas supply contracts for another 10–15 years and that a new 10-year accord had been agreed. France is the major importer of Algerian LNG and, following the new agreement, annual imports could rise to more than 10,000m. cu m. In June 1992 SONATRACH signed a contract with Enagas of Spain to supply 6,000m. cu m of natural gas per year over 25 years, starting in 1995. The gas will be carried through the Maghreb-Europe pipeline. Distrigaz of Belgium announced that its maximum level of contracted lifting would be reached in 1992/93 at 4,500m. cu m. In August 1992 doubts were expressed about the future of SONATRACH's contract to supply 2,300m. cu m of LNG a year to Columbia LNG's regasification plant at Cove Point in the USA, which had been due to begin in 1993, following Shell's decision not to take over Columbia LNG. In December 1992 Natgas signed an agreement with SONATRACH to supply natural gas to Portugal. Natgas, a Portuguese, French and German consortium, was developing a grid for Portugal to come into operation in the mid-1990s. Some 2,100m. cu m of Algerian LNG per year were scheduled to be imported, from January 1997, from the Bethioua LNG plant at Arzew. In February 1993 talks between Natgas and the Portuguese state electricity company were suspended after the two sides failed to agree on pricing. In April 1993 Portugal's assistant secretary of state for energy stated that Natgas would not be taking part in the project but that Portugal was committed to taking Algerian gas for its planned natural gas network, though this might involve piped gas through the new Europe-Maghreb pipeline, rather than LNG. In April 1994 the Portuguese consortium Transgas signed a 25-year contract with SONATRACH to take 2,500m. cu m of natural gas a year from late 1996.

In early 1990 contracts were signed for the renovation of gas liquefaction facilities at Skikda and Arzew which were constructed in the 1970s. The work is being undertaken by Sofregas of France, Bechtel UK and M. W. Kellogg of the USA. In January 1992 it was reported that the GL1-K plant at Skikda was operating at about 55% of its annual capacity of 8,500m. cu m. The three plants at Arzew, GL1-Z, GL2-Z and GL4-Z, with capacities of 10,580m. cu m, 10,700m. cu m and 1,400m. cu m, were operating at 60%, 85% and 90% of their respective capacities. In September 1992 it was announced that Tractebel of Belgium had been awarded a five-year contract to carry out supervisory work for the project to rehabilitate and extend the gas liquefaction plants at Arzew, Bethioua and Skikda. In July 1992 delays to the programme were reported because of financing problems due to the sharp rise in the cost of the rehabilitation and expansion schemes from an initial $600m. to more than $2,000m. However, by October 1992, credit lines had been agreed with Eximbank of America, Coface of France, Canada's Export Development Corporation and the Export-Import Bank of Japan to support the work. In May 1994 SONATRACH announced further delays in its plans to refurbish gas liquefaction plants at Skikda and Arzew due to financing and technical problems. If the revised schedule is met, LNG output is forecast to rise from 30,000m. cu m in 1993 to 32,834m. cu m in 1994 rising to 48,000m. cu m in 1996. Japanese companies are involved in the renovation of the GL1-Z gas liquefaction plant at Arzew, where Bechtel is the main contractor. In March 1993 Mitsubishi Corporation and Mitsubishi Heavy Industries signed a $129m.-contract to supply equipment to expand the Alrar field natural gas plant near the Libyan border. The project is expected to raise gas production at Alrar from 18.5m. cu m a day to 24.7m. cu m a day, condensate production from 3,650 tons a day to 4,828 tons a day and LPG output from 2,210 tons a day to 2,924 tons a day. Two more Japanese companies, JGC Corporation and Itochu Corporation, signed a $110m.-contract to refurbish the gas processing plant at Hassi R'Mel. Both projects are financed by export credits from the Export-Import Bank of Japan. In July 1993 SONATRACH signed a $270m.-contract with JGC Corporation and Itochu Corporation of Japan to build two units at LPG plants at Hassi Messaoud to process 21m. cu m of gas a year to produce 1.4m. tons of LPG. The new units will more than double LPG capacity at Hassi Messaoud, where the two existing plants, built in 1974, produced 1m. tons annually. The Director-General of SONATRACH announced that the project would allow Algeria to consolidate its major role in the world LPG market and to increase its export capacity to more than 7m. tons in 1996 and 8m. tons by 1998. In February 1994 it was reported that work on two new production lines at the LPG complex at Bethioua, due to start in April 1994, had been delayed because the Export-Import Bank of Japan and the Japanese Ministry of International Trade and Industry had suspended new operations until Algeria signed a new agreement with the IMF. When completed the $368m.-project will raise LPG production from 4.8m. tons a year to 7.2m. tons a year. In July 1993 French companies were awarded the contract to supply equipment for the 307 km-northern section of the 988 km-Alrar-Hassi R'Mel LPG pipeline. When completed the new pipeline will carry 6.1m. tons of LPG a year and double Algeria's LPG export capacity, making it the world's principal exporter of LPG. The trans-Mediterranean gas pipeline between Algeria and Italy, is being expanded at an estimated cost of $1,000m. Work on the Tunisian and Italian sections of the pipeline expansion has begun. Italy's SAE Sadelmi has won the $195m.-contract to build the Algerian section. The expansion will raise capacity from 16,000m. cu m to 24,000m. cu m a year. In April 1993 it was announced that the European Investment Bank would provide ECU 195.8m. ($232m.) to finance work on the Italian section of the pipeline expansion scheme. In May 1991 an agreement was signed with Spain and Morocco to build a 1,365 km-gas pipeline, running from Algeria's Saharan gas fields through Morocco to Spain. The pipeline was initially to carry 7,200m. cu m of natural gas a year with Spain taking 6,000m. cu m annually and Morocco 1,000m.

cu m. In April 1994, however, Portugal signed a contract to take 2,500m. cu m a year from 1996. Enagas of Spain has been the principal agent in the scheme, which, it is estimated, will cost $1,357m. SONATRACH estimated the total cost of the Algerian section to be $465m. The work was scheduled to be completed by January 1996. In April 1994 it was reported that work on the Algerian section had fallen behind schedule because export credit agencies were waiting for Algeria to finalize its agreement with the IMF and for the security situation to improve before providing credits.

In 1970 the local interests of Shell, Phillips, Elwerath and AMIF were nationalized, after protracted negotiations had failed to achieve agreement on tax reference prices, and SONATRACH thus became Algeria's largest producer. In 1971, Algeria nationalized the French oil companies operating in the country, as well as pipeline networks and natural gas deposits. Later in the year, President Boumedienne issued a decree banning concession-type agreements and laying down the conditions under which foreign oil companies could operate in Algeria. As a result, SONATRACH gained control of virtually all of Algeria's petroleum production, compared with only 31% in 1970. After 1979, SONATRACH attempted to bring foreign oil companies back to Algeria to explore, owing to its declining petroleum reserves. A surcharge of $3 per barrel was levied on oil sales, which foreign companies were to reinvest in exploration. Many decided to accept the loss of money through the levy, rather than start a programme of drilling, especially after the oil price began to weaken after 1982. However, some companies, such as Italy's Agip and France's Total, made small discoveries. In 1986 the Government passed a new oil exploration law, which offered better terms for foreign exploration companies, with the aim of encouraging those that had made discoveries to develop their finds. In addition, some new companies, including US oil firms, expressed an interest in acquiring rights to operate in Algerian concessions. In December 1987 Agip became the first foreign company to sign an exploration and production agreement with SONATRACH after the 1986 law. A further agreement was signed by the Spanish company, Cepsa, in January 1988, and a contract with the Australian group BHP Petroleum was concluded in December 1988. An agreement with the US company Anadarko Petroleum Corporation was signed in June 1989.

In December 1991 a new hydrocarbons law, passed by the ANP, aimed to encourage greater participation by foreign companies in Algeria's oil and gas industry and marked the most radical change in energy policy since the nationalizations carried out in 1971. The new legislation sought to stimulate exploration but the most notable feature was that it allowed foreign companies to participate in existing oil fields in order to improve recovery rates and thus increase output. The Government hoped to encourage the participation of the major oil companies which were expected to pay substantial front-end bonuses in return for a share of the output. Equally significant was the fact that foreign companies would be allowed a stake in gas reserves discovered under exploration and production-sharing agreements, though not in existing fields. Previously gas had been a national monopoly and foreign companies had been excluded from benefiting from the discovery of gas in their oil acreage. Opening the hydrocabons sector to foreign capital and expertise was the central pillar of the Ghozali administration's economic recovery programme. New investment from the participation of foreign companies was regarded as essential to reverse the falling oil output. The Minister of Energy, Nordine Ait-Laoussine, stated in August 1991 that SONATRACH could recover only about 20% of its 5,000m. tons of proven reserves. With the participation of foreign firms, recoverable reserves of crude oil could be increased from around 5,500m. barrels to 9,000m. barrels. In a later statement the minister added that new gas finds were essential to increase exports from around 32,000m. cu m per year to meet projected demand of around 65,000m. cu m in the next 10 years.

After the appointment of Belaid Abd es-Salam as Prime Minister in July 1992, it was emphasized that the investment-oriented oil and gas policy of the Ghozali Government would not be reversed. When Abd es-Salam appointed his Council of

Ministers, Hacen Mefti replaced Ait-Laoussine as Minister of Energy. Despite concern over the political situation, analysts argued that oil companies, because they take a longer view of political risk, would overcome their doubts and buy into the hydrocarbons sector. Nevertheless, the Ministry of Energy admitted that fewer companies had expressed interest than would have been the case if the country had enjoyed political stability and that talks on a range of projects had been delayed. A series of agreements, principally with US organizations, showed that international companies were prepared to invest in exploration and production-sharing activities, but hopes that large-scale capital inputs would be secured by foreign companies buying into existing fields proved less well-founded. Final offers were opened in November 1992, when the Minister of Energy reported interest from companies in eight fields. He admitted that the Government was disappointed by the money offered as entry fees, which were seen as an important method of raising new revenue. In July 1993 it was reported that two companies, Total of France and Atlantic Richfield of the USA, were still negotiating the purchase of shares in the Rhourde el-Baguel field, but that Aqip of Italy had withdrawn its interest. Several contracts with international companies had been concluded in 1992–93 for new exploration work. In 1994 the Anadarko (Algeria) Petroleum Corporation of the USA announced plans to drill two more exploration wells in the Hassi Berkine field. Cepsa and Repsol of Spain and BHP Petroleum of Australia were also engaged in drilling projects. In late 1993 British Petroleum announced that it would drill its first exploration well in 1994 as part of a nine-year programme during which the company is committed to drill five wells. Despite the deteriorating security situation and the withdrawal of some expatriate staff and dependents, international petroleum companies stated that they were continuing operations as normal. In January 1994 SONATRACH opened a second round of exploration bidding and announced that it was moving ahead with plans to allocate at least four new exploration permits. SONATRACH officials attempted to underplay the impact of the withdrawal of expatriates occasioned by the political crisis, and in May 1994 plans were announced to drill 51 exploration wells in 1994.

In early 1993 SONATRACH announced that it was planning to develop its natural gas, condensate, LPG and other hydrocarbon sectors, despite a fall in income in 1992. Some $2,700m. in development spending was forecast for 1993. In 1992 SONATRACH's revenues fell by $1,000m. to $10,900m., despite an increase in hydrocarbons production to a total of 107m. tons of oil equivalent, a 2.8% rise from the previous year. Exports rose in 1992, with crude oil, natural gas liquids and refined products totalling 47.4m. tons of oil equivalent, compared with 47.1m., in 1991. Piped gas and LNG exports rose to 34.4m. tons of oil equivalent, up from 32.7m. tons in 1991. LPG sales remained the same, at 4m. tons of oil equivalent. Lower world oil prices resulted in the fall in income from hydrocarbons. SONATRACH's Director-General, Abdelmak Bouhafs, announced that two new oil fields, Hassi Guettar and Hassi Chergui Nord, and two gas fields, Rhourde Chouff and Rhourde Hamra, commenced operation in 1992. He forecast higher output for most hydrocarbon sectors in 1993–97, as development projects were completed.

Following its establishment in 1963, SONATRACH expanded to become the largest, most complex and economically most important state company in Algeria. In May 1980 the Government decided that SONATRACH should be rationalized into smaller, specialized and more autonomous units. Thirteen such units were eventually formed, including SONATRACH itself. The others were: *Entreprise Nationale* (EN) *de Raffinage et de Distribution des Produits Pétroliers* (ENRDP), EN *de Raffinage des Produits Pétroliers* (ENRP), EN *des Plastiques et de Caoutchouc* (ENPC), EN *des Grands Travaux Pétroliers* (ENGTP), EN *de Forage* (ENAFOR), EN *de Géophysique* (ENAGEO), EN *de Travaux aux Puits* (ENTP), EN *de Génie Civil et Bâtiments* (ENGCB), EN *de Service aux Puits* (ENSP), EN *de Canalisation* (ENAC), EN *de Pétrochimie et d'Engrais* (ENPE) and EN *d'Engineering Pétrolier* (ENEP).

In April 1989 Algeria's first nuclear reactor came into operation. Following international press speculation in April 1991

that the 15-MW nuclear reactor at Ain Oussera was for military use, officials of the Ministry of Research and Technology stressed its peaceful application and Algeria's willingness to allow an inspection by the International Atomic Energy Agency. At the inauguration of the reactor in December 1993, Mohamed Saleh Dembri, the Minister of Foreign Affairs, announced that Algeria would sign the nuclear non-proliferation treaty. In early 1990 plans to build a helium and nitrogen plant in Bethioua, near Arzew, were announced. The plant will produce 16m. cu m of liquid helium and 33,000 tons of liquid and gaseous nitrogen per year, mainly for export, utilizing gas from SONATRACH's LNG 2 plant at Arzew. Algeria has proven helium reserves of 6,000m. cu m.

HOUSING AND SOCIAL INFRASTRUCTURE

A key feature of the 1980–84 and the 1985–89 Development Plans, and a priority for the regime of President Chadli, was a concerted effort to tackle Algeria's chronic housing shortage. More spending, too, was allocated for other aspects of social infrastructure, in particular health and education facilities, which, like housing, had been neglected in the 1970s. Under the 1985–89 Development Plan, 8% of total investment was allocated to transport infrastructure and nearly 16% to housing. More than 300,000 new homes were to be built and some 350,000 homes which had been started under the previous Plan were to be completed.

According to government estimates, at least 100,000 new homes were built in 1982 and in 1983. Building, traditionally the province of state concerns, was facilitated by two independent factors: firstly, the 30,000 and more homes believed to have been started—frequently without official permission—by the thriving private domestic construction industry; and, secondly, the prefabricated construction techniques which had been introduced by foreign companies under the aegis of a newly-created state concern, the *Office National de la Promotion de la Construction en Préfabrique* (ONEP). This was founded in March 1982, following the successful use of imported prefabricated building techniques to repair earthquake damage in el-Asnam. By the end of that year, ONEP had signed contracts for its entire construction programme of almost 5m. sq m, at a total cost of almost $2,800m. It was the world's largest prefabricated construction programme and was chosen as a costly, but speedy and efficient, way of satisfying urgent demand. ONEP drew most of its contractors from France, Spain, Italy, Denmark, Belgium, the United Kingdom, Switzerland, Portugal and Sweden, financing the bulk of its work through export credits. The 1982 programme included 21,000 homes (about one-half of that number being attached to hospitals), 34 fully-equipped hospitals, 60 polyclinics, 83 vocational training centres, 41 technical schools, 122 secondary schools, six biological research centres and six university housing 'cities'. ONEP contractors worked directly for local *wilayat* (administrative districts) but negotiated through ONEP and received tax and customs dispensations.

Although prefabricated construction was, on average, almost half the cost of traditional methods, it drained Algeria's foreign exchange because of the high proportion of imported work. ONEP awarded no new contracts in 1983, and was finally disbanded in the following year. By then, traditional construction methods were being used to build most of the extra housing.

In 1983 the Government launched its other main scheme to expedite building, namely the use of foreign contractors under bilateral agreements with foreign governments. In mid-1982 France signed a bilateral agreement with Algeria to build 60,000 homes as part of a general co-operation agreement which resulted from an improved relationship between the two countries, prompted by the gas price agreement of February. By late 1983, French firms had signed contracts to build almost 27,000 new homes. The largest contracts were awarded to Dumez, Bouygues, Fougerolle, Société Auxiliaire d'Entreprise and Société Parisienne d'Entreprise, providing a major boost for the depressed French construction industry. After the dissolution of ONEP, however, there was a general shift in government policy towards housing construction. Contracts were awarded to companies from Eastern Europe, often to accompany barter agreements, because they could complete the work more cheaply. The Government also urged local construction companies to become involved in the housing programme. Foreign companies were asked to form joint ventures with local companies if they wished to be awarded more work, but these requirements proved unpopular. After the collapse of oil prices in 1986, the Government began to search for cheaper methods of solving the housing crisis, encouraging local companies to undertake housing projects. The private sector was given more freedom to undertake developments on its own, and those who had built their houses illegally were offered an amnesty. However, the Government remained determined to prevent housing development on potential farming land. In 1989 it was estimated that about 100,000 new homes needed to be built each year in order to solve the housing crisis.

Announcing the outlines of the Government's recovery programme in February 1992, Prime Minister Ghozali stated that priority would be given to spending on imports for public works and construction and that foreign participation would be encouraged in the production of construction materials. There were plans to build 60,000 public homes within a year, with a total of 150,000 under construction within 30 months. The Government's stated aim was to eliminate shanty towns, especially in the major cities. According to government sources, 360,000 homes needed to be built in 1992–93, 210,000 for sale on the open market.

In April 1993 the World Bank approved a $200m.-loan to support the Government's emergency programme to build 130,000 public housing units. Some 105,000 units are in urban areas, 23,000 in rural areas and 3,000 for company employees. The loan is intended to cover the hard currency costs of the programme and most of it will go towards financing imports for the construction sector. The EU also approved a parallel structural adjustment grant of ECU 70m. ($83m.) to finance imports needed for the construction of 100,000 social housing units. Abd es-Salam admitted in August 1992 that the previous Government's plan to build 60,000 homes in 1992 could not be realized. Direct state involvement in the housing programme marked a break with recent government policy of leaving house construction to the private sector and autonomous state bodies. Nevertheless, the Government still appeared to support foreign investment in the construction sector. In May 1993 it was reported that the *Conseil de la Monnaie et du Crédit* had given approval to several joint venture applications, including plans by Chadwick International of the USA to produce prefabricated houses. In July 1993 a loan was agreed with the Saudi Fund for Development to finance the construction of 2,000 homes in the Dar el-Beida and Bir Mourad Rais districts of Algiers. Following agreement on a new accord with Algeria in April 1994 the IMF asked other donors to concentrate additional funding on social spending projects, especially housing.

TRANSPORT

Bilateral arrangements were applied to the ambitious plans of the *Société Nationale des Transports Ferroviaires* (SNTF) for its railway network. By 1990 up to $11,000m. had been invested in doubling the length and freight capacity of the existing 3,900-km network. About $3,000m. of this was spent on new equipment. The SNTF argued that rail transport was about 75% cheaper than road transport and should be developed to absorb up to 40% of freight, as in France, compared with about 15% in 1982. The aim was to create a new trunk-line, running east-west across Algeria's High Plateaux, which would facilitate the development of new industrial centres; and also to build a southern loop-line down to the oil towns of Hassi Messaoud and Ghardaia. New track, signalling equipment, stations and freight centres were also planned. Algerian conscripts were to provide cheap labour on much of the basic track, under the guidance of Indian designers and technicians. Assistance was also sought from the People's Republic of China for large sections of the new line, while European designers and contractors became involved in improving existing facilities; Austria, in particular, allocated substantial funds for SNTF's use at concessionary rates, and in 1983 Austrian firms began upgrading the Thenia–el-Harrach line in the suburbs of Algiers. Italian and French contrac-

tors were awarded substantial railway work in 1983. In 1991 the Abidjan-based African Development Bank approved a loan partially to finance the El-Achir railway tunnel project in Bordj Bou-Arreridj *wilaya*. The project was expected to cost $130m. and to take 40 months to complete.

As the economy encountered difficulties in 1985–86, the emphasis shifted away from major new projects. Instead, the Government planned to renew large stretches of the existing network. A new local company was established in 1986 to implement the upgrading programme in co-operation with foreign firms. Meanwhile, large projects were cancelled or postponed. The construction of a metro (rapid transit transport) system for Algiers, for instance, was suspended until 1989. Work began on the first two metro stations in August 1989, but by 1992 only one km of tunnel had been dug. In June 1993 the *Entreprise du Métro d'Alger* admitted that the project could not now be completed without the involvement of international companies. The first line is now scheduled for completion by 1998, and the total cost of the project is estimated at $800m. In view of Algerian difficulties obtaining export credits, financing is expected to be a major problem.

In September 1992 the Director-General of the SNTF announced that the company was to upgrade its services in 1992–93 and planned to complete several major projects by the year 2000. Rail projects would include a rail link between Tizi-Ouzau and Oued Aissi industrial zone, renewing the Relizane-Tiaret-Mahdia line, and transferring the company's workshops from Hamma in the capital to Rouiba. The SNTF carried 58m. passengers and 12m. tons of freight in 1991 when the company's losses increased by nearly AD 1,000m. ($49m.) Rail links with Morocco were resumed in September 1988 after a 12-year closure. In April 1989 part of a $211m.-loan from the World Bank was allocated to the reconstruction of Algeria's railways, but by October 1993 only $15m. of this had been utilized owing to a dispute concerning the reform of the SNTF.

The national airline, Air Algérie, was restructured in 1984, with domestic routes being passed to the newly formed Air Inter Services. Algeria purchased its first two European Airbus A310 aircraft in 1984. The number of passengers carried by Air Algérie fell from 4.2m. in 1986 to 3.7m. in 1991. The company's outstanding debt was calculated to have risen to AD 9,000m. in 1991 and debt due in 1992 equalled one-third of the company's turnover. The company's problems arose from the effects of devaluation, a fall in traffic due to the introduction of new visa regulations for Algerians visiting Europe, and increased operating costs. In April 1991 it was reported that Air Algérie had raised its international fares by 50% after losses of $340m. in 1990. The company's fleet is made up of older aircraft and a 10-year renewal programme, to cost an estimated $1,400m., has been suspended. In 1992 a three-year reform programme, designed to improve the management and performance of the airline, was initiated. Air Algérie reported profits of $14.5m. in 1992, but there was no indication that the company was about to make major purchases of new aircraft. Work began in early 1990 on the construction of a second runway at Tamanrasset airport. The Algiers airport terminal was reopened in June 1993 following a bombing incident in August 1992. A 2.4 km-runway at El-Achouet airport in Jijel province was scheduled for completion in 1994. Preliminary studies have been completed for an international airport to be built at Ain-Arnet, west of Sétif, to serve the region. The construction of a 2,000m-runway was scheduled to be completed in 1994.

In mid-1989 a $63m.-loan from the World Bank was approved for the Ports 3 scheme to upgrade the ports of Algiers, Oran and Annaba. In April 1991 it was reported that development work at Annaba port was to be accelerated in response to increased production at the nearby El-Hadjar steel plant. There were also plans to expand the port's cereals storage and handling facilities. In September 1990 an agreement was signed with the Japanese International Co-operation Agency to finance a $2.8m.-study for the development of the ports of Algiers, Oran and Annaba. The study, submitted in July 1993, recommended that container facilities should be upgraded, and road and rail connections improved at Algiers. It also recommended that facilities for unloading cereals and containers should be upgraded at the ports of Annaba and

Oran. In 1991 the three ports handled 71% of all traffic: Algiers 32%, Annaba 23% and Oran 16%. The opening of the new port of Djenddjen near Jijel has been delayed due to lack of essential equipment. The port was built, with financial assistance from Saudi Arabia, to serve the proposed Bellara steelworks, the future of which now appears to be in doubt. In December 1993 it was announced that the African Development Bank (ADB) was to lend $29.1m. to finance equipment for the port. Traffic through local ports fell from 83.8m. tons in 1990 to 82m. tons in 1991. Passenger traffic fell to 377,561 in 1990.

In June 1992 it was reported that the Government was to revive plans to build an east-west motorway system linking Annaba and Tlemcen and forming part of a trans-Maghreb motorway. About 100 km of the highway are already operational and another 55 km are under construction, although completion could take another 20 years. The Abd es-Salam Government made development of the road network central to its economic strategy. In December 1993 the Minister of Equipment announced road-building projects at an estimated cost of $1,820m. over four years. Of this total, $440m. was allocated to reinforcing the existing network of main roads, and the rest to rehabilitation and new projects.

MANUFACTURING

Industrialization has been the keynote of economic policy and the major investment effort in the 1970–73 Plan was devoted to this end. Under the 1974–77 Plan, industry received about 43.5% of total allocations. In the 1980–84 Plan it was allocated 38% of total investment, and 32% in the 1985–89 Plan.

At the time of independence the Algerian industrial sector was very small, being confined mainly to food processing, building materials, textiles and minerals. The departure of the French entailed loss of demand, capital and skill, thereby slowing down the industrialization process. Foreign firms became increasingly reluctant in the 1960s to invest in Algeria because of the danger of nationalization. By 1978 about 300 state-owned manufacturing plants had been set up, but productivity was very low, with some factories operating at only 15%–25% of design capacity. The early 1980s were a time of increasing emphasis on productivity and efficiency, and nowhere more so than in the manufacturing sector. The restructuring of the state mechanical manufacturing and supply monopoly, SONACOME, into 11 smaller and, in theory, more efficient units appears to have helped output, as did profit-sharing schemes.

In 1983 the Government began to encourage foreign and domestic manufacturers to supply the larger *sociétés nationales*, such as SONACOME. Foreign companies would be junior partners to state concerns, but local businesses would receive the finance from state banks which was normally available to state concerns. The Government was also interested in encouraging companies to establish joint ventures, in order to stimulate foreign investment and to ensure closer working relations with foreign companies, thus enabling Algerian companies to monitor the progress of projects and gain a genuine transfer of technology.

In the late 1980s the Ministry of Light Industries considered that the basic network of small-scale manufacturing was complete, and it intended to concentrate in future on improving the integration of the sector. The private sector was to be given a greater role in setting up manufacturing industries, to process raw materials produced in the state sector. Instead of investing in new cement works, the ministry was to concentrate on increasing output at existing works, and to carry out small extensions to satisfy any increase in demand. Beyond the year 1990 the ministry planned to develop high technology industries, such as clock manufacturing, and intended to promote industries to integrate the sector, such as the manufacture of synthetic fibres. In early 1992 the Government announced radical measures to open state sector industries, which account for some 80% of industrial production, to local private and to foreign participation. Officials acknowledged that many state industries were operating at below 50% capacity; and recognized that as income from oil and gas was not sufficient to finance the recovery of its industrial base, privatization was essential to provide investment and new

markets as well as technology. The only exceptions would be industries classified as strategic, such as the *Entreprise Nationale de Sidérurgie*, Sonelgaz and agroindustrial companies. New legislation would make provision for the transfer of shares in public companies and would require changes to the system of *fonds de participation* established in 1988. The Minister of Mines and Industry indicated that some shares might be transferred to workers in state industries. After an audit of major state companies carried out as part of Algeria's World Bank structural adjustment programme, the following were identified as viable, if non-profit-making: *Entreprise Nationale des Véhicules Industriels, Entreprise Nationale des Matériaux de Travaux Publics, Entreprise Nationale de Production de Matériel Agricole and Entreprise Nationale de Production de Matériel Hydraulique*. The plan was to transfer some of their responsibilities to small and medium-sized industrial companies, which were to be given an increased role with the introduction of a new industrial code in order to encourage new investors.

After taking office as Prime Minister in July 1992 Abd es-Salam proceeded to reverse many of the policies of his predecessor. He rejected privatization as a means of reviving public-sector industries and announced that the restructuring of loss-making public companies would be reversed. These policy changes appeared to mark a reassertion of state control over the economy. In August 1993 the new Government of Redha Malek gave notice of a return to the reform of state industries and of its commitment to attract foreign investment in the private manufacturing sector. In April 1994 it was reported that the World Bank was to finance studies to reform some of Algeria's least efficient public companies, including the state steel company. Further contracts to restructure 14 state companies were signed with Coopers & Lybrand and Ernst & Young of the United Kingdom. In April 1994 Mourad Benacherou was placed in charge of the newly-created Ministry of Industrial Restructuring and Participation. The new ministry was to oversee the restructuring of state companies as required by the latest IMF accord in order to reduce Algeria's budget deficit.

The iron and steel industry is crucial to the development of other industries. In 1988 the state-owned steel company, the *Entreprise Nationale de Sidérurgie* (SIDER), announced proposals to increase output of long-steel products to meet 70%, rather than 30%, of local demand and thus reduce imports of steel, which total 1.9m.–2m. tons per year. Plans were also made to increase SIDER's annual flat-steel capacity to 1.8m. tons from 1.4m. tons. Huge investments have been made in the el-Hadjar complex at Annaba. Liquid steel output rose slightly from 830,000 tons in 1991 to 841,115 tons in 1992. According to SIDER's projections output should have reached 1.25m. tons, well below design capacity of 2m. tons. Exports of steel products in 1992 reached 281,949 tons. Metalsider, Algeria's first private steel maker, started operations in 1992. A merchant bar mill with a capacity of 100,000 tons a year commenced production in 1993 and a third bar/rod combination mill is due to commence operations in 1996. In April 1993 it was reported that Metalsider was seeking joint-venture partners to build a 1.5m.-ton-a-year direct-reduced iron plant. Plans to construct an aluminium smelter and associated facilities at Mostagenem were announced in November 1989, but were delayed owing to problems of securing finance and to political uncertainties. In April 1992 it was reported that the Government had asked International Development Corporation (IDC) of Dubai to resume work on the project. A joint venture between IDC, the local partner, *Entreprise National de Métallurgie et de Transformation des Non-Ferreux*, and the Mediterranean Aluminium Company, has been established to operate the smelter, which will produce 220,000 tons annually with the potential to expand to 330,000 tons. In October 1992 it was reported that the project had been suspended to await clarification of the Government's policy towards industrial investment and an improvement in the attitude of export credit agencies towards Algeria.

Although ambitious plans have been announced to expand the country's petrochemical industries, technical and financial problems have hindered progress. A vast petrochemical complex at Skikda produces polyethylene, PVC, caustic soda and chlorine. In 1991 a project to build a high-density polyethylene (HDPE) plant at Skikda was announced. Its capacity will be 130,000 tons a year. It is estimated that the project will cost $120m. and will commence production in 1994. The project is a joint venture between the *Entreprise Nationale de la Pétrochimie* and Repsol Quimica of Spain. The partners have also set up a joint trading company to market part of the plant's production for export. In November 1992 Repsol Quimica announced that it was renegotiating its contracts for the project. In November 1991 it was reported that Rollechim Impianti of Italy together with *Entreprise Nationale de la Pétrochimie and Entreprise Nationale de Raffinage de Pétrole* had agreed to create a joint venture to build a petrochemicals plant at Skikda to produce 30,000 tons of orthoxylene, 71,000 tons of paraxylene and 25,000 tons of phthalic anhydride annually. There is a nitrogenous fertilizer plant at Arzew, utilizing natural gas, with an annual capacity of 800,000 tons, and a complex for the manufacture of intermediate petrochemical products. In May 1991 the *Entreprise Nationale de la Pétrochimie* established a joint venture with Repsol of Spain and Rhône-Poulenc of France to build a polyester resins plant at Arzew with an annual production of 10,000 tons. In August 1991 Total of France, Ecofuel of Italy and SONATRACH confirmed plans to build a $400m.-methyl tertiary butyl ether (MTBE) plant at Arzew, with an annual production capacity of 600,000 tons mainly for export to refineries in southern Europe. By July 1993 progress on the project had been limited, and it was reported that Total and Ecofuel were undecided about their continued participation. In December 1992 the *Entreprise Nationale de la Pétrochimie* invited international and local companies to apply to prequalify to rehabilitate the *Entreprise Nationale d'Industrie Pétrochimique* (ENIP)'s ethylene unit in the plastics complex at Skikda. The plant was to be expanded from 120,000 tons a year to 220,000 tons. At Annaba, a plant for phosphate fertilizers, with an annual capacity of 550,000 tons, was opened in 1972 but has suffered from technical difficulties. A new fertilizer complex began production in 1980, also at Annaba. New units starting up at Arzew and Annaba in 1981 and 1982, together with efforts to exploit existing productive capacity more fully, have provided a surplus of ammonium nitrate, phosphate fertilizers and urea for export.

Algeria suffers from a severe shortage of vehicles of all types but is expanding its vehicle and farm machinery industries rapidly. A large farm machinery complex was officially opened at Sidi-Bel-Abbès in 1976. An industrial vehicles plant at Rouiba, about 25 km from Algiers, started production in 1974 under a product-in-hand contract with Berliet of France. Assembly capacity is 7,000–10,000 vehicles per year, but mechanical shop capacity is sufficient to produce parts for only about 4,500 vehicles per year, and SONACOME has had to import kits to offset the deficit. Reductions in imports in 1988 led to a shortage of spare parts for vehicles and for industry in general. In its first expansion phase, SONACOME aimed to produce 7,200–7,500 vehicles per year with a 60% local content, compared with 6,000 in 1979, with about 50% local content. A second phase was to raise production to 10,000–11,000 vehicles per year and bring the rate of integration nearer to the original target of 75%.

In 1987 the Ministry of Heavy Industry concluded an agreement for the construction of a passenger car manufacturing plant by the Italian firm, Fiat. The plant is at Ain Bouchekif, near Tiaret. Fiat has taken a 35% equity share in the project. In May 1989 a financing agreement, worth $80m., was signed by Italy's Mediocredito Centrale and the Banque Algérienne de Développement (BAD), to go towards the $200m. capital of the car assembly plant. Construction of the plant eventually began in early 1992, but the project was delayed by financial difficulties. In late 1993 it was stated that the project was back on schedule and production of the new Punto model was to begin in July 1995. In July 1989 an agreement, which included provision for the construction of a second passenger car manufacturing plant, was concluded with the French firm, Peugeot. Peugeot's engine-overhaul plant near Algiers began operations in 1990. Local demand for private cars and light vehicles totals about 100,000 per year. French and Japanese manufacturers may be involved in later stages of the project.

SONATRACH is preparing studies for a factory to produce heavy-duty tyres for industrial vehicles, and several contractors, including subsidiaries of Michelin and Pirelli, have made offers for the contract. The new factory will supplement a pre-independence plant near Algiers. In 1987 the *Entreprise Nationale d'Articles de Quincaillerie et Serrurerie* invited companies to establish factories manufacturing vehicle parts at Ksar el-Boukhari and Mazouna, as part of the Government's strategy to establish a local car components industry, based on Algerian companies and joint ventures. In 1990/91 the Government approved the entry of several foreign car manufacturers into the local market under concessionaire agreements. Automobiles Peugeot has established a local subsidiary and under an agency agreement will establish a sale network to sell 8,000–10,000 cars a year in Algeria. Other agreements have been signed with Régie Nationale des Usines Renault, Fiat Auto, Daewoo Corporation, Honda and Nissan. Most of these companies have stated their intention to build car assembly plants in the future.

Other growth areas are the paper industry, textiles, electrical goods (including radio and television sets), flour milling and building materials. There are six cement works with a total installed capacity of about 9m. tons, but they have been operating at barely 50% of capacity. Plans to rehabilitate the cement industry were announced in early 1990. In July 1993 it was reported that the four national cement companies had created two new subsidiaries. The Société des Ciments de Tebessa was to manage the Tebessa factory, where there were plans to seek foreign capital for a project to double capacity. The Société de Maintenance et d'Equipment des Cimenteries was to deal with maintenance, subcontracting and the supply of parts to local cement companies. There are also plans to develop the manufacture of pharmaceuticals through a network of joint ventures with international partners. In 1991 Denmark's Novo-Nordisk Pharmaceuticals and *Entreprise Nationale d'Approvisionnement en Produits Pharmaceutiques* agreed to build a plant near Algiers to manufacture a range of drugs for local consumption and export. Other joint ventures have been agreed with Pfizer of the USA and Rhône-Poulenc Rohrer of France. The new plant, in which Rhône-Poulenc Rohrer will hold a 36% stake and the state-owned *Entreprise Nationale de Production Pharmaceutique* 40%, will produce a variety of basic pharmaceutical products. In 1992 the Caisse Française de Développement provided FF 160m. ($10.7m.) for the renovation of the Meftah asbestos cement plant, FF 35.4m. ($6.3m.) for upgrading the M'Sila aluminium plant and FF 19.6m. ($3.5m.) for reorganization and pollution reduction at the Ghazaouet zinc plant. In spite of all these efforts, it was estimated that total industrial production in 1991 was less than in 1984, while the country's population had increased by about 4m.

TRADE

Algeria had a consistent foreign trade deficit, with the exception of small surpluses recorded in 1967 and 1968, until the huge increases in petroleum prices in 1973. Exports of petroleum and natural gas have transformed the pattern of Algerian exports, previously limited to agricultural products and some minerals—mainly wine, citrus fruit and iron ore. Hydrocarbons accounted for over 96% of export earnings in 1990. Other exports include vegetables, tobacco, hides and skins, dates and phosphates. The Government sets an annual budget for imports, and the import requirements of public-sector companies are strictly controlled, allowing the state to adjust its trade policy relatively quickly. The value of imports was reduced to $7,683.3m. in 1991, while that of exports increased to $11,790m.

The visible trade account turned from a state of chronic deficit to surplus in 1974, alternating annually between deficit and surplus thereafter. Increases in the price of petroleum in 1979, however, put Algeria in credit and kept the trade balance in surplus. In order to preserve this surplus (which reached 16,500m. dinars in 1985), the Government introduced new import controls. However, the sharp fall in the price of petroleum in 1986 resulted in a trade deficit of AD 6,567m. for that year, according to figures released by the Algerian Office National des Statistiques. In 1987 the price of petroleum recovered slightly and there was a trade surplus of $2,413m. There was a trade surplus of $946m. in 1988. In 1990, although imports increased by almost 22%, exports increased further, by 42%. This produced a trade surplus of AD 11,497m., compared with a deficit of 1,835m. in 1989. Statistics from the Banque d'Algérie forecast the value of exports in 1991 at $11,740m. with that of imports rising to $10,070m. and a current account deficit of $270m. An improvement was projected in 1992, with the current account expected to register a $320m. surplus. The forecast for 1993 was a current account surplus of $1,200m. In September 1992 Abd es-Salam's Government moved to restore strict state control over imports and in a circular distributed to local companies it indicated that preference would be given in foreign exchange allocations to priority areas such as basic foods, spare parts and construction materials. When allocating hard currency, the Government would take account not only of a company's financial situation, but also of the state's wider economic and social priorities. A committee chaired by the Minister of Commerce, Tahar Hamdi, was established to decide on import priorities and set quotas. Imports which compete with locally-produced goods were banned and in November imports of luxury goods were suspended indefinitely in order to conserve foreign exchange. In spite of this austerity programme, the value of imports was forecast by the Banque d'Algérie to rise from $9,790m. in 1992 to $11,440m. in 1993 and to $12,300m. in 1994. The value of exports was forecast to rise very slowly, from $12,020m. in 1992 to $12,040m. in 1993 and to $12,220m. in 1994. The Banque d'Algérie has stated that it will use existing credits to finance imports. By 1996 a substantial trade surplus was projected, with the value of exports expected to rise to $15,630m. and that of imports to $14,460m. In November 1993 it was announced that the Government intended to ease the import controls imposed by Abd es-Salam's Government. The operations of the *ad hoc* committee which controlled imports were to be terminated by the end of 1993, although full import liberalization could not be implemented, particularly at a time when oil prices were low. In February 1994 officials of the Ministry of Commerce stated that a ban on imports of consumer goods imposed by Abd es-Salam's Government had been lifted.

Before independence France purchased 81% of Algeria's exports and provided 82% of its imports. This dominance declined steadily, particularly at the time of the 1971 oil nationalization crisis, and France's share of Algerian trade by 1977 had declined to only 12.7% of exports and 24% of imports. In 1977 France decided to import more of its crude oil from Saudi Arabia rather than Algeria, and Algeria retaliated by imposing a ban on the import of French goods in 1978. However, relations have improved steadily since 1979, and by 1983 France was providing 24% of Algeria's imports and taking 30% of exports. An economic co-operation agreement and, later, detailed sectoral protocols were signed from mid-1982, following the conclusion of a gas price agreement and a new political dialogue at presidential level. These agreements led to major orders for French business, and by 1985 France had achieved a surplus in its trade with Algeria, totalling FF 1,095m. In 1988 France was still the largest exporter, followed by the USA and Italy. Trade with France increased in 1989. The value of Algerian exports to France rose from FF 9,461m. in 1989 to FF 10,557m. in 1990, and that of imports from France rose from FF 12,775m. in 1989 to FF 14,774m. in 1990. The value of French exports to Algeria declined to FF 12,273m. in 1991, while that of French imports from Algeria rose to FF 11,995m. In July 1991 Coface, the French export credit agency, agreed to provide credits of FF 5,000m. in order to finance trade with Algeria. The agency reported in March 1992, however, that Algeria was at the top of its list of high-risk countries for trade and that while it would continue to make credits available, it would practice very great selectivity. The value of French exports to Algeria fell again in 1992, to FF 11,774m. ($2,114m.) and that of Algerian exports to France declined by 17.2% to FF 9,932.5m. francs ($1,783m.). Hydrocarbons accounted for 96.3% of Algerian exports to France, while capital goods remained the single largest element in French exports to Algeria, followed by agroindustrial products and consumer goods.

Since 1991 the German export credit agency Hermes has suspended credit lines to Algeria and this has been reflected in a decline in the value of German exports, from DM 1,479.9m. in 1990 to DM 1,220.4m. in 1991. Algerian exports to Germany, however, increased from DM 1,531.2m. in 1990 to DM 1,873.7m. in 1991. In November 1988 it was reported that Yugoslavia would supply 1,300 tractors with trailers in a deal worth $1.5m., and that the USSR had ordered 600,000 hectolitres of Algerian wine in a contract valued at $19m. Many symbolic agreements have been concluded with African states but, overall, Algeria's economy is heavily dependent on members of the Organization for Economic Co-operation and Development (OECD). It also has a preferential trade agreement with the EU.

In the mid-1980s the Government introduced measures to facilitate the growth of private-sector trade. An increasing role for entrepreneurs was one of the features of the 1985–89 Development Plan, and, in 1984 (as part of the Government's campaign to increase non-hydrocarbon exports) new regulations were introduced, with the aim of encouraging the growth of private-sector export companies. Agricultural produce, surplus manufactured goods, phosphates and other minerals were all to be privately exported, especially by use of barter or counter-trade with foreign suppliers. In July 1988 the Government announced new legislative proposals, intended to improve local companies' access to foreign markets. Whereas, previously, foreign companies had to be represented in Algeria by their own liaison offices or *bureaux de liaison* (BDLs), of which many had to be closed down (owing to their expense and inefficiency), the new proposals enabled companies to form joint BDLs. In order to improve communication and understanding between foreign and local companies, the proposals also allowed the heads of the BDLs to be of a different nationality from that of the companies which they represented. In May 1991 Algeria's official news agency reported that import licences had been abolished.

In February 1989 the Union of the Arab Maghreb (UAM) was formed by Algeria, Libya, Tunisia, Morocco and Mauritania, and the five countries are now working towards self-sufficiency and independence. In January 1989 the Ministers of Industry of the Maghreb countries met to discuss industrial unity and economic integration; co-operation in the mining, textiles, electronics, domestic appliances, leather and construction industries is also under consideration. The UAM aims to establish a customs union and a single monetary exchange currency. The ultimate aim is to allow all members of the UAM to establish industries in each of the five countries. In October 1993, during negotiations in Brussels, Belgium, the Minister of Foreign Affairs, Muhammad Saleh Dembri, asked the President of the European Commission to schedule talks on a free trade agreement between Algeria and the EU. Negotiations on similar agreements have already been opened by Algeria's neighbours, Morocco and Tunisia.

FINANCE

Before independence, Algeria was mostly dependent on France for its central banking and monetary system, though some of the usual central banking functions were carried out by the Banque d'Algérie. The Banque Centrale d'Algérie started its operations on 1 January 1963; it issues currency, regulates and licenses banks and supervises all foreign transactions. The banking system has been largely taken over by the state. A state monopoly on all foreign financial transactions was imposed in November 1967; this followed a similar monopoly imposed on insurance in June 1966. There are now five nationalized banks: the Banque Extérieure d'Algérie (BEA), which deals with the hydrocarbons sector; the Banque Nationale d'Algérie (BNA), which handles transport; the Crédit Populaire d'Algérie (CPA), responsible mainly for light industry, transport and tourism; Al-Baraka Bank of Algeria (ABA) and the Banque du Maghreb Arabe pour l'Investissement et le Commerce. The Banque Algérienne de Développement (BAD), founded in 1963, handles large-scale lending and arranges lines of credit with foreign banks. Legislation on banking and credit was introduced in 1986 to define the role of these institutions and of the Central Bank, and to improve their project-assessment capabilities, as well as guaranteeing banking secrecy. In 1987 legislation was introduced to enable local commercial banks to provide credit directly to state-owned enterprises, as well as to private companies. The criteria for authorizing credit were modified, requiring the bank to assess a project primarily by its economic viability (including the company's ability to make repayments), rather than its social value. This legislation allowed banks to compete against each other for business, although they were not allowed to determine their own interest rates. In the same year the *Conseil National de Crédit* (CNC) was established to supervise the implementation of the banking reforms and to determine the level of Algeria's foreign borrowing. In October 1988 banks were included in the group of more than 70 state-controlled companies which became *entreprises publiques économiques* (EPEs). The BEA was the first state bank to become fully autonomous under the scheme. All local banks reported a fall in profits in 1990 and faced serious problems as a result of debts incurred by public companies.

Algeria has also formed joint institutions with other countries. In 1974 an Algerian-Libyan bank, the Banque Internationale Arabe, was opened in Paris to finance trade and investment between France and Arab countries. Possible joint financial institutions have been discussed with Kuwait, Saudi Arabia and the United Arab Emirates. The Banque de Coopération du Maghreb Arabe was established with Tunisia, in order to promote joint projects. In 1988 Algeria and Libya agreed to establish a joint bank, the Banque du Maghreb Arabe pour l'Investissement et du Commerce. In March 1990 a banking and investment law was approved which, for the first time since independence, permitted foreign investors, in most sectors, to own up to 100% of companies and to repatriate all of their profits. Foreign banks were to be allowed to establish representative branches. Three French banks had already opened branches, with the status of BDLs, in Algiers. The new law also gave the banks greater powers of autonomy from the Ministry of Finance. In June 1991 the Al-Baraka Bank of Algeria, the country's first joint-venture bank, opened. It was also Algeria's first Islamic bank and the two partners are the local Banque de l'Agriculture et du Développement Rural (BADR) and Dallah Al-Baraka of Jeddah. In June 1993 the Banque d'Algérie reported that legislation permitting the establishment of local private banks was in place and that applications to set up new institutions were being considered. In July 1993 it was announced that First International Bank of Algeria, the country's first private bank, would shortly be open offering Islamic banking services.

In June 1992 the Governor of the Banque d'Algérie, Abderrahman Hadj-Nacer, stated that plans for the dinar to become convertible by 1993 remained feasible. However, Belaid Abd es-Salam, who became Prime Minister in July 1992, criticized the monetary policy overseen by Nacer, arguing that devaluation had been excessive and that the dinar should return to its 1987 value. Within two weeks of taking office Abd es-Salam replaced Nacer as Governor of the Banque d'Algérie with Abdelwahab Keramane. The devaluation of the dinar, undertaken since 1989, was halted and in a statement in March 1993 the Prime Minister confirmed his opposition to devaluation which, he maintained, resulted in the loss of jobs and hyperinflation. The Government announced that it would introduce a system of dual exchange rates in the second half of 1993. However, in June 1993 the Vice-Governor of the Banque d'Algérie, responsible for monetary policy, stated that plans for the dual system had been postponed until the end of the year. On 9 April 1994 the Government devalued the dinar by 40% days before an agreement was reached with the IMF on a new standby loan. The devaluation was announced as the Government submitted a package of monetary and fiscal measures for approval by the IMF.

According to official data published in April 1992, GDP, expressed in US dollars, declined by 26.9% in 1991 reflecting the sharp devaluation of the dinar. Per capita GDP fell from $2,752 in 1987 to $2,213 in 1990 and to $1,607 in 1991. According to the Banque d'Algérie, GDP amounted to an estimated AD 987,000m. ($43,025m.) in 1992, an increase of 2.9%. Growth rates for individual sectors were: agriculture 4.8%; industry 0.6% and building and public works 6%. Growth of 2% was forecast in 1993. In contrast, the Algiers-based

consultant, Ecotechnics, forecast a fall of 2%–3% in GDP in 1992. In May 1994 it was reported that, according to the projections included in Algeria's letter of intent to the IMF, there was no growth in GDP in 1993. Growth of 3% was forecast for 1994, and of 6% for 1995. The 1991 budget forecast an increase in revenue of 30%, to AD 195,300m., and current spending was to rise by 28% to AD 195,300m. The main objective of the 1991 budget was to control the level of current expenditure and to increase revenues, principally from the hydrocarbons sector. The 1991 budget was revised in August 1991 to reflect the Government's intention to reflate the economy with a controlled rise in public spending. Under the complementary budget, spending was due to rise to AD 230,800m., with revenues forecast at AD 250,800m., giving a budget surplus of AD 20,800m. Unemployment stood at 21% in 1991, according to the Government's recovery programme which was published in early 1992.

The 1992 budget set spending at AD 327,900m. of which, AD 203,900m. was for current expenditure and AD 124,000m. for investment. The higher investment spending was intended to revive the depressed economy and was to be concentrated on the agriculture, mining and energy sectors. Revenues were calculated at AD 328,400m. giving a surplus of AD 5,000m. Revenues from the hydrocarbons sector were forecast to rise to AD 200,000m., based on a favourable response to the new hydrocarbons law. The introduction of an income tax, corporation tax and value-added tax were central to the budget. Earnings from direct taxes were calculated at AD 38,000m. With a sharp rise in prices forecast as Algeria made the transition to a market economy, the 1992 finance act included plans for the introduction of a social security system to provide assistance for poor families. The budget also recommended the maintenance of subsidies at AD 53,100m. Price subsidies totalling AD 29,500m. were to be directed into 10 essential products, including vegetable oil, semolina, milk and dry vegetables. According to the finance law enacted in 1993, government spending was forecast to rise to AD 503,900m., with revenues forecast at AD 335,600m., leaving a deficit of AD 168,300m. Spending on security was to be substantially increased. Budgets for the ministries of defence, the interior and justice were more than doubled to AD 29,800m., AD 18,700m. and AD 2,900m. respectively. Higher allocations were also made to education, health, religious and social affairs. Some AD 83,500m. were allocated to support loss-making public companies and AD 24,000m. to provide social security payments to an estimated 7m. poor Algerians. A tax described as a contribution to national solidarity was to be levied on richer Algerians over the following three years. Fears were expressed that the massive budget deficit and the sharp reduction in imports would increase inflationary pressures. According to official figures, inflation was 33.6% in the year ending October 1992 and 30% in 1993. According to the official Algérie Presse Service (APS), reporting in January 1994, the budget deficit in 1993 amounted to AD 192,00m. APS also reported that a deficit of more than AD 74,000m. had been recorded in 1992, a year when the budget had been forecast to balance.

In 1994 it was estimated that total expenditure would rise by 6% to, AD 535,300m. Revenues were forecast to rise to AD 410,000m., resulting in a budget deficit of AD 125,300m., equivalent to 9.6% of forecast GDP. It was reported that the increase in state revenues was to be achieved through improved tax collection. Under the 1994 Finance Act, reforms to the tax system included changes in local company taxation, and a higher ceiling and lower rates for corporate tax. Some customs tariffs were to be modified to stimulate and protect local production. An export credit insurance scheme was also planned. It was reported that, despite criticisms of recent social welfare programmes, there were no plans to make major cuts in social spending. It was anticipated that, owing to the depressed price of petroleum, the actual budget deficit would be much higher than the figure forecast in the finance law.

During the 1970s Algeria borrowed heavily on the international markets to finance development, especially in its gas industry. Borrowing on the Euromarket, principally by SONATRACH, in one peak year, 1978, amounted to $2,515m. In 1979 total borrowing declined by almost one-third to around

$2,000m. The total borrowing requirement for the 1980–84 Plan was estimated at $10,000m.

Algeria avoided the Euromarkets between 1980 and 1983, but after 1983 the country again began to borrow heavily on the international markets, owing to a steady erosion of its earnings from hydrocarbons. It borrowed about $2,000m. in both 1984 and 1985, usually securing favourable repayment terms. However, towards the end of 1985, the banks became nervous over potential risks in lending to Algeria, and, subsequently, US banks, worried about their Latin American commitments, tended to avoid any new syndicated loans. With the collapse of energy prices in 1986, this nervousness became more acute. Despite being offered more generous terms for the loans arranged during the year, banks failed to provide the total amount sought by Algeria. The loans that the commercial banks agreed were used to finance imports. In 1987 Algeria attempted to gain official export credit lines to finance imports and succeeded in securing a three-year French loan of $514.5m. Oil prices did not rise and Algeria was forced to seek further international loans in 1988 and 1989. During 1988 Algerian bankers raised almost $3,500m. in new loans, and about $1,000m. in medium- and long-term syndicated loans. Algeria's standing with international bankers was unaffected by the riots in October 1988, since President Chadli rapidly regained control of the situation. In January 1989 France agreed a credit package of FF 7,500m. as part of the settlement of its dispute with Algeria over gas prices. Credit packages from Spain and Italy were also secured in early 1989. In April the World Bank allocated a development loan of $211m., and in June Algeria accepted for the first time an IMF loan, preferring this option to debt rescheduling. The EU became an increasingly important source of multilateral support. In September 1991 it agreed to provide a loan worth $471m. (ECU 400m.). The seven-year loan was to be disbursed in two instalments, of $294m. (ECU 250m.) and $177m. (ECU 150m.), and was agreed on condition that it would not be used to repay borrowing from commercial banks. In 1990 the Banque Nationale de Paris provided Algeria with a seven-year loan of FF 1,000m. to assist the Minister of Economic Affairs' plan to convert short-term borrowing into medium- or long-term loans. Fears of further instability in Algeria, and the possible repercussions for Western Europe, with its large North African communities, resulted in strong political pressure on financial institutions to offer substantial support to Algeria by refinancing loans to restructure existing debts, and by providing new export credits. In June 1991 Italy reaffirmed its commitment to provide the first $2,700m. of a planned $7,200m. debt-refinancing and credit package. After initial reluctance, the Italian export agency, SACE, agreed to underwrite the first phase of the package, which was to provide credits to cover mainly short-term debt to Italian creditors falling due in the two years to January 1993. In June 1991 the World Bank approved a $350m.-structural adjustment loan to Algeria, repayable over 17 years and to be disbursed in two instalments, the first available immediately. Michel Camdessus, the Managing Director of the IMF, visited Algiers in July 1991 and urged commercial banks to support the Government's search for new credits. The IMF had agreed a $404m.-standby loan package in June 1991 to run to March 1992. In spite of the balance-of-payments support offered by the EU and the IMF, in October 1991 creditors reported a rise in payment delays, which reflected a financing shortfall in 1991/92. In October 1991, after months of speculation, a group of eight international banks, led by Crédit Lyonnais of France, agreed, in principle, to refinance up to $1,500m. of short-term debt: the major part, in fact, of Algeria's outstanding commercial short-term debt. The refusal of several banks to participate delayed the signing of the final agreement for a $1,457m.-refinancing facility until March 1992. There was strong political pressure from Europe to mobilize support for the facility. The refinancing strategy was designed to avoid rescheduling at a time of peak debt repayment, since rescheduling would have excluded Algeria from the commercial markets it needed to cultivate in order to encourage investment. Until the refinancing package was in place, banks agreed to treat missed repayments as deferrals rather than as arrears or a default. In April 1992 it was reported that, following the March dis-

bursal of credits from the new refinancing facility, the Banque d'Algérie had repaid arrears of syndicated debt and had started to repay trade arrears. It was reported in March 1992 that France had rejected Algeria's request for bilateral refinancing (of FF 33,000m. ($5,830m.)) of debt, guaranteed by the French export credit agency, Coface, because it would have contravened orthodox debt management structures of the 'Paris Club'. The reports indicated that France favoured formal rescheduling instead. In April 1992 The Export-Import Bank of Japan signed a $300m.-untied loan to provide co-financing with the World Bank's financial sector structural adjustment loan. Following a visit to Algiers by the World Bank's Vice-President for North Africa and the Middle East in June 1992, the Bank approved two new project loans worth $58m.

Preliminary talks on a new IMF standby loan were scheduled to take place in mid-1992, but were delayed after the appointment of a new Government. Abdelwahab Keramane, the Governor of the Banque d'Algérie, stated that the new Government intended to continue the process of refinancing the country's debt as long as this did not require difficult economic and social policies. He requested additional debt relief, including a second reprofiling operation, but reiterated that the Government rejected formal rescheduling. In August Italian creditors announced that up to $4,500m. in new export credits, agreed in 1991, had been suspended. At the end of November, after speculation that the Algerian Government might seek rescheduling as the only solution to its economic crisis, the Prime Minister made it clear that he continued to reject formal rescheduling. After a visit to Algiers by the French Minister of Foreign Affairs, Roland Dumas, in early January 1993, France indicated that it would provide large-scale financial support, and an agreement for some FF 6,000m. ($1,072m.) in French aid and aid credits in 1993 was signed in February of that year. Nevertheless, France maintained its long-standing refusal to enter into bilateral debt negotiations, insisting that any rescheduling must be made through the 'Paris Club'. In April the Banque d'Algérie stated that it would be able to service existing debts in 1993 without signing a new IMF standby agreement, but that special assistance would be necessary in 1994, when a current account deficit was predicted. By 1996 the Banque d'Algérie forecast that increased gas exports would have reduced the burden of debt servicing and that they would permit a level of imports sufficient for economic growth. The Government reiterated its wish to avoid formal rescheduling, but did not rule out recourse to refinancing operations with certain partners, if these could be agreed. An IMF delegation visited Algeria in the second half of June 1993 in order to continue talks about a new facility to replace the standby credit that had expired in March 1992. However, no progress was achieved. Without a new agreement with the IMF, funds from other international agencies could not be released. Lack of confidence in government policy had already resulted in a serious reduction in credit support. After the appointment of Redha Malek as Prime Minister there was speculation that the new Government would favour the rescheduling of the country's external debt. In the new Council of Ministers, announced in September 1993, Mourad Benachenou, an economist known to support rescheduling, was appointed Minister of the Economy. In October Benachenou stated that the Government needed more time to establish a consensus on economic policy. In December the Banque d'Algérie announced revised figures for the external debt, which totalled $26,008m. at the end of 1992, and indicated that debt-service payments would total $9,400m. in 1993, and that the debt-service ratio would rise to 83%. In February 1994 it was reported that Algeria had stopped repaying most of its medium- to long-term debt insured by European export credit agencies, but was continuing to service its short-term debt and commodity credits. The Government continued to seek support for bilateral rescheduling, but most creditors were convinced that a 'Paris Club' rescheduling was inevitable. On 17 April the Banque d'Algérie announced that it had applied to the 'Paris Club' to reschedule debts of $13,500m., more than half the country's total external debt. It was estimated that rescheduling would reduce debt repayments by $4,000m. in 1994 and by $5,000m. in 1995. Agreement was expected from official creditors in June and talks would then follow to discuss final dates for debt to be rescheduled and the duration of the repayments. Algeria was reported to be seeking a minimum repayment period of 15 years as well as debt reduction. A new standby package had been agreed with the IMF a few days before the announcement, as part of which the IMF was to provide a $500m.-standby loan and a $300m.-compensatory and contingency financing facility over the following 12 months. The IMF agreement cleared the way for Algeria to utilize loans from the EU, the World Bank and Japan, worth a total of $475m. At the beginning of April the World Bank had announced that it was revising its lending strategy for Algeria to provide new financing once an agreement was signed with the IMF. The Banque d'Algérie, however, has calculated that even with the new IMF accord extending until March 1995, and a 'Paris Club' rescheduling, the economy will still lack some $5,000m. of the amount required to purchase imports in 1994.

Algeria's return to the international capital markets in 1983 ended a period during which the Government had managed to effect a net repayment of its external debt. The OECD estimated that total external debt rose from $17,924m. at the end of 1983 to $18,500m. at the end of 1985. Estimates published by the World Bank in December 1993, put Algeria's total external debt at $26,349m. at the end of 1992. The cost of servicing the debt was estimated at 71.9% of the value of exports of goods and services. The Government's economic recovery programme, published in February 1992, included data which showed rising levels of debt service. In October 1992 the *Conseil National de la Planification* issued revised targets for external payments in 1992. Repayments of medium- and long-term debt totalling $25,500m. were forecast at $6,990m. in 1992, compared with $7,290m. in 1991, and

$6,730m. in 1990. The Washington-based Institute of International Finance reported that net repayments of debt reached $15,000m. in 1991, with principal payments at $7,300m. According to statements by the Banque d'Algérie in early 1993, medium- and long-term debt totalled $25,690m. in 1992. Debt-service levels were forecast to fall from $9,360m. in 1992 to $8,250m. in 1996. The debt-service ratio was projected to fall from almost 78% in 1992 to 70.1% in 1994 and 52% in 1997. By early 1994 Algeria's external debt was estimated at $26,000m. and debt-service repayments were forecast at $9,500m. for that year. As a result of depressed petroleum prices, hydrocarbon revenues for 1994 were estimated at only $8,000m.

According to IMF data, Algeria's foreign exchange reserves minus gold amounted to only $404m. in July 1991, as the Government came under pressure to meet debt repayments, but rose to $791m. in August 1991. Official sources reported that foreign exchange reserves stood at $1,094m. at 31 October 1991. In June 1993 officials of the Banque d'Algérie stated that reserves had been increased to $2,000m., the highest level since 1986, as a result of the Government's austerity programme. The Banque d'Algérie has been criticized for its management of Algeria's gold reserves, which for many years have stood at 5.58m. fine troy ounces (with a market value of about $2,000m.). All gold reserves were formerly held in the USA to underpin the currency, but in August 1991 the Governor of the Banque d'Algérie told the ANP that some of the reserves had been transferred to Zürich, Basel and London, and that, in the form of London 'Good Delivery' gold (rather than US ingots), the deposits would be more liquid and could earn money through swap procedures. The policy was criticized by the Minister of the Economy, but it was supported by the president of the ANP's finance commission.

Statistical Survey

Source (unless otherwise stated): Office National des Statistiques, 8 rue des Moussebiline, BP 55, Algiers; tel. (2) 64-77-90; telex 52620.

Area and Population

AREA, POPULATION AND DENSITY

Area (sq km)	2,381,741*
Population (census results)†	
12 February 1977 (provisional)	16,948,000
20 April 1987	23,038,942
Population (official estimates at 1 January)†	
1991	25,324,000
1992	25,942,000
1993	26,581,000
Density (per sq km) at 1 January 1993 . . .	11.2

* 919,595 sq miles.
† Excluding Algerian nationals residing abroad, numbering an estimated 828,000 at 1 January 1978.

POPULATION BY WILAYA (ADMINISTRATIVE DISTRICT)
(provisional census results, April 1987)*

	Population
Adrar	216,931
el-Asnam (ech-Cheliff)	679,717
Laghouat	215,183
Oum el-Bouaghi (Oum el-Bouagul) . . .	402,683
Batna	757,059
Béjaia	697,669
Biskra (Beskra)	429,217
Béchar	183,896
Blida (el-Boulaïda)	704,462
Bouira	525,460
Tamanrasset (Tamenghest)	94,219
Tébessa (Tbessa)	409,317
Tlemcen (Tilimsen)	707,453
Tiaret (Tihert)	574,786
Tizi-Ouzou	931,501
Algiers (el-Djezaïr)	1,687,579
Djelfa (el-Djelfa)	490,240
Jijel	471,319
Sétif (Stif)	997,482
Saida	235,240
Skikda	619,094
Sidi-Bel-Abbès	444,047
Annaba	453,951
Guelma	353,329
Constantine (Qacentina)	662,330
Médéa (Lemdiyya)	650,623
Mostaganem (Mestghanem)	504,124
M'Sila	605,578

- continued							Population
Mascara (Mouaskar)	.	.	.	.	.	.	562,806
Ouargla (Wargla)	.	.	.	.	.	.	286,696
Oran (Ouahran)	.	.	.	.	.	.	916,678
el-Bayadh	.	.	.	.	.	.	155,494
Illizi	.	.	.	.	.	.	19,698
Bordj Bou Arreridj	.	.	.	.	.	.	429,009
Boumerdes	.	.	.	.	.	.	646,870
el-Tarf	.	.	.	.	.	.	276,836
Tindouf	.	.	.	.	.	.	16,339
Tissemsilt	.	.	.	.	.	.	227,542
el-Oued	.	.	.	.	.	.	379,512
Khenchela	.	.	.	.	.	.	243,733
Souk-Ahras	.	.	.	.	.	.	298,236
Tipaza	.	.	.	.	.	.	615,140
Mila	.	.	.	.	.	.	511,047
Ain-Defla	.	.	.	.	.	.	536,205
Naama	.	.	.	.	.	.	112,858
Ain-Temouchent	.	.	.	.	.	.	271,454
Ghardaia	.	.	.	.	.	.	215,955
Relizane	.	.	.	.	.	.	545,061
Total	.	.	.	.	.	.	22,971,558

* Excluding Algerian nationals abroad, estimated to total 828,000 at 1 January 1978.

PRINCIPAL TOWNS (estimated population at 1 January 1983)

Algiers (el-Djezaïr, capital) .	1,721,607	Tlemcen (Tilimsen)	146,089
Oran (Ouahran) .	663,504	Skikda . . .	141,159
Constantine (Qacen-		Béjaia . .	124,122
tina) . .	448,578	Batna . .	122,788
Annaba . .	348,322	El-Asnam (ech-	
Blida (el-Boulaïda)	191,314	Cheliff) . .	118,996
Sétif (Stif) .	186,978	Boufarik . .	112,000*
Sidi-bel-Abbès .	146,653	Tizi-Ouzou .	100,749
		Médéa (Lemdiyya)	84,292

* 1977 figure.

April 1987 (census results, not including suburbs): Algiers 1,483,000; Oran 590,000; Constantine 438,000.

BIRTHS AND DEATHS (UN estimates, annual averages)

	1975–80	1980–85	1985–90
Birth rate (per 1,000) . .	45.0	40.6	35.5
Death rate (per 1,000) . .	13.4	10.4	8.3

Expectation of life (UN estimates, years at birth, 1985–90): 64.1 (males 63.1; females 65.0).

Source: UN, *World Population Prospects: The 1992 Revision.*

1990 (provisional): Registered live births 758,533 (birth rate 30.3 per 1,000); Registered deaths 113,511 (death rate 4.5 per 1,000). Figures refer to the Algerian population only and exclude liveborn infants dying before registration of birth. Birth registration is estimated to be at least 90% complete, but death registration is incomplete.

ECONOMICALLY ACTIVE POPULATION
(1987 census)*

	Males	Females	Total
Agriculture, hunting, forestry and fishing . . .	714,947	9,753	724,699
Mining and quarrying . . .	64,685	3,142	67,825
Manufacturing. . . .	471,471	40,632	512,105
Electricity, gas and water . .	40,196	1,579	41,775
Construction	677,211	12,372	689,586
Trade, restaurants and hotels	376,590	14,399	390,990
Transport, storage and communications	207,314	9,029	216,343
Financing, insurance, real estate and business services	125,426	17,751	143,178
Community, social and personal services . . .	945,560	234,803	1,180,364
Activities not adequately defined	149,241	83,718	232,959
Total employed . . .	3,772,641	427,183	4,199,824
Unemployed	1,076,018	65,260	1,141,278
Total labour force . . .	4,848,659	492,443	5,341,102

* Employment data relate to persons aged 6 years and over; those for unemployment relate to persons aged 16 to 64 years. Estimates have been made independently, so the totals may not be the sum of the component parts.

Agriculture

PRINCIPAL CROPS ('000 metric tons)

	1990	1991	1992
Wheat	775	1,741	1,750†
Barley	800	1,751	1,370†
Oats	35	125	95†
Potatoes	809	900*	900*
Pulses	35	45*	47*
Rapeseed*	87	93	98
Olives*	90	130	130
Tomatoes	402	500*	500*
Pumpkins, squash and gourds*	57	61	63
Cucumbers and gherkins* . .	45	45	45
Chillies and peppers (green)* .	120	150	210
Onions (dry)	173	220*	231*
Carrots	101	120*	140*
Other vegetables* . . .	341	366	388
Melons and watermelons* . .	356	374	389
Grapes.	263	251	260*
Dates	206	208*	210†
Apples*	54	57	57
Oranges	184	190*	192*
Tangerines, mandarins, clementines and satsumas .	82	95*	95*
Apricots*	42	42	42
Other fruits*	208	214	228
Tobacco (leaves) . . .	4	5†	5*

* FAO estimate(s).   † Unofficial figure.

Source: FAO, *Production Yearbook.*

LIVESTOCK ('000 head, year ending September)

	1990	1991*	1992*
Sheep	17,698	18,500	18,600
Goats	2,472	2,480	2,500
Cattle	1,393	1,400	1,420
Horses	81	83	84
Mules	100	107	107
Asses	299	340	340
Camels	122	130	130

Poultry (FAO estimates, million): 74 in 1990; 75 in 1991; 76 in 1992.
* FAO estimates.

Source: FAO, *Production Yearbook.*

LIVESTOCK PRODUCTS ('000 metric tons)

	1990	1991	1992
Beef and veal	89	94	95
Mutton and lamb . . .	134†	144†	145*
Goat's meat*	10	10	10
Poultry meat*	185	189	193
Other meat*	9	9	10
Cows' milk*	630	640	650
Sheep's milk*	213	222	230
Goats' milk*	129	129	130
Hen eggs†	132.0	130.0	135.0
Wool:			
greasy*	45.9	48.6	48.6
clean*	24.0	25.4	25.4
Cattle hides*	7.0	7.2	7.3
Sheep skins*	17.0	18.0	18.1
Goat skins*	2.0	2.0	2.0

* FAO estimate(s). † Unofficial figure(s).

Source: FAO, *Production Yearbook.*

Forestry

ROUNDWOOD REMOVALS
('000 cubic metres, excluding bark)

	1990	1991	1992
Sawlogs, veneer logs and logs for sleepers	20*	39	46
Other industrial wood* . .	241	248	255
Fuel wood*	1,901	1,953	2,006
Total	2,162	2,240	2,307

* FAO estimate(s).

Sawnwood production ('000 cubic metres, incl. railway sleepers): 13 per year (FAO estimates) in 1980–92.

Source: FAO, *Yearbook of Forest Products.*

Fishing

('000 metric tons, live weight)

	1989	1990	1991
European pilchard (sardine) .	65.5	61.5*	52.5*
Other fishes . . .	30.7	26.3*	24.3*
Crustaceans and molluscs . .	3.5	3.3*	3.3*
Total catch	99.7	91.1	80.1
Inland waters	0.6	0.4	0.4
Mediterranean Sea. . . .	99.2	90.7	79.7

* FAO estimate.

Source: FAO, *Yearbook of Fishery Statistics.*

1992 (sea fishing): Total catch 95,274 metric tons.

Mining

('000 metric tons, unless otherwise indicated)

	1989	1990	1991
Hard coal	15	10*	15*
Crude petroleum . . .	34,064	37,021	37,698
Natural gas (petajoules) . .	1,489	1,615	1,738
Iron ore:			
gross weight. . . .	2,124*	n.a.	n.a.
metal content . . .	1,485	1,589	1,270
Lead concentrates† . . .	2.8	1.9	1.9
Zinc concentrates† . . .	12.0	8.0	7.9
Mercury (metric tons) . . .	587	637	430
Phosphate rock . . .	1,223	1,128	1,031
Salt (unrefined) . . .	129	117	103
Gypsum (crude)	65	49	152

* Provisional or estimated data.
† Figures refer to the metal content of concentrates.

Source: UN, *Industrial Statistics Yearbook* and *Monthly Bulletin of Statistics.*

1992 ('000 metric tons): Lead concentrates (metal content) 1.5; Zinc concentrates (metal content) 7.5; Phosphate rock 1,143.

Industry

SELECTED PRODUCTS
('000 metric tons, unless otherwise indicated)

	1989	1990	1991
Olive oil (crude) . . .	12	8	16
Refined sugar	214	209	217
Wine ('000 hectolitres) . .	1,000	490	460
Beer ('000 hectolitres). . .	365	325	301
Soft drinks ('000 hectolitres) .	1,233	1,067	938
Cigarettes (metric tons) . .	15,950	18,775	17,848
Cotton yarn—pure and mixed	28.1	27.4	26.6
Woven cotton fabrics (million metres)	62.9	63.1	53.7
Woven woollen fabrics (million metres)	5.9	8.1	9.9
Footwear—excl. rubber ('000 pairs)	14,943	16,376	11,824
Nitrogenous fertilizers (a)† .	88.0*	90.4	73.2
Phosphate fertilizers (b)† . .	45.3*	53.7	34.6
Naphthas	4,746	4,200	4,250
Motor spirit (petrol) . . .	1,860	1,900	2,233
Kerosene	110	120	100
Jet fuel	522	530	300
Distillate fuel oils . . .	7,510	8,052	7,800
Residual fuel oils . . .	5,926	5,948	5,645
Lubricating oils . . .	120	120	125
Petroleum bitumen (asphalt) .	220	210	220
Liquefied petroleum gas:			
from natural gas plants . .	4,216	4,533	4,600*
from petroleum refineries* .	710	900	900
Cement	6,819	6,337	6,323
Pig-iron for steel-making . .	1,300	1,037	879
Crude steel (ingots) . .	943	767	797
Zinc—unwrought . . .	16.8	15.0	24.9
Refrigerators for household use ('000)	381	387	388
Radio receivers ('000) . .	120	213	215
Television receivers ('000) . .	219	283	176
Buses and coaches—assembled (number)	577	727	654
Lorries—assembled (number)	3,946	3,564	3,164
Electric energy (million kWh)	15,358	16,104	17,345

* Provisional or estimated data.
† Production in terms of (a) nitrogen or (b) phosphoric acid. Phosphate fertilizers include ground rock phosphate. Source: FAO, *Quarterly Bulletin of Statistics.*

Source: mainly UN, *Industrial Statistics Yearbook.*

1992 ('000 metric tons, unless otherwise indicated): Olive oil* 8; Wine* 50; Footwear—excl. rubber ('000 pairs) 9,040; Cement 7,093; Pig-iron for steel-making 930; Crude steel (ingots) 768; Television receivers ('000) 218; Buses and coaches—assembled (number) 1,008; Lorries—assembled (number) 2,434; Electric energy (million kWh) 18,286.

*FAO estimates (Source: FAO, *Production Yearbook*).

Finance

CURRENCY AND EXCHANGE RATES

Monetary Units
100 centimes = 1 Algerian dinar (AD).

Sterling and Dollar Equivalents (31 May 1994)
£1 sterling = 55.914 dinars;
US $1 = 36.985 dinars;
1,000 Algerian dinars = £17.885 = $27.038.

Average Exchange Rate (dinars per US $)
1991   18.473
1992   21.836
1993   23.345

ADMINISTRATIVE BUDGET (estimates, million AD)

Expenditure	1985	1986	1987*
Presidency.	611.8	640.0	585.0
National defence	4,793.1	5,459.0	5,805.0
Foreign affairs	583.5	619.3	583.0
Light industry	137.6	149.5	132.0
Housing and construction	359.4	460.9	439.0
Finance	1,252.4	1,446.1	1,613.0
Home affairs	n.a.	3,543.0	4,003.0
Commerce	130.6	146.8	148.0
Youth and sport	403.6	446.6	396.0
Information	350.8	384.8	373.0
Ex-servicemen	2,984.5	3,289.0	3,192.0
Culture and tourism	218.3	258.2	226.0
Agriculture and fishing	766.0	838.1	772.0
Health	2,720.6	3,518.3	3,961.0
Transport	373.7	414.0	413.0
Justice	477.4	556.4	668.0
Professional training	1,397.9	1,539.8	1,562.0
Religious affairs	363.7	403.1	473.0
Public works	690.8	784.1	697.0
Education	11,026.7	13,626.7	15,886.0
Higher education and scientific research	2,764.4	2,931.6	3,494.0
Heavy industry	94.6	108.3	107.0
Water, environment and forests	798.3	866.0	810.0
Energy and petrochemicals industries	201.5	220.9	216.0
Planning and land development.	n.a.	165.9	—
Social protection	476.7	530.1	501.0
Extra expenditure	25,197.5	23,384.4	15,779.0
Total (incl. others)	**62,200.0**	**67,000.0**	**63,000.0**

* As announced in November 1985. A revised administrative budget, announced in April 1986, projected total expenditure of 59,500 million AD.

1988 (million AD): Revenue 103,000; Administrative expenditure 64,500.
1989 (million AD): Revenue 114,700; Administrative expenditure 71,900.
1990 (million AD): Revenue 136,500; Administrative expenditure 84,000.
1991 (million AD): Revenue 195,300; Administrative expenditure 118,300.
1992 (million AD): Revenue 322,700; Administrative expenditure 396,800.
1993 (million AD): Revenue 335,600; Administrative expenditure 503,900.
1994 (million AD): Revenue 474,100; Administrative expenditure 613,700.

INVESTMENT BUDGET (million AD)

Expenditure	1988
Hydrocarbons	700
Manufacturing industries	1,300
Mines and energy (incl. rural electrification)	1,000
Agriculture and water projects	7,450
Services	135
Economic and administrative infrastructure	8,369
Education and training	7,100
Social and cultural infrastructures	3,294
Construction	2,142
Infrastructure and training linked to the reform of state enterprises	470
Grants to new enterprises	150
Financial restructuring of state enterprises	3,400
Total (incl. others)	**47,500**

Source: *Al-Moudjahid*.

CENTRAL BANK RESERVES (US $ million at 31 December)

	1991	1992	1993
Gold*	280	269	268
IMF special drawing rights	2	1	7
Foreign exchange	1,484	1,456	1,468
Total	**1,766**	**1,726**	**1,743**

* Valued at 35 SDRs per troy ounce.
Source: IMF, *International Financial Statistics*.

MONEY SUPPLY (million AD at 31 December)*

	1991	1992	1993
Currency outside banks	157,200	184,610	211,410
Demand deposits at deposit money banks	133,110	140,840	186,510
Checking deposits at post office	31,950	39,830	40,980
Private sector demand deposits at treasury	2,210	4,200	5,280
Total money	**324,470**	**377,000†**	**447,600†**

* Figures are rounded to the nearest 10 million dinars.
† Including others.
Source: IMF, *International Financial Statistics*.

COST OF LIVING (Consumer Price Index for Algiers; average of monthly figures; base: 1989 = 100)

	1991	1992	1993
Food	147.3	184.8	230.4
All items (incl. others)	148.4	195.4	235.5

Source: UN, *Monthly Bulletin of Statistics*.

NATIONAL ACCOUNTS
National Income and Product (million AD at current prices)

	1987	1988	1989
Compensation of employees .	125,754.4	137,647.5	156,145.1
Operating surplus . . .	92,417.5	99,899.8	142,711.2
Domestic factor incomes.	218,171.9	237,547.3	298,856.3
Consumption of fixed capital .	32,525.2	32,621.8	33,050.1
Gross domestic product (GDP) at factor cost .	250,697.1	270,169.1	331,906.4
Indirect taxes, *less* subsidies .	62,009.0	64,437.5	71,553.8
GDP in purchasers' values .	312,706.1	334,606.6	403,460.2
Net factor income from abroad	−7,267.7	−11,744.7	−13,178.4
Reinsurance (net)	−76.0	—	—
Gross national product .	305,362.4	322,861.9	390,281.8
Less Consumption of fixed capital	32,525.2	32,621.8	33,050.1
National income in market prices	272,837.2	290,240.1	357,231.7
Other current transfers from abroad (net).	2,358.2	2,067.7	3,850.4
National disposable income	275,195.4	292,307.8	361,082.1

Expenditure on the Gross Domestic Product
('000 million AD at current prices)

	1991	1992	1993
Government final consumption expenditure	124.3	165.2	202.1
Private final consumption expenditure	390.1	512.8	594.7
Increase in stocks . . . }	230.1	279.3	300.3
Gross fixed capital formation }			
Total domestic expenditure	744.5	957.3	1,097.1
Exports of goods and services	244.3	263.6	251.9
Less Imports of goods and services	199.3	251.9	255.9
GDP in purchasers' values .	789.5	969.0	1,093.1

Source: IMF, *International Financial Statistics.*

BALANCE OF PAYMENTS (US $ million)

	1989	1990	1991
Merchandise exports f.o.b. .	9,534	12,964	12,330
Merchandise imports f.o.b. .	−8,372	−8,777	−6,852
Trade balance . . .	1,162	4,187	5,478
Exports of services . .	496	498	393
Imports of services . .	−1,231	−1,328	−1,172
Other income received . .	111	73	70
Other income paid . . .	−2,159	−2,343	−2,618
Private unrequited transfers (net).	535	332	239
Official unrequited transfers (net).	6	1	−23
Current balance . . .	−1,081	1,420	2,367
Direct investment (net) . .	4	−4	−39
Other capital (net). . .	751	−1,090	−982
Net errors and omissions .	−448	−336	−299
Overall balance . . .	−774	−10	1,047

Source: IMF, *International Financial Statistics.*

External Trade

Note: Data exclude military goods. Exports include stores and bunkers for foreign ships and aircraft.

PRINCIPAL COMMODITIES
(distribution by SITC, US $ million)

Imports c.i.f.	1989	1990	1991
Food and live animals . .	2,891.6	2,125.1	1,868.1
Dairy products and birds' eggs	556.3	506.5	452.5
Milk and cream . . .	439.1	392.5	379.1
Cereals and cereal preparations	1,320.3	824.7	593.3
Wheat and meslin (unmilled). . . .	738.2	417.3	247.5
Maize (unmilled) . . .	220.7	121.7	111.5
Vegetables and fruit . . .	206.9	176.1	187.0
Sugar, sugar preparations and honey	354.9	314.8	293.1
Refined sugars, etc. . .	345.6	313.1	291.6
Crude materials (inedible) except fuels	530.3	506.7	283.4
Cork and wood . . .	260.0	290.2	103.5
Simply worked wood and railway sleepers. . .	230.5	245.7	83.8
Sawn coniferous wood . .	219.9	240.6	80.5
Mineral fuels, lubricants, etc.	129.3	110.7	250.4
Animal and vegetable oils, fats and waxes . . .	318.5	169.1	117.8
Fixed vegetable oils and fats .	257.0	135.6	91.9
Chemicals and related products	1,118.6	798.2	705.5
Medicinal and pharmaceutical products.	457.0	340.3	217.3
Medicaments . . .	416.6	301.5	184.4
Artificial resins, plastic materials, etc. . . .	273.0	134.0	202.2
Products of polymerization, etc.	215.5	89.3	159.1
Basic manufactures . .	1,601.7	1,954.6	1,614.7
Rubber manufactures . .	173.0	363.3	126.0
Rubber tyres, tubes, etc .	129.7	308.9	89.1
Iron and steel	591.7	606.3	636.4
Bars, rods, angles, shapes and sections	394.2	298.2	255.8
Machinery and transport equipment	2,327.2	3,800.3	2,392.7
Power-generating machinery and equipment . . .	386.9	416.1	224.6
Internal combustion piston engines and parts . .	126.4	211.8	121.0
Machinery specialized for particular industries . .	325.4	603.6	487.5
Metalworking machinery . .	140.1	205.4	131.2
General industrial machinery, equipment and parts .	630.1	1,023.0	731.0
Heating and cooling equipment. . . .	94.9	259.6	145.8
Electrical machinery, apparatus and appliances .	451.3	575.8	398.6
Road vehicles and parts* . .	272.1	555.1	357.5
Parts and accessories for cars, buses, lorries, etc.*	133.9	233.2	121.9
Other transport equipment* .	34.4	327.6	14.1
Aircraft, associated equipment and parts* . .	13.2	279.3	3.7
Gliders, kites and rotochutes . . .	1.1	275.1	–
Miscellaneous manufactured articles	238.5	256.8	434.0
Baby carriages, toys, games and sporting goods . .	2.2	2.4	217.2
Roundabouts, swings and other fairground amusements . . .	1.0	0.8	215.0
Total (incl. others) . . .	9,187.5	9,735.9	7,683.3

* Excluding tyres, engines and electrical parts.

Exports f.o.b.	1989	1990	1991
Mineral fuels, lubricants, etc.	8,556.2	10,623.4	11,424.5
Petroleum, petroleum products, etc.	6,053.6	7,671.6	7,407.7
Crude petroleum oils, etc. .	4,179.0	5,385.4	5,060.0
Refined petroleum products	1,872.6	2,270.4	2,345.8
Motor spirit (petrol) and other light oils . .	577.4	704.6	812.6
Motor spirit (incl. aviation spirit) .	577.4	704.6	804.8
Gas oils (distillate fuels) .	677.3	802.7	882.3
Residual fuel oils . .	600.1	722.4	638.7
Gas (natural and manufactured) . .	2,500.0	2,951.5	4,016.8
Liquefied petroleum gases .	1,684.6	2,040.0	2,567.6
Petroleum gases, etc. in the gaseous state . . .	815.4	911.4	1,449.2
Total (incl. others) . . .	8,949.0	11,011.1	11,790.0

Source: UN, *International Trade Statistics Yearbook*.

1992 (million AD): Imports c.i.f. 188,406; Exports f.o.b. 243,087 (Source: IMF, *International Financial Statistics*).

PRINCIPAL TRADING PARTNERS (US $ million)*

Imports c.i.f.	1989	1990	1991
Austria	197.3	150.1	120.5
Belgium/Luxembourg . . .	297.1	361.1	253.7
Brazil	133.8	89.7	87.0
Canada	324.3	317.0	200.0
France	1,594.2	2,251.3	1,584.5
Germany, Federal Republic	887.0	1,045.1	750.7†
Indonesia	147.9	75.1	76.3
Italy	1,218.3	1,201.0	1,187.0
Japan	346.1	449.0	371.3
Netherlands . . .	298.3	170.3	116.7
Spain	368.1	607.2	647.1
Sweden	142.4	157.9	93.8
Switzerland . . .	128.7	114.3	95.6
Turkey	267.0	205.7	188.3
USSR	163.7	92.7	21.3
United Kingdom . .	162.3	143.3	104.7
USA	1,101.3	1,123.1	763.6
Yugoslavia	132.5	106.5	94.5
Total (incl. others) . . .	9,187.5	9,735.9	7,683.3

Exports f.o.b.	1989	1990	1991
Austria	161.7	216.9	273.7
Belgium/Luxembourg . . .	625.4	757.3	733.5
Brazil	149.4	166.7	232.2
France	1,667.2	1,910.1	2,215.1
Germany, Federal Republic .	375.4	236.4	275.1†
Italy	1,838.5	2,254.0	2,794.0
Japan	124.9	104.2	81.6
Korea Republic . . .	104.0	9.8	0.3
Netherlands . . .	792.3	1,027.1	991.2
Portugal	147.0	219.1	237.9
Spain	492.5	665.9	800.1
Tunisia	89.9	177.5	101.0
Turkey	144.6	177.1	53.7
USSR	124.3	143.1	130.5
United Kingdom . . .	116.3	238.2	309.0
USA	1,709.9	2,118.1	2,037.6
Total (incl. others) . . .	8,949.0	11,011.1	11,790.0

* Imports by country of production; exports by country of last consignment.
† Including trade with the former German Democratic Republic.
Source: UN, *International Trade Statistics Yearbook*.

Transport

RAILWAYS (traffic)

	1990	1991	1992
Passengers carried ('000) . .	53,664	57,841	58,422
Freight carried ('000 metric tons) . .	12,357	11,939	11,112
Passenger-km (million) . .	2,991	3,192	2,904
Freight ton-km (million) . .	2,690	2,710	2,523

ROAD TRAFFIC ('000 motor vehicles in use)

	1989	1990	1991
Passenger cars	705	720	740
Commercial vehicles . . .	341	348	349

Source: UN Economic Commission for Africa, *African Statistical Yearbook*.

INTERNATIONAL SEA-BORNE SHIPPING (estimated freight traffic, '000 metric tons)

	1988	1989	1990
Goods loaded	52,270	54,018	57,607
Goods unloaded	13,900	14,278	14,284

Source: UN, *Monthly Bulletin of Statistics*.

CIVIL AVIATION (traffic on scheduled services)

	1990	1991
Kilometres flown ('000)	32,000	27,000
Passengers carried ('000)	3,748	3,385
Passenger-km (million)	3,463	3,092
Freight ton-km ('000)	15,000	24,000
Total ton-km ('000)	330,000	303,000

Source: UN, *Statistical Yearbook*.

Tourism

FOREIGN TOURIST ARRIVALS BY COUNTRY OF ORIGIN*

	1989	1990	1991
France	107,589	122,554	86,602
Germany, Federal Republic .	16,227	19,577	11,692
Italy	13,873	22,881	13,280
Libya	23,373	23,330	18,060
Morocco	216,042	223,204	338,931
Spain	8,673	9,617	11,081
Tunisia	185,853	154,344	161,960
Total (incl. others) . .	661,079	700,321	722,682

* Excluding arrivals of Algerians resident abroad (545,786 in 1989; 451,103 in 1990).

Communications Media

	1989	1990	1991
Radio receivers ('000 in use) .	5,645	5,820	6,000
Television receivers ('000 in use)	1,700	1,840	1,900
Telephones ('000 in use) . .	1,051	1,103	n.a.

1990: Daily newspapers 10 (average circulation 1,274,000 copies); 37 non-daily newspapers (average circulation 1,409,000 copies); 48 other periodicals.

Sources: UNESCO, *Statistical Yearbook*, and UN, *Statistical Yearbook*.

Education

(1991/92)

	Institutions	Teachers	Pupils
Primary	13,461	154,685	4,357,352
Middle	2,498	86,610	1,490,035
Secondary			
General	845	44,622	742,743
Technical	145	5,541	96,025

Primary education (1992/93: Institutions 13,970; Teachers 162,066; Students 4,436,363; Middle: Pupils 1,558,046; Secondary (General): Pupils 747,152.

Source: Ministry of Education.

Higher education (1990): Teachers 20,562 (1989); Students 285,930 (Source: UNESCO, *Statistical Yearbook*).

Directory

The Constitution*

A new constitution for the Democratic and Popular Republic of Algeria, approved by popular referendum on 19 November 1976, was promulgated on 22 November 1976. The Constitution was amended by the National People's Assembly on 30 June 1979. Further amendments were approved by referendum on 3 November 1988, and on 23 February 1989. The main provisions of the Constitution, as amended, are summarized below:

The preamble recalls that Algeria owes its independence to a war of liberation which led to the creation of a modern sovereign state, guaranteeing social justice, equality and liberty for all. It emphasizes Algeria's Islamic heritage, and stresses that, as an Arab Mediterranean and African country, it forms an integral part of the Great Arab Maghreb.

FUNDAMENTAL PRINCIPLES OF THE ORGANIZATION OF ALGERIAN SOCIETY

The Republic

Algeria is a popular, democratic state. Islam is the state religion and Arabic is the official national language.

The People

National sovereignty resides in the people and is exercised through its elected representatives. The institutions of the State consolidate national unity and protect the fundamental rights of its citizens. The exploitation of one individual by another is forbidden.

The State

The State is exclusively at the service of the people. Those holding positions of responsibility must live solely on their salaries and may not, directly or by the agency of others, engage in any remunerative activity.

Fundamental Freedoms and the Rights of Man and the Citizen

Fundamental rights and freedoms are guaranteed. All discrimination on grounds of sex, race or belief is forbidden. Law cannot operate retrospectively and a person is presumed innocent until proved guilty. Victims of judicial error shall receive compensation from the State.

The State guarantees the inviolability of the home, of private life and of the person. The State also guarantees the secrecy of correspondence, the freedom of conscience and opinion, freedom of intellectual, artistic and scientific creation, and freedom of expression and assembly.

The State guarantees the right to form political associations, to join a trade union, the right to strike, the right to work, to protection, to security, to health, to leisure, to education, etc. It also guarantees the right to leave the national territory, within the limits set by law.

Duties of citizens

Every citizen must respect the Constitution, and must protect public property and safeguard national independence. The law sanctions the duty of parents to educate and protect their children, as well as the duty of children to help and support their parents.

The National Popular Army

The army safeguards national independence and sovereignty.

Principles of foreign policy

Algeria subscribes to the principles and objectives of the UN. It advocates international co-operation, the development of friendly relations between states, on the basis of equality and mutual interest, and non-interference in the internal affairs of states.

POWER AND ITS ORGANIZATION

The Executive

The President of the Republic is Head of State, Head of the Armed Forces and responsible for national defence. He must be of Algerian origin, a Muslim and more than 40 years old. He is elected by universal, secret, direct suffrage. His mandate is for five years, and is indefinitely renewable. The President embodies the unity of the nation. The President presides over joint meetings of the party and the executive. The President presides over meetings of the Council of Ministers. He decides and conducts foreign policy and appoints the Head of Government, who is responsible to the National People's Assembly. The Head of Government must appoint a Council of Ministers. He drafts, co-ordinates and implements his government's programme, which he must present to the Assembly for ratification. Should the Assembly reject the programme, the Head of Government and the Council of Ministers resign, and the President appoints a new Head of Government. Should the newly-appointed Head of Government's programme be rejected by the Assembly, the President dissolves the Assembly, and a general election is held. Should the President be unable to perform his functions, owing to a long and serious illness, the President of the National People's Assembly assumes the office for a maximum period of 45 days (subject to the approval of a two-thirds majority in the Assembly). If the President is still unable to perform his functions after 45 days, the Presidency is declared vacant by the Constitutional Council. Should the Presidency fall vacant, the President of the National People's Assembly temporarily assumes the office and organizes presidential elections within 45 days. He may not himself be a candidate in the election. The President presides over a High Security Council which advises on all matters affecting national security.

The Legislature

The National People's Assembly prepares and votes the law. Its members are elected by universal, direct, secret suffrage for a five-year term. The deputies enjoy parliamentary immunity. The Assembly sits for two ordinary sessions per year, each of not more than three months' duration. The commissions of the Assembly are in permanent session. The Assembly may be summoned to meet for an extraordinary session on the request of the President of the Republic, or of the Head of Government, or of two-thirds of the members of the Assembly. Both the Head of Government and the Assembly may initiate legislation. The Assembly may legislate in all areas except national defence.

The Judiciary

Judges obey only the law. They defend society and fundamental freedoms. The right of the accused to a defence is guaranteed. The Supreme Court regulates the activities of courts and tribunals. The Higher Court of the Magistrature is presided over by the President of the Republic; the Minister of Justice is Vice-President of the Court. All magistrates are answerable to the Higher Court for the manner in which they fulfil their functions.

The Constitutional Council

The Constitutional Council is responsible for ensuring that the Constitution is respected, and that referendums, the election of the President of the Republic and legislative elections are conducted in accordance with the law. The Constitutional Council comprises seven members, of whom two are appointed by the President of the Republic, two elected by the National People's Assembly and two elected by the Supreme Court. The Council's members serve for a six-year term of office.

Constitutional revision

The Constitution can be revised on the initiative of the President of the Republic by a two-thirds majority of the National People's Assembly, and must be approved by national referendum. The basic principles of the Constitution may not be revised.

* On 14 January 1992, following the dissolution of the National People's Assembly and the resignation of President Chadli, the High Security Council appointed a five-member High Council of State to fulfil the functions of the Head of State until December 1993, at the latest (subsequently extended to the end of January 1994). At the end of January 1994 the eight-member High Security Council appointed Gen. Lamine Zérroual as Head of State for a three-year period.

The Government

HEAD OF STATE

President and Minister of Defence: Gen. LAMINE ZÉRROUAL (appointed 30 January 1994 for a three-year period).

COUNCIL OF MINISTERS
(July 1994)

Prime Minister: MOKDAD SIFI.

Minister of the Economy: AHMED BENBITOUR.

Minister of Foreign Affairs: MUHAMMAD SALEH DEMBRI.

Minister of Justice: MUHAMMAD TEGUIA.

Minister of Industrial Restructuring and Participation: MOURAD BENACHENHOU.

Minister of Tourism and Handicrafts: MUHAMMAD BENSALEM.

Minister of Religious Affairs: SASSI LAMOURI.

Minister of the Interior, Local Authorities, Administrative Reform and the Environment : ABDERRAHMANE CHERIF.

Minister of Education: AMAR SAKHRI.

Minister of Youth and Sports: SID ALI LEBIB.

Minister of Labour and Social Affairs: MUHAMMAD LAICHOUBI.

Minister of Industry and Energy: AMAR MEKHLOUFI.

Minister of Agriculture: NOUREDDINE BAHBOUH.

Minister of Transport: MUHAMMAD AREZKI ISLI.

Minister of Equipment and of Regional Development: CHÉRIF RAHMANI.

Minister of Professional Training: HACÈNE LASKRI.

Minister of Housing: MUHAMMAD MAGHLAOUI.

Minister of Posts and Telecommunications: TAHAR ALLAN.

Minister of Culture: SLIMANE CHEIKH.

Minister of Health and Population: YAHIA KAIDOUM.

Minister of War Veterans: MUHAMMAD SAÏD ABADOU.

Minister of Communications: MUHAMMAD ZERHOUNI.

Minister of Commerce: SASSI AZIZA.

Minister of Light and Medium Industry: REDHA HAMIANI.

Minister of Universities and Scientific Research: BOUBEKEUR BENBOUZID.

Secretary of State for National Solidarity and the Family: LEILA ASLAOUI.

Secretary of State for the Local Communities and Administrative Reform: NOUREDDINE KASDALLI.

Secretary of State for the Budget: ALI BRAHITI.

Secretary of State for Co-operation and Maghreb Affairs: AHMED ATTAF.

Secretary-General of the Government: SAÏD BOUCHAIR.

MINISTRIES

Office of the President: Présidence de la République, el-Mouradia, Algiers; tel. (2) 60-03-60; telex 53761.

Office of the Prime Minister: rue Docteur Sâadone, Algiers; tel. (2) 73-23-40; telex 52073.

Ministry of Agriculture: 4 route des Quatre Canons, Algiers; tel. (2) 71-17-12; telex 52984.

Ministry of Communications: Palais de la Culture, Les Annassers, Kouba, Algiers; tel. (2) 67-24-20.

Ministry of the Economy: Immeuble Maurétania, Place du Pérou, Algiers; tel. (2) 71-13-66; telex 52062.

Ministry of Education: 14 rue Mahmoud Boudjaâtit, Algiers; tel. (2) 68-10-78; telex 52443.

Ministry of Equipment and of Regional Development: BP 86, le Grand Seminaire, Kouba, Algiers; tel. (2) 68-95-00; telex 62560; fax (2) 58-21-70.

Ministry of Foreign Affairs: 6 rue Ibn Batran, el-Mouradia, 16050 Algiers; tel. (2) 60-80-50; telex 52794.

Ministry of Health and Population: 125 rue Laala Abd ar-Rahmane, el-Madania, Algiers; tel. (2) 67-53-15; telex 51263.

Ministry of the Interior, Local Authorities, Administrative Reform and the Environment: 18 rue Docteur Saâdane, Algiers; tel. (2) 73-23-40; telex 52073.

Ministry of Justice: 8 place Bir Hakem, el-Biar, Algiers; tel. (2) 78-02-90; telex 52761.

Ministry of Posts and Telecommunications: 4 blvd Krim Belkacem, Algiers; tel. (2) 71-12-20; telex 52020.

Ministry of Religious Affairs: 4 rue de Timgad, Hydra, Algiers; tel. (2) 60-85-55; telex 66118; fax (2) 60-09-36.

Ministry of Transport: 119 rue Didouche Mourad, Algiers; tel. (2) 74-06-99; telex 52775.

Ministry of Youth and Sports: 3 rue Mohamed Belouizdad, Algiers; tel. (2) 68-33-50; telex 65054.

Legislature

ASSEMBLÉE NATIONALE POPULAIRE

First Round of Legislative Election, 26 December 1991

Party	Seats
Front Islamique du Salut (FIS)	188
Front des Forces Socialistes (FFS)	25
Front de Libération Nationale (FLN)	15
Independents	3

Under a new electoral law adopted in April 1991, elections to the Assembly were to comprise two rounds of voting, the second to take place in those constituencies in which no candidate obtained at least 50% of the votes cast in the first round. Legislation that was enacted in October 1991 raised the number of seats in the National People's Assembly from 295 to 430. The term of the Assembly remained unchanged at five years, and deputies were to be elected by universal suffrage.

On 26 December 1991, in the first round of voting in Algeria's first multi-party general election, the Front Islamique du Salut obtained 47.5%, the Front de Libération Nationale 23.5% and the Front des Forces Socialistes some 15% of the total votes cast. About 59% of Algeria's 13.3m. registered voters were reported to have participated in the first round of the election.

On 4 January 1992 the Assembly was dissolved by presidential decree, and on 12 January the High Security Council suspended the second round of voting in the 199 constituencies in which no candidate had gained an absolute majority in the first round. On 14 January the High Security Council appointed a five-member High Council of State to fulfil the functions of the Head of State until December 1993, at the latest (subsequently extended to the end of Januar 1994). On 22 April 1992 the High Council of State appointed a 60-member National Consultative Council, which was to meet each month in the building of the suspended National People's Assembly, although it had no legislative powers. In May 1994 a 178-member National Transition Council was appointed, which was intended to provide a forum for the debate of affairs of state, until such time as legislative elections—scheduled, provisionally, to be held in 1997—could be organized.

Political Organizations

Until 1989 the FLN was the only legal party in Algeria. The February 1989 amendments to the Constitution permitted the formation of other political associations, with some restrictions. Some 59 political parties contested the first round of the legislative election which took place in December 1991. The most important of these are listed below.

Alliance Centriste et Démocrate (ACD): Algiers; f. 1990 as an informal alliance to unite social-democratic and central candidates for electoral purposes; includes:

> **Association Populaire pour l'Unité et l'Action (APUA):** BP 85, Bachdjarah, 116 rue de Tripoli, Hussein-Dey, Algiers; tel. (2) 77-91-05; telex 65645; fax (2) 77-64-64; f. 1990 as a legal party; Leader AL-MAHDI ABBES ALLALOU.

> **Front National de Renouvellement (FNR):** Algiers; Leader ZINEDDINE CHERIFI.

> **Parti National pour la Solidarité et le Développement (PNSD):** Algiers; Leader RABAH BENCHERIF.

> **Parti Social-Démocrate (PSD):** Algiers; f. 1989; centre party; advocates economic liberalization; Leader ABDERRAHMANE ABJERID; Sec.-Gen. ABD AL-KADER BOUZAR.

> **Parti Social-Libéral (PSL):** Algiers; Leader AHMAD KHELIL.

El-Oumma (The Community): Algiers; f. 1990 as a legal party; advocates the application of Islam in political life; Leader BENYOUSSEF BEN KHEDDA.

Ettahaddi: Algiers; f. 1993 to replace Parti de l'Avant-Garde Socialiste (Communist); Leader HACHÉMI CHERIF.

Front des Forces Socialistes (FFS): 56 ave Souidani Boudjemaâ, 16000 Algiers; tel. (2) 59-33-13; f. 1963; revived 1990; Leader HOCINE AÏT AHMAD.

Front Islamique du Salut (FIS): Algiers; f. 1989; aims to emphasize the importance of Islam in political and social life; formally dissolved by the Algiers Court of Appeal in March 1992 (Leader ABBASI MADANI (sentenced to 12 years' imprisonment in July 1992)).

Front de Libération Nationale (FLN): blvd Zirout Yousuf, Algiers; telex 53931; f. 1954; sole legal party until 1989; socialist in outlook, the party is organized into a Secretariat, a Political Bureau, a Central Committee, Federations, Kasmas and cells; until November 1988, the Secretary-General (chosen by the Central Committee) automatically became the candidate for the presidency, but the revision of the Constitution in February 1989 formally separated the two roles; a new Central Committee of 272 mems. was elected at an extraordinary congress, held in November 1989, and a 15-mem. Political Bureau (replacing the Executive Secretariat of the Central Committee) was elected in December 1989; the 15-mem. Political Bureau was replaced by one with 14 members in July 1991; under the aegis of the FLN are various mass political organizations, including the Union Nationale de la Jeunesse Algérienne (UNJA) and the Union Nationale des Femmes Algériennes (UNFA); Sec.-Gen. ABD AL-HAMID MEHIRI.

Hamas: Algiers; moderate Islamic party, favouring the gradual introduction of an Islamic state; Leader Sheikh MAHFOUD NAHNAH.

Mouvement Algérien pour la Justice et le Développement: Algiers; tel. (2) 78-38-31; fax (2) 78-78-72; f. 1990; reformist party supporting policies of fmr Pres. Boumedienne; Leader ABD AL-KADER MERBAH.

Mouvement pour la Démocratie en Algérie (MDA): Algiers; f. 1990 as a legal party; Leader AHMAD BEN BELLA.

Nahdah: Algiers; fundamentalist Islamic group; Leader Sheikh ABDULLAH DJABALLAH.

Parti Démocratique Progressif (PDR): Algiers; f. 1990 as a legal party; Leader SACI MABROUK.

Parti Républicain Progressif (PRP): Algiers; f. 1990 as a legal party; Sec.-Gen. KADIR DRISS.

Parti d'Unité Arabe Islamique-Démocratique (PUAID): Menaa; f. 1990 as a legal party; advocates creation of a pan-Arab state under Islamic law; Leader BELHADJ KHALIL HARFI.

Rassemblement Arabique-Islamique (RAI): Algiers; f. 1990; aims to increase the use of Arabic in social and cultural life; Leader ME LAID GRINE.

Rassemblement pour la Culture et la Démocratie (RCD): 87A rue Didouche Mourad, Algiers; tel. (2) 73-62-01; telex 67256; fax (2) 73-62-20; f. 1989; secular party; advocates recognition of Berber as national language; Sec.-Gen. SAÏD SAADI.

Other political parties include the following: Hezbollah (Algerian Party for Maghreb Rebirth), Parti du Peuple Algérien (PPA), Parti National Algérien (PNA), Parti du Renouveau Algérien (PRA, Leader NOURREDDINE BOUKROUH), Parti Socialiste des Travailleurs (PST), Union des Forces Démocratiques (UFD).

Diplomatic Representation

EMBASSIES IN ALGERIA

Albania: Lot. Ben Haddadi, Villa No. 7, Cheraga, Algiers; tel. (2) 37-12-31; fax (2) 37-18-23; Ambassador: SULEJMAN TOMCINI.

Angola: 14 rue Curie, el-Biar, Algiers; tel. (2) 79-74-41; telex 61620; Ambassador: JOSÉ CÉSAR AUGUSTO.

Argentina: 7 rue Hamani, Algiers; tel. (2) 71-86-83; telex 56185; fax (2) 71-86-82; Ambassador: EDUARDO AIRALDI.

Austria: Les Vergers, rue 2, Villa 9, DZ-16330 Bir Khadem, Algiers; tel. (2) 56-26-99; telex 62302; fax (2) 56-73-52; Ambassador: CHRISTIAN BERLAKOVITS.

Bangladesh: 14 ave des Frères Oughlis, el-Mouradia, Le Golf, Algiers; tel. (2) 60-36-29; telex 66363; fax (2) 59-46-16; Ambassador: MAHBUBUL HUQ.

Belgium: 22 chemin Youcef Tayebi, el-Biar, Algiers; tel. (2) 78-57-12; telex 61365; Ambassador: DIRK LETTENS.

Benin: 36 Lot. du Stade, Birkhadem, Algiers; tel. (2) 56-52-71; telex 62307; Ambassador: LEONARD ADJIN.

Brazil: 48 blvd Muhammad V, Algiers; tel. (2) 63-21-46; telex 67156; fax (2) 63-17-47; Ambassador: SERGIO THOMPSON-FLORES.

Bulgaria: 13 blvd Col Bougara, Algiers; tel. (2) 69-15-14; telex 66087; Ambassador: MARIN DIMITROV TODOROV.

Cameroon: 34 rue Yahia Mazouni, 16011 el-Biar, Algiers; tel. (2) 92-11-24; telex 61356; fax (2) 92-17-71; Chargé d'affairs: Dr FRANCIS NGANICHA.

Canada: POB 225, 27 bis rue Ali Massoudi, Alger-Gare, 16000 Algiers; tel. (2) 60-66-11; telex 66043; fax (2) 60-59-20; Ambassador: MARC C. LEMIEUX.

Chad: Villa No. 18, Cité DNC, Chemin Ahmed Kara, Hydra, Algiers; tel. (2) 60-66-37; fax (2) 60-53-16; Ambassador: KOCHÉ ADOUM.

China, People's Republic: 4 blvd des Martyrs, Algiers; tel. (2) 60-27-24; telex 66193; fax (2) 59-29-62; Ambassador: WANG JIANBANG.

Congo: 111 Parc Ben Omar, Kouba, Algiers; tel. (2) 58-68-00; telex 52069; Ambassador: PIERRE N'GAKA.

Côte d'Ivoire: Immeuble 'Le Bosquet', Le Paradou, Hydra, Algiers; tel. (2) 60-23-78; telex 66152; Ambassador: GUSTAVE OUFFOUE-KOU-ASSI.

Cuba: 22 rue Larbi Alik, Hydra, Algiers; tel. (2) 59-21-41; telex 52963; Ambassador: RAFAEL POLANCO SIRAHOJOS.

Czech Republic: BP 999, Villa Malika, 7 chemin Zyriab, Algiers; tel. (2) 60-05-25; telex 66281; Ambassador: JAN KORBA.

Denmark: 12 ave Emile Marquis, Lot. Djenane el-Malik, 16035 Hydra, Algiers; tel. (2) 59-02-34; telex 66270; fax (2) 60-28-46; Ambassador: HERLUF HANSEN.

Egypt: POB 297, 8 chemin Abdel-Kader Gadouche, 16300 Hydra, Algiers; tel. 60-16-73; telex 66058; fax (2) 60-29-52; Ambassador: IBRAHIM YOUSSRI.

Finland: BP 256, 16035 Hydra, Algiers; tel. (2) 69-12-92; telex 66296; fax (2) 69-16-37; Ambassador: JAN GROOP.

France: 6 rue Larbi Alik, Hydra, Algiers; tel. (2) 60-44-88; telex 52644; fax (2) 60-53-69; Ambassador: JEAN AUDIBERT.

Gabon: 21 rue Hadj Ahmed Mohamed, Hydra, Algiers; tel. (2) 60-54-00; telex 61282; fax (2) 60-95-46; Ambassador: YVES ONGOLLO.

Germany: BP 664, 165 chemin Sfindja, Algiers; tel. (2) 74-19-56; telex 67343; fax (2) 74-05-21; Ambassador: Dr FRIEDRICH REICHE.

Ghana: 62 rue des Frères Bénali Abdellah, Hydra, Algiers; tel. (2) 69-24-44; telex 62234; fax (2) 69-28-56; Ambassador: GEORGE A. O. KUGBLENU.

Greece: 60 blvd Col Bougara, Algiers; tel. (2) 60-08-55; telex 66071; fax 69-16-55; Ambassador: LOANNIS DRAKOULARAKOS.

Guinea: 43 blvd Central Saïd Hamdine, Hydra, Algiers; tel. (2) 60-06-11; telex 66208; fax (2) 60-04-68; Ambassador: MAMADY CONDE.

Guinea-Bissau: Cité DNC, rue Ahmad Kara, Hydra, Algiers; tel. (2) 60-01-51; telex 62210; Ambassador: JOSÉ PREIRA BATISTA.

Holy See: 1 rue Nouredine Mekiri, 16090 Bologhine, Algiers (Apostolic Nunciature); tel. (2) 62-34-30; fax (2) 57-23-75; Apostolic Pro-Nuncio: Most Rev. EDMOND FARHAT, Titular Archbishop of Byblos.

Hungary: BP 68, 18 ave des Frères Oughlis, el-Mouradia, Algiers; tel. (2) 60-77-09; telex 62217; fax (2) 59-44-31; Ambassador: Dr TAMÁS HORVÁTH.

India: 119 rue Didouche Mourad, Algiers; tel. (2) 74-71-35; telex 66138; Ambassador: T. C. A. RANGACHARI.

Indonesia: BP 62, 6 rue Muhammad Chemlal, 16070 el-Mouradia, Algiers; tel. (2) 60-20-51; telex 62214; fax (2) 59-12-45; Ambassador: HAMID AL-HADAD.

Iraq: 4 rue Arezki Abri, Hydra, Algiers; tel. (2) 60-31-25; telex 66098; fax (2) 60-10-97; Ambassador: ABD AL-KARIM AL-MULLA.

Italy: 18 rue Muhammad Ouidir Amellal, el-Biar, Algiers; tel. (2) 78-33-99; telex 61357; Ambassador: ANTONIO BADINI.

Japan: 1 chemin el-Bakri, el-Biar, Algiers; tel. (2) 78-62-00; telex 61389; fax (2) 79-22-93; Ambassador: TERUO HAYAKAWA.

Jordan: 6 rue du Chenoua, Algiers; tel. (2) 60-20-31; telex 66089; Ambassador: KHALED ABIDAT.

Korea, Democratic People's Republic: 49 rue Hamlia, Bologhine, Algiers; tel. (2) 62-39-27; telex 61165; Ambassador: KIM CHANG RYONG.

Korea, Republic: 21 rue Abdel-Kader Stambouli, el-Mouradia, Algiers; tel. (2) 69-20-60; telex 66166; fax (2) 69-30-14; Ambassador: KWON IN HYUK.

Kuwait: chemin Abdelkader Gaddouche, Hydra, Algiers; tel. (2) 59-31-57; telex 66628; Ambassador: YOUSSEFF ABDULLAH AL-AMIZI.

Lebanon: 9 rue Kaïd Ahmad, el-Biar, Algiers; tel. (2) 78-20-94; telex 61354; Ambassador: SALHAD NASRI.

Libya: 15 chemin Cheikh Bachir Ibrahimi, Algiers; telex 52700; Ambassador: ABDEL-MOULA EL-GHADHBANE.

Madagascar: 22 rue Abd al-Kader Aouis Bologhine, Algiers; tel. (2) 62-31-96; telex 61156; fax (2) 57-71-69; Chargé d'affaires: RAVELOMANANTSOA RATSIMIHAH.

Mali: Villa no. 15, Cité DNC/ANP, chemin Ahmed Kara, Algiers; tel. (2) 60-61-18; telex 66109; Ambassador: MAHAMADOU DIAGOURAGA.

Mauritania: 107 Lot. Baranès, Air de France, Bouzaréah, Algiers; tel. (2) 79-21-39; telex 61455; fax (2) 78-42-74; Ambassador: SID AHMED OULD BABAMINE.

Mexico: BP 329, 21 rue du Commandant Amar Azzouz, el-Biar, Alger-Gare, Algiers; tel. (2) 79-40-23; telex 61641; fax (2) 78-24-51; Ambassador: ALFREDO BRAVO.

Mongolia: 4 rue Belkacem Amani, Hydra, Algiers; tel. (2) 60-26-12; Ambassador: BURENJARGALYN ORSOO.

Morocco: 8 rue des Cèdres, el-Mouradia, Algiers; tel. (2) 60-74-08; telex 66159; fax (2) 60-59-00; Ambassador: ABD AL-KRIM SEMMAR.

Netherlands: BP 72, 23 chemin Cheikh Bachir Ibrahimi, el-Biar, Algiers; tel. (2) 78-28-29; telex 61364; fax (2) 78-07-70; Ambassador: Dr PATRICK S. J. RUTGERS.

Niger: 54 rue Vercors Rostamia Bouzareah, Algiers; tel. (2) 78-89-21; telex 61371; fax (2) 78-97-13; Ambassador: GOUROUZA OUMAROU.

Nigeria: BP 629, 27 bis rue Blaise Pascal, Algiers; tel. (2) 59-32-98; telex 66093; Ambassador: ALIYU MOHAMMED.

Oman: 28 blvd Mohamed Khoudi, Algiers; tel. (2) 79-26-55; telex 61335; fax (2) 68-40-60; Ambassador: HELLAL AS-SIYABI.

Pakistan: 14 ave Souidani Boudjemâa, Algiers; tel. (2) 60-57-81; telex 66277; Ambassador: MUSHTAQ MEHR.

Philippines: Algiers; Ambassador: PACIFICO CASTRO.

Poland: 37 ave Mustafa Ali Khodja, el-Biar, Algiers; telex 52562; Ambassador: STANISŁAW STAWIARSKI.

Portugal: 67 chemin Mohamed Gacem, el-Mouradia, Algiers; tel. (2) 74-53-13; telex 61647; fax (2) 74-53-13; Ambassador: RUY G. DE BRITO E CUNHA.

Qatar: BP 118, 25 bis rue de l'Indépendance, Algiers; tel. (2) 36-80-56; telex 61280; Ambassador: HOCINE ALI EDDOUSRI.

Romania: 24 rue Arezki abri, Hydra, Algiers; tel. (2) 60-08-71; telex 66156; Ambassador: TUDOR ZAMFIRA.

Russia: chemin du Prince d'Annam, el-Biar, Algiers; tel. (2) 92-31-39; telex 61561; fax (2) 78-28-82; Ambassador: ALEXANDRE ADSENYONOK.

Saudi Arabia: 1 rue Doudou Mokhtar, Ben Aknoun, Algiers; tel. (2) 79-67-51; telex 61389; Ambassador: HASAN FAQQI.

Senegal: BP 720, Alger-Gare, Algiers; tel. (2) 60-72-00; telex 67743; fax (2) 60-26-84; Ambassador: SAïDOU NOUROU.

Slovakia: BP 84, 7 chemin du Ziryab, Didouche Mourad, 16006 Algiers; tel. (2) 69-35-25; fax (2) 69-21-97; Ambassador: IVAN SPIŠKA.

Somalia: 11 impasse Tarting, blvd des Martyrs, Algiers; telex 52140; Ambassador: ABD AL-HAMID ALI YOUCEF.

Spain: 10 rue Azil Ali, Algiers; tel. (2) 71-69-93; telex 67330; fax (2) 74-05-95; Ambassador: FRANCISCO UGARTE.

Sweden: rue Olof Palme, Nouveau Paradou, Hydra, Algiers; tel. (2) 69-23-00; telex 66046; fax (2) 69-19-17; Ambassador: GÖRAN WIDE.

Switzerland: 27 blvd Zirout Youcef, DZ-16000 Alger-Gare, Algiers; tel. (2) 63-39-02; telex 67342; Ambassador: H. REIMANN.

Syria: Domaine Tamzali, chemin A. Gadouche, Hydra, Algiers; tel. (2) 78-20-67; telex 61368; Ambassador: ABELJABER ALDAHAK.

Tunisia: 11 rue du Bois de Boulogne, Hydra, Algiers; tel. (2) 60-13-88; telex 66164; Ambassador: M'HEDI BACCOUCHE.

Turkey: Villa dar el Ouard, chemin de la Rochelle, blvd Col Bougara, Algiers; tel. (2) 60-12-57; telex 66244; Ambassador: UMIT PAMIR.

United Arab Emirates: POB 454, 26 rue Aouis Mokrane, el-Mouradia, Algiers; tel. (2) 78-05-60; telex 61616; fax (2) 79-14-42; Ambassador: TARIQ AL-HAIDAN.

United Kingdom: BP 43, Résidence Cassiopée, Bâtiment B, 7 chemin des Glycines, DZ-16000 Alger-Gare, Algiers; tel. (2) 69-24-11; telex 66151; fax (2) 69-24-10; Ambassador: C. D. CRABBIE.

USA: BP 549, 4 chemin Cheikh Bachir Brahimi, Alger-Gare, 16000 Algiers; tel. (2) 60-11-86; telex 66047; fax (2) 60-39-79; Ambassador: MARY ANN CASEY.

Venezuela: BP 813, 3 impasse Ahmed Kara, Algiers; tel. (2) 59-28-46; telex 66642; fax (2) 60-75-55; Ambassador: EDMUNDO GONZÁLEZ URRUTIA.

Viet Nam: 30 rue de Chenoua, Hydra, Algiers; tel. (2) 60-07-52; telex 66053; Ambassador: TRAN XUAN MAN.

Yemen: ave les Vergers, Résidence Djenane el-Malik, Villa 41, Said Hamdine, Algiers; tel. (2) 59-40-85; telex 66037; fax (2) 59-17-58; Ambassador: GACEM ASKAR DJEBRANE.

Yugoslavia: BP 209, 7 rue des Frères Benhafid, Hydra, Algiers; tel. (2) 60-47-04; telex 66076; Ambassador: DRAGOMIR VICICEVIĆ.

Zaire: 10 Lot. Cadat, Djenane Ben Omar, Kouba, Algiers; tel. (2) 58-06-79; telex 62545; Ambassador: IKAKI BOMELE MOLINGO.

Zimbabwe: BP 69, 5 chemin des Vieillards, Bouzaréah, Algiers; tel. (2) 79-82-50; telex 61281; Ambassador: GEORGES TSAURAI-VENGESA.

Judicial System

The highest court of justice is the Supreme Court (Cour suprême) in Algiers. Justice is exercised through 183 courts (tribunaux) and 31 appeal courts (cours d'appel), grouped on a regional basis. Three special Criminal Courts were established in Oran, Constantine and Algiers in 1966 to consider alleged economic crimes against the State. From these courts there is no appeal. In April 1975 a Cour de sûreté de l'état, composed of magistrates and high-ranking army officers, was established to try all cases involving state security. The Cour des comptes was established in 1979. A new penal code was adopted in January 1982, retaining the death penalty.

President of Supreme Court: A. MEDJHOUDA.

Procurator-General: Y. BEKKOUCHE.

Religion

ISLAM

Islam is the official religion, and the whole Algerian population, with a few rare exceptions, is Muslim.

President of the Superior Islamic Council: AHMAD HAMANI; place Cheik Abd al-Hamid ibn Badis, Algiers.

CHRISTIANITY

The European inhabitants, and a few Arabs, are generally Christians, mostly Roman Catholics.

The Roman Catholic Church

Algeria comprises one archdiocese and three dioceses (including one directly responsible to the Holy See). In December 1992 there were an estimated 26,000 adherents in the country.

Bishops' Conference: Conférence Episcopale Régionale du Nord de l'Afrique, 13 rue Khélifa-Boukhalfa, DZ-16000 Alger-Gare, Algiers; tel. (2) 63-42-44; fax (2) 64-05-82; f. 1985; Pres. Most Rev. HENRI TEISSIER, Archbishop of Algiers; Sec-Gen. Fr JEAN LANDOUSIES.

Archbishop of Algiers: Most Rev. HENRI TEISSIER, Archevêché, 13 rue Khélifa-Boukhalfa, DZ-16000 Alger-Gare, Algiers; tel. (2) 63-42-44; fax (2) 64-05-82.

Protestant Church

Protestant Church of Algeria: 31 rue Reda Houhou, 16000 Alger-Gare, Algiers; tel. (2) 71-62-38; fax (2) 65172; fax (2) 71-62-38; three parishes; 1,500 mems; Pastors (Algiers) Dr HUGH G. JOHNSON; Pastor (Oran) Dr DAVID W. BUTLER; Pastor (Constantine) KAYIJA-MUTOMBU.

The Press

DAILIES

Ach-Cha'ab (The People): 1 place Maurice Audin, Algiers; f. 1962; FLN journal in Arabic; Dir KAMEL AVACHE; circ. 24,000.

Al-Badil: Algiers; relaunched 1990; MDA journal in French and Arabic; circ. 130,000.

Al-Djeza'ir El-Youm: Algiers; Arabic; circ. 54,000.

Horizons: 20 rue de la Liberté, Algiers; tel. (2) 73-67-25; telex 66310; fax (2) 73-61-34; f. 1985; evening; French; circ. 200,000.

Al-Joumhouria (The Republic): 6 rue ben Senoussi Hamida, Oran; f. 1963; Arabic; Editor MOHAMED KAOUCHE; circ. 70,000.

Al-Massa: Algiers; f. 1985; evening; Arabic; circ. 100,000.

Al-Moudjahid (The Fighter): 20 rue de la Liberté, Algiers; f. 1965; FLN journal in French and Arabic; Dir ZOUBIR ZEMZOUM; circ. 392,000.

An-Nasr (The Victory): BP 388, Zone Industrielle, La Palma, Constantine; tel. (4) 93-92-16; f. 1963; Arabic; Editor ABDALLAH GUETTAT; circ. 340,000.

El Khabar: Algiers; Arabic; Dir CHERIF REZKI; circ. 52,000.

Le Journal: Algiers; f. 1992; French.

Le Soir d'Algérie: Algiers; f. 1990; evening; independent information journal in French; Editors ZOUBIR SOUISSI, MAAMAR FARRAH.

WEEKLIES

Algérie Actualité: 2 rue Jacques Cartier, 16000 Algiers; tel. (2) 63-54-20; telex 66475; f. 1965; French; Dir KAMEL BELKACEM; circ. 250,000.

Al-Hadef (The Goal): BP 388, Zone Industrielle, La Palma, Constantine; tel. (4) 93-92-16; f. 1972; sports; French; Editor-in-Chief LARBI MOHAMED ABBOUD; circ. 110,000.

Révolution Africaine: 5 place Emir Abdelkader, 16400 Algiers; tel. (2) 64-04-71; telex 56126; fax (2) 61-19-96; current affairs journal in French; socialist; Dir FERRAH ABDELALI; circ. 50,000.

OTHER PERIODICALS

Al-Acala: 4 rue Timgad, Hydra, Algiers; tel. (2) 60-85-55; telex 66118; fax (2) 60-09-36; f. 1970; published by the Ministry of Religious Affairs; fortnightly; Editor MUHAMMAD AL-MAHDI.

Algérie Médicale: 3 blvd Zirout Youcef, Algiers; f. 1964; publ. of Union médicale algérienne; 2 a year; circ. 3,000.

Alouan (Colours): 119 rue Didouche Mourad, Algiers; f. 1973; cultural review; monthly; Arabic.

Bibliographie de l'Algérie: Bibliothèque Nationale, 1 ave Docteur Fanon, Algiers 16000; tel. (2) 63-06-32; fax (2) 61-04-35; f. 1964; lists books, theses, pamphlets and periodicals published in Algeria; 2 a year; Arabic and French.

Ach-Cha'ab ath-Thakafi (Cultural People): Algiers; f. 1972; cultural monthly; Arabic.

Ach-Chabab (Youth): 2 rue Khélifa Boukhalfa; journal of the UNJA; bi-monthly; French and Arabic.

Al-Djeza'ir Réalités (Algeria Today): BP 95–96, Bouzareah, Algiers; f. 1972; organ of the Popular Assembly of the Wilaya of Algiers; monthly; French and Arabic.

Al-Djeza'iria (Algerian Woman): Villa Joly, 24 ave Franklin Roosevelt, Algiers; f. 1970; organ of the UNFA; monthly; French and Arabic.

Al-Djeich (The Army): Office de l'Armée Nationale Populaire, 3 chemin de Gascogne, Algiers; f. 1963; monthly; Algerian army review; Arabic and French; circ. 10,000.

Journal Officiel de la République Algérienne Démocratique et Populaire: 7, 9 and 13 ave A. ben Barek; f. 1962; French and Arabic.

Al-Kitab (The Book): 3 blvd Zirout Youcef, Algiers; f. 1972; bulletin of SNED; every 2 months; French and Arabic.

Nouvelles Economiques: 6 blvd Amilcar Cabral, Algiers; f. 1969; publ. of Institut Algérien du Commerce Extérieur; monthly; French and Arabic.

Révolution et Travail: 1 rue Abdelkader Benbarek, place du 1er mai, Algiers; tel. (2) 66-73-53; telex 65051; fax (2) 65-82-21; journal of UGTA (central trade union) with Arabic and French editions; monthly; Editor-in-Chief LAKHDARI MOHAMED LAKHDAR.

Revue Algérienne du Travail: Algiers; f. 1964; labour publication; quarterly; French.

Ath-Thakafa (Culture): BP 96, 2 place Cheikh ben Badis, BP 96, Algiers; tel. (2) 62-20-73; f. 1971; every 2 months; cultural review; Editor-in-Chief CHEBOUB OTHMANE; circ. 10,000.

NEWS AGENCIES

Algérie Presse Service (APS): 4 rue Zouieche, Kouba, Algiers; tel. (2) 77-79-28; telex 66577; fax (2) 59-77-59; f. 1962; Dir-Gen. MUHAMMAD SÉLOUA.

Foreign Bureaux

Agence France-Presse (AFP): 6 rue Abd al-Karim el-Khettabi, Algiers; tel. (2) 63-62-01; telex 67427; Chief YVES LEERS.

Agencia EFE (Spain): 4 ave Pasteur, Algiers; tel. (2) 73-56-80; telex 66458; fax (2) 74-04-56; Chief MANUEL OSTOS.

Agenzia Nazionale Stampa Associata (ANSA) (Italy): 4 ave Pasteur, Algiers; tel. (2) 63-73-14; telex 66467; fax (2) 61-25-84; Representative CARLO DI RENZO.

Associated Press (AP) (USA): BP 769, 4 ave Pasteur, Algiers; tel. (2) 63-59-41; telex 67365; fax (2) 63-59-42; Representative RACHID KHIARI.

Bulgarska Telegrafna Agentsia (BTA) (Bulgaria): Zaatcha 5, el-Mouradia, Algiers; Chief GORAN GOTEV.

Informatsionnoye Telegrafnoye Agentstvo Rossii—Telegrafnoye Agentstvo Suverennykh Stran (ITAR—TASS) (Russia): 21 rue de Boulogne, Algiers; Chief KONSTANTIN DUDAREV.

Reuters (UK): 117 rue Didouche Mourad, Algiers; tel. (2) 747053; telex 67756; fax (2) 74-53-75.

Rossiyskoye Informatsionnoye Agentstvo—Novosti (RIA—Novosti) (Russia): BP 24, el-Mouradia, Algiers; Chief Officer YURI S. BAGDASAROV.

Xinhua (New China) News Agency (People's Republic of China): 32 rue de Carthage, Hydra, Algiers; tel. (2) 60-76-85; telex 66204; Chief BAI GUORUI.

Wikalat al-Maghreb al-Arabi (Morocco) and the Middle East News Agency (Egypt) are also represented.

Publishers

Entreprise Nationale du Livre (ENAL): 3 blvd Zirout Youcef, BP 49, Algiers; tel. (2) 73-74-93; telex 53845; fax (2) 73-84-21; f. 1966 as Société Nationale d'Edition et de Diffusion, name changed 1983; publishes books of all types, and is sole importer, exporter and distributor of all printed material, stationery, school and office supplies; also holds state monopoly for commercial advertising; Pres. and Dir-Gen. HASSEN BENDIF.

Office des Publications Universitaires: 1 place Centrale de Ben, Aknoun, Algiers; tel. (2) 78-87-18; telex 61396; publishes university textbooks.

Radio and Television

In 1991 there were 6,000,000 radio receivers and 1,900,000 television receivers in use.

Radiodiffusion Télévision Algérienne (RTA): Immeuble RTA, 21 blvd des Martyrs, Algiers; tel. (2) 60-23-00; telex 52042; government-controlled; Dir of RTA MUHAMMAD OUZEGHDOU; Dirs of Radio FATHI SAIDI, RABEH ADDOUS; Dir of TV ZOUBIR ZEMZOUM.

RADIO

Arabic Network: transmitters at Adrar, Aïn Beïda, Algiers, Béchar, Béni Abbès, Djanet, El Goléa, Ghardaia, Hassi Messaoud, In Aménas, In Salah, Laghouat, Les Trembles, Ouargla, Reggane, Tamanrasset, Timimoun, Tindouf.

French Network: transmitters at Algiers, Constantine, Oran and Tipaza.

Kabyle Network: transmitter at Algiers.

TELEVISION

The principal transmitters are at Algiers, Batna, Sidi-Bel-Abbès, Constantine, Souk-Ahras and Tlemcen. The national network was completed during 1970. Television plays a major role in the national education programme. Plans for a second national television service were announced in early 1990. The new station was to broadcast in Arabic, French and English for 20 hours per day.

Finance

(cap. = capital; res = reserves; dep. = deposits; brs = branches; m. = million; amounts in Algerian dinars)

BANKING

Central Bank

Banque d'Algérie: 38 ave Franklin Roosevelt, Algiers; tel. (2) 60-10-44; telex 66499; fax (2) 60-37-77; f. 1962 as Banque Centrale d'Algérie; present name adopted 1990; cap. 40m.; bank of issue; Gov. ABDELWAHAB KERAMANE; Vice-Gov. BACHIR SAÏL; 50 brs.

Nationalized Banks

Al-Baraka Bank of Algeria (ABA): 12 blvd Col Amirouche, Algiers; tel. (2) 74-56-27; telex 55284; fax (2) 74-56-48; f. 1991; the bank is Algeria's first Islamic financial institution and is owned by the Jeddah-based Al-Baraka Investment and Development Co (50%) and the local Banque de l'Agriculture et du Développement Rural (BADR)(50%); Chair. MUHAMMAD AL-MAGHRIBI; Gen. Man. MUHAMMAD HAFID.

Banque Extérieure d'Algérie (BEA): BP 471, 11 blvd Col Amirouche, Algiers; tel. (2) 71-12-52; telex 56090; fax (2) 63-93-34; f. 1967; cap. 1,600m., res 45,240m., dep. 133,528m.; total assets 181,823.2m. (Dec. 1991); chiefly concerned with energy and maritime transport sectors; Chair. ABD AR-RAHMANE DJERIDI; Dir-Gen. HOCINE HANNACHI; 80 brs.

Banque du Maghreb Arabe pour l'Investissement et le Commerce: 21 blvd des Frères Bouaddou Bir Mourad Rais, Algiers; tel. (2) 56-04-46; telex 62266; fax (2) 56-60-12; owned by the Algerian Govt (50%) and the Libyan Govt (50%); Pres. HAKIKI; Dir-Gen. IBRAHIM ALBISHARY.

Banque Nationale d'Algérie (BNA): BP 713, 8 blvd Ernesto Ché Guévara, Alger-Gare, 1600 Algiers; tel. (2) 71-55-64; telex 61250; fax (2) 71-47-59; f. 1966; cap. 5,433m., res 34,056m. (1991); specializes in industry, transport and trade sectors; Chair. HOCINE MOUFFOK; Gen. Man. MUHAMMAD TERBECHE; 85 brs.

Crédit Populaire d'Algérie (CPA): BP 1031, 2 blvd Col Amirouche, 16000 Algiers; tel. (2) 61-13-34; telex 67147; fax (2) 64-40-41; f. 1966; cap. 800m., dep. 25,154m. (1990); bank for light industry, transport and tourism; Chair. and Gen. Man. OMAR BENDERRA; 93 brs.

Development Banks

Banque de l'Agriculture et du Développement Rural (BADR): BP 484, 17 blvd Col Amirouche, Algiers; tel. (2) 64-72-64; telex 62240; fax (2) 61-55-51; f. 1982; cap. 2,200m., res 3,356m., dep. 93,201m. (Dec. 1989); finance for the agricultural sector; Dir-Gen. MOURAD DAMARDJI; 241 brs.

Banque Algérienne de Développement (BAD): 12 blvd Col Amirouche, Algiers; tel. (2) 73-89-50; telex 55220; fax (2) 74-62-56; f. 1963; cap. 100m. (1989), dep. 3,596.5m. (Dec. 1984); a public establishment with fiscal sovereignty, to contribute to Algerian economic development through long-term investment programmes; Chair. SASSI AZIZA; Dir-Gen. DJELLOUL MABROUK; 4 brs.

Banque de Développement Local (BDL): 5 rue Gaci Amar Staouéli, Wilaya de Tipaza; tel. (2) 39-28-01; telex 63171; fax 39-34-75; f. 1985; regional development bank; cap. 500m. (1992); Dir-Gen. MUHAMMAD MALEK; 14 brs.

Caisse Nationale d'Epargne et de Prévoyance (CNEP): 42 rue Khélifa Boukhalfa, Algiers; tel. (2) 71-33-53; telex 65196; fax (2) 71-70-22; f. 1964; savings and housing bank; Man. ABDELWAHID BOUABDALLAH.

FOREIGN BANKS
(Representative offices)

Beogradska Banka (Yugoslavia): 12 rue Ali Azil, Algiers; tel. (2) 63-56-19; fax (2) 79-69-42.

Société Générale (France): 1 rue No 2, Le Paradou-Hydra, Algiers; tel. (2) 59-49-21; telex 66569; fax (2) 60-04-87; Dir JEAN-PAUL COURT.

INSURANCE

Insurance is a state monopoly.

Caisse Nationale de Mutualité Agricole: 24 blvd Victor Hugo, Algiers; tel. (2) 73-31-07; telex 56033; fax (2) 73-34-79; Sec.-Gen. NEDJARI AISSA.

Compagnie Algérienne d'Assurance: 48 rue Didouche Mourad, Algiers; tel. (2) 64-53-32; telex 56051; fax (2) 64-20-15; f. 1963 as a public corporation; Pres. ALI DJENIDI.

Compagnie Centrale de Réassurance: 21 blvd Zirout Youcef, Algiers; tel. (2) 73-80-20; telex 55091; fax (2) 73-80-60; f. 1973; general; Chair. DJAMEL-EDDINE CHOUAÏB CHOUITER; Gen. Man. AHMAD AL-AZHAR NECHACHBY.

Société Nationale d'Assurances (SNA): 5 blvd Ernesto Ché Guévara, Algiers; tel. (2) 71-47-60; telex 61216; fax (2) 71-23-39; f. 1963; state-sponsored company; Pres. KACI AISSA SLIMANE; Dir-Gen. HORRI MUHAMMAD BOUZIANE.

Trade and Industry

CHAMBERS OF COMMERCE

Chambre Française de Commerce et d'Industrie en Algérie (CFCIA): 1 rue Lieutenant Mohamed Touileb, Algiers; tel. (2) 73-28-81; telex 66505; fax (2) 63-75-33; f. 1965; Pres. MICHEL DE CAFARELLI; Dir CLAUDINE SERRE.

Chambre Nationale de Commerce (CNC): BP 100, Palais Consulaire, rue Amilcar Cabral, Algiers; tel. (2) 57-55-55; telex 61345; fax (2) 62-99-91; f. 1980; Dir-Gen. MOHAMED CHAMI.

TRADE AND INDUSTRIAL ORGANIZATIONS

Association Nationale des Fabrications et Utilisateurs d'Emballages Métalliques: BP 245, rue de Constantine, Algiers; telex 64415; Pres. OTHMANI.

Groupement pour l'Industrialisation du Bâtiment (GIBAT): BP 51, 1 et 3 ave Colonel Driant, 55102 Verdun; tel. 29-86-09; fax (2) 29-86-20; Dir ARMAND MANFE.

Institut Algérien de Normalisation et de Propriété Industrielle (INAPI): 5–7 rue Abou Hamou Moussa, 16000 Algiers; tel. (2) 63-51-80; telex 66409; fax (2) 61-09-71; f. 1973; Dir-Gen. DJENIDI BENDAOUD.

Institut National Algérien du Commerce Extérieur (COMEX): 6 blvd Anatole-France, Algiers; tel. (2) 62-70-44; telex 52763; Dir-Gen. SAAD ZERHOUNI.

Institut National des Industries Manufacturières (INIM): 35000 Boumerdès; tel. (2) 81-62-71; telex 68462; fax (2) 82-56-62; f. 1973; Dir-Gen. HOCINE HASSISSI.

DEVELOPMENT ORGANIZATIONS

Entreprise Nationale de Développement des Industries Alimentaires (ENIAL): 2 rue Ahmed Aït Muhammad, Algiers; tel. (2) 76-51-42; telex 54816; Dir-Gen. MOKRAOUI.

Entreprise Nationale de Développement des Industries d'Articles de Sport, Jouets et Instruments de Musique (DEJIMAS): 5 rue Abane Ramdane, Algiers; tel. (2) 63-22-17; telex 52873; Dir-Gen. FAROUK NADI.

Entreprise Nationale de Développement des Industries Manufacturières (ENEDIM): 22 rue des Fusillés, El Anasser, Algiers; tel. (2) 68-13-43; telex 65315; fax (2) 67-55-26; f. 1983; Dir-Gen. FODIL.

Entreprise Nationale de Développement et de Recherche Industriels des Matériaux de Construction (ENDMC): BP 78, 35000 Algiers; tel. (2) 41-50-70; telex 63352; f. 1982; Dir-Gen. A. TOBBAL.

Entreprise Nationale d'Engineering et de Développement des Industries Légères (EDIL): BP 1010, 50 rue Khélifa Boukhalfa, Algiers; tel. (2) 73-33-90; telex 65153; fax (2) 73-24-81; f. 1982; Dir-Gen. MUHAMMAD BENTIR.

Institut National de la Production et du Développement Industriel (INPED): 126 rue Didouche Mourad, Boumerdès; tel. (2) 41-52-50; telex 52488.

NATIONALIZED INDUSTRIES

A large part of Algerian industry is nationalized. Following the implementation of an economic reform programme in the 1980s, however, more than 300 of the 450 nationalized companies had been transferred to the private sector by late 1990.

The following are some of the most important nationalized industries, each controlled by the appropriate ministry.

Centre National d'Etudes de Recherches Appliquées et de Travaux d'Art (CNERATA): BP 279, 114 rue de Tripoli, Hussein Dey, Algiers; tel. (2) 77-50-22; telex 65402; Gen. Man. DJAMAL-EDDINE HELALI.

Entreprise Nationale d'Ammeublement et de Transformation du Bois (ENATB): BP 18, route de Hassainia, Bouinan; tel. (3) 39-40-63; telex 72848; fax (3) 39-40-10; f. 1982; furniture and other wood products; Dir-Gen. ALI SLIMANI.

Entreprise Nationale d'Ascenseurs (ENASC): 86 rue Hassiba Ben Bouali, Algiers; tel. (2) 65-99-40; telex 65222; f. 1989; manufacture of elevators; Dir-Gen. MUHAMMAD FERRAH.

Entreprise Nationale de Bâtiments Industrialisés (BATIMETAL): BP 89, Ain Defla; tel. (3) 45-24-31; telex 53312; f. 1983; study and commercialization of buildings; Dir-Gen. ABD AL-KADER RAHAL.

Entreprise Nationale de Cellulose et de Papier (CELPAP): BP 128, route de la Salamandre, Mostaganem; tel. (6) 26-54-99; telex 14058; fax (6) 22-42-64; pulp and paper; Dir-Gen. MUSTAPHA MERZOUK.

Entreprise Nationale de Charpentes et de Chaudronnerie (ENCC): BP 1547, 13 rue Marcel Cerdan, Oran; tel. (6) 33-29-32; telex 22107; f. 1983; manufacture of boilers; Dir-Gen. DRISS TANDJAOUI.

Entreprise Nationale de Commerce: 6–9 rue Belhaffat-Ghazali, Hussein Dey, Algiers; tel. (2) 77-43-20; telex 52063; monopoly of imports and distribution of materials and equipment; Dir-Gen. MUHAMMAD LAÏD BELARBIA.

Entreprise Nationale de Construction de Matériaux et d'Equipements Ferroviaires: BP 63, route d'El Hadjar, Annaba; tel. (8) 83-77-41; telex 81998; f. 1983; production, import and export of railway equipment; Dir-Gen. SEBIT OTHMANE BOUSSADIA.

Entreprise Nationale de Développement et de Coordination des Industries Alimentaires (ENIAL): Bab Ezzouar, 5 route nationale, Algiers; tel. (2) 76-21-06; telex 64112; fax (2) 75-59-84; f. 1965; semolina, pasta, flour and couscous; Dir-Gen. YOUNSI HACHEMI.

Entreprise Nationale de Distribution du Matériel Electrique (EDIMEL): 4 et 6 blvd Muhammad V, Algiers; tel. (2) 63-70-82; telex 67161; f. 1983; distribution of electrical equipment; Dir-Gen. ABD AR-RAZAK KEBBAB.

Entreprise Nationale des Engrais et Produits Phytosanitaires: BP 326, route des Salines, Annaba; tel. (8) 83-20-22; telex 81922; fax (8) 84-47-20; f. 1985; production of fertilizers and pesticides.

Entreprise Nationale de Production de Produits Pharmaceutiques: Aïn d'Heb, Médéa; tel. (3) 58-54-64; telex 74018; fax (3) 58-18-64; f. 1983; production of chemicals; Dir-Gen. HAMID HADDAJD.

Entreprise Nationale de Produits Métalliques Utilitaires: BP 25, Carrefour de Meftah, Algiers; tel. (2) 76-64-12; telex 64524; manufacture of metal products; Dir-Gen. MUHAMMAD SAID MOUACI.

Entreprise Nationale de Produits Miniers Non-Ferreux et des Substances Utiles (ENOF): 31 rue Muhammad Hattab, Belfort; tel. (2) 76-62-42; telex 64161; f. 1983; production and distribution of minerals; Dir-Gen. HOCINE ANANE.

Entreprise Nationale des Appareils de Mesure et de Contrôle (AMC): 248 route de Djeinila, El Eulma; tel. (5) 86-24-24; telex 86843; fax (5) 86-49-72; f. 1985; production of measuring equipment; Dir-Gen. MOKHTAR TOUIMER.

Entreprise Nationale des Corps Gras (ENCG): 13 ave Mustapha Sayed el-Ouali, Algiers; tel. (02) 74-49-99; telex 66075; f. 1982 to replace SOGEDIA; oils, margarines and soaps; Dir-Gen. RACHID HAMOUCHE.

Entreprise Nationale des Emballages en Papier et Cartons (ENEPAC): BP 490, route d'Alger, Bordj-Bou-Arreridj; tel. (5) 69-58-48; telex 86823; fax (5) 69-17-73; f. 1985; wrapping paper and cardboard containers.

Entreprise Nationale des Gaz Industriels (ENGI): BP 247, route de Baraki, Gué de Constantine, Algiers; tel. (2) 75-12-70; telex 64413; fax (2) 76-74-41; production and distribution of gas; Dir-Gen. ABD AR-RAHMANE MAKHOUKH.

Entreprise Nationale des Industries du Cable (ENICAB): BP 94, 62 blvd Salah Bouakouir, Algiers; tel. (2) 64-94-32; telex 66497; f. 1983; consortium of cable manufacturers; Dir-Gen. MUHAMMAD BELLAG.

Entreprise Nationale des Industries de Confection et de Bonneterie (ECOTEX): BP 324, Ihadaden, Bejaia; tel. (5) 21-28-84; telex 83030; fax (5) 22-00-08; consortium of textiles and clothing manufacturers; Dir-Gen. AMAR CHERIF.

Entreprise Nationale des Industries de l'Electro-Ménager (ENIEM): BP 71, 15000 Poste Chikhi; tel. (3) 40-29-71; telex 76954; fax (3) 20-54-98; consortium of manufacturers of household equipment; Dir-Gen. CHAABANE HAMMAD.

Entreprise Nationale des Jus et Conserves Alimentaires (ENAJUC): 1BP 108, route nationale, Boufarik; tel. (3) 48-22-13; telex 52437; f. 1982; manufacture of food products; Dir-Gen. OUSSALAH.

Entreprise Nationale de la Pêche Hauturière et Oceanique: Quai d'Aigues Mortes, Port d'Alger; tel. (2) 71-52-68; telex 61346; fax (2) 71-52-67; f. 1979, as Enterprise Nationale des Pêches, to replace (with ECOREP, which is responsible for fishing equipment) former Office Algérien des Pêches; production, marketing, importing and exporting of fish; Man. Dir HACHANI MADANI.

Entreprise Nationale de Sidérurgie (SIDER): BP 342, Chaiba, el-Hadjar, 23000 Annaba; tel. (8) 83-19-99; telex 81661; fax (8) 83-89-57; f. 1964 as Société Nationale de Sidérurgie, restructured 1983; steel, cast iron, zinc and products; Man. Dir MESSAOUD CHETTIH.

Entreprise Nationale de Transformation de Produits Longs (ENTPL): BP 1005, 19 ave Mekki Khelifa, El Manouar; tel. (6) 34-52-40; telex 22953; fax (6) 34-19-50; f. 1983; production and distribution of girders; Dir-Gen. MUHAMMAD BOUTCHACHA.

Entreprise Nationale de Travaux d'Electrification: Villa Malwall, Ain d'Heb, Médéa; tel. (3) 50-61-27; telex 74061; f. 1982; study of electrical infrastructure; Dir-Gen. ABD AL-BAKI BELABDOUN.

Entreprise Nationale de Tubes et de Transformation de Produits Plats (ENTTPP): BP 131, route de la Gare, Reghaia, Algiers; tel. (2) 80-91-86; telex 68116; f. 1983; manufacture and distribution of tubing; Dir-Gen. RACHID BELHOUS.

Entreprise Nationale du Fer et du Phosphate (FERPHOS): BP 122, Zhun 2, Tebessa; tel. (8) 97-49-58; telex 95004; f. 1983; production, import and export of iron and phosphate products; Dir-Gen. AHMAD BENSLIMANE.

Entreprise Publique Economique des Manufactures de Chaussures et Maroquinerie (EMAC): BP 150, route de Sidi Bel-Abbès, Sig 29300; tel. (6) 83-82-15; telex 13935; fax 83-84-51; f. 1983; manufacture of shoes and leather goods; Dir-Gen. DJELLOUL BENDJEDID.

Office Régional du Centre des Produits Oléicoles (ORECPO): route de Ain Bessem Bouira, 10000 Algiers; tel. (3) 92-92-11; telex 77098; fax (3) 92-00-88; f. 1982; production and marketing of olives and olive oil; Dir-Gen. CHABOUR MUSTAPHA.

Pharmacie Centrale Algérienne: 2 rue Bichat, Algiers; tel. (2) 65-18-27; telex 52993; f. 1969; pharmaceutical products; Man. Dir M. MORSLI.

Secrétariat d'Etat aux Forêts et au Reboisement: Immeuble des Forêts, Bois du Petit Atlas, el-Mouradia, Algiers; tel. (2) 60-43-00; telex 52854; f. 1971; production of timber, care of forests; Man. Dir DANIEL BELBACHIR.

Société Nationale de Véhicules Industriels (SNVI): BP 153, 5 route nationale, Rouiba 35300; tel. (2) 85-19-70; telex 68134; fax (2) 85-17-14; f. 1981; manufacture of vehicles; Dir-Gen. ALI BEKKOUCHE.

Société Nationale de Constructions Mécaniques (SONACOME): Birkhadem, Algiers; tel. (2) 65-93-92; telex 52800; f. 1967; to be reorganized into 11 smaller companies, most of which will specialize in manufacture or distribution of one of SONACOME's products; Dir DAOUD AKROUF.

Société Nationale de Constructions Métalliques (SN METAL): Algiers; tel. (2) 63-29-30; telex 52889; f. 1968; production of metal goods; Chair. HACHEM MALIK; Man. Dir ABD AL-KADER MAIZA.

Société Nationale des Eaux Minérales Algériennes (SN-EMA): 21 rue Bellouchat Mouloud, Hussein Dey, Algiers; tel. (2) 77-17-91; telex 52310; mineral water; Man. Dir TAHAR KHENEL.

Société Nationale de l'Electricité et du Gaz (SONELGAZ): 2 blvd Belkacem Krim, Algiers; tel. (2) 74-82-60; telex.66381; fax (2) 61-13-14; monopoly of production, distribution and transportation of electricity and gas; Gen. Man. ABDELBAKI BENABDOUN.

Société Nationale de Fabrication et de Montage du Matériel Electrique (SONELEC): 4 & 6 blvd Muhammad V, Algiers; tel. (2) 63-70-82; telex 52867; electrical equipment.

Société Nationale des Industries Chimiques (SNIC): BP 641, 4–6 blvd Muhammad V, Algiers; tel. (2) 64-07-73; telex 52802; production and distribution of chemical products; Dir-Gen. RACHID BEN IDDIR.

Société Nationale des Industries des Lièges et du Bois (SNLB): BP 61, 1 rue Kaddour Rahim, Hussein Dey, Algiers; tel. (2) 77-99-99; telex 52726; f. 1973; production of cork and wooden goods; Chair. MALEK BELLANI.

Société Nationale des Industries des Peaux et Cuirs (SONIPEC): BP 113, 100 rue de Tripoli, Hussein Dey, Algiers; tel. (2) 77-21-22; telex 52832; fax (2) 77-76-13; f. 1967; hides and skins; Chair. MUHAMMAD CHERIF AZI; Man. Dir NACERI ABDENOUR.

Société Nationale des Industries Textiles (SONITEX): 4–6 rue Patrice Lumumba, Algiers; tel. (2) 63-41-35; telex 52929; f. 1966; split in 1982 into separate cotton, wool, industrial textiles, silk, clothing and distribution companies; 22,000 employees; Man. Dir MUHAMMAD AREZKI ISLI.

Société Nationale des Matériaux de Construction (SNMC): Algiers; tel. (2) 64-35-13; telex 52204; f. 1968; production and import monopoly of building materials; Man. Dir ABD AL-KADER MAIZI.

Société Nationale de Recherches et d'Exploitations Minières (SONAREM): BP 860, 127 blvd Salah Bouakouiz, Algiers; tel. (2) 63-15-55; telex 52910; f. 1967; mining and prospecting; Dir-Gen. OUBRAHAM FERHAT.

Société Nationale pour la Recherche, la Production, le Transport, la Transformation et la Commercialisation des Hydrocarbures (SONATRACH): 10 rue du Sahara, Hydra, Algiers; tel. (2) 56-18-56; telex 62103; f. 1963; exploration, exploitation, transport and marketing of petroleum, natural gas and their products; Dir-Gen. ABDELMAK BOUHAFS.

In May 1980 SONATRACH was disbanded, and its functions were divided among 12 companies (including SONATRACH itself). The other 11 were:

Entreprise Nationale de Canalisation (ENAC): BP 514, ave de la Palestine, Algiers; tel. (2) 70-35-90; telex 42939; piping; Dir-Gen. HAMID MAZRI.

Enterprise Nationale de Commercialisation et de Distribution des Produits Pétroliers (ENCDP): BP 73, route des Dusses, Cheraga, Algiers; tel. (2) 36-09-69; telex 53876; f. 1987; internal marketing and distribution of petroleum products; Gen. Man. HAMID BENZIOUNI.

Entreprise Nationale d'Engineering Pétrolier (ENEP): 2 blvd Muhammad V, Algiers; tel. (2) 63-08-92; telex 66493; fax (2) 63-71-83; engineering; Gen. Man. MUSTAPHA MEKIDECHE.

Entreprise Nationale de Forage (ENAFOR): BP 211, 30500 Hassi Messaoud, Algiers; tel. (2) 73-71-35; telex 44077; fax (2) 73-22-60; drilling; Dir-Gen. ABD AR-RACHID ROUABAH.

Entreprise Nationale de Génie Civil et Bâtiments (GCB): BP 23, route de Corso, Boudouaou, Algiers; tel. (2) 84-65-26; telex 68213; fax (2) 84-60-09; civil engineering; Dir-Gen. ABD EL-HAMID ZERGUINE.

Entreprise Nationale de Géophysique (ENAGEO): BP 140, Hassi Messaoud, Ouargla; tel. (9) 73-77-00; telex 42703; fax (9) 73-72-12; geophysics; Dir-Gen. RABAH DJEDDI.

Entreprise Nationale des Grands Travaux Pétroliers (ENGTP): BP 09, Zone Industrielle, Reghaïa, Boumerdes; tel. (2) 80-06-80; telex 68150; fax (2) 80-59-20; major industrial projects; Dir-Gen. A. BENAMEUR; Asst Dir-Gen. M. BENAMEUR.

Entreprise Nationale de la Pétrochimie (ENIP): BP 215, Skikda; telex 87098; fax (8) 75-74-41; petrochemicals and fertilizers.

Entreprise Nationale des Plastiques et de Caoutchouc (ENPC): BP 452, rue des Frères Meslim, Aïn Turk, Sétif; tel. (5) 90-64-99; telex 86040; fax (5) 90-05-65; production and marketing of rubber and plastics; Dir-Gen. MAHIEDDINE ECHIKH.

Entreprise Nationale de Service aux Puits (ENSP): BP 83, Hassi Messaoud, Ouargla; tel. (9) 73-89-85; telex 44018; fax (9) 73-82-01; oil-well servicing; Dir-Gen. O. BENDAHOU.

Entreprise Nationale des Travaux aux Puits (ENTP): BP 71, In-Amenas, Illizi; telex 44052; oil-well construction; Dir-Gen. ABD AL-AZIZ KRISSAT.

Société Nationale des Tabacs et Allumettes (SNTA): 40 rue Hocine-Nourredine, Algiers; tel. (2) 66-18-68; telex 52780; monopoly of manufacture and trade in tobacco, cigarettes and matches; Dir-Gen. MUHAMMAD TAHAB BOUZEGHOUB.

STATE TRADING ORGANIZATIONS

Since 1972 all international trading has been carried out by state organizations, of which the following are the most important:

Entreprise Nationale d'Approvisionnement en Bois et Dérivés (ENAB): 2 blvd Muhammad V, Algiers; tel. (2) 63-85-32; telex 66470; fax (2) 61-10-89; wood and derivatives; Dir-Gen. El-Hadj REKHROUKH.

Entreprise Nationale d'Approvisionnement en Outillage et Produits de Quincaillerie Générale (ENAOQ): 6 rue Amar Semaous, Hussein-Dey, Algiers; tel. (2) 77-45-03; telex 65566; tools and general hardware; Dir-Gen. ALI HOCINE.

Entreprise Nationale d'Approvisionnements en Produits Alimentaires (ENAPAL): BP 659, 29 rue Larbi ben M'hidi, Algiers; tel. (2) 76-10-11; telex 64278; f. 1983; monopoly of import, export and bulk trade in basic foodstuffs; brs in more than 40 towns; Chair. LAID SABRI; Man. Dir BRAHIM DOUAOURI.

Entreprise Nationale d'Approvisionnement et de Régulation en Fruits et Légumes (ENAFLA): BP 42, 12 ave des 3 Frères Bouadou, Birmandreis, Algiers; tel. (2) 56-90-83; telex 62113; f. 1983; division of the Ministry of Commerce; fruit and vegetable marketing, production and export; Man. Dir ALI BENSEGUENI.

Office Algérien Interprofessionel des Céréales (OAIC): 5 rue Ferhat-Boussaad, Algiers; tel. (2) 73-26-59; telex 65056; fax (2) 73-22-11; f. 1962; monopoly of trade in wheat, rice, maize, barley and products derived from these cereals; Man. Dir M. DOUAOURI.

Office National de la Commercialisation des Produits Viti-Vinicoles (ONCV): 112 Quai-Sud, Algiers; tel. (2) 73-72-75; telex 56063; fax (2) 73-72-97; f. 1968; monopoly of importing and exporting products of the wine industry; Man. Dir S. MEBARKI.

TRADE FAIR

Foire Internationale d'Alger: BP 656, Palais des Expositions, Pins Maritimes, Algiers; tel. (2) 68-52-00; telex 64212; fax (2) 68-50-38; f. 1971; Dir-Gen. SADEK KERAMANE.

PRINCIPAL TRADE UNIONS

Union Générale des Travailleurs Algériens (UGTA): Maison du Peuple, place du 1er mai, Algiers; tel. (2) 66-89-47; telex 65051; f. 1956; 800,000 mems; Sec.-Gen. ABD AL-HAK BENHAMOUDA.

There are 10 national 'professional sectors' affiliated to UGTA. These are:

Secteur Alimentation, Commerce et Tourisme (Food, Commerce and Tourist Industry Workers): Gen. Sec. ABD AL-KADER GHRIBLI.

Secteur Bois, Bâtiments et Travaux Publics (Building Trades Workers): Gen. Sec. LAIFA LATRECHE.

Secteur Education et Formation Professionnelle (Teachers): Gen. Sec. SAÏDI BEN GANA.

Secteur Energie et Pétrochimie (Energy and Petrochemical Workers): Gen. Sec. ALI BELHOUCHET.

Secteur Finances (Financial Workers): Gen. Sec. MUHAMMAD ZAAF.

Secteur Information, Formation et Culture (Information, Training and Culture).

Secteur Industries Légères (Light Industry): Gen. Sec. ABD AL-KADER MALKI.

Secteur Industries Lourdes (Heavy Industry).

Secteur Santé et Sécurité Sociale (Health and Social Security Workers): Gen. Sec. ABD AL-AZIZ DJEFFAL.

Secteur Transports et Télécommunications (Transport and Telecommunications Workers): Gen. Sec. EL-HACHEMI BEN MOUHOUB.

Union Nationale des Paysans Algériens—UNPA: f. 1973; 700,000 mems; Sec.-Gen. AÏSSA NEDJEM.

Al-Haraka al-Islamiyah lil-Ummal al-Jazarivia (Islamic Movement for Algerian Workers): Tlemcen; f. 1990; based on teachings of Islamic faith and affiliated to the FIS.

Transport

RAILWAYS

A new authority, Infrafer (Entreprise Nationale de Réalisation des Infrastructures Ferroviares), was established in 1987 to take responsibility for the construction of new track. In February 1988 a project to build a 64-km underground railway network in Algiers was revived in a modified form. Work on the first 26-km line of the network, to be constructed by local companies with foreign assistance, began in 1990. It was projected that the line would take 10 years to complete.

Société Nationale des Transports Ferroviaires (SNTF): 21–23 blvd Muhammad V, Algiers; tel. (2) 74-81-90; telex 66333; fax (2) 74-81-90; f. 1976 to replace Société Nationale des Chemins de Fer Algériens; 4,290 km of track, of which 301 km are electrified and 1,081 km are narrow gauge; daily passenger services from Algiers to the principal provincial cities and services to Tunisia and Morocco; Dir-Gen. CHAÂBANE DEROUICHE.

ROADS

There are about 90,000 km of roads and tracks, of which 400 km are motorways, 26,000 km are main roads and 22,000 km are secondary roads. The French administration built a good road system, partly for military purposes, which since independence has been allowed to deteriorate in parts, and only a small percentage of roads are surfaced. New roads have been built linking the Sahara oil fields with the coast, and the Trans-Sahara highway is a major project. The first 360-km stretch of the highway, from Hassi Marroket to Aïn Salah, was opened in April 1973, and the next section, ending at Tamanrasset, was opened in June 1978.

Société Nationale des Transports Routiers (SNTR): 27 rue des Trois Frères Bouadou, Birmandreis, Algiers; tel. (2) 54-06-00; telex 62120; fax (2) 56-53-73; f. 1967; holds a monopoly of goods transport by road; Chair. El-Hadj HAOUSSINE; Dir-Gen. ESSAID BENDAKIR.

Société Nationale des Transports des Voyageurs (SNTV): 19 rue Rabah Midat, Algiers; tel. (2) 66-00-52; telex 52603; f. 1967; holds monopoly of long-distance passenger transport by road; Man. Dir M. DIB.

SHIPPING

Algiers is the main port, with anchorage of between 23 m and 29 m in the Bay of Algiers, and anchorage for the largest vessels in Agha Bay. The port has a total quay length of 8,380 m. There are also important ports at Annaba, Arzew, Béjaia, Djidjelli, Ghazaouet, Mostaganem, Oran, Skikda and Ténés. Petroleum and liquefied gas are exported through Arzew, Béjaia and Skikda. Algerian crude petroleum is also exported through the Tunisian port of La Skhirra.

Compagnie Algéro-Libyenne de Transports Maritimes (CAL-TRAM): 21 blvd des Trois Frères Bouaddou, Bir Mourad Rais, Algiers; tel. (2) 63-58-07; telex 62112; Chair. M. O. DAS.

Entreprise Nationale de Consignation et d'Activités Annexes aux Transports Maritimes (ENCATM): 2 rue de Béziers, Algiers; tel. (2) 64-27-82; telex 66577; fax (2) 63-24-98; f. 1987 as part of restructuring of SNTM-CNAN; responsible for merchant traffic.

Entreprise Nationale de Réparations Navales (ERENAV): Algiers; tel. (2) 64-00-10; telex 66650; fax (2) 63-45-79; f. 1987; ship repairs; Dir-Gen. TOURAB BRAHIM.

Entreprise Nationale de Transport Maritime de Voyageurs—Algérie Ferries (ENTMV): 5,6 Jawharlal Nehru, Algiers; tel. (2) 74-05-85; f. 1987 as part of restructuring of SNTM-CNAN; responsible for passenger transport; operates car ferry services between Algiers, Annaba, Skikda, Alicante, Marseille and Oran.

Entreprise Portuaire d'Alger: BP 830, 2 rue d'Anghur, Algiers; tel. (2) 71-54-36; telex 61275; fax (2) 62-44-98; Man. Dir M. KHELIFI.

Entreprise Portuaire de Annaba: BP 1232, Môle Cigogne-Quai nord, Annaba: tel: (8) 86-31-31; telex 81652; fax (8) 83-90-69; Man. Dir D. SALHI.

Entreprise Portuaire d'Arzew: 45 rue Aissat Iddir, Arzew; tel. 37-24-91; telex 12919; Man. Dir C. OUMEUR.

Entreprise Portuaire de Béjaia: BP 94, Môle de la Casbah, Béjaia; tel. (5) 21-18-07; telex 83055; fax (5) 22-25-79; Man. Dir M. RABOUHI.

Entreprise Portuaire de Djidjelli: BP 87, Djidjelli; tel. 45-94-63; telex 84060; fax (5) 45-90-72; f. 1984; Man. Dir M. ATHMANE.

Entreprise Portuaire de Ghazaouet: BP 217, Ghazaouet; tel. 32-13-45; telex 18836; fax (2) 32-12-55; Man. Dir M. MEHABI.

Entreprise Portuaire de Mostaganem: BP 131, Mostaganem; tel. (6) 26-59-38; telex 14086; Man. Dir M. TAHAR.

Entreprise Portuaire d'Oran: BP 106, blvd Mimouni Laucène, Oran; tel. (6) 39-26-25; telex 22422; Man. Dir M. S. LOUHIBI.

Entreprise Portuaire de Skikda: 46 rue Rezki Rahal, Skikda; tel. (8) 95-98-29; telex 87840; Man. Dir D. SALHI.

Entreprise Portuaire de Ténés: BP 18, Ténés; tel. 76-61-95; telex 78090; fax (2) 76-64-97; Man. Dir K. AL-HAMRI.

NAFTAL Direction Aviation Maritime: BP 70, Aéroport Houari Boumedienne, Dar-el-Beida, Algiers; tel. (2) 50-65-10; telex 64346; Dir Z. BEN MERABET.

Office National des Ports (ONP): BP 830, quai d'Arcachon, Algiers-Port; tel. (2) 62-57-48; telex 52738; f. 1971; responsible for management and growth of port facilities and sea pilotage; Man. Dir M. HARRATI.

Société Nationale de Manutention (SONAMA): 6 rue de Béziers, Algiers; tel. (2) 64-65-61; telex 52339; monopoly of port handling; Man. Dir AMOS BELALEM.

Société Nationale de Transports Maritimes et Compagnie Nationale Algérienne de Navigation (SNTM-CNAN): quai no. 9, Nouvelle Gare Maritime, Algiers; tel. (2) 71-16-10; telex 66580; f. 1963; state-owned company which has the monopoly of conveyance, freight, chartering and transit facilities in all Algerian ports; operates fleet of freight and passenger ships; office in Marseilles and reps. in Paris, most French ports and the principal ports in many other countries. In September 1987 the company was restructured, and two new shipping companies were formed to deal with passenger transport and merchant traffic; Man. Dir AMMAR BOUSBAH; Gen. Man. HANI LAZHAR.

Société Nationale de Transports Maritimes des Hydrocarbures et des Produits Chimiques (SNTM-HYPROC): BP 60, Arzew, 31200 Oran; tel. (6) 37-30-99; telex 12097; fax (6) 37-28-30; f. 1982; Dir-Gen. MOKRANE YATAGHENE.

CIVIL AVIATION

Algeria's main airport, Dar-el-Beïda, 20 km from Algiers, is a class A airport of international standing. At Constantine, Annaba, Tlemcen and Oran there are also airports which meet international requirements. There are also 65 aerodromes of which 20 are public, and a further 135 airstrips connected with the petroleum industry.

Air Algérie (Entreprise Nationale d'Exploitation des Services Aériens): BP 858, 1 place Maurice Audin, Immeuble el-Djazair, Algiers; tel. (2) 74-24-28; telex 55145; fax (2) 74-44-25; f. 1953 by merger; state-owned from 1972; internal services and extensive services to Europe, North, Central and West Africa, the Middle East and Asia; Dir-Gen. CHAKIB BELLEILI.

Air Maghreb: consortium of the national airlines of Algeria, Libya, Mauritania, Morocco and Tunisia; operates co-ordinated schedules within the region.

Tourism

Algeria's tourist attractions include the Mediterranean coast, the Atlas mountains and the desert. In 1991 a total of 722,682 tourists

visited Algeria. Receipts from tourism totalled about US \$64m. in 1990. In 1986 there were 200 hotels, with a total of 32,862 beds, and in 1987 a development programme planned to provide a further 120,000 beds by 1999, through joint ventures with foreign companies. The Government identified 19 potential tourist centres and aimed to attract 900,000 tourists per year by 1999.

Entreprise de Gestion Touristique du Centre (EGT CENTRE): Hotel Essafir, Algiers; tel. (2) 63-50-40; telex 52142; Dir-Gen. SALAH EDDINE SENNI.

Office National du Tourisme (ONT): 8 rue Ismail Kerrar, Algiers; tel. (2) 60-59-60; telex 66590; fax (2) 59-13-15; f. 1990; state institution; oversees tourism development policy; Dir-Gen. ATMAN SAHNOUN.

ONAT-TOUR (Opérateur National Algérien de Tourism): 25–27 rue Khélifa-Boukhalfa, 16000 Algiers; tel. (2) 74-33-76; telex 55250; fax (2) 74-32-14; f. 1962; Dir-Gen. ABID KERAMANE.

Société de Développement de l'Industrie Touristique en Algérie (SODITAL): 2 rue Asselah Hocine, Algiers; f. 1989; Dir-Gen. NOUREDDINE SALHI.

Defence

Commander-in-Chief of the Armed Forces: Maj.-Gen. KHALED NEZZAR.

Inspector-General of the Armed Forces: Maj.-Gen. TAYEB DERRADJI.

Chief of Staff of the Army: Gen. MUHAMMAD LAMARI.

Commander of the Land Force: Maj.-Gen. AHMED GAÏD.

Commander of the Air Force: Gen. MUHAMMAD BENSLIMANE.

Commander of the Naval Forces: Gen. ABDELMAJID TARIGHT.

Defence Budget (1993): AD 29,800m.

Military Service: 18 months national service (army only).

Total Armed Forces (June 1993): 121,700: army 105,000 (65,000 conscripts); navy 6,700; air force 12,000.

Paramilitary Forces: 41,200 (including a gendarmerie of 24,000).

Education

As a result of reforms that the government initiated in 1973, education in the national language (Arabic) is now officially compulsory for a period of nine years, for children between six and 15 years of age. Primary education begins at the age of six and lasts for six years. Secondary education begins at 12 years of age and lasts for a maximum of six years, comprising two cycles of three years each. In 1990 the total enrolment at primary and secondary schools was equivalent to 79% of the school-age population (males 86%; females 72%). Primary enrolment in that year included 88% of children in the relevant age-group (males 94%; females 83%). The comparable ratio for secondary enrolment was 53% (males 59%; females 46%). More than 14% of total planned expenditure in the 1990 budget was allocated to education and training.

There were 4,357,352 pupils at primary schools in 1991/92, compared with about 800,000 in 1962. Facilities for middle and secondary education are still very limited, although they have greatly improved since independence, accommodating 1,490,035 pupils at middle schools, and 838,768 pupils at secondary schools in 1991/92, compared with 48,500 at middle and secondary schools in 1962. Whereas before independence most teachers were French, in 1975/76 more than 95% of primary teachers were Algerian, as were about 65% of middle and secondary teachers. Most education at primary level is in Arabic, but at higher levels French is still widely used. The majority of foreign teachers in Algeria come from Egypt, Syria, Tunisia and other Arab countries.

In 1990 the number of students receiving higher education was 285,930. In addition to the 10 main universities there are seven other *centres universitaires* and a number of technical colleges. Several thousand students go abroad to study. Adult illiteracy, which, according to UNESCO estimates, averaged 42.6% (males 30.2%; females 54.5%) in 1990, has been combated by a large-scale campaign, in which instruction is sometimes given by young people who have only recently left school, and in which the broadcasting services are widely used.

Bibliography

Ageron, Charles-Robert. *Modern Algeria: A History from 1830 to the present.* London, Hurst, 1992.

Al-Ahnaf, M., Botiveau, B., and Frégosi, F. *L'Algérie par ses islamistes.* Paris, Karthala, 1992.

Alazard, J., and others. *Invitation à l'Algérie.* Paris, 1957.

Allais, M. *Les Accords d'Evian, le référendum et la résistance algérienne.* Paris, 1962.

Amin, Samir. *The Maghreb in the Modern World: Algeria, Tunisia, Morocco.* Harmondsworth, Penguin, 1970.

Aron, Raymond. *La Tragédie Algérienne.* Paris, 1957.

Bourdieu, Pierre. *The Algerians.* Boston, 1962.

　Sociologie de l'Algérie. Paris, Que Sais-je, 1958.

Brace, R. and J. *Ordeal in Algeria.* New York, 1960.

Chaliand, G. *L'Algérie, est-elle Socialiste?* Paris, Maspéro, 1964.

De Gaulle, Charles. *Mémoires d'espoir: Le Renouveau 1958–1962.* Paris, Plon, 1970.

Encyclopaedia of Islam. *Algeria.* New edition, Vol. I. London and Leiden, 1960.

Eveno, P., and Planchais, J. *La Guerre d'Algérie.* Paris, La Découverte, 1989.

Favrod, Ch.-H. *Le FLN et l'Algérie.* Paris, 1962.

First, Ruth. *The Barrel of a Gun: Political Power in Africa and the Coup d'Etat.* London, Allen Lane, The Penguin Press, 1970.

Francos, Avia, and Séréri, J.-P. *Un Algérien nommé Boumedienne.* Paris, 1976.

Gillespie, Joan. *Algeria.* London, Benn, 1960.

Gordon, David. *North Africa's French Legacy, 1954–1963.* London, 1963.

　The Passing of French Algeria. Oxford, 1966.

Henissart, Paul. *Wolves in the City: The Death of French Algeria.* London, Hart-Davis, 1971.

Horne, Alistair. *A Savage War of Peace: Algeria 1954–1962.* London, Macmillan, 1977.

Humbaraci, Arslan. *Algeria—A Revolution that Failed.* London, Pall Mall, 1966.

Ibrahimi, A. Taleb. *De la Décolonisation à la Révolution Culturelle (1962–72).* Algiers, SNED, 1973.

Jeanson, F. *La Révolution Algérienne; Problèmes et Perspectives.* Milan, 1962.

Joesten, Joachim. *The New Algeria.* New York, 1964.

Julien, Charles-André. *Histoire de l'Algérie contemporaine, conquête et colonisation, 1827–1871.* Paris, Presses Universitaires de France, 1964.

Kettle, Michael. *De Gaulle and Algeria.* London, Quartet, 1993.

Lacheraf, Mostepha. *L'Algérie, Nation et Société.* Paris, Maspéro, 1965.

Laffont, Pierre. *L'Expiation: De l'Algérie de papa à l'Algérie de Ben Bella.* Paris, Plon, 1968.

Lambotte, R. *Algérie, naissance d'une société nouvelle.* Paris, Editions Sociales, 1976.

Lebjaoui, Mohamed. *Vérités sur la Révolution Algérienne.* Paris, Gallimard, 1970.

Leca, Jean, and Vatin, Jean-Claude. *L'Algérie politique, institutions et régime.* Paris, Fondation nationale des sciences politiques, 1974.

Lyotard, Jean-François. *La Guerre des Algériens Ecrits 1956–1963.* Paris, Galilée, 1989.

Mallarde, Etienne. *L'Algérie depuis.* Paris, La Table Ronde, 1977.

Mandouze, André. *La Révolution Algérienne par les Textes.* Paris, 1961.

Martens, Jean-Claude. *Le modèle algérien de développement (1962–1972).* Algiers, SNED, 1973.

Martin, Claude. *Histoire de l'Algérie Française 1830–1962.* Paris, 1962.

Mouilleseaux, Louiz. *Histoire de l'Algérie.* Paris, 1962.

Nyssen, Hubert. *L'Algérie en 1970.* 1970.

Ottaway, David and Marina. *Algeria. The Politics of a Socialist Revolution.* Berkeley, University of California Press, 1970.

Ouzegane, Amar. *Le Meilleur Combat.* Paris, Julliard, 1962.

Quandt, William B. *Revolution and Political Leadership: Algeria, 1954–1968.* MIT Press, 1970.

Reudy, John D. *Land Policy in Colonial Algeria: The Origins of the Rural Public Domain.* Berkeley, University of California Press, 1967.

Robson, P., and Lury, D. *The Economics of Africa.* London, Allen & Unwin, 1969.

Sa'dallah, A. Q. *Studies on Modern Algerian Literature.* Beirut, Al Adab, 1966.

Sivan, Emmanuel. *Communisme et Nationalisme en Algérie (1920–1962).* Paris, 1976.

Smith, Tony. *The French Stake in Algeria 1945–1962.* Cornell University Press, 1978.

Sulzberger, C. L. *The Test, de Gaulle and Algeria.* London and New York, 1962.

Talbott, John. *France in Algeria, 1954–1962.* New York, Knopf, 1980.

Vatin, Jean-Claude. *L'Algérie politique, histoire et société.* Paris, Fondation nationale des sciences politiques, 1974.

Vidal-Naquet, Pierre. *L'Affaire Audin.* Paris, Les éditions de Minuit, 1989.

　Face à la Raison d'Etat: Un Historien dans la Guerre d'Algérie. Paris, La Découverte, 1989.

BAHRAIN

Geography

The State of Bahrain consists of a group of about 35 islands, situated midway along the Persian (Arabian) Gulf, about 24 km (15 miles) from the east coast of Saudi Arabia, and 28 km (17 miles) from the west coast of Qatar.

The total area of the Bahrain archipelago is 691.2 sq km (266.9 sq miles). Bahrain itself, the principal island, is about 50 km (30 miles) long and between 13 km and 25 km (8 miles and 15 miles) wide. To the north-east of Bahrain, and linked to it by a causeway and road, lies Muharraq island, which is approximately 6 km (4 miles) long. Construction commenced in 1993 of a second causeway linking Bahrain to Muharraq. A causeway also links Bahrain to Sitra island. Some of the other islands in the state are Nabih Salih, Jeddah, Hawar, Umm Nassan and Umm Suban. A causeway linking Bahrain and Saudi Arabia was opened in November 1986.

The total population of Bahrain increased from 216,078 in April 1971 to 508,037 at the census of November 1991. Of the 1991 total, 323,305 were Bahraini citizens. About 80% of the population are thought to be of Arab ethnic origin, and 20% Iranian. In 1991 the port of Manama, the capital and seat of government, had a population of 136,999. Bahrain's Muslim population (82% of the total in 1991) is estimated to consist of between 40% and 45% of the Sunni sect and between 55% and 60% of the Shi'ite sect. The Bahraini labour force, 60% of whom were estimated to be of non-Bahraini origin in 1993, was expected to double between 1989 and the end of the century. The ruling family are Sunnis.

History

Revised for this edition by RICHARD I. LAWLESS.

After several centuries of independence, Bahrain passed first under the rule of the Portuguese (1521–1602) and then under periodic Persian rule (1602–1782). The Persians were expelled in 1783 by the Utub tribe from Arabia, whose leading family, the al-Khalifas, became the independent sheikhs of Bahrain and have ruled Bahrain ever since, except for a short break before 1810. Nevertheless, claims, based on the Persian occupation of the islands in the 17th and 18th centuries, were renewed intermittently.

In the 19th century European powers began to take an interest in the Gulf area. Britain was principally concerned to prevent the French, Russian and German penetration towards India, and to suppress the trade in slaves and weapons. In 1861 the Sheikh of Bahrain undertook to abstain from the prosecution of war, piracy and slavery by sea in return for British support in case of aggression. In 1880 and 1892 the Sheikh further undertook not to cede, mortgage or otherwise dispose of parts of his territories to anyone except the British Government, nor to enter into a relationship with any other government without British consent. A convention acknowledging Bahrain's independence was signed by the British and Ottoman Governments in 1913, although the islands remained under British administration.

Under Sheikh Sulman bin Hamad al-Khalifa (who became ruler of Bahrain in 1942), social services and public works were considerably extended. Sheikh Sulman died on 2 November 1961 and was succeeded by his eldest son, Sheikh Isa bin Sulman al-Khalifa. In February 1956 elections were held for members of an Education and Health Council (the first election in Bahrain had been held in 1919 for the Municipal Council). Shortly after the 1956 elections, there was a strike in the petroleum refinery, alleged to be partly a protest against the paternalism of the British adviser to the Sheikh. There were further disturbances at the time of the Suez crisis. Other symbols of Bahrain's growing independence included the establishment of Bahraini, as opposed to British, legal jurisdiction over a wide range of nationalities (1957), the issue of Bahrain's own stamps (1960) and the introduction of a separate currency (1965). Bahrain also pioneered free education and health services in the Gulf region. In 1967 Britain transferred its principal Arabian military base from Aden to Bah-

rain, but by 1968 the British Government had decided to withdraw all forces 'East of Suez' before the end of 1971. In October 1973, at the time of the Arab-Israeli war, the Bahrain Government gave one year's notice to quit to the US Navy, whose ships had docking facilities in Bahrain. The evacuation did not, in fact, take place, but negotiations continued and Bahrain finally took over the base in July 1977.

Extensive administrative and political reforms came into effect in January 1970, when a 12-member Council of State was established. The formation of this new body, which became the state's supreme executive authority, represented the first formal derogation of the ruler's powers. Sheikh Khalifa bin Sulman al-Khalifa, the ruler's eldest brother, became President of the Council. Only four of the initial 12 'Directors' were members of the royal family, but all were Bahrainis, and the British advisers were reduced to the status of civil servants. Equal numbers of Sunni and Shi'ite Muslims were included (the royal family apart) to reflect Bahrain's religious balance. When Bahrain became fully independent, in August 1971, the Council of State became the Cabinet of the State of Bahrain (with Sheikh Khalifa as Prime Minister), with authority to direct the country's internal and external affairs.

After 1968 Bahrain was officially committed to membership of the embryonic Federation of Arab Emirates. The Bahraini Government, however, failed to negotiate an agreement on the terms of the federal constitution with the richer, but less developed, sheikhdoms further down the Gulf. Bahrain's position was strengthened in May 1970, when Iran accepted the findings of a UN report on Bahrain's future. The UN representatives had visited the island in April and found that popular opinion overwhelmingly favoured complete independence rather than union with Iran.

On 15 August 1971 Bahrain's full independence was proclaimed, a new treaty of friendship was signed with the United Kingdom, and Sheikh Isa took the title of Amir. Bahrain became a member of the Arab League and the UN later in the year. In December 1972 elections were held for a Constituent Assembly. This body drafted a new Constitution, which came into force on 6 December 1973. Elections to a 44-member National Assembly were held on the following day. Of the members, 30 were chosen by the all-male electorate, and the remaining 14 were members of the Government. A delay in the establishment of trade unions, for which the Constitution made provision, and a sharp rise in the cost of living provoked industrial unrest in 1974. In August 1975 the Prime Minister submitted his resignation, complaining that the National Assembly was preventing the Government from carrying out its functions. The Amir invited him to form a new government, and two days later dissolved the National Assembly and suspended the Constitution. Despite the arrest of 'leftists' in December 1975, sporadic unrest continued. The traditional administrative system of *majlis* (assembly), where citizens and non-citizens present petitions to the Amir, remains.

Bahrain joined other Arab states in condemning the Egyptian-Israeli peace treaty in March 1979, and suspended diplomatic relations with Egypt. In September 1979 Iranian Shi'ite elements exhorted Bahraini Shi'ites, who are in the majority and many of whom are of Iranian descent, to demonstrate against the Sunni Amir. Calm was restored but it was apparent that the new Iranian regime was interested in reviving the Iranian claim to Bahrain, which the Shah had not renounced until 1975. In December 1981 between 50 and 60 people, mainly Bahrainis, were arrested in Bahrain on charges of conspiring to overthrow the Government. Bahrain's Minister of the Interior alleged that the plot was the work of Hojatoleslam Hadi al-Mudarasi, an Iranian clergyman, who was operating in the name of the Islamic Front for the Liberation of Bahrain. In 1984 the discovery of a cache of weapons in a Bahraini village renewed fears of Iranian attempts to disrupt the island's stability, and in June 1985 there was increased concern over Bahrain's security when a further plot to overthrow the Government was discovered. Despite subsequent assurances from President Rafsanjani of Iran, Bahrain remains vigilant, watching carefully both the political situation in Teheran and domestic stability. Strict censorship is imposed, and political parties and trade unions are banned. The Government has been severely criticized by human rights organizations for its alleged use of torture and detention without trial.

Concern over security was one of the reasons why Bahrain joined five other Gulf states in forming the Gulf Co-operation Council (GCC: see p. 224) in March 1981. In 1984 the GCC granted $1,000m. to Bahrain and Oman for the improvement of defences. Fear of a possible escalation of the Iran–Iraq War led to further concern about the strength of Bahrain's defences. In January 1987 the USA agreed to sell 12 F-16 fighter aircraft to Bahrain as part of a contract, valued at $400m., to provide military equipment. Bahrain became the first Gulf nation to receive any of these aircraft, the delivery of which had been completed by mid-1990. In 1987 work began on the construction of an air-force base, in the south of the main island, to accommodate the F-16 aircraft. Bahrain's intention to maintain its security through collective defence has also been emphasized by the country's participation in joint naval manoeuvres with Qatar and other Gulf states, and in the GCC's 'Peninsula Shield' military exercises.

Bahrain provides onshore facilities for US forces, and there is a large US navy presence. In September 1987 the US President, Ronald Reagan, expressed his gratitude to Bahrain for its assistance in enabling US warships to escort 'reflagged' Kuwaiti merchant vessels in Gulf waters. In December 1987 a controversial sale of as many as 70 *Stinger* anti-aircraft missiles and 14 launchers, worth $7m., was agreed between Bahrain and the USA.

By February 1983 the GCC had concluded agreements for freer trade and for co-operative economic protection among Gulf states. Bahrain consolidated its links with the rest of the Gulf region when a 25-km causeway to Saudi Arabia was opened in November 1986. The causeway, financed wholly by Saudi Arabia, has increased trade and tourism between Bahrain and the other Gulf states.

Co-operation in the industrial sector was marked in 1983 by the election of the first officially recognized General Committee for Bahrain Workers. This is not a trade union but a joint management-worker committee, meeting in eight designated companies. A decree ordering equal pay for both sexes was issued in 1984, reflecting a less rigorous enforcement of Islamic principles than in many other Muslim countries. A new Gulf University was built in Bahrain in the late 1980s,

to serve all the Arab states, but was only partially opened, owing to financial difficulties; only Bahrain and Saudi Arabia have fully honoured their financial commitments to the project. On the completion of extension work to its international airport in mid-1992, Bahrain was established as an important centre of Gulf aviation.

In April 1986 a long-standing territorial dispute between Bahrain and Qatar erupted into a military confrontation. Qatari military forces raided the island of Fasht ad-Dibal, a coral reef situated midway between Bahrain and Qatar, over which both claim sovereignty. During the raid Qatar seized 29 foreign workers (all of whom were subsequently released), who were constructing a Bahraini coastguard station on the island. Officials of the GCC met representatives from both states in an attempt to reconcile them and avoid a split within the Council. Fasht ad-Dibal was the third area of dispute between the two countries, the others being Zubara, on mainland Qatar, and the Hawar islands. In July 1991 Qatar instituted proceedings at the International Court of Justice (ICJ) in The Hague in an attempt to resolve the dispute over the potentially oil-rich Hawar islands, the shoals of Dibal and Quitat Jaradah and the delineation of the maritime boundary. In mid-1992 Qatar rejected Bahrain's attempt to broaden the issue to include its claim to part of the Qatari mainland, around Zubara, which had been Bahraini territory until the early 20th century. However, in mid-1993 it was announced that the ICJ would consider the claims of each country to the Hawar islands in February 1994, before determining whether it had jurisdiction to decide the case, as Qatar had applied unilaterally to the Court. On 1 July 1994 the ICJ announced that it was requesting both Qatar and Bahrain to resubmit their dispute to the Court by 30 November 1994.

In 1989 Bahrain established diplomatic relations with the People's Republic of China and signed an agreement with Iraq on mutual non-interference. In 1990 Bahrain established diplomatic relations with the USSR and Czechoslovakia and upgraded its relations with Iran to ambassadorial level. Subsequently, in early 1992, Bahrain signed an important protocol for industrial co-operation with Iran. In November 1993 Bahrain raised sanctions against South Africa, and diplomatic relations were restored during a visit to Manama by the South African Minister of Foreign Affairs. The South African embassy in Bahrain was the first to be opened in the Arab world.

In August 1990 Bahrain, in common with the whole Gulf area, seemed likely to be drawn into a conflict as a result of Iraq's occupation and annexation of Kuwait. Following the annexation, Bahrain firmly supported the implementation of UN economic sanctions against Iraq, and permitted the stationing of US combat aircraft in Bahrain. British armed forces participating in the multinational force for the defence of Saudi Arabia and the liberation of Kuwait were also stationed in Bahrain in 1990/91. In May 1991 representatives of the Bahraini Government met defence officials from the USA, the United Kingdom and Germany to discuss post-war security arrangements, and the role that the USA should play in the implementation of any regional security plan. In June the Amir visited Kuwait for talks on regional security, and it was announced that Bahrain would remain a regional support base for the USA, but would not become the headquarters of a Gulf-based US military command and control centre. At the end of October Bahrain and the USA signed a defence co-operation agreement allowing for joint military exercises, the storage of equipment and the use of Bahraini port facilities by US forces. In January 1994 memoranda of military co-operation were signed with the USA and the United Kingdom.

In July 1992 Bahrain's Prime Minister expressed the hope that the country's relations with Iraq would improve and that, eventually, both Iraq and Iran would be incorporated into the GCC. This was the first time that a government of a GCC state had openly recommended the restoration of contacts with Iraq. At the GCC summit in Riyadh, however, in December 1993, there was criticism of both Iraq and Iran. In the final communiqué the Heads of State of the six GCC member countries demanded that international pressure on Iraq to observe all of the UN resolutions pertaining to it should be maintained, and that the sovereignty of Kuwait should be respected. It was also decided to double the size of the Saudi-based 'Peninsula Shield' joint defence force. There was no further reference to the stationing of Syrian and Egyptian soldiers in the Gulf region.

In November 1992 the Amir announced the formation of a new, 30-member Consultative Council. The Council's powers are limited and it has little scope to question or alter government policy. Power remains with the Amir and the ruling al-Khalifa family. The establishment of the Council met with little popular enthusiasm.

Fears of renewed unrest among Bahrain's Shi'ite majority have continued to preoccupy the ruling regime. In January 1994, when a crowd gathered at the Momin mosque in Manama to mourn the death of the highest-ranking Shi'ite cleric, Aya-

tollah Mohammad Reza Golpayegani of Iran, police immediately isolated the area and fired tear-gas canisters into the mosque compound. At least 20 people were arrested. The Government commented that the gathering had been unauthorized and had been dispersed by normal security measures. In December 1993 the human rights organization, Amnesty International, had published a report that was highly critical of the Bahraini Government, claiming that Bahraini Shi'ites had been deprived of their nationality and forcibly exiled by their own Government. In response to the criticism the Amir issued a decree in March 1994 pardoning several Bahrainis exiled since the 1980s and permitting them to return to Bahrain.

Economy

Dr P. T. H. UNWIN

Revised for this edition by RICHARD I. LAWLESS

INTRODUCTION

During the 1970s the exploitation of Bahrain's hydrocarbon resources was the basis for considerable economic diversification, particularly in the construction, industrial and banking sectors. Since then Bahrain has remained heavily dependent on its hydrocarbon resources, which by 1991 had begun to diminish. Nevertheless hydrocarbon sales constitute about 80% of Bahrain's export earnings. The collapse of the price of petroleum in the first half of 1986 revealed the fragility of the country's economic base. Although there was a recovery after the cease-fire in the Iran–Iraq War in 1988, the crisis in the Gulf region, following Iraq's occupation of Kuwait in August 1990, again cast doubt on the continued stability of Bahrain's economy. Bahrain lost US $2,000m. during the Gulf crisis and, since the liberation of Kuwait in February 1991, has striven to regain the momentum for economic growth. The official rate of unemployment in 1993 was 15% and the creation of new jobs is one of the Government's priorities, as the population is rising by more than 3% each year. Inflation averaged 1% in 1991.

Before the discovery of petroleum in Bahrain, the archipelago's economy was one of the most prosperous on the northern shores of the Arabian peninsula. Traditionally, the livelihood of most of the population depended on agriculture, pearling and trade, and Bahrain's offshore pearl banks were reputed to be the best in the region. However, with the discovery of commercially exploitable petroleum deposits in 1932 and the simultaneous growth of the Japanese pearl trade, Bahrain became increasingly reliant on its reserves of petroleum and natural gas. Traditional occupations, particularly agriculture, suffered, and the heavy demand for water led to a dramatic lowering of the aquifer levels. In some places this resulted in excessive salination of the soil and consequent loss of agricultural production. Pollution in the Gulf has adversely affected the islands' fishing industry.

Bahrain will be the first Gulf state to experience a future largely without petroleum. As a result, it has engaged in economic diversification in an attempt to become the major financial and trading centre in the Gulf region. Bahrain was a founder member of the Gulf Co-operation Council (GCC) in 1981, and by the mid-1980s had begun to benefit from a number of joint industrial projects, although the Council has never provided the support and trading opportunities envisaged by Bahrain. The construction of the King Fahd Causeway between Bahrain and Saudi Arabia was a further indication of Bahrain's commitment to close ties with other Gulf states. The causeway, costing about $900m., was officially opened in November 1986. The private sector has, since 1988, been encouraged to expand its role in economic development with considerable success. It was hoped that the wider credit facilities available through the new Bahrain stock exchange, which opened in June 1989, would stimulate investment in industry

and commerce. However, the Gulf crisis forced a scaling-down of privatization plans and lowered the immediate expectations of the private sector. One of the few successful examples of privatization is the Bahrain Aluminium Extrusion Company (BALEXCO). By 1994 the state was to have reduced its holding in BALEXCO to 40%. There are plans to offer shares to the general public and the eventual aim is complete privatization. Plans have also been revived to privatize Gulf Air, the regional airline, with proposals to sell 49% of the shareholding, beginning in 1995. In 1994 it was reported that the Government had sold 20% of its shares in Bahrain's principal food company, the General Trading and Food Processing Company. The Ministry of Development and Industry, through its industrial branch (the Industrial Development Directorate), has adopted a policy of encouraging foreign investment in Bahrain. In 1991 the Government established the Bahrain Development Bank to provide long-term loans and venture capital to attract investors, and the Bahrain Marketing and Promotions Office to encourage companies to establish a base in the region. Incentives to new investors introduced in the 1993 Government Incentive Programme included major tax concessions, rebates on rent and power charges to small and medium-sized companies, and a subsidy for every Bahraini national employed. Official procedures were simplified and full foreign ownership was extended to onshore companies provided they were industrial or were establishing a base for the sale of manufactured goods and services in the Gulf region. In March 1994 the director of the Stock Exchange announced that, subject to approval by the Consultative Council, a law would be passed allowing foreign residents to invest on the Bahrain Stock Exchange. Foreigners who have lived in Bahrain for at least three years will be permitted to buy up to 1% of a company's shares. The new regulation was to apply to individuals only, but legislation was also planned to open up the Stock Exchange to foreign companies registered in Bahrain for a minimum of three years. The Bahraini Government now believes that it has the best foreign investment incentive package in the Gulf region.

Efforts to attract foreign investors into the industrial and infrastructural sectors met with some success in 1993. Industrialization remains central to the Government's strategy of economic diversification away from oil, and a number of foreign investors have been attracted to Bahrain by its proximity to the Saudi Arabian market. Two major industrial projects are planned by foreign companies, a $33m.-tissue paper mill to be built as a joint venture between Kimberly-Clark of the USA and Olayan of Saudi Arabia, and a factory for prefabricated pipeline systems; and another joint venture between Shaw Industries of the USA and a local partner, Abdulla Ahmed Nass Industrial Services. Further development of the country's infrastructure is essential to sustain the process of industrialization. A new power station and desalination plant, originally planned by the Government, is now to be built by the private sector. British Gas, which is financing the project, is preparing a technical and financial plan for the plant which is scheduled to become operational in 1996. In May 1994, however, it was reported that the plant's capacity had been reduced from 500 MW to 300 MW. The Government has increased its efforts to get the private sector to invest in power generation since demand in July 1993 came close to installed capacity. Private capital is also being sought to finance the construction of additional desalination plants. In January 1994 it was reported that the local United Gulf Industries Corpn was considering a plan to establish a private desalination plant.

AGRICULTURE AND FISHING

Agriculture has declined rapidly since the 1960s, and in 1991 contributed less than 1% of gross domestic product (GDP). The Bahrain islands are largely barren and have never been able to support farming on more than a limited scale. The northern belt of date plantations, supplied with water by wells and underground canals, was a relatively well-developed region, agriculturally, but it is estimated that 75% of the total agricultural land of approximately 6,500 ha had been abandoned by the end of the 1970s. This reduction in agriculture was caused both by the increasing salinity of traditional supplies of water, and by the attractions of other sectors of the economy. (In 1988 Bahrain had 21 land and sea springs, compared with a total of 223 in 1954.) The Government is nevertheless keen to develop the archipelago's agricultural potential. By 1988 milk production had risen sufficiently to satisfy 50% of local demand, and vegetable production to 75% of requirements. Self-sufficiency in egg production had also been achieved. In order to increase the agricultural area, the Government initiated a two-stage irrigation project, costing an estimated BD 12m., that entailed ozonizing and storing treated sewage at the Tubli sewage works for distribution and application to fields. The first phase of this scheme, which was expected to double the plant's daily production capacity to 110,000 cu m of water, involved taking water to Adari, Buhayr, Buri and Hawrat Ali, while the second phase involved the connection of Saar, Sadad, Salmabad and Zallaq to the network, and the construction of a major reservoir at Buhayr. In April 1994 international consultants were invited to submit bids for a study to examine the feasibility of expanding the Tubli sewage treatment plant to process 140,000 cu m a day of waste water for reuse in agriculture. The increase in water supply would be used in the west of the country, which is the most severely affected by the depletion of underground water resources. The Bahrain National Dairy Company was founded in 1985, with a capital of BD 650,000. In 1984 a new five-year agricultural plan, which aimed to increase dairy production, was initiated. In 1992 there were 13,000 cattle, 20,000 sheep and 16,000 goats in the country. In 1979 the Bahrain Fishing Company was forced to cease its operations because of the virtual disappearance of shrimps from the Gulf, owing to pollution. In 1981 the Government initiated a five-year plan to revive the industry by acquiring more sophisticated equipment and establishing training schemes. In 1985 the Government announced an investment of BD 20,000 (US $54,000) to revive the pearling industry. In December 1988 a fisheries development programme, with a projected cost of BD 19m., was initiated, but in mid-1989 about 75% of the country's fish resources remained unexploited, and one-third of local fish requirements were being supplied by imports. In June 1993 the Ministry of Agriculture and Fisheries sold a government fishing project at Mina Salman to the private sector, the local Banz Group. There are plans to modernize the fishing fleet and processing facilities at Mina Salman, which could eventually supply 25% of the local market for fish products.

PETROLEUM AND GAS

Bahrain was the first state on the Arabian side of the Gulf to produce petroleum, in 1932, and the archipelago's recent prosperity has been based on the exploitation of its hydrocarbon reserves. By 1935 there were 16 wells in operation, and a small petroleum refinery had been established at Sitra. Bahrain's average prodcution of crude petroleum from the onshore Awali field, increased from 19,300 barrels per day

(b/d) in 1940 to 57,000 b/d in 1965, and to 76,639 b/d in 1970. Output subsequently decreased steadily, from an annual total of just less than 25m. barrels in 1973 to 16.06m. barrels in 1982, and to 15.26m. barrels (equivalent to 41,770 b/d) in 1984. Production averaged 44,000 b/d in 1991, 41,433 b/d in 1992 and 40,753 b/d in 1993. Output from the Awali field is refined at the Sitra refinery. At 1 January 1992 Bahrain's proven published reserves of petroleum were estimated at 200m. barrels which, at current rates of production, would be exhausted in 10–13 years. Between 1981 and 1984 the Government spent $20m. on exploration and drilling, but no significant discoveries resulted. In 1991 Bahrain signed a 35-year production sharing agreement with Harkon Energy Corpn of the USA which was to cover most of the country's offshore area. Wells drilled in 1991 and 1992 proved to be dry, but new drilling was to take place in 1994. In 1979 the state-owned Bahrain National Oil Company (BANOCO), which is responsible for exploration, drilling and oil production, took over the remaining 40%-stake in the Awali field from Texaco and Standard Oil of the USA.

Bahrain also has a share in the output of the offshore Abu Safa field which lies between Bahrain and Saudi Arabia and is operated by ARAMCO. Production has recently averaged 140,000 b/d, with Bahrain receiving a 70,000 b/d share. At the beginning of 1993 Saudi Arabia raised Bahrain's share to a fixed 100,000 b/d for two years. The additional 30,000 b/d was worth an extra $160m. in revenue to Bahrain at March 1993 prices.

Bahrain is the only GCC state to export only petroleum products and no crude oil. The Sitra refinery has a capacity of 250,000 b/d, but most of its supply of crude is piped from Saudi Arabia; domestic production can meet only 17% of the refinery's capacity. The refinery was originally owned by Caltex of the USA, but in 1981 the Government bought a 60% share in it. A light isomate plant was added in 1983.

Production was below capacity in the early 1980s, owing to the decline in demand for petroleum and to the rapid increase in the refining capacity of neighbouring countries. Since 1985 there has been a recovery in production, which rose to 238,000 b/d in 1987 and almost reached capacity in 1988. Production has averaged around 245,000 b/d in recent years. The Bahrain Petroleum Company (BAPCO) reported that production rose to a record 257,576 b/d in 1992 but fell to 246,128 b/d in 1993 as a result of reduced imports from Saudi Arabia. A 10-year strategic plan was announced by BAPCO in 1988, and a contract was awarded to the US company, Bechtel, to undertake the first stage of modernization at Sitra. However, the Gulf crisis of 1990–91 prolonged indecision over modernization plans, and it was not until 1992 that they were approved. In November 1993, however, BAPCO announced that plans to modernize the refinery were being revised as demand for certain products had changed. Exports of petroleum products earned $2,939m. in 1990, $2,725m. in 1991 and $2,605m. in 1992.

Bahrain has expanded production of natural gas. Proven reserves are estimated at 263,000m. cu m, sufficient to maintain output at present levels until 2050. Gas production totalled 22.6m. cu m a day in 1990, 22.4m. cu m a day in 1991 and 25.9m. cu m a day in 1992. In 1992 31.5% of gas production was used for reinjection into oil wells, 22.8% for electricity generation, 22.3% to power the Aluminium Bahrain (ALBA) smelter, 11.7% as feedstock for the Gulf Petrochemical Industries Company and 10.1% by the Sitra refinery. In mid-1986 the completion of a programme of expansion at the Bahrain National Gas Company (BANAGAS) plant producing liquefied petroleum gas (LPG) increased its capacity to 4.8m. cu m per day. The plant's production of gas liquids rose by 13.2% in 1992 to reach a total of 4.69m. barrels and BANAGAS exported 117,336 tons of propane, 109,254 tons of butane and 195,690 tons of naptha, earning a total of BD24.4m.

INDUSTRY

After independence, the Bahrain Government recognized that the flow of revenue from the petroleum sector would not last far beyond the end of the 20th century, and Bahrain began a programme of industrial diversification. As a result of the collapse of petroleum prices in 1986, these industries have become increasingly important. To expand industry, Bahrain needed to surmount structural disadvantages such as diminishing oil reserves and a shortage of raw materials, apart from gas. The Government has sought to expand existing industries, moving into both primary and secondary activities, establishing new ventures, such as a tyre industry, increasing inter-industry products and expanding production in the consumer goods sector. The main problem was, and remains, the financing of such projects. This has been greatly aggravated by the effects of the 1990–91 Gulf crisis. In 1989 $2,600m. was allocated to industrial projects for the period 1989–94. After the war between Iraq and the multinational force, however, only $700m. was pledged over the next two years. Important projects remain suspended, and other GCC member states seem unlikely to supply the capital necessary for their resumption. Government efforts are now concentrated on encouraging private foreign investment in the industrial sector to achieve greater diversification and to promote more export-oriented industries. Investment is being sought in downstream industries related to aluminium and pharmaceuticals, as well as in new activities. The Government's Incentive Programme, introduced in 1993, offers a wide range of concessions and incentives to attract foreign investment, and official procedures have been greatly simplified.

The aluminium industry remains central to the Government's strategy to expand the country's export-oriented industries. In 1994 some 23 projects were being promoted by the state and private sector in the downstream aluminium sector. The development of Bahrain's aluminium industry began in 1969 when the Government formed a consortium with British, Swedish, French and US companies to construct and operate an aluminium smelter with a capacity of 120,000 metric tons per year. Production at the new smelter of Aluminium Bahrain (ALBA) began in 1972 using alumina imported from Australia. The Bahrain Government, having perchased Kaiser Aluminium's share in 1989, now owns 77% of ALBA together with the Public Investment Fund of Saudi Arabia (20%) and Breton Investments of Germany (3%). By 1981 the smelter's annual capacity had been expanded to 170,000 tons. A $1,500m.-expansion programme to double the annual capacity of the smelter to 460,000 tons was completed in November 1992, making it one of the largest in the world. In April 1994 it was reported that ALBA was to issue $50m. of bonds to finance loans that it had taken out for the recent expansion programme. In January 1994 ALBA signed a $75m.-loan facility with a syndicate of 13 banks to cover the remaining financing requirements for its fourth potline and its new power station. In February ALBA invited international companies to bid for a contract to build a reverse osmosis desalination plant at the smelter. ALBA currently has two desalination plants in service, with a combined capacity of 3,000 cu m a day. The new plant will eventually have a capacity of 10,000 cu m a day, and will also supply the industrial area developing to its south.

Production at the plant in 1993, the first year since its expansion, was 450,000 tons and there are plans to raise production to 460,000 tons in 1995. In January 1994 an ALBA spokesperson stated that it would not reduce production despite low prices since 1991, but in March ALBA announced that it was going to reduce its annual production by 20,000 tons, together with European, Australian and US producers, in an effort to increase prices. In May ALBA's chief executive stated that the company would not consider further reductions until smelters in Asia, Africa and Latin America had agreed to reduce their production. ALBA operates as a cost centre, delivering at cost to its shareholders, who purchase its production on an agreed quota basis. Output is marketed by the Bahrain-Saudi Aluminium Marketing Company (BALCO). In 1992, when production totalled 289,056 tons, sales of 257,244 tons were recorded. Of total sales, 59% were to the Middle East, 27% to Australia and the Pacific Rim, and the remainder to other parts of Asia and to Europe. BALCO's sales income for 1992 was BD128.3m.

Five major secondary enterprises, related to aluminium, now exist in Bahrain. The first downstream venture was the International Bahrain Aluminium Atomizer Company, established in 1973 with 51% government ownership in association with Echart Werke of Germany. It produces 4,500 tons of atomized aluminium powder a year which is marketed in Japan, Germany, the United Kingdom and the USA. In addition, it plans to produce 2,000 tons of aluminium pellets a year, mainly for export to the USA. The new project was scheduled for completion in 1994 at an estimated cost of BD1.6m. The state-owned Bahrain Aluminium Extrusion Company (BALEXCO), inaugurated in 1977, produces aluminium rods for domestic and foreign markets. In January 1991 BALEXCO formally became a joint-stock company, following the Government's reduction of its shareholding to 80%. However, the process of privatization was hindered by the Gulf crisis in 1990/91. BALEXCO lost BD 1.5m.–2m.-worth of orders from Kuwait, and its privatization share issue was not fully subscribed. Prior to the 1990–91 Gulf crisis some 20% of the state's shareholding in the company had been privatized, and in June 1993 it was announced that the total privatization of BALEXCO was envisaged. The Government was to reduce its share from 63% to 40% and would offer shares worth BD2.6m ($6.9m) to the public. A second extrusion press was under construction in mid-1993 which was to double capacity by 1995. The company currently produces 6,000 tons of extruded products from the existing 2,000 ton-press. A 7,000 ton powder coating plant was also being constructed at a cost of $3.2m. There are also plans for a scrap metal recycling plant, capable of processing up to 7,000 tons of scrap metal a year, and third press. In order to finance its expansion plans BALEXCO was to increase its paid up capital to BD10m. ($31.8m.). In mid-1991 the Gulf Aluminium Industries Company (GAICO) was established as a joint venture between BALEXCO and Finleader of Italy in order to take advantage of the increase of production at ALBA. Middle East Aluminium Cable Ltd (Midal Cables) is a private company, established in 1978 with a target output of 15,000 tons of aluminium cables per year. A rod mill was added to the plant in 1985, increasing capacity by 75%, and in 1986 the Saudi Cable Company increased its share in Midal to 50%, with the remaining 50% being held by the A-Zayani Investments Group. In January 1986 the Gulf Aluminium Rolling Company (GARMCO), established under the auspices of the Gulf Organization for Industrial Consulting (GOIC), began production at its $100m.-plant at Sitra. The principal shareholders are the Bahrain Government (25.5%) and Saudi Basic Industries Corpn (20.75%). The mill's initial capacity was 40,000 tons a year of sheet and coil aluminium, but annual production in 1993 totalled more than 60,000 tons, most of which was exported to other Gulf states. A new, $69m.-expansion programme was to increase GARMCO's output of rolled products to more than 100,000 tons a year by 1996. In 1989 50,000 tons of rolled aluminium were produced. Forecast production for 1990 was 59,000 tons. In 1991 Bahrain's new investment policy attracted an aluminium wheel manufacturing company, Aluwheel, to the island. The company is a $32m.-joint venture between Al-Zayani Investments and BBS Kraftfahrzeugtechnik of Germany. Its new factory has an initial target capacity of 500,000 vehicle wheels per year, which is expected to increase to 1.5m. wheels within three years.

The Gulf Petrochemical Industries Corpn (GPIC) built a petrochemicals plant at Sitra in 1985 with a capacity of 1,200 tons a day each of ammonia and methanol. The complex is a joint venture between the Bahrain National Oil Company, the Saudi Basic Industries Corpn and Kuwait's Petrochemical Industries Corpn. Exports of ammonia and methanol totalled 803,000 tons in 1992. In February 1994 GPIC signd a $32m.-credit facility, syndicated by the Arab Investment Company, to be used for its expansion plans. In 1992 the company had announced that it would build a 1,700 tons-per-day urea plant using GPIC's ammonia production as feedstock. In February 1994 it was announced that a consultant was to be appointed for the plant, but that detailed design tenders were not expected until 1995. The new plant was expected to cost $140m.

In June 1993 the National Chemical Industries Corpn (NACIC) signed a $13.1m.-contract with United Engineers International of the USA to build a sulphur derivatives plant near the refinery at Sitra. The plant was to produce 18,000 tons of sodium sulphite and sodium metabisulphite each year.

Work is scheduled to be completed by 1995. NACIC is owned by the Bahraini United Gulf Industries Corpn (55%), together with the Qatar Industrial Manufacturing Company (15%), the Saudi Arabian Industry Development Company (10%), and the United Group for the Development of Riyadh (5%).

The Arab Shipbuilding and Repair Yard (ASRY) Company's dry dock, financed by the members of the Organization of Arab Petroleum Exporting Countries (OAPEC), was opened in 1977. It has a capacity of 450,000 dwt. The decline in oil markets and in world shipping led to severe problems for the company, and in 1983 revenues totalled only $13.3m., compared with $31m. in 1982. Nevertheless, in 1984 ASRY received renewed financial support from the OAPEC countries, and revenues rose slightly, to $16.6m. In 1985 ASRY's occupancy rate was 83%, and its operating costs were $27m. In 1987 ASRY's occupancy rate rose, as a result of an increase in demand (caused by attacks on shipping in the Gulf), and revenues amounted to $22m., compared with $11.3m. in 1986. ASRY's losses in 1985 were estimated at $10m., and in 1986 they were about $8m. The company's accounts showed its first full-year profits in 1987. ASRY's profits declined to approximately $1.5m. in 1990, compared with a record $9m. in 1989. Plans to build a second dry dock, with a capacity of 180,000 dwt, were suspended in August 1990. ASRY renewed its plans in March 1991 and intended to install a second-hand floating dock of up to 100,000 dwt capacity in the near future, with the construction of the dry dock to begin after the floating dock is in place. The company announced a profit for 1992, although the figure was less than had been forecast. The Bahrain Ship Repairing and Maintenance Company, which specializes in smaller-scale ship repairs, made a profit of $11.9m. in 1990, 3.2% lower than in 1989.

In 1981 the Bahrain Government attempted further to diversify the economy by forming the Arab Iron and Steel Company (AISCO), with shareholders from Bahrain, Kuwait, Jordan and the United Arab Emirates (UAE). The company opened the Gulf's first iron-pelletizing plant in December 1984, with a capacity of 4m. tons per year. Total production in 1985, AISCO's first full year of operation, reached 680,000 tons. However, AISCO recorded a financial loss of $31.6m. in 1986, representing a deficit $20m. greater than that incurred in 1985. In March 1988 the sale of AISCO to a newly-formed subsidiary of the Kuwait Petroleum Corpn (KPC), the Gulf Industrial Investment Company, was agreed, and production at the plant restarted. After an agreement was signed with Iran in 1992 the company announced plans to double output to 4m. tons a year.

In 1985 the Gulf Acid Industries Company began production of sulphuric acid and distilled water. Light industry, including the production of supplementary gas supplies, asphalt, prefabricated buildings, plastics, soft drinks, air-conditioning equipment and paper products, also continued to develop during 1986. In 1987 the Government imposed a 20% tariff on competing imported goods for a trial period of 12 months, as part of a programme to support the expansion of light industry. In 1987 Wires International became the first Bahraini company to export an industrial product, aluminium fly mesh, to the Far East. In 1988 the Government announced plans to increase import substitution to a level of 30%, with guaranteed state protection of markets. In 1989 Bahrain Berger Paints, in a joint venture with United Breweries of India, announced a new $3,000m.-project for a pharmaceuticals plant, the first of its kind in Bahrain. Following the introduction of the Government's Incentive Programme in 1993 two joint ventures were agreed. Kimberly-Clark of the USA and Olayam of Saudi Arabia were to build a $33m. tissue paper mill for completion by 1995. The new plant was to produce 15,000 tons of tissue products a year. Shaw Industries of the USA and the local Abdulla Ahmed Nass Industrial Services were to establish a factory producing prefabricated pipeline systems.

Industrial expansion and population growth have necessitated an increase in the provision of electricity and water. Bahrain's first power-station began production in 1931, and by the early 1980s there were major power-stations at al-Mahouz, al-Muharraq, Sitra and Rifa'a, with a combined generating capacity of 992 MW. After the war to liberate Kuwait ended in February 1991, plans for an increase in electricity supplies were activated. The refurbishment of Sitra power-station, in order to increase its life-expectancy, was begun, and a 200-km link between the ALBA power-station and the national grid was due to be completed by mid-1994. In the past ALBA has sold some of its generating surplus in times of shortage, but since its power-station was expanded to 800 MW the company has indicated that it wishes to sell 250 MW on a regular basis. The Government has tended to concentrate on the combined production of power and water, and the first multi-stage flash desalination project at Sitra was completed in 1976, with two units producing 5m. gallons per day. Water consumption rose by more than 50% between 1979 and 1983, and in order to meet rising demand the Government planned the further expansion of desalination units at Sitra. One such unit, with a capacity of 5m. gallons per day, came into operation in 1985. In 1984 contracts were exchanged for the construction of a reverse osmosis plant, with a capacity of 10m. gallons per day, at ad-Dir. It was intended that this plant should provide water for 22% of Bahrain's population. In November 1989 a $380m.-programme to expand water desalination by 30m. gallons per day and electric capacity by 180 MW was approved. In early 1991 it was announced that two 15m.-gallons-per-day sea water desalination plants at Manama and Muharraq, were to be built. These were intended to increase desalination capacity to 75,000m. gallons per day by 1994. By 1986 Bahrain's total daily output of desalinated water was 35m. gallons, sufficient to meet only 68% of the country's daily water consumption, and in 1987 average consumption rose to 54.3m. gallons. In February 1991 it was decided that emergency measures should be taken to protect Bahrain against the Gulf's largest-ever oil spillage. Booms were installed at Bahrain's main desalination plant at Sitra to protect its 25m.-gallons-per-day sea water intake. Power demand had been projected to rise by 5% annually. In mid-1993, however, peak demand increased by 13.5% over the 1992 equivalent, and in July demand approached the installed capacity of 925 MW. In May 1994 it was reported that the new power-station to be financed by British Gas was to be scaled down from the original 500 MW to 300 MW. The project was also to include a 15m.-gallons-per-day desalination plant. ALBA was also in the process of constructing a new desalination plant to increase its capacity to 9,000 cu m. a day.

BANKING, FINANCE AND TRADE

In the 1970s there was a considerable expansion in Bahrain's banking and financial sector, but it subsequently suffered considerable set-backs. Bahrain has always attracted foreign investors because of its freedom from taxation and its good communication links. In 1973 the Bahrain Monetary Agency (BMA) replaced the former Bahrain Currency Board, and in 1975 it assumed the full powers of a central bank. In 1976, however, the Government introduced a commercial law that required all companies registered in Bahrain to have a majority of Bahraini-owned shares. This law did not apply to banks or to similar organizations which could be registered as Exempt Companies. By creating offshore banking units (OBUs), the Government thus succeeded in attracting high-level foreign trade to the islands without detracting from local growth. The combined assets of Bahrain's OBUs increased from $23,441m. in 1978 to $62,741m. in 1983, before falling to $56,805m. in 1985. By the beginning of 1984 Bahrain's banking sector was beginning to feel the effects of the serious decline in spending by Arab petroleum-exporters since 1981, the rise in domestic banking elsewhere in the Gulf region, and increased protectionism in Saudi Arabia. By July 1985 a total of 74 OBUs, 60 banks with representative offices, 20 commercial banks, more than a dozen specially-licensed investment banks, six money-brokers, 43 money-changers and 19 insurance companies were operating in Bahrain. The problems of the banking sector continued into 1986, and, as the world's financial markets became increasingly located in London, New York and Tokyo, the future of Bahrain's financial market became increasingly uncertain. By mid-1986 the total assets of Bahrain's OBUs had fallen to $51,186m. In January 1988 there were 65 OBUs, 20 full commercial banks, 18 investment banks, 59 banks with representative offices and one specialized bank operating in

Bahrain. In November 1988 two UK-based groups, National Westminister Bank and the Scandinavian Banking Group, terminated their operations in Bahrain. At the end of 1988 the total assets of Bahrain's OBUs stood at a new peak of $68,100m. The offshore banks announced their best-ever results in 1988, attributable to renewed stability in the region, following the cease-fire in the Iran–Iraq War. Total profits in the banking sector rose in 1989. The Gulf crisis of 1990–91 dealt the banking sector another heavy blow. Some $1,000m. was lost by the banks, according to the Government. The BMA acted quickly to maintain dinar liquidity, however, and by October 1990 the outflow of capital had been stemmed. By the end of 1992, total OBU assets were $69,800m. The number of OBUs in June 1994 was 47.

Five banks dominate the domestic banking sector with 80% of local bank assets: the Al-Ahli Commercial Bank, Grindlays Bahrain, Bank of Bahrain and Kuwait, the Bahrain Saudi Bank and the National Bank of Bahrain. Their operations are regulated by the BMA. Bahrain's Islamic banks, the Bahrain Islamic Bank, Faisal Islamic Bank of Bahrain and the Al-Baraka Islamic Investment Bank of Bahrain, have been particularly successful in the field of short-term finance.

The Bahrain Government's budget relies heavily on revenues from the petroleum industry. In 1983 a 17.8% fall in these revenues caused a trade account deficit for the first time in five years. In 1984 a deficit was also recorded on the current account of Bahrain's balance of payments, for the first time in six years. In 1985 the trade deficit decreased by 18%, to BD 122.3m., as the value of exports fell to BD 1,056.6m., and the BMA announced an increase in the current account surplus of more than 300%, to BD 229.8m. In 1986–87 receipts from hydrocarbons were expected to provide about 61% of total budgetary revenue, but the collapse of international petroleum prices in 1986 led to a reduction of revenue, and consequently the Government announced a reduction of 15% in spending for that year. The budget deficit of BD 19.5m. was funded largely by the Government's drawing on its cash balances and by the issuing of bonds by the Treasury. In 1987 the economy became more stable, and the 1988 budget (issued for one year only, in an attempt further to stabilize the economy) envisaged expenditure of BD 490m. and revenue of BD 430m. In 1989/90 revenue totalled BD 438m. and expenditure totalled BD 496m., resulting in a deficit of BD 58m. The deficit was to be financed by a further Treasury bond issue, a 50% rise in cigarette tariffs and, possibly, increases in health, passport and immigration charges. A reduction of BD 20m. in development budget expenditure was also announced, even though plans to stimulate the economy included the expansion of trade and tourism. In 1990 government revenue totalled BD 498m. and expenditure was estimated at BD 536m. Deficits of BD 39m. and BD 22m. were recorded in 1990 and 1991 respectively. In 1992 revenues remained unchanged from the previous year with increased non-oil revenues compensating for lower oil receipts. The deficit increased, however, to BD 71.8m. as a result of an increase in both current and capital expenditure. In July 1993 the Minister of Finance predicted a reduction in the deficit for 1993 to BD 63m. following Saudi Arabia's decision to increase Bahrain's share from the Abu Safa field to 100,000 b/d. Both Saudi Arabia and Kuwait provide grant aid to Bahrain. This was suspended during the 1990–91 Gulf crisis, but each country is again contributing $50m. a year. Oil revenues are projected to contribute just less than two-thirds of total revenue in 1993 and 1994. Tourism contributed more than BD 50m. to foreign earnings in 1993.

Bahrain has traditionally acted as an entrepôt centre, but this role has been less significant since Saudi Arabia and the other Gulf states developed their own ports. Petroleum products accounted for about three-quarters of the value of total exports in 1992, but non-oil exports, in particular aluminium, have increased as industrialization has progressed. Bahrain's principal import is crude oil from Saudi Arabia for the Sitra refinery. The major suppliers of non-oil imports are the USA, the United Kingdom and Japan. Non-oil imports rose rapidly in 1992 resulting in a sharp increase in the trade deficit, from BD 226.4m. in 1991 to BD 273.5m. Machinery and transport equipment accounted for some 40% of all non-oil imports in 1992. A balance of payments deficit of BD 155.2m. was

recorded in 1992, compared with a surplus of BD 87.9m. in 1991. The value of oil exports declined by 6% in 1993, to BD 917.1m., but non-oil exports increased by 54%, to BD 469.9m. non-oil exports represented about one-third of total exports, which increased by 8% to BD 1,387m. Following a reduction in oil imports, the value of total imports decreased by 8% in 1993, to BD 1,438m., reducing the trade deficit to BD 51m.

Bahrain's stock exchange opened in June 1989 and it now includes some 30 Bahraini companies with a market capitalization of $5,000m. Trading of both local and foreign bonds and investment funds was to be introduced in 1994, and there are plans to allow foreign companies to be listed. GCC nationals are eligible to trade in shares on the exchange and it is planned to allow foreigners resident in Bahrain for a minimum of three years to do likewise.

Bahrain's domestic banks experienced problems between 1986 and 1988, as a result of an increase in bad debts and bankruptcies. In 1986 Bahrain's largest bank, the Bank of Bahrain and Kuwait (whose total assets amounted to BD 652.8m. in 1986), was unprofitable, and in 1987 it recorded a net loss of BD 23.4m., following a nine-fold increase in the provision for loan losses. In 1988 new banking initiatives in syndications and trade-financing led to a revival in the finance sector. Gulf International Bank (GIB) extended credits in Turkey and Libya, and doubled its authorized capital to $1,100m. Syndications were also led by GIB and the Arab Banking Corporation (ABC) in Morocco, Qatar and Jordan, and both banks announced record profits in 1988. The Islamic banks also extended their activities, led by the Faisal Islamic Bank of Bahrain, which had assets of $869.4m. in 1988. However, the Al-Bahrain Arab African Bank announced heavy losses, and this led to its restructuring and to the investment of capital by the Kuwait Investment Agency. The Manama-based Arab Insurance Group, which reported record profits in 1985, suffered a decline in profits of 33% in 1987, compared with 1986. In 1988, however, the Group's fortunes revived, with profits reaching a record level of $29.5m. In 1988 the total assets of Bahraini commercial banks declined by 4.2%.

TRANSPORT AND COMMUNICATIONS

Bahrain's role as a major financial centre has been associated with an expansion of the country's air and telephone services. The Bahrain International Airport was opened in 1971 on Muharraq island and it has also become the headquarters of Gulf Air, which is owned jointly by the Governments of Bahrain, Oman, Qatar and the UAE. The first phase of a programme to expand the international airport, involving the construction of a new passenger terminal capable of handling 10m. passengers a year, was completed in October 1991. A second phase, to expand and improve other facilities, began in 1992. In 1993 some 3m. passengers used the international airport. Gulf Air recorded a loss of BD 4m. in 1987. However, net profits recovered to BD 2.58m. in 1988, as flights to Baghdad and Teheran were resumed. In April 1989 Gulf Air announced plans to double the size of its fleet to 40 aircraft by 1994. The crisis in the Gulf region led to heavy losses in 1990 of BD 36m. Losses increased to BD 43m. in 1991, resulting in a scaling-down of expansion plans and the introduction of austerity measures in order to reduce costs. Gulf Air recorded profits of $40m. in 1993, a decline of 13.4% compared with the previous year's figure. The airline has announced plans to invest $10m. in various commercial enterprises in 1994 in order to diversify the scope of its investments. The company also plans to extend the number of destinations it serves from 51 to 80. A $134m.-loan for the purchase of two Boeing 767-300 ER aircraft was to be signed in May 1994 as part of a policy to expand the airline's fleet. The Bahrain Telecommunications Company (BATELCO) was formed in July 1981, with capital of BD 60m. (60% government-owned). BATELCO achieved a profit of BD 17.75m. in 1987, owing to a fall in tariffs. At the beginning of 1986 Bahrain became the 45th member of the London-based International Maritime Satellite Organization (INMARSAT), and during 1986 BATELCO also introduced a cellular telephone system. BATELCO's profits in 1990 amounted to $57m., mainly due to the presence in Bahrain of Western servicemen during the Gulf crisis. In 1992 BATELCO undertook a $3.5m.-expansion of its mobile telephone system, increasing capacity to 11,000 lines in order to satisfy rising demand. In the same year the digitalization of Bahrain's 120,000-line domestic system was completed.

A container terminal at the port of Mina Sulman was opened in 1979, with a 400-m quay, allowing two 180-m container ships to be handled simultaneously. At present the port has 14 conventional berths, two container terminals and a roll-on/roll-off berth. Plans for a new container port, industrial and free trade zone at Hidd have been under consideration for some time. A feasibility study was completed by Profabril of Portugal in August 1993, and the Government announced that it would accept tenders for the detailed design and construction supervision early in 1994. The most significant recent development in Bahrain's transport network has been the construction of the causeway linking Bahrain with Saudi Arabia, which was opened in February 1987. In its first year of operation, more than 4.5m. people and 1.3m. vehicles used the causeway. The prospect of increased traffic has also led to improvements in Bahrain's road network. The contract for the completion of the final stage of the second Manama to Muharraq causeway, Bahrain's largest construction project, was signed in April 1993. In 1991 a total of 104,453 passenger motor cars were estimated to be in use on the roads of Bahrain.

EDUCATION AND HEALTH

The high level of petroleum revenues during the 1970s enabled the Government to embark on an ambitious programme to expand education and health services. By the end of the 1950s there were 46 government schools in Bahrain, and between 1971 and 1991 the number of enrolled students increased from 50,049 to 100,658. In 1991 there was a total of 3,052 classes in government institutions. In 1968 the Gulf Technical College was founded, and in 1988 work on the first phase of the Arabian Gulf University (AGU) was completed. In 1992, however, there were only 368 students attending the AGU. In 1991 expenditure on education and training was BD 77.9m., and for 1992 expenditure on education was forecast at BD 72m. Despite such investments in education and technical training, Bahrain continues to rely heavily on expatriate labour. The Government has initiated a scheme to train Bahrainis to take over jobs from expatriates. At the census of November 1991 the non-Bahraini population in Bahrain was 184,732, equivalent to 36.4% of the total population.

Health services and housing have received considerable support. In 1982 there were 397 physicians working in Bahrain. By 1983 there were six hospitals, 27 health centres and 16 child welfare centres in Bahrain, which together treated 2,005,825 cases among out-patients during the year. In 1991 expenditure on health was BD 46.1m., and for 1992 it was forecast to rise to BD 49.3m. The Government provides a number of low-cost houses, particularly in the new towns. Saudi Arabian aid helped to fund a three-year project for the construction of low- and middle-cost housing, and in 1984 the first residents moved into the newly completed Hamad Town.

Statistical Survey

Source (unless otherwise stated): Central Statistics Organization, POB 5835, Manama; tel. 725725; telex 8853; fax 728989.

AREA AND POPULATION

Area (1991): 695.26 sq km (268.44 sq miles).

Population: 350,798 (males 204,793, females 146,005), comprising 238,420 Bahrainis (males 119,924, females 118,496) and 112,378 non-Bahraini nationals (males 84,869, females 27,509), at census of 5 April 1981; 508,037 (males 294,346, females 213,691), comprising 323,305 Bahrainis (males 163,453, females 159,852) and 184,732 non-Bahraini nationals (males 130,893, females 53,839), at census of 16 November 1991.

Density (1991): 730.7 per sq km.

Principal Towns (population in 1991): Manama (capital) 136,999; Muharraq Town 74,245.

Births, Marriages and Deaths (1991): Registered live births 13,229 (birth rate 26.0 per 1,000); Registered marriages 3,528 (marriage rate 6.8 per 1,000); Registered deaths 1,744 (death rate 3.4 per 1,000).

Expectation of Life (UN estimates, years at birth, 1985–90): 70.4 (males 68.6; females 72.9). Source: UN, *World Population Prospects: The 1992 Revision.*

Economically Active Population (1991 census, persons aged 15 years and over): Agriculture, hunting, forestry and fishing 5,108; Mining and quarrying 3,638; Manufacturing 26,618; Electricity, gas and water 2,898; Construction 26,738; Trade, restaurants and hotels 29,961; Transport, storage and communications 13,789; Financing, insurance, real estate and business services 17,256; Community, social and personal services 83,944; Activities not adequately defined 2,120; unemployed 14,378 (males 9,703; females 4,675); *Total labour force* 226,448 (males 186,857; females 39,591), comprising 90,662 Bahrainis (males 73,118, females 17,544) and 135,786 non-Bahraini nationals (males 113,739, females 22,047).

AGRICULTURE, ETC.

Principal Crops ('000 metric tons, 1992): Tomatoes 4.7; Other vegetables and melons 6.7; Dates 18 (FAO estimate).

Livestock ('000 head, 1992): Cattle 12; Sheep 22; Goats 18.

Livestock Products ('000 metric tons, 1992): Poultry meat 4.6; Cows' milk 14.0; Hen eggs 3.4.

Fishing ('000 metric tons, live weight): Total catch 9.2 in 1989; 8.1 in 1990; 7.6 in 1991.

MINING

Production (1993): Crude petroleum 14,874,845 barrels; Natural gas 333,428m. cu ft (1992).

INDUSTRY

Production ('000 barrels unless otherwise indicated, 1992): Liquefied petroleum gas 288; Naphtha 12,263; Motor spirit (Gasoline) 9,078; Kerosene 12,072; Jet fuel 5,832; Fuel oil 23,859; Diesel oil 37; Gas oil 29,903; Petroleum bitumen (asphalt) 523; Electric energy 3,896.3 million kWh; Aluminium (unwrought, '000 metric tons) 213.7 (1991).

FINANCE

Currency and Exchange Rates: 1,000 fils = 1 Bahrain dinar (BD). *Sterling and Dollar Equivalents* (31 May 1994): £1 sterling = 568.4 fils; US $1 = 376.0 fils; 100 Bahrain dinars = £175.92 = $265.96. *Exchange Rate:* Fixed at US $1 = 376.0 fils (BD 1 = $2.6596) since November 1980.

Budget (BD million, 1992): *Revenue:* Taxation 134.4 (Taxes on income and profits 22.7, Social security contributions 37.3, Domestic taxes on goods and services 19.4, Import duties 48.7); Entrepreneurial and property income 300.3 (Bahrain Petroleum Co dividends 82.9, Revenue from gas supplies 35.8, Abu Saafa oilfield receipts 168.4); Other current revenue 30.4; Capital revenue 0.3; Total 465.4, excl. grants from abroad (37.6). *Expenditure:* General public services 177.4; Defence 94.6; Education 72.0; Health 49.3; Social security and welfare 14.1; Housing and community amenities 13.0; Recreational, cultural and religious affairs and services 10.8; Economic affairs and services 109.0 (Fuel and energy 30.7, Road transport 36.1, Other transport and communication 35.1); Total (incl. others) 548.7 (Current 412.5, Capital 124.0), excl. lending minus repayments (−69.4). Source: IMF, *Government Finance Statistics Yearbook.* **1993** (estimates, BD million): Revenue 580; Expenditure 643.

International Reserves (US $ million at 31 December 1993): Gold (valued at cost of acquisition) 6.6; IMF special drawing rights 14.8; Reserve position in IMF 56.2; Foreign exchange 1,231.2; Total 1,308.8. Source: IMF, *International Financial Statistics.*

Money Supply (BD million at 31 December 1993): Currency outside banks 103.81; Demand deposits at commercial banks 261.14; Total money 364.95. Source: IMF, *International Financial Statistics.*

Cost of Living (Consumer Price Index for Bahraini nationals; base: 1990 = 100): 100.8 in 1991; 100.6 in 1992. Source: IMF, *International Financial Statistics.*

Gross Domestic Product by Economic Activitiy (BD million at current prices, 1991): Agriculture, hunting, forestry and fishing 14.7; Mining and quarrying 296.4; Manufacturing 264.1; Electricity, gas and water 24.3; Construction 91.7; Trade, restaurants and hotels 168.6; Transport, storage and communications 192.8; Finance, insurance, real estate and business services 274.2; Government services 322.9; Other community, social and personal services 81.2; Sub-total 1,730.9; *Less* Imputed bank service charge 133.1; GDP in purchasers' values 1,597.8.

Balance of Payments (US $ million, 1992): Merchandise exports f.o.b. 3,417.3; Merchandise imports f.o.b. –3,730.3; *Trade balance* –313.0; Exports of services 1,018.9; Imports of services –1,010.1; Other income received 245.2; Other income paid –763.6; Private unrequited transfers (net) –270.7; Government unrequited transfers (net) 100.0; *Current balance* –993.4; Direct investment (net) –8.5; Other capital (net) 374.7; Net errors and omissions 545.3; *Overall balance* –81.9. Source: IMF, *International Financial Statistics.*

EXTERNAL TRADE

Principal Commodities (US $ million, 1992): *Imports c.i.f.:* Mineral fuels etc. 1,553.0; Machinery and transport equipment 1,077.1; Total (incl. others) 4,144.7. *Exports f.o.b.:* Mineral fuels etc. 2,604.5; Basic manufactures 547.6; Total (incl. others) 3,417.3.

Principal Trading Partners (US $ million, 1992: *Imports c.i.f.:* Australia 160.2; France 145.5; Germany 268.8; India 72.4; Italy 111.7; Japan 274.4; Netherlands 61.8; Saudi Arabia 147.9; United Arab Emirates 78.7; United Kingdom 286.6; USA 346.0; Total (incl. others) 4,144.7. *Exports f.o.b.:* Japan 76.0; Republic of Korea 100.3; Kuwait 41.7; Netherlands 43.8; Saudi Arabia 142.6; USA 69.2; United Arab Emirates 36.2; Total (incl. others) 3,417.3.

TRANSPORT

Road Traffic (registered motor vehicles, 31 December 1991): Private cars 107,657; Buses and coaches 8,509; Goods vehicles 16,014; Motorcycles. 1,372. Source: International Road Federation, *World Road Statistics.*

Shipping (international sea-borne freight traffic, '000 metric tons, 1990): *Goods loaded:* Dry cargo 1,145; Petroleum products 12,140. *Goods unloaded:* Dry cargo 3,380; Petroleum products 132. Source: UN, *Monthly Bulletin of Statistics.*

Civil Aviation (1991): Kilometres flown (million) 11; Passengers carried ('000) 876; Passenger-km (million) 1,676; Freight ton-km (million) 51. Figures include an apportionment (equivalent to one-quarter) of the traffic of Gulf Air, a multinational airline with its headquarters in Bahrain. Source: UN, *Statistical Yearbook.*

TOURISM

Tourist arrivals (1993): 1,761,402.

Tourist receipts (1993): more than BD 50m.

COMMUNICATIONS MEDIA

Radio receivers (1991): 278,000 in use.

Television receivers (1991): 215,000 in use.

Telephones (1993): 124,500 in use.

Book production (1989, estimate): 150 titles.

Daily newspapers (1993): 3 (estimated circulation 82,000 copies).

Non-daily newspapers (1993): 7 (estimated circulation more than 60,000 copies).

Source: mainly UNESCO, *Statistical Yearbook.*

EDUCATION

Government Institutions (1991): *Primary:* 1,749 classes; 57,805 pupils. *Intermediate:* 703 classes; 24,436 pupils. *Secondary* (general): 384 classes, 12,537 pupils; (commercial): 86 classes, 2,416 pupils; (industrial): 130 classes, 3,464 pupils; *Colleges and Institutes:* 190 Institutions, 116,706 students.

Directory

The Constitution

A 108-article Constitution was ratified in June 1973. It states that 'all citizens shall be equal before the law' and guarantees freedom of speech, of the press, of conscience and religious beliefs. Other provisions include the outlawing of the compulsory repatriation of political refugees. The Constitution also states that the country's financial comptroller should be responsible to the legislature and not to the Government, and allows for national trade unions 'for legally justified causes and on peaceful lines'. Compulsory free primary education and free medical care are also laid down in the Constitution. The Constitution, which came into force on 6 December 1973, also provided for a National Assembly, composed of the members of the Cabinet and 30 members elected by popular vote, although this was dissolved in August 1975.

The Government

HEAD OF STATE

Amir: Sheikh ISA BIN SULMAN AL-KHALIFA (succeeded to the throne on 2 November 1961; took the title of Amir on 16 August 1971).

Crown Prince: Sheikh HAMAD BIN ISA AL-KHALIFA.

CABINET
(July 1994)

Prime Minister: Sheikh KHALIFA BIN SULMAN AL-KHALIFA.

Minister of Defence: Maj.-Gen. Sheikh KHALIFA BIN AHMAD AL-KHALIFA.

Minister of Finance and National Economy: IBRAHIM ABD AL-KARIM MUHAMMAD.

Minister of Foreign Affairs: Sheikh MUHAMMAD BIN MUBARAK BIN HAMAD AL-KHALIFA.

Minister of Education: Dr ALI MUHAMMAD FAKHRO.

Minister of Health: JAWAD SALIM AL-ARRAYEDH.

Minister of the Interior: Sheikh MUHAMMAD BIN KHALIFA BIN HAMAD AL-KHALIFA.

Minister of Information: TARIQ ABD AR-RAHMAN AL-MOAYED.

Minister of Justice and Islamic Affairs: Sheikh ABDULLAH BIN KHALIFA AL-KHALIFA.

Minister of Development and Industry: YOUSUF AHMAD ASH-SHI-RAWI.

Minister of Transport: Sheikh ALI BIN KHALIFA AL-KHALIFA.

Minister of Labour and Social Affairs: Sheikh ISA BIN ALI AL-KHALIFA.

Minister of Housing: Sheikh KHALID BIN ABDULLAH BIN KHALID AL-KHALIFA.

Minister of Public Works, Power and Water: MAJID JAWAD AL-JISHI.

Minister of Commerce and Agriculture: HABIB AHMAD QASSIM.

Minister of State for Cabinet Affairs: MUHAMMAD IBRAHIM AL-MUTAWWA.

Minister of State for Legal Affairs: Dr HUSSAIN MUHAMMAD AL-BAHARNA.

Minister of State, in charge of the Amiri Court: YOUSUF RAHMAN AD-DOSAN.

Secretary-General, Supreme Council for Youth and Sport: Sheikh ISA BIN RASHID AL-KHALIFA.

MINISTRIES

Amiri Court: POB 555, Riffa Palace, Manama; tel. 661451; telex 8666.

Office of the Prime Minister: POB 1000, Government House, Government Rd, Manama; tel. 252556; telex 9336; fax 246585.

Ministry of Commerce and Agriculture: POB 5479, Diplomatic Area, Manama; tel. 531531; telex 9171.

Ministry of Defence: POB 245, West Rifa'a; tel. 665599; telex 8429.

Ministry of Development and Industry: POB 1435, Manama; tel. 291511; telex 8344; fax 290302.

Ministry of Education: Isa Town; tel. 680071; telex 9094; fax 680161.

Ministry of Finance and National Economy: POB 333, Government House, Government Rd, Manama; tel. 530800; telex 8933; fax 532853.

Ministry of Foreign Affairs: POB 547, Government House, Government Rd, Manama; tel. 258200; telex 8228.

Ministry of Health: POB 12, Sheikh Sulman Rd, Manama; tel. 251360; telex 8511; fax 242485.

Ministry of Housing: POB 802, Diplomatic Area, Manama; tel. 533000; telex 8599; fax 534115.

Ministry of Information: POB 253, Isa Town; tel. 781888; telex 8399; fax 682777.

Ministry of the Interior: POB 13, Police Fort Compound, Manama; tel. 254021; telex 8333.

Ministry of Justice and Islamic Affairs: POB 450, Diplomatic Area, Manama; tel. 531333.

Ministry of Labour and Social Affairs: POB 32333, Isa Town, Manama; tel. 687800; telex 9062.

Ministry of Public Works, Power and Water: POB 6000, Muharraq Causeway Rd, Manama; tel. 533133; telex 8515; fax 533027.

Ministry of State for Cabinet Affairs: POB 1000, Government House, Government Road, Manama; tel. 262266; telex 7424.

Ministry of State for Legal Affairs: POB 790, Al-Hidaya Bldg, Government Rd, Manama; tel. 259990.

Ministry of Transport: POB 10325, Diplomatic Area, Manama; tel. 534534; telex 8989; fax 537537.

CONSULTATIVE COUNCIL

The Consultative Council is an advisory body of 30 members appointed by the ruling authorities, which is empowered to advise the Government but has no legislative powers. The Council held its inaugural session on 16 January 1993.

Chairman: IBRAHIM HUMAIDAN.

Legislature

NATIONAL ASSEMBLY

In accordance with the 1973 Constitution, elections to a National Assembly took place in December 1973. About 30,000 electors elected 30 members for a four-year term. Since political parties are not allowed, all 114 candidates stood as independents but, in practice, the National Assembly was divided almost equally between conservative, moderate and more radical members. In addition to the 30 elected members, the National Assembly contained the members of the Cabinet. In August 1975 the Prime Minister resigned because, he complained, the National Assembly was preventing the Government from carrying out its functions. The Amir invited the Prime Minister to form a new cabinet, and two days later the National Assembly was dissolved by Amiri decree. It has not been revived.

Diplomatic Representation

EMBASSIES IN BAHRAIN

Algeria: POB 26402, Villa 579, Rd 3622, Adliya, Manama; tel. 713783; telex 7775; Ambassador: MUHAMMAD GHALIB NEDJARI.

Bangladesh: POB 23434, House 159, Rd 2004, Area 320, Hoora; tel. 293371; telex 7029; fax 291272; Ambassador: AKHTER-UL-ALAM.

China, People's Republic: POB 3150, Villa 379, Rd 1912, Area 319, Hoora; tel. 293451; telex 9444; fax 293451; Ambassador: WANG SHIJIE.

Denmark: POB 45, Maersk Line, Manama; tel. 727896; telex 8676; fax 728797; Chargé d'affaires: FLEMMING JENSEN.

Egypt: POB 818, Adliya; tel. 720005; telex 8248; Ambassador: MAHMOUD SAMI AHMED ESMAT.

France: POB 11134, King Faisal Rd, Diplomatic Area, Manama; tel. 291734; telex 8323; fax 293655; Ambassador: ALBERT PAVEC.

Germany: POB 20287, Tariq Bldg, Government Ave, Manama; tel. 530210; telex 7128; fax 536282; Chargé d'affaires: ALFRED GERTH.

India: POB 26106, Bldg 182, Rd 2608, Area 326, Adliya, Manama; tel. 714520; telex 9047; fax 715527; Ambassador: RAJANIKANTA VERMA.

Iran: POB 26365, Entrance 1034, Rd 3221, Area 332, Mahooz, Manama; tel. 722400; telex 8238; fax 722101; Ambassador: JAVAD TORKABADI.

Iraq: POB 26477, Al-Raqeeb Bldg, No 17, Rd 2001, Comp 320, King Faisal Ave, Manama; tel. 290999; telex 8238; fax 291227; Chargé d'affaires: AHMAD TAYES ABDULLAH.

Japan: POB 23720, House 403, Rd 915, Area 309, Manama; tel. 243364; telex 7002; fax 230694; Ambassador: TERUO KIJIMA.

Jordan: POB 5242, Villa 43, Rd 915, Area 309, Hoora; tel. 291109; telex 7650; fax 291980; Chargé d'affaires: HASSAN AL-JAWARNA.

Korea, Republic: POB 11700, Bldg 69, Rd 1901, Block 319, Hoora; tel. 291629; telex 8736; fax 291628; Ambassador: HOI-JUNG KWAK.

Kuwait: POB 786, Rd 1703, Diplomatic Area, Rd 1703, Manama; tel. 534040; telex 8830; fax 536475; Ambassador: FAISAL M. AL-HAJJI.

Morocco: POB 26229, Villa 58, Rd 3404, Area 334, Manama; tel. 713687; telex 8018; fax 716251; Chargé de'affaires: MOHAMED LAMRID.

Oman: POB 26414, Diplomatic Area, Bldg 37, Rd 1901, Manama; tel. 293663; telex 9332; Ambassador: GHALIB BIN ABDULLAH BIN JUBRAN.

Pakistan: POB 563, Kuwait Rd, Adliya, Manama; tel. 712470; fax 742194; Ambassador: AFZAL AKBAR KHAN.

Philippines: POB 26681, Bldg 81, Rd 3902, Block 339, Umm Al-Hassan; tel. 725355; fax 729585; Ambassador: LEONIDES CADAY.

Russia: POB 26612, House 877, Rd 3119, Block 331, Zinj, Manama; tel. 725222; telex 7006; fax 725921; Ambassador: ALEXANDER NOVO-JILOV.

Saudi Arabia: POB 1085, Bldg 1450, Rd 4043, Area 340, Juffair, Manama; tel. 727223; telex 9871; fax 725199; Ambassador: Dr GHAZI ABD AR-RAHMAN AL-GOSAIBI.

South Africa: c/o Gulf Business Centre, Bahrain Tower, 1st Floor, Manama; tel. 214640; fax 214645; Chargé d'affaires: RUDI APPEL.

Tunisia: POB 26911, House 54, Rd 3601, Area 336, Manama; tel. 714149; telex 7136; fax 721678; Ambassador: MOHAMMAD KHU-NAYFAN.

Turkey: POB 10821, Flat 10, Bldg 81, Rd 1702, Area 317, Manama; tel. 533448; telex 7049; fax 536557; Ambassador: GUNALTAY SIBAY.

United Kingdom: POB 114, 21 Government Rd, Manama; tel. 534404; fax 531273; Ambassador: HUGH TUNNELL.

USA: POB 26431, Bldg 979, Rd 3119, Block 331, Zinj, Manama; tel. 273300; telex 9398; fax 272594; Ambassador: DAVID RANSOM.

Yemen: POB 26193, House 1048, Rd 1730, Area 517, Saar; tel. 277012; telex 8370; fax 262358; Ambassador: MUHAMMAD SHUKRI.

Judicial System

Since the termination of British legal jurisdiction in 1971, intensive work has been undertaken on the legislative requirements of Bahrain. The Criminal Law is at present contained in various Codes, Ordinances and Regulations. All nationalities are subject to the jurisdiction of the Bahraini courts which guarantee equality before the law irrespective of nationality or creed.

Directorate of Courts: POB 450, Government House, Government Rd, Manama; tel. 531333.

Religion

At the November 1991 census the population was 508,037, distributed as follows: Muslims 415,427; Christians 43,237; Others 49,373.

ISLAM

Muslims are divided between the Sunni and Shi'ite sects. The ruling family is Sunni, although the majority of the Muslim population (estimated at almost 60%) are Shi'ite.

CHRISTIANITY

The Anglican Communion

Within the Episcopal Church in Jerusalem and the Middle East, Bahrain forms part of the diocese of Cyprus and the Gulf. There are two Anglican churches in Bahrain, St Christopher's Cathedral in Manama and the Community Church in Awali, and the congregations are entirely expatriate. The Bishop in Cyprus and the Gulf is resident in Cyprus, while the Archdeacon in the Gulf is resident in the United Arab Emirates.

Provost: Very Rev. DEREK J. TAYLOR, St Christopher's Cathedral, POB 36, Al-Mutanabi Ave, Manama; tel. 253866; fax 253866.

The Press

DAILIES

Akhbar al-Khalij (Gulf News): POB 5300, Manama; tel. 620111; telex 8565; fax 621566; f. 1976; Arabic; Chair. IBRAHIM AL-MOAYED;

Man. Dir ANWAR M. ABD AR-RAHMAN; Editor-in-Chief AHMAD KAMAL; circ. 25,000.

Al-Ayam (The Days): POB 3232, Manama; tel. 727111; fax 729009; f. 1989; publ. by Al-Ayam Establishment for Press and Publications; Chair. and Editor-in-Chief NABIL YAQUB AL-HAMER; circ. 37,000.

Gulf Daily News: POB 5300, Manama; tel. 620222; telex 8565; fax 622141; f. 1978; English; Editor-in-Chief CLIVE JACQUES; Editor GEORGE WILLIAMS; circ. 20,000.

WEEKLIES

Al-Adhwaa' (Lights): POB 250, Manama; tel. 245251; telex 8564; fax 293166; f. 1965; Arabic; publ. by Arab Printing and Publishing House; Chair. RAID MAHMOUD AL-MARDI; Editor-in-Chief MUHAMMAD QASSIM SHIRAWI; circ. 7,000.

Akhbar BAPCO (BAPCO News): Bahrain Petroleum Co BSC, POB 25149, Awali; tel. 755055; telex 8214; fax 752924; f. 1981; formerly known as *an-Najma al-Usbou'* (The Weekly Star); Arabic; house journal; Editor KHALID F. MEHMAS; circ. 8,000.

Al-Bahrain: POB 26005, Isa Town; Arabic; tel. 683986; telex 8399; fax 686355; publ. by the Ministry of Information; Editor HAMAD AL-MANNAI; circ. 3,000.

BAPCO Weekly News: Awali; tel. 755047; telex 8214; fax 752924; publ. by the Bahrain Petroleum Co BSC; English; Wednesday; Editor SAMUEL KNIGHT; circ. 1,000.

Al-Mawakif (Attitudes): POB 1083, Manama; tel. 231231; fax 271720; f. 1973; Arabic; general interest; Editor-in-Chief MANSOOR M. RADHI; circ. 6,000.

Oil and Gas News: POB 224, Bldg 149, Exhibition Ave, Manama; tel. 293131; telex 8981; fax 293400; English; publ. by Al-Hilal Publishing and Marketing Co; Editor GURDIP SINGH.

Sada al-Usbou' (Weekly Echo): POB 549, Bahrain; tel. 291234; telex 8880; fax 290507; f. 1969; Arabic; Owner and Editor-in-Chief ALI SAYYAR; circ. 35,000 (in various Gulf states).

OTHER PERIODICALS

Arab Agriculture: POB 10131, Manama; tel. 213900; fax 211765; annually; English and Arabic; publ. by Fanar Publishing WLL.

Arab World Agribusiness: POB 10131, Manama; tel. 213900; fax 211765; nine per year; English and Arabic; publ. by Fanar Publishing WLL.

Discover Bahrain: POB 10704, Manama; f. 1988; publ. by G. and B. Media Ltd; Publr and Editor ROBERT GRAHAM.

Gulf Construction: POB 224, Exhibition Ave, Manama; tel. 293131; telex 8981; fax 293400; monthly; English; publ. by Al-Hilal Publishing and Marketing Group; Editor BINA PRABHU GOVEAS; circ. 10,166.

Gulf Economic Monitor: POB 224, Exhibition Ave, Manama; tel. 293131; fax 293400; weekly; English; published by Al-Hilal Publishing and Marketing Group; Editor PETER FAGIN.

Gulf Panorama: POB 1122, Manama; tel. 277677; monthly; Editor IBRAHIM BASHMI; circ. 15,000.

The Gulf Tourism Directory: POB 33770, Manama; tel. 244613; fax 731067; f. 1990; English; Publr RASHID BIN MUHAMMAD AL-KHALIFA.

Al-Hayat at-Tijariya (Commerce Review): POB 248, Manama; tel. 233913; telex 8691; fax 241294; monthly; English and Arabic; publ. by Bahrain Chamber of Commerce and Industry; Editor KHALIL YOUSUF; circ. 3,500.

Al-Hidayah (Guidance): POB 450, Manama; tel. 522384; f. 1978; monthly; Arabic; publ. by Ministry of Justice and Islamic Affairs; Editor-in-Chief ABD AR-RAHMAN BIN MUHAMMAD RASHID AL-KHALIFA; circ. 5,000.

Al-Mohandis (The Engineer): POB 835, Manama; f. 1972; quarterly; Arabic; English; publ. by Bahrain Association of Engineers; Editor KHALID AL-MOHANADI.

Al-Murshid (The Guide): POB 553, Manama; fax 293145; monthly; English and Arabic; includes 'What's on in Bahrain'; publ. by Arab Printing and Publishing House; Editor M. SOLIMAN.

Al-Musafir al-Arabi (Arab Traveller): POB 10131, Manama; tel. 213900; fax 211765; f. 1984; bi-monthly; Arabic; publ. by Fanar Publishing WLL; Editor-in-Chief ABD AL-WAHED AL-WANI.

Profile: POB 10243, Manama; tel. 291110; fax 294655; f. 1992; monthly; English; publ. by Bahrain Market Promotions; Editor HENNU GORDE.

Al-Quwwa (The Force): POB 245, Manama; tel. 665599; telex 8429; f. 1977; monthly; Arabic; publ. by Bahrain Defence Force; Editor-in-Chief Maj. AHMAD MAHMOUD AS-SUWAIDI.

Shipping and Transport News International: POB 224, Exhibition Ave, Manama; tel. 293131; telex 8981; fax 293400; monthly;

English; publ. by Al-Hilal Publishing and Marketing Group; Editor FERMIN D'SOUZA; circ. 5,500.

Travel and Tourism News Middle East: POB 224, Exhibition Ave, Manama; tel. 293131; telex 8981; fax 293400; monthly; English; travel trades; publ. by Al-Hilal Publishing and Marketing Group; Editor FREDERICK ROCQUE; circ. 5,130.

NEWS AGENCIES

Associated Press (AP) (USA): POB 11022, Al-Moosa Bldg, Manama; tel. 530101; telex 9470; fax 530249; Chief of Bureau ALI MAHMOUD.

Deutsche Presse-Agentur (dpa) (Germany): POB 26995, Rd 3435, Bldg 1464, Apt 2, Al-Mahouz, Manama; tel. 727523; telex 9542; fax 725440; Correspondent HUSSEIN DAKROUB.

Gulf News Agency: POB 301, Manama; tel. 687272; telex 9030; fax 687008; Editor-in-Chief KHALID ZAYANI.

Inter Press Service (IPS) (Italy): c/o Gulf News Agency, POB 301, Manama; tel. 532235; fax 687008.

Press Trust of India: POB 2546, Manama; tel. 713431; telex 8482; Chief of Bureau SHAKIL AHMAD.

Reuters (United Kingdom): UGB Bldg, 6th Floor, Diplomatic Area, Manama; tel. 536111; fax 536192; Chief of Bureau RANDALL PALMER.

Publishers

Arab Communicators: POB 551, Manama; tel. 211006; telex 8263; fax 210931; publrs of annual Bahrain Business Directory; Dirs AHMAD A. FAKHRI, HAMAD A. ABUL.

Gulf Advertising: POB 5518, Manama; tel. 250014; telex 8494; fax 230025.

Al-Hilal Publishing and Marketing Group: POB 224, Exhibition Ave, Manama; tel. 293131; telex 8981; fax 293400; specialist magazines of commercial interest; Chair. A. M. ABD AR-RAHMAN; Man. Dir R. MIDDLETON.

Al-Masirah Journalism, Printing and Publishing House: POB 5981, Manama; tel. 258882; telex 7421; fax 276178.

Tele-Gulf Directory Publications, WLL: POB 2738, 3rd Floor, Bahrain Tower, Manama; tel. 213301; telex 8917; fax 210503; Chair and Man. Dir ABD AN-NABI ASH-SHO'ALA.

Government Publishing House

Directorate of Publications: POB 26005, Manama; tel. 689077; Dir MUHAMMAD AL-KHOZAI.

Radio and Television

In 1991 there were 278,000 radio receivers and 215,000 television receivers in use. English language programmes, broadcast from Saudi Arabia by the US Air Force in Dhahran and by the Arabian-American Oil Co (Aramco), can be received in Bahrain, as can the television service provided by the latter.

Bahrain Broadcasting Station: POB 194, Manama; tel. 781888; telex 9259; f. 1955; state-owned and -operated enterprise; two 10 kW transmitters; programmes are in Arabic and English, and include news, plays and talks; Head of Station ABD AR-RAHMAN ABDULLAH.

Radio Bahrain: POB 702, Manama; tel. 781888; telex 8311; fax 780911; f. 1977; commercial radio station in English language; Head of Station AHMAD M. SULAIMAN.

Bahrain Radio and Television Corpn: POB 1075, Manama; tel. 781888; telex 8311; fax 681544; commenced colour broadcasting in 1973; broadcasts on five television channels, of which the main Arabic and the main English channel accept advertising, and three radio frequencies; covers Bahrain, eastern Saudi Arabia, Qatar and the UAE. An Amiri decree in early 1993 established the independence of the Corpn, which was to be controlled by a committee.

Finance

(cap. = capital; p.u. = paid up; dep. = deposits; m. = millions; res = reserves; brs = branches; amounts in Bahraini dinars unless otherwise stated)

BANKING

Central Bank

Bahrain Monetary Agency (BMA): POB 27, Manama; tel. 535535; telex 9191; fax 533342; f. 1973, in operation from January 1975; controls issue of currency, regulates exchange control and credit policy, organization and control of banking system and bank credit; cap. p.u. 100m., res 110.1m., dep. 64.9m., total assets 403.9m. (Dec. 1993); Governor ABDULLAH HASSAN SAIF; Chair. Sheikh KHALIFA BIN SALMAN AL-KHALIFA.

Locally Incorporated Commercial Banks

Al-Ahli Commercial Bank BSC: POB 5941, Manama; tel. 244333; telex 9130; fax 241301; f. 1977; full commercial bank; total assets 151.1m. (Dec. 1993); Chair. MUHAMMAD YOUSUF JALAL; Gen. Man. CEO MICHAEL J. FULLER.

Al-Baraka Islamic Investment Bank BSC (EC): POB 1882, Manama; tel. 274488; telex 8220; fax 274499; f. 1984; res 3.23m., dep. 163.8m., total assets 221.2m. (1991); Chair. MAHMOUD HAS-SOUBAH; Gen. Man. ABDULLA ABOLFATIH.

Arlabank International EC: POB 5070, Manama Centre, Manama; tel. 232124; telex 9345; fax 246239; f. 1977; wholly-owned subsidiaries: Arab-Latin American Bank (Banco Arabe Latinoamericano) in Peru, Alpha Lambda Investment and Securities Corpn in the British Virgin Islands; cap. p.u. US $90.3m., total assets US $620.7m. (Dec. 1991); Chair. ABDULLAH A. SAUDI; Dep. Gen. Man. FAROOK QADIR.

Bahrain Islamic Bank BSC: POB 5240, Manama; tel. 231402; telex 9388; fax 275734; f. 1979; cap. p.u. 11.5m., res 1.7m., dep. 111.5m., total assets 127.4m. (Dec. 1993); Chair Sheikh ABD AR-RAHMAN AL-KHALIFA; Gen. Man. ABD AL-LATIF JANAHI.

Bahrain Middle East Bank EC: POB 797, Manama; tel. 528101; telex 7866; fax 530987; f. 1982; owned by Burgan Bank (28%) and GCC nationals (72%); cap. and res US $90.3m., dep. US $400.3m., total assets US $499.9m. (Dec. 1993); Chair. ABDUL RAHMAN SALEM AL-ATEEQI; Gen. Man. and CEO ALBERT I. KITTANEH.

Bahraini Saudi Bank BSC (BSB): POB 1159, Manama; tel. 211010; telex 7232; fax 210989; f. 1983; commenced operations in early 1985; licensed as a full commercial bank; cap. 20.0m., res 3.1m., dep. 87m., total assets 110.7m. (Dec. 1993); Chair. Sheikh IBRAHIM BIN HAMAD AL-KHALIFA; Gen. Man. MANSOOR AS-SAYED.

Bank of Bahrain and Kuwait BSC (BBK): POB 597, Manama; tel. 253388; telex 8919; fax 275785; f. 1971; cap. 57m., dep. 576.8m., total assets 644.4m. (Dec. 1992); Chair. RASHID ABD AR-RAHMAN AZ-ZAYANI; Gen. Man. MURAD ALI MURAD; 22 local brs, 2 brs overseas.

Faisal Islamic Bank of Bahrain: Chamber of Commerce Bldg, POB 3005, King Faisal Rd, Manama; tel. 275040; telex 9411; fax 277305; f. 1982 as Massraf Faysal Al-Islami of Bahrain EC; renamed as above in 1987; cap. US $50m., res US $22.2m., dep. US $1,236m., total assets US $1,681.6m. (Dec. 1992); Chair. ABDULLAH AHMED ZAINAL ALIREZA; Gen. Man. IMTIAZ PERVEZ; 9 brs.

Gulf International Bank BSC (GIB): POB 1017, Al-Dowali Bldg, 3 Palace Ave, Manama; tel. 534000; telex 8802; fax 522633; f. 1975; owned by the Gulf Investment Corporation; cap. p.u. US $450m., total assets US $7,172m. (Dec. 1993); Chair. IBRAHIM ABDUL KARIM; Gen. Man. GHAZI M. ABD AL-JAWAD; 3 brs, 2 rep. offices.

National Bank of Bahrain BSC (NBB): POB 106, Government Rd, Manama; tel. 258800; telex 8242; fax 263876; f. 1957; commercial bank with Government of Bahrain as major shareholder; dep. 629.7m., total assets 734.5m. (Dec. 1993); Chair. AHMAD ALI KANOO; Gen. Man. and CEO HUSSAN ALI JUMA; 22 brs.

Foreign Commercial Banks

ABN AMRO Bank NV (Netherlands): POB 350, Manama; tel. 255420; telex 8356; fax 262241; Man. CALLENS FEL.

Arab Bank Ltd (Jordan): POB 395, Manama Centre, Manama; tel. 256398; telex 8658; fax 231640; Senior Man. J. W. TAKCHI; 4 brs.

Bank Melli Iran: POB 785, Government Rd, Manama; tel. 259910; telex 8266; fax 270768; Gen. Man. MUHAMMAD HASSAN NAJIMI; 1 br.

Bank Saderat Iran: POB 825, Manama; tel. 210003; telex 8363; fax 210398; Man. Y. M. SHENOY; 2 brs.

Banque du Caire (Egypt): POB 815, Manama; tel. 254454; telex 8298; fax 213704; Man. ES-SAYED MOUSTAFA EL-DOKMAWEY.

Banque Paribas FCB (France): POB 5241, Manama; tel. 253119; telex 8458; fax 242077; Gen. Man. M. APTHORPE.

British Bank of the Middle East (BBME): POB 57, Manama; tel. 242555; telex 8230; fax 256822; Area Man. ROGER J. JORDAN; 2 brs.

Chase Manhattan Bank NA (USA): POB 368, Manama; tel. 535388; telex 8286; fax 535135; Vice-Pres. and Man. MAHMOUD DIFRAWY; 1 br.

Citibank NA (USA): POB 548, Manama; tel. 257124; telex 8225; fax 210000; Vice-Pres. ROSS DI BACCO; 1 br.

Grindlays Bahrain Bank BSC: POB 793, Manama; tel. 250805; telex 8335; fax 272708; Chair. MUHAMMAD ABDULLAH AZ-ZAMIL; Gen. Man. NORMAN ANDERSON; 3 brs.

Habib Bank Ltd (Pakistan): POB 566, Manama Centre, Manama; tel. 271402; telex 9448; fax 213421; f. 1941; Sr Vice-Pres. and Gen. Man. ANWER CHAUDHRY.

National Bank of Kuwait: BMB Centre, Diplomatic Area, POB 5290, Manama; tel. 532225; fax 530603.

Rafidain Bank (Iraq): POB 607, Manama; tel. 255456; telex 8332; fax 255656; f. 1979; Man. ABBAS HADI AL-BAYATI; 1 br.

Saudi National Commercial Bank: POB 10363, Manama; tel. 531182; telex 9298; fax 530657; Gen. Man. SALEH HUSSAIN.

Standard Chartered Bank (United Kingdom): POB 29, Manama; tel. 255946; telex 8229; fax 230503; f. in Bahrain 1920; Gen. Man. GRAHAM HONEYBILL; 5 brs.

United Bank Ltd (Pakistan): POB 546, Government Rd, Manama; tel. 251580; telex 8247; fax 234143; Gen. Man. ZAFARUL HAQ MEMON; 3 brs.

Development Bank

Bahrain Development Bank (BDB): POB 20501, Manama; tel. 537007; telex 7022; fax 534005; f. 1992; investing in manufacturing, agribusiness, tourism, transport, fishing, distribution and services; auth. cap. 25m.; cap. p.u. 10m.; Chair. Sheikh EBRAHIM BIN KHALIFA AL-KHALIFA.

Specialized Financial Institutions

Arab Banking Corpn BSC: POB 5698, ABC Tower, Diplomatic Area, Manama; tel. 532235; telex 9432; fax 533163; f. 1980 by Amiri decree; jointly owned by Kuwait Ministry of Finance, Central Bank of Libya, Abu Dhabi Investment Authority and private investors; offers full range of commercial, merchant and investment banking services; cap. and res US $1,360m., total assets $18,433m. (Dec. 1993); Pres. and Chief Exec. ABDULLAH A. SAUDI; 7 brs.

Bahrain Housing Bank: POB 5370, Diplomatic Area, Manama; tel. 534443; telex 8599; f. 1979; fax 533437; provides finance for the construction industry; Chair. Sheikh KHALID BIN ABDULLAH BIN KHALID AL-KHALIFA; Gen. Man. ISA SULTAN ADH-DHAWADI.

Bahrain Islamic Bank BSC: POB 5240, Government Rd, Manama; tel. 231402; telex 9388; fax 275734; f. 1979; cap. and res 13.2m., total assets 127m. (1993); Pres. and Gen. Man. ABD AL-LATIF A. RAHIM JANAHI; 2 brs.

'Offshore' Banking Units

Bahrain has been encouraging the establishment of offshore banking units (OBUs) since October 1975. An OBU is not allowed to provide local banking services but is allowed to accept deposits from governments and large financial organizations in the area and make medium-term loans for local and regional capital projects. Prior to the Iraqi invasion of Kuwait in August 1990, there were 56 OBUs in operation in Bahrain. By mid-1993, however, the number of OBUs had declined to 47.

Representative Offices

In January 1988 a total of 59 banks maintained representative offices in Bahrain.

Investment Banks

Investment banks operating in Bahrain include the following: Arab Financial Services Co EC, Arab Multinational Investment Co (AMICO), Bahrain International Investment Centre (BIIC), Bahrain Investment Bank BSC, Bahrain Islamic Investment Co BSC, Bahraini Kuwaiti Investment Group (BKIG), Al-Baraka Islamic Investment Bank BSC, Citicorp Investment Bank (CIB), Elders IXL, Gulf Investments Co, EF Hutton International Inc., InvestBank EC, Islamic Investment Company of the Gulf (Bahrain) EC, Merrill Lynch Int. Inc., National Bank of Pakistan, Nikko Investment Banking (Middle East) EC, Nomura Investment Banking (Middle East) EC, Okasan Int. (Middle East) EC, Robert Fleming Holdings Ltd, Sumitomo Finance (Middle East) EC, Trans-Arabian Investment Bank EC (TAIB), United Gulf Investment Co, Yamaichi International (Middle East) EC, Az-Zayani Investments Ltd.

INSURANCE

Al-Ahlia Insurance Co BSC: POB 5282, Manama; tel. 258860; telex 8761; f. 1976; fax 245597; auth. cap. 5m.; Chair. QASSIM AHMAD FAKHRO.

Arab Insurance Group BSC (ARIG): POB 26992, Arig House, Diplomatic Area, Manama; tel. 531110; telex 9395; fax 530289; f. 1980; owned by Governments of Kuwait, Libya and the UAE; cap. p.u. US $150m. (June 1988); all non-life reinsurance; Chair. ABD AL-WAHAB A. AT-TAMMAR; Gen. Man. and CEO NOOR UD-DIN A. NOOR UD-DIN.

Arab International Insurance Co EC (AIIC): POB 10135, Manama; tel. 530087; telex 9226; fax 530122; f. 1981; cap. p.u. US $4m.; non-life reinsurance; Chair. and Man. Dir Sheikh KHALID J. AS-SABAH.

Bahrain Insurance Co BSC (BIC): POB 843, Suite 310, Sh. Mubarak Bldg, Government Ave, Manama; tel. 255641; telex 8463; fax

242389; f. 1969; all classes including life insurance; cap. 2.4m.; 80% Bahraini-owned, 19% Iraqi-owned; Gen. Man. PATRICK N. V. IRWIN; 3 brs.

Bahrain Kuwait Insurance Co BSC: POB 10166, Diplomatic Area, Manama; tel. 532323; telex 8672; fax 530799; f. 1975; cap. p.u. US $5.3m.; Gen. Man. A. HAMEED AN-NASSER.

National Insurance Co BSC (NIC): POB 1818, Unitag House, Government Rd, Manama; tel. 244181; telex 8908; fax 230228; f. 1982; cap. p.u. US $2.9m.; all classes of general insurance; Chair. J. A. WAFA; Gen. Man. SAMIR AL-WAZZAN.

STOCK EXCHANGE

Bahrain Stock Exchange: POB 3203, Manama; tel. 261260; telex 7937; fax 276181; f. 1989; nine mems; Dir-Gen. Dr FAWZI BEHZAD.

Trade and Industry

CHAMBER OF COMMERCE

Bahrain Chamber of Commerce and Industry: POB 248, Manama; tel. 233913; telex 8691; fax 241294; f. 1939; 4,350 mems (1993); Pres. ALI BIN YOUSEF FAKHROO; Sec.-Gen. JASSIM MUHAMMAD ASH-SHATTI.

STATE ENTERPRISES

Aluminium Bahrain BSC (ALBA): POB 570, Manama; tel. 830000; telex 8253; fax 830083; f. 1971; operates a smelter owned by the Governments of Bahrain (77%) and Saudi Arabia (20%), the remainder being held by Breton Investments; a major expansion, completed in 1993, increased capacity to 460,000 metric tons per year; Chief Exec. GUDVIN K. TOFTE.

Bahrain Aluminium Extrusion Co BSC (BALEXCO): POB 1053, Manama; tel. 730221; telex 8634; fax 731678; f. 1977; supplies aluminium profiles in mill finish; capacity 20,000 metric tons per year; was undergoing a process of progressive privatization in 1993; Chair. SALEH ALI AL-MADANI; Gen. Man. MAHMOUD AS-SOUFI.

Bahrain Atomizers International: POB 5328, Manama; tel. 830008; fax 830025; f. 1973; produces 7,000 metric tons of atomized aluminium powder per year; owned by the Government of Bahrain (51%) and Breton Investments (49%); Chair. Y. SHIRAWI.

Bahrain National Gas Co BSC (BANAGAS): POB 29099, Rifa'a; tel. 756222; telex 9317; fax 756991; f. 1979; responsible for extraction, processing and sale of hydrocarbon liquids from associated gas derived from onshore Bahrain fields; ownership is 75% Government of Bahrain, 12.5% Caltex and 12.5% Arab Petroleum Investments Corporation (APICORP); produced 243,801 metric tons of LPG and 196,589 tons of natural gasoline in 1992; Chair. Sheikh HAMAD BIN IBRAHIM AL-KHALIFA; Gen. Man. ALI A. GINDI.

Bahrain National Oil Co (BANOCO): POB 25504, Awali; tel. 754666; telex 8670; fax 753203; f. 1976; responsible for exploration, production, processing, transportation and storage of petroleum and petroleum products; distribution and sales of petroleum products (including natural gas), international marketing of crude petroleum and petroleum products, supply and sales of aviation fuels; produced an average of 40,753 barrels a day in 1993; CEO Sheikh ALI MUHAMMAD SALEH.

Bahrain Petroleum Co BSC (BAPCO): Awali; tel. 754444; telex 8214; fax 752924; f. 1980; a refining company owned by the Government of Bahrain (60%) and Caltex Bahrain (40%); refined 90.3m. barrels of crude petroleum in 1993; Chair. YOUSUF AHMAD ASH-SHIRAWI (Minister of Development and Industry); Chief Exec. DON F. HEPBURN.

Bahrain-Saudi Aluminium Marketing Co (BALCO): POB 20079, Manama; tel. 532626; telex 9110; fax 532727; f. 1976; to market ALBA products; owned by the Government of Bahrain (74.33%) and Saudi Basic Industries Corpn (25.67%); Gen. Man. ABD AL-MONIM ASH-SHIRAWI.

Bahrain Telecommunications Co BSC (BATELCO): POB 14, Manama; tel. 885529; telex 8790; fax 259006; f. 1981; operates all telecommunications services; cap. BD 60m.; 39% owned by Government of Bahrain, 20% by Cable and Wireless PLC (United Kingdom); Chair. Sheikh ALI BIN KHALIFA BIN SALMAN AL-KHALIFA; Gen. Man. ANDREW HEARN.

General Poultry Co: POB 5472, Bahrain; tel. 600716; telex 8678; fax 631001; 100% state-owned produces poultry feed and eggs; Chair. SIDDIQ AL-ALAWI.

Gulf Aluminium Rolling Mill Co (GARMCO): POB 20725, Manama; tel. 731000; telex 9786; fax 730542; f. 1980 as a joint venture between the Governments of Bahrain, Saudi Arabia, Kuwait, Iraq Oman and Qatar; produced 60,000 tons of rolled aluminium in 1991; Chair. and Man. Dir Sheikh IBRAHIM BIN KHALIFA AL-KHALIFA; Gen. Man. JOHN PATERSON.

Gulf Petrochemical Industries Co BSC (GPIC): POB 26730, Sitra; tel. 731777; telex 9897; fax 731047; f. 1979 as a joint venture between the Governments of Bahrain, Kuwait and Saudi Arabia, each with one-third equity participation; cap. p.u. BD 60m.; a petrochemical complex at Sitra, inaugurated in 1981; produces 1,200 tons of both methanol and ammonia per day (1990); Chair. Sheikh ISA BIN ALI AL-KHALIFA; Gen. Man. MUSTAFA AS-SAYED.

MAJOR INDUSTRIAL COMPANIES

Al-Khajah Establishment and Factories: POB 5042, Sitra Industrial Area; tel. 730611; telex 8619; fax 731340; f. 1972; sales BD 12m. (1992); cap. and res BD 2.3m.; contracting, trading and manufacture of switchgear and light fittings; numerous subsidiaries within the Gulf; Chair. AHMAD AL-KHAJAH; Man. Dir FAREED AL-KHAJAM; approx. 850 employees.

Az-Zamil Group of Cos: POB 285, Manama; tel. 253445; telex 8381; fax 231803; f. 1930; manufacture of prefabricated metal buildings, aluminium doors, windows and frames, plastic industrial and household products, marble fascias, stairways, floors, etc., nails and screws; services include a travel agency, ship repair, maintenance, camp accommodation and catering, high technology services to petroleum sector, processing of refrigerated and frozen foods, civil, mechanical and electrical engineering; a Commercial Division handles trading, representation and sponsorship activities and all dealings in real estate, land development and property leasing; Chair. MUHAMMAD AZ-ZAMIL; approx. 7,500 employees.

Bahrain Bedding Factory (Al-Ansari): POB 5648, Manama; tel. 727407; telex 9493; fax 729796; f. 1973; sales BD 750,000 (1983); cap. and res BD 1.5m.; manufacturers of quality beds with export openings in Saudi Arabia and all other GCC states; Chair. ABD AL-JALEEL AL-ANSARI; 51 employees.

Bahrain Danish Dairy Co WLL: POB 601, Manama; tel. 258500; telex 8590; f. 1963; sales BD 3.5m. (1983); cap. and res BD 1.5m.: processing, packaging and sale of milk, ice-cream and fruit juice; Gen. Man. PAUL MIKKELSEN; 165 employees.

Bahrain Light Industries Co BSC: POB 26700, Manama; tel. 830222; telex 8538; fax 830399; cap. and res BD 5m.; manufacture of solid wood and veneered furniture, internal partitions and doors; Chair. HAMID R. AZ-ZAYANI; Gen. Man. HAMID FALEH; 158 employees.

Gulf Acid Industries Co: POB 2770, Manama; tel. 730686; telex 7554; f. 1983; cap. BD 2m.; manufacture and sale of distilled water engine coolant, engine flush and sulphuric acid using double catalysis and double absorption; Man. Dir MUHAMMAD AHMAD NASS.

Gulf Aluminium Industries Co (GAICO): joint venture between BALEXCO and Finleader of Italy to expand production of aluminium; Chair. AHMAD HUBAIL.

Maskati Brothers and Co: POB 24, Manama; tel. 729911; telex 8621; fax 725454; f. 1957; sales BD 9.0m. (1992); cap. and res BD 9m.; paper converters, polyethylene manufacture, injection moulders; Gen. Man. KHALID H. MASKATI; 400 employees.

Midal Cables Ltd: POB 5939, Manama; tel. 830111; telex 9127; fax 830168; f. 1978; cap. US $4.08m.; sales US $70m. (1992); manufacture of aluminium and aluminium alloy electrical rods and conductors for overhead transmission and distribution lines; Man. Dir HAMID R. AZ-ZAYANI; Gen. Man. SALMAN ASH-SHEIKH; 125 employees.

TRADE UNIONS

There are no trade unions in Bahrain.

Transport

ROADS

In 1991 Bahrain had 2,671 km of roads, of which 2,011 km were surfaced roads. Most inhabited areas of Bahrain are linked by bitumen-surfaced roads. In the same year the number of private cars in Bahrain stood at 107,657. Public transport consists of taxis and privately-owned bus services. A national bus company provides public services throughout the country. A modern network of dual highways is being developed, and a 25-km causeway link with Saudi Arabia was opened in November 1986. A three-lane dual carriageway links the causeway to Manama. A joint Bahraini-Saudi bus company was formed in 1986, with capital of US $266,600, to operate along the causeway. Construction work began in 1993 on a second causeway, to link Manama with al-Muharraq at an estimated cost of $46m..

Directorate of Roads: POB 5, Exhibition Rd, Hoora, Manama; tel. 524870; telex 7129; fax 532565; responsible for road safety, maintenance and construction; Dir ISAM A. KHALAF.

SHIPPING

Numerous shipping services link Bahrain and the Gulf with Europe, the USA, Pakistan, India, the Far East and Australia. In 1988 a total of 14,316 vessels called at Bahraini ports.

The deep-water harbour of Mina Sulman was opened in April 1962; it has 14 conventional berths, two container terminals and a roll-on/roll-off berth. In the vicinity are two slipways able to take vessels of up to 1,016 tons and 73 m in length, with services available for ship repairs afloat. The second container terminal, which has a 400-m quay (permitting two 180-m container ships to be handled simultaneously), was opened in April 1979. Further development of Mina Sulman, to allow handling of larger quantities of container cargo, was completed in 1985. During 1992 Mina Sulman handled about 90,000 20-ft equivalent units. In 1989 plans were announced to build a new floating dry dock, with a capacity of 70,000 dwt.

Directorate of Customs and Ports: POB 15, Manama; tel. 725555; telex 8642; fax 725534; responsible for customs activities and acts as port authority; Director of Customs and Ports Sheikh DAIJ BIN KHALIFA AL-KHALIFA; Port Director EID ABDULLAH YOUSUF.

Arab Shipbuilding and Repair Yard Co (ASRY): POB 50110, Hidd; tel. 671111; telex 8455; fax 670236; f. 1974 by OAPEC members; 500,000-ton dry dock opened 1977; two floating dry docks in operation since 1992; repaired 90 ships in 1992; Chair. Sheikh DAIJ BIN KHALIFA AL-KHALIFA; Gen. Man. HANS G. FRISK.

CIVIL AVIATION

Bahrain International Airport has a first-class runway, capable of taking the largest aircraft in use. In 1991 there were 29,534 flights to and from the airport, carrying a total of 2.4m. passengers. In 1993 some 3m. passengers used the International Airport. Extension work to the airport's main terminal building was completed in mid-1992.

Department of Civil Aviation Affairs: POB 586, Bahrain International Airport, Muharraq; tel. 321094; telex 9186; fax 321139; Asst Under-Sec. IBRAHIM ABDULLAH AL-HAMER.

Gulf Air Co GSC (Gulf Air): POB 138, Manama; tel. 531166; telex 8255; fax 330466; f. 1950; jointly owned by the Governments of Bahrain, Oman, Qatar and the UAE; services to the Middle East, South-East Asia, Africa, Europe and North America; Chair. YOUSSEF AHMAD ASH-SHIRANI (Bahrain); Pres. and Chief Exec. SALIM BIN ALI BUN NASSER (Qatar).

Tourism

There are several archaeological sites of importance. Bahrain is the site of the ancient trading civilization of Dilmun. There is a wide selection of hotels and restaurants, and a new national museum opened in early 1989. In 1993 more than 1.76m. tourists visited Bahrain, and income from tourism totalled more than BD 50m..

Bahrain Tourism Co (BTC): POB 5831, Manama; tel. 530530; telex 8929; fax 530867.

Directorate of Tourism and Archaeology: POB 26613, Manama; tel. 211199; telex 8311; fax 210969; Dir Dr KADHIM RAJAB.

Defence

Chief of Bahraini Defence Force: Sheikh HAMAD BIN ISA AL-KHALIFA.

Defence Budget (1994): BD 93.3m.

Military Service: voluntary.

Total Armed Forces (June 1994): 8,100 (army 6,800; navy 600; air force 700).

Paramilitary Forces: Coast Guard 250; Police 9,000.

Education

In 1991 an estimated 86% of children aged six to 11 years (85% of boys; 86% of girls) attended primary schools, and 83% of those aged 12 to 17 (83% of boys; 84% of girls) were enrolled at secondary schools. Education is not compulsory in Bahrain, but state education is available free of charge. In 1986 85,867 children were receiving education in 139 government-operated schools, and by 1991 the total enrolment at such schools had increased to 100,658. Private and religious education is also available.

Education begins at six years of age. From the ages of six to 11, children attend primary school. Secondary education, beginning at the age of 12, lasts for six years and is divided into two stages, each lasting three years. In early 1988, according to the Ministry of Education, more than 65% of teachers were native Bahrainis. There are four higher educational establishments: the University College of Arts, Sciences and Education, the Gulf Polytechnic, the College of Health Sciences, and the Hotel and Catering Training Centre. In 1986 the University College of Arts, Sciences and Education and the Gulf Polytechnic were merged to form the University of Bahrain, which 4,050 students attended in 1993.

In the first three years of the 1982–88 Development Plan, the government allowed for a total capital outlay of BD 43.1m. on education, reflecting intense development within the area. The 1992 budget allocated BD 72m. to education, representing 13.1% of total spending. In 1987 four new schools and a technical institute, built at a cost of BD 8m., were opened. The 1989 building programme included plans for the construction of four schools and a teacher-training complex, at a cost of BD 4m.

The first phase of the Arabian Gulf University (AGU), funded by seven Arab governments, was completed in 1988. The University campus is due to be completed at the end of 2006, and will accommodate 5,000 students. In 1993 there were 368 students attending the AGU.

In 1981 the average rate of adult illiteracy among the indigenous Bahraini population was 31.3% (males 21.2%; females 41.4%). In 1990, according to UNESCO estimates, the illiteracy rate among all adults resident in Bahrain was 22.6% (males 17.9%; females 30.7%).

Bibliography

Adamiyat, Fereydoun. *Bahrain Islands: A Legal and Diplomatic Study of the British-Iranian Controversy.* New York, Praeger, 1955.

Faroughby, Abbas. *The Bahrain Islands.* New York, 1951.

Hakima, A. M. *The Rise and Development of Bahrain and Kuwait.* Beirut, 1965.

Hay, Sir Rupert. *The Persian Gulf States.* Washington, DC, Middle East Institute, 1959.

Khuri, F. I. *Tribe and State in Bahrain.* Chicago University Press, 1981.

Lawson, Fred H. *The Modernization of Autocracy.* Boulder, Colo, Westview Press, 1989.

Marlowe, John. *The Persian Gulf in the 20th Century.* London, Cresset Press, 1962.

Miles, S. B. *The Countries and Tribes of the Persian Gulf.* 3rd edition, London, Cass, 1970.

Nakhleh, Emile A. *Bahrain: Political Development in a Modernizing Society.* Lexington, Mass, Lexington Books, 1976.

Nugent, Jeffrey, and Thomas, Theodore. *Bahrain and the Gulf: Prospects for the Future.* London, Croom Helm, 1985.

Rumaihi, Mohammed al-. *Bahrain: Social and Political Change since the First World War.* Durham Univ., Bowker, in association with the Centre for Middle Eastern and Islamic Studies, 1977.

Ward, Philip. *Bahrain—A Travel Guide.* Cambridge, The Oleander Press, 1993.

Wilson, Sir A. T. *The Persian Gulf.* Oxford University Press, 1928.

CYPRUS

Physical and Social Geography

W. B. FISHER

The island of Cyprus, with an area of 9,251 sq km (3,572 sq miles), is situated in the north-eastern corner of the Mediterranean Sea, closest to Turkey (which is easily visible from its northern coast), but also less than 160 km (100 miles) from the Syrian coast. Its greatest length (including the long, narrow peninsula of Cape Andreas) is 225 km (140 miles). The census of 1 October 1982, which was held in Greek Cypriot areas only, recorded a total population (including an estimate for the Turkish-occupied region) of 642,731. According to an official estimate, the population was 725,000 at 31 December 1992.

PHYSICAL FEATURES

Cyprus owes its peculiar shape to the occurrence of two ridges that were once part of two much greater arcs running from the mainland of Asia westwards towards Crete. The greater part of these arcs has disappeared, but remnants are found in Cyprus and on the eastern mainland, where they form the Amanus range of Turkey. In Cyprus the arcs are visible as two mountain systems—the Kyrenia range of the north, and the much larger and imposing Troödos massif in the centre. Between the two mountain systems lies a flat lowland, open to the sea in the east and west and spoken of as the Mesaoria. Here also lies the chief town, Nicosia (Lefkoşa in Turkish).

The mountain ranges are actually very different in structure and appearance. The Kyrenia range is a single narrow fold of limestone, with occasional deposits of marble, and its maximum height is 900 m (3,000 ft). As it is mainly porous rock, rainfall soon seeps below ground; and so its appearance is rather arid, but very picturesque, with white crags and isolated pinnacles. The soil cover is thin. The Troödos, on the other hand, has been affected by folding in two separate directions, so that the whole area has been fragmented, and large quantities of molten igneous rock have forced their way to the surface from the interior of the earth, giving rise to a great dome that reaches 1,800 m (6,000 ft) above sea-level. As it is impervious to water, there are some surface streams, rounder outlines, a thicker soil, especially on the lower slopes, and a covering of pine forest.

CLIMATE

The climate in Cyprus is strongly 'Mediterranean' in character, with the usual hot dry summers and warm, wet winters. As an island with high mountains, Cyprus receives a fair amount of moisture, and up to 1,000 mm (40 in) of rain falls in the mountains, with the minimum of 300 mm–380 mm (12 in to 15 in) in the Mesaoria. Frost does not occur on the coast, but may be sharp in the higher districts, and snow can fall fairly heavily in regions over 900 m (3,000 ft) in altitude. In summer, despite the nearness of the sea, temperatures are surprisingly high, and the Mesaoria, in particular, can experience over 38°C (100°F). A feature of minor importance is the tendency for small depressions to form over the island in winter, giving a slightly greater degree of changeability in weather than is experienced elsewhere in the Middle East.

Cyprus is noteworthy in that between 50% and 60% of the total area is under cultivation—a figure higher than that for most Middle Eastern countries. This is partly to be explained by the relatively abundant rainfall; the expanses of impervious rock that retain water near the surface; and the presence of rich soils derived from volcanic rocks which occur around the Troödos massif. The potential of the tourist trade and the export markets in wine and early vegetables add to the incentives to development. In the southern (Greek) part of the island economic recovery after partition has been considerable: far less so in the north.

History

Revised for this edition by ALAN J. DAY.

EARLY HISTORY

Cyprus first became important in recorded history when the island fell under Egyptian control in the second millennium BC. After a long period during which the Phoenicians and the people of Mycenae founded colonies there, Cyprus, in the eighth century BC, became an Assyrian protectorate, at a time when the Greeks of the mainland were extending their settlements in the island. From the sixth century BC it was a province of the Persian empire and took part in the unsuccessful Ionian revolt against Persian rule in 502 BC. Despite the Greek triumph over Xerxes in 480 BC, subsequent efforts by the Greek city states of the mainland to free Cyprus from Persian control met with little success, largely because of dissension among the Greek cities of Cyprus itself. For more than two centuries after 295 BC the Ptolemies of Egypt ruled in Cyprus until it became part of the Roman Empire.

Cyprus prospered under the enlightened Roman rule of Augustus, for trade flourished while the Romans kept the seas free of piracy. When Jerusalem fell to the Emperor Titus in AD 70, many Jews found refuge in Cyprus where they became numerous enough to undertake a serious revolt in AD 115. Christianity, apparently introduced into the island in the reign of the Emperor Claudius (AD 41–54), grew steadily in the next three centuries, during which Cyprus, isolated from a continent frequently ravaged by barbarian inroads, continued to enjoy a relative degree of prosperity. From the time of Constantine the Great, Cyprus was a province governed by officials appointed from Antioch and formed part of the diocese of the East. In the reign of Theodosius I (379–395) the Greek Orthodox Church was firmly established there and in the fifth century proved strong enough to resist the attempts of the Patriarchs of Antioch to control the religious life of the island.

The Arab attack of 649 began a new period in the history of Cyprus which now became, for more than 300 years, the object of dispute between the Byzantines and the Muslims. Whenever the Byzantine fleet was weak, Cyprus remained a doubtful possession of the Empire. From the decisive Byzantine reconquest of 964–65, Cyprus enjoyed, for more than two centuries, a period of relative calm.

WESTERN RULE

In 1192 King Richard I of England, having taken the island from the Greek usurper Comnenus, sold it to the Knights

Templar, who, in turn, sold it to Guy de Lusignan, formerly King of Jerusalem. There now began almost 400 years of Western rule, which saw the introduction of Western feudalism and of the Latin Church into a land which hitherto had been Greek in its institutions and Orthodox in its religious beliefs.

In the period from 1192 to 1267 (when the direct line of the Lusignan house became extinct) the new regime was gradually elaborated. The Lusignan monarchy was limited in character, for the royal power was effective only in the military sphere, all other important business of state being decided in a high court which consisted of the nobles, the fief-holders, and the great officers of state. This court applied to the island a highly developed code of feudal law derived from the Assizes of Jerusalem, the Cypriots being allowed to retain their own laws and customs in so far as these did not conflict with the feudal law. The period was also marked by the determined efforts of the Latin clergy, supported by the Papacy, to establish complete control over the Orthodox Church, a policy carried out with much harshness, which the Crown and the feudal nobility often sought to mitigate in order to keep the loyalty of the subject population. The dominance of the Latin Church was finally assured by the Bulla Cypria of Pope Alexander IV (1260).

During the second half of the 13th century the kingdom of Cyprus (now ruled by the house of Antioch-Lusignan) played an important role in the last struggle to maintain the Latin states in Syria against the Mamluk offensive. The influence of the monarchy was further strengthened in this period, and when, in 1324, Hugues IV became king, the great age of feudal Cyprus had begun. Cyprus was now of great importance in the commerce which the Italian republics maintained with the East, and Famagusta became a flourishing port. The Papacy, however, always anxious to weaken the power of Mamluk Egypt, placed severe limitations on the trade of the Italian republics with that state and charged Cyprus and Rhodes with their enforcement. Thus began a conflict between the kings of Cyprus and the great republics of Venice and Genoa which did not endanger Cyprus so long as the Papacy could mobilize sentiment in the West to support the crusading state of the Lusignans. When, as the 14th century advanced, the Papacy lost its power to command such support in the West, Cyprus was left to face unaided the ambitions of Genoa and Venice, which she was powerless to withstand.

Before this decline began, Cyprus enjoyed a brief period of great brilliance under her crusading king, Peter I (1359–69). In 1361 he occupied the port of Adalia on the south coast of Asia Minor, then held by the Turkish emirate of Tekke; and in the years 1362–65 toured Europe in an effort to win adequate support for a new crusade. His most memorable exploit came in 1365, when he captured Alexandria in Egypt, sacking it so completely that even as late as the 16th century it had not recovered its former splendour. With his assassination in 1369 the great period of the Lusignan house was ended.

The reign of King Janus I (1398–1432) was a long struggle to drive out the Genoese, who had seized Famagusta during the war with Cyprus in 1372–74, and to repel the attacks of Mamluk Egypt, which had become weary of the repeated sea-raids undertaken from the ports of Cyprus. After plundering Larnaca and Limassol in 1425 the Mamluks crushed the army of Cyprus in a battle at Khoirakoitia in 1426, King Janus himself being captured, and his capital, Nicosia, sacked. The king was released in 1427, when he had promised the payment of a large ransom and of an annual tribute. The last years of Lusignan power were marked by dissension in the ruling house and by the increasing domination of Venice which, with the consent of Caterina Cornaro, the Venetian widow of the last Lusignan king, annexed Cyprus in 1489.

TURKISH RULE

Venice held Cyprus until 1570 when the Ottoman Turks began a campaign of conquest which led to the fall of Nicosia in September 1570 and of Famagusta in August 1571. The Turks now restored to the Orthodox Greek Church its independence and ended the former feudal status of the peasantry. The Cypriots paid a tax for their freedom to follow their own religion and were allowed to cultivate their land as their own

and to hand it to their descendants on payment of a portion of the produce. About 30,000 Turkish soldiers were also given land on the island, thus forming a Turkish element in the population which was later reinforced by immigration from Asia Minor.

The 17th and 18th centuries were a melancholy period in the history of Cyprus. Repeated droughts and ravages of locusts preceded a famine in 1640 and an outbreak of plague in 1641. In 1660 the Ottoman Government, in order to limit the extortions of its officials and of the tax-farmers, recognized the Orthodox Archbishop and his three suffragans as guardians of the Christian peasantry, but this step did not prevent revolts in 1665 and 1690. A great famine in 1757–58 and a severe attack of plague in 1760 reduced the numbers of the peasantry very considerably, causing a widespread distress which culminated in the revolt of 1764–66. Cyprus from 1702 had been a fief of the Grand Vizier who normally sold the governorship to the highest bidder, usually for a period of one year. This practice created great opportunities for financial oppression. Perhaps the most striking development of the period was the continued rise in the power of the Orthodox bishops whose influence was so great in the late 18th century that the Turkish administration depended on their support for the collection of the revenues. The Turkish elements in Cyprus, resenting the dominance of the Orthodox bishops, accused them in 1821 of having a secret understanding with the Greeks of the Morea (who had revolted against Turkish rule) and carried out a massacre of the Christians at Nicosia and elsewhere, which brought the supremacy of the bishops to an end.

In 1833 the Sultan granted Cyprus to Muhammad Ali, Pasha of Egypt, who was forced, however, to renounce possession of it in 1840 at the demand of the Great Powers. During the period of reforms initiated by Sultan Mahmud II (1808–39) and continued by his immediate successors, efforts were made to improve the administration of the island. The practice of farming out taxes was abolished (although later partially reintroduced) and the Governor became a salaried official ruling through a divan that was half-Turkish and half-Christian in composition.

BRITISH RULE

At the Congress of Berlin of 1878 the Great Powers endorsed an agreement between the United Kingdom (UK) and the Sultan by which Cyprus was put under British control, to be used as a base from which to protect the Ottoman Empire against the ambitions of Russia. Control of Cyprus was now regarded as vital, since the opening of the Suez Canal (1869) had made the eastern Mediterranean an area of great strategic importance. Under the agreement of 1878, Cyprus remained legally a part of the Ottoman Empire, to which a tribute was paid, consisting of the surplus revenues of the island, calculated at less than £93,000 per annum.

From 1882 until 1931 the island had a legislative council partly nominated and partly elected. Various reforms were carried out in this first period of British rule: the introduction of an efficient judicial system and of an effective police force, and considerable improvements in agriculture, roads, education and other public services.

When Turkey joined the Central Powers in World War I, Britain immediately annexed Cyprus (1914) and then offered it to Greece (1915) provided the latter joined the Allies: this offer was refused, however, and was not repeated when Greece eventually joined the hostilities in 1917. Under the terms of the Treaty of Lausanne of 1923, both Greece and Turkey recognized British sovereignty over Cyprus, which became a Crown Colony in 1925. Thereafter, discontent among the Greek Cypriots began to assume serious proportions, culminating in anti-British riots in 1931 and the suspension of constitutional rule.

In the period after 1931 the desire to achieve self-government within the British Commonwealth grew stronger, but the movement for Enosis (union with Greece) became the dominant influence in the political life of the island. Cypriot troops performed valuable services in the war of 1939–45, for example in Libya, under Lord Wavell, and in the Greek campaign of 1941. Later, Cyprus was used as a place of detention for illegal Jewish immigrants into Palestine, the last of such detention camps being closed in 1949. Following his election as head of the Orthodox Church of Cyprus in 1950, Archbishop Makarios III assumed the leadership of the Enosis movement. An unofficial plebiscite, conducted by the Church in that year, demonstrated overwhelming support for Enosis among Greek Cypriots.

CONSTITUTIONAL PROPOSALS

In July 1954 the UK made known its intention to prepare a restricted form of constitution for Cyprus, with a legislature containing official, nominated and elected members. The Greek Cypriots, insisting that their ultimate goal was Enosis, viewed the proposed constitution with disfavour, whereas the Turkish Cypriots declared their readiness to accept it. The Greek Government at Athens now brought the problem of Cyprus before the United Nations (UN). The UK, however, argued that the question was one with which it alone was competent to deal. The result was that, in December 1954, the UN resolved to take no immediate action in the matter.

The more extreme advocates of Enosis, grouped together in EOKA (National Organization of Cypriot Combatants) under the leadership of Gen. George Grivas (Dhigenis), now began a campaign of terrorist activities against the British administration. A conference including representatives from the UK, Greece and the Turkish Republic met in London in August 1955. The British offer of substantial autonomy for Cyprus failed to win the approval of Greece, since it held out no clear prospect of self-determination for the island, and the conference therefore ended in frustration.

A new and more violent wave of terrorism swept Cyprus in November 1955. A state of emergency was declared on 27 November whereby the death penalty was imposed for the bearing of arms, life imprisonment for sabotage and lesser sentences for looting and the harbouring of terrorists. All public assemblies of a political nature were forbidden; the British troops in Cyprus (about 10,000 in all) assumed the status of active service in war time. The Governor now ruled the island through an executive council consisting of four officials from the administration, two Greek Cypriots and one Turkish Cypriot.

At the beginning of 1956 the Governor, Sir John Harding, discussed the situation with Archbishop Makarios. Since the UK was now willing to accept the principle of ultimate independence for Cyprus, agreement seemed to be within reach. In March 1956, however, the discussions were suspended, and Archbishop Makarios, implicated in the activities of EOKA, was deported to the Seychelles Islands.

RELEASE OF MAKARIOS

In March 1957 Archbishop Makarios was released from detention in the Seychelles and, since he was not allowed to return to Cyprus, went to Athens. The British authorities also relaxed some of the emergency laws, such as the censorship of the press and the mandatory death penalty for the bearing of arms. These measures facilitated the holding of further discussions but little progress was made by the end of the year.

The tide of violence ran high in Cyprus during the first half of 1958. EOKA carried out an intensive campaign of sabotage, especially at Nicosia and Famagusta. At the same time strife between the Greek Cypriots and the Turkish Cypriots was becoming more frequent and severe, the outbreaks in June 1958 being particularly serious. There was increased tension, too, between the governments at Athens and at Ankara.

It was in this situation that in June 1958 the UK made public a new scheme for Cyprus, which came into force in October. The island was to remain under British control for seven years; full autonomy in communal affairs would be granted, under separate arrangements, to the Greek Cypriots and the Turkish Cypriots; internal administration was to be reserved for the Governor's Council, which would include representatives of the Greek Cypriot and Turkish Cypriot communities and also of the Greek and Turkish Governments in Athens and Ankara.

ACHIEVEMENT OF INDEPENDENCE

As a result of a conference held at Zürich, it was announced in February 1959, that Greece and Turkey had devised a compromise settlement concerning Cyprus. A further conference at London decided that Cyprus was to become an independent republic with a Greek Cypriot president and a Turkish Cypriot vice-president. There would be a Council of Ministers (seven Greeks, three Turks) and a House of Representatives (70% Greek, 30% Turkish) elected by universal suffrage for a term of five years. Communal Chambers, one Greek, one Turkish, were to exercise control in matters of religion, culture and education. The Turkish inhabitants in five of the main towns would be allowed to establish separate municipalities for a period of four years.

Cyprus was not to be united with another state, nor was it to be subject to partition. The UK, Greece and Turkey guaranteed the independence, the territorial integrity and the Constitution of Cyprus. Greece received the right to station a force of 950 men in the island, and Turkey a force of 650 men. The UK retained under its direct sovereignty two base areas in Cyprus—at Akrotiri and at Dhekelia.

In November 1959 agreement was attained in regard to the delimitation of the executive powers to be vested in the President and Vice-President of Cyprus. A further agreement defined the composition of the Supreme Constitutional Court. In December the state of emergency came to an end and Archbishop Makarios was elected to be the first President of Cyprus. The post of Vice-President was awarded, unopposed, to the Turkish Cypriot leader, Dr Fazil Küçük. After long negotiations, concluded in July 1960, the UK and Cyprus reached agreement over the precise size and character of the two military bases to be assigned to British sovereignty.

Cyprus formally became an independent republic on 16 August 1960, and, in September, a member of the UN. The Conference of Commonwealth Prime Ministers, meeting in London, resolved in March 1961 to admit Cyprus as a member of the Commonwealth.

CONSTITUTIONAL PROBLEMS

As Cyprus entered into its independence, serious problems began to arise over the interpretation and working of the Constitution. There was divergence of opinion between Greek and Turkish Cypriots over the formation of a national army, in accordance with provisions of the Zürich agreement of 1959 (2,000 men; 60% Greek, 40% Turkish); the main point of dispute being the degree of integration to be established between the two components. In October 1961 the Turkish Vice-President, Dr Küçük, used his power of veto to ban full integration, which President Makarios favoured at all levels of the armed forces.

Difficulties arose also over the implementation of the 70:30 ratio of Greek Cypriot to Turkish Cypriot personnel in the public services. There was friction too in the House of Representatives, about financial affairs, such as customs duties and income tax laws.

The year 1962 saw the growth of a serious crisis over the system of separate Greek and Turkish municipalities in the five main towns of Cyprus—Nicosia, Famagusta, Limassol, Larnaca and Paphos. In December 1962 the Turkish Communal Chamber passed a law maintaining the Turkish municipalities in the five towns from 1 January 1963, and also establishing a similar municipality in the predominantly Turkish town of Lefka. President Makarios now issued a decree stating that, from 1 January 1963, government-appointed bodies would control municipal organizations throughout the island—a decree which the Turkish Cypriots denounced as an infringement of the Constitution.

The Constitutional Court of Cyprus, sitting in judgement on the financial disputes, ruled in February 1963 that, in view of the veto exercised by the Turkish members of the House of Representatives since 1961, taxes could be imposed on the people of the island, but that no legal machinery existed for the collection of such taxes. In April the court declared that the Government had no power to control the municipalities through bodies of its own choosing and that the decision of the Turkish Communal Chamber to maintain the separate

Turkish municipalities in defiance of the Cyprus Government was likewise invalid.

Negotiations between President Makarios and Vice-President Küçük to resolve the deadlock broke down in May. Accordingly, in November, Archbishop Makarios put forward proposals for a number of reforms—e.g. that the President and Vice-President of Cyprus should lose their right of veto over certain types of legislation; that separate Greek Cypriot and Turkish Cypriot majorities in the House of Representatives should not be required for financial legislation; and that single municipal councils, with both Greek and Turkish Cypriot members, should replace the separate municipalities in the five chief towns of Cyprus. These proposals proved to be unacceptable to the Turkish Cypriots.

CIVIL WAR

Meanwhile, underground organizations, prepared for violence, had been formed both among the Greek and the Turkish communities. In December 1963 serious conflict broke out. The UK suggested that a joint force composed of British, Greek and Turkish troops stationed in Cyprus should be established to restore order. The governments at Nicosia, Athens and Ankara gave their assent to this scheme. At this same moment the forces of Turkey serving in the island occupied a strong position, north of Nicosia, which gave them control of the important road to Kyrenia on the northern coast of Cyprus— a road which was to become the scene of much conflict in the future. As a result of the December crisis co-operation between the Greek Cypriots and the Turkish Cypriots in government and in other sectors of public life came almost to an end, most notably in the Turkish Cypriot boycott of the House of Representatives.

There was renewed violence in February 1964, especially at Limassol. Arms in considerable quantities were being brought secretly into the island for both sides, and the number of armed 'irregulars' was increasing rapidly. These developments also gave rise to friction between Athens and Ankara.

ESTABLISHMENT OF UN PEACE-KEEPING FORCE

In January 1964, following a request by the Cyprus Government, the UN nominated Lt-Gen. Prem Gyani of India to act as its representative to the island. Later in the same month the Cyprus Government informed U Thant, the Secretary-General of the UN, that it would be glad to see a UN force established in the island. The UN Security Council debated the Cyprus question in February, finally adopting, on 4 March, a resolution to establish the UN Peace-keeping Force in Cyprus (UNFICYP). Advance units of the Canadian contingent reached the island on 27 March, and by 22 May the UN head-quarters at Nicosia controlled 6,931 men.

There was more fighting between Greek and Turkish Cypriots in March and April 1964. On 1 June the Cyprus House of Representatives approved legislation establishing a National Guard and rendering all male Cypriots between the ages of 18 and 59 liable to six months of service. Only members of the National Guard, of the regular police and of the armed forces would now have the right to bear arms. One purpose of the legislation was to suppress the irregular bands which, as extremist sentiment grew stronger, tended more and more to escape the control of the established regime.

Under the agreements concluded for the independence of Cyprus in 1959–60, Turkey maintained a contingent of troops on the island, the personnel of this force being renewed from time to time on a system of regular rotation. A new crisis arose in August–September 1964 when the Government at Nicosia refused to allow such a rotation of personnel. After much negotiation through the UN officials on the island the Cyprus Government agreed to raise its existing blockade of the Turkish Cypriots entrenched in the Kokkina district and to allow the normal rotation of troops for the Turkish force stationed at Cyprus. The Government at Ankara now con-sented that this force should come under the UN command in Cyprus.

LEGISLATIVE MEASURES

Towards the end of 1964 the Cyprus House of Representatives passed a number of important measures (despite the continued absence of Turkish Cypriot deputies), including a bill for the creation of unified municipalities in Nicosia, Larnaca, Limassol, Famagusta and Paphos; a law restoring to the Government the right to exact income tax (a right inoperative since 1961 as a result of the veto of the Turkish Cypriot members in the House); and a bill extending compulsory ser-vice in the National Guard for Greek Cypriots from six months to 12 months. In July 1965 a new law was approved for unified elections on the basis of a common electoral roll, the communal distinction between Greek Cypriots and Turkish Cypriots being thus abolished.

The UN mediator in Cyprus, Dr Galo Plaza, resigned in December 1965. In January 1967 U Thant announced that he had chosen Bibiano Osorio-Tafall, of Mexico, to be his personal representative in Cyprus, Carlos Bernardes, of Brazil, having resigned the appointment for personal reasons.

GENERAL GRIVAS

There was further tension in Cyprus during March 1966 over the position of Gen. Grivas, the former head of EOKA. Grivas had returned to the island in June 1964 at a time when it was felt that he might be able, with his high personal prestige, to bring to order the small 'private armies' and 'irregular bands' which had emerged among the Greek Cypriots and which were violently defying the Cyprus Government.

In March 1966 President Makarios attempted to limit the functions of Gen. Grivas in Cyprus and so to end a situation which saw political control vested in himself, while command of the armed forces (both the Greek Cypriot National Guard and also the 'volunteer' Greek troops stationed in Cyprus), rested with the General, who took his orders from Athens. The President suggested that the National Guard should be transferred to the control of the Cyprus Minister of Defence— a proposal which found favour neither with Gen. Grivas nor in Athens, where it provoked a serious political crisis. The whole affair underlined the distrust separating President Makarios and Gen. Grivas and the doubts existing in Athens regarding the ultimate intentions of the President.

In November 1966 the UK announced its intention to reduce its military establishment in Cyprus. Some 2,000 servicemen would be withdrawn by the summer of 1967. At the same time there was to be a reduction of stores at the Dhekelia base. The Royal Air Force (RAF) station at Nicosia had already been reduced to operating on a 'care and maintenance' basis, leaving Akrotiri to function as RAF headquarters in Cyprus.

The military coup in Greece in April 1967 was followed by a brief improvement in Greco-Turkish relations. The Prime Ministers and Foreign Ministers of Greece and Turkey met in Thrace in September 1967, but failed to come to an agreement on Cyprus, Greece rejecting any form of partition, which was implicit in the Turkish proposal to accept Enosis in return for military bases and 10% of the island's territory.

TURKISH CYPRIOT ADMINISTRATION

On 29 December 1967 the Turkish Cypriot community announced the establishment of a 'Transitional Administra-tion' to administer their affairs until the provisions of the 1960 Constitution were implemented. Measures were approved to establish separate executive, legislative and judicial authori-ties, and Dr Küçük, who remained the official Vice-President of Cyprus, was appointed President of the Transitional Admin-istration, with Rauf Denktaş as Vice-President. A legislative body was established, consisting of the Turkish Cypriot mem-bers of the House of Representatives elected in 1960 and the members of the Turkish Communal Chamber. The Executive Council's nine members functioned as the administration. President Makarios described the Transitional Administration as 'totally illegal', but it continued to function as the *de facto* Government of the Turkish community in Cyprus.

INTERCOMMUNAL TALKS, 1968–74

Between January and April 1968 the Cypriot Government gradually relaxed the measures it had taken against the Turk-ish community. With the exception of the Turkish area in Nicosia, freedom of movement for Turkish Cypriots was re-stored, checkpoints were removed and unrestricted supplies to

Turkish areas were allowed. In April Rauf Denktaş, the Vice-President of the Turkish Cypriot Administration, was permitted to return from exile, and in May he began talks with Glavkos Klerides, the President of the House of Representatives. These talks were intended to form the basis of a settlement of the constitutional differences between the Greek and Turkish communities, but very little progress was made. After years of intermittent discussion, there was still an impasse, the Turks demanding local autonomy, the Greeks rejecting any proposals tending towards a federal solution, fearing that it might lead to partition. In June 1972 Dr Kurt Waldheim, the UN Secretary-General, attended the talks, stressing the need for a peaceful settlement and expressing a hope that UNFICYP might be withdrawn in the near future. By the end of 1973 the Greek Cypriot representative seemed to have accepted the principle of local autonomy, but the talks still dragged on, with no acceptable compromise having been found on the scope of local autonomy or the degree of control to be exercised by the central government over local authorities. A statement by Bülent Ecevit, Prime Minister of Turkey, calling for a federal settlement of the constitutional problem, caused the talks to break down in April 1974. The Greek and Cypriot Governments claimed that the talks had been conducted on the understanding that any solution would be in terms of a unitary state; Mr Denktaş that federation would not necessarily mean partition. Mr Denktaş also feared that the Greek Government was giving support to the Enosis movement. Each side accused the other of trying to sabotage the talks.

TERRORISM AND ELECTIONS

While the talks between the Greek and Turkish communities continued, there was a marked reduction in intercommunal violence, but the Greek population of the island was divided between supporters of Makarios, and his aim of an independent unitary state, and those who demanded union with Greece. In 1969 the National Front, an organization advocating immediate Enosis, embarked on a campaign of terrorism, raiding police stations to steal arms, bombing British military buildings and vehicles, shooting and wounding the chief of police and making several unsuccessful bomb attacks on government ministers. Mr Papadopoulos, the Greek Prime Minister, denounced terrorism in Cyprus and the National Front in particular.

On 8 March 1970 there was an attempt to assassinate President Makarios, attributed to the National Front. A week later, Polykarpos Georghadjis, a former Minister of the Interior, was found shot dead. At the trial of the President's would-be assassins, Georghadjis was named as a party to the conspiracy.

Despite the activities of the National Front, the Government decided to hold a general election on 5 July 1970. The dissolved House of Representatives had been in existence since 1960, and the elections which should have been held in 1965, according to the Constitution, had been postponed from year to year, owing to the continuing crisis. The continued absence of the 15 Turkish members, who met as part of the Turkish Legislative Assembly, meant that the Greek Cypriot House of Representatives contained only 35 members. Fifteen of the Greek Cypriot seats were won by the Unified Party, led by Glavkos Klerides, with a policy of support for President Makarios and a united independent Cyprus. The communist party, AKEL, won nine seats, to become the second largest in the House. None of the candidates of DEK, the Democratic National Party (which advocated Enosis), won a seat. The elections held at the same time by the Turkish Cypriots resulted in a victory for the National Solidarity Party, led by Rauf Denktaş.

RETURN OF GRIVAS AND EOKA-B

The ideal of Enosis was still attractive to many Greek Cypriots, despite the lack of success for pro-Enosis candidates in the election. Greek Cypriot students condemned President Makarios' support for the creation of an independent unitary state, and called for an end to the intercommunal talks. Gen. Grivas attacked the President in an article in an Athens newspaper, calling for his resignation on the grounds that, by abandoning Enosis, the President had betrayed EOKA's struggle for freedom.

At the beginning of September 1971 Gen. Grivas returned secretly to Cyprus and began to hold meetings with the leaders of the National Front and his followers in the EOKA movement of the 1950s. President Makarios threatened to arrest the General for setting up armed bands, and declared his opposition to the achievement of Enosis by violent means. His opponents, pro-Enosis Greek Cypriots, condemned the intercommunal talks and rejected the idea of a negotiated compromise with the Turkish community. The Cyprus Government imported a considerable quantity of arms from Czechoslovakia as a precautionary measure, but after protests from the Greek and Turkish foreign ministries that the distribution of these arms would serve only to aggravate an already tense situation, the consignment was placed under the custody of UNFICYP.

The President had been under pressure for some time from the Greek Government to dismiss ministers considered hostile to Athens. In February 1972 it was suggested in Athens that a Cypriot government of national unity should be formed, including moderate representatives of Gen. Grivas. For some months the President resisted this pressure, and it seemed that the Greek Government, in alliance with dissident bishops and Gen. Grivas, was intent on forcing his resignation. In May Spyros Kyprianou, the Foreign Minister, who had been the main target of Greek hostility and one of the President's closest collaborators, resigned, and in June the President capitulated and carried out an extensive reorganization of his Cabinet.

Gen. Grivas organized a new guerrilla force, which became known as EOKA-B, and launched a series of attacks on the Makarios Government similar to those against British rule in the 1950s. While the Committee for the Co-ordination of the Enosis Struggle, Grivas' political front organization, demanded a plebiscite on Enosis and rejected intercommunal agreement as a means of settling the future of Cyprus, EOKA-B raided police stations, quarries and warehouses, stealing arms, ammunition, dynamite and radio transmitters.

1973 PRESIDENTIAL ELECTION

The demand for a plebiscite from supporters of Gen. Grivas was put forward as an alternative to the election for the presidency, called by President Makarios as a test of strength. The President's speech of 8 February 1973 explained his position. While believing in Enosis, he considered that talks with the Turkish community on the basis of an independent Cyprus were the only practical possibility. He condemned terrorism and violence as counter-productive, likely to lead to Turkish intervention and unsupported by the Greek and Cypriot authorities. The Greek Government also repudiated terrorism and expressed its support for a constitutional solution.

On 8 February 1973 Makarios was returned unopposed for a third five-year term as President, and in the Turkish quarter of Nicosia Rauf Denktaş was declared elected Vice-President, following the withdrawal of Ahmet Berberoğlu.

EOKA-B continued its terrorist activities throughout 1973, concentrating on bombings and raids on police stations. In July the Minister of Justice, Christos Vakis, was kidnapped, prompting an escalation in violence. The President refused to submit to violence or to blackmail, rejecting the terms put forward by Grivas for the release of Vakis. Numerous police and National Guard officers, suspected of being Grivas sympathizers, were dismissed, and Vakis was released in August. Action by security forces against secret EOKA bases resulted in many arrests, the seizure of quantities of munitions and the discovery of plans to assassinate the President. President Papadopoulos of Greece publicly condemned the activities of 'the illegal organization of Gen. Grivas', which undermined the Greek policy of 'support for the finding of a solution to the Cyprus problem through the enlarged local talks aimed at ensuring an independent, sovereign and unitary state'.

MAKARIOS AND THE BISHOPS

In March 1972 the three bishops of the Orthodox Church of Cyprus—Anthimos of Kitium, Yennadios of Paphos and Kyprianos of Kyrenia—called on Archbishop Makarios to divest himself of the temporal power of the presidency, on the ground that his political role was incompatible with his ecclesiastical position under the rules of the Church. This provoked massive popular demonstrations and a resolution in the House of Representatives in support of the President. It appeared that the bishops had the support and protection of Gen. Grivas. When the President rejected their demand for his resignation, they charged him with abandoning the ideal of Enosis, tolerating the growth of communism and permitting the rise of anti-Greek attitudes.

The clergy of the diocese of Paphos voted Bishop Yennadios out of office in June 1972, but he and the other two bishops refused to accept this decision and continued their campaign against Archbishop Makarios. In March 1973 they held what they called a Holy Synod of the Church of Cyprus, and announced that in view of the Archbishop's refusal to resign the presidency they would strip him of his episcopal titles. Makarios disregarded this move and the bishops' declaration in April that he had been reduced to the rank of layman. While the bishops were attempting to gain control of the administration and finances of the Church, claiming that Yennadios had been appointed to the vacant archiepiscopal throne, Makarios was taking counter-measures. He called an election for the diocese of Paphos in succession to Yennadios, and in July 1973 held a synod of the Orthodox churches in Nicosia. The synod, presided over by the Patriarch of Alexandria, gave its support to Archbishop Makarios. It ruled that the presidency and the archbishopric were not incompatible under canon law, that the bishops' attempt to depose the Archbishop was invalid and that the bishops were guilty of schism. The dissident bishops were replaced.

ABORTIVE 1974 MILITARY COUP

Following the deposition of the three bishops, and the demonstrations of popular support for the President which their actions provoked, the Cypriot Government was able to take strong measures against other supporters of Gen. Grivas. Forces loyal to the President waged guerrilla war against EOKA-B, and carried out a purge of the armed forces and police, some of whose members had collaborated with EOKA and helped in their raids on police stations in search of arms. The Grivas campaign of terrorism seemed to have been checked by the beginning of 1974, and when Gen. Grivas died of a heart attack in January 1974 the President granted an amnesty to 100 of his imprisoned supporters, hoping to restore normality in Cyprus.

In June 1974 President Makarios ordered a purge of EOKA supporters in the police, civil service, schools and National Guard, and on 2 July wrote to President Ghizikis of Greece, accusing the Greek military regime of giving arms and subsidies to EOKA and using the Greek army officers attached to the Cyprus National Guard for subversion. The President demanded that the Greek officers who had collaborated with EOKA should be withdrawn, and began to take steps to ensure that the Guard should be loyal to Cyprus, rather than to Greece and Enosis. The National Guard, apparently with Greek support, then staged a coup. On 15 July a former EOKA gunman, Nicos Sampson, was appointed President. Makarios fled to Britain, the resistance of his supporters was crushed, and Greece sent more officers to reinforce the National Guard.

Rauf Denktaş, the Turkish Cypriot leader, called for military action by the UK and Turkey, as guarantors of Cypriot independence, to prevent Greece imposing Enosis. Having failed to induce the UK to intervene, Turkey acted unilaterally. Turkish troops landed in Cyprus on 20 July, and seized the port of Kyrenia and a corridor connecting it to the Turkish sector in Nicosia. A cease-fire on 22 July did not prevent further Turkish advances, and the UN peace-keeping force had little success in its efforts to interpose itself between the two Cypriot communities. Massacres and other atrocities were reported from many bi-communal villages, reinforcing the hostility between the Greeks and Turks.

TURKEY OCCUPIES NORTHERN CYPRUS

The successful Turkish invasion had foiled Greek plans to take over Cyprus using the National Guard, and when the military Government of Greece resigned on 23 July 1974, Nicos Sampson did likewise. Glavkos Klerides, the moderate Speaker of the House of Representatives who had led the

Greek Cypriot delegation to the intercommunal talks, was appointed President, and began negotiations with Rauf Denktaş. In Geneva, the UK, Greece and Turkey also held talks, seeking a settlement, but negotiations broke down following Turkish demands for the establishment of a cantonal federation giving almost a third of the area of Cyprus to the Turkish Cypriots.

On 14 August, the day after the Geneva talks ended, the war was renewed. Turkish forces seized the whole of Cyprus north of what became the 'Attila line', running from Morphou through Nicosia to Famagusta, and the new civilian Government in Greece announced its inability to intervene. Turkey proclaimed that, by this *fait accompli*, the boundaries of an autonomous Turkish Cypriot administration had been established, while Denktaş spoke of establishing a completely independent Turkish Cypriot state north of the 'Attila line' and of encouraging the immigration of Turkish Cypriots from areas still under Greek Cypriot control, to produce a permanent ethnic and political partition of the island. The UN Secretary-General, Dr Kurt Waldheim, succeeded in arranging talks between Klerides and Denktaş, but was unable to bring about any constructive results from these negotiations. An important round of peace talks on the Cyprus problem began in Vienna between Klerides and Denktaş in January 1975, under the aegis of Dr Waldheim. The success of the talks depended on whether the two sides could reach agreement on the political future of the island: the Turkish Cypriots wanting a Greek-Turkish bi-regional federation with strong regional governments, whereas the Greeks, whilst not ruling out a bizonal solution, favoured a multi-regional or cantonal federation with strong central government. Both parties stressed the need for an independent, non-aligned, demilitarized Cyprus.

On 13 February 1975 a 'Turkish Federated State of Cyprus' ('TFSC') was proclaimed in the part of the island under Turkish occupation. The new State was not proclaimed as an independent republic but as a restructuring of the Autonomous Turkish Cypriot Administration, a body established after the invasion, 'on the basis of a secular and federated state until such time as the 1960 Constitution of the Republic . . . is amended in a similar manner to become the Constitution of the Federal Republic of Cyprus'. Rauf Denktaş was appointed President of the new 'state'. Greece denounced this move as a threat to peace and declared that the issue would be taken to the UN Security Council where a resolution was passed on 13 March, regretting the unilateral decision to set up a Federated Turkish State. Talks were resumed in April and the foundation laid for intercommunal reconciliation and co-operation, when the Cypriot leaders agreed to form an expert committee, under the auspices of Dr Luis Weckmann-Muñoz, Special Representative of the UN Secretary-General, to consider the powers and functions of a central government for Cyprus and present their findings in June to the Cypriot negotiators in Vienna.

The flight of Turkish Cypriots to British bases after the National Guard coup and the withdrawal of Greek Cypriot civilians before the advancing Turkish army had produced a major problem in Cyprus. In August 1974 the UN estimated that there were some 225,600 refugees in Cyprus, of whom 183,800 were Greek Cypriots. In the southern part of Cyprus, under Greek Cypriot control, were 198,800 of these refugees, of whom 35,000 were Turkish Cypriots, including prisoners of war. This problem remained unsolved in 1976, with an estimated 200,000 refugees on the island. However, 9,000 Turkish Cypriots were given the opportunity to move to the northern sector in August 1975. In return the Turkish Cypriot authorities allowed 800 relatives of Greeks who remained in the north to join them in the Turkish sector. The concern over the treatment of Greeks in the Turkish-occupied area gave rise in August 1975 to an investigation by the European Commission of Human Rights which, in a report published in January 1977, found Turkey guilty of committing atrocities in Cyprus.

In December 1974 Archbishop Makarios returned to Cyprus, and resumed the presidency. In January 1975 Britain decided to permit the resettlement of over 9,000 Turkish Cypriot refugees from the British Sovereign Base at Akrotiri. In retali-

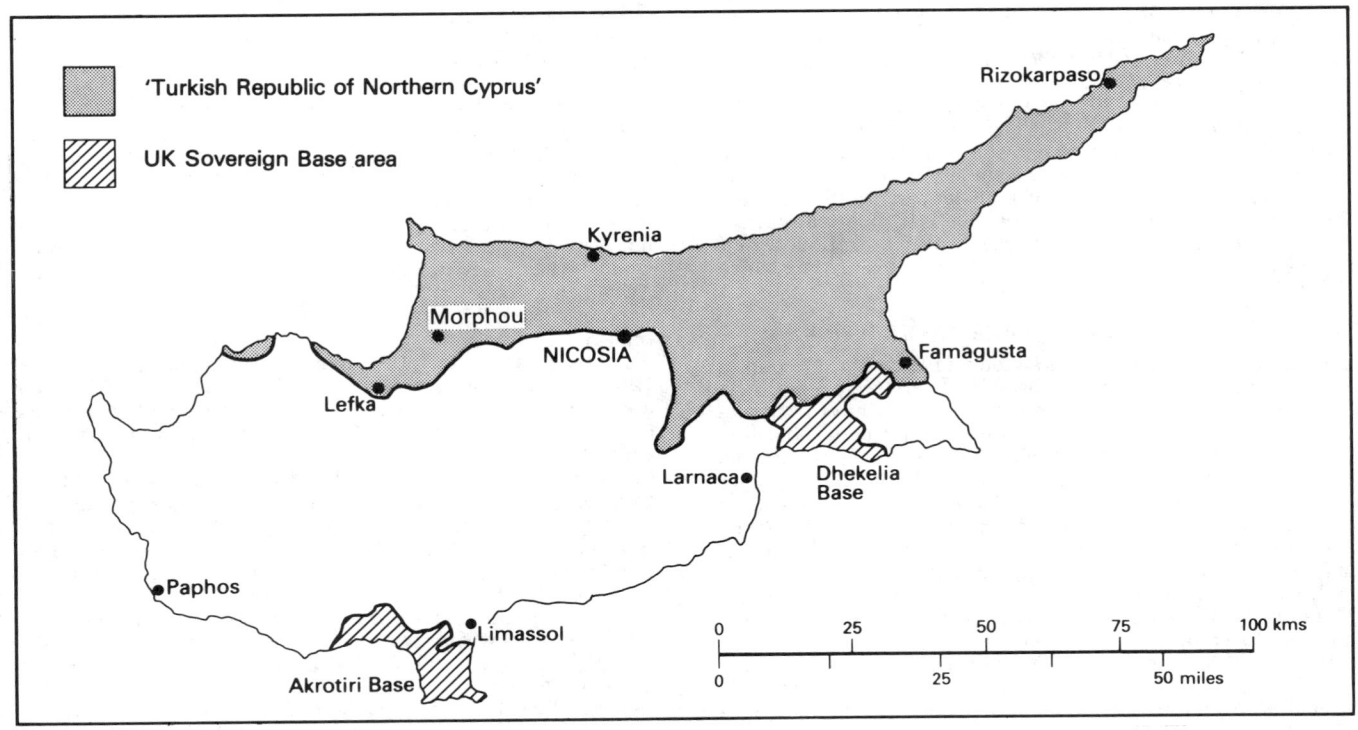

Cyprus, showing the 'Turkish Republic of Northern Cyprus'

ation for the alleged ill-treatment of Turkish Cypriots still living in Greek areas and in order to force a decision on the release of the refugees and their resettlement, the Turks threatened to expel all remaining Greek Cypriots in northern Cyprus and launched a massive scheme to colonize the area, bringing thousands of farmers and peasants from mainland Turkey and settling them in Greek-owned property. Before the Turkish invasion of July 1974, the population of Cyprus numbered 639,000 of whom 18% were Turkish Cypriots and 78% Greek Cypriots.

ELECTIONS AND INTERCOMMUNAL TALKS 1975–76

In September 1975 talks between the two sides were resumed in New York. However, these and further talks in February 1976 were completely unproductive. In April 1976 the divergence in the policies of Archbishop Makarios and Glavkos Klerides, the Greek Cypriot negotiator, eventually led to the resignation of the latter and his replacement by Tassos Papadopoulos. At the same time the Turkish Cypriot negotiator, Rauf Denktaş, was replaced by Umit Suleyman Onan.

During 1976 general elections were held on both sides of the 'Attila line'. In June Rauf Denktaş was elected President of the 'TFSC'. His election placed him constitutionally above party politics but in fact his position depended upon the support of the National Unity Party (UBP). Under the terms of the Constitution promulgated by the Turkish Cypriot authorities, 40 deputies were elected to a legislative assembly, with the UBP gaining a majority. Nejat Konuk, the Secretary-General of the UBP, was appointed Prime Minister. In September general elections were held in the government-controlled area. A new party under Spyros Kyprianou, the Democratic Front (supporting the policies of Archbishop Makarios), won a decisive victory, gaining 21 of the 35 seats. The party of Glavkos Klerides, the Democratic Rally (DISY), did not win any seats.

In January 1977 Rauf Denktaş initiated a meeting with Archbishop Makarios to establish preliminaries for resuming intercommunal talks (suspended since February 1976); Archbishop Makarios made it clear that he was prepared to accept bi-zonal federation provided the Turkish authorities made territorial concessions, and only if there was provision for a central government with adequate powers. A sixth round of talks, which opened in Vienna in March 1977, broke down, was resumed in Nicosia in May but was suspended until after the general elections in Turkey in June 1977.

DEATH OF MAKARIOS, ACCESSION OF KYPRIANOU

The death of Archbishop Makarios on 3 August 1977, put an end to hopes for an immediate continuation of negotiations and gave rise to fears about the stability of the Greek Cypriot regime in his absence, especially since there was no obvious successor. Spyros Kyprianou, the President of the House of Representatives, was elected on 31 August to serve the remainder of Makarios's term of office. In the elections of January 1978 he was re-elected unopposed and formed a new Cabinet with an increased membership of 13. Shortly afterwards the EOKA-B announced its dissolution, but in April 1978, after the discovery of a plot, 22 of its members were arrested. In the same month, following criticism in the Turkish Cypriot press about rising prices, Nejat Konuk resigned as Prime Minister of the 'TFSC' and was replaced by Osman Orek, former president of the National Assembly, who formed a new Cabinet.

In April and July 1978 President Kyprianou was subjected to criticism from within his own government, both from the powerful left wing and from the followers of Makarios. This resulted in the dismissal of his chief negotiator with the Turkish Cypriots, Tassos Papadopoulos. In December there was a crisis in the 'TFSC' as a result of factional disputes within the UBP. Amid widespread rumours about the establishment of a multinational company to which the Turkish Cypriot unions were opposed, all nine Cabinet ministers resigned, followed by the Prime Minister, Osman Orek. A new Cabinet was formed under Mustafa Çağatay, formerly Minister of Labour, Social Affairs and Health. In April 1979 a new party, the Democratic Party, was formed by Nejat Konuk, the former Prime Minister, as the UBP lost support in the legislature.

On 19 May 1979 Kyprianou and Denktaş agreed a 10-point agenda, based on the Makarios/Denktaş agreement. However, inter-communal talks in June were adjourned after a week over differences in the interpretation of the agreement, which Turkish Cypriots saw as providing for bi-zonality on the island. In November Süleyman Demirel became Prime Minister of Turkey, and in March 1980 Turkey signed a new defence agreement with the USA. Meanwhile, the mandate of the UN Peacekeeping Force (UNFICYP) continued to be extended at six-monthly intervals.

On 9 September 1980 the Greek Cypriot Government's reshuffle involved the appointment of seven new ministers. As a result, President Kyprianou was again attacked by AKEL and by the right-wing opposition under Klerides, thus losing his overall majority in the House of Representatives. During the next three months, three new 'centrist' political parties were established: the Pan-Cypriot Revitalization Front (PAME), the new Democratic Party (DIKO) and the Centre Union.

ELECTIONS AND FURTHER TALKS 1980–81

On 16 September 1980, in the shadow of the military coup in Turkey, the intercommunal peace-talks were resumed after a break of 15 months. These were to be held within the framework of a procedural formula proposed by Hugo Gobbi, the UN Special Representative for Cyprus. The negotiators for the Greek and Turkish sides were respectively George Ioannides and Umit Suleyman Onan. There were to be four main areas of discussion: the re-settlement of Varosha (the Greek area of Famagusta); constitutional aspects; territorial aspects; and 'initial practical measures by both sides to promote good will, mutual confidence and the return to normal conditions'. The talks continued intermittently, but by the spring of 1981 no concrete results had been achieved.

In March 1981 there was a resumption of negotiations with Britain about outstanding development payments to Cyprus, which, according to the Cypriots, amounted to £150m. since 1960. In the same month the Foreign Minister, Nikos Rolandis, expressed his opposition to the possible use of the British airbases at Akrotiri and Dhekelia by the USA's proposed Rapid Deployment Force.

Growing criticism of Kyprianou's Government for its failure to avert an economic crisis or to make any real progress in the intercommunal talks led the House of Representatives to vote almost unanimously on 16 April for the dissolution of the Government. In the subsequent parliamentary elections, held on 24 May 1981, under a system of proportional representation, the communist AKEL party and the DISY party of Glavkos Klerides each won 12 of the 35 Greek Cypriot seats in the House of Representatives, while President Kyprianou's DIKO party won only eight seats. In the elections held in the 'TFSC' in June 1981, President Rauf Denktaş was returned to office, but with only 52% of the vote. His right-wing UBP won 18 out of 40 seats, compared with 23 at the previous elections.

The intercommunal talks continued throughout 1981, but little progress was made. In August there were signs of hope when fresh proposals were put forward by the Turkish Cypriots. These envisaged handing back 3% to 4% of the 35.8% of land now controlled by them, plus the buffer zone between the two communities, and allowing some 40,000 of the 200,000 Greek Cypriot refugees to return to the Famagusta area. The constitutional issue remained the main problem: the Greek Cypriots wanted a federation with a strong central government and freedom of movement throughout the island; the Turkish Cypriots favoured something more like a partition within a confederation, equal representation in government and strong links with the mother country. The Greek Cypriots, although they agreed to the principle of an alternating presidency, objected to disproportionate representation of the Turkish community, who form less than 20% of the population. The Turkish proposals were rejected by the Greek Cypriots, but it was agreed that the talks should continue.

NEW UN PEACE PROPOSAL

In November 1981 the UN put forward a new peace plan, or 'evaluation', for a federal, independent and non-aligned Cypriot state. Although more favourable to the Greek side than the Turkish Cypriot proposals had been, this was only accepted reluctantly as a basis for negotiation by the Greek Cypriots, in the face of opposition from the Church and some political groups. The Turkish Cypriots accepted the plan.

The socialist Government of Greece, elected in October 1981, pledged more active support for the Greek Cypriots than their predecessors. Andreas Papandreou, the Greek Prime Minister, who visited Cyprus early in 1982, wanted to see the withdrawal of all Greek and Turkish troops from the island, and favoured an international conference on Cyprus rather than the continuation of the intercommunal talks.

With presidential elections in view, President Kyprianou and his DIKO party formed an alliance with the communist AKEL party in April 1982, based on a 'minimum programme' of continuance of the non-aligned *status quo*, defence of the mixed economy and support for the intercommunal talks. This put a strain on relations with the Greek Government by going against the policy which had recently been laid down by Athens and Nicosia. The alliance with AKEL involved a Cabinet reshuffle in which all but three ministers were replaced.

In the 'TFSC' the Çağatay Government resigned in December 1981. A three-month crisis followed until March 1982, when a coalition government was formed by Çağatay between his own UBP, the Democratic People's Party and the Turkish Unity Party.

In February 1983 President Kyprianou was re-elected for a five-year term by a comfortable 56.5% majority. Glavkos Klerides' DISY party polled 34%, and Vassos Lyssarides' socialist party, EDEK, 9.5%. President Kyprianou reiterated that communist policies would not be introduced and that no communists would be given cabinet rank.

In May the UN General Assembly voted overwhelmingly in favour of the withdrawal of Turkish troops from Cyprus, although the USA and the UK abstained in protest against the partisan wording of the resolution. In retaliation, Rauf Denktaş threatened to boycott any further intercommunal talks and to call a referendum in the 'TFSC' to decide whether to make a unilateral declaration of independence and seek international recognition. The Cyprus pound was replaced by the Turkish lira as legal tender in 'TFSC'.

Informal talks, under the auspices of the UN, continued in August 1983 but no agreement was reached, and in September the Greek Cypriot Minister of Foreign Affairs resigned because of policy differences with President Kyprianou over the proposed resumption of the intercommunal talks.

DECLARATION OF 'TURKISH REPUBLIC OF NORTHERN CYPRUS'

United Nations proposals for a 'summit' meeting between Denktaş and Kyprianou in late 1983 were unsuccessful. On 15 November the 'TFSC' made a unilateral declaration of independence as the 'Turkish Republic of Northern Cyprus' ('TRNC'), with Denktaş as President. Later that month, Mustafa Çağatay resigned as Turkish Cypriot Prime Minister and as leader of the UBP. On 2 December the Legislative Assembly of the 'TRNC' adopted legislation for the establishment of a 70-member constituent assembly (comprising the 40 elected members of the Legislative Assembly and 30 others appointed from representative groups within the community), which met for the first time on 6 December. On the following day, President Denktaş appointed Nejat Konuk (who had been Prime Minister of the 'TFSC' in 1976–78 and was then President of the 'TRNC' Legislative Assembly) to be Prime Minister in an interim Cabinet, pending elections in 1984. Like the 'TFSC', the 'TRNC' was recognised only by Turkey, and the declaration of independence was condemned by the UN Security Council in November. The EC decided against applying trade sanctions against the 'TRNC', and the mandate of UNFICYP continued to be extended at six-monthly intervals. Conciliatory proposals that were made by the 'TRNC', including the resettlement of 40,000 Greek Cypriot refugees, were rejected by the Cyprus Government in January 1984, while the 'TRNC', in turn, refused to accept President Kyprianou's proposal that the Turkish Cypriots should be allowed to administer 25% of the island (despite the fact that they comprised only 18% of the population) on condition that the declaration of independence be withdrawn before talks were re-opened.

In April 1984 Turkey and the 'TRNC' exchanged ambassadors, and plans were made for a referendum on 19 August to approve a new constitution, to be followed by a general election on 4 November to elect members for the Constituent

Assembly. (These elections were subsequently postponed.) The establishment of diplomatic links with Turkey was followed by a formal rejection of UN proposals for a 'freezing' of independence as a pre-condition of peace talks, along with a continued refusal to return the Varosha (Greek Cypriot) area of Famagusta. In May an offer by President Ronald Reagan of the USA to establish a 'peace and reconstruction' fund of US $250m., if the two sides would settle their differences, was ignored.

ABORTIVE 1985 KYPRIANOU—DENKTAŞ SUMMIT

In August and September 1984 the Greek and Turkish Cypriots conferred separately with the UN Secretary-General, Javier Pérez de Cuéllar, whose aim was to bring the two sides together for direct negotiations. The Turkish Cypriots reiterated that they would accept the proposed creation of a bi-zonal federation only if power were to be shared equally between the north and the south. The third round of negotiations, begun in November, were seen as being crucial to any long-term solution of the problem but, despite some concessions on the part of the Turkish Cypriots, an impasse was reached. In December 1984, after the third round of talks had ended, the leaders of the two communities, Spyros Kyprianou and Rauf Denktaş agreed to hold a 'summit' meeting in January 1985. No agreement was reached at the meeting, however, and Denktaş subsequently declared that a further 'summit' meeting could not be arranged until after the elections which were due to be held in the 'TRNC' in June. The new Constitution of the 'TRNC' was approved by a referendum in May 1985, and this was followed by a presidential election on 9 June, at which Rauf Denktaş was returned with over 70% of the vote. A general election followed on 23 June, with the UBP, led by Dr Derviş Eroğlu, winning more seats than any other party (24) but failing to win an overall majority in the 50-seat Legislative Assembly.

In July 1985 the UN Secretary-General drew up further proposals, which the Greek Cypriots accepted. The new UN proposals were for a bi-zonal federal Cyprus (with the Turkish Cypriots occupying 29% of the land) in which the government would be led by a Greek Cypriot president and a Turkish Cypriot vice-president, both having limited power of veto over federal legislation. Ministers would be appointed in a ratio of seven Greek Cypriots to three Turkish Cypriots. One 'major' ministry would always be held by a Turkish Cypriot, and a special working party would consider demands that the Minister of Foreign Affairs should always be a Turkish Cypriot. There would be two assemblies: an upper house, with a 50:50 community representation, and a lower house, weighted 70:30 in favour of the Greek Cypriots. Legislation on important issues would require 'separate majorities in both chambers'. A tripartite body, including one non-Cypriot voting member, would have the final say in constitutional clashes concerning the extent of federal power. However, serious problems remained over the crucial questions of a timetable for the withdrawal of Turkey's troops and the nature of international guarantees for a newly united Republic of Cyprus. This plan was underwritten by foreign governments (in effect the USA), which were to subsidize two funds: one to help the poorer Turkish Cypriot community, and the other to aid both Greek and Turkish Cypriots who had been displaced as a result of the events of 1974. However, the Turkish Cypriots did not accept the revised plan, as they wanted Turkish troops to remain on the island indefinitely, to protect their interests, and they felt that any peace settlement must include Turkey as a guarantor. They had also revised their opinion on allowing Greek Cypriot refugees to return to the 'TRNC'.

1985 GREEK CYPRIOT ELECTIONS

President Kyprianou had come under severe criticism, from within the House of Representatives, over the failure of the 'summit' in January 1985. He reshuffled the Council of Ministers and terminated his alliance with the communist party, AKEL. This alliance had become increasingly strained, mainly because of Kyprianou's unyielding attitude to the intercommunal talks. In November, following an acrimonious debate over Kyprianou's leadership, the House of Representatives was dissolved. A general election was not due until May 1986, but the two largest parties, AKEL and the conservative DISY, had formed an alliance with the intention of achieving a two-thirds majority in the House, which would enable them, under Article 44, to amend the Constitution and so force an early presidential election. However, they were one vote short of the required majority.

A general election was held on 8 December 1985 for an enlarged House of 56 Greek Cypriot seats (compared with 35 previously), while the nominal allocation of seats to the Turkish Cypriot community was increased from 15 to 24. Significant gains were made by Kyprianou's DIKO party, although it remained a minority party. It won 16 seats and increased its share of the vote to 27.6% (compared with 19.5% in the 1981 election). The AKEL party suffered a setback, gaining only 15 seats, while its share of the vote fell to 27.4% from 32.8% in 1981. This ended a communist ascendancy in Greek Cypriot politics which dated back to the independence of Cyprus from Britain in 1960 (although AKEL partially recovered its position in the local elections in May 1986). The DISY party replaced AKEL as the largest party in the House by winning 19 seats, with 33.6% of the vote, compared with 31.9% in 1981. The socialist party, EDEK, which supported Kyprianou's stand on peace negotiations, won six seats with 11.1% of the vote, compared with 8.2% in 1981. Campaigning was dominated by two issues: the proposed peace plan and Kyprianou's argument that, constitutionally, the President was not bound by the decisions of the House. The result of the election was interpreted as evidence of widespread support for President Kyprianou's policies.

Further meetings to discuss the UN peace plan were conducted in March 1986. On this occasion the Turkish Cypriots accepted the draft peace plan (which was, still, based on the idea of establishing a bi-zonal federal republic, with specified posts and ratios for the Greek and Turkish Cypriot participants in the federal government) while the Greek Cypriots stated that it was no different from that put forward in January 1985 (which they had rejected). The Greek Cypriots' principal objections were that the plan failed to envisage: the withdrawal of the Turkish troops prior to implementation of the plan; the removal from Cyprus of settlers from the Turkish mainland; the provision of suitable international guarantors for the settlement, with the exclusion of Turkey; and the assurance of the 'three basic freedoms', namely the right to live, move and work anywhere in Cyprus. Kyprianou and the other Greek Cypriot leaders, as well as Prime Minister Papandreou of Greece, were all opposed to the plan but were careful not to reject it absolutely. They wanted a 'summit' meeting between the two leaders (Kyprianou and Denktaş) or an international conference to discuss the matter. The latter suggestion was first proposed by the USSR, which also suggested a complete withdrawal of all foreign troops from the island, including UNFICYP. President Denktaş, however, later stated that he would not accept an international conference which treated the Greek Cypriots as the official government of Cyprus and the Turkish Cypriots as a minority population. He said that, should such a conference be arranged, he would seek international recognition of the 'TRNC'.

In July 1986 Turgut Özal, the Prime Minister of Turkey, paid his first visit to the 'TRNC' and urged the adoption of an economic model similar to that in Turkey. The Toplumcu Kurtuluş Partisi (Communal Liberation Party) disagreed with this policy, and in August it withdrew from the coalition Government of the 'TRNC'. In September the Prime Minister, Dr Derviş Eroğlu, formed a new administration in coalition with the Yeni Doğuş Partisi (New Dawn Party, YDP).

In July 1987 it was reported that the Cyprus Government had proposed to the UN Secretary-General that the Cypriot National Guard be dissolved, and orders for military equipment cancelled, in exchange for the withdrawal of Turkish forces from the island. In an address to the UN General Assembly in October, President Kyprianou proposed an international peace-keeping force to replace the armed forces of both the Greek and Turkish Cypriots. President Denktaş, however, maintained that negotiations on the establishment of a federal bi-zonal republic should precede any demilitarization.

ELECTION OF VASSILIOU AS PRESIDENT

The first round of voting in presidential elections took place in the Greek Cypriot zone on 14 February 1988. There were four main candidates, including the incumbent President Kyprianou, who was seeking his third consecutive five-year term. The three other main candidates were: Georghios Vassiliou, who presented himself as an independent, but who was unofficially backed by the communist party, AKEL (although he, himself, was not a communist), Glavkos Klerides, the leader of the conservative DISY, and Dr Vassos Lyssarides, leader of the socialist EDEK. Since no candidate received more than 50% of the total vote, a second round was held a week later, to decide between the two candidates who had received the most votes—Glavkos Klerides, with 33.3% of the total vote, and Georghios Vassiliou, with 30.1%. Kyprianou was third, with 27.3% of the total vote. This surprising defeat was widely interpreted as a result of the failure of Kyprianou's hardline policies for the reunification of Cyprus. The outgoing President decided not to support either of the remaining presidential candidates. In the second round of voting, Georghios Vassiliou, with the backing of EDEK and a significant number of Kyprianou supporters, was elected as the new President by a narrow margin, with 167,834 votes (51.6% of the total), whilst Glavkos Klerides gained 157,228 votes (48.4%).

Although it was predicted that President Vassiliou would promote his predecessor's policies regarding a settlement for the divided island, he, unlike Kyprianou, quickly expressed his willingness to enter into direct informal dialogue with the Turkish Cypriot leader. Vassiliou also promised to re-establish the National Council, which was to include representatives from all the main Greek Cypriot political parties, to negotiate plans for the settlement of the Cyprus problem. On 28 February 1988 Vassiliou was officially sworn in as the new President and named his new nine-member Council of Ministers. On the same day, President Vassiliou proposed a meeting with the Turkish Prime Minister, Turgut Özal, to discuss the withdrawal of Turkish troops from Cyprus. Özal responded by claiming that Vassiliou's priority, as regards the Cyprus problem, should be to talk with President Denktaş of the 'TRNC'. In March Denktaş submitted a series of goodwill proposals to President Vassiliou, via the new Special Representative of the UN Secretary-General, Oscar Camilión. Vassiliou immediately rejected the proposals, which included a plan to form committees to study the possibilities of intercommunal co-operation. In the same month, President Vassiliou held talks with the Greek Prime Minister, Andreas Papandreou, in Athens, to examine the prospects for a Cyprus settlement. Papandreou said that, despite the recent breakthrough in Greco-Turkish relations, there could be no overall improvement unless progress was made towards solving the Cyprus problem.

RESUMPTION OF INTERCOMMUNAL TALKS

After a meeting with the newly-revived National Council in June 1988, President Vassiliou agreed to a proposal by the UN Secretary-General, Javier Pérez de Cuéllar, to resume inter-communal talks, without preconditions, with President Denktaş of the 'TRNC', in the capacity of the leaders of two communities. Following a meeting with the Turkish Government in July, Denktaş also approved the proposal. Consequently, the impasse between the two sides was ended and a Cyprus 'summit' meeting took place in Geneva on 24 August, under the auspices of the UN. At this 'summit', which was the first such meeting between Greek and Turkish Cypriot leaders since January 1985, President Vassiliou and President Denktaş resumed direct talks on a settlement of all aspects of the Cyprus problem. As a result of this meeting, the two leaders began the first formal round of substantive direct negotiations, under UN auspices, in Nicosia on 15 September. A target date of 1 June 1989 was, rather optimistically, set for the conclusion of a comprehensive political settlement. Despite several rounds of intensive direct talks, under the supervision of the UN, in Nicosia and New York, however, it became apparent, by the end of June 1989, that no real progress had been achieved as a result of the discussions. The general consensus seemed to be that, although the two leaders expressed their willingness that Cyprus should be reunited as

a bi-zonal federation, they disagreed on what form a government should take. In addition, attitudes regarding three issues due to which former talks had broken down (i.e. the withdrawal of Turkish troops, the right of Turkey to intervene as a guarantor, and the assurance of the 'three basic freedoms'—see above) appeared irreconcilable. Vassiliou and Denktaş agreed to hold another meeting with Javier Pérez de Cuéllar to review the intercommunal talks in New York in September 1989.

In mid-May 1989, under the supervision of the UNFICYP, a deconfrontation agreement (reached at the end of March) was implemented, which involved the withdrawal of Greek-Cypriot and Turkish-Cypriot troops from 24 military posts along the central Nicosia sector of the 'Attila line'. It was hoped that this limited withdrawal would reduce the tension (there were five fatal shootings reported during the period May 1988–December 1988), which persisted in this troubled area. In July, however, crowds of Greek-Cypriot women held angry demonstrations at the buffer zone to protest against the continuing partition of Cyprus. There was a dramatic escalation in tension when more than 100 protesters were arrested by the Turkish-Cypriot forces during the demonstration and were detained for several days.

ABORTIVE 1990 VASSILIOU—DENKTAŞ SUMMIT

Despite a relaxation, in November 1989, of entry restrictions for Greek Cypriots with compelling reasons to travel to the 'TRNC', no significant progress was made towards a political settlement in the first half of 1990. A new round of UN-sponsored talks, which began in late February 1990 in New York, came to a premature end in early March, following disagreement arising from demands by Rauf Denktaş that the right to self-determination of the Turkish Cypriots be recognized by the Greek Cypriot community. President Vassiliou accused Denktaş of deliberately frustrating hopes of a settlement by introducing new conditions to the negotiations and implicitly advocating some form of partition or secession. Denktaş, in turn, accused Vassiliou of refusing to consider any form of compromise. A resolution approved by the UN Security Council later in the month rejected Denktaş' stance and reaffirmed the UN's commitment to a resolution based on a bicommunal federal republic.

Later in March 1990 Denktaş resigned the presidency in order to call early presidential elections on 22 April. Denktaş, standing as an independent, received 66.7% of the votes cast, while İsmail Bozkurt, who also stood as an independent, received about 32%, and Alpay Durduran of the Yeni Kıbrıs Partisi (New Cyprus Party, YKP) slightly more than 1%. Denktaş' victory was widely interpreted as a sign of public approval of the President's stance throughout the recent negotiations with President Vassiliou, although opposition parties advocating a more conciliatory approach commanded significant support in the 'TRNC'.

The UBP retained its majority in the 'TRNC' Legislative Assembly at a general election on 6 May when it received 55% of the votes cast, thereby securing 34 of the 50 available seats. In June Denktaş approved the appointment of several newcomers to the Council of Ministers, which Derviş Eroğlu continued to head as Prime Minister. In local elections on 24 June the UBP consolidated its position when its candidates were elected to 14 out of a total of 22 mayoral positions.

Rumours in the Greek Cypriot zone of widespread disaffection within the communist party, AKEL, were substantiated in early 1990, when resignations and dismissals from the party's central committee and politburo followed calls for democratic reform of the party structure. At least five of the party's 15 parliamentary representatives were thought to belong to the dissident faction. A new political party, the Ananeotiko Demokratiko Sosialistiko Kinima (Democratic Socialist Reform Movement, ADISOK), was formed in April 1990, and was expected to attract many dissatisfied supporters of AKEL.

In July 1990 Cyprus formally applied for full membership of the European Community, although any expansion of the EC before 1993 had been declared unlikely. International observers regarded the political division within the island as a major obstacle to Cyprus's achieving member status, while

President Denktaş declared that the 'unilateral' application by the Greek Cypriots on behalf of the whole island would further complicate the search for a political settlement for Cyprus.

In July and October 1990, in retaliation for the EC application, the 'TRNC' Government and Turkey signed an agreement envisaging the creation of a customs union, the abolition of passport controls and the introduction of a 'TRNC' currency backed by the Central Bank of Turkey. These 'unilateral' steps were condemned by the Greek Cypriot Government, which claimed that the 'TRNC' was also actively planning to settle sensitive northern areas, such as Varosha, with Palestinians and Bulgarian Turkish immigrants. (In June 1989 President Denktaş had publicly advocated the transfer of Bulgarian Turkish refugees from Turkey to the 'TRNC' but the Turkish Government had declined the offer.)

UN-sponsored efforts to revive intercommunal talks on the Cyprus question were hindered by international preoccupation with the conflict in the Persian (Arabian) Gulf after August 1990. As a supporter of the multinational coalition against Iraq, the Vassiliou Government drew parallels between the Iraqi invasion of Kuwait and the Turkish occupation of northern Cyprus in 1974. The 'TRNC' and Turkish authorities, however, maintained that any similarities lay rather with the attempted Greek military takeover of Cyprus in 1974, which had precipitated the Turkish action. Of the obstacles to an outline agreement as proposed by the UN, the most intractable remained the demands of the Turkish Cypriots for recognition as a 'people' with the right to self-determination in UN terms, a demand which was interpreted by the Greek Cypriots as a desire for distinct sovereignty. Another major point of contention remained each side's rejection of the other's preferred negotiating framework: whereas the Greek Cypriots, with support from Greece, advocated a UN-chaired conference to be attended by the five permanent members of the UN Security Council, the Turkish Cypriots, with Turkish support, favoured a conference at which participation would be limited to representatives of the Turkish and Greek Cypriot sectors as well as Turkey and Greece.

While efforts to resume the negotiating process revolved mainly around the UN and the US Government, the Greek Cypriots also attached importance to the potential role of the EC and the newly-institutionalized Conference on Security and Co-operation in Europe (CSCE). In November 1990 President Vassiliou urged the CSCE to consider the plight of Cyprus in the context of its situation as 'the only European country facing foreign occupation'. In April 1991 the EC Ministers of Foreign Affairs authorized Luxembourg (the presiding member nation at that time) to organize an independent diplomatic initiative for Cyprus, to be co-ordinated with that of the UN.

1991 GREEK CYPRIOT ELECTIONS

In general elections for the 56 Greek Cypriot seats in the House of Representatives, which took place on 19 May 1991, campaigning focused on economic and social issues, there being only marginal policy differences between the parties regarding the Cyprus issue. The conservative DISY party, in alliance with the Liberal Party (Komma Phileleftheron), received 35.8% of the votes cast (2.2% more than in 1985) and secured 20 seats, representing a gain of one seat. The AKEL communists, despite competition from ADISOK, unexpectedly achieved the biggest advance, with 30.6% of the vote and 18 seats, representing a gain of three seats. The EDEK socialists also gained ground by securing seven seats in the House, while support for the 'centrist' DIKO party decreased from 27.6% of votes cast and 16 seats in 1985 to 19.5% of the vote and just 11 seats in 1991. Both ADISOK and PAKOP (a new party representing refugees) failed to win a seat in the House.

On 30 May 1991, at the inaugural meeting of the newly-constituted House of Representatives, Alexis Ghalanos (the former parliamentary spokesman for DIKO) was elected President of the House in succession to the EDEK leader, Dr Vassos Lyssarides.

RESUMPTION OF UN-SPONSORED TALKS, 1991–92

US diplomatic efforts resulted in an announcement, made by President Bush on 2 August 1991, that the Greek and Turkish Prime Ministers had confirmed their willingness to attend a UN-sponsored conference in New York with the aim of finding a solution to the Cyprus question. However, although Presidents Vassiliou and Denktaş declared their support for this initiative, hopes of a breakthrough receded when the UN Secretary-General made it clear that the conference would not be convened unless progress had been made on resolving outstanding differences. No such progress being immediately apparent, the Bush schedule for a conference in September 1991 was not met. In a report to the UN Security Council in October 1991, the Secretary-General stated that in the latest discussions Denktaş has asserted 'that each side possessed a sovereignty which it would retain after the establishment of a federation, including the right of secession', and had sought 'extensive changes in the text of the ideas that were discussed'. Recalling that the UN Security Council had 'posited a solution based on the existence of one state of Cyprus comprising two communities', he concluded that the introduction of the Denktaş concept would 'fundamentally alter the nature of the solution' as envisaged previously.

On taking office on 1 January 1992, the new UN Secretary-General, Dr Boutros Boutros Ghali, initiated another attempt to establish the basis for a high-level conference on Cyprus. To this end, UN envoys visited Cyprus, Turkey and Greece in February, and Dr Boutros Ghali had meetings in New York with Presidents Vassiliou and Denktaş in January and March. However, in a report to the Security Council in April 1992, the UN Secretary-General advised that no progress had been made towards resolving basic disagreements and that 'there has even been regression'. Although there was a measure of agreement on the shape of a federal government structure, the issues of 'territorial adjustment' and the return of displaced persons remained serious problems. In a resolution adopted on 10 April, the Security Council reaffirmed that a settlement 'must be based on a state of Cyprus with a single sovereignty and international personality and a single citizenship, with its independence and territorial integrity safeguarded, and comprising two politically equal communities'.

In accordance with Security Council instructions, Dr Boutros Ghali had further separate talks with Presidents Vassiliou and Denktaş in New York in June 1992, when deliberations centred on UN proposals for the demarcation of Greek Cypriot and Turkish Cypriot areas of administration under a federal structure. In view of the reluctance of the parties to discuss lines on a map, the cartographic ideas put forward by Dr Boutros Ghali were described as a 'non-map'. Although both sides undertook to observe a news blackout on the talks, pending a further round in mid-July, the Boutros Ghali 'non-map' was published by the Turkish Cypriot press on 30 June. It showed that the area of Turkish administration would be about 25% smaller than the 'TRNC', from whose present territory the Greek Cypriots would recover the towns of Morphou and Varosha (although not old Famagusta) and a total of 34 villages. According to the published details, the new division would, among other things, create a Turkish enclave to the east of Nicosia and a Greek enclave in the north-east tip of the island. It was estimated that under the UN plan some 60,000 displaced Greek Cypriots would be able to return to their pre-1974 homes and remain under Greek Cypriot administration.

While denying that he had leaked details of the 'non-map' (which were eventually released by the UN in August), Denktaş seized the opportunity presented by its publication to assert that its proposals were totally unacceptable to the 'TRNC' Government. On the Greek Cypriot side, government spokesmen took the view that the disclosure of the UN plan was a ploy by which the Turkish Cypriots hoped to gain negotiating leverage. As regards the content of the 'non-map' and related ideas for a settlement, Greek Cypriot opinion was divided: whereas AKEL and DISY continued to express broad support for President Vassiliou's conduct of the negotiatons, DIKO and EDEK spokesmen declared that the UN plan would entrench an unacceptable partition of the island. Greek Cypriot critics of the emerging proposals also complained that there appeared to be no provision for the removal of post-1974 Turkish settlers from Cyprus. Among prominent opponents of the UN plan was Archbishop Chrysostomos, who stated that the Church of Cyprus could not accept any permanent surrender of Greek land to the Turks.

Following further unsuccessful UN-sponsored talks, conducted in New York during October and November 1992, the Secretary-General took the unusual step of publishing a tabulation of the respective responses to his settlement ideas. This revealed that, whereas the Greek Cypriot side accepted the proposals and the UN map as the basis for a negotiated settlement, the Turkish Cypriot side had reservations with regard to nine of the 100 articles, all of which dealt with crucial matters. The tabulation demonstrated that, apart from the basic issues of sovereignty and territorial division, the Turkish Cypriots were continuing to insist that the posts of federal President and Vice-President should rotate between the two communities and that the federal Government should contain an equal number of Greek Cypriot and Turkish Cypriot ministers. The Greek Cypriots proposed that the two premier positions should be decided by 'federation-wide and weighted universal suffrage', and also endorsed the UN proposal that there should be a 7:3 ratio of Greek Cypriot and Turkish Cypriot ministers, although they accepted that a Turkish Cypriot should normally hold one of the three main portfolios of foreign affairs, finance and defence. Moreover, while both sides accepted the 'security and guarantees' section of the UN proposition (including provisions for the withdrawal of all non-Cypriot forces), considerable disagreement persisted as to whether or not the 1959 treaty of guarantee afforded Turkey a unilateral right of intervention in Cyprus.

Reporting to the UN Security Council on the failure of the latest round of negotiations, the Secretary-General noted that a 'lack of political will . . . continues to block the conclusion of an agreement', adding that 'it is essential that the Turkish Cypriot side adjust its position'. This assessment was reflected in the resultant Security Council Resolution 789, adopted in late November, which also incorporated a set of proposed confidence-building measures. These included a reduction in the level of armed forces on both sides, the extension of the UN security zone to include the disputed Varosha suburb of Famagusta, the easing of restrictions on 'people to people' contacts and the reopening of Nicosia international airport.

GREEK AND TURKISH CYPRIOT ELECTIONS, 1993

The veteran DISY leader, Glavkos Klerides, was the unexpected victor in Greek Cypriot presidential elections conducted in two rounds on 7 and 14 February 1993, narrowly defeating Vassiliou's bid for a second term. Standing, once again, as an independent with AKEL support, Vassiliou headed the first-round voting with 44.2%, compared with 36.7% for Klerides and 18.6% for a joint DIKO-EDEK candidate, Paschalis Paschalides. Although DISY had previously declared its support for the Government's conduct of the settlement negotiations, in the election campaign Klerides distanced himself from Vassiliou's stance. This enabled DIKO and EDEK, both strongly opposed to the UN plan, to transfer their support to Klerides, who won 50.3% of the second-round vote compared with 49.7% for Vassiliou. The new Government, appointed by the President-elect on 25 February, contained six DISY ministers and five from DIKO.

Despite his long-standing personal relationship with Denktaş, Klerides failed to obtain any significant compromise in the Turkish Cypriots' declared objections to the measures at reconvened talks in New York during May and June 1993.

Denktaş tabled counter-proposals urging international recognition of certain other parts of Turkish-controlled northern Cyprus, but these were interpreted by Klerides as an attempt to obtain a degree of international acceptance of the division of Cyprus, in opposition to the Greek Cypriot (and UN) insistence that the island should remain a single state.

Despite the recommendation of the new Turkish President, Süleyman Demirel, that Denktaş should adopt a more conciliatory approach to the negotiations, Denktaş failed to meet the Secretary-General's proposed deadline of mid-June for acceptance of the confidence-building measures. A mission to Athens, Cyprus and Ankara, undertaken by the UN Secretary-General's new Special Representative in Cyprus, Joe Clark, failed to foster any significant new initiative for peace.

An early general election in the 'TRNC' on 12 December 1993 partially resolved a long power-struggle between Denktaş and the Prime Minister, Derviş Eroğlu, in the former's favour. The UBP, once led by Denktaş but now advocating Eroğlu's openly pro-partition stance, remained the largest party in the Legislative Assembly, but failed to win an overall majority. The pro-Denktaş Democrat Party (DP) and the left-wing Republican Turkish Party (CTP) thereupon agreed to form a coalition under the premiership of Hakki Atun, the DP leader (hitherto the Speaker of the Assembly). The new coalition supported the Denktaş policy that talks should continue, while at the same time confirming policy positions likely to ensure continued deadlock.

DEADLOCK ON CONFIDENCE-BUILDING MEASURES

Negotiations in the first half of 1994 on the UN-sponsored confidence-building measures (CBMs) centred on the proposed transfer to UN administration of the Turkish-held Varosha suburb of Famagusta (so that its former Greek Cypriot inhabitants might then return) and the reopening of Nicosia airport for use by both sides. Despite a further visit by Clark in May, no agreement could be reached, in particular because Denktaş claimed that the proposals envisaged greater concessions by the Turkish Cypriots than by the Greek Cypriots. In his report submitted to the Security Council in May, the UN Secretary-General again censured the Turkish Cypriot side for failing to show the political will needed to produce a settlement. In the following month, however, he amended this verdict by stating that there was 'a very substantial measure of agreement' and that the only obstacle to implementation of the CMBs was disputed methodology. The Greek Cypriots reacted angrily that this assessment did not give 'the true picture' of the persisting differences between the two sides.

In a concurrent deterioration, Denktaş warned, on 30 May 1994, that, if Greek Cyprus was admitted to the European Community (now Union—EU) without reference to the Turkish Cypriots, the 'TRNC' would opt for integration with Turkey. However, this warning did not deter Greek Cypriot spokesmen from welcoming an EU decision, in June, that Cyprus would be included in the next phase of enlargement (i.e. after the prospective admission of Austria, Finland, Norway and Sweden in January 1995). The Greek Cypriot Government was also gratified by a ruling of the European Court of Justice on 5 July, banning EU members from importing goods from the 'TRNC' (see Economy section). This ruling was condemned by the 'TRNC' authorities, who proceeded to organize large-scale public celebrations to commemorate the 20th anniversary of the 1974 Turkish invasion of the island. In late August the 'TRNC' Legislative Assembly voted to reject any solution to the Cyprus problem based on a federation.

Economy

Revised for this edition by ALAN J. DAY.

Geographically, Cyprus may be divided into four regions, distinguished by their natural and climatic features. These are the northern coastal belt, including the narrow Kyrenia mountain chain; the central plain, known as the Mesaoria, from Famagusta and Larnaca to Morphou Bay; the mountainous area of the south-centre, dominated by the Troödos massif, with the summit of Mt Olympus (1,951 m or 6,403 ft above sea-level) as its highest point; and the coastal plain of the south, running from a point west of Larnaca to Limassol and Paphos.

Since the middle of 1974, however, the most important division in Cyprus has been that between the areas to the north and south of the 'Attila line' which divides the island (see map, p. 327). The northern two-fifths of the country, under Turkish Cypriot control, is closely linked to the economy of Turkey, and has almost no economic contact with the south of the island. The unilateral declaration of independence by the Turkish Cypriots in November 1983 reinforced the economic embargo, which has caused serious problems for the northern sector. Both areas suffered severe disruption as a result of the events of 1974. As well as the physical damage caused by the fighting, more than one-third of the total population of around 640,000 became refugees, some 180,000 Greek Cypriots fleeing to the south and about 45,000 Turkish Cypriots moving to the north. The collapse of essential services in many places reduced economic activity to a low level. Crops were not harvested, tourism ceased, and industrial buildings and plant were destroyed or lost their workforce.

THE SOUTHERN ECONOMY

Since 1974 the economies to the north and the south of the 'Attila line' have diverged. The economy of the south made a remarkable recovery, despite having lost 38% of the island's territory, 70% of its productive resources, 30% of its factories, 60% of the tourist installations, the main port (Famagusta) and 80% of the citrus fruit groves, all of which were on the northern side of the line. In 1975 the gross domestic product (GDP) was only two-thirds of the 1973 level, but during 1976 and 1977 production rose at an average of 18% per year. Even with the growth rate falling to an average 7% annually during 1978 and 1979, at the end of that period, production in the southern part of the island was 12% higher than for the whole of Cyprus in 1973. Unemployment was reduced from almost 25% of the labour force in late 1974 to 1.8% in 1979, partly by the emigration of workers but largely through the promotion of labour-intensive industry and massive expansion of the construction sector, both for private housing and development projects.

By 1980, however, it was clear that the post-1976 boom in the Cypriot economy would not continue at the same level. This was partly the result of the disappearance of short-term factors which had favoured growth: in 1977 market conditions in the Middle East and Europe were advantageous to Cypriot exports, and petroleum prices were temporarily stable, whereas by 1979 it was becoming difficult for agricultural products from Cyprus to penetrate the European market, while petroleum prices were once more rising sharply. However, there was also a deeper instability in the economy. Recovery was based on labour-intensive production by a low-wage workforce—wages in 1976 were lower than in 1973—but, with full employment from 1977, wage rises escalated. Between 1976 and 1979 real wages increased by an average 10% annually, and in 1980 average wages rose by 20%, not allowing for inflation, or by 6.5% in real terms. Rising wages and the increasing cost of imported petroleum, among other factors, helped to increase inflation, from an annual average of 4% in 1976–77, to 9.8% in 1979 and 13.4% in 1980. The Cyprus Government was also faced with a growing balance-of-payments deficit and a budgetary deficit. Economic growth had been stimulated by tax incentives and direct government investment in development projects. Consequently, revenue

failed to keep pace with expenditure. Despite loans from international agencies and foreign governments and extensive borrowing abroad, Cyprus's reserves in 1980 were perilously low. The Government adopted a stabilization programme which was designed to reduce imports, to cut the budget deficit and to limit inflation. As a result, inflation declined from 10.8% in 1981 to 5% in 1985. The trade deficit continued to widen, however, despite a reduction in visible imports in 1985. It rose from C£345.2m. in 1983 to C£413.2m. in 1984, and to C£431.8m. in 1985. The deficit on the current account of the balance of payments, however, returned to 1983 levels, owing to an increase in earnings from tourism, which reduced the deficit to C£98.7m. in 1985, compared with C£116.7m. in 1984 and C£93.4m. in 1983.

Having grown by an annual average of 5.6% between 1980 and 1985, real GDP increased by 7.1% in 1987, by 8.6% in 1988, by 8.0% in 1989 and by 7.3% in 1990. The rate of growth was only 1.2% in 1991, but rose to 8.5% in 1992. The Government's Five-Year Economic Plan for the period 1989–93, adopted in June 1989, envisaged annual growth of 5%. However, in 1993 the rate was reduced to only 1%, owing to the effects on the Cyprus economy of the European recession. In 1992, according to estimates by the World Bank, Cyprus's gross national product (GNP), measured at average 1990–92 prices, was US $7,070m., equivalent to $9,820 per head, significantly greater than that of Greece and at least three times that of the 'TRNC'. According to independent estimates, Cyprus's GNP per head rose to $10,735 in 1993, more than six times the estimated figure of $1,642 in the 'TRNC'. In August 1991, in view of this encouraging economic performance, the World Bank removed Cyprus from its official list of developing countries, thereby ending Cyprus's qualification for development loans at preferential rates. The average level of unemployment decreased steadily from 3.6% of the registered labour force in 1986 to 1.8% in 1990, rising again to 2.3% in 1991, but falling to 1.8% in 1992, before rising to 2.5% on average in 1993, during the last months of which the rate rose to more than 3%. After a reduction in the annual rate of inflation to 1.2% in 1986 (its lowest point in 20 years), an increase in economic activity caused the rate to rise again, reaching 4.5% in 1990, 5% in 1991, 6.5% in 1992 and 4.9% in 1993.

The 1991 budget, adopted by the House of Representatives in December 1990, provided for total expenditure of C£835.7m. (including C£181.7m. for a supplementary defence budget) and aimed to reduce the budget deficit to 1.9% of GDP (from 2.6% in 1989). Among the provisions of the new budget were measures designed to encourage investment in industry, while the maximum rate of income tax was reduced to 40%. In fact, the 1991 budget deficit amounted to C£135m. (4.8% of GDP). The 1992 budget, in its final form, contained provision for total government expenditure of C£965.2m. and revenues of C£848.5m., thus envisaging a deficit of C£116.7m. (3.9% of GDP). The anticipated revenue total included receipts from value-added tax (VAT), which was introduced on 1 July 1992 at a rate of 5% on consumer goods and services (food and other basic items being zero rated). Under the terms of an austerity programme, introduced by the Government in May 1993 (see below), the rate of VAT was increased to 8%.

An 8% increase in the cost of imports caused the trade deficit to rise to C£413.4m. in 1987. An increase in revenues from tourism helped to reduce the current account deficit by 96% to C£3.5m. in 1986. In 1987 a surplus of C£50m. was recorded. This was the first current-account surplus for 20 years and was largely due to a 14% increase in exports and the continuing growth in tourism. In 1988 there was a current account surplus of C£3.7m., but in 1989 the trade deficit increased to C£587.8m. while the current account showed a surplus of C£15.8m. In 1990 the trade deficit widened to C£651.3m., but an increase in invisible earnings produced a current-account surplus of C£40.6m. In 1991 the trade deficit increased to C£687.6m., while lower receipts from tourism resulted in a current-account deficit of C£88m. Foreign exchange reserves increased by C£161m. in the 12 months to the end of 1990, totalling C£955m. A trade deficit of C£887m. was recorded in 1992, but income from non-merchandise transactions limited the deficit on the balance of payments to C£130m. (compared with C£32m. in 1991). By the end of 1992 gross reserves of foreign exchange totalled C£1,137.2m., compared with C£1,071.3m. at the end of 1991. In 1993 the trade deficit fell to C£829.6m. and the current-account deficit fell to C£33m. (1% of GDP) from C£275m. (9% of GDP) in 1992, as a result of which the overall balance of payment went into surplus. At the end of 1993 gross foreign exchange reserves totalled C£1,340m. and net reserves C£190m. (compared with C£131.6m. at the end of 1992).

The 1980s saw a diversification of the Greek Cypriot economy, with less reliance being placed on the agricultural sector, and increased emphasis on the development of more broadly-based services and industrial sectors, particularly tourism, shipping and financial services. One of the main problems facing the economy, however, is the continuing high level of foreign debt. Public and publicly-guaranteed medium- and long-term debt had increased to C£754m. by the end of 1989, rising to C£1,047m. (equivalent to 32.3% of annual GNP) at the end of 1993.

The Greek Cypriot economy was adversely affected by the crisis in the Persian (Arabian) Gulf region in 1990 and 1991 and the consequent embargo on trade with Iraq, which had supplied 70% of the island's oil imports. Disruption to the eastern Mediterranean significantly weakened the tourist, shipping and manufacturing sectors. Following the resolution of the crisis in February 1991, however, the economy recovered its forward impetus. Although overall growth in GDP declined to 1.2% in 1991, a rapid recovery, particularly of tourism and financial services, produced a growth rate of 8.5% in 1992. A feature of economic policy in 1992 was the gradual adaptation of economic practices and procedures to prepare for full membership of the European Community (EC, now the European Union—EU), for which the Cyprus Government had applied in July 1990 (having achieved customs union with the EC from 1 January 1988). In addition to the introduction of VAT (see above), in June 1992 the Government linked the Cyprus pound to the narrow band of the EC's exchange rate mechanism (ERM).

The departure of the United Kingdom (the island's principal trading partner) from the ERM in September 1992, and the subsequent devaluation of sterling, had an adverse effect on trade with the UK, and also contributed to a decline in tourist arrivals from the UK during 1993. Nevertheless, both the Vassiliou administration and its successor expressed support for a policy of economic harmonization with EC guidelines, including those detailed in the Treaty on European Union (which had been agreed by EC heads of government at Maastricht, the Netherlands, in December 1991) for eventual economic and monetary union. Full achievement of the Maastricht 'convergence' criteria was identified as a central objective of the proposed 1993–98 Five-Year Economic Plan. On 1 January 1993 the pensionable age for men in the government-controlled area was reduced from 65 to 63 years, thereby establishing parity with the existing pensionable age for women.

A feature of the election campaign which preceded the change of government in February 1993 was the contrast in assessment of the state of the economy expounded by Vassiliou and by the opposition. While the former stressed the high rate of growth and low rate of unemployment, the latter focused on the burgeoning budget deficit, claiming that Cyprus was heading for economic crisis. In May 1993 the new Government announced a programme of austerity measures designed to reduce the budget deficit and the public debt (which totalled C£2,400m.). An increase in the rate of VAT from 5% to 8% was to take effect from October 1993, while new, higher taxes were to be imposed on petrol and cigarettes. A proposed end to the index-linking of wages to inflation encountered considerable opposition from trade unions. However, the economic stance of the new Government received endorsement from an IMF report, published in July, which warned that wage increases were surpassing productivity gains and

eroding competitiveness, and from the Governor of the Central Bank of Cyprus, who, later in the month, urged broader deregulation of capital markets and speedier progress towards trade liberalization.

The aggregate budget for 1993 provided for total expenditure of C£1,060m., compared with anticipated revenue of C£815m. The comparable budget for 1994 envisaged expenditure of C£1,061m., also against revenue of C£815m. The main items of development expenditure under the 1994 budget were the road network (C£43.5m.), water development (C£19.4m.), education (C£17.5m.), public construction (C£13.6m.) and airports (C£10.2m.). The fiscal deficit in 1993 was estimated at 4.8% of GDP (about the same level as in 1992), the 1994 target being a reduction to 3.7% of GDP.

THE NORTHERN ECONOMY

Since 1974 the economy of the area north of the 'Attila line' has not made nearly as much progress as the Greek Cypriot area, despite an extensive programme of development, based on aid from Turkey (estimated to amount to some 20% of projected budget expenditure in recent years). Initial development priorities of the 'TRNC' authorities were the improvement of communications, irrigation, and the restoration of damaged citrus groves, in the pursuit of which the methods of central planning were used for some years. Beginning in 1978, successive development plans aimed, according to official statements, 'to secure the achievement of the highest rate of growth compatible with the maintenance of economic stability'. Other goals included increased capital investment, particularly in tourism and industry, balance-of-payments improvement, 'the more equitable distribution of economic burdens and national income', and 'the further expansion and improvement of the financial sector and social services'. From 1987, however, the emphasis switched to the encouragement of free-market economic activity, with priority being given to the development of trade, tourism, banking, education, transportation and the industrial sector.

Assessment of the real performance of the 'TRNC' economy has been notoriously difficult, because of the lack of objective data. Much of the statistical material issued by the northern authorities is not regarded as accurate by the Greek Cypriot side (or by many independent observers). According to official 'TRNC' figures, northern GNP increased by 87% in the period 1977–92, measured in constant 1977 prices. However, the annual growth target of 7.5% during the first Five-Year Plan (1978–82) was not thought to have been achieved: in 1980 and 1981, for example, the 'TRNC' economy was reported to have contracted. By the final year of the second Five-Year Plan (1983–87) GNP had officially risen to TL5,684m. (at 1977 prices), compared with TL4,038m. in 1977. The targets of the third Five-Year Plan (1988–92) included an annual growth rate of 7%, but the outturn was officially assessed at 4.6%. Measured in 1977 prices, total GNP reached TL7,125m. in 1992, according to official figures, which also claimed that GNP per head had increased by 66.4% over the period of the plan, to stand at US $3,343 in 1992 (compared with $2,009 in 1987). Independent observers, however, estimated annual GNP per head to be no higher than $1,650 in both 1992 and 1993. The sectors which were reported to have contributed most to economic growth in 1988–92 were manufacturing, construction, tourism and services, which yielded average annual growth rates of 9.2%, 7.7%, 9.6% and 7.2% respectively. GNP was officially projected to grow by 1.5% in 1993, while the 1994 Annual Programme aimed at 6.1% growth (at 1993 prices).

Total local revenues, according to official reports, showed 'an ascending tendency' during the period 1987–92, with an average annual growth rate of 5.9%. During the same period total budgetary expenditures increased by 3% annually, whereas as a proportion of GNP they declined from 36.7% to 33.9%. As a result, the ratio of budget deficit to GNP was reduced from 16.3% to 12.2%, and to total budget from 44.3% to 36%. On 1 July 1992, in partial parallel to Greek Cypriot policy, the 'TRNC' Government introduced VAT on consumer goods, at a rate of 10% (compared with the introductory rate of 5% in the south). The 1993 budget envisaged a 9.9% increase in total local revenues, while expenditure and the budget deficit were projected to increase by 7.6% and 3.5% respectively; these targets implied a ratio of revenue, expenditure and deficit to GNP of 23.5%, 35.9% and 12.4% respectively. In the 1994 Annual Programme total local revenues were projected to increase by 5.4% at 1993 prices, the growth targets for expenditure and budget deficit being 4.6% and 3% respectively.

The 'TRNC' has experienced a persistently high level of inflation, much of it 'imported' from Turkey, in that the Turkish lira is the currency in use and the local authorities have no control over the money supply. Having reached 93% in 1980, the annual inflation rate fell to 33% in 1982, but then rose again to an estimated 69% in 1990, before again dipping to 61% in 1993 and a projected 60% in 1994. Agreements that Turkey and the 'TRNC' signed in 1990 envisaged the eventual replacement of the Turkish lira in the north by a local currency, backed by the Turkish Central Bank (as well as the creation of a full customs union between the two entities), but no substantive progress had been made on these goals by mid-1994. The official unemployment rate remained low in the 'TRNC', despite an increase of 11.8% in the working population in the period 1987–92, to a total of 74,037 (projected to increase to 76,793 in 1994). According to official figures, the unemployment rate declined from 1.8% of the labour force in 1987 to 0.8% (or 568 persons) in 1993.

The liberal trade policies adopted by the 'TRNC' since 1987 have resulted in the establishment of trading relations with over 60 countries. Its volume of trade was officially said to have increased from US \$276.1m. in 1987 to \$426m. in 1992, with imports increasing by 68% from \$221m. to \$371.4m. and exports decreasing from \$55.1m. to \$54.6m., with the result that the trade deficit grew from \$165.9m. in 1987 to \$316.8m. in 1992. Net tourism revenues rose from \$103.5m. in 1987 to \$175.1m. in 1992 (i.e. by an annual average of 11%), while other invisible earnings increased by 15% per annum, so that the current-account deficit in 1992 was only \$23.4m. Moreover, a positive capital movements balance, of \$41.7m. in 1992, produced an overall balance-of-payments surplus of \$18.3m. in 1992, compared with \$23.1m. in 1987. The 1993 trade deficit was projected to decline by 12.5% to \$277.2m. in 1993, but was expected to rise to \$291.1m. in 1994, balanced by a projected increase in net tourism revenues to \$189.6m. in 1993 and to \$206.9m. in 1994.

From August 1990 the northern economy encountered major difficulties as a result of the collapse, with debts of some £1,300m., of Polly Peck International, a fruit-packaging, tourism and publishing conglomerate based in the United Kingdom but with substantial interests in the 'TRNC'. In December 1990 charges of theft and fraud were preferred against the Turkish Cypriot chairman of the conglomerate, Asil Nadir, whose various companies were estimated to have provided more than one-third of the GDP in the 'TRNC', accounting for 60% of total exports. Pending Nadir's trial, British administrators of the collapsed concern attempted to locate the conglomerate's assets in the 'TRNC', but encountered legal and political obstacles. Further complications arose when Greek Cypriot authorities claimed that several of Polly Peck's major properties in the 'TRNC' had been expropriated from Greek Cypriots after 1974. In May 1993 Nadir fled to the 'TRNC', claiming that he could not expect a fair trial from the British authorities. It was reported that he intended to revive the remnants of the Polly Peck empire in northern Cyprus. Whether or not he had the official support of the 'TRNC' authorities in this endeavour remained unclear.

Further prospective damage was done to the 'TRNC' economy by a European Court of Justice ruling on 6 July 1994, banning EU member states from importing goods originating from the 'TRNC'. Under an earlier decision, the Council of Ministers of the then EC had enjoined in 1983 that exports from the Turkish-controlled area of Cyprus would be allowed to enter EC countries only if accompanied by documents from the Greek Cypriot Government, and that such goods also had to pass through ports controlled by that administration. However, this restriction had been evaded by the 'TRNC' by use of Turkey as an export channel, and the United Kingdom, in particular, had been prepared to import goods from northern Cyprus as long as the export documents did not bear the stamp of the 'TRNC'. The Court ruling said, *inter alia*, that 'co-operation is excluded with the authorities of an entity such as that established in the northern part of Cyprus, which is recognized neither by the Community nor by the member states'.

AGRICULTURE

Until quite recently agriculture was the most important single economic activity in Cyprus, but in recent years, in the Greek Cypriot sector, agriculture has been superseded in importance by tourism, manufacturing and financial services. In 1974 agriculture employed 33% of the island's labour force. In 1992 some 25% of the northern sector's working population were engaged in agriculture, compared with about 13% of the employed labour force in the south. In the early 1990s the agricultural sector contributed about 12% of GDP in the north and around 6% in the south. The chief crops are citrus fruits, potatoes, carrots, grapes, carobs, tobacco, wheat and barley.

After the division of the island in 1974, the Government of the Republic of Cyprus initiated a series of emergency development plans in which agriculture and irrigation featured prominently. Loans were given to farmers, and agricultural production responded rapidly. Most of the island's citrus trees were in the north, so they were replaced as the main agricultural product in the south by potatoes and other vegetables. Total exports of agricultural products (mainly citrus fruits and potatoes) accounted for more than one-third of the value of all domestic exports from the government-controlled area in 1977. Following a disappointing year in 1978, exports of fruit and vegetables recovered in 1979, owing largely to an increase in the production and export of citrus fruits, grapes and wine. Although potatoes remained the single most important crop, the importance of fruits and wine continued to grow throughout the early 1980s. Record agricultural exports were achieved in 1984, owing principally to an outstanding potato crop, and agriculture's contribution to GDP increased by 9.3%. This was followed by a severe overall decline in 1985, owing to adverse climatic conditions which affected potato production in particular and reduced agriculture's share of GDP by 1%. Having declined again in 1986, the sector's contribution to GDP increased by 5.3%, in real terms, in 1987, although a significant increase in the volume of manufactured exports reduced the sector's share of the total value of domestic exports to 22%, compared with 26% in 1986. This share decreased again in 1988 to less than 20% but revived to 21% in 1989, when agricultural exports were valued at C£51.7m. In 1990 drought conditions restricted production to 1989 levels, but significantly higher export prices for potatoes and citrus fruits resulted in an increase in the value of agricultural exports to C£65m., representing 25% of the value of total domestic exports. Potato exports increased in value to some C£30m. in 1990 (from C£16m. in 1988 and C£21m. in 1989), while the value of exports of citrus fruits increased to C£21m. (from C£14m. in 1988 and C£17m. in 1989). In 1991 total agricultural exports were valued at C£59m., representing a decline in overall production of 12%.

Despite a damaging frost in the early months of 1992, agricultural production during the year increased by some 15%, although the value of exports, which reached C£47.5m. (including C£21.8m. for potatoes), was diminished by a marked deterioration in quality. Production of vegetables was sufficient to bring about a reduction in domestic prices, although the value of exports was 17% less than that registered in 1991. Exports of citrus fruit decreased from 102,411 tons in 1991 to 94,374 tons in 1992 (an increase in production of lemons and mandarines was undermined by a decline in exports of oranges and grapefruit). Production of grapes increased to 110,000 tons (from 90,000 tons in 1991), while cereal production trebled to a record level of more than 180,000 tons. Meanwhile, meat production increased by 4% during 1992. During the period 1989–92 agricultural production increased by an average of 1.5% annually. Failure to attain the planning target of 2.5% was due mainly to the effects of periodic drought conditions.

The Paphos project, completed in 1983 at a cost of C£24m., involved the irrigation of some 5,000 ha along the south-western coast, to facilitate the production of tropical fruits such as mango, avocado and papaya, as well as grapes and early vegetables. The Government is currently working on the Southern Conveyor Project, the completed first phase of which carries water from the mountainous region of western Cyprus to the main potato-growing area in the south-east of the island. The second phase of the project, scheduled for completion in 1993, will increase water supplies to Nicosia, Larnaca and Limassol. The project is the largest water treatment and irrigation programme ever undertaken on the island, and total costs are expected to amount to C£175m. Another major investment is the Pitsilia Integrated Rural Development Project, which aims to stem the tide of rural depopulation by doubling the irrigated area in the mountainous central regions of the island. In early 1992 the Greek Cypriot Government approved initial plans for the construction of a number of desalination plants, intended to compensate for the occasional shortfall in water resources resulting from inconsistent rainfall. The first such plant was scheduled for construction at Dhekelia.

The Turkish Cypriot north inherited about 80% of the island's citrus groves, all the tobacco fields, 40% of the carobs, 80% of carrots and 10%–15% of potatoes. Nevertheless, agriculture in the north has lagged behind that of the south. In the chaos which followed the fighting, many citrus trees were neglected and died, or contracted diseases. Production has resumed gradually, with exports of citrus fruit rising from 66,174 tons in 1976/77 to 96,637 tons in 1980 and 115,163 tons in 1982. The growing importance of citrus fruit in the Turkish Cypriot economy was reflected in the fact that the value of citrus fruit exports in 1986 totalled US $28.5m. (54.8% of total export revenue), although in 1987 the value of citrus fruit exports declined to $22.5m. and the proportion of total export revenue derived from citrus fruit decreased to 40.9%. Potatoes, carobs and tobacco are also exported. In 1990–91 the collapse of Polly Peck International (see above) seriously disrupted the northern citrus fruit industry, resulting in plant closures and severely reducing export volumes. In 1992 57% of northern exports (by value) were agricultural products.

INDUSTRY

Industry, also, was severely affected by the war of 1974. It was estimated that the Greek Cypriots lost 70% of gross domestic manufacturing output, yet the growth of this sector since 1975 has been spectacular. Government incentives for investment, combined with a decline in real wages, stimulated a rapid expansion of manufacturing industry, especially in small-scale labour-intensive plants which produce goods for export. The share of manufactured products in total exports increased from around 40% in 1975 to more than 62% in 1981, although it declined to 58% in 1982. During 1983 exports of manufactured goods were valued at C£134.3m., compared with a record of almost C£142m. in 1981. Largely owing to competition from south-east Asia, however, the revenue from manufactured exports (nearly 80% of which go to the Middle East) fell by almost 30%, from C£140m. in 1985 to C£98.4m. in 1986. The most striking success in manufacturing has been clothing and footwear, with exports rising from C£3.2m. in 1974 to C£82m. in 1991, representing some 30% of total domestic export earnings. A greater emphasis was placed on the sector in the late 1980s and, although manufacturing has gradually declined as a proportion of GDP, the sector continues to grow in real terms, and exports have recovered. Manufacturing and construction, combined, employed about 28% of the labour force in 1991 and accounted for 24% of GDP in 1990, when manufactured exports were valued at C£190m. and accounted for 72% of total domestic exports (compared with 60% in 1987). In 1991 exports of manufactured goods were valued at C£183m. The value of the output of manufactured goods increased from C£132.2m. in 1980 to C£366.7m. in 1990, representing 14.4% of GDP. Cement production increased from 338,000 metric tons in 1974 to 1,233,000 tons in 1980. It declined to 659,000 tons in 1985, but had recovered to 1,132,000 tons by 1992. In the late 1980s one of the main

areas of growth was the cigarette industry. Production of cigarettes increased from 3,718m. in 1987 to 4,601m. in 1990, and to 6,177m. in 1992. Export earnings from cement and cigarettes were valued at C£16.5m. in 1990 (compared with C£13.6m. in 1988). In 1991 manufacturing output was valued at C£289.2m. (equivalent to 14% of GDP), of which C£183m. was exported.

By 1992 the availability of footwear produced in Asia (utilising cheaper labour) had begun to pose a serious threat to the Cypriot shoe-manufacturing industry. In August 1992, therefore, the Government imposed a ban on the import of inexpensive shoes from non-EC countries, and placed restrictions on the import of more expensive footwear. In April 1993, moreover, the new Klerides administration agreed to extend 'substantial assistance' to the industrial sector, with the aim of increasing its competitiveness.

The construction sector grew rapidly after the 1974 Turkish invasion, with an average annual growth of 40% in 1975–79. The most important growth area was the housing sector, which provided accommodation for refugees. A record 9,449 units of housing were constructed in 1979, though the total declined to 6,327 units in 1984. The manufacturing and construction sectors were hampered, in the early 1980s, by the adverse effects of the Government's measures to deflate the economy and by the accumulated results of wage inflation over several years. However, the construction sector enjoyed a period of rapid growth in the late 1980s, contributing C£240m. (10%) to GDP in 1990, in which year issued building permits increased by 47% in value and by 22% in volume, in comparison with 1989. Annual investment in the construction of hotels rose by some 25% between 1990 and 1992, but thereafter began to contract, being some 7% lower in the first half of 1994 than in the corresponding period in 1993. In the period 1989–92 the manufacturing sector showed an average annual increase in output of 3%, in comparison with the planning target of 5% annually. Failure to attain the projected growth rate was attributed to adverse conditions in major markets, such as the UK and the Arab states. From the mid- to late 1980s the service industries, such as banking, insurance and consultancy, grew at a remarkable rate and emerged as an important part of the Greek Cypriot economy. By the end of 1993 more than 9,000 'offshore' companies were registered in the Greek Cypriot sector, although only about 10% maintained offices on the island. In the period 1989–92 the services sector expanded at an average annual rate of 8% in real terms, overshooting the original planning target of 5.7%. In this period all service areas, both those directly connected with tourism (e.g. hotels, restaurants and transport) and other activities (e.g. commerce, communications, banking and professional services), expanded at substantially higher rates than had been projected.

Although the labour market loosened somewhat in the early 1980s, an increase in economic activity, beginning in 1986, resulted in a shortage of skilled labour. In conditions of effective full employment in 1990, the Government authorized the recruitment of 1,600 additional foreign workers (mainly from Bulgaria and Poland) to fill vacancies in the construction and manufacturing sectors. In the early years after 1974, the Government encouraged the temporary emigration of workers as a solution to unemployment. Now the emphasis is more on encouraging workers to return, although their remittances are still important to Cyprus's foreign reserves. By mid-1992 renewed labour shortages had induced the Greek Cypriot Government to authorize the recruitment of another 8,000 foreign workers (some 2%–3% of the labour force). Owing to Government fears that permanent immigration might engender social problems, the maximum contract period was restricted to two years.

The Turkish-occupied area has few industrial resources. The share of industrial exports in total 'TRNC' exports, however, increased from 28.3% (US $14.7m.) in 1986 to 42.6% in 1987. Revenue from industrial exports in 1987 was, in fact, greater than that from citrus fruit exports. The textile and clothing industry has grown rapidly since the early 1980s (although most of the raw material has to be imported), and exports amounted to about $10m. in 1987, thus making it the area's second largest source of export revenue after citrus fruit. It is estimated that 90% of Cyprus's mining operations are in the Greek zone, while the Turkish zone has no petroleum refinery. Hitherto also lacking electricity-generating capacity, the 'TRNC' was reported, in May 1993, to be about to complete its first power plant, located near Kyrenia and financed by Turkey. Meanwhile, the Cyprus Electrical Authority was continuing to supply electricity to both zones and the Turkish north's debt for unbilled consumption had reached more than $250m. by mid-1992. A successful energy conservation programme is under way in the Greek Cypriot sector, involving the exploitation of solar and wind energy and the development of hydroelectricity potential.

TRADE, TOURISM AND COMMUNICATIONS

Cyprus has experienced a trade deficit for many years, but in 1977 the trade deficit* widened to C£124.3m., a rise of 74% from the previous year, and in 1978 it grew to C£154.3m. In 1979 both exports and imports exceeded the growth target of the Emergency Action Plan for 1979–81 but the deficit increased further to C£195.7m. Imports of fuel and raw materials increased, due to demands made by the restructuring of the industrial sector, but the value of imports of capital goods fell, as a result of a slackening in investment. In 1981 a continuing increase in the value of petroleum imports (up 34.8% to C£102.6m.) helped to produce a visible deficit of C£254.8m. Despite government efforts to stimulate exports, the trade deficit continued to widen, and by 1985 it had reached a record C£471.7m. In 1986, however, the trade deficit declined by 15%, to C£398.9m., owing to a 13.5% fall in the cost of imports (including a 39% reduction in the value of petroleum imports, due to the decrease in international petroleum prices). Despite the improved growth in exports of manufactured goods (following depressed figures in 1986), the trade deficit increased, reaching C£587.8m. in 1989. In 1992 the deficit was C£887m., compared with C£687m. in 1991 and C£651m. in 1990. In 1993 total imports (covering imports for home consumption and imports placed in bonded warehouses) declined by 15.4% (compared with 1992), to C£1,261m., while total exports increased to C£443m. (from C£431.5m. in 1992), yielding a trade deficit of C£829.6m.

There was a significant alteration in the Greek Cypriot trading pattern in the mid-1980s, with EC countries taking over the dominant role from Arab countries (chiefly Lebanon, Egypt, the states of the Arabian peninsula, and Libya). The Arab countries' share of total Greek Cypriot exports was reduced from 48% in 1985 to 25% in 1989, decreasing further in 1990, to less than 20%, as a result of the conflict in the Persian (Arabian) Gulf. Greek Cypriot exports to EC countries, on the other hand, increased from 32.4% of total domestic export revenue in 1985 to 55.5% in 1989 and more than 60% in 1990 and 1991. In 1987 the Greek Cypriot Government established a Council for the Promotion of Exports (COPE), one of the main aims of which was to promote exports to Europe. EC countries were also the main suppliers of goods to the Greek Cypriot sector, their share of imports, by value, increasing to 60.8% in 1986, before decreasing slightly, to 57% in 1987 and 54% in 1990, only to increase again to 58% in 1992. Imports from Arab countries, in turn, declined after 1985, when they accounted for 10.1% of total import costs, to 6.1% in 1987 and to 5% in 1990. In 1993 the UK strengthened its position as the largest individual trading partner of Cyprus, exporting 6% more to the island (by value) while importing over 40% of total Cypriot exports.

In November 1985 the EC Council of Ministers approved the admission of Cyprus to a customs union with the EC. The terms of this union were agreed by both sides and a protocol with the EC was signed in October 1987, which came into effect on 1 January 1988. The protocol defined an initial 10-year phase (1988-98), during which time tariffs on imports to Cyprus were to be reduced by 10% annually, leading to their complete removal by 1998. For some products, which are important to the island's economy (e.g. clothing and footwear), tariffs were to fall by only 4% annually in the first phase. The EC agreed to waive quantitative restrictions on exports

to the EC of Cypriot garments and to make concessions to Cypriot agricultural exports, particularly potatoes, grapes, wine and citrus fruit. Cyprus, in turn, agreed to dismantle its quantitative restrictions on imports on industrial products from EC countries. Cyprus, however, was to be allowed to retain a 20% tariff on up to 15% of imports that competed with local products. A second phase, lasting four to five years, which was to be introduced after a review of the first phase, was to lift all remaining restrictions and trade barriers on products covered by the agreement. Cyprus was, then, expected to adopt the EC's common customs tariff, in line with its third-country provisions, freeing it of restrictions within the EC.

The President of the 'TRNC', Rauf Denktaş, strongly attacked the customs union, claiming that the EC was not entitled to negotiate the agreement without consulting representatives of the Turkish sector of the island. The EC, however, made it clear that the union would apply to the whole of the island, a point which was reiterated in an EC report, published by the Commission in June 1993, which confirmed Cyprus's eligibility for EC membership (while recommending that accession to full member-state status should be dependent upon progress at UN-sponsored peace negotiations).

The Turkish sector's main exports are citrus fruit, potatoes and tobacco, the principal markets being the UK and Turkey. Exports in 1990 totalled US $65.5m., compared with $55.1m. in 1987. Imports were worth $381.5m. in 1990, compared with $221.1m. in 1987. In 1991, however, the value of exports declined to $52.5m., while the value of imports declined to $301.1m. The current account deficit averaged about $26m. per year between 1980 and 1986, despite a steady increase in exports. In 1990 the current account deficit declined to $16.4m. After Turkey, the UK is the principal export market. In 1987 exports to the UK, including agricultural, light industrial and textile goods, were worth about TL30.6m.

Tourism was one of the areas of the Greek Cypriot economy which was most adversely affected by the 1974 war, as 90% of the island's hotels came under Turkish Cypriot control. Following the introduction of a government loan plan, however, the number of hotel beds increased from a low point of 3,880 in 1975 to 18,197 in 1985. Tourist receipts rose to C£71m. in 1980, with 353,375 visitors. The sector continued to expand rapidly in the 1980s, and in 1986 the number of tourist arrivals rose to 900,727 and the tourist industry became the Republic of Cyprus's largest source of income, with receipts totalling C£257m. In 1988 tourist arrivals numbered 1,111,818, while total receipts from tourism in that year were C£386m. (equivalent to 36.2% of total receipts from exports of goods and services). In 1989 1,377,636 tourists visited the government-controlled part of the island. The total increased to 1,561,479 in 1990, when 44% of visitors were from the UK. Receipts from tourism totalled C£573m. in 1990, representing an increase of 13% over 1989's total (compared with a 27% increase between 1988 and 1989). There were an estimated 47,500 tourist beds (many of them in self-catering accommodation) in 1988, with projects to provide a further 15,500 already in progress. Employment in the hotels and restaurant sector increased to 24,000 in 1990, accounting for almost 10% of the employed labour force. In 1991 the number of tourist arrivals decreased to 1,385,000, owing to the negative impact of the political crisis in the Persian (Arabian) Gulf region, and receipts fell to C£467m. In 1992 the sector recovered, with 1,950,000 arrivals and receipts of C£665m., only to be followed by a 6.5% reduction in arrivals in 1993, as a result of the devaluation of the UK pound, and a general economic recession in Europe. The relative slump in tourism continued into 1994, although the Government predicted the start of a modest recovery. It also laid emphasis on the desirability of developing 'high-value' tourism (as opposed to the 'package' holiday trade) and on sustainable tourist development.

Tourism in the north has also expanded, giving rise to a shortage of hotel beds. The best hotels still exist in the Turkish sector but most remained unused and derelict after the invasion, although some have been taken over, much against the will of the Greek Cypriot owners. The number of non-Turkish visitors rose steadily from 8,172 in 1978 to 36,372 in

---

* The trade figures quoted in this chapter include re-exports and stores for ships and aircraft.

1987. Turkish visits from the mainland remained fairly steady between 1978 (when they totalled 104,738) and 1986, increasing to 147,965 in 1987, when income from tourism totalled US $56.1m. In 1990 a total of 375,491 tourists (including those from the Turkish mainland) visited the 'TRNC', generating total receipts of $130m. Non-Turkish tourist arrivals in 1992 were officially reported as 267,618 (yielding $175.1m.), compared with 220,237 in 1991 (yielding $153.6m.).

As part of a programme of economic diversification, the Greek Cypriot sector has become a major maritime trading centre. Shipping heads the 'offshore' sector in terms of turnover, providing some 30% of revenue receipts from 'offshore' activities. From 1989 to mid-1992 the number of shipping companies registered in Cyprus doubled to more than 700, making the Cyprus registry the fastest-growing in the world. By mid-1993 some 2,300 ships were registered in Cyprus (the world's third largest total, and the seventh largest registry in the world, by tonnage). In 1994 Cyprus climbed to fifth position in terms of displacement, which totalled more than 23m. grt.

Famagusta formerly handled 83% of Cyprus's freight traffic but, now that it is in Turkish hands, it has been largely superseded by Larnaca and Limassol. In 1989 a total of 5,725 vessels visited Greek Cypriot ports, this figure increasing to 5,732 in 1990. Limassol handled about three-quarters of all ships entered and cleared. Port development schemes for Larnaca and Limassol are expected to cost US $65m., and a new port is also planned for Paphos. There has been a suggestion that Cyprus should be used as an entrepôt for distributing food supplies to Saudi Arabia and the Gulf states. Cyprus has, to some extent, benefited from the paralysis of Beirut, although none of its ports has the capacity of Beirut.

PROSPECTS

The economy and its future are inextricably linked with the political deadlock in the island, which seems unlikely to be resolved by diplomacy in the near future. The Turkish Cypriot claim to equal representation to the EU aggravates the problem. Meanwhile, as negotiations continue, both sides are proceeding with their own plans for development on either side of the 'Attila line'.

Trade between the EU and the Greek Cypriots will retain its predominant share of both exports and imports, providing new opportunities for local industries, but, at the same time, presenting them with the challenge of competing with EU exports to Cyprus. The 1990–91 crisis in the Persian (Arabian) Gulf region proved to be a major set-back for the expanding Greek Cypriot economy, which had benefited from reconstruction activity in the Gulf region. For the Greek Cypriot Government, entry into the EU remains a cardinal goal, in which context it welcomed the decision, in June 1994, of the EU Council of Ministers that Cyprus would be included in the next phase of enlargement negotiations, probably beginning in 1995. Also considered to be significant was the EU's assertion that the division of the island, if it persisted, should not delay the start of negotiations.

A serious restraint on future economic growth is likely to be a shortage of labour. Rather than incur the social problems assumed to be associated with unrestricted immigration of foreign workers, the Greek Cypriot authorities prefer to maintain severe entry restrictions, despite the probable inhibition of economic expansion. A political solution to the island's division would release the labour potential of the stagnant north for the thriving south; meanwhile, the economic division of the two sectors of the island seems likely to worsen.

Statistical Survey

Source (unless otherwise indicated): Department of Statistics and Research, Ministry of Finance, Nicosia; tel. (2) 303286; telex 3399; fax (2) 366080.

Note: Since July 1974 the northern part of Cyprus has been under Turkish occupation. As a result, some of the statistics relating to subsequent periods do not cover the whole island. Some separate figures for the 'TRNC' are given on p. 340.

AREA AND POPULATION

Area: 9,251 sq km (3,572 sq miles), incl. Turkish-occupied region.

Population: 612,851 (males 306,144; females 306,707), incl. estimate for Turkish-occupied region, at census of 30 September 1976; 642,731 (males 319,562; females 323,169), incl. estimate for Turkish-occupied region, at census of 1 October 1982; 715,000 (official estimate for December 1991); 725,000 (official estimate for December 1992).

Ethnic Groups (estimates for 1992): Greeks 580,725 (80.1%), Turks 134,850 (18.6%), others 9,425 (1.3%); Total 725,000.

Principal Towns (population at 1 October 1982): Nicosia (capital) 149,100 (excl. Turkish-occupied portion); Limassol 107,200; Larnaca 48,300; Famagusta (Gazi Mağusa) 39,500 (mid-1974); Paphos 20,800; (estimated population at 31 December 1992): Nicosia 177,000; Limassol 137,000.

Births and Deaths (estimates, 1992): Live births 14,395 (birth rate 20.0 per 1,000); Deaths 6,417 (death rate 8.9 per 1,000).

Employment (government-controlled area, provisional figures, '000 persons, excl. armed forces, 1992): Agriculture, hunting, forestry and fishing 35.0; Mining and quarrying 0.7; Manufacturing 49.0; Electricity, gas and water 1.4; Construction 24.0; Trade, restaurants and hotels 65.8; Transport, storage and communications 15.9; Financing, insurance, real estate and business services 18.4; Community, social and personal services 56.4; Activities not adequately defined 3.7; Total 270.3 (males 162.8, females 107.5).

AGRICULTURE, ETC.

Principal Crops (government-controlled area, '000 metric tons, 1992): Wheat 11, Barley 171, Potatoes 195, Olives 19, Grapes 122, Oranges 60, Grapefruit 67, Lemons and limes 40.

Livestock (government-controlled area, '000 head, 1992): Cattle 56, Sheep 235, Goats 200, Pigs 342, Chickens 3,000.

Fishing (metric tons, live weight, government-controlled area): Total catch 2,621 in 1989; 2,694 in 1990; 2,690 (Fishes 2,412, Crustaceans and molluscs 278) in 1991. Source: FAO, *Yearbook of Fishery Statistics.*

MINING AND QUARRYING

Selected Products (metric tons, government-controlled area, 1992): Sand and gravel 5,750,000, Marble 58,000, Gypsum 34,470, Bentonite (activated) 58,840, Cement copper 473.

INDUSTRY

Selected Products (government-controlled area, 1992): Cement 1,131,604 metric tons, Bricks 62.2 million, Mosaic tiles 2.3 million sq metres, Cigarettes 6,177 million, Footwear (excluding plastic and semi-finished shoes) 5,117,000 pairs, Beer 37.0 million litres, Wines 46.4 million litres, Intoxicating liquors 4.8 million litres.

FINANCE

Currency and Exchange Rates: 100 cents = 1 Cyprus pound (Cyprus £). *Sterling and US Dollar Equivalents* (30 April 1994): £1 sterling = 76.4 Cyprus cents; US $1 = 50.40 Cyprus cents; Cyprus £100 = £130.85 sterling = $198.41. *Average exchange rate* (US $ per Cyprus £): 2.1670 in 1991; 2.2212 in 1992; 2.0120 in 1993.

Budget (estimates, Cyprus £ million, government-controlled area, 1992): *Revenue:* Taxation 693.42 (Taxes on income 160.11, Social security contributions 132.85, Taxes on payroll 14.73, Taxes on property 17.87, Excises 95.90, Value-added tax 36.48, Other domestic taxes on goods and services 47.66, Import duties 123.18, Other taxes 64.64); Entrepreneurial and property income 118.03; Administrative fees and charges, non-industrial and incidental sales 42.26; Other current revenue 19.50; Capital revenue 0.78; Total 873.99, excl. grants from abroad (1.14). *Expenditure:* General public services 69.52; Defence 29.90; Public order and safety 61.66; Education 104.33; Health 60.11; Social security and welfare 201.85; Housing and community amenities 34.26; Recreational, cultural and religious affairs and services 11.17; Economic affairs and services 138.51 (Agriculture, forestry, fishing and hunting 71.42, Road transport 31.26, Other transport and communication 18.85); Other purposes 151.45; Sub-total 862.77 (Current 761.76, Capital 101.01); Adjustment 144.61; Total 1,007.38, excl. lending minus repayments (15.32).

International Reserves (US $ million at 31 December 1993): Gold (national valuation) 14.2; IMF special drawing rights 0.1; Reserve position in IMF 35.0, Foreign exchange 1,061.6; Total 1,110.9. Source: IMF, *International Financial Statistics.*

Money Supply (Cyprus £ million at 31 December 1993, government-controlled area): Currency outside banks 229.4, Demand deposits at deposit money banks 317.2; Total money (incl. others) 549.1. Source: IMF, *International Financial Statistics.*

Cost of Living (Retail Price Index, government-controlled area; base: 1986 = 100): 115.3 in 1990; 121.1 in 1991; 129.0 in 1992.

Gross Domestic Product in Purchasers' Values (Cyprus £ million at current prices, government-controlled area): 2,547.4 in 1990; 2,670.5 in 1991; 3,011.8 in 1992. Source: IMF, *International Financial Statistics.*

Gross Domestic Product by Economic Activity (provisional, Cyprus £ million at current prices, government-controlled area, 1990): Agriculture, hunting, forestry and fishing 175.3; Mining and quarrying 6.7; Manufacturing 362.3; Electricity, gas and water 48.8; Construction 242.3; Trade, restaurants and hotels 539.0; Transport, storage and communications 226.7; Finance, insurance, real estate and business services 372.8; Government services 293.7; Other community, social and personal services 138.8; Other services 15.6; **Sub-total** 2,422.0; Import duties 171.8; *Less* Imputed bank service charges 74.5; **Total** 2,519.3. Source: UN, *National Accounts Statistics.*

Balance of Payments (US $ million, government-controlled area, 1992): Merchandise exports f.o.b. 903.2, Merchandise imports f.o.b. −2,989.9, *Trade balance* −2,086.8; Exports of services 2,616.5, Imports of services −818.3, Other income received 237.5, Other income paid −221.6, Private unrequited transfers (net) 22.0, Official unrequited transfers (net) 9.0, *Current balance* −241.7; Direct investment (net) 92.5, Portfolio investment (net) 54.0, Other capital 162.9, Net errors and omissions −284.7, *Overall balance* −217.1. Source: IMF, *International Financial Statistics.*

EXTERNAL TRADE

Principal Commodities (Cyprus £ '000, government-controlled area, 1992): *Imports c.i.f.:* Textile and textile articles 135,978 (Clothing and clothing accessories 19,615); Aircraft and parts 50,169; Road vehicles, parts and accessories 157,984; Mineral products 132,574 (Crude oil 47,847); Base metals and articles of base metal 121,566; Chemicals and related products 88,059 (Pharmaceutical products 19,340); Prepared foodstuffs, beverages, spirits and vinegar, tobacco and manufactured tobacco substitutes 161,745 (Beverages, spirits and vinegar 13,524; tobacco and manufactured tobacco substitutes 94,608); Plastics and plastic products 39,505; Paper, paperboard and derivatives 35,976; Live animals and animal products 30,571 (Meat and edible offal 10,322); Total (incl. others) 1,490,755. *Exports f.o.b.:* Clothing

64,501; Footwear 10,883; Potatoes 21,783; Citrus fruit 16,095; Cement 6,248; Pharmaceutical products 11,626; Alcoholic beverages 7,279; Total (incl. others) 230,831. Figures for exports exclude re-exports (Cyprus £222.6 million).

Total Trade (Cyprus £ million, government-controlled area): *Imports c.i.f.:* 1,215.83 in 1991; 1,490.76 in 1992; 1,260.05 in 1993. *Exports f.o.b.* (incl. re-exports): 441.79 in 1991; 453.41 in 1992; 439.08 in 1993. Source: IMF, *International Financial Statistics.*

Principal Trading Partners (Cyprus £ '000, government-controlled area, 1992): *Imports c.i.f.:* France 117,673; Germany 134,378; Greece 101,493; Italy 143,940; Japan 156,815; CIS 69,870; United Kingdom 165,598; USA 125,082; Total (incl. others) 1,490,755. *Exports f.o.b.:* Egypt 14,202; Germany 17,422; Greece 10,636; Israel 6,039; Lebanon 4,780; Saudi Arabia 9,578; Belgium and Luxembourg 4,962; United Kingdom 78,339; Total (incl. others) 230,831. Figures for exports exclude re-exports (Cyprus £222.6 million).

TRANSPORT

Road Traffic (licensed motor vehicles, government-controlled area, 1992): Private cars 189,199, Taxis and self-drive cars 7,612, Lorries and buses 88,892, Motor cycles 53,762, Total (incl. others) 352,690.

Shipping (freight traffic, '000 metric tons, government-controlled area, 1992): Goods loaded 2,066, Goods unloaded 5,783. In 1992 a total of 2,316 ships (displacement 22.3m. grt) were registered in Cyprus.

Civil Aviation (government-controlled area, 1992): Overall passenger traffic 4,304,390; Total freight transported 26,441 metric tons.

TOURISM

Foreign Visitors by Country of Origin (excluding one-day visitors and visitors to the Turkish-occupied zone, 1992): Germany 102,260, Greece 65,200, Lebanon 50,300, Scandinavian countries 240,090, United Kingdom 1,087,500, USA 27,800; Total (incl. others) 1,991,000.

Tourist Arrivals: 1,561,479 in 1990; 1,385,000 in 1991; 1,991,000 in 1992.

Tourist Receipts (Cyprus £ million): 573 in 1990; 476 in 1991; 694 in 1992.

COMMUNICATIONS MEDIA

Radio Receivers (government-controlled area): 180,000 in 1990; 190,000 in 1991.

Television Receivers (government-controlled area): 89,900 in 1990; 100,000 in 1991.

EDUCATION

1992/93 (government-controlled area): Kindergarten: 608 institutions, 1,225 teachers, 24,977 pupils; Primary schools: 391 institutions, 3,365 teachers, 64,313 pupils; Secondary schools (Gymnasia and Lyceums): 102 institutions, 3,563 teachers, 48,123 pupils; Technical: 11 institutions, 470 teachers, 3,518 pupils; Teacher-training: 1 institution, 33 teachers, 223 students; University of Cyprus: 64 teachers, 486 students; Other post-secondary: 29 institutions, 445 teachers, 5,554 students.

'Turkish Republic of Northern Cyprus'*

Sources: Office of the London Representative of the 'Turkish Republic of Northern Cyprus', 28 Cockspur St, London SW1 (tel. (71) 839-4577; telex 8955363); K. Rüstem and Brother, North Cyprus Almanack, 1987; *Kıbrıs* (Northern Cyprus Weekly); Prime Ministry, State Planning Organization, Statistics and Research Department.

AREA AND POPULATION

Area: 3,355 sq km (1,295 sq miles).

Population (official estimate, 1989): 169,272 (males 83,737; females 85,535); (official estimate, 1992): 176,127.

Ethnic Groups (estimates, 1985): Turks 158,225, Greeks 733, Maronites 368, Others 961; Total 160,287.

Principal Towns (estimated population within the municipal boundary, 1989): Lefkoşa (Nicosia) 39,496 (Turkish-occupied area only); Gazi Mağusa (Famagusta) 20,516; Güzelyurt (Morphou) 10,179 (1985); Girne (Kyrenia) 7,290.

Births, Marriages and Deaths (registered, 1989): Birth rate 14.8 per 1,000; Marriage rate 6.9 per 1,000; Death rate 3.4 per 1,000.

Note: Birth registration is estimated to be 95% complete, but death registration only 25% complete.

Employment (1986): Agriculture, forestry and fishing 20,320; Industry 6,497; Construction 4,581; Trade and tourism 5,923; Transport and communications 4,554; Financial institutions 1,564; Business and personal services 4,932; Public Services 14,881; *Total employed* 63,252. Total unemployed: 1,556; *Total labour force* 64,808. **1991:** *Total employed* 71,941; Total unemployed 1,027; *Total labour force* 72,968.

AGRICULTURE, ETC.

Principal Crops ('000 metric tons, 1989): Wheat 22.0, Barley 88.4, Chick-peas 0.3, Potatoes 17.0, Tomatoes 1.9, Artichokes 1.3,

Water melons 7.0, Sweet melons 1.2, Carobs 3.0, Olives 1.6, Lemons 21.2, Grapefruit 47.2, Oranges 118.5, Tangerines 0.8.

Livestock ('000 head, 1989): Cattle 12.1, Sheep 192.6, Goats 56.6, Chickens 1,659.4 (1988).

Livestock Products ('000 metric tons, unless otherwise indicated, 1989): Sheep's and goats' milk 10.6, Cows' milk 17.9, Mutton and lamb 2.7, Goats' meat 0.7, Beef 0.9, Poultry meat 2.8, Wool 0.3, Eggs (million) 15.2 (1988).

Fishing (metric tons, 1985); Total catch 300.

FINANCE

Currency and Exchange Rates: Turkish currency: 100 kuruş = 1 Turkish lira (TL) or pound. *Sterling and Dollar Equivalents* (31 May 1994): £1 sterling = 48,018 liras; US $1 = 31,762 liras; 100,000 Turkish liras = £2.083 = $3.148. *Average Exchange Rate* (liras per US dollar): 4,171.8 in 1991; 6,872.4 in 1992; 10,984.6 in 1993.

Draft Budget (estimates, million Turkish liras, 1993): *Revenue:* Internal revenue 1,337,000, Aid from Turkey 560,000, Loans 677,000, Total 2,574,000; *Expenditure:* Defence 130,000, Total 2,574,000.

Cost of Living (Retail Price Index; base: December 1984 = 100): 143.04 in 1985.

Gross Domestic Product (GDP) by Economic Activity (provisional figures, million Turkish liras, 1992): Agriculture, forestry and fishing 426,957.4; Mining and quarrying 31,580.7; Manufacturing 365,854.2; Electricity and water 64,827.6; Construction 264,832.9; Wholesale and retail trade 629,386.1; Restaurants and hotels 149,613.5; Transport and communications 317,598.8; Finance 242,450.0; Ownership of dwellings 67,381.0; Business and personal services 231,809.1; Government services 721,333.3; *Subtotal* 3,513,624.6; Import duties 216,784.2; *GDP in purchasers' values* 3,730,408.8.

Balance of Payments (US $ million, 1990): Merchandise exports f.o.b. 65.5; Merchandise imports c.i.f. −381.5; *Trade balance* −316.0; Services and unrequited transfers (net) 299.6; *Current balance* −16.4; Capital movements (net) 22.5; Net errors and omissions −2.3; *Total* (net monetary movements) 6.5.

EXTERNAL TRADE

Principal Commodities (US $ million, 1989): *Imports c.i.f.:* Food and live animals 25.5, Beverages and tobacco 7.5, Crude materials (inedible) except fuels 6.3, Mineral fuels, lubricants, etc. 18.2, Animal and vegetable oils and fats 1.4, Chemicals 17.7, Basic manufactures 87.0, Machinery and transport equipment 72.8, Mis-

cellaneous manufactured articles 26.2; Total 262.5. *Exports f.o.b.:* Food and live animals 34.0, Beverages and tobacco 1.1, Crude materials (inedible) except fuels 1.6, Chemicals 0.4, Basic manufactures 1.1, Miscellaneous manufactured articles 14.3; Total 55.2.

1991 (US $ million): Imports c.i.f. 301.1; Exports f.o.b. 52.5.

1992 (US $ million): Imports c.i.f. 348.2; Exports f.o.b. 54.3.

Principal Trading Partners (US $ million, 1989): *Imports:* Turkey 112.5, United Kingdom 49.6, other EC countries 45.1, Total (incl. others) 262.5; *Exports:* Turkey 9.2, United Kingdom 35.3, other EC countries 5.0, Total (incl. others) 55.2.

1991 (US $ million): *Imports c.i.f.:* Turkey 145.0; *Exports f.o.b.:* Turkey 7.3.

1992 (US $ million): *Imports c.i.f.:* Turkey 181.1; *Exports f.o.b.:* Turkey 9.8.

TRANSPORT

Road Traffic (licensed motor vehicles, 1989): Cars (incl. taxis and self-drive cars) 34,127, Lorries, vans and buses 9,780, Motor cycles 10,802, Tractors 4,823; Total (incl. others) 60,263.

Shipping (1989): Freight traffic ('000 metric tons): Goods loaded 229.9, Goods unloaded 509.3; Vessels entered 2,027.

Civil Aviation (Turkish Cypriot Airlines Co, Ltd, 1985): Kilometres flown 1,126,848, Passenger arrivals 67,693, Passenger departures 68,392 (1987), Freight landed (metric tons) 909, Freight cleared (metric tons) 1,030.

TOURISM

Visitors (1992): 242,506 (including 186,647 Turkish); **Accommodation** (1992): Hotels 33, Tourist beds (in all tourist accommodation, including pensions and hotel-apartments) 7,087; **Receipts** (US $ million, 1992) 175.

COMMUNICATIONS MEDIA

1985: 42,170 radio receivers, 75,000 television receivers.

EDUCATION

1991/92: Primary and pre-primary education: 155 institutions, 849 teachers, 19,400 pupils; *High schools:* 28 institutions, 963 teachers, 16,719 students; *Vocational schools:* 10 institutions, 254 teachers, 2,761 students; *Higher education:* 4 institutions, 6,145 students.

* Note: Following a unilateral declaration of independence in November 1983, the 'Turkish Federated State of Cyprus' became known as the 'Turkish Republic of Northern Cyprus'.

Directory

The Constitution

The Constitution, summarized below, entered into force on 16 August 1960, when Cyprus became an independent republic.

THE STATE OF CYPRUS

The State of Cyprus is an independent and sovereign Republic with a presidential regime.

The Greek Community comprises all citizens of the Republic who are of Greek origin and whose mother tongue is Greek or who share the Greek cultural traditions or who are members of the Greek Orthodox Church.

The Turkish Community comprises all citizens of the Republic who are of Turkish origin and whose mother tongue is Turkish or who share the Turkish cultural traditions or who are Muslims.

The official languages of the Republic are Greek and Turkish.

The Republic shall have its own flag of neutral design and colour, chosen jointly by the President and the Vice-President of the Republic.

The Greek and the Turkish Communities shall have the right to celebrate respectively the Greek and the Turkish national holidays.

THE PRESIDENT AND VICE-PRESIDENT

Executive power is vested in the President and the Vice-President, who are members of the Greek and Turkish Communities respectively, and are elected by their respective communities to hold office for five years.

The President of the Republic as Head of the State represents the Republic in all its official functions; signs the credentials of

diplomatic envoys and receives the credentials of foreign diplomatic envoys; signs the credentials of delegates for the negotiation of international treaties, conventions or other agreements; signs the letter relating to the transmission of the instruments of ratification of any international treaties, conventions or agreements; confers the honours of the Republic.

The Vice-President of the Republic, as Vice-Head of the State, has the right to be present at all official functions; at the presentation of the credentials of foreign diplomatic envoys; to recommend to the President the conferment of honours on members of the Turkish Community, which recommendation the President shall accept unless there are grave reasons to the contrary.

The election of the President and the Vice-President of the Republic shall be direct, by universal suffrage and secret ballot, and shall, except in the case of a by-election, take place on the same day but separately.

The office of the President and of the Vice-President shall be incompatible with that of a Minister or of a Representative or of a member of a Communal Chamber or of a member of any municipal council including a Mayor or of a member of the armed or security forces of the Republic or with a public or municipal office.

The President and Vice-President of the Republic are invested by the House of Representatives.

The President and the Vice-President of the Republic in order to ensure the executive power shall have a Council of Ministers composed of seven Greek Ministers and three Turkish Ministers. The Ministers shall be designated respectively by the President and the Vice-President of the Republic who shall appoint them by an instrument signed by them both. The President convenes and presides over the meetings of the Council of Ministers, while the

Vice-President may ask the President to convene the Council and may take part in the discussions.

The decisions of the Council of Ministers shall be taken by an absolute majority and shall, unless the right of final veto or return is exercised by the President or the Vice-President of the Republic or both, be promulgated immediately by them.

The executive power exercised by the President and the Vice-President of the Republic conjointly consists of:

Determining the design and colour of the flag.

Creation or establishment of honours.

Appointment of the members of the Council of Ministers.

Promulgation by publication of the decisions of the Council of Ministers.

Promulgation by publication of any law or decision passed by the House of Representatives.

Appointments and termination of appointments as in Articles provided.

Institution of compulsory military service.

Reduction or increase of the security forces.

Exercise of the prerogative of mercy in capital cases.

Remission, suspension and commutation of sentences.

Right of references to the Supreme Constitutional Court and publication of Court decisions.

Address of messages to the House of Representatives.

The executive powers which may be exercised separately by the President and Vice-President include: designation and termination of appointment of Greek and Turkish Ministers respectively; the right of final veto on Council decisions and on laws concerning foreign affairs, defence or security; the publication of the communal laws and decisions of the Greek and Turkish Communal Chambers respectively; the right of recourse to the Supreme Constitutional Court; the prerogative of mercy in capital cases; and addressing messages to the House of Representatives.

THE COUNCIL OF MINISTERS

The Council of Ministers shall exercise executive power in all matters, other than those which are within the competence of a Communal Chamber, including the following:

General direction and control of the government of the Republic and the direction of general policy.

Foreign affairs, defence and security.

Co-ordination and supervision of all public services.

Supervision and disposition of property belonging to the Republic.

Consideration of Bills to be introduced to the House of Representatives by a Minister.

Making of any order or regulation for the carrying into effect of any law as provided by such law.

Consideration of the Budget of the Republic to be introduced to the House of Representatives.

THE HOUSE OF REPRESENTATIVES

The legislative power of the Republic shall be exercised by the House of Representatives in all matters except those expressly reserved to the Communal Chambers.

The number of Representatives shall be 50, subject to alteration by a resolution of the House of Representatives carried by a majority comprising two-thirds of the Representatives elected by the Greek Community and two-thirds of the Representatives elected by the Turkish Community.

Out of the number of Representatives 70% shall be elected by the Greek Community and 30% by the Turkish Community separately from amongst their members respectively, and, in the case of a contested election, by universal suffrage and by direct and secret ballot held on the same day.

The term of office of the House of Representatives shall be for a period of five years.

The President of the House of Representatives shall be a Greek, and shall be elected by the Representatives elected by the Greek Community, and the Vice-President shall be a Turk and shall be elected by the Representatives elected by the Turkish Community.

THE COMMUNAL CHAMBERS

The Greek and the Turkish Communities respectively shall elect from amongst their own members a Communal Chamber.

The Communal Chambers shall, in relation to their respective Community, have competence to exercise legislative power solely with regard to the following:

All religious, educational, cultural and teaching matters.

Personal status; composition and instances of courts dealing with civil disputes relating to personal status and to religious matters.

Imposition of personal taxes and fees on members of their respective Community in order to provide for their respective needs.

THE PUBLIC SERVICE AND THE ARMED FORCES

The public service shall be composed as to 70% of Greeks and as to 30% of Turks.

The Republic shall have an army of 2,000 men, of whom 60% shall be Greeks and 40% shall be Turks.

The security forces of the Republic shall consist of the police and gendarmerie and shall have a contingent of 2,000 men. The forces shall be composed as to 70% of Greeks and as to 30% of Turks.

OTHER PROVISIONS

The following measures have been passed by the House of Representatives since January 1964, when the Turkish members withdrew:

The amalgamation of the High Court and the Supreme Constitutional Court (see Judicial System section).

The abolition of the Greek Communal Chamber and the creation of a Ministry of Education.

The unification of the Municipalities.

The unification of the Police and the Gendarmerie.

The creation of a military force by providing that persons between the ages of 18 and 50 years can be called upon to serve in the National Guard.

The extension of the term of office of the President and the House of Representatives by one year intervals from July 1965 until elections in February 1968 and July 1970 respectively.

New electoral provisions; abolition of separate Greek and Turkish rolls; abolition of post of Vice-President, which was re-established in 1973.

The Government*

HEAD OF STATE

President: GLAVKOS KLERIDES (took office 28 February 1993).

COUNCIL OF MINISTERS
(August 1994)

Minister of Foreign Affairs: ALEKOS MICHAELIDES.

Minister of Defence: KOSTAS ELIADES.

Minister of the Interior: DINOS MICHAELIDES.

Minister of Finance: PHEDROS EKONOMIDES

Minister of Justice and Public Order: ALEKOS EVANGELOU.

Minister of Commerce and Industry: STELIOS KILIARIS.

Minister of Education and Culture: KLERI ANGELIDOU.

Minister of Health: MANOLIS CHRISTOPHIDES.

Minister of Labour and Social Insurance: ANDREAS MOUSHIOUTAS.

Minister of Communications and Works: ADAMOS ADAMIDES.

Minister of Agriculture, Natural Resources and the Environment: KOSTAS PETRIDES.

* Under the Constitution of 1960, the vice-presidency and three posts in the Council of Ministers are reserved for Turkish Cypriots. However, there has been no Turkish participation in the Government since December 1963. In 1968 President Makarios announced that he considered the office of Vice-President in abeyance until Turkish participation in the Government is resumed, but the Turkish community elected Rauf Denktaş Vice-President in February 1973.

MINISTRIES

All ministries are in Nicosia.

Ministry of Agriculture, Natural Resources and the Environment: Loukis Akritas Ave, Nicosia; tel. (2) 302171; telex 4660; fax (2) 445156.

Ministry of Commerce and Industry: 6 Andreas Araouzos St, Nicosia; tel. (2) 303441; telex 2283; fax (2) 366120.

Ministry of Communications and Works: Dem. Severis Ave, Nicosia; tel. (2) 302161; telex 3678; fax (2) 465462.

Ministry of Defence: 4 Emmanuel Roides St, Nicosia; tel. (2) 303187; telex 3553; fax (2) 366225.

Ministry of Education and Culture: Greg. Afxentiou St, Nicosia; tel. (2) 303331; telex 5760; fax (2) 445021.

Ministry of Finance: Ex Secretariat Compound, Nicosia; tel. (2) 302779; telex 3399; fax (2) 366080.

Ministry of Foreign Affairs: 18–19 Dem. Severis Ave, Nicosia; tel. (2) 302157; telex 3001; fax (2) 451881.

Ministry of Health: Nicosia; tel. (2) 303243; telex 5734; fax (2) 303498.

Ministry of the Interior: Dem. Severis Ave, Ex Secretariat Compound, Nicosia; tel. (2) 302238; fax (2) 453465.

Ministry of Justice and Public Order: 1 Diogenes St, Engomi, Nicosia; tel. (2) 302355; fax (2) 461427.

Ministry of Labour and Social Insurance: Byron Ave, Nicosia; tel. (2) 303481; telex 6011; fax (2) 450993.

President and Legislature

PRESIDENT

Election, 7 February 1993* and 14 February 1993

Candidates	Votes	%
GLAVKOS KLERIDES (Democratic Rally)	178,858 (130,663)	50.3 (36.7)
GEORGHIOS VASSILIOU (Independent)	176,870 (157,270)	49.7 (44.2)
PASCHALIS PASCHALIDES (EDEK—Socialist Party/Democratic Party)	— (66,300)	— (18.6)
GEORGHIOS MAVROGENIS (Independent)	— (890)	— (0.3)
YIANNAKIS TALIOTIS (Independent)	— (755)	— (0.2)
Total	355,728 (355,878)	100.0 (100.0)

*Figures from the first round of voting appear in brackets.

HOUSE OF REPRESENTATIVES

The House of Representatives originally consisted of 50 members, 35 from the Greek community and 15 from the Turkish community, elected for a term of five years. In January 1964 the Turkish members withdrew and set up the 'Turkish Legislative Assembly of the Turkish Cypriot Administration' (see p. 344). At the 1985 elections the membership of the House was expanded to 80 members, of whom 56 were to be from the Greek community and 24 from the Turkish community (according to the ratio of representation specified in the Constitution).

President: ALEXIS GHALANOS.

Elections for the Greek Representatives, 19 May 1991

Party	Votes	% of Votes	Seats
Democratic Rally/Liberal Party	122,482	35.8	20
AKEL (Communist Party)	104,772	30.6	18
Democratic Party	66,864	19.5	11
EDEK (Socialist Party)	37,256	10.9	7
ADISOK	8,200	2.4	—
PAKOP	1,892	0.6	—
Independents	555	0.2	—
Total	342,021	100.0	56

Political Organizations

Ananeotiko Dimokratiko Sosialistiko Kinema (ADISOK) (Democratic Socialist Reform Movement): 19 Nikitaras St, Ayioi Omoloyitae, Nicosia; tel. (2) 367345; fax (2) 367611; f. 1990; supports settlement of the Cyprus problem based on UN resolutions; Pres. MICHAEL PAPAPETROU; Vice-Pres. COSTAS THEMISTOCLEOUS.

Anorthotiko Komma Ergazomenou Laou (AKEL) (Progressive Party of the Working People): POB 1827, 8 Akamas St, Nicosia; tel. (2) 441121; f. 1941; successor to the Communist Party of Cyprus (f. 1926); Marxist-Leninist; supports demilitarized, non-aligned and independent Cyprus; over 14,000 mems; Sec.-Gen. DEMETRIS CHRISTOFIAS.

Dimokratiko Komma (DIKO) (Democratic Party): POB 3979, 50 Grivas Dhigenis Ave, Nicosia; tel. (2) 472002; fax (2) 366488; f. 1976; absorbed Enosi Kentrou (Centre Union, f. 1981) in 1989; supports settlement of the Cyprus problem based on UN resolutions; Pres. SPYROS KYPRIANOU; Vice-Pres. ALEXIS GHALANOS; Sec.-Gen. STATHIS KITTIS.

Dimokratikos Synagermos (DISY) (Democratic Rally): POB 5305, 23 Pindarou St, Nicosia; tel. (2) 449791; fax (2) 449894; f. 1976; opposition party; absorbed Democratic National Party (DEK) in 1977 and New Democratic Front (NEDIPA) in 1988; advocates entry of Cyprus into the European Union and greater active involvement by the EU in the settlement of the Cyprus problem; 18,000 mems; Pres. YIANNAKIS MATSIS; Gen. Sec. DEMETRIS SYLLOURIS.

Ethniki Dimokratiki Enosi Kyprou (EDEK)—Socialistiko Komma (Cyprus National Democratic Union—Socialist Party): POB 1064, 2 Bouboulinas St, Nicosia; tel. (2) 458617; telex 3182; fax (2) 458894; f. 1969; supports independent, non-aligned, unitary, demilitarized Cyprus; advocates the establishment of a socialist structure; Pres. Dr VASSOS LYSSARIDES; Vice-Pres. TAKIS HADJIDEMETRIOU; Sec.-Gen. YIANNAKIS OMEROU.

Kinema ton Eleftheron Dimokraton (KED) (Movement of Free Democrats): 21 Akademia Ave, Aglanja, Nicosia; tel. (2) 336142; fax (2) 336301; Pres. GEORGHIOS VASSILIOU.

Komma Phileleftheron (Liberal Party): POB 7282, Nicosia Tryfon Bldg, Eleftheria Sq., Nicosia; tel. (2) 452117; telex 2483; fax (2) 368900; f. 1986; supports settlement of the Cyprus problem based on UN resolutions; Pres. NIKOS A. ROLANDIS; Vice-Pres. SOFOCLES MOUSSOULOS.

PAKOP (Refugee Party): Nicosia; f. 1991.

Diplomatic Representation

EMBASSIES AND HIGH COMMISSIONS IN CYPRUS

Australia: 4 Annis Komninis St, 2nd Floor, Nicosia; tel. (2) 473001; telex 2097; fax (2) 366486; High Commissioner: E. J. STEVENS.

Bulgaria: POB 4029, 13 Konst. Paleologos St, Engomi, Nicosia; tel. (2) 472486; telex 2188; fax (2) 456598; Ambassador: ALEXEI IVANOV.

China, People's Republic: 28 Archimedes St, Engomi, Nicosia; tel. (2) 352182; telex 6376; Ambassador: CHEN ZHENYOU.

Cuba: 39 Regas Phereos St, Acropolis, Nicosia; tel. (2) 427211; telex 2306; fax (2) 429390; Ambassador: JORGE RODRÍGUEZ GRILLO.

Czech Republic: POB 1165, 7 Kastorias St, Nicosia; tel. (2) 311683; telex 2490; fax (2) 311715.

Egypt: POB 1752, 3 Egypt Ave, Nicosia; tel. (2) 465144; telex 2102; Ambassador: N. M. MAHDY.

France: POB 1671, 6 Ploutarchou St, Engomi, Nicosia; tel. (2) 465258; telex 2389; Ambassador: PIERRE COUTURIER.

Germany: POB 1795, 10 Nikitaras St, Ay. Omoloyitae, Nicosia; tel. (2) 444362; telex 2460; fax (2) 365694; Ambassador: FRIEDRICH GARBERS.

Greece: POB 1799, 8/10 Byron Ave, Nicosia; tel. (2) 441880; telex 2394; fax (2) 473990; Ambassador: PAVLOS APOSTOLIDES.

Holy See: POB 1964, Holy Cross Catholic Church, Nicosia (Apostolic Nunciature); tel. (2) 462132; fax (2) 466767; Apostolic Pro-Nuncio: Most Rev. ANDREA CORDERO LANZA DI MONTEZEMOLO, Titular Archbishop of Tuscania.

Hungary: 13/a Princess Anne St, Nicosia; tel. (2) 366230.

India: POB 5544, 3 Indira Gandhi St, Engomi, Nicosia; tel. (2) 351741; telex 4146; fax (2) 350402; High Commissioner: YOGESH TIWARI.

Iran: 8 Elia Papakyriakou, Nicosia; tel. (2) 314459; telex 6416; fax (2) 315446.

Israel: POB 1049, 4 I. Gryparis St, Nicosia; tel. (2) 445195; fax (2) 453486; Ambassador: SHEMI TZUR.

Italy: POB 1452, Margarita House, 15 Themistoklis Dervis St, Nicosia; tel. (2) 473183; telex 3847; Ambassador: GUIDO RIZZO VENCI.

Lebanon: POB 1924, 1 Vasilissis Olgas St, Nicosia; tel. (2) 442216; telex 3056; Ambassador: ZAIDAN ZAIDAN.

Libya: POB 3669, 14 Estias St, Nicosia; tel. (2) 496511; Secretary of People's Bureau: ALI ABDULHAMED AS-SAGHAIER.

Poland: 55/57 St Mavrommatis St, Nicosia; tel. (2) 448410.

Romania: 37 Tombazis St, Nicosia; tel. (2) 445845; telex 2431; Chargé d'affaires: JOAN SBARNA.

Russia: 4 Gladstone St, Nicosia; tel. (2) 472141; telex 5808; fax (2) 464854; Ambassador: BORIS G. ZENKOV.

Slovakia: POB 1165, 7 Kastorias St, Nicosia; tel. (2) 311683; telex 2490; fax (2) 311715.

Switzerland: POB 729, 46 Themistokles Dervis St, Nicosia; tel. (2) 446261; fax (2) 446008.

Syria: POB 1891, Cnr Androcleous and Thoukidides Sts, Nicosia; tel. (2) 474481; telex 2030; fax (2) 446963; Chargé d'affaires a.i.: ABDUL FATTAH AMMOURAH.

United Kingdom: POB 1978, Alexander Pallis St, Nicosia; tel. (2) 473131; telex 2208; fax (2) 367198; High Commissioner: DAVID MADDEN.

USA: Dositheos St, and Therissos St, Lykavitos, Nicosia; tel. (2) 465151; telex 4160; fax (2) 459571; Ambassador: RICHARD A. BOUCHER.

Yemen: 25 Thermopylon St, Nicosia; tel. (2) 494598; Ambassador: AHMAD MOHAMMAD AL-MOUTAWAKIL.

Yugoslavia: 2 Vasilissis Olgas St, Nicosia; tel. (2) 445511; fax (2) 445910; Ambassador: PETAR BOSKOVIĆ.

Judicial System

Supreme Council of Judicature: Nicosia. The Supreme Council of Judicature is composed of the President and Judges of the Supreme Court. It is responsible for the appointment, promotion, transfer, etc., of the judges exercising civil and criminal jurisdiction in the District Courts and the Assize Courts.

SUPREME COURT

Supreme Court: Char. Mouskos St, Nicosia; tel. (2) 302398. The Constitution of 1960 provided for a separate Supreme Constitutional Court and High Court but in 1964, in view of the resignation of their neutral presidents, these were amalgamated to form a single Supreme Court.

The Supreme Court is the final appellate court in the Republic and the final adjudicator in matters of constitutional and administrative law, including recourses on conflict of competence between state organs on questions of the constitutionality of laws, etc. It deals with appeals from Assize Courts and District Courts as well as from the decisions of its own judges when exercising original jurisdiction in certain matters such as prerogative orders of *habeas corpus, mandamus, certiorari*, etc., and in admiralty cases.

President: ANDREAS N. LOIZOU.

Judges: I. C. CONSTANTINIDES, D. GR. DEMETRIADES, CHR. C. ARTEMIDES, D. STYLIANIDES, G. M. PIKIS, A. G. KOURRIS, I. Z. PAPADOPOULLOS, CHR. C. HADJITSANGARIS, I. CH. BOYADJIS, Y. CHR. CHRYSOSTOMIS, S. NIKITAS, P. CH. ARTEMIS.

Attorney-General: MICHALAKIS TRIANTAFYLLIDES.

OTHER COURTS

Assize Courts and District Courts: As required by the Constitution a law was passed in 1960 providing for the establishment, jurisdiction and powers of courts of civil and criminal jurisdiction, i.e. of six District Courts and six Assize Courts. In accordance with the provisions of new legislation, approved in 1991, a permanent Assize Court, with powers of jurisdiction in all districts, was established.

Ecclesiastical Courts: There are seven Orthodox Church tribunals having exclusive jurisdiction in matrimonial causes between members of the Greek Orthodox Church. Appeals go from these tribunals to the appellate tribunal of the Church. In accordance with the provisions of a constitutional amendment, approved in 1989, new jurisdiction was awarded to specially constituted Family Courts.

'Turkish Republic of Northern Cyprus'

The Turkish intervention in Cyprus in July 1974 resulted in the establishment of a separate area in northern Cyprus under the control of the Autonomous Turkish Cypriot Administration, with a Council of Ministers and separate judicial, financial, police, military and educational machinery serving the Turkish community.

On 13 February 1975 the Turkish-occupied zone of Cyprus was declared the 'Turkish Federated State of Cyprus', and Rauf Denktaş declared President. At the second joint meeting held by the Executive Council and Legislative Assembly of the Autonomous Turkish Cypriot Administration, it was decided to set up a Constituent Assembly which would prepare a constitution for the 'Turkish Federated State of Cyprus' within 45 days. This Constitution, which was approved by the Turkish Cypriot population in a referendum held on 8 June 1975, was regarded by the Turkish Cypriots as a first step towards a federal republic of Cyprus. The main provisions of the Constitution are summarized below:

The 'Turkish Federated State of Cyprus' is a democratic, secular republic based on the principles of social justice and the rule of law. It shall exercise only those functions which fall outside the powers and functions expressly given to the (proposed) Federal Republic of Cyprus. Necessary amendments shall be made to the Constitution of the 'Turkish Federated State of Cyprus' when the Constitution of the Federal Republic comes into force. The official language is Turkish.

Legislative power is vested in a Legislative Assembly, composed of 40 deputies, elected by universal suffrage for a period of five years. The President is Head of State and is elected by universal suffrage for a period of five years. No person may be elected President for more than two consecutive terms. The Council of Ministers shall be composed of a prime minister and 10 ministers. Judicial power is exercised through independent courts.

Other provisions cover such matters as the rehabilitation of refugees, property rights outside the 'Turkish Federated State', protection of coasts, social insurance, the rights and duties of citizens, etc.

On 15 November 1983 a unilateral declaration of independence brought into being the 'Turkish Republic of Northern Cyprus', which, like the 'Turkish Federated State of Cyprus', was not granted international recognition.

The Constituent Assembly, established after the declaration of independence, prepared a new constitution, which was approved by the Turkish Cypriot electorate on 5 May 1985. The new Constitution is very similar to the old one, but the number of deputies in the Legislative Assembly was increased to 50.

HEAD OF STATE

President of the 'Turkish Republic of Northern Cyprus': RAUF R. DENKTAŞ (assumed office as President of the 'Turkish Federated State of Cyprus' 13 February 1975; became President of the 'TRNC' 15 November 1983; re-elected for a five-year term 9 June 1985 and again on 22 April 1990).

COUNCIL OF MINISTERS
(August 1994)

A coalition of the Demokrat Parti (DP) and the Cumhuriyetçi Türk Partisi (CTP).

Prime Minister: HAKKI ATUN (DP).

Minister of State and Deputy Prime Minister: ÖZKER ÖZGÜR (CTP).

Minister of Foreign Affairs and Defence: ATAY A. RAŞIT (DP).

Minister of the Economy and Finance: ONUR BORMAN (DP).

Minister of Communications and Public Works: AHMET KAŞIF (DP).

Minister of the Interior: TANER ETKIN (DP).

Minister of Labour and Social Security: ÖZKAN MURAT (CTP).

Minister of Youth, Sports and Environment: SERDAR DENKTAŞ (DP).

Minister of Health: ERGIN İLKTAÇ (CTP).

Minister of Agriculture, Natural Resources and Energy: FERDI SABIT SOYER (CTP).

Minister of National Education and Culture: MEHMET ALI TALAT (CTP).

MINISTRIES

All Ministries are in Lefkoşa (Nicosia). Address: Lefkoşa (Nicosia), Mersin 10, Turkey.

Prime Minister's Office: tel. (22) 83141; telex 57444; fax (22) 77518.

Ministry of State and Deputy Prime Minister's Office: tel. (22) 83141; telex 5744; fax (22) 77518.

Ministry of Agriculture, Natural Resources and Energy: tel. (22) 83735; telex 57419; fax (22) 81031.

Ministry of Communications and Public Works: tel. (22) 83666; telex 57169; fax (22) 81891.

Ministry of the Economy and Finance: tel. (22) 83116; telex 57268; fax (22) 73049.

Ministry of Foreign Affairs and Defence: tel. (22) 83241; telex 57178; fax (22) 84290.

Ministry of Health: tel. (22) 83173; fax (22) 83893.

Ministry of the Interior: tel. (22) 85453; fax (22) 83043.

Ministry of Labour and Social Security: tel. (22) 78765.

Ministry of National Education and Culture: tel. (22) 83136; fax (22) 82334.

Ministry of Youth, Sports and Environment: tel. (22) 83911; telex 57178; fax (22) 83776.

PRESIDENT

Election, 22 April 1990

Candidates	Votes	%
RAUF R. DENKTAŞ (Independent) . . .	61,404	66.65
İSMAİL BOZKURT (Independent) . . .	29,568	32.09
ALPAY DURDURAN (YKP)	1,157	1.26
Total	92,129	100.00

LEGISLATIVE ASSEMBLY

Speaker: AYHAN H. ACARKAN (DP).

Deputy Speaker: OLGUN PAŞALAR (UBP).

General Election, 12 December 1993

Party	% of votes	Seats
Ulusal Bırlık Partisi	29.9	17
Demokrat Parti	29.2	15
Cumhuriyetçi Türk Partisi . . .	24.2	13
Toplumcu Kurtuluş Partisi . . .	13.3	5
Others*	3.5	—
Total	100.0	50

* The other parties that contested the election were the National Struggle Party, which won 2% of the votes; the Yeni Kıbrıs Partisi, which obtained 1.2%; and the Unity and Sovereignty Party, which won 0.3%.

POLITICAL ORGANIZATIONS

Cumhuriyetçi Türk Partisi (CTP) (Republican Turkish Party): 99A Şehit Salahi, Şevket St, Lefkoşa (Nicosia), Mersin 10, Turkey; tel. (22) 73300; f. 1970 by members of the Turkish community in Cyprus; socialist principles with anti-imperialist stand; district organizations at Famagusta, Kyrenia, Morphou and Nicosia; Leader ÖZKER ÖZGÜR; Gen. Sec. NACİ TALAT USAR.

Demokrat Parti (DP) (Democrat Party): Lefkoşa (Nicosia), Mersin 10, Turkey; tel. (22) 83795; fax (22) 87130; f. 1992 by disaffected UBP representatives; merged with the Yeni Doğuş Partisi (New Dawn Party; f. 1984) and Sosyal Demokrat Partisi (Social Democrat Party) in May 1993; Leader HAKKI ATUN.

National Struggle Party (MMP): Lefkoşa (Nicosia), Mersin 10, Turkey; f. 1993, as an opposition alliance of the Hür Demokrat Parti (Free Democrat Party; f. 1991; Leader ISMET KOTAK), the Nationalist Justice Party and the Homeland Party, to contest the December 1993 general election.

Toplumcu Kurtuluş Partisi (TKP) (Communal Liberation Party): 13 Mahmut Paşa St, Lefkoşa (Nicosia), Mersin 10, Turkey; tel. (22) 72555; f. 1976; merged with the Atılımcı Halk Partisi (Progressive People's Party, f. 1979) in 1989; left of centre; social democratic principles, social justice; believes in the leading role of organized labour; wants a solution of Cyprus problem as an independent, non-aligned, bi-zonal and bi-communal federal state; Leader MUSTAFA AKINCI; Gen. Sec. ERDAL SÜREÇ.

Ulusal Bırlık Partisi (UBP) (National Unity Party): 9 Atatürk Meydanı, Lefkoşa (Nicosia), Mersin 10, Turkey; tel. (22) 73972; f. 1975; right of centre; based on Atatürk's reforms, social justice, political equality and peaceful co-existence in an independent, bi-zonal, bi-communal, federal state of Cyprus; Leader Dr DERVİŞ EROĞLU.

Unity and Sovereignty Party (BEP): Lefkoşa (Nicosia), Mersin 10, Turkey; Leader ARIF SALIH KIRDAĞ.

Yeni Kıbrıs Partisi (YKP) (New Cyprus Party): Lefkoşa (Nicosia), Mersin 10, Turkey; tel. (22) 74917; fax (22) 71476; f. 1989; Leader ALPAY DURDURAN.

DIPLOMATIC REPRESENTATION

Embassy in the 'TRNC'

Turkey: Bedreddin Demirel Ave, Lefkoşa (Nicosia), Mersin 10, Turkey; tel. (22) 72314; fax (22) 82209; Ambassador: CAHIT BAYAR.

Turkey is the only country to have officially recognized the 'Turkish Republic of Northern Cyprus'.

JUDICIAL SYSTEM

Supreme Court: The highest court in the 'TRNC' is the Supreme Court. The Supreme Court functions as the Constitutional Court, the Court of Appeal and the High Administrative Court. The Supreme Court, sitting as the Constitutional Court, has exclusive jurisdiction to adjudicate finally on all matters prescribed by the

Constitution. The Supreme Court, sitting as the Court of Appeal, is the highest appellate court in the 'TRNC'. It also has original jurisdiction in certain matters of judicial review. The Supreme Court, sitting as the High Administrative Court, has exclusive jurisdiction on matters relating to administrative law.

The Supreme Court is composed of a president and seven judges.

President: SALİH S. DAYIOĞLU.

Judges: NAZIM ERGİN SALÂHİ, NİYAZİ FAZIL KORKUT, NEVVAR NOLAN, CELÂL KARABACAK, TANER ERGİNEL, METİN A. HAKKI, MUSTAFA ÖZKÖK.

Subordinate Courts: Judicial power other than that exercised by the Supreme Court is exercised by the Assize Courts, District Courts and Family Courts.

Supreme Council of Judicature: The Supreme Council of Judicature, composed of the president and judges of the Supreme Court, a member appointed by the President of the 'TRNC', a member appointed by the Legislative Assembly, the Attorney-General and a member elected by the Bar Association, is responsible for the appointment, promotion, transfer and matters relating to the discipline of all judges. The appointments of the president and judges of the Supreme Court are subject to the approval of the President of the 'TRNC'.

Attorney-General: SAİT AKIN.

Religion

Greeks form 77% of the population and most of them belong to the Orthodox Church. Most Turks (about 18% of the population) are Muslims. At the 1960 census, religious adherence was:

Greek Orthodox		441,656
Muslims		104,942
Armenian Apostolic		3,378
Maronite		2,752
Anglican	}	
Roman Catholic.	}	18,836
Other	}	

CHRISTIANITY

The Orthodox Church of Cyprus

The Autocephalous Orthodox Church of Cyprus, founded in AD 45, is part of the Eastern Orthodox Church; the Church is independent, and the Archbishop, who is also the Ethnarch (national leader of the Greek community), is elected by representatives of the towns and villages of Cyprus. The Church comprises six dioceses, and in 1985 had an estimated 442,000 members.

Archbishop of Nova Justiniana and all Cyprus: Archbishop CHRYSOSTOMOS, POB 1130, Arch. Kyprianos St, Nicosia; tel. (2) 474411; fax (2) 474180.

Metropolitan of Paphos: Bishop CHRYSOSTOMOS.

Metropolitan of Kitium: Bishop CHRYSOSTOMOS, Dem. Lipertis St, Larnaca; fax (41) 55588.

Metropolitan of Kyrenia: Bishop PAULUS.

Metropolitan of Limassol: Bishop CHRYSANTHOS.

Metropolitan of Morphou: Bishop CHRYSANTHOS.

Metropolitan of Salamis: Bishop BARNABAS.

The Roman Catholic Church

Latin Rite

The Patriarchate of Jerusalem covers Israel, Jordan and Cyprus. The Patriarch is resident in Jerusalem (see the chapter on Israel).

Vicar Patriarchal for Cyprus: Father UMBERTO BARATO.

Maronite Rite

Most of the Roman Catholics in Cyprus are adherents of the Maronite rite. Prior to June 1988 the Archdiocese of Cyprus included part of Lebanon. At December 1992 the archdiocese contained an estimated 10,500 Maronite Catholics.

Archbishop of Cyprus: Most Rev. BOUTROS GEMAYEL, POB 2249, Maronite Archbishop's House, 8 Favierou St, Nicosia; tel. (2) 458877; fax (2) 368260.

The Anglican Communion

Anglicans in Cyprus are adherents of the Episcopal Church in Jerusalem and the Middle East, officially inaugurated in January 1976. The Church has four dioceses, and the President is the Bishop in Jerusalem (see Israel). The diocese of Cyprus and the Gulf includes Cyprus, Iraq and the countries of the Arabian peninsula.

Bishop in Cyprus and the Gulf: Right Rev. JOHN EDWARD BROWN, POB 2075, Diocesan Office, 2 Grigoris Afxentiou St, Nicosia; tel. (2) 451220; fax (2) 466553.

Other Christian Churches

Among other denominations active in Cyprus are the Armenian Apostolic Church and the Greek Evangelical Church.

ISLAM

Most adherents of Islam in Cyprus are Sunni Muslims of the Hanafi sect. The religious head of the Muslim community is the Mufti.

Mufti of Cyprus: AHMET CEMAL İLKTAÇ (acting), PK 142, Lefkoşa (Nicosia), Mersin 10, Turkey.

The Press

GREEK CYPRIOT DAILIES

Agon (Struggle): POB 1417, Makarios Ave and Agapinoros St, Nicosia; tel. (2) 477181; fax (2) 457887; f. 1964; morning; Greek; independent, right of centre; Owner and Dir N. KOSHIS; Chief Editor GEORGE A. LEONIDAS; circ. 8,000.

Alithia (Truth): POB 1695, 5 Pindaros and Androklis St, Nicosia; tel. (2) 463040; fax (2) 463945; f. 1952 as a weekly, 1982 as a daily; morning; Greek; right-wing; supports DISY party; Dir SOCRATIS HASSIKOS; Chief Editor ALEKOS KONSTANTINIDES; circ. 8,000.

Apogevmatini (Afternoon): POB 5603, 5 Aegaleo St, Strovolos, Nicosia; tel. (2) 353603; fax (2) 353223; f. 1972; afternoon; Greek; independent, moderate; Dir M. HADJIEFTHIMIOU; Chief Editor ANTHOS LYKAVGHIS; circ. 10,000.

Cyprus Mail: POB 1144, 24 Vassilios Voulgaroktonos St, Nicosia; tel. (2) 462074; telex 2616; fax (2) 366385; f. 1945; morning; English; independent; Dir. KYRIACOS IAKOVIDES; Editor RACHAEL GIL-LETT; circ. 3,500.

Eleftherotypia (Free Press): POB 3821, 50 Grivas Dhigenis Ave, Nicosia; tel. (2) 454400; fax (2) 454413; f. 1981; morning; Greek; right of centre; organ of DIKO party; Dir and Chief Editor GEORGE ELIADES; circ. 7,000.

Haravghi (Dawn): POB 1556, ETAK Bldg, 6 Akamantos St, Nicosia; tel. (2) 476356; fax (2) 365154; f. 1956; morning; Greek; organ of AKEL (Communist Party); Dir and Chief Editor ANTONIS CHRISTO-DOULOU; circ. 13,000.

Machi (Battle): POB 1105, 231 Ledras, 2nd Floor, Nicosia; tel. (2) 477676; fax (2) 477701; f. 1960; morning; Greek; right-wing; Dir SOTIRIS SAMSON; Chief Editor DEMETRIS SAVVIDES.

Messimvrini (Midday): POB 1543, 40 Sofouli St, Nicosia; tel. (2) 366230; f. 1970; afternoon; Greek; independent, right-wing; Publr, Dir and Chief Editor ELLI HADJINICOLAOU; circ. 2,000.

Phileleftheros (Liberal): POB 1094, Commercial Centre, 1 Diogenous St, 6th–7th Floor, Engomi, Nicosia; tel. (2) 463922; telex 4999; fax (2) 366122; f. 1955; morning; Greek; independent, moderate; Dir N. PATTICHIS; Editorial Dir A. LYKAVGIS; Chief Editor T. KOUNNAFIS; circ. 20,100.

Simerini (Today): POB 1836, 31 Archangelos Ave, Strovolos, Nicosia; tel. (2) 353532; telex 3826; fax (2) 352298; f. 1976; morning; Greek; right-wing; supports DISY party; Dir COSTAS HADJI-COSTIS; Chief Editor SAVVAS IAKOVIDES; circ. 13,000.

TURKISH CYPRIOT DAILIES

Bırlık (Unity): 43 Yediler St, PK 841, Lefkoşa (Nicosia), Mersin 10, Turkey; tel. (22) 72959; fax (22) 83959; f. 1980; Turkish; organ of UBP; Editor MEHMET AKAR; circ. 4,500.

Halkın Sesi (Voice of the People): 172 Kyrenia St, Lefkoşa (Nicosia), Mersin 10, Turkey; tel. (22) 73141; telex 57173; f. 1942; morning; Turkish; independent Turkish nationalist; Editor REŞAT AKAR; circ. 6,000.

İstiklal (Independence): Lefkoşa (Nicosia), Mersin 10, Turkey; f. 1949, ceased publication 1954, recommenced publication 1993.

Kıbrıs: Dr Fazil Küçik Blvd, Lefkoşa (Nicosia), Mersin 10, Turkey; tel. (22) 81922; telex 57177; fax 81934; Editor MEHMET ALI AKPINAR; circ. 4,000.

Kıbrıs Postası (Cyprus Post): M. İrfan Bey Sok. 30, Lefkoşa (Nicosia); tel. (22) 75242; telex 57244; f. 1982; Turkish; independent; Owner and Chief Editor İSMET KOTAK; circ. 4,500.

Ortam (Political Conditions): 158A Girne St, Lefkoşa (Nicosia), Mersin 10, Turkey; tel. (22) 74872; Turkish; organ of the TKP; Editor KEMAL AKTUNÇ; circ. 1,250.

Vatan (Homeland): Lefkoşa (Nicosia), Mersin 10, Turkey; Editor ERTEN KASIMĞLU.

Yenidüzen (New System): Yeni Sanayi St, Lefkoşa (Nicosia), Mersin 10, Turkey; tel. (22) 74906; fax (22) 75240; Turkish; organ of the CTP; circ. 1,000.

GREEK CYPRIOT WEEKLIES

Ammochostos: 44 Egnatias, Plati, Eylenja; tel. 352918; Greek; right-wing; reflects views of Famagusta refugees; Dir and Chief Editor NIKOS FALAS; circ. 2,800.

Anexartitos (Independent): POB 1064, A. Karyos St, Engomi, Nicosia; tel. (2) 449766; f. 1973; Greek; organ of EDEK party; Chief Editor ANTONIS MAKRIDES; circ. 2,780.

Cyprus Financial Mirror: 80B Thermopylon St, Nicosia; tel. (2) 495790; fax (2) 495907; f. 1993; circ. 2,000.

Cyprus Weekly: POB 1992, 216 Mitsis 3 Bldg, Makarios Ave, Nicosia; tel. (2) 441433; telex 2260; fax (2) 458665; f. 1979; English; independent; Dirs and Editors GEORGES DER PARTHOGH, ALEX EFTHYVOULOS; circ. 12,000.

Eleftherotypia Tis Defteras (Monday's Free Press): POB 3821, Hadjisavvas Bldg, Eleftheria Sq, Nicosia; tel. (2) 454400; telex 3963; f. 1980; Greek; right of centre; organ of DIKO party.

Embros (Forward): Nicosia; tel. (2) 451280; f. 1987; Greek; left-wing, supports ADISOK; Chief Editor P. POLYDORIDES; circ. 2,500.

Epikeri (Current Affairs): POB 3786, 19 Bouboulinas St, Nicosia; tel. (2) 455788; f. 1987; Greek; independent; Dir and Chief Editor LAZAROS MAVROS; circ. 2,500.

Ergatiki Phoni (Workers' Voice): POB 5018, SEK Bldg, 23 Alkeou St, Engomi, Nicosia; tel. (2) 441142; telex 6180; fax (2) 476360; f. 1947; Greek; organ of SEK trade union; Chief Editor GREGORIS GREGORIADES; circ. 12,544.

Ergatiko Vima (Workers' Tribune): POB 1185, 31-35 Archemos St, Nicosia; tel. (2) 443382; telex 3073; fax (2) 349382; f. 1956; Greek; organ of the PEO trade union; Editor-in-Chief NIKODEMOS MELISSOS; circ. 14,000.

Exormisi (Starting Line): POB 1697, 87b Ayias Phylaxeos, Limassol; tel. (5) 332814; f. 1989; Greek; independent; Dir and Chief Editor G. EROTOKRITOU; circ. 2,500.

Flas (Flash): POB 4626, 11 Kolokotronis St, Kaimakli, Nicosia; tel. (2) 437887; fax (2) 434197; f. 1978; Greek; Chief Editor LOUCAS BARBAS; circ. 10,000.

Kyriakatikes Ores (Sunday Hours): POB 1450, 7 Androkleous St, Nicosia; tel. (2) 448548; Dir and Chief Editor PHIVOS MORIDES.

Official Gazette: Printing Office of the Republic of Cyprus, Nicosia; tel. (2) 302202; fax (2) 302205; f. 1960; Greek; published by the Government of the Republic of Cyprus.

Panorama: POB 7033, 20 Stassicratous St, Nicosia; tel. (2) 367367; f. 1990; Greek; Dir STELIOS MANDRIDES; Chief Editor TITOS KOLOTAS; circ. 7,000.

Paraskinio (Behind the Scenes): 39 Kennedy Ave, Nicosia; tel. (2) 313334; f. 1987; Greek; Dir and Chief Editor D. MICHAEL; cir. 4,900.

To Periodiko: POB 1836, Dias Bldg, 31 Archangelos Ave, Strovolos, Nicosia; tel. (2) 353646; telex 3826; fax (2) 352298; f. 1986; Greek; Chief Editor PHILIPPOS STYLIANOU; circ. 20,000.

Proina Nea (Morning News): POB 4349, 40 Vyronos Ave, Nicosia; tel. (2) 451000; fax (2) 448299; f. 1989; organ of EDEK (Socialist Party); Dir R. PRENZAS; Chief Editor L. LARKOU; circ. 3,000.

Selides (Pages): POB 1094, Nicosia; tel. (2) 467167; fax (2) 366122; f. 1991; Greek; Dir N. PATTICHIS; Chief Editor A. MICHAELIDES; circ. 20,000.

TURKISH CYPRIOT WEEKLIES

Cyprus Today: A. N. Graphics Ltd, 18 Server Somuncuuğlu Sokak, Köşklüçiftlik, Lefkoşa (Nicosia), Mersin 10, Turkey; tel. (22) 73892; fax (22) 72033; f. 1989; English; political, social, cultural and economic.

Ekonomi (The Economy): Bedrettin Demirel Ave, PK 718, Lefkoşa (Nicosia), Mersin 10, Turkey; tel. (22) 83760; telex 57511; fax (22) 83089; f. 1958; Turkish; published by the Turkish Cypriot Chamber of Commerce; Editor-in-Chief SAMI TAŞARKAN; circ. 3,000.

Ekspres: Lefkoşa (Nicosia), Mersin 10, Turkey; f. 1987; Editor-in-Chief ÖNDER ASLITÜRK.

Haber: Lefkoşa (Nicosia), Mersin 10, Turkey; tel. (22) 78188; Turkish; Chief Editor MEHMET AKAR.

Olay: 5 Hükümet St, Gazi Mağusa (Famagusta), Mersin 10, Turkey; tel. (536) 66111; telex 57244.

Söz (The Word): Sabri Orient Otel Alti, Lefkoşa (Nicosia), Mersin 10, Turkey; tel. (22) 76179.

Sportmence: Lefkoşa (Nicosia), Mersin 10, Turkey; tel. (22) 72212; Turkish; Chief Editor ERTAN BIRINCI.

Süper Spor: Lefkoşa (Nicosia), Mersin 10, Turkey; tel. (22) 74471; Turkish; Chief Editor İBRAHİM ÖZSOY.

OTHER WEEKLIES

Lion: British Forces Post Office 53; tel. (5) 263926; fax (5) 263181; British Sovereign Base Areas weekly with Services Sound and Vision Corpn programme guide; Editor K. FISH; circ. 5,000.

Middle East Economic Survey: Middle East Petroleum and Economic Publications (Cyprus), POB 4940, Nicosia; tel. (2) 445431; telex 2198; fax (2) 474988; f. 1957 (in Beirut); weekly review and analysis of petroleum, economic and political news; Publr BASIM W. ITAYIM; Editor IAN SEYMOUR.

GREEK CYPRIOT PERIODICALS

Avgherinos (Morning Star): 5th Floor, 18 Makarios Ave, Nicosia; tel. (2) 454466; f. 1983; children's magazine; every 2 months; Greek; Publr A. CHRISTODOULIDES; circ. 5,000.

Agrotis (Countryman): Nicosia; tel. (2) 446981; telex 2526; f. 1943; quarterly; Greek; published by the Cyprus Press and Information Office; circ. 6,000.

Cypria (Cypriot Woman): 56 Kennedy Ave, 11th Floor, Nicosia; tel. (2) 494907; f. 1984; every 2 months; Greek; Owner MARO KARAYIANNI; circ. 7,500.

Cyprus Bulletin: Nicosia; tel. (2) 446981; telex 2526; fax (2) 366123; f. 1964; fortnightly; Arabic, English, Greek, Spanish; published by the Cyprus Press and Information Office; Principal Officers P. TAKKOUSHIS, G. HADJISAVVAS; circ. 8,000.

Cyprus P.C.: POB 4989, 15 Dhigenis Ave, Nicosia; tel. (2) 343044; f. 1990; monthly; Greek; computing magazine; Dir PERIKLES VARNAVA; circ. 2,500.

Cyprus Time Out: POB 3697, 4 Pygmalion St, Nicosia; tel. (2) 452079; fax (2) 360668; f. 1978; monthly; English; Chief Editor ELLADA SOPHOCLEOUS; circ. 5,000.

Cyprus Today: c/o Ministry of Education and Culture, Nicosia; tel. (2) 454733; telex 2526; fax (2) 366123; f. 1963; quarterly; English; cultural and information review; published and distributed by Press and Information Office; Principal Officer YIANNIS KATSOURIS; circ. 15,000.

Dimosios Ypallilos (Civil Servant): 3 Dem. Severis Ave, Nicosia; tel. (2) 442278; fax (2) 465199; fortnightly; published by the Cyprus Civil Servants' Association (PASYDY); circ. 11,500.

Economiki Kypros (Economic Cyprus): 37 Onassagoras St, Nicosia; tel. (2) 472510; f. 1987; monthly; Dir and Chief Editor TASSOS ANASTASSIADES; circ. 4,000.

Endoskopisi: 31 Archangelos Ave, Strovolos, Nicosia; tel. (2) 353532; fax (2) 352298; f. 1984; monthly; Greek; Chief Editor NICOS HADJICOSTIS; circ. 3,000.

Enimerossi (Briefing): POB 1417, 37 Onassagoras St, Nicosia; tel. (2) 477181; fax (2) 457887; f. 1982; fortnightly; Greek; Dir NIKOS KOSHIS; Chief Editor ANDREAS KAOURIS; circ. 10,000.

Eso-Etimos (Ever Ready): POB 4544, Nicosia; tel. (2) 443587; f. 1913; quarterly; Greek; publ. by Cyprus Scouts' Asscn; Editor TAKIS NEOPHYTOU; circ. 2,500.

Gyneka ke Enimerossi (Women, Fashion, Briefing): POB 1417, Makarios Ave and Agapinoros St, Nicosia; tel. (2) 477181; fax (2) 457887; f. 1982; monthly; Greek; Dir. and Chief Editor LEONIDAS KOSSIS; circ. 3,000.

Katanalotis (Consumer): POB 4874, 28 Gladstone St, Nicosia 162; tel. (2) 451092; fax (2) 467080; f. 1977; every 2 months; Greek; circ. 3,000.

Nea Epochi (New Epoch): POB 1581, 8A Achillea Kyrou St, Nicosia; tel. (2) 444605; f. 1959; every 2 months; Greek; literary; Editor ACHILLEAS PYLIOTIS; circ. 2,000.

Nicosia This Month: POB 1015, Nikoklis Publishing House, Ledras and Pygmaleon St, Nicosia; tel. (2) 473124; telex 5374; fax (2) 463363; f. 1984; monthly; English; Chief Editor ELLADA SOPHOCLEOUS; circ. 3,000.

Oikogeneia Kai Scholeio (Family and School): 18 Archbishop Makarios III Ave, 5th Floor, Flat 8, Nicosia; tel. (2) 454466; f. 1970; every 2 months; Greek; for parents and teachers; publ. by the Pancyprian School for Parents; Editor A. D. CHRISTODOULIDES; circ. 7,000.

Paedikes Ores (Children's Time): POB 8205, 86 Iphigenias St, 2nd Floor, Acropolis, Nicosia; tel. (2) 378900; fax (2) 378916; f. 1990; monthly; Greek; children's magazine; Dir KYPROULA CHRISTOFIDOU; Chief Editor PROMITHEAS CHRISTOPHIDES; circ. 13,800.

Paediki Chara (Children's Joy): POB 136, 18 Archbishop Makarios III Ave, Nicosia; tel. (2) 442638; fax (2) 360410; f. 1962; monthly; for pupils; publ. by the Pancyprian Union of Greek Teachers; Editor SOFOCLES CHARALAMBIDES; circ. 14,000.

Pnevmatiki Kypros (Cultural Cyprus): Nicosia; tel. (2) 659001; f. 1960; monthly; Greek; literary; Owner Dr KYPROS CHRYSANTHIS.

Tele Ores: POB 8205, Nicosia; tel. (2) 378900; fax (2) 378916; fortnightly; television guide.

TV Radio Programme: POB 4824, Cyprus Broadcasting Corpn, Broadcasting House, Nicosia; tel. (2) 422231; telex 2333; fax (2) 314050; fortnightly; Greek and English; published by the CyBC; radio and TV programme news; circ. 23,000.

Success: POB 4706, Nicosia; tel. (2) 472510; f. 1985; monthly; English; Chief Editor TITOS KOLOTAS; circ. 4,000.

Synergatiko Vima (The Co-operative Tribune): Shanteclair Bldg, 4th Floor, No. 401, 2 Sofoulis St, Nicosia; tel. (2) 458757; fax (2) 458758; f. 1961; monthly; Greek; official organ of the Pancyprian Co-operative Confederation Ltd; circ. 5,000.

Synthesis (Composition): POB 3539, 22 Thessalonikis St, Limassol; tel. (5) 344154; fax (5) 357122; f. 1988; every 2 months; art; Dir YIANNOS KOUZARIDES; circ. 5,000.

Touristika Chronnica (Tourism Chronicle): POB 7083, Nicosia; tel. (2) 443240; f. 1986; every 2 months; Dir and Publr A. KAROUZIS; circ. 3,000.

Trapezikos (Bank Employee): POB 1235, 8 Prevezis St, Nicosia; tel. (2) 366993; f. 1960; Greek; monthly; Editor L. HADZICOSTIS; circ. 5,000.

TURKISH CYPRIOT PERIODICALS

Belge (Document): 6 Hurriyet Cad., Girne, Mersin 10, Turkey; monthly; Turkish; Chief Editor TIJEN ÖZDAVRIM.

Çengel: Lefkoşa (Nicosia), Mersin 10, Turkey; tel. (22) 75225; Turkish; Owner and Publr ERDAL ANDIZ.

Kuzey Kıbrıs—Northern Cyprus Monthly: Directorate of Press and Information, Kültür Dergisi, PK 828, Lefkoşa (Nicosia), Mersin 10, Turkey; tel. (22) 84133; telex 57177; fax (22) 84847; f. 1963; Chief Editors ESER BIREY (English), HAKKI YAZGAN (Turkish).

Kuzey Kıbrıs Kültür Dergisi (North Cyprus Cultural Journal): PK 828, Lefkoşa (Nicosia), Mersin 10, Turkey; monthly; Turkish; Chief Editor GÜNSEL DOĞASAL.

Kooperatif (Co-operative): Dept of Co-operative Development, Lefkoşa (Nicosia), Mersin 10, Turkey; tel. (22) 71207; f. 1970; monthly; Turkish; circ. 2,000.

New Cyprus: PK 327, Lefkoşa (Nicosia), Mersin 10, Turkey; tel. (22) 78194; telex 2585; fax (22) 72592; English; publ. by the North Cyprus Research and Publishing Centre; also Turkish edition *Yeni Kıbrıs*; Editor AHMET C. GAZIOĞLU.

Özgürlük: PK 327, Lefkoşa (Nicosia), Mersin 10, Turkey; Turkish; Owner and Publr HÜRREM TOLGA.

Uluslararası Kuzey Kıbrıs Magazin (International Northern Cyprus Magazine): Cengiz Han St, Yuva Apt, Köşklüçiftlik, Lefkoşa (Nicosia), Mersin 10, Turkey; f. 1987; quarterly; Turkish and English; publ. by YORUM Publishing House; Editor TANSU KONURALP.

OTHER PERIODICALS

The Blue Beret: POB 1642, HQ UNFICYP, Nicosia; tel. (2) 359550; fax (2) 359752; monthly; English; circ. 1,100.

International Crude Oil and Product Prices: Middle East Petroleum and Economic Publications (Cyprus), POB 4940, Nicosia; tel. (2) 445431; telex 2198; fax (2) 474988; f. 1971 (in Beirut); 2 a year; review and analysis of petroleum price trends in world markets; Publisher BASIM W. ITAYIM.

NEWS AGENCIES

Cyprus News Agency: POB 3947, 7 Kastorias St, Hilton Area, Nicosia; tel. (2) 319009; telex 4787; fax (2) 319006; f. 1976; English and Greek; Dir ANDREAS HADJIPAPAS.

Kuzey Kıbrıs Haber Ajansı (Northern Cyprus News Agency): 18 Server Somuncuoğlu St, Lefkoşa (Nicosia), Mersin 10, Turkey; tel. (22) 73892; telex 57536; fax (22) 72033; f. 1977; Dir-Gen. M. ALI AKPINAR.

Pan Basin Yayin Ajansi (Pan Press Agency): ATO Apt 4, Sht. İbrahim Yusuf Sok., Lefkoşa (Nicosia), Mersin 10, Turkey; tel. (22) 77813; f. 1980; Dir ARMAN RATIP.

Papyros Press Agency: 13 Dramas St, Nicosia; tel. (2) 376878; telex 4645; fax (2) 377157.

Türk Ajansı Kıbrıs (TAK) (Turkish News Agency of Cyprus): 9 Server Somuncuoğlu St, Lefkoşa (Nicosia), Mersin 10, Turkey; tel. (22) 71818; telex 57448; fax (22) 71213; f. 1973; Dir EMIR HÜSEYIN ERSOY.

Foreign Bureaux

Agence France-Presse (AFP) (France): POB 7242, Loizides Centre, 7th Floor, 36 Kypranoros St, Nicosia; tel. (2) 365050; telex 2824; fax (2) 365125; Bureau Chief JEAN-FRANÇOIS LE MOUNIER; Correspondent DIMITRI ANDREOU.

Agencia EFE (Spain): 10 Katsonis St, Nicosia; tel. (2) 461311; telex 6126; Correspondent MARIA SAAVEDRA.

Agenzia Nazionale Stampa Associata (ANSA) (Italy): Middle East Office, 10 Katsonis St, Ayii Omoloyites, Nicosia; tel. (2) 491699; telex 4139; fax (2) 492732; Rep. VITTORIO FRENQUELLUCI.

Associated Press (AP) Middle East Ltd (USA): POB 4853, Neo-elen Marina, 10 Katsonis St, Nicosia; tel. (2) 492599; telex 2459; fax (2) 491617; Rep. EARLEEN FISHER; Editor, Middle East ED BLANCHE.

Athinaikon Praktorion Eidiseon (Greece): 10 Andreas Patsalides St, Engomi, Nicosia; tel. (2) 441110; fax (2) 457418; Rep. GEORGE LEONIDAS.

Informatsionnoye Telegrafnoye Agentstvo Rossii-Telegraf-noye Agentstvo Suverennykh Stran (ITAR-TASS) (Russia): POB 2235, 6 Kipoupolis St, Archangelos, Nicosia; tel. (2) 382486; telex 2368; Rep. VIKTOR DOROSHENKO.

Iraqi News Agency: POB 1098, Flat 201, 11 Ippocratous St, Nicosia; tel. (2) 472095; telex 2197; fax (2) 472096; Correspondent AHMED SULEIMAN.

Jamahiriya News Agency (JANA) (Libya): 93 Kennedy Ave, Nicosia; tel. (2) 453933; Rep. MUHAMMAD ASH-SHWEIHDI.

Novinska Agencija Tanjug (Yugoslavia): 26 Methonis St, Lyca vitos, Nicosia; tel. (2) 450212; telex 3087; Rep. NADA DUGONJIĆ.

Polska Agencja Prasowa (PAP) (Poland): POB 2373, Prodromos St 24, Nicosia; Rep. MICHALAKIS PANTELIDES.

Prensa Latina (Cuba): 12 Demophon St, 5th Floor, Apt 501, Nicosia; tel. (2) 464131; telex 4505; Rep. LEONEL NODAL.

Reuters MEA (UK): POB 5725, 5th Floor, George and Thelma Paraskevaides Foundation Bldg, 36 Grivas Dhigenis Ave, Nicosia; tel. (2) 365087; telex 4922; fax (2) 475487; Rep. GRAHAM STEWART.

Sofia-Press Agency (Bulgaria): 9 Roumeli St, Droshia, Larnaca; tel. (4) 494484; Rep. IONKA VERESIE.

Syrian Arab News Agency (SANA): POB 1891, Nicosia; tel. (2) 474481; fax (2) 446963; Correspondent ALMALA MOUZAD.

United Press International (UPI) (USA): 24A Heroes Ave, Nicosia 171; tel. (2) 456643; telex 2260; fax (2) 458665; Rep. GEORGES DER PARTHOGH.

Xinhua (New China) News Agency (People's Republic of China): POB 7024, Flat 32, 6 Nafpaktos St, Nicosia; tel. (2) 349703; telex 5265; fax (2) 435741; Rep. ZHANG SHENPING.

Publishers

GREEK CYPRIOT PUBLISHERS

Action Publications: POB 4676, 35 Ayiou Nicolaou St, Engomi, Nicosia; tel. (2) 444104; telex 4455; fax (2) 450048; f. 1971; travel; Pres. TONY CHRISTODOULOU.

Alithia: POB 1695, 5 Pindaros and Adroklis St, Nicosia; tel. (2) 463040; fax (2) 463945.

Andreou Chr. Publications: POB 2298, 67a Regenis St, Nicosia; tel. (2) 466813; fax (2) 466649; f. 1979.

Chrysopolitissa: POB 5182, Nicosia; tel. (2) 351460.

MAM (The House of Cyprus Publications): POB 1722, Phaneromeni Library Building, 46 Phaneromeni St, Nicosia; tel. (2) 472744; fax (2) 465411; f. 1965.

Nikoklis Publishing House: POB 3697, Nicosia; tel. (2) 456544; fax (2) 360668; tourism; Man. ELLADA SOPHOCLEOUS.

Romantic Cyprus: POB 2375, Nicosia; fax (2) 445155.

TURKISH CYPRIOT PUBLISHERS

Birlik Gazetesi: Yediler St, Lefkoşa (Nicosia), Mersin 10, Turkey; tel. (22) 72959; f. 1980; Dir MEHMET AKAR.

Bolan Matbaası: 35 Pençizade St, Lefkoşa (Nicosia), Mersin 10, Turkey; tel. (22) 74802.

Devlet Basımevi (Turkish Cypriot Government Printing House): Şerif Arzik St, Lefkoşa (Nicosia), Mersin 10, Turkey; tel. (22) 72010; Dir S. KÜRŞAD.

Halkın Sesi Ltd: 172 Girne Cad., Lefkoşa (Nicosia), Mersin 10, Turkey; tel. (22) 73141.

Kema Matbaası: 1 Tabak Hilmi St, Lefkoşa (Nicosia), Mersin 10, Turkey; tel. (22) 72785.

K. Rüstem & Bro.: 22–24 Girne Cad., Lefkoşa (Nicosia), Mersin 10, Turkey; tel. (22) 71418.

Sebil International Press: 27 Agâh Efendi St, PK 7, Lefkoşa (Nicosia), Mersin 10, Turkey; tel. (22) 74254; telex 57565; fax (22) 83474; f. 1985; technical and scientific; Principal Officer E. BAŞARAN.

Tezel Matbaası: 35 Şinasi St, Lefkoşa (Nicosia), Mersin 10, Turkey; tel. (22) 71022.

Radio and Television

In December 1991, in the government-controlled area, it was estimated that there were 190,000 radio receivers and 100,000 television receivers (including about 90,000 colour receivers) in use; while, in December 1985, in the Turkish sector of Cyprus there were an estimated 42,170 radio receivers and 75,000 television receivers in use. In 1991, under an agreement between Cyprus and Greece, Cypriot viewers were to be given access to Greek television channels for several hours daily via satellite.

Cyprus Broadcasting Corporation (CyBC): POB 4824, Broad-casting House, Nicosia; tel. (2) 422231; telex 2333; fax (2) 314050; Chair. MARIOS ELIADES; Dir-Gen. G. POTAMITES (acting).

    Radio: f. 1952; Programme I in Greek, Programme II in Greek, Turkish, English, Arabic and Armenian, Programme III in Greek; two medium wave transmitters of 100 kW in Nicosia with relay stations at Paphos and Limassol; three 30 kW ERP VHF FM stereo transmitters on Mount Olympus; international service in English and Arabic.

    Television: f. 1957; **(Channel 1):** one Band III 200/20 kW transmitter on Mount Olympus. **Channel 2:** one Band IV 100/10kW ERP transmitter on Mount Olympus. **ET 1:** one Band IV 100/10 kW ERP transmitter on Mount Olympus for transmission of the ET1 Programme received, via satellite, from Greece.

    The above three TV channels are also transmitted from 65 transposer stations.

In 1993 there were, in addition, 27 small licensed radio broad-casting stations operating in the government-controlled area.

Bayrak Radio and TV Corpn (BRTK): Atatürk Square, Lefkoşa (Nicosia), Mersin 10, Turkey; tel. (22) 85555; telex 57264; fax (22) 81991; in July 1983 it became an independent Turkish Cypriot corpn, partly financed by the Govt; Dir MUAMMER YAĞCIOĞLU.

    Radio Bayrak: f. 1963; home service in Turkish, overseas ser-vices in Turkish, Greek, English, Arabic, Swedish and German; broadcasts 31 hours a day; Dir of Broadcasting HÜSEYIN ÇOBAN-OĞLU.

    Bayrak TV: f. 1976; transmits programmes in Turkish, Greek, English and Arabic on six channels; Dir of Programmes HÜSEYIN ÇOBANOĞLU.

Services Sound and Vision Corpn, Cyprus: Akrotiri, British Forces Post Office 58; tel. (5) 278518; fax (5) 278580; f. 1948; incorporates the British Forces Broadcasting Service, Cyprus; broadcasts a two-channel 24-hour radio service in English on VHF and a daily TV service; Station Man. CHARLES FOSTER; Engineering Man. JOHN DUNLOP.

Türkiye Radyo Televizyon (TRT): 2 channels of television pro-grammes in Turkish, transmitted to the Turkish sector of Cyprus.

Finance

(brs = branches; cap. = capital; p.u. = paid up; auth. = authorized; dep. = deposits; res = reserves; m. = million; amounts in Cyprus pounds)

BANKING
Central Bank

Central Bank of Cyprus: POB 5529, 36 Metochiou St, Nicosia; tel. (2) 445281; telex 2424; fax (2) 472012; f. 1963; cap. p.u. 0.1m., res 1m., dep. 705m. (Dec. 1992); Gov. A. C. AFXENTIOU.

Greek Cypriot Banks

Bank of Cyprus Ltd: POB 1472, 51 Stasinos St, Ayia Paraskevi, Strovolos 140, Nicosia; tel. (2) 378000; telex 4545; fax (2) 378111; f. 1899, reconstituted 1943 by the amalgamation of Bank of Cyprus, Larnaca Bank Ltd and Famagusta Bank Ltd; cap. p.u. 68m., res 25.6m. (Dec. 1993); Chair. SOLON A. TRIANTAFYLLIDES; Gov. ANDREAS C. PATSALIDES; 218 brs.

Co-operative Central Bank Ltd: POB 4537, Gregoris Afxentiou St, Nicosia; tel. (2) 442921; telex 2313; fax (2) 443088; f. 1937 under the Co-operative Societies Law; banking and credit facilities to member societies, importer and distributor of agricultural requi-sites, insurance agent; dep. 298m. (Dec 1993); Chair A. MAVRO-NICOLAS; Sec.-Gen. D. PITSILLIDES; 5 brs.

The Cyprus Popular Bank Ltd: POB 2032, Popular Bank Bldg, 39 Archbishop Makarios III Ave, Nicosia; tel. (2) 450000; telex 2494; fax (2) 453355; f. 1901; full commercial banking; cap. 73.9m., res 35.6m., total assets 1,362.7m. (Dec. 1992); Chair. and Group Chief Exec. KIKIS N. LAZARIDES; 135 brs.

Hellenic Bank Ltd: POB 4747, 92 Dhigenis Akritas Ave, Nicosia; tel. (2) 360000; telex 3311; fax (2) 454074; f. 1974; full commercial banking; cap. p.u. 11.3m., res 8.1m., dep. 290.2m. (Dec. 1992); Chair. PASCHALIS L. PASCHALIDES; Gen. Man. PANOS CHR. GHALANOS; 70 brs.

Housing Finance Corpn: POB 3898, 41 Themistoklis Dervis St, Hawaii Tower, Nicosia; tel. (2) 452777; telex 4134; fax (2) 452870;

f. 1980; provides long-term loans for home-buying; cap. 2.8m., dep. 38m., total assets 40m. (Dec. 1991); Chair. I. TYPOGRAPHOS; Gen. Man. CH. SHIAMBARTAS (acting); 7 brs.

Lombard NatWest Bank Ltd: POB 1661, Corner of Chilon and Gladstone St, Stylianos Lenas Square, Nicosia; tel. (2) 474333; telex 2262; fax (2) 457870; f. 1960; locally incorporated although foreign-controlled; cap. p.u. 3m., dep. 126.4m. (Sept. 1993); Chair. M. G. COLOCASSIDES; Man. Dir E. IOANNOU; 15 brs.

Turkish Cypriot Bankers' Association
Northern Cyprus Bankers' Association: Lefkoşa (Nicosia), Mersin 10, Turkey; f. 1987; tel. (22) 82216; fax (22) 82131; 15 mems.

Turkish Cypriot Banks
(amounts in Turkish liras)
Akdeniz Garanti Bankası Ltd: PK 149, 4 Iplik Pazan St, Lefkoşa (Nicosia), Mersin 10, Turkey; tel. (22) 86744; telex 57572; fax (22) 86741; f. 1989 as Mediterranean Guarantee Bank; cap. 5.4m., res 1.1m., dep. 73.6m. (Dec. 1991); Chair. and Gen. Man. SINAN H. SEMILER.

Asbank Ltd: 8 Mecidiye St, PK 448, Lefkoşa (Nicosia), Mersin 10, Turkey; tel. (22) 83023; telex 57305; fax (22) 81244; f. 1986; cap. and res 31,150.6m., dep. 225,126.1m. (Dec. 1993); Chair. MUSTAFA ALTUNER; Gen. Man. DERVİŞ TÜRKER; 5 brs.

Kıbrıs Endüstri Bankası (Industrial Bank of Cyprus): 81–83 Kyrenia Ave, Lefkoşa (Nicosia), Mersin 10, Turkey; tel. (22) 83770; telex 57397; fax (22) 71830; assets 'frozen' Oct. 1991; 8 brs.

Kıbrıs Kredi Bankası Ltd (Cyprus Credit Bank Ltd): 5–7 İplik Pazarı St, Lefkoşa (Nicosia), Mersin 10, Turkey; tel. (22) 75026; telex 57336; fax (22) 76999; f. 1978; cap. p.u. 15,262m., res 41,753m., dep. 773,785m. (Dec. 1992); Chair. SALİH BOYACI; Gen. Man. YÜKSEL YAZGIN; 14 brs in Cyprus, 1 in Turkey, 2 in UK.

Kıbrıs Ticaret Bankası Ltd (Cyprus Commercial Bank Ltd): 53 Kyrenia Ave, Lefkoşa (Nicosia), Mersin 10, Turkey; tel. (22) 83180; telex 57395; fax (22) 82278; f. 1982; cap. p.u. 10,068m., res 14,473m., dep. 422,788m. (Dec. 1993); Chair. YUKSEL AHMET RAŞİT; Gen. Man. PEKER M. TURGUD; 8 brs.

Kıbrıs Türk Kooperatif Merkez Bankası Ltd (Turkish Cypriot Co-operative Central Bank): 49–55 Mahmut Paşa St, PK 823, Lefkoşa (Nicosia), Mersin 10, Turkey; tel. (22) 83207; telex 57216; fax (22) 76787; cap. and res 74,621.0m., dep. 517,600.6m. (Dec. 1992); banking and credit facilities to member societies and individuals; assets 'frozen' in October 1991; Gen. Man. Dr TUNCER ARİFOĞLU; 14 brs.

Kıbrıs Vakiflar Bankası Ltd: 58 Yediler St, PK 212, Lefkoşa (Nicosia), Mersin 10, Turkey; tel. (22) 75109; telex 57122; fax (22) 75169; f. 1982; cap. and res 3,475m., dep. 54,631m. (Dec. 1990); Chair. MEHMET TAHİROĞLU; Gen. Man. ALPAY R. ADANIR; 4 brs.

Türk Bankası Ltd (Turkish Bank Ltd): 62 Girne Cad., PK 242, Lefkoşa (Nicosia), Mersin 10, Turkey; tel. (22) 83313; telex 2585; fax (22) 82432; f. 1901; cap. p.u. 70,009m., res 75,245m., dep. 783,053m. (Dec. 1992); Chair. and Gen. Man. M. TANJU ÖZYOL; 11 brs.

Investment Organization
Cyprus Investment and Securities Corpn: POB 597, Ghinis Bldg, 4th Floor, 58–60 Dhigenis Akritas Ave, Nicosia; tel. (2) 451535; telex 4449; fax (2) 445481; f. 1982 to promote development of capital market; issued cap. 1m. (1990); Chair. J. CL. CHRISTOPHIDES; Gen. Man. SOCRATES R. SOLOMIDES.

Development Bank
The Cyprus Development Bank Ltd: POB 1415, Alpha House, 50 Archbishop Makarios III Ave, Nicosia; tel. (2) 457575; telex 2797; fax (2) 464322; f. 1963; share cap. p.u. 9.4m. (Sept. 1993); res 3.4m. (Dec. 1991); aims to accelerate the economic development of Cyprus by providing medium- and long-term loans for productive projects, developing the capital market, encouraging joint ventures and providing technical and managerial advice to productive private enterprises; Chair. J. CHR. STRONGYLOS; Gen. Man. JOHN G. JOANNIDES; 1 br.

Savings Bank
Yialousa Savings Bank Ltd (Designated Financial Institution): POB 8510, 26 Santarosa St, Nicosia; tel. (2) 472972; fax (2) 450280; f. 1908 (closed 1974, reopened 1990); provides loan facilities and other banking services; cap. p.u. 1.1m., res 0.1m. (Dec. 1991); Chair. GEORGE SYRIMIS; Gen. Man. D. MESSIOS; 1 br.

Foreign Banks
Arab Bank PLC: POB 5700, 28 Santarosa St, Nicosia; tel. (2) 457111; telex 5717; fax (2) 457890; f. 1983; commercial; Area Exec. C. C. STEPHANI; 18 brs.

Barclays Bank PLC: POB 2081, Galaxias Bldg, 33 Archbishop Makarios III Ave, Nicosia; tel. (2) 461861; telex 3400; fax (2) 367269; f. 1937; Local Dir M. J. SHADRACH; 51 brs.

National Bank of Greece SA: POB 1191, 36 Archbishop Makarios III Ave, Nicosia; tel. (2) 441412; telex 2445; fax (2) 447089; f. 1907; Chief Gen. Man. V. DALAKIDES; 18 brs.

Türkiye Cumhuriyeti Halk Bankası AŞ: Osman Paşa Cad., Ümit Office, Lefkoşa (Nicosia), Mersin 10, Turkey; tel. (22) 72145; telex 57241.

Türkiye Cumhuriyeti Ziraat Bankası: Girnekapi Cad., Ibrahim-paşa Sok. 105, Lefkoşa (Nicosia), Mersin 10, Turkey; tel. (22) 83050; telex 57499; fax (22) 82041.

Türkiye İş Bankası AŞ: Lefkoşa (Nicosia), Mersin 10, Turkey; tel. (22) 83133; telex 57569; fax (22) 78315; f. 1924; Man. KEMAL AĞANOĞLU.

Offshore Banking Units
Cyprus-based Offshore Banking Units (OBUs) are fully-staffed units which conduct all forms of banking business from within Cyprus with other offshore or foreign entities and non-resident persons. (OBUs are not permitted to accept deposits from persons of Cypriot origin who have emigrated to the United Kingdom and taken up permanent residence there.) Although exempt from most of the restrictions and regulatory measures applicable to onshore banks, OBUs are subject to supervision and inspection by the Central Bank of Cyprus. OBUs may conduct business with onshore and domestic banks in all banking matters which the latter are allowed to undertake with banks abroad. OBUs are permitted to grant loans or guarantees in foreign currencies to residents of Cyprus (conditional on obtaining an exchange control permit from the Central Bank of Cyprus). Interest and other income earned from transactions with residents is subject to the full rate of income tax (20%), but the Minister of Finance is empowered by law to exempt an OBU from the above tax liability if satisfied that a specific transaction substantially contributes towards the economic development of the Republic. In November 1993 there were 19 OBUs operating in Cyprus.

Allied Business Bank SAL: POB 4232, 3rd Floor, Flat 31, Lara Court, 276 Archbishop Makarios III Ave, Limassol; tel. (5) 363759; telex 6040; fax (5) 372711; Sr Man. SAMIR BADR.

Arab Jordan Investment Bank SA (Cyprus Offshore Banking Unit): POB 4384, Libra Tower, 23 Olympion St, Limassol; tel. (5) 351351; telex 4029; fax (5) 360151; f. 1978; cap. and dep. US $63m., total assets 96m. (Dec. 1993); Man. ABED ABU-DAYEH.

Bank of Beirut and the Arab Countries SAL: POB 6201, Emelle Bldg, 1st Floor, 135 Archbishop Makarios III Ave, Limassol; tel. (5) 381290; telex 5444; fax (5) 381584; Man. O. S. SAAB.

Banque de l'Europe Méridionale SA: POB 6232, Doma Court, 1st-2nd Floors, 227 Archbishop Makarios III Ave, Limassol; tel. (5) 368628; telex 5575; fax (5) 368611; Local Man. N. A. HCHAIME.

Banque du Liban et d'Outre-Mer SAL: POB 3243, P. Lordos Centre Roundabout, Byron St, Limassol; tel. (5) 376433; telex 4424; fax (5) 376292; Local Man. S. FARAH.

Banque Nationale de Paris Intercontinentale SA: POB 4286, Hanseatic House, 111 Spyrou Araouzou Ave, Limassol; tel. (5) 360166; telex 5519; fax (5) 376519; Local Man. J. POIRIER.

Banque SBA (Cyprus Offshore Banking Unit): POB 4405, Iris House, Kanika Enaerios Complex, 8C Kennedy St, Limassol; tel. (5) 368650; telex 3569; fax (5) 351643; branch of Banque SBA (fmrly Société Bancaire Arabe), Paris; Local Man. N. DAGISTANI.

Barclays Bank PLC, Cyprus Offshore Banking Unit: POB 7320, Barclays House, 2nd and 3rd Floors, 88 Dhigenis Akritas Ave, Nicosia; tel. (2) 464777; telex 5200; fax (2) 464233; Local Man. J. B. S. CONNELL.

Beogradska Banka: POB 530, 34 Kennedy Ave, Nicosia; tel. (2) 453493; telex 6413; fax (2) 453207; Man. Dir B. VUCIC.

Byblos Bank SAL: POB 218, Loucaides Bldg, 1 Archbishop Kyprianou St/St Andrew St, Limassol; tel. (5) 341433; telex 5203; fax (5) 367139; Local Man. R. T. CHEMALY.

Crédit Libanais SAL (COBU): POB 3492, Chrysalia Court, 1st Floor, 206 Archbishop Makarios III Ave, Limassol; tel. (5) 376444; telex 4702; fax (5) 376807; Local Man. R. F. AWAD.

Federal Bank of the Middle East Ltd: POB 5566, Megaron Lavinia, Santa Rosa Ave and Mykinon St, Nicosia; tel. (2) 461716; telex 4700; fax (2) 461751; f. 1983; cap. and res US $30.2m., dep. $92.3m. (Dec. 1993); Chair. and Chief Exec. A. F. M. SAAB.

Jordan National Bank PLC, Cyprus Offshore Banking Unit: POB 3587, 1 Anexartissias St, Pecora Tower, 2nd Floor, Limassol; tel. (5) 356669; telex 5471; fax (5) 356673; f. 1984; Local Man. KHALIL NASR.

Karić Banka: Flat 22, Cronos Court, 66 Archbishop Makarios III Ave, Nicosia; tel. (2) 444977; telex 6510; fax (2) 447145; Man. Dir BILJANA CAMILOVIĆ.

Lebanon and Gulf Bank SAL: POB 337, Akamia Court, 3rd Floor, corner of G. Afxentiou and Archbishop Makarios III Ave, Larnaca; tel. (4) 620500; telex 5779; fax (4) 620708; Man. MOUNIR M. HAMMOUD.

Rosvneshtorgbank (Bank for Foreign Trade of Russia): POB 6868, 2 Amathuntos St, Limassol; tel. (5) 344290; telex 4561; fax (5) 342192; Local Man. O. I. LAPUSHKIN.

Société Générale Cyprus Ltd: POB 8560, 7–9 Grivas Dhigenis Ave, Nicosia; tel. (2) 464885; telex 5342; fax (2) 464471; Gen. Man. ROY M. HUTTON.

Wardley Cyprus Ltd: POB 5718, Laiki Tower, 3rd Floor, 11–13 Archbishop Makarios III Ave, Nicosia; tel. (2) 477515; telex 4980; fax (2) 464314; Man. Dir T. TAOUSHANIS.

STOCK EXCHANGE

Cyprus Stock Exchange: POB 1455, Chamber Bldg, 38 Grivas Dhigenis Ave, Nicosia; tel. (2) 449500; telex 2077; fax (2) 449098; Head N. METAXAS.

INSURANCE

Office of the Superintendent of Insurance: Treasury Department, Ministry of Finance, Nicosia; tel. (2) 303256; telex 3399; fax (2) 302938; f. 1969 to control insurance companies, insurance agents, brokers and agents for brokers in Cyprus.

Greek Cypriot Insurance Companies

Aegis Insurance Co Ltd: POB 3450, Iris Tower, Room 301, 58 Archbishop Makarios III Ave, Nicosia 137; tel. (2) 369180; fax (2) 369359; Man. PANTELAKIS SOUGLIDES.

Allied Assurance & Reinsurance Co Ltd: POB 5509, 66 Grivas Dhigenis Ave, Nicosia 151; tel. (2) 457131; telex 2064; fax (2) 441975; f. 1982; offshore company operating outside Cyprus; Chair. HENRI J. G. CHALHOUB; Principal Officer DEMETRIOS DEMETRIOU.

Alpha Insurance Ltd: 16 Kyriacou Matsis St, Eagle Star Bldg, 1st Floor, Nicosia 150; tel. (2) 449083; fax (2) 473925; Principal Officer IOANNIS LOIZOI.

Antarctic Insurance Co Ltd: 284 Archbishop Makarios III Ave, Fortuna Bldg, Block 'B', 4th Floor, Limassol 255; offshore captive company operating outside Cyprus; Principal Officer ANDREAS NEOCLEOUS.

Apac Ltd: POB 5403, 5 Mourouzi St, Apt 1, Nicosia 133; tel. (2) 455186; telex 2766; f. 1983; captive offshore company operating outside Cyprus; Chair. KYPROS CHRYSOSTOMIDES; Principal Officer GEORGHIOS POYATZIS.

APOL Insurance Ltd: 24 Perea St, Mocassino Centre, 3rd Floor, Strovolos, Nicosia; tel. (2) 425550; fax (2) 425147; offshore company operating outside Cyprus; Principal Officer STELIOS MICHAEL.

Asfalistiki Eteria I 'Kentriki' Ltd: POB 5131, Greg Tower, 3rd Floor, 7 Florinis St, Nicosia 136; tel. (2) 473931; telex 4987; fax (2) 366276; f. 1985; Chair. ARISTOS CHRYSOSTOMOU; Principal Officer GEORGHIOS GEORGALLIDES.

Atlantic Insurance Co Ltd: POB 4579, 37 Prodromou St, 2nd Floor, Nicosia 152; tel. (2) 444052; telex 6446; fax (2) 474800; f. 1983; Chair. and Man. Dir ZENIOS PYRISHIS; Principal Officer KONSTANTINOS MELISSAS.

Axioma Insurance (Cyprus) Ltd: 2 Ionni Klerides St, Demokritos No. 2 Bldg, Flat 83, Nicosia 134; offshore company operating outside Cyprus; Principal Officer CONSTANTINOS KYAMIDES.

Commercial Union Assurance (Cyprus) Ltd: POB 1312, Commercial Union House, 101 Archbishop Makarios Ave, Nicosia; tel. (2) 445045; telex 2547; fax (2) 459011; f. 1974; Chair. J. CHRISTOPHIDES; Gen. Man. CONSTANTINOS P. DEKATRIS.

Compass Insurance Co Ltd: POB 7501, 56–60 Kyriacos Matsis St, Engomi, Nicosia 161; tel. (2) 462492; telex 2270; fax (2) 354871; f. 1981; Chair. P. LOUCAIDES; Gen. Man. PHAEDON MAKRIS.

Cosmos (Cyprus) Insurance Co Ltd: POB 1770, 1st Floor, Flat 12, 6 Ayia Eleni St, Nicosia 135; tel. (2) 441235; telex 3433; fax (2) 457925; f. 1982; Chair. and Gen. Man. KYRIACOS M. TYLLIS.

Crown Insurance Co Ltd: POB 4690, Royal Crown House, 20 Mnasiadou St, Nicosia 136; tel. (2) 455333; fax (2) 455757; Principal Officer SAVVAS ZACHARIADES.

Eurolife Ltd: POB 1655, 40 Them. Dervis St, Eurolife House, Nicosia 136; tel. (2) 442044; telex 3313; fax (2) 451040; Principal Officer LAMBROS PRODROMOU.

Eurosure Insurance Co Ltd: POB 1961, 8 Michalaki Karaoli St, Anemomylos Bldg, 3rd Floor, Nicosia 162; tel. (2) 463439; telex 2302.

Financial and Mercantile Insurance Co Ltd: POB 132, 284 Archbishop Makarios III St, Fortuna Bldg, Block 'B', 2nd Floor, Limassol; offshore captive company operating outside Cyprus; Principal Officer CHR. GEORGHIADES.

General Insurance Co of Cyprus Ltd: POB 1668, 2–4 Themistoklis Dervis St, Nicosia; tel. (2) 450444; telex 2311; fax (2) 446682; f. 1951; Chair. A. PATSALIDES; Gen. Man. R. MEGALEMOS.

Geopolis Insurance Ltd: POB 8530, 6 Neoptolemou St, Nicosia 138; tel. (2) 490094; fax (2) 490494; Principal Officer NICOS DRYMIOTIS.

Granite Insurance Co Ltd: POB 613, 2nd Floor, Block 'A', Fortuna Bldg, 284 Archbishop Makarios III Ave, Limassol 255; tel. (5) 359262; telex 2948; captive offshore company operating outside Cyprus; Chair. and Gen. Man. KOSTAS KOUTSOKOUMNIS; Principal Officer ANDREAS NEOKLEOUS.

Greene Insurances Ltd: POB 132, 4th Floor, Vereggaria Bldg, 25 Spyrou Araouzou St, Limassol 202; tel. (5) 362424; telex 2566; f. 1987; Chair. GEORGHIOS CHRISTODOULOU; Principal Officer JOSIF CHRISTOU.

Hermes Insurance Co Ltd: POB 4828, 1st Floor, Office 101–103, Anemomylos Bldg, 8 Michalakis Karaolis St, Nicosia; tel. (2) 448130; telex 3466; fax (2) 461888; f. 1980; Chair. and Man. Dir P. VOGAZIANOS.

Interamerican Insurance Co Ltd: POB 570, 5 Santaroza St, Nicosia; Principal Officer PETROS ADAMIDES.

Iris Insurance Co Ltd: POB 4841, Flat A5–A6, 1st Floor, 'Aspelia' Bldg, 34 Costis Palamas St, Nicosia 136; tel. (2) 448302; telex 3675; fax (2) 449579; Chair. and Gen. Man. PAVLOS CL. GEORGHIOU.

Laiki Insurance Co Ltd: POB 2069, 6 Evgenias & Antoniou Theodotou St, Nicosia; tel. (2) 449900; telex 5916; fax (2) 466890; f. 1981; Chair. K. N. LAZARIDES; Man. Y. E. SOLOMONIDES.

LCF Reinsurance Co Ltd: POB 3589, 3 Themistoklis Dervis St, Julia House, Nicosia 136; tel. (2) 453053; telex 2046; f. 1984; Principal Officer SOPHIA XINARI.

Metropolitan Insurance Ltd: POB 6516, 2 Kretes St, Pelekanos Court, Of. 1, Nicosia; tel. (2) 360655; fax (2) 360483; Principal Officer PAVLOS DEKATRIS.

Minerva Insurance Co Ltd: POB 3554, 8 Epaminondas St, Nicosia 137; tel. (2) 445134; telex 2608; fax (2) 455528; f. 1970; Chair. and Gen. Man. K. KOUTSOKOUMNIS.

Pancypian Insurance Ltd: POB 1352, Mepa Tower, 66 Grivas Dhigenis Ave, Nicosia; Principal Officer DEMETRIOS DEMETRIOU.

Paneuropean Insurance Co Ltd: POB 553, 3rd, 4th and 5th Floor, 88 Archbishop Makarios III Ave, Nicosia 137; tel. (2) 449488; telex 3419; fax (2) 377396; f. 1980; Chair. N. K. SHACOLAS; Gen. Man. ZENIOS DEMETRIOU.

Philiki Insurance Co Ltd: POB 2274, 45 Byzantium St, Strovolos, Nicosia 152; tel. (2) 444433; telex 4523; fax (2) 442026; f. 1982; Chair. LOUKIS PETRIDES; Gen. Man. DOROS ORPHANIDES.

Progressive Insurance Co Ltd: POB 2111, 6 Themistoklis Dervis St, 3rd Floor, Office C1 and C2, Nicosia 136; tel. (2) 448787; fax (2) 453588; Principal Officer TAKIS HADJIANDREOU.

Saviour Insurance Co Ltd: POB 3957, 8 Michalakis Karaolis St, Anemomylos Bldg, Flat 204, Nicosia 162; tel. (2) 365085; fax (2) 445577; f. 1987; Chair. ROBERT SINCLAIR; Principal Officer KONSTANTINOS KITTIS.

Universal Life Insurance Company Ltd: POB 1270, Universal Tower, 85 Dhigenis Akritas Ave, Nicosia 135; tel. (2) 461222; telex 3116; fax (2) 461343; f. 1970; Chair. J. CHRISTOPHIDES; CEO ANDREAS GEORGHIOU.

Warwick Insurance Co Ltd: POB 1612, 3 Themistoklis Dervis St, Julia House, Nicosia 136; tel. (2) 453053; telex 2046; fax (2) 475446; f. 1987; Chair. CHARALAMBOS ZAVALLIS.

WOB Insurances Ltd: 2nd Floor, Block 'A', Fortuna Bldg, 284 Archbishop Makarios III Ave, Limassol 255; tel. (5) 359262; telex 2948; captive offshore company operating outside Cyprus; Chair. and Gen. Man. KOSTAS KOUTSOKOUMNIS.

Zako Insurance Ltd: POB 7106, 170 Ledra St, Nicosia; tel. (2) 454316; telex 2250.

Turkish Cypriot Insurance Companies

Aksigorta Insurance AŞ: 182 Girne Cad., PK 571, Lefkoşa (Nicosia), Mersin 10, Turkey; tel. (22) 72976; fax (22) 79001.

As-Can Ltd: Hasan Nihat, Apt Kat 1, Daire 5, Lefkoşa (Nicosia), Mersin 10, Turkey; tel. (22) 76444.

Atlantic Sigorta: Abdi Çavuş Sok., Bahire Küçük Apt, Lefkoşa (Nicosia), Mersin 10, Turkey; tel. (22) 71667.

Genel Sigorta: 11 Cumhuriyet Sok., Lefkoşa (Nicosia), Mersin 10, Turkey; tel. (22) 72658.

Güneş Sigorta: 42–46 Girne Cad., Lefkoşa (Nicosia), Mersin 10, Turkey; tel. (22) 71132; telex 57139.

Halk Sigorta: Memduh Asaf Sok., Lefkoşa (Nicosia), Mersin 10, Turkey; tel. (22) 71859; fax (22) 83099.

Sark Sigorta: 13A Türk Bankası Sok., Lefkoşa (Nicosia), Mersin 10, Turkey; tel. (22) 73150.

Şeker Sigorta: K.T. Kooperatif Merkez Bankası, 49–55 Mahmut Paşa Sok., PK 823, Lefkoşa (Nicosia), Mersin 10, Turkey; tel. (22) 71207; telex 57216.

Tam Sigorta: Vakıflar Bankası Ltd, Lefkoşa (Nicosia), Mersin 10, Turkey.

There were 33 foreign insurance companies operating in Cyprus in 1987.

Trade and Industry

GREEK CYPRIOT CHAMBERS OF COMMERCE AND INDUSTRY

Cyprus Chamber of Commerce and Industry: POB 1455, 38 Grivas Dhigenis Ave, Nicosia; tel. (2) 449500; telex 2077; fax (2) 449048; f. 1963; Pres. PHANOS EPIPHANIOU; Sec.-Gen. PANAYIOTIS LOIZIDES; 5,000 mems, 76 affiliated trade asscns.

Famagusta Chamber of Commerce and Industry: POB 3124, 339 Ayiou Andreou St, Andrea Chambers, 2nd Floor, Office No 201–202, Limassol; tel. (5) 370165; telex 4519; fax (5) 370291; f. 1952; Pres. T. KYRIAKIDES; Vice-Pres. P. PAPATHOMAS, A. MATSIS; 400 mems.

Larnaca Chamber of Commerce and Industry: POB 287, 12 Gregoris Afxentiou St, Skouros Bldg, Apt 43, 4th Floor, Larnaca; tel. (4) 655051; telex 3187; fax (4) 628281; Pres. IACOVOS DEMETRIOU; Vice-Pres. K. LEFKARITIS; 400 mems.

Limassol Chamber of Commerce and Industry: POB 347, 25 Spyrou Araouzou St, Veregaria Bldg, 3rd Floor, Limassol; tel. (5) 362556; fax (5) 371655; Pres. MICHAEL ROLYDORIDES; Vice-Pres. I. CHRISTODOULOU, S. PAPADAKIS; 650 mems.

Nicosia Chamber of Commerce and Industry: POB 1455, 38 Grivas Dhigenis Ave, Chamber Bldg, Nicosia; tel. (2) 456858; telex 2077; fax (2) 367483; Pres. COSTAS CONSTANTINIDES; Sec. PANIKOS MICHAELIDES; 1,200 mems.

Paphos Chamber of Commerce and Industry: POB 82, Grivas Dhigenis Ave, Demetra Court, Flat 22, 2nd Floor, Paphos; tel. (6) 235115; telex 2888; fax (6) 244602; Pres. THEODOROS ARISTODEMOU; Sec. KENDEAS ZAMBIRINIS; 400 mems.

TURKISH CYPRIOT CHAMBERS OF COMMERCE AND INDUSTRY

Turkish Cypriot Chamber of Industry: Osman Paşa Cad. 14, PK 563, Köşklüçiftlik, Lefkoşa (Nicosia), Mersin 10, Turkey; tel. (22) 84596; fax (22) 84595; Pres. VEDAT ÇELIK.

Turkish Cypriot Chamber of Commerce: Bedrettin Demirel Cad., PK 718, Lefkoşa (Nicosia), Mersin 10, Turkey; tel. (22) 83645; telex 57511; fax (22) 83089; f. 1958; more than 6,000 regd mems; Chair. SALIH BOYACI; Sec.-Gen. JANEL BURCAN.

EMPLOYERS' ORGANIZATIONS

Greek Cypriot Employers' Organizations

At 31 December 1980 there were 28 employers' associations with a total membership of 4,115 enterprises.

Cyprus Employers' & Industrialists' Federation: POB 1657, 30 Grivas Dhigenis Ave, Nicosia; tel. (2) 445102; telex 4834; fax (2) 459459; f. 1960; 33 member trade associations, 400 direct and 2,000 indirect members; Dir-Gen. ANTONIS PIERIDES; Chair. MICHALAKIS ZIVANARIS. The largest of the trade association members are: Cyprus Building Contractors' Association; Cyprus Hotel Keepers' Association; Clothing Manufacturers' Association; Cyprus Shipping Association; Shoe Makers' Association; Cyprus Metal Industries Association; Cyprus Bankers Employers' Association; Motor Vehicles Importers' Association.

Turkish Cypriot Employers' Organization

Kıbrıs Türk İşverenler Sendikası (Turkish Cypriot Employers' Association): PK 674, Lefkoşa (Nicosia), Mersin 10, Turkey; tel. (22) 76173; Chair. ALPAY ALI RIZA GÖRGÜNER.

TRADE UNIONS

At 31 December 1980 there were 97 trade unions with 240 branches, six union federations and five confederations.

Greek Cypriot Trade Unions

Cyprus Civil Servants' Trade Union: 3 Dem. Severis Ave, Nicosia; tel. (2) 442278; fax (2) 465199; f. 1949, registered 1966; restricted to persons in the civil employment of the Government and public authorities; 6 brs with a total membership of 15,383; Pres. N. PANAYIOTOU; Gen. Sec. A. POLYVIOU.

Demokratiki Ergatiki Omospondia Kyprou (Democratic Labour Federation of Cyprus): POB 1625, 40 Byron Ave, Nicosia; tel. (2) 456506; fax (2) 449494; f. 1962; 4 unions with a total membership of 4,407; Gen. Sec. RENOS PRENTZAS.

Pankypria Ergatiki Omospondia—PEO (Pancyprian Federation of Labour): POB 1885, 31–35 Archermos St, Nicosia; tel. (2) 349400; fax (2) 349382; f. 1946, registered 1947; previously the Pancyprian Trade Union Committee f. 1941, dissolved 1946; 10 unions and 176 brs with a total membership of 75,000; affiliated to the WFTU; Gen. Sec. AVRAAM ANTONIOU.

Pankyprios Omospondia Anexartition Syntechnion (Pancyprian Federation of Independent Trade Unions): 1 Menadrou St, Nicosia; tel. (2) 442233; f. 1956, registered 1957; has no political orientations; 8 unions with a total membership of 798; Pres. KOSTAS ANTONIADES; Gen. Sec. KYRIACOS NATHANAEL.

Synomospondia Ergaton Kyprou (Cyprus Workers' Confederation): POB 5018, 23 Alkaiou St, Engomi, Nicosia; tel. (2) 441142; telex 6180; fax (2) 476360; f. 1944, registered 1950; 7 federations, 5 labour centres, 47 unions, 12 brs with a total membership of 54,441; affiliated to the ICFTU and the ETUC; Gen. Sec. MICHAEL IOANNOU; Deputy Gen. Sec. DEMETRIS KITTENIS.

Union of Cyprus Journalists: POB 3495, 2 Kratinos St, Strovolos, Nicosia; tel. (2) 454680; fax (2) 464598; f. 1959; Chair. ANDREAS KANNAOUROS.

Turkish Cypriot Trade Unions

In 1986 trade union membership totalled 20,627.

Devrimci İşçi Sendikaları Federasyonu (Dev-İş) (Revolutionary Trade Unions' Federation): 30 Beliğ Paşa Sok., Lefkoşa (Nicosia), Mersin 10, Turkey; tel. (22) 72640; f. 1976; two unions with a total membership of 4,586 (1986); affiliated to WFTU; Pres. HASAN SARICA; Gen.-Sec. BAYRAM ÇELIK.

Kıbrıs Türk İşçi Sendikaları Federasyonu (TÜRK-SEN) (Turkish Cypriot Trade Union Federation): POB 829, 7-7A Şehit Mehmet R. Hüseyin Sok., Lefkoşa (Nicosia), Mersin 10, Turkey; tel. (22) 72444; f. 1954, regd 1955; 15 unions with a total membership of 9,307 (1986); affiliated to ICFTU, ETUC, CTUC and the Confederation of Trade Unions of Turkey (Türk-İş); Pres. HÜSEYİN CURCIOĞLU; Gen. Sec. (vacant).

TRADE FAIRS

Cyprus International (State) Fair: POB 3551, Macedonitissa, Nicosia; tel. (2) 352918; telex 3344; fax (2) 352316; f. 1976; 19th Fair scheduled for 26 May–5 June 1994.

MAJOR INDUSTRIAL COMPANIES

Greek Cypriot Companies

Covotsos Textiles Ltd: POB 1090, Limassol; tel. (5) 391344; telex 2672; fax (5) 390754.

Cyprus Canning Co Ltd: POB 21, Limassol; tel. (5) 392078; telex 3928; fax (5) 392083.

Cyprus Cement Co Ltd: POB 378, Limassol; telex 2684.

Cyprus Forest Industries Ltd: POB 4043, Nicosia; tel. (2) 832121; telex 2177; fax (2) 833564.

Cyprus Phassouri Plantations Ltd: POB 180, Limassol; tel. (5) 252211; telex 2396; fax (5) 252225.

Cyprus Pipes Industries Ltd: 172 St Andrew St, Limassol; telex 2496.

Cyprus Trading Corporation Ltd: POB 1744, Nicosia; tel. (2) 482800; telex 2415; fax (2) 485385.

Keo Ltd: POB 209, Limassol; tel. (5) 362053; telex 2449; fax (5) 373429; f. 1927; cap. C£5m; manufacturers of wine, beer and spirits, fruit juices, canned vegetables and mineral water; Chair. P. L. PASCHALIDES; Man. Dir M. POLYDORIDES; 500 employees.

Vassiliko Cement Works Ltd: POB 2281, Nicosia; tel. (2) 442005; telex 2448; fax (2) 442741; f. 1965; cap. C£5m; cement manufacturers; Chair. P. L. PASCHALIDES; Man. Dir Mr ST C. LOIZIDES; 350 employees.

Turkish Cypriot Companies

Cypfruvex Ltd: Güzelyurt, PK 433, Lefkoşa (Nicosia), Mersin 10, Turkey; tel. (22) 43495; telex 57131; state-owned; fruit exporters; Gen. Man. MUSTAFA REFIK.

Eti Ltd: Abdi İpekci Cad., PK 452, Lefkoşa (Nicosia), Mersin 10, Turkey; tel. (22) 71222; state-owned; import and distribution of foodstuffs.

Hilmi Toros Industries Ltd: Mehmet Akif Ave, PK 526, Lefkoşa (Nicosia), Mersin 10, Turkey; tel. (22) 72412; textile and clothing manufacturers.

Kıbrıs Türk Petrolleri Ltd, Şti (Turkish Cypriot Petroleum Co Ltd): Gazi Mağusa, PK 117, Mersin 10, Turkey; tel. (36) 63260; telex 57582; fax (36) 65230; import, storage and distribution of petroleum and petroleum derivatives.

Kıbrıs Türk Sanayi İşletmeleri Holding Ltd, Şti (Turkish Cypriot Industrial Enterprises Holding Ltd): PK 445, Lefkoşa (Nicosia), Mersin 10, Turkey; tel. (22) 83231; telex 57575; fax (22) 82441; state-owned; manufacturers and exporters of water pumps, metal pipes, paints, plastics, detergents, cosmetics, textiles, foodstuffs, furniture, polypropylene and polyethylene sacks, cables, polystyrene and polyurethane foam.

Kıbrıs Türk Tütün Endüstri Ltd (Turkish Cypriot Tobacco Industry Ltd): 27 Atatürk Cad., Lefkoşa (Nicosia), Mersin 10, Turkey; tel. (22) 73403; state-owned; cigarette manufacturers.

TAŞEL (Turkish Spirits and Wine Enterprises Ltd): Gazi Mağusa, PK 48, Mersin 10, Turkey; tel. (36) 65440; fax (36) 66330; f. 1961; state-owned; manufacturers of alcoholic beverages; Gen. Man. HASAN YUMUK.

Toprak Ürünleri Kurumu: 11 Şehit Mustafa Hacı Sok., Yenişehir, Lefkoşa (Nicosia), Mersin 10, Turkey; tel. (22) 71211; state-owned; potato exporters.

Transport

There are no railways in Cyprus.

ROADS

In December 1993 there were 20,300 km of roads in the government-controlled areas, of which 5,902 km were paved and the remainder were earth or gravel roads. The Nicosia–Limassol four-lane dual carriageway, which was completed in 1985, was subsequently extended with the completion of the Limassol and Larnaca bypasses. New highways between Nicosia and Larnaca, and Larnaca and Kophinou have been completed, as well as the Aradippo-Dhekelia and Larnaca Airport bypasses. The Nicosia–Anthoupolis–Kokkinotrimithia highway was scheduled for completion in 1994. The north and south are now served by separate transport systems, and there are no services linking the two sectors. In 1984 the road network in the Turkish Cypriot area consisted of about 5,278 km of paved and 838 km of unpaved roads. Between 1988 and 1990 some 250 km of new highways were constructed in the area.

SHIPPING

Until 1974 Famagusta, a natural port, was the island's most important harbour, handling about 83% of the country's cargo. Since its capture by the Turkish army in August 1974 the port has been officially declared closed to international traffic. However, it continues to serve the Turkish-occupied region.

The main ports which serve the island's maritime trade at present are Larnaca and Limassol, which were constructed in 1973 and 1974 respectively. Both ports have since been expanded and improved. There is also an industrial port at Vassiliko and there are three specialized petroleum terminals, at Larnaca, Dhekelia and Moni. A second container terminal, being constructed at Limassol, was scheduled to be operational by early 1995.

In 1992, 5,132 vessels, with a total net registered tonnage of 14,700,000, visited Cyprus, carrying 7,762,000 metric tons of cargo to and from Cyprus. In addition to serving local traffic, Limassol and Larnaca ports act as cargo distribution and consolidation centres for the Mediterranean area and as regional warehouse and assembly bases for the Middle East and the Persian (Arabian) Gulf. Containerized cargo handled at Cypriot ports amounted to 2,401,000 metric tons in 1992.

Both Kyrenia and Karavostassi are under Turkish occupation and have been declared closed to international traffic. Karavostassi used to be the country's major mineral port, dealing with 76% of the total mineral exports. However, since the war minerals have been passed through Vassiliko and Limni, which are open roadsteads. A hydrofoil service operates between Kyrenia and Mersin on the Turkish mainland. Car ferries sail from Kyrenia to Taşucu and Mersin, in Turkey.

The total number of merchant vessels registered in Cyprus on 31 December 1992 was 2,316, amounting to a total displacement of 22.3m. grt.

Cyprus Ports Authority: POB 2007, Nicosia; tel. (2) 450100; telex 2833; fax (2) 365420; f. 1973; Chair. KOSTAS EROTOKRITOU; Gen. Man. JOSEPH BAYADA.

Cyprus Shipping Council: POB 6607, Limassol; tel. (5) 360717; fax (5) 358642.

Greek Cypriot Shipping Companies

Amer Shipping Ltd: 6th Floor, Ghinis Bldg, 58–60 Dhigenis Akritas Ave, Nicosia; tel. (2) 451707; telex 6513; fax (2) 451460; Reps SHASHI K. MEHROTRA, DEMETRI ANGELOU.

C. F. Ahrenkiel Shipmanagement (Cyprus) Ltd: POB 3594, 4th Floor, O & A Tower, 25 Olympion St, Limassol; tel. (5) 359731; telex 6309; fax (5) 359714; Reps PETER DE JONGH, JOHN CONSTANTINOU.

Columbia Shipmanagement Ltd: POB 1624, Columbia House, Dodekanissou and Kolonakiou Corner, Limassol; tel. (5) 320900; telex 3206; fax (5) 320325; f. 1978; Chair H. SCHOELLER, Man. Dir D. FRY.

Hanseatic Shipping Co Ltd: POB 127, 111 Spyrou Araouzou St, Limassol; tel. (5) 345111; telex 3282; fax (5) 342879; f. 1972; Man. Dirs A. J. DROUSSIOTIS, B. BEHRENS.

Interorient Navigation Co Ltd: POB 1309, 3 Thalia St, Limassol; tel. (5) 341616; telex 2629; fax (5) 345895; Man. Dir JAN LISSOW.

Lefkaritis Bros Marine Ltd: POB 162, Lefkaritis House, 1 Kilkis St, Larnaca; tel. (4) 652142; telex 2222; fax (4) 657173; Chair. and Man. Dir TAKIS LEFKARITIS.

Marlow Navigation Co Ltd: POB 4077, 3rd Floor, Libra Tower, 23 Olympion St, Limassol; tel. (5) 367029; telex 2019; fax (5) 369623; Gen. Man. ANDREAS NEOPHYTOU.

Oldendorff Ltd, Reederei Nord Klaus E: POB 6345, Libra Tower, 23 Olympion St, Limassol; tel. (5) 370262; telex 5938; fax (5) 370263; Chair. and Man. Dir KLAUS E. OLDENDORFF.

Seatankers Management Co Ltd: POB 3562, Flat 411, Deana Beach Apartments, Promachon Eleftherias St, Limassol; tel. (5) 326111; telex 5606; fax (5) 323770; Man. Dir DANIEL IOANNIDES.

Turkish Cypriot Shipping Companies

Fergun Maritime Co: Kyrenia (Girne), Mersin 10, Turkey; ferries to Turkish ports; Owner FEHIM KUÇUK.

Kıbrıs Türk Denizcilik Ltd, Şti (Turkish Cypriot Maritime Co Ltd): Girne Cad., Adem Kaner İş Hanı, Lefkoşa (Nicosia), Mersin 10, Turkey.

Orion Navigation Ltd: Seagate Court, Famagusta, Mersin 10, Turkey; tel. (36) 62006; telex 57583; fax (36) 67093; f. 1976; shipping agents; Dir O. LAMA; Shipping Man. L. LAMA.

CIVIL AVIATION

There is an international airport at Nicosia, which can accommodate all types of aircraft, including jets. It has been closed since July 1974 following the Turkish invasion. A new international airport was constructed at Larnaca, from which flights operate to Europe, the Middle East and the Gulf. Another international airport at Paphos began operations in November 1983.

In 1975 the Turkish authorities opened Ercan (formerly Tymbou) airport, and a second airport was opened at Geçitkale (Lefkoniko) in 1986.

Cyprus Airways: POB 1903, 21 Alkeou St, Engomi, Nicosia; tel. (2) 443054; telex 2225; fax (2) 443167; f. 1947; jointly owned by Cyprus Government and local interests; wholly-owned charter subsidiaries Cyprair Tours Ltd and Eurocypria Airlines Ltd; Chair. VASSILIS ROLOGIS; CEO PANIKOS PAPADAKIS; services throughout Europe and the Middle East.

Kıbrıs Türk Hava Yolları (Turkish Cypriot Airlines): Bedreddin Demirel Ave, PK 793, Lefkoşa (Nicosia), Mersin 10, Turkey; tel. (22) 83901; telex 57350; fax (22) 81468; f. 1974; jointly owned by the Turkish Cypriot Community Assembly Consolidated Improvement Fund and Turkish Airlines Inc; Gen. Man. Dr FERDA ÖNEŞ; services to Turkey and London.

Tourism

In 1992 a total of 1,991,000 foreign tourists visited the Greek Cypriot area; in 1993 the number of tourist arrivals was estimated to be 1.8m. Receipts from tourism in that area were C£694m. in 1992, and were expected to be C£630m. in 1993. Receipts from tourism in the Turkish Cypriot area were estimated to have declined by around 50% in 1991, as a result of the Gulf War, but recovered to an estimated US $175m. in 1992, when the number of tourist arrivals reached 242,506. In 1993 an estimated 146,000 tourists visited the area, and revenue from tourism reached $173m.

Cyprus Tourism Organization (CTO): POB 4535, 19 Limassol Ave, Nicosia; tel. (2) 315715; telex 2165; fax (2) 313022; Chair. A. NICOLAOU; Dir-Gen. FRYNI MICHAEL.

Cyprus Turkish Tourism Enterprises, Ltd (CTTE): Kyrenia (Girne), Mersin 10, Turkey; tel. (81) 52165; telex 57128; fax (81) 52073; f. 1974; Chair. LEMI GALIP; Gen. Man. MEHMET KIRAL.

Defence

The National Guard was set up by the House of Representatives in 1964, after the withdrawal of the Turkish members. Men between the ages of 18 and 50 are liable to 26 months' conscription. In June 1993 it comprised an army of 10,000 regulars, mainly composed of Cypriot conscripts, but with some seconded Greek

Army officers and NCOs, and 88,000 reserves. There is also a Greek Cypriot paramilitary force of 3,700 armed police. In June 1993 the 'TRNC' had an army of about 4,000 regulars and 11,000 reserves. Men between the ages of 18 and 50 are liable to 24 months' conscription. In 1990 it was estimated that the 'TRNC' forces were being supported by about 30,000 Turkish troops. Cyprus also contains the UN Peace-keeping Force and the British military bases at Akrotiri and Dhekelia.

Commander of the Greek Cypriot National Guard: Lt-Gen. (retd) PANAYIOTIS MARKOPOULOS.

UNITED NATIONS PEACE-KEEPING FORCE IN CYPRUS
(UNFICYP)

Headquarters at POB 1642, Nicosia; tel. (2) 464000; telex 2329.

Set up for a three-month period in March 1964 by Security Council resolution (subsequently extended at intervals of three or six months by successive resolutions) to keep the peace between the Greek and Turkish communities and help to solve outstanding issues between them. In mid-1993, following an announcement by troop-providing countries that they were to withdraw a substantial number of troops, the Security Council introduced a system of financing UNFICYP by voluntary and assessed contributions. At 30 April 1994 the Force comprised 1,235 military and police personnel, drawn from nine countries, representing a reduction in strength of 44% since the end of 1990.

Commander: Maj.-Gen. AHTI TOIMI PAAVALI VARTIAINEN (Finland).

Chief of Mission: C. JOSEPH CLARK (Canada).

See p. 206.

BRITISH SOVEREIGN BASE AREAS
Akrotiri and Dhekelia

Headquarters British Forces Cyprus, British Forces Post Office 53; tel. (52) 63395.

Under the Cyprus Act 1960, the United Kingdom retained sovereignty in two sovereign base areas and this was recognized in the Treaty of Establishment signed between the UK, Greece, Turkey and the Republic of Cyprus in August 1960. The base areas cover 99 square miles. The Treaty also conferred on Britain certain rights within the Republic, including rights of movement and the use of specified training areas. In June 1993 an estimated 4,100 military personnel were resident in the sovereign base areas.

Administrator: Maj.-Gen. ALEXANDER HARLEY.

Chief Officer of Administration: A. J. H. ADAMS.

Senior Judge of Senior Judge's Court: Hon. Justice T. H. PIGOT.

Resident Judge of Judge's Court: F. WOOD.

Education

Until 31 March 1965 each community in Cyprus managed its own schooling through its respective Communal Chamber. Intercommunal education had been placed under the Minister of the Interior, assisted by a Board of Education for Intercommunal Schools of which the Minister was the Chairman. On 31 March 1965 the Greek Communal Chamber was dissolved and a Ministry of Education was established to take its place. Intercommunal education has been placed under this Ministry.

GREEK CYPRIOT EDUCATION

Primary education is compulsory and is provided free in six grades to children between $5\frac{1}{2}$ and 12 years of age. In some towns and large villages there are separate junior schools consisting of the first three grades. Apart from schools for the deaf and blind, there are also seven schools for handicapped children. In 1992/93 there were 694 Kindergartens (including privately run pre-primary schools) for children aged $3-5\frac{1}{2}$ years of age. There were 370 primary schools, with 3,132 teachers and 60,912 pupils in 1992/93.

Secondary education is also free for all years of study and lasts six years, three years at the Gymnasium being followed by three years at technical school or the Lyceum. Attendance for the first cycle of secondary education is compulsory. Pupils at the Lyceums may choose one of five main fields of specialization: classics, science, economics, commercial/secretarial and foreign languages. Three-year courses are also offered to students at technical schools and the school-leaving certificate awarded is equivalent to that of the Lyceum. In 1993/94 there were 103 secondary schools (gymnasia, lyceums and technical schools) with 3,900 teachers and 48,500 pupils. In addition, there were numerous privately-operated secondary schools.

Post-Secondary education is provided at the Pedagogical Academy, which organizes three-year courses for the training of pre-primary and primary school teachers, and at the Higher Technical Institute, which provides three and four-year courses for technicians in civil, electrical, mechanical and marine engineering. Specialized training is also provided at the Forestry College (administered by the Ministry of Agriculture), the Hotel and Catering Institute, the School of Nursing and the Mediterranean Institute of Management, all of which are State institutions. Adult education is conducted through Youth Centres in rural areas and Foreign Language Institutes in the towns, and in addition a number of private institutions offer courses in business administration, engineering, secretarial work etc. The University of Cyprus was inaugurated in September 1992, with 440 undergraduates, projected to increase to 4,000 undergraduates by 1998.

In 1990/91, 9,028 students were studying at universities abroad, mainly in Greece, the USA, the United Kingdom, Germany and Italy.

TURKISH CYPRIOT EDUCATION

With the exception of private kindergartens, a vocational school of agriculture attached to the Ministry of Agriculture, a training school for nursing and midwifery attached to the Ministry of Health and Social Welfare, and a school for hotel catering attached to the Ministry of Communications, Public Works and Tourism, all schools and educational institutes are administered by the Ministry of National Education and Culture.

Education in the Turkish Cypriot zone is divided into two sections, formal and adult education. Formal education covers nursery, primary, secondary and higher education. Adult (informal) education caters for special training outside the school system.

Formal education is organized into four categories: nursery, primary, secondary and higher education. Nursery education is provided by kindergartens for children between the ages of 4 and 6. In 1990/91 there were 5 public kindergartens with 26 teachers catering for 610 children. Primary education is provided at two stages. The first stage (elementary) lasts five years and caters for children aged 7–12. The second stage (junior), lasting three years, is intended for pupils aged 13–15. Both stages of primary education are free and compulsory. In 1989/90 there were 150 elementary primary schools with 790 teachers and 16,682 pupils. In the same academic year there were 22 junior primary schools with 529 teachers and 11,879 pupils. In 1991/92 there were 155 pre-primary and primary institutions with 849 teachers and 19,400 pupils. Secondary education consists of a three-year programme of instruction for pupils aged 16–18. Pupils elect either to prepare for higher education, to prepare for higher education with vocational training, or to prepare for vocational training only. Secondary education is free for those who cannot afford the fees of a minimum of £18 and is not compulsory. In 1991/92 there were 28 secondary schools and lycées, with 963 teachers and 16,719 pupils. There were also 10 technical lycées and technical secondary schools, with 254 teachers and 2,671 pupils.

In 1982 an Institute of Islamic Banking and Economics was opened to provide postgraduate training. Cyprus's first university, The Eastern Mediterranean University, which is located near Famagusta, was opened in October 1986. The university has four main faculties: Engineering, Arts and Sciences, Tourism and Hotel Management, and Economics and Business Administration. A total of 3,965 students attended the university in 1992. There are two higher education institutions in the Turkish Cypriot zone which are affiliated to the university: the Teachers' Training College in Lefkoşa (Nicosia), which trains teachers for the elementary school stage, and the Higher Technical Institute, which trains engineers in three major fields: electrical, mechanical and civil. Higher education is also provided by the Near East University College in Lefkoşa (Nikosia), with 1,049 students in 1992; the Cirne (Kyrenia) American University, with 353; and Lefke (Levka) University, with 418.

Bibliography

Alastos, D. *Cyprus in History.* London, 1955.

Arnold, Percy. *Cyprus Challenge.* London, Hogarth Press, 1956.

Barker, Dudley. *Grivas.* London, Cresset Press, 1960.

Byford-Jones, W. *Grivas and the Story of EOKA.* London, Robert Hale, 1960.

Casson, S. *Ancient Cyprus.* London, 1937.

Crawshaw, Nancy. *The Cyprus Revolt: An Account of the Struggle for Union with Greece.* London, Allen and Unwin, 1978.

Denktaş, Rauf R. *The Cyprus Triangle.* London, K. Rüstem and Bros, 1988.

Emilianides, Achille. *Histoire de Chypre.* Paris, 1963.

Esin, Emel. *Aspects of Turkish Civilization in Cyprus.* Ankara, Ankara University Press, 1965.

Foley, Charles. *Island in Revolt.* London, Longmans Green, 1962.

Legacy of Strife. London, Penguin, 1964.

Foot, Sylvia. *Emergency Exit.* London, Chatto and Windus, 1960.

Foot, Sir Hugh. *A Start in Freedom.* London, 1964.

Grivas (Dhigenis), George. *Guerrilla Warfare and EOKA's Struggle.* London, Longman, 1964.

Memoirs of General Grivas. London, Longman, 1964.

Harbottle, Michael. *The Impartial Soldier.* Oxford University Press, 1970.

Hill, Sir George. *A History of Cyprus.* 4 vols, London, 1940–1952.

Hitchens, Christopher. *Cyprus.* London, Quartet, 1984.

House, William J. *Cypriot Women in the Labour Market: An Exploration of Myths and Reality.* London, International Labour Office, 1985.

Kyle, Keith. *Cyprus.* London, Minority Rights Group, 1984.

Kyriakides, S. *Cyprus—Constitutionalism and Crisis Government.* Philadelphia, University of Pennsylvania Press, 1968.

Lavender, D. S. *The Story of Cyprus Mines Corporation.* San Marino, Calif., 1962.

Luke, Sir H. C. *Cyprus under the Turks 1571–1878.* Oxford, 1921.

Cyprus: A Portrait and an Appreciation. London, Harrap, 1965.

Meyer, A. J. (with S. Vassiliou). *The Economy of Cyprus.* Harvard University Press, 1962.

Newman, Philip. *A Short History of Cyprus.* 1940.

Panteli, Stavros. *The Making of Modern Cyprus.* Interworld, 1990.

Papadopoullos, T. *The Population of Cyprus (1570–1881).* Nicosia, 1965.

Purcell, H. D. *Cyprus.* London, Benn, 1969.

Richard, J. *Chypre Sous les Lusignan.* Paris, 1962.

Spyridakis, Dr C. *A Brief History of Cyprus.* Nicosia, 1964.

Storrs, Sir Ronald. *A Chronology of Cyprus.* Nicosia, 1930.

Stylianou, A. and J. *Byzantine Cyprus.* Nicosia, 1948.

Xydis, S. G. *Cyprus—Conflict and Conciliation 1945–58.* Columbus, Ohio, Ohio State University Press, 1967.

Official Books of Reference:

Cyprus: Documents relating to Independence of Cyprus and the Establishment of British Sovereign Base Areas. London, Cmnd 1093, HMSO, July 1960.

Cyprus: Treaty of Guarantee, Nicosia, 16 August 1960.

EGYPT

Physical and Social Geography

W. B. FISHER

SITUATION

The Arab Republic of Egypt occupies the north-eastern corner of the African continent, with an extension across the Gulf of Suez into the Sinai region which is usually, but not always, regarded as lying in Asia. The area of Egypt is 997,738.5 sq km (385,229 sq miles) but only 3.5% can be said to be permanently settled, the remainder being desert or marsh. Egypt lies between Lat. 22° and 32°N; and the greatest distance from north to south is about 1,024 km (674 miles), and from east to west 1,240 km (770 miles), giving the country a roughly square shape, with the Mediterranean and Red seas forming respectively the northern and eastern boundaries. Egypt has political frontiers on the east with Israel, on the south with the Republic of Sudan, and on the west with the Great Socialist People's Libyan Arab Jamahiriya. The actual frontiers run, in general, as straight lines drawn directly between defined points, and do not normally conform to geographical features. Between June 1967 and October 1973 the *de facto* frontier with Israel was the Suez Canal. As a result of the 1979 Peace Treaty, the frontier reverted to a line much further to the east (see map on p. 89).

Egypt occupies a significant place in the world as a region where, in all probability, the earliest developments of civilization and organized government took place. Though many archaeologists would not wholly subscribe to the view of Egypt as actually the first civilized country, there can be no doubt that from very early times the lower Nile Valley has been prominent as possessing strongly marked unity, with a highly specialized and characteristic way of life. Empires with fluctuating boundaries and with varying racial composition have arisen in neighbouring lands of the Middle East, but Egypt has seemed able to stand relatively unchanged, with the facility for absorbing immigrants and outside ideas, of surviving military occupation and defeat, and of maintaining its own culture, finally shaking off foreign rule and influence.

PHYSICAL FEATURES

The remarkable persistence of cultural cohesion amongst the Egyptian people may largely be explained by the geography of the country. Egypt consists essentially of a narrow, trough-like valley, some 3 km to 15 km wide, cut by the River Nile in the plateau of north-east Africa. At an earlier geological period a gulf of the Mediterranean Sea probably extended as far south as Cairo, but deposition of silt by the Nile has entirely filled up this gulf, producing the fan-shaped Delta region (22,000 sq km in area), through which flow two main distributary branches of the Nile—the eastern, or Damietta branch (240 km long), and the western, or Rosetta branch (235 km), together with many other minor channels. As deposition of silt takes place, large stretches of water are gradually impounded to form shallow lakes, which later become firm ground. At present there are four such stretches of water in the north of the Delta: from east to west, and, in order of size, lakes Menzaleh, Brullos, Idku and Mariut.

Upstream from Cairo the Nile Valley is at first 10 km to 15 km in width, and, as the river tends to lie close to the eastern side, much of the cultivated land, and also most of the big towns and cities, lie on the western bank. Towards the south the river valley gradually narrows until, at about 400 km from the frontier of Sudan, it is no more than 3 km wide. Near Aswan there is an outcrop of resistant rock, chiefly granite, which the river has not been able to erode as quickly as the rest of the valley. This gives rise to a region of cascades

and rapids which is known as the First Cataract. Four other similar regions occur on the Nile, but only the First Cataract lies within Egypt. The cataracts form a barrier to human movement upstream and serve to isolate the Egyptian Nile from territories farther south. In Ancient Egypt, when river communications were of paramount importance, there was a traditional division of the Nile Valley into Lower Egypt (the Delta), Middle Egypt (the broader valley above the Delta), and Upper Egypt (the narrower valley as far as the cataracts). Nowadays, it is usual to speak merely of Upper and Lower Egypt, with the division occurring at Cairo.

The fertile strip of the Nile Valley is isolated to the south by the cataracts and by the deserts and swamps of Sudan; to the north by the Mediterranean Sea; and to east and west by desert plateaux, about which a little more must be said. The land immediately to the east of the Nile Valley, spoken of as the Eastern Highlands, is a complex region with peaks that rise 1,800 m to 2,100 m but also much broken up by deep valleys which make travel difficult. Owing to aridity the whole region is sparsely populated, with a few partly nomadic shepherds, one or two monasteries and a number of small towns associated chiefly with the exploitation of minerals—petroleum, iron, manganese and granite—that occur in this region. Difficult landward communications mean that contact is mostly by sea, except in the case of the ironfields. The Sinai, separated from the Eastern Highlands by the Gulf of Suez, is structurally very similar, but the general plateau level is tilted, giving the highest land (again nearly 2,100 m in elevation) in the extreme south, where it rises in bold scarps from sea-level. Towards the north the land gradually slopes down, ultimately forming the low-lying sandy plain of the Sinai desert which fringes the Mediterranean Sea. Because of its low altitude and accessibility, the Sinai, in spite of its desert nature, has been for many centuries an important corridor linking Egypt with Asia. It is now crossed only by a motor road, the railway having been torn up in 1968 by occupying Israeli forces. Since its return to Egypt, efforts at development have been made by the Egyptian Government.

West of the Nile occur the vast expanses known as the Western Desert. Though by no means uniform in height, the land surface is much lower than that east of the Nile, and within Egypt rarely exceeds 300 m above sea-level. Parts are covered by extensive masses of light, shifting sand that often form dunes; but in addition there are a number of large depressions, some with the lowest parts actually below sea-level. These depressions seem to have been hollowed out by wind action, breaking up rock strata that were weakened by the presence of underground water, and most hollows still contain supplies of artesian water. In some instances (as, for example, the Qattara depression, and the Wadi Natrun, respectively south-west and south-east of Alexandria) the subterranean water is highly saline and consequently useless for agriculture; but in others—notably the oases of the Fayoum, Siwa, Dakhla, Behariya and Farafra—the water is sufficiently sweet to allow use for irrigation, and settlements have grown up within the desert. In the last few years, much attention has been given to irrigation development in these oases, which are sometimes spoken of as 'the New Territories'.

CLIMATE

The main feature of Egyptian climate is the almost uniform aridity. Alexandria, the wettest part, receives only 200 mm of rain annually, and most of the south has 80 mm or less. In many districts rain may fall in quantity only once in two or

354

three years, and it is apposite to recall that throughout most of Egypt, and even in Cairo itself, the majority of the people live in houses of unbaked, sun-dried brick. During the summer temperatures are extremely high, reaching 38°C to 43°C at times and even 49°C in the southern and western deserts. The Mediterranean coast has cooler conditions, with 32°C as a maximum; hence the wealthier classes move to Alexandria for the three months of summer. Winters are generally warm, with very occasional rain; but cold spells occur from time to time, and light snow is not unknown. Owing to the large extent of desert, hot dry sand-winds (called *khamsin*) are fairly frequent particularly in spring, and much damage can be caused to crops; it has been known for the temperature to rise by 20°C in two hours, and the wind to reach 150 km per hour. Another unusual condition is the occurrence of early morning fog in Lower Egypt during spring and early summer. This, on the other hand, has a beneficial effect on plant growth in that it supplies moisture and is a partial substitute for rainfall.

IRRIGATION

With a deficient rainfall over the entire country, human existence in Egypt depends closely on irrigation from the Nile; in consequence it is now necessary to consider the regime of the river in some detail. It may be stated, in summary, that the river rises in the highlands of East Africa, with its main stream issuing from lakes Victoria and Albert. In southern Sudan it wanders sluggishly across a flat, open plain, where the fall in level is only 1:100,000. Here the shallow waters become a vast swamp, full of dense masses of papyrus vegetation, and this section of the Nile is called the Sudd (Arabic for 'blockage'). Finally, in the north of Sudan, the Nile flows in a well-defined channel and enters Egypt. In Upper Egypt the river is in the process of cutting its bed deeper into the rock floor; but in the lower part of its course silt is deposited, and the level of the land is rising—in some places by as much as 10 cm per century.

The salient feature of the Nile is, of course, its regular, annual flood, which is caused by the onset of summer rains in East Africa and Ethiopia. The flood travels northward, reaching Egypt during August, and within Egypt the normal rise in river level was at first 6.4 m, which had declined to 4.6 m as irrigation works developed. This cycle of flood had been maintained for several thousand years until, in 1969, construction of the Aswan High Dam made it a feature of the past (see the section on the High Dam below) so far as Egypt is concerned.

Originally, the flood waters were simply retained in specially prepared basins with earthen banks, and the water could then be used for three to four months after the flood. Within the last century, the building of large barrages, holding water all the year round, has allowed cultivation at any season. The old (basin) system allowed one or two crops per holding per year; the newer (perennial) system, three or even four. In the past, barley and wheat were the main crops; under perennial irrigation maize and cotton, which can tolerate the great summer heat, provided they are watered, take first and second place.

The change-over from basin to perennial irrigation allowed a considerable population increase in Egypt, from about 2.5m. in 1800 to over 50m. in 1987, giving rural densities of over 2,500 per sq km in some areas; and, as 99% of all Egyptians live within the Nile valley (only 4% of the country's area), there is considerable pressure on the land.

With most Egyptians entirely dependent upon Nile water, the point has now been reached that almost all the water entering Egypt is fully utilized. However, there are enormous losses by evaporation which at present amount to some 70% of the total flow. A political problem is concerned with the effects of devoting an increased area of the Nile Valley to the growing of commodities for export: cotton, rice and vegetables. Such a change from agricultural self-sufficiency to a cash economy involves the purchase abroad of fertilizers and even foodstuffs, and is inducing considerable social changes within the country. Moreover, so long as only one or two crops were taken per year, the silt laid down by the annual floods maintained soil fertility, but now that three or four crops are taken the import of fertilizer is essential. Hence, Egypt has

become increasingly sensitive to world trade prices. The position of the merchant and capitalist has greatly improved, often at the expense of the peasant farmer. This was to some extent true in Nasser's time and is certainly true of the situation since 1970.

Difficulties and opportunities over use of Nile water are exemplified in the High Dam scheme at Aswan, which has created a lake 500 km (350 miles) in length and 10 km (6 miles) wide that has extended southwards across the Sudanese frontier and inundated the town of Wadi Halfa, whose 55,000–60,000 inhabitants were resettled at Kashm el-Girba, a district lying south-east of Khartoum, whilst displaced Egyptians were settled in 33 villages around Kom Ombo. Prior to 1959 technical and political objections delayed the High Dam scheme; and, as the cost of the dam (estimated at £E345m.–£E400m.) could not be met by the Egyptian Government alone, application was made to the World Bank, the USA and Britain for a loan. This was refused (Sudanese opposition being one, but only one, factor in this refusal), whereupon Egyptian reaction was to expropriate the Suez Canal Company, in order to finance part of the Aswan scheme.

Soviet offers to assist were made and accepted; and in 1959 a first Soviet credit of £E113m. allowed preliminary work to begin in December of the same year. In 1960 further agreement was reached by which the USSR supplied credits up to £E81m., together with technical and material assistance; and in 1964 further proposals for credit and loans were made by Nikita Khrushchev, then the Soviet head of government, leaving Egypt to find at least £E200m. in addition to repayments at a later stage of the Soviet credits.

In May 1964 the first phase of the High Dam was inaugurated by President Nasser and Mr Khrushchev. The High Dam is 3,600 m across, with a girth of 980 m at the river bed and 40 m at the top. It holds back the largest artificial lake in the world (Lake Nasser), and makes possible large-scale storing of water from year to year, and a regular planned use of all Nile water independently of the precise amount of annual flood. Its irrigation potential is 2m. feddans for Lower Egypt alone, and the total for the Nile valley (including Upper Egypt) is adding 30% to the total cultivable area of Egypt. Twelve generator units incorporated in the dam give considerable quantities of low-cost electric power. This power is already a most important aid to industrialization, especially for the new metal industries. The Dam was completed in July 1970 and officially inaugurated in January 1971.

Adverse effects have been noticed: scouring of the Nile bed below the dam; increased salinity in the lower stretches; reduced sedimentation below the dam and heavy deposition within the basin, resulting in the need for increasing use of artificial fertilizers, which must be imported; effects of blowing sand on the electric power lines; and, perhaps more seriously, the disappearance of fish (particularly sardines) off the Mediterranean coast of Egypt. It is hoped that this last can be compensated for by new fishing within Lake Nasser.

Possibly the most serious effect of all is a notable rise in the water-table in some areas, due to hydrostatic pressures, and the year-round presence of water. Besides disturbing irrigation systems (which are adapted to pre-existing conditions), salinity and gleying of a more permanent nature are appearing; bilharzia and other parasitic diseases are spreading; and there is the appearance of the plant water hyacinth, which, if uncleared, can choke irrigation systems.

LANGUAGE

Arabic is the language of almost all Egyptians, though there are very small numbers of Berber-speaking villages in the western oases. Most educated Egyptians also speak either French or English, often with a preference for the former. This is a reflection of the traditional French interest in Egypt, which is reciprocated: governmental decrees are sometimes published in French, as well as Arabic, and newspapers even in French have an important circulation in Cairo and Alexandria. Small colonies of Greeks and Armenians are also a feature of the larger Egyptian towns. It should perhaps be noted that the Arabic name for Egypt, Misr, is always used within the country itself.

History

PRE-ARAB EGYPT

Egypt's relative isolation, with the majority of the population living in the Nile Valley and the Nile Delta, with desert on either side, has produced a high degree of cultural individuality. Pharaonic Egypt lasted from the end of the fourth millennium BC until conquest by the Assyrians in 671 BC. The building of the pyramids and other works in the third millennium BC indicate a powerful monarchy commanding great resources. After the rule of Rameses II (c.1300–1234 BC), Egypt passed into a decline but, after the Assyrian conquest in 671, native rule was soon restored until 525, when Persia conquered Egypt.

The Persian kings patronized the religion of their subjects and were officially regarded as pharaohs. Another change occurred in 332 when the Persian satrap surrendered to Alexander the Great, who was recognized as a pharaoh and founded the city of Alexandria. After Alexander's death Egypt fell to his general, Ptolemy, and his dynasty was Greek in origin and outlook.

On the death of Cleopatra in 30 BC Egypt passed under Roman rule and became a province of a great Mediterranean empire. Christianity was introduced, and the Coptic church of Egypt clung to its monophysite beliefs in the face of Byzantine opposition.

THE COMING OF THE ARABS

Except for a brief Sasanian (Persian) invasion in 616, Egypt remained under Byzantine rule until, with the birth and advance of Islam in the seventh century AD, the Arab army under 'Amr ibn al-As invaded Egypt from Syria. The conquest was virtually complete by 641, but for some centuries Egypt remained an occupied rather than a Muslim country. The Copts, who disliked Byzantine rule, had not opposed the conquest. In the course of time, however, Egypt became an Arabic-speaking country with a Muslim majority, but there remained a Coptic Christian minority. For over two centuries Egypt was administered as part of the Abbasid caliphate of Baghdad, but the Tulunid and Ikshidid dynasties functioned in virtual independence of the caliph between 868 and 969. Ikshidid rule was ended in 969 by a Fatimid invasion from Tunisia. The Fatimids were Shi'a Muslims and Egypt was to remain under Shi'ite (as opposed to orthodox Sunni) rule until 1171.

Under the early Fatimids, Egypt enjoyed a golden age. The country was a well-administered absolute monarchy which, at its height, formed the central portion of an empire which, at its height, included North Africa, Sicily and western Arabia. The city of Cairo was developed and the mosque of al-Azhar founded. But, by the long reign of al-Mustansir (1035–94) decay had set in, and when the Kurdish Salah ad-Din ibn Ayyub, known to Europe as Saladin, rose to prominence as he opposed the Syrian Crusader states in the 12th century, he was able to become sultan over Egypt and almost the whole of the former Crusader territory.

When Saladin died in 1193, his Empire was divided amongst his heirs, one branch of which, the Egyptian Ayyubids, reigned in Cairo. Louis IX of France led an attack on Egypt in 1249, but was stopped at the battle of al-Mansura in 1250. Thereafter Egypt was ruled by Mamluk sultans until the Ottoman advance at the beginning of the 16th century.

OTTOMAN EGYPT: 1517–1798

By the beginning of the 16th century the Ottoman Turks had made dramatic advances. Constantinople was captured by them in 1453, and early in the 16th century the Turks were threatening Vienna. In their expansion southwards the Turks defeated the Mamluks at the battle of Marj Dabiq, north of Aleppo, in 1516, and overthrew the last Mamluk sultan at a second battle, outside Cairo, in 1517. Egypt became a province of the Ottoman Empire, but the Turks usually interfered little with the Egyptian administration. From time to time Mamluk grandees were virtually sovereign in Egypt.

At the end of the 18th century Egypt became a pawn in the war between France and Britain. Napoleon wanted to disrupt British commerce and eventually overthrow British rule in India. He landed at Alexandria in 1798, but in 1801 the French were forced to capitulate by a British and Ottoman force. French interest in Egyptian affairs and Egyptian culture continued, however.

INCREASED EUROPEAN INFLUENCE

The expulsion of the French was followed by a struggle for power in which the victor was an Albanian officer in the Ottoman forces, Muhammad Ali. In 1807 he defeated a British force which had occupied Alexandria, and between 1820 and 1822 his army conquered most of northern Sudan.

In 1824 Muhammad Ali sent his son Ibrahim with an Egyptian force to help the Sultan suppress the Greek struggle for independence, but European intervention in 1827 led to the destruction of the Turkish and Egyptian fleets at Navarino. On the rejection by the Sultan of Muhammad Ali's demand that he should be given Syria in recompense, Ibrahim invaded Syria in 1831. Ibrahim was eventually defeated and Muhammad Ali's dominion was restricted to Egypt and the Sudan, but his governorship was made hereditary. He died in 1849, having been predeceased by Ibrahim. Muhammad Ali introduced many features of Western intellectual life into Egypt, and a Western-educated class began to emerge. Muhammad Ali was succeeded by his grandson, Abbas I (1849–54), under whom Westernization was reduced, and he by Said (1854–64), Muhammad Ali's surviving son.

In 1854 Said granted a concession to a French engineer, Ferdinand de Lesseps, to build the Suez Canal, but work did not begin until 1859 and the canal was opened in 1869. By this time Said had been succeeded by Ibrahim's son, Ismail. Ismail extended his Sudanese dominions, built railways and constructed telegraph lines. Moreover, his personal expenses were high, and between 1863 and 1876 Egyptian indebtedness rose from £7m. to nearly £100m. In 1875 Ismail staved off a financial crisis by selling his Suez Canal shares to the British Government. As part of the Ottoman Empire, Egypt was bound by the Capitulations—treaties with European powers giving European communities in Ottoman territories a considerable degree of autonomy under the jurisdiction of their consuls, and, under conditions of indebtedness and the necessity of loans from the European powers, financial control by outsiders increased.

Ismail was succeeded by his son Tawfiq, who ostensibly governed through a responsible Egyptian ministry, but strict financial control was exercised by a French and a British controller. Meanwhile a nationalist outlook was developing among those Egyptians who had been touched by Western influences, many of whom regarded the Khedive, Tawfiq, as a puppet maintained by France and Britain. In 1881 a group of army officers, led by Arabi Pasha, forced Tawfiq to form a new ministry and to summon the Chamber of Notables, a consultative body originally set up by Ismail. France opposed any concessions to placate Egyptian opinion, and Britain concurred in this. Feelings in Egypt hardened, and in 1882 the Khedive had to appoint a nationalist ministry with Arabi as Minister for War. France and Britain sent naval squadrons, but France subsequently withdrew support and a British expeditionary force landed at Ismailia and routed the Egyptian army at Tel el-Kebir. Cairo was occupied and Tawfiq's prerogatives were restored, to be subsequently exercised under British control.

INCREASED BRITISH INFLUENCE

Britain hoped to set Egyptian affairs in order and then withdraw, but Egypt's financial difficulties contributed towards Britain prolonging its stay. From 1883 to 1907 the Egyptian Government was dominated by the British Agent and Consul-General, Sir Evelyn Baring, who in 1891 became Lord Cromer. Tawfiq was succeeded by his son Abbas II in 1892. He resented

Cromer's authority and a new nationalist movement developed under Mustafa Kamil, a young lawyer. A series of puppet governments preserved a façade of constitutionalism, but educated youth turned increasingly to opposition. British officials increased from about 100 in 1885 to over 1,000 in 1905, and were out of touch with the growing strength of nationalist feeling.

Cromer was succeeded in 1907 by Sir Eldon Gorst, who established better relations with the Khedive, and Gorst was in turn followed by Lord Kitchener in 1911. When Turkey entered the First World War in November 1914 on the side of Germany, Egypt was still nominally a province of the Ottoman Empire. Egypt was declared a British protectorate, with a British High Commissioner, and Britain assumed responsibility for the defence of the Suez Canal. In December Abbas II was deposed and the British Government offered the title of Sultan to Hussain Kamil, the brother of Tawfiq. When Hussain died in 1917 he was succeeded by his brother Fouad. The nationalist movement flourished under wartime conditions, and in November 1918 the nationalist leader Saad Zaghloul presented the High Commissioner, Sir Reginald Wingate, with a demand for autonomy, which Britain refused. The nationalists became known as the *Wafd* (Delegation), but a negotiated settlement was not forthcoming and on 28 February 1922 Britain unilaterally abolished the protectorate and recognized Egypt as an independent sovereign state. Britain, however, reserved to itself the security of the Suez Canal and the defence of Egypt. In March 1922 Fouad took the title of King of Egypt.

INDEPENDENCE

The years between independence and the Second World War brought a triangular struggle between the King, the Wafd and the British Government. The Wafd wanted a revolution, but the King owed his throne to the British. Elections usually gave the Wafd a majority, but a Wafd ministry was unacceptable to King Fouad, who normally had the concurrence of the British Government. In 1935 Fouad was succeeded by his son Farouk, and in 1936 an Anglo-Egyptian treaty of 20 years' duration was signed which terminated British occupation but empowered Britain to station forces in the Suez Canal Zone until the Egyptian army was in a position to ensure the security of the canal.

During the Second World War Egypt was a vital strategic factor as the British base in the Middle East. Egyptian support for the Allied cause was by no means total. The Wafd favoured co-operation with the British, and Britain forced Farouk's acquiescence in the formation of a Wafdist government under Nahas Pasha in 1942. Nahas became increasingly enthusiastic about Arab unity and was instrumental in setting up the Arab League. In 1944 his Government fell.

Egypt joined Iraq, Syria and Jordan in military action following the declaration of the State of Israel in May 1948. Military failure resulted. The King's early popularity had vanished. The Muslim Brotherhood, a puritanical religious body, had become a threat, and communism had gained new adherents. The discredited regime made a last bid for royal and popular support when Nahas, again in power, abrogated the 1936 Treaty with Britain. Terrorism and economic sanctions were then employed in an attempt to force the British forces to withdraw from the Canal Zone.

THE REVOLUTION: 1952–56

On 23 July 1952 a group of young army officers, the 'Free Officers', who had long been planning a *coup d'état*, seized power in Cairo. They invited the veteran politician, Ali Maher, to form a government under their control, and secured the abdication of King Farouk in favour of his infant son, Ahmad Fuad II, on 26 July. Farouk sailed to exile.

General Muhammad Neguib, an associate of the Free Officers who had incurred the enmity of King Farouk and who had earlier made himself popular by his condemnation of the British action in 1942, was made commander-in-chief of the armed forces and head of the military junta. A Council of Regency was formed in August. On 7 September, after an attempt by the Wafd and other parties to resume the political battle on their own terms, a new Cabinet, with Gen. Neguib

as Prime Minister, was substituted for that of Ali Maher. Real power, however, lay with the nine officers who formed the Revolutionary Command Council (RCC).

The Revolution soon gained momentum. In September 1952 land ownership was limited to 300 acres in any one family and the power of the feudal class, which had for so long dominated Egyptian political life, was destroyed. Land owned by the royal family was confiscated. On 10 December the Constitution was abolished, and on 16 January 1953 all political parties were dissolved. It was announced that there would be a three-year transition period before representative government was restored. On 18 June the monarchy was abolished and Egypt declared a republic, with Neguib as President and Prime Minister as well as Chairman of the RCC. Colonel Gamal Abd an-Nasser, who, although leader of the Free Officers, had hitherto remained in the background, became Deputy Prime Minister and Minister of the Interior, and Abd al-Hakim Amer was appointed commander-in-chief of the armed forces.

A struggle for power soon developed between Gen. Neguib, whose personal tendencies were Islamic and conservative, and Col Nasser. On 25 February 1954 Neguib was relieved of his posts as President, Prime Minister and Chairman of the RCC and accused of having attempted to concentrate power in his own hands. Nasser became Prime Minister and Chairman of the RCC in his place for a few days but Neguib was restored as President and took back both the other posts, only to be ousted again as Prime Minister by Nasser in April. Neguib had suffered a defeat and his liberal measures were rescinded. When in October a member of the Muslim Brotherhood attempted to assassinate Nasser, its leaders and several thousand alleged supporters were arrested and in subsequent trials a number of death sentences were passed. On 14 November 1954 Neguib was relieved of the office of President and accused of being involved in a Muslim Brotherhood conspiracy against the regime. He was placed under house arrest and Nasser became acting Head of State.

A settlement of the Sudan and Suez problems had been facilitated by the expulsion of King Farouk. The claim to the joint monarchy of Egypt and Sudan was dropped and negotiations with Sudanese leaders were helped by the fact that Neguib himself was half-Sudanese and popular in Sudan. An Anglo-Egyptian agreement, signed on 12 February 1953, ended the Condominium and offered the Sudanese the choice of independence or union with Egypt. Egyptian expectation that they would choose the latter was disappointed; the overthrow of Neguib and the suppression of the Muslim Brotherhood fed the century-old suspicion of Egyptian motives.

An Anglo-Egyptian agreement on Suez was signed on 19 October 1954; this provided for the withdrawal of British troops from the Canal Zone within 20 months. The agreement recognized the international importance of the Suez Canal (which was described as 'an integral part of Egypt') and expressed the determination of both parties to uphold the 1888 Constantinople Convention.

Under Nasser Egypt began to assert its importance in world affairs. He sought influence in three circles: the Islamic, the African and the Arab, and his visit to the Bandung conference in 1955 added a fourth: the 'non-aligned'. Egypt led the opposition among certain Arab states to the Baghdad Pact (later to become the Central Treaty Organization). In October 1955 Egypt concluded defence agreements with Syria and with Saudi Arabia and in April 1956 a military pact was signed between Egypt, Saudi Arabia and Yemen. Tension with Israel remained high, and raids and counter-raids across the border of the Gaza Strip called for unceasing vigilance on the part of the UN observers stationed on the frontier. In September 1955 Nasser announced an arms deal with Czechoslovakia which was to supply large quantities of military equipment, including Soviet tanks and aircraft, in return for cotton and rice.

In 1956 a constitutional basis for Col Nasser's authority was established. A new Constitution providing for a strong presidency was proclaimed in January and on 23 June approved in a plebiscite in which the citizens of the Egyptian Republic also elected Nasser as President.

THE SUEZ CRISIS AND ITS CONSEQUENCES: 1956–57

President Nasser's policy of non-alignment, which implied willingness to deal with both power blocs, was followed by the Egyptian attempt to obtain funds for the ambitious High Dam project at Aswan. By this project the Egyptian Government aimed to increase cultivable land and generate electricity for industrialization, which was seen as the main solution to Egypt's increasing population problem. Following offers of assistance from the USA and Britain and, separately, from the USSR, the International Bank for Reconstruction and Development (IBRD) offered a loan of $200m. in February 1956, on condition that the USA and Britain lent a total of $70m. and that the agreement of the riparian states to the scheme was obtained; Egypt was to provide local services and material.

The last British troops were withdrawn from Egypt in June 1956, in accordance with the 1954 agreement. Relations with the West were not helped, however, by Egyptian opposition to the Baghdad Pact and strong propaganda attacks on Britain, France and the USA. On 20 July the USA and Britain withdrew their offers of finance for the High Dam, pointing out that agreement between the riparian states had not been achieved and that Egypt's ability to devote adequate resources to the scheme was doubtful. The USSR made no compensating move. On 26 July President Nasser announced that the Suez Canal Company had been nationalized and that revenue from the Canal would be used to finance the High Dam.

Britain, France and the USA protested strongly at this action and after an international conference had met in London in August a committee under the chairmanship of Mr Menzies, the Prime Minister of Australia, went to Cairo to submit proposals for the operation of the Canal under an international system. These were rejected by the Egyptian Government. At a second London conference, in September, a Suez Canal Users' Association took shape and was later joined by 16 states. On 13 October the UN Security Council voted on an Anglo-French resolution embodying basic principles for a settlement agreed earlier between the British, French and Egyptian Ministers of Foreign Affairs in the presence of the UN Secretary-General. The first part of this, setting out the agreed principles, was adopted unanimously; the second, endorsing the proposals of the first London conference and inviting Egypt to make prompt proposals providing no less effective guarantees to users, was vetoed by the USSR.

Britain and France, thus frustrated in their attempts to retain some measure of control over the Suez Canal, at this stage reached a secret understanding with Israel involving military action. Following the disclosure on 24 October that a unified military command had been formed by Egypt, Jordan and Syria, Israeli forces crossed into Sinai on 29 October, ostensibly to attack Egyptian *fedayin* bases, and advanced towards the Suez Canal. On 30 October France and Britain called on Israel and Egypt to cease warlike action and withdraw their forces from either side of the Canal; Egypt was requested to agree to an Anglo-French force moving temporarily into key positions at Port Said, Ismailia and Suez. Israel agreed but Egypt refused. The same day in the UN Security Council Britain and France vetoed US and Soviet resolutions calling for an immediate Israeli withdrawal and calling on all UN members to refrain from the use of force or the threat of force.

Anglo-French air operations against Egypt began on 31 October but paratroops and seaborne forces landed in the Port Said area only on 5 November. Meanwhile, on 2 November, the UN General Assembly called for a cease-fire and two days later adopted a Canadian proposal to create a UN Emergency Force to supervise the ending of the hostilities. On 6 November, following considerable US pressure, the British Prime Minister, Sir Anthony Eden, announced that, subject to confirmation that Egypt and Israel had accepted an unconditional cease-fire, the armed conflict would end at midnight.

The organization of the UN force was rapidly put in hand and the first units reached Egypt on 15 November. The withdrawal of the Anglo-French forces was completed the following month. Israeli forces, which had occupied the entire Sinai peninsula, withdrew from all areas except the Gaza strip, which they wished to prevent becoming a base for more

raids, and Sharm esh-Sheikh at the entrance to the Gulf of Aqaba, which commanded the seaway to the port of Eilat. These areas were returned to Egyptian control in March 1957 after pressure on Israel by the USA.

The Suez Canal, which had been blocked by the Egyptians, was cleared by a UN salvage fleet and reopened at the end of March 1957. The terms under which the Canal reopened were full control by the Egyptian Canal Authority and respect for the Constantinople Convention of 1888, which provided that the Suez Canal should be open to vessels of all nationalities, in war and peace. Disputes would be settled in accordance with the UN Charter or referred to the International Court of Justice.

UNION OF EGYPT AND SYRIA

Elections to the Egyptian National Assembly, provided for in the 1956 Constitution, were held in July 1957. Only candidates approved by President Nasser and his colleagues were permitted to stand and it was clear that the 350 members elected (who included women) were not expected to exert much influence on the Government.

Following the defence agreement in 1955, discussions had been held in the following two years on union between Egypt and Syria. Both countries were aligned against the West and looked to the USSR and other communist states for support, and in Syria pro-Egyptian elements were in the ascendant. On 1 February 1958 the union of Egypt and Syria, under the title of the United Arab Republic (UAR), was announced, but it was not until 21 July 1960 that the first National Assembly of the UAR, consisting of deputies from both Egypt and Syria, was opened in Cairo by President Nasser.

EXTERNAL RELATIONS: 1958–61

During this period President Nasser was actively concerned with changes in the rest of the Arab world.

An invitation was extended to other Arab states to join the new union and in March 1958 the UAR and Yemen entered into a loose association referred to as the United Arab States. This association did not prosper, however, and was terminated by the UAR in December 1961.

The military revolution in Iraq in July, in which the royal family and the Prime Minister, Nuri as-Said, were murdered, destroyed the only Arab regime in the Middle East to have identified itself explicitly with the West. The immediate dispatch of American troops to Lebanon and of British forces to Jordan drew strong protests from the UAR which were echoed by the USSR. The USA and Britain gave warning of the grave consequences of any conflict between their forces and those under the control of Egypt and Syria. President Nasser visited Moscow and on his return received in Damascus a delegation from the new republican regime in Baghdad. A joint communiqué on 19 July declared that the UAR and Iraq would assist each other to repel any foreign aggression.

President Nasser's hostility to the West found favour with the USSR, with which the UAR established closer ties during these years. Soviet military and industrial aid was granted and in December 1958 an agreement was concluded which ensured Soviet assistance for the building of the Aswan High Dam. Work on the first stage of the High Dam began in January 1960.

Relations with the West improved during 1959 and 1960. Through the mediation of the IBRD an agreement with Britain was signed on 1 March 1959 providing for the payment by the UAR of £27.5m. as compensation for British private property taken over at the time of the Suez crisis in 1956. Diplomatic relations with Britain were resumed at chargé d'affaires level in December 1959 and raised to ambassadorial level early in 1961. A $56.5m. loan to improve the Suez Canal was obtained from the World Bank in 1959, and other aid came from the USA in 1960.

SYRIAN WITHDRAWAL FROM UAR

President Nasser replaced the two Regional Executive Councils and the Central Cabinet of the UAR with a single central government in August 1961. Syria had by now become dissatisfied with the union and on 28 September the Syrian army seized control in Damascus and Syria withdrew from the UAR. President Nasser at first called for resistance to the Syrian *coup d'état* but, when the rebels were seen to be in firm control, said on 5 October that he would not oppose recognition of Syria's independence. The loss of Syria was a bitter blow to President Nasser and his Egyptian colleagues who now set about a re-examination of their policies which resulted in a renewal of revolutionary fervour.

The UAR Government (Egypt retained the full title) was re-formed on 18 October and a National Congress of Popular Forces, consisting of 1,750 delegates, representing not geographical areas but economic and professional interests and other social groups, met in Cairo on 21 May 1962. President Nasser presented the National Congress with a draft National Charter outlining his programme for developing the UAR on Arab socialist lines. A new democratic system of government was introduced, based on the Arab Socialist Union (ASU) (replacing the National Union) and including popular councils at least half the members of which would be workers or *fellahin*.

MORE ATTEMPTS AT UNION

The Syrian *coup d'état* had been preceded by the overthrow in February 1963 of the regime of Gen. Qassim in Iraq. These changes in power brought Syria and Iraq into closer alignment with Egypt and it was announced on 17 April that agreement had been reached on the formation of a federation of the three countries under the name of the United Arab Republic. Rivalries, however, arose in both Baghdad and Damascus between supporters of the Baath Party and 'Nasserists', and by August President Nasser had withdrawn from the agreement, claiming that the Baathists had set up one-party dictatorships in Syria and Iraq and ignored his insistence on wider nationalist representation.

A month later President Arif of Iraq called for a Baathist union of the three countries, but after the expulsion of Baath leaders from Iraq in November 1963 and the consolidation of power in Arif's hands the unity movement between Iraq and Syria fell apart and Iraq and Egypt again moved closer together. A Unified Political Command between Iraq and Egypt began work in early 1965, but progress towards unity was slow.

During 1964 President Nasser took an important initiative in Arab League affairs by calling two Arab summit meetings in Egypt, which determined Arab policy on the use of water from the River Jordan and also strengthened the armies of Syria, Lebanon and Jordan. A further £E1m. was set aside for the formation of the Palestine Liberation Organization (PLO).

The Arab reconciliation and presentation of a united front lasted until the spring of 1965. Iraq, Kuwait, Yemen (Arab Republic), Algeria and Lebanon continued to follow President Nasser's lead, only Syrian critics complaining that UAR policy was not sufficiently anti-Israeli. UAR relations with Jordan improved strikingly and, after a conference of heads of Arab governments in Cairo in January 1965 to discuss co-ordination of Arab policies, King Hussein, previously the object of UAR attacks and derision, himself paid a visit to Cairo.

In Yemen, despite Egyptian support, the republican regime seemed no closer to victory over the royalists, who held the mountainous regions of the north-east and were assisted by Saudi Arabian finance and supplies of arms. This military stalemate and the financial burden of maintaining some 50,000 troops in Yemen moved President Nasser to attempt to disengage, but negotiations ended in deadlock and Egyptian troops remained in Yemen. On 22 February 1966, the day the British Government announced that British forces would leave Aden and South Arabia when that territory became independent in 1968, President Nasser stated that Egyptian troops would not be withdrawn until the Revolution in Yemen could 'defend itself against the conspiracies of imperialism and reactionaries'.

CHANGES OF INTERNATIONAL ALIGNMENT

The years 1964 and 1965 saw a deterioration of UAR relations with the West and increasing dependence on the Soviet Union.

Relations with the USA were adversely affected by UAR support for the Stanleyville rebels in the Congo during the winter of 1964–65. Diplomatic relations with Britain, already worsened by Egyptian encouragement of dissident elements in South Arabia, were severed by the UAR in December 1965 over the Rhodesia issue, in common with eight other members of the Organization of African Unity.

Relations with the USSR had been strengthened in May 1964 when the Soviet Premier, Nikita Khrushchev, made a 16-day visit to Egypt to attend the ceremony marking the completion of the first stage of the Aswan High Dam, being built with Soviet aid. President Nasser paid his third visit to the USSR in August 1965 and (Khrushchev having been overthrown) the new Soviet Premier, Alexei Kosygin, visited the UAR in May 1966, expressing support for UAR policies and again demonstrating Soviet interest in the Middle East.

DOMESTIC TROUBLES

Although President Nasser obtained over 99% of the votes cast in the presidential referendum in March 1965, there were subsequently more signs of discontent in the UAR than at any time since he had come to power. In a speech to Arab students during his visit to Moscow in August 1965, he disclosed that a plot against his life had been discovered, in which the banned Muslim Brotherhood was thought to have been involved.

In September 1965 a new government headed by Zakaria Mohi ed-Din replaced that of Ali Sabri, who became secretary-general of the ASU. Thereafter, administrative changes were made and the security system was tightened up. Taxation was increased and measures of retrenchment were introduced because of increasing economic difficulties, particularly the acute shortage of foreign exchange. US wheat supplies were continued, credits from France, Japan and Italy and a loan from Kuwait were obtained and there were increased drawings from the International Monetary Fund (IMF). Nevertheless the level of imports, particularly food to feed the growing population, and the debt service burden resulting from the first Five-Year Plan caused a continuing drain on foreign exchange reserves and the UAR faced a balance of payments crisis. The second Five-Year Plan was revised and extended over seven years and President Nasser gave public warnings that sacrifices were necessary in every field as Egypt lacked the foreign currency to pay for imports. He refused, however, to abandon the expensive commitment in Yemen. Zakaria Mohi ed-Din's replacement in September 1966 by Sidki Sulaiman (a technocrat who retained his post as Minister of the High Dam) was seen as the outcome of disagreement over retrenchment measures. When the UAR defaulted on repayments due to the IMF in December 1966, the country was on the verge of bankruptcy.

WIDENING RIFT WITH SAUDI ARABIA

The rift between the UAR and Saudi Arabia widened. President Nasser in February 1966 expressed opposition to an Islamic grouping which King Faisal was promoting, and in the succeeding months propaganda warfare between the two countries was intensified. In the middle of the year the President gave notice that he would not attend an Arab summit conference with Saudi Arabia and Jordan, both of whom he criticized for obtaining British and US military aid, and called for the indefinite postponement of the conference planned for September. A majority of Arab states agreed, but in October Tunisia broke off relations with the UAR over continued differences on Arab League policies.

In Yemen, Egyptian forces had been withdrawn from northern and eastern areas and concentrated in the triangle between San'a, Hodeida and Taiz. Egyptian control over the republican armed forces and administration was increased and when, in September 1966, after President Sallal had returned to Yemen from a year's absence in Cairo, the republican Prime Minister, Hassan al-Amri, and seven senior members of his Cabinet visited Egypt to make a plea for greater independence, they were arrested and detained there. The following month, about 100 senior Yemen officials were dismissed and arrests and executions were carried out.

WAR WITH ISRAEL

The events of May 1967 were to transform the Middle East. There had been an increase in Syrian guerrilla activities in

Israel during the previous six months and on 7 April the tension had led to fighting in the Tiberias area, in which six Syrian aircraft had been shot down. Israeli warnings to the Syrian Government, culminating on 12 May in the threat by Premier Eshkol of severe reprisals if terrorist activities were not controlled, evoked Syrian allegations that Israel was about to mount a large-scale attack on Syria. President Nasser, who had been reproached for not aiding Syria in the April fighting in accordance with the mutual defence agreement, responded immediately, moving large numbers of troops to the Israeli border. He secured the dissolution of the UN Emergency Force, whose presence on the Egyptian side of the frontier depended on Egyptian permission, and reoccupied the gun emplacement at Sharm esh-Sheikh on the Straits of Tiran. He later justified these steps by claiming that he had received Syrian and Soviet warnings that Israeli troops were concentrated on the Syrian border (an allegation subsequently disproved by reports of UN truce observers) and an invasion of Syria was imminent.

When on 23 May President Nasser closed the Straits of Tiran to Israeli shipping, thereby effectively blockading the Israeli port of Eilat, his prestige in the Arab world reached an unparalleled height. Britain and the USA protested that the Gulf of Aqaba was an international waterway; Israel regarded the blockade of the Straits as an unambiguous act of war. As tension increased, King Hussein of Jordan concluded a mutual defence pact with the UAR and was immediately joined by Iraq.

On the morning of 5 June Israel launched large-scale air attacks on Egyptian, Jordanian, Syrian and Iraqi airfields, and Israeli ground forces made rapid advances into the Gaza Strip, Sinai and western Jordan; there was also fighting on the Israeli-Syrian border. The outcome was decided within hours by the air strikes, which destroyed the bulk of the Arab air forces, and the Israeli ground forces were everywhere successful. By 10 June, when all participants had accepted the UN Security Council's call for a cease-fire, Israeli troops were in control of the Sinai peninsula as far as the Suez Canal (including Sharm esh-Sheikh), the West Bank of the Jordan (including the Old City of Jerusalem), the Gaza Strip and Syrian territory extending 12 miles from the Israeli border. The Suez Canal was blocked by Egypt in the course of the fighting. President Nasser offered to resign, but popular support led him to withdraw his resignation. He dismissed a number of senior army officers and took over himself the duties of Prime Minister and secretary-general of the ASU.

The implications of the catastrophe were only gradually realized. It was estimated that the loss of revenue from the Suez Canal, from oil produced in Sinai and from tourism amounted to some £E12.5m. per month, or almost half Egypt's foreign currency earnings. Also, the withdrawal of a large part of the Egyptian force in Yemen reduced Nasser's ability to influence affairs both in that country and in Aden and South Arabia (which became independent as the Republic of Southern Yemen on 30 November 1967, after the withdrawal of British troops).

The USSR, which had given the Arab cause strong verbal support throughout the crisis, continued to take a strong pro-Arab stand at the UN and President Podgorny paid a lengthy visit to Cairo to discuss future Egyptian policy. The USSR replaced about half the lost Egyptian aircraft and provided other military supplies and instructors. Further economic assistance was also offered by the USSR and in May 1968 an agreement was announced for the construction of a steel complex at Helwan.

Israel demanded direct negotiations with the Arab states for a peace settlement but the fourth conference of Arab heads of state, held in Khartoum at the end of August 1967, decided against recognition of, or negotiation with, Israel. At this conference, in which Syria did not participate, it was agreed that the embargo on oil supplies to Western countries (applied the previous June) should be lifted, that the Suez Canal should remain closed until Israeli forces were withdrawn, and that Saudi Arabia, Kuwait and Libya should give special aid of £95m. a year to the UAR (and also £40m. a year to Jordan) until the 'effects of the aggression' were eliminated. King Faisal and President Nasser announced their agreement on a peace plan for Yemen under which Egyptian troops were to

be withdrawn within three months and Saudi Arabia was to stop supplying the royalists; the withdrawal was subsequently completed by December (President Sallal being deposed by republican leaders in November).

After repeated violations of the cease-fire by both sides, the UN Security Council, on 22 November 1967, adopted a British resolution laying down the principles for a just and lasting peace in the Middle East and authorizing the appointment of a special UN representative to assist in bringing about a settlement. This was Resolution 242 (see Documents on Palestine p. 73) which has subsequently formed the basis of most attempts to restore peace to the Middle East. Dr Gunnar Jarring was appointed special UN representative, and quickly began discussions with Arab and Israeli leaders which continued for a number of years.

UAR AFTER THE JUNE WAR

Meanwhile President Nasser faced daunting economic difficulties and a disturbed political situation in Egypt. An austerity budget had been framed in July 1967. The cost of re-equipping the armed forces forced a cut in investment, in spite of Soviet aid and assistance from other Arab governments. Socialist policies were still followed, as was shown by the decision to nationalize the wholesale trade, announced in October. The continuing shortage of foreign exchange made it desirable to improve the UAR's relations with the West and in December diplomatic relations with Britain were resumed. A bridging loan from British, West German and Italian banks, obtained in February 1968, enabled the UAR to make the repayments to the IMF which had been due since the end of 1966, and in March the IMF approved further drawings.

Widespread demonstrations of students and workers took place in Cairo, Helwan and other centres, towards the end of February 1968. Initially in protest at the leniency of sentences on air force officers, they revealed widespread discontent. A number of persons were killed in clashes with police, and the universities were closed; nevertheless President Nasser realized the need for immediate conciliatory action. Retrials were ordered and sweeping Cabinet changes announced, a number of civilian experts in various fields being brought in. Ali Sabri, who had been reinstated as secretary-general of the ASU in January, was also included but Zakaria Mohi ed-Din left the Government. President Nasser continued to exercise the functions of Prime Minister.

On 30 March President Nasser announced a new plan for building a modern state in Egypt based on democracy, science and technology. The single party would remain but there would be free elections throughout the ASU and changes were promised among leaders in all spheres. An announcement of the distribution to the people of land taken over by the state or reclaimed was made on 6 April. In a plebiscite on 2 May the 'Declaration of 30 March' was overwhelmingly approved. The first ASU elections were held in June; the 75,000 persons chosen then elected a national congress in July; this in turn chose a central committee which then chose the party's higher executive. These proceedings, however, did not appear to arouse much public interest. Further student riots in November 1968 and the closure of the universities left Nasser increasingly isolated and exposed.

Deprived of foreign exchange by the continued closure of the Canal and the drop in the tourist trade, the UAR remained dependent on the regular aid payments from Saudi Arabia, Kuwait and Libya and on Soviet assistance, both humiliating to a people strongly nationalist in outlook. There were signs that the civilian economic ministers favoured some relaxation of over-rigid state control in industry and more encouragement of private enterprise and foreign investment. Military expenditure in 1968 and 1969 remained high. Soviet arms deliveries continued, as also did the presence of about 3,000 Soviet military advisers and instructors.

The efforts of Dr Jarring, the representative of the UN Secretary-General, to bring Israel, the UAR and Jordan closer together had, by the end of 1968, yielded little success. In April 1969, following initiatives by the USSR and France, those two countries, together with Britain and the USA, as permanent members of the Security Council, began talks at the UN in New York in an unsuccessful attempt to promote a settlement.

A pattern of sporadic action, involving artillery duels across the Suez Canal, commando raids and air combat developed throughout 1969 and into 1970, with growing Soviet involvement in Egypt's defence. In the summer of 1970 the US Secretary of State, William Rogers, put forward a set of proposals for solving the continuing Middle East crisis. An uneasy cease-fire, but no permanent solution, resulted.

EGYPT AFTER NASSER

Although President Nasser had had his differences with the Palestinian guerrillas over their rejection of the US peace proposals and the hijacking of western airliners at the beginning of September 1970, one of his last acts was to secure agreement in Cairo between King Hussein and Yasser Arafat for an end to the fighting between the Jordanian army and the guerrillas.

Nasser's death on 28 September 1970 came as a profound shock and it was feared by many that it would reduce chances of achieving peace in the Middle East. A close associate of Nasser, and Vice-President at the time of his death, Col Anwar Sadat, was immediately appointed provisional President by the Cabinet and the Party, being later elected President in a national referendum, and by mid-1971 he was firmly in control of the Government of Egypt.

In November 1970 President Sadat had agreed to the federation of the UAR with Sudan and Libya. Sudan, however, later postponed its membership of the union. In April 1971 Syria agreed to become the third member of the federation. The federation proposals, together with Sadat's plan for the reopening of the Canal, precipitated a crisis in the leadership, which led to a comprehensive purge by Sadat of opponents at all levels of the Government, including Ali Sabri, one of the two Vice-Presidents. In July new elections were held, not only for all levels of the Party, but also for trade unions and professional bodies. A new Constitution, the first permanent one since the 1952 revolution, was approved in September. It contained important clauses governing personal freedoms and discarded at last the name of United Arab Republic, the state being known henceforward as the Arab Republic of Egypt.

The year 1971 was marked by repeated Egyptian declarations of the intention to fight Israel—but only when the time was ripe—and Egypt mounted an extensive diplomatic campaign to state its case in the West. In September 1971 came the first large-scale military operations on the Canal since the August 1970 cease-fire and in December the UN passed a resolution calling for the resumption of the Jarring peace mission.

Dr Mahmoud Fawzi, who was appointed Prime Minister in October 1970, resigned in January 1972 and was made a joint Vice-President. His successor was Dr Aziz Sidqi, who had been first Vice-Premier since September 1971.

Egypt was becoming increasingly dependent on the USSR, both militarily and economically. Student riots at the beginning of 1972 brought assurances from President Sadat that an armed confrontation with Israel was definitely intended. Against this background of increasing internal uneasiness Egypt intensified efforts to diversify sources of development aid and armaments. The Suez-Alexandria (Sumed) pipeline received promises of Western backing and in May 1972 a five-year preferential trade agreement was concluded with the EC.

CRISIS IN EGYPTIAN-SOVIET RELATIONS

The most striking event of 1972 was the dismissal of Soviet military advisers from Egypt in July. This did not lead to a rupture in Egyptian-Soviet relations but neither did it result in any significant rapprochement with the West, anti-American feeling remaining very strong. A new round of diplomatic visits to state Egypt's case, particularly in the West and the Far East, was embarked upon and arms supplies requested from France and Britain. With the announcement on 2 August 1972 of Egypt's plan to merge with Libya, France stated that supplies of *Mirage* fighters to Libya would continue, Libya not being in direct conflict with Israel.

Contacts with the USSR continued and economic relations appeared unaffected by the events of July but it was clear that the USSR was looking elsewhere to maintain its presence in the Mediterranean. It was unclear to what extent Sadat's hand had been forced in ordering the Soviet withdrawal.

INTERNAL UNREST

A law passed in August 1972 provided for penalties up to life imprisonment for offences endangering national unity, including opposing the Government by force and inciting violence between Muslims and the Coptic minority. Clashes between these two communities were growing more frequent and, along with increasing student unrest, were seen as an expression of dissatisfaction with the state of 'no-peace-no-war'. The Government resorted to repeated assurances of military preparations. In December 1972 Sadat in fact ordered preparations for fighting, after strong criticism in the People's Assembly of the government's policies. Another cause of uneasiness was the proposed merger with Libya, which many people felt might give Col Muammar al-Qaddafi, the Libyan leader, excessive control over Egypt's destiny.

In January 1973 there were violent clashes between police and students. In February a number of left-wing elements, among them many journalists, were expelled from the ASU, student unrest continued and in March President Sadat took over from Aziz Sidqi as Prime Minister. The new administration's policies were approved by the Majlis ash-Sha'ab (People's Assembly) but the Government was criticized for failing to follow a clear-cut economic policy, particularly with regard to the five-year plan.

RELATIONS WITH LIBYA

Egypt and Libya had agreed on a programme of full union by stages at a meeting between the two Heads of State in Benghazi in August 1972, and a merger of the two countries was planned to take place on 1 September 1973. The Libyan leader, Col Qaddafi, showed more enthusiasm than President Sadat for total union, and in July 1973 Qaddafi organized a march of 40,000 Libyans on Cairo in order to bring pressure to bear on Egypt. The march was turned back about 200 miles from Cairo, however, and Sadat, although showing support for eventual union, stated that 'enthusiasm and emotional impulses are not a sufficient basis for unity'. An agreement in principle was nevertheless signed on 29 August, but few practical steps were taken to implement the agreement.

Throughout 1974 and early 1975 relations between the two countries deteriorated to such an extent that President Sadat asserted in a press interview in April 1975 that Qaddafi was '100% sick'. At the time Libya had been threatening to take action against Egyptians working in Libya. Relations worsened when a large Soviet-Libyan arms deal was revealed later in the month. President Sadat hastily accused Libya and the USSR of conducting an international campaign against him and his Middle East policy. Libya was among the Arab countries severely critical of the Second Interim Disengagement Agreement between Egypt and Israel in September 1975. In July 1977 open warfare took place on the border between Egypt and Libya, and when Sadat visited Israel in November 1977 (see below), relations deteriorated even further, with Egypt breaking off diplomatic relations with Libya in December. Libya joined the rest of the Arab world in condemning the Egyptian-Israeli peace treaty in March 1979, and it was reported that renewed outbreaks of war on the Egyptian-Libyan border were prevented only by the intervention of the USA. In March 1980 Libya constructed airfields and fortifications on the border with Egypt, and in June 1980 Egypt declared martial law in the border area with Libya for a period of one year.

THE OCTOBER WAR AND ITS AFTERMATH

Between the June 1967 war and October 1973 Egyptian leaders frequently stated that the war against Israel would be resumed, but when Egyptian forces crossed the Suez Canal on 6 October 1973, it came as a surprise to Israel and to the rest of the world. For President Sadat the war was a considerable triumph. It appeared to end the years of stalemate with Israel, and his personal reputation was greatly enhanced. As a result of the Disengagement Agreement which Israel and Egypt signed on 18 January 1974, Egyptian forces regained a strip of territory to the east of the Suez Canal (see map on p. 89).

After the war extensive and far-reaching changes took place in Egypt. An amnesty was extended to many important political prisoners in January 1974, and in April an amnesty was extended to more than 2,000 persons who had been imprisoned for political or criminal offences. Press censorship was lifted in February, and in April about 8.5m. voters gave a 99.95% endorsement to a programme of economic and social reform which concentrated on reconstruction, attracting foreign investment, limiting police interference in everyday life, and the introduction of a private enterprise sector in the economy while still maintaining the public sector (see Economy).

One result of the October war was Egypt's improved relations with the USA. Diplomatic relations between Egypt and the USA were restored in November 1973 and the US Secretary of State, Dr Henry Kissinger, had a cordial relationship with President Sadat during the disengagement talks. American initiatives in peacemaking were generally welcomed by Egypt, while the Americans became more conscious of the extent of their dependence on Arab oil. It was, therefore, in an atmosphere of *rapprochement* that President Nixon visited Cairo in June 1974.

RETURN TO STALEMATE

The euphoria which the crossing of the Suez Canal had produced began to disappear during 1974. Increases in the cost of living, and the slowness with which the promised economic reform was proceeding, led to riots in Cairo on 1 January 1975, and to further disturbances among textile workers in March 1975, when the textile complex at el-Mahalla el-Koubra was closed for several days after violent clashes over pay demands.

As a result of these disturbances Dr Abd al-Aziz Higazi, who had taken over the premiership from President Sadat in September 1974, resigned as Prime Minister and was replaced in April 1975 by Gen. Mamdouh Muhammad Salem, the former Minister of the Interior and Deputy Prime Minister. On 1 May 1975 President Sadat announced that all lower-paid public-sector employees would receive additional cost-of-living allowances equal to 30% of their pay, and later in May, in a speech to the People's Assembly, the Prime Minister, Salem, promised that steps would be taken to ensure that the economic programme of 1974 would be implemented and that foreign investors, whether from Western countries or from the Eastern bloc, would be given every facility.

During the first eight months of 1975 Dr Kissinger engaged in considerable 'shuttle diplomacy' and in September Egypt and Israel signed the Second Interim Disengagement Agreement. In brief, Israel withdrew from the Giddi and Mitla passes and Egypt recovered the Abu Rudeis oilfield in Sinai, while Article I of the Agreement stated that Egypt and Israel have agreed that 'the conflict between them and in the Middle East shall not be resolved by military force but by peaceful means'. This agreement brought upon President Sadat the strong disapproval of other Arab interests, particularly Syria, Jordan, Iraq and the PLO, as it appeared to them that Egypt was seeking to commit the whole Arab world to a policy of peace with Israel. The position had also been complicated by the fact that, at the Arab summit at Rabat in October 1974, the PLO had achieved the status of the sole legitimate representative of the Palestinian people. At the end of May 1976 Egypt attempted to consolidate an improvement in relations with the PLO by asking the Arab League to admit the PLO as a full member. Relations with Syria, at a particularly low ebb during the Lebanese civil war, improved after the Riyadh and Cairo summits in October 1976.

The rest of the Arab world was also aware that Egypt was drawing even closer to the USA. Certainly, Sadat was becoming disillusioned with the USSR. In March 1976 he abrogated the Treaty of Friendship with the USSR, which Egypt had signed in 1971. In a speech to the Egyptian People's Assembly, Sadat accused the USSR of exerting political, economic and military pressure on Egypt by criticizing his Middle East policies, refusing to reschedule Egypt's debts, and refusing supplies of weapons and spares. Egypt decided to expel about 40 Soviet diplomats in protest against the Soviet invasion of Afghanistan in December 1979.

POLITICAL ADVANCE AND DOMESTIC DIFFICULTIES

During 1976 and for most of 1977, President Sadat was forced to involve himself increasingly in domestic issues. In March 1976 three political 'platforms' were allowed to form within the ASU, and in the November 1976 elections to the People's Assembly the 'platforms' entered the contest as full-scale political parties. The Arab Socialists (a party of the centre, supporting Sadat) won 280 seats, while the Liberal Socialists (supporting political and economic liberalization) won 12 seats. The left-wing National Progressive Unionist Party won 2 seats. After the elections President Sadat announced that the ASU would fade into the background and would become merely a watchdog for the three parties' activities.

Egypt's economy, during 1976, was experiencing great difficulties (see Economy), and when in January 1977 Sadat announced a budget which, because of the withdrawal of subsidies, meant large increases in food and other prices, severe riots broke out in Cairo and other centres. In the face of this opposition Sadat had to revoke the price increases and in February he introduced a law which made a wide range of new offences punishable by hard labour for life. Among these offences were forming a political group other than the three legal parties; forming a group to destroy public or private property; failing to submit an accurate account of earnings and property; tax evasion; stirring up the people or impeding the Government, or public and private sectors, or the institutions of learning; and premeditated striking. These measures were put to a referendum in which 96.9% of the enfranchised population voted, and 99.4% of the votes cast approved of the measures.

By June 1977 Sadat considered the internal situation in Egypt to be sufficiently under control to regularize the current position on political parties. A law was adopted by the People's Assembly stating that each party must include at least 20 members of the People's Assembly (current parties excepted). This effectively excluded the Communist Party, the Muslim Brotherhood and the New Wafd Party.

PROGRESS TOWARDS A PEACE TREATY WITH ISRAEL

In November 1977, however, domestic questions were completely overshadowed by Sadat's visit to Israel and his address to the Knesset. It was by no means certain whether any tangible peace proposals would result from Sadat's talks with Menachem Begin, the newly elected Likud Premier of Israel, whose hitherto aggressive attitude did not seem to augur well for the cause of peace, but who might use his newly acquired power in putting forward a daring initiative. In the event, no significant breakthrough was made immediately. The status of any future Palestinian state presented the main obstacle. Talks continued in 1978, in spite of the opposition of much of the Arab world, which regarded Egypt's unilateral bid for peace with Israel as detrimental to Arab unity. Egypt had pre-empted action being considered by Syria, Libya, Algeria, Iraq and the People's Democratic Republic of Yemen, by breaking off diplomatic relations with these countries in December 1977. In September 1978 there came a somewhat unexpected breakthrough when, after talks at Camp David in the USA under the guidance of President Carter, Sadat and Begin signed two agreements. The first was a 'framework of peace in the Middle East' (see p. 90) and the second was a 'framework for the conclusion of a peace treaty between Egypt and Israel'. The first agreement provided for a five-year transitional period during which the inhabitants of the Israeli-occupied West Bank of the Jordan and the Gaza Strip would obtain full autonomy and self-government, and the second agreement provided for the signing of a peace treaty within three months. In the event the signing of the peace treaty was delayed because of the question of whether there should be any linkage between the conclusion of the peace treaty and progress towards autonomy in the Israeli-occupied areas, but on 26 March 1979, after another intervention by President Carter, the signing took place. The treaty (see p. 92) provided for a phased Israeli withdrawal from Sinai over a period of three years. This withdrawal went according to plan, and for the first time, diplomatic relations between Egypt and Israel were established on 26 February 1980 and the two countries exchanged ambassadors.

Proposals for Palestinian autonomy were contained in a separate letter published with the treaty, and provided for both sides to attempt to complete negotiations within 12 months. There would then be elections of Palestinian local councils and a five-year transitional period would follow during which the final status of the West Bank and Gaza would be negotiated. The autonomy negotiations began in May 1979, but the deadline of 26 May 1980 passed without agreement being reached. The main stumbling blocks were the presence and growth of Israeli settlements on the West Bank, the strengthening of Israel's insistence that Jerusalem was its eternal indivisible capital, and a fundamental difference between Egyptian ideas of Palestinian autonomy, which were tantamount to an independent state, and those of Israel, which envisaged a limited form of self-government.

The Camp David agreements and the subsequent peace treaty resulted in Egypt's isolation in the Arab world. Syria, Algeria, Libya and the PLO had met in Damascus in September 1978 and strongly condemned the Camp David agreements, and in March 1979, after the signing of the peace treaty, the Arab League Council met in Baghdad and passed a series of resolutions (see p. 93) comprising the withdrawal of Arab ambassadors to Egypt, the severing of economic and political links with Egypt, the withdrawal of Arab aid and the removal of the headquarters of the Arab League from Cairo to Tunis. Egypt had already been threatened with these sanctions at an earlier Arab summit in Baghdad in November 1978. Some Arab states were reluctant to honour these decisions, but when Saudi Arabia broke off diplomatic relations with Egypt in late April, Egypt's isolation became potentially serious, although private Arab investment continued. (In the event, only Oman, Sudan and Somalia continued to have diplomatic relations with Egypt.) As a result, Egypt came to rely even more heavily than before on financial and military aid from the USA. During 1980 it became evident that Egypt's isolation was having little practical effect. The economic measures taken against Egypt were balanced by the growing strength of Egypt's own economy, and the exchange of ambassadors between Egypt and Sudan in March 1981 was a recognition of its reduced isolation. Another sign of this was Egypt's sale of arms worth US $25m. to Iraq in the same month.

INTERNAL POLITICAL CHANGE

Since 1976 President Sadat had been trying to allow the formation of political parties while at the same time ensuring that dangerous opposition did not achieve too much influence. In a law of June 1977 political parties were legalized. Disturbed by the revival of the Wafd Party (as the New Wafd Party) and the criticisms of the National Progressive Unionist Party (NPUP), Sadat won approval in a referendum for a new set of regulations on political parties which resulted in the disbanding of the New Wafd Party and the suspension of the NPUP. In July Sadat announced the creation of a new political party, the National Democratic Party (NDP), with himself as leader, which in practice replaced the Arab Socialist Party (SLP). In September 1978 an official opposition party, the Socialist Labour Party (SLP), was formed.

The signing of the Camp David agreements in September 1978, although causing the resignation of the Egyptian Minister of Foreign Affairs, Muhammad Ibrahim Kamel, was popular in Egypt and in October Sadat appointed a new government, designed to further the peace process, with Mustafa Khalil as Prime Minister. Khalil also became Minister of Foreign Affairs in February 1979. The signing of the peace treaty in March was followed by a referendum in April in which 99.95% of the voters approved the treaty. A simultaneous referendum gave Sadat a mandate for fresh general elections and for future constitutional changes. The elections, held in June, resulted in a convincing win for Sadat's NDP, which obtained 302 seats in the 392-seat People's Assembly. On 30 April 1980 the People's Assembly passed a number of amendments to the Constitution (see p. 393), the most important of which gave Sadat the power to serve further

terms as President and which affirmed that Islamic jurisprudence was the basis of Egyptian law.

On 12 May 1980 the Prime Minister, Mustafa Khalil, offered his resignation because Egypt was 'on the threshold of a new stage of national construction', which required a new government. Two days later, Sadat appointed a government in which he himself became Prime Minister. The constitutional amendments then received the approval of more than 98% of the voters at yet another referendum. One of these amendments provided for the election of a 210-member Majlis ash-Shura (Advisory Council), to replace the former Central Committee of the ASU. Elections took place in September 1980 and the NDP won all 140 elected seats. The remaining 70 members were appointed by the President. The NDP also gained more seats in the People's Assembly in 1980 and early 1981, as at least 13 members of the official opposition SLP defected to the NDP or became independents.

MUBARAK SUCCEEDS SADAT

Although political parties had been allowed by Sadat, power had remained with his own NDP, and latent opposition was never far beneath the surface. In the summer of 1981 there had been clashes between Copts and Islamic fundamentalists, resulting in numerous arrests and the closure of various newspapers. Sadat was trying to stifle the opposition, of whatever religious or political persuasion.

On 6 October, however, Sadat was assassinated at a military parade by a group of Islamic fundamentalists led by Lt Khaled Islambouli, who was executed with four associates on 15 April 1982. An Islamic rebellion, which broke out in Asyut immediately after the assassination, was quickly suppressed, and Vice-President Muhammad Hosni Mubarak was confirmed as President at a referendum on 13 October.

Following his sudden rise to power, Mubarak demonstrated that he was not the nonentity which many believed him to be while he was Vice-President. Athough many of Sadat's religious and political detainees were released, Mubarak continued to arrest Muslim fundamentalists, several hundred of whom were tried on charges of belonging to the al-Jihad organization which plotted to overthrow the Government in 1981. In September 1984, 174 of the 302 people arrested in connection with Sadat's killing were acquitted of plotting to overthrow the Government; 16 were sentenced to hard labour for life; and the remainder received prison sentences ranging from two to 15 years. The state of emergency that had been declared after the assassination of President Sadat was extended for another year, in October 1982 and October 1983, for a further 18 months in October 1984 and for two more years in April 1986.

In his first government reshuffle, in January 1982, Mubarak replaced Dr Ali Abd ar-Razzaq Abd al-Majid (the architect of Egypt's 'open door policy') as Deputy Prime Minister for Finance and Economy, signalling a concern to correct the great inequalities of wealth in Egypt. A second reshuffle in August, including the dismissal of three deputy prime ministers, was intended to secure an improved economic performance. Nevertheless, opposition parties felt that the pace of economic and political reform was too slow, and their criticisms found an outlet in a press that was less fettered than during the last days of Sadat. Mubarak gained approval for his anti-corruption drive, a policy leading to the dismissal, in March 1983, of the Minister of Industry (Fouad Ibrahim Abu Zaglah) and the Minister of Supply (Ahmad Ahmad Nuh), who were implicated in the trial for fraud of Sadat's half-brother, Esmat.

In foreign affairs, the early months of Mubarak's presidency were preoccupied with the question of the return of Sinai by Israel under the 'Camp David process'. After many last-minute snags, the last section was returned to Egypt on 25 April 1982—although a dispute persisted until 1989 concerning the 1 sq km of the Taba enclave on the Egypt/Israel border, north of the Gulf of Aqaba, which was still occupied by Israel. Since then, relations between the two countries have been soured, most significantly, by Israel's invasion of Lebanon in June 1982, in protest at which Egypt withdrew its Ambassador from Tel-Aviv (and, since 1987, by Israeli suppression of the Palestinian uprising in the Occupied Territories) (see below). Of the formulae to secure the withdrawal of foreign forces from Lebanese territory, Mubarak urged Arab states to support the agreement between Israel and Lebanon which was sponsored by the US Secretary of State, George Shultz. Although, in so doing, Egypt was at variance with most of the Arab world, there were signs during 1983—such as the readiness of Iraq and the PLO to restore normal diplomatic links, the resumption of trade with Jordan, after four years, and with Iraq, and the increased flow of Arab money into Egyptian banks—that the period of the country's ostracism by other Arab states (with the exception of those with hardline regimes, such as Algeria, Libya and Syria) was drawing to a close. President Mubarak had openly supported Yasser Arafat when a Syrian-inspired revolt against his leadership of the PLO broke out in 1983, in the Beka'a Valley, in Lebanon. In recognition of Egypt's support, Arafat visited Mubarak for talks in Cairo in December 1983, his first visit to Egypt for six years, marking the end of the rift between Egypt and the PLO. Substantial proof of Egypt's rehabilitation was provided by its readmission to the Organization of the Islamic Conference (OIC) in March 1984, although several countries, notably Libya and Syria, opposed the move.

RELATIONS WITH SUDAN: 1982–87

A joint Egypt/Sudan Nile Valley Parliament, a Higher Integration Council and a Joint Fund, based on the two countries' common interests in the river Nile, were established by charter in October 1982. The Parliament, comprising 60 Egyptian and 60 Sudanese members, was inaugurated in May 1983. Relatively powerless in itself, it was designed to be the first step towards economic integration and an ultimate federation of the two states. The Higher Integration Council was to meet regularly to organize and review joint economic projects and to plan all aspects of the transition to the hoped-for federation. It was also to be used as a forum to co-ordinate policy on Pan-Arab questions and on matters of mutual concern such as the Iran–Iraq War, Lebanon, Palestinian autonomy, etc.

In October 1984 Egypt unilaterally withdrew from the confederation agreement for a 'Union of Arab Republics', which it had entered into with Syria and Libya in 1971, saying it was no longer of any relevance. In April 1985 President Nimeri of Sudan was deposed by Lt-Gen. Abd ar-Rahman Swar ad-Dahab in a bloodless coup, which was endorsed by Col Qaddafi of Libya, who urged Arabs to overthrow other 'reactionary' regimes, implicitly including Egypt. Lt-Gen. Swar ad-Dahab reaffirmed Sudan's commitment to the integration agreement of 1982 during a visit to Egypt in October, but the Sudanese Government, led by Sadiq al-Mahdi (who became Prime Minister in May 1986), sought to improve its relations with Libya. It was also feared that relations between Egypt and the new Sudanese regime would be embittered by the presence of ex-President Nimeri in Egypt, where he had been granted political asylum. (In July 1986 lawyers representing the Sudanese Government in Cairo requested Nimeri's extradition.) Bilateral links were placed on a more secure footing in February 1987, when Sadiq al-Mahdi and his Egyptian counterpart, Atif Sidqi, signed a 'Brotherhood Charter' in Cairo. This was understood to supersede the integration charter of October 1982 and to form the basis for future relations between the two countries. It was agreed in July 1987 that the issue of Nimeri's political asylum in Egypt should not be permitted to jeopardize bilateral links.

THE RE-EMERGENCE OF THE NEW WAFD PARTY

Politically, one of the most significant features of Mubarak's presidency has been the re-emergence of the New Wafd Party, perhaps the only opposition party with the prospect of wide popular support. The right-wing New Wafd, as the Wafd Party, had led the Egyptian nationalist movement against Britain between 1919 and 1952. In the slightly more liberal atmosphere developing under Mubarak, the New Wafd re-formed in August 1983, and Fuad Serag ed-Din was brought out of political retirement to lead the party. Alarmed, as Sadat had been in 1978, at the New Wafd's potential for popular support, Mubarak's Government refused to recognize the party, but its legality was finally established by the courts in January 1984. In its present form, the New Wafd is more heterogeneous than before, comprising Copts, Nasserites,

Muslim fundamentalists, former army officers (both pro- and anti-Nasser) and socialist and liberal businessmen.

THE GENERAL ELECTION OF 1984

In April 1984, in the hope that he could consolidate his authority and, at the same time (by restoring a measure of real democracy), establish himself as a popular leader, tolerant, within limits, of opposition, Mubarak promised the first 'free, honest and sincere' elections in Egypt for more than 30 years. Safe passage in these elections for his ruling National Democratic Party (NDP) had effectively been assured by an electoral law passed in July 1983, requiring parties to gain a minimum 8% of the total vote in order to be represented in the People's Assembly, which was to be increased from 392 elected seats to 448 from 48 constituencies. Elections to the People's Assembly took place on 27 May, and the NDP accordingly took 72.9% of the total vote (the turn-out was officially only 43.14% of those eligible to vote), entitling it to 389 members. Of the four other participating parties, only the New Wafd, with 15.1% of the vote, crossed the 8% threshold, winning 59 seats in the Assembly. The opposition parties claimed that the elections had been undemocratic, accusing the Government of widespread fraud and intimidation of voters. The electoral alliance of the New Wafd and the fundamentalist Muslim Brotherhood was thought to have alienated many of Egypt's 6m. Copts, potentially a major constituency for the New Wafd.

The Assembly elections left Mubarak firmly in power, with a viable, yet politically brittle, opposition in the New Wafd, and the subversive Muslim Brotherhood in a relatively open political role, in which their activities could more easily be monitored. The Prime Minister, Fuad Mohi ed-Din, died on 5 June, and on 16 July Mubarak reshuffled his Cabinet.

DIPLOMATIC DEVELOPMENTS

As if to signal its progress back into the Arab fold, Egypt severed diplomatic relations with El Salvador and Costa Rica in May 1984, in response to a call from the Jerusalem Committee of the OIC, after both countries had transferred their embassies in Israel from Tel-Aviv to Jerusalem (see The Jerusalem Issue, p. 72). Egypt and Morocco agreed, in principle, to resume diplomatic relations, while President Mubarak and King Hassan discussed moves to end Egypt's suspension from the Arab League, the last major obstacle to Egypt's reintegration into the Arab community of states.

The full resumption of diplomatic relations with the USSR was also achieved during 1984, following the visit to Cairo in May of Vladimir Polyakov, the last Soviet Ambassador to Egypt, who was expelled with 1,000 or more experts by President Sadat in 1981. Mubarak had previously allowed the experts to return, and had signed trade and cultural agreements with the USSR. Whilst it sought improved relations with the USSR, Egypt stood second only to Israel in the amount of economic and military aid which it received from the USA.

Relations with Israel have been strained since the latter's invasion of Lebanon, but Egypt's renewed commitment to issues affecting the entire Arab community (in particular, as concerning its relations with Israel, the Palestinian question) has given it the confidence to use its influence with both sides in the Arab-Israeli conflict to try to achieve a general peace in the Middle East. Israel has repeatedly accused Egypt of contraventions of the military provisions of the 1979 peace treaty, and the question of ownership of the disputed Taba region was a further obstacle to any improvement in bilateral relations. In January 1986 Israel agreed to submit the dispute to international arbitration, provided that this was preceded by a period of conciliation during which arbitrators would try to secure a compromise solution before delivering a binding decision. After the appointment of arbitrators (three independent and one each from Egypt and Israel) and the demarcation of the Taba enclave had been agreed, the arbitration document was finally approved by both countries on 10 September 1986. The process of arbitration began in December. In May 1987 each side presented its case for sovereignty to the arbitration panel, and, in September, a three-member 'conciliation chamber' was established. This failed to formulate a compromise solution in the 60 days allotted to it. In January 1988

Israel rejected a US plan, whereby Egypt would be granted sovereignty over Taba, while Israel was given access to the area, and in July Egypt rejected further attempts at compromise which failed to establish Egyptian sovereignty. The arbitration panel effectively awarded sovereignty to Egypt on 29 September, but left a key border undefined. Discussions on the final arrangements for the Taba enclave were held in January 1989, and Egypt assumed control over the area in March.

EGYPT'S REHABILITATION AND MIDDLE EAST PEACE INITIATIVES

In September 1984 Jordan decided to resume diplomatic relations with Egypt. The gradual rehabilitation of Egypt as a political force in the Middle East was deeply frustrating to Libya and Syria, as it was progressing without Egypt's being required to renounce the Camp David agreements or the 1979 treaty with Israel, which had been the cause of its ostracism, and in that it suggested the emergence of a moderate alignment in Arab politics which could bring its influence to bear on the seemingly intractable problems facing the region, in opposition to the particular aims of Syria. Egypt's confidence in its role in international affairs was demonstrated by Mubarak's active involvement in attempts to find a diplomatic solution to the Iran–Iraq War. (He made a surprise visit to Baghdad in March 1985, despite the fact that diplomatic relations between Egypt and Iraq had been cut in 1979.) The division of loyalties in this conflict reflected the wider split in the Arab world, with Egypt, Jordan, Saudi Arabia and, less vocally, the remaining Gulf states supporting Iraq, while Libya and Syria, who had hoped to usurp Egypt's traditional role as leader of the Arab community, backed Iran. Egypt accused Iran and Libya of laying mines in the Red Sea and the Gulf of Suez in order to disrupt traffic through the Suez Canal, after explosions damaged 19 merchant vessels in the area between July and September 1984. Relations with Libya continued to deteriorate. In July 1985 Col Qaddafi barred Egyptian workers (of whom there were some 100,000 in the country at the time) from Libya, in retaliation against a similar Egyptian measure preventing Libyans from working in Egypt.

Consolidating the contacts first made between them after Yasser Arafat's expulsion from Lebanon at the end of 1983, following the revolt against his leadership of Fatah, the PLO leader, King Hussein of Jordan and President Mubarak continued their discussions on the Palestinian issue during 1984 and 1985, in Cairo and Amman. In February 1985 King Hussein and Yasser Arafat agreed the principle of a joint Jordanian-Palestinian delegation taking part in a Middle East peace conference including the members of the UN Security Council, though the questions of the composition of such a delegation and the basis on which peace talks would proceed were not resolved. The PLO rejected the UN Resolution 242 as a basis for negotiation and it was not clear whether the Palestinian representation in the joint delegation would comprise members of the PLO. So that progress should not be brought to a complete halt, Mubarak suggested that, as a stage preliminary to direct negotiations with Israel, a joint Jordanian-Palestinian delegation (including PLO members, Mubarak finally conceded) should hold talks with the USA in Washington, after which Israel and other Arab parties would join the negotiations and make preparations for a full peace conference. The Reagan Administration in the USA, for its part, held by its refusal to negotiate with the PLO unless it accepted Resolution 242 and therefore, implicitly, Israel's right to exist; King Hussein, for his, voiced equivocal approval only, standing by the agreement he had made with Arafat. Mubarak's proposals were not adopted but he persisted in trying to smooth the way for ultimate negotiations between the Arabs and Israel.

A series of terrorist incidents during the second half of 1985, in which factions of the PLO loyal to Yasser Arafat were implicated, damaged the PLO's credibility as a participant in peace negotiations and virtually assured the failure of the Jordanian-PLO peace initiative. On 7 October, in the first of two incidents directly involving Egypt, an Italian cruise liner, the *Achille Lauro*, was 'hijacked' in the eastern Mediterranean by four Palestinians belonging to the Palestine Liberation Front (PLF—one of two factions of that name—led by Muhammad (Abu) Abbas, an Arafat loyalist). They murdered a Jewish American passenger before giving themselves up to the Egyptian authorities in Port Said. Rather than put the terrorists on trial in Egypt, President Mubarak gave them into the custody of Muhammad Abbas (who, as well as being leader of the PLF, was a member of the PLO Executive Committee) to be tried, as he thought, by the PLO. The USA accused Muhammad Abbas of planning the *Achille Lauro* operation and criticized Mubarak for allowing him to go free. On 10 October US fighter aircraft intercepted the Egyptian aircraft that was taking Muhammad Abbas and the four Palestinians to Tunis, forcing it to land at a US air force base in Sicily. This action aroused considerable anti-American feeling in Egypt. Then, in November, in the second incident involving Egypt, an EgyptAir airliner carrying 98 passengers was hijacked to Malta by Palestinians, whom Egypt immediately linked with the renegade PLO leader, Abu Nidal, and his Libyan backers, though the only clear claim of responsibility came from a group calling itself 'Egypt's Revolution'. Egyptian special forces were sent to Malta to release the hostages, but their assault on the aircraft resulted in the deaths of 61 passengers and strong criticism of Egypt's handling of the affair. Earlier in November, in Cairo, Yasser Arafat, responding to pressure from King Hussein and President Mubarak for the PLO to renounce violence, had reiterated a PLO decision of 1974 to confine military operations to Israel and the Occupied Territories, though this was hardly the unequivocal statement that the two leaders had sought and was immediately repudiated by Arafat's aides.

On 11 September 1986 President Mubarak of Egypt and Prime Minister Peres of Israel met in Alexandria, Egypt, to discuss ways of reviving the Middle East peace process. After the summit meeting (the first between Egypt and Israel since August 1981), and following the signing of the Taba arbitration agreement, President Mubarak appointed Muhammad Bassiouni, Egypt's former chargé d'affaires in Tel-Aviv, as Ambassador to Israel. The previous Egyptian Ambassador had been recalled from Israel in 1982, following the Israeli invasion of Lebanon.

It was largely as a result of its links with Israel that a new rift occurred between Egypt and the PLO in 1987. The crisis in relations was precipitated by the reunification of the Palestinian movement that took place at a session of the Palestine National Council (PNC) in Algiers in April 1987. One of the conditions that dissident PLO factions exacted as the price for their return to the mainstream of the movement, under Yasser Arafat's leadership, was the reduction of Arafat's links with Egypt. The Popular Front for the Liberation of Palestine (PFLP) initially demanded the immediate severance of relations but the PNC finally adopted a compromise resolution, urging the reappraisal of PLO links with Egypt, and making future contacts dependent on Egypt's abrogation of the Camp David accord and the 1979 Peace Treaty with Israel. President Mubarak responded by closing all the PLO's offices in Egypt at the end of April 1987.

INTERNAL DISSENSION

At home, President Mubarak had to tread warily to avoid confrontation with sections of the Egyptian population. While conscious of the need to relieve the country's finances of the crippling burden of state subsidies, he was also aware of the dangers to social stability inherent in increasing the prices of basic commodities. These dangers were demonstrated by riots in the town of Kafr ad-Dawar in September 1984, which were prompted by modest price increases in staple foodstuffs. The government, nevertheless, continued gradually to reduce subsidies on food, electricity and oil.

The campaign by Muslim fundamentalists for the legal system fully to adopt the principles of the *Shari'a* (Islamic holy law) intensified and became part of a wider resurgence of Islamic consciousness in Egypt. An amendment to the Constitution, passed by the People's Assembly in 1980, made Islamic law the basis of national law, and this was largely, but not fully, implemented. As well as taking account of the views of a potentially volatile puritan Islamic section of the community, Mubarak had to take care not to alienate the country's Coptic Christians (many of whom occupied important positions in commerce, industry and the professions). In May 1985 the People's Assembly rejected immediate changes in the legal system and advocated thorough study of the 2% of Egyptian law which did not conform to Islamic precepts before proceeding further. Mubarak did make concessions to purist doctrine by imposing tighter censorship on books and films and by restricting the progress of female emancipation: in May 1985 a Constitutional Court ruled that the law of 1979, which declared that polygamy was legally harmful to a first wife and awarded her limited freedom to divorce her husband, was invalid. In July the law was effectively reinstated, but with the provision that it constituted 'no encroachment on man's right to polygamy', so as not to offend Islamic fundamentalist feeling. However, Mubarak continued to take measures to prevent agitation by fundamentalists from destabilizing the country: banning Islamic rallies, arresting militant Islamic leaders and, in July 1985, placing all mosques under the control of the Ministry of Awqaf (Islamic Endowments).

A further threat to public order arose from Egypt's poor economic state, which exaggerated the already wide discrepancy in living standards between the vast and growing numbers of people who lived in great poverty, and a rich minority. The priority that President Mubarak placed on improving the economy was reflected in the appointment of Dr Ali Lutfi, a former Minister of Finance under President Sadat, as Prime Minister on 4 September 1985, following the resignation of Gen. Kamal Hassan Ali and his Council of Ministers. Ali Lutfi presided over a Council of Ministers containing nine new appointments and three members who, while retaining their portfolios, were elevated to the rank of deputy prime minister, making four in all.

On 25 February 1986, in reaction to a rumour that their period of service was to be extended by one year to four years, some 17,000 poorly-paid conscripts to the Central Security Force (CSF) went on the rampage in and around Cairo, destroying two luxury hotels and damaging other buildings used by tourists in the Pyramids area of the city. The disturbances lasted for three days and there were clashes between the conscripts and the army, which was trying to regain control of the city. According to government figures, 107 people died as a result of the mutiny, and 1,324 members of the CSF were arrested. There were reports of violence in other cities, including Asyut, Ismailia and Suhag. The Minister of the Interior, Ahmad Roushdi, held responsible for the failure of the intelligence services to detect signs of unrest in the CSF, was dismissed and replaced by Maj.-Gen. Zaki Badr.

In November 1986 President Mubarak accepted the resignation of the Prime Minister, Ali Lutfi. A new Council of Ministers, containing, among 11 changes, a new Minister of Finance and three other new ministers in positions related to the management of the economy, was appointed under a new Prime Minister, Dr Atif Sidqi. President Mubarak was believed to have been critical of Ali Lutfi's apparent readiness to accede to demands from the IMF for the introduction of far-reaching economic reforms, in return for financial aid (see Economy), and yet dissatisfied with the pace of reform to combat the continuing deterioration of the economy.

THE 1987 GENERAL ELECTION

Agitation by Islamic fundamentalists led to student riots in Asyut in October 1986 (in protest against the university authorities' refusal to allow women to veil their faces on university premises) and in February 1987. In December 1986 it was revealed that, three or four months earlier, four reserve army officers and 29 civilians, allegedly linked with the Islamic Jihad organization, had been arrested in Cairo, accused of plotting to overthrow the Government. This was the first known case of fundamentalist infiltration of the armed forces. Another, communist-inspired, coup plot was reportedly foiled in December.

A referendum was held on 12 February 1987, to decide whether the People's Assembly (Majlis ash-Sha'ab) should be dissolved, prior to the holding of a general election on the basis of a new electoral law, providing for a total of 48 seats for independent candidates in the 458-seat assembly. The new

law had been quickly adopted in December 1986 to pre-empt a ruling by the Supreme Constitutional Court that the general election of 1984 had been unconstitutional, as independent candidates had not been allowed to stand. An overwhelming vote in the referendum in favour of the dissolution of the People's Assembly facilitated the holding of a general election on 6 April. Mubarak hoped that the election would establish his Government on a firm constitutional basis and effectively secure him a second term as President. The SLP, the Liberal Socialist Party (LSP) and the Muslim Brotherhood (which was legally barred from forming its own political party) decided to form an electoral alliance, principally in order to overcome the requirement for political parties to win at least 8% of the total vote before they qualified for seats in the People's Assembly, that effectively prevented a single opposition party from gaining significant representation in the assembly. The influence of the Muslim Brotherhood was evident in the fact that the doctrine of wholesale application of Islamic law, the Brotherhood's principal tenet, was a prominent element in the alliance's campaign.

The election campaign was marred by sectarian clashes between Muslims and Christians in several towns, including Sohag and Beni Suef, in February and March, and the opposition parties accused the Government of electoral fraud, the intimidation of opposition candidates and other forms of corruption. On the eve of the election, hundreds of opposition party workers were arrested. They were understood to be mostly members of the Muslim Brotherhood, who, according to the authorities, were campaigning, illegally, on their own behalf.

The election resulted in a large, though reduced, majority for the ruling NDP in the People's Assembly. The NDP won 346 seats (compared with 389 at the previous election in 1984), the opposition parties won a total of 95, and independents seven. The SLP/LSP/Muslim Brotherhood alliance won a combined total of 60 seats, of which the Brotherhood took 37, making it the largest single opposition group in the new Assembly. The New Wafd Party, which, with 58 seats, had been the only opposition party to be represented in the previous Assembly, won only 35 seats in the election.

In July 1987 Mubarak was nominated by the necessary two-thirds majority of the members of the People's Assembly to seek a second six-year term as President. The only candidate, Mubarak was duly confirmed in office by national referendum on 5 October, polling 97.1% of the votes cast. Prime Minister Atif Sidqi submitted the resignation of the Egyptian Government on 12 October and formed a new Council of Ministers, with only minor changes in personnel.

The principal threat to Mubarak's position remained the activities of Muslim militants. More than 500 Islamic fundamentalists, mostly members of Islamic Jihad and Gamaat Islamiya (the Islamic Groups), were reportedly arrested after the attempted assassination of the former Minister of the Interior, Maj.-Gen. Hassan Abou Basha, and two US diplomats in May, and of a left-wing magazine editor in June. Egypt severed its remaining diplomatic ties with Iran in May, closing the Iranian interests section at the Swiss Embassy, which, it was alleged, maintained contacts with Muslim extremists.

MIDDLE EAST PEACE MOVES

President Mubarak and Yasser Arafat held two sessions of discussions in Addis Ababa, Ethiopia, in July 1987, beginning to heal the rift that led to the closure of the PLO's offices in Egypt in April. (They were reopened, unofficially, at the end of July and, formally, at the end of November.) Both leaders endorsed proposals (which were already supported by Egypt and Jordan) for the convening of an international peace conference on the Middle East, under UN auspices, involving the five permanent members of the UN Security Council and all parties to the conflict, including the PLO. President Mubarak and the Israeli Minister of Foreign Affairs, Shimon Peres, had agreed in principle on the need for an international conference when the latter visited Egypt in February, though the issue of PLO representation remained an obstacle to further progress. The Israeli Prime Minister, Itzhak Shamir, was opposed to a peace conference in any form, and suggested direct talks between Israel, Egypt, a Jordanian/Palestinian delegation, and the USA. President Mubarak urged the PLO to devise a formula for its inclusion in an international peace conference, and, during a visit to Israel in July (the first by a high-ranking Egyptian since 1982), the Egyptian Minister of Foreign Affairs, Dr Esmat Abd al-Meguid, appealed to the Israeli Government to participate in an international conference.

In November 1987, at a summit conference in Amman, Jordan, which was attended by the majority of Arab leaders (excluding Col Qaddafi of Libya), the Syrian President, Hafiz Assad, obstructed proposals to readmit Egypt to membership of the League of Arab States. However, recognizing Egypt's support for Iraq in its war against Iran and acknowledging the influence that Egypt (as the most populous and, militarily, the most powerful Arab nation) could bring to bear on the problems of the region, the conference approved a resolution putting the establishment of diplomatic links with Egypt at the discretion of member governments. One week after the end of the conference, nine Arab states (the United Arab Emirates, Iraq, Kuwait, Morocco, the Yemen Arab Republic, Bahrain, Saudi Arabia, Mauritania and Qatar) had re-established full diplomatic relations with Egypt. Of the remaining 12 members of the League, three (Sudan, Somalia and Oman) had maintained diplomatic links with Egypt throughout the period of the boycott, Jordan and Djibouti had re-established them in 1985 and 1986, respectively, and the PLO (to which the League accorded nation status) had recently begun to settle its differences with Egypt. In February 1988 the People's Democratic Republic of Yemen restored full diplomatic relations with Egypt, leaving Algeria, Lebanon, Libya and Syria as the only Arab League members not to have done so. Libya was the most outspoken critic of the change in the League's policy towards Egypt, complaining that the 1979 peace treaty with Israel, the original reason for Egypt's ostracism, remained in force. In November Algeria announced that it would re-establish diplomatic relations with Egypt, and in June 1989 full diplomatic relations with Lebanon were restored.

Following Jordan's decision, in July 1988, to sever its legal and administrative links with the West Bank region (annexed by Jordan in 1950 but, like the Gaza Strip, under Israeli occupation since 1967), President Mubarak urged the PLO to exercise caution in its plans to declare an independent Palestinian state and to form a government-in-exile. In September, however, during a tour of Western Europe, he sought support for proposals to convene an international conference on the Middle East. In November Egypt granted full recognition to the newly-declared Palestinian state.

The visit of King Fahd of Saudi Arabia to Cairo in March 1989 was a further sign of the rehabilitation of Egypt's standing in the Arab world. In May President Mubarak represented Egypt at an emergency summit meeting of the League of Arab States in Casablanca, Morocco. The meeting, convened to rally support for the diplomatic initiatives of Yasser Arafat following the Palestinian declaration of independence, was preceded by a meeting of the Ministers of Foreign Affairs of the majority of the members of the League, which endorsed Egypt's formal readmission to the Arab League after an absence of 10 years. Despite Libya's opposition to Egypt's readmission to the League, Col Qaddafi attended the meeting, and held separate talks with President Mubarak. In June 1989 it was announced that Egypt was preparing to reopen its border with Libya, and in October Col Qaddafi visited Egypt, the first such visit for 16 years, for further discussions with President Mubarak.

Egypt was hopeful that its improved standing in the Arab world would enhance its role as a mediator in the Middle East peace process. In February 1989, during a tour of five Middle Eastern countries, Eduard Shevardnadze paid the first visit to Egypt by a Soviet Minister of Foreign Affairs for 15 years, and held talks with both President Mubarak and Moshe Arens, the Israeli Minister of Foreign Affairs. In the wake of the Israeli peace initiative announced in April 1989 (see Documents on Palestine, p. 100), Egypt directed its diplomatic efforts towards bringing about preliminary negotiations between Palestinian and Israeli delegations. In September President Mubarak sought to persuade the Israeli Government to accept 10 points clarifying its peace initiative (the 'Mubarak

plan') so that direct Palestinian-Israeli negotiations could begin. The 10 points in question were: a commitment by Israel to accept the results of the elections proposed under its initiative; the supervision of the elections by international observers; the granting of immunity to elected representatives; the withdrawal of the Israeli Defence Force from the balloting area; a commitment by Israel to begin negotiations, within three to five years after the proposed elections; the ending of Israeli settlement of the West Bank; complete freedom as regards election propaganda; a ban on entry of all Israelis to the Occupied Territories on the day of the proposed elections; the participation of residents of East Jerusalem in the elections; a commitment by Israel to the principle of exchanging land for peace. An offer by President Mubarak to host talks between Palestinian and Israeli delegations was approved by the USA, but rejected by Israel's 'inner Cabinet' in early October. In early December, following two months of US diplomatic support for (and development of) the 'Mubarak plan', Egypt accepted a five-point US framework for the holding of elections in the Occupied Territories. It was reported that the US Secretary of State would meet the Egyptian and Israeli Ministers of Foreign Affairs in January 1990, with the aim of facilitating direct discussions between an Israeli and a Palestinian delegation.

By early 1990, however, there had been no appreciable progress in the peace process, which had been further complicated by Israel's apparent intention to settle in the Occupied Territories some of the Soviet Jewish immigrants who had arrived in the country in large numbers throughout 1989 and continued to do so in 1990. In February the death of nine Israelis in an attack on a tour bus in Egypt was regarded in Israel as a further blow to President Mubarak's credibility as a mediator between Israelis and Palestinians, and reduced the chances of an early meeting between the Egyptian and Israeli Ministers of Foreign Affairs.

Egypt's increasing frustration at the lack of progress in the peace process and its concern about the escalation of the Palestinian *intifada* (especially after the murder of seven Palestinians by an Israeli civilian at Rishon Le Ziyyon in May 1990) led it to assume a more critical stance towards the Israeli Government in the first half of 1990. In May President Mubarak warned that the increased immigration of Soviet Jews into Israel threatened to destroy the whole peace process and could lead to a new war in the Middle East. In June, after the formation of a new Israeli Government by Itzhak Shamir, the Egyptian Government condemned Israel in even harsher terms, suggesting that it was preparing for war in the region. Following the suspension by the US Government of its dialogue with the PLO in June 1990, Egypt again attributed the disintegration of the peace process to 'Israeli intransigence' and urged the resumption of the US-PLO dialogue.

President Mubarak undertook a tour of the six states of the Gulf Co-operation Council (GCC) in January 1988 but denied reports that Egypt had agreed to send troops to the Gulf as part of an Arab task-force to defend GCC states against Iranian attack, in return for payment of Egypt's military debt to the USA. However, military co-operation and financial assistance were discussed during President Mubarak's visit, and it was known that several hundred Egyptian military advisers had already been sent to Iraq and Kuwait.

In February 1989 Egypt was a founder member of the Arab Co-operation Council (ACC). The foundation agreement of the ACC was signed by the heads of state of Egypt, Iraq, Jordan and the Yemen Arab Republic, its aim being to increase economic ties between member states and, in the long term, to develop an integrated economy with a single market.

In March 1988 Egypt signed an arms co-operation agreement with the USA, replacing the memorandum of understanding signed in 1979. The new five-year agreement placed Egypt on the same footing with the USA as Israel and the members of NATO, giving it access to US defence contracts and to the latest weaponry, as well as exempting Egyptian military exports from US import duties. In April the US Government notified the Congress that it intended to proceed with controversial plans to sell 555 battle tanks to Egypt, at a cost of \$2,000m. Three months later, similar intentions were announced regarding the sale of 144 US *Maverick* air-to-ground missiles, costing $27m. The arrest, in July, of an Egyptian with American citizenship, who was charged with stealing US missile parts and attempting to smuggle them to Egypt, placed these and further sales of US arms to Egypt in doubt. Egypt's embarrassment at this arrest was cited as the main reason for President Mubarak's decision, in April 1989, to transfer the influential Minister of Defence, Field-Marshal Ghazalah, to the newly-created position of Presidential Assistant, which was widely regarded as a sinecure.

Further embarrassment was caused to Egypt by allegations in the US press that it had begun to produce chemical weapons. During a visit to the USA in April 1989, Mubarak strongly denied these allegations. However, he faced further criticism of the slow speed at which Egypt was implementing its programme of economic reform, and of its failure to conclude an agreement with the IMF as a prelude to the rescheduling of part of its $44,000m. foreign debt.

SOCIAL REPERCUSSIONS OF ECONOMIC CRISIS

The extreme caution with which Egypt has implemented economic reforms has been largely due to fears that they will provoke further social unrest and increase the threat to social stability posed by Islamic fundamentalists. The Government remains extremely sensitive to any such threat. In December 1988 it was reported that more than 500 militant Muslim students in Cairo and Asyut had been arrested on suspicion of involvement in 'anti-state activities'; and in April and May 1989, facing mounting popular discontent over price increases and food shortages, the Government acted to pre-empt disturbances during the month of Ramadan by detaining more than 2,000 Islamic fundamentalists. In June elections to the 210-member Shura Council were contested by opposition parties (the 'Islamic Alliance', consisting of the Muslim Brotherhood, the LSP and the SLP) for the first time since the establishment of the Council in 1980. Other political parties, however, boycotted the elections in protest at the prevailing state of emergency. None of the candidates from the 'Islamic Alliance' was elected, and it was subsequently alleged that the NDP had achieved its victory by fraudulent means.

In July and August 1989, in a further attempt by the Government to suppress political opposition, members of the proscribed Egyptian Communist Workers' Party and Shi'ite Muslims, including prominent members of the Muslim Brotherhood, were arrested on charges of subversion. By early September, following international protests, it was reported that most of the detainees had been released. In December there was speculation that Muslim fundamentalists had been responsible for the attempted assassination of the Minister of the Interior, Maj.-Gen. Zaki Badr, who had conducted the Government's campaign against political dissent. The ruthlessness of the campaign had not only alienated those targeted by it, but had also caused embarrassment within the Government itself. In January 1990 Badr was dismissed from his post and replaced by Muhammad Abd al-Halim Moussa. In the same month the Egyptian Organization for Human Rights condemned the violence which, it alleged, was routinely inflicted on political detainees by the Egyptian security forces.

In April three new political parties, the Green Party, the Democratic Unionist Party (DUP) and the Young Egypt Party (YEP), were legalized, bringing the total number of officially recognized political parties in Egypt to nine.

THE 1990 GENERAL ELECTION

In May a constitutional crisis arose after Egypt's Supreme Constitutional Court ruled that elections to the People's Assembly in 1987 had been unconstitutional because the electoral law promulgated in 1986 unfairly discriminated against independent candidates. Legislation which had subsequently been passed by the Assembly was deemed to be valid, but the Court declared that any new laws approved after 2 June 1990 could not enter into force. In September President Mubarak announced that a popular referendum would be held on 11 October in order to decide whether the People's Assembly should be dissolved; and that the electoral law would be amended with regard to the limited number of independent candidates previously permitted to participate in elections. (The People's Assembly, in recess since 4 June, had granted

the President permission to legislate by decree in its absence.) Some 58.6% of the electorate subsequently participated in the referendum, and, of these, 94.34% voted for the dissolution of the Assembly. The People's Assembly was duly dissolved on 12 October.

Campaigning for the elections took place in a tense atmosphere resulting from the crisis in the Gulf (see below) and the threat to Egypt's security posed by Islamic extremists hostile to the Government's pro-Western stance over Iraq's invasion of Kuwait. The assassination of Dr Rifa'at el-Mahgoub, the Speaker of the People's Assembly, on 12 October in Cairo, increased tensions and led to the most comprehensive security operation since the murder of President Sadat in 1981. Hundreds of Muslim fundamentalists were arrested and detained in the known centres of Muslim extremism in the suburbs of Cairo and the cities of Asyut and Beni Suef. The Ministry of the Interior claimed that eight members of an Islamic fundamentalist group, Al-Jihad (arrested at the end of October), had been responsible for the assassination.

At the legislative elections held on 29 November and 6 December 1990, the former requirement for political parties to win a minimum of 8% of the total vote in order to gain representation in the Assembly was abolished, and restrictions on independent candidates were removed. However, the Government refused to concede the opposition parties' demands that the elections be removed from the supervision of the Ministry of the Interior, and that the emergency regulations (in force since 1981) be repealed. The elections resulted in a clear victory for the ruling NDP: of the 444 elective seats in the new Assembly, the NDP won 348 (compared with 346 at the 1987 general election), the NPUP won six, and independent candidates (of which 56 were affiliated to the NDP, 14 to the New Wafd Party, eight to the SLP and one to the LSP) won 83. Voting in the remaining seven seats was suspended. President Mubarak exercised his right to appoint 10 additional deputies, including five Copts.

In a poll that was characterized by a low turnout of voters (estimated at no greater than 20%–30% of the electorate), four of the main opposition groups, the New Wafd Party, the SLP, the LSP and the banned—but officially tolerated—Muslim Brotherhood, boycotted the elections after the Government refused their demands concerning the conduct of the elections (see above). Several opposition members who ignored the boycott were subsequently dismissed by their party organizations, leaving the NPUP, with its six representatives, as leader of the official opposition. The new People's Assembly convened on 13 December and elected Dr Ahmad Fathi Surur, formerly Minister of Education, as its Speaker.

THE CRISIS IN THE GULF IN 1990–91

On 27 December 1989, in a move presaged by the restoration, earlier in that month, of air links between Cairo and Damascus, Egypt and Syria restored full diplomatic relations after a break lasting 12 years. In May 1990 President Mubarak made a visit to Damascus for talks with President Assad of Syria, and in July President Assad visited Egypt. The *rapprochement* between Egypt and Syria was widely regarded as signalling a shift away from the balance of power which had prevailed in the Arab world throughout the 1980s.

In November 1989 reports of widespread acts of violent discrimination against Egyptian expatriate workers in Iraq threatened the special relationship which had developed between Egypt and Iraq during the Iran–Iraq War, when Egypt provided Iraq with military equipment and advisers. Prior to the crisis in the Gulf precipitated by Iraq's invasion and annexation of Kuwait in August 1990, Egypt sought to mediate between Iraq and Kuwait, appealing for dialogue between the two sides in the interests of Arab solidarity. Following the invasion of Kuwait, Egypt sought initially to maintain its role as a mediator, immediately proposing the convening of—and subsequently hosting—a summit meeting of Arab leaders. At the summit meeting, held on 10 August, Egypt firmly demanded the withdrawal of Iraqi forces from Kuwait, and 12 of the 20 Arab League member states participating in the meeting voted to send an Arab deterrent force to the Gulf in support of the USA's effort to deter an Iraqi invasion of Saudi

Arabia. By late August about 5,000 Egyptian troops were reported to be in Saudi Arabia.

Egypt's quick success in mobilizing the support of 'moderate' Arab states for the economic sanctions imposed on Iraq by the UN, and for the defence of Saudi Arabia, emphasized the extent of the improvement in relations with Syria. While Iraq called on the Egyptian people to overthrow the Egyptian Government, there was no evidence of widespread popular support in Egypt for President Saddam Hussein of Iraq, and the Government's action was judged to have bolstered its domestic popularity. While it condemned Iraq's invasion of Kuwait, however, the Muslim Brotherhood, the largest opposition group in the People's Assembly, demanded the immediate withdrawal of US forces from the Gulf and opposed the dispatch of Egyptian troops to Saudi Arabia as part of an Arab deterent force. It was feared, too, that Egyptian expatriate workers (totalling some 800,000 in Iraq and some 100,000 in Kuwait before the Iraqi invasion), returning in large numbers from Iraq and Kuwait to almost certain unemployment in Egypt, might have a destabilizing effect. Some 85,000 were reported to have returned to Egypt by the end of August 1990, the total rising to more than 600,000, following the outbreak of hostilities between Iraq and the UN multinational force in January 1991.

On 28 August 1990 President Mubarak and President Assad of Syria met in Alexandria to discuss Arab efforts to avert war in the Gulf. An extraordinary meeting of Ministers of Foreign Affairs of Arab League member states took place in Cairo on 30 August, but it was attended by representatives of only 12 member states (those which had supported the proposal to send an Arab deterrent force to Saudi Arabia), reflecting the divisions which had arisen in the Arab world as a result of Iraq's invasion of Kuwait.

Following the outbreak of hostilities between Iraq and a UN multinational force in January 1991, the Egyptian Government continued to support the anti-Iraq coalition. Egypt's contingent within the multinational force, eventually boosted to 35,000 troops, sustained only light casualties in the fighting. On the domestic front, there were few disturbances during the war, and the opposition's predictions of popular unrest proved false. In fact, Egypt emerged from the conflict in the Gulf with its international reputation enhanced, largely as a result of President Mubarak's firm leadership of 'moderate' Arab opinion. Moreover, the economy benefited from the waiving of almost US $14,000m. of Egypt's debts to the USA and other Western and Gulf states at an early stage in the crisis, and by the signing of an agreement with the IMF in mid-May 1991, which, later in the same month, led to the rescheduling of $10,000m. of Egypt's debt to the 'Paris Club' of Western creditors, and the cancellation of the remaining $10,000m. over a three-year period.

Following the conclusion of the war in February 1991, Egypt took part in a meeting of the eight Arab nations (the six GCC member states, Egypt and Syria) that had participated in the UN multinational force, held on 5–6 March in Damascus. The statement issued after the meeting, known as the 'Damascus Declaration', called for 'a new Arab order to bolster joint Arab action'. It proposed, *inter alia*, that Egyptian and Syrian troops already deployed in Saudi Arabia and the Gulf states should constitute the nucleus of an Arab regional security force. However, in early May Egypt unexpectedly announced that its forces in Saudi Arabia and Kuwait were to be withdrawn and no Arab regional security force has since been formed.

Representatives from all the Arab League member states met in Cairo on 30 March 1991 for the first regular meeting of the Arab League since the outbreak of the crisis in the Gulf. The meeting was conciliatory in tone and attempted to establish an Arab consensus. A further meeting took place on 15 May, at which Dr Ahmad Esmat Abd al-Meguid, hitherto Egypt's Minister of Foreign Affairs, was endorsed as the League's new Secretary-General, in succession to Chedli Klibi who had resigned in September 1990. The holding of the League's meetings at its original headquarters in Cairo, and under its new Secretary-General, was a further indication of Egypt's return to centre-stage in the Arab world.

GOVERNMENT POLICY IN THE 1990s

President Mubarak reshuffled his Council of Ministers on 20 May 1991, dismissing the influential Minister of Petroleum and Mineral Resources, Abd al-Hadi Muhammad Kandil, who had been criticized by foreign oil companies for his Ministry's policies, in addition to having been at the centre of a series of disagreements with the Egyptian General Petroleum Corporation. Further new appointments were made at the Ministries of Defence, Foreign Affairs and Education.

Since the end of the crisis in the Gulf in 1990–91, the Government's foreign policy has continued to focus on the twin themes of Arab reconciliation and a settlement of the Arab–Israeli dispute, with particular emphasis being given to the Palestinian dimension. Egypt participated in the inaugural meeting of the Middle East peace conference in Madrid in October 1991. In later stages it attended bilateral sessions as an observer and multilateral sessions as a participant. Despite the procedural delays and the slow progress of the negotiations, Egypt felt that the conference represented the best hope for a durable peace in the region and that it had an important behind-the-scenes role to play in co-ordinating Arab strategy and providing diplomatic expertise. The choice of Egypt's former deputy Prime Minister, Dr Boutros Boutros-Ghali, as the new Secretary-General of the United Nations was regarded by Egypt as recognition of its moderating regional influence. President Mubarak welcomed the change of government in Israel in June 1992, and in July the Israeli Prime Minister, Itzhak Rabin, visited Cairo for talks with President Mubarak, who reportedly emphasized to him his opinion that progress in the peace process was dependent on a halt to Jewish settlements in the Occupied Territories.

Egyptian mediators played an active role during the secret negotiations which led to the Gaza–Jericho interim peace agreement between Israel and the PLO on 13 September 1993. The agreement made provision for limited Palestinian self-rule in the Gaza Strip and the town of Jericho on the West Bank. Once the agreement was announced, Egypt was the first Arab state that the PLO looked to for support. In October, PLO and Israeli negotiating teams began meeting regularly in Cairo, or at Taba on the Red Sea, to discuss the detailed implementation of the agreement. On the whole, the agreement was welcomed by the Egyptian press, although it was denounced by the Nasserites and the Muslim Brotherhood as a betrayal of the struggle for the Palestinians' homeland. In November King Hussain of Jordan visited Cairo for talks on the Middle East peace process, his first visit since the Gulf crisis of 1990–91 which had strained relations between the two countries. In December, when talks between the PLO and Israel became deadlocked, President Mubarak convened an emergency summit meeting in Cairo between the Israeli Prime Minister and the PLO leader, Yasser Arafat. However, the meeting failed to achieve an agreement on the withdrawal of Israeli armed forces from Gaza and Jericho which had been scheduled to start on 13 December.

The massacre of more than 40 Palestinians in Hebron on the West Bank by an Israeli settler on 25 February 1994 provoked several days of angry demonstrations in Cairo. Egypt withdrew its ambassador from Israel for consultations, but Egyptian diplomats tried to persuade both the PLO and Israel to resume their negotiations. Talks between Israel and the PLO recommenced in Cairo on 29 March. On 4 April President Assad of Syria visited Cairo for talks with President Mubarak, reportedly about Syria's dissatisfaction with Egypt's support for the Israeli–PLO agreement. On 4 May, after months of negotiations, an agreement on Palestinian self-rule in Gaza and Jericho was signed in Cairo by the Israeli Prime Minister and the PLO Chairman at a ceremony presided over by President Mubarak and attended by the US Secretary of State and the Russian Minister of Foreign Affairs. Under the terms of the agreement Israeli forces withdrew from Gaza on 13 May and from Jericho on 17 May.

Although the Middle East peace process continued to dominate Egyptian foreign policy, Egypt was also involved in mediation efforts involving Libya, Yemen and Somalia. Egypt's relations with Libya have been dominated by the repercussions of the Lockerbie affair. With an estimated 1m. Egyptians working in Libya, Egypt has used its diplomacy to try to avert a confrontation between Libya and the West, which could not only threaten the jobs of its workers, but also a steadily growing market for its exports. Egypt also regards the Qaddafi regime as a useful ally in its struggle against Islamist militancy in the region. At the beginning of November 1993, as the UN Security Council was being urged by the USA, the United Kingdom and France to impose tougher economic sanctions on Libya, President Mubarak met Col Qaddafi, but Egyptian mediation efforts failed to engineer a compromise. Egypt was deeply embarrassed when a leading opponent of the Libyan regime, Mansour al-Kikhia, disappeared in Cairo in December 1993 during a human rights conference. There was speculation that al-Kikhia, who was living in exile in the USA, had been kidnapped by Libyan agents, despite assurances regarding his safety from senior Egyptian officials. In March 1994 Egypt attempted to mediate between rival Yemeni leaders, and hosted peace talks in Cairo between rival Somali factions. Following an increase in commercial and economic exchanges with South Africa during 1993, in October Egypt announced that it would resume full diplomatic relations after South Africa's first multiracial elections in April 1994. President Mubarak is currently chairman of the Organization of African Unity (OAU). Egypt's relations with its southern neighbour, Sudan, deteriorated following the visit to Khartoum, in December 1991, of a large Iranian delegation led by President Rafsanjani. Acutely aware of the dangers posed by its own Islamist militants, Egypt has been alarmed by Iran's support for Sudan's military regime, which is dominated by the National Islamic Front, and by the dangerous escalation of Islamist violence in Algeria, which has virtually plunged that country into civil war. In June 1993 President Mubarak held private talks with the Sudanese President, Lt-Col al-Bashir, who was visiting Cairo for the annual meeting of the OAU, in an attempt to reduce tensions between Egypt and Sudan.

THE UPSURGE IN ISLAMIST VIOLENCE

Since the early part of 1992 militant Islamist groups have intensified their campaign to overthrow the Government and establish an Islamic state. Militant Islamists have been particularly active in Asyut governorate in Upper Egypt, the traditional stronghold of Islamic militancy, and also in the poorer districts of Cairo, such as Imbaba. For example, in May 1992 there was a violent confrontation in Asyut governorate between militant Islamists and Coptic Christians which resulted in the death of 14 people, mostly Copts. At the beginning of June some 5,000 members of the security forces were deployed in Asyut governorate in the most extensive military operation against militant Islamists for many years, and at the end of July the People's Assembly adopted a new law to combat terrorism which imposed the death sentence for some crimes. In October 1992 it was reported that terrorists would be tried by military courts. After the earthquake on 12 October which killed 500 people, Islamist organizations quickly came to the assistance of people made homeless in the poorer districts through the collapse of badly-built tenements, in sharp contrast to the slow response of state agencies. In December an Egyptian military court sentenced to death eight militant Islamists, after finding them guilty of conspiring to overthrow the Government. It was reported that over the previous 12 months some 70 people had been killed as a result of Islamist violence. Foreign tourists were targeted by militant Islamists for the first time in 1992 and several were killed. The leader of the Jama'ah al'Islamiyah, one of the two main groups of Islamist extremists, publicly attacked the very concept of foreign tourism in Egypt and threatened to destroy the country's major tourist attractions, the Pharaonic sites. Tourist numbers were reported to have fallen by 40% by the end of 1992, with a loss of foreign currency earnings of $1,500m. Among those killed during 1992 was the writer Farag Fouda, one of Egypt's most outspoken critics of militant Islam. He was murdered on 9 June by extremists belonging to Islamic Jihad, the group believed to have been responsible for the assassinations of President Sadat and the Speaker of the People's Assembly, Rifa'at el-Mahgoub. A year later, at the trial of those charged with Fouda's murder, Sheikh Mohamed el-Ghazali, a leading Islamist scholar, claimed that it was legitimate to kill any Muslim who opposed the application of Islamic law.

The problem of Islamist violence became more acute in 1993 and attempts to control it came to dominate the domestic political agenda. After several car bomb explosions in Cairo at the beginning of the year, there was a wave of attacks by militant Islamists throughout the year. According to an independent source, there were more than 250 separate terror operations between January and December 1993 resulting in 274 deaths. More than one-third of the attacks were directed against police and security forces. Cinemas, video shops and Coptic churches were also targeted. Several attacks were carried out against leading politicians and senior members of the security forces. In April, Safwat Mohammad ash-Sharif, the Minister of Information, narrowly escaped death when his car was ambushed. Ironically, the Minister had been criticized by liberals for filling the television schedules with religious programmes, which was regarded as a crude and unconvincing attempt to appease Islamist opinion. The Minister of the Interior, Hussain al-Alfi, was seriously wounded in an assassination attempt outside his office in the centre of Cairo in August. Officials stated that the attack was carried out by the Vanguards of Conquest, a faction of Islamic Jihad. It had been thought that this group had been eliminated after it assassinated President Sadat in 1981. In November the Prime Minister, Atif Sidqi, escaped unharmed when a car bomb exploded near his residence, killing a schoolgirl and injuring 18 other people. The police stated that the attack was once again the work of the Vanguards of Conquest, although Islamic Jihad claimed responsibility. Militant Islamists continued to target foreign tourists. Three tourists were killed in January in an attack on a tourist bus, and in February a bomb exploded in a cafe in Cairo killing two foreigners. In April there was an explosion near one of the pyramids at Giza and four Germans were injured in a bomb attack against a tourist bus in Cairo in June. At the end of December eight Austrian tourists and eight Egyptians were wounded when a tour bus was attacked in Cairo. According to official sources, the murder of four foreign tourists at the Cairo hotel in October was carried out by a lone gunman who was mentally disturbed and not by militant Islamists. Nevertheless the incident was yet another damaging blow to the country's declining tourist industry. The number of tourist nights fell by 30% during the first eight months of 1993 as a result of the Islamists' campaign of violence and many international tour operators withdrew from Egypt. Revenues from tourism fell by about $800m. in 1993 to $1,300m.

Harsh measures were employed by the security forces to counter the escalation in Islamist violence. During the early months of 1993 heavily armed security forces carried out operations in Asyut and in the popular quarters of Cairo resulting in the arrest of large numbers of Islamists. Violent confrontations were reported during which militant Islamists were killed or injured. In March, for example, during simultaneous operations in Upper Egypt and Cairo, 16 Islamists were killed and a large number injured. Those arrested by the security forces were increasingly tried by military courts which were seen as more effective than the civil courts in securing quick convictions. Severe sentences were imposed on Islamists convicted by the military tribunals. During 1993 military courts sentenced 38 militant Islamists to death and 29 were hanged. This was the largest number of political executions in Egypt's recent history.

In April 1993 President Mubarak dismissed the Minister of the Interior, Muhammad Abd al-Halim Moussa, because he had indicated that he was willing to start a dialogue with imprisoned leaders of Islamic Jihad and Jama'ah al'Islamiyah. He was replaced by Gen. Hussain Mohammad al-Alfi who immediately reaffirmed the Government's uncompromising commitment to suppressing militant Islamist groups. However, the new Minister won approval in some quarters for favouring a more subtle approach to the security question. He pledged to stop the security forces carrying out indiscriminate mass arrests—a policy strongly criticized by human rights organizations—and stressed the need for greater efforts to improve social conditions. The crude methods employed by the police were revealed in August when a panel of eight judges found the 24 defendants on trial for the assassination of Rifa'at el-Mahgoub not guilty of murder. The court strongly criticized police practices and revealed that medical reports had shown that 16 of the defendants had been tortured. One of the judges condemned the security forces for resorting to torture in order 'to justify their ineptness and impotence in catching the real culprits'. Safwat Abdel-Ghani, the political leader of Jama'ah al-Islamiyah, one of 10 defendants convicted of lesser offences, stated that the Mahgoub case highlighted the injustice of the military courts which accepted police evidence unchallenged. In December a civil court acquitted Abdel-Ghani on the charge of ordering the assassination of Farag Fouda from his prison cell. On his reappointment as Minister of the Interior in October 1993, Hassan al-Alfi stated that the new Government would confront terrorism 'with extreme force, resolution and firmness'. However, he denied that torture was used to extract confessions from Islamist suspects. It was the Minister's first public statement since the assassination attempt in August. Mass arrests began again—for example, around 30 suspected militant Islamists were arrested every day during a single week in mid-October—and the Government continued to use the so-called 'fast track' military courts for the trials of militant Islamists.

Policing methods and the use of military courts in the campaign against Islamist violence provoked widespread international criticism. In late May 1993 Amnesty International published a report in which it strongly condemned the 'frightening brutality' of the Egyptian security forces. Amnesty International alleged that, in response to the increased killings of police officers and others, the security forces appeared to have been given 'a licence to kill with impunity'. It labelled the military courts 'a travesty of justice'. In November the UN Committee against Torture accused the Egyptian security forces of carrying out systematic torture against suspects in security cases and in ordinary criminal cases. The Egyptian Organization for Human Rights (EOHR) issued a statement endorsing the UN's accusations and claimed that 13 people—nearly all suspected militant Islamists had died under torture in jails, police stations or state security headquarters during 1993. EOHR also drew attention to the 221 cases of torture the organization had documented since July 1986 when Egypt ratified the UN convention on torture. Nevertheless, in January 1994 the EOHR admitted that the major responsibility for all acts of violence in the country lay with militant Islamist groups, and they produced figures which showed that Islamist groups were responsible for the death of 137 people in 1993. They also accused the Government of acceding to Islamist pressure to ban books and of permitting the state-controlled media and education system to promote Islamist ideas. In November the Majlis ash-Shura, the Advisory Council, also warned that Islamist influence was increasing in the mass media and in the universities. Earlier in the year the leftist Tagammu, the only opposition party represented in the People's Assembly, accused the Government of allowing the message of Islamic intolerance to be widely disseminated in the media. The Government moved to take some action in these areas. Already in February 1993 a trade union election law had been passed requiring the participation of at least 50% of the members for an election to be valid. Earlier, the Muslim Brotherhood had gained control of the lawyers', engineers' and doctors' associations. Press censorship was increased and a number of high-profile corruption cases were prosecuted. In order to demonstrate the Government's determination to press ahead with social spending programmes in low income areas, President Mubarak announced in December that governors would now be made accountable for progress in slum improvements in their governorates.

Following the bombing of the International Trade Centre in New York in February 1993, FBI investigations led to the dismantling of some of the Islamist networks in the USA and the arrest of the influential militant Islamist, Sheikh Omar Abd ar-Rahman. At the beginning of July the Government requested the USA to extradite Sheikh Abd al-Rahman so that he could face charges of inciting violence in Egypt. But leaders of the Islamist militant groups continued to operate in some European countries. For example, it was reported that Tala'at

Mohammed Tala'at, one of the leaders of the Vanguards of Conquest, was living in Denmark and that Egyptian requests for his extradition had been rejected. Ayman al-Zawari, the leader of Islamic Jihad, sentenced to death *in absentia* for his part in the assassination of President Sadat, was reported to be living in Switzerland and to have applied for political asylum. Al-Zawahri was believed to be linked to Mohammed Mekawi, considered to be the field officer of the Vanguards of Conquest in Afghanistan, and responsible for the training of several hundred Egyptian militants there. Members of these extremist groups appeared to be able to travel without difficulty between Europe, the Middle East and Pakistan and Afghanistan. According to the police, the external leadership of the militant Islamist groups was responsible for planning some of the high profile operations such as the assassination attempts on government ministers. In November 1993 it was reported that a preliminary agreement had been reached between the leaderships of Islamic Jihad and Jama'ah al-Islamiyah, urging joint action and greater co-ordination between the two groups in confronting the security forces. It was also agreed that Sheikh Abd ar-Rahman should be the leader of the clandestine Islamic movement as a whole, including Islamic Jihad and Jama'ah al-Islamiyah, and that a committee composed of members of the *Majlis ash-shura* of both groups should be formed to overcome differences and strengthen co-operation.

MUBARAK'S THIRD TERM

President Mubarak was formally nominated for a third six-year term of office in July 1993. He received 439 of the 448 votes cast in the People's Assembly. None of the opposition parties, nor the banned but officially tolerated Muslim Brotherhood, endorsed his candidature for a third term of office, arguing that the people should be allowed to choose the president from a list of candidates and not just approve the decision of parliament. His nomination was approved by nationwide referendum on 4 October. According to official figures, Mubarak won 96.3% of the valid votes cast in an 84% turnout. However, despite a major publicity campaign by the ruling National Democratic Party (NDP), the general mood appeared to be one of apathy and independent observers commented on the small numbers of people voting. The following day President Mubarak promoted the Minister of Defence, Gen. Muhammad Hussain Tantawi, to the rank of Field Marshal, an honour accorded to only four other generals since the revolution. Senior air force and air defence officers were also promoted. Some observers saw this as a move to placate the army, the ultimate power behind the regime, after Mubarak's refusal to appoint a vice-president, a post that the military had traditionally regarded as its own. Others argued that Mubarak had drawn closer to the armed forces as the security situation had deteriorated as a result of Islamist violence. In a rare interview with *Al-Ahram* published on 11 October, Tantawi stated that he would send in the army against Islamist extremists if they threatened the security of the state. He hoped that it would not be necessary to deploy the armed forces to maintain internal security but they were the last line of defence against Islamist organizations bent on overthrowing the government and achieving power. This was the first time that the army had publicly stated that it was prepared to involve itself in the battle against militant Islamist groups. So far the campaign against Islamist extremists has been carried out by forces under the command of the Ministry of the Interior.

There was considerable internal and external pressure for fundamental changes to the government team in order to meet the challenge of economic reform and to counter the Islamist threat. But when the new Cabinet was sworn in on 14 October, Atif Sidqi—first appointed in 1986—was retained as Prime Minister and the key portfolios of foreign affairs, defence, the interior and information remained unchanged. Among the new faces were Mahmoud Mohamed Mahmoud, a former chairman of Misr International Bank, who replaced Yousri Mustapha as Minister of Economy and Foreign Trade; Ismail Hassan, the Chairman of the Bank of Alexandria, as governor of the Central Bank with ministerial rank; and Ibrahim Fawzi Abdel-Wahed, a former university professor, as Minister of Industry.

The public enterprise sector, previously the responsiblity of Sidqi, was transferred to Atef Obeid with promises to speed up the privatization process. Obeid was also given responsibility for environmental affairs, one of the priorities of some international aid agencies operating in Egypt. Youssef Boutros-Ghali moved from the Prime Minister's office to the new post of Minister of State for International Co-operation. Hassabalah al-Kafrawi, who had presided over the vast Ministry of Housing since 1977, departed and his ministry was divided into three parts. Mohamed Saleheddin Hassaballah, the former general manager of Arab Contractors, Egypt's largest construction company, was appointed to the new post of Minister of Housing and Utilities, while ministers of state were appointed with responsiblity for housing affairs and the family and for new communities, including the far from successful new industrial cities built around Cairo over the last 15 years. The President announced that the priorities of his third term would be security and stability, economic reform, social justice, educational reform, combating unemployment, dealing with the problem of high population growth and improving Egypt's unwieldy bureaucracy. He made no reference to political reform.

However, Mubarak did propose a 'broad national dialogue' involving all parties which rejected violence and terrorism and supported democracy. The idea was first broached by the president at the end of September 1993 and at the beginning of December Egypt's 10 main legal political parties, together with the Muslim Brotherhood and the Communists, issued a statement welcoming dialogue but insisting that the discussions should be comprehensive and focus on the question of political reform. Officials of the ruling NDP, headed by the deputy prime minister, Youssef Wali, eventually indicated that they would be willing to hold wide-ranging discussions covering political, social and economic reforms, but that the dialogue would be confined to the principal political parties in the first instance. There seemed little doubt that the decision not to include professional and trade unions was because several of them are controlled by the Muslim Brotherhood. The national dialogue meetings were scheduled to start in February 1994, but were postponed until April and then again until late May. In April President Mubarak stated that he would nominate a 25-member preparatory committee composed of party and trade union leaders to prepare a report on the terms of reference for dialogue. The Minister of Information indicated that the president had established three main guidelines for the proposed dialogue. These were that the discussions should include all legal political parties and forces, including the trade unions; that the NDP would not try to impose its views on other participants, and that the discusions would be wide-ranging and include political as well as economic and social issues. The reference to legal political parties indicated that the Muslim Brotherhood would remain excluded from direct participation in the deliberations. However, it was assumed that its views would be expressed through its electoral ally, the Socialist Labour Party (SLP), and union delegates. It was reported in March that the legal opposition parties had held a series of meetings to co-ordinate their positions in preparation for the first national dialogue meeting. An earlier attempt at national dialogue in 1991 foundered when the NDP and the opposition parties failed to agree on the scope of the discussions. Despite the latest initiative, there were serious doubts that the NDP was willing to share power.

Reports of corruption in high places continued to circulate. At the beginning of November 1993 the *Wall Street Journal* alleged that over the previous two years two former Egyptian generals had received substantial commissions from major US corporations in connection with military sales to Egypt. One of the generals was described as a former colleague of Mubarak when they were both in the air force. *Ash-Shaab*, the newspaper of the pro-Islamist SLP called for an investigation into the allegations. Over the previous two months, several journalists from *Ash-Shaab*, together with Helmi Murad, the vice-president of the SLP, had been detained for labelling the Mubarak regime as corrupt. *Ash-Shaab* later alleged that senior figures in the regime had received favours from property magnate Fawzi el-Sayyid which had enabled him to build several apartment blocks in Nasr City in violation of building codes. Following these allegations, the Prime Minister, Atif Sidqi, Omar Abdel-Akhter, the Governor of Cairo, and Zakaria Azmi, the head of the presidential office, filed libel suits against the SLP leader, Ibrahim Shukri, and the editor of *Ash-Shaab*, Magdi Hussain. In early February the public prosecutor referred Shukri and Hussain to the criminal court to face charges of libel and slander.

THE CAMPAIGN AGAINST MILITANT ISLAMISTS INTENSIFIES

In February 1994 militant Islamist groups intensified their attacks on tourists and also targeted foreign investors. Jama'ah al-Islamiyah sent a series of warnings by fax to international news agencies warning tourists and foreign investors to leave Egypt, and that anyone helping a regime that opposed Islam would receive 'the same punishment as the oppressors'. This policy, however, was condemned by the Vanguards of Conquest which, in a statement from Islamabad in Pakistan, declared that targeting foreigners and foreign investors was harmful to Muslim interests because it would increase the hardships of the Muslim people. Earlier there had been reports of differences between the two extremist groups and their failure to set up the joint *Majlis ash-Shura* as agreed in November 1993. In February and March 1994 there were several attacks on tourist trains in Upper Egypt, injuring a number of foreigners, and in early March a German tourist was killed when shots were fired at Nile cruise ships. Jama'ah al-Islamiyah also carried out a series of bomb attacks on banks in Cairo and towns in Upper Egypt. The biggest explosion was near a bank in Cairo on 19 March. Jama'ah al-Islamiyah had issued a warning to Egyptians to close their accounts at banks practising *riba* (usury) by 22 February. On 9 April Islamist militants assassinated Maj.-Gen. Raouf Khairat, the head of the state security Department for Combating Religious Activity and a key figure in the campaign against Islamist violence. Jama'ah al-Islamiyah claimed responsibility for the attack. In February suspected militant Islamists had shot dead the chief prosecution witness in the trial against those arrested for the attempted assassination of Prime Minister, Atif Sidqui.

The crackdown by the security forces was unrelenting. Figures released by the Ministry of the Interior showed that 29,000 Islamist militants had been jailed following mass arrests. The security forces claimed to have arrested 900 Islamist suspects in a single week in February. The EOHR criticized police action during a raid on an apartment in Zawiya al-Hamra on 1 February because there were witnessess who claimed that seven militants were killed in cold blood. The police stated that the men had been killed during a gun battle. The security forces claimed to have inflicted a serious blow against their opponents when they killed the military commanders of both Jama'ah al-Islamiyah and Islamic Jihad in April. Adil Awad Siyam, the military commander of Islamic Jihad, was killed during a security operation in Giza during which automatic rifles, small firearms and explosives were seized. Talaat Yasin Himam, believed to be the military commander of Jama'ah al-Islamiyah, was killed in a shoot-out in Asyut along with four of his comrades. In March two army officers were executed for their part in a plot to assassinate President Mubarak when he arrived at Sidi Barrani airport, near the Libyan border on his way to visit Col Qaddafi.

On 10 April a new law was passed abolishing local elections and giving the Ministry of the Interior powers to appoint village *omdas* or mayors. Answering criticisms from opposition deputies, the Government claimed that many *omdas* had refused to co-operate in security matters and were corrupt. The following day the emergency laws, which give the security forces wide powers to arrest and detain suspects, were renewed for another three years. The authorities also renewed their efforts to curb the activities of leaders of extremist groups living abroad. In early April an extradition treaty was signed with Pakistan and there were reports that the authorities in Yemen and Saudi Arabia were co-operating with Egypt in security matters. Local and Western journalists were warned to ensure that their articles on the Islamist challenge followed the official line or they would face arrest or expulsion. A propaganda offensive against the Islamists was launched in the state-controlled media including television broadcasts of confessions by former members of underground Islamist groups. A new Egyptian film entitled El-Irhabi (The Terrorist), denouncing Islamist militants, broke box office records during the first week it was screened. Allegations that several senior police officers were being investigated for supplying arms to Islamist militants were strongly denied by Hassan al-Alfi, the Minister of the Interior in March. The allegations had been made in the Majlis by Zaki Badr, a former Minister of the Interior, who had accused Muhammad Abd al-Halim Moussa, al-Alfi's predecessor, of being associated with a private security firm that had employed a number of Islamist militants arrested for security offences. There were reports that in recent years over 200 private security firms had been set up by serving or former police officers and that many of them had financial backing from Gulf business interests known to support the Islamist movement in Egypt.

The major battle between the security forces and the extremists continued to be waged unabated in the southern province of Asyut, one of the poorest in the country. The political violence there was believed to have intensified because of the widespread tradition of *thaar*, or blood feud, strongly rooted in local culture. Asyut was the scene of almost daily clashes between security forces and armed Islamists. The police claimed that 54 people had been killed in these clashes between January and March—30 policemen, 13 civilians and 11 Islamists—and 67 wounded. In February, after gunmen from Jama'ah al-Islamiyah attacked a bus carrying eight Romanian engineers working for the Asyut Cement Company, 23 Polish workers at the company announced that they had decided to leave Egypt. Most foreigners have quit the province. In March an Islamist gunman shot at a crowd of Coptic Christians outside the Muharraq monastery near Asyut killing five people and wounding three others in the most serious incident to date involving a Christian place of worship. In April the Minister of the Interior announced that the province was to be divided into four zones each headed by a senior officer in order to assist the security forces in controlling the area. At the same time, it was reported that several development projects were underway to improve basic services in the turbulent province.

Economy

Updated for this edition by ALAN J. DAY

INTRODUCTION

Over the last few decades, Egypt's economy has been fundamentally influenced by various political vicissitudes. In particular, the wars, and then peace, with Israel have had major repercussions on the nature of expenditure and foreign aid, while in recent years the Government has moved away from state socialism and towards a market economy. Underneath these changes of direction, however, lie the important physical constraints of a large and rapidly growing population, and the dearth of land available for agriculture and water for irrigation.

The total area of Egypt is 997,738.5 sq km, but 96% of the country is desert. With no forested land, and hardly any permanent meadows or pastures, the arable land available is greatly overcrowded. Relating the population, numbering 38.2m. at the 1976 census, to the inhabited area (about 35,200 sq km), a density of 1,085 persons per sq km gave 5.7 persons per acre of arable land, representing one of the highest man/land ratios in the world. Since then, the root of Egypt's poverty has remained the rapid rise in the population, of 2.8% per annum between 1978 and 1986, which added about 1.3m. people per year. According to the results of the 1986 census, the population had risen to 48.2m., and only 4% of the land area was occupied. By mid-1992, according to the World Bank, the population had risen to 54.8m., while in early 1993 official Egyptian estimates gave the total end-1992 population as 58,987,000, and the current rate of increase as just 2.1% per annum. World Bank figures showed that the average annual rise in population in the 1980s was 2.4%, compared with 2.1% in 1965–80, but this was projected to fall to 1.8% in the decade to 2000. Family planning has been heavily promoted by the Government since the establishment of a National Population Council in 1985. An estimated 48% of families were practising contraception in 1992, when the average number of births per mother fell below four for the first time since records have been kept. The Government's long-term aim is to extend the practice of contraception to 70% of Egyptian families by 2010.

Lack of employment opportunities drove people from the country into already overcrowded cities, which grew at a rate of 3.4% per annum in the late 1970s (the population of Greater Cairo increased from 7m. in 1976 to more than 10m. in 1985), and hastened the emigration of qualified personnel the country could ill afford to lose. In 1983 3.28m. Egyptians were working abroad. Many originally went to much better-paid jobs in the rich Gulf States and Libya, although a considerable number were forced to return from the former in the 1980s, owing to a downturn in the oil industry, and from the latter because of a government order of 1985, prohibiting the employment of Egyptian workers. Poor job prospects were not improved by

the return of thousands of expatriate workers (including about 5,000 from Libya in 1985, and about 250,000 who left Iraq in the first half of 1986, when new restrictions were imposed on the amount of money they were allowed to send home). This trend also helped swell the bureaucracy, since the Government had been committed to giving a post to every Egyptian graduate who could not find other employment. It was officially estimated that the number of Egyptians working abroad had fallen to about 2m. by 1986, and in mid-1991 government officials estimated that the number of unemployed was in the range of 20%–22% of the total labour force. In 1990 47% of the population was estimated to be urban, compared with the 43.8% comprising the urban population at the 1976 census and 41% in 1965. In 1990, according to estimates by the World Bank, Egypt's gross national product (GNP) per head was $600, having increased at an average rate of 4.1% per year, in real terms, since 1965. The average annual growth of overall gross domestic product (GDP), measured in constant prices, was 7.3% in 1965–80, slowing to 5.0% in 1980–90. In 1990/91 the crisis in the Gulf had a damaging short-term effect on the Egyptian economy, due in particular to a decline in tourism and the return of hundreds of thousands of Egyptian nationals from Iraq and Kuwait, which was only partially offset by higher revenues from oil exports. However, the Government's political and military alignment with the anti-Iraq coalition brought important post-war benefits in the form of generous debt relief and increased aid from major donors (see below). Tourism recovered strongly in 1991/92, but underwent a new decline in 1992/93 when foreign tourists were among the targets of a terrorist campaign by militant Islamist elements. At the end of 1993 the level of unemployment in Egypt was officially estimated to be between 1.4m. and 1.5m. (about 10% of the labour force), significantly below the lowest estimates of most independent analysts.

During the 1960s Egypt, under Nasser, followed an economic policy which was based on socialist planning. However, the wars with Israel in 1967 and 1973, and Nasser's death in 1970, heralded a major period of change in Egypt's economic relations, both with its Arab neighbours and with the superpowers. Since 1973 great efforts have been made to repair the war damage, and Sadat's Law No. 43 of 1974 led to the replacement of Nasser's socialist planning by an 'open door policy' (*infitah*), encouraging foreign investment. The economic implications of Sadat's assassination in October 1981 were slight at first, but his successor, Hosni Mubarak, gradually encouraged the private sector. Basic tax on company profits was reduced from 40% to 32% in early 1982, while the enactment in 1990 of Law No. 230, a revised and refined version of the 1974 Law, was regarded as a sign of the

Government's commitment to the growth of private enterprise and deregulation. This shift from an essentially centrally controlled economy to one that is much more open to private enterprise and foreign investment has itself caused considerable strain on, and problems in, the economy. Private investment increased sharply following the 'open door policy': it totalled £E1,025m. in 1983, compared with £E443m. in 1982, and by 1990 it had reached £E10,700m., of which 64% was Egyptian, 19% Arab and 17% from other sources. The 1970s also saw a great increase in aid from the oil-rich Arab states. In 1967–73 Arab aid to Egypt was estimated at an annual average of US $310m. In 1973 this increased to $720m., and in 1974 it rose to $1,260m., while by 1977 it had risen to between $1,700m. and $2,000m. Much of this aid came from the Gulf Organization for the Development of Egypt (GODE), set up by Saudi Arabia, Kuwait, the United Arab Emirates and Qatar in 1977. Saudi sources, in fact, claimed in May 1979 that Egypt had received more than US $13,000m. from the four GODE countries in the preceding six years.

By signing the peace treaty with Israel in March 1979, however, Sadat undertook the risk of losing this Arab aid. The Arab League Council which met in Baghdad immediately after the signing of the peace treaty, agreed on a policy of economic and political isolation of Egypt. At first it seemed unlikely that the economic sanctions would be stringently carried out by some of the Arab countries, but when in late April Saudi Arabia broke off diplomatic relations with Egypt some of the more 'moderate' Arab states implemented the boycott. The Arab Fund for Economic and Social Development suspended all future aid and credit relations with Egypt, although honouring transactions already in progress, and in May Saudi Arabia, Qatar and the United Arab Emirates withdrew from the Arab Organization for Industrialization (AOI), which was an Egypt-based Arab arms enterprise, causing its collapse. Egypt, however, responded by planning to set up its own arms industry with Western capital (see Manufacturing Industry, below). During 1980 Egypt and Israel signed agricultural, trade, aviation and health agreements, and their common border was opened to commercial and tourist traffic towards the end of the year. While the loss of Saudi military aid, estimated at an annual rate of just under $2,000m., was undoubtedly significant, the fact that only about 7% of Egypt's total trade was with Arab countries implied that the Arab trade boycott would probably not be of major importance. The loss of Arab aid from the GODE was significant, however, although Egypt ceased to pay interest due on sums already loaned in 1979. By 1987 the resulting arrears in interest on GODE loans totalled almost $2,000m. Sadat hoped that Egypt's economic difficulties would be alleviated by the 'Carter Plan', which he saw in the same light as the 'Marshall Plan', by which Egypt would receive US $12,250m. over a period of five years, mainly from the USA, Western Europe and Japan. The USA promised that it would be no less generous to Egypt after the peace treaty with Israel than it was to Israel itself in terms of economic aid; as a result, Egypt became the second largest recipient of US aid, after Israel. The return of multinationals such as Coca-Cola and Cadbury Schweppes, associated with the normalization of relations with Israel, clearly demonstrated the increased readiness of foreign capital to invest in Egypt. In the early 1980s the USA was providing around $1,000m. per year in aid, and by mid-1983 the US Agency for International Development (USAID) was involved in some 650 projects in Egypt. In the financial year 1984/85 (beginning in July) US aid rose to $2,200m. In 1985 the US Senate approved emergency economic aid of $500m., to be paid out over the fiscal years 1985/86 and 1986/87. Total aid for 1985/86 was set at about $2,340m. (including $1,300m. in economic assistance), after the US Congress, dissatisfied with Egypt's rate of economic reform, had refused an Egyptian request for aid totalling more than $3,000m. In 1986/87 US aid to Egypt was reduced to $2,115m. ($1,300m. in military aid; $815m. in economic support) but was held at this level for the following two years. Between 1975 and 1985, according to USAID, US economic assistance to Egypt totalled $10,897.8m. In June 1988, in order to comply with a congressional mandate which required the suspension of aid to

countries failing to meet terms imposed by the IMF as conditions for a debt-rescheduling agreement, the USA halted the disbursement of $230m. of financial aid allocated to Egypt in 1988/89. Egypt's total debt to the USA was by then estimated at $10,000m., of which $4,500m. was military debt. In April 1989, following the Government's decision to raise energy prices to industry by 30%–40%, the US Administration agreed to release the $230m. and several other categories of aid. In 1990 Egypt received a total of $5,604m. (or 15.9% of its GNP) in official development aid from OECD members, Arab countries and multilateral organizations, compared with $1,568m. in 1989, $1,537m. in 1988, $1,774m. in 1987 and $1,716m. in 1986. The principal OECD donors, apart from the USA, were the Federal Republic of Germany and Japan. In the 1989/90 US fiscal year USAID allocations to Egypt amounted to $815m.

In February 1989 Egypt was a founder member of the Arab Co-operation Council (ACC), together with Jordan, Iraq and the Yemen Arab Republic (YAR), and in May, Egypt was formally readmitted to the Arab League and its various economic committees. However, hopes that the ACC would provide a framework for increased economic co-operation were dissipated, at least temporarily, by the impact of the Gulf crisis of 1990–91.

ECONOMIC POLICY AND PLANNING

Between 1918 and 1939, when the Egyptian pound was tied to sterling and a fairly free trade policy was being pursued, manufacturing industry had little chance of developing and agricultural production, though expanding, could not keep up with the rapidly rising population. A gradual deterioration of living standards set in. This trend did not change direction until the immediate post-war period, when cotton prices improved. These reached their greatest heights during the Korean boom of 1951–52, when 'soft-currency cotton', including Egyptian cotton, enjoyed high premia over dollar-cotton. But the collapse of the boom, the easing of the world dollar scarcity and the beginning of American subsidization of cotton exports in the mid-1950s, marked a turning point in raw cotton terms of trade which, until quite recently, showed a declining trend.

The regime which assumed power in 1952 and ended the monarchy gave urgent attention to Egypt's economic problems. Its policies included measures of agrarian reform, land reclamation, the High Dam, and a programme of industrialization which was accelerated in 1960 by the formation of a comprehensive social and economic development plan.

According to the Permanent Constitution of 1971 the economy of Egypt was to be based on socialism with the people controlling all means of production. In practice this meant that the Government took ownership or control of practically every unit in the economy worth controlling. Although the doctrine of socialism was invoked from the first land reform in 1952, the economy remained largely in private hands until 1961, except for the nationalization of the Suez Canal Company in 1956 and that of British and French property during the Suez attack. During 1961 all cotton exporting firms were nationalized, and the Alexandria futures market was closed; 275 industrial and trading concerns were taken over by the state in whole or in part; taxation was made so progressive that individual income was virtually limited to the official maximum of £E5,000; the maximum limit on land ownership was reduced from 200 to 100 feddans (1 feddan is equivalent to 4,201 sq m, 1.038 acres or 0.42 ha), before it was reduced again in 1969; individual share-holding was limited to £E10,000; 25% of the net profits of industrial companies (later reduced to 10%) was to be distributed to the workers, who were to be represented on the boards of directors, and to work only a 42-hour week.

Other nationalization measures followed, so that the only sectors of the economy remaining outside complete government ownership were agriculture and urban real estate, but even these were overwhelmingly regulated by laws and decrees. Concerns were to be grouped under boards and boards under chairmen and ministers, and a constant stream of directives helped to bring the activities of all the controlled units in line with government policies. In June 1991 the Government introduced new legislation to reform public-sector companies, with the aim of reducing state intervention in such companies to a minimum. The reforms envisaged the establishment of state-owned holding companies to replace the general bodies hitherto in control of groups of state-owned companies. By May 1993 a total of 16 state-owned holding companies controlled a total of 317 subsidiary companies, grouped together in such a way as to minimize functional duplication and maximize administrative efficiency within the public sector.

Egypt's first Five-Year Development Plan aimed at increasing real national income by 40% between 1960 and 1965. The five-year growth target was virtually fulfilled, so that the second Plan was replaced by a more ambitious Seven-Year Plan (1965–72), which aimed to double real income by its end. Lack of finance, however, frustrated this new plan and after two years of uncertainty, a three-year 'accomplishment' plan, beginning July 1967, was proclaimed. This plan was dropped as a result of the 1967 war and was substituted by annual development appropriations. Apart from a few select new projects, the whole emphasis of Egyptian planning was turned towards rationalizing the existing industries, and introducing incentives to improve their performance.

After 1967 the Government introduced yet more restrictive measures aimed at curbing consumer demand, including a variety of taxes, forced savings and compulsory contributions out of wages and salaries. Following Nasser's death in 1970, however, President Sadat embarked on a gradual retreat from old-style socialist economic policies. Under what was termed 'denasserization', the sequestrations of the 1960s were ruled illegal, new laws were passed to allow private-sector participation in former state preserves such as exporting and importing and transport, and foreign investment was seen as the key to development.

In 1971 President Sadat proclaimed a decennial plan which aimed to double the national economy by 1982. This, however, was never fully implemented, and it was soon replaced by a transitional 18-month plan, to be followed by a more thorough five-year plan to cover the years 1976–80. Owing to the financial problems of 1976, this new plan was then postponed to cover 1978–82. It foresaw total expenditure at some £E12,000m. ($17,000m. at the parallel rate), and its main objective was to achieve annual economic growth rates of 8%. However, this was, in its turn, replaced by the 1980–84 five-year Peace Plan with planned investment of £E25,185m.; according to figures provided by the World Bank, the average annual growth of GDP in 1965–80 was 6.8%.

On 20 February 1982 the Prime Minister addressed the People's Assembly with a major statement on the economic policy to be followed by the country under its new leader, President Mubarak. In general terms, this policy was based on a clear strategy for economic development aimed at increasing exports and employment, through the comprehensive planning of the public, private and co-operative sectors. Particular attention was to be paid to social problems. Investment resources were to be increased through new channels for private investment, increasing the contribution of the banking sector, improving the efficiency of the tax system, increasing indigenous financial resources, cutting government expenditure, and limiting the consumption of imported goods. The Government's aim was to use the public sector as the main prop of production, regarding manpower as the real wealth of the country. The negative effects of subsidies (mainly on food, but also on oil, petrol, gas and electricity) were acknowledged, but the Government regarded the sole remedy to be increased rates of development and the promotion of productivity. It committed itself to strenuous efforts to reduce the level of imports, and all import operations in the future were to be undertaken through the banks without the transfer of currency. The Government planned to increase its export earnings, particularly through sales of petroleum, and the expansion of the war production sector. In agriculture, it envisaged reclamation as continuing to play an important role. Transport, communications, housing, tourism, health and education were also all to be boosted.

At the end of 1982 proposals were put forward for the next Five-Year Plan (1982–87), with a target for GDP growth in real terms of 7.9% per annum. The strategy behind the Plan

was to reduce the proportion of private consumption and of imports in total expenditure, so as to mobilize domestic resources for investment and to reduce the growing trade deficit, which had developed as a result of the policy of *infitah*. Planned investment was to be £E27,216m. ($32,790m.) in the public sector and £E8,271m. ($8,965m.) in the private sector. The Plan's objectives could be achieved, however, only if there was an improvement in Egypt's balance of payments. In this regard, the progressive decline in world oil demand (oil being Egypt's principal export commodity) cast doubts upon the viability of the Plan's targets. These doubts were confirmed by the collapse in the price of oil in 1986, when Egypt's net revenues from oil sales declined to less than $1,000m. The annual rate of growth of GDP during the Plan reached only about 5%, well short of its target of 7.9%. It was reported that only 15% of projects outlined in the Plan had actually been carried out when it ended in June 1987, owing to inadequate funding.

The next Five-Year Plan, which began in July 1987, provided for investment of £E46,500m. The Plan was designed to encourage public-sector production, to increase the manufacturing of commodities and to raise the level of exports. It also devoted more resources to the development of the private sector, which was to receive 39% of total investment (£E18,000m.), compared with 23% under the 1982–87 Plan. It was hoped to achieve annual growth in GDP of 5.8% during the Plan. Another important feature of the new Plan was the improvement of agricultural output, so as to minimize food imports, which account for 60% of Egypt's requirements. To this end, it was intended to bring an extra 100,000 feddans of land into production during each year of the Plan. However, even before the onset of the Gulf crisis in 1990, the Plan's targets had already been placed in serious doubt by the lack of funds available to finance development projects. According to one Egyptian newspaper, the shortage of foreign currency reserves forced the Government to order the National Investment Bank to halt financing of the Plan in March 1988 and to cancel imports of a number of foodstuffs.

Despite the non-fulfilment of the 1987–92 Plan and the general move to a market economy, a further Five-Year Plan was drawn up for the period beginning 1 July 1992. This document envisaged a 4% growth in GDP in the 1992/93 financial year, to £E131,000m., and thereafter by 5.1% per annum, to £E161,000m. in 1996/97 (at constant 1991/92 prices). Total investment of £E154,000m. was projected for the Plan period, of which 58% would come from the private sector, and it was envisaged that 2.5m. new jobs would be created (the current workforce numbering 14m., of whom 5.3m. were in the state sector).

One of the fundamental problems facing Egypt's economy remained the very high level of subsidies on basic consumer items, despite the Government's efforts—under pressure from the IMF—to reduce them as a proportion of budgeted expenditure. In 1983/84 food subsidies were cut by 16.3%, but they still amounted to £E2,055m. out of total subsidies of £E2,996m. (US $3,595m.), representing about 18% of overall budgeted expenditure. Moreover, in 1983 an additional estimated $3,600m. were spent on 'invisible' petroleum subsidies alone. Rioting in September 1984 forced President Mubarak to withdraw some food price increases, but the reduction of subsidies remained one of the Government's objectives.

ECONOMIC REFORM 1986–90

Under pressure from its main aid donor, the USA, and the IMF, to reform its economy, in June 1986 the Egyptian Government made a new effort to deal with the burden of subsidies. The new Prime Minister, Dr Ali Lutfi, proposed a system of cash benefits for those most affected by a 15% reduction in food subsidies under the 1986/87 budget, which set total expenditure for subsidies at £E1,746m. ($802m.) for the year, 12% less than the previous year. However, Dr Lutfi resigned as Prime Minister in November 1986, owing to President Mubarak's opposition to his apparent willingness to accede to proposals by the IMF for the introduction of economic reforms, in return for a stand-by credit arrangement. The IMF's demands included the adoption of a unified exchange rate (meaning an effective substantial devaluation), the progressive elimination of state subsidies, increases in real interest rates, tax reforms, and increases in customs duties as a means of reducing the level of imports.

The new Prime Minister, Dr Atif Sidqi, rejected the IMF's demands as too extreme, particularly those referring to the unification of the exchange rate system and a 75% reduction in subsidies. By May 1987, however, Dr Sidqi was himself beginning to yield to IMF pressure. Domestic energy prices rose by 60%–85% on 1 May, thereby reducing the 'hidden' energy subsidy. The exchange rate was allowed, partially, to 'float' in mid-May, with a daily rate, competitive with the 'black'-market rate, being fixed by a panel of commercial banks in order to attract remittances. Plans were also announced to reduce the budget deficit to 13% of GDP in 1987/88, compared with 15% in 1986/87, and to cut expenditure on subsidies to £E1,650m. In mid-May, following its approval of the Egyptian Government's programme of economic reform, the IMF indicated its support for the programme's aims by according Egypt a stand-by credit of $325m., of which $150m. was made available immediately. At the end of May an agreement was reached with the Paris Club group of Western creditor nations to reschedule, over 10 years, payments of $12,000m. in civilian and military debt from Egypt's estimated $44,000m. of foreign debt (Central Bank of Egypt estimate). One month earlier, the USSR had agreed to reschedule, over 25 years, without interest, more than $3,000m. in military debt, payment of which had been due since 1977. Military debt totalled an estimated $13,500m. in February 1988, including $4,500m. owed to the USA. In November 1987 Egypt signed an agreement rescheduling the payment of $1,600m. in military and civil debt to the USA. Similar agreements, covering debt repayments of $8,000m. up to the end of June 1988, had been concluded with the remaining 17 Paris Club members by the end of July 1988.

By mid-1988, however, the Egyptian Government was concerned that the pace of economic reform required by the IMF was such as to risk a repetition of earlier riots over rises in the price of food, and it urged the introduction of a new reform programme, which would be implemented at a more gradual rate and supported by financial assistance for the balance of payments. The Government opposed further reductions in state subsidies which, it claimed, would fuel an inflation rate that was already as high as 30%; it was resolved to maintain the artificially high fixed Central Bank exchange rate of US$1 = £E0.70 (used for imports of basic commodities), which acted as an indirect subsidy on food prices and which the IMF wished to be abolished. The Prime Minister, Dr Atif Sidqi, said that rises in energy prices of between 30% and 40% required by the IMF, were too great; that the Government refused to raise interest rates to 20%–25%; and that the budget deficit would not fall to the IMF's target of 10% of GDP in 1988/89 (in which year, budgeted expenditure on subsidies rose to £E1,813m.). The IMF conceded that a shortfall of about $1,400m. in the aid allocations needed to support a reform programme was a hindrance to its implementation. However, Egypt's request for further balance-of-payments support for the duration of a long-term programme of economic reform did not meet with a favourable response. The IMF's stand-by credit of $325m. was, accordingly, frozen after only one disbursement of $150m. in May 1987, owing to IMF dissatisfaction with the pace of reform in Egypt.

By June 1988 the Government's wages bill was estimated to have increased by 25%, and to have contributed greatly to a budget deficit equivalent to 16%–17% of GDP in 1987/88, compared with the IMF's target of 13%. The Government's public sector salary commitments were expected to rise by a further 42% in 1988/89. Negotiations between the Government and senior IMF officials, regarding the elaboration of a new economic reform programme, recommenced in mid-1988 and continued intermittently for the remainder of the year without success. While the Government argued that it had made significant achievements in its reform of the exchange rate and prices, the IMF pressed for faster, more wide-ranging reform, including an increase of 30%–40% in energy prices to industry.

Further negotiations between the Government and the Fund in January 1989 remained deadlocked over the timing of the economic reform programme. While the Government argued

that it should be allowed four years to implement the Fund's demands, the Fund refused to concede any more than two years for their implementation. In mid-April, however, despite further economic pressure in the form of a depreciation of 20% in the value of the Egyptian pound against foreign currencies since mid-March, the Government was reported to have undertaken to raise energy prices to industry by 30%–40%, and to be ready to begin a programme of public sector reform. The 1989/90 budget, announced in June, granted greater autonomy to public companies, and in September the Central Bank rate of US $1 = £E0.70 was raised to US $1 = £E1.10. Moreover, although budget expenditure on subsidies rose to £E2,061m., the overall budget deficit was set at 8% (in fact, a deficit of 7% was recorded). However, no further progress towards an agreement with the Fund was achieved during the remainder of 1989.

Technical discussions, as distinct from negotiations proper, between the IMF and the Government resumed in June 1990. In the first half of the year the Government had taken some steps towards fulfilling the conditions stated by the Fund; in particular, subsidies applicable to a wide range of basic commodities had been reduced—causing sharp price increases, and the 73% increase in their cost, to some £E3,500m. in 1990/91 was due mostly to effective devaluation of the Central Bank exchange rate to US $1 = £E2.00. Despite these steps, and provision for a budget deficit again within 10% of the country's GDP for 1990/91, the IMF remained dissatisfied with the level of interest rates, the size of the budget deficit provision and the slow speed at which energy prices were being raised. Further discussions were overtaken, however, by the onset of the Gulf crisis, precipitated by Iraq's invasion of Kuwait in August 1990.

THE GULF CRISIS AND THE 1991 IMF AGREEMENT

Egypt's economic reform programme was disrupted by the 1990/91 Gulf crisis, which most adversely affected foreign exchange earnings from tourism and remittances from Egyptian nationals working in Iraq and Kuwait. Losses in these two areas were officially estimated by the Government at, respectively, $1,500m. in the 1990/91 tourist season (see 'Transport and Tourism', below) and $2,400m. in the 1990 calendar year. After a decline in the mid-1980s, a new boom in the oil-producing Gulf states had resulted in total remittances increasing to $4,235m. in 1989, a large proportion of which derived from the estimated 1.5m. Egyptians then working in Iraq and Kuwait. By late 1990 about 400,000 workers had returned to Egypt (the total rising to more than 600,000 following the outbreak of hostilities between Iraq and the US-led multinational force in January 1991); their return caused serious social problems for the Egyptian authorities and led to an increase in the existing level of unemployment of around 20%. On the other hand, an anticipated fall in Suez Canal revenues in 1990, due to the UN embargo on trade with Iraq, failed to materialize; instead, earnings increased by 14% over 1989 (see 'Suez Canal', below). Moreover, increased world oil prices in the third quarter of 1990 almost doubled Egypt's revenues from oil exports to $210m. per month (compared with average monthly receipts of $138m. in 1989/90), thereby offsetting losses from suspended trade with Iraq and Kuwait. One further consequence of the crisis was an increase in the budget deficit, to 17% of GDP in 1990/91.

Initial fears that the Iraqi invasion of Kuwait would curtail Kuwait's important role in Egyptian investment plans proved to be largely unfounded: even before the liberation of their country in February 1991, the Kuwaiti authorities (then in exile) pledged that existing commitments would be honoured. Moreover, the crisis resulted in a sharp increase in aid to Egypt, in addition to the waiver or rescheduling of certain Egyptian debts to other countries. Emergency aid was allocated through the Gulf Financial Crisis Co-ordinating Group (GFCCG), which by March 1991 had arranged funding amounting to $11,741m. for Egypt, Turkey and Jordan. Saudi Arabia, Japan and Kuwait were the largest donors, while Saudi Arabia, which in 1990 made its first development loans to Egypt since the resumption of bilateral relations in 1988, also announced that it had written off outstanding Egyptian debts of $4,000m. Moreover, in November 1990 the US Congress finally consented to write off some $7,000m. in Egyptian debts for arms purchases in the 1970s (comprising $4,500m. in principal and $2,500m. in interest and penalties). With smaller amounts being written off by other Western and Gulf states, Egypt's debt was reduced from some $50,000m. before the Gulf crisis to around $36,000m. by early 1991.

The agreement of Western nations to reschedule Egypt's remaining debts depended on a new accord being concluded with the IMF. Negotiations resumed after the end of the Gulf war, and were conducted in a more sympathetic climate in view of Egypt's active participation in the anti-Iraq coalition. Progress was also expedited by the following factors: the introduction in February 1991 of new market-related currency exchange arrangements, as a prelude to a single unified rate and full convertibility no later than February 1992; trade liberalization measures, under which most existing tariff and other barriers were to be phased out over three years; publication in April of a further list of 60 state-owned enterprises which the Government sought to privatize; price increases in April, ranging from 14% to 66% on petroleum products, gas and electricity; the introduction in May of new sales taxes of between 5% and 30% on most goods and services (although certain basic items such as bread, meat, fish, petrol and gas were exempted); and the adoption of a budget for 1991/92 providing for a deficit of 9.3% of GDP, falling to 6.5% in 1992/93 and to 3.5% in 1993/94 (see National Budget, below). The new exchange rate arrangements resulted in an effective devaluation of some 38% by May 1991, while interest rates underwent a consequential significant rise (see 'Banking', below).

Against this background, a new stand-by facility was formally approved by the IMF in mid-May 1991, under which some $372m. would be made available to Egypt over a period of 18 months to provide balance-of-payments assistance for its economic reform programme. This was rapidly followed by a decision of the Paris Club of Western creditors to write off, over a three-year period, $10,000m. of the $20,000m. owed by Egypt to creditor nations and to reschedule repayment of the remaining $10,000m. on favourable terms. Defending the IMF agreement in a speech to the Egyptian people on 1 May, President Mubarak said that it provided the opportunity to put the country's economy in order and stressed that the required restructuring would be fully under Egyptian control.

In accordance with the IMF agreement, the commercial and Central Bank exchange rates for the Egyptian pound were unified on 8 October 1991 (several months ahead of schedule) at the prevailing market rate of $1 = £E3.31. This made the pound almost fully convertible, in that for the first time most state-owned enterprises could freely maintain foreign exchange accounts to finance their hard currency requirements. The only exceptions were state exporters of cotton and rice, and the state oil and gas sector (which was required to deposit any surplus revenue beyond what it needed to cover foreign currency requirements).

In early 1992 the World Bank concluded that the Egyptian economic reform programme was broadly on course. Their report noted: that real GDP had risen by 2% in 1990/91; that the current account was set to record a surplus in 1991/92; that inflation and the budget deficit were within the prescribed parameters; and that trade liberalization and subsidy reductions were on target. Remaining obstacles were the slow pace of privatization, investment authorization and deregulation. In March the General Authority for Investments, in response to the World Bank criticism, introduced five new measures to facilitate investment. An initial 15% of Egypt's $20,000m. Paris Club debt was cancelled shortly after the formal announcement of the 1991 IMF stand-by arrangement, with cancellation of a further 15% scheduled to take effect at such time as the IMF formally approved the terms of a follow-up arrangement. (The remainder of the promised write-off, amounting to 20% of the original debt, was scheduled to take effect half-way through the duration of such a follow-up arrangement, provided that the IMF was broadly satisified with government economic policy at that point).

Notwithstanding Egypt's announcement that it did not intend to draw on the final $180m. tranche of the 1991 stand-by facility because of strong growth in the country's foreign-exchange reserves during 1992, formal expiry of the facility (originally set for the end of November 1992) was postponed by the IMF for two successive periods of three months.

The World Bank, for its part, delayed from June 1992 to March 1993 the release of the second half of a $300m. structural adjustment loan, eventually announcing the release of the funds shortly after the Government had announced the start of the active phase of its long-awaited privatization programme. The 20 firms whose shares were offered to local and foreign private investors in this initial privatization exercise included hotels, a cement company, beverage producers and vineyards. Other liberalization measures announced in the first quarter of 1993 included a cut from 100% to 80% in Egypt's top rate of import tariffs.

On 19 March 1993 (one week after the World Bank's release of funds) the IMF's executive board formally declared that Egypt had fulfilled its commitments under the 1991 stand-by arrangement. This opened the way for negotiations on the terms of a follow-up arrangement.

Egyptian officials said in July 1993 that the Government would undertake to achieve a further reduction in the budget deficit, to maintain exchange-rate stability and to keep the annual rate of inflation below 8%. It would aim eventually to privatize public-sector assets with an estimated market value totalling £E40,000m., and it hoped to be able to complete around 25% of the privatization programme within three years. On trade liberalization (reportedly the most contentious issue in negotiations with the IMF), the Government's declared aim was to reduce Egypt's maximum import tariff from 80% to 50% over a four-year period. As an apparent gesture to IMF negotiators who had sought a much swifter cut in the top rate, the Government acted in mid-July to lift certain import restrictions (on timber, paints and household appliances) and to abolish preferential tariffs for public-sector industries.

On 21 September 1993 the IMF's executive board approved a $560m. extended fund facility, to be drawn down in six-monthly tranches over a period of three years. Earlier in September, the Egyptian Government had reached 'substantial agreement' with the World Bank on the monitoring of the process of structural economic reform over the same period. In view of the recent strengthening of the country's balance-of-payments position (attributed mainly to the attractive rates of return on local currency deposits), no new World Bank loan was associated with this agreement.

Having secured implementation of the second phase of the Paris Club debt write-off in September 1993, the Egyptian Government was in mid-1994 seeking formal IMF/World Bank approval for the current economic position and outlook in order to trigger the final phase of the promised debt write-off. The only perceived obstacle to the early achievement of this goal was a difference of opinion between the Government and the IMF on the currency exchange rate (which stood at $1 = £E3.38 in May 1994). In the Fund's economic judgement, some devaluation was desirable, whereas the Government regarded exchange-rate stability as an important factor in maintaining investor confidence in the economy.

In other respects, the Government's monetary and fiscal policies were broadly on course to satisfy IMF targets, while the World Bank-monitored restructuring programme was gathering momentum, with up to £E3,200m. of public-sector assets scheduled for sale during the second half of 1994. Privatization deals approved by mid-1994 involved the sale of two bottling companies and a boiler-making company (in each case to consortia of foreign and local interests and on terms which included guarantees to maintain employment levels for agreed periods), while negotiations for the sale of a large state-owned hotel were well advanced.

Many of the businesses offered for sale in the initial privatization exercise had, however, failed to attract adequate bids from single buyers, prompting the Government to modify its privatization strategy to include sales of shares in state enterprises through the local securities market. It was also decided that 10% of the shares in about 100 public-sector companies should be earmarked for sale to employee shareholders' associations over a period of years. The Government's overall target for sales of shares in the 1994/95 fiscal year was £E9,000m. The state shareholding in the Commercial

International Bank (Egypt) was reduced from 70% to 43% in September 1993 as a result of a heavily-oversubscribed issue of new shares. State-owned banks were recommended to reduce their shareholdings in joint-venture banks (i.e. those with mixed public and private ownership) to 25% by the end of 1995.

The maximum import tariff was cut to 70% in February 1994 as part of a wide-ranging reform package which included substantial tariff reductions for many raw materials, coupled with various fiscal incentives to exporters. Further trade liberalization measures, including cuts in import tariffs on capital goods, were due to come into effect in December 1994. By mid-1994 price subsidies had been eliminated or substantially reduced throughout the public sector, and timetables existed to remove the remaining subsidies (e.g. on electricity prices, which were due to rise from 90% to 100% of supply cost by the end of 1996).

THE NATIONAL BUDGET

The price increases and the new sales tax introduced in April–May 1991 (see above) were incorporated in the Government's budget for fiscal year 1991/92 (beginning 1 July), which provided for a gross deficit equivalent to 9.3% of GDP. In the event, the deficit was trimmed to 7.1% of GDP, compared with 17% of GDP in 1990/91. Budgeted expenditure in 1991/92 showed a notional increase of more than one-third compared with the previous year, but much of this rise reflected a 38% depreciation of the Egyptian pound since the move to market-determined exchange rates in February 1991 (a rate of US $1 = £E3.24 being used for the budget). The 1992/93 budget provided for total expenditure of £E62,533m. and total revenue of £E53,389m., the resulting deficit of £E9,144m. representing under 5% of GDP. This was to be achieved by measures affecting both revenue and expenditure sections of the budget, although ministers promised there would be no tax or customs increases. Calculated at an exchange rate of $1 = £E3.33 (virtually unchanged from 1992/93), the 1993/94 budget provided for expenditure totalling £E65,313m. and revenue totalling £E56,330m., leaving a gross deficit of £E8,983m. (3.5% of GDP). After financing, there remained a net deficit (to be covered by treasury bills) of £E1,338m., compared with £E2,298m. in 1992/93. Categories of expenditure in 1993/94 included public sector wages (£E11,300m.), defence (£E5,417m.), foreign debt servicing (£E4,850m.) and subsidies (£E3,600m.). Sources of budgeted revenue included general taxes (£E14,937m.), sales tax (£E8,000m.) and customs duties (£E6,070m.). By mid-1993 the annual inflation rate was around 9%, compared with an annual average of 11.8% in the decade to 1990 and a recent peak of over 20% in 1991. The Government's stated economic growth target for 1993/94 was 4%.

The 1994/95 budget (calculated at an exchange rate of $1 = £E3.38) provided for an 8.4% increase in total expenditure to £E70,790m. (broadly in line with the rate of inflation), coupled with a 4.3% reduction in the gross deficit (to £E8,600m.) and a 63.5% reduction (to £E488m.) in the net budget deficit after financing. The Government's target for GDP growth in 1994/95 was 4.3%. Real GDP growth in 1993/94 was provisionally estimated as 2%, compared with 0.5% growth in 1992/93. As at February 1994, the year-on-year rise in consumer prices was 7.3%, while the average inflation rate over the previous 12 months was 11.3%.

AGRICULTURE

Egyptian agriculture is dominated by the river Nile and the necessity for irrigation. The main summer crops are cotton, rice, maize and sorghum, and in winter the chief crops are wheat, beans, berseem (Egyptian clover, used for animal feed) and vegetables. While there is self-sufficiency in fruit and vegetables (some of which are exported to the EC), it is with the basic grains that shortages are encountered. During the 1970s agriculture's contribution to GDP remained fairly constant at just less than 30%, but fell steadily in the 1980s, to reach 17% by 1990. In 1978 the agricultural sector accounted for approximately 60% of total export earnings, but by 1979 this had fallen to 50%, and by 1990 to around 10%. During the 1970s the increase in agricultural production was clearly outstripped by population growth, and this reflected a diminishing emphasis on agriculture in government plans. Between 1970 and 1976 food imports, in terms of weight, increased by over two and a half times, and exports of rice declined to one-third of their former weight. Agricultural production averaged an annual increase of 2.6% in 1980–88 and this has meant a continued dependence on substantial imports of foodstuffs. From a position of self-sufficiency in food during the early 1970s, Egypt now has to import more than one-half of its food. The difficulties in the agricultural sector are well illustrated by the riots against the increases in the prices of basic foodstuffs in Kafr ed-Dawar in September 1984, and by the heavy subsidies on bread and flour. Although the riots were not as serious as those in Cairo in January 1977, they emphasized the critical problem which the Government faced in attempting to reduce basic subsidies (see 'Economic Policy and Planning', above).

The increase in the rate of wheat consumption exemplifies the problems faced by the agricultural sector. The annual consumption of wheat by Egyptians rose from 80 kg per head in 1960, to 197 kg in 1970 and 300 kg in 1986/87, making Egyptians the world's biggest consumers of wheat per head of population. National consumption rates are also amongst the highest in the world: Egypt consumed 8,850,000 tons of wheat in 1986/87, compared with 4,154,000 tons in 1970, an annual rate of increase of 7%. On several occasions during the 1980s Egypt bought wheat and wheat flour from the USA on preferential terms, although it also buys subsidized grain from the EC. Other grain suppliers have included Australia and Canada. Egyptian wheat production totalled 4.62m. tons in 1992 (the third successive record harvest), and was forecast to approach 5m. tons in 1993. The total wheat import requirement in 1992 was 5.9m. tons while the forecast requirement for 1993 was 5.5m. tons. In 1994 the Egyptian wheat harvest was expected to reach 5.2m. tons (another record), sufficient to cover just over half of consumption.

The overall value of Egyptian farm output was estimated by the US Department of Agriculture to amount to $9,526m. in 1992, of which $6,309m. was contributed by crops, and the balance of livestock. The 1992 total represented an annual increase of 4%, compared with a 2.2% increase in 1991 and a 7.2% increase in 1990. Strong growth in crop production from 1990 onwards was attributed to changes in producer price policy, greater use of multiple cropping and a shift in land use from berseem to vegetables, while the relative stagnation of livestock output over the same period was linked to problems in phasing in new supply and pricing arrangements for animal feedstuffs.

The arable area is 7m. feddans, about 4% of the total land area, and not much more than one-third of this is serviced by main and secondary drains. This deficiency is significant because an unforeseen effect of the High Dam (see below) has been to make the water-table rise (because of more abundant water and more intensive cropping) and lead to widespread waterlogging and high soil salinity. Insufficient attention to drainage has therefore been a serious problem with agricultural planning.

The extension of the cultivable area through reclamation has been slow, difficult and costly, but remains at the forefront of government policy. The increasing pressure of people on the land has led to an intensification of cultivation almost without parallel anywhere. Dams, barrages, pumps and an intricate network of canals and drains bring perennial irrigation to almost the whole area. The strict pursuit of crop rotation, lavish use of commercial fertilizer and pesticides, and the patient application of manual labour not only make multiple cropping possible, but also raise land yields to high levels. Despite the difficulties concerning reclamation, early in 1981 the Government announced plans to reclaim 1.2m. ha of land at a rate of 63,000 ha per year over the next 20 years. The largest planned development was at West Nuberiya near Alexandria where, in the first phase, 10,100 ha of land were to be irrigated and drained. A second major agricultural reclamation project has been in progress in the northern Tahrir region; a third project was intended for the region south of Port Said, and further long-term plans included the New Valley project from Aswan to the Qattara depression. While these developments look promising on paper, there is nevertheless much scepticism over official figures relating to the amount of land which has so far been reclaimed. Moreover, the reclamation programme is counterbalanced by the fact that about 20,000 ha of agricultural land are being lost every year owing to urban growth and the depredations of the red clay brick manufacturing industry, which pays farmers large sums for the rich, red topsoil from their fields, which it uses as raw material. A ban on the manufacture of red bricks was introduced in August 1985. In June 1989 the Government announced plans, within the framework of the socio-economic development plan for 1989/90, to reclaim a further 175,000 feddans of land for agriculture. A record cereal harvest in 1991 was officially attributed, in part, to the reclamation of some 125,000 feddans of land in Sinai and the Alexandria region.

The bulk of agricultural production from reclamation is intended for the market place and not for subsistence. Nearly three-quarters of agricultural income comes from field crops, the remainder deriving from fruit, vegetables, livestock and dairy products.

Long-staple cotton is the most important field crop but the area under cultivation has declined since the late 1960s. Egypt produces about one-third of the world crop of long-staple cotton (1.125 in and longer) and is the world's largest exporter of the premium grades that have been least affected by competition from man-made fibres. Cotton provides 15% of all agricultural employment and helps to support a substantial textile industry. Many factors combine to give the high yields and excellent quality of Egyptian cotton. Among these are climatic, soil and labour conditions, and a long experience of careful planting, watering and picking. Government assistance and supervision have always been important. Fertilizers and pesticides are distributed through the government-sponsored agricultural credit banks and agricultural co-operatives. However, investment in cotton has been inadequate to develop the full potential of the industry. Plans were announced at the beginning of 1993 to liberalize Egypt's internal trade in cotton and to end the public-sector monopoly of cotton exports which had been in force for over 30 years. Forming part of a deregulation programme agreed with the World Bank, the cotton industry reforms were designed to improve the crop's financial appeal to farmers and to encourage wider use of high-yield cultivation techniques. Total production in 1992 amounted to 348,000 tons. During recent years the Egyptian textile industry has absorbed about 80% of the country's cotton crop, and the volumes available for export have often fallen some way short of the prevailing levels of world demand.

Production of cotton in the 1993/94 marketing season (ending in August) was expected to be more than 25% higher than in the previous year, while the volume of cotton contracted for export was by early May 1994 over five times higher than the export volume for the entire 1992/93 season. The relevant export contracts—accounting for almost one-third of the season's forecast production—were worth an estimated £E700m. Draft legislation was introduced in mid-1994 to revive the Alexandria Cotton Exchange, which had been closed down in 1961.

Rice is another important crop and is now, after cotton, almost as important as fruit in the agricultural sector as a foreign currency earner. Production of rice in 1992 was a record 3.91m. tons, compared with the wheat harvest of 4.62m. tons and a maize harvest of 4.5m. tons. The total area planted with cereals in 1992 was approximately 3m. feddans. Rice output in 1993 amounted to 4m. tons, compared with local consumption of 2.2m. tons. Rice exporters were among the main beneficiaries of a lifting of export licensing regulations for farm produce in late 1993.

Another high yielding crop is sugar cane. In 1992 the state-owned sugar refining company (which currently supplies two-thirds of Egypt's annual consumption of 1.5m. tons) was 90% reliant on cane as a raw material, the balance of its input being beet and corn. Although the company's plans for the future expansion of sugar production were mainly based on beet rather than cane, it was also planning to add new value to its cane-based operations by developing a plant to manufacture newsprint from *bagasse* (cane waste). Production of sugar

cane was expected to reach 1.15m. tons in 1993. Other crops include lucerne (alfalfa), a nitrogen-fixing fodder, beans, potatoes and onion and garlic. A pilot project to produce palm oil in the Western Desert (currently imported from Malaysia and Indonesia) began in 1993.

The many kinds of fruit, vegetables and horticultural products grown are capable of some expansion and are increasingly important as exports. Particular efforts are being made to promote the production of these items, especially citrus fruit, and special areas are being allocated along the Mediterranean coast for their cultivation. Output of fruit totalled 3.5m. tons (including a record 2.2m. tons of citrus) in 1992, while tomato production totalled 4.3m. tons and other vegetable production 4.45m. tons. There was particularly rapid growth in production of high-value items for which there was strong export demand, such as peaches (over 35,000 tons) and strawberries (around 50,000 tons).

Recent attention has been given to animal husbandry in an attempt to raise dairy and meat production, but there has so far been little increase in either number of livestock or productivity. Egypt is a net importer of meats to supplement its own output of around 800,000 tons per year. Increases in animal feed prices to world levels were partly responsible for some well-publicized problems in 1992/93, including a fall in poultry production to as little as 55% of capacity as the industry adjusted to a new cost structure.

In May 1988 measures were announced to conserve water supplies owing to the fall in the level of the Nile. These included a reduction in the area planted with rice to 900,000 feddans; a moratorium on the allocation of land for the cultivation of sugar cane; and a ban on the extension of the area planted to crops requiring large amounts of water. Major irrigation and drainage projects in preparation in 1992 included the 'Suez Siphon', which was intended to convey Nile water under the Suez Canal into the Sinai desert, and a scheme to update the drainage of about 720,000 feddans of existing cultivated land (about 10% of the country's total cultivable area). The Siphon project, which was expected to be completed in late 1996, involved the construction of a system whereby water (mostly recycled from agricultural drainage) would be pumped into North Sinai at a rate of 160 cu m per second over a distance of 150 km.

AGRARIAN REFORM

Immediately after the Egyptian Revolution of 1952 an experiment in land reform was started. This was among the more successful of such attempts, though only the very large estates were dismembered while medium-sized estates remained untouched. Among other measures, a limit of 200 feddans was imposed on individual ownership of land. This limit was lowered to 100 feddans in 1961 and again to 50 feddans in 1969. The primary aim of this reform was the destruction of the feudal power of the old politicians, an aim which was easily realized. In 1952, 5.7% of all landowners held 64.6% of the total area, but only a quarter of the country's cultivable land (i.e. some 1.25m. feddans of a total of about 5m. feddans) was in plots of over 100 acres each. By 1961, however, this area had dwindled to about 1m. feddans, nearly all of which had been appropriated by the Ministry of Agrarian Reform and redistributed to landless peasants. The 1969 land reform affected a further 1.13m. feddans owned by 16,000 landowners.

Other measures of agrarian reform included rent control; the regulation of land tenure; consolidation of fragmented holdings for production purposes; and the drive to build co-operatives. In 1986 there were 5,150 agricultural co-operatives (compared with 1,727 in 1952 and 5,384 in 1984). However, in the process of dispossessing the large landowners and promoting co-operatives, the authorities unwittingly helped to eliminate many highly efficient medium-sized farmers. On balance, however, the redistribution of land was accompanied by improved land productivity and not the reverse.

By 1984 only 13.9% of the total cultivated area was held by owners with 50 feddans or more. However, since land reform affected only about one-sixth of the total land, the main structure of land-ownership remained unaffected; in 1984, 4.7% of the owners (i.e. those with more than 5 feddans) still held 47% of the land while 95.3% of the owners shared the remaining 53%. The fundamental land tenure problem is not so much one of distribution but of an overall scarcity.

Given the land shortage, special attention has naturally been paid to increasing the arable area. In view of the fact that the land to be reclaimed is often arid desert, reclamation is a costly process requiring substantial capital outlays, and the question has to be asked whether new investment should not be directed to the development of manufacturing industry instead, where returns to the scarce capital may well be higher. Between 1952 and 1976, 912,000 feddans were reported to have been reclaimed, 536,000 feddans being reclaimed during the 1960–65 Plan period. By 1985/86, 1,221,500 feddans were stated to have been reclaimed (though only one-half of this land is actually in production), and 1,072,000 feddans to have been redistributed to 440,000 families as a result of agrarian reform measures. Under the Five-Year Plan for 1982–87, only 325,000 feddans were reclaimed, compared with a target of 636,000 feddans. The 1987–92 Plan envisaged reclamation at a rate of not less than 150,000 feddans per year, which was considered unrealistic by most observers, given the water shortage caused by the fall in the level of the Nile to 1988. In 1986 President Mubarak, reviewing the situation, stated that since 1909 Egypt's agricultural land had increased by only 1m. feddans. At the same time, however, some attention should be paid to the high annual loss of arable land due to the expansion of towns and villages, which is currently about 20,000 feddans a year. Land is also being lost through increasing soil salinity, resulting from poor drainage.

In November 1993 the Government rescheduled some £E200m. of debts owed to agricultural credit institutions as part of an initiative to deal with growing arrears in the farm sector. In March 1994 the World Bank approved $121m. of financing (including $67m. in International Development Association credits) for a $269m. project designed to provide 250,000 farming families with improved access to agricultural credit facilities.

THE HIGH DAM

The decision to invest more than £E400m. in the Aswan High Dam project (including Russian credits of £E194m.) was taken with an eye also on the development of cheap hydroelectric energy for industry. The project was started in January 1960, completed in July 1970, and officially inaugurated in January 1971, with a generating capacity of 10,000m. kWh, compared with the 6,012m. kWh produced in all Egypt in 1967. By 1974 revenue from the dam had exceeded the cost of its construction. Transmission lines carry the current from the dam site to Cairo and further north, and a scheme aimed at the complete electrification of Egypt's villages is in progress. The Aswan II hydroelectric power station started up in early 1986, adding 270 MW of capacity to the national grid. In August 1991 a $140m.-contract was signed with a west European consortium for the renovation of the High Dam's older generating turbines and related installations.

The dam's primary purpose was to store the annual Nile flood which reaches its peak in August, allowing yearly control of the downstream flow, and, therefore, the possibility of perrenial irrigation and further land reclamation. Between 1964 and 1978 Lake Nasser (maximum capacity 169,000m. cu m) behind the dam, and the largest man-made lake in the world, gradually filled and ensured that Egypt did not suffer the worst effects of the drought experienced in much of northeast Africa. Under the terms of an agreement signed with Sudan in 1959, Egypt is allocated 55,500m. cu m of Nile water a year out of an estimated 84,000m. cu m annual average flow as measured at Aswan. Sudan receives 18,500m. cu m and the remainder is calculated to be the annual evaporation loss from Lake Nasser. By June 1988, more than 10 years of drought at the source of the Blue Nile in Ethiopia (which provides approximately 70% of the flow at Aswan), had reduced the water level in Lake Nasser to 153 m, just above the 150 m point at which the High Dam's hydroelectricity turbines would be affected, drastically reducing their generating capacity, and approaching the 147 m level at which they would have to be shut down completely. However, an exceptionally high flood after torrential rainfall on the Ethiopian plateau in

August 1988 raised the water beyond the danger level. In September 1990 the water level in Lake Nasser was 167 m and live storage was calculated to be 83,700m. cu m. In October 1993, following inflows from an above-average flood, the water level reached 174 m, while storage behind the dam amounted to 116,110m. cu m of water. The 500 km-long Lake Nasser is expected to become a major fisheries resource, the development of which would replace the sardine catch in the Mediterranean, lost as a result of the building of the dam.

When construction of the dam was agreed in 1958, a target of 1.2m. feddans was set for desert reclamation. However, costs have far outweighed returns and it has taken on average about 10 years to raise any reclaimed area up to even marginal levels of production. Reclamation has started on some 900,000 feddans, but each year over the last 15 years or so the Government has had to cover a deficit of around £E10m. on operations in reclaimed areas. In 1972 the Government stopped all new desert reclamation projects. However, the country's very limited options in the face of acute pressure of population on the land have brought the idea of reclamation back into the government plans (see 'Agrarian Reform', above).

THE SUEZ CANAL

After the October 1973 war, the most pressing need was to restore and reopen the Suez Canal and, at Sadat's initiative, the Canal was reopened on 5 June 1975, the eighth anniversary of the outbreak of war which led to its closure in 1967. Expansion was made even more urgent because of the vast increase in oil-tanker sizes after June 1967 which the closure of the Canal helped to provoke. The Canal Authority set the dues for ships using the Canal 90%–100% higher than in 1967, and revenue in the first year of operation was $230m. In December 1980 the first phase of work to widen and deepen the southern end of the Canal was completed at an estimated cost of $1,275m. Income reached $888m. in 1981, compared with $676m. in 1980. In 1982 Suez Canal revenue was reported to have reached $1,000m. for the first time, with $956m. being derived from transit tolls and $44m. coming from services to ships in transit. Earnings from Suez Canal tolls were reported to have been $974m. in fiscal 1983/84 (July–June) (other services raised the overall revenue to more than $1,000m.) but fell to $897m. in 1984/85. Despite an increase in transit rates in January 1984, revenue in 1984 totalled only $960m., $100m. less than had been projected, owing to reduced tanker traffic and the planting of mines in the Red Sea approaches to the Canal, which deterred shipping from using it in the summer of 1984. Transit rates were raised by an average of 5% in 1985 and 3.4% in 1986. In 1986 revenue totalled $1,107m., compared with $929m. in 1985. Transit rates were raised again on 1 January 1987, by 7.4% for the first 5,000 tons and by 3.8% for the next 15,000 tons and during the year total revenue from tolls and other services was a record $1,222m. (for fiscal 1988/89 the total was $1,340m., compared with $1,289m. in 1987/88). The chairman of the Suez Canal Authority attributed the increase to the Authority's success in attracting large oil tankers and container vessels by offering them a 17% reduction in transit fees. A $400m.-development scheme, which was nearing completion in mid-1993, was designed to allow passage of vessels of 56 ft draught, or up to 170,000 deadweight tons (dwt), compared with 130,000 dwt previously. A further scheme to deepen the canal to 72 ft (to accommodate vessels of up to 300,000 dwt) remained in abeyance in 1993 after feasibility studies had shown it to be uneconomic at current levels of world trade.

Reconstruction of the canal cities, some of them up to 80% destroyed, was also put in hand and by 1979 more than 1m. Egyptians had returned to Port Said, Ismailia and Suez. In November 1979 construction of the Salem canal, to take water from the East Nile to Sinai, was started and in October 1980 the 1.64-km Ahmad Hamdi tunnel was opened, thus providing the first road link under the Suez Canal.

Transit rates were increased by an average of 5% from 1 January 1990. Despite initial forecasts that the Gulf crisis of 1990/91 would adversely affect the Canal, revenue in 1990/91 increased by 14% compared with 1989/90, to reach $1,664m. From 1 January 1991 transit tolls were increased by 6% (4% for dry bulk carriers), while an average 3% increase in 1992 was below the rate of inflation of the Suez Canal Authority's operating costs. A carefully structured programme of selective discounts—e.g. for southbound tankers in ballast—kept the Canal keenly competitive with rival shipping routes in the first half of 1993, when a total of 8,670 ships generated revenue totalling $981m., compared with the January–June 1992 figures of 8,353 ships generating revenue of $927m. The Suez Canal Authority's 1994 tariff schedule incorporated average toll increases of about 4%, coupled with further refinements of the structure of selective discounts. In addition to the commercially determined discounts for different categories of cargo vessel, a 35% discount was introduced for passenger cruise ships in support of the Government's campaign to bolster the tourism industry.

MANUFACTURING INDUSTRY

During the 1970s manufacturing industry suffered from a lack of foreign exchange, and some excess capacity resulting from shortages of spare parts and raw materials. Food processing and textiles have traditionally dominated the industrial sector, contributing 55%–60% of the total value of industrial output in the mid-1970s. With the growing importance of oil, though, this situation has changed. Provisional employment data for 1989 indicated a work-force of 2,002,000 in manufacturing and mining, 990,200 in construction, and 99,900 in electricity, gas and water, totalling 21% of employed labour. In 1990 the manufacturing sector accounted for 16% of GDP, while industry as a whole accounted for 45% of GDP (compared with 27% in 1965).

The manufacturing sector has suffered from considerable inefficiency. A World Bank report, published in 1987, pointed out that returns on investment were low and that, despite considerable investment, the industrial sector was neither diversified nor efficient, and, therefore, was unable to compete in the international market-place. Among the problems identified by the report were overstaffing and excessive government protection from foreign competition. The Egyptian authorities have admitted that productivity is low, as is plant utilization (only 30% of capacity in some cases), but have blamed the international recession and the lack of foreign exchange, in addition to problems of poor incentives and low salary levels among the work-force. In addition, private sector investment has been attracted to service industries rather than manufacturing industry. Nevertheless, private firms were responsible for about 50% of Egypt's $2,000m.-worth of manufactured exports in 1992.

In the manufacturing industry textiles, having once accounted for about one-third of total output, contributed only 16% in 1989. However, exports of textile fibres and products contributed about 27% of total export revenue in 1990, compared with 26% in 1984. The Government has embarked on a three-stage rehabilitation of the cotton-ginning industry costing $40.4m. and assisted by an $18.5m. loan from the IDA. The Arab Fund for Economic and Social Development (AFESD) was to lend Egypt $40m. to finance a spinning and weaving project at Kafr ed-Dawar and Bayda. Recent developments in the food processing industry have included a major expansion of sugar refining, undertaken to reduce an import requirement of 600,000 tons per year, costing an estimated $60m. Annual consumption per head has more than doubled since the mid-1960s to 28 kg.

Within heavy industry the development of projects established in the 1970s has continued. The Egyptian Iron and Steel Company complex at Helwan, developed around a Soviet-built plant first opened in 1973, was by late 1993 producing at its design capacity of 1.2m. tons per year for the first time, following a 10-year upgrading programme financed by the World Bank and Germany. The Alexandria Iron and Steel Company complex at Dikheila—a Japanese-built plant, in production since the end of 1986—produced 1.1m. tonnes of high-quality steel reinforcing bars and wire rods in 1993, when the company made a net profit of £E112m. on sales of £E1,300m. (including exports worth $70m.). Plans were announced in early 1994 for an expansion scheme to add 400,000 tons of additional production capacity at Dikheila, one element in the proposed financial arrangements for the scheme being a fresh

injection of private capital which would reduce the public-sector shareholding in the company from 87.4% to about 60%. New steel industry projects under consideration in 1994 included a special products mill with a capacity of 140,000 tons per year, to be built at Sadat City, north of Cairo. Egypt's total manufacturing capacity in steel products in 1994 was around 3m. tons, compared with a total annual demand of about 4m. tons which was expected to rise sharply in coming years. A long-term growth strategy for the industry was under discussion by public- and private-sector experts in mid-1994.

The Aluminium Company of Egypt, whose complex at Naga Hammadi opened in 1975 (having been developed to take advantage of power supplied from the Aswan High Dam), was in 1993 in the process of upgrading its annual production capacity from 180,000 tons to 250,000 tons with no extra power use. Earlier development work had already brought the plant's operating efficiency into line with international norms. A contract to build a new rolling mill at the site was signed by a French company in 1991.

Egypt's cement industry underwent rapid expansion in the 1980s. Annual consumption of cement rose from 4.1m. tons in 1977 to about 16m. tons in 1986. Four cement works began production in 1985, adding 5.2m. tons per year and reaching an installed capacity of 7.7m. tons by 1987. Egypt produced 7.6m. tons of cement in 1985 but imported 9.1m. tons. The conversion of a Soviet-built cement works at Asyut created the largest production line in Africa, with a nominal output capacity of 5,000 tons per day. Under the 1987–92 Five-Year Plan, five new works were to be built, adding 5m. tons to Egypt's annual capacity, and steps have also been taken to expand output at existing plants. By the early 1990s local supply had been brought more closely into balance with demand, and, in mid-1993, an announcement of plans to triple the capacity of a Suez cement plant was coupled with plans to export part of the additional output.

Partly due to surprisingly buoyant foreign exchange earnings in the early 1980s and the freer availability of raw materials, there were signs that the construction industry was beginning to expand rapidly. Indeed, housing dominated construction during the 1982–87 Plan, with investment set at £E4,600m., 13.3% of the total. The private sector had been expected to provide 94% of investment in housing construction, itself 54% of total projected private-sector investment under the Plan. The housing programme constituted only about 25% of all construction activity, which has been dominated by the building of public utilities (mainly water and sewerage projects). The Plan provided for £E2,900m. to be invested in public utilities' construction but the projects involved, such as the Greater Cairo sewerage and the Alexandria waste-water schemes, are so vast that they are being funded outside the Plan and their duration will extend far beyond the Plan period.

Evidence of increased foreign investment in Egyptian industry was provided by the World Bank's loan of $69m. towards the $109.3m. cost of the National Weaving and Spinning Company's building programme at Alexandria, the Japanese interest in the ed-Dikheila steel plant, and the World Bank's $50m. loan towards the cost of expanding the National Paper Company.

Within the field of the motor industry, Egypt has been assembling and manufacturing parts of Italian Fiat passenger cars since the early 1960s. The El-Nasr Automotive Manufacturing Co (NASCO) produces these cars at a rate of 12,000 per year, as well as buses, trucks and other vehicles. General Motors Egypt (GME, owned 31% by General Motors of the USA, 20% by Isuzu of Japan and 49% by private Egyptian and Saudi investors), was established in 1985 to build light commercial vehicles at 6 October City, south-west of Cairo. By 1993 GME was producing 10,000 such vehicles per year, 10% of which were exported to Syria, Jordan and the Gulf region, and was due to start assembling a passenger car (the Opel Vectra) later in the year. Other companies were meanwhile developing local assembly plants for various other makes of car, including Hyundai, Suzuki, Peugeot and Citroen, while Daimler-Benz was studying the feasibility of setting up a truck factory in Egypt.

In 1994 GME's output of Opel Vectras was running at the rate of 1,000 a month, while Suzuki Egypt (51% owned by the local Suzuki dealer) was producing Suzuki Swifts at the rate of about 850 per month and Centre for Trade and Development (51% owned by Peugeot) was producing about 100 Peugeot 405s per month. Production of Hyundai Excels (licensed to the locally-owned bus and coach assembler, Ghabbour Brothers) was due to start in the last quarter of 1994 at an annual rate of 17,000 cars, some of them for export to neighbouring countries. Production of Citroen cars and vans (licensed to the locally-owned JAC Car Makers) was due to start at the end of 1994 at an initial annual rate of 4,000 AX models, to be increased to 24,000 vehicles (including other models) at the end of 1995. The local assembly of Nissan cars and vans was scheduled to begin at the end of 1995 at an annual rate of 10,000 vehicles. A plant to manufacture Pirelli radial tyres under licence was due to open in Alexandria at the end of 1994 with a workforce of 800 and a capacity of 350,000 tyres per year.

Early in 1983 the Egyptian Chief of Staff stated that Egypt was interested in the joint manufacture of weapons with other countries, and in November 1987 Egypt began to press its former partners in the Arab Organization for Industrialization (AOI) (Saudi Arabia, Qatar and the UAE) to revive their involvement in a regional Arab defence industry. The AOI was funded in 1974 to provide an Arab challenge to Israel's advanced defence industry but Egypt's three co-founders withdrew from the organization in 1979, after Egypt signed a peace treaty with Israel. The armaments industry is being seen in Egypt as a possible source of revenue to offset the decline in receipts from the traditional revenue earners, and the decision of its former partners to re-establish diplomatic relations with Egypt after the Arab League summit meeting in Amman, in November 1987, gave rise to hopes that new Arab investment in the AOI might be forthcoming. Sales of armaments earned a reported $1,000m. in 1982, when Iraq, at a critical stage in its war with Iran, turned to Egypt for spare parts and ammunition for its mainly Soviet-built equipment, and bought battle tanks from Egypt's strategic reserves. Egypt has acquired licences to rebuild and modify old Soviet tanks and its most ambitious project involves the assembly, under licence, of the US General Dynamics Land System's M1A1 Abrams battle tank. Some 75 of the latter had been produced by the beginning of 1994, when production was proceeding at the rate of 10 tanks per month towards a cumulative target of 540 tanks (all intended for use by the Egyptian armed forces).

According to a report by the General Organization for Industrialization, private investment in new industrial ventures totalled £E1,889m. in 1993, creating 30,000 new jobs in 799 projects.

The needs of heavy industry, and the plan to extend electric power to all Egypt's rural communities underlined the need for more power generation than that supplied by the Aswan High Dam. The dam represented some 2,000 MW of total installed capacity of 3,700 MW at the start of the 1982–87 Five-Year Plan. The Plan provided for the expansion of installed capacity by 3,430 MW, of which 270 MW was to be obtained through the Aswan II scheme, and the remainder from thermal power stations and eight nuclear plants, which were to be completed by 2005, at a cost of $36,000m. Total net installed capacity rose to 5,850 MW in 1985. However, the nuclear programme came under government reappraisal in the aftermath of the disaster at the Chernobyl plant in the USSR in April 1986, and the collapse of oil prices; while some of the thermal units, which were intended to be oil- and gas-fired, were redesigned to burn coal from Australia instead. It was proposed that a 2,600-MW plant, costing $1,800m. to construct, and ultimately using 15m. tons of Australian coal per year, would be built at Zaafarana on the Gulf of Suez during the 1987–92 Five-Year Plan, with an associated port, capable of handling 7m.–8m. tons of coal per year initially, rising to 12m.–15m. tons. Annual consumption of electricity was given at 34,000m. kWh in 1985—a figure that was expected to increase threefold by the end of the century. Hence, plans to implement the Qattara Depression scheme to generate energy by flooding the depression with waters from the Mediter-

ranean were given the final go-ahead late in 1980, at an estimated cost of at least $2,600m. In August 1980 the USA agreed to a $102m. loan to modernize the electricity grid, and plans for the implementation of complete rural electrification are in an advanced stage. In May 1985 USAID also agreed to provide $55m. of an estimated $156m. required for the fourth 315-MW power unit at Shoubra el-Kheima power station in Cairo. The station, whose first three units, costing $604m., became operational in early 1986, provides up to 75% of Cairo's electricity. The fourth unit was completed in the late 1980s, bringing total capacity to more than 1,000 MW. Since 1981, Egypt's total installed capacity has increased by 7,000 MW to reach 10,938 MW in 1991. It is planned to add a further 6,000 MW by 2000, including the commissioning of a 400 MW combined cycle plant at Damietta, east of Alexandria, and the rehabilitation of an old Soviet plant at Suez which will boost capacity by 185 MW. Annual output of electricity was estimated to have reached 75,000m. kWh in 1992. Power supplies were priced at about 90% of cost in mid-1994, a level of subsidy which the Government was pledged to eliminate by the end of 1996 as part of its economic reform programme. A further aim of the sector is to reduce oil consumption. In 1990 the sector accounted for 8.3m. tons of oil, equivalent to 16% of total production. Where possible, power stations were being converted to use natural gas in the early 1990s, the Government's target being to increase the contribution of gas to thermal power generation from 60% in 1992 to 80% by 1997 (thus minimizing domestic use of oil that could be used to generate valuable export revenue). Plans were being drawn up in 1993 to link the Egyptian and Jordanian electricity grids as part of a regional inter-connection project to be financed by the Arab Fund for Economic and Social Development.

In June 1981 the USA signed an agreement for nuclear co-operation with Egypt, which was to lead to the construction of two nuclear power stations. More recently, Egypt turned to France for additional assistance with its nuclear projects, and also to Italy, with whom a nuclear co-operation agreement was signed in March 1984. A Franco-Italian consortium was to build Egypt's first nuclear plant at ed-Dabaa, 160 km west of Alexandria but the French withdrew in early 1987, owing to export-credit problems. The Government initially planned to build eight nuclear power units at a cost of $36,000m., with a total capacity of 8,000 MW, to meet 40% of Egypt's energy needs by the year 2005, buying uranium from Niger. However, in April 1986, the Government announced that only three nuclear power units would be built up to the year 2005, the first of which, at el-Dabaa, was under review in early 1991. At the beginning of 1988 the USSR offered to build five nuclear power stations in Egypt. A plant for the production of nuclear fuel, using advanced technology, is to be established in co-operation with the Federal Republic of Germany's nuclear research centre under the agreement between the two countries on mutual assistance in the peaceful use of nuclear energy.

To guard against severe power shortages arising from low water levels at the Aswan High Dam (see above), the Government announced, in January 1988, that 20 thermal power plants, with a combined capacity of 5,500 MW, would be built by the end of 1992. Four 300-MW plants were to be built at Abu Qir (No. 5), Asyut, Suez (No. 4) and Damanhour; a 270-MW hydroelectric plant is under construction at Esmat, on the upper Nile; and a gas-fired plant, with a capacity of 700 MW, was planned for Damietta. It was subsequently announced that four plants, at Ayoun Mousa, Zaafarana, Sidi Krer and Kurimat, each of 1,200 MW generating capacity and originally designed to be coal-fired, would be oil- and gas-fired. In May 1989 the USSR granted Egypt a 'soft' loan (repayable over 12 years) for the construction of a 600-MW power station in the Sinai desert. In February 1991 it was confirmed that USAID funds of $200m. would be allocated to the Kurimat project, the total cost of which was estimated at $1,000m., and an initial consultancy contract was signed with a US firm, Ebasco Overseas, in October 1991.

Major urban redevelopment schemes are also under way. The first stage of an urban mass-transit railway system was completed in Cairo in August 1987 by a French consortium (see 'Transport and Tourism'). At the end of 1982 the first contract, worth $55m., was awarded for the Greater Cairo sewerage renewal scheme. The $3,000m. scheme involves the digging of a 10-mile tunnel which will connect Cairo's drains to the largest sewage-pumping station in the world in the northern suburb of al-Ameriya. Elsewhere, there are plans to build new towns to accommodate 5m. people by the year 2000 and relieve the pressures on existing urban centres of a rapidly increasing population, though even these provisions are in danger of becoming obsolete in the face of an ever accelerating birth rate. At the beginning of 1984 a 20-year Master Plan for Alexandria was announced. It envisaged growth of the city's population to 4.75m. by 2005. The urban development schemes which have so far been undertaken have not, however, been as successful as was anticipated. An example of this is the new town of 10 Ramadan, 30 km from Cairo, begun in 1978, which was estimated to have as few as 100,000 residents (a quarter of its intended residential population) by 1993. To provide for the large number of Egyptians returning from the Gulf in 1990–91, the Government announced the creation of eight project zones, some of them free zones for tariff purposes, designed to provide factory employment for displaced workers. By March 1994, the total population of new industrial cities around Cairo was officially given as 265,000, and plans were announced to encourage their further growth by providing incentives for workers to take up residence in them.

The Government's awareness that Egypt's urban slum areas were fertile breeding grounds for social unrest prompted a 1993/94 budget allocation of £E250m. to improve the housing conditions and basic amenities in such areas, the Government's eventual aim being to invest over £E3,000m. in a long-term development programme covering 404 districts in 10 provinces.

Egypt's mineral resources are now being reappraised. Iron ore has traditionally been mined from the Aswan area, but new and better quality reserves have recently been discovered in the Bahariya Oasis region. Phosphate production from mines at Isna, Hamrawein and Safaga exceeded 600,000 tons per annum in the 1980s, and exports reached around 300,000 tons in 1992/93. A new phosphate mine at Abu Tartur in the Western Desert was due to be brought into production at a rate of 2.2m. tons per year at the end of 1994, rising to twice that rate by 1996, when 600,000 tons of its output would be earmarked for export. Manganese is being mined in the Eastern Desert and Sinai, chromium is found in the Eastern Desert, and uranium has been discovered in Sinai. In 1985 a British company, Minex Minerals Egypt, was awarded concessions to prospect for gold in two areas at Barramiya and es-Sid. Bids for further concessions in the Eastern Desert were invited in 1987. There are extensive coal deposits in Sinai, including an estimated 21m. tons at Maghana, where a deep mine (disused since 1967), was due to reopen in 1994 on completion of redevelopment work to install an annual production capacity of 125,000 tons (to be expanded to 600,000 tons within five years).

PETROLEUM AND GAS

The development of Egypt's hydrocarbon sector has had a major impact on the economy, although petroleum production in Egypt remains relatively small by Middle Eastern standards. In 1974 petroleum exports accounted for only 4% of Egypt's export revenue, and it is only since 1976 that Egypt has become a petroleum surplus country. Production of crude petroleum at the end of 1980 averaged approximately 600,000 barrels per day (b/d), compared with 420,000 b/d in 1977, and continued to rise thereafter. Petroleum revenue rose to $3,431m. in 1981/82 (representing about 60% of total export earnings), compared with $960m. in 1979. In 1982/83 gross revenue from petroleum sales fell to $2,977m. It rose to $3,127m. in 1983/84 and to $3,340m. in 1984/85. Overall production averaged 785,000 b/d in 1983/84, rising to almost 900,000 b/d in 1985/86, compared with capacity of 1m. b/d. Of average daily output, about 50% is used locally and between 25%–30% is taken by foreign oil companies, which leaves only about one-quarter of output or less available for export. In 1986 the effect of the collapse in oil prices, coupled with Egypt's decision voluntarily to reduce production, was to limit

average output to about 770,000 b/d, while exports fell to a rate of only 150,000 b/d.

Domestic consumption of hydrocarbons, was, until 1984, rising at a rate of 12%–15% each year, while oil production was rising by only 7% annually. Subsidies on petroleum placed a considerable strain on the nation's finances: the estimated $3,600m. spent on them in 1983 kept oil products at less than one-fifth of their price on the world market. Substitution of natural gas for fuel oil helped to slow the rate of increase in domestic oil consumption during the latter part of the 1980s, while sharp reductions in price subsidies in 1991 helped to stabilize domestic hydrocarbon consumption at just under 27m. tons in both the 1990/91 and 1991/92 fiscal years. The most significant factors in explaining the great increases in oil production so far are the return by Israel of the Alma Oilfield, renamed the Sha'b Ali field, in the Gulf of Suez, in November 1979 and, in 1982, the Sinai oilfields (notably the Abu Rudeis area), and the increase in concessions and finds particularly in the Gulf of Suez and the Western Desert. At the beginning of 1993 Egypt's proven published oil reserves stood at 6,200m. barrels, sufficient to last for 16 and-a-half years at the 1992 level of production.

Egypt, not being a member of OPEC, is able to maintain a flexible pricing policy. In 1983 and 1984, by maintaining a higher price for its oil (as much as $28.50 per barrel for the premium Suez 33° API oil blend, which accounts for about 60% of all oil exports), Egypt's policy was consistent with its support for OPEC's programme to prevent a collapse in world oil prices. In February 1985, however, Egypt disassociated itself from OPEC's policies, steadily reducing the price of its oil, as demand remained slack. A decline in the value of the US dollar and a reduction in Iranian oil exports led to increases in all blends (including the 26° API Belayim blend and Ras Gharib, the heaviest Egyptian crude) during the last third of 1985. During 1986, however, the oil price, already weakened by the glut of oil on world markets, fell sharply after OPEC decided to increase production, in order to secure a 'fair' share of the reduced market. In order to remain competitive, Egypt was forced to cut production and make a series of reductions in the price of its oil. For the second half of July the Suez blend was valued at only $7.35 per barrel, compared with $11.30 in June and $26.70 in December 1985. Egypt's average output was cut by some 300,000 b/d in early 1986, and in April exports were reduced to about 50,000 b/d, compared with more than 250,000 b/d at the end of 1985. After OPEC decided in August 1986 to reintroduce a production 'ceiling', the price of petroleum on world markets began to increase again. Following several increases, the Suez and Ras Bahar blends were priced at $17.60 per barrel in the second half of January 1987. In February the price of Suez and Ras Bahar was reduced to $17.25 but there were no further alterations until July, when the prices rose to $17.75 per barrel. Egypt's production rose after August 1986, reaching 940,000 b/d in December, but it agreed to restrict its output to 870,000 b/d for the first half of 1987, in support of OPEC's new production and prices strategy. However, according to the Egyptian General Petroleum Corporation (EGPC), average output exceeded 900,000 b/d during this period, and reached 904,000 b/d in the year as a whole. By mid-July 1988, with the world market once more oversupplied with petroleum, the price of the Suez and Ras Bahar blends had been reduced to $12.75 per barrel. Net petroleum revenues, which totalled $2,630m. in 1985, declined to $704m. in 1986 and rose to $1,446m. in 1987, following an improvement in world oil prices; in the 1988/89 fiscal year they amounted to $1,451m., while in 1989/90 they rose to $1,651m. In 1990/91 oil exports totalled $2,539m. and oil imports $978m., making a surplus of $1,561m. In the calendar year 1992 Egypt's oil trade surplus totalled $1,253m., falling to $1,190m. in 1993 (when oil export earnings totalled $2,134m. and oil import costs totalled $944m.).

The plan for the hydrocarbon sector in 1982/83–86/87 envisaged an increase in oil and gas production by 85% from 34m. tons in 1981 to 63m. tons by 1987. However, these plans had to be revised owing to the crisis in the world oil market. Actual production totalled 48m. tons in 1985 (oil 44.3m. tons; gas 3.7m. tons), fell to 44.6m. tons in 1986 (oil 40.3m. tons; gas 4.3m. tons) but rose to 50m. tons in 1987 (oil 45.2m. tons;

gas 4.8m. tons). Production amounted to 49.6m. tons in 1988 and rose to 50.4m. tons in 1989, 50m. tons in 1990, 51.6m. tons in 1991 and 52m. tons in 1992 (oil 44.4m. tons; gas 7.6m. tons). Output in 1993 totalled 53.7m. tons (oil 45m. tons, gas 8.7m. tons). Average output of crude petroleum in the first half of 1990 was about 870,000 b/d, but in August the Government authorized an increase in production to more than 900,000 b/d, to take advantage of higher world oil prices arising from the Gulf crisis. This level of production was maintained in the first half of 1991, despite a fall in international oil prices, but fell back to 870,000 b/d in the third quarter. Following the decision by OPEC in July 1990 to set a new target price of $21 per barrel until the end of the year, Egypt announced that it would fix new prices for its own crude petroleum. At the time of this announcement, the price of Egypt's premium Suez blend was $12 per barrel. Following personnel changes at the EGPC, a more flexible oil pricing system was introduced from 1 October 1991, under which the premium Suez blend was priced against a basket of comparable crudes of other countries.

Egypt has made numerous oil concession and exploration agreements with foreign companies, among which Amoco of the USA was responsible for nearly 50% of all Egyptian crude output in the early 1990s. Exploration was greatly stimulated by the oil price rises of the early 1970s, leading to new oil finds in the Gulf of Suez, on the Red Sea coast and in the Eastern and Western Deserts. Western Desert oilfields contributed 6.5% of national output in 1987 (compared with more than 90% for the Gulf of Suez), when 41 of Egypt's oilfields were situated in the Gulf of Suez and 26 in the Western Desert. Twelve new finds were reported in the Gulf of Suez in 1980, leading to a doubling of Egypt's known oil reserves. These rates of discovery continued in 1981, when 12 main new oil discoveries, 10 of which were in the Gulf of Suez, were made.

Exploration continued in 1982, and early in 1983 four new major production sharing agreements were signed by the EGPC with Shell Winning, Getty Oil, Deminex, and a partnership of BP, Elf Aquitaine, Occidental Petroleum and IEOC. Expansion continued during 1984, with petroleum flowing ashore from the first of the Deminex Egyptian Oil Company's platforms in the Ras Fanar field, in the Gulf of Suez, in January. Further concessions were also signed with Deminex in the Zeit area; with Marathon, Aminoil and IEOC in the southern part of the Gulf of Suez; and with Shell Winning in the East Gamsa area of the Gulf of Suez and in the Qaraouan area of the Western Desert. The Zeit Bay oilfield came 'on stream' in 1984, with an initial output of 10,000 b/d, which had risen to 65,000 b/d by April 1985. The third oil field in the Gulf of Suez to begin production during 1984 was Ras al-Bihar, the largest field yet struck by EGPC. With an initial output of 12,000 b/d, it helped to push overall production up to the target of 1m. b/d in 1985. A consortium of Western oil companies, including Total-CFP and BP, discovered oil in Egyptian waters off the coast of North Sinai in early 1986; an exploration well yielded 5,000 b/d–10,000 b/d. Texas International Inc and Conoco made two discoveries of oil in a 200,000-ha concession 325 km west of Alexandria in mid-1985, one of which is of commercial quality. More than 350 exploratory wells have been drilled in the Gulf of Suez, and some 40 fields discovered. During 1986, new discoveries were reported in the Western Desert by Khalda Petroleum (a joint venture of EGPC, Texas International and Conoco). New exploration agreements were signed with BP, Shell, Amoco and Agip in mid-1987 for concessions in the Gulf of Suez and the Sinai desert, reflecting more advantageous production sharing terms being offered by EGPC to encourage foreign participation. In September 1987 the EGPC announced that 78 oil deposits had been discovered since 1982, of which 41 were in production and 31 were to begin production during the next five years. According to the EGPC, a record 49 exploration agreements with foreign oil companies were approved by the Egyptian Government in 1989.

The results of exploration in the late 1980s were generally disappointing, especially in the Western desert, and a new round of invitations to bid for concessions, issued by the EGPC in 1990, elicited only a limited response. Partly as a result, BP announced in November 1991 that it would sell its 16.6% stake in the Suez Petroleum Company (SUCO), while other

Western companies scaled down their activities in Egypt. Nevertheless, several new oil and gas finds were announced in 1990/92, one by British Gas in December 1990, in its offshore North Zaafarana concession in the Gulf of Suez, being described as 'the most significant in the area for nearly a decade'. Other finds announced in early 1992 included strikes of both oil and gas in the Western Desert, the Gulf of Suez and the Nile delta, close to existing fields. According to government sources, there was known potential for the proving of a further 2,000m. barrels of oil reserves in Egypt, although it was conceded that they were in relatively small pockets which would be difficult to exploit.

In June 1989 Egypt was readmitted to OAPEC, and it has since sought to increase co-operation with Libya, Syria, Jordan, Oman, Yemen and the other Gulf States. Companies from Kuwait and the UAE have invested in exploration concessions in Egypt.

In 1993 the EGPC made strenuous efforts to revitalize oil exploration activity, concluding seven new agreements in February for blocks in the Western Desert and the Gulf of Suez; the companies involved included British Gas, Amoco, Mobil and Agip. Bids for a further five blocks (two of them in the Delta region) were being evaluated in mid-1993, while bidding for 15 more blocks (five of them in the Mediterranean region) was to close near the end of the year. Reported improvements in terms included increased block sizes, improved cost-recovery formulae and flexible withdrawal options. Production-sharing terms (which were negotiable on a case-by-case basis) reportedly envisaged a reduction in the EGPC's share of output to between 70% and 80%, compared with its entitlements of between 80% and 89% under existing production-sharing agreements.

Egypt's Minister of Petroleum and Mineral Wealth said that in order to attract exploration dollars it was essential to adopt a flexible negotiating stance in an environment of 'intense international competition'. In a further demonstration of its pragmatic approach to oil development, the Government agreed in 1993 to allow Agip's local affiliate to merge a total of 14 separate agreements, of widely differing terms and lengths, into one unified agreement with an extended expiry date, thereby improving the viability of the company's capital investment programme. (The Agip-affiliated International Egyptian Oil Company was Egypt's second largest oil producer and largest gas producer in 1992.)

A 320-km Suez-Mediterranean (Sumed) crude pipeline, operated by the Arab Petroleum Pipeline Co (owned 50% by Egypt and 50% by Saudi Arabia, Kuwait, Qatar and Abu Dhabi, mostly through state oil companies), opened in 1977 with a throughput capacity of 1.6m. b/d. An expansion of capacity to 2.3m. b/d was due to be completed in March 1994. Terminals at Ain Sukhna (near Suez) and Sidi Kerir (near Alexandria) can accommodate tankers otherwise too large to navigate the Suez Canal. Oil storage capacity at these terminals in 1993 totalled 2.4m. barrels, which many users considered to be insufficient to ensure efficient utilization of the forthcoming increase in the throughput capacity of the pipeline. Proposals to build as much as 4.5m. barrels of additional storage capacity were under consideration in mid-1993. As well as providing an oil transit service, the Sumed company does some trading on its own account (buying crude at the Red Sea terminal for resale at the Mediterranean terminal).

Egypt has oil refineries at Suez (two), Mosturud (near Cairo), Ameriya and Mex (near Alexandria), Tanta and Wadi Feran. Annual output of refined products averaged just under 25m. tons in the period 1990 to 1992. The main population centres are served by an extensive network of product pipelines. Downstream development initiatives for the mid-1990s are expected to include refinery modernization to bring the local industry's product mix more closely into line with the pattern of domestic demand (e.g. by adding the capability to produce diesel fuel, one of several categories of oil product that were still being imported in 1993).

Having brought its first natural gas field on-stream in 1974 at a rate of 3.5m. cubic metres per day (cu m/d), Egypt was producing around 6m. cu m/d by the early 1980s, when the country's proven gas reserves totalled around 85,000m. cu m. Substantial new discoveries in succeeding years helped to boost proven reserves to 400,000m. cu m by the end of 1992, during which year Egyptian gas output averaged 31.15m. cu m/d (having increased by nearly 25% since 1990 and by nearly 50% since 1987). Until the late 1980s gas pipelines were developed primarily to serve industrial plants (including the Helwan iron and steel complex). Thereafter, power stations became the largest consumers of Egyptian gas, most of the steep rise in gas consumption in the early 1990s being attributable to a national strategy to substitute gas for oil wherever possible.

Almost 40% of Egypt's gas output in 1992 came from the Abu Madi and El Qaraa fields in the Nile Delta (foreign participant Agip), while about 25% came from the Badr el-Din field in the Western Desert (foreign participant Shell). The most important new gas discovery of 1992 was made by Shell Egypt in the coastal region of the Western Desert, involving the Obaiyed field, which was expected to add between 40,000m. cu m and 250,000m. cu m to the country's proven reserves when fully appraised. Other companies with major Egyptian gas interests include Amoco and Phillips Petroleum. Having significantly improved its financial terms for gas development and production in 1988, the Government further enhanced the return to producing companies in 1993, when it raised its main reference price by 12.5%, bringing it roughly into line with European gas prices.

There are five main fertilizer plants using Egypt's hydrocarbon feedstocks: Talkha I in Lower Egypt, which began in 1976 and produces 380,000 tons per year of nitrogenous fertilizers; Talkha II, opened in 1979 and producing 396,000 tons per year of ammonia, which is then used for making urea (both plants use gas from the Abu Madi field); Suez, producing 250,000 tons per year of nitrogenous fertilizer, using gas from Abu Gharadeq; the plant at Dikheila, using Abu Qir gas, which has a capacity of 500,000 tons per year of urea and 100,000 tons per year of ammonium nitrate; and the Abu Qir fertilizer works, in Alexandria, which produces 450,000 tons per year of ammonia/urea. An extension to the Abu Qir plant, which is being built by a West German company, Uhde, will have a daily production capacity of 1,000 tons of ammonia, 1,800 tons of nitric acid, and 2,300 tons of ammonium nitrate. Plans were announced in 1993 to develop Egypt's first ethylene/polyethylene complex at Alexandria, using natural gas feedstock piped in from the Western Desert. The first phase of the project would entail the construction of an ethylene plant with an annual capacity of 150,000 tons.

BANKING

In late 1971, reorganization of the banking system resulted in the merger of three of the banks into others, with each of the rest being entrusted with specialized functions. The National Bank of Egypt was entrusted with foreign trade, the Bank of Port Said merged into Misr Bank which was to deal with home trade, including agricultural finance, the Industrial Bank merged into the Bank of Alexandria which was to deal with manufacturing, the Mortgage Credit Bank merged with the Crédit Foncier Egyptien and was to deal with construction and housing and the Bank of Cairo was left to deal with operations of the public sector. In 1975, in line with the liberalization of the banking system, these restrictions on sectoral operations of the major banks were removed. A new bank, the Nasser Social Bank, was created to deal with pensions and other forms of social security. The Egyptian International Bank for Foreign Trade and Development was also created in 1971 to promote foreign trade and attract foreign investment but was later transformed into the Arab International Bank for Foreign Trade and Development with Egypt, Libya and other Arab investors holding shares. These banks are additional to the Central Bank of Egypt, which was created from the issue department of the National Bank of Egypt in 1960, and the Public Organization for Agricultural Credit and Co-operatives, which the Crédit Agricole became in 1964.

Foreign banks are welcome in Egypt since it began liberalizing its economy in earnest in 1974, and about 50 of them now operate in the country. The biggest impact on the Egyptian banking system from foreign banks, however, has come from the joint ventures established with Egyptian banks. These include Misr International Bank, which partners Misr Bank with First National Bank of Chicago, Banco di Roma and UBAF Bank (London); Egyptian-American Bank, which pairs American Express and Bank of Alexandria; Cairo Barclays International Bank, a venture between Banque du Caire and Barclays Bank International; Misr-America International Bank, part-owned by Bank of America, the Kuwait Real Estate Bank and the First Arabian Corporation on the foreign partners' side, and by the Development Industrial Bank and Misr Insurance Company on the Egyptian side; and Banque du Caire et de Paris, a pairing of Banque Nationale de Paris and Banque du Caire. All these, with the exception of Cairo Barclays, were established as 51/49 ventures in favour of the Egyptian side. Cairo Barclays, being a 50/50 venture, was not permitted domestic banking activity under the banking regulations in force at the time of its establishment. Other developments include the opening in Cairo in July 1979 of the Faisal-Islamic bank, with 49% Saudi and Gulf equity participation. This was the first Egyptian bank to do business according to the Shari'a (Islamic Law). By 1987, however, the major public-sector banks (National Bank of Egypt, Banque Misr, Banque du Caire, and Bank of Alexandria) all had Islamic banking facilities. Some Islamic investment companies also appeared, although they encountered problems owing to excessive dividend payments. As a result, the Central Bank tightened its control over the banking sector in early 1987.

During 1980 a number of changes took place in the banking structure. In December Egypt's first international bank, the Egyptian International Bank, was opened with a capital of $100m. Of this capital 50% was subscribed by the country's four main banks: the National Bank of Egypt, Bank of Alexandria, Banque de Caire, and Banque Misr, with the other half being provided by the Central Bank of Egypt. In addition a National Investment Bank was established earlier in the year to monitor public investment, and there were also plans to establish an import-export bank. The fiscal year was also changed in 1980 to begin in July and not January.

An incentive exchange rate was introduced in December 1984 in an effort to check a slide in the value of the Egyptian pound against the US dollar and to undercut the 'black' market in currency, which had grown following a major devaluation of the Egyptian pound, by one-half, against the US dollar in 1979. (Egypt maintained different exchange rates for specific purposes, e.g. for basic commodity transactions, for workers' remittances, for public sector purchases etc.) A series of measures by successive finance ministers, including the authorization of preferential exchange rates at Egypt's four public sector banks, failed to attract remittances from Egyptians working abroad who preferred to deal on the 'black' market, where the rate of exchange on the US dollar remained above the official level. Only about 40% of the estimated $4,000m. which is generated annually in remittances reaches Egyptian banks. In January 1985 the Minister of Finance, Dr Mustafa as-Said, established a 'floating' exchange rate to reflect more accurately the value of the Egyptian pound against the US dollar, to restrain rising imports, and to counter 'black' market transactions by attracting remittances to the banks. The official rate of exchange remained some 10% below the free market level and failed to divert remittances. Meanwhile, measures restraining imports, including the obligation to purchase letters of credit in Egyptian pounds, proved too restrictive, causing long delays for importers, particularly in the private sector, who were competing for short supplies of currency in the banks. Dr as-Said resigned at the end of March 1985 after a banking scandal, which was the direct result of his 1983 decree banning banks from dealing with certain 'black' market operators. His replacement, Dr Sultan Abu Ali, immediately withdrew the currency regulations of his predecessor: importers were once again able to fund imports by securing hard currency from the 'black' market without having to declare the source; and in June 112 items were removed from the list of restricted imports.

By 1987, Egypt was under considerable pressure, particularly from the IMF, to unify its multiple exchange rates. The IMF wanted the change to be effected within one year but the Government required 18 months. In May 1987, however, the Government acted to curb the 'black' market in currency and announced the partial 'flotation' of its currency, with a daily ('free pool') exchange rate being set by a panel consisting of representatives of eight banks, in order to attract foreign currency. The unofficial market rate persisted but the new 'floating' rate was much closer to it and made the federal banking system more accessible to foreign exchange. The fixed Central Bank rate was adjusted from US $1 = £E0.70 to US $1 = £E1.10 in September 1989. However, the old rate was still applied to revenues from the Suez Canal and the EGPC. The commercial bank exchange rate ($1 = £E1.35 in May 1987), which was used to finance public sector imports and customs duties, was phased out by the end of March 1988, having been allowed to depreciate to merge with the 'free pool' rate, which was set every day by a committee of Central Bank and commercial bank officials ($1 = £E2.708 at 30 June 1990). Before the doubts expressed by the Egyptian Government over the reforms required of it, the IMF expected the unification of the remaining exchange rates (the Central bank rate; the bank 'free pool' rate; the $1 = £E0.40 rate, used for barter deals with the Communist bloc; and a new rate of $1 = £E1.89, introduced in April 1988, for customs duties) to have been achieved by the end of 1988.

In May 1989, as part of a comprehensive adjustment of the interest rate structure, the Central Bank raised interest rates by three percentage points. The measure was designed to encourage savings in the local currency and facilitate a renewed agreement with the IMF. Under reforms agreed with the IMF, which became operative in late February 1991, a new currency exchange system was introduced. It provided for the determination by the commercial banks of a free-market rate of exchange, although an 'official' Central Bank rate continued to be set at not more than 5% less (in terms of the Egyptian pound's free-market value) than the commercial bank rate. This two-tier system resulted in an effective devaluation of nearly 40% compared with the official rate in the previous year, and was officially stated to be a prelude to a unified exchange rate and full currency convertibility commencing in February 1992. By May 1991 the exchange rate was US $1 = £E3.24. Moreover, the new exchange system also resulted in an increase in the Central Bank's interest rates, which rose from 16.2% to more than 20% by May 1991.

For some years the Government has been concerned about the growth of Islamic investment companies, which have been attracting a significant proportion of private savings, including remittances from Egyptians working abroad, and channelling domestic funds and vital foreign exchange away from the official banking system. According to the Islamic precepts under which these investment companies operate, they are not permitted to charge or pay interest. Instead, they pay depositors out of profits, at a high rate of return (up to 24%, compared with the 13% interest available from banks), from their speculations and investments at home and abroad. There are four or five major companies and more than 100 smaller ones, with 2m.–3m. customers (mostly small investors), which effectively constitute a large, unregulated financial sector in competition with the official banking institutions. The largest Islamic investment house, Al-Rayan, holds deposits of $2,000m.–$3,500m. (more than all but the largest banks), and estimates of the combined deposits of all the Islamic companies are in the range of $12,000m.–$20,000m., compared with total commercial bank deposits of $15,000m. at the end of 1987.

In 1987 the Government announced plans to regularize the activities of Islamic investment companies, and in June 1988 the Majlis passed a law requiring them to become regular shareholding companies (issuing share certificates in exchange for deposits, rather than simple receipts) and placing a limit of £E50m. on their authorized capital. All companies were forbidden to take new deposits for three months, while they decided whether to comply with the new regulations or to go into liquidation. The measures provoked strong resistance among the Islamic investment companies, and many leading executives protested that they would not be able to continue in business if they complied with them (see 'Islamic Banking and Finance', p. 166).

It was feared that the collapse of several of Egypt's Islamic investment companies in late 1988 would lead to the loss of several thousand depositors' funds. There was also evidence,

by mid-1989, that the resulting loss of confidence in the economy had led to a sharp decline in Egyptian workers' remittances from abroad, which was exacerbated by Iraq's invasion of Kuwait in August 1990. The Government estimated, too, that Egyptian deposits worth $14,000m. in Kuwaiti banks, and $540m. in Iraqi banks, had been lost as a result of the invasion. A new banking law, presented to parliament in November 1991, tightened the financial regulations relating to banks and strengthened the supervisory powers of the Central Bank. Under the measure (which attracted some criticism in financial circles), Egyptian banks were required to have paid-up capital of at least £E50m. (as against £E500,000 previously), while foreign banks had to have at least $10m.

An amendment was introduced in March 1993 to allow branches of foreign banks to take deposits and give loans in Egyptian pounds, regardless of whether they were locally incorporated or had local shareholders. A total of 22 foreign banks had branches in Egypt at this time, and several of them were expected to develop a full range of services, placing particular emphasis on the introduction of new products and the creation of modern capital market structures in Egypt.

Total deposits in the Egyptian banking system stood at £E159,000m. (nearly two-thirds of this in local currency) at the beginning of February 1993, an increase of almost 50% over the previous six months as depositors took advantage of the first opportunity for decades to earn a positive return on their money (Egypt's inflation rate having fallen to around 10% while bank deposit rates stood at 15%). The attractiveness of the local currency (which had maintained a stable exchange rate for over a year in conditions of virtually free convertibility) was such that the Central Bank was buying about $1,000m. of 'surplus' foreign exchange each month—a development which helped to boost Egypt's foreign exchange reserves to a record $14,300m. during the first quarter of 1993. By mid-1994 the country's foreign-exchange reserves had reached $16,600m., and were forecast by the Government to rise to around $20,000m. by the end of 1995. The amount of surplus liquidity in the Egyptian banking system was estimated at around £E4,400m. in the first half of 1994.

FOREIGN TRADE AND PAYMENTS

The Government keeps a constant vigil on all external payments, but the pressure of population on resources is a critical factor in keeping the balance of payments in a precarious state. Although the development of the petroleum sector has alleviated the difficulties to some extent, food imports have continued to be substantial, accounting for 31% of the value of total imports in 1990 (compared with 26% in 1965), while imports of machinery and transport equipment increased from 23% in 1965 to 29% in 1988, before falling back to 23% in 1990. Exports have traditionally been agricultural goods, with raw cotton accounting for almost one-third of the value in 1977. However, by 1979 a change was apparent, with crude petroleum accounting for 30% of the exports against raw cotton's 21%. By 1982 crude petroleum accounted for 55% of exports, but this proportion had fallen to 40% by 1990, as domestic requirements outstripped production.

The external trade deficit has persisted almost without interruption since before the Second World War. The trade deficit increased from $3,980m. in 1980/81 to $4,620m. in 1981/82. The situation did not improve in 1982/83 and the trade deficit was $5,559m. (imports $9,519m., exports $3,960m.) in 1983/84. By 1984/85 the trade deficit had risen to $7,000m. (imports $10,800m., exports $3,800m.), but fell to around $6,000m. in 1985/86 and to $5,200m. in 1986/87. The decline in imports was largely due to a shortage of convertible currency and to limitations on the importation of luxury items, such as passenger motor cars and sound reproduction equipment. In discussions with senior IMF officials in mid-1988, the Government cited improvements in the export sector as one of its major economic achievements: non-oil exports increased by 14% in 1986/87 and rose by a further 25% in 1987/88. Nevertheless, by 1989/90 the trade deficit had increased to $8,295m., before contracting to $7,537m. in 1990/91. The deficit on the current account of the balance of payments rose to $1,527m. in 1984/85 from $1,421m. in 1983/84. Including imports of US military equipment, which did not figure in Central Bank calculations, the deficit was $2,500m. in 1983/84 and $2,950m. in 1984/85. The Central Bank estimated that the deficit on the current account rose to $1,936m. in 1985/86. In both 1986/87 and 1987/88 the deficit remained below $1,000m., owing mainly to an increase in earnings from tourism and transfers of expatriate workers' remittances through the banking system. In 1988/89 the current account deficit increased to $1,600m., but declined to $634m. in 1989/90, and in 1990/91 showed a surplus of $1,391m., the first for many years. The main factors in the turn-around were debt relief and increased aid transfers, although a significant rise in export values and buoyant remittances from workers abroad ($3,667m. in 1990/91) also contributed. From 1990 Egypt's foreign exchange reserves increased sharply, to reach $5,300m. by May 1992.

In 1991/92 there was a sharp rise in Egypt's current-account surplus to about $3,737m., with income rising to some $18,779m. (including $1,727m. from tourism) while a $1,370m. fall in the value of imports (to $10,054m) helped to contain total expenditure. In 1992/93 the current-account surplus reached $4,774m. Visible export earnings totalled $3,417m. (53% of this from crude oil), while import spending totalled $10,732m. (one-fifth of this for foodstuffs), leaving a visible trade deficit of $7,315m. Income from services amounted to $9,173m. (21% of this from Suez Canal charges and 14% from tourism), while outgoings totalled $5,701m. (25% of this being interest payments and 18% repayments of principal under loan agreements). Inward private transfers, including both remittances from workers abroad and deposits attracted by high interest rates, totalled $7,260m. (almost enough to offset the visible trade deficit), while inward official transfers amounted to $1,357m.

TRANSPORT AND TOURISM

Egypt's principal ports are at Alexandria, Port Said and Suez. The Government is aiming to expand both the Mediterranean and Red Sea port capacities to cope with traffic passing through the Suez Canal. Alexandria port is being expanded, aided by a $95m. loan from the World Bank, and a completely new port is planned, west of Alexandria, at Dikheila, with a capacity of 20m. tons per year, compared with Alexandria's present capacity of 13m. tons. Safaga on the Red Sea is also being developed but mainly to handle mineral imports and exports. The first stage of a port situated 10 miles west of the Nile's Damietta tributary, and capable of handling up to 16m. tons of cargo per year, was opened in July 1986. A second stage will increase the port's capacity to 25m. tons per year.

River transport is being expanded to relieve the load on roads and railways for internal distribution. Navigable waterways total about 3,100 km, of which about one-half is the Nile and the rest canals. Canals such as the Nubariya canal in the delta and the Bahr Yousuf, between Fayoum and Asyut, make it possible to link Alexandria with Upper Egypt through Cairo.

Egypt has over 5,000 km of railway and modernization is urgently needed. A project using loans from various sources is being undertaken to modernize the railway system and expand its carrying capacity, as well as to draw up a comprehensive national transport survey. This includes modernization of the line from Cairo to Upper Egypt, for which funding of $300m. was sought from the World Bank in 1990. Earlier modernization plans have not been carried out. Plans are in hand to repair 300 km of the railway network in the south of the country and to replace all locomotives in the country with modern rolling stock. Under active consideration in late 1991 was a plan to upgrade the 160-km railway link between the Tabbia industrial zone to the south of Cairo and areas of mineral deposits in the Western Desert. Construction of the first stage of the French-designed Cairo metro system, consisting of a 42.5-km line, which runs from el-Marg in the north to Helwan in the south, began in 1982. Incorporating 33 stations, including six underground, on a 4.2-km line tunnelled beneath the centre of Cairo (the first underground transport system in the Middle East and North Africa), this section connected with an existing line to Helwan; it was completed in July 1987 (18 months later than originally planned) and was opened in September. Traffic on the metro reached a record 988,000 passengers per day in March 1993. Construc-

tion work began in mid-1993 on Cairo's second metro line (which will run north to the suburb of Shoubra el-Khaima, and, eventually, south to within a few hundred metres of the Greater Cairo ring road, south of Giza railway station). The second line will serve a total of 21 stations.

Good roads connect Cairo with Alexandria, the canal towns and Upper Egypt. Output of motor vehicles from local assembly plants was expected to increase sharply after 1993 (see Manufacturing Industry, above).

EgyptAir, the state airline, operates a network of domestic and international routes. It made a profit of £E82.7m. in 1991/92, following a loss of £E257.3m. in 1990/91 because of severe problems caused by the regional security crisis. The company made a net loss of £E30.5m. in 1992/93 after experiencing a 50% fall in its Western tourist traffic which contributed to a decision in March 1993 to suspend its current five-year expansion plans. EgyptAir's existing debt in respect of past aircraft purchases amounted to $545m. in early 1993. The number of tourists visiting Egypt reached 1.3m. in 1986 and rose to 2.5m. in 1990, slightly above the 1989 level, but below the original target of 2.9m. because of the impact of the Gulf crisis. Revenue from tourism was about $800m. in 1984/85, and rose to about $2,500m. by 1989/90, making tourism one of the most dynamic sectors of the Egyptian economy. The management of several public-sector hotels has been transferred to international groups, legislation to reduce land speculation enacted, and the aviation industry liberalized. However, the industry is one of the most immediately vulnerable to instability in the region. An increase in terrorist activity in the Middle East during the second half of 1985 and the anti-American reaction in the region, following the bombing of Libyan cities by US forces in April 1986, combined to deter tourists, particularly Americans, from visiting Egypt. The prospect of renewed and protracted instability in the region, following the Iraqi invasion of Kuwait in August 1990 and the subsequent international response, accordingly posed a serious threat to the sector's vital contribution to Egypt's limited supplies of foreign exchange. In February 1991 tourist arrivals slumped to 57,000, compared with 208,000 in February 1990. By April 1991, however, the resolution of the Gulf crisis had led to a recovery in the number of tourist arrivals, which increased to 276,000 in August 1991 and reached the record figure of some 3m. in the 12 months to June 1992, over which period tourism's total contribution to the economy (including the indirect benefits not quantified in simple balance-of-payments analyses) was officially estimated at $3,500m.

Having planned for a 1m. rise in visitor numbers in 1992/93, the tourism industry instead experienced a sharp downturn when an Islamist terrorist campaign included foreign tourists as targets. The number of tourists visiting Egypt fell by about 22% in 1993, while revenue fell by 38% because the length of the average stay was shorter. Having failed to eliminate the problem of terrorism through its harsh crackdown on militant Islamists, the Government allocated $25m. for a campaign to promote tourism in 1994, with the aim of restoring revenue from this sector to its 1992 level. However, the number of visitors in the first three months of 1994 was 15% down on the 1993 level, while the average length of stay was rather shorter than in 1993. Upper Egypt (hardest hit by the terrorist campaign) reported little sign of a recovery, whereas Cairo hotels had a 60% occupancy rate and most Red Sea and Sinai resorts reported some upturn in tourist business.

Egypt's tourism expansion plans for the rest of the decade envisaged an annual inflow of 4.4m. visitors by the year 2000, by which time an additional 32,000 local jobs were expected to have been created in the industry. In January 1993 the World Bank approved a $130m.-loan for the development of new tourism infrastructure within the framework of a $805m.-programme involving also $330m. of private-sector equity financing, $300m. of commercial bank lending, $40m. of Egyptian government funding and $5m. from the World Bank's global environment facility. The main focus of the programme was the development of new resorts on Egypt's Red Sea coast as part of a policy of diversification into the seaside holiday market.

Statistical Survey

Sources (unless otherwise stated): Central Agency for Public Mobilization and Statistics, POB 2086, Nasr City, Cairo; tel. (2) 604632; telex 92395; Research Department, National Bank of Egypt, Cairo.

Area and Population

AREA, POPULATION AND DENSITY

Area (sq km)	997,738.5*
Population (census results)	
22–23 November 1976	36,626,204†
17–18 November 1986‡	
Males	24,709,274
Females	23,544,964
Total	48,254,238
Population (official estimates at mid-year)§	
1990	52,690,000
1991	53,918,000
1992	55,163,000
Density (per sq km) at mid-1992	55.3

* 385,229 sq miles. Inhabited and cultivated territory accounts for 35,189 sq km (13,587 sq miles).
† Excluding Egyptian nationals abroad, totalling 1,572,000.
‡ Including Egyptian nationals abroad, totalling an estimated 2,250,000.
§ Including Egyptian nationals abroad.

GOVERNORATES (population at 1986 census*)

Governorate	Area (sq km)	Population ('000)	Capital
Cairo	214.2	6,052.8	Cairo
Alexandria . . .	2,679.4	2,917.3	Alexandria
Port Said	72.1	399.8	Port Said
Ismailia	1,441.6	544.4	Ismailia
Suez	17,840.4	326.8	Suez
Damietta	589.2	741.3	Damietta
Dakahlia	3,470.9	3,500.5	Mansoura
Sharkia	4,179.5	3,420.1	Zagazig
Kalyubia	1,001.1	2,514.2	Benha
Kafr esh-Sheikh . .	3,437.1	1,800.1	Kafr esh-Sheikh
Gharbia	1,942.2	2,871.0	Tanta
Menufia	1,532.1	2,227.1	Shibin el-Kom
Behera	10,129.5	1,770.6	Damanhur
Giza	85,153.2	3,700.1	Giza
Beni Suef . . .	1,321.7	1,443.0	Beni Suef
Fayum	1,827.2	1,544.0	Fayum
Menia	2,261.7	2,648.0	Menia
Asyut	1,553.0	2,223.0	Asyut
Suhag	1,547.2	2,455.1	Suhag
Qena	1,850.7	2,252.3	Qena
Aswan	678.5	801.4	Aswan
Al-Bahr al-Ahmar .	203,685.0	90.5	Al-Ghaurdaqah
Al-Wadi al-Jadid .	376,505.0	113.8	Al-Kharijah
Matruh	212,112.0	160.6	Matruh
North Sinai* . .	} 60,714.0 {	171.5	El-Arish
South Sinai* . .		29.0	Et-Toor

* Preliminary results.

PRINCIPAL TOWNS (estimated population at 1 July 1991)

El-Qahira (Cairo, the capital) .	6,663,000	Asyut . . .	313,000
		Zagazig . .	279,000
El-Iskandariyah (Alexandria) .	3,295,000	Ismailia . .	247,000
		El-Fayoum . .	244,000
El-Giza . .	2,096,000	Kafr ed-Dawar .	221,000
Shoubra el-Kheima	812,000	Damanhur . .	216,000
Bur Sa'id (Port Said)	449,000	Aswan . .	215,000
El-Mahalla el-Koubra	400,000	El-Minya (Menia) .	203,000
Es-Suweis (Suez) .	376,000	Beni Suef . .	174,000
Tanta . . .	372,000	Shebin el-Kom .	153,000
El-Mansoura . .	362,000	Sohag . . .	152,000

Source: UN, *Demographic Yearbook*.

BIRTHS AND DEATHS

	Registered live births		Registered deaths	
	Number	Rate (per 1,000)	Number	Rate (per 1,000)
1981 . . .	1,593,698	36.8	432,264	9.9
1982 . . .	1,601,265	36.0	441,621	9.9
1983* . .	1,710,000	37.2	412,700	9.0
1984* . .	1,820,000	38.6	400,600	8.5
1985 . . .	1,817,297	37.5	442,258	9.1
1986 . . .	1,907,975	40.1	455,888	9.6
1987 . . .	1,902,604	38.8	466,161	9.5
1988 . . .	1,912,765	37.9	427,018	8.5

* Figures are provisional.

Marriages (registrations): 384,941 (marriage rate 9.1 per 1,000) in 1980; 385,095 (marriage rate 8.9 per 1,000) in 1981; 370,000 (marriage rate 8.1 per 1,000) in 1983; 442,280 (marriage rate 9.1 per 1,000) in 1985.
1989: Registered live births 1,722,934 (birth rate 33.5 per 1,000); Registered deaths 414,214 (death rate 8.0 per 1,000).
1992: Registered live births 1,669,836 (birth rate 30.3 per 1,000); Registered deaths 429,494 (death rate 7.8 per 1,000).

Source: UN, *Demographic Yearbook* and *Population and Vital Statistics Report*.

ECONOMICALLY ACTIVE POPULATION
(Labour Force Sample Survey of Egyptians aged 12–64 years only, December 1989, provisional results)

	Males	Females	Total
Agriculture, hunting, forestry and fishing	3,734,600	2,600,600	6,335,200
Mining and quarrying . .	41,900	1,400	43,300
Manufacturing	1,614,100	344,600	1,958,700
Electricity, gas and water . .	88,700	11,200	99,900
Construction	973,000	17,200	990,200
Trade, restaurants and hotels	1,102,600	237,400	1,340,000
Transport, storage and communications . .	734,300	45,900	780,200
Finance, insurance, real estate and business services .	209,000	46,300	255,300
Community, social and personal services . .	2,302,400	813,100	3,115,500
Activities not adequately defined	7,400	—	7,400
Total employed . . .	10,808,000	4,117,700	14,925,700
Unemployed	615,900	492,000	1,107,900
Total labour force . .	11,423,900	4,609,700	16,033,600

Source: ILO, *Year Book of Labour Statistics*.

Agriculture

PRINCIPAL CROPS ('000 metric tons)

	1990	1991	1992
Wheat	4,266	4,483	4,618
Rice (paddy) . . .	3,167	3,448	3,908
Barley	129	110	213
Maize	4,799	5,122	5,226*
Sorghum . . .	630	676	736
Potatoes . . .	1,638	1,786	1,800†
Sweet potatoes . .	102	128	90
Taro (Coco yam) . .	99	118	128
Dry broad beans . .	451	466	390*
Soybeans (Soya beans) .	107	120	59
Cottonseed. . . .	504	483	485*
Cotton (lint) . . .	303	302	324*
Cabbages . . .	381	424	436
Tomatoes . . .	4,234	3,796	4,694
Cauliflowers . . .	86	83	96
Pumpkins, squash and gourds .	347	396	342
Cucumbers and gherkins . .	267	250	270
Aubergines . . .	385	415	343
Chillies and peppers . .	271	282	285†
Onions (dry) . . .	577	555	500†
Garlic	185	220	186
Green beans . . .	123	148	129
Carrots	92	93	90
Watermelons . . .	1,007	894	711
Melons. . . .	417	463	480†
Grapes. . . .	585	527	550†
Dates	542	603	610†
Sugar cane. . . .	11,144	11,095	11,624
Sugar beets . . .	575	1,106	744
Oranges	1,574	1,624	1,690*
Tangerines, mandarins, clementines and satsumas .	278	298	300†
Lemons and limes . .	408	411	435†
Mangoes	144	152	155†
Bananas	415	393	400†

* Unofficial figure. † FAO estimate.

Source: FAO, *Production Yearbook*.

LIVESTOCK ('000 head, year ending September)

	1990	1991	1992*
Cattle	2,618	2,973	3,016
Buffaloes . . .	2,897	2,994	3,036
Sheep	4,146	4,270	4,350
Goats	4,442	4,697	4,800
Pigs	102	109	115
Horses*	10	10	10
Asses	1,380*	1,530	1,550
Camels	197	208	210

Chickens (million): 34 in 1990; 35 in 1991; 36* in 1992.
Ducks (million): 7 in 1990; 8 in 1991; 8* in 1992.
* FAO estimate(s).

Source: FAO, *Production Yearbook*.

LIVESTOCK PRODUCTS ('000 metric tons)

	1990	1991	1992
Beef and veal*	151	152	155
Buffalo meat*	160	170	180
Mutton and lamb* . . .	67	69	72
Goats' meat*	32	32	33
Pig meat*	2	3	3
Poultry meat . . .	233	219	200
Other meat . . .	78	82	83
Edible offals* . . .	78	81	83
Cows' milk. . . .	910*	850*	691†
Buffaloes' milk . . .	1,250†	1,256*	1,330*
Sheep's milk* . . .	7	7	8
Goats' milk* . . .	17	17	18
Butter and ghee* . . .	79.0	79.6	80.1
Cheese*	311.3	318.8	323.8
Hen eggs†	141.5	138.0	127.4
Honey	10.0	9.0	10.0*
Wool: greasy* . . .	1.9	2.0	2.0
Cattle and buffalo hides* . .	47.2	48.4	49.8
Sheep skins* . . .	8.1	8.4	8.6
Goat skins* . . .	4.5	4.6	4.8

* FAO estimate(s). † Unofficial figure(s).

Source: FAO, mainly *Production Yearbook*.

Forestry

ROUNDWOOD REMOVALS
(FAO estimates, '000 cubic metres, excluding bark)

	1990	1991	1992
Industrial wood . . .	104	107	109
Fuel wood	2,144	2,193	2,243
Total	2,248	2,300	2,352

Source: FAO, *Yearbook of Forest Products*.

Fishing

('000 metric tons, live weight)

	1989	1990	1991
Marine. . . .	79.3	75.3	82.1
Freshwater . . .	214.3	237.7	215.9
Total catch . . .	293.6	313.0	298.0

Source: FAO, *Yearbook of Fishery Statistics*.

Mining

('000 metric tons, unless otherwise indicated)

	1989	1990	1991
Crude petroleum . .	42,960*	44,032*	45,581
Iron ore† . . .	1,290	1,202	1,072
Salt (unrefined) . . .	1,162	1,125	891
Phosphate rock‡ . . .	1,347	1,505	1,865
Gypsum (crude) . . .	1,309	1,279	1,239
Natural gas (petajoules) .	250	265	303

* Provisional.
† Figures refer to the metal content of ores.
‡ Source: US Bureau of Mines.

Source: UN, *Industrial Statistics Yearbook*.

Industry

SELECTED PRODUCTS
('000 metric tons, unless otherwise indicated)

	1989	1990	1991
Wheat flour	3,629	3,532	3,392
Raw sugar*	946	971	1,064
Cottonseed oil (refined) . .	355	317	357
Beer ('000 hectolitres). .	490	500	440
Cigarettes (million) . .	43,208	39,837	40,154
Cotton yarn (pure)† . .	248.7	259.0	260.3
Jute yarn	26.2	25.1	24.1
Jute fabrics	20.7	20.1	19.2
Wool yarn	19.0	15.8	20.4
Paper and paperboard* . .	216	223	208
Rubber tyres and tubes ('000)‡	3,391	3,334	3,609
Sulphuric acid (100%). . .	60	92	101
Caustic soda (Sodium hydroxide) . . .	51	53	58
Nitrogenous fertilizers§ . .	678	676	824
Phosphate fertilizers‖ . .	217	195	168
Motor spirit (petrol) . .	3,514	3,714	3,783
Kerosene	2,424	2,327	2,271
Distillate fuel oils . . .	3,743	3,934	4,146
Residual fuel oil (Mazout) . .	10,576	11,315	11,675
Petroleum bitumen (asphalt) .	593	655	613
Cement	12,480	14,111	16,427
Pig-iron	112	108	113
Radio receivers ('000) . .	43	59	39
Television receivers ('000) .	194	333	264
Passenger motor cars— assembly (number) . .	13,000	10,000	9,000
Electric energy (million kWh) .	33,349	39,425	40,460

1992 ('000 metric tons): Wheat flour 3,435; Raw sugar 1,077*.
1993 ('000 metric tons): Raw sugar 1,092*.

* Data from the FAO.
† Figures refer to the year ending 30 June.
‡ Tyres and inner tubes for road motor vehicles (including motorcycles) and bicycles.
§ Production in terms of nitrogen (Source: FAO).
‖ Production in terms of phosphoric acid (Source: FAO).

Source: mainly UN, *Industrial Statistics Yearbook*.

Finance

CURRENCY AND EXCHANGE RATES

Monetary Units
 1,000 millièmes = 100 piastres = 5 tallaris = 1 Egyptian pound (£E).

Sterling and Dollar Equivalents (31 May 1994)
 £1 sterling = £E5.119;
 US $1 = £E3.386;
 £E100 = £19.535 sterling = $29.533.

Note: The official rate of the Central Bank was fixed at US $1 = 700 millièmes (£E1 = $1.4286) between January 1979 and August 1989. It was adjusted to $1 = £E1.100 in August 1989, and to $1 = £E2.000 in July 1990. The latter rate remained in force until February 1991. However, a system of multiple exchange rates was in operation, and the official rate was applicable only to a limited range of transactions, including payments for selected imports and exports. At 30 September 1991 the banks' free market rate, applicable to most other transactions, was $1 = £E3.318. The average of this secondary rate (£E per US $) was: 2.223 in 1988; 2.517 in 1989; 2.707 in 1990. From February 1991 foreign exchange transactions were conducted through only two markets, the primary market and the free market. With effect from 8 October 1991, the primary market was eliminated, and all foreign exchange transactions are effected through the free market. For external trade purposes, the average value of the Egyptian pound was 30.75 US cents in 1991 and 30.2 US cents in 1992.

STATE PUBLIC BUDGET (£E million, year ending 30 June)

Revenue	1989/90	1990/91
Current budget	20,342,2	27,845.1
Taxes on income . . .	5,730.0	7,915.0
Customs duties	3,600.0	3,780.0
Tax on consumption. . .	3,920.0	4,200.0
Petroleum surplus . . .	780.9	1,697.7
Suez Canal surplus . . .	351.4	1,245.2
Central Bank surplus . .	749.7	3,181.7
Investment budget . . .	2,231.3	2,110.6
External and domestic grants . .	846.1	779.2
Transfer budget	2,842.7	2,566.8
External grants . . .	2,215.0	1,735.0
Total	25,416.2	32,522.5

Expenditure	1989/90	1990/91*
Current budget	18,749.1	27,245.1
Wages	6,250.0	7,140.0
Subsidies	2,061.0	3,579.2
Armed forces . . .	2,711.5	3,132.7
Interest on domestic public debt . .	2,851.9	6,140.0
Interest on external public debt .	761.7	2,222.1
Pensions.	1,511.0	2,042.5
Investment budget . . .	6,350.5	6,750.9
Administrative system . .	1,601.5	1,713.3
Service authorities . .	1,272.5	1,333.6
Economic authorities . .	3,099.9	3,320.3
Transfer budget	5,206.9	7,251.8
Domestic public debt . .	956.5	1,138.1
External public debt . .	1,339.8	3,120.4
Capital transfer to economic authorities	2,325.8	2,229.8
Total	30,306.5	41,247.8

* Figures are provisional.

1991/92 (estimates £E million, year ending 30 June): Revenue 45,083; Expenditure 54,431.
1992/93 (estimates £E million, year ending 30 June): Revenue 53,389; Expenditure 62,533.

CENTRAL BANK RESERVES (US $ million at 31 December)

	1991	1992	1993
Gold*	656	616	616
IMF special drawing rights .	1	59	69
Reserve position in IMF . .	—	74	74
Foreign exchange . . .	5,324	10,677	12,761
Total	5,981	11,426	13,520

* Valued at market-related prices.
Source: IMF, *International Financial Statistics*.

MONEY SUPPLY (£E million at 31 December)

	1991	1992	1993
Currency outside banks . .	13,524	15,241	17,818
Demand deposits at deposit money banks . . .	12,703	13,985	14,940

Source: IMF, *International Financial Statistics*.

COST OF LIVING (Consumer Price Index; base: 1980 = 100)

	1988	1989	1990
Food	373.8	473.3	548.3
Fuel and light	133.5	137.2	n.a.
Clothing	274.3	315.3	374.1
Rent	122.4	128.7	150.0
All items (incl. others) . .	337.1	408.8	477.3

1991: Food 639.0; All items 571.5.

Source: ILO, *Year Book of Labour Statistics.*

1992: Food 692.4; All items 649.3. Source: UN, *Monthly Bulletin of Statistics.*

NATIONAL ACCOUNTS
(£E million, year ending 30 June)

Expenditure on the Gross Domestic Product (at current prices)

	1989/90	1990/91	1991/92
Government final consumption expenditure	10,850	12,450	14,500
Private final consumption expenditure	68,950	80,900	101,000
Increase in stocks	1,800	−1,200	−1,200
Gross fixed capital formation .	26,500	27,850	28,700
Total domestic expenditure .	108,100	120,000	143,000
Exports of goods and services	19,400	31,000	40,400
Less Imports of goods and services	31,400	39,800	44,300
GDP in purchasers' values .	96,100	111,200	139,100

Source: IMF, *International Financial Statistics.*

Gross Domestic Product by Economic Activity
(at constant 1986/87 factor cost)

	1987/88	1988/89	1989/90
Agriculture, hunting, forestry and fishing	8,930.0	9,180.0	9,440.0
Mining and quarrying . . . }	9,234.2	9,726.7	10,292.2
Manufacturing . . . . }			
Electricity, gas and water . .	745.6	796.3	905.4
Construction	2,145.0	2,259.0	2,381.0
Trade, restaurants and hotels .	10,150.6	10,618.2	11,110.0
Transport, storage and communications	3,995.8	4,368.4	4,678.0
Other services	8,047.7	8,654.7	9,104.0
Total	43,248.9	45,603.3	47,910.6

Source: UN, *National Accounts Statistics.*

BALANCE OF PAYMENTS (US $ million)

	1990	1991	1992
Merchandise exports f.o.b. .	3,604	3,856	3,400
Merchandise imports f.o.b. .	−10,303	−9,831	−8,901
Trade balance	−6,699	−5,975	−5,501
Exports of services . .	6,285	7,086	7,968
Imports of services . .	−3,788	−3,364	−4,867
Other income received . . .	862	865	933
Other income paid . . .	−1,879	−2,143	−2,797
Private unrequited transfers (net)	4,284	4,054	6,104
Official unrequited transfers (net)	1,119	1,380	972
Current balance . . .	184	1,903	2,812
Direct investment (net) . .	722	191	455
Portfolio investment (net) . .	15	21	6
Other capital (net) . . .	−11,776	−4,554	−629
Net errors and omissions . .	631	730	716
Overall balance . . .	−10,224	−1,709	3,360

Source: IMF, *International Financial Statistics.*

External Trade

Note: Figures exclude trade in military goods.

PRINCIPAL COMMODITIES
(distribution by SITC, £E million)

Imports c.i.f.	1989	1990	1991
Food and live animals . .	4,498.7	6,877.4	5,475.4
Meat and meat preparations .	460.6	595.4	469.3
Fresh, chilled and frozen meat	439.5	563.4	437.0
Meat of bovine animals .	389.8	554.0	432.3
Dairy products and birds' eggs	460.6	554.0	407.4
Cereals and cereal preparations	2,231.4	3,310.8	2,404.5
Wheat and meslin (unmilled)	1,307.7	2,128.5	1,614.6
Maize, unmilled . . .	423.6	513.7	428.5
Wheat, etc., meal or flour .	460.0	634.0	334.2
Flour of wheat or meslin .	444.0	621.0	317.2
Sugar, sugar preparations and honey	412.1	n.a.	n.a.
Coffee, tea, cocoa and spices .	283.7	n.a.	n.a.
Tea	232.2	415.4	n.a.
Crude materials (inedible) except fuels . . .	1,432.9	2,172.2	2,380.0
Cork and wood . . .	852.6	1,147.5	1,097.4
Simply worked wood and railway sleepers . . .	804.2	1,088.9	1,050.8
Simply worked coniferous wood	782.1	1,073.5	1,032.3
Sawn coniferous wood .	775.5	1,066.7	1,045.3
Mineral fuels, lubricants, etc. (incl. electric current) .	385.5	662.2	563.8
Animal and vegetable oils, fats and waxes . . .	548.7	603.6	420.8
Fixed vegetable oils and fats .	398.3	475.0	347.0
Soft fixed vegetable oils . .	330.4	363.9	231.0
Chemicals and related products	2,092.9	3,137.4	3,618.8
Organic chemicals . . .	328.5	n.a.	n.a.
Medicinal and pharmaceutical products	288.3	386.8	496.4
Artificial resins, plastic materials, etc. . . .	505.3	819.6	1,106.5
Products of polymerization, etc.	381.3	616.0	842.8
Basic manufactures . . .	3,037.6	4,638.9	5,531.2
Paper, paperboard and manufactures	476.3	775.3	1,060.2
Paper and paperboard (not cut to size or shape) ..	439.2	721.9	982.9
Non-metallic mineral manufactures	231.9	286.8	356.1
Iron and steel	1,141.7	1,596.7	1,671.7
Bars, rods, angles, shapes, etc.	438.1	468.8	291.3
Machinery and transport equipment . . .	3,845.9	5,661.1	5,972.4
Machinery specialized for particular industries . .	788.9	n.a.	n.a.
General industrial machinery, equipment and parts . .	944.7	n.a.	n.a.
Telecommunications and sound equipment	266.5	357.0	355.3
Other electrical machinery, apparatus, etc.	684.0	n.a.	n.a.
Road vehicles and parts* . .	673.2	1,053.4	916.3
Parts and accessories for cars, buses, lorries, etc.* .	287.8	472.7	368.3
Miscellaneous manufactured articles	594.2	794.9	860.4
Total (incl. others) . . .	16,623.6	24,823.2	25,216.3

* Excluding tyres, engines and electrical parts.

Exports f.o.b.	1989	1990	1991
Food and live animals . .	492.3	642.2	937.8
Vegetables and fruit . . .	322.9	386.1	514.9
Fresh or simply preserved vegetables. .	121.7	168.3	277.7
Fresh and dried fruit and nuts (excl. oil nuts) . .	177.8	173.4	177.3
Oranges, mandarins, etc. .	155.0	148.3	141.7
Oranges . . .	154.6	148.3	141.7
Crude materials (inedible) except fuels . .	674.4	690.7	335.8
Textile fibres and waste . .	608.7	578.1	213.1
Cotton . . .	594.7	562.7	193.4
Raw cotton (excl. linters) .	594.2	562.2	193.3
Mineral fuels, lubricants, etc.	1,747.6	2,051.0	6,348.5
Petroleum, petroleum products, etc. . . .	1,691.6	2,006.0	5,881.2
Crude petroleum . .	1,212.8	1,290.0	n.a.
Refined petroleum products .	464.3	n.a.	n.a.
Kerosene and other medium oils . .	286.8	496.4	754.4
Residual fuel oils . .	155.8	n.a.	n.a.
Chemicals and related products	256.0	331.0	534.2
Basic manufactures . .	2,103.3	2,505.8	2,571.5
Textile yarn, fabrics, etc. .	1,272.0	1,492.0	1,599.0
Textile yarn. . .	1,003.2	1,054.3	989.0
Cotton yarn . .	990.2	1,045.8	n.a.
Woven cotton fabrics (excl. narrow or special fabrics).	176.9	224.9	345.2
Non-ferrous metals . .	573.8	603.9	514.2
Aluminium and aluminium alloys . . .	554.6	n.a.	n.a.
Aluminium bars, wire, etc.	513.3	534.2	431.9
Miscellaneous manufactured articles	424.2	668.0	864.1
Clothing and accessories (excl. footwear) . . .	289.2	389.0	557.8
Total (incl. others) . .	5,734.7	6,953.8	11,764.7

PRINCIPAL TRADING PARTNERS
(countries of consignment, £E million)

Imports c.i.f.	1989	1990	1991
Australia	428.2	1,038.0	858.4
Austria	128.0	216.6	284.2
Belgium/Luxembourg . .	363.9	468.5	502.7
China, People's Repub. .	133.0	276.9	n.a.
Czechoslovakia . . .	160.2	249.9	338.3
Finland	177.0	294.2	256.5
France.	1,489.0	2,329.3	1,745.4
Germany, Fed. Repub.. .	1,613.4	2,621.1	2,631.0
Greece	169.5	174.3	182.9
India	135.0	184.8	213.4
Italy	964.4	1,620.0	1,709.1
Japan	642.6	923.6	1,026.0
Netherlands . . .	537.7	761.3	864.4
Romania	496.5	256.0	210.3
Saudi Arabia . . .	102.1	205.9	433.8
Spain	205.0	298.0	391.4
Sweden	374.7	559.2	590.5
Switzerland . . .	456.0	674.5	600.9
Turkey	275.7	386.2	426.7
USSR	576.6	733.0	458.3
United Kingdom . .	690.5	991.4	1,141.0
USA	2,930.7	3,502.9	4,056.7
Yugoslavia. . . .	269.2	463.8	457.6
Total (incl. others) . .	16,623.6	24,823.2	25,216.3

Exports f.o.b.	1989	1990	1991
Belgium/Luxembourg . .	140.8	164.8	162.8
Czechoslovakia . .	92.5	153.5	8.8
France. . . .	408.0	278.4	695.3
Germany, Fed. Repub.. .	296.8	386.0	439.2
Greece . . .	131.3	104.5	448.2
Israel	364.8	451.5	1,186.8
Italy	792.8	849.3	1,743.8
Japan	206.2	189.0	165.1
Netherlands . . .	328.4	440.2	450.0
Romania . . .	7.7	75.2	399.3
Saudi Arabia . . .	169.8	206.2	366.1
Sudan	47.1	55.8	81.8
Switzerland . . .	70.6	56.3	90.4
USSR	764.4	1,097.5	745.8
United Kingdom . .	150.0	208.0	255.4
USA	288.9	596.7	894.7
Yugoslavia. . . .	48.8	64.9	42.5
Total (incl. others) . . .	5,734.7	6,953.8	11,764.7

Transport

RAILWAYS (year ending 30 June)

	1987/88	1988/89	1989/90
Total freight (million ton-km) .	3,029	2,853	3,045
Total passengers (million passenger-km) . . .	28,743	27,083	28,684
Track length (km)	7,106	7,736	8,600

ROAD TRAFFIC (motor vehicle licences at 31 December)

	1989	1990	1991
Passenger cars. . . .	1,018,806	1,053,599	1,081,268
Buses and coaches. . .	30,409	32,832	32,065
Goods vehicles . . .	322,229	346,875	356,512
Motor cycles	318,176	330,521	339,217

SHIPPING (Suez Canal traffic)

	1991	1992	1993
Transits (number) . . .	18,326	16,629	17,317
Displacement ('000 net tons) .	426,449	369,779	396,550
Northbound goods traffic ('000 metric tons) . .	153,220	152,522	149,027
Southbound goods traffic ('000 metric tons) . .	119,322	122,505	147,887
Net tonnage of tankers ('000) .	156,809	118,154	137,879

Source: Suez Canal Authority.

CIVIL AVIATION (traffic on scheduled services)

	1989	1990	1991
Kilometres flown (million). .	42	43	35
Passengers carried ('000) . .	3,419	3,239	2,602
Passenger-km (million) . .	6,186	5,998	5,230
Freight ton-km (million) . .	138	144	132

Source: UN, *Statistical Yearbook*.

Tourism

TOURIST ARRIVALS BY REGION ('000)

	1987/88	1988/89	1989/90
Arabs	638.7	940.3	1,132.9
OECD nationals . . .	1,102.1	1,274.6	1,215.1
Nationals of socialist countries	51.3	50.0	58.0
Others	177.2	238.5	194.2
Total	1,969.3	2,503.4	2,600.2

Source: Ministry of Tourism.

Education

	Teachers		Pupils/Students	
	1989	1990	1989	1990
Pre-primary . .	5,094	8,015	177,740	198,742
Primary* . . .	261,613	279,315	6,155,100	6,402,472
Secondary:				
General* . . .	175,864	204,063	3,982,806	4,125,252
Teacher training* .	6,683	6,159	65,676	25,335
Vocational . .	65,554	79,167	950,133	1,110,184
Higher:				
Universities, etc.* .	34,240	34,553	548,099	520,496
Others	n.a.	n.a.	105,360†	n.a.

* Excluding Al-Azhar education.
† Figure refers to 1988.
Source: UNESCO, *Statistical Yearbook*.

Directory

The Constitution

A new constitution for the Arab Republic of Egypt was approved by referendum on 11 September 1971.

THE STATE

Egypt is an Arab Republic with a democratic, socialist system based on the alliance of the working people and derived from the country's historical heritage and the spirit of Islam.

The Egyptian people are part of the Arab nation, who work towards total Arab unity.

Islam is the religion of the State; Arabic is its official language and the Islamic code is a principal source of legislation. The State safeguards the freedom of worship and of performing rites for all religions.

Sovereignty is of the people alone which is the source of all powers.

The protection, consolidation and preservation of the socialist gains is a national duty: the sovereignty of law is the basis of the country's rule, and the independence of immunity of the judiciary are basic guarantees for the protection of rights and liberties.

THE FUNDAMENTAL ELEMENTS OF SOCIETY

Social solidarity is the basis of Egyptian society, and the family is its nucleus.

The State ensures the equality of men and women in both political and social rights in line with the provisions of Muslim legislation.

Work is a right, an honour and a duty which the State guarantees together with the services of social and health insurance, pensions for incapacity and unemployment.

The economic basis of the Republic is a socialist democratic system based on sufficiency and justice in a manner preventing exploitation.

Ownership is of three kinds, public, co-operative and private. The public sector assumes the main responsibility for the regulation and growth of the national economy under the development plan.

Property is subject to the people's control.

Private ownership is safeguarded and may not be sequestrated except in cases specified in law nor expropriated except for the general good against fair legal compensation. The right of inheritance is guaranteed in it.

Nationalization shall only be allowed for considerations of public interest in accordance with the law and against compensation.

Agricultural holding may be limited by law.

The State follows a comprehensive central planning and compulsory planning approach based on quinquennial socio-economic and cultural development plans whereby the society's resources are mobilized and put to the best use.

The public sector assumes the leading role in the development of the national economy. The State provides absolute protection of this sector as well as the property of co-operative societies and trade unions against all attempts to tamper with them.

PUBLIC LIBERTIES, RIGHTS AND DUTIES

All citizens are equal before the law. Personal liberty is a natural right and no one may be arrested, searched, imprisoned or restricted in any way without a court order.

Houses have sanctity, and shall not be placed under surveillance or searched without a court order with reasons given for such action.

The law safeguards the sanctities of the private lives of all citizens; so have all postal, telegraphic, telephonic and other means of communication which may not therefore be confiscated, or perused except by a court order giving the reasons, and only for a specified period.

Public rights and freedoms are also inviolate and all calls for atheism and anything that reflects adversely on divine religions are prohibited.

The freedom of opinion, the Press, printing and publications and all information media are safeguarded.

Press censorship is forbidden, so are warnings, suspensions or cancellations through administrative channels. Under exceptional circumstances, as in cases of emergency or in war time, censorship may be imposed on information media for a definite period.

Egyptians have the right to permanent or provisional emigration and no Egyptian may be deported or prevented from returning to the country.

Citizens have the right to private meetings in peace provided they bear no arms. Egyptians also have the right to form societies which have no secret activities. Public meetings are also allowed within the limits of the law.

SOVEREIGNTY OF THE LAW

All acts of crime should be specified together with the penalties for the acts.

Recourse to justice, it says, is a right of all citizens, and those who are financially unable, will be assured of means to defend their rights.

Except in cases of *flagrante delicto*, no person may be arrested or their freedom restricted unless an order authorizing arrest has been given by the competent judge or the public prosecution in accordance with the provisions of law.

SYSTEM OF GOVERNMENT

The President, who must be of Egyptian parentage and at least 40 years old, is nominated by at least one-third of the members of the People's Assembly, approved by at least two-thirds, and elected by popular referendum. His term is for six years and he 'may be re-elected for another subsequent term'. He may take emergency measures in the interests of the State but these measures must be approved by referendum within 60 days.

The People's Assembly, elected for five years, is the legislative body and approves general policy, the budget and the development plan. It shall have 'not less than 350' elected members, at least half of whom shall be workers or farmers, and the President may appoint up to 10 additional members. In exceptional circumstances the Assembly, by a two-thirds vote, may authorize the President to rule by decree for a specified period but these decrees must be approved by the Assembly at its next meeting. The law governing the composition of the People's Assembly was amended in May 1979 (see People's Assembly, below).

The Assembly may pass a vote of no confidence in a Deputy Prime Minister, a Minister or a Deputy Minister, provided three days' notice of the vote is given, and the Minister must then resign. In the case of the Prime Minister, the Assembly may 'prescribe' his responsibility and submit a report to the President: if the President disagrees with the report but the Assembly persists, then the matter is put to a referendum: if the people support the President the Assembly is dissolved; if they support the Assembly the President must accept the resignation of the Government. The President may dissolve the Assembly prematurely, but his action must be approved by a referendum and elections must be held within 60 days.

Executive Authority is vested in the President, who may appoint one or more Vice-Presidents and appoints all Ministers. He may also dismiss the Vice-Presidents and Ministers. The President has 'the right to refer to the people in connection with important matters related to the country's higher interests.' The Government is described as 'the supreme executive and administrative organ of the state'. Its members, whether full Ministers or Deputy Ministers, must be at least 35 years old. Further sections define the roles of Local Government, Specialized National Councils, the Judiciary, the Higher Constitutional Court, the Socialist Prosecutor General, the Armed Forces and National Defence Council and the Police.

POLITICAL PARTIES

In June 1977 the People's Assembly adopted a new law on political parties, which, subject to certain conditions, permitted the formation of political parties for the first time since 1953. The law was passed in accordance with Article Five of the Constitution which describes the political system as 'a multi-party one' with four main parties: 'the ruling National Democratic Party, the Socialist Workers (the official opposition), the Liberal Socialists and the Unionist Progressive'. (The legality of the re-formed New Wafd Party was established by the courts in January 1984.)

1980 AMENDMENTS

On 30 April 1980 the People's Assembly passed a number of amendments, which were subsequently massively approved at a referendum the following month. A summary of the amendments follows:

(i) the regime in Egypt is socialist-democratic, based on the alliance of working people's forces.

(ii) the political system depends on multiple political parties; the Arab Socialist Union is therefore abolished.

(iii) the President is elected for a six-year term and can be elected for 'other terms'.

(iv) the President shall appoint a Consultative Council to preserve the principles of the revolutions of 23 July 1952 and 15 May 1971.

(v) a Supreme Press Council shall safeguard the freedom of the press, check government censorship and look after the interests of journalists.

(vi) Egypt's adherence to Islamic jurisprudence is affirmed. Christians and Jews are subject to their own jurisdiction in personal status affairs.

(vii) there will be no distinction of race or religion.

The Government

THE PRESIDENCY

President: MUHAMMAD HOSNI MUBARAK (confirmed as President by referendum, 13 October 1981, after assassination of President Sadat; re-elected and confirmed by referendum, 5 October 1987 and 4 October 1993).

COUNCIL OF MINISTERS
(September 1994)

Prime Minister and Minister of International Co-operation: Dr ATIF SIDQI.

Deputy Prime Minister and Minister of Planning: Dr KAMAL AHMAD AL-GANZOURI.

Deputy Prime Minister and Minister of Agriculture, Livestock, Fisheries and Land Reclamation: Dr YOUSUF AMIN WALI.

Minister of Transport, Communications and Civil Aviation: Eng. SULAYMAN MUTAWALLI SULAYMAN.

Minister of Defence and Military Production: Field Marshal MUHAMMAD HUSSAIN TANTAWI.

Minister of Electricity and Energy: Eng MUHAMMAD MAHIR ABAZAH

Minister of Information: MUHAMMAD SAFWAT MUHAMMAD YOUSUF ASH-SHARIF.

Minister of Foreign Affairs: AMR MUHAMMAD MOUSSA.

Minister of Supply and Internal Trade: AHMED GUEILY

Minister of Finance: Dr MUHAMMAD AHMAD AR-RAZZAZ.

Minister of Awqaf (Islamic Endowments): Dr MUHAMMAD ALI MAHGOUB.

Minister of Justice: FAROUK SAYF AN-NASR.

Minister of Culture: FAROUK HOSNI.

Minister of Cabinet Affairs: AHMAD RADWAN JUM'AH MANSUR.

Minister of Local Administration: MAHMOUD SAYED AHMED SHARIF.

Minister of Education: HUSSAIN KAMAL BAHAEDDIN.

Minister of Petroleum: Dr Eng. HAMDY AL-BANBI.

Minister of the Interior: HUSSAIN MUHAMMAD AL-ALFI.

Minister of Housing and Public Utilities: Eng. MUHAMMAD SALAH ED-DIN HASSAB-ALLAH.

Minister of Tourism: Dr MAMDOUH EL-BELTAGI.

Minister of Economy and Foreign Trade: MUHAMMAD MAHMOUD BAIOUMI.

Minister of Public Works and Water Resources: Eng. ISAM RADI ABD AL-HAMID RADI.

Minister of Health: Dr ALI ABD AL-FATTAH.

Minister of Industry and Mineral Resources: Dr Eng. IBRAHIM FAWZI ABD AL-WAHED.

Minister of Labour: AHMED AHMED EL-AMAWI.

Minister of Insurance and Social Affairs: Dr AMAL ABD AR-RAHIM OSMAN.

Minister of the Public Sector and Minister of State for Administrative Development and for the Environment: Dr ATIF MUHAMMAD OBEID.

Minister of State for International Co-operation: Dr YOUSSEF BOUTROS GHALI.

Minister of State for Population and Family Affairs: Dr MAHER AHMED MAHRAN.

Minister of State for People's Assembly and Shura (Advisory) Council Affairs: Dr MUHAMMAD ZAKI ABOU-AMER.

Minister of State for New Communities: Dr Eng. MUHAMMAD IBRAHIM SULAYMAN.

Minister of State for Scientific Research: Dr VINIECE KAMEL GOUDA.

Minister of State for Military Production: Dr Eng. MUHAMMAD EL-GHAMRAWI DAWOUD.

MINISTRIES

Ministry of Agriculture: Sharia Wizaret az-Ziraa, Dokki, Giza; tel. (2) 702677; telex 93006.

Ministry of Awqaf (Islamic Endowments): Sharia Sabri Abu Alam, Ean el-Luk, Cairo; tel. (2) 746305.

Ministry of Civil Aviation: Sharia Matar, Cairo (Heliopolis); tel. (2) 969555.

Ministry of Communications: 26 Sharia Ramses, Cairo; tel. (2) 909090.

Ministry of Culture: 110 Sharia al-Galaa, Cairo; tel. (2) 971995.

Ministry of Development, New Communities, Housing and Public Utilities: 1 Ismail Abaza, Qasr el-Eini, Cairo; tel.: Development (2) 3540419; New Communities (2) 3540590; Public Utilities (2) 3540110; telex: Development and New Communities 20807; Public Utilities 92188.

Ministry of Economic Co-operation: 9 Sharia Adly, Cairo; telex 348.

Ministry of Economy: 8 Sharia Adly, Cairo; tel. (2) 907344.

Ministry of Scientific Research: 4 Sharia Ibrahim Nagiv, Cairo (Garden City).

Ministry of Electricity and Energy: Cairo (Nasr City); tel. (2) 829565.

Ministry of Finance: Sharia Maglis esh-Sha'ab, Lazoughli Sq., Cairo; tel. (2) 24857; telex 22386.

Ministry of Foreign Affairs: Tahrir Sq., Cairo; telex 92220.

Ministry of Foreign Trade: Lazoghli Sq., Cairo; tel. (2) 25424.

Ministry of Health: Sharia Magles esh-Sha'ab, Cairo; tel. (2) 903939; telex 94107.

Ministry of Industry: 2 Sharia Latin America, Cairo (Garden City); tel. (2) 3550641; telex 93112.

Ministry of Information: Radio and TV Bldg, Corniche en-Nil, Cairo (Maspiro); tel. (2) 974216.

Ministry of International Co-operation: 8 Sharia Adly, Cairo; tel. (2) 3909707; fax (2) 3915167.

Ministry of Irrigation: Sharia Qasr el-Eini, Cairo; tel. (2) 3552120.

Ministry of Justice: Justice Bldg, Cairo (Lazoughli); tel. (2) 31176.

Ministry of Land Reclamation: Land Reclamation Bldg, Dokki, Giza; tel. 703011.

Ministry of Manpower and Vocational Training: Sharia Yousuf Abbas, Nasr City, Abbasia, Cairo.

Ministry of Military Production: 5 Sharia Ismail Abaza, Kasr el-Eini, Cairo; tel. (2) 3553063; telex 92167.

Ministry of National Education: Sharia el-Falaky, Cairo; tel. (2) 8544805.

Ministry of Naval Transport: 4 Sharia el-Bataisa, Alexandria; tel. 35763; telex 54147.

Ministry of Petroleum and Mineral Resources: el-Mokhayem el-Dayem St, Cairo (Nasr City); tel. (2) 2622237; telex 92197; fax (2) 2636060.

Ministry of Planning: Sharia Salah Salem, Cairo (Nasr City); tel. (2) 604489.

Ministry of Social Affairs: Sharia Sheikh Rihan, Cairo; telex 94105.

Ministry of Social Insurance: 3 Sharia el-Alfi, Cairo; tel. (2) 922717; fax (2) 5922717.

Ministry of Supply and Internal Trade: 99 Sharia Qasr el-Eini, Cairo; tel. (2) 3552600; telex 93497.

Ministry of Tourism: Misr Travel Tower, Abbassia Sq., Cairo; tel. (2) 2828430; telex 94040; fax (2) 2829771.

Ministry of Transport: Sharia Qasr el-Eini, Cairo; tel. (2) 3555566; telex 92802; fax (2) 3555564.

Legislature

MAJLIS ASH-SHA'AB
(People's Assembly)

The law governing election to, and the composition of, the People's Assembly was amended in October 1990. In May 1990 the Supreme Constitutional Court had ruled that the previous elections to the People's Assembly, held in 1987, had been unconstitutional because amendments to the 1972 electoral law discriminated against independent candidates. There are now 222 constituencies, which each elect two deputies to the Assembly. Ten deputies are appointed by the President, giving a total of 454 seats. Parties are no longer required to gain a minimum of 8% of the total vote in order to be represented in the Assembly.

On 12 October 1990, following a popular referendum, the People's Assembly was dissolved. A new Assembly was elected, in accordance with the provisions of the new electoral law, on 29 November.

Speaker: Dr AHMAD FATHI SURUR.

Deputy Speakers: Dr ABD AL-AHAD GAMAL AD-DIN, AHMAD ABU ZEID.

Elections, 29 November and 6 December 1990

Party	% of votes received	Seats
National Democratic Party . . .	79.6	348
National Progressive Unionist Party . .	1.4	6
Independents*	19.0	83
Total	**100.0**	**437†**

* The elections were boycotted by the principal opposition parties (the Socialist Labour Party, the Muslim Brotherhood and the New Wafd Party), which refused to offer candidates unless legislation providing for the declaration of states of emergency was repealed, and the elections were supervised by magistrates.

† Voting was suspended in three constituencies, and for one of the seats of a fourth. There are, in addition, 10 deputies appointed by the President.

MAJLIS ASH-SHURA
(Advisory Council)

In September 1980 elections were held for a 210-member **Shura (Advisory) Council,** which replaced the former Central Committee of the Arab Socialist Union. Of the total number of members, 140 are elected and the remaining 70 are appointed by the President. The National Democratic Party holds all the elected seats. The opposition parties boycotted elections to the Council in October 1983, and again in October 1986, in protest against the 8% electoral threshold. In June 1989 elections to 153 of the Council's 210 seats were contested by opposition parties (the 'Islamic Alliance', consisting of the Muslim Brotherhood, the LSP and the SLP). However, all of the seats in which voting produced a result (143) were won by the National Democratic Party. A supplementary poll was to be held at a later date to elect a further 10 members.

Speaker: Dr ALI LUTFI.

Deputy Speakers: THARWAT ABAZAH, AHMAD AL-IMADI.

Political Organizations

Democratic Unionist Party: f. 1990; Pres. MUHAMMAD ABD AL-MONEIM TURK.

Green Party: f. 1990; Chair. HASSAN RAGEB.

Ikhwan (Brotherhood): f. 1928; officially illegal, the (Muslim) Brotherhood advocates the adoption of the *Shari'a*, or Islamic law, as the sole basis of the Egyptian legal system; Sec.-Gen. MAAMOUN AL-HODAIBY.

Liberal Socialist Party: Cairo; f. 1976; advocates expansion of 'open door' economic policy and greater freedom for private enterprise; Leader MUSTAFA KAMEL MURAD.

Nasserist Party: Cairo; f. 1991.

National Democratic Party: Cairo; f. July 1978; government party established by Anwar Sadat; has absorbed Arab Socialist Party; Leader MUHAMMAD HOSNI MUBARAK; Sec.-Gen. Dr YOUSUF AMIN WALI; Political Bureau: Chair. MUHAMMAD HOSNI MUBARAK; mems: KAMAL HASSAN ALI, Dr MUSTAFA KHALIL, Dr RIFA'AT EL-MAHGOUB, Dr SUBHI ABD AL-HAKIM, Dr MUSTAFA KAMAL HILMI, FIKRI MAKRAM OBEID, Dr ISMAT ABD AL-MEGUID, Dr AMAL OSMAN, SAFWAT ASH-SHARIF, Dr YOUSUF AMIN WALI, HASSAN ABU BASHA, KAMAL HENRY BADIR, Dr AHMAD HEIKAL.

National Progressive Unionist Party (Tagammu): 1 Sharia Karim ed-Dawlah, Cairo; f. 1976; left wing; Leader KHALED MOHI ED-DIN; Sec. Dr RIFA'AT ES-SAID; 160,000 mems.

New Wafd Party: Cairo; original Wafd Party f. 1919; banned 1952; re-formed as New Wafd Party February 1978; disbanded June 1978; re-formed August 1983; Leader FOUAD SERAG ED-DIN; Sec.-Gen. IBRAHIM FARAG.

Socialist Labour Party: 12 Sharia Awali el-Ahd, Cairo; f. September 1978; official opposition party; Leader IBRAHIM SHUKRI.

Umma (National) Party: Islamic religious party, based in Khartoum, Sudan; Leader SADIQ AL-MAHDI (fmr Prime Minister of Sudan).

Young Egypt Party: f. 1990; Chair. ALI ALDIN SALIH.

Diplomatic Representation

EMBASSIES IN EGYPT

Afghanistan: *Interests served by India.*

Albania: 29 Sharia Ismail Muhammad, Cairo (Zamalek); tel. (2) 3415651; Ambassador: ARBEN PANDI CICI.

Algeria: 14 Sharia Bresil, Cairo (Zamalek); tel. (2) 3418527; Ambassador: MUHAMMAD ABRAHIMI EL-MILY.

Angola: 12 Midan en-Nasr, Cairo (Dokki); tel. (2) 707602; Ambassador: DANIEL JULIO CHIPENDA.

Argentina: 8 Sharia as-Saleh Ayoub, Cairo (Zamalek); tel. (2) 3401501; telex 92260; fax (2) 3414355; Ambassador: ALBINO GOMEZ.

Australia: World Trade Centre, Corniche en-Nil, Cairo; tel. (2) 777900; telex 92257; fax (2) 768220; Ambassador: COLIN McDONALD.

Austria: Sharia en-Nil, Cnr of Sharia Wissa Wassef, Cairo (Giza); tel. (2) 5702975; telex 92258; fax (2) 5702979; Ambassador: PETER PRAMBERGER.

Bahrain: 8 Sharia Gamiet an-Nisr; tel. (2) 706202.

Bangladesh: 47 Sharia Ahmed Heshmat, Cairo (Zamalek); tel. (2) 3412642; Ambassador: M. NURUN NABI CHOWDHURY.

Belgium: 20 Sharia Kamel esh-Shennawi, Cairo (Garden City); tel. (2) 3547494; telex 92264; Ambassador: ALAIN RENS.

Bolivia: Cairo; tel. (2) 3546390; fax (2) 3550917; Ambassador: ALBERTO SALAMANCA PRADO.

Brazil: 1125 Corniche en-Nil, 11561 Cairo (Maspiro); tel. (2) 756938; telex 92044; fax (2) 761040; Ambassador: MARCIO DE OLIVEIRA DIAS.

Brunei: 11 Sharia Amer, Cairo (Dokki); tel. (2) 3485903; Dato Paduka Haji SUNI BIN Haji IDRALS.

Bulgaria: 141 Sharia Tahrir, Cairo (Dokki); tel. (2) 982691; Ambassador: PETER VALKANOV.

Burkina Faso: POB 306, Ramses Centre, 3 el-Fawakeh St, Mohandessin, Cairo; tel. (2) 3608480; telex 93871; fax (2) 3495310; Chargé d'affaires a.i.: MAMADOU SANGARE.

Burundi: 13 Sharia el-Israa, Madinet el-Mohandessin, Cairo (Dokki); tel. (2) 3419940; telex 20091; Ambassador: GERVAIS NDIKUMAGNEGE.

Cambodia: 2 Sharia Tahawia, Cairo (Giza); tel. (2) 3489966; Ambassador: IN SOPHEAP.

Cameroon: POB 2061, 15 Sharia Israa, Madinet el-Mohandessin, Cairo (Dokki); tel. (2) 3441101; telex 92088; fax (2) 3459208; Ambassador: MOUCHILI NJI MFOUAYO.

Canada: POB 1668, 6 Sharia Muhammad Fahmy es-Sayed, Cairo (Garden City); tel. (2) 3543110; telex 92677; fax (2) 3563548; Ambassador: MICHAEL BELL.

Central African Republic: 13 Sharia Chehab, Madinet el-Mohandessin, Cairo (Dokki); tel. (2) 713291; Ambassador: HENRY KOBA.

Chad: POB 1869, 12 Midan ar-Refaï, 11511 Cairo (Dokki); tel. (2) 703232; telex 92285; fax (2) 704726; Ambassador: Al-Haji MAHMOUD ADJI.

Chile: 5 Sharia Chagaret ed-Dorr, Cairo (Zamalek); tel. (2) 3408711; telex 92519; fax (2) 3403716; Ambassador: EDUARDO TRABUCCO.

China, People's Republic: 14 Sharia Bahgat Aly, Cairo (Zamalek); tel. (2) 3417691; Ambassador: ZHU YINGLU.

Colombia: 20/A Gamal ed-Din Aboul Mahassen, Cairo (Garden City); tel. (2) 3546152; telex 3036; fax (2) 3557087; Ambassador: MARIO GUTIÉRREZ CÁRDENAS.

Côte d'Ivoire: 39 Sharia el-Kods esh-Sherif, Madinet el-Mohandessin, Cairo (Dokki); tel. (2) 699009; telex 2334; Ambassador: Gen. FÉLIX ORY.

Cuba: 6 Fawakeh St, Madinet el-Mohandessin, Cairo (Dokki); tel. (2) 710390; telex 93966; fax (2) 3612739; Ambassador: ORLANDO MARINO LANCIS SUÁREZ.

Cyprus: 23A Sharia Ismail Muhammad, Cairo (Zamalek); tel. (2) 3411288; telex 92059; fax (2) 3415299; Ambassador: GEORGE GEORGIADES.

Czech Republic: 4 Sharia Dokki, 12511 Cairo (Giza); tel. (2) 3485531; fax (2) 3485892.

Denmark: 12 Sharia Hassan Sabri, Cairo (Zamalek); tel. (2) 3407411; telex 92254; fax (2) 3411780; Ambassador: STEN LILHOLT.

Djibouti: 157 Sharia Sudan, Madinet el-Mohandessin, Cairo (Dokki); tel. (2) 709787; telex 93143; Ambassador: ADEN Sheikh HASSEN.

Ecuador: Suez Canal Bldg, 4 Sharia Ibn Kasir, Cairo (Giza); tel. (2) 3496782; telex 93464; fax (2) 3609327; Chargé d'affaires a.i.: Dr GERMÁN ALEJANDRO ORTEGA.

Ethiopia: 3 Sharia Ibrahim Osman, Mohandessin, Cairo (Dokki); tel. (2) 3477805; fax (2) 3479002; Ambassador: TESHOME TOGA.

Finland: 3 Abu el-Feda St, Cairo (Zamalek); tel. (2) 3411487; fax (2) 3405170; Ambassador: GARTH CASTRÉN.

France: 29 ave en-Nil, Cairo (Giza); tel. (2) 728346; telex 92032; Ambassador: ALAIN DEJAMMET.

Gabon: 15 Sharia Mossadek, Cairo (Dokki); tel. (2) 702963; telex 92323; Ambassador: MAMBO JACQUES.

Germany: 8B Sharia Hassan Sabri, Cairo (Zamalek); tel. (2) 3410015; telex 92023; fax (2) 3410530; Ambassador: Dr WOLF-DIETRICH SCHILLING.

Ghana: 24 Sharia el-Batal Ahmad Abd al-Aziz, Cairo (Dokki); tel. (2) 704275; Ambassador: BON OHANE KWAPONG.

Greece: 18 Sharia Aicha et-Taimouria, Cairo (Garden City); tel. (2) 551074; telex 92036; Ambassador: PANDEUS MENGLIDIS.

Guatemala: POB 8062, 8 Muhammad Fahmi el-Mohdar St, Primer Zone, Madinet Nasr, Cairo; tel. (2) 2611813; fax (2) 2611814; Ambassador: RODOLFO ROSALES MURALLES.

Guinea: 46 Sharia Muhammad Mazhar, Cairo (Zamalek); tel. (2) 3411088; Ambassador: LANSANA KOUYATE.

Guinea-Bissau: 37 Sharia Lebanon, Madinet el-Mohandessin, Cairo (Dokki).

Holy See: Apostolic Nunciature, Safarat al-Vatican, 5 Sharia Muhammad Mazhar, Cairo (Zamalek); tel. (2) 3402250; fax (2) 3406152; Pro-Nuncio: Most Rev. ANTONIO MAGNONI, Titular Archbishop of Boseta.

Hungary: 29 Sharia Muhammad Mazhar, Cairo (Zamalek); tel. (2) 3400653; fax (2) 3408648; Ambassador: ERNŐ JÚHÁSZ.

India: 5 Sharia Aziz Abaza, Cairo (Zamalek); tel. (2) 3413051; telex 92081; fax (2) 3414038; Ambassador: ARUNDHAI GHOSE; also looks after Afghanistan interests at 39 Sharia Orouba (Heliopolis) (tel. (2) 666653); and Iraqi interests at 1 Abd al-Moneim St, Mohandessin, Cairo (tel. (2) 706188).

Indonesia: POB 1661, 13 Sharia Aicha at-Taimouria, Cairo (Garden City); tel. (2) 3547200; Ambassador: R. ACHMAD DJUMIRIL.

Iraq: *Interests served by India.*

Ireland: POB 2681, 3 Sharia Abu el-Feda, Cairo (Zamalek); tel. (2) 3408264; telex 92778; fax (2) 3412863; Ambassador: HUGH SWIFT.

Israel: 6 Sharia ibn el-Malek, Cairo (Giza); tel. (2) 3610545; telex 93363; fax (2) 3610414; Ambassador: DAVID SULTAN.

Italy: 15 Sharia Abd ar-Rahman Fahmi, Cairo (Garden City); tel. (2) 3543974; telex 94229; Ambassador: PATRIZIO SCHMIDLIN.

Japan: Immeuble Cairo Centre, 2nd and 3rd Floors, 2 Sharia Abd al-Kader Hamza or 106 Sharia Kasr el-Eini; tel. (2) 3553962; telex 92226; fax (2) 3546347; Ambassador: TAIZO WATANABE.

Jordan: 6 Sharia Juhaini, Cairo; tel. (2) 3487543; Ambassador: NABIH AN-NIMR.

Kenya: POB 362, 7 el-Mohandess Galal St, Cairo (Dokki); tel. (2) 3453907; telex 92021; fax (2) 3443400; Ambassador: ALI MOHAMED ABDI.

Korea, Democratic People's Republic: 6 Sharia es-Saleh Ayoub, Cairo (Zamalek); tel. (2) 650970; Ambassador: KIM YONG SOP.

Korea, Republic: 3 Sharia Boolos Hanna, Cairo (Dokki); tel. (2) 3611234; fax (2) 3611238.

Kuwait: 12 Sharia Nabil el-Wakkad, Cairo (Dokki); tel. (2) 701611; ABD AR-RAZAK ABD AL-KADER AL-KANDRI.

Lebanon: 5 Sharia Ahmad Nessim, Cairo (Giza); tel. (2) 3610474; telex 92227; fax (2) 3610463; Ambassador: HISHAM DIMASHKIEH.

Liberia: 11 Sharia el-Brasil, Cairo (Zamalek); tel. (2) 3419866; telex 22474; fax (2) 3473074; Ambassador: Dr BRAHIMA D. KABA.

Libya: 7 es-Saleh Ayoub, Cairo (Zamalek); tel. (2) 3401864; Secretary of People's Bureau: AHMAD GADDAF'ADDAM.

Malaysia: 7 Sharia Wadi en-Nil, Mohandessin, Cairo (Agouza); tel. (2) 699162; Ambassador: Dato RAJA MANSUR RAZMAN.

Mali: 3 Sharia al-Kawsar, Cairo (Dokki); tel. (2) 701641; telex 94319; fax (2) 701841; Ambassador: ALLAYE ALPHADY CISSE.

Malta: 7A Sharia 20, Ma'adi, Cairo; tel. (2) 3503014; telex 22689; fax (2) 3754452; Ambassador: IVES DE BARRO.

Mauritania: 31 Sharia Syria, Cairo (Dokki); tel. (2) 707229; telex 92274; MUHAMMAD LEMINE OULD.

Mauritius: 72 Sharia Abd el-Moneim Riad, Cairo (Agouza) 11111; tel. (2) 3470929; telex 93631; fax (2) 3452425; Ambassador: (vacant).

Mexico: 5 Sharia Dar es-Shifa, Cairo (Garden City); tel. (2) 3543422; telex 92277; fax (2) 3557953; Ambassador: Prof. GRACIELA DE LA LAMA.

Mongolia: 3 Midan en-Nasr, Cairo (Dokki); tel. (2) 650060; Ambassador: SONOMDORJIN DAMBADARJAA.

Morocco: 10 Sharia Salah Eddine, Cairo (Zamalak); tel. (2) 3409849; Ambassador: ABD AL-LATIF LARAKI.

Myanmar: 24 Sharia Muhammad Mazhar, Cairo (Zamalek); tel. (2) 3404176; telex 20957; fax (2) 3416793; Ambassador: U AUNG GYI.

Nepal: 9 Sharia Tiba, Cairo (Dokki); tel. (2) 3603426; fax (2) 704447; Ambassador: JITENDRA RAJ SHARMA.

Netherlands: 18 Sharia Hassan Sabri, Cairo (Zamalek); tel. (2) 3406434; telex 92028; fax (2) 3415249; Ambassador: Dr N. VAN DAM.

Niger: 28 Sharia Pahlaw, Cairo (Dokki); tel. (2) 987740; telex 2880; Ambassador: MAMANE OUMAROU.

Nigeria: 13 Sharia Gabalaya, Cairo (Zamalek); tel. (2) 3406042; telex 92038; Chargé d'affaires a.i.: P. S. O. EROMOBOR.

Norway: 8 Sharia el-Gezireh, Cairo (Zamalek); tel. (2) 3403340; telex 92259; fax (2) 3420709; Ambassador: PER T. HAUGESTAD.

Oman: 30 Sharia el-Montazah, Cairo (Zamalek); tel. (2) 3407811; telex 92272; Ambassador: ABDULLA BIN HAMED AL-BUSAIDI.

Pakistan: 8 Sharia es-Salouli, Cairo (Dokki); tel. (2) 3487677; fax (2) 3480310; Ambassador: GUL HANEEF.

Panama: POB 62, 4A Sharia Ibn Zanki, 11211 Cairo (Zamalek); tel. (2) 3411093; telex 92776; fax (2) 3411092; Chargé d'affaires a.i.: ROY FRANCISCO LUNA GONZÁLEZ.

Peru: 8 Kamel esh-Shenawi St, Cairo (Garden City); tel. (2) 3562973; telex 93663; fax (2) 3557985; Ambassador: MANUEL VERAMENDI I. SERRA.

Philippines: 5 Sharia ibn el-Walid, Cairo (Dokki); tel. (2) 3480396; telex 92446; Ambassador: KASAN A. MAROHOMBSAR.

Poland: 5 Sharia el-Aziz Osman, Cairo (Zamalek); tel. (2) 3417456; Ambassador: ROMAN CZYZYCKI.

Portugal: 15A Sharia Mansour Muhammad, Cairo (Zamalek); tel. (2) 3405583; telex 20325; Ambassador: FRANCISCO DO VALLE.

Qatar: 10 Sharia ath-Thamar, Midan an-Nasr, Madinet al-Mohandessin, Cairo; tel. (2) 704537; telex 92287; Ambassador: BADIR AL-DAFA.

Romania: 4 Sharia Aziz Abaza, Cairo (Zamalek); tel. (2) 3410107; telex 93807; fax (2) 3410851; Ambassador: RADU ONOFREI.

Russia: 95 Sharia Giza, Cairo (Giza); tel. (2) 731416; Ambassador: VLADIMIR POLYAKOV.

Rwanda: POB 485, 9 Sharia Ibrahim Osman, Mohandessin, Cairo; tel. (2) 3461126; telex 92552; fax (2) 3461079; Ambassador: CÉLESTIN KABANDA.

Saudi Arabia: 12 Sharia al-Kamel Muhammad, Cairo (Zamalek); tel. (2) 819111; Ambassador: ASSAD ABD AL-KAREM ABOU AN-NASR.

Senegal: 46 Sharia Abd al-Moneim Riad, Mohandessin, Cairo (Dokki); tel. (2) 3458479; telex 92047; Ambassador: SHAMS ED-DINE NDOYE.

Sierra Leone: *Interests served by Saudi Arabia.*

Singapore: POB 356, 40 Sharia Babel, Cairo (Dokki); tel. (2) 704744; telex 21353; fax (2) 3481682; Ambassador: Dr CHIANG HAI DING.

Slovakia: 3 Sharia Adel Hussein Rostom, 12511 Cairo (Giza); tel. (2) 718240; telex 22029; fax (2) 718240.

Somalia: 38 Sharia esh-Shahid Abd el-Moneim Riad, Cairo (Dokki); tel. (2) 704038; Ambassador: ABDALLA HASSAN MAHMOUD.

Spain: 9 Hod el-Laban, Cairo (Garden City); tel. (2) 3547069; telex 92255; Ambassador: EUDALDO MIRAPEIX.

Sri Lanka: POB 1157, 8 Sharia Sri Lanka, Cairo (Zamalek); tel. (2) 3417138; telex 23375; fax (2) 3417138; Ambassador: NORMAN JAMES WAIDYARATNE.

Sudan: 4 Sharia el-Ibrahimi, Cairo (Garden City); tel. (2) 3549661; Ambassador: IZZ AD-DIN HAMID.

Sweden: POB 131, 13 Sharia Muhammad Mazhar, Cairo (Zamalek); tel. (2) 3414132; telex 92256; Ambassador: JAN STAHL.

Switzerland: POB 633, 10 Sharia Abd al-Khalek Saroit, Cairo; tel. (2) 5758133; telex 92267; fax (2) 5745236; Ambassador: MARIANNE VON GRÜNIGEN.

Syria: 14 Ahmad Hechmar St, Cairo (Zamalek); Ambassador: ISSA DARWISH.

Tanzania: 9 Sharia Abd al-Hamid Lotfi, Cairo (Dokki); tel. (2) 704155; telex 23537; Ambassador: MUHAMMAD A. FOUM.

Thailand: 2 Sharia al-Malek el-Afdal, Cairo (Zamalek); tel. (2) 3410094; telex 94231; fax (2) 3400340; Ambassador: RANGSAN PHAHOLYOTHIN.

Tunisia: 26 Sharia el-Jazirah, Cairo (Zamalek); tel. (2) 3404940; Ambassador: ABD AL-HAMID AMMAR.

Turkey: ave en-Nil, Cairo (Giza); tel. (2) 726115; Ambassador: CANDEMIR ONHON.

Uganda: 9 Midan el-Messaha, Cairo (Dokki); tel. (2) 3485544; telex 92087; Ambassador: AHMAD SSENYOMO.

United Arab Emirates: 4 Sharia Ibn Sina, Cairo (Giza); tel. (2) 729955; Ambassador: HAMED HILAL SABIT EL-KUWAITI.

United Kingdom: 7 Sharia Ahmad Raghab, Cairo (Garden City); tel. (2) 3540852; fax (2) 3540859; Ambassador: CHRISTOPHER LONG.

USA: 8 Sharia Kamal ed-Din, Cairo (Garden City); tel. (2) 3557371; telex 93773; fax (2) 3573200; Ambassador: EDWARD S. WALKER, Jr.

Uruguay: 6 Sharia Lotfallah, Cairo (Zamalek); tel. (2) 3415137; telex 92435; fax (2) 3418123; Ambassador: JOSÉ LUIS BRUNO.

Venezuela: 15A Sharia Mansour Muhammad, Cairo (Zamalek); tel. (2) 3413517; telex 93638; fax (2) 3417373; Ambassador: Dr JOSÉ RAFAEL ZANONI.

Viet Nam: 39 Sharia Kambiz, Cairo (Dokki); tel. (2) 701494; fax (2) 3496597; Ambassador: TRAN TAM GIAP.

Yemen: 28 Sharia Amean ar-Rafai, Cairo (Dokki); tel. (2) 3604806; Ambassador: ABD AL-GHALIL GHILAN AHMAD.

Yugoslavia: 33 Sharia Mansour Muhammad, Cairo (Zamalek); tel. (2) 3404061; telex 21046; Ambassador: Dr IVAN IVEKOVIĆ.

Zaire: 5 Sharia Mansour Muhammad, Cairo (Zamalek); tel. (2) 3403662; telex 92294; Ambassador: KAMIMBAYA WA DJONDO.

Zambia: POB 253, Dokki; 6 Abd ar-Rahman Hossein, Mohandessin, 12311 Cairo; tel. (2) 3610282; telex 92262; fax (2) 3610833; Ambassador: Dr ANGEL ALFRED MWENDA.

Zimbabwe: 36 Sharia Wadi an-Nil, Mohandessin, Cairo; tel. (2) 3471217; telex 21876; fax (2) 3474872; Ambassador: MOSES JACKSON MVENGE.

Judicial System

The Courts of Law in Egypt are principally divided into two juridical court systems: Courts of General Jurisdiction and Administrative Courts. Since 1969 the Supreme Constitutional Court has been at the top of the Egyptian judicial structure.

THE SUPREME CONSTITUTIONAL COURT

The Supreme Constitutional Court is the highest court in Egypt. It has specific jurisdiction over: (i) judicial review of the constitutionality of laws and regulations; (ii) resolution of positive and negative jurisdictional conflicts and determination of the competent court between the different juridical court systems, e.g. Courts of General Jurisdiction and Administrative Courts, as well as other bodies exercising judicial competence; (iii) determination of disputes over the enforcement of two final but contradictory judgments rendered by two courts each belonging to a different juridical court system; (iv) rendering binding interpretation of laws or decree laws in the event of a dispute in the application of said laws or decree laws, always provided that such a dispute is of a gravity requiring conformity of interpretation under the Constitution.

COURTS OF GENERAL JURISDICTION

The Courts of General Jurisdiction in Egypt are basically divided into four categories, as follows: (i) The Court of Cassation (ii) The Courts of Appeal; (iii) The Tribunals of First Instance; (iv) The District Tribunals; each of the above courts is divided into Civil and Criminal Chambers.

(i) Court of Cassation: Is the highest court of general jurisdiction in Egypt. Its sessions are held in Cairo. Final judgments rendered by Courts of Appeal in criminal and civil litigation may be petitioned to the Court of Cassation by the Defendant or the Public Prosecutor in criminal litigation and by any of the parties in interest in civil litigation on grounds of defective application or interpretation of the law as stated in the challenged judgment, on grounds of irregularity of form or procedure, or violation of due process, and on grounds of defective reasoning of judgment rendered. The Court of Cassation is composed of the President, 41 Vice-Presidents and 92 Justices.

President: Hon. ABD AL-BORHAN NOOR.

(ii) The Courts of Appeal: Each has geographical jurisdiction over one or more of the governorates of Egypt. Each Court of Appeal is divided into Criminal and Civil Chambers. The Criminal Chambers try felonies, and the Civil Chambers hear appeals filed against such judgment rendered by the Tribunals of First Instance where the law so stipulates. Each Chamber is composed of three Superior Judges. Each Court of Appeal is composed of President, and sufficient numbers of Vice-Presidents and Superior Judges.

(iii) The Tribunals of First Instance: In each governorate there are one or more Tribunals of First Instance, each of which is divided into several Chambers for criminal and civil litigations. Each Chamber is composed of: (a) a presiding judge, and (b) two sitting judges. A Tribunal of First Instance hears, as an Appellate Court, certain litigations as provided under the law.

(iv) District Tribunals: Each is a one-judge ancillary Chamber of a Tribunal of First Instance, having jurisdiction over minor civil and criminal litigations in smaller districts within the jurisdiction of such Tribunal of First Instance.

PUBLIC PROSECUTION

Public prosecution is headed by the Attorney General, assisted by a number of Senior Deputy and Deputy Attorneys General, and a sufficient number of chief prosecutors, prosecutors and assistant prosecutors. Public prosecution is represented at all levels of the Courts of General Jurisdiction in all criminal litigations and also in certain civil litigations as required by the law. Public prosecution controls and supervises enforcement of criminal law judgments.

Attorney General: GAMAL SHOMAN.

Prosecutor-General: MUHAMMAD ABD AL-AZIZ EL-GINDI.

ADMINISTRATIVE COURTS SYSTEM (CONSEIL D'ETAT)

The Administrative Courts have jurisdiction over litigations involving the state or any of its governmental agencies. The Administrative Courts system is divided into two courts: the Administrative Courts and the Judicial Administrative Courts, at the top of which is the High Administrative Court. The Administrative Prosecutor investigates administrative crimes committed by government officials and civil servants.

President of Conseil d'Etat: Hon. MUHAMMAD HILAL QASIM.

Administrative Prosecutor: Hon. RIFA'AT KHAFAGI.

THE STATE COUNCIL

The State Council is an independent judicial body which has the authority to make decisions in administrative disputes and disciplinary cases within the judicial system.

THE SUPREME JUDICIAL COUNCIL

The Supreme Judicial Council was reinstituted in 1984, having been abolished in 1969. It exists to guarantee the independence of the judicial system from outside interference and is consulted with regard to draft laws organizing the affairs of the judicial bodies.

Religion

About 90% of Egyptians are Muslims, and almost all of these follow Sunni tenets. According to government figures from 1986, there are about 2m. Copts (a figure contested by Coptic sources, whose estimates range between 6m. and 7m.), forming the largest religious minority, and about 1m. members of other Christian groups. There is also a small Jewish minority.

ISLAM

There is a Higher Council for the Isamic Call, on which sit: the Grand Sheikh of al-Azhar (Chair); the Minister of Awqaf (Islamic Endowments); the President and Vice-President of Al-Azhar University; the Grand Mufti of Egypt; and the Secretary-General of the Higher Council for Islamic Affairs.

Grand Sheikh of al-Azhar: Sheikh JAD AL-HAQ ALI JAD AL-HAQ.

Grand Mufti of Egypt: Dr MUHAMMAD SAYED ATTIYAH TANTAWI.

CHRISTIANITY

Orthodox Churches

Coptic Orthodox Church: St Mark Cathedral, POB 9035, Anba Ruess, 222 Ramses St, Abbasiya, Cairo; telex 23281; fax (2) 2825983; f. AD 61; Leader Pope SHENOUDA III; c. 10m. followers in Egypt, Sudan, other African countries, the USA, Canada, Australia, Europe and the Middle East.

Greek Orthodox Patriarchate: POB 2006, Alexandria; tel. (3) 4835839; f. AD 64; Pope and Patriarch of Alexandria and All Africa His Beatitude PARTHENIOS III; 350,000 mems.

The Roman Catholic Church

Armenian Rite

The Armenian Catholic diocese of Alexandria, with an estimated 1,800 adherents at 31 December 1992, is suffragan to the Patriarchate of Cilicia. The Patriarch is resident in Beirut, Lebanon.

Bishop of Alexandria: BOUTROS TAZA, Patriarcat Arménien Catholique, 36 Sharia Muhammad Sabri Abou Alam, Cairo; tel. (2) 3938429; fax (2) 3932025.

Chaldean Rite

The Chaldean Catholic diocese of Cairo had an estimated 500 adherents at 31 December 1992.

Bishop of Cairo: YOUSSEF IBRAHIM SARRAF, Evêché Chaldéen, Sanctuaire Notre Dame de Fatima, 141 Sharia Nouzha, 11361 Heliopolis, Cairo; tel. (2) 2455718.

Coptic Rite

Egypt comprises the Coptic Catholic Patriarchate of Alexandria and five dioceses. At May 1993 there were an estimated 210,000 adherents in the country.

Patriarch of Alexandria: His Beatitude STEPHANOS II (ANDREAS GHATTAS), Patriarcat Copte Catholique, POB 69, 34 Sharia Ibn Sandar, Koubbeh Bridge, Cairo; tel. (2) 2571740; fax (2) 4545766.

Latin Rite

Egypt comprises the Apostolic Vicariate of Alexandria (incorporating Heliopolis and Port Said), containing an estimated 6,739 adherents at 31 December 1992.

Vicar Apostolic: Fr EGIDIO SAMPIERI (Titular Bishop of Ida in Mauretania), 10 Sharia Sidi El-Metwalli, Alexandria; tel. (3) 4836065; fax (2) 4833169; also at 2 Sharia Banque Misr, Cairo; tel. (2) 41280.

Maronite Rite

The Maronite diocese of Cairo had an estimated 5,800 adherents at 31 December 1992.

Bishop of Cairo: JOSEPH DERGHAM, Evêché Maronite, 15 Sharia Hamdi, Daher, Cairo; tel. (2) 923327.

Melkite Rite

His Beatitude MAXIMOS V HAKIM (resident in Damascus, Syria) is the Greek-Melkite Patriarch of Antioch, of Alexandria and of Jerusalem.

Patriarchal Exarchate of Egypt and Sudan: Patriarcat Grec-Melkite Catholique, 16 Sharia Daher, Cairo; tel. (2) 905790; 7,500 adherents (31 December 1992); Exarch Patriarchal Mgr PAUL ANTAKI, Titular Archbishop of Nubia.

Syrian Rite

The Syrian Catholic diocese of Cairo had an estimated 2,115 adherents at 31 December 1992.

Bishop of Cairo: BASILE MOUSSA DAOUD, Evêché Syrien Catholique, 46 Sharia Daher, Cairo; tel. (2) 901234.

The Anglican Communion

The Anglican diocese of Egypt, suspended in 1958, was revived in 1974 and became part of the Episcopal Church in Jerusalem and the Middle East, formally inaugurated in January 1976. The Church has four dioceses, and its President is the Bishop in Jerusalem (see the chapter on Israel). The Bishop in Egypt has jurisdiction also over the Anglican chaplaincies in Algeria, Djibouti, Ethiopia, Libya, Somalia and Tunisia.

Bishop in Egypt: Rt Rev. GHAIS ABD AL-MALIK, Diocesan Office, POB 87, 5 Michel Lutfalla St, Zamalek, Cairo; tel. (2) 3414019; fax (2) 3408941.

Other Christian Churches

Armenian Apostolic Church: 179 ave Ramses, Cairo, POB 48-Faggalah; tel. 901385; fax (2) 906671; Archbishop ZAVEN CHINCHINIAN; 10,000 mems.

Protestant Churches of Egypt: POB 1304, 11511 Cairo; tel. (2) 904995; f. 1854, independent since 1926; 200,000 mems (1985); Gen. Sec. Rev. Dr SAMUEL HABIB.

Other denominations active in Egypt include the Coptic Evangelical Church (Synod of the Nile) and the Union of the Armenian Evangelical Churches in the Near East.

JUDAISM

The 1976 census recorded 1,631 Jews in Egypt.

Jewish Community: Office of the Chief Rabbi, Rabbi HAIM DOUEK, 13 Sharia Sebil el-Khazindar, Abbassia, Cairo.

The Press

Despite a fairly high illiteracy rate in Egypt, the country's press is well developed. Cairo is one of the biggest publishing centres in the Middle East and Africa.

Legally all newspapers and magazines come under the guidance of the Supreme Press Council. The four major publishing houses of al-Ahram, Dar al-Hilal, Dar Akhbar al-Yawm and Dar at-Tahrir, operate as separate entities and compete with each other commercially.

The most authoritative daily newspaper is the very long-established *Al-Ahram*. Other popular magazines are *Rose al-Yousuf*, *Sabah al-Kheir* and *Al-Iza'a wat-Television*.

A Press Law of July 1980 liberalized the organization of the major papers and, while continuing to provide for 49% ownership by the employees, arranged for the transfer of the remaining 51% from the defunct Arab Socialist Union to the new Shura (Advisory) Council. The editorial board of a national newspaper should consist of 15 members, nine of whom (including the chairman and the editor-in-chief) are appointed, while the remaining six are elected by staff members. In June 1984 the Shura Council approved a proposal made by the Supreme Press Council that the posts of chairman of the board and editor-in-chief be held separately and not by one individual.

DAILIES

Alexandria

Bareed ach-Charikat (Companies' Post): POB 813, Alexandria; f. 1952; Arabic; evening; commerce, finance, insurance and marine affairs, etc.; Editor S. BENEDUCCI; circ. 15,000.

Al-Ittihad al-Misri (Egyptian Unity): 13 Sharia Sidi Abd ar-Razzak, Alexandria; f. 1871; Arabic; evening; Propr ANWAR MAHER FARAG; Dir HASSAN MAHER FARAG.

Le Journal d'Alexandrie: 1 Sharia Rolo, Alexandria; French; evening; Editor CHARLES ARCACHE.

As-Safeer (The Ambassador): 4 Sharia as-Sahafa, Alexandria; f. 1924; Arabic; evening; Editor MUSTAFA SHARAF.

Tachydromos-Egyptos: 4 Sharia Zangarol, Alexandria; tel. 35650; f. 1879; Greek; morning; liberal; Publr PENY COUTSOUMIS; Editor DINOS COUTSOUMIS; circ. 2,000.

Cairo

Al-Ahram (The Pyramids): Sharia al-Galaa, Cairo; tel. (2) 5747011; telex 92002; fax (2) 5747089; f. 1875; Arabic; morning; incl. Sundays (international edition published in London, England; North American edition published in New York, USA); Editor and Chair. IBRAHIM NAFEH; circ. 900,000 (weekdays), 1.1m. (Friday).

Al-Akhbar (The News): Dar Akhbar al-Yawm, Sharia as-Sahafa, Cairo; tel. (2) 5748100; telex 20321; f. 1952; Arabic; Chair. IBRAHIM ABU SADAH; Managing Editor GALAL DEWIDAR; circ. 980,000.

Arev: 3 Sharia Soliman Halaby, Cairo; tel. 754703; f. 1915; Armenian; evening; official organ of the Armenian Liberal Democratic Party; Editor AVEDIS YAPOUDJIAN.

Egyptian Gazette: 24–26 Sharia Zakaria Ahmad, Cairo; tel. (2) 751511; telex 92475; f. 1880; English; morning; Editor-in-Chief MOHAMED EL-EZABI; circ. 35,000.

Al-Gomhouriya (The Republic): 24 Sharia Zakaria Ahmad, Cairo; tel. (2) 751511; telex 92475; f. 1953; Arabic; morning; Chair. SAMIR RAGAB; Editor MAHFOUZ AL-ANSARI; circ. 650,000.

Le Journal d'Egypte: 1 Sharia Borsa Guédida, Cairo; f. 1936; French; morning; Gen. Man. LITA GALLAD; Editor-in-Chief MUHAMMAD RACHAD; circ. 72,000.

Mayo (May): Sharia al-Galaa, Cairo; organ of National Democratic Party; Supervisor MUHAMMAD SAFWAT ASH-SHARIF; Chair. ABDULLAH ABD AL-BARY; Chief Editor SAMIR RAGAB; circ. 500,000.

Al-Misaa' (The Evening): 24 Sharia Zakaria Ahmad, Cairo; telex 92475; f. 1956; Arabic; evening; Editor-in-Chief SAMIR RAGAB; circ. 105,000.

Misr (Egypt): Cairo; f. 1977; organ of the Arab Socialist Party.

Phos: 14 Sharia Zakaria Ahmad, Cairo; f. 1896; Greek; morning; Editor S. PATERAS; Man. BASILE A. PATERAS; circ. 20,000.

Le Progrès Egyptien: 24 Sharia Zakaria Ahmad, Cairo; tel. (2) 741611; telex 92475; f. 1890; French; morning including Sundays; Editor-in-Chief KHALED ANWAR BAKIR; circ. 21,000.

PERIODICALS

Alexandria

Al-Ahad al-Gedid (New Sunday): 88 Sharia Said M. Koraim, Alexandria; tel. 807874; f. 1936; Editor-in-Chief and Publr GALAL M. KORAITEM; circ. 60,000.

Alexandria Medical Journal: 4 G. Carducci, Alexandria; f. 1922; English, French and Arabic; quarterly; publ. by Alexandria Medical Asscn; Editor AMIN RIDA; circ. 1,500.

Amitié Internationale: 59 avenue Hourriya, Alexandria; tel. 23639; f. 1957; publ. by Asscn Egyptienne d'Amitié Internationale; Arabic and French; quarterly; Editor Dr ZAKI BADAOUI.

L'Annuaire des Sociétés Egyptiennes par Actions: 23 Midan Tahrir, Alexandria; f. 1930; annually in December; French; Propr ELIE I. POLITI; Editor OMAR ES-SAYED MOURSI.

L'Echo Sportif: 7 Sharia de l'Archevêché, Alexandria; French; weekly; Propr MICHEL BITTAR.

Egypte-Sports-Cinéma: 7 avenue Hourriya, Alexandria; French; weekly; Editor EMILE ASSAAD.

Egyptian Cotton Gazette: POB 433, Alexandria; fax 809482; organ of the Alexandria Cotton Exporters Association; English; 2 a year; Chief Editor AHMAD HASSAN YOUSSEF.

Informateur des Assurances: 1 Sharia Sinan, Alexandria; f. 1936; French; monthly; Propr ELIE I. POLITI; Editor SIMON A. BARANIS.

Sina 'at en-Nassig (L'Industrie Textile): 5 rue de l'Archevêché, Alexandria; Arabic and French; monthly; Editor PHILIPPE COLAS.

Voce d'Italia: 90 Sharia Farahde, Alexandria; Italian; fortnightly; Editor R. AVELLINO.

Cairo

Al-Ahali (The People): 23 Sharia Abd al-Khalek, Tharwat, Cairo; tel. (2) 3923306; fax (2) 3909114; f. 1978; weekly; published by the National Progressive Unionist Party; Chair. LOTFI WAKID; Editor-in-Chief ABD EL-BAKOURY.

Al-Ahram al-Iqtisadi (The Economic *Al-Ahram*): Sharia al-Galaa, Cairo; telex 20185; fax (2) 745888; Arabic; weekly; economic and political affairs; owned by Al-Ahram publrs; Chief Editor ISSAM RIFA'AT; circ. 67,000.

Al-Ahram Weekly (The Pyramids): Al-Ahram Bldg, Sharia al-Galaa, Cairo; tel. (2) 5786064; telex 20185; fax (2) 5786833; f. 1989; English; weekly; published by Al-Ahram publications; Editor-in-Chief HOSNY GUINDY; circ. 150,000.

Al-Ahrar (The Liberals): Cairo; f. 1977; weekly; published by Liberal Socialist Party; Editor WAHID GHAZI.

Akhbar al-Yaum (Daily News): 6 Sharia as-Sahafa, Cairo; f. 1944; Arabic; weekly (Saturday); Chair. and Editor-in-Chief IBRAHIM ABU SEDAH; circ. 1,158,000.

Akher Sa'a (Last Hour): Dar Akhbar al-Yawm, Sharia as-Sahafa, Cairo; telex 92215; f. 1934; Arabic; weekly (Wednesday); independent; Editor-in-Chief MUHAMMAD WAJDI KANDIL; circ. 150,000.

Al-Azhar: Idarat al-Azhar, Sharia al-Azhar, Cairo; f. 1931; Arabic; Islamic monthly; supervised by the Egyptian Council for Islamic Research of Al-Azhar University; Dir MUHAMMAD FARID WAGDI.

Al-Bitrul (Petroleum): Cairo; monthly; published by the Egyptian General Petroleum Corporation.

Contemporary Thought: University of Cairo, Cairo; quarterly; Editor Dr Z. N. MAHMOUD.

Ad-Da'wa (The Call): Cairo; Arabic; monthly; organ of the Muslim Brotherhood.

Ad-Doctor: 8 Sharia Hoda Shaarawy, Cairo; f. 1947; Arabic; monthly; Editor Dr AHMAD M. KAMAL; circ. 30,000.

Echos: 1–5 Sharia Mahmoud Bassiouni, Cairo; f. 1947; French; weekly; Dir and Propr GEORGES QRFALI.

The Egyptian Mail: 24–26 Sharia Zakaria Ahmad; telex 92475; weekly; Saturday edition of *The Egyptian Gazette*; English; circ. 35,000.

Al-Fusoul (The Seasons): 17 Sharia Sherif Pasha, Cairo; Arabic; monthly; Propr and Chief Editor SAMIR MUHAMMAD ZAKI ABD AL-KADER.

Al-Garidat at-Tigariyat al-Misriya (The Egyptian Business Paper): 25 Sharia Nubar Pasha, Cairo; f. 1921; Arabic; weekly; circ. 7,000.

Hawa'a (Eve): Dar al-Hilal, 16 Sharia Muhammad Ezz el-Arab, Cairo; telex 92703; women's magazine; Arabic; weekly; Chief Editor SUAD AHMAD HILMI; circ. 160,837.

Al-Hilal Magazine: Dar al-Hilal, 16 Sharia Muhammad Ezz el-Arab, Cairo; telex 92703; f. 1895; Arabic; literary monthly; Editor MOUSTAFA NABIL.

Industrial Egypt: POB 251, 26A Sharia Sherif Pasha, Cairo; tel. (2) 3928317; telex 92624; fax (2) 3928075; f. 1924; quarterly bulletin and year book of the Federation of Egyptian Industries in English and Arabic; Editor ALI FAHMY.

Informateur Financier et Commercial: 24 Sharia Soliman Pasha, Cairo; f. 1929; weekly; Dir HENRI POLITI; circ. 15,000.

Al-Iza'a wat-Television (Radio and Television): 13 Sharia Muhammad Ezz el-Arab, Cairo; f. 1935; Arabic; weekly; Editor and Chair. SAKEENA FOUAD; circ. 80,000.

Al-Kerazeh (The Sermon): Cairo; Arabic; weekly newspaper of the Coptic Orthodox Church.

Al-Kawakeb (The Stars): Dar al-Hilal, 16 Sharia Muhammad Ezz el-Arab, Cairo; tel. (2) 27954; f. 1952; Arabic; weekly; film magazine; Editor HOSN SHAH; circ. 86,381.

Kitab al-Hilal: Dar al-Hilal, 16 Sharia Muhammad Ezz el-Arab, Cairo; monthly; Founders EMILE and SHOUKRI ZEIDAN; Editor MOUSTAFA NABIL.

Al-Liwa' al-Islami (Islamic Standard): 11 Sharia Sherif Pasha, Cairo; f. 1982; Arabic; weekly; government paper to promote official view of Islamic revivalism; Propr AHMAD HAMZA; Editor MUHAMMAD ALI SHETA; circ. 30,000.

Lotus Magazine (Afro-Asian Writings): 104 Sharia Qasr el-Eini, Cairo; f. 1968; quarterly; English, French and Arabic.

Magallat al-Mohandeseen (The Engineer's Magazine): 28 avenue Ramses, Cairo; f. 1945; published by The Engineers' Syndicate; Arabic and English; 10 a year; Editor and Sec. MAHMOUD SAMI ABD AL-KAWI.

Al-Magallat az-Zira'ia (The Agricultural Magazine): Cairo; monthly; agriculture; circ. 30,000.

Medical Journal of Cairo University: Manyal University Hospital, Sharia Qasr el-Eini, Cairo; f. 1933; Kasr el-Eini Clinical Society; English; quarterly.

The Middle East Observer: 41 Sherif St, Cairo; tel. (2) 3926919; fax (2) 3939732; f. 1954; English; weekly; specializing in economics of Middle East and African markets; also publishes supplements on law, foreign trade and tenders; agent for IMF, UN and IDRC publications, distributor of World Bank publications; Man. Owner AHMAD FODA; Chief Editor MUHAMMAD ABDULLAH HESHAM A. RAOUF; circ. 30,000.

Al-Musawar: Dar al-Hilal, 16 Sharia Muhammad Ezz el-Arab, Cairo; tel. (2) 27954; telex 92703; f. 1924; Arabic; weekly; Editor-in-Chief MAKRAM MUHAMMAD AHMAD; circ. 130,423.

October: 1119 Sharia Corniche en-Nil, Cairo; tel. (2) 777077; telex 847031; fax (2) 5744999; monthly; Chair. and Editor-in-Chief SALAH MONTASSIR; circ. 140,500.

Al-Omal (The Workers): 90 Sharia Galal, Cairo; telex 93255; published by the Egyptian Trade Union Federation: Arabic; weekly; Chief Editor AHMAD HARAK.

Progrès Dimanche: 24 Sharia Galal, Cairo; tel. 741611; telex 92475; French; weekly; Sunday edition of *Le Progrès Egyptien*; Editor-in-Chief KHALED ANWAR BAKIR.

Rose al-Yousuf: 89A Sharia Qasr el-Eini, Cairo; f. 1925; Arabic; weekly; political; circulates throughout all Arab countries; Chair. of Board and Editor MAHMUD TUHAMI; circ. 35,000.

As-Sabah (The Morning): 4 Sharia Muhammad Said Pasha, Cairo; f. 1922; Arabic; weekly; Editor MUSTAFA EL-KACHACHI.

Sabah al-Kheir (Good Morning): 18 Sharia Muhammad Said Pasha, Cairo; Arabic; weekly; light entertainment; Chief Editor MOFEED FAWZI; circ. 70,000.

Ash-Shaab (The People): 313 Sharia Port Said, Cairo; organ of Socialist Labour Party; weekly; Editor-in-Chief ADEL HUSSEIN; circ. 130,000.

At-Tahrir (Liberation): 5 Sharia Naguib, Rihani, Cairo; Arabic; weekly; Editor ABD AL-AZIZ SADEK.

At-Taqaddum (Progress): c/o 1 Sharia Jarim ed-Dawlah, Cairo; f. 1978; organ of National Progressive Unionist Party.

Tchehreh Nema: 14 Sharia Hassan el-Akbar (Abdine), Cairo; f. 1904; Iranian; monthly; political, literary and general; Editor MANUCHEHR TCHEHREH NEMA MOADEB ZADEH.

Up-to-Date International Industry: 10 Sharia Galal, Cairo; Arabic and English; monthly; foreign trade journal.

Al-Wafd: Cairo; f. 1984; weekly; organ of the New Wafd Party; Editor-in-Chief GAMAL BADAWI; circ. 360,000.

Watani (My Country): Cairo; French; weekly newspaper of the Coptic Orthodox Church; Editor MEGUID ATTAIA.

Yulio (July): July Press and Publishing House, Cairo; f. 1986; weekly; Nasserist; Editor ABDULLAH IMAM; and a monthly cultural magazine, Editor MAHMOUD AL-MARAGHI.

NEWS AGENCIES

Middle East News Agency: 17 Sharia Hoda Sharawi, Cairo; tel. (2) 3933000; telex 92252; fax (2) 3935055; f. 1955; regular service in Arabic, English and French; Chair. and Editor-in-Chief MOUSTAFA NAGUIB.

Foreign Bureaux

Agence France-Presse (AFP): POB 1437-15511, 2nd Floor, 10 Misaha Sq, Cairo; tel. (2) 3481236; telex 92225; fax (2) 3603282; Correspondent DAVID DAUR.

Agencia EFE (Spain): 35a Sharia Abul Feda, 4th Floor, Apt 14, Cairo (Zamalek); Correspondent DOMINGO DEL PINO.

Agenzia Nazionale Stampa Associata (ANSA) (Italy): 19 Sharia Abd al-Khalek Sarwat, Cairo; tel. (2) 3929821; telex 93365; fax (2) 3938642; Chief ANTONELLA TARQUINI.

Allgemeiner Deutscher Nachrichtendienst (ADN) (Germany): 17 Sharia el-Brazil, Apt 59, Cairo (Zamalek); tel. (2) 3404006; telex 92339; Correspondent RALF SCHULTZE.

Associated Press (AP) (USA): POB 1077, 33 Sharia Qasr en-Nil, Cairo 11511; tel. (2) 3936096; telex 92211; fax (2) 3939089; Chief WILLIAM C. MANN.

Deutsche Presse-Agentur (dpa) (Germany): 14th Floor, 1125 Corniche en-Nil, Cairo; tel. (2) 5780351; telex 92054; fax (2) 5780354; Chief JÖRG FISCHER.

Informatsionnoye Telegrafnoye Agentstvo Rossii-Telegrafnoye Agentstvo Suverennykh Stran (ITAR-TASS) (Russia): 30 Sharia Muhammad Mazhar, Cairo (Zamalek); tel. 3419784; telex 93008; fax (2) 3417268; Dir MIKHAIL I. KROUTIKHIN.

Jiji Press (Japan): Room 2, 1st Floor, 3 Gezira el-Wosta, Cairo (Zamalek); tel. (2) 3411411; telex 20940; fax (2) 3405244; Chief SATORU YAMAMOTO.

Kyodo News Service (Japan): Flat 2, 9 Sharia el-Kamel Muhammad, Zamalek, Cairo; tel. (2) 3411571; telex 20435; fax (2) 3406105; Correspondent SHIN SASAKI.

Magyar Távirati Iroda (MTI) (Hungary): 6A el-Malek el-Afdal St, Cairo (Zamalek); tel. (2) 3402892; fax (2) 3402898; Chief GYÖRGY RAKOS.

Reuters (United Kingdom): POB 2040, 21st Floor, Bank Misr Tower, 153 Sharia Muhammad Farid, Cairo; tel. (2) 777121; telex 92210; fax (2) 771133; Chief Correspondent JONATHAN WRIGHT.

United Press International (UPI) (USA): POB 872, 4 Sharia Eloui, Cairo; tel. (2) 3928106.

Xinhua (New China) News Agency (People's Republic of China): 2 Moussa Galal Sq., Mohandessin, Cairo; tel. (2) 3448950; telex 93812.

The Iraqi News Agency (INA) reopened its office in Cairo in October 1985.

Publishers

General Egyptian Book Organization: 117 Sharia Corniche en-Nil, Boulak, Cairo; tel. (2) 775000; telex 93932; f. 1961; affiliated to the Ministry of Culture; Chair. Dr SAMIR SARHAN.

Alexandria

Alexandria University Press: Shatby, Alexandria.

Egyptian Printing and Publishing House: Ahmad es-Sayed Marouf, 59 Safia Zaghoul, Alexandria; f. 1947.

Maison Egyptienne d'Editions: Ahmad es-Sayed Marouf, Sharia Adib, Alexandria; f. 1950.

Maktab al-Misri al-Hadith li-t-Tiba wan-Nashr: 7 Sharia Noubar, Alexandria; also at 2 Sharia Sherif, Cairo; Man. AHMAD YEHIA.

Cairo

Al-Ahram Establishment: Sharia al-Galaa, Cairo; tel. (2) 758333; telex 92001; fax 745888; f. 1875; publishes newspapers, magazines and books, incl. *Al-Ahram*; Chair. IBRAHIM NAFEA.

Akhbar al-Yawm Publishing Group: 6 Sharia as-Sahafa, Cairo; tel. (2) 5748100; telex 20321; fax (2) 5748895; f. 1944; publishes *Al-Akhbar* (daily), *Akhbar al-Yawm* (weekly), and colour magazine *Akher Sa'a* (weekly); Pres. IBRAHIM SAAD.

Al-Arab Publishing House: 28–29 Sharia Faggalah, 11271 Cairo; tel. (2) 908025; fax 771140; f. 1900; fiction, poetry, history, biography, philosophy, Arabic language, literature, politics, religion, etc.; Man. Dir Dr SALADIN BOUSTANY.

Argus Press: 10 Sharia Zakaria Ahmad, Cairo; Owners KARNIG HAGOPIAN and ABD AL-MEGUID MUHAMMAD.

Dar al-Gomhouriya: 24 Sharia Zakaria Ahmad, Cairo; affiliate of At-Tahrir Printing and Publishing House; publications include the dailies, *Al-Gomhouriya*, *Al-Misaa'*, *Egyptian Gazette* and *Le Progrès Egyptien*; Pres. MOHSEN MUHAMMAD.

Dar al-Hilal Publishing Institution: 16 Sharia Muhammad Ezz el-Arab, Cairo; tel. (2) 20610; telex 92703; f. 1892; publishes *Al-Hilal, Riwayat al-Hilal, Kitab al-Hilal, Tabibak al-Khass* (monthlies); *Al-Mussawar, Al-Kawakeb, Hawaa, Samir, Mickey* (weeklies); Chair. MAKRAN MUHAMMAD AHMAD.

Dar al-Kitab al-Arabi: Misr Printing House, Sharia Noubar, Bab al-Louk, Cairo; f. 1968; Man. Dir Dr SAHAIR AL-KALAMAWI.

Dar al-Kitab al-Masri: POB 156, 33 Sharia Kasr en-Nil, Cairo; tel. (2) 3922168; telex 23081; fax (2) 3924657; f. 1929; religion, history, books for children, general interest, etc.; Man. Dir HASSAN EL-ZEIN.

Dar al-Maaref: 1119 Sharia Corniche en-Nil, Cairo; tel. (2) 777077; telex 92199; fax (2) 5744999; f. 1890; publishing, printing and distribution of all kinds of books in Arabic and other languages; publishers of *October* magazine; Chair. and Man. Dir SALAH MUNTASSAR.

Dar an-Nashr (formerly Les Editions Universitaires d'Egypte): POB 1347, 41 Sharia Sherif, 11511 Cairo; tel. (2) 3934606; fax (2) 3921997; f. 1947; university textbooks, academic works, encyclopaedia.

Dar ash-Shorouk: 16 Sharia Gawad Hosni, Cairo; tel. (2) 3929333; telex 93091; fax (2) 3934814; f. 1968; publishing, printing and distribution; publishers of books on modern Islamic politics, philosophy and art, and books for children; Chair. M. I. EL-MOALLIM.

Editions Horus: 1 Midan Soliman Pasha, Cairo.

Editions le Progrès: 6 Sharia Sherif Pasha, Cairo; Propr WADI SHOUKRI.

Egyptian Co for Printing and Publishing: 40 Sharia Noubar, Cairo; tel. (2) 21310; Chair. MUHAMMAD MAHMOUD HAMED.

Higher University Council for Arts, Letters and Sciences: University of Cairo, Cairo.

Lagnat at-Taalif wat-Targama wan-Nashr (Committee for Writing, Translating and Publishing Books): 9 Sharia el-Kerdassi (Abdine), Cairo.

Librairie La Renaissance d'Egypte (Hassan Muhammad & Sons): POB 2172, 9 Sharia Adly, Cairo; f. 1930; religion, history, geography, medicine, architecture, economics, politics, law, philosophy, psychology, children's books, atlases, dictionaries; Man HASSAN MUHAMMAD.

Maktabet Misr: POB 16, 3 Sharia Kamal Sidki, Cairo; tel. (2) 5898553; fax (2) 907593; f. 1932; publs wide variety of fiction, biographies and textbooks for schools and universities; Man. AMIR SAID GOUDA ES-SAHHAR.

National Centre for Educational Research and Development: 12 Sharia Waked, el-Borg el-Faddy, POB 836, Cairo; tel. (2) 3930981; f. 1956; formerly Documentation and Research Centre for Education (Ministry of Education); bibliographies, directories, information and education bulletins; Dir Prof. ABD EL-FATTAH GALAL.

National Library Press (Dar al-Kutub): Midan Ahmad Maher, Cairo; bibliographic works.

Senouhy Publishers: 54 Sharia Abd al-Khalek Sarwat, Cairo; f. 1956; Dirs LEILA A. FADEL, OMAR RASHAD.

At-Tahrir Printing and Publishing House: 24 Sharia Zakaria Ahmad, Cairo; tel. (2) 5749999; telex 92475; f. 1953; affil. to Shura (Advisory) Council; Chair. and Man. Dir SAMIR RAGAB.

Radio and Television

In 1991 there were an estimated 17.5m. radio receivers and 6.2m. television receivers in use.

RADIO

Egyptian Radio and Television Union (ERTU): Radio and TV Building, POB 504, Sharia Maspiro, Corniche en-Nil, Cairo; tel. (2) 749508; telex 22609; fax (2) 746989; f. 1928; 450 hours daily. Home Service radio programmes in Arabic, English and French; foreign services in Arabic, English, French, Swahili, Hausa, Bengali, Urdu, German, Spanish, Armenian, Greek, Hebrew, Indonesian, Malay, Thai, Hindi, Pushtu, Persian, Turkish, Somali, Portuguese, Fulani, Italian, Zulu, Shona, Sindebele, Lingala, Afar, Amharic, Yoruba, Wolof, Bambara; Pres. Eng. FATHI AL-BAIOUMI.

Middle East Radio: Société Egyptienne de Publicité, 24–26 Sharia Zakaria Ahmad, Cairo; f. 1964; commercial service with 500-kW transmitter; UK Agents: Radio and Television Services (Middle East) Ltd, 21 Hertford St, London, W1.

TELEVISION

Egyptian Television Organization: POB 1186, Radio and TV Bldg, Sharia Maspiro, Corniche en-Nil, Cairo; tel. (2) 755721; telex 92466; f. 1960; 42 hours of programmes daily (2 main channels, 3 regional channels); Pres. ABDEL SALAM EL-NADI.

Finance

(cap. = capital; auth. = authorized; p.u. = paid up; dep. = deposits; res = reserves; m. = million; brs = branches; amounts in £ Egyptian unless otherwise stated)

BANKING

The whole banking system was nationalized in 1961. Since 1974 foreign and private sector banks have been allowed to play a role in the economy, and about 100 joint-venture banks, branches of foreign banks and private banks have been established. More than 200 financial institutions are now operating in Egypt.

Central Bank

Central Bank of Egypt: 31 Sharia Qasr en-Nil, Cairo; tel. (2) 3931514; telex 92237; fax (2) 3904232; f. 1961; state-owned; cap. 100m., dep. 84,113m., res 2,161m., total assets 101,388m. (June 1993); Gov. and Chair. ESMAIEL HASSAN MUHAMMAD; 3 brs.

Commercial and Specialized Banks

Alexandria Commercial and Maritime Bank: POB 2376, 85 avenue el-Hourriya, Alexandria 21519; tel. (3) 4921556; telex 54553; fax (3) 4913706; f. 1981; the National Investment Bank has 10% interest, Bank of Alexandria 9.71%, National Bank of Egypt 9.52%, Misr Insurance Co 8.83%, Other interests 61.94%; cap. 32,078.3m., dep. 455.4m., total assets 582.7m. (Dec. 1991); Chair. MUHAMMAD ADEL EL-BARKOUKI; Man. Dir MUHAMMAD MAHMOUD FAHMY; 3 brs.

Bank of Alexandria, SAE: 6 Sharia Salah Salem, Alexandria; and 49 Sharia Kasr en-Nil, Cairo; tel. (3) 4831460 (Alexandria), (02) 3913822 (Cairo); telex 54107 (Alexandria), 92069 (Cairo); f. 1957; state-owned; cap. p.u. 650m., total assets 12,307m. (Dec. 1992); Chair. ISMAIL HASSAN MUHAMMAD; 184 brs.

Bank of Commerce and Development: POB 1373, 13 Midan 26 July Sq., Sphinx, Mohandessin, Cairo; tel. (2) 3479461; telex 21607; fax (2) 3450581; f. 1980; cap. 100m., dep. 416.3m., total assets 736m. (Dec. 1992); Chair. and Man. Dir SAMIR MUHAMMAD FOUAD EL-QASRI; 6 brs.

Banque du Caire, SAE: POB 1495, 30 Roushdy St, Cairo; tel. (2) 3904554; telex 92838; fax (2) 3908922; f. 1952; state-owned; cap. p.u. 803m., dep. 11,477m., total assets 14,044m. (June 1992); Chair. MUHAMMAD ABD EL-FATH ABDEL AZIZ; 208 brs.

Banque Misr: 151 Sharia Muhammad Farid, Cairo; tel. (2) 3912711; telex 92242; fax (2) 3919779; f. 1920; state-owned since 1960; cap. p.u. 1,000m., dep. 26,696m. (June 1992); Chair. MUHAMMAD Ali HAFEZ; 380 brs.

Crédit Foncier Egyptien: 11 Sharia el-Mashadi, POB 141, Cairo; tel. (2) 3911977; telex 93863; f. 1880; state-owned; cap. p.u. 30.5m., dep. 24.3m., res 32.9m., total assets 1,182.6m. (June 1989); Chair. ADEL MAHMOUD ABD AL-BAKI; Gen Man. IBRAHIM ABD AL-HALIM KHOR ED-DIN; 9 brs.

Egyptian British Bank: POB 126 D, Abu el-Feda Bldg, 3 Sharia Abu el-Feda, Zamalek, Cairo; tel. (2) 3404849; telex 20471; fax (2) 3414010; f. 1982; the Hongkong and Shanghai Banking Corporation has a 40% shareholding, Egyptian interests 51%, other Arab interests 9%; auth. cap. 18.5m., dep. 291m. res 4m., total assets 574m. (Dec. 1993); Chair. Dr HAMED ES-SAYEH; 4 brs.

Egyptian Workers Bank: 10 Muhammad Hilmy Ibrahim, Cairo; tel. (2) 763622; telex 23520; f. 1983; Workers Union has a 70% interest, Banque Misr and other Egyptian interests 30%; cap. p.u. 9.9m., dep. 45.4m., res 6.2m., total assets 77.5m. (June 1989); Chair. AHMED MUHAMMAD AMAWY; 3 brs.

Export Development Bank of Egypt: Evergreen Bldg, 10 Sharia Talaat Harb, Cairo; f. 1983 to replace National Import-Export Bank; tel. (2) 777003; telex 20850; fax (2) 774553; cap. p.u. 69m., dep. 718.5m., res 67.2m., total assets 1,080.8m. (June 1992); Chair. Dr HAZEM EL-BEBLAWY; 3 brs.

Industrial Development Bank of Egypt: 110 Sharia el-Galaa, Cairo; tel. (2) 779087; telex 23377; fax (2) 777324; f. 1975; cap. p.u. 146.2m.; total assets 1,403m. (June 1991); Chair. Dr KAMAL ABOU EL-EID; 8 brs.

National Bank for Development: POB 647, 5 Sharia el-Borsa el-Gedida, Cairo; tel. (2) 3936191; telex 20878; fax (2) 3936719; f. 1980; cap. p.u. 80.4m., dep. 1,690.9m., res 36.2m., total assets 2,228.3m. (Dec. 1992); Chair. MUHAMMAD ZAKI EL-ORABI; 12 brs; there are affiliated National Banks for Development in 16 governorates.

National Bank of Egypt: 24 Sharia Sherif, Cairo; tel. (2) 3924143; telex 92238; f. 1898; nationalized 1960; handles all commercial banking operations; cap. 1,000m., dep. 37,075m., total assets 44,319m. (June 1992); Chair. MAHMOUD ABD EL-AZIZ; 283 brs in Egypt, 2 in London.

Commercial International Bank (Egypt), SAE: POB 2430, Nile Tower Bldg, 21-23 Sharia Giza, Giza; tel. (2) 5703043; telex 20201; fax (2) 5703172; f. 1975; National Bank of Egypt has 79.997% interest; name changed 1987; cap. 150m., dep. 2,943m., total assets 4,405m. (Dec. 1991); Exec. Chair. MAHMOUD ABD AL-AZIZ MUHAMMAD; 15 brs.

Principal Bank for Development and Agricultural Credit: POB 11612, 110 Sharia Qasr el-Eini, Cairo; tel. (2) 3551204; telex 93045; f. 1976 to succeed former Credit organizations; state-owned; cap. p.u. 114.3m., dep. 11,611m., res 77.8m., total assets 1,054.7m. (June 1989); Chair. HASSAN KHIDR; Gen. Man. ABED AR-RAOUF DEKHEL; 8 brs.

Société Arabe Internationale de Banque: POB 124, 56 Sharia Gamet ed-Dowal al-Arabia, Mohandessin, Cairo (Giza); tel. (2) 3499463; telex 22087; fax (2) 3603497; f. 1976; the Arab International Bank has a 39.3% share, other interests 60.7%; cap. p.u. US $28m., dep. US $92.2m., total assets 148.7m. (Dec. 1992); Chair. Dr HASSAN ABBAS ZAKI; 4 brs.

Social Bank

Nasser Social Bank: POB 2552, 35 Sharia Qasr en-Nil, Cairo; tel. (2) 744377; telex 92754; f. 1971; state-owned; interest-free savings and investment bank for social and economic activities, participating in social insurance, specializing in financing co-operatives, craftsmen and social institutions; cap. p.u. 20m.; Chair. NASSIF TAHOON.

Multinational Banks

Arab African International Bank: 5 Midan es-Saray al-Koubra, Garden City, POB 60, Majlis ash-Sha'ab, 11516 Cairo; tel. (2) 3545094; telex 93531; fax (2) 3558493; f. 1964; cap. p.u. US $100.0m., dep. US $611.1m., total assets US $1,090m. (Dec. 1992); commercial investment bank; shareholders are Governments of Kuwait, Egypt, Algeria, Jordan and Qatar, Bank Al-Jazira (Saudi Arabia), Rafidain Bank (Iraq), individuals and Arab institutions; Chair. Dr FAHED F. AR-RASHED; Deputy Chair. and Man. Dir MUHAMMAD IBRAHIM FARID; 4 brs in Egypt, 4 abroad.

Arab International Bank: POB 1563, 35 Sharia Abd al-Khalek Sarwat, Cairo; tel. (2) 3918794; telex 92098; fax (2) 3916233; f. 1971 as Egyptian International Bank, renamed 1974; cap. p.u. US $175m., res US $95.5m., dep. US $1,925m., total assets US $2,271.9m. (June 1993); offshore bank; aims to promote trade and investment in shareholders' countries and other Arab countries; owned by Egypt, Libya, UAE, Oman, Qatar and private Arab shareholders; Chair. Dr MUSTAFA KHALIL; 5 brs in Egypt, 1 in Bahrain.

Commercial Foreign Venture Banks

Alexandria-Kuwait International Bank: POB 92, 4th Floor, Evergreen Bldg, 10 Sharia Talaat Harb, Majlis ash-Sha'ab, Cairo; tel. (2) 779766; telex 21394; fax (2) 764844; f. 1978; Bank of Alexandria 71.68%, Kuwaiti Egyptian Real Estate Development Consortium 1.8%, Principal Bank for Development and Agric. Credit 1.62%, Kato Aromatic 1.07%, Other interests 23.83%; cap. 50m., dep.

615m., res 11.5m., total assets 855.4m. (Dec. 1993); Chair. and Man. Dir MOHAMED EL-ASFAR; 7brs.

Alwatany Bank of Egypt: POB 750, 1113 Sharia Corniche en-Nil, Cairo; tel. (2) 753479; telex 93268; fax (2) 772959; f. 1980; cap. p.u. 28.0m., dep. 466.7m., res 17.1m., total assets 665.2m. (Dec. 1992); Chair. ADEL HUSSEIN EZZI; 5 brs.

Arab Land Bank: Emoubilia Bldg, 26 Sharia Sherif, Cairo; tel. (2) 3928506; telex 21208; f. 1958; Egyptian/Jordanian joint venture; cap. 20.0m., dep. 187.8m., res 22.1m., total assets 864.7m. (June 1989); Chair. ABD EL-RABMAN ALI EL-NAD; 5 brs in Egypt, 13 in Jordan.

Bank of Credit and Commerce (Misr), SAE: POB 788, 56-A Gameat ed-Dowal al-Arabia St, Mohandessen Yiza; tel. (2) 3607361; telex 93806; fax (2) 3609054; f. 1981; member of BCC Group; cap. p.u. 20m., dep. 1,662m., total assets 1,973m. (Dec. 1990); Chair. Dr ALY ABD AL-MEGUID ABDOU; Man. Dir GHULAM HANNANI; 19 brs.

Banque du Caire Barclays International, SAE: POB 10, 12 Midan esh-Sheikh Yousuf, Garden City, Cairo; tel. (2) 3542195; telex 93734; fax (2) 3552746; f. 1975 as Cairo Barclays Int. Bank; name changed 1983; Banque du Caire has 51%, Barclays Bank 49%; cap. 20m., dep. 1,118.2m., total assets 1,322.9m. (Dec. 1991); Chair. MUHAMMAD ABO EL-FATH ABD AL-AZIZ; 3 brs.

Banque du Caire et de Paris: POB 2441, 3 Sharia Latin America, Garden City, Cairo; tel. (2) 3548323; telex 93722; fax (2) 3540619; f. 1977; Banque du Caire has 51% interest and Banque Nationale de Paris 49%; cap. p.u. 30.3m., dep. 325.7m. (Dec. 1992); Chair. SAMIR MANSOUR; 2 brs.

Cairo Far East Bank: POB 757, 104 Corniche en-Nil, Cairo (Dokki); tel. (2) 710280; telex 93977; fax (2) 3483818; f. 1978; cap. p.u. 7m., dep. 290.3m., total assets 349.9m. (Dec. 1991); Chair. MAMDOUH EN-NADOURY; 2 brs.

Crédit International d'Egypte: 46 Sharia el-Batal Ahmed Abd al-Aziz, Mohandessen, Cairo; tel. (2) 712823; telex 21216; fax (2) 712744; f. 1977; National Bank of Egypt has 51% interest, Crédit Commercial de France 39% and Berliner Handels und Frankfurter Bank 10%; cap. 15m., dep. 422.9m., res 26.3m., total assets 464.1m. (Dec. 1991); Chair. ALY NOUR ED-DIN SHAHIN; Gen. Man. SHAKER HANNA SAWIRES; 3 brs.

Delta International Bank: POB 1159, 1113 Corniche en-Nil, Cairo; tel. (2) 750989; telex 933833; fax (2) 762851; f. 1978; cap. p.u. 15m., dep. 969m. (Dec. 1992); Chair. and Man. Dir ALI MUHAMMAD NEGM; Gen. Man. FOUAD EL-KOMMOS SIDRAK; 16 brs.

Egyptian American Bank: POB 1825, 4 Sharia Hassan Sabri, Zamalek, Cairo; tel. (2) 3416150; telex 92683; fax (2) 3420265; f. 1976; Bank of Alexandria has 51% interest and American Express Ltd 49%; cap. p.u. 22.0m., dep. 2,523.8m., res 170.3m., total assets 2,964.2m. (Dec. 1992); Chair. ABD AL-GHANI GAMEH; Man. Dir GARY L. JOHNS; 26 brs.

Egyptian Gulf Bank: POB 56, El-Orman Plaza Bldg, 8–10 Sharia Ahmad Nessim, el-Orman, Cairo (Giza); tel. (2) 3606457; telex 20214; fax (2) 3606512; f. 1981; Banque du Caire has 14% interest, Misr Insurance Co 9.5%, Other interests 76.5%; cap. p.u. 49.6m., dep. 529m., res 11.0m., total assets 1,178m. (Dec. 1993); Chair. SALAH ED-DIN MUHAMMAD MAHMOUD; 5 brs.

Egyptian-Saudi Finance Bank: Es-Sabbah Tower, 8 Sharia Ibrahim Naguib, Garden City, Cairo; tel. (2) 3546208; telex 20623; fax (2) 3542911; f. 1980 as Pyramids Bank; cap. p.u. 60.2m. (Dec. 1992); Chair. Sheikh SALEH ABDULLAH KAMEL; Gen. Man. ABD AL-LATIF YOUSEF ABD AL-LATIF; 3 brs.

Faisal Islamic Bank of Egypt: POB 2446, 1113 Corniche en-Nil, Cairo; tel. (2) 5753109; telex 93877; fax (2) 777301; f. 1979; all banking operations conducted according to Islamic principles; cap. p.u. US $131.9m., dep. US $1,296.5m. (July 1993); Chair. Prince MUHAMMAD AL-FAISAL AS-SAOUD; Gov. ABDEL HAMID ABOU MOUSA; 13 brs.

Misr Exterior Bank, SAE: POB 272, Cairo Plaza Bldg, Corniche en-Nil, Ataba, Cairo; tel. (2) 778380; telex 94061; fax (2) 762806; f. 1981; Banco Exterior de España has 40% interest, Banque Misr 40%, Egyptian/Arab private investors 20%; cap. p.u. 16.1m., dep. 897.6m., res 50.1m., total assets 963.9m. (Dec. 1990); Chair. MUHAMMAD NABIL IBRAHIM; 7 brs.

Misr International Bank, SAE: POB 218, 54 Sharia al-Batal Ahmed Abd al-Aziz, Mohandessen, Cairo 12411; tel. (2) 3497091; telex 22840; fax (2) 3498072; f. 1975; the Banque Misr has 44% interest, Banco di Roma 7.375%, First National Bank of Chicago 20%, Other interests 28.625%; total assets 4,518m. (Dec. 1990); Chair. MAHMOUD MUHAMMAD MAHMOUD; Vice-Chair. and Man. Dir MUHAMMAD ALI HAFEZ; 11 brs.

Misr-America International Bank: POB 1003, 12 Nadi es-Seid St, Dokki, Giza, Cairo; tel. (2) 3616623; telex 23505; fax (2) 3616610; f. 1977; Banque du Caire has 33% interest, Misr Insurance Co 33%, Development Industrial Bank 17%, Red Sea Enterprises 17%; cap. p.u. 45m., dep. 544.8m., total assets 698.1m. (Dec. 1991); Chair. and Man. Dir ISMAIL HASSAN MUHAMMAD; 5 brs.

Misr-Romanian Bank, SAE: POB 35, 15 Sharia Abu al-Feda, Zamalek, Cairo; tel. (2) 3418045; telex 93653; fax (2) 3420481; f. 1977; Banque Misr has 51% interest, Romanian Bank for Foreign Trade (Bucharest) 19%, Bank of Agriculture (Bucharest) 15%, and Romanian Bank for Development (Bucharest) 15%; cap. p.u. 58m., dep. 436.3m., res 93.4m. (Dec. 1993); Chair. Dr BAHAA ED-DIN HELMY ISMAIL; 3 brs in Egypt, 1 in Romania.

Mohandes Bank: POB 2778, 30 Sharia Ramses, 199095 Cairo; tel. (2) 5756004; telex 93950; f. 1979; Engineers' Syndicate has 31% interest, Suez Canal Bank 9%, Suez Canal Authority 10%, Arab International Company for Investment 8%, Other interests 42%; cap. p.u. 20m., dep. 321m., total assets 527m. (Dec. 1991); Chair. AHMED ALI MAZEN; 8 brs.

Nile Bank, SAE: POB 2741, 35 Sharia Ramses, Cairo; tel. (2) 5741417; telex 22344; fax (2) 756296; f. 1978; cap. p.u. 32.2m., dep. 917.2m., total assets 1,032.5m. (Dec. 1991); Chair. and Man. Dir ISSA EL-AYOUTY; 16 brs.

Suez Canal Bank: POB 2620, 11 Sharia Muhammad Sabry Abu Alam, Cairo; tel. (2) 3931033; telex 93852; fax (2) 3913522; f. 1978; cap. p.u. 15m., dep. 2,294.7m., res 115.2m., total assets 3,192.1m. (Dec. 1991); Chair. and Man. Dir AHMAD FOUAD; 12 brs.

Non-Commercial Banks

Egypt Arab African Bank: POB 61, Maglis esh-Shaab, 5 Midan es-Saray, el-Koubra, Garden City, Cairo; tel. (2) 3550948; telex 20965; fax (2) 3556239; f. 1982; Arab African International Bank has 49% interest, Egyptian businessmen have 15.2%, Egyptian Reinsurance Co has 7.8%, Arab African International Bank Pension Fund, Bank of Alexandria, Banque du Caire and Industrial Development Bank each have 7%; cap. p.u. 20m., dep. 781m., res 45m., total assets 1,121m. (Dec. 1992); merchant and investment bank services; Chair. MUHAMMAD SAMI EL-HALAWANY; Dep. Chair. and Man. Dir GAMIL BALBAA HUSSEIN BALBAA; 5 brs.

Housing and Development Bank: POB 234, 12 Syria St, Mohandessen, Cairo; tel. (2) 3492013; telex 94075; fax (2) 3600712; f. 1979; cap. p.u. 18m., dep. 172.5m., res. 59.7m. (Dec. 1991); Chair. and Man. Dir MUHAMMAD MOHI ED-DIN ET-TAYEB EN-NAGGAR; 17 brs.

Islamic International Bank for Investment and Development: POB 180, 4 Sharia Ali Ismail, Mesaha Sq., Dokki, Cairo; tel. (2) 3489983; telex 94248; fax (2) 3600771; f. 1980; cap. p.u. 133.8m., dep. 406.9m., res 1.6m., total assets 908.9m. (Dec. 1991); Chair. KHALIL IBRAHIM ELAKANY; 8 brs.

Misr Iran Development Bank: POB 219, The Nile Tower, 21–23 Sharia Giza, El-Orman; tel. (2) 727311; telex 20474; fax (2) 5701185; f. 1975; the Bank of Alexandria has 37.5% interest, Misr Insurance Co 37.5%, Iranian banks 25%; cap. p.u. 110m., res 95m., dep. 872m. (Dec. 1991); Chair. FATHI MUHAMMAD IBRAHIM; Gen. Man. Dr IBRAHIM MOKHTAR; 7 brs.

National Investment Bank: 18 Sharia Abd el-Meguid er-Remaly, Bab el-Louk, Cairo; tel. (2) 3541336; telex 23414; fax (2) 3557399; f. 1980; state-owned; responsible for government projects; Chair. GAMAL AL-GANZOURI.

National Société Générale Bank, SAE: POB 2664, 10 Talaat Harb, Cairo; tel. (2) 747396; telex 22307; fax (2) 776249; f. 1978; the National Bank of Egypt has 51% interest, Société Générale de Paris 49%; cap. p.u. 40m., dep. 785.9m., res 41.6m., total assets 1,321.8m. (June 1989); Chair. MAHMOUD ABD AL-AZIZ; 4 brs.

Union Arab Bank for Development and Investment: POB 826, Cairo Sky Center Bldg, 8 Abd el-Khalik, Sharia Sarwat, Cairo; tel. (2) 760031; telex 20191; fax (2) 770329; f. 1978; Egyptian/Syrian/Libyan joint venture; cap. p.u. 18.5m., dep. 625m., res 31.8m., total assets 977m. (Dec. 1990); Chair. Prof. FOUAD HASHEM AWAD; 13 brs.

STOCK EXCHANGES

Capital Market Authority: 20 Sharia Emad ed-Din, Cairo; tel. (2) 779696; telex 94282; fax (2) 755339; f. 1979; Chair. Dr MUHAMMAD HASSAN FAG AN-NOUR.

Cairo Stock Exchange: 4 Sharia esh-Sherifein, Cairo; tel. (2) 3921447; fax (2) 3928526; f. 1904; Chair. Dr MUHAMMAD HAMED.

Alexandria Stock Exchange: 11 Sharia Talaat Harb, Alexandria; tel. (3) 4824015; fax (3) 4823039; f. 1861; Chair. EDWARD ANIS GEBRAYIL.

INSURANCE

Arab International Insurance Co: POB 2704, 28 Sharia Talaat Harb, Cairo; tel. (2) 5746322; telex 92599; fax (2) 760053; f. 1976; a joint-stock free zone company established by Egyptian and foreign insurance companies; Chair. and Man. Dir HASSAN MUHAMMAD HAFEZ.

Ach-Chark Insurance Co, SAE: 15 Sharia Kasr en-Nil, Cairo; tel. (2) 5753265; telex 92276; fax (2) 766973; f. 1931; Chair. EZZAT M. ABD AL-BARY; general and life.

Egyptian Reinsurance Co, SAE: POB 950, 7 Sharia Dar esh-Shifa, Cairo (Garden City); tel. (2) 3543354; telex 92245; fax (2) 3557483; f. 1957; Chair. MUHAMMAD MUHAMMED AHMED ET-TEIR.

L'Epargne, SAE: POB 548, Immeuble Chemla, Sharia 26 July, Cairo; all types of insurance.

Al-Iktisad esh-Shabee, SAE: POB 1635, 11 Sharia Emad ed-Din, Cairo; f. 1948; Man. Dir and Gen. Man. W. KHAYAT.

Misr Insurance Co: 44A Sharia Dokki, Giza; tel. 700158; telex 93320; fax 700428; f. 1934; all classes of insurance and reinsurance; res 1,650m. (June 1993); Chair. ABD EL-AZIZ MOUSTAFA.

Mohandes Insurance Co: POB 363, 36 Sharia Batal Ahmad Abd al-Aziz, Mohandesin, Giza; tel. 701074; telex 93392.

Al-Mottahida: POB 804, 9 Sharia Soliman Pasha, Cairo; f. 1957.

National Insurance Co of Egypt, SAE: 41 Sharia Kasr en-Nil, Cairo; tel. (2) 3910731; telex 92372; fax (2) 3909133; f. 1900; cap. 58m.; Chair. MUHAMMAD ESH-SHAZLY.

Provident Association of Egypt, SAE: POB 390, 9 Sharia Sherif Pasha, Alexandria; f. 1936; Man. Dir G. C. VORLOOU.

Trade and Industry

CHAMBERS OF COMMERCE

Federation of Chambers of Commerce: 4 el-Falaki Sq., Cairo; tel. (2) 3551164; telex 92645; Pres. MAHMOUD EL-ARABY.

Alexandria

Alexandria Chamber of Commerce: 31 Sharia el-Ghorfa Altogariya, Alexandria; tel. (3) 809339; telex 4180; Pres. MOSTAFA EL-NAGGAR.

Cairo

Cairo Chamber of Commerce: 4 el-Falaki Sq., Cairo; tel. (2) 3558261; telex 927753; fax (2) 3563603; f. 1913; Pres. MAHMOUD EL-ARABY; Sec.-Gen. MOSTAFA ZAKI TAHA.

In addition, there are 20 local chambers of commerce.

INVESTMENT ORGANIZATION

General Authority for Investment and Free Zones: POB 1007, 8 Sharia Adly, Cairo; tel. (2) 3906163; telex 92235; fax (2) 3907315; Exec. Pres. MOHI ED-DIN EL-GHAREB.

NATIONALIZED ORGANIZATIONS

In November 1975 a Presidential Decree ratified the establishment of Higher Councils for the various sectors of industry. During 1978, however, various government ministries took increasing control of industries. In 1980 it was estimated that the Government controlled about 350 companies. The majority of the larger, more important industrial and commercial companies are now either state-owned or operate under government supervision.

MINERALS

Egyptian Geological Survey and Mining Authority (EGSMA): 3 Sharia Salah Salem, Abbassiya, Cairo; tel. (2) 831242; telex 22695; fax (2) 820128; f. 1896; state supervisory authority concerned with geological mapping, mineral exploration and other mining activities; Chair. GABER M. NAIM.

PETROLEUM

Egyptian General Petroleum Corporation (EGPC): POB 2130, 4th Sector, Sharia Palestine, New Maadi, Cairo; tel. (2) 3531340; telex 92049; state supervisory authority generally concerned with the planning of policies relating to petroleum activities in Egypt with the object of securing the development of the petroleum industry and ensuring its effective administration; Chair. MUSTAFA SHAARAWI.

Belayim Petroleum Co (PETROBEL): Sharia Gharb el-Istad, Nasr City, Cairo; tel. (2) 608456; telex 92449; f. 1978; capital equally shared between EGPC and International Egyptian Oil Co, which is a subsidiary of ENI of Italy; petroleum and gas exploration, drilling and production.

General Petroleum Co (GPC): 8 Sharia Dr Moustafa Abou Zahra, Nasr City, Cairo; f. 1957; wholly-owned subsidiary of EGPC; operates mainly in Eastern Desert.

Gulf of Suez Petroleum Co (GUPCO): POB 2400, 4th Sector, Sharia Palestine, New Maadi, Cairo; tel. (2) 3520985; telex 92248; fax (2) 3521286; f. 1965; partnership between EGPC and Amoco-Egypt Oil Co, which is a subsidiary of Amoco Corpn, USA; developed the el-Morgan oilfield in the Gulf of Suez, also holds other exploration concessions in the Gulf of Suez and the Western Desert; Chair. AHMED SHAWKY ABDINE.

Western Desert Petroleum Co (WEPCO): POB 412, Alexandria; tel. (3) 4928710; telex 54075; f. 1967 as partnership between EGPC (50% interest) and Phillips Petroleum (35%) and later Hispanoil (15%); developed Alamein, Yidma and Umbarka fields in the Western Desert and later Abu Qir offshore gas field in 1978 followed by NAF gas field in 1987; Chair. Eng. MUHAMMAD MOHI ED-DIN BAHGAT.

Arab Petroleum Pipelines Co (SUMED): POB 158 es-Saray, 431 el-Geish Ave, Loran, Alexandria; tel. (3) 5864138; telex 55446; fax (3) 5871295; f. 1974; Suez-Mediterranean crude petroleum transportation pipeline (capacity: 117m. tons per year) and petroleum terminal operators; Chair. and Man. Dir Dr ALI NAZEIH ABBAS.

Numerous foreign petroleum companies are prospecting for petroleum in Egypt under agreements with EGPC.

EMPLOYERS' ORGANIZATION

Federation of Egyptian Industries: POB 251, 26A Sharia Sherif Pasha, Cairo, and 65 Gamal Abdel Nasser Ave, Alexandria; tel. (2) 3557642 (Cairo), (03) 28622 (Alexandria); f. 1922; Pres. Dr ADEL GAZAREIN; represents the industrial community in Egypt.

TRADE UNIONS

Egyptian Trade Union Federation (ETUF): 90 Sharia Galaa, Cairo; tel. (2) 740362; telex 93255; f. 1957; 23 affiliated unions; 5m. mems; affiliated to the International Confederation of Arab Trade Unions and to the Organization of African Trade Union Unity; Pres. AHMED AHMED EL-AMMAWI; Gen. Sec. ABD AL-RAHMAN KEDR.

General Trade Union of Air Transport: 5 Sharia Ahmad Sannan, St Fatima, Heliopolis; 11,000 mems; Pres. ABD AL-MONEM FARAG EISA; Gen. Sec. SHEKATA ABD AL-HAMID.

General Trade Union of Banks and Insurance: 2 Sharia el-Kady el-Fadel, Cairo; 56,000 mems; Pres. MAHMOUD MUHAMMAD DABBOUR; Gen. Sec. ABDOU HASSAN MUHAMMAD ALI.

General Trade Union of Building Workers: 9 Sharia Emad ed-Din, Cairo; 150,000 mems; Pres. HAMID HASSAN BARAKAT; Gen. Sec. SALEM ABD AR-RAZEK.

General Trade Union of Chemical Workers: 90 Galaa St, Cairo; telex 93255; 120,000 mems; Pres. AHMED AHMED EL-AMMAWI; Gen. Sec. GAAFER ABD EL-MONEM.

General Trade Union of Commerce: 70 Sharia el-Gomhouriya, Cairo; tel. (2) 914124; f. 1903; more than 100,000 mems; Pres. ABD AR-RAZEK ESH-SHERBEENI; Gen. Sec. KAMEL HUSSEIN A. AWAD.

General Trade Union of Food Industries: 3 Sharia Housni, Hadaek el-Koba, Cairo; 111,000 mems; Pres. SAAD M. AHMAD; Gen. Sec. ADLY TANOUS IBRAHIM.

General Trade Union of Health Services: 22 Sharia esh-Sheikh Qamar, es-Sakakiny, Cairo; 56,000 mems; Pres. IBRAHIM ABOU EL-MUTI IBRAHIM; Gen. Sec. AHMAD ABD AL-LATIF SALEM.

General Trade Union of Maritime Transport: 36 Sharia Sharif, Cairo; 46,000 mems; Pres. THABET MUHAMMAD ES-SEFARI; Gen. Sec. MUHAMMAD RAMADAN ABOU TOR.

General Trade Union of Military Production: 90 Sharia el-Galaa, Cairo; telex 93255; 64,000 mems; Pres. MOUSTAFA MUHAMMAD MOUNGI; Gen. Sec. FEKRY IMAM.

General Trade Union of Mine Workers: 5 Sharia Ali Sharawi, Hadaek el-Koba, Cairo; 14,000 mems; Pres. ABBAS MAHMOUD IBRAHIM; Gen. Sec. AMIN HASSAN AMER.

General Trade Union of Petroleum Workers: 5 Sharia Ali Sharawi, Koba Hadek, Cairo; tel. (2) 820091; telex 93255; fax (2) 834551; 60,000 mems; Pres. MUHAMMAD ZAD ED-DIN; Gen. Sec. ABD AL-KADER HASSAN ABD AL-KADER.

General Trade Union of Postal Workers: 90 Sharia el-Galaa, Cairo; telex 93255; 80,000 mems; Pres. HASSAN MUHAMMAD EID; Gen. Sec. SALEM MAHMOUD SALEM.

General Trade Union of Press, Printing and Information: 90 Sharia el-Galaa, Cairo; tel. (2) 740324; telex 93255; 55,000 mems; Pres. MUHAMMAD ALI EL-FIKKI; Gen. Sec. AHMED ED-DESSOUKI.

General Trade Union of Public and Administrative Workers: 2 Sharia Muhammad Haggag, Midan et-Tahrir, Cairo; tel. (2) 742134; telex 93255; 210,000 mems; Pres. ABD AR-RAHMAN KHEDR; Gen. Sec. MAHMOUD MUHAMMAD ABD EL-KHALEK.

General Trade Union of Public Utilities Workers: 30 Sharia Sharif, Cairo; tel. (2) 3938293; telex 93255; fax (2) 753427; 290,000 mems; Pres. MUHAMMAD ES-SAYED MORSI; Gen. Sec. MUHAMMAD TALAAT HASSAN.

General Trade Union of Railway Workers: POB 84 (el-Fagalah), 15 Sharia Emad ed-Din, Cairo; tel. (2) 930305; 89,000 mems; Pres. SABER AHMED HUSSAIN; Gen. Sec. YASIN SOLUMAN.

General Trade Union of Road Transport: 90 Sharia el-Galaa, Cairo; tel. (2) 7403254; telex 93255; 245,000 mems; Pres. MUHAMMAD KAMAL LABIB; Gen. Sec. MOUNIR BADR SHETA.

General Trade Union of Textile Workers: 327 Sharia Shoubra, Cairo; 244,000 mems; Pres. ALI MUHAMMAD DOUFDAA; Gen. Sec. HASSAN TOULBA MARZOUK.

General Trade Union of Hotels and Tourism Workers: 90 Sharia el-Galaa, Cairo; 50,000 mems; Pres. MUSTAFA IBRAHIM; Gen. Sec. MUHAMMAD HILAL ES-SHARKAWI.

General Trade Union of Workers in Agriculture and Irrigation: 31 Sharia Mansour, Bab el-Louq, Cairo; tel. (2) 3541419; 150,000 mems; Pres. MUKHTAR ABD AL-HAMID; Gen. Sec. FATHI A. KURTAM.

General Trade Union of Workers in Engineering, Metal and Electrical Industries: 90 Sharia el-Galaa, Cairo; tel. (2) 742519; telex 93255; 160,000 mems; Pres. SAID GOMAA; Gen. Sec. MUHAMMAD FARES.

General Trade Union of Telecommunications Workers: POB 651, Cairo; telex 93255; 60,000 mems; Pres. KHAIRI HACHEM; Sec.-Gen. IBRAHIM SALEH.

Transport

RAILWAYS

The area of the Nile Delta is well served by railways. Lines also run from Cairo southward along the Nile to Aswan, and westward along the coast to Salloum.

Egyptian Railways: Station Bldg, Midan Ramses, Cairo; tel. (2) 751000; telex 92616; fax (5) 540000; f. 1852; length 8,600 km; 42 km electrified; a 346-km line to carry phosphate and iron ore from the Bahariya mines, in the Western Desert, to the Helwan iron and steel works in south Cairo, was opened in August 1973, and the Quena–Safaga line (length 223 km) came into operation in May 1989; Chair. Eng. HUSSEIN MUHAMMAD HALIM.

Alexandria Passenger Transport Authority: POB 466, 3 Sharia Aflatone, Shatby, Alexandria; tel. (3) 5975223; telex 54637; f. 1860; controls City Tramways (30 km), Ramleh Electric Railway (14.7 km), suburban buses (430.2 km); 129 tram cars, 36 light railway three-car sets; Chair. Eng. MUHAMMAD SALEH ED-DIN ABD AL-MONEIM; Tech. Dir Eng. ABD AL-MONEIM ABD AL-GHANI.

Cairo Metro: National Authority for Tunnels, Ministry of Transport, Sharia Qasr el-Eini, Cairo; construction of the first underground transport system in Africa and the Middle East began in Cairo in 1982; connects electrified Helwan line of Egyptian railways with Koubri el-Lamoun to el-Marg line, via a 4.2-km tunnel with five stations beneath central Cairo, making a 42.5-km regional line with a total of 33 stations; gauge 1,435 mm, electrified; work on the first stage of the system was completed in July 1987, and it was opened in September; the second and final stage was completed in April 1989; Gen. Dir H. ABD ES-SALAM.

Cairo Transport Authority: POB 254, Madinet Nasr, Cairo; tel. (2) 830533; length 78 km (electrified); gauge 1,000 mm; operates 16 tram routes and 24 km of light railway; 441 cars.

Heliopolis Co for Housing and Inhabiting: 28 Sharia Ibrahim el-Lakkany, Heliopolis, Cairo; 50 km, 148 railcars; Gen. Man. ABD AL-MONEIM SEIF.

Lower Egypt Railway: Mansura; f. 1898; length 160 km; gauge 1,000 mm; 20 diesel railcars.

ROADS

There are good metalled main roads as follows: Cairo–Alexandria (desert road); Cairo–Benna–Tanta–Damanhur–Alexandria; Cairo–Suez (desert road); Cairo–Ismailia–Port Said or Suez; Cairo–Fayum (desert road); in 1993 there were some 38,000 km of roads, including more than 18,000 km of highways. The Ahmad Hamdi road tunnel (1.64 km) beneath the Suez Canal was opened in October 1980. A 320-km macadamized road linking Mersa Matruh, on the Mediterranean coast, with the oasis town of Siwa was completed in 1986.

General Authority for Roads and Bridges, Ministry of Transport: 105 Sharia Qasr el-Eini, Cairo; tel. (2) 3556409; telex 92802; fax (2) 3555564; Chair. FOUAD ABD AL-AZIZ KHALIL.

SHIPPING

Egypt's principal ports are Alexandria, Port Said and Suez. A port constructed at a cost of £E315m. and designed to handle up to 16m. tons of grain, fruit and other merchandise per year (22% of the country's projected imports by the year 2000) in its first stage of development, was opened at Damietta in July 1986. The second stage will increase handling capacity to 25m. tons per year. A ferry link between Nuweibah and the Jordanian port of Aqaba was opened in April 1985.

Alexandria Port Authority: 66 ave Gamal Abd an-Nasser, Alexandria; Head Office: 106 Sharia el-Hourriya, Alexandria; tel. (3) 34321; telex 54147; Chair. Adm. ANWAR HEGAZI.

Major Shipping Companies

Alexandria Shipping and Navigation Co: POB 812, 557 ave el-Hourriya, Alexandria; tel. (3) 62923; telex 54029; services between Egypt, N. and W. Europe, USA, Red Sea and Mediterranean; 9 vessels; Chair. and Man. Dir Eng. MAHMOUD ISMAIL; Man. Dir ABD AL-AZIZ QADRI.

Arab Bridge Maritime Co: Aqaba, Jordan; tel. (3) 316307; telex 62354; fax (3) 316313; f. 1987; joint venture by Egypt, Iraq and Jordan to improve economic co-operation; an expansion of the company that established a ferry link between the ports of Aqaba, Jordan, and Nuweibeh, Egypt, in 1985; Chair. HANI HUSNI.

Egyptian Navigation Co: POB 82, 2 Sharia en-Nasr, Alexandria; tel. (3) 800050; telex 54131; fax (3) 4831345; f. 1930; owners and operators of Egypt's mercantile marine; services Alexandria/Europe, USA, Black Sea, Adriatic Sea, Mediterranean Sea, Indian Ocean and Red Sea; 42 vessels; Chair. BADR ED-DIN IBRAHIM.

Pan-Arab Shipping Co: POB 39, 404 El Horreya Ave, Rouchdy, Alexandria; tel. (3) 5468680; telex 54123; fax (3) 5469533; f. 1974; Arab League Co; 6 vessels; Chair. Adm. SHERIF ES-SADEK; Gen. Man. Capt. MAMDOUH EL-GUINDY.

THE SUEZ CANAL

In 1992 a total of 16,629 vessels, with a net displacement of 407.9m. tons, used the Suez Canal, linking the Mediterranean and Red Seas.

Length of Canal 195 km; maximum permissible draught: 16.2 m (53 ft); breadth of canal at water level and breadth between buoys defining the navigable channel 365 m and 225 m respectively in the northern section and 305 m and 160 m in the southern section.

Suez Canal Authority (Hay'at Canal as-Suess): Irshad Bldg, Ismailia; tel. (64) 220000; telex 63238; fax (64) 320784; Cairo Office: 6 Sharia Lazoghli, Garden City, Cairo; f. 1956; Chair. MUHAMMAD EZZAT ADEL.

CIVIL AVIATION

The main international airports are at Heliopolis (23 km from the centre of Cairo) and Alexandria (7 km from the city centre). A second terminal was opened at Cairo International Airport in July 1986. An international airport was opened at Nuzhah in December 1983.

EgyptAir: Cairo International Airport, Heliopolis, Cairo; tel. (2) 3902444; telex 92221; fax (2) 3901557; f. 1932 as Misr Airwork; known as United Arab Airlines 1960–1971; operates internal services in Egypt and external services throughout the Middle East, Far East, Africa, Europe and the USA; Chair. Gen. MUHAMMAD FAHIM RAYAN.

Egyptian Civil Aviation Authority: 31 Sharia 26 July, Cairo; tel. (2) 742853; telex 24430; fax (2) 2475473; Chair. ALI OSMAN ZIKO.

Zarkani Air Services (ZAS): Cairo; operates internal services and external services to Amsterdam, Belgrade, Kampala, Lisbon, Mogadishu and Valletta, *inter alia*.

Tourism

Ministry of Tourism: Misr Travel Tower, Abbassia Sq., Cairo; tel. (2) 2828430; telex 94040; fax (2) 2829771; f. 1965; brs at Alexandria, Port Said, Suez, Luxor and Aswan; Minister of Tourism and Civil Aviation Dr FOUAD SULTAN.

Egyptian General Authority for the Promotion of Tourism: Misr Travel Tower, Abbassia Sq., Cairo; tel. (2) 823570; telex 20799; Chair. SAYED MOUSSA.

Egyptian General Co for Tourism and Hotels: 4 Latin America St, Garden City, Cairo; tel. (2) 3026470; telex 92363; fax (2) 3024456; f. 1961; affiliated to the holding co for Housing, Tourism and Cinema.

Authorized foreign exchange dealers for tourists include the principal banks and the following:

American Express of Egypt Ltd: POB 2160, 15 Sharia Qasr en-Nil, Cairo; tel. (2) 750444; telex 92715; f. 1919; 7 brs.

Thomas Cook Overseas Ltd: POB 165, 12 Midan Esh Sheikh Youssef, Garden City, 11511 Cairo; tel. (2) 3564650; telex 21031; fax (2) 3545886.

Defence

Supreme Commander of the Armed Forces: President MUHAMMAD HOSNI MUBARAK.

Commander-in-Chief of the Armed Forces: Field-Marshal MUHAMMAD ABD AL-HALIM ABU GHAZALAH.

Chief of Staff of the Armed Forces: Lt-Gen. SAFIY AD-DIN ABU SHINAF.

Commander of the Air Force: Air Marshal MUHAMMAD ABD AL-HAMID HELMI.

Commander of Air Defence: Maj.-Gen. MUSTAFA AHMAD ASH-SHADHILI.

Commander of the Navy: Admiral MUHAMMAD SHARIF AS-SADIQ.

Estimated Defence Expenditure (1993): £E9,090m. (US $2,730m.).

Military service: Three years, selective.

Total armed forces (June 1994): 440,000; army 310,000; air defence command 80,000; navy 20,000; air force 30,000. Reserves 254,000. Paramilitary forces: 374,000 (Central Security Forces 300,000, National Guard 60,000, etc.).

Education

Education is compulsory for eight years between six and 14 years of age. Secondary education, beginning at 11 years of age, lasts for a further six years, comprising two equal cycles of three years each. Enrolment at primary and secondary schools in 1990 was equivalent to 91% of children in the relevant age-groups (boys 100%; girls 83%). There are 13 universities. Education is free at all levels. In 1990, according to UNESCO estimates, the rate of adult illiteracy was 51.6% (males 37.1%; females 66.2%), compared with 61.8% (males 46.4%; females 77.6%) in 1976. A new campaign to combat adult illiteracy was launched in 1988.

ADMINISTRATION

Responsibility for education and training lies with the Ministry of Education and Scientific Research, except for the ministries which train manpower for their own specialized needs. The 13 universities are outside ministerial jurisdiction.

The Ministry of Education is responsible for primary, preparatory, secondary general, secondary technical (commercial, agricultural and industrial), primary teacher training and higher education.

The universities, however, maintain their individual independence even though the President of the Supreme Council is the Minister of Education. The Council is a planning and co-ordinating body and comprises the Rectors, Vice-Rectors and some representatives of different disciplines of university education.

Bibliography

GENERAL

Abdel-Malek, Anwar. *Egypte, société militaire.* Paris, 1962.
Idéologie et renaissance nationale/L'Egypte moderne. Paris, 1969.

Ahmed, J. M. *The Intellectual Origins of Egyptian Nationalism.* London, Royal Institute of International Affairs, 1960.

Aldridge, James. *Cairo: Biography of a City.* London, Macmillan, 1970.

Ayrout, H. H. *The Egyptian Peasant.* Boston, 1963.

Baddour, Abd. *Sudanese-Egyptian Relations. A Chronological and Analytical Study.* The Hague, Nijhoff, 1960.

Badeau, J. S. *The Emergence of Modern Egypt.* New York, 1953.

Baer, Gabriel. *A History of Landownership in Modern Egypt 1800–1950.* London, Oxford University Press, 1962.
The Evolution of Landownership in Egypt and the Fertile Crescent, the Economic History of the Middle East 1800–1914. Chicago and London, University of Chicago Press, 1966.
Studies in the Social History of Modern Egypt. Chicago and London, University of Chicago Press, 1969.

Baker, Raymond William. *Egypt's Uncertain Revolution under Nasser and Sadat.* Harvard University Press, 1979.

Berger, Morroe. *Bureaucracy and Society in Modern Egypt: a Study of the Higher Civil Service.* Princeton University Press, 1957.
Islam in Egypt Today: Social and Political Aspects of Popular Religion. Cambridge University Press, 1970.

Berque, Jacques. *Egypt: Imperialism and Revolution.* London, Faber, 1972.

Boktor, Amin. *The Development and Expansion of Education in the UAR.* Cairo, The American University, 1963.

Cannuyer, Christian. *Les Copres.* Turnhout, Editions Brepol 1991.

Chevillat, Alain and Evelyne. *Moines du désert d'Egypte.* Lyons, Editions Terres du Ciel, 1991.

Coult, Lyman H. *An Annotated Bibliography of the Egyptian Fellah.* University of Miami Press, 1958.

Cromer, Earl of. *Modern Egypt.* 2 vols, London, 1908.

Dawisha, A. I. *Egypt in the Arab World.* London, Macmillan, 1976.

Dodwell, H. *The Founder of Modern Egypt.* Cambridge, 1931, reprinted 1967.

Driault, E. *L'Egypte et l'Europe.* 5 vols, Cairo, 1935.

Garzouzi, Eva. *Old Ills and New Remedies in Egypt.* Cairo, Dar al-Maaref, 1958.

Harris, C. P. *Nationalism and Revolution in Egypt: the Role of the Muslim Brotherhood.* The Hague, Mouton and Co, 1964.

Harris, J. R. (Ed.). *The Legacy of Egypt.* 2nd edn Oxford University Press, 1972.

Holt, P. M. *Egypt and the Fertile Crescent.* London, Longman, 1966.

Hopkins, Harry. *Egypt, The Crucible.* London, Secker and Warburg, 1969.

Hurst, H. E. *The Nile.* London, 1952.
The Major Nile Projects. Cairo, 1966.

Kepel, Gilles. *The Prophet and the Pharaoh: Muslim Extremism in Egypt.* London, Al Saqi Books, 1985.

King, Joan Wucher (Ed.). *An Historical Dictionary of Egypt.* Metuchen, NJ, Scarecrow Press, 1984.

Lacouture, Jean and Simonne. *Egypt in Transition.* London, Methuen, 1958.

Lauterpacht, E. (Editor). *The Suez Canal Settlement.* London, Stevens and Sons, 1960, under the auspices of the British Institute of International and Comparative Law.

Lengye, Emil. *Egypt's Role in World Affairs.* Washington, DC, Public Affairs Press, 1957.

Little, Tom. *Modern Egypt.* London, Ernest Benn, 1967, New York, Praeger, 1967.

Lloyd, Lord. *Egypt since Cromer.* 2 vols, London, 1933–34.

Marlowe, J. *Anglo-Egyptian Relations.* London, 1954.

Nasser, Gamal Abdel. *Egypt's Liberation: The Philosophy of the Revolution.* Washington, 1955.

Neguib, Mohammed. *Egypt's Destiny: A Personal Statement.* New York, 1955.

Owen, Robert, and Blunsum, Terence. *Egypt, United Arab Republic, The Country and its People.* London, Queen Anne Press, 1966.

Pick, Christopher. *Egypt: A Traveller's Anthology.* London, John Murray, 1991.

Riad, Hassan. *L'Egypte Nassérienne.* Paris, Editions de Minuit, 1964.

Robin, Barry. *Islamic Fundamentalism in Egyptian Politics.* London, Macmillan, 1990.

Stewart, Desmond. *Cairo.* London, Phoenix House, 1965.

Vaucher, G. *Gamal Abdel Nasser et son Equipe.* 2 vols, Leiden, Brill, 1950.

Viollet, Roger, and Doresse, Jean. *Egypt.* New York, Cromwell, 1955.

Waterfield, Gordon. *Egypt.* London, Thames and Hudson, 1966.

Watt, D. C. *Britain and the Suez Canal.* London, Royal Institute of International Affairs, 1956.

Wavell, W. H. *A Short Account of the Copts.* London, 1945.

Wilbur, D. N. *The United Arab Republic.* New York, 1969.

Wilson, John A. *The Burden of Egypt.* Chicago, 1951.

Wynn, Wilton. *Nasser of Egypt: The Search for Dignity.* Cambridge, Mass., 1959.

ANCIENT EGYPT

Aldred, Cyril. *Egypt to the End of the Old Kingdom.* London, Thames and Hudson, 1965.

Bernard, Jean-Louis. *Aux origines de l'Egypte.* Paris, Laffont, 1976.

Breasted, James Henry. *A History of Egypt from the Earliest Times to the Persian Conquest.* New York, Harper and Row, 1959.

De Lubicz, A. S. *The Temples of Karnak.* 2 vols, London, 1961.

Fischel, Walter J. *Ibn Khaldun in Egypt.* University of California Press, 1967.

Forster, E. M. *Alexandria: a History and a Guide.* New York, Doubleday, 1961.

Gardiner, Sir Alan Henderson. *Egypt of the Pharaohs.* Oxford, Clarendon Press, 1961.

Glanville, S. R. K. (Ed.). *The Legacy of Egypt.* Oxford, 1942.

Greener, L. *The Discovery of Egypt.* London, Cassell, 1966, New York, Viking Press, 1967.

James, T. G. H. *Howard Carter—The Path to Tutankhamun.* London, Kegan Paul International, 1993.

Johnson, Allan C. *Egypt and the Roman Empire.* Ann Arbor, 1951.

Meyer-Ranke, Peter. *Der Rote Pharao.* Hamburg, Christian Wegner Verlag, 1964.

Montet, Pierre. *Das Leben der Pharaonen.* Frankfurt/ Berlin/Vienna, 1970.

Murnane, William J. *The Penguin Guide to Ancient Egypt.* London, Penguin, 1984.

Pirenne, Jacques. *Histoire de la Civilization de l'Egypte antique.* Neuchâtel, 1966.

   La Religion et la Morale de l'Egypte antique. Neuchâtel, La Baconnière, 1966.

Posener, G. (Ed.). *A Dictionary of Egyptian Civilization.* London, Methuen, 1962.

Rice, Michael. *Egypt's Making: the origins of Ancient Egypt 5,000–2,000BC.* London, Routledge, 1990.

MODERN HISTORY

Avram, Benno. *The Evolution of the Suez Canal State 1869–1956. A Historico-Juridical Study.* Geneva, Paris, Librairie E. Droz, Libraire Minard, 1958.

Baker, Raymond William. *Sadat and After: struggles for Egypt's political soul.* London, I. B. Tauris, 1990.

Baraway, Rashed El-. *The Military Coup in Egypt.* Cairo, Renaissance Bookshop, 1952.

Barraclough, Geoffrey (Ed.). *Suez in History.* London, 1962.

Blunt, Wilfred Scawen. *Secret History of the English Occupation of Egypt.* London, Martin Secker, 1907.

Brown, Nathan J. *Peasant Politics in Modern Egypt: the struggle against the state.* New Haven and London, Yale University Press, 1990.

Carter, B. L. *The Copts in Egyptian Politics.* London, Croom Helm, 1986.

Connell, John. *The Most Important Country. The Story of the Suez Crisis and the Events leading up to It.* London, Cassell, 1957.

Cooper, Mark N. *The Transformation of Egypt.* London, Croom Helm, 1982.

Efendi, Husein. *Ottoman Egypt in the Age of the French Revolution* (trans. and with introduction by Stanford J. Shaw). Cambridge, Mass., Harvard Univ. Press, 1964.

Farnie, D. A. *East and West of Suez. The Suez Canal in history, 1854–1956.* Oxford, Clarendon Press, 1969.

Fawzi, Mahmoud. *Suez 1956.* London, Shorouk International, 1986.

Heikal, Muhammad. *The Road to Ramadan.* London, Collins, 1975.

   Sphinx and Commissar: The Rise and Fall of Soviet Influence in the Arab World. London, Collins, 1978.

   Autumn of Fury: The Assassination of Sadat. London, André Deutsch, 1983.

   Cutting the Lion's Tail: Suez through Egyptian eyes. London, André Deutsch, 1986.

Hirst, David, and Beeson, Irene. *Sadat.* London, Faber, 1981.

Holt, P. M. *Political and Social Change in Modern Egypt.* Oxford University Press, 1967.

Hussein, Mahmoud. *La Lutte de Classes en Egypte de 1945 à 1968.* Paris, Maspero, 1969.

Ismael, Tareq Y., and El-Said, Rifa'at. *The Communist Movement in Egypt 1920–1988.* Syracuse University Press, 1990.

Issawi, Charles. *Egypt in Revolution.* Oxford, 1963.

Joesten, Joachim. *Nasser: The Rise to Power.* London, Odhams, 1960.

Kamel, Muhammad Ibrahim. *The Camp David Accords: A Testimony by Sadat's Foreign Minister.* London, Routledge and Kegan Paul, 1986.

Kinross, Lord. *Between Two Seas: The Creation of the Suez Canal.* London, John Murray, 1968.

Kyle, Keith. *Suez.* London, Weidenfeld, 1991.

Lacouture, Jean. *Nasser: A Biography.* London, Secker and Warburg, 1973.

Lane-Poole, S. *History of Egypt in the Middle Ages.* 4th edn, reprinted, London, Frank Cass, 1967.

Love, K. *Suez: the Twice-fought War.* Longman, 1970.

Mansfield, Peter. *Nasser's Egypt.* London, Penguin Books, 1965.

   Nasser. London, Methuen, 1969.

   The British in Egypt. London, Weidenfeld and Nicolson, 1971.

Marlowe, John. *Cromer in Egypt.* London, Elek Books, 1970.

Marsot, Afaf Lutfi as-Sayyed. *A Short History of Modern Egypt.* Cambridge University Press, 1985.

Nutting, Anthony. *No End of a Lesson; the Story of Suez.* London, Constable, 1967.

   Nasser. London, Constable, 1972.

O'Ballance, E. *The Sinai Campaign 1956.* London, Faber, 1959.

Quandt, William B. *Camp David: Peacemaking and Politics.* Washington, DC, Brookings Institution, 1986.

Raymond, André. *Artisans et commerçants au Caire au XVIIIe siècle.* 2 vols Paris, Librairie Adrien-Maisonneuve 1973–74.

Richmond, J. C. B. *Egypt, 1798–1952: Her Advance towards a Modern Identity.* London, Methuen, 1977.

Sadat, Anwar Al-. *Revolt on the Nile.* London, Allen Wingate, 1957.

Safran, Nadav. *Egypt in Search of Political Community. An analysis of the intellectual and political evolution of Egypt, 1804–1952.* Cambridge, Mass., Harvard University Press, London, Oxford University Press, 1961.

Sayyid, Afaf Lutfi Al-. *Egypt and Cromer: A Study in Anglo-Egyptian Relations.* London, John Murray, New York, Praeger, 1968.

Schonfield, Hugh A. *The Suez Canal in Peace and War, 1869–1969.* London, Vallentine, Mitchell, 2nd revised edn, 1969.

Shazly, Gen. Saad El-. *The Crossing of Suez: The October War (1973).* London, Third World Centre for Research and Publishing, 1980.

Stephens, R. *Nasser.* London, Allen Lane, The Penguin Press, 1971.

Tignor, R. L. *Modernization and British Colonial Rule in Egypt 1882–1914.* Princeton, 1966.

Vatikiotis, P. J. *A Modern History of Egypt.* New York, Praeger, 1966; London, Weidenfeld and Nicolson, 1969, revised edn, 1980.

   The Egyptian Army in Politics. Bloomington, Indiana University Press, 1961.

Waterbury, John. *The Egypt of Nasser and Sadat: The Political Economy of Two Regimes.* Princeton University Press, 1983.

Zaki, Abdel Rahman. *Histoire Militaire de l'Epoque de Mohammed Ali El-Kebir.* Cairo, 1950.

ECONOMY

El Ghonemy, M. Riad. *Economic and Industrial Organization of Egyptian Agriculture since 1952, Egypt since the Revolution.* London, Allen and Unwin, 1968.

El Kammash, M. M. *Economic Development and Planning in Egypt.* London, 1967.

Kardouche, G. S. *The UAR in Development.* New York, Praeger, 1967.

Mabro, Robert. *The Egyptian Economy 1952–1972.* London, Oxford University Press, 1974.

Mead, Donald C. *Growth and Structural Change in the Egyptian Economy.* Homwood, Ill., Irwin, 1967.

O'Brien, Patrick. *The Revolution in Egypt's Economic System 1952–65.* Oxford, 1966.

Saab, Gabriel S. *The Egyptian Agrarian Reform 1952–1962.* London and New York, Oxford University Press, 1967.

Warriner, Doreen. *Land Reform and Economic Development.* Cairo, 1955.

   Land Reform and Development in the Middle East—A Study of Egypt, Syria and Iraq. 2nd edn London, Oxford University Press, 1962.

IRAN

(PERSIA)

Physical and Social Geography

W. B. FISHER

SITUATION

The Islamic Republic of Iran is bounded on the north by the Caspian Sea, Azerbaijan and Turkmenistan, on the east by Afghanistan and Pakistan, on the south by the Persian Gulf and Gulf of Oman, and on the west by Iraq and Turkey.

PHYSICAL FEATURES

Structurally, Iran is an extremely complex area and, owing partly to political difficulties and partly to the difficult nature of the country itself, complete exploration and investigation have not so far been achieved. In general, Iran consists of an interior plateau, 1,000 m to 1,500 m (3,000 ft to 5,000 ft) above sea-level, ringed on almost all sides by mountain zones of varying height and extent. The largest mountain massif is that of the Zagros, which runs from the north-west of Iran, where the frontiers of Iran, Azerbaijan, Turkmenistan, Turkey and Iraq meet, first south-westwards to the eastern shores of the Persian Gulf, and then eastwards, fronting the Arabian Sea, and continuing into Baluchistan. Joining the Zagros in the north-west, and running along the southern edge of the Caspian Sea, is the narrower but equally high Elburz range; whilst along the eastern frontier of Iran are several scattered mountain chains, less continuous and imposing than either the Zagros or the Elburz, but sufficiently high to act as a barrier.

The Zagros range begins in north-west Iran as an alternation of high tablelands and lowland basins, the latter containing lakes, the largest of which is Lake Urmia. This lake, having no outlet, is saline. Further to the south-east the Zagros becomes much more imposing, consisting of a series of parallel hog's-back ridges, some of which reach over 4,000 m in height. In its southern and eastern portions the Zagros becomes distinctly narrower, and its peaks much lower, though a few exceed 3,000 m. The Elburz range is very much narrower than the Zagros, but equally, if not more abrupt, and one of its peaks, the volcanic cone of Mt Damavand, at 5,604 m (18,386 ft), is the highest in the country. There is a sudden drop on the northern side to the flat plain occupied by the Caspian Sea, which lies about 27 m below sea-level, and is shrinking rapidly in size. The eastern highlands of Iran consist of isolated massifs separated by lowland zones, some of which contain lakes from which there is no outlet, the largest being the Hirmand Basin, on the borders of Iran and Afghanistan.

The interior plateau of Iran is partly covered by a remarkable salt swamp (termed *kavir*) and partly by loose sand or stones (*dasht*), with stretches of better land mostly round the perimeter, near the foothills of the surrounding mountains. In these latter areas much of the cultivation of the country is carried on, but the lower-lying desert and swamp areas, towards the centre of the plateau, are largely uninhabited. The Kavir is an extremely forbidding region, consisting of a surface formed by thick plates of crystallized salt, which have sharp, upstanding edges. Below the salt lie patches of mud, with, here and there, deep drainage channels—all of which are very dangerous to travellers, and are hence unexplored. Because of this great handicap from the presence of an unusually intractable 'dead heart', it has proved difficult to find a good central site for the capital of Iran—many towns, all peripheral to a greater or lesser degree, have in turn fulfilled this function, but none has proved completely satisfactory. The choice of the present capital, Teheran, dates only from the end of the 18th century.

Iran suffers from occasional earthquakes, which cause severe loss of life, damage to property and disruption of communications. A particularly bad example occurred around Tabas in the north-eastern Khurasan province in September 1978; estimates put the toll from this disaster at up to 20,000 deaths, with severe damage extending over 2,000 sq km. Even more devastating was the major earthquake which struck north-western Iran (principally the provinces of Gilan and Zanjan) in June 1990. Estimates put the number of those killed during the first quake and a series of severe tremors and aftershocks at between 35,000–40,000, while more than 60,000 were reported to have been injured in the disaster.

The climate of Iran is one of great extremes. Owing to its southerly position, adjacent to Arabia and near the Thar Desert, the summer is extremely hot, with temperatures in the interior rising possibly higher than anywhere else in the world—certainly over 55°C has been recorded. In winter, however, the great altitude of much of the country and its continental situation result in far lower temperatures than one would expect to find for a country in such low latitudes. Minus 30°C can be recorded in the north-west Zagros, and −20°C is common in many places.

Another unfortunate feature is the prevalence of strong winds, which intensify the temperature contrasts. Eastern Iran in particular has a violent visitation in the so-called 'Wind of 120 Days', which blows regularly throughout summer, reaching at times over 160 km per hour and often raising sand to such an extent that the stone walls of buildings are sometimes scoured away and turn to ruins.

Most of Iran is arid; but in contrast, parts of the north-west and north receive considerable rainfall—up to 2,000 mm along parts of the Caspian coast, producing very special climatic conditions in this small region, recalling conditions in the lower Himalayas. The Caspian coast has a hot, humid climate and this region is by far the most densely populated of the whole country. Next in order of population density comes the north-west Zagros area—the province of Azerbaijan, with its capital, Tabriz, the fourth city of Iran. Then, reflecting the diminished rainfall, next in order come the central Zagros area, and adjacent parts of the interior plateau, round Isfahan, Hamadan, Shiraz and Kermanshah, with an extension as far as Teheran. The extreme east and south, where rainfall is very scanty, were for long extremely lightly populated, except in the few parts where water is available, by nomadic groups. Over the past few years, however, a development programme has been initiated, and the effects are seen in the expansion of the towns, some of which have grown by 30%–40% since 1972.

ECONOMIC LIFE

Owing to the difficulties of climate and topography, there are few districts, apart from the Caspian plain, that are continuously cultivated over a wide area. Settlement tends to occur in small clusters, close to water supplies, or where there are especially favourable conditions—a good soil, shelter from winds, or easy communications. Away from these cultivated areas, which stand out like oases among the barren expanses of desert or mountain, most of the population live as nomads, by the herding of animals. The nomadic tribesmen have had great influence on the life of Iran. Their principal territory is the central Zagros, where the tribal system is strongly developed; but nomads are found in all the mountain zones, though their numbers are very few in the south and east. Reza Shah (see History) made considerable efforts to break the power of the nomadic tribes and to force them to settle as agriculturalists. Now, with the development of the economy, many nomads have moved into towns (though some still remain).

Economic activity has suffered from the handicaps of topography and climate, prolonged political and social insecurity (with constant pressure by foreign powers), and widespread devastation in the later Middle Ages by Mongol invaders, from which Iran has never fully recovered. Agricultural methods in particular are primitive, so that yields are low; but the drawbacks to efficient production—archaic systems of land tenure, absentee landlords, lack of education, and shortage of capital—are gradually being overcome. In the north and west, which are by far the most productive regions, a wide variety of cereals (including wheat, barley and rice) and much fruit are grown, but in the south and east the date is the principal source of food.

Iran has a number of mineral resources, some of which are exploited on a commercial scale. The recently discovered copper deposits at Sar Cheshmeh are the second largest in the world. Iran also has the second largest natural gas deposits in the world; and there are large deposits of good-quality coal and iron ore near Kerman. Iranians have always had a high reputation as craftsmen—particularly in metal-work and in carpet making. Although Reza Shah attempted to develop modern mechanized industry by placing state-owned factories in most large towns—some of which proved successful, others not—bazaar manufactures have retained their importance. Teheran is now a major manufacturing centre, with a considerable spread of activities from the processing of foodstuffs to the manufacture of consumer and construction goods and an increasing range of more complex items: electronics, motor manufacturing and high-grade chemicals.

The adverse nature of geographical conditions has greatly restricted the growth of communications in Iran. The country is very large in relation to its size of population—it is 2,250 km from north-west to south-west—and, because of the interior deserts, many routes must follow a circuitous path instead of attempting a direct crossing. Then, too, the interior is shut off by ranges that are in parts as high as the Alps of Europe, but far less broken up by river valleys. Road construction is generally difficult, but since the mid-1960s increasing effort has been devoted to providing all-weather trunk routes between major cities for which special allocations have been made in the five-year plans. An important link is the railway constructed with great effort before the Second World War between the Caspian coast, Teheran and the Persian Gulf. Other rail links with bordering countries already exist or are under construction. Although there are mountain streams, many flowing in deep, inaccessible gorges, only one, the Karun river, is at all navigable. The Caspian ports are subject to silting, while most of the harbours in the south are either poorly sheltered or difficult of access from the interior. However, there has been a deliberate focusing of development on the Gulf, in response to the enhanced economic and political status of the region, now one of the wealthiest parts of the world. Development occurred in the region of the Shatt al-Arab in the last years of the Shah's regime. However, the war between Iran and Iraq, beginning in September 1980, greatly impeded economic prospects, both there and in the Persian Gulf. Overall, the effect of the Revolution of 1979 was to reduce, though not entirely to terminate, the sophisticated industrial developments that were initiated under the Shah, and to shift external trading more towards imports of basic raw materials and food, balanced (often by direct exchange approaching barter) by exports of petroleum which, though reduced (in part because of war in the Gulf), are still considerable.

RACE AND LANGUAGE

Iran has numerous ethnic groups of widely differing origin. In the central plateau there occurs a distinctive sub-race, termed by some anthropologists Iranian or Irano-Afghan. In the mountain districts there are many other smaller groups of separate racial composition. A number of nomads, including the Bakhtiari tribes, would seem to be of Kurdish stock; whilst Turki (Mongoloid) strains are apparent in others, such as the Qashqai tribes. Smaller groups from the Caucasus (Georgians and Circassians) are represented in Azerbaijan and the Caspian provinces, whilst Turki influence is again apparent in the racial composition of the eastern districts of Iran, especially round Meshed. The southern Zagros near the Arabian Sea has a small population that tends to be of mixed Iranian, Afghan, and Hindu stock. Some observers have suggested that in this region there may also be representatives of a primitive negrito race, related to the hill-tribes of India and of south-east Asia.

With so many differing ethnic groups, it is not surprising to find that several languages are current in Iran. Persian (Farsi), an Indo-Aryan language related to the languages of western Europe, is spoken in the north and centre of the country, and is the one official language of the state. As the north is by far the most densely peopled region of Iran, the Persian language has an importance somewhat greater than its territorial extent would suggest. Various dialects of Kurdish are current in the north and central Zagros mountains, and alongside these are found several Turki-speaking tribes. Baluchi occurs in the extreme south-east. English and French are spoken by most of the educated classes.

History

Updated for this edition by JON LUNN

EARLY HISTORY

The Achaemenid empire, the first Persian empire, was founded by Cyrus who revolted against the Median empire in 533 BC. After the defeat of the Median empire, Babylon was taken in 529 BC, and in 525 BC under Cambyses, the successor of Cyrus, Egypt was conquered. The period of conquest was rounded off by Darius who reduced the tribes of the Pontic and Armenian mountains and extended Persian dominion to the Caucasus. The main work of Darius, however, lay not in the conquest but in the organization which he gave to the empire. During his reign wars with Greece broke out and in 490 BC the Persian army suffered a major defeat at Marathon; an expedition under Xerxes, the successor of Darius, which set out to avenge this defeat was, after initial successes, defeated at Salamis in 480 BC. The empire was finally overthrown by Alexander who defeated the Persian army at Arbela in 331 BC and then burnt Persepolis, the Achaemenid capital; the last Darius fled and was killed in 330 BC. Alexander thereafter regarded himself as the head of the Persian empire. The death of Alexander was followed by a struggle between his generals, one of whom, Seleucus, took the whole of Persia, apart from northern Media and founded the Seleucid empire. About the year 250 BC a reaction against Hellenism began with the rise of the Parthian empire of the Arsacids. Although by origin nomads from the Turanian steppe, the Arsacids became the wardens of the north-east marches and were largely preoccupied in defending themselves in the east against the Scythians who, with the Tocharians and Sacae, repeatedly attacked the Parthian empire, while in the west they were engaged in fending off attacks by the Romans.

The Arsacids were succeeded by the Sasanians, who, like the Achaemenids, came from Fars and, like them, were Zoroastrians. Ardashir b. Babak, after subduing the neighbouring states (c. AD 212), made war on the Arsacid, Artabanus V, whom he eventually defeated. The empire which he founded largely continued the traditions of the Achaemenids, although it never equalled the Achaemenid empire in extent. The monarchy of the Sasanian period was a religious and civil institution. The monarch, who ruled by divine right, was absolute but his autocracy was limited by the powers of the Zoroastrian hierarchy and the feudal aristocracy. In the reign of Qubad (AD 488–531) a movement of revolt, partly social and partly religious, led by Mazdak, gained ground. Under Qubad's successor Anushiravan (531–79) orthodoxy was restored, but at the cost of the imposition of a military despotism. Like the Arsacids before them the Sasanians were occupied in the west with wars with Rome and in the east with repelling the advances of nomads from Central Asia.

MUSLIM PERSIA

By the beginning of the seventh century AD Persia had been greatly weakened by these wars, and when the Muslim Arabs attacked, little effective resistance was offered. The decisive battles were fought at Qadisiyya (AD 637) and Nihavand (*c.* AD 641). Persia did not re-emerge as a political entity until the 16th century AD, although with the decline of the Abbasid empire semi-independent and independent dynasties arose in different parts of Persia and at times even incorporated under their rule an area extending beyond the confines of present-day Iran. As a result of the Arab conquest Persia became part of the Muslim world. Local administration remained largely in the hands of the indigenous population and many local customs continued to be observed. In due course a new civilization developed in Persia, the unifying force of which was Islam.

With the transfer of the capital of the Islamic empire from Damascus to Baghdad (*c.* AD 750) Persian influence began to be strongly felt in the life of the empire. Islam had already replaced Zoroastrianism and by the 10th century modern Persian, written in the Arabic script and including a large number of Arabic words in its vocabulary, had established itself. Its emergence was of immense importance; the literary tradition for which it became the vehicle has perhaps more than any other factor kept alive a national consciousness among the Iranians and preserved the memory of the great Persian empires of the past.

By the eighth century AD the Abbasid caliphate had begun to disintegrate and when in the 11th century control of the north-eastern frontiers broke down, the Ghuzz Turks invaded Persia. This movement, of which the Seljuqs became the leaders, was ethnologically important since it altered the balance of population, the Turkish element from then on being second only to the Persian in numbers and influence. Secondly, it was in the Seljuq empire that the main lines of the politico-economic structure, which was to last in Persia in a modified form down to the 20th century AD, were worked out. The basis of this structure was the land assignment, the holder of which was often virtually a petty territorial ruler, who was required, when called upon to do so, to provide the ruler with a military contingent.

The Seljuq empire itself broke up in the 12th century into a number of succession states; the 13th century saw the Mongol invasion and in 1258 Hulagu, the grandson of Chinghiz (Jenghiz) Khan, sacked Baghdad and destroyed the caliphate. For some years the Ilkhan dynasty, founded by Hulagu, ruled Persia as vassals of the Great Khan in Qaraqorum, but from the reign of Abaqa (1265–81) onwards they became virtually a Persian dynasty. Their empire, like that of the Seljuqs before them—and for very much the same reason—broke up at the beginning of the 14th century into a number of succession states. Towards the end of the century Persia again fell under the dominion of a military conqueror, when Timur, who had started his career as the warden of the marches in the Oxus-Jaxartes basin against the nomads of Central Asia, undertook a series of military campaigns against Persia between 1381 and 1387. The kingdom founded by him was shortlived and rapidly disintegrated on the death of his son Shahrukh, the western part falling first to the Turkomans of the Black Sheep and then to the Turkomans of the White Sheep, while Transoxania passed into the hands of the Uzbegs.

THE PERSIAN MONARCHY

The 16th century saw the foundation of the Safavid empire, which was accompanied by an eastward movement of the Turkomans from Asia Minor back into Persia. For the first time since the Muslim conquest Persia re-emerged as a political unit. The foundations of the Safavid empire were laid by

Isma'il Safavi (1502–24). He deliberately fostered a sense of separateness and of national unity *vis-à-vis* the Ottoman Turks with whom the Safavids were engaged in a struggle for supremacy in the west, and the main weapon he used to accomplish his purpose was Shi'ism. Not only the Turks but the majority of his own subjects were at the time Sunni Muslims—nevertheless he imposed Shi'ism upon them by force and created among the population of his dominions, many of whom, especially among his immediate followers, were Turks, a sense of national unity as Persians. Apart from a brief interlude under Nadir Shah, Shi'ism has since then remained the majority rite in Persia and is the official rite of the country at the present day. Under Shah Abbas (1587–1629) the Safavid empire reached its zenith and Persia enjoyed a power and prosperity which it has not achieved since.

GREAT POWER RIVALRY

During the Safavid period, contact with Europe increased. Various foreign embassies interested mainly in the silk trade reached the Safavid court via Russia and via the Persian Gulf. In the latter area in the early years of the 16th century a struggle for supremacy developed between the British and the Dutch. 'Factories' were established by the East India Company in the Gulf from the early 16th century.

Under the later Safavids internal decline set in and from 1722–30 Persia was subject to Afghan invasion and occupation while in the west and north it was threatened by Turkey and Russia. After the death of Peter the Great there was a temporary slackening of Russian pressure, but the Turks continued to advance and took Tabriz in 1725, peace being eventually made at Hamadan in 1727. The Afghans were finally evicted by Nadir Shah Afshar whose reign (1736–47) was remarkable chiefly for his military exploits. The Afsharids were succeeded by Karim Khan Zand (1750–79) whose relatively peaceful reign was followed by the rise of the Qajars who continued to reign until 1925. Under them the capital was transferred from Isfahan to Teheran. During the Qajar period events in Persia became increasingly affected by Great Power rivalry until not only Persia's foreign policy was dominated by this question, but its internal politics also.

With the growth of British influence in India in the late 18th and early 19th centuries the main emphasis in Anglo-Persian relations, which during the 16th and 17th centuries had been on commerce, began to shift to strategy. The region of Persia and the Persian Gulf came to be regarded as one of the main bastions protecting British India, and the existence of an independent Persia as a major British interest. In the early 19th century fear of a French invasion of India through Persia exercised the minds of the British in India and Whitehall. French envoys were active in Persia and Mesopotamia from 1796 to 1809, and to counter possible French activities Captain (afterwards Sir) John Malcolm was sent to Persia in 1800 by the Governor-General of India. He concluded a political and commercial treaty with Fath Ali Shah, the main purpose of which was to ensure that the Shah should not receive French agents and would do his utmost to prevent French forces entering Persia. With the defeat of Napoleon in Egypt the matter was no longer regarded as urgent and the agreement was not ratified. Subsequently the French made proposals to Persia for an alliance against Russia and in 1807 Persia concluded the Treaty of Finkenstein with France after which a military mission under General Gardanne came to Persia. In 1808 another British mission was sent under Malcolm. Its object was 'first, to detach the Court of Persia from the French alliance and to prevail on that Court to refuse the passage of French troops through the territories subject to Persia, or the admission of French troops into the country. If that cannot be obtained, to admit English troops with a view of opposing the French army in its progress to India, to prevent the creation of any maritime post, and the establishment of French factories on the coast of Persia'. Malcolm's task was complicated by the almost simultaneous arrival of a similar mission from Whitehall. In 1809 after the Treaty of Tilsit, which debarred the French from aiding the Shah against Russia, Gardanne was dismissed.

WARS WITH RUSSIA AND TURKEY

Meanwhile the formal annexation of Georgia by Russia in 1801 had been followed by a campaign against Russia. This proved disastrous to Persia and was temporarily brought to an end by the Treaty of Gulistan (1813) by which Persia ceded Georgia, Qara Bagh and seven other provinces. British policy continued to be concerned with the possibility of an invasion of India via Persia and in 1814 the Treaty of Teheran was concluded with Persia by which Great Britain undertook to provide troops or a subsidy in the event of unprovoked aggression against Persia. Although the treaty provided for defence against any European power it was primarily intended to counteract the designs of Russia. In fact it proved ineffective and when the Perso-Russian war recommenced in 1825 Great Britain did not interfere except as a peacemaker and discontinued the subsidy to Persia, which was technically the aggressor. The war was concluded in 1828 by the Treaty of Turkomanchai, under the terms of which Persia ceded Erivan and Nakhjivan and agreed to pay an indemnity; in addition, it was prohibited from having armed vessels on the Caspian.

During this period Persia was also engaged in hostilities with Turkey. Frontier disputes in 1821 culminated in the outbreak of war, which was concluded by the Treaty of Erzerum (1823).

By the 19th century the Persian Government had ceased to exercise effective control over the greater part of Khurasan. Russian policy, which became conciliatory towards Persia during the 25 years or so after the Treaty of Turkomanchai, encouraged the Shah to reimpose Persian rule on the eastern provinces. British policy, on the other hand, having come to regard Afghanistan as an important link in the defence of India, urged moderation upon the Persian Government. After the accession of Muhammad Shah in 1834, an expedition was sent against Herat. The siege of Herat began in 1837 but was raised when the Shah was threatened with British intervention. Subsequently local intrigues enabled the Persians to enter Herat. The seizure of the city by Persia led to the outbreak of the Anglo-Persian war in 1856, which was terminated by the Treaty of Paris (1857) after a British force had occupied the island of Kharg in the Persian Gulf.

In the second half of the century the subjection of the Turkoman tribes by Russia, its capture of Marv in 1854, and the occupation of the Panjeh, meant that Russian influence became dominant in Khurasan in the same way as the advance of Russia to the Araxes after the Persian wars in the early part of the 19th century had made Russian influence dominant in Azerbaijan.

INCREASED FOREIGN INTERVENTION

Internally the second half of the 19th century was remarkable chiefly for the beginnings of the modernist movement, which was stimulated on the one hand by internal misgovernment and on the other by increased intervention in the internal affairs of the country by Russia and Britain. Towards the end of the century numerous concessions were granted to foreigners largely in order to pay for the extravagances of the court. The most fantastic of these was the Reuter concession. In 1872 a naturalized British subject, Baron de Reuter, was given by the Shah a monopoly for 70 years of railways and tramways in Persia, all the minerals except gold, silver and precious stones, irrigation, road, factory and telegraph enterprises, and the farm of customs dues for 25 years. Eventually this concession was cancelled and permission instead given for the foundation of a Persian state bank with British capital, which was to have the exclusive right to issue banknotes; and accordingly in September 1889 the Imperial Bank of Persia began business. In the same year Dolgoruki obtained for Russia the first option of a railway concession for five years. In November of the following year the railway agreement with Russia was changed into one interdicting all railways whatsoever in Persia. By the turn of the century there had been 'a pronounced sharpening of Anglo-Russian hostility as a consequence of a whole series of Russian actions, not only in northern Persia, where Russian ascendancy to a large extent had to be admitted, but as well in southern and eastern Persia which had hitherto been predominantly British preserves'. In 1900 a Russian loan was given. Subsequently

various short-term advances and subsidies from the Russian treasury including advances to the heir apparent, Muhammad Ali, were made so that by 1906 some £7.5m. was owing to the Russians. Under the 1891 Russo-Persian tariff treaty, trade between the two countries had increased, and when, under the 1901 Russo-Persian commercial treaty, a new customs tariff was announced in 1903, Russian exports to Persia were considerably aided, and, up to 1914, Russian commerce with Persia continued to grow.

The grant of these various concessions to foreigners and the raising of foreign loans gave rise to growing anxiety on the part of the Persian public. Further, large numbers of Persians had fled the country and were living in exile. When a tobacco monopoly was granted to a British subject in 1890, various elements of the population, including the intellectuals and the religious classes, combined to oppose it. Strikes and riots threatened and the monopoly was rescinded. No effective steps, however, were taken to allay popular discontent. In 1901 protests were made against the loans and mortgages from Russia which were being contracted to pay for Muzaffar ud-Din Shah's journeys to Europe. By 1905–6 the demand for reform had grown in strength and finally on 5 August 1906, after 12,000 persons had taken sanctuary in the British legation, a constitution was granted. A long struggle then began between the constitutionalists and the Shah. The Cossack Brigade, formed during the reign of Nasir ud-Din Shah, which was under Russian officers and was the most effective military force in the country, played a major part in this struggle and was used by Muhammad Ali Shah to suppress the National Assembly in 1908. Civil war ensued and Muhammad Ali Shah's abdication was forced in 1909.

Meanwhile in 1907 the Anglo-Russian convention had been signed. The convention, which included a mutual undertaking to respect the integrity and independence of Persia, divided the country into three areas, that lying to the north of a line passing from Qasr-e-Shirin to Kakh, where the Russian, Persian and Afghan frontiers met in the east, that lying to the south of a line running from Qazik on the Perso-Afghan frontier through Birjand and Kerman to Bandar Abbas on the Persian Gulf, and that lying outside these two areas. Great Britain gave an undertaking not to seek or support others seeking political or economic concessions in the northern area; Russia gave a similar undertaking with reference to the southern area. In the central area the freedom of action of the two parties was not limited and their existing concessions (which included the oil concession granted to D'Arcy in 1901) were maintained. The conclusion of this convention—which had taken place partly because of a change in the relative strength of the Great Powers and partly because the British Government hoped thereby to terminate Anglo-Russian rivalry in Persia and to prevent further Russian encroachments—came as a shock to Persian opinion which had hoped for much from the support which the British Government had given to the constitutional movement. It was felt that Persian interests had been bartered away by Great Britain for a promise of Russian support in the event of a European war. In fact, the convention failed in its object. Russian pressure continued to be exercised on Persia directly and indirectly. In 1911, as a result of Russian pressure, the National Assembly was suspended, and the resignation forced of the American Administrator-General of the Finances, Shuster, who had been appointed in the hope of bringing order to the finances of Persia.

THE FIRST WORLD WAR

During the First World War Persia was nominally neutral but, in fact, pro-Turkish. By the end of the war the internal condition of Persia was chaotic. To the British Government the restoration of order was desirable and with this end in view the Agreement of 1919 was drawn up whereby a number of men were to be lent to reorganize the Persian army and to reform the Ministry of Finance and a loan of £2m. was to be given. There was opposition to this agreement in the USA and France and in Persia, and the treaty was not ratified. A *coup d'état* took place in 1921, Reza Khan (later Reza Shah) becoming Minister of War. In February 1921 the Soviet-Persian Treaty was signed whereby the USSR declared all treaties and conventions concluded with Persia by the Tsarist Government null and void. Under Article VI the USSR was permitted 'to advance her troops into the Persian interior for the purpose of carrying out the military operations necessary for its defence' in the event of a third party attempting 'to carry out a policy of usurpation by means of armed intervention in Persia, or if such a Power should desire to use Persian territory as a base of operations against Russia. . .'

REZA SHAH, 1925–41, AND AFTER

In 1923 Reza Khan became Prime Minister and finally in 1925 the crown of Persia was conferred upon him. His first task was to restore the authority of the central Government throughout the country, and the second to place Persia's relations with foreign countries on a basis of equality. All extra-territorial agreements were terminated from 1928. Lighterage and quarantine duties on the Persian littoral of the Persian Gulf, hitherto performed by Great Britain, were transferred to the Persian Government in 1930. The Indo-European Telegraphy Company, which had been in operation since 1872, had almost entirely been withdrawn by 1931 and the British coaling stations were transferred from Basidu and Henjam to Bahrain in 1935.

In 1932 the cancellation of the Anglo-Persian Oil Company's concession was announced by Persia. The original concession obtained by D'Arcy in 1901 had been taken over by the Anglo-Persian Oil Company (later the Anglo-Iranian Oil Company) in 1909 and the British Government had acquired a controlling interest in the company in 1914. The Persian Government's action in cancelling the concession was referred to the League of Nations. Eventually an agreement was concluded in 1933 for a new concession whereby the concession area was materially reduced and the royalty to be paid to the Persian Government increased. The concession was to run to 1993.

Internally Reza Shah's policy aimed at modernization and autarchy. In the later years of his reign the Government became increasingly totalitarian in nature. Compulsory military service was introduced and the army much increased in size. Communications were greatly improved; the construction of a trans-Persian railway was begun. Education was remodelled on western lines. Women were no longer obliged to wear the veil after 1936. Foreign trade was made a state monopoly, and currency and clearing restrictions were established. These arrangements fitted in with the economy of Germany and, by the outbreak of the Second World War, Germany had acquired considerable commercial and political influence in Persia.

On the outbreak of war Persia declared its neutrality. In 1941 the Allies demanded a reduction in the number of Germans in the country, and when no satisfaction was obtained sent another communication demanding the expulsion of all German nationals, except such as were essential to the Persian economy and harmless to the Allies. This demand was not complied with and on 26 August 1941, Persia was invaded. Hostilities lasted some two days. On 16 September Reza Shah abdicated in favour of his son Muhammad Reza. In January 1942 a Tripartite Treaty of Alliance was concluded with Great Britain and the USSR whereby Great Britain and the USSR undertook jointly and severally 'to respect the territorial integrity, sovereignty and political independence of Persia' and 'to defend Persia by all means in their command from aggression'. The Persian Government undertook to give the Allies, for certain military purposes, the unrestricted right to use, maintain and guard, and in the case of military necessity, to control, all means of communications in Persia. Allied forces were to be withdrawn not later than six months after the conclusion of hostilities between the Allied Powers and Germany and its associates. In so far as the establishment of communications with the USSR was concerned the Treaty was effective; its operation in other respects was less satisfactory. In the Russian zone of occupation the Persian authorities were denied freedom of movement and effective administration made impossible. American advisers were appointed by the Persian Government in 1942 and 1943 in the hope of reorganizing certain aspects of the administration, but little success was achieved.

In 1943 a British company applied for an oil concession in south-east Persia and in 1944 the Socony Vacuum and Sinclair Oil Companies made various proposals to the Persian Government. In September the Persian Cabinet issued a decree deferring the grant of oil concessions till after the war. The USSR meanwhile asked for an oil concession in the north and brought heavy, though unavailing, pressure to bear on the Persian Government to accede to this demand. Persian security forces were prevented by Soviet forces from entering Azerbaijan or the Caspian provinces, and an autonomous government was set up in Azerbaijan, with Soviet support, in December 1945. In January 1946 the Persian Government had recourse to the UN Security Council. In March the Tripartite Treaty expired and British and American forces evacuated Persia, Soviet forces remaining. The Persian Government again presented a note to the Security Council. In April an understanding, whereby a joint Soviet-Persian company to exploit the oil in the northern provinces was to be formed. In May Soviet forces evacuated the country. Soviet pressure, however, continued to be exerted through the communist Tudeh party, the Democrat movement in Azerbaijan, and the Kurdish autonomy movement, and the Persian Government was unable to re-enter Azerbaijan until December. In the following October, the Soviet Oil Agreement was presented to the National Assembly but was not ratified. In October 1947 an agreement was signed with the USA, providing for a US military mission in Persia to co-operate with the Persian Ministry of War in 'enhancing the efficiency of the Persian army'.

NATIONALIZING THE OIL INDUSTRY

Meanwhile unrest and discontent at internal misgovernment increased, culminating in the nationalist movement of 1950–51. In July 1949 a Supplemental Oil Agreement with the Anglo-Iranian Oil Company was initialled. Opposition to this agreement (whereby Persia was offered considerable financial gains) was strong. In November 1950 the oil commission of the National Assembly recommended its rejection. Meanwhile Persia had received a loan of $25m. from the Export & Import Bank of Washington and a grant of $500,000 under the Point IV allocation. Subsequently in 1952 the Point IV aid programme was expanded. In April 1951 the National Assembly passed a Bill for the nationalization of the oil industry, and in May Dr Muhammad Musaddiq, who had led the campaign for nationalization of oil, became Prime Minister. In spite of efforts to involve the International Court of Justice, the status quo could not be maintained in Persia and the Anglo-Iranian Oil Company evacuated the country, being unable to continue operations.

On 22 July 1952, the International Court found that it had no jurisdiction in the oil dispute. This decision, however, was not a decision on the merits of the case. The Company accordingly maintained its claim to be entitled to all crude oil and oil products derived from the area covered by its concession agreement, and stated its intention to take such action as was necessary to protect its interests. US policy showed an increasing interest in Persian affairs. During the period August to October 1952, considerable correspondence passed between the British, American and Persian Governments in the oil dispute, culminating in a joint offer by Sir Winston Churchill and President Truman, concerning proposals to assess the compensation to be paid to the Anglo-Iranian Oil Company and the resumption of the flow of oil to world markets. The Persian Government rejected these proposals and put forward counter proposals which were unacceptable. On 22 October the Persian Government broke off diplomatic relations with Great Britain. Further Anglo-American proposals for an oil settlement were put forward in February 1953, which the Persian Government rejected. Meanwhile dissension between Musaddiq and some of his supporters broke out, and a rift also developed between him and the Shah. The economic situation of the country began to deteriorate rapidly, culminating in the overthrow of Musaddiq by General Zahedi in August 1953. Musaddiq was tried and sentenced to three years solitary confinement for allegedly trying to overthrow the regime and illegally dissolving the Majlis-e-Shura (Consultative Assembly).

The new Government resumed diplomatic relations with Great Britain in December 1953, and negotiations with British and American oil interests began for the solution of the oil problem. In September 1954 an agreement was signed, and ratified by the Majlis and Senate in October, granting a concession to a consortium of eight companies (subsequently increased to 17) on a percentage basis.

It was also agreed that the claims of the Anglo-Iranian Oil Company and the Persian Government against each other were to be settled by the payment of a lump sum to the Company, which was also to receive compensation from the other members of the consortium. The profits arising within Persia from the oil operations were to be equally shared between the Persian Government and the consortium. The agreement was for a period of 25 years with provision for three five-year extensions, conditional upon a progressive reduction of the original area. The National Iranian Oil Company (NIOC) was to operate the Naft-i Shahr oilfield and the Kermanshah refinery to meet part of Persia's own needs and to handle the distribution of oil products in Persia and to be responsible for all facilities and services not directly part of the producing, refining, and transport operations of the two operating companies set up under the agreement. The greater part of the cost of these facilities and services, which would include industrial training, public transport, road maintenance, housing, medical care, and social welfare, would be recovered by the NIOC from the operating companies.

GROWING POWER OF THE SHAH

Internally, order was restored. The communist Tudeh Party was proscribed, but continued to exist underground. The failure of the Government to push forward actively with reform, however, led, in due course, to a reappearance of unrest and discontent. In April 1955 Zahedi resigned and was succeeded by Hussein Ala, the Shah henceforward taking a more active part in the administration. In October, Persia joined the Baghdad Pact. In November an attempt was made on the Prime Minister's life. The country had not recovered from the financial difficulties brought on by the Musaddiq regime, in spite of considerable financial aid granted by the USA to enable the country to carry on until oil revenues were received. More than US $800m. were poured into Iran between the end of the Second World War and September 1960. On 5 March 1959 a bilateral defence agreement was signed in Ankara between the USA and Iran. Under the agreement, the Government of the USA would 'in case of aggression, take such appropriate action, including the use of armed force, as may be mutually agreed, and as envisaged in the Joint Resolution to promote peace and security in the Middle East'. (The Joint Resolution refers to the 'Eisenhower Doctrine'.)

Relations with the USSR in the years following the fall of Musaddiq were not cordial, but in December 1954 an agreement providing for (1) the repayment by the USSR of its war debts to Persia for goods supplied and services rendered, and (2) mapping of the revised frontiers was signed.

On 3 April 1957, Hussein Ala resigned and was succeeded as Prime Minister by Dr Manoutchehr Egbal, who formed a new government. Immediately after taking office Dr Egbal issued a decree ending martial law and declared his intention of forming a democratic two-party system, in accordance with the wishes of the Shah. In February 1958 a pro-government Nation Party was formed. An opposition People's Party had been formed in 1957. Elections contested by both these political parties disclosed electoral irregularities, and in August 1960 Jaafar Sharif-Emami replaced Dr Egbal as Prime Minister.

In May 1961, however, Dr Emami resigned as a result of criticism of his handling of a teachers' strike, and the Shah called upon Dr Ali Amini, the leader of the opposition, to form a new government.

Dr Amini quickly took stern measures to halt the political and economic chaos in Iran. A drive against corruption in the government and civil service was coupled with policies of land reform, decentralization of administration, control of government expenditure and limitation of luxury imports. Both houses of Parliament were dissolved pending the passing of a new electoral law which would make free and fair elections possible. Postponement of elections, in July 1962, led to disorder in Teheran, and the added difficulty of producing

a reasonably balanced budget led Dr Amini to tender his resignation.

A new government was quickly formed by Mr Assadollah Alam, the leader of the Mardom (People's) Party. Mr Alam, one of Iran's largest landowners and administrator of the Pahlavi Foundation, had previously distributed much of his land voluntarily amongst the peasants. He stated that Iran would remain closely linked to the West, and that he would continue the land reform programme and the struggle against internal political corruption. A reform programme was approved by a national referendum held in January 1963.

REFORMS OF THE SHAH

In 1950 the Shah began distributing his estate amongst the peasants. By the end of 1963 he had disposed of all his Crown Properties. The Pahlavi Foundation was established in 1958 and received considerable gifts from the Shah for the purpose of improving standards of education, health and social welfare amongst the poorer classes. In October 1961 the Shah created the £40m. Pahlavi Dynasty Trust, the income of which was used for social, educational and health services for the Iranian people.

In January 1963 a referendum was held, as a result of which overwhelming approval was given to the Shah's six-point plan for the distribution of lands among the peasants, the promotion of literacy, the emancipation of women, etc. The break-up of great estates began almost immediately, and the programme was finally completed in September 1971. Another important measure was the formation of the Literacy Corps (and later of the Health Corps), in which students could serve their period of national service as teachers, working in the villages.

Elections in September 1963 resulted in an overwhelming victory for the National Union of Mr Alam. The elections, in which, for the first time, women were allowed to vote, were held in the face of strong opposition from the left-wing parties of Iran, notably the National Front and the Tudeh Party, which called unsuccessfully for a boycott. The Shah called on the new Parliament to inaugurate a 20-year programme of economic and social reform and political development and he also announced a second phase of the land reform programme, whereby it was hoped that another 20,000 villages would be added to the 10,000 already handed over to the tenants. The Alam Government continued until March 1964, when, without offering any reason, Mr Alam resigned. The new leader was Hassan Ali Mansur, a former minister and founder of the Progressive Centre, which had played a prominent part in the coalition of Mr Alam the previous year. In December 1963 he had formed the New Iran Party, which by now had the support of some 150 members of the Majlis. The second stage of the land reform plan was placed before the Majlis in May and this aimed to break down the great estates more thoroughly; the maximum permissible size was to be from 120 ha in arid regions to 30 ha in more fertile areas.

On 21 January 1965 Mr Mansur was assassinated by members of the right-wing religious sect Fedayin Islam. The assassins were reportedly followers of the Ayatollah Ruhollah Khomeini, a Shi'ite Muslim religious leader who had been exiled in 1964 for his opposition to the Shah's reforms.

Amir Abbas Hoveida, the Minister of Finance, was immediately appointed acting premier, and became Prime Minister on the day following Mr Mansur's death, retaining his post at the Ministry of Finance. He pledged himself to the continuation of his predecessor's policies, and was given the massive support of the Majlis. Elections took place in 1967, 1971 and 1975. Mr Hoveida continued as Prime Minister until August 1977, when he was succeeded by Dr Jamshid Amouzegar.

FOREIGN RELATIONS

Iran began a period of good relations with the USSR in 1964–65 when various mutually beneficial trading and technical agreements were signed, and a regular air service between Teheran and Moscow was inaugurated. It had been an avowed part of Mr Mansur's policy that Iran should be as much interested in maintaining links with the USSR as with the West. In June 1965 the Shah visited Moscow, and in October an agreement was signed for the construction by Soviet engineers of a steel mill. Relations with Iraq in early 1966 became strained when the long-standing disagreement over the Shatt al-Arab waterway erupted into a series of border incidents.

The coronation of the Shah in October 1967 seemed to augur forthcoming prosperity and the apparent stability of Iran was emphasized, not only by economic development and by the organization of international gatherings, but also by the formal ending in November of US economic aid under the Point IV allocation. Iran, which had been the first country to accept this aid in 1951, was now the second (after the Republic of China) to find itself able to dispense with it. Military aid, however, was to continue. At the same time economic co-operation with the USSR was developed, and an agreement was made for the purchase of £40m. of munitions, the first occasion on which the USSR had concluded an arms transaction with a member of the Western bloc.

In January 1968 the British Government announced its decision to withdraw all its forces from the Gulf by the end of 1971. Since these forces had apparently helped to preserve the local status quo, a revival of the ancient rivalry between Arabs and Persians over supremacy in the Gulf then seemed a likely prospect following their removal. The Iranian Government's reiteration of its claim to Bahrain in February 1968 did not help relations with the Arab world, but Iran cautiously welcomed the proposed Federation of Arab Emirates (which it was thought would incorporate Bahrain).

A UN Mission visiting Bahrain in early 1970 found that the large Arab majority overwhelmingly preferred full independence to joining Iran or remaining a British protectorate. Iran had previously agreed to accept the mission's findings, and it did so without complaint, though expressing concern for the future of Iranians in the Gulf states. In June 1970 a dispute with other Gulf states also arose over Iran's claim to the islands of Abu Musa and the Tumbs belonging to Sharjah and Ras al-Khaimah respectively. The dispute was only settled at the beginning of December 1971. The Sheikh of Sharjah agreed to share his island of Abu Musa with Iran. The Sheikh of Ras al-Khaimah was less accommodating, so Iran invaded his possessions of the Greater and Lesser Tumbs and took them by force. After occupying Abu Musa and the Tumbs, Iran has developed them as military bases to command the Strait of Hormuz at the neck of the Gulf. Iran regarded the maintenance of freedom of passage through the Strait of Hormuz as vital to its strategic and economic interests.

Iran's relations with the more radical Arab states were less friendly under the Shah. These states had long been suspicious of Iran's close ties with the West, and especially of the generous US military aid to the powerful Iranian armed forces. Moreover, the Arab states distrusted Iran's attitude to Israel. Although no formal diplomatic links existed, trade, particularly in oil, was conducted with Israel. One of the first actions of the Khomeini regime in early 1979 was to end any ties with Israel and to align Iran firmly behind the Arab cause, by allowing, for example, the opening of a PLO office in Teheran.

Iran's only frontier with an Arab state is with Iraq. Near the Gulf the border is delineated by the 185-km Shatt al-Arab waterway, the estuary of the Tigris and Euphrates, which flows into the Gulf, and, by the terms of the 1937 treaty, the frontier followed the eastern, i.e. Iranian, bank; thus, Iraq legally had sovereignty over the whole waterway. For many years, Iran resented this provision, and in April 1969 it decided to abrogate the treaty by sending Iranian vessels, flying the national flag, through the waterway, while heavy naval forces stood ready to intervene. The aim was apparently to force a renegotiation of the treaty. In September 1969 there were further armed clashes on the border. In January 1970 Iraq accused the Iranian Government of supporting an abortive coup in Iraq, and diplomatic relations between the two countries were severed.

Diplomatic relations between Iran and Iraq were restored soon after the outbreak of the Arab-Israeli War in October 1973, but border incidents continued. In March 1975, however, it was announced at an OPEC meeting in Algiers that the Shah and Saddam Hussain (then Vice-President of the Iraqi Revolution Command Council) had signed an agreement which 'completely eliminated the conflict between the two brotherly countries'. Not only did this agreement settle the outstanding

border differences, but it also deprived the Kurds in Iraq of the help which they had been receiving from Iran in their struggle against the Iraqi Government, thus causing a Kurdish collapse and a virtual end to the Kurdish War.

The border agreement provided that Iran and Iraq would define their frontiers on the basis of the Protocol of Constantinople of 1913 (which allowed the Ottoman Empire to retain control over the Shatt al-Arab but granted sovereignty over the east bank to Persia) and the verbal agreement on frontiers of 1914, and that the Shatt al-Arab frontier would be defined according to the Thalweg Line (i.e. the middle of the deepest shipping channel). The treaty giving effect to this agreement was signed on 15 June 1975 and later became one of the key issues of the war with Iraq which broke out in September 1980 (see below).

INTERNAL PROBLEMS

Internally, signs of opposition to the Shah's regime, never far from the surface of Iranian life, became more and more evident as the celebrations for the 2,500th anniversary of the Persian monarchy were in preparation for October 1971. The combination of the very unequal distribution of the enormous earnings from oil and the suppression of any sign of dissent was made more politically explosive as the lavishness of the celebrations and the huge extent of the accompanying security precautions became apparent. From then, until the final fall of the Shah in early 1979, there were countless stories of the stifling of opposition by the ruthless activities of SAVAK, the government security agency.

In March 1975 the Shah, dissatisfied with the current structure of party politics in Iran and wanting to weld together all those who supported the principles of his 'White Revolution' policy (later known as the 'Revolution of the Shah and People'), announced the formation of a single party system, the Iran National Resurgence Party (Rastakhiz), with the Prime Minister, Amir Abbas Hoveida, as Secretary-General. By 1978 it became clear that the single-party Rastakhiz system was not solving the problem of internal opposition in Iran, but few people in early 1978 would have forecast that, within a year, a completely new political system would take its place.

FALL OF THE SHAH

During 1977 and 1978 demonstrations centred around the universities and acts of political violence increased. Attempts by the Shah to control the situation, first by greater liberalization and then through firmer suppression, proved ineffective. In August 1977 Dr Jamshid Amouzegar, who had become secretary-general of Rastakhiz, replaced the long-serving Amir Abbas Hoveida as Prime Minister but he resigned a year later. In August 1978 Jaafar Sharif-Emami was appointed Prime Minister (an office he had previously held in 1960–61) and, in response to the emerging mood of the country, promised that his Government would observe Islamic tenets. Unrest continued, however. Martial law was introduced in September, and in November the Shah set up a military government headed by the army Chief of Staff, General Gholamreza Azhari. Censorship was imposed, but strikes in the oil industry and public services left the Shah in a desperate situation, and in early January 1979 he charged Dr Shapour Bakhtiar, a former deputy leader of the National Front, with forming a 'last-chance' government. Dr Bakhtiar undertook to dissolve SAVAK (the security police), stop the export of oil to South Africa and Israel and support the Palestinians. However, opposition to the Shah continued to such an extent that he left the country on 15 January, never to return.

The opposition within Iran had stemmed from two main sources, with little in common except their desire to overthrow the Shah. By the time the Shah left Iran opposition from the left and the more liberal National Front had been overshadowed by the success of the opposition coming from the exiled religious leader Ayatollah Khomeini. He conducted his campaign from France where he had arrived in early October after 14 years of exile in Iraq for opposing the Shah's 'White Revolution' (1963) because it conflicted with traditional Islamic values.

In January Khomeini formed an Islamic Revolutionary Council from his base near Paris and pressure in Iran grew for his return. The Bakhtiar Government tried to delay his return for as long as possible, but on 1 February Khomeini arrived in Teheran from Paris to a tumultuous welcome from the Iranian people. Bakhtiar refused to recognize Khomeini but, after several demonstrations and outbreaks of violence, the army withdrew its support from Dr Bakhtiar and he resigned on 11 February. Dr Mehdi Bazargan, who had been named 'Provisional Prime Minister' by Khomeini on 6 February, formed a provisional government later in the month but it soon became clear that real power rested with Khomeini's 15-man Islamic Revolutionary Council.

IRAN UNDER AYATOLLAH KHOMEINI

Although Khomeini became the *de facto* leader of Iran riding on the crest of a wave of public euphoria, the difficulties of putting into practice the ideals of the Islamic Revolution severely tested the Revolutionary Government.

From the very outset conflict arose between the Islamic Revolutionary Council, which gave effect to its policies through a network of Komitehs, and the Prime Minister, Dr Bazargan.

Tension over Iran's ethnic minorities, either not in evidence or stifled under the Shah, became a problem after the Revolution. Most serious was the demand for autonomy from the Kurds in the north-west, which often led to open warfare in that area. Other minorities also demanded autonomy. These included the Baluchis in the south-east, the Turkomans in the north-east and the Azerbaijanis in the north-west. Conflict with the Arabs in the south-west also interacted with hostile relations with Iraq, which later developed into the Iran–Iraq War in September 1980 (see below). The position was complicated by the fact that these minorities were Sunni Muslims, while the Khomeini regime and the majority of Iranians were Shi'ite.

Another major difficulty was Iran's relations with the USA and, as an extension of that, with the Western world. Khomeini's regime from the outset had condemned previous US interference in Iranian affairs, and when, on 4 November 1979, Iranian students seized 53 hostages in the US Embassy in Teheran, Khomeini was quite ready to offer his support to the students who demanded the return of the Shah (then in the USA) to Iran to face trial. This problem dominated relations with the USA for the next 14 months, and was not resolved by the death of the Shah in Egypt on 27 July 1980. The USA launched an airborne military operation to free the hostages, landing a commando force in eastern Iran. The operation was cancelled at an early stage, however, owing to equipment failure, and eight men died when a helicopter collided with a transport aircraft as the force prepared to abandon the mission. Internal disagreements meant that the first Islamic Majlis, elected in March and May 1980, was slow to grapple with the problem of the hostages, who were not released until 20 January 1981.

Another problem was the intensity of Islamic fervour in Iran. Ayatollah Khalkhali, at one time Chief Justice of the Islamic Revolutionary Courts, set about his task with extraordinary zeal and by May 1980 claimed to have ordered more than 300 executions. Moreover, in May 1980 he destroyed the tomb of Reza Shah, an action which was later condemned by President Bani-Sadr, who pointed out that such actions worked against the Revolution. Not all Iranians approved of the ardour with which the 'Bureau to Stop Bad Acts' set about cleaning up the moral lapses in Iranian society.

CONSTITUTIONAL DEVELOPMENT

At the end of March 1979 Khomeini held a referendum on the question, 'Do you favour an Islamic Republic?' The result was an almost unanimous 'yes' and on 1 April an Islamic Republic was declared. A draft constitution proposed that Iran be governed by a president, prime minister and a single-chamber Islamic Consultative Assembly (Majlis-e-Shura) of 270 deputies. Although there was pressure in Iran to submit the draft constitution to a newly-elected Constituent Assembly, Khomeini submitted it for revision to a 'Council of Experts' consisting of 75 members who were elected on 3 August. After prolonged deliberations the revised constitution was submitted to a referendum at the beginning of December 1979.

The most important change from the draft constitution was provision for a *wali faqih* (religious leader), whose extensive powers (see The Constitution) secured for him the most important levers of power in Iran. Votes against the Constitution were negligible.

Presidential elections followed on 25 January 1980, and resulted in a convincing win for Abolhasan Bani-Sadr, who polled about 75% of the votes. All this time the Islamic Revolutionary Council had effectively been administering the country, although there was a government headed by Dr Mehdi Bazargan until his resignation in mid-November 1979 over Khomeini's support for the retention of the US hostages. Thereafter the Islamic Revolutionary Council, with President Bani-Sadr becoming its chairman in February 1980, ruled more openly, and appointed ministers to run the country until elections to the Majlis in the spring of 1980.

The elections took place in two rounds, on 14 March and 9 May 1980. A total of 3,300 candidates contested 270 seats, 30 of which were in Teheran. Disturbances in Kurdish areas and various allegations of fraud resulted in the fact that, when the Majlis began its first session on 28 May 1980, only 234 deputies had been decided, and, of those, only 213 had received their credentials. It was clear, however, that the Islamic Republican Party (IRP), the party identified with the policies of Ayatollah Khomeini and led by Ayatollah Beheshti, was in a majority, claiming 130 seats. Ayatollah Beheshti presented a threat to the leadership of President Bani-Sadr. On 7 May Khomeini had given Bani-Sadr authority to appoint a prime minister until the Majlis convened, but Beheshti successfully prevented this, insisting that this appointment be the responsibility of the Majlis.

The Islamic Revolutionary Council was dissolved on 18 July 1980, but there followed a delay in forming a government. Many of the candidates for ministerial office who were proposed by the Majlis and supported by the IRP were unacceptable to President Bani-Sadr. The President agreed to the appointment of Muhammad Ali Rajai as Prime Minister only with reluctance, doubting his competence. The ministries of finance and economic affairs, commerce and foreign affairs were left without ministers for some months, and a feud developed between President Bani-Sadr, on the one hand, and Rajai and the IRP, on the other. An abortive three-man commission tried to resolve these differences in March 1981, but on 10 June Khomeini dismissed Bani-Sadr as Commander-in-Chief of the Armed Forces. A few days later, Bani-Sadr was deprived of the presidency, and he later fled to France, where he formed a 'National Council of Resistance' in alliance with Massoud Rajavi, the former leader in Iran of the opposition guerrilla group, the Mujahidin-e-Khalq. (Bani-Sadr left the council in 1984 because of his objection to Rajavi's increasing co-operation with the Iraqi Government—see Political Organizations, p. 455.) A three-man Presidential Council replaced Bani-Sadr after his dismissal, until new presidential elections could be held on 24 July. On 28 June, however, a bomb exploded at the headquarters of the IRP, killing Ayatollah Beheshti (the Chief Justice and Head of the IRP), four cabinet ministers, six deputy ministers and 20 parliamentary deputies.

On 24 July 1981 the presidential election took place and resulted in a win for the Prime Minister, Muhammad Ali Rajai. Muhammad Javad Bahonar then became Prime Minister of a government introduced to the Majlis on 13 August. A further bomb outrage occurred on 29 August, this time killing both the President (Rajai) and the Prime Minister (Bahonar). Ayatollah Muhammad Reza Mahdavi Kani became Prime Minister in September, and another round of presidential elections was held on 2 October. Hojatoleslam Ali Khamenei, a leading figure of the IRP, was elected President, winning more than 16m. of the 16.8m. votes cast. At the end of October, after the resignation of Ayatollah Muhammad Reza Mahdavi Kani, Mir Hossein Moussavi was appointed Prime Minister.

THE IRAN–IRAQ WAR

It was generally thought by outsiders at this time that the whole Iranian Islamic Revolution was about to crumble. In addition to internal troubles, Iran had been at war with Iraq for over a year. Fighting between the two countries had begun after Iran ignored Iraqi demands for the withdrawal of Iranian forces from Zain ul-Qos, in Diali province on the border between the two countries. Iraq maintained that this territory should have been returned to Iraq under the 1975 agreement with Iran. Iraq therefore abrogated the 1975 Shatt al-Arab agreement and invaded Iran on 22 September 1980. Most observers now believe that this was no more than a pretext on Iraq's part, the real objective of its President, Saddam Hussain, being to topple what he regarded as the threatening but vulnerable Iranian regime.

Iranian resistance was spirited, and a position of stalemate was soon reached along a 480-km front. Various international peace missions all proved of no avail, and in the spring of 1982 the Iranian forces broke the stalemate by launching two offensives, the first in the Shush-Dezful area in March, and the second on a 60-mile front south of Susangerd to the port of Khorramshahr at the end of April. Both offensives achieved considerable success, with Iran recapturing Khorramshahr in the middle of May. It then carried the war into Iraqi territory, but a speedy conclusion to the war, for which Iran had hoped, did not materialize. In February 1983 Iran began a major offensive in the area of Iraq's Misan province, but the impetus was soon lost, and a fresh Iranian offensive in April similarly proved indecisive. A further Iranian offensive in July (combined with operations to suppress renewed activity by Kurdish guerrillas in the area) saw its forces entrenched 15 km within northern Iraq. The attack seemed to be consistent with Iran's policy of waging a war of attrition, keeping Iraq on a war footing and thereby exerting pressure on the weakening Iraqi economy which might topple the regime of Saddam Hussain. Action by Iran prevented Iraq from exporting oil through the Gulf and a pipeline through Syria was cut off. Iraq was able to continue the war only with financial aid from Saudi Arabia and Kuwait.

During the second half of 1983 Iraq stepped up missile and aircraft raids against Iranian towns and petroleum installations and, in the autumn, took delivery of five French-built *Super Etendard* fighter aircraft. With these, and with the *Exocet* missiles already in its possession, Iraq threatened to destroy Iran's oil export industry, centred on Kharg Island in the Gulf, which financed the Iranian war effort. Iran countered by promising to make the Gulf impassable to all shipping (one-sixth of the Western world's petroleum requirement passed through the Gulf) if Iraqi military action rendered it unable to export oil from the Gulf via the Strait of Hormuz. In retaliation for the sale of *Super Etendard* aircraft to Iraq, Iran severed most of its economic ties with France.

In March 1984 a further Iranian offensive succeeded in taking part of the marshlands around the southern Iraqi island of Majnoun, the site of rich oilfields, though only at a great cost in lives. Iraq subsequently retook some of the territory which they had lost, but seemed more intent on consolidating their defences than making further ground. A team of UN observers, sent in at the request of the Iranian Government, found that Iraq had used mustard gas to counter the offensive. A long-awaited Iranian offensive against Basra failed to materialize. While Iran delayed, Iraq developed a formidable network of defensive fortifications along its southern border.

Although it had earlier declared a maritime exclusion zone at the north-east end of the Gulf around Kharg Island and made spasmodic attacks against shipping (not only oil tankers), which in some cases was well outside the zone, Iraq refrained from attacking tankers using the Kharg Island oil terminal until May 1984. Iran retaliated with attacks against Saudi and Kuwaiti tankers in the Gulf.

INTERNAL DEVELOPMENTS

At the time of the bomb outrages in mid-1981 the Iranian regime appeared to the rest of the world to be on the point of collapse. Subsequent events, however, demonstrated that it possessed greater resilience than was at one time thought possible. An extended campaign against the main anti-government guerrilla group, the Mujahidin-e-Khalq, waged sometimes with savage ferocity, eventually achieved some success, and in February 1982 the Mujahidin leader in Iran, Musa Khiabani, was killed.

In April 1982 an anti-government plot was uncovered in which Ayatollah Shariatmadari, one of Iran's leading mullahs, was accused of being involved. He subsequently denied this, but admitted knowledge of the plot, in which the former Minister of Foreign Affairs, Sadeq Ghotbzadeh, was deeply implicated. Ghotbzadeh was subsequently tried and executed in September. Ayatollah Shariatmadari died in April 1986, having been under house arrest in Qom for two years.

In 1983 the Iranian Government turned its attention to the Iranian communist party, the Tudeh Party. The party had been banned under the Shah, but had come into the open after the 1979 revolution. In February the party's Secretary-General, Nour ed-Din Kianuri, was arrested on charges of spying for the USSR. Kianuri was subsequently the first of a number of Tudeh members publicly to confess on TV to this and other crimes against the state. Further arrests of Tudeh Party members followed, bringing the total of arrests to about 1,000, and 18 Soviet diplomats were expelled. The party was officially banned again in April.

An intense rivalry within the Government, reflecting a wider divergence of views in the country, became increasingly apparent after the Revolution. The two rival groups were the right-wing Hojjatieh, identified with the traditionalist clerical and merchant ('bazaari') communities, and the radical technocrats. The Hojjatieh were opposed on grounds of religion and self-interest to radical economic reforms such as the nationalization programme and the reform of the laws governing land ownership (the clergy are extensive land owners), which were advocated by the technocrats, who were motivated by more secular, socialist concerns. The resignation, in August 1983, of the Ministers of Commerce, and of Labour, and the subsequent dismissal of three other members of the Council of Ministers and of nine of the 27 provincial governors, were directly attributable to this factional rivalry. The Hojjatieh had extensive representation in the first Majlis.

Elections to the second Majlis took place on 15 April and 17 May 1984, significantly altering the distribution of influence in the assembly. Slightly more than one-half of the outgoing first Majlis were clerical men and that majority had given them the power to determine policy according to largely religious considerations. A high proportion of the 1,230 or more candidates who contested the elections were of a more secular cast; doctors, scientists, engineers; people with a practical economic background. The elections were boycotted by former Prime Minister Dr Mehdi Bazargan's Liberation Movement opposition party (the only party recognized by the ruling IRP), in protest against what he considered to be the undemocratic conditions prevailing in Iran. Some 60%–70% of the 24m.–25m. electorate voted in the two-round election and the second Majlis was opened on 28 May. It was estimated that more than 50% of the seats in the new assembly were filled by new members giving rise to speculation that a more sympathetic Majlis might allow Moussavi greater success in implementing his economic programme. However, the Council of Guardians, which exists to determine whether Majlis legislation is both constitutional and Islamic, was of a conservative, clerical character and proved to be a major obstacle to economic reform.

Islamic codes of correction were introduced in 1983, including the dismembering of a hand for theft; flogging for more than 50 offences including forgery, consumption of alcohol, fornication and violations of the strict code of dress for women; and stoning to death for adultery. These began to be more rigidly enforced in 1985, in response to demonstrations in April by young Muslim fundamentalists demanding stricter adherence to Islamic law. There were clashes between opponents of the regime and fanatical *hezbollahi* (members of the Party of God) who supported the continuation of the Iran–Iraq War and the rigid observance of Islamic codes of behaviour. Widespread active popular opposition to the Teheran regime was not conspicuous until 1985. Dissatisfaction with the conduct of the war with Iraq and with austere economic conditions sparked demonstrations and rioting in several Iranian cities, including Teheran. Government supporters staged numerous counter-demonstrations.

Active suppression of opposition to the Government continued. In 1985, according to Amnesty International, 399 people were executed in Iran in the period to the end of

October, bringing the total to 6,426 since the Revolution. A UN Human Rights Commission report, published in February 1987, estimated the number of executions at a minimum of 7,000 between 1979 and 1985.

President Ali Khamenei was due to complete his four-year term of office in September 1985, and a presidential election was held on 16 August, with only three candidates, including Ali Khamenei, taking part. The Council of Guardians rejected the candidature of nearly 50 people who had applied to stand in the election, including Dr Mehdi Bazargan, leader of the Liberation Movement of Iran, the only legally recognized opposition party. Ali Khamenei was re-elected President, gaining 85.7% of the 14,244,630 votes cast.

Although 99 deputies either voted against him or abstained, Hossein Moussavi was confirmed as Prime Minister by the Majlis on 13 October 1985. A dispute over the composition of the new Council of Ministers, which President Khamenei considered to be too radical, initially withholding his approval from half of Moussavi's appointees, was not resolved until the intervention of Ayatollah Khomeini on Moussavi's behalf, so that the list submitted to the Majlis contained only two changes. All but seven of the new Council of Ministers had served in the previous Government.

DEVELOPMENTS IN THE IRAN–IRAQ WAR IN 1985–86

A resumption of Iraqi attacks on shipping in the Gulf in December 1984 had the effect of reducing Iranian oil exports to an estimated 1.1m. b/d and causing the Teheran Government to suspend imports temporarily. Although Iraqi raids on Iranian petroleum installations and oil tankers in the Gulf undeniably affected the level of oil exports, they failed to halt them altogether, the Kharg Island oil terminal remained in operation, largely undamaged, and Iran's economy appeared to be capable of sustaining the cost of continuing the war, albeit under severe pressure. Iran managed to keep up its oil exports by offering discounts and rebates on purchases to its customers, and by tactical evasions such as the introduction of temporary floating oil terminals, such as that at Sirri Island, out of range of most Iraqi war planes, whence oil was shuttled from the more exposed Kharg Island terminal. Iraq had an estimated 580 combat aircraft and 130 armed helicopters at the beginning of 1985, compared with Iran's 110 combat aircraft, of which only 50–60 were thought to be operational, but it failed fully to exploit its superiority. The People's Republic of China became the leading supplier of military equipment to Iran during the war, and it was estimated that businesses or governments in 44 countries, including both the USA and the USSR, had sold armaments to Iran during the war. Other major suppliers included the Democratic People's Republic of Korea and Israel.

Iran mounted an assault in the region of the al-Hawizah marshes in southern Iraq, east of the Tigris, in March 1985. This did not appear to be the long-awaited decisive thrust, as it involved, at the most, only 50,000 troops. The Iranian forces crossed the Tigris and succeeded, for a time, in closing the main road between Baghdad and Basra. The Iraqis launched a counter-offensive, repulsing the Iranians, with heavy casualties sustained by both sides. Iraq was again accused of using chemical weapons during this battle.

The UN had painstakingly engineered an agreement between Iran and Iraq in June 1984, suspending attacks on civilian targets, but, after the failure of the Iranian offensive in March 1985, and with the war on the ground once more at stalemate, Iraq resumed its air attacks on Iranian cities from the ground and from the air. The first Iraqi air raid on Teheran in four years took place in March. Iran retaliated, shelling Basra and other Iraqi towns, and hit Baghdad with ground-launched missiles, but Iraq, in this instance making full use of its air superiority, hit more than 30 Iranian population centres in the first half of 1985, killing hundreds of civilians. President Saddam Hussain's stated intention was to carry the war to every part of Iran until Khomeini decided to come to the negotiating table.

In April 1985 the UN Secretary-General, Javier Pérez de Cuéllar, visited both Teheran and Baghdad, in an attempt to establish a basis for peace negotiations, but Iran's terms remained the same. The Iranian claim for Iraqi war reparations

was US $350,000m., and, though there was less official insistence on the removal of Hussain and his Baathist regime from power as a condition of peace, it was accepted by the Iranian Government that, if all the other conditions (the payment of reparations, an Iraqi admission of responsibility for starting the war, and the withdrawal of Iraqi troops from all Iranian territory) were met, he would fall anyway.

Also in April 1985, Saddam Hussain ordered the suspension of air raids on Iranian towns in order to give Iran the opportunity to declare a cease-fire and begin negotiations. Iran did not respond. After six weeks, Iraqi air raids resumed with greater intensity at the end of May, with Iran retaliating in kind. A 16-day moratorium in June achieved the same result.

Until mid-1985 Iraq had failed to launch attacks against the main Iranian oil export terminal on Kharg Island of sufficient frequency or intensity seriously to threaten the continuation of oil exports. In August, however, Iraq made the first of a concentrated series of raids upon Kharg, causing a reduction in Iranian oil exports from 1.2m.–1.5m. barrels per day (b/d), in the months leading up to the raids, to less than 1m. b/d in September. Exports from Kharg were temporarily halted altogether during the latter half of September. By the end of 1985 exports from Kharg had reportedly been reduced to a trickle compared with its 6.5m. b/d capacity. In February 1986 Iraq announced an expansion of the area from which it would try to exclude Iranian shipping. Previously confined to the waters around Iran's Gulf ports, the area was broadened to include the coast of Kuwait. Attacks on tankers and other commercial vessels in the Gulf were increased by both sides during 1986, and Iran intensified its practice of intercepting merchant shipping and confiscating goods which it believed to be destined for Iraq. Iraq, meanwhile, was successful in damaging the alternative oil export facilities which Iran had established at the islands of Sirri and Larak, despite their remoteness near the mouth of the Persian Gulf.

The next important engagement, in terms of land gained, did not occur until 1986. On 9 February Iran launched the Wal-Fajr (Dawn) 8 offensive, so called to commemorate the month of Ayatollah Khomeini's return to Iran in 1979 from exile in France. Iranian forces (some 85,000 troops were thought to be involved in the operation) crossed the Shatt al-Arab waterway and, on 11 February, occupied the disused Iraqi port of Faw, on the Persian Gulf, and, according to Iran, about 800 sq km of the Faw peninsula. From this position, within sight of the Kuwaiti island of Bubiyan, commanding the Khor Abdullah channel between the Faw peninsula and the island, Iran threatened Iraq's only access to the Gulf and, if it could extend the offensive to the west, Iraq's Umm Qasr naval base. However, the marsh and then desert terrain to the west was not conducive to further Iranian gains, and the position on the Faw peninsula was defensible only with difficulty, given the problem of maintaining supply lines across the Shatt al-Arab. At the same time as the attack upon Faw, Iran began a complementary operation along the Faw–Basra road to divert Iraqi forces. When Iraq launched a counter-offensive on Faw in mid-February, Iran opened up a second front in Iraqi Kurdistan, hundreds of miles to the north, with the Wal-Fajr 9 offensive.

At the end of February 1986 the UN Security Council, while urging a cease-fire, blamed Iraq for starting the war for the first time. Despite heavy fighting, Iraq's counter-offensive made little progress and failed to dislodge an estimated 30,000 Iranian troops, now firmly entrenched in and around Faw. The proximity of Kuwaiti territory to the hostilities notwithstanding, Iran promised not to involve Kuwait in the war, provided that it did not allow Iraq the use of its territory (part of which, Bubiyan Island, is claimed by Iraq) for military purposes.

In May 1986 Iraq adopted different tactics by making its first armed incursions into Iran since withdrawing its forces from Iranian territory in 1982. About 150 sq km of land, including the deserted town of Mehran (about 160 km east of Baghdad), were occupied. (Iran recaptured Mehran in July.) Also in May, in the first Iraqi air raid on Teheran since June 1985, Iran's second largest oil refinery was bombed, signalling a renewal of reciprocal attacks on urban and economic targets, which continued for the remainder of 1986 and into 1987.

According to the *Washington Post* in December 1986, for the previous two years Iraq had received US intelligence assistance in targeting attacks on Iranian oil terminals and power plants. However, in the following month, US intelligence sources were reported as saying that both Iran and Iraq had been supplied with deliberately distorted or misleading information to assist the policies of the Reagan administration.

On 24 December 1986 Iran mounted an offensive (named Karbala-4 after the holy Shi'ite city in Iraq) in the region of Basra but failed to penetrate Iraqi defences on four islands in the Shatt al-Arab waterway. On 8 January 1987 a two-pronged attack (Karbala-5) was launched towards Basra. Iranian forces, attacking from the east, established a bridgehead inside Iraq, between the Shatt al-Arab, to the west, and the artificial Fish Lake to the east, and advanced gradually towards Basra, sustaining heavy casualties, while an assault from the southeast secured a group of islands in the Shatt al-Arab. Iran opened a second front, 400 km to the north, with the Karbala-6 offensive, on 13 January. By mid-February, Iranian forces from the east had advanced to within about 10 km of Basra, but no further gains were made and the Karbala-5 offensive was officially terminated at the end of the month.

In November 1986 it emerged that the USA, despite its official discouragement of arms sales to Iran by other countries, had been conducting secret negotiations with the Islamic Republic since July 1985, and had made three shipments of weapons and spare parts (valued at an estimated $100m.) to Iran, through Israeli and Saudi intermediaries, in September 1985, and July and October 1986. The shipments were allegedly in exchange for Iranian assistance in securing the release of US hostages who had been kidnapped by Shi'ite extremists in Lebanon, and an Iranian undertaking to abstain from involvement in international terrorism. The talks were reportedly conducted on the Iranian side by the Speaker of the Majlis, Hojatoleslam Hashemi Rafsanjani, with Ayatollah Khomeini's consent but without the knowledge of other senior government figures, including the Prime Minister and the President.

THE IRAN–IRAQ WAR: 1987

Iran rejected the offer of a cease-fire and peace talks, which was made by President Hussain of Iraq in January 1987, and in the following months demonstrated its ability to launch attacks from one end to the other of its 1,200-km frontier with Iraq. The Karbala-7 offensive, in March, penetrated northeastern Iraqi territory to a depth of about 20 km in the Gerdmand mountains, near Rawanduz, itself only some 100 km from Iraq's largest oilfields, at Kirkuk. On the southern front, in April, Iran launched the Karbala-8 offensive from the salient 10 km east of Basra, which had been secured in Karbala-5. The Iranians claimed that the attack established a new front line about 1 km towards Basra, west of the artificial Twin Canals water barrier, though Iraq claimed that it had been repulsed. An almost simultaneous offensive, Karbala-9, was mounted in the central sector of the Iran-Iraq border, from near the Iranian town of Qasr-e-Shirin.

The Iran–Iraq War entered a potentially explosive new phase in 1987. Once more, the danger of an escalation of the conflict was focused on the shipping lanes of the Persian Gulf. During 1986 there were about 100 attacks by Iran and Iraq on shipping in the Gulf. Iran had begun to use squads of high-speed patrol boats, crewed by Islamic Revolutionary Guards (*Pasdaran Inqilab*), stationed on islands in the Gulf, in attacks on commercial ships. Reflecting its anger at Kuwait's support for Iraq, Iranian attacks were concentrated on Kuwaiti shipping and on neutral vessels and tankers carrying oil or other cargoes to and from Iraq, via Kuwait. Between October 1986 and April 1987 15 ships bound to or from Kuwait were attacked by Iran in the Gulf, and several Kuwaiti cargoes were seized. Alarmed by the repeated attacks on its merchant ships and by the apparent indifference of the outside world to the war, Kuwait sought the protection of the leading powers for its shipping in the Gulf, and, by involving them more closely, hoped to persuade them of the urgent need for international co-operation in achieving a peaceful end to the conflict. The USSR and, subsequently, the USA were asked to re-register Kuwaiti ships under their flags, which they would then be obliged to defend if they came under attack. On 24

March, the day after the USA had made its navy available to escort Kuwaiti tankers, Iran threatened to halt the traffic in oil through the Gulf. In April the USSR allowed Kuwait to charter three Soviet tankers and proposed international talks on the protection of commercial shipping in the Gulf. The USA rejected the Soviet proposal but in May agreed to re-register 11 Kuwaiti tankers under the US flag and to increase its naval presence in the Gulf in order to protect them. This decision followed the apparently accidental attack in the Gulf by an Iraqi *Mirage* F-1 fighter plane on the *USS Stark* on 17 May, only hours after one of the Soviet tankers chartered by Kuwait had struck a mine while approaching a Kuwaiti port. Iraq desisted from attacks on tankers for the next five weeks.

At the end of June 1987, following a hiatus of five weeks, and one week after Iraq, Iran resumed its attacks on Gulf shipping using high speed launches based on the islands of Minou, Farsi and Abu Musa. Iran made it clear that it considered the US naval presence in the Gulf to be provocative, and fears of a military confrontation grew.

The escalation of tension in the Gulf resulted in a rare display of unanimity in the UN Security Council, which adopted a 10-point resolution (No. 598) on 20 July 1987, urging an immediate cease-fire in the Iran–Iraq War; the withdrawal of all forces to internationally recognized boundaries; and the co-operation of Iran and Iraq in mediation efforts to achieve a peace settlement. Iraq said that it would abide by the resolution if Iran did so (Iraqi attacks on tanker traffic had been halted in mid-July). Iran criticized the resolution for failing to identify Iraq as the original aggressor in the war, and claimed that the belligerent US naval presence in the Gulf (which rose to a peak of 48 vessels in 1987) rendered it null and void, but failed to deliver an official, unequivocal response.

The *USS Bridgeton* and the *USS Gas Prince*, the first Kuwaiti tankers to be re-registered under the US flag, passed unharmed through the Strait of Hormuz with a US naval escort on 22 July 1987. However, on 24 July the *Bridgeton* struck a mine (probably Iranian) near the Iranian island of Farsi, and struggled to port in Kuwait. The US naval force in the Gulf was ill-equipped to deal with mines and US Government requests for minesweeping assistance were initially refused by its main NATO allies, who were anxious to avoid a confrontation with Iran. In August, however, the UK and France announced that they were to send minesweepers to the Gulf region and, in September, these were followed by minesweeping vessels from Belgium, the Netherlands and Italy. Iran was believed to have laid mines on the shipping routes to Kuwait, including the al-Ahmadi channel, the approach to Kuwait's main oil ports.

POLITICAL AND DIPLOMATIC DEVELOPMENTS IN 1987–88

During 1987 the conviction grew among the international community that Iran was attempting to spread the Islamic Revolution through a network of agents operating in its diplomatic missions abroad, and controlled by the Iranian Ministry of Intelligence and Internal Security. In March Tunisia broke off diplomatic relations with Iran, accusing it of fomenting Islamic fundamentalist opposition to the Government, and of recruiting Tunisians for terrorist operations abroad through its embassy in Tunis. Eight suspected terrorists (six of whom held Tunisian passports) were arrested in Paris in March. They were believed to be members of a network of 'sleeper' terrorist cells co-ordinated by Iran and established several years before. In June the French authorities sought to interview Wahid Gordji, who was officially listed as a translator at the Iranian Embassy in Paris, in connection with a bombing campaign in the city in 1986. Although Gordji did not have diplomatic status the Iranians refused to give him up, and armed French police surrounded the embassy. The Iranian Government retaliated by throwing a cordon of armed Revolutionary Guards around the French Embassy in Teheran. On 17 July France severed its diplomatic relations with Iran. The embassy siege was lifted at the end of November, when Gordji was permitted to leave France. Two days after his release, two French hostages, held by Iranian-backed groups in Lebanon, were set free. The French Prime Minister, Jacques Chirac, denied that a ransom had been paid to the hostages' captors but admitted that negotiations were continuing between France and Iran over the repayment of the $670m. balance on the $1,000m. loaned by the Shah to France in 1978. It was also rumoured that France had agreed to supply arms to Iran in order to secure the hostages' release. France and Iran resumed diplomatic relations and exchanged ambassadors in June 1988.

In June 1987 Ayatollah Khomeini approved a proposal by Hashemi Rafsanjani, the Speaker of the Majlis, which was reluctantly supported by President Khamenei, to disband the IRP. In a letter to Khomeini, the two leaders said that, the institutions of the Islamic Republic having been established, contrary to the IRP's intended function, 'party polarization under the present conditions may provide an excuse for discord and factionalism'.

On 31 July 1987 attention was diverted from the Gulf by the deaths in riots in Mecca of 402 people, including 275 Iranian pilgrims (the majority of them women) engaged in the *Hajj* (pilgrimage) to the city's Muslim shrines. The Saudi authorities maintained that most of the victims had been trampled to death when some 150,000 Iranians (who, in contravention of Saudi laws governing the *Hajj*, had been demonstrating in support of Ayatollah Khomeini) went on the rampage, attacking Saudi security forces. The Iranians, on the other hand, alleged that the Saudi police had opened fire on the pilgrims, and accused Saudi Arabia and the USA of planning the incident. Mass demonstrations took place in Teheran on 1 August, and the Saudi and Kuwaiti embassies were ransacked by the mob. A 'day of hatred' was proclaimed by the Government on 2 August, and Hashemi Rafsanjani (the Speaker of the Majlis) promised vengeance. Iranian naval and military manoeuvres, dubbed 'Operation Martyrdom', began on 4 August, prefaced by a warning to foreign ships and planes to keep clear of Iranian territorial waters and airspace for the duration of the exercises, which lasted for four days.

In August 1987 Hojatoleslam Mehdi Hashemi, a close associate of Ayatollah Montazeri (Ayatollah Khomeini's designated successor), was tried by a specially-appointed Islamic court and convicted of murder, the kidnapping of a Syrian diplomat in Teheran, of forming a private army (with the aim of overthrowing the Government and installing a more rigorous Islamic regime), and of planning explosions in Mecca during the *Hajj*. It was Hashemi who, in an attempt to disrupt the planned sale of US arms to Iran, had revealed to a Lebanese magazine, *Ash-Shira'*, details of the secret visits of the then US National Security Adviser, Robert McFarlane, and Col Oliver North to Teheran in May 1986. Hashemi was executed on 28 September 1987.

In April 1988, following further Iranian attacks on Saudi and other neutral shipping in the Gulf, Saudi Arabia severed its diplomatic relations with Iran. Iran had been insisting on sending up to 150,000 pilgrims on the *Hajj* to the holy places in Saudi Arabia in 1988 (the same number as in 1987), despite the events of July 1987 and the subsequent deterioration in bilateral relations. A meeting of the Organizations of the Islamic Conference, in Amman, had agreed a formula for 1988, whereby each Muslim nation would be permitted to send 1,000 pilgrims per 1m. citizens, giving Iran a quota of 45,000. Finally, Iran decided that it would send no pilgrims on the *Hajj* at all.

THE UN FAILS TO ENFORCE RESOLUTION 598

Frustrated by Iran's temporizing over a definitive response to UN Security Council Resolution 598, on 29 August 1987 Iraq, contrary to advice from Western governments, resumed attacks on Iranian oil installations and industrial targets, and on tankers in the Gulf transporting Iranian oil. Iran had exploited the 45-day lull in Iraqi attacks by raising the level of oil production and exports. Resolution 598 made provision for unspecified sanctions in the event of the failure of either or both sides to comply with its terms for a cease-fire. However, the resumption of Iraqi attacks weakened the UN's position in its attempts to secure a cease-fire through diplomacy, and made it less likely that the USSR, if it would accept the principle at all, could be persuaded that the arms embargo proposed by the USA and the UK should apply only to Iran.

Iranian threats of reprisals against Saudi Arabia and Kuwait for their support of Iraq ceased to be purely rhetorical when Iran fired three *Silkworm* missiles into Kuwaiti territory at the beginning of September 1987 (and a further three before the end of the year). Kuwait expelled five Iranian diplomats on 5 September. The visit of the UN Secretary-General, Pérez de Cuéllar, to Iran and Iraq between 11 and 15 September, was preceded by an intensification of Iraqi attacks on Iranian economic targets. In Teheran Iranian leaders told Pérez de Cuéllar that they supported the provision in Resolution 598 for the setting up of an 'impartial body' to apportion responsibility for starting the war, but that Iraq's guilt in this matter had to be established before Iran would observe a cease-fire. For its part, Iraq was prepared to accept the ruling of a judicial body in determining responsibility for the war but stated that a formal cease-fire, according to the terms of Resolution 598, should precede the setting up of such a body.

Signs of an apparent willingness on Iran's part to modify its stand on Resolution 598 forestalled attempts by the USA, the UK and France to promote their proposal of an arms embargo against Iran, and also pre-empted the adoption of diplomatic or other sanctions by the Arab League, at its meeting in Tunis on 20 September 1987.

On 25 September 1987 Iran presented a plan to the UN Security Council, according to which it would observe a *de facto* cease-fire while a UN-appointed commission of enquiry determined which side was responsible for starting the war. An official cease-fire would take effect when the commission had identified the aggressor (by implication, Iraq). Iraq rejected these proposals as being a deviation from the terms of Resolution 598.

By mid-October 1987 the number of tankers being employed by Iran to shuttle oil from Kharg Island to Sirri and Larak Islands had declined to an estimated 20 vessels, owing to damage sustained during Iraq's intensified campaign of attacks in the Gulf. On 19 October four US naval vessels destroyed Iran's Rostam and Rakhsh oil platforms, about 100 km east of Qatar, which were, the USA alleged, being used to launch military operations against shipping.

The extraordinary session of the Arab League in Amman, Jordan, from 8 to 11 November 1987, produced a final communiqué which unanimously condemned Iran for prolonging the war with Iraq and for its occupation of Arab (i.e. Iraqi) territory, and urged Iran to implement Resolution 598 as it stood, without preconditions. Syria announced that it had succeeded in blocking an Iraqi proposal for Arab states to sever diplomatic relations with Iran, and that the good relations between Syria and Iran were unimpaired.

On 22 December 1987 the USSR itself proposed discussions within the Security Council to consider a mandatory ban on the sale of arms to Iran. According to the Soviet proposal, these talks would take place at the same time as discussions on the introduction of an international naval force in the Gulf, under the control of the UN, which would replace the various national forces patrolling the region. Although all the five permanent members of the Security Council subsequently agreed on the need for further measures to be taken to ensure the compliance of both combatants with Resolution 598, the USSR's insistence on the withdrawal of foreign navies and the deployment of a UN naval force in the Gulf as a complementary measure, and the USA's growing military involvement in the area during 1988 (see below), prevented the adoption of an arms embargo.

CEASE-FIRE AND NEGOTIATIONS: 1988–89

During the first half of 1988 Iran suffered a series of military set-backs in the war with Iraq, which offset the gains that it had made during the previous few years. Meanwhile, divisions within the Government over the conduct of the war became more apparent, as Ayatollah Khomeini grew more frail and the political struggle for the succession intensified. However, the world was taken by surprise in July 1988 when, after 12 months of prevarication, Iran agreed, unconditionally, to accept Resolution 598 in all its parts.

In January 1988 Ayatollah Khomeini had intervened in a debate over the role of the government in an Islamic Republic to reject a narrow interpretation of its competence by President Khamenei, who had said that the government operated 'within the limits of Islamic law and Islamic principles'.

Khomeini had replied that, on the contrary, the government was the primary instrument of Islamic rule and was competent to override certain aspects of Islam, even such practices as prayer (*salat*), fasting and the *Hajj* (three of the five 'pillars' of Islam), if it was in the interests of the state. In asserting the primacy of the government, Khomeini was believed to have strengthened the position of reformers, identified with Hashemi Rafsanjani, the Speaker of the Majlis, and Prime Minister Moussavi, who were attempting to enact legislation hitherto obstructed by the conservative clerics on the Council of Guardians.

The elections to the third Majlis in April and May 1988 provided a further boost for the reformers. The elections were the first not to be contested by the IRP, which had been dissolved in June 1987. Instead, all 1,600 candidates for the 270 seats in the Majlis were examined for eligibility by local committees and sought election as individuals. A record 16,988,799 people (68% of the electorate) voted in the first round of the elections on 8 April (when the majority of seats were contested), compared with 15.8m. in 1984 and 10.8m. in 1980. In June Hashemi Rafsanjani was re-elected as Speaker of the Majlis and Hossein Moussavi was overwhelmingly endorsed as Prime Minister. He presented a new Council of Ministers to the Majlis in July.

In January 1988 Iraq resumed the so-called 'tanker war'. During 1987, according to Lloyds of London, Iran and Iraq had damaged 178 vessels in the Gulf (34 in December alone), compared with 80 during 1986. Although the US Navy continued safely to escort reflagged Kuwaiti vessels, traffic not under its protection, including Kuwaiti shipping, remained a target for Iranian attack. (When a cease-fire was proclaimed in July, a total of 546 vessels had been attacked since 1981, when the 'tanker war' began in earnest.)

At the end of February 1988 Iraq resumed the so-called 'war of the cities' (which, apart from sporadic attacks, had not been pursued in earnest since early 1987), by bombing a petroleum refinery on the outskirts of Teheran. Iran retaliated by bombing a petrochemicals plant in Basra. This was the beginning of a series of reciprocal attacks on civil and economic targets in the two countries which lasted for several months.

During 1987/88, for the first time in six years, owing to poor mobilization, disorganization and a shortage of volunteers, Iran was unable to launch a major winter offensive and began to lose ground to Iraqi advances along the length of the war front. In mid-April 1988 Iraqi forces regained control of the Faw peninsula, where the Iranians, who had been unable to strike out to make further gains since capturing the area in 1986, had scaled down their presence. Iran accused Kuwait of allowing Iraqi forces to use Bubiyan Island during the offensive. In March the Mujahidin Iranian National Liberation Army (NLA), supported by Iraq, undertook a major offensive for the first time since its creation in 1987, attacking Iranian units in Iran's south-western province of Khuzestan. In May Iraq recaptured the Shalamcheh area, south-east of Basra, driving Iranian forces across the Shatt al-Arab into Iran.

Identifying military inefficiency as the principal cause of these reverses, Ayatollah Khomeini appointed Hashemi Rafsanjani as acting Commander-in-Chief of the Armed Forces on 2 June 1988 and gave him the task of unifying the command structure and improving co-ordination between the regular armed forces, the Revolutionary Guards Corps (*Pasdaran*) (with its own land, naval and air forces) and the Mobilization (*Basij*) Volunteers Corps. At the beginning of July Rafsanjani announced the creation of a general command headquarters to rationalize the disjointed military command structure, but a merger of the army and the Revolutionary Guards was ruled out.

The changes came too late to prevent further Iranian defeats. Having won back more territory from the Iranian army in the north of Iraq near Sulaimaniya, in mid-June 1988, at the end of the month Iraq recaptured Majnoun Island and the surrounding area (the site of one of the world's biggest oilfields) in the al-Hawizah marshes, on the southern front.

In the Gulf, fears of a serious military confrontation between Iran and the USA were realized on 18 April 1988, when the US navy destroyed two Iranian oil platforms (Sassan and

Nasr) in the southern Gulf, and six Iranian warships (a guided-missile boat, three speedboats and two frigates) were either sunk or badly damaged, in retaliation for damage allegedly inflicted on a US frigate by an Iranian mine on 14 April. On 3 July the USS *Vincennes*, the US navy's most sophisticated guided-missile destroyer, which had only recently been deployed in the Gulf to counter the threat to shipping of Iran's *Silkworm* missiles (which, the USA believed, were soon to become operational from a permanent site near the Strait of Hormuz), mistakenly shot down an Iran Air Airbus A300B over the Strait of Hormuz, having assumed it to be an attacking F-14 fighter-bomber. All 290 passengers and crew on board the scheduled flight to Dubai were killed.

Iranian forces were expelled from more Iraqi territory in Kurdistan during June and July 1988. Iraqi troops forced Iranian units back over the international border in the central sector of the war front, crossing into Iranian territory on 13 July for the first time since 1986, and capturing the Iranian border town of Dehloran. In mid-July the last pockets of Iranian occupation in southern Iraq were cleared by Iraqi troops. On 18 July Iran officially announced its unconditional acceptance of Resolution 598. The first clause of the resolution required the combatants to withdraw to international borders and to observe a cease-fire. Iraqi troops advanced further into Iran before retiring behind the border on 24 July. On the other hand, the NLA, over which Iraq claimed to have no control, launched a three-day offensive on 25 July, penetrating as far as 150 km into Iranian territory, before being forced to withdraw. Iraq professed to have no designs on Iranian territory, but was possibly using the NLA as a proxy to prevent the Iranian forces from regrouping during a cease-fire which might prove to be only temporary. The implementation of a cease-fire was delayed by Iran's refusal to accede to an Iraqi demand for direct peace talks, under UN auspices, to commence prior to a cessation of hostilities. Iran protested that Resolution 598 did not require this. However, Iraq withdrew its demand and a cease-fire finally came into force on 20 August, monitored by a specially-created UN observer force of 350 officers, the UN Iran-Iraq Military Observer Group (UNIIMOG).

Negotiations between Iran and Iraq for a comprehensive peace settlement began at foreign ministerial level in Geneva on 25 August 1988, under the aegis of the UN. One of the most contentious issues to be decided at these talks was the status of the Algiers Agreement of 1975 between Iran and Iraq, which Iran insisted should be the basis for negotiations, but which Iraq rejected. According to the terms of the Algiers Agreement, which defined the southern border between Iran and Iraq as running along the deepest channel of the Shatt al-Arab waterway (the Thalweg line), the two countries exercise joint sovereignty over the waterway. However, President Saddam Hussein of Iraq publicly tore up the agreement (to which he had been a signatory) immediately prior to the Iraqi invasion of Iran in 1980, demanding full Iraqi sovereignty over the waterway, which Iraq held under previous agreements in 1847, 1913 and 1937. The matter of determining responsibility for starting the war was another potential obstacle to the negotiation of a lasting peace. It was generally accepted that Iraq initiated the conflict by invading Iran on 22 September 1980. Iraq, however, maintained that the war began on 4 September with Iranian shelling of Iraqi border posts. Resolution 598 provides for the establishment of an impartial body to apportion responsibility for the war. Finally, Iraq rejected Iranian demands for the payment of reparations, for which Resolution 598 did not provide.

The peace negotiations soon became deadlocked in disputes concerning sovereignty over the Shatt al-Arab, and the right of navigation in the waterway and the Gulf, the exchange of prisoners of war, and the withdrawal of troops to within international borders. By August 1989 progress in the negotiations, at least as far as the border issue was concerned, had been insignificant, although some exchanges of prisoners of war had taken place. In November, in an attempt to unblock the negotiations, Iran proposed an immediate exchange of prisoners of war, accompanied by the withdrawal of troops to within international borders. By the end of the year, however, the cease-fire remained the only element of Resolution 598 to have been successfully implemented.

THE RUSHDIE AFFAIR

On 14 February 1989 Ayatollah Khomeini issued a religious edict, pronouncing a sentence of death on the British author Salman Rushdie and his publishers, and exhorting all Muslims to carry out the sentence. Khomeini's edict followed demonstrations in India and Pakistan in protest at the imminent publication in the USA of Rushdie's novel, *The Satanic Verses,* the content of which was considered to be blasphemous by some Muslims. (Rushdie, born a Muslim himself, was therefore guilty of apostasy, an offence punishable by death under Shari'a law.) The novel had first been published in the UK in September 1988. Khomeini's edict, which, despite an apology by Rushdie for any offence his novel had given to Muslims, was reiterated on 19 February, led to a sharp deterioration in relations between Iran and the UK and other Western countries. On 20 February Khomeini's sentence on Rushdie was condemned at a meeting of the Ministers of Foreign Affairs of the 12 EC member states. Senior-level diplomatic contacts between the member states and Iran were suspended, while the UK announced the withdrawal of its diplomatic representatives and personnel in Teheran. Iran, in turn, announced the withdrawal of all diplomatic representatives and staff in EC member countries on 21 February, and on 7 March severed diplomatic relations with the UK.

While the significance of the Rushdie affair was initially defined in terms of its effect on Iran's foreign relations, it soon became apparent that the issue was being used tactically by vying factions within the Iranian leadership. In a speech on 22 February 1989 Khomeini referred explicitly to a division in the Iranian leadership (between 'liberals' who sought Western participation in Iran's post-war reconstruction, and 'conservatives' who opposed Western involvement) in terms which implied that *The Satanic Verses* was the culmination of a Western conspiracy against Islam, and declared that he would never allow the 'liberal' faction within the leadership to prevail.

By late March 1989 it was clear that Khomeini's intervention had decisively strengthened the hand of the 'conservatives'. In early April the 'liberal' Ayatollah Montazeri, who had been elected as successor to Ayatollah Khomeini by the Council of Experts in 1985, resigned. It was reported that, in the absence of any individual with sufficient authority to assume the role, the Council of Experts had established a five-member leadership council to replace Montazeri as Khomeini's successor. On 24 April a 20-member council was appointed by Ayatollah Khomeini to draft amendments to the Iranian Constitution.

IRAN AFTER KHOMEINI

The death of Ayatollah Khomeini, long anticipated by manoeuvres within the Iranian leadership, occurred on 3 June 1989. In an emergency session on 4 June the Council of Experts elected President Khamenei to succeed Ayatollah Khomeini as Iran's spiritual leader, and on 5 June the Iranian Prime Minister, Hossein Moussavi, declared his support, and that of all government institutions, for Khamenei. On 8 June Hashemi Rafsanjani reiterated his intention to stand as a candidate at the forthcoming presidential election, and on 12 June he was re-elected for a further one-year term as Speaker of the Majlis.

Despite the apparent intensification in the struggle for power within the Iranian leadership in the months preceding Ayatollah Khomeini's death both 'conservatives' and 'liberals' gave their support to the candidacy of Hashemi Rafsanjani for the Presidency. The presidential election, held on 28 July, was contested by only Rafsanjani and Abbas Sheibani, a former minister who was widely regarded as a 'token' candidate. According to official figures, Rafsanjani received some 15.5m. (95.9%) of a total 16.2m. votes cast. Abbas Sheibani received 632,247 (3.9%) of the total votes cast. A total of 24m. people had been eligible to vote. At the same time, 95% of those who voted approved the 45 proposed amendments to the Constitution, the most important of which were the elevation of the President to the Government's Chief Executive and the abolition of the post of Prime Minister. Rafsanjani was sworn

in as President on 17 August. The new Council of Ministers was regarded as a balanced coalition of 'conservatives', 'liberals' and technocrats, and its endorsement by the Majlis was viewed as a mandate for Rafsanjani to conduct a more conciliatory foreign policy towards the West, in particular with regard to the Western hostages held captive by pro-Iranian Shi'ite groups in Lebanon; and to introduce reforms designed to stimulate economic reconstruction.

While the amendments to the Constitution increased the power of the Presidency, it was anticipated that Rafsanjani's leadership would be challenged by several factions, including Ahmad Khomeini, son of the late Ayatollah Khomeini, and by the Minister of the Interior, Ali Akbar Mohtashami, and the Minister of Intelligence, Muhammad Muhammadi Reyshahri, both of whom were known to be advocates of a doctrine of 'permanent revolution' and to approve of international terrorism to achieve this aim. Both Mohtashami and Reyshahri were excluded from the Council of Ministers that the Majlis endorsed in August 1989.

While Western support was regarded as vital to Iran's economic reconstruction by Rafsanjani and his supporters within the Iranian leadership, it was regarded as anathema by his opponents, who feared that it would lead to the erosion of Islamic values and the betrayal of the Revolution. Rafsanjani's fundamental problem on assuming the Presidency was to find a way of gaining Western support without alienating the 'conservative' faction within the leadership, which remained too powerful to be directly confronted. The urgency of the need for economic reform was demonstrated by increased incidents of popular protest against food shortages and high prices in early 1990. In May 1990 an 'open letter' was addressed to Rafsanjani by 90 prominent clerics, professionals and retired soldiers associated with the Liberation Movement of Iran, which was legal but did not enjoy official approval. The 'open letter' criticized government policies, complained of massive corruption and regretted Iran's international isolation. It led to widespread arrests, which appeared to indicate that Rafsanjani was unable to control his 'conservative' opponents. Divisions within ruling circles were exemplified by the dispute between Rafsanjani and his opponents over whether to accept Western aid following an earthquake in Gilan and Zanjan provinces in June 1990, in which more than 40,000 people died. After some initial hesitations, Western aid was accepted in what was regarded as an important victory for Rafsanjani.

FOREIGN RELATIONS

Although the death sentence on the British author Salman Rushdie remained in force, the tension created by its initial pronouncement in February 1989 lessened somewhat in the ensuing months. On 20 March EC Ministers of Foreign Affairs, meeting in Brussels, agreed that member states should be allowed to reinstall their ambassadors in Teheran. There was evidence, too, of an improvement in relations between Iran and the communist countries. In late June Rafsanjani visited the USSR, where he and the Soviet leader, Mikhail Gorbachev, signed a 'declaration on the principles of relations' between Iran and the USSR. These relations were strained in January 1990, however, when Iranian politicians voiced support for the Muslim Azerbaijani revolt against the Soviet central Government in the Nekhichevan enclave on the Iranian border.

In mid-July 1989 the USA unexpectedly offered to pay compensation directly to the families of the 290 passengers and crew of the Iran Air Airbus A300B mistakenly shot down by the USS *Vincennes* in July 1988. However, the Iranian Government insisted that the compensation should be distributed through its agencies, rather than privately, and took the dispute to the International Court of Justice (ICJ). The fragility of Iran's relations with the USA was underlined in early August when, in response to the abduction by Israeli forces of the Lebanese Shi'a Muslim leader, Sheikh Abdul Karim Obeid, a US hostage in Lebanon, Lt-Col William Higgins, was executed by his captors, who threatened the execution of more hostages if Sheikh Obeid was not released. While Iran denied any involvement in the killing of Lt-Col Higgins, it was widely suspected of complicity. Whatever its role, the USA immediately engaged in urgent negotiations with Iranian leaders in order to prevent further killings. In November 1989 the USA agreed to release US $567m. of the total of $810m. of Iranian assets that had been seized 10 years previously, at the time of the siege of the US Embassy in Teheran, in order to secure US bank claims on Iran. At the same time, while denying that the release of the assets was linked to the question of US hostages in Lebanon, the USA expressed the hope that Iran would use its influence with pro-Iranian groups in Lebanon to facilitate their release.

In April 1990, following the release of two US citizens who had been held hostage by pro-Iranian groups in Lebanon, the USA thanked both the Syrian and the Iranian Governments for the part that they had played in securing the hostages' release. In March 1990 a report in an Iranian newspaper had assured the USA that Iran would do what it could to secure the release of hostages, while elsewhere it had been reported that indirect contacts between the USA and Iran were taking place with regard to their release. Two Iranian diplomats were reported to be acting as liaison officers between Teheran and the pro-Iranian Hezbollah. In May 1990 the USA and Iran concluded a 'small claims agreement', whereby US claimants were to be repaid for losses that they had incurred during the Iranian Revolution in 1979; and in June 1990 Iran agreed to pay the US company Amoco $600m. in compensation for US oil operations which had been expropriated during the Revolution.

Relations between Iran and the United Kingdom fluctuated during the first half of 1990. In February the United Kingdom expelled nine Iranian diplomats for reasons of national security, and, as a retaliatory gesture, Iran closed the BBC office in Teheran. In the same month, however, President Rafsanjani described the *fatwa* that had been pronounced against Rushdie as an exclusively Islamic issue (implying that it ought not to interfere with the re-establishment of normal relations between Iran and the United Kingdom), while trade between the United Kingdom and Iran was reported to be increasing. In May 1990 it was reported that the United Kingdom was involved in indirect contacts with Iran concerning four UK nationals held hostage by pro-Iranian groups in Lebanon, and the United Kingdom announced that it was prepared to resume direct talks with the Iranian Government. In June, however, Ayatollah Khamenei declared that the *fatwa* could never be repealed.

Iran's position of strict neutrality during the Kuwait conflict (see below) brought rapid dividends. On 27 September 1990 Iran and the United Kingdom resumed diplomatic relations after, in an exchange of letters, Iran had assured the United Kingdom of its respect for international law and of its commitment to achieving the release of Western hostages held in Lebanon. The United Kingdom assured Iran of its respect for Islam and stated that it understood the offence which Salman Rushdie's novel, *The Satanic Verses*, had caused to Muslims. In October 1990 the EC revoked its ban on senior-level diplomatic contacts with Iran.

In May 1990 an Iranian delegation met EC officials in Dublin (Ireland). During the meeting Iran reiterated its pledge to work towards securing the release of Western hostages in Lebanon. A diplomatic initiative by the Irish Government was believed to have brought about the release, in August 1990, of an Irish citizen held hostage for four years by a pro-Iranian group in Lebanon. In July 1990, having boycotted the *Hajj* for the third successive year, Iran accused Saudi Arabia of being unfit to administer Islam's shrines, following an incident in which more than 1,400 pilgrims were trampled to death in a stampede in a tunnel near Mecca.

IRAQ CONCEDES IRAN'S PEACE TERMS

In early 1990 Iran and Iraq agreed to resume negotiations in the USSR, at the invitation of the Soviet Ministry of Foreign Affairs. In July the Iraqi and Iranian Ministers of Foreign Affairs conferred at the UN's European headquarters in Geneva. It was the first such direct meeting between them since the cease-fire in the war had taken effect. It had been facilitated by an exchange of letters between Presidents Saddam Hussain and Rafsanjani in May. This breakthrough in the peace process was quickly overtaken by the conse-

quences of Iraq's invasion and annexation of Kuwait in August 1990.

On 16 August 1990 Saddam Hussain abruptly sought an immediate, formal peace with Iran by accepting all the claims that Iran had pursued since the declaration of a cease-fire, including the reinstatement of the Algiers Agreement of 1975, dividing the Shatt al-Arab. While these concessions were transparently dictated by expediency (on 17 August Iraq began to redeploy in Kuwait troops hitherto positioned on its border with Iran) and thus left the conflicts underlying the Iran–Iraq War unresolved, they were welcomed by Iran, although it insisted that the issue of peace with Iraq was separate from that of Iraq's occupation of Kuwait. Exchanges of an estimated 80,000 prisoners of war commenced on 17 August, and on 18 August Iraq began to withdraw troops from the central border areas of Ilam, Meymak, Mehran and Naft Shahr. On 11 September Iran and Iraq re-established diplomatic relations.

The withdrawal of all armed forces to the internationally recognized boundaries was verified and confirmed as complete on 20 February 1991 by the UNIIMOG, whose mandate was terminated on 28 February 1991 by the UN Security Council. Iran and Iraq subsequently initiated a 'confidence-building' process of reducing the levels of troops and military equipment in the border areas. Exchanges of prisoners of war continued until 16 January 1991, when the multinational force commenced military operations to expel Iraqi armed forces from Kuwait. At this time Iran still held 30,000 Iraqi prisoners of war. Preliminary negotiations on the full implementation of Resolution 598 were also curtailed. Relations between Iran and Iraq again deteriorated after March 1991, when Iraqi Shi'ite Muslims participated in a rebellion against the Baath regime in the aftermath of Iraq's decisive military defeat by the multinational force.

The publication in August 1991 of the report of a UN delegation sent to Iran—in accordance with the terms of Resolution 598—to assess the level of human and material damage caused by the war with Iraq seemed to indicate that the UN was once again considering the need for a comprehensive peace settlement. The Iranian Government released its own assessment of the damage caused by the war with Iraq. It estimated that during the war Iran experienced direct damage amounting to 30,811,000m. Iranian rials; that 50 towns and 4,000 villages were destroyed or badly damaged; and that 14,000 civilians were killed and 1.25m. people displaced.

IRAN AND THE CONFLICT OVER KUWAIT

Iran condemned Iraq's invasion of Kuwait in August 1990 and offered to defend other Gulf states from Iraqi aggression, but it welcomed Iraq's offer of a formal settlement of the Iran–Iraq War on Iran's terms (see above). While Iran stated that it would observe the economic sanctions imposed on Iraq by the UN, Iraq was believed to have tried to persuade Iran to trade oil for food. However, the Iranian Government adhered to its pledge to implement economic sanctions for the duration of the conflict over Kuwait, sending only supplies of food and medicine to Iraq on a humanitarian basis.

As the deployment of a multinational force (assembled in accordance with Article 51 of the UN Charter) for the defence of Saudi Arabia gathered pace, Iran urged the simultaneous and unconditional withdrawal of Western—above all of US—armed forces from the Gulf region, and of Iraqi armed forces from Kuwait. In September 1990 Ayatollah Khamenei almost endorsed the demands of 'conservatives', such as Hojatoleslam Ali Akbar Mohtashemi, for Iran to ally itself with Iraq in a *jihad* against Western forces in the Gulf. President Rafsanjani's position was that the presence of these forces was tolerable on condition that they withdrew as soon as the conflict in Kuwait had been resolved.

Following the outbreak of military hostilities between Iraq and the multinational force in January 1991, Iran attempted, unsuccessfully, to intercede. After having consulted with Algeria, Yemen, France, the USSR and the Non-Aligned Movement (NAM), Iran urged an 'Islamic solution' to the conflict. On 4 February 1991 President Rafsanjani announced that the terms of an Iranian peace proposal had been conveyed to President Saddam Hussain of Iraq during the visit to Teheran, on 1–3 February, of Iraq's Deputy Prime Minister, Dr Sa'adoun Hammadi; and claimed that the terms of the proposal were consistent with resolutions adopted by the UN Security Council. An immediate cease-fire was to be followed by the simultaneous and complete withdrawal of Iraqi armed forces from Kuwait, and of all foreign forces from the Gulf region. In deference to Iraq's insistence on the 'linkage' of the conflict in Kuwait with other conflicts in the Middle East (in particular the continuing Israeli occupation of the West Bank and the Gaza Strip), Iran also urged the immediate cessation of new Israeli settlements in the Occupied Territories.

While the Iranian peace proposal was welcomed by the USSR, it was rejected by the USA, and on 8 February 1991, in a letter to President Rafsanjani, Saddam Hussain dismissed it, stating that Iraq had no intention of withdrawing from Kuwait, and accusing the USA of seeking to dominate the Middle East by destroying Iraq. There was no clear expression of support for the Iranian peace proposal at a closed session of the NAM, held in Belgrade, Yugoslavia, on 11–12 February, and thereafter Soviet diplomacy came to the fore in attempting to find peace terms which might avert a ground war. Iran claimed some of the credit for the concessions offered in an Iraqi peace proposal on 15 February, and urged the multinational force not to initiate hostilities on the ground until the limits of Iraq's flexibility had been determined. However, the countries contributing to the multinational force were unwilling, by this stage, to allow Iraq the opportunity to procrastinate.

As the air bombardment of Iraq and occupied Kuwait continued, Iran accused the multinational force of exceeding the terms of resolutions adopted by the UN Security Council by seeking to destroy Iraq's military and industrial facilities. However, when, in late January 1991, more than 100 Iraqi fighter aircraft landed in Iran without having sought permission to do so, Iran lodged a protest with Iraq and impounded both the aircraft and their pilots for the duration of the conflict.

Relations between Iran and Iraq deteriorated after the conclusion of hostilities between Iraq and the multinational force on 28 February 1991. In response to the suppression, by Iraqi armed forces loyal to President Saddam Hussain, of a Shi'a-led rebellion against the Baath regime in southern and central Iraq, Iran declared its commitment to the territorial integrity of Iraq, but demanded the resignation of Saddam Hussain and protested at the damage inflicted by Iraqi armed forces on Shi'a shrines at Najaf, Karbala and Samarra. Iraq accused Iran of providing material and human support for the southern and central rebellions, citing the involvement of the Teheran-based Supreme Council of the Islamic Revolution in Iraq. In a clear indication of deteriorating relations, Iraq later resumed support for the military activities of the largest Iranian dissident groups, the Mujahidin-e-Khalq and the Kurdish Democratic Party (KDP). Iraq's suppression of the internal rebellions led to a mass flight of Iraqi Kurds and Shi'a Muslims across the Iranian border. By May 1991 more than 1m. Iraqi Kurds had fled to Iran, while the number of Shi'a refugees in Iran was estimated at 65,000.

Iran supported the Western initiative to establish 'safe havens' for Iraqi Kurds in northern Iraq, and urged, unsuccessfully, similar support for Iraqi refugees in Iran. Throughout June and July 1991 Iran accused the Iraqi armed forces of harassing Iraqi Shi'a Muslims who had fled into the marshes of southern Iraq after the defeat of the southern rebellion in March. There were conflicting reports regarding the accuracy of these allegations and of the number—estimated by Iran at 600,000—of Shi'a Muslims who had sought refuge in the marshes.

REFORM UNDER RAFSANJANI

While the onset of the crisis in the Gulf in August 1990 led to further friction between the rival factions in the Iranian leadership, President Rafsanjani gradually asserted his authority and began the difficult process of marginalizing the power-bases of the 'conservatives'. At times his relationship with Ayatollah Khamenei became tense, especially with regard to foreign policy issues. However, in October 1990 they formed an alliance to prevent the election of many powerful 'conserva-

tives' to the 83-seat Council of Experts, which chooses Iran's supreme leader and interprets the Constitution. Hojatoleslam Ali Akbar Mohtashemi and Ayatollah Khalkhali were amongst those rejected as candidates by Khamenei, on the grounds that their expertise in the Koran was inadequate. In December 1990 the Majlis enacted legislation which allowed defendants legal representation. The new legislation was thought to signal a move towards the less rigorous application of Islamic law.

In April 1991 it was announced that Iran's internal security services—the police, the gendarmerie and the Islamic *Komitehs*—were to be merged. The *Komitehs* had hitherto acted as the chief enforcers of 'Islamic behaviour' within post-revolutionary Iranian society. In the same month the release of a British businessman, Roger Cooper, who had been imprisoned without trial since 1985 for alleged espionage, was regarded as a further sign of Rafsanjani's ascendancy. In May 1991 the human rights organization, Amnesty International, was allowed access to Iran for the first time since the Revolution, despite having published, in December 1990, a report which condemned the thousands of executions (many of which, it alleged, had, in fact, been executions of political dissidents) for drug-related offences which had been carried out in Iran.

However, the assassination in Paris in August 1991 of Dr Shapour Bakhtiar, Iran's last pre-revolutionary Prime Minister who had been living in exile since 1980, indicated that the Islamic regime had far from entirely abandoned the persecution of its opponents.

Disturbances and demonstrations in Teheran and other parts of the country in the same month indicated significant levels of popular discontent. In April and May 1992 further demonstrations occured, most notably in Teheran and Mashad. Eight protestors were executed by the authorities. An important factor in the unrest was municipal action in many cities against squatter settlements.

Elections to the fourth Majlis in April and May 1992 seemed to provide Rafsanjani with the opportunity finally to shift the balance of power decisively against the 'conservatives'. Prior to the elections, in January 1992, a budget was announced which doubled food subsidies for the poor. Of those who applied to contest the forthcoming elections, about one-third were disqualified by the Council of Guardians. Most of those disqualified were considered to be opponents of Rafsanjani.

In the first round of voting in the elections, in which 65% of the electorate participated, it was reported that 136 candidates were elected to the Majlis, having gained at least 30% of the total vote in their respective constituencies. Of the newly-elected deputies, some 55 were regarded as supporters of Rafsanjani, while the remainder were independents who, it was thought, would align themselves with the President. Most of the remaining seats were allocated in a second round of voting in May. It was estimated that about 70% of the deputies in the new Majlis were supporters of Rafsanjani. The new deputies appeared to be more highly educated, younger and more technocratic in orientation than their predecessors and had received a theological education. Rafsanjani installed a new, sympathetic Speaker of the Majlis, Ali Akbar Nateq Nouri, who replaced the 'conservative', Mahdi Karrubi.

The new Government indicated that it wished to push ahead rapidly with measures to end all subsidies and the system of multiple foreign exchange rates; and to allow full foreign ownership of companies. In fact, the pace of economic reform in the months following the election to the fourth Majlis remained cautious. Rafsanjani remained constrained by tensions within his own policies, not least by the fact that economic reform was lowering the standard of living of the traditional constituency of the Islamic regime, the urban lower classes. The middle classes, supposedly one of the engines of reform, remained deeply distrustful of the regime. Rafsanjani quickly discovered, too, that the deputies in the new Majlis who were in favour of reform were far from uncritical in their support for his policies.

The extent to which Rafsanjani had lost popular support became clear when he stood for re-election to the presidency on 11 June 1993. Competing against three ostensibly 'token' candidates, Rafsanjani received 63.2% of the vote in a low electoral turn-out of 56%. His nearest rival, former Minister of Labour, Ahmed Tavakkoli, received 24% of the vote, a performance widely attributed to his stringent criticisms of state corruption, social injustice and economic mismanagement. Rafsanjani's re-election was regarded as a popular comment on there being no realistic alternative rather than as a positive endorsement of his record in office. There was further evidence of possible opposition to Rafsanjani's policies from within the Majlis when the assembly refused, in August, to endorse his nomination of Mohsen Nourbakhch as Minister of Economy and Finance in a reshuffled Council of Ministers. Rafsanjani and the Majlis ultimately agreed upon the appointment of Morteza Muhammadkhan.

During 1994 there were numerous signals that the problems encountered by Rafsanjani in carrying through his reform programme were emboldening 'conservative' forces, encouraged by Ayatollah Khamenei, to challenge the President more directly. In February 1994 there was an attempt on his life during a speech he made at Khomeini's tomb. In the same month Rafsanjani's brother, Muhammad Mashemi, was dismissed by Ayatollah Khamenei as head of state radio and television after 13 years in the post. In March 1994, perhaps reading the political runes, Rafsanjani announced that he would not seek a constitutional amendment to allow him to stand for a third term of office. In June 1994 the Government agreed to reduce economic subsidies at a slower rate in order to appease a Majlis in which demands had been raised for powers over prices to be wrested from the Government.

The atmosphere of political malaise was further deepened in June 1994 by the bombing of the Imam Reza shrine in Mashad which left at least 24 dead. The Government blamed the Mujahidin-e-Khalq; others speculated that it might be the work of militant members of the Sunni minority in Iran, angered by the destruction of a Sunni mosque earlier in the year. The atmosphere of malaise turned to one of near crisis in the following month when, in the space of a few days, two Iranian Christian leaders were assassinated in Teheran and bombs wrought havoc against Jewish targets in London, United Kingdom, and Buenos Aires, Argentina. Rafsanjani's political authority and his reform agenda both appeared in serious jeopardy.

FOREIGN POLICY SINCE 1991

Domestic reforms have been accompanied by diplomatic initiatives by Iran, aimed at securing its reintegration into the international community. Despite further acts to improve relations with Western countries, such as the release of the British businessman, Roger Cooper, and the freeing of hostages in Lebanon (see below), the religious edict against Rushdie remains unrevoked and Iran remains a sponsor of international terrorism in Western eyes. A round of retaliatory diplomatic expulsions between the United Kingdom and Iran in July 1992 showed how far from full normalization relations between the two countries remained.

The greatest single obstacle to improved relations with Western countries was Iran's perceived continued complicity in the holding of Western hostages in Lebanon by groups linked to the pro-Iranian Hezbollah. Between August and December 1991, with Iran, Syria, Israel and the UN diplomatically active, all remaining UK and US hostages were released. While the aim of the captors was to trade the release of the UK and US hostages for the release of Shi'a hostages held by Israel, it was decided ultimately to release the UK and US hostages unconditionally. The last remaining Western hostages were released in June 1992.

There has been no formal *rapprochement* between the USA and Iran, but the release of US hostages and some progress at the US-Iran Claims Tribunal in the Hague, Netherlands, temporarily removed some of the tension between the two countries. In September 1990 the USA paid Iran $200m. for armaments not delivered after the Revolution of 1979. In December 1991 a further $278m. was paid by the USA. In March 1992 the USA was ordered to compensate Iran for property frozen in the USA after 1979. The total value of Iran's claims against the USA amounts to $12,000m., a figure which the USA claims to be grossly inflated. Iran is still pursuing efforts through the ICJ to compel the USA to pay the compensation it has offered for the shooting down of the Iran Air flight by the USS *Vincennes* in 1988 to the Government rather than directly to the victims. It has also consistently opposed the US-sponsored Middle East peace process that began in October 1991. Relations between the USA and Iran again deteriorated after President Clinton took office in January 1993. The USA has expressed anxiety over Iran's nuclear ambitions and has alleged that the country is engaged in a rapid conventional military build-up which has included the purchase of submarines from Russia. The International Atomic Energy Agency has repeatedly stated, however, that it has no evidence of an Iranian nuclear weapons programme.

Throughout 1993 the USA pressed initially reluctant Western allies to reduce levels of economic assistance to Iran. The USA sought to block Iranian efforts to reschedule its international debts. In May 1994 American pressure was evident when it emerged that no new loans would be made to Iran by the World Bank in the forseeable future. In the same month relations between Iran and the United Kingdom again deteriorated. There was a further round of diplomatic expulsions as Iran accused the United Kingdom of having links with the Mujahidin-e-Khalq and of bugging its embassy in London. In turn, the United Kingdom claimed that Iran was supporting the Irish Republican Army (IRA). In July 1994 bomb attacks—widely believed to be Iranian-inspired—in London and Buenos Aires, Argentina, reinforced Iran's pariah status. Iran had condemned the US-brokered peace agreement between the PLO and Israel in September 1993. Ninety-six people died in the bomb attack in Buenos Aires and in August 1994 arrest warrants were issued in Argentina for four Iranian diplomats.

During the conflict over Kuwait in 1990/91 Iran normalized its relations with Egypt, Tunisia, Jordan and the Gulf states. In March 1991 it re-established diplomatic relations with Saudi Arabia, and about 115,000 Iranian pilgrims were subsequently able to participate in the 1991 *Hajj*. In August 1991 Iran and Iraq met directly for talks on a comprehensive settlement to the 1980–88 war. The repatriation of prisoners of war has not yet been completed. The International Committee of the Red Cross claims that virtually all Iranian prisoners have been returned by Iraq. Iran asserts that Iraq continues to hold 5,000. Iran still holds at least 20,000 prisoners. A UN Commission has formally blamed Iraq for starting the Iran–Iraq War; Iran now expects a proposed UN conference to award US $100,000m. in reparations. In April 1992 Iran launched airstrikes against Mujahidin-e-Khalq camps in Iraq. Iraq protested to the UN Security Council. The treatment by the Iraqi government of its southern Shi'a population has continued to obstruct relations between Iran and Iraq.

In the aftermath of the Kuwait conflict, Iran sought to assert itself as a regional power. It reacted negatively to efforts based on the Damascus Declaration of March 1991 to create a regional security structure in the Gulf from which it was itself excluded. Its disapproval played an important part in ensuring that the Declaration remained a 'dead letter'. While opposing the defence agreements which the Gulf states subsequently negotiated with the USA, Iran focused its diplomatic efforts on improving its relations with them. Significant progress in that sphere was thwarted by a dispute between Iran and the United Arab Emirates (UAE) over the island of Abu Musa after August 1992. Since 1971 the status of Abu Musa had been governed by an agreement giving the two countries joint sovereignty. In August 1992 the Iranian authorities on the island restricted the movement of third country nationals and expelled some residents on security grounds, prompting the UAE to accuse Iran of annexing Abu Musa. By April 1993, after Syrian mediation and several rounds of talks, the *status quo ante* had been restored. However, although the dispute awaits a formal settlement. Iran has stated that it is willing to engage in talks without preconditions about Abu Musa with the UAE, but insists on acceptance of Iranian sovereignty over the island.

The dramatic developments in the USSR after August 1991 opened up a new arena for Iranian diplomacy in Central Asia. Iran, Saudi Arabia and Turkey are vying for influence in the newly-independent states of Central Asia. While well-placed geopolitically, Iran lacks the money to pursue its ambitions and is further disadvantaged by the fact that Central Asia is Sunni Muslim, with the exception of Azerbaijan, and speaks languages belonging to the Turkic family, with the exception of Tajikistan. Iran is seeking to strengthen its position in Central Asia through bilateral agreements and institutions such as the revived Economic Co-operation Organisation (ECO), comprising the states of Central Asia, Iran, Turkey and Pakistan. Iran has called the ECO the basis for a future 'Islamic Common Market'. In early 1992 Iran announced the formation of the Caspian Sea Zone, which includes Russia, Azerbaijan, Turkmenistan and Kazakhstan. A source of anxiety for Iran may be the encouragement which indepen-

dence for the former Soviet republic of Azerbaijan may give to those who advocate the secession of Iranian Azerbaijan. Iran attempted, with little success, to mediate between Azerbaijan and Armenia in the armed conflict over the future of the enclave of Nagorny Karabakh. Iran is viewed as a close ally of Azerbaijan by Armenia, which looks to Russia for support. Iran has enjoyed more success in its mediation efforts in the civil war which erupted in Tajikistan in 1994, hosting peace talks in Teheran in June.

Economy

Updated for this edition by RICHARD I. LAWLESS

At the census of November 1966 the population of Iran was recorded as 25,788,722. Of this total, about 9.8m. were urban residents. The November 1976 census enumerated a total population of 33,708,744, and the October 1986 census recorded 49,445,010 inhabitants (including 2.6m. refugees), of whom 26,844,561 resided in urban areas, an increase of 70% since 1976. In early 1992 the Statistical Centre of Iran reported that the population had increased by almost 40% since 1979, to more than 58m. The rate of growth in urban areas was twice that recorded in rural areas. The population of Teheran was reported to have more than doubled since the late 1970s, exceeding 10m. Much of the Iranian population is concentrated in the fertile northern areas of the country, while the central desert lands are sparsely populated. In mid-1992 the Statistical Centre of Iran reported that the annual rate of population growth over the previous five years was 3.28%, lower than the record level of 3.9% estimated for the first-half of the 1980s. It was forecast by some official sources that the annual rate of population growth would have fallen to 2.5% by the end of 1992, the lowest rate recorded in more than a decade. However, other sources have suggested that the Iranian population could reach 140m. by the year 2020. In September 1993 the Minister of Health, addressing a conference on family planning, stated that the annual rate of population growth had fallen from 3.2% in 1992 to 2.3% in 1993. In March 1994 the head of the Civil Status Registration Organization announced that Iran's total population grew by 1.5m in 1993 compared with 1.7m. in 1991. In 1989 the Government introduced a campaign of birth control, intended to reduce population growth, designating the Iranian year beginning 21 March 1989 'Birth Control Year'. In October 1990 the Ministry of Health announced that free birth control facilities would be made available to all women. The Government has continued to encourage family planning and in addition to free contraceptives the Ministry of Health announced in July 1991 that new measures to take effect in July 1992, would prevent families with more than three children from receiving ration coupons. Local production of contraceptives is to be increased and village family planning units are to be expanded. In July 1992 the Minister of Health reported that the country's family planning programme involved 15,500 rural and urban health centres. Officials have warned that the high rate of population growth and extensive migration from rural to urban areas are straining public utilities in the cities. In September 1988 the Minister of Planning and Budget recommended government controls on the movement of rural residents. In June 1989 the Minister of Housing and Urban Development announced plans to construct 12 new towns, over the next five years, for 300,000–500,000 people. The reconstruction of the towns of Abadan and Khorramshahr, which were destroyed during the war with Iraq, was also to be accelerated. Confrontations between municipal officials and people occupying land or building houses illegally have become widespread. Municipal officials have tried either to remove the squatters or to force them to pay for construction permits. Action by municipal authorities against the large number of squatters who have built houses illegally on the fringes of Iran's major cities

provoked widespread rioting in mid-1992 in Arak, Shiraz, Khorramabad and Mashad. It is estimated that half of present-day Teheran has been built on land occupied illegally since 1979. Government officials have cited Iran's expanding population as a major constraint on economic development. In July 1992 the head of the Population and Family Planning Department of the Ministry of Health stated that if the population continued to grow at a rapid rate, 600,000 new jobs would have to be created each year, and 40,000 classroooms and 500,000 houses constructed. The country's farmers would not be able to meet the demand for food and half the population would face starvation. Unemployment in 1990 was officially estimated to affect 14.2% of the labour force. However, the Plan and Budget Organization indicated that a further 3.5m. people were engaged only in temporary work or were underemployed. Indeed, other sources suggest that the rate of unemployment may be as high as 20%. Only 2.2m. new jobs were created between 1980 and 1990: an inadequate total, in view of the rising demand for employment. Following the 1991 population census the Plan and Budget Organization estimated the economically active population at 25.2% of the total and unemployment at less than 10%. The size of the nomadic population, estimated at 248,463 in October 1986, has declined dramatically since the 1940s (it was estimated to be 641,937 at the 1966 census), as a result of government attempts to settle the nomads in villages. These tribes are, in fact, semi-nomadic, moving between traditional winter quarters in the plains and summer pastures in the mountains.

Iran has received a large number of refugees in recent years. After the Soviet intervention in Afghanistan in 1979 possibly as many as 3m. Afghans sought refuge in Iran. Some 1m.–2m. Iranians became refugees during the Iran-Iraq War, and large numbers of Iraqi refugees, mainly Kurds, fled to Iran. Iran's refugee programme has cost between $50m. and $100m. annually. In November 1991 the Ministry of the Interior announced that the number of refugees in the country was falling. More than 1m. refugees had returned to Iraq, leaving only 150,000 Iraqi Kurds in Iran. In December 1992 it was announced that thousands of Afghan refugees had recently been sent home under repatriation schemes. In October an agreement for a UN co-ordinated repatriation programme had been signed with the UN High Commissioner for Refugees and the Government of Afghanistan. The UN World Food Programme also allocated $23.7m.-worth of food aid to support 260,000 refugees living in border provinces and to help repatriate 1m. people during 1993. Between 600,000 and 750,000 Afghan refugees are believed to have returned to Afghanistan during 1993. In January 1994 the Minister of the Interior stated that some 750,000 Afghan refugees and 50,000 Iraqi refugees were expected to return home during the Iranian year beginning in March 1994 with the help of the UN High Commissioner for Refugees. In August 1993 the Ministry of the Interior reported that 4,500 Iraqis had fled to Iran as a result of the Iraqi Government's policy of draining the country's southern marshes, and that a further 15,000 Iraqis might seek refuge in Iran. In October 1993 President Rafsanjani visited Baku in Azerbaijan for urgent discussions about the return and resettlement of some 20,000 Azeris reported to have taken refuge in Iran as a result of fighting between Azeri and Armenian forces. The previous month, Iran is reported to have signed an agreement with Azerbaijan to assist in setting up camps in Azerbaijan itself for an estimated 100,000 Azeri refugees displaced by the fighting and living close to the Iranian border. Iran was believed to be anxious to prevent large numbers of Azeri refugees from crossing its borders because of the implications for its own Azeri population.

In 1978, the last year of the Shah's reign, per caput income was calculated at about US $2,500, up from about $200 in 1963. During the period of the Fourth Development Plan (1968–73), Iran's gross national product (GNP) rose at an annual average of 11.2% in real terms. Over the period of the 1973–78 Plan, GNP rose in real terms from $17,000m. to $55,300m. The growth rate of GNP, which was as much as 41% in 1974/75, slowed to about 17% in the following year, owing to declining revenues from petroleum (which provided about 40% of the total GNP). In real terms, the gross domestic product (GDP) was estimated to have grown by as little as 2.6% in 1975/76 (the Iranian year runs from 21 March–20 March). In 1976/77 GDP grew at over 14% in real terms, but during 1977 the economy showed signs of further deceleration. Total GDP for 1977/78 was estimated at $56,500m., representing growth in real terms of about 10% over the previous year.

The revolutionary Government that followed the Shah's downfall reassessed nearly all Iran's economic and social strategies. The new leaders announced that priority would be given to low growth rates, a concentration on small-scale projects in industry, emphasis on traditional agriculture and stringent control of petroleum exports. Three years after the Revolution, however, Iran's economy was in deep crisis. The war with Iraq, loss of forecast petroleum revenues in mid-1980 as the world went into economic recession, and failure of public utilities (mainly electricity) were among the problems advanced to account for a deteriorating economic situation. The war had taken its toll of physical damage in the south, with major settlements reduced to rubble and the destruction of oil installations and factories. However, political conflicts and confusion over the management of the economy aggravated these problems and resulted in contradictions in policy and economic mismanagement.

In early 1981 the then President, Bani-Sadr, reported that agricultural output remained static, industrial production had declined dramatically and even the minimum petroleum output that Iran required for national survival was not being attained. The disappointing performance of the major economic sectors had resulted in declines in real GDP of 13% in 1979/80 and 10% in 1980/81, and in a further fall in 1981/82. At the same time, Ayatollah Khomeini warned Iranians that there would be 10 years of austerity ahead before the country became productive enough to fulfil its needs from domestic sources.

Some real growth in the economy did take place as a result of developments in the construction sector and some expansion in industrial output. However, as both were at low base levels, real gains were small. In reality it was the petroleum sector which was responsible for the improvement in the country's economic prospects in 1982 and 1983. An increase in sales of crude petroleum during 1982, by means of discounts and special incentives to purchasers, resulted in rising revenues, which, in turn, stimulated economic activity. The Iranian economy remained petroleum-based, and the pattern of growth reflected the performance of that sector. The oil sector fared badly in 1984, with production down by 13% in a deteriorating market oversupplied with oil and subject to falling world prices. Production costs have always been higher for Iran than for its regional competitors, and the situation was aggravated by the escalation of the conflict with Iraq, with the consequent rise in the costs of insurance, storage and transport. As a result of the continuing decline in international prices for crude petroleum, government income was seriously reduced during 1986, and income from oil exports totalled $6,600m. in 1986/87, according to OPEC. This downward trend was halted in early 1987, when the volume of exports of oil increased and prices rose. In 1987/88 oil exports were

estimated at $8,000m.–$9,000m., with a further $1,100m. in earnings from rising non-oil exports.

From September 1980 until the August 1988 cease-fire, the war with Iraq dominated all economic and political life in Iran. War needs dictated planning priorities, distorting the economy and forcing long-term objectives to be sacrificed to expediency. It has been estimated that annual expenditure of foreign exchange on the war was $5,000m.–$9,000m. After the announcement of the cease-fire, attempts were made to assess the extent of the damage inflicted on the Iranian economy during the war and widely diverging figures were quoted for the cost of reconstruction. The cost of repairing industrial plant alone was estimated at $40,000m. Positive leadership often appeared to be lacking, resulting in the inability or unwillingness to resolve fundamental issues of principle. One crucial issue affecting the economy after the Revolution was disagreement over the degree of government involvement in business. After 1981 the Government appeared to favour an increase in state control, particularly the nationalization of foreign trade. However, conservative religious leaders, businessmen, the Council of Guardians (which ensures that legislation conforms with Islamic precepts) and many members of the Majlis maintained that the Government should play a minimal role. Although new appointments to the Council of Ministers and the changing character of the Majlis strengthened those elements in government favouring more control of the economy by the state (in particular more land reform, nationalization of trade and the spread of collective organization among the industrial work-force), the conservative elements in government (in particular, the Council of Guardians) succeeded in delaying radical reform. In a vigorous press campaign at the end of 1985 the radicals alleged that the courts were overturning revolutionary measures and allowing expropriated industries to be returned to their former owners. In January 1988 Ayatollah Khomeini decreed that government policies could overrule Islamic law where this was in the interest of the state. In the following month a 13-member assembly was appointed to settle disputes by majority vote whenever the Majlis and the Council of Guardians could not agree on the direction of policy. However, despite the strength of the radicals in the third Majlis, the assembly proceeded cautiously, seeking to maintain a consensus between conservatives and radicals.

In the agricultural sector, the problem of rights of ownership has affected about 1.2m. ha, or one-quarter of Iran's prime cultivable land, since the Revolution, and government plans for land reform have been consistently obstructed by the Council of Guardians, making long-term planning difficult. As a result, the technocrats in government have concentrated on industry and other areas of the economy where quick results are easier to obtain. In February 1989 the Minister of Oil, Gholamreza Aqazadeh, announced the end of a six-month debate concerning the future structure of the Iranian economy. The Council of Ministers had decided, he reported, to approve a limited number of foreign loans for infrastructural schemes, and to encourage private enterprise. In May 1989 the then Minister of Planning and Budget, Massoud Roghani Zanjani, outlined the Government's plans for development and economic trends over the next five years. He confirmed that the plans included 'privatization' of non-strategic state-owned industries. It was also revealed that Imam Khomeini had approved foreign borrowing to finance major projects if it did not result in political dependence. Foreign-financed projects should lead to savings in convertible currency or generate new revenue in convertible currency.

On his election to the Presidency on 28 July 1989, Hashemi Rafsanjani announced that his immediate economic aims would be to combat inflation and unemployment by increasing industrial output. Existing factories would receive more foreign exchange to raise production, which was running at only 40% of capacity; and, in an attempt to generate more productive investment, the private sector was to be given a bigger role in the economy. In the long term, Rafsanjani indicated, his Government would concentrate on developing energy, transport and basic industrial and educational resources. Some experts have suggested that, in order to achieve a rapid economic recovery, Rafsanjani would have to resort to large-scale foreign financing. However, this would expose the President to accusations of compromising Iran's revolutionary ideology and independence. In August 1989 it was announced that the Government had allocated $4,800m. for imports of food and consumer goods during the following year, to improve standards in the short term. Short-term measures to revive the economy included the privatization of state enterprises, the reopening of the Teheran stock exchange and the liberalization of regulations controlling the availability of foreign exchange. The introduction of a new Five-Year Development Plan, in January 1990, was expected to help to revive the economy. The new plan, together with the announcement of the annual budget in March 1990, strengthened economic activity, resulting in increased imports of raw materials, equipment and spares. In May 1990 the IMF agreed to extend technical assistance to Iran.

An IMF report on Iran, compiled in 1990, was favourable; it estimated an increase in real GDP of 2% in 1989 and 4% in 1990; economic growth of more than 4% was forecast for 1991.

As a consequence of Iraq's invasion of Kuwait in August 1990, Iran's economic prospects improved momentarily. According to official sources, earnings from exports of petroleum rose to $18,400m. in 1990–91 as a result of an increase in volume and price triggered by the conflict over Kuwait. With his leadership strengthened, President Rafsanjani took advantage of extra oil revenues to accelerate the implementation of economic reforms which have resulted in the rapid dismantlement of the state-controlled economy created during the years of war with Iraq. The private sector expanded and came to play a significant role in trade and investment. Imports by the private sector rose, non-petroleum exports doubled and considerable investment occurred in housing construction and industry after the deregulation of price and trade controls. However, his reforms to revive the economy caused widespread hardship and contributed to the riots and urban unrest in mid-1992. Moreover, the economy remains excessively dependent on oil, while bureaucratic inefficiency and a serious shortage of skilled workers and managers continues to obstruct the realization of optimistic plans.

At the start of his second term of office in August 1993, President Rafsanjani vowed to press on with economic reforms so that Iran would no longer be dependent on other countries for their markets and products. He stated that during his first term of office the old state economy had been transformed, production had increased and unemployment had fallen from 16% to 10%–11%. Outlining his policies for the next four years to the Majlis on 4 August, Rafsanjani declared that his Government would not embark on adventures abroad but would concentrate on reforming and rebuilding the economy. He stressed that costly state subsidies had to be reduced but promised that this would be done gradually so as not to disrupt peoples' lives. In the Majlis and the press, however, there was strong criticism of the Government for mishandling the economy and allowing the country to accumulate some $20,000m. in external debts. On 16 August the Majlis refused to approve the reappointment of Mohsen Nourbakhsh as Minister of the Economy. *Jomhuri Eslami,* the Persian language daily, accused the Government's economic team of being 'deceived by liberal Western economic theories', argued that the reforms had been introduced too rapidly and urged the reintroduction of some state controls. Since mid-1992 Iran had faced problems in paying its external debts as low oil prices resulted in falling oil revenues. Much of the short-term debt resulted from high levels of imports in the early 1990s. Oil revenues for 1993–94 were projected at around $18,000m., but in August 1993 the Minister of Oil, Aqazadeh, told the Majlis that they would probably reach only $16,500m. By January 1994 officals estimated that revenues would not exceed $12,000m. Oil revenues were projected at only $10,150m. for 1994–95. By the end of 1993 at least $7,000m. of debt payments were in arrears. Acute shortages of some essential imports occurred as foreign companies held back deliveries when Iranian banks fell behind with their payments. There were reports that some factories had been forced to shut down and others to cut production and lay off workers. Prices and unemployment rose rapidly. During the last quarter of 1993 the rial's free market value fell by about one-third

due to reduced supplies of foreign exchange to importers. Growth in GDP, which had been projected at 6%–7% in 1993–94, was estimated to have slowed to 4%–5%.

In response to these criticisms, in August the Bank Markazi relaxed some import restrictions to ease pressures on industry and consumers. However, Rafsanjani rejected calls in the Majlis to postpone the second Five-Year Plan until 1996 because of the economic crisis. The President presented the plan document to the Majlis on 21 December and asked approval for higher spending based on increased domestic revenues. The day before, Ayatollah Khamenei had announced new guidelines for economic and social planning, urging a reduction in the country's dependence on foreign finance and special efforts to settle outstanding obligations. He also urged caution in privatizing state enterprises and emphasized that privatization should promote the aims of the development plan and of the constitution of the Islamic Republic. He stressed that social equity should be central to the Government's development policy. Deprived regions should receive more attention and development policies should benefit those who had worked hard for the revolution. Priority should be given to promoting domestic production, particularly agriculture, in order to satisfy the basic needs of the people. Imports of consumer goods should be reduced and non-oil exports increased. Corruption should be eliminated and waste and extravagance discouraged. At the same time Khamenei gave his support to the president and attempted to underplay the scale of the country's economic problems.

In early January 1994 Rafsanjani declared that the Iranian economy was no longer totally dependent on oil revenues and could survive even if oil exports were completely cut off; falling oil prices would not hurt Iran so much as other oil exporters. He pointed to Iran's success in increasing its non-oil exports, which he estimated would earn $5,000m. in 1993–94, nearly one-third of total hard currency revenues. In contrast, Mohammad Reza Bahonar, a member of the Majlis economy and finance committee, argued that Iran must shake off its addiction to oil revenues during the next few years because low oil prices and a rapidly growing population had resulted in a fall in per capita oil income to about $15 a month. Rafsanjani also repeated accusations made by other Iranian officials that the 30% fall in oil prices during 1993 had been orchestrated by hostile countries, principally the USA, because they were alarmed by Iran's economic recovery. Later in the year Khamenei accused Saudi Arabia of helping 'international thieves' to keep oil prices low. In March 1994 the Majlis reduced projected revenue and expenditure before approving the Government's 1994–95 budget because of concern over low oil prices and the high level of foreign debt. Announcing the decision, Ali Akbar Nateq Nouri, the Speaker of the Majlis, stated that economic reforms, including the reduction of subsidies, should be slowed down to protect the vulnerable strata of society. Yet despite opposition from within the Majlis, in April Rafsanjani renewed his attack on some state subsidies which he stated cost the country $15,000m. every year. He declared that energy subsidies alone cost $11,000m. a year, more than projected oil revenues for 1994–95. He argued that subsidies for agriculture and for assisting the families of those killed during the revolution and the war with Iraq were justified, whereas bread subsidies for the general population and energy subsidies were unjust and should be eliminated. This programme was a matter of urgency because subsidies were preventing the country's economic recovery. After the failure of an attempt within the Majlis in May to remove control over price-setting from the Government, Rafsanjani appeared to compromise and promised that subsidy reforms would be introduced gradually. Nothing would be done until the new Five-Year Development Plan was ready because subsidy cuts directly affected the people's standard of living and could cause resentment against the Government. The president stated that 'It needs at least 10 years for us to remove the iniquities that exist in fuel and bread consumption', suggesting that the comprehensive phasing out of subsidies that appears to have been included in the new Five-Year Plan will now take place over a much longer period.

Inflation is estimated to have risen sharply to well above the official figure of 22% announced in 1993. The Government's plans to accelerate the privatization programme appear to be going ahead. In March 1994 Massoud Roghani Zanjani, vice-president of the Plan and Budget Organization, announced that the sale of state factories through the Teheran stock exchange had proved unsatisfactory so that in future factories could be sold by auction and negotiation. There was speculation that while falling oil revenues might delay some economic reforms, the crisis might accelerate the pace of change in other areas.

AGRICULTURE

Out of a total surface area of 165m. ha, the 1988 agricultural census reported that there were 56m. ha of cultivable farm land, of which 16.8m. ha were actually being cultivated. Some 9m. ha of the cultivated area are dry-farmed, while rain-fed agriculture is important in the western provinces of Kermanshah, Kurdistan and Azerbaijan. Irrigated areas are fed from modern water-storage systems or from the ancient system of *qanat* (underground water channels), although these have fallen into disrepair in recent years. In 1986 Iran had 17 operational dams which provided irrigation for 871,200 ha of land. In 1989 the $170m. 15th Khordad dam near Qom, which will hold 200m. cu m of water, was reportedly nearing completion. Irrigated land currently accounts for nearly 80% of food output excluding livestock. People are moving from the countryside to the towns, and only one-quarter of Iran's population was expected to be based in the countryside by 1990. In February 1994 Isa Kalantari, the Minister of Agriculture stated that agriculture had accounted for 26% of GNP during the previous four years. The average annual growth of the sector during that period had been 6%. The minister reported that in 1992–93 the value of agricultural exports was $700m., representing one-quarter of Iran's non-oil exports. According to the export promotion centre, agricultural exports grew by 17% to $900m. in 1993/94. The chief factors limiting the size of agricultural production are: inadequate communications, which limits access to markets; poor seeds, implements and techniques of cultivation; scarcity of water and under-capitalization, chiefly the result of the low incomes of peasant households. About four-fifths of all farms have an area of less than 11 ha. Iran was self-sufficient in foodstuffs until the late 1960s but then began importing vast quantities, owing to the failure of agricultural output to keep pace with increasing domestic consumption and the failure of the Government to produce a really sound agricultural policy. Natural disasters have also taken their toll. Early in 1992 nearly 5% of cultivated land, mostly in the north of the country, was damaged by floods.

A large variety of crops are cultivated in the diverse climatic regions of Iran. Grains are the chief crops, including wheat (the major staple), barley and rice. According to the 1988 agricultural census, the area sown to wheat rose to 5.3m. ha during the previous six years, while the average yield per hectare reached 1,082 kg. Under the Five-Year Development Plan (introduced in January 1990), it was aimed to increase wheat production to 11m. metric tons per year by 1995, although it appears unlikely that this will be achieved. In 1991 Iran's deputy minister of agriculture declared that wheat yields would rise significantly, from 1.96 tons per hectare to 3.2 tons per hectare, through the expansion of irrigation; and that by 1993 wheat production would reach 12.5m. tons, making self-sufficiency possible. However, the use of scarce water resources for the cultivation of cereals rather than of crops that would give higher yields has been questioned. Moreover, given the current trend away from wheat cultivation to more profitable cash crops, expectations regarding the achievement of self-sufficiency appear to be misplaced. According to the FAO, Iranian production rose from a low of 5.79m. tons in the drought year 1989 to 7m. tons in 1990. Production was estimated at 8.9m. tons in 1991. The 1992 wheat harvest totalled 10.3m. tons, 17% more than forecast in the Five-Year Plan. The Ministry of Agriculture stated that production would meet 80% of domestic requirements and that 2.5m. tons only would be imported. Under the new Five-Year Plan due to begin in 1994, annual wheat production is

projected to rise by 40% to 14m. tons. Barley production reached 2.6m. tons in 1989, while the yield per hectare was 1,040 kg; production was estimated at 3.6m. tons in 1991. In 1988 rice production rose to more than 1.5m. tons, although the yield per hectare improved only slightly, to 2,700 kg. After falling to 1.2m. tons in 1989, rice production rose to 1.7m. tons in 1990, declining, however, to 1.4m. tons in 1991. Production rose again, to 2.5m. tons, in 1992. Between 1982 and 1988 the area sown with sugar beet declined by 65,000 ha, to 131,890 ha, but annual production remained steady at 3.4m. tons. Production was estimated at 3.4m. tons again in 1989. In 1991/92 sugar beet production rose to 5m. tons, 1.4m. tons more than in the previous year, according to the Ministry of Agriculture. Sugar beet provides 50% of Iran's sugar requirements. Between 1982 and 1988 the area under cotton also declined, by 26,000 ha, but output rose by 63,000 tons per year to 332,000 tons. The output of potatoes declined from 2.3m. tons in 1987 to an estimated 1.4m. tons in 1989, while the planted area remained almost the same, at 77,000 ha. Tea, almonds, pistachios and dates are of commercial importance, while olives and a variety of fruits and vegetables, as well as tobacco, are also cultivated. Sugar cane is being cultivated at Haft Teppeh, in the southern province of Khuzestan (production reached an estimated 2m. tons in 1991), and a paper plant has been established in association with the plantation. Food requirements, as a result of improved living standards and increased population, have been rising by more than 11.5% per year. Estimates suggest that grain imports alone could increase to 30m. tons per year by 2022, when Iran's population is projected to reach 140m.

Despite the early social and political benefits of land reform, which the Shah had vigorously pursued in the 1960s and 1970s, agriculture in general suffered under the Shah, to the point where it became one of the principal issues raised against him by his opponents. Typical of the Shah's grandiose projects were four joint ventures set up with foreign companies in 1970 on over 60,000 ha of land in Khuzestan, in the southwest, involving the removal of some 6,500 peasant families. Despite massive infusions of funds, the projects began to collapse within a few years owing to inadequate planning, a lack of skilled manpower and delays in irrigation schemes. By the time that the Revolution ousted the Shah the projects were in the process of being wound up.

Having made such an issue of agriculture in the political battle against the Shah, the victorious revolutionaries made its revival one of their priorities. Self-sufficiency in foodstuffs, above all else, became central to their economic philosophy, but the authorities have acknowledged that, unlike the former regime, they do not have the money to extend the cultivated area through building dams and irrigation schemes. Instead of spending capital, the Government has emphasized the intensification of agriculture, i.e. the improvement of farming on existing lands. To this end, the Government increased support prices for grains and other crops. The biggest subsidies have gone to wheat, the country's most important crop. The Government increased its support to IR53 ($0.74) per kg, compared with the pre-Revolution price of IR18 ($0.20). Since March 1983 the Government has been providing further subsidies in kind as well as giving tax exemption for 10 years to all farmers who follow official guidelines. For each ton of wheat produced, the Government offers 100 kg of fertilizer, 4 kg of cube sugar, and 1 kg of tea. Farmers have also been told that they can pay for a tractor at cost price in wheat delivered to the local grains and cereals organization. Subsidies, though less generous, have been introduced for rice and other grains. However, many farmers can sell their wheat on the unofficial market for as much as IR60–IR70 ($0.65–$0.75). It has been estimated that the government teams that tour the country, buying up surplus wheat, purchase less than 15% of Iran's total production. Towards the end of 1991 the Government announced that it had purchased 1.82m. tons of wheat in the current farming year, and announced its intention to purchase 20% more wheat from farmers the following season in order to encourage the cultivation of the crop after the high production and modest prices of the previous season. In early 1994 President Rafsanjani stated that the $350m. spent on subsidizing the agricultural sector were justified and should be maintained. Rural projects, such as the building of schools, mosques, public baths, silos, roads and irrigation networks and the extension of electricity to villages, have been undertaken by the Construction Jihad Ministry, which combines the roles of three agencies of the Shah's White Revolution, the Literacy, Health and Agricultural Extension corps. It was constituted as a Ministry at the end of 1983, and in July 1984 announced a plan to commit 1m. ha to dry farming. Delays in implementing these projects have added to rural insecurity and are an additional cause of rural-to-urban migration.

The Construction Jihad Ministry and the Ministry of Agriculture are known to hold conflicting views on almost every aspect of policy, with the Jihad strongly in favour of a more far-reaching land reform. Proposals for the merger of the two Ministries in 1987 encountered resistance inside both organizations. While the Ministry of Agriculture favours an essentially advisory and technical role in the agricultural sector, the Jihad promotes the creation of collective farming organizations and a reduction in the role of the private land-owner. Although the Jihad has achieved spectacular success in some villages, there are fears that an extension of its authority could impede production, with ideological factors taking precedence over sound farm management.

Short-term credit to farmers has been greatly increased. In the last year of the old regime the Agricultural Bank lent some $600m.; in 1982–83 it lent $11,900m., and in 1983–84 $2,300m. In spite of expanded credit facilities, farmers have been reluctant to start long-term, high-value cultivation of perennial crops. Instead, they have put their effort into annual crops that yield a quick return, particularly wheat. Moreover, the impact has been uneven, with big changes in the centre of the country, around Teheran, but in other areas, those disrupted by the war and those where tribe-state relations are bad, the villages have hardly been touched by the new policies. More than a decade after the Revolution, Iran is no more self-sufficient than it was in the latter days of the Shah's rule. In spite of successes claimed in increasing agricultural output, US Department of Agriculture estimates revealed that Iranian imports of foodstuffs reached $3,670m. in 1984 and were only modestly reduced in 1985. Agricultural imports reached $1,900m. in 1987/88, according to the Minister of Agriculture. The allocation for agricultural imports in 1988/89 was $2,000m. In the Iranian year 1990/91 the value of food imports through government agencies was $5,300m. Imports by the private sector are not officially recorded. Imports of wheat were estimated at 4.5m. tons, those of rice at 800,000 tons and those of coarse grains at 1.3m. tons. There are doubts that significant increases in farm productivity can be achieved in the short term. Agriculture has suffered massive losses of labour (5m. people since 1982), the land ownership question is still unresolved, provision of farm inputs is poor and the state marketing system ineffective.

Problems of land ownership and uncertainty about the Government's land reform policies have added to the difficulties affecting the agricultural sector. After the fall of the Shah, when the authority of the central Government was weak, land seizures began in many villages. The most dramatic examples occurred in Turkoman and Kurdish areas, where concentrations of large absentee land-holdings were especially pronounced, but other areas were also affected. In some cases the Government did not intervene but, where it did, it tended to oppose land seizures. The events were accompanied by mass migration from the countryside to the cities—nearly 1.5m. rural dwellers migrated to Teheran alone during the first year of the Revolution. The regime recognized the economic disaster that this migration threatened. Nearly one-quarter of the most fertile farm land awaits settlement of ownership claims between big landlords and the farmers who have taken over their lands. The redistribution of these lands is decreed by the Revolution but, according to the rules of Islam, property is sacred and the right to it absolute. The issue has been complicated by the radical element in the Government which advocates the appropriation of more land by the state. A land reform programme, prepared by the Ministry of Agriculture, was submitted to the Revolutionary Council at the end of 1979. The programme planned to limit the size of holdings to three times the average in an area. The large landowners were

accused of influencing the clergy to oppose the new measures, but the necessary legislation was eventually introduced. It was approved by the Majlis in 1981, but was later rejected by the Council of Guardians as un-Islamic. The form of the land reform bill was then altered considerably. Land was to be confiscated only from former enemies of the Revolution and only if it was barren or uncultivated. After many months before the Majlis and deep controversy over the acceptability of the law in the light of Islamic principles, the bill was again rejected by the Council of Guardians. A compromise law, giving farmers, peasants and squatters rights to land (amounting to some 800,000 ha) settled by them after the Revolution, but allowing big landlords who avoided the redistribution of land to retain their estates, was approved by the Majlis in May 1985, though it was not ratified by the Council of Guardians. The law would affect about 630,000 ha of farmland belonging to some 5,300 landlords who fled the country or whose lands were appropriated. Some 800,000 ha of land, confiscated from officers and others linked with the Shah's regime, have been redistributed since the Revolution. (More than 50% of this land is uncultivable or grazing land, but 200,000 ha of cultivable land have been given to poor or landless peasants.) For more than a decade the authorities have been trying to reconcile Islamic principles with revolutionary goals and expectations, while a comprehensive settlement of the land ownership reform question is still awaited.

In early 1990 changes in government policy on the utilization of agricultural land were announced. Instead of granting confiscated and unused land to small farmers, henceforth official teams (consisting of seven members) were to grant land in blocks to groups of investors, in order to ensure its rapid development. Consequently, some 200,000 ha of land have been leased to farmers for temporary cultivation, and it is aimed to lease a further 250,000 ha under the new terms.

Agriculture has been described as the weakest spot in the Iranian economy and the biggest impediment to progress. Although it was given high priority by the Islamic Republic in the 1983/84–1987/88 Five-Year Development Plan (see Development Plans, p. 447), the Government has been unable to make it fulfil its designated role. The Five-Year Development Plan, introduced in January 1990, envisaged investment of $64,000m. in agriculture. Of this sum, one-third was to be invested by the Government and the remainder by the private sector. Some $340m. were to be spent on increasing the output of cotton, sugar cane and maize, on animal husbandry and on schemes to mechanize the farming of wheat on 2m. ha of irrigated land. Plans also included the development of major agro-industrial complexes in Mazandaran and Khuzestan.

The war with Iraq imposed numerous constraints. Between 1980 and 1982 10% of agricultural land fell under Iraqi occupation; a disproportionate number of volunteers for the war effort were drawn from the villages; and the heavy financial burden of the war imposed limits on spending. Since the end of the war, recovery has been hampered by drought in the western rain-fed areas and by the earthquake of June 1990, which destroyed irrigation works, orchards and farms in the fertile north-west provinces of Gilan and Zanjan. Within the Government, some ministers have criticized the subsidies to farmers, while others wish to provide greater assistance to farmers in order to reduce imports, which are regarded as a form of subsidy to foreign farmers. Stability of land ownership, skilled management of the commodity market by the state and professional support systems for agriculture are essential if this sector is to recover. They have been lacking for more than a decade and this deficiency will not be easily remedied. Very little information has been released by the Government on the role of agriculture in the 1990–94 Five-Year Plan, but it was reported that in the 1992/93 budget the Ministry of Agriculture and the Construction Jihad Ministry had been allocated $116m. in hard currency to spend on imported equipment to improve agricultural output. Most of the allocation was devoted to the Ministry of Agriculture to spend on the improvement of wheat and rice yields, and for pumps and electrical equipment for water wells. The allocation for the Construction Jihad Ministry was for animal husbandry, dairy products and the construction of fodder storage facilities. According to Iran's export promotion centre, the value of agricultural exports during the term of the 1990–94 Five-Year Plan amounted to $3,500m., some $500m. more than had been projected.

The principal products of the nomad sector of Iranian agriculture are livestock products—dairy produce, wool, hair and hides. According to the 1988 agricultural census, nomads' herds included 40.7m. sheep and lambs, of which more than one-third were in the provinces of Khorassan and east and west Azerbaijan. About 40% of sheep and goats are raised by semi-nomadic tribal herdsmen. Production is limited by the prevalence of animal pests and the apparently inevitable poor productivity of pastoral stock breeding compared with its domestic counterpart. However, account must be taken of the fact that most of the land grazed by the nomads' herds is land which could not be made economically viable in any other way. During the reign of Reza Shah (1925–41) the Iranian Government tried to enforce settlement on the nomads but the tribes rebelled. Since the early 1960s, government 'encouragement' and economic pressures have resulted in significant settlement. By contrast, the Revolutionary Government accepts the tribes as part of the social structure and is providing the nomads with support to expand meat production. Local output of red meat increased by 35% in 1991/92 to 575,000 tons, with imports totalling 225,000 tons according to the Minister of Construction Jihad.

About 11.5% of Iran is under forest or woodland, including the Caspian area—the main source of commercial timber—and the Zagros mountains. Forestry in an economic sense is a recent activity and it is only since the nationalization of forest land in 1963 that effective attempts have been made, under the Forestry Commission, at protection, conservation and re-afforestation. Total roundwood output in 1990 was estimated at 6.7m. cu m.

Although Iran has direct access to both the Caspian Sea and the Gulf, fishing remains poorly developed in both areas. The total Iranian catch amounted to an estimated 250,000 tons in 1990. With the assistance of new investment, the Government hopes to increase the annual catch to 730,000 tons per year. The Caspian fisheries are chiefly noted for the production of caviar, mostly for export. Caviar exports in recent years have been estimated at around 100 tons, but in 1993 exports were projected to rise to 200 tons. During the 1990s prices have fallen by about one-third due to an increase in smuggling through Russia. In August 1993 Iran, Russia, Azerbaijan, Kazakhstan and Turkmenistan agreed to establish a cartel to regulate international prices of caviar, to co-ordinate exports and to protect stocks of sturgeon. Pollution and the steadily falling water-level of the Caspian Sea are two serious problems being tackled under a Soviet–Iranian agreement signed in 1973. One survey estimated that, if fully developed, Iran's southern fisheries could earn as much as $200m. annually, chiefly from high-grade shrimps and prawns. At the end of 1982 a $1,300m. five-year plan for the development of the fishing industry was announced. The first phase of a giant fishing port at Javad al-A'emeh, in Hormozgan Province, was completed in June 1986, at a cost of $3m. Under a $20m.-protocol signed in August 1987, Iran agreed to buy 36 trawlers from the People's Republic of China, 18 of which were to be assembled in Iran from Chinese parts. China was also to assist in the construction of factories producing canned fish at three Iranian ports. Government expenditure of $4,520m. on the sector is planned over the period 1990–95; projects include the construction of 13 new fishing ports along the Gulf and the Sea of Oman, and the purchase or charter of fishing vessels. In May 1993 a new fishing port, which was to be equipped with cold storage facilities, opened on Hormuz Island. At the end of November 1993 a $1.4m.-fish canning plant was opened in the Qeshm Island free zone, with a daily capacity of 40,000 cans. As a result of pollution caused by the war in the Gulf in 1991, Iran's shrimp catch was reported to have fallen by almost two-thirds to 4,000 tons in the Iranian year 1991/92.

PETROLEUM

The major economic activity in Iran is the petroleum industry. The history of commercial exploitation dates back to 1901, when W. K. D'Arcy was granted a 60-year monopoly of the

right to explore for and exploit petroleum in Iran, with the exception of the five northern provinces, which fell within the sphere of Russian influence. Petroleum was eventually discovered in commercial quantities at Masjid-i-Sulaiman in 1908 and the Anglo-Persian Oil Company was formed in 1909. The Company was renamed Anglo-Iranian in 1935. A long series of disputes between the Iranian Government and Anglo-Iranian ended with the nationalization of the petroleum industry by Iran in 1951 and the replacement in 1954 of Anglo-Iranian by what became known as the Consortium until it was dissolved in March 1979. The Consortium was an amalgam of interests (British Petroleum 40%; Royal Dutch Shell 14%; Gulf Oil, Socony, Mobil, Exxon, Standard Oil of California and Texaco each with 7%; Compagnie Française des Pétroles 6%; a group of independents under the umbrella of the Iricon Agency 5%) which was formed to extract petroleum in the area of the old Anglo-Iranian concession as redefined in 1933. The Consortium's concession was to have lasted until 1979, with the possibility of a series of extensions under modified conditions for a further 15 years. Ownership of petroleum deposits throughout Iran and the right to exploit them, or to make arrangements for their exploitation, was vested in the National Iranian Oil Company (NIOC), an Iranian state enterprise. According to official figures, Iran's proven oil reserves in 1993 were 92,000m. barrels. In August 1993 the Ministry of Oil announced the discovery of a new oil reservoir at Darkhorin in Khozistan, containing an estimated 7,000m. barrels of light crude.

Until 1973 Iran had a leasing agreement with the Consortium, but the Iranian Government then insisted that the companies should either continue under existing arrangements until 1979 and then become ordinary 'arm's-length buyers', or else negotiate an entirely new 'agency' agreement immediately. The Consortium opted for the latter plan, and on 31 July 1973 a contract was signed in Teheran under which NIOC formally took over ownership and control of the petroleum industry in the Consortium area, while the Consortium was to set up a new operating company, Oil Service Company of Iran, which would act as production contractor for NIOC. In return, the western companies were granted a 20-year supply of crude petroleum as privileged buyers, which they would take in proportion to their shareholding in the Consortium.

Strikes at the petroleum installations, halting petroleum exports, constituted one of the difficulties which forced the Shah to leave Iran in January 1979. The strikers announced that exports would not resume until the Shah left the country; Iran did not restore supplies to the rest of the world until 5 March 1979. The first shipments were sold on the spot market, fetching prices as high as $20 per barrel, but NIOC announced that this was a temporary measure. Within a matter of weeks, three dozen long-term contracts were signed with international companies for the supply of Iranian petroleum.

NIOC cancelled the 1973 agreement to market Iranian petroleum through the Consortium, and since 5 March 1979 has sold petroleum directly to individual companies and countries. After initial resistance, the former members of the Consortium accepted the new arrangement and signed new nine-month supply agreements effective from 1 April. The role of the Consortium effectively came to an end on 1 July 1981, when Kala Ltd, a subsidiary of NIOC which had been established to undertake purchasing and service functions for Iran's petroleum industry, replaced the Iranian Oil Service Co (IROS), one of the subsidiaries of the Consortium.

Iran's greatest difficulty after November 1979, however, was finding customers willing to pay the high prices that it demanded. Supplies of about 900,000 barrels per day (b/d) to the USA were stopped in November, and by May 1980 deliveries of about 800,000 b/d to Japan and British Petroleum and Royal Dutch Shell were also halted. The USA stopped taking delivery for political reasons in order to put pressure on Iran for the release of its hostages in the US Embassy in Teheran, taken over by Iranian students in November 1979; BP and Shell, themselves under pressure from the USA, refused to buy Iranian petroleum from 21 April, when the Ministry of Oil raised the price of its lightest crude to $35 per barrel, retroactive from 1 April. Including surcharges and other conditions Iran's oil was costing its customers closer to $37.50

per barrel, perhaps the highest for any OPEC country (this price compared with $17.17 per barrel less than a year earlier). With the (at least temporary) loss of its major Western customers, Iran began to investigate the Eastern bloc and developing countries for its principal markets.

The Government targeted average exports of crude petroleum for the Iranian year 1360 (March 1981–March 1982) at 2.5m. b/d: within the 3m. b/d ceiling which had been set after the Revolution as the optimum production level. Before the Revolution, Iran was producing 5m. to 6m. b/d, of which around 800,000 b/d were required for domestic consumption. Political action in late 1978 brought production almost to a standstill but it recovered to around 3m. b/d during the following 18 months. Average production in 1979 was just over 3m. b/d, and in 1980 declined to 1.5m. b/d, 49.5% less than the 1979 level, owing to price disputes and the crisis in relations with the West.

After the Prime Minister, Muhammad Ali Rajai, presented his April 1981 budget, with expenditure set at an ambitious US $44,000m., NIOC was apparently instructed to raise production to 2.5m. b/d to generate foreign exchange for the budget requirements. A special effort was made by NIOC to improve performance in petroleum exports by seeking contract customers as quickly as possible. By mid-1981 contracts for sales totalling 1m. b/d had been signed (207,000 b/d to Eastern bloc countries). Not all of these contracts, however, yielded foreign exchange. Crude contracts with CMEA countries (including the USSR) during the 1980s, and subsequently with other countries, including Turkey and India, were normally on a barter basis, with only the balance being made up in hard currency. In return for petroleum, these countries exported industrial goods and services, plus some food.

In October 1981, as a result of growing internal political violence and the war damage caused by Iraq, the main purchasers of Iranian petroleum announced that they would cease to lift Iranian crude. The contracts held by BP for 65,000 b/d, Mitsubishi for 40,000 b/d, Daikyo Oil for 10,000 b/d and Showa Oil for 18,000 b/d lapsed as from the end of September 1981. A group of nine Japanese firms also stopped purchases from Iran; only Shell retained its contract. In September 1981 the Government announced that all agreements and contracts signed under the Shah's regime had been abrogated. At the beginning of 1982 Japanese buyers re-entered the Iranian market.

The pricing of Iranian crude petroleum also had an adverse effect on exports, as both Iranian Light and Iranian Heavy have been priced towards the upper end of the market for similar API crudes. In April 1980 the price for Light was raised from $32.5 to $35 per barrel, with an additional premium of $2.5 per barrel. The Japanese, who had been taking 520,000 b/d, suspended purchases, while Shell and BP refused to buy until the price was below $35 per barrel. In July 1980 differentials between Iranian and similar Gulf crudes narrowed as Iraq and Kuwait raised prices up to the $32 benchmark agreed at the OPEC meeting in Algiers. In January 1981 prices were raised by $1.63 to $37 for Light and $36 for Heavy, with an additional premium of $1.8 per barrel. However, against this pricing policy, Iran was reported in early 1981 to have offered discounts of up to 20% to offset the very high insurance rates of loading in the war zone of Kharg Island and to have offered 60 days' credit instead of 30 days'.

In July and August 1981 Iran refused requests by its main customers for negotiations on prices of crude petroleum despite a difference of $5.50 per barrel between the Saudi reference price and the $37.50 per barrel charged by Iran. After the OPEC meeting in Abu Dhabi in December 1981, Iran reduced its prices to $34.20, just 20 cents above the reference price charged by Saudi Arabia, and in February 1982, as part of its drive to increase petroleum exports, NIOC announced two price cuts, each of $1. Taking into account 30 days' credit, the NIOC prices were $32.20 for 34° API crude and $30.30 for 31° API crude. These reductions made Iran's petroleum the cheapest in the Middle East.

The period April 1980 to June 1981 was, in almost every way, very poor for the Iranian petroleum industry. Apart from the factors already mentioned, the country was in a continuous state of political ferment, which spilled over into the hydrocarbon industry. Stoppages, strikes, go-slows and sabotage seriously hindered production. The loss of foreign personnel for oilfield maintenance on the onshore fields was compounded by the May 1980 EC sanctions, imposed in support of the USA over the American hostages in Iran. The EC's action prevented Iran from purchasing some of the sophisticated spares and components required for repairs and maintenance. Iran's response, however, deprived the country of some petroleum customers, since it suspended supplies to any country supporting the sanctions.

The Iraqi attack on Iran across the Shatt al-Arab in September 1980 and the consequent expanded and prolonged hostilities further weakened the industry. Iraqi shelling of the 628,000 b/d Abadan refinery put the plant out of action. Spasmodic attacks on shipping in the Gulf caused some disruption, but the movement of ultra-large cargo carriers and other vessels was virtually uninterrupted until May 1984, when Iraq began to concentrate its attacks on ships using Iran's main terminal for crude oil exports, at Kharg Island, and on the terminal itself. Only part of the terminal's export capacity was damaged, and, with an installed capacity of 6.5m. b/d, the loss of an estimated 2.5m. b/d capacity still enabled the terminal to deal effectively with Iran's levels of export in early 1983, which remained well below pre-Revolution figures. During periods of concerted Iraqi action in the Gulf, there were massive increases in insurance charges for tankers, followed by sharp falls during periods of relative military inactivity. Iraqi raids disrupted the product lines extending from Bandar Mahshahr along the length of the country, and delayed construction of the giant petrochemical complex at Bandar Khomeini, a joint Iranian-Japanese project expected to cost $4,000m.

From the depressed levels of early 1982, Iran's output of petroleum rose significantly during the first half of 1983. In January 1983 oil rationing for domestic consumers was ended. Domestic consumption in mid-1982 was believed to be between 600,000 b/d and 700,000 b/d, of which some 300,000 b/d was being refined outside Iran, leaving exports at between 1.6m. b/d and 1.7m. b/d. In the second half of 1983, output dropped to 2.6m. b/d, compared with an OPEC production quota of 2.4m. b/d, under which exports of 1.7m. b/d were possible, after domestic consumption. Petroleum exports in June 1984 rose to 1.4m. b/d after falling below 1m. b/d in May, following Iraqi attacks on tankers in the Gulf. Japanese companies, the principal customers for Iranian crude oil, lifted more than 400,000 b/d in early 1984. Between May and July 1984 Japan banned its tankers from Kharg Island, and Iran offered lower prices to certain customers to bolster sales in the absence of its largest customer.

In 1982/83, with its oil priced at $34 per barrel, export earnings reached $23,000m.; in 1983/84, when Iran's oil was priced at $28 per barrel, earnings totalled $21,500m., about $4,000m. more than the OPEC quota (which was reduced by 100,000 b/d, to 2.3m. b/d, in October 1984) would have allowed. Iran responded to the need to increase earnings by breaking OPEC production limits (Iran repeatedly pressed for an increase in its OPEC production quota, until the crisis of 1985–86, when prices fell precipitously in a glutted market (see below)) and by energetic price-cutting policies, actions which offended its OPEC partners. It was reliably reported that Iran priced its crude petroleum in 1984 considerably below the official market level of $29 per barrel, as it was known to have done with the previous official price of $34. Some liftings were reportedly offered at approximately $26.50 per barrel in September and October 1984. Special insurance rates were made available to offset Iraqi threats to tanker traffic in the Gulf, and extended credit was also reportedly used as an incentive. Some customers, in particular Japan, began to turn to Saudi Arabia and Kuwait for their oil, as the risk of attacks on tankers and, commensurately, the rate of insurance were lower. Barter trading continued, but there was some evidence of Iran's dissatisfaction with such arrangements, owing to the failure of partners to deliver materials which had been promised, and to supply goods according to specification. In 1985, despite its stated wish to abide by OPEC's official pricing structure, Iran continued to offer discounts on its oil, below official OPEC prices, to attract customers otherwise deterred by risks to shipping in the Gulf from Iraqi air attacks, and by the increased rates of insurance charged on vessels using the Kharg Island oil terminal. In January Iran brought its prices into line with those of OPEC by raising the price of its light crude oil by $1.11 to $29.10 per barrel. In February, when OPEC prices were reduced, Iran cut the price of its light crude by $1.05 to $28.05 per barrel. By mid-1985, however, Iran was again offering discounts on its oil. Despite efforts to remain competitive (which included rebate incentives, discounts and the shuttling of oil from Kharg Island by tanker to a safer lifting point, see below), Iran's revenue from oil exports (of 1.68m. b/d) fell to $17,000m. in 1984/85, 15% less than had been predicted. The Government blamed the war with Iraq and the OPEC decision to reduce its prices by $1.00 per barrel.

During 1985 Iran achieved an output of some 2.3m. b/d, in spite of heavy Iraqi bombing of the Kharg Island terminal in the last third of the year, with exports running at some 1.5m. b/d–1.7m. b/d. Falling oil prices severely affected Iran, and in January 1986 the Minister of Oil offered to halve Iranian exports, in an attempt to curb the fall in the price of crude, if other OPEC states would do the same. The Ministry of Oil argued publicly against the use of barter deals to stimulate oil exports while the Ministry of Foreign Affairs adopted barter and bilateral agreements as one of the main features of Iran's foreign policy. New barter deals were agreed in 1985 but their profitability was low and often fell short of the country's real needs; bartering returned to favour, however, with the appointment of a new Council of Ministers in January 1986.

A suggested long-term solution to the threat to oil exports, posed by Iraqi attacks on Kharg Island, was the construction of a new oil terminal, either at the end of a pipeline outside the Gulf area, or at Sirri Island, close to the mouth of the Gulf, 450 km south-east of Kharg Island, safer from Iraqi attack. An immediate and cheaper alternative, more a short-term solution to the problem of Iraqi air raids on Kharg, involved the establishment of a tanker shuttle service between Kharg and a makeshift floating oil terminal at Sirri Island, using tankers anchored off shore, where the oil was stored and reloaded. The Sirri facility began operating in March 1985 and proved its worth between August 1985 and January 1986, when Iraq launched a series of some 60 attacks against the Kharg Island terminal (which was still responsible for more than 80% of Iran's oil exports). The frequency and effectiveness of these attacks diminished during October, but at the beginning of the month exports were reported to be only 750,000 b/d–800,000 b/d, compared with an average of 1.5m. b/d in August and 1m. b/d in September. However, by dint of rapid repairs, employing the ample spare capacity on Kharg and exploiting alternative means of export, such as the shuttle to Sirri, Iran could claim that exports in October finally averaged 1.7m. b/d. However, further Iraqi raids were said to have reduced exports from Kharg to a trickle by January 1986. In June 1986, as a precaution against possible Iraqi attacks on the Sirri facility, a new floating terminal, called Wal-Fajr 2 (Dawn 2), was established at Larak Island, 210 km east of Sirri, using at least three of the supertankers formerly based at Sirri.

Average oil production in Iran at the end of 1985 was between 2.2m. b/d and 2.5m. b/d, while exports averaged about 1.6m. b/d. The rate of export fell from about 1.5m. b/d in January 1986 to 1.2m. b/d in February. At the end of January Iran offered to halve its oil production, and in February pressed OPEC to suspend oil exports for two weeks in an attempt to force prices up again. It was perhaps no coincidence that Iran's most vehement advocacy of production discipline within OPEC occurred at a time when the depredations of war prevented it from producing and exporting sufficient oil in excess of its OPEC quota to obviate the effects of falling prices. In fact, it could barely meet its quota in early 1986. In July prices fell below $10 per barrel (following six months of unrestrained production by OPEC in pursuit of a 'fair' market share), and in August OPEC members, at Iran's suggestion, agreed to cut output for two months from 1 September, effectively reverting to the production quotas imposed in October 1984, giving Iran a quota of 2.3m. b/d. Although

Iraq refused to participate in the agreement, considering its quota of less than 1.5m. b/d to be too low, and demanding one commensurate with its production capacity or, at least, the equal of Iran's, Iran averred that military action in the Gulf would effectively restrain Iraqi oil production.

In October 1986, when the price of oil had risen to about $15 per barrel, OPEC members agreed to increase collective production by some 200,000 b/d. In December all OPEC members (with the exception of Iraq, which, once more, since it was not expected to comply, received a notional quota) accepted a 7.25% reduction in their output, effective for the first half of 1987. It was hoped that this measure would enable the organization to support a fixed price of $18 per barrel, effective from 1 February, replacing the policy of pricing according to spot market rates, which prevailed in 1986. The reduction gave Iran a production quota of 2.26m. b/d, compared with 2.32m. b/d in November 1986–January 1987. Iran's average output of crude oil was estimated by OPEC to be 2.04m. b/d in 1986, compared with 2.19m. b/d in 1985, well below its OPEC quota. Production fluctuated during the first half of 1987 between 1.7m. b/d in February and 2.6m. b/d in June.

The OPEC production programme succeeded in sustaining the price of its oil at $18 per barrel during the first half of 1987, and during the month of July prices on the spot market rose above $20 per barrel, in response to alarm over the growing threat to oil supplies posed by developments in the Iran–Iraq War. In June OPEC members agreed to retain the $18 per barrel benchmark, but to increase their collective production by 800,000 b/d during the second half of the year to 16.6m. b/d (including a notional quota for Iraq). Iran's quota was raised to 2.37m. b/d, an increase of 111,000 b/d. In August, however, output averaged 2.8m. b/d, according to oil industry sources, despite having counselled restraint at the June meeting. Iran had, since 1985, urged a return to a price of $28 per barrel, as OPEC's ultimate goal, in tandem with lower production—obviously with regard to its own difficulties in sustaining production levels.

In June 1987 Iraqi aircraft attacked the Kharg Island terminal for the first time since January. It was reported that, in the interim, three oil-loading berths at Kharg had been made operational again. Exports averaged 2.2m. b/d in August and 1.6m. b/d in September, according to oil industry sources, compared with an OPEC quota of 1.7m. b/d. By mid-October Iraqi attacks had reduced the number of tankers shuttling oil from Kharg to 20.

At the OPEC meeting which was held in December 1987, Iran demanded an increase in the central reference price of at least $2 per barrel and output reductions by members, and refused to participate in a new agreement which awarded Iraq the same quota as that given to Iran. It was finally agreed to retain the $18 per barrel reference price and the ceiling of 16.6m. b/d (15.06m. b/d excluding Iraq) on collective production for a further six months from 1 January 1988. Prices remained well below the OPEC reference level during the first half of 1988, owing to member states' flouting of their quotas, but in May OPEC decided to retain the 16.6m. b/d ceiling and the $18 reference price for a further six months. In August, when the cease-fire in the Iran–Iraq War took effect, Iran was producing at its quota level of about 2.37m. b/d, though, owing to Iraqi attacks on oil installations (including the first on Larak Island for five months in May), it had rarely been able to produce so much during the preceding six months. While Iranian representatives at OPEC meetings strongly urged reductions in output, to defend the $18 benchmark, Iran was allegedly so desperate for oil revenue that it was selling oil at less than $10 per barrel.

At a meeting of OPEC's Long-Term Strategy Committee in November 1988 (at which Iran reluctantly adopted a more flexible approach to Iraq's demand for quota parity), member states agreed a production ceiling of 18.5m. b/d for the first half of 1989. By December it was apparent that world demand for oil had surged, and prices strengthened to a level close to the $18 per barrel reference price which remained in force. According to oil industry sources, Iranian production averaged 2.27m. b/d in 1988, while OPEC's provisional estimate of Iranian petroleum revenues in 1988 was $8,170m.

In early 1989 the agreement that had been signed in November 1988 was undermined when Kuwait rejected the quota assigned to it within the 18.5m. b/d ceiling. By the time that the next full OPEC meeting was held, at the beginning of June 1989, prices had weakened considerably. To take account of the increased volume of Kuwaiti production, which OPEC member states regarded as inevitable, the production ceiling was raised by only 1m. b/d, to 19.5m. b/d, thus reducing the extra volume to which other members were entitled.

At the meeting of OPEC's Long-Term Strategy Committee (subsequently redesignated a full-scale quota and pricing meeting) in June 1989, Iran demanded a redistribution of quotas, to favour Kuwait, the UAE, Ecuador and Gabon, within a ceiling of 21.5m. b/d. In the event, a ceiling of 20.5m. b/d was set; Kuwait duly rejected its quota of 1.149m. b/d for the final quarter of 1989, and overproduction continued to such an extent that by the end of 1989 total OPEC output had reached almost 24m. b/d. According to oil industry sources, Iranian production averaged 2.87m. b/d during 1989, while Iran's petroleum revenues were estimated at $13,600m. At the next full OPEC meeting, held in November 1989, the production ceiling was raised to 22m. b/d, although most members regarded this as inadequate, since the *de facto* level of production was already 24m. b/d.

In early 1989 the Ministry of Oil issued a number of contracts for the construction and repair of offshore oil platforms destroyed during the Iran-Iraq War as part of a major $2,000m.-expansion programme. Offshore production had totalled some 500,000 b/d before the war but by 1986 it was estimated that production had fallen to 250,000 b/d. Offshore production may have fallen to 50,000 b/d by the end of the war. In April 1988 US warships severely damaged Salman, one of three rigs 150 km west of Sirri Island, feeding the Lavan Island terminals, and installations in the Nasr oilfield off Sirri. Rigs in the Reshadat and Risala'at oilfields, and the Raksh and Rostan platforms, had been destroyed by US attacks in April and October 1987.

By January 1990, prompted by optimistic demand estimates issued by OPEC and by members' closer adherence to their quotas, the price of crude petroleum had risen to its highest level for two years. Between January and May 1990, however, prices fell steadily, as quotas were largely ignored. In May 1990, at a meeting of OPEC's Monitoring Committee, it was agreed to reduce production by 1.445m. b/d, bringing it just within the previously agreed ceiling. A report issued by the IEA in July, however, showed that this reduction had not been implemented.

In June 1990 it was reported that Iran had agreed to pay the US oil company Amoco $600m. in compensation for operations which had been expropriated during the Revolution. This was the first major settlement of US corporate oil claims totalling $1,800m., and was regarded as a step towards the re-establishment of oil trade between Iran and the USA. In December it was announced that a US company, Atlantic Richfield, had secured compensation of $9m. from Iran for its share in the former international oil Consortium; this represented the last in a series of settlements (totalling $320m.) made by Iran to US members of the former Iranian international oil Consortium. At the end of 1990 the USA eased the three-year ban on purchases of Iranian crude, but Iran objected to the US Administration's stipulation that all payments had to be made into a security account in The Hague, Netherlands, for use by the special US–Iran Claims Tribunal. However, in early 1991 Iran approved two sales to US companies, Coastal Corpn and Mobil Corpn. Coastal Corpn, Chevron and Amerada Hess purchased shipments of Iranian oil for the US market in 1991. Mobil and other US oil firms have also purchased Iranian crude petroleum, but for delivery outside of the USA. In August 1992 Atlantic Richfield and Sun Oil agreed to accept $130m. each in compensation for their share in the joint venture, Lavan Petroleum Company, nationalized after the Revolution. Two other US shareholders, Murphy and Union, settled in 1986. Payment was to be made from the special security account created by Iran at The Hague under the 1981 Algiers agreement. This compensation payment settled the last of the US oil company claims.

By mid-July 1990 prices had fallen as low as $14.40 per barrel, and both Iran and Iraq were demanding that a minimum reference price of $25 per barrel be fixed at the full OPEC meeting scheduled for the end of July. At the meeting, however, a minimum reference price of $21 per barrel was set, within a 22.5m. b/d ceiling. Nevertheless, the agreement apparently indicated a new political alliance between Iran, Iraq and Saudi Arabia, and its immediate effect was to raise prices.

Iraq's invasion and annexation of Kuwait in August 1990 gave rise to a further, dramatic rise in the price of crude petroleum. It also created serious divisions within OPEC. Iran criticized those member states, principally Saudi Arabia, which, in the aftermath of the Iraqi invasion, sought to raise OPEC production in order to compensate for the loss of Iraqi and Kuwaiti supplies, due to the economic sanctions imposed by the UN. At an emergency OPEC meeting convened in late August and attended by the oil ministers of all member states except Iraq and Libya, a draft agreement was signed which effectively allowed for a suspension of the production quotas agreed in July. Iran refused to support the agreement, however, and proposed that oil companies and industrialized countries release petroleum stocks in order to relieve pressure on prices, which had risen above $30 per barrel during August. However, it appeared likely in late August that production quotas would be ignored until a resolution of the Gulf conflict made it possible to convene an OPEC meeting in which all 13 members could participate.

In October 1990 the Iranian Ministry of Oil announced that, since August, output of crude oil had been averaging 3.2m. b/d, slightly above the OPEC quota of 3.14m. b/d. It was further reported that exports of crude oil to Japan had trebled and that exports to the Republic of Korea and the Philippines had also increased. Sales to Asian countries accounted for nearly 60% of total oil exports. For the first time, contracts in convertible currency were signed with several eastern European countries that had previously bought oil from Iran through clearing accounts linked to reciprocal purchases of goods. In addition, in late 1990 and early 1991 revenue from oil exports increased by between $700m. and $800m. per month, as a result of the rise in prices for oil (precipitated by the crisis in the Gulf region).

Sustainable output of crude oil from both onshore and offshore fields was estimated at 3.5m. b/d in mid-1991. Domestic consumption has risen rapidly, and in mid-1991 it was reported to exceed 1m. b/d. In January 1991 the Ministry of Oil announced a revision of long-term investment plans for the sector, including additional investment of $2,000m. over two years, aimed at increasing output from the southern fields on the mainland. Under the Five-Year Development Plan (introduced in January 1990), projected onshore output was set at 3.5m. b/d–3.7m. b/d, but was later revised to between 4.1m. b/d and 4.6m. b/d. The Ministry projected a combined onshore and offshore capacity of some 5m. b/d by the end of the Plan's term. However, some Western experts believed that such a significant increase in capacity was not technically feasible. NIOC has emphasized that its ambitious development plans can only be achieved through major inputs of technology, funding and personnel from abroad, and has stressed the scope it offers for joint ventures and foreign technical co-operation. In August 1992 the head of the Southern oil fields stated that the crude output expansion programme required the drilling of nearly 300 new wells. Most of the wells had been drilled during the previous 12 months and when the programme was completed there would be a total of 600 wells in 47 fields. He estimated onshore production capacity at 3.4m. b/d, compared with 2.4m. b/d at the end of the Iran–Iraq War, with a further 250,000 b/d in offshore capacity, to be raised to more than 500,000 b/d in 1993. Most of Iran's crude oil exports go through Kharg Island. Loading capacity was reduced to 2.5m. b/d as a result of Iraqi air attacks, but in August 1992 it was reported that capacity would be restored to 5m. b/d within two years. It was also reported that storage capacity at the terminal had been restored to nearly 50% of its pre-war level of 22m. barrels and further reconstruction would raise capacity to 16m. barrels. Reconstruction of the main oil export terminal at Kharg Island is being undertaken by French, Italian and South Korean companies.

Iran's production of crude petroleum in 1991 is reported to have averaged 3,238,000 b/d, with exports averaging 2.41m. b/d, of which 2.35m. b/d were from onshore fields and 65,000 b/d from offshore fields. Iran's production capacity was estimated to have increased from 3.5m. b/d in 1991 to almost 4m. b/d in 1992. On 20 January 1992 the Ministry of Oil announced that it was reducing petroleum production by 50,000 b/d in an attempt to increase the international price of crude petroleum. In March the Ministry stated that, as of 1 March, oil production had been reduced to 3.184m. b/d in line with new OPEC quota allocations. However, the Minister of Oil reaffirmed Iran's intention of expanding production capacity to 4.5m. b/d by March 1993—including an increase of 500,000 b/d in the course of 1992. Many observers doubt whether export capacity can be raised significantly above the level of 2.4m. b/d. To increase onshore capacity involves drilling new wells and injecting gas into depleting reservoirs, notably at the Gachsaran, Karanj, Pars, Marun and Ahwaz fields.

When NIOC began to negotiate prepaid sales in order to raise short-term finance, a ceiling of $2,000m. was placed on these sales, but in 1991 the Minister of Oil announced that this limit had been removed. This appeared to indicate a return to significant prepaid sales of crude petroleum which, in the past, have involved payment up to 18 months in advance of delivery. It has been argued that prepaid, or usance, sales are inefficient and that they can undermine future sales prospects; but for Iran they are more acceptable, ideologically, than raising direct foreign loans. Four Japanese trading houses arranged prepaid packages worth $600m. in 1991 and in November 1991 it was announced that a group of more than 25 banks, led by Banque Nationale de Paris and Crédit Lyonnais, had concluded a similar package involving several supply contracts between NIOC and international oil companies, worth $1,000m.

Early in 1992 repairs to the offshore Nasr platform were completed and initial production of 35,000 b/d was due to rise to 85,000 b/d after the installation of new pumps. The rebuilt Salman platform was due to commence production at an initial rate of 180,000 b/d in mid-1992. Offshore production was scheduled to rise to 500,000 b/d by early 1993, although some sources considered this projection to be over-optimistic. It was reported that in 1993, the Lavan Island facilities, with a capacity of 220,000 b/d, became fully operational and would export crude oil piped from the Salman offshore field. In October 1992 the head of the Iran Offshore Oil Company announced that agreements were being negotiated with several international oil companies for the development of a number of offshore fields, Balal, and Sirri E and A fields, and for new installations at the Abuzar field, which would together add about 300,000 b/d to national production. Bids were also to be invited for the exploration and development of the Hormuz reservoir at the mouth of the Gulf, following the withdrawal of the Japanese consortium, Japex. However, little progress was made, largely due to financial and political problems, but in early 1994 a number of international oil companies showed renewed interest in Iran's offshore fields in the Gulf. In March 1994 the Minister of Oil, Aqazadeh, confirmed that talks were being held with several US companies and that Conoco of Houston, USA, had submitted a proposal to develop the offshore Sirri E crude oil field.

According to Gholamreza Aqazadeh, the Minister of Oil, oil production was officially raised to 3.5m. b/d–3.6m. b/d from 23 September 1992 following divisions within OPEC over production policy. In mid-October oil production was temporarily raised to 4m. b/d to demonstrate Iran's improved capacity and to establish Iran's position as OPEC's biggest producer after Saudi Arabia, and to support its claims for a larger share of OPEC's market. The well-publicized increase in output, 3.6m. b/d from onshore fields and 400,000 b/d from offshore fields, was maintained for a week. Normal production in previous months had averaged about 3.5m. b/d with about 1m. b/d designated for domestic consumption. Officials stated that production capacity would be raised to 4.5m. b/d in March 1993—equivalent to about 50% of Saudi Arabia's capacity—though actual production would be in line with OPEC quotas.

Observers argued that export capacity would be limited to about 2.5m. b/d until work on the reconstruction of the Kharg Island terminal is completed in 1994. In December 1992 the Minister of Oil announced that crude oil production would average 3.5m. b/d from 1 December 1992 to 31 March 1993, representing a cutback of 400,000 b/d from the November level of 3.9m. b/d. Oil exports during the Iranian year beginning March 1993 were forecast at 2.7m. b/d, about 10% higher than in the previous year. In March 1993 the Minister of Oil announced that output had been cut to 3.34m. b/d on 1 March in line with OPEC's new quota, but explained that the reduction would be compensated for by higher prices. About 2.4m. b/d would be available for export. A Plan and Budget Organization report released in April 1993 revealed that oil exports during the first nine months of 1992/93 averaged 2.386m. b/d, 448,000 b/d less than the budget level and 265,000 b/d less than the Ministry of Oil's export timetable. Observers estimated oil revenues for the Iranian year ending 20 March 1993 at $14,500m., $2,000m. below the budget projection. At a conference in April 1993, Mehdi Hossaini, an adviser to the Minister of Oil, presented figures which cited maximum 1993 capacity as 4.2m. b/d, 300,000 b/d below the 4.5m. b/d target. He indicated that capacity would be raised to 4.6m. b/d in 1994, 5m. b/d in 1995, rising to above 5.5m. b/d in the year 2000. Some Western experts doubted that the 4.2m. b/d capacity could be sustained because of the poor condition of the Southern oil fields and argue that Iran could only achieve higher targets with the involvement of the international oil companies in field maintenance and secondary recovery programmes. The involvement of foreign companies in mainland fields has been limited because of legal and political constraints.

Following the OPEC meeting at Geneva in September 1993 the Minister of Oil, Aqazadeh, announced that from 1 October Iran's quota would be 3.6m. b/d, 240,000 b/d more than the previous level, allowing exports to rise to 2.6m. b/d. However, international traders stated that actual exports had averaged 2.7m. tons in 1993, with production estimated at some 200,000 b/d more than Iran's earlier OPEC quota of 3.34m. b/d. Aqazadeh reiterated previous claims that output was scheduled to rise to 4.6m. b/d in 1994, with a further rise to 5.5m.–6m. b/d by the year 2000. It is interesting to note that this was the level of production before the Revolution. He also stated that Iran planned to produce an average of 4.5m. b/d during the second Five-Year Plan due to begin in March 1994. Early in 1994 reports suggested that Iran was having difficulty producing crude to the level of its OPEC quota of 3.6m. b/d, but these were denied by the Minister of Oil. In January 1994 Mostafa Khoee, managing director of the Iranian Offshore Oil Company, stated that crude capacity was 4.2m. b/d; 3.8m. b/d on shore and 400,000 b/d off shore. He did not indicate whether these figures were sustainable. Actual output during 1993 averaged 3.6m. b/d. Defending his record as Minister of Oil before the Majlis in August 1993, Aqazadeh stated that during the first 52 months of the Five-Year Plan ending in March 1994, oil revenues totalled $61,720m., slightly higher than the Plan's target. He predicted that high sales would raise total annual revenues for 1993/94 to about $16,500m., about 10% below the target of $18,000m. By January 1994 these figures had been revised downwards because of low oil prices and ministry officials estimated that revenues would not exceed $12,000m. The budget for 1994/95 projected oil revenues at only $10,150m.

Early in 1994 the Minister of Oil, Aqazadeh, announced that 9,530m. barrels of oil, worth $45,000m. had been discovered during the term of the Five-Year Plan ending in March 1994. In January 1994 it was reported that production of 5,000 b/d had begun at the Qal-e Nar oilfield near Andimeshk and was scheduled to increase to 15,000 b/d. During the debate in the Majlis on the draft of the new Five-Year Plan to begin in 1994, the Minister of Oil, Aqazadeh, stated that oil revenues during the plan period were projected at $64,000m. This figure was $13,600m. lower than that given in mid-November 1993, when the Council of Ministers reviewed the draft plan. The projections, based on oil prices of between $14 and $16 a barrel over the plan period, were criticised in the Majlis as too optimistic. Aqazadeh also stated that domestic fuel subsidies would be reduced over the following five years because an increase in fuel prices was needed to help finance the ministry's development projects. However, in May 1994 it appeared that Rafsanjani, faced with opposition in the Majlis to his plans to cut subsidies, had been forced to compromise and to promise that the phasing out of energy subsidies would now take place over a much longer period. During the new Five-Year Plan the Ministry of Oil has declared that it hopes to invest $16,600m. of government funds and $9,000m. in foreign credits in the country's oil industry, together with an additional $3,800m. in government funds in gas, in order to increase production. However, officials admitted that the programme might be delayed because of low oil prices.

The loss of the Abadan refinery, destroyed in the early stages of the war with Iraq, with a production capacity which had reached 628,000 b/d, affected the already difficult situation in Iran for oil products. Iran has traditionally imported some refined products, such as kerosene in winter, and has had shortages in the middle distillates range (diesel oil, kerosene and heating oil). The loss of Abadan denied Iran the flexibility of changing product volumes to meet market or seasonal variations of demand. Abadan was a highly sophisticated and flexible refinery, capable of substantial product conversion. It was also one of the main sources of aviation fuel and gasoline. With the Abadan refinery destroyed, Iran's refining capacity stood at 555,000 b/d in 1980; this had risen to 574,000 b/d by mid-1985, produced at Isfahan (200,000 b/d), Teheran (254,000 b/d), Tabriz (80,000 b/d) and Shiraz (40,000 b/d). However, Iran succeeded in raising its refinery output to levels far above rated capacity. Refinery output was 642,000 b/d in 1983/84 and 685,310 b/d in 1984/85, and at the end of 1985 it was reported that the refineries were operating at 31% above design capacity, giving a total output of 728,000 b/d. The refineries at Isfahan (its capacity increased to 380,000 b/d by 1986) and Shiraz were said to be producing at 50% and 35% above their respective capacities. However, Iraqi air attacks were believed to have reduced capacity to about 500,000 b/d by 1988, resulting in the re-imposition of petrol rationing and the need to import some petroleum products. Further attacks in 1988 resulted in damage to the Isfahan, Shiraz and Tabriz refineries.

Following the cease-fire, the Government started to rebuild its oil facilities. The Abadan oil refinery is symbolic of this reconstruction, and the first phase was completed in April 1989, allowing production of 130,000 b/d. The second phase was completed in April 1991, bringing the plant's capacity to 250,000 b/d. In March 1991 President Rafsanjani announced that the refinery would eventually be restored to its pre-War capacity of 628,000 b/d. In March 1992 it was reported that the Plan and Budget Organization had been asked to approve a third phase of reconstruction at the refinery which would double its present capacity. In February 1994 the Ministry of Oil reported that the refinery's capacity was being expanded to 330,000 b/d. The reconstruction of the Abadan refinery brought the total output of domestic refineries to about 800,000 b/d. On 1 April 1993 President Rafsanjani stated that imports of petroleum products amounting to 300,000 b/d were a wasteful expenditure, costing up to $1,800m. a year. He predicted that the newly installed refinery capacity would allow the country to stop importing refined products by early 1994. The Minister of Oil told a press conference on 14 April 1993 that Iran's refining capacity would reach 1,285m. b/d in early 1994, and could be raised to 1.6m. b/d in emergencies. He stated that 1993 was the last year that refined products would have to be imported. In September 1989 it was announced that the reconstruction of the Tabriz and Isfahan oil refineries was complete and that they were supplying almost 50% of Iran's domestic oil requirements. Expansion work at the Teheran and Kermanshah refineries was also reported to have begun. Bids for a continuous catalytic reforming unit for the Teheran refinery commenced in April 1992. The construction of new refineries at Bandar Abbas, Bandar Taheri and Arak, and the expansion of the Isfahan refinery, were designated priority projects by the NIOC, but the programme has experienced considerable delays. The contract for the 150,000 b/d-Arak refinery was awarded to an Italian-Japanese consortium in May 1989. The $1,100m.-

refinery was inaugurated by President Rafsanjani in September 1993, and in April 1994 it was reported to be producing 165,000 b/d, 10% more than its nominal capacity. Construction of the 250,000 b/d export refinery at Bandar Abbas should have been completed in 1993, but financial problems delayed work on the project. In October 1993 it was reported that a group of four Japanese trading houses was negotiating a $250m.-financial package for the refinery so that the NIOC could go ahead and invite tenders. The NIOC is seeking funding on a buy-back basis, as required by the Majlis, and repayment is expected to be made through the supply of the refinery's products. In March 1994 the Director-General of the National Iranian Tanker Company announced that six 80,000-ton tankers would be purchased in order to supply the Bandar Abbas refinery, which would come on stream in 1996. The refinery planned for Bandar Taheri will now be sited at the port of Asaluyeh and will process 70,000 b/d of condensates from the nearby Nar-Kangan and Agar-Dalan gas fields. It was reported that international companies would be asked to submit tenders in June 1994. The $600m.–$700m. project is to be financed on a buy-back basis involving financing through the export of half of the refinery's output. With the increase in domestic refinery capacity, petrol rationing was ended in February 1991. Three years after the end of the war with Iraq NIOC's inability to meet growing domestic demand for petroleum products provoked strong criticism. Iran continues to experience fuel shortages during the winter months of most years because of insufficient refinery capacity and transportation problems. In January 1994 the Minister of Oil stated that there was a stockpile of some 1,700m. litres of fuel so that no serious shortages were envisaged that year. It was also reported that Iran expected to resume oil supplies to the Sasolburg refinery in South Africa, in which the NIOC has had a 17.5% share since 1970. Until 1979, when oil supplies were suspended, Iran was supplying 70% of the refinery's crude oil under a 20 year-agreement. The NIOC has retained its shareholding despite the suspension in oil supplies. Negotiations between Iran and South Africa began early in 1994 for South African refineries to resume purchases of Iranian crude after the multi-racial elections in April. Iran was South Africa's major supplier of crude until 1979. In April 1992 it was reported that NIOC might lose its monopoly status and that eight refineries were to be transformed into separate business units.

The country's internal pipeline network currently handles 1.2m. b/d of crude and oil products for domestic use. A 14-in pipeline is being constructed between the Teheran refinery and Tabriz and another line is to be built from the new Bandar Abbas refinery to cities such as Rafsanjan, Kerman and Yazd. In early 1988 the Government revived the Moharram pipeline project, which had been abandoned in mid-1986. However, only one of two planned 320-km export pipelines, running from the Gurreh pumping station on the mainland, just north of the main Kharg Island export terminal, to export facilities at Taheri, near the central Gulf, was to be built. The project was intended to provide a safer alternative to the Kharg terminal. The pipeline was expected to have a capacity of 600,000 b/d, just over one-third of Iran's total exports (1.7m. b/d), as stipulated by OPEC. Tank farms and single-buoy moorings off the coast, as terminals for tankers, are being built at Taheri. Plans have also been approved to extend the line a further 700 km to Jask, outside the Gulf, construction of which would take about two years. Formerly a major priority, work on the Moharran export scheme proceeded more slowly after the cease-fire. While there appear to be differences of opinion about the restructuring of the export pipeline system, plans to reorient the system to a terminal close to the Strait of Hormuz will depend on the availability of foreign exchange. Discussions on the proposed export pipeline through Turkey to the port of Dortyol on the Mediterranean, development of which had been postponed since 1986 for financial reasons, resumed in 1988, with the result that the pipeline was expected to be operative in 1992, two years later than originally planned. The construction of the 1,900-km pipeline, which has a capacity of 1m. b/d, was estimated to have cost $4,300m. Iran's share of the cost is $3,500m., for the construction of the pipeline from the outfields at Ahwaz to the Turkish border, a distance of 1,020 km.

NATURAL GAS

With proven reserves of 20,000,000m. cu m, Iran is the world's second richest country in gas resources after Russia, with 12.6% of the global total. According to a statement by the Minister of Oil in February 1994, 3,200,000m. barrels of gas, worth $200,000m., were discovered during the term of the Five-Year Plan ending in March 1994. In August 1988 it was announced that a large reservoir of natural gas had been discovered near Asaluyeh on the Gulf coast, 70 km south-east of Kangan. NIOC has announced a $1,000m. scheme to develop the Aghar Dalan fields, 120 km north-east of Kangan, and plans have been announced to construct a gas refinery there at a cost of $900m. Gas discoveries have also been made in the Caspian Sea area. The first phase of the $1,000m. Nar-Kangan gas treatment plant, 260 km east of Bushehr, began operating in June 1989. It will produce 34m. cu m per day, and the second phase, which began production in May 1990, was expected to increase output to 80m. cu m per day by exploiting the nearby Kangan field, whose reserves are estimated at 820,000m. cu m. Gas from the Nar-Kangan field will be piped north to Teheran via the IGAT-2 trunkline. Plans to quadruple gas-refining capacity, and to lay 3,000 km of gas pipeline by 1994, have been announced in order to reduce consumption of petroleum products and make more crude petroleum available for export. It is planned to raise gas-refining capacity from just over 10,000m. cu m in 1990 to 46,000m. cu m by 1994 and, eventually, to 80,000m. cu m.

The main gas pipeline projects concern the extension of the IGAT-2 trunkline from Nar-Kangan to Teheran and the west; the extension of the third trunkline from Khangiran to the west along the Caspian coast; and the laying of a pipeline from Sarkhun northwards to Rafsanjan.

In 1980 Iran suspended daily deliveries of some 30m. cu m of natural gas to the USSR, from the Nar and Kangan fields, via the IGAT-1 gas trunkline, which had been carrying natural gas from the southern oilfields to northern Iran and the USSR, a total distance of 1,130 km. In 1983 Iran's Ministry of Oil announced that it was no longer interested in gas export projects, in spite of the country's huge resources, and indicated that the gas industry would seek to satisfy the rapidly growing energy requirements of the industrial, commercial and residential markets within Iran. In August 1986 the Ministry announced that gas exports to the USSR would resume before the end of the year but, in November, the date for their resumption was postponed to mid-1987. Plans to convert IGAT-1 to carry 700,000 b/d of oil appear also to have been abandoned, and the pipeline is used to satisfy domestic demand only. Only the southern section of the 56-in diameter IGAT-2 natural gas pipeline, which was started before the Revolution, also to supply gas to the USSR, has been completed, and extends only as far as Isfahan. The 632-km pipeline from Kangan to Isfahan, costing $200m., was completed at the end of 1985 by the Italian contractors Saipem, who have also been involved in the construction of a $1,000m. gas-gathering complex at Kangan and the smaller neighbouring gasfield of Nar (with combined reserves of 720,000m. cu m), which will supply IGAT-2. In November 1989 an agreement was concluded to resume natural gas exports to the USSR, and the first supplies were piped in April 1990. Some 3,000m. cu m per year were to be supplied via the IGAT-1 trunkline, rising eventually to the pre-Revolution level of 10,000m. cu m. The agreement also permitted Iranian gas to be exported to eastern Europe via the Soviet pipeline system. Revenues from these exports, estimated at about $300m. annually, were to be used to pay for nine Soviet-assisted projects in the Iranian power, gas, mining and metallurgy sectors. In October 1990 a further agreement was reached with the USSR to export natural gas to eastern Europe, starting in 1991. Under the scheme, the capacity of IGAT-1 was to be increased and the possible completion of the IGAT-2 trunkline was also envisaged. In return for the supply of Iranian gas to the southern Soviet republics, the USSR was to deliver an equivalent quantity of gas to eastern European countries, using its own pipeline system. In October 1991 the Minister of Oil stated that exports of gas would be restricted to the USSR, which was purchasing some $200m.-worth annually; and that gas exports would not become a significant source of foreign currency until the second half of the 1990s. He announced that by 2000 Iran expected to be exporting some 50,000m. cu m of gas annually if pipeline projects currently envisaged were realized. More than half of the exports would be to Europe and the remainder to Pakistan. Exports of liquefied natural gas (LNG) have been resumed and reports suggest that some 400,000 tons were exported in 1991/92. Since the disintegration of the USSR, Iran has established economic agreements with the newly-independent former Soviet republics. In February 1992 the Iranian Minister of Oil announced details of an agreement, signed in January, to supply gas to the Ukraine via Azerbaijan. Some 3,000m. cu m of gas were to be supplied during 1992 through the existing IGAT-1 pipeline. Over the four years covered by the agreement gas exports are to total 75,000m. cu m. It is planned to construct three new gas pipelines by 1996. In February 1993 Iran and Ukraine agreed to build a gas pipeline from Iran to Ukraine through Azerbaijan and Russia, with a capacity of 25,000m. cu m a year. In March 1993 it was reported that the gas project had failed to gain formal consent from Russia. In November 1992 an agreement was signed with Azerbaijan for Iran to supply 300m. cu m of gas a year in exchange for 100,000 tons of gas-oil. Gas is to be supplied through the IGAT-1 trunkline. Gas-oil from Azerbaijan will supply Iran's northwestern provinces to make up for shortages in domestic distribution. In January 1994 officials of the Iranian Institute for Political and International Studies announced that they had proposed a major gas pipeline loop system around Iran from which spurs could be constructed to India, the Central Asian republics, Turkey and, eventually, Europe through Turkey. They had named it PEACE: 'Pipeline extending from Asian Countries to Europe'. More than half of the loop was already in existence. One of the officials commented that liquefied natural gas schemes were not economical while oil prices remained below $20 a barrel. In spite of the resumption of gas exports, the use of gas is still being encouraged for domestic purposes, in order to save oil and to reduce pollution. More than 13,000 km of gas distribution lines have been built in cities since 1979, but implementation of the residential gas programme has been delayed by a shortage of regulators. The Five-Year Plan scheduled to begin in 1994 proposes greater domestic use of gas resources in order to allow more oil to be exported. According to the draft of the new plan, daily domestic gas consumption is projected to rise from 115m. cu m in 1994 to 192m. cu m in 1999. The draft plan states that about one third of Iranian households now use piped gas and that 200 towns and cities will be connected to the network by March 1994. Natural gas also fuels half of the country's power stations. The draft plan makes provision for the investment of $3,800m. in government funds in the gas sector over the next five years.

In October 1990 NIOC announced a joint study with Gaz de France to assess the cost of transporting natural gas to France and other European countries. In April 1993 it was reported that Ruhrgas of Germany, Austria's ONV and Enagas of Spain would take part in the consortium with Gaz de France. If the plans go ahead central and eastern European countries could be supplied first by pipeline, but for western Europe it is unclear at this stage whether transport by pipeline or ship would be preferred. In November 1993 Iran and India signed a memorandum of understanding regarding a gas pipeline from Bandar Abbas to the Indian state of Gujerat. The construction of the 1,100 km. pipeline, with a capacity of 50m. cu m of gas per day, has been estimated at $4,000m.–$5,000m. In June 1994 it was reported that technical details for the project would be finalized in July and that a feasibility study would be completed by November. Iran has also shown interest in joining Crescent Petroleum Company International's Qatar-to-Pakistan pipeline project. This $3,500m.-project requires a 1,600 km, 48-in pipeline from Qatar along the Iranian coast to Pakistan. Under the Five-Year Development Plan (introduced in January 1990), some $3,400m. in foreign funding were to be allocated to the development of the Pars and South Pars fields for export to Japan or Europe. In 1992 the NIOC awarded the $17,000m.-contract to develop the gas reserves of the offshore South Pars field to a consortium led by TPL of Italy and including Saipam of Italy, Machinoimport of Russia and Mitsubishi Corpn of Japan. This was the largest offshore gas project awarded since the Revolution. The South Pars field is an extension into Iranian waters of Qatar's North field, the largest gas field in the world. Production of up to 35m. cu m of gas a day for domestic consumption and up to 60,000 b/d of condensate for export was planned to commence in 1996. By the end of 1993, when the consortium had completed nearly all the basic engineering and had drilled two wells in the field, the NIOC announced that it was suspending the project because of cash shortages. Payment arrears on Iran's external debt appear to have made foreign banks reluctant to finance the project, which may not be revived for some time. In April 1993 preliminary discussions began between the National Iranian Gas Company and a number of foreign companies on the development of the offshore Pars field, often referred to as North Pars, as distinct from South Pars. Plans to develop the field, based on exports of liquefied natural gas, were first discussed in the 1970s, but were abandoned after the Revolution. Under the revised scheme gas would be treated for domestic use only. In January 1994 it was reported that negotiations were under way with Royal Dutch Shell for an agreement on engineering studies for the North Pars field. Shell appeared to be insisting on equity participation in the project, but foreign ownership of national hydrocarbon resources is not permitted under the Iranian constitution. However, in March it was reported that the Majlis had authorized the NIOC to raise up to $3,500m. in foreign finance on a buy-back basis in order to develop oil and gas fields together with two refineries. There was speculation that this decision might lead to a compromise with Shell over financing arrangements for the North Pars field. In early 1994 the Minister of Oil announced the discovery of a new offshore gas field 50 km west of the South Pars field and 180 km south-east of Bushehr, estimated to contain 566,000m. cu m of gas and 1,000m. barrels of condensate.

OTHER MINERALS

According to the Minister of Mines and Metals, in June 1988 there were 780 producing mines in Iran, employing 73,500 people. Some 870 exploration permits were awarded during 1990/91. Deposits of lead-zinc ore are mined at Bafq near Yazd, at Khomeini, west of Isfahan, and at Ravanj near Qom, with a combined potential of 600 tons of concentrates daily, though current plans for development are limited to Bafq. In June 1992 a German/Canadian consortium won a $250m.-contract to build a zinc plant at Zanjan with an annual capacity of 60,000 tons. Construction was due to be completed within three and a half years after financial credits had been finalized. Another zinc plant is to be built at Bafq, with an annual output capacity rising to 24,000 tons. Iran's largest lead mine is at Nakhlak, near Isfahan. Chromium from the Elburz mountains and near Bandar Abbas, red oxide from Hormuz in the Persian Gulf and turquoise from Nishapur are all produced for export. Sulphur and salt are produced on the coast of the Gulf, near Bandar Abbas, and Iran exported 105,000 tons in the year 1985/86 (21 March–20 March). Iran is also the second largest exporter of strontium, after Mexico, and during the second half of 1985/86 and the first half of 1986/87 exported 25,000 tons, valued at $2.9m. Strontium reserves are estimated at 1.1m. tons. In 1986 Iran's phosphate resources were calculated at 220m. tons. Annual imports of phosphate fertilizers total 1m. tons, worth $300m., so a major portion of domestic demand would be met by developing the country's phosphate reserves. In July 1992 it was announced that the country's largest phosphate deposit, with reserves of 400m. tons, had been discovered in Charam in the southern province of Yasuj.

The major iron ore deposits are in Kerman province in southeast Iran, in particular at Bafq, where proven reserves total 911m. tons of ore, and at Chadormelo mine, in Yazd province, which has proven reserves of 500m. tons. In February 1992 it was reported that Bafq was producing 4m. tons a year. In December 1991 a Japanese consortium signed a contract to build an ore concentrator at Chadormelo, with a projected annual production rate of 5m. tons. The concentrator will supply the Mobarakeh steel complex. In late 1991 the Ministry

of Mines and Metals invited bids to expand the existing Chogart iron ore complex near Yazd at an estimated cost of $200m. The ore from Bafq will be carried 540 km by a specially developed railway to the $4,700m. Mobarakeh steel plant at Isfahan. In July 1986 the Government claimed that the mine at Sangan, in Khorassan Province, with reserves of 127m. tons, would supply Isfahan with iron ore for the next 200 years. The Gol-e-Gohar iron ore mining complex in Kerman province, originally planned before the Revolution, was officially opened in March 1994 by President Rafsanjani. Production at the $114m. complex began in December 1993. Output of 2.5m. tons of concentrate will be used to supply the Mobarakeh steel plant at Isfahan. Production will eventually be expanded to 5m. tons per year.

Coal reserves are estimated at 6,000m. tons, of which about one-third are capable of exploitation. The main mines are around Kerman and in Mazandaran, Semnan and Tabas, where output is to be expanded. An 85-km railway is being built from Kerman, the major mining area, to supply coal shale to the Zarand refinery. At the Shahroud mines in Semnan output of 232,000 tons per year was to be increased to a projected 360,000 tons per year by 1989. The mines supply 15% of the requirements of the Isfahan steel mill. In 1987/88 Iran produced 95,706 tons of melted cast iron and 1,471,699 tons of steel. Coal production in 1985 recovered to the pre-revolutionary level of 900,000 tons per year, but remains insufficient for domestic consumption, and imports of around 400,000 tons per year are required. Production declined to 722,000 tons in 1986, and was 791,000 tons in 1987.

Deposits of copper ore have been found in Azerbaijan, Kerman and in the Yazd and Anarak areas. A number of very important deposits have been discovered since 1967 in the Kerman area, the most important being at Sar Cheshmeh. However, of the 330 copper mines in Iran, with combined reserves of an estimated 1,600m. tons, only those at Sar Cheshmeh and Birjand are currently being exploited. The reserves at Sar Cheshmeh are estimated at 1,200m. tons (the second largest deposit in the world), including perhaps 600m. tons of 1.12% copper content, with another 600m. tons of lower grade beneath. The giant project includes the construction of road and rail links to connect the mine with Bandar Abbas 400 km away on the Gulf, a training school, and a new town for the families of the 3,000 men who will work the mine. The construction of a large smelter/refinery and associated rolling mill and two continuous casting mills was halted during the Revolution. The mine was officially opened in May 1982. Initially the plant operated at substantially below its capacity of 158,000 tons of refined copper per year but, since production began in mid-1984, output has risen to 40,000 tons in 1985/86, and to 50,000 tons in 1986/87. Following the opening of new units in February 1989, output rose to 100,000 tons a year by mid-1992. The mine is expected to reach full capacity by 1996. Techpro Mining and Metallurgy of the United Kingdom have been appointed general consultants by the National Iranian Copper Industries Company to advise on expanding production at Sar Cheshmeh. Production is projected to increase, eventually, to 200,000 tons a year. A molybdenum production unit started operating at the Sar Cheshmeh copper refinery in June 1983. A copper extrusion plant was installed at the Shahid Bahonar copper complex, in Kerman, in 1987. Output of copper and copper alloy semi-finished products—tube, sheet, bar and rods from the plant, which opened in 1989, has risen from less than 10,000 tons a year to 18,000 tons a year. The plant expects to reach full capacity of 55,000 tons in 1996. One-third of the output is exported, mainly to Japan and other countries in the Far East, earning some $10m. a year. There are plans to export half of the plant's production in the future. In 1986/87 28,000 tons of copper and molybdenum from Sar Cheshmeh were exported in the form of copper wire and molybdenite, and a further 6,000 tons of blister copper. A much smaller copper mine at Minakhan, developed in association with Japanese interests, has been brought under complete Iranian ownership.

In March 1976 it was announced that important uranium deposits had been found in Iran's northern and western regions, and in 1978 agreements were signed with Federal German and French companies to carry out surveys. The scope and pace of exploration were reduced after the Revolution, but deposits of more than 5,000 tons of uranium ore were discovered in the Saghand region of Yazd in central Iran in 1984 and there were plans to develop the site. Long-term plans, proposed during the reign of the Shah, for a network of 20 nuclear power stations were abandoned because the project was too expensive, too dependent on Western technology and unnecessary in view of the availability of cheap natural gas.

In mid-1988 construction work began on a gold-processing plant at Muteh, near Isfahan. The plant, Iran's second, was scheduled to start producing in 1991, using ore from an estimated 1.2m.-ton deposit, which, it is hoped, will yield 5 tons of gold.

Two rich mineral deposits were discovered in the northern provinces of Gilan and Mazandaran in the first half of 1985: one consisted of an estimated 51,000 tons of mica and the other of 20m. tons of silica. Further discoveries of reserves of silica, limestone, granite and iron, totalling an estimated 194m. tons, were made in Gilan during the last quarter of 1985. Proven reserves of bauxite at Jafarm are estimated at 22m. tons, with an average purity of 48%, and annual production of 280,000 tons of alumina is planned to commence in 1994. A $300m. contract has been signed with Technoexport of Czechoslovakia.

Iran's exports of non-hydrocarbon minerals in 1985/86, mainly copper, coal, chromite and metal concentrates, were valued at $70m., and the total was increased to $85m. in 1986/87, when, of the 50m. tons of minerals extracted, 230,000 tons were exported. Mineral exports reached 486,413 tons in 1987/88, worth $90.2m., although total mineral extraction from Iran's 780 active mines declined to 45m. tons. During the five years to March 1993 it was planned to spend some $5,000m. in order to increase the mining sector's share of GDP from 1% to 5%. This represented the fulfilment of one of the Iranian Government's stated aims: the development of the country's non-hydrocarbon raw materials to supply the demands of the country's expanding metal manufacturing facilities. In April 1994 Hossein Mahloodji, the Minister of Mines and Metals, announced that exports of metal concentrates and minerals had earned $1,400m. during the three years to March 1994.

INDUSTRY

After the Revolution, no clear policy was formulated for the industrial sector. Of the modern manufacturing plants that were established under the Shah's regime, those which remained in production (estimated at only 20% of the total by value of output) have encountered serious difficulties. Raw materials have been in short supply, as have spare parts and other inputs. In March 1981 the then President, Bani-Sadr, estimated that in the period March 1979–March 1980 industrial and related output declined by 34% and was still falling, possibly at an even faster rate. In 1982 some reports indicated that increased reserves of foreign exchange and larger imports of raw materials had allowed production in many factories to be expanded. They also noted that factories producing goods for the war effort were working overtime, with Iranian engineers and technicians learning to repair, adapt and make items that had formerly been imported. Nevertheless, officials admitted that only a small number of factories were properly operational. Many factories were operating at only 30% capacity in the late 1980s, although considerable improvement has been reported in state-owned industrial producers since 1990.

Official thinking about the future of this sector appears confused. The stated policies of the revolutionary Government favour small-scale, traditional or bazaar-related enterprises. It is estimated that private industry is responsible for 20%–30% of Iran's industrial output. Yet, in sharp contrast, financial allocations to industry have tended to follow the pattern which was formulated by the previous regime. In late 1982 Khomeini lectured ministers and post-revolutionary technocrats on their preoccupation with modern industry.

Reports on industrial production have provided confusing conclusions. The National Iranian Industries Organization (NIIO) claimed that output rose by 23% during 1983/84. Other sources indicate that 1985/86 was a poor year for industry.

Investment declined in most sectors because of limited access to credits and to imported raw materials and capital goods. In May 1985 the Majlis approved legislation granting permanent status to the Ministry of Heavy Industry. The Ministry was to take over all aspects of heavy industry (formerly the responsibility of the Ministry of Industry), including iron and steel, foundry, engine, motor vehicle, machine-building and general engine plants. In April 1994 the Majlis approved legislation to merge the ministries of industry, heavy industries and mines and metals as part of an effort to reduce bureaucracy.

Since the end of the war with Iraq the 1989–94 Five-Year Plan has placed emphasis on the development of heavy industry and this sector has been given priority access to reserves of foreign exchange. In spite of debate about the privatization of Iranian industry, until 1991 almost all industrial projects were state-sponsored. However, in February 1991 the Minister of Economic Affairs and Finance announced that 400 state-controlled light industrial companies would be sold during the next three years as part of the Government's plans for privatization. It was also announced that heavy industry, previously monopolized by the state, would be opened to private investment. In May 1991 the Minister of Industries announced that the NIIO was to offer shares to the value of IR100,000m. in its companies for acquisition by the public during 1991–92. In April the Ministry of Oil invited the private sector to invest in petrochemical projects and gave an assurance that other sectors of the oil industry would be made accessible to private investors. In addition, foreign companies are now able to invest in heavy industries. On 5 May 1992 the Supreme Council for Investment approved new regulations which removed the 49% share ceiling held by foreign partners in joint ventures, removed nearly all restrictions on the repatriation of profits and provided guarantees against nationalization. There was speculation that the Government would face criticism—on purely political grounds—for opening the door to foreign capital even though the Constitution does not forbid foreign investment or ownership. In July 1992 it was reported that the International Finance Corporation (IFC) was entering the private-sector market in Iran with possible equity participation or finance for two large industrial projects. The IFC's involvement followed the return to Iran of the World Bank. Privatization of state industries appears to have made only slow progress. In March 1994 Massoud Roghani Zanjani of the Plan and Budget Organization stated that privatization through the Teheran stock exchange had not proved satisfactory. The Government planned to sell factories by auction or negotiation in order to speed up the privatization process. In August 1993 shares were offered on the Teheran stock exchange in Iran Khodrow, the country's largest car assembly plant. The plant was nationalized after the Revolution. Some 33% of the shares have been reserved for workers, with employees at the plant offered preferential terms. Despite legal changes introduced in the 1990s allowing foreign shareholdings, only a few joint ventures with foreign investors have been agreed. One example is a joint venture between Elin Anwendung of Austria and the local company, Joyain, who propose to build a $63m.-plant at Sabezevar to make electromotors and generators. Financial arrangements were expected to be completed in 1994. Another is the joint venture between the Ministry of Mines and Metals and the International Development Corpn of Dubai to build a $1,400m.–aluminium smelter at Bandar Abbas. Despite difficulties arranging the necessary finance, it was reported in early 1994 that the plant should be in production in late 1995, a year behind schedule.

Steel, petrochemicals and copper remain the country's three basic industries. Other important branches are automobile manufacture (many assembled from kits, under licence from Western and Japanese manufactures, such as Nissan), which has expanded rapidly in recent years, machine tools, construction materials, pharmaceuticals, textiles and food processing. With the exception of one major petrochemical plant and a number of textile and construction materials ventures, all these industries were nationalized after the Revolution. Annual cement production doubled between 1976 and 1986, reaching 13m. tons in the latter year. Output declined to

12.5m. tons in 1988. In early 1989 a $40m. foreign exchange allocation was announced to equip a cement works. Two plants have been built in Kurdistan and Hormuzgan, and a 2,300 tons-per-day plant at Orumiyah commenced operations in 1989. In 1990 the Ministry of Industries announced plans to increase the total national output of cement to 33m. tons per year by the late 1990s. Some 27 new cement works were to be built, at a cost of $800m., in the five years to 1995. In 1990 the annual capacity of the existing 15 cement plants was 17m. tons, but only 12m. tons per year was being produced, owing to shortages of foreign exchange and electricity. Production in the Iranian year ending 20 March 1993 was estimated at 16m. tons and annual domestic demand at 20m. tons. In November 1992 the Ministry of Industries stated that 19 cement plants, costing $555m., were under construction and another 31 'in-principle' agreements had been signed. During 1993 the International Finance Corpn was involved in negotiations concerning investment in or lending to at least four cement schemes and was negotiating with several European equipment suppliers as potential investors.

Electricity generation was severely restricted by Iraqi attacks on power stations during the Iran–Iraq War, reducing viable capacity from 8,000 MW to 5,000 MW, according to one estimate. In December 1988 the Minister of Energy stated that the generating capacity of the national grid was deficient by 2,500 MW, owing to war damage, lack of fuel and inadequate rainfall. Parts of Teheran and other cities have experienced interruptions to the power supply lasting around six hours per day. It is reported that electricity demand increased from 2,876 MW to 7,850 MW between 1979 and 1989. The Government plans to increase generation by 1,000 MW annually during the period 1989–94, and has allocated $7,500m. to this end. In 1989 $1,200m. in foreign exchange was set aside for the reactivation of dormant contracts and for the completion of repairs to damaged power stations. Installed capacity was reported to be 14,630 MW in 1990. In September 1992 the head of the state power generation and transmission company, Tavanir, stated that the national grid needed to be expanded by more than 1,000 MW a year for the foreseeable future in order to meet increasing demand, particularly at peak times in winter and summer when there are frequent power cuts. It is forecast that consumption will have reached 109,000m. kWh in 1998. Residential consumption currently accounts for about 40% of total consumption and industry for about one-quarter. However, industrial demand is forecast to rise dramatically and to account for almost one-half of total consumption by 1998. During the term of the Five-Year Plan beginning in March 1994 all new power plants will supply the growing demands of the industrial sector. Two-thirds of total capacity in 1998 will be provided by steam power and about one-fifth by hydroelectricity. By 1998 it is planned to build more than 20,000 km of transmission lines to supply electricity to 5m. new customers and 16,000 new villages. Only one-half of Iran's villages currently have electricity, but supplies are expected to reach more than two-thirds by 1998. In June 1991 Kraftwerk Union AG of Germany was awarded a $1,450m. contract to construct a 2,080 MW-combined-cycle plant south of Teheran, the largest single power contract to be awarded since the Revolution. The company had earlier won a $700m. contract to construct a smaller plant in Guilan. In January 1992 a Canadian-European consortium won a $770m. contract to build a 1,100-MW gas/oil/fired-power station at Arak, to be completed in 1996. Work was due to start in late 1992, but more than a year after the contract was awarded implementation of the project was still delayed because of financing problems. In early 1992 it was also reported that repairs to the country's biggest power plant at Neka on the Caspian Sea, damaged during the war with Iraq, had been completed. In November 1992 it was reported that Bharat Heavy Electricals of India had been selected to build a 1,000-MW thermal power station in Kerman. Some of the major hydroelectric power schemes require large amounts of foreign exchange and it is unclear whether the development programme will remain on schedule. The programme may also be affected by the disintegration of the USSR which formerly participated in several major dam projects. In May 1992 a consortium led by Asea Brown Boveri was awarded a $1,250m.-contract to build a

2,000-MW hydroelectric dam on the Karun river, designated as Karun-3, but the financing arrangements were still to be completed. In March 1994 it was reported that Japan's Overseas Economic Co-operation Fund had advanced a concessionary loan of $350m. to partly finance the Godar-e Bandar hydroelectric dam on the Karun river, 160 km north of Ahwaz, in Khuzistan, previously known as Karun 4. The dam, which is to be operational by 2001, will have a capacity of 1,000 MW and a further 1,000 MW will be added in the second phase. Preconstruction work started in 1992 and the contract for the main construction work was expected to be awarded towards the end of 1994. In March 1993 the World Bank approved a loan of $165m. for converting the Qom power-station to combined cycle. The conversion will double the plant's capacity to 600 MW. In April 1994 the contract for the conversion work was awarded to ABB, Asea Brown Boveri. The World Bank loan also covers the cost of constructing 400-kV substations and transmission lines to strengthen the country's north–south connection. In September 1992 it was announced that the Government plans to extend the privatization programme to electricity generation plants. Most power stations will be run as independent companies, and 51% of shares in power plants are to be transferred to the staff.

In May 1987 Iran and Argentina signed a nuclear power co-operation agreement, the details of which were not disclosed, but were thought to include an Argentine letter of intent to supply a $5.5m. reactor core and enriched uranium for a nuclear research centre to be established in Teheran University. Kraftwerk Union AG of the Federal Republic of Germany (FRG) began building a 2,400-MW twin reactor nuclear plant at Bushehr before the Revolution; most of the work on the plant had been completed by the time of the outbreak of the Iran–Iraq War. After several Iraqi air attacks on the plant, however, the company withdrew its staff in 1987. The FRG Government refused to issue export licences for machinery and equipment until a peace agreement had been signed between Iran and Iraq. More than $3,700m. have already been spent on the plant. Iran wishes to complete at least one of the 1,200-MW reactors and has estimated the cost of this at about $1,000m. Independent sources, however, have argued that the true cost is more likely to be $3,000m. and have advised against proceeding. The Ministry of Energy does not have responsibility for the Bushehr nuclear facility, and a decision to complete what could be one of Iran's largest power plants could divert scarce financial resources from other parts of the country's ambitious energy programme. Iran is believed to have received technical advice and training for its atomic engineers from Pakistan. In November 1989 the head of the Atomic Energy Organization of Iran announced that work on the Bushehr nuclear power plant had recommenced, and it is thought that vital equipment, placed in storage during the Iran–Iraq War, has been reinstalled. In January 1992 it was reported that Brazil had offered to resell to Iran equipment purchased from West Germany for the construction of its third nuclear plant, which had been delayed as a result of financial problems. Such equipment could be used in the construction of the Bushehr plant. On 15 February 1993, during a tour of the facility, President Rafsanjani stated that the Bushehr plant would be completed, whatever the cost. In August 1992 the Atomic Energy Organization of Iran (AEOI) announced that it had filed international suits against Siemens of Germany (Kraftwerk Union AG's parent company), for breaking the contract to complete the Bushehr reactor. Kraftwerk Union maintained that it was unable to do so because of a German Government-ban on the export of sensitive equipment. For some years negotiations with Indian, Russian and other suppliers ended in failure because of opposition from the USA which suspects that Iran is trying to develop a nuclear weapon. However, in December 1993 the Russian ambassador in Teheran stated that Russia had agreed in principle, to complete the Bushehr plant and to build a conventional power plant at Bushehr. A spokesman for Siemens stated that the main building at Bushehr would not be suitable for a Russian-designed reactor and there was speculation that Iran may be planning to use some of the facilities at Bushehr to reduce the cost of the Russian reactor. In 1993 Iran signed an agreement with China for at least one 300-MW nuclear reactor and despite pressure from the USA China has indicated that it plans to proceed with the agreement. Teams from the International Atomic Energy Agency (IAEA) visited nuclear sites in Iran in February 1992 and November 1993 and reported that they had found no evidence that Iran was developing nuclear weapons. A 5-kV solar power plant, built by the Atomic Energy Organization, opened in Ardakan, near Teheran, in November 1993. It was reported in October 1993 that new funds would be allocated to research into solar energy during the Five-Year Plan due to begin in 1994. In May 1994 President Rafsanjani stated that there should be greater investment in new sources of energy in order to reduce dependence on oil. Iran's first wind-powered electricity plant is being constructed at Manjil in the north-west of the country.

Steel

The Government's target, like that of the Shah, is to achieve self-sufficiency in steel production and to end dependence on imports. In 1980 steel accounted for almost one-sixth of total imports. Consumption was estimated at 6m. metric tons per year in mid-1981 and was expected to rise to 10m. tons by 1983. Domestic production and development plans were severely affected by the Revolution and the war with Iraq. By early 1983, output had been raised to 58,000 tons per month, equivalent to about 700,000 tons per year, produced by an old-fashioned coal-fired steel mill which was built by the USSR in Isfahan (formerly known as the Aryamehr Steel Mill), where installed capacity before the Revolution was claimed to be 1.1m. tons per year. Built under a $286m. credit arrangement which had been concluded with the USSR in 1965, the mill came into operation in March 1973. Subsequently, however, the mill has been beset by technical and production problems. For some time output has been running at about 50% of its design capacity of 1.9m. tons a year. Agreements with the former USSR to expand the obsolete facility appear to have been abandoned and in January 1992 Danieli of Italy won a $600m. contract to expand steel-making and rolling capacity at the plant. In October 1992 it was reported that Japan's Nippon Steel Company had won a contract to overhaul and expand three converters at the plant and was preparing bids for further work as part of the National Iranian Steel Company's plan to increase capacity to 5.5m. tons by 1998. Hylsa of Mexico has a similar contract at Iran's second largest production facility, the Ahwaz steel plant, to expand the unit's capacity to 1.1m. tons a year and, eventually, to 1.7m. tons a year. The National Iranian Steel Company reported that the plant produced 805,000 tons of steel in the Iranian year ending 20 March 1993, an increase of 54% over the previous year. In December 1993 it was reported that production at the plant had improved and that it was now producing quality steel for export. In September 1991 President Rafsanjani opened the first stage of the Mobarakeh steel mill. When all five furnaces at the plant are completed it will have an annual production capacity of 2.4m. tons. In June 1989 the construction of a $192m. steel-rolling complex at Miyaneh, in East Azerbaijan, was announced. In February 1992 a Japanese-Italian consortium won a $550m. contract to build a steel plant near Yazd. Owing to financing and technical problems, work was not scheduled to start until October 1993. The plant was due to open in 1995, with an initial capacity of 140,000 tons a year of engineering and special steels, to be expanded within three years to 260,000 tons a year. In March 1993 it was announced that Italy's Simimpianti had won a $112m.-contract to supply equipment, supervision, expertise and training for a specialized steel mill near Mashad which will have an annual capacity of 250,000 tons. As in the past, it seems likely that these plans will proceed slowly and much below scheduled capacities. Between 1981 and 1986 Iranian steel production officially totalled 5.3m. tons, of which 1.2m. tons were produced in 1986. According to the Ministry of Mines and Metals, Iran's steel production in the year ending March 1989 totalled 1.4m. tons and rose to 3.8m. tons in 1992–93. Output for 1993–94 was projected at 4.5m. tons and the Minister of Mines and Metals stated in August 1993 that a target of 12m. tons had been set for 1999. The Ministry of Mines and Metals had earlier forecast an expansion in output to 5.5m. tons a year by March 1994 when the first Five-Year Plan ended. Actual

output was well below target even according to the Ministry's own figures. Somewhat lower output figures have been given by the National Steel Company and the target figures for 1999 appear wildly optimistic. In October 1992 it was reported that the International Institute of Iron and Steel had accepted Iran as a full member, as its raw steel production exceeded 2m. tons a year. For many years Iran has been a major purchaser of steel on the world market, and imports, principally from Spain and Japan, have averaged 2m.–5m. tons a year. Domestic consumption of steel was estimated at 3.5m. tons a year in early 1989 and was projected to rise to 7m. tons annually as post-war reconstruction got under way. In January 1994 the Ministry of Mines and Metals announced that 1.35m. tons of steel had been exported during the first nine months of the Iranian year beginning March 1993. Even though Iran is now exporting steel, it seems unlikely that imports have ceased, given the level of domestic consumption and failure to meet output targets. As part of its plan to increase production, Japan's Nippon Steel Company was awarded a $1.8m.-contract in May 1993 to improve the management of the Company.

Petrochemicals

The Shah had planned a huge petrochemical sector that would not only meet local demand, but also provide $2,000m. worth of exports by 1983. Development of the industry was paralysed after the Revolution. However, in 1983 the Ministry of Oil announced that it would place greater emphasis on further development and expansion of the petrochemicals industry. Several new plants are to be built during the forthcoming Five-Year Plans, aimed at making Iran not only self-sufficient but also an exporter of surplus nitrogenous fertilizer, plastics and other products; indeed, Iran intends to become a leading world producer of petrochemicals during the 1990s. At present the sector comprises the following major ventures: the Iran Fertilizer Company, the Razi Chemical Company (formerly Shahpour), the Abadan Petrochemical Company, the Kharg Chemical Company, Iran Carbon Company, the Iran Nippon Chemical Company, Aliaf Company and Polyacryl Corporation. All these companies were nationalized in 1979 and are administered by the National Petrochemical Company (NPC) under the Ministry of Oil.

Under the Shah the cornerstone of the petrochemical industry, was the Iran-Japan petrochemical complex at Bandar Khomeini, which had a planned capacity of 300,000 tons per year of olefins and aromatics. This began in 1973 as a joint venture shared equally between NIOC and a Mitsui-led consortium, the Iran Chemical Development Company (ICDC). It was originally projected to cost $300m., but this estimate had increased to $3,000m. by 1979. The immense 13-unit complex was 85% finished at the time of the Revolution. Work was resumed briefly in the summer of 1980, but was halted again after Iraqi bombers attacked the plant several times in late September and early October. Disputes between NPC and its Japanese partners have been numerous. In mid-1984 Iran stopped a $10.8m. interest payment on a loan because the Japanese consortium, concerned with safety in the war zone, had withdrawn its technicians from the site. After renewed Iraqi bombings in September 1984, ICDC again withdrew all its technicians. In February 1986 Iran decided to end all repayments on credits and loans received from Japan. In the late 1980s Mitsui estimated that it would cost at least $2,000m. to complete the scheme, taking into account extensive war damage and the fact that some of the original units were obsolete. Iran disputed these estimates. The Japanese consortium expressed its desire to withdraw from the scheme, but Iran stated that it wished to complete the project and claimed that the Japanese estimates were pessimistic and that the cost would be about $1,000m. In November 1989, after prolonged negotiations, the Japanese consortium agreed to dissolve the $4,500m. partnership for the complex, and in February 1990, as part of the agreement, it paid the Iranian Government $910m. Dutch and German companies are helping the NPC to reconstruct some of the complex's 13 units. In November 1990 the Daelim Industrial Company, a South Korean venture, secured a $150m. contract to reconstruct the olefins plant. In April 1994 the head of the National Petrochemical Company stated that test production would start that month on the second phase of the complex which would treble annual production capacity to 3m. tons. Three-quarters of the plant's output had been sold in advance to German, French and Finnish companies to help finance its construction. The complex is the country's biggest petrochemical plant.

The expanded Shiraz petrochemical complex, located next to a smaller 20-year-old unit at Marvdasht, 50 km from the city, was opened in February 1986. The plant's daily output has been increased nearly 10-fold to produce 1,200 tons of ammonia, 1,500 tons of urea, 100 tons of nitric acid and 750 tons of ammonium nitrate. The initial capacity of the Shiraz plant was 500,000 tons per year, rising to 850,000 tons in 1987. A chloro-alkali unit with a capacity of 60,000 tons per year was completed in February 1989 at Shiraz, and the Shiraz methanol plant commenced production in May 1990. Contracts worth $33m. have been awarded to expand a dense soda ash plant and the ammonia plant. In September 1993 NPC officials reported that the Razi fertilizer complex near Bandar Khomeini was operating at only three-quarters of its planned capacity of 2m. tons a year. As part of the NPC's ambitious petrochemicals expansion programme a $2,200m. complex has been constructed at Arak using feedstocks from the Isfahan refinery and the new Arak refinery. The first phase of the complex was opened in July 1993 and planned output is 550,000 tons of products a year. Another project was the petrochemicals complex at Isfahan to produce benzene and toluene as well as polyethylene, polystyrene and polyols. In April 1994 it was reported that the Ministry of Heavy Industry had taken over responsibility for a $1,900m.-olefins petrochemical complex at Isfahan from the NPC. The project will be financed by a buy-back arrangement. In October 1993 it was reported that the benzene plant would start production in March 1994 with an annual capacity of 50,000 tons. Japan's Kawasaki Corpn and MW Kellog Company of the USA are building a petrochemical complex in Khorassan in the northeast of the country. Work on the plant, which will produce 330,000-tons a year of ammonia and 495,000-tons a year of urea, began in 1988 and production is scheduled to start in 1995. A $1,000m.-petrochemical complex is also being built at Tabriz, near to the Tabriz refinery. A $80m.-private sector petrochemical plant is also to be built at Tabriz, producing 50,000 tons of polypropylene, half of which will be exported. In October 1993 two German companies, Lurgi and BASF, were awarded the contract to set up and equip the plant for Polynar, a subsidiary of Narhan, a private consulting firm involved in local petrochemical and oil industries. The financial package should be concluded in 1994 and construction is due to be completed in three years. Polynar was given the concession in 1992 by the NPC as part of its programme to encourage more private sector investment in petrochemicals. The Tabriz plant is reported to be one of nine petrochemical projects handed over to the private sector, including a 660,000-ton a year methanol plant and a 500,000-ton a year methyl tertiary butyl ether facility. The total import bill for petrochemicals was $1,500m. in 1987. During the 1990s, if its plans are completed, Iran hopes to be able to satisfy internal demands and have a surplus output to export a range of products. Output has risen steadily since the end of the war with Iraq, reaching 2.1m. tons in 1989/90 and more than 3.5m. tons in 1990/91. Output in 1991/92 totalled 4.3m. tons, according to the NPC, and 970,000 tons of petrochemicals were exported, worth $100m. About 5.4m. tons of petrochemicals were produced in 1992/93. In February 1994 the managing director of the NPC stated that annual production had reached 5.5m. tons, well below the target figure of 9m. tons planned for March 1994. Annual output by the end of the Five-Year Plan beginning in 1994 is projected at 12m. tons, with 60% of production being exported. In August 1993 the head of the NPC urged the Majlis to approve new incentives to encourage private and foreign investment in petrochemical projects during the term of the Five-Year Plan due to start in 1994. He reported that 14 projects started under the Five-Year Plan which ended in March 1994 had been delayed because of the shortage of funds. Foreign finance and expertise were urgently needed if the petrochemical sector was to be developed successfully over the next five years. The NPC was seeking approval from the Majlis to guarantee foreign loans and secure concessionary domestic credit for private projects from March 1994. In 1992 around 1.5m. tons of petrochemicals were exported, earning $150m. Petrochemical exports were due to earn nearly $200m. in 1993/94 and the NPC forecasts that revenues will rise to $300m. in 1994/95. Nevertheless, the head of the NPC stated in September 1993 that Iran was still spending $3,000m. a year on petrochemical imports. The NPC states that annual production in 1993/94 was worth $1,000m. and was expected to rise to $1,800m. in 1994/95.

TRADE AND COMMUNICATIONS

Iran's exports of crude petroleum or petroleum products account for the major part of the country's export revenue. Non-oil exports rose from $283.7m. in 1982/83 to $1,002m. in 1986/87, and $1,158m. in 1987/88 (a record $485m. of which accrued from sales of carpets), but fell to $1,021m. in 1988/89. In 1984/85 (the Iranian year runs from 21 March to 20 March) oil exports of 1.68m. b/d were worth $17,000m. However, oil exports declined to $13,100m. in 1985/86, and to $6,600m. in 1986/87. The value of oil exports in 1987/88 rose to $8,600m. and total earnings of foreign exchange were $9,600m. The Government's utilization, from early 1989, of pre-financed oil sales has increased oil exports and has raised vital foreign exchange for post-war reconstruction. Pre-financing involves the delivery of crude oil 12–18 months after payment and thus amounts, in effect, to the raising of short-term foreign credit. Non-military imports fell sharply to $5,600m. in 1986/87, reflecting the decline in revenue from oil. As a result of the sharp decline in income from oil exports in 1986, the Government decided to place greater emphasis on increasing non-oil exports and thereby reduce dependence on oil. In 1986/87, according to the Governor of the Central Bank, 24% of state revenue was provided by sales of petroleum, compared with 74% in 1975/76 and 63% in 1983/84. During the same period, the proportion of revenue deriving from non-oil exports rose from 2% to 8.5%. The Government is committed to increasing the value of non-oil exports. Official figures reveal that non-oil exports are experiencing a boom. In 1991/92 the value of non-oil exports nearly doubled to $2,500m. Earnings from carpet exports totalled $1,000m., with most of the balance provided by pistachios, caviar and other traditional items. However, there are doubts that the Government's ambitious projections for further dramatic increases by the end of the current Five-Year Plan can be achieved. Nevertheless, in the budget for the Iranian year beginning 21 March 1992 the Government set a target of $4,248m. for the value of non-oil export revenues. The value of industrial exports was projected at $2,043m., that of carpets at $1,152m. and that of agricultural exports at $660m. Figures released in December 1992 for the first eight months of the Iranian year, starting on 21 March 1992, show that although the value of non-oil exports rose to $1,771m. during that period, it was still below the Government's target. Carpets accounted for 40.7% of earnings. According to official sources, the value of non-oil exports in 1993/94 rose to $3,500m. Carpets and handicrafts accounted for 39% of the value of non-oil exports, industrial products for 26%, farm products for 24% and minerals and other goods for 11%. Oil revenues fell sharply in 1993 due to low oil prices and in the year 1993/94 it was estimated that they would not exceed $12,000m. Oil revenues for 1994/95 were projected at only $10,150m. Consequently, non-oil exports have become a more important source of foreign exchange. Non-oil exports for 1994/95 are projected at $4,500m.–$5,000m. The Government's concern about the continuing dependence on oil as the major source of foreign exchange was reflected in the establishment in 1991 of the Export Development Bank, the first new bank set up since the 1979 Revolution. It provides state credit guarantees and invests in export-oriented schemes. A priority is to increase the export of industrial goods and fruits.

After the Revolution, the Government declared that it would pursue an increase in trade with Islamic and developing countries. New trading patterns have emerged, but Iran remains heavily dependent on the advanced industrial economies.

Iran's imports in 1980/81 were valued at IR776,841m. ($10,844m.), an increase of 13.5% over the 1979/80 level, despite the imposition of sanctions by the USA, the EC and

Japan, and the outbreak of war with Iraq in September 1980. This compares with a total of $14,100m. in 1978/79, the year immediately before the Revolution began to affect trade levels. Despite efforts to reduce the import bill, the value of imports rose from $11,845m. in 1982/83 to $24,200m. in 1983/84. With the tightening of import controls, the value of imports declined to $17,500m. in 1984/85 and to an estimated $15,000m. in 1985/86. Further controls, introduced in 1987, permitted the import of basic commodities only. As a result, imports were reported to have fallen to $10,000m. in 1986/87. However, they rose in 1987/88 to $12,760m., considerably more than the budgeted maximum of $9,000m.

Following the seizure of the US hostages and the almost complete embargo on US sales to Iran, imports from the USA plunged dramatically in 1980/81, falling to almost nothing, compared with $2,200m. in 1977/78. As a result of the suspension of US imports and the imposition of EC and Japanese sanctions, Iran began to find new sources of supply in the Third World and among non-aligned countries in Western Europe. There was also a considerable increase in imports from East European countries such as the USSR, Romania and Bulgaria. A protocol which envisaged the development of economic relations between Iran and the USSR was signed in Moscow in September 1985. Under an economic co-operation agreement signed in October 1987, Iran was to supply 5m. tons of crude oil to the USSR annually, 2m. tons of which were to be returned as refined products. Major imports are foodstuffs, equipment and raw materials for industry, power transmission and generating equipment, and purchases of armaments and refined oil products.

During 1981/82 the USA re-emerged as a significant trading partner. Direct US sales rose to $300m. in 1981, making the USA the eighth highest OECD exporter to Iran. However, US exports to Iran in 1986 fell to $34m., compared with US purchases of Iranian goods totalling $600m. In 1987 the USA became the largest purchaser of Iranian oil (with exports reaching $1,592m., 14.6% of total Iranian exports), closely followed by Japan (with exports of $1,426m., 13% of market share). In October 1987 the USA placed a ban on all imports of Iranian goods, and in November imposed tighter restrictions on US exports to Iran. It had earlier been revealed that, in July, Iran had become the second largest supplier of petroleum to the USA, and that, by October, Iranian exports to the USA (valued at some $1,000m.) were already at a higher level than in any year since the Islamic Revolution, except 1983. These measures were taken by the USA as a 'direct result' of Iranian policy in the Iran–Iraq War. In support of the US measures, Japanese companies agreed not to increase their purchases of Iranian oil during the first quarter of 1988.

The sanctions that the EC imposed in 1989, as a result of the Rushdie affair (see History), were repealed in October 1990, and in early November the USA eased its three-year ban on imports of Iranian oil. The increase in oil revenues that followed Iraq's invasion of Kuwait in August 1990 precipitated a sharp rise in imports. Imports are reported to have exceeded $20,000m. in 1990. Exports by Iran's leading suppliers increased by 50% during 1991 compared to 1990, with Germany, Italy and the USA registering the biggest increases. Germany, which remains Iran's major supplier, increased its share of the market in 1991, with exports totalling $4,000m., an increase of some 60%. Japan, the second biggest supplier, reported exports of over $2,500m., an increase of some 56%. Italian exports increased by 64% to $1,800m. US sales rose from a mere $166m. in 1990 to $546m. in 1991. Imports and import commitments in the Iranian year ending 20 March 1991 were almost at a record high of $22,000m. Despite the Government's stated intention to set a ceiling of about $16,000m. on the value of imports in the year beginning 21 March 1991, according to the Bank Markazi, the value of imports in the Iranian year ending 20 March 1992 rose dramatically, to $28,000m. According to the Iranian Customs Office, the value of imports in the year to the end of March 1993 fell to $17,000m. though it was reported that there was still a glut of foreign products on the market, such as textiles and rice. The Central Bank, however, which uses a different method in its calculations, estimated the value of imports at the higher level of $21,000m. In 1993/94, as oil revenues

declined sharply and Iran experienced problems servicing its external debt, imports fell dramatically to around $10,000m. and it has been predicted that Iran will have to keep its imports at around this level for another two years in order to clear payment arrears. Early in 1994 the Majlis voted to reduce hard currency spending on essential imports during the year beginning March 1994 and in May 1994 an advisor to the Bank Markazi stated that imports during 1994/95 would be kept at the same level as the previous year. He stated that this was necessary in order to release extra funds to repay foreign debts at a time when oil revenues were low. The agreements reached in mid-1994 to reschedule about half of the country's external debt (see Finance) and revenue from the increase in non-oil exports may ease the import situation somewhat during 1994/95. Imports from Iran's leading suppliers declined by about one-half in 1993. Japan experienced the biggest fall with the value of its exports down by more than 50% to about $1,500m. Iran's exports to Japan declined by 18% to $2,500m. Germany, still Iran's major supplier, reported that its exports fell by slightly less than 50% in the first 10 months of 1993 to $2,000m. The value of Iran's exports to Germany, however, rose by more than 20% to about $1,000m. The value of Italian exports to Iran declined by 20% during the first nine months of 1993 to $960m., but Italian imports from Iran remained at about the same level of $1,000m. The value of the United Kingdom's exports to Iran fell by only 12% to $742m., while that of its imports from Iran doubled to $365m. France was the only major supplier to record an increase in the value of its exports to Iran, which totalled $725m., an increase of 4.5%. Iranian exports to France rose by 41% in value, to $1,430m. The value of US exports to Iran fell by 18% to $616m. and that of its imports from Iran was only $200,000.

Increased trade led to the revival, in October 1984, of the Regional Co-operation for Development pact with Pakistan and Turkey, which had been inaugurated at the instigation of the late Shah in 1964. Under a new name, the Economic Co-operation Organization, the pact was ratified in January 1985. In February 1992 the pact was expanded to include five Muslim republics of the former USSR: Azerbaijan, Turkmenistan, Uzbekistan, Tajikistan and Kyrgyzstan, all of which need new communication links with the outside world, access to new markets and sources of investment and expertise. A 10% cut in trade tariffs has been agreed and there are plans eventually to remove all tariff and non-tariff barriers. At a summit in Teheran on 16–17 February 1992, the importance of developing transport and communications links and co-operation in the fields of energy, industry and agriculture within the ECO was stressed. Talks are in progress for new rail links and ambitious gas and oil pipeline projects. In April 1992 the ECO announced the setting up of a new trade and development bank, jointly owned by Iran, Turkey and Pakistan, with a capital of $320m.

For several years following the Revolution, government policy concerning foreign trade favoured forms of trade other than cash payments. Straight barter—a direct exchange of goods for oil—was rare; much more common were the countertrade triangle and the clearing account. During the early part of 1985, though, the Government pressed foreign suppliers to take payment for goods in crude oil in order to maintain oil exports at a time of weak demand, and to conserve reserves of foreign exchange. The shift in policy caused argument within the establishment. The Ministry of Oil would have preferred to sell petroleum for cash, as it foresaw an improvement in the market. In the second half of April, partly owing to barter deals, oil exports reached a post-revolutionary peak of more than 2.3m. b/d and the practice of barter trading lost some of its appeal. From May, customers for bartered oil were required to refine it in their own countries and to supply it to their domestic markets alone. By 1991 existing barter arrangements, mainly with east European countries, were being progressively terminated, in favour of cash transactions.

After the Revolution, the new Government declared itself in favour of the nationalization of foreign trade, and progress has been made towards its achievement. Nearly all foreign trade is now channelled through government-controlled purchasing and distribution companies (PDCs), of which 13 were established during the 1980s for chemicals, electrical appliances, electronic and surgical instruments, food processing, a variety of light industrial products, machinery and spare parts, metals, plastics materials, textiles, tools and hardware, and wood and paper. Their main aim was to exercise strict controls over prices and import levels. In spite of the nationalization measures, the Government found it difficult, in practice, to exercise proper control over all aspects of imports and distribution. Consequently, by 1991 the PDCs were being progressively dissolved, and efforts were under way to simplify regulations and to eliminate bureaucratic obstacles to international trade. The PDCs were officially abolished in August 1991. In part, responsibility for foreign trade now lies with the Ministry of Commerce and in part with the Central Bank which exerts considerable control over foreign trade through constraints on letters of credit and the issue of regulations.

In September 1981 the Central Bank of Iran stopped the issue of all letters of credit and imposed more stringent controls on the activities of the new import centres. In January 1982 the Government, faced with a poor rate of foreign exchange earnings from petroleum exports and a deteriorating foreign reserves position, announced that restrictions on imports, other than vital commodities, would remain in force. Foodstuffs, medicines, agricultural goods and industrial supplies were permitted but all other items were classified as luxury goods and excluded. A dramatic improvement in external accounts, as a result of the aggressive petroleum pricing policy, transformed a $2,000m. trade deficit in 1981 into a $5,000m. surplus in 1982. It was thought that import restrictions on certain goods might be lifted but controls were tightened towards the end of 1985/86 in response to the decline in oil revenues, and further controls were introduced in 1987, which permitted the import of only basic commodities. In spite of these efforts, estimates of the trade deficit vary from $1,500m. to $4,000m. In December 1988 the Government eased restrictions on private-sector imports of several pharmaceutical products and foodstuffs. In December 1991 it was announced that some import regulations would be simplified so that a number of goods, including electrical and electronic equipment, tools and construction items and other tools for industrial use, could be imported without a foreign exchange licence. In January 1991 some of the restrictions on foreign currency transactions were removed, as a result of which convertible currency could be legally exchanged by foreign visitors at the 'floating' free-market rate. Iran's non-oil exports were also expected to benefit from the ending of restrictions. After January 1991 the 12 exchange rates were reduced to three: the official rate of $1 = IR70 for food, defence and other strategic imports; the competitive rate of $1 = IR600 for imports of raw materials and spares; and the free floating rate of about $1 = IR1,350 for other imports and exports and for travellers. According to official sources, private importers are no longer required to obtain hard currency from government sources, or special permits for their imports, but instead simply paid 10% of the value of the goods to the Government as trading profit. In October 1991 the Governor of the Central Bank announced that the official exchange rate was being phased out and that only the competitive and free-floating rates would apply to all transactions until the final unification of the two exchange rates. On 13 April 1993 the Central Bank declared the rial fully convertible. The Governor of the Bank, Muhammad Hossain Adeli, announced that all those who needed foreign currency should refer to the banking system for their various needs. Importers of authorized goods and services could open letters of credit and buy foreign exchange without limitations from state banks. Some 32 bank branches in Teheran would sell up to $5,000 to anyone who asked, without requiring any documents. These measures were reversed in November 1993 when the Government imposed limits on hard currency sales by state banks in order to stabilize the rial and conserve foreign exchange. Under these new regulations state banks could only sell hard currency to importers, travellers, students and government personnel on missions abroad. Before their goods could be released from customs, importers had to prove that they had obtained hard currency from banks and not on the open market. Further restrictions on the availability of hard

currency for imports were announced by Bank Markazi in February 1994 (see Finance).

In July 1993 Bank Markazi relaxed restrictions on imports of primary raw materials and spare parts and at the same time restrictions were tightened on cheap consumer imports through the country's free zones. These measures were designed to assist local industry, following complaints from industrialists. However, the Central Bank governor urged industrialists to restrict their cash imports to the most urgent commodities and to use medium term rather than short-term credit facilities. The new measures were welcomed by industrialists, but they also increased the demand for foreign exchange resulting in a fall in the rial's free-market value. In October 1993 it was reported that the Majlis had authorized the Government to increase customs tariffs to help protect local industry from cheap imports. The devaluation of the rial by 95% in March 1993 effectively cut import duties. The import tax on primary raw materials for industry, together with machinery and spare parts that cannot be manufactured locally, would not be raised. It was expected to take some months to prepare the necessary export-import legislation. In March 1994 the Government made the Ministry of Commerce responsible for the administration of export-import regulations.

Since the late 1980s Qeshm and Kish Islands in the Gulf have been developed as free-trade and industrial zones. Kish Island was designated a free zone before the Revolution. Other free zones are Bandar Enzeli on the Caspian Sea and the southeastern port city of Chah Bahar. Sirjan in Kerman province is designated as a special trade zone aimed to promote the re-export of foreign goods to Central Asia and the Caucasus. The chairman of the board for the zone stated in February 1994 that it had an annual capacity to process 20m. tons of goods and could earn revenues of some $2,000m. a year. After a prolonged debate and amendments demanded by the Council of Constitutional Guardians, the legislation confirming the special status of the free zones was ratified in September 1993 and was due to come into effect in March 1994 after detailed regulations had been drafted. The free zones are intended to act as centres of production, export and tourism attracting foreign investment and promoting non-oil exports. They are exempt from most restrictions in force on the mainland. All foreign investments in these zones are guaranteed, profits can be repatriated and disputes taken to international arbitration. Foreign ownership is allowed up to 100%. Foreign banks and foreign credit institutions are also allowed to set up branches in the free zones where the exchange rate will be determined by the free market. In 1993, however, there was criticism that the free zones were using their special status to import some $1,500m. of finished consumer products into Iran every year. In July 1993 business people and government agencies were banned from purchasing individual travellers' rights to bring in goods from the free zones to form large-scale commercial import operations. In November 1993 the amount of goods travellers can bring into Iran from the free zones was reduced from $700 to $200 from Kish and $80 from Qeshm. In December 1993 it was reported that President Rafsanjani had sacked the heads of the country's free zones and there was speculation that this action was taken because of their opposition to these new restrictions. A number of foreign companies have expressed interest in investing in the new zones but were waiting for detailed regulations. In 1993 Kobe Steel of Japan formed a joint venture company for a possible hot-briquetted iron plant on Qeshm Island.

The threat of a US naval embargo in the Gulf at the time of the hostage crisis in 1980 focused attention on land supply lines through the USSR and Turkey and air routes from Pakistan. A protocol with the USSR, including arrangements for land supply lines across the border, was approved by the Islamic Revolutionary Council in May 1980. However, after the Revolution, there was little investment in the transport and communication sector, and in many areas the low level of maintenance of roads and railways led to the reduction in the efficiency of existing routes. Conflicts of interest over resource allocation affected the planning of new roads, and there was pressure to give priority to improving transport in rural areas. The Ministry of Roads and Transport and the

Construction Jihad Ministry built thousands of kilometres of primary roads and about 20,000 km of secondary roads in the provinces. In contrast, plans to improve road access to the ports suffered. Ministry officials have criticized the annual allocation of $150m. for road construction as inadequate. They argue that two-thirds of the $30,000m. spent on transporting goods within the country is wasted because of inadequate transport facilities and poor co-ordination. This situation appears to be changing, however, and in 1990 the Ministry of Roads and Transport announced that expenditure on the transport system during the 1990–1994 Development Plan's term would total some $16,000m., including $4,300m. in convertible currency. In August 1993 it was reported that the Government planned to denationalize a wide range of transport activities and that a detailed plan would be completed by the Ministry of Roads and Transport early in 1994. The involvement of the private sector in the country's transportation system has been encouraged by the Government since 1991 and a number of projects have already been offered to the private sector. These include the new Teheran international airport, the proposed motorway from Teheran to the Caspian Sea and a railway line from Mashad to Baqf. The Supreme Administrative Council wants to reduce state expenditure on transport in the future by involving the private and co-operative sectors in developing and maintaining all parts of the transport network. In December 1992 the Ministry of Roads and Transport stated that more than 1,400 km of roads had been repaired since March and that another 11,000 km were under construction. In November 1993 it was reported that the Ministry of Roads and Transport had approved the $800m.-motorway from Teheran to Chalus on the Caspian Sea and that the private sector had been invited to participate in its construction.

The State Railways Organization is extending and upgrading the country's 6,000 km-rail network with the assistance of several international firms. The major improvement since the Revolution has been the opening of the final section of electrified track on the 146-km link between Tabriz and Djulfa, used to bring imports from the former USSR. Priority is being given to completing a 730-km line connecting Bandar Abbas to Bafq and the national network, and to constructing a 560-km line from Kerman to Zahedan, providing a link with Pakistan. In August 1992 Iran and Pakistan agreed to establish a joint venture to lay track between Baqf and Bandar Abbas. In September 1992 Pakistan Railways engineers were due to visit Teheran in order to discuss the rehabilitation of the 540 km Kerman-Zahedan, and the 500 km Kerman to Bandar Abbas, lines. The 112-km line from Bandar Khomeini to Ahwaz is to be double-tracked, in order to reduce congestion at the port, and long-term projects include double-tracking the line from Teheran to Ahwaz and the construction of new lines. The first phase of construction of a 175 km line from Mashad to Sarakhs by the Engineering Corps of the Islamic Revolutionary Guards Corps began in May 1992. Since the disintegration of the USSR the line now forms part of a plan to link the rail systems of the newly independent Central Asian republics to the Iranian national network and the Gulf. The Mashad-Sarakhs line will connect Turkmenistan to the Gulf port of Bushehr via Teheran. When the Baqf-Bandar Abbas line is completed by Iran early in 1995, Turkmenistan will have access to the Strait of Hormuz. A direct line is also planned from Mashad to Bandar Abbas. The 110-km line from Ahwaz to Khorramshahr reopened in July 1989. The State Railways Organization has proposed a high-speed rail line between Teheran and Isfahan, involving a possible investment of $2,500m., and proposals from German, French and Japanese firms are also being considered. The highest speed rail service at present is on the Teheran-Qazvin line. The electrification of the Teheran-Tabriz line is expected to go ahead soon and it has been proposed to shorten and improve the Tabriz line to the Turkish border. Several foreign companies are involved in the construction of the 40 km-Teheran–Karaj rapid transit line. Under the Five-Year Development Plan which commenced in January 1990, $6,800m. has been allocated to the State Railways Organization. It is aimed to increase annual transport capacity to 10m. passengers and 25m. tons of freight. About 1,000 km of new track are to be completed by 1995 and 1,750 km of existing track

are to be renovated during the same period. In February 1994 the deputy director of the State Railways Organization stated that the railways carried 9m. passengers a year and 19m. tons of freight. During preliminary discussions about the second Five-Year Plan, due to start in 1994, the Minister of Roads and Transport stated that the allocation to railways should be doubled to $17,700m. Tunnelling and other work on the Teheran underground network is almost complete, but it was reported in March 1993 that orders for rolling stock and electrical and other equipment had not been placed. The first line of the new underground was due to open in 1993, but there have been long delays in completing the project which was started before the Revolution, abandoned in 1979 and begun again in the late 1980s. There are plans to introduce similar networks in other major cities.

In the ports sector a decision was taken in September 1981 to complete work on a major extension of Bandar Abbas, a project designed before the Revolution but scaled down after the fall of the Shah. Because of war damage at the traditional seaports of Bandar Khomeini and Khorramshahr, Iran became heavily dependent on Bandar Abbas for its sea-borne imports. A new port, Bandar Shahid Rajai, was inaugurated in 1983 handling 9m. tons of the total of 12m. tons of cargo passing through Iran's Persian Gulf ports every year. Work on the port development at Bandar Abbas began in February 1985. However, only two of the original three phases of the project have been completed. There are plans to build a new jetty at the port for mineral exports, at a cost of $770m. When completed in 1994, the jetty will have a handling capacity of 10m. tons per year. Two new ports at Chah Bahar (the first called Shahid Beheshti, costing $37m.) were opened in February 1984 and September 1988, respectively, while Bushehr port is being expanded. The Ganaveh oil export port, with an export capacity of 2m. b/d, was opened in August 1988. Before the cease-fire in the Iran–Iraq War was announced, in preparation for a possible international economic embargo and closure of the Gulf to shipping, Iran made arrangements to use ports and oil refineries in neighbouring countries. Agreements were signed with Pakistan, Turkey and the USSR. Pakistan agreed in October 1987 to permit Iran's use of Karachi and Qasim ports to import up to 2m. tons of goods. In August 1992 it was announced that the port of Khorramshahr, destroyed in the Iran–Iraq War, had been reopened to freight traffic. The port of Abadan, also destroyed by Iraqi forces, was due to reopen in February 1993.

One of Iran's major transport projects is the construction of the Imam Khomeini international airport south-west of Teheran. When the first phase is completed in 1997 the airport will be capable of handling 12m. passengers a year, according to the head of the Civil Aviation Organisation and it will eventually have a capacity of 30m. passengers a year. The new airport will replace Mehrabad Airport for all international flights by 1997 and it will be linked to Teheran by a special underground railway system. In July 1992 it was announced that some $800m. in foreign credits had been allocated towards the cost of completing Imam Khomeini International Airport, and another $350m. to other airports. The Civil Aviation Organisation plans to construct 21 new airports by 1995 and the modernization of another 42 airports. Some IR30,000m. was spent on airport modernization during 1991/92. Abadan airport reopened in 1991 and started handling international traffic in January 1994.

FINANCE

The first post-Revolutionary budget, for the Iranian year 1979/80, was set at $34,000m., a little more than one-half of the target that was set during the previous year by the Shah's regime. The following year's budget (1980/81) reached $40,000m., including provisions for a $6,500m. deficit. In fact, the deficit came to almost $12,000m., mainly because of the fall in the Government's petroleum revenues from an estimated $23,000m. to $11,900m. For 1981/82 the then Prime Minister, Muhammad Ali Rajai, drew up a $44,000m. budget which, he claimed, would be a non-deficit budget, the entire expenditure plan being financed through petroleum revenues and taxes, and petroleum production being boosted to the point where sufficient revenue was earned. He was immediately criticized by President Bani-Sadr and the Governor of the Central Bank, Ali Reza Nobari, who attacked the use of non-replenishable resources to finance excessive current expenditures, as a matter of principle, and also pointed out that, with the current world glut of oil, it would be practically impossible to raise enough money from petroleum. Their vehement opposition to the budget was one of the key factors which led Islamic fundamentalists to push them out of power. Many other members of the Majlis also attacked the budget strongly. In July 1981 the Majlis reduced total allocations to $37,000m. Some $2,500m. were reduced from defence expenditure, and $3,100m. from the Development Plan. An overall cut of 5% in the expenditure by government departments was also demanded. Even so, a deficit of $8,500m. was forecast.

For the year March 1982 to March 1983 the Government proposed a $39,050m. budget to the Majlis. Revenues were estimated at $31,902m., leaving a deficit of $7,150m. Priority for expenditure was given to the reconstruction of war-damaged areas in the south, and great emphasis was placed on restoring the existing agricultural and industrial base in order to create employment, to reduce dependency on petroleum and to limit imports. A supplementary budget of $4,856m. was approved on 13 October 1982, the principal increases being allotted to the war effort and reconstruction projects ($1,820m.), current government expenditure ($1,200m.), and the remainder mostly to power, road and port construction, government building and other infrastructural projects.

According to the then Prime Minister, Mir Hossein Moussavi, some 30% of the 1983/84 budget, totalling an estimated IR3,600,000m. ($42,400m.), was spent on the war effort. A budget of $48,300m. for the fiscal year beginning in March 1984 was presented to the Majlis. Budgeted spending was about 14% higher than in 1983/84, and allowed for a deficit of $3,600m. Prime Minister Moussavi stated that government revenues were projected at $44,600m., of which more than one-half ($23,400m.) would come from sales of petroleum. The war effort was given a direct budget of $4,000m., but war-related allocations totalled some 31% of the entire budget expenditure. Planned current expenditure by the Government accounted for $30,000m. of the total. Education was the biggest single item of government spending. Development expenditure was put at $15,200m. The Construction Jihad Ministry was allocated more than $2,500m. However, before being approved by the Majlis, which traditionally considers government spending to be excessive and inflationary, proposed budgetary expenditure was reduced by 15%.

A budget of $42,000m. for the year 1985/86 was presented to the Majlis. It envisaged a 25% fall in the deficit, compared with the 1984/85 projected level ($10,000m.). Of the total projected budget spending, 30.6% was devoted to the war effort and war-related costs, with education receiving the next largest sectoral allocation. The Plan and Budget Committee of the Majlis cut the budget to $38,300m., almost the entire reduction being made in current expenditure, to bring it in line with the expected fall in revenue from oil sales. The Majlis approved the revised budget at the end of February 1985.

The budget for 1986/87 was presented to the Majlis in December 1985. With total spending of IR4,049,700m. ($50,600m.), it provided for an increase of 12.5% in defence spending, while allocations to all other sectors were to be lower than those for 1985/86. In a debate in February 1986 the Government was criticized for not taking full account of the rapid fall in oil prices, and for overestimating oil revenues in preparing the budget. An additional problem was the accumulated deficit on foreign exchange receipts and payments from 1985/86, when oil revenues, budgeted at $19,700m., reached only $13,000m.–$15,000m. Contrary to expectations, however, in March 1986 the Majlis increased planned expenditure under the 1986/87 budget to IR4,249,700m. ($53,100m.). Although projected oil revenue was revised downwards to IR1,500,000m. ($18,600m.), even this proved to be an appreciable over-estimate, with actual revenue failing to reach one-half of that figure.

In March 1987 the Majlis approved a budget of IR4,000,000m. ($55,555m.) for 1987/88 (an increase of 15% compared with 1986/87), of which IR3,000,000m. ($41,670m.) were allocated to current expenditure and IR704,700m.

($9,788m.) to development. The rise in current expenditure reflected the demands of the war effort and was at the expense of domestic development. War-related expenditure was budgeted to absorb IR700,000m. ($9,722m.), or 24% of current expenditure. The Government had originally allocated IR430,000m. ($5,972m.) to war costs, but the Majlis Plan and Budget Committee increased the figure to IR660,000m. ($9,167m.), and a further IR118,000m. ($1,639m.) were allocated from the development budget. In the late 1980s, actual expenditure on the war was much greater than budget allocations. For 1987/88 a budget deficit of some $13,820m. was predicted, mainly as a result of the low volume of foreign exchange earnings, with oil revenues projected at only $11,740m. It was reported in early 1989 that the deficit was as high as $18,200m. in 1987/88. Expenditure of $57,000m. for the year 1988/89 was approved in March 1988, and proposals for expenditure of $55,000m. in 1989/90 were presented to the Majlis in December 1988. After a long debate and much criticism of the Government for its lack of direction in economic affairs, the Assembly approved a budget of $70,000m., including $9,814m. in foreign exchange for export earnings. A detailed analysis of planned expenditure was not disclosed, but there appears to be provision for a high level of domestic borrowing to finance a deficit of as much as $20,000m. Approval for foreign credit of as much as $2,500m. was given. Allocations for annual defence spending were not announced, but it was reported informally in Teheran that these had been almost halved, from $10,000m. to $5,850m.

The budget for 1990/91, approved by the Majlis in March 1990, projected overall expenditure of $79,900m. and revenue of $57,300m., leaving a deficit of $22,600m. An additional $21,000m. were to be invested by state enterprises. Major projects were allocated $5,400m. in foreign credits. In July 1990 the Majlis authorized an amendment to the annual budget, whereby the allocations for disaster relief and post-war reconstruction were doubled; in addition, it approved a $300m. emergency fund for provinces devastated by the earthquake of 21 June 1990; the cost of damage to the provinces of Gilan and Zanjan was believed to exceed $7,000m. Moreover, an estimated 35,000 people were killed, and 500,000 left homeless, as a result of the disaster. In March 1991 the World Bank approved an emergency loan of $250m. for reconstruction projects to repair damage caused by the earthquake. A supplementary budget was introduced in November 1990 to cover the remaining five months of the year; the revised estimates assumed higher revenues than had been previously forecast. Total government revenue in the period March–September 1990 was reported as $37,700m., and expenditure as $46,400m., leaving a deficit of $8,700m. Oil and gas revenues over the same period were estimated at $8,000m. With oil and gas revenues expected to rise (owing to increases in both prices and output), the 1991/92 budget forecast total government revenue of IR7,300,000m. and expenditure of IR8,640,000m. (an increase of 54% from the 1990/91 total), leaving a deficit of IR1,340,000m. A further budget of IR11,440,000m. was agreed for state-owned companies, bringing overall planned expenditure in the general budget for 1991/92 to IR20,080,000m. The budget in convertible currency, set at $24,000m., was the highest ever introduced. On 30 January 1992 the Majlis approved the budget law for 1992/93 despite criticism by deputies of its inflationary aspects. The general budget remains at the level requested by the Government, IR28,800,000m., but within it, the Government budget has been increased from around IR10,000,000m. to IR12,400,000m. Deficit financing remains unchanged at IR623,000m. The Majlis increased the proportion of revenues from taxation in order to reduce dependence on oil revenues. In addition it reduced the proportion of current spending (i.e. that on education, health and social security) and increased that of development expenditure, which now accounts for one-third of the total. In October 1992 the Minister of Economy and Finance forecast that the budget deficit for 1992/93 would be $10,570m. The Government's budget for 1993/94 finally received approval from the Majlis on 2 February 1993. The general budget was set at IR54,400,000m. and the Government's budget at IR25,400,000m. Efforts by the Majlis to reduce expenditure by 10% appear to have been reversed.

The Government set aside $3,800m. at the existing official exchange rate of about $1 = IR70 to subsidize essential imports and prices. Among the subsidized allocations were $1,200m. for oil product imports, the same amount for basic food items, $452m. for medicine and baby food, $80m. for Iranian students abroad and $850m. for defence. The Majlis authorized the National Iranian Oil Company to use up to $2,600m. in foreign finance to build and expand the Bandar Abbas oil refinery and its lubricants unit, and for five offshore oil fields in the Gulf.

The Majlis, concerned about low oil prices and debt repayment problems, secured cuts in both projected expenditure and revenue before the Government's budget for the year beginning March 1994 was approved. Projected revenue was reduced by 10% and expenditure cut by between 7% and 13% in various sectors. Revenue is projected at IR30,700,000m. ($17,700m.), including oil revenues of $10,150m. The overall budget was set at IR69,800,000m. ($36,900m.), of which government expenditure is IR32,300,000m. ($18,500m.), with the balance to state banks and companies. Despite the cutbacks secured by the Majlis, the overall budget is still substantially higher than the level approved for the year 1993/94. The Government's proposal to reduce subsidies on fuel prices in order to raise revenues was rejected by the Majlis.

Inflation has become a persistent problem for the economy. Import controls have tended to feed inflation in a situation of growing shortages and especially in view of a policy favouring wage increases for the lower paid without increases in productivity. The annual rate of inflation officially fell from 32.5% in 1980/81 to 17% in 1983/84, and in May 1985 the Central Bank reported that wholesale prices rose by only 7.6% in 1984/85 (year to 20 March). IMF figures suggest that inflation for the year ended September 1984 was approximately 13%–14%. In October 1985 the Government continued to maintain that inflation was falling, and that the annual rate was a mere 5.5%. In the first half of 1987, when the annual rate of inflation was unofficially estimated at between 30% and 50%, the Government appeared tacitly to admit the seriousness of the problem by announcing that, henceforth, the prices of 22 basic commodities would be controlled to halt the rise in inflation. In an interview in November 1991 the Governor of the Central Bank stated that inflation was running at 15%. Given the reconstruction and development programmes and the adjustment of a war-stricken economy that were taking place, as an economist he did not regard the level of inflation as a matter for very much concern. According to the Governor of the Bank Markazi, the rate of inflation rose to 22% in 1993/94 when the rial was devalued and oil prices fell sharply. He declared 1994/95 a year of 'monetary discipline' and predicted that a tight monetary policy would reduce inflation to less than 20%. He reported that the Majlis had imposed a 15% ceiling on the growth of liquidity in 1994/95 in order to control inflation. He also stated that rates charged by state banks on loans to various sectors would remain unchanged.

The state offers a wide range of subsidies on basic food-stuffs. In an interview in November 1991 the Minister of Economic Affairs and Finance stated that the Government would continue subsidizing essential goods, notably food, such as bread, rice, cooking oil, sugar, and medicines, until 1994. Other subsidies would gradually be reduced. Figures produced by the Consumer and Producer Protection Organization indicate that prices of local goods are rising much faster than claimed by the Central Bank. Rising prices in the extensive 'black market' in goods are not taken into account in official price indices, while rents in the housing market have increased substantially in urban areas throughout the country. A recent survey has suggested that between one-half and two-thirds of income among low-income families is being absorbed by housing rental costs. At the beginning of his second term of office in August 1993, President Rafsanjani warned the country to expect a gradual reduction of some state subsidies and the elimination of others, particularly those on fuel and electricity. He stated that subsidies were wasting public funds, distorting the economy and preventing the growth of a healthy private sector. Furthermore, he believed that the system of subsidies was unjust. The rich were the main beneficiaries because of their high level of consumption. The result was that the majority of Iranians were in effect subsidizing the living standards of the richest 10% of the population. Some subsidies had been removed during 1992/93, but a comprehensive programme to phase out subsidies was incorporated in the draft second Five-Year Plan due to start in 1994. These proposals were greeted with strong opposition in the Majlis, largely because of the political risks involved. In February 1994 the Majlis rejected proposed price increases for petroleum products and domestic gas supplies. Nevertheless, the President renewed his attack on subsidies in April 1994, stating that energy subsidies alone cost the Government $11,000m. a year, which was more than projected oil revenues for 1994/95. He estimated that the total cost of subsidies was $15,000m. a year. He acknowledged that some subsidies were justified; these included the $360m. for agriculture, and $230m. for assistance to families of those killed in the Revolution and the Iran-Iraq War. However, he condemned bread subsidies and energy subsidies as unjust because the rich benefited most. In April some deputies proposed a bill to cancel all price rises announced since 21 March and to transfer price-setting powers from the Supreme Economic Council, which is headed by the President, to the Majlis. Since February 1994 the Supreme Economic Council had authorized increases in telephone charges, postal rates and domestic air fares, while there were also increases in inter-city bus and train fares. The motion was postponed indefinitely as other deputies rallied to the Government's support, but at the end of May Rafsanjani announced that the Government would act cautiously on subsidies and indicated that those on bread and fuel, in particular, would not be removed during the next five years. He stated that 'it needs at least 10 years for us to remove the iniquities that exist in fuel and bread consumption'.

In June 1990, under pressure to reduce inflation, President Rafsanjani's Government enacted major reforms of the foreign exchange market and import-export regulations. Foreign currency dealings outside authorized money-changing houses became illegal and restrictions on importers and exporters were relaxed. A new rate for the rial against the US dollar was intended to encourage exports by giving industrialists access to hard currency for raw materials and machinery. In February 1993 the Minister of Economy and Finance announced that the Government would use a variety of financial instruments, including forward selling, to keep the rial stable after the planned currency devaluation at the beginning of the new Iranian year on 21 March. Public sector demand for hard currency would be controlled in order to create a hard currency surplus to support the rial in the free market. The rial was declared fully convertible by the Central Bank on 13 April 1993. Since devaluing the rial by more than 96% in April 1993 Bank Markazi responded to downward market pressures by further devaluing its floating rate. The value of the rial fell to record lows from late 1993. After April 1994, when new restrictions were introduced requiring nearly all importers to use limited official supplies of hard currency earned from non-oil exports, the rial's value on the open market plunged dramatically. On 7 May 1994 Bank Markazi introduced a new currency exchange rate, known as the import-against-export rate, which applied to most imports. The rate announced on 7 May was $1=IR2,585, compared with a floating rate of $1=IR1,748. The Central Bank stated that the new rate would be IR50 below the open market rate which had fluctuated between IR2,500–IR2,800. The new rate effectively devalued the rial by 32%. A bank official stated that very limited funds had been allocated by the Government to some ministries for essential imports such as machinery and medicine, but that most goods would have to be imported at the new rate.

Following the June 1979 nationalization of banking and insurance, the Government announced in 1980 the establishment of an Islamic banking system, which officially came into force from 21 March 1984. Interest on loans (*riba*, which is prohibited under Islamic law) was replaced by a commission—4% per year, compared with the traditional 14%—and interest on deposits was replaced with profits—estimated at a minimum 7%–8.5% per year. The banks would become temporary shareholders in major industrial enterprises to which they lent money.

More than 10% of total private deposits, mainly short- and medium-term funds, are now subject to Islamic rules. Longer-term deposits will be Islamized as they mature. On 21 March 1985 the whole process became more stringent when all bank loans and advances were Islamized. In March 1980 the 22 small commercial banks were merged into two major new institutions, Bank Tejarat and Bank Mellat. Today the Iranian commercial banking system is composed of eight institutions: Bank Keshavarzi, Bank Mellat, Bank Melli Iran, Bank Refah Kargaran, Bank Saderat Iran, Bank Sepah, Bank Tejarat and the Islamic Economy Organization.

In 1992 rumours that state banks might be privatized were strongly denied by the Central Bank. Nevertheless, in recent years the state banks have been encouraged to operate on more commercial lines and competition between them for customers is now intensive. As commercial state banks have not produced statements for several years, they are being urged by the Central Bank to bring their accounting up to date. In May 1994 the Council of Ministers authorized the establishment of private savings and loan associations which were described by the Governor of Bank Markazi as 'non-banking credit associations' which will be able to take deposits and make loans, but will not be permitted to offer current accounts. He stated that the aim of these associations was to encourage savings by providing a range of institutions able to take deposits. It was not clear whether the interest-free Islamic banking law would be applied to the new associations. For some years there has been pressure, mainly from business and industry, for the reintroduction of a private commercial banking system along international lines. The existing system is regarded as an impediment to developing business and industry. Some officials are believed to acknowledge that the banking system needs to be changed, but that this would pose serious constitutional and religious obstacles. There was speculation that the new associations may represent the first step towards the reform of the entire banking system.

The US–Iran Claims Tribunal in The Hague, Netherlands, deliberated over the claims by Iran for compensation for its assets in the USA worth $9,000m., which were 'frozen' by President Carter, and by US interests (mostly companies) for the loss of $6,000m. in assets after the Islamic Revolution. The tribunal awarded, and helped to settle, more than $972m. (including $905m. to American claimants) by 24 October 1988.

No official information regarding Iran's reserves of foreign exchange was released between 1982 and 1994. In 1982 reserves were recorded at $5,700m. (excluding gold), representing less than 50% of the level prevailing before the Revolution. In March 1984 the Majlis approved legislation preventing the Government from spending more than it earned. As a result, drawings on foreign reserves were believed to have been limited in 1984 and 1985. About $3,000m. were withdrawn by the Government during 1986, when the price of oil collapsed, but there followed a steady improvement in reserve holdings. In mid-1988 Iran's foreign exchange reserves were estimated at $6,000m.–$7,000m. (including gold holdings) compared with $3,000m.–$4,000m. in mid-1986. In June 1991 the Bank for International Settlements (BIS) reported that the value of Iranian assets had fallen by 25% during the previous 12 months to $5,019m., while, during the same period, the extent of Iran's liabilities had risen to $3,784m. The BIS reported that liabilities to OECD commercial banks were at an all-time high of $9,105m. in March 1993, when Iranian deposits with the same banks were estimated at $5,935m. By the final quarter of 1993 the BIS reported that liabilities to foreign banks and other financial institutions were $8,553m., with assets at $5,561m.

According to the World Bank, reporting for the first time since 1979, Iran's total external debt had risen to just over $9,000m. by December 1990, of which one-fifth consisted of long-term commitments. Figures from the BIS and the OECD indicated that Iran's external debt rose from $5,560m. in December 1989 to $6,469m., in June 1990 and to $10,000m. by the end of that year. According to the BIS external debts rose rapidly in 1991 to an estimated $13,653m. by December. By June 1992 they had increased to about $15,000m. A lower figure of $11,500m. was reported by the World Bank for December 1991. The World Bank estimate showed a $2,500m. increase compared to December 1990 and a $5,000m. increase compared to December 1989. According to the World Bank, $8,775m. of the total external debt was in short-term borrowing and $2,775m. in long-term borrowing. Debt servicing cost $777m. a year—$578m. in short-term borrowing and $199m. in long-term commitments. However, in February 1993 the chairman of the Majlis Plan and Budget Committee declared that Iran had accumulated about $30,000m. in short-term external debts by March1992—the first official acknowledgement of the country's high external indebtedness. He reported that $18,000m. had been added to the external debt since 1989. The World Bank gave a lower estimate of $14,166m. in December 1992, of which $11,102m. consisted of short term debts. The Bank estimated that total debt servicing was $810m. The Bank for International Settlements (BIS) estimated Iran's total external debt at $16,107m. in mid-1993, made up of $8,826m. in external bank claims and $7,281m. of non-bank credits.

The exact size of Iran's external debt is unclear and estimates during early 1994 varied from $17,000m., to over $30,000m. A realistic figure was thought to be around $20,000m., much of it in the form of short-term credits accumulated during the early years of President Rafsanjani's first term when government spending was at a high level. From mid-1992 Iran experienced problems paying its external debts as oil revenues fell. During 1993 Western creditors became increasingly concerned about arrears on repayments. During the early part of the year a series of rescheduling agreements were concluded regarding letters of credit payment not covered by export guarantee organizations. In April 1993 German, French and Japanese banks holding over $2,000m. of Iranian letters of credit agreed to defer payment for one year to allow Iran time to bring its short-term debt repayments back on schedule. Belgian creditors followed and by the end of the year agreement had been reached to reschedule debts totalling $3,000m. In November 1993 total payment arrears were estimated to have reached at least $7,000m. Early in 1994 it was rumoured that Iran was exploring the possibility of bilateral government-to-government deals with Germany and France in order to avoid a Paris Club rescheduling, the implications of which would be politically unacceptable to the Iranian Government. Despite opposition from the USA, agreements of bilateral rescheduling were made with several European creditors and with Japan during the first half of 1994. In February 1994 Germany agreed to restructure about $2,400m. of short-term debts into medium-term ones. Similar agreements followed with Japan, Austria, Switzerland, Denmark, Spain, Belgium, Italy and France. The package includes a two-year grace period, with payments spread over four years starting in 1996. The agreements reached with Italy and France in June 1994 brought the amount of debt rescheduled to about $8,000m. and there was speculation that further negotiations could bring the figure to $10,000m. A Bank Markazi official stated in May that the refinancing deals were arranged so that the annual repayments beginning in 1996 would not exceed 25% of projected government revenue. Some European creditors indicated that if Iran could show that it had the debt problem under control, some new money might be available by late 1994.

Early in 1994 the USA succeeded in its campaign to stop further World Bank loans to Iran. In April the Bank's lending programme to Iran was frozen at $850m. A $150m.-loan proposal to develop livestock and arable land and a $125m.-proposal to develop basic education were shelved indefinitely. Earlier, in September 1993, Iran had been told to seek alternative sources of funding for two proposals for gas flaring reduction and rail and ports rehabilitation because the Bank considered them to be controversial. No new loans have been approved since March 1993 and the Bank claimed to be waiting for Iran to finalize its rescheduling agreements before proceeding. However, the loan programme was blocked at the same time as Iran succeeded in completing agreements on rescheduling with its major creditors. The USA has an 18.4% shareholding in the World Bank.

DEVELOPMENT PLANS

The five-year development planning concept, started in 1947 by the Shah's regime, was abandoned after the Revolution. The fifth and last Plan ended in March 1978, and the projected sixth Plan, never published, was overtaken by the Revolution.

The Islamic Republic's first Five-Year Development Plan, covering the period 1983/84–1987/88, was drafted in 1981–82 but was overtaken by the war with Iraq. Its stated aims were: the expansion of education and culture; securing the interests of the *mostazafin* (the deprived or downtrodden people); and the development of the agricultural sector. The long-term objective of development planning is to secure economic independence by achieving self-sufficiency in food and reducing the economy's dependence on the petroleum sector (crude oil's share of GNP was 20% in 1982/83, and oil exports accounted for 97% of all sales by value in 1983/84). The Republic's first Plan was criticized for being too optimistic. Projected oil revenues were based on a price of $33.25 per barrel at a time when the price of Iranian crude had fallen to $28. The planners were also accused of giving industry priority over agriculture. The Majlis forced a revision of the Plan, which was presented in late 1983, whereby expenditure was reduced by 10%. Agriculture's share of investment was raised to 16.7%, while the share of non-oil industry declined to around 50%. In early 1984 the Plan was returned once again to the Plan and Budget Organization for revision. The Majlis appeared to prefer the broader 20-year strategic plan that the Government had presented at the same time. In January 1985 the Majlis approved a law that transformed the Plan and Budget Organization into a Ministry. In January 1986 the Majlis approved the outline of the revised Five-Year Development Plan for 1983/84–1987/88, redrafted by the Ministry of Planning and Budget after being rejected by the Majlis in 1984. Following the end of the Iran–Iraq War, a draft Five-Year Development Plan was announced in November 1988, with spending projected at $324,000m. over the period 1989–94. The Plan's stated aims were to free the economy from its dependence on oil and to give priority to defence, physical infrastructure, employment and education.

The draft Five-Year Development Plan was placed under urgent review by President Rafsanjani, into whose office the Ministry of Planning and Budget has been incorporated. A new Plan was implemented in January 1990, after having been ratified by the Majlis and the Council of Guardians. Over the period 1990/91–1994/95 it provides for total investment of $394,000m., including $119,000m. in convertible currency ($27,000m. in foreign credits). The new Plan is regarded as the focus of President Rafsanjani's efforts to rebuild the Iranian economy. It aims, among other things, to achieve an average annual economic growth rate of 8%; to create 2m. new jobs; and to reduce the annual rate of inflation to below 10%. More than two-thirds of convertible currency earnings during the Plan's term are to be provided by petroleum and gas reserves. Some $10,000m. in foreign financing will be used to revive existing industries, while $9,000m. will be devoted to new industries, mining and agricultural projects. The Chairman of the Plan and Budget Committee of the Majlis, Morkeza Alviri, has denied that the Plan's aims are unrealistic, stating that its aims are based on an estimated rise in the price of oil, from $15.60 per barrel to $21.60 per barrel, over its five-year term. An important feature of the Plan is to encourage private sector participation in reviving the economy. Planned targets for private sector investment may not be achieved but it is clear that the private sector has responded positively and is playing a more important role in the economy.

On 15 January 1993 President Rafsanjani commented that the Government would concentrate on completing existing projects during the second Five-Year Plan due to start in March 1994 and there would be no new large-scale public investment. He stated that the second Plan would create more jobs and result in industrial self-sufficiency. The plan document was approved by the Supreme Economic Council and was due to be presented to the Majlis for approval in December 1993. However, there were calls from some deputies for the plan to be delayed for a year because of the economic crisis resulting from low oil prices and the fall in the value of the rial. They argued that there should be a pause between the first and second plans to provide time for reassessment and for reviewing the results of the first plan. Nevertheless, the Government declared that it was going ahead with the second Five-Year Plan and the President presented the plan document to the Majlis on 21 December 1993, together with the budget for the year beginning March 1994. Total government spending under the new plan is set at IR238,500,000m. ($151,900m. at the exchange rate of $1=IR1,570), some 26% higher than in the first draft of the plan. Projected oil revenues, which remain unchanged at $77,600m, will meet just over half of expenditure with the balance coming from increased domestic revenues. The plan envisages an average annual growth in GDP of between 5.45%–6%. There was no reference at this stage to the controversial subject of foreign finance. The day before the president submitted the plan document to the Majlis, Supreme Leader Ayatollah Khamenei had spoken out against reliance on foreign loans although he did not make it clear whether he was opposed to all foreign loans.

Statistical Survey

The Iranian year runs from 21 March to 20 March.

Source (except where otherwise stated): Statistical Centre of Iran, Dr Fatemi Ave, Cnr Rahiye Moayeri, Opposite Sazeman-e-Ab, Teheran 14144; tel. (21) 655061; telex 213233.

Area and Population

AREA, POPULATION AND DENSITY

Area (sq km)	1,648,000*
Population (census results)†	
22 September 1986	
Males	25,280,961
Females	24,164,049
Total	49,445,010
September 1991	55,837,163
Density (per sq km) at September 1991 . . .	33.9

* 636,296 sq miles.
† Excluding adjustment for underenumeration.

PRINCIPAL TOWNS (population at 1986 census)

Tehran (Teheran,		Zahedan . .	281,923
the capital) .	6,042,584	Karaj . . .	275,100
Mashad (Meshed)	1,463,508	Hamadan . .	272,499
Esfahan (Isfahan) .	986,753	Arak . . .	265,349
Tabriz . . .	971,482	Kerman . .	257,284
Shiraz . . .	848,289	Qazvin . . .	248,591
Ahwaz. . . .	579,826	Yazd . . .	230,483
Bakhtaran		Zanjan . . .	215,261
(Kermanshah) .	560,514	Eslamshahr	
Qom	543,139	(Islam Shahr) .	215,129
Orumiyeh . .	300,746	Khorramabad .	208,592
Rasht . . .	290,897	Sanandaj . .	204,537
Ardabil (Ardebil) .	281,973	Bandar-e-Abbas .	201,642

BIRTHS AND DEATHS (UN estimates, annual averages)

	1975–80	1980–85	1985–90
Birth rate (per 1,000) . .	44.7	46.1	43.1
Death rate (per 1,000). . .	11.8	10.4	8.2

Expectation of life (UN estimates, years at birth, 1985–90): 65.2 (males 65.0; females 65.5).

Source: UN, *World Population Prospects: The 1992 Revision.*

1991: Registered live births 1,885,649 (birth rate 33.8 per 1,000); Registered deaths 461,443 (death rate 8.3 per 1,000).
Note: Registration is incomplete.

ECONOMICALLY ACTIVE POPULATION
(persons aged 6 years and over, 1986 census)

	Males	Females	Total
Agriculture, hunting, forestry, and fishing	2,945,793	262,820	3,208,613
Mining and quarrying . . .	31,839	538	32,377
Manufacturing.	1,243,812	216,320	1,460,132
Electricity, gas and water . .	88,812	2,252	91,064
Construction	1,198,018	9,441	1,207,459
Trade, restaurants and hotels .	861,190	14,729	875,919
Transport, storage and communications . . .	622,136	8,568	630,704
Financing, insurance, real estate and business services.	103,826	10,476	114,302
Community, social and personal services . . .	2,636,551	414,392	3,050,943
Activities not adequately defined	316,882	47,567	364,449
Total employed . . .	10,048,859	987,103	11,035,962
Unemployed	1,486,138	332,602	1,818,740
Total labour force . . .	11,534,997	1,319,705	12,854,702

Source: ILO, *Year Book of Labour Statistics.*

Agriculture

PRINCIPAL CROPS ('000 metric tons)

	1990	1991	1992
Wheat	8,012	8,793	10,200
Rice (paddy)	1,981	2,357	2,500
Barley	3,548	3,102	3,700
Maize	130*	188	190*
Potatoes	2,516	2,612	2,800*
Pulses	355	576	600
Soybeans	89	115†	115*
Cottonseed.	262	247	240
Cotton (lint)†	120	114	120
Tomatoes	1,530*	1,642	1,600*
Onions (dry)	1,213	1,125	930*
Other vegetables . . .	3,384	2,227	2,475*
Watermelons	2,646	1,235	2,300*
Melons.	1,247	776	830*
Grapes.	1,424	1,626	1,650*
Dates	516	634	635*
Apples.	1,524	1,365	1,520*
Pears	148	153	150*
Oranges	1,334	1,285	1,300*
Other citrus fruits . . .	975	1,187	715*
Apricots	85	81	82*
Other fruits	1,158	1,137	1,120*
Sugar cane.	1,659	1,374	1,600*
Sugar beets	3,641	5,000	6,000
Almonds	70.0	66.0	66.0*
Pistachios	162.8	182.5	170.0*
Walnuts	44.5	73.2	63.0*
Tea (made)	37.0	42.0	45.0*
Tobacco (leaves) . . .	19.0	20.0	22.0*

* FAO estimate. † Unofficial figures.
Source: FAO, *Production Yearbook.*

LIVESTOCK ('000 head, year ending September)

	1990	1991	1992
Horses	255	255	270*
Mules*	135	134	134
Asses	1,860	1,860	1,935*
Cattle	7,532	6,697	6,900†
Buffaloes	383	383	300†
Camels	143	143	130†
Sheep	44,581	44,681	45,000†
Goats	24,748	24,748	23,500†

Chickens (FAO estimates, million): 160 in 1990; 165 in 1991; 170 in 1992.

* FAO estimate(s).   † Unofficial figure.

Source: FAO, *Production Yearbook.*

LIVESTOCK PRODUCTS ('000 metric tons)

	1990	1991	1992
Beef and veal†	210	235	270
Buffalo meat*	10	10	10
Mutton and lamb†	231	240	249
Goats' meat†	100	100	101
Poultry meat	315*	373	444
Other meat	16	17	17
Cows' milk	1,632†	1,892†	1,449*
Buffaloes' milk*	100	100	90
Sheep's milk	810†	810†	810*
Goats' milk	945†	945†	897*
Cheese*	196.0	204.2	184.9
Butter*	73.0	80.0	68.0
Hen eggs	295	342	350
Honey*	7.4	7.7	7.8
Wool:			
greasy	32†	32*	32*
clean	17.6†	17.6*	17.6*
Cattle and buffalo hides*	37.8	38.6	39.1
Sheep skins*	43.2	45.0	46.7
Goat skins*	17.8	17.9	18.0

* FAO estimate(s).   † Unofficial figure(s).

Source: FAO, *Production Yearbook.*

Forestry

ROUNDWOOD REMOVALS ('000 cu metres, excl. bark)

	1990	1991	1992*
Sawlogs, veneer logs and logs for sleepers	267	320	320
Other industrial wood*†	4,007	4,007	4,007
Fuel wood*	2,483	2,495	2,513
Total	6,757	6,822	6,840

* FAO estimates.
† Assumed to be unchanged since 1974.
Source: FAO, *Yearbook of Forest Products.*

SAWNWOOD PRODUCTION
('000 cu metres, incl. railway sleepers)

	1990	1991	1992*
Total	169	173	173

* FAO estimate.
Source: FAO, *Yearbook of Forest Products.*

Fishing

('000 metric tons, live weight)

	1989	1990	1991
Freshwater fishes	30.1	47.4	48.6
Diadromous fishes	17.8	22.1	31.3
Marine fishes	201.7	190.9	189.1
Marine crustaceans and molluscs	10.8	10.7	8.4
Total catch	260.5	271.0	277.4
Inland waters	50.3	71.0	82.4
Indian Ocean	210.2	200.0	195.0

Source: FAO, *Yearbook of Fishery Statistics.*
Production of caviar (metric tons, year ending 20 March): 281 in 1988/89; 310 in 1989/90; 233 in 1990/91.

Mining

CRUDE PETROLEUM
(net production, '000 barrels per day, year ending 20 March)

	1988/89	1989/90	1990/91
Southern oilfields	2,454	2,716	2,987
Offshore oilfields	103	231	244
Doroud–Forouzan–Abouzar–Soroush	58	162	166
Salman–Rostam–Resalat	23	40	46
Sirri–Hendijan–Bahregan	22	29	32
Total	2,557	2,947	3,231

1991/92 ('000 barrels per day): Total production 3,366.
1992/93 ('000 barrels per day): Total production 3,502.
Source: Ministry of Oil.

NATURAL GAS (million cu metres, year ending 20 March)

	1990/91	1991/92	1992/93
Consumption (domestic)*	23,500	32,200	33,900
Flared	11,400	11,100	12,800
Exports	2,100	2,900	500
Total production	37,000	46,200	47,200

* Includes gas for household, commercial, industrial, generator and refinery consumption.

OTHER MINERALS ('000 metric tons, year ending 20 March)

	1986/87	1987/88	1988/89
Hard coal	722*	791	885
Iron ore†	1,156	953	1,045
Copper ore†	50.0	59.4	54.2
Lead ore†	25.0	13.3	15.4
Zinc ore†	17.0	41.1	10.3
Chromium ore†	30.0‡	25.2	31.6
Magnesite (crude)	4,400.0	2,400.0	1,200
Barytes	41.2	42.3	57.0
Salt (unrefined)	539	813	912
Gypsum (crude)	6,082*	6,571	6,676

* Figures refer to calendar year 1986.
† Figures refer to the metal content of ores.
‡ Year ending 30 June.

Industry

PETROLEUM PRODUCTS
(million litres, unless otherwise indicated, year ending 20 March)

	1988/89	1989/90	1990/91
Liquefied petroleum gas ('000 metric tons)*	900	1,096	1,220
Naphtha ('000 metric tons)*	150	150	160
Motor spirit (petrol)	5,551	7,006	7,307
Aviation gasoline ('000 metric tons)*	100	100	150
Kerosene	4,659	6,812	6,062
White spirit ('000 metric tons)*	80	90	100
Jet fuel	485	470	637
Distillate fuel oils	10,751	13,118	13,739
Residual fuel oils	11,721	15,211	15,773
Lubricating oils	153	143	144
Petroleum bitumen (asphalt—'000 metric tons)*	1,700	1,670	1,644

* Figures refer to calendar years 1988, 1989 and 1990. Source: UN, *Industrial Statistics Yearbook*.

OTHER PRODUCTS (year ending 20 March)

	1988/89	1989/90	1990/91
Refined sugar ('000 metric tons)	418	339	385
Cigarettes (million)	13,790	9,923	12,319
Paints ('000 metric tons)	24	31	54
Cement ('000 metric tons)	11,926	12,587	14,429
Refrigerators ('000)	326	351	651
Gas stoves ('000)	131	87	140
Telephone sets ('000)	351	216	189
Radios and recorders ('000)	344	217	232
Television receivers ('000)	303	407	598
Motor vehicles (assembled) ('000)	95	48	88
Footwear (million pairs)	34	37	45
Machine-made carpets ('000 sq m)	4,408	4,867	7,198

Production of Electricity (million kWh): 47,599 in 1988/89; 52,712 in 1989/90; 59,102 in 1990/91.

Finance

CURRENCY AND EXCHANGE RATES
Monetary Units
100 dinars = 1 Iranian rial (IR).

Sterling and Dollar Equivalents (31 May 1994)
£1 sterling = 2,640.1 rials;
US $1 = 1,746.3 rials;
10,000 Iranian rials = £3.788 = $5.726.

Average Exchange Rate (rials per US $)
1991	67.51
1992	65.55
1993	1,267.77

Note: Prior to March 1993, the data on exchange rates refer to the basic official rate of the Central Bank. From 22 May 1980 this valuation of the Iranian rial was linked to the IMF's special drawing right (SDR) at a mid-point rate of SDR 1 = 92.30 rials. However, a system of multiple exchange rates was in operation. Exchange reforms that took effect in January 1991 reduced the number of official rates to three. In addition to the basic rate, there was a 'competitive' rate and a 'floating' rate. In March 1993 the multiple exchange rate system was unified, and since then the exchange rate of the rial has been market-determined.

BUDGET ('000 million rials, year ending 20 March)*

Revenue	1990/91†	1991/92‡	1992/93‡
Taxation	4,912	5,996	4,197
Taxes on income, profits, etc.	656	931	1,294
Individual	157	259	325
Corporate	499	670	967
Social security contributions	538	433	728
Taxes on payroll and work force	128	122	205
Taxes on property	145	244	248
Taxes on financial and capital transactions	82	99	110
Domestic taxes on goods and services	277	544	574
Excises	93	98	100
Profits of fiscal monopolies	120	359	165
Motor vehicle taxes	44	35	243
Taxes on international trade and transactions	3,148	3,690	1,106
Import duties	495	511	1,064
Exchange profits	2,257	3,137	—§
Other current revenue	1,705	2,117	6,307
Entrepreneurial and property income	1,148	1,411	5,157
From non-financial public enterprises and public financial institutions	1,144	1,374	5,123
Oil revenue	1,118	1,329	5,042§
Administrative fees and charges, non-industrial and incidental sales	319	511	702
Total	6,617	8,113	10,504
Budgetary receipts	5,631	7,498	9,518
Social security funds	530	425	720
Extrabudgetary accounts	457	190	266

Expenditure‖	1990/91†	1991/92‡	1992/93‡
General public services	182	233	317
Defence	749	892	969
Public order and safety	318	434	505
Education	1,585	1,938	2,392
Health	556	730	938
Social security and welfare	1,014	1,019	1,406
Housing and community amenities	435	421	601
Recreational, cultural and religious affairs and services	125	178	179
Economic affairs and services	1,576	1,497	1,560
Fuel and energy	191	197	167
Agriculture, forestry, fishing and hunting	396	335	369
Mining and mineral resources, manufacturing and construction	295	295	262
Transport and communications	439	553	649
Other purposes	749	1,929	2,390
Total	7,288	9,271	11,257
Current	5,480	6,534	7,962
Capital	1,808	2,737	3,295

* Figures refer to the consolidated accounts of the central Government, comprising the General Budget, the operations of the Social Insurance Organization and special (extrabudgetary) revenue and expenditure. Data for 1990/91 also include the operations of the Organization for Protection of Consumers and Producers, a central government unit with its own budget.
† Provisional figures.
‡ Estimates.
§ For 1992/93 exchange profits, previously included in taxation, are included in oil revenue.
‖ Excluding lending minus repayments ('000 million rials): −6 in 1990/91.

Source: IMF, *Government Finance Statistics Yearbook*.

CENTRAL BANK RESERVES (US $ million at 31 December)

	1991	1992	1993
Gold	217	209	n.a.
IMF special drawing rights .	309	10	144
Reserve position in IMF . .	—	144	—
Foreign exchange*	—	—	—
Total	526	363	144

* Figures not available since 1982, when the value of reserves was US$5,287m.
Source: IMF, *International Financial Statistics*.

MONEY SUPPLY ('000 million rials at 20 December)

	1991	1992	1993
Currency outside banks . .	3,861.8	4,088.0	4,924.8
Official entities' deposits at Central Bank . . .	553.0	559.3	861.8
Demand deposits at commercial banks	7,850.9	9,433.6	12,518.8
Total money	12,2365.7	14,080.9	18,305.4

Source: IMF, *International Financial Statistics*.

COST OF LIVING (Consumer Price Index; base: 1986 = 100)

	1988	1989	1990
Food	140.5	169.2	174.4
Fuel and light	130.4	127.1	130.5
Clothing	206.9	293.4	364.8
Rent	117.5	132.1	152.3
All items (incl. others) . .	165.4	202.4	217.7

1991: Food 212.9; All items 255.2.
Source: ILO, *Year Book of Labour Statistics*.
1992: Food 284.9; All items 313.7. **1993**: Food 348.2; All items 375.6 (Source: UN, *Monthly Bulletin of Statistics*).

NATIONAL ACCOUNTS
('000 million rials at current prices, year ending 20 March)
National Income and Product

	1990/91	1991/92	1992/93*
Domestic factor incomes† . .	30,312.4	41,064.1	55,419.8
Consumption of fixed capital .	5,442.6	7,600.8	10,585.7
Gross domestic product (GDP) at factor cost . .	35,755.0	48,664.9	66,005.5
Indirect taxes . . . . } *Less* Subsidies . . . . }	889.6	1,434.8	1,805.3
GDP in purchasers' values .	36,644.6	50,099.7	67,810.8
Factor income from abroad . } *Less* Factor income paid abroad . . . }	−263.4	462.5	235.2
Gross national product (GNP)	36,381.2	50,562.2	68,046.0
Less Consumption of fixed capital	5,442.6	7,600.8	10,585.7
National income in market prices	30,938.6	42,961.4	57,460.3

* Provisional figures.
† Compensation of employees and the operating surplus of enterprises.

Expenditure on the Gross Domestic Product

	1990/91	1991/92	1992/93*
Government final consumption expenditure	4,054.2	5,367.1	7,988.4
Private final consumption expenditure	24,070.7	31,676.8	41,294.6
Increase in stocks . . .	4,827.0	5,805.7	6,440.7
Gross fixed capital formation .	5,662.6	10,844.0	15,690.9
Statistical discrepancy . .	−573.0	−1,284.4	−1,802.4
Total domestic expenditure .	38,041.5	52,409.2	69,612.2
Exports of goods and services .	5,395.1	7,439.3	9,644.8
Less Imports of goods and services	6,792.0	9,748.8	11,446.2
GDP in purchasers' values .	36,644.6	50,099.7	67,810.8
GDP at constant 1982/83 prices	10,930.2	12,181.2	12,910.6

* Provisional figures.

Gross Domestic Product by Economic Activity (at factor cost)

	1990/91	1991/92	1992/93*
Agriculture, hunting, forestry and fishing	8,419.1	11,221.6	15,392.0
Mining and quarrying . . .	3,967.0	4,251.2	6,030.9
Manufacturing.	4,413.9	6,833.2	9,218.0
Electricity, gas and water . .	395.2	554.4	834.3
Construction	1,437.5	2,129.1	2,618.8
Trade, restaurants and hotels .	6,541.6	8,645.8	11,308.0
Transport, storage and communications . . .	2,652.4	4,371.0	5,273.9
Finance, insurance, real estate and business services . .	4,296.1	5,898.7	8,095.4
Government services . . .	3,091.6	4,193.2	6,504.9
Other services	817.2	1,076.2	1,403.4
Sub-total	36,031.6	41,174.4	66,679.6
Less Imputed bank service charge	276.6	509.5	674.1
Total	35,755.0	48,664.9	66,005.5

* Provisional figures.

BALANCE OF PAYMENTS (US $ million, year ending 20 March)

	1990/91	1991/92*	1992/93*
Merchandise exports f.o.b. .	19,305	18,415	19,279
Merchandise imports f.o.b. .	−18,330	−23,941	−21,150
Trade balance . . .	975	−5,532	−1,871
Exports of services . .	436	896	741
Imports of services . .	−3,962	−5,583	−5,699
Other income received . .	456	472	340
Other income paid . .	−78	−85	−162
Unrequited transfers (net) .	2,500	2,000	2,000
Current balance . .	327	−7,826	−4,651
Long-term capital (net) . .	49	n.a.	n.a.
Short-term capital (net) . .	305	n.a.	n.a.
Net errors and omissions .	−981	n.a.	n.a.
Overall balance . . .	−300	n.a.	n.a.

* Provisional figures.

External Trade

PRINCIPAL COMMODITIES
(US $ million, year ending 20 March)

Imports c.i.f.	1988/89	1989/90	1990/91
Food and live animals . . .	1,374	2,779	2,138
Beverages and tobacco . .	47	77	47
Crude materials (inedible) except fuels . . .	243	392	753
Mineral fuels, lubricants, etc. .	347	319	422
Animal and vegetable oils and fats	130	359	323
Chemicals and chemical products	1,304	2,048	2,876
Paper, textiles, iron and steel, mineral products, etc. . .	1,623	2,553	5,153
Machinery and motor vehicles .	2,804	3,842	6,264
Miscellaneous manufactured articles . . .	271	381	683
Other commodities. . . .	34	57	63
Total	**8,177**	**12,807**	**18,722**

Exports f.o.b. (excl. petroleum and gas)	1990/91	1991/92	1992/93*
Agricultural and traditional goods	1,038.4	1,959.9	2,076.6
Carpets	509.1	1,125.3	1.133.3
Fruit (fresh and dried) . .	333.0	477.9	503.5
Animal skins and hides, and leather	56.8	57.6	74.2
Caviar	43.5	39.0	23.3
Casings	21.9	36.9	42.7
Others	74.1	223.2	299.6
Metal ores	32.3	39.2	35.6
Industrial manufactures	241.5	474.1	682.2
Shoes	0.2	15.1	25.4
Textile manufactures .	11.7	56.9	77.7
Cements	4.2	6.3	28.2
Motor vehicles . .	4.7	20.4	72.3
Others	220.7	375.4	478.6
Total	**1,312.2**	**2,612.8**	**2,936.5**

* Figures refer to the first 11 months of the Iranian year.

PETROLEUM EXPORTS
('000 barrels per day, year ending 20 March)

	1990/91	1991/92	1992/93
Crude petroleum* . . .	2,224	2,460	2,397
Refined petroleum products .	60	n.a.	n.a.

* Does not include crude oil exported for refining or exchange ('000 barrels per day, year ending 20 March): 170 in 1990/91; 136 in 1991/92; 149 in 1992/93.

Source: Ministry of Oil.

Value of crude petroleum exports ('000 million rials, year ending 20 December; estimates): 731.5 in 1981; 1,508.3 in 1982; 1,621.0 in 1983; 1,065.9 in 1984; 1,364.0 in 1985; 488.7 in 1986; 721.6 in 1987; 632.6 in 1988; 778.4 in 1989 (Source: IMF, *International Financial Statistics*).

Total Exports ('000 million rials, year ending 20 December; estimates): 980.8 in 1981; 1,632.4 in 1982; 1,684.7 in 1983 (Source: IMF, *International Financial Statistics*).

PERCENTAGE GEOGRAPHICAL DISTRIBUTION OF CRUDE PETROLEUM EXPORTS

	1988/89	1989/90	1990/91
Western Europe	39.4	60.5	50.8
Japan	12.4	18.0	20.2
Asia and Far East (excluding Japan)	20.2	15.4	18.1
Africa	0.9	—	0.4
Others (incl. North, Central and South America, and Eastern Europe). . . .	27.1	6.1	10.5

Source: Ministry of Oil.

PRINCIPAL TRADING PARTNERS
(US $ million, year ending 20 March)

Imports c.i.f.	1988/89	1989/90	1990/91
Argentina	159	457	545
Australia	216	451	684
Austria	161	226	450
Belgium	393	493	797
Brazil	343	362	645
Canada	79	384	414
France	243	266	489
Germany, Fed. Republic . .	1,472	2,024	3,430
Italy	417	803	1,499
Japan	836	973	1,933
Korea, Republic . .	127	477	635
Netherlands . . .	286	410	576
Spain	110	219	287
Sweden	80	112	281
Switzerland . . .	215	306	546
Turkey	425	699	726
USSR	217	200	305
United Arab Emirates . .	276	949	971
United Kingdom . . .	556	567	1,015
Yugoslavia. . . .	124	169	210
Total (incl. others) . .	**8,177**	**12,807**	**18,722**

Exports f.o.b.*	1988/89	1989/90	1990/91
France	19.2	25.7	36.1
Germany, Fed. Republic . .	289.3	359.2	399.8
Italy	106.9	134.4	159.0
Japan	36.9	52.9	52.1
Switzerland . . .	77.8	80.3	106.1
Turkey	3.4	5.5	106.1
USSR	63.7	22.8	26.9
United Arab Emirates . . .	145.8	143.6	152.5
United Kingdom . . .	99.3	18.3	50.1
Total (incl. others) . .	**1,035.8**	**1,043.9**	**1,312.2**

* Excluding petroleum products and hydrocarbon solvents obtained from petroleum.

Transport

RAILWAYS (traffic, year ending 20 March)

	1988/89	198/90	1989/90
Passenger-km (million) . .	3,674	4,661	4,752
Freight ton-km (million) . .	8,625	12,334	7,963

ROAD TRAFFIC ('000 vehicles in use)

	1987/88	1988/89	1989/90
Cars	1,966	1,989	2,008
Buses	73	74	76
Trucks.	382	390	396
Ambulances	1,531	10	2
Motor cycles	578	591	605

MERCHANT SHIPPING FLEET
('000 gross registered tons)

	1988/89	1989/90	1990/91
Oil tankers.	120	120	120
Other vessels	2,009	2,012	1,995
Total	**2,129**	**2,132**	**2,115**

INTERNATIONAL SEA-BORNE SHIPPING
(estimated freight traffic, '000 metric tons)

	1988	1989	1990
Goods loaded . . .	87,392	98,404	113,207
Crude petroleum and petroleum products . .	87,162	97,189	112,005
Goods unloaded . .	13,782	15,735	16,719
Petroleum products . .	2,930	2,920	3,161

Source: UN, *Monthly Bulletin of Statistics.*

CIVIL AVIATION (traffic on scheduled services)

	1989	1990	1991
Kilometres flown (million) .	29	33	33
Passengers carried ('000) .	4,883	5,633	5,353
Passenger-km (million) .	4,691	5,755	5,551
Freight ton-km (million) .	92	114	86

Source: UN, *Statistical Yearbook.*

Tourism

	1988	1989	1990
Tourist arrivals ('000). .	66	89	154

Source: UN, *Statistical Yearbook.*

Communications Media

	1989	1990	1991
Radio receivers ('000 in use) .	13,000	13,500	13,860
Television receivers ('000 in use)	3,500	3,800	3,750
Telephones ('000 in use)* . .	2,104	2,270	n.a.
Book production: titles† . .	6,289	n.a.	5,018
Daily newspapers . . .	n.a.	21	n.a.
Periodicals.	n.a.	50	n.a.

* At 21 March of each year.
† Excluding pamphlets (133 in 1988).
Sources: UNESCO, *Statistical Yearbook*; UN, *Statistical Yearbook.*

Education
(1991)

	Institutions	Teachers	Students
Pre-primary	4,114	8,841	252,513
Primary	59,280*	312,273	9,787,593
Secondary:			
General	n.a.	199,451	5,311,988
Teacher training. . .	n.a.	1,222	46,493
Vocational	n.a.	18,258	260,576
Higher:			
Universities, etc. . .	n.a.	19,564	256,212
Distance-learning . .	n.a.	1,691	339,272
Others	n.a.	3,953	40,770

* 1990.
Source: UNESCO, *Statistical Yearbook.*

Directory

The Constitution

A draft constitution for the Islamic Republic of Iran was published on 18 June 1979. It was submitted to a 'Council of Experts', elected by popular vote on 3 August 1979, to debate the various clauses and to propose amendments. The amended Constitution was approved by a referendum on 2–3 December 1979. A further 45 amendments to the Constitution were approved by a referendum on 28 July 1989.

The Constitution states that the form of government of Iran is that of an Islamic Republic, and that the spirituality and ethics of Islam are to be the basis for political, social and economic relations. Persians, Turks, Kurds, Arabs, Balochis, Turkomans and others will enjoy completely equal rights.

The Constitution provides for a President to act as chief executive. The President is elected by universal adult suffrage for a term of four years. Legislative power is held by the Majlis (Islamic Consultative Assembly), with 270 members who are similarly elected for a four-year term. Provision is made for the representation of Zoroastrians, Jews and Christians.

All legislation passed by the Islamic Consultative Assembly must be sent to the Council for the Protection of the Constitution (Article 94), which will ensure that it is in accordance with the Constitution and Islamic legislation. The Council for the Protection of the Constitution consists of six religious lawyers appointed by the Faqih (see below) and six lawyers appointed by the High Council of the Judiciary and approved by the Islamic Consultative Assembly. Articles 19–42 deal with the basic rights of individuals, and provide for equality of men and women before the law and for equal human, political, economic, social and cultural rights for both sexes.

The press is free, except in matters that are contrary to public morality or insult religious belief. The formation of religious, political and professional parties, associations and societies is free, provided they do not negate the principles of independence, freedom, sovereignty and national unity, or the basis of Islam.

The Constitution provides for a Wali Faqih (religious leader) who, in the absence of the Imam Mehdi (the hidden Twelfth Imam), carries the burden of leadership. The amendments to the Constitution that were approved in July 1989 increased the powers of the Presidency by abolishing the post of Prime Minister, formerly the Chief Executive of the Government.

PROVINCIAL DIVISIONS

According to the state division of May 1977, Iran was divided into 23 provinces (Ostans), 472 counties (shahrestan) and 499 municipalities (bakhsh).

The Government

WALI FAQIH (RELIGIOUS LEADER)

Ayatollah SAYED ALI KHAMENEI.

HEAD OF STATE

President: Hojatoleslam ALI AKBAR HASHEMI RAFSANJANI (took office 17 August 1989; re-elected 11 June 1993).

First Vice-President: Dr HASSAN HABIBI.

Vice-President in charge of Economic Affairs: MOHSEN NOUR-BAKHCH.

Vice-President in charge of the Plan and Budget Organization: MASSOUD ROGHANI ZANJANI.

COUNCIL OF MINISTERS
(September 1994)

Minister of Foreign Affairs: Dr ALI AKBAR VELAYATI.

Minister of Education and Training: MUHAMMAD ALI NAJAFI.

Minister of Culture and Islamic Guidance: MOSTAFA MIRSALIM.

Minister of Information: ALI FALAHIAN.

Minister of Commerce: YAHYA AL-E ESHAQ.

Minister of Health: ALI REZA MARANDI.

Minister of Posts, Telegraphs and Telephones: Eng. SAYED MUHAMMAD GHARAZI.

Minister of Justice: ISMAÏL CHOUCHTARI.

Minister of Defence and Logistics: MUHAMMAD FOROUZANDEH.

Minister of Roads and Transport: ALI AKBAR TORKAN.

Minister of Industries: Eng. MUHAMMAD REZA NEEMATZADEH.

Minister of Higher Education: MUHAMMAD REZA HASHEMI GOLPAYE-GANI.

Minister of Mines and Metals: HOSSEIN MAHLOUDJI.

Minister of Labour and Social Affairs: HOSSEIN KAMALI.

Minister of the Interior: ALI MUHAMMAD BESHARATI.

Minister of Agriculture: ISA KALANTARI.

Minister of Housing and Urban Development: ABBAS AHMAD AKHUNDI.

Minister of Energy: NAMDAR ZANGANEH.

Minister of Oil: GHOLAMREZA AQAZADEH.

Minister of Economic Affairs and Finance: MORTEZA MUHAMMAD-KHAN.

Minister of Construction Jihad: GHOLAMREZA FOROUZESH.

Minister of Co-operatives: GHOLAMREZA SHAFEI.

MINISTRIES

Ministry of Mines and Metals: 248 Somayeh Ave, Teheran; tel. (21) 836051; telex 212718.

Ministry of Roads and Transport: 49 Taleghani Ave, Teheran; tel. (21) 646770.

All ministries are in Teheran. The Plan and Budget Organization, which was made a ministry, was returned to its former status, under the Presidency, in 1989.

President and Legislature

PRESIDENT

Election, 11 June 1993

Candidates	Votes	%
Hojatoleslam ALI AKBAR HASHEMI RAFSANJANI	10,553,644	63.2
AHMED TAVAKKOLI	3,976,165	23.8
ABDULLAH JASBI	1,515,632	9.1
RAJABALI TAHERI	401,579	2.4
Invalid	253,230	1.5
Total	**16,700,250**	**100.0**

MAJLIS-E-SHURA E ISLAMI—ISLAMIC CONSULTATIVE ASSEMBLY

Elections to the fourth Majlis took place in two rounds, on 10 April and 8 May 1992. In the first round of voting 136 candidates gained a sufficiently large proportion (at least 30%) of the total votes cast in their constituencies to take up seats in the 270-member Majlis. In the second round of voting a further 132 deputies were elected to the Assembly. The elections in two single-member constituencies were declared to be invalid by the Council of Guardians and were to be contested again during the term of the new Majlis.

Speaker: ALI AKBAR NATEQ NOURI.

Deputy Speakers: Hojatoleslam HOSSEIN HASHEMIAN, ASADOLLAH BAYAT.

SHURA-YE ALI-YE AMNIYYAT-E MELLI—SUPREME COUNCIL FOR NATIONAL SECURITY

Formed in July 1989 to co-ordinate defence and national security policies, the political programme and intelligence reports, and social, cultural and economic activities related to defence and security. The Council is chaired by the President and includes two representatives of the Wali Faqih, the Head of the Judiciary, the Speaker of the Majlis, the Chief of Staff, the General Command of the Armed Forces, the Minister of Foreign Affairs, the Minister of the Interior, the Minister of Information and the Head of the Plan and Budget Organization.

MAJLIS-E KHOBREGAN—COUNCIL OF EXPERTS

Elections were held on 10 December 1982 to appoint a Council of Experts which was to choose an eventual successor to the Wali Faqih, Ayatollah Khomeini, after his death. The Constitution provides for a three- or five-man body to assume the leadership of the country if there is no recognized successor on the death of the Wali Faqih. The Council comprises 83 clerics. Elections to a second term of the Council were held on 8 October 1990.

Speaker: Ayatollah ALI MESHKINI.

First Deputy Speaker: Hojatoleslam ALI AKBAR HASHEMI RAFSANJANI.

Secretaries: Hojatoleslam HASSAN TAHERI-KHORRAMABADI, Ayatollah MUHAMMAD MOME-QOMI, Ayatollah IBRAHIM AMINI.

SHURA-E-NIGAHBAN—COUNCIL OF GUARDIANS

The Council of Guardians, composed of six qualified Muslim jurists and six lay Muslim lawyers, appointed by Ayatollah Khomeini and the Supreme Judicial Council, respectively, was established in 1980 to supervise elections and to examine legislation adopted by the Majlis, ensuring that it accords with the Constitution and with Islamic precepts.

Chairman: Ayatollah MUHAMMAD MUHAMMADI GUILANI.

SHURA-YE TASHKHIS-E MASLAHAT-E NEZAM— COMMITTEE TO DETERMINE THE EXPEDIENCY OF THE ISLAMIC ORDER

Formed in February 1988, by order of Ayatollah Khomeini, to arbitrate on legal and theological questions in legislation passed by the Majlis, in the event of a dispute between the latter and the supervisory Council of Guardians. The Committee comprises the six qualified religious jurists on the Council of Guardians and seven leading government officials.

Chairman: Hojatoleslam ALI AKBAR HASHEMI RAFSANJANI.

Political Organizations

The Islamic Republican Party was founded in 1978 to bring about the Islamic Revolution under the leadership of AYATOLLAH KHOMEINI. After the revolution the IRP became the ruling party in what was effectively a one-party state. In June 1987 AYATOLLAH KHOMEINI officially disbanded the IRP at the request of party leaders, who said that it had achieved its purpose and might only 'provide an excuse for discord and factionalism' if it were not dissolved. Of the parties listed below, only the Nehzat-Azadi (Liberation Movement of Iran) has enjoyed official recognition and been allowed to participate in elections.

Democratic Party of Iranian Kurdistan: f. 1945; seeks autonomy for Kurdish area; mem. of the National Council of Resistance; 54,000 mems.

Fedayin-e-Khalq (Warriors of the People): urban Marxist guerrillas; Spokesman FARRAKH NEGAHDAR.

Hezb-e-Komunist Iran (Communist Party of Iran): f. 1979 on grounds that Tudeh Party was Moscow-controlled; Sec.-Gen. 'AZARYUN'.

Komala: f. 1969; Kurdish wing of the Communist Party of Iran; Marxist-Leninist; Leader IBRAHIM ALIZADEH.

Mujahidin-e-Khalq (Holy Warriors of the People): Islamic guerrilla group; since June 1987 comprising the National Liberation Army; mem. of the National Council of Resistance; Leaders MASSOUD RAJAVI and MARYAM RAJAVI (in Baghdad 1986–).

National Democratic Front: f. March 1979; Leader HEDAYATOLLAH MATINE-DAFTARI (in Paris, January 1982–).

National Front (Union of National Front Forces): comprises Iran Nationalist Party, Iranian Party, and Society of Iranian Students; Leader Dr KARIM SANJABI (in Paris, August 1978–).

Nehzat-Azadi (Liberation Movement of Iran): f. 1961; emphasis on basic human rights as defined by Islam; Gen. Sec. Dr MEHDI BAZARGAN; Principal Officers Prof. SAHABI, Dr YAZDI, S. SADR, Dr SADR, Eng. SABAGHIAN, Eng. TAVASSOLI.

Pan-Iranist Party: extreme right-wing; calls for a Greater Persia; Leader Dr MOHSEN PEZESHKPOUR.

Sazmane Peykar dar Rahe Azadieh Tabaqe Kargar (Organization Struggling for the Freedom of the Working Class): Marxist-Leninist.

Tudeh Party (Communist): f. 1941; declared illegal 1949; came into open 1979, banned again April 1983; First Sec. Cen. Cttee ALI KHAVARI.

The National Council of Resistance (NCR) was formed in Paris in October 1981 by former President ABOLHASAN BANI-SADR and the Council's current leader, MASSOUD RAJAVI, the leader of the Mujahidin-e-Khalq in Iran. In 1984 the Council comprised 15 opposition groups, operating either clandestinely in Iran or from exile abroad. BANI-SADR left the Council in 1984 because of his objection to RAJAVI'S growing links with the Iraqi Government. The French Government asked RAJAVI to leave Paris in June 1986 and he is now based in Baghdad, Iraq. On 20 June 1987 RAJAVI, Secretary of the NCR, announced the formation of a National Liberation Army (10,000–15,000-strong) as the military wing of the Mujahidin-e-Khalq. There is also a National Movement of Iranian Resistance, based in Paris. Dissident members of the Tudeh Party founded the Democratic Party of the Iranian People in Paris in February 1988.

Diplomatic Representation

EMBASSIES IN IRAN

Afghanistan: Dr Beheshi Ave, Pompe Benzine, Corner of 4th St, Teheran; tel. (21) 627531; Ambassador: Dr MOHAMMAD AKRAM OSMAN.

Albania: Teheran; Ambassador: GILANI SHEHU.

Angola: Teheran; Ambassador: MANUEL BERNARDO DE SOUSA.

Argentina: 4th Floor, 7 Argentina Sq., Teheran; tel. (21) 628294; Ambassador: NORBERTO AUGUSTO AUGE.

Australia: POB 15875-4334, 123 Khaled al-Islambuli Ave, Teheran 15138; tel. (21) 626202; telex 212459; fax (21) 626415; Ambassador: JOHN G. W. OLIVER.

Austria: POB 15115-455, 3rd Floor, 78 Africa Sq., Teheran; tel. (21) 620753; telex 212872; fax (21) 620778; Ambassador: ERICH MARTIN BUTTENHAUSER.

Azerbaijan: Teheran; Ambassador: (vacant).

Bahrain: Khaled al-Islambuli Ave, Teheran; tel. (21) 682079; Ambassador: HAMAD AHMAD ABDOLAZIZ AL-AMER.

Bangladesh: POB 11365-3711, Gandhi Ave, 5th St, Building No. 14, Teheran; tel. (21) 682979; telex 212303; Ambassador: SHAHEED FALLAHI ZAFRANIYEH SHAHEED BAGHDADI.

Belgium: POB 11365-115, Fereshteh Ave, Shabdiz Lane, 3 Babak St, Teheran 19659; tel. (21) 294574; telex 212446; Ambassador: LOUIS FOBE.

Brazil: Vanak Sq., Vanak Ave No. 58, Teheran 19964; tel. (21) 685175; telex 212392; Ambassador: SERGIO TUTIKIAN.

Bulgaria: POB 11365-7451, Vali Asr Ave, Tavanir St, Nezami Ganjavi St, No. 82, Teheran; tel. (21) 685662; telex 212789; Ambassador: STEFAN POLENDAKOV.

Canada: POB 11365-4647, 57 Shahid Sarafraz St; tel. 622623; fax 623202; Ambassador: DONALD P. MCLENNAN.

China, People's Republic: Pasdaran Ave, Golestan Ave 1, No. 53, Teheran; tel. (21) 245131; Ambassador: HUA LIMING.

Colombia: Teheran; Ambassador: EDUARDO A. BARAJAS SANDÓVAL.

Cuba: Teheran; tel. (21) 685030; Ambassador: ENRIQUE TRUJILLO RAPALLO.

Czech Republic: POB 11365-4457, Enghelab Ave, Sarshar St, No. 61, Teheran; tel. (21) 828168; Ambassador: (vacant).

Denmark: POB 11365-158, 18 Dashti Ave, Teheran; tel. (21) 261363; telex 212784; fax (21) 294085; Ambassador: ERLING HARILD NIELSEN.

Ethiopia: Teheran; Ambassador: MOHAMMED HASAN KAHIM.

Finland: POB 15115-619, Vali Asr Ave, Vanak Sq., Nilou St, Teheran; tel. (21) 4889151; telex 212930; fax (21) 4889107; Ambassador: E. SAARKOSKI.

France: 85 ave Neauphle-le-Château, Teheran; tel. (21) 676005; Ambassador: HUBERT COLIN DE VERDIÈRE.

Gabon: Teheran; tel. (21) 823828; telex 215038; Ambassador: J. B. ESSONGUE.

Gambia: Teheran; Ambassador: OMAR JAH.

Germany: POB 11365-179, 324 Ferdowsi Ave, Teheran; tel. 3114111; telex 212488; Ambassador: Dr REINHOLD SCHENK.

Ghana: Teheran; Ambassador: Mr AL-HASSAN.

Greece: POB 11365-8151, Africa Expressway (Ex. Jordan Ave), Esfandiar St No. 43, Teheran 19686; tel. (21) 2272348; Ambassador: JOHN THOMOGLOU.

Guinea: Teheran; Ambassador: MAMDGU SOALIOU SYLLA.

Holy See: Apostolic Nunciature, POB 11365-178, Razi Ave, No. 97, ave Neauphle-le-Château, Teheran; tel. (21) 6403574; fax (21) 6419442; Apostolic Pro-Nuncio: ROMEO PANCIROLI.

Hungary: Abbas Abad Park Ave, 13th St, No. 18, Teheran; tel. (21) 622800; Ambassador: Dr GÉZA PALMAI.

India: POB 11365-6573, Saba-e-Shomali Ave, No. 166, Teheran; tel. (21) 894554; telex 212858; Ambassador: S. K. ARORA.

Indonesia: POB 11365-4564, Ghaem Magham Farahani Ave, No. 210, Teheran; tel. (21) 626865; telex 212049; Ambassador: BAMBANG SUDARSONO.

Iraq: Vali Asr Ave, No. 494, Teheran.

Ireland: 8 Mirdamad Blvd, 8 North Razan St, Teheran; tel. (21) 222731; telex 213865; fax (21) 2222731; Ambassador: ANTHONY EDWARD MANNIX.

Italy: POB 11365-7863, 81 ave Neauphle-le-Château, Teheran; tel. (21) 6496955; telex 214171; fax (21) 6496961; Ambassador: GIOVANNI CASTELLANETA.

Japan: POB 11365-814, Bucharest Ave, N.W. Corner of 5th St, Teheran; tel. (21) 623396; telex 212757; Ambassador: TSUNEO OYAKE.

Jordan: POB 19395-4666, No. 6, 2nd Alley, Shadavar St, Mahmoodieh Ave, Teheran; tel. (21) 291432; telex 226899; fax (21) 2007160; Ambassador YASIN ISTANBULI.

Kazakhstan: Teheran; Ambassador: MURZATAY ZHOLDASBEKOV.

Kenya: 60 Hormoz Satari St, Africa Ave, Teheran; tel. (21) 2270795; telex 213652; fax (21) 2270160; Ambassador: SALIM JUMA.

Korea, Democratic People's Republic: Fereshteh Ave, Sarvestan Ave, No. 11, Teheran; tel. (21) 298610; Ambassador: HWANG SUN MUK.

Korea, Republic: 37 Bucharest Ave, Teheran; tel. (21) 621125; telex 212693; fax (21) 627917; Chargé d'affaires a.i.: KYUNG YIL JHUNG.

Kuwait: Dehkadeh Ave, 3–38 Sazman-Ab St, Teheran; tel. (21) 636712; Ambassador: AHMAD ABD AL-AZIZ AL-JASSIM.

Kyrgyzstan: Teheran.

Laos: Teheran; Ambassador: CHANPHENG SIHAPHOM.

Lebanon: Teheran; Ambassador: JAOUDAT YOUSEF NOUREDDINE.

Libya: Ostad Motahhari Ave, No. 163, Teheran; tel. (21) 859191; Sec.-Gen. Committee of People's Bureau: MAHDI AL-MABIRASH.

Malaysia: Africa Expressway, 21 Golghasht St, Teheran; tel. (21) 297791; Ambassador: MOHAMMAD AZHARI BIN ABDUL KARIM.

Mauritania: Teheran.

Mexico: POB 15875-4636, No. 24, Shabnam Alley, Africa Expressway, Teheran; tel. (21) 2225374; telex 216557; fax (21) 2225375; Ambassador: ANTONIO DUENAS PULIDO.

Mongolia: Teheran; Ambassador: L. KHASHOAT.

Morocco: Teheran; tel. (21) 2582365; fax (21) 2551551; Ambassador: MOHAMMAD AZAROUAL.

Mozambique: Teheran; Ambassador: MURADE ISAC MIGUIGY MURARGY.

Myanmar: Teheran; Ambassador: U SAW HLAING.

Namibia: Teheran; Ambassador: MWAILEPENI T. P. SHITILIFA.

Nepal: Teheran; Ambassador: Gen. ARJUN NARSING RONA.

Netherlands: POB 11365-138, Vali Asr Ave, Ostad Motahhari Ave, Sarbederan St, Jahansouz Alley, No. 36, Teheran; tel. (21) 896011; telex 212788; fax (21) 8892083; Ambassador: H. HEŸEN.

New Zealand: POB 11365-436, Mirza-e-Shirazi Ave, Kucheh Mirza Hassani, No. 29, Teheran; tel. (21) 625061; telex 212078; fax (21) 8861715; Ambassador: (vacant).

Nigeria: POB 11365-7148, Khaled Islamboli Ave, 31st St, No. 9, Teheran; tel. (21) 684921; telex 213151; fax (21) 684936; Ambassador: ANO SANUSI.

Norway: POB 15875-4891, Bucharest Ave, 6th St, No. 23, Teheran 15146; tel. (21) 624644; telex 213009; Ambassador: JAN NAERBY.

Oman: POB 41-1586, Pasdaran Ave, Golestan 9, No. 5 and 7, Teheran; tel. (21) 286021; telex 212835; Chargé d'affaires a.i.: RASHID BIN MUBARAK BIN RASHID AL-ODWALI.

Pakistan: Dr Fatemi Ave, Jamshidabad Shomali, Mashal St, No. 1, Teheran; tel. (21) 934332; AHMAD SHAMSHAD.

Panama: Teheran; Ambassador: G. MOVAGA.

Philippines: POB 19395-4797, 2 Bahar St Corner, Vali Asr Ave, Zafaranieh, Teheran; tel. (21) 8019619; telex 212510; fax (21) 274039; Ambassador OSCAR G. VALENZUELA.

Poland: Africa Expressway, Piruz St, No. 1/3, Teheran; tel. (21) 227262; Ambassador: STEFAN SZYMCZYKIEWICZ.

Portugal: Vali Asr Ave, Tavanir Ave, Nezami Ghanjavi Ave, No. 30, Teheran; tel. (21) 681380; telex 212588; Ambassador: CARLOS MARIA DAVID CALDER.

Qatar: Africa Expressway, Golazin Ave, Parke Davar, No. 4, Teheran; tel. (21) 221255; telex 212375; Ambassador: ALI ABDULLAH ZAID AL-MAHMOOOD.

Romania: Fakhrabad Ave 12, Darvaze Shemiran, Teheran; tel. (21) 7509309; telex 212791; fax (21) 7509841; Ambassador: IOAN EMIL VASILIU.

Russia: 39 ave Neauphle-le-Château, Teheran; tel. (21) 671163; Ambassador: SERGEI TRETYAKOV.

Saudi Arabia: 10 Saba Blvd, Africa Ave, Teheran; tel. (21) 2220081; fax (21) 2220083; Ambassador: ABD AL-LATIF ABDULLAH AL-MEIMANI.

Singapore: Teheran; Ambassador: GOPINATH PILLAI.

Slovakia: POB 11365-4451, No. 24, Babak Markazi St, Africa Ave, Teheran; tel. (21) 2271058; fax (21) 2271057; Chargé d'affaires a.i.: ALEXANDER BAJKAI.

Somalia: Shariati Ave, Soheyl Ave, No. 20, Teheran; tel. (21) 272034; Ambassador: ABDI SHIRE WARSAME.

Spain: Ghaem Magham Farahani Ave, Varahram St, No. 14, Teheran; tel. (21) 624575; telex 212980; Ambassador: FERNANDO JOSÉ BELLOSO.

Sudan: Khaled Islambouli Ave, 23rd St, No. 10, Teheran; tel. (21) 628476; telex 213372; Ambassador: Dr ABDEL RAHANA MOHAMMED SAID.

Sweden: POB 15875-4313, 78 Argentine Sq., Teheran; tel. (21) 620514; telex 212822; fax (21) 8861241; Ambassador: HANS ANDERSSON.

Switzerland: POB 19395-4683, 13/1 Boustan Ave, 19649 Teheran; tel. (21) 268227; telex 212851; fax 269448; Ambassador: RUDOLF WEIERSMÜLLER.

Syria: Africa Ave, 19 Iraj St, Teheran; tel. (21) 229032; Ambassador: AHMAD AL-HASSAN.

Tajikistan: Teheran.

Thailand: POB 11495-111, Baharestan Ave, Parc Amin ed-Doleh, No. 4, Teheran; tel. (21) 7531433; telex 214040; fax (21) 7532022; Ambassador: PRIDA APIRAT.

Tunisia: Teheran; Ambassador: Dr NOUREDDINE AL-HAMDANI.

Turkey: Ferdowsi Ave, No. 314, Teheran; tel. (21) 3115299; telex 213670; fax (21) 3117928; Ambassador: A. MITHAT BALKAN.

Turkmenistan: Teheran.

Ukraine: Hefez Avenue, Teheran 487; tel. (21) 675148; telex 112574; Chargé d'affaires: IVAN GRIGOROVICH MAYDAN.

United Arab Emirates: Zafar Ave, No. 355–7, Teheran; tel. (21) 221333; telex 212697; Ambassador: AHMAD MOHAMMED BORHEIMAH.

United Kingdom: POB 11365-4474, 143 Ferdowsi Ave, Teheran 11344; tel. (21) 675011; telex 212493; fax (21) 678021; Chargé d'affaires a.i.: JEFFREY JAMES.

Uruguay: Africa Expressway, 49 Golzin Blvd; tel. (21) 4275130; Ambassador: Dr DUPETIT.

Venezuela: POB 15875-4354, Bucharest Ave, 9th St, No. 31, Teheran; tel. (21) 625185; telex 213790; fax (21) 622840; Ambassador: Dr HERNÁN CALCURIAN.

Viet Nam: Teheran; Ambassador: VUXNAN ANG.

Yemen: Bucharest Ave, No. 26, Teheran; Chargé d'affaires a.i.: Dr AHMED MOHAMED ALI ABDULLAH.

Yugoslavia: POB 11365-118, Vali Asr Ave, Fereshteh Ave, Amir Teymour Alley, No. 12, 19659 Teheran; tel. (21) 294127; telex 214235; fax (21) 294978; Chargé d'affaires: ZORAN BOJOVIĆ.

Zaire: Teheran; tel. (21) 222199; Chargé d'affaires a.i.: N'DJATE ESELE SASA.

Judicial System

In August 1982 the Supreme Court revoked all laws dating from the previous regime which did not conform with Islam. In October 1982 all courts set up prior to the Islamic Revolution were abolished. In June 1987 Ayatollah Khomeini ordered the creation of clerical courts to try members of the clergy opposed to government policy. A new system of *qisas* (retribution) was established, placing the emphasis on speedy justice. Islamic codes of correction were introduced in 1983, including the dismembering of a hand for theft, flogging for fornication and violations of the strict code of dress for women, and stoning for adultery. One hundred and nine offences may be punished by the death penalty. In 1984 there was a total of 2,200 judges. The Supreme Court has 16 branches.

SUPREME COURT

Chief Justice: Hojatoleslam MUHAMMAD MUHAMMADI GUILANI.

Prosecutor-General: Hojatoleslam MORTEZA MOQTADAI.

Religion

According to the 1979 constitution, the official religion is Islam of the Ja'fari sect (Shi'ite), but other Islamic sects, including Zeydi, Hanafi, Maleki, Shafe'i and Hanbali, are valid and will be respected. Zoroastrians, Jews and Christians will be recognized as official religious minorities. According to the 1976 census, there were then 310,000 Christians (mainly Armenian), 80,000 Jews and 30,000 Zoroastrains.

ISLAM

The great majority of the Iranian people are Shi'a Muslims, but there is a minority of Sunni Muslims. Persians and Azerbaijanis are mainly Shi'i, while the other ethnic groups are mainly Sunni.

CHRISTIANITY

The Roman Catholic Church

At 31 December 1992 there were an estimated 14,000 adherents in Iran, comprising 6,350 of the Chaldean Rite, 2,650 of the Armenian Rite and 5,000 of the Latin Rite.

Armenian Rite

Bishop of Isfahan: Dr VARTAN TEKEYAN, Armenian Catholic Bishopric, Khiaban Ghazzali 22, Teheran; tel. (21) 677204.

Chaldean Rite

Archbishop of Ahwaz: HANNA ZORA, Archbishop's House, POB 61956, Naderi St, Ahwaz; tel. (61) 24890.

Archbishop of Teheran: YOUHANNAN SEMAAN ISSAYI, Archevêché, Forsat Ave 91, Teheran 15819; tel. (21) 8823549.

Archbishop of Urmia (Rezayeh) and Bishop of Salmas (Shahpour): THOMAS MERAM, Khalifagari Kaldani Katholiq, POB 338, Orumiyeh 57135; tel. (441) 22739.

Latin Rite

Archbishop of Isfahan: IGNAZIO BEDINI, Consolata Church, POB 11365-445, 75 France Ave, Teheran; tel. (21) 673210.

The Anglican Communion

Anglicans in Iran are adherents of the Episcopal Church in Jerusalem and the Middle East, formally inaugurated in January 1976. The Rt Rev. HASSAN DEHQANI-TAFTI, the Bishop in Iran from 1961 to 1990, was President-Bishop of the Church from 1976 to 1986. Following an assassination attempt against him in October 1979, the Bishop went into exile (he now resides in the United Kingdom and was Assistant Bishop of Winchester, in the Church of England, between 1982 and 1990).

Bishop in Iran: Rt Rev. IRAJ MOTTAHEDEH, Abbas-abad, POB 81465-135, Isfahan; tel. (31) 234675; diocese founded 1912.

Presbyterian Church

Synod of the Evangelical (Presbyterian) Church in Iran: Assyrian Evangelical Church, Khiaban-i Hanifnejad, Khiaban-i Aramanch, Teheran; Moderator Rev. ADEL NAKHOSTEEN.

ZOROASTRIANS

There are about 30,000 Zoroastrians, a remnant of a once widespread sect. Their religious leader is MOUBAD.

OTHER COMMUNITIES

Communities of Armenians, and somewhat smaller numbers of Jews (an estimated 30,000 in 1986), Assyrians, Greek Orthodox Christians, Uniates and Latin Christians are also found as officially recognized faiths. The Bahá'í faith, which originated in Iran, has about 300,000 Iranian adherents, although at least 10,000 are believed to have fled since 1979 in order to escape persecution. The Government banned all Bahá'í institutions in August 1983.

The Press

Teheran dominates the press scene as many of the daily papers are published there and the bi-weekly, weekly and less frequent publications in the provinces generally depend on the major metropolitan dailies as a source of news. A press law which was announced in August 1979 required all newspapers and magazines to be licensed and imposed penalties of imprisonment for insulting senior religious figures. Offences against the Act will be tried in the criminal courts. In the Constitution which was approved in December 1979, the press is free, except in matters that are contrary to public morality, insult religious belief or slander the honour and reputation of individuals. In August 1980 Ayatollah Khomeini issued directives which indicated that censorship would be tightened up, and several papers were closed down in 1981. In 1985, however, a policy of relative liberalization of the press was introduced.

PRINCIPAL DAILIES

Abrar (Rightly Guided): Apadan Ave 198, Abbasabad, Teheran; tel. (21) 859971; f. 1985 after closure of *Azadegan* by order of the Prosecutor-General; morning; Farsi; circ. 75,000.

Alik: POB 11365-953, Jomhoori Islami Ave, Alik Alley, Teheran 11357; tel. (21) 676671; f. 1931; afternoon; political and literary; Armenian; Propr A. AJEMIAN; circ. 3,400.

Bahari Iran: Khayaban Khayham, Shiraz; tel. 33738.

Ettela'at (Information): Khayyam St, Teheran; tel. (21) 3281; telex 212336; fax (21) 3115530; f. 1925; evening; Farsi; political and literary; owned and managed by Mostazafin Foundation from October 1979 until 1 January 1987, when it was placed under the

direct supervision of Wilayat-e-Faqih (religious jurisprudence); Editor S. M. DOAEI; circ. 500,000.

Kayhan (Universe): Ferdowsi Ave, Teheran; tel. (21) 310251; telex 212467; f. 1941; evening; Farsi; political; also publishes *Kayhan International* (f. 1959; daily and weekly; English; Editor HOSSEIN RAGHFAR), *Kayhan Arabic* (f. 1980; daily and weekly; Arabic), *Kayhan Persian* (f. 1942; daily; Persian), *Kayhan Turkish* (f. 1984; monthly; Turkish), *Kayhan Havaie* (f. 1950; weekly for Iranians abroad; Farsi), *Kayhan Andishe* (World of Religion; f. 1985; 6 a year; Farsi), *Zan-e-Ruz* (Woman Today; f. 1964; weekly; Farsi), *Kayhan Varzeshi* (World of Sport; f. 1955; weekly; Farsi), *Kayhan Bacheha* (Children's World; f. 1956; weekly; Farsi), *Kayhan Farhangi* (World of Culture; f. 1984; monthly; Farsi); *Kayhan Yearbook* (yearly; Farsi); *Period of 40 Years, Kayhan* (series of books; Farsi); owned and managed by Mostazafin Foundation from October 1979 until 1 January 1987, when it was placed under the direct supervision of Wilayat-e-Faqih (religious jurisprudence); Chief Editor HOSSEIN SHARIATMADARI; circ. 350,000.

Khorassan: Meshed; Head Office: Khorassan Daily Newspapers, 14 Zohre St, Mobarezan Ave, Teheran; f. 1948; Propr MUHAMMAD SADEGH TEHERANIAN; circ. 40,000.

Rahnejat: Darvazeh Dowlat, Isfahan; political and social; Propr N. RAHNEJAT.

Risala'at (The Message): Teheran; organ of right-wing group of the same name; political; Propr Ayatollah AHMAD AZARI-QOMI; circ. 40,000.

Salam: Farsi; Editor ABBAS ABDI.

Teheran Times: Nejatullahi Ave, 32-Kouche Bimeh, Teheran; tel. (21) 839900; telex 213662; fax (21) 822951; f. 1979; independent; English; Editor-in-Chief M. B. ANSARI.

PRINCIPAL PERIODICALS

Acta Medica Iranica: Faculty of Medicine, Enghelab Ave, Teheran Medical Sciences Univ., Teheran 14-174; tel. (21) 6112743; f. 1960; quarterly; English, French; under the supervision of the Research Vice-Dean (G. POURMAND) and the Editorial Board; Editor-in-Chief PARVIZ JABAL-AMELI (Dean, Faculty of Medicine); circ. 2,000.

Akhbar-e-Pezeshki: 86 Ghaem Magham Farahani Ave, Teheran; weekly; medical; Propr Dr T. FORUZIN.

Ashur: Ostad Motahhari Ave, 11-21 Kuhe Nour Ave, Teheran; tel. (21) 622117; f. 1969; Assyrian; monthly; Founder and Editor Dr W. BET-MANSOUR; circ. 8,000.

Auditor: 77 Ferdowsi Ave North, Teheran; quarterly; financial and managerial studies.

Ayandeh: POB 19575-583, Niyavaran, Teheran; tel. (21) 283254; fax (21) 6406426; monthly; Iranian literary, historical and book review journal; Editor Prof. IRAJ AFSHAR.

Bulletin of the National Film Archive of Iran: POB 5158, Baharestan Sq., Teheran 11365; tel. 311242; telex 214283; f. 1989; English periodical; Editor M. H. KHOSHNEVIS.

Daneshkadeh Pezeshki: Faculty of Medicine, Teheran Medical Sciences University; tel. (21) 6112743; f. 1947; 10 a year; medical magazine; Propr Dr HASSAN AREFI; circ. 1,500.

Daneshmand: POB 15875-3649, Teheran; tel. (21) 854969; f. 1963; monthly; scientific and technical magazine; Editor AHMAD FARMAD.

Donaye Varzesh: Khayyam Ave, Ettela'at Bldg, Teheran; tel. (21) 3281; telex 212336; fax (21) 3115530; weekly; sport; Editor G. H. SHABANI; circ. 200,000.

Echo of Islam: POB 14155-3987, Teheran; monthly; English; published by the Foundation of Islamic Thought.

Ettela'at Elmi: 11 Khayyam Ave, Teheran; tel. (21) 3281; telex 212336; fax (21) 3115530; f. 1985; fortnightly; sciences; Editor Mrs GHASEMI; circ. 75,000.

Ettela'at Haftegi: 11 Khayyam Ave, Teheran; tel. (21) 3281; telex 212336; fax (21) 3115530; f. 1941; general weekly; Editor F. JAVADI; circ. 150,000.

Ettela'at Javanan: POB 11335-9365, 11144 Khayyam Ave, Teheran; tel. (21) 3281, telex 212336; fax (21) 3115530; f. 1966; weekly; youth; Editor M. J. RAFIZADEH; circ. 120,000.

Farhang-e-Iran Zamin: POB 19575-583, Niyavaran, Teheran; tel. (21) 283254; annual; Iranian studies; Editor Prof. IRAJ AFSHAR.

Film International: POB 5875, Teheran 11365; tel. (21) 679374; fax (21) 6459971; f. 1993; quarterly in English; Editor B. RAHIMIAN.

Iran Press Digest (Economic): POB 11365-5551, Hafiz Ave, 4 Kucheh Hurtab, Teheran; tel. (21) 668114; telex 212300; weekly; Editor J. BEHROUZ.

Iran Press Digest (Political): POB 11365-5551, Hafiz Ave, 4 Kucheh Hurtab, Teheran; tel. (21) 668114; telex 212300; weekly.

Iranian Cinema: POB 5158, Baharestan Sq., Teheran 11365; tel. 311242; f. 1985; annually; English; Editor B. REYPOUR.

Javaneh: POB 15875-1163, Motahhari Ave, Cnr Mofatteh St, Teheran; tel. (21) 839051; published by Soroush Press; quarterly.

Kayhan Bacheha (Children's World): Shahid Shahsheragi Ave, Teheran; tel. (21) 310251; telex 212467; f. 1956; weekly; Editor AMIR HOSSEIN FARDI; circ. 150,000.

Kayhan Varzeshi (World of Sport): Ferdowsi Ave, Teheran; tel. (21) 310251; telex 212467; f. 1955; weekly; Dir MAHMAD MONSETI; circ. 125,000.

Mahjubah: POB 14155-3897, Teheran; tel. (21) 844092; fax (21) 898295; Islamic women's magazine; published by the Islamic Thought Foundation.

Majda: POB 14155-3695, 94 West Pirouzi St, Kooye Nasr, Teheran; tel. (21) 639591; telex 212918; fax (21) 639592; f. 1963; four a year; medical; journal of the Iranian Dental Association; Pres. Dr ALI YAZDANI.

Music Iran: 1029 Amiriye Ave, Teheran; f. 1951; monthly; Editor BAHMAN HIRBOD; circ. 7,000.

Negin: Vali Asr Ave, Adl St 52, Teheran; monthly; scientific and literary; Propr and Dir M. ENAYAT.

Pars: Alley Dezhban, Shiraz; f. 1941; irregular; Propr and Dir F. SHARGHI; circ. 10,000.

Salamate Fekr: M.20, Kharg St, Teheran; tel. (21) 223034; f. 1958; monthly; organ of the Mental Health Soc.; Editors Prof. E. TCHEHRAZI, ALI REZA SHAFAI.

Soroush: POB 15875-1163, Motahhari Ave, Corner Mofatteh St, Teheran; tel. (21) 830771; f. 1972; two monthly magazines in Farsi, one for children and one for adolescents; Editor MEHDI FIROOZAN.

Zan-e-Ruz (Woman Today): Ferdowsi Ave, Teheran; telex 212467; f. 1964; weekly; women's; circ. over 100,000.

NEWS AGENCIES

Islamic Republic News Agency (IRNA): POB 764, 873 Vali Asr Ave, Teheran; tel. (21) 892050; telex 212827; f. 1936; Man. Dir HOSSEIN NASIRI.

Foreign Bureaux

Agence France-Presse (AFP): POB 513, Office 207, 8 Vanak Ave, Vanak Sq., Teheran 19919; tel. (21) 687509; telex 212475; fax (21) 8886289; Correspondent LAURENT MAILLARD.

Agenzia Nazionale Stampa Associata (ANSA) (Italy): Khiabane Shahid Bahonar (Niavaran) Kuche Mina No. 16, Teheran 19367; tel. (21) 276930; telex 213629; Chief of Bureau LUCIANO CAUSA.

Anatolian News Agency (Turkey): Teheran.

Informatsionnoye Telegrafnoye Agentstvo Rossü—Telegrafnoye Agentstvo Sovetskovo Soyuza (ITAR—TASS) (Russia): Kehyaban Hamid, Kouche Masoud 73, Teheran; Correspondent (vacant).

Kyodo Tsushin (Japan): No. 23, First Floor, Couche Kargozar, Couche Sharsaz Ave, Zafar, Teheran; tel. (21) 220448; telex 214058; Correspondent MASARU IMAI.

Novinska Agencija Tanjug (Yugoslavia): Teheran.

Reuters (UK): POB 15875-1193, Teheran; tel. (21) 847700; telex 212634.

Xinhua (New China) News Agency (People's Republic of China): 75 Golestan 2nd St, Pasdaran Ave, Teheran; tel. (21) 241852; telex 212399; Correspondent CHEN MING.

Publishers

Amir Kabir: 28 Vessal Shirazi St, Teheran; f. 1950; historical, social, literary and children's books; Dir ABD AR-RAHIM JAFARI.

Ebn-e-Sina: Meydane 25 Shahrivar, Teheran; f. 1957; educational publishers and booksellers; Dir EBRAHIM RAMAZANI.

Eghbal Printing & Publishing Organization: 15 Booshehr St, Dr Shariati Ave, Teheran; tel. (21) 768113; f. 1903; Man. Dir DJAVAD EGHBAL.

Iran Chap Co: Khayyam Ave, Teheran; tel. (21) 3281; telex 212336; fax (21) 3115530; f. 1966; newspapers, books, magazines, book binding, colour printing and engraving; Man. Dir M. DOAEI.

Iran Exports Publication Co Ltd: POB 15815-3373, 27 Eftekhar St, Vali Asr Ave, Teheran 15956; tel. (21) 8801800; telex 215017; fax (21) 890547; f. 1987; business and trade.

Khayyam: Jomhoori Islami Ave, Teheran; Dir MOHAMMAD ALI TARAGHI.

Majlis Press: Ketab-Khane Majlis-e-Showraie Eslami No. 1, Baharistan Sq., Teheran 11564; tel. (21) 3124257; f. 1924; Dir ABD AL-HOSSEIN HAIERI; Ketab Khane Majlis-e-Showraie Eslami No. 2, Imam Khomeini Ave, Teheran 13174; tel. (21) 6462906; f. 1950; Dir ABD AL-HOSSEIN HAIERI.

Sahab Geographic and Drafting Institute: POB 11365-617, 30 Somayeh St, Hoquqi Crossroad, Dr Ali Shariati Ave, Teheran 16517; tel. (21) 7535670; telex 222584; fax (21) 7535876; maps, atlases, and books on geography, science, history and Islamic art; Founder and Pres. ABBAS A. SAHAB.

Scientific and Cultural Publications Co: tel. (21) 685457; f. 1974; Iranian and Islamic studies and scientific and cultural books; Pres. Sayed JAVAD AZHARS.

Teheran University Press: 16 Kargar Shomali Ave, Teheran; tel. (21) 632062; fax (21) 632063; f. 1944; university textbooks; Man. Dir A. RASTGOU.

Radio and Television

In 1992, according to UNESCO, there were an estimated 13.5m. radio receivers and 3.8m. television receivers in use.

Islamic Republic of Iran Broadcasting (IRIB): POB 19395-3333, Vali Asr Ave, Jame Jam St, Teheran; tel. (21) 21961; telex 213910; semi-autonomous government authority; non-commercial; operates three national television and three national radio channels, as well as local provincial radio stations throughout the country; Dir-Gen. ALI LARIJANI.

RADIO

Radio Network 1 (Voice of the Islamic Republic of Iran): there are three national radio channels: Radio Networks 1 and 2 and Radio Quran, which broadcasts recitals of the Quran (Koran) and other programmes related to it; covers whole of Iran and reaches whole of Europe, the Central Asian republics of the CIS, whole of Asia, Africa and part of USA; medium-wave regional broadcasts in local languages; Arabic, Armenian, Assyrian, Azerbaijani, Balochi, Bandari, Dari, Farsi, Kurdish, Mazandarani, Pashtu, Turkoman, Turkish and Urdu; external broadcasts in English, French, German, Spanish, Turkish, Arabic, Kurdish, Urdu, Pashtu, Armenian, Bengali, Russian and special overseas programme in Farsi; 53 transmitters.

TELEVISION

Television (Vision of the Islamic Republic of Iran): 625-line, System B; Secam colour; two production centres in Teheran producing for two networks and 28 local TV stations.

Finance

(cap. = capital; p.u. = paid up; dep. = deposits; res = reserves; brs = branches; m. = million; amounts in rials)

BANKING

Prior to the Islamic Revolution, the banking system comprised 36 banks. Banks were nationalized in June 1979 and a revised banking system has been introduced consisting of nine banks. Three banks were reorganized, two (Bank Tejarat and Bank Mellat) resulted from mergers of 22 existing small banks, three specialize in industry and agriculture and one, the Islamic Bank (now Islamic Economy Organization), set up in May 1979, was exempt from nationalization. A change-over to an Islamic banking system, with interest being replaced by a 4% commission on loans, began on 21 March 1984. More than 10% of short- and medium-term private deposits are subject to Islamic rules, and in 1985 all bank loans and advances were Islamized.

Although the number of foreign banks operating in Iran has fallen dramatically since the Revolution, some 30 are still represented. Since the exclusion of French banks from the Iranian market at the end of 1983, German, Swiss, Japanese and British banks have been responsible for about 30% of total trade financing.

Central Bank

Bank Markazi Jomhouri Islami Iran (Central Bank): POB 11365-8551, Ferdowsi Ave, Teheran; tel. (21) 3110101; telex 213965; fax (21) 390323; f. 1960; Bank Markazi Iran until Dec. 1983; central note-issuing bank of Iran, government banking; cap. p.u. 159,000m., total assets 18,807,000m. (March 1992); Gov. MOHSEN NOURBAKHSH.

Commercial Banks

Bank Keshavarzi (Agricultural Bank): POB 14155-6395, 129 Patrice Lumumba Ave, Jalal al-Ahmad Expressway, Teheran; tel. (21) 9121; telex 212058; f. 1979 as merger of the Agricultural Development Bank of Iran and the Agricultural Co-operative Bank of Iran; state-owned; cap. 208,186m., dep. 394,720m. (March 1993); 576 brs; Man. Dir SAYED ALI MILANI HOSSEINI.

Bank Mellat (Nation's Bank): POB 11365-5964, Park Shahr, Varzesh Ave, Teheran; tel. (21) 32491; telex 212619; fax (21) 892868; f. 1980 as merger of the following: International Bank of Iran, Bank Bimeh Iran, Bank Dariush, Distributors' Co-operative Credit Bank, Iran Arab Bank, Bank Omran, Bank Pars, Bank of Teheran, Foreign Trade Bank of Iran, Bank Farhangian; state-owned; cap. p.u. 33,500m. (March 1989), dep. 2,478,173m., total assets 2,644,929m. (March 1990); 1,288 brs throughout Iran; Chair. and Man. Dir M. ARAMINIA.

Bank Melli Iran (The National Bank of Iran): POB 11365-171, Ferdowsi Ave, Teheran; tel. (21) 3231; telex 212890; fax (21) 302813; f. 1928; state-owned; cap. 25,000m., res 21,459m., dep. 7,658,105m., total assets 8,101,169m. (March 1992); 2,232 brs throughout Iran, 24 brs abroad; Chair. and Man. Dir ASSADOLLAH AMIRASLANI.

Bank Refah Kargaran: POB 15815/1866, 125 Ayatollah Shahid Dr Moffateh Ave, Teheran; tel. (21) 825000; telex 213786; f. 1960; state-owned; cap. p.u. 10,000m., dep. 795,309m. (March 1992); 177 brs throughout Iran.

Bank Saderat Iran (The Export Bank of Iran): Sepehr Tower, Somayyeh Ave, Teheran; tel. (21) 8826122; telex 212352; fax (21) 88095391; f. 1952, reorganized 1979; state-owned; cap. p.u. and res. 107,873m., dep. 3,982,475m., total assets 4,358,756m. (March 1990); 2,937 brs in Iran, 22 foreign brs; Man. Dir VALIOLLAH SEIF.

Bank Sepah (Army Bank): POB 11364, Imam Khomeini Sq, Teheran; tel. (21) 3111090; telex 212462; fax (21) 3112138; f. 1925, reorganized 1979; state-owned; cap. p.u. 8,000m., dep. 3,077,075m., total assets 4,273,808m. (March 1992); 1,117 brs throughout Iran and 5 brs abroad; Chair. and Man. Dir ABOLGHASEM DJAMSHIDI.

Bank Tejarat (Commercial Bank): POB 11365-5416, 130 Taleghani Ave, Teheran 15994; tel. (21) 81041; telex 212077; fax (21) 8828215; f. 1979 as merger of the following: Irano-British Bank, Bank Etebarate Iran, The Bank of Iran and the Middle East, Mercantile Bank of Iran and Holland, Bank Barzagani Iran, Bank Iranshahr, Bank Sanaye Iran, Bank Shahriar, Iranians' Bank, Bank Kar, International Bank of Iran and Japan, Bank Russo-Iran; state-owned; cap. p.u. 66,226m., dep. 3,648,123m., total assets 3,886,696m. (March 1992); 1,280 brs; Pres. and Chair. MUHAMMAD JAFAR EFTEKHAR.

Islamic Economy Organization (formerly Islamic Bank of Iran): Ferdowsi Ave, Teheran; f. February 1980; cap. 2,000m.; provides interest-free loans and investment in small industry.

Development Banks

Bank Sanat va Madan (Bank of Industry and Mines): POB 15875-4456, 593 Hafiz Ave, Teheran; tel. (21) 893271; telex 212816; fax (21) 895052; f. 1979 as merger of the following: Industrial Credit Bank (ICB), Industrial and Mining Development Bank of Iran (IMDBI), Development and Investment Bank of Iran (DIBI), Iranian Bankers Investment Company (IBICO); cap. p.u. 80,770m., res 102,276m., total assets 709,432m. (1992); Man. Dir Dr MORAD KHODABANDEHLOU.

Export Development Bank of Iran: POB 15875-5964, 129 Khaled Eslambouli St, 15139 Teheran; tel. (21) 626916; telex 226895; fax (21) 626979; cap. p.u. 50,000m.

Housing Bank

Bank Maskan (Housing Bank): Ferdowsi Ave, Teheran; tel. (21) 675021; telex 213904; f. 1980; state-owned; cap. p.u. 42,663.8m., dep. 221,153.4m., total assets 1,313,708m. (June 1985); provides mortgage and housing finance; 187 brs; Chair. and Man. Dir ABDULLAH EBTEHAJ.

STOCK EXCHANGE

Teheran Stock Exchange: 228 Hafez Ave, 11380 Teheran; tel. (21) 674981; telex 223282; fax (21) 672524; f. 1966; Sec.-Gen. ALLAHVIRDI RAGAI SALMASSI.

INSURANCE

The nationalization of insurance companies was announced on 25 June 1979.

Bimeh Alborz (Alborz Insurance Co): POB 4489-15875, Alborz Bldg, 234 Sepahbod Garani Ave, Teheran; tel. (21) 893201; telex 214134; fax (21) 898088; f. 1959; state-owned insurance company; all types of insurance; Man. Dir ALI FATHALI.

Bimeh Asia (Asia Insurance Co): POB 1365-5366, Asia Insurance Bldg, 297-299 Taleghani Ave, Teheran; tel. (21) 836040; telex 213664; fax (21) 827196; all types of insurance; Man. Dir MASOUM ZAMIRI.

Bimeh Dana (Dana Insurance Co): POB 11365-7473, 898 Ferdowski Sq., Engelab Ave, opposite Ostad-Nejatol-Alhi, Teheran;

tel. (21) 679041; telex 224396; life, personal accident and health insurance; Man. Dir. M. TEHRANI.

Bimeh Iran (Iran Insurance Co): POB 11365-9153, Saadi Ave, Teheran; tel. (21) 304026; telex 212782; fax (21) 313510; all types of insurance; Man. Dir ALI MOSAREZA.

Bimeh Markazi Iran (Central Insurance of Iran): POB 15875-4345, 149 Ayatollah Taleghani Ave, Teheran 15914; tel. (21) 6409912; telex 212888; fax (21) 6405729; supervises the insurance market and tariffs for new types of insurance cover; the sole state reinsurer for domestic insurance companies, which are obliged to reinsure 50% of their direct business in life insurance and 25% of business in non-life insurance with Bimeh Markazi Iran; Pres. ABDOL NASSER HEMMATI.

Trade and Industry

CHAMBER OF COMMERCE

Iran Chamber of Commerce, Industries and Mines: 254 Taleghani Ave, Teheran; tel. (21) 8360319; telex 213382; fax (21) 8825111; supervises the affiliated 20 Chambers in the provinces; Pres. ALINAQI KHAMOUSHI.

STATE ENTERPRISES

Iranian Offshore Oil Co (IOOC): POB 15875-4546, 339 Dr Beheshti Ave, Teheran; tel. (21) 624102; telex 212707; fax (21) 627420; wholly owned subsidiary of NIOC; f. 1980; development, exploitation and production of crude petroleum, natural gas and other hydrocarbons in all offshore areas of Iran in Persian Gulf; Chair. M. HASHEMIAN; Man. Dir S. M. KHOEE.

National Iranian Copper Industries Co (NICEC): MAHMUD SHIRI.

National Iranian Drilling Co: POB 61635-138, Ahwaz; tel. (61) 442197; telex 612025; fax (61) 442456; Chair. MANSOUR PARVINIAN.

National Iranian Gas Co (NIGC): Man. Dir MOHAMMAD ISMAIL KARACHIAN.

National Iranian Industries Organization (NIIO): POB 14155-3579, 133 Dr Fatemi Ave, Teheran; tel. (21) 656031-40; telex 214176; fax (21) 658070; f. 1979; owns 400 factories in Iran.

National Iranian Industries Organization Export Co (NECO): No. 8, Second Alley, Bucharest Ave, Teheran 15944; tel. (21) 4162384; telex 212429.

National Iranian Lead and Zinc Co (NILZC).

National Iranian Mines and Metal Smelting Co (NIMMSC).

National Iranian Mining Explorations Co (NIMEC).

National Iranian Oil Co (NIOC): POB 1863, Taleghani Ave, Teheran; tel. (21) 6151; telex 212514; a state organization controlling all 'upstream' activities in the petroleum and natural gas industries; incorporated April 1951 on nationalization of petroleum industry to engage in all phases of petroleum operations; in February 1979 it was announced that, in future, Iran would sell petroleum direct to the petroleum companies, and in September 1979 the Ministry of Oil assumed control of the National Iranian Oil Company, and the Minister of Oil took over as Chairman and Managing Director; Chair. of Board and Gen. Man. Dir GHOLAMREZA AQAZADEH (Minister of Oil); Directors: HABIB AMIN FAR (Engineering and Construction), HAMDOLLAH MUHAMMAD-NEJAD (Refining, Pipelines and Communications), FATHINEJAD (Administration), GANIMI FARD (International Affairs), VAZIRI HAMANEH (Corporate Planning Affairs), MOVAHEDIZADEH (Commercial Affairs), NIYACAN (Exploration Affairs).

National Iranian Steel Co (NISC): POB 15875-4469, Teheran; tel. (21) 8162243; telex 212334; fax (21) 893715; Man. Dir MUHAMMAD HOSSEIN MOQIMI.

National Petrochemical Co of Iran (NPC): POB 7484, Karimkhan Zand Blvd, Teheran; tel. (21) 839060-74; telex 213520; fax (21) 822087; f. 1965; wholly owned by Iranian Govt; Pres. AHMAD RAHGOZAR.

National Refining and Distribution Co (NRDC): f. 1992 to assume responsibility for refining, pipeline distribution, engineering, construction and research in the petroleum industry from the NIOC; Chair. and Man. Dir GHOLAMREZA AQAZADEH.

CO-OPERATIVES

Central Organization for Co-operatives of Iran: Teheran; in October 1985 there were 4,598 labour co-operatives, with a total membership of 703,814 and capital of 2,184.5m. rials, and 9,159 urban non-labour co-operatives, with a total membership of 262,118 and capital of 4,187.5m. rials.

Central Organization for Rural Co-operatives of Iran (CORC): Teheran; Man. Dir SAYED HASSAN MOTEVALLI-ZADEH.

The CORC was founded in 1963, and the Islamic Government of Iran has pledged that it will continue its educational, technical, commercial and credit assistance to rural co-operative societies and unions. At the end of the Iranian year 1363 (1984/85) there were 3,104 Rural Co-operative Societies with a total membership of 3,925,000 and share capital of 25,900m. rials. There were 181 Rural Co-operative Unions with 3,097 members and capital of 7,890m. rials.

TRADE FAIR

Export Promotion Centre of Iran (EPCI): POB 11-48, Tajrish, Teheran; tel. (21) 21911; telex 213397; fax (21) 292858; international trade fairs and exhibitions; Chair. ALI SAEEDLOO.

Transport

RAILWAYS

Iranian Islamic Republic Railway: Shahid Kalantary Bldg, Rahe-Ahan Sq., Teheran 13185; tel. (21) 555120; telex 213103; f. 1934; Pres. Eng. SADEGH AFSHAR; Vice-Pres. ESMAEIL MUHAMMAD (Admin. and Finance), Vice-Pres. NASSER POURMIRZA (Technical and Operations), Vice-Pres. REZA IRANKHAH (Planning and Technical Studies), Vice-Pres. Eng. VAHAB JAMSHIDI (Construction and Renovation), Vice-Pres. ABOLGHASSEM SAEEDI (Commerce and Economic Affairs), Vice-Pres. HAMID-REZA MEHRAZMA (Manpower).

The total length of main lines in the Iranian railway system, which is generally single-tracked, is 4,847 km (4,751 km of 1,435 mm gauge and 96 km of 1,676 mm gauge). The system includes the following main routes:

Trans-Iranian Railway runs 1,392 km from Bandar Turkman on the Caspian Sea in the north, through Teheran, and south to Bandar Imam Khomeini on the Persian Gulf.

Southern Line links Teheran to Khorramshahr via Qom, Arak, Dorood, Andimeshk and Ahwaz; 937 km.

Northern Line links Teheran to Gorgan via Garmsar, Firooz Kooh and Sari; 499 km.

Teheran–Kerman Line via Kashan, Yazd and Zarand; 1,106 km.

Teheran–Tabriz Line linking with the Azerbaijan Railway; 736 km.

Tabriz–Djulfa Electric Line: 146 km.

Garmsar–Meshed Line connects Teheran with Meshed via Semnan, Damghan, Shahrud and Nishabur; 812 km.

Qom–Zahedan Line when completed will be an intercontinental line linking Europe and Turkey, through Iran, with India. Zahedan is situated 91.7 km west of the Balochistan frontier, and is the end of the Pakistani broad gauge railway. The section at present links Qom to Kerman via Kashan, Sistan, Yazd, Bafq and Zarand; 1,005 km. A branch line from Sistan was opened in 1971 via Isfahan to the steel mill at Zarrin Shahr; 112 km. A broad-gauge (1,976-mm) track connects Zahedan and Mirjaveh, on the border with Pakistan; 94 km.

Zahedan-Quetta (Pakistan) Line: 685km; not linked to national network.

Ahwaz–Bandar Khomeini Line connects Bandar Khomeini with the Trans-Iranian railway at Ahwaz; this line is due to be double-tracked; 112 km.

Azerbaijan Railway extends from Tabriz to Djulfa (146.5 km), meeting the Caucasian railways at the Azerbaijani frontier. Electrification works for this section have been completed and the electrified line was opened in April 1982. A standard gauge railway line (139 km) extends from Tabriz (via Sharaf–Khaneh) to the Turkish frontier at Razi.

Bandar Abbas-Bafq: a 630-km double-track line to link Bandar Abbas and Bafq has been under construction since 1982. The first phase, linking Bafgh to Sirjang (260 km), was opened in May 1990; the second phase was expected to be completed by 1994. The aim of the project is to provide access to the copper mines at Sarcheshmeh and the iron ore mines at Gole-Gohar.

Underground Railway. An agreement was signed in March 1976 between the Municipality of Teheran and French contractors for the construction of a subway. Four lines are to be built with a total length of 143 km. Construction began during 1978, but the project was suspended after the revolution in 1979. Work on two of the lines resumed in September 1986 and was due to be completed during the early 1990s, when work on the remaining two lines will begin.

ROADS

In 1989 there were 490 km of motorways, 18,044 km of paved main roads, 33,275 km of paved feeder roads, 49,398 km of gravel roads and 52,120 km of earth roads. There is a paved highway (A1, 2,089 km) from Bazargan on the Turkish border to the Afghanistan border. The A2 highway runs 2,473 km from the Iraqi border to Mir Javeh on the Pakistan border; 2,422 km of the A2 has been completed, and the remaining 51 km are under construction.

Ministry of Roads and Transport: 49 Taleghani Ave, Teheran; tel. (21) 661034; telex 213381.

INLAND WATERWAYS

Principal waterways:

Lake Rezaiyeh (Lake Urmia) 80 km west of Tabriz in North-West Iran; and River Karun flowing south through the oilfields into the River Shatt al-Arab, thence to the head of the Persian Gulf near Abadan.

Lake Rezaiyeh: From Sharafkhaneh to Golmankhaneh there is a twice-weekly service of tugs and barges for transport of passengers and goods.

River Karun: Regular cargo service is operated by the Mesopotamia-Iran Corpn Ltd. Iranian firms also operate daily motorboat services for passengers and goods.

SHIPPING

Persian Gulf: The main oil terminal is at Kharg Island. The principal commercial non-oil ports are Bandar Shahid Rajai (which was officially inaugurated in 1983 and handles 9m. of the 12m. tons of cargo passing annually through Iran's Persian Gulf ports), Bandar Khomeini, Bushehr, Bandar Abbas and Chah Bahar. A project to develop Bandar Abbas port, which predates the Islamic Revolution and was originally to cost IR 1,900,000m., is now in progress. Khorramshahr, Iran's biggest port, was put out of action in the war with Iraq, and Bushehr and Bandar Khomeini also sustained war damage, which has restricted their use. In August 1988 the Iranian news agency (IRNA) announced that Iran was to spend $200m. on the construction of six 'multi-purpose' ports on the Arabian and Caspian Seas, while ports which had been damaged in the war were to be repaired.

Caspian Sea: Principal port Bandar Anzali (formerly Bandar Pahlavi) and Bandar Nowshahr.

Irano–Hind Shipping Co: No. 3, 13th St, Miremad Ave, Dr Beheshti Ave, Teheran; tel. (21) 850213; telex 215233; joint venture between the Islamic Republic of Iran and the Shipping Corpn of India; Chair. M. H. DAJMAR; Vice-Chair. J. C. SHETH; Man. Dir K. R. SACHAR.

Islamic Republic of Iran Shipping Lines (IRISL): POB 15875-4646, 675 North East Corner of Vali Asr Sq., Teheran 15896; tel. (21) 833061; telex 212794; fax (21) 837555; f. 1967; affiliated to the Ministry of Commerce Jan. 1980; liner services between the Persian (Arabian) Gulf and Europe, the Far East and South America and the Caspian Sea and Central Asia; Chair. and Man. Dir MAHMOOD F. TARJOMAN.

National Iranian Tanker Co: POB 16765-947, 67–88 Atefi St, Africa Ave, Teheran; tel. (21) 21939; telex 213937; fax (21) 2228065; Chair. and Man. Dir MUHAMMAD SOURI.

Ports and Shipping Organization: 751 Enghelab Ave, Teheran; tel. (21) 837041; telex 212271; Man. Dir Eng. MUHAMMAD MADAD.

CIVIL AVIATION

The two main international airports are Mehrabad (Teheran) and Abadan. An international airport was opened at Isfahan in July 1984 and the first international flight took place in March 1986. Work on a new international airport, 40 km south of Teheran, abandoned in 1979, resumed in the mid-1980s, and work on three others, at Tabas, Ardebil and Ilam was under way in mid-1990. The airports at Urumiyeh, Ahwaz, Bakhtaran, Sanandaz, Abadan, Hamadan and Shiraz were to be modernized and smaller ones constructed at Lar, Lamard, Rajsanjan, Barm, Kashan, Maragheh, Khoy, Sirjan and Abadeh.

Iran Air (Airline of the Islamic Republic of Iran): Iran Air Bldg, Mehrabad Airport, Teheran; tel. (21) 9111; telex 212795; fax (21) 6003248; f. 1962; Chair. and Man. Dir S. H. SHAFTI; serves the Middle East and Persian Gulf area, Europe, Asia and the Far East.

Iran Asseman Airlines: POB 13145-1476, Mehrabad Airport, Teheran; tel. (21) 661967; telex 212575; fax (21) 6404318; f. after Islamic Revolution as result of merger of Air Taxi Co (f. 1958), Pars Air (f. 1969), Air Service Co (f. 1962) and Hoor Asseman; Man. Dir ALI ABEDZADEH; domestic routes and charter services.

Kish Air: Kish Island; f. 1991 under the auspices of the Kish Development Organization (Man. Dir. MOHSEN MEHR ALIZADEH); serves Persian Gulf area, Teheran, Dubai, Frankfurt, London and Paris.

Saha Airline: f. 1990; weekly cargo service between Teheran and Singapore.

Tourism

Tourism has been adversely affected by political upheaval since the Revolution. Iran's chief attraction for tourists is its wealth of historical sites, notably Isfahan, Rasht, Tabriz, Susa and Persepolis. There were 250,000 visitors to Iran in the year to March 1992.

Defence

Estimated defence expenditure (1992): 527,700m. rials (US $2,300m.).

Chairman of the Supreme Defence Council: Hojatoleslam SAYED ALI KHAMENEI.

Commander-in-Chief of the Armed Forces: (vacant).

Chief of Staff of the Armed Forces and Commander of the Gendarmerie: Brig.-Gen. ALI SHAHBAZI.

Commander of the Army: Brig.-Gen. HOSSEIN HASSANI-SAADI.

Commander of the Air Force: Brig.-Gen. MANSOUR SATTARI.

Commander of the Navy: Cdre MUHAMMAD HOSSEIN MALEK-ZADEGAN.

Chief of Staff of the Revolutionary Guards Corps (Pasdaran): ALI-REZA AFSHAR.

Commander of the Islamic Revolutionary Guards Corps: MOHSEN REZAI.

Commander of Basij (Mobilization) War Volunteers Corps: MUHAMMAD ALI RAHMANI.

Military service: 24 months.

Total armed forces: At the beginning of the Iran–Iraq War in September 1980 Iran's army was estimated to total between 120,000 and 150,000 men, and the navy to total 30,000. In June 1994 it was estimated that the armed forces totalled 513,000 men: army 345,000 men; navy 18,000; air force 30,000; reserves 350,000; revolutionary guard corps (Pasdaran, which has its own army, navy and marines units) 120,000.

Education

PRIMARY AND SECONDARY EDUCATION

Primary education, beginning at age six and lasting for five years, is compulsory for all children and is provided free of charge. In 1991 more than 9.5m. pupils were enrolled in primary education. Secondary education may last for a further seven years, divided into two cycles; one of three, and another of four, years. In 1991 some 5.6m. pupils were receiving secondary education.

According to the Government, 24,000 schools were built between the Revolution in 1979 and 1984.

HIGHER EDUCATION

Iran has 29 universities of various types, including nine in Teheran. Universities were closed by the government in 1980 but have been reopened gradually since 1983. According to official sources, 250,709 students (71,822 women) were enrolled at Iran's colleges and universities in the 1988/89 academic year. Candidates for entrance examinations for courses in higher education in 1989/90 numbered 752,343, of whom 61,000 were successful. Apart from Teheran, there are universities in Bakhtaran, Isfahan, Hamadan, Tabriz, Ahwaz, Babolsar, Meshed, Kermanshah, Rasht, Shiraz, Zahedan, Kerman, Shahrekord and Urmia. There are c. 50 colleges of higher education, c. 40 technological institutes, c. 20 teacher training colleges, several colleges of advanced technology, and colleges of agriculture in Hamadan, Zanjan, Sari and Abadan. Vocational training schools also exist in Teheran, Ahwaz, Meshed, Shiraz and other cities.

In recent years much emphasis has been put on agriculture and vocational programmes in higher education.

Bibliography

GENERAL

Abdalian, S. *Damavand (Iran)*. Teheran, 1943.

Amirahmadi, Hooshang, and Entessar, Nader. *Iran and the Arab World*. Basingstoke, The Macmillan Press Ltd, 1993.

Barth, F. *Nomads of South Persia*. London, 1961.

Cambridge History of Iran.
Volume I: *The Land of Iran*.
Volume V: *The Seljuq and Mongol Periods*.
Both Cambridge University Press, 1968.

Cottam, Richard W. *Iran and the United States: A Cold War Case Study*. Pittsburgh, Pa, University of Pittsburgh Press, 1990.

Curzon, Lord. *Persia and the Persian Question*. 2 vols, London, 1892.

De Planhol, X. *Recherches sur la Géographie humaine de l'Iran Septentrional*. Paris, 1964.

Elwell-Sutton, L. P. *Modern Iran*. London, 1941.

A Guide to Iranian Area Study. Ann Arbor, 1952.

Persian Oil: A Study in Power Politics. London, 1955.

Eskelund, Karl. *Behind the Peacock Throne*. New York, Alvin Redman, 1965.

Frye, Richard N. *Persia*. London, Allen and Unwin, 3rd ed. 1969.

Furon, Raymond. *L'Iran*. Paris, 1952.

Géologie du Plateau iranien. Paris, 1941.

La Perse. Paris, 1938.

Haeri, Shahla. *Law of Desire: temporary marriage in Iran*. London, I. B. Tauris, 1990.

Huot, Jean Louis. *Persia*, Vol. I. London, Muller, 1966.

Iqbal, Muhammad. *Iran*. London, 1946.

Iran Almanac. Teheran, Echo of Iran, annually.

Iran: A Selected and Annotated Bibliography. Washington, 1951.

Iran Research Group (Ed.). *Who's Who in Iran*. Wisbech, Menas Associates, 1990.

Keddie, Nikki R. *Historical Obstacles to Agrarian Change in Iran*. Claremont, 1960.

Iran. Religion, Politics and Society. London, Frank Cass, 1980.

(Ed. with Gasiorowski, Mark). *Neither East nor West: Iran, the Soviet Union and the United States*. New Haven, Conn., Yale University Press, 1990.

Kemp, N. *Abadan*. London, 1954.

Khomeini, Ayatollah Ruhollah. *A Clarification of Questions*. Boulder, Westview Press, 1985.

Lambton, A. K. S. *Landlord and Peasant in Persia*. New York, 1953.

Islamic Society in Persia. London, 1954.

A Persian Vocabulary. Cambridge, 1961.

The Persian Land Reform 1962–66. Oxford, Clarendon Press, 1969.

Marlowe, John. *Iran, a Short Political Guide*. London and New York, Pall Mall Press, 1963.

Mehdevi, A. S. *Persian Adventure*. New York, 1954.

Persia Revisited. London, 1965.

Millspaugh, A. C. *Americans in Persia*. Washington, 1946.

Motter, T. H. Vail. *The Persian Corridor and Aid to Russia*. Washington, 1952.

Ramazani, Rouhollah K. *The Persian Gulf: Iran's Role*. Charlottesville, University Press of Virginia, 1972.

Sabahi, Hushang. *British Policy in Persia 1918–1925*. London, Frank Cass, 1990.

Sanghvi, Ramesh. *Aryamehr: The Shah of Iran*. London, Macmillan, 1968.

Savory, Roger. *Iran under the Safavids*. Cambridge University Press, 1980.

Shah of Iran. *Mission for My Country*. London, Hutchinson, 1961.

Shearman, I. *Land and People of Iran*. London, 1962.

Sirdar, Ikbal Ali Shah. *Persia of the Persians*. London, 1929.

Stark, Freya. *The Valleys of the Assassins*. London, 1934.

East is West. London, 1945.

Tharaud, Jérôme. *Vieille Perse et Jeune Iran*. Paris, 1947.

Wickens, G. M., and Savory, R. M. *Persia in Islamic Times, a practical bibliography of its history, culture and language*. Montreal, Institute of Islamic Studies, McGill University, 1964.

Wilber, Donald N. *Iran: Past and Present*. Princeton University Press, 1955, 8th edn 1977.

 Iran: Oasis of Stability in the Middle East. New York, Foreign Political Association, Inc., 1959.

Zabih, Sepehr. *The Communist Movement in Iran*. University of California Press, 1967.

CIVILIZATION AND LITERATURE

Arberry, A. J. (Ed.). *The Legacy of Persia*. London and New York, 1953.

 Shiraz: The Persian City of Saints and Poets. Univ. of Oklahoma Press, 1960.

 Tales from the Masnavi. London, 1961.

 More Tales from the Masnavi. London, 1963.

 (Ed.). *The Cambridge History of Iran*. Cambridge University Press, 1969.

Bausani, A. *Der Perser: von den Anfängen bis zur Gegenwart*. Stuttgart, Kohlhammer, 1965.

Bell, Gertrude L. *Persian Pictures*. London, 1928.

Browne, E. G. *A Literary History of Persia*. 4 vols, Cambridge, 1928.

Colledge, M. A. R. *The Parthians*. London, Thames and Hudson, 1968.

Culican, William. *The Medes and the Persians*. 1965.

Duchesne-Guillemin, Jacques. *The Hymns of Zarathustra* (trans. with commentary). Beacon, L. R., Boston, Mass., 1963.

Ghirshman, R. *L'Iran: des Origines à Islam*. Paris, 1951.

 Iran from the Earliest Times to the Islamic Conquest. London, 1954.

 Arts of Ancient Persia from the Origins to Alexander the Great. London, 1963.

 Iran. New York, 1964.

Herzfeld, E. *Iran in the Ancient East*. Oxford, 1941.

Levy, Reuben. *The Persian Language*. New York, 1952.

 Persian Literature. 1928.

Lockhart, L. *Famous Cities of Iran*. London, 1939.

 The Fall of the Safavi Dynasty and the Afghan Occupation of Persia. Cambridge University Press, 1958.

Milani, Farzaneh. *Veils and Words: The Emerging Voices of Iranian Women Writers*. London, I. B. Tauris, 1990.

Monteil, V. *Les Tribus du Fars et la sédentarisation des nomades*. Paris and The Hague, Mouton, 1966.

Olmstead, A. T. *History of the Persian Empire, Achaemenid Period*. Chicago, 1948.

Pope, Arthur. *Survey of Persian Art from Prehistoric Times to the Present*. Vols 1–6. Oxford University Press, 1938–58.

Rice, Cyprian. *The Persian Sufis*. London, Allen and Unwin, 1964.

Ross, Sir Denison. *Eastern Art and Literature*. London, 1928.

 The Persians. London, 1931.

Storey, C. A. *Persian Literature*. London, 1927.

Sykes, Sir Percy. *Persia*. Oxford, 1922.

 A History of Persia (2 vols; 3rd edition, with supplementary essays). London, 1930.

Teague-Jones, Reginald. *Adventures in Persia*. London, Gollancz, 1990.

Widengren. *Die Religionen Irans*. Stuttgart, Kohlhammer, 1965.

Wulfe, H. E. *The Traditional Crafts of Persia*. Cambridge, Mass., M.I.T. Press, 1966.

RECENT HISTORY

Akhavi, Shahrough. *Religion and Politics in Contemporary Iran*. State University of New York Press, 1980.

Amirahmadi, Hooshang, and Entessar, Nader. *Reconstruction and Regional Diplomacy in the Persian Gulf*. London, Routledge, 1992.

Amirsadeghi, Hossein. *Twentieth Century Iran*. London, Heinemann, 1977.

Assadollah, Alam. *The Shah and I: The Confidential Diaries of Iran's Royal Court, 1969–77*. London, I. B. Tauris, 1991.

Azimi, Fakhreddin. *Iran: The Crisis of Democracy 1941–1953*. London, I. B. Tauris, 1990.

Bakhash, Shaul. *The Reign of the Ayatollahs*. London, I. B. Tauris, 1984.

Bani-Sadr, Abol-Hassan. *My Turn to Speak: Iran, the revolution and secret deals with the US*. New York, Brassey's, 1991.

Balta, Paul. *Iran-Irak: une guerre de 5,000 ans*. Paris, Editions Anthropos, 1987.

Banani, Amin. *The Modernization of Iran, 1921–1924*. Stanford, 1961.

Benard, Cheryl, and Zalmay Khalilzad. *The Government of God: Iran's Islamic Republic*. New York, Columbia University Press, 1984.

Bill, James A. *The Lion and the Eagle: the Tragedy of American-Iranian Relations*. New Haven, Conn., Yale University Press, 1988.

Bullard, Render. *Letters from Tehran: a British ambassador in World War II Persia*. London, I. B. Tauris, 1991.

Bunya, Ali Akbar. *A Political and Diplomatic History of Persia*. Teheran, 1955.

Chubin, Shahram, and Tripp, Charles. *Iran and Iraq at War*. London, I.B. Tauris, 1988.

Chubin, Shahram, and Zabih, Sepehr. *The Foreign Relations of Iran: A Developing State in the Zone of a Great-Power Conflict*. University of California Press, 1975.

Cordesman, Anthony H. *The Iran-Iraq War and Western Security 1984–87*. London, Jane's Publishing Company, 1987.

Cottam, R. W. *Nationalism in Iran*. Pittsburgh University Press, 1964.

 Iran and the United States: a cold war case study. Pittsburgh, University of Pittsburgh Press, 1988.

Delannoy, Christian. *Savak*. Paris, Editions Stock, 1991.

Farsoon, Samih K., and Mashayekhi, Mehrdad. *Iran: Political Culture in the Islamic Republic*. London, Routledge, 1993.

Fischer, M. J. *Iran: From Religious Dispute to Revolution*. Harvard University Press, 1980.

Goode, James F. *The United States and Iran, 1946–51: The Diplomacy of Neglect*. New York, St. Martin's Press, 1989.

Halliday, Fred. *Iran: Dictatorship and Development*. London, 1978.

Hamzavi. A. H. K. *Persia and the Powers: An Account of Diplomatic Relations, 1941–46*. London, 1946.

Heikal, Muhammad. *The Return of the Ayatollah*. London, André Deutsch, 1981.

Hiro, Dilip. *Iran under the Ayatollahs*. London, Routledge and Kegan Paul, 1984.

Hoveyda, Ferydoun. *The Fall of the Shah*. London, Weidenfeld and Nicolson, 1979.

Humphreys, Eileen. *The Royal Road: a popular history of Iran*. London, Scorpion, 1991.

Huyser, General Robert E. *Mission to Tehran*. London, André Deutsch, 1986.

Ismael, Tareq Y. *Iran and Iraq: Roots of Conflict*. Syracuse, N.Y., Syracuse University Press, 1983.

Issawi, Charles. *The Economic History of Iran, 1800–1919*. University of Chicago Press, 1972.

Kapuscinski, Ryszard. *Shah of Shahs*. San Diego, Harcourt Brace Jovanovich, 1985.

Katzman, Kenneth. *The Warriors of Islam: Iran's Revolutionary Guard*. Boulder, Co, and Oxford, United Kingdom, Westview Press, 1994.

Keddie, Nikki. *Roots of Revolution*. Yale University Press, 1982.

Khomeini, Ayatollah Ruhollah. *Islam and Revolution: Writings and Declarations of Imam Khomeini, trans. and ed. by Hamid Algar*. Berkeley, Calif., Mizan Press, 1982.

Laing, Margaret. *The Shah*. London, Sidgwick and Jackson, 1977.

Lenczowski, George. *Russia and the West in Iran*. Cornell University Press, 1949.

Lenczowsci, G. (Ed.). *Iran under the Pahlavis*. Stanford, Hoover Institution Press, 1978.

Mottahedeh, Roy. *The Mantle of the Prophet: Religion and Politics in Iran*. London, Chatto and Windus, 1985.

Nakhai, M. *L'Evolution Politique de l'Iran*. Brussels, 1938.

Naraghi, Ehsan. *Des Palais du Chah aux prisons de la révolution*. Paris, Editions Balland, 1993.

Omid, Homa. *Islam and the Post-Revolutionary State in Iran*. London, Macmillan, 1993.

Parsa, Misagh. *Social Origins of the Iranian Revolution*. New Brunswick, New Jersey and London, Rutgers University Press, 1989.

Parsons, Sir Anthony. *The Pride and the Fall: Iran 1974–79*. London, Jonathan Cape, 1984.

Pelletiere, Stephen. *The Iran–Iraq War: chaos in a vacuum*. London and New York, Praeger Publishers, Inc., 1992.

Rahnema, Ali, and Nomani, Farhad. *The Sewlar Miracle: religion, politics and economic policy in Iran*. London, Zed Books, 1990.

Rajaee, Farhang (Ed.). *The Iran-Iraq War: The Politics of Aggression*. Gainsville, University Press of Florida, 1994.

Ramazani, Rouhollah K. *The Foreign Policy of Iran 1500–1941*. University Press of Virginia, 1966.

Rezun, Miron (Ed.). *Iran at the Crossroads: global relations in a turbulent decade*. Oxford, Westview Press, 1990.

Roosevelt, Kermit. *Countercoup: the Struggle for the Control of Iran*. McGraw-Hill, 1980.

Sick, Gary. *All Fall Down: America's Tragic Encounter with Iran*. New York, Random House, 1985.

October Surprise. New York, Random House, 1991.

Stempel, John D. *Inside the Iranian Revolution*. Indiana University Press, 1982.

Steppat, Fritz. *Iran zwischen den Grossmächten, 1941–48*. Oberursel, 1948.

Taheri, Amir. *The Spirit of Allah: Khomeini and the Iranian Revolution*. London, Hutchinson, 1985.

Upton, Joseph M. *The History of Modern Iran: An Interpretation*. Harvard University Press, 1960.

Villiers, Gerard de. *The Imperial Shah: An Informal Biography*. London, Weidenfeld and Nicolson, 1977.

Wroe, Ann. *Lives, Lies and the Iran-Contra Affair*. London, I. B. Tauris, 1991.

Zonis, Marrin. *Majestic Failure: The Fall of the Shah*. University of Chicago Press, 1991.

ECONOMY AND PETROLEUM

Amid, Mohammad Javad. *Poverty, Agriculture and Reform in Iran*. London, Routledge, 1990.

Amuzegar, Jahangir. *Technical Assistance in Theory and Practice: the Case of Iran*. New York, Praeger Special Studies in International Economics, 1966.

Amuzegar, Jahangir, and Ali Fekrat, M. *Iran: Economic Development under Dualistic Conditions*. University of Chicago Press, 1971.

Baldwin, George B. *Planning and Development in Iran*. Baltimore, Johns Hopkins Press, 1967.

Bharier, Julian. *Economic Development in Iran 1900-1970*. London, Oxford University Press, 1971.

Elm, Mostafa. *Oil, Power and Principle: Iran's oil nationalization and its aftermath*. Syracuse, Syracuse University Press, 1992.

Ghosh, Sunil Kanti. *The Anglo-Iranian Oil Dispute*. Calcutta, 1960.

Gupta, Raj Narain. *Iran: An Economic Study*. New Delhi, 1947.

Mason, F. C. *Iran: Economic and Commercial Conditions in Iran*. London, HMSO, 1957.

Mofid, Kamran. *The Economic Consequences of the Gulf War*. London, Routledge, 1990.

Nahai, L., and Kibell, C. L. *The Petroleum Industry of Iran*. Washington, US Department of the Interior, Bureau of Mines, 1963.

Nirumand, Bahman. *Persien, Modell eines Entwicklungslande, oder Die Diktatur der freien Welt*. Reinbek-bei-Hamburg, Rowohlt-Verlag, 1967.

Sotoudeh, H. *L'Evolution Economique de l'Iran et ses Problèmes*. Paris, 1957.

IRAQ

Physical and Social Geography

W. B. FISHER

Iraq is bounded on the north by Turkey, on the east by Iran, on the south by Kuwait and the Persian Gulf, on the south-west by Saudi Arabia and Jordan, and on the north-west by Syria. The actual frontier lines present one or two unusual features. In the first place, there exists between Iraq, Kuwait, and Saudi Arabia a 'neutral zone', rhomboidal in shape, which was devised to facilitate the migrations of pastoral nomads, who cover great distances each year in search of pasture for their animals and who move regularly between several countries. Hence the stabilization or closing of a frontier could be for them a matter of life and death. Secondly, the frontier with Iran in its extreme southern portion below Basra follows the course of the Shatt al-Arab channel (the confluence of the Tigris and Euphrates), which flows into the Persian Gulf, but from 1936 until March 1975 the frontier was at the left (east) bank, placing the whole of the river within Iraq. This situation had become increasingly unacceptable to Iran, and under the Algiers Agreement of March 1975 the border was restored to the Thalweg Line in the middle of the deepest shipping channel in the Shatt al-Arab estuary. The dispute over the precise position of this border was one of the causes of the war with Iran which began in 1980. Thirdly, the inclusion of the northern province of Mosul within Iraq was agreed only in 1926. Because of its petroleum deposits, this territory was in dispute between Turkey, Syria and Iraq. Again, the presence of large numbers of migratory nomads, journeying each season between Iran, Turkey, Syria and Iraq, was a further complicating factor. In March 1984 a treaty was signed by Jordan and Iraq which finally demarcated the border between the two countries and under which Iraq ceded some 50 sq km to Jordan.

PHYSICAL FEATURES

The old name of Iraq (Mesopotamia = land between the rivers) indicates the main physical aspect of the country—the presence of the two river valleys of the Tigris and Euphrates, which merge in their lower courses. On the eastern side of this double valley the Zagros Mountains of Persia appear as an abrupt wall, overhanging the riverine lowlands, particularly in the south, below Baghdad. North of the latitude of Baghdad the rise to the mountains is more gradual, with several intervening hill ranges, such as the Jebel Hamrin. These ranges are fairly low and narrow at first, with separating lowlands, but towards the main Zagros topography becomes more imposing, and summits over 3,000 m in height occur. This region, lying north and east of Baghdad, is the ancient land of Assyria; and nowadays the higher hill ranges lying in the extreme east are called Iraqi Kurdistan, since many Kurdish tribes inhabit them.

On the western side of the river valley the land rises gradually to form the plateau which continues into Syria, Jordan, and Saudi Arabia, and its maximum height in Iraq is about 1,000 m. In places it is possible to trace a cliff formation, where a more resistant bed of rock stands out prominently, and from this the name of the country is said to be derived (Arabic: Iraq = cliff). There is no sharp geographical break between Iraq and its western neighbours comparable with that between Iraq and Iran; the frontier lines are artificial.

THE RIVERS

It remains to describe the valley region itself and the two rivers. The Tigris, 1,850 km (1,150 miles) in length, rises in Turkey, and is joined by numerous and often large tributaries both in Turkey and Iraq. The Euphrates, 2,350 km (1,460 miles) in length, also rises in Turkey and flows first through Syria and then Iraq, joining the Tigris in its lower course at Qurna, to form the stream known as the Shatt al-Arab (or Arvand river, as it is called by the Iranians), which is 185 km (115 miles) in length. Unlike the Tigris, the Euphrates receives no tributaries during its passage of Iraq. Above the region of Baghdad both rivers flow in well-defined channels, with retaining valley walls. Below Baghdad, however, the vestiges of a retaining valley disappear, and the rivers meander over a vast open plain with only a slight drop in level—in places merely 1.5 m or 2 m in 100 km. Here the rivers are raised on great levees, or banks of silt and mud (which they themselves have laid down), and now lie several feet above the level of the surrounding plain. One remarkable feature is the change in relative level of the two river beds—water can be led from one to the other according to the actual district, and this possibility, utilized by irrigation engineers for many centuries, still remains the basic principle of present-day development. At the same time, the courses of both rivers can suddenly alter. A flood may breach the wall of the levee, and the water then pours out on to the lower-lying plain, inundating large areas of land. Ultimately, the river finds a new course and builds a fresh levee. Old river channels, fully or partially abandoned by the river, are thus a feature of the Mesopotamian lowland, associated with wide areas of swamp, lakes, and sandbars. The Tigris, though narrower than the Euphrates, is swifter, and carries far more water.

As the sources of both rivers lie in the mountains of Turkey, the current is very fast, and upstream navigation is difficult in the middle and upper reaches. In spring, following the melting of snows in Asia Minor, both rivers begin to rise, reaching a maximum in April (Tigris) and May (Euphrates). The spring is a very anxious time, since floods of 3.6 m to 6.0 m occur, and 10 m is known—this in a region where the land may fall only 4 m or less in level over 100 km. Immense areas are regularly inundated, levees often collapse, and villages and roads, where these exist, must be built on high embankments. The Tigris is particularly liable to sudden flooding, and can rise at the rate of one foot per hour. Contrasts with the Nile of Egypt will be noted. The latter river is confined in a steep-sided valley over most of its length, and floods do not spread far away from the river. In lower Iraq, on the other hand, wide expanses are inundated every year, e.g. as in early 1954 when a flood of 9 m occurred and many thousands were rendered homeless. Construction of the Wadi Tharthar control scheme has, however, greatly reduced the incidence of severe flooding, particularly along the Tigris, and continued expansion of irrigation schemes (which has been a feature of Iraq since the late 1960s) is having a further effect.

Roads were formerly difficult to maintain because of floods, and the rail system was of different gauges. New standard-gauge rail links have now been constructed: north-south from Mosul to Basra via Baghdad; various cross-country lines; and an extension along the Euphrates valley towards north-eastern Syria.

Because of the former difficulties in communication, many communities of differing cultures and ways of life have persisted. Minority groups have thus been a feature in Iraq.

CLIMATE AND ECONOMIC ACTIVITY

The summers are overwhelmingly hot, with shade temperatures of over 43°C; and many inhabitants retire during the heat of the day to underground rooms. Winters may be surprisingly cold: frost, though very rare in the south, can be severe in the north. Sudden hot spells during winter are another feature in the centre and south of Iraq. Rainfall is scanty over all of the country, except for the north-east (Assyria), where annual falls of 400 mm–600 mm occur—enough to grow crops without irrigation. Elsewhere farming is entirely dependent upon irrigation from river water. The great extent of standing water in many parts of Iraq leads to an unduly high air humidity, which explains the notorious reputation of the Mesopotamian summer.

The unusual physical conditions outlined present a number of obstacles to human activity. The flood waters are rather less 'manageable' than in Egypt, and there is less of the regular deposition of thick, rich silt that is such a feature of the Nile. The effects of this are strikingly visible in the relatively small extent of land actually cultivated—at most, only one-sixth of the potentially cultivable territory and 3% of the total area of the country. The population (16.3m. at the census of October 1987) is about one-third that of Egypt. Because of the easy availability of agricultural land, wasteful, 'extensive' farming methods are often followed, giving a low yield. On the whole, Iraq is underpopulated, and could support larger numbers of inhabitants.

A feature of the last few years has been the use of oil royalties for development schemes, particularly in irrigation. Various early plans allocated up to £30m. annually, but this was not always used. Now, with much higher oil revenues, the figure has been revised upward, and far more extensive development is planned. A further favourable factor is the discovery in 1975 of a major new oilfield, which made Iraq the second largest Middle Eastern oil producer.

The unusual physical conditions have greatly restricted movement and the development of communications of all kinds. In the upper reaches of the rivers boat journeys can only be made downstream, whilst nearer the sea the rivers are wider and slower but often very shallow. Roads are difficult to maintain because of the floods, and the railways have two differing gauges—standard and metre; the latter is, however, in process of replacement; and, with decreasing risk of flooding, standard gauge has been laid between Baghdad and Basra via Kut.

THE PEOPLE

In the marshes of the extreme south there are communities of Arabs who spend most of their lives in boats and rafts. Other important minorities live in, or close to, the hill country of the north: the Kurds, who number an estimated 3.5m. and migrate extensively into Syria, Turkey and Iran (see History); the Yazidis of the Jebel Sinjar; the Assyrian Christians (the name refers to their geographical location, and has no historical connection); and various communities of Uniate and Orthodox Christians. As well, there were important groups of Jews—more than in most other Muslim countries—though, since the establishment of the State of Israel, much emigration has taken place. It should be noted that, while the majority of the Muslims follow Shi'a rites, the wealthier Muslims are of Sunni adherence.

Ethnically, the position is very complicated. The northern and eastern hill districts contain many racial elements—Turki, Persian, and proto-Nordic, with Armenoid strains predominating. The pastoral nomads of western Iraq are, as might be expected, of fairly unmixed Mediterranean ancestry, like the nomads of Syria, Jordan, and Saudi Arabia; but the population of the riverine districts of Iraq shows a mixture of Armenoid and Mediterranean elements. North of the Baghdad district the Armenoid strain is dominant, but to the south, it is less important, though still present.

Arabic is the official and most widely used language, Kurdish and dialects of Turkish are current in the north, whilst variants of Persian are spoken by tribesmen in the east. An estimate, probably over-generous to the Arabic speakers, puts the relative proportions at: Arabic 79%, Kurdish 16%, Persian 3%, and Turkish 2% of the total population.

History

EARLY HISTORY

By the time that Islam burst forth in the seventh century AD Iraq had already experienced over 3,500 years of civilization. The Sumerians were in turn succeeded by the Elamites, the Amorites, the Mittani, the Hittites, and the Assyrians, until in 612 BC the subject peoples rose and sacked Nineveh. Iraq then became the centre of a neo-Babylonian state, which, under Nebuchadnezzar (604–538 BC), included much of the Fertile Crescent, but soon fell to the Persians, who seized Babylon in 539–538 BC.

Iraq then became a province of the Achaemenid Empire until the military successes of Alexander the Great in 334–327 BC. After about 100 years of Seleucid rule Iraq became a frontier province of the Parthian Empire against the might of Rome. Between AD 113 and 117 Trajan conquered much of Iraq but his successor Hadrian withdrew. Roman reoccupation later took place. Parthian rule eventually gave way before the emergence of the Sasanid regime in the second century AD. Frontier wars with Rome broke out from time to time, but by the seventh century both Persia and Byzantium were exhausted, and the way was open to conquest from the south.

THE RISE OF ISLAM

The spectacular birth and growth of Islam in the first quarter of the seventh century set the Arabs on the path of conquest outside Arabia. In 637, at the battle of Jalula, the Arabs virtually ended Sasanid power in Iraq. There immediately followed a period of struggle between Ali, the son-in-law of the Prophet, and Mu'awiya, who had been governor of Syria. Ali fell in battle, however, in 661, making way for the Umaiyad dynasty, under Syrian hegemony, until 750. A party arose known as the Shi'atu Ali (i.e. the party of Ali) and most new converts gave their allegiance to the Shi'a, partly as an expression of their social and political grievance against the established order. In 750 Umaiyad rule was replaced by that of the Abbasid dynasty, with Iraq becoming the dominant and most prosperous part of the empire. The second Abbasid, al-Mansour (754–775), quickly abandoned the Shi'ite extremists who had brought the Abbasids to power. Abbasid power waned, and Baghdad fell under the rule of the Shi'ite Buwaihids from the middle of the 10th to the middle of the 11th century, when effective power passed to the Seljuq Turks, although the Abbasid Caliph was, in name, the Head of State.

MONGOL INVASIONS

In 1253 Hulagu, a grandson of Chinghiz (Jenghiz) Khan, moved westward in force, captured Baghdad in 1258 and thus made an end of the Abbasid Caliphate. Now subordinate to the Mongol Khan of Persia, Iraq became a mere frontier province. After the death of the Mongol Khan Abu Sa'id in 1335, Iraq passed to the Jala'irids who ruled until the early years of the 15th century. Iraq then passed successively under the power of two rival Turcoman confederations (the Black Sheep and the White Sheep) until, in the years 1499–1508, the White Sheep regime was destroyed by the Safavid Ismail, who made himself Shah of Persia. The Sunni Ottoman Turks saw a great threat in the Shi'ite Ismail, and the Sultan Suleyman, in the course of his campaign against Persia, conquered Baghdad in 1534–35.

OTTOMAN IRAQ

Although Persian control was restored for a brief period between 1623 and 1638, Iraq was to remain, at least nominally, under Turkish control until the First World War. A series of Mamluk pashas in the 18th century engaged in wars with Persia, and, towards the end of the century, had to deal with Kurdish insurrection in the north and raids by Wahhabi tribesmen from the south. In the early 19th century the Ottoman Sultan decided to regain direct possession of Iraq and end the Mamluk system. Sultan Mahmoud II sent Ali Ridha Pasha to perform this task in 1831. A severe outbreak of plague hampered the Mamluks, Da'ud Pasha was deposed, and the Mamluk regiments were exterminated.

WESTERN INFLUENCE

Although some of the European nations had long been in contact with Iraq through their commercial interests in the Persian Gulf, Western influences were slow to penetrate into the province. By 1800 there was a British Resident at Basra and two years later a British Consulate at Baghdad. France also maintained agents in these cities. French and Italian religious orders had settlements in the land. It was not, however, until after 1831 that signs of more rapid European penetration became visible, such as steamboats on the rivers of Iraq in 1836, telegraph lines from 1861 and a number of proposals for railways, none of which was to materialize for a long time to come. The Ottoman Government did much in the period between 1831 and 1850 to impose direct control over Kurdistan and the mountainous areas close to the Persian border, but the introduction of reforms was not, in fact, begun until in 1869 Midhat Pasha arrived at Baghdad. Much of his work, performed in the brief space of three years, proved to be superficial and ill-considered, yet he was able to set Iraq on a course from which there could be no retreat in the future. A newspaper, military factories, a hospital, an alms-house, schools, a tramway, conscription for the army, municipal and administrative councils, comparative security on the main routes and a reasoned policy of settling tribesmen on the land—these achievements, however imperfect, bear solid witness to the vigour of his rule. After his departure in 1872, reform and European influence continued to advance, although slowly. Postal services were much developed, a railway from Baghdad to Samarra was completed in 1914 (part of the projected *Baghdad-bahn* which betokened the rapid growth of German interest in the Ottoman Empire) and the important Hindiya Barrage on the Euphrates was rebuilt between 1910 and 1913. The measures of reform and improvement introduced between 1831 and 1914 must indeed be judged as belated and inadequate—the Iraq of 1900 differed little from that of 1500—yet a process of fundamental change had begun, which no regime, however inept, could reverse.

In November 1914 Britain and the Ottoman Empire were at war. British troops occupied the Shatt al-Arab region and, under the pressure of war needs, transformed Basra into an efficient and well-equipped port. A premature advance on Baghdad in 1915 ended in the retreat of the British forces to Kut, their prolonged defence of that town and, when all attempts to relieve it had failed, the capitulation to the Ottomans in April 1916. A new offensive launched from Basra in the autumn of that year brought about the capture of Baghdad in March 1917. Kirkuk was taken in 1918, but, before the Allies could seize Mosul, the Ottoman Government sought and obtained an armistice in October. For two years, until the winter of 1920, the Commander-in-Chief of the British Forces, acting through a civil commissioner, continued to be responsible for the administration of Iraq from Basra to Mosul, all the apparatus of a modern system of rule being created at Baghdad—e.g. departments of land, posts and telegraphs, agriculture, irrigation, police, customs, finance, etc. The new regime was Christian, foreign and strange, resented by reason of its very efficiency, feared and distrusted no less by those whose loyalties were Muslim and Ottoman than by important elements who desired self-determination for Iraq.

The last phase of Ottoman domination in Iraq, especially during the years after the Young Turk Revolution in 1908, had witnessed a marked growth of Arab nationalist sentiment. Local circles in Iraq now made contact with the Ottoman Decentralization Party at Cairo, founded in 1912, and with the Young Arab Society, which moved from Paris to Beirut in 1913. Basra, in particular, became a centre of Arab aspirations

and took the lead in demanding from Istanbul a measure of autonomy for Iraq. A secret organization, al-'Ahd (the Covenant), included a number of Iraqi officers serving in the Ottoman armies. The prospect of independence which the Allies held out to the Arabs in the course of the war strengthened and extended the nationalist movement. In April 1920 Britain received from the conference at San Remo a mandate for Iraq. This news was soon followed by a serious insurrection amongst the tribesmen of the south. The revolt, caused partly by instinctive dislike of foreign rule but also by vigorous nationalist propaganda, was not wholly suppressed until early in the next year. In October 1920 military rule was formally terminated in Iraq. An Arab Council of State, advised by British officials and responsible for the administration, now came into being and in March 1921 the Amir Faisal ibn Husain agreed to rule as King at Baghdad. His ceremonial accession took place on 23 August 1921.

The Najdi (Saudi Arabian) frontier with Iraq was defined in the Treaty of Mohammara in May 1922. Saudi concern over loss of traditional grazing rights resulted in further talks between Ibn Saud and the British Civil Commissioner in Iraq, and a Neutral Zone of 7,000 sq km was established adjacent to the western tip of the Kuwait frontier. No military or permanent buildings were to be erected in the zone and the nomads of both countries were to have unimpeded access to its pastures and wells. A further agreement concerning the administration of this zone was signed between Iraq and Saudi Arabia in May 1938.

MODERN IRAQ

Despite the opposition of the more extreme nationalists, an Anglo-Iraqi Treaty was signed on 10 October 1922. It embodied the provisions of the mandate, safeguarded the judicial rights of foreigners and guaranteed the special interests of Britain in Iraq. An electoral law prepared the way for the choice of a constituent assembly, which met in March 1924 and, in the face of strong opposition by the nationalists, ratified the treaty with Britain. It accepted, too, an organic law declaring Iraq to be a sovereign state with a constitutional hereditary monarchy and a representative system of government. In 1925 the League of Nations recommended that the *wilaya* (administrative district) of Mosul, to which the Turks had laid claim, be incorporated into the new kingdom, a decision finally implemented in the treaty of July 1926 between the interested parties, Britain, Turkey and Iraq. By this year a fully constituted Parliament was in session at Baghdad and all the ministries, as well as most of the larger departments of the administration, were in effective control. In 1930 a new treaty was signed with Britain, which established between the two countries a close alliance for a period of 25 years and granted Britain the use of airbases at Shuaiba and Habbaniya. On 3 October 1932 Iraq entered the League of Nations as an independent power, the mandate being now terminated.

The difficulties which confronted the Kingdom in the period after 1932 required much time and effort for their solution: e.g. the animosities between the Sunni Muslims and the powerful Shi'ite tribes on the Euphrates, which tended to divide and embitter political life; the problem of relations with the Kurds, some of whom wanted a state of their own, and with other minorities like the Assyrians; the complicated task of reform in land tenure and of improvement in agriculture, irrigation, flood control, public services and communications. As yet, the Government itself consisted of little more than a façade of democratic forms concealing a world of faction and intrigue. The realities of the political scene were a xenophobic press often ill-informed and irresponsible; 'parties' better described as cliques gathered around prominent personalities; a small ruling class of tribal sheikhs; landowners; and the intelligentsia—lawyers, students, journalists, doctors, ex-officers—frequently torn by sharp rivalries. It is not surprising, therefore, that the first years of full independence showed a rather halting progress towards efficient rule. The dangerous nature of the tensions inside Iraq was revealed in the Assyrian massacre of 1933 carried out by troops of the Iraqi army. Political intrigue from Baghdad had much to do with the outbreak of tribal revolt along the Euphrates in 1935–36. The army crushed the insurrection without much trouble and then, under the leadership of General Bakr Sidqi and in alliance with disappointed politicians and reformist elements, brought about a *coup d'état* in October 1936. The new regime failed to fulfil its assurances of reform, its policies alienated the tribal chieftains and gave rise to serious tensions even within the armed forces, tensions which led to the assassination of Bakr Sidqi in August 1937.

Of vast importance for Iraq was the rapid development of the oil industry during these years. Concessions were granted in 1925, 1932 and 1938 to the Iraq, Mosul and Basra Petroleum Companies. Oil had been discovered in the Kirkuk area in 1927 and by the end of 1934 the Iraq Petroleum Company was exporting crude oil through two 30-cm (12-inch) pipelines, one leading to Tripoli and the other to Haifa. Exploitation of the Mosul and Basra fields did not begin on a commercial scale until after the Second World War.

In 1937 Iraq joined Turkey, Persia and Afghanistan in the Sa'dabad Pact, which arranged for consultation in all disputes that might affect the common interests of the four states. A treaty signed with Persia in July 1937 and ratified in the following year provided for the specific acceptance of the boundary between the two countries as it had been defined in 1914. Relations with Britain deteriorated in the period after 1937, mainly because of the growth of anti-Zionist feeling and of resentment at British policy in Palestine. German influence increased very much at this time in Iraq, especially among those political and military circles associated with the army group later to be known as the Golden Square. Iraq severed its diplomatic connections with Germany at the beginning of the Second World War, but in 1941 the army commanders carried out a new *coup d'état*, establishing, under the nominal leadership of Rashid 'Ali al-Gaylani, a regime which announced its non-belligerent intentions. A disagreement over the passage of British troops through Iraq left no doubt of the pro-German sympathies of the Gaylani Government and led to hostilities that ended with the occupation of Basra and Baghdad in May 1941. Thereafter, Iraq co-operated with the Allies and declared war on the Axis powers in 1943.

Iraq, during the years after the Second World War, was to experience much internal tension and unrest. Negotiations with Britain led to the signing, at Portsmouth in January 1948, of a new Anglo-Iraqi agreement designed to replace that of 1930 and incorporating substantial concessions, amongst them the British evacuation of the airbases at Shuaiba and Habbaniya and the creation of a joint board for the co-ordination of all matters relating to mutual defence. The animosities arising from the situation in Palestine called forth riots at Baghdad directed against the new agreement with Britain, which were sufficiently disturbing to oblige the Iraqi Government to repudiate the Portsmouth settlement.

ARAB-ISRAEL WAR 1948

With anti-Jewish and anti-Western feeling so intense, it was inevitable that troops should be sent from Iraq to the Arab-Israeli war which began on 15 May 1948. The Iraqi troops shared in the hostilities for a period of just over two months, their participation terminating in a truce operative from 18 July. Their final withdrawal from Palestine did not commence, however, until April 1949. Subsequently, there was a considerable emigration of Jews from Iraq to Israel, especially in the years 1951–52.

The expense of the war against Israel, bad harvests, the general indigence of the people—all contributed to bring about serious tensions resulting in rioting at Baghdad in November 1952 and the imposition of martial law until October 1953. None the less, there were some favourable prospects for the future—notably a large expansion of the oil industry. New pipelines were built to Tripoli in 1949 and to Banias in Syria in 1952; the oilfields of Mosul and Basra were producing much crude petroleum by 1951/52. A National Development Board was created in 1950 and became later, in 1953, a national ministry. An agreement of February 1952 gave to the Iraqi Government 50% of the oil companies' profits before deductions for foreign taxes. Abundant resources were thus available for development projects of national benefit (e.g. the flood control and irrigation works opened in April 1956 on the Tigris at Samarra and on the Euphrates at Ramadi).

THE BAGHDAD PACT

Iraq, in the field of foreign relations, was confronted during these years with a choice between the Western powers, eager to establish in the Middle East an organized pattern of defence, and the USSR, entering at this time into a diplomatic propaganda and economic drive to increase its influence in the Arab lands. In February 1955, Iraq made an alliance with Turkey for mutual co-operation and defence. Britain acceded to this pact in the following April, agreeing also to end the Anglo-Iraqi agreement of 1930 and to surrender its air bases at Shuaiba and Habbaniya. With the adherence of Pakistan in September and of Iran in October 1955, the so-called Baghdad Pact was completed: a defensive cordon now existed along the southern fringe of the USSR.

CONSEQUENCES OF THE SUEZ CRISIS

The outbreak of hostilities between Israel and Egypt on 29 October 1956, and the armed intervention of British and French forces against Egypt (31 October–6 November) led to a delicate situation in Iraq, where strong elements were still opposed to all connections with the Western Powers. Iraq, indeed, broke off diplomatic relations with France on 9 November and announced that, for the immediate future at least, it could give no assurance of taking part in further sessions of the Council of the Baghdad Pact, if delegates from Britain were present.

The equivocal attitude of the Baghdad Government during the Suez crisis had provoked unrest in Iraq. Disturbances at Najaf and Mosul resulted in some loss of life. Student demonstrations against the Anglo-French intervention in Egypt and the Israeli campaign in Sinai led the Iraqi Government to close colleges and schools. Martial law, imposed on 31 October 1956, was not raised until 27 May 1957.

The tension born of the Suez crisis persisted for some time to come. President Eisenhower, concerned over the flow of Soviet arms to Syria and Egypt, sought from Congress permission to use the armed forces of the USA to defend nations exposed to danger from countries under the influence of international communism. He also secured authorization to disburse economic and military aid to the Middle East states prepared to co-operate with the West. This programme became known as the 'Eisenhower Doctrine'.

RELATIONS WITH SYRIA AND JORDAN

At the time of the Suez crisis there had been sharp tension between Iraq and Syria. Pumping-stations located inside Syria and belonging to the Iraq Petroleum Company were sabotaged in November 1956 with the result that Iraq suffered a large financial loss through the interruption in the flow of oil to the Mediterranean coast. Not until March 1957 did Syria allow the Iraq Petroleum Company to begin the repair of the pipelines.

Since the Suez crisis of 1956 troops of Iraq and Syria had been stationed in Jordan as a precaution against an Israeli advance to the east. Iraq, in December 1956, announced that its troops would be withdrawn; the Syrian forces, however, still remained in Jordan. The fear that Syria might intervene in favour of the elements in Jordan opposed to King Hussein brought about further recriminations between Baghdad and Damascus. The danger of an acute crisis receded in April 1957, when the USA declared that the independence of Jordan was a matter of vital concern and underlined this statement by sending its Sixth Fleet to the eastern Mediterranean. In February 1958 King Faisal of Iraq and King Hussein of Jordan joined together in an abortive Arab Federation.

OVERTHROW OF THE MONARCHY

King Faisal II, together with the Crown Prince of Iraq and Gen. Nouri as-Said, lost their lives in the course of a *coup d'état* begun on 14 July 1958 by units of the Iraqi army. Iraq was now to become a republic. Power was placed in the hands of a council of sovereignty exercising presidential authority and of a Cabinet led by Brig. Abd al-Karim Kassem, with the rank of Prime Minister.

A struggle for power was now to develop between the two main architects of the July *coup d'état*—Brig. (later Gen.)

Kassem, the Prime Minister, and Col (later Field-Marshal) Abd as-Salam Muhammad Aref, the Deputy Prime Minister and Minister of the Interior. Colonel Aref was associated with the influential Baath Party and had shown himself to be a supporter of union between Iraq and the United Arab Republic (UAR), the union of Egypt and Syria. Now, in September 1958, he was dismissed from his offices and, in November, was tried on a charge of plotting against the interests of Iraq. As reconstituted in February 1959 the new regime might be described as hostile to the UAR and inclined to favour a form of independent nationalism with left-wing tendencies.

General Kassem announced the withdrawal of Iraq from the Baghdad Pact on 24 March 1959. Since the revolution of July 1958 Iraq's adherence to the Pact had been little more than nominal. One result of this withdrawal was the termination of the special agreement existing between Britain and Iraq since 1955 under the first article of the Baghdad Pact. On 31 March it was made known that the Royal Air Force contingent at Habbaniya would be recalled.

PROBLEMS OF THE KASSEM REGIME

Earlier in 1959 the communist elements in Iraq had been refused representation in the Government. The communists operated through a number of professional organizations and also through the so-called People's Resistance Force. Communist elements had infiltrated into the armed forces of Iraq and into the civil service. General Kassem now began to introduce measures which would limit communist influence inside the Government and administration of the country. In July 1959 fighting occurred at Kirkuk between the Kurds (supported by the People's Resistance Force) and the Turcomans, with the result that Kassem disbanded the People's Resistance Force. Much more important for the Government at Baghdad was the fact that, in March 1961, a considerable section of the Kurdish population in northern Iraq rose in rebellion under Mustafa Barzani, the President of the Democratic Party of Kurdistan— a party established in 1958 after the return of Barzani from an exile occasioned by an earlier unsuccessful revolt in 1946. The refusal of the central regime at Baghdad to grant the reiterated Kurdish demands for autonomous status had contributed greatly to bringing about the new insurrection. Mustafa Barzani in March 1961 proclaimed an independent Kurdish state. By September 1961 the rebels controlled some 250 miles of mountainous territory along the Iraqi-Turkish and Iraqi-Persian frontiers, from Zakho in the west to Sulaimaniya in the east. The Kurds were able to consolidate their hold over much of northern Iraq during the course of 1962. The Kurds used guerrilla tactics with much success to isolate and deprive the government garrisons in the north of supplies. By December 1963 Kurdish forces had advanced south towards the Khanaqin area and the main road linking Iraq with Iran. The government troops found themselves in fact confined to the larger towns such as Kirkuk, Sulaimaniya and Khanaqin. Negotiations for peace began near Sulaimaniya in January 1964 and led to a cease-fire on 10 February. The national claims of the Kurds were to be recognized in a new provisional constitution for Iraq. Moreover, a general amnesty would be granted by the Iraqi Government. The Kurdish tribesmen, however, refused to lay aside their arms until their political demands had been given practical effect. Despite the negotiation of this settlement it was soon to become clear that no final solution of the Kurdish problem was in sight.

FALL OF KASSEM

A military coup, carried out in Baghdad on 8 February 1963, overthrew the regime of Gen. Kassem, the General himself being captured and shot. The coup arose out of an alliance between nationalist army officers and the Baath Party. Colonel Aref was now raised to the office of President and a new Cabinet created under Brig. Ahmad al-Bakr. The Baath Party, founded in 1941 (in Syria) and dedicated to the ideas of Arab unity, socialism and freedom, drew its main support from the military elements, the intellectuals and the middle classes. It was, however, divided in Iraq into a pro-Egyptian wing advocating union with the UAR and a more independent wing disinclined to accept authoritarian control from Egypt. The coup of February 1963 was followed by the arrest of pro-

Kassem and of communist elements, by mass trials and a number of executions, by confiscations of property and by a purge of the officer corps and of the civil service.

A number of efforts were made, during the years 1963–65, to further the cause of Arab unification, but agreements made between Syria and Iraq, and between Egypt, Syria and Iraq, had little practical effect.

MANOEUVRES OF THE BAATH PARTY

These same years saw in Iraq itself a conflict for control between the extremist and the more moderate Baath elements. At the end of September 1963 the extremists dominated the Baath Regional Council in Iraq. An international Baath conference held at Damascus in October 1963 strengthened the position of the extremists through its support of a federal union between Syria and Iraq and its approval of more radical social and economic policies. A further Baathist conference at Baghdad in November 1963 enabled the moderates to elect a new Baath Regional Council in Iraq with their own adherents in control. At this juncture the extremists attempted a *coup d'état*, in the course of which air force elements attacked the Presidential Palace and the Ministry of Defence.

On 18 November 1963 President Aref assumed full powers in Iraq, with the support of the armed forces, and a new Revolutionary Command was established at Baghdad. Sporadic fighting occurred (18–20 November) between government troops and the pro-Baathist National Guard. A main factor in the sudden fall of the Baathists was the attitude of the professional officer class. Officers with communist, Kassemite or pro-Nasser sympathies, or with no strong political views, or of Kurdish origin, had all been removed from important commands and offices. The privileged position of the National Guard caused further resentment in the army. The long drawn-out operations against the Kurds, the known dissensions within the Baathist ranks in Iraq and the intervention of Baath politicians from abroad in Iraqi affairs also contributed to discredit the extreme elements amongst the Baathists. On 20 November 1963, a new Cabinet was formed at Baghdad, consisting of officers, moderate Baathists, independents and non-party experts.

THE ARAB SOCIALIST UNION

On 14 July 1964 President Aref announced that all political parties would be merged in a new organization known as the 'Iraqi Arab Socialist Union'. At the same time it was revealed that all banks and insurance companies, together with 32 important industrial concerns, would undergo nationalization.

In July 1965 a number of pro-Nasser ministers handed in their resignations. At the beginning of September 1965 a new administration came into being with Brig. Aref Abd ar-Razzaq as Prime Minister. The Brigadier, reputed to be pro-Nasser in his sympathies, attempted to seize full power in Iraq, but his attempted *coup d'état* failed and, on 16 September he himself, together with some of his supporters, found refuge in Cairo. On 13 April 1966 President Abd as-Salam Aref of Iraq was killed in a helicopter crash. His brother Maj.-Gen. Abd ar-Rahman Aref succeeded him as President with the approval of the Cabinet and of the National Defence Council. In late June 1966 Brig. Aref Abd ar-Razzaq, who had staged the unsuccessful *coup d'état* of September 1965, led a second abortive coup, which was foiled by the prompt action of President Aref.

KURDISH NATIONALISM

The war against the Kurds, halted only for a short while by the cease-fire of February 1964, dragged out its inconclusive course during 1964–66. Some of the fighting in December 1965 occurred close to the Iraq-Iran border, leading to a number of frontier violations which gave rise to sharp tension between the two states during the first half of 1966. In June 1966 Dr Abd ar-Rahman al-Bazzaz, Prime Minister of Iraq since September 1965, formulated new proposals for a settlement of the conflict with the Kurds. Kurdish nationalism and language would receive legal recognition; the administration was to be decentralized, allowing the Kurds to run educational, health and municipal affairs in their own districts; the Kurds would have proportional representation in Parliament and in the Cabinet and the various state services; the Kurdish armed forces (some 15,000 strong) were to be dissolved. Mustafa Barzani, the Kurdish leader, declared himself to be well disposed towards these proposals.

This entente was implemented only to a limited extent. The Cabinet formed in May 1967 contained Kurdish elements, and President Aref, after a visit to the north in late 1967, reaffirmed his intention to make available to the Kurds appointments of ministerial rank, to help with the rehabilitation of the war-affected areas in Kurdistan, and to work towards effective co-operation with the Kurds in the Government of Iraq. This state of quiescence was, however, broken in the first half of 1968 by reports of dissension amongst the Kurds themselves, with open violence between the adherents of Mustafa Barzani and the supporters of Jalal Talabani, who had co-operated with the Government.

OIL DISPUTES AND THE JUNE WAR

Although the winter of 1966–67 brought an improvement in relations with Iran, it also witnessed a dispute between Syria and the Iraq Petroleum Company (IPC) over alleged losses of revenue on oil from Iraq passing through Syria by pipeline. The flow of oil was halted for a time and settlement was not reached until well into 1967.

When the Arab-Israeli war broke out in June 1967, the movement of Iraqi oil was again affected. Problems connected with its production and export constituted a major preoccupation of the Baghdad Government during the period immediately following the war. Iraq had at the outset severed diplomatic relations with the USA and Britain after Arab charges that the two states had aided Israel in the war and it also banned the export of oil to them. When, at the end of June, supplies of Iraqi oil began to be moved once more from the pipeline terminals on the Mediterranean, this embargo remained. In August Iraq, Syria and Lebanon resolved to allow the export of Iraqi oil to most of the countries of Europe, the UK being still subject, however, to the embargo.

Relations with the West improved slightly during the autumn and winter of 1967. The remaining oil embargoes were gradually removed, and in December Gen. Sabri led a military delegation to Paris. This was followed by President Aref's official visit to France in February 1968, and in April France agreed to supply Iraq with 54 *Mirage* aircraft over the period 1969–73. In May diplomatic relations with the UK were resumed.

THE 1968 COUP AND ITS AFTERMATH

Throughout the first half of 1968 the regime conspicuously lacked popular support, being commonly thought to be both corrupt and inefficient, and the sudden bloodless *coup d'état* of 17 July did not surprise many observers. General Ahmad Hassan al-Bakr, a former Prime Minister, became President; the deposed President Aref went into exile and his Prime Minister, Taher Yahya, was imprisoned on corruption charges. A new government was soon dismissed by the President, who accused it of 'reactionary tendencies'. He then appointed himself Prime Minister and Commander-in-Chief of the armed forces.

During the second half of 1968 the internal political situation deteriorated steadily. By November there were frequent reports of a purge directed against opponents of the new regime, and freedom of verbal political comment seemed to have disappeared. A former Minister of Foreign Affairs, Dr Nasser al-Hani, was found murdered, and a distinguished former Prime Minister, Dr al-Bazzaz, and other members of former governments were arrested as 'counter-revolutionary leaders'; most were later sentenced to long terms of imprisonment. Open hostilities with the Kurds broke out in October 1968 for the first time since the June 1966 cease-fire, and continued on an extensive scale throughout the winter. Iraqi army and air force attempts to enforce the writ of the Baghdad Government had little success; the regime claimed that the rebels were receiving aid from Iran and Israel. Fighting continued unabated through 1969, the Kurds demanding autonomy within the state and asking for UN mediation.

SETTLEMENT WITH THE KURDS

The most important event of 1970 was the settlement with the Kurds when, in March, a 15-article peace plan was announced by the Revolutionary Command Council (RCC) and the Kurdish leaders. The plan conceded that the Kurds should participate fully in the Government; that Kurdish officials should be appointed in areas inhabited by a Kurdish majority; that Kurdish should be the official language, along with Arabic, in Kurdish areas; that development of Kurdish areas should be implemented; and that the provisional constitution should be amended to incorporate the rights of the Kurds.

The agreement was generally accepted by the Kurdish community and fighting ceased immediately. The war had been very expensive for Iraq and it had seriously delayed the national development programme. The Kurdish settlement, although not entirely satisfactory, did introduce an element of stability into life in Iraq and allowed a number of reforms to be initiated. In October 1970 the state of emergency, in operation almost continuously since July 1958, was lifted. Many political detainees, including former ministers, were released. Censorship of mail was abolished at the end of the year, having lasted for over 13 years, and a month later the censorship of foreign correspondents' cables was brought to an end after a similar period.

Kurdish unity was boosted in February 1971 by the decision of the Kurdish Revolutionary Party to merge with the Democratic Party of Kurdistan (DPK), led by Masoud Barzani, and in July 1971 a new provisional constitution was announced, which embodied many of the points contained in the 1970 settlement. The Kurds were directed by the Supreme Committee for Kurdish Affairs to give up their arms by August 1971 and the situation in the north continued to be normal.

Evidence of unrest, however, was growing both in Kurdistan and in the Government itself. In July 1971 an attempted coup by army and air force officers was put down by the Government but dissatisfaction continued to be reported. The Kurds were beginning to show discontent with the delays in implementing the 1970 agreement. Their demand for participation in the RCC was refused and in September 1971 an attempt was made on Barzani's life.

THE CONTINUING KURDISH PROBLEM

During 1972, possibly because of increasing preoccupation with foreign affairs, dissension within the Government was less in evidence. Clashes with the Kurds, however, became more frequent and there was another plot to assassinate Barzani in July. The Baath Party's deteriorating relations with the Kurds brought a threat from the DPK to renew the civil war. One of the main Kurdish grievances was that the census agreed upon in 1970 had still not taken place. The two sides met to discuss their differences, the Kurdish side pointing to the unfulfilled provisions of the 1970 agreement and the Baath reiterating the various development projects carried out in Kurdish areas. In December 1972 a break appeared in the Kurdish ranks when it was reported that a breakaway party was to be set up in opposition to Barzani's party.

FOREIGN RELATIONS 1968–71

The more radical section of the Arab world had initially greeted the July 1968 coup with disfavour and the new regime was at pains to prove itself as militant an exponent of Arab nationalism as its predecessor. The regime gradually became an accepted member of the nationalist group, but there was some Arab criticism of its policies, notably the public hangings and their effect on world opinion.

Like Algeria, on the opposite flank of the Arab world, Iraq adopted an uncompromising attitude to the Palestinian problem. All peace proposals—US, Egyptian and Jordanian—were rejected. In theory, total support was given to the Palestine liberation movement. However, despite a threat to the Jordanian Government at the beginning of September 1970 to intervene in Jordan on behalf of the Palestinian guerrillas, the Iraqi forces stationed there did not take part in the fighting. In January 1971 most of Iraq's 20,000 troops were withdrawn from both Jordan and Syria. In March it was reported in Cairo that Iraq's monthly contribution to the Palestine Liberation Army had ceased. Iraq's attitude to Middle East peace proposals opened up a rift with Egypt even before President Nasser's death, and Iraq's contempt for the proposed Egypt-Libya-Syria federation, as well as for any negotiated settlement with Israel, kept it well isolated from Egypt and almost all the other Arab states. In July 1971 there were signs that Iraq wished to reduce its isolation, offering to co-operate again with the Arab states if they abandoned attempts to negotiate with Israel, but the renewal of hostilities between the Jordanian Government and the guerrillas caused a break in relations with Jordan. Iraq closed the border, demanded Jordan's expulsion from the Arab League and banned it from participating in the Eighth International Baghdad Fair.

Meanwhile, relations with Iran continued to be poor. Iraq frequently accused the Teheran Government of assisting the Kurdish rebellion and in April 1969 the Shatt al-Arab waterway again caused a minor confrontation. Iraq had benefited by a 1937 treaty which gave it control of the waterway. Iran tried to force a renegotiation of the treaty by illegally sending through vessels flying the Iranian flag. Being unwilling (or politically unable) to yield any of its sovereignty, and unable to challenge Iran militarily, Iraq was obliged to accept this situation. Iraq proposed referring the dispute to the International Court of Justice, but Iran rejected the suggestion. Minor border clashes between the two sides' forces continued to occur sporadically and both Iran and Iraq accused each other of attempting to foment coups. Not surprisingly, the two countries were also divided on policy towards the Gulf states. Iraq broke off diplomatic relations with Iran (and Britain) after Iran's seizure of the Tumb Islands in the Persian (Arabian) Gulf in November 1971.

Relations with the Western world, and the USA in particular, remained poor, and several people were arrested or expelled in late 1968, after having been accused of spying for the USA. The friendship with the Soviet Union remained the major factor in Iraq's foreign policy, particularly since the USSR was supplying the major portion of Iraq's military equipment.

THE PROBLEM OF OIL

In June 1972 Iraq nationalized IPC's interests and agreement on outstanding points of dispute was finally reached on 28 February 1973. The company agreed to settle Iraqi claims for back royalties by paying £141m., and to waive its objections to Law No. 80 under which the North Rumaila fields were seized in 1961. The Government agreed to deliver a total of 15m. tons of crude from Kirkuk, to be loaded at Eastern Mediterranean ports, to the companies as compensation. The Mosul Petroleum Company agreed to relinquish all its assets without compensation and the Basrah Petroleum Company, the only one of the group to remain operational in Iraq, undertook to increase output from 32m. tons in 1972 to 80m. tons in 1976. This agreement was regarded on the whole as a victory for the Iraqi Government, although the companies were by no means net losers by it.

With the IPC dispute out of the way, Iraq showed its unwillingness to continue indefinitely with exporting oil on a barter basis to the Eastern bloc countries. The Government made it clear that it would press for a cash basis to future agreements.

FOREIGN RELATIONS 1972–73

The nationalization of IPC brought expressions of approval from a number of countries, including Arab states and the USSR. The 15-year friendship treaty with the USSR, signed in March 1972, was ratified in July, and Iraq's relations with the Eastern bloc continued to be good. Despite this, the Government was well aware of the dangers of too close and exclusive a relationship with the Soviet bloc. France was specifically singled out as the Western country most friendly towards the Arabs, and the President's fourth anniversary speech in July revealed that Iraq would not be unwilling to initiate friendly relations with Western countries. Although diplomatic relations with the USA remained severed, the USA established an 'interests section' in Baghdad.

CONSTITUTIONAL CHANGE

In July 1973 an abortive coup took place, led by the security chief, Nazim Kazzar, in which the Minister of Defence, Gen. Hammad Shehab, was killed. It is thought that it was an attempt by a civilian faction within the Baath Party to get rid of President Bakr and the military faction. One result of the attempted coup was an amendment to the Constitution giving more power to the President, and the formation of a National Front between the Baath Party and the Iraqi Communist Party.

CLIMAX AND END OF KURDISH WAR

According to the agreement made between the Iraqi Government and the Kurds in March 1970 the deadline for implementation of the agreement was 11 March 1974. An uneasy peace between the Kurds and the Iraqis existed between those two dates. When 11 March 1974 arrived, Saddam Hussain Takriti, the Vice-President of the RCC and the 'strong man' of the regime, announced the granting of autonomy to the Kurds. Barzani and his Democratic Party of Kurdistan (DPK) felt that the Iraqi offer fell short of their demands for full government representation, which included membership of the RCC. A minority of Kurds, who belonged to Abd as-Satter Sharif's Kurdish Revolutionary Party welcomed the proposals, however. Barzani and his militia, the *peshmerga* (literally, 'those who confront death'), began armed resistance in north Iraq. In April 1974 the Iraqi Government replaced five Kurdish ministers known to support Barzani by five other Kurds who supported the government plan for giving the Kurds a measure of autonomy. Later in April the Iraqi Government appointed a Kurd, Taha Mohi ed-Din Marouf, as Vice-President of Iraq, but since he had long been a supporter of the Baghdad Government, it seemed unlikely that this would mollify the Kurds of the DPK.

By August 1974 the Kurdish war had reached a new level of intensity. The Baghdad Government was directing large military resources against the *peshmerga*, and was deploying tanks, field guns and bombers. About 130,000 Kurds, mainly women, children and old men, took refuge in Iran. The *peshmerga* were able to keep up their resistance in Iraq only with the help of arms and other supplies from Iran. When, therefore, an agreement to end their border dispute was signed by Iraq and Iran at the OPEC meeting in Algiers on 6 March 1975, both countries also agreed to end 'infiltrations of a subversive character' and the Kurdish rebellion collapsed. Barzani felt that he could not continue his struggle without Iran's aid, and fled to Teheran. A cease-fire was arranged on 13 March and a series of amnesties granted to Kurds who had fled to Iran encouraged most of them to return to Iraq. By February 1976, however, it was reported that the DPK was secretly reorganizing inside Iraqi Kurdistan and preparing to resume its struggle. In March there were reports of clashes between Kurds and Iraqi security forces in the Rawanduz area, after Iraqi attempts to clear the frontier area with Iran and resettle Kurds in less sensitive areas of Iraq. A new political organization, the National Union of Kurdistan, was also set up in Damascus quite separately from the DPK, which, in the opinion of the National Union of Kurdistan, had become discredited. Renewed Kurdish activity occurred in 1976 but was not serious enough to weaken the Iraqi claim that the Kurdish problem had been solved. Reconstruction and school-building was certainly undertaken in Kurdish areas in 1977, and in April 1977 the Iraqi authorities allowed 40,000 Kurds who had been compulsorily settled in the south in 1975 to return to their homes in the north. It was also decided in April 1977, by the Executive Council of the Kurdish Autonomous Region, that Kurdish should become the official language to be used in all communications and by all government departments in the Kurdish Autonomous Region which had no connection with the central Government.

FOREIGN AFFAIRS 1973–76

On the outbreak of the October 1973 war between the Arabs and Israel, Iraq sent considerable land forces to the Syrian front and took advantage of Iran's offer to resume diplomatic relations. The Iraqi Government, however, had taken offence because President Sadat of Egypt had not consulted Iraq in advance, and, therefore, Iraqi forces were withdrawn from Syria as soon as the cease-fire went into effect, and Iraq boycotted the Arab summit meeting in Algiers in November.

Relations deteriorated with Iran in the early months of 1974, when frontier fighting broke out, and it was only after the appointment of a UN Mediator in March that 'normal' relations on the frontier were restored, and they deteriorated again in August in spite of talks in Istanbul between Iraqi and Iranian diplomats. Further border clashes took place in December 1974, and secret talks in Istanbul between the Iraqi and Iranian ministers of foreign affairs in January 1975 failed to prevent the outbreak of fresh clashes in February. It was therefore something of a surprise when, at the OPEC meeting at Algiers in March 1975, it was announced that Saddam Hussain Takriti, Vice-President of the RCC, and the Shah of Iran had signed an agreement which 'completely eliminated the conflict between the two brotherly countries'. This agreement also ended the Kurdish war (see above), and was embodied in a treaty signed between the two countries in June 1975. The frontiers were defined on the basis of the Protocol of Constantinople of 1913 and the verbal agreement on frontiers of 1914. The Shatt al-Arab frontier was defined according to the Thalweg Line, which runs down the middle of the deepest shipping channel.

THE BAATH PARTY AND RELATIONS WITH SYRIA

Iraq was one of the many Arab states which were severely critical of the second interim disengagement agreement signed between Egypt and Israel in September 1975. Iraqi reaction to the agreement was similar to that of Syria, but this condemnation was perhaps the only thing upon which the two countries agreed between 1975 and 1978. Rivalry between the two wings of the Baath party in Baghdad and Damascus, and a dispute over the sharing of the water from the Euphrates were just two areas of contention. In February 1976 Iraq was reported to be diverting much of its oil from pipelines to the Mediterranean to terminals near Basra, thus depriving Syria of valuable pipeline revenues. Iraq was also very critical of Syria's intervention in Lebanon. Syrian agents were also blamed for violence which took place in the Shi'a holy cities of Najaf and Karbala in February 1977. Relations with Syria deteriorated even further in late 1977, and Iraq became somewhat isolated after President Sadat of Egypt's peace initiative in visiting Jerusalem in November 1977. At the Tripoli Conference, summoned by the states which disagreed with President Sadat's approach, Iraq wanted a specific rejection of UN Security Council Resolution 242 (see Documents on Palestine, p. 86). The stand taken by the other participants (Syria, Libya, the People's Democratic Republic of Yemen, Algeria and the Palestine Liberation Organization) seemed too moderate for Iraq, which walked out of the conference. Iraq subsequently boycotted the Algiers conference of 'rejectionist' states in February 1978, hoping, unsuccessfully, to form its own 'steadfastness and liberation front' at a Baghdad conference.

NEW ALIGNMENTS

Iraq opposed the Camp David agreements made between Egypt and Israel in September 1978, but, continuing its attitude of boycott, it stayed away from the Damascus Arab summit which immediately followed the Camp David agreements. Iraq's period of isolation was almost at an end, however. In October President Assad of Syria visited Baghdad and, as a result, Iraq and Syria signed a Charter outlining plans for political and economic union between the two countries. Old rivalries and animosities were set aside in an effort to form a political and military power which would be a sizeable counterweight to Egypt in Middle Eastern affairs. In November Iraq successfully called a Pan-Arab summit which threatened sanctions against Egypt if a peace treaty with Israel should be signed, and in March 1979, when the peace treaty became a fact, Baghdad was the venue for the meeting of the Arab ministers of foreign and economic affairs which resolved to put into practice the threats made to Egypt in the previous November.

The plans for complete political and economic union of Iraq and Syria were pursued with enthusiasm but little real practical application by both countries until July 1979. On 16 July 1979 Saddam Hussain replaced Bakr as President of Iraq and chairman of the RCC. A few days later, an attempted coup was reported, and several members of the RCC were sentenced to death for their alleged part in the plot. Saddam Hussain believed Syria to be implicated, in spite of Syrian denials, and the newly-formed alliance foundered. Another aspect of this political unrest in Iraq was the breakdown of the alliance between the Baath Party and the Communist Party. In the summer of 1978 21 army personnel were executed for conducting political activity in the army, and relations with the communists continued to deteriorate. They withdrew from the National Progressive Front in March 1979, and in early 1980 President Hussain referred to them in a speech as 'a rotten, atheistic, yellow storm which has plagued Iraq'. This led to a decrease in dependence on the USSR and to tentative moves to improve relations with the West. Hussain joined in the general Arab condemnation of the Soviet invasion of Afghanistan at the end of 1979.

In February 1980 President Hussain announced his 'National Charter', which reaffirmed the principles of non-alignment, rejecting 'the existence of foreign armies, military forces, troops and bases in the Arab Homeland', and made a plea for Arab solidarity. With Sadat compromised by his *rapprochement* with Israel, Hussain saw himself in a position of virtual pre-eminence in the Arab world and, with the Non-Aligned Summit due to take place in Baghdad in 1982, he would be in a position to present himself as the responsible leader of the non-aligned world.

Domestically, Hussain was engaged in restoring parliamentary government to Iraq. The intention had been announced for some years, but on 16 March 1980 laws were adopted for the election of an Iraqi National Assembly of 250 deputies for a four-year session, and also for a Legislative Council for the Autonomous Region of Kurdistan, consisting of 50 members elected for a three-year session. Elections took place on 20 June 1980, and deputies were elected by a direct, free and secret ballot. The first session of the National Assembly opened on 30 June, and one of the deputy premiers, Naim Haddad, was elected chairman and speaker. Elections to a 50-member Kurdish Legislative Council took place in September 1980.

WAR WITH IRAN

Although the 1975 peace agreement with Iran virtually ended the Kurdish rebellion, Iraq was dissatisfied and wanted a return to the Shatt al-Arab boundary whereby it controlled the whole waterway, and also the withdrawal of Iranian forces from Abu Musa and Tumb Islands, which Iran occupied in 1971. Conflict also became evident after the Iranian Revolution over Arab demands for autonomy in Iran's Khuzestan (termed 'Arabistan' by Arabs), which Iran accused Iraq of encouraging. In addition, Iraq's Sunni leadership was suspicious of Shi'ite Iran and fearful that the Islamic Revolution in Iran might spread to its own Shi'ites, who are in the majority in Iraq. Border fighting between Iran and Iraq frequently occurred as 1980 progressed, and open warfare began on 22 September when Iraqi forces advanced into Iran along a 300-mile front. Iran had ignored Iraqi diplomatic efforts demanding the withdrawal of Iranian forces from Zain ul-Qos on the border. Iraq maintained that this territory should have been returned by Iran under the 1975 agreement. Iraq therefore abrogated the Shatt al-Arab agreement on 16 September.

Most commentators agree that Saddam Hussain's real intention when he invaded Iran was to topple the Islamic revolutionary regime in Iran. Resistance was fiercer than he expected, however, and stalemate was soon reached along a 300-mile front, while various international peace missions sought in vain for a solution. In the spring of 1982 Iranian forces launched successful counter-offensives, one in the region of Dezful in March, and another in April which resulted in the recapture of Khorramshahr by the Iranians in May.

By late June 1982 Saddam Hussain had to acknowledge that the invasion of Iran had been a failure, and he arranged for the complete withdrawal of Iraqi troops from Iranian territory. In July the Iranian army crossed into Iraq, giving rise to the heaviest fighting of the war, thus far.

INTERNAL OPPOSITION TO SADDAM HUSSAIN

As well as the deteriorating military situation, Saddam Hussain faced a number of other threats to his position from within Iraq. The 'Iraqi Front of Revolutionary, Islamic and National Forces', consisting of Kurds, exiled Shi'ites and disaffected Baath party members, had been formed in 1981 with the backing of Syria, whose President Assad was as anxious as Ayatollah Khomeini to see the downfall of Saddam Hussain, his Baathist rival. In northern Iraq, Kurdish rebels were becoming active again and there existed the possibility that Iraq's majority Shi'ite community (55% of the population) would turn against the Sunnis (the sect of the Iraqi leadership). However, the bulk of Iraq's Shi'ites seemed to distrust the harsh fundamentalism of Khomeini's Iran. Against this background, Hussain was re-elected chairman of the RCC and regional secretary of the Arab Baath Socialist Party, and in July 1982, having purged his administration, was apparently more firmly in control than ever.

In November 1982 new opposition arose from the Supreme Council of Iraqi Opposition Groups, under the leadership of an exiled Shi'ite leader, Hojatoleslam Muhammad Baqir Hakim, in Teheran. However, as the war with Iran degenerated into a conflict of attrition after the first Iranian advance into Iraq, the severe burden which it placed upon the country's economy emerged as the most critical concern for Hussain in 1983. Petroleum revenues had been slashed by almost 75%, following the destruction of Iraq's Gulf terminals, the closure of the pipeline across hostile Syria and the decline in oil prices. Iraq was searching for ways to avoid defaulting on payments for foreign construction contracts and was already borrowing money from friendly Gulf states.

In October 1983 there were rumours of an attempted coup in Baghdad, led by the recently dismissed head of intelligence, Barzan at-Takriti (the President's half-brother), and a number of senior army officers, who were later reported to have been executed.

An abiding problem for Iraqi governments has been the question of Kurdish autonomy within Iraq. The drain on military and financial resources, resulting from efforts to contain Kurdish secessionist forces, had a particular significance for Saddam Hussain. Costly equipment and manpower was being diverted from critical areas in the war with Iran to control Kurdish rebellion. Unable to fight wars on two fronts, Hussain sought an accommodation with the Kurds. A series of talks with Jalal Talibani, leader of the Patriotic Union of Kurdistan (PUK) and of an estimated 40,000 Kurdish soldiers, began in December 1983, after a cease-fire was agreed. The PUK demanded the release of 49 Kurdish political prisoners, the return of 8,000 Kurdish families, moved from Kurdistan to southern Iraq, and the extension of the Kurdish autonomous area to include the oil town of Kirkuk. The talks could have provided only a partial solution, as they did not include the DPK, which sought to further the cause of Kurdish autonomy by siding with Iran (and which was antipathetic towards the PUK). Thoughts of a government of national unity, including the PUK and the Communist Party of Iraq, were short-lived. Hussain's attitude changed, possibly prompted by the greater international support for Iraq which was forthcoming in the first half of 1984, and the talks broke down in May. The dialogue between the two sides was resumed and continued on a sporadic basis, with Hussain trying to persuade the PUK to join the National Progressive Front. To win its support, Hussain would have had to make major concessions to the PUK, such as granting Kurdish control of Kirkuk province, where Iraq's main oilfields are situated, and giving the Kurds a fixed share of national oil revenues (perhaps 20%–30%), and this he was unlikely to do. Negotiations on Kurdish autonomy collapsed again in January 1985 and fighting broke out in Kurdistan between PUK guerrillas and government troops after a 14-month cease-fire. The PUK blamed the Government's continued persecution and execution of Kurds; its refusal to include consideration of the one-third of Kurdistan containing the Kirkuk oilfields in autonomy talks; and an agreement with Turkey to act jointly to quell Kurdish resistance, which had been made in October 1984. The PUK then rejected the offer of an amnesty for President Hussain's political opponents at home and abroad in February, and fighting has continued.

THE IRAN–IRAQ WAR OCTOBER 1983–DECEMBER 1984

Beginning in October 1983, Iran launched a series of attacks across its northern border with Iraq. About 700 sq km (270 square miles) of Iraqi territory were gained, threatening the last outlet for Iraqi exports of petroleum through the Kirkuk pipeline. Iraq intensified its missile attacks and bombing raids against Iranian towns and petroleum installations. During the autumn of 1983 Iraq took delivery of five French-built *Super Etendard* fighter aircraft. With these, and with the *Exocet* missiles already in its possession, Iraq threatened to destroy Iran's petroleum export industry, centred on the Kharg Island oil terminal in the Gulf. (In fact, Iraq did not use the *Super Etendards* and *Exocet* missiles in tandem until the end of March 1984 in the Gulf.) Iran responded by promising to make the Gulf impassable to all traffic (including exports of one-sixth of the West's petroleum requirements) by blocking the Strait of Hormuz, if Iraqi military action made it impossible for Iran to export its own petroleum by that route.

Despite approaches from the UN and various governments (Egypt, Saudi Arabia and Syria among them), Iran refused to negotiate with Iraq and was adamant that nothing less than the removal of the regime of Saddam Hussain, the withdrawal of Iraqi troops from Iranian territory and the agreement to pay reparations for war damages could bring hostilities to an end.

In August 1982 Iraq declared a maritime exclusion zone in the Gulf, extending from the Khor Abdullah channel, at the mouth of the Shatt al-Arab waterway, to a point south of the Iranian port of Bushehr. This zone included the Kharg Island oil terminal. Iraq carried out sporadic attacks on shipping (not only tankers) making for Kharg or returning from it, or fired indiscriminately on ships well outside the zone. The aim was to make the export of petroleum from Iran as difficult and expensive as possible and, by the threat of military action, to deter shipping from using Iranian ports, thus starving Iran of vital oil revenues. These tactics succeeded to a limited extent. Rates of insurance for shipping using the Gulf rose dramatically, and Japan, the largest customer for Iranian oil, briefly ordered its tankers not to use Iranian ports in mid-1984. Iraq refrained, however, from implementing its threat to attack Kharg Island itself and tankers loading there until May 1984. When the attack came, it was not immediately followed up, and the sequence of isolated attacks of limited effectiveness seemed to be continuing. The dangers of the war's spreading to other Gulf states were shown when Iran retaliated by attacking Saudi Arabian and Kuwaiti tankers, and tankers using oil terminals belonging to those countries. During 1984 the conviction grew that neither Iran nor Iraq possessed the capability to give effect to its worst threats.

Iraq certainly had no shortage of financial and military supporters. Egypt is estimated to have supplied military equipment and spare parts worth more than US $2,000m.; according to *The Washington Post*, the People's Republic of China sold arms to Iraq worth $3,100m. between 1981 and 1985 (compared with sales to Iran, over the same period, worth $575m.); Brazil and Chile sold weapons to Iraq; the USSR (previously officially neutral in the war) increased its aid, following a *rapprochement* with Iraq in March 1984, and had already sold SS-12 missiles to Iraq; and the USA supplied helicopters and other heavy military equipment, though it remained officially neutral. (Both the USA and the USSR also sold arms to Iran.) Saudi Arabia and Kuwait supported Iraq with loans and the revenue from sales of up to 310,000 barrels of petroleum per day (250,000 b/d from the Neutral Zone and the remainder from Saudi Arabia), sold on Iraq's behalf.

In February 1984 Iran launched an offensive in the marshlands around Majnoon Island, the site of rich oilfields in southern Iraq, near the confluence of the rivers Tigris and Euphrates. Iraq failed to regain control of this territory and was condemned for using mustard gas in the fighting. Iraq subsequently established extensive and formidable defences, including a system of dams and embankments, along the southern front, near Basra, in anticipation of a possibly decisive offensive by Iran, which massed some 500,000 men there.

In 1984 the balance of military power moved in Iraq's favour, and the USA and the USSR, both officially neutral in the war with Iran, provided aid. The USSR increased its military aid following a *rapprochement* in March between the two Governments, precipitated by Iran's anti-Soviet stance, and was responsible for supplying an estimated two-thirds of Iraq's total armaments and much of its ammunition. At the end of 1987 it was estimated that the USSR had supplied Iraq with military aid worth $10,000m. since lifting a ban on arms sales in 1982. The USA assisted Iraq with the financing of crucial oil export pipeline projects and with an increasing allocation of commodity credits. Iraq and the USA re-established full diplomatic relations on 26 November 1984, more than 17 years after they had been broken off by Iraq following the Arab-Israeli war of 1967.

Iraq had a substantial advantage in the strength of its air force. At the end of 1984 Iraq had 580 combat aircraft and 130 armed helicopters, while Iran had 110 combat aircraft, only 50 to 60 of which were thought to be operational. On the ground, Iraq's tank force was superior in numbers and sophistication.

THE IRAN–IRAQ WAR 1985–86

A resumption in December 1984 of Iraqi attacks on shipping in the Gulf, in particular on oil tankers using the terminal at Kharg Island caused hull insurance rates to rise sharply. Iran's oil exports fell to a record low level in January 1985 as a result of Iraqi action but, after another lull in military activity, in a pattern which became familiar during the next four years, insurance rates were reduced and custom returned. Attacks on shipping continued but Iraq failed decisively to exploit its superiority in the air. The Kharg Island oil terminal remained operational and largely undamaged for much of 1985 and Iran was quite successful in circumventing Iraqi attempts to debilitate its oil export industry. It consistently offered oil at discount and rebate deals to attract customers deterred by the high cost of war insurance, and in February established a makeshift floating export terminal at Sirri Island, militarily a much less exposed location (journeys to which commanded lower rates of insurance), 800 km (500 miles) south-east of Kharg, from where it received its oil by tanker shuttle.

In March Iran committed an estimated 50,000 troops to an offensive on the southern front in the region of the Hawizah marshes, east of the Tigris. Iranian forces succeeded in crossing the Tigris and for a time closed the main road connecting Baghdad and Basra before being repulsed. Iraq was again accused of using chemical weapons during this engagement.

In June 1984 the UN engineered the suspension by Iran and Iraq of attacks on civilian targets. However, in March 1985, with the war on the ground at stalemate, Iraq resorted to air raids on Iranian towns and declared Iranian airspace a war zone. Saddam Hussain's stated intention was to carry the war to every part of Iran until Ayatollah Khomeini should decide to come to the negotiating table. The first Iraqi air raid on Teheran in four years took place in March. Although Iraq initially identified its targets as industrial, government and military installations only, thousands of civilians inevitably were killed as Iraqi aircraft attacked more than 30 Iranian towns with bombs, missiles and shellfire. Iran retaliated with shelling and air raids of its own on Iraqi economic, industrial and civilian targets, and with ground-based missile attacks on Baghdad itself. In this instance, Iraq was taking full advantage of its military superiority. In March King Hussein of Jordan and President Mubarak of Egypt unexpectedly visited Baghdad to show their support for Saddam Hussain, despite the fact that full diplomatic relations had not existed between Egypt and Iraq since Egypt's signing of the peace treaty with Israel in 1979.

The UN Secretary-General, Javier Pérez de Cuéllar, visited both Teheran and Baghdad in April to try to establish a basis for peace negotiations. Iraq made it clear that it was interested only in a permanent cease-fire and immediate peace negotiations; while Iran, though placing less official emphasis on the removal of Saddam Hussain's regime as a pre-condition of peace, accepted that, if he acquiesced in the other conditions,

including the payment of reparations calculated by Iran at $350,000m. in March 1985, he would fall anyway.

Twice during 1985 (in April and June) President Saddam Hussain ordered a suspension of air raids on Iranian cities, as an inducement to Iran to begin peace negotiations. On both occasions Iran ignored the gesture and Iraqi air raids were resumed.

In response to a joint Irano-Libyan strategic alliance which was becoming more open in character, Iraq withdrew its diplomatic mission from Tripoli in June 1985 and asked the Libyans to withdraw theirs from Baghdad. Iraq had severed its diplomatic links with Libya in late 1980, accusing Col Qaddafi of assisting Iran in the war, but limited diplomatic contact was restored and Libya was said to have had diplomatic representatives in Baghdad since 1984.

Until mid-1985 Iraq had failed to launch attacks against the main Iranian oil export terminal on Kharg Island of sufficient frequency or intensity seriously to threaten the continuation of oil exports. In August, however, Iraq made the first of a concentrated series of raids on Kharg, causing a reduction in Iranian oil exports from 1.2m.–1.5m. barrels per day (b/d), in the months leading up to the raids, to less than 1m. b/d in September. Exports from Kharg were temporarily halted altogether during the latter half of September. During October–December the raids became progressively less frequent and less damaging in their effect, and, by dint of rapid repairs and the taking up of Kharg's ample spare capacity, the Iranian Ministry of Oil was able to claim in October, with little exaggeration, that exports of oil had risen to 1.7m. b/d. Between August and the end of 1985 some 60 attacks on Kharg Island were reported. Despite Iran's earlier success in minimizing the effect of Iraqi raids and in developing alternative means of exporting oil (such as the floating terminal at Sirri Island), by the end of 1985 exports from Kharg had reportedly been reduced to a trickle compared with its 6.5m. b/d capacity, and Iraq had turned its attention to the tankers shuttling oil to Sirri Island for transhipment.

In February 1986 Iraq announced an expansion of the area of the Gulf from which it would try to exclude Iranian shipping. Previously confined to the waters around Iran's Gulf ports, the area was broadened to include the coast of Kuwait. Attacks on tankers and other commercial vessels in the Gulf were intensified by both sides during 1986, and they totalled 105 during the year. In the first half of 1986 Iraq continued to attack Kharg Island and tankers shuttling oil to Sirri Island, and in August an Iraqi raid demonstrated that the Sirri export facility itself was vulnerable to attack, bringing about an immediate doubling of insurance rates for vessels travelling there. Iran was forced to transfer more of its oil export operations to the remoter floating terminal at Larak Island, at the mouth of the Gulf, but this, too, proved accessible to Iraqi aircraft, employing mid-air refuelling facilities, and was itself attacked in November. Loading berths, refining facilities, and several tankers docked at Iran's Lavan Island oil terminal, were destroyed or badly damaged by an Iraqi raid in September 1986.

In the land war, the next important engagements, in terms of land gained, occurred in 1986, when, on 9 February, Iran launched the Wal-Fajr (Dawn) 8 offensive. Some 85,000 Iranian troops (leaving about 400,000 uncommitted on the southern front) crossed the Shatt al-Arab waterway and, on 11 February, occupied the disused Iraqi oil port of Faw, on the Persian Gulf, and, according to Iran, about 800 sq km of the Faw peninsula. From this position, within sight of the Kuwaiti island of Bubiyan, commanding the Khor Abdullah channel between the Faw peninsula and the island, Iran threatened Iraq's only access to the Gulf and, if it could extend the offensive to the north-west, Iraq's Umm Qasr naval base. However, the marsh and then desert terrain to the west was not conducive to further Iranian gains, and the position on the Faw peninsula was defensible only with difficulty, given the problem of maintaining supply lines across the Shatt al-Arab. At the same time as the attack upon Faw, Iran began a complementary operation along the Faw-Basra road to divert Iraqi forces. When Iraq launched a counter-offensive on Faw in mid-February, Iran opened up a second front in Iraqi Kurdistan, hundreds of miles to the north, with the Wal-Fajr 9 offensive. Iranian forces drove Iraqi and counter-revolutionary Iranian Kurds out of some 40 villages in the area of Sulaimaniya.

At the end of February the UN Security Council, while calling for a cease-fire, effectively blamed Iraq for starting the war. Despite heavy fighting, Iraq failed to dislodge an estimated 30,000 Iranian troops from in and around Faw. The proximity of Kuwaiti territory to the hostilities notwithstanding, Iran promised not to involve Kuwait in the war, provided that it did not allow Iraq the use of its territory (part of which, Bubiyan Island, is claimed by Iraq) for military purposes.

The Faw offensive prompted a change in tactics by Iraq. In May 1986 Iraq made its first armed incursions into Iran since withdrawing its forces from Iranian territory in 1982. An area of about 150 sq km of Iranian land was occupied, including the deserted town of Mehran (about 160 km east of Baghdad), but Iran recaptured the town in July and forced the Iraqis back across the border. Also in May, Iraqi aircraft raided Teheran for the first time since June 1985, signalling a new wave of reciprocal attacks on urban and industrial targets in Iran and Iraq that continued for the remainder of 1986. For perhaps the first time during the war, Iraq took full advantage of its aerial superiority to damage Iran's industry and to limit its oil production, with numerous attacks on oil installations and tankers shuttling oil to floating terminals near the mouth of the Gulf.

In July the ruling Arab Baath Socialist Party held an extraordinary regional conference, the first since June 1982. Three new members were elected to the party's Regional Command, increasing its number to 17. Naim Haddad, who had been a member of the Regional Command and of the ruling RCC since their formation in 1968, was not re-elected to the Regional Command and was subsequently removed from the RCC, on which he was replaced by Sa'adoun Hammadi, the Chairman, or Speaker, of the National Assembly. These changes effectively strengthened Saddam Hussain's position as leader of the party.

A meeting between the ministers of foreign affairs of Iraq and Syria, scheduled for June 1986, which was heralded as the beginning of a reconciliation between the two countries, was cancelled at the last minute by President Assad of Syria. However, rumours of a *rapprochement* were revived by reports that President Hussain and President Assad had met in secret in Jordan in April 1987. Ministers from both countries met on several occasions in the ensuing weeks, and the reopening of the oil pipeline from Haditha, in Iraq, to the Syrian port of Banias, was discussed. There were, however, no public statements from either side to confirm the improvement in relations.

THE IRAN–IRAQ WAR 1987

From mid-1986 onwards, Iran was reported to be reinforcing its army at numerous points along the Iraqi border. When an Iranian offensive (Karbala-4: after the holy Shi'te city in Iraq) was launched on 24 December, it came, as anticipated, in the region of Basra, but failed to penetrate Iraqi defences on four islands in the Shatt al-Arab waterway. On 8 January 1987 a two-pronged attack (Karbala-5) was launched towards Basra. Iranian forces, attacking from the east, established a bridgehead inside Iraq, between the Shatt al-Arab, to the west, and the artificial water barrier, Fish Lake, to the east, and slowly advanced towards Basra, sustaining heavy casualties; while an assault from the south-east secured a group of islands in the Shatt al-Arab. (On 13 January Iran mounted the Karbala-6 offensive in north-east Iraq.) By mid-February Iranian forces from the east had advanced to within about 10 km of Basra but no further gains were made and the Karbala-5 offensive was officially terminated at the end of the month.

In January 1987, at the height of the Karbala-5 offensive, President Hussain of Iraq offered Iran a cease-fire and peace negotiations. Iran rejected the offer, and in the following months demonstrated its ability to launch attacks at several points from one end to the other of the 1,200-km war front. The Karbala-7 offensive, in March, penetrated north-eastern Iraqi territory to a depth of about 20 km in the Gerdmand heights, near Rawanduz, only some 100 km from Iraq's largest oilfields, at Kirkuk. In April, on the southern front, Iran launched the Karbala-8 offensive from the salient, 10 km east of Basra, which had been secured in Karbala-5. The Iranians claimed that the attack established a new front line about 1 km nearer Basra, west of the artificial Twin Canals water barrier, though Iraq claimed that it had been repulsed. At the same time, another offensive, Karbala-9, was mounted in the central sector of the war front, from near the Iranian border town of Qasr-e-Shirin.

Iraq announced a two-week moratorium on its bombing of Iranian towns and cities on 18 February, which Iraq agreed to observe in respect of its artillery and missile bombardment of Iraqi cities. In April, following new Iranian attacks east of Basra, and well after the initially stipulated two-week period had expired, Iraq said that it was no longer bound by the unofficial agreement. However, Iraqi air raids did not resume in earnest until May.

Iraq continued to attack tankers shuttling Iranian oil from Kharg Island to the floating terminals at Sirri and Larak islands during the first half of 1986. However, an apparently accidental attack in the Gulf by an Iraqi *Mirage* F-1 fighter plane on the frigate USS *Stark*, part of the US naval force, which had been deployed in the Gulf to protect shipping, created a crisis in Iraqi-US relations. The fighter fired two *Exocet* missiles at the *Stark*, only one of which exploded, killing 37 US sailors. Iraq apologized for the 'error' and desisted from attacks on tankers for the next five weeks. Although it is plausible that the attack was the result of error and inexperience on the part of the Iraqi pilot, Iraq had recently had occasion to record its displeasure at US policy regarding the war. In November 1986 it had emerged that the USA, contrary to its official policy of neutrality, and of discouraging sales of arms to Iran by other countries, had made three shipments of weapons and military spare parts to the Islamic Republic since September 1985. Then, in December, it was reported in *The Washington Post* that the USA had been supplying Iraq with detailed intelligence information for at least two years, to assist it in the war with Iran. In particular, the USA's Central Intelligence Agency was said to have provided satellite reconnaissance data, to assist Iraq in its raids on Iranian oil installations and power plants. One month later, US intelligence sources revealed that the USA had, in fact, provided both Iran and Iraq with deliberately misleading or inaccurate information. The explanation of the apparent contradictions in US policy seemed to be that the USA had been trying to engineer a stalemate in the Iran–Iraq War, to prevent either side from gaining a decisive advantage. Iraq subsequently attributed the loss of the disused oil port of Faw in February 1986 to false intelligence reports supplied by the USA.

Tension in the Gulf escalated in May 1987 after the USA's decision to accede to a request from Kuwait for 11 Kuwaiti tankers to be reregistered under the US flag, entitling them to US naval protection. Apart from the financial aid it gave Iraq, Kuwait was a transit point for goods (including military equipment) destined for Iraq, and for exports of oil sold on Iraq's behalf. Iran warned Kuwait on several occasions of the dire consequences of its continued support for Iraq, and between October 1986 and April 1987 15 ships bound to or from Kuwait were attacked in the Gulf by Iran, and several Kuwaiti cargoes were seized. After the USA made its navy available to escort reregistered Kuwaiti tankers through the Gulf, Iran announced that it would not hesitate to sink US warships if provoked.

The possibility of a confrontation between the USA and Iran resulted in a rare display of unanimity in the UN Security Council, which, on 20 July, adopted a resolution (No. 598) urging an immediate cease-fire in the Iran–Iraq War; the withdrawal of all forces to internationally recognized boundaries; and the co-operation of Iran and Iraq in mediation efforts to achieve a peace settlement. Iraq agreed to abide by the terms of the resolution if Iran did so. Iran said that the resolution was 'unjust', and criticized it for failing to identify Iraq as the original aggressor in the war. Moreover, it maintained that the belligerent US naval presence in the Gulf, effectively in support of Iraq, rendered the resolution null and void. However, by mid-September Iran had still not delivered an unequivocal response to the resolution. Iraq, meanwhile, had halted its attacks on tankers in the Gulf in mid-July and Iran had exploited the lull by raising the level of its oil production and exports.

THE UN FAILS TO ENFORCE RESOLUTION 598

Contrary to advice from Western governments, Iraq resumed attacks on Iranian oil installations and industrial targets, and on tankers in the Gulf transporting Iranian oil, on 29 August. Resolution 598 made provision for unspecified sanctions in the event of the failure of either or both sides to comply with its terms. However, the resumption of Iraqi attacks weakened the UN's position in its attempts to secure a cease-fire through diplomacy, and made it less likely that the USSR could be persuaded to agree to the imposition of an arms embargo, whether against Iran alone or against both protagonists.

During the remainder of the year the UN Secretary-General, Javier Pérez de Cuéllar, sought a cease-fire formula which would be acceptable to Iran. His visit to the Gulf region, for talks in Iran and Iraq, between 11 and 15 September, was preceded by an intensification of Iraqi attacks on Iranian economic targets. In Teheran, Iranian leaders told Pérez de Cuéllar that they supported the provision in Resolution 598 for the setting up of an 'impartial body' to apportion responsibility for starting the war, but that Iraq's guilt in this matter had to be established before Iran would observe a cease-fire. For its part, Iraq was prepared to accept the ruling of a judicial body in determining responsibility for the war but refused to countenance any deviation from the original terms of Resolution 598, which stated that a formal cease-fire should precede the setting up of such a body.

Signs of an apparent willingness on Iran's part to modify its stand on Resolution 598 forestalled attempts by the USA, the UK and France to promote their proposal of an arms embargo against Iran, and also pre-empted the adoption of diplomatic or other sanctions by the Arab League, at its meeting in Tunis on 20 September 1987. An extraordinary session of the Arab League in Amman, Jordan, from 8–11 November, produced a final communiqué which unanimously condemned Iran for prolonging the war with Iraq and for its occupation of Arab (i.e. Iraqi) territory, and urged Iran to implement Resolution 598 without preconditions.

Following the summit meeting in Amman, the Iraqi Government, in common with a number of other Arab countries, re-established diplomatic relations with Egypt. During the summit, a meeting had taken place between President Hussain and President Assad, reviving speculation of a *rapprochement* between Iraq and Syria, which had supported Iran in war. President Assad, however, obstructed the League's adoption of an Iraqi proposal that member states should sever their diplomatic links with Iran, and Syria subsequently averred that its good relations with Iran were unimpaired.

On 3 November 1987 the Iranian Deputy Minister of Foreign Affairs, Muhammad Javad Larijani, stated that Iran would observe a cease-fire if the UN Security Council were to identify Iraq as the aggressor in the Iran–Iraq War. The USA and the UK interpreted this announcement as a device to forestall a change in Soviet policy on the question of an arms embargo. The USSR had persistently refused to consider an embargo, and argued that Iran should be allowed more time in which to accept Resolution 598. At the beginning of December, during further discussions with Pérez de Cuéllar in New York, Larijani made the additional condition that Iraq should agree to pay war reparations prior to the introduction of a cease-fire, and cited Iraqi intransigence and the presence of US ships in the Gulf as the principal obstacles to peace.

On 22 December the USSR itself proposed discussions within the Security Council to consider a mandatory ban on the sale of arms to Iran, which would take place at the same time as discussions on the introduction of an international naval force in the Gulf, under the control of the UN, to replace the various national forces patrolling the region. Although all the five permanent members of the Security Council subsequently agreed on the need for further measures to be taken to ensure the compliance of both combatants with Resolution 598, the USSR's insistence on the withdrawal of foreign navies followed by the deployment of a UN naval force in the Gulf, and

the USA's growing military involvement in the area during 1988, prevented the adoption of an arms embargo.

CEASE-FIRE IN THE IRAN–IRAQ WAR

During the first half of 1988 Iraq regained much of the territory which it had lost to Iran in previous years, taking advantage of Iranian military inefficiency and the confused aims of a divided Iranian leadership. However, the world was taken by surprise in July 1988 when, after 12 months of prevarication, Iran agreed, unconditionally, to accept Resolution 598.

In January 1988 Iran and Iraq rebuffed a Syrian initiative to engineer a diplomatic end to the war by opening a dialogue between Iran and the Gulf states. After a lull of 10 days, Iraq resumed the so-called 'tanker war', accusing Syria of violating Arab solidarity against Iran. During 1987, according to Lloyds of London, Iranian and Iraqi attacks had damaged 178 vessels in the Gulf (including 34 in December alone), compared with 80 during 1986. (When a cease-fire was proclaimed in July, a total of 546 vessels had been hit since 1981, when the 'tanker war' began in earnest.)

At the end of February 1988 Iraq resumed the 'war of the cities' (which, apart from sporadic attacks, had been halted in early 1987), signalling the beginning of a series of reciprocal raids on civil and economic targets in the two countries which lasted for several months.

During 1987/88, for the first time in six years, owing to poor mobilization, disorganization and a shortage of volunteers, Iran was unable to launch a major winter offensive and began to lose ground to Iraqi advances along the length of the war front. However, this was not before Kurdish guerrillas, in February 1988, had succeeded in making inroads into government-controlled territory in Iraqi Kurdistan, where Iranian forces, with Kurdish assistance, had established bridgeheads, particularly in the Mawat region, along the Iranian border. The Kurdish part in these operations represented the largest Kurdish offensive since 1974/75, uniting forces from the DPK and the PUK, which, in November 1986, had agreed to co-ordinate their military and political activities and were in the process of forming a coalition of Kurdish nationalist groups (see below). In March 1988, in a retaliatory attack against the captured town of Halabja, Iraq is believed to have used chemical weapons, killing 4,000 Kurdish civilians. (In July Iraq admitted its use of chemical weapons during the war. A UN report compiled in April had concluded that there were victims of chemical weapons on both sides; a team of UN experts reported in August that Iraq had used mustard gas against Iranian civilians.)

After the success of the Iranian/Kurdish offensive, the following months provided a catalogue of Iraqi victories over Iranian forces. In March the National Liberation Army (NLA), the military wing of the Iranian resistance group, Mujahidin Khalq, supported by Iraq, undertook a major offensive for the first time since its creation in 1987, attacking Iranian units in Iran's south-western province of Khuzestan. In mid-April Iraqi forces regained control of the Faw peninsula, where the Iranians, who had been unable to strike out to make further territorial gains since capturing the area in 1986, had scaled down their presence. (Iran accused Kuwait of allowing Iraqi forces to use the nearby Bubiyan Island during the Faw offensive.) Then, in May, Iraq recaptured the Shalamcheh area, south-east of Basra, driving the Iranians back across the Shatt al-Arab.

A radical military re-organization by Iran, undertaken in June and July, failed to reverse the tide of defeat. Having won back more territory in the north of Iraq, near Sulaimaniya, in mid-June, Iraq recaptured Majnoon Island and the surrounding area in the al-Hawizah marshes (the site of one of the world's biggest oilfields), on the southern front, at the end of the month. Also at the end of June, and in July, Iraq expelled Iranian forces from Iraqi territory in Kurdistan, recapturing the border town of Mawat and key mountain areas to the north-east of Halabja. On 13 July, in the central sector of the front, Iraqi forces crossed into Iranian territory for the first time since 1986, and captured the Iranian border town of Dehloran. The last pockets of Iranian occupation in southern Iraq were cleared by Iraqi troops in mid-July and, on 18 July, Iran officially announced its unconditional acceptance of Resolution 598. Iraqi troops in the central sector advanced further into Iran before retiring behind the border on 24 July. However, the NLA, over which Iraq claimed to have no control, launched a three-day offensive on 25 July, penetrating as far as 150 km into Iranian territory, before being forced to withdraw. Iraq professed to have no designs on Iranian territory but it was suggested that the NLA was being used as a proxy by Iraq to prevent Iranian forces from reorganizing during a cease-fire which might prove to be only temporary. At the beginning of August, owing to uncertainty over the war, Iraq's general elections, which had been scheduled to take place at the end of the month, were postponed for six months.

The implementation of a cease-fire was delayed by an Iraqi demand for the initiation of direct peace talks with Iran, under UN auspices, prior to a cessation of hostilities. Iran protested that Resolution 598 did not require this. However, on 6 August Iraq withdrew its insistence on the necessity for direct talks to take place before a cease-fire and, on the following day, Iran agreed to direct talks following the end of hostilities. Accordingly, a cease-fire finally came into force on 20 August, monitored by a specially-created UN observer force of 350 officers, the UN Iran-Iraq Military Observer Group (UNIIMOG).

PEACE TALKS

Negotiations between Iran and Iraq for a comprehensive peace settlement, based on the full implementation of Resolution 598, began at foreign ministerial level in Geneva on 25 August 1988, under the aegis of the UN. With the question of the location of frontiers a matter of dispute, the requirement in Clause One of Resolution 598 for military forces to retire behind internationally recognized borders was causing problems before the talks began, and, once started, they soon reached stalemate. Iran insisted that the Algiers Agreement of 1975 between the two countries should be the basis for negotiations. According to the terms of the Algiers Agreement, which defined the southern border between Iran and Iraq as running along the deepest channel of the Shatt al-Arab waterway (the Thalweg Line), the two countries exercise joint sovereignty over the waterway. However, President Hussain of Iraq, who had been a signatory to the agreement, publicly tore it up immediately prior to the Iraqi invasion of Iran in 1980, claiming that it had been made under duress, and demanded full Iraqi sovereignty over the Shatt al-Arab, which Iraq held under previous agreements in 1847, 1913 and 1937. Iraq also claimed the right of navigation through the Shatt al-Arab and the Gulf during the cease-fire, unhindered by Iranian vessels. When Iran claimed to have stopped and searched an Iraqi cargo vessel which was making its way through the Strait of Hormuz into the Gulf on 20 August, Iraq (though it denied the Iranian claim) threatened to resume hostilities if Iraqi vessels were harassed in this way. It also insisted that an agreement for the dredging of the Shatt al-Arab and the removal of sunken ships be finalized before the discussion of final (mainly Iraqi) troop withdrawals and the exchange of prisoners of war could proceed. Iran claimed that it was, technically, still at war with Iraq and was, therefore, entitled, under international law, to search Iraqi and other vessels for war supplies, for as long as Iraqi troops were in occupation of Iranian territory (an estimated 1,500 sq km, according to Iran).

These disputes, largely concerning issues for which there was no provision in Resolution 598, delayed the implementation of the resolution beyond the introduction of a cease-fire. Clause Three, for example, urged the repatriation of prisoners of war. By mid-1988 the Red Cross had registered 50,182 Iraqi prisoners of war held in Iran, and 19,284 Iranians held in Iraq, although the actual figures were thought to be higher, as the Red Cross had not been allowed access to all prisoners. In November Iran and Iraq agreed to exchange all sick and wounded prisoners of war. The first exchanges took place in the same month, but the arrangements collapsed shortly afterwards, following a dispute over the number of prisoners involved. Resolution 598 also provided for the creation of an impartial judicial body to determine where the responsibility for starting the war lay, and, when and if it is established, its conclusions may also prove to be a considerable

obstacle to a peace settlement. It is generally accepted that Iraq initiated the conflict by invading Iran on 22 September 1980. Iraq, however, maintains, that the war began on 4 September with Iranian shelling of Iraqi border posts. The negotiations for a comprehensive peace settlement remained deadlocked for two years.

On 16 August 1990 President Hussain of Iraq abruptly sought an immediate, formal peace with Iran (for full details, see chapter on Iran, History, p. 421) by accepting almost all of the claims that Iran had pursued since the declaration of a cease-fire in the war in August 1988. On 10 September 1990 Iran and Iraq formally agreed to resume diplomatic relations.

IRAQI SUPPRESSION OF THE KURDS

Since 1987, when the Iranian military threat began to wane, Iraq had concentrated more resources in the north of the country to deal with the Kurdish separatist movement, which claimed to control a 'liberated zone' of 10,000 sq km. It had stepped up its 'scorched earth' policy, which is believed first to have been employed in Kurdistan in 1975 when, following the suppression of a Kurdish guerrilla campaign, 800 Kurdish villages along the border with Iran were razed to create a 'security belt', and Kurds were resettled inside Kurdistan or deported to the south of Iraq. The systematic depopulation of Kurdish areas, achieved by the destruction of Kurdish villages and the resettlement elsewhere in the country of those inhabitants who were not driven into more remote mountain areas, or into neighbouring Iran, was intensified in early 1988, in response to Kurdish support for new Iranian offensives in Iraqi Kurdistan. It was estimated at this time that, with the destruction of some 1,000 villages during the previous year, only about 1,000 of the 4,000 Kurdish villages which had existed before were still standing, and more than one-third of the area of Iraqi Kurdistan was completely depopulated.

In May 1988 the two principal Kurdish dissident groups, the DPK and the PUK, announced the formation of a coalition of six organizations, which would continue the struggle for Kurdish self-determination and co-operate militarily with Iran. Apart from the DPK and the PUK, the new front consisted of the Socialist Party of Kurdistan, the People's Democratic Party of Kurdistan, the United Socialist Party of Kurdistan, and the predominantly Kurdish Iraqi Communist Party.

The introduction of a cease-fire in the Iran–Iraq War in August 1988 allowed Iraq to divert more troops and equipment to Kurdistan, apparently in an attempt to effect a final military solution to the problem of the Kurdish separatist movement. At the end of August an estimated 60,000–70,000 Iraqi troops launched a new offensive to overrun guerrilla bases near the borders with Iran and Turkey, bombarding villages, allegedly using chemical weapons, and forcing thousands of Kurdish civilians and fighters (*peshmerga*) to escape into Iran and Turkey. By mid-September more than 100,000 Kurdish refugees were believed to have fled across the border into Turkey, while Iraqi Kurds seeking refuge in Iran joined an estimated 100,000 of their countrymen, some 40,000 of whom had escaped from Halabja, after the chemical attack on the city in March. The number of dead in the new offensive was estimated at 15,000 in early September.

On 26 August 1988 the UN Security Council adopted a resolution (No. 620) unanimously condemning the use of chemical weapons in the Iran–Iraq War. However, Iraq was not censured by name and continued to deny that it was using chemical weapons against the Kurds, despite what the USA, in September, called 'compelling evidence' to the contrary. On 9 September the US Senate voted to impose economic sanctions against Iraq, which, if they were legally adopted, would cut off US credits and exports of US goods worth $800m., prohibit US imports of Iraqi oil, and require US representatives on international financial bodies to vote against all loans and aid to Iraq. Reacting to the vote of the US Senate, an estimated 150,000 Iraqis took part, in Baghdad, in the largest anti-US demonstration ever staged in Iraq.

On 6 September 1988, with its army effectively in control of the border with Turkey, the Iraqi Government offered a full amnesty to all Iraqi Kurds inside and outside the country (excluding only Jalal Talibani, the leader of the PUK), inviting those Kurds abroad to return within 30 days and promising to release all Kurds held on political grounds. The offer was generally dismissed by Kurds as a propaganda ploy, although the Government subsequently claimed that more than 60,000 Kurdish refugees had taken advantage of the amnesty to return to Iraq.

On 17 September 1988 the Government began to evacuate inhabitants of the Kurdish autonomous region to the interior of Iraq, as the first step towards the creation of a 30-km.-wide uninhabited 'security zone' along the whole of Iraq's border with Iran and Turkey. In June 1989 Kurdish opposition groups appealed for international assistance to halt the evacuations, claiming that they were, in fact, forcible deportations of Kurds to areas more susceptible to government control, and that many of the evacuees (reported to number 300,000 by August 1989) did not reside in the border strip which was to be incorporated into the 'security zone', but in other areas of the Kurdish autonomous region. However, the Iraqi Government apparently remained impervious to international criticism of the 'evacuation' programme.

PROPOSED POLITICAL REFORMS

While the cease-fire in the Iran–Iraq War in August 1988, which was precipitated by Iraqi military successes, strengthened Saddam Hussain's position, it also allowed domestic conflicts to find expression again. Hussain's regime is widely regarded as one of the most autocratic in the Arab world, and in February 1989 there were reports of a further attempt by senior army officers to stage a coup. In November 1988 Hussain announced a programme of political reforms, including the introduction of a multi-party political system, and in January 1989 he declared that a committee was to be established to draft a new constitution. These developments were regarded as attempts to retain the loyalty of Iraq's Shi'ite community, which sought the liberalization of Iraqi society as a reward for its role in the war against Iran.

In April 1989 elections were held to the 250-member National Assembly for the third time since its creation in 1980. The 250 seats were reportedly contested by 911 candidates, one-quarter of whom were members of the Baath Party. The remaining candidates were reported to be either independent or members of the National Progressive Front. It was estimated that 75% of Iraq's electorate (totalling about 8m.) voted in the elections, and that more than 50% of the newly-elected deputies were members of the Baath Party. A new, draft Constitution was completed in January 1990, and approved by the National Assembly in July, when its provisions were published in the Iraqi press. It allowed for a multi-party political system, and there was speculation that defunct political parties, such as the National Democratic Party, would be permitted to re-form and participate in future elections. Under the terms of the draft Constitution, a Consultative Assembly was to be established. This, together with the National Assembly, was to assume the duties of the RCC, which was to be abolished after a presidential election (to be held within two months of the draft Constitution's approval by the National Assembly) had taken place. Following its approval by the National Assembly, the draft Constitution was to be subjected to a popular referendum before ratification by the President.

FOREIGN RELATIONS

From late 1989 there was increased concern in Western countries about the scale of a military expansion programme apparently under way in Iraq; about the involvement of Western companies in the programme; and about covert attempts by Iraq to obtain advanced military technology from the West. International attention focused on Iraq in September 1989, following an explosion at an Iraqi defence industry complex which was thought to be a major installation in a missile development programme.

In March 1990 Iraq's conviction for espionage, and subsequent execution, of an Iranian-born UK journalist, Farzad Bazoft, provoked international outrage and damaged relations with the UK. The incident emphasized the sensitivity of the Iraqi Government to the question of its military capabilities: in his defence, Bazoft claimed that, as a *bona fide* journalist, he had been investigating the explosion at the Iraqi defence

industry complex in September 1989. At the end of March 1990 the British Government claimed to have thwarted attempts by Iraq to import prohibited military devices from the UK, and in April it alleged that steel tubes which Iraq had ordered from a British company were to be used to construct a 'supergun'.

In April 1990 the US President, George Bush, also urged Iraq to abandon production of chemical weapons, and in June the US media alleged that France had helped to extend the range, and improve the accuracy, of Iraqi missiles. At the end of July the US Congress voted to impose sanctions on Iraq, which formally prohibited sales of weapons and military technology to Iraq.

As its relations with the West deteriorated, Iraq's standing in the Arab world improved. The outrage that was provoked by Iraq's execution of Farzad Bazoft, together with more general criticisms in Western media of its human rights record, elicited expressions of support for Iraq from the Arab League and from individual Arab states. In April 1990, after Saddam Hussain had referred to Iraq's chemical weapons as a deterrent against a nuclear attack by Israel, there were further expressions of support, even from Iraq's staunchest Arab rival, Syria, for Iraq's right to defend itself.

IRAQ'S INVASION OF KUWAIT

Prior to a meeting of the OPEC ministerial council in Geneva on 25 July 1990, Iraq had implied that it might take military action against countries which continued to flout their oil production quotas. It had also accused Kuwait of violating the Iraqi border in order to steal Iraqi oil resources worth $2,400m., and suggested that Iraq's debt to Kuwait, accumulated largely during the Iran–Iraq War, should be waived. On the eve of the OPEC meeting in Geneva, Iraq stationed two armoured divisions (about 30,000 troops) on its border with Kuwait.

The Iraqi threat and military mobilization led to a sharp increase in regional tension. Before the OPEC meeting in Geneva on 25 July 1990, President Mubarak of Egypt and Chedli Klibi, the Secretary-General of the Arab League, travelled to Baghdad in an attempt to calm the situation. The USA, meanwhile, placed on alert its naval forces stationed in Bahrain. At the conclusion of the OPEC meeting, however, the threat of Iraqi military action appeared to recede: both Kuwait and the UAE agreed to reduce their petroleum production, while OPEC agreed to raise its 'benchmark' price of crude petroleum from US $18 to $21 per barrel.

Direct negotiations between Iraq and Kuwait commenced in Saudi Arabia at the end of July 1990, with the aim of resolving disputes over territory, oil pricing and Iraq's debt to Kuwait. Kuwait was expected to accede to Iraqi demands for early negotiations to draft a border demarcation treaty, and Iraq was expected to emphasize a claim to the strategic islands of Bubiyan and Warbah, situated at the mouth of the Shatt al-Arab. (After Kuwait obtained independence in 1961—it had formerly been under the protection of the UK—Iraq claimed sovereignty over the country. Kuwait was placed under the protection of British troops, who were later withdrawn and replaced by Arab League forces. On 4 October 1963 the Iraqi Government formally recognized Kuwait's complete independence and sovereignty within its present borders.) On 1 August, however, the talks collapsed, and on 2 August Iraq invaded Kuwait, taking control of the country and establishing a (short-lived) Provisional Free Government.

There was no evidence at all to support Iraq's claim that its forces had entered Kuwait at the invitation of insurgents who had overthrown the Kuwaiti Government. The invasion appeared more likely to have been motivated by Iraq's financial difficulties in the aftermath of the Iran–Iraq War; by strategic interests—Iraq had long sought the direct access to the Persian Gulf which it gained by occupying Kuwait; and by Iraq's pursuit of regional hegemony.

The immediate response, on 2 August 1990, of the UN Security Council to the invasion of Kuwait was to convene and to adopt unanimously a resolution (No. 660), which condemned the Iraqi invasion of Kuwait; demanded the immediate and unconditional withdrawal of Iraqi forces from Kuwait; and appealed for a negotiated settlement of the conflict. On 6 August the UN Security Council convened again and adopted a further resolution (No. 661), which imposed mandatory economic sanctions on Iraq and on occupied Kuwait, affecting all commodities with the exception of medical supplies and foodstuffs 'in humanitarian circumstances'.

As early as 3 August 1990 it was feared that the economic sanctions being imposed on Iraq and Kuwait would be superseded by international military conflict. On 3 August Iraqi troops began to deploy along Kuwait's border with Saudi Arabia, and the USA and the UK announced that they were sending naval vessels to the Gulf. On 7 August, at the request of King Fahd of Saudi Arabia, the USA dispatched combat troops and aircraft to Saudi Arabia, in order to secure the country's border with Kuwait against a possible attack by Iraq. US troops began to occupy positions in Saudi Arabia on 9 August, one day after Iraq announced its formal annexation of Kuwait. On the same day, the UN Security Council convened and adopted a unanimous resolution (No. 662), which declared the annexation of Kuwait to be null and void, and urged all states and institutions not to recognize it.

The dispatch of US troops signified the beginning of 'Operation Desert Shield' for the defence of Saudi Arabia, in accordance with Article 51 of the UN Charter. By the end of January 1991 some 30 countries had contributed ground troops, aircraft and warships to the multinational force in Saudi Arabia and the Gulf region. By far the biggest contributor was the USA, which, it was estimated, had deployed some 500,000 military personnel. Arab countries participating in the multinational force were Egypt, Syria, Morocco and the members of the Co-operation Council for the Arab States of the Gulf—Bahrain, Kuwait, Oman, Qatar, Saudi Arabia and the United Arab Emirates. It was estimated that Iraq had deployed some 555,000 troops in Kuwait and southern Iraq by the end of January 1991.

Iraq's invasion and annexation of Kuwait altered the pattern of relations prevailing in the Arab world. In the immediate aftermath of the invasion, individual Arab states condemned Iraq's action, and on 3 August 1990 a hastily-convened meeting of the Arab League in Cairo agreed a resolution (endorsed by 14 of the 21 member states and opposed by Iraq, Jordan, Mauritania, Sudan, Yemen and the PLO) which condemned the invasion of Kuwait and demanded the immediate and unconditional withdrawal of Iraqi forces. At a summit meeting of Arab League Heads of State, held in Cairo on 10 August, the demand for Iraq to withdraw from Kuwait was reiterated, and 12 of the 20 members participating in the meeting voted to send an Arab deterrent force to the Gulf in support of the US-led effort to deter potential aggression against Saudi Arabia.

As the crisis in the Gulf developed, Western diplomacy strove to maintain Iraq's isolation. The invasion of Kuwait had provoked widespread popular support for Iraq, notably in Jordan, where there was a huge Palestinian population, and also in the Maghreb states. Although conducted with the approval of the UN, in pursuit of aims formulated in specific UN resolutions, and with the active support of Egypt, Syria, Morocco and the Gulf states, both 'Operation Desert Shield' and its successor, 'Operation Desert Storm', were widely perceived, in parts of the Arab world, to be US-led campaigns to secure US interests in the Gulf region.

On 12 August 1990 Saddam Hussain proposed an initiative for the resolution of the conflict in the Gulf, linking Iraq's occupation of Kuwait with other conflicts in the Middle East, in particular the continuing Israeli occupation of the West Bank of Jordan and the Gaza Strip, and the Palestinian question. This was the first explicit example of so-called 'linkage' in diplomatic efforts to resolve the crisis in the Gulf. Practically, 'linkage' would have amounted to the trading of an Iraqi withdrawal from Kuwait for, at least, the convening of an international conference on the Palestinian issue, and it was repeatedly rejected by the USA, which considered that 'linkage' would reward Iraq's aggression and enhance the country's reputation in the Arab world.

The authority for the deployment of a multinational force for the defence of Saudi Arabia was contained in Article 51 of the UN Charter, which affirms 'the inherent right of individual or collective self-defence if an armed attack occurs against a member of the United Nations, until the Security Council has taken measures necessary to maintain international peace and security'. The UN Security Council warned, however, that its authorization would be necessary for the use of force to implement the economic sanctions imposed on Iraq and Kuwait. Article 42 of the UN Charter provided for the taking of 'such action by air, sea or land forces as may be necessary to maintain international peace and security', including the use of a blockade. In order to clarify the Charter's provisions, the USA drafted a resolution which would allow the UN to use legitimately the force necessary to maintain a blockade against Iraq. On 25 August 1990 the UN Security Council adopted a resolution (No. 665) which requested, with immediate effect, member states deploying maritime forces in the area to use 'such measures commensurate to the specific circumstances as may be necessary under the authority of the Security Council to halt all inward and outward maritime shipping in order to inspect and verify the cargoes and destinations' and ensure the implementation of the mandatory economic sanctions against Iraq and Kuwait. The resolution also invited all states to co-operate, by political and diplomatic means, to ensure compliance with sanctions.

Successive diplomatic efforts to achieve a peaceful solution to the crisis in the Gulf—undertaken, at different times, by the UN and by numerous individual countries—between August 1990 and mid-January 1991 foundered, virtually without exception, on Iraq's steadfast refusal to withdraw its forces from Kuwait. Diplomacy was initially complicated by the treatment of Western citizens residing in Iraq and Kuwait. On 9 August 1990 Iraq closed its borders to foreigners, and on 13 August all US and UK nationals in Kuwait were ordered to assemble at hotels prior to their removal to Iraq. Iraq subsequently announced that Westerners would be housed near military locations in order to deter an attack on Iraq by the multinational force in Saudi Arabia. On 28 August, however, Iraq announced that all foreign women and children were free to leave Iraq and Kuwait, extending this permission to all foreigners on 6 December.

On 29 November 1990 the UN Security Council convened and adopted a resolution (No. 678), drafted by the USA, which, with reference to its previous resolutions regarding Iraq's occupation of Kuwait, authorized 'all member states co-operating with the Government of Kuwait, unless Iraq on or before 15 January 1991, fully implements ... the foregoing resolutions, to use all necessary means to uphold and implement Security Council Resolution 660 and all subsequent relevant resolutions and to restore international peace and security in the area'. Iraq denounced Resolution 678, the first UN resolution since 1950 which authorized the use of force, as a threat, and reiterated its demand for the UN Security Council to address equally all the problems of the Middle East.

'Operation Desert Storm'—in effect, war with Iraq—in pursuance of the liberation of Kuwait, as demanded by UN Resolution 660, commenced on the night of 16–17 January 1991. It was preceded by intense diplomatic activity to achieve a peaceful solution to the crisis in the Gulf, in particular a visit, on 10 January, by the UN Secretary-General, Javier Pérez de Cuéllar, to Baghdad for talks with Saddam Hussain. The failure of this mission was widely regarded as signalling the inevitability of military conflict. On 14 January Iraq's National Assembly approved a resolution which afforded the President all constitutional powers to respond to any 'US-led' attack.

The declared aim of the multinational force in Saudi Arabia, in the initial phase of 'Operation Desert Storm', was to gain air superiority, and then air supremacy, over Iraqi forces, in order to facilitate air attacks on Iraqi military and industrial installations. Hostilities commenced with air raids on Baghdad, and by late February 1991 a total of 91,000 attacking air missions were reported to have been flown over Iraq and Kuwait by the multinational air forces.

The multinational force claimed air supremacy over Iraq and Kuwait on 30 January 1991, and air attacks were refocused on the fortified positions of Iraqi ground troops in Kuwait, in preparation for a ground offensive. During the initial phase of the air campaign, the Iraqi air force appeared to have offered surprisingly little resistance. Indeed, by 8 February it was reported that more than 100 Iraqi fighter aircraft had sought refuge in Iran, and the apparent good faith of Iran's reaffirmation of its neutrality in the conflict prompted speculation that they had been directed there deliberately in an attempt to prevent the total destruction of the Iraqi air force.

Iraq's most serious response to the military campaign waged against it was attacks with *Scud* missiles on Israel. While these were of little military significance, they threatened to provoke Israeli retaliation against Iraq and the consequent disintegration of the multinational force, since it would have been politically impossible for any Arab state to fight alongside Israel against Iraq. US diplomacy, together with the installation in Israel of advanced US air defence systems, averted the threat of Israeli retaliation for the attacks by the missiles, 37 of which had been launched by late February 1991. In addition, Iraq launched 35 *Scud* missiles against Saudi Arabia.

On 6 February 1991 Iraq formally severed diplomatic relations with the USA, the UK, France, Italy, Egypt and Saudi Arabia. Between August 1990 and January 1991 many foreign embassies in Baghdad had closed, and most countries had withdrawn their diplomatic staff before the outbreak of hostilities in the Gulf.

On 15 February 1991 the Iraqi Government abruptly expressed its willingness to 'deal with' the UN Security Council resolutions pertaining to its occupation of Kuwait. However, its offer to do so was conditional upon the fulfilment of a long list of requirements (including an assurance that the as-Sabah family would not be restored to power in Kuwait) and was accordingly unacceptable to the countries contributing to the multinational force. The offer to 'deal with' the UN resolutions was nevertheless thought to indicate a new flexibility on the part of the Iraqi leadership.

Soviet diplomacy came to the fore in seeking to persuade Iraq to alter its offer to withdraw from Kuwait into one which the multinational force could accept. On 21 February 1991 Iraq agreed to an eight-point Soviet peace plan which stipulated that: Iraq should make a full and unconditional withdrawal from Kuwait; that the withdrawal was to begin on the second day of a cease-fire; that the withdrawal should take place within a fixed time-frame; that, after two-thirds of Iraq's forces had withdrawn from Kuwait, the UN-sponsored economic sanctions were to be repealed; that the relevant UN Security Council resolutions should be waived following Iraq's withdrawal; that all prisoners of war were to be released following a cease-fire; that the withdrawal was to be monitored by observers from neutral countries following a cease-fire; that other details were to be discussed at a later stage.

The eight-point Soviet peace plan remained unacceptable to the multinational force, not least because it stipulated that a cease-fire should take effect before Iraq began to withdraw from Kuwait. On 22 February 1991, in response, the USA, representing the multinational force, demanded that Iraq commence a large-scale withdrawal of its forces from Kuwait by noon (US Eastern Standard Time) on 23 February, and that the withdrawal should be completed within one week. In response to this ultimatum, the USSR proposed a further plan for peace, this time containing six points—subsequently formally approved by Iraq—in a final attempt to avert a ground war in Kuwait and Iraq. However, once again the plan was rejected by the multinational force because it did not amount to the unconditional withdrawal of Iraqi forces from Kuwait which UN Security Council Resolution 660 demanded.

During the night of 23–24 February 1991 the multinational force launched a ground offensive for the liberation of Kuwait. Iraqi troops defending Kuwait's border with Saudi Arabia were quickly defeated, offering little resistance to the multinational force. One of the biggest problems which confronted the multinational force was that of coping with the very large number of Iraqi troops who surrendered at the onset of the ground war.

A flanking movement, far to the west, by French units and elements of the 101st US Airborne Division succeeded in severing the main road west from Basra, while the road leading north from Basra was breached by repeated bombing. Divisions of Iraq's élite Republican Guards in the Kuwait area were thus isolated to the south of the Tigris and Euphrates rivers and prevented from retreating towards Baghdad. On

28 February 1991 President Bush announced that the war to liberate Kuwait had been won, and he declared a cease-fire. Iraq had agreed to renounce its claim to Kuwait, and to release all the prisoners of war whom it was holding. It also indicated that it would comply with the remaining relevant UN Security Council resolutions. On 3 March Iraq accepted the cease-fire terms that had been dictated, at a meeting with Iraqi military commanders, by the commander of the multinational force, Gen. Norman Schwarzkopf of the US army.

On 3 April 1991 the UN Security Council adopted a resolution (No. 687) which stipulated the terms for a full cease-fire in the Gulf. These terms were accepted on 5 April by Iraq's RCC, and on the following day by the National Assembly. A separate UN Security Council resolution (No. 689), adopted on 9 April, created a demilitarized zone between Iraq and Kuwait, to be monitored by military personnel from the five permanent members of the UN Security Council.

INTERNAL REVOLT

Following the rout of the Iraqi army by the UN-sponsored multinational force in February 1991, armed rebellion broke out among the largely Shi'ite population of southern Iraq and among the Iraqi Kurds in the Kurdish northern provinces of the country. In the south the town of Basra was the centre of the rebellion. On 4 March it was reported that suppporters of the Teheran-based Supreme Council for the Islamic Revolution in Iraq (SCIRI) had gained control of the towns of Basra, Amarah, Samawah and Nasiriyah. At a conference of Iraqi groups opposed to the Government of Saddam Hussain, in Beirut on 11–13 March, it was claimed that, despite the prominent role of the SCIRI, the uprising in the south was secular in character and was not an attempt to establish an Iranian-style Islamic republic in Iraq. Already, on 5 March, the assessment of US intelligence sources, that the southern rebellion lacked sufficient organization to succeed, appeared to be corroborated: armed forces loyal to the Government were reported to be regaining control of the cities which had fallen to the rebels. On the same day it was announced that Ali Hassan al-Majid had been appointed Minister of the Interior, with express instructions to suppress the southern rebellion; and on the following day the Government announced financial bonuses for certain elements of the armed forces, in order to stem disaffection. Crucially, there was no military intervention by the multinational force in support of the rebellion. In this respect there appeared to have been a fundamental shift in the policy of the US Government: claiming that actively to support the southern rebellion would constitute unjustified interference in Iraq's internal affairs, its principal aim now seemed to be to prevent the disintegration of Iraq, rather than to oust Saddam Hussain from power. By contrast, at the conference of Iraqi opposition groups held in Beirut in mid-March, it was agreed to seek the overthrow of Saddam Hussain; the abolition of the Arab Baath Socialist Party; and the establishment of a democratic system of government in Iraq.

By mid-March 1991 armed forces loyal to the Government had effectively crushed the rebellion in the south, but their deployment there had allowed a simultaneous revolt by Kurdish guerrilla groups in the Kurdish northern provinces of Iraq to gather momentum. In late March it was reported that Kurdish rebels had gained control of Kirkuk and of important oil installations to the west of the city, and in early April Kurdish leaders claimed that as many as 100,000 guerrillas were involved in hostilities against government forces. The various Kurdish factions appeared to have achieved greater unity of purpose through their alliance, in May 1988, in the Kurdistan Iraqi Front (KIF). Rather than seeking the creation of an independent Kurdish state (which would not be tolerated by the Turkish and Iranian Governments), the KIF claimed that the objective of the northern insurrection was the full implementation of the 15-article peace plan which had been concluded between Kurdish leaders and the Iraqi Government in 1970. At the same time, however, the KIF invited the leaders of other Iraqi groups opposed to the Government to join it in the newly captured areas of northern Iraq in order to establish a unified anti-government movement.

Lacking military support from the multinational force— which was denied to them for the same reasons that it had been denied to the southern insurgents—the Kurdish guerrillas were unable to resist the onslaught of the Iraqi armed forces, which were redeployed northwards as soon as they had crushed the uprising in southern Iraq. By early April 1991 government forces had recaptured Kirkuk, Arbil, Dohok and Zakho. Some 50,000 Kurds were reported to have been killed in the hostilities, and, fearing genocide, an estimated 1m.–2m. Kurds fled before the Iraqi army across the northern mountains into Turkey and Iran. On 5 April, as Saddam Hussain offered an amnesty to all Kurds with the exception of 'criminal elements', the UN Security Council adopted a resolution (No. 688) which condemned 'the repression of the Iraqi civilian population in many parts of Iraq' and demanded that the Iraqi Government permit the immediate access of international humanitarian organizations to persons in need of assistance. As relief operations were subsequently mounted, the means were sought whereby the Kurdish refugees could return to Iraq without fear of a renewed onslaught by the Iraqi armed forces.

As the 'Kurdish crisis' had developed, France, the United Kingdom and the USA had all committed troops to maintain a 'safe haven' for the Kurds in northern Iraq. On 8 April 1991 a proposal by the UK Prime Minister, John Major, that a UN-supervised enclave should be created in northern Iraq, for the protection of the Kurdish population, was approved by the leaders of the EC member states. The US Government withheld its formal approval of the proposal, but on 10 April it warned Iraq that any interference in relief operations north of latitude 36°N would prompt military retaliation. The UN response to the proposal to create Kurdish 'safe havens' under its auspices also remained cautious. On 17 April the UN Secretary-General, Javier Pérez de Cuéllar, warned that the Iraqi Government's permission would have to be obtained before foreign troops were deployed in northern Iraq, and that the UN Security Council would need to approve the policing of the Kurdish enclave by a UN-backed force. Nevertheless, in late April UN relief agencies reported that Kurdish refugees were returning to Iraq in large numbers.

In mid-May 1991 the UN reported that progress had been achieved in the implementation of Security Council Resolution 688, and the Secretary-General announced that the UN was negotiating with the Iraqi Government over the deployment of a 'UN police force' to safeguard the Kurdish enclave. By mid-June UN agencies and other non-governmental organizations were reported to have assumed responsibility for the provision of essential services in the Kurdish enclave, and the transition from military to UN-backed security was under way.

As international diplomacy sought to create secure conditions for Iraqi Kurds within Iraq, the leaders of Kurdish groups began negotiations with the Iraqi Government on the future status of Iraqi Kurds. In late April 1991 the leader of the PUK, Jalal Talabani, announced that President Saddam Hussain had agreed in principle to implement the provisions of the Kurdish peace plan of 1970. By mid-June, however, negotiations with the Iraqi Government were reported to be in deadlock over the question of the frontiers of the Kurdish autonomous area, and at the end of August leaders of Kurdish groups announced their decision to suspend further negotiations with the Iraqi Government until various issues relating to an autonomy agreement had been clarified. Renewed clashes between government forces and Kurdish guerrillas in northern Iraq in September were succeeded, in late October, by the Iraqi Government's withdrawal of all services from Iraqi Kurdistan, effectively subjecting it to an economic blockade.

In the absence of a negotiated autonomy agreement with the Iraqi Government, the KIF organized elections to a 105-member Kurdish National Assembly, and for a paramount Kurdish leader. The result of the elections to the Assembly, held on 19 May 1992 and in which virtually the whole of the estimated 1.1m.-strong electorate participated, was that the DPK and the PUK were entitled to an almost equal number of seats. None of the smaller Kurdish parties achieved representation and the DPK and the PUK subsequently agreed to share equally the seats in the new Assembly. The election for an overall Kurdish leader was inconclusive, Masoud Barzani, the leader of the DPK, receiving 47.5% of the votes cast; and Jalal

Talabani, the leader of the PUK, 44.9%. A run-off election was to be held at a future date. In December a member of the Kurdish Cabinet, elected by the Kurdish National Assembly in July 1992, appealed for increased Western aid for the Kurdish-controlled area of northern Iraq, and criticized the UN for its use of Saddam Hussain's regime as an intermediary in the provision of humanitarian relief. At the end of the year it was announced that relief supplies entering the Kurdish-controlled north from Turkey or central Iraq would be protected by UN forces in order to prevent the recurrence of acts of sabotage allegedly perpetrated by agents of Saddam Hussain's regime. The Iraqi Government was reported to have agreed, in principle, to allow UN forces to escort food convoys into Kurdish-controlled areas.

In March 1993 the Kurdish Cabinet elected in July 1992 was dismissed by the Kurdish National Assembly for its failure effectively to deal with the crisis in the region. A new Cabinet was appointed at the end of April. In late December armed conflict was reported to have taken place between fighters of the PUK and the Islamic League of Kurdistan (ILK, also known as the Islamic Movement of Iraqi Kurdistan (IMIK). The two parties were reported to have signed a peace agreement in February 1994 following mediation by the Iraqi National Congress (INC). More serious armed conflict, between fighters belonging to the PUK and the KDP, was reported in May to have led to the division of the northern Kurdish-controlled enclave into two zones. The two parties were reported to have concluded a peace agreement in early June.

OTHER POST-WAR DEVELOPMENTS

By mid-August 1991, despite the failure of his Kuwaiti adventure and the outbreak of internal revolts in its aftermath, the overthrow of President Saddam Hussain, which had been widely predicted during the crisis in the Gulf, seemed unlikely in the short term. Indeed, it was arguable that his position was more secure than it had been at the time of the invasion of Kuwait: opponents of the Government in the south of the country had been ruthlessly suppressed; a negotiated settlement of the Kurdish question was under discussion; and, in the wake of several alleged attempts to mount a military *coup d'état*, the Government appeared to have strengthened its control of the army, which remained the key to its survival in power. A reshuffle of the Council of Ministers in March 1991 had placed the President's closest supporters and members of his family in the most important positions of government and additional governmental adjustments later in the year, and in February and August 1992, furthered this process. Above all, it had become clear that the US Government was not willing actively to seek Saddam Hussain's overthrow at the expense of the integrity of Iraq.

The survival of the Iraqi Government in the long term depended on three factors: its continued control of the armed forces; the length of time and the stringency with which economic sanctions would continue to be applied against Iraq; and the degree to which popular disaffection, created by the economic sanctions, could be appeased by the granting of limited political reform.

In September 1991 the Government introduced legislation providing for the establishment of a multi-party political system, in accordance with the draft of the new permanent Constitution. New political parties were to be subject to stringent controls, however, and later in the month the President stated that the Baath Party would retain its leading role in Iraqi political life. In early September the Baath Party held its 10th Congress—the first such Congress since 1982—at which Saddam Hussain was re-elected Secretary-General of the Party's powerful RC.

Iraq's post-war relations with the international community have been dominated by conflicts over the way in which the Iraqi regime has apparently sought to circumvent demands by the UN—as stipulated by UN Security Council Resolution 687—that it should disclose the full extent of its programmes to develop chemical weapons, nuclear weapons and missiles, and should eliminate its weapons of mass destruction. One consequence of the conflicts over Iraqi compliance with Resolution 687 was that there was no easing of the economic sanctions that were first imposed on Iraq on 6 August 1990, under the terms of UN Security Council Resolution 661.

In May 1991 the UN Security Council decided to establish a compensation fund for victims of Iraqi aggression (both governments and individuals), to be financed by a levy (subsequently fixed at 30%) on Iraqi petroleum revenues. In August the UN Security Council adopted a resolution (No. 706, subsequently approved in Resolution 712 in September) proposing that Iraq should be allowed to sell petroleum worth up to US $1,600m. over a six-month period, the revenue from which would be paid into an escrow account controlled by the UN. Part of the sum thus realized was to be made available to Iraq for the purchase of food, medicines and supplies for essential civilian needs.

Iraq rejected the terms proposed by the UN for the resumption of exports of petroleum, and in February 1992 withdrew from further negotiations on the issue. In April the UN reiterated its demand that Iraq should comply with the terms of Security Council Resolutions 706 and 712 before resuming petroleum exports. In late June a further session of negotiations between Iraq and the UN on the resumption of petroleum exports ended indecisively. On 2 October the UN Security Council adopted a resolution (No. 778) permitting it to confiscate up to $500m.-worth of oil-related Iraqi assets. By so doing, the Security Council was believed to be seeking to place further pressure on Iraq to accept the UN's terms for renewed exports of petroleum. In late October the UN commission responsible for the supervision of the destruction of Iraqi weapons proposed a relaxation of the embargo on sales of Iraqi oil in return for increased co-operation by Iraq with the UN. However, this suggestion did not gain the support of Western governments or of Iraqi opposition movements, and in late November the UN Security Council refused a request by an Iraqi delegation to repeal the economic sanctions in force against Iraq.

In January 1993 a 52-member team of UN weapons inspectors arrived in Iraq, the Government having revoked a ban on all UN flights into the country, in response to renewed air attacks by Western forces (see below). In early July, however, another team of UN weapons inspectors departed abruptly from Baghdad after the Government had refused to allow them to station surveillance equipment at missile-testing locations. Iraq continued to refuse the terms of UN Security Council Resolution 715, which governed the long-term monitoring of its weapons programmes. In early July a further session of negotiations between Iraq and the UN on the resumption of petroleum exports ended inconclusively, and later in the month the UN Security Council renewed the economic sanctions in force against Iraq. At the beginning of September Iraq's Deputy Prime Minister, Tareq Aziz, met the UN Secretary-General to discuss the resumption of Iraqi petroleum sales and the lifting of the economic sanctions. The UN was reportedly anxious to raise funds from such sales in order to finance its own operations in Iraq. The talks were inconclusive, however, and at the end of September the economic sanctions in force against Iraq were renewed. In early October the Government agreed to UN demands that it should release details of its weapons suppliers. In the absence of any progress on the issue of UN Security Council Resolution 715, however, economic sanctions were extended for a further 60 days in late November. Shortly after their renewal, the Iraqi Government was reported to have agreed to the provisions for weapons-monitoring contained in Resolution 715, and the UN to have begun plans for their implementation. However, it was clear by the end of December that neither the UN Security Council nor the US Government would be willing to allow even a partial easing of sanctions until Iraq had demonstrated its commitment to the dismantling of its weapons systems for a period of at least six months. Moreover, the US Government insisted that Iraq must first also comply with all other relevant UN resolutions, recognize the newly-demarcated border with Kuwait and cease the repression of its Kurdish and southern Shi'ite communities. In September hundreds of inhabitants of Iraq's southern marshlands were reported to have been killed by government forces using chemical weapons; and in November the UN accused the Government of indiscriminate attacks on civilians in that area.

From March 1994 the Iraqi Government engaged in a campaign of diplomacy to obtain the lifting of economic sanctions. In early May Deputy Prime Minister Tareq Aziz took part in discussions with ambassadors to the UN in an attempt to achieve this aim. However, the Governments of the United Kingdom and the USA were reported to have insisted that any easing of the sanctions should be conditional on an end to the repression of Iraq's Kurdish and southern Shi'ite communities. In mid-June it was announced that the destruction of Iraq's chemical weapons had been completed. In mid-July evidence emerged of a division within the UN Security Council regarding the continuation of the economic sanctions in force against Iraq. Russia, France and China were reported to be in favour of the Security Council issuing a statement acknowledging Iraq's increased co-operation with UN agencies. In mid-August the Russian ambassador to the UN stated that Iraq had promised to recognize Iraq's sovereignty and the UN-demarcated border with Kuwait. In September, however, the UN Security Council agreed to extend the international sanctions against Iraq for a further period. Russia and France had proposed that the Security Council should draw up a timetable for the lifting of sanctions, but had not obtained the agreement of the other permanent members of the Council. On 6 October the leader of the UN's Special Commission on Iraq (responsible for inspecting the country's weapons) announced that a system for monitoring Iraqi defence industries was ready to begin operating. On the same day, however, there was a large movement of Iraqi forces towards the border with Kuwait, apparently to draw attention to Iraq's demands for swift action to ease UN sanctions. In response, Kuwait deployed most of its army to protect its side of the border on 9 October, and the USA sent reinforcements to Kuwait and other parts of the Gulf region to support the 12,000 US troops already stationed there. On 10 October Iraq announced that it would withdraw its troops northward from their positions near the Kuwaiti border. On 13 October, after Russian mediation, the Iraqi Government reportedly offered to comply with the Security Council's demands to recognize the UN-demarcated border with Kuwait and to acknowledge Kuwait's sovereignty. In return, the Russian Government agreed to urge the relaxation of the UN sanctions against Iraq. On the following day the US Secretary of Defense arrived in Kuwait and warned that the USA might take military action against Iraq if heavily armoured Iraqi units were not removed from the area near the Kuwaiti border. On 15 October the Security Council adopted a resolution demanding that Iraq grant unconditional recognition to Kuwait and that all the Iraqi forces recently transferred to southern Iraq be redeployed to their original positions. Two days later, addressing the Security Council, Iraq's Deputy Prime Minister, Tareq Aziz, made clear that the Iraqi Government would recognize Kuwait only in return for assurances that the UN embargo on Iraq's sales of petroleum (other than for the purchase of emergency supplies) would be revoked.

On 26 August 1992 the Governments of the USA, the UK, France and Russia announced their decision to establish a zone in southern Iraq, south of latitude 32°N, from which all flights by Iraqi fixed-wing and rotary-wing aircraft were to be excluded. Although the air exclusion zone was not formally established by a UN Security Council Resolution, the UN Secretary-General subsequently indicated his own support for the measure and stated that it enjoyed that of the Security Council. The exclusion zone was established in response to renewed attacks by Iraqi government forces on southern Iraqi Shi'ite communities and on the inhabitants of the marshlands of southern Iraq. In April 1992 Saddam Hussain had ordered the evacuation of the marshlands and the resettlement of their inhabitants; and in June Iraqi armed forces were reported to have encircled the areas and to have intensified their attacks on the communities there. The Iraqi Government reacted with predictable anger to the establishment of the air exclusion zone, but it was reported in early September to have withdrawn all flights over the area. However, large numbers of troops remained there and continued to attack the civilian population. Other Arab governments, notably those of Algeria, Jordan, Sudan, Syria and Yemen, also condemned the establishment of the air exclusion zone as a step towards the disintegration of Iraq, which, as a result of the other, UN-authorized exclusion zone north of latitude 36°N (see above), was now effectively divided into three parts.

In late December 1992 a US combat aircraft shot down an Iraqi fighter aircraft which had allegedly entered the southern air exclusion zone; and on 6 January 1993 the USA, with the support of the British and French Governments, demanded that Iraq should withdraw anti-aircraft missile batteries from within the zone. Iraq was reported to have complied with this demand, but subsequent Iraqi military operations inside Kuwaiti territory, to recover military equipment, provoked air attacks by Western forces on targets in southern Iraq on 13 January. A ban which the Iraqi Government had imposed on UN flights into the country was cited as a further justification for the attacks. Further air raids by Western forces on targets in northern and southern Iraq took place in late January. In late May, in response to the deployment of Iraqi armed forces close to the UN-authorized exclusion zone north of latitude 36°N, the USA warned Iraq that it might suffer military reprisals in the event of any incursion into the Kurdish-held north. In late June the USA launched an attack against intelligence headquarters in Baghdad, in retaliation for Iraq's role in an alleged conspiracy to assassinate former US President Bush in Kuwait in April 1993. Iraq made a formal protest to the UN Security Council over the attack, which provoked widespread international condemnation, not least because it was regarded by many observers as an attempt by the Clinton Administration to increase its domestic popularity. In early July Iraqi armed forces were reported to have renewed the Government's offensive against the inhabitants of the marshlands of southern Iraq, and the London-based Iraqi National Congress (INC) urged the UN Security Council to send emergency supplies of food and medicine to the communities there.

In late July the Food and Agriculture Organization (FAO) of the UN warned that pre-famine conditions existed in much of Iraq and appealed for the economic sanctions in force against the country to be either alleviated or lifted. In late August it was reported that the Government had drained some 70% of the southern marshlands and that some 3,000 of their inhabitants had fled to Iran.

ECONOMIC CRISIS

By October 1994 the living standards of large sections of the Iraqi population had reportedly been reduced to subsistence level. The Iraqi Government appeared increasingly desperate to maintain order in the face of this economic crisis. In May 1994 Saddam Hussain himself had assumed the post of Prime Minister in a reshuffle of the Council of Ministers in which the Ministers of Finance and Agriculture were dismissed. In June, and again in September, harsh new punishments for those convicted of theft were announced by the RCC. Also in September a substantial reduction in the daily ration of some staple food items was announced. There were no signs, other than these, however, that the fall of Saddam Hussain's regime was any closer, nor any clear indications of what might happen if it were to fall. Iran, Syria and Turkey, whose Ministers of Foreign Affairs have met at regular intervals since November 1992 in order to discuss the situation in Iraq, continued to emphasize their commitment to Iraq's territorial integrity, while urging the Iraqi Government to end its economic blockade of the northern Kurdish and southern Shi'ite populations. In September the Iranian Minister of Foreign Affairs was reported to have stated that Iran was now in favour of lifting the UN economic sanctions applied against Iraq. It was clear, however, that this would not take place until Iraq had made a sustained effort to comply with the various relevant UN resolutions (see above).

Economy

Revised for this edition by ALAN J. DAY

INTRODUCTION

Having begun to recover from the effects of the 1980–88 war with Iran, the Iraqi economy entered a new period of trauma in August 1990, as a result of the UN sanctions that were imposed because of Iraq's invasion of Kuwait. It then suffered substantial material damage in the war with the US-led multinational force in early 1991; a UN report suggested that aerial bombardment had reduced Iraq to a 'pre-industrial' state in the immediate aftermath of the 1991 hostilities. Although the authorities succeeded in restoring a measure of basic infrastructural viability by early 1992, having given priority to the rapid rebuilding of key installations and facilities, there was no prospect of a full normalization of economic life while Iraq remained subject to UN trade sanctions. Having relied on petroleum for 98% of export earnings over the previous decade, the country suffered a massive loss of revenue when it was excluded from the world oil market in 1990. In September 1993 Iraq's Minister of Trade estimated that three years of sanctions had cost the country $60,000m. in lost oil revenues. The UN trade sanctions remained in force in October 1994, by which time the living standards of large sections of the Iraqi population had been reduced to subsistence level by the prolongation of conditions of acute economic hardship.

The earlier war with Iran had itself severely affected Iraq's economic development, which had been steadily gaining momentum since 1977, forcing expenditure on former priority areas, such as water and electricity, to be reduced, with funds being transferred to defence. Towards the end of that conflict, the Government initiated, in March 1987, an economic reform programme which was supposed to reduce the extent of state control over industry, this having previously been an article of faith of the Baath Socialist Party regime which came to power in 1968. Many state organizations were abolished, and others sold to the private sector, the emphasis being placed on securing greater efficiency in the industrial and agricultural

sectors and on the performance of workers and management, rather than on the state bureaucracy. More liberal import regulations—including the use of 'offshore' foreign currency funds—were introduced to enable private companies to become more involved in foreign trade. The campaign for economic reform also resulted in changes in personnel in important ministries, and in the reorganization of others, including the merging of the Ministries of Irrigation and Agriculture (1987) and numerous reorganizations of industrial responsibilities. The latter culminated in the creation, in July 1988, of a combined Ministry of Industry, Minerals and Military Industrialization, which, notwithstanding the declared intentions of the 1987 reforms, enshrined continued state control and direction of the industrial and oil sectors.

As it emerged from the 1980–88 war, Iraq was generally considered to have strong development prospects, despite its continuing allocation of huge sums to military expenditure. Unlike other Arab states in the region, Iraq had the advantage of a relatively large population (16,335,199 at the census of October 1987), giving it the labour force necessary for industrial development. It also placed considerable emphasis on education and the creation of a skilled work-force. Moreover, Iraq continued to have an extensive and productive agricultural sector, assisted by substantial investment funds, ample supplies of irrigation water and availability of fertile land. However, by the late 1980s agriculture had become overshadowed by large-scale production of petroleum and natural gas. Both the 1970–75 and the 1976–80 development plans had given priority to the petroleum and industrial sectors, the aim being not only to maximize earnings from exports of oil and gas, but also to diversify into other industrial exports. These objectives were maintained in the 1981–85 development plan, but this was abandoned amid the exigencies of the 1980–88 war with Iran, after which planning was conducted on an annual basis. The country's increasing industrialization was reflected in the population distribution: according to World Bank estimates, 71% of the population were classed as urban at mid-1990, compared with 51% in 1965 and 64% in 1977, when only 30% of the labour force were employed in agriculture, compared with 53% in 1960. Nevertheless, the industrial sector remained totally dominated by oil and gas production, which accounted for more than 99% of export earnings in 1989.

Lack of reliable official data has prevented the World Bank from publishing recent statistics for Iraq's overall national output and income. According to the Statistical Office of Iraq, gross domestic product (GDP) at factor cost increased from ID 1,139m. in 1970 to ID 15,647m. in 1980, while GDP per caput rose from ID 120 to ID 1,181 over the same period. The Iran–Iraq War resulted in a decline in GDP to ID 11,215m. in 1981, and in GDP per caput to ID 820, but thereafter GDP rose steadily, to ID 15,551m. in 1987 and to ID 20,811m. in 1989, while GDP per caput recovered to ID 1,186 by 1989, just above the pre-war level. The effect of the 1980–88 war was particularly apparent in the decline in oil export revenues, from ID 7,718.4m. in 1980 to ID 5,982.4m. in 1982, although by 1988 revenue from this source had recovered to ID 7,223.9m. National income increased from ID 10,589m. (ID 826 per caput) in 1979 to ID 17,290m. (ID 986 per caput) in 1989. According to Iraqi officials, overall GDP in dinar terms rose by 16% in 1989, compared with 1988 (and per caput GDP by 20%) and by 78% during 1979–89 (in which period national income grew by 63%), despite the adverse effects of the Iran–Iraq War. According to Western estimates, the real growth in GDP in 1989 was 6.5%, following zero growth in 1988, an increase of 7.7% in 1987, an actual decline of 2.9% in 1986, an increase of 3.2% in 1985 and an increase of 15.7% in 1984.

Iraq's development plans were, however, seriously compromised by a continuing shortage of foreign exchange (reserves were estimated at between zero and $2,000m. in 1987) and the accumulation of massive foreign debts during the 1980–88 war. Estimated at more than $50,000m. at the end of 1986, Iraq's total foreign debt was thought to have risen to about $65,000m. by mid-1990, including some $30,000m. in the form of loans from neighbouring Gulf states, about $13,000m. in civil debt guaranteed by export credit agencies and a further $6,000m. owed to Western companies and not covered by export credit guarantees; some $3,000m. per year was required to service the Western portion of the debt. In the late 1980s Iraq successfully negotiated a number of debt-rescheduling agreements, enabling it to proceed with major development projects in the petroleum, industrial and water-management sectors, with foreign contractors accepting deferred payment terms or using credit lines to finance contracts. Nevertheless, Iraq's international financial standing continued to be eroded by the decline in international petroleum prices in 1989 and early 1990, which, in turn, explained the country's fierce criticism of Kuwait and other Gulf states for exceeding OPEC production quotas (see Petroleum and Natural Gas, below). Against this background, Iraq's invasion of Kuwait in August 1990 had a powerful economic motivation, although in the event it was to lead to economic catastrophe.

CONSEQUENCES OF THE 1990/91 GULF CRISIS

The mandatory economic sanctions that were imposed on Iraq (and Iraqi-controlled Kuwait) by the UN Security Council on 6 August 1990 included bans on the purchase or transhipment of Iraqi oil and other commodities and on the sale or supply of all goods and products to Iraq (with possible humanitarian exceptions for medical supplies and foodstuffs). Also prescribed were an interdiction of new investment in Iraq and Kuwait and the 'freezing' of Iraqi and Kuwaiti assets abroad. Adopted unanimously and applied by virtually the whole international community, these sanctions were tightened on 25 September to cover interdiction of air traffic and obligatory detention of Iraqi-registered ships violating the trade embargo. Their effect was to place the Iraqi economy in almost total isolation, except that the land route from Jordan remained open for certain supplies. Particularly damaging for Iraq was the abrupt cessation of its oil and gas exports,

including those via pipelines through Saudi Arabia and Turkey, which were closed. With its prime source of revenue thus interrupted, the Government responded by introducing rationing for basic food items and by taking various emergency measures to promote economic self-sufficiency. It also sought to counter the damaging effects of the flight from Iraq and Kuwait of hundreds of thousands of foreign workers, mostly from other Arab countries and the Indian sub-continent. Moreover, under Law 57 of 1990, announced on 18 September but backdated to 8 August, the Government declared Iraq's non-recognition of all seizures of Iraqi assets and decreed the seizure of the assets of all countries and organizations which 'issued arbitrary decisions' against Iraq. As part of this strategy, Iraq suspended debt repayments to the USA and other members of the anti-Iraq coalition.

Western reports indicated that, despite some shortages and steeply rising prices, the Iraqi economy continued to function on an emergency basis in the latter months of 1990. The situation changed dramatically, however, during the active hostilities of January–February 1991, particularly as a result of the massive allied bombing campaign against both military and strategic economic targets. According to an official UN report compiled in mid-March 1991, the conflict 'wrought near-apocalyptic results on the economic infrastructure', destroying or damaging most modern means of life support and relegating Iraq for some time to come to a 'pre-industrial age but with all the disabilities of post-industrial dependency on an intensive use of energy and technology'. The report went on to detail the effects of the war in the various economic sectors (see separate sections, below) and warned, in particular, of the danger of famine and epidemics spreading because of the collapse of water-distribution and sewerage systems. Of various forecasts made of the potential cost of repairing the war damage, US officials estimated in April that some $30,000m. would be required for the reconstruction of roads, power plants and oil installations. Other Western esimates assessed the total cost of the conflict to Iraq at some $50,000m. as at mid-May 1991, including the loss of 50% of GDP since August 1990 as well as war damage. The Iraqi Government, in April 1991, estimated the cost of reconstruction at $25,800m., excluding repairs in the private sector and damage to the military and nuclear industries.

Faced with the maintenance of most UN sanctions after the cease-fire agreement of 3 March 1991 (except those on food and medical supplies), the Iraqi Government was obliged to begin its reconstruction efforts within those constraints, involving the continued non-availability of crucial oil revenues. An emergency six-month reconstruction budget, announced on 2 May, incorporated a reduction of state expenditure in 1991 to the equivalent of $44,760m. (from the original total of $47,080m.) but still assumed a partial resumption of oil revenues in the second half of the year. As a result of the consequential Iraqi campaigning for the removal of the UN embargo, the sanctions committee agreed on 9 May to a partial 'unfreezing' of Iraqi assets abroad, officially estimated at $4,000m., so that Iraq could pay for essential civilian items. However, Iraqi requests for the repeal of the oil export embargo were complicated by the UN Security Council's decision, on 20 May, to establish a Geneva-based Compensation Fund for victims of Iraq's aggression (governments, corporations and individuals), to be financed by a percentage levy on Iraqi oil revenues. With Western estimates valuing the possible extent of claims for damages at between $50,000m. and $100,000m., Iraq appealed for a five-year moratorium on payments from the Fund and also urged that the country be permitted to export at least $1,000m. worth of oil in 1991 to pay for urgently-needed imports. It also opposed, as unrealistic, the level of 'up to 30%' which the Security Council eventually set for the Compensation Fund level, on the proposal of the UN Secretary-General.

In support of its requests to the UN for more lenient treatment, the Iraqi Government, on 29 April 1991, took the unprecedented step of submitting a report on its external debt position. This showed that at the end of 1990 outstanding debts totalled $43,320m., excluding interest already due (of some $32,350m.) and what Iraq termed 'grants' from other Gulf states (estimated at between $30,000m. and $40,000m.).

The report calculated that a total of $75,450m. would be required to service the debt in the 1991–95 period (during which 97% of the outstanding amount fell due) and that the foreign currency requirement for imports, development and reconstruction would total $140,000m. Export earnings over this period were forecast at $65,455m., on the assumption of progress to approaching pre-war oil export levels by 1993, so that an overall external deficit of $150,000m. was expected to accumulate by 1995. Western analysts pointed out that these calculations were based on the conservative assumption of a constant nominal price for crude petroleum of $16 per barrel. They nevertheless agreed that, if any substantial proportion of Iraqi oil revenues were diverted to war reparations in this period, an even greater deficit would accumulate and that the other commitment categories would not be fulfilled as specified.

In the event, Iraqi resistance to full observance of the UN cease-fire resolution terms meant that, as at end-September 1994, the UN embargo was still in force. Moreover, UN Security Council Resolutions 706 and 712 of 16 August and 19 September 1991 respectively, authorizing Iraq to export oil to the value of $1,600m. to pay for emergency food and medical imports, were not utilized by Iraq, which claimed that the stringent terms attached thereto amounted to an infringement of the country's sovereignty. The Security Council's decision was prompted by an FAO study of Iraq, warning that a 'widespread and acute food supply crisis' threatened 'massive starvation throughout the country', and describing the effects of the economic blockade as 'alarming'. Iraq's rejection of Resolutions 706 and 712 was reaffirmed in February 1994 by a government spokesman, who said that no oil would be sold on terms which constituted 'a flagrant violation of Iraq's sovereignty'.

Countries which 'unfroze' part of the Iraqi assets under their jurisdiction included the United Kingdom (in November 1991) and Italy (in January 1992). Such relaxations enabled Iraq to import some urgently-needed items, although the country relied mainly on overland supplies, in breach of UN sanctions. According to a US report of January 1992, substantial 'seepage' through the sanctions net had resulted in Iraq being able to import goods worth some $2,000m. since the end of the war, representing about 25% of the pre-crisis level. An official Iraqi report claimed in May 1992 that food and medicine shortages had caused the deaths of over 19,000 people since March 1991.

During the first half of 1993 it was clear that Iraq's economic position was rapidly deteriorating; hyper-inflation in the market prices of most goods, including basic foodstuffs, was accompanied by a collapse in the value of the currency and sharp rises in unemployment and destitution. Even in the central regions, where the Government was most concerned to underpin minimum living standards, growing numbers of people lacked the means to supplement the official ration of subsidized staple foods. Increases in this ration entitlement in early 1993 raised its estimated calorific value to about two-thirds of the minimum subsistence level defined by UN humanitarian agencies. The Government claimed in March 1993 that nearly 234,000 people, including 83,000 children under the age of five, had died 'as a result of sanctions' between August 1990 and January 1993, over which period the provision of basic health care had been compromised by an 85% shortfall in medical supplies. A UNICEF report estimated that Iraq's infant mortality rate had tripled over this period. Subsequent reports from UN agencies re-emphasized the human costs of the situation. The FAO and the World Food Programme issued a statement on 26 May 1994 describing present-day Iraq as a country crippled by 'massive deprivation, chronic hunger, endemic under-nutrition for the vast majority of the population, collapse of personal incomes and rapidly increasing numbers of destitute people'.

By the end of May 1994 (two months before its scheduled closing date for claims) the UN's Compensation Fund for victims of Iraq's aggression had received claims totalling $81,000m. (including $15,000m. claimed by the Kuwait Government). The Fund's resources at this time totalled about $43m., derived from frozen Iraqi assets and voluntary contributions by Saudi Arabia and the USA. These resources were expected to be significantly depleted by payments to priority claimants, namely individuals who had been severely injured and families of those who had been killed. The first awards in this category (to 670 persons from 16 countries) were approved on 26 May and totalled $2.7m.

It was estimated that funds held in the escrow account established under Security Council Resolution 778 (see 'Finance and Banking' section below) might be sufficient to meet an estimated $150m. in claims by workers forced to leave Kuwait as a result of the invasion, and might also cover the slightly lower estimate for aggregate claims by individuals who had suffered personal losses of up to $100,000, including loss of earnings or assets held in Kuwait. However, the claims which made up the greater part of the total—those submitted by governments and businesses and by individuals with losses exceeding $100,000—stood no chance of even partial settlement while the intended funding mechanism remained inoperable for want of any Iraqi oil revenues to appropriate. Consideration of large claims was not expected to begin before 1995.

AGRICULTURE AND FOOD

Despite the increasing dominance of oil and gas production, the Government continued, through the 1980s, to allocate substantial resources to the development of agriculture, with the aim of achieving food self-sufficiency and even surpluses for export. At the same time, state control of the agricultural sector was steadily relaxed in favour of allowing a greater role for private initiative and for private-sector investment from both Iraqi and other Arab sources. The total area under cultivation rose from 3.2m. ha in 1984 to about 3.7m. in 1989, it being estimated that a further 20% increase was required to achieve self-sufficiency. Like the rest of the economy, however, agriculture suffered major disruption in the Gulf crisis and hostilities of 1990–91, one consequence of which was a return to state control and direction.

Until the 1958 revolution, agricultural improvement was often inhibited by the need for adequate land reform. In October 1958 the incoming Government announced a new and more radical land reform project. This provided for the break-up of large estates whose owners were to be compelled to forfeit their 'excess' land to the Government, which would redistribute the land to new peasant owners. Landowners losing land were to be compensated in state bonds (in 1969 all the state's liabilities to recompense land-owners were cancelled). It was hoped that the reform would take only five years to complete but the application of the law was initially mismanaged and the expropriation of land consistently ran ahead of the ability of the administration to distribute it. By the end of 1972 some 4.73m. dunums (1 dunum = 0.25 ha approx.) had been requisitioned from landlords and distributed to 100,646 families. By 1988, more than 300,000 families had received 10.8m. dunums. The Government has been promoting the growth of co-operatives and collective farms since 1967. By the end of 1987 there were 857 agricultural co-operatives, with a total of 376,329 members. In 1984 there were 23 state farms, covering 188,000 ha. By 1989 the percentage of the labour force engaged in agriculture had fallen to about 21%, compared with 50% in 1965 and 53% in 1960.

Government awareness that the rate of progress in the agricultural sector had been disappointing encouraged measures to be taken to allow greater private involvement in agriculture. By 1986, the land area occupied by state farms had fallen to only 52,925 ha, and by 1988 more than 220,000 ha had been leased—a total investment estimated at ID 72m.—as a result of the 1983 law enabling local and other Arab companies or individuals to lease land at nominal rates. Other incentives included encouragement for agriculturists and graduates working for the Ministry of Agriculture and Agrarian Reform to take up farming, and there was a more liberal attitude towards profit-making. Farmers could now bypass the state marketing system and sell direct, either to public wholesale markets or to private shops which were licensed for wholesale trade. Higher procurement prices were now paid by the state. These concessions were intended to ease supply difficulties, and to encourage local farmers.

In May 1987 came belated recognition of criticism voiced in 1982, at the Baath Party regional congress, that state intervention had often proved more of a hindrance than a help to small farms, and that state and collective farms were frequently unprofitable. It was announced that all state farms (including six dairy farms) were for sale or lease to local or Arab investors or companies, providing that the land continues to be used for agriculture. In July 1987 the Ministry of Agriculture and Agrarian Reform was re-organized, and in September the ministry was merged with the Ministry of Irrigation to become the Ministry of Agriculture and Irrigation.

A wide variety of crops is grown but the most important are barley and wheat. Production estimates vary considerably. In the case of wheat, annual output fluctuated around 950,000 metric tons in the 1980s, although drought severely affected the 1984 crop, which slumped to 471,000 tons. A good crop is dependent on favourable rains, and 1988 saw an estimated 1.2m. tons of wheat produced, while barley production was estimated at 1.2m. tons, compared with 743,000 tons in 1987.

Other crops are rice, vegetables, maize and millet, sugar cane and beet, oil seeds, pulses, dates and other fruits (the main fruit being melon), fodder, tobacco and cotton. Drought caused production to fall in 1984, but output has recovered since 1986. In 1988 Iraq produced an estimated 250,000 metric tons of paddy rice and 62,000 tons of maize, compared with 196,000 tons and 61,000 tons in 1987. Total vegetable output (including cabbages, spinach, carrots, tomatoes, okra, beans, cauliflowers and potatoes), which had been about 3m. tons per year in 1982 and 1983, fell to an estimated 1.8m. tons in 1984. In 1988 production of vegetables was 2.5m. tons.

Production of dates, the country's main export after petroleum, was also affected by drought. During 1983–88 production of dates averaged 350,000 tons per year. Iraq had about 29m. date palms in 1987, compared with 25m. in 1985. In 1986/87 some 150,000 metric tons were exported to Japan, France, Canada, India and to Arab and Asian countries. Exports rose to 163,000 tons in 1988/89, and to 373,000 tons (worth $75m.) in 1989/90. Dates are not only a lucrative export, but are also being put to industrial use. Several years ago, the Ministry of Industry and Minerals (as it then was) started a major programme to produce sugar, dry sugar alcohol, vinegar and concentrated protein from dates. Such factories together with the private sector, will use up to 100,000 tons of dates per year when operating at full capacity. As part of the Government's programme for economic reform, a new mixed-sector company, the Iraqi Date Processing and Marketing Company (IDPMC), was established to replace the Iraqi Dates Commission, which was formerly responsible for production and marketing. Deliveries to the IDPMC in the 1990/91 season were estimated at 350,000 tons.

The livestock and poultry sector was developed in the 1980s with the assistance of Dutch, British, West German and Hungarian companies. Iraq's annual output of eggs was 1,274m. in 1988, almost enough to meet local demand which is estimated at about 1,350m. eggs per year. White meat production amounted to 199,000 tons in 1988.

Provision has also been made to develop a fishing industry and the private sector has been encouraged to establish fish farms on many of the lakes and reservoirs which have been created by the construction of new dams. It is estimated that, up to the mid-1990s, freshwater fish resources will exceed marine resources, with annual potential catches estimated at between 80,000 and 100,000 metric tons. In 1987 catches of freshwater fish amounted to 16,430 tons. Development of a $160m. fisheries port complex near Basra was delayed by the Iran–Iraq War, however.

Aid to farmers is channelled through the Agricultural Co-operative Bank, which loaned ID 570m. over the period 1980–87 and increased its lending after the cease-fire in the Iran–Iraq War. To encourage farmers to use its services, the bank offers a low interest rate and has raised its maximum credit limit.

The country's food import bill, which reached $3,100m. in 1984, declined to $2,712m. in 1986, and remains at about $2,500m. per year. The USA was formerly a major agricultural supplier, retaining a large share of the market under a credit programme. The EC supplied some $345m. worth of farm products in 1986, equivalent to a 12.7% market share, compared with 16% in 1984. Canada and Australia were long-term wheat suppliers. Cuba is a long-standing sugar supplier and Thailand supplies rice.

Following the implementation of UN economic sanctions against Iraq in August 1990, the Government announced the introduction, from 1 September, of rationing for flour, tea, sugar and rice; other items, such as cooking oil, children's milk and salt, were later added to the list. The Government also steadily raised the official purchase prices for important crops, with the aim of encouraging greater production, and initiated an urgent programme to increase the cultivated area, especially in northern Iraq. From October 1990 it became compulsory for cereal farmers to deliver their output to state collection centres within two weeks of harvesting. The Government also took emergency powers to confiscate land from farmers who failed to fulfil production quotas, and from November 1990 it introduced the death penalty for hoarding of cereals. According to Iraqi officials, the 1990 cereal harvest was the best for several years, including nearly 1.2m. tons of wheat (an increase of 75% compared with 1989), more than 1.8m. tons of barley and 500,000 tons of rice. These figures were, however, questioned by US government officials, who estimated that Iraq would need to import some 1.75m. tons of grain in 1991 to feed its population.

The combined effect of rationing, increased local production, use of reserves and imports through Jordan was to prevent the development of serious food shortages in Iraq until the outbreak of actual hostilities in January 1991, although prices rose steeply. Thereafter, the devastation resulting from allied bombing seriously disrupted not only agricultural production but also food distribution, and food stocks declined to a record low in the war's immediate aftermath. On 23 March 1991 the UN Security Council's sanctions committee eased restrictions on food exports to Iraq, following which several countries agreed in principle to resume supplies. However, the continuing UN embargo on Iraqi oil exports rendered payment for imported food problematical, even though the UN committee decided, on 9 May, to 'unfreeze' sufficient Iraqi assets to pay for emergency food and medical supplies (see Consequences of the 1990/91 Gulf Crisis, above).

As part of its post-war reconstruction plans, the Government launched a national agricultural campaign on 12 April 1991, involving new incentives for farmers, priority allocation of fuel and machinery, and the creation of a special ministerial committee to supervise the 1991 harvest and to maintain the state's monopoly of food sales. The emergency six-month reconstruction budget, announced on 2 May, included provision for substantial state subsidies on cereal production in order to reduce consumer prices.

An FAO report of August 1991 found that Iraq would have to spend about $500m. to restore the country's agricultural output. The FAO estimated the latest grain harvest at only 1.25m. tons, about a third of the 1990 yield, while other crops, as well as the livestock and poultry sectors, had been devastated by the war. Prospects of speedy recovery were regarded as bleak, in that seed stocks were deficient and much of the sector's machinery and irrigation system were out of commission. The Iraqi Minister of Agriculture, speaking in May 1992, estimated that 50% of the country's cereal and seed stocks had been destroyed during the 1991 war, as had 95% of the breeding stock of the poultry and livestock industry. Efforts by the Government to bring in food supplies from abroad included the signing of agreements with Thailand (for rice), Malaysia (for palm oil), Sri Lanka (for tea), France and Australia (for wheat) and Morocco (various items).

In July 1993 the FAO estimated that Iraq's food import requirement for the coming year would amount to 5.4m. tons, valued at $2,500m. FAO experts said that the threat of famine had moved ever closer during the prolonged deadlock over utilization of the emergency oil export quota authorized by the UN Security Council on humanitarian grounds in summer 1991. Western observers had earlier reported that the Government had started using gold reserves to fund essential food imports in the latter part of 1992, having virtually exhausted its hard-currency resources.

The execution in July 1992 of 42 merchants accused of 'profiteering' served only to exacerbate the problem of persistent food price inflation, as a consequent drop in the volume of trade with Jordan added further scarcity value to items in short supply. The market prices of such staple items as wheat flour reached up to 500 times their mid-1990 levels at some points during the first half of 1993, while the estimated ratio between the average urban wage and the average market price of a typical family's food requirements widened from about 1:3 to 1:9 between April and July 1993.

Following increases in January and April 1993, the monthly ration of state-subsidized foodstuffs comprised 9 kg of flour, 2.25 kg of rice, 1.75 kg of oil and 1.5 kg of sugar. The Government implicitly acknowledged the seriousness of the food supply situation when it distributed an extra month's rations (in September 1992), brought forward a scheduled distribution date (in February 1993) and announced a supplementary Ramadan distribution of one chicken per family (in March 1993). So-called 'economic crime squads' were established in March 1993 to enforce harsh laws against overcharging for price-controlled basic foods.

Efficient administration of the rationing system was reported throughout most of Iraq, with the main exceptions in government-controlled Kurdish areas to the south of the Kurdish-controlled 'safe-havens'. The availability of subsidized supplies in these areas was reported to represent no more than 10% of the ration entitlement. There were also reports of some supply shortfalls in southern cities, attributed by Shia spokesmen to a government policy of moving food-processing operations and storage facilities out of the southern no-fly zone.

The prices of a wide range of food items outside the rationing system, including meat, eggs and dairy produce, were well beyond the reach of the average Iraqi worker in mid-1993. Government efforts to stimulate domestic food production included price incentives for farmers to sell staple crops through state marketing channels, coupled with penalties for such offences as failing to harvest crops.

There were reports in May 1993 that Kurdish farmers were being harassed by troops based in Iraqi-controlled cities south of the Kurds' northern safe haven, but it was not clear whether there was any systematic government campaign to commandeer local agricultural production. Within the Kurdish-controlled safe haven, there was a heavy dependence on international relief supplies in mid-1993, when early efforts to rebuild local agriculture were being hampered by shortages of fertilizer and other inputs. Agricultural rehabilitation projects and the provision of food supplements remained high on the UN's list of aid priorities for the safe haven in 1994.

Against a background of worsening hyper-inflation, the Iraqi Government ordered the official rations of rice, cooking oil and tea (but not flour or sugar) to be increased by up to one-third from February 1994. However, supplies of food to supplement the still-meagre ration were priced even further beyond the reach of most wage-earners as the depreciation of the Iraqi dinar accelerated in subsequent months. By mid-May the average monthly salary of a schoolteacher would buy about 800 grams of meat, or 21 eggs or 70 centrilitres of cooking oil, at current market prices. It was not unusual for middle-class households to sell or barter valuable possessions in order to buy food, while Iraq's crime rate (once very low by regional standards) increased dramatically as theft became a major problem.

In early May the Government announced that the theft of goods worth more than ID 5,000 (about $12 at the prevailing unofficial exchange rate) would henceforth be punishable by the amputation of a hand, while in early June branches of the Baath party were empowered to incarcerate shopkeepers or traders who violated official price guidelines. The Minister of Agriculture was dismissed on 25 May for having 'failed to check the rise in food prices', and on 22 June the Government banned the import of many foodstuffs, including canned meat, fish, eggs, potatoes, spaghetti and chicken, in order to conserve foreign exchange. Traders who failed to clear their shelves of banned goods within two months would be subject to 'stringent penalties'. The Iraqi business community was urged to make voluntary financial contributions to the Government (repay-able after the lifting of UN sanctions) to finance government food imports. Public-sector wages, pensions and allowances were increased from July 1994, bringing little real benefit against a background of spiralling price inflation.

RIVER CONTROL AND IRRIGATION

River control policy in Iraq has three main objects: the provision of water for irrigation, the prevention of devastating floods, and the creation of hydroelectric power. An extensive dam-building programme has been instituted on the River Tigris and its tributaries in northern Iraq, with the aim of using stored water to irrigate land which has traditionally been rain-fed. However, such installations were among those which suffered serious damage and dislocation in the 1991 Gulf hostilities.

When operational, the main systems providing flow irrigation are based in the Euphrates (serving nearly 3m. dunums), the Tigris (1.7m. dunums), the Diyalah river and the Lesser Zab river. Pumps are used extensively along both the Euphrates and the Tigris. A series of dams, barrages or reservoirs (at Samarra, Dokan, Derbendi Khan, and Habbaniya) provide security against flood dangers. When the waters of the Euphrates and Tigris are fully utilized through dams and reservoirs, the area of cultivated land in Iraq will be almost doubled.

After delays during the Iran–Iraq War, the Government evinced renewed determination to proceed with its programme of water control and storage. In the summer of 1984 the Government was able to release stored water to farmers, to offset the low levels of the Euphrates. It was hoped that the completion of the Mosul (on the Tigris) and Haditha (on the Euphrates) dams (renamed the Saddam and Qadisiya dams) would ease concern over Syrian and Turkish dam-building plans for the upper reaches of the Tigris and Euphrates, which were expected to reduce the flow of water significantly. The Qadisiya dam and its associated 600-MW hydroelectric power plant were opened in 1986. By 1990, however, the distribution of these water resources had become a fundamental issue in Iraq's relations with Syria and Turkey, following Turkey's diversion of the Euphrates in order to fill the reservoir of its new Atatürk dam. Discussions between Iraq, Syria and Turkey, held in June 1990, failed to resolve the issue, and Iraq subsequently announced that future water shortages might create the need for water rationing. In early 1993 Turkey appointed a German-led consortium to implement a major hydroelectric project at Birecik on the Euphrates. Iraq, which had condemned this project as an infringement of its water rights under international law, announced its intention to take legal action against the contractors.

In September 1986 a $1,485m. contract to build the Bekme dam, in the north-east, 40 km from the Iranian border, on the Greater Zab, a tributary of the Tigris, was awarded to a joint venture of Turkey's Enka and Yugoslavia's Hidrogradnja companies. Work on the dam commenced in 1987, and the first phase of the diversion of the Greater Zab had been completed by June 1990. In November 1990 the Bekme dam was renamed 'Al-Faris' (Knight), an appellation which the Iraqi media often used for Saddam Hussain. Another Yugoslav company, Energoprojekt, has been chosen to design dams at Badush, also on the Tigris, and at Mandawa, on the Greater Zab. There are also plans to construct dams at Taqtaq, Dujala and Farha. River control projects are also under way at Hindiya, Kifl-Shinafiya and Baghdadi.

In December 1983 the 87,500-ha first stage of the massive Kirkuk irrigation project (now renamed Saddam) was opened. More than 300,000 ha will eventually be irrigated at a cost of more than ID 1,000m. Contracts have been awarded to Chinese and South Korean companies to work on the North Jazira irrigation project, which will be fed with water stored by the Saddam dam; and to local and international companies for work on the East Jazira irrigation project, involving the installation of irrigation networks on more than 70,000 ha of rain-fed land near Mosul. These projects are part of an ID 820m. scheme to irrigate 250,000 ha of the Jazira plain. South of Baghdad, completed land reclamation schemes include Lower Khalis, Diwaniya-Dalmaj, Ishaqi, Dujaila and much of Abu Ghraib. The massive Dujaila project is intended to produce about 22% of Iraq's output of crop and animal products. Consultants have designed irrigation schemes for Kifl-Shinafiya, East Gharraf, Saba Nissan, New Rumaitha, Zubair, Bastora, Greater Musayyib and Makhmour. The project's main outfall canal, completed in December 1992, is known as the 'third river'. It runs for 565 km from Mahmudiya, south of Baghdad, to Qurna, north of Basra, and carries saline water (flushed away from 1.5m. ha of reclaimed land) to an outlet on the Gulf.

A 120-km 'fourth river', designed to irrigate an area of 250,000 ha, and the 140-km Qadissiyah canal, branching off from the Euphrates and designed to irrigate an area of 125,000 ha, were under construction in early 1993. Political opponents of the Iraqi Government claimed that this major programme of irrigation works, together with a number of drainage schemes in the southern marshes in 1992/93, was partly aimed at Shi'ite dissidents living in the area. However, the Government was able to provide numerous economic justifications for its policy (including, on the issue of marsh drainage, the fact that the area contained large untapped oil reserves).

Since 60% of Iraq's land area has no access to the major river irrigation schemes, a programme of well-drilling has been initiated under the direction of the State Company for Water Wells Drilling (SCWWD). In November 1990 the SCWWD announced that it had drilled 1,615 wells and supplied 1,159 pumps since its creation in 1987.

In the war with the multinational force in 1991, several dams were hit in the bombing campaign, but the wholesale dislocation of the country's river control and irrigation systems was mainly attributable to the multinational force's destruction of Iraq's power supply network. Restoration of such installations to proper functioning became a major priority of the Government's post-war reconstruction programme, as did restoration of drinking water supplies and sewerage systems in Baghdad and other major cities. Many of the failures of urban sewerage systems in 1992/93 were attributed to shortages of imported spare parts for pump motors. The UN Development Programme, which had a $4m.-budget for projects in Iraq, said in June 1994 that $1m. had been allocated for the rehabilitation of two major sewage plants in Baghdad and $1m. for the repair of water treatment plants in southern population centres.

PETROLEUM AND NATURAL GAS

Following the nationalization of the hydrocarbons sector in the early 1970s, Iraq rapidly increased its output of crude petroleum, becoming, by 1979, the world's second largest exporter of oil, after Saudi Arabia. Production in 1979 totalled 170.6m. metric tons (compared with 83.5m. tons in 1971, the last full year before nationalization, and 47.5m. tons in 1960). Exports in 1979 and 1980 averaged 3.3m. barrels per day (b/d), producing revenues of $21,300m. and $26,300m. respectively. However, because of the outbreak of the Iran–Iraq War in September 1980, output went into sharp decline in 1981 and exports fell to 800,000 b/d by 1982 (worth $10,000m.), before rising to 1.4m. b/d in 1986, although lower world oil prices reduced revenues in that year to $7,000m. The end of the war with Iran in 1988 facilitated further recovery in oil production, from 127.4m. tons (2.6m. b/d) in 1988 to 138.6m. tons (2.8m. b/d) in 1989, earning export revenues of some $13,000m. and $12,000m. respectively. In the first half of 1990 production was averaging about 3.1m. b/d (almost back to the pre-1980 level) and 1990 export earnings from oil were expected to total $15,400m. However, Iraq's oil exports were then brought to a virtual halt by the UN embargo, imposed as a consequence of its invasion of Kuwait, and in the Gulf hostilities of early 1991 the massive damage sustained by Iraqi oil installations brought production to a standstill. In June 1993 Iraq's proven oil reserves were officially estimated at 112,000m. barrels, placing it second only to Saudi Arabia in the extent of its reserves and sufficient to maintain production at the 1989 level for 109 years.

Iraq's petroleum industry has been highly dependent on pipelines carrying Iraqi oil through neighbouring territories or to the Gulf coast. In 1980 these were the 'strategic' reversible-flow pipeline (with a capacity of 1m. b/d) from Rumaila

to Haditha and Kirkuk which links oilfields in the north and south of Iraq; a pipeline running for 980 km (609 miles) from Kirkuk, through Turkey, to Dörtyol, on the Mediterranean coast in the Gulf of Iskenderun; another from Haditha, via Syria, to Tripoli, in Lebanon and Banias, in Syria; and lines running from the southern oilfields near Basra to the offshore Gulf export terminals of Mina al-Bakr and Khor al-Amaya, with capacities of 2.7m. b/d and 1.8m. b/d, respectively, which were exporting up to 2.9m. b/d before the Iran–Iraq War.

Following Iranian air raids on key installations in the early stages of the war, however, exports soon ceased from Iraq's offshore oil terminals in the Gulf, and production declined to 900,000 b/d in 1981. Refineries, pipelines, pumping stations and petrochemical plants were all damaged. Exports of petroleum were, at first, diverted to Mediterranean ports via Iraq's reversible pipeline pumping network, but these were then brought to a halt by an explosion on the line through Turkey, reportedly the work of Kurdish guerrillas, and by Iranian bombing of the K-1 pumping station at the Kirkuk oilfield in the north.

By December 1980 petroleum exports through the Mediterranean ports had resumed but total exports consisted only of petroleum being pumped through the pipeline across Turkey at a rate of around 650,000 b/d, supplemented by 60,000 b/d–80,000 b/d transported by road to Jordan. Not all of this was for worldwide exports, however, since Turkey was taking 250,000 b/d as its entitlement under the pipeline transit agreement. Preference for sales was given to countries which were major customers for Iraqi petroleum before the war and which had suffered most from the cessation of petroleum exports in the fourth quarter of 1980. These included Japan and France.

Pumping through the Banias pipeline resumed in early December 1981, despite tense political relations between Iraq and Syria and the Iraqi decision of April 1976 to suspend deliveries through the pipeline because of a dispute over transit fees and other political issues. The long period of disuse limited the throughput to 350,000 b/d, compared with the full capacity of 1.4m. b/d, and pumping soon halted, not to be resumed until the end of February 1982. On 10 April 1982, however, Syria closed the pipeline, depriving Iraq of a possible $17m. per day in revenues and leaving the Turkish pipeline as Iraq's only outlet for petroleum exports. The loss of the Gulf terminals and the vulnerability of the Turkish and Syrian pipelines forced Iraq to consider alternative pipelines.

To complement the pipeline through Turkey, which was pumping about 1m. b/d by mid-1987, the Government decided to build new export pipelines across Turkey (to run parallel to the existing line), Saudi Arabia and Jordan. In September 1984 a $507m. order to build the first (640 km) phase of the Saudi Arabian project (IPSA-1)—to link Iraq's southern oilfields with Saudi Arabia's east-west Petroline to the terminal at Yanbu—was awarded to an Italian consortium, led by Saipem and including France's Spie-Capag. The French and Italian Governments provided credit to support the project, and the contractors agreed to accept Iraqi oil in part-payment. The spur line began pumping in September 1985. Although Japanese and Indian customers were secured, through-put was limited to 350,000 b/d–400,000 b/d by the Saudi Arabian Government. In March 1987, however, Saudi Arabia agreed to allow Iraq to export oil through its terminal at Yanbu at the spur line's full capacity of 500,000 b/d, on condition that it charged OPEC's official prices for crude. The second phase (IPSA-2), for which a contract was awarded in September 1987 to a consortium led by Italian and Japanese companies, envisaged an independent 970-km Iraqi pipeline (with a capacity of 1.15m. b/d) across Saudi Arabia, parallel to the Saudi line, to a new export terminal on the Red Sea coast, near Yanbu, providing a total through-put via Saudi Arabia of 1.65m. b/d.

A consortium of Italian and Turkish companies began work in February 1986 on the second 980-km trans-Turkey line, parallel to the existing line from Kirkuk to the Mediterranean port of Yumurtalik in Turkey. With a capacity of 500,000 b/d, this boosted total possible exports through Turkey to 1.5m. b/d, when it became operational at the end of July 1987, and there were plans to double the capacity of this line. Plans for an oil pipeline to Aqaba, in Jordan, were suspended in

1984, as Iraq could secure no guarantee of compensation from the US Bechtel Corporation, the project's managing contractor, for loss of earnings in the event of Israeli sabotage of the pipeline, which would have terminated near the Israeli border. In April 1987 Turkey and Iraq agreed plans to construct a third trans-Turkish pipeline, with a capacity of 70,000 b/d, from oilfields at Ain Zalah, near Mosul, to the Batman oil refinery in Turkey, a distance of 240 km. With its promised new export capacity, Iraq now had less need for the reopening of the pipeline across Syria, despite speculation in 1987 of a possible reconciliation with Damascus. When the new lines across Turkey and the two phases of the trans-Saudi Arabia development are in full operation, Iraq's export capacity will be about 3.2m. b/d. The facilities in the south, which were put out of action by the war with Iran, could provide another 3m. b/d in exports. Repair work started in March 1989, and by July tankers were lifting 200,000 b/d from the Mina al-Bakr terminal. Iraq has also exported between 100,000 b/d and 250,000 b/d of refined petroleum products by road through Jordan and Turkey. In 1986 Saudi Arabia and Kuwait, through the Arabian Oil Company which operates in the Neutral Zone, renewed an agreement whereby they sold as much as 310,000 b/d (250,000 b/d from the Zone and the remainder from Saudi Arabia), with the proceeds going to Iraq to compensate it for lost export capacity. This agreement was terminated at the end of 1988.

When war broke out with Iran in September 1980, many major oil and gas development projects were in progress. War damage was not as extensive as was originally believed, although the Basra petroleum refinery, with a capacity of 140,000 b/d, was bombed early in the war. Repair work began in 1988, and by mid-1989 the refinery was again producing oil products for export. Iraq was already short of refining capacity, so the damage to the Basra refinery had a severe impact on the domestic supply of petroleum products. The country was left with the 70,000 b/d Dawra refining facility, near Baghdad, which also came under attack, and some 100,000 b/d topping capacity at a number of other locations. At 1 January 1981, refinery capacity stood at 118,000 b/d. The 150,000 b/d north Baiji refinery (Baiji II), built by Chiyoda of Japan, was opened in 1983, complementing the 71,000 b/d Czechoslovak-built refinery (Baiji I) already in operation. In the first quarter of 1987, the Baiji lubricating oil refinery, built by Technip of France, began operations. During its first year of operations, about 70,000 metric tons were expected to be available for export, rising subsequently to 200,000 metric tons per year. Plans were also announced to quadruple refining capacity. In mid-1988 international companies submitted offers to construct a 140,000 b/d refinery south of Baghdad.

Before the outbreak of war in 1980, the Federal German-US consortium of Thyssen Rheinstahl Technik and C.E. Lummus completed a petrochemicals complex at Khor az-Zubair, near Basra. The plant sustained minor damage during the war, but recommissioning began in 1988, and by 1989 some units had resumed operations. The complex was intended to produce 150,000 tons per year of low- and high-density polyethylene and PVC, and 40,000 tons per year of caustic soda, using 90m. cu ft per day of natural gas as feedstock. The Government also approved plans for a second petrochemicals complex about 60 km south of Baghdad, near the new refinery referred to above.

Other projects in the Basra area include a gas liquefaction and treatment plant at Zubair, which was constructed by a French company, Technip, under a $239m. 'turnkey' contract, awarded in March 1980. The recommissioning of this plant began in 1989, with the intention that it would use as feedstock 6,000m. cu m of associated gas from the Rumaila oilfields to produce 4m. tons of propane and butane and 1.5m. tons per year of condensate. The plant is part of the southern gas project, which entails gathering and compression facilities that will be capable of handling 16,000m. cu m of gas per year from the Rumaila oilfields. Part of the project, a southern gas-gathering complex with the capacity to process and export as much as 4m. tons of associated gas annually, commenced operations in July 1990. A similar scheme exists in the north.

Both are part of a government programme to increase its use of gas as an energy resource.

Total gas reserves, three-quarters of which are associated with oil, were estimated at 3,100,000m. cu m at 1 January 1992. Gas production rose from 5,900m. cu m in 1966 to 20,160m. cu m in 1979, but declined, owing to the war with Iran, to 5,290m. cu m in 1984. By 1986 output had recovered to 8,270m. cu m, and in 1989 it totalled 10,680m. cu m. Whereas 80% of gas production was flared in 1979, projects to make wider use of gas, particularly in industry, resulted in a decline in this proportion to 40% by 1989. Gas exports also increased, from 8.3% of production in 1986 to some 30% in 1989. Shortly before the onset of the August 1990 Gulf crisis, Petrobrás of Brazil shipped Iraq's first export cargo of liquefied petroleum gas (LPG).

In 1986 a Soviet contractor, Tsvetmetpromexport (TSMPE), was awarded a $154m. contract to construct the first section, 345 km in length, of the trans-Iraq dry gas pipeline. This section runs from Nasiriya, in the south, to Baghdad, and will initially carry 4.2m. cu m of gas per day. TSMPE is also expected to win the contract for the second stage of the trans-Iraq gas pipeline project, which will extend the line to the border with Turkey. After being linked to the northern gas-gathering network, the pipeline will supply a national gas grid. Eventually, power stations and industrial plants will be connected to the gas grid.

In the late 1970s and early 1980s the Iraq National Oil Company (INOC), then the supreme state body exercising control over the hydrocarbons sector, pursued a programme of further exploration for oil and gas reserves. Five major fields were identified in 1981 for future development—Majnoon, Nahr-Umr, Halfaya, East Baghdad and West Qurnah. These fields are likely to increase production capacity by some 2m. b/d. Exploitation of the East Baghdad field (with estimated reserves of 5,000m. barrels) began at the end of 1984, with the award of a $60m. contract to establish a plant to process and degas an initial 30,000 b/d to Italy's Snamprogetti and its British affiliate. Production began in April 1989, and capacity will eventually be increased to 150,000 b/d. The main contractor at West Qurnah is Technoexport of the USSR, with TPL of Italy. The Soviet company also undertook development work at the North Rumaila field, which was producing at a rate of 500,000 b/d in 1987, compared with potential capacity of 800,000 b/d. Development of Halfaya and Nahr-Umr was delayed by the war with Iran. In the north, exploitation of the Sfaya oilfield is under way. In 1988 experimental production started at Nasiriya, Gharraf, Subba, Balad and West Tikrit. Contracts were awarded in 1988 to Technip, of France, and Mannesmann, of the Federal Republic of Germany, to develop the Khabbaz and Saddam oilfields to produce 30,000 b/d and 45,000 b/d respectively; both came into production in 1990. The recapture from Iran of Majnoon Island and the surrounding area of the al-Hawizah marshes, in June 1988, restored to Iraq oilfields containing reserves estimated at 30,000m. barrels. Plans for a second reversible-flow pipeline, parallel to the first, 670 km in length, linking new oilfields in the south with northern petroleum installations, and capable of pumping 900,000 b/d, were announced in April 1988. Plans for a $500m. oil-products storage complex at Khor az-Zubair have also been announced.

INOC's activities extended beyond exploration for, and production of, crude petroleum. In 1972 it established an autonomous company to be responsible for the operation and management of a tanker fleet. In May 1987, however, INOC and the Ministry of Oil were merged as part of a programme to reorganize the oil industry and make it more efficient. At the same time, a number of state organizations, hitherto responsible for, among other functions, oil-refining, distribution and industrial training, under the auspices of INOC, were removed from INOC control and converted into separate national companies, responsible to the ministry.

Iraq is one of the founder members of the Organization of the Petroleum Exporting Countries (OPEC). It was not required to make a reduction in its output in October 1984, when OPEC cut production by 1.5m. b/d in order to prevent a further fall in prices on the world market, which was over-supplied with oil. With new export outlets becoming available, Iraq frequently lobbied for an increase in its OPEC production quota, while consistently exceeding its allocation. During 1986 oil prices continued to decline, falling below $10 per barrel in July. When, in August, OPEC decided to reduce production to a maximum 16.7m. b/d for two months from 1 September, effectively reverting to the quota restrictions imposed in October 1984, in order to raise oil prices, Iraq declined to be a party to the decision, demanding at least parity with Iran, and continued to produce as much as it could to finance its war effort. The proposal for a reduction in output was made by Iran, whose Minister of Oil said that Iran would 'act in a way to prevent Iraq getting its desired quota'. Iraq then opted out of a succession of OPEC production agreements, between October 1986 and May 1988 (though it was allocated notional quotas in each), and stated that it would continue to do so while its quota allocations were lower than those allotted to Iran, and failed to take account of Iraq's increased export capacity. For the second half of 1987 a 'ceiling' of 16.6m. b/d was placed on OPEC production, including a notional quota for Iraq of 1.54m. b/d, compared with actual export capacity of about 2.7m. b/d in August, and the 2.37m. b/d allocated to Iran. A reference price for OPEC oil of $18 per barrel had been in force since February 1987. At OPEC's meeting in December 1987 Iraq declined to participate in the agreement covering production in the first half of 1988, whereby the 'ceiling' on collective output and Iraq's notional quota were unchanged.

The cease-fire in the Iran–Iraq War prompted preliminary efforts by OPEC to accommodate Iraq in future production agreements by raising its quota to take account of increased export capacity, even though Iran had clearly stated that it would not participate in an agreement which awarded Iraq quota parity with itself. In late 1988 OPEC granted Iraq parity with Iran and set its production quota at 2.64m. b/d. Iraqi production had reached 2.8m. b/d in November 1987, and was subject to government reviews during 1988, when output was maintained at about 2.6m. b/d. By the end of 1988 production had risen to about 2.7m. b/d, and exports were running at about 2.3m. b/d. On 1 January 1989 Iraq temporarily reduced production to match its quota, halting the bulk of its crude oil exports by road to Jordan and Turkey. In mid-1989 Iraq's quota was raised to 2.783m. b/d, still maintaining parity with Iran, and average output in 1989 amounted to some 2.8m. b/d.

In view of its need to reconstruct its economy, Iraq sought, following the cease-fire in the Iran–Iraq War, to maximize its oil revenues and to raise the OPEC minimum reference price. At the OPEC meeting held in June 1989, Kuwait claimed a quota of 1.35m. b/d, rather than the 1.12m. b/d which would have been allocated to it under a simple pro-rata distribution of the 20m. b/d 'ceiling' which the majority of members judged to be reasonable in order to stabilize prices. Since Kuwaiti overproduction was now regarded as inevitable (it had already been overproducing by some 800,000–900,000 b/d in May and June), the new production 'ceiling' was raised by only 1m. b/d, to 19.5m. b/d. In September a new 'ceiling' of 20.5m. b/d was fixed, but Kuwait rejected its quota of 1.149m. b/d for the final quarter of 1989. Overproduction continued, and by the end of 1989 total OPEC output had reached almost 24m. b/d, with a consequential depressive effect on world oil prices.

At the next OPEC meeting, held in November 1989, the production 'ceiling' was raised to 22m. b/d, although the *de facto* level of production was already 24m. b/d. Quotas were redistributed, with Kuwait being allocated 6.82% of total output, compared with 5.61% previously. Owing to optimistic estimates of demand, and closer adherence to quotas by member states, prices rose following the November meeting, reaching their highest level for two years in January 1990. By May, however, quotas were again largely being ignored, and prices had slumped. Iraq's crude oil production at this time was estimated at about 3.14m. b/d—approximately its quota level.

By May 1990 overproduction had continued to such an extent that increasing numbers of tankers were being chartered for floating storage. At a meeting of OPEC's ministerial monitoring committee, held on 2 May, it was agreed to reduce production by 1.445m. b/d from an average level of 23.5m.

b/d. However, the effect of this on prices was negligible. In June 1990 an Iraqi Deputy Prime Minister, Dr Sa'adoun Hammadi, condemned Kuwait and the UAE for producing above their quota levels, and stated that there should be no further review of quotas until a 'fair' price for crude petroleum—$25 per barrel—had been achieved. Kuwaiti overproduction was regarded as an attempt to wreck efforts within OPEC to raise the minimum reference price above $18 per barrel, and Iraq claimed to be losing $1,000m. annually for every reduction of $1 per barrel in the price of oil. In July President Saddam Hussain blamed overproduction for low oil prices, and warned of action against those states—Kuwait and the UAE—which persistently flouted their quotas. He claimed that the decline in the price of oil in the first half of 1990 had cost Iraq $14,000m. Iraq subsequently accused Kuwait of violating the Iraqi border in order to steal oil resources worth more than $2,400m. from Iraq's section of the Rumaila oilfields.

At the full OPEC meeting held in Geneva in late July 1990, Iraq sought to raise the minimum reference price for crude petroleum to $25 per barrel. Although the agreement that was achieved at the meeting raised the reference price to only $21 per barrel until the end of 1990, and fixed the production 'ceiling' at 22.5m. b/d, it was regarded as OPEC's most serious attempt to address the problem of overproduction for many years. However, oil markets were thrown into turmoil by Iraq's invasion and annexation of Kuwait at the beginning of August 1990 and by the consequential imposition of mandatory UN sanctions on all trade with Iraq and Iraqi-controlled territory. By late August, prices had risen as high as $30 per barrel, and an emergency OPEC meeting was held in an attempt to restore stability to the market. At the meeting, which was attended by the oil ministers of all OPEC member states except Libya and Iraq, draft agreement to suspend the production quotas that had been agreed in July (and thus compensate for the loss of Iraqi and Kuwaiti production) was endorsed by all member states attending except Iran.

Faced with the UN embargo and the closure of its pipeline outlets through Saudi Arabia and Turkey, Iraq reduced its oil production to less than 400,000 b/d in the latter months of 1990, sufficient to supply its domestic refining capacity. Although consumer prices rose sharply, a move by the Minister of Oil to introduce petrol rationing on 19 October 1990 was countermanded by the Revolutionary Command Council 10 days later (and the Minister was dismissed). The situation deteriorated rapidly with the onset of hostilities in January 1991, when the allied bombing campaign resulted in the destruction of most of Iraq's oil and gas installations, both upstream and downstream. By mid-February petrol was officially rationed (but virtually unobtainable), as were heating oil and gas. A UN report, compiled in March 1991, estimated that restoration of 25% of pre-war refinery capacity—the minimum needed for survival—would take from four to 13 months. Some refineries resumed limited production in April–May, enabling the Government to end petrol rationing on 28 April and to reduce consumer prices, but government claims that oil exports of 1.5m. b/d could be resumed in July 1991 (if UN sanctions were repealed), rising to 2m. b/d in 1992, were not put to the test, because the UN embargo remained in place. In its emergency six-month reconstruction budget, announced on 2 May, the Government identified the restoration of oil production, refining and pipeline facilities as a central priority. The appointment of a new Minister of Oil on 27 May confirmed the dominance over the hydrocarbons sector of the Ministry of Industry, Minerals and Military Industrialization.

By-mid 1992 Iraq appeared to have made substantial progress in restoring its oil production, refining and storage capacity, in accordance with the priorities laid down in the reconstruction plan. Annual average oil production (including natural gas liquids) rose from 235,000 b/d in 1991 to 480,000 b/d in 1992 (compared with average production of 2.01m. b/d in 1990 and a production level of over 3m. b/d before the August 1990 invasion of Kuwait). Output averaged 495,000 b/d in 1993 and 555,000 b/d in the first half of 1994. In the first half of 1992, Iraq claimed that it had restored its output capacity to 3m. b/d, although the non-availability of export markets (and Iraq's refusal to utilize the UN concession of limited, authorized exports to pay for emergency imports) precluded an early attempt to bring the bulk of this capacity back on stream.

In April 1993 the head of oil operations in the south of the country announced that available productive capacity in this region amounted to 1.8m. b/d (compared with production of 2.25m. b/d from the southern fields in August 1990), and that facilities were in place to export up to 800,000 b/d via the Mina al-Bakr terminal and 1m. b/d via the strategic pipeline to the north. Mina al-Bakr was Iraq's preferred export point for UN-authorized oil exports, whereas the sanctions administrators proposed that any shipments should be made via Turkey to facilitate strict monitoring. The Turkish authorities also declared their anxiety about possible corrosion problems associated with a prolonged pipeline shut-down. Technical arrangements for repairing and flushing Iraq's Turkish pipeline were agreed in principle between the two Governments in the first half of 1994, with Turkey proposing to use the resulting outflow of trapped oil on its domestic market and to arrange for 30% of the payment due to Iraq to be deposited in the UN Compensation Fund for victims of Iraq's aggression, while the remaining 70% would be used to finance Iraqi imports of essential foodstuffs and medical supplies. It was estimated that 12m. barrels of oil (of which 3.8m. barrels were already owned by Turkey) would be discharged in the course of the proposed maintenance operation. Iraq made it clear that the scheme (for which Turkey was hoping to obtain early UN clearance) could not proceed if the UN sought to attach the same conditions that had caused Iraq to reject Security Council Resolutions 706 and 712.

Although the resumption of its own oil exports remained in abeyance, Iraq continued to attend OPEC meetings to express formal opposition to pricing and production decisions adopted by the other member countries from 1991 to mid-1993. At the end of 1992 the Iraqi Minister of Oil accused OPEC of failing to uphold 'the interests of producing countries'. In June 1993 the Deputy Prime Minister, Tareq Aziz, indicated that Iraq's eventual return to the oil export market would be geared to the country's revenue needs, and that the Government would be prepared to see oil prices fall to $5 per barrel if necessary, 'since now we get nothing'. He pointed out that the UN had defined the proposed emergency export quota in cash terms, setting no limit on the volume of oil that could be exported to generate income of $1,600m. By early 1994 Iraqi ministers and officials had moderated their criticism of OPEC, and appeared to be laying the foundations for a reasoned claim for a high OPEC quota allocation at such time as Iraq was able to rejoin the export market.

INDUSTRY

Until the 1970s Iraq had few large industries apart from petroleum. In greater Baghdad the larger enterprises were concerned with electricity and water supply and the building materials industry. In addition, there was a large number of smaller-unit industries concerned with food and drink processing (date-packing, breweries, etc.), cigarette-making, textiles, chemicals, furniture, shoe-making, jewellery and various metal manufactures.

In recent years greater priority has been given to industrial developments, as the Government has sought to reduce Iraq's dependence on the petroleum industry. Between 1970 and 1986 more than ID 14,000m. was invested in the industrial sector. Iraq now has some major industrial plants, with others under construction. An iron and steel works at Khor az-Zubair, built by Creusot-Loire of France, began operations in 1978 and should eventually have a maximum annual output of 1.2m. tons of sponge iron and 400,000 tons of steel. Plans for a second iron and steel works were announced at the beginning of 1988. Khor az-Zubair is also the site of a major petrochemicals complex (see Petroleum and Natural Gas, above).

Iraq's mineral resources, apart from hydrocarbons, include sulphur and phosphate rock. Sulphur has been mined at Mishraq, near Mosul, since 1972. The mining complex, which includes a sulphuric acid plant, has a design capacity of 1.25m. tons per year. However, a record 1.4m. tons were produced in 1989, of which 1.2m. tons were for export, compared with

950,000 tons and 750,000 tons, respectively, in 1988. A new sulphur recovery and sulphuric acid plant, built by Japanese contractors, uses Mishraq sulphur. Production began in 1988 and has raised exports of sulphur by more than 50%, from their former level of 500,000 tons per year. Some 500,000 tons of sulphur are sent for sulphuric acid production at the phosphate processing plant at al-Qaim, but Iraq hopes to maintain sulphur exports by increasing the rate of sulphur recovery (currently 90%) during hydrocarbon processing. A new recovery unit is being built at Kirkuk. In 1988 proven reserves of sulphur stood at 515m. tons, the largest in the world according to the Iraqi Government.

Phosphate rock reserves, mostly in the Akashat area, and in the Marbat region, north-west of Baghdad, were estimated at 10,000m. tons in 1988. The phosphate fertilizer plant at al-Qaim was built by Sybetra of Belgium, which also installed the phosphate mine in Akashat. The mine, which has reserves estimated at 3,500m. tons, opened in 1981 and was intended to produce 3.4m. metric tons per year of phosphate rock for the al-Qaim plant, which received the first loads from the mine by rail in 1982. Iraq is now self-sufficient in fertilizers, producing slightly more than 1.2m. tons in 1989. Of this, some 766,000 tons were exported. The al-Qaim plant started production in 1984, and is scheduled to export 75% of its output. A $400m. programme to double production at al-Qaim began in 1989. Daily production of 1,000 tons of ammonia and 1,700 tons of urea also commenced at a fourth nitrogenous fertilizer factory at Baiji. One of the contractors, the M. W. Kellogg Company, was appointed in 1988 to double capacity at the Baiji plant. There are also plans to build a new ammonia/urea factory at al-Qaim, and work to expand capacity at the Basra fertilizer plant commenced in early 1990.

Major state factories also include a textile factory at Mosul, producing calico from local cotton; three sugar refineries, at Karbala, Sulaimaniya and Mosul, with another four planned; a tractor assembly plant which produced 2,500 tractors in 1975; a paperboard factory at Basra, a synthetic fibres complex, at Hindiya; and a number of flour mills. Shoe and cigarette factories serve the domestic market. Other developments in the manufacturing sector have included factories to produce pharmaceuticals, electrical goods, telephone cables and plastics, together with additional food-processing plants. In 1984 Iraq's annual capacity for cement production was 11m. tons; this is expected to reach 20m. tons when the country's newest cement works operate at full capacity. Two cement works, a plant at al-Qaim with a capacity of 1m. tons per year, and another at Sinjar, in Nineveh governorate, with a capacity of 2m. tons, were built by Uzinexportimport of Romania. Exports of 1m. tons of cement to Egypt began in 1986. Production of cement reached 13m. tons in 1989, when 5.4m. tons were exported, mainly to other Arab countries. Brick production in 1984 reached 1,607m. units, rising to 1,773m. in 1986. Much of the output was used to build homes. Up to 4m. homes are expected to be built in the years 1981–2000. According to official plans, the local construction industry would also be supplied by three new factories—a steel foundry, a central moulds factory and a steel formworks—built on at-Taji industrial estate. Trucks and buses designed by the Swedish firm Saab-Scania have been assembled under licence in Iskandariya since 1973.

The latest developments in the manufacturing sector have been in the production of pharmaceuticals, electrical goods, telephone cables and plastics, and in the establishment of more food processing plants.

The USSR has assisted with the construction of 11 factories, including a steel mill and an electrical equipment factory at Baghdad, a drug factory at Samarra and a tractor plant at Musayib. A large share of industrial development is taking place in co-operation with Eastern bloc countries and several agreements have been signed, including one at the end of 1984 with Bulgaria's Bulgartabac to extend the northern tobacco industry. Other projects include the establishment of an electronics industry, by Thomson CSF of France.

Local industry came under increasing scrutiny during 1987 and 1988 and a wide improvement was sought both in the quantity and the quality of production, while particular emphasis was placed on import substitution by local production and on producing surpluses for export. Priority continued to be given to meeting local demands for raw materials, spare parts, new machinery and equipment. There has also been official recognition of private and mixed-sector companies' ability to meet vital consumer needs more effectively than the state.

In July 1988, following a number of earlier attempts to reorganize the government departments responsible for industry in Iraq, responsibility for all civilian and military industry was placed under the control of a single Ministry of Industry, Minerals and Military Industrialization. This was to run large-scale and strategic industries such as power generation, minerals and petrochemicals, and military industrial production, through the Military Industries Commission which was attached to it. Some state factories producing light industrial goods were auctioned off to private companies, or to newly established mixed-sector firms. In August 1988 the new ministry announced that it was to sell 47 factories to the private sector by the end of the year. Iraq allocated the equivalent of $11,500m. to investment in development projects in fiscal 1988, some 42% of which was to be devoted to industrial and agricultural schemes. Some 229 light industrial schemes (involving investment of ID 234m.) were listed in the Five-Year (1986-90) Industrial Development Plan and were also open to private and Arab investment. In April 1988, the Arab Investment Law No. 46 was passed, offering Arab investors tax exemptions and profit remittances.

Industrial production was valued at a record $8,500m. in 1987, owing, said government sources, to optimum use of production facilities and greater use of local, rather than imported, raw materials, which was estimated to have saved $130m. By 1987 the proportion of the labour force employed in industry was just over 21%. The foreign labour force was reduced by one-third during 1987, saving an additional $50m., according to government announcements. Some 218 development projects worth a total of ID 2,496m. ($8,051m.) were completed in 1987, according to the Ministry of Planning, including 50 agricultural schemes (worth $2,319m.) and 33 industrial schemes ($1,574m.). During 1989 the Ministry of Industry, Minerals and Military Industrialization emerged as the leading client for new business. Danieli of Italy was awarded a contract to construct a special steel factory at Taji, and a rolling mill for flat steel products at Khor az-Zubair. Contracts for new pipe factories were awarded to companies from Italy and the Federal Republic of Germany. The Ministry's Technical Corporation for Special Projects also assumed responsibility for the new petrochemicals complex and for the new central oil refinery in mid-1989. The Ministry also announced plans in 1989 to manufacture cars, tractors, trucks and buses. A licensing agreement for the production of cars has been signed with General Motors of the USA, and an agreement for the production of trucks and buses has been signed with Mercedes-Benz of Germany.

Investment in the power generation sector, which was severely disrupted during the early years of the Iran–Iraq War, has been given a high priority by the Government. In 1981 a large number of contracts—worth more than $2,000m.—were awarded for additional generation and transmission facilities (including a 600-MW power station at Haditha), as well as for the expansion and renovation of local and national networks, and the supply of emergency back-up systems. Since 1982, contracts for 400-kV 'supergrid' and 132-kV transmission lines and substations have been awarded to South Korean, French, Italian, Yugoslav and Japanese companies. The first of three 1,200-MW thermal power stations planned during the early 1980s was to be built at al-Musayyib, under a $730m. contract awarded to the Hyundai Engineering and Construction Company of South Korea. The second, at Yousufia, on the Euphrates, comprising six 200-MW units, was to be built by the USSR's Technopromexport under the terms of a Soviet-Iraq agreement covering the period 1986–90, which also provided for co-operation on an 800-MW power plant in Mosul; and a 300–400-MW hydroelectric plant and dam, costing $200m., in Baghdadi, on the Euphrates. The USSR also helped to build an 840-MW thermal power plant in Nasiriya; a 400-MW hydroelectric plant in Dukan; and a 200-MW thermal power plant in Najibiya. A West German consultant, Fichtner,

was chosen to design the third 1,200-MW power station, the al-Anbar plant, which was to be built near Ramadi, on the Euphrates. Italy's GIE has completed expansion of Baghdad's Dawra power station, and was appointed in 1989 to add two 350-MW units to al-Musayyib power station. Another new plant, the 1,400-MW oil-fired power station at ash-Shamal, on the Tigris, is being designed by Energoprojekt of Yugoslavia, and four 350-MW turbine generators are to be supplied by Northern Engineering Industries of the UK.

In 1987 six new hydroelectric plants, one power station and 18 transformer units went into operation raising Iraq's generating capacity by 6% to 8,538 MW. By mid-1990 capacity had reached 9,000 MW and was expected to double by the end of the century. However, it was estimated that demand for power would increase four-fold by the year 2000. By 1990 about 95% of the population had access to electricity, with millions connected to the network since the rural supply scheme began in 1975. Consumption was 1,450 kWh per head in 1987, compared with 1,344 kWh per head in 1986. The connection with the Turkish grid has been completed, and wider inter-Arab power connections have also been discussed. Supplies for Turkey were scheduled to flow in December 1988, making Iraq the first exporter of electricity in the Middle East.

Iraq's experimental 70-MW Osirak nuclear reactor was destroyed by an Israeli air force bombing attack in June 1981. In 1990, according to official sources, Iraq had only one nuclear reactor: the 5-MW reactor at Temmuz, supplied by the USSR in the 1960s. Nevertheless, the US and allied governments remained convinced that Iraq was pursuing a large-scale nuclear development programme with the aim of producing nuclear weapons. During the 1991 hostilities, it was reported that Iraqi nuclear installations had been bombed to destruction. However, the issue resurfaced in the post-war period, when it became apparent that Iraq's nuclear potential had partially survived, although the Government continued to insist that only civilian nuclear research was being conducted.

The UN embargo that was imposed on Iraq in August 1990 resulted in the suspension of most industrial development projects involving foreign co-operation. The industrial sector was also adversely affected by the loss of technicians from Western countries. The outbreak of actual hostilities in January 1991 led to massive destruction of Iraq's heavy industrial capacity and infrastructure, including as much as 90% of its electricity generating and transmission facilities as well as oil refineries, oil export terminals, petrochemical plants, iron and steel foundries, engineering factories, and phosphate and cement plants. The light industrial sector, which normally supplied the domestic market, was also badly disrupted by the general infrastructural collapse, chronic shortages of fuel and power, and destruction of communications. By early 1992 the Government claimed that 75% of the national power grid had been restored.

A major priority in the Government's six-month emergency reconstruction budget, announced on 2 May 1991, was the restoration of sufficient industrial production to ensure self-sufficiency in certain basic areas. Sectors that were identified for special attention included drug manufacturing, geological surveys and mining, phosphate, fertilizer and sulphur production, and electricity generation and transmission. Priority repairs were also to be undertaken to factories making electrical fittings, bricks, cigarettes and textiles. According to the minister responsible, the rebuilding of civilian industry would have priority over military production (which had traditionally absorbed a large, albeit undisclosed, proportion of resources); however, Western reports of urgent Iraqi moves to re-establish its armaments production capacity (to as much as 87% of the pre-war level by September 1992) cast doubt on this stated policy. Also in May 1991, the Government approved the replacement of Arab Investment Law No. 46 of 1988 by new rules that were designed to encourage greater Arab investment in the private and mixed industrial sectors by granting Arab nationals the right to implement industrial projects and offering them tax and other incentives. Moreover, in August 1991 Law 115 of 1982 was replaced by Law 25 of 1991, which aimed to accelerate industrial development in the private and mixed sectors through the provision of state assistance to selected projects. Strategic and export-oriented industries using local raw materials were to be targeted under the new policy, which specified that a project must involve the use of plant worth at least ID 100,000.

In April 1993 the Iraqi Minister of Labour stated that the prolonged UN embargo was causing many factories to close or to shed labour, with the result that 'for the first time in Iraqi's modern history we have registered a large number of unemployed people'. In September 1993 the Ministry of Industry and Minerals, which was responsible for thousands of state enterprises in areas other than oil production and arms manufacture, was authorized to incorporate these enterprises as limited companies and to offer up to 75% of their shares for sale on the Baghdad stock exchange. Companies which passed into majority private ownership would enjoy tax exemptions for 10 years. About 150m. shares in four of the largest companies—producing textiles, bricks and cement— were offered for sale later in the year, but the level of public indifference to this exercise was such that less than 1m. shares were taken up. In the case of a major cement company, the reported take-up was 40,000 shares, each priced at ID 125, out of 75m. shares offered.

COMMUNICATIONS

The communications sector was considered to be of major importance under the provisions of the 1981–85 Plan, and there was considerable activity in this sector during 1981. In May a consortium of British consultants was awarded a $129m. contract to design an extensive underground public transport system for Baghdad. It was believed to be the largest design contract ever awarded in Iraq, and the full cost of constructing the system was estimated to be up to $10,000m. The consortium, known as the British Metro Consultants Group, was to act as overall designers. Contracts for detailed designs for the various sections have so far been awarded to a German consortium of JV Dorsch, to the US company DeLeuw Cather International, to a Brazilian consortium, led by Promon Engenharia, and to Belgium's Transurb Consult; and the contract for soil investigation has been tendered. However, the project had already been reduced in priority before the 1991 hostilities rendered its future even more uncertain.

Another major project is construction of the new Baghdad international airport. In April 1979 a $900m. contract was awarded to two French companies—Spie Batignolles and Fourgerolle Construction—to build this airport for the State Organization for Roads and Bridges. The first stage has been completed and is used by Western European airlines and Iraqi Airways. In preparation for the substantial increase in traffic that the opening of the new airport is expected to bring, Iraqi Airways began expanding its fleet and network, acquiring two Boeing 747s and three 727s from the USA in 1981 at a cost of $183.6m. Passenger traffic was expected to rise by 10% per year, but was limited by regulations which permitted only night flights in and out of Baghdad airport. In 1989 Iraqi Airways carried 1,171,600 passengers, compared with 695,538 in 1988 and 525,948 in 1987. The airline normally flies to about 42 cities in Iraq and abroad.

A new international airport was built at Basra during the Iran–Iraq War by Federal German contractors and was opened in August 1988, after the cease-fire. The airport has a 4,000 m runway which will be capable of taking the biggest wide-bodied aircraft now available. Consultants have designed the country's third international airport, at Mosul, and a local airport at Arbil. The latter is intended to form part of a domestic network which will also include Amara, Kirkuk and Najaf. It was reported in mid-1990 that Airbus Industries had concluded the sale of five Airbus A310-300 aircraft to Iraq, but discussions concerning the financing of the sale were cancelled following the imposition of UN economic sanctions against Iraq. The two aircraft scheduled for delivery to Iraq in 1992 were allocated to other customers and no work was undertaken on the remainder of the contract.

Total freight carried by Iraqi Airways amounted to 31,539 tons in 1989, compared with 24,752 tons in 1988 and 16,833 tons in 1987. In 1990 plans were announced to establish a separate freight airline, Iraqi Airways Cargo.

Iraq's main port is at Basra but it was not able to operate during the Iran–Iraq War, and its future depends on there being a lasting political decision over the ownership and use of the Shatt al-Arab waterway. Before the war, two new ports were developed, at Umm Qasr and Khor az-Zubair. The latter is linked with Umm Qasr and the Gulf by a 40-km ship canal. Clandestine operations to clear this canal began before the end of the war with Iran, and after August 1988 extensive dredging operations were begun in order to clear navigation channels to both ports. Deep-water channels were certified free from hazards in early 1990, and the ports now have the capacity to handle general cargo, sulphur, petrochemicals, iron ore, grain, sugar and fertilizers. Dredging work on the ports' approach channels was continuing in early 1990, and, as soon as restrictions on shipping draught have been repealed, the ports should be able to handle about 6m. tons of cargo annually. A further 13 berths are to be constructed at Umm Qasr, at a projected cost of more than $500m. Just before the Iraqi invasion of Kuwait in August 1990, work commenced on the construction of two floating docks at Khor az-Zubair. The first cargo to be unloaded at Umm Qasr since 1990 was a food shipment in November 1993. In March 1994 the United Arab Emirates announced its intention to apply to the UN sanctions committee for permission to set up a direct shipping link with Umm Qasr to ferry in approved supplied from the UAE port of Jebel Ali.

River transport has been given increasing prominence. Dredging of several stretches of the Tigris between Baghdad and Basra has been completed, and navigation channels are being laid out. A French consultant, Sogreah, was appointed to study the navigation possibilities on the Euphrates between Haditha and Qurna, and Iraq has invited consultants to bid for a navigation development study of the Tigris as a whole— from Mosul to Basra. The artificial 'third river', completed in December 1992, is navigable by 5,000-ton cargo barges.

The Government sought to go ahead with plans to build some 2,400 km of railways between 1981 and 1985. The two major existing lines (between Baghdad and Basra, and from Baghdad north to Mosul and Tel Kotchek) will eventually be superseded by more modern, high-speed tracks. The cost of the Baghdad-to-Basra line, for which companies were reported in August 1990 to be preparing bids, has been estimated at $6,000m. The contract for the building of the first stage of the new Baghdad-Umm Qasr line has been delayed. Designs for the new line north from the capital to the Turkish border, via Mosul, Arbil and Kirkuk, have been completed by French consultants. A 273-km (170-mile) line between Kirkuk, Baiji and Haditha, built by South Korean firms, and the 550-km (342-mile) line from Baghdad to Husaibah, on the Syrian border, built by Construction Mendes of Brazil, were both opened in 1986. An Indian company has built the third and fourth stages of the Musayyib-Samarra line. All lines entering Baghdad will eventually be connected to the 112-km (70-mile) Baghdad loop line. Designs have been completed for the project, which involves the expansion of the capital's two main passenger stations, the development of a new freight terminal, and the building of three new bridges. Again, however, shortage of funds may enforce a scaling-down of the scheme.

Negotiations with Kuwait and Saudi Arabia over the establishment of rail links have taken place over a number of years. A working link and joint operation with Turkey may be developed first. The Government hopes eventually to link its rail system with Kuwait, Saudi Arabia and Turkey as part of a European-Gulf network.

Considerable emphasis is also being put on road construction. A 137-km section, from Tulaiha to Rutba, of the six-lane 1,200-km international Expressway Number One, was opened in August 1987. It is the main section in a project designed to create a road link between the Gulf states and the Mediterranean. The bulk of the project had been completed by 1989. In Baghdad, a South Korean company is working on the Abu Ghraib expressway, which will connect the capital with Expressway Number One.

A second expressway is intended to link Baghdad with the Turkish border via Samarra, Kirkuk, Arbil, Mosul, Dohuk and Zakho. Cowiconsult of Denmark has completed designs for the project, which will cost an estimated $6,000m. A six-lane highway, running from Safwan, on the Kuwaiti border, to

Baghdad, via Zubair and Nasiriya, was completed in 1987. Several urban expressways and bridges have been built in Baghdad, though further work on the capital's planned motorway network may be delayed for some years. A three-stage programme to build 10,000 km of rural roads is also being implemented.

Iraq has been modernizing its telecommunications system for some years and has introduced crossbar telephone switching, a telex system, a microwave link between major cities and an earth satellite connection for international communications. By 1985 more than 1m. lines had been added to the network. Iraq is also investigating the potential of fibre optics, and awarded a contract to a Japanese firm at the end of 1982. At the end of 1985 bids were invited for a 1,000-km cable to link Baghdad and Basra. The addition of a further 1m. telephone lines is also planned.

Iraq's communications infrastructure was a prime target of the multinational force's bombing campaign during the 1991 hostilities and suffered massive damage therefrom. According to an official UN report compiled in March 1991, all modern communications systems were destroyed, including the internal and external telephone networks, and heavy damage was inflicted on roads, railways and ports. Of 123 bridges hit by allied bombs, about one-third were totally destroyed, and in the war's immediate aftermath the only viable surface transport link to the outside world was through Amman (Jordan) to the port of Aqaba. In June the Government estimated the cost of repairing bridges and other installations that had been built by the Ministry of Housing and Construction at $1,450m. Repair of roads and bridges was given priority in the post-war reconstruction programme, it being claimed that 35 bridges had been repaired by the end of June 1991. By January 1992 the Government claimed that 99 bridges had been repaired, while the colossal damage to the telephone system (including the destruction of nearly half of the country's 900,000 telephone lines) was also being remedied. Completion of a new 190-metre telecommunications tower in Baghdad, to replace the tower destroyed in the 1991 war, was scheduled for November 1993. In January 1992 Iraqi Airways resumed regular commercial flights between Baghdad and Basra. However, around 37 Iraqi Airways aircraft, which were flown out of the country during the 1990/91 Gulf Crisis, remained abroad in mid-1994, their return to Iraq being prohibited by UN sanctions administrators.

FINANCE AND BANKING

Owing to Iraq's inability to export large quantities of petroleum during the early years of the Iran–Iraq War, the fall in petroleum prices, the heavy cost of the conflict (estimated at $600m.–$1,000m. per month at the beginning of 1986) and the additional burden of funding economic development, the country's official reserves of foreign exchange had declined to below $5,000m. by mid-1983. This was to be compared with the pre-war estimate of $35,000m. Little new information has become available since, and 1989 estimates were between zero and $2,000m. To minimize the continuing annual deficits on the current account of the balance of payments (an estimated $1,571m. in 1986), the Iraqi Government imposed stringent controls on foreign currency payments and imports. In the absence of Iraqi statistics, Western sources estimated, before the 1990/91 Gulf crisis, that the current account deficit would be about $1,500m. in 1990, declining to $200m. per year by 1992 and then going into increasing surplus in the mid-1990s. However, the combined effects of the UN embargo, the 'freezing' of Iraqi assets abroad, the physical destruction of the 1991 war and the post-war requirement on Iraq to pay reparations served to reduce Iraq's national finances to a state of total disarray (see Consequences of the 1990/91 Gulf Crisis, above).

In comparison with other Arab countries, Iraq has few banks and all are state-controlled, although in May 1991 the Government adopted an amendment to the banking laws, enabling the creation of private banks, provided that they undertook to operate under the supervision of the Central Bank. The Central Bank of Iraq, founded in 1947 as a successor to the National Bank of Iraq, was one of the first Arab monetary authorities.

For many years, the only commercial bank was Rafidain Bank, which was founded in 1941. Rafidain is the biggest Arab commercial bank in terms of deposits and gross assets. In 1986 its total assets reached ID 12,800m., up from ID 10,379m. in 1985; profits rose for the third successive year, to ID 348.3m. Rafidain has about 228 local branches and 10 branches abroad. Rafidain is also permitted to take part in the Arab and international markets for syndicated loans and bonds. It is a shareholder in several European-Arab consortia banks, such as the Paris-based Union de Banques Arabes et Françaises (UBAF), and development agencies. It is also one of the seven shareholders in Gulf International Bank, established in Bahrain in 1977 as a regional commercial bank. At the end of 1981, Rafidain established a joint venture bank with Banco do Brasil. Its capital was set at $17.5m.; each bank has an equal share. In 1987 Rafidain's capital was doubled to ID 100m. in the first stage of a programme to upgrade and expand the banking system. In May 1988 the Government announced that a second commercial bank, Rashid Bank, would be established, with capital of ID 100m., to compete with Rafidain Bank. Competition was also to be encouraged in the insurance sector. The three companies in this sector have all been absorbed into the Finance Ministry, as have the country's three specialist banks. The ministry is encouraging them to expand, and the banks are being given administrative and financial autonomy, bound only by the Government's fiscal policy.

The oldest specialized bank is the Agricultural Co-operative Bank, established in 1936, which provides medium- and long-term credits to farmers and agricultural development organizations. It has 47 local branches, including four in Baghdad. After 1981, when a record ID 186m. was loaned, lending levels fell as a consequence of the war. In 1987 the bank loaned a total of ID 25.4m., compared with ID 43.2m. in 1986. Total lending by the bank over the period 1980–87 amounted to ID 570m. There are two other specialized banks. The Industrial Bank, set up in 1940, has eight branches and provides short-, medium- and long-term loans to public and private industrial companies. Between 1980 and 1987 the bank extended ID 52m. in loans and credits. During 1987 total loans amounted to ID 1.5m., compared with ID 14.9m. in 1982. The bank holds shares worth $62.9m. in 14 mixed-sector joint-stock companies and has been instructed to become more involved in offering finance to both local and Arab investors, as private and mixed-sector companies are encouraged to play a wider role in the development of the economy. The bank is also administering a $28m. loan for the Kuwait-based Arab Fund for Economic and Social Development to assist in the development of light industry. The Real Estate Bank, founded in 1949, now has 27 branches providing credits for housing, construction and tourism. Because of the high demand for housing, the bank has expanded rapidly in recent years. Lending over the period 1980–87 totalled ID 2,770m., although annual levels have declined since the 1982 peak of ID 750.5m. In mid-1988 the bank's capital was raised by ID 50m., to ID 800m. to enable it to play a wider role in encouraging people to build their own houses. A government decree of June 1991 established a new state-owned Socialist Bank, with an initial capital of ID 500m., its principal stated role being to make interest-free loans to civil servants and decorated veterans of the war with Iran.

Iraq was also a major aid donor before the Iran–Iraq War, being the third biggest among Arab states, after Saudi Arabia and Kuwait. In 1979, according to OECD figures, its disbursements totalled $861.5m., representing about 3% of GNP. Most of this was channelled through the Iraqi Fund for External Development (IFED) which had a capital of $677m. In mid-1979 Iraq decided to compensate poorer customers for its oil for any future oil price increases by granting them long-term interest-free loans. Under this system, 12 developing countries (Bangladesh, India, Madagascar, Morocco, Mozambique, Pakistan, the Philippines, Senegal, Somalia, Sri Lanka, Tanzania and Viet Nam) received over $200m. in the second half of 1979. No further loans were extended; IFED is now concentrating on the implementation and management of existing loans.

Donations of aid had resumed by 1990, and in June Iraq announced that it would grant Jordan $50m. (for 1990) and the

PLO $25m. In September 1990 the Iraqi Government offered to supply free petroleum to developing countries, but this was widely seen as a public relations exercise, intended to undermine international support for the UN embargo that had been imposed on Iraq in the previous month because of its invasion of Kuwait.

An amendment to Law 64 of 1976, introduced in May 1991, authorized the operation of private banks and thus ended the state monopoly of banking dating from 1964. Applications were subsequently lodged by four prospective new banks, namely the Alitimad Bank, the Baghdad Bank, the Iraqi Commercial Bank and the Private Bank. The step was intended to encourage a wider private-sector role in the economy, in accordance with the Government's post-1989 liberalization policy. However, observers commented that the authorization of private banks was unlikely to affect the banking system substantially until the Central Bank relaxed its tight control of monetary policy. A stock exchange was established in Baghdad in March 1992.

Having acted as the Iraqi Government's main means of paying external debts before the country was isolated from the international financial system, Rafidain Bank was exposed to numerous claims from overseas creditors after 1990. However, a creditors' meeting held in London in April 1993 was informed by British liquidation experts that liquidation of Rafidain's international operations would yield only a minimal recovery, as these operations currently showed a net deficiency of funds totalling £5,560m. ($8,800m.).

UN Security Council resolution 778 of 2 October 1992 authorized the impounding of oil-related Iraqi assets (frozen in overseas accounts since August 1990) for the purpose of funding UN programmes connected with the Gulf crisis and its aftermath, including humanitarian relief operations, administration of war victims' compensation claims and inspection and destruction of Iraqi weapons. Assets so impounded were to be transferred to a UN escrow account in New York, disbursements from which would be refundable to Iraq if the Iraqi Government agreed to sell oil under UN supervision.

Notwithstanding an Iraqi Government threat to take legal action against foreign banks transferring funds to the escrow account, a total of $101.5m. had been so transferred by 30 April 1993. In response to a UN appeal for further transfers to meet ongoing programme costs, the US Government said that it was prepared to authorize the transfer of $200m. of the $637.4m. of impounded Iraqi assets within its jurisidiction, provided that transfers of US-based funds never exceeded 50% of total transfers. Among other overseas fund holders, the Bank of Tokyo said that assets totalling $44.88m. could not be transferred in view of third-party rights over them, while Tunisia indicated that $15.8m. in locally-held assets had been used to offset outstanding Iraqi debts to Tunisia.

The black-market value of the Iraqi dinar, already worth only a fraction of the official exchange rate of $1 = ID 0.31, was further depressed by the UN decision on external asset transfers. Punctuated by occasional extreme fluctuations (e.g. from $1 = ID 23 in February 1993 to $1 = ID 95 in April 1993), the underlying decline of the currency continued during the first half of 1993, taking the average market rate to around $1 = ID 65 during July.

In early May 1993 the Iraqi Government announced a six-day deadline for the exchange of old-style Swiss-printed 25-dinar notes for locally-printed equivalents, introduced after the 1990/91 Gulf crisis. The old-style notes were not exchangeable outside the country, and the border with Jordan, where speculators and currency traders held notes with an estimated market value of $200m., was closed during the exchange period. Within Iraq, this exercise highlighted the problematical status of the Kurdish-controlled area in the north, which was effectively deprived of the exchange facility yet unable to relinquish its formal currency link with Baghdad. It led to a marked rise in Kurdish use of the Turkish lira as a preferred medium of exchange within the safe haven, this arrangement being presented as a strictly practical (i.e. politically neutral) matter.

Western observers had difficulty in discerning a clear-cut economic motive for the May 1993 currency initiative. It was readily accepted in Iraqi government circles that the post-war reconstruction drive had been accompanied by rapid growth in the money supply, making price inflation and currency depreciation inevitable while the external position continued to deteriorate. Moreover, the Government had virtually institutionalized the unofficial currency trade by itself relying on the black market to supply part of its hard currency requirement (estimated at $90m. per month in the first half of 1993) to maintain the food rationing system.

The unofficial exchange rate fell below $1 = ID 100 for the first time on 26 October. The Government responded to this development by halting its own purchases of dollars on the black market. At the beginning of December, when the unofficial rate had fallen below $1 = ID 150, the Government authorized its ministries to deal in hard currency with the private sector. At the beginning of January 1994 Iraqis were permitted to deal legally in foreign exchange and to open foreign cash accounts in domestic banks, while 28 firms were licensed by the Central Bank to buy and sell foreign currency at rates determined by 'daily supply and demand'. On 5 February, after the unofficial exchange rate had fallen below $1 = ID 200, state banks were authorized to buy and sell hard currency outside the official rate of $1 = ID 0.31. As Iraq's chronic economic crisis intensified, the rate of currency depreciation accelerated, taking the unofficial rate per dollar to around 250 dinars in March, 300 dinars in April, 400 dinars in mid-May and 500 dinars by the beginning of June. The Central Bank, which had previously issued no currency notes above 25 dinars, announced the launch of a 50-dinar note in March and a 100-dinar note in May.

FOREIGN TRADE

Exports of petroleum have been, by far, Iraq's most important source of revenue, providing more than 95% of the country's earnings of foreign exchange. Receipts from these exports rose sharply in the mid- and late 1970s, partly because of higher production, but mainly because of the rise in prices. By 1979, Iraq's petroleum exports were earning three times as much as in 1974, and by 1980 these exports were worth $26,278m. However, owing to Iraq's inability to export sufficient petroleum, because of the war with Iran, and to the drop in prices, exports fell to $9,198m. in 1981. Revenues from oil exports were in the range $9,000m.–$11,000m. per year in 1982–85, and declined to an estimated $6,813m. in 1986. The higher oil prices recorded in the first half of 1987 were believed to have brought about a revival in the value of petroleum sales to more than $11,000m. in 1987, to about $13,000m. in 1988 and to about $12,000m. in 1989. While earnings declined in 1981 and 1982, Iraq continued to spend, importing goods worth more than $18,000m. in 1981 and $19,000m. in 1982, before imposing a sharp decrease in the level of imports, to about $12,000m. per year in 1983, 1984 and 1985. Imports were reduced to between $8,000m. and $9,000m. per year in 1986 and 1987 (though Western analysts estimate that they reached $9,700m. in 1987), and to $7,146m. in 1988. In 1989, according to Western calculations, total exports were worth $12,080m., while imports rose to $10,290m.

Most trade is normally with Western Europe, the USA and Japan, but Iraq also exports significant amounts of oil to Brazil, Yugoslavia, eastern Europe and Turkey. Trade with the USSR, until recently, consisted mainly of Soviet military supplies. Among Western countries, France has been one of Iraq's most important trading partners. It is estimated that, after the outbreak of war with Iran, Iraq bought more than $5,500m. worth of French armaments in the 1980s, while French contractors won orders worth more than $4,500m.

Although several countries experienced a decline in exports to Iraq during the second half of the 1980s, imports from Western countries generally rose during 1988 and 1989. The value of Japanese exports rose to $406m. in 1988 and to $490m. in 1989, compared with $391m. in 1987. French exports were worth $445m. in 1988 and $478m. in 1989, compared with $391m. in 1987, while the value of the UK's exports rose from $445m. in 1987 to $720m. per year in both 1988 and 1989. The value of Federal German exports rose from $457m. in 1987 to $884m. in 1988 and to $1,168m. in

1989. The value of imports from Italy declined to $174m. in 1988, compared with $225m. in 1987, but rose to $372m. in 1989, while that of imports from Brazil fell to $228m. in 1988, compared with $305m. in 1987. The value of imports from the USSR declined from $511m. in 1987 to $509m. in 1988 and to $405m. in 1989. In 1988 the USA supplanted Turkey as Iraq's leading trading partner, exporting $1,156m. worth of goods (mainly agricultural products), compared with $683m. in 1987. US exports to Iraq were valued at $1,173m. in 1989. Like the UK, the USA extended a credit line to Iraq in 1988 in order to guarantee the volume of its exports. The value of Turkish exports to Iraq increased from $945m. in 1987 to $986m. in 1988, but fell to $445m. in 1989.

The value of Iraq's exports to the USA, at $2,408m., more than quadrupled in 1989, compared with 1987, as a result of Iraq's decision to market its crude petroleum more attractively in the USA. Another leading importer of Iraqi petroleum was the USSR, the value of whose total imports from Iraq rose from $1,243m. in 1987 to $1,585m. in 1988, but declined to $1,549m. in 1989. The value of Turkish imports from Iraq was $1,650m. in 1989, compared with $1,154m. in 1987, while the value of Italian imports declined from $1,214m. in 1987 to $996m. in 1988 and to $674m. in 1989.

In the first half of 1990 there were increased efforts by Iraq's trading partners to prevent exports of industrial goods which might possibly serve as components for missiles and atomic weapons. In March 1990 the UK and the USA claimed to have frustrated Iraqi attempts to import nuclear detonators, and in April two UK companies were prevented from exporting to Iraq steel cylinders which were later proved to be components for a planned supergun. The USA has also claimed that Iraq planned to use loans made improperly by the Atlanta (USA) branch of Italy's Banca Nazionale del Lavoro to acquire military technology.

The imposition of the UN trade embargo on Iraq in August 1990 and the subsequent Gulf hostilities brought about the total disruption of Iraq's external trade, subsequently prolonged by disagreements between the Iraqi Government and UN sanctions administrators (see Consequences of the 1990/91 Gulf Crisis, above). The IMF estimated the value of Iraq's total imports in 1992 as ID 78.2m., compared with ID 118.9m. in 1991 and ID 2,042.4m. in 1990. The estimated 1992 total was equivalent to about $250m. at the official exchange rate, but only a fraction of this at prevailing black-market rates.

DEVELOPMENT AND PLANNING

At the beginning of the 1980s Iraq did not need to seek external loans, economic development having been funded mainly from the State's petroleum revenues. The sustained rise in petroleum prices gave Iraq a major opportunity to increase its development spending. Despite the heavy costs incurred by the war with Iran, the 1982 expenditure programme allocated an estimated ID 7,000m. to the ordinary budget and ID 7,000m. to investment spending. The import programme was allocated ID 5,000m. Iraq was unable to maintain the early momentum of its development programme, however, in the face of falling petroleum revenues and the heavy cost of the Iran–Iraq war. No detailed budget figures were disclosed from 1982 to 1989, and the 1981–85 Development Plan had to be abandoned,

although longer-term plans were published for specific sectors.

In the Government's published budget for 1990, expenditure was forecast at ID 24,400m. The new 'consolidated general budget' reportedly projected a deficit of ID 6,600m., compared with a deficit of ID 7,200m. in 1989. The budget proposals also incorporated a total investment allocation of ID 5,600m., of which industry was to receive ID 2,965m. Because of the Gulf crisis, no details were disclosed of the 1991 budget until it was substantially revised to take account of damage sustained in the hostilities. A six-month emergency reconstruction budget, announced on 2 May 1991, reduced planned expenditure in the general consolidated budget to ID 13,876m. (from the original total of ID 14,596m.) and cut the investment budget to ID 1,660m. (from ID 2,340m.). It was stated that non-essential development projects had been postponed until 1992, and available resources diverted to the reconstruction effort. Nevertheless, over the five-year period 1991–95, it was envisaged that ID 28,700m. ($92,580m.) would be spent on development projects, of which the foreign currency component would be some $56,000m.

In the 1980s Iraq attracted substantial foreign investment for its development projects, notably from West European countries, Japan and the USSR. In 1984 the USSR pledged $2,000m. in long-term credits for Iraq, which also obtained lines of credit or other credit facilities from the UK, the USA and the Federal Republic of Germany (the latter two agreeing in 1987–88 to restore export credit guarantees which had earlier been withdrawn when Iraq defaulted on debt repayments). Nevertheless, as a result of persistent repayment problems, much of the credit—and the goodwill—had again ceased by the end of the decade, despite the conclusion of various inter-governmental refinancing agreements. By mid-1990 the claims of BIS-reporting banks on Iraq were calculated as totalling $7,690m. worldwide, while national credit guarantee agencies with major exposure to outstanding Iraqi debts were headed by Coface of France (some $3,200m.) and included those of Japan and Italy (each some $3,000m.) and of Germany ($2,000m.).

On a multilateral basis, loans worth more than $250m. were agreed with the Islamic Development Bank to fund imports and hospital work. The Arab Monetary Fund also loaned money ($523m. between 1983 and mid-1989) to support Iraq's balance of payments. Loans to support a coldstore project, telecommunications, an earthquake warning system, agricultural and industrial development and the upgrading and extension of power generation units were made by the Kuwait-based Arab Fund for Economic and Social Development. Iraq secured two Euroloans of $500m., in 1983 and 1985, to finance foreign trade and development projects, but was forced to reschedule payments due on them, owing to a shortage of foreign exchange.

Against this background, there was considerable doubt regarding continued foreign investment in Iraqi development projects even before the onset of the Gulf crisis in August 1990 brought about the suspension of virtually all such co-operation and of Iraqi repayments on outstanding debts. In September 1990 Iraq's total foreign debt was estimated at $65,000m., a total which the Iraqi Government itself appeared to revise upwards in a post-war submission to the UN in April 1991 (see Consequences of the 1990–91 Gulf Crisis, above).

Statistical Survey

Source (unless otherwise indicated): Central Statistical Organization, Ministry of Planning, Karradat Mariam, ash-Shawaf Sq., Baghdad; tel. 537-0071; telex 212218.

Area and Population

AREA, POPULATION AND DENSITY*

Area (sq km)	438,317†
Population (census results)‡	
17 October 1977	12,000,497
17 October 1987	
Males	8,395,889
Females	7,939,310
Total	16,335,199
Population (official estimate at mid-year)†	
1991	17,903,000
Density (per sq km) at mid-1991	40.8

* No account has been taken of the reduction in the area of Iraq as a result of the adjustment to the border with Kuwait that came into force on 15 January 1993.

† 169,235 sq miles. This figure includes 924 sq km (357 sq miles) of territorial waters but excludes the Neutral Zone, of which Iraq's share is 3,522 sq km (1,360 sq miles). The Zone lies between Iraq and Saudi Arabia, and is administered jointly by the two countries. Nomads move freely through it but there are no permanent inhabitants.

‡ Figures exclude Iraqis abroad, estimated at 129,000 in 1977.

GOVERNORATES (estimated population at October 1986)

	Area* (sq km)	Population† ('000)	Density (per sq km)
Nineveh	37,698	1,393	37.0
Salah ad-Din	29,004	454	15.7
At-Ta'meem	10,391	674	64.9
Diala	19,292	706	36.6
Baghdad	5,159	4,868	943.6
Al-Anbar	137,723	598	4.3
Babylon	5,258	759	144.4
Karbala	5,034	337	66.9
An-Najaf	27,844	484	17.4
Al-Qadisiya	8,507	524	61.6
Al-Muthanna	51,029	259	5.1
Thi-Qar	13,626	741	54.4
Wasit	17,308	494	28.5
Maysan	14,103	417	29.6
Basrah (Basra)	19,070	1,346	70.6
Autonomous Regions:			
D'hok	6,120	343	56.0
Arbil	14,471	774	53.5
As-Sulaimaniya . . .	15,756	939	59.6
Total	437,393	16,110	36.8

* Excluding territorial waters (924 sq km).
† Not adjusted to take account of the 1987 census results.

Population (at census of 17 October 1987): 1,507,926 in Nineveh governorate; 1,108,773 in Babylon governorate; more than 750,000 in each of five other governorates (Diala, al-Anbar, Thi-Qar, Basrah and as-Sulaimaniya).

PRINCIPAL TOWNS (population at 1977 census)

Baghdad (capital) .	3,236,000*		Mosul	1,220,000
Basrah (Basra) .	1,540,000		Kirkuk . . .	535,000

* The population of Baghdad at the 17 October 1987 census was 3,844,608.

BIRTHS AND DEATHS (UN estimates, annual averages)

	1975–80	1980–85	1985–90
Birth rate (per 1,000) . .	41.9	41.0	40.3
Death rate (per 1,000). . .	8.8	8.4	7.2

Expectation of Life (UN estimates, years at birth, 1985-90): 64.9 (males 63.5; females 66.5).

Source: UN, *World Population Prospects: The 1992 Revision.*

1989: Registered live births 641,791 (birth rate 36.8 per 1,000); Registered deaths 92,255 (death rate 5.3 per 1,000). Note: Registration is incomplete.

ECONOMICALLY ACTIVE POPULATION*
(persons aged 7 years and over, 1987 census)

	Males	Females	Total
Agriculture, forestry and fishing	422,265	70,741	493,006
Mining and quarrying . .	40,439	4,698	45,137
Manufacturing. . . .	228,242	38,719	266,961
Electricity, gas and water . .	31,786	4,450	36,236
Construction	332,645	8,541	341,186
Trade, restaurants and hotels .	191,116	24,489	215,605
Transport, storage and communications . . .	212,116	12,155	224,271
Financing, insurance, real estate and business services.	16,204	10,811	27,015
Community, social and personal services . .	1,721,748	233,068	1,954,816
Activities not adequately defined	146,616	18,232	167,848
Total labour force . . .	3,346,177	425,904	3,772,081

* Figures exclude persons seeking work for the first time, totalling 184,264 (males 149,938, females 34,326), but include other unemployed persons.

Source: ILO, *Year Book of Labour Statistics.*

Agriculture

PRINCIPAL CROPS ('000 metric tons)

	1990	1991	1992
Wheat	1,196	1,476	600*
Rice (paddy)	229	189	150†
Barley	1,854	768	400*
Maize	172	297	100†
Potatoes	195	167	195†
Dry broad beans . . .	8	16	12*
Sunflower seed . . .	59	21	25*
Sesame seed . . .	14	13	14†
Cabbages	19	8	21†
Tomatoes	722	438	480†
Pumpkins, etc.. . . .	72	59	60*
Cucumbers. . . .	362	298	320*
Aubergines	144	127	145†
Green peppers . . .	38	22	30*
Onions (dry)	119	44	50†
Carrots	13	9	10*
Watermelons . . .	561	394	450†
Melons.	312	122	175†
Grapes†	455	460	470
Dates	545	566	580*
Sugar cane. . . .	71	12*	13*
Apples.	75†	65*	75*
Peaches and nectarines* .	29	24	27
Plums*.	35	27	30
Oranges†	176	180	185
Tangerines, etc.* . . .	79	70	60
Apricots*	33	25	30
Tobacco (leaves) . . .	4	1	3*
Cotton seed*	12	5	9
Cotton (lint)*	6	2	5

* FAO estimate(s).   † Unofficial figure(s).

Source: FAO, *Production Yearbook.*

LIVESTOCK (FAO estimates, '000 head, year ending September)

	1990	1991	1992
Horses	60	18	40
Mules	27	10	22
Asses	416	150	355
Cattle	1,675	1,150	1,400
Buffaloes	148	110	130
Camels.	59	10	10
Sheep	9,600	7,800	9,000
Goats	1,650	1,350	1,500

Poultry (FAO estimates, million): 75 in 1990; 15 in 1991; 35 in 1992.
Source: FAO, *Production Yearbook.*

LIVESTOCK PRODUCTS ('000 metric tons)

	1990	1991	1992
Beef and veal*	42	32	38
Buffalo meat*	2	2	2
Mutton and lamb* . . .	19	14	17
Goats' meat*	8	7	8
Poultry meat	192	17	60*
Cows' milk. . . .	297†	235†	278*
Buffalo milk*	27	22	24
Sheep's milk*	175	140	160
Goats' milk*	77	62	69
Cheese*	34.4	27.0	31.5
Butter*	8.0	6.4	7.4
Hen eggs*	81.6	20.0	45.0
Wool:			
greasy	22.8†	20.3†	18.0*
clean	12.5	11.1	9.0*
Cattle and buffalo hides* .	6.0	4.5	5.5
Sheep skins*	3.5	2.7	3.2
Goat skins* . . .	1.7	1.4	1.7

* FAO estimate(s).   † Unofficial figure(s).

Source: FAO, *Production Yearbook.*

Forestry

ROUNDWOOD REMOVALS
(FAO estimates, '000 cubic metres, excluding bark)

	1990	1991	1992
Sawlogs, veneer logs and logs for sleepers	20	20	20
Other industrial wood . .	30	30	30
Fuel wood	99	99	105
Total	149	149	155

Sawnwood production ('000 cubic metres, incl. railway sleepers): 8 per year (FAO estimates) in 1988–92.

Source: FAO, *Yearbook of Forest Products.*

Fishing

(FAO estimates, '000 metric tons, live weight)

	1989	1990	1991
Inland waters	13.2	10.5	9.0
Indian Ocean	5.0	3.5	3.0
Total catch	18.2	14.0	12.0

Source: FAO, *Yearbook of Fishery Statistics.*

Mining

('000 metric tons, unless otherwise indicated)

	1989	1990	1991
Crude petroleum . . .	136,603	100,638	13,365
Natural gas (petajoules) . .	191	110	46
Native sulphur* . . .	900	800	400

* Estimates by the US Bureau of Mines.
Source: UN, *Industrial Statistics Yearbook.*

Industry

SELECTED PRODUCTS
('000 metric tons, unless otherwise indicated)

	1989	1990	1991
Cigarettes (million) . . .	27,000	26,000	13,000
Cement	12,500	13,000	5,000*
Liquefied petroleum gas*† . .	1,428	1,110	170
Naphtha	700	600	450
Motor spirit (petrol) . . .	2,600	2,500	1,600
Kerosene	790	600	560
Jet fuel	500	410	250
Distillate fuel oils . . .	5,700	5,100	4,500
Residual fuel oils . . .	8,200	7,200	5,000
Lubricating oils	200	180	175
Paraffin wax*	90	70	10
Petroleum bitumen (asphalt) .	460	450	350
Electric energy (million kWh) .	28,900	29,160	20,810

* Estimated production.
† Includes estimated production ('000 metric tons) from natural gas plants: 1,128 in 1989; 900 in 1990; 0 in 1991; and from petroleum refineries: 300 in 1989; 210 in 1990; 170 in 1991.

Footwear (excluding rubber): 4,600,000 pairs in 1989; 4,400,000 pairs in 1990.

Source: UN, *Industrial Statistics Yearbook.*

Finance

CURRENCY AND EXCHANGE RATES

Monetary Units

1,000 fils = 20 dirhams = 1 Iraqi dinar (ID).

Sterling and Dollar Equivalents (31 May 1994)

£1 sterling = 469.95 fils;

US $1 = 310.86 fils;

100 Iraqi dinars = £212.79 = $321.69.

Exchange Rate

From February 1973 to October 1982 the Iraqi dinar was valued at US $3.3862. Since October 1982 it has been valued at $3.2169. The dinar's average value in 1982 was $3.3513. The aforementioned data refer to the official exchange rate. There is, in addition, a special rate for exports and also a free-market rate.

BUDGET ESTIMATES (ID million)

Revenue	1981	1982
Ordinary	5,025.0	8,740.0
Economic development plan . . .	6,742.8	7,700.0
Autonomous government agencies. . .	7,667.8	n.a.
Total	19,434.9	n.a.

Petroleum revenues (estimates, US $ million): 9,198 in 1981; 10,250 in 1982; 9,650 in 1983; 10,000 in 1984; 11,900 in 1985; 6,813 in 1986; 11,300 in 1987.

Expenditure	1981	1982
Ordinary	5,025.0	8,740.0
Economic development plan . . .	6,742.0	7,700.0
Autonomous government agencies. . .	7,982.4	n.a.
Total	19,750.2	n.a.

1991 (ID million): General consolidated state budget expenditure 13,876; Investment budget expenditure 1,660.

CENTRAL BANK RESERVES

(US $ million at 31 December)

	1975	1976	1977
Gold	168.0	166.7	176.1
IMF special drawing rights .	26.9	32.5	41.5
Reserve position in IMF . .	31.9	31.7	33.4
Foreign exchange . . .	2,500.5	4,369.8	6,744.7
Total	2,727.3	4,600.7	6,995.7

IMF special drawing rights (US $ million at 31 December): 132.3 in 1981; 81.9 in 1982; 9.0 in 1983; 0.1 in 1984; 7.2 in 1987.

Reserve position in IMF (US $ million at 31 December): 130.3 in 1981; 123.5 in 1982.

Note: No figures for gold or foreign exchange have been available since 1977.

Source: IMF, *International Financial Statistics*.

COST OF LIVING

(Consumer Price Index; base: 1988 = 100)

	1990	1991*
Food	176.0	640.4
Fuel and light	108.9	147.5
Clothing	157.1	394.4
Rent	108.4	116.0
All items (incl. others) . . .	161.2	461.9

* May to December only.

Source: ILO, *Year Book of Labour Statistics*.

NATIONAL ACCOUNTS (ID million at current prices)

National Income and Product

	1987	1988	1989
Compensation of employees .	5,697.0	6,300.9	5,604.2
Operating surplus*. . .	10,319.0	11,382.4	12,364.0
Domestic factor incomes. .	16,016.0	17,683.3	17,968.2
Consumption of fixed capital .	1,584.0	1,748.9	1,777.1
Gross domestic product (GDP) at factor cost . .	17,600.0	19,432.2	19,745.3
Indirect taxes	708.2	1,019.6	692.2
Less Subsidies	407.6	419.3	427.7
GDP in purchasers' values .	17,900.6	20,032.5	20,009.8
Factor income received from abroad	23.7	40.8	37.6
Less Factor income paid abroad	728.4	741.2	715.8
Gross national product . .	17,195.9	19,332.1	19,331.6
Less Consumption of fixed capital	1,584.0	1,748.9	1,777.1
National income in market prices	15,611.9	17,583.2	17,554.5
Net current transfers from abroad	−84.0	−18.7	−149.3
National disposable income .	15,527.9	17,564.5	17,405.2

* Obtained as a residual.

Source: UN, *National Accounts Statistics*.

Expenditure on the Gross Domestic Product

	1987	1988	1989
Government final consumption expenditure	5,673.8	6,260.0	6,578.7
Private final consumption expenditure	9,204.4	10,101.4	11,232.4
Increase in stocks . . .	−124.1	−118.3	−4,123.9
Gross fixed capital formation .	3,657.8	4,396.6	5,735.8
Total domestic expenditure .	18,411.9	20,639.7	19,423.0
Exports of goods and services .	4,087.1	3,825.7	5,342.7
Less Imports of goods and services	4,598.4	4,432.9	4,755.9
GDP in purchasers' values .	17,900.6	20,032.5	20,009.8

Source: UN, *National Accounts Statistics*.

Gross Domestic Product by Economic Activity (at factor cost)

	1987	1988	1989*
Agriculture, hunting, forestry and fishing . . .	2,518.7	2,834.3	3,358.1
Mining and quarrying . . .	3,594.8	3,639.0	4,712.8
Manufacturing. . . .	2,071.1	2,641.0	2,288.4
Electricity, gas and water† .	298.5	325.7	382.0
Construction	1,430.8	1,527.9	1,519.9
Trade, restaurants and hotels†	2,182.7	2,524.2	2,368.6
Transport, storage and communications . . .	1,269.7	1,295.1	1,411.1
Finance, insurance and real estate‡	1,788.6	1,981.0	1,961.0
Government services . . .	3,228.0	3,557.2	2,529.6
Other services	200.4	230.2	279.3
Sub-total	18,583.3	20,555.6	20,810.8
Less Imputed bank service charge	983.3	1,123.4	1,065.4
Total	17,600.0	19,432.2	19,745.4
GDP at constant 1975 prices .	6,912.7	7,123.7	6,611.5

* Figures are provisional.

† Gas distribution is included in trade.

‡ Including imputed rents of owner-occupied dwellings.

Source: UN, *National Accounts Statistics*.

External Trade

PRINCIPAL COMMODITIES (ID million)

Imports c.i.f.	1976	1977*	1978
Food and live animals . .	159.6	154.0	134.5
Cereals and cereal preparations	70.0	79.9	74.9
Sugar, sugar preparations and honey	37.2	24.1	10.2
Crude materials (inedible) except fuels . . .	33.7	20.5	25.1
Chemicals	58.5	47.4	58.7
Basic manufactures . .	293.3	236.7	285.2
Textile yarn, fabrics, etc. . .	44.3	69.4	72.7
Iron and steel	127.5	44.3	73.2
Machinery and transport equipment . . .	557.4	625.8	667.4
Non-electric machinery . .	285.4	352.5	368.1
Electrical machinery, apparatus, etc. . . .	106.9	120.2	160.5
Transport equipment . . .	165.2	153.1	138.8
Miscellaneous manufactured articles	33.2	49.4	51.7
Total (incl. others) . . .	1,150.9	1,151.3	1,244.1

* Figures are provisional. Revised total is ID 1,323.2 million.

Total imports (official estimates, ID million): 1,738.9 in 1979; 2,208.1 in 1980; 2,333.8 in 1981.
Total imports (IMF estimates, ID million): 6,013.0 in 1981; 6,309.0 in 1982; 3,086.2 in 1983; 3,032.4 in 1984; 3,222.8 in 1985; 2,714.3 in 1986; 2,241.2 in 1987; 2,867.2 in 1988; 3,059.2 in 1989; 2,022.6 in 1990; 132.6 in 1991; 201.1 in 1992 (Source: IMF, *International Financial Statistics*).

Total exports (ID million): 5,614.6 (crude petroleum 5,571.9) in 1977; 6,422.7 (crude petroleum 6,360.5) in 1978; 12,522.0 (crude petroleum 12,480.0) in 1979.

Exports of crude petroleum (estimates, ID million): 15,321.3 in 1980; 6,089.6 in 1981; 5,982.4 in 1982; 5,954.8 in 1983; 6,937.0 in 1984; 8,142.5 in 1985; 5,126.2 in 1986; 6,988.9 in 1987; 7,245.8 in 1988.

Source: IMF, *International Financial Statistics*.

PRINCIPAL TRADING PARTNERS (ID million)

Imports	1983	1984	1985
Australia	10.7	35.2	45.7
Austria	33.7	49.0	53.3
Brazil	32.7	67.0	118.9
China, People's Republic . .	22.1	11.5	40.5
France	118.7	117.1	112.5
Germany, Fed. Republic . .	323.6	236.3	211.0
Italy	162.9	116.5	128.2
Japan	369.4	258.3	352.1
Jordan	18.0	50.2	34.2
Korea, Republic . . .	54.1	39.5	68.8
Malaysia	35.0	16.9	49.9
Netherlands	42.7	57.9	37.2
Sweden	52.0	37.7	46.2
Switzerland	55.2	26.8	36.5
Turkey	101.7	218.6	259.2
United Kingdom . . .	118.6	118.2	109.8
USA	45.1	153.6	126.0
Yugoslavia	40.8	50.8	71.0
Total (incl. others) . . .	2,062.8	2,080.7	2,266.0

Exports (excl. petroleum)	1983	1984	1985
China, People's Repub. .	—	—	0.9
Hong Kong	—	—	0.7
India	1.7	0.8	0.6
Japan	—	0.3	0.5
Jordan	3.4	2.1	6.8
Kuwait	5.3	4.0	2.0
Saudi Arabia	1.0	0.7	0.5
Turkey	8.2	16.5	21.8
United Arab Emirates . .	2.5	0.4	2.3
United Kingdom . . .	0.9	0.5	0.8
Total (incl. others) . .	81.8	82.7	46.9

Note: Since 1975 no official figures have been available for the destination of petroleum exports.

Transport

RAILWAYS (traffic)

	1987	1988	1989
Passenger-km (million) . .	1,150	1,570	1,643
Freight ton-km (million) . .	1,584	2,079	2,678

ROAD TRAFFIC (motor vehicles in use at 31 December)

	1987	1988	1989
Passenger cars	573,990	630,319	672,205
Buses and coaches . . .	50,877	43,005	47,200
Goods vehicles*	117,630	117,100	128,550

* Including vans.
Source: International Road Federation, *World Road Statistics*.

CIVIL AVIATION (revenue traffic on scheduled services)

	1989	1990	1991
Kilometres flown (million) . .	20	12	—
Passengers carried ('000) . .	1,161	702	28
Passenger-km (million) . .	2,269	1,370	17
Freight ton-km (million) . .	73	43	—

Source: UN, *Statistical Yearbook*.

Tourism

FOREIGN VISITORS BY ORIGIN ('000)

	1988	1989	1990
Africa	—	340	96
North and South America . .	5	10	7
Europe	94	85	55
East and South-East Asia and Oceania	4	11	11
Southern Asia	11	46	33
Western Asia	109	473	512
Total	224	966	714

Source: UN, *Statistical Yearbook*.

Communications Media

	1989	1990	1991
Radio receivers ('000 in use) .	3,700	3,880	4,020
Television receivers ('000 in use)	1,250	1,300	1,350
Daily newspapers . . .	n.a.	6	n.a.

Non-daily newspapers: 12 in 1988.

Source: UNESCO, *Statistical Yearbook.*

Telephones ('000 in use): 886 in 1985 (Source: UN, *Statistical Yearbook*).

Education

	Teachers		Pupils/Students	
	1988	1990*	1988	1990*
Pre-primary . .	4,654	4,908	85,096	86,508
Primary . . .	130,777	134,081	3,023,132	3,328,212
Secondary:				
General . .	42,829	44,772	981,409	1,023,710
Teacher training . .	1,367	n.a.	25,172	n.a.
Vocational . .	9,741	n.a.	160,278	n.a.
Higher . . .	11,072	n.a.	209,818	n.a.

* Figures for 1989 are unavailable.

Schools: Pre-primary: 614 in 1988; 646 in 1990. Primary: 8,052 in 1988; 8,917 in 1990.

Source: UNESCO, *Statistical Yearbook.*

Directory

The Constitution

The following are the principal features of the Provisional Constitution, issued on 22 September 1968:

The Iraqi Republic is a popular democratic and sovereign state. Islam is the state religion.

The political economy of the State is founded on socialism.

The State will protect liberty of religion, freedom of speech and opinion. Public meetings are permitted under the law. All discrimination based on race, religion or language is forbidden. There shall be freedom of the Press, and the right to form societies and trade unions in conformity with the law is guaranteed.

The Iraqi people is composed of two main nationalities: Arabs and Kurds. The Constitution confirms the nationalistic rights of the Kurdish people and the legitimate rights of all other minorities within the framework of Iraqi unity.

The highest authority in the country is the Council of Command of the Revolution (or Revolutionary Command Council—RCC), which will promulgate laws until the election of a National Assembly. The Council exercises its prerogatives and powers by a two-thirds majority.

Two amendments to the Constitution were announced in November 1969. The President, already Chief of State and Head of the Government, also became the official Supreme Commander of the Armed Forces and President of the RCC. Membership of the latter body was to increase from five to a larger number at the President's discretion.

Earlier, a Presidential decree replaced the 14 local government districts by 16 governorates, each headed by a governor with wide powers. In April 1976 Tekrit (Saladin) and Karbala became separate governorates, bringing the number of governorates to 18, although three of these are designated Autonomous Regions.

The 15-article statement which aimed to end the Kurdish war was issued on 11 March 1970. In accordance with this statement, a form of autonomy was offered to the Kurds in March 1974, but some of the Kurds rejected the offer and fresh fighting broke out. The new Provisional Constitution was announced in July 1970. Two amendments were introduced in 1973 and 1974, the 1974 amendment stating that 'the area whose majority of population is Kurdish shall enjoy autonomy in accordance with what is defined by the Law'.

The President and Vice-President are elected by a two-thirds majority of the Council. The President, Vice-President and members of the Council will be responsible to the Council. Vice-Presidents and Ministers will be responsible to the President.

Details of a new, permanent Constitution were announced in March 1989. The principal innovations proposed in the permanent Constitution, which was approved by the National Assembly in July 1990, were the abolition of the RCC, following a presidential election, and the assumption of its duties by a 50-member Consultative Assembly and the existing National Assembly; and the incorporation of the freedom to form political parties. The new, permanent Constitution is to be submitted to a popular referendum for approval.

In July 1973 President Bakr announced a National Charter as a first step towards establishing the Progressive National Front. A National Assembly and People's Councils are features of the Charter. A law to create a 250-member National Assembly and a 50-member Kurdish Legislative Council was adopted on 16 March 1980, and the two Assemblies were elected in June and September 1980 respectively.

The Government

HEAD OF STATE

President: SADDAM HUSSAIN (assumed power 16 July 1979).

Vice-Presidents: TAHA YASSIN RAMADAN, TAHA MOHI ED-DIN MARUF.

REVOLUTIONARY COMMAND COUNCIL

Chairman: SADDAM HUSSAIN.

Vice-Chairman: IZZAT IBRAHIM.

Other Members:

TAHA YASSIN RAMADAN	MUHAMMAD HAMZAH AZ-ZUBAYDI
TAREQ AZIZ	
Gen. ALI HASSAN AL-MAJID	TAHA MOHI ED-DIN MARUF
	SA'ADOUN HAMMADI MAZBAN KHADR HADI

COUNCIL OF MINISTERS
(September 1994)

Prime Minister: SADDAM HUSSAIN.

Deputy Prime Ministers: TAREQ AZIZ, TAHA YASSIN RAMADAN, MUHAMMAD HAMZAH AZ-ZUBAYDI.

Minister of the Interior: WATBAN IBRAHIM AL-HASSAN.

Minister of Defence: Gen. ALI HASSAN AL-MAJID.

Minister of Foreign Affairs: MUHAMMAD SAEED AS-SAHAF.

Minister of Finance: AHMAD HUSSEIN KHUDAYER.

Minister of Culture and Information: HAMAD YOUSSEF HAMMADI.

Minister of Justice: SHABIB AL-MALKI.

Minister of Irrigation and Acting Minister of Agriculture: NIZAR JUMAH ALI AL-QASIR.

Minister of Industry and Minerals: HUSSEIN KAMEL.

Minister of Oil: SAFA HADI JAWAD.

Minister of Education: HIKMAT ABDULLAH AL-BAZZAZ.

Minister of Health: UMEED MADHAT MUBARAK.

Minister of Labour and Social Affairs: LATIF NUSAYYIF JASIM.

Minister of Planning: SAMAL MAJID FARAJ.

Minister of Higher Education and Scientific Research: HUMAM ABD AL-KHALIQ ABD AL-GHAFUR.

Minister of Housing and Construction: MAHMOUD DIYAB AL-AHMAD.

Minister of Transport and Communications: Dr AHMAD MURTADA AHMAD KHALIL.

Minister of Awqaf (Religious Endowments) and Religious Affairs: Dr ABD AL-MUNIM AHMAD SALIH.

Minister of Trade: MUHAMMAD MAHDI SALIH.

Minister of State for Military Affairs: Gen. ABD AL-JABBAR KHALIL ASH-SHANSHAL.

Ministers of State: ARSHAD MUHAMMAD AHMAD MUHAMMAD AZ-ZIBARI, ABD AL-WAHHAB UMAR MIRZA AL-ATRUSHI.

Presidential Advisers: ABD AS-SATTAR AHMAD AL-MAINI, ABD AL-WAHHAB ABDULLAH AS-SABBAGH, ABDULLAH FADEL-ABBAS, AMER HAMMADI AS-SAADI.

MINISTRIES*

Office of the President: Presidential Palace, Karradat Mariam, Baghdad.

Ministry of Agriculture and Irrigation: Khulafa St, Khullani Sq., Baghdad; tel. 887-3251; telex 212222.

Ministry of Awqaf (Religious Endowments) and Religious Affairs: North Gate, St opposite College of Engineering, Baghdad; tel. 888-9561; telex 212785.

Ministry of Culture and Information: Nr an-Nusoor Sq., fmrly Qasr as-Salaam Bldg, Baghdad; tel. 551-4333; telex 212800.

Ministry of Defence: North Gate, Baghdad; tel. 888-9071; telex 212202.

Ministry of Education: POB 258, Baghdad; tel. 886-0000; telex 2259.

Ministry of Finance: Khulafa St, Nr ar-Russafi Sq., Baghdad; tel. 887-4871; telex 212459.

Ministry of Foreign Affairs: Opposite State Org. for Roads and Bridges, Karradat Mariam, Baghdad; tel. 537-0091; telex 212201.

Ministry of Health, Labour and Social Affairs: Khulafa St, Khullani Sq., Baghdad; tel. 887-1881; telex 212621.

Ministry of Industry and Minerals: Nidhal St, Nr Sa'adoun Petrol Station, Baghdad; tel. 887-2006; telex 212205.

Ministry of Local Government: Karradat Mariam, Baghdad; tel. 537-0031; telex 212568.

Ministry of Oil: POB 6178, al-Mansour, Baghdad; tel. 443-0749; telex 212216.

Ministry of Planning: Karradat Mariam, ash-Shawaf Sq., Baghdad; tel. 537-0071; telex 212218.

Ministry of Trade: Khulafa St, Khullani Sq., Baghdad; tel. 887-2682; telex 212206.

Ministry of Transport and Communications: Nr Martyr's Monument, Karradat Dakhil, Baghdad; tel. 776-6041; telex 212020.

* In January 1991 the Government announced its intention to relocate the principal ministries to the city of Ramadi, west of Baghdad.

KURDISH AUTONOMOUS REGION

Executive Council: Chair. MUHAMMAD AMIN MUHAMMAD (acting).

Legislative Council: Chair. AHMAD ABD AL-QADIR AN-NAQSHABANDI.

In May 1992, in the absence of a negotiated autonomy agreement with the Iraqi Government, the KIF (see below) organized elections to a 105-member Kurdish National Assembly. The DPK and the PUK were the only parties to achieve representation in the new Assembly and subsequently agreed to share seats equally between them. Elections held at the same time as those to the National Assembly, to choose an overall Kurdish leader, were inconclusive and were to be held again at a later date. In July the Assembly elected a 16-member Cabinet.

Legislature

NATIONAL ASSEMBLY

No form of National Assembly existed in Iraq between the 1958 revolution, which overthrew the monarchy, and June 1980. (The existing provisional Constitution, introduced in 1968, contains provisions for the election of an assembly at a date to be determined by the Government. The members of the Assembly are to be elected from all political, social and economic sectors of the Iraqi people.) In December 1979 the RCC invited political, trade union and popular organizations to debate a draft law providing for the creation of a 250-member National Assembly (elected from 56 constituencies) and a 50-member Kurdish Legislative Council, both to be elected by direct, free and secret ballot. Elections for the first National Assembly took place on 20 June 1980, and for

the Kurdish Legislative Council on 11 September 1980, 13 August 1986 and 9 September 1989. The Assembly is dominated by members of the ruling Baath Party.

Elections for the second National Assembly were held on 20 October 1984. The total number of votes cast was 7,171,000 and Baath Party candidates won 73% (183) of the 250 seats, compared with 75% in the previous Assembly. The number of women elected rose to 33.

Elections for the third National Assembly, which were originally scheduled to be held in late August 1988 but were subsequently postponed on three occasions, were held on 1 April 1989. It was estimated that 75% of Iraq's 8m.-strong electorate participated in the elections, and that Baath Party candidates won more than 50% of the 250 seats.

Chairman: SAADI MAHDI SALIH.

Chairman of the Kurdish Legislative Council: AHMAD ABD AL-QADIR AN-NAQSHABANDI.

Political Organizations

National Progressive Front: Baghdad; f. July 1973, when Arab Baath Socialist Party and Iraqi Communist Party signed a joint manifesto agreeing to establish a comprehensive progressive national and nationalistic front. In 1975 representatives of Kurdish parties and organizations and other national and independent forces joined the Front; the Iraqi Communist Party left the National Progressive Front in mid-March 1979; Sec.-Gen. NAIM HADDAD (Baath).

Arab Baath Socialist Party: POB 6012, al-Mansour, Baghdad; revolutionary Arab socialist movement founded in Damascus in 1947; has ruled Iraq since July 1968, and between July 1973 and March 1979 in alliance with the Iraqi Communist Party in the National Progressive Front; founder MICHAEL AFLAQ; Regional Command Sec.-Gen. SADDAM HUSSAIN; Deputy Regional Command Sec.-Gen. IZZAT IBRAHIM; mems. of Regional Command: TAHA YASSIN RAMADAN, TAREQ AZIZ, MUHAMMAD HAMZAH AZ-ZUBAYDI, ABD AL-GHANI ABD AL-GHAFUR, SAADI MAHDI SALIH, SA'ADOUN HAMMADI MAZBAN KHADR HADI, ALI HASSAN AL-MAJID, KAMIL YASSIN RASHID, MUHAMMAD ZIMAM ABD AR-RAZZAQ, MUHAMMAD YOUNIS AL-AHMAD, KHADER ABD AL-AZIZ HUSSAIN, ABD AR-RAHMAN AHMAD ABD AR-RAHMAN, NOURI FAISAL SHAHIR, MIZHER MATNI AL-AWWAD, FAWZI KHALAF; approx. 100,000 mems.

Kurdistan Democratic Party: Aqaba bin Nafi's Sq., Baghdad; f. 1946; Kurdish Party; supports the National Progressive Front; Sec.-Gen. MUHAMMAD SAEED AL-ATRUSHI.

Kurdistan Revolutionary Party: f. 1972; succeeded Democratic Kurdistan Party; admitted to National Progressive Front 1974; Sec.-Gen. ABD AS-SATTAR TAHER SHAREF.

There are several illegal opposition groups, including:

Ad-Da'wa al-Islamiya (Voice of Islam): f. 1968; based in Teheran; mem. of the Supreme Council of the Islamic Revolution in Iraq; guerrilla group; Leader Sheikh AL-ASSEFIE.

Iraqi Communist Party: Baghdad: f. 1934; became legally recognized in July 1973 on formation of National Progressive Front; left National Progressive Front March 1979; proscribed as a result of its support for Iran during the Iran–Iraq War; First Sec. AZIZ MUHAMMAD.

Umma (Nation) Party: f. 1982; opposes Saddam Hussain's regime; Leader SAAD SALEH JABR.

There is also a breakaway element of the Arab Baath Socialist Party represented on the Iraqi National Joint Action Cttee (see below); the Democratic Gathering (Leader SALEH DOUBLAH); the Iraqi Socialist Party (ISP; Leader Gen. HASSAN AN-NAQUIB); the Democratic Party of Kurdistan (DPK; f. 1946; Leader MASOUD BARZANI); the Patriotic Union of Kurdistan (PUK; f. 1975; Leader JALAL TALIBANI); the Socialist Party of Kurdistan (SPK; f. 1975; Leader RASSOUL MARMAND); the United Socialist Party of Kurdistan (USKP; Leader MAHMOUD OSMAN), a breakaway group from the PUK; the Kurdistan People's Democratic Party (KPDP; Leader SAMI ABD AR-RAHMAN); and the Kurdish Hezbollah (Party of God; f. 1985; Leader Sheikh MUHAMMAD KALED), a breakaway group from the DPK and a member of the Supreme Council of the Islamic Revolution in Iraq (SCIRI), which is based in Teheran under the leadership of the exiled Iraqi Shi'ite leader, Hojatoleslam MUHAMMAD BAQIR AL-HAKIM.

Various alliances of political and religious groups have been formed to oppose the regime of Saddam Hussain in recent years. They include the Kurdistan Iraqi Front (KIF; f. 1988), an alliance of the DPK, the PUK, the SPK, the KPDP and other, smaller Kurdish groups; the Iraqi National Joint Action Cttee, formed in Damascus in 1990 and grouping together the SCIRI, the four principal Kurdish parties belonging to the KIF, Ad-Da'wa al-Islamiya, the Movement of the Iraqi Mujahidin (based in Teheran; Leaders Hojatoleslam MUHAMMAD BAQIR AL-HAKIM and SAID MUHAMMAD AL-HAIDARI), the Islamic Movement in Iraq (Shi'ite group based in

Teheran; Leader Sheikh MUHAMMAD MAHDI AL-KALISI), Jund al-Imam (Imam Soldiers; Shi'ite; Leader ABU ZAID), the Islamic Action Organization (based in Teheran; Leader Sheikh TAQI MODARESSI), the Islamic Alliance (based in Saudi Arabia; Sunni; Leader ABU YASSER AL-ALOUSI), the Independent Group, the Iraqi Socialist Party, the Arab Socialist Movement, the Nasserite Unionist Gathering and the National Reconciliation Group. There is also the London-based Iraqi National Congress (INC; Presidential Council: MASOUD BARZANI, Gen. HASSAN AN-NAQUIB, MUHAMMAD BAHR AL-OLOUM), which has sought to unite the various factions of the opposition and in November 1992 organized a conference in Iraqi Kurdistan, at which a 25-member executive committee and a three-member presidential council were elected. In September 1992 the KPDP, the SPK and the Kurdish Democratic Independence Party were reported to have merged to form the Kurdistan Unity Party (KUP).

Diplomatic Representation

EMBASSIES IN IRAQ

Afghanistan: Maghrib St, ad-Difa'ie, 27/1/12 Waziriya, Baghdad; tel. 5560331; Ambassador: ABD AR-RASHID WASEQ.

Albania: Baghdad; Ambassador: GYLANI SHEHU.

Algeria: ash-Shawaf Sq., Karradat Mariam, Baghdad; tel. 537-2181; Ambassador: AL-ARABI SI AL-HASSAN.

Argentina: POB 2443, Hay al-Jamia District 915, St 24, No. 142, Baghdad; tel. 776-8140; telex 213500; Ambassador: GERÓNIMO CORTES-FUNES.

Australia: POB 661, Masba 39B/35, Baghdad; tel. 719-3434; telex 212148; Ambassador: P. LLOYD.

Austria: POB 294, Hay Babel 929/2/5 Aqaba bin Nafi's Sq., Masbah, Baghdad; tel. 719-9033; telex 212383; Ambassador: Dr ERWIN MATSCH.

Bahrain: POB 27117, al-Mansour, Hay al-Watanabi, Mah. 605, Zuqaq 7, House 4/1/44, Baghdad; tel. 5423656; telex 213364; Ambassador: ABD AR-RAHMAN AL-FADHIL.

Bangladesh: 75/17/929 Hay Babel, Baghdad; tel. 7196367; telex 2370; Ambassador: MUFLEH R. OSMARRY.

Belgium: Hay Babel 929/27/25, Baghdad; tel. 719-8297; telex 212450; Ambassador: MARC VAN RYSSELBERGHE.

Brazil: 609/16 al-Mansour, Houses 62/62–1, Baghdad; tel. 5411365; telex 2240; Ambassador: MAURO SERGIO CONTO.

Bulgaria: POB 28022, Ameriya, New Diplomatic Quarter, Baghdad; tel. 556-8197; Ambassador: ASSEN ZLATANOV.

Canada: 47/1/7 al-Mansour, Baghdad; tel. 542-1459; telex 212486; Ambassador: DAVID KARSGAARD.

Central African Republic: 208/406 az-Zawra, Harthiya, Baghdad; tel. 551-6520; Chargé d'affaires: RENÉ BISSAYO.

Chad: POB 8037, 97/4/4 Karradat Mariam, Baghdad; tel. 537-6160; Ambassador: MAHAMAT DJIBER AHNOUR.

China, People's Republic: New Embassy Area, International Airport Rd, Baghdad; tel. 556-2740; telex 212195; Ambassador: ZHANG DAYONG.

Cuba: St 7, District 929 Hay Babel, al-Masba Arrasat al-Hindi; tel. 719-5177; telex 212389; Ambassador: JUAN ALDAMA LUGONES.

Czech Republic: Dijlaschool St, No. 37, Mansour, Baghdad; tel. 541-7136.

Denmark: POB 2001, Zukak No. 34, Mahallat 902, Hay al-Wahda, House No. 18/1, Alwiyah, Baghdad; tel. 719-3058; telex 212490; Ambassador: TORBEN G. DITHMER.

Djibouti: POB 6223, al-Mansour, Baghdad; tel. 551-3805; Ambassador: ABSEIA BOOH ABDULLA.

Finland: POB 2041, Alwiyah, Baghdad; tel. 776 6271; telex 212454; Ambassador: HENRY SÖDERHOLM.

Germany: Zuqaq 2, Mahala 929, Hay Babel (Masbah Square), Baghdad; tel. 719-2037; telex 212262; fax 7180340; Ambassador: Dr RICHARD ELLERKMANN.

Greece: 63/3/913 Hay al-Jamia, al-Jadiriya, Baghdad; tel. 776-6572; telex 212479; Ambassador: EPAMINONDAS PEYOS.

Holy See: POB 2090, as-Sa'adoun St 904/2/46, Baghdad (Apostolic Nunciature); tel. 719-5183; Apostolic Pro-Nuncio: Most Rev. MARIAN OLEŚ, Titular Archbishop of Ratiaria.

Hungary: POB 2065, Abu Nuwas St, az-Zuwiya, Baghdad; tel. 776-5000; telex 212293; Ambassador: TAMÁS VARGA.

India: Taha St, Najib Pasha, Adhamiya, Baghdad; tel. 422-2014; telex 212248; Ambassador: K. N. BAKSHI.

Indonesia: 906/2/77 Hay al-Wahda, Baghdad; tel. 719-8677; telex 2517; Ambassador: A. A. MURTADHO.

Iran: Karradat Mariam, Baghdad; Ambassador: (vacant).

Ireland: 913/28/101 Hay al-Jamia, Baghdad; tel. 7768661; Ambassador: PATRICK MCCABE.

Japan: 929/17/70 Hay Babel, Masba, Baghdad; tel. 719-5156; telex 212241; fax 7196186; Ambassador: TAIZO NAKAMARA.

Jordan: POB 6314, House No. 1, St 12, District 609, al-Mansour, Baghdad; tel. 541-2892; telex 2805; Ambassador: HILMI LOZI.

Korea, Republic: 915/22/278 Hay al-Jamia, Baghdad; tel. 7765496; Ambassador: BONG RHUEM CHEI.

Libya: Baghdad; Head of the Libyan People's Bureau: ABBAS AHMAD AL-MASSRATI (acting).

Malaysia: 6/14/929 Hay Babel, Baghdad; tel. 7762622; telex 2452; Ambassador: K. N. NADARAJAH.

Malta: 2/1 Zuqaq 49, Mahalla 503, Hay an-Nil, Baghdad; tel. 7725032; Chargé d'affaires a.i.: NADER SALEM RIZZO.

Mauritania: al-Mansour, Baghdad; tel. 551-8261; Ambassador: MUHAMMAD YEHYA WALAD AHMAD AL-HADI.

Mexico: 601/11/45 al-Mansour, Baghdad; tel. 719-8039; telex 2582; Chargé d'affaires: VÍCTOR M. DELGADO.

Morocco: POB 6039, Hay al-Mansour, Baghdad; tel. 552-1779; Ambassador: ABOLESLAM ZENINED.

Netherlands: POB 2064, 29/35/915 Jadiriya, Baghdad; tel. 776-7616; telex 212276; Ambassador: Dr N. VAN DAM.

New Zealand: POB 2350, 2D/19 az-Zuwiya, Jadiriya, Baghdad; tel. 776-8177; telex 212433; Ambassador: JOHN CLARKE.

Nigeria: POB 5933, 2/3/603 Mutanabi, al-Mansour, Baghdad; tel. 5421750; telex 212474; Ambassador: A. G. ABDULLAHI.

Norway: 20/3/609 Hay al-Mansour, Baghdad; tel. 5410097; telex 212715; Ambassador: HARALD LONE.

Oman: POB 6180, 213/36/15 al-Harthiya, Baghdad; tel. 551-8198; telex 212480; Ambassador: KHALIFA BIN ABDULLA BIN SALIM AL-HOMAIDI.

Pakistan: 14/7/609 al-Mansour, Baghdad; tel. 541-5120; Ambassador: KHALID MAHMOUD.

Philippines: Hay Babel, Baghdad; tel. 719-3228; telex 3463; Ambassador: AKMAD A. SAKKAN.

Poland: POB 2051, 30 Zuqaq 13, Mahalla 931, Hay Babel, Baghdad; tel. 719-0296; Ambassador: KRZYSZTOF SLOMINSKI.

Portugal: POB 2123, 66/11 al-Karada ash-Sharqiya, Hay Babel, Sector 925, St 25, No. 79, Alwiya, Baghdad; tel. 776-4953; telex 212716; Ambassador: GABRIEL MESQUITO DE BRITO.

Qatar: 152/406 Harthiya, Hay al-Kindi, Baghdad; tel. 551-2186; telex 2391; Ambassador: MUHAMMAD RASHID KHALIFA AL-KHALIFA.

Romania: Arassat al-Hindia, Hay Babel, Mahalla 929, Zukak 31, No 452/A, Baghdad; tel. 7762860; telex 2268; Ambassador: IONEL MIHAIL CETATEANU.

Russia: 4/5/605 al-Mutanabi, Baghdad; tel. 541-4749; Ambassador: VIKTOR J. MININ.

Senegal: 569/5/10, Hay al-Mansour Baghdad; tel. 5420806; Ambassador: DOUDOU DIOP.

Slovakia: Dijlaschool St, No. 37, Mansour, Baghdad; tel. 541-7136.

Somalia: 603/1/5 al-Mansour, Baghdad; tel. 551-0088; Ambassador: ISSA ALI MOHAMMED.

Spain: POB 2072, ar-Riyad Quarter, District 908, Street No. 1, No. 21, Alwiya, Baghdad; tel. 719-2852; telex 212239; Ambassador: JUAN LÓPEZ DE CHICHERI.

Sri Lanka: POB 1094, 07/80/904 Hay al-Wahda, Baghdad; tel. 719-3040; Ambassador: N. NAVARATNARAJAH.

Sudan: 38/15/601 al-Imarat, Baghdad; tel. 542-4889; Ambassador: ALI ADAM MUHAMMAD AHMAD.

Sweden: 15/41/103 Hay an-Nidhal, Baghdad; tel. 719-5361; telex 212352; Ambassador: HENRIK AMNEUS.

Switzerland: POB 2107, Hay Babel, House No. 41/5/929, Baghdad; tel. 719-3091; telex 212243; Ambassador: HANS-RUDOLF HOFFMANN.

Thailand: POB 6062, 1/4/609, al-Mansour, Baghdad; tel. 5418798; telex 213345; Ambassador: CHEUY SUETRONG.

Tunisia: POB 6057, Mansour 34/2/4, Baghdad; tel. 551-7786; Ambassador: LARBI HANTOUS.

Turkey: POB 14001, 2/8 Waziriya, Baghdad; tel. 422-2768; telex 214145; Ambassador: SÖNMEZ KÖKSAL.

Uganda: 41/1/609 al-Mansour, Baghdad; tel. 551-3594; Ambassador: SWAIB M. MUSOKE.

United Arab Emirates: al-Mansour, 50 al-Mansour Main St, Baghdad; tel. 551-7026; telex 2285; Ambassador: HILAL SA'ID HILAL AZ-ZU'ABI.

Venezuela: al-Mansour, House No. 12/79/601, Baghdad; tel. 552-0965; telex 2173; Ambassador: FREDDY RAFAEL ALVAREZ YANES.

Viet Nam: 29/611 Hay al-Andalus, Baghdad; tel. 551-1388; Ambassador: TRAN KY LONG.

Yemen: Jadiriya 923/28/29, Baghdad; tel. 776-0647; Ambassador: MOHAMMED ABDULLAH ASH-SHAMI.

Yugoslavia: POB 2061, 16/35/923 Hay Babel, Jadiriya, Baghdad; tel. 776-7887; telex 213521; Ambassador: STOJAN ANDOV.

Judicial System

Courts in Iraq consist of the following: The Court of Cassation, Courts of Appeal, First Instance Courts, Peace Courts, Courts of Sessions, *Shari'a* Courts and Penal Courts.

The Court of Cassation: This is the highest judicial bench of all the Civil Courts; it sits in Baghdad, and consists of the President and a number of vice-presidents and not fewer than 15 permanent judges, delegated judges and reporters as necessity requires. There are four bodies in the Court of Cassation, these are: (*a*) the General body, (*b*) Civil and Commercial body, (*c*) Personal Status body, (*d*) the Penal body.

Courts of Appeal: The country is divided into five Districts of Appeal: Baghdad, Mosul, Basra, Hilla, and Kirkuk, each with its Court of Appeal consisting of a president, vice-presidents and not fewer than three members, who consider the objections against the decisions issued by the First Instance Courts of first grade.

Courts of First Instance: These courts are of two kinds: Limited and Unlimited in jurisdiction.

Limited Courts deal with Civil and Commercial suits, the value of which is 500 Iraqi dinars and less; and suits, the value of which cannot be defined, and which are subject to fixed fees. Limited Courts consider these suits in the final stage and they are subject to Cassation.

Unlimited Courts consider the Civil and Commercial suits irrespective of their value, and suits the value of which exceeds 500 Iraqi dinars with first grade subject to appeal.

First Instance Courts consist of one judge in the centre of each *Liwa*, some *Qadhas* and *Nahiyas*, as the Minister of Justice judges necessary.

Courts of Sessions: There is in every District of Appeal a Court of Sessions which consists of three judges under the presidency of the President of the Court of Appeal or one of his vice-presidents. It considers the penal suits prescribed by Penal Proceedings Law and other laws. More than one Court of Sessions may be established in one District of Appeal by notification issued by the Minister of Justice mentioning therein its headquarters, jurisdiction and the manner of its establishment.

Shari'a Courts: A *Shari'a* Court is established wherever there is a First Instance Court; the Muslim judge of the First Instance Court may be a *Qadhi* to the *Shari'a* Court if a special *Qadhi* has not been appointed thereto. The *Shari'a* Court considers matters of personal status and religious matters in accordance with the provisions of the law supplement to the Civil and Commercial Proceedings Law.

Penal Courts: A Penal Court of first grade is established in every First Instance Court. The judge of the First Instance Court is considered as penal judge unless a special judge is appointed thereto. More than one Penal Court may be established to consider the suits prescribed by the Penal Proceedings Law and other laws.

One or more Investigation Court may be established in the centre of each *Liwa* and a judge is appointed thereto. They may be established in the centres of *Qadhas* and *Nahiyas* by order of the Minister of Justice. The judge carries out the investigation in accordance with the provisions of Penal Proceedings Law and the other laws.

There is in every First Instance Court a department for the execution of judgments presided over by the Judge of First Instance if a special president is not appointed thereto. It carries out its duties in accordance with the provisions of Execution Law.

Religion

ISLAM

About 95% of the population are Muslims, more than 50% of whom are Shi'ite. The Arabs of northern Iraq, the Bedouins, the Kurds, the Turkomans and some of the inhabitants of Baghdad and Basra are mainly of the Sunni sect, while the remaining Arabs south of the Diyali belong to the Shi'i sect.

CHRISTIANITY

There are Christian communities in all the principal towns of Iraq, but their principal villages lie mostly in the Mosul district. The Christians of Iraq comprise three groups: (*a*) the free Churches, including the Nestorian, Gregorian and Syrian Orthodox; (*b*) the churches known as Uniate, since they are in union with the Roman Catholic Church, including the Armenian Uniates, Syrian Uniates and Chaldeans; (*c*) mixed bodies of Protestant converts, New Chaldeans and Orthodox Armenians.

The Assyrian Church

Assyrian Christians, an ancient sect having sympathies with Nestorian beliefs, were forced to leave their mountainous homeland in northern Kurdistan in the early part of the 20th century. The estimated 550,000 members of the Apostolic Catholic Assyrian Church of the East are now exiles, mainly in Iraq, Syria, Lebanon and the USA. Their leader is the Catholicos Patriarch, His Holiness MAR DINKHA IV.

The Orthodox Churches

Armenian Apostolic Church: Bishop AVAK ASADOURIAN, Primate of the Armenian Diocese of Iraq, Younis as-Saba'awi Sq., Baghdad; tel. 885-5066; nine churches (four in Baghdad); 23,000 adherents, mainly in Baghdad.

Syrian Orthodox Church: about 12,000 adherents in Iraq.

The Greek Orthodox Church is also represented in Iraq.

The Roman Catholic Church

Armenian Rite

At 31 December 1992 the archdiocese of Baghdad contained an estimated 2,200 adherents.

Archbishop of Baghdad: Most Rev. PAUL COUSSA, Archevêché Arménien Catholique, Karrada Sharkiya, POB 2344, Baghdad; tel. 719-1827.

Chaldean Rite

Iraq comprises the patriarchate of Babylon, five archdioceses (including the patriarchal see of Baghdad) and five dioceses (all of which are suffragan to the patriarchate). Altogether, the Patriarch has jurisdiction over 21 archdioceses and dioceses in Iraq, Egypt, Iran, Lebanon, Syria, Turkey and the USA, and the Patriarchal Vicariate of Jerusalem. At 31 December 1992 there were an estimated 190,489 Chaldean Catholics in Iraq (including 149,220 in the archdiocese of Baghdad).

Patriarch of Babylon of the Chaldeans: His Beatitude RAPHAËL I BIDAWID, Patriarcat Chaldéen Catholique, Baghdad; tel. 887-9604.

Archbishop of Arbil: Most Rev. STÉPHANE BABACA, Archevêché Catholique Chaldéen, Ainkawa, Arbil; tel. 0665-26681.

Archbishop of Baghdad: the Patriarch of Babylon (see above).

Archbishop of Basra: Most Rev. YOUSIF THOMAS, Archevêché Chaldéen, POB 217, Ahsar-Basra; tel. 219455.

Archbishop of Kirkuk: Most Rev. ANDRÉ SANA, Archevêché Chaldéen, Kirkuk; tel. 050-213978.

Archbishop of Mosul: Most Rev. GEORGES GARMO, Archevêché Chaldéen, Mayassa, Mosul; tel. 060-762149.

Latin Rite

The archdiocese of Baghdad, directly responsible to the Holy See, contained an estimated 3,300 adherents at 31 December 1992.

Archbishop of Baghdad: Most Rev. PAUL DAHDAH, Archevêché Latin, Hay al-Wahda—Mahalla 904, rue 8, Imm. 44, POB 35130, Baghdad; tel. 719-9537.

Melkite Rite

The Greek-Melkite Patriarch of Antioch (MAXIMOS V HAKIM) is resident in Damascus, Syria.

Patriarchal Exarchate of Iraq: Rue Asfar, Karrada Sharkiya, Baghdad; tel. 719-1082; 340 adherents (31 December 1988); Exarch Patriarchal: Archimandrite NICOLAS DAGHER.

Syrian Rite

Iraq comprises two archdioceses, containing an estimated 49,050 adherents at 31 December 1992.

Archbishop of Baghdad: Most Rev. ATHANASE MATTI SHABA MATOKA, Archevêché Syrien Catholique, Baghdad; tel. 719-1850; fax 7190166.

Archbishop of Mosul: Most Rev. CYRILLE EMMANUEL BENNI, Archevêché Syrien Catholique, Mosul; tel. 060-762160.

The Anglican Communion

Within the Episcopal Church in Jerusalem and the Middle East, Iraq forms part of the diocese of Cyprus and the Gulf. Expatriate congregations in Iraq meet at St George's Church, Baghdad (Hon. Sec. GRAHAM SPURGEON). The Bishop in Cyprus and the Gulf is resident in Cyprus.

JUDAISM

Unofficial estimates assess the present size of the Jewish community at 2,500, almost all residing in Baghdad.

OTHERS

About 30,000 Yazidis and a smaller number of Turkomans, Sabeans and Shebeks reside in Iraq.

Sabean Community: 20,000 adherents; Head Sheikh DAKHIL, Nasiriyah; Mandeans, mostly in Nasiriyah.

Yazidis: 30,000 adherents; Leader TASHIN BAIK, Ainsifni.

The Press

DAILIES

Al-Baath ar-Riyadhi: Baghdad; sports; Propr and Editor UDAI SADDAM HUSSAIN.

Babil (Babylon): Baghdad; f. 1991; Propr and Editor UDAI SADDAM HUSSAIN.

Baghdad Observer: POB 624, Karantina, Baghdad; f. 1967; English; state-sponsored; Editor-in-Chief NAJI AL-HADITHI; circ. 22,000.

Al-Iraq: POB 5717, Baghdad; f. 1976; Kurdish; formerly *Al-Ta'akhi*; organ of the National Progressive Front; Editor-in-Chief SALAHUDIN SAEED; circ. 30,000.

Al-Jumhuriya (The Republic): POB 491, Waziriya, Baghdad; f. 1963, refounded 1967; Arabic; Editor-in-Chief SAMI MAHDI; circ. 150,000.

Al-Qadisiya: Baghdad; organ of the army.

Ar-Riyadhi (Sportsman): POB 58, Jadid Hassan Pasha, Baghdad; f. 1971; Arabic; published by Ministry of Youth; circ. 30,000.

Tariq ash-Sha'ab (People's Path): as-Sa'adoun St, Baghdad; Arabic; organ of the Iraqi Communist Party; Editor ABD AR-RAZZAK AS-SAFI.

Ath-Thawra (Revolution): POB 2009, Aqaba bin Nafi's Square, Baghdad; tel. 719-6161; f. 1968; Arabic; organ of Baath Party; Editor-in-Chief HAMEED SAEED; circ. 250,000.

WEEKLIES

Alif Baa (Alphabet): POB 491, Karantina, Baghdad; Arabic; Editor-in-Chief KAMIL ASH-SHARQI; circ. 150,000.

Al-Idaa'a wal-Television (Radio and Television): Iraqi Broadcasting and Television Establishment, Karradat Mariam, Baghdad; tel. 537-1161; telex 212246; radio and television programmes and articles; Arabic; Editor-in-Chief KAMIL HAMDI ASH-SHARQI; circ. 40,000.

Majallati: Children's Culture House, POB 8041, Baghdad; telex 212228; Arabic; children's newspaper; Editor-in-Chief FAROUQ SALLOUM; circ. 35,000.

Ar-Rased (The Observer): Baghdad; Arabic; general.

Sabaa Nisan: Baghdad; f. 1976; Arabic; organ of the General Union of the Youth of Iraq.

Sawt al-Fallah (Voice of the Peasant): Karradat Mariam, Baghdad; f. 1968; Arabic; organ of the General Union of Farmers Societies; circ. 40,000.

Waee ul-Ummal (The Workers' Consciousness): Headquarters of General Federation of Trade Unions in Iraq, POB 2307, Gialani St, Senak, Baghdad; Arabic; Iraq Trades Union organ; Chief Editor KHALID MAHMOUD HUSSEIN; circ. 25,000.

PERIODICALS

Afaq Arabiya (Arab Horizons): POB 2009, Aqaba bin Nafi's Sq., Baghdad; monthly; Arabic; literary and political; Editor-in-Chief Dr MOHSIN J. AL-MUSAWI.

Al-Aqlam (Pens): POB 4032, Adamiya, Baghdad; tel. 443-3644; telex 214135; f. 1964; publ. by the Ministry of Culture and Information; monthly; Arabic; literary; Editor-in-Chief Dr ALI J. AL-ALLAQ; circ. 7,000.

Bagdad: Dar al-Ma'mun for Translation and Publishing, POB 24015, Karradat Mariam, Baghdad; tel. 538-3171; telex 212984; fortnightly; French; cultural and political.

Al-Funoon al-Ida'iya (Fields of Broadcasting): Cultural Affairs House, Karradat Mariam, Baghdad; quarterly; Arabic; supervised by Broadcasting and TV Training Institute; engineering and technical; Chief Editor MUHAMMAD AL-JAZA'RI.

Gilgamesh: Dar al-Ma'mun for Translation and Publishing, POB 24015, Karradat Mariam, Baghdad; tel. 538-3171; telex 212984; quarterly; English; cultural.

Hurras al-Watan: Baghdad; Arabic.

L'Iraq Aujourd'hui: POB 2009, Aqaba bin Nafi's Sq, Baghdad; f. 1976; bi-monthly; French; cultural and political; Editor NADJI AL-HADITHI; circ. 12,000.

Iraq Oil News: POB 6178, al-Mansour, Baghdad; tel. 541-0031; telex 2216; f. 1973; monthly; English; publ. by the Information and Public Relations Div. of the Ministry of Oil.

The Journal of the Faculty of Medicine: College of Medicine, University of Baghdad, Jadiriya, Baghdad; tel. 93091; f. 1935; quarterly; Arabic and English; medical and technical; Editor Prof. YOUSUF D. AN-NAAMAN.

Majallat al-Majma' al-'Ilmi al-'Iraqi (Iraqi Academy Journal): Iraqi Academy, Waziriyah, Baghdad; f. 1947; quarterly; Arabic; scholarly magazine on Arabic Islamic culture; Gen. Sec. Dr NURI HAMMOUDI AL-QAISI.

Majallat ath-Thawra az-Ziraia (Magazine of Iraq Agriculture): Baghdad; quarterly; Arabic; agricultural; published by the Ministry of Agriculture and Irrigation.

Al-Maskukat (Coins): State Organization of Antiquities and Heritage, Karkh, Salihiya St, Baghdad; tel. 537-6121; f. 1969; annually; the journal of numismatics in Iraq; Chair. of Ed. Board Dr MUAYAD SA'ID DAMERJI.

Al-Masrah wal-Cinema: Iraqi Broadcasting, Television and Cinema Establishment, Salihiya, Baghdad; monthly; Arabic; artistic, theatrical and cinema.

Al-Mawrid: POB 2009, Aqaba bin Nafi's Sq, Baghdad; f. 1971; monthly; Arabic; cultural.

Al-Mu'allem al-Jadid: Ministry of Education, al-Imam al-A'dham St, A'dhamaiya, Nr Antar Sq., Baghdad; tel. 422-2594; telex 212259; f. 1935; quarterly; Arabic; educational, social, and general; Editor in Chief KHALIL I. HAMASH; circ. 190,000.

An-Naft wal-Aalam (Oil and the World): Ministry of Oil, POB 6178, Baghdad; f. 1973; monthly; Arabic; Editor-in-Chief USAMA ABD AR-RAZZAQ HAMMADI AL-HITHI (Minister of Oil).

Sawt at-Talaba (The Voice of Students): al-Maghreb St, Waziriyah, Baghdad; f. 1968; monthly; Arabic; organ of National Union of Iraqi Students; circ. 25,000.

As-Sina'a (Industry): POB 5665, Baghdad; every 2 months; Arabic and English; publ. by Ministry of Industry and Minerals; Editor-in-Chief ABD AL-QADER ABD AL-LATIF; circ. 16,000.

Sumer: State Organization of Antiquities and Heritage, Karkh, Salihiya St, Baghdad; tel. 537-6121; f. 1945; annually; archaeological, historical journal; Chair. of Ed. Board Dr MUAYAD SA'ID DAMERJI.

Ath-Thaqafa (Culture): Place at-Tahrir, Baghdad; f. 1970; monthly; Arabic; cultural; Editor-in-Chief SALAH KHALIS; circ. 5,000.

Ath-Thaqafa al-Jadida (The New Culture): Baghdad; f. 1969; monthly; pro-Communist; Editor-in-Chief SAFA AL-HAFIZ; circ. 3,000.

At-Turath ash-Sha'abi (Popular Heritage): POB 2009, Aqaba bin Nafi's Sq., Baghdad; monthly; Arabic; specializes in Iraqi and Arabic folklore; Editor-in-Chief LUTFI AL-KHOURI; circ. 15,000.

Al-Waqai al-Iraqiya (Official Gazette of Republic of Iraq): Ministry of Justice, Baghdad; f. 1922; Arabic and English weekly editions; circ. Arabic 10,500, English 700; Dir HASHIM N. JAAFER.

NEWS AGENCIES

Iraqi News Agency (INA): POB 3084, 28 Nissan Complex—Baghdad, Sadoun; tel. 5383199; telex 2267; f. 1959; Dir-Gen. ADNAN AL-JUBOURI.

Foreign Bureaux

Agence France-Presse (AFP): POB 190, Apt 761-91-97, Baghdad; tel. 551-4333; Correspondent FAROUQ CHOUKRI.

Agenzia Nazionale Stampa Associata (ANSA) (Italy): POB 5602, Baghdad; tel. 776-2558; Correspondent SALAH H. NASRAWI.

Associated Press (AP) (USA): Hay al-Khadra 629, Zuqaq No. 23, Baghdad; tel. 555-9041; telex 213324; Correspondent SALAH H. NASRAWI.

Deutsche Presse-Agentur (dpa) (Germany): POB 5699, Baghdad; Correspondent NAJHAT KOTANI.

Informatsionnoye Telegrafnoye Agentstvo Rossii—Telegrafnoye Agentstvo Suverennykh Stran (ITAR—TASS) (Russia): 67 Street 52, Alwiya, Baghdad; Correspondent ANDREI OSTALSKY.

Reuters (UK): House No. 8, Zuqaq 75, Mahalla 903, Hay al-Karada, Baghdad; tel. 719-1843; telex 213777; Correspondent SUBHY HADDAD.

Xinhua (New China) News Agency (People's Republic of China): al-Mansour, Adrus District, 611 Small District, 5 Lane No. 8, Baghdad; tel. 541-8904; telex 213253; Correspondent ZHU SHAOHUA.

Publishers

National House for Publishing, Distribution and Advertising: Ministry of Culture and Information, POB 624, al-Jumhuriya St, Baghdad; tel. 425-1846; telex 212392; f. 1972; publishes books on politics, economics, education, agriculture, sociology, commerce and science in Arabic and other Middle Eastern languages; sole importer and distributor of newspapers, magazines, periodicals and books; controls all advertising activities, inside Iraq as well as outside; Dir-Gen. M. A. ASKAR.

Afaq Arabiya Publishing House: POB 4032, Adamiya, Baghdad; tel. 443-6044; telex 214135; fax 4448760; publisher of literary monthlies, *Al-Aqlam* and *Afaq Arabiya*, periodicals, *Foreign Culture*, *Art*, *Folklore*, and cultural books; Chair. Dr MOHSIN AL-MUSAWI.

Dar al-Ma'mun for Translation and Publishing: POB 24015, Karradat Mariam, Baghdad; tel. 538-3171; telex 212984; publisher of newspapers and magazines including: the *Baghdad Observer* (daily newspaper), *Bagdad* (monthly magazine), *Gilgamesh* (quarterly magazine).

Al-Hurriyah Printing Establishment: Karantina, Sarrafia, Baghdad; tel. 69721; telex 212228; f. 1970; largest printing and publishing establishment in Iraq; state-owned; controls *Al-Jumhuriyah* (see below).

Al-Jamaheer Press House: POB 491, Sarrafia, Baghdad; tel. 416-9341; telex 212363; fax 416-1875; f. 1963; publisher of a number of newspapers and magazines, *Al-Jumhuriyah*, *Baghdad Observer*, *Alif Baa*, *Yord Weekly*; Pres. SAAD QASSEM HAMMOUDI.

Al-Ma'arif Ltd: Mutanabi St, Baghdad; f. 1929; publishes periodicals and books in Arabic, Kurdish, Turkish, French and English.

Al-Muthanna Library: Mutanabi St, Baghdad; f. 1936; booksellers and publishers of books in Arabic and oriental languages; Man. ANAS K. AR-RAJAB.

An-Nahdah: Mutanabi St, Baghdad; politics, Arab affairs.

Kurdish Culture Publishing House: Baghdad; f. 1976; attached to the Ministry of Culture and Information.

Ath-Thawra Printing and Publishing House: POB 2009, Aqaba bin Nafi's Sq., Baghdad; tel. 719-6161; telex 212215; f. 1970; state-owned; Chair. TARIQ AZIZ.

Thnayan Printing House: Baghdad.

Radio and Television

In 1991 there were an estimated 4m. radio receivers and 1.4m. television receivers in use.

RADIO

State Organization for Broadcasting and Television: Broadcasting and Television Bldg, Salihiya, Karkh, Baghdad; tel. 537-1161; telex 212246.

Iraqi Broadcasting and Television Establishment: Salihiya, Baghdad; tel. 31151; telex 2446; f. 1936; radio broadcasts began 1936; home service broadcasts in Arabic, Kurdish, Syriac and Turkoman; foreign service in French, German, English, Russian, Azeri, Hebrew and Spanish; there are 16 medium-wave and 30 short-wave transmitters; Dir-Gen. HAMID SAID; Dir-Gen. of Radio ADNAN RASHID SHUKR; Dir of Engineering and Technical Affairs MUHAMMAD FAKHRI RASHID.

Idaa'a Baghdad (Radio Baghdad): f.1936; 22 hours daily.

Idaa'a Sawt al-Jamahir: f. 1970; 24 hours.

Other stations include **Idaa'a al-Kurdia**, **Idaa'a al-Farisiya** (Persian).

TELEVISION

Baghdad Television: Ministry of Culture and Information, Iraqi Broadcasting and Television Establishment, Salihiya, Karkh, Baghdad; tel. 537-1151; telex 212446; f. 1956; government station operating daily on two channels for 9 hours and 8 hours respectively; Dir-Gen. Dr MAJID AHMAD AS-SAMARRIE.

Kirkuk Television: f. 1967; government station; 6 hours daily.

Mosul Television: f. 1968; government station; 6 hours daily.

Basra Television: f. 1968; government station; 6 hours daily.

Missan Television: f. 1974; government station; 6 hours daily.

Kurdish Television: f. 1974; government station; 8 hours daily.

There are 18 other TV stations operating in the Iraqi provinces.

Finance

(cap. = capital; p.u. = paid up; dep. = deposits; res = reserves; brs = branches; m. = million; amounts in Iraqi dinars)

All banks and insurance companies, including all foreign companies, were nationalized in July 1964. The assets of foreign companies were taken over by the state. In May 1991 the Government announced its decision to end the state's monopoly in banking, and by mid-1992 three private banks had commenced operations.

BANKING
Central Bank

Central Bank of Iraq: POB 64, Rashid St, Baghdad; tel. 886-5171; telex 212558; f. 1947 as National Bank of Iraq; name changed as above 1956; has the sole right of note issue; cap. and res 125m. (Sept. 1988); Gov. TARIQ AT-TUKMACHI (acting); brs in Mosul and Basra.

Nationalized Commercial Banks

Rafidain Bank: POB 11360, New Banks' St, Massarif, Baghdad; tel. 887-0521; telex 2211; f. 1941; state-owned; cap. p.u. 100m., res 710.4m., dep. 14,962m., total assets 20,593.1m. (Dec. 1988); Chair. and acting Gen.-Man. TARIK H. AL-KHATEEB; 113 brs in Iraq.

Rashid Bank: 7177 Haifa St, Baghdad; tel. 888-3505; telex 214357; f. 1988; state-owned; cap. 100m., res 110.6m., dep. 9,048.1m., total assets 9,258.7m. (Dec. 1991); Pres. A. MAJID H. AL-ANI; 3 brs.

Private Commercial Banks

Baghdad Bank: f. 1992; cap. 100m.; Chair. HASSAN AN-NAJAFI.

Dula Bank: f. 1991; cap. 100m.

Iraqi Commercial Bank: f. 1991; cap. 150m.; Chair. SHAWQI AL-KUBAISI.

Specialized Banks

Agricultural Co-operative Bank of Iraq: POB 5112, Rashid St, Baghdad; tel. 888-9081; f. 1936; state-owned; cap. p.u. 295.7m., res 14m., dep 10.5., total assets 351.6m. (Dec. 1988); Dir Gen. HDIYA H. AL-KHAYOUN; 32 brs.

Industrial Bank of Iraq: POB 5825, al-Khullani Sq., Baghdad; tel. 887-2181; telex 2224; f. 1940; state-owned; cap. p.u. 59.7m., dep. 77.9m. (Dec. 1988); Dir-Gen. BASSIMA ABD AL-HADDI ADH-DHAHIR; 5 brs.

Real Estate Bank of Iraq: POB 14185, Yaffa St, al-Salhiya, Baghdad; tel. 537-5165; telex 2635; f. 1949; state-owned; gives loans to assist the building industry; cap. p.u. 800m., res 11m., total assets 2,593.6m. (Dec. 1988); acquired the Co-operative Bank in 1970; Dir Gen. ABD AR-RAZZAQ AZIZ; 18 brs.

Socialist Bank: f. 1991; state-owned; gives interest-free loans to civil servants and soldiers who obtained more than three decorations in the Iran–Iraq War; cap. 500m.; Dir-Gen. ISSAM HAWISH.

INSURANCE

Iraqi Life Insurance Co: POB 989, Aqaba Bin Nafie Sq, Khalid Bin Wileed St, Baghdad; tel. 7192184; telex 213818; f. 1959; Chair. and Gen. Man. ABD AL-KHALIQ RAUF KHALIL.

Iraq Reinsurance Company: POB 297, Aqaba bin Nafi's Sq., Khalid bin al-Waleed St, Baghdad; tel. 719-5131; telex 214407; fax 791497; f. 1960; transacts reinsurance business on the international market; total assets 93.2m. (1985); Chair. and Gen. Man. K. M. AL-MUDARIES.

National Insurance Co: POB 248, Al-Khullani St, Baghdad; tel. 886-0730; telex 2397; f. 1950; cap. p.u. 20m.; state monopoly for general business and life insurance; Chair. and Gen. Man. MOWAFAQ H. RIDHA.

STOCK EXCHANGE

Capital Market Authority: Baghdad; Chair. MUHAMMAD HASSAN FAG EN-NOUR.

Trade and Industry

CHAMBERS OF COMMERCE

Federation of Iraqi Chambers of Commerce: Mustansir St, Baghdad; tel. 888-6111; f. 1969; all Iraqi Chambers of Commerce are affiliated to the Federation; Chair. ABD AL-MOHSEN A. ABU ALK-AHIL; Sec.-Gen. FUAD H. ABD AL-HADI.

EMPLOYERS' ORGANIZATION

Iraqi Federation of Industries: Iraqi Federation of Industries Bldg, al-Khullani Sq., Baghdad; f. 1956; 6,000 mems; Pres. HATAM ABD AR-RASHID.

INDUSTRIAL ORGANIZATIONS

In 1987 and 1988, as part of a programme of economic and administrative reform, to increase efficiency and productivity in industry and agriculture, many of the state organizations previously responsible for various industries were abolished or merged, and new state enterprises or mixed-sector national companies were established to replace them. For example, all the state organizations within the Ministries of Industry and of Heavy Industries were abolished and their functions and responsibilities combined in a smaller number of state enterprises; the five state organizations, grouped under the Ministry of Irrigation, were replaced by 14 national companies; and the number of state enterprises serving the farming sector was halved to six (see Agricultural Organizations). In 1987 and 1988 (up to June) 811 state organizations and departments were abolished. In August 1988 some 32 state enterprises were attached to the newly created Ministry of Industry and Military Industrialization, in addition to 11 under the aegis of the Military Industries Commission (MIC), which was, itself, attached to the new ministry. In July 1991 the MIC was detached from the Ministry of Industry and Military Industrialization (which reverted to its former title of Ministry of Industry and Minerals) and placed under the jurisdiction of the Ministry of Defence. The status of the state enterprises which had been attached to the MIC remained unclear. State enterprises include the following:

Iraqi State Enterprise for Cement: f. 1987 by merger of central and southern state cement enterprises.

National Company for Chemical and Plastics Industries: Dir-Gen. RAJA BAYYATI.

The Rafidain Company for Building Dams: f. 1987 to replace the State Org. for Dams.

State Enterprise for Battery Manufacture: f. 1987; Dir-Gen. ADEL ABBOUD.

State Enterprise for Communications and Post: f. 1987 from State Org. for Post, Telegraph and Telephones, and its subsidiaries.

State Enterprise for Construction Industries: f. 1987 by merger of state orgs for gypsum, asbestos, and the plastic and concrete industries.

State Enterprise for Cotton Industries: f. 1988 by merger of State Org. for Cotton Textiles and Knitting, and the Mosul State Org. for Textiles.

State Enterprise for Drinks and Mineral Water: f. 1987 by merger of enterprises responsible for soft and alcoholic drinks.

State Enterprise for the Fertilizer Industries: f. by merger of Basra-based and central fertilizer enterprises.

State Enterprise for Generation and Transmission of Electricity: f. 1987 from State Org. for Major Electrical Projects.

State Enterprise for Import and Export: f. 1987 to replace the five state organizations responsible to the Ministry of Trade for productive commodities, consumer commodities, grain and food products, exports and imports.

State Enterprise for Leather Industries: f. 1987; Dir Gen. MUHAMMAD ABD AL-MAJID.

State Enterprise for Sugar Beet: f. 1987 by merger of sugar enterprises in Mosul and Sulaimaniya.

State Enterprise for Textiles: f. 1987 to replace the enterprise for textiles in Baghdad, and the enterprise for plastic sacks in Tikrit.

State Enterprise for Tobacco and Cigarettes.

State Enterprise for Woollen Industries: f. by merger of state orgs for textiles and woollen textiles and Arbil-based enterprise for woollen textiles and women's clothing.

AGRICULTURAL ORGANIZATIONS

The following bodies are responsible to the Ministry of Agriculture and Irrigation:

State Agricultural Enterprise in Dujaila.

State Enterprise for Agricultural Supplies: Dir-Gen. MUHAMMAD KHAIRI.

State Enterprise for Developing Animal Wealth.

State Enterprise for Fodder.

State Enterprise for Grain Trading and Processing: Dir-Gen. ZUHAIR ABD AR-RAHMAN.

State Enterprise for Poultry (Central and Southern Areas).

State Enterprise for Poultry (Northern Area).

State Enterprise for Sea Fisheries: POB 260, Basra; telex 7011; Baghdad office: POB 3296, Baghdad; tel. 92023; telex 212223; fleet of 3 fish factory ships, 2 fish carriers, 1 fishing boat.

TRADE UNIONS

General Federation of Trade Unions of Iraq (GFTU): POB 3049, Tahrir Sq, Rashid St, Baghdad; tel. 887-0810; telex 212457; f. 1959; incorporates six vocational trade unions and 18 local trade union federations in the governorates of Iraq; the number of workers in industry is 536,245, in agriculture 150,967 (excluding peasants) and in other services 476,621 (1986); GFTU is a member of the International Confederation of Arab Trade Unions and of the World Federation of Trade Unions; Pres. FADHIL MAHMOUD GHAREB.

Union of Teachers: Al-Mansour, Baghdad; Pres. Dr ISSA SALMAN HAMID.

Union of Palestinian Workers in Iraq: Baghdad; Sec.-Gen. SAMI ASH-SHAWISH.

There are also unions of doctors, pharmacologists, jurists, artists, and a General Federation of Iraqi Women (Chair. MANAL YOUNIS).

CO-OPERATIVES

At the end of 1986 there were 843 agricultural co-operatives, with a total of 388,153 members. At the end of 1985 there were 67 consumer co-operatives, with 256,522 members.

PEASANT SOCIETIES

General Federation of Peasant Societies: Baghdad; f. 1959; has 734 affiliated Peasant Societies.

PETROLEUM AND GAS

Ministry of Oil: POB 6178, al-Mansour City, Baghdad; tel. 551-0031; telex 212216; solely responsible until mid-1989 for petroleum sector and activities relevant to it; since mid-1989 these responsibilities have been shared with the Technical Corpn for Special Projects of the Ministry of Industry and Military Industrialization (Ministry of Industry and Minerals from July 1991); the Ministry was merged with INOC in May 1987; the state organizations responsible to the ministry for petroleum refining and gas processing, for the distribution of petroleum products, for training personnel in the petroleum industry, and for gas were simultaneously abolished, and those for northern and southern petroleum, for petroleum equipment, for petroleum and gas exploration, for petroleum tankers, and for petroleum projects were converted into companies, as part of a plan to reorganize the petroleum industry and make it more efficient; Minister of Oil USAMA ABD AR-RAZZAQ HAMMADI AL-HITHI.

Iraq National Oil Company (INOC): POB 476, al-Khullani Sq., Baghdad; tel. 887-1115; telex 212204; f. in 1964 to operate the petroleum industry at home and abroad; when Iraq nationalized its petroleum industry, structural changes took place in INOC, and it became solely responsible for exploration, production, transportation and marketing of Iraqi crude petroleum and petroleum products. INOC was merged with the Ministry of Oil in 1987, and the functions of some of the organizations under its control were transferred to newly-created ministerial departments or to companies responsible to the ministry.

Iraqi Oil Drilling Co: f. 1990.

Iraqi Oil Tankers Company: POB 37, Basra; tel. 319990; telex 207007; fmrly the State Establishment for Oil Tankers; re-formed as a company in 1987; responsible to the Ministry of Oil for operating a fleet of 17 oil tankers; Chair. MUHAMMAD A. MUHAMMAD.

National Company for Distribution of Oil Products and Gas: POB 3, Rashid St, South Gate, Baghdad; tel. 888-9911; telex 212247; fmrly a state organization; re-formed as a company in 1987; fleet of 6 tankers; Dir-Gen. ALI H. IJAM.

National Company for Manufacturing Oil Equipment: fmrly a state organization; re-formed as a company in 1987.

National Company for Oil and Gas Exploration: INOC Building, POB 476, al-Khullani Sq, Baghdad; fmrly the State Establishment for Oil and Gas Exploration; re-formed as a company in 1987; responsible for exploration and operations in difficult terrain such as marshes, swamps, deserts, valleys and in mountainous regions; Dir-Gen. RADHWAN AS-SAADI.

Northern Petroleum Company (NPC): POB 1, at-Ta'meem Governorate; f. 1987 by the merger of the fmr Northern and Central petroleum organizations to carry out petroleum operations in northern Iraq; Dir-Gen. GHAZI SABIR ALI.

Southern Petroleum Company (SPC): POB 240, Basra; fmrly the Southern Petroleum Organization; re-formed as the SPC in 1987 to undertake petroleum operations in southern Iraq; Dir-Gen. ASRI SALIH (acting).

State Company for Oil Marketing (SCOM): Dir-Gen. ADEL AL-HASSOUN (acting).

State Company for Oil Projects (SCOP): POB 198, Oil Compound, Baghdad; tel. 774-1310; telex 212230; fmrly the State Org. for Oil Projects; re-formed as a company in 1987; responsible for construction of petroleum projects, mostly inside Iraq through direct execution, and also for design supervision of the projects and contracting with foreign enterprises, etc.; Dir-Gen. FALIH AL-KHAYYAT.

State Enterprise for Oil and Gas Industrialization in the South: f. 1988 by merger of enterprises responsible for the gas industry and petroleum refining in the south.

State Enterprise for Petrochemical Industries.

State Establishment for Oil Refining in the Central Area: Dir-Gen. KAMIL AL-FATLI.

State Establishment for Oil Refining in the North: Dir-Gen. TAHA HAMOUD.

State Establishment for Pipelines: Dir-Gen. SABAH ALI JOUMAH.

Transport*

RAILWAYS

The metre-gauge line runs from Baghdad, through Khanaqin and Kirkuk, to Arbil. The standard gauge line covers the length of the country, from Rabia, on the Syrian border, via Mosul, to Baghdad (534 km), and from Baghdad to Basra and Umm Qasr (608 km), on the Arabian Gulf. A 404-km standard-gauge line linking Baghdad to Husaibah, near the Iraqi-Syrian frontier, was completed in 1983. The 638-km line from Baghdad, via al-Qaim (on the Syrian border), to Akashat, and the 252-km Kirkuk-Baiji-Haditha line, which was designed to serve industrial projects along its route, were opened in 1986. The 150-km line linking the Akashat phosphate mines and the fertilizer complex at al-Qaim was formally opened in January 1986 but had already been in use for two years. Lines totalling some 2,400 km were planned at the beginning of the 1980s, but by 1988 only 800 km had been constructed. All standard-gauge trains are now hauled by diesel-electric locomotives, and all narrow-gauge (one-metre) line has been replaced by standard gauge (1,435 mm). As well as the internal service, there is a regular international service between Baghdad and Istanbul. A rapid transit transport system is to be established in Baghdad, with work to be undertaken as part of the 1987–2001 development plan for the city.

Responsibility for all railways, other than the former Iraq Republic Railways (see below), and for the design and construction of new railways, which was formerly the province of the New Railways Implementation Authority, was transferred to the newly created State Enterprise for Implementation of Transport and Communications Projects.

State Enterprise for Iraqi Railways: Baghdad Central Station Bldg, Damascus Sq., Baghdad; tel. 537-30011; telex 212272; fmrly the Iraqi Republic Railways, under the supervision of State Org. for Iraqi Railways; re-formed as a State Enterprise in 1987, under the Ministry of Transport and Communications; total length of track (1986): 2,029 km, consisting of 1,496 km of standard gauge, 533 km of one-metre gauge; Dir-Gen. MUHAMMAD Y. AL-AHMAD.

New Railways Implementation Authority: POB 17040, al-Hurriya, Baghdad; tel. 537-0021; telex 2906; f. to design and construct railways to augment the standard-gauge network and to replace the metre-gauge network; Sec.-Gen. R. A. AL-UMARI.

ROADS

At the end of 1989, according to the Central Statistical Organization, there were 36,438 km of new paved roads; 10,776 km of earth roads; and 4,039 km of roads under construction.

The most important roads are: Baghdad–Mosul–Tel Kotchuk (Syrian border), 521 km; Baghdad–Kirkuk–Arbil–Mosul-Zakho (border with Turkey), 544 km; Kirkuk–Sulaimaniya, 160 km; Baghdad–Hilla–Diwaniya–Nasiriya–Basra, 586 km; Baghdad–Kut-Nassirya, 186 km; Baghdad–Ramadi-Rurba (border with Syria), 555 km; Baghdad–Kut–Umara–Basra–Safwan (border with Kuwait), 660 km; Baghdad–Baqaba–Kanikien (border with Iran). Most sections of the six-lane 1,264-km international Express Highway, linking Safwan (on the Kuwaiti border) with the Jordanian and Syrian borders, had been completed by June 1990. The Diwaniya–Nasiriya section remains under construction, and is due to be completed in 1993. Studies have been completed for a second, 525-km Express Highway, linking Baghdad and Zakho on the Turkish border. The estimated cost of the project is more than US $4,500m. and is likely to preclude its implementation in the immediate future. An elaborate network of roads was constructed behind the war front with Iran in order to facilitate the movement of troops and supplies during the 1980–88 conflict.

Iraqi Land Transport Co: Baghdad; f. 1988 to replace State Organization for Land Transport; fleet of more than 1,000 large trucks; Dir Gen. AYSAR AS-SAFI.

Joint Land Transport Co: Baghdad; joint venture between Iraq and Jordan; operates a fleet of some 750 trucks.

State Enterprise for Implementation of Expressways: f. 1987; Dir-Gen. FAIZ MUHAMMAD SAID.

State Enterprise for Roads and Bridges: POB 917, Karradat Mariam, Karkh, Baghdad; tel. 32141; telex 212282; responsible for road and bridge construction projects to the Ministry of Housing and Construction.

SHIPPING

The ports of Basra and Umm Qasr are usually the commercial gateway of Iraq. They are connected by various ocean routes with all parts of the world, and constitute the natural distributing centre for overseas supplies. The Iraqi State Enterprise for Maritime Transport maintains a regular service between Basra, the Gulf and north European ports. The Iran-Iraq War caused the closure of the port of Basra. There is also a port at Khor az-Zubair, which came into use during 1979, although it too was closed, owing to the war with Iran.

At Basra there is accommodation for 12 vessels at the Maqal Wharves and accommodation for seven vessels at the buoys. There is one silo berth and two berths for petroleum products at Muftia and one berth for fertilizer products at Abu Flus. There is room for eight vessels at Umm Qasr. There are deep-water tanker terminals at Khor al-Amaya and Faw for three and four vessels respectively. The latter port, however, was abandoned during the early part of the Iran-Iraq War.

For the inland waterways, which are now under the control of the General Establishment for Iraqi Ports, there are 1,036 registered river craft, 48 motor vessels and 105 motor boats.

General Establishment for Iraqi Ports: Maqal, Basra; tel. 413211; telex 207008; f. 1987, when State Org. for Iraqi Ports was abolished; Dir-Gen. ABD AR-RAZZAQ ABD AL-WAHAB.

State Enterprise for Iraqi Water Transport: POB 23016, Airport St, al-Furat Quarter, Baghdad; telex 212565; f. 1987 when State Org. for Iraqi Water Transport was abolished; responsible for the planning, supervision and control of six nat. water transportation enterprises, incl.:

State Enterprise for Maritime Transport (Iraqi Line): POB 13038, al-Jadiriya al-Hurriya Ave, Baghdad; tel. 776-3201; telex 212565; Basra office: 14 July St, POB 766, Basra; tel. 210206; telex 207052; f. 1952; Dir-Gen. JABER Q. HASSAN; Operations Man. M. A. ALI.

Shipping Company

Arab Bridge Maritime Navigation Co: Aqaba, Jordan; tel. (03) 316307; telex 62354; fax (03) 316313; f. 1987; joint venture by Egypt, Iraq and Jordan to improve economic co-operation; an expansion of the company that established a ferry link between the ports of Aqaba, Jordan, and Nuweibeh, Egypt, in 1985; cap. US $6m.; Chair. NABEEH AL-ABWAH.

CIVIL AVIATION

There are international airports near Baghdad, at Bamerni, and at Basra. A new airport, Saddam International, is under construction at Baghdad. Internal flights connect Baghdad to Basra and Mosul. Civilian, as well as military, airports sustained heavy damage during the war with the multinational force in 1991. Basra airport reopened in May 1991.

National Company for Civil Aviation Services: al-Mansour, Baghdad; tel. 551-9443; telex 212662; f. 1987 following the abolition of the State Organization for Civil Aviation; responsible for the provision of aircraft, and for airport and passenger services.

Iraqi Airways Co: Saddam International Airport, Baghdad; tel. 551-9999; telex 212297; f. 1948; Dir-Gen. NOUR ED-DIN AS-SAFI HAMMADI; formerly Iraqi Airways, prior to privatization in September 1988; regular services from Baghdad to destinations throughout Asia, Europe, the Middle East and North Africa.

* Much of Iraq's transport infrastructure, including roads, bridges, civil aviation and port facilities, was destroyed or damaged in the war with the multinational force in 1991.

Tourism

The Directorate-General for Tourism was abolished in August 1988 and the various bodies under it and the services that it administered were offered for sale or lease to the private sector. The directorate was responsible for 21 summer resorts in the north, and for hotels and tourist villages throughout the country. These were to be offered on renewable leases of 25 years or sold outright.

Defence

Defence Expenditure (1993): an estimated $2,600m.

Military service: 18 months–2 years.

Total armed forces (June 1994): 382,000 (mostly conscripted): army 350,000; air force 30,000; navy 2,000; army reserves 650,000.

Commander-in-Chief of the Armed Forces: SADDAM HUSSAIN.

Chief of the General Staff: Gen. AYAD FITAYEH KHALIFA AR-RAWI.

Deputy Commander of Armed Forces: (vacant).

Commander of the Popular Army: Taha Yassin Ramadan.
Commander of the Air Force: Lt-Gen. Muzahim Sa'b Hasan.

Education

Since the establishment of the Republic in 1958, there has been a marked expansion in education at all levels. Spending on education has increased substantially since 1958, reaching ID 211m. in the 1980 budget. During 1974–75 two decisions were promulgated which constitute a landmark in the history of the Iraqi educational system. The first was a decision of the Revolutionary Command Council announcing free education in all stages from pre-primary to higher. The second decision abolished private education and transformed all existing private schools into state schools. Pre-school education is expanding, although as yet it reaches only a small proportion of children in this age-group. Primary education, lasting six years, is now officially compulsory, and there are plans to extend full-time education to nine years as soon as possible. Primary enrolment of children aged six to 11 reached 100% in 1978, but the proportion had declined to 84% by 1988. At present,

secondary education, which is expanding rapidly, is available for six years. About 39% of children aged 12 to 17 (48% of boys; 31% of girls) attended secondary schools in 1988. A US $22m. anti-illiteracy campaign began during the 1978/79 academic year. There are seven teacher training institutes in Iraq. Teacher training schools were abolished at the end of the 1985/86 academic year.

Science, medical and engineering faculties of the universities have undergone considerable expansion, although technical training is less developed. Two branches of Baghdad University at Basra and Mosul became independent universities in 1967. There are seven universities—the universities of Baghdad, Basra, Mosul, Salah ad-Din (in Arbil), al-Mustansiriya (in Baghdad), Tikrit and a university of technology (in Baghdad). Preliminary designs of two new universities at Salah ad-Din and ar-Rashid have been completed, and in February 1988 plans were announced for a further four to be established in Tikrit, al-Kufa, Ramadi (in al-Anbar governorate) and Diwaniya (in al-Qadisiya governorate). The Foundation for Technical Institutes incorporates 18 institutes of technology throughout the country. The number of students enrolled in higher education increased from 86,111 in 1975 to 183,608 in 1987.

Bibliography

GENERAL

Al-Khalil, Samir. *The Monument: Art, Vulgarity and Responsibility in Iraq.* London, André Deutsch, 1991.

Bell, Lady Florence (Ed.). *The Letters of Gertrude Lowthian Bell.* 2 vols, London, 1927.

Burgoyne, Elizabeth (Ed.). *Gertrude Bell, from her personal papers, 1914–26.* London, 1961.

Korn, David A. *Human Rights in Iraq.* New Haven, CT, Yale University Press, 1990.

Lloyd, Seton, F. H. *Iraq: Oxford Pamphlet.* Bombay, 1943.

Twin Rivers: A Brief History of Iraq from the Earliest Times to the Present Day. Oxford, 1943.

Foundations in the Dust. Oxford, 1949.

Longrigg, S. H., and Stoakes, F. *Iraq.* London, Ernest Benn, 1958.

Salter, Lord, assisted by Payton, S. W. *The Development of Iraq: A Plan of Action.* Baghdad, 1955.

Stark, Freya. *Baghdad Sketches.* London, John Murray, 1937.

Stewart, Desmond, and Haylock, John. *New Babylon: a Portrait of Iraq.* London, Collins, 1956.

ANCIENT HISTORY

Braidwood, R. J., and Howe, B. *Prehistoric Investigation in Iraqi Kurdistan.* Chicago, 1961.

Cambridge Ancient History. Vols I and II, New Ed., Cambridge, 1962.

Chaterji, S. *Ancient History of Iraq.* Calcutta, M. C. Sarkar Ltd, 1961.

Frankfort, H. *Archaeology and the Sumerian Problem.* Chicago, 1932.

The Birth of Civilization in the Near East. New York, Anchor, 1951.

Lloyd, Seton F. H. *The Art of the Ancient Near East.* London, 1961.

Ruined Cities of Iraq. Oxford, 1945.

Mesopotamia. London, 1936.

Mounds of the Near East. Edinburgh, 1964.

Mallowan, M. E. L. *Early Mesopotamia and Iran.* London, Thames and Hudson, 1965.

Oates, E. E. D. M. *Studies in the Ancient History of Northern Iraq.* London, British Academy, 1967.

Oppenheim, A. Leo. *Ancient Mesopotamia.* Chicago U.P., 1964.

Letters from Mesopotamia. Chicago U.P., 1967.

Parrot, A. *Nineveh and Babylon.* London, 1961.

Sumer. London, 1961.

Piggott, S. (Ed.). *The Dawn of Civilization.* London, 1962.

Roux, Georges. *Ancient Iraq.* London, 1964.

Saggs, H. W. F. *The Greatness that was Babylon.* London, Sidgwick and Jackson, 1962.

Stark, Freya. *Rome on the Euphrates.* London, John Murray, 1966.

Woolley, Sir C. L. *Abraham.* London, 1936.

Mesopotamia and the Middle East. London, 1961.

The Sumerians. Oxford, 1928.

Ur of the Chaldees. London, 1950.

Ur Excavations. 8 vols. Oxford, 1928–.

ISLAMIC PERIOD

Creswell, K. A. C. *Early Muslim Architecture.* 3 vols, Oxford, 1932–50.

Hitti, P. K. *A History of the Arabs.* 2nd edn, London, 1940.

Le Strange, Guy. *The Lands of the Eastern Caliphate.* Cambridge, 1905.

RECENT HISTORY

Al-Khalil, Samir. *Republic of Fear: Saddam's Iraq.* London, Hutchinson Radius, 1989.

Al-Marayati, Abid A. *A Diplomatic History of Modern Iraq.* New York, Speller, 1961.

Anderson, Ewan W., and Rashidian, Khalil. *Iraq and the Continuing Middle East Crisis.* London, Printer Publishers, 1991.

Baram, Amatzia. *Culture, History and Ideology in the Formation of Baathist Iraq, 1968–89.* Basingstoke, Macmillan, 1991.

Batatu, Hanna. *The Old Social Classes and the Revolutionary Movements of Iraq.* Princeton University Press, 1978.

Bennis, Phyllis, and Moushabeck, Michael (Eds). *Beyond the Storm: A Gulf Crisis Reader.* Edinburgh, Canongate Press, 1992.

Chubin, Shahram, and Tripp, Charles. *Iran and Iraq at War.* London, I. B. Tauris, 1988.

Cordesman, Anthony H. *The Iran-Iraq War and Western Security 1984–87.* London, Jane's Publishing Company, 1987.

Dann, Uriel. *Iraq under Qassem: A Political History 1958–63.* New York, Praeger, 1969.

Darwish, Adel, and Alexander, Gregory. *Unholy Babylon: the secret history of Saddam's war.* London, Gollancz, 1991.

Dauphin, Jacques. *Incertain Irak: Tableau d'on royaume avant la tempête.* Paris, Geuthner, 1993.

Editions du Monde Arabe. *The Iraq-Iran Conflict.* Trans. from French, Paris, 1981.

Farouk-Slugett, Marion, and Slugett, Peter. *Iraq since 1958: from Revolution to Dictatorship.* London, KPI Limited, 1988.

Foster, H. A. *The Making of Modern Iraq.* London, 1936.

Gallman, W. J. *Iraq under General Nuri.* Johns Hopkins Press, 1964.

Gittings, John (Ed.). *Beyond the Gulf War: The Middle East and the New World Order.* London, Catholic Institute for International Relations, 1991.

Heikal, Mohammed. *Illusions of Triumph: An Arab View of the Gulf War.* London, HarperCollins, 1992.

Henderson, Simon. *Instant Empire: Saddam's Ambition for Iraq*. San Francisco, Mercury House, 1991.

Hiro, Dilip. *Desert Shield to Desert Storm*. London, HarperCollins, 1992.

Ismael, Tareq Y. *Iran and Iraq: Roots of Conflict*. Syracuse, New York, Syracuse University Press, 1983.

Karsh, Efraim, and Ravtsi, Inari. *Saddam Hussein: A Political Biography*. London, Brasseys (UK), 1992.

Kent, Marian. *Oil and Empire: British Policy and Mesopotamian Oil, 1900–1920*. London, Macmillan, 1976.

Khadduri, Majid. *Independent Iraq 1932–58, A Study of Iraqi Politics*. 2nd edition, Oxford University Press, 1960.

   Republican Iraq: A study in Iraqi Politics since the Revolution of 1958. Oxford University Press, 1970.

   Socialist Iraq: A Study in Iraqi Politics since 1968. Washington, The Middle East Institute, 1978.

Kienle, Eberhard. *Ba'th versus Ba'th: The Conflict between Iraq and Syria*. London, I. B. Tauris, 1990.

Leigh, David. *Betrayed*. London, Bloomsbury, 1993.

Longrigg, S. H. *Four Centuries of Modern Iraq*. Oxford, 1925.

   Iraq 1900–1950: A Political, Social and Economic History. London, 1953.

Lowther, William. *Arms and the Man: Dr Gerald Bull, Iraq and the Supergun*. London, Macmillan, 1991.

MacArthur, Brian (Ed.). *Despatches from the Gulf War*. London, Bloomsbury, 1991.

Mark, Phoebe. *The History of Modern Iraq*. London, Longman, 1983.

Millar, Ronald. *Kut: The Death of an Army*. London, 1969.

Moberly, F. J. *The Campaign in Mesopotamia, 1914–1918*. 4 vols, London, 1923–27.

PAIFORCE: the official story of the Persia and Iraq Command, 1941–1946. London, 1948.

Penrose, Edith and E. F. *Iraq: International Relations and National Development*. Benn, Tonbridge, 1978.

Simpson, John. *From the House of War*. London, Hutchinson, 1991.

Sweeney, John. *Trading with the Enemy*. London, Pan Macmillan, 1993.

Timmerman, Kenneth R. *The Death Lobby*. London, Fourth Estate, 1992.

Wilson, Sir A. T. *Loyalties: Mesopotamia, 1914–17*. London, 1930.

   Mesopotamia, 1917–20: a Clash of Loyalties. London, University Press, 1931.

Zaki, Salih. *Origins of British Influence in Mesopotamia*. New York, 1941.

ECONOMY

Ainsrawy, Abbas. *Finance and Economic Development in Iraq*. New York, Praeger, 1966.

Gabbay, R. *Communism and Agrarian Reform in Iraq*. London, Croom Helm, 1978.

Jalal, Ferhang. *The Role of Government in the Industrialization of Iraq 1950–1965*. London, Frank Cass, 1972.

Longrigg, S. H. *Oil in the Middle East*. London, 1954.

MINORITIES

Arfa, Hassan. *The Kurds*. Oxford, Oxford University Press, 1966.

Badger, G. P. *The Nestorians and their Rituals*. 2 vols, London, 1888.

Blunt, A. T. N. *Bedouin Tribes of the Euphrates*. 2 vols, London, 1879.

Damluji, S. *The Yezidis*. Baghdad, 1948 (in Arabic).

Drower, E. S. *Peacock Angel (Being some account of Votaries of a Secret Cult and their Sanctuaries)*. London, 1941.

   The Mandeans of Iraq and Iran. Oxford, 1937.

Field, H. *Arabs of Central Iraq: Their History, Ethnology, and Physical Characters*. Chicago, 1935.

   The Anthropology of Iraq. 4 vols, 1940, 1949, 1951, 1952, Chicago (first 2 vols), Cambridge, Mass. (last 2 vols).

Kinnane, Dirk. *The Kurdish Problem*. Oxford, 1964.

   The Kurds and Kurdistan. Oxford, 1965.

Luke, Sir H. C. *Mosul and its Minorities*. London, 1925.

O'Ballance, Edgar. *The Kurdish Revolt 1961–1970*. London, Faber and Faber, 1974.

Salim, S. M. *Marsh Dwellers of the Euphrates Delta*. New York, 1961.

Short, Martin, and McDermott, Anthony. *The Kurds*. London, Minority Rights Group, 1975.

Thesiger, Wilfred. *The Marsh Arabs*. London, 1964.

Van Bruinessen, Martin. *Agha, Sheikh and State. The Social and Political Structures of Kurdistan*. London, Zed Books, 1992.

ISRAEL

Physical and Social Geography

W. B. FISHER

The pre-1967 frontiers of Israel are defined by armistice agreements signed with neighbouring Arab states, and represent the stabilization of a military front as it existed in late 1948 and early 1949. These boundaries are thus, in many respects, fortuitous, and have little geographical basis. It may be pertinent to recall that, prior to 1918, the whole area which is now partitioned between Syria, Israel and the Kingdom of Jordan formed part of the Ottoman Empire, and was spoken of as 'Syria'. Then, after 1918, came the establishment of the territories of Lebanon, Syria, Palestine and Transjordan—with the frontier between the last two lying, for the most part, along the Jordan river.

The present state of Israel is bounded on the north by Lebanon, on the north-east by Syria, on the east by the Hashemite Kingdom of Jordan, and on the south and south-west by the Gulf of Aqaba and the Sinai Desert, occupied in 1967 and returned in April 1982 to Egyptian sovereignty. The so-called 'Gaza Strip', a small piece of territory some 40 km long, formed part of Palestine but was, under the Armistice Agreement of February 1949, then left in Egyptian control. The territories which were occupied after the war of June 1967 are not recognized as forming part of the State of Israel, although it seems unlikely that Israel will reverse its annexation of the Old City of Jerusalem. The geographical descriptions of these territories are, therefore, given in the supplementary section at the end of the chapter.

Because of the nature of the frontiers, which partition natural geographical units, it is more convenient to discuss the geography of Israel partly in association with that of its neighbour, Jordan. The Jordan Valley itself, which is divided territorially between the two states, is dealt with in the chapter on Jordan, but the uplands of Samaria-Judaea, from Jenin to Hebron, and including Jerusalem, which form a single unit, will be discussed below, though a part of this territory lies outside the frontiers of Israel.

PHYSICAL FEATURES

The physical geography of Israel is surprisingly complex and, though the area of the state is small, a considerable number of regions are easily distinguished. In the extreme north the hills of the Lebanon range continue without break, though of lower altitude, to form the uplands of Galilee, where the maximum height is just over 1,200 m. The Galilee hills fall away steeply on three sides: on the east to the well-defined Jordan Valley (see Jordan), on the west to a narrow coastal plain, and to the south at the Vale of Esdraelon or 'Emek Yezreel'. This latter is a rather irregular trough formed by subsidence along faults, with a flat floor and steep sides, and it runs inland from the Mediterranean south-eastwards to reach the Jordan Valley. At its western end the vale opens into the wide Bay of Acre, 25 km to 30 km in breadth, but it narrows inland to only a few km before opening out once again where it joins the Jordan Valley. This lowland area has a very fertile soil and an annual rainfall of 400 mm, which is sufficient, with limited irrigation, for agriculture. Formerly highly malarial and largely uncultivated, the vale is now very productive. For centuries it has been a corridor of major importance linking the Mediterranean coast and Egypt with the interior of south-west Asia, and has thus been a passage-way for ethnic, cultural and military invasions.

South of Esdraelon there is an upland plateau extending for about 150 km. This is a broad upfold of rock, consisting mainly of limestone and reaching 900 m in altitude. In the north, where there is a moderate rainfall, the plateau has been eroded into valleys, some of which are fertile, though less so than those of Esdraelon or Galilee. This district, centred on Jenin and Nablus, is the ancient country of Samaria, until 1967 part of Jordan. Further south rainfall is reduced and erosion is far less prominent; hence this second region, Judaea proper, stands out as a more strongly defined ridge, with far fewer streams and a barer open landscape of a more arid and dusty character. Jerusalem, Bethlehem and Hebron are the main towns. Towards the south-east rainfall becomes scanty and we reach the Wilderness of Judaea, an area of semi-desert. In the extreme south the plateau begins to fall in altitude, passing finally into a second plateau only 300 m to 450 m above sea-level, but broader, and broken by occasional ranges of hills that reach 900 m in height. This is the Negev, a territory comprising nearly half of the total area of Israel, and bounded on the east by the lower Jordan Valley and on the west by the Sinai Desert. Agriculture, entirely dependent on irrigation, is carried on in a few places in the north, but for the most part the Negev consists of steppe or semi-desert. Irrigation schemes have been developed in those areas where soils are productive.

Between the uplands of Samaria-Judaea and the Mediterranean Sea there occurs a low-lying coastal plain that stretches southwards from Haifa as far as the Egyptian frontier at Gaza. In the north the plain is closely hemmed in by the spur of Mount Carmel (550 m), which almost reaches the sea; but the plain soon opens out to form a fertile lowland—the Plain of Sharon. Still further south the plain becomes broader again, but with a more arid climate and a sandier soil—this is the ancient Philistia. Ultimately the plain becomes quite arid, with loose sand dunes, and it merges into the Sinai Desert.

One other area remains to be mentioned—the Shephelah, which is a shallow upland basin lying in the foothills of the Judaean plateau, just east of the Plain of Sharon. This region, distinguished by a fertile soil and moister climate, is heavily cultivated, chiefly in cereals.

CLIMATE

Climatically Israel has the typical 'Mediterranean' cycle of hot, dry summers, when the temperature reaches 32°C to 38°C, and mild, rainy winters. Altitude has a considerable effect, in that though snow may fall on the hills, it is not frequent on the lowlands. Jerusalem can have several inches of snow in winter, and Upper Galilee several feet. The valleys, especially Esdraelon and adjacent parts of the upper Jordan, lying below sea-level, can become extremely hot (over 40°C) and very humid.

Rainfall varies greatly from one part of Israel to another. Parts of Galilee receive over 1,000 mm annually, but the amount decreases rapidly southwards, until in the Negev and Plain of Gaza, it is 250 mm or less. This is because the prevailing south-westerly winds blow off the sea to reach the north of Israel, but further south they come from Egypt, with only a short sea track, and therefore lack moisture.

RACE AND LANGUAGE

Discussion of the racial affinities of the Jewish people has continued for many years, but there has been little agreement on the subject. One view is that the Jewish people, whatever their origin, have now taken on many of the characteristics of the peoples among whom they have lived since the Dispersal—e.g. the Jews of Germany were often quite similar in anthropological character to the Germans; the Jews of Iraq resembled the Arabs; and the Jews of Ethiopia had black skin.

Upholders of such a view would largely deny the separateness of ethnic qualities amongst the Jews. On the other hand, it has been suggested that the Jews are really a particular and somewhat individual intermixture of racial strains that are found over wider areas of the Middle East: a special genetic 'mix' with ingredients by no means restricted to the Jews themselves. The correctness of either viewpoint is largely a matter of personal interpretation.

Under British mandatory rule there were three official languages in Palestine—Arabic, spoken by a majority of the inhabitants (all Arabs and a few Jews); Hebrew, the ancient language of the Jews; and English. This last was considered to be standard if doubt arose as to the meaning of translation from the other two.

Since the establishment of the State of Israel the relative importance of the languages has changed. Hebrew is now dominant, Arabic has greatly declined following the flight of Arab refugees, and English is also less important, though it remains the first foreign language of most Israelis.

Hebrew, widely current in biblical days, was largely eclipsed after the dispersal of Jewish people by the Romans, and until fairly recently its use was largely restricted to scholarship, serious literature and religious observance. Most Jews of Eastern and Southern Europe did not employ Hebrew as their everyday speech, but spoke either Yiddish or Ladino, the former being a Jewish-German dialect current in East and Central Europe, and the latter a form of Spanish. Immigrants into Israel since 1890 have, however, been encouraged to use Hebrew in normal everyday speech, and Hebrew is now the living tongue of most Israeli Jews. The revival has been a potent agent in the unification of the Israeli Jewish people because, in addition to the two widely different forms of speech, Yiddish and Ladino, most Jewish immigrants spoke yet another language according to their country of origin, and the census of 1931 recorded more than 60 such languages in habitual use within Palestine. Now, as the proportion of native-born Israelis increases, Hebrew is dominant, and the use of other languages diminishes.

It is only by a revival of Hebrew that the Jewish community has found a reasonable *modus vivendi*—yet this step was not easy, for some devout Jews opposed the use of Hebrew for secular speech. Furthermore, there was controversy as to the way Hebrew should be pronounced, but the Sephardic pronunciation was finally adopted.

History

TOM LITTLE

(with subsequent revisions by the Editor)

For most Jews, the creation of the State of Israel in 1948 was the fulfilment of Biblical prophecy; to some, in this more secular age, it is a country justifiably won by political skill and force of arms in a world that denied them one for nearly 2,000 years; but, however regarded, it is seen as the fulfilment of Jewish history.

Although clearly a more ancient people from east of the Euphrates, the Jews trace their descent from Abraham, the first of the Patriarchs, who departed from Ur, the centre of the ancient Chaldean civilization, about 2,000 years BC. Oral tradition, as recorded in the Old Testament, states that he was instructed by God to leave Chaldea with his family and proceed to Canaan (Phoenicia), or Palestine, the land of the Philistines, where he would father a great nation which would play an important part in human history. The authors of the Old Testament were primarily concerned to establish the descent of the Jewish people from Abraham under the guidance of God but, in so doing, they preserved the ancient history of the Jews which archaeology has tended to confirm within a debatable chronology.

Abraham's nomad family eventually reached Canaan and grazed their flocks there for a time before crossing Sinai to the richer pastures of Egypt. They remained in Egypt for probably about 400 years and multiplied greatly, but their separateness in race, religion and customs at last excited the fears of the pharaohs, who enslaved them. Moses, who had escaped this slavery because he was brought up as an Egyptian, fled with the Jews from the country (c. 1200 BC) and gave them his law (the Torah), proclaiming the absolute oneness of God and establishing the disciplines for worship.

They wandered for some decades in the wilderness before reaching the River Jordan. Moses' successor, Joshua, led some of the families (or tribes) across it and conquered Canaan. It was a stormy occupation of constant conflict with the indigenous peoples until the warrior Saul triumphed and became the first 'king'. His successor, David, completed the subjugation of the Israelites' enemies and briefly united all the tribes. King Solomon, his son, raised the country to its peak and built the Temple of Jerusalem which came to be recognized as the temple of all the Jews and the focal point of worship. His magnificence burdened the people, and this and his tolerance of the worship of idols provoked a successful revolt of the 10 northern tribes under Jereboam who established Israel as his own kingdom. This division into two parts, Israel and Judah (which contained Jerusalem), was disastrous, for Israel was soon overcome by the Assyrians and its people were taken into captivity and lost to history. About 100 years later Judah fell victim to the Babylonians and its people were also taken captive, but their community endured to become an important element in the future of Judaism. The Babylonians destroyed Solomon's temple.

When the Persian leader Cyrus conquered Babylon he gave the Jews permission to return to Jerusalem, and some did so. There they set about rebuilding the Temple which was completed about 500 BC and in 200 years of relative tranquillity their religion was consolidated by a series of great teachers. Palestine was in turn conquered by Alexander the Great and it and the Jews became part of his empire; but Alexander was tolerant, as were his successors in Egypt, the Ptolemies, with the result that Alexandria became the centre of a learned school of Hellenic Judaism.

This tolerant policy was reversed under the Roman empire, which succeeded the Ptolemies. The Jews rebelled against the oppressive Roman rule and Nero sent his greatest general, Vespasian, and his son, Titus, to suppress them. The conquest was completed by Titus; Jerusalem and the second temple were destroyed (c. AD 70), and the Diaspora which began with the Assyrian conquest of Israel was complete. A small community of Jews remained in Jerusalem and the surrounding countryside, and devoted themselves to their religion, producing their version of the Talmud, the repository of Judaic history, learning and interpretation which, with the Torah and the Old Testament became the essence of the faith, but it was the version of the Talmud produced by the Babylonian scholars which became the accepted document.

Scattered across the world, throughout Arabia, Asia as far as China, North Africa and Europe as far as Poland and Russia, Jewish communities continued to exist, sometimes powerful, often persecuted, but united by religion and certain central themes: their belief in the oneness of God, His promise to Abraham, the promise of the 'return', and the Temple as the temple of all Jews. In terms of time their occupation of Palestine was relatively short and for even less of that time did they hold or rule it all, but the scattered communities continued to look towards Jerusalem.

THE ZIONIST MOVEMENT

In the late 19th century there were affluent and even powerful groups of Jews in Europe but the people as a whole were usually treated as second-class citizens in the countries where they lived. The large, pious and orthodox groups in Eastern Europe, in particular, were subject intermittently to persecution, and in 1881 there was a series of pogroms in Russia which stirred the conscience of world Jewry into forming plans for their escape. For the Eastern Jews there could be only one destination: Palestine. The pogroms led directly to the formation in Russia of a movement called the Lovers of Zion (Hovevei Zion), and within that movement another was formed, called the Bilu, by a large community of young Jews in the Kharkov region. In 1882 a Bilu group in Constantinople issued a manifesto demanding a home in Palestine. They proposed that they should beg it from the Sultan of Turkey, in whose empire Palestine lay.

The word Zionism was coined by a Russian about a decade later as a spiritual-humanitarian concept but Theodor Herzl, who became the leader of the movement, defined its aim specifically at the Basle Congress of 1897 (see Documents on Palestine, p. 79): 'Zionism', he said, 'strives to create for the Jewish people a home in Palestine secured by public law.' He wrote in his journal after the congress: 'At Basle I founded the Jewish State . . . perhaps in five years, and certainly fifty, everyone will know it.' He is recognized as the founder of political Zionism.

He was concerned essentially with the creation of a safe refuge for the suffering communities of Eastern Europe and thought that their migration and settlement could and should be financed by prosperous Jews. When he failed to get help from the Sultan he considered other possible 'homes' as far apart as Uganda and Latin America, but even safe places could never have the same appeal to orthodox Jews as Palestine, sanctioned in their scriptures and 'promised' to them by God. Some of the Jews of Russia and Poland escaped persecution to make their own way to Palestine and became the earliest immigrant communities there.

When the Turkish Empire was destroyed by Allied forces in the 1914–18 war new possibilities of getting their 'home' or state in Palestine opened up before the Zionists. In the years 1915–16 Sir Mark Sykes for Britain and M. Charles Georges-Picot for France had, in fact, drafted an agreement (see Documents on Palestine, p. 79) in which, while undertaking 'to recognize and protect an independent Arab State or Confederation of Arab States', the two powers in effect carved the Middle East into their respective spheres of influence and authority pending the time of its liberation from Turkey. Influential Zionists, notably Dr Chaim Weizmann, saw their opportunity to press Britain for a commitment to provide a home for the Jews in Palestine and secured the help of Judge Louis Brandeis, a leading US Zionist and principal adviser to President Woodrow Wilson, in bringing the USA into the war on the side of the Allies in April 1917. The outcome was the Balfour Declaration (see Documents on Palestine, p. 80) which was contained in a letter from Arthur James Balfour to Lord Rothschild on behalf of the Zionist Federation, dated 2 November 1917. It stated:

'His Majesty's Government view with favour the establishment in Palestine of a national home for the Jewish people, and will use their best endeavours to facilitate the achievement of this object, it being clearly understood that nothing shall be done which may prejudice the existing civil and religious rights of existing non-Jewish communities in Palestine, or the rights and political status of Jews in other countries.'

The San Remo Conference decided on 24 April 1920 to give the Mandate under the newly formed League of Nations to Britain (the terms of which were approved by the USA, which was not a member of the League, before they were finally agreed by the League Council on 24 July 1922). The terms (see Documents on Palestine, p. 82) included a restatement of the Balfour Declaration and provided that 'an appropriate Jewish agency' should be established to advise and co-operate with the Palestine Administration in matters affecting the Jewish national home and to take part in the development of the country. This gave the Zionist Organization a special position because the Mandate stipulated that it should be recognized as such an agency if the mandatory authority thought it appropriate. Britain took over the Mandate in September 1923.

THE MANDATE

Herzl's first aim had thereby been achieved: the national home of the Jewish people had been 'secured by public law'; but major obstacles were still to be overcome before the home, or state, became a reality. When the Mandate was granted, the Arabs constituted 92% of the population and owned 98% of the land in Palestine, and it could clearly not be a home unless the demography and land ownership were changed in favour of the Jews. It was to these ends that the Zionist movement now directed itself, but Britain had different views concerning what was meant by 'favouring' the establishment of the home, both in the matter of boundaries and immigration, even while it remained sympathetic to the enterprise. This was important, for although nominally under the supervision of the Mandates Commission of the League, Britain was able to run Palestine very much as a Crown Colony and administered it through the Colonial Office.

The World Zionist Organization had presented a memorandum to the Paris Peace Conference in 1919 setting forth its territorial concept of the home, as follows:

The whole of Palestine, southern Lebanon, including the towns of Tyre and Sidon, the headwaters of the Jordan river on Mount Hermon and the southern portion of the Litani river; the Golan Heights in Syria, including the town of Quneitra, the Yarmuk river and Al-Himmeh hot springs; the whole of the Jordan valley, the Dead Sea, and the eastern highlands up to the outskirts of Amman, thence in a southerly direction along the Hedjaz railway to the Gulf of Aqaba; in Egypt, from El-Arish, on the Mediterranean coast, in a straight line in a southerly direction to Sharm el-Sheikh on the Gulf of Aqaba.

The League of Nations and the Peace Settlement did not accept these boundaries but the Mandate given to Britain included Transjordan, the territory east of the river and beyond Amman. Britain allotted Transjordan as an Emirate to Emir Abdullah in 1921 and with the grant of full independence in 1946 it became a kingdom.

The Arabs bitterly opposed the Balfour Declaration and Jewish immigration and called for the prohibition of land sales to Jews. Britain would neither accede to their demands nor to Jewish claims to a majority in Palestine. There were intermittent outbreaks of Arab violence, notably in 1922 and 1929, which brought the Arabs into conflict with the mandatory government and there were four British Commissions of Inquiry and two White Papers were issued (see Documents on Palestine, p. 82) on the situation before 1936, none of which envisaged a Jewish majority. In 1936 there was an effective six-month general strike of the Arab population followed by a large-scale rebellion which lasted until the outbreak of the Second World War and in 1939 another Commission issued the third White Paper (see Documents on Palestine, p. 84) which stated that Britain would not continue to develop the Jewish national home beyond the point already reached, proposed that 75,000 more Jews should be admitted over five years and then Jewish immigration would cease. Finally, it proposed that self-governing institutions should be set up at the end of the five years. This would have preserved the Arab majority in the country and its legislature.

THE BILTMORE PROGRAMME AND AFTER

International opinion at that time was conditioned by the horrifying Nazi policy of exterminating Jews—a policy which was to reach even more frightful proportions after the outbreak of war. Zionists and Jews generally regarded the White Paper as a betrayal of the terms of the Mandate and when David Ben Gurion, Chairman of the Jewish Agency Executive, was in New York in 1942 an Extraordinary Zionist Conference held at the Biltmore Hotel utterly rejected the White Paper and reformulated Zionist policy. The declaration of the conference (see Documents on Palestine, p. 85), issued on 11 May 1942, concluded as follows:

The conference urges that the gates of Palestine be opened; that the Jewish Agency be vested with control of immigration into Palestine and with the necessary authority for upbuilding the country, including the development of its unoccupied and uncultivated lands; and that Palestine be established as a Jewish Commonwealth integrated into the new structure of the democratic world.

This policy brought the Jews into direct conflict with the Palestine Government before the war was over. Those in Europe who escaped the Nazi holocaust were herded into refugee camps and some who could do so with organized Zionist help tried to reach Palestine, but the British authorities, in accordance with the 1939 policy, tried to prevent their entry.

The British failed. The Jewish population which had been 56,000 at the time of the Mandate was 608,000 in 1946 and was estimated to be 650,000 on the eve of the creation of Israel, or about two-fifths of the entire population. Further, the Jewish Agency had formed its own military organizations, the Haganah, and its units of shock troops, the Palmach, which were strengthened by those Jews who had fought on the side of the British during the war, and supported by two smaller extremist groups, the Irgun Zvaei Leumi and the Stern Gang. Towards the end of the war they embarked on a policy of violence designed to impose the Biltmore programme. They successfully made the Mandate unworkable and Britain referred it to the United Nations (which had replaced the League) on 2 April 1947.

The UN General Assembly sent a Special Commission (UNSCOP) to Palestine to report on the situation, and its report, issued on 31 August 1947, proposed two plans: a majority plan for the partition of Palestine into two states, one Jewish and one Arab, with economic union; and a minority plan for a federal state. The Assembly adopted the majority plan (see Documents on Palestine, p. 86) on 29 November by 33 votes for and 13 against, with 10 abstentions. The plan divided Palestine into six principal parts, three of which, comprising 56% of the total area, were reserved for the Jewish state, and three (with the enclave of Jaffa), comprising 43% of the area, for the Arab state. It provided that Jerusalem would be an international zone administered by the UN as the holy city for Jews, Muslims and Christians. The Arabs refused to accept this decision and, in the subsequent disorders, about 1,700 people were killed. In April 1948 the Jewish forces swung into full-scale attack and, by the time the Mandate was terminated on 14 May, 400,000 Arabs had evacuated their homes to become refugees in neighbouring Arab countries.

THE STATE ESTABLISHED

The Mandate was relinquished by Britain at 6 p.m. Washington time; at 6.01 the State of Israel was officially declared by the Jewish authorities in Palestine; at 6.11 the USA accorded it recognition and immediately afterwards the USSR did likewise. Thus Israel came into existence only one year later than Herzl's 50-year diary prophecy. The Arab states belatedly came to the help of the Palestinian Arabs but their attempt to overthrow the new state failed and Israel was left in possession of more territory than had been allotted to it under the UN partition plan, including new (non-Arab) Jerusalem. Israel rejected the proposed internationalization of the city, for the Jews considered the return to Jerusalem to be central to their divine legacy.

A provisional government was formed in Tel-Aviv the day before the Mandate ended, with Ben Gurion as Prime Minister and other members of the Jewish Agency Executive in leading ministerial posts. The constitution and electoral laws had already been prepared and the first general elections were held in January 1949 for a single-chamber Knesset (or Parliament) elected by proportional representation. This enabled several parties to gain representation, with Mapai usually in the majority but never predominant. As a result, government has usually been conducted by uneasy coalitions.

After the war another 400,000 Arabs fled from the additional territory conquered by Israel and in the course of another year about 300,000 more left the impoverished Arab West Bank for Transjordan. (In 1950 King Abdullah held a referendum in which the West Bank Arabs agreed to be part of his kingdom which then became known as Jordan.) The Israeli Government maintained the mandatory military control, established in the earlier disorders, over those Arab populations which remained within its territory but allowed

'co-operative' Arabs to be elected to the Knesset; four were elected to the first Parliament.

A gigantic programme of immigration was launched immediately the Provisional Government took over and within three years the Jewish population was doubled. This result, unparalleled in history, was assisted by Iraq which expelled the larger part of its age-old Jewish communities. The 1961 census gave Israel's population as 2,260,700, of whom 230,000 were Arabs. The two-millionth Jew arrived in May 1962 and the three-millionth early in 1972. A massive plan for land development to provide for the new people was executed concomitantly with the early immigration programme; the Jewish National Fund took over 3m. dunums of former Arab land and used heavy mechanical equipment to bring it rapidly back into production. This was made possible by the stupendous support from abroad which came in the form of private gifts from world Jewry, state loans and aid, and private Jewish investments. The USA was both privately and publicly the major contributor, but at the Hague in 1952 West Germany agreed to pay reparations for Nazi crimes, and these payments amounted to £216m. in Deutsche Marks before they were concluded in 1966. One effect of this influx of unearned money from all sources was to cause serious inflation which was still a problem in the 1990s (see Economy).

Israel was admitted to the UN, albeit on conditions concerning Jerusalem and refugees which were contrary to its overall policy and were never fulfilled. Its relations with the Arab states were governed by a series of armistice agreements reached in Rhodes in 1949 which, in effect, established an uneasy truce without an Arab commitment to permanent peace. The Arabs continued to insist that the creation of Israel was a usurpation of Arab territory and right and a denial of UN principles. Defence policy therefore dominated Israel's political thinking and firmly established the principle that it would remain militarily superior to any combination of Arab states. In the early 1950s, however, it was the Palestinian refugees who caused intermittent frontier trouble, mainly from Syria and Jordan, but to some extent from the Gaza Strip which, since the 1948 war, had been administered by Egypt.

Whenever one of the frontiers became too troublesome, Israel mounted a retaliatory raid *pour décourager les autres*. Acting on the principle that Nasser's Egypt was the only serious danger, Ben Gurion ordered a raid which on 28 February 1955, wiped out the small Egyptian garrison at Gaza and the reinforcements travelling by road to its support. The result was contrary to Ben Gurion's intention; Nasser determined to secure adequate military strength and to that end entered into the 'Czech' arms agreement in August 1955, by which he bartered cotton and took credits from the USSR for substantial quantities of arms and planes which began to arrive quickly. The threat to Israel was therefore increased.

SUEZ

On 26 July 1956 Nasser nationalized the Suez Canal Company of which Britain and France were the principal shareholders (see Egypt) and the two European powers prepared to retake control of it. Neither could expect any support from the two superpowers, or from world opinion in general, for open invasion, but in October Ben Gurion entered into a secret pact with them by which Israel would invade Sinai and thus justify Britain and France intervening to keep the combatants apart. Israel invaded on 29 October, with powerful armoured columns, and rapidly advanced towards the Canal. The following day Britain and France issued their ultimatum that both sides should withdraw to 20 miles from the Canal. Israel, which had by this time taken almost all of the Sinai, including the Gaza Strip and Sharm esh-Sheikh at the entrance to the Gulf of Aqaba, readily agreed to comply with the ultimatum, but Egypt refused on the grounds that it was being asked to withdraw from its own territory.

The Anglo-French force thereupon invaded the Port Said area and advanced some miles along the Suez Canal. There it was halted by Sir Anthony Eden, the British Prime Minister, in face of the forthright condemnation of the UN and financial sanctions threatened by the USA; a decision which the French Prime Minister, M. Guy Mollet, reluctantly accepted. Both countries withdrew their troops before the year was out. This was a severe blow to Ben Gurion who had counted on holding at least a security buffer zone on a line from el-Arish, on the Mediterranean coast, to Sharm esh-Sheikh (the Zionist 1919 frontier proposal). Therefore Israel delayed its final withdrawal from Egypt until January, and from the Gaza Strip until March 1957 when a UN Emergency Force was safely established on the Sinai frontier and at Sharm esh-Sheikh.

A development of great consequence to Israel at this time was the increasing involvement of the Soviet Union in the Middle East, especially in Egypt. The USSR took no less than 50% of Egyptian exports in 1957, and in 1958 agreed to finance and direct the building of the mammoth High Dam at Aswan. In keeping with this policy, the Soviet Union adopted a strongly pro-Arab and anti-Israeli line and steadily rearmed Nasser's forces.

Ben Gurion resigned 'for personal reasons' in June 1963 and was succeeded by Levi Eshkol, his minister of finance, who had been a minister continuously since joining the Provisional Government from the Jewish Agency in 1948. He was in modern terminology a 'dove', inclined to a more conciliatory policy which he hoped would in time erode Arab enmity. This was opposed by many in the ruling hierarchy, notably the veteran Ben Gurion and Gen. Moshe Dayan, who had commanded the Israeli forces in their brilliant victory in 1956.

There was a notable increase in Arab guerrilla activity across the frontiers of Egypt, Jordan and Syria in the mid-1960s. The Palestinians formed a guerrilla organization called al-Fatah for which the Syrian Prime Minister publicly declared his support in 1966. Mutual accusations of frontier violations followed, and President Nasser warned that he would have to activate the Egypt-Syrian Joint Defence Agreement if Israel's 'aggression' did not cease. In May 1967 King Hussein brought Jordan into the agreement and in that same month Nasser received information, which later proved to be untrue, that Israeli troops were massing on the Syrian frontier. In response Nasser ordered the withdrawal of the UN Emergency Force from the Gaza Strip, the Sinai Desert and Sharm esh-Sheikh. U Thant, the Secretary-General of the UN, immediately obeyed, and Nasser then imposed a total blockade on Israeli shipping in the Straits of Tiran, although Israel had always made it plain that this would be considered a *casus belli*.

U Thant flew to Cairo on 22 May 1967 but, by that time, Nasser had already strengthened his forces in the Sinai and called up his reserves. Israel, Jordan and Syria had also mobilized. Israel formed a national government by bringing into the Cabinet one representative of each of the three opposition parties. Gen. Moshe Dayan, the leader of the 1956 Sinai campaign, was brought in as Minister of Defence.

THE JUNE WAR

Israel made its pre-emptive strike in the early hours of 5 June when its armoured forces moved into Sinai. At 0600 hours GMT Israeli planes attacked 25 airfields in Egypt, Jordan, Syria and Iraq, destroying large numbers of planes on the ground and putting the runways out of action, thus effectively depriving the Egyptian and Jordanian ground forces of air cover. There were some fierce armoured battles in the Sinai but Israeli forces were in position along the Suez Canal on 8 June. They took Sharm esh-Sheikh without a fight. On the eastern front, they reached the Jordan river on 7 June and entered and conquered Old (Arab) Jerusalem on the same day. Their main forces destroyed, President Nasser and King Hussein accepted a cease-fire on 8 June. Israel then turned its attention to the Syrian fortifications on the Golan Heights from which Israeli settlements were being shelled. In a brilliant but costly action, armour and infantry captured the heights. Syria accepted a cease-fire on 9 June but Israel ignored it until 10 June, by which time its troops were in possession of Quneitra, on the road to Damascus. The 'six-day war', as it became known, was over; Israel had achieved a victory more sweeping even than that of 1956.

Israel had recovered Jerusalem and access to the Western Wall of the Temples of Solomon and Herod, which were the most sacred places of worship for all Jews but to which they had been denied access since the partition of the city between the Arabs and Israel in 1948. Israel immediately tore down the barriers, reunited the city, put the administration of Arab Jerusalem under its existing city administration, and effectively annexed it. The UN General Assembly passed a resolution on 4 July which Israel disregarded, calling on it to rescind all the measures taken and to desist from any further action that would change the status of the holy city. Israel made it plain from the outset that there could be no question of returning Old Jerusalem to Arab possession in any peace settlement.

The UN and the world powers busied themselves with the peace process. On 29 August the heads of the Arab states began a summit conference in Khartoum at which they decided to seek a political settlement but not to make peace with or recognize Israel or to negotiate directly with it, and meanwhile 'to adopt necessary measures to strengthen military preparation to face all eventualities'. On 22 November, after many attempts, the UN Security Council agreed to Resolution 242, which stated that the establishment of a just and lasting peace in the Middle East should include the application of the following principles:

(i) withdrawal of Israeli armed forces from territories occupied in the recent conflict; and (ii) termination of all claims or states of belligerency and respect for and acknowledgement of the sovereignty, territorial integrity, and political independence of every State in the area, and their right to live in peace within secure and recognized boundaries free from threats or acts of force. The Council affirmed also the necessity for (*a*) guaranteeing freedom of navigation through international waterways in the area, and (*b*) achieving a just settlement of the refugee problem.

The Secretary-General designated Ambassador Gunnar Jarring of Sweden as Special Representative to assist the process of finding a peaceful settlement on this basis.

The essential ambiguity of the Council resolution was contained in the phrase 'withdrawal . . . from territories occupied . . .' (which in the French translation became 'les territoires'), and the Israeli Government contended that it meant an agreed withdrawal from some occupied territories 'to secure and recognized boundaries'. This was, in Israel's view, precluded by the Arab states' Khartoum Resolution and their insistence that Resolution 242 meant total withdrawal from the 1967 occupied territories. Further, Israel insisted that it would only negotiate withdrawal directly with Egypt and the Arab states as part of a peace settlement and that the function of Jarring was to bring this about and not to initiate proposals of his own for a settlement.

UNEASY SECURITY

Meanwhile Israel based its policy on retention of the Occupied Territories as warranty for its security. The 1967 defeat had severely damaged the USSR's prestige in the Arab world, and to repair its position it began immediately to restore the Egyptian armed forces, including the air force. Meanwhile in 1967 President de Gaulle imposed an arms embargo on Israel and refused to deliver 50 supersonic *Mirage* IV fighters which Israel had ordered and paid for. Israel therefore turned to the USA arguing that the balance of military power must, for its security, be maintained in its favour. This point was conceded by the USA in 1968 with a contract to deliver 50 Phantom jet fighter-bombers, which brought Cairo within range and were more powerful than any MiGs in Egypt.

Using powerful artillery installed by the USSR west of the Canal, Nasser began in 1968 a 'war of attrition' in order to force Israel to accept his terms. Relatively heavy casualties were inflicted on the Israeli troops, notably in July and October, and throughout the period Israel retaliated with air and artillery attacks which forced Egypt to evacuate the Canal zone towns. Suez and its oil refineries were destroyed. The zone remained unsettled until 1970.

Israel's Prime Minister, Levi Eshkol, died on 26 February 1969, and was succeeded in the following month by Mrs Golda Meir, who had been Minister for Foreign Affairs from 1956 to 1966.

President Nixon, who had taken office in the USA, supported an initiative by his Secretary of State, William Rogers, 'to encourage the parties to stop shooting and start talking'. This was announced on 25 June 1970, and was unfavourably received in the Arab world. Nasser flew to Moscow with a proposal to accept it on condition that Russia supplied SAM-III missiles capable of destroying low-flying aircraft. He returned to Cairo and stunned Egypt and the Arab world with an unconditional acceptance of the Rogers plan and its related Canal zone 90-day cease-fire. King Hussein immediately associated Jordan with Nasser's acceptance. Israel accepted the Rogers plan on 7 August but immediately complained that Egypt had broken the cease-fire agreement by moving SAM-III missile sites into the 30-mile wide standstill area along the canal.

President Nasser died suddenly on 28 September 1970, but President Sadat, who succeeded him, sustained his policy. Although he only agreed to extend the cease-fire for another 90 days, it continued indefinitely. The US effort was directed towards securing an interim agreement by which Israel would withdraw from the Suez Canal and allow it to be reopened, but Israel, again on the basic principle of its security, would only consider a limited withdrawal and would not agree that Egyptian troops should cross the Canal, terms which Egypt would not accept. US-Israeli relations, vital to Israel, were uneasy during most of 1971 while the Department of State pressed the Israeli Government to concede unacceptable terms of withdrawal from the Canal. President Sadat gave the end of the year as a deadline for 'peace or war', but before the year was out Mrs Golda Meir secured a commitment to Israeli security from President Nixon firmer than any obtained in the past; the Rogers plan was thereby abandoned, but 1972 began without the threatened outbreak of war with Egypt. Instead, there was a series of terrorist acts by various Palestinian groups, which in turn provoked punitive raids by Israeli forces.

The stated objective of Israeli raids on Syria and Lebanon was to compel both countries to prevent the Palestinian resistance groups from mounting raids from within their borders, whether against Israel or in other countries. This objective seemed most successfully achieved in Lebanon on 10 April 1972 by a daring commando raid into the heart of Beirut, where the raiders killed three resistance leaders, while other commando units attacked two refugee camps outside the city and destroyed the PDFLP headquarters, killing one of its leaders. The Israeli authorities were able to make a number of arrests in the Occupied Territories from information gained in this raid.

THE OCCUPIED TERRITORIES

About 380,000 Arabs fled from the West Bank to Jordan, but nearly one million remained under Israeli occupation; of these, the 70,000 in East (Arab) Jerusalem, which was annexed, were treated as Israeli citizens and the remainder brought under military administration. This was of necessity strict for the first three years because of help given to Palestinian guerrillas by the Arabs in the Occupied Territories and, in some instances, in Israel proper. The Gaza Strip was by far the most troublesome and it was not until the end of 1971 that Israeli security operations, including the clearance of one large refugee camp which had proved particularly difficult, brought the area under control. It was announced in March 1973 that the strip would be incorporated into Israel, that Jewish settlement in the strip would continue and that Arab inhabitants could circulate freely in Israel during the day. Higher living standards enjoyed by the Arabs under the occupation, 60,000 of whom found work in Israel itself, the inevitable growth of collaboration with the Israeli authorities and, finally, the disarray in which the Palestinian movement found itself by late 1970, rendered the security problem inside the country minimal during 1971. In March of the following year the Israeli military authorities successfully held elections for the mayors and municipalities in the main Arab towns, despite guerrilla threats of reprisals against any Arabs taking part.

Government policy was officially that in a peace settlement there would be substantial territories returned to the Arabs but there was no clear consensus in the Government or the country as to what they would amount to, except to the extent that Israel should have 'secure frontiers'. However, statements by ministers made it clear that in addition to East Jerusalem and the Gaza Strip, which had been effectively annexed, the Golan Heights of occupied Syria and parts of the Jordanian West Bank would not be returned. There was also increasing evidence on the ground. An extensive building programme to house immigrants was rapidly being executed in and around Jerusalem; 42 settlements had been established by January 1973 although, according to Israeli figures, only 3,150 Israeli civilians had been allowed to take up permanent residence in the areas.

Israel radio announced on 18 August 1973 that another 35 settlements would be built in the Occupied Territories, bringing the total to 77. The Jewish National Fund and the Israeli Lands Administration had between them acquired 15,000 acres (6,070 ha) of Arab land and the army was in occupation of another 20,000 acres (8,100 ha). A plan advanced by Deputy Prime Minister Yigal Allon, although not publicly approved by the Government, seemed to be in process of *de facto* execution. He proposed that a chain of Israeli settlements should be established along the Jordan river, which was effectively being done, a second chain along the Samarian hills on the West Bank, and a third along the road from Jerusalem to Jericho, in order to establish Israel's security. The rest of the West Bank and the main towns, excepting Jericho, would then be returned to Jordan.

The virtue of the Allon plan for most Israelis was that it would absorb few Arabs, for the core of the dispute within Israel remained the question of demographic balance between Arabs and Jews which would be changed in the Arabs' favour by the absorption of territory in which there were many of them resident. For that reason, the Government refused the request, submitted by the newly-elected mayors of the Arab towns on the West Bank, that those Arabs who had fled the area after the 1967 war should be allowed to return. To restore the population balance the Jewish Agency, which was responsible for organizing immigration, concentrated upon Jews in the USSR, who were the largest reservoir of would-be immigrants. The USSR began to relax its stringent opposition to Jewish emigration in 1971, with the result that thousands of Soviet Jews began to arrive in Israel.

THE YOM KIPPUR WAR

Although the Arab world had been urging Sadat to attack Israel, it was firmly believed that Egypt was afraid to go to war again and that the Bar-Lev defences along the eastern bank of the Suez Canal could not be overcome. In fact Sadat was working steadily towards war, against the advice of his Soviet ally. He secured the financial support of King Faisal of Saudi Arabia to buy arms for hard currency, the agreement of Syria's President Hafiz Assad to a limited war for the recovery of territories lost in 1967, made his peace with King Hussein of Jordan and finally secured the arms required from the USSR.

By the late summer of 1973 he was ready for war on two fronts, Syria and Egypt, with King Hussein standing aside to tie up a part of Israeli forces facing Jordan. At 2 p.m. on 6 October—the most important religious festival in Israel, Yom Kippur—the Egyptians launched their attack, breaking down the supposedly impregnable sand banks of the Bar-Lev line with powerful water-jets, throwing pontoon bridges across the Suez Canal and breaking into Sinai. By midnight that day, the Egyptians had 500 tanks and missiles across the Canal and destroyed 100 Israeli tanks. Almost simultaneously the Syrian armed forces had broken through the Israeli lines on the Golan Heights.

Israel began the rapid mobilization of its reserve forces, the highly trained and numerically most important part of its defensive system, but before they could play an effective part Egyptian armed forces had occupied the east bank of the Canal to a depth of several miles and by the third day were advancing to the strategic Mitla pass in Sinai. The Syrian forces had by that time reached a point five miles from the Israeli frontier in Golan.

While fierce tank battles, said to be bigger than any in the Second World War, raged in Sinai, Israel halted the Syrian forces on its vulnerable northern frontier and counter-attacked successfully, driving them in a fighting retreat back over the 1967 cease-fire lines to within 20 miles of Damascus, where its forces were halted on the Syrian second line of defence. The Egyptian forces held their positions in Sinai but did not reach the Mitla pass.

The Egyptian High Command blundered on the twelfth day when it allowed a small Israeli commando force to cross to the west bank of the Suez Canal near Deversoir at the northern end of the Great Bitter Lake. The Israeli force was able to reinforce the bridgehead with a force strong enough to swing southwards to Suez and endanger the Egyptian Third Army on the east bank. Losses were very heavy on both sides.

After three UN Security Council resolutions, a precarious cease-fire came into effect on 25 October, but even this was honoured more in the breach than the observance until the end of the year. The US Secretary of State, Dr Henry Kissinger, did much to maintain a peace-making momentum by tours of the Arab countries to secure negotiations for a permanent settlement in Geneva on 18 December and in November Israel had accepted 'in principle' the terms of an agreement Dr Kissinger had reached with President Sadat for the 'scrupulous' observance of the cease-fire.

Talks were soon adjourned to an unspecified date in order to allow time for the Israeli general elections, which had been postponed from 30 October to 31 December 1973 because of the war. Dr Henry Kissinger returned to the Middle East in January and after days of intensive diplomatic activity, shuttling back and forward between Israel and Egypt, he secured the agreement of both countries to a disengagement of their forces which was announced on 17 January 1974 (see Documents on Palestine, p. 89). Israel agreed to withdraw its troops in Sinai to a line approximately 20 miles from the Suez Canal and Egypt to reduce its forces on the east bank. There was to be a neutral buffer zone between the two armies manned by troops of the UN Emergency Force.

Agreement for the disengagement of forces on the northern front was not signed until 31 May (see Documents on Palestine, p. 89) and then only after further shuttle diplomacy by Dr Kissinger. Israel and Syria agreed to withdraw their troops to lines on each side of the 1967 cease-fire line, and the ruined town of Quneitra, capital of the Golan Heights, was handed back to Syria.

Two important factors weakened Israel's position. In the last days of the war the Arab oil-producing states banned the supply of oil to the USA and the Netherlands, and reduced supplies to Western Europe. (Britain and France were exempted but, in fact, were unable to obtain their full supplies.) This, combined with steep increases in oil prices which caused serious balance-of-payments problems for the European countries—although this had nothing to do with the war—led the EC to issue a joint declaration in the Arab favour. Even more damaging to Israel was the confrontation which almost developed between the USSR and the USA when they both began delivering heavy supplies of war equipment to the Arabs and Israel respectively. Dr Kissinger made it clear to Israel that the USA would continue to support Israel, but only within the limits imposed by *détente* with the USSR. It was unquestionably a form of pressure on Israel, although this was denied. President Nixon went on a peace-making mission to the Middle East in June, and shortly afterwards Israel's Minister of Finance, Shimon Peres, visited Washington. The outcome was the conversion of a $500m. loan into a gift and an undertaking to supply a powerful force of warplanes to ensure Israel's security.

THE AFTERMATH

The war had a profoundly disturbing effect on Israeli public opinion. The country had never suffered such losses before; nearly 3,000 dead and missing, which was a substantial proportion of so small a population. The ease with which the Egyptian forces had crossed the Canal and overrun the Bar-Lev line and the firmness with which the Syrian forces held the second line of defence 20 miles from Damascus were not offset in Israeli eyes by the fact that Israeli troops had broken through and recrossed the Canal and had made territorial gains in Syria; the Arab forces had fought with hitherto unknown determination and had used their sophisticated Soviet weaponry with great skill. The public's confidence in the overwhelming superiority of their own army and air force was severely shaken, with the result that a sharp division of

opinion occurred between those who thought the war emphasized the need to keep defensible frontiers at all costs and those, less numerous, who viewed it as an argument for a more diligent search for a permanent peace. There was widespread dissatisfaction with the Government and a public debate ensued over the failure to anticipate the outbreak of war and the breakdown of military intelligence. There were mutual recriminations among the generals and the Minister of Defence Moshe Dayan's popularity in the country slumped. General Ariel Sharon, whose forces had made the breakthrough and Canal crossing in Egypt, resigned from the army to join the right-wing Likud Party—the 'hawks' of Israeli politics.

The elections of December 1973 reflected this confusion. The Labour Alignment, led by Mapam, emerged as the strongest party, with 51 seats. Likud, the main opposition, made substantial gains and won 39 seats. Mrs Golda Meir reformed her coalition but resigned in April 1974, when the report on the 1973 war was published. She was succeeded in June by Gen. Itzhak Rabin, whose Cabinet contained neither Moshe Dayan nor Abba Eban, who had been Minister of Foreign Affairs since 1966. General Rabin and his Minister of Foreign Affairs, Yigal Allon, were both willing to make territorial sacrifices to achieve a settlement with the Arabs, and in September 1975 Israel and Egypt signed a Second Disengagement Agreement, whereby Israeli forces withdrew from some territory in the Sinai peninsula.

Meanwhile the PLO had achieved recognition by the Arabs as 'sole representative of the Palestinian people' at the Rabat summit of November 1974, but Rabin asserted Israeli policy, which he was to maintain throughout his premiership, of refusing to recognize a PLO delegation at any renewed Geneva peace talks.

Rabin was never able to command the support that he needed as Prime Minister. Moreover, Israel's economic difficulties (described in the Economy) cost Rabin considerable popularity, and it seemed that the austerity measures that he was forced to introduce to combat inflation won him few hearts, discouraged immigration, and made little visible progress towards a sounder economy.

In December 1976 the National Religious Party (NRP) abstained in a confidence vote in the Knesset arising from charges that the Sabbath had been desecrated at a ceremony marking the arrival of three US aircraft. Rabin subsequently dismissed two of the NRP ministers from the Cabinet, and the consequent withdrawal of NRP support left the Government in a minority in the Knesset, thus precipitating Rabin's resignation.

Rabin carried on in a caretaker capacity until the election of May 1977, but in April 1977 he resigned as leader of the Labour Party. On 10 April the Labour Party selected Shimon Peres as its new leader. Peres had earlier been narrowly defeated by Rabin in the February poll for the leadership of the Labour Party.

ISRAEL UNDER BEGIN

When the elections for the ninth Knesset took place on 17 May 1977, the result was a surprise victory for the Likud, under Menachem Begin, who won 43 out of the 120 seats—the largest single total. The Likud victory removed the Labour Party from the predominant position it had held in Israel since 1949. With the support of the NRP, Agudat Israel and Shlomzion, Begin was able to form a government on 19 June, and his position was strengthened in October 1977 when the Democratic Movement for Change (DMC) joined the Likud coalition. In September 1978, however, the DMC split into two factions, with seven Knesset members leaving Begin's coalition because they felt that his policy of announcing plans for further Israeli settlements on the West Bank was endangering prospects for peace.

A permanent peace settlement suddenly seemed possible when President Sadat of Egypt visited Jerusalem in November 1977 and addressed the Knesset. Talks between Sadat and Begin continued, and after various delays an unexpected breakthrough occurred in September 1978 after talks at Camp David in the USA under the guidance of President Carter, when Begin and Sadat signed two agreements. The first was a 'framework of peace in the Middle East' (see p. 91) and the second was a 'framework for the conclusion of a peace treaty between Egypt and Israel'. The first agreement provided for a five-year transitional period during which the inhabitants of the Israeli-occupied West Bank and Gaza would obtain full autonomy and self-government, and the second agreement provided for the signing of a peace treaty between Egypt and Israel, which was finally signed on 27 March 1979. The treaty provided for a phased withdrawal from Sinai which was successfully completed on 25 April 1982. Diplomatic relations between Israel and Egypt were opened on 26 January 1980.

Proposals for Palestinian autonomy provided for negotiations to be completed by 26 May 1980. That date passed with no agreement in sight. It became clear during the negotiations that Egypt and the Palestinians were considering 'autonomy' in terms of an independent Palestinian state, whereas Israel had in mind only some form of administrative self-government for the Palestinian Arabs in the West Bank. The announcement of fresh Israeli settlements in the West Bank, and a Knesset Bill making East Jerusalem an integral part of the Jewish capital, gave Arabs little ground for hope that their concept of Palestinian autonomy would ever emerge from the negotiations, though both Israel and Egypt maintain their adherence to the 'Camp David process'.

BEGIN'S PROBLEMS

After becoming Prime Minister, Begin had to contend with two opposing factions in his Cabinet. Ariel Sharon, then Minister of Agriculture and the Minister responsible for Settlements, followed the policy of the Gush Emunim movement, which endeavoured to push the maximum number of Israeli settlements into the West Bank as quickly as possible. Sometimes voices calling for moderation prevailed, but more often settlements went ahead unopposed. As the deadline for the autonomy talks (26 May) approached, plans for more settlements were announced. Begin prevaricated on the subject of the settlements, but more often than not he supported them. The uncertainty of his exact position on many policy matters led to strains in the Cabinet. Begin's health was also a cause for concern at times. In October 1979 Moshe Dayan resigned as Minister of Foreign Affairs, because he considered the Israeli Government stand on Palestinian autonomy to be too intransigent, and at the end of May 1980 Ezer Weizman resigned as Minister of Defence, ostensibly because of reductions in planned expenditure on defence, but his dissatisfaction with the settlements position and with the autonomy talks was well-known. Begin encountered difficulty when trying to arrange the consequent Cabinet reshuffle. He was hoping to appoint the Minister of Foreign Affairs, Itzhak Shamir, to the post of Minister of Defence but, when this proposal encountered opposition, Begin assumed the defence portfolio himself.

Begin's biggest problem, however, was the state of the Israeli economy (see Economy). Rampant inflation called for austerity measures, and the Minister of Finance, Yigael Hurwitz, resigned in early January 1981 when the Knesset voted to award pay increases to teachers. Hurwitz took his Rafi Party, with three Knesset members, out of the Likud coalition and the Government could no longer command a majority. General elections were then called for 30 June. It was thought in early 1981 that Begin was certain to be defeated in the forthcoming elections, but his position grew stronger as they approached. The tax-cutting policies of the new Minister of Finance, Yoram Aridor, proved popular. Begin's support for the Christians in Lebanon, in their struggle with the Syrians, who had stationed SAM missiles on Lebanese soil, also proved electorally popular.

A SECOND TERM FOR BEGIN

Although the election results were close, Begin was able to present a new coalition to the Knesset in early August. This was possible only by making an agreement with the religious parties, in particular Agudat Israel, by which numerous undertakings on religious observance, affecting most aspects of everyday life, were guaranteed. Although these measures were welcomed by zealots, more secular elements in Israeli society found them unpalatable.

Begin's majority was precarious, and it is remarkable that his Government survived as long as it did. In December he formally annexed the strategically important Golan Heights, a step which pleased the 'hawks' in Israel, but which angered the USA enough to cause it to suspend the strategic co-operation agreement which it had signed with Israel less than a month before.

As the time for withdrawal from Sinai drew nearer, there was increasing pressure from settlers in Sinai (particularly Yamit) to remain there. Squatters from the extreme right-wing Tehiya Party adopted a belligerent stance, but they were eventually removed and the withdrawal took place as planned on 25 April 1982.

ADVANCE INTO LEBANON

During 1982 and the first half of 1983, Arab disturbances on the West Bank became more severe, and there were even Jewish demonstrations against Israel's settlement of the area. The number of Jewish settlements in the West Bank rose to more than 100 in 1983, and more land was expropriated. The event which provoked another major Middle East crisis, however, was Israel's 'Operation Peace for Galilee', an armed incursion into Lebanon which was launched on 6 June 1982 and intended as a brief and limited campaign. By the end of June, however, Israeli forces had advanced across Lebanon and surrounded West Beirut, where 6,000 PLO fighters had become trapped. Israel's action met with disapproval from most of the world, and the support of the USA became questionable after Secretary of State Haig's resignation at the end of June, and his replacement by George Shultz. Israel declared a cease-fire and demanded that the Palestinians lay down their heavy arms and leave Lebanon.

Intensive diplomatic efforts, hampered by repeated outbreaks of fighting, were made between June and August to find an acceptable basis for the supervised withdrawal of the trapped Palestinian and Syrian forces. With the help of a US envoy, Philip Habib, their evacuation began on 21 August and was completed by 1 September (estimates put the number of evacuees at 14,500–15,000).

Israeli forces remained in effective control of Beirut, although, under the terms of the evacuation agreement, an international peace-keeping force (predominantly comprising US, French and Italian troops) was stationed in various parts of the city until early September. Despite US protests, Israeli forces moved into West Beirut again on 15 September, taking up positions around Palestine refugee camps located in the Muslim sectors. On 17 September reports began to emerge of a massacre committed in the Sabra and Chatila camps by armed men who were ostensibly seeking PLO guerrillas. The identity of the killers was uncertain but evidence pointed to their being Christian Phalangist militiamen, whose entry into the camps had been facilitated by Israeli troops. Israel rejected the charge of responsibility for the massacre, which was laid at its door by the Arab world, but on 28 September the Government initiated a full judicial inquiry, led by the Chief Justice of the Supreme Court, Itzhak Kahan. Published on 8 February 1983, the report of the inquiry placed actual responsibility for the massacre on Lebanese Phalangists, but concluded that Israel's political and military leaders bore indirect responsibility for the tragic events by failing properly to supervise the militiamen in the area. Begin was censured merely for showing indifference to reports reaching him of Phalangists entering the camps. As recommended by the inquiry, Ariel Sharon resigned as Minister of Defence (though he remained in the Government as Minister without Portfolio), to be replaced by the Ambassador to the USA, Moshe Arens.

Direct talks between Israel and Lebanon for the withdrawal of foreign forces began on 28 December. Progress was slow but a 12-article agreement, formulated by US Secretary of State Shultz and declaring the end of hostilities, was finally signed on 17 May 1983. Syria rejected the agreement and its forces held their positions in the Beka'a valley, raising the possibility of open war with Israel, which, in turn, refused to withdraw while the Syrians remained. On the same day that Israel signed its agreement with Lebanon, it concluded another secret one with the USA which recognized Israel's right, despite the accord with Lebanon, to retaliate against terrorist attacks in Lebanon and to delay its withdrawal, beyond the date (three months from the date of signing) which had been agreed in that accord, if Syrian and PLO forces remained there.

In July, Israel, with its casualties from guerrilla attacks increasing, decided to redeploy its forces south of Beirut along the Awali river.

BEGIN'S RESIGNATION

Support for Begin's Government had been sustained throughout the early weeks of 'Operation Peace for Galilee' but, as the planned, limited incursion developed into a costly occupation, opposition to government policy increased, not only among the Israeli public but also in the army.

By the summer of 1983, Israel was sliding into an economic crisis and the involvement in Lebanon had become an expensive stalemate. The Government's prestige had been badly damaged by the Beirut massacres and by a capitulation to wage demands by the country's doctors, whose four-month strike for higher pay had taken medical services to the brink of collapse. Begin, already depressed by the death of his wife in November and by the events in Lebanon, announced his resignation as Prime Minister and leader of the Likud bloc on 30 August 1983. Itzhak Shamir, the Minister of Foreign Affairs since 1980, was elected leader of Likud on 2 September. Begin withheld his formal resignation until 15 September, while a period of political wrangling ensued to find a viable coalition government. Although Labour was the largest single party in the Knesset, Shamir was asked to form a government on 21 September, his Likud grouping having a theoretical majority of seven seats with the support of minority religious parties. Shamir pronounced himself committed to the Israeli presence in Lebanon, to the continuation of the West Bank settlement programme and to tackling the country's economic problems.

During the second half of 1983 the monetary crisis (see Economy) emerged as the main cause of the Government's declining popularity. The lack of a single-minded approach to the crisis led to the resignation in October of the minister of finance, Yoram Aridor, whose policies, diluted by the Cabinet, failed to prevent inflation from soaring. The more thoroughly pursued austerity measures of Aridor's successor, Yigal Cohen-Orgad, only threatened to alienate elements of Shamir's shaky coalition (in particular the Tami Party), concerned over the effects of cuts in social services and increases in the price of food, and caused growing labour unrest. Further uproar greeted a plan virtually to 'freeze' the programme of creating Jewish settlements on Israeli-occupied territory in the West Bank and the Gaza Strip, in order to save money, at the beginning of 1984. Although the rate of settlement had slowed down (owing to Israel's economic recession and the shortage of government funds with which to finance new communities), the number of settlements established since 1967 had risen to 129 (114 in the West Bank) by March 1985, and the number of Israeli settlers to 46,000 (42,500 in the West Bank). By March 1985, Israel had direct control of more than 50% of the 490,000 ha of land in the West Bank. The depth of feeling on the issue was illustrated by the exposure in April 1984 of a Jewish anti-Palestinian terrorist organization operating in the West Bank, some of whose members were active in Gush Emunim, the main West Bank settlement organization.

THE 1984 GENERAL ELECTION

Inflation continued to rise sharply in 1984 and in January the Government narrowly survived a vote of no confidence in the Knesset. Its position was further weakened by the resignation from the Cabinet (and the loss of the guaranteed vote) of the Minister without Portfolio, Mordechai Ben-Porat, one week later. Finally, in March, the Government failed by 61 votes to 58 to prevent the passage of a bill, sponsored by the Labour Party, calling for the dissolution of the Knesset prior to a general election. In this vote the Tami Party sided with the opposition. The general election was set for 23 July.

The election campaign was conducted against a background of strikes as the state of the economy continued to deteriorate. The overall rate of inflation passed 400% in July and it was apparent that the main issue determining voters' likely preference in the election was the economy. Bans which had been imposed by the parliamentary election committee on the

ultra-right-wing Kach and the left-wing Progressive List for Peace parties, preventing them from contesting the election, were overturned by the Supreme Court so that 27 parties (including 16 new groupings, mostly splinter groups from existing parties) were due to be competing for seats on 23 July.

Although an opinion poll conducted three weeks before the election indicated a clear Labour lead, the election produced no conclusive result. The Labour Alignment won 44 seats in the Knesset (an insufficient number to enable it to form Israel's first single-party government), while Likud gained 41. The balance of power lay, once again, with the minority parties which won the remaining 35 seats in the 120-seat assembly. When what was required was the swift establishment of a new government to deal with the deteriorating economy, both Labour and Likud were embroiled in negotiations to win the support of the minority parties for a viable coalition administration. These talks provided no clear majority in the Knesset for either side, and it became increasingly likely that a government of national unity, comprising both Labour and Likud, presented the only way out of the political impasse, short of calling a second election. President Herzog nominated the Labour leader, Shimon Peres, as Prime Minister-designate on 5 August and invited him to form a government of national unity. The eleventh Knesset was inaugurated on 13 August in an atmosphere of great uncertainty as to whether Labour and Likud could bridge the political gap between them and could agree on the formation of a national government.

THE ISRAELI OCCUPATION OF SOUTHERN LEBANON

The withdrawal in September 1983 of Israeli forces in Lebanon to the Awali river, south of Beirut, produced a *de facto* partition of the country. Israeli troops (reduced to some 10,000 by the end of 1983) faced about 50,000 Syrian troops and 2,000–4,000 Palestinian guerrillas entrenched in the Beka'a valley to the north. The 2,500 men of Maj. Sa'ad Haddad's Israeli-controlled southern Lebanese militia, the so-called 'South Lebanon army' (SLA), were employed to police the occupied area, with the Israeli troops, and to combat guerrilla attacks on the occupying forces. Israel also armed other, independent, militias (including Shi'ite Muslim groups) so that they could control their own areas of influence. Despite these measures and, perhaps, partly because of them, Israeli soldiers continued to be the target of guerrilla attacks (the Israeli death toll in the 'Peace for Galilee' operation approached 600 by July 1984). Although, after the withdrawal to the Awali river, the Israeli air force and navy were involved in attacks on Syrian targets in north Lebanon and against the PLO in the port of Tripoli (in November and December 1983), there were no serious land-based exchanges between Israeli and Syrian forces in Lebanon during the first half of 1984. Some isolated Israeli shelling of Palestinian positions in the Beka'a took place in retaliation against the activities of Palestinian guerrilla squads which infiltrated the Israeli-occupied areas to make their attacks.

Major Sa'ad Haddad died in December 1983 and Maj.-Gen. Antoine Lahad replaced him as leader of the southern Lebanese militia in March 1984. In the same month, under the influence of Syria, President Gemayel abrogated the 17 May agreement with Israel. Although the agreement had effectively been a 'dead-letter' for some time, the rising cost of involvement in Lebanon and the unpopularity of that policy at home disposed the Israelis at least to consider withdrawing. It was clear, however, that, much as Israel would prefer to spare the expense of occupation and the lives of its people by leaving the policing of southern Lebanon to Maj.-Gen. Lahad's and other militias, it would not withdraw either until it felt secure within its existing boundaries against terrorist attacks launched from Lebanese territory, or until it was politically impossible for it to remain. The official policy of the Shamir Government was that Syrian withdrawal from Lebanon was a precondition of Israeli withdrawal. Shimon Peres, the Labour Party leader, had pledged to adopt a more flexible pragmatic approach to negotiations on an Israeli withdrawal if he came to power. However, Labour's failure to win an overall majority in the election, and the likely formation of a government of national unity with Likud, meant that Labour might have to make compromises, over controversial issues, in the very policies which distinguished it from Likud.

THE GOVERNMENT OF NATIONAL UNITY

Six weeks of negotiation were required before Peres and Itzhak Shamir could agree on the composition and policy of a coalition government. The new Government, whose component parties accounted for 97 of the 120 Knesset seats, was formed on 13 September. It contained representatives of the two major party groupings (Labour and Likud), four religious parties (the NRP, Shas, Agudat Israel and Morasha) and the Shinui, Yahad and Ometz parties. Under the terms of the coalition agreement, Shimon Peres was to hold the premiership for the first two years and one month of the government, while Itzhak Shamir served as Deputy Prime Minister and Minister of Foreign Affairs, after which time they were to exchange their respective posts for a further period of two years and one month. Within the Cabinet of 25 ministers, an inner Cabinet of 10 (including five members each from Labour and Likud) was formed.

The only Cabinet post not to be allocated was that of Minister of Religious Affairs, for which the NRP and Shas were vying. They agreed to leave this portfolio, and that of minister of the interior which went with it, in the hands of the Prime Minister for one month, while a solution to the problem was worked out. Eventually, in December, a proposal was made whereby the religious affairs portfolio (and all religious matters previously dealt with by the Ministry of the Interior) was to be awarded to the NRP, and the Ministry of the Interior to Shas. The spiritual leaders of Shas baulked at this loss of the Ministry of the Interior's religious responsibilities. Rabbi Itzhak Peretz, Shas's leader and Minister without Portfolio in the Government, resigned on 16 December, and the coalition was faced with collapse, as Likud threatened to leave the Government if Shas, its ally, were not more considerately dealt with. On 20 December, however, the NRP and Shas accepted a formula whereby the NRP controlled the Ministry of Religious Affairs and 60% of the budget for the activities of the Jewish Religious Councils, while Shas (in the person of Rabbi Peretz) controlled the Ministry of the Interior and the remaining 40% of the budget.

ISRAEL'S WITHDRAWAL FROM LEBANON

The Government of national unity pledged itself to withdrawing the Israel Defence Force (IDF) from Lebanon, and to tackling the problems of the economy. Any withdrawal agreement with Lebanon was not to be without conditions. To ensure the security of its northern border, ideally, Israel sought Syrian commitments not to redeploy its forces in areas evacuated by the IDF; to prevent the infiltration of PLO terrorists into the south of Lebanon; to grant freedom of operation to the SLA; and to allow the UN Interim Force in Lebanon (UNIFIL) to deploy north of the SLA area up to Syrian lines in the Beka'a valley. Lebanon, for its part, demanded $10,000m. in reparations, and the unconditional withdrawal of the IDF. More realistically, Israel dropped its demand for simultaneous Syrian withdrawal, provided satisfactory military arrangements could be made, and Syria approved a series of talks, under UN auspices, between Lebanese and Israeli army representatives, to agree the terms of withdrawal. The talks began in Naqoura (Lebanon) in November but repeatedly foundered on the question of which forces should take the place of the IDF, to prevent inter-communal fighting. The Lebanese, influenced by Syria, wanted UNIFIL to police the Israel-Lebanon border (as it had been mandated to do in 1978), and the Lebanese army to deploy north of the Litani river, between UNIFIL and the Syrian forces. Israel was not convinced of the competence of the Lebanese army, and wanted UNIFIL to be deployed north of the Litani while the SLA patrolled the southern Lebanese border. In the absence of any agreement, Israel withdrew from talks, and on 14 January 1985 the Israeli Cabinet voted to take unilateral steps towards withdrawal, arousing fears of civil war in southern Lebanon when they departed. The Cabinet agreed a three-phase withdrawal plan whose final aim was the return of the IDF to the international border. The first phase took place in February 1985 and involved the evacuation of the IDF from the western occupied sector, around Sidon, to the Litani river area, around Nabatiyah. The UN force was asked to police the vacated area with the Lebanese army. In the second phase, the IDF was to leave the occupied central and eastern sector (including the southern Beka'a valley), and redeploy around Hasbayyah. The third and final phase, taking the IDF behind Israel's northern border and leaving an apparatus of control inside southern Lebanon (based on the SLA, with IDF backing), was to be completed some nine months after the first.

The cost of the withdrawal was estimated at $100m., and that of the entire 'Operation Peace for Galilee' at some $3,500m. The second stage of the withdrawal began on 3 March 1985, with no fixed duration. The Shi'ites of southern Lebanon, antipathetic towards the PLO, had initially welcomed the IDF, but now they attacked it in retreat. Guerrilla attacks increased the Israeli death toll in Lebanon during the invasion and occupation to more than 650 by April, with about 50 of these deaths having occurred during the withdrawal. In retaliation, Israel pursued an 'Iron Fist' policy, purging Shi'ite villages of suspected guerrillas or attacking them indiscriminately, killing innocent inhabitants. Instead of decreasing, the number of attacks on Israeli forces, orchestrated by the Shi'ite National Resistance Movement, Amal and Hezbollah (the Party of God), multiplied, and during March Israel accelerated the process of withdrawal. The second stage was completed with the evacuation of Tyre on 29 April.

On 4 April 1985 Israel released 750 Shi'ite prisoners, detained as part of the 'Iron Fist' policy, from Ansar camp, prior to withdrawing from that part of western Lebanon. At the same time, contrary to international conventions (as they were not prisoners of war), 1,200 Lebanese and Palestinian detainees were transferred to prisons in Israel. Then, on 20 May, 1,150 Lebanese and Palestinian prisoners were exchanged for three Israeli prisoners of war. The release of 766 Shi'ite prisoners, transferred from Lebanon to Atlit prison in Israel, became the central demand of Amal guerrillas who hijacked a TWA airliner and held it and its largely US crew and passengers at Beirut airport in June. Israel refused to release the prisoners unless requested to do so by the USA. Some 450 of them were freed at the end of June and in early July, though Israel denied that their release was related to the hostage crisis, and the rest by 10 September.

Israel announced the completion of the third and final stage of the withdrawal of the IDF, ahead of the original schedule, at the beginning of June, though it was common knowledge that about 500 Israeli troops and advisers remained in Lebanon to support the SLA in patrolling the defensive buffer zone which formed a strip, between 11 km and 20 km wide, inside the border. The SLA had been depleted by desertion and defections to the Shi'ite resistance during the withdrawal. Syria, the Lebanese Government and leaders of the Shi'ite and Druze communities in Lebanon did not recognize the SLA's role in policing the border with Israel. Despite a continued Israeli presence in Lebanon, Syria withdrew 10,000 of its troops from the Beka'a valley at the end of June and the beginning of July, leaving fewer than 25,000 men in the country. Attacks on the security zone, and on the SLA policing it, were frequent, but the zone remained intact.

After the initial euphoria of the Israeli withdrawal from Sidon in February, fighting erupted between the Christian Phalange (allegedly incited by Israel), the Lebanese army, Amal, and other Shi'ite groups, and Palestinians in the refugee camps. From the Israeli point of view, the return of some 2,000 PLO fighters to the Palestinian refugee camps around Sidon was a serious development. However, the Shi'ites of southern Lebanon and the Syrians had no desire to see a pro-Arafat PLO re-establish itself militarily in the region, and tried to prevent it from doing so.

Israel was confronted by a more firmly entrenched enemy in the Shi'ite community just across its northern border. After the final stage of the Israeli evacuation was completed, Shi'ite guerrilla attacks on the SLA continued and the PLO steadily re-established itself in southern Lebanon. Israeli forces repeatedly pursued PLO fighters across the border and raided PLO positions in Lebanon by land and air in retaliation for attacks on Israeli territory made by PLO guerrillas. According to Israel the 'frequency' of attempts by guerrillas to infiltrate northern

Israel increased significantly after December 1987, when the Palestinian uprising in the Occupied Territories began (see below).

DOMESTIC AND DIPLOMATIC ISSUES

The state of the economy presented the main domestic problem to the Government of national unity and was the cause of considerable argument within the Cabinet between those convinced of the necessity for strict budgetary control and those concerned at the consequences such control might have for Israel's defensive capability and for civil order (see Economy).

On the question of Jewish settlement of the occupied West Bank and Gaza Strip, the document establishing the Government of national unity effectively allowed Shimon Peres and his fellow Labour ministers in the Cabinet to obstruct plans for new settlements. The coalition agreement provided for the establishment of five or six new settlements in each of the Government's four years in office. However, between October 1984 and October 1986 only two new settlements were opened in the West Bank, though the population of the 114 existing settlements increased from 42,500 in October 1984 to about 60,000 in mid-1986. Before his two-year period of office as Prime Minister terminated in October 1986, Shimon Peres said that no new settlements would be established in 1986/87, and that the budget for investments would be used to consolidate existing settlements. However, on assuming the premiership, Itzhak Shamir stated that the settlement programme would be carried out in accordance with the coalition agreement. By the end of 1987, the number of settlements in the Occupied Territories had risen to 139 (118 in the West Bank) and the number of Jewish settlers to 70,023 (67,648 in the West Bank). Of the total land area of the West Bank, 52% had been expropriated.

After 1974 and the fall of Emperor Haile Selassie, Israel had smuggled Falashas (Ethiopian Jews) out of Ethiopia. Between 1980 and 1982 some 2,000 were brought to Israel. In 1984 and 1985 respectively, with the co-operation of international Jewish organizations, 7,800 and 2,035 Falashas were airlifted via Europe to resettlement camps in Israel from Sudan, to which they travelled from famine-stricken Ethiopia. Owing to international publicity, criticism of the operation from Ethiopia's Marxist regime and the possibility of Arab opposition to it, the Sudanese Government suspended the airlift in January 1985, leaving 1,000 Falashas awaiting transportation in Sudan and a further 12,000 stranded in Ethiopia. The USA secretly completed the airlift of Falashas from Sudan at the end of March.

In January 1985 Israel and Egypt embarked on a series of talks, the first for two years, to determine the sovereignty of the minute Taba coastal strip on the Red Sea, which Israel had not vacated when it left Sinai in 1982. The Taba issue threatened the survival of the fragile coalition on several occasions. Negotiations were not finally concluded until February 1989, when Israel agreed to return Taba to Egyptian control by 15 March. Israel was to continue providing Taba with water, electricity and telephone lines, and Israeli citizens with valid passports were to be granted free access.

THE FAILURE OF THE JORDANIAN-PALESTINIAN PEACE INITIATIVE

In 1984 Israel rejected a call by King Hussein of Jordan for a peace conference involving all the concerned parties in the Arab-Israeli conflict. The formal establishment by King Hussein and Yasser Arafat of a combined Jordanian-Palestinian position on future peace talks, on 23 February 1985 in Amman, providing for a joint Jordanian-Palestinian delegation to such talks, gave new impetus to the search for a diplomatic solution to the Palestinian question. Although Israel supported the involvement of the five permanent members of the UN Security Council in the peace process, it rejected the call for an international peace conference, which was reiterated in 1985 by King Hussein and President Mubarak of Egypt, and also their suggestion of preliminary talks between the USA, Egypt and a joint Jordanian-Palestinian delegation, if it contained PLO members. Israel was interested only in direct talks once an acceptable Palestinian delegation was agreed on. In July Israel rejected a list of seven Palestinians, all members

or supporters of Yasser Arafat's Fatah, nominated by the PLO as members of a joint delegation with Jordan to hold talks with the USA prior to direct negotiations with Israel. Israel refused to talk to any members of the PLO or the Palestine National Council (PNC) and considered US participation in talks with them as a violation of their commitment not to deal with the PLO until it recognized Israel's right to exist. Peres subsequently accepted two men on the list who satisfied his requirement for 'authentic Palestinian representatives' from the Occupied Territories. The other major obstacle to progress at this time was the PLO's position regarding UN Security Council Resolution 242. The PLO consistently refused to accept this resolution as a basis for negotiations as it referred only to a Palestinian refugee problem and not to the right of Palestinians to self-determination and a state of Palestine. The PLO Executive Committee repudiated Resolution 242 again after the Amman agreement with Jordan, although it was King Hussein's contention that Arafat had privately acknowledged (and would, in time, publicly accept) the resolution. However, despite persistent cajoling by King Hussein, Arafat made no public declaration.

The peace process was further hampered by a series of terrorist incidents in which the PLO was implicated. Firstly, in September 1985, three Israelis were murdered by terrorists in Larnaca, Cyprus. Israel held the PLO's élite Force 17 responsible, and, at the beginning of October, bombed the organization's headquarters in Tunis. Then, in October, an Italian cruise ship, the *Achille Lauro*, was 'hijacked' in the eastern Mediterranean by members of the Palestine Liberation Front (PLF; one of two groups of that name, this being the pro-Arafat PLF, led by Muhammad Abbas—'Abu Abbas'). They killed a Jewish American passenger before surrendering to the Egyptian authorities in Port Said.

These incidents gave Israel further cause to reject the PLO as a prospective partner in peace negotiations, and raised doubts as to Arafat's desire for a peaceful settlement. Meanwhile, Jewish settlers in the Occupied Territories had made it clear that any attempt to negotiate Israeli sovereignty over the disputed areas would be met by a campaign of civil disobedience.

In November, in Cairo, Yasser Arafat, under pressure from King Hussein of Jordan and President Mubarak of Egypt to renounce the use of violence, reiterated a PLO decision of 1974 to confine military operations to the Occupied Territories and Israel, though his aides immediately repudiated the statement.

In December 17 people were killed when terrorists, believed to belong to Abu Nidal's anti-Arafat Fatah Revolutionary Council, attacked passengers at the desks of the Israeli state airline, El Al, in Rome and Vienna airports.

King Hussein, who had already prepared the ground for an alternative approach to the Palestinian question by initiating a *rapprochement* with Syria, formally severed political links with the PLO on 19 February 1986, 'until such time as their word becomes their bond, characterized by commitment, credibility and constancy'. It emerged that, in January, the USA (without Israel's knowledge) had undertaken to invite the PLO to an international peace conference, on condition that the PLO publicly accepted UN Security Council Resolutions 242 and 338 as the basis for negotiation. Arafat refused to make such a commitment without a similar US acceptance of the Palestinians' right to self-determination.

After the collapse of the Jordanian-Palestinian peace initiative, Jordan resisted Israeli requests for direct talks excluding the PLO, and there was little prospect of a speedy revival of the peace process.

CABINET DISCONTENT

The coalition Government continued its precarious existence in 1986, beset by a number of contentious issues which divided Labour and Likud, its largest constituents. In February, after the success of the first seven months of the Government's economic stabilization programme, Prime Minister Peres drew criticism from the Minister of Finance, Itzhak Modai of Likud, when he expressed support for various reflationary measures (see Economy). Their difference of opinion culminated in April, when Modai accused Peres of being a 'flying Prime

Minister' with no understanding of economics. Peres demanded Modai's resignation as Minister of Finance (though he said that Modai could stay in the Government), and the Likud members of the Cabinet threatened to resign *en masse* if Modai was dismissed or replaced. Modai offered to resign, rather than endanger the existence of the Government, but Likud refused to countenance this. The crisis lasted for 10 days until a compromise was agreed, whereby Modai exchanged Cabinet portfolios with Moshe Nissim, the Minister of Justice. Itzhak Shamir, the leader of Likud, asserted that the exchange of Cabinet posts would remain valid only until he took over the premiership from Peres in October.

SHAMIR ASSUMES THE PREMIERSHIP

In accordance with the terms of the agreement under which the coalition Government of national unity was formed in September 1984, Shimon Peres, the leader of the Labour Party, resigned as Prime Minister on 10 October 1986, to allow Itzhak Shamir, the Minister of Foreign Affairs, to assume the premiership on 14 October. The transfer of power was delayed while the coalition parties negotiated the composition of the new Cabinet, which was approved by the Knesset on 20 October. The Labour group had objected to the reinstatement of Itzhak Modai, but his name was finally included in the Cabinet, in which he was one of five ministers without portfolio. The only unscheduled changes in the Cabinet were the replacement of Dr Josef Burg, who resigned as Minister of Religious Affairs, by Zvulun Hammer, and the naming of Shoshana Arbeli-Almoslino as Minister of Health, instead of Mordechai Gur, who refused to serve under Itzhak Shamir. (Mordechai Gur returned to the Cabinet in April 1988.) The composition of the inner Cabinet was unchanged. Peres and Shamir duly exchanged posts on 20 October.

THE SHIN BET CONTROVERSY

The activities of Shin Bet, the Israeli internal military intelligence agency, came under scrutiny in 1986, when it was suggested that the deaths, under interrogation, of two Palestinians in April 1984 had been deliberately concealed. The official Shin Bet version of events was that all four Palestinians involved in the 'hijacking' of an Israeli bus had been killed at the time of the incident. Photographs revealed that two terrorists were captured alive. Two subsequent official inquiries, between April 1984 and August 1985, confirmed that the two terrorists had 'died at a later stage', and identified Brig.-Gen. Itzhak Mordechai as the prime suspect in their deaths. Mordechai was acquitted by a military court in August 1985, and the Attorney-General, Itzhak Zamir, initiated investigations into the affair. He was told by leading Shin Bet officials that Avraham Shalom, the director of the agency, had ordered the prisoners' execution and had falsified evidence and suborned witnesses at the two official inquiries. Zamir insisted on a police investigation into the affair. In May 1986 the Cabinet refused to suspend Shalom, the Shin Bet director, and (though the Labour group, with the exception of Shimon Peres, supported some form of investigation) continued to resist the suggestion of a police inquiry. Likud, in particular, feared that such an investigation would reveal too much about the operations of Shin Bet, thus preventing the organization from functioning effectively and so endangering national security. On 1 June Itzhak Zamir, who had wanted to resign in February, was replaced as Attorney-General by Josef Harish. At the end of June Avraham Shalom resigned as director of Shin Bet, he and three of his deputies having been assured of a pardon and immunity from prosecution by the President of Israel, Chaim Herzog. In a letter to President Herzog, Shalom stated that his actions had been taken 'on authority and with permission', presumably from Itzhak Shamir, to whom, as Prime Minister at the time of the killings and the cover-up, he was responsible. In August a further seven Shin Bet agents were granted a presidential pardon for their alleged involvement in the killings or the subsequent cover-up.

In July the Supreme Court challenged the Government to explain why it had not instituted a police investigation into the affair. The Cabinet then voted, by a narrow margin, for a police inquiry (which was supported by Likud and the small religious parties), rather than a full judicial inquiry (supported by Labour). Later that month, after criticizing Shimon Peres for his handling of the Shin Bet affair, Itzhak Modai resigned from the Cabinet.

In December a secret report, compiled by the Ministry of Justice and based on a three-month-long police investigation into the affair, absolved Itzhak Shamir from any blame for the deaths of the two Palestinians or for the subsequent attempts by Shin Bet to conceal the truth of the incidents in question; it also exonerated Shimon Peres and Moshe Arens, respectively the Prime Minister during one of the official inquiries, and the Minister of Defence when the killings occurred. Following further revelations of illegal Shin Bet practices in 1987, the Government established a commission of inquiry in June, under Moshe Landau, the former Supreme Court President, to investigate the agency.

In October 1986, using information supplied by Mordechai Vanunu, a former technician at Israel's nuclear research establishment at Dimona, *The Sunday Times* of London claimed that Israel had succeeded in developing thermonuclear weapons and was stockpiling them at Dimona. Vanunu subsequently disappeared from London, and at the end of October Israeli authorities admitted that he was in their custody and would be tried for breaching national security. It was alleged that Vanunu had been lured to Rome, by a female agent of Mossad (the Israeli external security agency), where he was kidnapped and smuggled to Israel. His trial began in September 1987.

Following the revelation in a Lebanese magazine, in November 1986, that the USA had made three deliveries of military equipment to Iran since September 1985, it emerged that the sale of weapons and spare parts had been effected through Israeli intermediaries, with the knowledge, and even partly at the instigation, of Prime Minister Peres. According to some reports, Israel had itself been supplying armaments to Iran since the outbreak of the Iran-Iraq war in 1980.

ATTEMPTS TO REVIVE THE MIDDLE EAST PEACE PROCESS

On 11 September 1986 President Mubarak of Egypt and Prime Minister Peres of Israel met in Alexandria, Egypt, to discuss ways of reviving the Middle East peace process. They agreed to form a committee to prepare for an international peace conference (though Peres did not have Cabinet endorsement for this initiative), but failed to agree on the nature of the Palestinian representation at such a conference. Following the summit meeting (the first between Egypt and Israel since August 1981) and the signing of the Taba arbitration agreement, President Mubarak appointed Muhammad Bassiouni as Egyptian ambassador to Israel. The previous ambassador had been recalled from Israel in 1982, following the Israeli invasion of Lebanon.

Under the premiership of Itzhak Shamir, however, official Israeli policy regarding a Middle East peace settlement remained divided. Shamir opposed the concept of an international peace conference, involving the five permanent members of the Security Council, and instead proposed direct negotiations between Israel, Egypt, the USA and a joint Jordanian-Palestinian delegation, excluding the PLO. Although King Hussein resisted Shamir's advances, Jordan and Israel appeared to have a common interest in fostering a Palestinian constituency in the West Bank, which was independent of the PLO and with which they could deal, and, to this extent, their policy in the region coincided after the demise of the joint Jordanian-PLO peace initiative. In 1986, under the premiership of Shimon Peres (who said that the 'freeze' in the building of new Jewish settlements in the West Bank would continue), Israel revived a programme of limited Palestinian autonomy, with the appointment of Palestinians to replace Israeli officials in municipal government, though this resulted in civil protests by pro-PLO Palestinians and the intimidation or assassination of Israeli appointees. In August Jordan announced a major five-year investment programme in the Occupied Territories and gave its approval to an Israeli proposal for the establishment of branches of the Amman-based Cairo-Amman Bank in Nablus, under dual Jordanian/Israeli authority, to provide financial services to the Palestinian community. However, support for Yasser Arafat and the PLO remained strong in the West Bank.

In the less influential role of Minister of Foreign Affairs, Shimon Peres continued to pursue his own diplomatic initiative to secure international agreement on the terms for a peace conference.

In February 1987, although Prime Minister Shamir warned him that he had no authority to enter into agreements with a foreign power on Israel's behalf, Shimon Peres revisited President Mubarak in Egypt, and, at the conclusion of their discussions, Peres and the Egyptian Minister of Foreign Affairs issued a joint statement urging 'the convening in 1987 of an international conference leading to direct negotiations' between the main protagonists in the Middle East conflict. The outstanding issues to be resolved remained those of Palestinian representation and the participation of the USSR. On the Israeli side, the main obstacle to any negotiated settlement remained the refusal of any Israeli leader to accept the participation of the PLO in peace negotiations. In May Peres claimed to have made significant progress on the issue of Palestinian representation with King Hussein of Jordan, and to have the consent of Egypt, Jordan and the USA for convening an international peace conference, including a delegation of Palestinians (presumably not PLO members) who rejected terrorism and violence and accepted UN Security Council resolutions 242 and 338 as the basis for negotiations. King Hussein continued publicly to insist on the need for the PLO to be represented, but he appeared to have accepted (contrary to his long-standing view) that the conference would have no decision-making powers and be only a preliminary to direct negotiations.

However, Peres failed to gain the approval of the 10-member inner Israeli Cabinet for his plan, and his Labour bloc did not have the necessary support in the Knesset to force an early general election on the issue, or to be sure of being able to form a coalition government, thereafter, which excluded Shamir's Likud bloc. Likud and other right-wing Israeli groups remained implacably opposed to the principle of an Israeli offer to exchange territory taken in 1967 for peace with its Arab opponents, which Peres would have sought to apply at a peace conference.

In July 1987 Egypt's Minister of Foreign Affairs, Dr Esmat Abd al-Meguid, on the first visit to Israel by a leading member of the Egyptian Government since the Israeli invasion of Lebanon in 1982, appealed to the Israeli Government to participate in an international peace conference, which must, he said, inevitably include a PLO delegation. He rejected Prime Minister Shamir's alternative proposal of direct peace negotiations between Israel, Egypt, Jordan, the USA and Palestinian representatives.

PALESTINIAN UPRISING

The frequency of anti-Israeli demonstrations and violent incidents in the Occupied Territories increased during 1987, in particular following the reunification of the PLO and its abrogation of the 1985 Jordanian-PLO accord in Algiers in April. However, the authorities were not prepared for the wave of violent demonstrations against Israeli rule (the worst since Israel occupied the Territories in 1967) which began in December. The rioting was apparently precipitated by the deaths of four Palestinians on 8 December 1987, when the two vehicles in which they were travelling were in collision with an Israeli army truck at a military checkpoint in the Gaza Strip. Rioting in the Gaza Strip soon spread to the other Occupied Territories, and the number of Palestinians shot dead by the heavily reinforced Israeli army and security forces rose to 38 by mid-January 1988. There was widespread international condemnation of the 'iron fist' tactics that Israeli forces employed to control rioters who hurled bricks, stones and petrol bombs. A series of strikes was widely observed in the Occupied Territories, and many of the estimated 120,000 Palestinians who commute to work in Israel stayed at home. The uprising (*intifada*), which had probably begun more as a spontaneous expression of accumulated frustration at 20 years of occupation, degrading living conditions, overcrowding and declining opportunities in education and employment, than as a politically co-ordinated demonstration, was

soon being exploited and orchestrated by an underground leadership, the Unified National Leadership of the Uprising (UNLU), comprising elements from across the Palestinian political spectrum (the PLO, the Communist Party and Islamic Jihad). The UNLU organized strikes, the closure of shops and businesses, and other forms of civil disobedience, including the non-payment of taxes. It also distributed regular newssheets, exhorting Palestinians to continue the struggle and instructing them in means of revolt.

On 22 December 1987 the USA abstained from a UN Security Council Resolution (No. 605) deploring Israel's violent methods of suppressing Palestinian demonstrations. On 5 January 1988, however, the USA voted in support of Resolution 607, which urged Israel to comply with the International Red Cross's fourth Geneva Convention of 1949, concerning the treatment of civilians in wartime, and to abandon its plans to deport nine Palestinian political activists from the Occupied Territories. (This was the first time since 1981 that the USA had supported a UN resolution which was critical of Israel.) However, on 13 January during a fact-finding mission to the Occupied Territories by a UN Under-Secretary-General, Marrack Goulding, four of the Palestinians were deported to Lebanon. By mid-January up to 1,000 Palestinians had been arrested, and 24-hour curfews were in force around 12 or more refugee camps in the Gaza Strip and the West Bank, preventing the entry of food and supplies. The Israeli Cabinet repeatedly endorsed the security forces' 'iron fist' policy but was divided over the long-term solution to the Palestinian question. Shimon Peres, in contrast to Itzhak Shamir's Likud bloc (which considered the Occupied Territories to be a nonnegotiable part of 'Greater Israel'), believed that only a political solution could end the uprising, and favoured a demilitarization of those areas and the removal of Jewish settlements prior to a negotiated agreement.

At the end of January, by order of Itzhak Rabin, the Minister of Defence, Israeli security forces adopted a policy of indiscriminate, pre-emptive beatings of Palestinians, allegedly to avoid shootings, which was internationally condemned. The new policy, combined with the periodic imposition of curfews on refugee camps, towns and villages, far from quelling unrest, appeared to provoke it and encouraged greater self-reliance and organization among the Palestinians, who set up committees to oversee the collection and distribution of food and other supplies, and to co-ordinate resistance. In addition, the Israeli economy began to feel the effects of an absence of labour, as Palestinian workers from the Occupied Territories either boycotted their jobs in Israel or were prevented from travelling to them by curfew, so that production at industrial plants and fruit plantations declined. Equally worrying for the Israeli authorities was the prominent role which was adopted by Islamic fundamentalists in organizing demonstrations and appealing for a *jihad* (holy war) against Israel. Meanwhile, Israeli Arabs (and some Jews) demonstrated in Nazareth and Tel-Aviv in opposition to the Government's treatment of the Palestinians in the Occupied Territories.

THE SHULTZ PLAN

At the end of February 1988 the US Secretary of State, George Shultz, embarked on a tour of Middle Eastern capitals, in an attempt to elicit support for a new peace initiative. The Shultz Plan, as the initiative came to be known, proposed the convening of an international peace conference, involving all parties to the Arab-Israeli conflict and the five permanent members of the UN Security Council, with the Palestinians represented in a joint Jordanian/Palestinian delegation, excluding the PLO. However, this conference would have no power to impose a peace settlement and would act only as a consultative forum prior to and during subsequent direct talks between Israel and each of its Arab neighbours, and between Israel and a joint Jordanian/Palestinian delegation. The latter talks would determine the details of a three-year transitional period of autonomy for the 1.5m. Palestinians in the Occupied Territories, leading (before the transitional period began) to negotiations to determine the final status of government in the Territories.

When Shultz returned to the USA at the beginning of March, his plan appeared to be, already, a dead letter. The plan's failure to provide for the participation of the PLO immediately made it impossible for the Arab nations to accept, while the divisions within the Israeli Government precluded a coherent response from that quarter. Having expressed initial reservations over the Shultz proposals, Shimon Peres had generally endorsed them. For Itzhak Shamir, however, they had 'no prospect of implementation'.

THE INTIFADA CONTINUES

Meanwhile, the demonstrations against Israeli occupation of the West Bank and the Gaza Strip continued, apparently unabated. The uprising had demonstrated a surprising resilience and, at the end of March, Israel redoubled its efforts to extinguish the Palestinian revolt by economic as well as military means. The flow of money into the Occupied Territories was restricted to prevent PLO funds from reaching the Palestinian resistance movement; a partial ban was imposed on the export of goods from the Occupied Territories to Jordan and Israel; telephone links between the Territories and the outside world were cut; access to the Territories for the media and the press was strictly curtailed; restrictions were placed on the freedom of movement between areas within the Territories; a 24-hour curfew was imposed on the entire Gaza Strip for three successive days; and the Occupied Territories were sealed off from each other and from Israel, for the first time since 1967, and declared 'closed military areas'. The restrictions on movement within, and on access to and from the West Bank and the Gaza Strip were primarily introduced as a temporary measure to prevent Palestinians in the Territories and Arabs in Israel joining forces in a massive demonstration which the UNLU had planned for Land Day on 30 March (commemorating the killing of six Israeli Arabs in 1976, who had been demonstrating against Israeli land seizures) and were lifted on 1 April. However, they could be reintroduced at any time and used in combination with the other economic and administrative sanctions as part of Israel's long-term strategy to starve the *intifada* of publicity and to force it into submission by depriving Palestinians of the funds and supplies they required to compensate for losses incurred by them in a campaign of strikes, shop and business closures, and civil disobedience. By the end of March more than 100 Palestinians had been killed during the uprising and an estimated 4,000 had been arrested and detained without trial for six months, under martial law. Once more, however, the result of these measures seemed to be to steel the Palestinians' resolve to continue the uprising.

George Shultz returned to the Middle East in mid-April but, in talks with Israeli leaders, with President Assad of Syria and with King Hussein of Jordan, he made no further progress towards the acceptance of his peace plan. His lack of success in Israel was partly due to the obstinacy of Israeli Prime Minister Shamir and partly to the unwillingness of Shultz to exert persuasive pressure on him.

THE ASSASSINATION OF 'ABU JIHAD'

On 16 April 1988, in Tunis, an Israeli assassination squad murdered Khalil al-Wazir (alias 'Abu Jihad'), the military commander of the Palestine Liberation Army (PLA). Although there was satisfaction in Israeli political circles at the success of the operation, the incident provoked the most violent demonstrations in the Occupied Territories since the uprising began, and 16 Palestinians were reportedly killed in a single day. New curfews were introduced in 17 towns and villages in the Occupied Territories for one week after the disturbances.

At the beginning of June 1988 an extraordinary summit of the League of Arab States was held in Algiers to discuss the *intifada* and the prospects for peace in the Middle East. The communiqué issued at the end of the summit effectively rejected the Shultz Plan by demanding the participation of the PLO in any future international peace conference and insisting on the Palestinians' right to self-determination and the establishment of an independent Palestinian state in the Occupied Territories. The summit hailed the 'heroic' *intifada* and pledged all necessary assistance (including an unspecified amount of financial aid) to ensure its continuance.

JORDAN SEVERS ITS LINKS WITH THE WEST BANK

During the Algiers summit, Bassam Abu Sharif, a close adviser of the PLO leader, Yasser Arafat, distributed a paper entitled *PLO View: Prospects of a Palestinian-Israeli Settlement*, which clearly stated that the PLO was seeking peace with Israel through direct negotiations within the context of a UN-sponsored international conference, on the basis of all relevant UN Security Council Resolutions, including 242 and 338. Although Arafat did not publicly endorse the document and it provoked fierce arguments within the PLO, it did rise to speculation that a PLO peace initiative might be forthcoming. The suggestion that the PLO might be ready to take political responsibility for its own future and that of the Palestinian people, reflected the new confidence it had acquired since the *intifada* began and was substantiated by subsequent developments which affected the status of the West Bank.

The *intifada* increased Palestinian aspirations to statehood and reinforced support in the Occupied Territories for the PLO. The endorsement of the uprising that was expressed at the Arab summit in Algiers finally persuaded King Hussein of Jordan to end the speculation as to his intentions regarding the West Bank and to grant the PLO the larger role in determining the future of Palestine that it had sought. On 28 July 1988 Jordan cancelled its Five-Year Development Plan for the West Bank and, on 31 July, King Hussein officially severed Jordan's legal and administrative links with the West Bank. The House of Representatives, in which deputies representing the West Bank held 30 of the 60 seats, was dissolved (for further details, see chapter on Jordan).

King Hussein's action appeared finally to end hopes that the Shultz Plan could be implemented and to damage the prospects of a victory for Shimon Peres' Labour Alignment in the Israeli general election, which was scheduled to take place in November 1988. The peace plans of both Shultz and Peres had relied on the Palestinians being represented at negotiations in a joint Jordanian-Palestinian delegation (the so-called 'Jordanian option'). Without the participation of Jordan, which had voluntarily withdrawn from the West Bank and renounced any pretension to represent the Palestinians, the PLO could make a stronger claim to be, in the eyes of the world, as well as the Arab nations, the sole legitimate representative of the Palestinian people. The Israeli Government, however, was united in refusing to negotiate with the PLO. The possibility did exist, though, that the PLO might make the sort of concessions which would persuade Israel to reconsider its position. The severance of Jordanian links with the West Bank stimulated a heated debate within the PLO on the issues of recognizing Israel's right to exist, declaring an independent Palestinian state in the West Bank and proclaiming a Palestinian government-in-exile. To have done so would, by implication, have been to place the emphasis of the Palestinian independence movement on a diplomatic and political search for a solution, rather than on armed struggle. Israel's Prime Minister Shamir, however, immediately announced that he would use an 'iron fist' to prevent the creation of such a government or state. The Labour Party of Shimon Peres, on the other hand, bereft of the 'Jordanian option', offered to talk to 'any Palestinians' who renounced the use of violence and recognized the Jewish state.

NEW INITIATIVES BY THE PLO

In continuation of the spirit expressed at the June 1988 Arab summit, the Palestine National Council met in Algiers in November and the PLO declared an independent Palestinian state (notionally on the West Bank) and endorsed UN Security Council Resolution 242, thereby implicitly granting recognition to Israel. A month later, Yasser Arafat stated explicitly in Stockholm that 'the Palestine National Council accepted two states, a Palestinian state and a Jewish state, Israel'. Later in December, Arafat presented a three-point peace initiative to the UN General Assembly in Geneva. He proposed the convening of an international conference under UN auspices, the creation of a UN force to supervise Israeli withdrawal from the Occupied Territories, and the implementation of a comprehensive settlement based on UN Security Council Resolutions 242 and 338. Although the USA refused to accept the PLO proposals (alleging ambiguities), the PLO's explicit rejection of violence encouraged the US Government to open a dialogue with the PLO, implying a change in the direction of US-Israeli policy over Palestine. The United Kingdom and the USSR, among other countries, urged Israel to make a positive response to the change in the PLO's position.

ISRAELI PEACE PLANS

Meanwhile, the *intifada* continued unabated, and by the time of the Israeli general election on 1 November 1988, it had claimed the lives of an estimated 300 Palestinians and six Israelis. (By September 1989 the death toll had risen to 638 Palestinians and 42 Israelis.) The election once again produced a result whereby neither Likud (which won 40 of the 120 seats in the Knesset) nor Labour (with 39 seats) secured enough seats to be able to form a coalition with groups of smaller parties. The religious parties won 18 seats, gaining potential significance in the formation of a government either by Likud or Labour. After two changes of direction, Peres and the Labour Party eventually agreed to the formation in December of another government of national unity under the Likud leader, Itzhak Shamir, with Peres as Deputy Prime Minister and Minister of Finance. The protracted wrangling over forming a coalition had diverted attention from the PLO's peace initiative, and in the coalition accord no mention was made of an international peace settlement, nor were any new proposals advanced for solving the Arab-Israeli problem.

When municipal elections took place at the end of February 1989, Likud made sweeping gains, obtaining control of six of the 10 largest cities and also of many middle-sized towns. Likud regarded these election results as a vindication of their bitter opposition to the PLO. Shamir continued to maintain that the PLO remained a terrorist organization and presented his own four-point proposals for peace when he visited Washington in April. The proposals comprised: (i) reaffirmation by Egypt, Israel and the USA of their dedication to the 1978 Camp David accords; (ii) abandonment by Arab states of their hostility towards Israel; (iii) efforts to solve the Arab refugee problem; (iv) free democratic elections in the West Bank and Gaza to elect delegates who could negotiate self-rule under Israeli authority, but only if the violence ceased. A 20-point programme, developed from these proposals, was endorsed by both the Cabinet and the Knesset in May.

Although Palestinian activists dismissed these proposals as unacceptable (because direct negotiations with the PLO were excluded), many observers felt that they offered a chance for negotiations to begin.

After a meeting of the Likud Central Committee on 5 July 1989, however, Shamir agreed to attach stringent conditions to the Government's peace initiative. He stated that Israel would never allow the establishment of a Palestinian state on the West Bank nor negotiate peace with the PLO, nor would it end Jewish settlements in the territories. This tougher approach threatened to cause the dissolution of the coalition, as Labour considered that it destroyed any chance of the plan's success. This threat was averted, however, when the Cabinet reaffirmed the original peace initiative on 23 July.

The USA was, by now, exerting pressure on the PLO to consider the Israeli plan for elections in the West Bank and Gaza, but in August 1989 Yassir Abed Rabbo, a senior PLO spokesman, declared that 'the PLO does not consider, in any way, that elections can establish the basis for a political settlement'. In mid-September 1989 President Mubarak of Egypt invited Israeli clarification on 10 points connected with Shamir's election plans and at the same time offered to convene an Israeli-Palestinian meeting to discuss election details. Mubarak's 10-point plan was accepted by the Labour Party members of the inner Cabinet, but was vetoed in early October by the Likud ministers on the grounds that they did not want any direct contact with a Palestinian delegation. In early November the inner Cabinet provisionally accepted a five-point initiative proposed by the US Secretary of State, James Baker, regarding a preliminary Israeli-Palestinian meeting to discuss the holding of elections in the West Bank and Gaza Strip, on condition that Israel would not be required to negotiate directly with a Palestinian delegation, and that the talks would be concerned only with Israel's election proposals.

However, the PLO continued to demand a direct role in talks with the Israelis.

At the end of July 1989, Israeli agents abducted Sheikh Obeid, a leading Shi'a Muslim, from a village in South Lebanon, with the aim of securing the release of three Israeli soldiers held by Hezbollah (see chapter on Lebanon). Col William Higgins, a US hostage held by Hezbollah, was murdered in retaliation. World attention was then focused on the position of all Middle East hostages, and it seemed at first that some agreement leading to their release was imminent. However, no final solution to the problem was forthcoming.

In January 1990 the dismissal from the Government of Ezer Weizman, the Labour Minister of Science and Technology, for unauthorized contact with the PLO, endangered the fragile Likud-Labour coalition. The Labour Party claimed that, under the coalition agreement, Prime Minister Shamir was not allowed to dismiss Labour ministers. A compromise was eventually reached, whereby Weizman resigned from the 12-member inner Cabinet, but retained the Science and Technology portfolio. The coalition was further undermined on 28 January when five disaffected members of the Knesset, led by Itzhak Modai, the Minister of Economic Affairs, split from the Likud to form an independent party, the Movement for the Advancement of the Zionist Idea.

In February 1990 Ariel Sharon launched a campaign for the premiership after resigning the post of Minister of Trade and Industry in protest at Shamir's peace policy and the Government's failure to suppress the *intifada*. One obstacle to the progress of the peace negotiations was the question of whether residents of East Jerusalem should be allowed to participate in proposed elections in the Occupied Territories. On 28 February the USA suggested a compromise solution, which would allow East Jerusalem residents with second homes in the West Bank and some deported activists to stand in the elections. The USA attempted to apply further pressure to Israel to accelerate the pace of the peace process at the beginning of March, when President Bush opposed the grant to Israel of a \$400m. loan for the housing of Soviet immigrants, since Israel would give no assurances that the housing in question would not be in the Occupied Territories, including East Jerusalem.

On 11 March Shimon Peres and five Labour colleagues walked out of a cabinet meeting in protest at further delays of a proposed vote on US plans for talks between an Israeli and a Palestinian delegation. Two days later Prime Minister Shamir dismissed Peres, the Labour leader and Minister of Finance, from the Government, prompting the resignation of all the Labour ministers. On 15 March a vote of no confidence was passed against Prime Minister Shamir, the first such vote against an Israeli Government to have succeeded. Shamir was left in charge of a transitional administration, since he had managed to ensure he would retain the premiership by preventing the vote of no confidence from being brought forward to when the Labour ministers remained in office (all resignations and dismissals take 48 hours to come into effect). On 20 March President Herzog invited Peres to form a new coalition government after he had received assurances of the support of five members of the Knesset belonging to Agudat Israel. A two-month period of political wrangling ensued, however, during which both Likud and the Labour Party tried to establish a viable coalition government by soliciting the support of the minor religious parties represented in the Knesset.

On 8 April 100,000 people demonstrated in Jerusalem, calling for the reform of the electoral system (based on proportional representation). The concessions extracted by the minor religious parties during the period of political wrangling had aroused public resentment, and public pressure had subsequently led to a ruling by the Supreme Court requiring all political parties to make public the details of coalition agreements before a government could be formed.

On 12 April violence erupted in the Christian quarter of Jerusalem's Old City when 150 Orthodox Jewish settlers occupied the St John's Hospice, a Greek patriarchate building. Revelations that Israel's Ministry of Housing had financed the occupation of the building by providing the settlers with funds to lease it, increased public resentment and damaged relations with Greece, which warned that failure to evict the settlers might affect the Greek Government's decision to recognize Israel. On 26 April the Israeli High Court ruled that the settlers must leave the building by 1 May, and the Greek Government formally recognized Israel on 22 May, being the last member of the EC to do so.

On 25 April Shimon Peres acknowledged that he had failed to form a new government. President Herzog accordingly invited Itzhak Shamir to form an administration within 21 days. On 14 May, however, Shamir was granted a 21-day extension of his mandate to do so owing to disputes with potential coalition partners over the distribution of cabinet posts.

Violence erupted throughout Israel and the Occupied Territories on 19 May when seven Palestinians were murdered by an Israeli civilian gunman at Rishon le Zion. During the ensuing three days of rioting 21 Palestinians were killed. On 30 May an attack by members of the PLF on a beach near Tel-Aviv led the USA to demand that the PLO condemn the attack. When it failed to do so in terms satisfactory to the USA, the USA suspended its dialogue with the PLO. On 31 May the USA vetoed a UN Security Council resolution calling for international observers to be despatched to the Occupied Territories.

On 8 June Itzhak Shamir announced the formation of a new government following the signing of a coalition agreement which gave him the support of 62 of the 120 members of the Knesset. In a policy document Shamir emphasized the right of Jews to settle in all parts of Greater Israel; his opposition to the creation of an independent Palestinian state; and his refusal to negotiate with the PLO, indeed with any Palestinians other than those resident in the Occupied Territories (excluding East Jerusalem). On 11 June the new Government won a vote of confidence in the Knesset, by 62 votes to 57 with one abstention. The Government thus empowered was a narrow, right-wing coalition of Likud and five small parties (the MAZI, the NRP, Shas and the Tzomet and Tehiya parties), together with three independent members of the Knesset. Ariel Sharon was appointed Minister of Housing in the new Government; Moshe Arens Minister of Defence; and David Levy Minister of Foreign Affairs.

On 18 June Prime Minister Shamir invited President Assad of Syria to visit Israel for the purpose of peace negotiations, and on 22 June Jean-Claude Aimé, the special envoy of the UN Secretary-General, visited Israel to discuss issues related to the Occupied Territories. Shamir was believed to be seeking to appease the USA after US Secretary of State, James Baker, had expressed impatience at the lack of progress in the peace process. However, on 27 June Shamir wrote to US President Bush rejecting the principal elements of US proposals for direct talks between Israeli and Palestinian delegations.

Controversy surrounding the settlement of Soviet Jewish immigrants in the Occupied Territories intensified in June when Moshe Arens, the Minister of Defence, ordered the creation of a civil guard in the West Bank in order to protect Jewish settlers. The huge influx of immigrants from the USSR (250,000 were expected to arrive in 1990 and 1m. by 1992, increasing Israel's population by one-fifth) gave rise to fears of the further erosion of Arab rights. On 16 June the EC criticized Israel for failing to respect the human rights of the Palestinian community in the Occupied Territories. Israel rejected the criticism, however, and on 18 July refused to sanction the establishment of an EC consulate in East Jerusalem. By the beginning of August 1990 it was estimated that 683 Palestinians had been killed by Israeli forces since the onset of the *intifada*.

Israel's relations with African countries, the USSR and other eastern European countries improved significantly in late 1989 and 1990. In September 1989 Hungary became the first 'eastern bloc' country to restore diplomatic relations (severed in 1967) with Israel. In January 1990 the USSR upgraded its diplomatic links with both Israel and the PLO, while Israeli and East German officials held secret talks on establishing diplomatic relations. In February Israel restored diplomatic relations with Poland and Czechoslovakia, and with Bulgaria in May.

ISRAEL AND THE CONFLICT OVER KUWAIT

Iraq's invasion of Kuwait on 2 August 1990 led to improved relations between Israel and the USA, because it was vital, if a broad coalition of Western and Arab powers opposed to Iraq were to be maintained, that Israel did not become actively involved in the new conflict in the region of the Persian (Arabian) Gulf. On 12 August President Saddam Hussain of Iraq offered to withdraw his forces from Kuwait if Israel would withdraw from the Occupied Territories. Israel firmly rejected any analogy between the occupation of Kuwait and its presence in the Occupied Territories. As a crisis developed in the Gulf region, as a result of Iraq's invasion and annexation of Kuwait, there was support for Iraq from both Palestinians resident in the Occupied Territories and from the PLO. The PLO's support for Iraq led left-wing Israeli groups to cancel scheduled meetings with PLO representatives and other Palestinian leaders.

The improvement taking place in US-Israeli relations was seriously jeopardized in October 1990, when Israeli police shot and killed some 17 Palestinians on the Temple Mount in Jerusalem, after they had clashed with Jewish worshippers there. The killings provoked international outrage and sustained the arguments of those who, like Saddam Hussain, sought to link Iraq's occupation of Kuwait with the Israeli presence in the Occupied Territories in any solution to the crisis in the Gulf region. There was intense pressure on the UN to respond to this outrage, since it was with UN authority that a multinational force had been deployed in Saudi Arabia for the protection of the Kingdom. To many Arabs, the disparity between the vigour with which the UN was seeking to implement successive resolutions pertaining to the occupation of Kuwait and its long-standing impotence with regard to successive resolutions pertaining to the Occupied Territories was now more conspicuous than before.

The UN Security Council voted to send a mission to the Occupied Territories to investigate the Temple Mount killings, but the Israeli Cabinet announced that it would not co-operate with any such UN delegation and rejected the UN's criticism of its decision. In early November 1990 the UN Secretary-General asked the Security Council to request the convening of an unprecedented international conference, with the aim of forcing Israel to accept that Palestinians in the Occupied Territories were protected by the provisions of the Fourth Geneva Convention (concerning the protection of civilians during wartime). On 13 November the Israeli Government announced that it would permit a UN emissary to visit Israel to discuss the situation in the Occupied Territories.

In late November 1990 there was increased concern in Israel about the security of its borders with Lebanon and Jordan, and about improvements in relations between the USA and Syria, which, it was feared, might damage Israel's interests.

In mid-December 1990 the USA resisted attempts by the UN Security Council to draft a resolution advocating the convening of a Middle East peace conference and an increase in the UN presence in the Occupied Territories. The USA feared that the holding of a peace conference, at this time, could be construed as a concession to Saddam Hussain's concept of 'linkage'.

In mid-December 1990 Shamir visited the USA to confer with President Bush. He was reported to have sought, and received, assurances from President Bush that any diplomatic solution of the crisis in the Gulf region would protect Israeli interests. Nevertheless, only days later, the USA proposed a UN Security Council resolution condemning Israel's reinstatement of a policy of deporting Palestinians, in response to violence in the Occupied Territories, as a violation of the Fourth Geneva Convention. The USA also supported further criticism by the UN of Israel's treatment of the Palestinian population in the Occupied Territories and supported a separate UN appeal for an 'active negotiating process' in the Middle East 'at an appropriate time'. However, in view of the crisis in the Gulf, the USA did not believe that such a time had arrived.

Attacks on Israel by Iraqi *Scud* missiles, beginning on 18 January 1991, created the most serious threat to the integrity of the multinational force which had commenced hostilities against Iraq on 16–17 January. It was widely expected that

Israel would retaliate immediately, so risking the withdrawal of Arab countries from the multinational force. While Egypt implied that it would accept a measured degree of retaliation, Syria stated bluntly that it would change sides in response to any Israeli attacks on Iraq which violated Jordanian airspace. Graver still was the possibility of Iranian involvement on the side of Iraq in response to Israeli military action. US diplomacy, supported by the installation in Israel of advanced US air defence systems, succeeded in averting an immediate Israeli military response, although Israel vowed that it would, ultimately, retaliate for the attacks. By late February Iraq had launched 39 *Scud* missiles against Israel, killing two people and injuring more than 200.

Wider strategic considerations apart, a policy of restraint appeared to be in Israel's best interest. The Iraqi missile attacks, together with fears that similar attacks using chemical warheads might be launched, provoked a rare, open outburst of international sympathy for Israel. They also strengthened the Israeli case for rejecting any 'linkage' between the occupation of Kuwait and the Occupied Territories, and undermined the PLO's claim to be the only credible interlocutor in a future dialogue with the Israeli Government. In response to the widespread support, expressed by ordinary Palestinians and in the official policy of the PLO, for Saddam Hussain, the attitude of the Israeli Government hardened. Its new mood was symbolized by the appointment by Shamir, in February 1991, of Gen. Rechavam Ze'evi, the leader of the Moledet (Homeland) Party, as Minister without Portfolio and a member of the policy-making inner Cabinet. The appointment was strongly opposed by some cabinet members, as Ze'evi was known to advocate a policy of 'transfer' (i.e. the forcible, mass deportation of Palestinians) as a solution to the Arab-Israeli conflict. In early February, in a speech to the Knesset, Shamir again rejected, with more authority than he had been able to muster for many months, proposals for convening an international conference on the Palestinian issue, and promoted his own peace plan, formulated in 1989 (see above), as the only starting-point for any peace dialogue involving the Israeli Government.

RENEWED ATTEMPTS TO CONVENE A PEACE CONFERENCE

For Israel the defeat of Iraq by the multinational force in February 1991 was a double-edged sword, since it left President Saddam Hussain in power—Israel had openly urged his removal—as a potential threat to Israel's security. Israel's greatest gain from the conflict over Kuwait had been the renewed goodwill of the USA: in late February the US Secretary of State, James Baker, signed a guarantee for a loan to Israel—previously approved by the US Congress—of $400m. for the housing of immigrants. (Baker had previously refused to sign the guarantee, owing to his concern that the funds would be used to establish communities of immigrants in the Occupied Territories.) However, it was clear that the USA would seek to use its increased influence in the Middle East to achieve a resolution of the Arab–Israeli conflict, and that the USA's continued extension of goodwill and financial aid would require concessions by the Shamir Government.

At the beginning of March 1991 President Bush of the USA stated that a settlement of the Arab-Israeli conflict was one of the principal aims of US foreign policy in the post-war period, and in mid-March James Baker made his first visit, as US Secretary of State, to Israel, where he sought to initiate a 'confidence-building' process between Israelis and Arabs, as a preparatory step towards peace negotiations. The visit to Israel was followed by one to Syria, where Baker held talks with President Assad.

The USA's diplomatic efforts to initiate peace negotiations intensified in April 1991. In the first half of the month the US Secretary of State returned to the Middle East, visiting Israel, Egypt and Syria, in order to promote the idea of a regional peace conference. The proposal gained only limited support. While the Israeli Government tentatively endorsed the idea of a regional conference—comprising an initial, symbolic session, to be followed by direct negotiations with Arab states and a joint Jordanian-Palestinian delegation—its continued refusal to negotiate with any Palestinian delegation

which comprised either residents of East Jerusalem or members of the PLO appeared to present an insurmountable obstacle to any further progress towards a settlement of the Arab-Israeli conflict. Syria, Egypt and the PLO, meanwhile, rejected the proposed regional conference outright, favouring instead an international conference fully supported by the UN and with the full participation of the PLO.

After the US Secretary of State had again failed, following further talks with Shamir in mid-April 1991, to extract any flexibility from the Israeli Government, the question of a settlement to the Arab-Israeli conflict appeared as intractable as it had before Iraq's invasion of Kuwait in August 1990. It was generally accepted that Shamir would seek to prevaricate to a degree which would allow him to continue to enjoy both the goodwill—and financial aid—of the USA and the support of the extreme right-wing elements of his coalition Government, which remained firmly opposed to peace negotiations. The continued settlement of Soviet Jewish immigrants to Israel in the Occupied Territories became increasingly controversial. Visiting the USA in late April 1991, the Israeli Minister of Housing and Construction, Ariel Sharon (with whom the settlement policy was most closely identified), was rebuffed when he sought meetings with senior members of the US Government. The US Secretary of State described the settlement of the immigrants in the Occupied Territories as the biggest obstacle to the convening of a Middle East peace conference.

On 18 July 1991, in a remarkable *volte-face*, President Assad of Syria agreed for the first time, following a meeting with the US Secretary of State, to participate in direct negotiations with Israel at a regional conference, for which the terms of reference would be a comprehensive peace settlement based on UN Security Council Resolutions 242 (see Documents on Palestine, p. 86) and 338 (ibid, p. 88). By agreeing to participate in a peace conference on the terms proposed by the USA, Syria decisively increased the intense diplomatic pressure on Israel to do likewise: the US initiative already enjoyed the express support of the 'G7' group of industrialized countries, the USSR, the UN Security Council and the EC; and, following Syria's concession, Egypt and Jordan indicated that they would also be willing to participate in direct negotiations with Israel.

On closer examination, however, substantive progress towards a resolution of the Arab-Israeli conflict appeared illusory. The publicly-stated positions of the Israeli and Syrian Governments remained as far apart as ever. Each claimed, towards the end of July 1991, to have received confidential (and incompatible) assurances from the USA: Israel with regard to the composition of a Jordanian-Palestinian delegation to the peace conference; and Syria with regard to the return of the Israeli-occupied Golan Heights. For its part, the US Government insisted that there were no preconditions for attending the peace conference, and that, with regard to the composition of the Jordanian-Palestinian delegation, only members of the PLO were excluded.

On 31 July 1991, at the conclusion of a summit meeting between Presidents Bush and Gorbachev, the USA and the USSR announced their intention to act as joint chairmen of a Middle East peace conference which they had scheduled—without having received the prior, formal consent of the Israeli Government—to take place in October 1991, and which representatives of the UN and the EC would attend in the capacity of observers. On 4 August 1991 the Israeli Cabinet formally agreed to attend a peace conference on the terms proposed by the USA and the USSR.

OTHER POST-WAR DEVELOPMENTS

The signing, in May 1991, by Syria and Lebanon of a treaty of 'fraternity, co-operation and co-ordination' was immediately denounced by Israel as a further step towards the formal transformation of Lebanon into a Syrian protectorate. The signing of the treaty appeared to reduce the likelihood that, in response to the deployment of the Lebanese army in southern Lebanon, Israel would comply with UN Security Council Resolution 425 (adopted in March 1978) and withdraw its forces from its self-declared security zone in southern Lebanon. As the Lebanese army began to deploy east of the coastal town of Sidon in July 1991, Israel continued to launch attacks on

Palestinian and Hezbollah militia units which, it claimed, the Lebanese army (which it regarded as little more than a Syrian proxy force) was unable to suppress. A serious escalation of the conflict endemic to southern Lebanon occurred in February 1992, when Israeli armed forces advanced beyond Israel's self-declared security zone to attack the alleged positions of Hezbollah; and again in May, when the Israeli air force attacked Hezbollah villages to the north and west of Israel's self-declared security zone, in response to attacks by Hezbollah units on positions occupied by the South Lebanon Army.

In August 1991 Israel claimed that one of a number of conditions to which the USA had agreed in return for Israel's participation in the regional peace conference scheduled for October was the re-establishment of full diplomatic relations with the USSR. Soviet promotion of the USA's proposed regional peace conference had already led to closer contacts between Israel and the USSR. In April 1991 Shamir met the Soviet Prime Minister, Valentin Pavlov, in London, UK; and in May the Soviet Minister of Foreign Affairs, Aleksandr Bessmertnykh, made a visit to Israel, where he met the Israeli Prime Minister and the Minister of Foreign Affairs, David Levy. Full diplomatic relations with the USSR—superseded by the establishment of relations with some of the newly-independent, former Soviet republics—were formally re-established, after an interval of 24 years, in November; and in January 1992 Israel established diplomatic relations with the People's Republic of China for the first time.

DEADLOCKED NEGOTIATIONS

By March 1992—following an initial, 'symbolic' session of the conference, held in Madrid, Spain, in October 1991, four sessions of negotiations between Israeli, Syrian, Lebanese and Palestinian-Jordanian delegations had been held, but little progress had been achieved with regard to the substantive issues which the conference was intended to address, in particular the question of transitional Palestinian autonomy in the West Bank and Gaza Strip, pending negotiations on the 'permanent status' of those territories. Rather, these bilateral talks had become deadlocked over procedural issues. Israeli delegations, wary of making any gesture which might be construed as recognition of Palestinian independence, consistently questioned the status of the Palestinian-Jordanian delegation and the right of the Palestinian component to participate separately in negotiations; while Israel's refusal to halt the construction of new settlements in the Occupied Territories posed a constant threat to the faltering peace process. Israel's continued refusal to concede over the settlement issue further damaged its relations with the USA. As early as May 1991 the US Secretary of State, James Baker, had identified this issue as the main obstacle to US efforts to achieve a Middle Eastern peace settlement. In February 1992, immediately prior to the fourth session of the peace negotiations, Baker demanded a complete halt to Israeli settlement in the Occupied Territories as a condition for the granting of US $10,000m. in US-guaranteed loans for the housing of Jewish immigrants from the former USSR.

While the Israeli Government's refusal to halt the construction of new settlements was regarded as provocative by all the other parties to the peace conference, and by the US Government, the right-wing minority members of Israel's governing coalition, which opposed any Israeli participation in the peace conference at all, threatened to withdraw from the coalition if funds were not made available for the settlement programme. In December 1991 the Government's majority in the 120-seat Knesset was reduced when the Minister of Agriculture, Rafael Eitan (a member of the right-wing, nationalist Tzomet Party), resigned his portfolio in protest at the Prime Minister's opposition to electoral reform; and in mid-January 1992 the majority was lost entirely when two other right-wing, nationalist political parties, Moledet and Tehiya (which together held five seats in the Knesset) withdrew from the coalition. Their withdrawal was a deliberate attempt to obstruct the third session of the Middle East peace conference in Moscow, Russia, where delegates had begun to address the granting of transitional autonomy to Palestinians in the West Bank and Gaza Strip. A general election was subsequently scheduled to be held in June 1992, and Itzhak

Shamir remained the head of a transitional, minority government.

In late February 1992 Shamir retained the leadership of the Likud, receiving 46.4% of the votes cast at a party convention. At the same time, Itzhak Rabin, a former Israeli Prime Minister, was elected Chairman of the Labour Party, replacing Shimon Peres. Rabin's election was regarded as having significantly improved the Labour Party's prospects at the forthcoming general election, since, while he favoured the continuation of peace negotiations, he also enjoyed more popular confidence than Peres with regard to issues affecting Israel's security. A future Likud-Labour government of national unity, with Rabin as head of the Labour component, was thus viewed as more capable of conducting peace negotiations—and more likely to receive international, especially US, support—than another coalition composed of the Likud and minority, right-wing, nationalist and religious parties.

A fifth round of bilateral negotiations, between Israeli, Syrian, Lebanese and Palestinian-Jordanian delegations, was held in Washington, USA, at the end of April. In this latest session of the peace conference procedural issues were reported to have been resolved, and, in its talks with the Palestinian component of the Palestinian-Jordanian delegation, the Israeli delegation presented proposals for the holding of municipal elections in the West Bank and Gaza Strip; and for the transfer of control of health amenities there to Palestinian authorities. The Palestinian delegation, for its part, did not reject the proposals outright, although they fell far short of Palestinians' ambition for full legislative control of the Occupied Territories. No progress was made in the meetings between Israeli and Syrian delegations to discuss the principal dispute between Israel and Syria—Israel's continued occupation of the Golan Heights.

In May 1992 the first multilateral negotiations between the parties to the Middle East peace conference commenced, as had been arranged at the third session of bilateral talks in Moscow in January. However, these negotiations were boycotted by Syria and Lebanon, which argued that they were futile until progress had been made in the bilateral negotiations. Various combinations of delegations attended meetings convened to discuss regional economic co-operation; regional arms control; the question of Palestinian refugees; water resources; and environmental issues. A Jordanian delegation, for instance, attended all five meetings, and the Palestinian component all except the one on regional arms control. Israel boycotted the meetings on Palestinian refugees and regional economic development after the USA approved Palestinian proposals to allow exiles (i.e. non-residents of the Occupied Territories) to be included in the Palestinian delegations to these two meetings. The session of talks on Palestinian refugees became especially controversial after both the Palestinian and the Jordanian components of the Palestinian-Jordanian delegation asserted at it the right of Palestinian refugees to return to the Occupied Territories, in accordance with UN General Assembly Resolution 194 of 1948. However, the US Government subsequently indicated that the terms of reference for the peace conference were UN Security Council Resolutions 242 and 338 only.

A NEW LABOUR COALITION

In the general election, held on 23 June, the Labour Party won 44 seats in the Knesset and Likud 32. Meretz—an alliance of Ratz (Civil Rights and Peace Movement), Shinui and the United Workers' Party which had won 12 seats in the Knesset—formally confirmed its willingness to form a coalition government with the Labour Party on 24 June. However, even with the support of the two Arab parties—the Arab Democratic Party and Hadash—which together had won five seats in the Knesset, such a coalition would have enjoyed a majority of only two votes over the so-called 'right bloc' (Likud, Tzomet, Moledet and Tehiya) and the religious parties which had allied themselves with Likud in the previous Knesset. Formally invited to form a government on 28 June, the Labour leader, Itzhak Rabin, was accordingly obliged to solicit support among those religious parties which, he had indicated on 24 June, he was willing to incorporate into a coalition led by Labour in return for their support of Labour's policies.

On 13 July Rabin was able to present a new government for approval by the Knesset. The new coalition, an alliance of Labour, Meretz and the ultra-orthodox Jewish party, Shas, had a total of 62 seats in the 120-seat Knesset; and also enjoyed the unspoken support of five deputies from the two Arab parties.

Immediately after the election the Labour Party had re-affirmed its commitment to granting Palestinian autonomy within nine months, while maintaining Israel's control of defence and security measures in the Occupied Territories, and its responsibility for existing settlements there; and its desire for improved relations with the USA. However, it remained unclear precisely what the Party's policy would be *vis-à-vis* the occupied Golan Heights and occupied areas of southern Lebanon. As it strove to form a coalition that included right-wing religious parties, the Labour Party became of necessity less outspoken in its commitment to some of its stated aims, giving rise to fears that improved relations with the USA might ultimately force Palestinians to accept limited autonomy entirely on Israel's terms.

A sixth round of bilateral negotiations between Israeli, Syrian, Lebanese and Palestinian-Jordanian delegations, the first since the new Israeli Government had taken office, commenced in Washington in late August. Again, little progress was achieved on substantive issues. The Israeli delegation and the Palestinian component of the Palestinian-Jordanian delegation, for instance, were unable to agree terms for negotiating an initial, five-year period of Palestinian autonomy in the West Bank and Gaza Strip prior to a permanent settlement. Talks between the Israeli and the Syrian delegations remained deadlocked over the issue of the Golan Heights, and in private delegates were reported to have admitted that they were likely to remain so without the eventual diplomatic intervention of the USA.

In early October, in a clear gesture of support for the new Israeli Government, the USA granted Israel the US $10,000m. in US-guaranteed loans for the housing of immigrants that it had previously withheld, owing to Israel's housing construction programme in the Occupied Territories. In late October a seventh round of bilateral negotiations between the parties to the Middle East peace conference commenced in Washington, USA. The negotiations were adjourned, pending the conclusion of the US presidential election, but multilateral negotiations on regional economic co-operation, in which an Israeli delegation participated, took place in Paris, France, at the end of October. The seventh round of bilateral negotiations resumed in early November, but, again, no tangible progress was achieved. Multilateral negotiations on the issue of refugees took place in Ottawa, Canada, on 11–12 November.

In spite of the hopes that had been expressed for the prospects of the peace process since the election of the Labour-led Israeli Government, the months of October and November were marked by violent clashes between Palestinians and members of the Israeli security forces in the Occupied Territories. At the end of November it was reported that, since 1987, 959 Palestinians, 543 alleged Palestinian 'collaborators' and 103 Israelis had died in the Palestinian *intifada*.

In early December an eighth round of bilateral negotiations between Israeli and Arab delegations commenced in Washington. However, the talks were quickly overtaken by events in the Occupied Territories, which led to the withdrawal of the Arab delegations. On 16 December, in response to the deaths in the Occupied Territories of five members of the Israeli security forces, and to the abduction and murder by the Islamic Resistance Movement (Hamas) of an Israeli border policeman, the Israeli Cabinet ordered the deportation to Lebanon of more than 400 alleged Palestinian supporters of Hamas. Owing to the Lebanese Government's refusal to co-operate in this action, the deportees were stranded in the territory between Israel's self-declared southern Lebanese security zone and Lebanon proper.

The deportations caused international outrage, and intense diplomatic pressure was placed on Israel to revoke the expulsion order. On 18 December the UN Security Council unanimously approved a resolution (No. 799) condemning the deportations and demanding the return of the deportees to Israel. At the end of December, however, the Israeli Govern-

ment announced that only 10 of the deportees had been unjustifiably expelled and could return to Israel. The remainder would continue in exile. The future of the Middle East peace process, meanwhile, remained in doubt. The Palestinian delegation to the eighth round of bilateral negotiations had indicated that it would not resume negotiations until all of the deportees had been allowed to return to Israel, and the PLO formally expressed the same position in mid-January 1993. At the beginning of February the Israeli Government was reported to have indicated its willingness to allow some 100 of the deportees to return to Israel, but insisted that the remainder should serve a period of exile lasting at least until the end of 1993. On 5 February the ninth round of bilateral negotiations was formally suspended, but later in the month the UN Security Council was reported to have welcomed the Israeli Government's decision to permit 100 of the deportees to return to Israel, and to be ready to take no further action over the issue. Palestinians party to the peace negotiations, however, insisted that UN Security Council Resolution 799 should be implemented in full before a Palestinian delegation would resume negotiations. In late February the US Secretary of State, Warren Christopher, made a tour of the Middle East, visiting Syria, Saudi Arabia, Kuwait, Lebanon and Israel, in an attempt to revive the peace negotiations.

During March 1993 the number of violent confrontations between Palestinians and the Israeli security forces in the Occupied Territories—especially in the Gaza Strip—increased to such an extent that, at the end of the month, the Israeli Cabinet responded by sealing off the West Bank and the Gaza Strip indefinitely. Also, in late March the Knesset elected Ezer Weizman, leader of the Yahad political party, to replace Chaim Herzog as President of Israel in May 1993; and Binyamin Netanyahu was elected leader of the opposition Likud in place of Itzhak Shamir.

On 27 April the ninth round of bilateral negotiations in the Middle East peace process, which had been formally suspended in February, resumed in Washington. It was reported that the Palestinian delegation had only agreed to attend the ninth round of talks under pressure to do so from Arab governments, and after Israel had agreed to allow Faisal Husseini, the nominal leader of the Palestinian delegation, to participate in the talks. Israel had previously refused to grant this concession because Husseini was a resident of East Jerusalem, the status of which Israel regards as distinct from that of the West Bank, the Gaza Strip and the Golan Heights. Israel was also reported to have agreed that it would not, in future, resort to deportations as a punitive measure, and to have restated, together with the USA, its commitment to UN Security Council Resolutions 242 and 338 as the terms of reference for the peace process. However, as previously, the ninth round of bilateral talks achieved no progress on substantive issues. In particular, Israel and the Palestinian delegation were reported to have failed to agree on a statement of principles regarding Palestinian self-rule in the Occupied Territories.

In mid-May Ezer Weizman formally assumed the presidency of Israel. At the end of the month a minor reshuffle of the Cabinet averted the defection of the ultra-orthodox Jewish party, Shas, from the governing coalition.

A tenth round of bilateral negotiations, held in Washington on 15 June–1 July, concluded in deadlock, having achieved no progress on a statement of principles concerning Palestinian self-rule in the Occupied Territories, which was now regarded as the key element in the Middle East peace process. However, it was reported that a committee had been established in an attempt to facilitate progress on this issue. By the same token, there was no progress on the issues of contention between the Israeli delegation and its Syrian, Lebanese and Jordanian counterparts.

UNEXPECTED BREAKTHROUGH IN THE PEACE PROCESS

In late July Israeli armed forces mounted the most intensive air and artillery attacks on targets in Lebanon since 'Operation Peace for Galilee' in 1982. The attacks were mounted in retaliation for attacks by Hezbollah fighters on settlements in northern Israel, and provoked widespread international criticism for the high number of civilian casualties that they caused and for the perceived threat they posed to the Middle East peace process. At the eleventh round of bilateral negotiation, however, which commenced in Washington on 31 August, a major, unexpected breakthrough was achieved between Israel and the Palestinian delegation, which culminated in the signing, on 13 September, by Israel and the PLO, of a declaration of principles on Palestinian self-rule in the Occupied Territories. The agreement, which entailed mutual recognition by Israel and the PLO, had been elaborated during a series of secret negotiations mediated by Norwegian diplomacy. The declaration of principles established a detailed timetable for Israel's disengagement from the Occupied Territories and stipulated that a permanent settlement of the Palestinian question should be in place by December 1998. From 13 October 1993 Palestinian authorities were to assume responsibility for education and culture, health, social welfare, direct taxation and tourism in the Gaza Strip and the Jericho area of the West Bank, and a transitional period of Palestinian self-rule was to begin on 13 December 1993. (For full details of the declaration of principles on Palestinian self-rule, see Documents on Palestine, p. 100.)

While it was welcomed as a major breakthrough in the Middle East peace process, the declaration of principles was nevertheless regarded as only a tentative first step towards the resolution of the region's conflicts that could be threatened from many directions. Although the Israeli Prime Minister was able to obtain the ratification of the declaration of principles, and of Israel's recognition of the PLO, by the Knesset on 23 September, there was widespread opposition to it from right-wing Israeli political groups. By the same token, the conclusion of the agreement aggravated divisions within the PLO and the wider Palestinian liberation movement. Within the PLO some senior officials, hitherto loyal to Yasser Arafat's leadership, now declared their opposition to him, while dissident groups, such as the Democratic Front for the Liberation of Palestine, denounced the declaration of principles as treason. Most observers regarded the future success of the agreement between Israel and the PLO as dependent on the ability of the mainstream PLO to gain popular support for it from Palestinians residing in the West Bank and the Gaza Strip.

The reaction to the declaration of principles by the other Arab Governments engaged in peace negotiations with Israel was mixed. King Hussein welcomed the agreement between Israel and the PLO, and Jordan immediately agreed an agenda for direct negotiations with Israel, which was also ratified by the Knesset on 23 September. Lebanon, however, feared that the divisions that the declaration of principles had provoked within the Palestinian movement might in future lead to renewed conflict in Lebanese territory. It remained unclear, too, whether Syria—which neither condemned nor welcomed the declaration of principles—would continue to support those Palestinian groups opposed to the PLO's position.

In mid-September 1993 the resignation of Arye Deri as Minister of the Interior, following allegations of corruption, provoked the resignation of other members of Shas from the Cabinet and meant that the governing coalition was now effectively reduced to an alliance between the Labour Party and Meretz; and the Government's majority in the Knesset to only two. It followed that it might prove more difficult to obtain the Knesset's approval for any controversial measures associated with the Middle East peace negotiations. In mid-March 1994, however, the Labour Party and Shas were reported to have concluded a new coalition agreement. In early February 1994 the Minister of Health, Haim Ramon, resigned after the Government refused to endorse a health insurance bill that he had drawn up. Ephraim Sneh was appointed as his replacement in early June.

BEGINNING OF PALESTINIAN SELF-RULE

In early October 1993 Itzhak Rabin and Yasser Arafat held their first meeting in the context of the Declaration of Principles in Cairo, Egypt, where they agreed to begin talks on the implementation of the Declaration of Principles on 13 October, and to establish general liaison, technical, economic and regional co-operation committees.

On 13 October 1993 the PLO-Israeli joint liaison committee met for the first time, the delegations to it headed, respectively, by Mahmoud Abbas and by Shimon Peres, the Israeli Minister of Foreign Affairs. It was agreed that the committee should meet at regular, short intervals to monitor the implementation of the Declaration of Principles. The technical committee also held three meetings during October in the Egyptian coastal resort of Taba. Its task was to establish the precise details of Israel's military withdrawal from the Gaza Strip and Jericho, which, under the terms of the Declaration of Principles, was scheduled to take place between 13 December 1993 and 13 April 1994. At the meetings that took place in October progress was reported to have been made on the creation of a Palestinian police force, although the issue of security measures to protect Israeli settlers in the Gaza Strip remained unresolved. Israel was also reported to have agreed to the gradual release of some of the Palestinian prisoners that it held. Also in early October the Central Council of the PLO formally approved the Declaration of Principles by a large majority.

The joint PLO-Israel technical committee met on several occasions during November 1993, but by the end of the month it appeared unlikely that it would have made sufficient progress for Israel's military withdrawal from the Gaza Strip and from Jericho to begin by 13 December. In particular, it was proving difficult to reach agreement on three issues: arrangements for border security; the delineation of the Jericho area; and the release of Palestinian prisoners.

At the beginning of October 1993 talks had taken place in Washington between Crown Prince Hassan of Jordan and Shimon Peres. Despite reports of subsequent secret negotiations, King Hussein of Jordan insisted, during visits to Egypt and Syria in November, that Jordan would not conclude a separate peace agreement with Israel.

As had been feared, it proved impossible satisfactorily to negotiate the details of Israel's military withdrawal from the Gaza Strip and Jericho by 13 December 1993. This failure cast doubt on the whole of the September agreement between Israel and the PLO. The main cause of the failure remained the issue of security arrangements for border crossings between the Gaza Strip and Jericho and Jordan and Egypt. The PLO continued to insist that the border crossings should come under full, exclusive Palestinian control. Israel opposed this claim since to grant it would imply at least a partial recognition of something like Palestinian sovereignty.

Following meetings between the US Secretary of State, Warren Christopher and President Assad of Syria and the Syrian Minister of Foreign Affairs in Damascus in early December 1993, Syria announced its willingness to resume bilateral negotiations with Israel in early 1994. Syrian Jews wishing to leave Syria were also to be granted exit visas. In early January 1994, before a meeting between US President Clinton and Syria's President Assad took place, Israel appeared to indicate, tentatively, that it might be prepared to execute a full withdrawal from the Golan Heights in return for a comprehensive peace agreement with Syria. On 17 January it was reported that the Government would put the issue to a referendum before making such a withdrawal. This was interpreted as an attempt by the Government to deflect in advance any pressure for a swift move towards a peace agreement with Syria which might emerge at the forthcoming summit meeting between the US and Syrian Presidents. There was likely to be far less support in the Knesset for a peace agreement with Syria—in particular, for concessions regarding the Golan Heights—than there had been for an agreement with the PLO. Bilateral negotiations between Israeli and Syrian delegations resumed in Washington on 24 January after a four-month hiatus.

On 9 February 1994 Israel and the PLO appeared to achieve a breakthrough in their stalled negotiations when they signed an agreement to share control of the two future international border crossings. It was reported that security arrangements for Jewish settlers in the Gaza Strip had also been decided: three access routes to Jewish settlements there were to remain under Israeli control. However, the boundaries of the Jericho enclave remained undefined. Further talks began on 14 February to address the issues of the implementation of the first stage of Palestinian autonomy in the Gaza Strip and the Jericho area; the size, structure and jurisdiction of a future Palestinian police force; control of sea and air space; and the delineation of the Jericho enclave.

In late February 1994 the PLO, together with the other Arab parties, withdrew from the peace process with Israel, following the murder, by a right-wing Jewish extremist, of some 30 Muslim worshippers in a mosque in Hebron on the West Bank. Negotiations between the PLO and Israel resumed at the end of March, when the two sides signed an agreement on security in Hebron and the whole of the Occupied Territories. Israel agreed, among other things, to allow a team of international observers to travel to Hebron, where they were to monitor efforts to restore stability. Earlier in the month the UN Security Council had adopted a resolution (No. 904) condemning the killings in Hebron, prompting Syria, Jordan and Lebanon to agree to resume negotiations with Israel in April.

In late April Israel and the PLO signed an agreement concerning economic relations between Israel and the autonomous Palestinian entity during the five-year period leading to self-rule. At the end of the month it was reported that the US Secretary of State, Warren Christopher, had submitted to President Assad of Syria Israel's proposals regarding a withdrawal from the occupied Golan Heights in exchange for a full peace agreement with Syria.

On 4 May in Cairo, Egypt, Israel and the PLO signed an agreement which set forth detailed arrangements for Palestinian self-rule in Gaza and Jericho. The agreement provided for Israel's military withdrawal from Gaza and Jericho and the deployment there of a 9,000-strong Palestinian police force. A nominated Palestine National Authority (PNA, see below) was to assume the responsibilities of the Israeli military administration in Gaza and Jericho, although Israeli authorities were to retain control in matters of external security and foreign affairs. It was also announced that elections for a Palestinian Council, which, under the terms of the Declar-

ation of Principles, were to have taken place in Gaza and the West Bank in July 1994, had been postponed until October. Israel's military withdrawal from Gaza and Jericho was reported to have been completed on 13 May, and on 17 May the PLO formally assumed control of the Israeli Civil Administration's departments in Gaza and Jericho. On 18 May Yasser Arafat held talks with Israel's Minister of Foreign Affairs, Shimon Peres, regarding future negotiations on the extension of Palestinian self-rule in the West Bank. On 26–28 May an incomplete PNA held its inaugural meeting in Tunis, Tunisia, setting out a political programme and distributing ministerial portfolios. It had originally been Arafat's intention to appoint 24 members to the PNA (12 from within the Occupied Territories and 12 from the Palestinian diaspora). In the event, some of his chosen appointees refused to serve on the PNA—reflecting the extent of divisions within the mainstream Palestinian movement regarding the terms of the peace with Israel—and only 20 members assembled in Tunis. The PNA held its first meeting in Gaza in late June.

On 1 July Yasser Arafat returned to Gaza City, a homecoming that had far more symbolic than practical significance. Negotiations with Israel continued on the extension of Palestinian authority, the redeployment of Israeli armed forces in the West Bank and on the holding of Palestinian elections. In late July Israel and Jordan signed a joint declaration that formally ended the state of war between them and further defined the arrangements for future negotiations between the two sides. In late August Israel and the PLO signed an agreement which extended the authority of the PNA to include education, health, tourism, social welfare and taxation. In September the PNA was reported to have approved plans in preparation for elections in Gaza and the West Bank within three months. However, the size of the future Palestinian legislature remained unclear. The PLO was reported to wish to elect a 100-member council, while Israel insisted that its size should be restricted to no more than 25 members.

Economy

The shekel (which replaced the Israeli pound in 1980) was supported in 1982 and 1983 as part of a strategy to curb an inflation rate which exceeded 100% in every year between 1980 and 1983, soaring, in the latter year, above the previous record rate of 131.5% which was experienced in 1980. During 1983 a major economic crisis, which had been threatening to occur for some time, finally arrived. There were a number of reasons for this. Partly responsible was the policy of the Minister of Finance, Yoram Aridor, in maintaining an artificially high valuation of the shekel, with the result that exports became less profitable and failed to increase in 1982 and 1983, while imports rose as the exchange rate made them cheaper. Excessive spending by the Government was also a significant factor. Israel's gross national product (GNP), measured in constant prices, registered no growth in 1982 and increased by less than 1% in 1983. The country's foreign debt at the end of 1983 was, at $22,566m., the highest per head of population ($5,550) in the world. The cost of servicing this debt amounted to the total sum of US aid for the 1984 fiscal year ($2,400m.)—and Israel was already the largest recipient of US military and economic aid. The current deficit on the balance of payments rose to a record $1,944m. in 1983.

A number of more immediate factors exacerbated the deleterious effect on the economy of long-term government policy during 1983. Defence expenditure, already absorbing one-quarter of the budget, increased as a result of commitments in Lebanon, costing about $1m. per day; the West Bank settlement programme and a four-month strike of the nation's doctors added to the economic burden.

From September 1982 the Treasury had made the reduction of inflation its priority, using heavy subsidization in an attempt to keep increases in the price of basic commodities down to 5% per month, and allowing a gradual, monthly depreciation of the shekel of no more than 5% against the US

dollar. Any impact which these measures may have had on inflation was effectively dissipated by the quarterly cost-of-living increment which was received by every salaried employee as a result of the indexation of wages (as well as savings, mortgages, pensions, etc.) to inflation. In addition the artificially high exchange rate of the shekel was affecting the balance of trade at the expense of exports.

The shekel was devalued by 7.5% in August 1983, and Yoram Aridor announced cuts in government spending, with the heaviest reductions intended for the defence budget. This met with opposition in the Cabinet and approval was gained for only two-thirds of the proposed $1,000m. in cuts. With a major devaluation of the shekel apparently inevitable, Israelis rushed to buy dollars, selling even their bank shares. This trend continued during the period of uncertainty following Begin's resignation as Prime Minister in September, and trading on the stock exchange was suspended for two weeks in October. The shekel was devalued by 23% in October, and food subsidies were reduced by 50%, followed by cuts in financial support for electricity, water and public transport. Aridor, in proposing the temporary use of the US dollar as legal tender (to undercut the inflationary effect of the system of cost-of-living increments and to give his austerity measures a chance to reduce inflation), was forced to resign. His replacement, Yigal Cohen-Orgad, made a reduction in the balance-of-payments deficit his priority and embarked on pruning $2,000m. from current budget expenditure by the end of the year.

Besides Cabinet opposition, Cohen-Orgad's policies were greeted with increasing labour unrest as inflation accelerated to 190% at the end of 1983. A new round of price increases in January 1984, coupled with the reduction of food subsidies, meant that food prices had trebled in three months. To avert a new wave of strikes, the Government approved a 46.5% cost-of-living increment for wage-earners in January, amounting to 85% of the increase in inflation during the preceding quarter. The budget for the fiscal year ending 31 March 1985 cut some 10% (more than US $600m.) from the defence budget, although $300m. of this was to be in the form of redistributed US defence aid. The budget proposals envisaged total expenditure of $22,700m.

The real value of wages fell by 25% up to March 1984 in response to Cohen-Orgad's economies. He allowed the shekel to depreciate in line with inflation. The control of inflation, however, was no longer the Government's principal aim and, as a result, the annual rate of inflation had risen from under 150%, when Cohen-Orgad assumed office in October 1983, to about 400% in July 1984. It was clear that some form of social contract between government and unions including price-, wage- and tax-freezes, was required if inflation was to be reduced. Preparations for the July general election, followed by political uncertainty after its inconclusive result, fore-stalled serious negotiations on the issue.

The new Government (which included a new Minister of Finance, Itzhak Modai) immediately requested more aid from the USA, including $1,000m., unrelated to Israel's annual grant (set at $2,600m. in the year ending 30 September 1985 and comprising $1,200m. in economic and $1,400m. in military aid), to be paid at once. The US Government refused to give additional aid until Israel reduced government spending and introduced a comprehensive programme of economic austerity to curb inflation and reduce the balance-of-payments deficit. The Histadrut (the National Labour Federation), whose co-operation was needed for any such programme to have a chance of success, opposed a planned 'freeze' of wages and prices, and refused to accept a reduction in the cost-of-living increment, which amounted to 80% of inflation. Planned expenditure cuts were reduced to $250m. by dissenting ministers. The Government did devalue the shekel by 9% in Sep-tember, but the principal effect of the removal of subsidies on oil, the reduction of those on electricity and foodstuffs, and consequent price increases (of 30% on oil), to compensate for pre-election liberality, was that inflation rose even more sharply than before. The retail price index rose by 21.4% in September, the highest monthly rise in Israel's history, until October, when the rate was 24.3% (equivalent to an annual rate of 1,260%).

The Government's economic programme was approved by the representatives of employers and labour in November 1984. The aim of the three-month 'package' was to cut the standard of living by 10%–12% and to reduce the rate of inflation to 10% per month (still equivalent to an annual rate of 214%). Prices, wages, taxes and profits were 'frozen', while the shekel was held at its existing value against the US dollar. In addition, one-third was cut from the cost-of-living increment, reducing it to 55% of inflation, and it was decided to shed 14,000 jobs from the public sector (10% of its work-force). The negative effects of these measures were that unem-ployment, traditionally 2%–3% of the labour force, rose to almost 6%; a degree of social unrest was discernible, and special courts had to be established to enforce the 'freeze'. However, the monetary policy had an almost immediate effect. Inflation fell to 19.5% in November (equivalent to an annual rate of 748%), and to only 3.7% in December, though it rose to 5.3% in January 1985. Inflation in the year to December 1984 was 444.9%, compared with 190% in 1983.

Lengthy negotiations between government, unions and employers led to the signing of an agreement for a second economic programme, which was due to come into operation on the expiry of the term of its predecessor on 31 January 1985. In anticipation of the second 'package', and as part of a plan to make savings of $1,000m., subsidies on many essential goods were heavily cut. The eight-month second plan aimed to allow prices of unsubsidized goods to rise by an average of 3%–5% per month, while most subsidized goods would not be allowed to rise by more than 13%. Subsidies on oil, electricity and water were either to be reduced or removed altogether, so that prices would rise by between 25% and 50%. To offset these increases, wage-earners were to receive a flat-rate cash compensation and 5% monthly tax relief, but the cost-of-living

increment was not to take into account increases in the price of subsidized goods.

Israel's two-stage austerity programme had been intended to clear the way for reductions in planned expenditure of some $1,000m. There was general acceptance of the necessity of spending cuts if the economy was to make progress but the Treasury and the Ministry of Defence disagreed, to the extent of some $500m., on the scale of cuts in the defence budget. Apart from the traditional Israeli sensitivity to issues affecting its ability to defend itself, the defence industry was a major employer (10% of total Israeli manpower) and exporter.

On the eve of the introduction of the new 'package', the Cabinet agreed a budget for the year 1985/86, involving planned expenditure of $23,300m., somewhat more than that for 1984/85, with the cuts in spending ($1,300m.) considerably less than the amount for which Itzhak Modai had been arguing. The Knesset approved the budget on 30 March. However, the USA repeatedly stressed the need for more stringent measures to be introduced in order to control the economy before it would consider meeting in full Israeli requests for aid. In January 1985 Israel's foreign debt was $24,500m., of which $9,600m. were owed to the USA. For the year beginning in October 1985, Israel was seeking an increase in US aid to $4,100m. (comprising $1,900m. in economic aid and $2,200m. in military aid). President Reagan gained the approval of Congress for military aid of $1,800m. but the condition of concerted action to reform the economy (including more budget cuts, a large devaluation of the shekel, and a sharp cut in the index-linked salaries system) still attached to any increase in economic aid.

The second 'package' of economic measures was introduced on 4 February 1985. However, consumer prices rose by 13.5% in February, 12.1% in March, 19% in April, 6.8% in May and 14.9% in June—an annual rate of more than 300%. The country's reserves of foreign exchange, which fell to $2,601m. at the end of 1984, continued to dwindle. In March the US Administration agreed to provide economic aid of $1,200m. for 1985/86, and in June the US House of Representatives approved emergency aid of $750m. in both 1985/86 and 1986/87, despite its dissatisfaction with Israel's tentative econ-omic reforms.

The sharp rise in inflation recorded in April prompted the Government to implement a new set of austerity measures in May. Value-added tax was increased from 15% to 17%; the tax on foreign travel was doubled to $300; purchase tax on imported goods was increased from 10% to 20%; wages and contracts in the public sector were 'frozen' for three months; and a law was approved which limited the Government's power to cover the budget deficit by ordering the Central Bank to print money, the intention being to eliminate the practice entirely within two years. Then, at the end of the month, the prices of goods and services, from bread to petrol, were increased by between 14% and 41%, and 'frozen' for two months. The prices of basic foods, subsidized by the Government, were increased by 25%; the price of many ser-vices was increased by 14%, and that of petrol went up by 41%. The Histadrut considered these measures to be too harsh and opposed any attempt to alter existing wage arrangements, which continued, though at a lower level than in the past, to undercut government attempts to reduce spending by compen-sating salaried employees for price increases.

A wave of strikes, in protest at rising prices, disrupted the country in June 1985, but the Cabinet approved a new three-month programme of emergency measures, to reduce proposed government expenditure, at the beginning of July. Food sub-sidies were drastically reduced, so that prices were to rise by between 45% and 75%; wages, prices and the currency exchange rate were to be 'frozen' until October; the shekel was to be devalued by 18.8%, to about $1 = 1,500 shekels, and 'frozen' at that level; 3% of the public-sector work-force (some 10,000 jobs) were to be laid off; spending on health, education and welfare was reduced, and ministry budgets were decreased by a total of $750m., despite strong opposition in the Cabinet. The Knesset approved the measures, and on the same day (2 July) more than 1m. Israelis participated in a general strike, organized by the Histadrut, in protest.

Two weeks of negotiation produced an agreement between the Government, employers and the Histadrut on 16 July, and averted a prolonged general strike. The Histadrut and private-sector employers settled on a level of wage erosion which was acceptable to the Histadrut while remaining within the framework of the Government's economic stabilization programme. The Government, which had also been urging a 6% reduction in public-sector labour costs, abandoned a plan to cut wages in the sector by 3%.

The rate of inflation in July was, at 27.5%, a new record for a single month, corresponding to an annual rate of 380% and a cumulative rate for 1985 of 150%. The three-month programme was designed to reduce inflation to between 4% and 6% per month, and in August, the first month in which its effects could be felt, the rate of inflation was 3.9%, while in September it was a mere 3%. However, the Government was engaged upon a cost-saving programme which involved the shedding of more than 26,000 public-sector jobs, while about 1,000 companies were believed to be in serious financial difficulties, placing a further 40,000 jobs at risk. Unemployment rose by 2% during the July–September plan, and by November some 120,000 people, or 8.3% of the working population, were out of work, compared with about 72,000 in April. However, the rate of unemployment fell to below 7% during the first half of 1986.

At the end of September the three-month price 'freeze' was extended until the end of June 1986. The Histadrut was opposed to the further suspension of wage indexation but offered to forego all pay increases until April 1986, in return for the preservation of the principle of free collective bargaining. A new shekel, worth 1,000 of the old units, was officially introduced on 1 January 1986, partly as a financial practicality (the old shekel had become unwieldy in calculation, owing to inflation) and to restore faith in the currency in the face of the widespread use of the US dollar as an alternative currency, in barter and on the 'black' market. The Cabinet reduced planned expenditure in the budget for the fiscal year 1986/87 by $580m. in December 1985, compared with the $600m. for which Itzhak Modai had been arguing. The proposed budget totalled $21,200m. (30,300m. new shekels), with defence spending claiming the biggest share, after the Minister of Defence had resisted demands by the Ministry of Finance for reductions in its allowance totalling $180m. Subsidies on basic foodstuffs, public transport and services were to be reduced by $120m. The Knesset approved the budget proposals at the end of March 1986.

The effect of the economic stabilization programme, launched in July 1985, continued to be felt in controlling the rate of inflation, which in October was 4.7%, in November 0.5% and in December 1.4%, giving an overall rate for 1985 of 185.2%. Between July 1985 and the end of the year the real value of wages fell by about 25%, and in February 1986 the Histadrut called a strike of public-sector employees to protest against the continuation of stringent monetary policy in the 1986/87 budget. Inflation, however, remained under control, with consumer prices falling by 1.3% in January (the first monthly decline for more than a decade) and rising by 1.6% in February.

In February the Prime Minister, Shimon Peres, unexpectedly advocated economic growth, the establishment of a reflationary fund of $500m., and emergency spending to support large companies experiencing financial difficulties. The Minister of Finance, Itzhak Modai, criticized Peres, accusing him of endangering the success of the economic stabilization programme. The subsequent recriminations threatened the survival of the coalition Government (see History), but the crisis ended when Modai exchanged portfolios with Moshe Nissim, the Minister of Justice, in April.

The rate of inflation remained below 2% from March 1986 until the end of June, and in July there was no rise in prices, resulting in an annual rate of 15%. The success of the economic programme was indicated by the announcement of a surplus (the first ever) of $1,100m. on the current account of the balance of payments in fiscal 1985, following deficits of $1,400m. in 1984 and $2,100m. in 1983. Even without emergency economic aid of $750m. from the USA, the current account would have been in surplus. Meanwhile, Israel's

reserves of foreign exchange increased by 60% between July 1985 and July 1986, to about $3,500m., or the equivalent of the cost of two and a half months' imports, and the trade deficit fell by 17% during 1985. In June the Knesset approved an extension of the price 'freeze' until the end of 1986, while the Government sought the co-operation of the Histadrut in 'freezing' public-sector wages for a further 12 months. During 1986, with lower inflation, compensation payments, and the partial indexation that was still in operation, wages rose to a level higher than that prevailing prior to the introduction of the economic austerity programme in July 1985. Average real wages in 1986 were 5.1% above their 1985 equivalent, although 3.8% below the level of 1984.

In December 1985 Israel requested the US Administration to provide $3,550m. in economic and military aid in 1986/87. The USA approved aid for Israel in 1986/87 totalling $3,000m. ($1,200m. in economic assistance and $1,800m.—a slight increase compared with 1985/86—for military purposes). Responding to pressure from the USA to persevere with its programme of economic stringency the Israeli budget for 1986/87, then $19,000m., was cut by a further $215m. in August 1986.

A combination of wage rises, a 10% fall in exports during the last quarter of 1986, and an increase in the level of imported consumer goods, threatened to offset the benefits of the Government's austerity measures. The rate of inflation rose to 2.4% in October, and to 2.9% in November; it fell to 1.5% in December, but rose to 2.1% in January 1987. However, the success of the Government's austerity programmes and the injections of US aid into the economy was evidenced by an overall inflation rate of 19.7% in 1986 (compared with 185.2% in 1985 and 444.9% in 1984), a surplus of $1,371m. in the current account of the balance of payments in fiscal 1986, and an increase in reserves of foreign exchange, to $4,200m. After initial opposition, a new programme of measures was introduced in January 1987, with the approval of the manufacturers' association and the Histadrut. The new 10-point programme was devised by Moshe Nissim, the Minister of Finance. Total recommended reductions of planned expenditure by 500m. new shekels in the 1987/88 budget were restricted to 400m. new shekels, after a proposed reduction of 180m. new shekels in the defence budget had been successfully resisted in the Cabinet, but they included a cut of more than 100m. new shekels in government subsidies on basic commodities. In addition, there were to be large reductions in spending on health, education and social welfare; a major reform of the tax system to encourage capital investment; a wages 'freeze'; a partial de-indexation of cost-of-living payments, reducing the level of compensation from 70% to 43% of rises in prices; and reductions in the public-sector work-force. The programme was introduced in two stages, in January and on 1 April, and the arrangements for controlling prices were to remain in force until April 1988. On 12 January the Cabinet approved a budget of 39,300m. new shekels for the fiscal year 1987/88, incorporating spending cuts of 400m. new shekels, which still left a substantial deficit of 1,400m. new shekels. Two days later, the shekel was devalued by 10.2% in relation to a 'basket' of five international currencies. (The shekel, which had formerly been aligned with the US dollar, was linked with a 'basket' of currencies in July 1986, in an attempt to prevent wide fluctuations in the exchange rate and to stabilize returns from foreign trade.) In April 1987 the Knesset approved the state budget for 1987/88 in the form in which it had been presented by the Government.

The Government's economic programme continued to restrain inflation during 1987. At the end of the year, according to the Central Bureau of Statistics, the overall rate of inflation for the preceding 12 months was 16.1%, the lowest annual rate for 15 years. Israel's reserves of foreign exchange rose to $5,700m. in November 1987, on receipt of the US economic aid grant for the fiscal year 1987/88, totalling $1,200m. In November the Minister of Finance, Moshe Nissim, claimed that Israel's real GDP was growing at a rate of more than 4% per year, compared with only 2.2% in 1986. Unemployment, which, as a result of the shedding of thousands of public-sector jobs by the Government in a cost-saving exercise, had risen to the equivalent of 7.9% of the civilian labour force during the second quarter of 1986, declined to 5.6%, its lowest level since 1985, during the same period of 1987. During the whole of 1987, employment in the industrial sector rose by 3%, and industrial output rose by 5%. The budget deficit, which had reached a record level of 13% of GDP in 1984, declined to 2% of GDP in 1987. However, the visible trade deficit increased by 36.5%, to $3,228.6m. (compared with $2,361m. in 1986), incorporating an 18.6% rise in the level of exports and a 23.3% rise in imports. The overall deficit on the balance of payments rose by 55%, to $6,200m., largely owing to a 200% increase in the cost of security imports, to $2,700m. Israel's foreign debt rose to $33,000m. at the end of 1987.

The success that was achieved was made possible only by a continuing policy of financial stringency. According to the Bank of Israel's report for 1986, defence spending, expressed as a percentage of national income, was lower than at any time since 1967. This reflected the success of Moshe Nissim in securing cuts in the defence budget, traditionally the largest portion of government expenditure, though these had been limited by vigorous resistance in the Cabinet. Nissim was strongly opposed to the continuation of the Lavi fighter aircraft project, owing to its enormous cost. The project was finally cancelled by the Government in August 1987, under pressure from the USA, which, as part of its annual military aid to Israel, had contributed about 95% of the $1,500m. spent on the development of the Lavi between 1980 and 1987. Moshe Arens, a Minister without Portfolio in the Cabinet, resigned in protest against the decision (he returned to the Cabinet in April 1988).

The budget for 1988/89 was approved by the Cabinet in January 1988. Total expenditure was fixed at 47,800m. new shekels ($29,900m.), incorporating cuts totalling 742m. new shekels ($463m.), only 13m. new shekels ($8.1m.) less than those originally proposed by Moshe Nissim. Spending on defence was to remain the same as in the previous year, at 8,200m. new shekels ($5,100m.), but state subsidies on food, public transport, health and education were all reduced. Debt servicing was to absorb 17,000m. new shekels. Government revenue was to include $3,000m. in aid from the USA (comprising $1,200m. in economic and $1,800m. in military aid), the same as in 1987/88. The Knesset approved the budget for 1988/89 in March 1988.

In February 1988 the Cabinet approved a supplementary budget, allowing for additional expenditure of 1,160m. new shekels in the period December 1987 to March 1988, which was made necessary by increased spending on security in the Occupied Territories, wage rises, an increase in state subsidies and the failure to implement decisions to reduce spending on health and education. Although expenditure had risen beyond the limits of the original budget, income had meanwhile risen by 1,500m. new shekels, largely owing to an increase in tax collection and a growth in economic activity.

After three years of relatively rapid growth, 1988 was characterized by a deceleration in the rate of economic expansion. GDP increased by only 1.6%, compared with growth of 5.2% in 1987, while in the commercial sector production rose by a mere 1%, compared with an increase of 7% in 1987. These were the lowest rates of growth since 1982. The principal factor behind this stagnation was a decline of 3% in the volume of exports (the result of the Government's decision to 'freeze' the exchange rate), which combined with a substantial rise in real wages to impair the competitiveness of local manufacturers on both external and domestic markets. In 1988 the value of the new shekel, measured against the 'basket' of five international currencies (see above), declined by 10% compared with its average value in 1987. Unrest in the Occupied Territories continued to exert a harmful effect on the Israeli economy in 1988: it was estimated that additional expenditure on security and the cost of lost exports to the Occupied Territories (normally worth $70m. per month) absorbed 1.5%–2% of GDP, equivalent to $700m. Against this background of unrest, and uncertainty regarding exchange rate policy, investment declined by some 4% in 1988, after having increased by about 14% in 1987. This, in turn, contributed to a fall in aggregate demand and the slowing of economic activity. Industrial production declined by 3% in 1988, while agricultural output fell by 7%.

Real wages increased, on average, by around 7% in 1988. In the private sector they increased by approximately 6%, and in the public sector by around 10%. These increases were inconsistent with the recessionary trend in the economy and resulted from rigidities in the mechanisms used to determine wage increments, which have not been adjusted to the lower rate of inflation. A further contributory factor was the enactment of legislation establishing a minimum wage. There was a moderate increase in public spending in 1988. Spending on public consumption rose by about 3%, while domestic defence spending increased by 3%, compared with a rise of 2% in 1987.

Owing to excessive reliance on the 'frozen' exchange rate policy, the economy lapsed into an unplanned recession in 1988. However, this policy failed to achieve its main target of reducing the rate of inflation, which, at 16.4%, was close to that of 1987. In November and December expectation of a devaluation of the shekel intensified. The reaction of the private sector was to make purchases of foreign currency, financed mainly by drawing on shekel deposits. This gave rise to an increase in short-term credit, causing the Bank of Israel to abandon its policy of reducing interest rates. In an attempt to prevent the devaluation of profits financed by short-term borrowings, the rate of interest on Bank of Israel monetary tenders was raised to a record level of 48%. A wave of foreign currency purchases in the second half of December led to a 5% devaluation of the new shekel on 27 December, and to the cessation of foreign currency trading on 29 December. When trade was resumed on 3 January 1989, a further devaluation, of 8%, was implemented, and the cumulative devaluation of 13.4% was presented as part of a new economic policy. During the ensuing months to May 1989, most of the private sector's foreign currency purchases were reconverted to shekels.

The trade deficit on goods and services (excluding defence imports) amounted to $3,250m. in 1988, similar to that recorded in 1987. The stability of the deficit was due, in part, to a decline in imports of investment goods, a major component of total imports. There was also an improvement in the terms of international trade, not least an 18% reduction in fuel prices.

Israel's net foreign debt stood at $17,100m. at the end of March 1989, its lowest level since 1982, having fallen by more than $1,000m. during 1988. Foreign debts, excluding commercial banks' net assets in foreign currency, amounted to $24,350m. at the end of 1988, compared with $25,440m. at the end of 1987. Commercial banks also repaid debts of about $800m. during 1988.

In 1988 unemployment increased to 6.4% of the labour force, compared with 6.1% in 1987. The increase was especially noticeable in the second half of the year, when it rose from 5.9% to 6.9%. In the first quarter of 1989 unemployment rose further, to 8.2%. The number of persons seeking employment increased from around 36,000 in the first quarter of 1988 to some 59,000 in the corresponding period of 1989. The rise in unemployment was due to a substantial increase in the labour force participation rate, from an average of 50.4% in 1987 to 51.4% in 1988, reaching 52% at the end of the year. This rise in the labour force occurred when children born during the 1960s joined the working-age population. It was also due to a higher participation rate among women; to the continued implementation of efficiency measures and lay-offs in the private sector; and to the renewed participation of workers from the Occupied Territories in the Israeli labour force.

A new economic programme was presented in January 1989 by the newly-appointed Minister of Finance, Shimon Peres. Under this, the shekel was devalued by 13.4% (see above) and exchange rate policy was made more flexible by permitting an adjustment of up to 3% above and below the basic exchange rate. In addition, the commitment to non-intervention in the exchange rate, which had prevailed since 1985, was abandoned. Import duties were reduced in accordance with trade agreements, and exchange rate insurance for exporters was lowered from 12% to 10%. The new programme envisaged a reduction of about 1,000m. new shekels in the budget deficit, in an attempt to reduce the domestic deficit from some 3.5% of GNP in 1988 to 1.5%–2% in 1989. This was to be achieved through reductions in planned expenditure and increases in revenue.

A cost-of-living agreement (COLA) was signed at the same time as the presentation of the new programme, in an attempt to neutralize the inflationary effects on real wage rises. The COLA was also intended to maintain the exchange rate at a level appropriate to the renewal of export growth. Within the framework of the new economic programme, the Bank of Israel adopted various expansionary measures, intended to reduce the cost of credit. Despite all these measures, 1989 was characterized by relatively slack economic activity for the second consecutive year. Real GDP rose by a mere 0.4%, following an increase of 1.6% in 1988.

At the same time, the efficiency drive in the business sector continued, with a substantial reduction in unit costs of production. In addition, the adverse economic effect of the uprising in the Occupied Territories weakened; from an estimated 1.5% contraction of GDP in 1988, equivalent to $600m., it decreased to a 0.7% loss of output in 1989. A further contribution to better business profitability came from the capital market, as financing costs through the various channels declined. At the same time, however, there was an exceptionally high unemployment rate of 8.9%, compared with 6.4% in 1988. This rise was mainly due to an increase in the number of new entrants into the labour force.

An analysis of the economic developments during 1989 shows that in the first half of the year GDP rose by 0.6%, compared with the second half of 1988, and the second half of 1989 recorded a 1.5% increase over the first half of the year. Similar indications of accelerated economic activity can be seen in the trend of private consumption, which declined by 1.7% in the first half of 1989, and rose by 1.8% in the second half. Likewise, public consumption (excluding direct defence imports) fell by 1.5% in the first half of 1989, and rose by 1.1% in the second half.

Improved business sector profitability brought a transformation in the development of industrial production, which has been on an upward trend since the second quarter of 1989. Exports of goods also recorded a significant increase (9.2%). Towards the end of 1989, a rise in fixed investment became apparent, following a two-year decline. Investment in construction expanded in the third quarter of 1989, and an increase in imports of capital goods was recorded in the last quarter. Private consumption remained stable. Consumer prices rose by 20.7% in the 12 months to December 1989.

One major challenge facing the Israeli economy is mass immigration from the former USSR. As part of its policy of *glasnost*, the Soviet Union, after 1989, allowed the virtually unrestricted emigration of Soviet Jews. The number of Jewish immigrants to Israel from the USSR rose from 2,283 in 1988 to 12,932 in 1989, and to an estimated 185,000 in 1990.

During 1990 the Israeli economy began to emerge from recession. GDP expanded, in real terms, by 5.1%, following the low growth rates of 1988 and 1989, and totalled 103,269m. new shekels. This improvement was given impetus by the mounting wave of immigration from the USSR. The second important development to affect the Israeli economy was the crisis in the Persian (Arabian) Gulf region during the second half of the year. The Iraqi invasion of Kuwait in August 1990 and its aftermath affected prospects for economic growth in Israel in a number of areas: there was a drastic decline in the number of tourist arrivals; a substantial rise in fuel prices; a significant increase in expenditure on defence; and a postponement of investment projects. The capital market's reaction to the Iraqi invasion of Kuwait was made evident by a fall in share prices similar to that recorded in the capital markets of most Western countries. Indeed, the war in the Gulf region between Iraq and the multinational force, and, in particular, Iraqi attacks with *Scud* missiles on Israel during January and February 1991, paralysed part of the economy and for a few days brought it to an almost complete standstill. Even after a return to normal activity was declared, only partial stability was achieved.

The third factor to influence economic development was the political crisis which erupted in March 1990 and was to last for two months (see History). The crisis ended in April, when President Herzog invited Itzhak Shamir to form a new coalition government, without the participation of the Labour Party. The new Government was eventually formed in early June, resulting in a considerable delay in the formulation of policies for the construction industry and immigration.

In 1990 domestic consumption rose by 5%, to 64,702m. new shekels. This increase was recorded primarily in the second half of the year and was prompted by the need to supply services (mainly in the areas of housing, education and health) to new immigrants. The consumer price index rose by 17.6% in 1990, with the cost of housing being the dominant accelerating factor. By contrast, most of the other components of the index showed a slackening in the rate of price increases. Deducting the rising cost of housing, the index increased by only 14.3% in 1990. Towards the end of the year, however, a slight rise in the pace of price increases of the other components was recorded, largely attributable to the increase in fuel prices and the reduction in government subsidies, together with the easing of price controls on many products.

At the end of February 1990 the Bank of Israel announced a devaluation of 6% in the 'fixed median rate' of the shekel in relation to the 'basket' of foreign currencies, compared with the 'fixed median rate' set at the time of the last devaluation in June 1989. The maximum permitted range of daily fluctuation of the representative rate of exchange—above and below the median rate (which is based on the supply and demand of foreign currency)—was extended from 3% to 5%. In March 1991 the Bank of Israel devalued the 'fixed median rate' of the shekel against the basket of foreign currencies by a further 6.7%. Moreover, in 1990 the exchange rate of the shekel in relation to the US dollar rose by only 4.5%, in contrast to its 16% rise against the 'basket' of currencies (including the US dollar). This increase was the result of the weak performance of the US dollar on international currency markets in 1990.

As new immigrants rapidly entered the labour market, the projected increase in the available labour force was expected to accelerate, giving rise to fears that unemployment might undermine the recovery of the Israeli economy. During 1990 the average rate of unemployment was 9.6%, representing some 164,000 people; a rate of more than 10% was anticipated in 1991. (Under an agreement signed on 24 May 1991 between the Government, the Histadrut and the employer's organization, the Government pledged that it would create some 36,000 jobs over the following months at a cost of 2,000m. new shekels, of which 1,960m. new shekels were to be allocated to infrastructure projects. In addition, the Government undertook to give preference to Israeli goods with regard to public expenditure projects. For their part, representatives of the employers' organization agreed to engage a further 150,000 workers over the following four years.)

Industrial exports, excluding diamonds, increased by 11.3% in terms of US dollars (by 5% in real terms), to reach $7,868m. in 1990. Increases were recorded in most industrial sectors, including those where technology is not used extensively, such as food, textiles and leather. This improvement in industrial exports was a result of the greater competitiveness of the sector. During 1990, for example, industrial production rose by 6.3%, while the sector's work-force declined by 0.8%.

Rising demand and intensified economic activity in 1990 resulted in an increase in imports of goods, by 16.6% in US dollar terms, and in imports of services, by 8.8% in US dollar terms. The increase in imports of capital goods was spectacular, amounting to 38.2% in US dollar terms. Overall, imports of goods exceeded exports by US $2,379m., producing an increase in the trade deficit.

In September 1990 the Government approved an economic programme that was designed to permit the efficient absorption of immigrants into the Israeli economy. The programme was based on a reform of the capital and labour markets and the granting of incentives to the business sector by means of changes in taxes and customs duties. By early 1991, however, most of the provisions had not been put into effect, hence the particular significance of the agreement between the Government, the Histadrut and the employers' organization, signed in May 1991 (see above).

During 1991 the Israeli economy continued to grow and it became apparent that damage caused by the 1990/91 crisis in the Persian (Arabian) Gulf region had been only temporary. (It is estimated that the conflict in the Gulf cost the Israeli economy some $2,000m., but this was made good during the course of 1991.) GDP expanded, in real terms, by 5.9%, totalling 134,756m. new shekels. Immigration remained the principal cause of economic growth—during 1991 some 176,000 immigrants arrived in Israel and, overall, the population rose by 5.8%. Investment in fixed assets increased substantially, by 41.8%, reaching 31,958m. new shekels, while stocks rose by 134%. Private consumption, which accounted for 61% of GDP, increased by 7.6%. About one-fifth of the increase in private consumption was due to purchases of consumer durables. Public consumption—including expenditure on public services and defence—increased by 43.4%, accounting for 20% of all domestic expenditure.

As a result of the expansion of economic activity in 1991 there was a sharp rise, of 15.8%, in imports of goods and services. The value of exports, however, expressed in real terms, declined by 2.3%. Meanwhile, the rapid absorption of immigrants into the labour force caused unemployment to rise and the erosion of salaries in real terms.

Consumer prices rose by 18% in 1991 and during the first three-quarters of the year loans by the Bank of Israel bore rates of interest which were lower than the rate of inflation. In October 1991, however, owing to a huge demand for money in anticipation of a devaluation of the shekel, the Bank of Israel raised the interest rates it charged to commercial banks and interest rates on unindexed assets rose sharply as a consequence. The Bank of Israel's persistence in restrictive monetary policies succeeded in taming excessive demand for foreign currency and interest rates were reduced in November. In December the new Governor of the Bank of Israel announced a new policy regarding the exchange rate of the shekel. The mid-point of the range within which the exchange rate was allowed to fluctuate was to be devalued daily, at an annual rate of 9%; while the representative rate was to be allowed to fluctuate as before, within a range of 5% relative to the mid-point, and was to be determined according to daily demand for foreign currency. At the same time the Bank of Israel announced a target rate for inflation of 14%–15% in 1992.

In 1992 the Israeli economy grew at a rate not recorded since the early 1970s. Fuelled by high levels of demand for Israeli exports and high rates of public and private consumption, GDP expanded by 6.6% and business-sector GDP by 7.9%. The cumulative growth of the business sector during 1990–92 totalled 24%. An exceptional 48.8% growth in the export of tourism services and a 10.1% rise in industrial exports (excluding diamonds) largely accounts for the 14.1% increase in exports in real terms over 1991. The rise in private consumption from 7.6% in 1991 to 7.8% in 1992—including a 22% increase in the consumption of consumer durables, following a similar rise in the previous two years—is evidence of the growth of the Israeli population and the integration of immigrants into the national economy. The 4.7% growth in public consumption (excluding defence imports) also reflects expenditure on the absorption of immigrants, of whom 437,352 entered the country during 1990–92. Approximately 113,000 new jobs were created during 1992, but, despite this increase, the overall unemployment rate rose for the sixth consecutive year, to 11.2%. Growth in salaried employment occurred mainly in the financial and business services sector, the trade, restaurants and hotels sector, and in the public sector.

Consumer prices rose by 9.4% in 1992, the first time since 1969 that a single-digit rate had been recorded. Since the implementation of the 1985 economic stabilization programme, rates had been in the range of 16%–20%. The drastic reduction in the inflation rate can be attributed to the erosion in the real value of wages (0.5% in the public sector), caused by the high level of unemployment, a substantial decline—in real terms—in housing prices, a low budget deficit, a greater exposure to imports (which rose by 13%), continued reforms in the capital market and greater liberalization in the foreign currency market. Nineteen ninety-two was the first full year in which the 'diagonal band' exchange rate regime was implemented. In line with this policy, the shekel was devalued by 16.3% against a basket of currencies and by 21.1% against the US dollar. However, in contrast to the experience of previous years, devaluation did not lead to an immediate rise in inflation.

Gross investment increased by 7.6% in 1992, reaching 39,814m. new shekels (at current prices) after a spectacular 45% increase in 1991. Investment in fixed assets, however, increased by only 4.9% to reach 37,580m. new shekels (at current prices).

High economic growth rates and other positive economic developments generated a bullish trend in the stock market, 1992 being a record year for securities trading. The Tel-Aviv Stock Exchange share index (excluding banks) rose by 91%. The daily volume of shares traded on the Stock Exchange reached $45m., an increase of 56% over 1991.

Israel's GDP increased by 3.5% in 1993. This was below the annual average for the previous three years of more than 6%, owing to a 27% decline in activity in the housing construction sector compared with 1992. It should be noted that during the second quarter of 1993 GDP declined by 0.8% due, among other things, to the closure of the administered territories, which seriously affected the agriculture and construction sectors. In the second half of the year, however, GDP grew at a rate equivalent to an annual increase of 8%. Economic growth in 1993 was mainly export-oriented, exports of goods and services increasing by 12%. Industrial exports—excluding diamonds—rose by 18%, while exports of electronic goods increased by 30% in dollar terms. This growth was achieved in spite of the economic difficulties of many of the industrialized countries which are responsible for the bulk of Israel's foreign trade. An impressive growth in tourism, for the second consecutive year, was also recorded, leading to a rise of 16% in earnings from exports of tourist services. The number of tourists rose by 8% in 1993 to approximately 2m. The trade deficit in the civilian sector increased to $5,900m. in 1993, while imports in the military sector also rose, to some $2m., bringing the total deficit to almost $8,000m. Investment in the economy was equivalent to about 17% of GDP in 1993.

Private consumption continued to grow at a high rate, increasing by 7.6% in 1993. During the past four years private consumption has increased by an annual average of 7%, representing an annual average increase of 3% in per capita consumption. The growth in private consumption in the previous three years had been mainly due to sales of consumer durables, which rose annually by 16%. In 1993, however, sales of consumer durables rose by only 2.2%.

In 1993 the budget deficit, which totalled 7,300m. new Israeli shekels (4% of GDP), was financed by revenue from the privatization of government corporations (3,200m. new Israeli shekels); borrowing on the capital markets (2,500m. new Israeli shekels); and by deposits at the Bank of Israel.

Inflation reached 11.2% in 1993. The price of housing was the fastest growing component of the consumer price index during the year and in the first half of 1994. Employment expanded by 6.1% in 1993. The number of job seekers declined by some 20% in the first half of the year, remaining stable in the second half.

During 1993 the value of the new Israeli shekel fell by 6.3% against the currency basket, and by 8% against the US dollar. The main devaluation took place in the second half of the year, owing to increases in the consumer price index towards the end of the year.

The money market was characterized by rapid growth in monetary aggregates during 1993. Nevertheless, towards the end of the year—in order to curb growth in inflation—there was a change in the expansionary monetary policy and the interest on funds made available to the banking system by the Central Bank was raised. This rise was continued into 1994. An increase in interest rates at the end of June was sharply criticized by the Minister of Finance, who feared that too high a rate would obstruct economic growth.

As at the end of 1993, there was rapid economic growth during the first quarter of 1994. In the second quarter, however, as a consequence of the closure of the administered territories, the rate of growth declined.

AREA AND POPULATION

The total area of the State of Israel, within its 1949 armistice frontiers, amounts to 20,700 sq km. This compares with the area of Palestine under the British mandate, which totalled 27,090 sq km. At the census of 4 June 1983 the population of

Israel (including East Jerusalem and the Golan Heights) was 4,037,620, of whom 3,349,997 (83%) were Jews. In addition, there were about 1m. persons in other areas which were brought under Israeli administration as a result of the 1967 war, and after the Sinai peninsula was evacuated at the end of April 1982. According to official estimates, the population (*de jure*) of Israel at 31 December 1993 was 5,322,000, of whom 4,335,000 (81%) were Jews.

The population density of Israel was 184 per sq km at the June 1983 census and 220.4 per sq km at the end of 1990. The population is heavily concentrated in the coastal strip, with about three-quarters of the Jewish inhabitants and nearly two-thirds of the non-Jewish population located between Ashkelon and Naharia. According to the official estimates at the end of 1992, the Tel-Aviv District had a population of 1,142,200, accounting for 22% of the total population. A further 1,112,000 (21.4%) lived in the Central District, 691,000 (13%) in the Haifa District, 651,700 (12.5%) in the Southern District (comprising almost two-thirds of Israel's land area, but including the Negev Desert, which is largely uninhabited except for nomads), 877,400 (17%) in the Northern District (including 27,200 in the Golan Heights) and 616,000 (12%) in the Jerusalem District. The remaining 105,400 were Israelis residing at Jewish localities in the West Bank and the Gaza Strip. Of the 1993 population, 4,695,000 (comprising 3,824,900 Jews and 870,000 non-Jews), or 90% of the total, were defined as urban, i.e. resident in localities with 2,000 or more inhabitants. The remaining 417,700 Jews and 83,200 non-Jews were rural residents. Within this total there were 51,900 persons (12,900 Jews and 39,000 non-Jews), including Bedouin tribes, who were living outside localities.

The main reason for the growth of the Jewish population was immigration, accounting for 58% of the yearly increase in the Jewish population between 1948 and 1977. On 31 December 1992, 39% of the Jewish population had been born abroad. These included 1,068,800 born in Europe and America, 335,800 in Africa and 263,800 in Asia. Of the 2,574,200 Israeli-born Jews, 979,000 were second-generation Israelis. Immigration up to 1948 totalled 452,158 persons, of whom nearly 90% came from Europe and America. The biggest wave of immigrants—more than 576,000—arrived within six years of the founding of the new state. These were refugees from war-torn Europe, followed by Jews emigrating from the Arab states. Large numbers have come from North Africa as a result of political developments there, and during 1955–64 more than 200,000 emigrated from Africa into Israel. Since 1956 immigration from Eastern Europe has resumed. In the mid-1960s immigration declined, falling from 54,716 in 1964 to 14,327 in 1967, but the level of immigration rose considerably after the 1967 war, bringing the total numbers of immigrants between 1965 and 1974 to more than 300,000. Almost 70% of these came from Europe and America. After the Yom Kippur war, immigration declined again, falling from 54,886 in 1973 to 31,979 in 1974, and to 19,754 in 1976. Immigrants totalled 12,599 in 1981, rising to 18,766 in 1984, including 7,800 Ethiopian Jews (Falashas). In 1988 the number of people who emigrated from Israel totalled 18,900 (including Israelis who had spent more than one year abroad), while 13,034 people settled in Israel. In 1989 the number of immigrants, mainly from the USSR, rose sharply, to 24,000 people; a further increase, to 194,500 people, was reported in 1990; in 1993 the number totalled only 68,716.

The Jewish birth rate was 18.5 per 1,000 in 1993, compared with a rate of 37.2 per 1,000 for Muslims, but the infant mortality rate was much higher for the latter. The total yearly rate of increase (including immigration) of the Jewish population was only 2% in 1975, compared with 3.1% in 1973 and a peak annual rate of increase of 23.7% during 1949–51.

The Israeli civilian labour force at the end of 1993 (seasonally adjusted) totalled 1,946,000, or 53% of the population aged 15 years and over, and comprised approximately 37% women and 63% men. The growth in the labour force from 735,800 in 1960 was due chiefly to the rise in total population, since the participation rate declined slightly.

An important characteristic is the relatively high proportion of dependants in the population, with one-third aged 14 years and under. As a result of this, the ratio of the labour force to total population—under 35%—is low by European and American standards. Unemployment affected 10% of the labour force in 1993, and totalled 195,000 individuals.

During 1993, of 1,751,000 employees, some 62,000 were employed in agriculture, forestry and fishing; 371,300 in mining and manufacturing; 17,500 in electricity and water; 118,300 in construction; 250,700 in trade, restaurants and hotels; 106,100 in transport, storage and communications; 183,900 were engaged in financing and business services; 500,200 in public and community service, and the remainder (131,800) in personal and other services.

AGRICULTURE

The agricultural sector is relatively small, accounting for about 6% of domestic product in 1986 and employing 4.1% of the labour force in 1990. In spite of this, Israeli agriculture has attracted a great deal of international attention. Agriculture, more than any other sector of the economy, has been the focus of ideological pressure. For centuries, Jews in the Diaspora were barred from owning land and the Zionist movement therefore saw land settlement as one of the chief objectives of Jewish colonization. Since the establishment of the state, government agricultural policy has centred chiefly on the attainment of self-sufficiency in foodstuffs, in view of military considerations and Israel's possible isolation from its chief foreign food supplies; on the saving of foreign exchange through import substitution and the promotion of agricultural exports; and on the absorption of the large numbers of immigrants in the agricultural sector. In line with these objectives, the promotion of mixed farming and of co-operative farming settlements has also been an important element in government policy. Although the increase in agricultural production (which rose by an annual average of 3% during 1980–90, but declined by almost 5% in 1991) has resulted in Israel becoming largely self-sufficient in foodstuffs—it is seriously deficient only in grains, oils and fats—and important savings have been made in foreign exchange, government intervention in the agricultural sector has been criticized as having resulted in a misallocation of resources and in the impairment of the economic efficiency of agriculture.

Cultivation has undergone a profound transformation and from an extensive, primitive and mainly dry-farming structure it has developed into a modern intensive irrigated husbandry. A special feature of Israel's agriculture is its co-operative settlements which have been developed to meet the special needs and challenges encountered by a farming community new both to its surroundings and its profession. While there are a number of different forms of co-operative settlements, all are derived from two basic types: the *moshav* and the *kibbutz*. The *moshav* is a co-operative smallholders' village. Individual farms in any one village are of equal size and every farmer works his own land to the best of his ability. He is responsible for his own farm, but his economic and social security is ensured by the co-operative structure of the village, which handles the marketing of his produce, purchases his farm and household equipment, and provides him with credit and many other services. On 31 December 1991 a total of 155,700 people inhabited 410 *moshavim*.

The *kibbutz* is a collective settlement of a unique form developed in Israel. It is a collective enterprise based on common ownership of resources and on the pooling of labour, income and expenditure. Every member is expected to work to the best of his ability; he is paid no wages but is supplied by the *kibbutz* with all the goods and services he needs. The *kibbutz* is based on voluntary action and mutual liability, equal rights for all members, and assumes for them full material responsibility. On 31 December 1992 a total of 269 *kibbutzim* were inhabited by 125,800 people (2.4% of the total population). Both the *moshavim* and the *kibbutzim* have experienced severe financial difficulties. In 1987 the Knesset approved a plan to cancel about $265m. of the estimated $1,000m. debt accumulated by the *moshavim*, which had borrowed heavily during the hyperinflation of the late 1970s and early 1980s.

During the years following the establishment of the State of Israel, a large-scale expansion of the area under cultivation took place. This was caused by the heavy influx of immigrants and the recultivation and rehabilitation of land from which Arabs had been forced to flee. The cultivated area increased from 1,650,000 dunums (1 dunum = 1,000 sq m) in the 1948/49 agricultural year to 4,110,000 dunums in 1958/59 and to 4,402,000 dunums in 1978/79. The cultivated area in 1991 totalled 4,320,000 dunums, including 1,815,000 dunums of unirrigated crops. Production of water in 1992 reached 1,527m. cu m, of which 62% was consumed by agricultural users.

Without taking into consideration the cost or availability of irrigation water, it is estimated that the land potential ultimately available for farming under irrigation is 5.3m. dunums, while an estimated 4.1m. dunums are potentially available for dry farming. There are also 8.5m. dunums available for natural pasture and 0.9m. dunums for afforestation.

The main factor limiting agricultural development is not land, but the availability of water. Since, on average, 800 cu m of water are needed per annum to irrigate one dunum of cultivated area, it is obvious that Israel must harness all water resources. For this reason, the Government established a special Water Administration, headed by a Water Commissioner who has statutory powers to control and regulate both the supply and the consumption of water.

The Water Administration has been charged, among other tasks, with the implementation of the national water project. The purpose of this project is to convey a substantial part of the waters of the River Jordan and of other water sources from the north to southern Judaea and to the Negev, to store excess supplies of water from winter to summer and from periods of heavy rainfall to periods of drought, and to serve as a regulator between the various regional water supply systems. Essential to the national water project is the main conduit from Lake Tiberias to Rosh Haayin (near Tel-Aviv), known as the National Water Carrier, which has an annual capacity of 320m. cu m. Two other large schemes, also in operation, are the Western Galilee-Kishon and the Yarkon-Negev projects. Small desalination plants have been built at Eilat and elsewhere, and will be used more extensively if costs are eventually reduced. Desert farming in the Negev, using brackish water found underground, has achieved considerable success on an experimental basis.

In 1993 agricultural production generated revenue of 5,983m. new shekels. Agricultural exports totalled US $550.9m. in 1992 and $558m. in 1993.

In 1993 wheat production reached 148,614 metric tons, a 22% fall in comparison with 1992, while potato crops fell by 3% to an output of 188,672 tons. Tomato production rose by 31% during 1993, to 364,904 tons. Cucumber production rose to 69,769 tons, and the output of carrots totalled 77,699 tons. Avocado production fell by 41% in 1992/93, to reach 45,959 tons, while banana production declined in the same crop year by 55%, to 32,998 tons.

During 1993 the apple harvest rose by 3%, to 118,135 tons. In 1993 the harvest of table grapes totalled 36,336 tons, and that of wine grapes 32,000 tons.

Cultivation of citrus fruit is one of the oldest and principal agricultural activities, and produces the main export crop. In 1993 Israel exported 256,914 tons of citrus fruit, valued at $180m., a decrease of 10% in comparison with 1992. Total area under cultivation in 1991 was 333,833 dunums. The Citrus Marketing and Control Board supervises all aspects of the growing and marketing of the fruit, particularly exports. Principal markets were the United Kingdom, the Federal Republic of Germany and France.

Increasing emphasis is being laid on the cultivation of floral plants. About 90% of production is usually exported to the EU. In 1993 Israel exported 1,028m. flowers and ornamental branches (mainly roses, carnations and gypsophilia), earning $160m., a 3% increase over the previous year. The state-owned Flower Marketing Board is increasing the number of its packing-houses, and is investing heavily in modern equipment. In 1991, 27,100 dunums were under glasshouse cultivation.

In 1993 production of cotton lint and seed cotton fell by 8%, to 69,651 tons, 25% of which were exported, earning $27m. In 1993 Israel exported an estimated $11m.-worth of potatoes.

In 1993 production of cows' milk reached 1,031m. litres.

In the poultry sector, egg production reached 1,469m. in 1993. In the same year Israel's output of poultry meat totalled 258,154 tons (247,151 in 1992). During 1993 beef production (live weight) totalled 22,929 tons in 1993 (23,092 tons in 1992). Fish production reached 12,604 tons in 1993, a decline of 14% compared with the previous year.

CONSTRUCTION AND INDUSTRY

As a unit, construction is the leading sector in Israel since, with affiliated industries (cement, wood, glass and ceramics), it accounts for 20% of GNP. During 1993 there were 7,430,000 sq m of building area completed, of which 2,300,000 sq m were public buildings and 5,130,000 sq m private constructions.

Israel derives more of its national income—some 30%—from industry than does any other Middle Eastern country. In the period 1968–77 industrial production rose by 85%. Gross domestic capital formation in machinery and equipment increased from 23,539m. shekels in 1980 to 24,776m. shekels at 1980 prices in 1982, a rise of 6.2%. Industrial growth was particularly vigorous after 1967. Output in the period 1968–72, in real terms, rose by 80%, while exports rose over five years by 124%. The expansion was particularly rapid in the more sophisticated industries—electrical and electronic equipment, transport equipment, machinery, metal and polished diamonds. Value of industrial exports rose by 26% during 1974, but declined the following year.

In 1992 there were 17,928 establishments, which engaged employees whose number totalled 344,400. Of these establishments, 364 engaged between 100 and 300 persons, and 129 more than 300 persons. In the latter category 109,600 were employed. On the other hand, 8,227 establishments engaged four or fewer persons, and 4,238 between five and nine persons; 17,403 establishments belonged in 1992 to the private sector, 497 to the Histadrut (the National Labour Federation) and 28 to the public sector (mainly government companies). The main branches of these establishments were: metal products; wood and its products; clothing and made-up textiles; food, beverages and tobacco.

Israel's industry originally developed by supplying such basic commodities as soap, vegetable oil and margarine, bread, ice, printing and electricity. It used raw materials available locally to produce citrus juices and other citrus by-products, canned fruit and vegetables, cement, glass and bricks. In order to save foreign exchange, imports of manufactured goods were curtailed, thus giving local industry the opportunity of adding local labour value to the semi-manufactures imported from abroad.

To stimulate investment and encourage the inflow of foreign capital, the Law for the Encouragement of Capital Investments was enacted in 1950, broadened in 1959 and amended in 1967 and 1977. The Law created an Investment Centre and provided for the approval of projects contributing to the development of industrial potential, the exploitation of natural resources, the creation of new sources of employment—particularly in development areas—and to the absorption of new immigrants. Among the concessions granted to approved projects, particularly those financed in foreign currency, are remittance of profits and withdrawal of capital, and tax benefits in respect of income tax, indirect taxes and depreciation allowances.

Although most of Israel's industrial production continues to be for domestic consumption, industrial exports (excluding diamonds) constituted 91% of total exports in 1985. In this area also, there has been a very rapid expansion as a result of tax and investment incentives from the Government. Israeli industrial exports, worth $18m. in 1950, had risen to $780m. by 1971, and by 1993 had reached $13,824.5m.

Israel's most important industrial export product is cut and polished diamonds, most of the expertise for the finishing of which was supplied by immigrants from the Low Countries. In 1993 Israel exported $3,645m.-worth of cut diamonds, 13% more than the $3,210m.-worth supplied in 1992, and was one of the world's largest traders, second only to Belgium in processing diamonds, with approximately three-quarters of the international market in medium-sized stones, Israel's speciality. Israel obtains about 50% of its rough diamonds directly from the Central Selling Organization (the marketing arm of De Beers). Israel bought diamonds worth $532m. in this way in 1987, and an additional $1,000m. worth on the open market, mostly from dealers in Antwerp.

Apart from diamonds (which accounted for almost 26% of industrial exports in 1993), exports were constituted of 4% foodstuffs; 7% textiles, clothing and leather; 2% mining and quarrying products; 14% chemical and oil products; 36% metal products, machinery and electrical and electronic equipment. The value of all exports rose by 161% between 1980 and 1993.

Israel Aircraft Industries (IAI), employing some 15,000, is Israel's largest single industrial enterprise. At its main plant, adjacent to Lod Airport, it produces the *Kfir* combat and multi-mission aircraft, the *Arava*, a twin-turboprop passenger/cargo transport, the Commodore Jet, a 10-place twin-jet executive aircraft, the *Gabriel* sea-to-sea missile, as well as other weapons. The development, with US assistance, of the *Lavi* fighter aircraft was abandoned in September 1987.

The food, beverage and tobacco industries accounted in 1991 for 12% of manufactures. About 90% of output was sold on the local market; the rest, such as juices, wines, chocolate and coffee, was sold abroad. Exports totalled $551m. during 1993, compared with $558m. in 1992.

The textiles and clothing industry, which was developed chiefly because of its low capital-labour ratio, constituted 9% of industrial production during 1993, when it exported goods worth some $930m.

There is also a rapidly expanding electronics industry, specializing in equipment for military and communications purposes. Exports by this sector and by that of metal products and machinery rose from $12.8m. in 1970 to $5,042m. in 1993.

In view of the heavy power needs of irrigation and the water installations, agriculture as well as industry is a large-scale consumer of electricity. Total installed generating capacity at the end of 1992 was 5,835 MW. Generation during 1992 totalled 24,019.2m. kWh. Out of 22,319m. kWh total sales of electricity, industry used 30%. Total water production during 1992 reached 1,527m. cu m, of which industry used 7% while agriculture consumed 61%, and domestic use accounted for 32%.

MINERALS

The Petroleum Law of 1952 regulates the conditions for the granting of licences for petroleum prospecting, divides the country into petroleum districts and fixes a basic royalty of 12.5%. Petroleum was discovered in 1955 at the Heletz-Bror field on the coastal plain and later at Kokhav, Brur and Negba. Signs of petroleum were also discovered near Ashdod. Some 33 wells in Israel are now producing, and their output was 16.6m. litres in 1987. Since 1983, when oil exploration began, the four small fields have produced only 16.6m. barrels. From the time of the 1967 war to the 1975 disengagement agreement, Israel was able to exploit the petroleum resources of the Sinai and, during 1978–79, those of the Suez Gulf (Alma Fields). In July 1988 the Israeli Government awarded an offshore oil-prospecting concession of 7,000 sq km, about 16 km from Israel's southern Mediterranean coast, to a consortium of local and foreign companies headed by the late Dr Armand Hammer, chairman of Occidental Petroleum Inc. The consortium, Negev Joint Venture, was investing $25.5m. in test drilling over a three-year period from autumn 1988.

Output of natural gas from Rosh-Zohar in the Dead Sea area, Kidod, Hakanaim and Barbur is transported through a 29 km pipeline (diameter 15 cm) to the Dead Sea potash works at Sodom and through a 49 km line (diameter 10 cm or 15 cm) to towns in the Negev and to the Oron phosphate plant. Production totalled 23.8m. cu m in 1993.

Lacking large scale resources of fuel and power, Israel is forced to import more than 90% of its energy requirements. Imports of petroleum and petroleum products, which rose in value from $210.6m. in 1973 to $597m. in the following year and to $775m. in 1978, reached about $2,000m. in 1980 and cost $1,741m., at current prices, in 1993. In the same year petroleum constituted 9% of all goods imports (or 31% of the trade deficit). The large increases in the petroleum import bill since 1979 are directly attributable to the peace agreement with Egypt. In 1978 Israel produced one-quarter of its oil requirements from the Alma oilfields which it discovered in Sinai. The Alma fields were handed over to Egypt in 1979, in accordance with the terms of the peace treaty. Israel now imports most of its crude oil requirements of about 48m. barrels per year under long-term contracts with Egypt (which provides about 25% of the total), Mexico (35%) and Norway (10%), and buys the remainder on the 'spot' market. Most imported crude oil is refined at the Haifa oil refinery, which has a capacity of more than 6m. tons per year.

The Dead Sea, which contains potash, bromides, magnesium and other salts in high concentration, is the country's chief source of mineral wealth. The potash works on the southern shore of the Dead Sea are owned by Dead Sea Works Ltd. The works are linked by road to Beersheba, from where a railway runs northward. Phosphates are mined at Oron in the Negev, and in the Arava. A total of 2.66m. tons of phosphate rock was produced in 1993. In the same year Israel produced 11,817 tons of sodium hydrochlorate, 29,851 tons of caustic soda, 35,241 tons of chlorine, 144,147 tons of polyethylene, and 5,837 tons of potassium carbonate.

At Timna, in the southern Negev near Eilat, geological surveys have located proven reserves of 20m. tons of low-grade copper ore (about 1.5% Cu). The building of a mill to make use of these ores and for producing copper-cement was completed in 1958. The ore was mined by open-cast and underground methods until 1975, when copper production from the Timna complex totalled 8,000 tons. Owing to the decline in copper prices on international markets, and following accumulated losses, the Government closed the mines in 1976 (copper imports during 1988 were worth $17m.). Gold in potentially commercial quantities was discovered near the Negev copper mines in 1988, and further exploration is under way.

GDP, CURRENCY AND FINANCE

In 1993 Israel's gross domestic product (GDP) increased, in real terms, by 3.4% (following a 6% growth in 1992), to reach 184,078m. new shekels; in the business sector the rate of growth was identical.

In 1993, on the Tel-Aviv Stock Exchange, issues linked to the consumer price index (which rose by 11.2%) were augmented by 9.3%, and those linked to foreign currency rose by 5%.

Shares and convertible bonds registered at the Exchange increased by 41%. Commercial banks' shares rose by 22%, while shares in industrial establishments rose by 27%. Increases were also reported in the shares of investment and maintenance companies (51%), and in real estate, construction and agriculture (81.2%).

During 1993 the new Israeli shekel depreciated (on the basis of the average annual exchange rate) by 6% against the pound sterling, by 10% against the US dollar, by 1% against the Deutsche Mark, by 1% against the French franc and by 24% against the Japanese yen.

BALANCE OF PAYMENTS AND TRADE

Israel's balance-of-payments deficit on trade in goods and services stood at $8,120m. in 1993. Total trade in goods and services rose by 8% in 1993, to $52,406m., almost as much as total GNP. Exports of goods and services in 1993 amounted to $22,143m., compared with $20,779m. in 1992, while the value of imports amounted to $30,263m., compared with $27,446m. in 1992.

Israel's deficit on merchandise trade, which relates to goods only, amounted to $5,607m. in 1993, an increase of 13% from the deficit of $4,946m. recorded in 1992. In 1993 the deficit on civilian imports totalled $3,501m., compared with $3,498m. in 1992.

Net transfer payments, most of which consisted of US aid, were worth $6,747m. in 1993, a decline of 2% compared with 1992. They covered 83% of the deficit on goods and services, compared with 103% in 1992. Israel's foreign liabilities totalled $15,693m. at the end of 1993, and $15,229m. at the end of 1992.

Israel's deficit on trade in services rose by $792m. in 1993 to $2,513m. The revenue from tourism rose by 14% to $2,1091m.

Net exports of goods in 1993 increased by 13%, to $14,082m., while the value of net imports totalled $20,244m. Imports included production inputs worth $14,390.5m. (of which diamonds accounted for $3,541m.) and investment goods valued at $3,576m. The value of industrial exports amounted to $13,824m., while that of agricultural exports totalled $547m.

The focus of Israel's foreign trade is mainly the EC and North America. In 1984 about 62% of total exports were destined for these countries but efforts are being made to penetrate Central and South America. A free trade agreement between Israel and the USA, which provides for the progressive dismantling of all tariff and quota barriers on industrial goods between the participants over a 10-year period, took effect from 1 September 1986. During the first full year of the agreement, Israeli exports to the USA rose by $100m. to $1,800m. Under a similar financial and economic protocol concluded with the EC in 1976, the EC agreed to cut tariffs on some 85% of Israeli exports. In this domain, some difficulties (relative to agricultural exports) arose with competitors for the European market, following Greece's entry to the EC in 1981 and the entry of Spain and Portugal in 1986. An Israeli-EC Chamber of Commerce was founded in June 1986. Duties on goods imported from the EC and the USA were reduced by an average of 60% on 1 January 1987, under the terms of separate bilateral trade agreements. Spain refused to sign the draft agricultural goods access agreement between the EC and Israel in December 1986, demanding the reduction by Israel of tariffs on Spanish industrial exports in line with the reductions on EC goods implemented on 1 January 1987. In October 1988 the European Parliament approved three trade protocols, giving Israel privileged access to EC markets, having withheld its approval in March and July and delayed further votes, in protest against Israel's treatment of Palestinians during the *intifada* in the Occupied Territories. The Israeli Government, in an attempt to placate the EC, had undertaken to allow Palestinian farmers in the West Bank to export their produce directly to the EC, unimpeded by the occupation authorities.

BANKING, TRANSPORT AND COMMUNICATIONS

Israel possesses a highly developed banking system, consisting of the central bank (Bank of Israel), 26 commercial banks and credit co-operatives, 16 mortgage banks, and other financial institutions. Nevertheless, three bank-groups—namely Bank Leumi group, Bank Ha-Poalim and Bank Discount—hold 92% of the total assets of the banking system. Their subsidiaries are represented all over the world and enjoy a growing reputation; due to devaluation their share in the consolidated balance sheet is increasing markedly. Long-term credits are granted by mortgage banks, the Israel Agricultural Bank, the Industrial Development Bank and the Maritime Bank. By the end of 1993 the amount of outstanding credit allocated by the banks to the public reached the sum of 106,607m. new shekels in Israeli currency and 17,135m. new shekels in foreign currency.

The function of the central bank is to issue currency (and commemorative coins), to accept deposits from banking institutions and extend temporary advances to the Government, to act as the Government's sole fiscal and banking agent and to manage the public debt. Its Governor supervises the liquidity position of the commercial banks and regulates the volume of bank advances.

The significant changes that have characterized the financial world and international capital markets in recent years have also affected the Israeli banking system. The banks are gradually losing their traditional monopoly as financial intermediaries, as other financial entities assume this role. One consequence of this development has been to encourage the banks to enter other fields of financial activity, hitherto closed to them.

The continued severance of nearly all lines of communication with its Arab neighbours (except Egypt and the open bridges on the Jordan River) has not only intensified Israel's dependence on maritime and air communications, but has also given great impetus to the establishment of a national merchant marine and airline.

Since 1949 Israel has operated its own international air carrier—El Al Israel National Airlines Ltd. Regular scheduled services to Europe, the USA, Canada, Cyprus, and parts of Africa and Asia are maintained. In 1976 a new private company—CAL, which specializes in cargo air transportation to Europe—was constituted. In addition, 14 international airlines call at Ben Gurion Airport, near Tel-Aviv. The number of passengers carried in 1992 reached 4.5m. Israel's merchant navy has been undergoing expansion, while the passenger fleet has been practically abolished. The number of ships under the Israeli flag in 1992 totalled 68. Their combined displacement was 1,674,000 gross tons. Israel Shipyards Ltd, at Haifa, can build ships with a capacity of as much as 10,000 dwt. In the north, the port of Haifa and its Kishon harbour extension provide Israel's main port facilities. The south is served by the port at the head of the Gulf of Aqaba, and mainly by the deep-water port at Ashdod, some 50 km south of Tel-Aviv. Gaza port assures the needs of the Gaza Strip. The amount of cargo loaded at seaports in 1993 totalled 8.4m. tons, while the amount unloaded was 21m. tons (including coal).

Israeli railways operate some 573 km of main lines and 366 km of branch lines. The service extends from Nahariya, north of Haifa to Jerusalem and Tel-Aviv and then southwards through Beersheba. In 1965 it reached Dimona and in 1970 the phosphate works at Oron; the construction of a huge bridge over Tsin Valley will enable the extension to Eilat. Traction is wholly by diesel locomotives. In 1992 traffic consisted of 3.4m. passengers and 8.4m. tons of freight.

Roads are the chief means of transport. At the beginning of 1993 there were 13,461 km of paved roads, of which 4,229 km were inter-urban, out of which 300 km were motorways with four or more lanes. Travelling them at the end of 1992 were 923,041 private vehicles, 9,309 buses, 185,737 trucks and 9,325 taxis.

TOURISM

The drop in the number of tourists entering Israel which began in 1973 (a slowdown had already been recorded in the second half of 1972), continued in 1975; 1976 witnessed a recovery, and the number of tourists rose, reaching 1,175,800 in 1980. Then, in 1981, a slight drop to 1,137,055 was recorded, and in 1982 the industry slumped by 12%, with only 997,510 tourists entering Israel. The war in Lebanon, labour disputes at El Al and the less attractive exchange rates for tourists were all responsible for the situation. These reasons also contributed to the number of Israeli tourists leaving the country; in 1982 they totalled about 600,000, spending some $600m. abroad. Nevertheless, 1984 witnessed a recovery, when 1,260,000 tourists visited the country, and income from tourism doubled in the six years up to 1984, reaching $1,000m. per year. In 1985 a total of 1,264,367 tourists visited Israel. In 1986 the total declined by 13%, to 1,101,481, and revenue from tourism fell by $107m. In 1987 the number of tourists rose by 25%, to 1,378,742, and revenue increased to a record $1,635m. In 1988, however, the number of tourists declined to 1,169,582, mainly as a result of continued unrest in the Occupied Territories. In 1989 the number of tourists rose slightly, to reach 1,176,500, with revenue totalling $1,467.7m. This increase continued throughout the first half of 1990. However, following Iraq's invasion of Kuwait in August 1990 and the ensuing crisis in the Persian (Arabian) Gulf region, the number of tourist arrivals declined sharply. The total for the year was 1,131,700. Revenue amounted to $1,381.7m. Tourism revived again in 1992, when some 1,502,092 tourist arrivals were recorded, and revenue from tourism amounted to $1,891m. In 1993 tourist arrivals totalled 1,655,700, an increase of 9.6% on the previous year's figure.

Overall administration of Israeli tourism is sponsored by the Ministry of Tourism which maintains 20 offices abroad. It is also in charge of regulating tourist services in Israel, including arrangement of 'package' tours and the provision of multilingual guides. In 1976 the Ministry promoted the inauguration of charter-flights from the USA and Europe to Israel. During 1992 a total of 2,795 charter-flights landed in Israel, bringing some 733,761 passengers into the country.

Statistical Survey

Source: Central Bureau of Statistics, POB 13015, Hakirya, Romema, Jerusalem 91130; tel. (2) 553553; fax (2) 553325.

Area and Population

AREA, POPULATION AND DENSITY

Area (sq km)	
Land .	21,501
Inland water .	445
Total .	21,946*
Population (*de jure*; census results)†	
20 May 1972 .	3,147,683
4 June 1983	
Males .	2,011,590
Females	2,026,030
Total .	4,037,620
Population (*de jure*; official estimates at 31 December)†	
1990 .	4,821,700
1991	5,058,800
1992	5,195,900
Density (per sq km) at 31 December 1992 .	241.7

* 8,473.4 sq miles. Area includes East Jerusalem, annexed by Israel in June 1967, and the Golan sub-district (1,176 sq km), annexed by Israel in December 1981.
† Including the population of East Jerusalem and Israeli residents in certain other areas under Israeli military occupation since June 1967. Beginning in 1981, figures also include non-Jews in the Golan sub-district, an Israeli-occupied area of Syrian territory. Census results exclude adjustment for underenumeration.

ADMINISTERED TERRITORIES*

	Area (sq km)	Estimated population (31 December 1992)
Golan .	1,176	28,100
Judaea and Samaria .	5,879	1,051,500‡
Gaza Area† .	378	716,800‡
Total .	7,433	1,796,400

The area figures in this table refer to 1 October 1973. No later figures are available.

* The area and population of the Administered Territories have changed as a result of the October 1973 war.
† Not including El-Arish and Sinai which, as of April 1979 and April 1982 respectively, were returned to Egypt.
‡ Excluding Israelis in Jewish localities. The population in this category at 31 December 1992 totalled 101,100 in Judaea and Samaria, and 4,300 in the Gaza Area.

POPULATION BY RELIGION (estimates, 31 December 1992)

	Number	%
Jews .	4,242,500	81.65
Muslims .	725,400	13.96
Christians .	140,000	2.71
Druze and others .	87,100	1.68
Total .	5,195,900	100.00

PRINCIPAL TOWNS (estimated population at 31 December 1992)

Jerusalem (capital)	556,500*	Bat Yam .	145,300
Tel-Aviv—Jaffa .	356,900	Netanya .	141,800
Haifa .	249,800	Beersheba .	134,700
Holon .	162,800	Bene Beraq .	124,400
Petach-Tikva .	150,900	Ramat Gan .	124,100
Rishon LeZiyyon .	150,400		

* Including East Jerusalem, annexed in June 1967.

BIRTHS, MARRIAGES AND DEATHS*

	Registered live births		Registered marriages		Registered deaths	
	Number	Rate (per 1,000)	Number	Rate (per 1,000)	Number	Rate (per 1,000)
1985 .	99,376	23.5	29,158	6.9	28,093	6.6
1986 .	99,341	23.1	30,113	7.0	29,415	6.8
1987 .	99,022	22.7	30,116	6.9	29,244	6.7
1988 .	100,454	22.6	31,218	7.0	29,176	6.6
1989 .	100,757	22.3	32,303	7.1	28,600	6.3
1990 .	103,349	22.2	31,746	6.8	28,734	6.2
1991 .	105,725	21.4	32,291	6.5	31,266	6.3
1992 .	110,062	21.5	33,147	6.5	33,311	6.5

* Including East Jerusalem.

IMMIGRATION*

	1990	1991	1992
Immigrants:			
on immigrant visas .	192,017	168,697	70,580
on tourist visas† .	2,924	4,235	5,825
Potential immigrants:			
on potential immigrant visas	3,484	2,472	103
on tourist visas† .	1,091	696	522
Total .	199,516	176,100	77,057

* Excluding immigrating citizens (2,033 in 1990; 2,075 in 1991; 2,868 in 1992) and Israeli residents returning from abroad.
† Figures refer to tourists who changed their status to immigrants or potential immigrants.

ECONOMICALLY ACTIVE POPULATION (annual averages, '000 persons aged 15 years and over, excluding armed forces)*

	1990	1991	1992
Agriculture, forestry and fishing .	62.0	55.5	57.8
Mining and quarrying .	4.8	4.5	4.5
Manufacturing .	317.5	335.2	344.3
Electricity and water .	16.6	16.8	14.5
Construction .	76.2	96.2	107.6
Trade, restaurants and hotels	216.5	224.0	229.1
Transport, storage and communications .	92.5	96.6	104.1
Financing and business services .	148.4	160.8	172.3
Public and community services	439.2	468.3	483.2
Personal and other services .	109.8	114.9	122.1
Activities not adequately defined .	8.7	10.4	10.7
Total employed .	1,491.9	1,583.1	1,650.2
Unemployed .	158.0	187.2	207.6
Total civilian labour force	1,649.9	1,770.3	1,857.8
Males .	979.9	1,042.7	1,080.9
Females .	669.5	727.9	776.6

* Figures are estimated independently, so the totals may not be the sum of the component parts.

Agriculture

PRINCIPAL CROPS ('000 metric tons)

	1990	1991	1992
Wheat .	291	180	260*
Barley .	8	6	10*
Potatoes .	214	173	215†
Groundnuts (in shell) .	21	21	21†
Cottonseed .	83	34	49*
Cotton (lint) .	51	21	31*
Olives .	42	17	40†
Cabbages .	51	56	57†
Tomatoes .	521	328	400†
Cucumbers .	94	95	95†
Peppers (green) .	53	52	53†
Onions (dry) .	62	65	67†
Carrots .	77	75	77†
Watermelons .	94	110	120†
Melons .	68	64	66†
Grapes .	99	71	90†
Apples .	113	116	117†
Peaches .	41	41	42†
Oranges .	871	564	513*
Tangerines, mandarins, clementines and satsumas .	167	108	127*
Lemons and limes .	48	39	36†
Grapefruit .	404	379	345*
Avocados .	48	53	53†
Bananas .	61	83	84†
Strawberries .	14.3	12.9	13.5†

* Unofficial estimate.   † FAO estimate.

Source: FAO, *Production Yearbook.*

LIVESTOCK ('000 head)

	1990	1991	1992
Cattle .	331	349	357
Poultry .	27,680	27,200	32,680
Sheep .	375	360	330
Goats .	115	111	100

Pigs (FAO estimates, '000 head, year ending September): 115 in 1990; 100 in 1991; 70 in 1992. (Source: FAO, *Production Yearbook.*)

LIVESTOCK PRODUCTS ('000 metric tons)

	1990	1991	1992
Beef and veal .	36	38†	37†
Mutton and lamb† .	5	5	5
Pig meat .	9	8*	7*
Poultry meat .	178	193	198
Cows' milk .	952	998	998†
Sheep's milk .	18	18	20†
Goats' milk .	16	14	15†
Cheese .	75.6	76.7	77.9*
Butter .	7.1	7.1*	7.1*
Hen eggs .	98.4	103.8	108.6†
Honey .	2.7	2.0	2.2*

* FAO estimate.   †Unofficial estimate(s).

Source: FAO, *Production Yearbook.*

Forestry

ROUNDWOOD REMOVALS ('000 cubic metres, excl. bark)

	1990	1991*	1992*
Sawlogs, veneer logs and logs for sleepers .	36	36	36
Pulpwood .	32	32	32
Other industrial wood .	32*	32	32
Fuel wood .	13	13	13
Total .	113	113	113

*FAO estimate(s).

Source: FAO, *Yearbook of Forest Products.*

Fishing

(metric tons, live weight)

	1989	1990	1991
Inland waters .	16,466	16,718	17,335
Mediterranean and Black Sea	3,855	4,025	3,388
Atlantic Ocean .	6,170	2,875	—
Total catch .	26,491	23,618	20,723

Source: FAO, *Yearbook of Fishery Statistics.*

Mining

	1990	1991	1992
Crude petroleum (million litres) .	13	9.4	7.8
Natural gas (million cu m) .	33	27	2.3
Phosphate rock ('000 metric tons) .	2,472	2,267	2,372
Potash ('000 metric tons) .	2,124	1,958	2,086

Industry

SELECTED PRODUCTS
('000 metric tons, unless otherwise stated)

	1990	1991	1992
Refined vegetable oils (metric tons) .	84,058	81,512	56,463
Margarine .	30.9	33.8	35.1
Wine ('000 litres) .	12,795	11,972	12,373
Beer ('000 litres) .	56,736	53,180	51,078
Cigarettes (metric tons) .	5,440	5,590	5,742
Newsprint (metric tons) .	642	152	0
Writing and printing paper (metric tons) .	63,991	66,116	66,334
Other paper (metric tons) .	44,159	30,953	32,368
Cardboard (metric tons) .	92,864	84,911	92,072
Rubber tyres ('000) .	778	786	892
Ammonia (metric tons) .	77,582	55,056	41,072
Ammonium sulphate (metric tons) .	35,441	14,875	12,444
Sulphuric acid .	154	136	138
Chlorine (metric tons) .	36,342	36,105	33,912
Caustic soda (metric tons) .	31,575	32,180	29,459
Polyethylene (metric tons) .	106,599	124,613	128,739
Paints (metric tons) .	46,341	48,242	58,963
Cement .	2,868	3,340	3,960
Commercial vehicles (number)	1,074	864	852
Electricity (million kWh) .	20,269	20,857	24,019

Finance

CURRENCY AND EXCHANGE RATES

Monetary Units
100 agorot (singular: agora) = 1 new sheqel (plural: sheqalim) or shekel.

Sterling and Dollar Equivalents (31 May 1994)
£1 sterling = 4.591 new shekels;
US $1 = 3.037 new shekels;
100 new shekels = £21.78 = $32.93.

Average Exchange Rate (new shekels per US $)
1991	2.2791
1992	2.4591
1993	2.8301

Note: The new shekel, worth 1,000 of the former units, was introduced on 1 January 1986.

CENTRAL GOVERNMENT BUDGET
(estimates, million new shekels)

Revenue	1991*	1992	1993
Ordinary budget	45,230	74,090	73,418
Income tax and property tax	14,090	23,310	25,840
Customs and excise	1,240	2,165	2,360
Purchase tax	2,960	4,610	5,340
Employers' tax	660	900	380
Value added tax	11,145	18,325	18,570
Other taxes	4,270	6,780	6,670
Interest	741	1,350	1,248
Transfer from development budget	8,920	14,011	10,957
Other receipts	1,204	−2,639	2,053
Development budget	22,368	34,500	29,029
Foreign loans	8,937	17,144	13,152
Internal loans	14,228	22,385	18,449
Transfer to ordinary budget	−8,920	−14,011	−10,956
Other receipts	8,123	8,982	8,384
Total	67,598	108,590	102,447

Expenditure†	1991*	1992	1993
Ordinary account	45,230	74,090	73,418
Ministry of Finance	343	560	586
Ministry of Defence	11,152	17,579	17,945
Ministry of Health	694	1,186	1,308
Ministry of Education and Culture	4,620	7,753	9,056
Ministry of Police	878	1,431	1,509
Ministry of Labour and Social Welfare	6,490	10,276	10,464
Other ministries‡	4,235	5,853	5,118
Interest	9,663	14,125	13,522
Pensions and compensations	921	1,498	1,659
Transfers to local authorities	759	1,284	1,261
Subsidies	1,556	3,772	2,988
Reserves	2,957	4,257	3,048
Other expenditures	962	4,516	4,954
Development budget	22,368	34,500	29,029
Agriculture	142	2,324	1,930
Industry, trade and tourism	1,028	198	278
Housing	5,668	6,430	4,594
Public buildings	396	806	609
Development of energy resources	40	49	—
Debt repayment	11,625	19,840	16,783
Other expenditures	3,469	4,853	4,835
Total	67,598	108,590	102,447

* Figures refer to April–December.
† Does not include the entire defence budget.
‡ Includes the President, Prime Minister, State Comptroller and the Knesset.

CENTRAL BANK RESERVES (US $ million at 31 December)

	1991	1992	1993
Gold*	21.1	0.4	0.4
IMF special drawing rights	0.4	0.3	0.5
Foreign exchange	6,278.7	5,127.1	6,382.1
Total	6,300.2	5,127.8	6,383.0

* Valued at 35 SDRs per troy ounce.
Source: IMF, *International Financial Statistics*.

MONEY SUPPLY (million new shekels at 31 December)

	1991	1992	1993
Currency outside banks	3,228	4,113	n.a.
Demand deposits at deposit money banks	4,680	6,319	8,506

Source: IMF, *International Financial Statistics*.

COST OF LIVING
(Consumer Price Index, annual averages; base: 1980 = 100)

	1990	1991	1992
Food	60,231	68,518	77,389
Fuel and light	47,600	54,659	58,328
Clothing	42,306	45,751	49,978
Rent	91,041	124,169	147,219
All items (incl. others)	65,418	77,838	87,144

Source: International Labour Office, *Year Book of Labour Statistics*.
1993: All items 96,689 (Source: UN, *Monthly Bulletin of Statistics*).

NATIONAL ACCOUNTS (million new shekels at current prices)
National Income and Product (provisional)

	1989	1990	1991
Compensation of employees	45,866	54,786	68,101
Operating surplus	17,807	22,625	29,754
Domestic factor incomes	63,673	77,411	97,855
Consumption of fixed capital	12,908	15,854	19,596
Statistical discrepancy	−102	−870	851
Gross domestic product at factor cost	76,479	92,395	118,302
Indirect taxes	16,539	21,146	28,456
Less Subsidies	3,060	3,290	3,889
GDP in purchasers' values	89,958	110,251	142,869
Factor income received from abroad	2,670	3,204	4,043
Less Factor income paid abroad	6,532	7,274	7,649
Gross national product	86,096	106,181	139,263
Less Consumption of fixed capital	12,908	15,854	19,596
National income in market prices	73,188	90,327	119,667
Other current transfers received from abroad	9,352	11,251	14,444
Less Other current transfers paid abroad	271	333	443
National disposable income	82,269	101,245	133,668

Source: UN, *National Accounts Statistics*.

Expenditure on the Gross Domestic Product

	1991	1992	1993
Government final consumption expenditure	40,182	45,180	53,010
Private final consumption expenditure	82,177	98,513	116,315
Increase in stocks	1,258	2,234	2,589
Gross fixed capital formation .	32,575	37,580	41,615
Total domestic expenditure .	156,192	183,507	213,529
Exports of goods and services	40,610	50,124	61,836
Less Imports of goods and services	61,167	72,352	91,287
GDP in purchasers' values	135,635	161,279	184,078
GDP at constant 1990 prices	111,787	119,157	122,736

Source: IMF, *International Financial Statistics.*

Net Domestic Product by Economic Activity (at factor cost)

	1989	1990	1991
Agriculture, hunting, forestry and fishing	2,095	2,492	2,398
Manufacturing, mining and quarrying	14,552	16,924	21,488
Electricity, gas and water .	1,579	1,899	2,299
Construction	3,885	4,933	7,777
Wholesale and retail trade, restaurants and hotels . .	6,911	8,185	9,665
Transport, storage and communications . . .	5,162	6,379	7,560
Finance, insurance, real estate and business services . .	14,811	18,257	24,065
Government services . .	15,031	18,295	22,894
Other community, social and personal services . . .	2,892	3,432	4,110
Statistical discrepancy . .	571	572	587
Sub-total	67,489	81,368	102,843
Less Imputed bank service charge	3,817	3,958	4,988
Other adjustments (incl. errors and omissions) . . .	−102	−870	851
Total	63,570	76,540	98,706

Source: UN, *National Accounts Statistics.*

BALANCE OF PAYMENTS (US $ million)

	1991	1992	1993
Merchandise exports f.o.b. .	12,029	13,314	14,804
Merchandise imports f.o.b. .	16,149	18,260	20,411
Trade balance . . .	−4,918	−4,946	−5,607
Exports of services . .	4,466	5,536	5,870
Imports of services . .	−5,334	−5,611	−6,753
Other income received . .	2,065	1,930	1,469
Other income paid . . .	−3,370	−3,575	−3,099
Private unrequited transfers (net)	2,282	2,722	2,853
Official unrequited transfers (net)	4,392	4,163	3,894
Current balance . . .	−416	218	−1,373
Direct investment (net) . .	−73	−112	−374
Portfolio investment (net) . .	548	−740	1,750
Other capital (net) . . .	−564	−1,268	624
Net errors and omissions . .	332	445	854
Overall balance . . .	−173	−1,457	1,481

Source: IMF, *International Financial Statistics.*

External Trade

PRINCIPAL COMMODITIES (US $ '000)

Imports c.i.f.*	1990	1991	1992
Diamonds, rough . . .	2,895,200	2,557,800	2,910,400
Machinery and parts . . .	2,022,500	2,603,900	2,810,600
Electrical machinery and parts	829,100	1,015,100	1,180,200
Iron and steel	478,600	587,900	545,200
Metal products n.i.e. . . .	312,900	386,200	420,300
Vehicles	893,900	1,291,500	1,673,100
Chemicals and related products	1,507,900	1,547,000	1,807,800
Crude petroleum and petroleum products . .	1,348,900	1,310,900	1,452,200
Cereals	332,000	319,800	370,800
Textiles and textile articles .	474,500	531,800	629,600
Total (incl. others) . .	15,325,500	16,915,000	18,813,600

* Figures exclude military goods. Total imports (in US $ million) were: 16,794 in 1990; 18,855 in 1991; 20,261 in 1992; 22,619 in 1993 (Source: IMF, *International Financial Statistics*).

Exports f.o.b.	1990	1991	1992
Diamonds, worked. . . .	2,783,400	2,469,600	2,641,300
Clothing	482,400	506,000	593,600
Textiles and textile articles .	269,900	310,900	329,800
Fruit and vegetables . .	793,700	662,800	573,600
Fertilizers	253,800	253,500	296,300
Organic chemicals . . .	440,200	471,200	488,600
Inorganic chemicals . .	288,400	289,700	269,300
Chemical products. . . .	1,007,000	986,900	1,112,900
Transport equipment . .	385,400	403,400	350,500
Machinery and parts . .	2,056,100	1,846,300	2,497,200
Electrical machinery and parts.	506,800	609,400	744,000
Metals and metal products .	394,700	398,300	416,000
Total (incl. others) . . .	12,079,800	11,891,300	13,082,300

PRINCIPAL TRADING PARTNERS (US $ '000)

Imports (excl. military goods)	1990	1991	1992
Argentina	66,700	66,600	41,500
Australia	36,400	47,400	55,000
Austria	62,200	68,300	85,000
Belgium/Luxembourg . .	2,029,000	1,878,400	2,391,600
Brazil	18,600	46,800	59,700
Canada	133,800	129,200	113,500
Denmark	68,700	83,400	139,700
Finland	97,000	77,800	90,300
France.	593,900	716,400	844,800
Germany, Fed. Rep. . .	1,794,000	2,012,700	2,246,900
Greece.	48,000	46,600	73,400
Hong Kong	119,700	142,500	183,500
India	69,600	62,200	74,700
Ireland	40,900	44,100	55,700
Italy	934,800	1,093,100	1,308,700
Japan	546,500	733,400	998,200
Netherlands	529,400	568,000	615,700
Romania	22,500	28,000	36,600
Singapore	57,500	84,100	92,000
South Africa	221,700	234,500	267,400
Spain	154,100	172,400	203,800
Sweden	149,200	203,000	206,400
Switzerland	1,409,100	1,436,500	1,353,000
Turkey	36,200	82,000	79,600
United Kingdom . . .	1,317,300	1,401,000	1,509,400
USA	2,722,800	3,261,000	3,234,400
Uruguay	33,300	50,400	54,000

Exports	1990	1991	1992
Australia	96,400	103,500	115,600
Austria	62,100	60,500	68,900
Belgium/Luxembourg . .	691,800	680,600	650,500
Brazil	78,600	78,000	66,500
Canada	101,600	94,700	85,300
France	579,900	566,700	620,500
Germany, Fed. Rep. . .	711,900	797,800	762,500
Greece	104,900	125,200	109,100
Hong Kong	536,100	548,600	666,400
Italy	502,900	460,600	459,600
Japan	874,300	722,200	689,100
Netherlands	546,300	529,600	553,800
Singapore	106,500	80,600	121,000
South Africa	96,800	95,700	122,600
Spain	170,200	197,200	242,800
Sweden	69,100	62,800	57,100
Switzerland	301,200	270,100	231,100
Turkey	88,700	111,400	114,500
United Kingdom . . .	848,100	795,100	1,005,200
USA	3,488,100	3,602,400	3,995,700
Venezuela	90,700	29,900	27,300

Transport

RAILWAYS (traffic)

	1990	1991	1992
Passengers ('000) . . .	2,524	2,883	3,439
Freight ('000 metric tons) . .	7,219	7,742	8,403

ROAD TRAFFIC, 1992 (motor vehicles)

Private cars (incl. station wagons)	923,041
Trucks, trailers	185,737
Buses	9,309
Taxis	9,325
Motor cycles, motor scooters	43,762
Other vehicles	4,702
Total	1,175,876

SHIPPING
(international sea-borne freight traffic, '000 metric tons)*

	1990	1991	1992
Goods loaded	7,924	7,702	8,023
Goods unloaded	13,752	16,205	19,767

* Excluding petroleum.

CIVIL AVIATION (El Al revenue flights only, '000)

	1990	1991	1992
Kilometres flown . . .	45,664	48,860	51,064
Revenue passenger-km . .	7,472,000	7,747,000	8,492,000
Mail (tons)	1,185	1,623	1,353

Tourism

	1990	1991	1992
Tourist arrivals	1,063,400	951,200	1,509,500

Communications Media

	1989	1990	1991
Radio receivers ('000 in use) .	2,115	2,165	2,290
Television receivers ('000 in use)	1,200	1,225	1,310
Telephones ('000 in use) . .	2,285	2,425	n.a.
Daily newspapers . . .	n.a.	30	n.a.

Book production (1985): 2,214 titles; 8,872,000 copies.
Non-daily newspapers (1988): 80.
Other periodicals (1985): 807.

Source: mainly UNESCO, *Statistical Yearbook.*

Education

(1992/93)

	Schools	Pupils	Teachers
Jewish			
Kindergarten	n.a.	291,900	n.a.
Primary schools . . .	1,238	523,755	43,329
Intermediate schools . .	330	131,855	15,670
Secondary schools . .	588	238,972	28,968
Vocational schools . .	311	105,703	n.a.
Agricultural schools . .	23	6,121	n.a.
Teacher training colleges .	n.a.	17,746	n.a.
Others (handicapped) . .	202	12,006	3,287
Arab			
Kindergarten	n.a.	24,600	n.a.
Primary schools . . .	335	135,547	7,992
Intermediate schools . .	89	36,815	2,672
Secondary schools . .	94	41,765	3,082
Vocational schools . .	50	9,883	n.a.
Agricultural schools . .	2	516	n.a.
Teacher training colleges . .	n.a.	801	n.a.
Others (handicapped) . .	31	1,761	406

Directory

The Constitution

There is no written constitution. In June 1950 the Knesset voted to adopt a state constitution by evolution over an unspecified period. A number of laws, including the Law of Return (1950), the Nationality Law (1952), the State President (Tenure) Law (1952), the Education Law (1953) and the 'Yad-va-Shem' Memorial Law (1953), are considered as incorporated into the state Constitution. Other constitutional laws are: The Law and Administration Ordinance (1948), the Knesset Election Law (1951), the Law of Equal Rights for Women (1951), the Judges Act (1953), the National Service and National Insurance Acts (1953), and the Basic Law (The Knesset) (1958). The provisions of constitutional legislation that affect the main organs of government are summarized below:

THE PRESIDENT

The President is elected by the Knesset for a maximum of two five-year terms.

Ten or more Knesset members may propose a candidate for the Presidency.

Voting will be by secret ballot.

The President may not leave the country without the consent of the Government.

The President may resign by submitting his resignation in writing to the Speaker.

The President may be relieved of his duties by the Knesset for misdemeanour.

The Knesset is entitled to decide by a two-thirds majority that the President is too incapacitated owing to ill health to fulfil his duties permanently.

The Speaker of the Knesset will act for the President when the President leaves the country, or when he cannot perform his duties owing to ill health.

THE KNESSET

The Knesset is the parliament of the state. There are 120 members.

It is elected by general, national, direct, equal, secret and proportional elections.

Every Israeli national of 18 years or over shall have the right to vote in elections to the Knesset unless a court has deprived him of that right by virtue of any law.

Every Israeli national of 21 and over shall have the right to be elected to the Knesset unless a court has deprived him of that right by virtue of any law.

The following shall not be candidates: the President of the state; the two Chief Rabbis; a judge (shofet) in office; a judge (dayan) of a religious court; the State Comptroller; the Chief of the General Staff of the Defence Army of Israel; rabbis and ministers of other religions in office; senior state employees and senior army officers of such ranks and in such functions as shall be determined by law.

The term of office of the Knesset shall be four years.

The elections to the Knesset shall take place on the third Tuesday of the month of Cheshven in the year in which the tenure of the outgoing Knesset ends.

Election day shall be a day of rest, but transport and other public services shall function normally.

Results of the elections shall be published within 14 days.

The Knesset shall elect from among its members a Chairman and Vice-Chairman.

The Knesset shall elect from among its members permanent committees, and may elect committees for specific matters.

The Knesset may appoint commissions of inquiry to investigate matters designated by the Knesset.

The Knesset shall hold two sessions a year; one of them shall open within four weeks after the Feast of the Tabernacles, the other within four weeks after Independence Day; the aggregate duration of the two sessions shall not be less than eight months.

The outgoing Knesset shall continue to hold office until the convening of the incoming Knesset.

The members of the Knesset shall receive a remuneration as provided by law.

THE GOVERNMENT

The Government shall tender its resignation to the President immediately after his election, but shall continue with its duties until the formation of a new government. After consultation with representatives of the parties in the Knesset, the President shall charge one of the members with the formation of a government. The Government shall be composed of a Prime Minister and a number of ministers from among the Knesset members or from outside the Knesset. After it has been chosen, the Government shall appear before the Knesset and shall be considered as formed after having received a vote of confidence. Within seven days of receiving a vote of confidence, the Prime Minister and the other ministers shall swear allegiance to the State of Israel and its Laws and undertake to carry out the decisions of the Knesset.

The Government

HEAD OF STATE

President: Ezer Weizman (took office 13 May 1993).

THE CABINET
(September 1994)

Prime Minister, Minister of Defence, Minister of the Interior and Minister of Religious Affairs: Itzhak Rabin (Labour).

Minister of Foreign Affairs: Shimon Peres (Labour).

Minister of Trade and Industry: Michael Harish (Labour).

Minister of Finance: Avraham Shohat (Labour).

Minister of Housing and Construction: Binyamin Ben-Eliezer (Labour).

Minister of Justice: David Libai (Labour).

Minister of Communications and of Science and Technology: Shulamit Aloni (Meretz).

Minister of Transport: Israel Kessar (Labour).

Minister of Economy and Social Development: Shimon Sheetrit (Labour).

Minister of Health: Ephraim Sneh (Labour).

Minister of Tourism and Minister in charge of Religious Affairs: Uzi Baram (Labour).

Minister of Immigrant Absorption: Yair Tsaban (Meretz).

Minister of Education, Culture and Sport: Amnon Rubenstein (Meretz).

Minister of the Environment: Yossi Sarid (Labour).

Minister of Agriculture: Yaakov Tsur (Labour).

Minister of Energy, Infrastructure and Police: Moshe Shahal (Labour).

Minister of Labour and Social Affairs: Ora Namir (Labour).

MINISTRIES

Office of the Prime Minister: 3 Rehov Kaplan, Hakirya, Jerusalem 91007; tel. 2-705555; fax 2-664838.

Ministry of Agriculture: POB 7011, 8 Arania St, Tel-Aviv 61070; tel. 3-6955473; fax 3-6971603.

Ministry of Communications: POB 29515, Tel-Aviv; tel. 3-5198247; fax 2-5198109.

Ministry of Defence: Kaplan St, Hakirya, Tel-Aviv 61909; tel. 3-6975546; telex 32147; fax 3-6977285.

Ministry of Economy and Planning: POB 13158, 3 Rehov Kaplan, Kiryat Ben-Gurion, Jerusalem 91007; tel. 2-705353; fax 2-536101.

Ministry of Education and Culture: POB 292, 34 Shivtei Israel St, Jerusalem 91911; tel. 2-292222; fax 2-292223.

Ministry of Energy and Infrastructure: POB 13106, 234 Rehov Yafo, Jerusalem 91130; tel. 2-316111; fax 2-381444.

Ministry of the Environment: POB 6234, 2 Rehov Kaplan, Kiryat Ben-Gurion, Jerusalem 91061; tel. 2-701606; telex 25623; fax 2-513945.

Ministry of Finance: POB 883, 1 Rehov Kaplan, Kiryat Ben-Gurion, Jerusalem 91008; tel. 2-317111; telex 25216; fax 2-610049.

Ministry of Foreign Affairs: Hakirya, Romema, Jerusalem 91950; tel. 2-303111; telex 25223; fax 2-303367.

Ministry of Health: POB 1176, 2 Ben-Tabai St, Jerusalem 91010; tel. 2-705705; telex 26138; fax 2-781456.

Ministry of Housing and Construction: POB 18110, Kiryat Hamemshala (East), Jerusalem 91180; tel. 2-277211; fax 2-822114.

Ministry of Immigrant Absorption: POB 883, 2 Rehov Kaplan, Kiryat Ben-Gurion, Jerusalem 91006; tel. 2-752691; fax 2-669244.

Ministry of the Interior: POB 6158, 2 Rehov Kaplan, Kiryat Ben-Gurion, Jerusalem 91061; tel. 2-701411; fax 2-639368.

Ministry of Justice: 29 Rehov Salahadin, Jerusalem 91010; tel. 2-708511; fax 2-869473.

Ministry of Labour and Social Affairs: POB 915, 2 Rehov Kaplan, Kiryat Ben-Gurion, Jerusalem 91008; tel. 2-752311; fax 2-666385.

Ministry of Police: POB 18182, 3 Sheikh Jarrah, Kiryat Hamemshala (East), Jerusalem 91181; tel. 2-309921; fax 2-826770.

Ministry of Religious Affairs: POB 13059, 236 Rehov Yafo, Jerusalem 91130; tel. 2-388605; fax 2-551146.

Ministry of Science and Technology: POB 18195, Kiryat Hamemshala, Hakirya Hamizrachit, Government Offices, Bldg 3, Jerusalem 91181; tel. 2-847096; fax 2-820591.

Ministry of Tourism: POB 1018, 24 Rehov King George, Jerusalem 91000; tel. 2-754811; fax 2-253407.

Ministry of Trade and Industry: POB 229, 30 Rehov Agron, Jerusalem 91002; tel. 2-750111; fax 2-245110.

Ministry of Transport: Klal Bldg, 97 Rehov Jaffa, Jerusalem 94342; tel. 2-319211; fax 2-319206.

Legislature

KNESSET

General Election, 23 June 1992

Party	Seats
Labour	44
Likud	32
Meretz (an alliance of Ratz, Shinui and the United Workers' Party)	12
Tzomet	8
Shas	6
National Religious Party	6
United Torah Judaism	4
Hadash	3
Moledet	3
Arab Democratic Party	2
Total	**120**

Political Organizations

Agudat Israel: POB 513, Jerusalem; tel. 2-385251; fax 2-385145; orthodox Jewish party; stands for strict observance of Jewish religious law; Leaders AVRAHAM SHAPIRO, MENACHEM PORUSH.

Agudat Israel World Organization (AIWO): POB 326, Hacherut Sq., Jerusalem 91002; tel. 2-384357; f. 1912 at Congress of Orthodox Jewry, Kattowitz, Germany (now Katowice, Poland), to help solve the problems facing Jewish people all over the world; more than 500,000 mems in 25 countries; Pres. Rabbi Dr I. LEWIN (New York); Chair. Rabbi J. M. ABRAMOWITZ (Jerusalem), Rabbi M. SHERER (New York); Gen. Sec. ABRAHAM HIRSCH (Jerusalem).

Arab Democratic Party: Nazareth; tel. 06-560937; f. 1988; aims: to unify Arab political forces so as to influence Palestinian and Israeli policy; international recognition of the Palestinian people's right to self-determination; the holding of an international peace conference in the Middle East, with the participation of all parties to the conflict, including the PLO, as sole representative of the Palestinian people, on an equal footing; the withdrawal of Israel from all territories occupied in 1967; Chair. ABD AL-WAHAB DARAWSHAH.

Council for Peace and Security: f. 1988 by four retd Israeli generals: Maj.-Gen. AHARON YARIV, Maj.-Gen. ORI ORR, Brig.-Gen. YORAM AGMON and Brig.-Gen. EPHRAIM SNEH; MOSHE AMIRAV of Centre Party a founder mem.; aims: an Israeli withdrawal from the Occupied Territories in return for a peace treaty with the Arab nations.

Degel Hatora: 103 Rehov Beit Vegan, Jerusalem; tel. 2-418167; fax 2-438105; f. 1988 as breakaway from Agudat Israel; orthodox Western Jews; Chair. AVRAHAM RAVITZ.

Gush Emunim (Bloc of the Faithful): f. 1967; engaged in unauthorized establishment of Jewish settlements in the occupied territories; Leader Rabbi MOSHE LEVINGER.

Hadash (Democratic Front for Peace and Equality): POB 26205, 3 Rehov Hashikma, Tel-Aviv; tel. 3-827492; descended from the Socialist Workers' Party of Palestine (f. 1919); renamed Communist Party of Palestine 1921, Communist Party of Israel (Maki) 1948; pro-Soviet anti-Zionist group formed New Communist Party of Israel (Rakah) 1965; Jewish Arab membership; aims for a socialist system in Israel, a lasting peace between Israel and the Arab countries and the Palestinian Arab people, favours full implementation of UN Security Council Resolutions 242 and 338, Israeli withdrawal from all Arab territories occupied since 1967, formation of a Palestinian Arab state in the West Bank and Gaza Strip, recognition of national rights of state of Israel and Palestine people, democratic rights and defence of working class interests, and demands an end to discrimination against Arab minority in Israel and against oriental Jewish communities; Sec.-Gen. MEIR VILNER.

Israel Labour Party: 110 Ha'yarkon St, Tel-Aviv 61032; tel. 3-5209222; fax 3-5271744; f. 1968 as a merger of the three Labour groups, Mapai, Rafi and Achdut Ha'avoda; a Zionist democratic socialist party, was in government from 1948 to 1977; with the United Workers' Party (Mapam), formed the main opposition bloc under name of Labour-Mapam Alignment until elections of July 1984; formed national unity government with Likud in 1984 and again in 1988; formed coalition govt with the Meretz alliance and Shas in July 1992; Yahad (Together) (f. 1984; advocates a peace settlement with the Arab peoples and the Palestinians) joined the Labour bloc in Jan. 1987; Chair. of Israel Labour Party ITZHAK RABIN; Sec.-Gen. NISSIM ZVILI.

Kahane Chai (Kahane Lives): POB 5379, 111 Agripas St, Jerusalem; tel. 2-231081; f. 1977 as 'Kach' (Thus); right-wing religious nationalist party; advocates creation of a Torah state and expulsion of all Arabs from Israel and the annexation of the Occupied Territories; Leader Rabbi BINYAMIN ZEEV KAHANE.

Likud (Consolidation): 38 Rehov King George, Tel-Aviv 61231; tel. 3-5630666; fax 3-5282901; f. September 1973; is a parliamentary bloc of Herut (Freedom; f. 1948; Leader ITZHAK SHAMIR; Sec.-Gen. MOSHE ARENS), the Liberal Party of Israel (f. 1961; Chair. AVRAHAM SHARIR), Laam (For the Nation) (f. 1976; fmrly led by YIGAEL HURWITZ, who left the coalition to form his own party, Ometz, before the 1984 general election), Ahdut (a one-man faction, HILLEL SEIDEL), Tami (f. 1981; represents the interests of Sephardic Jews; Leader AHARON UZAN), which joined Likud in June 1987, and an independent faction (f. 1990; Leader ITZHAK MODAI), which formed the nucleus of a new Party for the Advancement of the Zionist Idea; Herut and the Liberal Party formally merged in August 1988 to form the Likud-National Liberal Movement; aims: territorial integrity (advocates retention of all the territory of post-1922 mandatory Palestine); absorption of newcomers; a social order based on freedom and justice, elimination of poverty and want; development of an economy that will ensure a decent standard of living; improvement of the environment and the quality of life. Likud was the sole government party from June 1977 until September 1984, when it formed the national unity government with the Israel Labour Party; a new government of national unity was formed after the 1988 election; Leader of Likud BINYAMIN NETANYAHU.

Meretz (Vitality): an alliance of Ratz, Shinui and the United Workers' Party; stands for civil rights, electoral reform, welfarism, Palestinian self-determination, separation of religion from the state and a halt to settlement in the Occupied Territories; formed coalition government with the Israel Labour Party and Shas in July 1992; Leader Mrs SHULAMIT ALONI.

Moledet (Homeland): 14 Rehov Yehuda Halevi, Tel-Aviv; tel. 3-654580; f. 1988; right-wing nationalist party; aims: the expulsion ('transfer') of the 1.5m. Palestinians living in the West Bank and Gaza Strip; supported the government of national unity formed after the 1988 election, but withdrew from the coalition in January 1992; Leader Gen. RECHAVAM ZE'EVI.

Movement for the Advancement of the Zionist Idea (MAZI): f. 1990 as breakaway group of Likud; supported the government of national unity formed after the 1988 election; Leader ITZHAK MODAI.

National Religious Party (NRP): 166 Ibn Gavirol St, Kastel Bldg, Tel-Aviv; tel. 3-5442151; fax 3-5468942; f. 1956; stands for strict adherence to Jewish religion and tradition, and strives to achieve the application of religious precepts of Judaism in everyday life; it is also endeavouring to establish the Constitution of Israel on Jewish religious law (the Torah); supported the government of national unity formed after the 1988 election; 135,000 mems; Leader Prof. ZEVULUN HAMER; Sec.-Gen. RAVINO ITZHAK LEVY.

New Liberal Party: Tel-Aviv; f. 1987 as a merger of three groups: Shinui-Movement for Change (f. 1974 and restored 1978, when Democratic Movement for Change split into two parties; centrist; Leader AMNON RUBINSTEIN), the Centre Liberal Party (f. 1986 by members of the Liberal Party of Israel; Leader ITZHAK BERMAN), and the Independent Liberal Party (f. 1965 by 7 Liberal Party of Israel Knesset mems, after the formation of the Herut Movement and Liberal Party of Israel bloc; 20,000 mems; Chair. MOSHE KOL; Gen. Sec. NISSIM ELIAD); Leaders AMNON RUBINSTEIN, ITZHAK BERMAN and MOSHE KOL.

Poale Agudat Israel: f. 1924; working-class Orthodox Judaist party; Leader Dr KALMAN KAHANE.

Political Zionist Opposition (Ometz): f. 1982; one-man party, YIGAEL HURWITZ.

Progressive List for Peace: 5 Simtat Lane, Nes Tziona, Tel-Aviv; tel. 3-662457; fax 3-659474; f. 1984; Jewish-Arab; advocates recognition of the PLO and the establishment of a Palestinian state in the West Bank and the Gaza Strip; Leader MUHAMMAD MI'ARI.

Ratz (Civil Rights and Peace Movement): 21 Tchernihovsky St, Tel-Aviv 63291; tel. 3-5101847; fax 3-5100008; f. 1973; concerned with human and civil rights, opposes discrimination on basis of religion, gender or ethnic identification and advocates a peace settlement with the Arab countries and the Palestinians; formed coalition government, as part of the Meretz alliance, with the Israel Labour Party and Shas in July 1992; Leader Mrs SHULAMIT ALONI.

Religious Zionism Party (Matzad): Tel-Aviv; f. 1983; breakaway group from the National Religious Party; also known as Morasha (Heritage); Leader Rabbi HAIM DRUCKMAN.

Shas (Sephardic Torah Guardians): Beit Abodi, Rehov Hahida, Bene Beraq; tel. 3-579776; f. 1984 by splinter groups from Agudat Israel; ultra-orthodox Jewish party; supported the government of national unity formed after the 1988 election; formed coalition government with the Israel Labour Party and the Meretz alliance in July 1992; Spiritual Leader Rabbi ELIEZER SHACH.

Shinui (Centre Party): 19 Rehov Levontin, Tel-Aviv 65112; tel. 3-5604737; fax 3-5601396; f. 1974; as a new liberal party, led by AMNON RUBINSTEIN, which withdrew from the coalition government of national unity in May 1987; formed coalition government, as part of the Meretz alliance, with the Israel Labour Party and Shas in July 1992; combines a moderate foreign policy with a free-market economic philosophy.

Tehiya—Zionist Revival Movement: POB 355, 34 Rehov Hahaluts, Jerusalem; tel. 2-259385; f. 1979; aims: Israeli sovereignty over Judaea, Samaria, Gaza; extensive settlement programme; economic independence; uniting of religious and non-religious camps; opposes Camp David accords; supported the government of national unity formed after the 1988 election, but withdrew from the coalition in January 1992; Leaders GERSHON SHAFAT, GEULA COHEN, ELYAKIM HAEZNI, DAMI DAYAN.

Tzomet Party: 22 Rehov Huberman, Tel-Aviv; tel. 3-204444; f. 1988; right-wing nationalist party; breakaway group from Tehiya party; supported the government of national unity formed after the 1988 election, but withdrew from the coalition in December 1991; Leader RAFAEL EITAN.

United Arab List: Arab party affiliated to Labour Party.

United Torah Judaism: electoral list of four minor ultra-orthodox parties (Moria, Degel Hatora, Poale Agudat Israel, Agudat Israel) formed, prior to 1992 election, to overcome the increase in election threshold from 1% to 1.5% and help to counter the rising influence of the secular Russian vote; Spiritual Leader Rabbi ELIEZER SHACH.

United Workers' Party (Mapam): POB 1777, 4 Rehov Itamar Ben-Avi, Tel-Aviv 61016; tel. 3-6972111; fax 3-6910504; f. 1948; left-wing socialist-Zionist Jewish-Arab party; grouped in Labour-Mapam Alignment with Israel Labour Party from January 1969 until Sept. 1984 when it withdrew in protest over Labour's formation of a government with Likud; formed coalition government, as part of the Meretz alliance, with the Israel Labour Party and Shas in July 1992; member of the Socialist International; 77,000 mems; Chair. CHANAN EREZ; Sec.-Gen. VICTOR BLIT.

Yahad (Together): f. 1984; advocates a peace settlement with the Arab peoples and the Palestinians; joined the Labour Party parliamentary bloc in January 1987.

Diplomatic Representation

EMBASSIES IN ISRAEL

Albania: Tel-Aviv.

Argentina: 22nd Floor, Diamond Tower, 3A Jabolinsky Rd, Ramat Gan, Tel-Aviv 63571; tel. 3-5759173; telex 33730; fax 3-5759178; Ambassador: JOSÉ MARÍA V. OTEGUI.

Australia: Beit Europa, 4th Floor, 37 Shaul Hamelech Blvd, Tel-Aviv 64928; tel. 3-6950451; telex 33777; fax 3-6968404; Ambassador: PETER RODGERS.

Austria: POB 11095, 11 Rehov Hermann Cohen, Tel-Aviv 61110; tel. 3-246186; telex 33435; fax 3-5244039; Chargé d'affaires: Dr KURT HENGL.

Belgium: 266 Rehov Hayarkon, Tel-Aviv 63504; tel. 3-6054164; telex 342211; fax 3-5465345; Ambassador: MARC OTTE.

Bolivia: 10th Floor, Industry House, 29 Rehov Hamered, Tel-Aviv 68125; tel. 3-662583; Ambassador: Dr MARCELO OSTRIA TRIGO.

Brazil: 14 Rehov Hei Be'Iyar, Kikar Hamedina, 5th Floor, Tel-Aviv 62093; tel. 3-6919292; telex 33752; fax 3-6916060; Ambassador: IVAN CANNABRAVA.

Bulgaria: 9th Floor, 124 Ibn Gvirol, Tel-Aviv 62308; tel. 3-5241751; fax 3-5241798; Ambassador: SVETLOMIR BAEV.

Cameroon: POB 50252, Dan Panorama Hotel, 10 Rehov Kaufman, Tel-Aviv 61500; tel. and fax 3-5190011; Chargé d'affaires a.i.: ETONNDI ESSOMBA.

Canada: 220 Rehov Hayarkon, Tel-Aviv 63405; tel. 3-5272929; telex 341293; fax 3-5272333; Ambassador: NORMAN SPECTOR.

Chile: 54 Rehov Pinkas, Apt 45, Tel-Aviv 62261; tel. 3-440414; telex 342189; Ambassador: MARCOS ALVAREZ GARCÍA.

China, People's Republic: Tel-Aviv.

Colombia: 52 Rehov Pinkas, Apt 26, Tel-Aviv 62261; tel. 3-449616; telex 342165; Chargé d'affaires a.i.: Dr EUFRACIO MORALES.

Costa Rica: 13 Rehov Diskin, Apt 1, Kiryat Wolfson, Jerusalem 92473; tel. 2-666197; telex 33533; fax 2-638469; Ambassador: (vacant)

Côte d'Ivoire: POB 14371, Dubnov Tower, 3 Rehov Daniel Frisch, Tel-Aviv 64371; tel. 3-6962211; telex 341143; fax 3-6962008; Ambassador: JEAN-PIERRE BONI.

Czech Republic: POB 16361, 23 Rehov Zeitlin, Tel-Aviv 61664; tel. 3-6918282; fax 3-6918286.

Denmark: POB 21080, 23 Rehov Bnei Moshe, Tel-Aviv 61210; tel. 3-5442144; telex 33514; fax 3-5465502; Ambassador: JAKOB RYTTER.

Dominican Republic: 4 Sderot Shaul Hamelech, Apt 81, Tel-Aviv 64733; tel. 3-6957580; fax 3-9723; Ambassador: JÓSE BATTLE-NICOLÁS.

Ecuador: POB 30, Room 211, 'Asia House', 4 Rehov Weizman, Tel-Aviv 64239; tel. 3-258764; telex 342179; fax 3-269437; Ambassador: PAULINA GARCÍA DE LARREA.

Egypt: 54 Rehov Bazel, Tel-Aviv 62744; tel. 3-5464151; telex 361289; fax 3-5441615; Ambassador: MUHAMMAD ABD AL-AZIZ BASSIOUNI.

El Salvador: POB 4005, 16 Kovshei Katamon, Jerusalem 93663; tel. 2-633575; Ambassador: ENRIQUE GUTTFREUND HANCHEL.

Ethiopia: Dan Panorama Hotel, 10 Rehov Kaufman, Tel-Aviv 61500; tel. 3-519019; Chargé d'affaires a.i.: Dr TESHOME TEKLU.

Finland: POB 20013, 8th Floor, Beith Eliahu, 2 Rehov Ibn Gvirol, Tel-Aviv 61201; tel. 3-6950527; telex 33552; fax 3-6966311; Ambassador: ARTO TANNER.

France: 112 Tayelet Herbert Samuel, Tel-Aviv 36572; tel. 3-245371; telex 33662; fax 3-5440062; Ambassador: ALAIN PIERRET.

Gabon:

Germany: POB 16038, 19th Floor, 3 Rehov Daniel Frisch, Tel-Aviv 61160; tel 03-5421313; telex 33621; fax 3-269217; Ambassador: OTTO VON DER GABLENTZ.

Greece: 35 Sderot Shaul Hamelech, Tel-Aviv 64927; tel. 3-6959704; telex 341227; fax 3-6955423; Ambassador: CONSTANTINE TSOKOS.

Guatemala: 74 Rehov Hei Be'Iyar, Apt 6, Tel-Aviv 62198; tel. 3-5467372; Ambassador: STELLA R. DE GARCÍA-GRANADOS.

Haiti: 16 Rehov Bar Giora, Tel-Aviv 64336; tel. 3-280285; Ambassador: FRANCK M. JOSEPH.

Holy See: Tel-Aviv; Apostolic Pro-Nuncio: Mgr ANDREA CORDERO LANZA DI MONTEZEMELO.

Honduras: 46 Rehov Hei Be'Iyar, Apt 3, Kikar Hamedina, Tel-Aviv 62093; tel. 3-5469506; fax 3-5469505; Ambassador: FRANCISCO ZEPEDA ANDINO.

Hungary: 18 Rehov Pinkas, Tel-Aviv 62662; tel. 3-5466860; Ambassador: Dr JÁNOS GOROG.

India: 4 Rehov Koifman, Tel-Aviv; tel. 3-5101431; telex 371583; fax 3-5101434; Ambassador: P. K. SINGH.

Italy: 'Asia House', 4 Rehov Weizman, Tel-Aviv 64239; tel. 3-6964223; telex 342664; fax 3-6918428; Ambassador: PIER LUIGI RACHELE.

Japan: 'Asia House', 4 Rehov Weizman, Tel-Aviv 64239; tel. 3-257292; telex 242202; fax 3-265069; Ambassador: SADAKAZU TANIGUCHI.

Liberia: 6 Shimon Frug, Ramat-Gan, Tel-Aviv 524282; tel. 3-728525; telex 361637; Ambassador: Maj. SAMUEL B. PEARSON, Jr.

Mexico: 3 Rehov Bograshov, Tel-Aviv 63808; tel. 3-5230367; telex 32352; fax 3-5237399; Ambassador: RODRÍGUEZ BARRERA.

Myanmar: 12 Zalman Schneor St, 47239 Ramat Hasharon, Tel-Aviv 52376; tel. 3-5400948; telex 371504; fax 3-5493866; Ambassador: U AUNG GYI.

Netherlands: 'Asia House', 4 Rehov Weizman, Tel-Aviv 64239; tel. 3-6957377; telex 342180; fax 3-6957370; Ambassador: CHRISTIAAN M. J. KRÖNER.

Nigeria: Tel-Aviv.

Norway: 40 Rehov Hei Be'Iyar, Tel-Aviv, Tel-Aviv 62093; tel. 3-295207; telex 33417; fax 3-5442034; Ambassador: JOHN EGIL GRIEG.

Panama: 10 Rehov Hei Be'Iyar, Kikar Hamedina, Tel-Aviv 62998; tel. 3-6956711; Ambassador: MOISÉS A. MIZRACHI.

Peru: 52 Rehov Pinkas, Apt 31, 8th Floor, Tel-Aviv 62261; tel. 3-5442081; telex 371351; fax 3-5465532; Ambassador: JORGE TORRES.

Philippines: POB 50085, Textile Centre Bldg, 13th Floor, 2 Rehov Kaufmann, Tel-Aviv 68012; tel. 3-5102231; telex 32104; fax 3-5102229; Ambassador: AMANTE R. MANZANO.

Poland: 16 Rehov Soutine, Tel-Aviv; tel. 3-5240186; telex 371765; fax 3-5237806; Ambassador: JAN DOWGIALLO.

Romania: 24 Rehov Adam Hacohen, Tel-Aviv 64585; tel. 3-247379; Chargé d'affaires a.i.: MIRCEA MIRONENCO.

Russia: 120 Rehov Hayarkon, Tel-Aviv 63573; tel. 3-5226733; fax 3-5226713; Ambassador: ALEKSANDR BOVIN.

Slovakia: POB 6459, Tel-Aviv 61064; tel. 3-5440066; fax 3-5440069.

South Africa: 16th Floor, Top Tower, 50 Dizengoff St, Tel-Aviv 64332; tel. 3-5252566; telex 341355; fax 3-5253230; Ambassador: MALCOLM G. FERGUSON.

Spain: Dubnov Tower, 3 Rehov Daniel Frisch, 16th Floor, Tel-Aviv 64731; tel. 3-6965210; telex 361415; fax 3-6952505; Ambassador: JOSÉ LUIS CRESPO.

Sweden: 'Asia House', 4 Rehov Weizman, Tel-Aviv 64239; tel. 3-258111; telex 33650; Ambassador: MATS BERGQUIST.

Switzerland: 228 Rehov Hayarkon, Tel-Aviv 63405; tel. 3-5464455; telex 342237; fax 3-5464408; Ambassador: GASPARD BODMER.

Togo: POB 50222, Beit Hatassianim, 29 Rehov Hamered, Tel-Aviv 68125; tel. 3-652206; Ambassador: KOFFI-MAWUENAM KOWOUVI.

Turkey: 34 Rehov Amos, Tel-Aviv 62495; tel. 3-6054155; fax 3-6054156; Ambassador: ONUR GÖKÇE.

Ukraine: 12 Stricker St, Tel-Aviv 62006; tel. 3-6040242; fax 3-6042512; Ambassador: YURI MIKOLAYOVICH SHERBAK.

United Kingdom: 192 Rehov Hayarkon, Tel-Aviv 63405; tel. 3-5249171; telex 33559; fax 3-5243313; Ambassador: ROBERT ANDREW BURNS.

USA: 71 Rehov Hayarkon, Tel-Aviv 63903; tel. 3-5174338; telex 33376; fax 3-663449; Ambassador: EDWARD P. DJEREJIAN.

Uruguay: 52 Rehov Pinkas, Apt. 10, 2nd Floor, Tel-Aviv 62261; tel. 3-440411; telex 342669; Ambassador: ANÍBAL DÍAZ MONDINO.

Venezuela: Textile Center, 2 Rehov Kaufmann, 16th Floor, Tel-Aviv 61500; tel. 3-656287; telex 342172; Ambassador: NESTOR COLL BLASINI.

Viet Nam: Tel-Aviv.

Yugoslavia: 3rd Floor, Shaul Hamelech 8, Tel-Aviv 64733; tel. 3-6938412; fax 3-6938411; Charge d'affaires a.i.: MIRKO STEFANOVIĆ.

Zaire: Apt 5, 60 Hei Be'Iyar, Kikar Hamedina, Tel-Aviv 62198; tel. 3-452681; telex 371239; Ambassador: Gen. ELUKI MONGA AUNDU.

Zambia: Tel-Aviv.

The Jewish Agency for Israel

POB 92, Jerusalem 91920; tel. 2-202222; fax 2-202303.

Organization: The governing bodies are the Assembly which determines basic policy, the Board of Governors which sets policy for the Agency between Assembly meetings and the Executive responsible for the day-to-day running of the Agency.

Chairman of Executive: SIMCHA DINITZ.

Chairman of Board of Governors: MENDEL KAPLAN.

Director-General: MOSHE NATIV.

Secretary-General: HOWARD WEISBAND.

Functions: According to the Agreement of 1971, the Jewish Agency undertakes the immigration and absorption of immigrants in Israel, including absorption in agricultural settlement and immigrant housing; social welfare and health services in connection with immigrants; education, youth care and training; neighbourhood rehabilitation through project renewal.

Budget (1993): US $500m.

Judicial System

The law of Israel is composed of the enactments of the Knesset and, to a lesser extent, of the acts, orders-in-council and ordinances that remain from the period of the British Mandate in Palestine (1922–48). The pre-1948 law has largely been replaced, amended or reorganized, in the interests of codification, by Israeli legis-

lation. This legislation generally follows a pattern which is very similar to that operating in England and the USA.

Attorney-General: MICHAEL BEN-YAIR.

CIVIL COURTS

The Supreme Court: Sha'arei Mishpat St, Kiryat David Ben Gurion, Jerusalem 91909; tel. 2-759666; fax 2-759648. This is the highest judicial authority in the state. It has jurisdiction as an Appellate Court over appeals from the District Courts in all matters, both civil and criminal (sitting as a Court of Civil Appeal or as a Court of Criminal Appeal). In addition it is a Court of First Instance (sitting as the High Court of Justice) in actions against governmental authorities, and in matters in which it considers it necessary to grant relief in the interests of justice and which are not within the jurisdiction of any other court or tribunal. The High Court's exclusive power to issue orders in the nature of *habeas corpus, mandamus*, prohibition and *certiorari* enables the court to review the legality of and redress grievances against acts of administrative authorities of all kinds and religious tribunals.

President of the Supreme Court: MEIR SHAMGAR.

Deputy-President of the Supreme Court: AHARON BARAK.

Justices of the Supreme Court: Y. KEDMI, SH. LEVIN, D. LEVIN, G. BACH, M. CHESHIN, E. GOLDBERG, Mrs T. STRASSBERG-COHEN, T. OR, E. MAZZA, Z. TAL, Mrs D. DORNER.

Registrar: Judge A. GILLON (magistrate).

The District Courts: There are five District Courts (Jerusalem, Tel-Aviv, Haifa, Beersheba, Nazareth). They have residual jurisdiction as Courts of First Instance over all civil and criminal matters not within the jurisdiction of a Magistrates' Court, all matters not within the exclusive jurisdiction of any other tribunal, and matters within the concurrent jurisdiction of any other tribunal so long as such tribunal does not deal with them. In addition, the District Courts have appellate jurisdiction over appeals from judgments and decisions of Magistrates' Courts and judgments of Municipal Courts and various administrative tribunals.

Magistrates' Courts: There are 28 Magistrates' Courts, having criminal jurisdiction to try contraventions, misdemeanours and certain felonies, and civil jurisdiction to try actions concerning possession or use of immovable property, or the partition thereof whatever may be the value of the subject matter of the action, and other civil claims not exceeding 450,000 new shekels.

Labour Courts: Established in 1969. Regional Labour Courts in Jerusalem, Tel-Aviv, Haifa, Beersheba and Nazareth, composed of judges and representatives of the public. A National Labour Court in Jerusalem, presided over by Judge M. Goldberg. The Courts have jurisdiction over all matters arising out of the relationship between employer and employee or parties to a collective labour agreement, and matters concerning the National Insurance Law and the Labour Law and Rules.

RELIGIOUS COURTS

The Religious Courts are the courts of the recognized religious communities. They have jurisdiction over certain defined matters of personal status concerning members of their respective communities. Where any action of personal status involves persons of different religious communities the President of the Supreme Court decides which Court will decide the matter. Whenever a question arises as to whether or not a case is one of personal status within the exclusive jurisdiction of a Religious Court, the matter must be referred to a Special Tribunal composed of two Justices of the Supreme Court and the President of the highest court of the religious community concerned in Israel. The judgments of the Religious Courts are executed by the process and offices of the Civil Courts. Neither these Courts nor the Civil Courts have jurisdiction to dissolve the marriage of a foreign subject.

Jewish Rabbinical Courts: These Courts have exclusive jurisdiction over matters of marriage and divorce of Jews in Israel who are Israeli citizens or residents. In all other matters of personal status they have concurrent jurisdiction with the District Courts.

Muslim Religious Courts: These Courts have exclusive jurisdiction over matters of marriage and divorce of Muslims who are not foreigners, or who are foreigners subject by their national law to the jurisdiction of Muslim Religious Courts in such matters. In all other matters of personal status they have concurrent jurisdiction with the District Courts.

Christian Religious Courts: The Courts of the recognized Christian communities have exclusive jurisdiction over matters of marriage and divorce of members of their communities who are not foreigners. In all other matters of personal status they have concurrent jurisdiction with the District Courts.

Druze Courts: These Courts, established in 1963, have exclusive jurisdiction over matters of marriage and divorce of Druze in

Israel, who are Israeli citizens or residents, and concurrent jurisdiction with the District Courts over all other matters of personal status of Druze.

Religion

JUDAISM

Judaism, the religion of the Jews, is the faith of the majority of Israel's inhabitants. On 31 December 1992 Judaism's adherents totalled 4,242,500, equivalent to 81.65% of the country's population. Its basis is a belief in an ethical monotheism.

There are two main Jewish communities: the Ashkenazim and the Sephardim. The former are the Jews from Eastern, Central, or Northern Europe, while the latter originate from the Balkan countries, North Africa and the Middle East.

There is also a community of about 10,000 Falashas (Ethiopian Jews) who have been airlifted to Israel at various times since the fall of Emperor Haile Selassie in 1974.

The supreme religious authority is vested in the Chief Rabbinate, which consists of the Ashkenazi and Sephardi Chief Rabbis and the Supreme Rabbinical Council. It makes decisions on interpretation of the Jewish law, and supervises the Rabbinical Courts. There are 8 regional Rabbinical Courts, and a Rabbinical Court of Appeal presided over by the two Chief Rabbis.

According to the Rabbinical Courts Jurisdiction Law of 1953, marriage and divorce among Jews in Israel are exclusively within the jurisdiction of the Rabbinical Courts. Provided that all the parties concerned agree, other matters of personal status can also be decided by the Rabbinical Courts.

There are 195 Religious Councils, which maintain religious services and supply religious needs, and about 405 religious committees with similar functions in smaller settlements. Their expenses are borne jointly by the State and the local authorities. The Religious Councils are under the administrative control of the Ministry of Religious Affairs. In all matters of religion, the Religious Councils are subject to the authority of the Chief Rabbinate. There are 365 officially appointed rabbis. The total number of synagogues is about 7,000, most of which are organized within the framework of the Union of Israel Synagogues.

Head of the Ashkenazi Community: The Chief Rabbi ISRAEL MEIR LAU.

Head of the Sephardic Community: Jerusalem; tel. 2-244785; The Chief Rabbi ELIAHU BAKSHI-DORON.

Two Jewish sects still loyal to their distinctive customs are:

The Karaites, a sect which recognizes only the Jewish written law and not the oral law of the Mishna and Talmud. The community of about 12,000, many of whom live in or near Ramla, has been augmented by immigration from Egypt.

The Samaritans, an ancient sect mentioned in 2 Kings xvii, 24. They recognize only the Torah. The community in Israel numbers about 500; about half of them live in Holon, where a Samaritan synagogue has been built, and the remainder, including the High Priest, live in Nablus, near Mt Gerizim, which is sacred to the Samaritans.

ISLAM

The Muslims in Israel are mainly Sunnis, and are divided among the four rites of the Sunni sect of Islam: the Shafe'i, the Hanbali, the Hanafi and the Maliki. Before June 1967 they numbered approx. 175,000; in 1971, approx. 343,900. On 31 December 1992 the total Muslim population of Israel was 725,400.

Mufti of Jerusalem: POB 19859, Jerusalem; tel. 2-283528; (vacant) (also Chair. Supreme Muslim Council for Jerusalem).

There was also a total of 87,100 Druzes in Israel at 31 December 1992.

CHRISTIANITY

The total Christian population of Israel (including East Jerusalem) at 31 December 1992 was 140,900.

United Christian Council in Israel: POB 116, Jerusalem 91000; tel. 052-432832; fax 052-432081; f. 1956; 21 mems (churches and other bodies); Chair. TOM HOCUTT; Gen. Sec. DAVID ALLEN.

The Roman Catholic Church

Armenian Rite

The Armenian Catholic Patriarch of Cilicia is resident in Beirut, Lebanon.

Patriarchal Exarchate of Jerusalem: POB 19546, Via Dolorosa 41, Third and Fourth Stations of the Cross, Jerusalem; tel. 2-284262; fax 2-272123; f. 1885; Exarch Patriarchal ANTREAS BEDOGH-OLIAN.

Chaldean Rite

The Chaldean Patriarch of Babylon is resident in Baghdad, Iraq.

Patriarchal Exarchate of Jerusalem: Chaldean Patriarchal Vicariate, Saad and Said Quarter, Nablus Rd, Jerusalem; Exarch Patriarchal Mgr PAUL COLLIN.

Latin Rite

The Patriarchate of Jerusalem covers Palestine, Jordan and Cyprus. At 31 December 1992 there were an estimated 140,000 adherents.

Bishops' Conference: Conférence des Evêques Latins dans les Régions Arabes, Patriarcat Latin, POB 14152, Jerusalem; tel. 2-282323; f. 1967; Pres. His Beatitude MICHEL SABBAH; Patriarch of Jerusalem.

Patriarchate of Jerusalem: Patriarcat Latin, POB 14152, Jerusalem; tel. 2-282323; Patriarch: His Beatitude MICHEL SABBAH; Vicar General for Israel: Mgr HANNA KALDANY (Titular Bishop of Gaba), Vicariat Patriarcal Latin, Nazareth; tel. 06-554075.

Maronite Rite

The Maronite community, under the jurisdiction of the Maronite Patriarch of Antioch (resident in Lebanon), has about 7,000 members.

Patriarchal Exarchate of Jerusalem: Vicariat Maronite, Maronite St 25, Jerusalem; tel. 2-282158; fax 2-280073; Exarch Patriarchal Mgr AUGUSTIN HARFOUCHE (also representing the Archbishop of Tyre, Lebanon, as Vicar General for Israel).

Melkite Rite

The Greek-Melkite Patriarch of Antioch (Maximos V Hakim) is resident in Damascus, Syria.

Patriarchal Vicariate of Jerusalem: Vicariat Patriarcal Grec-Melkite Catholique, POB 14130, Porte de Jafa, Jerusalem 91141; tel. 2-282023; fax 2-286652; about 3,000 adherents (1992); Vicars Patriarchal Mgr HILARION CAPUCCI (Titular Archbishop of Caesarea in Palestine), Mgr LUTFI LAHAM (Titular Archbishop of Tarsus).

Archbishop of Akka (Acre): Most Rev. MAXIMOS SALLOUM, Archevêché Grec-Catholique, POB 279, 33 Hagefen St, Haifa; tel. 04-523114; 43,000 adherents (1992).

Syrian Rite

The Syrian Catholic Patriarch of Antioch is resident in Beirut, Lebanon.

Patriarchal Exarchate of Jerusalem: Vicariat Patriarcal Syrien Catholique, POB 19787, Chaldean St No. 6, Nablos Road, Jerusalem 91190; tel. 2-282657; fax 2-284217; 1,051 adherents in Palestine and Jordan (Dec. 1992); Exarch Patriarchal Mgr PIERRE ABD AL-AHAD.

The Armenian Apostolic (Orthodox) Church

Patriarch of Jerusalem: TORKOM MANOOGIAN, St James's Cathedral, Jerusalem; tel. 2-894853; fax 2-894862 .

The Greek Orthodox Church

The Patriarchate of Jerusalem contains an estimated 260,000 adherents in Israel, the Israeli-Occupied Territories, Jordan, Kuwait, the United Arab Emirates and Saudi Arabia.

Patriarch of Jerusalem: DIODOROS I, POB 19632-633, Greek Orthodox Patriarchate St, Old City, Jerusalem; tel. 2-282048; fax 2-282048.

The Anglican Communion

Episcopal Church in Jerusalem and the Middle East: POB 1248, St George's Close, Jerusalem; tel. 2-271670; fax (2) 273847; President-Bishop The Most Rev. SAMIR KAFITY, Bishop in Jerusalem.

Other Christian Churches

Other denominations include the Coptic Orthodox Church (700 members), the Russian Orthodox Church, the Ethiopian Orthodox Church, the Romanian Orthodox Church, the Lutheran Church and the Church of Scotland.

The Press

Tel-Aviv is the main publishing centre. Largely for economic reasons, there has developed no local press away from the main cities; hence all papers regard themselves as national. Friday editions, issued on Sabbath eve, are increased to as much as twice the normal size by special weekend supplements, and experience a considerable rise in circulation. No newspapers appear on Saturday.

Most of the daily papers are in Hebrew, and others appear in Arabic, English, French, Polish, Yiddish, Hungarian and German. The total daily circulation is 500,000–600,000 copies, or 21 papers per hundred people, although most citizens read more than one daily paper.

Most Hebrew morning dailies have strong political or religious affiliations. *Al-Hamishmar* is affiliated to Mapam, *Hatzofeh* to the National Religious Front—World Mizrahi. *Davar* is the long-established organ of the Histadrut. Most newspapers depend on subsidies from political parties, religious organizations or public funds. The limiting effect on freedom of commentary entailed by this party press system has provoked repeated criticism.

An increasing number of Israeli Arabs are now reading Hebrew dailies. The daily, *Al-Quds*, was founded in 1968 for Arabs in Jerusalem and the West Bank; the small indigenous press of occupied Jordan has largely ceased publication or transferred operations to Amman. Two of the four Arabic newspapers which are published in occupied East Jerusalem, the daily, *Al-Mithaq*, and the weekly, *Al-Ahd*, were closed by the Israeli authorities in August 1986. It was alleged that they were financed and managed by the Popular Front for the Liberation of Palestine. The Palestinian news agency in the West Bank town of Nablus was closed for two years in October 1987. Since the Palestinian uprising in the Occupied Territories began in December 1987, further action has been taken by the Israeli authorities to curb allegedly pro-PLO press activities. In February 1988 the left-wing newspaper, *Derech Hanitzotz*, was closed for its alleged links with the Democratic Front for the Liberation of Palestine; in March the Palestine Press Service in East Jerusalem (the only remaining Arab news agency in the Occupied Territories) was closed by military order for six months; and in April the minor weekly magazine *Al-Awdah* (The Return) (also based in East Jerusalem) was closed, on the grounds that it was being funded by the PLO.

There are around 400 other newspapers and magazines including some 50 weekly and 150 fortnightly; over 250 of them are in Hebrew, the remainder in eleven other languages.

The most influential and respected dailies, for both quality of news coverage and commentary, are *Ha'aretz* and the trade union paper, *Davar*, which frequently has articles by government figures. These are the most widely read of the morning papers, exceeded only by the popular afternoon press, *Ma'ariv* and *Yedioth Aharonoth*. The *Jerusalem Post* gives detailed and sound news coverage in English.

The Israeli Press Council (Chair. ITZHAK ZAMIR), established in 1963, deals with matters of common interest to the Press such as drafting the code of professional ethics which is binding on all journalists.

The Daily Newspaper Publishers' Association represents publishers in negotiations with official and public bodies, negotiates contracts with employees and purchases and distributes newsprint.

DAILIES

Davar (The Word): POB 199, 45 Sheinkin St, Tel-Aviv; tel. 3-286141; telex 33807; fax 3-294783; f. 1925; morning; Hebrew; official organ of the General Federation of Labour (Histadrut); Editor Dr YORAM PERI; circ. 39,000; there are also weekly magazine editions.

Al-Fajr (The Dawn): POB 19315, Jerusalem; tel. 2-271649; fax 2-273521; daily version in Arabic, weekly version in English; Publr PAUL AJILOUNY; Editor HANNAH SINIORA.

Globes: 127 Igal Alon St, Tel-Aviv 67443; tel. 3-6979797; fax 3-6917573; f. 1983; evening; business, economics; Editor A. BARUCH; circ. 29,000.

Ha'aretz (The Land): POB 233, 21 Salman Schocken St, Tel-Aviv 61001; tel. 3-5121212; fax 3-810012; f. 1918; morning; Hebrew; liberal, independent; Editor HANOCH MARMARI; circ. 55,000 (weekdays), 65,000 (weekends).

Hadashot (The News): Tel-Aviv; late morning; Hebrew.

Hamodia (The Informer): POB 1306, Yehuda Hamackabbi 3, Jerusalem; fax 2-539108; morning; Hebrew; organ of Agudat Israel; Editors M. A. DRUCK, H. M. KNOPF; circ. 15,000.

Hatzofeh (The Watchman): 66 Hamasger St, Tel-Aviv; tel. 3-5622951; fax 3-5621502; f. 1938; morning; Hebrew; organ of the National Religious Party; Editor M. ISHON; circ. 16,000.

Israel Nachrichten (News of Israel): 49 Czlenow St, Tel-Aviv 66048; tel. 3-5371395; fax 3-377142; f. 1974; morning; German; Editor ALICE SCHWARZ-GARDOS; circ. 20,000.

Israelski Far Tribuna: 113 Givat Herzl St, Tel-Aviv; tel. 3-3700; f. 1952; Bulgarian; circ. 6,000.

Al-Ittihad (Unity): POB 104, Haifa; tel. 4-511296; fax 4-511297; f. 1944; Arabic; organ of the Israeli Communist Party (Maki); Chief Editor NAZIR MJALLI ZUBIEDAT.

The Jerusalem Post: POB 81, Romema, 91000, Jerusalem; tel. 2-315666; telex 26121; fax 2-389527; f. 1932; morning; English; independent; Pres. and Pblr YEHUDA LEVY; Editor DAVID BAR-ILLAN; circ. 30,000 (weekdays), 50,000 (weekend edition); there is also a

weekly international edition, circ. 70,000, and a weekly French-language edition, circ. 7,500.

Le Journal d'Israel: POB 28330, 26 Agra St, Tel-Aviv; f. 1971; French; independent; Chief Editor J. RABIN; circ. 10,000; also overseas weekly selection; circ. 15,000.

Letzte Nyess (Late News): POB 28034, 52 Harakevet St, Tel-Aviv; f. 1949; morning; Yiddish; Editor S. HIMMELFARB; circ. 23,000.

Ma'ariv (Evening Prayer): 2 Carlebach St, Tel-Aviv 61200; tel. 3-5632111; telex 33735; fax 3-5610614; f. 1948; mid-morning; Hebrew; independent; published by Modiin Publishing House; Editor OFFER NIMRODI; circ. daily 160,000, weekend 270,000.

Mabat: 8 Toshia St, Tel-Aviv 67218; tel. 3-5627711; fax 3-5627719; f. 1971; morning; economic and social; Editor S. YARKONI; circ. 7,000.

Al-Mawqif: Jerusalem; Arabic; owned by the Arab Council for Public Affairs.

Al-Mithaq (The Covenant): Jerusalem; Arabic; Editor MAHMOUD KHATIB; (closed down by Israeli authorities August 1986).

An-Nahar (Day): Jerusalem; Arabic; pro-Jordanian; Editor OTHMAN HALLAQ.

Nasha Strana (Our Country): 52 Harakeret St, Tel-Aviv 67770; tel. 3-370011; fax 3-5371921; f. 1970; morning; Russian; Editor S. HIMMELFARB; circ. 35,000.

Al-Quds (Jerusalem): POB 19788, Jerusalem; tel. 2-272663; fax 2-272657; f. 1968; Arabic; Publr MAHMOUD ABU ZALAF; Editor-in-Chief MARWAN ABU ZALAF; circ. 50,000.

Ash-Sha'ab (The People): Jerusalem; f. 1972; Arabic; circ. 15,000; Editor SALAH ZUHAIKA.

Uj Kelet: 49 Tchlenor St, Tel-Aviv; tel. 3-5371395; fax 3-377142; f. 1918; morning; Hungarian; independent; Editor D. DRORY; circ. 20,000.

Viata Noastra: 49 Tchlenor St, Tel-Aviv; tel. 3-5372059; fax 3-377142; f. 1950; morning; Romanian; Editor ISEF ROTEM; circ. 30,000.

Yated Ne'eman: POB 328, Bnei Brak; tel. 3-5709171; fax 3-5709181; f. 1986; morning; religious; Editors Y. ROTH and N. GROSSMAN; circ. 25,000.

Yedioth Ahronoth (The Latest News): 2 Yehuda and Noah Mozes St, Tel-Aviv 61000; tel. 3-6972222; telex 33847; fax 3-6953950; f. 1939; evening; independent; Editor-in-Chief MOSHE VARDI; circ. 300,000, Friday 600,000.

WEEKLIES AND FORTNIGHTLIES

Al-Ahd (Sunday): Jerusalem; weekly; Arabic; (closed down by Israeli authorities August 1986).

Al-Awdah (The Return): East Jerusalem; weekly; Arabic and English; Proprs IBRAHIM QARA'EEN, Mrs RAYMONDA TAWIL; circ. 10,000; (closed down by Israeli authorities April 1988).

Bama'alah: 120 Kibbutz Gabuyot St, Tel-Aviv; tel. 3-817788; fax 3-816852; Hebrew; journal of the young Histadrut Movement; Editor ODED BAR-MEIR.

Bamahane (In the Camp): Military POB 1013, Tel-Aviv; f. 1948; military, illustrated weekly of the Israel Armed Forces; Hebrew; Editor-in-Chief YOSSEF ESHKOL; circ. 70,000.

Bitaon Heyl Ha'avir (Air Force Magazine): Doar Zwai 01560, Zahal; tel. 3-5693886; fax 3-5695806; f. 1948; bi-monthly; Hebrew; Man. Editor D. MOLAD; Editor-in-Chief MERAV HALPERIN; Technical Editor SHARON SADEH; circ. 30,000.

Davar Hashavua (The Weekly Word): 45 Shenkin St, Tel-Aviv; tel. 2-286141; f. 1946; weekly; Hebrew; popular illustrated; published by Histadrut, General Federation of Labour; Editor TUVIA MENDELSON; circ. 43,000.

Ethgar (The Challenge): 75 Einstein St, Tel-Aviv; twice weekly; Hebrew; Editor NATHAN YALIN-MOR.

Gesher (The Bridge): Jerusalem; fortnightly; Hebrew; Editor ZIAD ABU ZAYAD.

Glasul Populurui: Tel-Aviv; weekly of the Communist Party of Israel; Romanian; Editor MEÏR SEMO.

Haolam Hazeh (This World): POB 136, 3 Gordon St, Tel-Aviv 61001; tel. 3-5376804; fax 3-5376811; f. 1937; weekly; independent; illustrated news magazine; Editor-in-Chief RAFFI GINAT.

Harefuah (Medicine): 39 Shaul Hamelech Blvd, Tel-Aviv 64928; tel. 3-6969639; fax 3-6956103; f. 1920; fortnightly journal of the Israeli Medical Association; Hebrew with English summaries; Editor Y. ROTEM; circ. 7,500.

Hotam: Al-Hamishmar House, Choma U'Migdal St, Tel-Aviv; Hebrew.

Al-Hurriya (Freedom): 38 King George St, Tel-Aviv; Arabic weekly of the Herut Party.

Illustrirte Weltwoch: Tel-Aviv; f. 1956; weekly; Yiddish; Editor M. KARPINOVITZ.

Jerusalem Post International Edition: POB 81, Romema, Jerusalem 91000; tel. 2-315666; telex 26121; fax 2-385070; f. 1959; weekly; English; overseas edition of the *Jerusalem Post* (q.v.); circ. 60,000 to 95 countries.

Kol Ha'am (Voice of the People): Tel-Aviv; f. 1947; Hebrew; organ of the Communist Party of Israel; Editor B. BALTI.

Laisha (For Women): POB 28122, 35 Bnei Brak St, Tel-Aviv 67132; tel. 3-371464; fax 3-378071; f. 1946; Hebrew; women's magazine; Editor ZVI ELGAT.

Ma'ariv Lanoar: 2 Carlebach St, Tel-Aviv 67132; tel. 3-5632111; fax 3-5632030; f. 1957; weekly for youth; Hebrew; Editor AVI MORGENSTERN; circ. 100,000.

Magallati (My Magazine): Arabic Publishing House, POB 28049, Tel-Aviv; tel. 3-371438; f. 1960; young people's fortnightly; Man. JOSEPH ELIAHOU; Editor-in-Chief IBRAHIM MUSA IBRAHIM; Editor MISHEL HADDAD; circ. 3,000.

MB (Mitteilungsblatt): POB 1480, Tel-Aviv; tel. 3-664461; fax 3-664435; f. 1932; German monthly journal of the Irgun Olei Merkas Europa (The Association of Immigrants from Central Europe); Editor Prof. PAUL ALSBERG.

Al-Mirsad (The Telescope): POB 1777, Tel-Aviv; tel. 3-6972111; fax 3-6910504; f. 1948; Arabic; Mapam.

Otiot: Beit Orot, Hordes Post, Jerusalem 95908; tel. 2-895097; fax 2-895196; f. 1987; weekly for children; English; Editor URI AUERBACH.

Reshumot: Ministry of Justice, Jerusalem; f. 1948; Hebrew, Arabic and English; official government gazette.

Sada at-Tarbia (The Echo of Education): published by the Histadrut and Teachers' Association, POB 2306, Rehovot; f. 1952; fortnightly; Arabic; educational; Editor TUVIA SHAMOSH.

OTHER PERIODICALS

Ariel: Cultural and Scientific Relations Division, Ministry for Foreign Affairs, Jerusalem; Publisher and Distributor: Youval Tal Ltd, POB 2160, Jerusalem 91021; tel. 2-248897; fax 2-254896; Editorial Office: 214 Jaffa Road, Jerusalem 91130; tel. 2-381515; fax 2-380626; f. 1962; quarterly review of the arts and letters in Israel; regular edns in English, Spanish, French, German and Russian; occasional edns in other languages; Editor ASHER WEILL; Asst Editor ALOMA HALTER; circ. 30,000.

Avoda Urevacha Ubituach Leumi: POB 915, Jerusalem; f. 1949; monthly review of the Ministry of Labour and Social Affairs, and the National Insurance Institute, Jerusalem; Hebrew; Chief Editor AVNER MICHAELI; Editor MICHAEL KLODOVSKY; circ. 2,500.

Al-Bushra (Good News): POB 6088, Haifa; f. 1935; monthly; Arabic; organ of the Ahmadiyya movement; Editor FALAHUD DIN O'DEH.

Business Diary: 37 Hanamal St, Haifa; f. 1947; weekly; English, Hebrew; shipping movements, import licences, stock exchange listings, business failures, etc.; Editor G. ALON.

Challenge: POB 32107, Jerusalem 91320; tel. 2-225382; fax 2-251614; f. 1989; magazine of Israeli-Palestinian coexistence, published by Hanitzotz Publishing House; bi-monthly in English; circ. 2,000; Editor LIZ LEYH LEVAC.

Christian News from Israel: 30 Jaffa Rd, Jerusalem; f. 1949; half-yearly; English, French, Spanish; issued by the Ministry of Religious Affairs; Editor SHALOM BEN-ZAKKAI; circ. 10,000.

Di Goldene Keyt: 30 Weizmann St, Tel-Aviv; f. 1949; literary quarterly; Yiddish; published by the Histadrut; Man. Editor MOSHE MILLIS; Editor A. SUTZKEVER.

Divrei Haknesset: c/o The Knesset, Jerusalem; f. 1949; Hebrew; records of the proceedings of the Knesset; published by the Government Printer, Jerusalem; Editor DVORA AVIVI (acting); circ. 350.

The Easy Way to do Business with Israel: POB 20027, Tel-Aviv; published by Federation of Israeli Chambers of Commerce; Editor Y. SHOSTAK.

Folk un Zion: POB 7053, Tel-Aviv 61070; tel. 3-5423317; f. 1950; bi-monthly; current events relating to Israel and World Jewry; circ. 3,000; Editor MOSHE KALCHHEIM.

Frei Israel: POB 8512, Tel-Aviv; progressive monthly; published by Asscn for Popular Culture; Yiddish.

Gazit: POB 4190, 8 Zvi Brook St, Tel-Aviv; f. 1932; monthly; Hebrew and English; art, literature; Publisher G. TALPHIR.

Hameshek Hahaklai: 21 Melchett St, Tel-Aviv; f. 1929; Hebrew; agricultural; Editor ISRAEL INBARI.

Al-Hamishmar (The Guardian): POB 61999, 2 Rehov Ghoma U'migdal, Tel-Aviv 67771; tel. 3-378833; telex 341652; fax 3-

5370037; f. 1943; morning; Hebrew; published by the Kibbutz Artsi Movement; Editor ZVI TIMOR; circ. 25,000.

Hamizrah Hehadash (The New East): Israel Oriental Society, The Hebrew University, Mount Scopus, Jerusalem 91905; tel. 2-883633; f. 1949; annual of the Israel Oriental Society; Middle Eastern, Asian and African Affairs; Hebrew with English summary; Editor JACOB LANDAU; circ. 1,500–2,000.

Hamionai (The Hotelier): POB 11586, Tel-Aviv; f. 1962; monthly of the Israel Hotel Association; Hebrew and English; Editor Z. PELTZ.

Hapraklit: POB 14152, 8 Wilson St, Tel-Aviv 61141; tel. 3-5614695; fax 3-561476; f. 1943; quarterly; Hebrew; published by the Israel Bar Association; Editor-in-Chief A. POLONSKI; Editor ARNAN GAVRIELI; circ. 9,000.

Hassadeh: POB 40044, 8 Shaul Hamelech Blvd, Tel-Aviv 61400; tel. 3-6929976; fax 3-6929979; f. 1920; monthly; review of Israeli agriculture; English; Publr GUY KLUG; circ. 10,000.

Hed Hagan: 8 Ben Saruk St, Tel-Aviv 62969; tel. 3-5432958; f. 1935; Hebrew; educational; Editor Mrs ZIVA PEDAHZUR; circ. 6,300.

Hed Hahinukh: 8 Ben Saruk St, Tel-Aviv 62969; tel. 3-5432911; fax 3-5432928; f. 1926; monthly; Hebrew; educational; published by the Israeli Teachers' Union; Editor DALIA LACHMAN; circ. 40,000.

Israel Economist: POB 7052, 6 Hazanowitz St, Jerusalem 91070; tel. 2-234131; fax 2-246569; f. 1945; monthly; English; independent; political and economic; Editor BEN MOLLOV; Publisher ISRAEL KELMAN; also publishes *Keeping Posted* (diplomatic magazine), *Mazel and Brucha* (jewellers' magazine); annuals: *Travel Agents' Manual, Electronics, International Conventions in Israel, Arkia, In Flight,* various hotel magazines.

Israel Environment Bulletin: Ministry of the Environment, POB 6234, Jerusalem 91061; tel. 2-701606; telex 25629; fax 2-513945; f. 1973; Editor SHOSHANA GABBAY; circ. 2,800.

Israel Export and Trade Journal: POB 11586, Tel-Aviv; f. 1949; monthly; English; commercial and economic; published by Israel Periodicals Co Ltd; Man. Dir ZALMAN PELTZ.

Israel Journal of Mathematics: f. 1951; monthly, three vols of four issues per year; published by Magnes Press; Editor Prof. A. LUBOTZKY.

Israel Journal of Medical Sciences: 2 Etzel St, French Hill, 97853 Jerusalem; tel. 2-817727; fax 2-815722; f. 1965; monthly; Editor-in-Chief Dr M. PRYWES; Exec. Sec. Mrs S. NOY; circ. 5,500.

Israel Journal of Occupational Therapy: Gefen Publishing House Ltd, POB 6065, Jerusalem 91060; tel. 2-380247; fax 2-388423; f. 1992; quarterly; Editor-in-Chief NAOMI KATZ.

Israel Journal of Psychiatry and Related Sciences: Gefen Publishing House Ltd, POB 6056, Jerusalem 91060; tel. 2-380247; fax 2-388423; f. 1963; quarterly; Editor-in-Chief Dr DAVID GREENBERG.

Israel Journal of Veterinary Medicine: POB 3076, Rishon Le-Zion 75130; f. 1943; quarterly of the Israel Veterinary Medical Asscn; formerly *Refuah Veterinarith*; Editor Prof. E. KUTTIN.

Israel Scene: POB 92, Jerusalem 91920; tel. 2-527156; telex 26436; fax 2-513542; f. 1980 as continuation of Israel Digest; bi-monthly; English; published by the World Zionist Organization; news, features and analysis; circ. 50,000; Editor LISA GANN-PERKAL.

Israel-South Africa Trade Journal: POB 11587, Tel-Aviv; f. 1973; bi-monthly; English; commercial and economic; published by Israel Publications Corpn Ltd; Man. Dir Z. PELTZ.

Israels Aussenhandel: POB 11586, Tel-Aviv 61114; tel. 3-5280215; telex 341118; f. 1967; monthly; German; commercial; published by Israel Periodicals Co Ltd; Editor PELTZ NOEMI; Man. Dir ZALMAN PELTZ.

Al-Jadid (The New): POB 104, Haifa; f. 1951; literary monthly; Arabic; Editor SALEM JUBRAN; circ. 5,000.

Journal d'Analyse Mathématique: f. 1955; 2 vols per year; published by Magnes Press; Editor Prof. L. ZALCMAN.

Kalkala Ubamishar (Economics and Trade): POB 20027, Tel-Aviv 61200; tel. 3-5612444; telex 33484; fax 3-5612614; f. 1919; monthly; Hebrew; published by Federation of Israeli Chambers of Commerce; Editor Z. AMIT.

Kalkalan: POB 7052, 8 Akiva St, Jerusalem; f. 1952; monthly; independent; Hebrew commercial and economic; Editor J. KOLLEK.

Kibbutz Trends: Yad Tabenkin, Ramat Efal 52960; tel. 3-5343311; fax 3-5346376; quarterly; English journal of the Federation of Kibbutz Movements; Editors RUTH LACEY, IDIT PAZ; circ. 1,500.

Labour in Israel: 93 Arlosorof St, Tel-Aviv 62098; tel. 3-6921111; telex 342488; fax 3-6969906; quarterly; English, French, German and Spanish; bulletin of the Histadrut (General Federation of Labour in Israel); circ. 28,000.

Leshonenu: Academy of the Hebrew Language, POB 3449, Jerusalem 91034; tel. 2-632242; fax 2-617065; f. 1929; 4 a year; for the study of the Hebrew language and cognate subjects; Editor J. BLAU.

Leshonenu La'am: Academy of the Hebrew Language, POB 3449, Jerusalem 91034; tel. 2-632242; fax 2-617065; f. 1945; popular Hebrew philology; Editors S. BAHAT, D. TALSHIR, Y. OFER.

Ma'arachot (Campaigns): POB 7026, Hakirya, 3 Mendler St, Tel-Aviv 61070; tel. 3-5694343; f. 1939; military and political bi-monthly; periodical of Israel Defence Force; Editors EVIATHAR BEN-ZEDEFF, Lt Col R. ROJANSKI.

Melaha Vetaassiya (Trade and Industry): POB 11587, Tel-Aviv; f. 1969; bi-monthly review of the Union of Artisans and Small Manufacturers of Israel; Hebrew; Man. Dir Z. PELTZ.

Molad: POB 1165, Jerusalem 91010; f. 1948; annual; Hebrew; independent political and literary periodical; published by Miph'ale Molad Ltd; Editor EPHRAIM BROIDO.

Monthly Bulletin of Statistics: Israel Central Bureau of Statistics, POB 13015, Jerusalem 91130; tel. 2-553553; fax 2-553325; f. 1949.

> **Foreign Trade Statistics:** f. 1950; Hebrew and English; appears annually, 2 vols; imports/exports.
>
> **Foreign Trade Statistics Quarterly:** f. 1950; Hebrew and English.
>
> **Judea, Samaria and Gaza Area Statistics:** f. 1971; irregular; Hebrew and English.
>
> **Tourism and Hotel Services Statistics Quarterly:** f. 1973; Hebrew and English.
>
> **Price Statistics Monthly:** f. 1959; Hebrew.
>
> **Transport Statistics Quarterly:** f. 1974; Hebrew and English.
>
> **Agricultural Statistics Quarterly:** f. 1970; Hebrew and English.
>
> **New Statistical Projects:** f. 1970; quarterly; Hebrew and English.

Moznaim (Balance): POB 7098, Tel-Aviv; tel. 3-6953256; f. 1929; monthly; Hebrew; literature and culture; Editors ORTSION BARTANA, MOSHE BEN-SHAUL; circ. 2,500.

Na'amat-Urim Lahorim: 93 Arlozorov St, Tel-Aviv 62098; tel. 3-5221207; fax 3-5249746; f. 1934; monthly journal of the Council of Women Workers of the Histadrut; Hebrew; Editor ZIVIA COHEN; circ. 16,500.

Nekuda: Hebrew; organ of the Jewish settlers of the West Bank and Gaza Strip.

New Outlook: 9 Gordon St, Tel-Aviv 63458; tel. 3-5236496; fax 3-5232252; f. 1957; bi-monthly; Israeli and Middle Eastern Affairs; dedicated to the quest for Arab-Israeli peace; Editor-in-Chief CHAIM SHUR; Senior Editor DAN LEON; circ. 10,000.

Proche-Orient Chrétien: POB 19079, Jerusalem 91190; tel. 2-283285; fax 2-280764; f. 1951; quarterly on churches and religion in the Middle East; circ. 1,000.

Quarterly Review of the Israel Medical Association (Mif'al Haverut Hutz—World Fellowship of the Israel Medical Association): POB 33289, 39 Shaul Hamelech Blvd, Tel-Aviv 61332; tel. (3) 6955521; fax 3-6956103; quarterly; English; Editor-in-Chief YEHUDA SHOENFELD.

The Sea: POB 33706, Hane'emanim 8, Haifa; tel. 04-529818; every six months; published by Israel Maritime League; review of marine problems; Pres. M. POMROCK; Chief Editor M. LITOVSKI; circ. 5,000.

Shdemot: 10 Dubnov, Tel-Aviv 64732; tel. 3-342513; three a year; Hebrew; Editor JOEL MAGID; circ. 2,500.

Shituf (Co-operation): POB 7151, 24 Ha'arba St, Tel-Aviv; f. 1948; bi-monthly; Hebrew; economic, social and co-operative problems in Israel; published by the Central Union of Industrial, Transport and Service Co-operative Societies; Editor L. LOSH; circ. 12,000.

Shivuk (Marketing): POB 20027, Tel-Aviv 61200; tel. 3-5612444; fax 3-5612614; monthly; Hebrew; publ. by Federation of Israeli Chambers of Commerce; Editor SARA LIPKIN.

Sinai: POB 642, Jerusalem; tel. 2-526231; f. 1937; Hebrew; Torah science and literature; Editor Dr YITZCHAK RAPHAEL.

Sindibad: POB 28049, Tel-Aviv; f. 1970; children's monthly; Hebrew; Man. JOSEPH ELIAHOU; Editor WALID HUSSEIN; circ. 7,000.

Spectrum: Jerusalem; monthly of the Israel Labour Party; Editor DAVID TWERSKY.

At-Ta'awun (Co-operation): POB 303, 93 Arlosoroff St, Tel-Aviv 62098; tel. 3-431813; telex 342488; fax 3-267368; f. 1961; Arabic; published by the Arab Workers' Dept of the Histadrut; co-operatives irregular; Editor ZVI HAIK.

Terra Santa: POB 186, Jerusalem 91001; tel. 2-282354; f. 1921; every two months; published by the Custody of the Holy Land (the official custodians of the Holy Shrines); Italian, Spanish, French, English and Arabic editions published in Jerusalem, by the Franciscan Printing Press, German edition in Munich, Maltese edition in Valletta.

Tmuroth: POB 23076, 48 Hamelech George St, Tel-Aviv; f. 1960; monthly; Hebrew; organ of the Liberal Labour Movement; Editor S. MEIRI.

WIZO Review: Women's International Zionist Organization, 38 Sderot David Hamelech Blvd, Tel-Aviv 64237; tel. 3-6923805; fax 3-6958267; f. 1947; English edition (quarterly), Spanish and German editions (two a year); Editor HILLEL SCHENKER; circ. 20,000.

Zion: POB 4179, Jerusalem 91041; tel. 2-637171; fax 2-662135; f. 1935; quarterly; published by the Historical Society of Israel; Hebrew, with English summaries; research in Jewish history; Editors R. I. COHEN, A. OPPENHEIMER, J. HACKER; circ. 1,000.

Zraim: POB 40027, 7 Dubnov St, Tel-Aviv; tel. 3-691745; fax 3-6953199; f. 1953; Hebrew; journal of the Bnei Akiva (Youth of Tora Va-avoda) Movement; Editor URI AUERBACH.

Zrakor: Haifa; f. 1947; monthly; Hebrew; news digest, trade, finance, economics, shipping; Editor G. ALON.

The following are all published by Laser Pages Publishing Ltd of Israel, POB 50257, 40/18 Levi Eshkol Blvd, Jerusalem 97665; tel. 2-829770; fax 2-818782.

Israel Journal of Chemistry: f. 1951; quarterly; Editor Prof. H. LEVANON.

Israel Journal of Earth Sciences: f. 1951; quarterly; Editors Dr Y. BARTOV, Y. KOLODNY.

Israel Journal of Plant Sciences: f. 1994; quarterly; Editor Prof. A. M. MAYER.

Israel Journal of Zoology: f. 1951; quarterly; Editor Prof. D. GRAUER.

Lada'at (Science for Youth): f. 1971; Hebrew; ten issues per vol.; Editor Dr M. ALMAGOR.

Mada (Science): POB 801, 8A Horkanya St, Jerusalem 91007; tel. 2-783203; fax 2-783784; f. 1955; popular scientific bi-monthly in Hebrew; Editor-in-Chief Dr YACHIN UNNA; circ. 10,000.

PRESS ASSOCIATIONS

Daily Newspaper Publishers' Association of Israel: POB 51202, 74 Petach Tikva Rd, Tel-Aviv 61200; fax 3-5617938; safeguards professional interests and maintains standards, supplies newsprint to dailies; negotiates with trade unions, etc.; mems all daily papers; affiliated to International Federation of Newspaper Publishers; Pres. SHABTAI HIMMELFARB; Gen. Sec. BETZALEL EYAL.

Foreign Press Association: Govt. Press Office Bldg, 9 Rehov Itamar Ben Avi, Tel-Aviv; tel. 3-6916143; fax 3-6961548; Pres. C. MUS.

Israel Press Association: Sokolov House, 4 Kaplan St, Tel-Aviv.

NEWS AGENCIES

Jewish Telegraphic Agency (JTA): Israel Bureau, Jerusalem Post Bldg, Romema, Jerusalem; Dir DAVID LANDAU.

ITIM, News Agency of the Associated Israel Press: 10 Tiomkin St, Tel-Aviv; f. 1950; co-operative news agency; Dir and Editor ALTER WELNER.

Palestine Press Service: Salah ad-Din St, East Jerusalem; Proprs IBRAHIM QARA'EEN, Mrs RAYMONDA TAWIL; only Arab news agency in the Occupied Territories; (closed down by Israeli authorities for six months, March 1988).

Foreign Bureaux

Agence France-Presse: POB 1507, 17th Floor, Migdal Haïr Tower, 34 Ben Yehuda St, Jerusalem 91014; tel. 2-242005; telex 26401; fax 2-6793623; Correspondent SAMY KETZ.

Agencia EFE (Spain): POB 3279, Avizohar 2, Apt 9, Bet Ha'Kerem, Jerusalem 91032; tel. 2-436658; telex 26446; fax 2-436658; Correspondent ELÍAS-SAMUEL SCHERBACOVSKY.

Agenzia Nazionale Stampa Associata (ANSA) (Italy): 30 Dizengoff St, Tel-Aviv 64332; tel. 3-299319; telex 341704; fax 3-5250302; Bureau Chief LUIGI SANDRI; c/o Associated Press, Jerusalem 92233 (see below); tel. 2-250571; fax 2-258656; Correspondent GIORGIO RACCAH.

Associated Press (AP) (USA): POB 20220, 30 Ibn Gavirol St, Tel-Aviv 61201; tel. 3-262283; telex 341411; POB 1625, 18 Shlomzion Hamalcha, Jerusalem; tel. 2-224632; telex 25258; Chief of Bureau NICHOLAS TATRO.

Deutsche Presse-Agentur (dpa) (Germany): POB 6311, 30 Ibn Gavirol St, Tel-Aviv 61062; tel. 3-6959007; telex 33416; fax 3-6963594; Correspondents THOMAS P. SPIEKER, ANDY GOLDBERG.

Jiji Tsushin-Sha (Japan): 9 Schmuel Hanagld, Jerusalem 94592; tel. 2-232553; fax 2-232402; Correspondent HIROKAZU OIKAWA.

Kyodo News Service (Japan): 19 Lessin St, Tel-Aviv 62997; tel. 3-6958185; telex 361568; fax 3-6917478; Correspondent HAJIME OZAKI.

Reuters (UK): 38 Hamasger St, Tel-Aviv 67211; tel. 3-5372211; telex 361567; fax 3-5372045; Jerusalem Capital Studios (JCS) 206, Jaffa Road, Jerusalem 91131; tel. 2-370502; fax 2-374241.

United Press International (UPI) (USA): 138 Petah Tikva Rd, Tel-Aviv; Bureau Man. BROOKE W. KROEGER; Bureau Man. in Jerusalem LOUIS TOSCANO.

Informatsionnoye Telegrafnoye Agentstvo Rossii—Telegrafnoye Agentstvo Suverennykh Stran (ITAR—TASS) (Russia) is also represented.

Publishers

Achiasaf Ltd: POB 4810, 13 Yosef Hanassi St, Tel-Aviv 65236; tel. 3-5283339; fax 3-5286705; f. 1933; general; Man. Dir MATAN ACHIASAF.

Am Hassefer Ltd: 9 Bialik St, Tel-Aviv; tel. 3-53040; f. 1955; Man. Dir DOV LIPETZ.

'Am Oved' Ltd: POB 470, 22 Mazah St, POB 470, Tel-Aviv; tel. 3-291526; fax 3-298911; f. 1942; fiction, non-fiction, reference books, school and university textbooks, children's books, poetry, classics, science fiction; Man. Dir AHARON KRAUS.

Amichai Publishing House Ltd: 5 Yosef Hanassi St, Tel-Aviv 65236; tel. 3-284990; f. 1948; Man. Dir YITZHAK ORON.

Arabic Publishing House: POB 28049, 17A Hagra St, Tel-Aviv; tel. 3-371438; f. 1960; established by the Histadrut (trade union) organization; periodicals and books; Dir JOSEPH ELIAHOU; Editor-in-Chief IBRAHIM M. IBRAHIM.

Carta, The Israel Map and Publishing Co Ltd: POB 2500, Yad Haruzim St, Jerusalem 91024; tel. 2-733501; fax 2-734882; f. 1958; the principal cartographic publisher; Chair. EMANUEL HAUSMAN; Pres. and CEO SHAY HAUSMAN.

Dvir Publishing Co Ltd: POB 22383, 32 Schocken St, Tel-Aviv; tel. 3-6812244; f. 1924; literature, science, art, education; Publrs O. ZMORA, A. BITAN.

Eked Publishing House: POB 11138, 29 Bar-Kochba St, Tel-Aviv; tel. 3-5283648; fax 3-5283648; f. 1959; poetry, belles lettres, fiction; Man. Dir MARITZA ROSMAN.

Encyclopedia Publishing Co: 29 Jabotinski St, Jerusalem; tel. 2-632310; fax 2-611699; f. 1947; Hebrew Encyclopedia and other encyclopaedias; Chair. ALEXANDER PELI.

Rodney Franklin Agency: POB 37727, 5 Karl Netter St, Tel-Aviv 61376; tel. 3-5600724; fax 3-5600479; exclusive representative of various British and USA publishers; Dir RODNEY FRANKLIN.

Gazit: POB 4190, 8 Zvi Brook St, Tel-Aviv; tel. 3-53730; art publishers; Editor GABRIEL TALPHIR.

Hakibbutz Hameuchad Publishing House Ltd: POB 16040, 27 Sutin St, Tel-Aviv 64684; tel. 3-5452228; fax 3-5230022; f. 1940; general; Dir UZI SHAVIT.

Hanitzotz A-Sharara Publishing House: POB 1575, Jerusalem; tel. 2-255382; fax 2-251614; 'progressive' booklets and publications in Arabic, Hebrew and English.

Israeli Music Publications Ltd: POB 7681, 25 Keren Hayesod St, Jerusalem 91076; tel. 2-251370; fax 2-241378; f. 1949; books on music and musical works; Dir of Music Publications MANDY FEINGERS.

Izre'el Publishing House Ltd: 76 Dizengoff St, Tel-Aviv; tel. 3-285350; f. 1933; Man. ALEXANDER IZRE'EL.

The Jerusalem Publishing House Ltd: POB 7147, 39 Tchernechovski St, Jerusalem 91071; tel. 2-636511; fax 2-634266; f. 1967; biblical research, history, encyclopaedias, archaeology, arts of the Holy Land, cookbooks, guide books, economics, politics; Dir SHLOMO S. GAFNI; Man. Editor RACHEL GILON.

Jewish History Publications (Israel 1961) Ltd: POB 1232, 29 Jabotinski St, Jerusalem; tel. 2-632310; fax 2-611699; f. 1961; encyclopaedias, World History of the Jewish People series; Chair. ALEXANDER PELI; Editor-in-Chief Prof. J. PRAWER.

Karni Publishers Ltd: POB 22383, 32 Schocken St, Tel-Aviv 61223; tel. 3-6812244; fax 3-6826138; f. 1951; children's and educational books; Publrs O. ZMORA, A. BITAN.

Keter Publishing House Jerusalem Ltd: POB 7145, Givat Shaul B, Jerusalem 91071; tel. 2-521201; telex 25275; fax 2-536811; f. 1959; original and translated works in all fields of science and humanities, published in English, French, German, other European languages and Hebrew; publishing imprints: Israel Program for Scientific Translations, Israel Universities Press, Keter Books, Encyclopedia Judaica; Man. Dir BARRY LIPPMAN.

Kiryat Sefer: 15 Arlosoroff St, Jerusalem; tel. 2-521141; f. 1933; concordances, dictionaries, textbooks, maps, scientific books; Dir AVRAHAM SIVAN.

Ma'ariv Book Guild Ltd: 3 Rehov Hilazon, Ramat-Gan 52522; tel. 3-5752020; fax 3-7525906; f. 1954 as Sifriat-Ma'ariv Ltd; Man. Dir IZCHAK KFIR; Editor-in-Chief ARYEH NIR.

Magnes Press: The Hebrew University, POB 7695, Jerusalem 91076; tel. 2-660341; telex 25391; fax 2-633370; f. 1929; biblical studies, Judaica, and all academic fields; Dir DAN BENOVICI.

Rubin Mass Ltd: POB 990, 7 Haaynhet St, Jerusalem 91009; tel. 2-277863; telex 26144; fax 2-277864; f. 1927; Hebraica, Judaica, export of all Israeli publications; Dir OREN MASS.

Massada Press Ltd: POB 1232, 29 Jabotinski St, Jerusalem; tel. 2-632310; fax 2-611699; f. 1961; encyclopaedias, the arts, educational material, children's books; Chair. ALEXANDER PELI.

Ministry of Defence Publishing House: 27 David Elazar St, Hakiriya, Tel-Aviv 67673; tel. 3-6917940; fax 3-6975509; f. 1939; military literature, Judaism, history and geography of Israel; Dir YOSI PERLOVITZ.

M. Mizrachi Publishing House: 106 Allenby Rd, Tel-Aviv; tel. 3-621492; fax 3-5660274; f. 1960; children's books, novels; Dir MEIR MIZRACHI.

Mosad Harav Kook: POB 642, Jerusalem; tel. 2-526231; f. 1937; editions of classical works, Torah and Jewish studies; Dir Rabbi M. KATZENELENBOGEN.

Otsar Hamoreh: POB 303, 8 Ben Saruk, Tel-Aviv; tel. 3-260211; f. 1951; educational.

Alexander Peli Jerusalem Publishing Co Ltd: POB 1232, 29 Jabotinski St, Jerusalem; tel. 2-632310; fax 2-611699; f. 1977; encyclopaedias, Judaica, history, the arts, educational material; Chair. ALEXANDER PELI.

Schocken Publishing House Ltd: POB 2316, 24 Nathan Yelin Mor St, Tel-Aviv 67015; tel. 3-5610130; fax 3-5622668; f. 1938; general; Dir Mrs RACHELI EDELMAN.

Shikmona Publishing Co Ltd: POB 7145, Givat Shaul B, Jerusalem 91071; tel. 2-521201; telex 25275; fax 2-536811; f. 1965; Zionism, archaeology, art, guide-books, fiction and non-fiction; Man. Dir BARRY LIPPMAN.

Sifriat Poalim Ltd: 2 Choma Umigdal St, Tel-Aviv 67771; tel. 3-376845; fax 3-378948; f. 1939; general literature; Gen. Man. NATHAN SHAHAM.

Sinai Publishing Co: 72 Allenby St, Tel-Aviv 65172; tel. 3-663672; f. 1853; Hebrew books and religious articles; Dir MOSHE SCHLESINGER.

World Zionist Organization Torah Education Dept: POB 7044, Jerusalem 91070; tel. 2-632584; telex 25236; fax 2-202697; f. 1945; education, Jewish philosophy, studies in the Bible, children's books published in Hebrew, English, French, Spanish, German, Swedish and Portuguese.

Yachdav United Publishers Co Ltd: POB 20123, 29 Carlebach St, Tel-Aviv; tel. 3-5614121; fax 3-5611996; f. 1960; educational; Chair. EPHRAIM BEN-DOR; Exec. Dir AMNON BEN-SHMUEL.

Yavneh Publishing House Ltd: 4 Mazeh St, Tel-Aviv 65213; tel. 3-297856; telex 35770; fax 3-293638; f. 1932; general; Dir AVSHALOM ORENSTEIN.

S. Zack and Co: 2 King George St, Jerusalem 94429; tel. 2-257819; fax 2-252493; f. c. 1930; fiction, science, philosophy, Judaism, children's books, educational and reference books, dictionaries; Dir MICHAEL ZACK.

PUBLISHERS' ASSOCIATION

Israel Book Publishers Association: POB 20123, 29 Carlebach St, Tel-Aviv 67132; tel. 3-5614121; fax 3-5611996; f. 1939; mems: 84 publishing firms; Chair. RACHELI EDELMAN and OHAD ZMORA; Man. Dir AMNON BEN-SHMUEL.

Radio and Television

In 1991 there were an estimated 2,290,000 radio receivers and 1,310,000 television receivers in use.

RADIO

Israel Broadcasting Authority (IBA) (Radio): POB 6387, Jerusalem; tel. 2-222121; telex 26488; f. 1948; station in Jerusalem with additional studios in Tel-Aviv and Haifa. IBA broadcasts six programmes for local and overseas listeners on medium, short-wave and VHF/FM in 16 languages: Hebrew, Arabic, English, Yiddish, Ladino, Romanian, Hungarian, Moghrabit, Persian, French, Russian, Bucharian, Georgian, Portuguese, Spanish and Amharic; Chair. MICHA YINON; Dir-Gen. URI PORAT; Dir of Radio (vacant);Dir External Services VICTOR GRAJEWSKY.

Galei Zahal: MPOB 01005, Zahal; tel. 3-814888; fax 3-814697; f. 1950; Israeli defence forces broadcasting station, Tel-Aviv, with studios in Jerusalem; broadcasts music, news and other programmes on medium-wave and FM stereo, 24-hour in Hebrew; Dir MOSHE SHLENSKY; Dir of Engineering G. KERNER.

TELEVISION

Israel Broadcasting Authority (IBA): POB 7139, Jerusalem 91071; tel. 2-301333; telex 25301; fax 2-301345; broadcasts began in 1968; station in Jerusalem with additional studios in Tel-Aviv; one colour network (VHF with UHF available in all areas); broadcasts in Hebrew, Arabic and English; Dir of Television J. BAR-EL; Dir of Engineering D. YOGEV.

Israel Educational Television: Ministry of Education and Culture, 14 Klausner St, Tel-Aviv; tel. 3-6466666; telex 342325; fax 3-6429291; f. 1966 by Hanadiv (Rothschild Memorial Group) as Instructional Television Trust; began transmission in 1966; school programmes form an integral part of the syllabus in a wide range of subjects; also adult education; Gen. Man. YAAKOV LORBERBAUM; Dir of Engineering A. KAPLAN.

In September 1986 the Government approved the establishment of a commercial radio and television network to be run in competition with the state system.

Finance

(cap. = capital; p.u. = paid up; dep. = deposits; m. = million; res = reserves; brs = branches)

BANKING

Central Bank

Bank of Israel: POB 780, Bank of Israel Bldg, Kiryat Ben Gurion, Jerusalem 91007; tel. 2-552211; telex 25214; fax 2-528805; f. 1954 as the Central Bank of the State of Israel; cap. and res 320m. new shekels, dep. 42,633m. new shekels (April 1994); Gov. Prof. JACOB A. FRENKEL; 2 brs.

Principal Israeli Banks

American Israel Bank Ltd: POB 1346, 62 Rothschild Blvd, Tel-Aviv 61013; tel. 3-5647021; telex 341217; fax 3-5647114; f. 1933; subsidiary of Bank Hapoalim BM; total assets 2,509m. new shekels, dep. 2,328m. new shekels (Dec. 1993); Chair. Y. ELINAV; Man. Dir M. TSAFRIR; 19 brs.

Bank Hapoalim BM: POB 27, 50 Rothschild Blvd, Tel-Aviv 66883; tel. 3-5673333; telex 342342; fax 3-5607028; f. 1921 as the Workers' Bank, name changed as above 1961; total assets 94,134m. new shekels, dep. 70,772m. new shekels (Dec. 1992); Chair. Bd of Man. AMIRAM SIVAN; 351 brs in Israel and abroad.

Bank Leumi le-Israel BM: POB 2, 24–32 Yehuda Halevi St, Tel-Aviv 65546; tel. 3-5148111; telex 33586; fax 3-664496; f. 1902 as Anglo-Palestine Co; renamed Anglo-Palestine Bank 1930; reincorporated as above 1951; total assets 88,286m. new shekels, dep. 76,257m. new shekels (Dec. 1993); Chair. MOSHE SANBAR; Gen. Man. DAVID FRIEDMANN; 329 brs.

First International Bank of Israel Ltd: POB 29036, Shalom Mayer Tower, 9 Ahad Ha'am St, Tel-Aviv 65251; tel. 3-5196111; telex 341252; fax 3-5100316; f. 1972 as a result of a merger between The Foreign Trade Bank Ltd and Export Bank Ltd; total assets 17,556m. new shekels, cap. 11,341m. new shekels, dep. 13,429m. new shekels (Dec. 1993); Chair. YIGAL ARNON; Man. Dir SHLOMO PIOTRKOWSKY; 78 brs.

Industrial Development Bank of Israel Ltd: POB 33580, 2 Dafna St, Tel-Aviv 61334; tel. 3-6972727; telex 033646; fax 3-6972893; f. 1957; cap. 138.1m. new shekels, dep. 2,849.7m. new shekels, total assets 3,220.3m. new shekels (Dec. 1992); Chair. ARIE SHEER; Gen. Man. YEHOSHUA ICHILOV.

Israel Bank of Agriculture Ltd: POB 2440, 83 Hahashmonaim St, Tel-Aviv 61024; tel. (3) 285141; telex 35739; f. 1951; total assets 809.2m. new shekels, cap. p.u. 20.2m. new shekels, dep. 726.3m. new shekels (Dec. 1990); Chair. GIDON MAKOFF; Gen. Man. ISRAEL RAUCH.

Euro-Trade Bank Ltd: POB 37318, 41 Rothschild Blvd, Tel-Aviv 61372; tel. 3-5643813; telex 371530; fax 3-5602483; f. 1953; total assets 67.5m. new shekels, dep. 44.8m. new shekels (Dec. 1992); Chair. SHOSHANA VAYINSHEL; Man. Dir MENAHEM WEBER.

Israel Continental Bank Ltd: POB 37406, 65 Rothschild Blvd, Tel-Aviv 61373; tel. 3-5641616; telex 341447; fax 3-200399; f. 1974; capital held jointly by Bank Hapoalim BM (62%) and Bank für Gemeinwirtschaft AG (38%); total assets 994.1m. new shekels, cap. and res 125.6m. new shekels, dep. 859.4m. new shekels (Dec. 1993); Chair. A. SIVAN; Man. Dir P. HOREV; 3 brs.

Israel Discount Bank Ltd: 27-31 Yehuda Halevi St, Tel-Aviv 65136; tel. 3-5145555; telex 33724; fax 3-5145346; f. 1935; cap. p.u. 933,944 new shekels, dep. 45,921m. new shekels (Dec. 1993);

Chair. GIDEON LAHAV; Man. Dir AVRAHAM ASHERI; some 250 brs in Israel and abroad.

Israel General Bank Ltd: POB 677, 38 Rothschild Blvd, Tel-Aviv 61006; tel. 3-5645645; telex 33515; fax 3-5645210; f. 1934 as Palestine Credit Utility Bank Ltd, name changed as above 1964; total assets US $497.1m., dep. US $456.44m. (Dec. 1992); Chair. Baron EDMOND DE ROTHSCHILD; Man. Dir ELIEZER YONES; 3 brs.

Leumi Industrial Development Bank Ltd: POB 2, 19 Rothschild Blvd, Tel-Aviv 65121; tel. 3-5148111; telex 33586; fax 3-5148560; f. 1944; subsidiary of Bank Leumi le-Israel BM; cap. and res 24m. new shekels, dep. 410m. new shekels (Dec. 1992); Chair. J. HURWITZ; Gen. Man. M. ZIV.

Maritime Bank of Israel Ltd: POB 29373, 16 Ahad Ha'am St, Tel-Aviv 65142; tel. 3-663111; telex 33507; fax 3-661735; f. 1962; total assets 370.6m. new shekels, dep. 311.2m. new shekels (Dec. 1992); Chair. SHIMON TOPOR; Man. Dir JOSEPH WEGRZYN.

Union Bank of Israel Ltd: POB 2428, 6–8 Ahuzat Bayit St, Tel-Aviv 65143; tel. 3-5191631; telex 33493; fax 3-5191274; f. 1951; subsidiary of Bank Leumi le-Israel BM; total assets 4,080.5m. new shekels, dep. 3,753.1m. new shekels (Dec. 1991); Chair. D. FRIEDMANN; Gen. Man. and CEO A. KACHERGINSKI; 25 brs.

United Mizrahi Bank Ltd: POB 309, 13 Rothschild Blvd, Tel-Aviv 61002; tel. 3-629211; telex 03-3625; fax 3-614780; f. 1923 as Mizrahi Bank Ltd; 1969 absorbed Hapoel Hamizrahi Bank Ltd and name changed as above; total assets 19,866.2m. new shekels, dep. 17,457.6m. new shekels (Dec. 1991); Chair. CHAIM KUBERSKY; Man. Dir ITZHAK JAEGER; 80 brs.

Mortgage Banks

Discount Mortgage Bank Ltd: 16–18 Simtat Beit Hashoeva, Tel-Aviv 65814; tel. 3-5643111; fax 3-5661104; f. 1959; subsidiary of Israel Discount Bank Ltd; cap. p.u. 1.3m. new shekels, res 183.7m. new shekels (Dec. 1993); Chair. G. LAHAV; Jt Gen. Mans M. ELDAR, J. SHEMESH.

Leumi Mortgage Bank Ltd: POB 69, 31–37 Montefiore St, Tel-Aviv 61000; tel. 3-5648444; fax 3-5684334; f. 1921; subsidiary of Bank Leumi le-Israel BM; cap. and res 111m., dep. 5,354m. new shekels, total assets 5,490.6m. new shekels (Dec. 1992); Chair. A. ZELDMAN; Gen. Man. B. AVITAL; 102 brs.

Mishkan-Hapoalim Mortgage Bank Ltd: POB 1610, 2 Ibn Gvirol St, Tel-Aviv 64077; tel. 3-6970505; fax 3-6959662; f. 1950; subsidiary of Bank Hapoalim BM; total assets 8,289m. new shekels, dep. 10,268.3m. new shekels (Dec. 1993); Chair. M. OLENIK; Man. Dir A. KROIZER; 131 brs.

Mortgage and Savings Bank Ltd: POB 116, 49 Rothschild Blvd, Tel-Aviv 61000; f. 1922; subsidiary of First International Bank of Israel Ltd; cap. and res 1,558m. shekels (Dec. 1990); Chair. A. SACHAROV; Man. Dir E. SHANOON; 36 brs.

Tefahot, Israel Mortgage Bank Ltd: POB 93, 9 Heleni Hamalka St, Jerusalem 91000; tel. 2-755222; fax 2-755344; f. 1945; subsidiary of United Mizrahi Bank Ltd; cap. and res 542m. new shekels, total assets 12,081m. new shekels (Dec. 1993); Chair. C. KUBERSKY; Man. Dir URI WÜRZBURGER; 60 brs.

Foreign Banks

Barclays Discount Bank Ltd: POB 1292, 103 Allenby Rd, Tel-Aviv 65134; tel. 3-5143333; telex 33550; fax 3-5143444; f. 1971 by Barclays Bank International Ltd and Israel Discount Bank Ltd to incorporate Israel brs of Barclays; total assets 3,129m. new shekels, dep. 2,846.3m. new shekels (Dec. 1991); Chair. GIDEON LAHAV; Gen. Man. MOSHE NEUDORFER; 69 brs; wholly owned subsidiary: **Mercantile Bank of Israel Ltd,** POB 512, 24 Rothschild Blvd, Tel-Aviv; tel. 3-622541; telex 341344; fax 3-622949; f. 1924; total assets 124.6m. new shekels, cap. and res 15.3m. new shekels, dep. 107.1m. new shekels, (Dec. 1990); Dep. Chair. IAN D. POLTON; Gen. Man. LEON GERSHON.

Four branches of the Jordan-based **Cairo-Amman Bank** were opened in the occupied West Bank, between November 1986 and August 1987 to provide financial services for the Palestinian community. The branches operated in both Jordanian dinars and Israeli shekels and were subject to dual Jordanian and Israeli regulatory authority. The Palestinian uprising in the Occupied Territories and Jordan's severance of legal and administrative links with the West Bank in July 1988 may result in the closure of these branches.

STOCK EXCHANGE

Tel-Aviv Stock Exchange: POB 29060, 54 Ahad Ha'am St, Tel-Aviv 65202; tel. 3-5677411; telex 341762; fax 3-5105379; f. 1953; Chair. HAIM STOESSEL; Gen. Man. SAUL BRONFELD.

INSURANCE

The Israel Insurance Association lists 35 companies, a selection of which are listed below; not all companies are members of the association.

Ararat Insurance Co Ltd: Ararat House, 13 Montefiore St, Tel-Aviv 65164; tel. 3-640888; telex 341484; f. 1949; Co-Chair. AHARON DOVRAT, PHILIP ZUCKERMAN; Gen. Man. PINCHAS COHEN.

Aryeh Insurance Co of Israel Ltd: 9 Ahad Ha'am St, Tel-Aviv 65251; tel. 3-5172671; telex 342125; fax 3-5179337; f. 1948; Chair. YEDIDIA GREENBERG.

Clal Insurance Co Ltd: POB 326, 42 Rothschild Blvd, Tel-Aviv 61002; tel. 3-627711; telex 341701; fax 3-622666; f. 1962; Man. Dir R. BEN-SHAOUL.

Hassneh Insurance Co of Israel Ltd: POB 805, 115 Allenby St, Tel-Aviv 61007; tel. 3-5649111; telex 341105; f. 1924; Man. Dir M. MICHAEL MILLER.

Israel Phoenix Assurance Co Ltd: 30 Levontin St, Tel-Aviv 65116; tel. 3-5670111; telex 341199; fax 3-5601242; f. 1949; Chair. of Board JOSEPH D. HACKMEY; Man. Dir Dr ITAMAR BOROWITZ.

Maoz Insurance Co Ltd: Tel-Aviv; f. 1945; formerly Binyan Insurance Co Ltd; Chair. B. YEKUTIELI.

Menorah Insurance Co Ltd: Menorah House, 73 Rothschild Blvd, Tel-Aviv 65786; tel. 3-5260771; telex 341433; fax 3-5618288; f. 1935; Gen.-Man. SHABTAI ENGEL.

Migdal Insurance Co Ltd: POB 37633, 26 Sa'adiya Ga'on St, Tel-Aviv 61375; tel. 3-5637637; telex 32361; part of Bank Leumi Group; f. 1934; Chair. S. GROFMAN; CEO U. LEVY.

Palglass Palestine Plate Glass Insurance Co Ltd: Tel-Aviv 65541; f. 1934; Gen. Man. AKIVA ZALZMAN.

Sahar Israel Insurance Co Ltd: POB 26222, Sahar House, 23 Ben-Yehuda St, Tel-Aviv 63806; tel. 3-5140311; telex 33759; f. 1949; Chair. Y. HAMBURGER (acting); Gen. Man. M. HARPAZ.

Samson Insurance Co Ltd: POB 33678, Avgad Bldg, 5 Jabotinski Rd, Ramat-Gan 52520, Tel-Aviv; tel. 3-7521616; fax 3-7516644; f. 1933; Chair. E. BEN-AMRAM; Gen. Man. GIORA SAGI.

Sela Insurance Co Ltd: 53 Rothschild Blvd, Tel-Aviv 65124; tel. 3-61028; telex 35744; f. 1938; Man. Dir E. SHANI.

Shiloah Co Ltd: 2 Pinsker St, Tel-Aviv 63322; f. 1933; Gen. Man. Dr S. BAMIRAH; Man. Mme BAMIRAH.

Yardenia Insurance Co Ltd: 22 Maze St, Tel-Aviv 65213; f. 1948; Man. Dir H. LEBANON.

Zion Insurance Co Ltd: POB 1425, 41–45 Rothschild Blvd, Tel-Aviv 61013; f. 1935; Chair. A. R. TAIBER.

Trade and Industry

CHAMBERS OF COMMERCE

Federation of Israeli Chambers of Commerce: POB 20027, 84 Hahashmonaim St, Tel-Aviv 67011; tel. 3-5612444; telex 33484; fax 3-5612614; co-ordinates the Tel-Aviv, Jerusalem, Haifa and Beer-sheba Chambers of Commerce; Dir ZVI AMIT.

Jerusalem Chamber of Commerce: POB 2083, 10 Hillel St, Jerusalem 91020; tel. 2-254333; fax 2-254335; f. 1908; c. 300 mems; Pres. JOSEPH PERLMAN; Dir-Gen. SHLOMO NAHMIAS.

Haifa Chamber of Commerce and Industry (Haifa and District): POB 33176, 53 Haatzmaut Rd, Haifa 31331; tel. 4-626364; fax 4-645428; f. 1921; 700 mems; Pres. S. GANTZ; Man. Dir C. WINNYKAMIN.

Chamber of Commerce, Tel-Aviv-Jaffa: POB 20027, 84 Hahashmonaim St, Tel-Aviv 61200; tel. 3-5612444; telex 33484; fax 3-5612614; f. 1919; 1,800 mems; Pres. DAN GILLERMAN; Man. Dir ZVI AMIT.

Federation of Bi-National Chambers of Commerce and Industry with and in Israel: 76 Ibn Gvirol St, Tel-Aviv; tel. 3-264790; telex 342315; fax 3-221783; federates: Israel-America Chamber of Commerce and Industry; Israel-British Chamber of Commerce; Australia-Israel Chambers of Commerce; Chamber of Commerce and Industry Israel-Asia; Chamber of Commerce Israel-Belgique-Luxembourg; Canada-Israel Chamber of Commerce and Industry; Israel-Denmark Chamber of Commerce; Chambre de Commerce Israel-France; Chamber of Commerce and Industry Israel-Germany; Camera di Commercio Israeli-Italia; Israel-Japan Chamber of Commerce; Israel-Latin America, Spain and Portugal Chamber of Commerce; Netherlands-Israel Chamber of Commerce; Israel-Yugoslavia Chamber of Commerce; Israel-Greece Chamber of Commerce; Israel-Bulgaria Chamber of Commerce; Israel-Ireland Chamber of Commerce; Handelskammer Israel-Schweiz; Israel-South Africa Chamber of Commerce; Israel-Sweden Chamber of Commerce; Israel-Hungary Chamber of Commerce; Israel-Romania Chamber of Commerce; Israel-Russia Chamber of Commerce; Israel-Poland Chamber of Commerce; also incorporates Bi-National Chamber of Commerce existing in 20 foreign countries with Israel; Chair. J. ZIV; Vice-Chair. BEZALEL BLEI.

Israel-British Chamber of Commerce: POB 4610, 65 Allenby Road, Tel-Aviv 61046; tel. 3-5252232; telex 342315; fax 3-203032; f. 1951; 350 mems; Chair. GAD PROPPER; Exec. Dir FELIX KIPPER.

TRADE AND INDUSTRIAL ORGANIZATIONS

Agricultural Export Co (AGREXCO): Tel-Aviv; state-owned agricultural marketing organization; Dir-Gen. AMOTZ AMIAD.

The Agricultural Union: Tchlenov 20, Tel-Aviv; consists of more than 50 agricultural settlements and is connected with marketing and supplying organizations, and Bahan Ltd, controllers and auditors.

Central Union of Artisans and Small Manufacturers: POB 4041, Tel-Aviv 61040; f. 1907; has a membership of more than 40,000 divided into 70 groups according to trade; the union is led by a 17-man Presidium; Chair. JACOB FRANK; Sec. ITZHAK HASSON; 30 brs.

Citrus Marketing Board: POB 80, Beit Dagan 50250; tel. 3-9683811; fax 3-9683838; f. 1942; the growers' institution for the control of the Israel citrus industry; jointly owned by the Government and the growers. Functions: control of plantations, supervision of picking and packing operations, marketing of the crop overseas and on the home markets; shipping; supply of fertilizers, insecticides, equipment for orchards and packing houses and of packing materials, technical research and extension work; long-term financial assistance to growers; representing the citrus industry in international organizations; Chair. Y. KAPLAN; Gen. Man. M. DAVIDSON.

Cotton Production and Marketing Board: POB 384, Herzlia B'46103; tel. 3-509491; telex 32120; fax 3-509159.

Farmers' Union of Israel: POB 209, 8 Kaplan St, Tel-Aviv; tel. 3-69502227; fax 3-6918228; f. 1913; membership of 7,000 independent farmers, citrus and winegrape growers; Pres. PESACH GRUPPER; Dir-Gen. SHLOMO REISMAN.

General Association of Merchants in Israel: 6 Rothschild Blvd, Tel-Aviv; the organization of retail traders; has a membership of 30,000 in 60 brs.

Israel Diamond Exchange Ltd: POB 3222, Ramat-Gan, Tel-Aviv; tel. 3-5760211; fax 3-5750652; f. 1937; production, export, import and finance facilities; estimated exports (1993) US $3,011m.; Pres. ITZHAK FOREM.

Israel Export Institute: POB 50084, 29 Rehov Hamered, Tel-Aviv 61500; tel. 3-5142830; fax 3-5142902; Dir-Gen. DAVID LITVAK.

Israel Fruit Production Board: 119 Rehov Hahashmonaim, Tel-Aviv 61070; tel. 3-5610811; fax 3-5614672; Dir-Gen. EZRA MEIR.

Israel Journalists' Association Ltd: 4 Kaplan St, Tel-Aviv; tel. 3-256141; Sec. YONA SHIMSHI.

Kibbutz Industries Association: 8 Rehov Shaul Hamelech, Tel-Aviv 64733; tel. 3-6955413; fax 3-6951464; responsible for marketing and export of the goods produced by Israel's kibbutzim; Pres. MILHA HERTZ.

Manufacturers' Association of Israel: POB 50022, Industry House, 29 Hamered St, Tel-Aviv 61500; tel. 3-5198787; fax 3-662026; 1,000 mem.-enterprises employing nearly 72% of industrial workers in Israel; Pres. DAN PROPPER; Dir-Gen. YORAM BLIZOVSKY.

MAJOR INDUSTRIAL COMPANIES

Elbit Ltd: POB 539, Haifa 31053; tel. 04-315315; telex 46586; fax 04-550002; producers of computers and defence electronics; subsidiary of ELRON Electronic Industries; sales $176m., profits $16m. (1986/87); Pres. and CEO EMMANUEL GILL.

Elscint Ltd: Haifa; tel. 310310; telex 46656; fax 525608; f. 1969; designers and mfrs of electronic medical diagnostic equipment (body and brain scanners), nuclear medicine cameras and processors, whole body computerized tomographers, magnetic resonance imagers (MRI) and ultrasound scanners; Pres. SHMUEL PARAG; 1,800 employees.

Israel Aircraft Industries Ltd (IAI): Lod; telex 37114; f. 1953; 96% govt-owned; designers and mfrs of military and civil aircraft; Dir-Gen. MOSHE KERET; 21,000 employees.

Israel Chemicals: frmly largest State-owned industrial concern; privatized 1988.

Koor Industries Ltd: Tel-Aviv; telex 33758; Israel's largest industrial company; subsidiary of Hevrat Haovdim, the Histadrut's (the National Labour Federation) industrial arm; Man. Dir BENNY GAON; 31,000 employees (June 1988).

Polgat Industries: mfrs of textiles; Chair. ISRAEL POLLACK.

Scitex Ltd: Herzliya; telex 341939; f. 1968; mfr of computerized imaging equipment for the publishing industry; Chair. and CEO ARIE ROSENFELD.

Soltam: mfr of artillery; Man. Dir ELAZAR BARAK.

Tadiran Israel Electronics Industries Ltd: Givat Shmuel; telex 341692; Israel's leading mfr of civil and military electronics; subsidiary of Koor Industries Ltd.

The Histadrut

Hahistadrut Haklalit shel Haovdim Beeretz Israel (General Federation of Labour in Israel): 93 Arlosoroff St, Tel-Aviv 62098; tel. 3-6921111; telex 342488; fax 3-6969906; f. 1920; publs *Labour in Israel* (quarterly) in English, French, Spanish and German.

The General Federation of Labour in Israel, usually known as the Histadrut, is the largest voluntary organization in Israel, and the most important economic body in the state. It is open to all workers, including the self-employed, members of co-operatives and of the liberal professions, as well as housewives, students, pensioners and the unemployed. Members of two small religious labour organizations, Histadrut Hapoel Hamizrahi and Histadrut Poalei Agudat Israel, also belong to the trade union section and social services of the Histadrut, which thus extend to *c*. 85% of all workers. Dues—between 3.6% and 5.8% of wages—cover all its trade union, health insurance and social service activities. The Histadrut engages in four main fields of activity: trade union organization (with some 50 affiliated trade unions and 65 local labour councils operating throughout the country); social services (including a comprehensive health insurance scheme 'Kupat Holim', pension and welfare funds, etc.); educational and cultural activities (vocational schools, workers' colleges, theatre and dance groups, sports clubs, youth movement); and economic development (undertaken by Hevrat Ovdim (Labour Economy), which includes industrial enterprises partially or wholly owned by the Histadrut, agricultural and transport co-operatives, workers' bank, insurance company, publishing house etc.). A women's organization, Na'amat, which also belongs to the Histadrut, operates nursery homes and kindergartens, provides vocational education and promotes legislation for the protection and benefit of working women. The Histadrut publishes its own daily newspaper, *Davar*, in Hebrew. The Histadrut is a member of the ICFTU and its affiliated trade secretariats, APRO, ICA and various international professional organizations.

Secretary-General: HAIM RAMON.

ORGANIZATION

In 1989 the Histadrut had a membership of 1,630,000. In addition some 110,000 young people under 18 years of age belong to the Organization of Working and Student Youth, a direct affiliate of the Histadrut.

All members take part in elections to the Histadrut Convention (Veida), which elects the General Council (Moetsa) and the Executive Committee (Vaad Hapoel). The latter elects the 41-member Executive Bureau (Vaada Merakezet), which is responsible for day-to-day implementation of policy. The Executive Committee also elects the Secretary-General, who acts as its chairman as well as head of the organization as a whole and chairman of the Executive Bureau. Nearly all political parties are represented on the Histadrut Executive Committee.

The Executive Committee has the following departments: Trade Union, Organization and Labour Councils, Education and Culture, Social Security, Industrial Democracy, Students, Youth and Sports, Consumer Protection, Administration, Finance and International.

TRADE UNION ACTIVITIES

Collective agreements with employers fix wage scales, which are linked with the retail price index; provide for social benefits, including paid sick leave and employers' contributions to sick and pension and provident funds; and regulate dismissals. Dismissal compensation is regulated by law. The Histadrut actively promotes productivity through labour management boards and the National Productivity Institute, and supports incentive pay schemes. There are some 50 trade unions affiliated to the Histadrut.

There are unions for the following groups: clerical workers, building workers, teachers, engineers, agricultural workers, technicians, textile workers, printing workers, diamond workers, metal workers, food and bakery workers, wood workers, government employees, seamen, nurses, civilian employees of the armed forces, actors, musicians and variety artists, social workers, watchmen, cinema technicians, institutional and school staffs, pharmacy employees, medical laboratory workers, X-ray technicians, physiotherapists, social scientists, microbiologists, psychologists, salaried lawyers, pharmacists, physicians, occupational therapists, truck and taxi drivers, hotel and restaurant workers, workers in Histadrut-owned industry, garment, shoe and leather workers, plastic and rubber workers, editors of periodicals, painters and sculptors and industrial workers.

Histadrut Trade Union Department: Dir HAIM HABERFELD.

ECONOMIC ACTIVITIES AND SOCIAL SERVICES

These include Hevrat Haovdim (Economic Sector, literally, 'the Workers' Company', employing 260,000 workers in 1983), Kupat

Holim (the Sick Fund, covering almost 77% of Israel's population), seven pension funds, and NA'AMAT (women's organization which runs nursery homes and kindergartens, organizes vocational education and promotes legislation for the protection and benefit of working women).

Other Trade Unions

General Federation of West Bank Trade Unions: Sec.-Gen. SHAHER SAAD.

Histadrut Haovdim Haleumit (National Labour Federation): 23 Sprintzak St, Tel-Aviv 64738; tel. 3-6958351; fax 3-261753; f. 1934; 170,000 mems.

Histadrut Hapoel Hamizrahi (National Religious Workers' Party): 166 Even Gavirol St, Tel-Aviv 62023; tel. 3-5442151; fax 3-5468942; 150,000 mems in 85 settlements and 15 kibbutzim; Sec.-Gen. ELIEZER ABTABI.

Histadrut Poale Agudat Israel (Agudat Israel Workers' Organization): POB 11044, 64 Frishman St, Tel-Aviv; tel. 3-5242126; fax 3-5230689; has 33,000 members in 16 settlements and 8 educational insts.

Transport

RAILWAYS

Freight traffic consists mainly of grain, phosphates, potash, containers, petroleum and building materials. Rail service serves Haifa and Ashdod ports on the Mediterranean Sea, while a combined rail-road service extends to Eilat port on the Red Sea. Passenger services operate between the main towns: Nahariya, Haifa, Tel-Aviv and Jerusalem. In 1988 the National Ports Authority assumed responsibility for the rail system.

Israel Railways: POB 18085, Central Station, Tel-Aviv 61180; tel. 3-6937401; telex 46570; fax 3-5421488; the total length of main line is 530 km and there are 170 km of branch line; gauge 1,435 mm; Gen. Man. JACOV SHEN-ZUR; Deputy Gen. Mans DORON IZRAELI, HANOCH BEN-ELIAHU.

Underground Railway

Haifa Underground Funicular Railway: 122 Hanassi Ave, Haifa 34633; tel. 04-376861; fax 04-376875; opened 1959; 2 km in operation; Man. D. SCHARF.

ROADS

In 1990 there were 13,181 km of paved roads, of which 7,790 km were urban roads, 4,088 km non-urban roads and 1,303 km access roads.

Ministry of Housing and Construction: POB 13198, Public Works Dept, 23 Hillel St, Jerusalem; tel. 2-277211; fax 2-823532.

SHIPPING

In 1990 Israel had a merchant fleet of 69 ships.

Haifa and Ashdod are the main ports in Israel. The former is a natural harbour, enclosed by two main breakwaters and dredged to 45 ft below mean sea-level. In 1965 the deep water port was completed at Ashdod which had a capacity of about 8.6m. tons in 1988.

The port of Eilat is Israel's gate to the Red Sea. It is a natural harbour, operated from a wharf. Another port, to the south of the original one, started operating in 1965. Gaza port fulfils the needs of the Gaza Strip.

The Israel Ports and Railways Authority: POB 20121, Maya Building, 74 Petach Tikva Rd, Tel-Aviv 61201; tel. 3-5657070; fax 3-5617142; f. 1961; to plan, build, develop, administer, maintain and operate the ports and railways. In 1988/89 investment plans amounted to US $68m. for the development budget in Haifa, Ashdod and Eilat ports. Cargo traffic April 1989–March 1990 amounted to 16.2m. tons (oil excluded); Chair. ZVI KEINAN; Dir-Gen. Ing. SHAUL RAZIEL.

ZIM Israel Navigation Co Ltd: POB 1723, 7–9 Pal-Yam Ave, Haifa 31000; tel. 04-652111; telex 46501; fax 04-652956; f. 1945; runs cargo and container services in the Mediterranean and to northern Europe, North, South and Central America, the Far East, Africa and Australia; operates 79 ships (including 6 general cargo ships, 23 container ships, 7 multipurpose ships, 1 bulk carrier and 1 pure car carrier); total cargo carried: more than 10.7m. metric tons in 1993; Chair. SHOUL N. EISENBERG; Pres. and CEO MATTY MORGENSTERN.

CIVIL AVIATION

Israel Airports Authority: Ben-Gurion International Airport, Tel-Aviv; tel. 3-9712804; telex 381050; fax 3-9721722; Dir-Gen. MOTI DABI.

El Al Israel Airlines Ltd: POB 41, Ben Gurion International Airport, Tel-Aviv; tel. 3-9716111; telex 381007; fax 3-9721442; f. 1948; the Government is the major stockholder; daily services to most capitals of Europe; over 20 flights weekly to New York; services to the USA, Canada, China, Egypt, Kenya, South Africa, Thailand and Turkey; Pres. RAPHAEL HARLEV.

Arkia Israeli Airlines Ltd: POB 39301, Sde-Dov Airport, Tel-Aviv 61392; tel. 3-6902222; telex 341749; fax 3-6991390; f. 1980 through merger of Kanaf-Arkia Airlines and Aviation Services; scheduled passenger services linking Tel-Aviv, Jerusalem, Haifa, Eilat, Rosh Pina and Masada; charter services to European destinations; Chair. Y. ARNON; Pres. ISRAEL BOROVICH.

Tourism

In 1992 some 1.6m. tourists visited Israel.

Ministry of Tourism: POB 1018, 24 King George St, Jerusalem 91000; tel. 2-754811; telex 26115; fax 2-250890; Minister of Tourism UZI BARAM; Dir-Gen. ELI GONEN.

Defence

The General Staff: This consists of the Chiefs of the General Staff, Manpower, Logistics and Intelligence Branches of the Defence Forces, the Commanders of the Air Force and the Navy, and the officers commanding the three Regional Commands (Northern, Central and Southern). It is headed by the Chief of Staff of the Armed Forces.

Chief of Staff of the Armed Forces: Lt-Gen. EHUD BARAK.

Head of Ground Forces Command: Maj.-Gen. ISRAEL TAL.

Commander of the Air Force: Maj.-Gen. AVIHU BIN-NUN.

Commander of the Navy: Rear-Admiral AVRAHAM BEN SHOSHAN.

Defence Budget (1994): 20,200m. new shekels (US $7,200m.).

Military Service (Jewish and Druze population only; Christians and Arabs may volunteer): Officers are conscripted for regular service of 48 months, men 36 months, women 21 months. Annual training as reservists thereafter, to age 45 for men (54 for some specialists), 24 (or marriage) for women.

Total Armed Forces (June 1994): 172,000: including 138,500 conscripts; this can be raised to 602,000 by mobilizing the 430,000 reservists within 48–72 hours; army 134,000 (114,700 conscripts; navy 6,000–7,000 (2,000–3,000 conscripts); air force 32,000 (21,800 conscripts).

Paramilitary Forces (June 1994): 6,000.

Education

The present-day school system is based on the Compulsory Education Law (1949), the State Education Law (1953), the School Inspection Law (1969) and on certain provisions of the 1933 Education Ordinance dating back to the British Mandatory Administration. The first of these introduced free compulsory primary education for all children aged between the ages of 5 and 13 (one year kindergarten, eight years' elementary schooling). This law was extended, with the school reform of 1968, to include the ninth and tenth grades. In the 1979/80 school year free, but not compulsory, education was extended up to and including the twelfth grade.

The State Education Law abolished the old complicated Trend Education System, and vested the responsibility for education in the Government, thus providing a unified state-controlled elementary school system. The law does, however, recognize two main forms of Primary Education—(a) State Education; (b) Recognized Non-State Education. State Education can be sub-divided into two distinct categories of schools—State Schools and State Religious Schools where the language of instruction is Hebrew, and State Schools where the language of instruction is Arabic. Schools and kindergartens of the state system are in the joint ownership of the state and the local authorities, while the recognized non-state institutions are essentially privately-owned and mainly religious, although they are subsidized, and supervised by the state and the local authorities.

The largest 'recognized' school system is the Agudat Israel Schools (ultra-orthodox religious). The others are mainly Christian denominational schools.

State Primary Education is financed by a partnership of the central government and the local authorities. Since 1953 the salaries of all teachers of State Schools have been paid by the central government, whilst the cost of maintenance and of maintenance services, and the provision of new buildings and equip-

ment have been the responsibility of the local authorities. The state does not impose an Education Tax but local authorities may, with the Ministry's approval, levy a rate on parents for special services.

The state provides schools in which the language of instruction is either Hebrew or Arabic according to the language spoken by the majority of the local population. Nevertheless, some Arab children attend Jewish secondary, vocational, agricultural and teacher-training colleges. In the Jewish sector there is a distinct line of division between the secular state schools and the Religious State Schools, which are established on the demand of parents in any locality, provided that a certain minimum number of pupils have first been enrolled. In the Arab Schools all instruction is in Arabic, and there is a special department for Arabic Education in the Ministry of Education and Culture. The administration of Arab education is in the process of being decentralized. Some 90% of the Arab children attend school regularly.

The Compulsory Education Law and the institutions it established for absorbing weak students have cancelled the need for special systems for working youth. The law provides special education for emotionally or physically handicapped children. In addition, special attention is given to those children who are culturally deprived and a great variety of methods are being devised to bring them up to the level of the other children.

Post-Primary Education is free, lasts six years, four of which are compulsory, and is divided into an intermediate and a higher level. The intermediate level provides general education and the higher level is roughly divided into academic; technical and vocational; and agricultural. The last two categories also have pre-academic streams lasting from one to two years and receive all the benefits of the regular post-primary schools. The pupils graduating from academic high school receive either a school leaving certificate or *bagrut* (matriculation). The *bagrut* certificate entitles the pupil to enter university, although the university is not obliged to accept him or her.

The frameworks offered by vocational and technical schools can be divided into three types: practical-technical; general-technical; and secondary technical. All three types are of three or four years' duration, depending on whether they are run under the Reform or under the old system. Very few of the practical-technical schools still offer a two-year course, i.e. a total of 11 years' schooling. The practical-technical schools train their pupils mainly for a profession and the ratio between general studies and vocational-technical studies is 40:60. The general-technical schools award a School Leaving Certificate to those pupils who complete the course successfully. This entitles them to continue their studies in the third level of education after some complementary examinations, either for one additional year to obtain a technician's certificate (Techna'i), or for two additional years to obtain the certificate of a practical engineer (Handessa'i). The ratio between general studies and vocational studies in these schools is 50:50. All graduates of the secondary technical schools may sit for the *bagrut* examinations. Even without achieving the *bagrut* certificate the pupils may continue their studies in the short-cycle post-secondary schools, described above, without further examination and obtain the technician or practical engineer certificate. The ratio between general studies and technical-vocational studies in these schools is 60:40. Those who graduate and complete their matriculation (*bagrut*) examinations are eligible for admission to any Israeli university.

Agricultural post-primary courses are of either three or four years' duration (again depending on the Reform) and some schools offer an additional year or year and a half (13th and 14th grade) leading to a practical engineer certificate. The holders of this certificate are eligible, without further examinations, for study in agricultural engineering or general agricultural higher studies in the Technion (the Israel Institute of Technology) at Haifa or the Faculty of Agriculture at the Hebrew University of Jerusalem. Unlike pupils at vocational-technical post-primary schools, all those completing agricultural courses may sit for the bagrut examinations. By and large, agricultural post-primary schools are boarding schools although some, mainly those of the kibbutz and the moshav movements, are regional day schools.

Adult Education. There is an extensive adult education programme. Programmes extend from literacy courses through primary and secondary level studies up to second-chance university facilities. There are post-army preparatory courses for entry into the university. High school courses may be completed in the army and in 1976 the Everyman's University began, based on the British model of Open University.

Teacher Training. Almost all kindergarten and primary school teachers are trained in three to three and a half year courses at post-secondary teacher training institutions (Mossadot Le-Hakhsharat Morim Ve Gananot). The Ministry's policy is to have only three-year teacher training colleges and to extend the training period to four years for a B.Ed. degree. Government regulations require that teachers for grades 7 to 10 have a BA and a university teaching certificate, while for grades 11 and 12 they are required to have a master's degree and a university teaching certificate. The *bagrut* certificate and a passing grade in the psychometric examination are required for admittance to the above teacher training institutions. In some of the teacher training schools there are special courses for instruction in Arabic education, in addition to separate Arab teacher training schools.

Bibliography

GENERAL

Avnery, Uri. *Israel without Zionists*. London, Collier-Macmillan, 1969.

Black, Ian, and Morris, Benny. *Israel's Secret Wars: History of Israel's Intelligence Services*. New York, Grove Weidenfeld, 1992.

Burr, Gerald. *Behind the Star: inside Israel today*. London, Constable, 1990.

Eban, Abba. *Personal Witness: Israel through my eyes*. London, Jonathan Cape, 1993.

Ellis, Mark H. *Beyond Innocence and Redemption: Confronting the Holocaust and Israeli Power*. San Francisco, Harper and Row, 1990.

Glueck, Nelson. *The River Jordan*. Philadelphia, 1946. *Rivers in the Desert*. London, 1959.

Hersh, Seymour. *The Samson Option: Israel, America and the Bomb*. London, Faber and Faber, 1991.

Koestler, Arthur. *The Thirteenth Tribe*. London, Random House, 1976.

Kohn, Hans. *Nationalism and Imperialism in the Hither East*. London, 1932.

Kollek, Teddy, and Pearlman, Moshe. *Jerusalem, Sacred City of Mankind*. London, Weidenfeld and Nicolson, 1968.

Marmorstein, Emile. *Heaven at Bay: The Jewish Kulturkampf in the Holy Land*. Oxford University Press, 1969.

Orni, E., and Efrat, E. *The Geography of Israel*. New York, Darey, 1965.

Parkes, J. W. *The Emergence of the Jewish Problem, 1878–1939*. Oxford, 1946.

    A History of Palestine from AD *135 to Modern Times*. London, Gollancz, 1949.

    End of Exile. New York, 1954.

    Whose Land? A History of the Peoples of Palestine. Harmondsworth, Pelican, 1970.

Patai, R. *Israel Between East and West*. Philadelphia, 1953.

    Culture and Conflict. New York, 1962.

Raviv, Dan, and Melman, Yossi. *Every Spy a Prince: the complete history of Israel's intelligence community*. Boston, Houghton Mifffin, 1990.

Shapiro, Harry L. *The Jewish People: a biological history*. UNESCO, 1960.

Tuchman, Barbara W. *Bible and Sword*. London, Redman, 1957; New York, Minerva, 1968.

Weingrod, Alex. *Reluctant Pioneers, Village Development in Israel*. New York, Cornell University Press, 1966.

Zander, Walter. *Israel and the Holy Places of Christendom*. Weidenfeld and Nicolson, 1972.

ANCIENT HISTORY

De Vaux, R. *Ancient Israel: Its Life and Institutions*. New York, 1961.

Orlinsky, H. M. *Ancient Israel*. Cornell University Press.

Smith, Sir G. A. *Historical Geography of the Holy Land*. 24th edn, London, 1931.

Yadin, Yigael. *Message of the Scrolls*. New York, Grosset and Dunlap.

    Masada. London, Weidenfeld and Nicolson, 1966.

RECENT HISTORY

Allon, Yigal. *The Making of Israel's Army*. London, Vallentine, Mitchell, 1970.

Barbour, Nevill. *Nisi Dominus: a survey of the Palestine Controversy*. London, Harrap, 1946, reprinted by the Institute for Palestine Studies, Beirut, 1969.

Bentwich, Norman and Helen. *Mandate Memories, 1918–1948*. London, Hogarth Press, 1965.

Bermant, Chaim. *Israel*. London, Thames and Hudson, 1967.

Berger, Earl. *The Covenant and the Sword, Arab-Israel Relations 1948–56*. Toronto, University of Toronto Press, 1965.

Bethell, Nicholas. *The Palestine Triangle: the Struggle Between the British, the Jews and the Arabs, 1935–48*. London, André Deutsch, 1979.

Cattan, Henry. *Palestine, the Arabs and Israel*. London, Longmans Green, 1969.

    The Palestine Question. London, Croom Helm; New York, Methuen, 1987.

Cohen, Michael J. *Palestine, Retreat from the Mandate: The Making of British Policy*. London, Elek, 1978.

Crossman, R. H. S. *Palestine Mission*. London, 1947.

Draper, T. *Israel and World Politics: Roots of the Third Arab-Israeli War*. London, Secker and Warburg, 1968.

Esco Foundation for Palestine. *Palestine: A Study of Jewish, Arab and British Policies*. 2 vols, New Haven, 1947.

Gabbay, Rony E. *A Political Study of the Arab-Jewish Conflict, the Arab Refugee Problem*. Geneva and Paris, 1959.

Green, Stephen. *Taking Sides: America and Israel in the Middle East, 1948–1967*. London, Faber and Faber, 1984.

    Living by the Sword: America and Israel in the Middle East, 1968–1987. London, Faber and Faber, 1988.

Grossman, David. *The Yellow Wind*. London, Jonathan Cape, 1988.

Howard, M., and Hunter, R. *Israel and the Arab World*. Beirut, Institute for Palestine Studies.

Jansen, Michael. *The Battle of Beirut*. London, Zed Press, 1982.

Jiryis, Sabri. *The Arabs in Israel*. Beirut, Institute for Palestine Studies, 1968.

Kader, Razzak Abdel. *The Arab-Jewish Conflict*. 1961.

Katz, Samuel M. *Guards without Frontiers: Israel's war against terrorism*. London, Arms and Armour Press, 1990.

Khalidi, Walid. *From Haven to Conquest: Readings in Zionism and the Palestine Problem until 1948*. Beirut, Institute for Palestine Studies, 1971.

Kimche, Jon. *Palestine or Israel*. London, Secker & Warburg, 1973.

Kimche, Jon and David. *Both Sides of the Hill: Britain and the Palestine War*. London, Secker and Warburg, 1960.

Koestler, Arthur. *Promise and Fulfilment: Palestine, 1917–1949*. London, 1949.

    Thieves in the Night. New York and London, 1946.

Landau, Jacob M. *The Arabs in Israel*. London, Oxford University Press, 1969.

Laqueur, Walter. *The Road to War 1967*. London, Weidenfeld and Nicolson, 1968.

    The Israel-Arab Reader. London, Weidenfeld and Nicolson, 1969.

Lilienthal, Alfred M. *The Other Side of the Coin: An American Perspective of the Arab-Israeli Conflict*. New York, 1965.

Lorch, N. *The Edge of the Sword: Israel's War of Independence 1947–49*. New York, Putnam, 1961.

Lucas, Noah. *The Modern History of Israel*. London, Weidenfeld and Nicolson, 1974–75.

McDowall, David. *Palestine and Israel: the uprising and beyond*. London, I.B. Tauris, 1989.

Marlowe, John. *The Seat of Pilate, An Account of the Palestine Mandate*. London, Cresset, 1959; Philadelphia, Dufour, 1958.

O'Ballance, E. *The Arab-Israeli War*. New York, Praeger, 1957.

    The Third Arab-Israeli War. London, Faber & Faber, 1972.

Oz, Amos. *In the Land of Israel*. London, Chatto and Windus, 1983.

Peretz, Don. *Israel and the Palestine Arabs*. Washington, The Middle East Institute, 1958.

    Intifada. Oxford, Westview Press, 1990.

Perlmutter, Amos. *Military and Politics in Israel, 1948–1967*. 2nd edn. London, Frank Cass, 1977.

    Politics and the Military in Israel, 1967–1976. London, Frank Cass, 1977.

Rabin, Yitzhak. *The Rabin Memoirs*. London, Weidenfeld and Nicolson, 1979.

Rizk, Edward. *The Palestine Question, Seminar of Arab Jurists on Palestine, Algiers, 1967*. Beirut, Institute for Palestine Studies, 1968.

Rodinson, Maxime. *Israel and the Arabs*. Harmondsworth, Penguin Books, 1968; New York, Pantheon, 1969.

Rouleau, Eric, and Held, Jean-Francis. *Israël et les Arabes*. Paris, Editions du Seuil, 1967.

Royal Institute of International Affairs. *Great Britain and Palestine 1915–45*. London, 1946.

Sachar, Howard M. *A History of Israel: Vol. I: From the Rise of Zionism to Our Time; Vol. II: From the Aftermath of the Yom Kippur War*. Corby, Oxford University Press, 1987.

Schiff, Ze'ev, and Ehud Ya'ari. *Israel's Lebanon War*. New York, Simon and Schuster, 1984.

   Intifada: the Palestinian uprising—Israel's third front. London, Simon and Shuster, 1990.

Schindler, Colin. *Ploughshares into Swords?: Israelis and Jews in the Shadow of the Intifada*. London, I. B. Tauris, 1992.

Sharabi, Hisham B. *Palestine and Israel: The Lethal Dilemma*. New York, Van Nostrand Reinhold, 1969.

Shipler, David K. *Arab and Jew: Wounded Spirits in a Promised Land*. London, Bloomsbury, 1987.

Sykes, Christopher. *Crossroads to Israel*. London, Collins, 1965.

Timerman, Jacob. *The Longest War*. London, Chatto and Windus, 1982.

Weizman, Ezer. *The Battle for Peace*. New York, Bantam Books, 1981.

Yaniv, Avner. *Dilemmas of Security—Politics, Strategy and the Israeli Experience in Lebanon*. Oxford, Oxford University Press, 1987.

THE STATE

Al-Haj, Majid, and Rosenfeld, Henry. *Arab Local Government in Israel*. Boulder, San Francisco and London, Westview Press, 1990.

Avi-hai, Avraham. *Ben Gurion, State Builder*. Israel Universities Press, 1974.

Badi, Joseph. *Fundamental Laws of the State of Israel*. New York, 1961.

Bar-Zohar, Michael. *Ben-Gurion: A Biography*. London, Weidenfeld and Nicolson, 1978.

Baruth, K. H. *The Physical Planning of Israel*. London, 1949.

Ben Gurion, D. *Rebirth and Destiny of Israel*. New York, 1954.

   Israel: A Personal History. London, New English Library, 1972.

Bentwich, Norman. *Fulfilment in the Promised Land 1917–37*. London, 1938.

   Judaea Lives Again. London, 1944.

   Israel Resurgent. Ernest Benn, 1960.

   The New-old Land of Israel. Allen and Unwin, 1960.

   Israel, Two Fateful Years 1967–69. London, Elek, 1970.

Brecher, Michael. *The Foreign Policy System of Israel*. London, Oxford University Press, 1972.

Comay, Joan, and Pearlman, Moshe. *Israel*. New York, 1965.

Crossman, R. H. S. *A Nation Reborn*. London, Hamish Hamilton, 1960.

Davis, Moshe (Ed.). *Israel: Its Role in Civilisation* New York, 1956.

Davis, Uri. *Israel: An Apartheid State*. London, Zed Press, 1987.

Dayan, Shmuel. *The Promised Land*. London, 1961.

De Gaury, Gerald. *The New State of Israel*. New York, 1952.

Eban, Abba. *The Voice of Israel*. New York, Horizon Press, 1957.

   The Story of Modern Israel. London, Weidenfeld and Nicolson, 1973.

Edelman, Maurice. *Ben Gurion, a Political Biography*. London, Hodder and Stoughton, 1964.

Frankel, William. *Israel Observed: An Anatomy of the State*. London, Thames and Hudson, 1980.

Hollis, Rosemary. *Israel on the Brink of Decision: division, unity and cross-currents in the Israeli body politic*. London, Research Institute for the Study of Conflict and Terrorism, 1990.

Janowsky, Oscar I. *Foundations of Israel: Emergence of a Welfare State*. Princeton, Anvil Nostrand Co, 1959.

Kraines, O. *Government and Politics in Israel*. London, Allen and Unwin, 1961.

Likhovski, Eliahu S. *Israel's Parliament: The Law of the Knesset*. Oxford, Clarendon Press, 1971.

Medding, Peter. *Mapai in Israel: Political Organisation and Government in a New Society*. London, Cambridge University Press, 1972.

Meir, Golda. *This is our Strength*. New York, 1963.

Merhav, Peretz. *The Israeli Left: History, Problems, Documents*. Tantivy Press, 1981.

Nusseibeh, Sari, and Heller, Mark A. *No Trumpets, No Drums: A Two-State Settlement of the Israeli-Palestinian Conflict*. London, I. B. Tauris, 1992.

Perlmutter, Amos. *The Times and Life of Menachem Begin*. New York, Doubleday, 1987.

Preuss, W. *Co-operation in Israel and the World*. Jerusalem, 1960.

Sachar, Howard M. *The Peoples of Israel*. New York, 1962.

Safran, Nadav. *The United States and Israel*. Harvard University Press, 1963.

Samuel, The Hon. Edwin. *Problems of Government in the State of Israel*. Jerusalem, 1956.

Segre, V. D. *Israel: A Society in Transition*. London, Oxford University Press, 1971.

Shatil, J. *L'Économie Collective du Kibboutz Israélien*. Paris, Les Editions de Minuit, 1960.

Teveth, Shabtai. *Ben-Gurion*. Boston, Houghton Mifflin, 1987.

ZIONISM

Avishai, Bernard. *The Tragedy of Zionism*. Farrar Strauss Giroux, 1986.

Bein, Alex. *Theodor Herzl*. London, East and West Library, 1957.

Cohen, Israel. *A Short History of Zionism*. London, Frederick Muller, 1951.

Dieckhoff, Alain. *Les Espaces d'Israël*. Paris, Fondation pour les études de la défense nationale, 1987.

Fisch, Harold. *The Zionist Revolution: A New Perspective*. London, Weidenfeld and Nicolson, 1978.

Frankl, Oscar Benjamin. *Theodor Herzl: The Jew and Man*. New York, 1949.

Laqueur, Walter. *A History of Zionism*. London, Weidenfeld and Nicolson, 1972.

Lowenthal, Marvin (Ed. and trans.). *Diaries of Theodor Herzl*. New York, Grosset and Dunlap, 1965.

O'Brien, Conor Cruise. *The Siege: The Saga of Israel and Zionism*. London, Weidenfeld and Nicolson, 1986.

Rose, Norman. *Chaim Weizmann*. London, Weidenfeld and Nicolson, 1987.

Schama, Simon. *Two Rothschilds and the Land of Israel*. London, Collins, 1978.

Schechtman, J. *Rebel and Statesman: the Jabotinsky Story*. New York, Thomas Yoseloff, 1956.

Sober, Moshe. *Beyond the Jewish State: confessions of a former Zionist*. Toronto, Summerhill Press, 1990.

Sokolow, Nahum. *History of Zionism*. 2 vols, London, Longmans, 1919; New York, Ktav, 1969.

Stein, Leonard and Yogev, Gedilia (Editors). *The Letters and Papers of Chaim Weizmann; Volume I 1885–1902*. Oxford University Press, 1968.

Vital, David. *The Origins of Zionism*. Oxford University Press, 1975, re-issued 1980.

   Zionism: The Formative Years. Oxford University Press, 1981.

Weisgal, Meyer, and Carmichael, Joel. *Chaim Weizmann—a Biography by Several Hands*. London, Weidenfeld and Nicolson, 1962.

Weizmann, Dr Chaim. *The Jewish People and Palestine*. London, 1939.

   Trial and Error: the Autobiography of Chaim Weizmann. London, Hamish Hamilton, 1949; New York, Schocken, 1966.

ECONOMY

Aharoni, Yair. *The Israeli Economy: Dreams and Realities*. London, Routledge, 1991.

OFFICIAL PUBLICATIONS

Report of the Palestine Royal Commission, 1937. Cmd 5479, London.

Report of the Palestine Partition Commission, 1938. Cmd 5854, London.

Statement of Policy by His Majesty's Government in the United Kingdom. Cmd 3692, London, 1930; Cmd 5893, London, 1938; Cmd 6019, London, 1939; Cmd 6180, London, 1940.

Government Survey of Palestine. 2 vols, 1945–46, Jerusalem. Supplement, July 1947, Jerusalem.

Report of the Anglo-American Committee of Enquiry. Lausanne, 1946.

Report to the United Nations General Assembly by the UN Special Committee on Palestine. Geneva, 1947.

Report of the UN Economic Survey Mission for the Middle East. December 1949, United Nations, Lake Success, NY; HM Stationery Office.

Annual Yearbook of the Government of Israel.

Jewish Agency for Palestine. Documents Submitted to General Assembly of UN, relating to the National Home, 1947.

The Jewish Plan for Palestine. Jerusalem, 1947.

Statistical Survey of the Middle East. 1944.

Statistical Abstract of Israel. Central Bureau of Statistics, annual.

Israeli-Occupied Territories and Emerging Palestinian Autonomous Areas

THE WEST BANK

Location, Climate

The West Bank (Judaea and Samaria) covers an area of 5,879 sq km (2,270 sq miles) and can be divided into three major sub-regions: the Mount Hebron massif, approximately 45 km long by 20 km wide, the peaks of which rise to between 700 m and 1,000 m above sea-level; the Jerusalem mountains, which extend to the northernmost point of the Hebron-Bethlehem massif; and the Mount Samaria hills, the central section of which—the Nablus mountains—reaches heights of up to 800 m before descending to the northern, Jenin hills, of between 300 m and 400 m. The eastern border of the West Bank is bounded by the valley of the River Jordan, leading to the Dead Sea (part of the Syrian-African rift valley), into which the River Jordan drains. The latter is 400 m below sea-level. Precipitation ranges between 600 mm–800 mm on the massif and 200 mm in the Jordan Valley; 36% of the area is classified as cultivable land, 32% grazing land, 27% desert or rocky ground and 5% natural forest. Apart from the urban centres of Bethlehem and Hebron to the south, the majority of the Palestinian population is concentrated in the northern districts around Ramallah, Nablus, Jenin and Tulkaram.

Administration

Until the end of the 1948 Arab-Israeli War, the West Bank formed part of the British Mandate of Palestine, before becoming part of the Hashemite Kingdom of Jordan under the Armistice Agreement of 1949. It remained under Jordanian sovereignty, despite Israeli occupation in 1967, until King Hussein of Jordan formally relinquished legal and administrative control on 31 July 1988. Under Israeli military occupation the West Bank was administered by a military government, which divided the territory into seven sub-districts. The Civil Administration, as it later became known, did not extend its jurisdiction to the many Israeli settlements which were established under the Israeli occupation; settlements remained subject to the Israeli legal and administrative system. By 1992 approximately 67% of the West Bank was under direct Israeli control, either resulting from settlement building (believed to have covered some 10% of the total area of the West Bank) on what has become Israeli 'state land', or through areas being declared closed military areas. Palestinians are believed to be in control of less than 5% of the total area of the West Bank.

In accordance with the Declaration of Principles on Palestinian Self-Rule (see Documents on Palestine, p. 100) and the Cairo Agreement on the Gaza Strip and Jericho, the PLO took control of the Jericho Area of the West Bank on 17 May 1994. Its jurisdiction there is exercised through the Palestine National Authority (appointed in May 1994) and will eventually be extended throughout the whole of the West Bank. Israel will retain responsibility for external security and foreign affairs.

Demography and Economy

In September 1967 the only census, to date, of the Arab population of the West Bank since the territory's occupation was conducted by the Israeli military administration, and the number of Palestinians was recorded at 589,000. The most recent estimates suggest that the population has subsequently doubled to between 1.0m. and 1.1m.; this compares with an estimated 110,000 Jewish settlers by the end of 1992 (approximately 10% of the Palestinian population), who inhabit some 128 settlements.

Despite concerted attempts during the Palestinian *intifada* to escape from Israeli economic domination, the relationship of the economy of the West Bank is still one of dependence. Israel remains by far the largest market for goods and services from the West Bank and is the most important employer of the burgeoning Palestinian labour force. In 1991 the gross

national product (GNP) of the West Bank was $2,134m., compared with Israel's GNP of $58,989m. GNP per caput showed a similarly wide margin, at $2,175 and $10,878, respectively. Even prior to the *intifada*, in 1987, the West Bank recorded a balance-of-trade deficit with Israel of $420.2m.; the value of exports to Israel amounted to $160.5m., compared with imports worth $580.7m. During 1988–90 the export of goods and services from the West Bank fell at an annual average rate of 16%, and the overall trade deficit was aggravated by the 1990/91 crisis in the Persian (Arabian) Gulf region, when the closure of borders and reduced demand affected the export of agricultural goods and manufactures to Arab markets.

Agriculture is the largest economic sector in the West Bank. In 1990 this sector was estimated to have contributed 737m. new Israeli shekels to total GDP of 3,251m.–3,376m. new Israeli shekels. In spite of a slight increase in production in recent years, amongst other constraints, further expansion is severely limited by a lack of water for irrigation. The proportion of irrigated land in the West Bank is estimated to be less than 5%, compared with 45% within Israel. Of the total annual average water consumption by Palestinians of 115m. cu m, approximately 100m. cu m is for use in agriculture. The imbalance in allocation of this resource between the Palestinian inhabitants and Israeli settlers is reflected in figures for 1990, which show that the West Bank Palestinian population of approximately 1m. was allocated 137m. cu m by the Israeli authorities, compared with an allocation of 160m. cu m for 30 Israeli agricultural settlements and a population of approximately 100,000 settlers.

Attempts by the Palestinians in the early years of the *intifada* to disengage from the Israeli economy through the boycott of taxes levied by the Israeli authorities provoked a severe response. By the end of 1989, after two years of boycotts during which revenues for Israel declined by one-third, forced collections by the military authorities and intensive 'tax raids' had almost re-established the pre-1988 tax collection level. Israeli tax collection policy, as a form of collective punishment and a means of asserting Israeli control, caused a decline in the standard of living, constrained business expansion and reduced the personal savings of Palestinians in the territory. However, perhaps the strongest link with the Israeli economy, and the one which has proved the most difficult to break, is the employment that Palestinians find within the 'Green Line', which provides many families with their livelihoods. In 1990 some 37% of the West Bank's labour force was employed in Israel, mainly in skilled and semi-skilled occupations—especially in the construction industry. In 1993, following a series of attacks on Jews within Israel, the Israeli Prime Minister, Itzhak Rabin, ordered the closure of Israel's borders with the West Bank and the Gaza Strip, preventing an estimated 70,000 West Bank Palestinians from travelling to work. Palestinian leaders claim that some $1.6m. in income was lost as a result of the closure. Significantly, controls on cross-border movement were relaxed only after considerable pressure from Israeli employers; the 'reserve labour force' of 100,000 or so unemployed Israelis had been reluctant to do the Palestinians' work, which is often of a low-paid, menial nature.

Following the signing of the Declaration of Principles on Palestinian self-rule in the Occupied Territories in September 1993, hopes were raised in the West Bank that future economic reconstruction would be financed from abroad. A World Bank report on the Occupied Territories estimated that a 10-year programme to construct essential infrastructure and social facilities would cost $3,000m. The PLO, with a more ambitious Palestine Development Programme (PDP), estimated that the reconstruction of the Palestinian economy during 1994–2000 would cost $11,600m. The planners expected $2,000m. to come from domestic savings, and the remainder from external donors; however, it was unclear how much of the total would be allocated to the West Bank if the plan were to be implemented.

THE GAZA STRIP

Location, Climate

The Gaza Strip, lying beside the Mediterranean Sea and the border with Egypt, is approximately 45 km long by 8 km wide at its widest point. Crossed only by two shallow valleys, the 378 sq km area is otherwise almost entirely flat, and has no surface water. Annual average rainfall is 300 mm. Most notable for its high population density, the Gaza Strip has, after East Jerusalem, the largest Palestinian urban centre in the Occupied Territories—Gaza City—with an estimated population of 273,000 at 31 December 1991.

Administration

An administrative province under the British Mandate of Palestine, Gaza was transferred to Egypt after the 1949 Armistice and remained under Egyptian administration until June 1967, when it was invaded and occupied by Israel. Following Israeli occupation the Gaza Strip, like the West Bank, became an 'administered territory'. Until the provisions of the Declaration of Principles on Palestinian self-rule in the Occupied Territories took effect, the management of day-to-day affairs was the responsibility of the area military commander. Neither Israeli laws nor governmental and public bodies—including the Supreme Court—could review or alter the orders of the military command to any great extent. By 1993 it was estimated that approximately 50% of the land area was under Israeli control, either through Jewish settlements having been established or through areas being closed by the military.

The PLO assumed control of the Gaza Strip on 17 May 1994 and exercises its jurisdiction there through the Palestine National Authority, which meets alternately in Gaza City and Jericho.

Demography and Economy

The Gaza Strip is one of the most densely-populated areas in the world. In 1986 the number of inhabitants per sq km was estimated to be 1,730, compared with 198 in Israel and 193 in the West Bank. At the last census conducted by the Israeli military administration, in 1967, a population of 380,800 was recorded. By the end of 1992 the population was estimated to be approximately 760,000 (including residents temporarily abroad). The high crude birth rate in Gaza of 55–56 per 1,000 is reflected in the extremely high annual population growth rate of 4%. Among the refugee population, which accounts for more than 60% of the total population, the annual population growth rate is 7.3%. In 1986 59% of the population were estimated to be under 19 years of age and 77% under 29 years of age. Out of a total Palestinian refugee population of approximately 354,700, it is estimated that 260,000 inhabit one of eight refugee camps in the Gaza Strip. By mid-1991 there were 18 Jewish settlements, housing approximately 5,000 settlers.

As a result of a combination of proximity to Israeli industry, the poor local labour market and a large population, the Gaza Strip has provided Israel with a source of cheap labour for many years. Until restrictions were imposed on the movement of Palestinians from the Occupied Territories into Israel in 1993, approximately 30,000 of the Gaza Strip labour force (45% of the total labour force) regularly commuted to Israel to find work, usually being hired by the day to perform semi-skilled or unskilled tasks for Israeli industry. However, the gradual closure of the Israeli labour market to Palestinians from Gaza in recent years has seriously affected the Gaza Strip economy. Before the crisis in the Persian (Arabian) Gulf in 1990/91, 45,000–50,000 employees, supporting an estimated 250,000 people worked in Israel, some 20,000–30,000 fewer than had worked in Israel prior to the *intifada*. Since 1991 a further 20,000 jobs have been lost, and the unemployment rate is estimated to be as high as 40%. According to one estimate, closure of the border with Israel in March 1993 cost the Gaza Strip economy as much as $2.5m. per day.

Rising salinity in the ground water supply has begun seriously to affect the irrigation of the important citrus crop, on which much of the local economy depends. In central Gaza ground-water salinity levels are three times the level regarded by the World Health Organization (WHO) as safe. Coupled with the decline in water quality is a rising water deficit. Estimated annually at approximately 50m. cu m, the water deficit could rise to 150m. cu m by 2000. The fishing industry, formerly one of the Gaza Strip's most profitable industries, has been severely constricted by Israeli military control over the area in which Palestinian boats may fish, including the prohibition of any fishing beyond a 19-mile radius established by the Israeli authorities.

The dismal state of the economy of the Gaza Strip is evident from the decline in GNP of 30%–50% that has occurred since the beginning of the *intifada*. The decline in indigenous industry and the loss of remittances from expatriate workers and other external sources of income during the Gulf War of 1991—the latter had contributed as much as 50% of GNP—further exacerbated the economic malaise. By mid-1993 the formal sector of the economy had all but collapsed, leading to a rapid growth in informal income-generating activities. Purchases of basic foodstuffs are estimated to have decreased by as much as 50% over recent years, a decline which is reflected in the widespread malnourishment of some sections of the population. Between June 1990 and June 1991, families receiving food aid from the United Nations Relief and Works Agency (UNRWA) increased eleven-fold, from 9,838 to 120,000. Although the UNRWA's mandate is to aid Palestinian refugees, the latter figure included substantial numbers of non-refugee families as well.

THE GOLAN HEIGHTS

Location, Climate

The Golan Heights, a mountainous plateau which formed most of Syria's Quneitra Province (1,710 sq km) and parts of Dera'a Province, was occupied by Israel after the 1967 Arab-Israeli War. Following the Disengagement Agreement of 1974 (see below), Israel continued to occupy some 70% of the territory (1,176 sq km), valued for its strategic position and abundant water resources (the headwaters of the River Jordan have their source on the slopes of Mount Hermon). The average height of Golan is approximately 1,200 m above sea-level in the northern region and about 300 m above sea-level in the southern region, near Lake Tiberias (the Sea of Galilee). Rainfall ranges from about 1,000 mm per year in the north to less than 600 mm per year in the southern region.

Administration

Prior to the Israeli occupation, the Golan Heights were incorporated by Syria into a provincial administration of which the city of Quneitra, with a population at the time of 27,378, was capital. The disengagement agreement that was mediated in 1974 by the US Secretary of State, Henry Kissinger, after the 1973 Arab-Israeli War, provided for the withdrawal of Israeli forces from Quneitra. Before they withdrew, however, Israeli army engineers destroyed the city. In December 1981 the Israeli Knesset enacted the Golan Annexation Law, whereby Israeli civilian legislation was extended to the territory of Golan, now under the administrative jurisdiction of the Commissioner for the Northern District of Israel. The Arab-Druze community of the Golan immediately responded by declaring a three-day strike and appealed to the UN Secretary-General to force Israel to rescind the annexation decision. At the seventh round of multilateral talks between Israeli and Arab delegations in Washington in August 1992, the Israeli Government of Itzhak Rabin for the first time accepted that UN Security Council Resolution 242, adopted in 1967, applied to the Golan Heights. The withdrawal of Israel from the Golan Heights is one of President Assad of Syria's primary objectives in any future peace agreement with Israel.

Demography and Economy

As a consequence of the Israeli occupation, an estimated 93% of the ethnically diverse Syrian population of 147,613, distributed across 163 villages and towns and 108 individual farms, was expelled. The majority were Arab Sunni Muslims, but the population also included Alawite and Druze minorities and also some Circassians, Turcomen, Armenians and Kurds. Approximately 9,000 Palestinian refugees from the 1948 Arab-Israeli War also inhabited the area. At the time of the occupation, the Golan was a predominantly agricultural province, 64% of the labour force of which was employed in agriculture. Only one-fifth of the population resided in the administrative centres. By 1991 the Golan Heights had a Jewish population of approximately 12,000, living in 21 Jewish settlements (four new settlements had been created by the end of 1992), and a predominantly Druze population of approximately 16,000 living in the only six remaining villages, of which Majd ash-Shams is by far the largest. The Golan Heights have remained predominantly an agricultural area, and, although large numbers of the Druze population now work in Israeli industry in Eilat, Tel-Aviv and Jerusalem, the indigenous economy relies almost solely on the cultivation of apples, for which the area is famous. The apple orchards benefit from a unique combination of fertile soils, abundance of water and a conducive climate.

EAST JERUSALEM

Location, Climate

Greater Jerusalem includes Israeli West Jerusalem (99% Jewish), the Old City and Mount of Olives, East Jerusalem (the Palestinian residential and commercial centre), Arab villages declared to be part of Jerusalem by Israel in 1967 and Jewish neighbourhoods constructed since 1967, either on land expropriated from Arab villages or in areas requisitioned as 'government land'. Although the area of the Greater Jerusalem district is 627 sq km, the Old City of Jerusalem covers just 1 sq km.

Administration

Until the 1967 Arab-Israeli War, Jerusalem had been divided into the new city of West Jerusalem—captured by Jewish forces in 1948—and the old city, East Jerusalem, which was part of Jordan. Israel's victory in 1967, however, reunited the city under Israeli control. Two weeks after the fighting had stopped, on 28 June, Israeli law was applied to East Jerusalem and the municipal boundaries were extended by 45 km (28 miles). Jerusalem had been, in effect, annexed. Israeli officials, however, still refer to the 'reunification' of Jerusalem.

Demography and Economy

In June 1993 the deputy mayor of Jerusalem, Avraham Kahila, declared that the city now 'had a majority of Jews', based on population projections which estimated the Jewish population at 158,000 and the Arab population at 155,000. This was a significant moment for the Israeli administration, as this had been a long-term objective. Immediately prior to the June 1967 Arab-Israeli War, East Jerusalem and its Arab environs had an Arab population of approximately 70,000, and a small Jewish population in the old Jewish quarter of the city. By contrast, Israeli West Jerusalem had a Jewish population of 196,000. As a result of this population imbalance, in the Greater Jerusalem district as a whole the Jewish population was in the majority even prior to the occupation of the whole city in 1967. Israeli policy following the occupation of East Jerusalem and the West Bank consisted of encircling the eastern sector of the city with Jewish settlements. In contrast to the more politically sensitive siting of Jewish settlements in the old Arab quarter of Jerusalem, the Government of Itzhak Rabin has concentrated on the outer circle of settlement building. Greater Jerusalem was recently reported to have a Jewish majority of 73%.

The Old City, within the walls of which are found the ancient quarters of the Jews, Christians, Muslims and Armenians, has a population of approximately 25,500 Arabs and 2,600 Jews. In addition, there are some 600 recent Jewish settlers in the Arab quarter.

Many imaginative plans have been submitted with the aim of finding a solution to the problem of sharing Jerusalem between Arabs and Jews, including the proposal that the city be placed under international trusteeship, under the auspices of the United Nations (see The Jerusalem Issue, p. 72). However, to make the implementation of such plans an administrative as well as a political quagmire, the Israeli administration, after occupying the whole city in June 1967, began creating 'facts on the ground'. Immediately following the occupation, all electricity, water and telephone grids in West Jerusalem were extended to the East. Roads were widened and cleared, and the Arab population immediately in front of the 'Wailing Wall' was forcibly evicted. Arabs living in East Jerusalem became 'permanent residents' and could apply for Israeli citizenship if they wished (in contrast to Arabs in the West Bank and Gaza Strip). However, few chose to do so. None the less, issued with identity cards (excluding the estimated 25,000 Arabs from the West Bank and Gaza Strip living illegally in the city), the Arab residents were taxed by the Israeli authorities, and their businesses and banks became subject to Israeli laws and business regulations.

Now controlling approximately one-half of all land in East Jerusalem and the surrounding Palestinian villages (previously communally, or privately, owned by Palestinians), the Israeli authorities allowed Arabs to construct buildings on only 10%–15% of the land in the city; and East Jerusalem's commercial district has been limited to three streets. The Palestinian economy has been quite seriously affected by the drop in tourism during the *intifada* and by curfews, enforced tax collections and confiscations of property exercised by the Israeli authorities.

PALESTINE NATIONAL AUTHORITY

Appointed in May 1994, the Palestine National Authority (PNA) has assumed the civil responsibilities formerly exercised by the Israeli Civil Administration in the Gaza Strip and the Jericho Area of the West Bank.

Chairman and Minister of the Interior: YASSER ARAFAT.

Secretary-General: TAYYIN ABD AR-RAHIM.

Minister of Planning and Economic Co-operation: NABIL SHAATH.

Minister of Finance: MUHAMMAD ZOHDI AN-NASHASHIBI.

Minister of Education: YASSER AMR.

Minister of Social Affairs: INTISAR AL-WAZIR.

Minister of Justice: FURAYH ABU MIDDAYN.

Minister of Housing: ZAKARIYA AL-AGHA.

Minister of Local Government: SAEB URAYQAT.

Minister of Tourism and Antiquities: ELIAS FURAYJ.

Minister of Health: RIAYD AL-ZAANOUN.

Minister of Youth and Sports: AZMI ASH-SHUAIBI.

Minister of Communications and Posts: ABD AL-AZIZ AL-Hajj AHMAD.

Minister of Transport: ABDEL HAFIDH AL-ACHHAB.

Minister of Economy and Trade: AHMED QURIE.

Minister of Culture and Arts: YASSER ABD AR-RABBUH.

Minister of Labour: SAMIR GHOUSHA.

Ministers without Portfolio: FAISAL HUSSEINI, MUNIB AL-MASRI.

LEBANON

ISRAELI SECURITY ZONE

1974 ceasefire lines

S Y R I A

Mediterranean

Sea

Haifa

Sea of Galilee

GOLAN HEIGHTS

I S R A E L

Jenin

Tulkarm

Nablus

Qalqiliya

J O R D A N

Tel Aviv

WEST BANK

Ramallah

Jericho

Jerusalem

Bethlehem

Halhul

Dead Sea

Hebron

Gaza

GAZA STRIP

Israeli occupied areas

Palestinian semi-autonomous areas

0   50 kilometres

0   50 miles

E G Y P T

JORDAN

Physical and Social Geography

W. B. FISHER

The Hashemite Kingdom of Jordan (previously Transjordan) came officially into existence under its present name in 1947 and was enlarged in 1950 to include the districts of Samaria and part of Judaea that had previously formed part of Arab Palestine. The country is bounded on the north by Syria, on the north-east by Iraq, on the east and south by Saudi Arabia, and on the west by Israel. The total area of Jordan is 97,740 sq km (37,738 sq miles). The territory west of the Jordan river (the West Bank)—some 5,600 sq km (2,160 sq miles)—has been occupied by Israel since June 1967. The population of the East and West Banks at mid-1991 was estimated by the UN to be 4,145,000. According to a census in November 1979, the population of the East Bank (area 89,206 sq km—34,442 sq miles) was 2,100,019. The total had risen to an estimated 2,796,100 at the end of 1986. In April 1994 there were 1,176,208 Palestinian refugees registered with the United Nations Relief and Works Agency (UNRWA) in Jordan, and a further 324,250 in the West Bank.

PHYSICAL FEATURES

The greater part of the State of Jordan consists of a plateau lying some 700 m–1,000 m above sea-level, which forms the north-western corner of the great plateau of Arabia (see Saudi Arabia). There are no natural topographical frontiers between Jordan and its neighbours Syria, Iraq, and Saudi Arabia, and the plateau continues unbroken into all three countries, with the artificial frontier boundaries drawn as straight lines between defined points. Along its western edge, facing the Jordan Valley, the plateau is uptilted to give a line of hills that rise 300 m–700 m above plateau-level. An older river course, the Wadi Sirhan, now almost dry with only occasional wells, fractures the plateau surface on the south-east and continues into Saudi Arabia.

The Jordanian plateau consists of a core or table of ancient rocks, covered by layers of newer rock (chiefly limestone) lying almost horizontally. In a few places (e.g. on the southern edge of the Jordan Valley) these old rocks are exposed at the surface. On its western side the plateau has been fractured and dislocated by the development of strongly marked tear faults that run from the Red Sea via the Gulf of Aqaba northwards to Lebanon and Syria. The narrow zone between the faults has sunk, to give the well-known Jordan rift valley, which is bordered both on the east and west by steep-sided walls, especially in the south near the Dead Sea, where the drop is often precipitous. The valley has a maximum width of 22 km (14 miles) and is now thought to have been produced by lateral shearing of two continental plates that on the east have been displaced by about 80 km (50 miles).

The floor of the Jordan Valley varies considerably in level. At its northern end it is just above sea-level; the surface of Lake Tiberias (the Sea of Galilee) is 209 m below sea-level, with the deepest part of the lake over 200 m lower still. Greatest depth of the valley is at the Dead Sea (surface 400 m below sea-level, maximum depth 396 m).

Dislocation of the rock strata in the region of the Jordan Valley has had two further effects: firstly, earth tremors are still frequent along the valley (Jerusalem has minor earthquakes from time to time); and secondly, considerable quantities of lava have welled up, forming enormous sheets that cover wide expanses of territory in the state of Jordan and southern Syria, and produce a desolate, forbidding landscape. One small lava flow, by forming a natural dam across the Jordan Valley, has impounded the waters to form Lake Tiberias.

The River Jordan rises just inside the frontiers of Syria and Lebanon—a fruitful source of dispute between the two countries and Israel. The river is 251 km (156 miles) long, and after first flowing for 96 km (60 miles) in Israel it lies within Jordanian territory for the remaining 152 km (94 miles). Its main tributary, the Yarmouk, is 40 km (25 miles) long, and close to its junction with the Jordan forms the boundary between the state of Jordan, Israel and Syria. A few km from its source, the River Jordan used to open into Lake Huleh, a shallow, marsh-fringed expanse of water which was for long a breeding ground of malaria, but which has now been drained. Lake Tiberias, also, like the former Huleh, in Israel, covers an area of 316 sq km (122 sq miles) and measures 22 km (14 miles) from north to south, and 26 km (16 miles) from east to west. River water outflowing from the lake is used for the generation of hydroelectricity.

The river then flows through the barren, inhospitable country of its middle and lower valley, very little of which is actually, or potentially, cultivable, and finally enters the Dead Sea. This lake is 65 km (40 miles) long and 16 km (10 miles) wide. Owing to the very high air temperatures at most seasons of the year evaporation from the lake is intense, and has been estimated as equivalent to 8.5m. tons of water per day. At the surface the Dead Sea water contains about 250 grams of dissolved salts per litre, and at a depth of 110 m the water is chemically saturated (i.e. holds its maximum possible content). Magnesium chloride is the most abundant mineral, with sodium chloride next in importance; but commercial interest centres on the less abundant potash and bromide salts.

Climatically, Jordan shows close affinity to its neighbours. Summers are hot, especially on the plateau and in the Jordan Valley, where temperatures up to 49°C have been recorded. Winters are fairly cold, and on the plateau frost and some snow are usual, though not in the lower Jordan Valley. The significant element of the climate of Jordan is rainfall. In the higher parts (i.e. the uplands of Samaria and Judaea and the hills overlooking the eastern Jordan Valley) 380 mm to 630 mm of rainfall occur, enough for agriculture; but elsewhere as little as 200 mm or less may fall, and pastoral nomadism is the only possible way of life. Only about 25% of the total area of Jordan is sufficiently humid for cultivation.

Hence the main features of economic life in Jordan are subsistence agriculture of a marginal kind, carried on in Judaea-Samaria and on the north-eastern edge of the plateau, close to Amman, with migratory herding of animals—sheep, goats, cattle and camels—over the remaining and by far the larger portion of the country. As a result, the natural wealth of Jordan is small and tribal ways of life exist in parts. Before the June 1967 war, tourism (with which must be included religious pilgrimage, mainly to the holy Christian places of Jerusalem) had developed into a very important industry but this has been seriously jeopardized by the Israeli occupation of the West Bank territory and annexation of Jerusalem. However, the civil war in Lebanon and the reopening of the Suez Canal (which greatly affects the Jordanian port of Aqaba) were very favourable factors. The war between Iran and Iraq also had a very beneficial effect at first, since Aqaba, with the denial of Gulf ports to Iraq, became a major supply base. Iraq was Jordan's most important export market between 1980 and 1983 but the cost of continuing the war later severely curtailed the purchase by Iraq of goods from Jordan. By August 1990, when Iraq temporarily occupied Kuwait, Iraq had again become Jordan's principal trading partner; and the economic sanctions imposed on Iraq as a consequence of its invasion of Kuwait had a disastrous effect on the Jordanian economy (see Economy).

The shift of trade from Lebanon, a very much better economic and political relationship with Egypt and Iraq, continuing (though cool) relations with Syria, the inflow of remittances from Jordanians working abroad, and subventions from Arab funds together greatly improved the Jordanian economy. However, the growth of the economy slowed in the 1980s. Foreign aid of various kinds continues to account for more than 40% of budgetary revenues, and workers in the service sector greatly outnumber those in directly productive activities. With so many Jordanians working abroad, local activities are hampered by lack of managerial and technical skills.

RACE, LANGUAGE AND RELIGION

A division must be drawn between the Jordanians living east of the River Jordan who, in the main, are ethnically similar to the desert populations of Syria and Saudi Arabia, and the Arabs of the Jordan Valley and Samaria-Judaea. These latter are slightly taller, more heavily built, and have a broader head-form. Some authorities suggest that they are descendants of the Canaanites, who may have originated far to the north-east, in the Zagros area. An Iranian racial affinity is thus implied—but this must be of very ancient date, as the Arabs west of the Jordan Valley have been settled in their present home for many thousands of years. Besides the two groups of Arabs, there are also small colonies of Circassians from the Caucasus of Russia, who settled in Jordan as refugees during the 19th and 20th centuries AD.

Arabic is spoken everywhere, except in a few Circassian villages, and, through contacts with Britain, some English is understood in the towns.

Over 80% of the population are Sunni Muslims, and King Hussein can trace unbroken descent from the Prophet Muhammad. There is a Christian minority, and there are smaller numbers of Shi'a Muslims.

History

Revised for this edition by RICHARD I. LAWLESS.

Jordan, as an independent state, is a 20th-century development. Before then it was seldom more than a rugged and backward appendage to more powerful kingdoms and empires, and indeed never had any separate existence. In Biblical times the area was covered roughly by Gilead, Ammon, Moab and Edom, and the western portions formed for a time part of the kingdom of Israel. During the sixth century BC the Arabian tribe of the Nabateans established their capital at Petra in the south and continued to preserve their independence when, during the fourth and third centuries, the northern half was incorporated into the Seleucid province of Syria. It was under Seleucid rule that cities such as Philadelphia (the Biblical Rabbath Ammon and the modern Amman) and Gerasa (now Jerash) rose to prominence. During the first century BC the Nabateans extended their rule over the greater part of present-day Jordan and Syria; they then began to recede before the advance of Rome, and in AD 105–6 Petra was incorporated into the Roman Empire. The lands east of the Jordan shared in a brief blaze of glory under the Palmyrene sovereigns Odenathus (Udaynath) and Zenobia (az-Zabba') in the middle of the third century AD, and during the fifth and sixth centuries formed part of the dominions of the Christian Ghassanid dynasty, vassals of the Byzantine Empire. Finally, after 50 years of anarchy in which Byzantine, Persian and local rulers intervened, Transjordania was conquered by the Arabs and absorbed into the Islamic Empire.

For centuries nothing more is heard of the country; it formed normally a part of Syria, and as such was generally governed from Egypt. From the beginning of the 16th century it was included in the Ottoman *vilayet* (administrative district) of Damascus, and remained in a condition of stagnation until the outbreak of the First World War in 1914. European travellers and explorers of the 19th century rediscovered the beauties of Petra and Gerasa, but otherwise the desert tribes were left undisturbed. Even the course of the war in its early stages gave little hint of the upheaval that was to take place in Jordan's fortunes. The area was included in the zone of influence allocated to Britain under the Sykes-Picot Treaty of May 1916 (see Documents on Palestine, p. 79), and Zionists held that it also came within the area designated as a Jewish National Home in the promise contained in the Balfour Declaration of November 1917. Apart from these somewhat remote political events the tide of war did not reach Jordanian territory until the capture of Aqaba by the Arab armies under Faisal, the third son of King Hussein of the Hedjaz, in July 1917. A year later, in September 1918, they shared in the final push north by capturing Amman and Deraa.

The end of the war thus found a large area, which included almost the whole of present-day Jordan, in Arab hands under the leadership of Faisal. To begin with, the territory to the east of the River Jordan was not looked on as a separate unit. Faisal, with the assistance of British officers and Iraqi nationalists, set up an autonomous government in Damascus, a step encouraged by the Anglo-French Declaration of 7 November 1918, favouring the establishment of indigenous governments in Syria and Iraq. Arab demands, however, as expressed by Faisal at the Paris Peace Conference in January 1919, went a good deal further in claiming independence throughout the Arab world. This brought them sharply up against both French and Zionist claims in the Near East, and when, in March 1920, the General Syrian Congress in Damascus declared the independence of Syria and Iraq, with Faisal and Abdullah, Hussein's second son, as kings, the decisions were denounced by France and Britain. In the following month the San Remo Conference awarded the Palestine Mandate to Britain, and thus separated it effectively from Syria proper, which fell within the French share. Faisal was forced out of Damascus by the French in July and left the country.

THE KINGDOM OF TRANSJORDAN

The position of Transjordania was not altogether clear under the new dispensation. After the withdrawal of Faisal the British High Commissioner informed a meeting of notables at es-Salt that the British Government favoured self-government for the territory with British advisers. In December 1920 the provisional frontiers of the Mandates were extended eastwards by Anglo-French agreement so as to include Transjordania within the Palestine Mandate, and therefore presumably within the provisions regarding the establishment of a Jewish National Home. Yet another twist of policy came as the result of a conference in Cairo in March 1921 attended by Winston Churchill, the new British Colonial Secretary, Abdullah, T. E. Lawrence and Sir Herbert Samuel, High Commissioner for Palestine. At this meeting it was recommended that Faisal should be proclaimed King of Iraq, while Abdullah was persuaded to stand down in his favour by the promise of an Arab administration in Transjordania. He had in fact been in effective control in Amman since his arrival the previous winter to organize a rising against the French in Syria. This project he now abandoned, and in April 1921 was officially recognized as *de facto* ruler of Transjordan. The final draft of the Palestine Mandate confirmed by the Council of the League of Nations in July 1922 contained a clause giving the Mandatory Power considerable latitude in the administration of the territory east of the Jordan (see Documents on Palestine, p. 82). On the basis of this clause a memorandum was approved in the following September expressly excluding Transjordan from the clauses relating to the establishment of the Jewish National Home, and although many Zionists continued to press for the reversal of this policy, the country thenceforth remained in practice separate from Palestine proper.

Like much of the post-war boundary delineation, the borders of the new state were somewhat arbitrary. Although they lay mainly in desert areas, they frequently cut across tribal areas and grazing grounds, with small respect for tradition. Of the 300,000–400,000 inhabitants, only about one-fifth were town-dwellers, and these confined to four small cities ranging in population from 30,000 to 10,000. Nevertheless, Transjordan's early years were destined to be comparatively peaceful. On 15 May 1923 Britain formally recognized Transjordan as an independent constitutional state under the rule of the Amir Abdullah with British tutelage, and with the aid of a British subsidy it was possible to make some slow progress towards development and modernization. A small but efficient armed force, the Arab Legion, was built up under the guidance of Peake Pasha and later Glubb Pasha; this force distinguished itself particularly during the Iraqi rebellion of May 1941. It also played a significant role in the fighting with Israel during 1948. Other British advisers assisted in the development of health services and schools.

The Amir Abdullah very nearly became involved in the fall of his father, King Hussein, in 1924. It was in Amman on 5 March 1924, that the latter was proclaimed Caliph, and during the subsequent fighting with Ibn Sa'ud Wahhabi troops penetrated into Transjordanian territory. They subsequently withdrew to the south, and in June 1925, after the abdication of Hussein's eldest son Ali, Abdullah formally incorporated Ma'an and Aqaba within his dominions. The move was not disputed by the new ruler of the Hedjaz and Najd, and thereafter the southern frontier of Transjordan remained unaltered.

INDEPENDENCE

In February 1928 a treaty was signed with Great Britain granting a still larger measure of independence, though reserving for the advice of a British Resident such matters as financial policy and foreign relations. The same treaty provided for a constitution, and this was duly promulgated in April 1928, the first Legislative Council meeting a year later. In January 1934 a supplementary agreement was added permitting Transjordan to appoint consular representatives in Arab countries, and in May 1939 Britain agreed to the conversion of the Legislative Council into a regular Cabinet with ministers in charge of specified departments. The outbreak of war delayed further advances towards independence, but this was finally achieved in name at least by the Treaty of London of 22 March 1946. On 25 May 1946 Abdullah was proclaimed king and a new constitution replaced the now obsolete one of 1928.

Transjordan was not slow in taking its place in the community of nations. In 1947 King Abdullah signed treaties with Turkey and Iraq and applied for membership of the United Nations (UN); this last, however, was thwarted by the Soviet veto and by lack of US recognition of Transjordan's status as an independent nation. In March 1948 Britain agreed to the signing of a new treaty in which virtually the only restrictive clauses related to military and defence matters. Britain was to have certain peace-time military privileges, including the maintenance of airfields and communications, transit facilities and co-ordination of training methods. It was also to provide economic and social aid.

Transjordan had, however, not waited for independence before making its weight felt in Arab affairs in the Middle East. It had not been very active before the war, and, in fact its first appearance on the international scene was in May 1939, when Transjordanian delegates were invited to the Round Table Conference on Palestine in London. Transjordan took part in the preliminary discussions during 1943 and 1944 that finally led to the formation of the Arab League in March 1945, and was one of the original members of that League. During the immediately following years it seemed possible that political and dynastic differences would be forgotten in this common effort for unity. Under the stresses and strains of 1948, however, the old contradictions began to reappear. Abdullah had long favoured the project of a 'Greater Syria',

that is, the union of Transjordan, Syria and Palestine, as a step towards the final unification of the Fertile Crescent by the inclusion of Iraq. This was favoured on dynastic grounds by various parties in Iraq, and also by some elements in Syria and Palestine. On the other hand it met with violent opposition from many Syrian nationalists, from the rulers of Egypt and Saudi Arabia—neither of whom were disposed to favour any strengthening of the Hashemite house—and of course from the Zionists and the French. It is in the light of these conflicts of interest that developments subsequent to the establishment of the State of Israel must be seen.

FORMATION OF ISRAEL

On 14–15 May 1948 British troops were withdrawn into the port of Haifa as a preliminary to the final evacuation of Palestine territory, the State of Israel was proclaimed, and Arab armies entered the former Palestinian territory from all sides. Only those from Transjordan played any significant part in the fighting, and by the time that major hostilities ceased in July they had succeeded in occupying a considerable area. The suspicion now inevitably arose that Abdullah was prepared to accept a *fait accompli* and to negotiate with the Israeli authorities for a formal recognition of the existing military boundaries. Moreover, whereas the other Arab countries refused to accept any other move that implied a tacit recognition of the status quo—such as the resettlement of refugees—Transjordan seemed to be following a different line. In September 1948 an Arab government was formed at Gaza under Egyptian tutelage, and this was answered from the Transjordanian side by the proclamation in December at Jericho of Abdullah as King of All Palestine. In the following April the country's name was changed to Jordan and three Palestinians were included in the Cabinet. In the mean time, armistices were being signed by all the Arab countries, including Jordan, and on 31 January 1949 Jordan was at last recognized by the United States of America (USA).

On the three major problems confronting the Arab states in their dispute with Israel, Jordan continued to differ more or less openly with its colleagues. It refused to agree to the internationalization of Jerusalem, it initiated plans for the resettlement of the Arab refugees, and it showed a disposition to accept as permanent the armistice frontiers. In April 1950, after rumours of negotiations between Jordan and Israel, the Arab League Council in Cairo succeeded in getting Jordan's adherence to resolutions forbidding negotiations with Israel or annexation of Palestinian territory. Nevertheless, in the same month elections were held in Jordan and Arab Palestine, the results of which encouraged Abdullah formally to annex the latter territory on 24 April 1950. This step was immediately recognized by Britain.

At the meeting of the Arab League that followed, Egypt led the opposition to Jordan, who found support, however, from Iraq. The decisions reached by the Council were inconclusive; but thereafter Jordan began to drift away from Arab League policy. Jordan supported the UN policy over Korea, in contradistinction to the other Arab states, and signed a four-point agreement with the USA in March 1951. Although there was at the same time constant friction between Jordan and Israel, the unified opposition of the Arab states to the new Jewish state seemed to have ended, and inter-Arab differences were gaining the upper hand.

ABDULLAH ASSASSINATED

On 20 July 1951 King Abdullah was assassinated in Jerusalem. Evidence brought out at the trial of those implicated in the plot showed that the murder was as much as anything a protest against his Greater Syria policy and it was significant that Egypt refused to extradite some of those convicted. Nevertheless, the stability of the young Jordanian state revealed itself in the calm in which the King's eldest son Talal succeeded to the throne, and the peaceful elections held shortly afterwards. In January 1952 a new constitution was promulgated. Even more significant, perhaps, was the dignity with which, only a year after his accession, King Talal, whose mental condition had long been giving cause for anxiety, abdicated in favour of his son, Hussein, still a minor. In foreign policy Talal had shown some signs of a reaction against his father's ideas in favour of a *rapprochement* with Syria and Egypt, one step being Jordan's signature of the Arab Collective Security Pact which it had failed to join in the summer of 1950.

This policy was continued during the reign of his son, King Hussein, notably by the conclusion of an economic and financial agreement with Syria in February 1953, and a joint scheme for the construction of a dam across the Yarmouk River to supply irrigation and hydroelectric power. One problem which became pressing in 1954 was the elaborate scheme sponsored by the USA for the sharing of the Jordan waters between Jordan, Iraq, Syria and Israel, which could make no progress in the absence of political agreement.

During December a financial aid agreement was signed in London with the United Kingdom, and the opportunity was taken to discuss the revision of the Anglo-Jordanian Treaty of 1946. Agreement over this was not possible owing to British insistence that any new pact should fit into a general Middle East defence system. In May 1955 Premier Abu'l-Huda was replaced by Sa'id al-Mufti, while an exchange of state visits with King Sa'ud hinted at a *rapprochement* with Saudi Arabia. Nevertheless, in November Jordan declared its unwillingness to adhere either to the Egyptian-Syrian-Saudi Arabian bloc or to the Baghdad Pact.

DISMISSAL OF GLUBB PASHA

On 15 December 1955, following a visit to General Sir G. Templer, Chief of the Imperial General Staff, Sa'id al-Mufti resigned and was replaced by Hazza al-Majali, known to be in favour of the Baghdad Pact. The following day there were violent demonstrations in Amman, and on 20 December Ibrahim Hashim became Prime Minister, to be succeeded on 9 January 1956 by Samir Rifai. In February the new Prime Minister visited Syria, Lebanon, Iraq, Egypt and Saudi Arabia, and shortly after his return, on 2 March, King Hussein announced the dismissal of Glubb Pasha, Commander-in-Chief of the Jordanian armed forces, and replaced him with Maj.-Gen. Radi Annab. The Egyptian-Syrian-Saudi Arabian bloc at this juncture offered to replace the British financial subsidy to Jordan; but the latter was not in fact withdrawn, and King Hussein and the Jordanian Government evidently felt that they had moved far enough in one direction, and committed themselves to a policy of strict neutrality. In April, however, the King and the Prime Minister paid a visit to the Syrian President in Damascus, and in May Maj.-Gen. Annab was replaced by his deputy, Lt-Col Ali Abu Nuwar, generally regarded as the leader of the movement to eliminate foreign influence from the Jordanian army and government. This coincided with the reappointment of Sa'id al-Mufti as Prime Minister. During the same period discussions culminated in agreements for military co-operation between Jordan and Syria, Lebanon and Egypt, and in July Jordan and Syria formed an economic union. At the beginning of the same month al-Mufti was replaced by Ibrahim Hashim.

RELATIONS WITH ISRAEL AND WITH THE OTHER ARAB STATES

Meanwhile relations with Israel, including the problem of the Arab refugees, the use of Jordan waters, the definition of the frontier, and the status of Jerusalem, continued to provide a standing cause for anxiety. Tension between Jordan and Israel was further increased after the Israeli, British and French military action in Egypt. A new Cabinet, headed by Suleiman Nabulsi, had taken office in October, and new elections were followed by the opening of negotiations for the abrogation of the Anglo-Jordan Treaty of 1948, and the substitution of financial aid from the Arab countries, notably Saudi Arabia, Egypt and Syria. Owing to subsequent political developments, however, the shares due from Egypt and Syria were not paid. On 13 March 1957, an Anglo-Jordanian agreement was signed abrogating the 1948 treaty, and by 2 July the last British troops had left. In the mean time, Nabulsi's evident leanings towards the Soviet connection, clashing with the recently enunciated Eisenhower doctrine, led to his breach with King Hussein and his resignation on 10 April, to be succeeded by Ibrahim Hashim. All political parties were suppressed, and plans to establish diplomatic relations with the USSR were dropped. Gen. Ali Abu Nuwar was removed from the post of

Commander-in-Chief, and the USA announced its determination to preserve Jordan's independence—a policy underlined by a major air-lift of arms to Amman in September in response to Syria's alignment with the USSR. In May Syrian troops serving under the joint Syro-Egypto-Jordanian command were withdrawn from Jordanian territory at Jordan's request, and in June there was a partial rupture of diplomatic relations with Egypt.

On 14 February 1958 the merger of the kingdoms of Iraq and Jordan in a federal union to be called the Arab Federation was proclaimed in Amman by King Faisal of Iraq and King Hussein. This new federation proved abortive. Samir Rifai became Prime Minister of Jordan in May, on the resignation of Ibrahim Hashim who took up the appointment of vice-premier in the short-lived Arab Federation.

British troops were flown to Amman from Cyprus on 17 July, in response to an appeal by King Hussein. They had all been withdrawn by the beginning of November—under UN auspices—and in the two years that followed Jordan settled down to a period of comparative peace. Hazza al-Majali succeeded Rifai as Prime Minister on 6 May 1959. Firm measures were taken against communism and subversive activities and collaboration with the West was, if anything, encouraged by the country's isolation between Iraq, Israel and the two halves of the United Arab Republic (UAR). American loans continued to arrive at the rate of about $50m. per year, and there was also technical aid of various kinds from Britain, West Germany and other countries. An important development was the official opening of the port of Aqaba on the Red Sea, virtually Jordan's only outlet.

Relations with Jordan's Arab neighbours continued to be uneasy, though diplomatic relations with the UAR, broken off in July 1958, were resumed in August 1959. Incidents on the Syrian border were almost as frequent as on the Israeli, and there were no signs of a *rapprochement* with Iraq. In January 1960 both the King and the Prime Minister condemned the Arab leaders' approach to the Palestine problem, and in February Jordanian citizenship was offered to all Arab refugees who applied for it. On the other side of the balance sheet, King Hussein paid a flying visit to King Sa'ud in February 1960, and in March strongly anti-Zionist statements appeared in the Jordanian press. Nevertheless, there seemed to be no change in the general position that Jordan wished for formal recognition of its absorption of the Palestinian territory west of the Jordan, while the UAR and other Arab countries favoured the establishment of an independent Palestine Arab government.

On 29 August 1960 the Jordanian Prime Minister, Hazza al-Majali, was assassinated. He was followed by a succession of prime ministers during the next five years. In April 1965 a constitutional uncertainty was resolved, with the nomination of the King's brother Hassan as Crown Prince; the King's own children were thus excluded from the succession to the throne.

Meanwhile, in September 1963 the creation of a unified 'Palestinian entity' was approved by the Council of the Arab League, despite opposition from the Jordanian Government, which regarded the proposal as a threat to Jordan's sovereignty over the West Bank. The first congress of Palestinian Arab groups was held in the Jordanian sector of Jerusalem in May–June 1964, when the participants unanimously agreed to form the Palestine Liberation Organization (PLO) as 'the only legitimate spokesman for all matters concerning the Palestinian people'. The PLO was to be financed by the Arab League and was to recruit military units, from among refugees, to constitute a Palestine Liberation Army (PLA). From the outset, King Hussein refused to allow the PLA to train forces in Jordan or the PLO to levy taxes from Palestinian refugees in his country.

WAR WITH ISRAEL

During the latter part of 1966 Jordan's foreign relations were increasingly worsened by the widening breach with Syria. Charges and counter-charges were made of plots to subvert each other's governments, and while the UAR and the USSR supported Syria, Jordan looked for backing to Saudi Arabia and the USA. This situation made it increasingly difficult for Jordan's relations with Israel to be regularized. In July 1966

Jordan suspended support for the PLO, accusing its secretary, Ahmad Shukairi, of pro-communist activity. In November an Israeli reprisal raid aroused bitter feeling in Jordan and elsewhere. While Jordan introduced conscription and Saudi Arabia promised military aid, Syria and the PLO appealed to Jordanians to revolt against King Hussein. Negotiations to implement the resolution of the Supreme Council for Arab Defence that Iraqi and Saudi troops should be sent to Jordan, to assist in its defence, collapsed in December. This was followed by clashes on the Jordan/Syria frontier, by PLO-sponsored bomb outrages in Jordan (resulting in the closure of the PLO headquarters in Jerusalem), and by worsening relations between Jordan and the UAR and a ban by the latter on aircraft carrying British and American armaments to Jordan. In retaliation, Jordan withdrew recognition of the Sallal regime in Yemen, and boycotted the next meeting of the Arab Defence Council. On 5 March Wasfi at-Tal resigned and was succeeded by Hussein bin Nasser at the head of an interim government.

As the prospect of war with Israel drew nearer, King Hussein composed his differences with Egypt, and personally flew to Cairo to sign a defence agreement. Jordanian troops, together with those of the UAR, Iraq and Saudi Arabia, went into action immediately on the outbreak of hostilities in June. By the end of the Six-Day War, however, all Jordanian territory west of the River Jordan had been occupied by Israeli troops, and a steady stream of West Bank Jordanians began to cross the River Jordan to the East Bank. Estimated at between 150,000 and 250,000 persons, they swelled Jordan's refugee population and presented the government with intractable social and economic problems.

In August 1967 King Hussein formed a nine-man Consultative Council, composed of former premiers and politicians of varying sympathies, to meet weekly and to participate in the 'responsibility of power'. Later a Senate was formed, consisting of 15 representatives from the inhabitants of the West Bank area and 15 from eastern Jordan. Several changes of government took place and the King took over personal command of the country's armed forces.

Meanwhile, the uneasy situation along the frontier with Israel persisted, aggravated by the deteriorating economic situation in Jordan. Reprisal actions by Israel, after numerous commando raids directed against its authority in Jerusalem and the West Bank and operating from Jordanian territory, provoked Jordan to appeal for UN intervention. In June 1969 Israeli commandos blew up the diversion system of the Ghor Canal, Jordan's principal irrigation project.

THE GUERRILLA CHALLENGE

The instability in Amman after the June war was reflected in the short life of Jordanian Cabinets—it became rare for one to remain unchanged for more than three months. A careful balance had to be struck between the Palestinians and the King's traditional supporters. Thus, in the new Cabinet announced after the June 1970 crisis, Palestinians were given more of the key ministries, including that of the interior. Abd al-Munem Rifai, Jordan's senior diplomat, became Prime Minister for the second time.

The main factor in Jordan's internal politics between June 1967 and 1971 was the rivalry between the Government and Palestinian guerrilla organizations, principally the Palestine National Liberation Movement, known as al-Fatah ('Conquest'), which was led by Yasser Arafat, the Chairman of the PLO. These organizations gradually assumed effective control of the refugee camps and commanded widespread support amongst the Palestinian majority of Jordan's present population. They also received armaments and training assistance from other Arab countries, particularly Syria, and finance from the oil-rich states bordering the Persian (Arabian) Gulf. Some camps became commando training centres, the younger occupants of these, almost all unemployed, welcoming the sense of purpose and relief from idleness and boredom that recruitment into a guerrilla group offered. The *fedayeen* ('martyrs') movement virtually became a state within a state. Its leaders stated that they 'have no wish to interfere in the internal affairs of Jordan provided it does not place any obstacles in the way of our struggle to liberate Palestine'. In

practice, however, its popularity and influence represented a challenge to the Government, whilst its actions attracted Israeli reprisals that did serious damage to the East Bank, now the only fertile part of Jordan, and generally reduced the possibilities of a peace settlement on which Jordan's long-term future depended.

A major confrontation between the two forces occurred in November 1968, after massive demonstrations in Amman on the anniversary of the Balfour Declaration. Extensive street fighting broke out between guerrillas and the army, and for a short period a civil war seemed possible, but both sides soon backed down. Similar confrontations followed in February and June 1970, and on both occasions the Government was forced to yield to Palestinian pressures. King Hussein and Arafat (whose own position was threatened by the rise of small extremist groups in Jordan) concluded an agreement redefining their respective spheres of influence. The guerrillas appeared to have granted little or nothing, but Hussein was forced to dismiss his Commander-in-Chief and a Cabinet minister, both relatives. These were regarded as the leaders of the anti-*fedayeen* faction, which remained strong amongst the Bedouin sheikhs. Despite the agreement, the tension between the Government and the guerrillas continued, aggravated by opposition to the Government's concessions from intransigent army officers.

A new and dangerous stage in the relations between the two sides in Jordan was reached in July 1970 with the acceptance by the Government of the American peace proposals for the Middle East. The guerrilla groups, with few exceptions, rejected these, and, as the cease-fire between the UAR and Israel came into operation on 7 August, it was clear that the Jordanian Government was preparing for a full-scale confrontation with them.

CIVIL WAR

Bitter fighting between government and guerrilla forces broke out at the end of August 1970. This escalated into full civil war in the latter half of September, with thousands of deaths and injuries. On 16 September a military Cabinet was formed under Brig. Muhammad Daoud—in any case martial law had been in force since the end of the June 1967 war—and immediately Field Marshal Habis Majali replaced as commander-in-chief Lt-Gen. Mashour Haditha, who had been sympathetic to the commandos and had tried to restrain their severest opponents in the army.

In the fighting that followed, the guerrillas claimed full control in the north, aided by Syrian forces and, it was later revealed, three battalions of the PLA sent back by President Nasser from the Suez front. The Arab states generally appealed for an end to the fighting. Libya threatened to intervene and later broke off diplomatic relations; Kuwait stopped its aid to the Government; but the Iraqi troops stationed on the eastern front against Israel notably failed to intervene. On the government side talks were held with the USA about direct military assistance. In the event such a dangerous widening of the Palestinian confrontation was avoided by the scale of the casualties in Jordan and by the diplomacy of Arab Heads of State (reinforced by President Nasser's reported threat to intervene on the guerrillas' behalf) who prevailed upon King Hussein and Yasser Arafat to sign an agreement in Cairo on 27 September 1970, ending the war. The previous day a civilian Cabinet had been restored under Ahmad Toukan. Five military members were retained.

A definitive agreement, very favourable to the liberation organizations, was signed by Hussein and Arafat on 13 October in Amman, but this proved to be simply the beginning of a phase of sporadic warfare between the two parties, punctuated by new agreements, during which the commandos were gradually forced out of Amman and driven from their positions in the north back towards the Syrian frontier. At the end of October a new government, still containing three army officers, was formed under Wasfi at-Tal. By January 1971 army moves against the Palestine guerrillas had become much more blatant, and the UAR, Syria and Algeria all issued strong protests at the Jordanian Government's attempt to 'liquidate' the liberation movements. All but two brigades of Iraqi troops were, however, withdrawn from Jordan.

By April 1971 the Jordanian Government seemed strong enough to set a deadline for the guerrillas' withdrawal of their remaining men and heavy armaments from the capital. On 13 July a major government attack began on the guerrillas entrenched in the Jerash-Ajloun area. Four days later it was all over. The Government claimed that all the bases had been destroyed and that 2,300 of 2,500 guerrillas in them had been captured. Most of the Palestinians taken prisoner by the Jordanian Government were released a few days later, either to leave for other Arab states or to return to normal life in Jordan.

The 'solution' (in King Hussein's word) of the guerrilla 'problem' provoked strong reaction from other Arab governments. Iraq and Syria closed their borders with Jordan; Algeria suspended diplomatic relations; and Egypt, Libya, Sudan and both Yemens voiced public criticism. Relations with Syria deteriorated fastest of all, but normal trading and diplomatic relations were restored by February 1972.

In the mean time, Saudi Arabia had been attempting to bring together guerrilla leaders and Jordanian Government representatives to work out a new version of the Cairo and Amman agreements. Meetings did take place in Jeddah but were fruitless, and the Palestinians responded in their own way to the events of July. Three unsuccessful attempts were made in September to hijack Jordanian airliners. Then, on 28 September 1971, Wasfi at-Tal, the Prime Minister and Minister of Defence, was assassinated by members of a Palestinian guerrilla group, the Black September Organization, and other assassination attempts were made.

HUSSEIN'S ANSWER

Throughout the period since the liquidation of the guerrillas in July 1971 Hussein had been seeking to strengthen his political position. In August he announced the creation of a tribal council—a body of sheikhs or other notables, appointed by him and chaired by the Crown Prince—which was to deal with the affairs of tribal areas. A month later the formation of the Jordanian National Union was announced. This (renamed Arab National Union in March 1972) was to be Jordan's only legal political organization. It was not a party in the usual sense; proponents of 'imported ideologies' were debarred from membership; the King became president, and the Crown Prince vice-president, and appointed the 36 members of the Supreme Executive Committee.

However, the King's boldest political move, and an obvious attempt to regain his standing in the eyes of Palestinians, was his unfolding of plans for a United Arab Kingdom in March 1972. This Kingdom was to federate a Jordanian region, with Amman as its capital and also federal capital, and a Palestinian region, with Jerusalem as its capital. Each region was to be virtually autonomous, though the King would rule both and there would be a federal Council of Ministers.

Outside Jordan there was almost universal criticism of this plan from interested parties—Israel, the Palestinian organizations and Egypt, which in the following month broke off diplomatic relations. Jordan's isolation in the Arab world had never been more complete.

Throughout the rest of 1972 and the first half of 1973 Hussein continued to adhere to his original plans for a United Arab Kingdom, but at the same time he insisted that peace with Israel could be arrived at only within the framework of UN Security Council Resolution 242 (see Documents on Palestine, p. 86) and strongly denied suggestions from other Arab states that he was considering signing a separate peace treaty with Israel.

The internal security of Jordan was threatened in November 1972 when an attempted military coup in Amman by Major Rafeh Hindawi was thwarted. In February 1973 Abu Daoud, one of the leaders of al-Fatah, and 16 other guerrillas were arrested on charges of infiltrating into Jordan for the purpose of subversive activities.

The latter affair took place while King Hussein was on a visit to the USA requesting defence and financial aid. On his return he commuted the death sentences passed on the guerrillas by a Jordanian military court and previously confirmed by himself, to life imprisonment. In May 1973 Hussein's Prime Minister, Ahmad Lauzi, resigned for health reasons and

a new government under Zaid ar-Rifai, who was known as an opponent of the Palestinian guerrillas, was formed.

In September 1973 Hussein attended a 'reconciliation summit' with Presidents Sadat of Egypt and Assad of Syria. This was Jordan's first official contact with the two states since they had broken diplomatic relations, and they were restored after the summit. The meeting was condemned by al-Fatah, Libya and Iraq, but Jordan regained some stature in the Arab world after Hussein's general amnesty for all political prisoners; among those released was Abu Daoud.

During the Middle East War in October 1973 Jordan sent troops to support Syria on the Golan Heights but was otherwise not actively involved, and did not open a third front against the Israelis as in the 1967 war. Jordan was represented at the Geneva talks in December 1973. During February 1974 there was considerable unrest among sections of the army, although this was settled by increases in pay, ordered by Hussein, who was out of the country when the disturbances started. In April Hussein announced that the Arab National Union, which was then the sole political organization in Jordan, was to be reorganized with an executive and council of reduced numbers.

During most of 1974 the main characteristic of Hussein's policy towards the PLO and the status of the West Bank was extreme ambiguity. He continued to try to preserve the West Bank as part of his Kingdom despite strong pressure from other Arab states and the increasing influence of the PLO. In September 1974 after a meeting between Egypt, Syria and the PLO expressing support for the PLO as the 'only legitimate representative of the Palestinian people', Jordan refused to participate in further Middle East peace talks. However, in October 1974 at the Arab Summit Conference at Rabat (see Documents on Palestine, p. 89), representatives of twenty Arab Heads of State unanimously recognized the PLO as the sole legitimate representative of the Palestinians, and its right to establish a national authority over any liberated Palestinian territory. Effectively ceding Jordan's claim to represent the Palestinians and reincorporate the West Bank, when recaptured, into the Hashemite Kingdom, Hussein reluctantly assented to the resolution. He said that Jordan would continue to strive for the liberation of the West Bank and recognize the full rights of citizenship of Palestinians in Jordan. The prospect of a separate, independently-ruled Palestinian state was strongly condemned by Israel.

JORDAN AFTER THE RABAT SUMMIT

Following the Rabat Conference Hussein was given more extensive powers in revisions to the Jordanian Constitution approved by the National Assembly in November. He was allowed to rule without the National Assembly for a year, and to reorganize his Kingdom in order to lessen the numbers of Palestinians in the executive and legislative branches of government, his 1972 plan for a United Arab Kingdom now being wholly defunct. The National Assembly was dissolved and a new government formed in November, with Zaid ar-Rifai remaining Prime Minister. Palestinian representation was decreased, and the question of citizenship of the estimated 800,000 Palestinians on the East Bank became contentious. Elections in Jordan were postponed in March 1975 and when the National Assembly was briefly reconvened in February 1976 a constitutional amendment was enacted to suspend elections indefinitely.

The success of the PLO at the Rabat Conference had, despite internal feuds, considerably strengthened its position. This was further the case when the UN acknowledged the PLO as the sole legitimate representative of the Palestinians by an overwhelming majority in November. The PLO was also granted observer status at the UN.

One of the most notable results of the Rabat Summit Conference, and of Hussein's virtual abandonment of his claim to the West Bank, was an improvement in relations with the Arab world in general, and with Syria in particular. During 1975 various links with Syria were forged and strengthened. Early in the year Hussein visited Damascus and President Assad visited Jordan in June. A supreme joint committee was set up to co-ordinate military and political planning, with the two countries' Prime Ministers as chairmen. In August a

Supreme Command Council, headed by the King and President Assad, was formed to direct military and political action against Israel, and in December 1976 it was announced that a form of political union between the two countries was to be elaborated.

This close relationship, however, was jeopardized by President Sadat's visit to Israel in November 1977, and subsequently threatened by Syria's proposed *rapprochement* with Iraq. Jordan, unlike Syria, was anxious not to condemn Sadat's peace initiative, but did not want to destroy its growing relationship with Syria. King Hussein, therefore, remained uncommitted and tried to act as a conciliator between Egypt on the one hand and the 'rejectionist' states (Algeria, Libya, Iraq, Syria and the People's Democratic Republic of Yemen) on the other. Jordan, however, emphatically rejected Israel's peace proposals which were put forward by Prime Minister Begin in December 1977, and maintained its policy of demanding an Israeli withdrawal from Gaza and the West Bank, including East Jerusalem, leaving no Jewish settlements. Jordan also wanted the creation of a Palestinian homeland, the nature of whose link with Jordan should be decided by a referendum.

It was these factors which helped to determine Jordan's attitude to the Camp David agreements (see Documents on Palestine, p. 90) in September 1978 and the subsequent peace treaty between Egypt and Israel (see Documents on Palestine, p. 92) in March 1979. Jordan refused to be drawn into the Camp David talks by the USA, and joined the other Arab states at the Baghdad Arab summit in drawing up a list of sanctions against Egypt.

Immediately prior to the signing of the peace treaty, Jordan showed its commitment to the PLO by welcoming Yasser Arafat on an official visit, and after the treaty was signed Jordan was the first Arab country still having diplomatic relations with Egypt to break them off. In the months that followed the signing of the peace treaty, however, Jordan's hostility to Egypt subsided, and was replaced by the souring of relations with Syria. In spite of Jordanian denials, Syria was convinced that the Muslim Brotherhood (allowed limited freedom in Jordan) was fostering treachery inside Syria. Syria also disapproved of Jordan's support for Iraq in the Iran–Iraq War. These factors led to a build-up of Syrian and Jordanian troops on the frontier in December 1980, and to mediation between the two sides by Saudi Arabia. Relations did not improve in February 1981 when the Jordanian Chargé d'affaires in Beirut was abducted (allegedly by Syrians), and Jordan responded by abrogating a six-year economic and customs agreement with Syria.

Throughout 1981 Jordan continued with its policy of supporting Iraq, and in January 1982 Hussein announced that he was prepared to take charge of a special 'Yarmuk Force' of Jordanians to give military help to Iraq. In April, however, as Iraq's position in the war with Iran grew weaker, Hussein tried, unsuccessfully, to encourage a negotiated settlement between Iran and Iraq (by 1984 Hussein was, once more, offering troops and other military assistance to Iraq) and a revival of Saudi Arabia's Fahd plan for a resolution of the Arab-Israeli question. After the Israeli invasion of Lebanon in June 1982, Hussein found himself a key part of President Reagan's peace plan, involving the creation of an autonomous Palestinian authority on the West Bank in association with Jordan (see Documents on Palestine, p. 95). Hussein discussed the matter in Washington in December, and in January 1983 held talks with the PLO leader, Yasser Arafat, in Amman.

Opinion within Jordan was very sceptical of the supposed advantages that would accrue to Jordan if Hussein associated himself too deeply with President Reagan's peace plan. As well as a military threat from Syria, there was the possibility of the withdrawal of aid from other Arab countries. Talks between Hussein and Arafat again took place in early April, however, when Arafat stressed his commitment to the Fez plan which had been agreed at the Arab summit in September 1982 (see Documents on Palestine, p. 95). By the middle of April the Reagan peace plan seemed dead, when Arafat rejected the draft agreement which Hussein had prepared. In the weeks that followed, Hussein still claimed to support the Reagan plan. Much of his time, however, was spent in taking

steps to control emigration of Palestinians from the West Bank in Jordan.

In domestic affairs, Hussein had dissolved the House of Representatives in 1974, but in April 1978 he formed a 60-member National Consultative Council (NCC) appointed by Royal Decree. The third term of the NCC began on 20 April 1982. In December 1979 Sharif Abd al-Hamid Sharaf replaced Mudar Badran as Prime Minister. Sharaf, however, died of a heart attack on 3 July 1980, and was replaced as Prime Minister by the former Minister of Agriculture, Qassim ar-Rimawi. In August, however, a new government under former Prime Minister Mudar Badran was introduced, although little change of policy resulted.

THE RECALL OF THE NATIONAL ASSEMBLY

Despite the failure to agree a formula for the creation of a Palestinian state on the West Bank with Yasser Arafat, Jordan gave diplomatic support to Arafat when a Syrian-backed revolt against his leadership of al-Fatah, the major guerrilla group within the PLO, erupted in Lebanon in May 1983. During the last three months of 1983, Jordanian diplomats in several European countries, and targets in Amman, came under attack from terrorists who were thought to be members of a radical Arab group, based in Syria, which was angered by Jordan's call for Egypt to be readmitted to the community of Arab states, by its backing for Arafat and by the prospect of a revival of President Reagan's peace plan which their improved relations raised.

With a view to recovering something from the West Bank before Jewish settlement there produced a *de facto* extension of Israel, King Hussein dissolved the National Consultative Council on 5 January 1984 and reconvened the National Assembly, which had been suspended in 1974, for its first session since 1967. At the same time, he embarked upon a series of talks with Yasser Arafat, dealing with the Palestinian question, which sought to consolidate their good relations and to establish a moderate core of opinion as a counter-weight to the intransigent Syrian, Libyan and extremist PLO position, that a solution could only be achieved by armed struggle. Hussein, moreover, could not forget that some 60% of his subjects were Palestinians. By recalling the National Assembly, Hussein seemed, effectively, to be creating the kind of Palestinian forum which was called for in the Reagan plan. This was not, as it turned out, a prelude to a concerted move by Hussein and Arafat towards establishing a Palestinian state on the West Bank. The National Assembly provided a focus for a debate which revealed strong opposition among Jordanian Palestinians to the Reagan plan. As the talks between Hussein and Arafat progressed, they were at pains to stress that they stood by the resolution of the Rabat Summit Conference in 1974, which recognized the PLO as the sole legitimate representative of the Palestinian people.

Israel allowed the surviving West Bank deputies to attend the reconvened House of Representatives (the Lower House), which unanimously approved constitutional amendments enabling elections to the House to be held in the East Bank alone but giving itself the right to elect deputies from the West Bank, without whom the House would have been inquorate. The first elections in Jordan for 17 years, and the first in which women were allowed to vote, took place on 12 March 1984 (although political parties were still banned). The House of Representatives had already, in January, elected seven deputies from the West Bank by majority vote to fill the places of members who had died since 1974, bringing the membership of the House up to 52. The 12 March elections filled the remaining 8 seats from the East Bank. Any thought that Hussein, in reviving the National Assembly, might, in the absence of agreement with the PLO on the Reagan plan, seek a mandate from the West Bank deputies to begin talks with Israel on Palestinian autonomy, was set further aside by the election of three Muslim fundamentalists and an Arab nationalist in the eight East Bank by-elections. The extent of the opposition to a solution based on the Reagan plan was apparent.

The nucleus of a moderate body of Arab opinion on the Palestinian question did, none the less, give the impression of being formed around Jordan and Yasser Arafat, with likely support to come from Saudi Arabia, Egypt and the Gulf states. The opposition to these developments of other Arab groups was reaffirmed when the Jordanian Embassy in Tripoli, Libya, was burnt down in February 1984. Jordan responded by severing diplomatic relations with Libya. Sporadic attacks on Jordanian diplomats, principally in European countries, continued throughout 1984 and 1985, for which responsibility was claimed by various extremist Arab groups including the Islamic Jihad and the re-emergent Black September organization, which was formed after the expulsion of the PLO from Jordan in September 1970. Jordan suspected Syria and Libya of being behind these attacks.

In January 1984 the Jordanian Cabinet resigned, and a new one, containing a higher proportion of Palestinians and led by Ahmad Ubeidat, as Prime Minister, took office.

RELATIONS WITH THE SUPERPOWERS

At the beginning of 1984 the US Government tried to renew its efforts to gain congressional approval for a $220m. plan to supply Jordan with arms and equipment for an 8,000-strong Jordanian strike force. King Hussein tried to distance Jordan from any interest or involvement in the creation of such a force. Plans for a Jordanian strike force were abandoned by the Reagan Administration in June.

Hussein, frustrated by the unwillingness of the USA to use its influence with Israel to 'freeze' Jewish settlement of the West Bank and unable to buy arms from the USA, began to look to the USSR for diplomatic backing in solving the problem of Palestinian autonomy and for armaments with which to defend his country. In January 1985 Jordan purchased an air defence system from the USSR, having already made an agreement to buy French anti-aircraft missiles in September 1984. The need to re-equip the Jordanian air force was acute: in 1984 the Jordanians possessed only about 100 effective fighter aircraft, compared with the 630 and 600 aircraft respectively of Israel and Syria, according to 1982/83 figures.

Although US President Reagan was advocating the sale of arms worth $500m.–$750m. to Jordan in 1985, there was still considerable opposition to the proposal, and he was advised not to put it before Congress and risk a Senate veto. Instead, on 12 June, King Hussein was offered extra economic aid of $250m., to be spread over 1985 and 1986, by Secretary of State Shultz, as a token of US support for his efforts to achieve a peace settlement between the Arabs and Israel. Jordan received US aid of $136m. in 1984, and the level of aid in 1985 and 1986 had originally been set at $111.7m. and $117m. respectively. The Senate authorized the aid but spread it over 27 months, not 15, as the Reagan Administration had requested.

JOINT JORDANIAN-PALESTINIAN PEACE PROPOSALS

In September 1984, to the anger of radical Arab states, Jordan decided to re-establish diplomatic relations with Egypt, five years after breaking them off in protest at the Egypt-Israel peace treaty of 1979. Hussein rejected the Israeli offer of direct negotiations, excluding the PLO, in October, calling instead for a conference of all the concerned parties in the Middle East, including, on an equal footing with nation states in the region, the PLO. He required Israel to accept the principle of 'land for peace'—this is, talks leading to the restoration of occupied territories (including East Jerusalem) to Jordan, in return for a comprehensive Arab-Israeli peace treaty. Negotiations, according to Hussein, should proceed on the basis of UN Security Council Resolution 242 of November 1967. This last point was the impediment to Jordanian and PLO agreement to a programme for peace talks. Resolution 242 had not been acceptable to the PLO as it referred to the Palestinian Arabs as refugees, implicitly denying the existence of a Palestinian nation and Palestinians' right to self-determination, and recognized Israel's right to exist. The Palestine National Council (PNC), which finally convened in Amman in November 1984, replied non-committally to King Hussein's

offer of a joint Jordanian-Palestinian peace initiative, without explicit rejection or acceptance of the principles embodied in Resolution 242, and referred the proposal to the PLO Executive Committee for examination.

On 23 February 1985, in Amman, King Hussein and Yasser Arafat announced the terms of a joint Jordanian-Palestinian agreement on the framework for a peace settlement in the Middle East, which the two leaders had finalized on 11 February. It held that peace talks should take the form of an international conference including the five permanent members of the UN Security Council and all parties to the conflict, including the PLO, representing the Palestinian people in a joint Jordanian-Palestinian delegation. The Palestinian people would in future exercise their right to self-determination in the context of a proposed confederated state of Jordan and Palestine. The Jordanian Government claimed that the agreement was based on a number of UN resolutions and not solely UN Security Council Resolution 242, though the published text of the accord (see Documents on Palestine, p. 96) gave land in exchange for peace, a central tenet of that resolution, as its first principle. The PLO Executive Committee, in approving the terms of the accord (providing that they received full Arab support) on 20 February, complicated the position by stressing that the joint position stemmed, in fact, from a rejection of Camp David, the Reagan plan and Resolution 242 as well. According to King Hussein, Arafat subsequently accepted Resolution 242 as the basis for future peace negotiations, but Arafat made no public declaration of acceptance. Argument over the implications of the agreement persisted, and the PLO adopted a new position on the status of the Palestinian representation at future peace negotiations, which, it said, should be within a united Arab, not merely a Jordanian-Palestinian, delegation. Syria and Libya and the rebel PLO factions predictably rejected the Amman agreement.

In March 1985 President Mubarak of Egypt called for talks between Egypt, the USA and a joint Jordanian-Palestinian delegation. The PLO Executive Committee rejected the proposal as it deviated from the accord with Jordan. Israel rejected the idea of preliminary talks and any suggestion that the USA might negotiate with the PLO, as it had always refused to do unless the PLO renounced terrorism and accepted Israel's right to exist. In May King Hussein, still averring that the PLO accepted UN Security Council Resolutions 242 and 338 as the basis for negotiations, put foward a four-stage plan in Washington. Under the terms of the plan, the USA would first meet a Jordanian-Palestinian delegation, not including PLO representatives. Arafat would then be prepared to make a formal declaration of the PLO's readiness to recognize and negotiate with Israel if the USA publicly stated its support for Palestinian self-determination within the context of a Jordanian-Palestinian confederation, as proposed in the 11 February agreement between King Hussein and Arafat. The USA would then hold a second meeting with a Jordanian-Palestinian delegation, including PLO representatives, at which the terms of the third and fourth stages of the plan, an international conference under the auspices of the five permanent members of the UN Security Council, leading to direct negotiations between Israel and a Jordanian-Palestinian delegation, would be discussed. Israel rejected the plan and the call for an international peace conference, and instead proposed enlisting the support of the permanent members of the Security Council for direct talks between Israel and a joint Jordanian-Palestinian delegation including 'authentic Palestinian representatives' from the Occupied Territories who were not members of the PLO or the PNC. In July Israel rejected a list of seven Palestinians, five of whom were members of the PLO loyal to Yasser Arafat or had links with the PNC, whom King Hussein had presented to the USA as candidates for inclusion in a joint Jordanian-Palestinian delegation to hold preliminary talks with the USA. The Israeli Prime Minister, Shimon Peres, later conceded that two of the seven fulfilled his requirements.

The Prime Minister, Ahmad Ubeidat, resigned in April 1985. On 5 April a new Cabinet, only four of whose 23 members were retained from the previous Government, was sworn in under the premiership of Zaid ar-Rifai, who had served as Prime Minister during the 1970s.

THE COLLAPSE OF THE JORDANIAN-PALESTINIAN PEACE INITIATIVE

King Hussein and Yasser Arafat continued to seek Arab support for their peace initiative, but an extraordinary meeting of the Arab states in Casablanca, in August 1985 (which was boycotted by Syria, Libya, Lebanon, the PDRY and Algeria), merely noted the existence of the Jordanian-Palestinian agreement and reaffirmed Arab allegiance to the Fez plan of September 1982.

Further progress was then hampered by a series of terrorist attacks, carried out by Palestinian organizations. In September three Israelis were murdered by terrorists in Larnaca, Cyprus. Israel blamed the PLO's élite Force 17 and retaliated by bombing the PLO's headquarters in Tunis on 1 October. Later in October an Italian cruise ship, the *Achille Lauro*, was 'hijacked' in the eastern Mediterranean by members of the Palestine Liberation Front (the faction of that name led by 'Abu' Abbas, nominally loyal to Arafat), who killed an elderly American Jewish passenger.

King Hussein was under increasing pressure to advance the peace process, if necessary without the participation of the PLO. In September President Reagan revived a plan to sell US arms worth $1,900m. to Jordan. The proposal was approved by Congress on the condition that Jordan entered into direct talks with Israel before 1 March 1986. However, a *rapprochement* developed between Jordan and Syria, which made such a development even more unlikely. In February 1986 the administration of President Reagan in the USA indefinitely postponed its proposed arms sale to Jordan (worth $1,500m., with the withdrawal of *Hawk* missiles from the package) when it became clear that it would not be approved by the Senate. King Hussein said that he would look instead to European countries and the USSR for arms supplies.

Relations between Jordan and Syria had been poor since 1979, when Syria had accused Jordan of harbouring anti-Syrian groups. Their policies also diverged in respect of the Iran–Iraq War, in which Syria supported Iran, and Jordan Iraq. In November 1985 King Hussein admitted that Jordan had, unwittingly, been a base for the Sunni fundamentalist Muslim Brotherhood in its attempts to overthrow Syria's President Assad, but stated that members of the group would no longer receive shelter there. The Prime Ministers of the two countries met in Damascus in November and agreed on the need for 'joint Arab action' to achieve peace in the Middle East. At previous talks in Saudi Arabia in October, Jordan and Syria had rejected 'partial and unilateral' solutions and affirmed their adherence to the Fez plan, omitting all mention of the Jordanian-Palestinian peace initiative. President Assad and King Hussein confirmed the improved state of Syrian-Jordanian relations when they met in Damascus in December.

By pursuing a reconciliation with Syria, which was opposed to Yasser Arafat's leadership of the PLO, King Hussein may have hoped to exert pressure on Arafat to take the initiative in the peace process and finally signal PLO acceptance of Resolution 242. Arafat was also under pressure from King Hussein and President Mubarak of Egypt to promote the PLO's credibility as a prospective partner in peace talks by renouncing terrorism. He responded to their appeals in November, in Cairo, by effectively reiterating a PLO decision of 1974 to confine military operations to the Occupied Territories and Israel. Any credence that this declaration may have won was immediately dispelled by Arafat's aides, who repudiated it. Then, in December, the PLO Executive Committee reiterated its opposition to Resolution 242.

Shimon Peres, the Israeli Prime Minister, although he remained opposed to the idea of preliminary negotiations excluding Israel, intimated in a speech at the UN in October that he would not rule out the possibility of an international conference on the Palestinian question. Rumours of a secret meeting between King Hussein and Peres were followed at the end of October by the disclosure to the Israeli press of a document, drawn up by the Israeli Prime Minister's office, which purported to summarize the state of negotiations between Israel and Jordan. The document suggested the establishment of an interim Israeli-Jordanian condominium of the West Bank, granting a form of Palestinian autonomy, and recorded mutual agreement on the need for an international forum for peace talks. Israel would consent to the participation of the USSR in such a forum (on the condition that it re-established diplomatic relations with Israel), and of Syria, but not of the PLO, on whose involvement King Hussein still insisted.

Given Yasser Arafat's persistent refusal to accept UN Security Council Resolutions 242 and 338 as the basis for peace talks, the demise of the Jordanian-Palestinian peace initiative had been forecast for some time. On 19 February 1986 King Hussein publicly severed political links with the PLO 'until such time as their word becomes their bond, characterized by commitment, credibility and constancy'. Arafat was ordered to close his main PLO offices in Jordan by 1 April. The activities of PLO members in the country were henceforth to be restricted to an even greater extent than before, and a number of officers of al-Fatah, loyal to Arafat, were expelled. King Hussein made efforts to strengthen Jordanian influence and create a Palestinian constituency in the Occupied Territories, independent of Arafat's PLO, including: the passing of a draft law by the House of Representatives in March 1986, increasing the number of seats in the House from 60 to 142 (71 seats each for the East and West Bank), thereby providing for greater West Bank Palestinian representation in the House; and the introduction, in August 1986, with Israeli support, of a $1,300m. five-year development plan for the West Bank and the Gaza strip.

This last measure provoked strong criticism from Yasser Arafat and from West Bank Palestinians, who claimed that it represented a normalization of relations between Jordan and Israel. There was considerable support for Arafat among Palestinians in Jordan and in the West Bank, and this was consolidated after he re-established himself at the head of a reunified PLO at the PNC session in Algiers in April 1987 (when the Jordan-PLO accord of 1985 was formally abrogated). As criticism of King Hussein mounted in Jordan and in the West Bank, the authorities responded by imposing new security measures, arresting dissidents (in particular members of the fundamentalist Muslim Brotherhood and the banned Jordanian Communist Party), tightening press censorship and 'blacklisting' journalists deemed too critical of the government.

After the termination of political co-ordination with the PLO, Jordan continued to reject Israeli requests for direct peace talks which excluded a form of PLO representation. However, Jordan's subsequent efforts to strengthen its influence in Israeli-occupied territories and to foster a Palestinian constituency there which was independent of the PLO, complemented Israeli measures to grant limited autonomy to the Palestinian community in the West Bank, by appointing Arab mayors instead of Israeli military administrators in four towns. In May 1987, after a number of secret meetings with King Hussein, Peres (who was now the Israeli Minister of Foreign Affairs) claimed to have made significant progress on the critical issue of Palestinian representation at a peace conference, and to have the consent of Egypt, Jordan and the USA for convening an international conference, including the five members of the UN Security Council and a delegation of Palestinians (presumably not PLO members) who 'reject terrorism and violence' and accept UN Security Council resolutions 242 and 338 as the basis for negotiations. King Hussein continued publicly to insist on the need for the PLO to be represented, but he appeared to have accepted (contrary to his long-standing official policy) that the conference would have no power to impose a peace settlement, and would be only a preliminary to direct talks between the main protagonists in the Middle East conflict. However, the prospect of an international peace conference remained academic for as long as there was no majority in the Israeli Cabinet in favour of Peres' plan and, therefore, for as long as the Israeli coalition Government of National Unity remained in power. The Prime Minister, Itzhak Shamir, was opposed in principle to an international conference, which would negotiate on the basis of an Israeli offer of the return of occupied territory in exchange for peace. He reiterated his alternative proposal to Peres' plan, namely, direct regional talks involving Israel, Egypt, Jordan, Palestinian representatives and the USA.

ARAB LEAGUE SUMMIT IN AMMAN

During 1987 King Hussein pursued his efforts, begun in 1986, to reconcile Syria and Iraq, with the wider aim of securing Arab unity. He was instrumental in arranging the first full summit meeting of the Arab League (excluding Egyptian representation) for eight years, which took place in Amman in November, principally to discuss the Iran–Iraq War. In September Jordan had restored diplomatic relations with Libya, which had modified its support for Iran and now urged a cease-fire. The Arab summit meeting unanimously adopted a resolution of solidarity with Iraq, which condemned Iran for its occupation of Arab territory and for prolonging the war (although Syria obstructed the adoption of diplomatic or other sanctions). King Hussein's appeal for Egypt to be restored to membership of the League was successfully resisted by Syria and Libya, but nine Arab states re-established diplomatic relations with Egypt soon after the summit, and these were followed by Tunisia in January 1988 and by the People's Democratic Republic of Yemen in February. President Saddam Hussain of Iraq and President Assad of Syria held two sessions of talks at the summit, and the resumption of co-operation between Jordan and the PLO was announced.

THE INTIFADA AND THE SHULTZ PLAN

In December 1987 a violent Palestinian uprising (*intifada*), against Israeli occupation of the West Bank and Gaza Strip, erupted in the Occupied Territories. Despite intensive and often brutal security measures, Israel was unable to suppress the revolt. Public demonstrations in Jordan (60% of whose population were of Palestinian origin) in support of the *intifada* were muted, owing mainly to security precautions taken by the authorities to prevent unrest. In April the Palestinian extremist group, Black September, claimed responsibility for a series of bomb attacks in Amman, which, it said, were directed against the 'client Zionist regime in Jordan'.

The intensity of the *intifada* and the world-wide condemnation of Israeli security tactics, and revulsion at the degrading conditions in which many Palestinians were forced to live in the Occupied Territories, alerted the international community to the need for a revival of the efforts to secure an Arab-Israeli peace agreement. At the end of February 1988 the US Secretary of State, George Shultz, embarked on a tour of Middle East capitals, in an attempt to elicit support for a new peace initiative. The Shultz plan, as the initiative came to be known, proposed the convening of an international peace conference, involving all parties to the Arab-Israeli conflict and the five members of the UN Security Council, with the Palestinians represented in a joint Jordanian-Palestinian delegation, excluding the PLO. This conference would have no power to impose a settlement and would act only as a consultative forum prior to and during subsequent direct talks between Israel and each of its Arab neighbours, and between Israel and a joint Jordanian-Palestinian delegation. The latter talks would determine the details of a three-year transitional period of autonomy for the 1.5m. Palestinians in the Occupied Territories, leading (before the start of the transitional period) to negotiations to determine the final status of government in the Territories. (For full details of the Shultz plan, see Documents on Palestine, p. 96.)

The plan's refusal to contemplate the participation of the PLO, the Palestinians' right to self-determination, and the establishment of an independent Palestinian state in the West Bank (i.e. the principles of the plan formulated at the Arab summit in Fez in 1982), made it impossible for the Arab nations to accept. Jordan, which had initially welcomed a renewal of the USA's commitment to peace in the Middle East, became disillusioned by its failure to apply persuasive pressure on Israel's Prime Minister, Itzhak Shamir, to modify his opposition to the Shultz plan. King Hussein pronounced himself sceptical that Israel would withdraw militarily from the West Bank prior to the transitional autonomy period, as the plan would require it to do, and reiterated his opposition, in accordance with Arab summit resolutions, to 'partial or interim solutions'. He welcomed the USA's acceptance, on 1 March 1988, of the concept of the Palestinians' 'legitimate rights', although he asked the USA to clarify its definition of

those 'rights'. However, given the resumption of Jordanian political co-operation with the PLO, the enhanced status conferred on the organization by the *intifada*, and the potentially threatening reaction of Palestinians in Jordan, King Hussein was effectively constrained from supporting the Shultz plan.

An extraordinary summit meeting of the Arab League was held in Algiers in June 1988 to discuss the continuing *intifada* and the Arab-Israeli conflict in general. Addressing the summit, King Hussein gave his unconditional support to the *intifada* and disclaimed any ambition to restore Jordanian rule in the West Bank. He insisted that the PLO must represent the Palestinians at any future peace conference, and repeatedly stressed the PLO's status as 'the sole legitimate representative of the Palestinian people'. The Shultz plan, he claimed, had been launched only because the *intifada* had taken on the appearance of a Palestinian war against Israel.

The summit hailed the 'heroic' Palestinian uprising and its final communiqué effectively rejected the Shultz plan by endorsing the Palestinians' right to self-determination and the establishment of an independent Palestinian state in the West Bank, and insisting on the participation of the PLO in future peace talks.

JORDAN SEVERS ITS LINKS WITH THE WEST BANK

The effect of the *intifada* had been to increase international support for Palestinian national rights, to heighten Palestinian aspirations to statehood and to reinforce support for the PLO (which was helping to organize the uprising) as the Palestinians' representative in achieving it. From King Hussein's point of view, the *intifada* had created a new set of conditions in which Jordan could no longer realistically present itself as an alternative to the PLO. The King's subsequent actions were entirely consistent with his acknowledgement of the new realities, as expressed at the Algiers summit, yet they were still greeted with surprise.

On 28 July 1988 Jordan cancelled its $1,300m. Development Plan for the West Bank, which had been opposed by the PLO since its launch in 1986 and had remained substantially underfunded. Then, two days later, King Hussein severed Jordan's legal and administrative links with the West Bank, dissolving the lower house of the Jordanian Parliament (the House of Representatives), where Palestinian representatives for the West Bank occupied 30 of the 60 seats. The King explained that his actions were taken in accordance with the wishes of the PLO and with the resolutions of the Rabat and Fez Arab summits in 1974 and 1982, and the positions adopted at the recent Algiers summit, which recognized the PLO as 'the sole legitimate representative of the Palestinian people'.

The extent to which Jordan was actually disengaging from the West Bank was uncertain and it appeared that King Hussein was leaving the way open for the resumption of political co-ordination between Jordan and the PLO in the future. For example, King Hussein stopped short of formally and irrevocably repealing the 'union agreement' of 1950 (Jordan's annexation of the West Bank) uniting the East and West Banks of the River Jordan; while the notion that, by dissolving the House of Representatives and dismantling Jordanian civil institutions, the King was actually transferring administrative responsibility for the West Bank to the PLO was difficult to take seriously: the Jordanian legislature had exercised little or no practical influence over the affairs of the West Bank since the Israeli occupation began in 1967, and Israel soon introduced measures to restrict the activities of Palestinian institutions, in order to prevent the PLO from filling the administrative vacuum left by the dismissal of about 20,000 Jordanian teachers and civil servants who had continued to run public services in the West Bank after the Israeli occupation. It was suggested that, in placing responsibility for the Palestinians in the West Bank and for furthering the peace process in the hands of the PLO, King Hussein foresaw the inevitable failure of the PLO to finance and administer public services, and a political and diplomatic impasse that would demonstrate to Palestinians the necessity of Jordanian involvement if their hopes for self-government were to be realized. For its part, the PLO leadership complained that King Hussein had not consulted it prior to announcing the removal of Jordanian links, but the move was generally welcomed by the 850,000 Palestinians in the West Bank. According to the Jordanian Government, Palestinians residing in the West Bank were no longer considered to be Jordanian citizens. They were still entitled to hold a Jordanian passport, but this would, in future, only have the status of a 'travel document'.

Jordan's withdrawal from the West Bank appeared finally to make the Shultz plan redundant and to damage the prospects of a victory for Shimon Peres' Labour Party in the Israeli general election, which was scheduled to take place in November 1988. The peace plans of both Shultz and Peres had relied on the Palestinians' being represented at negotiations by a joint Jordanian-Palestinian delegation. Deprived of the so-called 'Jordanian option', the Israeli Labour Party signalled its willingness to negotiate with 'any Palestinians' who renounced the use of violence and recognized Israel's right to exist.

On 15 November 1988 the PNC proclaimed the establishment of an independent State of Palestine and, for the first time, endorsed UN Security Council Resolution 242 as a basis for a Middle East peace settlement, thus implicitly recognizing Israel. Jordan and 60 other countries recognized the new state. In December Yasser Arafat addressed a special session of the UN General Assembly in Geneva, where he renounced violence on behalf of the PLO. Subsequently, the USA opened a dialogue with the PLO, and (although the Israeli Prime Minister, Itzhak Shamir, denounced Arafat's renunciation of terrorism as deceitful) it appeared that Israel would have to negotiate directly with the PLO if it wished to seek a solution to the Palestinian question.

In December 1988 Marwan al-Qassim was appointed Minister of Foreign Affairs, replacing Taher al-Masri, who had been the principal opponent of King Hussein's decision to withdraw from the West Bank and also of the severe economic measures which the Prime Minister, Zaid ar-Rifai, had introduced. In April 1989 riots erupted in several cities in southern Jordan, spreading rapidly to areas near the capital, Amman, after the Government had imposed price rises of between 15% and 50% on basic goods and services. The gravity of the situation was emphasized by reports that only Bedouin and native Jordanians, from whom the Government traditionally drew most of its support, had participated in the riots, while the Palestinians, who formed an estimated 60% of the country's population, were uninvolved; and by the early return to Jordan of King Hussein, who had been making an official visit to the USA when the riots began. The riots led to the resignation of the Prime Minister and his Cabinet. On 24 April Field Marshal Sharif Zaid ibn Shaker, who had been Commander-in-Chief of the Jordanian Armed Forces between 1976 and 1988, was appointed Prime Minister, at the head of a new 24-member Cabinet. While King Hussein refused to make any concessions regarding the price increases which had provoked the disturbances (and which had been implemented in accordance with an agreement with the IMF), he had announced, immediately prior to the appointment of the new Prime Minister, that a general election would be held for the first time since 1967.

TOWARDS DEMOCRACY

A general election to the 80-seat House of Representatives took place on 8 November 1989 and was contested by 647 candidates, most of whom were independent, as the ban on political parties (in force since 1963) had not been withdrawn. However, it was possible for the Muslim Brotherhood (MB) to present candidates for election, owing to its legal status as a charity rather than a political party. At the election, in which 63% of the total electorate (including, for the first time, women) of 877,475 voted the MB won 20 seats, while independent Islamic candidates, who supported the Muslim Brotherhood, won a further 14 seats. It was estimated that Palestinian or Arab nationalist candidates won seven seats and that candidates who were supporters of 'leftist' political groupings won four seats. The remaining seats were won by candidates who were broadly considered to be supporters of the Government. The strength of support for the opposition candidates was regarded as surprising, both in Jordan and abroad, especially since a disproportionately large number of seats had been assigned to rural areas, from which the Government had traditionally drawn most support.

On 4 December 1989 Mudar Badran was appointed Prime Minister by King Hussein. Badran had served as Prime Minister twice previously, during 1976–79 and 1980–84. The new Government did not include any members of the MB who had been elected to the House of Representatives, the MB having declined participation after its demand for the education portfolio had been rejected. Included in the new Cabinet, however, were three independent Muslim deputies and three 'leftists', all of whom were regarded as members of the opposition. The Government received a vote of confidence from the House of Representatives on 1 January 1990. The Prime Minister affirmed continuing support for prevailing austerity measures, and at the end of January announced the abolition of the 1954 anti-communism law.

The discovery of fraud and embezzlement at Petra Bank, Jordan's second largest commercial bank, had led to the seizure of its assets in August 1989 and the subsequent arrest of 22 former employees and business associates of the bank. The scandal spread to the national airline, Alia, and some 37 other companies. Following the 1989 election, King Hussein, under increasing pressure to initiate constitutional reform, promised to allow political parties more freedom and to tighten controls on corruption. In April 1990 he appointed a 60-member Royal Commission to draft a National Charter to regulate political life in Jordan. A former Prime Minister, Ahmad Ubeidat, was appointed Chairman of the commission, whose members included figures from the country's various political and religious groupings, including left-wingers and religious fundamentalists, and whose influence in all areas of public life became increasingly evident during the course of the year. In October 1990 a National Islamic Bloc was formed by more than one-half of the deputies in the House of Representatives. In a Cabinet reshuffle in January 1991 Taher al-Masri, a leading Palestinian who was to be a strong supporter of Iraq's position in the Gulf crisis (see below), was appointed Minister of Foreign Affairs (a post that he had held between 1984 and 1988), in succession to Marwan al-Qassim. Four members of the MB were given portfolios in the new Cabinet.

On 9 June 1991 the National Charter to regulate political life was endorsed by the King and Leading political figures. Among other things, the Charter revoked the ban on Jordanian political parties (which had been imposed since 1963) in return for their allegiance to the monarchy. On 19 June the King accepted the resignation of the Government headed by Mudar Badran and appointed a new Cabinet, with Taher al-Masri, the erstwhile Minister of Foreign Affairs, as Prime Minister. Taher al-Masri was Jordan's first Palestinian-born Prime Minister and, in spite of his support for Saddam Hussain during the 1990–91 Gulf crisis, was known for his liberal, pro-Western views. Badran's resignation was attributed to the King's disapproval of his sympathy for the MB, which had urged that *Shari'a* (Islamic) law should govern the new National Charter and whose members were again excluded from the Cabinet. The new Government obtained a vote of confidence in the House of Representatives on 18 July.

On 7 July 1991 the King issued a decree repealing the provisions of martial law which had been in force since 1967, reportedly at the request of the new Prime Minister, who sought to continue the progress towards greater political freedom and democracy.

ARAB LEAGUE SUMMIT IN BAGHDAD

An emergency summit meeting of the Arab League was held in Baghdad on 28–30 May 1990. Convened under pressure from Jordan and the Palestinians to discuss the 'threat to pan-Arab security' that was presented by the mass emigration of Soviet Jews to Israel, the meeting was boycotted by President Assad of Syria, a long-term adversary of Iraq's President Saddam Hussain, and by four other Arab Heads of State. In October 1989 King Hussein had warned against further Jewish colonization of the Occupied Territories, claiming that Israel was seeking to settle the Soviet immigrants there, thus causing more Palestinians (who already comprised 60% of the population of his country) to flee to Jordan and effectively transform it into a surrogate Palestinian state. The *intifada* had already resulted in a net movement of Palestinians into Jordan. King Hussein urged other Arab nations to provide economic and military assistance to Jordan, declaring that mass Jewish immigration into Israel and the Occupied Territories posed a threat to Jordan which it could not afford to confront alone. Israel had selected Jordan as 'the point through which to penetrate . . . . the Arab Nation', he declared. The PLO leader, Yasser Arafat, urged other Arab states, in vain, to impose economic sanctions on countries involved in the transfer of Jews to Arab lands. President Saddam Hussain of Iraq, supported by King Hussein (who rejected the more moderate stance of both Egypt and Saudi Arabia), vehemently denounced Israel and threatened to use weapons of mass destruction against it. In a final statement, issued at the end of the summit, Arab leaders criticized US economic and military assistance to Israel and reaffirmed their commitment to the defence of Jordanian sovereignty and national security. The question of financial aid for Jordan would be a matter for bilateral negotiations. An Iraqi promise of US \$50m. on 1 June was followed by further promises of aid from Saudi Arabia (\$100m.) and from Kuwait and the UAE (\$200m.).

The issue of Soviet-Jewish emigration to Israel figured prominently in discussions between the British Secretary of State for Foreign and Commonwealth Affairs, Douglas Hurd, and Prime Minister Badran during the former's visit to Jordan on 30–31 May 1990. In May 1991 the then Soviet Minister of Foreign Affairs, Aleksandr Bessmertnykh (visiting Amman for talks with King Hussein), emphasized that Israel's policy of building Jewish settlements in the Occupied Territories was obstructing progress towards peace in the Middle East. Later that month, King Hussein declared that the Arab-Israeli conflict had reached its most critical point since the formation of Israel in 1948, and he urged the world to act decisively to prevent a drift towards extremism.

JORDAN'S POSITION IN THE GULF CRISIS

Even before Iraq's invasion of Kuwait on 2 August 1990, Jordan's economy was in severe difficulties; the country's foreign debt of \$800m. was equivalent to one-quarter of annual GDP. Of all the Arab states affected, Jordan was probably the nation which was most likely to suffer from the effects of the conflict and the imposition of economic sanctions against Iraq, as stipulated by UN Security Council Resolution 661 of 6 August 1990. The loss of remittances from thousands of Jordanian workers who returned, destitute, from Iraq and Kuwait; the increased cost of importing petroleum products (almost all of Jordan's oil had been imported from Iraq); the threatened loss of as much as one-quarter of the country's exports and its transit trade with Iraq and Kuwait; the sudden decline in activity at the Red Sea port of Aqaba, as a result of the naval blockade and increases in insurance rates for shipping in the war zone; the enormous cost of humanitarian aid to refugees fleeing the conflict through its territory: all these were potentially disastrous for Jordan, which was embroiled in events beyond its control.

Following Iraq's invasion of Kuwait, the Palestinians and the PLO supported Saddam Hussain. Officially Jordan, in its own interests, remained neutral in the conflict. King Hussein 'regretted', but did not condemn, the action of Saddam Hussain in invading Kuwait, and Jordanian public opinion was solidly pro-Iraq for the duration of the crisis. Arab League ministers, attending a meeting of the Organization of the Islamic Conference in Cairo on 3 August 1990, issued a statement, opposed by Jordan, condemning the invasion and demanding Iraq's immediate and unconditional withdrawal. At the emergency summit meeting of the Arab League, held in Cairo on 10 August, Jordan abstained in a vote to denounce the annexation of Kuwait and to advocate the deployment of a pan-Arab force to defend Saudi Arabia and neighbouring states from invasion by the forces of Saddam Hussain. King Hussein welcomed Saddam Hussain's proposal, on 12 August, to link Iraq's occupation of Kuwait with the continued Israel occupations, and he held talks with the Iraqi leader in Baghdad on the following day. Another Arab League meeting in Cairo (30–31 August) was boycotted by Jordan and other Arab nations which supported Iraq. King Hussein persistently argued in favour of an

Arab solution to the crisis and opposed the deployment of a multinational armed force in the Gulf region.

In the West, which had always regarded King Hussein as one of its chief allies in the region, there was much criticism of the King's pro-Iraq stance, though this was tempered with acknowledgement of the extremely difficult position in which he found himself. Talks in the USA between the King and President Bush, at Kennebunkport on 16 August, resulted in promises of US financial assistance in return for Jordanian observance of the economic embargo imposed on Iraq. A report by a UN envoy in October 1990 estimated that the crisis would cost Jordan some 30% of its GDP in 1990 and as much as 50% in 1991.

Following the Iraqi invasion of Kuwait, Jordan was overwhelmed by an influx of refugees, who included thousands of migrant workers from Egypt and the Indian sub-continent, fleeing the conflict. The congestion was such that Jordan was forced temporarily to close its border with Iraq in late August 1990, in an attempt to cope with the accumulation of refugees who could not immediately be transported to the Red Sea port of Aqaba or airlifted to their countries of origin. On 3 September Jordan issued an urgent appeal for international aid, partially to offset the costs of caring for the refugees. By October some 800,000 refugees had passed through the country, at a cost of some \$40m. to the Jordanian authorities. About 700 still awaited repatriation.

In mid-September 1990 two of King Hussein's former Palestinian opponents, George Habbash of the Popular Front for the Liberation of Palestine (PFLP) and Nayef Hawatmeh of the Democratic Front for the Liberation of Palestine (DFLP), who had been expelled during the civil war in 1970, were allowed to return to Amman for a pro-Iraqi conference of 'Arab Popular Forces'. The two Damascus-based leaders were received by the King in a display of unity and reconciliation fostered by the Gulf crisis. The conference, which was opened by the Speaker of the Jordanian House of Representatives (although not attended by the King), heard severe criticisms of governments opposed to Saddam Hussain and ended with pledges to wage a *jihad* against foreign forces in the Gulf region if Iraq were attacked. This led to a denunciation of King Hussein by the Saudi Arabian Ambassador in Washington, and Saudi Arabia subsequently expelled Jordanian diplomats and many Jordanian immigrant workers. It also halted oil supplies to the Kingdom, claiming that Jordan had not paid for earlier deliveries.

King Hussein invested considerable personal effort in the search for a peaceful solution to the crisis, visiting London, Paris and Washington. In late August 1990 he arrived in Libya at the start of a peace mission among Arab leaders. He continued to advocate an Arab solution to the crisis and, in a televised message to the US Congress and people on 23 September, he urged the immediate withdrawal of the multinational force from the Gulf region. Speaking at the World Climate Conference in Geneva on 6 November, the King warned of the potentially disastrous environmental consequences of war in the Gulf region (a fear which was subsequently realized when Iraq released oil into the waters of the Gulf and ignited Kuwait's oil installations).

Following talks in Baghdad with Saddam Hussain on 4 December 1990, the King proposed a peace plan linking the Iraqi–Kuwait dispute and the Arab-Israeli conflict. He urged the convening of a peace conference on the Middle East, and that all Arab leaders should take part in a dialogue on the crisis, to take place simultaneously with the talks between the USA and Iraq, which had been proposed by President Bush at the end of November.

THE 1991 GULF WAR

The King's diplomatic efforts continued into 1991, when he embarked, in January, on a fresh tour of European capitals in a final attempt to avert war in the Gulf region. Diplomatic ties with Iran, severed in 1981 after the start of the Iran–Iraq War, were resumed in mid-January 1991, and Jordan was later reported to be supporting Iranian proposals to end the crisis. On 10 January Jordan had closed its ar-Ruweishid border post, on the frontier with Iraq, to all except Jordanian refugees. As war became imminent, Jordan feared a further influx of refugees from Iraq and Kuwait, and claimed that it had still not received UN aid promised for the August 1990 exodus. However, after receiving assurances of UN assistance with the cost of caring for the refugees, the border was reopened on 18 January.

Following the outbreak of hostilities between Iraq and a multinational force on 16 January 1991, the Jordanian Government condemned the bombardment of Iraq as a 'brutal onslaught against an Arab and Muslim nation'. Large-scale anti-Western and anti-Israeli demonstrations occurred throughout the country, and overwhelming popular support for Iraq was expressed in all sections of society. Sentiments were further aroused when air attacks on goods vehicles (including tanker-trucks carrying oil) on the Baghdad-Ruwei-shid highway in late January killed at least six Jordanian civilians. Jordan had been entirely dependant on Iraqi oil since Saudi Arabian supplies were suspended in September 1990. Now these consignments were halted, and Jordan, which introduced petrol-rationing in February, was obliged to obtain more expensive supplies from Syria and Yemen. Oil imports from Iraq were eventually resumed in April 1991.

In a televised address in February 1991, King Hussein paid tribute to the people and armed forces of Iraq, describing them as victims of this 'savage and large-scale war' and claiming that the war was directed against all Arabs and Muslims. The speech was condemned by the US Administration, which accused Jordan of abandoning its neutrality and threatened to review its economic aid. In March the US Congress approved legislation cancelling a $57m. aid programme. The law was signed by President Bush in April. However, the effects were offset, to some extent, by the announcement of a $450m. Japanese concessionary loan. As the multinational force launched a ground offensive to liberate Kuwait on 24 February, Prime Minister Badran announced that the conflict had at that point cost Jordan some $8,000m.

Fears that Iraq would provoke Israel into entering the conflict, thus making Jordan part of the combat zone, were not realized, owing to the Israeli decision not to retaliate in response to the *Scud* missile attacks launched by Iraq against its territory. At the end of December 1990, Jordan had deployed 80,000 troops in defensive positions facing Israel. King Hussein declared, in mid-January 1991, that Jordan would defend its territory and air space against any incursions. In early February a Jordanian air force officer and a truck-driver were executed, having been convicted by a military court of spying for Israel.

On 1 March 1991, following the liberation of Kuwait and the end of hostilities between Iraq and the multinational force, King Hussein, in a televised address to the nation, advocated regional reconciliation. In late March he travelled to Damascus, for the first time for one year, for talks with President Assad, and subsequently sought to improve relations with the West, visiting President Mitterrand in Paris later that month.

MIDDLE EAST PEACE PROCESS 1991–94

US Secretary of State James Baker visited Jordan on 20–21 July 1991, when King Hussein announced his intention to accept an invitation to Jordan to attend a Middle East peace conference sponsored by the USA and the USSR. It was hoped that the conference would be attended by delegations from Israel, Egypt, Syria and Lebanon, and by a joint Jordanian-Palestinian delegation; and that it would thus become the first occasion when Israel, the Palestinians and the Arab nations would participate in direct negotiations. The Jordanian House of Representatives opposed the plan, however, demanding Israeli withdrawal from the Occupied Territories and East Jerusalem as a precondition for Jordan's attendance, and rejecting Israel's insistence that neither Palestinians from East Jerusalem nor overt supporters of the PLO should be allowed to attend. James Baker visited Amman again in September and October—he had visited the region eight times since the end of the Gulf War—for further rounds of pre-conference diplomacy, and on 12 October King Hussein announced that a Jordanian delegation would attend the conference, in spite of intense opposition from the MB and leftist political groupings. He stated that he had received assurances from the USA that it would do its utmost to ensure that a transitional period of

Palestinian 'autonomy' in the Occupied Territories would be negotiated within one year of the opening of the conference; and that he had considered abdicating over the Arab-Israeli confrontation, but believed that attending the conference would increase international pressure on Israel to withdraw from the Occupied Territories. The Central Council of the PLO, meeting in Tunis on 16–17 October, approved the formation of a joint Jordanian-Palestinian delegation, a decision strongly criticized by the leader of the PFLP, George Habbash.

The opening session of the historic Middle East peace conference, convened within the framework of UN Security Council Resolutions 242 and 338, and chaired by President Bush of the USA and the Soviet President, Mikhail Gorbachev, was held in Madrid, Spain, during 30 October–1 November 1991. The joint Jordanian-Palestinian delegation was led by Kamel Abu Jaber, a US-educated professor of political science, who had been appointed Jordan's Minister of Foreign Affairs following the resignation, on 3 October, of Abdullah Nusur and two other ministers opposed to Jordan's participation. The delegation included diplomats, civil servants and academics. In his speech, calling for the withdrawal of Israeli forces from all occupied lands, Abu Jaber stated that King Hussein would have preferred a separate Palestinian delegation but 'we have no objection to providing an umbrella for our Palestinian brethren . . . the Palestinian people must be allowed to exercise their right of self-determination in their ancestral homeland'. 'Let me speak plainly', he added, 'Jordan has never been Palestine and will not be so.'

Subsequent negotiations in Washington and Moscow between the Israeli and the joint Jordanian-Palestinian delegations remained deadlocked, with regard to substantive issues. However, secret talks between the PLO and the Israeli Government in Norway, which had begun early in 1993, led to an agreement on a Declaration of Principles on 19 August 1993 which involved a degree of Palestinian self-government in the Occupied Territories. The Declaration of Principles was signed in Washington on 13 September 1993. News of the agreement apparently came as a surprise to King Hussein who had not been informed that negotiations were taking place in Oslo and the agreement is reported to have caused grave embarrassment to the Palestinian negotiators in Washington. Despite the King's initial irritation at the Israeli-PLO accord, which presents a socio-economic as well as a political challenge for Jordan, he quickly accepted the Declaration of Principles. On 14 September, the day after the Washington signature of the accord, Jordan and Israel concluded a 'common agenda' for subsequent negotiations between the two countries. The agenda aimed to achieve 'a just, lasting and comprehensive peace' between the Arab States, the Palestinians and Israel. Jordan and Israel agreed to respect each other's security and to discuss future co-operation on territorial and economic issues. The signing of the agenda was publicized as being the first agreement between an Arab state and Israel since the peace agreement between Egypt and Israel in 1979. King Hussein, however, stressed that the agenda was not a peace agreement but an outline of topics to be discussed at future talks. Much of the agenda had already been agreed in 1992 but an official signing was delayed because of objections by the Palestinians.

Within Jordan, news of the Israeli-PLO accord was greeted with considerable cynicism. Opposition to the accord appeared to be strongest in the vast Palestinian refugee camp at Baqaa. Most Islamist and leftist politicians condemned the accord. (Following the Hebron massacre on 25 February 1994, it was reported that any support for the peace process among Palestinians in Jordan had almost entirely disappeared and that in their frustration many were turning to the Islamist movements.) The agreement between the PLO and Israel in September 1993 initiated a sometimes acrimonious debate on the vexed question of Palestinian identity and the future of Palestinians in Jordan. Since October 1993 Jordan had become increasingly frustrated with the PLO over its failure to implement agreements on closer co-operation. In particular Jordan was concerned that the PLO Chairman, Yasser Arafat, appeared to be unwilling to sign a draft economic agreement that had been drawn up earlier in the year. At the beginning of 1994 King Hussein publicly criticized Arafat because Jordan had not been continuously advised about the progress of talks between the PLO and Israel concerning the implementation of Palestinian self-rule in Gaza and Jericho and economic co-operation. He requested that Arafat stop making references to a future Jordanian-Palestinian confederation because this was an issue on which no decision had yet been made. In the past King Hussein had appeared to favour such an arrangement, but more recently Jordan had decided not to discuss the final relationship with the Occupied Territories. Following the King's criticisms, a PLO delegation led by Farouq Qaddoumi, the head of the PLO's political department, visited Amman and an agreement on economic co-operation, covering tourism, agriculture, infrastructure, investment promotion, and private sector co-operation, was signed on 7 January 1994. Just over a week later, Jordan and the PLO drew up a draft accord on security and the exchange of intelligence information. Jordan was particularly concerned about who would control the bridges across the river Jordan after the establishment of Palestinian autonomy. At a meeting of the Higher Jordanian-Palestinian Committee in February it was agreed that a number of joint committees, originally set up in 1993 to discuss relations between Jordan and the Occupied Territories during the period of transitional Palestinian self-rule, would be reconvened. Jordanian experts were reported to be present as observers at talks between the PLO and Israel in Paris on economic and monetary questions. Yet in spite of a personal visit by Arafat to Amman to brief King Hussein on the Cairo talks with Israel, relations between Jordan and the PLO remained strained. At the end of March King Hussein blamed the PLO for mishandling the negotiations leading up to Security Council Resolution 904 which had allowed the USA to abstain on the paragraph in the preamble concerning Jerusalem. The King argued that the American vote could have been avoided if the PLO had consulted Jordan. There was a relatively low-key reaction from the Jordanian Government to the Cairo accord between Israel and the PLO signed on 4 May. Arafat visited Amman on 5 May to brief King Hussein on the Cairo agreement but the King remained disillusioned by Arafat's failure to liaise with Jordan in the peace process.

Following a secret meeting in November 1993 between King Hussein and Shimon Peres, the Israeli Minister of Foreign Affairs, there was optimism in Israeli government circles that Jordan would soon sign a formal peace agreement with Israel. These hopes were dashed in late January 1994 when King Hussein insisted that the key issues which lay behind the Arab-Israeli conflict must be discussed before any accord could be signed and that it was unacceptable to leave negotiations until after the signing. Jordan, together with Syria and Lebanon, withdrew temporarily from the current round of bilateral talks with Israel in Washington immediately after the Hebron massacre in February, although the gesture appeared to be largely symbolic and aimed at appeasing public anger at the incident. The King firmly rejected calls made by Islamist deputies for Jordan to withdraw permanently from the peace talks.

The National Assembly requested that the Government link Jordan's resumption of peace negotiations with new arrangements for inspecting ships with cargo bound for Iraq through Aqaba port. There had been growing criticism of the policy of intercepting and searching ships bound for Aqaba in the Tiran Straits by a multinational inspection force led by the US navy. The system of inspection, introduced in August 1991 in order to verify compliance with international sanctions against Iraq, resulted in long delays and loss of revenue to the Jordanian authorities. When the USA failed to respond to Jordanian requests for new arrangements, this was interpreted in Amman as a means of putting pressure on Jordan to finalize a peace agreement with Israel. King Hussein took up the Assembly's recommendation and in late March told the ambassadors of the five Permanent Members of the Security Council that Jordan would not resume peace negotiations with Israel unless the naval blockade of Aqaba was lifted. The USA agreed to examine ways of easing the impact of the naval blockade on the Jordanian economy but made no promises. Jordan repeated its demands and sent only a low-level observer to two meetings between the Arab and Israeli delegations for multilateral negotiations. It was not until the end of April that the USA accepted a Jordanian proposal for a new land-based system of inspection. Subject to what the US Secretary of State, Warren Christopher described as 'fine-tuning', the system of intercepting ships bound for Aqaba at sea would be replaced by the inspection of cargo at port by an independent non-government organization, Lloyd's Register of London. Prime Minister Majali told the press on 25 April that his Government was now willing to sign agreements on all individual items on the Jordan-Israel agenda and to participate in all multilateral talks in the hope that the negotiations would lead eventually to a peace treaty. He emphasized that a peace treaty could only be achieved in this way.

At a ceremony at the White House on 25 July 1994 King Hussein and the Prime Minister of Israel, Itzhak Rabin, signed the 'Washington Declaration' ending the state of war which had existed between the two countries since 1948. After years of secret meetings, it was the first time that King Hussein had publicly met an Israeli Prime Minister. The declaration stopped short of a full peace treaty, but US Secretary of State, Warren Christopher, stated that he expected it to speed the process for formal peace agreement 'within a matter of months'. There was speculation that King Hussein's failing health might accelerate the peace process as he alone is seen by some to have the authority to sign a formal peace treaty with Israel. Both leaders addressed the US Congress on 26 July. King Hussein needs strong Congressional support if President Clinton's promise to cancel Jordan's $700m.-debt to the USA is to be realized. The US Secretary of State stated that a gradual clearance of the debt was likely to depend on the progress of the peace process. In Jordan Islamists declared 'a day of sadness and mourning' and at a modest protest meeting at the central mosque in Amman, Bahjat Abu-Gharbiah, head of the Arab-Jordanian Popular Committee Against Normalization, told the demonstrators that the peace was 'an attempt to consolidate the hegemony of the Zionist entity through normalization that allows its cancerous spread until the shores of the Arabian Gulf'. From Gaza, PLO Chairman Arafat sent his congratulations to the Israeli and Jordanian leaders on the declaration and expressed the hope that Syria and Lebanon would also make peace with Israel.

POLITICAL REFORM AND MULTI-PARTY ELECTIONS

On 6 October 1991 an alliance of 49 deputies in the House of Representatives, from the MB, the 'constitutional bloc', the 'Democratic Alliance', and some independent Islamic deputies, signed a petition in protest at the terms of Jordan's participation in the Middle East peace conference. They urged the resignation of the Government, and on 16 November Taher al-Masri resigned as Prime Minister, having lost the confidence of the House. The King appointed his cousin, Field Marshal Sharif Zaid ibn Shaker, who had led a transitional government in 1989, as Prime Minister, and a new, broader-based government received a vote of confidence on 16 December. Kamel Abu Jaber retained his position as Minister of Foreign Affairs. The MB was again excluded from the Cabinet and 18 of its members voted against the new Government in the confidence motion.

In June 1992 an extraordinary session of the House of Representatives was convened in order to debate new laws regarding political parties and the press. In early July the House adopted new legislation whereby, subject to certain conditions, political parties were formally legalized, in preparation for the country's first multi-party elections since 1956, which were to be held before November 1993. The new legislation was approved by royal decree at the end of August, and by March 1993 nine political parties had received the Government's formal approval of their activities.

In May King Hussein appointed a new cabinet, in which Abd as-Salam al-Majali, the leader of the Jordanian delegation to the Middle East peace conference, replaced Field Marshal Sharif Zaid ibn Shaker as Prime Minister. The new Government was regarded as a transitional administration, pending the country's first multi-party election.

At the beginning of August 1993 King Hussein unexpectedly dissolved the House of Representatives, provoking criticism from some politicians who had expected the House to debate proposed changes to the country's electoral law. Changes in voting procedures at the general election, which was scheduled to be held on 8 November, were subsequently announced by the King in mid-August. Voters were to be allowed to cast one vote only, rather than a number equal to that of the number of candidates contesting a given constituency, as before.

After the announcement of the Israeli-PLO accord in September 1993 King Hussein appeared to be unsure whether or not to proceed with the elections, fearing that they might be dominated by the debate about the peace process. In the end the King decided to hold the elections as planned on 8 November 1993. The election campaign went smoothly and peacefully. Some 820,000 Jordanian (52% of elegible voters and 68% of registered voters) cast ballots at one of the 2,906 polling stations in the 20 electoral districts. However, the independent New Jordan Research Centre estimated that 70% of Jordanians of Palestinian origin abstained. This low level of participation was attributed to the fact that Jordanians of Palestinian origin did not feel part of the Jordanian political system and also that the current system of electoral districts favoured areas dominated by East Bankers. For example, the predominantly Palestinian second electoral district of Amman, which has some 220,000 elegible voters, elects three deputies, whereas the southern district of Tufeila, with only c. 24,000 eligible voters (few of whom are of Palestinian origin), also elects three deputies.

In all some 534 candidates contested the election and half of the 20 registered political parties fielded candidates. The majority of candidates, however, stood as independents. The political parties, which had been legal for less than a year, had little time to organize and amass public support. With the exception of the Islamic Action Front, most political parties had a low profile in the elections. Abdul Hadi Al-Majali of the Pledge Party admitted that the political parties were not rooted in the political system and that successful candidates won because of their own qualities, personalities and relationships rather than the support of political parties. Domestic issues, such as unemployment, were the main issues in the electoral campaign, with traditionalist candidates focusing on local issues and promising to improve the provision of public services in their constituencies. Of the 80 deputies returned, 45 were independents. With the traditions of tribalism deeply rooted in the customs of the country, they won largely because of their tribal affiliations and personal influence. Talal Al-Ramhi, the Secretary-General of the Popular Unity Party, dubbed the new parliament a *majlis 'ashairi*—a tribal council.

The Islamic Action Front, an alliance between the Muslim Brotherhood and other Islamist groups, won 16 seats, the largest number of any political party, but six fewer than in the 1989 elections. This reversal was largely thought to result from the new electoral law which embodies the one-man one-vote principle. Indeed, the new law was widely interpreted as an attempt to weaken the Islamic Action Front. Others felt that the Islamists had misjudged the mood of the country and had not devoted enough attention in their campaign to basic issues related to the impact of the economic recession on the lives of ordinary Jordanians. The IAF's Secretary-General, Dr Ishaq Farhan, however, stated that his party did not consider the election a setback. It has been calculated that successful Islamist candidates won almost a third of all votes cast for the 80 elected deputies. Of the other political parties, leftists and Arab nationalists won eight seats while five conservative and right-of-centre parties claimed a total of 14 seats. Only 14 of the 80 new deputies were of Palestinian origin. Among the new deputies was the first woman to be elected to the Assembly, Toujan al-Faisal, who won one of the seats reserved for the Circassian minority.

Soon after the election a number of political groupings were formed in addition to the Islamic Action Front. The Progressive Democratic Coalition, made up of liberal deputies together with the leftist and Arab nationalists, claimed the support of 22 deputies; the National Action Front and the Jordan Action Front, both groupings of conservative parties and their allies, claimed 18 and 9 seats respectively. The Islamic Action Front remained the largest single political organization in the country. Some deputies saw the emergence of parliamentary

blocs as the first step in a move towards the formation of larger political parties.

Taher al-Masri, widely regarded as the most influential Palestinian in Jordanian politics and a former Prime Minister, was elected Speaker of the National Assembly on 23 November 1993. Al-Masri won an overwhelming victory against his rival, an IAF deputy. An IAF deputy held the post of Speaker in the last Parliament. Dr Abd as-Salam al-Majali remained Prime Minister and although he made few significant changes to his cabinet, there was some surprise that for the first time it did not include any parliamentary deputies. His new Government won a vote of confidence on 8 December after a prolonged debate during which the Prime Minister was criticized for changes to the country's electoral law and for not making an independent statement of government policy but simply adopting the King's speech from the throne at the opening of Parliament.

In January 1994 there were bomb attacks on cinemas in Amman and Zarqa which were attributed to Islamist extremists. Several arrests were made and the Interior Ministry claimed that it had successfully thwarted further outrages. It was reported that some of those arrested were men who had fought with the *mujahidin* in Afghanistan and the Government implied that the cinema bombings were the work of the Prophet Muhammad's Army, an organization set up by militant Islamists who had defected from the MB. The attacks were embarrassing for the moderate IAF which condemned political violence but at the same time demanded better treatment for the 72 detainees which it claimed were still in custody in April. In February and March Islamists won control of the Engineers Association and the Agricultural Engineers Association but failed to win control over the Contractors Association.

In another cautious move towards democratization, in March the National Assembly approved legislation to allow municipal elections in Greater Amman, where some two-fifths of the country's population live. The Government, no doubt concerned about the strength of Palestinian and Islamist opposition in the capital, had originally proposed that only half of the municipal council should be elected but this was increased to two-thirds by the National Assembly. The remaining one third of the council together the mayor will continue to be appointed by the Government.

RELATIONS WITH THE USA

On 20 June 1991 the US House of Representatives voted to withhold US $27m. in military aid, pending assurances that 'the Government of Jordan has taken steps to advance the peace process in the Middle East'. However, the US Department of State indicated that the Bush administration opposed legislation to prohibit the sending of US aid to Jordan. In October, following Jordan's acceptance of an invitation to attend the opening session of the Middle East peace conference in Madrid (see above), President Bush announced the USA's intention to resume military aid to Jordan.

In June 1992 the USA postponed a joint military exercise with Jordan in order to express its disapproval of the assistance that Jordan was allegedly providing to Iraq to enable it to circumvent the UN trade embargo. The USA subsequently proposed that UN observers should be dispatched to Jordan in order to suppress the smuggling of goods to Iraq. Jordan rejected the proposal outright as an infringement of its sovereignty. In late August both the Jordanian Government and the House of Representatives condemned Western plans to establish an air exclusion zone in southern Iraq. In January 1993 King Hussein strongly criticized renewed air attacks on targets in Iraq by Western air forces, but did not express support for the Iraqi President, Saddam Hussain. At the same time he emphasized that Jordan would remain on friendly terms with the USA under the newly-elected Clinton Administration. In June King Hussein visited the USA, where he held talks, for the first time, with President Clinton. Although relations between the USA and Jordan were described as good, the USA was reported to be continuing to withhold financial aid from fiscal 1992 in retaliation for Jordan's alleged assistance to Iraq during the 1991 Gulf War. Prior to his visit to the USA, King Hussein had stated publicly that he did not support the Iraqi leadership or its policies. At the end of July the USA was reported to have informed Jordan that it must make payments to the UN's Compensation Fund for Kuwait if it continued to receive deliveries of petroleum from Iraq. In mid-September, however, US President Clinton announced that some $30m. in economic and military aid to Jordan was to be released, in recognition of the country's enforcement of sanctions against Iraq and of its role in the Middle East peace process.

As part of his plans to improve relations with the USA, King Hussein visited Washington in late January 1994 where he met President Clinton and the Secretary of State, Warren Christopher. Their talks included discussions about the Arab-Israeli peace process and future American arms sales to Jordan. During the visit the King confirmed that he had met every Israeli Prime Minister, except Menachem Begin, and stated publicly that he would be willing to meet, Itzhak Rabin, the current Prime Minister. For the first time openly, he also met with a group of leading Jewish Americans through Project Nishma, a Jewish organization that promotes peace between the Arab states and Israel. In March, however, new tensions emerged with the USA over Jerusalem and over the US-led naval blockade of Jordan's only port at Aqaba. After the adoption of Resolution 904 by the UN Security Council on 18 March 1994, Jordan protested strongly about the US position on the status of Jerusalem. The USA had insisted that voting on the resolution should take place paragraph by paragraph and in this way had abstained on two paragraphs in the preamble concerning Jerusalem. In one of the paragraphs East Jerusalem was referred to as part of the Occupied Territories. Jordan was worried about the legal and political implications of what appeared to be an important change in US policy towards Jerusalem. However, most of King Hussein's fury over this reversal was directed towards PLO Chairman Yasser Arafat who was accused of mishandling the negotiations which preceded the resolution by failing to consult with Jordan on the wording of the resolution (see Middle East Peace Process 1991–94).

At the end of March 1994 the Jordanian Government told the USA that the interception of ships bound for Aqaba by the US-led multilateral inspection force as part of UN sanctions against Iraq was seriously damaging the Jordanian economy. Jordan pointed out that since August 1991, when the inspection started, not one violation of sanctions had been discovered although some 1,700 ships had been stopped and searched. Jordan warned that unless this problem was resolved, it would not return to the peace negotiations. After months of deliberations, the US administration announced on 25 April that it had accepted a Jordanian proposal for a new system of monitoring cargo bound for Aqaba. The announcement followed a meeting in London between King Hussein and US Secretary of State, Warren Christopher (see Middle East Peace Process 1991–94).

RELATIONS WITH ARAB STATES

Since the end of the 1990–91 Gulf War, Jordan has continued to distance itself from Saddam Hussain's regime in Iraq and has tried to improve relations with the Gulf states. In 1992 King Hussein spoke publicly of the need for change in Iraq, but denied that he had discussed ways of removing the Iraqi leader with the director of the CIA. Jordan protested at the harassment of Iraqi refugees in Jordan by the Iraqi secret

service and at the execution of Jordanian merchants in Iraq accused of economic crimes. At the end of November 1993 King Hussein made his first official visit to Egypt since the Gulf crisis. Relations with Egypt had slowly improved after diplomatic efforts by the King who made an unofficial visit to Cairo in October 1992 to offer condolences just after the Egyptian captial suffered a serious earthquake. During a visit to Amman by the Egyptian Minister of Foreign Affairs in October 1993 it was agreed to reconvene the Higher Jordanian-Egyptian Joint Committee which had not met since the Gulf crisis. Following visits by Crown Prince Hassan to Doha in late 1993 and by Sheikh Hamad bin Jaber ath-Thani, the Qatari Minister of Foreign Affairs, to Amman at the beginning of 1994, normal relations between Jordan and Qatar were restored after being strained by Jordan's support for Saddam Hussain in the Gulf War. In March 1994 King Hussein made his first visit to Doha since the Gulf crisis. However, the normalization of relations with Qatar did not include the resumption of financial aid to Jordan from the emirate. King Hussein also visited Oman, where discussions included the efforts by both countries to mediate between the two factions in Yemen, but visits to Bahrain and the UAE were cancelled.

Relations with Saudi Arabia and Kuwait remained particularly strained. When King Hussein visited Saudi Arabia on 8 March 1994 to perform the *umra* or minor pilgrimage, King Fahd refused to meet him, although it is usual for the Saudi King to receive Heads of State of Muslim countries on such occasions. The King has not visited Saudi Arabia since the Gulf crisis. According to some reports, King Fahd has sworn never to talk to Hussein so long as he lives. The background to the visit is unclear. In the months before the visit, King Hussein had stated repeatedly that he was willing to apologize if he had caused any personal offence to King Fahd but refused to apologize for the position that Jordan adopted during the Gulf crisis. The Saudi monarch is believed to have demanded a full apology for Jordan's support of Iraq. After King Fahd received Yasser Arafat in February, King Hussein may have decided to take a calculated risk that his visit would lead to a reconciliation with the Saudi monarch. The fact that Fahd snubbed Hussein after meeting Arafat suggested that the Saudi monarch may have a special animosity towards the Jordanian King because of the long rivalry between the Hashemites and the House of Saud. King Fahd may also have been angered by King Hussein's efforts to mediate between the rival factions in Yemen. Saudi Arabia is known to have been concerned that the reunification of the two Yemens in 1990 created a potentially powerful new state on its southern border and apprehension when the Arabian peninsula's first multi-party general elections were held there in April 1993. There were persistent rumours in early 1994 that Saudi Arabia had been providing military assistance to the southerners in the factional struggles in Yemen. King Hussein and the Jordanian Government played down the snub by Fahd and there was no public debate about it. King Hussein no doubt decided that it was not in Jordan's interests at this time to escalate tensions with its powerful neighbour. Jordan's efforts to mediate between rival factions in Yemen were unsuccessful. Although the leaders of the two factions signed an agreement in Amman in February 1994, the accord was never implemented, and as the situation in Yemen deteriorated in April Jordan withdrew from the multinational commission which had been trying to bring the two sides together.

Economy

Revised for this edition by ALAN J. DAY

Having twice been completely disrupted by war between the Arabs and the Israelis (first in 1948, and then in 1967), Jordan's economy was again severely affected by a regional conflict during the Gulf crisis and hostilities of 1990–91. This latest dislocation of established patterns of trade, aid and labour migration had a negative short-term impact on the vulnerable Jordanian economy, but failed to produce the sustained downturn that was widely predicted at the height of the crisis. By 1992 a strong recovery was under way, and it was clear that the restored Kuwaiti Government's expulsion of large numbers of Palestinians in 1991 had (because these 'returnees' were relatively affluent) provided Jordan with a timely economic stimulus. For its part, the Jordanian Government had, by adhering closely to IMF-approved economic policies, exerted a strong stabilizing influence throughout the crisis and its aftermath. From September 1993 onwards, Jordan's planners had to modify all medium- and long-term forecasts to take account of the implications of the PLO-Israel peace agreement.

In the 1948–49 Arab–Israeli war, Jordan acquired some 5,600 sq km of new territory—the vast salient which juts out into Israel west of the River Jordan, and the country's population increased more than threefold. Before the war broke out, the country's population was perhaps 400,000. The number of those living on the West Bank of the River Jordan in the territory acquired in 1948 was well over 800,000. This territory was occupied by the Israelis in 1967, and perhaps 350,000 of the inhabitants fled to non-occupied Jordan. It is extremely difficult to evaluate population estimates for the years between the census of 1961 and the most recent census, undertaken on 10 November 1979. This gave a total population for the East Bank of 2,100,019, which implied an annual growth rate between 1961 and 1979 of 4.8%. Natural increase accounted for 3.8% and immigration for 1.0%. The rate of growth in the mid-1980s was estimated at 4%. By the end of 1986 the population of the East Bank was officially estimated to have risen to 2,796,100 and by 1992 to 3.9m., the annual rate of increase in 1980–90 being 3.7%, compared with 4.3% in 1965–80. Of the present population, 32% reside in the capital Amman, and a further 15% in the cities of Zarqa and Irbid. The World Bank assessed the urban population proportion as 61% in 1990, in which year the crude birth rate was 43 per 1,000 (compared with 53 per 1,000 in 1965) and the crude death rate, 6 per 1,000 (compared with 21 per 1,000 in 1965). These levels of population increase are making themselves felt particularly in the major towns, where water shortages are becoming one of the most severe of the country's economic problems. The World Bank estimated Jordan's 1992 GNP per caput at $1,120.

The total work-force was estimated at 535,444 in 1986 by the government's Department of Statistics, with a further 276,000 working in Arab countries and 52,000 elsewhere abroad. As of the end of 1986 it was reported that there were about 180,000 non-Jordanians working in the country and 80% of those were Arab nationals. At the end of 1987 the Jordanian Government announced that it was to stop issuing work permits, in order to stem the growth in unemployment. The rate of unemployment was unofficially estimated at 17% of the work-force in September 1987 and at just under 20% in August 1990, when Iraq occupied Kuwait.

The absorption of the refugees of 1948 and of 1967 caused problems which were accentuated by ethnic, cultural and religious differences. Jordanians before 1948 were mainly Bedouin and mostly engaged in pastoral, and even nomadic, activities. They therefore had little in common with the Palestinians, many of whom established themselves in Jordan as traders and professional men. In April 1994 there were 1,176,208 Palestinian refugees registered with the United Nations Relief and Works Agency (UNRWA) in Jordan, and a further 324,250 in the West Bank. The vast majority of the country's inhabitants are Sunni Muslims, but about 6% are Christians, mostly Greek Orthodox.

The loss of the West Bank of Jordan to Israel in the summer of 1967 created a whole series of new economic problems. The result was the loss not only of some efficiently farmed agricultural land, but also of a large part of the important and growing tourist industry, and the large sums in foreign exchange received from the people who annually visited the old city of Jerusalem and Bethlehem. Some of the immediate problems caused by the war of 1967 were met by aid from Arab countries, but Jordan's economic future, in the long term, obviously depended on the evolution of the Arab-Israeli dispute and of regional relations generally.

During 1979 and the early part of 1980, Jordan moved closer to Iraq in both political and economic terms. The war between Iran and Iraq, which began in September 1980, further strengthened this alliance, notably by increasing trade for Iraq through Aqaba. Towards the end of 1980, Iraq and Jordan signed agreements to confirm their closer economic links, which were strengthened by various trade and aid protocols in 1981, in which year Jordanian exports to Iraq increased to US $186.8m. (compared with $42.3m. in 1979). Owing to war-induced cutbacks in Iraq, Jordanian exports declined to $180m. in 1982 and to $72.9m. in 1983. At Jordan's proposal, an oil-for-goods barter system was instituted. This facilitated a rise in Jordanian exports to $176.5m. in 1984 and, after a further downturn in 1986–87 (due to lower world oil prices and the continuing Iran-Iraq War), a further rise, to $216m., in 1989.

Jordan, its economy underpinned by foreign aid and by remittances from Jordanian workers abroad, enjoyed sustained economic growth from the mid-1970s into the early 1980s, although difficulties were encountered thereafter. Between 1974 and 1984 it had one of the highest growth rates in the world, with the East Bank region's GDP expanding, in real terms, at an average annual rate of more than 8%. In spite of the problems brought about by the conflicts with Israel and the uncertainty caused by the Iran-Iraq War, real GDP increased by 17.6% in 1980 and by 9.8% in 1981, but the growth rate slowed to 5.6% in 1982, 2.5% in 1983 and 0.8% in 1984. A major cause of this deceleration was the non-receipt of three-quarters of the special development aid of $1,250m. per year that was promised to Jordan at the 1978 Baghdad Arab 'Summit' Conference, which had condemned the Camp David accords between Israel and Egypt: of the seven Arab states party to the pledge, only Saudi Arabia honoured its commitments to Jordan in full. In consequence, the targets of Jordan's 1981–85 Development Plan were not attained, while in 1981 Jordan recorded its first current account deficit for five years and continued to record deficits in 1982–85. These shortfalls, combined with Jordan's customary trade deficit (generally in excess of $2,000m. per year during the 1980s), obliged the Government to obtain new foreign development loans, which, in turn, assisted a partial recovery of GDP growth to 2.7% in 1985, 2.4% in 1986 and 1.9% in 1987. Meanwhile, the annual rate of inflation had fallen steadily, from 12% in 1981 to 0% in 1986, but then rose steeply to 14% in 1988, in which year the national budget deficit increased to 24% of GDP. Moreover, the current account balance, having recorded a small surplus in 1986, showed deficits of 7% and 6% of GDP in 1987 and 1988 respectively. Against this background, the Government submitted to the disciplines of the IMF in mid-1989, agreeing to a five-year structural adjustment programme aiming, by 1993, to bring inflation down to 7%, to reduce the budget deficit to 5% of GDP and to eliminate the current account deficit (see Finance, below).

Immediate slippage on these targets included, in 1989, a rise of inflation to 25% and a budget deficit still around 20% of GDP, compared with the IMF target of 12.4%. Nevertheless, the current account recorded a surplus of $335m. in 1989 and the Government was able to conclude interim debt-rescheduling agreements with its major foreign creditors. Jordan's foreign debt remained high, at $8,400m. in early 1990, but by then the Government believed that economic prospects had brightened, in that inflation was running at only 8%, the budget deficit was on course to fall and substantial GDP growth was expected. Moreover, exports, particularly of vegetables, were buoyant, while remittances and foreign aid were expected to exceed budgeted figures. This relatively hopeful scenario was, however, changed dramatically by the onset of the new Gulf crisis in August 1990.

EFFECTS OF 1990–91 GULF CRISIS

At the time of Iraq's occupation of Kuwait, in August 1990, Iraq was Jordan's principal trading partner, taking at least 23% of Jordan's exports and supplying more than 80% of Jordan's petroleum. Total adherence by Jordan to the UN sanctions against Iraq, imposed by UN Security Council Resolution 661 on 6 August, therefore threatened the whole basis of Jordan's already troubled economy. On 25 August the Jordanian Ministry of Transport issued a circular stating that Jordan adhered to UN Security Council Resolution 661, but Jordan continued to import oil from Iraq by road tanker. Indeed, following the cessation of Saudi Arabian oil deliveries in late September, Jordanian imports from Iraq increased, until the outbreak of hostilities in the Gulf, in mid-January 1991, forced Jordan to find alternative suppliers and also to introduce petrol rationing (see Industry and Mining, below).

Loss of trade with Iraq was not the only problem facing Jordan's economy as a result of the Gulf crisis. Remittances from Jordanians working in the Gulf states (estimated at JD 470m. in 1989) dwindled to almost nothing as activity in Kuwait slowed or ceased, and business in the other Gulf states became affected. Moreover, many of these Jordanians returned to Jordan, as did thousands of Palestinians with Jordanian passports, raising the level of unemployment to 30%, increasing the population by 10% and putting an additional strain on health and education budgets. A further problem was the passage of thousands of migrants through Jordan, many of them attempting to return to the Indian sub-continent and South-East Asia. According to Jordanian officials, about 470,000 foreigners fled to Jordan in the five weeks following the Iraqi invasion of Kuwait on 2 August 1990. Many of these, particularly non-Arab Asians, remained stranded in overcrowded camps on the Iraqi-Jordanian border, suffering severe privations (including shortages of food, water and medical supplies), while awaiting repatriation. Conditions improved in early September, as new camps were established and chartered aircraft carried some of the refugees to their countries of origin. Moreover, fears that the outbreak of hostilities in January 1991 would lead to a furthur massive influx of refugees proved to be unfounded: although confirmed figures were scarce, it appeared that not more than a further 20,000 refugees were processed through Jordanian border camps in January-February.

Official Jordanian statistics showed that other negative effects of the crisis included a rise in inflation to more than 16% in 1990 as a whole and a nominal GDP growth rate of only 1.1%, which, according to the IMF, amounted to a fall in real terms of 7.9%, while GNP fell by 4% in nominal terms and by 17% in dollar terms. According to a UNICEF survey published in March 1991, nearly one-third of the Jordanian population were living in poverty (defined as a family income of less than JD 86 per month), compared with 20% before the crisis. Because of the crisis, disbursements to Jordan under the IMF stand-by facility, and under an associated $150m. World Bank structural loan, were suspended from September 1990. Subsequent negotiations resulted in a new agreement with the IMF in October 1991, through which Jordan was to undertake a seven-year economic reform programme (1992–98) and as part of which the 1992 budget envisaged a reduced deficit and GDP growth of 3% compared with 1% in 1991 (see Finance, below).

A 'worst-case' forecast, produced by the Jordanian Ministry of Finance in October 1990, put the country's possible crisis-related losses in the 12 months from August 1990 at $2,144m., itemized as follows: exports to Iraq and Kuwait, $280m.; exports to other countries, $160m.; budget support from

Kuwait and Iraq, $185m.; repayment of Iraqi loans, $169m.; transit business, $250m.; tourism, $230m.; remittances from Jordanians in Kuwait, $320m.; increased import bill, $220m.; oil imports, $180m.; increased freight and insurance premiums, $120m.; emergency relief for evacuees, $30m. By the beginning of 1991 new estimates had inflated the potential loss over the same period to as much as $8,300m. (equivalent to twice Jordan's GDP), by assuming much higher oil import costs and allowing for a total write-off of the assets of Jordanians resident in Kuwait. By March 1991 pledges of special aid for Jordan in 1991, channelled mainly through the Gulf Financial Crisis Co-ordination Group (GFCCG), totalled $1,230m., of which $470m. had already been received. Having weathered the 1990/91 crisis and its immediate aftermath with the help of external emergency aid, Jordan experienced an unexpectedly strong recovery in 1992, prompting a radical, reappraisal of the medium-term economic outlook. The effective fiscal deficit, estimated to have equalled 14% of GDP in 1991, was cut to about 6% of GDP in 1991 (when domestic revenue exceeded current expenditure for the first time in Jordan's history), while GDP increased by 10.1% in real terms in 1992, as against 1.6% in 1991. The return of some 300,000 Palestinians, expelled by Kuwait in 1991, brought new capital resources into Jordan and helped to boost construction activity to 220% of its 1990 level by 1992, with consequential growth in many related areas of the economy. As UN sanctions against Iraq continued into a third year, it was clear that Jordan's external trading position had not been undermined to the extent that many 'worst-case' scenarios had predicted.

While acknowledging that serious structural problems remained, including an external debt burden equivalent to 140% of GDP (down from 200% of GDP in the late 1980s) and an unemployment rate of around 25%, Jordanian ministers and business leaders were generally optimistic in mid-1993 about the prospects for continued progress in meeting IMF economic targets. The IMF subsequently extended substantial new assistance to support the process of structural reform, while Jordan's main creditors arranged a major debt rescheduling package (see 'Finance' section below).

THE REGIONAL PEACE PROCESS

A wide-ranging economic co-operation agreement between Jordan and the PLO was signed in Amman on 7 January 1994 to provide a framework for future approaches to specific issues 'as the peace process progresses'. It was agreed in principle that trade, investment, industry, agriculture, energy, water, electricity, telecommunications and private-sector enterprises were all fields of activity in which Jordan might be expected to co-operate closely with a developing PLO administration. It was predicted that Jordan could develop new trade flows of the order of $250m. to $500m. per year if Israel relinquished its dominant role in the Palestinian market.

On an issue of immediate concern to Jordan, the agreement in principle confirmed the Jordanian dinar as legal tender in the West Bank, gave the Central Bank of Jordan (CBJ) supervisory powers over Jordanian banks operating in the West Bank, and set up a joint Jordan-PLO committee to co-ordinate financial policy in the occupied territories.

A follow-up meeting in May 1994 re-examined the outlook for Jordanian-Palestinian co-operation in the light of a recently signed Israeli-Palestinian economic agreement which gave the Palestinian economy a measure of independence from Israel. The latter agreement's provision for the creation of a Palestinian Monetary Authority (PMA) had raised many questions in Jordan about the PMA's role and intended relationship with the CBJ. Jordan maintained that CBJ supervision of banking in the occupied territories was essential as long as the Jordanian currency was in use, in order to preserve control over the expansion of credit and ensure proper regulation of the money supply in Jordan. However, economists at the Palestinian Economic Council for Development and Reconstruction insisted that the PMA must assume a genuinely influential position within the regulatory process, and that key issues of bank licensing, currency management and payments administration should be examined in great detail before any binding agreements were concluded. Other topics discussed at this inconclusive meeting included trade, tariffs, tourism, transit rights and private Jordanian investment in the occupied territories.

In June 1994 Jordanian and Israeli delegations held two days of talks in Washington as part of the US-sponsored peace process, resulting in agreement in principle that all aspects of the emerging economic arrangements for the area needed to be discussed constructively between Jordan and Israel (and later in a tripartite forum with Palestinian representatives) with due regard for the long-term interests of all parties involved.

AGRICULTURE

The loss of the relatively fertile West Bank in the 1967 war, and subsequent events on the East Bank, caused major disruption to the agricultural sector, which was compounded by severe drought conditions from 1974 to late 1979. In the 1980s, however, major investment in irrigation, particularly in the Jordan Valley, began to show results, and agricultural output increased by an average of 6% per year in 1980–88, owing mainly to the rapid expansion in the output of vegetables and of dairy and poultry products, much of it exported. Whereas the 1981–85 Five-Year Plan had originally envisaged a decline in agriculture's share of GDP from 8.5% to 7.2%, non-attainment of industrial growth targets in that period, combined with greater emphasis on agricultural expansion in the 1986–90 Plan, in fact resulted in agriculture's retaining an average 10% share of GDP through the 1980s, although the proportion later fell to 8% in 1990, and to less than 7% in 1991 and 1992. Under the 1986–90 Plan, increases in the output of cereals, red meat and dairy produce were the major targets, and spending on agricultural projects was estimated at JD 337m. (about 10% of total investment), supplemented by JD 130m. for dam construction and JD 105m. for irrigation. A specific objective was to reduce the share of food imports (mainly cereals) in domestic consumption, which in the late 1970s had risen to 66% and in the late 1980s remained above 50%. In the 1980s migration away from the agricultural sector reduced its importance as an employer within the economy: in the late 1970s approximately 18% of the labour force were employed in agriculture, but by the late 1980s the proportion had declined to 10%.

A contrast can be drawn between the rain-fed upland zone (comprising about 90% of the cultivable land) and the irrigated Jordan Valley, which, since 1973, has been subject to its own development plan. As a result of irrigation and the production of high-value crops, the productivity of the Jordan Valley is far higher than that of the uplands, where cultivation is concentrated mainly on wheat and barley. Before the Jordan Valley Development Plan, only about 10% of the country's land was considered suitable for cultivation because of the low rainfall and vast areas of desert or semi-desert. The Jordan Valley, with its more favourable sub-tropical climate and available water, has been intensively exploited by small farmers who, using plasticulture and drip irrigation, obtained huge increases in production (particularly of fruit and vegetables). The development of irrigation in the Jordan Valley began in 1958, and between then and 1963 work on the East Ghor canal, carrying water from the Yarmouk river and running parallel to the Jordan, added about 120,000 ha to the country's irrigated area. The installations were severely damaged by Israeli bombardment in 1967 and repairs were not carried out until after the 1970–71 civil war. Stage I of the Jordan Valley Development Plan, funded by a great variety of foreign aid bodies, finished at the end of 1979. Irrigation projects centred mainly on the extension of the East Ghor canal and the Zarqa river complex. The King Talal dam was constructed between 1972 and 1978, the East Ghor canal extended between 1975 and 1978, and the Zarqa Triangle Irrigation Project finished in 1978. Other irrigation works include the Hisban Kafrein project, constructed between 1976 and 1978, and the North-East Ghor complex. Many of the irrigation projects undertaken in stage II of the Plan have been completed or are under implementation. Projects under way include the construction of the Wadi al-Arab dam, the raising of the King Talal dam, the extension of the 98-km East Ghor main canal, and the irrigation of 4,700 ha in the Southern Ghor (see below). The Jordan Valley Development scheme is,

however, more than just a complex of irrigation projects, and includes the development of transport links, grading, packing and marketing centres, the development of schools and health centres, and also a housing programme. In 1981 the Jordan Valley Authority (JVA) was responsible for 22,000 ha of irrigated land. The use of plastic tunnels, greenhouses and drip-irrigation has greatly expanded within the valley and by 1978 6,000 dunums (1 dunum = 1,000 sq m) had plastic tunnels and 741 dunums had greenhouses. Most of the JD 42m. allocated to agricultural development in the 1976–80 Five-Year Plan was to be used for development of the valley. As well as irrigation, crop-raising has also been improved by the introduction of special strains of seed, inorganic fertilizers and mechanization.

Attempts to alleviate the critical problems of water supply, most recently highlighted by severe drought in 1984 (the worst for 37 years), have been given high priority by the government. Developments begun by the JVA in 1983 include the beginning of the second phase of the Southern Ghor project, costing JD 30m., which involves the construction of a diversion weir on the Mujib river and the building of a 3.5-km canal to irrigate 4,000 ha. A dam is to be constructed in Wadi Hasa, at Tanur, to store water which will be used to irrigate the upland area to the east of the Jordan Valley. In 1983 work started on the $50m. project to raise the height of the King Talal dam by 16 m to 108 m. This has increased the capacity of the dam to 85m.–90m. cu m and, in addition to the construction of a 2.5-MW hydroelectric power station, has enabled 8,200 ha to be irrigated. Following the discovery of a major artesian well, estimated to be capable of producing 75m. cu m of water per year, at al-Muhaibeh in the north during 1982, an 11.6-km canal was rapidly constructed to take the water to join the East Ghor canal at Adasiya. This was opened in March 1983 at a cost of JD 3m. South Korea's Hanbo Corporation, who built this canal, are also constructing a dam of 20m. cu m capacity in the Wadi al-Arab, which will cost JD 17m. The dam is part of the Wadi al-Arab irrigation project, which began in early 1986 and is planned to increase the irrigated area between Wadi al-Arab, the Yarmouk river and the Jordan Valley by 2,800 ha. Elsewhere in the country, the National Resources Authority drilled 54 wells in 1982 in its search for new supplies of water. In 1989 the Ministry of Water and Irrigation announced plans to invest $20m. in a water exploration project in southern Jordan. It was estimated that by the year 2000 daily consumption of water per person (for all purposes) would rise to 300 litres.

The largest of 18 new agricultural projects to be started is a scheme to develop 830,000 dunums in the Zarqa river catchment area, at an estimated cost of JD 18.6m. The Water Authority of Jordan was established in 1984, and JD 521.7m. of the 1981–85 Development Plan budget was allocated to increase the irrigated area by 180,000 dunums. One of the major schemes for the 1980s was to have been the construction of the Maqarin dam and an associated hydroelectric power station on the Yarmouk river. However, plans for the dam were deferred. Under the 1986–90 Plan, an additional 114,000 dunums (11,400 ha) were to be brought under irrigation in the Jordan Valley, the Southern Ghor and the Wadi al-Arab. The Maqarin dam project was revived in 1988 as the al-Wahdeh ('Unity') dam and hydroelectric power station scheme, a joint Jordanian-Syrian venture to build a dam 100 m high on the Yarmouk river, to store 225m. cu m of water for drinking, irrigation and electricity generation. Plans were finalized in September 1988. Concern was expressed that the cost of building the dam was to be borne exclusively by Jordan but water stored therein was to be used to irrigate both Jordanian and Syrian land and 78% of the electricity to be generated by the dam was to be taken by Syria. The official estimate of the project's cost is $230m., compared with $450m. allocated in the 1975–80 Plan, and independent estimates of $300m.–$500m. In mid-1990 Jordan was seeking assistance from Arab and Islamic organizations in financing the al-Wahdeh dam.

Programmes initiated in 1991 included the North Ghor Conversion Project, involving the conversion of 7,300 ha in the Jordan Valley from surface to pressurized irrigation (with a consequential 20% water saving) at an estimated cost of

$25m.–$30m., of which 80% was to be provided by Japan. Final preparations were under way in 1993 to implement a programme to raise the storage capacity of the Kafrein dam on the Jordan river, from 4.3m. cu m to 7.5m. cu m, and to construct new dams at Walah, Mujib, Karameh and Tannour. The overall goal of this programme was to create a total of 115m. cu m of additional storage capacity by 1996, at an estimated cost of over $200m. The Kafrein dam project, and an associated scheme to reduce leakage from irrigation canals, was expected to bring an additional 1,830 ha of land into cultivation.

In early 1992 a series of contracts for water projects included the Marhib wells scheme, involving the pumping of water from the wells to the existing Marhib and Awaja reservoirs and to a projected new reservoir at Berain. There was a further project to research water-harvesting at Muwaqar, east of Amman.

Describing the water supply outlook in early 1993, the Secretary-General of the Water Authority of Jordan said that 60% of current supply came from groundwater reserves, mainly in the desert areas in the east of the country; that farmers currently used two-thirds of Jordan's total water supply; and that the total supply was expected to increase from 550m. cu m per year to 700m. cu m per year during the decade 1990 to 2000, over which period the underlying level of annual demand was expected to rise from 900m. cu m to 1,600m. cu m, necessitating increasingly harsh restrictions on water use (already rationed for up to seven months of the year). He added that there was considerable scope for improving the efficiency of water use in the agricultural sector (e.g. by discouraging diversification into water-intensive crops like bananas, which currently provided farmers with higher profit margins than crops requiring far less irrigation).

Cereals, fruit and vegetables are the mainstays of Jordan's agriculture. Production levels vary widely, depending on the prevailing weather conditions. For example, after 1974 (a record year) yields of wheat and barley (which is used as animal fodder) were severely reduced, owing to drought, so that by 1979, despite similar areas being under cultivation, wheat production on the East Bank fell to what was then a record low of only 16,500 tons. As a result of the rains in November 1979, there was a great increase in the cultivated area and, following the excellent harvest produced in 1980, the government banned imports of wheat, barley and lentils, and paid farmers almost double the normal price for imports. Field crop production rose appreciably from 32,400 tons in 1979 to 204,000 tons in 1980. In January 1980 the King Talal dam was full for the first time since its completion in 1978. In addition, the heavy rainfall also replenished depleting groundwater resources. Towards the end of 1980 grain storage was also greatly improved with the opening of new silos at Aqaba, with a storage capacity of 50,000 tons. The 1981 harvest, though, was 60% down on that of 1980, with a wheat production of 50,600 tons and barley, 19,200 tons. The 1982 harvest was generally worse and production in subsequent years continued to fluctuate as conditions alternated between rainfall and drought. Following favourable winter rains, annual production of wheat reached 80,000 tons in 1987/88 and in 1988/89. Although this was a relatively high yield, compared with the all-time low of less than 10,000 tons in 1983/84, it was still less than one-quarter of Jordan's annual requirement of 450,000 tons, which by 1990 had risen to 500,000 tons. The barley crop reached 40,000 tons in 1988/89, compared with an all-time low of 3,500 tons in 1983/84. Jordan continued to rely heavily on imports of food, which cost about $400m. per year (JD 155.7m.–$450m.—in 1987). Wheat consumption reached 627,000 tons in 1993 (50% higher than in 1988), owing partly to the increase in population after the Kuwait crisis and partly to Jordan's low bread prices.

The loss of the West Bank had a serious effect on cereal production, but its effect on fruit and vegetable cultivation was disastrous, removing some 80% of the fruit-growing area and 45% of the area under vegetables, and depriving Jordan of an important and expanding source of some of its major export commodities. Production of fruit and vegetables on the East Bank fluctuated widely in the 1970s, partly because of the weather and partly as a result of political instability.

However, the general trend recently has been for increases in fruit and vegetable production, particularly in citrus fruits, tomatoes, melons and cucumbers. Between 1973 and 1986, overall vegetable production increased by 149%, fruit production by 546% and field crops by 88%, according to the US Agency for International Development. Under the 1986–90 Plan, up to 200,000 dunums (20,000 ha) of government land in southern and eastern Jordan were to be cultivated for the first time to produce cereals, forage and red meat, while output of fruit was set to increase as areas planted since 1979 began to produce. Increases in fruit and vegetable production, however, were not matched by a corresponding development in the areas of sales and marketing. The country was also faced with the problem of excessive production of tomatoes, cucumbers and aubergines, which cost the Ministry of Agriculture substantial sums each year in support for growers who could not sell their produce. In early 1985 the Ministry introduced an optional cropping system for irrigated vegetable growing. Under the system, farmers could be fined if they exceeded their allocation of tomato production, and the maximum production of tomatoes for 1985 was fixed at 242,000 tons, 158,000 tons less than production in 1984. Emphasis has been placed on the growing of other crops and Jordan is now self-sufficient in potatoes and 80% self-sufficient in onions. The establishment of a government-owned public marketing organization (the Agricultural Marketing and Processing Company) to handle agricultural produce, which had been decided on in March 1983, was achieved in 1984.

Production of fruit and vegetables increased in the late 1980s, as did exports, especially after the devaluation of the currency in 1988. Moreover, the signature of the Iran–Iraq cease-fire agreement of August 1988 led to a rapid expansion of deliveries to Iraq, Kuwait and other gulf markets. A record 522,000 tons of vegetables were exported in the 1989/90 season, and a further record of 650,000 tons had been anticipated in 1990/91, before trade was disrupted by the latest Gulf crisis in August 1990. The value of vegetable exports in 1991 was JD 43.5m., compared with JD 36.8m. in 1990 and JD 27.9m. in 1989.

In a crisis-induced move to increase domestic agricultural production, the Government decided in November 1990 to offer unused state-owned land for lease at a rent of JD 1 per dunum. Another measure affecting farmers was the enactment, in December 1990, of a law specifying that women could inherit only half as much land as their brothers could, rather than an equal share. The Government explained that equal shares for women, which had been guaranteed under legislation dating from the Ottoman period, was contrary to Islamic law.

The Jordanian Minister of Agriculture said in January 1993 that dependence on uncertain rainfall patterns had helped to engender a 'low-risk' approach to farming, and that higher levels of productivity could be achieved if Jordan improved its standards of resource management. Endorsing the findings of a policy study drawn up with FAO assistance, he accepted that there had been excessive state regulation of agriculture in the past, and that farmers' interests would be better served if the Government devoted itself more to broad policy-making and co-ordination. He advocated a further shift from cereals into the growing of 'off-season' vegetables for export; criticized the spread of restrictive trade policies in many export markets; and called for an expansion of local food-processing capacity to provide new market outlets for farmers, particularly those producing highly perishable commodities.

INDUSTRY AND MINING

Manufacturing industry, which is almost entirely of recent origin, is concentrated around Amman (following the loss of the Nablus industrial centre on the West Bank in 1967). During the 1976–80 Plan period, it experienced an average growth rate of 13.6% per annum, which was only one-half of the planned rate. Moreover, the targets of the 1981–85 Plan period, during which manufacturing and mining were, together, expected to achieve an annual growth rate of 17.8%, fell even further short of being achieved. By 1990, according to World Bank figures, industry (including mining, manufacturing, construction and power) still contributed only 26% of GDP (compared with 66% from services and 8% from agriculture). Industrial investment in 1993 totalled JD 271m., up from JD 161m. in 1992, and remained buoyant in the first half of 1994, helping to allay Jordanian concern about the possible diversion of new investment to the West Bank and Gaza. The majority of factories produce food products, clothing or consumer goods but the major industrial income derives from the three heavier industries—phosphate extraction, cement manufacture and petroleum refining.

In a country which is short of natural resources, Jordan's mineral wealth lies predominantly in its phosphate reserves, which are estimated at more than 2,000m. tons, providing the country with its main export commodity, accounting for 24.5% of export value in 1987. The proportion was 40% in 1983 but later returns were affected by the low world price for phosphates. Jordan is the fifth largest producer of phosphate rock, after the USA, the countries of the former USSR, Morocco and China, and the third largest exporter, after Morocco and the USA. The mining and marketing of phosphate is handled by the Jordan Phosphate Mines Company (JPMC). The expansion of the phosphate industry has been a major element in successive Development Plans. Quantities of uranium and vanadium are now known to be mixed in with the phosphate reserves. There are also known to be deposits of good-quality copper ore at Wadi Arabeh. Other minerals include gypsum, manganese ore, abundant quantities of glass sand and the clays and feldspar required for manufacturing ceramics. Foreign investors have been found to finance the establishment of companies to produce ceramics and sheet glass and also to exploit potash deposits in the Dead Sea. The Arab Potash Company (APC), formed in 1956 as one of the earliest Arab joint ventures, is 57% owned by the Jordanian Government. The company was reconstituted in 1983 and produced 486,868 tons of potash in 1984, its first full year of operation, selling 450,000 tons, worth $36.4m. In 1986 production reached 1.1m. tons, compared with 932,000 tons and revenue of $77m. in 1985. In 1990 the APC recorded its first profit (of JD 39.6m.) since it began commercial operations in 1983, owing to production of 1.4m. tons (compared with 1.3m. tons in 1989). Export sales in 1990 were 21% higher than in 1989, India being Jordan's most important customer, followed by China and Indonesia. In 1993 the annual capacity of the APC's Ghor as-Safi extraction plant on the Dead Sea totalled 1.4m. tons, using the hot leach process. Work was under way to add 400,000 tons of cold crystallization capacity by 1995, after which there were plans to double the cold crystallization capacity to bring the plant's total capacity to 2.2m. tons per year by 1998. The value of potash exports amounted to $140m. in 1992.

Diversification plans under active consideration by the APC in 1993 included a salt plant on the Dead Sea with a capacity of 1.2m. tons of industrial salt and 31,000 tons of table salt per year; a chemical plant at Aqaba with a capacity of 75,000 tons of potassium sulphate and 50,000 tons of dicalcium phosphate; a $140m. scheme to produce bromine derivatives from the Dead Sea (the world's richest bromine lake); and a plant to produce 50,000 tons of magnesium oxide per year. The APC holds a 20% interest in a joint-venture project set up in 1993 in partnership with a Japanese consortium (60%) and the JPMC (20%). Scheduled for completion in late 1995, the project involves the establishment of plant at Aqaba to produce 300,000 tons of compound fertilizers and ammonium phosphates per year, the fertilizers to be produced using 80,000 tons of potash and 50,000 tons of imported ammonia.

Rich beds of phosphates exist at Rusaifa, a few km northeast of Amman, and, from 1963 onwards, were exploited by a local company financed partly by the Government. Other deposits in the Wadi Hasa area, south of Amman, have been developed by American and Italian interests, and phosphates are also produced at Wadi al-Abyad. For many years production was centred on these three sites. However, in mid-1985 the JPMC was forced to close its Rusaifa mine because of falling demand for low-grade phosphate. In the longer term, the industry will focus on a major new, low-cost, mine at Shidiya, near Ma'an, in the south-east, which the JPMC is developing in two stages. The World Bank is contributing

$31m. to the $71m. first stage and a further $25m. loan was announced in February 1990. The Shidiya mine has proven phosphate reserves of 1,200m. tons, and started production in the second half of 1988, the aim being to achieve an annual output of 9.6m. tons by the year 2000.

In 1968 the country's total production of natural phosphates was 1,162,000 tons, more than five times the production in 1956. By 1976 annual production exceeded 1.76m. tons. Export earnings from phosphates, constant in 1974 and 1975 at JD 19.5m., dropped to JD 19.2m. in 1976. This was due to a fall in the international price of phosphate rock and prompted Jordan in 1976 to join with Morocco, Tunisia and Senegal in an association of phosphate exporters. In 1985, when the Rusaifa mine was closed, output totalled 5.92m. tons. At the beginning of 1986 the JPMC secured a 10-year contract with Thailand to supply 650,000 tons of phosphates per year. Phosphates output rose to 6.25m. tons (exports 5.2m. tons) in 1986 and 6.7m. tons (exports 5.7m. tons) in 1987. Production in 1988 was 6.5m. tons (exports 5.5m. tons). Revenue from exports of phosphates amounted to $262m. in 1988, compared with $176m. in 1986. In 1989 the JPMC exported 6.4m. tons of phosphates and reported profits of JD 107.2m., but in 1990 exports fell to 4.9m. tons and profits to JD 41.4m. (compared with a target of JD 108m.). While the Gulf crisis was a factor in this decline in 1990, its major cause was a sharp fall in demand in Eastern Europe, exports to which were only 580,000 tons, compared with 2m. tons in 1989. By 1992 the JPMC's phosphate exports amounted to only 4.26m. tons (out of its total production of 5.2m. tons), although the company's share of the shrinking world market was, at 15.2%, slightly higher than before. The value of exports in 1992 was JD 206.1m. ($300m.), while the JPMC's net profit was JD 16.1m.

Allied industries form an important part of Jordan's industrial development programme. A $400m. phosphate fertilizer plant south of Aqaba began production in June 1982. The 1981–85 Five-Year Plan allocated JD 15m. to the development of the plant. It was designed to produce 750,000 tons of diammonium phosphate and 105,000 tons of phosphoric acid per year, but has failed to produce to more than 65% of its phosphoric acid capacity. The plant is now undergoing restructuring to take production beyond present design capacity. The original project, which was managed by the Jordan Fertilizer Industries Company (JFIC), cost $410m. and included an aluminium fluoride plant with an annual capacity of 12,000 tons, which entered production in mid-1984. The JFIC made a JD 12.9m. loss in 1984, its first full year of trading, owing to a slump in world fertilizer prices; production reached 568,968 tons, of which 524,900 tons were sold. However, in 1986 the JPMC bought the JFIC (which had accumulated losses of JD 40.3m. by the end of 1985) for JD 60m. A loss of JD 1.3m. ($1.9m.) at the Aqaba plant in 1992 was attributed by the JPMC partly to depressed world prices (blamed on dumping by US and Russian producers), and partly to the plant's high staffing level.

The JPMC's plans for future 'downstream' development are centred on joint ventures with foreign partners who would provide investment funds and guarantee long-term export markets. The ventures would be designated as 'free-zone' industries in order to allow foreign majority participation. The Indo-Jordan Chemicals Company (60% Southern Petrochemical Industries Corporation of India, 40% JPMC) was established in 1993 to set up a plant at Shidiya capable of producing 200,000 tons of phosphoric acid from an annual imput of 750,000 tons of rock phosphate, to create a 20,000-ton storage facility at Aqaba, and to export the acid to India for on-processing into fertilizer. Completion was scheduled for 1995. A similar scheme was under discussion in 1993 with Fauji Fertilizer of Pakistan to produce sufficient phosphoric acid in Jordan to support annual production of 445,000 tons of diammonium phosphate and 346,000 tons of urea in Pakistan. It was envisaged that the Jordanian end of this project would be developed in parallel with the Indo-Jordan venture.

Jordan is almost wholly dependent on imports of crude petroleum for its energy needs. Its main sources, before the onset of the Gulf crisis in August 1990, were Iraq and Saudi Arabia, the former having replaced the latter as Jordan's main supplier in the late 1980s. Output of petroleum products from Jordan's only oil refinery, at Zarqa, increased steadily from 445,800 tons in 1970 to 748,000 tons in 1974, and to 1,114,600 tons in 1976. Production capacity was scheduled to reach 3.5m. tons per year by the end of 1979. This would have been more than sufficient to satisfy Jordan's domestic requirements. In 1980 the refinery, in fact, produced only 1,760,000 tons, but by 1982 it had an output capacity of 3m. tons per year (60,000 b/d). Between 1982 and 1984, maximum daily throughput was raised to 12,300 tons (about 86,000 b/d), an annual capacity of about 4.3m. tons, probably enough to satisfy domestic demand until 2000. In 1985, when the refinery's capacity was raised to 5m. tons (100,000 b/d), output rose to 2.6m. tons, compared with 2.3m. tons in 1984. Of this total, 1.8m. tons came from Saudi Arabia, 698,600 tons from Iraq and 2,800 tons from Jordan's Hamzah oilfield. In addition, 10,000 tons of LPG and 395,000 tons of fuel oil were imported from Iraq for domestic needs. The country's oil import bill was $8m. in 1974, but higher prices and greater domestic consumption caused the cost to increase to $540m. in 1983, and to $610m. in 1984. Under an agreement designed to relieve pressure on reserves of foreign exchange, Jordan imported from Iraq, in payment for goods, about one-sixth of its crude oil requirements in 1984 and 395,000 tons of fuel oil in 1985. Imports of crude petroleum amounted to 2.5m. tons, averaging 48,743 b/d, in 1988. Of this, 33,415 b/d was imported from Iraq and 15,000 b/d from Saudi Arabia.

In an attempt to reduce petroleum imports, attention has been given to the possibility of exploiting the estimated 40,000m. tons of shale oil deposits in the south of the country. Consequently, in September 1980 an agreement was signed with Technopromexport of the USSR for an oil-shale survey at Lajjoun. By the end of 1983 15 of the 55 wells to be drilled, to extract the oil from the shale, were reported to have been finished. In March 1984 the Qarma One oil-well, in the field near Azraq, was reported to be producing at a rate of 600 b/d. In November 1984 a Ministry of Energy and Mineral Resources was created, and in the following month the Government announced a plan to double investment in oil exploration, following promising oil strikes in the Azraq area on the border with Iraq and Saudi Arabia, and to reduce oil consumption by cutting oil subsidies and by increasing the prices of electricity and petroleum-based products. However, no commercial oil discoveries were made in the late 1980s, while production from the Azraq area declined to 315 b/d in 1988 and to only 40 b/d by mid-1990. Over this period, the cost of imported oil declined in relative terms, owing to reductions in world prices and to the availability of Iraqi oil at preferential prices.

The deferment, in 1985, of plans to construct a pipeline to convey crude petroleum from Iraq to Aqaba contributed to the decision to renew an agreement to receive Saudi Arabian crude petroleum, via the Trans-Arabian Pipeline (Tapline), at the Zarqa refinery. Tapline had been due to close in November 1983 and, again, in 1985. Transit dues rose threefold, however, and the total annual cost of the agreement to Jordan was calculated at $26m. In mid-1985 the Jordanian Ports Corporation awarded a $20m. contract to Sosema Matex (a consortium of international firms) for the construction and management of an oil terminal at Aqaba port. The terminal consists of a permanently docked oil tanker, capable of exporting 7,000–10,000 b/d, and became operational before the end of 1985. In July 1990 Jordan opened talks on the construction of a new pipeline linking the Iraq-Saudi Arabia Petroline with Tapline, which would save Jordan the $50m. per year that it spent on importing Iraqi oil by road tanker. However, the subsequent Gulf conflict resulted in the suspension of this plan, at least temporarily.

At the outbreak of the Gulf crisis in August 1990, Jordan was importing more than 80% of its oil requirements from Iraq, with almost all the remainder coming from Saudi Arabia. When Jordan, in late August, announced its acceptance of the UN trade embargo on Iraq, Saudi Arabia pledged itself to supply at least half of Jordan's oil needs through Tapline. However, Jordan's reluctance to apply the UN embargo resulted in Saudi Arabia's suspension of all oil supplies to Jordan in late September (the official reason given was non-payment of outstanding oil bills of $46m.). Jordan accordingly

became entirely dependent on Iraqi supplies by road tanker, which rose to some 60,000 b/d by mid-January 1991. The start of hostilities then resulted in the virtual cessation of such supplies, obliging Jordan to impose petrol rationing and to conclude emergency agreements to import oil from Yemen and Syria (at a higher price than the preferential rate charged by Iraq). In April 1991 it was announced that Iraqi supplies to Jordan would be resumed, but the after-effects of the war in Iraq were expected to inhibit normal trade for some time. Official Jordanian figures, issued in April 1991, showed that Iraq had supplied 86% (2.3m. tons) of Jordan's oil imports in 1990, and Saudi Arabia 13.2%, and that the Zarqa refinery had processed 2.7m. tons in the year, an increase of 11% over the 1989 level. Jordan's domestic oil production remained minimal, although it rose to 120,000 barrels in 1990, as against 75,000 barrels in 1989. In mid-1993 the only commercial oil exploration activity was being carried out by Hanbo Corporation of South Korea. Some stated-funded exploration was being undertaken by the Natural Resources Authority.

The discovery of reserves of natural gas at locations around ar-Risha in north-east Jordan in 1987 and 1988 encouraged speculation that the deposits would be sufficient to satisfy a significant proportion of Jordan's energy requirements in the future. By 1989 gas from the new discoveries was fuelling a 60-MW electricity generating plant at ar-Risha, employing two 30-MW gas turbines (ultimately to rise to six, producing 180 MW), which is connected to the main grid by a 220-km high-voltage transmission line. The plant was supplying 15% of national power requirements by 1990, when plans were announced to transfer to it two turbines from the South Amman station, with the aim of increasing its capacity to 25% of national power requirements. Domestic gas production in 1990 rose to 340m. cu m (compared with 160m. cu m in 1989). Production capacity at the ar-Risha field was due to reach 475m. cu m per year in mid-1993.

Jordan also has a thermal power station at Aqaba, which currently consists of two 130 MW oil-fired steam units, and is undergoing a $75m. expansion with the addition of two more 130 MW units capable of burning coal as well as oil, which will give a potential reduction in operating costs of 28% when the scheme is completed. A 400 kV transmission line, extending for 320 km, has been constructed, joining the power plant to Amman. The total cost of the plant's expansion is estimated at $324m., of which $60m.–$65m. has been loaned by the World Bank. The country's total power generation capacity will rise to about 950 MW with the installation of the two new units at Aqaba. A plan to add two more 130 MW dual-capability units has been postponed until 1993 in the light of the gas finds in the north-east. Under the 1986–90 Five-Year Plan, the government planned expenditure of $555m. on electricity distribution and production. Plans were in hand in 1993 to link the Jordanian and Egyptian electricity grids as the first phase of a regional inter-connection project.

Cement production reached 964,300 tons in 1981. Within the 1981–85 Plan, 37% of the money allocated to mining and manufacturing was set aside for four cement projects, including the construction of a cement works in the south, at Rashidiya. The existing plant at Fuheis, near Amman, owned by the Jordan Cement Factories Company (JCFC), has undergone an expansion, bringing its capacity up to 4.2m. tons per year. By the end of 1983 the first production line at the South Cement Company (SCC) works at Rashidiya was completed, and the second line was finished in the autumn of 1984, giving a total plant capacity of 2m. tons per year. The production of cement, having declined to 793,400 tons in 1982, rose in each of the subsequent three years, reaching 2,023,000 tons in 1985. Local demand rose by 5% in 1987, to 1.6m. tons. In 1987 and 1988 Egypt agreed to buy 750,000 tons of cement annually from Jordan. Total exports, which reached 800,000 tons in 1987, increased to 1m. tons in 1988. The struggling SCC merged with the JCFC in September 1985. The discovery in the Tafila area of gypsum reserves totalling an estimated 1.5m. tons, sufficient to satisfy demand for 10 years, was announced in March 1985. In 1990 the JCFC achieved record exports of 1.4m. tons of cement and clinker, and also sold 1.5m. tons of cement in the domestic market.

Construction was the fastest growing sector of the economy in 1993, when its share of GDP reached 8.3% (up from 7.6% in 1991). Stimulated mainly by the influx of 'returnees' from Kuwait, new building projects totalled 5.9m. sq m in 1992, as against 4.4m. sq m in 1991 and 2.7m. sq m in 1990.

In 1981 construction began on the 225-ha Sahab industrial estate, 18 km south-east of Amman, which is being built at a cost of JD 18m. The first phase of the estate, covering 85 ha, was opened at the end of 1982, and will include 15 ready-built factories and 15 other factories that are being built by the companies which are to use them. Work on the second phase of the Sahab industrial estate began in 1985. Nevertheless, the main focus of the 1981–85 and 1986–90 Plans appeared to be decentralization, putting emphasis on locating industries in geographically underdeveloped areas, especially the Soputj. An example of this is the Encouragement of Investment Law, which was enacted in February 1984. This divides the country into the following three zones: (a) Amman and its suburbs; (b) the other major cities; and (c) the remainder of the country. The government hopes to encourage dispersal of investment by regulating the amount of assets required by companies setting up in each zone, with the minimum requirement of fixed assets for zone (a) being almost three times that for zone (c). The 1981–85 Plan, with a centrepiece in the construction of the $1,000m. Yarmouk University (which received its first students in 1985), concentrated on manpower, technology transfer and regional development. Export industries were also to be promoted. The industrial plans for the region around Irbid (where an industrial estate is to be built at a cost of $20m.) and the Ma'an-Aqaba area will form magnets for attracting benefits away from the industrial core of Amman. However, plans to build an iron and steel plant at Irbid were postponed in November 1990.

In an effort to boost Jordan's role as an entrepôt, a free trade zone was introduced at Aqaba in 1976, and a second free trade zone was opened at Zarqa in February 1983. The amount of goods which passed through these zones totalled 350,000 tons in 1984. In March 1985 it was announced that two more duty-free zones would be established, at Queen Alia international airport and at the port of Aqaba. There is another free trade zone at Ramtha, on the Syrian border, while an industrial free zone was planned for the Shidiya phosphates-producing area (see above). All the zones are operated by the Free Zone Corporation under the aegis of the Ministry of Finance.

A severe lack of water is rapidly becoming one of Jordan's most crucial problems (see also Agriculture, above). One scheme to resolve this situation is a project being discussed with Iraq to pipe water from the Euphrates River to Amman at a cost of $1,000m. However, there are obvious strategic complications attached to being dependent for water on a pipeline from Iraq.

Four other schemes were outlined in the 1981–85 Five-Year Plan: the pumping of water to Amman and Irbid from the Jordan River; an increase in the search for groundwater; the expansion of the dam-building programme in the west; and the establishment of a central water authority. In the short term a 100-km pipeline is planned to bring water to Amman from the eastern oasis of Azraq. In July 1989 the EC granted Jordan 3m. ECUs to finance a study to examine the possibility of drawing water from the deep aquifer at Azraq, as demand on the shallow aquifer there was creating environmental problems. A new $36m. water supply scheme for Aqaba was formally opened in February 1982. A desalination plant with a daily capacity of 18m. litres has been constructed at Alamadi by the Japanese joint venture of the Marubeni Corporation and Sumimoto Heavy Industries. The allocation for water and irrigation in the 1981–85 Plan was JD 500m., making this sector second only to industry in importance.

In 1993 an extensive programme of water and sewerage works in the main urban areas included the first stage of a complete rehabilitation of the water supply system in Amman, where about half of the input volume was wasted through leakage. In all, about 500 km of water mains and 700 km of house connections were expected to require renewal in the capital. Meanwhile, proposals were being studied to pump water to Amman from the Disi aquifer, near the Saudi border, in a project costing up to $350m.

TRANSPORT

The transport sector has contributed around 15% of Jordan's GDP since the early 1970s, and provided direct or indirect employment for over 20% of the private-sector workforce in the early 1990s.

Jordan's only seaport is situated at Aqaba on the country's 20-km Red Sea coastline. Cargo-handling facilities expanded rapidly during the 1980s, an important factor being the re-routing through Aqaba of much Iraqi trade when the Iran–Iraq War of 1980–88 severely dislocated trade through Iraq's own Gulf outlets. In 1989 Aqaba handled 2,446 vessels and 18.7m. tons of cargo, of which 8.7m. tons were Jordanian exports and 2.5m. tons were Jordanian imports. In mid-1990 the port had over 20 berths, one container terminal, two 40-ton gantry cranes and 299,000 sq m of storage facilities.

Aqaba's transit trade was severely affected by the imposition of UN sanctions against Iraq from August 1990. According to the Jordan Shipping Agents Association, the cumulative loss of transport revenues (including government port fees) amounted to $570m. by the end of 1992. The total cargo loaded at Aqaba in 1992 was 13.4m. tons, of which only 2.1m. tons was transit cargo (mainly Iraqi government imports of basic foods). Iraqi exports via Aqaba, which had amounted to about 1.15m. tons a year before the imposition of sanctions, ceased entirely. The estimated reduction in Aqaba's Iraq-bound imports as a result of sanctions was about 3.5m. tons per year, while up to 2.85m. tons of transit cargo for countries other than Iraq were being re-routed to non-Jordanian ports by shippers who did not wish to suffer the delays and inconveniences of UN monitoring of Aqaba-bound cargoes. For the same reason, some shippers were also routing part of Jordan's own import trade via Mediterranean ports in Syria and Lebanon. Although the number of ships calling at Aqaba in 1992 was, at 2,430, only 16 fewer than in 1989, the proportion of cargo vessels in the total fell from 64% in 1989 to 52% in 1992, while the number of shipping lines calling regularly at Aqaba fell from 41 to 26.

The US-led naval patrol responsible for enforcing the UN monitoring of shipping at Aqaba was discontinued in late April 1994 in favour of land-based inspections by agents of Lloyd's Register of Shipping. The change occurred after repeated and vigorous protests to the US Government by King Hussein, citing estimates that diversions and delays caused by the naval blockade had cost the port about US $440m. in lost revenue in 1993. A US spokesman acknowledged in April 1994 that only six of the 460 ships turned away from Aqaba by the naval patrol had been carrying embargoed goods, while the remainder had merely lacked correct documentation.

A ferry service between Aqaba and the Egyptian port of Nuweibeh, opened in 1985, is one of the main low-cost passenger links between North Africa and the Gulf region (and as such carried most of the Egyptian workers who left Kuwait and Iraq in August 1990). In 1992 this service carried a total of 1.2m. passengers (many of them *en route* to Saudi Arabia), and its operator (the Arab Bridge Maritime Company) made a record profit of $9m.

The Jordanian section of the narrow-gauge Hedjaz railway runs from the Syrian border, via Amman and Ma'an, to the Saudi border. A 115-km link to a phosphate export terminal at Aqaba was added in the 1970s. A further 68 km of track, including a 48-km link to the Shidiya phosphate mines, is to be added in the mid-1990s. Freight (mainly phosphates) accounts for virtually all Jordan's current rail traffic, but future diversification into passenger services has not been ruled out. Plans to build a 1,000-km standard-gauge railway from Aqaba to Baghdad were approved in principle in 1989 but were shelved in the following year when Iraq's development plans were overtaken by political events.

The Jordanian road system includes a number of major national and international transit routes, among which the main north-south desert highway from Amman to Aqaba had, by 1993, been upgraded along all but 71 km of its 330-km length. Improvements to the dilapidated section of the highway, between Ras an-Naqb and Wadi Yutm in a mountainous area in the south, were scheduled for completion by the end of 1996. Even after the suspension of much of Iraq's trade through Aqaba, an estimated 300,000 trucks were using the port in 1991, due in part to the fact that all of Jordan's potash exports, and about half of its phosphate exports, are transported to Aqaba by road. The proportion of phosphates carried by road was not due to decline until the mid-1990s, on completion of the planned rail link to the Shidiya mines. An estimated 22,000 Turkish trucks used Jordan as a freight transit route in 1992, while Jordan's own sizeable haulage fleet was increasingly active on routes to North Africa, Turkey and Eastern Europe to replace export business lost through the UN embargo on Iraq and a decline in some Jordanian markets in other Gulf states. The Iraqi-Jordanian Land Transport Company, operating exclusively between these two countries, cut its fleet from 900 to 336 trucks in 1992.

The national airline, Royal Jordanian, operates passenger and freight services from Queen Alia international airport at Zizya, 40 km south of Amman. It carried 44,520 tons of freight in 1992 (compared with a peak of 55,170 tons in 1990 and a decline to 41,637 tons in 1991 as a result of the Gulf crisis). Passenger numbers in 1992 totalled 1,109,000, compared with 798,000 in 1991 and a recent peak of 1,226,800 in 1988. The airline's operating profit reached a 5-year peak of JD 37.9m. in 1992, but its (unpublished) net profit position was believed to reflect an annual debt service requirement of around $40m. (which would have been even greater had the airline not cancelled an option on four additional European Airbus aircraft in 1991). Plans to privatize Royal Jordanian, first put forward in 1987, had still to be finalized in 1993, when a consultants' report recommended a major increase in capital to resolve cash-flow problems.

EXTERNAL TRADE

For a long time, phosphates have dominated Jordan's exports but, in spite of increasing in overall value, they fell in relative importance, accounting for only 22.6% of total export earnings in 1981 and 1982, compared with 43.6% in 1979. The proportion rose to 32.2% in 1983 (though this was principally due to a 40% fall in total export earnings), but fell to 26.6% (JD 69.6m.) in 1984 and 25.9% (JD 66.1m.) in 1985. It rose again to 28.7% (JD 64.8m.) in 1986 but fell to 24.5% (JD 61m.) in 1987. Phosphates and potash together accounted for 38.5% (JD 146.9m.) of total exports in 1988 and 35.2% (JD 224.9) in 1989. In 1992, phosphates valued at JD 206.1m. (24.9% of total exports), and potash valued at JD 95.3m. (11.5% of exports), together accounted for 36.4% of Jordan's export earnings. The overall contribution of mineral resources to 1992 exports was estimated to exceed 60% after taking account of processed derivatives (fertilizers and fertilizer inputs). Jordan's exports of phosphoric acid and other derivatives were forecast to increase substantially after the mid-1990s, when joint ventures with several Asian importers were scheduled to come into production. Cement, tomatoes, vegetables and fruit are other important exports.

Saudi Arabia was Jordan's principal supplier between 1979 and 1985. Saudi Arabia's share of imports rose to a peak of 20.4% in 1982, when it sold goods to Jordan worth JD 233.5m. The proportion declined to 5.8% in 1986, when sales to Jordan were valued at JD 49.7m. and the USA became Jordan's principal supplier, though its share of total imports in that year declined from 11.9% (JD 128m.) in 1985 to 8.9% (JD 75.5m.). The USA's share rose to 10.2% (JD 93.4m.) in 1987 but Iraq became Jordan's leading supplier with 10.9% (JD 99.4m.) of total imports. Other leading suppliers are, traditionally, the Federal Republic of Germany, Italy, Japan and the United Kingdom. Iraq overtook Saudi Arabia as the largest purchaser of Jordan's exports in 1980, when it accounted for 23.6% of the total. Iraq's share rose to 26% (valued at JD 63.5m.) in 1981 and declined slightly to 25.2% (worth JD 66.6m.) in 1982. Jordan's exports to Iraq slumped to only 16% (JD 26m.) of the total in 1983, and Saudi Arabia once more became the principal customer for Jordanian exports, though only for one year, as Iraq accounted for 26% (JD 67.8m.) of Jordanian imports in 1984 and 25.8% (JD 65.9m.) in 1985. Iraq's share declined to 18.8% in 1986 and rose to 24.1% in 1987. Iraq, Saudi Arabia (with 10.5% of the total, in 1987) and India

(8.9%) are by far the most important purchasers of Jordanian exports.

Iraq's position as Jordan's main trading partner made it inevitable that the UN sanctions against trade with Iraq, imposed after Iraq's occupation of Kuwait in August 1990, would be fulfilled only with reluctance by Jordan. In 1989 Jordan exported approximately JD 147.9m. worth of goods to Iraq (about 23% of its total commodity exports), while imports from Iraq totalled approximately JD 221.8m. (mainly petroleum). More than 80% of Jordan's petroleum is normally imported from Iraq. By the end of August 1990 transit trade with Iraq through the port of Aqaba had virtually ceased (see Transport, above), and the outbreak of hostilities in January 1991 resulted in the virtual cessation of Iraqi oil deliveries. Following the end of hostilities, Iraq declared in April that it wished to resume normal trade with Jordan, which it proposed to make its main channel to the outside world. However, while some Jordanian food exports resumed to Iraq, a restoration of full bilateral trading links depended on the repeal of the UN embargo.

In mid-1993 Jordan's full oil import requirement was supplied by road from Iraq under a bilateral arrangement (then in its third year) which was deemed by Jordan to fall outside UN sanctions because it involved no financial transfers. Just over half of the supply was free of charge, while the remainder (valued at $16 per barrel, inclusive of transport) was counted as a repayment of Iraqi debt to Jordan. The agreement, which was understood to cover 55,000 b/d of crude oil in 1993, was informally monitored by UN sanctions administrators but did not have the formal approval of the UN sanctions committee. Following widespread reports in early 1993 that there was a growing barter element (mainly involving the supply of Jordanian food to Iraq) in this trade, the US Government began to exert pressure on Jordan to contribute 30% of the value of its oil imports to the UN-administered compensation fund for claims arising out of the Iraqi invasion of Kuwait. (This was the percentage levy which the UN intended to impose on UN-supervised oil exports from Iraq under a scheme which Iraq had so far declined to implement.) Iraq continued to supply all of Jordan's oil imports in 1994.

Jordan's trade with Egypt has increased annually since the two countries resumed diplomatic relations in 1984. Trade protocols with Egypt set bilateral trade at $250m. in 1988, compared with JD 150m. in 1985, and the two countries aimed to increase trade to $350m. in 1989, in which year Jordan and Egypt joined Iraq and the Yemen Arab Republic to form the Arab Co-operation Council. Although this organization effectively disintegrated amid the Gulf crisis of 1990–91, Jordan and Egypt remained committed to increased bilateral trade in the 1990s.

Jordan's traditionally large trade deficit is offset, somewhat variably, by expatriate remittances, re-exports, international aid and tourism. In 1985 import duties were raised by between 11% and 50% in an effort to cut the import bill by $30m. Exports declined by 2.2% in 1985 to JD 255.3m., and imports rose by 0.3%, to JD 1,074,445m., giving a visible trade deficit of JD 819.1m. In 1986 exports declined by 11.6% to JD 225.6m., and imports declined by 20.9% to JD 850.2m., a deficit of JD 624.6m. In 1987 the trade deficit narrowed to JD 596.9m. (exports JD 315.7m., imports JD 912.6m.), but in 1988 it widened again, to JD 638.5m. (exports JD 381.5m., imports JD 1,020m.). In 1989 a rise in exports of phosphates and chemicals was largely responsible for narrowing the trade deficit to JD 576.5m. (exports JD 637.6m., imports JD 1,214.2m.). Devaluations of the Jordanian dinar in 1988–89 made Jordanian exports more competitive and restricted Jordanian consumers' ability to buy imported goods. From a deficit of JD 1,008.6m. in 1990, the visible trade balance improved slightly to a deficit of JD 994.1m. in 1991, when exports totalled JD 770.7m. and imports JD 1,764.8m. In 1992 imports rose sharply to JD 2,291m. ($3,363.2m.), mainly because of additional demand generated by 'returnees' from Kuwait, leaving a visible trade deficit of JD 1,461.7m. ($2,144m.) after taking account of exports worth JD 829.3m. ($1,217.4m.). In 1993 the visible trade deficit reached JD 1,593m. (imports totalling JD 2,234m. while exports totalled JD 641m.).

FINANCE

Today, Jordan's main exports are phosphates, potash and fertilizer, but before 1967 net earnings from the tourist trade and income from private donations constituted the only important invisible export. After 1967 income from tourism and private transfers fell dramatically. In 1974, however, the Jordanian Government decided to allow its visitors to cross over the West Bank and the number of tourists arriving in the country that year rose by 79% on the 1973 total to reach 554,913, nearly regaining the 1966 level of 617,000, while income from tourism exceeded it, reaching JD 17.3m., compared with JD 11.3m. Tourism continued to expand during the 1970s and 1980s, reaching 2,677,021 in 1985. Earnings from tourism reached a record JD 310m. ($546m.) in 1989, when the number of European long-stay visitors totalled 130,000. In 1990 the Gulf crisis effectively ended all tourism from September onwards, while a slow recovery in the latter part of the following year took total European arrivals to 57,000 in 1991. In 1992, when European arrivals rose to 121,000, a strong revival of tourism (at least among non-Arab visitors) generated estimated net receipts of around $300m. Average tourism growth of 15% per year was officially forecast for 1993 and 1994 following strong overseas marketing campaigns by the government, private-sector tour operators and the national airline, Royal Jordanian. A main aim of government tourism development policy for the 1990s is to provide a varied range of attractions in different parts of the country, while taking steps to prevent over-development of Jordan's world heritage site at Petra.

An important source of foreign exchange in recent years has been remittances from Jordanians working abroad. In 1979 these totalled JD 180.4m. (including transfers through the banking system but not those through 'black market' money changers or by hand, which, it is estimated, would increase the total by 50%) and by 1981 had risen to $987m. In real terms the income from foreign remittances fell in 1982, but rose by 5% (JD 20m.) to JD 402m. ($1,040m.) in 1983. In 1984 remittances from the 340,000 Jordanians working abroad were worth JD 475m. ($1,228m.). However, the world oil glut and a fall in oil prices have adversely affected the economies of oil-producing countries in the Middle East, in particular the Gulf states where 85% of expatriate Jordanian workers are employed, and this, in turn, has affected the level of remittances. These fell, accordingly, by 17%, to JD 403.5m. ($1,204m.) in 1985. Although they recovered to JD 414.5m. ($1,243.5m.) in 1986, they declined to JD 317.7m. ($953.1m.) in 1987. The decline in Gulf economies also added to the number of the unemployed as workers returned from abroad. Remittances rose to JD 335.7m. in 1988, and to an estimated JD 470m. in 1989. Statistics issued by the Central Bank in May 1993 gave remittances in the years 1990, 1991 and 1992 as JD 331.8m., JD 306.3m. and JD 573.1m. respectively. The 1992 total was believed to include a large element of deferred transfers by workers who had returned to Jordan from Kuwait in 1991.

For many years, Jordan's trade deficit has been offset, mainly by capital imports and subventions. Before 1967 these came principally from the United Kingdom and the USA, but since 1967 there have been similar payments from Saudi Arabia and other Arab states. These subventions enabled the country's exchange reserves to be maintained and even increased. At the end of 1979 net foreign assets stood at JD 363.9m., compared with JD 177.4m. at the end of 1976, and international reserves (excluding gold) were $1,140m., compared with $458.9m. at the end of 1976. The JD 57.4m. balance-of-payments surplus in 1979 was increased to a surplus of JD 144.9m. in 1980. However, aid from Arab states fixed at the Baghdad summit meeting in 1978 was not maintained at the agreed level (see below). The first balance-of-payments deficit for five years was recorded in 1981, followed by further small deficits in 1982, 1983, 1984 ($219m.) and 1985 ($260.5m.). These deficits led the Government to seek new loans. In 1984 and 1985 it obtained Euroloans of $200.8m. and $215m., respectively, both with eight years' credit, and in 1987 one of $150m., with seven years' credit. Consequently, the burden of debt financing was expected to increase over the next few years. The level of government debt and government

guaranteed foreign debt rose to JD 1,100m. in 1986. By May 1987, as a result of debt servicing and reduced aid from other Arab countries, reserves of foreign exchange held by the Central Bank had fallen to JD 51m. ($153m.), sufficient to cover the cost of imports for less than one month. In 1986, owing to an increase in the level of remittances and Arab grant aid, a surplus of JD 35m. ($104.6m) was recorded in the balance of payments. Total foreign aid, however, declined from JD 377m. ($1,127m.) in 1985 to JD 304m. ($908m.) in 1986. The continuing decline in Arab aid, remittances from Jordanians working abroad, and low world prices for phosphates and potash contributed to a balance-of-payments deficit of JD 42.4m. ($140m.) in 1987. Jordan's reserves of foreign exchange stood at JD 72.5m. ($212m.) in January 1988 but declined to $128.1m. in March and $27.7m. in April. Jordan's economic problems created a lack of confidence in the Jordanian dinar on the currency market and the dinar declined in value from US $1 = JD 0.33 in May 1988 to US $1 = JD 0.39 in June. On 4 June, in support of the dinar, the Government established a special committee to consider new foreign exchange regulations. Two days later, a fixed exchange rate system was introduced, with a commercial bank rate of US $1 = JD 0.356/0.360 and a rate of $1 = JD 0.370/0.375 for money-changers. Foreign currency reserves rose to $36m. in May and an aid instalment of $60m. from Saudi Arabia helped to calm the market. New regulations, introduced in June, permitted Jordanians working abroad to bring back as much foreign currency as they wished and to dispose of it as they chose; allowed citizens to import any amount of local or foreign currency; and increased the amount that local residents were allowed to hold in foreign currencies, from JD 30,000 to JD 50,000.

In early November 1988 the combination of a shortage of foreign currency reserves, a decline of more than 30% in the value of the dinar since mid-October, and the deteriorating balance-of-payments position prompted the Government to introduce various austerity measures. Bans were imposed on the import of several luxury items, and customs duties on non-essential items, airport tax and fees payable for work permits were increased. The Government hoped to save at least US $350m. by the measures. In February 1989, amid increasing pressure on the currency, the Government cancelled all licences for money-changers.

In March 1989 representatives of the International Monetary Fund (IMF) visited Jordan to discuss the Government's efforts to revive the economy and reschedule its foreign debt, which was estimated at $6,500m. The Government had reportedly been reluctant to enter into negotiations with the IMF, but had concluded that an agreement with the IMF was the only means by which it could maintain its reserves of foreign exchange and finance its budget deficit. The cost of servicing the foreign debt in 1989 was estimated at $900m., including interest payments of $500m. As a result of these negotiations, the IMF granted Jordan a stand-by credit of $125m. in mid-July 1979, conditional upon the implementation of a five-year economic adjustment programme, drafted in consultation with the Fund. The adjustment programme aimed to reduce Jordan's budget deficit from 24% of GDP in 1988 to 5%, to reduce the annual rate of inflation from 14% to 7%, and to achieve a current account surplus. In order to achieve this, the Government agreed to reduce state expenditure, to increase revenues and to reduce imports. In late April, however, the Government's announcement of substantial increases in taxes and in the prices of some commodities (staples such as bread, milk and rice were not affected) led to widespread rioting throughout the country and to the resignation of the Prime Minister, Zaid ar-Rifai, and his Cabinet. Nevertheless the new Government, under the leadership of Field Marshal Sharif Zaid ibn Shakar, remained committed to the programme agreed with the IMF.

Although the former Prime Minister, Zaid ar-Rifai, had assured bankers that the agreement between Jordan and the IMF would not affect the value of the dinar, a further devaluation, of 5.5%, was announced in May 1989, bringing the total devaluation of the dinar against the US dollar since October 1988 to 42.5%. It was announced that the value of the dinar would henceforth be determined against a 'basket' of currencies, although the dollar would remain the most important of these currencies. At the same time, it was reported that as much as one-third of the Central Bank's gold reserves had been exchanged for foreign currency in 1988, and the Governor of the Bank, Muhammad Said Nabulsi, confirmed reports that Jordan's foreign debt amounted to $8,100m.

On 31 July 1989 the Central Bank introduced a two-tier exchange rate for the dinar, formalizing a system that had already been operating informally. While the Government continued to provide dollars at a fixed rate for imports of basic commodities, commercial banks were permitted to trade dollars at free-market rates for other foreign currency requirements.

By September 1989 a renewed influx of financial aid from Arab states, together with the intervention of the Central Bank, had enabled the dinar to stabilize at around $1.20, and it was hoped to be able to maintain its value at about $1.60 by the end of 1989. On 11 September the Ministry of Finance announced that the 'London Club' of commercial bank creditors had agreed to reschedule $575m. of Jordan's debts, which were due to be repaid between the beginning of 1989 and mid-1991. Reserves of foreign currency were reported to have risen to $500m. by September. In July the 'Paris Club' of creditor countries had agreed to the rescheduling of Jordan's debt for 1989 and 1990 ($656m. and $622m. respectively) over a 10-year period. As a result of these financial measures, and increased aid from abroad, Jordan recorded a JD 223m. surplus on its current account for 1989, although the annual rate of inflation increased to 25%, and little impression was made on the budget deficit.

The Jordanian Minister of Finance, Basil Jardaneh, visited London in April 1990 to work for the completion of Jordan's debt-rescheduling arrangements with the 'London Club'. Foreign debt had by then reached $8,400m. and there was a probable deficit of $95m. on foreign reserves. The country's problems were subsequently exacerbated by the onset of the latest regional crisis in August 1990. Having immediately stopped all repayments on its foreign debts, Jordan had to cope with the suspension, from September 1990, of disbursements to it under the 1989 IMF agreement. When it became clear, in December 1990, that the original 1993 target for completion of the structural adjustment programme was not feasible, a two-year extension to 1995 was provisionally agreed with IMF negotiators. However, rescheduling of foreign debt due for repayment by mid-1991 was contingent upon a formal reactivation of the IMF agreement, with revised content and timetable. An agreement was concluded in October 1991, involving an IMF stand-by credit of SDR 44m. over 18 months in support of an economic and financial reform programme covering the seven-year period 1992–98. Elements of the new IMF agreement included cuts in state subsidies of food and other basic commodities and a progressive reduction of the budget deficit. This enabled Jordan, in early 1992, to reach new debt-rescheduling agreements with both the 'Paris Club' and the 'London Club', involving in the former case the deferral of payments due in 1991–93 on total foreign debt estimated at $7,200m.

Jordan's balance of payments showed a current-account deficit of JD 148.2m. in 1990, a surplus of JD 269m. in 1991 and a deficit of JD 520m. in 1992. The main factor in the 1991 surplus was a sharp dip in outgoings on the invisibles account, while the main factor in the 1992 deficit was the steep rise in spending on visible imports (see External Trade, above). External debt was reduced to $6,600m. by the end of 1992, when the country's foreign exchange reserves exceeded $800m.

Jordan's persistent financial problems in the 1980s had culminated in a budget deficit of 24% of GDP in 1988, but thereafter, in accordance with IMF prescriptions, efforts were made to improve matters. Budget proposals for 1989 envisaged total expenditure of JD 1,035.0m. (a reduction of 16% compared with the budget for 1988, due mainly to the decline in the value of the dinar), incorporating development spending of JD 346.5m., compared with JD 451.5m. in 1988, a reduction of 23%. The budget deficit was originally projected at JD 122.3m., but the Government subsequently introduced measures to reduce the budget deficit by 4.5% of GDP in 1989. Budget estimates for 1990 envisaged expenditure at JD 1,105.8m. and revenue at JD 906.7m., resulting in a deficit of JD 199.1m. Capital and development expenditure was reduced to only JD 253.3m., compared with JD 346.5m. in 1989. Projected current expenditure was subsequently reduced by JD 15.1m., before the budget proposals received legislative approval. A further revision in the course of 1990 reduced total budgeted expenditure to JD 1,033.7m. and increased forecast revenues to JD 938.7m. resulting in a deficit of JD 182.4m. after loan repayments of JD 87.4m. up to August 1990. The 1991 budget, as adopted by the House of Representatives, envisaged total expenditure of JD 1,109.2m. and loan repayments of JD 135.2m., compared with revenues of JD 902.5m., resulting in a projected deficit of JD 341.9m. It was noted, however, that the expenditure total excluded certain debit items (notably oil subsidies), which, if included, would produce a deficit of at least 16% of GDP. The Government also presented a separate emergency budget of JD 120m., intended to assist the economy to overcome the effects of the Gulf crisis, its implementation being dependent on receipts of special aid (see below).

The 1992 budget proposals reflected the terms of the October 1991 IMF agreement; government subsidies being cut by 30%, and new consumption taxes imposed, in order to reduce the deficit to JD 107m. In the event, there was an overall budget surplus of JD 149m. in 1992 (due mainly to additional revenue from 'returnees'), total domestic revenue (JD 1,098m.) being higher than current expenditure (JD 932m.) for the first time in Jordan's history. The 1993 budget envisaged an excess of domestic revenue over current expenditure of JD 87m. and an overall budget deficit of JD 55m. Despite the achievement of a budget surplus in 1992, the effective fiscal deficit for the year (as cited in discussions with international financial institutions) was put at about 6% of GDP. Total GDP was JD 3,189m. ($4,600m.) in 1992, up 10.1% in real terms on 1991 after allowing for inflation of 3%. Pledges of $380m. in aid to close Jordan's 1993 financing gap were made by international donors at a meeting organized by the World Bank in January 1993.

Of the structural reform measures proposed in the 1993 budget, price increases on selected oil products (including fuel for electricity generation and aviation fuel supplied to Royal Jordanian) were implemented in June. However, a new sales tax, which should have superseded existing consumption taxes in May 1993, was deferred following strong protests from private businesses which claimed that they would be subject to an unfair burden, notwithstanding the Government's intention to raise only an extra JD 30m. per year, as against JD 100m. when the sales tax was first proposed. In the event the Government amended the scope of the consumption tax system to raise an additional JD 3.5m., a step that was accepted by the IMF as 'a temporary alternative'.

The 'London Club' of commercial bank creditors signed a debt rescheduling agreement in December 1993 covering US $740m. in principal and $150m. in interest owed by the Jordan Government to more than 80 lenders. The details of the agreement had been negotiated in July of that year.

The 1994 budget provided for revenue of JD 1,488m. (including domestic revenue of JD 1,311m.) and expenditure of JD 1,488m. (JD 1,124m. on current account and JD 364m. on capital account). Excluded from the budget were an unspecified amount of military spending, to be met by 'friendly Arab states', and the cost of servicing Jordan's foreign debt, which would have to be covered by fresh domestic and foreign borrowing to raise some JD 300m. In addition to the normal budget, the Government drew up an emergency budget providing for JD 66m. of development expenditure if sufficient foreign grants and/or soft loans could be raised. The controversial sales tax, after being strongly attacked during parliamentary debates, was finally approved on 14 May 1994 and took effect at the beginning of July 1994.

The parliamentary passage of the sales tax legislation paved the way for the IMF executive board to announce on 25 May 1994 its formal approval of a three-year extended fund facility (EFF) to support the next stage of the Government's structural adjustment programme. Worth SDR 127.8m. ($178.9m.), the EFF would be used to further a programme whose main 1994 objectives were stated as real GDP growth of 5.5%, an annual inflation rate held at 5%, a reduction of the current-account deficit to 9.7% of GDP (compared with 12.5% in 1993), and an increase in the Central Bank's foreign exchange reserves to $665m. or the equivalent of 2.4 months' import cover. The aim of fiscal policy should be 'to enhance efficiency and revenue-elasticity' through tax reform. Areas of structural change which the Government should address more convincingly included the formulation of action plans for the agriculture and water sectors. The IMF said that the Government's on-target achievements in 1993 had included real growth of 5.8% of GDP, an inflation rate of 4.8% and a fiscal deficit of 6.4% of GDP.

The IMF agreement paved the way for successful negotiations with the 'Paris Club' of official creditors, culminating in an agreement on 29 June 1994 to reschedule $1,215m. of debt payments over 20 years, including 10 years' grace. Jordan's Prime Minister described the terms as very favourable and designed to alleviate pressure on the Jordanian economy during the EEF period. World Bank statistics for 1992 gave Jordan's total debt as $6,914m., of which $3,454m. (including $2,704m. in concessional loans) was owed to official bilateral creditors. Prior to the IMF and 'Paris Club' announcements, the Government had, on 18 May, obtained $200m. of aid from the Jordan consultative group of donors to finance the 1994 balance-of-payments deficit.

Jordan's financial viability has always been dependent on aid from Arab and other external sources, so that fluctuations in the levels of such transfers have been a major factor in changing domestic expenditure patterns.

Arab budget assistance rose after 1971, and in November 1978 at the Baghdad Arab Summit Conference there was an agreement to provide a $35,000m. 'war chest' for parties confronting Israel, and one-third of this sum was allotted to Jordan. From 1979 Jordan was thus to receive $1,250m. annually for 10 years. This figure was never achieved, though budgetary assistance from Arab countries increased from JD 19.3m. in 1976 to JD 198.7m. in 1979. In 1981 it reached JD 244m., and commitments on which Algeria and Libya had reneged were being covered by several other Gulf states. Jordan's stance on regional issues, such as the split within the PLO, relations with Egypt, and the Palestinian question, was, undoubtedly, largely responsible for the failure of certain Arab countries to fulfil their aid commitments (namely Algeria, Libya and Syria). However, the decline of the economies of Gulf states in the 1980s was also an important factor. By 1983 less than one-half of the Baghdad allocation had actually been given to Jordan, with the full amount received only from Saudi Arabia and Kuwait, and totalling $668m. However, this was only marginally less than the amount allowed for in the Jordanian budget. The total fell to $322.4m. in 1984, when Qatar and UAE failed to pay. Kuwait reduced the amount of its aid by 40% in 1984, and in August 1985 suspended its payments, putting all future aid under the Baghdad agreement on a discretionary basis. This left Saudi Arabia as the only one of the original seven Arab donor countries continuing completely to fulfil its obligations under the Baghdad agreement.

Following the Camp David Accords, in which Jordan did not co-operate, budgetary contributions from the USA were temporarily suspended in 1981. However, in March 1981 the USSR signed an agreement with Jordan for a loan of $1m., re-emphasizing the links between Jordan and the then Communist bloc. In addition, the cutbacks in Arab and US financial assistance meant that Jordan turned increasingly to the European financial market. In July 1984 Jordan arranged an eight-year syndicated Euroloan of $200.8m. but only $150m. was raised, as the Kuwait Government blocked the share being contributed by the National Bank of Kuwait. A Euroloan of $200m., made on similar terms, was finalized in April 1985 and increased to $215m. in June. Jordan was allocated $55.74m. in aid disbursements from the USA in fiscal 1987 (beginning October 1986), $46.25m. in fiscal 1988 and $67.8m. in fiscal 1989. According to OECD statistics, net disbursements of official development aid (ODA) to Jordan by OECD members, Arab countries and multilateral organizations increased from $564m. in 1986 to $579m. in 1987, but fell to $415m. in 1988

and to $280m. in 1989. Including non-ODA categories, Arab aid totalled about $400m. in 1989 and was budgeted at $360m. in 1990, in which year Jordan had originally expected to receive some $750m. from all sources. However, Jordan's aid needs and expectations were radically altered by the 1990–91 Gulf crisis, in light of which substantial additional commitments were made by a number of countries and organizations. Most of the special assistance was channelled through the 27-nation Gulf Financial Crisis Co-ordination Group (GFCCG), which by mid-March 1991 had received pledges totalling $11,741m. for Egypt, Turkey and Jordan, of which $5,482m. had been disbursed. In Jordan's case, whereas its 1991 ordinary and recovery budgets assumed aid receipts of about $1,050m., actual commitments for the year totalled $1,360m. by late March.

However, the donors did not include the USA, where Congress voted on 22 March 1991 to discontinue aid to Jordan because of King Hussein's pro-Iraqi stance. Affecting a total of $113m. in US aid allocated for 1990 and 1991, the relevant law was signed by President Bush on 10 April, after insertion of a clause allowing him to reinstate aid if Jordanian policy became more helpful. An improvement in relations with the USA was apparent when King Hussein visited President Clinton in Washington in June 1993, and it was reported in the following month that $30m. of aid (part of a $65m. economic assistance allocation for fiscal 1992) had been unfrozen. In August 1993, however, the US Senate Foreign Relations Sub-committee attached an amendment to the 1994 foreign aid bill to make aid disbursements to Jordan conditional on Jordan's compliance with UN sanctions against Iraq. The amendment required the US State Department to report at six-monthly intervals on Jordan's observance of the sanctions.

Jordan's banking sector grew with the economy, but recent changes in the country's economic fortunes have enforced a new caution. The number of institutions grew nearly three-fold to 36 between 1973 and 1983. In January 1984 the Central Bank announced measures to 'Jordanize' foreign banks operating in Amman. They were given three (later extended to five) years to comply with regulations requiring that 51% of their equity be held by Jordanian nationals. The only foreign bank to respond was the Arab Land Bank. However, in April 1985, the new Government of Prime Minister Zaid ar-Rifai abandoned the regulation, though this did not affect another requirement for all banks to raise their capital from JD 3m. to JD 5m. in line with local commercial banks. ('Jordanization' would have taken the capital of foreign banks above the new minimum requirement.) In July Said Nabulsi resigned as governor of the Central Bank of Jordan, a decision thought to have been influenced by the Government's rejection of his measures to 'Jordanize' foreign banks. The Chase Manhattan Bank decided to withdraw from Jordan in 1986, rather than comply with the direction to increase its capital. In February 1984 new Central Bank regulations stated that all banks must invest at least 4% of their total deposits either in government bonds or in government-guaranteed public corporation bonds, together with a further 4% in treasury bills. In addition, banks must now also invest at least 15%, but not more than 75%, of paid-up capital and domestic reserves in public shares. In July 1990 the financially-troubled Petra Bank went into liquidation, as did the Syrian-Jordanian Bank in May 1991, only 12 years after its creation as a joint venture of the Damascus and Amman Governments.

In January 1986 the Government lifted most of the restrictions preventing non-Jordanian Arabs from investing in the Jordanian economy. The only restriction to remain in force was that permitting a 49% maximum shareholding for non-Jordanian Arabs in retail trade, banking, finance and insurance companies. The change of policy was seen as an attempt to attract private capital to Jordan to offset the decline in Arab aid.

In December 1984 insurance companies were instructed to raise their capital to JD 600,000 by the end of 1986 or to merge with other companies. The regulation affected nine of the country's 21 insurance companies. Two mergers, between the Arab Belgium Insurance Co and the United Insurance Co, and the National Insurance Co and Al-Ahlia (Jordan)

Insurance Co took place between October 1985 and August 1986.

In August 1991 the Central Bank imposed new credit ceilings in accordance with the IMF-decreed reforms. These included a 9% per annum limit on the increase in commercial credit and a specification that, in extending credit, commercial banks should not exceed ten times their captial and reserves, or 90% of total customer deposits. In May 1993 an overall ceiling of JD 400m. was imposed on the growth of bank credit in the current year. This followed a surge in lending as banks sought to make profitable use of the strong inflow of deposits from 'returnees' over the previous two years. By the beginning of July the 1993 loan total already exceeded JD 300m. The Central Bank had earlier imposed restrictions on bank lending to finance customers' share purchases following signs that the Amman stock market was overheating in mid-June 1993 (when daily trading volumes of JD 16m. were recorded, compared with the normal average of JD 4m.).

At the beginning of 1993 the Central Bank ordered commercial banks to increase their bad debt provisions on around JD 2,200m. of outstanding loans. This move (which occurred at a time when bank profits were at record levels) effectively paved the way for the writing off of nearly JD 400m. of bad debts dating from the late 1980s. The banks had until 1995 to bring their loan cover up to new minimum levels.

DEVELOPMENT

Jordan's first Five-Year Development Plan, for 1962–67, aimed to invest JD 137m. in the economy, to raise GDP to JD 144m. This plan, however, was superseded by a Seven-Year Plan that was due to run from 1964 to 1970. In its turn, this was disrupted and abandoned after the loss of the West Bank in 1967, and a new Three-Year Plan, covering the period 1973–75, was introduced, with a total proposed expenditure of JD 179m. The three largest items of expenditure were transport, housing and government buildings and mining and industry. The 1976–80 Plan, which followed the 1973–75 Plan, envisaged a total expenditure of JD 756m., with the public and private sectors contributing in equal proportions. The Government felt that the Jordanian economy was too heavily biased towards the services sector, and one of the chief aims of the plan was the development of the commodity producing sector and its increased contribution to GDP. In the event, although GDP failed to rise at the planned rate of 11.9% per annum, by 1980 it had risen by a substantial 62% compared with its 1976 value.

During the 1976–80 Plan period, the growth of agriculture was below target, but the 1981–85 Five-Year Plan still set goals. Agriculture was planned to have an annual growth rate of 7.5%, mining and manufacturing 17.8%, electricity and water supply 18.9% and construction 12.6%. These compare with an annual industrial growth rate of 13.6% during the 1976–80 Plan. In contrast, investment during the period 1976–80 overshot planned levels by 150%, largely owing to high levels of private investment. The initial planned investment for the 1981–85 Plan was JD 2,800m. ($8,446m.). Industry was to account for 21%, water and irrigation 18%, transport 18% and housing 11%. By October 1981, however, Iraq had promised financial support of JD 500m., and this led to an increase in the planned level of investment to JD 3,300m., of which JD 1,162m. was to be from overseas assistance. Over the period there was planned to be an annual growth rate in GDP of 10.4%, compared with the 8.5% rate of the 1976–80 Plan. However, the targets of the 1981–85 Plan were not met.

Under the 1986–90 Plan, expenditure was set at JD 3,115m. ($9,727m.), 52% of which was allocated to projects in the public sector and 48% to the private sector. Of total expenditure, 33% was to be provided by foreign borrowing. The Plan aimed for real economic growth of 5% per year and, with 39% of total investment to be allocated to the services sector (compared with less than 30% in the previous Plan), it was hoped that as many as 100,000 jobs would be created during its term. Agriculture was allocated 10% of total investment, compared with 5% and 7% in the previous two Plans, and agricultural production was expected to increase at an annual

rate of 7%–8%. The phosphate industry was to be expanded with development plans focusing on the Shidiya phosphate deposits (see Industry and Mining), while potash mining and other important export industries were also to be developed with the aim of increasing the value of exports by an annual rate of 8.3%. At the same time, it was planned to reduce the annual growth of imports to 2.8% for goods and 3.6% for services. These measures were intended to reduce the deficit on the current account of the balance of payments—one of the Plan's key objectives. However, major slippages on the Plan's targets were compounded towards the end of its term by the onset of the 1990–91 Gulf crisis. According to World Bank figures, Jordan's GDP increased, in real terms, by an annual average of 4.2% in 1980–88, in which period agricultural output increased by 6% per year, industry by 3.6% and services by 4.4%.

A five-year development plan for the Occupied Territories (1986–90) was launched in November 1986. With total required investment of JD 461.5m. ($1,292.3m.) for projects in the West Bank and the Gaza strip, the aim of the plan was to enable the 1.3m. Palestinians living in these areas to achieve a greater degree of economic independence; creating 20,000 jobs, constructing 8,500 homes and limiting the movement to Israel and, more especially, to Jordan (where immigrants might contribute to social, economic and political problems) of Palestinians deprived of work and opportunities. (About 850,000 West Bank Palestinians are entitled to Jordanian citizenship.) About 654,000 residents of the Occupied Territories left or were forced to leave between 1967 and 1984 (most of them to Jordan), and more than 100,000 Arab workers from the Territories, about one-third of the labour force, work in Israel. Israel took measures to facilitate the implementation of the Plan, such as the appointment in September 1986 of Arab mayors in four West Bank towns, and agreeing to the opening of four branches of the Cairo-Amman Bank, which were to provide the main channel for the transfer of funds to development projects. The Plan had singularly failed to attract sufficient investment from abroad and appeared to be struggling for financial viability when, on 28 July 1988, it was abandoned by King Hussein on political grounds (see History, above). On 31 July King Hussein severed Jordan's legal and administrative links with the West Bank. The practical effects of this were that 5,300 teachers and civil servants, and other government workers employed by Jordan in the West Bank before the Israeli occupation in 1967, and fully paid by Jordan, were retired on full pension; subsidies from the Jordanian Government, including salaries, to some 10,000 teachers and 5,000 civil servants, employed since 1967, were removed (although most of these received a salary from Israel and only a monthly bonus from Jordan). An additional 2,000 employees, working in departments of religious affairs and Islamic law, were to continue to be employed in order to preserve an Islamic cultural identity in the area. It was estimated that the removal of subsidies would save Jordan $60m. per year. The PLO undertook to compensate all former Jordanian employees for the loss of their jobs but, owing to the restrictions imposed by Israel on the movement of funds into the Occupied Territories, this promise has proved difficult to honour.

Following the 1990–91 Gulf crisis, Jordan's 1991 budget estimates included an allocation of JD 230.2m. for capital expenditure, as well as an emergency budget of JD 120m., intended to assist the recovery of important economic sectors such as industry, transport, agriculture and tourism. Substantial additional aid commitments from external sources (see Finance, above) made it possible to implement this emergency budget, but the Government came under domestic criticism for using the extra aid to reduce the budget and external deficits, as required by the IMF, rather than to compensate the sectors that had been damaged during the recent crisis.

In May 1991 Jordan signed its fourth financial co-operation protocol with the EC, which undertook to provide a total of 126m. ECUs in development grants and loans over a five-year period from November 1991. Under the three previous protocols, covering the period 1977–91, Jordan had received a total of 203m. ECUs.

Statistical Survey

Source: Department of Statistics, POB 2015, Jabal Amman, 1st Circle, POB 2015, Amman; tel. 24313.

Area and Population

AREA, POPULATION AND DENSITY (East and West Banks)

Area (sq km)	97,740*
Population (UN estimates at mid-year)†	
1989	3,878,000
1990	4,009,000
1991	4,145,000
Density (per sq km) at mid-1991	42.4

* 37,738 sq miles.

† Source: UN, *World Population Prospects 1990*. The estimates are projections that assume stable growth and take no account of migration.

East Bank: Area 89,206 sq km; population 2,100,019 (males 1,086,591; females 1,013,428) at census of 10–11 November 1979; estimated population 3,888,000 (males 2,005,400; females 1,882,600) at 31 December 1991.

GOVERNORATES

(East Bank only; estimated population at 31 December 1991)

Amman	1,573,000
Irbid	950,000
Zarqa	601,000
Balqa	239,000
Karak	163,000
Mafraq	156,000
Ma'an	144,000
Tafiela	62,000
Total	3,888,000

PRINCIPAL TOWNS (including suburbs)

Population at 31 December 1991: Amman (capital) 965,000; Zarqa 359,000; Irbid 216,000; Russeifa 115,500.

BIRTHS, MARRIAGES AND DEATHS (East Bank only)*

	Live Births	Marriages	Deaths
1986	112,451	19,397	8,853
1987	107,519	23,208	8,591
1988	116,346	28,247	9,416
1989	115,742	31,508	9,695
1990	116,920	32,706	10,659
1991	150,177	35,926	11,268

* Data are tabulated by year of registration rather than by year of occurrence. Registration of births and marriages is reported to be complete, but death registration is incomplete. Figures exclude foreigners, but include registered Palestinian refugees.

Expectation of life (UN estimates, years at birth, 1985–90): 65.9 (males 64.2; females 67.8). Source: UN, *World Population Prospects: The 1992 Revision.*

ECONOMICALLY ACTIVE POPULATION (Jordanians only)

	1984	1985	1986
Agriculture	34,850	36,833	37,436
Mining and manufacturing .	47,414	49,869	52,706
Electricity and water . .	4,585	5,195	5,418
Construction	52,733	51,947	54,183
Trade	46,487	47,225	49,258
Transport and communications	41,178	44,391	46,302
Financial and insurance services	14,444	16,104	16,748
Social and administrative services	216,848	220,635	230,525
Total employed . . .	458,539	472,199	492,576
Unemployed	n.a.	n.a.	42,864
Total civilian labour force .	n.a.	n.a.	535,440

Agriculture

PRINCIPAL CROPS (East Bank only; '000 metric tons)

	1990	1991	1992
Barley	42	40	65*
Wheat	83	62	80*
Pumpkins, squash and gourds .	35	30†	34†
Oranges	26	26*	27†
Tangerines, mandarins, clementines, satsumas . .	72	71*	80†
Lemons and limes . . .	51	50*	50†
Grapefruit	3	3*	3†
Bananas	19	26	27†
Grapes	46	39	44†
Olives	64	41	60†
Tomatoes	377	276	300†
Eggplants (Aubergines) . .	59	61	60†
Cauliflowers	26	24*	25†
Cabbages	18	17*	19†
Watermelons	50	58*	50†
Melons	31	36*	30†
Potatoes	90	45†	59†
Green beans	11	9†	13†
Cucumbers and gherkins . .	54	56	55†

* Unofficial figure.   † FAO estimate.

Source: FAO, *Production Yearbook.*

LIVESTOCK

(East Bank only; '000 head, year ending September)

	1990	1991	1992
Horses*	4	4	4
Mules*	3	3	3
Asses*	19	19	19
Cattle*	29	31	32
Camels*	18	18	18
Sheep	1,556	1,700*	2,000*
Goats*	500	540	600
Poultry*	41,000	45,000	55,000

* FAO estimate(s).

Source: FAO, *Production Yearbook.*

Forestry

ROUNDWOOD REMOVALS (FAO estimates, '000 cubic metres)

	1990	1991	1992
Industrial wood	4	4	4
Fuel wood	6	7	7
Total	10	11	11

Source: FAO, *Yearbook of Forest Products.*

Fishing

(metric tons, live weight)

	1989	1990	1991
Total catch	57	62	22

Source: FAO, *Yearbook of Fishery Statistics.*

Mining

('000 metric tons)

	1989	1990	1991
Crude petroleum . .	11	16	7
Phosphate rock . . .	6,642	5,925	4,000
Potash salts* . . .	1,315	790	810
Salt (unrefined) . .	18	18	18

* Figures refer to the K_2O content.
† Provisional figure.
Source: UN, *Industrial Statistics Yearbook.*

Industry

SELECTED PRODUCTS
('000 metric tons, unless otherwise indicated)

	1989	1990	1991
Liquefied petroleum gas .	96	102	99
Motor spirit (petrol) .	359	400	427
Aviation gasoline . .	15	15	14
Kerosene	168	205	228
Jet fuels	232	250	96
Distillate fuel oils . .	692	745	717
Residual fuel oils . .	693	772	590
Lubricating oils . . .	12	12	14
Petroleum bitumen (asphalt)	89	120	134
Nitrogenous fertilizers (a)* .	108.5	107.3	107.8
Phosphate fertilizers (b)* .	277.2	274.2	275.5
Potassic fertilizers (c)* .	810.4	841.6	818.4
Cement	1,930	1,780	1,800†
Cigarettes (million) . .	2,926	4,100	3,800
Electricity (million kWh) .	3,434	3,688	3,723

* Production in terms of (a) nitrogen; (b) phosphoric acid; and (c)
potassium oxide.
† Estimated production.
Source: mainly UN, *Industrial Statistics Yearbook.*

Finance

CURRENCY AND EXCHANGE RATES
Monetary Units
   1,000 fils = 1 Jordanian dinar (JD).

Sterling and Dollar Equivalents (31 May 1994)
   £1 sterling = JD 1.0567;
   US $1 = 699.0 fils;
   JD 100 = £94.63 = $143.06.

Average Exchange Rates (US $ per JD)
   1991   1.4689
   1992   1.4712
   1993   1.4434

BUDGET ESTIMATES (East Bank only; JD million)

Revenue	1990	1991
Local revenues (taxes, etc)	746.1	702.5
Grants and loans	162.6	150.0
Unused loans	30.0	50.0
Total	938.7	902.5

Expenditure	1990	1991
Capital and development expenditure . .	188.3	230.0
Recurrent expenditure	845.4	889.2
Loan repayments	87.4	135.2
Total	1,121.1	1,254.4

1992 (estimates): Revenue JD 1,353m., Expenditure JD 1,204m.
1993 (estimates): Revenue JD 1,273m., Expenditure JD 1,328m.
1994 (estimates): Revenue JD 1,488m., Expenditure JD 1,488m.
Source: *Middle East Economic Digest.*

CENTRAL BANK RESERVES (US $ million at 31 December)

	1991	1992	1993
Gold*	103.8	101.4	99.8
IMF special drawing rights .	1.1	0.6	5.5
Foreign exchange	824.7	750.2	588.6
Total	929.6	852.2	693.9

* National valuation.
Source: IMF, *International Financial Statistics.*

MONEY SUPPLY (JD million at 31 December)

	1991	1992	1993
Currency outside banks . .	992.4	1,003.9	1,047.9
Demand deposits at commercial banks	640.3	685.9	780.0

Source: IMF, *International Financial Statistics.*

COST OF LIVING (Consumer Price Index; base: 1980 = 100)

	1990	1991	1992
Food	185.7	206.3	212.5
Fuel and light	132.0	143.2	147.6
Clothing	290.1	323.0	350.7
Rent	136.7	140.9	144.2
All items (incl. others) . .	202.1	218.6	227.3

Source: ILO, *Year Book of Labour Statistics.*

NATIONAL ACCOUNTS
(East Bank only; JD million at current prices)
Expenditure on the Gross Domestic Product

	1989	1990	1991
Government final consumption expenditure	615.4	663.2	713.0
Private final consumption expenditure	1,766.4	2,374.1	2,574.7
Increase in stocks	54.9	60.1	—
Gross fixed capital formation .	547.4	691.4	610.1
Total domestic expenditure .	2,984.1	3,788.8	3,897.8
Exports of goods and services .	1,150.2	1,296.9	1,196.2
Less Imports of goods and services	1,804.4	2,474.3	2,303.2
GDP in purchasers' values .	2,329.9	2,611.4	2,790.9
GDP at constant 1985 prices	1,898.4	1,910.5	1,927.5

Gross Domestic Product by Economic Activity*

	1989	1990	1991
Agriculture, hunting, forestry and fishing	131.7	179.6	174.3
Mining and quarrying . . .	154.5	158.8	145.7
Manufacturing.	254.7	345.2	371.6
Electricity, gas and water . .	52.8	53.3	59.8
Construction	106.7	111.6	122.5
Trade, restaurants and hotels .	180.6	207.9	287.3
Transport, storage and communications	359.1	362.0	358.3
Finance, insurance, real estate and business services . .	378.7	374.5	410.2
Government services . . .	427.8	443.8	471.2
Other community, social and personal services . .	45.6	51.2	55.9
Non-profit private services .	25.2	20.0	21.5
Domestic services of households	6.0	6.2	5.3
Sub-total	2,123.4	2,314.1	2,483.6
Less Imputed bank service charge	55.3	39.9	42.8
GDP at factor cost . .	2,068.1	2,274.2	2,440.8
Indirect taxes . . . . } *Less* Subsidies . . . . }	261.8	337.2	350.0
GDP in purchasers' values .	2,329.9	2,611.4	2,790.8

* Figures are provisional.

BALANCE OF PAYMENTS (US $ million)

	1991	1992	1993
Merchandise exports f.o.b. .	1,129.5	1,218.9	1,246.3
Merchandise imports . . .	−2,302.2	−2,998.7	−3,145.2
Trade balance . . .	−1,172.7	−1,779.7	−1,898.8
Exports of services . . .	1,351.2	1,449.2	1,573.8
Imports of services . . .	−1,122.5	−1,324.7	−1,347.2
Other income received. . .	114.3	112.4	99.0
Other income paid. . . .	−447.7	−390.0	−250.2
Private unrequited transfers (net).	408.1	781.3	997.1
Official unrequited transfers (net).	475.7	386.3	356.6
Current balance . . .	−393.5	−765.2	−469.7
Direct investment (net) . .	−25.6	44.1	19.5
Other capital (net). . . .	2,122.9	952.2	−699.3
Net errors and omissions . .	321.4	160.9	777.6
Overall balance . . .	2,025.2	392.0	−372.0

Source: IMF, *International Financial Statistics.*

External Trade

PRINCIPAL COMMODITIES (JD '000)

Imports	1989	1990	1991
Food and live animals . . .	232,408	403,907	417,668
Beverages and tobacco . .	8,522	9,800	9,505
Crude materials (inedible) except fuels	30,336	43,251	58,916
Mineral fuels, lubricants, etc.	227,476	312,110	247,454
Animal and vegetable oils and fats	9,341	21,896	23,676
Chemicals	128,629	190,205	218,764
Basic manufactures . . .	227,627	301,967	327,848
Machinery and transport equipment	243,384	327,207	299,085
Miscellaneous manufactured articles	83,003	89,850	93,958
Other commodities and transactions	39,416	25,635	13,589
Total	1,230,142	1,725,828	1,710,463

Exports	1989	1990	1991
Phosphates	146,270	138,668	123,092
Potash	71,176	88,526	96,764
Chemicals	150,204	188,967	177,045
Cement	7,476	22,209	26,103
Vegetables, fruit and nuts .	25,477	43,329	49,068
Cigarettes	503	1,592	4,126
Basic manufactures . . .	49,057	55,892	37,308
Machinery and transport equipment	10,758	14,283	7,442
Miscellaneous manufactured articles	24,425	31,105	26,627
Total (incl. others) . . .	534,159	612,263	598,627

PRINCIPAL TRADING PARTNERS (JD '000)

Imports	1989	1990	1991
Belgium	25,573	50,548	44,428
China, People's Republic . .	21,995	25,020	29,149
France.	72,721	97,892	73,601
Germany, Fed. Republic . .	77,360	96,887	133,182
Iraq	212,807	273,152	187,787
Italy	51,126	67,621	73,630
Japan	45,759	54,320	61,115
Korea, Republic . . .	15,612	17,558	24,771
Kuwait	29,722	25,777	363
Netherlands	34,834	47,800	57,711
Romania	12,427	15,597	22,313
Saudi Arabia	31,629	76,408	27,667
Spain	9,838	18,436	18,048
Switzerland	18,523	21,404	15,532
Taiwan	22,085	30,198	40,128
Turkey	28,551	46,110	57,140
United Kingdom . . .	73,849	89,378	77,570
USA	170,007	299,480	178,158

Exports	1985	1986	1987
China, People's Republic . .	2,278	7,570	10,044
Egypt	3,033	3,979	13,448
France.	5,252	7,070	5,187
India	45,310	34,126	22,034
Indonesia	9,081	7,606	7,993
Iraq	65,850	42,458	59,865
Italy	3,655	7,099	9,266
Japan	5,815	5,690	7,435
Kuwait	7,738	8,813	8,614
Pakistan	5,941	3,456	10,253
Poland.	3,287	3,721	7,068
Romania	10,015	7,524	6,418
Saudi Arabia	39,083	27,817	26,204
Syria	3,901	4,570	7,201
United Arab Emirates . .	805	845	4,861
Yugoslavia.	3,069	7,689	6,923

Transport

RAILWAYS (traffic)

	1988	1989	1990
Passenger-km (million) . .	1	1	2
Freight ton-km (million) . .	625	610	711

Source: UN, *Statistical Yearbook*.

ROAD TRAFFIC ('000 motor vehicles in use)

	1988	1989	1990
Passenger cars. . . .	158.9	159.9	172.0
Commercial vehicles . . .	63.2	63.4	68.3

Source: UN, *Statistical Yearbook*.

INTERNATIONAL SEA-BORNE SHIPPING
(freight traffic, '000 metric tons)

	1988	1989	1990
Goods loaded	913	832	739
Goods unloaded	762	725	514

Source: UN, *Monthly Bulletin of Statistics*.

CIVIL AVIATION (traffic on scheduled services)

	1989	1990	1991
Kilometres flown (million). .	32	28	23
Passengers carried ('000) . .	1,148	931	782
Passenger-km (million) . .	3,665	2,773	2,435
Freight ton-km (million) . .	206	223	162

Source: UN, *Statistical Yearbook*.

Tourism

	1988	1989	1990
Foreign tourist arrivals . .	2,368,347	2,257,660	2,629,500
Tourist receipts (million US dollars)	617	551	500

Source: UN, *Statistical Yearbook*.

Communications Media
(East Bank only)

	1984	1985	1986
Telephones in use	113,666	147,873	177,894

Radio receivers (1991): 1,060,000 in use.
Television receivers (1991): 330,000 in use.

Education
(East Bank, 1991)

	Teachers	Pupils
Pre-primary	1,933	44,856
Primary	36,930	926,445
Secondary	6,940	100,953
Universities	1,931	39,668
Other higher	1,838	40,774

Directory

The Constitution

The revised Constitution was approved by King Talal I on 1 January 1952.

The Hashemite Kingdom of Jordan is an independent, indivisible sovereign state. Its official religion is Islam; its official language Arabic.

RIGHTS OF THE INDIVIDUAL

There is to be no discrimination between Jordanians on account of race, religion or language. Work, education and equal opportunities shall be afforded to all as far as is possible. The freedom of the individual is guaranteed, as are his dwelling and property. No Jordanian shall be exiled. Labour shall be made compulsory only in a national emergency, or as a result of a conviction; conditions, hours worked and allowances are under the protection of the state.

The Press, and all opinions, are free, except under martial law. Societies can be formed, within the law. Schools may be established freely, but they must follow a recognized curriculum and educational policy. Elementary education is free and compulsory. All religions are tolerated. Every Jordanian is eligible for public office, and choices are to be made by merit only. Power belongs to the people.

THE LEGISLATIVE POWER

Legislative power is vested in the National Assembly and the King. The National Assembly consists of two houses: the Senate and the House of Representatives.

THE SENATE

The number of Senators is one-half of the number of members of the House of Representatives. Senators must be unrelated to the King, over 40, and are chosen from present and past Prime Ministers and Ministers, past Ambassadors or Ministers Plenipotentiary, past Presidents of the House of Representatives, past Presidents and members of the Court of Cassation and of the Civil and *Shari'a* Courts of Appeal, retired officers of the rank of General and above, former members of the House of Representatives who have been elected twice to that House, etc. ... They may not hold public office. Senators are appointed for four years. They may be reappointed. The President of the Senate is appointed for two years.

THE HOUSE OF REPRESENTATIVES

The members of the House of Representatives are elected by secret ballot in a general direct election and retain their mandate for four years. General elections take place during the four months preceding the end of the term. The President of the House is elected by secret ballot each year by the Representatives. Representatives must be Jordanians of over 30, they must have a clean record, no active business interests, and are debarred from public office. Close relatives of the King are not eligible. If the House of Representatives is dissolved, the new House shall assemble in extraordinary session not more than four months after the date of dissolution. The new House cannot be dissolved for the same reason as the last.

GENERAL PROVISIONS FOR THE NATIONAL ASSEMBLY

The King summons the National Assembly to its ordinary session on 1 November each year. This date can be postponed by the King for two months, or he can dissolve the Assembly before the end of its three months' session. Alternatively, he can extend the session up to a total period of six months. Each session is opened by a speech from the throne.

Decisions in the House of Representatives and the Senate are made by a majority vote. The quorum is two-thirds of the total number of members in each House. When the voting concerns the Constitution, or confidence in the Council of Ministers, 'the votes shall be taken by calling the members by name in a loud voice'. Sessions are public, though secret sessions can be held at the request of the Government or of five members. Complete freedom of speech, within the rules of either House, is allowed.

The Prime Minister places proposals before the House of Representatives; if accepted there, they are referred to the Senate and finally sent to the King for confirmation. If one house rejects a law while the other accepts it, a joint session of the House of Representatives and the Senate is called, and a decision made by a two-thirds majority. If the King withholds his approval from a law, he returns it to the Assembly within six months with the reasons for his dissent; a joint session of the Houses then makes a decision, and if the law is accepted by this decision it is promulgated. The Budget is submitted to the National Assembly one month before the beginning of the financial year.

THE KING

The throne of the Hashemite Kingdom devolves by male descent in the dynasty of King Abdullah Ibn al Hussein. The King attains his majority on his eighteenth lunar year; if the throne is inherited by a minor, the powers of the King are exercised by a Regent or a Council of Regency. If the King, through illness or absence, cannot perform his duties, his powers are given to a Deputy, or to a Council of the Throne. This Deputy, or Council, may be appointed by Iradas (decrees) by the King, or, if he is incapable, by the Council of Ministers.

On his accession, the King takes the oath to respect and observe the provisions of the Constitution and to be loyal to the nation. As Head of State he is immune from all liability or responsibility. He approves laws and promulgates them. He declares war, concludes peace and signs treaties; treaties, however, must be approved by the National Assembly. The King is Commander-in-Chief of the navy, the army and the air force. He orders the holding of elections; convenes, inaugurates, adjourns and prorogues the House of Representatives. The Prime Minister is appointed by him, as are the President and members of the Senate. Military and civil ranks are also granted, or withdrawn, by the King. No death sentence is carried out until he has confirmed it.

MINISTERS

The Council of Ministers consists of the Prime Minister, President of the Council, and of his ministers. Ministers are forbidden to become members of any company, to receive a salary from any company, or to participate in any financial act of trade. The Council of Ministers is entrusted with the conduct of all affairs of state, internal and external.

The Council of Ministers is responsible to the House of Representatives for matters of general policy. Ministers may speak in either House, and, if they are members of one House, they may also vote in that House. Votes of confidence in the Council are cast in the House of Representatives, and decided by a two-thirds majority. If a vote of 'no confidence' is returned, the ministers are bound to resign. Every newly-formed Council of Ministers must present its programme to the House of Representatives and ask for a vote of confidence. The House of Representatives can impeach ministers, as it impeaches its own members.

AMENDMENTS

Two amendments were passed in November 1974 giving the King the right to dissolve the Senate or to take away membership from any of its members, and to postpone general elections for a period not to exceed a year, if there are circumstances in which the Council of Ministers feels that it is impossible to hold elections. A further amendment in February 1976 enabled the King to postpone elections indefinitely. In January 1984 two amendments were passed, allowing elections 'in any part of the country where it is possible to hold them' (effectively, only the East Bank) and empowering the National Assembly to elect deputies from the Israeli-held West Bank.

The Government

HEAD OF STATE

King HUSSEIN IBN TALAL (proclaimed King on 11 August 1952; crowned on 2 May 1953).

CABINET
(October 1994)

Prime Minister, Minister of Defence and Minister of Foreign Affairs: ABD AS-SALAM AL-MAJALI.

Deputy Prime Minister: DHUQAN AL-HINDAWI.
Minister of Higher Education: RATIB AS-SUUD.
Minister of Transport: SAMIR QOWAR.
Minister of the Interior: SALAMEH HAMMAD.
Minister of Information: JAWAD AL-ANANI.
Minister of Labour: KHALID AL-GHAZAWI.
Minister of Social Development: MUHAMMAD AS-SAQOUR.
Minister of Municipal, Rural and Environmental Affairs: TAWFIQ QURAYSHAN.
Minister of Religious Affairs: ABD AS-SALAM AL-ABBADI.
Minister of Public Works and Housing: ABD AR-RAZZAQ AN-NUSUR.
Minister of Trade and Industry: RIMA KHALAF.
Minister of Supply: ADIL AL-QUDAH.
Minister of Culture: JUMAA HAMMAD.
Minister of Finance: SAMI GAMMO.
Minister of Communications and Postal Affairs: HISHAM AD-DABBAS.
Minister of Energy and Mineral Resources: TALAL URAQAT.
Minister of Planning: HISHAM AL-KHATIB.
Minister of Agriculture: MANSOUR BIN TARIF.
Minister of Justice: HISHAM AT-TALL.
Minister of Education and Minister of State for Cabinet Affairs: ABDEL RAUF AR-RAWABIDAH.
Minister of Health: ARIF BATAYNAH.
Minister of Youth: FAWWAZ ABU AL-GHANNAM.
Minister of Tourism and Antiquities: MUHAMMAD AFFASH AL-ADWAN.
Minister of Water and Irrigation: SALIH IRSHAIDAT.
Minister of State for Foreign Affairs: TALAL AL-HASSAN.
Minister of State for Legal Affairs: Sheikh ABDEL BAQI JAMMU.
Minister of State for Administrative Development: MUHAMMAD ADH-DHUNAIBAT.
Ministers of State: YUSUF AD-DALABIH, ABDULLAH AL-JAZI.
Chief of the Royal Court: Field Marshal Sharif ZAID IBN SHAKER.

MINISTRIES

Office of the Prime Minister: POB 80, 35216, Amman; tel. 641211; telex 21444.
Ministry of Agriculture: POB 961043, Amman; tel. 686151; telex 24176; fax 686310.
Ministry of Awqaf (Religious Endowments) and Islamic Affairs: POB 659, Amman; tel. 666141; telex 21559.
Ministry of Communications: POB 71, Amman; tel. 624301; telex 21666.
Ministry of Defence: POB 1577, Amman; tel. 644361; telex 21200.
Ministry of Education: POB 1646, Amman 11118; tel. 607181; telex 21396; fax 666019.
Ministry of Finance: POB 85, Amman; tel. 636321; telex 23634; fax 643132.
Ministry of Foreign Affairs: POB 1577, Amman; tel. 644361; telex 21255; fax 648825.
Ministry of Health: POB 86, Amman; tel. 665131; telex 21595.
Ministry of Information: POB 1794, Amman; tel. 661147; telex 21749.
Ministry of the Interior: POB 100, Amman; tel. 663111; telex 23162.
Ministry of Justice: POB 6040, Amman; tel. 663101.
Ministry of Labour: POB 9052, Amman; tel. 630343.
Ministry of Municipal, Rural and Environmental Affairs: POB 1799, Amman; tel. 641393.
Ministry of Public Works and Housing: POB 1220, Amman; tel. 668481; telex 21944.
Ministry of Social Development: POB 6720, Amman; tel. 673191; fax 673198.
Ministry of Supply: POB 830, Amman; tel. 602121; telex 21278; fax 604691.
Ministry of Tourism: POB 224, Amman; tel. 642311; telex 21741; fax 648465.
Ministry of Trade and Industry: POB 2019, Amman; tel. 663191; telex 21163; fax 603721.
Ministry of Transport: POB 1929, 35214 Amman; tel. 641461; telex 21541.

Legislature

MAJLIS AL-UMMA
(National Assembly)

Senate

The Senate (House of Notables) consists of 40 members, appointed by the King. A new Senate was appointed by the King on 18 November 1993.

President: AHMAD AL-LOUZI.

House of Representatives

Elections to the then 60-seat House of Representatives (30 from both the East and West Banks) took place in April 1967. There were no political parties. The House was dissolved by Royal Decree on 23 November 1974, but reconvened briefly on 15 February 1976. Elections were postponed indefinitely.

In April 1978 a National Consultative Council was formed by Royal Decree. It consisted of 60 members appointed by the King, and served terms of two years. The third term began on 20 April 1982. The King, by his constitutional right, dissolved the Council on 7 January 1984 and reconvened the House of Representatives. Eight members from the East Bank had died since the House was last convened and by-elections to fill their seats took place on 12 March 1984. The seven vacant seats of members from the Israeli-occupied West Bank, where elections could not take place, were filled by a vote of the members of the House in accordance with a constitutional amendment unanimously approved on 9 January 1984.

In March 1986 the House of Representatives approved a draft electoral law providing for the number of seats in the House to be increased from 60 to 142 (71 from the East Bank and 71 from the West Bank, including 11 from the refugee camps in the East Bank) at the next election. In October 1987, while opening a new session of the National Assembly, King Hussein announced that elections to the House of Representatives were to be postponed for two years. On 30 July 1988 King Hussein dissolved the House of Representatives, (one-half of whose 60 seats were held by deputies for the West Bank) and on 31 July he severed Jordan's legal and administrative links with the West Bank. (Theoretically, the Senate cannot legislate without the House of Representatives.) Legislative elections were postponed in October 1988, pending a revision of the 1986 electoral laws.

Electoral laws, announced in April 1989, propounded plans for a new, 72-seat House of Representatives. The increase in the number of seats was to take into account expansion in the major population centres of Amman, Zarqa and Irbid. A further eight seats were subsequently allocated to the governorates of Amman, Zarqa and Balqa, bringing the total to 80. A general election to the new House took place in November 1989. In July 1992 legislation was adopted that permitted the formation of political parties (see below). In August 1993 King Hussein dissolved the House of Representatives, pending the holding of the country's first multi-party general election, which took place on 8 November 1993.

General Election, 8 November 1993

Party	Seats
Independent centrists	44
Islamic Action Front	16
Independent Islamists	6
Independent leftists	4
Al-Ahd	2
Jordanian Arab Democratic Party	2
Others	6
Total	80

Speaker: TAHER AL-MASRI.

Political Organizations

Political parties were banned before the elections of July 1963. In September 1971 King Hussein announced the formation of a Jordanian National Union. This was the only political organization allowed. Communists, Marxists and 'other advocates of imported ideologies' were ineligible for membership. In March 1972 the organization was renamed the Arab National Union. In April 1974 King Hussein dissolved the executive committee of the Arab National Union, and accepted the resignation of the Secretary-General. In February 1976 the Cabinet approved a law abolishing the Union. Membership was estimated at about 100,000. A royal commission was appointed in April 1990 to draft a National Charter, one feature of which was the legalization of political

parties. In January 1991 King Hussein approved the National Charter, which was formally endorsed in June. In July 1992 the House of Representatives adopted draft legislation which formally permitted the establishment of political parties, subject to certain conditions. In the same month a joint session of the Senate and the House of Representatives was convened to debate amendments to the new legislation, proposed by the Senate. The political parties which achieved representation in the general election in November 1993 were: the Islamic Action Front (Sec.-Gen. Dr ISHAQ FARHAN); al-Mustaqbal; the Jordanian Arab Socialist Baath Party; al-Yakatha; al-Ahd; the Jordan National Alliance; the Jordan People's Democratic Party (Leader TAYSIR AZ-ZABRI); the Jordan Social Democratic Party; and the Jordan Arab Democratic Party.

Diplomatic Representation

EMBASSIES IN JORDAN

Algeria: 3rd Circle, Jabal Amman; tel. 641271; Ambassador: ABDERRAHMAN SHRAYYET.

Australia: POB 35201, 4th Circle, Jabal Amman; tel. 673246; telex 21743; fax 673260; Ambassador: J. P. SHEPPARD.

Austria: POB 815368, Amman; tel. 644635; telex 22484; Ambassador: Dr MICHAEL STIGELBAUER.

Bahrain: Amman; tel. 664148; Ambassador: IBRAHIM ALI IBRAHIM.

Belgium: Amman; tel. 675683; telex 22340; fax 697487; Ambassador: JOHAN BALLEGEER.

Brazil: POB 5497, Amman; tel. 642183; telex 23827; fax 612964; Ambassador: FERNANDO SILVA ALVES.

Bulgaria: POB 11195-950578, Amman; tel. 699391; telex 23246; fax 699393; Ambassador: (vacant).

Canada: POB 815403, Pearl of Shmeisani Bldg, Shmeisani, Amman; tel. 666124; telex 23080; fax 689227; Ambassador: A. PERCY SHERWOOD.

Chile: 73 Suez St, Abdoun, Amman; tel. 814263; telex 21696; Ambassador: NELSON HADAD-HERESIM.

China, People's Republic: Shmeisani, Amman; tel. 666139; telex 21770; Ambassador: ZHANG DELIANG.

Egypt: POB 35178, Zahran St, 3rd Circle, Jabal Amman; tel. 641375; Ambassador: IHAB SEID WAHBA.

France: POB 374, Jabal Amman; tel. 641273; telex 21219; fax 659606; Ambassador: DENIS BAUCHARD.

Germany: POB 183, 25 Benghazi St, Jabal Amman; tel. 689351; telex 21235; fax 685887; Ambassador: Dr HEINRICH REINERS.

Greece: POB 35069, Jabal Amman; tel. 672331; telex 21566; fax 696591; Ambassador: THEODOROS N. PANTZARIS.

Holy See: Amman.

Hungary: POB 3441, Amman; tel. 815614; telex 21815; fax 815836; Chargé d'Affaires: Dr TIBOR TÓTH.

India: POB 2168, 1st Circle, Jabal Amman; tel. 637262; telex 21068; fax 659540; Ambassador: A. K. BUDHIRAJA.

Iran: POB 173, Jabal Amman; tel. 641281 telex 21218.

Iraq: POB 2025, 1st Circle, Jabal Amman; tel. 639331; telex 21277; Ambassador: NORI AL-WAYES.

Italy: POB 9800, Jabal Luweibdeh, Amman; tel. 638185; telex 21143; fax 659730; Ambassador: ROMUALDO BETTINI.

Japan: POB 2835, Jabal Amman; tel. 672486; telex 21518; fax 672006; Ambassador: AKIRA NAKAYAMA.

Korea, Democratic People's Republic: Amman; tel. 666349; Chargé d'affaires: KIM YONG HO.

Korea, Republic: POB 3060, 3rd Circle, Jabal Amman, Abu Tamman St, Amman; tel. 660745; telex 21457; Ambassador: TAE JIN PARK.

Kuwait: POB 2107, Jabal Amman; tel. 641235; telex 21377; Ambassador: SULEIMAN SALEM AL-FASSAM.

Lebanon: 2nd Circle, Jabal Amman; tel. 641381; Ambassador: PIERRE ZIADÉ.

Morocco: Jabal Amman; tel. 641451; telex 21661; Chargé d'affaires: SALEM FANKHAR ASH-SHANFARI.

Oman: Amman; tel. 661131; telex 21550; Ambassador: KHAMIS BIN HAMAD AL-BATASHI.

Pakistan: POB 1232, Amman; tel. 638352; fax 611633; Ambassador: TARIQ KHAN AFRIDI.

Philippines: POB 925207, Amra Commercial Centre, 6th Circle, Umm Uthaina, Amman; tel. 827001; fax 827003; Ambassador: RAFAEL E. SEGUIS.

Poland: POB 2124, 3rd Circle, 1 Mai Zeyadeh St, Jabal Amman; tel. 637153; telex 21119; fax 618744; Chargé d'affaires: Dr EDMUND PAWLAK.

Qatar: Amman; tel. 644331; telex 21248; Ambassador: Sheikh HAMAD BIN MUHAMMAD BIN JABER ATH-THANI.

Romania: Amman; tel. 663161; Ambassador: TEODOR COMAN.

Russia: Amman; tel. 641158; Ambassador: ALEKSANDR VLADIMIRO-VICH SALTANOV.

Saudi Arabia: POB 2133, 5th Circle, Jabal Amman; tel. 644154; Ambassador: Sheikh IBRAHIM MUHAMMAD AS-SULTAN.

Spain: Zahran St, POB 454, Jabal Amman; tel. 614166; telex 21224; fax 614173; Ambassador: JUAN MANUEL CABRERA HERNÁNDEZ.

Sudan: Jabal Amman; tel. 624145; telex 21778; Ambassador: AHMAD DIAB.

Sweden: POB 830536, 4th Circle, Jabal Amman; tel. 669177; telex 22039; fax 669179; Ambassador: CHRISTIAN BAUSCH.

Switzerland: Jabal Amman; tel. 644416; telex 21237; Ambassador: HARALD BORNER.

Syria: POB 1377, 4th Circle, Jabal Amman; tel. 641935; Chargé d'affaires: MAJID ABOU SALEH.

Tunisia: Jabal Amman; tel. 674307; telex 21849; Ambassador: MONGI LAHBIB.

Turkey: POB 2062, Islamic College St, 2nd Circle, Jabal Amman; tel. 641251; telex 23005; fax 612353; Ambassador: OKTAY AKSOY.

United Arab Emirates: Jabal Amman; tel. 644369; telex 21832; Ambassador: ABDULLAH ALI ASH-SHURAFA.

United Kingdom: POB 87, Abdoun, Amman; tel. 823100; telex 22209; fax 813759; Ambassador: PETER HINCHCLIFFE.

USA: POB 354, Amman 11118; tel. 820101; fax 820121; Ambassador: WESLEY W. EGAN.

Yemen: Amman; tel. 642381; telex 23526; Ambassador: ALI ABDULLAH ABU LUHOUM.

Yugoslavia: POB 5227, Amman: tel. 665107; telex 21505; Ambassador: ZORAN S. POPOVIĆ.

Judicial System

With the exception of matters of purely personal nature concerning members of non-Muslim communities, the law of Jordan was based on Islamic Law for both civil and criminal matters. During the days of the Ottoman Empire, certain aspects of Continental law, especially French commercial law and civil and criminal procedure, were introduced. Due to British occupation of Palestine and Transjordan from 1917 to 1948, the Palestine territory has adopted, either by statute or case law, much of the English common law. Since the annexation of the non-occupied part of Palestine and the formation of the Hashemite Kingdom of Jordan, there has been a continuous effort to unify the law.

Court of Cassation. The Court of Cassation consists of seven judges, who sit in full panel for exceptionally important cases. In most appeals, however, only five members sit to hear the case. All cases involving amounts of more than JD100 may be reviewed by this Court, as well as cases involving lesser amounts and cases which cannot be monetarily valued. However, for the latter types of cases, review is available only by leave of the Court of Appeal, or, upon refusal by the Court of Appeal, by leave of the President of the Court of Cassation. In addition to these functions as final and Supreme Court of Appeal, the Court of Cassation also sits as High Court of Justice to hear applications in the nature of habeas corpus, mandamus and certiorari dealing with complaints of a citizen against abuse of governmental authority.

Courts of Appeal. There are two Courts of Appeal, each of which is composed of three judges, whether for hearing of appeals or for dealing with Magistrates Courts' judgments in chambers. Jurisdiction of the two Courts is geographical, with the Court for the Western Region (which has not sat since June 1967) sitting in Jerusalem and the Court for the Eastern Region sitting in Amman. The regions are separated by the River Jordan. Appellate review of the Courts of Appeal extends to judgments rendered in the Courts of First Instance, the Magistrates' Courts, and Religious Courts.

Courts of First Instance. The Courts of First Instance are courts of general jurisdiction in all matters civil and criminal except those specifically allocated to the Magistrates' Courts. Three judges sit in all felony trials, while only two judges sit for misdemeanour and civil cases. Each of the seven Courts of First Instance also exercises appellate jurisdiction in cases involving judgments of less than JD20 and fines of less than JD10, rendered by the Magistrates' Courts.

Magistrates' Courts. There are 14 Magistrates' Courts, which exercise jurisdiction in civil cases involving no more than JD250 and in criminal cases involving maximum fines of JD100 or maximum imprisonment of one year.

Religious Courts. There are two types of religious court: The *Shari'a* Courts (Muslims): and the Ecclesiastical Courts (Eastern Orthodox, Greek Melkite, Roman Catholic and Protestant). Jurisdiction extends to personal (family) matters, such as marriage, divorce, alimony, inheritance, guardianship, wills, interdiction and, for the Muslim community, the constitution of Waqfs (Religious Endowments). When a dispute involves persons of different religious communities, the Civil Courts have jurisdiction in the matter unless the parties agree to submit to the jurisdiction of one or the other of the Religious Courts involved.

Each *Shari'a* (Muslim) Court consists of one judge (*Qadi*), while most of the Ecclesiastical (Christian) Courts are normally composed of three judges, who are usually clerics. *Shari'a* Courts apply the doctrines of Islamic Law, based on the Koran and the *Hadith* (Precepts of Muhammad), while the Ecclesiastical Courts base their law on various aspects of Canon Law. In the event of conflict between any two Religious Courts or between a Religious Court and a Civil Court, a Special Tribunal of three judges is appointed by the President of the Court of Cassation, to decide which court shall have jurisdiction. Upon the advice of experts on the law of the various communities, this Special Tribunal decides on the venue for the case at hand.

Religion

Over 80% of the population are Sunni Muslims, and the King can trace unbroken descent from the Prophet Muhammad. There is a Christian minority, living mainly in the towns, and there are smaller numbers of non-Sunni Muslims.

ISLAM

Chief Justice and President of the Supreme Muslim Secular Council: Sheikh MUHAMMAD MHELAN.

Director of Shari'a Courts: Sheikh SUBHI AL-MUWQQAT.

Mufti of the Hashemite Kingdom of Jordan: Sheikh MUHAMMAD ABDO HASHEM.

CHRISTIANITY
The Roman Catholic Church

Latin Rite

Jordan forms part of the Patriarchate of Jerusalem (see chapter on Israel).

Vicar-General for Transjordan: Mgr SELIM SAYEGH (Titular Bishop of Aquae in Proconsulari), Latin Vicariate, POB 1317, Amman: tel. 637440.

Melkite Rite

The Greek-Melkite archdiocese of Petra (Wadi Musa) and Philadelphia (Amman) contained 18,288 adherents at 31 December 1991.

Archbishop of Petra and Philadelphia: Most Rev. GEORGES EL-MURR, Archevêché Grec-Melkite Catholique, POB 2435, Jabal Amman; tel. 624757.

Syrian Rite

The Syrian Catholic Patriarch of Antioch is resident in Beirut, Lebanon.

Patriarchal Exarchate of Jerusalem: Mont Achrafieh, Rue Barto, POB 10041, Amman; Exarch Patriarchal Mgr PIERRE ABD AL-AHAD.

The Anglican Communion

Within the Episcopal Church in Jerusalem and the Middle East, Jordan forms part of the diocese of Jerusalem. The President Bishop of the Church is the Bishop in Jerusalem (see the chapter on Israel).

Assistant Bishop in Amman: Rt Rev. ELIA KHOURY, POB 598, Amman.

Other Christian Churches

The Coptic Orthodox Church, the Greek Orthodox Church (Patriarchate of Jerusalem) and the Evangelical Lutheran Church in Jordan are also active.

The Press

Jordan Press Association: Amman; Pres. RAKAN AL-MAJALI.

DAILIES

Al-Akhbar (News): POB 62420, Amman; f. 1976; Arabic; publ. by the Arab Press Co; Editor RACAN EL-MAJALI; circ. 15,000.

Ad-Dustour (The Constitution): POB 591, Amman; tel. 664153; telex 21392; f. 1967; Arabic; publ. by the Jordan Press and Publishing Co; owns commercial printing facilities; Chair. KAMEL ASH-SHERIF; Editor-in-Chief and Dir-Gen. MAHMOUD ASH-SHERIF; circ. 90,000.

Al-Mithaq: Amman; f. 1993; Arabic.

Ar-Rai (Opinion): POB 6710, Amman; tel. 667171; telex 21496; fax 661242; f. 1971; Arabic; independent; published by Jordan Press Foundation; Chair. Dr KHALIL AL-SALEM; Gen. Dir Dr RADI WAQFI; Editor-in-Chief RAKAN AL-MAJALI; circ. 90,000.

The Jordan Times: POB 6710, Amman; tel. 667171; telex 21497; fax 661242; f. 1975; English; published by Jordan Press Establishment; Editor-in-Chief GEORGE HAWATMEH; circ. 15,000.

Sawt ash-Shaab (Voice of the People): Amman; f. 1983; Arabic; circ. 30,000.

PERIODICALS

Akhbar al-Usbou (News of the Week): POB 605, Amman; tel. 677881; telex 21644; fax 677882; f. 1959; weekly; Arabic; economic, social, political; Chief Editor and Publr ABD AL-HAFIZ MUHAMMAD; circ. 100,000.

Al-Aqsa (The Ultimate): POB 1957, Amman; weekly; Arabic; armed forces magazines.

Al-Ghad al-Iqtisadi: Media Services International, POB 9313, Amman; tel. and fax 648298; telex 21392; fortnightly; English; economic; Chief Editor RIAD AL-KHOURI.

Huda El-Islam (The Right Way of Islam): POB 659, Amman; tel. 666141; telex 21559; f. 1956; monthly; Arabic; scientific and literary; published by the Ministry of Awqaf and Islamic Affairs; Editor Dr AHMAD MUHAMMAD HULAYYEL.

Jordan: POB 224, Amman; telex 21497; f. 1969; published quarterly by Jordan Information Bureau, Washington; circ. 100,000.

Al-Liwa' (The Standard): Amman; f. 1972; weekly; Arabic; Chief Editor HASSAN ATTEL.

Military Magazine: Army Headquarters, Amman; f. 1955; quarterly; dealing with military and literary subjects; published by Armed Forces.

As-Sabah (The Morning): POB 2396, Amman; weekly; Arabic; circ. 6,000.

Shari'a: POB 585, Amman; f. 1959; fortnightly; Islamic affairs; published by Shari'a College; circ. 5,000.

Shehan: Al-Karak; Editor REYAD AL-HROUB.

The Star: Media Services International, POB 9313 Amman; tel. and fax 648298; telex 21392; f. 1982, formerly The Jerusalem Star; weekly; English; Publr and Editor-in-Chief OSAMA ASH-SHERIF; circ. 10,000.

NEWS AGENCIES

Jordan News Agency (PETRA): POB 6845, Amman; tel. 644455; telex 21220; f. 1965; government-controlled; Dir-Gen. KHALED MAHADIN.

Foreign News Bureaux

Agence France-Presse (AFP): POB 3340, Amman; tel. 642976; telex 21469; fax 654680; Bureau Man. Mrs RANDA HABIB.

Agenzia Nazionale Stampa Associata (ANSA) (Italy): POB 35111, Amman; tel. 644092; telex 21207; Correspondent JOHN HALABI.

Associated Press (AP) (USA): POB 35111, Amman; tel. 614660; telex 23514; fax 614661; Correspondent JAMAL HALABY.

Deutsche Presse Agentur (dpa) (Germany): POB 35111, Amman; tel. 623907; telex 21207; Correspondent JOHN HALABI.

Reuters (UK): POB 667, Amman; tel. 623776; telex 21414; fax 619231; Bureau Chief, News and Television JACK REDDEN.

Informatsionnoye Telegrafnoye Agentstvo Rossii-Telegrafnoye Agentstvo Suverennykh Stran (ITAR-TASS) (Russia): Jabal Amman, Nabich Faris St, Block 111/83 124, Amman; Correspondent NIKOLAI LEBEDINSKY.

Central News Agency (Taiwan), Iraqi News Agency, Middle East News Agency (Egypt), Qatar News Agency, Saudi Press Agency and UPI (USA) also maintain bureaux in Amman.

Publishers

Jordan Press and Publishing Co Ltd: POB 591, Amman; tel. 664153; telex 21392; fax 667170; f. 1967 by *Al-Manar* and *Falastin* dailies; publishes *Ad-Dustour* (daily), and *The Star* (English weekly); Chair. KAMEL ASH-SHARIF; Dir-Gen SEIF ASH-SHERIF.

Jordan Press Foundation: POB 6710, Amman; tel. 667171; telex 21497; fax 661242; publishes *Ar-Rai* (daily) and the *Jordan Times* (daily); Chair. MAHMOUD AL-KAYED; Gen. Dir MOHAMAD AMAD.

Other publishers in Amman include: Dairat al-Ihsaat al-Amman, George N. Kawar, Al-Matbaat al-Hashmiya and The National Press.

Radio and Television

In 1991 there were an estimated 1,060,000 radio receivers and 330,000 television receivers in use (East Bank only).

Jordan Radio and Television Corporation (JRTV): POB 909, Amman; tel. 773111; telex 23544; f. 1968; government TV station broadcasts for 90 hours weekly in Arabic and English; in colour; advertising accepted; Dir-Gen. RADI ALKHAS; Dir of TV MUHAMMAD AMIN; Dir of Radio I. SHAHZADH.

Finance

(cap. = capital; p.u. = paid up; dep. = deposits; m. = million; res = reserves; brs = branches; JD = Jordanian dinars)

BANKING
Central Bank

Central Bank of Jordan: POB 37, King Hussein St, Amman; tel. 630301; telex 21250; fax 638889; f. 1964; cap. p.u. JD 6m., dep. JD 907.7m., res JD 12m., total assets JD 2,012.8m. (Dec. 1992); 2 brs; Gov. Dr MUHAMMAD SAID NABULSI.

National Banks

Arab Bank PLC: POB 950545, Shmeisani, Amman; tel. 660131; telex 23091; fax 606793; f. 1930; cap. p.u. JD 44m., dep. JD 6,944m., res JD 388m., total assets JD 7,570 (Dec. 1993); 68 brs in Jordan, 50 brs abroad; Chair. ABD AL-MAJID SHOMAN.

Bank of Jordan PLC: POB 2140, South Sayegh Commercial Centre, Jabal Amman; tel. 644327; telex 22033; fax 656642; f. 1960; cap. p.u. JD 10.5m., dep. JD 225.6m., total assets JD 284.3m. (Dec. 1993); 38 brs; Chair. TAWFIK SHAKER FAKHOURI; Gen. Man. FAYEZ ABUL ENEIN.

Cairo Amman Bank: POB 715, Shabsough St, Amman; tel. 639321; telex 21240; fax 639328; f. 1960; cap. p.u. JD 5m., dep. JD 305.8m., res JD 12.2m., total assets JD 333.1m. (Dec. 1992); 24 brs; Chair. KHALIL TALHOUNI; Gen. Man. YAZID MUFTI.

Jordan Islamic Bank for Finance and Investment: POB 926225, Amman; tel. 677377; telex 21125; fax 666326; f. 1978; dep. JD 395.9m., cap. and res JD 14.1m., total assets JD 435.3m. (Dec. 1992); 22 brs; Chair. Sheikh SALEH A. KAMEL; Gen. Man. MUSA A. SHIHADEH.

Jordan Kuwait Bank: POB 9776, Amman; tel. 688814; telex 21994; fax 687452; f. 1976; cap. p.u. JD 10m., dep. JD 178.9m. (Dec. 1993); 22 brs; Chair. SUFIAN IBRAHIM YASSIN SARTAWI; Gen. Man. M. YASSER AL-ASMER.

Jordan National Bank PLC: POB 1578, Amman; tel. 642391; telex 21820; fax 628809; f. 1955; cap. p.u. JD 9.1m., dep. JD 231m., res JD 13.9m., total assets JD 285m. (1993); 35 brs in Jordan, 4 brs in Lebanon, 1 br. in Cyprus; Chair. ABD AL-KADER TASH; Deputy Chair. YOUSUF I. MOU'ASHER.

Foreign Banks

ANZ Grindlays Bank: POB 9997, Shmeissani, Amman; tel. 660201; telex 21980; fax 679115; cap. p.u. JD 5m., dep. JD 127m., total assets JD 140m. (Dec. 1993); brs in Amman (8 brs), Aqaba, Irbid (2 brs), Zerka, Northern Shouneh and Kerak; Gen. Man. in Jordan ADNAN AHMAD SALLAKH.

Arab Banking Corporation (Jordan): POB 926691, Amman; tel. 664183; telex 22258; fax 686291; f. 1980; cap. p.u. JD 10m., dep. JD 26.7m., total assets JD 51.5m. (Dec. 1990); Arab Banking Corpn, Bahrain, holds 60% share; Chair. MUHAMMAD AL-MERAIKHI; Vice-Chair. and Gen. Man. JAWAD HADID.

Arab Land Bank (Egypt): POB 6729, Amir Muhammad St, Amman; tel. 628357; telex 21208; fax 646274; wholly-owned subsidiary of the Central Bank of Egypt; cap. JD 6m., dep. JD 106.8m., res JD 5.5m., total assets JD 122.2m. (Dec. 1992); 18 brs in Jordan; Chair. ABD AR-RAHMAN AN-NADI; Gen. Man. SAMIR MAHDI.

The British Bank of the Middle East (Hong Kong): POB 922376, Jebel Hussein, Amman; tel. 660471; telex 21253; fax 682047; f. 1889; cap. p.u. JD 5m., dep. JD 138.9m., total assets JD 157.6m. (Dec. 1993); 5 brs; Chair. W. PURVES; Area Man. J. S. GIBSON.

Citibank NA (USA): POB 5055, Jordan Insurance Bldg, 3rd Circle, Jabal Amman; tel. 644065; telex 21314; fax 658693; cap. p.u. JD 5m., dep. JD 56.2m., total assets JD 75.4m. (Dec. 1992); Gen. Man. WALID R. ALAMUDDIN.

Rafidain Bank (Iraq): POB 1194, Amman; tel. 624365; telex 21334; fax 658698; f. 1941; cap. p.u. JD 5m., res JD 2.1m., dep. JD 31.4m. (Dec. 1992); 3 brs; Gen. Man. ADNAN AL-AZAWI.

Bank Al-Mashrek (Lebanon) also has a branch in Amman.

Specialized Credit Institutions

Agricultural Credit Corporation: POB 77, Amman; tel. 661105; telex 24194; fax 698365; f. 1959; cap. p.u. JD 24m., res JD 2.2m., total assets JD 65.1m. (Dec. 1992); 16 brs; Chair. Dr MARWAN RASEM KAMAL.

The Arab Jordan Investment Bank: POB 8797, Amman; tel. 607126; telex 21719; fax 681482; f. 1978; cap. p.u. JD 10m., dep. JD 188m., res JD 11m., total assets JD 217m. (Dec. 1993); 10 brs; Chair. and Gen. Man. ABD AL-KADER AL-QADI.

Cities and Villages Development Bank: POB 1572, Amman; tel. 668151; telex 22476; fax 668153; f. 1979; cap. p.u. JD 11.5m., gen. res JD 15.4m., total assets JD 67.5m. (Dec. 1993); 1 br. in Irbid; Gen. Man. Dr ZUHAIR KHALIFAH.

Housing Bank: POB 7693, Parliament St, Abdali, Amman; tel. 667126; telex 21693; fax 678121; f. 1973; cap. p.u. JD 12m., dep. JD 746m., total assets JD 892m. (Dec. 1993); 114 brs; Chair. and Dir-Gen. ZUHAIR KHOURI.

Industrial Development Bank: POB 1982, Jabal Amman, Schools of the Islamic College St, Amman; tel. 642216; telex 21349; fax 647821; f. 1965; cap. p.u. JD 6m., total assets JD 106.8m. (Dec. 1992); Chair. ROUHI EL-KHATIB; Gen. Man. Dr TAHER KANAAN.

Jordan Co-operative Organization: POB 1343, Amman; tel. 665171; telex 21835; f. 1968; cap. p.u. JD 5.2m., dep. JD 11.5m., res JD 6.8m. (Nov. 1992); Chair. and Dir-Gen. JAMAL AL-BEDOUR.

Jordan Investment and Finance Bank: POB 950601, Shmeisani, Amman; tel. 665145; telex 23181; fax 681410; f. 1982 as Jordan Investment and Finance Corpn, name changed 1989; cap. p.u. JD 4.5m., res JD 10.8m., dep. JD 142.9m., total assets JD 245.3m. (Dec. 1993); Chair. NIZAR JARDANEH.

Social Security Corporation: POB 926031, Amman; tel. 643000; telex 22287; fax 610014; f. 1978; Dir-Gen. MUHAMMAD S. HOURANI.

STOCK EXCHANGE

Amman Financial Market: POB 8802, Amman; tel. 660170; telex 21711; fax 686830; f. 1978; Gen. Man. UMAYYAH TOUKAN.

INSURANCE

Jordan Insurance Co Ltd: POB 279, Company's Bldg, 3rd Circle, Jabal Amman, Amman; tel. 634161; telex 21486; fax 637905; f. 1951; cap. p.u. JD 5m.; Chair. and Man. Dir KHALDOUN AL-HASSAN; 7 brs (3 in Saudi Arabia, 3 in the United Arab Emirates, 1 in Lebanon).

Middle East Insurance Co Ltd: POB 1802, Shmeisani, Yaqoub Sarrouf St, Amman; tel. 605144; telex 21420; fax 605950; f. 1963; cap. p.u. US $3.3m.; Chair. SAMIR KAWAR; 1 br. in Saudi Arabia.

National Ahlia Insurance Co: POB 6156-2938, Sayed Qutub St, Shmeisani, Amman; tel. 681979; telex 21309; fax 684900; f. 1965; cap. p.u. JD 1.25m.; Chair. MUSTAFA ABU GOURA; Gen. Man. GHALEB ABU GOURA.

United Insurance Co Ltd: POB 7521, United Insurance Bldg, King Hussein St, Amman; tel. 625828; telex 23153; fax 629417; f. 1972; all types of insurance; cap. JD 1.5m.; Chair. RAOUF SA'AD ABUJABER; Gen. Man. NAZEH K. AZAR.

There are 17 local and one foreign insurance company operating in Jordan.

Trade and Industry

CHAMBERS OF COMMERCE AND INDUSTRY

Amman Chamber of Commerce: POB 287, Amman; tel. 666151; telex 21543; f. 1923; Pres. MUHAMMAD ASFOUR; Sec.-Gen. MUHAMMAD AL-MUHTASSEB.

Amman Chamber of Industry: POB 1800, Amman; tel. 643001; telex 22079; fax 647852; f. 1962; 7,000 industrial companies registered (1992); Pres. KHALDUN ABUHASSAN; Dir.-Gen. WALID KHATIB.

PUBLIC CORPORATIONS

Jordan Valley Authority: POB 2769, Amman; tel. 642472; telex 21692; projects in Stage I of the Jordan Valley Development Plan were completed in 1979. In 1988 about 26,000 ha was under intensive cultivation. Infrastructure projects also completed include 1,100 km of roads, 2,100 housing units, 100 schools, 15 health centres, 14 administration buildings, 4 marketing centres, 2 community centres, 2 vocational training centres. Electricity is now provided to all the towns and villages in the valley from the national network and domestic water is supplied to them from tube wells. Contributions to the cost of development came through loans from Kuwait Fund, Abu Dhabi Fund, Saudi Fund, Arab Fund, USAID, Fed. Germany, World Bank, EC, Italy, Netherlands, UK, Japan and OPEC Special Fund. Many of the Stage II irrigation projects are now completed or under implementation. Projects under way include the construction of the Wadi al-Arab dam, the raising of the King Talal dam and the 14.5-km extension of the 98-km East Ghor main canal. Stage II will include the irrigation of 4,700 ha in the southern Ghor. The target for the Plan is to irrigate 43,000 ha of land in the Jordan Valley. Future development in irrigation will include the construction of the Maqarin dam and the Wadi Malaha storage dam; Pres. MUHAMMAD BANI HANI.

Agricultural Marketing and Processing Co of Jordan: POB 7314, 38 Muhammad Ali-Janah St, Amman; tel. 819161; telex 23796; fax 819164; f. 1984; govt-owned; Chair. Dr ABDULHADI ALAWEEN; Gen. Man. SALEH AR-REFAI.

PHOSPHATES

Jordan Phosphate Mines Co Ltd (JPMC): POB 30, Amman; tel. 660141; telex 21223; f. 1930; engaged in production and export of rock phosphate; absorbed Jordan Fertilizer Industries 1991; Chair. HUSSAIN AL-QASIM; Gen. Man. WASIF AZAR; three mines in operation; production 6.5m. tons (1988); exports 4.3m. tons (1992).

MAJOR INDUSTRIAL COMPANIES

Adnan Sha'lan & Co: POB 1428, King Hussein St, Amman; tel. 621122; telex 21613; fax 626946; f. 1953; manufacturers of paints, glues, refrigerators, gas cookers, dairy products and cosmetics; sales US $10m. (1982); cap. US $3m.; Chair. ADNAN SHA'LAN; Man. Dir GHALEB SHA'LAN; 400 employees.

Arab Breweries Co Ltd: POB 168, Amman; tel. 660730; telex 24303; f. 1969; brewers of Henninger beer under licence; sales JD 1m. (1982); cap. p.u. JD 220,000; Chair. SAID I. MUASHER; Brewmaster MUHAMMAD ABED FATTAH.

Arab Centre for Pharmaceutical and Chemical Industries (ACPC): POB 22, Sahab; tel. 782470; telex 23728; fax 722473; f. 1984; manufacturers of pharmaceuticals and chemicals; auth. cap. JD 4m., cap. p.u. JD 4m.; Man. Dir ADNAN FARAJ.

Arab Investment and International Trade Co Ltd: POB 94, ar-Raqim, Amman; tel. 731191; telex 23216; f. 1976; manufacturers of toiletries; sales JD 6.2m. (1992); cap. p.u. JD 3.5m.; Chair. RAJAB ELSAAD; Gen. Man. OMAR HIKMAT; 150 employees.

Arab Pharmaceutical Manufacturing Co Ltd: POB 1695, Amman; tel. 685121; telex 21315; fax 685131; f. 1962; manufacturers of pharmaceuticals; sales JD 18m. (1990); cap. p.u. JD 5m.; Chair. AMIN SHOUQAIR; 362 employees.

Arab Potash Co Ltd: POB 1470, Amman; tel. 666165; telex 21683; f. 1956; production of potash and potassium chloride, with a by-product of salt; production 1.2m. tons (1987); 51% State-owned; Chair. OMAR ABDULLAH DAQHAN; Dir-Gen. ALI NSOUR; 1,200 employees.

Elba House Co: POB 3449, Amman; tel. 842600; telex 22060; fax 842603; f. 1976; manufacturers of prefabricated buildings, caravans, steel structures, vehicle bodies and construction plant; 500 employees.

General Investment Co Ltd: POB 312, Prince Muhammad St, Amman; tel. 625161; telex 21323; f. 1986 by merger of Jordan Brewery Co (f. 1955) and its subsidiary the General Investment Co; producers of beer and soft drinks and investment and real estate brokers; sales JD 2.5m. (1987); cap. p.u. JD 3.4m.; Chair. FARHAN ABUJABER; Gen. Man. RAOUF ABUJABER.

Industrial, Commercial and Agricultural Co Ltd (ICA): POB 6066, Amman; tel. 951945; telex 41434; fax 951198; f. 1961; industrial, commercial and agricultural investment; operates factories producing (under licence) soap, detergents, toiletries, paints, biscuits, ice-cream and containers; sales JD 31m. (1993); cap. p.u. JD 5m.; Chair. MOHD. A. R. ABU HASSAN; Man. Dir Eng. YAHYA AL-ALAMI; 584 employees.

International Contracting and Investment Co: POB 19170, Amman; tel. 666133; telex 21977; f. 1977; building, civil construction, etc.; sales JD 10m. (1982); cap. p.u. JD 4m.; Chair. FAKHRY ABU SHAKRA; Vice-Pres. HASSAN SHIHABI; 176 employees.

Jordan Cement Factories Co: Amman; merged with South Cement Co Sept. 1985; annual production at two works 3.5m. tons (1987).

Jordan Petroleum Refinery Co: POB 1079, Amman; tel. 657600; telex 21246; fax 657934; f. 1956; petroleum refining and distribution of refined petroleum products (lube oil blending and canning; fmr of LPG cylinders); production 2.4m. tons (1991); sales 2.77m. tons (JD 307.6m.), profits JD 5.1m. ($7.5m.) (1991); Chair. ABD AL-MAJID SHOMAN; Gen. Man. SAAD TELL; Refinery Man. B. ABD AL-HADI; 2,983 employees.

Jordan Plastics Co: POB 2394, Amman; tel. 793144; telex 21712; manufacturers of plastics (household goods); Chair. TAWFIQ G. ABUEITA.

Jordan Tobacco and Cigarette Co Ltd: POB 59, Ras El-Ain St, Amman; tel. 677112; telex 21204; f. 1931; manufacturers of cigarettes; tobacco growers; Chair. HE FARID SA'AD.

Metal Industries Co Ltd: POB 134, Amman Industrial Estate, Amman; tel. 723015; fax 723621; f. 1976; manufacturers of steel panel radiators, boilers, scaffolding, hot water cylinders, solar panels, etc.; sales US $3.25m. (1992); cap. p.u. US $448,000; Chair. M. A. JARDANEH; Gen. Man. M. GHARAIBEH; Prodn Eng. S. OMRAN.

TRADE UNIONS

The General Federation of Jordanian Trade Unions: POB 1065, Amman; tel. 675533; f. 1954; 33,000 mems; member of Arab Trade Unions Confederation; Chair. KHALIL ABU KHURMAH; Gen. Sec. ABDUL HALIM KHADDAM.

There are also a number of independent unions, including:

Drivers' Union: POB 846, Amman; Sec.-Gen. SAMI HASSAN MANSOUR.

Engineers' Association: Amman; Sec.-Gen. LEITH SHUBELLAT.

Union of Petroleum Workers and Employees: POB 1346, Amman; Sec.-Gen. BRAHIM HADI.

Transport

RAILWAYS

Aqaba Railway Corporation: POB 50, Ma'an; tel. 332234; telex 64003; fax 341861; f. 1975; length of track 292 km (1,050-mm gauge); Dir-Gen. MUHAMMAD M. KRISHAN.

Formerly a division of the Hedjaz–Jordan Railway (see below), the Aqaba Railway was established as a separate entity in 1979; it retains close links with the Hedjaz but there is no regular through traffic between Aqaba and Amman. It comprises the 169-km line south of Menzil (leased from the Hedjaz–Jordan Railway) and the 115-km extension to Aqaba, opened in October 1975, which serves phosphate mines at el-Hasa and Wadi el-Abyad. A development programme is being implemented to increase the transport capacity of the line to 4m. tons of phosphate per year.

Hedjaz–Jordan Railway (administered by the Ministry of Transport): POB 582, Amman; tel. 689541; telex 21541; f. 1902; length of track 496 km (1,050-mm gauge); Dir-Gen. A. H. AD-DJAZI.

This was formerly a section of the Hedjaz Railway (Damascus to Medina) for Muslim pilgrims to Medina and Mecca. It crosses the Syrian border and enters Jordanian territory south of Dera'a, and runs for approximately 366 km to Naqb Ishtar, passing through Zarka, Amman, Qatrana and Ma'an. Some 844 km of the line, from Ma'an to Medina in Saudi Arabia, were abandoned for over sixty years. Reconstruction of the Medina line, begun in 1965, was scheduled to be completed in 1971 at a cost of £15m., divided equally between Jordan, Saudi Arabia and Syria. However, the reconstruction work was suspended at the request of the Arab states concerned, pending further studies on costs. The line between Ma'an and Saudi Arabia (114 km) is now completed, as well as 15 km in Saudi Arabia as far as Halet Ammar Station. A new 115-km extension to Aqaba (owned by the Aqaba Railway Corporation (see above) was opened in 1975. In 1987 a study conducted by Dorsch Consult (Federal Republic of Germany) into the feasibility of reconstructing the Hedjaz Railway to high international specifications to connect Saudi Arabia, Jordan and Syria, concluded that the reopening of the Hedjaz line would be viable only if it were to be connected with European rail networks.

ROADS

Amman is linked by road with all parts of the kingdom and with neighbouring countries. All cities and most towns are connected by a two-lane paved road system. In addition, several thousand km of tracks make all villages accessible to motor transport. In 1991, the latest inventory showed the East Bank of Jordan to have 1,712 km of motorways, 497 km of main roads, 1,657 km of secondary roads (both types asphalted) and 1,814 km of other roads. In 1989 the Ministry of Public Works and Housing announced plans to introduce tolls on main roads in order to raise funds for road maintenance.

Joint Land Transport Co: Amman; joint venture of Govts of Jordan and Iraq; operates about 750 trucks.

Jordanian-Syrian Land Transport Co: POB 20686, Amman; tel. 661134; telex 21384; fax 669645; f. 1976; transports goods between ports in Jordan and Syria; Chair. and Gen. Man. HAMDI AL-HABASHNEH.

SHIPPING

The port of Aqaba is Jordan's only outlet to the sea and has more than 20 modern and specialized berths, and one container terminal (540 m in length). The port has 299,000 sq m of storage area, and is used for Jordan's international trade and regional transit trade (mainly with Iraq). Transit cargo formed 39% of total cargo traffic in 1989. Total cargo handled in 1989 was 18.7m. metric tons.

There is a ferry link between Aqaba and the Egyptian port of Nuweibeh.

Arab Bridge Maritime Co: Aqaba; f. 1987; joint venture by Egypt, Iraq and Jordan to improve economic co-operation; an extension of the company that established a ferry link between Aqaba and the Egyptian port of Nuweibeh in 1985; Chair. Eng. KHALID SALEH AMAR; Dir-Gen. TAWFIQ GRACE AWADALLA.

T. Gargour & Fils: POB 419, 4th Floor, Da'ssan Commercial Centre, Wasfi at-Tal St, Amman; tel. 690626; telex 21213; fax 690512; f. 1928; shipping agents and owners; Chair. JOHN GARGOUR.

Jordan Maritime Navigation Co: Amman; privately owned.

Jordan National Shipping Lines Co Ltd: POB 5406, Shmeisani, Amman; tel. 6664214; telex 21730; POB 657, Aqaba; tel. 315342; telex 62276; owned 75% by the Government; service from Antwerp, Bremen and Tilbury to Aqaba; daily passenger ferry service to Egypt; land transportation to destinations in Iraq and elsewhere in the region; Chair. Dr FOTI KHAMIS; Gen. Man. Y. ET-TAL.

Jordanian Shipping Transport Co: Amman; f. 1984.

Amin Kawar & Sons Co W.L.L.: POB 222, 24 Abd al-Hamid Sharaf St, Shmeisani, Amman 11118; tel. 603703; telex 21212; fax 672170; chartering and shipping agents; Chair. TAWFIQ A. KAWAR; Gen. Man. GHASSOUB F. KAWAR; Shipping Man. ABD AL-AZIZ AL-KASAJI.

Petra Navigation and International Trading Co Ltd: POB 8362, White Star Bldg, Amman; tel. 662421; telex 21755; fax 601362; general cargo, ro/ro and passenger ferries; Chair. AHMAD H. ARM-OUSH.

Syrian-Jordanian Shipping Co: rue Port Said, BP 148, Latakia, Syria; tel. 316356; telex 451002; Chair. OSMAN LEBBADI.

PIPELINES

Two oil pipelines cross Jordan. The former Iraq Petroleum Company pipeline, carrying petroleum from the oilfields in Iraq to Haifa, has not operated since 1967. The 1,717-km (1,067-mile) pipeline, known as the Trans-Arabian Pipeline (Tapline), carries petroleum from the oilfields of Dhahran in Saudi Arabia to Sidon on the Mediterranean seaboard in Lebanon. Tapline traverses Jordan for a distance of 177 km (110 miles) and has frequently been cut by hostile action. Tapline stopped pumping to Syria and Lebanon at the end of 1983, when it was first due to close. It was later scheduled to close in 1985, but in September 1984 Jordan renewed an agreement to receive Saudi Arabian crude oil through Tapline. The agreement can be cancelled by either party at two years' notice.

CIVIL AVIATION

There are international airports at Amman and Aqaba. The new Queen Alia International Airport at Zizya, 40 km south of Amman, was opened in May 1983.

Civil Aviation Authority: POB 7547, Amman; tel. 892282; telex 21325; fax 891653; f. 1950; Dir-Gen. AHMAD JUWEIBER.

Royal Jordanian Airline: Head Office: Housing Bank Commercial Centre, Shmeisani, POB 302, Amman; tel. 672872; telex 21501; fax 672527; f. 1963; government-owned; services to Middle East, North Africa, Europe, USA and Far East; Pres. and CEO MAHMOUD BALQEZ.

Arab Wings Co Ltd: POB 341018, Amman; tel. 891994; telex 21608; fax 893158; f. 1975; subsidiary of Royal Jordanian; executive jet charter service, air ambulances, priority cargo; Chair. and Man. Dir HE Sharif GHAZI RAKAN NASSER.

Tourism

The ancient cities of Jerash and Petra, and Jordan's proximity to biblical sites, have encouraged tourism. In 1990 there were 3,909,800 foreign visitors to Jordan. Income from tourism in 1990 was JD 339.8m.

Ministry of Tourism and Antiquities: Ministry of Tourism, POB 224, Amman; tel. 642311; telex 21741; fax 648465; f. 1952; Minister of Tourism and Antiquities YANAL HIKMAT; Sec.-Gen. Ministry of Tourism MUHAMMAD AFFASH AL-ADWAN.

Defence

Commander-in-Chief of the Armed Forces: Maj.-Gen. FATHI ABU TALIB.

Assistant Commander-in-Chief of the Armed Forces: Brig. TAYSEER ZAROUR.

Commander of the Royal Jordanian Air Force: Lt-Gen. IHSAN HAMID SHURDUM.

Chief of Staff of the Armed Forces: (vacant).

Chief of the General Staff: Lt-Gen. ABDEL HADI AL-MAJAH.

Defence Budget (1994): JD 288m. (US $411.1m.).

Military Service: conscription, two years authorized.

Total Armed Forces (June 1994): 98,600: army 90,000; navy 600; air force 8,000. Reserves 35,000 (army 30,000).

Paramilitary Forces: 210,000 (10,000 Public Security Force, 200,000 Civil Militia).

Education

The Ministry of Education adopted the principle of decentralization from the beginning of 1980. It divided the East Bank into 18 districts, called Offices of Education, distributed over five Directorates of Education, each one run by a Director-General who is in charge of implementing educational policies and procedures in his own area. The Ministry of Education's Central Office is still responsible for all major educational decisions related to planning curricula, projects and examinations.

Education in Jordan is provided by public and private sectors. In 1982/83, 70.6% of school enrolment was provided by the Ministry of Education, 1% by other governmental agencies (such as the Ministries of Defence, Health, Labour and Islamic Affairs), 9.9% by the private sector and 15.9% by UNRWA, which offers educational facilities and services for Palestinian refugees in collaboration with UNESCO. The University of Jordan, Yarmouk University and Mo'ata University provided 2.6% of total school enrolment. In 1985/86 there were 3,205 schools in the East Bank, attended by 894,695 pupils and staffed by 37,516 teachers.

A child is admitted to the first grade of the elementary school at the age of five years and eight months. The duration of this cycle is six years. Most of the students are promoted to the seventh grade, which, with the eighth and ninth grades, constitutes the preparatory cycle.

The secondary school cycle, which follows the preparatory cycle, lasts three years, and is divided into three types: general school, vocational school and comprehensive school. At the end of this cycle all students sit the General Secondary Examination, and those who pass are entitled to continue their higher education by enrolling either in the universities of Jordan (at Amman, Irbid and Mo'ata) or in Community Colleges—or in foreign universities and colleges. In 1991 a total of 36,668 students were enrolled at Jordan's universities. In 1986 Yarmouk University, at Irbid, was divided into two separate institutions to create the University of Science and Technology. An open university, Al-Quds University, opened in October 1988.

Community Colleges, of two-year post-secondary duration, include 12 colleges controlled by the Ministry, 22 colleges controlled by the private sector and supervised by the Ministry, and seven other colleges controlled by other governmental agencies such as the Ministries of Health and Social Development, the armed forces, the Department of Statistics and the Central Bank of Jordan.

Education was allocated a total of JD 215m. (US $620m.) under the 1986–90 Development Plan.

The Ministry of Education, in accordance with law No. 16 of 1964, provides textbooks free of charge for the compulsory cycle, and at cost price for the secondary cycle.

In 1989 a 10-year programme to reform the state education system was announced. The programme, which was to be implemented in three phases (1989–92, 1993–95 and 1996–98), aimed to revise curricula; to produce new textbooks and teaching aids; to train 4,000 new primary school teachers, 1,500 new secondary school teachers and 360 new school principals and supervisors; and to construct 420 schools.

Bibliography

Abdullah of Transjordan, King. *Memoirs,* trans. G. Khuri, ed. P. Graves. London and New York, 1950.

Abidi, A. H. H. *Jordan, a Political Study 1948–1957.* Delhi, Asia Publishing House, 1966.

Day, Arthur. *East Bank, West Bank.* Council on Foreign Relations, 1986.

Dearden, Ann. *Jordan.* London, Hale, 1958.

Foreign Area Studies. *Jordan: A Country Study.* Washington, DC, American University, 1980.

Glubb, J. B. *The Story of the Arab Legion.* London, 1948.

> *A Soldier with the Arabs.* Hodder and Stoughton, 1957.

> *Britain and the Arabs: A Study of Fifty Years 1908–1958.* London, Hodder and Stoughton, 1959.

> *War in the Desert.* London, 1960.

> *The Middle East Crisis—A Personal Interpretation.* London 1967.

> *Syria, Lebanon, Jordan.* London, 1967.

> *Peace in the Holy Land.* London, 1971.

Goichon, A. M. *L'Eau: Problème Vital de la Région du Jourdain.* Brussels, Centre pour l'Etudes des Problèmes du Monde Musulmane Contemporain, 1964.

> *Jordanie réelle.* Paris, Maisonneuve et Larose, 1972.

Gubser, Peter. *Jordan: Crossroads of Middle Eastern Events.* Boulder, Colorado, Westview Press, 1983.

Hussein, His Majesty King. *Uneasy Lies the Head.* London, 1962.

> *Ma guerre avec Israel.* Paris, Albin Michel, 1968.

> *Mon métier de roi.* Paris, Laffont, 1975.

International Bank for Reconstruction and Development. *The Economic Development of Jordan.* Baltimore, Johns Hopkins Press, 1957.

Jarvis, C. S. *Arab Command: the Biography of Lt-Col. F. W. Peake Pasha.* London, 1942.

Johnston, Charles. *The Brink of Jordan.* London, Hamish Hamilton, 1972.

Kohn, Hans. *Die staats- und verfassungsrechtliche Entwicklung des Emirats Transjordanien.* Tübingen, 1929.

Konikof, A. *Transjordan: An Economic Survey.* 2nd edn, Jerusalem, 1946.

Luke, Sir Harry C., and Keith-Roach, E. *The Handbook of Palestine and Transjordan.* London, 1934.

Lunt, James. *Hussein of Jordan.* London, Macmillan, 1989.

Lyautey, Pierre. *La Jordanie Nouvelle.* Paris, Juillard, 1966.

Mishal, Shaul. *West Bank/East Bank: The Palestinians in Jordan 1949–67.* New Haven, London, Yale University Press.

Morris, James. *The Hashemite Kings.* London, Faber, 1959.

Patai, R. *The Kingdom of Jordan.* Princeton, 1958.

Peake, F. G. *History of Jordan and Its Tribes.* Univ. of Miami Press, 1958.

Perowne, Stewart. *The One Remains.* London, 1954.

> *Jerusalem and Bethlehem.* South Brunswick, New Jersey, A. S. Barnes Ltd, 1966.

Phillips, Paul G. *The Hashemite Kingdom of Jordan: Prolegomena to a Technical Assistance Programme.* Chicago, 1954.

Sanger, Richard H. *Where the Jordan Flows.* Washington, DC, Middle East Institute, 1965.

Shipler, David K. *Arab and Jew: Wounded Spirits in a Promised Land.* London, Bloomsbury, 1987.

Shlaim, Avi. *Collusion Across the Jordan.* Oxford, Oxford University Press, 1988.

Shwadran, B. *Jordan: A State of Tension.* New York, Council for Middle Eastern Affairs, 1959.

Smith, Sir G. A. *Historical Geography of the Holy Land.* 25th edn, London, 1931.

Snow, Peter. *Hussein: A Biography.* London, Barrie and Jenkins, 1972.

Sparrow, Gerald. *Hussein of Jordan (the authorized biography).* London, Harrap, 1961.

> *Modern Jordan.* Allen and Unwin, 1961.

Toukan, Baha Uddin. *A Short History of Transjordan.* London, 1945.

US Government Printing Office. *Area Handbook for the Hashemite Kingdom of Jordan.* Washington, DC, 1970.

Vatikiotis, P. J. *Politics and the Military in Jordan 1921–57.* New York, Praeger, 1967.

Verdes, Jacques Mansour. *Pour les Fidayine.* Paris, 1969.

Wilson, Rodney (Ed.). *Politics and Economy in Jordan.* London, Routledge, 1991.

KUWAIT

Physical and Social Geography

Kuwait lies at the head of the Persian (Arabian) Gulf, bordering Iraq and Saudi Arabia. The area of the State of Kuwait is 17,818 sq km (6,880 sq miles), including the Kuwaiti share of the Neutral or Partitioned Zone (see below).

Although, for some time, the Gulf was thought to extend much further north, geological evidence suggests that the coastline has remained broadly at its present position, while the immense masses of silt brought down by the Tigris and Euphrates cause irregular downwarping at the head of the Gulf. Local variation in the coastline is therefore likely, with possible changes since ancient times. Kuwait (which means 'little fortress') developed because it has a zone of slightly higher, firmer ground, giving access from the Gulf inland to Iraq, and because it has a reasonably good and sheltered harbour, away from nearby sandbanks and coral reefs.

The territory of Kuwait is mainly almost flat desert with a few oases. With an annual rainfall of 1 cm to 37 cm, almost entirely between November and April, there is a spring 'flush' of grass. Summer shade temperature may reach 49°C (120°F), although in January, the coldest month, temperatures range between −2.8°C and 28.3°C (27°F to 85°F), with a rare frost. There is little drinking water within the country, and supplies are largely distilled from sea-water, and brought by pipeline from the Shatt al-Arab waterway, which runs into the Gulf.

According to census results, the population of Kuwait increased from 206,473 in February 1957 to 1,357,952 by April 1980 and to 1,697,301 by April 1985. Based on the results of the 1985 census, the population was estimated to be 1,979,149 at mid-1989, increasing to 2,062,275 at mid-1990. It was estimated that in 1991, following the war to end the Iraqi occupation, the population had declined to only 1.2m., mainly as a result of the departure of a large proportion of the former non-Kuwaiti residents, who had previously formed a majority of the inhabitants (see below). The estimated population at mid-1993 was 1,433,205. Between 1963 and 1970 the average annual increase in Kuwait's population was 10%, the highest growth rate recorded in any independent country. The average annual increase between 1970 and 1980 was 6.3%, although between 1985 and 1990 the rate decreased to 4.0%. Between 1990 and 1992 the population was estimated to have declined by an average of 17.8% per year.

Much of Kuwait's population growth has resulted from immigration, though the country also has one of the highest natural increase rates in the world. Between 1957 and 1983 the non-Kuwaiti population grew from less than 93,000 (45% of the total) to about 870,000 (57.4%), most of them from other Arab states. At mid-1993 the non-Kuwaiti population, based on the definition of citizenship in use in 1992, totalled an estimated 955,948. In 1993, according to provisional figures, there were 36,235 recorded births (25.3 per 1,000 inhabitants) and only 3,311 deaths (2.3 per 1,000). In 1985 females comprised only 43% of the country's population, including non-Kuwaitis. The birth rate for the Kuwaiti population alone exceeded 50 per 1,000 each year in 1973–76.

At the 1985 census Kuwait City, the capital and principal harbour, had a population of 44,335 (compared with 60,525 in 1980), although the largest town was Salmiya, with 153,369 inhabitants. Other sizeable localities, all at that time in Hawalli Governorate, were Hawalli (population 145,126), Farwaniya (68,701) and Abraq Kheetan (45,120). In all these towns, non-Kuwaitis formed a large majority. A separate Farwaniya Governorate was subsequently formed.

Apart from the distinction between Kuwaiti citizens and immigrants, Kuwaiti nationals can be divided into six groups. These groups reflect the tribal origins of Kuwaiti society. The first tribe of settlers, the Anaiza (led by the Sabah family) and later settlers, including the Bahar, Hamad and Babtain families, originated in the Nejd (central Arabia). Another group, the Kenaat (including the Mutawa family and its offshoot, the Saleh), came to Kuwait from Iraq, and remain distinct from the Nejdi families. There are also a few large families of Persian (Iranian) origin, including the Behbanis. The remaining citizens may be described as 'new Kuwaitis'; a few are former Palestinians, although most are bedouin who have been granted second-class citizenship. The majority of the Kuwaitis (including the ruling family) are Sunni Muslims, but most of the Persian families belong to the Shi'a sect. They, together with other Persians, comprise an estimated 150,000 (or one-quarter) of all Kuwaiti citizens. About 30% of the total population are thought to be Shi'ites.

Kuwait is the only Gulf country with a National Assembly entirely elected by popular vote. Suffrage, however, is confined to first-class male citizens (those who can prove Kuwaiti ancestry from before 1920), who in 1981 comprised only 6.4% of the population.

Immediately to the south of Kuwait, along the Gulf, is a Neutral or Partitioned Zone of 5,700 sq km (2,200 sq miles), which is divided between Kuwait and Saudi Arabia. Each country administers its own half as an integral part of the state. However, the oil wealth of the whole Zone remains undivided and production from the onshore concessions in the Neutral/Partitioned Zone is shared equally between the two states.

History

The origin of the present city of Kuwait is usually placed about the beginning of the 18th century, when a number of families of the Anaiza tribe migrated from the interior to the Arabian shore of the Gulf. The foundation of the present Sabah ruling dynasty dates from about 1756, when the settlers of Kuwait decided to appoint a sheikh to administer their affairs, provide them with security and represent them in their dealings with the Ottoman Government. The town prospered and in 1765 it was estimated to contain some 10,000 inhabitants possessing 800 vessels and living by trading, fishing and pearling.

Between 1776 and 1779, during the Persian occupation of Basra, the East India Company moved the southern terminal of its overland mail route to Aleppo from Basra to Kuwait, and much of the trade of Basra was diverted to Kuwait. At around the same time Kuwait was repeatedly threatened by raids from the Wahhabis, fanatical tribesmen from central Arabia, and the need for protection led to closer contacts with the East India Company, which had a depot in the town. Ottoman dominion over the mainland was accepted in return for recognition of British trading interests along the route from the Mediterranean to India through the Gulf. The depredations of pirates and the threat from the Wahhabis caused a decline in prosperity during the early years of the 19th century, but the British navy restored peace to the Gulf, and by 1860 prosperity had returned.

In order to retain their autonomy the Kuwaitis had to maintain good relations with the Turks. Although not under direct Turkish administration, the Sheikh of Kuwait recognized a general Ottoman suzerainty over the area by the payment of tribute and Sheikh Abdullah bin Sabah al-Jabir (1866–92) accepted the title of Qa'immaqam (commandant) under the Turkish Vali (Governor) of Basra in 1871. His successor, Sheikh Mubarak 'the Great', feared that the Turks would occupy Kuwait, and in 1899, in return for British protection, he signed an agreement with the British not to cede, mortgage or otherwise dispose of parts of his territories to anyone except the British Government, nor to enter into any relationship with a foreign government other than the British without British consent.

The reign of Sheikh Mubarak, from 1896 to 1915, was notable for the development of Kuwait from a sheikhdom of undefined status to an autonomous state. In 1904 a British political agent was appointed, and in 1909 Great Britain and Turkey discussed proposals which, although never ratified because of the outbreak of the First World War, in practice secured the autonomy of Kuwait.

Sheikh Mubarak's second son, Sheikh Salim, who succeeded to the sheikhdom in 1917, supported the Turks in the World War, thus incurring a blockade of Kuwait. Sheikh Salim was succeeded in 1921 by his nephew, Sheikh Ahmad al-Jabir. Kuwait prospered under his rule, and by 1937 the population had risen to about 75,000.

Under Sheikh Ahmad the foundation of Kuwait's great petroleum industry was laid. After considerable prospecting, he granted a joint concession in 1934 to the Gulf Oil Corporation of the USA and the Anglo-Persian Oil Co of Great Britain, which formed the Kuwait Oil Co Ltd. Deep drilling started in 1936, and was just beginning to show promising results when the Second World War began in 1939. The oil wells were plugged in 1942 and drilling was suspended until the end of the war.

After the war the petroleum industry in Kuwait was revived on an extensive scale (see Economy) and in a few years Kuwait Town had developed from an old-fashioned dhow port to a thriving modern city, supported by the revenues of the petroleum industry. In 1950 Sheikh Ahmad died and was succeeded by Sheikh Abdullah as-Salim. His policy was to use the petroleum revenues substantially for the welfare of his people, and in 1951 he inaugurated a programme of public works and educational and medical developments which transformed Kuwait into an organized and well-equipped country.

THE MODERN STATE

Kuwait has gradually built up what are probably the most comprehensive welfare services in the world, and for the most part free of charge, at least to native Kuwaitis. Education is completely free in Kuwait, and, despite the introduction of health charges in 1984, the country's health service is considered to be of a very high standard. A heavily subsidized housing programme has provided accommodation for many residents who satisfy the country's generous criteria of 'poverty'.

In 1961 the United Kingdom (UK) and Kuwait terminated the 1899 agreement which had given the UK responsibility for the conduct of Kuwait's foreign policy; Kuwait became a fully independent state on 19 June of that year. The ruling Sheikh took the title of Amir, and Kuwait was admitted to the Arab League.

Shortly after attaining independence, Kuwait was threatened by an Iraqi claim to sovereignty over the territory. In response to a request from the Amir for assistance British troops landed in Kuwait. The Arab League met in July and agreed that an Arab League Force should be provided to replace the British troops as a guarantor of Kuwait's independence. This force, composed of contingents from Saudi Arabia, Jordan, the United Arab Republic (UAR) and Sudan, arrived in Kuwait in September 1961. The UAR contingent was withdrawn in December 1961, and those of Jordan, Saudi Arabia and Sudan before the end of February 1963. On 14 May 1963 Kuwait became the 111th member of the United Nations.

In December 1961, for the first time in Kuwait's history, an election was held to choose 20 members of the Constituent Assembly (the other members being ministers). This Assembly drafted a new Constitution under which a National Assembly of 50 members was elected in January 1963, and the first session was held, with Sheikh Sabah as-Salim as-Sabah, brother of the Amir and heir apparent, as the Prime Minister of a new Council of Ministers.

In October 1963 the new Iraqi Government announced its decision to recognize Kuwait's complete independence, in an attempt to dispel the tense atmosphere between the two countries, created by the previous regime. Kuwait was thought to have made a substantial grant to Iraq at this juncture.

In January 1965 a constitutional crisis, reflecting the friction between the ruling house and the National Assembly, resulted in the formation of a strengthened Council of Ministers under the heir apparent, Sheikh Sabah as-Salim as-Sabah. In July 1965 Kuwait decided not to ratify the agreement to establish an Arab common market with Iraq, Jordan, Syria and the UAR. On 24 November 1965 Sheikh Abdullah died and was succeeded by Sheikh Sabah. His post as Prime Minister was assumed by another member of the ruling family, Sheikh Jaber al-Ahmad, who became heir apparent in May 1966.

Kuwait played a neutral role in the conflicts of 1966 and 1967 within the Arab community, and in particular tried to act as mediator in inter-Arab disputes such as the Yemen and South Arabian problems. Sheikh Sabah visited Iraq and Lebanon, and Kuwait supported Syria in the dispute with the Iraq Petroleum Company.

Kuwait declared its support for the Arab countries in the 1967 war with Israel, and joined in the oil embargo on the USA and the UK. However, the cease-fire had been announced before any Kuwaitis entered the conflict. The Government donated KD25m. to the Arab war effort. At the Khartoum Conference in September 1967 Kuwait joined Saudi Arabia and Libya in offering financial aid to the UAR and Jordan to help their economies to recover from the June war. The Kuwaiti share of this amounted to KD55m. annually.

In 1968 it was announced that the agreement of June 1961—whereby Britain had undertaken to give military assistance to Kuwait if asked to do so by its ruler—would terminate by 1971. This followed an earlier announcement that Britain would withdraw all troops from the Gulf region by the end of 1971. At this time, Kuwait continually solicited support for the formation of a federation of Bahrain, Qatar and the Trucial States, but it failed to convince the first two states to join what eventually became the United Arab Emirates (UAE).

Following the June 1967 war, Kuwait ceased to be a target of radical Arab criticism, largely because of its financial support for the countries affected by war, and of the Palestinian guerrillas. A factor in this assistance was the large Palestinian community, totalling more than 350,000, in Kuwait; many of the most able and educated Palestinians had made a career in the country. Financial aid to Jordan, on the other hand, was suspended in September 1970, following the armed conflict between the Jordanian Government and Palestinian guerrilla forces.

During the 1960s the Kuwaiti leadership's policies led to extensive redistribution of income, through the use of oil revenues in public expenditure and through the land compensation scheme. At the same time, however, there was popular discontent about corruption and inefficiency in public services and the manipulation of the press and the National Assembly.

In response to public opinion, the ruling family permitted the assembly elections of January 1971 to be held on the basis of a free vote, although women, illiterates and all non-Kuwaitis were excluded, and remain so today. There was a lively election campaign, with 184 candidates contesting the 50 seats, despite the absence of political parties, which were still illegal. Several members and supporters of the Arab Nationalist Movement, founded in the 1950s by Dr George Habash (now leader of the Popular Front for the Liberation of Palestine), were elected. This radical group, led by Dr Ahmad al-Khatib, was generally regarded as the principal opposition to the Government.

After the 1971 elections the Crown Prince was reappointed Prime Minister and formed a new Council of Ministers. The representation of the ruling family was reduced from five to three and, for the first time, the Council of Ministers included two ministers drawn from the elected members of the National Assembly.

In August 1976 the Amir suspended the National Assembly for four years on the grounds that, amongst other things, it had been delaying legislation. A committee was ordered to be formed to review the Constitution.

On 31 December 1977 the Amir (Sheikh Sabah) died and was succeeded by his cousin, the Crown Prince, Sheikh Jabir al-Ahmad as-Sabah, who had been Prime Minister since 1966. The new heir apparent was Sheikh Saad al-Abdullah as-Sabah, who became Prime Minister as well as Crown Prince. Both the Amir and the Prime Minister publicly reaffirmed the Government's intention to reconvene the National Assembly and to restore democratic government by August 1980. In response to increasing public pressure, a 50-member committee was established in early 1980 to consider constitutional amendments and a revised form of legislature. Following its recommendations, an amiri decree provided for the election of a new assembly before the end of February 1981. Despite the uncertainty generated by the Iran–Iraq War, the election campaign proceeded, with 448 candidates contesting the 50 seats. The franchise was limited to 90,000 'first-class' Kuwaiti citizens, and, of these fewer than half (or about 3% of the population) registered to vote. A moderate assembly was returned, containing 23 conservative tribal leaders, sympathetic to the ruling sheikhs, and 13 young technocrats. The radical Arab nationalists, the fiercest opposition to the Government in the previous Assembly, failed to win any seats, while the Shi'a minority's representation was reduced to four seats. However, five Islamic fundamentalists of the Sunni sect were elected.

The Crown Prince was subsequently reappointed Prime Minister and formed a new 15-member Council of Ministers in which the ruling family retained the major posts. There were seven new ministers, including the only member of the Council of Ministers to have been elected to the new Assembly, and the finance and planning ministries were merged.

Of all the Gulf states, Kuwait has been the most vulnerable to regional disruption. In March 1973 Iraqi troops and tanks occupied a Kuwaiti outpost at Samtah, on the border with Iraq. Iraq later withdrew its troops, but a source of potential dispute remained over Iraq's territorial claim on Bubiyan Island. Following the crisis in 1973, Kuwait allocated larger sums for the expansion of its armed forces and established its own navy. Legislation to introduce conscription was approved in 1975.

During the Arab-Israeli war of October 1973 Kuwaiti forces stationed along the Suez Canal were involved in fighting, and Kuwait contributed considerable financial aid, totalling KD100m., to other Arab states. While the war was still in progress, Kuwait called for a meeting of OAPEC to draw up a common Arab policy for the use of oil as a weapon to put pressure on Western countries, particularly the USA, to force an Israeli withdrawal from occupied Arab territory. Kuwait also joined other Gulf states in announcing a unilateral increase of 70% in the posted price of crude petroleum (the reference price used for tax and royalty purposes) from 1 November 1973. The OAPEC meeting took place in Kuwait, where the organization's 10 member states decided to reduce petroleum production by at least 5% progressively each month. Kuwait also imposed a total embargo on petroleum shipments to the USA and, later, to the Netherlands.

In November, at a further meeting in Kuwait, oil ministers from the Arab states agreed on an extra 5% reduction in output, which effectively led to an overall drop in supply of 25% compared with September levels, to be followed by further reductions. Later in November the Arab group in OPEC agreed on the next 5% cut for December, but exempted EC countries except the Netherlands.

At the next OAPEC meeting, held in Kuwait in December, an additional 5% cut, without exemptions, was agreed for January 1974. A second December meeting, also in Kuwait, partly reversed earlier decisions to reduce oil production. Just before this, the Gulf states belonging to OPEC had agreed on

a further sharp increase in the posted price of oil, effective from 1 January 1974.

Kuwait played a leading part in all these moves and made considerable reductions in national oil output. Monthly production (in million metric tons) fell from 13.4 in September 1973 to 12.0 in October and 9.8 in November. There was later a reversal in this trend and monthly output was more than 10m. tons in the first half of 1974.

Following the conclusion in January of a disengagement agreement between Egypt and Israel and the consequent improvement in Arab relations with the USA, seven of the Arab oil-producing states (including Kuwait) agreed in March to lift the embargo on supplies to the USA. In July 1974 the Arab countries also lifted the oil embargo on the Netherlands. None the less, Kuwait's policy of conserving petroleum reserves, and the fall in the world demand, meant that production fell from a peak of 3.3m. barrels per day (b/d) in 1972 to an average of 1.5m. b/d in 1980, and below 1m. b/d in 1981. Since then, OPEC agreements have imposed a maximum quota on every member country's production (see Economy).

Following the division of the Ministry of Finance and Oil, petroleum affairs became the sole responsibility of the Ministry of Oil. In April 1975 the Government decided to take over the Kuwait National Petroleum Company (KNPC), which was already 60% government-owned. The KNPC came under the authority of the Supreme Oil Council and its co-ordinating committee and controlled all oil operations. The state-owned Kuwait Oil Co (KOC) was therefore limited to production. Nationalization of the oil industry was almost complete when, in 1977, the Government acquired Aminoil and created the Kuwait Wafra Oil Company.

Until 1973 Kuwait's financial support for the leading Palestinian organizations had protected the country from active involvement in the guerrilla struggle. However, the activities of extremist groups resulted in embarrassing incidents for the Government. In September 1973 Arab gunmen occupied the Saudi Arabian embassy in Paris and later flew to Kuwait with five hostages. The gunmen surrendered to the Kuwaiti authorities, who later handed them over to the Palestine Liberation Organization (PLO), which had condemned the incident.

At the Baghdad Arab summit in November 1978 Kuwait pressed for unanimity among the Arab nations in condemning the Egypt-Israeli peace agreement and supported the use of sanctions against Egypt. The Kuwaiti Ambassador was recalled from Cairo and all aid, except for specific development projects, was withdrawn. Anxious to preserve Arab unity, Kuwait mediated successfully in the conflict between the Yemen Arab Republic and the People's Democratic Republic of Yemen in 1979, eventually bringing about a ceasefire, and was instrumental in resolving the crisis in the UAE. In the war between Iran and Iraq, which began in September 1980, Kuwait supported Iraq, allowing access to its strategic ports to enable Iraqi petroleum exports to continue, and, with Saudi Arabia, exporting up to 310,000 b/d (250,000 b/d from the Neutral Zone and the remainder from Saudi Arabia), on Iraq's behalf, and providing generous financial aid, which by the end of 1983 was thought to have reached $30,000m. (donated by both Kuwait and Saudi Arabia). Relations with Iran were, however, maintained. In May 1981 Kuwait became, with Saudi Arabia, the UAE, Qatar, Oman and Bahrain, a founder-member of the Gulf Co-operation Council (GCC). By encouraging economic and social integration, it was hoped that the GCC would increase the security of the small oilproducing states of the Gulf.

In September 1981 Kuwaiti oil installations at Umm al-Aish, near the Iraqi border, were bombed by Iran. Kuwait's Ambassador to Iran was temporarily withdrawn, but in February 1982 Kuwait announced its willingness to mediate in the continuing conflict between Iran and Iraq. Attempts at mediation were, however, unsuccessful.

Events at the end of 1983 and in early 1984 highlighted Kuwait's vulnerability to attack, and increased concern for the country's security. In December 1983 six bombs exploded in Kuwait City, killing five people and wounding 61. The principal targets were the French and US embassies, but a power station and an airport were also bombed. Responsibility was claimed by the al-Jihad al-Islami (Islamic Holy War) organization, a group of militant Shi'ite Muslims with widely acknowledged connections in Iran. The potential threat of domestic agitation by the country's own fundamentalist Shi'-ites was coupled with the authorities' suspicion that the attacks were directed by Iran in retaliation for Kuwaiti support of Iraq in the Iran–Iraq War. As a result of the bombings, more than 600 Iranian workers were deported from Kuwait in early 1984.

In May 1984 two Kuwaiti and several Saudi Arabian tankers were bombed in a series of attacks by unidentified aircraft on shipping in the Gulf. Although both Iran and Iraq were known to have been firing at shipping, Iran was blamed for the attacks on Kuwaiti tankers. The bombings were seen as a warning to Kuwait to reduce its aid to Iraq and to put pressure on Iraq to desist from attacking tankers carrying Iranian oil. The GCC withdrew offers to mediate in the Iran–Iraq War and condemned Iran. Much concern arose as to whether the GCC countries could defend themselves unaided, and at the GCC summit conference in November 1984 the member states agreed to form a joint military force, capable of rapid deployment and aimed at combating any spread of the Iran–Iraq War.

Throughout 1984 Iranian Muslims were arrested and deported from Kuwait, and new measures were introduced, restricting free passage within the country. In December tension between Iran and Kuwait was heightened when a Kuwaiti airliner was hijacked and forced to land at Teheran airport. The hijackers demanded the release of the Shi'a Muslims who had been imprisoned as a result of the bomb attacks in 1983. The terrorists were later overwhelmed by Iranian security forces after murdering two American passengers. The airliner was eventually returned to Kuwait in May 1986.

Kuwait's attempts to mediate in the Iran–Iraq War in 1984 were hampered by Iran's increasing suspicion about the outcome of outstanding border disputes between Iraq and Kuwait. Iran believed that Kuwait was about to transfer three strategically important islands (Bubiyan, Warba and Failaka) to Iraq. In January 1985, however, Kuwait announced plans to build its own military bases on Bubiyan and Warba, and two months later Bubiyan was declared an out-of-bounds war zone. Kuwaiti forces were put on alert in February 1986, when Iranian forces crossed the Shatt al-Arab waterway and captured the Iraqi port of Faw, near Kuwait's north-eastern border. Iran pledged that Kuwait would not become embroiled in its war with Iraq provided that it maintained its military neutrality.

In an attempt to improve its own defences, Kuwait approached the USA in 1984 concerning the purchase of armaments, but, although it was prepared to sell other weapons, the USA refused to provide the *Stinger* anti-aircraft missiles which Kuwait had particularly requested. In July 1984 Kuwait signed a military training agreement with the USSR, and by January 1985, despite unwillingness among the GCC countries to allow either of the superpowers to become directly involved, Kuwait had taken delivery of a consignment of Soviet surface-to-air missiles. In November 1985 a trade agreement was signed between Kuwait and the USSR, and in early 1986 a $230m. arms sale was agreed between the two countries.

In May 1985 an Iraqi member of the banned ad-Dawa al-Islamiya (the Voice of Islam) organization attempted to assassinate the Amir of Kuwait, Sheikh Jaber al-Ahmad as-Sabah, by driving a car-bomb into a royal procession. The attack resulted in appeals for even greater security measures in Kuwait, and the Government responded by agreeing to introduce appropriate legislation and by temporarily suspending the issue of entry visas and residence permits. In July the National Assembly unanimously approved legislation to impose the death penalty for terrorist acts which result in loss of life, and the Government announced plans to establish popular security committees in all districts. In June 1986 four simultaneous explosions occurred at Kuwait's main oil export refinery at Mina al-Ahmadi. A hitherto unknown organization, calling itself the 'Arab Revolutionaries Group', later claimed responsibility for the attacks, which had been intended to force Kuwait to reduce its petroleum output. In July 1986

several arrests were made in connection with the attempted assassination of the Amir in 1985.

In 1985 and 1986 almost 27,000 expatriates, many of whom were Iranian, were deported, and concern over the security of the country continued. In June 1987 six Kuwaiti Shi'a Muslims were sentenced to death for their part in sabotaging oil installations and plotting against the Government. There were further explosions in May and July.

The Council of Ministers submitted its resignation to the Amir in July 1986, following 15 months of increasing confrontation with the National Assembly. The Amir subsequently issued a decree accepting the Council's resignation, dissolving the National Assembly and suspending some articles of the Constitution. Crown Prince Sheikh Saad al-Abdullah as-Sabah was immediately reappointed to the post of Prime Minister and charged with the task of nominating a new government, which would be given greater powers of censorship, including the right to close down newspapers for up to two years. Ten days later the Amir named a 22-man Council of Ministers, which included seven new ministers and three new portfolios. The former Minister of Education, Hassan Ali al-Ibrahim (who had been considered too liberal by Kuwait's Muslim fundamentalists), was the only minister not to be reappointed.

Between October 1986 and April 1987 Iranian forces attacked merchant ships sailing to or from Kuwait and seized cargoes, as a punishment for loading petroleum sold on Iraq's behalf and for the use of Kuwait's ports for Iraqi imports. In an attempt to deter Iranian attacks in the Gulf, Kuwait re-registered most of its fleet of oil tankers under the flags of the USA, Liberia, the USSR and the UK. Kuwait received help from the USA and Saudi Arabia in clearing mines from the channel leading to its main oil-loading facilities at Mina al-Ahmadi. On 24 July the *Bridgeton*, the first tanker to be re-registered by the USA, struck a mine in the Gulf, 30 km from Farsi Island, while under US naval escort to Mina al-Ahmadi. The US naval force in the Gulf was ill-equipped for minesweeping operations, and in August France and the UK, having initially refused a request for assistance to clear the shipping lanes, sent minesweeping vessels to the Gulf. These were followed in September by vessels from the Netherlands, Belgium and Italy.

Six Iranian diplomats were expelled from Kuwait in September 1987, following Iranian attacks on Kuwaiti installations. Kuwait's main offshore oil-loading terminal, at Sea Island, was closed between October and December, after an Iranian missile attack in which three workers were injured. In November Kuwait resumed full diplomatic relations with Egypt, following a decision taken by the League of Arab States that permitted member states to restore relations with Egypt at their own discretion. The GCC held a summit meeting in December 1987, when the six member states urged the UN Security Council to enforce its Resolution 598, which ordered a cease-fire to be observed in the Iran–Iraq War, and approved a pact to increase security co-operation between the member states.

Two Kuwaiti soldiers were wounded in March 1988 as Iranian and Kuwaiti armed forces clashed for the first time during the eight-year Iran–Iraq War, when three Iranian gunboats attacked Bubiyan island, situated 25 km from the southern coast of Iraq. In the following month an Iranian missile landed at al-Wafra oilfield, 80 km south of Kuwait City. The launching of the missile was believed to represent an Iranian warning to Kuwait for allegedly permitting Iraqi armed forces to use Bubiyan island in an attempt to recapture the Iranian-occupied Faw peninsula.

In April 1988 a Kuwaiti airliner was hijacked over the Arabian Sea by a group believed to belong to pro-Iranian Shi'ite Muslim organizations in Lebanon. The hijackers demanded the release of 17 Shi'ite Muslims who were imprisoned in Kuwait. Two hostages were killed during the 15-day hijack, which ended when the Algerian Government negotiated the release of the hostages and the safe passage of the hijackers to an unknown destination in the Middle East. In the same month a bomb exploded outside the offices of Saudia (the Saudi Arabian national airline) in Kuwait City. In May it was reported that a hitherto unknown group, calling itself

'Kuwaiti Hezbollah', had announced that it intended to commence a 'holy war' against Kuwait's ruling family and other pro-Western rulers in the Gulf region. Two bomb explosions followed this announcement, one of which killed two Kuwaitis.

The cease-fire in the Iran–Iraq War in August 1988 brought stability to the region and a revival of economic growth in Kuwait. Relations between Kuwait and Iran improved, despite Kuwait's support for Iraq in the war, and in April 1989 the Prime Minister, Saad al-Abdullah as-Salim as-Sabah, announced that relations with Iran were 'moving towards stability and normalization'. Co-operation with Iraq appeared to increase, despite the continuing dispute over Bubiyan island. In domestic affairs, concern about Iranian influence over the Shi'ite minority (about 30% of the population) led to severe measures to curb subversion. In June 1989 a Kuwaiti court sentenced 22 people, accused of plotting to overthrow the royal family, to prison terms of up to 15 years. However, it was recognized that the established Shi'ite families form part of the merchant aristocracy in Kuwait, with a financial commitment to the country, which ensures their loyalty. A programme of 'Kuwaitization' was vigorously pursued; the aim was to achieve a majority of Kuwaitis in the population by the year 2000. The programme was most successful in the public sector, where 90% of Kuwaiti workers were employed, but the private ssector continued to be dominated by expatriates, who formed 60% of the population.

In December 1989 a number of former members of the National Assembly campaigned for its re-establishment. In mid-January 1990 the Amir appealed for political dialogue, and in March the Prime Minister declared that he would welcome the restoration of an elected legislature. On 10 June 62% of the electorate voted at a general election for 50 members of a new National Council. The Council was to be an interim body and its members were to hold office for four years. It comprised 75 members, of whom 25 were appointed by the Amir.

Following the election, the Kuwaiti Government resigned. On 13 June 1990 the Amir reappointed the Crown Prince, Sheikh Saad al-Abdullah as-Salim as-Sabah, as Prime Minister. Sheikh Ali al-Khalifa as-Sabah became Minister of Finance, and Rashed Salim al-Ameeri became Minister of Oil. On 23 June a government reshuffle resulted in ten new appointments to the Council of Ministers. Only three ministers not belonging to the as-Sabah family retained their posts, while the new members of the Council were technocrats with no previous experience of government. The Council was believed to have been reshuffled in an attempt to satisfy domestic demands for new government policies. However, the fact that the as-Sabah family retained the majority of important positions in the Government, and that restoration of the National Assembly did not seem a realistic prospect, undermined the attempt to placate critics of the Government. In late June it was announced that five ministers from the reshuffled Council of Ministers had been appointed by the Amir to the National Council, the first session of which was held on 9 July.

IRAQ'S INVASION OF KUWAIT: THE GULF CRISIS

In July 1990 President Saddam Hussain of Iraq publicly criticized unspecified states for exceeding the petroleum production quotas that had been established by OPEC in May in order to increase prices. He accused Kuwait of having 'stolen' US $2,400m. worth of Iraqi oil reserves from a well in disputed territory. The Iraqi Minister of Foreign Affairs, Tareq Aziz, declared that Kuwait should not only cancel Iraq's war debt, but also compensate it for losses of revenue incurred during the war with Iran, and as a result of Kuwait's overproduction of oil, to which he attributed a decline in prices. Later in July Iraq began to deploy armed forces on the Kuwait-Iraq border, immediately before a meeting of the OPEC ministerial council in Geneva, Switzerland. At the meeting the minimum reference price for petroleum was increased, as Iraq had demanded. On 31 July representatives of Kuwait and Iraq conferred in Jeddah, Saudi Arabia, in an attempt to resolve the dispute over Iraq's territorial claims and demands for financial compensation. Kuwait was reportedly prepared to contribute one-half of the amount demanded, but would not concede any territory. Consequently, the negotiations collapsed.

On 2 August 1990 Iraq invaded Kuwait with 100,000 troops (compared with Kuwait's total military strength of about 20,000). The Iraqi Government claimed that its forces entered Kuwait at the invitation of insurgents who had overthrown the Kuwaiti Government, but there was no evidence to verify this. The Amir and other members of the Government escaped to Saudi Arabia, along with many other Kuwaiti citizens. The immediate response of the UN Security Council to the invasion of Kuwait was to adopt a series of resolutions. Resolution 660 condemned the invasion, demanded the immediate and unconditional withdrawal of Iraqi forces from Kuwait, and appealed for a negotiated settlement of the conflict. Resolution 661 imposed a trade embargo on Iraq and Kuwait. Immediately after the invasion, the USA and the members of the EC 'froze' all Kuwaiti assets to prevent an Iraqi-imposed regime from transferring them back to Kuwait.

On 7 August 1990, at the request of the Saudi Arabian Government, President Bush of the USA ordered the deployment of US troops and aircraft in Saudi Arabia, stating that his aim was to secure the country's borders with Kuwait in the event of an Iraqi attack. The British and other European Governments, together with some members of the Arab League, agreed to provide military support for the US forces (see chapter on Iraq). On 8 August the Iraqi Government announced the formal annexation of Kuwait, and ordered the closure of foreign diplomatic missions there. On 28 August most of Kuwait was officially declared to be the 19th governorate of Iraq, while a northern strip was incorporated into the Basra governorate. During August many thousands of Arab and Asian expatriates had fled from Iraq and Kuwait into Jordan. Kuwait had thus lost a large proportion of its foreign work-force. Successive diplomatic efforts to achieve a peaceful solution to the crisis in the Gulf region, undertaken by the UN and by numerous individual governments, proved futile. Attempts to pursue a diplomatic solution were complicated by the detention of Western citizens resident in Kuwait and Iraq. At the end of August, however, Iraq announced that foreign women and children were free to leave Iraq and Kuwait. By early December all hostages had been released.

Following the Iraqi invasion, there were widespread reports that Iraqi forces were plundering Kuwait City, looting goods from shops and warehouses, and searching for Kuwaiti resistance fighters and Westerners in hiding. Iraqi troops, in an attempt to subjugate the population of Kuwait, reportedly burned houses and tortured or summarily executed persons suspected of opposing the occupation forces. Many installations were dismantled and removed to Iraq. By early October an estimated 430,000 Iraqi troops had been deployed in southern Iraq and Kuwait. There was evidence of attempts to alter the demographic character of Kuwait, by settling Iraqis and Palestinians in the country, and by forcing Kuwaiti citizens to assume Iraqi citizenship. By October it was believed that a considerable number of Kuwaitis had died as a result of acts of brutality perpetrated by Iraqi occupation forces. The population was estimated to have decreased from approximately 2m., prior to the invasion, to about 700,000, of whom Kuwaitis constituted an estimated 300,000 and Palestinians 200,000, while the remainder comprised other Arab expatriate workers and Asians.

In early October 1990 a conference was held in Jeddah, Saudi Arabia, where the exiled Crown Prince and Prime Minister of Kuwait, Sheikh Saad al-Abdullah as-Salim as-Sabah, addressed approximately 1,000 distinguished Kuwaiti citizens, including 'opposition' members of the dissolved National Assembly. He agreed to establish committees to advise the Government on political, social and financial matters, and pledged that, after the liberation of Kuwait, the country's constitution and legislature would be restored, and that free elections would be held.

In late November 1990 the UN Security Council adopted a resolution (No. 678) which authorized the multinational force, stationed in Saudi Arabia and the Gulf region, to use 'all necessary means' to liberate Kuwait. Iraq was allowed until 15 January 1991 to begin to implement the 10 resolutions that had so far been adopted, including that stipulating unconditional withdrawal from Kuwait. Upon the expiry of this period, it was implied, military force would be employed against Iraq in order to remove its troops from Kuwait. In the interim various unsuccessful diplomatic attempts were made, by the UN Secretary-General and the Governments of the USA, the USSR, the EC members and Arab states, to avert a military confrontation between the multinational and Iraqi forces. On 17 January 1991 the UN-backed, US-led multinational force launched its military campaign to liberate Kuwait by an intensive aerial bombardment of Iraq, with the aim of disabling that country's airfields and strategic installations. In February the Soviet Government proposed a peace plan to Iraq, in an attempt to avoid the launching of a land offensive by the multinational force. The eight-point peace plan was deemed unacceptable by the USA and its allies, because it stipulated that a cease-fire should be declared before Iraq began to withdraw from Kuwait. On 24 February the US-led ground forces entered Kuwait, encountering relatively little effective Iraqi opposition. Within three days the Iraqi Government had agreed to accept all the resolutions of the UN Security Council concerning Kuwait, and on 28 February the US Government announced a suspension of military operations. In March the UN Security Council adopted a resolution (No. 686) which dictated the terms to Iraq for a permanent cease-fire. These included the release of all allied prisoners of war and of Kuwaitis who had been detained as potential hostages. A further resolution required Iraq to repeal all laws and decrees concerning the annexation of Kuwait. Iraq promptly announced its compliance with both resolutions. Another resolution, adopted in April, provided for the establishment of a demilitarized zone, supervised by the UN Iraq–Kuwait Observer Mission (UNIKOM, see p. 206), between the two countries.

In mid-January 1991 a conference in Jeddah, Saudi Arabia, was attended by members of the Kuwaiti Government-in-exile, including the Prime Minister, and opposition delegates. Islamic and Arab nationalist groups had collaborated in forming a 'National Constitutional Front' and demanded an immediate return of parliamentary and press freedom, while the more radical elements in the movement demanded the resignation of the as-Sabah family from all important positions in the Government, and the establishment of a constitutional monarchy. In February, despite the expression of discontent among the exiled Kuwaiti community, the Kuwaiti Government-in-exile excluded the possibility of early elections after Kuwait had been liberated, on the grounds that the need to rebuild and repopulate the country took precedence. The opposition parties were further frustrated by the stated aim of the UN resolutions to reinstate Kuwait's 'legitimate' Government prior to the invasion by Iraq, namely the as-Sabah family. In late February, immediately after the liberation of Kuwait, the Amir decreed that martial law would be enforced in Kuwait for the subsequent three months. The decree was contested by some members of Kuwait's opposition in exile, who expressed the need for the legislature to reconvene before any such decision could be made. In early March the opposition groups in exile made public their intention to form a coalition against the Government of the as-Sabah family. In the same month, the Amir announced the formation of a committee to administer martial law and to supervise the state's security internally and abroad. The committee's domestic objectives were to identify people who had collaborated with Iraq, to prevent the formation of 'vigilante' groups, and to identify civilians brought by the Iraqi authorities to settle in the emirate. On 4 March the Prime Minister and other members of the exiled Government returned to the emirate, followed by the Amir 10 days later. The country was in a condition of instability because of the enormous structural and environmental damage caused by the war, and also owing to the bitter resentment felt by the Kuwaiti people against many members of the Palestinian community who were suspected of having collaborated with Iraq; it was alleged by human rights groups that Palestinians suspected of collaboration were being tortured by the Kuwaiti security forces. Later in March the Government announced that elections would take place within six to 12 months, following the return of Kuwaiti exiles and the compilation of a new electoral roll. The Government also declared its intention to reduce the number of foreign workers in Kuwait. On 20 March the Council of Ministers resigned,

apparently in response to public discontent at the Government's failure to restore supplies of electricity, water and food.

In mid-April 1991 the Amir of Kuwait announced that elections to restore the National Assembly, which had been dissolved in 1986, would be held in 1992 after the gradual return of the 400,000 Kuwaiti citizens who remained abroad. Illegal opposition groups, such as the Popular Islamic Congress, the Islamic Constitutional Movement, the National Islamic Coalition and Salafeen, responded to the Amir's announcement by demanding the cessation of the nepotism towards members of the as-Sabah family; the legalization of political parties; the separation of the government and the as-Sabah family; the restoration of the freedom of the press; and an independent judiciary.

On 20 April 1991 the formation of a new Council of Ministers by the Crown Prince was announced. Although several technocrats were appointed to important positions within the Council (in charge of the economic portfolios), the major portfolios—foreign affairs, defence and the interior—were all retained by members of the as-Sabah family. Members of illegal opposition groups immediately denounced the new Council of Ministers as 'unrepresentative'.

Following the liberation of Kuwait, the repatriation of the national population became one of the Government's highest priorities. Prior to the Iraqi invasion, the national (i.e. Kuwaiti) population had been estimated at 800,000, representing 40% of the total population. By late April 1991 the Government had initiated a programme to register all non-Kuwaiti nationals resident in the country. However, the process of registration was complicated by the fact that two-thirds of the total pre-invasion population remained abroad. According to an official report, former non-Kuwaiti residents were not to be permitted to return to Kuwait until the Government had calculated its future labour requirements. However, it appeared inevitable that foreign workers would be allowed to return, in view of the Government's pledge to provide basic services for 1.25m. people by September 1991.

In May 1991 it was reported that 900 people were under investigation in connection with crimes committed during the Iraqi occupation. In late May the human rights organization, Amnesty International, alleged that trials were being conducted in Kuwait without the provision of adequate defence counsel, and that, in some cases, torture had been used in order to extract confessions from defendants. In the same month, the Prime Minister admitted that the abduction and torture of non-Kuwaiti nationals resident in Kuwait was taking place. He promised that the matter would be investigated.

In May 1991 it was announced that 3,700 US troops were to be transferred from Germany to Kuwait, where they would remain until September. The Minister of Defence, Ali Sabah as-Salim as-Sabah, stated that contingents belonging to the multinational force which had liberated Kuwait would remain in the country until June, when they would be replaced by a united Arab force. On 26 May martial law was extended for one month, in view of the prevailing civil unrest in many areas of Kuwait.

In June 1991 the Amir formally decreed that elections to a new National Assembly would be held in October 1992, and he ordered the National Council (which had been elected in a provisional capacity in June 1990) to reconvene on 9 July 1991 in order to prepare for the elections. However, the announcement failed to satisfy the illegal opposition groups, whose members continued to demand the immediate introduction of democracy into Kuwait.

In June 1991 it was reported that 29 of a total of 200 defendants in trials for alleged collaboration during the occupation of Kuwait had been sentenced to death. The sentences were condemned by international human rights organizations as having resulted from the abuse of the judicial system. On 26 June, however, the Government repealed martial law and quashed all of the death sentences which had been imposed in recent trials. Subsequent trials of those accused of collaboration were to be referred to civilian courts.

In late June 1991, with British and US armed forces expected to leave Kuwait in July and September respectively, the Minister of Defence announced that an agreement had been reached for their replacement by a united Arab force, to comprise contingents from the GCC states, Egypt and Syria. In September, however, it was announced that US armed forces would remain in the country for several more months, owing to the slow progress that Kuwait had made in rebuilding its own security forces.

In July 1991 it was estimated that the Kuwaiti population had fallen to about 600,000 since August 1990. The Palestinian population, which had totalled an estimated 400,000 prior to the Iraqi invasion, was estimated to have declined to 150,000. International human rights organizations produced a report critical of the continued deportation of non-Kuwaiti nationals, citing the Fourth Geneva Convention, which prohibits such action against civilians who are justified in fearing persecution for their political or religious beliefs.

THE AFTERMATH OF THE GULF CRISIS

In August 1991 Kuwait protested against the alleged landing of 80 Iraqi troops on Bubiyan island and appealed for further international safeguards. The Government also ordered that the trials of all detainees should be completed within six months and that courts of appeal be established, following international criticism of recent war trials. Further Palestinians were airlifted to Jordan (bringing the total to 3,000 by mid-August), as part of a policy of limiting non-Kuwaitis to less than 50% of the population.

On 19 September 1991 the Kuwaiti Defence Minister signed a 10-year defence pact with the USA. The agreement included provisions for the stockpiling of US military equipment in Kuwait, the use of Kuwaiti ports by US troops, and joint training exercises. US companies were awarded lucrative contracts to 'rebuild' Kuwait. Kuwait was accused of serious violations of human rights over its conduct of trials and deportations in its 'quest . . . to restructure Kuwaiti society in a fashion deemed more reliable politically.' The Amir made visits to the Governments of Saudi Arabia, Oman, the UAE, Qatar, Egypt and Syria to discuss defensive and economic co-operation. In the following month he visited Washington, London and Paris, where he expressed his country's gratitude and proposed closer defence ties. The Government protested at Iraq's lack of co-operation with the UN Iraq–Kuwait Boundary Demarcation Commission and failure to release prisoners. According to estimates, only 80,000 Palestinians (less than 25% of the pre-war total) were still resident in Kuwait, and there was international criticism of official sanctions and aggression against Palestinians, especially those suspected of collaboration.

In January 1992 the Government finally revoked its pre-publication censorship of written (but not broadcast) media. However, it retained the right to close publications printing articles to which it objected. The following month was the deadline for registration for the October elections to the National Assembly. Only first-class Kuwaiti male citizens, who number 82,000 (just under 15% of the adult population), are eligible to vote. The Minister for Justice and Legal Affairs excluded the possibility of foreign observers at the elections. On 11 February Kuwait signed a defence pact (similar to that with the USA) with the UK. A defence pact with France was also signed in August 1992. On 16 April the UN Iraq–Kuwait Boundary Demarcation Commission adjudged that the border should be set 570m to the north of its present position. This had the effect of awarding part of the port of Umm Qasr and several of the Rumaila oilwells to Kuwait. This decision, the validity of which was now rejected by Iraq, seemed certain to provoke further conflict between the two countries.

The first half of 1992 was characterized by an unprecedented breakdown of law and order in Kuwait, with regular shootings and other incidents of violence. Many of these were directed against expatriate communities, especially the Palestinians. On 25 June there was a bomb attack on the home of Sheikh Mubarak Sabah an-Nasser, a member of the ruling family. One man was killed in the incident, which was the culmination of two months of violence. There were widespread allegations that the Government was using the shootings, and the fear of further Iraqi aggression, as a pretext to restrict the press and opposition meetings.

In August 1992, after the Iraqi Government had refused to allow inspections of weapons facilities by the UN (as stipulated by the 1991 cease-fire agreement), the US Government deployed missiles in Kuwait, and some 7,500 US troops participated in a military exercise in the emirate. At the end of the month, the UN Security Council adopted a resolution guaranteeing the new land frontier between Kuwait and Iraq. Demarcation was to take place before the end of the year, and the new border was to come into force on 15 January 1993. In the week leading up to this deadline, however, Iraqi forces made several incursions into Kuwaiti territory. In the course of these they recovered armaments left behind at the end of the Gulf War. At the same time, as US aircraft led air attacks on Iraq, more than 1,000 US troops were dispatched to Kuwait. Following the deadline for enforcement of the border, Iraqi operatives began to dismantle installations on what was now Kuwaiti territory. Nevertheless, the US Government deployed further missiles in Kuwait, and in early February the UN Security Council agreed to strengthen UNIKOM by approving the dispatch of an initial 750-strong multinational contingent of armed troops (in addition to the existing unarmed personnel in the force) to patrol the Kuwaiti border with Iraq. In the same month Kuwait and Russia signed a memorandum of understanding, which, in the following month, led to a defence pact between the two countries.

In March 1993 the UN Iraq-Kuwait Boundary Demarcation Commission announced that it had completed demarcation of the maritime border between the two countries along the median line of the Khor Abdullah waterway. In May Kuwait announced that construction was to begin of a trench, to be protected by mines and a wall of sand, along the entire length of the land border. Allegations by Kuwait of Iraqi violations of the border intensified during the second half of 1993, and there were reports of exchanges of fire in the border region. In mid-November it was reported that some 300 Iraqi civilians had crossed the border in the Umm Qasr region to protest against the digging of the trench, while Iraqi troops were reported to have attacked a border post. These incursions coincided with the commencement of the evacuation, under UN supervision, of Iraqi nationals and property from the Kuwaiti side of the border. In November a 775-strong armed UNIKOM reinforcement was deployed in northern Kuwait, with authorization (under specific circumstances) to use its weapons, to assist the unarmed force already in the demilitarized zone.

In April Kuwaiti authorities announced that 14 men had been arrested on suspicion of plotting to assassinate the former US President, George Bush, who was due to visit the emirate. The suspects, 11 Iraqis and three Kuwaitis, had entered Kuwait across the frontier with Iraq and were allegedly found to be in possession of weapons and explosives. An application for the extradition of the 14 assassination suspects for trial in the USA was rejected by the Kuwaiti Government, and their trial began at Kuwait's State Security Court in early June, although hearings were subsequently adjourned on several occasions. Kuwait refuted reports that the detainees had been subjected to torture, and rejected assertions made by Amnesty International that the accused had been denied adequate access to defence counsel. On 4 June 1994, the State Security Court sentenced six of the defendants to be executed for the conspiracy, and the remainder to terms of imprisonment ranging from six months to 12 years.

In September 1994 the UN Security Council agreed to extend the international sanctions against Iraq for a further period. On 6 October the leader of the UN's Special commission on Iraq (responsible for inspecting the country's weapons) announced that a system for monitoring Iraqi defence industries was ready to begin operating. On the same day, however, there were reports of a large movement of Iraqi forces towards the border with Kuwait, apparently to draw attention to Iraq's demands for speedy action to ease UN sanctions (not due to be considered by the Security Council until mid-November). Over the next few days, the accumulation of Iraqi military units in the border area reached as much as 70,000 troops and 700 tanks. In response to the apparent threat, Kuwait moved about 15,000 troops (most of its army) to protect its side of the border on 9 October, and the USA sent reinforcements (including combat aircraft and warships) to Kuwait and other parts of the Gulf region, to support the 12,000 US troops already stationed there. On 10 October, as the first unit of additional US forces arrived in Kuwait, Iraq announced that it would withdraw its troops northward from their positions near the Kuwaiti border. On 13 October, as a result of mediation by the Russian Minister of Foreign Affairs, the Iraqi Government reportedly offered to comply with the Security Council's demands to recognize the UN-demarcated border with Kuwait and to acknowledge Kuwait's sovereignty. In return, the Russian Government agreed to urge the relaxation of the UN sanctions against Iraq. On the following day the US Secretary of Defence arrived in Kuwait and warned that the USA might take military action against Iraq if heavily armoured Iraqi units were not removed from the area near the Kuwaiti border. He had previously announced that the USA planned to deploy 30,000 troops in the Gulf region even if Iraq continued to withdraw its troops from the Kuwaiti border area. On 15 October the Security Council adopted a resolution demanding that Iraq grant unconditional recognition to Kuwait and that all the Iraqi forces recently transferred to southern Iraq be redeployed to their original positions. Two days later, in an address to the Security Council, Iraq's Deputy Prime Minister, Tareq Aziz, made clear that the Iraqi Government would recognize Kuwait only if there were assurances that, in return, the UN embargo on Iraq's sales of petroleum (other than for the purchase of emergency supplies) would be revoked.

In mid-1993 it was announced that Kuwait was willing to restore relations with Arab states that had supported Iraq during the Gulf crisis, with the exception of Jordan and the leadership of the PLO. Despite the lack of progress towards a wider Gulf-Arab defence force, ministers responsible for defence in the GCC countries, meeting in Abu Dhabi (United Arab Emirates) in November, agreed on the need to strengthen and extend the capabilities of the Peninsula Shield Force (the GCC's Saudi-based rapid deployment force). In the same month Kuwait signed a defence co-operation agreement with Russia, and in December the two countries participated in joint naval exercises in the Gulf. In mid-1994 the Kuwait National Committee for Missing People and Prisoners of War claimed that 625 Kuwaiti nationals were still in detention, or missing in Iraq.

THE ELECTIONS OF 1992 AND BEYOND

A total of 280 candidates, many of them affiliated to one of several quasi-political organizations, contested elections to the new National Assembly on 5 October 1992. The franchise was restricted to about 81,400 male citizens, and groups of women staged protests against their exclusion from the political process. Anti-Government candidates, in particular representatives of Islamic groups, secured 31 of the Assembly's

50 seats, and several of those elected had been members of the legislature dissolved in 1986. The Prime Minister submitted the resignation of his Government, and in the following week named a new administration. The revised Council of Ministers included six members of the new National Assembly. Among these was Ali Ahmad al-Baghli, the new Minister of Oil and a critic of the economic policy of the previous Government; members of the Assembly were also given responsibility for education, Islamic affairs and justice. The ruling family, however, retained control of the important defence, foreign affairs and interior portfolios.

In December 1992 the National Assembly voted to set up a commission of inquiry into the circumstances surrounding the 1990 invasion and Kuwait's preparedness for it. In January 1993, in an attempt to curb financial corruption, the Assembly adopted a law that all state companies and investment organizations must produce accounts for the auditor-general, who must pass them on to a commission of members of the Assembly. The law also provided for harsher penalties for those who misused public funds. In February a delegation of members of the Assembly travelled to London to investigate allegations that millions of dollars had been embezzled via the Kuwait Investment Office (KIO) in London. In March the Assembly voted to rescind a law of secrecy, which had been regarded as a cover for corruption. In the same month there were reports of criticism from members of the Assembly after the Government estimated defence spending for 1992/93 at US $6,200m. Moreover, in July a report of the National Assembly's finance and economy commission was highly critical of the Government's management of overseas investments and its failure to ensure the accountability of officials. In mid-August the Prime Minister submitted a proposal to the National Assembly, according to which future budgets will contain, for the first time, details of purchases of defence equipment. In January 1994 the National Assembly abrogated an earlier decree demanding that, in the case of legal proceedings, government ministers be tried by a special court. In the same month Sheikh Ali al-Khalifah as-Sabah, a former Minister of Finance and of Oil, and Abd al-Fatr al-Bader, a former Chairman of the company, were among five people brought to trial in connection with alleged embezzlement from the Kuwait Oil Tanker Company; hearings were subsequently adjourned until March. In June the assembly approved legislation designed to increase the electorate by amending the 1959 nationality law to allow sons of naturalized Kuwaitis to vote.

On 9 April 1994 the Prime Minister submitted the resignation of his Government, and in the following week named a new administration. The revised Council of Ministers included five new members, the ministers of Defence and of the Interior exchanged portfolios, and a new Minister of Oil was appointed. In a statement issued on 17 April, it was announced that the new Government would persevere with economic reforms including privatization.

Economy

Dr P. T. H. UNWIN

Revised for this edition by the Editor

Kuwait is a relatively small, arid country with a severe climate. Fresh water is scarce, and agriculture extremely limited (only 0.1% of the land is arable). However, the discovery of extremely rich deposits of petroleum transformed the economy and gave the country a high level of material prosperity. Kuwait's population increased from approximately 200,000 in 1957 to 1,697,301 in 1985, of whom only 40% were Kuwaiti nationals, while the remainder were non-Kuwaitis, mainly immigrant workers and their families. At mid-1990 the population was estimated to be 2,062,275, of whom 1,473,054 were non-Kuwaiti nationals (based on the definition of citizenship in use in 1992). Twelve months later the estimated population had fallen to 1.2m., at mid-1992 it was 1,395,000, and

at mid-1993 it had increased to 1,433,205 (of whom 43.3% were Kuwaiti nationals), according to the Ministry of Finance and Planning. The proportion of Kuwaiti nationals in the work-force rose from 12.9% in 1980 to 18.6% in 1985; this expansion was mainly due to an increase in the number of Kuwaiti women in employment. The high number of immigrants gave rise to increasing concern as political tensions in the area increased, and, following the attempted assassination of the Amir in May 1985, there were large-scale deportations, with an estimated 27,000 people being forced to leave the country during 1985 and 1986. The population increase also intensified demands on the infrastructure of the country; for example, total water consumption in Kuwait increased from

255m. gallons in 1954 to 40,306m. gallons in 1987. In August 1987 the Government initiated a five-year plan to reduce the number of expatriates in the Kuwaiti work-force. Taking advantage of the displacement caused by the Iraqi invasion, the Government subsequently announced its intention to restrict the level of non-Kuwaiti residents to less than 50% of the pre-crisis total. In pursuit of this policy, the Government attracted censure for its use of deportation and the treatment of expatriate groups, especially Palestinians, within the country. In March 1994 it was officially reported that a total of 34,000 persons had been deported from Kuwait since June 1991. In 1993 it was reported that non-Kuwaiti workers were being encouraged to leave the emirate on the expiry of their contracts and that unskilled workers would no longer be allowed to invite their families to join them unless they were earning a fixed minimum monthly salary. (For the demographic effects of the Iraqi occupation of Kuwait, see History.)

Kuwait's level of gross national product (GNP) per head was the third highest in the world in 1980 and 1981, exceeded only by that of Qatar and the United Arab Emirates (UAE). This was despite a deliberate reduction in petroleum output. According to estimates by the World Bank, Kuwait's GNP was US $33,150m. (equivalent to $24,160 per head) in 1980 and $30,600m. ($20,900 per head) in 1981 (at 1979–81 prices). By 1986 Kuwait ranked fourth (behind Bermuda, Switzerland and the USA), with a GNP of $29,472m. ($16,600 per head, at average 1984–86 prices). In 1992 Kuwait's GNP (at current prices) was KD 7,009m. (about $23,900m.), equivalent to about KD 5,025 ($17,125) per head. In 1993 current GNP increased to KD 8,594m. ($28,500m.), or KD 5,995 ($19,875) per head. Since 1980 Kuwait's overall gross domestic product (GDP) has fluctuated, falling over the period 1980–89 by 0.7% per year. After 1984, the decline of the economy became more pronounced, in particular after the collapse of petroleum prices in 1986. GDP, at current prices, was KD 5,203m. in 1986, and increased to KD 6,233m. in 1987, as a result of a rise in petroleum revenues. GDP was KD 5,773m. in 1988 and KD 7,143m. in 1989, before falling to KD 5,307m. in 1990 and KD 3,130m. in 1991. In 1992, however, GDP at current prices was KD 5,518m., and in 1993 it rose to KD 7,344m. The value of petroleum exports was KD 2,767.7m. in 1985, falling to KD 1,853.4m. in 1986. From the end of 1988 there was an upturn in the Kuwaiti economy, due to the cease-fire in the Iran–Iraq War and an increase in oil prices. Total exports rose to KD 3,378m. in 1989. Following the Iraqi occupation, exports increased from KD 248.6m. in 1991 to KD 1,967.5m. in 1992, and to KD 3,180.5m. in 1993.

In 1992 Kuwait's proven recoverable reserves of petroleum were 94,000m. barrels. This situation afforded Kuwait some insulation against the effects of falling petroleum prices, as production levels could be increased significantly without greatly affecting overall reserves. After 1972 (the year of Kuwait's peak petroleum production of 1,201.6m. barrels), output fluctuated, rising from 760.8m. barrels in 1975 to 911.2m. barrels in 1979, accounting for 4.5% of the world's oil output, and falling to 607m. barrels in 1980, 3% of world oil output. The oil glut and the implementation of OPEC quota allocations led to lower prices and fluctuating production after 1982. Oil production fell from 1.78m. barrels per day (b/d) in 1980 to 820,000 b/d in 1982, with the oil sector's contribution to GDP falling from KD 5,062m. to KD 2,767m. over the same period. In common with most OPEC members, Kuwait tended to exceed its petroleum production quota. In 1987 Kuwait's production (excluding output from the Neutral/Partitioned Zone, shared with Saudi Arabia) averaged 1.1m. b/d, compared with 1.2m. b/d in 1986. In early 1988 Kuwait's production levels were only marginally above its OPEC quota, but during the summer they rose steeply again, to more than 2m. b/d in October and November. Average production for 1988 was 1.4m. b/d. In November Kuwait's quota was increased to 1,037,000 b/d, but almost twice this amount was being produced. During the first half of 1989 Kuwait consistently exceeded its OPEC quota. At the beginning of June the oil ministers of OPEC member states convened and agreed on a quota increase of 5.8% for Kuwait. Kuwait rejected this allocation on the basis that it did not take into consideration the situation in early 1989, when, in terms of percentage,

Kuwait had made the most substantial sacrifices throughout the 1980s in OPEC. Kuwait requested a quota of 1.35m. b/d, but was allocated 1.12m. b/d under a pro-rata distribution of the 18.5m. b/d 'ceiling' then in force, which was judged to be sufficient to stabilize prices. The then Kuwaiti Minister of Oil, Sheikh Ali al-Khalifa as-Sabah, presented a claim for an amendment to the final OPEC resolution, excluding Kuwait from the accepted production quotas. The production 'ceiling' was raised by 1m. b/d to 19.5m. b/d.

In September 1989 the previous pro-rata format was reintroduced, within a new 'ceiling' of 20.5m. b/d. Kuwait nevertheless rejected its quota of 1.149m. b/d for late 1989. Overproduction persisted, and by the end of 1989 total OPEC output amounted to approximately 24m. b/d. At the following OPEC meeting, held in late November, Kuwait was authorized to produce 6.82% of the organization's entire output, compared with 5.61% previously.

Kuwait's production of crude petroleum averaged 1.34m. b/d in 1988, rising by 16.25% to 1.6m. b/d in 1989. In August 1990 Kuwait's OPEC production quota was fixed at 1.5m. b/d, but, owing to the invasion by Iraq, output averaged 1.065m. b/d for that year. In the aftermath of the Gulf crisis, Kuwait argued persistently within OPEC for a rise in the production 'ceiling' and an increase in the country's quota, in order to offset losses and to finance reconstruction.

Income from Kuwait's petroleum sales has mainly been channelled to five areas: industrial diversification, the development of substantial social service provision, the creation of the Reserve Fund for Future Generations (RFFG), overseas investment, and aid to poorer countries through the Kuwait Fund for Arab Economic Development (KFAED). In 1982 income from overseas investment yielded, for the first time, a higher revenue than petroleum sales. During the mid-1980s the domestic financial and banking sector was in crisis, and a government report in November 1985 revealed that the domestic economy was at its lowest ebb since the early 1950s. Nevertheless, Kuwait's diversification of industry and its considerable foreign investments enabled it to withstand a period of economic uncertainty.

Following the liberation of Kuwait from the Iraqi occupation in February 1991, it was estimated that some 800 of the country's 950 oil wells had been damaged, some 600 having been set alight by Iraqi troops shortly before their retreat. The rehabilitation of the petroleum sector became the Government's highest economic priority, but it was expected that all the burning wells would not be extinguished before early 1992. According to official reports, the cost of damage to the country's petroleum installations—including the value of lost petroleum revenues, extinguishing the well fires and repairing the wells—may amount to $40,000m.–$50,000m. By June 1991 about 140 of the burning wells had been 'capped', and by late July onshore production of crude petroleum had resumed at a level 115,000 b/d, while offshore production from fields in the Neutral/Partitioned Zone was estimated at 70,000 b/d. Exports of petroleum had also resumed by late July.

By the end of 1991 total production had reached 500,000 b/d and was increasing at a monthly rate of 100,000 b/d. By mid-1992 production had exceeded 1m. b/d, and was projected to reach 1.5m. by 1993 and 2m. thereafter. In June 1993 a meeting of OPEC oil ministers was obliged to exempt Kuwait from an agreement on production quotas, effectively allowing Kuwait to increase production to 2m. b/d in the third quarter of that year. In September, at the following OPEC meeting, this allocation was confirmed for a further period of six months. Kuwait, however, rejected suggestions that it was seriously jeopardizing its reserves by forcing such a rapid rise in output. At the same time, the major work of repairing Kuwait's infrastructure had been completed. By mid-1994 it was reported that Kuwait's current capacity had reached 2.4m. b/d, and that the emirate was likely to seek an increase in its quota to 2.2m. b/d, equal to that of the United Arab Emirates, at the next OPEC meeting.

In 1994 it was reported that the Kuwaiti economy had fully recovered from the effects of the Gulf crisis and rebuilding, and that the Government did not envisage further international borrowing. The economy had grown by 8% in 1993, as oil production increased, and inflation remained stable at

0.6% per year. The major difficulty facing the emirate was a budget deficit that was equivalent to 19% of GDP in 1993. To remedy this, the Government proposed a programme of privatization over five years, and established a privatization office. It was anticipated that candidates for privatization would be found in the telecommunications sector, the 'downstream' petroleum industry, and public utilities. A reduction in the level of government spending on state benefits was also forecast.

PETROLEUM

In 1938 the Kuwait Oil Company (KOC), operated jointly by the Anglo-Persian Oil Company (now the British Petroleum Company PLC) and the Gulf Oil Corporation, discovered a large oilfield at Burgan, about 40 km south of the town of Kuwait. The onset of the Second World War delayed development until 1945. In 1948, however, 6m. metric tons of crude petroleum were produced, although the main impetus to development was the Abadan affair in 1951, which effectively denied Iranian production to the rest of the world for three years. By 1956 Kuwait's annual production had increased to 54m. tons, and was then the largest in the Middle East. Further fields were discovered, notably at Raudhatain, north of Kuwait, and annual production had reached over 148m. tons by 1972. To handle this vast production, a huge tanker port was constructed at Mina al-Ahmadi, not far from the Burgan field. From a terminal about 15 km off shore, the port can now handle the largest tankers. Kuwait was the first Arab petroleum-producing nation to achieve complete control of its own output, buying out Gulf Oil and BP in March 1975 for approximately £32m.

Kuwait was the first OPEC state to restrict petroleum production for reasons of conservation. Until December 1976, when Kuwait (together with 10 other OPEC countries) decided to raise petroleum prices by 10% (compared with a 5% increase by Saudi Arabia and the UAE), the country was generally regarded as moderate with regard to oil pricing. Since then, Kuwait has become increasingly 'hawkish', and during 1979 and 1980 the country was one of the first to set still higher prices every time that Saudi Arabia raised its prices in an attempt to achieve some kind of parity within OPEC.

The petroleum industry was reorganized in 1980, when the Kuwait Petroleum Corporation (KPC) was established to co-ordinate the four companies involved: the KOC, the Kuwait National Petroleum Company (KNPC), the Petrochemical Industries Company (PIC), and the Kuwait Oil Tanker Company (KOTC). This has led to the centralization of oil sales and has improved Kuwait's market competitiveness. The KPC is the twelfth largest petroleum company in the world. In addition to its oil refineries in Kuwait, it owns three refineries abroad (in the Netherlands, Denmark and Italy), with a capacity of 210,000 b/d. The sale of KPC stocks of oil was vital in supporting the Kuwaiti community in exile during the Iraqi occupation. In 1987/88 profits were KD 120.7m., and in 1988/89 profits reached a record KD 341m. In 1989/90 profits were KD 136.5m. In 1990/91 KPC's budgeted profits were KD 177.5m.

There are three oil refineries in Kuwait: one at Mina al-Ahmadi, built in 1946, which had a capacity of 288,000 b/d in January 1988; one at Mina Abdullah, built in 1958, with a capacity of 75,000 b/d; and one at Shuaiba, completed in 1969, with a capacity of 195,000 b/d. Expansion of Mina al-Ahmadi was completed in February 1986, and a programme of modernization at Mina Abdullah, costing $2,100m., was completed in February 1989. This project increased the refinery's capacity to 200,000 b/d, and raised total capacity in Kuwait to 670,000 b/d, mainly in high-quality products for export. Plans by KPC subsidiaries to expand and upgrade production prior to the Iraqi invasion are now being revised, but the Government has committed itself to increasing Kuwait's petroleum assets as part of its reconstruction and development strategy. The Mina al-Ahmadi refinery had resumed operations by June 1991, but the Mina Abdullah and Shuaiba refineries were reported to be more seriously damaged. By May 1992 local refining capacity exceeded 300,000 b/d, still less than half of the pre-invasion level. The projected target was 450,000 b/d by mid-1993, and restoration of full capacity by 1995. The $47m. contract for

repairs to the refineries was awarded to a US company, Foster Wheeler. Refined petroleum products accounted for an estimated 65% of total petroleum exports in 1987, and 71% in 1988.

A further development in Kuwait's petroleum industry has been the expansion of 'downstream' interests overseas, which can process about 450,000 b/d. In 1981 the Kuwait Foreign Petroleum Exploration Co (KUFPEC) was established as a new subsidiary of KPC. Later that year, it purchased a 22.5% interest in a 22,000-sq km concession in Morocco. KPC purchased the Santa Fe International Corporation, allowing the country to secure wider rights and facilities in exploration, and to develop 'downstream' facilities. Through KUFPEC and Santa Fe, Kuwait now has interests in concessions in Australia, China, Egypt, Oman, the North Sea and the USA. In 1984 an agreement was signed for an offshore concession in Bahrain, and in February 1985 the USA reversed a two-year-old ruling by allowing Kuwait to acquire mineral leases on federal land.

Since 1981, Kuwait has been expanding facilities for the distribution, marketing and retail of its refined products. A joint venture to supply petroleum products to the Pacific area was agreed with Pacific Resources of Honolulu, Hawaii, in that year. In 1982 a 24% stake in a West German petrochemicals company, Hoechst, was acquired, and in 1983 KPC purchased Gulf Oil's network of petrol stations in Belgium, the Netherlands and Luxembourg, distribution outlets in Sweden and Denmark, and the refineries at Rotterdam (75,000 b/d), in the Netherlands, and at Skaelskor (85,000 b/d), in Denmark. In 1984 KPC acquired Gulf Oil's Italian interests, including a 75% share of the Bertonico refinery, near Sarni, and 1,500 service stations. In August 1985 the Belgian subsidiary of KPC acquired a further 53 retail service stations from Elf, bringing its total to more than 400. Kuwait Petroleum International (KPI), a subsidiary of KPC, was established at the end of 1983 to manage the newly-acquired distribution outlets (see Oil in the Middle East and North Africa, p. 119). Already successful in Scandinavia and other parts of Europe, KPI is seeking to extend its operations to Asia. In 1986 KPC adopted a new trade name, Q8, for its petroleum products distributed in Europe, and in March 1987 KPI acquired the UK marketing branch of Ultramar, Golden Eagle Petroleum, thereby bringing its total number of petrol stations in Europe to 4,800. In 1988 Kuwait Petrolia Italia, a KPC subsidiary, enlarged the company's portfolio by purchasing the lubricants divisions of Italy's Raffineria Olii Lubrificante and Feruzzi-Montedison, despite their operating losses in 1987. KPC's 'downstream' overseas expansion programme continued during the occupation. KPC is studying the possibility of investing in a refinery in Hungary with a capacity of 150,000 b/d. In 1991 an agreement was signed with KPC to provide Hungary with 17 Q8 petrol stations. This agreement is in accordance with KPC's plans to expand its East European and Far Eastern operations.

NATURAL GAS

In November 1976 the Amir inaugurated the KOC's Gas Project. This involves the construction of extensive facilities to make use of the gas associated with the output of crude petroleum for the production of liquefied natural gas (LNG) and such derivatives as propane and butane. A three-train plant for the production of liquefied petroleum gas (LPG), together with a gas-gathering system (which came into operation in 1979), collects the gas, which is produced together with petroleum, at well-heads, removes LPG components and natural gasoline, then treats and distributes them to fuel users and to pressure-maintenance facilities.

The plant, built at a cost of over US $1,000m., has a capacity of 2.2m. metric tons of LPG per year (60% propane, 40% butane) at a crude oil production rate of 1.5m. b/d. It was originally designed to take crude oil production of 3m. b/d. However, Kuwait's production of gas is limited by the absence of any known reserves independent of petroleum. Owing to the association of gas with petroleum, much of the gas produced is flared to facilitate oil production, or reinjected, to maximize the production of petroleum by maintaining pressure in the reservoir. Gross gas production (including gas flared or re-injected) rose to 7,200m. cu m, in 1987, and commercial production to 6,450m. cu m. However, flaring declined from 9,330m. cu m in 1973 to 700m. cu m in 1987. The LPG plant has been forced to operate at substantially below capacity in recent years, exporting 1.05m. metric tons of products in 1982/83 (compared with 1.7m. tons per year previously). In 1985 one in three of the trains at the plant was operating at a level below capacity. Although exploration for further resources of gas is under way, only crude petroleum, with its associated gas, has been discovered to date.

Other projects which suffered as a result of decreased production of gas include the expansion of an ammonia and urea plant, where the annual capacity had been increased to about 900,000 tons of ammonia and various by-products. The lack of feedstock, however, meant that in early 1984 the plant was operating at about 50% of capacity, and certain lines had been suspended. A gas-gathering grid to produce 2,500m. cu m per year from the Neutral/Partitioned Zone was due for completion by 1989. Gross gas production in 1989 was 9,130m. cu m. In 1992 gas reserves totalled 1,500,000m. cu m.

OTHER INDUSTRIES

Between 1974 and 1984 the manufacturing sector in Kuwait registered an average annual rate of growth of 6.4%, but in 1985 a decline of 4.2% was recorded. An average annual rate of decline of 0.2% was recorded between 1980 and 1989. In 1992 manufacturing contributed an estimated 14.4% of Kuwait's GDP. The Government has done much to foster other industries in order to diversify the economy and to provide alternative sources of employment. During the period of the 1976–81 Five-Year Plan, three industrial zones were established: at Shuaiba, Shuwaikh and Ahmadi. However, oil-related activities still contribute the overwhelming proportion of Kuwait's total industrial output. Despite efforts to diversify, petroleum's share of GDP rose from 61.1% in 1977 to 69.9% in 1980, before falling to around 50% in 1983. Since then GDP has remained at approximately the same level: according to provisional figures, in 1992 the petroleum sector contributed an estimated KD 2,720m. of GDP, and the non-petroleum sector KD 3,732m., of which the manufacturing sector contributed about 25%. Two fertilizer manufacturers were set up in the mid-1960s and, with a new fertilizer plant at Shuaiba (owned by KNPC), Kuwait could have a potential production capacity of 1.65m. tons per year, mainly in the form of urea and ammonia products. The profitability of these products is, however, proving difficult to maintain because of technical problems and a weak market. In addition, at the beginning of 1986 the EC imposed an 11% tariff on imports of urea from Kuwait after it had exceeded its duty-free allocation. Two new projects were approved in 1985: the construction of a 150,000-ton capacity salt plant in Shuaiba, and a chlorine plant with an annual capacity of 27,000 tons. In 1993 Union Carbide of the USA agreed to form a joint-venture with PIC of Kuwait to develop a major petrochemical complex (including a 650,000 tons-per-year ethylene cracker), at an estimated cost of KD 700m., in Shuaiba.

Unlike its neighbours, Kuwait has hesitated to undertake heavy industrial projects, fearing both for their viability and the excess of foreign labour which they involve. It has favoured, instead, joint projects with Bahrain, Saudi Arabia and other Gulf countries, including agreements with the Gulf Aluminium Rolling Company and Gulf Petrochemical Industries Co to establish aluminium, ammonia and methanol plants in Bahrain. At the end of 1982 a joint venture was also set up between PIC and the Tunisian state-owned Maghrebia Chemical Industries to build a 1,000 ton-per-day diammonium phosphate fertilizer plant in Kuwait, at a cost of KD 16m. Towards the end of 1987, KPC also agreed to take a majority shareholding in Bahrain's ailing Iron and Steel Company (see chapter on Bahrain). In early 1989 Kuwait Petrochemicals Industries Co announced a joint venture, with Union Carbide of the USA, for the production of polypropylene.

Several factories supply consumer goods, such as processed food and soft drinks, and there is a flour milling company. Kuwait's major branch of manufacturing, however, has been the production of building materials and related projects such as aluminium extrusion. The construction industry is considerable, owing to the vast amount of infrastructural development

since the early 1970s. During the 1970s major projects were carried out by foreign contractors, but in February 1981 the National Housing Authority (NHA) announced that 80% of future housing contracts would be awarded to local firms. In other sectors of construction, however, foreign companies continued to predominate. Between 1974 and 1989 the NHA recorded 27,000 housing units built. An indication of Kuwait's heavy reliance on foreign labour is the 2.4-km bridge from Subiya to Bubiyan island, completed in 1982 by Chinese migrant workers. The economic recession of the mid-1980s damaged the construction industry considerably, and the collapse of petroleum prices in 1986 exacerbated the situation. In 1988, however, there was a distinct recovery, particularly in the private residential sector, where expansion was stimulated by the availability of cheap bank credits, as well as the completion of highway improvements in suburban Kuwait. The NHA's budget for 1988/89 was KD 142.3m. of which KD 124.3m. was allocated to construction and maintenance work. The Al-Qurain complex, which will comprise 12,415 dwelling units, was under construction prior to the Iraqi invasion. In 1989 work began on the Amiri Diwan, a government facility which was to cost an estimated KD 65m.–80m. and was completed in 1992. In the aftermath of the Iraqi occupation, the Kuwaiti Government worked with the international construction companies with which it was familiar, in particular US companies, in order to rebuild Kuwait's infrastructure. In mid-1944 the Government approved the construction of two new border cities, at Subiya and Khiran, in order to alleviate the state's housing shortage. The cities were to be built by private-sector companies, and were scheduled for completion in 1998.

Many of the smaller industrial projects have been promoted by the Industrial Bank of Kuwait (IBK), founded in 1973, which is 49% government-owned. By 1984, however, four leading commercial banks had combined with IBK to form a more specific concern, the Industrial Investment Company (IIC), to make new investments. During 1985 the Government took a further step in assisting local industry when it announced the introduction of protectionist trade measures for local industries which satisfy three criteria. Such industries should meet at least 40% of domestic requirements; should have a substantial added value and should contribute to national income; and the consumer should not be affected by any inflationary results of tariff protection.

In accordance with its aim of diversifying the economy, Kuwait has entered the international hotel industry at an accelerated rate. The country has been estimated to own or part-own approximately 60 hotels. Following the occupation of Kuwait by Iraq, it was reported that a number of hotels had been destroyed or partially damaged. In 1988 Kuwait began to consolidate its assets by collecting them under one group, namely the Kuwait Hotels Co (KHC). The company was founded in 1962, soon after independence, and its main objectives were to assume control of all hotel management duties, and to take charge of all financial holdings. KHC will initially concentrate on Kuwait and other Arab countries, before venturing into the wider international market. Substantial staff-training will be a determining factor of the Government's intention to have all Kuwait-owned hotels managed by KHC in the next 10–15 years.

PUBLIC UTILITIES AND TRANSPORT

All of the industrial developments referred to above, and the demographic growth associated with the necessary immigration, have required great increases in power generation. By the end of 1987 the five power stations, at Shuwaikh, Shuaiba North, Shuaiba South, Doha East and Doha West, had a total installed capacity of 5,230 MW. A sixth power station, with an installed capacity of 2,511 MW, came into full production at az-Zour South in 1988. In mid-1990 the Ministry of Electricity and Water decided to provide desalination units for the Subiyah thermal power station. Two 6m.-gallons-per-day units are required for the 2,400-MW station. Subiya's first unit began operation in 1992. Substantial damage to Kuwait's power stations was reported as a result of the Iraqi occupation; az-Zour South was the least damaged power station. By mid-1993 installed generating capacity remained 30% below the pre-invasion level of 7,100 MW, although Shuaiba North was the only station not to have resumed operations. The increasingly harsh economic climate led the Government to introduce higher electricity rates in April 1986. This was the first increase since 1966 and meant that consumers would pay 27% of actual power costs, compared with their previous payment of about 6%.

Increased water demands have been met by the distillation plants at Shuwaikh, Shuaiba North, Shuaiba South, Doha East and Doha West, which, in 1986, gave Kuwait a total installed capacity of 35,286m. gallons per year. The rapid increase in water demand was reflected in the rise in average daily water consumption, from 3.8m. gallons in 1960, to 18.2m. gallons in 1970, 64.1m. gallons in 1980, and 110.4m. gallons in 1987. Traditionally, Kuwait had concentrated on distillation methods for obtaining fresh water, but at the end of 1984 the Doha reverse osmosis plant was inaugurated, with an annual capacity of 220m. gallons. The pumping of fresh water from underground aquifers declined from 700m. gallons in 1970 to 126m. gallons in 1980, and to 21m. gallons in 1987. The pumping of brackish water, however, increased from 11,319m. gallons in 1980 to 24,070m. gallons in 1987. The fresh water and brackish water systems are piped through separate networks, and the latter is used primarily for blending with distilled water, for irrigation, watering livestock, construction and in the household. Oil released into the Persian (Arabian) Gulf by Iraq caused considerable damage to Kuwait's desalination facilities.

The harbour of Kuwait City was completely reconstructed to accommodate the surge in imports after 1973. In 1992 the Government considered a proposal for a Free Trade Zone near the port, with a view to restoring Kuwait's role as a re-export centre. A new international airport was opened in 1980, and there is a national airline with an international service, Kuwait Airways Corpn (KAC). In 1990 KAC owned 19 aircraft, flying to 41 destinations. Passenger traffic declined in the mid-1980s, but revived in 1988, when record profits were achieved by the corporation. KAC has announced its intention to purchase 15 aircraft, valued at $1,900m., and three Boeing 747-400 airliners from the then Airbus Industrie consortium. KAC lost two-thirds of its fleet during the Iraqi occupation, and KAC airliners were held by Iran, which demanded reparation for their upkeep. The airport infrastructure was also seriously damaged, but by 1993 the refurbished airport was operating normally. The six Kuwaiti airbuses were finally returned to Kuwait at the end of July 1992.

The Kuwait Oil Tanker Co (KOTC) was fully nationalized in 1979. The oil ministry then started to include the use of Kuwaiti tankers in the terms of sale of its crude petroleum. In 1983 the displacement of Kuwait's merchant fleet was 2,542,490 gross tons, and this included 23 oil tankers and 47 general cargo ships, as well as a considerable number of smaller vessels. In January 1987 the company signed a contract, valued at $131m., with the Samsung Heavy Industries Corporation of the Republic of (South) Korea for the purchase of six new product carriers, two of 120,000 dwt and four of 35,000 dwt, to be delivered in 1988 and 1989. In early 1990 KOTC commissioned South Korea to supply a third 280,000-dwt very large crude carrier (VLCC) by 1992. Similarly, the company has finalized a contract with Japan for the supply of two liquefied gas carriers, each with a capacity of 78,000 cu m, under a plan to enlarge its fleet of 28 oil tankers and 6 gas carriers, in order to enhance its position in the world tanker market. Kuwait's two main container ports are at Shuwaikh and Shuaiba. Despite the devastation caused by the Iraqi forces during their occupation of Kuwait, the Shuaiba port resumed operations in March 1991. Both commercial ports have been expanded, with Shuaiba's container terminal opening in 1982. However, the recession meant that plans for expansion at Shuwaikh had to be deferred. The 1990–95 Ports Public Authority programme contained plans to expand both ports. During 1981 the conflict between Iraq and Iran led to greatly increased trade between Iraq and Kuwait, with ports becoming severely congested, but in 1983 exports to Iraq fell by 73.3%. This was largely due to a cessation of cement sales, but it nevertheless caused a reappraisal of plans for port expansion. Worsening relations with Iran had a serious influ-

ence on Kuwaiti shipping, and between October 1986 and April 1987, 15 Kuwaiti ships were attacked in the Gulf. As a result of these attacks, Kuwaiti ports were given similar status to those of Iran and Iraq for insurance purposes, and 11 Kuwaiti tankers were re-registered under the US and British flags. Since the ending of hostilities, most of these have been reflagged to Kuwait. The Government undertook a $2,000m. expressway road development (despite a recorded decline of 6.3% in traffic in 1983), which was completed in 1988. Plans were announced for a new KD 300m. causeway to link Shuwaikh with Bubiyan Island.

In recent years telecommunications have become increasingly important in Kuwait, and in 1987 construction work had begun on a 13-storey building for use as a telecommunications headquarters. The number of telephone lines totalled 362,000 in 1988. In mid-1989 plans were being made to install new telephone networks in Mishref and South Subiya, and the city area and Shuwaikh. It was reported that two 10,000-line telephone exchanges, at South Subiya and Umm al-Hannan, were destroyed—as were 1,000-line exchanges at Failaka, Abdali and Wafra—during the Iraqi occupation. The estimated cost of repairing damage was $400m. In 1994 it was reported that the telecommunications sector would be the first to be privatized under the new Government's programme.

AGRICULTURE AND FISHERIES

Owing to the scarcity of water in Kuwait, little grain is produced, and, as a result, most of the country's food has to be imported. In 1983 the total cultivable area was estimated at 150,000 ha, of which fruit and vegetables occupied 1,200. In 1992 agriculture contributed only about 0.3% of Kuwait's GDP. The principal agricultural crops are tomatoes, melons, onions and dates.

A five-year development plan for agriculture, initiated in 1982, was intended to increase the area under vegetables to 3,500 ha by 1986. This would increase overall vegetable production from 42,000 tons in 1981—supplying 24% of vegetable requirements—to 98,000 tons, which would provide 40% of projected demand. Experiments with hydroponics gave Kuwait the confidence to set these optimistic targets, and the Public Authority for Agriculture and Fish Resources agreed to continue to subsidize agricultural products during 1986 and 1987. A considerable amount was also invested in the development of methods of using treated effluent for irrigation purposes.

The Government has also encouraged animal husbandry, the main activity of the bedouin before the development of the oilfields. Subsidies were introduced in 1983 to assist farmers using artesian wells and greenhouses, and for the owners of small fishing boats. The Government also owned a 36-ha experimental farm, and in the private sector the poultry and dairy industries had increased, as had the cultivation of dates, production of which totalled 1,000 tons in 1990. In 1985 production of milk rose to 30,000 tons, compared with 9,000 tons in 1980. In 1992 production was estimated at 8,000 tons. Government figures for livestock indicate dramatic increases in the numbers of sheep and poultry, with sheep rising from 21,000 head in 1979 to 253,000 in 1981, and poultry from 1,432,000 in 1979 to 12,028,000 in 1981. In 1992 there were an estimated total of 5,000 cattle, 297,000 sheep, 1,000 goats and 1m. poultry in Kuwait. Kuwait also invested in livestock overseas, but it still needed to import considerable numbers of livestock. In 1985 the Kuwait Livestock Transport and Trading Company imported approximately 3m. sheep from Australia. By 1988 the country's 65 poultry farms were reported to be producing 30m. chickens and 200m. eggs per year. In 1989 plans were announced to develop self-sufficiency in food production by expanding irrigated farms and agricultural facilities in the north of Kuwait.

Fishing, particularly of prawns and shrimps, is also widely practised. Four fishing companies were amalgamated into Kuwait United Fisheries in 1972. A 20-year plan to develop the industry, at an estimated cost of $1m., was announced in 1987, when local production was sufficient to satisfy only 25% of domestic demand. The Public Authority for Agriculture and Fish Resources was allocated KD 8.6m. for construction projects in its 1988/89 budget. The total catch in 1992 was 7,689 tons, compared with 10,796 tons in 1988.

FOREIGN TRADE AND BALANCE OF PAYMENTS

Kuwait's total exports were valued at KD 3,631.5m. in 1984, compared with KD 5,527.3m. in 1980. The value of exports of crude petroleum and petroleum products in 1985 was KD 2,767.7m. The total value of imports was KD 1,805.3m. in 1985, declining to KD 1,661.2m. in 1986 and to KD 1,530.7m. in 1987. In 1985 the total value of exports was KD 3,185.1m. According to the IMF, total export earnings declined to KD 2,105.0m. in 1986 and were KD 2,304.4m. in 1987. The total fell to KD 2,166.2m. in 1988, but rose to KD 3,378.0m. in 1989. Of the latter total, petroleum and petroleum products provided KD 3,064.9m. (90.7%). In 1990, the year of the Iraqi invasion, Kuwait's exports were reduced to KD 2,031.4m. (of which petroleum accounted for KD 1,842.0m.), and in 1991 the total slumped to KD 248.6m. Kuwait was liberated from Iraqi occupation at the end of February in that year, but the country's petroleum-production facilities were severely damaged, and it was not possible to resume exports at pre-war levels. In 1992, however, export revenue recovered to KD 1,967.5m., with the petroleum sector providing KD 1,824.9m. (92.8% of the total). In 1993 total export earnings increased to KD 3,180.5m., of which petroleum accounted for KD 3,017.9m.

The total value of imports reached KD 1,714.2m. in 1988, advancing to KD 1,849.4m. in 1989. According to the IMF, Kuwait's imports fell to KD 1,145.7m. in 1990, but rose to KD 1,353.7m. in 1991 and to KD 2,201.2m. in 1992. Imports declined to KD 1,986.0m. in 1993. The most important commodity group in Kuwait's imports is usually machinery and transport equipment (which, according to provisional figures, accounted for 43.8% of total imports in 1992), followed by miscellanous manufactured articles (18.6% in 1992). In 1992 Kuwait's main source of imports was the USA, which supplied 20.4% of total imports, Japan supplied 12.7%, Germany 9.2% and the UK 6.1%. In 1987, 16.8% of Kuwait's exports were delivered to Japan, 8.9% to Italy and 7.9% to the Netherlands. Details concerning the destination of Kuwait's petroleum exports are not available for recent years. In 1992 the main customers for the country's non-petroleum exports (totalling KD 106.2m.) included Saudi Arabia (which took 25.8% of the total) and the United Arab Emirates (25.4%). In 1992 KPC signed an agreement with the National Iranian Oil Co to supply 700,000 tons of petroleum products per year. This was the first such agreement since the outbreak of the Iran–Iraq war in 1980. In February Kuwait took delivery of the first of 40 F-18 aircraft from the USA. Agreements were also concluded for the purchase of tanks, armoured vehicles and more aircraft from the allies. In mid-1992 Kuwait purchased a number of *Ammon* missiles from Egypt.

The current surplus on the balance of payments was US $4,543m. in 1987, increasing to $5,028m. in 1988 and to $9,688m. in 1989. The surplus declined to $4,042m. in 1990, when trade was disrupted by the Iraqi invasion and occupation. In 1991 Kuwait paid huge amounts to the countries that contributed to ending the occupation, resulting in a current deficit of $25,891m. In 1992 a deficit of $873m. was recorded. The rise in 1988 was a result of increased income from investments, although the sharp decline in world petroleum prices caused a reduction in the visible trade surplus from $3,449m. in 1987 to $2,261m. in 1988. The surplus rose to $5,872m. in 1989, but was reduced to $3,540m. in 1990. In 1991 Kuwait registered a visible trade deficit of $3,226m., but this was reversed in 1992, when a surplus of $85m. was recorded. The trade surplus increased further in 1993.

BANKING AND FINANCE

Following the Iraqi invasion of Kuwait, all Kuwaiti bank deposits were 'frozen', paralysing the operations of the country's banks. The Bank of England allowed individuals and organizations from Kuwait to operate in Britain, but all of the banks had to seek permission from the Bank of England to pay out Kuwait-controlled assets. Kuwait's largest bank, the National Bank of Kuwait (NBK), was instrumental in efforts to resume operations. With the support of the Kuwait Investment

Office (KIO), it was able to 'unfreeze' most of its blocked accounts, and to restore its liquidity position, by quickly selling US $2,000m. of its loan portfolio at little or no discount. The NBK played a central role in stabilizing the position of the other Kuwaiti banks. By early 1991 the Commercial Bank of Kuwait, the Al-Ahli Bank, the Industrial Bank of Kuwait (IBK), the Gulf Bank, the Kuwait Real Estate Bank, the Bank of Kuwait and the Middle East and Burgan Bank had resumed operations outside Kuwait and Iraq, as had Kuwait's main investment banks, the Kuwaiti Investment Co (KIC), the Kuwaiti Foreign Trading, Contracting and Investing Co (KFT-CIC) and the Kuwait International Investment Co (KIIC).

Following the liberation of Kuwait, the Kuwaiti banks resumed domestic operations, but NBK was the only bank able to participate in the reconstruction process. The Government encouraged rationalization and the merger of some of the numerous domestic banks. By mid-1994, however, little progress had been made in this direction. In March 1991 some branches of banks began to reopen, mainly to distribute the Government's cash grant to Kuwaiti citizens who had remained in the country during the occupation. Depositors were initially limited to cash withdrawals of $14,000 per month until the end of June. By August all currency restrictions had been removed. In April 1991 an Amiri decree instructed the banks to cancel debts totalling $4,900m., and so cleared the debts of 180,000 people. As a result, many local bad debts that had been incurred in the stock market crisis of the mid-1980s were cancelled. On 20 May 1992 it was announced that the Government was to buy the entire domestic loan portfolio of the domestic banking system, covering credits to residents worth $20,400m. In the first half of 1993 there was intense debate between the Government and the National Assembly over the terms under which the loans should be repaid. As long as the issue remained unresolved, Kuwaiti banks were unwilling to approve loans, and investment outside the petroleum industry was very limited. This had the effect of delaying full economic recovery by means of a revitalized public sector. Throughout August 1993 a joint parliamentary committee deliberated on a proposed draft law to establish a debt resettlement programme. At the end of the month the National Assembly approved a loan whereby the 9,546 corporate and individual borrowers were allowed six months in which to choose one of two alternatives for repayment.

In 1979 the Central Bank of Kuwait imposed tighter controls on the banking sector and demanded a significant reduction in overdrafts. Despite this, the banking sector continued to flourish in the early 1980s, with a 20% rise in total assets during 1982. However, the collapse of the Souk al-Manakh in 1982 (see below), the uncertainties caused by the Iran–Iraq War, and the problems associated with the falling price of oil led to severe difficulties for Kuwait's banking sector in the mid-1980s. In 1983 the banks' total assets rose by only 9.3%, and the decline in the commercial banking sector also led to the introduction of a two-tier exchange rate between April and August 1984. The foreign exchange market was effectively closed in June, when the Central Bank halted sales of US dollars, except for genuine commercial transactions.

In 1985 the banks faced a burgeoning debt crisis. Court cases involving bank debtors rose from 169 in 1981 to 437 in 1984, and in May 1985 bad debts held by commercial banks amounted to approximately KD 2,200m. ($7,200m.). At the end of 1984 the Central Bank asked for full documentation on all commercial bank loans in excess of KD 250,000. By the end of 1985 its survey of the country's financial institutions revealed that, as of 11 September 1985, Kuwait's banks had gross claims against foreign banks totalling KD 1,534m. ($5,192m.), a sum which exceeded their corresponding obligations by KD 93m. The survey also revealed that Kuwait's banks had lent a total of KD 275.9m. to their own directors. At the end of 1985 three banks recorded zero net profits, and the NBK was the only bank to record an increase (of 11.1%) in net profits over the previous year's figure. The dissolution of the National Assembly was widely regarded as providing an opportunity for seeking a solution to the debt crisis, and a series of measures, approved by the Council of Ministers in August 1986, facilitated a 'rescue programme' whereby debtors should repay as much as they could afford, and the

Government would pay the remainder of the debt. In 1989 the majority of the commercial banks in Kuwait remained dependent on this scheme for debt-restructuring. A range of other radical changes in the policy of the Central Bank were made between 1987 and 1989, promoting the further revival of the banking sector.

In 1987 Kuwait's largest bank, the NBK, had total assets of KD 3,017m. and estimated profits of KD 26.7m. The remaining banks all recorded an increase in assets in 1987, with the exception of the Central Bank, the Gulf Bank and the IBK. In 1988 the NBK increased profits by 15.9%, to KD 30.9m., while total assets grew by 15%, to KD 3,476m. Total assets of the Central Bank fell to KD 1,443m. at the end of the year, from KD 1,649m. in December 1987. A fall of 63% in foreign assets was partially offset by an increase in holdings of local bonds and public debt instruments. By 1989 the NBK had increased its total assets by 10.1%, to KD 3,867m., and had recorded a profit of KD 35m., representing an increase of 11.4% in comparison with the previous year. The other principal banks of Kuwait all reported an increase in assets and profits in 1989. NBK was the only commercial bank able to issue balance sheet figures for 1990. It announced that its total assets, excluding amounts booked through its Kuwait offices, were $5,630m. The assets of the NBK at the end of 1993 totalled KD 3,267m.

In July 1989 it was announced that legislation was being drafted to permit local banks and investment companies to manage money on behalf of non-Kuwaiti clients. Prior to the Iraqi invasion, there were plans to develop Kuwait as an international, rather than a regional, financial centre. Such plans have been severely disrupted. KIC incurred losses of $195m. over the period 1983–85, and, following a small recovery in 1986, foreign stocks were adversely affected by the world-wide decline in share prices in October 1987. Its total assets rose dramatically in 1988, from KD 9.8m. to KD 60.9m. KFTCIC announced losses of $213m. in the same year, bringing total losses to $613m. over four years. A capital injection in November 1988 helped to improve the situation. KIIC has been involved in the property market, and recent operations include a $40m. investment in real estate in Portugal, through the Kuwait-Portugal Fund.

CAPITAL MARKET

A significant, though (by international standards) still minor, capital market has been developed in Kuwait through the activities of the leading investment companies and the IBK, and with the encouragement of the Government. An active bond market developed after 1973, mostly for international borrowers from the Third World and Eastern Europe. The Central Bank then closed the new issue market in November 1979 as part of its efforts to boost liquidity in Kuwait's money market, but by July 1981 the Kuwaiti dinar international bond market had reopened. Despite the issue of a number of new bonds, the market was to close again in September 1982. It reopened in June 1983 with a KD 5m. floating rate note bond for the United Bank of Kuwait's subsidiary, UBK Finance, and there followed a KD 14m. two-tranche bond offer for KFTCIC in November. However, following the collapse of the stock market (see below), the bond market also lost its appeal, and in 1985 and 1986 only solitary domestic bonds were issued. In the last quarter of 1987 and the first quarter of 1988 the Government issued a series of bonds and treasury bills, in an attempt to finance the budget deficit. During 1987 the Central Bank's total assets fell by 31%, to KD 1,458.7m., mainly as a result of a decline in foreign deposits, which decreased by 44%, to KD 681.8m., by the end of the year. In May 1988 the Council of Ministers approved a measure allowing citizens of all GCC member states to purchase shares on the Kuwaiti stock exchange. (Previously only Kuwaiti citizens had been permitted to buy shares on the exchange.) In 1992 the Kuwaiti stock exchange was opened to international firms for the first time.

In 1952 Kuwait had established what was, prior to the Iraqi invasion of August 1990, the world's twelfth largest stock exchange. The amount of capital holders seeking investment outlets in Kuwait, and the innate entrepreneurial spirit of locals, generally pushed the prices of shares far above their real value. In April 1978, in an attempt to stem this unhealthy trend, the Government sanctioned the reduction in nominal value of shares to one dinar, a move which resulted in a split of share values to 10%–13% of their current value. This broadened the base of the market. In 1981 247m. shares worth US $6,854m. were traded in Kuwait's stock market, representing a 72% increase by volume, and a 47% increase by value, over 1980's figures.

Alongside the official market, an unofficial stock market, the Souk al-Manakh, also developed. After 1978 many Kuwaitis had invested in Iraq, and, as a result of the Iran-Iraq War, a severe cash-flow crisis emerged in Kuwait. In 1982 the liquidity shortage which this caused was particularly severe for the Souk al-Manakh. The unofficial market had been based on the use of post-dated cheques and the hope of continuously rising share prices. Then in September 1982 the system collapsed, as smaller creditors prematurely presented their post-dated cheques (perfectly legal under Kuwaiti law) at a time when many dealers were unable to pay. The collapse of the Souk al-Manakh initiated a major crisis in Kuwait's financial system, the impact of which lasted for several years.

Government measures to alleviate the crisis involved the immediate formation of the Kuwait Clearing Company, to register and process all cheques involved, and the establishment of a KD 500m. fund to protect, and pay, the smaller debtors whose investors were bankrupt. In August 1983 the Government urged the settlement of debts at the market price at the time of transaction, and set a maximum premium of 25% on post-dated cheques. Disagreement over the handling of the crisis led to the resignation of the Minister of Finance, Abd al-Latif Yousuf al-Hamad. In October the Government appointed an arbitration panel to revalue the debts of the 17 leading dealers in the Souk al-Manakh. These accounted for about US $78,000m., or 82% of the estimated total of outstanding debts at the time of the crisis, and the dealers' assets were valued at between 20% and 30% of their liabilities. Since then, a new investment company has been established, with a capital of KD 300m. (in which the Government has a 40% share), to convert the debtors' non-liquid assets into payment for the creditors. In April 1984 the Council of Ministers announced further financial measures to resolve the crisis, including the division of assets into three categories. Bonds to repay creditors were issued in July, and, of the 254 people referred to the receivership, 88 were declared bankrupt, three restored their solvency and 163 reached agreements with their creditors.

In August 1984 the official stock exchange moved to new premises, and its permanent floor officially opened in April 1985. The Souk al-Manakh stock market was closed on 1 November 1984, and trading in shares was restricted to the official stock exchange and to a parallel market which it operated. To avoid a repetition of the Souk al-Manakh crisis, measures were introduced to limit the activities of brokers on the official market. Before being allowed on the floor, brokers had to pay a registration fee and provide a guarantee for KD 1m., while a percentage of brokers' commissions had to be paid to the exchange. By mid-January 1985 creditors who had been owed money by Souk al-Manakh defaulters had received cash and bonds totalling KD 759m., accounting for about three-quarters of the net debts. At the end of 1987, however, 17% of the debts resulting from the collapse of the Souk al-Manakh remained outstanding.

The Government bore the brunt of the crisis and was forced to inject large sums into the banking system to restore liquidity. However, its share-supporting operation after the collapse of the Souk al-Manakh, when it spent KD 755m. on shares worth KD 230m. at the beginning of 1986, led to losses of KD 528m. ($1,820m.).

At the end of November 1985, the Minister of Finance and Economy made the following recommendations: 33 companies should be dissolved; a number of the remaining 47 companies should be merged; from March 1986 the KIC was to purchase the companies that closed, on behalf of the Government; and companies registered in the Gulf that fell outside the jurisdiction of Kuwait were urged to comply with the Government's recommendations. These measures appeared to be necessary, owing to the fact that 24 of the 36 companies that had closed, and were under consideration for purchase by the Government, had incurred losses exceeding 50% of the paid-up capital invested in them. It was estimated that by mid-1986 this scheme had cost the Government approximately KD 121m. In May 1989 it was reported that stock market activity was disappointing, and measures to deregulate the stock market to some extent were to be introduced before the end of the year. It was hoped that a reduction in restrictions would encourage investors. In May it was announced that the Souk al-Manakh stock exchange was to be re-opened in June, to allow trading in companies that had failed to meet the minimum capital requirements of the official stock exchange. Hopes for a recovery in the stock market were shattered by the invasion of Kuwait by Iraq in August 1990.

PUBLIC FINANCE

The cumulative costs of the Gulf conflict (1990–91) to the Kuwaiti Government will inevitably increase its budget deficits. By the end of July 1991 the cost to Kuwait of paying the expenses of Kuwaitis living abroad during the Iraqi occupation, and of financing 'Operation Desert Storm', had increased to $22,000m., which had been drawn from its reserves with further expenditure expected. A further $6,000m.–$7,000m. has been spent since liberation on stabilization measures, such as the cancellation of personal debts and cash grants to nationals who remained in Kuwait during the Iraqi occupation. While there have been some sales of overseas investments, the Kuwaiti Government has stated that it has no intention of making large-scale sales of investments in order to save revenues. Nevertheless, it has been estimated that 25% of Kuwait's foreign assets, which total more than $100,000m., were liquidated during and after the invasion. In mid-1993 it was reported that the value of Kuwait's overseas investments had more than halved in the previous three years. However, Kuwait has begun discussions with international banks with regard to a syndicated loan of $2,000m.–$3,000m. Kuwait's intention to request a loan was formally announced in July 1991, when the Ministry of Finance was authorized to borrow $35,000m., of which $10,000m. was to fulfil short-term commitments. It was envisaged that only in the long term would there be a revived effort to reduce the relative level of public expenditure, in particular in the social services sector. At the end of 1991 a $5,500m. Euroloan was announced, as well as export credit facilities, worth the same amount, with the USA, Japan, the UK, the Netherlands and France.

Kuwait's public finances suffered, owing to declining oil revenues in the latter part of the 1980s, and the Government sought ways of reducing expenditure. In 1982, as a result of a decrease in subsidies, the price of petrol doubled, and in 1983 the supply of free school meals and uniforms was withdrawn. Charges for other formerly free services, such as health, were introduced, and the price of electricity was increased. The 1985/86 budget contained the first projected spending cut in Kuwait's recent history. Expenditure and revenue were both lower than anticipated, totalling KD 2,871.5m. and KD 2,343.1m., respectively, resulting in a deficit of KD 528.4m. The 1987/88 budget deficit was only KD 554m., as expenditure for the year was 20% below the projected figure, while overproduction of petroleum led to a 30% rise in revenues, to KD 2,252m. In September 1987 the Council of Ministers approved legislation enabling the Government to borrow as much as KD 1,400m. over 10 years through direct loans, treasury bills and medium- and long-term treasury bonds, to finance its budget deficit. However, the limit of KD 1,400m. was reached by June 1988 and was raised in March 1989 to KD 3,000m. The 1988/89 budget envisaged revenue of KD 2,054m. and expenditure of KD 3,400.2m., resulting in a deficit of KD 1,346.2m., which was to be financed by drawing on the general reserve fund. In March 1989 it was announced that a separate defence budget, of $5,500m. over the next 10 years, would be drawn from the general reserve. In 1991 the US Department of Defense awarded the McDonnell Douglas Corpn a contract valued at $153m. for advance acquisition work to be undertaken on 40 F-18 fighter aircraft for Kuwait. The 1989/90 budget envisaged a 4.4% increase in revenue, to KD 2,230.5m., of which 87.1% was to be provided by the petroleum sector, and a rise in expenditure to

KD 3,326m., resulting in a deficit of KD 1,095.5m., 18.6% less than in the previous year. The 1990/91 budget resulted in a deficit of KD 1,469m., and the deficit for 1991/92 was more than $18,600m., even allowing for the negotiation of a higher quota with OPEC. In 1992/93 the budget deficit decreased to KD 1,718.3m. Projected total revenue for 1993/94 was KD 2,713m., and expenditure KD 3,867.8m. It was subsequently reported, however, that the actual budget deficit for 1993/94 totalled KD 1,400m. In March 1994 the finance and economy committee of the National Assembly approved KD 3,500m. in extraordinary defence spending over the 12 years from 1992 to 2004. At the same time an increase in the budget deficit to KD 2,106m. was forecast, although much of this was accounted for by the inclusion in the budget for the first time of allocations for arms procurement.

INVESTMENT

Kuwait's main priority for spending its income from petroleum has been the development of its own economy and the provision, through the investment of surplus funds, of an income for its citizens in the future when the oil-wells have run dry. In the mid-1970s, in addition to the general reserve, the Government established a Reserve Fund for Future Generations (RFFG), to which at least 10% of total revenue must be added annually, by law, and which was not intended to be used until the year 2001. Since the beginning of the 1984/85 fiscal year the National Investment Authority has begun to assume the management of all of Kuwait's reserves. By the end of 1986 it was clear that Kuwait's investments were not performing as well as had been expected. Income from investments declined to KD 1,154m. in 1985, from a total of KD 1,288.6m. in 1984. The interest on investments held by the RFFG totalled KD 747m. in 1985, which was equivalent to a return of 6.9%. During 1985 it was reported that, of its total reserves of KD 23,027.1m., Kuwait held 44% in non-Arab countries. The RFFG was estimated at KD 14,000m. before the world-wide collapse of prices on stock markets in October 1987. The 1988/89 budget allocated KD 205.4m. to the RFFG.

Kuwait had a budget surplus for some years before 1973 and therefore developed an investment strategy considerably earlier than other petroleum-producing countries did. This strategy was implemented when Kuwait established the Kuwait Investment Office (KIO) in the 1950s, with the aim of providing for its future generations by investing its oil profits. The KIO in London, a branch of the Ministry of Finance, handles much of the nation's investment in Europe and elsewhere. In 1979 the KIO also started to buy small interests in leading Japanese electronics companies. Many of Kuwait's investments are in the USA, and involve almost every one of the 500 leading US companies. Kuwait also has some major real estate projects there. Exceptions to Kuwait's traditional preference for small shares in foreign companies include its outright purchase of the St Martin's Property Corpn of the UK, its purchase of a 25% holding in Daimler-Benz of Germany, a 51% share in the USA's Korf Industries, and a 30% share in a Canadian copper-molybdenum mine. During 1983 it was announced that the Kuwait Real Estate Investment Consortium, together with the Arab General Investment Co of Dubai and other private investors, were to establish an offshore investment company in the Cayman Islands, with a capital of $25m., in order to invest mainly in advanced technology industries in the USA. However, in June 1985 the Kuwait Real Estate Investment Consortium defaulted on a $60m. syndicated loan, signed in 1981, and had to be rescued by the KIO, which bought KD 30m. of its assets and increased its capital by 50%. In 1984 the KIO acquired one-fifth of the Hong Leong Co in Hong Kong. Investments made in 1986 included the purchase of a share of 5% in the Banco Central of Spain through a Spanish holding company, Cartera Central.

Investment income from abroad increased to $8,074m. in 1986, overtaking income from petroleum for the first time. In 1987 the KIO acquired further considerable shareholdings in Europe: in particular, it acquired a major stake in BP, and by August 1988 had obtained 21.68% of BP's total shares. In October 1988, after a report by the Monopolies and Mergers Commission in Britain, the KIO was forced to reduce its interest in BP to 9.9%. This disposal produced a profit of

$700m. for the KIO, as the BP management raised its buy-back price for the shares in response to hostile bids from rival oil companies. Nevertheless, the KIO remained the largest single shareholder in BP. By October 1987 the KIO had accumulated investments in Spain with a value of $2,400m., and, as a result of its acquisition of 37% of Torras Hostench, it established itself as a major force in Spain's chemicals industry; it also acquired 35% of Explosivos Rio Tinto (ERT) and further shares in several Spanish media groups. In 1988 ERT was merged with Cros to form a new company, Ercros, with capital of $225m. ERT has been listed as unacceptable by the Arab League Boycott Office, causing some embarrassment to the KIO. The KIO has also purchased Ebro, a large Spanish food manufacturer, bringing total investment in Spain to $1,000m. in only four years. Other recent investments by the KIO include the purchase of a 51% share in First Capital Corpn, a Singapore property developer, and a 10% interest in Avimo Singapore, a manufacturer of military optics. In June 1989 the KIO disclosed a 5.2% share in the UK's Midland Bank. In early 1989 the KIO sold its interest in Cartera Central, which included shares in three Spanish banks, for $360m., following considerable public pressure in Spain.

In 1993 the dealings of the KIO were the subject of an inquiry by a commission comprising members of the new National Assembly. It was alleged that officials of the KIO had lost $5,000m. in Spain since 1986, of which some $1,000m. had been embezzled through the collapsed Grupo Torras company. In mid-1993 it was reported that legal proceedings were being prepared against fomer KIO officials in the UK and Spain. In July a report of the National Assembly's finance and economy commission was critical of the Government for failing to ensure the accountability of KIO officials. A series of legislative measures in 1993 attempted to ensure greater accountability from state investment organizations and to increase penalties for the misuse of public funds.

Kuwaiti private investment is substantial. It is predominantly in real estate and high-yielding equities. Although this investment is concentrated in the USA, Europe and Japan, Kuwaitis have shown an interest in investment in other non-Arab countries in Asia, Africa and South America, as well as in the Arab world. In June 1988 a three-member committee was formed by the Ministry of Finance to assess the country's future investment policy, and to deliver its reports directly to the Amir. From August 1990 until July 1991, Kuwait's sole sources of income were earnings from its international financial investments and profits from Kuwait Petroleum International, which operates Kuwaiti petroleum companies in Europe and Asia. It was estimated that Kuwait's international investments in August 1990 were worth as much as $100,000m., comprising the RFFG and the State General Reserve. The rate of return on these investments was estimated at 5% per year. Although the Kuwaiti Government refused to disclose any details concerning the sale of assets

to fund its activities during the 1990–91 Gulf crisis, it was estimated that by late 1990 proceeds totalled more than $5,000m. By mid-1993 it was estimated that the value of Kuwait's overseas investments had more than halved since August 1990. Following the liberation of Kuwait, the Government indicated that it did not envisage the sale of large-scale investments, especially of important strategic assets such as its interests in Daimler-Benz (14%), Hoechst (20%), Metallgesellschaft (20%), Hogg Robinson (11%), Midland Bank UK (10.2%) and BP. In mid-1994 Kuwait submitted a claim of almost $41,000m. to the UN Compensation Committee for losses incurred by the KIA during the Iraqi invasion. The claim was part of a total of $94,800m. worth of compensation claims made by Kuwait by the end of June 1994, with further submissions expected.

After its own development, Kuwait's next priority is that of the rest of the Arab and Islamic world, and then of the Third World in general. It pioneered foreign aid in the Arab world, setting up the Kuwait Fund for Arab Economic Development (KFAED) in 1961. Kuwait later raised the KFAED's capital considerably, and extended operations to Africa and Asia. Its capital in 1989 was KD 970m. The country also helped set up the Arab Fund for Economic and Social Development in Kuwait, and it is a member of various Arab, Islamic and OPEC aid organizations, notably the Islamic Development Bank, the Arab Bank for Economic Development in Africa (BADEA) and the OPEC Fund for International Development. It has also contributed to IMF and World Bank facilities.

Kuwait's total foreign aid, which was substantially more than that given on projected aid by the KFAED, ranged between about 8% and 15% of GNP during the second half of the 1970s. As a proportion of GNP, Kuwait gave more aid than any other country, at 4.86% of GNP in 1982. Overall, between 1962 and 1984 it was estimated that the KFAED disbursed 280 loans, valued at US $4,233m. A further $230m. were disbursed in 1985 to part-finance 20 schemes in 18 countries. However, Kuwait's official contribution to development assistance declined over the period 1984–87. It stood at $325m. in 1987. The KFAED made 22 loans, worth KD 69.7m. ($249m.), in 1987/88, with a grant element of between 27.5% and 61.4%. In January 1989 Burkina Faso received a loan of $23m. for a dam project, and in March a loan of $25m. was provided for the development of fisheries in Kerala state, India. Kuwait has pledged $3,684m., through the US-organized Gulf Financial Crisis Co-ordination Group (GFCCF), to assist those countries (in particular Egypt, Jordan and Turkey) which have been most severely affected by the economic repercussions of the 1990–91 Gulf crisis. It is believed, however, that levels of Kuwaiti foreign aid will decrease during the post-liberation period of reconstruction. The political stance that was adopted by countries during the Gulf crisis is likely to condition the levels of foreign aid to be granted to those countries in the future.

Statistical Survey

Source (unless otherwise stated): Central Statistical Office, Ministry of Planning, POB 26188, 13122 Safat, Kuwait City; tel. 2428200; telex 22468; fax 2430464.

Note: Unless otherwise indicated, data refer to the State of Kuwait as constituted at 1 August 1990, prior to the Iraqi invasion and annexation of the territory and its subsequent liberation. Furthermore, no account has been taken of the increase in the area of Kuwait as a result of the adjustment to the border with Iraq that came into force on 15 January 1993.

Area and Population

AREA, POPULATION AND DENSITY

Area (sq km)	17,818*
Population (census results)†	
21 April 1980	1,357,952
20–21 April 1985	
Males	965,297
Females	732,004
Total	1,697,301
Population (official estimates at mid-year)†	
1992	1,395,000
1993	1,433,205
1994	1,620,086
Density (per sq km) at mid-1994	90.9

* 6,880 sq miles.

† Figures include Kuwaiti nationals abroad. Based on the definition of citizenship in use in 1992, the total population at the 1985 census included 474,200 Kuwaiti nationals (240,068 males; 234,132 females). On the same basis, the estimated population at mid-1990 comprised 589,221 Kuwaitis (295,039 males; 294,182 females) and 1,473,054 non-Kuwaitis (839,675 males; 633,379 females). At mid-1993 the estimated population included 955,948 non-Kuwaitis.

GOVERNORATES (population at 1985 census)

Governorate	Area (sq km)*	Population	Capital
Capital . .	199.8	241,356	Kuwait City
Hawalli . .	} 368.4	493,127	Hawalli
Farwaniya . .		420,020	Farwaniya
Al-Jahra . .	11,230.2	241,285	Jahra
Al-Ahmadi . .	5,119.6	301,513	Ahmadi City

* Excluding the islands of Bubiyan and Warba (combined area 900 sq km).

PRINCIPAL TOWNS (population at 1985 census)

Kuwait City		South Kheetan	.	69,256
(capital) . .	44,335	Farwaniya .	.	68,701
Salmiya . .	153,369	Sabahiya. .	.	60,787
Hawalli . .	145,126	Fahaheel. .	.	50,081
Jaleeb al-Shuyukh	114,771	Abraq Kheetan	.	45,120
Jahra . .	111,222			

BIRTHS, MARRIAGES AND DEATHS

	Registered live births		Registered marriages		Registered deaths	
	Number	Rate (per 1,000)	Number	Rate (per 1,000)	Number	Rate (per 1,000)
1986 .	53,845	30.1	9,829	5.5	4,390	2.5
1987*	51,983	27.7	9,842	5.3	4,287	2.3
1988*	53,080	27.1	10,283	5.3	4,315	2.3
1989*	51,296	25.9	11,051	5.4	4,498	2.3
1990†	12,358	n.a.	n.a.	n.a.	1,177	n.a.
1991*	17,207	n.a.	4,241	n.a.	3,372	n.a.
1992*	34,204	24.5	4,616	3.3	3,138	2.2
1993*	36,235	25.3	5,144	3.6	3,311	2.3

* Provisional.

† Figures relate only to the first quarter of year.

Expectation of life (UN estimates, years at birth, 1985–90): 74.5 (males 72.6; females 76.3) (Source: UN, *World Population Prospects: The 1992 Revision*).

ECONOMICALLY ACTIVE POPULATION
(sample survey, persons aged 15 years and over, March 1988)*

	Males	Females	Total
Agriculture, hunting and fishing	9,122	132	9,254
Mining and quarrying . . .	6,329	201	6,530
Manufacturing. . . .	53,231	1,433	54,664
Electricity, gas and water . .	7,527	86	7,613
Construction	112,926	1,608	114,534
Trade and restaurants. . .	79,278	4,057	83,335
Transport, storage and communications . . .	35,119	2,653	37,772
Finance, insurance, real estate and business services . .	17,780	3,782	21,562
Other services (including defence).	224,328	159,256	383,584
Total	545,640	173,208	718,848
Kuwaitis	81,270	31,689	112,959
Non-Kuwaitis	464,370	141,519	605,889

* Figures exclude persons seeking work for the first time, totalling 11,067 (males 6,930; females 4,137), but include other unemployed persons.

Agriculture

PRINCIPAL CROPS (FAO estimates, '000 metric tons)

	1989	1990	1992*
Tomatoes	40	34	3
Onions (dry)	25	15	10
Melons	7	5	4
Dates	1	1	n.a.

* Figures for 1991 are not available.

Source: FAO, *Production Yearbook*.

LIVESTOCK (FAO estimates, '000 head, year ending September)

	1989	1990	1992*
Cattle	28	25	5
Camels	8	6	1
Sheep	260	200	297
Goats	32	25	1

Poultry (FAO estimates, million): 30 in 1989; 21 in 1990; 1 in 1992*.
* Figures for 1991 are not available.
Source: FAO, *Production Yearbook*.

LIVESTOCK PRODUCTS
(FAO estimates, '000 metric tons)

	1990	1991	1992
Beef and veal	2	n.a.	n.a.
Mutton and lamb	27	n.a.	3
Poultry meat	27	n.a.	1
Cows' milk	25	n.a.	8
Goats' milk	1	n.a.	n.a.
Hen eggs	8.0	0.1	0.6
Sheep skins	9.6	0.0	0.9

Source: FAO, *Production Yearbook*.

Fishing

('000 metric tons, live weight)

	1990*	1991*	1992
Fishes	2.7	1.2	4.2
Shrimps and prawns	1.8	0.8	3.5
Total catch	4.5	2.0	7.7

* FAO estimates (Source: FAO, *Yearbook of Fishery Statistics*).

Mining*

('000 metric tons, unless otherwise indicated)

	1989	1990	1991
Crude petroleum	74,051	59,550	9,766
Natural gas (petajoules)	212	204	19
Salt (refined)	73	30	n.a.

* Including an equal share of production with Saudi Arabia from the Neutral/Partitioned Zone.
Source: UN, *Industrial Statistics Yearbook*.

Industry

SELECTED PRODUCTS
('000 metric tons, unless otherwise stated)

	1989	1990	1991
Wheat flour	153	n.a.	n.a.
Sulphur (by-product)*	475	300	300
Chlorine	16	n.a.	n.a.
Caustic soda (Sodium hydroxide)	18	n.a.	n.a.
Nitrogenous fertilizers‡	386	204	n.a.
Jet fuels§	1,510	1,110	600
Motor spirit (petrol)§	2,510	1,880	900
Naphthas§	3,800	3,200	126
Kerosene§	1,890	1,700	600
Distillate fuel oils§	9,900	7,300	900
Residual fuel oils§	14,100	12,000	2,000
Petroleum bitumen (asphalt)§	160	110	70
Liquefied petroleum gas†§	2,710	2,410	100
Quicklime*	65	50	60
Cement	1,108	800	299†
Electric energy (million kWh)§	21,179	20,610	9,100

* Data from the US Bureau of Mines.
† Provisional or estimated figure(s).
‡ Production in terms of nitrogen.
§ Including an equal share of production with Saudi Arabia from the Neutral/Partitioned Zone.

Source: mainly UN, *Industrial Statistics Yearbook*.

1992 ('000 metric tons): Wheat flour 105; Chlorine 1.1; Caustic soda 12.2.
1993 ('000 metric tons): Wheat flour 127; Chlorine 9.2; Caustic soda 15.5)

Finance

CURRENCY AND EXCHANGE RATES
Monetary Units
    1,000 fils = 10 dirhams = 1 Kuwaiti dinar (KD).

Sterling and Dollar Equivalents (31 May 1994)
    £1 sterling = 449.8 fils;
    US $1 = 297.5 fils;
    100 Kuwaiti dinars = £222.32 = $336.10.

Average Exchange Rate (US $ per KD)
    1989   3.4049
    1992*   3.4087
    1993   3.3147

* Figures for 1990 and 1991 are not available (see below).

Note: During the Iraqi occupation of Kuwait, between August 1990 and February 1991, the Kuwaiti dinar was replaced (at par) by the Iraqi dinar. As a result, Kuwaiti coins and notes were withdrawn from circulation. In March 1991, following the liberation of Kuwait, the Kuwaiti dinar was reintroduced, with the exchange rate set at the same level as on 1 August 1990, namely US $1 = 287.5 fils (KD1 = $3.4782).

GENERAL BUDGET
(estimates, KD million, year ending 30 June)*

Revenue	1991/92	1992/93	1993/94
Oil revenues	495.9	2,000.3	2,419.8
Taxes on non-oil companies	2.8	5.0	8.0
Custom duties and fees	0.1	45.6	50.1
Service charges	134.0	146.6	202.7
Electricity and water	12.6	46.9	52.3
Transport and communications	32.9	49.7	77.5
Total revenue (incl. others)	647.4	2,218.0	2,713.0

Expenditure	1991/92	1992/93	1993/94
Ministries and departments			
Foreign affairs . . .	31.0	41.8	33.9
Finance	3,985.8	1,632.8	1,265.3
Oil	3.4	9.1	35.1
Defence	476.3	493.0	478.8
Interior	214.5	282.3	266.9
Education . . .	279.2	301.2	320.6
Information . . .	59.3	61.2	58.9
Public health . . .	207.5	241.7	273.6
Social affairs and labour .	78.2	87.2	48.0
Electricity and water .	207.1	302.5	252.7
Communications . .	72.9	86.7	86.4
Public works . .	56.0	130.7	107.0
National Guards . . .	43.8	51.8	55.8
Complementary credit .	n.a.	n.a.	371.5
Total expenditure (incl. others)	6,115.0	3,936.3	3,867.8

* Figures exclude investment income.

1994/95 (estimates, KD million, year ending 30 June): Total revenue 2,537; (of which Oil revenues 2,234); Total expenditure 4,303.

CENTRAL BANK RESERVES (US $ million at 31 December)

	1991	1992	1993
Gold*	111.5	104.7	106.2
IMF special drawing rights .	183.5	179.2	67.4
Reserve position in IMF .	158.9	132.9	230.5
Foreign exchange . . .	3,066.6	4,834.8	3,916.3
Total	3,520.5	5,251.6	4,320.3

* National valuation of gold reserves (2,539,000 troy ounces in each year).

Source: IMF, *International Financial Statistics*.

MONEY SUPPLY (KD million at 31 December)

	1991	1992	1993
Currency outside banks . .	446.0	389.7	365.7
Demand deposits at commercial banks	784.0	652.6	731.3
Total money	1,230.0	1,042.3	1,097.0

Source: IMF, *International Financial Statistics*.

COST OF LIVING
(Consumer Price Index, Kuwait City; base: 1978 = 100)

	1989	1990	1991
Food	128.4	144.2	158.9
Beverages and tobacco . .	177.8	201.9	226.7
Housing	169.6	172.4	175.4
Clothing and footwear .	158.9	180.7	198.3
Education and medical care .	193.9	205.3	222.9
All items (incl. others) . .	151.8	166.7	181.8

NATIONAL ACCOUNTS
(KD million at current prices, provisional figures)
Expenditure on the Gross Domestic Product

	1990	1991	1992
Government final consumption expenditure	2,074	5,209	2,408
Private final consumption expenditure	2,834	2,132	2,517
Increase in stocks	−21	156	130
Gross fixed capital formation .	957	1,616	2,141
Total domestic expenditure .	5,844	9,113	7,196
Exports of goods and services	2,382	489	2,280
Less Imports of goods and services	2,978	6,418	3,109
GDP in purchasers' values .	5,247	3,184	6,367

Gross Domestic Product by Economic Activity

	1990	1991	1992
Agriculture, hunting, forestry and fishing	32	8	22
Mining and quarrying . . .	1,978	448	2,720
Manufacturing	628	226	932
Electricity, gas and water* .	−38	−100	−95
Construction	109	192	127
Trade, restaurants and hotels .	402	528	489
Transport, storage and communications . . .	198	87	128
Finance, insurance, real estate and business services . .	728	628	707
Community, social and personal services . . .	1,251	1,245	1,422
Sub-total	5,288	3,262	6,452
Import duties	35	19	38
Less Imputed bank service charges	76	97	123
Total	5,247	3,184	6,367

* Value added is negative because of the inclusion of expenditure on fuel in the cost of production.

BALANCE OF PAYMENTS (US $ million)

	1990	1991	1992
Merchandise exports f.o.b. .	6,989	869	6,650
Merchandise imports f.o.b. .	−3,449	−4,095	−6,565
Trade balance . . .	3,540	−3,226	85
Exports of services . .	1,324	985	1,477
Imports of services . .	−3,359	−4,943	−3,796
Other income received . .	8,223	5,822	3,936
Other income paid . .	−735	−654	−638
Private unrequited transfers (net)	−770	−503	−870
Official unrequited transfers (net)	−4,181	−23,372	−1,067
Current balance . . .	4,042	−25,891	−873
Direct investment (net) . .	−10	−7	−532
Portfolio investment (net) .	62	−450	317
Other capital (net) . .	725	39,167	14,525
Net errors and omissions .	−5,716	−11,652	−11,562
Overall balance . . .	−897	1,167	1,875

Source: IMF, *International Financial Statistics*.

External Trade

PRINCIPAL COMMODITIES (distribution by SITC, KD '000)*

Imports c.i.f.	1990	1991	1992
Food and live animals . .	146,112	89,427	253,485
Live animals	19,863	13,780	35,922
Cereals and cereal preparations . . .	16,626	8,400	32,774
Fruit and vegetables . .	41,265	17,852	64,714
Chemicals	71,308	35,868	107,040
Basic manufactures . .	215,807	108,281	364,027
Paper, paperboard and manufactures . .	21,588	11,974	28,765
Textile yarn, fabrics, etc. . .	49,423	31,238	88,580
Non-metallic mineral manufactures . . .	38,946	11,477	39,167
Iron and steel . . .	46,034	15,876	102,531
Machinery and transport equipment . . .	321,526	578,123	933,148
Non-electric machinery . .	n.a.	n.a.	n.a.
Electrical machinery, apparatus, etc. .	n.a.	n.a.	n.a.
Transport equipment . .	152,052	326,030	473,345
Miscellaneous manufactured articles	165,684	144,803	395,675
Clothing (excl. footwear) .	60,178	33,765	90,497
Scientific instruments, watches, etc. . . .	22,469	29,066	54,607
Total (incl. others) . . .	847,346	992,346	2,129,238

* Figures are provisional or incomplete. Total imports (KD million) were: 1,145.7 in 1990; 1,353.3 in 1991; 2,201.2 in 1992; 1,986.0 in 1993 (Source: IMF, *International Financial Statistics*).

Exports f.o.b.	1983	1984	1985
Mineral fuels, lubricants, etc.	2,938,207	3,256,939	2,845,178
Petroleum and petroleum products .	2,837,440	3,179,648	2,767,692
Crude petroleum . . .	1,578,171	1,920,958	n.a.
Refined petroleum products	1,259,269	1,258,690	n.a.
Gas (natural and manufactured) . . .	100,752	77,287	77,486
Chemicals	50,385	68,409	53,219
Basic manufactures . .	122,136	86,757	76,036
Machinery and transport equipment	144,547	125,487	130,895
Transport equipment . .	95,580	80,108	78,024
Total (incl. others) . . .	3,363,757	3,631,470	3,185,068

1986 (KD million): Petroleum and petroleum products 1,853.4; Chemicals 47.8; Basic manufactures 56.2; Machinery and transport equipment 90.9; Total (incl. others) 2,105.0.
1987 (KD million): Petroleum and petroleum products 2,096.7; Chemicals 51.0; Basic manufactures 39.1; Machinery and transport equipment 56.7; Total (incl. others) 2,304.4.
1988 (KD million): Petroleum and petroleum products 1,908.4; Chemicals 64.7; Basic manufactures 55.7; Machinery and transport equipment 71.5; Total (incl. others) 2,166.2.
1989 (KD million): Petroleum and petroleum products 3,064.9; Chemicals 83.5; Basic manufactures 63.0; Machinery and transport equipment 84.6; Total (incl. others) 3,378.0.
1990 (KD million): Petroleum and petroleum products 1,842.0; Chemicals 37.5; Basic manufactures 29.7; Machinery and transport equipment 46.3; Total (incl. others) 2,031.4.
1991 (KD million): Machinery and transport equipment 43.8; Total (incl. others) 248.6.
1992 (KD million): Petroleum and petroleum products 1,824.9; Chemicals 16.6; Basic manufactures 16.7; Machinery and transport equipment 50.6; Total (incl. others) 1,967.5.
1993 (KD million): Petroleum and petroleum products 3,017.9; Total (incl. others) 3,180.5.

PRINCIPAL TRADING PARTNERS (KD '000)*

Imports c.i.f.	1990	1991	1992
Australia	15,698	10,537	30,376
China, People's Republic . .	31,068	10,153	36,467
France	32,661	25,183	108,624
Germany	87,778	90,566	196,247
India	21,128	12,945	49,293
Italy	53,981	43,423	122,940
Japan	119,058	161,183	269,494
Korea, Republic . . .	28,720	20,209	39,576
Netherlands	34,104	15,839	31,892
Saudi Arabia	49,983	53,938	93,573
Switzerland	25,595	9,650	37,592
Taiwan	22,054	13,026	41,440
Turkey	23,388	3,495	26,057
United Kingdom . . .	58,703	69,278	130,660
USA	127,599	291,383	433,486
Total (incl. others) . . .	978,929	992,346	2,129,218

* Figures are provisional or incomplete. Total imports (KD million) were: 1,145.7 in 1990; 1,353.3 in 1991; 2,201.2 in 1992; 1,986.0 in 1993 (Source: IMF, *International Financial Statistics*).

Exports f.o.b.	1983	1984	1985
Australia	103,390	108,027	69,294
Brazil	65,748	43,878	10
Egypt	23,997	39,607	48,376
France	50,430	59,409	92,518
Germany, Federal Republic .	74,161	45,531	22,115
India	79,007	103,983	66,892
Iran	56,502	19,629	10,320
Iraq	106,106	90,066	76,726
Italy	284,735	313,175	360,555
Japan	610,722	598,996	586,959
Korea, Republic . . .	192,594	135,980	138,966
Netherlands	327,560	377,001	409,077
Pakistan	138,472	151,368	168,119
Philippines	79,225	117,822	69,141
Saudi Arabia	114,814	99,754	88,395
Singapore	201,378	288,608	78,811
Taiwan	296,908	231,331	233,893
Turkey	47,061	24,872	28,884
United Arab Emirates . .	56,833	31,347	28,543
United Kingdom . . .	35,207	40,309	60,737
USA	58,496	92,812	60,084
Total (incl. others) . . .	3,363,757	3,631,470	3,185,068

Transport

ROAD TRAFFIC (motor vehicles in use at 31 December)

	1988	1989	1992*
Passenger cars	469,280	498,388	591,565
Buses and coaches . . .	10,411	10,775	13,508
Goods vehicles	100,081	99,814	113,246

* Data for 1990 and 1991 are not available.

SHIPPING
Merchant Fleet (at 30 June)

	1990	1991	1992
Number of vessels . . .	225	197	209
Displacement ('000 grt) . .	1,855	1,373	1,910

Source: Lloyd's Register of Shipping.

International Sea-borne Freight Traffic*
('000 metric tons)

	1988	1989	1990
Goods loaded	61,778	69,097	51,400
Goods unloaded	7,123	7,015	4,522

* Including Kuwait's share of traffic in the Neutral/Partitioned Zone.
Source: UN, *Monthly Bulletin of Statistics.*

CIVIL AVIATION (traffic on scheduled services)

	1989	1990	1991
Kilometres flown (million) .	28	18	14
Passengers carried ('000) .	1,641	966	840
Passenger-km (million) . .	3,893	2,300	1,908
Freight ton-km (million) .	233	145	116
Mail ton-km (million) . . .	6	3	1

Source: UN, *Statistical Yearbook.*

Communications Media

	1989	1990	1991
Radio receivers ('000 in use) .	660	700	715
Television receivers ('000 in use)	550	580	590
Daily newspapers Number	n.a.	9	n.a.
Estimated average circulation ('000 copies) .	n.a.	450	n.a.

Telephones ('000 in use): 362 in 1988.
Book production (titles published): 793 in 1988.
Sources: UNESCO, *Statistical Yearbook*; UN, *Statistical Yearbook.*

Education

(state-controlled schools, 1993/94)

	Schools	Teachers	Students
Kindergarten	126	2,311	37,112
Primary	169	6,180	88,304
Intermediate	153	7,030	81,968
Secondary	106	7,330	59,815
Religious institutes . .	3	179	1,102
Special training institutes . .	12	471	1,422

Private education (1990/91): 35 kindergarten schools (165 teachers, 3,509 students); 51 primary schools (1,204 teachers, 31,222 students); 53 intermediate schools (818 teachers, 19,168 students); 33 secondary schools (606 teachers, 11,508 students).

Directory

The Constitution

The principal provisions of the Constitution, promulgated on 16 November 1962, are set out below. On 29 August 1976 the Amir suspended four articles of the Constitution dealing with the National Assembly, the Majlis al-Umma. On 24 August 1980 the Amir issued a decree ordering the establishment of an elected legislature before the end of February 1981. The new Majlis was elected on 23 February 1981, and fresh legislative elections followed on 20 February 1985. The Majlis was dissolved by Amiri decree in July 1986, and some sections of the Constitution, including the stipulation that new elections should be held within two months of dissolving the legislature (see below), were suspended. A new Majlis was elected on 5 October and convened on 20 October 1992.

SOVEREIGNTY

Kuwait is an independent sovereign Arab State; its sovereignty may not be surrendered, and no part of its territory may be relinquished. Offensive war is prohibited by the Constitution.

Succession as Amir is restricted to heirs of the late MUBARAK AS-SABAH, and an Heir Apparent must be appointed within one year of the accession of a new Amir.

EXECUTIVE AUTHORITY

Executive power is vested in the Amir, who exercises it through the Council of Ministers. The Amir will appoint the Prime Minister 'after the traditional consultations', and will appoint and dismiss ministers on the recommendation of the Prime Minister. Ministers need not be members of the Majlis al-Umma, although all ministers who are not members of parliament assume membership ex officio in the legislature for the duration of office. The Amir also formulates laws, which shall not be effective unless published in the *Official Gazette*. The Amir establishes public institutions. All decrees issued in these respects shall be conveyed to the Majlis. No law is issued unless it is approved by the Majlis.

LEGISLATURE

A National Assembly, the Majlis al-Umma, of 50 members will be elected for a four-year term by all natural-born Kuwaiti males over the age of 21 years, except servicemen and police, who may not vote. Candidates for election must possess the franchise, be over 30 years of age and literate. The Majlis will convene for at least eight months in any year, and new elections shall be held within two months of the last dissolution of the outgoing legislature.

Restrictions on the commercial activities of ministers include an injunction forbidding them to sell property to the Government.

The Amir may ask for reconsideration of a bill that has been approved by the Majlis and sent to him for ratification, but the bill would automatically become law if it were subsequently adopted by a two-thirds majority at the next sitting, or by a simple majority at a subsequent sitting. The Amir may declare martial law, but only with the approval of the legislature.

The Majlis may adopt a vote of 'no confidence' in a minister, in which case the Minister must resign. Such a vote is not permissible in the case of the Prime Minister, but the legislature may approach the Amir on the matter, and the Amir shall then either dismiss the Prime Minister or dissolve the Majlis.

CIVIL SERVICE

Entry to the civil service is confined to Kuwait citizens.

PUBLIC LIBERTIES

Kuwaitis are equal before the law in prestige, rights and duties. Individual freedom is guaranteed. No one shall be seized, arrested or exiled except within the rules of law.

No punishment shall be administered except for an act or abstaining from an act considered a crime in accordance with a law applicable at the time of committing it, and no penalty shall be imposed more severe than that which could have been imposed at the time of committing the crime.

Freedom of opinion is guaranteed to everyone, and each has the right to express himself through speech, writing or other means within the limits of the law.

The press is free within the limits of the law, and it should not be suppressed except in accordance with the dictates of law.

Freedom of performing religious rites is protected by the State according to prevailing customs, provided it does not violate the public order and morality.

Trade unions will be permitted and property must be respected. An owner is not banned from managing his property except within the boundaries of law. No property should be taken from anyone, except within the prerogatives of law, unless a just compensation be given.

Houses may not be entered, except in cases provided by law. Every Kuwaiti has freedom of movement and choice of place of residence within the state. This right shall not be controlled except in cases stipulated by law.

Every person has the right to education and freedom to choose his type of work. Freedom to form peaceful societies is guaranteed within the limits of law.

The Government

HEAD OF STATE

Amir of Kuwait: His Highness Sheikh JABER AL-AHMAD AS-SABAH (succeeded on the death of his cousin, 31 December 1977).

COUNCIL OF MINISTERS
(August 1994)

Crown Prince and Prime Minister: Sheikh SAAD AL-ABDULLAH AS-SALIM AS-SABAH.

First Deputy Prime Minister and Minister of Foreign Affairs: Sheikh SABAH AL-AHMAD AL-JABER AS-SABAH.

Second Deputy Prime Minister and Minister of Finance: NASSER ABDULLAH AR-RODHAN.

Minister of Defence: AHMAD AL-HMOUD AS-SABAH.

Minister of Oil: Dr ABD AL-MOHSIN MUDAEJ AL- MUDAEJ.

Minister of the Interior: Sheikh ALI SABAH AS-SALEM AS-SABAH.

Minister of Labour and Social Affairs: AHMAD KHALED AL-KOLAIB.

Minister of Education and Higher Education: Dr AHMAD ABDULLAH AR-RAB'I.

Minister of Public Works and Minister of State for Housing: HABIB JAWHAR HAYAT.

Minister of Communications, Electricity and Water: JASSEM MUHAMMAD AL-AOUN.

Minister of Information: SA'UD NASIR SA'UD AS-SABAH.

Minister of State for Cabinet Affairs and Minister of Planning: ABD AL-AZIZ AD-DAKHIL.

Minister of Health: Dr ABD AR-RAHMAN AL-MEHILAN.

Minister of Awqaf (Religious Endowments) and Islamic Affairs: ALI FAHAD AZ-ZUMAI'.

Minister of Justice and Administrative Affairs: MISHARI JASEM AL-ANJARI.

Minister of Commerce and Industry: HELAL AL-MUTAIRI.

PROVINCIAL GOVERNORS

Ahmadi: MUHAMMAD KHALED AL-HAMAD AS-SABAH.

Farwaniya: IBRAHIM JASSEM AL-MUDHAF.

Hawalli: DAUD MUSAED AS-SALIH.

Jahra: IBRAHIM DUALJ AL-IBRAHIM AS-SABAH.

Kuwait: Sheikh ALI ABDULLAH AS-SALIM AS-SABAH.

MINISTRIES

Ministry of Awqaf and Islamic Affairs: POB 13, 13001 Safat, al-Morkab St, Ministries Complex, Kuwait City; tel. 2466300; telex 44735; fax 2449943.

Ministry of Commerce and Industry: POB 2944, 13030 Safat, Kuwait City; tel. 2463600; telex 22682; fax 2424411.

Ministry of Communications, Electricity and Water: POB 318, 13004 Safat, Kuwait City; tel. 4819033; telex 22197; fax 4818696.

Ministry of Defence: POB 1170, 13012 Safat, Kuwait City; tel. 4848300; telex 22784.

Ministry of Education and Higher Education: POB 7, 13001 Safat, Hilali St, Kuwait City; tel. 2455454; telex 23166; fax 2445946.

Ministry of Finance: POB 9, 13001 Safat, al-Morkab St, Ministries Complex, Kuwait City; tel. 2468200; telex 22527; fax 2404025.

Ministry of Foreign Affairs: POB 3, 13001 Safat, Gulf St, Kuwait City; tel. 2425141; telex 22042.

Ministry of Health: POB 5, 13001 Safat, Arabian Gulf St, Kuwait City; tel. 2462900; telex 22729; fax 2458584.

Ministry of Information: POB 193, 13002 Safat, as-Sour St, Kuwait City; tel. 2415300; telex 46151; fax 2421926.

Ministry of the Interior: POB 11, 13001 Safat, Kuwait City; tel. 4818000; telex 22507.

Ministry of Justice and Administrative Affairs: POB 6, 13001 Safat, al-Morkab St, Ministries Complex, Kuwait City; tel. 2465600; telex 44660; fax 2466957.

Ministry of Labour and Social Affairs: POB 563, 13006 Safat, al-Morkab St, Ministries Complex, Kuwait City; tel. 2464500; telex 30329; fax 2419877.

Ministry of Oil: POB 5077, 13051 Safat, Fahd as-Salem St, Kuwait City; tel. 2415201; telex 22363; fax 2417088.

Ministry of Public Works and Housing: POB 12, 13001 Safat, Kuwait City; tel. 4896000; telex 30060; fax 4897484.

Legislature

MAJLIS AL-UMMA
(National Assembly)

Speaker: AHMAD ABD AL-AZIZ AS-SAADUN.

Elections to the restored Majlis took place on 5 October 1992, at which candidates who were known to oppose the outgoing Government secured 31 of the legislature's 50 seats.

Political Organizations

Political parties are not permitted in Kuwait. However, several quasi-political organizations are in existence. Among those that secured representation in the Majlis at the October 1992 elections were:

Islamic Constitutional Movement: Sunni Muslim; moderate.

Kuwait Democratic Forum: secular; liberal.

Salafeen: Sunni Muslim; fundamentalist.

National Islamic Coalition: Shi'a Muslim.

Constitutional Group: supported by merchants.

Diplomatic Representation

EMBASSIES IN KUWAIT

Afghanistan: POB 33186, 73452 Rawdah, Block 1, 7 Mishref St, House 17, Kuwait City; tel. 5396916; Chargé d'affaires: TAZAKHAN WIAL.

Algeria: POB 578, 13006 Safat, Istiqlal St, Kuwait City; tel. 2519987; telex 44750; Ambassador: MUHAMMAD QADRI.

Austria: POB 33259, 73453 Rawdah, Kuwait City; tel. 2552532; telex 23866; Ambassador: Dr FERDINAND MAULTASCHL.

Bahrain: POB 196, 13002 Safat, Surra, Block 1, St 1, Villa 24, Kuwait City; tel. 5317351; fax 5330882; Ambassador: ABDUL RAHMANN AL-FADHEL.

Bangladesh: POB 22344, 13084 Safat, Khaldya, Block 1, St 14, House 3, Kuwait City; tel. 4834078; telex 22484; fax 4831603; Chargé d'affaires: MOHSIN ALI KHAN.

Belgium: POB 3280, 13033 Safat, Salmiya, Baghdad St, House 15, Kuwait City; tel. 5722014; telex 22535; fax 5748389; Ambassador: GUIDO SONCK.

Bhutan: POB 1510, 13016 Safat, Mishref St, Block 15, St 14, Villa 19, Rd 55, Kuwait City; tel. 5382873; telex 30185; Ambassador: TOBGYE S. DORJI.

Bolivia: POB 3115, 13032 Safat, Yarmouk, Area 3, Block 170, Ave 16, House 7, Kuwait City; tel. 5339964; telex 44016; fax 5320046; Ambassador MIGUEL A. DUERI.

Brazil: POB 39761, 73058 Safat, Nuzha, Plot 2, Damascus St, House 12, Kuwait City; tel. 2561029; telex 22398; fax 2562153; Ambassador: ADERBAL COSTA.

Bulgaria: POB 12090, 71651 Shamiya, Salwa, Parcel 10, Plot 312, Kuwait City; tel. 5643877; telex 22122; Ambassador: ANGEL N. MANTCHEV.

Canada: POB 25281, 13113 Safat, Daiya, Block 4, Al-Motawakell St, Villa 4, Kuwait City; tel. 2563025; telex 23549; fax 2564167; Ambassador: J. CHRISTOPHER POOLE.

China, People's Republic: POB 2346, 13024 Safat, Jabriya, Block 12, St 101, Villa 24, Kuwait City; tel. 5333340; fax 5333341; Ambassador: WANG JINGQI.

Cuba: POB 26385, 13124 Safat, Bayan, Block 5, St 5, House 16, Kuwait City; tel. 5382024; telex 44703; Ambassador: JORGE L. MANFUGAS LAVIGNE.

Czech Republic: POB 1151, 13012 Safat, Nuzha, Block 3, Kassima No. 56, St 34, House 13, Kuwait City; tel. 2548206; telex 22243.

Egypt: POB 11252, 35153 Ad-Desmah, Istiqlal St, Kuwait City; tel. 2519955; telex 22610; Ambassador: AMIN NAMMAR.

Finland: POB 26699, 13127 Safat, Surra, Block 4, St 1, Villa 8, Kuwait City; tel. 5312890; fax 4324198; Ambassador: PERTTI KAUKONEN.

France: POB 1037, 13011 Safat, Jabriya, Block 12, Parcel 156–158, Kuwait City; tel. 5312000; telex 22195; Ambassador: JEAN BRESSOT.

Gabon: POB 23956, 13100 Safat, Khaldiya, Block 2, Kuwait City; tel. 4830975; telex 22735.

Germany: Plot 1, St 14, Villa 13, Kuwait City; tel. 2520857; fax 2520763; Ambassador: GÜNTER MULACK.

Greece: POB 23812, 13099 Safat, Khaldiya, Block 4, St 44, House 4, Kuwait City; tel. 4817101; fax 4817103; Ambassador: STELIOS MALLIKOURTIS.

Hungary: POB 23955, 13100 Safat, Shamiya, Block 8, St 84, Villa 6, Kuwait City; tel. 4814080; telex 22662; Ambassador: BALINT GAL.

India: POB 1450, 13015 Safat, 34 Istiqlal St, Kuwait City; tel. 2530600; telex 22273; Ambassador: PREM SINGH.

Indonesia: POB 21560, 13076 Safat, Keifan, Block 5, ash-Shebani St, Building 21, Kuwait City; tel. 4839927; telex 22752; fax 4819250; Ambassador: ACHMAD HIDAYAT KUSUMANEGARA.

Iran: POB 4686, 13047 Safat, 24 Istiqlal St, Kuwait City; tel. 2533220; telex 22223; Ambassador: HUSSEIN SADEGHI.

Italy: POB 4453, 13045 Safat, Sharq, F. Omar Bin al-Khattab St, al-Mulla Bldgs, Villa 6, Kuwait City; tel. 2445120; telex 22356; Ambassador: Dr LUCIO FORATTINI.

Japan: POB 2304, 13024 Safat, Jabriya, Block 9, Plot 496, Kuwait City; tel. 5312870; telex 22196; Ambassador: TSUYOSHI KUROKAWA.

Jordan: POB 15314, 35305 Diiyah, Istiqlal St, Embassies Area, Kuwait City; tel. 2533500; telex 30412; Ambassador: NABIL TAWFIQ AT-TAHOUNI.

Korea, Republic: POB 4272, 13043 Safat, Nuzha, Block 2, Div. 42, Damascus St, Villa 12, Kuwait City; tel. 2531816; telex 22353; Ambassador: SAE HOON AHN.

Lebanon: POB 253, 13003 Safat, 31 Istiqlal St, Kuwait City; tel. 2619765; telex 22330; Ambassador: MUHAMMAD ISA.

Libya: POB 21460, 13075 Safat, Diiyah, Block 1, Plot 2, ar-Roumi St, Kuwait City; tel. 2520814; telex 22256; Ambassador: (vacant).

Malaysia: POB 4105, 13042 Safat, Faiha, Block 7, St 70, Villa 1, Kuwait City; tel. 2546022; telex 22540; Ambassador: ZAINAL ABIDIN BIN ALIAS.

Mauritania: POB 23784, 13098 Safat, Mishrif, Parcel 6, Villa 37, Kuwait City; tel. 5384849; telex 22643; Ambassador: MUHAMMAD A. DIDI.

Morocco: Kuwait City; tel. 4813912; telex 22074; Ambassador: ABD AL-WAHED BEN MASOUD.

Netherlands: POB 21822, 13079 Safat, Jabriya, Block 9, Parcel 40A, Kuwait City; tel. 5312650; telex 22459; Ambassador: JOSEPHUS F. R. M. VELING.

Niger: POB 44451, 32059 Hawalli, Salwa, Area 10, Plot 447, Kuwait City; tel. 5652639; telex 23365; Ambassador: ADAMOU ZADA.

Nigeria: POB 6432, 32039 Hawalli, Surra, Area 1, St 14, House 25, Kuwait City; tel. 5320794; telex 22864; Ambassador: MUSTAFA SHEIKH SALEH.

Oman: POB 21975, 13080 Safat, Udailia, Block 3, Parcel 123, House 25, Kuwait City; tel. 2561962; telex 22057; Ambassador: SALIM BIN ABDULLAH BA'OMAR.

Pakistan: POB 988, 13010 Safat, Diiyah, Hamza St, Villa 29, Kuwait City; tel. 2532101; telex 44117; Ambassador: ZAHID SAID KHAN.

Paraguay: POB 886, 13009 Safat, Shuwaikh, Kuwait City; tel. 4814462; telex 22071.

Philippines: POB 26288, 13123 Safat, Rawdah, Area 3, St 34, Villa 24, Kuwait City; tel. 2524398; telex 22434; Ambassador: MAUYAG TAMANO.

Poland: POB 5066, 13051 Safat, Rawdah, Block 4, 3rd Ring Rd, Villa 13, Kuwait City; tel. 2510355; telex 50080; fax 2524760; Ambassador: JAN NATKANSKI.

Qatar: POB 1825, 13019 Safat, Diiyah, Istiqlal St, Kuwait City; tel. 2513599; telex 22038; Ambassador: AHMAD G. AR-RUMAIHI.

Romania: POB 11149, Dasmah, 35152 Kifan, Zone 4, Mouna St, House 34, Kuwait City; tel. 843419; telex 22148; Ambassador: GHEORGHE SERBANESCU.

Russia: POB 1765, 13018 Safat, Ad-Da'yia, Embassies Campus, Block 17, Kuwait City; tel. 2560427; Ambassador: PYOTR STEGNY.

Saudi Arabia: POB 20498, 13065 Safat, Arabian Gulf St, Kuwait City; tel. 2531155; telex 23458; Ambassador: Sheikh ABDULLAH ABDU-AZIZ AS-SUDAIRY.

Senegal: POB 23892, 13099 Safat, Rawdah, Parcel 3, St 35, House 9, Kuwait City; tel. 2542044; telex 22580; Ambassador: ABDOU LAHAD MBACKE.

Somalia: POB 22766, 13088 Safat, Diiyah, Block 1, ar-Roumi St, Bldg 41, Kuwait City; tel. 2555567; telex 23280; Ambassador: MUHAMMAD S. M. MALINGUR.

Spain: POB 22207, 13083 Safat, Surra, Block 3, St 14, Villa 19, Kuwait City; tel. 5325827; telex 22341; Ambassador: CÉSAR ALBA Y FUSTER.

Sri Lanka: POB 16296, 35853 Qadisiah, Keifan, Plot 6, Al-Andalus St, House 31, Kuwait City; tel. 4844862; telex 46564; Ambassador: LATIF SHARIFDIN.

Sudan: POB 1076, 13011 Safat, Rawdah, Block 3, Abu Hayan St 26, Kuwait City; tel. 2519299; telex 22528; Ambassador: MUHAMMAD EL-AMIN ABDULLAH.

Sweden: POB 21448, 13075 Safat, Kuwait City; tel. 2523588; fax 2572157; Ambassador: TOMMY ARWITZ.

Switzerland: POB 23954, 13100 Safat, Qortuba, Area 2, St 1, House 122, Kuwait City; tel. 5340175; telex 22672; fax 5340176; Ambassador: DANIEL VON MURALT.

Syria: POB 25600, 13115 Safat, Rawdah, Plot 4, St 43, Villa 5, Kuwait City; tel. 2531164; telex 22270; Ambassador: Dr ISA DAR-WISH.

Thailand: POB 66647, 43757 Bayan, Surra, Area 3, Block 49, Ali bin Abi-Taleb St, Kuwait City; tel. 5317530; telex 44339; fax 5317532; Ambassador: MAITRI CHULADUL.

Tunisia: POB 5976, 13060 Safat, Faiha, Plot 9, St 91, Villa 10F, Kuwait City; tel. 2542144; telex 22518; Ambassador: MUHAMMAD AL-HABIB KAABASHI.

Turkey: POB 20627, 13067 Safat, Block 16, Plot 10, Istiqlal St, Kuwait City; tel. 2531785; telex 44806; Ambassador: GUNER OZTEK.

United Arab Emirates: POB 1828, 13019 Safat, Plot 70, Istiqlal St, Kuwait City; tel. 2518381; telex 22529; Ambassador: YOUSUF A. AS-SIRKAL.

United Kingdom: POB 2, 13001 Safat, Arabian Gulf St, Kuwait City; tel. 2403334; telex 44614; fax 2407395; Ambassador: WILLIAM H. FULLERTON.

USA: POB 77, 13001 Safat, Arabian Gulf St, Kuwait City; tel. 2424151; Ambassador: RYAN C. CROCKER.

Venezuela: POB 24440, 13105 Safat, Surra, Parcel 2, 11 Ali bin Abi-Taleb St, Kuwait City; tel. 5334578; telex 22782; Ambassador: RAFAEL OSUNA LOZADA.

Yemen: Abdullah as-Salam area, near school help, Ar-Riyad St, Kuwait City.

Yugoslavia: POB 20511, 13066 Safat, Shuwaikh 'B', al-Mansour St, Villa 15, Kuwait City; tel. 4813140; telex 46107; Ambassador: Dr HASAN DERVISBEGOVIĆ.

Zaire: POB 3998, 13040 Safat, Rawdah, Parcel 3, St 34, Villa 24, Kuwait City; tel. 2543688; telex 22460.

Judicial System

Kuwait adopted a unified judicial system, covering all levels of courts, in 1960. The different types of court operating in the country include:

Courts of Summary Justice: There is a Summary Court in each administrative district of Kuwait, comprising one or more divisions, each with one judge. These courts judge civil and commercial disputes (their verdict being final in cases where the amount involved does not exceed KD 500), urgent cases, lease problems and misdemeanours where the penalty is not more than three years' imprisonment.

Court of the First Instance: Judges lawsuits in which the amount involved is more than KD 1,000. Seven divisions consider disputes related to personal, civil, commercial, labour and rent affairs, and also cases of felony and appeals concerning misdemeanours. Chief Judge GHAZI OBAID AS-SAMMAR.

High Court of Appeal: tel. 2432131. Considers appeals against rulings of the Court of the First Instance. Chief Judge MUHAMMAD YOUSUF AR-RIFA'I.

Court of Cassation: Independent department in the High Court of Appeal, composed of five advisers. Considers cases of alleged discrimination, whether commercial, labour, civil, personal or criminal.

Constitutional Court: Composed of five advisers. Interprets the articles of the Constitution and judges disputes related to the constitutionality of laws, statutes and by-laws, and challenges to the election and legitimate membership of deputies in the National Assembly (when that body is in session). The verdict of this court is binding on all courts.

Criminal Courts, including the **State Security Court** (Pres. SALAH AL-FAHD), which tries specified crimes against the State.

Attorney-General: DHARI ABDULLAH AL-UTHMAN.

Advocate-General: MUHAMMAD ABD AL-HAIH AL-BANNAIY.

Religion

ISLAM

The Kuwaiti inhabitants are mainly Muslims of the Sunni and Shi'a sects. The Shi'ites comprise about 30% of the total.

CHRISTIANITY
The Roman Catholic Church

Latin Rite

For ecclesiastical purposes, Kuwait forms an Apostolic Vicariate. At 31 December 1992 there were an estimated 80,000 adherents in the country.

Vicar Apostolic: Mgr FRANCIS ADEODATUS MICALLEF (Titular Bishop of Tinisa in Proconsulari), Bishop's House, POB 266, 13003 Safat, Kuwait City; tel. 2434637; fax 2409981.

Melkite Rite

The Greek-Melkite Patriarch of Antioch is resident in Damascus, Syria. The Patriarchal Vicariate (now Exarchate) of Kuwait had an estimated 4,500 adherents at 31 December 1984.

Exarch Patriarchal: Archimandrite BASILIOS KANAKRY, Vicariat Patriarcal Melkite, POB 1205, Salmiya; tel. 615721.

Syrian Rite

The Syrian Catholic Patriarch of Antioch is resident in Beirut, Lebanon. The Patriarchal Exarchate of Iraq and Kuwait, with an estimated 1,250 adherents at 31 December 1992, is based in Basra, Iraq.

The Anglican Communion

Within the Episcopal Church in Jerusalem and the Middle East, Kuwait forms part of the diocese of Cyprus and the Gulf. The Anglican congregation in Kuwait is entirely expatriate. The Bishop in Cyprus and the Gulf is resident in Cyprus, while the Archdeacon in the Gulf is resident in the United Arab Emirates.

Other Christian Churches

National Evangelical Church in Kuwait: Rev. JERRY A. ZANDSTRA, pastor of the English-speaking congregation; pastoral vacancy in the Arabic-language congregation, POB 80, 13001 Safat, Kuwait City; tel. 2407195; fax 2431087; an independent Protestant Church founded by the Reformed Church in America; services in Arabic, English, Korean, Malayalam and other Indian languages; weekly congregation of some 7,000.

The Armenian, Greek, Coptic and Syrian Orthodox Churches are also represented in Kuwait.

The Press

Freedom of the press and publishing is guaranteed in the Constitution, although press censorship was in force between mid-1986 and early 1992 (when journalists adopted a voluntary code of practice). The Government provides financial support to newspapers and magazines.

DAILIES

Al-Anbaa (The News): POB 23915, Safat, Kuwait City; tel. 4830322; telex 22622; f. 1976; Arabic; general; Editor-in-Chief FAISAL YOUSUF AL-MARZOOQ; circ. 80,000.

Arab Times: POB 2270, 13023 Safat, Kuwait City; tel. 4813566; telex 22332; fax 4833628; f. 1977; English; Editor-in-Chief AHMAD ABD AL-AZIZ AL-JARALLAH; Man. Editor MISHAL AL-JARALLAH; circ. 31,134.

Kuwait Times: POB 1301, Safat, Kuwait City; tel. 4833199; telex 23843; f. 1963; (weekend edition also published); English; political; Owner and Editor-in-Chief YOUSUF ALYYAN; Man. Editor CLEMENT MESENAS; circ. 30,000.

Al-Qabas (Firebrand): POB 21800, 13078 Safat, Kuwait City; tel. 4812822; telex 23370; fax 4834320; f. 1972; Arabic; independent; Gen. Man. FOUZAN AL-FARES; circ. 90,000.

Ar-Ra'i al-'Aam (Public Opinion): POB 695, International Airport Rd, Shuwaikh Industrial Area, Kuwait City; tel. 4813134; telex 22636; fax 4849298; f. 1961; Arabic; political, social and cultural; Editor-in-Chief FAHAD A. AL-MUSSAEED; circ. 86,900.

As-Seyassa (Policy): POB 2270, Shuwaikh, Kuwait City; tel. 4816326; telex 22332; fax 4833628; f. 1965; Arabic; political; Editor-in-Chief AHMAD ABD AL-AZIZ AL-JARALLAH; circ. 126,616.

Al-Watan (The Homeland): Dar al-Watan KSC, POB 1142, Safat, Kuwait City; tel. 4840950; telex 22565; f. 1962; Arabic; political; Editor-in-Chief FATIMA HUSSEIN; Deputy Gen. Man. ABDULLAH ALI HINDI; circ. 56,758.

WEEKLIES AND PERIODICALS

'Alam al-Fann (World of Art): POB 13341, 71953 Keifan; tel. 4810526; Editor-in-Chief MUHAMMAD A. NASHMI DAWASH.

Arab Business Report: POB 6000, Safat, Kuwait City; telex 3511; fortnightly; English; business management.

Al-'Arabi (The Arab): POB 748, 13008 Safat, Kuwait City; telex 44041; f. 1958; monthly; Arabic; cultural; publ. by the Ministry of Information for distribution throughout the Arab world; Editor-in-Chief Dr MUHAMMAD AR-RUMAIHI; circ. 350,000.

Al-Balagh (Communiqué): POB 4558, 13046 Safat, Kuwait City; tel. 4818606; telex 44389; fax 4819008; f. 1969; weekly; Arabic; general, political and Islamic; Editor-in-Chief ABD AR-RAHMAN RASHID AL-WALAYATI; circ. 29,000.

Ad-Dakhiliya (The Interior): POB 12500, Shamiah, Kuwait City; monthly; Arabic; official reports, transactions and proceedings; publ. by Public Relations Dept, Ministry of the Interior; Editor-in-Chief FAHD KHALID AL-MUKHLID.

Al-Hadaf (The Objective): POB 2270, 13023 Safat, Kuwait City; tel. 4813566; telex 22332; fax 4833628; f. 1961; weekly; Arabic; literary, political and cultural; Editor-in-Chief AHMAD ABD AL-AZIZ AL-JARALLAH; Chair. M. M. AS-SALEH; circ. 210,123.

Hayatuna (Our Life): POB 1708, Safat, Kuwait City; f. 1968; fortnightly; Arabic; medicine and hygiene; publ. by Al-Awadi Press Corporation; Editor-in-Chief YOUSUF ABD AL-AZIZ AL-MUZINI; circ. 6,000.

Iftah Ya Simsim (Open Sesame): POB 44247, Safat, Kuwait City; telex 44090; monthly; Arabic; children.

Al-Iqtisadi al-Kuwaiti (Kuwaiti Economist): POB 775, 13008 Safat, Kuwait City; tel. 2433854; telex 22198; fax 2404110; f. 1960; monthly; Arabic; commerce, trade and economics; publ. by Kuwait Chamber of Commerce and Industry; Editor MAJED JAMAL UD-DIN.

Journal of the Gulf and Arab Peninsula Studies: POB 17073, Khaldiya, Kuwait University, Kuwait City; quarterly; English.

Journal of the Kuwait Medical Association: POB 1202, 13013 Safat, Kuwait City; tel. 5333278; fax 5333276; f. 1967; quarterly, English; case reports, articles; Editor-in-chief Dr A. A. AR-RASHID; circ. 6,000.

Al-Kuwait: POB 193, Safat, Kuwait City; tel. 2415300; telex 46151; f. 1961; monthly; Arabic; Islamic culture; publ. by Ministry of Information; Editor HAMED Y. AL-GHARABALLY; circ. 50,400.

Kuwait al-Youm (Official Gazette): POB 193, 13002 Safat, Kuwait City; tel. 2415300; telex 46151; fax 2421926; f. 1954; weekly; Arabic; statistics, Amiri decrees, laws, govt announcements, decisions, invitations for tenders, etc.; publ. by the Ministry of Information; circ. 5,000.

Al-Kuwaiti (The Kuwaiti): Information Dept, POB 9758, 61008 Ahmadi, Kuwait City; tel. 3982747; telex 44211; fax 3981602; f. 1961; monthly journal of the Kuwait Oil Co (KOC); Arabic; Editor-in-Chief SALEM R. AR-ROOMI; circ. 6,000.

The Kuwaiti Digest: Information Dept, POB 9758, 61008 Ahmadi, Kuwait City; tel. 3982747; telex 44211; fax 3981602; f. 1972; quarterly journal of Kuwait Oil Co (KOC); English; Editor-in-Chief SALEM R. AR-ROOMI; circ. 8,000.

Kuwaiti Economist: POB 775, 13008 Safat; tel. 2433854; telex 22198; fax 2433858; f. 1960; monthly; Arabic; commerce and economics; publ. by Kuwait Chamber of Commerce and Industry; Editor MAJED JAMAL UD-DIN; circ. 35,000.

Al-Majaless (Meetings): POB 5605, Safat, Kuwait City; tel. 814429; telex 44728; weekly; Arabic; current affairs; circ. 60,206.

Mejallat al-Kuwait (Kuwait Magazine): POB 193, 13002 Safat, Kuwait City; tel. 2415300; telex 46151; f. 1961; fortnightly; Arabic; illustrated magazine; science, arts and literature; publ. by Ministry of Information.

Mirat al-Umma (Mirror of the Nation): POB 2270, Shuwaikh, Kuwait City; telex 22332; weekly; Arabic; Editor-in-Chief ALI BIN YOUSUF AR-ROUMI; circ. 79,500.

An-Nahdha (The Renaissance): POB 695, Shuwaikh, Kuwait City; telex 22636; f. 1967; weekly; Arabic; social and political; Editor YOUSUF AL-MASSAID; circ. 148,500.

Osrati (My Family): POB 2995, Safat, Kuwait City; tel. 816928; telex 44438; f. 1978; weekly; Arabic; women's magazine; publ. by Fahad al-Marzouk Establishment; Editor GHANIMA F. AL-MARZOUK; circ. 76,450.

Ar-Ressaleh (The Message): POB 2490, Shuwaikh, Kuwait City; f. 1961; weekly; Arabic; political, social and cultural; Editor JASSIM MUBARAK.

Ar-Riyadhi al-'Arabi (The Arab Sportsman): POB 1693, 13017 Safat, Kuwait City; tel. 4845307; telex 44728; weekly; Arabic; sports; circ. 101,822.

Sa'd (Good Luck): POB 695, Ismail Wasi, ar-Racalam, Kuwait City; tel. 813133; telex 22636; weekly; Arabic; children's magazine; Editor MANAL AL-MOSAFED; circ. 60,000.

Sawt al-Khaleej (Voice of the Gulf): POB 659, Safat, Kuwait City; telex 2636; f. 1962; politics and literature; Arabic; Editor-in-Chief SALAH BAKER KHRIEBET; Owner BAKER ALI KHRIEBET; circ. 20,000.

At-Tali' (The Ascendant): POB 1082, Mubarak al-Kabir St, Kuwait City; tel. 2439376; f. 1962; weekly; Arabic; politics and literature; Editor SAMI AHMAD AL-MUNAIS; circ. 10,000.

Al-Yaqza (The Awakening): POB 6000, Safat, Kuwait City; tel. 6831318; telex 44513; fax 2414102; f. 1966; weekly; Arabic; political, economic, social and general; Editor-in-Chief AHMAD YOUSUF BEHBEHANI; circ. 91,340.

NEWS AGENCIES

Kuwait News Agency (KUNA): POB 24063, 13101 Safat, Kuwait City; tel. 2412044; telex 22758; fax 2414102; f. 1976; public corporate body; independent; also publishes research digests on topics of common and special interest; Chair. and Dir-Gen. YOUSUF AS-SUMAIT.

Foreign Bureaux

Informatsionnoye Telegrafnoye Agentstvo Rossii—Telegrafnoye Agentstvo Suverennykh Stran (ITAR—TASS) (Russia): POB 1455, Safat, Kuwait City; Correspondent MIKHAIL KOZHEVNIKOV.

Middle East News Agency (MENA) (Egypt): POB 1927, Safat, Fahd as-Salem St, Kuwait City; Dir REDA SOLIMAN.

Reuters (UK): POB 5616, 13057 Safat, Kuwait City; tel. 2431920; telex 22428; fax 22420617.

Xinhua (New China) News Agency (People's Republic of China): POB 22168, Safat, Sheikh Ahmad al-Jaber Bldg, 10 Dasman St, Kuwait City; Correspondent HUANG JIANMING.

Agence Arabe Syrienne d'Information, Anatolian News Agency (Turkey), JANA (Libya), QNA (Qatar) and RIA—Novosti (Russia) are also represented in Kuwait.

PRESS ASSOCIATION

Kuwait Journalist Association: POB 5454, Safat, Kuwait City; tel. 4843351; fax 4842874; Chair. YOUSUF ALYYAN.

Publishers

Gulf Centre Publishing and Publicity: POB 2722, 13028 Safat, Kuwait City; telex 46174; Propr HAMZA ISMAIL ESSLAH.

Al-Jeel Publishing Co: POB 44247, 32057 Hawalli, Kuwait City; tel. 4843183; telex 46443; children's education; Chair. and Gen. Man. OSSAMA EL-KAOUKJI.

Kuwait Publishing House: POB 5209, 13053 Safat, Kuwait City; tel. 2414697; telex 22771; Dir AMIN HAMADEH.

At-Talia Printing and Publishing Co: POB 1082, Airport Rd, Shuwaikh, 13011 Safat, Kuwait City; tel. 4840470; Man. AHMAD YUSEF AN-NAFISI.

Government Publishing House

Ministry of Information: POB 193, 13002 Safat, as-Sour St, Kuwait City; tel. 2415300; telex 46151; fax 2421926.

Radio and Television

In 1991, according to UNESCO, there were an estimated 715,000 radio receivers and 590,000 television receivers in use.

RADIO

Kuwait Broadcasting SCE: POB 397, 13004 Safat, Kuwait City; tel. 2423774; telex 46285; fax 2415946; f. 1951; broadcasts for 70 hours daily in Arabic, Farsi, English and Urdu, some in stereo;

Dir of Radio Dr ABD AL-AZIZ ALI MANSOUR; Dir of Radio Programmes ABD AR-RAHMAN HADI.

TELEVISION

Kuwait Television: c/o POB 621, 13007 Safat, Kuwait City; tel. 2423774; telex 22169; fax 2419659; f. 1961 (transmission began privately in Kuwait in 1957); transmits in Arabic; colour television service began in 1973; has a total of five channels; Dir-Gen. of TV BADR AL-MODAF.

Finance

(cap. = capital; p.u. = paid up; dep. = deposits; res = reserves; m. = million; brs = branches; amounts in Kuwaiti dinars unless otherwise stated)

BANKING

Central Bank

Central Bank of Kuwait: POB 526, 13006 Safat, Abdullah as-Salem St, Kuwait City; tel. 2449200; telex 22101; fax 2433461; f. 1969; cap. 5.0m., res 179.0m., total assets 1,435.3m. (Feb. 1994); Governor Sheikh SALEM ABD AL-AZIZ SA'UD AS-SABAH.

National Banks

Al-Ahli Bank of Kuwait KSC: POB 1387, 13014 Safat, Mubarak al-Kabir St, Safat Sq., Kuwait City; tel. 2400900; telex 22067; fax 2424557; f. 1967; wholly owned by private Kuwaiti interests; total assets US $5,600m. (Dec. 1990); Chair. MORAD YOUSUF BEHBEHANI; Dep. Chair. and Man. Dir ABD SALAM ABDULLAH AL-AWADI; 9 brs in Kuwait, 1 br. in Dubai.

Bank of Bahrain and Kuwait: POB 24396, 13104 Safat, Kuwait City; tel. 2417140; fax 2440937; f. 1977; owned equally by the Governments of Bahrain and Kuwait; Chair. RASHED AZ-ZAYANI; Gen. Man. MURAD ALI MURAD.

Bank of Kuwait and the Middle East KSC: POB 71, 13001 Safat, Darwazat Abd ar-Razzak, Kuwait City; tel. 2459771; telex 22045; fax 2461430; began operations in Dec. 1971; 49.4% state-owned; cap. 49.5m., res 17.2m., dep. 794.0m., total assets 861.8m. (Dec. 1992); Chair. SALIH MUBARAK AL-FALAH; Gen. Man. SAUD AL-GHARABALLY; 10 brs.

Burgan Bank SAK: POB 5389, 13054 Safat, Ahmad al-Jaber St, Kuwait City; tel. 2439000; telex 22730; fax 2461148; f. 1975; 51% state-owned, 49% owned by private Kuwaiti interests; cap. 68.8m. res 69.8m., dep. 629.4m, total assets 771.2m. (Dec. 1993); Chair. and Man. Dir Sheikh AHMAD ABDULLAH AL-AHMAD AS-SABAH; Gen. Man. MUHAMMAD AQEEL TAWFIQI; 12 brs.

Commercial Bank of Kuwait SAK: POB 2861, 13029 Safat, Mubarak al-Kabir St, Kuwait City; tel. 2411001; telex 22004; fax 2450150; f. 1960 by Amiri decree; cap. 64.1m., res 23.0m., dep. 1,187.5m., total assets 1,323.6m. (Dec. 1992); Chair. HAMAD AHMAD ABD AL-LATIF AL-HAMAD; Chief Gen. Man. MUHAMMAD ABD AR-RAHMAN AL-YAHYA; 36 brs.

Gulf Bank KSC: POB 3200, 13032 Safat, Mubarak al-Kabir St, Kuwait City; tel. 2449501; telex 22001; fax 2445212; f. 1960; cap. 78.2m., res 72.2m., dep. 1,099.5m., total assets 1,249.9m. (Dec. 1993); Chair. Dr ALI AL-HILAL AL-MUTAIRI; Chief Gen. Man. JOHN CARLOUGH; 15 local brs, offices in Singapore and London.

Industrial Bank of Kuwait KSC: POB 3146, 13032 Safat, Joint Banking Centre, Commercial Area 9, Kuwait City; tel. 2457661; telex 22469; fax 2462057; 31.4% state-owned; f. 1973; cap. 20m., res 27.5m., dep. 241.2m., total assets 290.5m. (Dec. 1992); Chair. and Man. Dir SALEH MUHAMMAD AL-YOUSUF.

Kuwait Finance House KSC (KFH): POB 24989, 13110 Safat, Abdullah al-Mubarak St, Kuwait City; tel. 2445050; telex 23331; fax 2455135; f. 1977; Islamic banking and investment company; 49% state-owned; cap. 142.0m., res 55m., dep. 3,319m., total assets 3,866m. (Dec. 1993); Chair. BADER AL-MUKHAISEEM; Gen. Man. ADNAN AL-BAHAR; 17 brs.

Kuwait Real Estate Bank KSC: POB 22822, 13089 Safat, West Tower—Joint Banking Centre, Darwazat Abd ar-Razzak, Kuwait City; tel. 2458177; telex 22321; fax 2462516; f. 1973; wholly owned by private Kuwaiti interests; cap. 29.7m., res 37.1m., dep. 397.3m., total assets 464.2m. (Dec. 1992); Chair. and Man. Dir SAAD ALI AN-NAHEDH; 2 brs.

National Bank of Kuwait SAK (NBK): POB 95, 13001 Safat, Abdullah as-Salem St, Kuwait City; tel. 2422011; telex 22451; fax 4310089; f. 1952; cap. 121.6m., res 192.0m., dep. 2,941.4m., total assets 3,267.1m. (Dec. 1993); Chair. MUHAMMAD ABD AR-RAHMAN AL-BAHAR; Chief Gen. Man. IBRAHIM S. DABDOUB; 32 brs.

Savings and Credit Bank: POB 1454, 13015 Safat, al-Hilali St, Kuwait City; tel. 2411301; telex 22211; f. 1965; nominal cap. 1,000m.; Chair. and Gen. Man. YOUSUF ALI AL-HOUTI.

INSURANCE

Al-Ahleia Insurance Co SAK: POB 1602, as-Sour St, Safat, Kuwait City; tel. 2448870; telex 23585; fax 2430308; f. 1962; all forms of insurance; cap. 9.7m.; Chair. YOUSUF IBRAHIM AL-GHANIM; Man. Dir OSAMAH MUHAMMAD AN-NISF; Gen. Man. Dr RAOUF H. MAKAR.

Al-Ittihad al-Watani Insurance Co for the Near East SAL: POB 781, 13008 Safat; tel. 2441830; telex 22442; fax 2432424.

Arab Commercial Enterprises (Kuwait): POB 2474, 13025 Safat; tel. 2413854; telex 22076; fax 2409450.

Gulf Insurance Co KSC: POB 1040, 13011 Safat, Kuwait City; tel. 2423384; telex 22203, fax 2422320; f. 1962; cap. 11.3m.; 75% state-owned; all forms of insurance; Chair. SULAIMAN HAMAD AD-DALALI.

Kuwait Insurance Co SAK (KIC): POB 769, Safat, Abdullah al-Salem St, Kuwait City; tel. 2420135; telex 22104; fax 2428530; f. 1960; cap. p.u. 17.6m.; all life and non-life insurance; Chair. MUHAMMAD SALEH BEHBEHANI; Gen. Man. ALI HAMAD AL-BAHAR.

Kuwait Reinsurance Co KSC: POB 21929, 13080 Safat, Al-Khaleejia Complex, 13th Floor, Al-Chark, Kuwait City; tel. 2432011; telex 22058; fax 2427823; Gen. Man. FATHI HAMAM.

Kuwait Technical Insurance Office: POB 25349, 13114 Safat; tel. 2413986; telex 23583; fax 2413986.

Mohd Saleh Behbehani & Co: POB 370, 13004 Safat; tel. 2412085; telex 22194; fax 2412089.

New India Assurance Co: POB 370, 13004 Safat; tel. 2412085; telex 22194; fax 2412089.

The Northern Insurance Co Ltd: POB 579, 13006 Safat; tel. 2427930; telex 22367; fax 2462739.

Oriental Insurance Co Ltd (Al Mulla Group): POB 22431, 13085 Safat; tel. 2424016; telex 22012; fax 2424017.

Sumitomo Marine & Fire Insurance Co (Kuwait Agency): POB 3458, 13055 Safat; tel. 2433087; telex 23754; fax 2430853.

Warba Insurance Company SAK: POB 24282, 13103 Safat; tel. 2445140; telex 22779; fax 2466131; f. 1976; Chair. and Man. Dir TEWFIK A. AL-GHARABALLY; 1 br.

Some 20 Arab and other foreign insurance companies are active in Kuwait.

STOCK EXCHANGE

Kuwait Stock Exchange: POB 22235, 13083 Safat, Kuwait; tel. 2423130; telex 44015; fax 2420779; f. 1984; 47 companies listed in 1993; Pres. HISHAM AL-OTAIBI; Vice-Pres. ABDULLAH AS-SDAIRAWI.

Trade and Industry

PETROLEUM

Kuwait Petroleum Corporation (KPC): POB 26565, 13126 Safat, Salhia Complex, Fahed as-Salem St, Kuwait City; tel. 2455455; telex 44875; fax 2423371; f. 1980; co-ordinating organization to manage the petroleum industry; controls companies listed below; Chair. Dr ABD AL-MOHSIN MUDAEJ AL-MUDAEJ (Minister of Oil); Deputy Chair. NADER SULTAN.

Kuwait Aviation Fuelling Co KSC: POB 1654, 13017 Safat, Kuwait City; tel. 4330482; telex 23056; fax 4330475; Gen. Man. ABD AL-AZIZ AS-SIRIE.

Kuwait Foreign Petroleum Exploration Co KSC (KUFPEC): POB 26565, 13126 Safat, Kuwait City; tel. 2455455; telex 44875; fax 2423371; f. 1981; state-owned; overseas oil exploration and development; Chair. FAISAL AL-KAZMAWI.

Kuwait National Petroleum Co KSC (KNPC): POB 70, 13001 Safat, Ali as-Salem St, Kuwait City; tel. 2420121; telex 22006; fax 2433839; f. 1960; oil refining, production of liquefied petroleum gas, and domestic marketing and distribution of petroleum by-products; output of 189,000 b/d of refined petroleum in 1991/92; Chair. and Man. Dir AHMAD ABD AL-MOHSIN AL-MUTAIR.

Kuwait Oil Co KSC (KOC): POB 9758, 61008 Ahmadi; tel. 3989111; telex 44211; fax 3983661; f. 1934; state-owned; Chair. and Man. Dir KHALID AL-FULAIJ.

Kuwait Oil Tanker Co SAK (see Transport—Shipping).

Kuwait Petroleum International Ltd (KPI): 80 New Bond St, London, W1, England; tel. (071) 491-4000; marketing division of KPC; controls 6,500 petrol retail stations in Europe, under the trade name 'Q8' (adopted in 1986), and European refineries with capacity of 235,000 b/d; Pres. KAMEL HARAMI.

Petrochemical Industries Co KSC (PIC) (see Development Organizations).

Arabian Oil Co: Head Office: Tokyo; Kuwait Office: POB 1641, 13017 Safat, Kuwait City; tel. 2439201; telex 22095; fax 2421936; Field Office Ras al-Khafji, Partitioned Zone, Saudi Arabia; f. 1950;

a Japanese company which holds concessions granted by Govts of Saudi Arabia and Kuwait in 1957 and 1958 respectively.

CHAMBER OF COMMERCE

Kuwait Chamber of Commerce and Industry: POB 775, 13008 Safat, Chamber's Bldg, Ali as-Salem St, Kuwait City; tel. 2433864; fax 2404110; f. 1959; 16,000 mems; Pres. ABD AL-AZIZ HAMAD AS-SAQR; Dir-Gen. HILAL MISHARI AL-MUTAIRI.

DEVELOPMENT ORGANIZATIONS

Arab Planning Institute (API): POB 5834, 13059 Safat, Kuwait City; tel. 4843130; telex 22996; fax 4842935; f. 1966; 50 mems; publishes annual directory and proceedings of seminars and discussion group meetings, offers research, training programmes and advisory services; Dir EBRAHIM ASH-SHAREEDAH.

General Board for the South and Arabian Gulf: POB 5994, Safat, Kuwait City; tel. 2424461; wholly state-owned; provides assistance to developing countries in the Arab world; Del. Mem. AHMAD AS-SAKKAF.

Industrial Investment Company (ITC): POB 26019, 13121 Safat, Kuwait City; tel. 2429073; telex 23132; fax 2448850; invests directly in industry; partly owned by the Kuwait Investment Authority.

Kuwait Foreign Trading, Contracting and Investment Co SAK (KFTCIC): POB 5665, 13057 Safat, Omar Bin al-Khattab St, Sharq, Kuwait City; tel. 2449031; telex 22021; fax 2446173; f. 1965 by Amiri decree; private banking, investments and real estate; 99.2% state-owned; Chair. and Man. Dir ABDULLAH AHMAD AL-GABANDI.

Kuwait Fund for Arab Economic Development (KFAED): POB 2921, 13030 Safat, cnr Mubarak al-Kabir St and al-Hilali St, Kuwait City; tel. 2468800; telex 22613; fax 2419091; f. 1961; cap. KD 2,000m.; state-owned; provides and administers financial and technical assistance to the countries of the developing world; Chair. NASSER ABDULLAH AR-RODHAN (Minister of Finance); Dir-Gen. BADER M. AL-HUMAIDHI.

Kuwait Investment Authority (KIA): POB 64, 13001 Safat, Kuwait City; tel. 2439595; telex 46089; fax 2454059; oversees the Kuwait Investment Office (London); responsible for the Kuwaiti General Reserve; Chair. NASSER ABDULLAH AR-RODHAN (Minister of Finance); Man. Dir ALI RASHID AL-BADR.

Kuwait International Investment Co SAK (KIIC): POB 22782, 13088 Safat, as-Salhia Commercial Complex, Kuwait City; tel. 2420762; fax 2454931; 30% state-owned; cap. p.u. 31.9m., total assets KD 146.9m. (1988); domestic real estate and share markets; Chair. and Man. Dir JASSIM MUHAMMAD AL-BAHAR.

Kuwait Investment Co SAK (KIC): POB 1005, 13011 Safat, Kuwait City; tel. 2438111; telex 22115; fax 2444896; f. 1961; 50% state-owned, 50% owned by private Kuwaiti interests; total resources KD 312.7m. (1988); international banking and investment; Chair. and Man. Dir BADER A. AR-RUSHAID AL-BADER.

Kuwait Planning Board: c/o Ministry of Planning, POB 15, 13001 Safat, Kuwait City; tel. 2428200; telex 22468; fax 2407326; f. 1962; supervises long-term development plans; through its Central Statistical Office publishes information on Kuwait's economic activity; Dir-Gen. AHMAD ALI AD-DUAIJ.

National Industries Co SAK: POB 417, 13005 Safat, Kuwait City; tel. 4849466; telex 22165; fax 4839582; f. 1960; 59.2% state-owned; cap. p.u. KD 24.3m.; has controlling interest in various construction enterprises; Chair. and Man. Dir MUFARREJ I. AL-MUFARREJ.

Petrochemical Industries Co KSC (PIC): POB 1084, 13011 Safat, Khalid Bin al-Walid St, Kuwait City; tel. 2422141; telex 22042; fax 2447159; f. 1963; state-owned; produced 851,700 metric tons of urea and 569,800 tons of ammonia in 1987/88; Chair. and Man. HANI HUSSAIN.

Fertilizer Plants: POB 1084, 13011 Safat, Kuwait City; tel. 2422141; telex 44212; fax 2447159; production of ammonia, urea, sulphuric acid and ammonium sulphate; four ammonia plants, three urea plants and one ammonium sulphate plant.

Salt and Chlorine Plants: POB 10277, 65453 Shuaiba, Kuwait; tel. 3263310; telex 46925; fax 3261587; f. 1963; production of salt, chlorine, caustic soda, hydrochloric acid, sodium hypochlorite, compressed hydrogen and distilled water; Operations Man. HAMAD AL-MISHWAT.

Shuaiba Area Authority SAA: POB 4690, 13047 Safat, Kuwait City; POB 10033, Shuaiba; tel. 3260903; telex 44205; f. 1964; an independent governmental authority to supervise and run the industrial area and Port of Shuaiba; has powers and duties to develop the area and its industries which include an oil refinery, cement factory, fishing plant, power stations and distillation plants, chemical fertilizer and petrochemical industries, sanitary ware factory, asbestos plant and sand lime bricks plant; Dir-Gen. SULEIMAN K. AL-HAMAD.

MAJOR INDUSTRIAL COMPANIES

Kirby Building Systems Kuwait: POB 23933, 13100 Safat, Mina Abdullah Industrial Area, Kuwait City; tel. 3260325; telex 44240; fax 3261798; f. 1976; pre-engineered steel buildings for industrial and commercial use; an affiliate of Alghanim Industries; Gen. Man. EDWARD G. EDGREN.

Kuwait Aluminium Co KSC: POB 5335, Safat ar-Rai Industrial Area, Plot 1636, St No. 13, Kuwait City; tel. 734600/800; telex 1730751; fax 734419; f. 1968; sales about KD 3.5m.; cap. p.u. KD 6m.; design, manufacture, erection and maintenance of aluminium and glass works for construction industry; Chair. NASSER NAKI; 250 employees.

Kuwait Cement Co KSC: POB 20581, Safat New Exhibition Bldg, 1st Floor, as-Sour St, Salhiya, Kuwait City; tel. 2422071; telex 22205; f. 1968; 34.6% govt-owned; manufacture and marketing of cement; cap. p.u. KD 25.6m.; Chair. ABD AL-MOHSIN ABD AL-AZIZ AR-RASHID; 525 employees.

Kuwait Food and Beverage Co WLL: POB 22528, Safat, Kuwait City; tel. 818862; canned food, soft drinks, juices, mineral water; Chair. MUHAMMAD RADWAN LUTHFI.

Kuwait Food Co (Americana) SAK: POB 5087, Safat Shuwaikh and Sabhan Industrial Area, Kuwait City; tel. 815900; telex 22125; f. 1963; cap. p.u. KD 11.3m.; chain of restaurants, meat industry, bakery plant for oriental sweets and English cakes; Chair. NASSER M. KHARAFI; 2,000 employees.

Kuwait Metal Pipe Industries Co KSC: POB 3416, Safat, Kuwait City; tel. 4675622; telex 23064; f. 1966; sales KD 10.8m. (1982); 16.6% govt-owned; manufacture of various pipes, tanks and coatings; cap. p.u. KD 15.2m.; Chair. KHALID FULAIJ AL-ALI FULAIJ; Vice-Chair. and Man. Dir AHMED YOUSUF M. AR-ROUDAN.

Kuwait Pharmaceutical Industries Co (KPICO): POB 5846, Safat, Kuwait City; tel. 4748011; telex 23091; fax 4714150; f. 1980; cap. KD 10m. (1987); began production in 1987; owned 34.9% by the govt, 25% by ACDIMA (Arab Co for Drug Industries and Medical Appliances), 20% by GIC (Gulf Investment Corporation) and 20.1% by private shareholders; cap. p.u. KD 5.5m.; Chair. Dr NA'IL AN-NAQIB; Man. Dir SULAIMAN S. ATH-THERBAN.

Kuwait Prefabricated Building Co SAK: POB 5132, Safat, Kuwait City; tel. 2438075; telex 22201; f. 1964; sales KD 18.5m. (1982); cap. p.u. KD 6m.; design and manufacture of precast structures, prestressed hollowcore slabs, claddings, beams, welded wire mesh, terrazzo tiles, structural steel items; hot dip galvanization; Chair. ABDULLAH J. AR-RUJAIB; 1,446 employees.

Kuwaiti Danish Dairy Co WLL: POB 835, 13009 Safat, Kuwait City; tel. 4717911; telex 23054; dairy products, ice cream, fruit juices and tomato paste.

Packaging and Plastic Industries Co: POB 10044, Shuwaikh Industrial Area, Kuwait City; tel. 3261322; telex 44219; f. 1974; production of polypropylene woven bags for packaging fertilizers, polyethylene agricultural sheets, co-extruded flexible film packaging; Chair. Dr ABD AL-AZIZ SULTAN AL-ESSA; 280 employees.

United Fisheries of Kuwait KSC: Shuwaikh Industrial Area, Shuwaikh, Kuwait; tel. 4833699; fax 4843701; f. 1972; sales KD 6.2m. (1989); cap. KD 7m.; production, export and import of frozen fish and shrimps; Chair. and Man. Dir ABD AL-LATIF AL-ASFOOR; 500 employees.

TRADE UNIONS

General Confederation of Kuwaiti Workers: Kuwait City; f. 1968; central authority to which all trade unions are affiliated.

KOC Workers Union: Kuwait City; f. 1964; Chair. JASSIM ABD AL-WAHAB AT-TOURA.

Federation of Petroleum and Petrochemical Workers: Kuwait City; f. 1965; Chair. JASSIM ABD AL-WAHAB AT-TOURA.

Transport

ROADS

Roads in the towns are metalled, and the most important are motorways or dual carriageways. There are metalled roads linking Kuwait City to Ahmadi, Mina al-Ahmadi and other centres of population in Kuwait, and to the Iraqi and Saudi Arabian borders, giving a total road network of 4,273 km in 1989 (280 km of motorways, 1,232 km of other major roads and 2,761 km of secondary roads).

Kuwait Public Transport Co SAK (KPTC): POB 375, 13004 Safat, Hilali St, Kuwait City; tel. 2469420; telex 22246; fax 2401265; f. 1962; state-owned; provides internal bus service; regular service to Iraq; Chair. of Board BARRAK K. AL-MARZOUK; Man. Dir ABD AL-WAHAB AL-HAROUN.

SHIPPING

Kuwait has three commercial seaports. The largest, Shuwaikh, situated about 3 km from Kuwait City, was built in 1960. By 1987 it comprised 21 deep-water berths, with a total length of 4 km, three shallow-water berths and three basins for small craft, each with a depth of 3.35m. In 1988 3.6m. metric tons of cargo were imported and 133,185 tons were exported through the port. A total of 1,189 vessels passed through Shuwaikh in 1988.

Shuaiba Commercial Port, 56 km south of Kuwait City, was built in 1967 to facilitate the import of primary materials and heavy equipment, necessary for the construction of the Shuaiba Industrial Area. By 1987 the port comprised a total of 20 berths, plus two docks for small wooden boats. Four of the berths constitute a station for unloading containers. Shuaiba handled a total of 3,457,871 metric tons of dry cargo, barge cargo and containers in 1988.

Doha, the smallest port, was equipped in 1981 to receive small coastal ships carrying light goods between the Gulf states. It has 20 small berths, each 100 m long. Doha handled a total of 20,283 metric tons of dry cargo, barge cargo and containers in 1988.

The oil port at Mina al-Ahmadi, 40 km south of Kuwait City, is capable of handling the largest oil tankers afloat, and the loading of over 2m. barrels of oil per day. By 1987 the port comprised 12 tanker berths, one bitumen-carrier berth, two LPG export berths and bunkering facilities.

Arab Maritime Petroleum Transport Co (AMPTC): POB 22525, 13086 Safat, Gulf Bank Bldg, Mubarak al-Kabir St, Kuwait City; tel. 2411815; telex 22180; fax 2437468; f. 1973; 3 tankers and 4 LPG carriers; sponsored by OAPEC and financed by Algeria, Bahrain, Iraq, Kuwait, Libya, Qatar, Saudi Arabia and the UAE; Chair. Sheikh RASHID AWAIDA ATH-THANI (Qatar); Vice-Chair. and Gen. Man. ABD AR-RAHMAN AHMAD AS-SULTAN.

Kuwait Maritime Transport Co KSC: POB 22595, 13086 Safat, Nafisi and Khatrash Bldg, Jaber al-Mubarak St, Kuwait City; tel. 2420519; telex 30967; fax 2420513; f. 1981.

Kuwait Oil Tanker Co SAK (KOTC): POB 810, 13009 Safat, as-Salhia Commercial Complex, Blocks 3, 5, 7 and 9, Kuwait City; tel. 2406805; telex 44766; fax 2445907; f. 1957; state-owned; operates 8 crude oil tankers, 26 other tankers and 4 LPG vessels; sole tanker agents for Mina al-Ahmadi, Shuaiba and Mina Abdullah and agents for other ports; LPG filling and distribution; Chair. and Man. Dir ABDULLAH AR-ROUMI.

Kuwait Shipbuilding and Repairyard Co SAK (KSRC): POB 21998, 13080 Safat, Kuwait City; tel. 4835488; telex 22438; fax 4830291; ship repairs and engineering services, underwater services, maintenance of refineries, power stations and storage tanks; maintains floating dock for vessels up to 35,000 dwt; synchrolift for vessels up to 5,000 dwt with transfer yard; five repair jetties up to 550 m in length and floating workshop for vessels lying at anchor; Chair. and Man. Dir MUSA J. MARAFI.

Ports Public Authority: POB 3874, 13039 Safat, Kuwait City; tel. 4812774; telex 22740; fax 4819714; there are plans to expand the ports to handle the increased cargo traffic projected for the 1990s; Chair. JASSEM AL'OUN; Dir-Gen. ABDUL RAHMAN AN-NAIBARI.

United Arab Shipping Co SAG (UASC): POB 3636, 13037 Safat, Shuwaikh, Airport Rd, Kuwait City; tel. 4843150; telex 22176; fax 4845388; f. 1976; national shipping company of six Arabian Gulf countries; services between Europe, Far East, Mediterranean ports, Japan and east coast of USA and South America, and ports of participant states on Persian (Arabian) Gulf and Red Sea; 47 vessels; subsidiary cos: Kuwait Shipping Agencies, Arab Transport Company (Aratrans), United Arab Chartering Company (London), Middle East Container Repair Company (Dubai), and United Arab Shipping Agencies Company; Chair. M. H. AR-RAYYES.

CIVIL AVIATION

Kuwait International Airport opened in 1980, and was designed to receive up to 4.5m. passengers per year. In 1991 Kuwait Airways carried a total of 840,000 passengers.

Directorate-General of Civil Aviation: POB 17, 13001 Safat, tel. 735599; telex 23038; Dir-Gen. Sheikh JABER AL-ATHBY AS-SABAH.

Kuwait Airways Corporation (KAC): POB 394, Kuwait International Airport, 13004 Safat; tel. 4740166; telex 23036; fax 4314726; f. 1954; services to the Arabian peninsula, Asia, Africa and Europe; Chair. AHMAD AL-MISHARI; Dir-Gen. AHMAD AZ-ZABIN.

Tourism

Department of Tourism: Ministry of Information, POB 193, 13002 Safat, Kuwait City; tel. 2436644; telex 44041; fax 2429758.

Touristic Enterprises Co: POB 23310, 13094 Safat, Kuwait City; tel. 5652775; telex 22801; fax 5657594; 92% state-owned; manages

23 tourist facilities; Chair. BADER AL-BAHAR; Vice-Chair. YACOUB AR-RUSHAID.

Defence

In June 1994 the armed forces numbered an estimated 16,600, including 10,000 in the army, 2,500 in the air force, and 2,500 in the navy. The latter includes a coastguard force of 500, administered by the Ministry of the Interior. Paramilitary forces include a National Guard of 5,000. The defence budget for 1994 was KD 500m. In August 1992 an Amiri decree authorized the Government to withdraw KD 3,500m., from state reserves to cover potential expenditure on defence over the following 12 years. There is a period of military service lasting two years (one year for university students), compulsory since March 1979.

Chief of Staff of Armed Forces: Gen. ALI AL-MOUMEN.

Education

In recent years a comprehensive system of kindergarten, primary, intermediate and secondary schools has been developed, and compulsory education for children between 6 and 14 years of age was introduced in 1966–67. However, many children spend two years prior to this in a kindergarten, and go on to complete their general education at the age of 18 years. It is government policy to provide free education to all Kuwaiti children from kindergarten stage to the University. In 1993/94 a total of 269,723 pupils attended 569 government schools (162 primary, 148 intermediate and 105 secondary). In 1990/91 a total of 65,407 pupils attended 172 private schools. Education was allocated an estimated KD 320.6m. in the Government's 1993/94 budget, or 8.3% of total expenditure.

Primary education lasts four years, after which the pupils move on to an intermediate school for another four years. Secondary education, which is optional and lasts four more years, is given mainly in general schools. There are also commercial institutes, a Faculty of Technological Studies, a health institute, religious institutes (with intermediate and secondary stages) and 11 institutes for handicapped children.

Two-year courses at post-secondary teacher training institutes provide teachers for kindergartens and primary schools and the University provides for intermediate and secondary schools. The number of graduates is not enough to meet all the teaching staff requirements and so the Ministry of Education meets this shortage by recruiting teachers from other Arab countries.

Scholarships are granted to students to pursue courses which are not offered by Kuwait University. In 1978/79 there were 2,925 Kuwaiti scholarship students studying abroad, mainly in Egypt, Lebanon, the UK and the USA. There were also pupils from Arab, African and Asian states studying in Kuwait schools on Kuwait Government scholarships. Kuwait University has about 12,500 students, and also provides scholarships for a number of Arab, Asian and African students. In 1989 a national library was being built, at an estimated cost of KD 4m. Following the Iraqi occupation of Kuwait, and the country's subsequent liberation, it was reported that 300 schools and colleges were in need of repair.

Between 1969 and 1985, 60,000 men and women graduated from the country's centres for illiteracy eradication and adult education, which in 1986 totalled 105, catering for 32,000 students. In 1990 the average rate of adult illiteracy was estimated by UNESCO at 27.0% (males 22.9%; females 33.3%).

Bibliography

Chisholm, A. H. T. *The First Kuwait Oil Concession: A Record of the Negotiations 1911–1934*. London, Cass.

Daniels, John. *Kuwait Journey*. Luton, England, White Crescent Press, 1972.

Department of Social Affairs. *Annual Report*. Kuwait.

Dickson, H. R. P. *Kuwait and her Neighbours*. London, Allen and Unwin, 1956.

El Mallakh, Ragaei. *Economic Development and Regional Co-operation: Kuwait*. University of Chicago Press, 1968.

Finnie, David. *Shifting Lines in the Sand*. London, I. B. Tauris, 1992.

Gardiner, Stephen, and Cook, Ian. *Kuwait: The Making of a City*. London, Longman, 1983.

Government Printing Press. *Education and Development in Kuwait*. Kuwait.

 Port of Kuwait Annual Report. Kuwait.

Hakima, Abu A. M. *The Modern History of Kuwait: 1750–1966*. UK, The Westerham Press, 1983.

Hay, Sir Rupert. *The Persian Gulf States*. Washington, DC, Middle East Institute, 1959.

International Bank for Reconstruction and Development. *The Economic Development of Kuwait*. Baltimore, Johns Hopkins Press, 1965.

Khouja, M. W., and Sadler, P. G. *The Energy of Kuwait: Development and Role in International Finance*. London, Macmillan, 1978.

Kochwasser, Friedrich H. *Kuwait. Geschichte, Wesen und Funktion eines modernen Arabischen Staates*. Tübingen, Eldmann, 1961.

Kuwait Oil Co Ltd. *The Story of Kuwait*. London.

Mansfield, Peter. *Kuwait: Vanguard of the Gulf*. London, Hutchinson, 1990.

Marlowe, John. *The Persian Gulf in the 20th Century*. London, Cresset Press, 1962.

Mezerik, Avraham G. *The Kuwait-Iraq Dispute, 1961*. New York, 1961.

Ministry of Planning. *Kuwait in Figures: Twenty-Five Years of Independence*. Kuwait, Central Statistical Office, 1986.

Rush, Alan. *Al-Sabah History and Genealogy of Kuwait's Ruling Family 1752–1987*. London, Ithaca Press, 1987.

Al-Sabah, Y. S. F. *The Oil Economy of Kuwait*. Henley-on-Thames, Routledge and Kegan Paul, 1981.

Saldanha, J. A. *The Persian Gulf: Administration Reports 1873–1957*. London, Archive Editions, 1986.

 The Persian Gulf Precis 1903–1908. London, Archive Editions, 1986.

Sandwick, John A. *The Gulf Co-operation Council: Moderation and Stability in an Interdependent World*. London, Mansell Publishing Ltd.

Winstone, H. V. F., and Freeth, Zahra. *Kuwait: Prospect and Reality*. London, Allen and Unwin, 1972.

LEBANON

Physical and Social Geography

W. B. FISHER

The creation, after 1918, of the modern state of Lebanon, first under French mandatory rule and then as an independent territory, was designed to recognize the nationalist aspirations of a number of Christian groups that had lived for many centuries under Muslim rule along the coast of the eastern Mediterranean and in the hills immediately adjacent. At least as early as the 16th century AD there had been particularist Christian feeling that ultimately resulted in the granting of autonomy, though not independence, to Christians living in the territory of 'Mount Lebanon', which geographically was the hill region immediately inland and extending some 30 km–45 km north and south of Beirut. The territory of Mount Lebanon was later expanded, owing to French interest, into the much larger area of 'Greater Lebanon' with frontiers running along the crest of the Anti-Lebanon mountains, and reaching the sea some miles north of Tripoli to form the boundary with Syria. In the south there is a frontier with Israel, running inland from the promontory of Ras an-Naqoura to the head of the Jordan Valley. In drawing the frontiers so as to give a measure of geographical unity to the new state, which now occupies an area of 10,452 sq km (4,036 sq miles), large non-Christian elements of Muslims and Druzes were included, so that at the present day the Christians of Lebanon form less than one-half of the total population.

PHYSICAL FEATURES

Structurally, Lebanon consists of an enormous simple upfold of rocks that runs parallel to the coast. There is, first, a very narrow and broken flat coastal strip—hardly a true plain—then the land rises steeply to a series of imposing crests and ridges. The highest crest of all is Qurnet as-Sauda, just over 3,000 m high, lying south-east of Tripoli; Mount Sannin, north-east of Beirut, is over 2,700 m. A few miles east of the summits there is a precipitous drop along a sharp line to a broad, troughlike valley, known as the Beka'a (Biqa), about 16 km wide and some 110 km to 130 km long. The eastern side of the Beka'a is formed by the Anti-Lebanon mountains, which rise to 2,800 m, and their southern continuation, the Hermon Range, of about the same height. The floor of the Beka'a valley, though much below the level of the surrounding mountain ranges, lies in places at 1,000 m above sea-level, with a low divide in the region of Baalbek. Two rivers rise in the Beka'a—the Orontes, which flows northwards into Syria and the Gharb depression, ultimately reaching the Mediterranean through the Turkish territory of Antioch; and the River Litani (Leontes). This latter river flows southwards, and then, at a short distance from the Israeli frontier, makes a sudden bend westwards and plunges through the Lebanon mountains by a deep gorge.

There exists in Lebanon an unusual feature of geological structure which is not present in either of the adjacent regions of Syria and Israel. This is the occurrence of a layer of non-porous rocks within the upfold forming the Lebanon mountains; and, because of this layer, water is forced to the surface in considerable quantities, producing large springs at the unusually high level of 1,200 m to 1,500 m. Some of the springs have a flow of several thousand cu ft per second and emerge as small rivers; hence the western flanks of the Lebanon mountains, unlike those nearby in Syria and Israel, are relatively well watered and cultivation is possible up to a height of 1,200 m or 1,500 m.

With its great contrasts of relief, and the configuration of the main ranges, which lie across the path of the prevailing westerly winds, there is a wide variety in climatic conditions.

The coastal lowlands are moderately hot in summer, and warm in winter, with complete absence of frost. But only 10 km or so away in the hills there is a heavy winter snowfall, and the higher hills are covered from December to May, giving the unusual vista for the Middle East of snow-clad peaks. From this the name Lebanon (laban—Aramaic for 'white') is said to originate. The Beka'a has a moderately cold winter with some frost and snow, and a distinctly hot summer, as it is shut off from the tempering effect of the sea.

Rainfall is generally abundant but it decreases rapidly towards the east, so that the Beka'a and Anti-Lebanon are definitely drier than the west. On the coast, between 750 mm and 1,000 mm (30 in to 40 in) fall annually, with up to 1,250 mm (50 in) in the mountains; but only 380 mm (15 in) in the Beka'a. As almost all of this annual total falls between October and April (there are three months of complete aridity each summer), rain is extremely heavy while it lasts, and storms of surprising intensity sometimes occur. Beirut, for example, has slightly more rain than Manchester, in England, but only about one-half of the number of rainy days. Another remarkable feature is the extremely high humidity of the coastal region during summer, when no rain falls.

ECONOMIC LIFE

The occurrence of high mountains near the sea, and the relatively abundant supplies of spring water, had a significant influence on economic development within Lebanon. Owing to the successive levels of terrain, an unusually wide range of crops can be grown, from bananas and pineapples on the hot, damp coastlands, olives, vines and figs on the lowest foothills, cereals, apricots and peaches on the middle slopes, to apples and potatoes on the highest levels. These latter are the aristocrats of the Lebanese markets, since they are rarest, and, with the growing market in the oilfield areas of Arabia and the Persian (Arabian) Gulf, they are sold for the highest price. Export of fruit is therefore an important item. In addition, abundant natural water led to the development of pinewoods and evergreen groves, which add greatly to the already considerable scenic beauty of the western hill country. Prior to the prolonged civil conflict in Lebanon (see History), there was an important tourist trade in the small hill villages, some of which have casinos, luxury hotels and cinemas. The greatest activity was during the summer months, when wealthy Middle Easterners and others arrived; but there was a smaller winter sports season, when skiing was pursued.

In addition, the geographical situation of Lebanon, as a 'façade' to the inland territories of Syria, Jordan, and even northern Iraq and southern Turkey, enabled the Lebanese ports to act as the commercial outlet for a very wide region. The importance of Beirut as a commercial centre was due in large part to the fact that Lebanon was a free market. More than one-half of the volume of Lebanon's former trade was transit traffic, and Lebanon used to handle most of the trade of Jordan. Byblos claims to be the oldest port in the world; Tyre and Sidon were for long world-famous, and the latter was reviving as the Mediterranean terminal of the Tapline (Trans-Arabian Pipeline) from Saudi Arabia until the Lebanese branch of the pipeline was closed at the end of 1983. Another ancient centre, Tripoli, was also a terminal of the pipeline from Iraq. Beirut is now, however, the leading town of the country, and contains more than one-half of the total population, including many displaced persons. Although local resources are not in general very great (there are no minerals or important raw materials in Lebanon), the city in normal times lived by commercial activity on a surprising scale, developed by the ingenuity and opportunism of its merchant class.

Beirut, of recent years, came to serve as a financial and holiday centre for the less attractive but oil-rich parts of the Middle East. Transfer of financial credit from the Middle East to Zürich, Paris, London, New York and Tokyo; a trade in gold and diamonds; and some connection with the narcotic trade of the Middle East—all these gave the city a very special function. Whether the traditional economic basis of the country—extreme individualism and 'laissez-faire' for entrepreneurs—can revive is uncertain, but strenuous efforts began in 1977 to bring about reconstruction and redevelopment, assisted by loans from outside. During 1980 a large contribution of 'front-line aid' was made by Arab League states, and this showed signs of producing significant economic recovery. However, the abrupt intensification of military activity in 1981–82, the effects of the subsequent Israeli invasion and the prolonged sectarian conflict negated these hopes. Production declined because of damage and disruption; the south was virtually disconnected from the remainder of the Lebanese state until Israeli forces withdrew to just inside the border in June 1985; such was the extent of factional division within the country that, in the early years of the recent civil conflict, the Government's authority was barely felt outside Beirut; by the late 1980s, if not before, even the capital had effectively lapsed into anarchy; the impossibility of controlling customs

and tax collection caused a substantial reduction in government income.

RACE AND LANGUAGE

It is difficult to summarize the racial affinities of the Lebanese people. The western lowlands have an extremely mixed population possibly describable only as 'Levantine'. Basically Mediterranean, there are many other elements, including remarkably fair individuals—Arabs with blonde hair and grey eyes, who are possibly descendants of the Crusaders. The remaining parts of the country show a more decided tendency, with darker colouring and more pronounced facial features. In addition, small refugee groups, who came to the more inaccessible mountain zones in order to escape persecution, often have a different racial ancestry, so that parts of Lebanon form a mosaic of highly varying racial and cultural elements. Almost all Middle Eastern countries are represented racially within Lebanon.

Arabic is current over the whole country, but owing to the high level of education (probably the highest in any Middle Eastern country) and to the considerable volume of temporary emigration, English, French and even Spanish are widely understood. French is probably still the leading European language (though English is tending to replace it) and some of the higher schools and one university teach basically in this language. In addition, Aramaic is used by some religious sects, but only for ritual—there are no Aramaic speaking villages as in Syria.

History

ANCIENT AND MEDIEVAL HISTORY

In the Ancient World Lebanon was important for its pine, fir and cedarwood, which neighbouring powers, poorly supplied with timber resources, coveted so much that during the long period of Egyptian, Assyrian, Persian and Seleucid rule, the exploitation of the forests of Lebanon was normally a royal privilege. The area was also mined for its iron and copper in the time of the Ptolemies and the Romans. Gradually Lebanon came to have a distinct history of its own, for the mountainous character of the region prevented any complete subjugation to outside authority. It is probable that the Arab conquest of Syria did not include the 'Mountain', to which fled all those who, for one reason or another, were opposed to the Arab domination. The Caliph Mu'awiya (661–80) made some effort to assert a greater control, but the resistance of the native Aramaean Christians was reinforced by the arrival of the Mardaites from the fastnesses of the Taurus and the Amanus. These Christian nomads, led by Byzantine officers, made determined advances into Lebanon, late in the seventh century, and seem to have united with the Maronite Christians who were later to become a Uniate Church of the Roman communion and to have a predominant role in the history of Lebanon. The Caliph Abd al-Malik (685–705) paid tribute to Byzantium in return for a withdrawal of most of the Mardaite forces; but it is clear that the 'Mountain' had begun to assume its historic function of providing a sure refuge for racial and religious minorities.

Lebanon maintained its Christian character until the ninth century when, amongst other elements, the Arab tribe of Tanukh established a principality in the region of al-Gharb, near Beirut, and acted as a counterpoise to the Maronites of northern Lebanon, and as a bulwark against Byzantine threats from the sea. Gradually, Islam and, more slowly still, the Arabic language penetrated the 'Mountain' where, however, Syriac lingered on in the Maronite districts until the 17th century (it is still spoken in three villages of the Anti-Lebanon). In the ninth and 10th centuries Muslim sects began to take root in the 'Mountain' as, for example, the Shi'a, known in Lebanon under the name of Mitwali, and, in the 11th

century, the Druze faith, which won a firm hold in southern Lebanon.

The Crusaders established in this area the County of Tripolis and the lordships of Gibelet and Batron, which enjoyed considerable support from the Christian population of northern Lebanon and were protected by a network of fortresses, the most famous of which is Hisn al-Akrad (Crac des Chevaliers). In the Mamluk period the rulers of Lebanon continued to practise the art of political manoeuvring, thus maintaining for themselves a considerable degree of autonomy. The Tanukhid amirs, after a long period in which they had played off the Crusaders against the Islamic amirates, had eventually taken the Mamluk side. In northern Lebanon the Maronites, under their bishop, maintained contact with the Italian republics and also with the Roman Curia. Less fortunate were the Druzes and the Mitwali who, in the last years of the 13th century, took advantage of the Mamluk preoccupation with the Mongol threat from Persia and began a protracted revolt which led to widespread devastation in central Lebanon.

THE OTTOMAN PERIOD

In the 16th century the Turcoman family of Assaf and, after them, the Banu Saifa rose to prominence in the area from Beirut to the north of Tripoli; while in the south the Druze house of Ma'an supplanted the Tanukhid amirs. After the conquest of 1516–17, the Ottoman Sultan Selim I had confirmed the amirs of Lebanon in their privileges and had imposed only a small tribute; yet not infrequently there was open conflict with the Ottomans, as in 1584–85 when, after an attack on a convoy bearing the tribute from Egypt to Constantinople, the Sultan Murad III sent a punitive expedition to ravage the lands of the Banu Saifa and of the Druzes.

The power of the House of Ma'an now reached its zenith in the person of Fakhr ad-Din II (1586–1635), who by every possible means—bribery, intrigue, foreign alliance, and open force—set out to establish an independent power over the whole of Lebanon and parts of Palestine to the south. To this end he entered into close relations with the Grand Duke of Tuscany, negotiating in 1608 a commercial agreement which contained a secret military clause directed against the Sultan. In 1613 a naval and military expedition sent from the Porte compelled Fakhr ad-Din to seek refuge with his Tuscan ally; but, returning in 1618, he rapidly restored his power and within a few years was virtual ruler from Aleppo to the borders of Egypt. The Sultan, heavily engaged in repressing revolt in Anatolia, and in waging a long struggle with Persia, could do no more than recognize the *fait accompli*. Fakhr ad-Din now embarked on an ambitious programme of development for Lebanon. He sought to equip a standing army with arms imported from Tuscany. Italian engineers and agricultural experts were employed to promote a better cultivation of the land and to increase the production of silk and olives. The Christian peasantry were encouraged to move from northern to southern Lebanon. Beirut and Sidon flourished as a result of the favour he showed to commerce, and religious missions from Europe—Capuchins, Jesuits, Carmelites—were allowed to settle throughout Syria, a development of great importance for France which strove to assert a 'protectorate' over all the Catholic and other Christian elements in the Ottoman Empire. However, the ambitions of Fakhr ad-Din were doomed to failure when by 1632 the Sultan Murad IV assumed effective control at Constantinople. The Pasha of Damascus, supported by a naval squadron, began a campaign to end the independent power of Lebanon, and in 1635 Fakhr ad-Din was executed at Constantinople.

In 1697 the Ma'an family became extinct and was succeeded by the House of Shihab, which maintained its predominance until 1840. In the course of the 18th century, the Shihab amirs gradually consolidated their position against the other factions of the 'Mountain' and for a while recovered control of Beirut. While normally they took care to remain on good terms with the Turkish pashas of Tripoli, Sidon and Damascus, the pashas, for their part, strove to exercise an indirect control by fomenting the family rivalries and religious differences which always marked the course of Lebanese politics. With the advent of Bashir II (1788–1840) the House of Shihab attained the height of its influence. Not until the death of Ahmad Jazzar, Pasha of Acre (1804), was he free to develop his power, which he maintained by the traditional methods of playing off one pasha against the other, and by bribing the officials of the Porte whenever it seemed expedient. In 1810 he helped the Ottomans to repel an invasion by the Wahhabi power of Arabia; but in 1831 he sided openly with Muhammad Ali of Egypt, when that ruler invaded Syria. Holding Lebanon as the vassal of Egypt, he was compelled, however, to apply to the 'Mountain' the unpopular policy imposed by Ibrahim Pasha, the son of Muhammad Ali, with the result that a revolt broke out, which, after the Egyptian withdrawal of 1840, led to his exile. The age of the Lebanese amirs was now at an end, for the Ottomans assumed control of the 'Mountain', appointing two Kaimakams to rule there, one Druze and the other Maronite, under the supervision of the pashas of Sidon and Beirut.

The period of direct Ottoman rule saw the rapid growth, between the Druzes and the Maronites, of a mistrust already visible during the time of the Egyptian dominance, and now fostered by the Ottomans as the only means of maintaining their influence over Lebanon. As a result of social and economic discontent, due to the slow disintegration of the old feudal system which had existed in Lebanon since the Middle Ages, the Maronite peasantry revolted in 1858 and destroyed the feudal privileges of the Maronite aristocracy, thus clearing the way for the creation of a system of independent smallholdings. The Druze aristocracy, fearing the consequences of a similar discontent among their own Maronite peasantry, made a series of attacks on the Maronites of northern Lebanon, who, owing to their own dissensions, could offer no effective resistance. The dubious attitude of the Turkish pashas, in the face of these massacres of 1860, led to French intervention, and in 1864 to the promulgation of an organic statute for Lebanon, which was now to become an autonomous province under a non-Lebanese Ottoman Christian governor, appointed by the Sultan and approved by the Great Powers. He was to be aided by an elected administrative council and a locally recruited police force. The statute also abolished legal feudalism in the area, thus consolidating the position won by the Maronite peasantry in 1858. The period from 1864 to 1914 was one of increasing prosperity, especially among the Christian elements, who also played an important role in the revival of Arab literature and Arab national feeling during the last years of the 19th century.

THE FRENCH MANDATE

The privileged position of Lebanon ended when the Turks entered the war of 1914–18; and by 1918 the coastal areas of Lebanon were occupied by British and French forces. In September 1920 the French created the State of Greater Lebanon which included not only the former autonomous province but also Tripoli, Sidon, Tyre and Beirut, some of which had in earlier times been under the control of the amirs of Lebanon. The period from 1920–36 was for Lebanon one of peaceful progress. A Constitution was devised in 1926, which proved unworkable and was suspended in 1932, from which time the President of the republic carried on the administration. He was, by convention, a Christian, while the Prime Minister was a Muslim, and both worked towards the achievement of a careful balance between the various religious communities of the new state. Lebanon was not unaffected by the growth of the nationalist movement in Syria, some sections of which demanded the reduction of Lebanon to its pre-war limits and even the abolition of its existence as a separate state. These demands found some support amongst the Sunni Muslims of the areas added to Lebanon proper in 1920, with the result that the Syrian revolt of 1925–26 spread to parts of southern Lebanon. The Maronite Christians, on the whole, supported the idea of a separate Lebanon, but were not united in their attitude towards France on the one hand, and the Arab states on the other. The Franco-Lebanese Treaty of 1936 differed little from that which France negotiated at the same time with Syria, the chief difference being that the military convention gave France wider military powers in Lebanon than in Syria. A reformed Constitution was promulgated in 1937; but the French refusal to ratify the treaty in 1938, and the advent of war prolonged a situation which, if outwardly calm, concealed a considerable discontent beneath the surface. In November 1941 the Free French Commander, General Catroux, formally proclaimed Lebanon a sovereign independent state. In September 1943 a new Parliament which had a strong nationalist majority soon came into conflict with the French authorities over the transfer of the administrative services. When, in November 1943, the Lebanese Government insisted on passing legislation which removed from the Constitution all provisions considered to be inconsistent with the independence of Lebanon, the French delegate-general arrested the President and suspended the Constitution. The other Arab states, together with the United Kingdom (UK) and the USA supported the Lebanese demands and in 1944 France began to transfer to Lebanese control all important public services, save for the Troupes Spéciales, i.e. local levies under French command, whose transfer the French authorities at first made conditional on the signing of a Franco-Lebanese Treaty. But in 1945 the Troupes Spéciales were handed over to Lebanon without such conditions, and an agreement between France and the Lebanese Government in 1946 provided for the withdrawal of French troops.

ECONOMIC DIFFICULTIES

Since 1946 Lebanon has continued to view with great reserve all projects for a Greater Syria, or for the union of Syria and Iraq. Like the other Arab states, Lebanon was at war with the new State of Israel from May 1948; but negotiated an armistice in March 1949. Just as in Syria the failure of the Arab arms had led eventually to the *coup d'état* of March 1949, so in Lebanon the widespread disillusionment of Arab nationalist hopes prepared the ground for a conspiracy against the Government. This conspiracy was easily suppressed in June 1949 and its leader, Antun Sa'ade, was executed.

In internal affairs, the Lebanese Government had to face considerable economic and financial difficulties soon after the end of the 1939–45 war. When, in January 1948, France devalued the franc (to which both the Lebanese and the Syrian currencies were linked) Lebanon, economically weaker than Syria, felt obliged to sign a new agreement with France (February 1948). Syria refused to do so and began a long and complicated dispute with Lebanon over the precise nature of the economic and financial arrangements which were to exist between the two states. In March 1950 the Lebanese Government refused a Syrian demand for full economic and financial union between Syria and Lebanon. The severance of economic relations which now ensued did not end until the signing, in February 1952, of an agreement which arranged for the division of royalties due from oil companies, and for the status, for customs purposes, of agricultural and industrial products passing between the two states.

In September 1952 Lebanon experienced a severe crisis in its internal affairs. Political and economic unrest brought about the fall of the Lebanese Government and the resignation of President al-Khouri, who had held office since 1943. Charges of corruption were made against the President. During his long tenure of power he had indeed used all the arts of political influence and manoeuvre in order to impose a real degree of unity on a state where the divergent interests of Maronites, Sunni and Shi'a Muslims, Druzes and other religious communities underlined the need for firm and coherent rule.

To an even greater degree, however, the crisis was due to causes of an economic order. Lebanon had attained its independence in the period of war-time prosperity. The end of the war meant a progressive diminution of foreign expenditure in Lebanon, and the gradual disappearance of war shortages which had favoured Lebanese trade. The devaluation of the French franc, the unsuccessful war with Israel, and above all the economic rupture with Syria gave rise to further difficulties. The break with Syria hit Lebanon hard, for Syria was the chief provider of agricultural goods to Lebanon and the chief customer for Lebanese industrial products. By 1952 there was much discontent arising from the high cost of living and from considerable unemployment. It was in fact a loose coalition of all the elements of opposition, both political and economic, which brought about the fall of the al-Khouri regime.

CONSTITUTIONAL REFORM

As a result of the crisis Camille Chamoun became the new President of the republic. The new administration, with the Amir Khalid Chehab as Prime Minister, bound itself to introduce reforms, including changes in the electoral laws, the grant of the vote to women, revision of the press laws and the reorganization of justice. The elections held in July 1953 led to the formation of a 44-member chamber of deputies composed on a sectarian basis according to the electoral law of 1952.

Since the foundation of the republic, all seats in the Chamber of Deputies had been distributed among the various religious communities in proportion to their numerical strength. The chamber was thus an institution reflecting in itself the religious and social structure of the state and capable of harmonious function, provided that the electoral system which maintained a delicate balance between the communities suffered no violent and prejudicial change. At the same time, it contained a strong 'feudal' element—the tribal and religious leaders who, with their trusted retainers, formed powerful groups within the chamber and were often criticized as being 'anti-national' in their aims and methods. To end or at least weaken this 'feudalization' of Lebanese political life, without, however, impairing the vital equilibrium between the Muslim and Christian communities, had long been the purpose of those who advocated a reasonable and well-considered policy of reform. The law of 1952 created 33 electoral districts (during the previous life of the republic the number had been, as a rule, five) and allotted to 11 of them two seats, and to the remainder one seat each. Of the total of 44 seats, the Maronites were now to receive 13, the Sunni Muslims nine, the Shi'a Muslims eight, the Greek Orthodox Christians five, the Druzes three, the Greek-Melkite Catholics three, the Armenian Catholics two, and the other confessions (Protestant, Jewish, Nestorian, etc.) one seat.

FOREIGN RELATIONS 1953–56

In the period 1953–56 financial and economic relations with Syria remained on a provisional basis much the same as that which had prevailed in the years 1950–53, earlier short-term arrangements being renewed from time to time, as the need arose. Discussions with Syria in November 1953 over problems of currency, loan policy, banks and exchange difficulties made no effective progress. The Lebanese Government was more successful, however, in its efforts to promote internal development. It was announced in August 1955 that the World Bank had granted to Lebanon a loan of $27m. for the Litani river scheme which, when completed, was expected to more than double the electric power available within the republic and also to irrigate a large area in the coastal region. Lebanon signed a number of commercial treaties at this time, which bore witness to the growing penetration of the Eastern bloc into Arab lands.

THE EISENHOWER DOCTRINE

A state of emergency was declared in Lebanon during the Sinai-Suez crisis at the end of October 1956. The Chamber of Deputies announced its support for Egypt, but Lebanon did not break off diplomatic relations with Great Britain and France. In November there were disturbances, however, at Tripoli and Beirut against the attitude of the Government. The 'Eisenhower Doctrine', a new programme, announced in January 1957, of financial, economic and military aid by the USA to those countries of the Middle East which were prepared to accept it, evoked a favourable response in Lebanese official circles. The foreign minister of Lebanon declared that the Government was willing to collaborate closely with the USA in the implementation of the programme, and it was later announced that Lebanon would co-operate with the USA in the task of opposing the growth of communist influence in the area and would receive, under the new programme, assistance to the amount of some $20m. The USA was also to help in the strengthening of the Lebanese armed forces. Some of the political groups in Lebanon protested against this pro-Western alignment, asserting that it could not fail to isolate Lebanon from the other Arab states and thus impair Arab solidarity. None the less, in April, the Government obtained from the Chamber of Deputies a vote of confidence in its policies.

The problem of electoral reform had been under consideration in Lebanon in the course of 1956. The main proposal now to be given effect was that the number of seats in the Chamber of Deputies should be raised from 44 to 66. As election time drew near in the summer of 1957, riots occurred in Beirut, the Government being compelled to call out troops for the maintenance of order. According to reports current at this time more than 100 communists were arrested for their part in the disturbances. The tense electoral campaign of June 1957 resulted in a marked triumph for the Government. A first provisional estimate suggested that it might count on the adherence of some three-quarters of the deputies in the new chamber. Of the total of 66 seats, the Maronites now received 20, the Sunni Muslims 14, the Shi'a Muslims 12, the Greek Orthodox Christians seven, the Druzes four, the Greek-Melkite Catholics four, the Orthodox Armenians three, the Armenian Catholics one, and the other religious minorities (Protestants, Jews, etc.) also one seat.

It was announced in July 1957 that Lebanon would receive from the USA, under the Eisenhower Doctrine, economic and military aid to the value of approximately $15m. in the course of the fiscal year 1958. Military equipment granted under the Doctrine had in fact begun to reach Beirut in June 1957. The Lebanese Government reiterated in August 1957 its firm desire to continue co-operation with the USA.

There had been serious disturbances in Lebanon at the time of the elections held in June 1957. It became clear that unrest, especially among those elements of the population which opposed the pro-Western policies of the Lebanese Government and favoured an alignment with Egypt and Syria, had not been quelled, when further incidents (bomb outrages and assassinations) occurred in November 1957. The Government, in its desire to halt these subversive activities, now imposed a close control over all Palestinian refugees in Lebanon. Indeed, after renewed outbreaks of violence in December, the northern area of Lebanon was declared to be a military sector.

The Lebanese Government stated in March 1958 that it would not join the United Arab Republic (Egypt and Syria), the

Arab Federation (Iraq and Jordan) or indeed any association which might limit its own independence and sovereignty. Large sections of the Muslim population, both in the north (at Tripoli) and in the south (at Tyre and Sidon), were inclined to be pro-Arab rather than pro-Lebanese in sentiment—a mood greatly stimulated by the emergence of the new United Arab Republic (UAR) and by the propaganda emitted from Cairo and Damascus for the return to Syria of those predominantly Muslim areas which had been joined to the old Lebanon in the time of the French mandate. There was conflict, too, between those who, although reluctant to see Lebanon lose its separate political existence, were none the less strongly opposed to the pro-Western attitude of the Lebanese Government and those who, fearing the possible absorption of Lebanon into the framework of a larger Arab state, felt themselves bound to support fully the policies of the Beirut regime. The danger was real that these complex tensions might explode in the form of a 'confessional' conflict between Muslims and Christians, in which, if not the continued independence, then at least the entire political orientation of Lebanon would be at stake.

THE CRISIS OF 1958

A reorganization of the Government, carried out in March 1958 and designed to remove those who were critical of the pro-Western policies of Lebanon and favoured closer co-operation with the UAR, brought no relief to the grave situation then developing. Serious disturbances, originating in Tripoli and the northern areas adjacent to the Syrian border, broke out in the second week of May and spread rapidly to Beirut and also to Tyre and Sidon in southern Lebanon. The Druze population in the south-east was involved, too, in the disorders, being sharply divided into pro- and anti-government factions. Hostile demonstrations led to the destruction of the US information service centres at Tripoli and Beirut. At the request of the Lebanese Government, the USA agreed to dispatch in all haste supplies of arms and police equipment and decided at the same time to reinforce the American Sixth Fleet stationed in the Mediterranean. The USSR now accused the USA of interference in Lebanese affairs and declared that Western intervention might have grave consequences. The Lebanese Government itself charged the UAR with interference in its internal affairs and appealed for redress to the Arab League which, meeting at Benghazi in June, failed to agree on a course of action. The problem was brought before the United Nations (UN), which resolved to send an observer corps to Lebanon.

The Lebanese Government was now, in fact, confronted with a widespread insurrection, in which the Muslim elements in the population were ranged against the Christian elements. The forces opposed to the existing regime controlled parts of Beirut, Tripoli and Sidon, as well as large areas in the north and the south of Lebanon. Attempts to negotiate a settlement led to no favourable result. The Prime Minister, Sami as-Sulh, gave an assurance that President Chamoun did not intend to ask for a constitutional amendment which would enable him to seek re-election to his office in September 1958, the date when his present tenure was due to end. To this assurance the leaders of the insurrection replied with a firm demand for the immediate resignation of the President, who made it clear, however, that he would not relinquish his office until September.

On 14 July—the date of the *coup d'état* which led to a change of regime in Iraq—President Chamoun requested the USA to send US troops into Lebanon to maintain security and preserve Lebanese independence. About 10,000 US troops were sent to the Beirut area. The USA also made it known that action on the part of forces under the control of the UAR against US troops in Lebanon might lead to most serious consequences. At this juncture, the USSR and China made strong protests against the US intervention and asked for the prompt withdrawal of the US forces landed in Lebanon. On 18 August the USA gave a written undertaking to withdraw its troops, either at the request of the Lebanese Government, or in the event of the UN's taking appropriate measures to ensure the integrity and peace of the country. The UN General Assembly thereupon adopted a resolution, framed by its Arab members, which provided for the evacuation of US troops under the auspices of the UN and of the Arab League.

PRESIDENT CHEHAB, 1958–64

Meanwhile, the Lebanese Chamber of Deputies had, on 31 July, elected as the new President of the state Gen. Fouad Chehab, the Commander-in-Chief of the Lebanese army—a choice supported by members from both sides involved in the internal conflict. He assumed office on 23 September, in succession to President Chamoun, and at once invited Rashid Karami, the leader of the insurgents at Tripoli, to become Prime Minister. An agreement was made on 27 September to the effect that the US forces were to leave Lebanon by the end of October.

In October 1959 the Lebanese Cabinet was increased from four to eight members, so that greater representation might be given to the various political groups. The Chamber of Deputies approved in April 1960 an Electoral Reform Bill, which imposed for the first time the principle of the secret ballot in Lebanese elections and also enlarged the chamber itself from 66 to 99 deputies—a total figure that maintained the existing ratio (laid down in 1943) of six Christian to every five Muslim (including Druze) deputies in the chamber. The chamber was dissolved by the President of Lebanon on 5 May 1960, the Government of Rashid Karami resigning nine days later. A general election was then held in four separate stages on 12, 19 and 26 June and 3 July 1960.

The election took place in an atmosphere of complete calm, strict security measures being enforced throughout the various stages of the electoral process. In the new Chamber of Deputies there were 30 Maronite Christians, 20 Sunni Muslims, 19 Shi'a Muslims, 11 Greek Orthodox Christians, six Greek-Melkite Catholics, six Druzes, four Armenian Orthodox Christians, one Armenian Catholic, one Protestant and one member representing other elements. A large number of the 'rebel' personalities prominent in the events of 1958 and hitherto not seated in the chamber were now returned as members.

A new government, under the leadership of Saeb Salam, took the oath of office on 2 August 1960. The Cabinet, which included several personalities active on one side or the other in the troubles of 1958, was prompt to reaffirm the traditional policies of non-expropriation, of minimal government intervention in private enterprise, of encouragement for private investment both foreign and domestic, and of currency convertibility. By 1960 Lebanon had recovered, in economic terms, almost completely from the disturbances in 1958.

CABINET REFORM

It had come to be felt, since August 1960, that the Lebanese Cabinet, 18 members strong, was too large for the maintenance of an efficient administration and so, on 22 May 1961, the Prime Minister established a new Cabinet consisting of eight ministers only. However, on 24 October, as the result of a dispute with some members of his Government (notably Kamal Joumblatt, the Druze leader, who was Minister of Works and Planning), Salam resigned. Rashid Karami, a former Prime Minister, formed a new government on 31 October 1961.

Military elements, acting in conjunction with civilians described as supporters of the extremist National Social Party, made an unsuccessful attempt, on 31 December 1961, to overthrow the Lebanese Government. The National Social Party was in fact the old Parti Populaire Syrien, founded in the 1930s by Antoine Saadé with the aim of uniting several Arab states into a Greater Syria. Its current leader, Dr Abdallah Saadé, was now arrested and the party itself dissolved by the Lebanese Government on 1 January 1962. The Lebanese Government took firm action against all the elements suspected of involvement in the revolt, and crushed it within a few days.

On 19 February 1964 the Cabinet led by Rashid Karami (which had held office for the last two years) resigned, after President Chehab had signed a decree dissolving the Chamber of Deputies (elected in 1960) and ordering elections to be held on four successive Sundays from 5 April to 3 May 1964. A caretaker Cabinet was appointed to supervise the elections for the new Chamber of Deputies.

PRESIDENT HÉLOU

General Chehab, whose six-year term of office as President of the republic was due to end in September 1964, rejected all appeals that he should submit himself as a candidate for a second time. Even when the Chamber of Deputies passed a motion in favour of an amendment to the Constitution which would enable him to stand for a further term of office, Gen. Chehab persisted (3 June 1964) in his refusal. On 18 August 1964 Charles Hélou, Minister of Education in the caretaker administration, succeeded Gen. Chehab as President. President Hélou pledged himself to follow the policies and reforms introduced under Gen. Chehab.

On 25 September 1964 Hussein Oweini, the head of the caretaker Cabinet in office since February of that year, formed an administration at the request of President Hélou. The new administration aroused dissatisfaction, however, in the Chamber of Deputies, since, deriving from the Cabinet appointed originally to act as a caretaker during the period of the 1964 elections, it was in fact composed wholly of non-members of the chamber. Having resigned on 13 November, Oweini now, on 18 November, gathered together a new Cabinet which, save for himself and the Minister of Foreign Affairs, consisted of members drawn from the Chamber of Deputies and reflected in itself all the main trends of opinion within the chamber.

FOREIGN RELATIONS

On 20 July 1965 the Prime Minister, Hussein Oweini, resigned. There had been much debate in the Chamber of Deputies about a proposed agreement to guarantee private US investment in Lebanon against expropriation, war or revolution—an agreement construed in some political circles as giving to the USA a possible excuse for intervention, at need, in Lebanese affairs. On 26 July Rashid Karami became the new Prime Minister, with nine Cabinet ministers to assist him, all chosen from outside the Chamber of Deputies.

There was friction during the first months of 1965 between Federal Germany and the Arab states because of the decision by Bonn to enter into formal diplomatic relations with Israel. Anti-German demonstrations occurred at Tripoli and Beirut, and on 13 May 1965 Lebanon severed diplomatic relations with Federal Germany. In May 1965 Lebanon signed an agreement on trade and technical co-operation with the European Economic Community (EEC). There was some friction between Israel and Lebanon over border incidents during the summer and autumn of 1965. Members of the main Palestinian guerrilla organization, al-Fatah (the Palestine National Liberation Movement), made raids into Israel, provoking Israeli reprisals against the Lebanese village of Noule.

FINANCIAL CRISIS

Rashid Karami modified his Cabinet in December 1965 and January 1966, these changes arising from difficulties which hindered the full implementation of an administrative and judicial reform programme, one of the main advocates of which was President Hélou. Between December 1965 and March 1966 an estimated 150 officials including 100 civil servants were compelled to withdraw from public life. This sustained attempt to curb corruption and the abuse of office in government circles and to ensure efficient and honest administration inevitably caused considerable tension. There was strong pressure in the Chamber of Deputies for a return to a Cabinet chosen mainly from the chamber itself. This and other difficulties obliged Karami to offer his resignation to President Hélou who appointed Dr Abdallah al-Yafi as the new Prime Minister.

Dr al-Yafi assembled a 10-man Cabinet drawn entirely from the Chamber of Deputies with the exception of himself and Philippe Takla, the new Minister of Foreign Affairs. The constitution of the Cabinet represented a balance between the various religious interests and, from the point of view of politics, between the left-wing and right-wing elements in the Chamber of Deputies.

In October 1966 the Intra Bank of Lebanon was compelled to close its doors because of a run of withdrawals amounting to more than £11m. in the preceding month. One result of that financial crisis was that the Government resolved to discourage the creation of new commercial banks, foreign or Lebanese, for a period of five years. Hitherto there had been an almost complete freedom to establish new banks in Lebanon and there had been a large expansion of the banking system based on the flow into Lebanon of vast oil revenues from Saudi Arabia and from the states of the Persian Gulf.

On 2 December the Prime Minister of Lebanon Dr Abdallah al-Yafi, offered the resignation of his Government to President Hélou. Rashid Karami formed a new administration on 7 December 1966. It was composed of men drawn from outside Parliament, six of whom held ministerial posts for the first time.

In June 1967 the Lebanese Government aligned itself with the Arab states then engaged in war against Israel. On 8 June the Government asked the ambassadors of the UK and the USA to leave Lebanon. Pro-Egyptian demonstrations at Beirut in June caused some damage to British and US properties there. Some trouble was also reported from Tripoli, where a West German cultural centre was subjected to attack. However, the months following the war witnessed a gradual easing of the tensions arising out of the conflict, and in September 1967 the Lebanese Cabinet agreed to reinstate its ambassadors in Washington and London.

POLITICAL INSTABILITY

Rashid Karami's Cabinet resigned from office in February 1968. President Hélou then asked Dr Abdallah al-Yafi to form an interim administration, whose main task was to be the preparation and conduct of the general election in March 1968. The two most successful parties elected in the Chamber of Deputies were the Maronite-dominated Triple Alliance, of a right-wing complexion, and the Democratic Block aligned further to the left. However, Dr al-Yafi's interim administration remained in office until October, when it was forced to resign, owing to bitter rivalry between the two main political groups, the 'Chamounists' and the 'Chehabists' (both named after former presidents), disputes over sectional representation in the Cabinet, and the Government's inability to command a majority in the Chamber of Deputies. After a week of confusion, a new four-man government was announced on 20 October, still headed by Dr al-Yafi.

THE GUERRILLAS AND ISRAEL

The first clash between Lebanese and Israeli forces on the border for over two years took place in May 1968. As the activities of the Palestinian guerrillas intensified, however, Lebanon became increasingly involved as a target for Israel's grievances against the Palestinians. On 26 December an Israeli airliner was machine-gunned by Arab guerrillas at Athens airport. Two days later, Israeli commandos raided Beirut airport and destroyed 13 aircraft, all belonging to Lebanese airlines. The Israeli Government stated that the raid should be regarded as a reprisal for the Athens attack, a warning to the Arab world not to make any repetition of it, and a further warning to Lebanon to police more effectively the activities of Palestinian *fedayin* (freedom fighters) in the country. The financial cost to Lebanon was relatively small, as most of the aircraft were insured abroad. The major after-effects of the raid were, firstly, the widespread criticism that it attracted even from countries normally favourable to Israel. Lebanon was viewed as a country which had taken little active part in the campaign against Israel, while the Palestinian *fedayin* within it were only enjoying the freedom available to them in Lebanon's open, tolerant society. The UN Security Council unanimously condemned Israel for the raid. The second effect was the fall of the Government on 7 January 1969, its alleged lack of preparedness for Israeli aggression dealing the final blow to a weak administration. On 20 January, after much political manoeuvring, a new Government was formed, headed by Rashid Karami, who thus became Prime Minister for the seventh time.

This Government was immediately confronted with the basic problems underlying the Lebanese situation, foremost among these being the Christian-Muslim balance. In theory, both religions were equally represented in Lebanon, but no census had been held since 1939 mainly because the authorities feared that the balance had shifted to a 60% Muslim predominance, which would seriously affect the political situation. (Indeed, according to 1983 estimates, the Muslim population of Lebanon, both Shi'a and Sunni, was 1.95m., while the combined Maronite and Greek Orthodox Christian communities numbered 1.15m.) The Christian community had a disproportionate share of the wealth and important positions, was generally conservative by Arab standards and took a moderate position on the Israel question. The less privileged Muslim majority was more in favour of both domestic reform (Lebanon had, for example, only the beginnings of a welfare state) and of a more militant position towards Israel. Early in 1969 numbers of Syrian guerrillas entered the country and spent as much time in action against the Lebanese army as against Israel. Unrest also appeared amongst the 260,000 Palestinian refugees in the Sidon camp; part of the frontier with Syria was eventually closed. Numerous strikes and demonstrations continued. The Karami Government felt unable to maintain the necessary coalition from the two communities and their various factions and resigned on 25 April. However, it continued to function as a caretaker administration as no stronger government could be formed.

In the late summer of 1969 a number of guerrilla groups were reported to have moved to new bases better sited for attacks on Israel, which continued to raid these bases in reprisal; the combination of these factors created some friction between the guerrillas and the Lebanese army. In October the army apparently attacked some of these camps in an attempt to restrict or direct their activities. This caused a political crisis in which the caretaker Government resigned, claiming that it had not authorized the army's actions, and the President and the armed forces administered the country directly. Radical elements and guerrillas took over Tripoli, the second largest city, for several days, and most of the Palestinian refugee camps were fully converted into military training and equipment centres. Militant support for the guerrillas was voiced throughout the Arab world, and there were threats of military intervention by Syria and Iraq.

On 2 November the Lebanese Commander-in-Chief and Yasser Arafat, the leader of al-Fatah, signed a cease-fire agreement in Cairo. This limited the guerrillas' freedom of movement to certain areas; as further defined in January 1970, it also provided that camps had to be set up some distance from towns, that military training must cease in refugee camps, and that guerrillas must enter Israel before engaging in hostilities. The intention was not to impede guerrilla attacks, but to prevent innocent Lebanese from being injured, and their property from being damaged, by Israeli counter-attacks.

The calmer atmosphere that followed the cease-fire enabled Karami to form another Cabinet towards the end of November. There was much concern about the weakness of the country's southern defences, and in January 1970 the new ministry felt strong enough to dismiss the Commander-in-Chief of the army, appointing instead Brig. Jean Njeim. In March there was a series of street battles in the Beirut area between the Palestinian guerrillas and militant right-wing Phalangist groups, but the Government and the army managed to avoid becoming involved. In May Israel launched a major air and ground attack on guerrilla positions in southern Lebanon, a substantial area being occupied for nearly two days. Syria sent air assistance for the small Lebanese air force.

POLITICAL CRISES

Sulayman Franjiya was elected President in August 1970, and a new Cabinet was formed by Saeb Salam. Some measures of political liberalization, such as the relaxation of press, radio and television censorship and the removal of the ban on extremist parties did little to curb domestic unrest. Strikes and demonstrations against unemployment and inflation, student disorders and fighting between Phalangists and the Parti Populaire Syrien continued throughout 1971. The parliamentary elections of April 1972 reflected a marked swing towards left-wing political groups.

The Palestinian guerrillas remained Lebanon's major problem. Their bases in the refugee camps became more important following the expulsion of the guerrillas from Jordan in July 1971, and guerrilla operations against Israel produced violent Israeli reprisals in which both Palestinians and Lebanese suffered. The villages of southern Lebanon bore the brunt of Israeli raids, and their inhabitants secured a greater measure of Lebanese army control over guerrilla activities in March 1972. Arab terrorist actions still provoked Israeli reprisals against Lebanon, even when there was little connection between the terrorists and Israel's vulnerable northern neighbour. The killing of Israeli athletes at the Olympic Games in Munich in September 1972 led to Israeli ground and air attacks on guerrilla bases, in which the Lebanese army suffered a number of casualties. The Lebanese Government was unable to persuade the guerrillas to suspend their activities against Israel, and several clashes between the Lebanese army and the guerrillas occurred.

In February 1973 Israeli commandos attacked guerrilla training bases in refugee camps about 160 km north of the Lebanese frontier, and escaped virtually unopposed. A further Israeli raid, in which three guerrilla leaders were shot in their homes in the centre of Beirut, and an attempt to blow up oil storage tanks at the Zahrani terminal, attributed to Palestinian extremists, resulted in the fall of the Salam Government. Salam resigned, dissatisfied with the inability of the Lebanese armed forces to prevent an Israeli military action in the capital, and Dr Amin Hafez formed a new government. Several members of the Salam Cabinet remained in office, the new Government including representatives of most of the major political and religious groups.

Tension between the Lebanese army and the guerrillas culminated in May 1973 in Lebanese ground and air attacks on the refugee camps. An invasion by guerrillas based in Syria was repulsed and a cease-fire was brought about by the mediation of other Arab states. The guerrillas apparently agreed to stop their terrorist activities within Lebanon and to cease using the camps as bases for training guerrillas.

The Hafez Government lasted only seven weeks. The Prime Minister resigned on 14 June, unable to settle the Sunni Muslim claim for a greater share in the allocation of government posts, and it was not until 8 July that Taki ed-Din Solh was able to form a new administration. A moderate, Mr Solh enjoyed the support of many Sunni factions, and his Cabinet included representatives of all the main religious blocs. Outside Parliament, however, violent disorders continued, with industrial disputes resulting in demonstrations and clashes with police.

The potential religious hostility within Lebanon, and the political implications of the division of government and administrative posts on a confessional basis were again demonstrated in February 1974. Civil service reforms, intended to overcome the sectarian nature of certain appointments, were opposed by Maronites who feared that they would lose posts traditionally reserved for their community. The National Liberal Party threatened to withdraw its three Cabinet members, and the proposed reforms were also condemned by the Phalange and the Bloc National. The Shi'a Muslims of southern Lebanon also made demands for increased representation and more investment and development in the south. The Shi'a leader, Imam Moussa as-Sadr, implied that he would organize his followers and arm them as protection against Israeli raids, as, indeed, he later did.

Although Lebanon was not directly involved in the October 1973 Arab-Israeli war, southern regions had continued to serve as a guerrilla base and to suffer Israeli reprisals. Southern villages were shelled intermittently, and small-scale raids across the border and acts of terrorism became commonplace.

In July 1974 there were clashes between Palestinians and Phalangists who continued to demand more government controls on guerrilla activities. Throughout 1974 and into 1975 Israeli shelling, air raids and incursions into Lebanon continued, together with guerrilla attacks against the Israelis. Consequently the situation on the border remained tense. In September 1974, unable to curb internal sectarian violence by its ineffective ban on the possession of firearms, Taki ed-Din Solh's Cabinet resigned. In October a new government was formed under Rashid Solh, although violence continued, finally erupting in a bloody clash between troops and citizens of the port of Sidon. The Cabinet split over the granting of a

Muslim demand to confer citizenship to long-time residents of the country. Letter bomb and dynamite explosions and further border fighting between the Israelis and guerrilla groups were followed by further fierce conflict between the Phalangists and Palestinians, in which over 150 died and 300 were wounded. Much damage was caused in Beirut and, after an agreement by Solh to normalize relations with the Palestinians and the fact that the security forces had not intervened in the fighting, the Phalangists appeared to be on the defensive.

CIVIL WAR

Intercommunal strife had never been far from the surface in Lebanon (see under The Guerrillas and Israel, p. 600). Following an incident in April 1975, when Palestinians made an attack on some Phalangists, the Phalangists killed the passengers of a bus, who were mainly Palestinians. From this incident inter-communal fighting between Christians and Muslims quickly spread, and continued, with short interruptions, until October 1976. At this point the official policy of the Palestine Liberation Organization (PLO), led by Yasser Arafat, was to stand aloof from the conflict, and Arafat himself was, in fact, instrumental in securing some of the many cease-fires.

In May 1975, shortly after the fighting began, Rashid Solh resigned as Prime Minister, and was replaced by Rashid Karami, who continued as Prime Minister through an exceedingly turbulent period until December 1976. In September 1975 a national dialogue committee was formed, consisting of 20 members from all political and confessional groups, to try to restore 'normal life'—a task in which they were unsuccessful. By October 1975 there was evident dissatisfaction with President Franjiya and his inability to bring the fighting to an end, and it also became increasingly evident that in spite of the official policy of the PLO not to interfere in the internal affairs of Lebanon, members of extremist Palestinian groups, particularly those of the 'rejectionist front', were being drawn into the fighting on the side of the Muslims. It was also, at this point, the official policy of the Lebanese army not to intervene, although, later, breakaway groups became involved in the fighting.

By the middle of January 1976 the PLO was becoming increasingly drawn into the conflict, and several Syrian-based units of the Palestine Liberation Army were fighting in Lebanon on the side of the Muslims. Under these increasingly ominous conditions the term of the Chamber of Deputies was extended by a year (later increased to two years) and the general elections scheduled for April 1976 were postponed for up to 26 months. In January 1978 the chamber's term was extended until June 1980. In March 1979 the Chamber was renamed the National Assembly and in April 1980 its term was further extended to the middle of 1983.

A temporary cease-fire gave a brief respite in January 1976, but by March no agreement had been reached on political reforms, fighting had flared up again, and 70 deputies signed a petition asking President Franjiya to resign. Further weight was given to this request in April, when a parliamentary session took place and 90 deputies voted unanimously to amend Article 73 of the Constitution to allow presidential elections to be held up to 6 months before the expiry of the incumbent's term of office. President Franjiya signed this amendment on 23 April but, in spite of the election of his successor, refused to resign until the completion of his term of office in September 1976, when he was succeeded by Elias Sarkis, who had been governor of the Central Bank.

INCREASED SYRIAN INTERVENTION

By May 1976 Syria was becoming increasingly involved in Lebanese affairs. By 20 May it was estimated that about 40,000 Syrian-controlled troops were in Lebanon. Yasser Arafat had ordered pro-Damascus Palestinian units to withdraw, and it now became clear that Arafat and the PLO had become entirely sympathetic to the Lebanese left-wing. In early June Syria launched a full-scale invasion of Lebanon officially to end the civil war and restore peace, but unofficially, it became clear, to crush the Palestinians. The conflict threatened to acquire international proportions, and an emergency meeting of Arab ministers of foreign affairs met in Cairo

under the sponsorship of the Arab League. It was agreed to send a joint Arab peace-keeping force to Lebanon, to be accompanied by a phased, but not complete, withdrawal of Syrian troops. The Arab peace-keeping force was to include participants from Syria, Libya, Algeria, Sudan, Saudi Arabia and the PLO, under an Egyptian Commander-in-Chief, but by the end of June 1976 the 1,000-man force was made up of 500 Syrian troops merely under a different guise, and 500 Libyans. Meanwhile, fierce fighting broke out in the area of two Palestinian refugee camps, Tal az-Zaatar and Jisr al-Basha, and most of Beirut was without water or electricity. The Arab League took steps to hasten the arrival of further contingents of the peace-keeping force, and the Secretary-General, Mahmoud Riad, headed another mediation mission, but fighting continued unabated until October 1976, when Arab summit meetings in Riyadh and Cairo secured a lasting cease-fire. During the course of the fighting there had been more than 50 abortive cease-fires and it was estimated that up to 60,000 people had been killed and up to 100,000 injured.

The Riyadh and Cairo summits arranged for a 30,000-strong Arab deterrent force (mainly Syrians) to police Lebanon, and a four-party disengagement committee was set up to attempt to implement the terms of the 1969 Cairo agreement between the Lebanese Government and the Palestinian guerrillas, as this was considered to be one of the keys to a lasting peace. The disengagement committee consisted of Col Muhammad Khouli (Syria), Abd al-Hamid Buaijan (the Kuwaiti Ambassador in Beirut), Gen. Ali ash-Shaer (Saudi Arabian Ambassador in Beirut), and Ahmad Loutfi Moutawalli, the Egyptian Ambassador in Beirut. The committee began by restricting the level of heavy weapons allowed to the various factions, and then sought an agreement on the proportion of armed men allowed in the Palestinian guerrilla camps. The Shtaura Agreement of July 1977 attempted to settle this problem, by endeavouring to regulate the Palestinian base camps and to introduce a reconstituted Lebanese army into the border area.

In December 1976 President Sarkis appointed as Prime Minister Dr Selim al-Hoss, who formed a Cabinet of eight technocrats charged with rebuilding and reconstruction; and the Government was granted the power to rule by decree for six months, subsequently extended. A reconstruction and development council was set up under the chairmanship of Muhammad Atalla, and this council took over the functions of the former ministry of planning. In January 1977 censorship was imposed on the press, initially both on Lebanese and foreign journalists, but the restrictions on foreign dispatches were soon removed.

The Druze chief and leader of the Lebanese left, Kamal Joumblatt, was assassinated on 16 March 1977. Although his murder was followed by a wave of revenge killings, it did not lead to any renewed outbreak of major fighting. However, the southern area of Lebanon, between the Litani river and the Israeli border, became the scene of renewed fighting during 1977. This area was largely spared during the civil war, and fighting developed when the Palestinians moved to the hills of southern Lebanon after being subdued by the Syrians in the civil war. A war 'by proxy' developed, with Syria allied with the Palestine guerrillas and Israel supporting the Lebanese Government. The Shtoura Agreement in July 1977 and a later cease-fire in September 1977, arranged with the intervention of the USA, was ineffective.

The volatile situation flared up in March 1978 as a result of a raid by al-Fatah guerrillas into Israel on 11 March, when, in an attack on a bus near Tel-Aviv, more than 35 people were killed. In retaliation, and in order to prevent further raids, Israeli forces advanced into southern Lebanon three days later. The UN Security Council demanded an Israeli withdrawal and established a United Nations Interim Force in Lebanon (UNIFIL) of 6,000 to maintain peace in the area. Israeli forces withdrew from southern Lebanon in June 1978, but relinquished control to a right-wing, mainly Christian Lebanese militia which maintained links with the Israelis.

In July 1978 fighting erupted again in Beirut between the Syrian troops of the Arab deterrent force and right-wing Christian militias. A cease-fire was proclaimed in early October and the Ministers of Foreign Affairs of the states participating in the Arab deterrent force (Kuwait, Lebanon, Qatar, Saudi Arabia, Sudan, Syria and the UAE) met at Beiteddin, near Beirut, and agreed on a declaration which was intended to bring peace to the area. It maintained that Lebanese central authority must be imposed, that armed militias must be curbed and that a truly national army must be formed.

LEBANON AFTER THE BEITEDDIN DECLARATION

The aims of the Beiteddin Declaration were not realized. In April 1979 Major Saad Haddad, a right-wing Lebanese army officer, proclaimed 'independent free Lebanon'—a slice of territory, covering about 1,800 sq km, next to the Israeli border. Encouraged and supplied by Israel, Haddad was able to maintain his independence. In July 1980 the Phalangist Commander, Bachir Gemayel, consolidated his power by overcoming the militia of the National Liberal Party. This led to a strengthening of the Phalangist militia, with the result that Phalangist forces occupied the town of Zahle in the Beka'a valley. In April 1981 fighting developed between Syrian troops and Christian militias in the Beirut area, and Syrian and Palestinian forces besieged Zahle. Syria maintained that Zahle and the Beka'a valley were essential for the security and defence of Syria against Israel, whereas the Phalangist forces sought the removal of Syrian forces from Lebanon.

During the remainder of April Israeli forces made frequent raids into southern Lebanon and Israeli aircraft strafed Palestinian guerrilla targets. When, at the beginning of May, two Syrian helicopters were destroyed by Israeli planes, Syria introduced SAM surface-to-air missiles into the Beka'a valley. Although it was thought that Israeli planes already had the capacity to withstand the outdated SAM missiles, the Israeli Prime Minister, Menachem Begin, adopted a very belligerent stance and threatened to destroy the SAM missiles. An international crisis developed but on 30 June Syrian forces lifted the siege on Zahle, after mediation by the Saudi and Kuwaiti Ambassadors to Lebanon. Regular troops of the Lebanese army then occupied positions in the town, as the Phalangist militia withdrew. The US Middle East peace envoy, Mr Philip Habib, was able to arrange a cease-fire which became effective on 24 July 1981.

The Lebanese Government was not able to exert its authority. In July 1979 the Prime Minister, Dr al-Hoss, introduced a Cabinet of 12 members, seven of whom were deputies, to replace the Government of eight technocrats which had been in office since December 1976. In April 1980 the National Assembly voted to extend its term by three years, to 30 June 1983, rather than by 18 months as the Government desired. President Sarkis tried to formulate a national accord. On 5 March he issued a 'message to the nation' which reiterated his policy for the future: the unity, independence and sovereignty of the whole territory; total opposition to mini-states and militias; allegiance to parliamentary democracy; acknowledgement that Lebanon was an Arab country; rejection of the Camp David agreements between Egypt and Israel; support for a future Palestinian state; co-operation with Syria; and support for UN resolutions concerning Lebanon.

On 7 June 1980 Dr al-Hoss offered his resignation on the grounds that no progress had been made towards achieving accord on those principles. On 16 July President Sarkis accepted al-Hoss's resignation, requesting him to continue in a transitional capacity. On 20 July Sarkis appointed Takieddin Solh as Prime Minister, but he soon resigned, being unable to form a government, and it was not until October 1980 that Chafic al-Wazzan was able to form a Cabinet.

ISRAEL'S 1982 INVASION OF LEBANON

The 1981 cease-fire lasted until the following spring, when fresh Israeli air raids, which led to the PLO shelling of northern Israel, culminated in a full-scale invasion of Lebanon by the Israeli army. On 6 June 1982 Israeli forces attacked on three fronts. While one column pursued the Syrian army, which was retreating up the Beka'a valley, the most serious fighting took place against PLO forces around Beaufort Castle and along the coast. The Israelis preceded their attacks with bombardments that devastated many Lebanese towns and villages. Parts of Tyre, Sidon, Damour and Nabatiyah were almost obliterated

by Israeli bombing raids. Civilian casualties among both Lebanese and Palestinians were enormous—according to *The Times* of London's correspondent in Beirut, about 14,000 people, at least 80% of them civilians, were killed during the first fortnight of the war.

The confrontation between the Maronite Christians and the alliance of radical Arab nationalists and Palestinians, which had been at the heart of the civil war of 1975–76, survived the Israeli invasion. The militia of the National Movement, in particular the Sunni Murabitoun and the Shi'ite Amal, fought alongside the PLO in the south and later in Beirut. The Phalangists, however, welcomed the invasion, although they did not take part in the actual fighting. During Israel's siege of west Beirut, which lasted two months, the Phalangists and the militiamen of Saad Haddad acted as auxiliaries for the Israelis. The Maronites also shared Israel's political aims, demanding the expulsion of the PLO from Lebanon and the removal of Syrian troops. During July and August, while the Israelis kept up an almost continuous bombardment of west Beirut, negotiations took place between Americans, Israelis, Lebanese and Palestinians. The PLO commitment to withdrawal from the city, which took place at the end of August, was negotiated by US diplomats through the mediation of the former Lebanese Prime Minister, Saeb Salam.

THE PRESIDENTIAL ELECTIONS

Bachir Gemayel, the younger son of the founder of the Phalangist Party and commander of the Lebanese Forces (LF) militia, had announced his presidential ambitions well in advance of the election. In peace-time there would have been no chance of his winning, but in the aftermath of the Israeli invasion he emerged as the obvious candidate. He was the strongest Maronite leader and the one most acceptable to the Israelis. Although Gemayel faced considerable opposition from the Muslim deputies, many of whom boycotted the election, he succeeded in being elected on 23 August. Three weeks later, before he had assumed power, he (with up to 60 others) was killed in a bomb explosion at the Phalangist Party headquarters. On the following day, 15 September, the Israeli army moved into Beirut, and on 16 September Phalangist militiamen, with Israeli knowledge, entered the Palestinian refugee camps of Sabra and Chatila and began a massacre of their inhabitants (see Arab-Israeli Confrontation 1967–94, p. 23).

A week after the assassination of Bachir Gemayel, his elder brother Amin was elected President. Amin was a Phalangist deputy with a reputation as a moderate and his election was welcomed by many Muslims who hoped that he would be able to control the extremist elements inside the Phalangist Party. The problems he faced were enormous. Lebanon was still occupied by two foreign armies and violence was continuing in many areas. After the Sabra/Chatila massacre the Israelis withdrew from Beirut but only as far as the airport, slightly south of the city, from where they consolidated their hold on the southern half of the country. The north of Lebanon was still dominated by the Syrian army which refused to withdraw from the country until the Israelis did so. Towards the end of the year there was savage fighting between pro- and anti-Syrian forces in Tripoli while in the Chouf area, where the Israelis were in control, there were frequent battles between Phalangists and Druze militiamen. The Government was in control of only a small area of central Lebanon but even there it was often unable to assert itself.

TALKS BETWEEN ISRAEL AND LEBANON

After insistent pressure from the US Government, talks between the Israeli and Lebanese Governments finally commenced at the beginning of 1983. The Israelis eventually dropped their insistence that talks should take place in Jerusalem and it was agreed that the two sides would meet alternately at Khalde in Lebanon and Kiryat Shmona in Israel. Israel's demands included security arrangements that would allow Israel to keep military bases inside Lebanon, a predominant role for Saad Haddad in the reconstituted Lebanese army, and relations with Lebanon that stopped only just short of a formal peace treaty. All these demands were rejected by the Lebanese, and the USA also considered them to be excessive. On 22 February President Reagan offered to guarantee the security of Israel's northern border once the army had withdrawn, but the proposal was rejected by the Israeli Government.

The negotiations remained stalled until the end of April, when the US Secretary of State, George Shultz, made his first visit to the area. He was able to persuade the two sides to sign an agreement on 17 May which provided for the withdrawal of Israeli forces from Lebanon. However, the Israeli Government announced that it would not be bound by the agreement unless Syria also agreed to withdraw its forces from the Beka'a valley. Mr Shultz returned to the Middle East in July, but during a visit to Damascus he was unable to persuade President Assad to agree to a withdrawal. The Syrian Government declared that it would not accept an agreement which it believed was in the interest only of Israel and the USA; nor was it prepared to support President Gemayel's attempt to extend his control over the areas occupied by Syrian and Israeli forces. In July, as violence between Phalangist and Druze militiamen intensified in the Chouf, an opposition front was set up to confront Gemayel. Calling itself the National Salvation Front, and relying entirely on Syrian support, it consisted of Walid Joumblatt, the Druze leader, Rashid Karami, the former Prime Minister, and Sulayman Franjiya, a former President and one of the chief opponents of the Gemayel family.

ISRAELI REDEPLOYMENT

In July Israel, its casualties at the hands of the contending militias increasing, decided to redeploy its forces (comprising 30,000 troops but reduced to 10,000 by the end of 1983) south of Beirut along the Awali river. The Israeli redeployment took place at the beginning of September but, owing to a lack of co-ordination between the Israeli and Lebanese armies in the handing over of military control of the vacated areas, a full-scale war flared up between the Druze and Christian militias in the Chouf mountains. In the southern, Israeli-occupied part of what had become, effectively, a partitioned country, Maj. Saad Haddad's militia (the so-called 'South Lebanon Army' (SLA), armed and trained by Israel) was employed as a police force, intended progressively to assume the duties of the Israeli forces, which were gradually reduced. (Major Haddad died in December 1983 and his successor, Maj.-Gen. Antoine Lahad, was appointed in March 1984.) Israeli personnel were a constant target of guerrilla attacks and, in order to reduce their exposure, as well as the burden of military supervision, the Israelis resorted to arming local militias, of whatever religious character, so that they could be responsible for the policing of their own areas. This policy frequently backfired when arms provided by the Israelis were turned on them. In eradicating armed resistance to its presence in Lebanon, Israel was accused of considerable brutality. Israel launched several punitive air raids against Palestinian positions in the Syrian-controlled Beka'a valley, in retaliation against the attacks of PLO guerrillas infiltrating from the north, and there were rumours that PLO fighters were returning to Beirut.

THE REVOLT AGAINST ARAFAT

From September 1983 the struggle for control of al-Fatah between the forces of its leader, Yasser Arafat (Chairman of the PLO), and those of the Syrian-backed rebels Abu Musa and Abu Saleh, which had begun in the Beka'a valley the previous May, was concentrated around Arafat's last stronghold, the northern Lebanese port of Tripoli. After months of bitter fighting, in which many Lebanese civilians, as well as Palestinian guerrillas, were killed or wounded, a truce was arranged through Saudi and Syrian mediation. This allowed Arafat and 4,000 of his supporters to leave Tripoli in December aboard five Greek ships, under UN protection, bound for Algeria, Tunisia and the Yemen Arab Republic.

THE NATIONAL RECONCILIATION CONFERENCE

After the Israeli withdrawal, the 5,800-strong multinational force (c. 2,000 French, 2,000 Italians, 1,600 Americans and 100 British), left to keep the peace between the various factions in Beirut, in the absence of an effective Lebanese army, was gradually drawn into the fighting. It came under attack from

Muslim militiamen who were suspicious of its role in bolstering a Christian-led government, and of the presence off shore of massive, predominantly US, naval support. In the two most devastating incidents, 241 US and 58 French marines were killed in almost simultaneous suicide bombings, carried out by Muslims on 23 October 1983.

The inter-factional fighting in Beirut was punctuated by numerous short-lived cease-fires. The most successful of these began on 26 September and was accompanied by the resignation of Chafic al-Wazzan, who hoped to make way for a government of national unity. He was persuaded to remain in office, but these events were the prelude to a Conference of National Reconciliation, held in Geneva, Switzerland, from 31 October to 4 November. These talks were attended by most of the interested Lebanese parties, including the Shi'ite Amal militia, led by Nabih Berri, and the representatives of the National Salvation Front, which had been proclaimed, with Syrian backing, in July 1983 by the Druze leader Walid Joumblatt (the son of Kamal Joumblatt, who had been assassinated in 1977) in alliance with ex-President Franjiya, a pro-Syrian Maronite Christian, and former Prime Minister Rashid Karami, a Sunni Muslim. The conference effectively foundered on President Gemayel's refusal to do more than 'freeze' the 17 May agreement with Israel, rather than to abrogate the pact (as Syria wished) and risk losing American support for his Government. Broad agreement was reached, however, on the need for constitutional changes which would give Muslims representation in the Government commensurate with their majority status in the country.

In early February 1984, following abortive Saudi-mediated attempts to implement a comprehensive security agreement in Beirut, factional fighting developed on an even more intense level than before, with the multinational force and the Lebanese army apparently impotent to prevent it. To the Muslim community, the reconstituted Lebanese army, armed and trained by the USA, appeared to be nothing more than an instrument to be used against them by the Christian President in co-operation with the Christian Phalangist militia. Amin Gemayel had refused to give Nabih Berri, the leader of Amal, a post in the Cabinet, while Walid Joumblatt was openly committed to the President's removal. Muslim members of the army, unwilling to fight against their coreligionists, began to defect to the militias, while the Druze and Shi'ite forces co-operated in fighting the army. The Sunni Muslim Prime Minister, Chafic al-Wazzan, and the entire Cabinet resigned on 5 February. Shortly afterwards, the USA, Italy and the UK decided to withdraw their peace-keeping troops from the multinational force. (The French troops were withdrawn in March.)

LEBANON ABROGATES THE 17 MAY AGREEMENT

By February, Beirut was divided by the militias, east and west, along the so-called 'Green Line', into Christian- and Muslim-controlled sectors. On 16 February, with West Beirut in Shi'ite hands, with the army sustaining defeats south of the capital, and with his Government in effective control only of the eastern part of the city, Amin Gemayel offered to abrogate the 17 May agreement with Israel and to give greater government representation to Muslims. President Gemayel also called for a UN peace-keeping force to replace the multinational one, while a government of national unity began to institute the planned reforms of the Constitution. These proposals, conditional on the simultaneous withdrawal of all foreign forces from Lebanon, proved to be unacceptable, not only to Syria and to Gemayel's Muslim opponents, who largely took their lead from Syria (which equipped the Druze militia), but also to the Christian parties which were committed to the agreement with Israel as a means to preserve their dominance in Lebanese politics.

Finally, on 5 March, bowing to Syria's influence in Lebanese affairs, President Gemayel abrogated the 17 May agreement in return for guarantees of internal security from President Assad of Syria. On the same day, Chafic al-Wazzan's Cabinet withdrew its resignation, and one week later the National Reconciliation Conference was reconvened in Lausanne, Switzerland. It failed to produce the results for which Syria had hoped and it saw the beginning of the disintegration of the Lebanese National Salvation Front. One of the Front's representatives, former President Sulayman Franjiya, vetoed Syrian plans for constitutional changes in Lebanon involving the diminution of the powers of the President, traditionally a Maronite Christian post. The Conference broke up, having agreed another cease-fire and recommended the formation of a government of national unity—though the composition of such a government was still undecided. (A movement replacing the National Salvation Front was announced in Damascus in March, including Walid Joumblatt, George Hawi, leader of the Lebanese Communist Party, Assem Qansou, leader of the Lebanese Baath Party, Inaam Raad, leader of the Syrian Nationalist Party, and representatives of the Socialist Union and Arab Democratic parties, but not Nabih Berri of Amal.)

THE GOVERNMENT OF NATIONAL UNITY

At talks in Damascus in April, President Assad of Syria approved plans for a Lebanese government of national unity, giving equal representation to Christians and Muslims, put to him by President Gemayel. Gemayel chose Rashid Karami, who had held the post on 10 previous occasions, as Prime Minister of the new Government, which was proclaimed on 30 April. Karami announced his principal aims as being the ending of the Israeli occupation of the south; the restoration of civil order; and the reformation of the Constitution to reflect the majority status of Lebanon's Muslims. On 30 April, without first consulting the appointees, Prime Minister Karami announced a 10-member Cabinet consisting of five leading members each from the Christian and Muslim communities. Nabih Berri, who was appointed Minister of Water and Electrical Resources and Justice, refused to participate in the Government unless some provision were made in it for dealing with the predominantly Shi'ite area of southern Lebanon occupied by the Israelis. A Ministry of State for Affairs of the South and Reconstruction was duly created to which Nabih Berri was appointed on 7 May. The other appointees having accepted their posts, the Cabinet thus included the leaders of all Lebanon's main religious groups and only former President Sulayman Franjiya, who was bitterly opposed to Pierre Gemayel and Camille Chamoun, both of whom were Cabinet members, refused to give his support to the Government. His son-in-law, Abdullah ar-Rassi, who had been made Minister of the Interior, boycotted Cabinet meetings in support of Franjiya's call for the dismissal of Pierre Gemayel and Camille Chamoun.

The new Government won the approval of the National Assembly in June. Fighting in Beirut between Christian and Muslim militias had not ceased, however, and it was not until Syrian Vice-President Abd al-Halim Khaddam intervened to mediate between the two sides that a cease-fire began which allowed the terms of a security plan providing for the reorganization of the army and the disengagement of the rival militias finally to be drawn up. An all-party Military Council, consisting of one member from each of the main religious groups, was set up to supervise the reintegration of the 37,000-strong army and the disengagement of the militias. Brigadier-Gen. Michel Awn (a Maronite Christian) was made Commander-in-Chief of the armed forces, while his chief of staff, Maj.-Gen. Nadim Hakim, was a Druze (Maj.-Gen. Nadim Hakim died in a helicopter crash in August and was replaced by Maj.-Gen. Abu Dargham). A new body, the Directorate of Internal Security, was placed under the control of a Shi'ite general, Uthman Uthman. In future, it was decided, appointments in the army would be distributed equally between Christians and Muslims.

The security plan, which had been elaborated between Abd al-Halim Khaddam and the Cabinet, was put into operation at the beginning of July. Three army brigades began to take control of militia positions along the 'Green Line' and in the port and airport of Beirut. The militias had earlier removed their heavy weaponry from the area and there was virtually no opposition to the implementation of the plan, even from the Phalangist militia which had bitterly opposed what it viewed as pro-Syrian, anti-Christian developments in Lebanese politics. The port and airport, which had been closed since 6 February, were reopened in the middle of July, and more crossing points between the east and west of Beirut were also cleared.

The security plan met with limited success. Muslim and Druze dissatisfaction with the Government's lack of progress on constitutional reform, despite the Syrian influence on President Gemayel, led to sporadic fighting between rival Muslim and Christian militias and, occasionally, between Shi'a and Sunni Muslims belonging, respectively, to the Amal and Murabitoun militias. Troops of the Lebanese army failed to gain control of the city, although they reduced fighting along the 'Green Line'. President Gemayel's efforts to gain agreement on constitutional reform, already constrained by his fear of alienating his Christian supporters, were further handicapped by disagreements within the Cabinet. Walid Joumblatt sustained a torrent of vituperation against Gemayel, and vetoed the extension of the security plan in September along the southern coastal road and into the Druze bastion of the Chouf mountains, as he regarded the Lebanese army as merely a tool of the Christian Phalangists.

In September 1984 the Cabinet, which was agreed on the principle of increasing the number of members in the National Assembly from 99, to allow an equal representation for Christians and Muslims, appeared to have approved a total membership of 122 but then failed to reach agreement on the number of members who would represent the various groups within the two major religious communities. Joseph Hashim, who became Minister of Posts, Telecommunications, Health and Social Affairs in September (succeeding Pierre Gemayel, who had died in August), caused further protest by demanding that the Maronite Christians form the largest single group in the Assembly. A 40-member committee, representing Muslims and Christians in equal numbers, was appointed to draw up proposals for political reforms. Ex-president Franjiya agreed to be represented on this committee, thus ending his boycott of the government of national unity.

Also in September, Syrian mediation settled a feud in the northern port of Tripoli between the pro-Syrian Arab Democratic Party (known as the 'Red Knights') and the anti-Syrian, Sunni Muslim, Tawheed Islami (the Islamic Unification Movement), enabling a security plan, drawn up in Damascus, to be implemented.

In Beirut, sporadic violence continued and, at the end of October, Walid Joumblatt (who was boycotting Cabinet meetings) and Nabih Berri threatened to resign from the Cabinet unless more progress was made on constitutional reform. A new security plan, effectively dictated by Syria, was introduced at the end of November. It was designed initially to put the whole of Beirut under the control of the Lebanese army, and then to extend the Government's authority north to Tripoli, south to Israeli-occupied territory and east to the Chouf mountains, demonstrating to the Israelis the ability of the Lebanese army to maintain security in the event of an Israeli withdrawal from the south of the country. Walid Joumblatt's Druze militia repeatedly objected to the eastward deployment, and obstructed the implementation of the plan. The army moved into Tripoli on 21 December, but a plan for the coastal areas to the north and south of Beirut was not agreed by all parties until 31 December. The army was deployed along the coast road to southern Lebanon in mid-January 1985.

ISRAEL'S WITHDRAWAL FROM LEBANON

With the cost of keeping a force in southern Lebanon proving a drain on a drastically weakened economy, and with its personnel increasingly the target of attacks by Lebanese resistance groups, Israel's government of national unity, which was formed in September 1984, pledged itself to a withdrawal from Lebanon. Israel abandoned an unrealistic demand for a simultaneous withdrawal of Syrian forces from north-east Lebanon and, in November, entered into a series of talks at an-Naqoura, in southern Lebanon, with representatives of the Lebanese Government, who participated with Syrian approval. Israel's concern was that adequate security arrangements should be agreed, which would prevent the areas which it vacated from becoming bases for terrorist attacks on Israeli soldiers or territory, while the Lebanese Government wished to co-ordinate the withdrawal so as to prevent inter-communal fighting, such as occurred in the Chouf mountains in September 1983. The talks repeatedly foundered on the question of which forces should take the place of the Israeli Defence Force (IDF). The Lebanese, influenced by Syria, wanted UNIFIL to police the border with Israel (as it had been mandated to do in 1978), and the Lebanese army to deploy north of the Litani river, between UNIFIL and the Syrian army. Israel did not consider the Lebanese army to be a credible security force, and wanted UNIFIL to deploy north of the Litani while the southern Lebanese border was patrolled by the Israeli-backed SLA. In the absence of any agreement, Israel withdrew from talks, and on 14 January 1985 the Israeli Cabinet voted to take unilateral steps towards a complete withdrawal, which was to be effected in three phases. The first phase involved the evacuation of the IDF from the western occupied sector, covering about 500 sq km around Sidon, to the Litani river area, around Nabatiyah, and was carried out in February 1985. Israel was prepared to test the competence of the Lebanese army in handing over responsibility for security in the evacuated area to it, operating in tandem with UNIFIL. The Lebanese Government, however, rejected a peace-keeping role for the UN force, and the Lebanese army moved into Sidon in mid-February.

The second phase of the Israeli withdrawal, designed to evacuate the IDF from the occupied central and eastern sector, including the Beka'a valley, to redeploy around Hasbayyah, began on 3 March with no fixed deadline. The process was accelerated during April as the majority Shi'ite community of the south, which, antipathetic towards the PLO, had initially welcomed the IDF, now attacked it in retreat. To defend itself, the Israelis pursued an 'Iron Fist' policy, attacking Shi'ite villages, killing many innocent inhabitants in the process, and detaining hundreds of suspected guerrilla fighters. Instead of abating, the level of guerrilla activity, directed against the IDF and orchestrated by the Shi'ite National Resistance Movement, intensified. After the evacuation of Tyre, the second phase of the Israeli withdrawal was completed on 29 April. The third and final phase, taking the IDF behind Israel's northern border and leaving a buffer zone between 10 km and 20 km wide along the border controlled by the SLA, was completed on 10 June, three months ahead of the original schedule. However, several hundred Israeli troops remained inside Lebanon to support the SLA, whose numbers had been depleted since the start of the withdrawal operation by desertion and defection to the southern Lebanese resistance movement. The Lebanese Government, Syria and Lebanese Muslims did not recognize the role of the SLA, and friction between it and UNIFIL increased. The Israeli invasion succeeded, in that (at the cost of 654 Israeli lives) it temporarily removed the threat of attack launched by the PLO from within Lebanon (although internal divisions contributed equally to the diminution of PLO strength) and, by a strange coincidence of interest, the Shi'tes of southern Lebanon were unwilling to allow the PLO to re-establish a military power-base in the region. In the Shi'ites themselves, though, Israel created an enemy across its northern border which was more firmly entrenched and, potentially, more dangerous. In July, less than one month after Israel completed its withdrawal from southern Lebanon, Syria withdrew 10,000–12,000 troops from the Beka'a valley, leaving some 25,000 in position.

CHRISTIAN REVOLT

After the initial euphoria of the Israeli departure from Sidon in February, during the first phase of the IDF's withdrawal, fighting broke out between Christian Phalangists on one side and Druze and Shi'ite militiamen on the other, with the Lebanese army manifestly unable to keep the peace. In early March President Gemayel had approved a Syrian security plan which had the long-term aim of granting more political and constitutional power to Lebanon's Muslim majority, and which would immediately deprive Christian militias of revenues from illegal ports and the control of a key checkpoint on the road from Beirut to Tripoli. Samir Geagea, a commander in the LF militia, rebelled against what he viewed as a capitulation to Syrian and Muslim influence, and attracted substantial support from units of the LF in east Beirut and north of the capital. Geagea demanded the end of party control of the LF and the introduction of a collective leadership for the Phalange. He also called for a democratically elected council to be

set up in areas controlled by the LF, to decide on any political reforms. Geagea soon controlled most of the LF in east Beirut, and street battles were fought between pro- and anti-Gemayel Christian factions. At the same time, fighting was renewed between Christian and Muslim militias along the 'Green Line' dividing east and west Beirut. The split in the Christian militia and the partitionist sentiments implicit in Geagea's proposals raised the possibility of Syrian military intervention in Beirut, to bolster President Gemayel and prevent the first stage in what might prove to be the inexorable sectarian fragmentation of Lebanon, creating a threat to Syria's internal stability. However, Geagea's revolt ended, as suddenly as it had begun, on 9 May, when Elie Hobeika was elected commander of the LF. He pronounced himself ready to open a dialogue with Druze and Shi'ite leaders, acknowledged the role of Syria in creating a stable Lebanon, and pledged to evacuate the LF from the last Christian enclave in southern Lebanon at Jezzine.

It was to Jezzine that at least 60,000 Christian refugees from Sidon had gone, to escape the fighting around Sidon which began after the Israeli withdrawal. At the end of March, units of the rebel Christian militia had launched an offensive, allegedly with Israeli encouragement, against the Palestinian refugee camp of Ain al-Hilweh (to which PLO guerrillas had been returning) and Muslim militiamen and troops of the Lebanese army in Muslim suburbs of Sidon. The exodus of Christians from Sidon began when, at the end of April, prior to the evacuation of the IDF from Jezzine, leaving them isolated, the LF removed some 300 men from the area to reinforce Christian forces involved in battles with Muslim militias in Beirut, and the remaining Christian militiamen retreated. The retiring IDF were followed into the buffer zone along the Lebanese border by 60,000 Christians from Jezzine.

On 10 April Prime Minister Rashid Karami, angered by the Government's inability to restore peace to Sidon and its failure to reinforce the beleaguered Lebanese army there, announced that he would boycott Cabinet meetings until a cease-fire was agreed. Then, on 17 April, he both announced and was persuaded to withdraw his resignation after west Beirut had been overwhelmed by fighting, instigated by the Shi'ite Amal militia and their Druze allies to crush the Sunni Murabitoun militia and its Palestinian allies, and to prevent the revival of a pro-Arafat PLO force in Beirut. Just before Karami made his announcement, Dr Selim al-Hoss, the Minister of Labour, National Education and Fine Arts, a Sunni member of the Cabinet, had resigned, though he, too, was persuaded to remain in office.

ATTEMPTED SYRIAN SUPPRESSION OF THE PLO IN BEIRUT

In May and June 1985, through its proxy, the Shi'ite Amal militia, and with the assistance of the largely Shi'ite sixth Lebanese army brigade, Syria renewed its attempt to prevent Yasser Arafat from re-establishing a power-base in Lebanon. Most of the estimated 5,000 PLO guerrillas who returned to Lebanon in anticipation of and after the Israeli withdrawal from the south were thought to be loyal to Yasser Arafat. The Palestinian refugee camps of Sabra, Chatila and Bourj el-Barajneh in Beirut were besieged by Amal guerrillas (without the assistance of the Druze militia, who helped the Palestinians to take in supplies and reinforcements), but they failed to gain control of the camps or to quell PLO resistance. In an unexpected development, Palestinians belonging to the Palestine National Salvation Front of pro-Syrian guerrilla organizations joined with Arafat supporters in resisting the Shi'ites, many of whom were among the 640 people killed in the fighting. An uneasy cease-fire agreement was achieved in Damascus on 17 June between Amal and the pro-Syrian Palestinian element in the camps, but it subsequently collapsed repeatedly.

HIJACK CRISIS IN BEIRUT

On 14 June two Lebanese Shi'ite Muslims, reputedly members of the Hezbollah (the Party of God), hijacked a TWA passenger aircraft, with 153 people on board, on a flight from Athens to Rome. After twice taking it to Beirut and Algiers, and releasing more than 100 hostages, the hijackers landed for the third time in Beirut on 16 June. On 17 June Nabih Berri, who was acting as spokesman for the hijackers, announced that the remaining 42 hostages, mostly Americans, had been taken to secret locations in Beirut, to await the response to the hijackers' demand for the release of 766 Lebanese prisoners, mostly Shi'ites, who were being held in Israeli prisons. Israel said that it would not release its prisoners unless asked to do so by the US Government. The USA renounced the use of force to secure the release of the hostages on 23 June, but threatened to impose sanctions against Lebanon. President Assad of Syria became involved in the negotiations for the release of the hostages (now reduced to 39 after further releases), through his links with Nabih Berri and Amal, and his influence was crucial in securing their freedom on 30 June.

ANOTHER SECURITY PLAN FOR BEIRUT

Weeks of fighting between Shi'ite, Sunni and Druze militias in west Beirut preceded another attempt by Syria to initiate the process of political reform. A security plan was introduced in July, after 13 spiritual and temporal leaders of the Lebanese Muslim community had met for talks with Syrian leaders in Damascus. Under the terms of the plan, west Beirut was to be divided into five security zones, each controlled by its own security committee. The Muslim militias were asked to leave the streets and to close their offices. The plan was designed to lay the basis for its extension to Christian east Beirut, and for a renewal of inter-sectarian dialogue on political and constitutional reform, but its implementation was almost immediately disrupted by further fighting.

On 6 August, in the central Lebanese town of Shtoura, representatives of most of the religious communities in the country (but, crucially, no one of stature representing the Sunni population and no Maronite Christians) announced the formation of a pro-Syrian national unity front. It had first been proclaimed in July, after meetings between the Syrian Vice-President, Abd al-Halim Khaddam, the Druze leader, Walid Joumblatt, and the leader of Amal, Nabih Berri. The front was committed to the end of the civil war and 'to the final liquidation of the sectarian regime' under disproportionate Maronite control.

In mid-July the LF settled its differences with ex-President Sulayman Franjiya, President Gemayel's Christian rival in northern Lebanon, in order to oppose any attempt to implement political reforms without the consent of the Christian community.

Four weeks of intensive fighting between rival militias in Tripoli in September and October were interpreted as part of Syria's campaign to prevent the re-emergence in Lebanon of the pro-Arafat wing of the PLO. The pro-Arafat, Sunni Muslim Tawheed Islami (Islamic Unification Movement) and the pro-Syrian, Alawite, Arab Democratic Party fought for control of the city and its port, which was allegedly being used to distribute armaments and supplies to Arafat loyalists in other parts of the country. More than 500 people were killed and 500,000 were driven from their homes in Tripoli before a cease-fire was agreed in Damascus at the beginning of October, and the Syrian army moved into the city.

THE ABORTIVE NATIONAL AGREEMENT

One month of negotiations between the three main Lebanese militias (the Druze forces, Amal and the LF), which began in October, led to the preparation of a draft accord for a politico-military settlement of the civil war. Objections by the Christians to the curbing of presidential powers and a reduction in their political influence delayed approval of the accord, but on 28 December it was finally signed in Damascus by the three militia leaders (Walid Joumblatt, Nabih Berri and Elie Hobeika). It provided for an immediate cease-fire and for an end to the state of civil war within one year; the militias would be disarmed and disbanded, and the responsibility for security would pass to a reconstituted and religiously integrated Lebanese army, supported by Syrian forces. The accord envisaged the immediate establishment of a national coalition government under a council of six ministers representing the main religious sects, for a transitional period of three years, after which the confessional system of power-sharing government would be abolished, and a secular administration created. A new National Assembly would be elected

within the three-year period to enact the necessary legislation. The number of deputies in the new assembly would be increased from 99 to 198, with the total divided equally between Christians and Muslims, and an upper house would be added to the legislature. For the period of transition, a Maronite would continue to hold the office of President, but some of his executive powers would pass to the Prime Minister. The agreement recognized Lebanon's community of interest with Syria and envisaged a 'strategic integration' of the two countries in the fields of military relations, foreign policy and security.

The agreement seemed to offer some hope for Lebanon, as it had been negotiated by the actual combatants in the civil war and not merely by politicians. However, the Shi'ite Hezbollah and the Sunni Murabitoun militias were not parties to the agreement, the Christian community was divided over it, and it made no provision for dealing with the problem of Palestinian refugees. Muslim support for the agreement was not widespread. The Sunni community had been virtually ignored during negotiations, and under the agreement the Druzes (although their leader, Walid Joumblatt, had signed the agreement) would be likely to lose their autonomy in the Chouf region. Only Amal appeared to be wholly in favour of the accord. President Gemayel, who had not been involved in drafting the agreement, refused to endorse it, and at the end of December 1985 clashes erupted in east Beirut between elements of the LF who supported the agreement and those who resented the concessions that had been made on their behalf by Elie Hobeika. In January 1986 Hobeika was forced into exile. Samir Geagea, the LF's chief of staff, was elected chairman of the Executive Committee of the LF on 24 January, and urged the renegotiation of the Damascus accord. This effectively ended all hope that the peace agreement with the Muslim militias could be implemented.

President Gemayel, who regained much support among the Christian community for his opposition to the Damascus accord, was blamed for its failure by Muslim leaders. By January 1986 the Cabinet had not met for five months, and Muslim ministers subsequently refused to have any dealings with President Gemayel. They rejected his request for the Damascus agreement to be referred to the National Assembly and persisted in attempts to engineer his downfall. The long round of inter-sectarian clashes in Beirut resumed in earnest on 22 January.

THE RESURGENCE OF THE PLO CONTINUES

In the south of the country Israel was faced with the consequences of the failure of its invasion. During 1986 rocket attacks on Israeli settlements in northern Israel were resumed by Palestinian guerrillas, who had been gradually returning to the refugee camps around Tyre and Sidon after the Israeli withdrawal in 1985, and had established a number of mobile bases in the south. Israel responded with a total of 18 air raids on Palestinian targets in southern Lebanon, mostly in the Syrian-occupied Beka'a valley, during 1986 (and 23 in 1987). The Amal militia, while contributing to the southern Lebanese resistance movement within the Israeli-imposed security zone, north of the international border, was more concerned to liberate south Lebanon than to carry the struggle against Israel into Israel itself. It attempted, therefore, to keep PLO guerrillas and radical Lebanese groups as far away from the zone as possible, in order to prevent them from launching rocket and mortar attacks against Israeli territory or from infiltrating the zone and then Israel itself, which might provoke Israeli reprisals inside Lebanon. Amal's controlling influence in the south was coming under threat from the pro-Iranian Hezbollah, which was attracting increasing support. Hezbollah intensified resistance to the SLA, attacking its positions within the security zone along the border with Israel, and fired rockets into Israel itself. Despite the backing of Amal, the role of UNIFIL was cast into doubt by the increasing number of clashes between the peace-keeping force and the SLA and, in particular, Hezbollah, which viewed UNIFIL as an obstacle to the pursuit of war against Israel. In May it was reported that the Syrians, ignoring Israeli warnings, were constructing fortifications and tank and gun emplacements in the Lake Karoun area, in the southern Beka'a, immediately to the north of the SLA-patrolled security zone.

Fighting between Palestinian guerrillas and Shi'ite Amal militiamen for control of the refugee camps in the south of Beirut, which had continued sporadically ever since a cease-fire nominally took effect in June 1985, erupted into major exchanges on 19 May 1986. The refugee camps of Sabra, Chatila and Bourj el-Barajneh were increasingly under the control of guerrillas loyal to Yasser Arafat, who were continuing to return to Lebanon. Senior PLO officials claimed that the number of guerrillas in Lebanon in 1986 exceeded the 14,300 who, according to their figures, had been evacuated from Beirut in 1982. Independent estimates assessed the number in Beirut at several thousands. Sunni and Druze militias continued to lend discreet support to the Palestinians, and serious fighting took place in June between Sunni forces and the Syrian-backed Amal.

THE SYRIAN ARMY'S RETURN TO BEIRUT

Leaders of the Muslim communities in Lebanon met Syrian government officials in Damascus, and agreed to impose a cease-fire around the Beirut refugee camps on 14 June 1986. The cease-fire, which succeeded in reducing the fighting to the level of sniper exchanges, proved to be the first element in a Syrian-sponsored peace plan for Muslim west Beirut. About 1,000 Lebanese troops were deployed in west Beirut at the end of June. The Amal, Druze and Sunni militias were ordered to close their offices and to remain off the streets. Crucial to their co-operation was the appearance in Beirut, for the first time since 1982, of uniformed Syrian soldiers (several hundred of them), supported by members of the Syrian *Muhabarat* (security service) under the command of Brig.-Gen. Ghazi Kena'an. The security plan was temporarily successful in its limited objective of curbing the activities of militias in west Beirut, but the plan (and Syria's active involvement in it) was strongly opposed in Christian east Beirut, and only in August, after lengthy negotiations with Amal and Hezbollah, was it tentatively extended to the predominantly Shi'ite southern suburbs, which contained the majority of the city's Palestinian refugees. The Syrian presence failed to end fighting across the 'Green Line', or to prevent a wave of car bombings and abductions of Westerners by extremist Islamic groups.

On 19 August 1986 the Prime Minister, Rashid Karami, urged the resumption of peace talks between the various Lebanese communities, and on 2 September, after a meeting of government ministers (excluding President Gemayel), a new truce (reportedly the 191st since the civil war broke out in April 1975) was agreed. At the same time, the drafting of a national charter, aiming to end the civil war and to reform the confessional system of political representation, was to be put in train.

THE WAR OF THE CAMPS

Resistance to the re-emergence of the pro-Arafat PLO in Lebanon spread from Beirut to the Palestinian refugee camps around Tyre and Sidon at the beginning of October 1986. Amal forces besieged Rashidiyah camp to the south of Tyre, and the camps at Miyeh Miyeh and Ain al-Hilweh, outside Sidon, cutting off access to food and medical supplies. According to the Palestine Red Crescent relief organization, 1,924 Palestinians died in the Beirut camps between November 1986, when the fighting resumed, and the following February. In February 1987, after the plight of the Palestinians in Beirut, Tyre and Sidon had attracted worldwide sympathy, Amal agreed to allow supplies into Bourj el-Barajneh and to permit women from Rashidiyah to leave the camp to buy food. Syria reportedly asked Amal to abandon the siege of the camps but the respite for the inhabitants of Bourj el-Barajneh and Rashidiyah proved to be brief, and the siege of the other camps remained strictly in force.

PAX SYRIANA

In February 1987 fierce fighting took place in west Beirut between Amal forces and an alliance of the Druze, Murabitoun and Communist Party militias. Muslim leaders appealed for

Syria to intervene to restore order, and, with the consent of Prime Minister Karami, Nabih Berri (the leader of Amal) and Walid Joumblatt (the Druze leader), about 4,000 Syrian troops were deployed in west Beirut on 22 February. The Syrian force (which was soon increased to some 7,500 troops) succeeded in enforcing a cease-fire in the central and northern districts of west Beirut, but, once again, its leaders hesitated to attempt to extend its control to the predominantly Shi'ite southern suburbs, which Syrian-backed Lebanese security forces had failed to secure in July 1986, when Syrian troops first re-entered Beirut. President Gemayel initially opposed the latest deployment of Syrian troops in Beirut as being 'unconstitutional', but in March he welcomed several clauses in a Syrian-sponsored agreement on political reform, which had been approved by Lebanese Muslim leaders and which would give Lebanon's Muslim majority a greater role in the government of the country and reduce the powers of the Christian President.

On 24 February 1987 Syrian troops moved into areas of west Beirut occupied by Hezbollah militiamen, killing 23 of them, but did not venture into the southern suburbs where Hezbollah had its greatest influence. On the following day, Syria claimed that all 75 militia offices in west Beirut had been closed. The remaining Hezbollah fighters in west Beirut moved to the group's stronghold in the southern suburbs, while hundreds of Amal militiamen left Beirut to pursue the struggle against Israel in the south of Lebanon.

A Syrian-supervised cease-fire at all the embattled Palestinian refugee camps in Beirut began on 6 April 1987, and the siege of Chatila and Bourj el-Barajneh was suspended to allow supplies to be taken into the camps. The cease-fire agreement was negotiated by representatives of Syria, Amal and the pro-Syrian Palestine National Salvation Front (PNSF), who had made common cause with pro-Arafat PLO members to defend the camps. However, in Sidon, outside effective Syrian jurisdiction, renewed fighting broke out between Amal and members of the PLO loyal to Yasser Arafat. Amal maintained that it would only agree fully to lift the siege of the Beirut camps and of Rashidiyah, near Tyre, if Arafat loyalists withdrew from villages near Sidon which they had captured from Amal in October and November 1986. Some 150 Syrian troops were deployed around Sidon in mid-April.

The Lebanese Prime Minister, Rashid Karami, resigned on 4 May 1987, following the failure of the Cabinet (which had held its first meeting for seven months, two weeks before) to agree on a course of action to alleviate Lebanon's acute economic problems. Under the terms of the Constitution the resignation of the Government followed automatically upon the President's acceptance of the Prime Minister's resignation. President Gemayel rejected Karami's resignation (although Karami, who had refused to have any dealings with President Gemayel since January 1986, did not formally submit it), and it seemed that he would remain in office until a suitable (i.e. Sunni) replacement could be found. On 1 June 1987, however, Karami was killed when a bomb exploded in the helicopter in which he was travelling. President Gemayel appointed the Minister of Labour, Education, and Fine Arts, Dr Selim al-Hoss, as acting Prime Minister. It was not clear who was responsible for Karami's assassination, though the Christian section of the divided Lebanese army and the Christian LF were considered by the Muslim community to be the leading suspects. Karami, a Sunni Muslim, had been a firm ally of Syria and had been instrumental in the deployment of Syrian troops in Beirut in February. On 5 June Hussain al-Hussaini, the Shi'ite President of the National Assembly, resigned because he suspected that President Gemayel was trying to conceal the truth about the circumstances of Karami's death and the identity of his assassins. Muslim leaders demanded a full investigation into the assassination.

On 21 May 1987 the National Assembly had voted to abrogate the agreement, signed by Lebanon and Yasser Arafat (for the PLO) in Cairo in 1969, which defined and regulated the PLO's activities and legitimized its presence in Lebanon. The annulment cancelled any theoretical right that the PLO had to official Lebanese protection while it operated in Lebanon. In practice any such protection had long been withheld or had been impracticable. The abrogation of the Cairo accord was strongly suspected of being Syrian-inspired, coming, as it did, in the wake of the reunification of the PLO under Arafat's leadership at the 18th session of the Palestine National Council in Algiers in April, which had deprived the Syrian-sponsored PNSF of the support of the largest groups that had rebelled against Arafat in 1983. Although the divided Lebanese security forces were incapable of enforcing a withdrawal of PLO forces from Lebanon, in line with the abrogation of the Cairo accord, Syria, which had effectively assumed responsibility for security in Beirut, through its own forces and those of its proxy, Amal, was certainly in a position to attempt to do so. Such a policy would be merely a logical continuation of Syria's attempt to prevent the re-establishment of the PLO in Lebanon, and one which Syria could claim was sanctioned by the Lebanese National Assembly. (The Assembly also finally and formally cancelled the peace treaty of 17 May 1983 between Lebanon and Israel, which President Gemayel had abrogated in March 1984, but on which the Assembly had never voted.)

Although the most intense fighting between Amal and PLO guerrillas had ended, and the removal of the blockade of the Palestinian refugee camps had been proclaimed in April 1987, they remained effectively under siege, apparently under the supervision of Syrian troops, and freedom of movement in and out of them was confined to women and children. On 11 September an agreement was announced between Amal (as part of the largely Muslim Unification and Liberation Front, which had been formed under Syrian auspices in July, and also included Walid Joumblatt's mainly Druze Parti Socialiste Progressiste—PSP) and the PLO in the camps, purportedly ending the 'war of the camps', in which more than 2,500 people had died. The agreement provided for the ending of the siege of the camps and for the withdrawal of Palestinian fighters from strategic positions outside the Ain al-Hilweh refugee camp, to the east of Sidon. However, neither measure was implemented, and in October differences over the withdrawal of some 5,000–8,000 Palestinian guerrillas led to renewed fighting around the disputed positions to the east of Sidon. On 16 January 1988, avowedly as a gesture of support for the uprising by Palestinians resident in Israeli-occupied territories, which had begun in December 1987, Nabih Berri, the leader of Amal, announced the ending of the siege of the Palestinian refugee camps in Beirut and southern Lebanon: Amal fighters and soldiers from the predominantly Shi'ite Sixth Brigade of the Lebanese army withdrew their positions around Bourj el-Barajneh and Chatila camps, to be replaced by Syrian troops, and the 14-month siege of Rashidiyah camp, near Tyre, was ended. However, PLO guerrillas loyal to Yasser Arafat continued to refuse to withdraw from their positions overlooking Ain al-Hilweh camp near Sidon, interrupting the withdrawal of Amal from around Rashidiyah.

The political crisis that was brought about by the assassination of Rashid Karami (on 1 June 1987) was believed to be partly responsible for an acceleration in the depreciation of the local currency during the summer. The increase in poverty, huge rises in the prices of basic commodities, and the lack of a solution to the country's sectarian conflict were, in turn, responsible for a wave of strikes and demonstrations by people of all religions in Beirut, protesting against the decline in living standards.

AMAL AND HEZBOLLAH CLASH

Cynically speaking, it was politically inexpedient for Syria to continue to employ its proxy, Amal, in its attempt to suppress the PLO in Lebanon, at a time when the Palestinian uprising in the Israeli-occupied territories was attracting the sympathy of the world (in particular, the Arab world) to the plight of the Palestinians. By suspending Amal's campaign against the pro-Arafat PLO, Nabih Berri's Amal forces could be deployed against the Iranian-backed Hezbollah, whose ultimate aim was to establish an Islamic state in Lebanon on the Iranian model and whose strength was viewed by Syria as a threat to its own ambitions to control Lebanon.

Amal's attacks were initially directed against Hezbollah bases in southern Lebanon, and clashes (the first military confrontation between the two groups) occurred at the end of March in the Nabatiyah area. On 9 April 1988 Amal claimed to have captured Hezbollah's last stronghold in the south, at

Siddiqin, while Iranian Revolutionary Guards stationed at Sharqiyah and Jibshit had been ordered to leave the area. According to Reuters news agency, thousands of people took to the streets of Tyre in April to celebrate the expulsion of Hezbollah and the Revolutionary Guards.

In Beirut, Syria had demonstrated its opposition to hostage-taking by preventing a Kuwaiti Boeing 747, which had been hijacked by Islamic fundamentalists (alleged to be Lebanese), from landing at the city's airport in early April. On 5 May 1988 fighting broke out between the Amal and Hezbollah militias (the latter supported by Iranian Revolutionary Guards) in the southern suburbs of Beirut. Attempts to impose a cease-fire through Iranian and Syrian mediation failed, and Syrian troops became involved in the fighting on 13 May when Hezbollah guerillas, who had wrested control of about 90% of the 36-sq-km southern suburbs from Amal, briefly advanced into a Syrian-controlled area of west Beirut. On 15 May Syrian troops encircled the southern suburbs, while intensive negotiations took place between Syria and Iran. On 27 May several hundred Syrian troops moved into the southern suburbs of Beirut to enforce a cease-fire agreement reached by Syria, Iran and their militia proxies on the previous day. When the Syrian deployment was complete, Amal and Hezbollah were to close down their military operations in all parts of the southern suburbs, except in areas adjoining the Green Line which separated west Beirut from the Christian-controlled east of the city, where they would continue to be allowed to post their men. On 3 June, in accordance with the agreement, Nabih Berri announced the disbandment of the Amal militia in Beirut and the Beka'a valley (areas under Syrian control) and all other areas of the country except the south (which was not controlled by Syrian troops).

ARAFAT LOYALISTS DRIVEN OUT OF BEIRUT

At the end of April 1988, following a partial reconciliation between Yasser Arafat and President Assad of Syria, Arafat loyalists in the Palestinian refugee camps of Chatila and Bourj el-Barajneh in Beirut, attempted to drive out the fighters belonging to the Syrian-backed group, al-Fatah Intifada (Fatah Uprising), led by PLO dissident 'Abu Musa'. The Syrian troops who had surrounded the camps in April 1987 did not attempt to intervene in the fighting but, with Syria's other surrogate in Lebanon's factional conflict, the Amal militia, otherwise occupied, they allowed reinforcements to reach the rebel Fatah group. On 27 June 1988 the Arafat loyalists in the camp of Chatila were overrun and surrendered to the forces of 'Abu Musa'. On the following day, Syria granted 100 PLO guerrillas safe passage from Chatila to the Palestinian camp at Ain al-Hilweh, near Sidon, although their entry into the camp was allowed by the local Sunni Muslim militia (the Popular Liberation Army, led by Mustafa Saad) only after the personal intervention of the Libyan leader, Col Qaddafi. On 7 July Bourj el-Barajneh, Yasser Arafat's last stronghold in Beirut, was captured by the forces of 'Abu Musa', and 120 Arafat loyalists were evacuated to Ain al-Hilweh.

LEBANON FAILS TO ELECT A NEW PRESIDENT

President Gemayel's term of office was due to expire on 23 September 1988 and the National Assembly was required to elect a new President before that date. As the election approached, political manoeuvring began in an attempt to find a candidate for the post (traditionally a Maronite Christian) who would be acceptable to both Christians and Muslims. The question was complicated by divisions within the Maronite community and the unwillingness of most Christians to accept a candidate who was thought to represent the interests of Syria. Discussions between Syria and the USA (in the person of Richard Murphy, the US Under-Secretary of State for Near East Affairs), seeking a suitable candidate, failed to produce a compromise choice.

By mid-August 1988 more than two dozen candidates for the presidency had declared themselves, but the three main contenders were: Gen. Michel Awn, the Commander-in-Chief of the Lebanese army; Raymond Eddé, the leader of the Maronite Bloc National, who had been in exile in France since 1976; and Sulayman Franjiya, who was President of Lebanon between 1970 and 1976. The latter did not announce his candidacy until 16 August 1988, two days before the date of the election, and the news immediately united President Gemayel and Samir Geagea, the commander of the LF, who opposed Franjiya's candidature on the grounds that he represented Syrian interests. It was Franjiya who, as President, had invited Syria to intervene militarily in Lebanon to end the civil war in 1976. President Gemayel and Dr Samir Geagea asserted that they would do everything in their power legally to prevent Franjiya from being elected. The reaction of Walid Joumblatt, the Druze leader, was to withdraw the presidential candidate of his own PSP and to support Franjiya's candidacy.

Votes for the presidency were to be cast in two ballots. To be elected, the successful candidate had to receive a majority vote of two-thirds of the members of the National Assembly in the first ballot and a simple majority in the second. Prior to the session at which the election was to be held, a quorum of the Assembly was deemed by its President, Hussain al-Hussaini, to be 51, or two-thirds of the surviving 76 members of the original 99-member National Assembly (whose mandate had been repeatedly renewed since 1972, owing to the impossibility of holding parliamentary elections). In the event, only 38 members (10 of the 41 Christian deputies and 28 of the 35 Muslim deputies) attended the session on 18 August 1988 at the temporary parliamentary premises on the 'Green Line'—the President of the Assembly declared the session to be inquorate, and the election was postponed. It was strongly alleged that several of the Christian absentees had been intimidated, threatened or forcibly prevented from attending the election by the Christian LF and soldiers under the command of Gen. Awn, while it was thought that the failure of some Muslim deputies to arrive was due to the perennial difficulty of travelling across factional boundaries in Beirut.

On 2 September 1988 the acting Prime Minister, Dr Selim al-Hoss, withdrew the Government's resignation which had been tendered by the late Rashid Karami in May 1987 but not accepted by President Gemayel. Gemayel claimed that al-Hoss's action was unconstitutional and insisted that his Government held office only in a caretaker capacity.

Consultations between Syria and the USA resumed during September 1988 in an attempt to agree upon a compromise presidential candidate who might be acceptable to the majority in Lebanon. It was reported that they had agreed to support the candidacy of Mikhail ad-Daher, a parliamentary deputy, but Christian army and LF leaders repeated their rejection of any candidate imposed upon Lebanon by foreign powers.

A second attempt to stage the presidential election was scheduled for 22 September 1988 but, again, the session of the National Assembly failed to achieve a quorum. Only 14 deputies gathered for the vote in the old parliament building in west Beirut. Christian deputies assembled, instead, at a villa in east Beirut to repeat their opposition to a Syrian-imposed presidential candidate (i.e. Mikhail ad-Daher) and to the siting of the venue for the election in Syrian-controlled, Muslim, west Beirut.

President Gemayel's term of office expired at midnight on 22 September 1988, and, only minutes before, in accordance with his constitutional privilege, he appointed a six-member interim military government, composed of three Christian and three Muslim officers, led by Gen. Awn, to rule until a new President was elected. His choice of a military government was made after Muslim politicians had refused to participate in an interim civilian government which was to be headed, contrary to the National Covenant of 1943 (which divided power between the Christian and Muslim communities), by a Maronite Prime Minister, Pierre Hélou, instead of by a Sunni Muslim. The three Muslim officers whom the outgoing President had appointed to the interim military Government refused to accept their posts (which were assumed by the remaining Christian ministers on 4 October), while the two Christian members of the Government of Dr Selim al-Hoss (Joseph Hashim and Victor Qasir) surrendered their posts in recognition of the authority of the interim military administration. Dr al-Hoss appointed a Greek Orthodox Christian, Abdullah ar-Rassi, as Deputy Prime Minister on 24 September.

Lebanon was plunged into a constitutional crisis, with two governments (one Christian, in east Beirut, and one predominantly Muslim, in west Beirut) claiming legitimacy. Syria refused to recognize the interim military Government and there were fears that the fact of dual-authority would formalize what was already an effective partition of the state into Christian and Muslim cantons. Concern over the stability of Lebanon's central institutions increased in October 1988, when the National Assembly failed to elect a successor to Hussain al-Hussaini, its President, or to renew his one-year mandate. Meanwhile, each of the two Governments claiming legitimacy warned the other not to encroach upon its jurisdiction. The authority of Gen. Awn's military administration was regarded as having been strengthened when the LF (the Christian militia commanded by Dr Samir Geagea) seized control of Gemayel's base in the Metn region, north of Beirut, in early October.

In November 1988 Gen. Awn was dismissed as Commander-in-Chief of the army by Adel Osseiran, the Minister of Defence in Dr Selim al-Hoss's Government. Of Lebanon's central institutions, only the central bank remained intact, and it continued to make funds available to both governments for basic supplies of food and fuel.

Fighting broke out in southern Beirut between rival Shi'a groups of the Syrian-supported Amal in November 1988, and between Amal and the Iranian-sponsored Hezbollah in January 1989. In the latter instance the two militias were reported to have agreed to a cease-fire on 30 January. In February a major confrontation occurred between the LF and the Lebanese army, when Gen. Awn attempted to restore the Government's authority over the illegal, militia-controlled ports. While neither side achieved a decisive victory, the authority of the Lebanese army, which had been steadily eroded, was restored as a result of the clashes. The balance of power in Beirut was perceived as gradually altering, and there were hopes that the success of the Lebanese army in its encounters with the LF would lead to the reunification of Beirut.

AWN'S ATTEMPT TO EXPEL SYRIAN FORCES FROM LEBANON

In March 1989, however, the most violent clashes for two years erupted in Beirut between Christian and Muslim forces, positioned on either side of the 'Green Line'. While the immediate cause of the fighting was the blockade of illegal ports in west and south Beirut by Christian forces, it was Gen. Awn's declared intention to take all measures for the immediate expulsion of Syrian forces from Lebanon. Exchanges of artillery fire between Awn's army and Syrian forces continued on a daily basis. On 29 March a cease-fire, agreed in response to an appeal from a six-member Arab League committee on Lebanon, was declared. However, exchanges of artillery fire resumed within a matter of hours.

Throughout most of April 1989, Gen. Awn's forces and Syrian troops exchanged artillery fire on an almost daily basis, and by the end of the month almost 300 people had been killed. On 19 April, despite Awn's claim that he had a popular mandate to pursue the expulsion of Syrian forces from Lebanon, 23 Christian members of the National Assembly demanded an immediate cease-fire and appealed to the Arab League, the UN and the EC to intervene to end the fighting. In late April, following an emergency meeting of Arab League Ministers of Foreign Affairs, further proposals for a comprehensive peace plan were announced, recommending a cease-fire, to take effect from 28 April, under the supervision of an Arab cease-fire monitoring force. The plan also proposed that blockades being imposed on sea, land and air facilities should be withdrawn, and that a conference should be held to arrange elections for a new President, and to consider political reforms and the withdrawal from Lebanon of Syrian and Israeli forces. Both Syria and the Syrian-supported Government of Dr Selim al-Hoss announced their support for the plan, and Gen. Awn announced that his forces would co-operate with the Arab cease-fire monitoring force. The cease-fire took effect on 28 April, but renewed exchanges of fire were reported on 30 April.

RENEWED DIPLOMATIC INITIATIVES AS THE CONFLICT ESCALATES

Further fighting between Christian and Muslim forces erupted at the beginning of May 1989, and on 3 May a delegation from the Arab League (consisting of the League's Assistant Secretary-General, Lakhdar al-Ibrahimi, and the Kuwaiti Ambassador to Syria, Ahmed Abd al-Aziz Jassem) arrived in Beirut with the aim of enforcing the cease-fire (declared on 28 April) and to arrange for the arrival of an Arab force to monitor it. The delegation met the leaders of each of the rival Lebanese Governments, who were reported to have consented to the withdrawal of all land, sea and air blockades. Following a further outbreak of fighting, an urgent meeting was held between the Arab League delegation, the Syrian Government and the leaders of the rival Lebanese Governments. On 11 May it was announced that a further cease-fire had been agreed, but this collapsed on the same day.

At an emergency summit meeting of Arab leaders, held in Casablanca between 23 May and 26 May 1989 (subsequently extended by two days in order to achieve a unified position on the Lebanese question), a tripartite Arab Committee, consisting of King Hassan of Morocco, King Fahd of Saudi Arabia and President Chadli of Algeria, was formed to supplement the efforts of the Arab League Committee on Lebanon. Its aims were: to implement a cease-fire agreement in Lebanon within six months; to install an Arab observer force to supervise the cease-fire; and to act as an intermediary between the conflicting forces in Lebanon in order to facilitate an agreement on the question of political reform and the election of a new President. However, many observers doubted that the newly-formed Committee, presided over by King Hassan, could achieve these aims, not least because there had been no indication at the summit meeting in Casablanca of any willingness on the part of either Syria or Iraq to resolve their conflicting interests in Lebanon. Since the cease-fire in the Iran–Iraq War of August 1988, the traditional enmity between Iraq and Syria (which had intensified as a result of Syria's support for Iran during the war) had increasingly found expression by proxy in the conflict within Lebanon. By mid-1989, as Gen. Awn pursued his campaign to expel Syrian forces from Lebanon, Iraq had become the principal supplier of weapons to the Lebanese army.

At the emergency summit meeting in Casablanca, Iraq had demanded the withdrawal of Syrian troops from Lebanon, but in this, as well as in its attempt to persuade other Arab leaders to condemn Syria's role in Lebanon, it was unsuccessful. Other Arab leaders, while reportedly willing to condemn Syria's 'negative' role in Lebanon in private, were believed to fear Iraqi ambitions and to have sought to maintain a balance between Iraq and Syria. Egypt, Iraq, Jordan and the PLO all supported a proposal for the withdrawal of Syrian troops from Lebanon and for their replacement by an Arab peace-keeping force, but the plan was abandoned, in response to Syrian opposition.

At the beginning of June 1989 the Tripartite Arab Committee on Lebanon issued a renewed appeal for a cease-fire, but further exchanges of artillery fire took place the following day. At the same time, King Hassan of Morocco, King Fahd of Saudi Arabia and President Chadli of Algeria were reported to have instructed their Ministers of Foreign Affairs to begin the implementation of a 'plan of action' for Lebanon. On 10 June the three ministers travelled to Damascus, delivering to President Assad a letter from the Tripartite Arab Committee and receiving assurances from President Assad of Syria's willingness to co-operate with the Committee. The Assistant Secretary-General of the Arab League, Lakhdar al-Ibrahimi, also made further attempts to mediate between the opposed parties in Lebanon in June, holding talks with both President Assad of Syria and Gen. Awn. By mid-June, however, it had not been possible to reach an agreement regarding the composition of the proposed Arab cease-fire monitoring committee.

On 28 June 1989 the Tripartite Committee renewed its appeal for a cease-fire and announced details of its peace plan for Lebanon. The new plan proposed a cease-fire, the removal of blockades of Muslim and Christian ports in Lebanon and the opening of roads between east and west Beirut prior to a meeting of the Lebanese National Assembly in an unspecified foreign country. The last component of the new plan for peace was immediately rejected by Gen. Awn, however, on the grounds that such a meeting would 'contradict the principles of

sovereignty and national unity'. Despite the appeal for a cease-fire, exchanges of artillery fire continued.

Evidence of Soviet support for the new peace plan emerged in early July 1989, when Aleksandr Bessmertnykh, the USSR's First Deputy Minister of Foreign Affairs, travelled to Damascus with a message to President Assad from President Gorbachev, which reportedly appealed for an end to the fighting in Beirut. Iraq had previously responded to a similar communication by stating that it was prepared to halt all supplies of armaments to Gen. Awn's forces. However, while some observers optimistically attached their hopes for the salvation of Lebanon to the USSR, the extent of Soviet influence on Syria, as its principal supplier of arms, was limited. Despite the prolonged ferocity of the hostilities since March, it had long been inconceivable that either of the superpowers would commit itself to the resolution of the Lebanese conflict. On 31 July the Tripartite Committee abruptly suspended its work and blamed Syrian intransigence for the lack of progress on the Lebanese question. The Committee issued a communiqué accusing Syria of having a concept of Lebanese sovereignty which was inconsistent with the independence of Lebanon.

By August 1989 more than 600 people had been killed since Gen. Awn had begun his attempt to expel Syrian forces from Lebanon. In mid-August France despatched senior government envoys to Middle Eastern capitals in a new diplomatic initiative to halt the fighting. Since the escalation of hostilities in March, France had evacuated badly-wounded victims from both Christian and Muslim communities and had urged its partners in the EC to join forces in an urgent humanitarian mission. Since a substantial number of Lebanese Christians enjoyed dual French-Lebanese nationality, the French Government was faced with increasing domestic pressure to send such a mission. However, the suspicions of Muslim Lebanese regarding France's true intentions, and its possible future extension of military support to Gen. Awn's forces, were only partially allayed by the French policy of providing aid to both Muslim and Christian communities. The new French diplomatic moves were made in response to a further, dramatic escalation of the fighting in Beirut. On 13 August Syrian forces made their first attempt for more than 14 years to penetrate Christian-held territory, launching an attack on the town of Souk el-Gharb. This assault, combined with increased artillery bombardments of east Beirut, was regarded as an attempt by Syria to compensate, by military means, for its increasing diplomatic isolation. At the end of July the Arab League had formally referred to Syria as the principal obstacle to a settlement in Lebanon, while the USA had condemned Syria's renewed use of heavy-calibre weapons in Beirut. Syria, however, claimed that Gen. Awn bore full responsibility for the escalation of hostilities since he had earlier rejected an offer of a cease-fire by Lebanese militias allied to Syria. While the disingenuity of Syria's claim (on many occasions) that it was not directly involved in the fighting in Beirut was widely recognized, there were many observers who doubted whether Gen. Awn had ever realistically expected to expel the Syrian forces from Lebanon. Rather, he was believed to seek the 'internationalization' of the Lebanese conflict as a prelude to their withdrawal, and regarded the new French initiative, provoked by the escalation in the hostilities, as precisely the kind of diplomatic gain that he had hoped to achieve.

The French diplomatic initiative was strongly condemned by the Iranian-backed Hezbollah militia, which described it as a French 'military adventure' to assist Gen. Awn. While France emphasized repeatedly that it was not considering any military intervention in Lebanon, the Beirut-based Revolutionary Justice Organization warned that such intervention by French forces (eight French naval vessels had been dispatched towards Lebanon by 22 August 1989, in anticipation of a renewed onslaught against Christian-held positions in Beirut) would rebound upon US hostages held in Beirut.

On 16 August 1989 the UN Secretary-General, Javier Pérez de Cuéllar, summoned an emergency meeting of the UN Security Council to discuss means of achieving a cease-fire in Lebanon. This meeting, convened under emergency powers of the Secretary-General which had been invoked on only two previous occasions, followed reports that both Syrian- and

Iranian-backed militias in Beirut were preparing to join regular Syrian forces to defeat the Lebanese army.

In late August 1989 French diplomatic pressure was reported to have led to an offer by Gen. Awn to meet his Muslim rivals at a conference, with no reference to his previous condition that political reform in Lebanon could be discussed only after Syrian forces had withdrawn from the country. On 27 August a French peace plan for Lebanon was formally presented to Syria's Minister of Foreign Affairs, Farouk ash-Shara', by the Director-General of the French Ministry of Foreign Affairs, François Scheer. The plan proposed: a cease-fire; a halt to deliveries of armaments to either side involved in the conflict; the introduction of political reforms to end the dominant role of the Christians in Lebanon; and the phased withdrawal of foreign forces from Lebanon, beginning with the withdrawal of Syrian forces from west Beirut. While there was no immediate official response to these proposals by Gen. Awn's Government, Christian Lebanese sources in Beirut dismissed the proposals as 'Syrian-inspired' and as seeking to distract the international community from the primary issue of ending the siege of east Beirut.

On 7 September 1989, following allegations by the USA that its Ambassador to Lebanon, John McCarthy, and his staff had been threatened with 'Christian terrorism', the USA announced its decision to evacuate its ambassador to Cyprus and to close its embassy in Beirut. (The US Embassy had been under a peaceful siege, the population demonstrating in favour of increased US involvement in solving the problems of Lebanon.) Prior to the embassy's closure, meetings between US diplomats and the head of the LF, Dr Samir Geagea, had prompted accusations by Gen. Awn that the USA was seeking to divide Lebanese Christians as a prelude to concluding an agreement with Syria to end the fighting in Lebanon. The withdrawal of US diplomatic representation was regarded as signalling the failure of Gen. Awn's attempt to 'internationalize' the Lebanese conflict and to win Western support to expel Syrian forces.

On 18 September 1989 the Tripartite Arab Committee on Lebanon resumed its efforts to bring peace to Lebanon, following a meeting in Tripoli, Libya, at the beginning of September between President Assad of Syria and President Chadli of Algeria, at which Assad agreed to have the Syrian presence in Lebanon debated. The Committee appealed for an 'immediate and comprehensive cease-fire'. A new peace plan was announced, under the terms of which a Lebanese security committee was to be established (under the auspices of the Assistant Secretary-General of the Arab League, Lakhdar al-Ibrahimi) to supervise the cease-fire. The new plan envisaged the removal of the Syrian naval blockade of Beirut's Christian enclave, while the committee would retain the right to inspect any ship reported to be carrying arms. At the same time, Beirut's international airport was to be reopened. Finally, the plan envisaged a meeting of the Lebanese National Assembly to discuss a 'charter of national reconciliation' drafted by the Tripartite Arab Committee. Members of the National Assembly were to assemble on 30 September at a venue to be announced. Unlike the Committee's previous plan for peace in Lebanon, the new plan made no appeal for the withdrawal of Syrian troops, and the new initiative was therefore welcomed by the Syrian Government. Gen. Awn rejected the proposal for an exclusively Lebanese security committee, arguing that, since Syrian forces were directly involved in the conflict, Syria should be represented on any committee established to supervise a cease-fire. However, due to his diplomatic isolation (the charter was supported by the USA, the USSR, the UK, France and almost every Arab nation), Awn subsequently relented. The cease-fire accordingly took effect from 23 September.

THE TAIF AGREEMENT

At the end of September the Lebanese National Assembly met in Taif, Saudi Arabia, to discuss the charter of national reconciliation. The session was attended by 31 Christian deputies and 31 Muslim deputies. (Of the 99 deputies elected in May 1972, only 73 still survived.) At a further meeting on 22 October, the charter of national reconciliation was endorsed by 58 of the 62 deputies attending the session. Subsequent to its first being announced, the charter had been amended at

informal sessions of the National Assembly. However, the section dealing with Syria's role in Lebanon was the result of a prior agreement between the Tripartite Committee and Syria, and Lebanese deputies were prohibited from altering it. With regard to political reform, the charter now provided for the transfer of executive power from the presidency to a Cabinet, with portfolios divided equally among Christian and Muslim ministers. The appointment of the Prime Minister would remain the prerogative of the President, to be exercised in consultation with the members and President of the National Assembly. The charter further provided for an increase in the number of seats in the National Assembly, from 99 to 108, to be divided equally among Christian and Muslim deputies. A further provision was the implementation of two security plans in Lebanon, one within six months and the other within 24 months. Following the endorsement of the charter, the election of a President and the formation of a new government, all Lebanese and non-Lebanese militias were to be disbanded within six months, while the internal security forces were to be strengthened. For a maximum period of two years the Syrian army would then assist the new government in implementing the security plan.

The endorsement of the charter of national reconciliation (the Taif agreement) by the National Assembly was immediately denounced by Gen. Awn as a betrayal of Lebanese sovereignty. Prior to their departure for Taif, Christian deputies to the Assembly had reportedly assured Gen. Awn that they would permit concessions on the question of political reform only in exchange for a full withdrawal of Syrian forces from Lebanon. While there was some support for Gen. Awn's position in east Beirut, the agreement had, to a large extent, been facilitated by the co-operation of Lebanon's Maronite leaders, most notably Georges Saadé, the leader of the Phalangist Party, who had played an important role in the Taif negotiations.

In an annex to the Taif agreement, the Tripartite Arab Committee on Lebanon had appealed to the National Assembly to meet in November 1989 to ratify the charter and to elect a new President. This session of the Assembly was duly held in the northern town of Qlaiaat on 5 November, when René Mouawad, a Maronite Christian deputy and a former Minister of Education and Arts, was elected as President. (Of the 58 votes cast in the second round of voting in the presidential election, Mouawad received 52; Georges Saadé and Elias Hrawi, another Maronite Christian deputy, withdrew after the first round of voting.) Deputies also unanimously endorsed the Taif agreement and re-elected Hussain al-Hussaini as President of the National Assembly. Prior to the meeting, Gen. Awn had appealed to all Christian deputies to consult with him before attending. In response to the news that Muslim deputies had departed for Qlaiaat, Gen. Awn had announced the dissolution of the National Assembly. His reaction to the presidential election was to declare it unconstitutional, and the result null and void.

On 13 November 1989 President Mouawad invited Dr Selim al-Hoss to form a 'government of national reconciliation'. However, Maronite leaders were reluctant to participate in such an administration and thus openly oppose Gen. Awn. On 22 November, only 17 days after his election, President Mouawad was assassinated in a bomb explosion. Two days later, in the town of Shtaura, 52 deputies of the National Assembly convened and elected Elias Hrawi as the new President. At the same session, deputies voted to extend the term of office of the National Assembly until the end of 1994. A new Government was formed by Dr al-Hoss on 25 November 1989, and received a unanimous vote of confidence from the National Assembly.

Following a meeting of the new Cabinet on 28 November 1989, it was announced that Gen. Awn had again been dismissed as Commander-in-Chief of the Lebanese army, and that Gen. Emile Lahud had been appointed in his place. It was feared that Syrian forces would now launch a major assault on Awn's stronghold in Baabda, east Beirut. Dr Samir Geagea, the commander of the LF, announced that, in the event of such an assault, the LF would fight beside Gen. Awn. In December, in an attempt to isolate Gen. Awn further, the Central Bank of Lebanon halted all transfers of funds to areas of Beirut controlled by him, and the Ministry of Defence was reported to have ceased paying the salaries of Awn's troops and officials.

On 31 January 1990 Gen. Awn ordered his forces to close all the barracks of the LF in east Beirut. There followed intense fighting between Awn's forces and the LF for control of the Christian enclave, precipitated by the refusal of Geagea to reject the Taif agreement, thus isolating Gen. Awn within the Christian community. Awn had accordingly declared the LF to be an ally of Syria. (Maronite leaders had sought to avoid open conflict with Gen. Awn by minimizing their approval of the Taif agreement, and on 29 January Georges Saadé, who had been appointed Minister of Posts and Telecommunications in November, announced that he would not serve in the administration, thus damaging its credibility as a government of national unity.) By early March more than 800 people had been killed, and more than 2,500 wounded, in the inter-Christian fighting since 31 January. In March Gen. Awn declared a halt to the conflict between Christian factions, and expressed willingness to negotiate with his opponents, implying that he was willing to accept the Taif agreement in a modified form. Inter-Christian fighting resumed, however, later in the month.

In April 1990 Dr Samir Geagea announced his recognition of the Government led by Dr Selim al-Hoss, formally accepting the Taif agreement, and in June Georges Saadé resumed his duties in the same administration as Minister of Posts and Telecommunications. In early June President Hrawi visited Egypt, Libya and Tunisia, where he reportedly sought Arab backing for the implementation of the resolutions agreed at Taif.

In July 1990 there were reports of renewed, fierce fighting between Amal and Hezbollah in southern Lebanon. Clashes between the rival Shi'ite groups had occurred in March in southern Beirut, prompting the intervention of Syrian forces. The renewed fighting in southern Lebanon was reportedly over the issue of control of the area's Shi'ite population. At the beginning of August Israel warned that it would intervene if its interests were endangered by the hostilities.

Meanwhile, at the end of July, the al-Hoss administration began an attempt to pressurize Gen. Awn into relinquishing his power base in east Beirut by seeking to prevent essential supplies from reaching his forces. In the last week of July Awn had conferred with the Assistant Secretary-General of the Arab League, Lakhdar al-Ibrahimi, but had rejected the suggestion—which had already been proposed in a diplomatic initiative pursued by the French Government and the Vatican in June—of joining the al-Hoss Government under the terms of the Taif agreement.

THE IMPLEMENTATION OF THE TAIF AGREEMENT

The crisis in the Persian (Arabian) Gulf region, which was precipitated by Iraq's invasion of Kuwait in August 1990, had serious repercussions for Lebanon. Iraq's Lebanese allies— Gen. Awn and the PLO—hoped that Iraq's challenge to US and Saudi power would serve to weaken that power and subsequently undermine the regional and international consensus which supported the Taif agreement. The pro-Taif parties in Lebanon were apprehensive about the fate of the agreement, in view of the crisis developing in the Gulf region. In response, they succeeded, on 21 August, in convening a session of the National Assembly at which the Constitution was amended to incorporate the reforms which had been agreed at Taif.

The reforms included increasing from 99 to 108 the number of seats in the National Assembly, which were to be divided equally between Christian and Muslim deputies (rather than according to a 5:6 ratio in favour of Christian deputies, as previously). New deputies (40 in all, taking account of the 32 vacant seats in the old assembly) were to be appointed, rather than elected, for one term, owing to the 'extraordinary situation' in the country. The powers of the National Assembly were increased to the point where it became virtually impossible to dissolve it. The term of office of the President of the National Assembly was increased from one to four years, and the holder of that office would in future play a role in appointing the Prime Minister. The President, meanwhile, was divested of his autonomous prerogatives. Presidential

decisions now required the co-signature of the Prime Minister, except in two instances: the appointment of a Prime Minister; and when accepting the Government's resignation. Nominally the President continued to be Commander-in-Chief of the armed forces, but the army remained subject to the full authority of the Cabinet. In appointing a Prime Minister, the President could only follow the choice of deputies to the National Assembly. He no longer enjoyed the right to chair meetings of the Cabinet, to determine the agenda of such meetings or to vote at them.

With the stipulations of the Taif agreement incorporated into the Constitution, executive power was effectively transferred to the Lebanese Cabinet. The main beneficiary of the changes was the office of the Prime Minister, who became the head of the Government, speaking in its name, implementing its policies and co-ordinating the various ministries. In the event of a vacancy in the office of the President, the Cabinet, under the chairmanship of the Prime Minister, would assume the privileges and responsibilities of the presidency. The speed with which the National Assembly was convened on 21 August 1990 reflected an evolution in Syria's attitude towards the process of constitutional reform. Syria's renewed interest in the Taif agreement came in response to US assurances, given during the course of a visit by the US Assistant Secretary of State for Middle Eastern Affairs, regarding Syria's continued dominance in Lebanon and US support to that end.

On 28 September 1990 units of the Lebanese army loyal to the Government imposed an economic blockade on the areas of Beirut which were under the control of Gen. Awn. The blockade, which enjoyed Syrian and US support, was designed to force Awn into either co-operating with the al-Hoss Government, or evacuating the presidential palace at Baabda, where he was based. On 13 October Syrian forces commenced a military assault against the presidential palace at Baabda and other strategic areas under Awn's control. In a clear breach of the 'Red Lines' agreement between Syria and Israel, which regulated the parameters within which each country could operate in Lebanon, the Syrian air force shelled the presidential palace which had, for many months, been protected by a human shield. That Israel did not retaliate in response to such a breach of the agreement reflected the USA's support of the Syrian offensive. The Syrian military operation was the first of the repercussions of the Gulf crisis in Lebanon, where Syria had been granted freedom of action as a reward for its participation in the US-led multinational force deployed in Saudi Arabia. Awn's forces were completely defeated, and the areas under his control overrun. During the fighting Awn had departed for the French Embassy in Beirut, in order to negotiate a cease-fire. As soon as Baabda had fallen under Syrian control, he was advised to remain in the embassy for his own safety, and the French Government, considering his protection to be a matter of honour, offered him and his family political asylum. The Lebanese Government, however, refused to allow Awn to depart for France, wishing to place him on trial for embezzlement of funds and crimes against the state.

Following Awn's defeat, the Government began to implement a security plan for the Greater Beirut area. On 24 December 1990 a new government of national reconciliation was formed under Omar Karami, hitherto the Minister of Education and Arts. It was the first Lebanese administration to be formed since the amendment of the Constitution in August 1990 and was intended to continue with the implementation of the Taif agreement, begun under the previous Government. The former Prime Minister, Dr Selim al-Hoss (who had enjoyed the strong support of the Gulf states), was dismissed. The new Prime Minister enjoyed exclusive Syrian support. The 30-man Cabinet, comprising 12 Ministers of State and 18 ministers with portfolios, included various militia and party leaders as well as traditional political figures. Cabinet posts were divided equally among Muslims and Christians: six Sunni Muslims, six Maronite Christians, six Shi'a Muslims, three Druzes, four Greek Orthodox Christians, three Greek Catholics, one Armenian Catholic and one Armenian Orthodox Christian.

The composition of the new Government attracted considerable criticism. Deputies in the National Assembly complained at their under-representation in the Cabinet, while the Lebanese press questioned the merits of ministers whose only qualifications for office were those of being either a military leader or the son of a prominent politician. Other commentators accused the President of nepotism. The Phalangist Party and the LF complained that the Government lacked 'national balance'. Druze representatives complained at the dilution of their influence, while Hezbollah, the Lebanese Communist Party and the National Liberal Party were not represented in the Cabinet at all.

The new Cabinet presented a statement of policy to the National Assembly and received a vote of confidence on 4 January 1991. However, representatives of the Phalangist Party and the LF boycotted sessions of the Cabinet, complaining that more than two-thirds of its members were, either directly or indirectly, susceptible to Syrian influence. However, their boycott of the sessions did not result in their outright resignation and was intended, rather, to gain certain assurances and guarantees. By the same token, on 11 January the Druze leader, Walid Joumblatt, resigned from the Cabinet in protest at the dilution of Druze influence in the Government, and at the fate of the so-called 'people's army' and the civilian administration that had been established in the Chouf mountains by his PSP. The Government, meanwhile, adhered to the four-point programme which it had presented to the National Assembly, aiming to extend its authority over the whole of Lebanon; to disband the militias; to formalize Lebanon's 'special relations' with Syria; and to appoint deputies to the vacant seats in the National Assembly and fill senior military and civilian posts.

On 6 February 1991 Lebanese army battalions were dispatched to the south of the country for the first time since the Israeli invasion of 1978. They were deployed in the wake of a serious escalation in Palestinian guerrilla operations in the south, and consequent Israeli retaliation, as a 'buffer' between the 6,000 Palestinian fighters in and around Sidon and units of the Israeli-backed SLA. However, the inadequacy of the army's *matériel*, in relation to the size of the area which it was meant to patrol, meant that its deployment was largely symbolic. Its presence was nevertheless welcomed by the Shi'ite militia, Amal. The Iranian-backed Hezbollah reacted cautiously. Israel welcomed the deployment of the army in principle, but warned that swift and severe retaliation would ensue if it failed to suppress attacks against Israel.

On 28 March 1991 a full session of the Cabinet approved a plan to dissolve all Lebanese and non-Lebanese militias in the country and to appoint 40 new deputies to the National Assembly. All militias were to surrender their weapons and *matériel* to the Government during the period 28 March–30 April. Between the end of April and 20 June the army was to deploy in the region of Mount Lebanon, outside Greater Beirut, and to assume responsibility for the security of the rest of the country during 20 June–20 September. The new momentum in the Government's extension of its authority was a result of the defeat of Iraq by the multinational force in February. The USA, Saudi Arabia, Egypt and Syria, which had all contributed to the multinational force, were all also proponents of the Taif agreement. Ministers in the Government who had boycotted sessions of the Cabinet while awaiting the outcome of the war in the Gulf region (Samir Geagea, Georges Saadé, Michel Sassine and Walid Joumblatt) now began to adjust their positions. On 7 March Joumblatt retracted his resignation, and by 20 March the representatives of the LF in the Government—Michel Sassine and Georges Saadé—had ended their boycott of the Cabinet sessions. Dr Samir Geagea refused to accept a post in the Cabinet, but nominated an adviser, Roger Deeb, in his stead.

Not surprisingly, the larger militias viewed their own disbandment with little enthusiasm. The LF urged the creation of a national guard to assume responsibility for the security of certain regions, while the PSP argued that the militias should be incorporated into official military structures. Palestinian representatives, meanwhile, announced that they would not comply with the Government's decision, as the presence of Palestinian militias was a regional, rather than a domestic, issue. However, strong regional and international pressure ultimately compelled Lebanon's three major militias to comply

with the Government's order to disband, and army units were deployed in areas previously controlled by the LF and the PSP.

Despite the enthusiasm generated by the disbandment of the militias, apprehension remained with regard to armed groups which had refused to disband. These included the 6,000-strong pro-Arafat PLO; the 2,000-strong Iranian Revolutionary Guards, stationed in and around the town of Ba'albeck in the Beka'a valley; the 5,000-strong, Iranian-backed Hezbollah in the Beka'a valley and the south; and the 3,000-strong, Israeli-backed SLA. Arafat's al-Fatah group, based in Sidon, refused to disband, on the grounds that it did not constitute a militia, but, rather, a 'resistance movement' or, even, the regular army of the Palestinian state. It accordingly refused to surrender its weapons, but indicated its willingness to negotiate an agreement with the Lebanese Government regarding their location and use. The Government, for its part, refused to negotiate an agreement similar to the one signed in Cairo in 1969 and abrogated by the National Assembly in 1987. It also rejected the PLO's demands for its own embassy in Beirut; for a Palestinian brigade within the Lebanese army, with responsibility for the security of the Palestinian refugee camps; and for the right to launch attacks against Israel. After much pressure, however, the PLO finally declared that it would not impede the deployment of Lebanese troops in the south of the country.

The commander of the Iranian Revolutionary Guards, Hadi Rida Askari, insisted that they did not constitute a militia within Lebanon and that their withdrawal could take place only following a decision by the Iranian Government, made in consultation with Syria. Hezbollah, meanwhile, agreed to dismantle its military structure in Beirut, but insisted on maintaining armaments in the Beka'a valley and in southern Lebanon, in order to continue the struggle against Israel's occupation. The SLA rejected any suggestion that it would disarm or that Israel was ready to comply with the appeals of the Lebanese Government for the implementation of UN Security Council Resolution 425, which demanded the unconditional withdrawal of Israeli forces from Lebanon. Indeed, the fact that the Government had begun to disband Lebanese militias before their non-Lebanese counterparts aroused fears that its decision would be only partially applied and that the extension of its authority would encounter the perennial obstacle of the armed Palestinian presence in Lebanon, exacerbated by the presence of armed groups backed by Iran.

In accordance with the four-point political programme of the Government of national reconciliation, relations between Lebanon and Syria became closer, culminating in the signing, in May 1991, of a treaty of 'fraternity, co-operation and co-ordination'. The treaty was the natural outcome of the stipulations of the Taif agreement, establishing a formal structure for developing and implementing policies on a wide range of issues, and creating links between Lebanon and Syria in political, military, security and economic affairs. It received a mixed welcome, however. Georges Saadé and Roger Deeb, representing, respectively, the Phalangist Party and the LF in the Cabinet, abstained from voting at the Cabinet session at which the treaty was approved, and refused to join the official delegation which travelled to Damascus for its signing. The Maronite Patriarch, Nasrallah Sfeir, complained that such a treaty should not have been negotiated or signed before the Government had regained full sovereignty over the whole of Lebanon. He further warned that the treaty contravened the National Covenant of 1943.

The treaty declared that Syria and Lebanon had 'distinctive brotherly relations', based on their 'geographic propinquity, similar history, common belonging, shared destiny and common interests'. Moreover, the treaty specified the executive mechanism by which these 'distinctive relations' were to be managed and developed. Five joint councils were established, which were to meet regularly in order to develop and execute policies affecting Lebanon. The most important of these was the Higher Council, comprising the Presidents of Lebanon and Syria, their Prime Ministers, Deputy Prime Ministers and the presiding officers of their respective legislatures. The Higher Council assumed responsibility for the co-ordination and co-operation of the two states in political, economic, security, military and other spheres. Its decisions were to be binding, albeit within the constitutional and legal frameworks of both countries. Opponents of the treaty claimed that the joint councils constituted a violation of Lebanese sovereignty and amounted, in effect, to Syria's annexation of Lebanon. In view of Syria's military strength, they regarded the treaty as unbalanced, and predicted grave consequences for Lebanon's independence, its democratic practices and its traditional freedoms. They considered to be even more alarming the Syrian Government's refusal to formalize its recognition of Lebanese independence through the establishment of diplomatic relations. The supporters of the treaty, however, argued that it did not affect Lebanese freedoms, and that close relations with Syria were necessary for Lebanon's stability and prosperity.

On 9 May 1991 the National Assembly approved an amendment to Lebanon's electoral law, which allowed the exceptional appointment by the Cabinet of 40 deputies to the National Assembly. The appointments were made to the 31 seats in the assembly which had become vacant since 1972, and to the nine new seats created in accordance with the Taif agreement. On 7 June the 40 deputies were selected from a list of 384 candidates who had presented their credentials for office to the Ministry of the Interior. The deputies were selected by the President, the Prime Minister and the President of the National Assembly, in close consultation with Syria. The term of office of the new assembly was to be four years. The appointed deputies were representative of the political and confessional breadth of the Cabinet. All except four (who represented the Phalangist Party and the LF) enjoyed close relations wtih Syria. Hezbollah and a new, popular 'Awnist' grouping remained unrepresented in the National Assembly.

Following the appointments to the National Assembly, the Government began to compile a list of militia members who would be enrolled into the state's security and administrative structures, and to establish a schedule and locations for their 'rehabilitation'. On 29 May 1991 the Government had decided that some 20,000 militia members would be incorporated into the structures of the state. The decision stipulated that equal numbers of Muslims and Christians would be assimilated, among them 6,500 members of the LF, 2,800 members of Amal and 2,800 members of the PSP. The remainder would be absorbed from other militias. Their assimilation was to take place in three stages: 6,000 in June, 7,000 in July and 7,000 in August. All were to undergo retraining courses, lasting up to six months, before being assigned to employment in the service of the state. Initially, each militia member was to receive a monthly salary of US \$100.

In early June 1991 Israel launched its fiercest attacks on Palestinian bases in southern Lebanon since its invasion of the country in 1982. The attacks coincided with statements by Israeli officials that Israel had no intention of withdrawing from its self-declared 'security zone', nor of reducing its support for the SLA. The escalation of the fighting in the south appeared to serve the interests of both Israel and the Palestinians. It supported the Palestinians' assertion that they needed to retain their weapons in order to fight a war against Israel; and it allowed Israel to claim that its northern border remained insecure and that it needed to maintain an armed presence in southern Lebanon.

On 1 July 1991 the Lebanese army began to deploy in and around Sidon, encountering some armed resistance from pro-Arafat Palestinian guerrillas. On 4 July the Government and the PLO concluded an accord whereby the PLO agreed to allow the army peacefully to impose the Government's authority in the area. The deployment of the army in southern Lebanon was subsequently reported to have proceeded according to plan, although its jurisdiction did not include the village of Jezzine, where, although the locality was technically outside Israel's buffer zone, units of the SLA occupied positions.

The release in August 1991 of John McCarthy, a UK citizen who had been held hostage in Lebanon by Islamic Jihad (a pro-Iranian fundamentalist guerrilla group) since 1986, represented the beginning of intensive diplomatic efforts by the UN to achieve a comprehensive exchange of hostages who were being detained, respectively, by Israel and by various sectarian groups in Lebanon. By June 1992 the release of all of the Western hostages being held in Lebanon had been secured.

On 29 August 1991 Gen. Michel Awn, the head of the interim military administration that President Gemayel had appointed in September 1988, left Lebanon for France, where he had been granted political asylum. The Lebanese Government had granted him an amnesty, allowing him to leave his refuge in the French embassy in Beirut, on condition that he remained in exile for at least five years and refrained from political activities during that time.

At the beginning of September 1991 Lebanon and Syria formally concluded a security agreement, as foreseen in the bilateral treaty of May 1991. The agreement permitted Lebanon and Syria to seek mutual military aistance in the event of a challenge to the stability of either country. In mid-October President Hrawi travelled to Damascus for the first session of the Lebanese-Syrian Supreme Council, established by the May accord and comprising the Presidents of Lebanon and Syria, their Prime Ministers, Deputy Prime Ministers and the presiding officers of their respective legislatures. The chief topic of discussion at the first session of the Council was reportedly the opening session (in October) of the Middle East peace conference in Madrid, Spain, which Lebanese and Syrian delegations had been invited to attend.

In early November 1991 Karami announced that the USA had requested Israel to cease military activity in southern Lebanon, since it jeopardized the newly-begun peace process. However, Israeli military activity intensified in late November, in response to alleged attacks by Hezbollah fighters. A further, more serious, escalation of the conflict in southern Lebanon was precipitated in February 1992 by the assassination, by the Israeli air force, of Sheikh Abbas Moussawi, the Secretary-General of Hezbollah. Retaliation by Hezbollah fighters prompted an incursion by Israeli armed forces beyond the southern Lebanese buffer zone in order to attack alleged Hezbollah positions. Although the Lebanese army had begun to occupy positions in southern Lebanon that had been vacated by the UNIFIL, Hezbollah had retained its freedom to conduct military operations, in an apparent reflection of Syria's belief that only by continued coercion would Israel withdraw from occupied Arab territories.

In late March 1992 Syrian forces began to withdraw from Beirut, in preparation for their withdrawal to eastern Lebanon by September 1992 (in accordance with the Taif agreement).

During the early months of 1992 Lebanon's economic situation worsened dramatically, and general strikes took place in April and May. There were widespread allegations of corruption and incompetence within the Government, and on 6 May the Prime Minister, Omar Karami, and his Cabinet were forced to resign. Following discussions in Damascus between President Hrawi and Syrian leaders, Rashid Solh was appointed Prime Minister, and on 13 May his appointment was approved by 70 of the National Assembly's 108 deputies. A new Cabinet, announced on 16 May, included 15 members of its predecessor. It was regarded as insufficiently different in character from Karami's Government to modify the widespread perception of Lebanon as a Syrian protectorate, which many, including Karami, had blamed for the reluctance of Western countries to provide the country with significant economic assistance.

The President was reported to have instructed the new Government to make the alleviation of the country's economic crisis its priority. However, its attention was diverted by a serious escalation of the conflict in southern Lebanon in late May 1992. The prospect of improved relations with Western countries was enhanced by the release, in mid-June of the last two Western hostages being held in Lebanon.

ELECTIONS TO THE NATIONAL ASSEMBLY

The other principal task of the Lebanese Government in mid-1992 was to prepare the country for its first legislative election since 1972. In order to comply with the terms of the Taif agreement (see above), this had to take place before November 1992, and in early April the Government had indicated that the election would be held in the summer of 1992, although it was not certain that Syrian forces would have withdrawn to the eastern area of the Beka'a valley by this time, as the Taif agreement stipulated that they should. Lebanese Christian groups accordingly threatened to boycott the election, on the grounds that the continued Syrian presence would prejudice its outcome. The USA, too, urged the withdrawal of Syrian armed forces, in accordance with the Taif agreement, before the election took place. The Lebanese Government, for its part, argued that the Lebanese army was still unable to guarantee the country's security in the absence of Syrian armed forces. As new electoral laws were debated in the National Assembly in June and July, Hezbollah, in marked contrast to the country's Christian groups, indicated that it favoured the holding of an election as soon as possible.

On 16 July the National Assembly approved a new electoral law whereby the number of seats in the Assembly was raised from 108 (as stipulated by the Taif agreement) to 128, to be divided equally between Christian and Muslim deputies. On 24 July the timetable for the election was announced. Voting was to take place in three phases: on 23 August in constituencies in North Lebanon and the Beka'a area; on 30 August in Beirut and Mount Lebanon governorates; and on 6 September in constituencies in the South and in Nabatiyah.

In mid-August the Government stated its determination to hold the election to the National Assembly as planned, although it was clear by this time that most Maronite Christian groups, in particular the Phalangist Party, would not present candidates. In July Syria had indicated that its troops would not withdraw to the Beka'a area until the process of constitutional reform was complete, in accordance with its interpretation of the Taif agreement. Christian groups continued to maintain that a fair election could not take place until the Syrian armed forces had withdrawn. As the Lebanese Prime Minister and Cabinet had been chosen in close consultation with Syrian leaders, the Government continued to invoke the inability of the Lebanese army to guarantee the country's security in the absence of Syrian armed forces; and the position of Christian ministers in the Cabinet appeared more compromised than ever.

The first round of the election to the National Assembly took place, as planned, on 23 August. Voting in the first round was to elect a total of 51 deputies—28 to represent North Lebanon and 23 the Beka'a area. A total of 273 candidates contested the first round, in which the participation of the estimated 900,000-strong electorate was described as high in Muslim districts and very low in Christian ones. There were widespread allegations of electoral malpractice both during and after the first round, prompting the resignation of the incumbent President of the National Assembly, Hussain al-Hussaini. All the candidates presented by the Iranian-backed Hezbollah, which contested the election as a political party, were elected. The religious denominations of the deputies elected to the National Assembly in the first round of voting were as follows: 16 Maronite Christians; 16 Sunni Muslims; 8 Shi'ite Muslims; 8 Greek Orthodox; 3 Greek Catholics; 2 Alawites; 1 Druze and 1 Armenian Orthodox.

The second round of voting in the election to the National Assembly—to elect 54 deputies to represent constituencies in the Beirut and Mount Lebanon areas—took place on 30 August and was again characterized by the low participation of the electorate, especially in Christian districts. Indeed, in the Maronite district of Kesrouan voting was postponed, owing to a boycott by all candidates for election to its five seats. (All five seats were subsequently won by Maronite candidates in a by-election held on 11 October.) As in the first round of voting, there were widespread allegations of bribery and intimidation of the electorate. The religious denominations of the deputies elected to the National Assembly in the second round of voting were: 20 Maronite Christians; 8 Sunni Muslims; 6 Druze; 5 Shi'ite Muslims; 5 Greek Orthodox; 4 Armenian Orthodox; 1 Greek-Melkite Catholic; 1 Armenian Catholic; and 4 minority denominations.

The third round of voting, in constituencies in the South and in Nabatiyah, took place on 6 September. The religious denominations of the deputies elected to the National Assembly in the third round of voting were as follows: 14 Shi'ite Muslims; 3 Sunni Muslims; 2 Maronite Christians; 2 Greek-Melkite Catholics; 1 Greek Orthodox; and 1 Druze.

Following the elections to the National Assembly, the USA again urged Syria to withdraw its armed forces to the Beka'a area. After a meeting between President Hrawi and President

Assad of Syria, it was announced that a timetable for the withdrawal of Syrian armed forces would be compiled in October 1992. However, by late 1993 no such withdrawal had taken place.

LEBANON UNDER HARIRI

On 22 October 1992 Rafik Hariri was invited by President Hrawi to form a government. A new, 30-member cabinet was appointed on 31 October. Hariri, a Lebanese-born Saudi Arabian entrepreneur, included many technocrats in his new Cabinet, and offices were not, as previously, distributed on an entirely confessional basis. His appointment was viewed as likely to restore some confidence in the country's economy and to facilitate its reconstruction. On 12 November the new Government gained a vote of confidence in the National Assembly.

On 16 December 1992, in response to the deaths in the Occupied Territories of five members of the Israeli security forces, and to the abduction and murder by the Islamic Resistance Movement (Hamas) of an Israeli border policeman, the Israeli Cabinet ordered the deportation to Lebanon of more than 400 alleged Palestinian supporters of Hamas. Owing to the Lebanese Government's refusal to co-operate in this action, the deportees were stranded in the territory between Israel's self-declared southern Lebanese security zone and Lebanon proper.

Serious escalations of the conflict in southern Lebanon between Hezbollah fighters, the SLA and Israeli armed forces occurred in October and November 1992, and fighting continued at a lower degree of intensity during the early months of 1993. In July the Government was reported to be attempting to curtail the activities of the Damascus-based Popular Front for the Liberation of Palestine-General Command (PFLP-GC), which had begun to mount guerrilla attacks on the positions of Israeli armed forces and Israeli-backed militias from southern Lebanon. On 25 July Israeli armed forces launched their heaviest artillery and air attacks on targets in southern Lebanon since 1982, with the declared aim of eradicating the threat posed by Hezbollah and Palestinian guerrillas. The positions of Syrian troops in Lebanon were also reported to have come under fire, and the Israeli operation displaced as many as 300,000 civilians towards the north and caused many civilian casualties. In August Hezbollah fighters were reported to have mounted further attacks on positions of the pro-Israeli SLA in southern Lebanon. The violence remained at a high level in October and November. A sudden cessation of attacks by Hezbollah units on Israeli targets in January 1994, during the approach to a meeting between US President Clinton and President Assad of Syria, was cited as evidence, by Israeli observers, of Syrian control of Hezbollah. Hezbollah resumed attacks on Israeli targets in February, giving rise to the usual pattern of Israeli reprisals against Hezbollah targets. In June Israeli forces mounted an air attack on an alleged Hezbollah training camp in the Beka'a valley, close to the Syrian border. In early August further Israeli attacks by Israeli forces against Hezbollah targets in southern Lebanon caused the death of eight civilians, for which Israel subsequently made a formal apology. Israel claimed that Hezbollah had been involved in the planning of bomb attacks against Jewish targets in the United Kingdom and Argentina in July.

In March 1994, following terrorist attacks on Christian targets in Beirut, the Government proscribed the LF—the military wing of the Phalangist Party—for allegedly having promoted the establishment of a Christian enclave and, hence, the country's partition. In early May Hariri withdrew from all his official duties owing to a dispute with the President, and with the Speaker of the National Assembly, who both reportedly opposed his proposals to give the Government a measure of credibility with Lebanon's Maronite community by incorporating some of its representatives into the Cabinet. The dispute appeared to be resolved by President Assad of Syria's reported assurance to Hariri that pro-Syrian ministers within the Lebanese Cabinet would not seek to undermine the efficiency of the Government. Hariri resumed his duties later in May. At the beginning of September there was a minor reorganization of the Cabinet in which Michel Murr, the Deputy Prime Minister, replaced Beshara Merhej as Minister of the Interior. It was reported that this change represented an attempt to increase the unity of the Government.

LEBANON AND THE PEACE CONFERENCE

The Government's decision to send a Lebanese delegation to the opening session of a Middle East peace conference, held in Madrid, Spain, in October 1991, and to participate in subsequent rounds of bilateral negotiations, was criticized in both governmental and non-governmental circles. Critics argued that, since the terms of reference for the conference were UN Security Council Resolutions 242 and 338 only, Lebanon's participation was tantamount to a repudiation of UN Security Council Resolution 425, which demanded a comprehensive withdrawal of all Israeli armed forces from southern Lebanon; and that the implementation of Resolution 425 would henceforth be linked to the implementation of other UN resolutions. They asserted, moreover, that Lebanon had nothing to discuss in bilateral negotiations with Israel, since its relations with that country were regulated by the Armistice agreement of 1949, which remained valid.

Before the opening session of the Middle East peace conference was convened, Lebanon sought assurances from the USA on the following issues: that the implementation of UN Security Council Resolution 425 would not be linked to the implementation of other UN resolutions; that the country would receive support for the establishment of an international fund for Lebanon; that restrictions imposed by the US Government on its citizens with regard to travelling and investing in Lebanon would be removed; that the US Consulate in Beirut would be reopened; that the Lebanese national carrier, Middle East Airlines, should be allowed to resume flights to New York; and that arms paid for by the Government during Amin Gemayel's presidency would be delivered by the USA, and US-based training programmes for Lebanese army officers would be resumed.

With regard to Resolution 425, Lebanon's diplomacy was rewarded by a written US commitment to support its implementation in isolation from the wider Middle East peace process. On the other issues that Lebanon had raised, however, the USA remained non-committal, pending the release of all Western hostages being held in Lebanon. Some observers, too, regarded the US assurance on Resolution 425 to be unclear, since the US Government's letter of intent failed to distinguish between the nature of the Israeli and the Syrian armed presence in Lebanon. Another potential point of contention was the USA's demand that the activities of the Hezbollah militia in southern Lebanon should cease before the peace conference commenced, while the Government insisted that Hezbollah's resistance would continue until the Israeli armed forces had withdrawn from Lebanese territory.

Lebanon reacted cautiously to the Declaration of Principles on Palestinian Self-Rule in the Occupied Territories, signed by Israel and the PLO on 13 September 1993 (for details of the Declaration of Principles, see Documents on Palestine, p. 100). Fears were expressed, for instance, that, if the Declaration of Principles were to provoke violent confrontations between rival Palestinian factions, most of the violence would be likely to occur in Lebanon, endangering the country's reconstruction. There was also concern about the ultimate fate of the estimated 350,000 Palestinian refugees residing in Lebanon.

In late February 1994 Lebanon, together with the other Arab parties, withdrew from the Middle East peace process, following the murder, by a right-wing Jewish extremist, of some 30 Muslim worshippers in a mosque in Hebron on the West Bank. Together with Syria and Jordan, Lebanon agreed to rejoin the peace process in March. As before, any significant progress in negotiations between Lebanon and Israel remained dependent on the conclusion of a peace agreement between Syria and Israel.

Economy

Revised for this edition by ALAN GEORGE

Lebanon's role as the Middle East's leading centre for trade and financial services was destroyed by the civil war which erupted in 1975. Attempts to prepare plans for reconstruction were frustrated by recurring outbreaks of violence, culminating in the Israeli invasion of June 1982, which added a new dimension to the country's devastation. Lebanon's gross domestic product (GDP) expanded, in real terms, at an average annual rate of 6%–6.5% between 1964 and 1974. Average income per head in 1974 was estimated at US $1,300, one of the highest levels among developing countries at the time. With the outbreak of the civil war, however, real GDP declined sharply. Expressed in constant 1974 prices, it was estimated to have averaged £L4,800m. per year in 1975–81. The Israeli invasion caused a further sharp decline in GDP, which, again expressed in constant 1974 prices, was estimated at £L3,080m. in 1982. Despite the intervening years of turmoil, Lebanon's GDP, expressed in constant 1974 prices, was estimated to have recovered to £L8,600m. in 1987. However, although the banking sector actually thrived after 1975, the development of alternative Middle East banking and financial centres, particularly in the Persian (Arabian) Gulf region, made it unlikely that an unstable Lebanon would regain its position as the commercial centre of the Arab world. After Amin Gemayel became president in September 1982 and formed a Cabinet comprising technical experts, it was hoped that the process of rehabilitating the country could begin in earnest. Although detailed programmes were prepared, they could not be implemented, owing to the continued civil conflict and to the unwillingness of potential aid donors to commit themselves before the restoration of stability. In the late 1980s, after years of relative resilience to political events, the deterioration of the political situation, combined with a high level of unemployment, major shifts in population, the breakdown of the infrastructure and the perpetual postponement of reconstruction and development projects, plunged the economy to new depths of depression, and it teetered on the verge of collapse. Those who could afford to leave the country made efforts to establish themselves abroad, often in Cyprus, the USA or Australia. For those with no escape route, however, the outlook was grim. Hopes of an economic revival were raised when the civil war effectively ended in 1991. GDP for the year was estimated at US $3,000m., compared with an estimated $2,300m. in 1990, and $2,600m. in 1989. In 1992, however, the Government failed to narrow the budget deficit and, amid allegations of corruption and incompetence on the part of ministers, the value of the local currency collapsed, leading to a sharp rise in inflation and the resignation of Omar Karami's Government. The legislative elections held in mid-1992 and the subsequent appointment of the entrepreneur, Rafik Hariri, as Prime Minister paved the way for a serious start to economic reconstruction, which was to be based on higher receipts of foreign aid.

INTRODUCTION

Lebanon's economic life since the outbreak of the civil war in 1975 has been intimately shaped by the violence, which has included the Israeli invasions of the south in March 1978 and of the area up to and including Beirut in 1982. According to the Lebanese authorities, of a total of more than 100,000 people killed between 1975 and 1982, up to and including the Israeli invasion, 19,085 people were killed and 30,302 wounded between 4 June and 31 August 1982, and the Council for Development and Reconstruction (CDR—created in 1977 as the main co-ordinator of reconstruction efforts) estimated the cost of material damage at US $1,900m., with damage to housing alone of $670m. The fighting in the Chouf in September 1983 was claimed to have retarded efforts at reconstruction by at least a year, and the violence of 1984 and 1985, combined with the Israeli occupation of (and subsequent withdrawal from) southern Lebanon, was a further blow to the economy.

Further serious damage was sustained in 1989 during Gen. Awn's six-month 'war of liberation' against the Syrian presence in Lebanon. Some 800 people died in the fighting between March and September and the financial cost of the 'war' in the period 14 March–10 May alone was estimated at $400m., of which two-thirds was borne by Christian areas. Lost profits accounted for $150m. of the losses, while the balance comprised damage to property and infrastructure. Of the cost of damage to infrastructure, $50m. was accounted for by the destruction of a fuel depot in the east Beirut district of Dora. In addition, the fighting prompted the departure of thousands of people from the battle zones, including more than 4,500 highly-qualified professionals, many of whom left the country permanently. East Beirut and the surrounding Christian area suffered further destruction during the battles which took place between the LF and Gen. Awn's forces in 1990.

In 1979 the CDR disclosed proposals for a five-year reconstruction programme that envisaged expenditure of £L22,000m. However, following the Israeli invasion, the CDR produced a revised, 10-year programme, covering the period 1982–91, with plans for estimated spending of £L68,000m. The CDR's proposals stressed that the private sector would continue to be the main generator of economic activity, and that credit programmes for the private sector would be strengthened. Of the total planned expenditure, one-quarter was to be raised locally, and the rest from Arab oil states, international lending agencies and foreign governments. As a result of fighting from September 1983, however, and the consequences of the Israeli invasion of the south, the cost of the 10-year plan had to be revised on more than one occasion: in mid-1984 it was estimated by the CDR at more than £L100,000m. (US $17,000m.), compared with the March 1983 revision (£L62,200m. or $13,000m.) of the original 1978 plan (see below); and at the beginning of 1985 the estimated cost had soared to £L530,000m. ($33,000m.), taking account of new damage and the fall in the value of the Lebanese pound. In March 1983 the World Bank published a report on the country's reconstruction needs and detailed a programme which allocated £L4,130m. to telecommunications, £L3,854m. to energy £L2,941m. to roads, £L2,121m. to urban development and £L2,222m. to education. The Bank also emphasized the need for a separate, $223.5m.-reconstruction project to cover urgent requirements, especially in Greater Beirut. In late 1991 the US engineering company, Bechtel, and the Lebanese consultancy, Dar al-Handasah, completed a government-commissioned plan for the country's emergency reconstruction needs. The $3,000m.-plan covered 133 projects, most of them for completion within three years. Of the total, $819m. was allocated to road schemes, $461.9m. to housing, $320m. to sewerage schemes, $234.9m. to health sector schemes and $200m. to water supply projects. The emergency reconstruction plan, covering 1992 to 1995, forms part of a 10-year programme called the Horizon 2000 plan. This involves public expenditure totalling $11,700m. (at constant prices of 1992). Of the total, $10,200m. is for physical infrastructure, $300m. for investments in institutions and planning and $1,200m. for grant and credit support for private sector enterprises. Horizon 2000 aims to restore real GDP to its 1974 level by 1995 and to double real per capita GDP in the 1992–2002 period.

Mobilizing resources for investment is one of the greatest challenges facing the Lebanese Government. Flows of aid have been far smaller than the amounts pledged. A CDR report of early 1985 stated that, of $3,136m. pledged in grants and loans since 1977, only $1,207m., or less than 40%, had actually been received. The grants pledged included $2,000m. which had been promised, over five years, at the Arab summit meeting in Tunis in November 1979, of which only $417m. had been received. The Arab oil states tended, however, to link their aid to efforts by Lebanon to reach a satisfactory internal political settlement. Libya and Algeria declined to pay any part of their share of the scheduled aid. Funding shortfalls severely hampered the CDR's work, and in mid-1986 forced the agency to suspend work on a number of major construction projects. However, supplies of aid were forthcoming from a number of sources. In 1985, for example, the USA offered a loan of $2,000m. and the Federal Republic of Germany one of $800m., while Czechoslovakia agreed to lend $50m. on concessionary terms, and Iran allocated $10.4m. in reconstruction aid.

Other assistance was provided by the EC and by individual European countries. In the mid-1970s Lebanon signed a co-operation agreement with the EC whereby aid was allocated under the terms of five-year protocols. Under the 1977–81 protocol, Lebanon received 30m. European Units of Account (EUAs), but by the end of 1981 EUA 7.5m. of these had not been allocated to specific projects. Under the 1982–86 protocol, the EC committed itself to giving a total of 50m. EUAs, comprising 16m. in loans and grants from the EC budget and 34m. from the European Investment Bank (EIB). Of the total, 40% was allocated to infrastructure, 30% to energy schemes, 21% to health, housing and education, 5% to agriculture, 2% to commerce and industry and 2% as aid to the CDR.

In mid-1985 the EC agreed to divert 16m. European Currency Units (ECUs) from development projects in southern Lebanon, which had been frustrated by the Israeli occupation, for the repair of 350 schools countrywide. The EIB agreed to provide 84m. ECUs in loans.

In 1986–88 further development aid was pledged, but the sums involved were not large. In 1986, for example, the Federal Republic of Germany pledged DM40m. for disbursement before the end of the year, and a similar amount was promised for 1987. In April 1988 the EC announced a grant and loan totalling 2m. ECUs to fund the establishment of a printing plant for school books. In May France agreed to lend the CDR $33m. under a Franco-Lebanese financial protocol. The US Congress, however, reduced the US aid allocation for Lebanon to $380,000 for 1988, compared with the already minimal $980,000 for 1987.

In May 1990, at the summit meeting of Arab leaders in Baghdad, it was agreed to establish an International Fund for Assisting Lebanon, with donations of $1,000m. However, the formation of the Fund was delayed by the crisis in the Gulf region, caused by Iraq's invasion of Kuwait in August. In September the Kuwaiti Government-in-exile and Saudi Arabia granted Lebanon loans of, respectively, $150m. and $100m. The end of Lebanon's civil war in early 1991 seemed likely to lead to an increase in foreign aid.

In December 1991 the World Bank sponsored a meeting of potential donors to Lebanon in Paris, at which the Lebanese Prime Minister, Omar Karami, reportedly requested $4,450m. for urgent projects in the subsequent three to five years. After the meeting it was confirmed that up to $700m. in 'soft' loans and grants had been pledged for the 1992–94 period, albeit mainly in earlier, bilateral meetings.

In late 1991 and early 1992 Lebanon secured a series of other aid commitments, although it was unclear whether these were included in the $700m. figure which had emerged after the Paris donors' meetings. In November 1991, for example, the Kuwait Fund for Arab Economic Development (KFAED) had agreed to make a $36.2m.-loan for the power projects, and in the following month the Arab Fund for Economic and Social Development (AFESD) granted a $73m.-loan, also for power shemes. In February 1992 it was announced that Italy had agreed to provide $460m. in loans and grants for electricity, water, telecommunications, refuse collection, health, agricultural and transport projects. Italy thus emerged as by far the biggest Western contributor to Lebanon's reconstruction.

By mid-1992 the International Fund for Assisting Lebanon had still not been formed, although in October 1991 the Minister of Foreign Affairs, Faris Bouez, announced that the Fund would have a capital of $2,000m., of which $500–$600m. would come from Gulf states and a further $500m. from Japan, France, Germany and Italy. Subsequently, however, Lebanon descended into a deep economic crisis which, the Government claimed, was partly due to the fact that foreign aid had not been arriving at the rate anticipated.

The Government's hopes that expatriate Lebanese might use some of their substantial funds to invest in their country's reconstruction meanwhile appeared too optimistic. In 1991 the IMF estimated that between $10,000m. and $15,000m. was held abroad by expatriates. Although there was a significant influx of private funds after the end of the fighting in 1991, these were mainly invested in property rather than in more directly productive areas.

The end of the civil war in 1991 did, nevertheless, allow the launch of some reconstruction work, although this was constrained by shortage of funds. The Italian company Emit, for example, began work on a $30m.-Italian government-funded project to improve Beirut's water supply system, and in February 1992 French companies submitted offers for three French government-funded contracts to repair and upgrade telecommunications and power installations. Local and international contracting firms were meanwhile preparing studies for a range of other schemes. There was a marked increase in the amount of foreign aid granted to Lebanon following the legislative elections which took place in mid-1992, and the appointment of a new government under Rafik Hariri. In March 1993 the World Bank agreed to grant the country $175m. for the reconstruction of its infrastructure. While this loan encouraged other lenders to grant aid, the World Bank made clear its concern at the Government's continued inability to bring state finances under control. In particular, the Bank was concerned at its failure to reduce the country's budget deficit. During 1993 and 1994 international confidence in Lebanon's new-found stability increased, and was reflected in a major influx of development aid from governments and lending agencies. During a visit to London in early 1994 Prime Minister Hariri said that the country had secured about $1,500m. in foreign funding and that a further $920m. was being negotiated. He commented that the Horizon 2000 programme could be completed in as little as five years if sufficient funding was available.

Private capital, mostly from expatriate Lebanese, has also returned on a large scale. Within one month of Hariri's appointment as Prime Minister and during the first nine months of 1993 aggregate bank deposits increased by a further $1,500m.

POPULATION

No proper census has been held in the country since 1932 for fear of upsetting the delicate political balance between the various sects or confessions. Until 1991 all political and administrative offices were allocated on the basis of the 1932 census, which showed Christians in the majority by six to five over non-Christians. It has been widely recognized for many years, however, that Muslims account for about 60% of the total population. (In 1983 the combined Shi'a and Sunni Muslim population was estimated at 1.95m., while the combined Maronite and Greek Orthodox Christian communities were numbered at 1.15m.) The increase in the Muslim proportion occurred partly because of the higher ratio of Muslims in the Palestinian population in Lebanon and partly because Muslims tended to have a higher birth rate and to emigrate less than Christians. Demographic changes strained to the limit the delicate system of allocating offices on a sectarian basis which was adopted under the National Covenant of 1943. They were finally recognized in the Taif agreement of 1989, which stipulated, among other things, that Christians and Muslims should be represented by an equal number of deputies in the National Assembly.

The effects of the civil war on the size, composition and geographical distribution of Lebanon's population have been dramatic. From an estimated 3.1m. inhabitants in 1974 (which made Lebanon one of the most densely populated countries of the Middle East), the total is believed to have declined to 2.7m. in 1979, thereafter rising slightly, to reach about 2.9m. in 1990. By mid-1991, owing to the return of many Lebanese from exile, the population was estimated to have increased to 3.2m.

The total of those killed or disabled during 1975–76 was estimated by the Lebanese Chamber of Commerce, Industry and Agriculture at 30,000 but other estimates were as high as 60,000, while thousands more were killed or wounded during the spring and autumn of 1978. By the Lebanese Government's

reckoning, a further 19,085 people died as a result of the Israeli invasion of 1982. Each round of violence tended to trigger a fresh wave of movement of population, whether within Lebanon, for example from the south into Beirut, or abroad. Those who went abroad often joined relatives or friends already there, for Lebanese emigration was considerable from the 1890s onwards, and by 1960 an estimated 2.5m. Lebanese, or people of Lebanese descent, were living outside the country. The biggest migrant community has traditionally been in the USA, and other favourite settling places were West Africa, Latin America and Australia. Remittances from Lebanese working abroad have traditionally been a staple source of national income. On average, the remittances from the 250,000–300,000 Lebanese workers abroad provided up to 35% of Lebanon's gross national product (GNP). However, returns slumped in 1983, according to US observers, with the usual monthly remittance of $125m.–$200m. falling to $75m.–$100m., reflecting the recession in the Gulf, where many Lebanese worked, caused by the world oil glut.

A study carried out at the American University of Beirut (AUB) showed the impact of the civil war and its aftermath on the labour force. It stated that in 1974 the non-agricultural labour force was 597,778, and had there been no civil war, the number would have reached 791,354 in 1979, instead of which it was only 426,239. The number of Lebanese working abroad in 1975 was 98,000, but by 1979 the number had risen to 210,000. Of these, 73,400 were in Saudi Arabia, 15,800 in Kuwait, and smaller numbers in other Arab states. Outside the Arab world, 17,300 were in West Africa, 27,000 in Europe, 17,000 in Latin America, 11,600 in North America and 14,000 in Australia. While Lebanon's recovery was hampered by the drain of skills and brains, there was at the same time a pool of unemployed, estimated at more than 200,000 in 1979. The sectors in which there was the greatest contraction of the work-force between 1974 and 1979 were industry (from 138,359 to 86,941), construction (from 46,517 to 18,942) and transport and communications (from 47,113 to 25,256). Many of those not in regular employment were engaged in paramilitary activities, or were part of the thriving 'black' economy. The exodus of thousands of Palestinian and Syrian workers from Lebanon, as a result of the Israeli invasion, caused a shortage of skilled and unskilled labour. The construction industry, in particular, was seriously affected. In 1985 it was estimated that 28% of the active population (18–68 years old) were unemployed, whereas before the civil war the rate had been 5%. Unemployment was estimated at almost 50% in 1987 and at 35% in 1990.

AGRICULTURE

Of the total area of the country, about 52% consists of mountain, swamp or desert, and a further 7% of forest. Only 23% of the area is cultivated, although a further 17% is considered cultivable. The coastal strip enjoys a Mediterranean climate and is exceedingly fertile, producing mainly olives, citrus fruits and bananas. Many of the steep valleys leading up from the coastal plain are carefully terraced and very productive in olives and soft fruit. In the Zahleh and Shtoura regions there are vineyards, while cotton and onions are grown in the hinterland of Tripoli. The main cereal-growing district is the Beka'a, the fertile valley between the Lebanon and the Anti-Lebanon ranges, to the north of which lies the source of the river Orontes. The River Litani also flows southwards through the Beka'a before turning west near Marjayoun to flow into the Mediterranean just north of Tyre. This valley is particularly fertile and cotton is now grown there with some success. Throughout the country the size of the average holding is extremely small and, even so, a small-holding, particularly in the mountains, may be broken up into several fragments some distance apart. The agricultural sector contributed over 9% of the GDP between 1972 and 1974 but this declined to about 8.5% during the civil war, when depopulation of the countryside occurred and both public and private investment in agriculture declined. The number of people employed in the agricultural sector fell from 147,724 in 1975 to an estimated 103,400, or 23% of the labour force, in 1985.

In 1963 the Government launched a 'Green Plan' involving land reclamation and agricultural development. Under the plan, more than 170,000 dunums of land was reclaimed, although this was less than has been devoured by urban development. In May 1980, the UN Food and Agricultural Organization (FAO) recommended a land and agricultural strategy to the Ministry of Agriculture. This involved preserving the 100,000 ha of land under cultivation, protecting grazing lands, and halting the encroachment of housing on agricultural land. The FAO also recommended that afforestation should be extended to cover 20% of the total land area.

In early 1983 a technical support project for agricultural and rural development planning was approved by the FAO. The objective was to rehabilitate the agricultural sector, and the project cost of $680,000 was provided by Saudi Arabia within the framework of its contribution to the FAO Near East Co-operation Programme. The project started in April 1983 and lasted 30 months. It included the training of Lebanese personnel to take over from the international consultants.

The International Fund for Agricultural Development (IFAD), the UN agency which specializes in helping small farmers, was keen to become involved in Lebanon. In 1980 it proposed a rural rehabilitation project with four components: rural roads, dairy farming, distribution of apple boxes to farmers and agricultural credit. The intention was to increase farmers' incomes and reduce imports of cereals, meat and milk, thus improving the trade balance. The civil conflict delayed a final agreement on the project, but in early 1983 an IFAD team visited the country to discuss it further. By that time the cost of the project had risen from an estimated $32m. in 1980 to $40m.

Lebanon's wheat crop totalled an estimated 52,000 metric tons in 1992, compared with 59,000 tons in 1991. Fruit-growing increased substantially from the early 1950s and played an important part in the economy during the civil conflict. A rush to plant apple trees in the 1950s resulted in gluts, followed by a reduction in output in the late 1960s. Production of apples was estimated at 190,000 metric tons in 1992, compared with an estimated 214,000 tons in 1991. Production of grapes was estimated at 290,000 metric tons in 1992, compared with an estimated 358,000 metric tons in 1991.

Other crops include sugar beet and tobacco, the cultivation of which declined as a result of the civil war and the Israeli invasions of 1978 and 1982. In 1980, only 3,273 ha were under tobacco cultivation, compared with about 8,000 ha before the civil war.

The Israeli invasion of 1982 cost farmers in the south an estimated £L800m., largely because Israeli agricultural products flooded the local market. Although direct damage to the orange groves in the south was not great, there were problems in finding labour following the killing of some Palestinians and the departure of others with the PLO. Before the invasion, a large proportion of the citrus work-force was Palestinian, and the Lebanese workers who replaced them cost their employers almost double the wages. Another difficulty was the increasing output of orange groves in Syria, which formerly imported almost three-quarters of the Lebanese crop. Orange growers complained at the lack of government assistance in the marketing of their produce, while the dangers of transport through areas of armed conflict was a further problem. The spring of 1983 saw a decline in fruit exports. In February, for example, they were down to 19,622 metric tons from 26,132 tons in the same month of 1982. Exports of apples were down by 45% and those of watermelons by 59%. In the spring of 1983 a boycott of Lebanese crops was imposed by some Arab states, which feared that they originated in Israel. In 1984 Saudi Arabia, the largest export market for local industries, banned all Lebanese imports for this reason. By June 1985, however, the number of Lebanese firms permitted to export to Saudi Arabia once again had risen to 319. Owing to Israeli interference with traffic between the south and Beirut, large quantities of produce perished from exposure to the sun.

The relative lack of security in Lebanon has allowed two crops to prosper: hemp (*Cannabis sativa*), the source of hashish; and the opium poppy (*Papaver somniferum*), the source of opium and its derivatives, heroin and morphine.

Before the civil war, Lebanon's annual hashish production was estimated at 100 tons. Between 1987 and 1989 output averaged 700–900 tons, although this fell to 100 tons in 1990–91 owing to inclement weather. In 1988–91 opium production was running at an annual average of 40 tons.

INDUSTRY

Until the time of the first sudden increase in petroleum prices, in 1973–74, the only minerals which were exploited in Lebanon were lignite and some iron ore, smelted in Beirut. There have been hopes of petroleum discoveries for a number of years but, so far, these hopes have been unfulfilled.

Even before hopes of a petroleum discovery were raised Lebanon was of considerable importance to the petroleum industry. Two of the world's most important oil pipelines cross the country, one from the Kirkuk oil wells in Iraq to Tripoli and the other from Saudi Arabia to Zahrani near Sidon. At each terminal there is an important petroleum refinery. Both the pipelines and the refineries have, however, been the subject of disputes.

Revenues from the Kirkuk-Tripoli pipeline, which was managed by the Iraq Petroleum Company (IPC), were reduced after both Iraq and Syria nationalized IPC assets in their countries on 1 June 1972. After the Iraqi Government and IPC had reached a settlement on the nationalization in 1973, a dispute over the ownership of the IPC refinery in Lebanon followed, as a result of which the Lebanese Government appropriated the refinery and agreed to compensate IPC. In April 1976, however, Iraq suspended pumping, choosing to direct its Kirkuk petroleum to the Persian (Arabian) Gulf instead. Lebanon was thus faced with a loss of around £L30m. per year in royalties as well as the loss of cheap petroleum. During the early part of 1977 the refinery at Tripoli was processing only 5,000 barrels per day (b/d), compared with an average of 36,000 b/d in 1975. By 1978, however, it was operating at around 75% of capacity on petroleum which reached Tripoli by sea or from nearby Zahrani. Iraq finally resumed pumping to Syria through the former IPC pipeline in early 1979, but the transfer of Kirkuk crude petroleum via Lebanon remained dependent on the conclusion of a new bilateral transit and supply agreement. It was reported in March 1981 that Iraq had agreed to start re-pumping after a break of five years. The initial rate of delivery was to be about 200,000 b/d, doubling after two months. Of this, 35,000 b/d were to be used domestically, with the remainder exported. At the time of the agreement, the Tripoli refinery was using 26,000 b/d of Saudi crude petroleum, which was pumped to Zahrani and then transported to Tripoli by tanker.

On 24 December 1981 Iraqi petroleum started to flow through the pipeline, but within days it was damaged by a bomb blast. Although the pipeline was repaired, its vulnerability to sabotage was underlined when, in March 1982, it was blown up again. Politics intervened when, on 10 April, the trans-Syria pipeline was closed and Iraqi deliveries to Tripoli were suspended. The refinery subsequently processed Iraqi petroleum which had been transported via Turkey. The fighting between PLO loyalists and anti-Arafat factions in Tripoli in December 1983 caused damage to the refinery which was estimated at $120m., while $60m.-worth of petroleum products were destroyed when 29 of the refinery's 36 major tanks, and 16 of its smaller tanks, were hit. The refinery began to receive shipments of Iraqi oil again in April 1984, when repairs were completed. Supplies of Iraqi oil ceased in 1990, as a result of the economic sanctions imposed on Iraq. In October 1990 Syria agreed to supply Lebanon with 20,000 b/d of light crude petroleum, to be delivered through the pipeline linking Tripoli with the Syrian oil terminal at Banias. In early 1991, after the completion of repairs and modifications, the Tripoli refinery resumed operations.

The Zahrani refinery was, until 1986, operated by the Mediterranean Refinery Company (Medreco), jointly owned by Caltex and Mobil. Mobil, Caltex's two parent firms (Texaco and Standard Oil of California) and Exxon also own the Trans-Arabian Pipeline Company (Tapline), which formerly operated the Saudi-Lebanese pipeline. Tapline suspended its pumping operations in early February 1975 because oil tankers found it cheaper to load petroleum directly from the Saudi terminal at Ras Tanura in the Gulf. This suspension cost Lebanon more than £L20m. in royalties. The company also demanded that the Lebanese Government pay for the higher cost of Saudi petroleum (previously supplied to the Zahrani refinery at a price of $5 per barrel), claiming that it was owed $100m. in back payments. A settlement was reached in August 1975 but, when the refinery which had been out of action for much of 1976, recommenced operations at the end of November 1976, the question of back payments arose again. Accumulated debts for 1975/76 were estimated at $120m., and in August 1977 it was finally agreed that these would be settled by the Saudi Government. However, it was not until early 1979, in the wake of the Iranian Revolution and the decline in Iran's exports of petroleum, that Tapline resumed operations on its former scale.

In early August 1981 Tapline suspended all deliveries of crude petroleum to the Zahrani refinery because of non-payment of debts for petroleum, but a few weeks later Saudi Arabia announced that it would pay most of Lebanon's petroleum bill. The Israeli invasion of Lebanon in 1982 presented further complications. The Zahrani refinery was out of action from June to November, after being bombed by the Israelis. Tapline's oil pipeline passed through Israeli-held territory, so Saudi crude petroleum was delivered by tanker. In February 1982 Tapline announced that it had lost some $350m. on its Lebanese operations since 1975, and that it had decided to close the damaged pipeline, which, for political and security reasons, would not be repaired. In September 1983 Tapline gave 90 days' notice that it was to stop operating in Lebanon and Syria and in early 1984 the Government took control of Tapline's installations. In 1986 Medreco ceased operations and the Government took control of the Zahrani refinery. In 1991, with the civil war apparently concluded, the Government announced its intention to bring the Zahrani refinery back into operation. During 1993 the French company Total confirmed an interest in participating in the renovation of the Tripoli refinery. In mid-1994 a French firm, BEICIP, was appointed by the Oil and Industry Ministry to conduct a six-month study into the refining sector.

Manufacturing industry in Lebanon was, for many years, highly developed in comparison with other states in the area, although it suffered from political disruptions and strikes even before the civil war. Industrial exports increased by 90% between 1973 and 1974 to reach just under £L846m., and the industrial sector in 1974 provided £L1,040m., or 16% of national income. The number of workers employed in industry was 139,471 in 1975.

The civil war had a dramatic impact on Lebanese industry. Between 1975 and 1982, up to and including the Israeli invasion, some 400 industrial units were destroyed or seriously damaged, according to the CDR. During their invasion, Israeli forces were said to have destroyed 25 of the country's major industrial units and to have damaged many smaller enterprises. Damage to the textile industry was particularly severe. Before the invasion, fewer than 50% of the 1,200 textile factories which were operating before 1975 remained active, and during the invasion a further 70 enterprises were completely destroyed and more than 150 others damaged.

The Chouf war of autumn 1983 cost local industry an estimated £L10m. per day; 140 factories, employing 25,000 workers, in the Choueifat-Kfarchima district of southern Beirut were forced to close. The Israeli occupation of southern Lebanon also posed serious problems for industrialists, who had to compete with a large influx of Israeli goods entering the country. This not only meant that local goods were competing with cheaper Israeli items, but it also led to problems between Lebanon and its Arab neighbours, who suspected that Israeli goods were being exported to them via Lebanon and imposed an embargo on some Lebanese products. Other factors which hampered industrial development were the shortage of skilled workers (owing to emigration to the Gulf), ageing machinery, and the weak and damaged infrastructure.

Much of Lebanon's remaining industry is located in the Christian Zone, which until 1989 had been relatively free of widespread violence. During the period 14 March–10 May 1989, however, 170 Lebanese factories were damaged in Gen. Awn's 'war of liberation' against Syria, 20 of them being completely destroyed. Factories sustained further damage during inter-Christian fighting in early 1990.

Industry in Lebanon traditionally consisted of small-scale operations run by individuals who employed a handful of people. Before the disruption of 1975, however, the number of limited liability companies had risen to 44. Food processing, yarn and textile firms accounted for about 44% of industrial output and furniture and woodworking factories for about 29%. Mechanical industries accounted for only about 7% of total production and the remainder was contributed by the cement, ceramics, pharmaceutical and plastic industries. New factories licensed in 1980 showed a similar bias. In all 77 were licensed, most of them small: 12 for bottling oxygen and other substances, 7 for food and drink processing, 6 for mineral water bottling, 5 for plastics and 5 for film manufacture and processing. Most of the others produced construction materials. A marked feature of the new factories was their decentralized distribution. Beirut was only the third most popular location, having 9 of the new factories compared with Zahleh's 13 and the Chouf's 10. Tripoli had 7, the western Beka'a 7 and the north Metn 6.

With the exception of petroleum companies, the largest industrial employers prior to the civil conflict were probably the food-processing industries, followed by the well-developed textile industries. The inflow into real estate of funds from Lebanese abroad, mainly those whose property was sequestrated in West Africa, also helped to stimulate the building industry, bringing a sharp rise in land prices and construction activity in 1974. The production capacity of the country's cement factories was sufficient to leave a surplus for export. In late 1981 the new cement plant at Sibline, in the south, was completed, with an annual capacity of 300,000 tons. However, the plant was damaged during the Israeli invasion of 1982. In 1986 it was announced that repairs would be undertaken, following a £L270m. investment in the plant by Sidon-born Saudi entrepreneur, Rafiq Hariri. It was hoped that production would resume in July 1986.

In 1977, at the conclusion of the first phase in the civil conflict, the government sought to regain investors' confidence by creating the National Establishment for Investment Insurance, which provided investments taking the form of fixed assets with insurance cover at low premiums against hazards of civil war, revolutions, dissension and acts of violence. In addition, legislation applying to foreign banks was amended to encourage them to contribute to reconstruction by investing in the Housing Bank and the National Bank for the Development of Industry and Tourism. The Housing Bank, in turn, embarked on a large-scale lending programme providing 15-year loans at an interest rate of only 2% per annum.

The civil conflict prevented any sustained revival of industry during the 1980s. The value of industrial exports in 1980 was 15% higher than in 1979, and in 1981 there was a further increase, of 25%, to £L2,290m. However, these increases were mainly due to the depreciation of the Lebanese pound. The major buyers of Lebanese industrial exports in 1981 were Iraq, Syria, Saudi Arabia and Jordan, which together accounted for 86% of all sales. The invasion of Lebanon by Israel in 1982 caused the value of industrial exports to decline to £L1,924m. in 1982 and to £L1,296.4m. in 1983. In 1984 their value fell to £L984m. Assisted by the rapid depreciation in the value of the Lebanese pound, the value of industrial exports subsequently increased sharply: to $372m. in 1985, $438m. in 1986 and $690m. in 1987. In 1988, however, it amounted to only $274m., and in 1989—a year in which factories in east Beirut sustained particularly heavy damage—only $174m. The 1990 figure was $127m. With the end of the fighting in 1991, the value of industrial exports recovered to $206m.; the 1992 figure was $210m. The Israeli occupation of the south, the cumulative effect of years of violence, the recession in the Gulf, which was Lebanon's principal export market, and competition from cheap, smuggled goods, all contributed to the decline of industry. The new industrial zone around Sidon, which developed after 1976, was effectively throttled by the Israeli presence and the influx of subsidized Israeli goods. Lebanon's industrial sector was estimated to be operating at only 40% of capacity in early 1986, with textiles, leather goods and finished wood products accounting for the bulk of production, while the labour force employed in manufacturing industry had declined to an estimated 45,000 in 1985.

The lack of adequate sources of power hindered industrial development in the 1960s but Lebanon gradually achieved the position of having excess capacity. In 1972 it began to supply power through a 100-kWh line to southern Syria, and in March 1976 the two countries agreed on the exchange of power through a similar line between Tripoli and Tartous. Work on implementing the power link-up project began in 1977 as part of moves to repair the country's badly damaged electricity network. A seven-year electrification scheme costing some £L1,260m. was drafted, which was expected to be financed by the World Bank and the Arab Fund for Economic and Social Development. An important feature of the plan was the upgrading of the Zouk power station, and in 1980 the EIB lent around $4.3m. for two 125-MW generators for the station. In early 1982 Electricité du Liban (EDL) obtained a further loan of 7m. ECUs to help to finance the expansion of the Zouk power station. Generating capacity in 1990 totalled 515 MW, with thermal stations accounting for 465 MW and hydroelectric plants for 50 MW. By comparison, a capacity of 1,200 MW was required to meet 1991 peak demand. In early 1991 officials from EDL outlined plans for a series of projects to expand existing power facilities and establish new ones. The projects included the construction of a 200-MW gas turbine station in the Beka'a valley; the installation of a 200-MW gas turbine and a 100-MW steam turbine at Zahrani; the addition of a 150-180-MW steam turbine at the Zouk station; the installation of 100-MW and 150-MW steam turbines at the Jiyyeh power station; the construction of a 100-MW steam turbine at the Harisha power station; and the construction of a new power station, with a 250-MW steam turbine, at Batroun. According to EDL, Lebanon required an additional 2,400 MW of capacity in order to satisfy projected demand in the 1990s. Owing to the decline in the value of the local currency and the ending of fuel oil and electricity subsidies to industry, raw materials and energy now cost more, and this will hamper any industrial recovery. In 1993 the Italian firm Ansaldo Energia, South Korea's Hyundai Corporation and two French firms, Bouygues and Clemessy, won contracts to repair and rehabilitate the electricity sector. The work is being financed by the AFESD, the KFAED and the World Bank. Also in 1993 Electricité de France was appointed to prepare tender documents for the construction of two 415-MW-combined-cycle power stations, one in the south, at Zahrani, the other in the north, at Beddawi.

EXTERNAL TRADE

Lebanon's trade deficit has grown rapidly in recent years. In 1982 it rose to some £L9,000m. from £L6,000m. in 1981 and £L5,800m. in 1980. However, the 1982 deficit was more than covered by remittances from abroad, which totalled an estimated $2,000m. in 1982 and helped give a balance-of-payments surplus of £L1,321m. in 1982. The comparable surpluses were £L1,200m. in 1981 and £L1,490m. in 1980. There was great concern in 1983 when a large deficit on Lebanon's balance of payments was recorded for the first time, as the country usually had a surplus. The deficit was $933m. in 1983, and the situation worsened in 1984, when a balance-of-payments deficit of $1,353m. was recorded. In both instances, the deficit was largely due to large purchases of weapons by the Government from the USA and France. Exports in 1983 totalled £L2,694m., compared with £L3,110m. in 1982, while imports rose from £L14,326m. ($3,770m.) to approximately £L15,000m. ($2,750m.). Allowing for inflation (about 17% in 1983), this represented a modest fall in real terms. Workers' remittances from abroad showed an alarming drop, to only $75m.–$100m. per month, compared with former levels of $125m.–$200m. In 1985, however, a balance-of-payments surplus of $249m. was recorded. This was believed to reflect an influx of funds from abroad for the militias, and reduced spending on imports (particularly arms) and foreign travel, caused by the weakness of the Lebanese pound. In 1984 the value of exports remained steady, at £L2,462m., and that of imports declined to £L14,800m. In 1985, however, although the value of exports rose to £L4,973m., that of imports, despite

the imposition of new controls, soared to £L23,000m., owing mainly to the depreciation in the local currency—in dollar terms, imports were worth only $1,270.7m. Reflecting the accelerating decline in the pound's value, IMF figures (based on data from partner countries) indicated that the value of exports in 1986 totalled £L15,936m. and that of imports £L76,600m., while in 1987 the value of exports amounted to £L107,345m. and that of imports to £L406,919m. The value of exports in 1988 was estimated at £L246,911m. and that of imports at £L957,946m. In 1989 the value of Lebanese exports amounted to £L249,483m. and that of imports to £L1,115,620m. In 1990, according to the IMF, the value of Lebanon's exports totalled $496m. and that of its imports $2,578m. Reflecting the post-war increase in reconstruction activity, the value of exports in 1991 totalled $490m., and that of imports $3,748m. The position continued to improve during 1992 and 1993. Although imports surged, reflecting the gathering pace of reconstruction, these were more than offset by capital inflows. The balance of payments (defined as net change in foreign assets of the banking system) was $1,100m. in surplus in 1993.

According to the Beirut Chamber of Commerce and Industry, the Israeli invasion and subsequent occupation of southern Lebanon cost Lebanon £L1,300m. in lost export earnings. A report, issued by the Chamber, said that the value of exports in the first nine months of 1982 was more than 16% less than the £L4,050m. which had been achieved in the same period of 1981. Before the Israeli invasion in June 1982, export earnings had been more than 50% above those in 1981 and the figure of £L1,300m. in losses allowed for an increase in value which could have been expected if the invasion had not occurred. About 35% of Lebanon's exports went to Saudi Arabia in 1982, compared with 31%, in 1981. Iraq's share dropped from 33% to 29.5%, but it remained Lebanon's second largest market.

The Government's anxiety to increase trade was reflected in the creation, in early 1983, of the National Council for External Economic Relations (NCEER), headed by Sami Maroun, a businessman and banker who had close links with President Gemayel. The NCEER was instructed to promote foreign trade, tourism and contacts with Lebanese émigrés. Within a few months of its creation, the NCEER had proposed an ambitious series of projects, including the creation of an export-oriented industrial free zone; the transfer of the country's energy imports away from petroleum towards coal; the establishment of an export credit guarantee agency; the internationalization of the Beirut stock exchange; and the development of offshore banking facilities. However, the NCEER became defunct within three years of its creation.

CURRENCY AND FINANCE

The importance of Beirut as the commercial and financial centre of the Middle East derived, in the 1950s and onwards, from the almost complete absence of restrictions on the free movement of goods and capital, and from the transference of the Middle Eastern headquarters of many foreign concerns from Cairo to Beirut after 1952. Moreover, large sums were earned in the Gulf by Arabs who sought to invest locally, especially in property, and for them Beirut was a convenient centre. Its dominance was further strengthened later by the massive increases in surplus oil revenue earned by the producing states, much of which was channelled through Lebanon.

By June 1975 the number of representative offices opened by foreign banks in Beirut had reached 72. But in February 1976, when a lull in the fighting encouraged the banks to open again after a two-month closure, 26 of these branches had been partially or totally destroyed. The calm was short-lived, but it was just long enough to quell fears of massive withdrawals. Another 10-month closure followed, however. The banks formally reopened again in Beirut in mid-January 1977. By this time damage and losses through the looting of vaults and safety deposit boxes were estimated, conservatively, at $500m. Fears of a flood of withdrawals again proved unfounded. Instead, the liquidity which had accumulated outside the banking system during the war began to flow back, to the extent that, by 1979, total bank deposits had reached more than £L19,000m., far exceeding the previous peak of £L11,500m. recorded in February 1975. At the end of June 1981 commercial bank deposits amounted to £L31,583m. having increased, in terms of the Lebanese pound, by 16% since December 1980. In terms of the US dollar, however, they had declined by 1.4%.

Private sector deposits moved increasingly out of Lebanese pounds and into foreign currencies. In 1974 deposits in Lebanese pounds were more than 70% of the total, but by 1981 they accounted for only 5.5%, largely because of high interest rates in foreign currencies. In an effort to stem the flow away from the Lebanese pound, the Central Bank lifted the prime rate of interest to 16.5% in early 1982.

In 1981 commercial bank lending to the private sector was less than that to the public sector and lending overseas. Lending to the public sector and overseas rose by 57% to £L24,774m., but private sector lending grew by only 29%, to £L23,286m.—44% of total lending. The immediate aftermath of the Israeli invasion of June 1982 proved the resilience of the Lebanese banking system. In March 1982 commercial banks' private sector deposits amounted to £L38,822m., and by the end of the year they were reported to have increased. However, banking activity fell by 30% in the first half of 1983 as restrictions on trade and industry (imposed by the Israeli occupation of the south and the Syrian presence in the north), and continued civil conflict, began to affect the economy.

The growing competitiveness of financial centres in Europe and the Gulf region had, even before the disruption caused by the civil conflict, led the Government to seek ways of enhancing Beirut's attractions as a banking centre. A banking free-zone law which took effect in April 1977, exempted non-residents' foreign currency accounts from taxes on interest earned, from payment of a deposit guarantee tax and from reserve requirements. Moreover, in June 1977 the Government decided to lift the moratorium on new bank licences which had been imposed in the wake of the collapse of the Intra Bank in 1966. In 1977 a new specialized bank, the Banque de l'Habitat, was set up and in 1978 two new commercial banks, the International Commerce Bank and Universal Bank, were granted licences bringing the total number of banks operating in Lebanon to 81 as of mid-1979. In April 1980 the American Express International Banking Corporation became the first foreign bank to open a new branch in Beirut since 1975. In the spring of 1983 the Central Bank raised the minimum capital requirement for new banks from £L50m. to £L75m., and that for new financial institutions from £L5m. to £L15m. This was the third such increase since 1977.

The banking system withstood the years of conflict surprisingly well, but by 1985 the strains were evident: non-performing loans accounted for 45% of banks' total loan portfolios, compared with 25% in 1984; costs were rising, while revenues were static or falling; and interest rates were extremely high, as a result of fierce competition in a depressed market. In addition, robberies were a serious problem. In 1985 50 banks were robbed, with losses of £L4,000m. The number of banks operating in Lebanon rose to 88 in 1986. The balance sheet of Beirut's commercial banks for 1985 and 1986 looked impressive, but it had to be interpreted with care. Total assets/liabilities amounted to £L455,614m. in 1986, a rise of 181% compared with 1985 (during which a rise of 61.9%, compared with 1984, had been recorded). Loans to the private sector rose by 120.3%, and treasury bill holdings by 32.8%. Loans to non-resident banks rose by 446.4%, private-sector deposits by 184.2%, and liabilities to non-resident banks rose by 281.7% compared with 1985. Even more impressive apparent growth was recorded between the first quarter of 1986 and the first quarter of 1987. Total assets/liabilities rose by 229.3%. Loans to the private sector increased by 158%, and treasury bill holdings by 82.6%. Loans to non-resident banks rose by 452.9%, private sector deposits by 22.7% and liabilities to non-resident banks by 389.9%. However, the rise in private-sector deposits was almost entirely attributable to the collapse in the value of the Lebanese pound, as almost all such deposits were in foreign currencies. The rise in loans to the private sector were more indicative of the high rate of inflation than of any general economic recovery. Loans to non-residents and non-resident banks had risen (hugely) because these advances

were almost all in foreign currencies. The expansion in treasury bill holdings merely reflected the government's increasing use of such bills to finance its growing deficits.

The remarkable resistance of the Lebanese pound to the pressures of the civil conflict was chiefly due to the absence of restrictions on withdrawals or foreign exchange transactions, to an increase in the supply of foreign currencies to finance the conflict, and to the pound's strong gold backing and the flow of remittances safeguarding the balance of payments. Shortly before the war, in October 1974, the pound had reached a record high value, standing at £L2.22 against the US dollar. It lost just over 30% of this value during the war in 1975–76, but quickly recovered to £L3 after the cease-fire. Although the Lebanese pound declined in value in the two months following the beginning of the Israeli invasion in June 1982, from £L5.00 to the US dollar to £L5.20, it had strengthened to £L4.11 to the dollar by mid-November. Although officially valued at $389.4m. in March 1982, the 9.22m. ounces of gold that were held by the Central Bank were worth some $4,000m. at mid-1987 market prices. In view of the legendary strength of the Lebanese pound, the rapid erosion of its value from late 1983 onwards was a considerable psychological blow. In July 1983 the exchange rate stood at $1 = £L4.15; by late June 1984 it had dropped below $1 = £L6, and by March 1985 it stood at $1 = £L20.00, at that time its lowest level ever. Excluding gold, Lebanon's official reserves declined from $1,903m. to $672m. in 1984. They recovered to $1,074m. at the end of 1985, owing to new import controls and a net inflow of capital, but fell to $488m. at the end of 1986, as imports began to rise again, and totalled only $368m. at the end of 1987. The appreciation of the Lebanese pound during much of 1988 prompted a recovery. By the end of 1988 reserves stood at $978m. They exceeded $1,000m. for most of the first three quarters of 1989, but by the end of the year they had declined to $938m. After further falls in the value of the Lebanese pound, the value of reserves was only $659.9m. by the end of 1990. During 1991 the stabilization of the exchange rate, the growth in exports and an influx of private funds from expatriate Lebanese combined to produce an increase in reserves to $1,276m. by the end of the year. At the end of November 1992 the value of reserves was $1,588m. During 1993 reserves continued to expand, to reach $1,900m.; and the April 1994 figure was $1,300m.

Government deficits have risen. In 1986 the shortfall was an estimated £L81,719m., while the 1987 deficit was projected at £L65,000m.; that for 1988 at £L60,300m.; that for 1989 at £L89,500m.; and that for 1990 at £L387,000m. The Government accordingly borrowed heavily from the Central Bank and the commercial banks. At the end of May 1984 the public debt amounted to £L35,529m. ($2,250m.). By the end of 1986 it stood at £L81,719m. and by the end of 1987 it had risen to £L194,100m., of which £L127,200m. represented outstanding treasury bills. At 31 October 1988 the debt totalled £L504,500m., but one year later it had risen to £L755,000m. By November 1990 it had reached £L1,442,000m., by March 1992 it was reportedly £L2,800,000m., and by the end of 1993 it had reached £L5,100,000m. Debt servicing has become a heavy burden on state finances, costing £L900,000m. in 1994 alone. Meanwhile, the Lebanese pound's decline has continued. By July 1986 it had fallen to $1 = £L38, or by about 50% since the end of 1985. This included an official devaluation of the pound by 16.35% against the US dollar in March 1986. The exchange rate fell below $1 = £L100 for the first time in February 1987 and continued to fall, reaching $1 = £L455 at the end of 1987 and $1 = £L530 at the end of 1988, following the failure to elect a new President in September of that year.

During much of 1989 the exchange rate was stable, at about $1 = £L510, despite the violence of Gen. Awn's 'war of liberation' against Syria. With Awn's acceptance of the Arab League peace plan in September, however, the pound strengthened, to $1 = £L460, and it appreciated further, to $1 = £L410, after the approval of the Taif agreement on 23 October and the election of President Mouawad. This was the highest level that the pound had reached since the spring of 1988. By mid-January 1990, following President Mouawad's assassination, the pound had declined again, to $1 = £L544. The continuing political deadlock between east and west Beirut;

the inter-Christian fighting in east Beirut; and the impact of the crisis in the Gulf region from August all caused further deterioration in the value of the Lebanese pound. In September the average rate of exchange was $1 = £L1,080. Following the defeat of Gen. Awn in October, the reunification of Beirut and the disbandment of the militias, the Lebanese pound gained in strength. In January and February 1991 the exchange rate averaged $1 = £L1,000, but by the end of the year it had strengthened to about $1 = £L880. On 19 February 1992, however, the Central Bank resolved to cease its currency support operations, prompting a dramatic slide in the value of the Lebanese pound. By 5 May the exchange rate was $1 = £L1,600. The Central Bank claimed that it had withdrawn its support from the pound because the currency had become overvalued. It was widely believed, however, that the real reason was the Bank's concern over the Government's inability to reduce its deficit. Rising tensions in the prelude to the legislative elections held in mid-1992, and the implications of the Maronite boycott of the elections, gave rise to a further decline in the value of the currency. On 21 July 1992 the exchange rate was $1 = £L2,050, and on 7 September it was almost $1 = £L2,800. Post-electoral stability and the establishment of the Government of Rafik Hariri caused the currency to strengthen, and during most of the first half of 1993 the exchange rate ranged between $1 = £L1,730 and $1 = £L1,750. Since then it has appreciated slightly, to about $1 = £L1,700.

In October 1987, for the first time in Lebanese history, the commercial banks refused to co-operate with the monetary policies of the Central Bank (Banque du Liban). For the previous two years the Central Bank had tried to increase its control over the banking sector, in a vain attempt to halt the depreciation in the Lebanese pound. The commercial banks refused to continue to subscribe to treasury bills, which financed the majority of government spending, and initiated legal proceedings against the Central Bank, in respect of fines imposed on them in 1986 and 1987. The Central Bank was forced to concede, cancelling the fines and revoking some of its recently-promulgated measures.

Renewed signs of problems in the banking sector emerged in late 1988, when rumours of a liquidity crisis caused a sudden withdrawal of deposits from Bank al-Mashrek, the banking arm of the partly state-owned Intra Investment Company. The bank's chairman, Roger Tamraz, was forced to resign and, amid controversy over Tamraz's role, the Central Bank agreed to underwrite only the claims of local non-institutional depositors. In early 1989 the Swiss and French banking authorities withdrew the licences of two of Bank al-Mashrek's affiliates, the Paris-based Banque de Participations et de Placement (BPP) and the Lugano-based BPP, because of their failure to satisfy liquidity requirements. In May 1989 another Lebanese-controlled French bank, United Banking Corporation, had its licence withdrawn because of an apparent fraud combined with over-lending to high-risk countries. In July the French authorities rescinded the licence of a third Lebanese-controlled bank, the Lebanese Arab Bank, again because of over-lending to high-risk creditors. The difficulties in France seriously undermined confidence in the entire Lebanese banking system, and in early August it was disclosed that more than $200m. had been withdrawn from Lebanese banks, most of the funds having been transferred to France.

Currency speculation had become a major source of profit for commercial banks, especially the smaller ones, and the relative stability of the exchange rate in 1991 and the first weeks of 1992 caused renewed problems in the banking sector. In 1991 some 20 of Beirut's 90 banks were reported to be in serious difficulty and late in the year four small banks ceased operations. In February 1992 the Banque Libano-Brésilienne and the Banque Tohme both closed, and in March the Globe Bank also ceased trading.

In late 1991 the Central Bank ordered commercial banks to increase their capital and reduce their 'hard' currency loan exposure by restricting lending to 55% of their 'hard' currency deposits by mid-September 1992. Beirut newspaper reports, however, suggested that the banks' foreign currency loans in September 1991 totalled $1,380m.—equivalent to 48% of their 'hard' currency deposits. The banks were also instructed to make extra capital provisions for their head offices and for

each branch. At the same time, the Central Bank informed commercial banks that they would soon be able to revalue their fixed assets. Their nominal value had remained constant for several years and had been rendered virtually meaningless by inflation.

In 1991 the Lebanese Bankers' Association proposed a series of reforms, including new procedures for the liquidation and merging of banks. By mid-1993, however, these measures had not taken effect.

Well before the civil war, inflationary pressures had been one of the country's most serious economic problems, and the conflict removed all vestiges of price restraint. The minimum monthly wage was increased to £L310 in 1977, then to £L415, and from that to £L525 in 1979, but this did little to relieve the chronic post-war hardship afflicting much of the population. In April 1982 the Cabinet approved a 17% pay rise for private and public sector workers. In 1983 the minimum wage was raised by 18.9% to £L1,100 per month, and by January 1987 it had been raised to £L3,200 per month. Inflation, which was estimated at 20% in 1982, fell marginally, to between 16% and 18%, in 1983, but reached an annual rate of 50% or more in early 1985. The 1986 figure was well over 100%. By the end of August 1987, the annual rate of inflation was about 200% (though the cost of many basic consumer items, such as sugar, milk, meat and cheese, was estimated to have risen by 300% since the beginning of the year), and the disastrous depreciation in the value of the Lebanese pound meant that the minimum monthly wage of £L4,300 was worth only $15. Demonstrations combining protests against poverty and against the continuing civil conflict became more frequent. Lebanon's reserves of foreign exchange declined to $300m. in August, but the Government was reluctant to reduce state subsidies on basic commodities (which cost about $100m. per year) for fear of provoking greater unrest. Despite substantial increases in the heavily subsidized domestic prices of petroleum products in June 1986 and January 1987, the IMF estimated that the cumulative deficit on the oil trade account would reach about £L17,000m. by the end of 1986, while the deficit for 1986 alone was expected to reach about £L4,000m. In September 1987 the government subsidy on petroleum was substantially reduced with the result that the price of petrol more than doubled. At the beginning of October the minimum monthly salary was raised to £L8,500 in order to compensate for the high rate of inflation, but in the same month the prices of bread and fuel were raised by 43% and 15%, respectively. Declines in standards of living prompted the Confédération Générale des Travailleurs du Liban (CGTL) to call a five-day general strike in November, which was generally supported in an unprecedented display of national unity. During 1987, according to official estimates, the consumer price index rose by 420% (though a survey of the prices of 30 basic commodities showed that they had risen by an average of 624% up to mid-December).

In 1988–93 the value of the Lebanese pound continued to fall, giving rise to further price increases. In two months, from mid-February 1992, the value of the currency declined by 65%, causing the price of food and that of many other commodities to double. Strikes and street demonstrations followed, culminating in the resignation, in May, of Omar Karami's Government. During 1992 the inflation rate was estimated to have averaged 100%. In March 1991 the Government finally removed subsidies on bread and fuel, although, at the same time, it levied a tax of 18% on petrol. In August 1991 public sector salaries were increased by 60% (the increase backdated to the beginning of the year) and in December they were increased again, by 120%. In the same month the remaining subsidies on wheat and flour were removed.

The stabilization of the exchange rate in 1992–93 resulted in lower inflation. In 1993 prices rose by about 10%. As of January 1994 the minimum monthly wage was increased to £L200,000, from £L118,000.

In June 1994 a secondary share market opened, dealing mainly in shares of Solidère, a company established to redevelop Beirut's war-ravaged commercial centre. It was the first time that stock had been traded in Lebanon since before the civil war. In order to counter speculation, no stock is permitted to rise or fall by more than 5% in one day. Solidère, sponsored by Rafik Hariri before he became Prime Minister, has a capital of $1,820m. Of this, $1,170m. has been allocated to the owners and tenants of properties affected by the development, which covers 160 ha. The other $650m. was raised by public subscription in January 1994. Solidère planned to start work on its redevelopment programme in 1994. A detailed masterplan has been prepared by local consultants Dar Al-Handasah. On completion in 2018, the development should have 40,000 residents and accommodate businesses and government offices employing 100,000 people.

TOURISM AND COMMUNICATIONS

Beirut's hotels, its port and airport as well as Lebanon's largest non-government employer, Middle East Airlines (MEA), were all severely affected by the civil conflict, which erupted just as tourism was beginning to recover from the effects of the October 1973 war. As the civil conflict progressed the prosperous hotel district in the centre of Beirut became the scene of some of the fiercest fighting. According to the Lebanese Hotel Owners' Association, 145 hotels were damaged, incurring losses of some £L218m. In Beirut alone the number of hotels had fallen from 130 (with 10,486 beds) in 1975 to 44 (with 4,631 beds) by 1979. The contribution of tourism to GNP, which was 20% before 1975 declined to 7.4% in 1977. Visitors spent only 469,272 nights in Beirut in 1979, compared with 2,307,122 nights in 1974. In 1980 there was some improvement, with a 15% rise in the number of visitors to 135,548, who spent a total of 585,531 nights in Beirut. Overall occupancy was only 27%, however. The cost of damage sustained by Beirut's hotels during the Israeli invasion in 1982 was estimated at £L400m.

The National Council for Tourism in Lebanon (NCTL) undertook a massive promotional campaign through its nine offices in Europe, the USA and the Middle East, issuing a glossy monthly bulletin and preparing brochures, books and other materials. In the spring of 1983 the newly formed NCEER took over all the activities of the NCTL (until the disbandment of the NCEER in 1985). The Ministry of Tourism and the Council for Development and Reconstruction drew up plans to rebuild the four international-class seaside hotels in Beirut at a cost of around $100m. They also outlined schemes to clean up the beaches. Although the security problem made it difficult to move from area to area within Lebanon, inside those areas domestic tourism flourished during the years of the civil conflict.

Middle East Airlines (MEA) suffered a loss of £L14m. in 1975, and of £L69.1m. in 1976. A recovery occurred in 1977, with profits reaching £L22m., but 1978 was again disappointing, with staff prevented by the fighting from reporting for duty and passenger traffic some 16% lower than had been expected. In 1979 MEA made a startling recovery, recording a profit of £L51.14m., its highest ever. However, the MEA Chairman, Asad Nasr, warned that inflation and increases in fuel prices meant the airline must expect narrower profit margins in the future. In 1980 profits slumped to £L9m., and in 1981 the airline's losses were £L88m. In May 1982 Asad Nasr resigned after a 27-year career with MEA and was succeeded by the airline's managing director, Salim Salaam.

In October 1981 MEA increased its capital from £L100m. to £L150m. Shortly beforehand, plans had been announced to introduce new routes, including a service to New York.

The Israeli invasion in 1982 plunged MEA into its worst-ever crisis. The airline was closed for 115 days, losing almost £L140m., and five aircraft were destroyed. The airline recorded a loss of £L187.5m. in 1982. The fighting in the Chouf in September 1983 led to the closure of Beirut airport. In that year MEA made a loss of about £L250m., and its problems continued in 1984. In that year Beirut airport was closed from February until July, during which time MEA lost $250,000 per day.

MEA's losses in 1985 amounted to £L454m., and they were expected to total £L50m. in 1986. In 1987 the airline's losses were £L452m., and in 1988 they totalled £L500m. In 1989 MEA was badly affected by a further, prolonged closure of Beirut airport during Gen. Awn's 'war of liberation' against

the Syrian presence in Lebanon. Losses of $15m. were forecast for 1990.

In 1987 MEA suffered from a dispute over the new, privately-developed Halat airport, sited in Christian-held territory to the north of Beirut and intended to enable Christians to travel to and from the country without having to enter Muslim-controlled west Beirut. The Government refused to recognize Halat as an international airport, and in January 1987 Christian LF militiamen closed Beirut airport by shellfire, in order to put pressure on the Government over the issue of Halat. One of MEA's Boeing 707s was destroyed and the airline dispersed its fleet outside the country for fear of further losses. Beirut airport reopened in May, after the LF accepted assurances from the Minister of Transport that a newly established government commission, examining the feasibility of converting military airstrips to civilian use, would grant Halat airport official status. The destruction of the 707 in 1987 reduced MEA's active fleet to 11 aircraft. In addition, the company owns three Boeing 747s which, for several years, have been leased to other airlines, generating annual revenues of about $17m. In November 1989, however, the company decided to take the 747s back into service with MEA. One of the leased aircraft was returned in 1990, and another in 1991, when, the civil conflict apparently having concluded, MEA was achieving high occupancy rates for its services to and from Beirut. In 1991 the airport handled 825,000 passengers, compared with 638,000 in 1990. In early 1992 it was reported that MEA had leased two Airbus A310s from the Dutch airline KLM for three years. In 1992 MEA's losses amounted to $6m., but in mid-1993 the company's chairman, Yousuf Lahoud, announced that it was hoping to make a small profit in 1993.

There was an increase in airfreight, due to companies' reluctance to store goods in Lebanon, which in turn necessitated a faster turnaround that could be provided only by air. Lebanon's chief cargo-carrier, Trans-Mediterranean Airways (TMA), in operation since 1953, hoped to profit from this transport trend, although in 1982 the company made a loss of £L57m., of which £L50m. was attributable to the Israeli invasion. The airline was also badly affected by the discontinuation of its round-the-world service as a result of disputes over lost traffic rights in northern Europe, the USA and Japan. In 1983 TMA's losses totalled £L61m., and in May 1984 the company asked for immediate government financial assistance to assure its survival. In mid-1985 TMA suffered serious losses as a result of a three-week ban on its aircraft entering Saudi airspace. It failed to recapture the lost volume of freight when the ban was lifted, and was forced to request further financial help from the Government. Flights were suspended in July, when pilots struck in protest at the company's failure to pay salaries. In August the airline was placed under government control. In July 1986 a majority stake in TMA was acquired by Jet Holdings, an east Beirut group headed by the financier Roger Tamraz. In December the airline resumed flights between Europe and the Middle and Far East. Following the collapse in late 1988, of Roger Tamraz' business interests, the Lebanese Central Bank effectively took control of Jet Holdings and, through it, TMA. The move was resisted by Tamraz' partners in Jet Holdings, and in early 1990 TMA's ownership was still disputed. In early 1991 it was reported that a committee, established by the Ministry of Transport to decide TMA's future, had estimated the company's debts at $80m., while its assets amounted to only $45m. The committee proposed three options for TMA: a merger with MEA; the company's takeover by MEA; or a substantial grant of funds by the Government to enable the airline to resume operations in its own right. In March 1993 the 74% stake in TMA, formerly controlled by Roger Tamraz, was bought for $8m. by a holding company, the Lebanese Company for Aviation Investment (LCAI). The main shareholder in LCAI is Banque Libano-Française SAL. In approving the acquisition, the court handling the bankruptcy of the Tamraz-controlled Al-Mashrek Bank also waived TMA's $39m.-debt to the bank. TMA's fleet comprises seven Boeing 707s, one of which is on lease to Saudi Arabian Airlines and another to the Kuwait Airways Corporation. In mid-1994 a joint venture comprising the German company Hochtief and Athens-based Consolidated

Contractors International Company won an estimated $490m.-contract to expand Beirut international airport. The two-year project will include the construction of a 3.5 km-runway, a control tower, an extension to the terminal building and a 90-room hotel.

During the early 1970s Beirut port suffered substantial congestion, owing, mainly, to the volume of goods bound for Saudi Arabia, Kuwait and Iraq, where petroleum revenues had boosted development expenditure. Shortly before the outbreak of the civil conflict in 1975 British consultants Peat, Marwick Mitchell & Co. and consulting engineers Coode & Partners conducted a major study of Beirut and Tripoli ports and drafted a master plan. In 1977, the British consultants revised their forecasts to include reconstruction, and the CDR appointed a port committee in August 1977 to oversee the reconstruction and modernization process, the total cost of which was estimated at more than $144m. Although work on the port continued, there were frequent disruptions, owing to the civil conflict.

With the reunification of Beirut after the siege of 1982, the reign of snipers and political factions at the port was ended for a while. A temporary strengthening of government authority began to ease the problem of illegal ports, of which at least 17 had begun operating as a result of the civil war. These ports imposed tariffs which were only a fraction of those payable at the official ports, and the official ports, for their part, were seriously affected by smuggling. Of particular significance was the appropriation by the Lebanese army, in March 1983, of the notorious fifth basin of Beirut port, which had been a valuable source of revenue for right-wing Lebanese militias for a number of years. According to some sources, it had accounted for 90% of the country's illegal trade. Import duties and airport and seaport charges, which had formerly accounted for more than 45% of government revenues, contributed less than 15% in 1983. Tripoli port remained under the control of pro-Syrian militias or was the scene of fierce fighting between rival groups, while Israeli forces continued to occupy the ports of Sidon and Tyre in the south. Fighting between rival militias intensified, however, and, after the withdrawal from Beirut of the multinational peace-keeping force in March 1984, the Government was unable to impose its authority over the operation of the ports. A brief expansion of government control took place during 1984, after the formation of an administration that was more representative of the country's diverse factions. This helped to increase customs' revenues from the ports, but the improvement was short-lived (see Public Finance and Development, below). In February 1989 Gen. Awn, the head of Lebanon's Christian Government, ousted the LF militia from the fifth basin of Beirut port and then, acting in the name of state legitimacy, moved to close illegal militia ports in the Muslim parts of the country, imposing an aerial and maritime blockade. Several weeks of bitter Christian-Muslim battles followed, and during Gen. Awn's 'war of liberation' against Syrian forces ports were a major target. The port of Tripoli made a significant recovery following the deployment there of Syrian troops at the end of 1985. After a two-year closure, Beirut port reopened on 15 March 1992 and in the first half of the year it handled 671 vessels and just over one million tons of cargo. This represented about one-quarter of pre-civil war traffic levels.

In late 1980 the CDR recommended to the Cabinet that the concession for a new port at Sidon should be granted to a Sidon businessman, Rafik Hariri. The CDR advised that Hariri should be granted the concession for 30 years, and that he should set up a joint company with the CDR, with capital of £L250m. It was a controversial decision, because the UK consultants who had prepared the plans for Beirut port said that in a politically unified Lebanon only two ports, Beirut and Tripoli, were needed, and that if the South must have a port, then Tyre, further south, would be more suitable than Sidon. In 1985, however, Hariri's Paris-based company, Oger International, invited bids for the construction of the first phase of a new port at Sidon. The problem of illegal ports seemed, finally, to have been solved in May 1991, when, in an assertion of its authority, the new Government of national reconciliation disbanded the country's militias, and units of the Lebanese army were deployed in the ports. In November

1993 Port Autonome de Marseille, of France, won a $1m.-contract to advise on an estimated $126m., three-year scheme to redevelop Beirut port. The project will include the renovation of general cargo basins two and three, the completion of construction of a fourth basin and the construction of a deep-water container dock. The scheme will raise the port's capacity by 70%, to 4.3m. tonnes.

In April 1983 the Ministry of Posts and Telecommunications confirmed that it intended to establish an autonomous body to administer the country's telephone and telecommunications services, as recommended by the World Bank. The deterioration of the telecommunications system during the civil war led many businesses to turn to private satellite communications systems. In early 1990 it was reported that 85 such systems were in use. In addition, international links were being maintained via cellular telephone systems operating through Cyprus, while private telephone systems were also in use for internal communications. In 1993 a major telecommunications rehabilitation project was launched, involving the replacement of existing exchanges and the installation of more than one million lines. As part of this, Siemens of Germany won an estimated $40m.-contract to install 420,000 new lines in and around Beirut, while the French company Alcatel is installing telephone exchanges with 270,000 new lines in the Beirut and Tripoli areas. Sweden's Ericsson was appointed to repair telephone switching systems in the south, the Beka'a Valley and parts of Mount Lebanon. In mid-1994 France Telecom and Finnish Telecom signed contracts to establish global systems for mobiles (GSM) networks on a build-operate-transfer basis. Each network will have 30,000 lines.

In 1994 plans were announced for a $500m.-scheme to rebuild Lebanon's coastal railway. The 170 km line links Tyre and Sidon in the south with Beirut and Tripoli in the north. The southern section of the line ceased operating in 1948, during the first Arab-Israeli War. Services on the section from Beirut to Tripoli stopped at the start of the Lebanese civil war. An east-west railway line from Beirut to the Syrian border also ceased operating during the civil war, but no plans have been announced for its reconstruction.

PUBLIC FINANCE AND DEVELOPMENT

The draft state budget for 1987 forecast total expenditure of £L27,250m., compared with £L17,937m. in 1986, an increase of 52%. In addition, there was a supplementary budget of £L42,000m., covering posts and telecommunications, the national lottery, and wheat, fuel and sugar subsidies. Moreover, the supplementary budget allocated £L20,000m. for the undersubscription of treasury bills. Revenue was expected to total £L4,250m., compared with £L12,712m. in the 1986 budget. In previous years, the Government's estimates of customs revenues had been wildly optimistic, given the authorities' continuing inability to wrest control of the ports from militias. The sharp fall in revenues projected in the draft 1987 budget indicated greater realism. The 1987 draft budget forecast a deficit of £L65,000m., about twice the actual shortfall during 1986.

In some years there was an alarming discrepancy between the budget proposals and the actual course of economic events, largely as a result of the political turbulence in the country. Thus, in 1986, the actual deficit was an estimated £L34,000m. (expenditure £L36,000m.; revenue £L2,000m.), compared with the £L5,225m. for which the budget had allowed. This was largely due to a huge shortfall in customs revenues. In more settled times, these would have been a major source of government revenue. From the mid-1970s, losses of revenue from taxation and customs duties, caused by the inability of the Government to impose taxes and the proliferation of illegal ports, deprived it of valuable income. As a result of stricter government control of the ports in 1983, customs revenues rose to £L1,280m. in that year, compared with only £L403m. in 1982. However, in 1984, when the Government might have expected to earn some £L3,000m. in customs duty, income from this source amounted to only £L452m., or nearly 65% less than in 1983. The Government introduced further measures to close illegal ports in October 1984, but parts of Beirut port were again under the control of the Christian militias by April 1985. In 1985 customs receipts totalled £L481m., compared with the budget projection of more than £L3,000m. (about 35% of total revenue). The 1986 budget estimate for customs revenue (about £L4,000m.) proved equally unrealistic. In the event, customs receipts for the year totalled only £L373m. The draft 1987 budget allocated £L8,836m., or one-third of the ordinary budget (the largest single portion of expenditure), to servicing the national debt (an estimated £L98,000m. in March 1987), while a further £L20,000m. was allocated in a supplementary budget for the undersubscription of treasury bills.

The draft budget for 1988 estimated expenditure at £L70,000m. with a deficit of £L38,030m. A revised budget set expenditure at £L167,000m. and revenue at £L106,700m. The increase in revenue was occasioned by Central Bank earnings which were much higher than had been anticipated. The draft budget for 1989 was presented by the Cabinet of Prime Minister Dr Selim al-Hoss at the beginning of October 1988, despite the appointment of a military government by President Gemayel to administer the country during the transition from the end of his tenure until the election of a new President. Such was the political uncertainty during 1989, however, that the actual spending and revenue of the country's two governments probably bore only a slight resemblance to the al-Hoss draft budget. However, it forecast total expenditure during 1989 of £L219,500m. and total revenue of £L130,000m., leaving a deficit of £L89,500m. (the figures, as in the 1988 budget, were distorted by the huge depreciation in the value of the Lebanese pound). The allocation for servicing the national debt (£L194,100m. in January 1988) was again the largest single item of expenditure, accounting for 32% (£L70,240m.) of the total. In April 1990 Ali Khalil, the Minister of Finance in the Cabinet of Dr Selim al-Hoss, presented a draft budget for 1990, in which expenditure was fixed at £L597,000m. and revenues at £L210,000m., leaving a deficit of £L387,000m. Debt service was, again, by far the biggest spending category, accounting, at £L183,557m., for 30% of the total. Defence was the second largest spending category, at £L97,486m., and education, at £L66,454m., the third largest. The 1991 budget, approved by the National Assembly in September of that year, set spending of £L1,158,000m., of which one-quarter was allocated to debt-servicing, 17% to public works and 12% to defence. After criticism, the Government, in February 1992, recalled a draft 1992 budget which had projected spending at £L2,500,000m.

It was subsequently replaced by a draft budget that forecast spending at £L1,550,190m. A draft budget for 1993, prepared before the appointment of Rafik Hariri's Government, projected spending at £L2,271,791m. and forecast revenues of more than £L1,500,000m., giving a deficit of about £L770,000m. The biggest spending category in the draft budget for 1993 was debt-servicing, which accounted for 26.3% of projected total spending. The 1993 budget, approved in December 1993, set spending at £L3,400,000m. and provided for a deficit of £L1,698,700m. Actual revenues in 1993 totalled £L1,800,000m., which was 82% higher than in 1992. Customs duties accounted for £L662,000m. (twice the 1992 figure), while income tax receipts, at £L126,000m., were three times higher than the year before, underlining the Government's success in establishing its authority.

Spending in the 1994 budget has been set at £L4,080,000m. and revenues at £L2,250,000m.

With the establishment of two rival Governments after the failure to elect a President to succeed Amin Gemayel in September 1988, the Central Bank provided funds, to both administrations. In November 1989, however, the Bank suspended payment of funds to Gen. Awn's Government, ostensibly because of his failure to account for earlier disbursements. In December it was reported that the Ministry of Defence had suspended wage payments to Awn's troops. To counter the financial squeeze, Gen. Awn's administration escalated its tax collection operations in the Christian enclave.

The CDR's budget for 1985 totalled £L4,030m., of which £L1,000m. was allocated to housing, while roads received £L800m., schools £L285m. and industry £L200m.; 15% was allocated to the north, 15% to the south, 13% to the Beka'a valley, 25% to Mount Lebanon and 20% to Beirut.

With the exception of the Palestinian refugee camps, the standard of living in Lebanon before 1975 was generally high. According to World Bank social indicators, published in 1983, Lebanon had an average life expectancy of 66 years at birth in 1980, compared with a regional average of 57 years, and an infant mortality rate of 41.2 deaths per 1,000 live births, compared with 104.3 per 1,000 for the whole of the Middle East. In 1975 Lebanon's national income per caput was an estimated $1,250, aligning the country more closely with certain of the more populous petroleum-producing countries of the Middle East than with other non-oil states. An estimate assessed national income at $800 per caput in 1985/86.

Statistical Survey

Source (unless otherwise stated): Direction Centrale de la Statistique, Ministère du Plan, and Direction Générale des Douanes, Beirut.

Area and Population

AREA, POPULATION AND DENSITY

Area (sq km)	10,452*
Population (official estimate)	
15 November 1970†	
Males	1,080,015
Females	1,046,310
Total	2,126,325
Population (UN estimates at mid-year)‡	
1990	2,740,000
1991	2,784,000
1992	2,838,000
Density (per sq km) at mid-1992	271.5

* 4,036 sq miles.
† Figures are based on the results of a sample survey, excluding Palestinian refugees in camps. The total of registered Palestinian refugees was 325,886 at March 1993.
‡ Source: UN, *World Population Prospects: The 1992 Revision.*

PRINCIPAL TOWNS (estimated population in 1975)

Beirut (capital) 1,500,000; Tarabulus (Tripoli) 160,000; Zahleh 45,000; Saida (Sidon) 38,000; Sur (Tyre) 14,000.

BIRTHS AND DEATHS (UN estimates, annual averages)

	1975–80	1980–85	1985–90
Birth rate (per 1,000) . . .	30.1	29.3	27.9
Death rate (per 1,000) . . .	8.7	8.8	7.8

Expectation of life (UN estimates, years at birth, 1985–90): 67.0 (males 65.1; females 69.0).
Source: UN, *World Population Prospects: The 1992 Revision.*

EMPLOYMENT (ISIC Major Divisions)

	1975	1985*
Agriculture, hunting, forestry and fishing	147,724	103,400
Manufacturing	139,471	45,000
Electricity, gas and water	6,381	10,000
Construction	47,356	25,000
Trade, restaurants and hotels . . .	129,716	78,000
Transport, storage and communications .	45,529	20,500
Other services	227,921	171,000
Total	744,098	452,900

* Estimates.
Source: National Employment Office.

Agriculture

PRINCIPAL CROPS ('000 metric tons)

	1990	1991	1992
Wheat	57*	59	52†
Barley	20†	19	18*
Sugar beet	93	6	9*
Potatoes	240*	268	250*
Onions (dry)	60*	65	60*
Tobacco	2	1	1*
Oranges	260*	261	245*
Tangerines, mandarins,			
clementines and satsumas .	53*	58	50*
Lemons and limes* . . .	78	90	80
Grapefruit and pomelo . .	50*	55	50*
Apples	200*	214	190*
Grapes	280*	358	290*
Olives	62	44	40*
Tomatoes	210*	213	200*

* FAO estimate(s). † Unofficial figure.
Source: FAO, *Production Yearbook.*

LIVESTOCK
('000 head, year ending September)

	1990*	1991	1992*
Goats	445	472	465
Sheep	220	238	230
Cattle	65	70	72
Asses	19	21	22
Pigs	45	44	42

Chickens (FAO estimates, million): 23† in 1990; 17 in 1991; 20 in 1992.
* FAO estimates. † Unofficial figure.
Source: FAO, *Production Yearbook.*

LIVESTOCK PRODUCTS ('000 metric tons)

	1990	1991	1992*
Beef and veal*	14	15	14
Mutton and lamb* . . .	5	10	10
Goats' meat*	4	5	5
Poultry meat	50†	53*	55
Cows' milk	93*	123	125
Sheep's milk	10†	17	18
Goats' milk	25*	32	34
Cheese*	9.6	13.1	13.4
Hen eggs*	55	57.5	60.0

* FAO estimates. † Unofficial figures.
Source: FAO, *Production Yearbook.*

Forestry

ROUNDWOOD REMOVALS
(FAO estimates, '000 cubic metres, excluding bark)

	1990	1991	1992
Industrial wood*	7	9	7
Fuel wood	463	468	481
Total	470	477	488

* Official estimates.
Source: FAO, *Yearbook of Forest Products*.

SAWNWOOD PRODUCTION
('000 cubic metres, including railway sleepers)

	1990	1991	1992
Total	13	11	9

Source: FAO, *Yearbook of Forest Products*.

Fishing

(metric tons, live weight)

	1989	1990	1991
Inland waters	100	80*	100
Mediterranean Sea . .	1,700	1,420	1,700
Total catch . . .	1,800	1,500	1,800

* FAO estimate.
Source FAO, *Yearbook of Fishery Statistics*.

Mining

('000 metric tons)

	1989	1990	1991
Salt (unrefined) . . .	3	3	3

Source: US Bureau of Mines.

Industry

SELECTED PRODUCTS
(estimates, '000 metric tons, unless otherwise indicated)

	1989	1990	1991
Olive oil	3	5*	6
Wine ('000 hectolitres)* . .	110	100	110
Cigarettes (million)† . .	4,000	4,000	4,000
Plywood ('000 cubic metres)* .	34	34	34
Paper and paperboard . .	37*	37*	42
Jet fuels	90	0	0
Kerosene	12	1	6
Motor spirit (petrol) . .	75	87	93
Distillate fuel oils . . .	72	102	133
Residual fuel oils . . .	229	226	283
Liquefied petroleum gas‡ . .	3	4	4
Quicklime§	10	10	10
Cement§	900	907	907
Electric energy (million kWh) .	4,585	4,735	4,750

* Estimate(s) by the FAO.
† Estimates by the US Department of Agriculture.
‡ Estimates.
§ Estimates by the US Bureau of Mines.
Source: UN, *Industrial Statistics Yearbook*.

1992 (FAO estimates): Olive oil 6,000 metric tons; Wine 90,000 hectolitres (Source: FAO, *Production Yearbook*).

Finance

CURRENCY AND EXCHANGE RATES
Monetary Units
100 piastres = 1 Lebanese pound (£L).

Sterling and Dollar Equivalents (31 May 1994)
£1 sterling = £L2,545.9;
US $1 = £L1,684.0;
£L10,000 = £3.928 sterling = $5.938.

Average Exchange Rate (£L per US $)
1991   928.2
1992   1,712.8
1993   1,741.4

ORDINARY BUDGET ESTIMATES (£L million)

Revenue	1985	1986
Direct taxation	1,375	1,375
Income tax	1,000	1,000
Property tax	300	300
Indirect taxation	3,721	4,737
Customs and excise duties . .	3,000	4,000
Car tax	300	300
Fuel tax	300	300
National insurance	150	175
Other income*	3,927	5,299
Total	9,567	12,712

* Including income from public enterprises and land revenues.
Source: Ministry of Finance.

Expenditure	1985	1986
President's office	17.5 ⎫	
Chamber of deputies	54.4 ⎬	322.7
Prime Minister's office	240.5 ⎭	
Ministry of justice	77.1	95.3
Ministry of foreign affairs	187.5	361.6
Ministry of interior	739.9	900.4
Ministry of finance	147.0	184.8
Ministry of national defence	2,447.8	3,740.1
Ministry of national education	1,639.5	2,162.9
Ministry of health	360.3	578.1
Ministry of labour and social affairs	175.9	175.7
Ministry of information	63.0	81.9
Ministry of public works and transport	729.0	1,630.7
Ministry of agriculture	123.0	153.0
Ministry of national economy	160.5	760.5
Ministry of posts and telecommunications	60.1	80.3
Ministry of hydroelectric resources	559.9	754.7
Ministry of tourism	38.8	60.7
Ministry of industry and oil	6.0	6.4
Ministry of housing and co-operatives	53.0	60.6
Payments on debt	2,812.0	5,364.0
Reserves	684.4	462.4
Total	**11,377.0**	**17,937.0**

1987 (estimates, £L million): Revenue 15,750; Expenditure 27,250.
1988 (estimates, £L million): Revenue 31,700; Expenditure 70,000.
1989 (estimates, £L million): Revenue 130,000; Expenditure 219,500.
1990 (estimates, £L million): Revenue 210,000 (direct taxes and duties 66,600; indirect taxes 40,598); Expenditure 597,000 (debt service 183,557; defence 97,486; education 66,454; internal security 36,960).
1991 (estimates, £L million): Total expenditure 1,150,000.
1992 (estimates, £L million, net of supplementary items): Total expenditure 1,470,000.
1993 (estimates, £L million): Revenue 1,700,000; Expenditure 3,800,000.
1994 (estimates, £L million): Total expenditure 4,700,000.

CENTRAL BANK RESERVES (US $ million at 31 December)

	1991	1992	1993
Gold*	3,260.1	3,066.4	3,603.6
IMF special drawing rights	11.8	13.0	14.4
Reserve position in IMF	26.9	25.9	25.9
Foreign exchange	1,236.7	1,457.5	2,220.0
Total	**4,535.6**	**4,562.8**	**5,863.9**

* Valued at $353.50 per troy ounce in 1991, at $332.50 per ounce in 1992 and at $390.75 per ounce in 1993.
Source: IMF, *International Financial Statistics*.

MONEY SUPPLY (£L '000 million at 31 December)

	1991	1992	1993
Currency outside banks	484.6	798.0	714.7
Demand deposits at commercial banks	202.0	393.5	422.4
Total money*	**689.4**	**1,199.4**	**1,143.2**

* Including private-sector demand deposits at Bank of Lebanon.
Source: IMF, *International Financial Statistics*.

NATIONAL ACCOUNTS
Expenditure on the Gross Domestic Product
(official estimates, £L million at current prices)

	1980	1981	1982
Government final consumption expenditure	3,515	4,219	4,850
Private final consumption expenditure	12,905	15,488	15,840
Increase in stocks ⎫			
Gross fixed capital formation ⎬	2,196	3,459	1,179
Total domestic expenditure	18,616	23,166	21,869
Exports of goods and services	5,460	5,724	5,255
Less Imports of goods and services	10,076	12,090	14,525
GDP in purchasers' values	14,000	16,800	12,599
GDP at constant 1974 prices	4,900	4,923	3,082

Gross Domestic Product by Economic Activity
(official estimates, £L million at current prices)

	1980	1981	1982
Agriculture, hunting, forestry and fishing	1,288	1,435	1,076
Manufacturing	1,702	2,192	1,644
Electricity, gas and water	708	911	683
Construction	447	575	431
Trade, restaurants and hotels	4,008	4,753	3,565
Transport, storage and communications	530	628	471
Finance, insurance, real estate and business services	2,349	2,785	2,089
Government services	1,443	1,712	1,284
Other community, social and personal services	1,526	1,809	1,357
GDP in purchasers' values	14,000	16,800	12,600

(Unofficial estimates, US $ million at current prices*)

	1987
Agriculture	287
Manufacturing	483
Energy and water	28
Construction	158
Commerce	1,127
Financial services	286
Non-financial services	756
Public administration	171
GDP in purchasers' values	**3,296†**

* Source: Gaspard, Toufic. *The Gross Domestic Product of Lebanon in 1987* in Bank of Lebanon Quarterly Bulletin, July–December 1988–December 1989.
† £L740,743 million.

External Trade

PRINCIPAL COMMODITIES (£L'000)

Exports	1984	1985	1986
Food products	51,767	113,103	321,300
Beverages	58,714	65,781	80,742
Clothing	121,346	257,946	660,542
Textiles	9,571	17,046	84,594
Carpets	23,221	4,714	14,193
Tanned hides and leather	12,881	35,727	129,734
Footwear	3,546	9,465	55,571
Wooden products	15,884	32,839	68,096
Paints	33,045	77,042	62,073
Chemical products	49,643	71,974	85,907
Pharmaceutical products	51,737	244,132	355,119
Paper and paper and cardboard products	62,371	155,538	312,362
Ceramics and sanitary ware	—	49,799	120,734
Glassware	—	33,732	27,378
Cement	12,471	28,606	6,815
Non-metal mineral products	49,370	—	—
Metal products	115,681	241,068	558,829
Aluminium products	44,744	138,244	362,344
Machinery and electrical apparatus	86,521	219,065	447,398
Plastic products	32,074	55,289	110,515
Jewellery	—	507,238	1,160,263
Total (incl. others)	2,462,000	4,973,000	n.a.

Source: Ministry of Economy.

Total imports (£L million): 5,100 in 1978; 7,500 in 1979; 10,000 in 1980; 12,500 in 1981; 13,100 in 1982; 15,500 in 1983; 14,800 in 1984; 23,000 in 1985.

PRINCIPAL TRADING PARTNERS (£L'000)

Imports	1980	1981	1982
Belgium	401,100	456,600	478,900
France	1,315,900	1,571,300	1,660,700
Germany, Fed. Rep.	907,000	1,025,500	1,222,200
Greece	232,500	252,100	332,100
Iraq	296,400	369,000	340,200
Italy	1,729,800	2,041,800	2,446,000
Japan	711,600	728,800	793,300
Netherlands	265,700	355,100	374,100
Romania	748,600	973,200	894,900
Saudi Arabia	1,444,900	1,752,700	919,100
Spain	279,800	329,000	383,700
Switzerland	521,200	777,900	904,500
Turkey	269,600	364,400	627,200
United Kingdom	605,500	596,500	586,900
USA	1,117,800	1,359,100	1,460,800
Total (incl. others)	12,775,400	15,374,700	16,123,800

Source: Chamber of Commerce and Industry, Beirut.

Exports	1981	1982	1983
CMEA	61,000	43,000	19,300
EEC	230,000	160,000	44,600
Iraq	1,440,000	1,163,000	190,500
Jordan	284,000	568,000	193,500
Kuwait	245,000	272,000	220,600
Saudi Arabia	1,478,000	1,559,000	1,293,500
Syria	610,000	390,000	305,800
United Arab Emirates	162,000	170,000	155,100
Total (incl. others)	5,444,000	5,256,000	2,694,200

Source: Chamber of Commerce and Industry, Beirut.

Transport

ROAD TRAFFIC (motor vehicles in use)

	1980	1981	1982
Passenger cars (incl. taxis)	362,013	403,532	473,372
Buses	2,980	3,161	3,348
Lorries	37,696	41,570	46,212
Motor cycles	15,903	16,253	16,797

SHIPPING
(international sea-borne freight traffic, '000 metric tons)

	1988	1989	1990
Goods loaded	148	150	152
Goods unloaded	1,120	1,140	1,150

Source: UN, *Monthly Bulletin of Statistics*.

CIVIL AVIATION (revenue traffic on scheduled services)

	1989	1990	1991
Kilometres flown (million)	15	16	18
Passengers carried ('000)	183	572	536
Passenger-km (million)	324	941	1,150
Freight ton-km (million)	284	167	170
Mail ton-km (million)	1	1	2
Total ton-km (million)	314	254	276

Source: UN, *Statistical Yearbook*.

Communications Media

	1989	1990	1991
Radio receivers ('000 in use)	2,247	2,270	2,320
Television receivers ('000 in use)	880	890	905
Daily newspapers (number)	n.a.	14	n.a.

Source: UNESCO, *Statistical Yearbook*.

Education

	Teachers			Pupils		
	1982	1984†	1986†	1982	1984†	1986†
Pre-primary	n.a.	n.a.	5,257	120,873	116,344	129,590
Primary*	22,810‡	n.a.	n.a.	382,500	329,340	399,029
Secondary:						
General*	21,344§	n.a.	n.a.	258,353	230,934	279,849
Teacher training	392§	n.a.	n.a.	1,663§	n.a.	n.a.
Vocational	3,866	3,506	n.a.	39,933	37,036	30,407
Higher	7,976	7,460	n.a.	73,052	70,510	n.a.

* Including schools operated by the UN Relief and Works Agency for Palestine Refugees in the Near East (UNRWA). The number of pupils at UNRWA primary schools in Lebanon was: 23,221 (with 770 teachers) in 1982; 24,001 in 1984; 23,481 in 1986. The number of pupils enrolled in general education at UNRWA secondary schools was: 9,425 in 1982; 10,564 in 1984; 10,521 in 1986.

† Figures for 1983 and 1985 are not available.

‡ Data refer to 1981.

§ Data refer to 1980.

In 1988 the number of pupils at pre-primary schools was 131,217, that at primary schools 346,534 and that at all secondary schools 241,964. In 1991 there were 85,495 students in higher education and 5,400 teachers.

Source: UNESCO, *Statistical Yearbook*.

Note: In the academic year 1988/89 an estimated 32,826 pupils were enrolled at 76 UNRWA schools in Lebanon.

Directory

The Constitution

The Constitution was promulgated on 23 May 1926 and amended by the Constitutional Laws of 1927, 1929, 1943, 1947 and 1990.

According to the Constitution, the Republic of Lebanon is an independent and sovereign state, and no part of the territory may be alienated or ceded. Lebanon has no state religion. Arabic is the official language. Beirut is the capital.

All Lebanese are equal in the eyes of the law. Personal freedom and freedom of the press are guaranteed and protected. The religious communities are entitled to maintain their own schools, on condition that they conform to the general requirements relating to public instruction, as defined by the state. Dwellings are inviolable; rights of ownership are protected by law. Every Lebanese citizen who has completed his twenty-first year is an elector and qualifies for the franchise.

LEGISLATIVE POWER

Legislative power is exercised by one house, the National Assembly, with 108 seats (raised, without amendment of the Constitution, to 128 in 1992), which are divided equally between Christians and Muslims. Members of the National Assembly must be over 25 years of age, in possession of their full political and civil rights, and literate. They are considered representative of the whole nation, and are not bound to follow directives from their constituencies. They can be suspended only by a two-thirds majority of their fellow-members. Secret ballot was introduced in a new election law of April 1960.

In normal times the National Assembly holds two sessions yearly, from the first Tuesday after 15 March to the end of May, and from the first Tuesday after 15 October to the end of the year. The normal term of the National Assembly is four years; general elections take place within 60 days before the end of this period. If the Assembly is dissolved before the end of its term, elections are held within three months of dissolution.

Voting in the Assembly is public—by acclamation, or by standing and sitting. A quorum of two-thirds and a majority vote is required for constitutional issues. The only exceptions to this occur when the Assembly becomes an electoral college, and chooses the President of the Republic, or Secretaries to the National Assembly, or when the President is accused of treason or of violating the Constitution. In such cases voting is secret, and a two-thirds majority is needed for a proposal to be adopted.

EXECUTIVE POWER

With the incorporation of the Taif agreement into the Lebanese Constitution in August 1990, executive power was effectively transferred from the presidency to the Cabinet. The President is elected for a term of six years and is not immediately re-eligible. He is responsible for the promulgation and execution of laws enacted by the National Assembly, but all presidential decisions (with the exception of those to appoint a Prime Minister or to accept the resignation of a government) require the co-signature of the Prime Minister, who is head of the Government, implementing its policies and speaking in its name. The President must receive the approval of the Cabinet before dismissing a minister or ratifying an international treaty. The ministers and the Prime Minister are chosen by the President of the Republic in consultation with the members and President of the National Assembly. They are not necessarily members of the National Assembly, although they are responsible to it and have access to its debates. The President of the Republic must be a Maronite Christian, and the Prime Minister a Sunni Muslim; the choice of the other ministers must reflect the level of representation of the communities in the Assembly.

The Government

HEAD OF STATE

President: ELIAS HRAWI (elected 24 November 1989).

CABINET
(October 1994)

Prime Minister and Minister of Finance: RAFIK HARIRI (Sunni).
Deputy Prime Minister and Minister of the Interior: MICHEL MURR (Greek Orthodox).
Minister of Foreign and Emigrant Affairs: FARIS BOUEZ (Maronite).

Minister of Defence: MUHSIN DALLOUL (Shi'ite).
Minister of Agriculture: ADEL KORIAS (Greek Orthodox).
Minister of Information: MICHAEL SAMAHA (Greek Catholic).
Minister of Education and Fine Arts: MICHAEL DAHER (Maronite).
Minister of Labour: ABDULLAH AL-AMIN (Shi'ite).
Minister of Health and Social Affairs: MARWAN HAMADEH (Druze).
Minister of Public Works and Transport: MOHAMMED BASSAM MORTADA (Shi'ite).
Minister of Industry and Oil: ASAAD RIZK (Greek Orthodox).
Minister of Economy and Trade: HAGOP DEMERJIAN (Armenian Orthodox).
Minister of Housing and Co-operatives: MAHMOUD ABU HAMDAN (Shi'ite).
Minister of Justice and Administrative Reform: BAHIJ TABBARA (Sunni).
Minister of Tourism: NICHOLAS FATOUSH (Greek Catholic).
Minister of Posts and Telecommunications: MOHAMMED GHAZIRI (Sunni).
Minister of State for Displaced Persons: WALID JOUMBLATT (Druze).
Minister of State for Social Affairs and the Handicapped, and for Electricity and Water Resources: ELIE HOBEIKA (Maronite).
Minister of State for Municipal and Village Affairs: SULEIMAN TONY FRANJIEH (Maronite).
Minister of State for Emigrant Affairs: REDA WAHID (Shi'ite).
Minister of State for Culture and Higher Education: MICHEL EDDÉ (Maronite).
Minister of State for Transport: OMAR MISKAWI (Sunni).
Minister of State for Vocational and Technical Education: HASSAN EZZ ED-DIN (Sunni).
Minister of State for the Environment: SAMIR MOKBEL (Greek Orthodox).
Ministers of State without portfolio: SHAHE BARSOUMIAN (Armenian Orthodox), ANWAR AL-KHALIL (Druze), ALI OSSEIRAN (Shi'ite), FUAD SINIORA (Sunni), JEAN OBEID (Maronite).

MINISTRIES

All ministries are in Beirut.

Legislature

MAJLIS ALNWAB
(National Assembly)

The first election to the National Assembly since 1972 was held in three rounds in August and September 1992, and in October there was a by-election to choose deputies for one district in which voting had earlier been postponed. Constitutional amendments, introduced in 1990, had raised the number of seats in the Assembly from 99 to 108. Prior to the election in 1992, the Government adopted legislation that further increased the number of seats, to 128. The equal distribution of seats among Christians and Muslims is determined by law, and the Cabinet must reflect the level of representation achieved by the various religious denominations within that, principal division. Deputies of the same religious denomination do not necessarily share the same political, or party allegiances. Many Christian, especially Maronite, voters refused to participate in the general election of 1992. The term of office of the National Assembly is four years.

President: NABIH BERRI.

Vice-President: ELIE FERZLI.

Religious Groups in the National Assembly (General election, 23 August, 30 August, 6 September and 11 October 1992)

Maronite Catholics	34
Sunni Muslims	27
Shi'a Muslims	27
Greek Orthodox	14
Druzes	8
Greek-Melkite Catholics	6
Armenian Orthodox	5
Alawites	2
Armenian Catholics	1
Protestants	1
Others	3
Total	**128**

Political Organizations

Armenian Revolutionary Federation (ARF): POB 11–587, rue Spears, Beirut; f. 1890; principal Armenian party; also known as Tashnag Party, which was the dominant nationalist party in the independent Armenian Republic of Yerevan of 1917–21, prior to its becoming part of the USSR; socialist ideology; collective leadership.

Al-Baath: f. in Syria, 1940, by MICHEL AFLAK; secular pro-Syrian party with policy of Arab union, branches in several Middle Eastern countries; Sec.-Gen. ABDULLAH AL-AMIN, Beirut.

Al-Baath: pro-Iraqi wing of Al-Baath party; Sec.-Gen. ABD AL-MAJID RAFEI.

Bloc National Libanais: rue Pasteur, Gemmayze, Beirut; tel. (1) 584585; fax (1) 584591; f. 1943; right-wing Lebanese party with policy of power-sharing between Christians and Muslims and the exclusion of the military from politics; Leader RAYMOND EDDÉ; Pres. SÉLIM SALHAB; Sec.-Gen. JEAN HAWAT.

Ad-Dustur (Constitutional Party): rue Michel Chiha, Kantari, Beirut; f. 1943; led struggle against French mandate, established 1943 National Covenant; party of the political and business élite; Leader MICHEL BECHARA AL-KHOURY.

Al-Harakiyines al-Arab: Beirut; f. 1948 by GEORGES HABASH; Arab nationalist party, with Marxist tendencies.

Al-Hayat al-Wataniya: Beirut; f. 1964 by AMINE ARAYSSI.

Al-Hizb ad-Damuqratiya al-Ishtiraqi al-masihi (Christian Social Democratic Party): Beirut; f. 1988; formerly Christian Social Democratic Union; Sec.-Gen. WALID FARIS.

Al-Jabha al-Damuqratiya al-Barlamaniya (Parliamentary Democratic Front): Beirut; advocates maintenance of traditional power-sharing between Christians and Muslims; mainly Sunni Muslim support; Leader (vacant).

Al-Kata'eb (Phalanges Libanaises, Phalangist Party): POB 992, place Charles Hélou, Beirut; tel. (1) 338230; telex 42245; f. 1936 by the late PIERRE GEMAYEL; nationalist, reformist, democratic social party; largest Maronite party; 100,000 mems; announced merger with Parti National Libéral, May 1979; Leader GEORGES SAADÉ; Vice-Pres. GEORGES UMAYRAH; Sec.-Gen. KARIM PAQRADUNI.

Mouvement de l'Action Nationale: POB 5890, Centre Starco, Bloc Sud, Beirut; f. 1965; Founder and Leader OSMAN MOSBAH AD-DANA.

An-Najjadé (The Helpers): c/o Sawt al-Uruba, POB 3537, Beirut; f. 1936; Arab socialist unionist party; 3,000 mems; Founder and Pres. ADNANE MUSTAFA AL-HAKIM.

An-Nida' al-Kawmi (National Struggle): Immeuble Chammat, Ramlet el Beida, Beirut; f. 1945; Founder and Leader KAZEM AS-SOLH.

Parti Communiste Libanais (Lebanese Communist Party): POB 633, Immeuble du Parti Communiste Libanais, rue al-Hout, Beirut; f. 1924; officially dissolved 1948–71; Marxist, much support among intellectuals; Leader and Sec.-Gen. FARUQ DAHRUJ (acting).

Parti Démocrate: Immeuble Labban, rue Kantari, Beirut; f. 1969; supports a secular, democratic policy, private enterprise and social justice; Sec.-Gen. JOSEPH MUGHAIZEL; Co-founder ÉMILE BITAR.

Parti National Libéral (Al-Wataniyin al-Ahrar): rue du Liban, Beirut; f. 1958; liberal reformist party; announced merger with Phalanges Libanaises, May 1979; Pres. DORY CHAMOUN; Deputy Leader KAZEM KHALIL.

Parti Socialiste Nationaliste Syrien: f. 1932, banned 1962–69; advocates a 'Greater Syria', composed of Lebanon, Syria, Iraq, Jordan, Palestine and Cyprus; Leader DAWOUD BAZ; Chair. HAFIZ AS-SAYEH; Sec.-Gen. ANWAR AL-FATAYRI.

Parti Socialiste Progressiste (At-Takadumi al-Ishteraki): POB 2893, Zkak el-Blat, Beirut; f. 1949; progressive party, advocates constitutional road to socialism and democracy; over 25,000 mems; mainly Druze support; Pres. WALID JOUMBLATT; Sec.-Gen. SHARIF FAYAD.

Wa'ad Party: Beirut; Leader ELIE HOBEIKA.

The **Lebanese Front** (f. 1976; Sec. DORY CHAMOUN) is a grouping of right-wing parties (mainly Christian). The **National Front** (f. 1969; Sec.-Gen. KAMAL SHATILA) is a grouping of left-wing parties (mainly Muslim). Other parties include the **Independent Nasserite Movement** (Murabitoun; Sunni Muslim Militia; Leader IBRAHIM QULAYAT) and the **Union of Working People's Forces** (Sec.-Gen. KAMAL SHATILA). The **Nasserite Popular Organization** and the **Arab Socialist Union** merged in January 1987, retaining the name of the former (Sec.-Gen. MUSTAFA SAAD). **Amal** (Hope) is a Shi'ite politico-military organization (Principal Controller of Command Council Sheikh MUHAMMAD MANDI SHAMS AD-DIN, Chair. SADR AD-DIN AS-SADR, Leader NABIH BERRI). The **Islamic Amal** is a breakaway group from Amal, based in Baalbek (Leader HUSSEIN MOUSSAVI). **Islamic Jihad** (Islamic Holy War) is a pro-Iranian fundamentalist guerrilla group (Leader IMAAD MOUGNIEH). **Hez-**bollah (the Party of God) is a militant Shi'ite faction which was founded by Iranian Revolutionary Guards who were sent to Lebanon (Spiritual Leader Sheikh MUHAMMAD HUSSEIN FADLALLAH). The **Popular Liberation Army** is a Sunni Muslim faction, active in the south of Lebanon (Leader MUSTAFA SAAD). **Tawheed Islami** (the Islamic Unification Movement; f. 1982; Sunni Muslim; Leader Sheikh SAYED SHABAN) and the **Arab Democratic Party** (or the Red Knights; Alawites; pro-Syrian; Leader ALI EID) are based in Tripoli.

Diplomatic Representation

EMBASSIES IN LEBANON

Algeria: POB 4794, Hôtel Summerland, Jnah, Beirut; tel. (1) 868433; telex 27382; Ambassador: IBRAHIM ISSA.

Argentina: POB 11-5245, 5th Floor, Immeuble Antoun Saad, rue de l'Eglise Mar-Takla, Hazmieh, Beirut; tel. and fax (1) 428960; telex 40687; Ambassador: JUAN ANGEL FARALDO.

Armenia: Beirut.

Australia: Hôtel Mayflower, Hamra, Beirut; telex 21754; Ambassador: PAUL ROBILLIARD.

Austria: 9th Floor, Tour Sadat, rue Sadat, Ras Beirut, Beirut; tel. (1) 801574; telex 23255; Ambassador: ANTON PROHASKA.

Bahrain: Sheikh Ahmed ath-Thani Bldg, Raoucheh, Beirut; tel. (1) 805495; telex 21686; Ambassador: MUHAMMAD BAHLOUL.

Belgium: Immeuble Hélou, Baabda, Beirut; tel. (1) 420585; telex 44040; Ambassador: PAUL PONJAERT.

Brazil: POB 166175, rue des Antonins, Baabda, Beirut; tel. (1) 421256; telex 41330; Ambassador: MAURÍCIO CARNEIRO MAGNAVITA.

Bulgaria: Immeuble Hibri, rue de l, Australie, Beirut; Ambassador: KRASTIO KRASTEV.

Chad: Immeuble Kalot Frères, Pine Forest, ave Sami Solh, Beirut; Ambassador: (vacant).

Chile: 5th Floor, Immeuble Edouard Abou Jaoudé, Beirut; tel. (1) 404745; telex 41421; Chargé d'affaires a.i.: ALEX GEIGER.

China, People's Republic: rue Nicolas Ibrahim Sursock 72, Mar Elias, Beirut; tel. (1) 830314; telex 21344; Ambassador: ZHU PEIQING.

Colombia: POB 1496, Corniche Chouran, Immeuble Jaber al-Ahmad as-Sabbah, Beirut; tel. (1) 810416; telex 44260; Ambassador: ROBERTO DELGADO SAÑUDO.

Cuba: Immeuble Ghazzal, rue Abd as-Sabbah between rue Sakiet el-Janzir and rue de Vienne, Beirut; tel. (1) 866641; Ambassador: SEVERINO MANSUR JORGE.

Czech Republic: POB 40195, Baabda, Beirut.

Egypt: POB 690, rue Thomas Eddison, Beirut; tel. (1) 801769; Ambassador: SAYED ABUZEID OMAR.

Finland: POB 113-5966, 11th Floor, Sadat, rue Sadat, Ras Beirut, Beirut; tel. (1) 802276; telex 20568; Ambassador: ARTO KURITTU.

France: Mar-Takla, Beirut; tel. (1) 429629; telex 41530; Ambassador: JEAN-PIERRE LAFON.

Germany: POB 2820, Hôpital Notre Dame du Liban, Jounieh, Beirut; tel. (1) 830021; telex 45445; Ambassador: WOLFGANG ERCK.

Greece: 11th Floor, Immeuble Sarras, ave Elias Sarkis, Achrafiyé, Beirut; tel. (1) 219217; telex 40131; fax (1) 201324; Ambassador: ATHANASSIOS KANILLOS.

Haiti: Immeuble Sarkis, rue du Fleuve, Beirut; Ambassador: (vacant).

Holy See: POB 1882, rue Georges Picot, Beirut (Apostolic Nunciature); tel. (1) 903102; fax (1) 903763; Apostolic Nuncio: Most Rev. PABLO PUENTE, Titular Archbishop of Macri.

Hungary: POB 90618, Immeuble Ahmavani, Cornet Chahnian, Montana, Beirut; tel. (1) 922490; telex 41503; Ambassador: BALAIZS BOKOR.

India: POB 113-5240, Immeuble Sahmarani, rue Kantari 31, Hamra, Beirut; tel. (1) 353892; telex 20229; Ambassador: S. SIVASWAMI.

Iran: Immeuble Sakina Mattar, Jnah, Beirut; tel. (1) 300007; Ambassador: HOMAYOUN ALIZADEH.

Italy: POB 211, Immeuble Cosmidis, rue de Rome, Beirut; tel. (1) 868301; telex 48347; Ambassador: GIUSEPPE DE MICHELIS.

Japan: POB 3360, Immeuble Olfat Nagib Salha, Corniche Chouran, Beirut; tel. (1) 810408; telex 20864; Ambassador: MATSUME TAKAO.

Jordan: Immeuble Sodeco, rue Vienna, Beirut; tel. (1) 864950; telex 22228; Ambassador: FAKHRI ABU TALEB.

Korea, Democratic People's Republic: rue Selim Salaam, Moussaitbé, Beirut; tel. (1) 311490; Ambassador: LI YONG SOP.

Kuwait: The Stadium Roundabout, Bir Hassan, Beirut; tel. (1) 345631; telex 22105; Ambassador: AHMAD GHAITH ABDALLAH.

Libya: Hôtel Beau Rivage, Ramlet el-Baida, Beirut; tel. (1) 866240; telex 22181; Chair. of People's Bureau: ASHOUR ABD AL-HAMID AL-FOURTAS.

Morocco: Bir Hassan, Beirut; tel. (1) 832503; telex 20867; Ambassador: MUHAMMAD FREDJ DOUKKALI.

Norway: Immeuble Taher et Fakhry, rue Bliss, Ras Beirut, Beirut; tel. (1) 353730; telex 22690; Ambassador: PER HANGESTAD.

Oman: Bir Hassan, Beirut; Ambassador: (vacant).

Pakistan: 11th Floor, Immeuble Shell, Raoucheh, Beirut; tel. (1) 869706; Ambassador: MUHAMMAD QURBAN.

Poland: POB 3667, Immeuble Nassif, rue Souraty, Hamra, Beirut; tel. (1) 860618; Chargé d'affaires a.i.: PIOTR KOWALSKI.

Qatar: POB 6717, Beirut; tel. (1) 865271; telex 23727; Ambassador: MOHAMED ALI SAEED AN-NUAIMI.

Romania: Manara, Beirut; tel. (1) 867895; telex 21661; Ambassador: ION BESTELIU.

Russia: rue Mar Elias, Wata, Beirut; tel. (1) 867560; telex 20775; Ambassador: GENNADY IRITCHEV.

Saudi Arabia: rue Bliss, Manara, Beirut; tel. (1) 804272; telex 20830; Ambassador: AHMAD IBN MAHMOUD MAHMOUD AL-KAHEIMI.

Spain: Palais Chehab, Hadath Antounie, 3039 Beirut; tel. (1) 464120; telex 44346; Ambassador: CARLOS BARCENA PORTOLES.

Switzerland: POB 2008, 9th Floor, Centre Debs, Kaflik, Beirut; tel. (1) 916279; telex 45585; Ambassador: GIANFREDERICO PEDOTTI.

Tunisia: Hazmieh, Mar-Takla, Beirut; tel. (1) 453481; telex 44429; Ambassador: MOHAMED HADI BELKHODJA.

Turkey: Beirut; tel. (1) 412080; telex 43331; Ambassador: AYDAN KARDAHAN.

United Arab Emirates: Immeuble Wafic Tanbara, Jnah, Beirut; tel. (1) 646117; Ambassador: MUHAMMAD ABDULLAH AMER EL-FILACI.

United Kingdom: POB 60180, Immeuble Middle East Airlines, Tripoli Autostrade, Jal ed-Dib, Beirut; tel. (1) 402035; telex 44204; fax (1) 402032; Ambassador: MAEVE GERALDINE FORT.

USA: Aoucar, Beirut; tel. (1) 417774; Ambassador: MARK HAMBLEY.

Uruguay: Immeuble Mohamad Hussein Ben Moutahar, rue Verdun, Ain et-Tine, Beirut; tel. (1) 803620; telex 45280; Ambassador: MANUEL SOLSONA-FLORES.

Venezuela: POB 603, Immeuble Sahmarani, rue Kantari, Beirut; tel. (1) 372394; telex 44599; Ambassador: NELCEN VALERA.

Yemen: Bir Hassan, Beirut; tel. (1) 832688; Ambassador: ABDALLAH NASSER MOUTHANA.

Yugoslavia: Beirut; tel. 866552; Chargé d'affaires: ZORAN VEJNOVIĆ.

Note: Lebanon and Syria have very close relations but do not exchange formal ambassadors.

Judicial System

Law and justice in Lebanon are administered in accordance with the following codes, which are based upon modern theories of civil and criminal legislation:

(1) Code de la Propriété (1930).

(2) Code des Obligations et des Contrats (1932).

(3) Code de Procédure Civile (1933).

(4) Code Maritime (1947).

(6) Code de Procédure Pénale (Code Ottoman Modifié).

(7) Code Pénal (1943).

(8) Code Pénal Militaire (1946).

(9) Code d'Instruction Criminelle.

The following courts are now established:

(*a*) Fifty-six **'Single-Judge Courts'**, each consisting of a single judge, and dealing in the first instance with both civil and criminal cases; there are seventeen such courts at Beirut and seven at Tripoli.

(*b*) Eleven **Courts of Appeal,** each consisting of three judges, including a President and a Public Prosecutor, and dealing with civil and criminal cases; there are five such courts at Beirut.

(*c*) Four **Courts of Cassation,** three dealing with civil and commercial cases and the fourth with criminal cases. A Court of Cassation, to be properly constituted, must have at least three judges, one being the President and the other two Councillors. The First Court consists of the First President of the Court of Cassation, a President and two Councillors. The other two civil courts each consist of a President and three Councillors. If the Court of Cassation reverses the judgment of a lower court, it does not refer the case back but retries it itself.

First President of the Court of Cassation: AMIN NASSAR.

(*d*) **The Council of State,** which deals with administrative cases. It consists of a President, Vice-President and four Councillors. A Commissioner represents the Government.

President of the Court of the Council of State: YOUSUF SAAVOLLAH EL-KHOURY.

(*e*) **The Court of Justice,** which is a special court consisting of a President and four judges, deals with matters affecting the security of the state.

In addition to the above, Islamic, Christian and Jewish religious courts deal with affairs of personal status (marriage, death, inheritance, etc.).

Religion

The largest single religious community in Lebanon was formerly the Maronite Christians, a Uniate sect of the Roman Catholic Church. Estimates for 1983 assessed the sizes of communities as: Shi'a Muslims 1.2m., Maronites 900,000, Sunni Muslims 750,000, Greek Orthodox 250,000, Druzes 250,000, Armenians 175,000. The Maronites inhabited the old territory of Mount Lebanon, i.e. immediately east of Beirut. In the south, towards the Israeli frontier, Shi'a villages are most common, while between the Shi'a and the Maronites live the Druzes (divided between the Yazbakis and the Joumblatis). The Beka'a valley has many Greek Christians (both Roman Catholic and Orthodox), while the Tripoli area is mainly Sunni Muslim. Altogether, of all the regions of the Middle East, Lebanon probably presents the closest juxtaposition of sects and peoples within a small territory. As Lebanese political life has traditionally been organized on a sectarian basis, the Maronites have also enjoyed considerable political influence (disproportionate to their actual numbers, according to the other religious communities), including a predominant voice in the nomination of the President of the Republic.

CHRISTIANITY
The Roman Catholic Church
Armenian Rite

Patriarchate of Cilicia: Patriarcat Arménien Catholique, rue de l'Hôpital Libanais, Jeitawi, 2400 Beirut; tel. (1) 329391; f. 1742; established in Beirut since 1932; includes patriarchal diocese of Beirut, with an estimated 12,000 adherents (31 December 1992); Patriarch JEAN-PIERRE XVIII KASPARIAN; Vicar-Gen. Mgr ANDRÉ BEDOGLOUYAN, Titular Bishop of Comana.

Chaldean Rite

Diocese of Beirut: Evêché Chaldéen-Catholique, POB 373, Hazmieh, Beirut; tel. (1) 429088; 10,000 adherents (31 December 1992); Bishop of Beirut (vacant); Patriarchal Administrator Mgr LOUIS AD-DAIRANY.

Latin Rite

Apostolic Vicariate of Beirut: Vicariat Apostolique, POB 11–4224, Beirut; tel. (9) 909420; 20,000 adherents (31 December 1992); Vicar Apostolic PAUL BASSIM, Titular Bishop of Laodicea in Lebanon.

Maronite Rite

Patriarchate of Antioch and all the East: Patriarcat Maronite, Bkerké; tel. (9) 915441; telex 45140; fax (9) 938844; includes patriarchal diocese of Batrun, Jobbé and Sarba; Patriarch NASRALLAH PIERRE SFEIR. The Maronite Church in Lebanon comprises four archdioceses and six dioceses. In December 1992 there were an estimated 1,854,017 adherents in the country.

Archbishop of Antelias: Mgr JOSEPH MOHSEN BÉCHARA, Archevêché Maronite, Cornet-Chahouane (summer); POB 40700, Antelias, Beirut (winter); tel. (2) 925005 (summer), 410020 (winter).

Archbishop of Beirut: KHALIL ABINADER, Archevêché Maronite, rue Collège de la Sagesse, Beirut; tel. (1) 200234; fax (1) 424727; also representative of the Holy See for Roman Catholics of the Coptic Rite in Lebanon.

Archbishop of Tripoli: GABRIEL TOUBIA, Archevêché Maronite, rue al-Moutran, Karm Saddé, Tripoli; tel. (6) 624324.

Archbishop of Tyre: MAROUN SADER, Archevêché Maronite, Tyre; tel. (7) 740059.

In addition, the Bishop of Sidon, IBRAHIM EL-HELOU, has the personal title of Archbishop.

Melkite Rite

Patriarchate of Antioch: Patriarcat Grec-Melkite-Catholique, POB 50076, Beirut, or BP 22249, Damascus, Syria; tel. (Beirut) (01) 413111; jurisdiction over an estimated 1.5m. Melkites throughout the world; Patriarch of Antioch and all the East, of

Alexandria and of Jerusalem MAXIMOS V HAKIM. The Melkite Church in Lebanon comprises seven archdioceses. At 31 December 1992 there were an estimated 343,195 adherents in the country.

Archbishop of Baalbek: CYRILLE SALIM BUSTROS, Archevêché Grec-Catholique, Baalbek; tel. 870200.

Archbishop of Baniyas: ANTOINE HAYEK, Archevêché de Panéas, Jdeidet Marjeyoun; tel. 770016.

Archbishop of Beirut and Gibail: HABIB BACHA, Archevêché Grec-Melkite-Catholique, Sabdeh-Firdaous, Beirut; tel. 880866.

Archbishop of Sidon: GEORGES KWAÏTER, Archevêché Grec-Melkite-Catholique, POB 247, rue el-Moutran, Sidon; tel. (7) 720100; fax (7) 722055.

Archbishop of Tripoli: ELIAS NIJMÉ, Archevêché Grec-Catholique, POB 72, Tripoli; tel. (6) 431602.

Archbishop of Tyre: JEAN ASSAAD HADDAD, Archevêché Grec-Melkite-Catholique, Tyre; tel. (7) 740015.

Archbishop of Zahleh and Furzol: ANDRÉ HADDAD, Archevêché Grec-Melkite-Catholique, Saidat en-Najat, Zahleh; tel. (8) 820540.

Syrian Rite

Patriarchate of Antioch: Patriarcat Syrien-Catholique, rue de Damas, POB 116–5087, Beirut; tel. (1) 381532; jurisdiction over about 150,000 Syrian Catholics in the Middle East; Patriarch IGNACE ANTOINE II HAYEK.

Patriarchal Exarchate of Lebanon: Vicariat Patriarcal Syrien, rue de Syrie, Beirut; tel. (1) 226725; 23,000 adherents (31 December 1992); Exarch Patriarchal (vacant).

The Anglican Communion

Within the Episcopal Church in Jerusalem and the Middle East, Lebanon forms part of the diocese of Jerusalem (see the chapter on Israel).

Other Christian Groups

Armenian Apostolic Orthodox: Armenian Catholicosate of Cilicia, Antelias, POB 70317, Beirut, Lebanon; tel. (1) 410001; f. 1441 in Cilicia (now in Turkey), transferred to Antelias, Lebanon, 1930; Leader His Holiness KAREKIN II (SARKISSIAN), Catholicos of Cilicia; jurisdiction over an estimated 1m. adherents in Lebanon, Syria, Cyprus, Kuwait, Greece, Iran, the United Arab Emirates, the USA and Canada.

Greek Orthodox: Leader His Beatitude IGNATIUS IV, Patriarch of Antioch and all the East, Patriarcat Grec-Orthodoxe, POB 9, Damascus, Syria.

National Evangelical Synod of Syria and Lebanon: POB 70890, Antelias, Beirut; tel. (1) 411100; 70,000 adherents (1987); Gen. Sec. Rev. Dr SALIM SAHIOUNY.

Protestants: Leader Rev. Habib Badr, Pres. of Nat. Evangelical Union of the Lebanon, POB 5224, rue Maurice Barrès, Beirut; tel. (1) 341285.

Syrian Orthodox: Leader IGNATIUS ZAKKA I IWAS, Patriarch of Antioch and all the East, Patriarcat Syrien Orthodoxe, Bab Toma, POB 22260, Damascus, Syria; tel. 432401; telex 411876; fax 432400.

Union of the Armenian Evangelical Churches in the Near East: POB 11–377, Beirut; tel. (1) 443547; fax (1) 582191; f. 1846 in Turkey; comprises about 30 Armenian Evangelical Churches in Syria, Lebanon, Egypt, Cyprus, Greece, Iran and Turkey; 7,500 mems (1990); Pres. Rev. HOVHANNES KARJIAN; Gen. Sec. Rev. KRIKOR YOUMSHAJEKIAN.

ISLAM

Shi'a Muslims: Leader Imam SAYED MOUSSA AS-SADR (went missing in August 1978, while visiting Libya), President of the Supreme Islamic Council of the Shi'a Community of Lebanon, Dar al-Iftaa al-Jaafari, Beirut; Deputy Pres. Sheikh MUHAMMAD MAHDI SHAMS AD-DIN.

Sunni Muslims: Leader SG Sheikh Dr MUHAMMAD RASHID QABBANI (acting), Grand Mufti of Lebanon, Dar el-Fatwa, Ilewi Rushed St, Beirut.

Druzes: Leader SG Sheikh MUHAMMAD ABOUCHACRA, Supreme Spiritual Leader of the Druze Community, rue Abou Chacra, Beirut.

Alawites: a schism of Shi'ite Islam; there are an estimated 50,000 Alawites in northern Lebanon, in and around Tripoli.

JUDAISM

Jews: Leader CHAHOUD CHREIM, Beirut.

The Press

The most important dailies are *Al-Anwar* and *An-Nahar*, which have the highest circulations, *Al-Jarida* and *L'Orient-Le Jour*, the

foremost French paper. The latter two are owned by Georges Naccashe, former Lebanese Ambassador to France, and tend to take a pro-Government line. In a country where most of the élite speak French, the other French daily, *Le Soir*, is also influential, and, for the same reason, the twice-weekly publication *Le Commerce du Levant* occupies an important place in the periodical press.

Political upheavals have hindered the operation of the press, but even at the height of the civil conflict about two dozen newspapers and magazines appeared, reflecting every shade of political opinion. In January 1977, however, censorship was imposed on all publications. Some papers ceased publication, if only temporarily. Before this, Lebanon enjoyed the reputation of having one of the freest presses in the Middle East and was an important base for foreign correspondents. Some Lebanese papers have since introduced London and Paris editions.

DAILIES

Al-Amal (Hope): POB 959, rue Libérateur, Beirut; tel. (1) 382992; telex 22072; f. 1939; Arabic; organ of the Phalangist Party; Chief Editor ELIAS RABABI; circ. 35,000.

Al-Anwar (Lights): POB 1038, Beirut; tel. (1) 450933; telex 44224; f. 1959; Arabic; independent; supplement, Sunday, cultural and social; published by Dar Assayad SAL; Propr SAID FREIHA; Editor ISSAM FREIHA; circ. 75,200.

Ararat: POB 756, Nor Hagin, Beirut; f. 1937; Armenian; Communist; Editor KRIKOR HAJENIAN; circ. 5,000.

Aztag: POB 11–587, rue Selim Boustani, Beirut; tel. (1) 366607; f. 1927; Armenian; circ. 6,500.

Al-Bairaq (The Standard): POB 1800, rue Monot, Beirut; f. 1911; Arabic; published by Soc. Libanaise de Presse; Editor RAYMOND KAWASS; circ. 3,000.

Bairut: POB 7944, Beirut; f. 1952; Arabic.

Ach-Chaab (The People): POB 5140, Beirut; f. 1961; Arabic; Nationalist; Propr and Editor MUHAMMAD AMIN DUGHAN; circ. 7,000.

Ach-Chams (The Sun): POB 7047, Beirut; f. 1925; Arabic.

Ach-Charq (The East): POB 838, rue Verdun, Beirut; f. 1945; Arabic; Editor AOUNI AL-KAAKI.

Ad-Diyar (The Homeland): Immeuble Shawki Dagher, Hazmieh, Beirut; tel. (1) 427440; Arabic.

Ad-Dunya (The World): POB 4599, Beirut; f. 1943; Arabic; political; Chief Editor SULIMAN ABOU ZAID; circ. 25,000.

Al-Hakika (The Truth): Beirut; Arabic; published by Amal.

Al-Hayat (Life): POB 11–987, Immeuble Gargarian, rue Emil Eddé, Hamra, Beirut; tel. (1) 352674; telex 43415; fax (1) 866177; f. 1946; Arabic; independent; circ. 31,034.

Al-Jarida (The News) Paper): POB 220, place Tabaris, Beirut; f. 1953; Arabic; independent; Editor ABDULLA SKAFF; circ. 22,600.

Al-Jumhuriya (The Republic): POB 7111, Beirut; f. 1924; Arabic.

Journal al-Haddis: POB 300, Jounieh; f. 1927; Arabic; political; Owner GEORGES ARÈGE-SAADÉ.

Al-Khatib (The Speaker): POB 365, rue Georges Picot, Beirut; Arabic.

Al-Kifah al-Arabi (The Arab Struggle): POB 5158–14, Immeuble Rouche-Shams, Beirut; f. 1974; Arabic; political, socialist, Pan-Arab; Publr and Chief Editor WALID HUSSEINI.

Lisan ul-Hal (The Organ): POB 4619, rue Châteaubriand, Beirut; f. 1877; Arabic; Editor GEBRAN HAYEK; circ. 33,000.

Al-Liwa' (The Standard): POB 2402, Beirut; tel. 865080; telex 43409; f. 1963; Arabic; Propr ABD AL-GHANI SALAM; Editor SALAH SALAM; circ. 79,000.

An-Nahar (The Day): POB 11–226, rue Banque du Liban, Hamra, Beirut; tel. (1) 340960; telex 22322; fax (1) 348448; f. 1933; Arabic; independent; Publr, Pres. GHASSAN TUENI; circ. 100,000.

An-Nas (The People): POB 4886, ave Fouad Chehab, Beirut; tel. (1) 308695; f. 1959; Arabic; Editor-in-Chief HASSAN YAGHI; circ. 22,000.

An-Nida (The Appeal): POB 4744, Beirut; f. 1959; Arabic; published by the Lebanese Communist Party; Editor KARIM MROUÉ; circ. 10,000.

Nida' al-Watan (Call of the Homeland): POB 6324, Beirut; f. 1937; Arabic.

An-Nidal (The Struggle): POB 1354, Beirut; f. 1939; Arabic.

L'Orient-Le Jour: POB 166495, rue Banque du Liban, Beirut; tel. (1) 340560; telex 42590; f. 1942; French; independent; Chair. MICHEL EDDÉ; Dir CAMILLE MENASSA; Editorial Dir AMINE ABOU-KHALED; Editor ISSA GORAÏEB; circ. 23,000.

Raqib al-Ahwal (The Observer): POB 467, rue Patriarche Hoyek, Beirut; f. 1937; Arabic; Editor SIMA'N FARAH SEIF.

Rayah (Banner): POB 4101, Beirut; Arabic.

Le Réveil: POB 8383, blvd Sinn el-Fil, Beirut; f. 1977; French; Editor-in-Chief JEAN SHAMI; Dir RAYMOND DAOU; circ. 10,000.

Ar-Ruwwad: POB 2696, rue Mokhalsieh, Beirut; f. 1940; Arabic; Editor BESHARA MAROUN.

Sada Lubnan (Echo of Lebanon): POB 7884, Beirut; f. 1951; Arabic; Lebanese Pan-Arab; Editor MUHAMMAD BAALBAKI; circ. 25,000.

As-Safeer (The Ambassador): POB 113-5015, rue Mnaimneh, Beirut; tel. (1) 802520; telex 21484; Arabic; Editor-in-Chief TALAL SALMAN.

Sawt al-Uruba (The Voice of Europe): POB 3537, Beirut; f. 1959; Arabic; organ of the An-Najjadé Party; Editor ADNANE AL-HAKIM.

Le Soir: POB 1470, rue de Syrie, Beirut; f. 1947; French; independent; Dir DIKRAN TOSBATH; Editor ANDRÉ KECATI; circ. 16,500.

At-Tayyar (The Current): POB 1038, Beirut; Arabic; independent; circ. 75,000.

Telegraf—Bairut: POB 1061, rue Béchara el-Khoury, Beirut; f. 1930; Arabic; political, economic and social; Editor TOUFIC ASSAD MATNI; circ. 15,500 (5,000 outside Lebanon).

Al-Yaum (Today): POB 1908, Beirut; f. 1937; Arabic; Editor WAFIC MUHAMMAD CHAKER AT-TIBY.

Az-Zamane: POB 6060, rue Boutros Karameh, Beirut; f. 1947; Arabic.

Zartonk: POB 617, rue Nahr Ibrahim, Beirut; tel. (1) 226611; f. 1937; Armenian; official organ of Armenian Liberal Democratic Party; Man. Editor BAROUYR H. AGHBASHIAN; Editor P. TOMASSIAN.

WEEKLIES

Al-Alam al-Lubnani (The Lebanese World): POB 462, Ministry of Foreign Affairs, Beirut; f. 1964; Arabic, English, Spanish, French; politics, literature and social economy; Editor-in-Chief FAYEK KHOURY; Gen. Editor CHEIKH FADI GEMAYEL; circ. 45,000.

Achabaka (Network): POB 1038, Dar Assayad, Beirut; f. 1956; Arabic; society and features; Founder SAID FREIHA; Editor GEORGE IBRAHIM EL-KHOURY; circ. 126,500.

Al-Ahad (Sunday): POB 1462, rue Andalouss, Chourah, Beirut; Arabic; political; organ of Hezbollah (the Party of God); Editor RIAD TAHA; circ. 32,000.

Al-Akhbar (The News): Beirut; f. 1954; Arabic; published by the Lebanese Communist Party; circ. 21,000.

Al-Anwar Supplement: POB 1038, Beirut; cultural-social; every Sunday; supplement to daily *Al-Anwar*; Editor ISSAM FREIHA; circ. 90,000.

Argus: Bureau of Lebanese and Arab Documentation, POB 16–5403, Beirut; tel. (1) 219113; Arabic, French and English; economic bulletin; circ. 1,000.

Assayad (The Hunter): POB 1038, Dar Assayad, Beirut; f. 1943; news magazine; Propr SAID FREIHA; Editor RAFIQUE KHOURY; circ. 94,700.

Le Commerce du Levant: POB 687, Immeuble de Commerce et Financement, rue Kantari, Beirut; tel. (1) 297770; f. 1929; weekly and special issue quarterly; French; commercial and financial; Editor: Société de la Presse Economique; Pres. MAROUN AKL; circ. 15,000.

Dabbour: POB 5723, place du Musée, Beirut; f. 1922; Arabic; Editors MICHEL RICHARD and FUAD MUKARZEL; circ. 12,000.

Ad-Dyar: POB 959, Immeuble Bellevue, rue Verdun, Beirut; f. 1941; Arabic; political; circ. 46,000.

Al-Hadaf (The Target): POB 212, Immeuble Esseilé, rue Béchir, Beirut; f. 1969; tel. (1) 420554; organ of Popular Front for the Liberation of Palestine (PFLP); Arabic; Editor-in-Chief SABER MOHI ED-DIN; circ. 40,000.

Al-Hawadess (Events): POB 1281, rue Clémenceau St, Beirut; published from London (183–185 Askew Rd, W12 9AX; tel. 081-740 4500; telex 261601; fax 081-749 9781); f. 1911; Arabic; news; Editor-in-Chief MELHIM KAVAM; circ. 120,000.

Al-Hurriya (Freedom): POB 857, Beirut; f. 1960; Arabic; voice of the Democratic Front for the Liberation of Palestine (DFLP) and the Organization for Communist Action in Lebanon (OCAL) 1969–81, of DFLP 1981–; Editor DAOUD TALHAME; circ. 30,000.

Al-Iza'a (Broadcasting): POB 462, rue Selim Jazaerly, Beirut; f. 1938; Arabic; politics, art, literature and broadcasting; Editor FAYEK KHOURY; circ. 11,000.

Al-Jumhur (The Public): POB 1834, Moussaitbé, Beirut; telex 21541; f. 1936; Arabic; illustrated weekly news magazine; Editor FARID ABU SHAHLA; circ. 45,000, of which over 20,000 outside Lebanon.

Kul Shay' (Everything): POB 3250, rue Béchara el-Khoury, Beirut; Arabic.

Al-Liwa' (The Standard): POB 11-2402, Immeuble Saradar, ave de l'Indépendence, Beirut; tel. (1) 865050; telex 43409; fax (1) 644761; Arabic; Editor-in-Chief SALAH SALAM; Propr ABD AL-GHANI SALAAM.

Magazine: POB 1404, rue Sursock, Beirut; tel. (1) 202070; telex 41362; fax (1) 202070; f. 1956; French; political and social; published by Les Editions Orientales SAL; Pres. and Editor-in-Chief CHARLES ABOU ADAL; circ. 18,000.

Massis: c/o Patriarcat Arménien Catholique, rue de l'Hôpital Grec Orthodoxe, Jeitawi, 2400 Beirut; Armenian; Catholic; Editor Father ANTRANIK GRANIAN; circ. 2,500.

Middle East Economic Survey: Middle East Petroleum and Economic Publications (Cyprus), POB 4940, Nicosia, Cyprus; tel. (2) 445431; telex 2198; fax (2) 474988; f. 1957 (in Beirut); review and analysis of petroleum, finance and banking sectors, and of political developments; Publr BASIM W. ITAYIM; Editor IAN SEYMOUR.

Al-Moharrir (The Liberator): POB 5366, Beirut; f. 1962; Arabic; circ. 87,000; Gen. Man. WALID ABOU ZAHR.

Al-Ousbou' al-Arabi (Arab Week): POB 1404, rue Sursock, Beirut; f. 1959; tel. (1) 202070; telex 41362; fax (1) 202070; Arabic; political and social; Publrs Les Editions Orientales, SAL; Gen. Man. CHARLES ABOU ADAL; circ. 88,407 (circulates throughout the Arab World).

Ar-Rassed: POB 11–2808, Beirut; Arabic; Editor GEORGE RAJJI.

Revue du Liban: POB 165612, rue Issa Maalouf, Beirut; tel. (1) 339960; telex 20303; f. 1928; French; political, social, cultural; Publr MELHEM KARAM; Gen. Man. MICHEL MISK; circ. 22,000.

Sabah al-Khair (Good Morning): Beirut; Arabic; published by the Syrian Nationalist Party.

Sahar: POB 1038, Beirut; telex 22632; Arabic.

Samar (Conversation): POB 1038, Beirut; Arabic; photorama magazine; circ. 50,000.

Ash-Shira' (The Sail): POB 13-5250, Beirut; tel. (1) 862556; telex 42073; fax (1) 866050; Arabic; Editor HASSAN SABRA; circ. 40,000.

OTHER SELECTED PERIODICALS

Alam at-Tijarat (Business World): Immeuble Strand, rue Hamra, Beirut; f. 1965 in association with Johnston International Publishing Corpn, New York; monthly; commercial; Editor NADIM MAKDISI; international circ. 17,500.

Arab Defense Journal: POB 1038, Beirut; tel. (1) 452700; monthly; published by Dar Assayad SAL.

Arab Economist: POB 11–6068, Beirut; telex 21071; monthly; published by Centre for Economic, Financial and Social Research and Documentation SAL; Chair. Dr CHAFIC AKRAS.

The Arab World: POB 567, Jounieh; tel. (9) 935096; f. 1985; 24 a year; published by Dar Naaman lith Thaqafa; Editor NAJI NAAMAN.

L'Economie Arabe: POB 11–6068, Beirut; f. 1958; monthly; French; published by Centre d'Etudes et de Documentation Economiques Financières et Sociales SAL; Chair. Dr CHAFIC AKRHAS.

Fairuz: POB 1038, Hazmieh, Beirut; tel. (1) 452700; telex 444224; fax (1) 429884; f. 1982; monthly; Arabic; for women; published by Dar Assayad SAL; international circ. 84,000.

Fikr (Idea): monthly; Arabic; published by the Syrian Nationalist Party.

Al-Idari (The Manager): POB 918-1038, Beirut; tel. (1) 452700; telex 44224; fax (1) 452957; f. 1975; monthly; Arabic; business management and public administration; published by Dar Assayad International; Pres. and Gen. Man. BASSAM FREIHA; Chief Editor HASSAN EL-KHOURY; circ. 25,819.

International Crude Oil and Product Prices: Middle East Petroleum and Economic Publications (Cyprus), POB 4940, Nicosia, Cyprus; tel. (2) 445431; telex 2198; fax (2) 474988; f. 1971 (in Beirut); 2 a year; review and analysis of oil price trends in world markets; Publisher BASIM W. ITAYIM.

Al-Intilak (Outbreak): c/o Michel Nehme, Al-Intilak Printing and Publishing House, POB 4958, Beirut; f. 1960; monthly; Arabic; literary; Chief Editor MICHEL NEHME.

Al-Khalij Business Magazine: POB 11-8440, Beirut; tel. (1) 811149; telex 20680; fmrly based in Kuwait; every two months; Arabic; Editor-in-Chief ZULFICAR KOBFISSI; circ. 16,325.

Lebanese and Arab Economy: POB 11–1801, Sanayeh, Beirut; tel. (1) 349530; telex 42241; fax (1) 865802; f. 1951; monthly; Arabic, English and French; Publr Beirut Chamber of Commerce and Industry.

Majallat al-Iza'at al-Lubnaniat (Lebanese Broadcasting Magazine): Radio Lebanon, Ministry of Information, Sanayeh, Beirut; tel. (1) 863016; telex 20786; f. 1959; monthly; Arabic; broadcasting affairs.

Al-Mouktataf (The Selection): POB 11–1462, rue Andalous, Chouran, Beirut; monthly; Arabic; general.

Qitâboul A'lamil A'rabi (The Arab World Book): POB 567, Jounieh; tel. (9) 935096; f. 1991; 6 a year; Arabic; published by Dar Naaman lith Thaqafa; Editor NAJI NAAMAN.

Rijal al-Amal (Businessmen): POB 6065, Beirut; f. 1966; monthly; Arabic; business; Publr and Editor-in-Chief MAHIBA AL-MALKI; circ. 16,250.

As-Sahafa wal I'lam (Press and Information): POB 567, Jounieh; tel. (9) 935096; f. 1987; 12 a year; Arabic; published by Dar Naaman lith Thaqafa; Editor NAJI NAAMAN.

Siyassa was Strategia (Politics and Strategy): POB 567, Jounieh; tel. (9) 935096; f. 1981; 36 a year; Arabic; published by Dar Naaman lith Thaqafa; Editor NAJI NAAMAN.

Tabibok (Your Doctor): POB 90434, Beirut; tel. (11) 212980; fax (11) 711316; f. 1956; monthly; Arabic; medical, social, scientific; Editor Dr SAMI KABBANI; circ. 90,000.

At-Tarik (The Road): Beirut; monthly; Arabic; cultural and theoretical; published by the Lebanese Communist Party; circ. 5,000.

Welcome to Lebanon and the Middle East: POB 4204, Centre Starco, Beirut; f. 1959; monthly; English; on entertainment, touring and travel; Editor SOUHAIL TOUFIK ABOU-JAMRA; circ. 6,000.

NEWS AGENCIES
Foreign Bureaux

Agence France-Presse (AFP): POB 4868, Immeuble Najjar, rue de Rome, Beirut; tel. (1) 347460; telex 20819; fax (1) 350318; Dir M. GAY-PARA; POB 166827, Immeuble Georges Massoud, rue d'Athènes, Achrafiye, east Beirut; tel. (1) 422445; telex 44279.

Agenzia Nazionale Stampa Associata (ANSA) (Italy): POB 1525, 2nd Floor, Immeuble Safieddine, rue Rashid Karame, Beirut; tel. (1) 810155; telex 20539; fax (1) 810201; cellular tel. 001212-4783734; Correspondent VITTORIO FRENQUELLUCCI.

Allgemeiner Deutscher Nachrichtendienst (ADN) (Germany): POB 114–5100, Immeuble Bitar-Rawas, Ramat el-Beida, Beirut; Correspondent HARALD DITTMAR.

Associated Press (AP) (USA): POB 3780, Immeuble Commodore, rue Ne' Meh Yafet, Beirut; tel. (1) 352310; telex 20636; Chief Middle East Correspondent (vacant).

Česká tisková kancelár (ČTK) (Czech Republic): POB 5069, Beirut; tel. (1) 305712; Chief Middle East Correspondent MARTIN JANKOVEC.

Informatsionnoye Telegrafnoye Agentstvo Rossii—Telegrafnoye Agentstvo Suverennykh Stran (ITAR—TASS) (Russia): Immeuble Diab, Dar el Fatwa, Beirut; Chief MIKHAIL I. KROUTIKHIN.

Kyodo Tsushin (Japan): POB 13-5060, Immeuble Makarem, rue Makdessi, Ras Beirut, Beirut; tel. (1) 863861; telex 21203; Correspondent IBRAHIM KHOURY.

Middle East News Agency (MENA) (Egypt): POB 2268, 72 rue al-Geish, Beirut.

United Press International (UPI) (USA): Immeuble An-Nahar, Hamra, Beirut; telex 20724; Bureau Man. RIAD KAJ.

Xinhua (New China) News Agency (People's Republic of China): POB 114-5075, Beirut; tel. (1) 830359; telex 21313.

BTA (Bulgaria), INA (Iraq), JANA (Libya) and Prensa Latina (Cuba) are also represented in Lebanon.

PRESS ASSOCIATION

Lebanese Press Syndicate: POB 3084, Immeuble Press Order, ave Saeb Salam, Beirut; tel. (1) 865519; f. 1911; 18 mems; Pres. MUHAMMAD AL-BAALBAKI; Vice-Pres. FADEL SAID AKL; Sec. BASSEM AS-SABEH.

Publishers

Dar al-Adab: POB 11-4123, Beirut; tel. and fax (1) 861633; f. 1953; literary and general; Man. RANA IDRISS.

Dar Assayad SAL: POB 1038, Hazmieh, Beirut; tel. and fax (1) 4783410; telex 44224; f. 1943; publishes in Arabic *Al-Anwar* (daily, plus weekly supplement), *Assayad* (weekly), *Achabaka* (weekly), *Background Reports* (three a month), *Arab Defense Journal* (monthly), *Al-Idari* (monthly), *Fairuz* (monthly), *Computers* (monthly), *Al-Fares* (monthly), *Middle East Observer* (quarterly); has offices and correspondents in Arab countries and most parts of the world; Chair. ISSAM FREIHA; Pres. and Man. Dir BASSAM FREIHA.

Arab Institute for Research and Publishing (Al-Mouasasah al-Arabiyah Lildirasat Walnashr): POB 11–5460, Tour Carlton, Saqiat el-Janzeer, Beirut; tel. (1) 807900; telex 40067; fax (1) 685501; f. 1969; Dir. MAHER KAYYALI; works in Arabic and English.

Editions Orientales SAL: POB 1404, Immeuble Sayegh, rue Sursock, Beirut; tel. and fax (1) 202070; telex 41362; political and social newspapers and magazines; Pres. GEORGES ABOU ADAL; Gen. Man. and Editor-in-Chief CHARLES ABOU ADAL.

Dar al-I'lam Lilmalayin: POB 1085, rue Bitar, Mar Elias, Beirut; tel. (1) 863474; telex 23166; fax (1) 825272; f. 1945; dictionaries, encyclopaedias, reference books, textbooks, Islamic cultural books; Editorial Dir Dr ROHI BAALBAKI.

Institute for Palestine Studies, Publishing and Research Organization: POB 11–7164, rue Nsouli-Verdun, Beirut; tel. and fax (1) 868387; telex 23317; f. 1963; independent non-profit Arab research organization; to promote better understanding of the Palestine problem and the Arab–Israeli conflict; publishes books, reprints research papers, etc.; Chair. Dr HISHAM NASHABE; Exec. Sec. Prof. WALID KHALIDI.

The International Documentary Center of Arab Manuscripts: POB 2668, Immeuble Hanna, Ras Beirut, Beirut; f. 1965; publishes and reproduces ancient and rare Arabic texts; Propr ZOUHAIR BAALBAKI.

Dar al-Kashaf: POB 112091, rue A. Malhamee, Beirut; tel. (1) 815527; f. 1930; publishers of *Al-Kashaf* (Arab Youth Magazine), maps and atlases; printers and distributors; Propr M. A. FATHALLAH.

Khayat Book and Publishing Co SAL: 90–94 rue Bliss, Beirut; Middle East, Islam, oil, Arab publications and reprints; Man. Dir PAUL KHAYAT.

Librairie du Liban: POB 945, place Riad Solh, Beirut; tel. (1) 258259; telex 21037; f. 1944; fiction, children's books, dictionaries, Middle East, travel, Islam; Proprs KHALIL and GEORGE SAYEGH.

Dar al-Maaref Liban SAL: POB 2320, Immeuble Esseilé, place Riad Solh, Beirut; f. 1959; children's books and textbooks in Arabic; Gen. Man. JOSEPH NASHOU.

Dar al-Machreq SARL: c/o Librairie orientale, POB 946, Beirut; tel. (1) 202423; telex 42733; fax (1) 200297; f. 1853; religion, art, Arabic and Islamic literature, history, languages, science, philosophy, school books, dictionaries and periodicals; Man. Dir CAMILLE HÉCHAIMÉ.

Dar Naaman lith-Thaqafa: POB 567, Jounieh; tel. (9) 935096; f. 1979; publishes *Encyclopedia of Contemporary Arab World*, *Qitâboul A'lamil A'rabi*, *Siyassa was Strategia*, *As-Sahafa wal I'lam* in Arabic and *The Arab World* in English; Propr NAJI NAAMAN; Exec. Man. MARCELLE AL-ASHKAR.

Dar an-Nahar SAL: POB 55-454, rue Zahret el-Ihsan, Achrafiyé, Beirut; f. 1967; tel. (1) 335530; telex 22322; a Pan-Arab publishing house; Pres. GHASSAN TUENI.

Naufal Group: POB 11-2161, Immeuble Naufal, rue Mamari, Beirut; tel. (1) 354394; telex 22210; f. 1970; subsidiary cos Macdonald Middle East Sarl, Les Editions Arabes; encyclopaedias, fiction, children's books, history, law and literature; Man. Dir. SAMI NAUFAL.

Rihani Printing and Publishing House: rue Jibb en-Nakhl, Beirut; f. 1963; Propr ALBERT RIHANI; Man. DAOUD STEPHAN.

Dar as-Safir: POB 113-5015, Immeuble As-Safir, Monimina, Hamra, Beirut; tel. (1) 802444; telex 21484; fax (1) 861806; f. 1974.

Radio and Television

In 1991, according to UNESCO, there were an estimated 2,320,000 radio receivers and 905,000 television receivers in use.

RADIO

Radio Lebanon: rue Arts et Métiers, Beirut; part of the Ministry of Information; tel. (1) 346880; telex 29786; f. 1937; Dir-Gen. QASSEM HAGE ALI; Technical Dir LOUIS RIZK; Dir of Programmes NIZAR MIKATI; Head of Administration A. AOUN.

The Home Service broadcasts in Arabic on short wave, and the Foreign Service broadcasts in Portuguese, Armenian, Arabic, Spanish, French and English.

TELEVISION

Lebanese Broadcasting Corporation: POB 111, Jounieh; tel. (9) 938938; telex 45949; f. Aug. 1985 by the 'Lebanese Forces' Christian militia; programmes in Arabic, French and English on two channels; Chair. PIERRE ED-DAHER.

Télé-Liban (TL) SAL: POB 11-5054, Beirut; tel. (1) 450100; telex 20923; f. 1959; commercial service; programmes in Arabic, French and English on three channels, and relays on three channels; Chair. and Dir-Gen. GEORGES SKAFF; Deputy Dir-Gen MUHAMMAD S. KARIMEH.

Télé-Management SARL: POB 113–5310, Beirut; tel. (1) 353510; telex 40529; f. 1972; exclusive airtime sales and programmes sales contractor to Télé-Liban SAL (channels 5, 7 and 9); Gen. Man. CLAUDE SAWAYA.

There are 50 'private' television and more than 100 'private' radio stations, usually of a sectarian nature.

Finance

(cap. = capital; auth. = authorized; p.u. = paid up; dep. = deposits; m. = million; £L = Lebanese £; res = reserves; brs = branches)

BANKING

Beirut was, for many years, the leading financial and commercial centre in the Middle East, but this role was destroyed by the civil conflict. At the end of 1993 only about 25 of Lebanon's 77 banks were fully active. New banking and investment legislation is planned to create more favourable conditions for the sector and mergers will be necessary to enable many Lebanese banks to meet the Bank for International Settlements' capital-asset ratio of 8%.

Central Bank

Banque du Liban: POB 11-5544, rue Masraf Loubnane, Beirut; tel. (1) 341230; telex 20744; fax (1) 782740; f. 1964 to take over the banking activities of the Banque de Syrie et du Liban in Lebanon; cap £L15m., total assets £L355,957m. (Dec. 1991); Gov. RIFAD SALAMEH.

Principal Commercial Banks

Adcom Bank SAL: POB 11-2431, Immeuble Ammar, rue Verdun, Beirut; tel. (1) 860160; telex 20884; f. 1960 as Advances and Commerce Bank; cap. p.u. £L50m., dep. £L19,600.9m. (Dec. 1990); Chair. and Gen. Man. HENRI R. SFEIR.

Allied Business Bank: POB 113, Immeuble Diab, rue Makdissi, 7165 Beirut; tel. (1) 860692; telex 21708; fax (1) 864551; f. 1982; cap. £L400m., dep. £L52,683.3m., res £L595.5m., total assets £L57,415.1m. (Dec. 1991); Chair. ABDULLAH S. ZAKHEM.

Al Moughtareb Bank SAL: POB 11-5508, Immeuble Sehnaoui, rue Banque du Liban, Beirut; tel. (1) 350060; telex 21406; fax (1) 602009; f. 1974; cap. p.u. £L4,000m., dep. £L36,166.8m., total assets £L42,176.8m. (Dec. 1993); Chair. HANI SAFI ED-DINE.

Bank of Beirut and the Arab Countries SAL: POB 11-1536, Immeuble de la Banque, 250 rue Clémenceau, Beirut; tel. (1) 867142; telex 20761; f. 1956; cap. £L15,000m., dep. £L232,106m., total assets £L340,699m. (Dec. 1992); Chair. and Gen. Man. TOUFIC S. ASSAF.

Bank of Kuwait and the Arab World SAL: Immeuble Intra Investment Co, rue Omar Ben Abd al-Aziz, Hamra, Beirut; tel. (1) 293890; telex 21524; f. 1959; cap. p.u. £L95m., res £L13.2m., dep. £L11,307.1m. (Dec. 1989); Chair. and Gen. Man. Dr AHMAD HAGE.

Bank of Lebanon and Kuwait SAL: POB 11-5556, Immeuble al-Hoss, rue Emile Eddé, Hamra, Beirut; tel. (1) 340270; telex 23013; fax (1) 340270; f. 1964; cap. p.u. £L150m., res £L10.5m., dep. £L8,093.8m. (Dec. 1989); Chair. Sheikh ALI SABAH-AS SALEM AS-SABAH; Gen. Man. T. SHWAYRI.

Bank al-Madina SAL: POB 113-7221, Immeuble Banque al-Madina, rue Commodore, Beirut; tel. (1) 351296; telex 23105; fax (1) 348305; f. 1982; cap. £L60m., res £L22.7m., dep. £L65,877m. (Dec. 1992); Chair. and Gen. Man. IBRAHIM ABOU AYASH.

Banque Audi SAL: POB 11-2560, ave Charles Malek, St Nicolas, Beirut; tel. (1) 331600; telex 43012; fax (1) 200955; f. 1962; cap. p.u. £L1,500m., dep. £L1,031,559m. (Dec. 1993); Chair. and Gen. Man. GEORGES W. AUDI; 20 brs.

Banque de la Beka'a SAL: POB 117, Centre Fakhoury, Zahleh; tel. (8) 803099; telex 21214; fax (8) 803217; f. 1965; cap. p.u. £L1,400m., dep. £L287,926m. (April 1992); Pres. and Gen. Man. CHAOUKI W. FAKHOURY.

Banque Beyrouth pour le Commerce SAL: POB 11-0216, Immeuble de la Banque Arabe, rue des Banques, Place Riad Solh, Beirut; tel. (1) 867459; telex 21457; fax (1) 865073; f. 1961; cap. p.u. £L3,000m., dep. £L239,442m., total assets £L243,311m. (Dec. 1992); Chair. and Gen. Man. RIFAAT EN-NIMR.

Banque de Crédit National SAL: Centre Moucarri, Autostrade Dora, Beirut; tel. (1) 582345; telex 42093; fax (1) 4782387; f. 1920 as Banque Jacob E. Safra, name changed 1959; cap. £L100m., dep. £L5,186.8m., total assets £L5,418.5m. (Dec. 1992); Chair. and Gen. Man. EDMOND J. SAFRA.

Banque du Crédit Populaire SAL: POB 11-5292, Immeuble Al-Ittihadia, ave Charles Malek, St Nicolas, Beirut; tel. (1) 200352; telex 40123; fax (1) 200354; f. 1963; cap. £L100m., res £L305.2m., dep. £L19,846.5m. (Dec. 1992); Chair. and Gen. Man. NEDIM B. DEMESHKIEH; 7 brs.

Banque de l'Essor Economique Libanais SAL: POB 80938, Centre Moucarri, Autostrade Dora, Beirut; tel. (1) 582420; telex

42887; cap. p.u. £L2,000m., dep. £L5,075m. (Dec. 1992); Chair. and Gen. Man. IMAD M. JAFFAL.

Banque de l'Industrie et du Travail SAL: POB 11-3948, Immeuble BIT, rue Riad Solh, Beirut; tel. (1) 200524; telex 44274; fax (1) 602806; f. 1960; cap. p.u. £L500m., dep. £L72,000m., total assets £L107,808m. (Dec. 1992); Chair. and Gen. Man. Sheikh FOUAD JAMIL EL-KHAZEN; Man. Dir NABIL N. KHAIRALLAH; 12 brs in Lebanon.

Banque Joseph Lati et Fils SAL: Immeuble Dr Elie Karam, ave de l'Indépendance, Achrafiyé, Beirut; tel. (1) 336316; telex 21702; f. 1924; cap. £L30m., dep. £L3,129.1m. (Dec. 1989); Chair. and Gen. Man. ISAAC LATI.

Banque du Liban et d'Outre-Mer SAL: POB 11-1912, Centre Daher, rue Omar Ben Abd al-Aziz, Hamra, Beirut; tel. (1) 346290; telex 22483; fax (1) 364133; f. 1951; cap. p.u. £L18,000m. (Dec. 1992); Chair. and Gen. Man. Dr NAAMAN AZHARI.

Banque Libanaise pour le Commerce SAL: POB 11-1126, rue Riad Solh, Beirut; tel. (1) 445450; telex 42650; fax (1) 951546; f. 1950; cap. p.u. £L80m., dep. £L129,671.7m., res £L13,098.8m., total assets £L160,863.8m. (Dec. 1991); Chair. and Gen. Man. JEAN F. S. ABOUJAOUDE; 31 brs.

Banque Libano-Française SAL: POB 11-808, Immeuble Sehnaoui, rue Riad Solh, Beirut; tel. (1) 200420; telex 42317; fax (1) 337262; f. 1968; cap. £L5,000m., dep £L891,424m. (Dec. 1992); Chair. FARID RAPHAEL.

Banque de la Méditerranée SAL: POB 11-348, rue Verdun, Ain et-Tine, Beirut; tel. (1) 866925; telex 20826; fax (1) 4782462; f. 1944; cap. £L100m., res £L17,865.4m., dep. £L886,574m., total assets £L979,052m. (Dec. 1992); Chair. and Gen. Man. Dr MUSTAPHA H. RAZIAN.

Banque Misr-Liban SAL: POB 11-7, rue Riad Solh, Beirut; tel. (1) 301575; telex 20537; fax (1) 868490; f. 1929; cap. £L3,000m., dep. £L194,122.3m., res £L6,090.4m. (Dec. 1992); Chair. MOHAMMED ALI HAFEZ; Dep. Chair. and Gen. Man. IBRAHIM NOUR ED-DINE; 14 brs.

Banque Saradar SAL: POB 11-1121, Immeuble Saradar, Rabyé, Beirut; tel. (1) 416804; telex 41806; fax (1) 404490; f. 1948 as Banque Marius Saradar, name changed 1956; cap. £L5,000m., dep. £L355,115.8m. (Dec. 1993); Chair. and Gen. Man. MARIO JOE SARADAR; 6 brs.

Beirut-Riyad Bank SAL: POB 11-4668, Immeuble de la Banque Beirut-Riyad, rue Riad Solh, Beirut; tel. (1) 867360; telex 20610; f. 1959; cap. £L600m., res £L28.9m., dep. £L157,712.2m. (Dec. 1990); Pres. and Gen. Man. HUSSEIN MANSOUR; Dep. Chair. and Man. Dir ANWAR M. EL-KHALIL; 11 brs.

Byblos Bank SAL: POB 11-5605, Centre Commercial Aya, Beirut; tel. (1) 898200; telex 41601; fax (1) 898209; f. 1959; cap. p.u. £L2,772m., dep. £L479,172m., total assets £L567,956m. (Dec. 1992); Chair. and Gen. Man. Dr FRANÇOIS SEMAAN BASSIL; 21 brs.

Crédit Commercial du Moyen-Orient SAL: POB 11-8271, Street No. 4, Rabyé, Beirut; tel. (1) 405950; fax (1) 601957; cap. £L1,000m., res £L2,198m., dep. £L100,854m. (Dec. 1992); Chair. Dr GEORGES ACHI.

Crédit Libanais SAL: POB 166729, Centre Sofil, blvd Fouad Chehab, Beirut; tel. (1) 200028; telex 40706; fax (1) 376807; f. 1961; cap. £L31,000m., dep. £L429,529m. (Dec. 1992); Chair. and Gen. Man. Dr JOSEPH M. TORBEY; 33 brs.

Federal Bank of Lebanon SAL: POB 11-2209, Immeuble Antoine Gebara, Dora, Beirut; tel. (1) 896183; telex 42307; fax (1) 268711; f. 1952; cap. £L10m., dep. £L19,695m. (Dec. 1992); Pres. and Chair. MICHEL A. SAAB; 7 brs.

First Phoenician Bank SAL: POB 90-1160, Centre Montelibano, New Jdeideh, Beirut; tel. (1) 887779; telex 43571; fax (1) 897078; f. 1958; fmrly First National Bank of Chicago (Lebanon) SAL, wholly-owned subsidiary of First National Bank of Chicago, USA, sold Dec. 1982; cap. £L5m., dep. £L3,019.2m. (Dec. 1991); Chair. and Gen. Man. GEORGES M. HATEM.

Fransabank SAL: POB 11-0393, Centre Sabbag, rue Hamra, Hamra, Beirut; tel. (1) 340180; telex 20631; f. 1978 as merger of Banque Sabbag and Banque Française pour le Moyen Orient SAL; cap £L8,800m., res £L6,077.4m., dep. £L650,205.5m. (Dec. 1992); Chair. ADNAN KASSAR; Dep. Chair. ADEL KASSAR; 33 brs.

Intercontinental Bank of Lebanon SAL: POB 90263, Immeuble Ghantous, Beirut; tel. (1) 883464; telex 44423; fax (1) 483119; f. 1961; subsidiary of Continental Bank, Chicago; cap. £L8m., res £L267m. (Dec. 1992); Chair. and Gen. Man. FADY GEORGES AMATOURY.

Jammal Trust Bank SAL: POB 11-5640, Immeuble Jammal, rue Riad Solh, Beirut; tel. (1) 800360; telex 20959; fax (1) 807381; f. 1963 as Investment Bank, SAL; cap. p.u. £L200m., dep. £L20,705.3m. (Dec. 1989); Chair. and Gen. Man. ALI A. JAMMAL.

Lebanese Swiss Bank SAL: POB 11-9552, 57 rue Riad Solh, Beirut; tel. (1) 221720; telex 21072; fax (1) 893497; f. 1973; cap. p.u. £L2,000m., res £L12,187.2m. (Dec. 1992); Chair. and Gen. Man. Dr TANAL SABBAH; 3 brs.

MEBCO Bank—Middle East Banking Co SAL: POB 11–3540, Centre Continental, ave Charles de Gaulle, Beirut; tel. (1) 810600; telex 20729; f. 1959; cap. p.u. £L60m., dep. £L64,408.4m., res £L6,027m., total assets £L83,999.2m. (Dec. 1989); Chair. and Gen. Man. JAWAD CHALABI; 10 brs.

Metropolitan Bank SAL: POB 70216, Immeuble Nihaco, Autostrade Antelias, Beirut; tel. (1) 415824; telex 42130; fax (1) 406861; f. 1979; cap. £L3,000m., res £L14.6m., dep. £L18,564.7m. (Dec. 1990); Chair. and Gen. Man. MERSHED BAAKLINI.

Near East Commercial Bank SAL: POB 16-5766, Immeuble SNA, Place Tabaris, St Maron, Beirut; tel. (1) 200770; telex 41161; fax (1) 422234; f. 1978; cap. p.u. £L1,500m., res £L27.2m., dep. £L37,170m. (Dec. 1993); Chair. and Gen. Man. HABIB J. HAKIM; 3 brs.

North Africa Commercial Bank SAL: POB 11–9575, Centre Piccadilly, rue Hamra, Hamra, Beirut; tel. (1) 370425; telex 21582; fax (1) 346322; f. 1973 as Arab Libyan Tunisian Bank; adopted present name 1989; subsidiary of Libyan Arab Foreign Bank; cap. p.u. £L25m., dep. £L141,537m., res £L404.6m., total assets £L154,765m. (Dec. 1992); Chair. REJEB MISELLATI.

Prosperity Bank of Lebanon SAL: Immeuble Accra, Place des Canons, Beirut; tel. (1) 402211; telex 43355; f. 1963; cap. p.u. £L150m., total assets £L16,104.3m. (Dec. 1988); Pres. and Gen. Man. NAJIB ELIAS CHOUFANI; 7 brs.

Rifbank SAL: POB 11-5727, rue Kantari, Beirut; tel. (1) 362495; telex 22083; fax (1) 4781644; f. 1965; in association with The National Bank of Kuwait SAK, Kuwait Foreign Trading Contracting and Investment Co SAK, The Commercial Bank of Kuwait SAK, Kuwait Investment Co SAK; cap. p.u. £L2,160m., dep. £L124,233m., total assets £L137,417m. (Dec. 1993); Chair. IBRAHIM DABDOUP; Gen. Man. RIAD TAKY; 5 brs..

Société Bancaire du Liban SAL: POB 165192, place Sassine, Achrafiyé, Beirut; tel. (1) 215660; telex 48265; fax (1) 200455; f. 1899; cap. p.u. £L2,200m., dep. £L51,785m., res £L762.3m., total assets £L60,515.2m. (Dec. 1993); Chair. SELIM LEVY; Vice Chair. and Gen. Man. ANDRÉ BOULOS.

Société Générale Libano-Européenne de Banque SAL: POB 11–2955, Rond Point Salomé, Sin el-Fil, Beirut; tel. (1) 499813; telex 44453; fax (1) 512872; f. 1953; cap. p.u. £L1,250m., dep. £L646,968.8m., res £L9,356.7m., total assets £L657,576m. (Dec. 1992); Pres. MAURICE SEHNAOUI; Gen. Man. GÉRARD HANNOTIN; 16 brs.

Société Nouvelle de la Banque de Syrie et du Liban SAL (SNBSL): POB 11-957, rue Riad Solh, Beirut; tel. (1) 405563; telex 44060; fax (1) 405564; f. 1963; cap. p.u. £L350m., res £L2,910.2m., dep. £L125,938.7m. (Dec. 1992); Chair. NADIA EL-KHOURY; Gen. Man. ANTOINE ADM; 22 brs.

Syrian Lebanese Commercial Bank SAL: POB 11-8701, Immeuble Fakhros Darwiche, rue Hamra, Hamra, Beirut; tel. (1) 341261; telex 20853; f. 1974; cap. £L1,250m., res. £L1,484.3m., dep. £L17,420.5m. (Dec. 1991); Gen. Man. MOHAMMED EL-KASSEM.

Transorient Bank SAL: POB 11–6260, Bauchrieh, rue Serail, Beirut; tel. (1) 881198; telex 44925; fax (1) 897705; f. 1966; cap. p.u. £L6,095m., dep. £L135,404.5m., res £L17m., total assets £L157,209.3m. (Dec. 1993); joint venture with Lebanese private investors; Chair. ADIB S. MILLET; Gen. Man. GABRIEL M. ATALLAH; 8 brs.

United Bank of Lebanon & Pakistan SAL: POB 11–5600, Centre TAYAR, Sin el-Fil, Beirut; tel. (1) 499776; telex 20823; f. 1964; cap. £L600m., dep. £L16,485m. (Dec. 1989); Chair. SAEB JAROUDI; Vice-Chair. ANIS YASSINE.

Universal Bank SAL: POB 217, Immeuble Unigroup, Place Sayyad, Hazmieh, Beirut; tel. (1) 429603; telex 43404; fax (1) 429312; f. 1978; cap. p.u. £L1,000m., dep. £L102,000m. (Dec. 1993); Chair. and Gen. Man. GEORGE H. HADDAD.

Wedge Bank Middle East SAL: POB 16-5852, Centre Sofil, ave Charles Malek, Achrafiyé, Beirut; tel. (1) 201182; telex 43570; fax (1) 201184; f. 1983; cap. £L215m., dep. £L45.1m. (Dec. 1993); Chair. MICHEL I. FARES.

Development Banks

Banque Nationale pour le Développement Industriel et Touristique SAL: POB 11-8412, Immeuble Concorde, rue Rashid Karame, Beirut; tel. (1) 861990; telex 23086; f. 1973; cap. £L1,518m., res £L467m. (Dec. 1993); Chair. and Gen. Man. Dr OMAR HALABLAB.

INFIBANK SAL: POB 16–5110, ave Fouad Chehab, St Nicolas, Beirut; tel. (1) 200951; telex 42297; f. 1974 as Investment and Finance Bank; medium- and long-term loans, 100% from Lebanese sources; owned by Banque Audi SAL (99.5%); cap. £L300m., res £L594,679m., dep. £L193,538.1m., total assets £L201,993.6m. (Dec. 1993); Chair. and Gen. Man. RAYMOND WADIH AUDI.

Principal Foreign Banks

Algemene Bank Nederland NV (Netherlands): POB 113–5162, Beirut; tel. (1) 362821; telex 43984; cap. £L5m., res £L76.9m., dep. £L21,255m. (Dec. 1989); Man. Dir. E. NAHAS.

American Express Bank (USA): POB 113–5160, Centre Mirna Chalouhi, rue Sin el-Fil, Beirut; tel. (1) 480048; telex 21759; fax (1) 4783589; cap. £L15m., res £L2.8m., dep. £L14,380.6m. (Dec. 1989); Gen. Man. GABY KASSIS.

Arab African International Bank (Egypt): POB 11–6066, Centre Ivoire, rue Commodore, Beirut; tel. (1) 350360; telex 22758; cap. £L25m., res £L2.1m., dep. £L3,205.7m. (Dec. 1989); Chief. Gen. Man. HUSSAIN B. ALDARWICHE.

Arab Bank plc (Jordan): POB 11–1015, rue Riad Solh, Beirut; tel. (1) 643412; telex 22893; fax (1) 868130; f. 1930; cap. and res £L4,775m., dep. £L961,741m., total assets £L1,017,157m.; Regional Man. Dr HISHAM BSAT.

Banco di Roma SpA (Italy): POB 11–968, Immeuble Borj el-Ghazal, place Tabaris, ave Fouad Chehab, Beirut; tel. (1) 335445; telex 42091; fax (1) 897958; cap. £L3,296.3m., dep. £L115,351m. (Dec. 1993); brs in Saida and Tripoli; Gen. Man. FRANCO MORETTI.

Bank Saderat Iran (Iran): POB 113-6717, Immeuble Sabbagh et Daaboul, rue Hamra, Hamra, Beirut; tel. (1) 866860; telex 20738; fax (1) 866860; cap. £L32.5m., res £L20.8m., dep. £L1,365.5m. (Dec. 1989); Gen. Man. ALI AKBAR KAZEMI.

Banque Nationale de Paris Intercontinentale SA (France): POB 11–1608, rue de l'Archevêché Orthodoxe, Sursock, Beirut; tel. (1) 444389; telex 41401; fax (1) 200604; f. 1944; cap. £L157.1m., dep. £L118,620m. (Dec. 1989); 4 brs in Lebanon; Gen. Man. HENRI TYAN.

British Bank of the Middle East (Hong Kong): POB 90408, Immeuble Ghantous, Autostrade Dora, Beirut; tel. (1) 894300; telex 40462; f. 1946; cap. p.u. £L50m., res £L189.1m., dep. £L64,859.7m. (Dec. 1989); brs at Ras Beirut, Dora, Jounieh and Tripoli; Lebanon Area Man. C. CHONEIRY.

Chase Manhattan Bank NA (USA): POB 11–3684, rue Riad Solh, Beirut; tel. (1) 368460; telex 20357; cap. £L5m., dep. £L30.4m., total assets £L742.2m.; Vice-Pres. and Gen. Man. ELIE WAKIM.

Citibank NA (USA): POB 11–3648, Immeuble Zard Zard, rue Jounieh, Beirut; tel. (1) 413222; telex 22029; cap. £L5m., dep. £L5m., res £L1.5m., total assets £L774.4m.; Resident Vice-Pres. ANTOINE BOUSTANY.

Habib Bank (Overseas) Ltd (Pakistan): POB 5616, Centre Sabbag, rue Hamra, Hamra, Beirut; tel. (1) 340215; telex 20873; cap. £L5m., dep. £L1,002m. (Dec. 1989); Sr Vice-Pres. and Man. MASOOD ALAM.

Jordan National Bank SA: POB 5186, Immeuble Sehnaoui, rue Banque du Liban, Hamra, Beirut; tel. (1) 340451; telex 20512; fax (1) 353185; cap. £L2,171m., dep. £L46,586m. (Dec. 1993); Tripoli and Saida; Regional Gen. Man. Dr ABED H. BARBIR.

Moscow Narodny Bank Ltd (UK): rue de Rome, Hamra, Beirut; cap. £L5m., res £L8.1m., total assets £L32.7m. (Dec. 1985); Asst. Gen. Man. S. MAKKOUK.

Saudi National Commercial Bank (Saudi Arabia): POB 11-2355, Al-Kaaki Bldg, Sakiet al-Janzir, Beirut; tel. (1) 809353; telex 43619; fax (1) 867728; cap. £L6,625m., total assets £L66,224m. (Dec. 1992); Man. ABDULLAH HASSAN ABDAT.

Numerous foreign banks have representative offices in Beirut.

Banking Association

Association des Banques du Liban: POB 80536, Centre Moucarri, Autostrade Dora, Beirut; tel. (1) 582346; telex 43069; f. 1959; serves and promotes the interests of the banking community in Lebanon; mems: 79 banks and 11 banking rep. offices; Pres. RAYMOND AUDI; Gen. Sec. Dr MAKRAM SADER.

INSURANCE

In 1985 110 insurance companies (58 national, 52 foreign) were registered in Lebanon, but a large number were not operating. The total number of companies that conducted operations in 1984 was 67 (46 Lebanese, 21 foreign).

Arabia Insurance Co Ltd SAL: POB 11–2172, rue de Phénicie, Beirut; tel. (1) 363610; telex 40060; fax (1) 365139; f. 1944; Chair. and Gen. Man. BADR S. FAHOUM.

Commercial Insurance Co SAL: POB 84, Jounieh; tel. (9) 917169; telex 45994; fax (9) 917214; f. 1962; Chair. MAX R. ZACCAR.

Compagnie Libanaise d'Assurances SAL: POB 3685, rue Riad Solh, Beirut; tel. (1) 868988; telex 20379; f. 1951; cap. p.u. £L3,000m. (1991); Chair. JEAN F. S. ABOUJAOUDÉ; Gen. Man. MAMDOUH RAHMOUN.

Al-Ittihad al-Watani: POB 1270, Immeuble Al-Ittihadia, ave Fouad Chehab, St Nicolas, Beirut; tel. (1) 330840; telex 20839; f. 1947; cap. £L30m.; Chair. JOE I. KAIROUZ; Exec. Dir TANNOUS FEGHALI.

Al-Mashrek Insurance and Reinsurance SAL: POB 16-6154, Immeuble Amir, 65 rue Aabrine, Beirut; tel. (1) 200541; telex 43244; fax (1) 888078; f. 1962; cap. (auth. and p.u.) £L500m., (1992); Chair. and Gen. Man. ABRAHAM MATOSSIAN.

Libano-Suisse Insurance Co SAL: Immeuble Cité Dora, Dora, Beirut; tel. (1) 890439; telex 43766; f. 1959; cap. £L405m. (1991);

Pres. and Gen. Man. MICHEL PIERRE PHARAON; Man. Lebanon Branch NAJI HABIS.

'La Phénicienne' SAL: POB 11-5652, Immeuble Hanna Haddad, rue Amine Gemayel, Sioufi, Beirut; tel. (1) 425484; telex 42357; fax (1) 424532; f. 1964; Chair. and Gen. Man. TANNOUS C. FEGHALI.

Trade and Industry

DEVELOPMENT ORGANIZATION

Council for Development and Reconstruction: POB 116-5351, Tallet es-Serail, Beirut; f. 1976; aimed to achieve reconstruction after 1975–76 civil war, subsequently engaged in repairs to damage caused by inter-communal fighting; central tendering committee for the world's largest construction programme in any one city; acts on behalf of the Cabinet, reporting directly to the Prime Minister; Chair. FADL ALI SHALAQ.

CHAMBERS OF COMMERCE AND INDUSTRY

Beirut Chamber of Commerce and Industry: POB 11-1801, Sanayeh, Beirut; tel. (1) 349530; telex 22269; fax (1) 865802; f. 1898; 32,000 mems; Pres. ADNAN KASSAR; Dir-Gen. Dr MOHI ED-DIN KAISSI.

Tripoli Chamber of Commerce and Industry: POB 27, blvd Tripoli, Tripoli; tel. 622790; telex 46024; Pres. HASSAN EL-MOUNLA.

Chamber of Commerce and Industry in Sidon and South Lebanon: POB 41, rue Maarouf Saad, Sidon; tel. 720123; telex 20402; fax 722986; f. 1933; Pres. MOHAMAD ZAATARI.

Zahleh Chamber of Commerce and Industry: POB 100, Zahleh; tel. (8) 802602; telex 48042; fax (8) 800050; f. 1939; 2,350 mems; Pres. EDMOND JREISSATI.

EMPLOYERS' ASSOCIATION

Association of Lebanese Industrialists: POB 1520, Chamber of Commerce and Industry, rue Justinian St, Beirut; Pres. JACQUES SARRAF.

TRADE UNION FEDERATION

Confédération Générale des Travailleurs du Liban (CGTL): POB 4381, Beirut; f. 1958; 300,000 mems; only national labour centre in Lebanon and sole rep. of working classes; comprises 18 affiliated federations including all 150 unions in Lebanon; Chair. ELIAS ABU RIZQ.

MAJOR INDUSTRIAL COMPANIES

Arabian Construction Co Group: POB 11-6876, 1st Floor, Sucam Bldg, Ain al-Tineh, Beirut, Beirut; tel. (1) 861962; telex 20385; f. 1971; construction of multi-storey buildings, hotels, houses, etc.; cap. p.u. $1m.; Chair. GHASSAN ABDALLAH AL-MEREHBI; Man. Dirs TAHA MIKATI, ANAS MIKATI; 1,500 employees.

Caves de Ksara: General Fouad Chehab Ave, POB 16-6184, Beirut; tel. (1) 200715; telex 41456; f. 1857; wines and spirits (incl. Ksarak); Pres. ZAFER CHAOUI; Gen. Man. CHARLES GHOSTINE; 75 employees.

Contracting and Trading Co (CAT): CAT Bldg, el-Arz St, Saifi Quarter, POB 11-1036, Beirut; tel. (1) 1449910; telex 44275; f. 1942; civil, mechanical and electrical engineering, pipeline and marine works contractors; sales £L36.7m. (1984); cap. p.u. £L5m.; total assets £L238.6m.; Man. Partners SHOUKRI H. SHAMMAS, Mrs LAURA BUSTANI, Mrs NADIA EL-KHOURY; 5,000 employees.

Filature Nationale de Coton SAL, Asseily & Cie: Immeuble Asseily, place Riad es-Solh, POB 11-4126, Beirut; tel. (1) 890610; telex 20018; production of textiles; Dir. G. ASSEILY.

Fonderies Ohannes H. Kassardjian SAL: POB 11-4150, Beirut; tel. (1) 464645; telex 44062; fax (1) 464645; f. 1939; production of bronze, brass and chromium-plated bathroom fixtures, cast iron pipes, manhole covers, sluice valves, etc.; Chair. OHANNES H. KASSARDJIAN; Pres. JOSEPH O. KASSARDJIAN; 675 employees.

Al-Hamra Engineering Co SAL: POB 116040, Beirut; tel. (1) 340640; telex 22211; f. 1966; part of the Al-Hamra Group; construction work on industrial projects, airports, hospitals, housing schemes, reservoirs, power stations, etc.; sales US $75m. (1981/82); cap. p.u. $4.8m.; total assets $70m.; Chair. Y. AL-HAMAD; Gen. Man. MUNIR SHALHOUB; 600 employees.

Industrial Development Co SARL (INDEVCO): Tabbara Bldg, Dora Roundabout, POB 11-2354, Beirut; tel. (1) 217530; telex 45736; f. 1963; mfrs of pulp and paper, corrugated containers, folding cartons, multi-wall sacks, aluminium foil, diapers, sanitary towels; polyethylene and agrifilm extrusion, injection moulding, tissue converting; sales US $266.8m. (1987); Chair. GEORGES FREM; 2,732 employees (Lebanon, Saudi Arabia, Brazil and the USA).

Karoun Dairies SAL: Baghdassarian Bldg, Bauchrieh Industrial City, POB 11-9150, Beirut; tel. (1) 497080; f. 1931; dairy products; Chair. and Gen. Man. ARA BAGHDASSARIAN.

Lahoud Engineering Co Ltd: POB 55366, ave Charles de Gaulle, Sin el-Fil, Beirut; tel. (1) 424828; telex 40469; fax (1) 496540; construction of industrial plants.

Mothercat Ltd: POB 11-1036, Beirut; tel. (1) 449910; telex 44275; f. 1963; civil, mechanical and electrical engineering, pipeline, storage tanks and marine works contractors; sales £L55.2m. (1984); cap. p.u. £L5m.; total assets £L101.4m.; Chair. Mrs LAURA BUSTANI; Man. Dir SHUKRI H. SHAMMAS; 3,000 employees.

Société Industrielle des Produits Pioneer-Jabre SAL: POB 369, Beirut; tel. (1) 395053; telex 20988; f. 1874; production of wafers, chocolates, halva, pasta, biscuits, confectionery, cartons, tins; Chair. EDWARD NASSAR; 250 employees.

Zahrani Oil Installations: POB 11-1925, Beirut; tel. (1) 345702; telex 20442; oil refining; Gen. Man. G. A. AHMAD; 300 employees.

Transport

RAILWAYS

Office des Chemins de Fer de l'Etat Libanais et du Transport en Commun de Beyrouth et de sa Banlieue: POB 109, Souk el-Arwam, Beirut; tel. (1) 443619; telex 43088; since 1961 all railways in Lebanon have been state-owned. Of the original network of some 412 km, no lines were known to be working in early 1994; in March 1994 tenders were invited for the reconstruction of the coastal line between Tyre-Beirut-Tripoli; Pres. RABIH AMMASH.

ROADS

Lebanon has 7,100 km of roads, of which 1,990 km are main roads. Most are generally good by Middle Eastern standards. The two international motorways are the north–south coastal road and the road connecting Beirut with Damascus in Syria. Among the major roads are that crossing the Beka'a and continuing south to Bent-Jbail and the Shtaura–Baalbek road. Hard-surfaced roads connect Jezzine with Moukhtara, Bzebdine with Metn, Meyroub with Afka and Tannourine.

SHIPPING

A two-phase programme to rehabilitate the port of Beirut is currently under way. In the first phase a new breakwater and a fourth basin are to be constructed, damaged and stolen equipment replaced and a new container area constructed, at an estimated cost of US $126m. In the second phase, due to commence in 1996, the construction of an industrial free zone, a fifth basin and a major container terminal are envisaged, at an estimated cost of $1,000m. The port of Beirut is currently administered by a 12-member committee appointed by the Cabinet, but its future status remains to be decided. Tripoli, the northern Mediterranean terminus of the oil pipeline from Iraq (the other is Haifa, Israel—not in use since 1948), is also a busy port, with good equipment and facilities. Jounieh, north of Beirut, is Lebanon's third most important port. Saida is still relatively unimportant as a port. The reconstructed port of an-Naqoura, in the South Lebanon Army-occupied security zone along the border with Israel, was inaugurated in June 1987.

Siège Provisoire de la Commission Portuaire: Immeuble de l'Electricité du Liban, rue du Fleuve, Beirut.

There are many shipping companies and agents in Beirut. The following are some of the largest:

'Adriatica' di Nav. SpAN: POB 11-1472, rue du Port, Immeuble Ras, Beirut; tel. (1) 580181; telex 44875; Gen. Man. J. WEHBE.

Ameaster Tanker Services: a division of American Lebanese Shipping Co SAL, POB 113-5388, Beirut; tel. (1) 354827; telex 20863; Pres. PAUL PARATORE; Man. N. BALTAGI.

American Levant Shipping & Distributing Co: POB 11-2736, Immeuble Andalusia, Gourand St, Gemmayze, Beirut; agents for: Holland America Line, Lykes Bros Steamship Co; correspondents throughout Middle East: Man. Dir SAMIR ISHAK.

Arab Shipping and Chartering Co: POB 1084, Beirut; tel. (1) 866386; telex 20768; agents for China National Chartering Corpn, China Ocean Shipping Co.

Barrad Shipping Co SAL: POB 181, Beirut; refrigerated tramp services; 3 cargo reefer vessels; Chair. P. H. HELOU.

O. D. Debbas & Sons: Head Office: POB 166678, Immeuble Debbas, Corniche du Fleuve Blvd, Beirut; tel. (1) 585253; telex 44651; fax (1) 602515; f. 1892; Man. Dir OIDIH ELIE DEBBAS.

Ets Derviche Y. Haddad: POB 11-42, rue Derviche Haddad, Beirut; tel. (1) 447879; telex 44987; fax (1) 447875; agents for: Armement Deppe, Antwerp and Compagnie Maritime Belge, Antwerp.

Fauzi Jemil Ghandour: POB 1084, Beirut; tel. (1) 866386; telex 20711; agents for: Denizçlik Bankasi TAO (Denizyollari), DB Deniz Nakliyati TAŞ (Dbcargo), Iraqi Maritime Transport Co, United Arab Shipping Co.

T. Gargour & Fils: POB 110–371, Garage Mercedes, Dora, Beirut; tel. (1) 899775; telex 43994; f. 1928; agents for: Assoc. Levant Lines SAL; Dirs NICOLAS T. GARGOUR, HABIB T. GARGOUR.

General United Trading and Shipping Co SARL: POB 36, Tripoli; tel. (6) 600530; telex 23889; 6 cargo vessels.

Henry Heald & Co SAL: POB 64, Beirut; tel. (1) 893184; telex 42364; temporary address: c/o Orphanides and Murat, POB 24, Larnaca, Cyprus; f. 1837; agents for: Nippon Yusen Kaisha, P. & O. Group, Swedish Orient Line, Finncarriers, Niver Lines, Greek South America Lines, Nordana, Shipping Corpn of India, Vanderzee Shipping Agency; Chair. J. L. JOLY; Dir H. JOLY.

Hitti Frères: POB 511, rue de Phénicie, Beirut; airlines and shipping agents.

Mediterranean Maritime Co SAL: POB 165658, Immeuble de la Bourse, rue Hoyek, Beirut; tel. (1) 249655; telex 42403; 1 tanker, 1 cargo vessel; managers for National Maritime Agencies Co W.LL., Kuwait.

Mena Shipping and Tourist Agency: POB 11–884, rue el Arz, Beirut; telex 20670; 5 cargo vessels; Man. Dir W. LEHETA.

Rassem Trading: POB 11–8460, Immeuble Shams, ave du Général de Gaulle, Raoucheh, Beirut; tel. (1) 866372; telex 21719; fax (1) 515485; 5 livestock transportation vessels, 3 general cargo vessels; Dirs F. R. W. MOUKAHAL, A. H. ZEIDO.

Rodolphe Saadé & Co SAL: POB 16–6526, Immeuble BUROTEC, rue Pasteur, Beirut; tel. (1) 583313; telex 41120; fax (1) 583319; agents for CMA, R. Farrell Lines; f. 1964; Travel Office: POB 11–2279, Union Bldg, Spears St, Beirut; tel. (1) 342047; telex 48396; fax (1) 346985; Pres. JACQUES R. SAADÉ.

G. Sahyouni & Co SAL: POB 175452, Immeuble Hafiz el-Hashem, Pont Karantina, Corniche an-Nahr, Beirut; tel. (1) 582601; telex 41322; fax (1) 582601; f. 1989; agents for Lloyd's, Pand OCL and Baltic Control; Financial Man. HENRY CHIDIAC; Man. Dir. GEORGE SAHYOUNI.

Union Shipping and Chartering Agency: POB 1084, Beirut; tel. (1) 866386; telex 20768; agents for Jugolinija (Rijeka), Jadroslobodna, Jugo Oceania, Atlanska Plovidba, Jadrolinija, Mediteranska Plovidba, Slobodna Plovidba.

CIVIL AVIATION

Services from the country's principal airport, in Beirut, were subject to frequent disruptions after 1975; its location in predominantly Muslim west Beirut made it virtually inaccessible to non-Muslims. In 1986 a new airport, based on an existing military airfield, was opened at Halat, north of Beirut, by Christian concerns, but commercial operations from the airport were not authorized by the Government. Services to and from Beirut by Middle East Airlines (MEA) were suspended, and the airport closed, at the end of January 1987, after the Christian LF militia shelled the airport and threatened to attack MEA aircraft if services from their own airport, at Halat, did not receive official authorization. Beirut airport was reopened in May, after the LF accepted government assurances that Halat would receive the necessary authorization for civil use. However, the commission concluded that Halat did not possess the facilities to cater for international air traffic.

MEA (Middle East Airlines, Air Liban SAL): POB 206, Immeuble MEA, blvd de l'Aéroport, Beirut; tel. (1) 316316; telex 20820; f. 1945; took over Lebanese International Airways in 1969; regular services throughout Europe, the Middle East, North and West Africa and the Far East; Chair. ABD AL-HAMID FAKHOURI; Man. Dir YOUSUF LAHOUD.

Trans-Mediterranean Airways SAL (TMA): Beirut International Airport, POB 11–3018, Beirut; tel. (1) 820550; telex 20637; f. 1953; worldwide cargo services between Europe, the Middle East, South-East Asia, the Far East and the USA; Chair. CHAFIC MOHARRAM.

Tourism

Before the civil war, Lebanon was a major tourist centre, and its scenic beauty, sunny climate and historic sites attracted some 2m. visitors annually. In 1974 tourism contributed about 20% of the country's income. Since the end of the civil conflict tourist facilities, in particular hotels, have begun to be reconstructed, and the Arab Tourist Organization has designated 1994 as the International Year of Tourism in Lebanon.

Ministry of Tourism: Beirut; f. 1966; official organization; Head of International Relations and Conventions Dept ANTOINE ACCAOUI; Head of Speleological Service SAMI KARKABI.

National Council of Tourism in Lebanon (CNTL): POB 11–5344, rue Banque du Liban, Beirut; tel. (1) 864532; telex 20898; taken over by Board of Foreign Economic Relations in 1983; re-established as a separate body 1985; government-sponsored autonomous organization responsible for the promotion of tourism; overseas offices in London, Paris, Brussels, Rome, Iraq and Cairo; Pres. SAMY MAROUN; Dir-Gen. NASSER SAFIEDDINE.

Defence

Commander-in-Chief of the Armed Forces: Gen. EMILE LAHUD (Maronite Christian).

Chief of Staff of Armed Forces: Maj.-Gen. ABU DIRGHAM (Druze).

Commander of the Air Force: Brig.-Gen. FAHIM AL-HAJJ.

Director-General of the Internal Security Forces: Brig.-Gen. UMAR MAKHZUMI (Shi'ite) (acting).

Total armed forces (June 1994): 44,300: army (estimated) 43,000; air force (estimated) 800; navy 500.

There is also an internal security force of some 13,000 (under reorganization), attached to the Ministry of the Interior. The strengths of the principal sectarian militias (before they, with the exception of Hezbollah, began to disband in March 1991) were estimated as follows: Lebanese Forces (Christian) 18,500 regulars (16,500 reserves); Druze 8,500 regulars (6,500 reserves); Amal (Shi'ite) 10,200 regulars (4,800 reserves); Hezbollah (Shi'ite) 3,500 regulars (11,500 reserves). The Israeli-backed South Lebanon Army, patrolling the buffer zone along the border with Israel, numbered an estimated 2,500. In March 1978 a 6,000-strong UN Interim Force in Lebanon (UNIFIL), (increased to 7,000 in February 1982 but numbering some 5,200 in June 1993), was deployed to try to keep the peace near the border with Israel. An estimated 30,000 Syrian troops remain in Lebanon.

Education

Education is not compulsory. Primary education has been available free of charge in state schools since 1960, but private institutions still provide the main facilities for secondary and university education. Private schools enjoy almost complete autonomy, except for a certain number which receive government financial aid and are supervised by inspectors from the Ministry of National Education.

Primary education begins at six years of age and lasts for five years. It is followed either by the four-year intermediate course or the three-year secondary course. The baccalaureate examination is taken in two parts at the end of the second and third years of secondary education, and a public examination is taken at the end of the intermediate course. Technical education is provided mainly at the National School of Arts and Crafts, which offers four-year course in electronics, mechanics, architectural and industrial drawing, and other subjects. There are also public vocational schools providing courses for lower levels.

Higher education is provided by 12 institutions, including six universities. Lebanon's newest university, the Notre Dame University of Louaize, run by the Maronite order of Louaize, was opened in mid-1988. Teacher training is given at various levels. A three-year course which follows the intermediate course trains primary school teachers and another three-year course which follows the second part of the baccalaureate trains teachers for the intermediate school. Secondary school teachers are trained at the Higher Teachers' College at the Lebanese University. Two agricultural schools provide a three-year course for pupils holding the intermediate school degree.

Bibliography

Abouchdid, E. E. *Thirty Years of Lebanon and Syria (1917–47).* Beirut, 1948.

Agwani, M. S. (Ed.). *The Lebanese Crisis, 1958: a documentary study.* Asia Publishing House, 1965.

Ajami, Fouad. *The Vanished Imam: Musa al-Sadr and the Shi'a of Lebanon.* London, I.B. Tauris; New York, Cornell University Press, 1986.

Atiyah, E. *An Arab tells his Story.* London, 1946.

The Beirut Massacre: the complete Kahan Commission Report. New York, Karz-Cohl, 1983.

Besoins et Possibilités de Développement du Liban. Étude Préliminaire, 2 Vols. Lebanese Ministry of Planning, Beirut, 1964.

Binder, Leonard (Ed.). *Politics in Lebanon.* New York, Wiley, 1966.

Bulloch, John. *Death of a Country: The Civil War in Lebanon.* London, Weidenfeld and Nicolson, 1977.

    Final Conflict: The War in Lebanon. London, Century Publishing Co.

Burckhard, C. *Le Mandat Français en Syrie et au Liban.* Paris, 1925.

Catroux, G. *Dans la Bataille de Méditerranée.* Paris, Julliard, 1949.

Chamoun, C. *Les Mémoires de Camille Chamoun.* Beirut, 1949.

Fisk, Robert. *Pity the Nation: Lebanon at War.* London, André Deutsch, 1990.

France, Ministère des Affaires Etrangères. *Rapport sur la Situation de la Syrie et du Liban.* Paris, annually, 1924–39.

Gaunson, A. B. *The Anglo-French Clash in Lebanon and Syria, 1940–45.* London, Macmillan, 1987.

Ghattas, Emile. *The monetary system in the Lebanon.* New York 1961.

Giannou, Chris. *Besieged: a doctor's story of life and death in Beirut.* Toronto, Key Porter, 1990.

Gilmour, David. *Lebanon: the Fractured Country.* London, Martin Robertson, 1983.

Glass, Charles. *Tribes with Flags: A Journey Curtailed.* London, Secker and Warburg, 1990.

Gulick, John. *Social Structure and Culture Change in a Lebanese Village.* New York, 1955.

Haddad, J. *Fifty Years of Modern Syria and Lebanon.* Beirut, 1950.

Halawi, Majed. *A Lebanon Defied: Mosa al-Sadr and the Shi'a community.* Oxford, Westview Press, 1993.

Harik, Iliya F. *Politics and Change in a Traditional Society— Lebanon 1711–1845.* Princeton University Press, 1968.

Hepburn, A. H. *Lebanon.* New York, 1966.

Himadeh, Raja S. *The Fiscal System of Lebanon.* Beirut, Khayat, 1961.

Hitti, Philip K. *Lebanon in History.* 3rd edn, London, Macmillan, 1967.

Hourani, Albert K. *Syria and Lebanon.* London, 1946.

Hudson, Michael C. *The Precarious Republic: Political Modernization in the Lebanon.* New York, Random House, 1968.

Kapeliouk, Amnon. *Sabra et Chatila: enquête sur un massacre.* Paris, Editions du Seuil.

Longrigg, S. H. *Syria and Lebanon under French Mandate.* Oxford University Press, 1958.

Mills, Arthur E. *Private Enterprise in Lebanon.* American University of Beirut, 1959.

Puaux, G. *Deux Années au Levant; souvenirs de Syrie et du Liban.* Paris, Hachette, 1952.

Qubain, Fahim I. *Crisis in Lebanon.* Washington, DC, Middle East Institute, 1961.

Randal, Jonathan. *The Tragedy of Lebanon.* London, Chatto and Windus, 1983.

Rondot, Pierre. *Les Institutions Politiques du Liban.* Paris, 1947.

Saba, Elias S. *The Foreign Exchange Systems of Lebanon and Syria.* American University of Beirut, 1961.

Safa, Elie. *L'Emigration Libanaise.* Beirut, 1960.

Salibi, K. S. *The Modern History of Lebanon.* New York, Praeger, and London, Weidenfeld and Nicolson, 1964.

    Cross Roads to Civil War: Lebanon 1958–76. New York, Caravan Books, 1976.

Sayigh, Y. A. *Entrepreneurs of Lebanon.* Cambridge, Mass., 1962.

Stewart, Desmond. *Trouble in Beirut.* London, Wingate, 1959.

Suleiman, M. W. *Political Parties in Lebanon.* Ithaca, NY, Cornell University Press, 1967.

Sykes, John. *The Mountain Arabs.* London, Hutchinson, 1968.

Tibawi, A. L. *A Modern History of Greater Syria, including Lebanon and Palestine.* London, Macmillan, 1969.

Vallaud, Pierre. *Le Liban au Bout du Fusil.* Paris, Librairie Hachette, 1976.

Zarmi, Meir. *The Foundation of Modern Lebanon.* London, Croom Helm, 1985.

Ziadeh, Nicola. *Syria and Lebanon.* New York, Praeger, 1957.

LIBYA

(THE GREAT SOCIALIST PEOPLE'S LIBYAN ARAB JAMAHIRIYA)

Physical and Social Geography

W. B. FISHER

The Great Socialist People's Libyan Arab Jamahiriya (as Libya has been known since April 1986) is bounded on the north by the Mediterranean Sea, on the east by Egypt and Sudan, on the south and south-west by Chad and Niger, on the west by Algeria, and on the north-west by Tunisia. The three component areas of Libya are: Tripolitania, in the west, with an area of 285,000 sq km (110,000 sq miles); Cyrenaica, in the east, area 905,000 sq km (350,000 sq miles); and the Fezzan, in the south, area 570,000 sq km (220,000 sq miles)—total for Libya, 1,760,000 sq km (680,000 sq miles). The independence of Libya was proclaimed in December 1951; before that date, following conquest from the Italians, Tripolitania and Cyrenaica had been ruled by a British administration, at first military, then civil; and the Fezzan had been administered by France. The revolutionary Government which came to power in September 1969 renamed the three regions: Tripolitania became known as the Western provinces, Cyrenaica the Eastern provinces, and the Fezzan the Southern provinces.

The political and economic capital of Libya is Tripoli. However, as part of a radical government decentralization programme undertaken in September 1988, all but two of the secretariats of the General People's Committee (ministries) were relocated in other parts of the country.

PHYSICAL FEATURES

The whole of Libya may be said to form part of the vast plateau of North Africa, which extends from the Atlantic Ocean to the Red Sea; but there are certain minor geographical features which give individuality to the three component areas of Libya. Tripolitania consists of a series of regions of different levels, rising in the main towards the south, and thus broadly comparable with a flight of steps. In the extreme north, along the Mediterranean coast, there is a low-lying coastal plain called the Jefara. This is succeeded inland by a line of hills, or rather a scarp edge, that has several distinguishing local names, but is usually alluded to merely as the Jebel. Here and there in the Jebel occur evidences of former volcanic activity—old craters, and sheets of lava. The Jefara and adjacent parts of the Jebel are by far the most important parts of Tripolitania, since they are better watered and contain most of the population, together with the capital town, Tripoli.

South of the Jebel there is an upland plateau—a dreary desert landscape of sand, scrub, and scattered irregular masses of stone. After several hundred km the plateau gives place to a series of east-west running depressions, where artesian water, and hence oases, are found. These depressions make up the region of the Fezzan, which is merely a collection of oases on a fairly large scale, interspersed with areas of desert. In the extreme south the land rises considerably to form the mountains of the central Sahara, where some peaks reach 3,500 m in height.

Cyrenaica has a slightly different physical pattern. In the north, along the Mediterranean, there is an upland plateau that rises to 600 m in two very narrow steps, each only a few km wide. This gives a bold prominent coastline to much of Cyrenaica, and so there is a marked contrast with Tripolitania where the coast is low-lying, and in parts fringed by lagoons. The northern uplands of Cyrenaica are called the Jebel Akhdar (Green Mountain), and here, once again, are found the bulk of the population and the two main towns, Benghazi and Derna. On its western side the Jebel Akhdar drops fairly steeply to the shores of the Gulf of Sirte; but on the east it falls more gradually, and is traceable as a series of ridges, about 100m

in altitude, that extend as far as the Egyptian frontier. This eastern district, consisting of low ridges aligned parallel to the coast, is known as Marmarica, and its chief town is Tobruk.

South of the Jebel Akhdar, the land falls in elevation, producing an extensive lowland, which except for its northern fringe, is mainly desert. Here and there occur a few oases—Aujila (or Ojila), Jalo and Jaghbub in the north; and Jawf, Zighen and Kufra (the largest of all) in the south. These oases traditionally supported only a few thousand inhabitants and were less significant than those of the Fezzan, though some are now in petroleum-producing areas and, consequently, increasing in importance. In the same region, and becoming more widespread towards the east, is the Sand Sea—an expanse of fine, mobile sand, easily lifted by the wind into dunes that can sometimes reach about 100 m in height and more than 150 km in length. Finally, in the far south of Cyrenaica, lie the central Saharan mountains—the Tibesti Ranges, continuous with those to the south of the Fezzan.

The climate of Libya is characterized chiefly by its aridity and by its wide variation in temperatures. Lacking mountain barriers, the country is open to influences both from the Sahara and from the Mediterranean Sea, and, as a result, there can be abrupt transitions from one kind of weather to another. In winter it can be fairly raw and cold in the north, with sleet and even light snow on the hills. In summer it is extremely hot in the Jefara of Tripolitania, reaching temperatures of 40°C–45°C. In the southern deserts, conditions are hotter still. Garian once (incorrectly) claimed the world record in temperature, but figures of over 49°C are known. Several feet of snow can also fall here in winter. Northern Cyrenaica has a markedly cooler summer of 27°C–32°C, but with high air humidity near the coast. A special feature is the *ghibli*—a hot, very dry wind from the south that can raise temperatures in the north by 15°C or even 20°C in a few hours, sometimes giving figures of 20°C or 25°C in January. This sand-laden, dry wind may blow at any time of the year, but spring and autumn are the usual seasons. Considerable damage is done to growing crops, and the effect even on human beings is often marked.

The hills of Tripolitania and Cyrenaica annually receive as much as 400 mm to 500 mm of rainfall, but in the remainder of the country the amount is 200 mm or less. A special difficulty is that once in every five or six years there is a pronounced drought, sometimes lasting for two successive seasons. Actual falls of rain can also be erratic.

ECONOMIC LIFE

Such conditions imposed severe restriction on all forms of economic activity. Although petroleum was discovered in considerable quantities in Libya, physical and climatic conditions made exploitation difficult and, until the closing of the Suez Canal in 1967, the remote situation of the country, away from the currents of international trade, was a further handicap. However, production of crude petroleum increased rapidly and proximity to southern and central Europe presented a considerable advantage (no Suez dues) that was reflected in the price. The introduction of petroleum revenues transformed the economic situation of Libya. Extensive development has been in progress, with the aim of improving housing, and the fostering of industries to produce consumer goods. Roads, electricity, better water supplies, telecommunications links and reorganized town planning are in the process of being achieved, and a number of sizeable industrial plants are under construction.

In the better-watered areas of the Jefara and, to a smaller extent, in northern Cyrenaica, there is cultivation of barley, wheat, olives and Mediterranean fruit.

The Fezzan and the smaller oases in Cyrenaica are almost rainless, and cultivation depends entirely upon irrigation from wells. Millet is the chief crop, and there are several million date palms, which provide the bulk of the food. Small quantities of vegetables and fruit—figs, pomegranates, squashes, artichokes and tubers—are produced from gardens. Along the northern coast, and especially on the lower slopes both of the Tripolitanian Jebel and the Jebel Akhdar, vines are grown, though less so than formerly because of the prohibition of wine-making since independence.

Over much of Libya, pastoral nomadism, based on the rearing of sheep and goats (and some cattle and camels), is the only possible activity. In Cyrenaica, nomads outnumbered the remainder of the population for many years, but in Tripolitania the main emphasis is on agriculture, although herding is still practised. Several industries have developed—petroleum refining, of course, plus some petrochemical activity, iron and steel production and some light industries. Overall, the scale of industrial activity is still small, but growing. Major efforts have been made to improve agriculture, with debatable suc-cess. One increasing difficulty is the exodus of rural workers to jobs in the developing towns, and foreign labour has had to be introduced on some rural development schemes. Another limitation is over-use of artesian water in the Jefara. In certain areas near the coast, the water-table has fallen by 3 m–5 m per year, resulting in invasion of the aquifers by sea-water.

The population of Libya seems to have been Berber in origin, i.e. connected with many of the present-day inhabitants of Morocco, Algeria, and Tunisia. The establishment of Greek colonies, from about 650 BC onwards, seems to have had little ethnic effect on the population; but in the ninth and 10th centuries AD there were large-scale immigrations by Arabic-speaking tribes from the Najd of Arabia. This latter group, of relatively unmixed Mediterranean racial type, is now entirely dominant, ethnically speaking, especially in Cyrenaica, of which it has been said that no other part of the world (central Arabia alone excepted) is more thoroughly Arab.

A few Berber elements do, however, survive, mainly in the south and west of Libya; while the long-continued traffic in Negro slaves (which came to an end in the 1940s) has left a visible influence on peoples throughout Libya and especially in the south.

Arabic, brought in by the 10th century invaders, is the one official language of Libya, but a few Berber-speaking villages remain.

History

Revised for this edition by RICHARD I. LAWLESS

PRE-ISLAMIC LIBYA

In earliest historical times two races inhabited Libya—the 'Libyans' and the 'Ethiopians'—the former, of Mediterranean stock, inhabited the coastal areas; the latter, of negroid and African stock, inhabited the interior. Phoenician sailors began to visit Libya in about 1000 BC to trade for gold and silver, ivory, apes and peacocks, and established the permanent colonies of Leptis, Uai'at (Tripoli) and Sabratha on the coast. A more famous Phoenician colony, Carthage, was established to the west of what is now called Libya, and by 517 BC had come to dominate the others. During the Punic wars between Rome and Carthage the Tripolitanian half of Libya fell under the control of the Numidians until Julius Caesar created the province of Africa Nova.

In about 600 BC the Greeks had colonized Cyrene, and raised it to be a powerful city. Cyrene later fell under the domination of Alexander the Great, came under the Ptolemies in about 322 BC and was bequeathed to Rome in 96 BC. Libya then enjoyed several centuries of prosperity under Roman rule, but, by the middle of the fourth century AD, decline had set in. In AD 431 the vandals, under Genseric, conquered the country, but a hundred years later the Emperor Justinian's general Belisarius reconquered the country for the Byzantine Empire. Repeated rebellions by Berber tribes, however, soon reduced the country to anarchy.

ARAB INVASION

Arab invaders overran the country and captured Tripoli in 643. The majority of the invaders embraced Islam, but mainly in its schismatic forms as Kharijites, Ibadites and Shi'ites. Continual rebellion induced the Caliph of Baghdad, Haroun ar-Rashid, to appoint, in 800, Ibrahim ibn al-Aghlabid as governor, with his capital at Qairawan (Kairouan now in Tunisia). This Aghlabid dynasty, virtually independent of the Abbasid caliphate of Baghdad, ended in the 10th century when a Shi'ite uprising founded the Shi'ite Fatimid Dynasty, which from Tunisia conquered Egypt, transferring the seat of government to Cairo in 972. Bulukkin ibn Ziri was made governor of Ifriqiya, and at the beginning of the 11th century the Zirid Amir returned to orthodox Sunnism and acknowledged the sovereignty of the Caliph of Baghdad.

The Fatimid Caliph of Baghdad reacted by invading Libya in 1049, and the next five centuries witnessed little but inter-tribal wars. By the 16th century the northern coast of Africa had become infested with the dens of pirates, and was attracting the crusading and imperialistic designs of Christian Spain. Ferdinand the Catholic sent an expedition which took Tripoli in 1510. The Muslim world had now become, under the Ottoman Turks, more united than it had been for 600 years, and Sinan Pasha was able to wrest Tripoli from the Knights Hospitallers of St John (to whom it had been confided by Charles V) in 1551. Ottoman rule was loose but oppressive. The professional soldiers, the Janissaries, became a power within the state, and the activities of the pirate corsairs, often with the blessing of the Ottoman pashas, attracted reprisals from the European naval powers.

In 1711 a local notable, Ahmad Karamanli, of Ottoman origin and an officer in the Janissaries, was proclaimed *dey*, (originally, deys were high officers of the Ottoman army of occupation) and eventually recognized as pasha. The Karamanli dynasty lasted until 1835. Piracy had again contributed much to its finance, and when European naval action suppressed piracy after the Napoleonic wars, the Karamanlis were ruined. In 1835, probably through fear of the extension of French power in Algiers and Tunis, the Sultan decided to reoccupy Libya and to bring it once more under the direct rule of the Porte. The years that followed were marked by corruption, oppression and revolts, but also by the rise of the Sanusi religious brotherhood.

ITALO-TURKISH CONFLICTS

On 29 September 1911 Italy declared war on Turkey for reasons even more trivial than those which 24 years later led to the war with Ethiopia and Italy's subsequent denunciation as an aggressor. After a short bombardment, Italian troops landed at Tripoli on 3 October. Italy knew the Turks to be involved in the Balkans, and knew, through its commercial infiltration of Libya, their weakness in Africa. But the attack on Libya was not the easy exercise which Italy expected. The Turks withdrew inland but the Libyans organized themselves and joined the Turks, to whom the Porte sent assistance in the form of arms and of two senior officers, Ali Fethi Bey and Enver Pasha. The presence in the Italian army of Eritrean troops was a spur to the pride of the Libyans. In October and November a number of actions were fought around Tripoli in which the Italians had little success. A seaborne Italian force then descended on Misurata and seized it, but could make no progress inland. At ar-Rumeila they suffered a considerable reverse. Turkey, however, defeated in the Balkan War, was anxious for a peace, which was signed on 18 October 1912. One of the conditions of this peace was that the Libyans should be allowed 'administrative autonomy'. This was never realized.

Peace with Turkey did not, however, mean peace in Libya for the Italians. Although most of the Tripolitanians submitted and were disarmed within two years, the Sanusiya of Cyrenaica under Said Ahmad ash-Sharif, and their adherents in the Fezzan and Tripolitania, refused to yield. The Sanusiya maintained a forward post at Sirte under Sayyid Ahmad's brother, Sayyid Safi ad-Din as-Sanusi. The extent of contact between this Sayyid and one Ramadan as-Sueihli of Misurata is not clear. Ramadan had been in the resistance to the Italians and two years later had appeared to be submissive. At all events, he found himself commanding Libyans in an action started by the Italians at al-Qaradabia in 1914, to push back Said Safi ad-Din. Ramadan and his Misuratis changed sides in this action to the discomfiture of the Italians. By the time that the First World War had started, the Italians held only the coastal towns of Tripoli, Benghazi, Derna and Tobruk, and a few coastal villages near Tripoli.

The First World War gave Turkey and its German allies the opportunity of fomenting trouble against Italy in Libya. Arms and munitions were sent by submarine. Nuri Pasha from Turkey and Abd ar-Rahman Azzam (late Secretary-General of the Arab League) from Egypt joined Said Ahmad ash-Sharif in Cyrenaica. Ramadan as-Sueihli became head of a government at Misurata. The Sultan, to prevent quarrels, sent Osman Fu'ad, grandson of Sultan Mourad, as Amir, and Ishaq Pasha as commander-in-chief in Tripolitania. The strategic objective of these efforts was to tie up Italian forces in Libya and British forces in the Western Desert. The climax of Nuri Pasha's efforts with the Sanusi was their disastrous action in the Western Desert against the British, as a result of which Said Ahmad ash-Sharif handed over the leadership to Said Muhammad Idris. He was compelled to make the treaty of az-Zawiatna with the British and the Italians who recognized him as Amir of the interior of Cyrenaica, provided he desisted from attacks on the coastal towns and on Egypt.

The end of the war in 1918 left Italy weak and the Libyans, deserted by the Turks, weary. The Tripolitanians attempted to form a republic with headquarters at Gharian and with Abd ar-Rahman Azzam as adviser. The Italians made a truce with them at Suani ibn Adam, permitting a delegation to go to Rome and entertaining the idea of 'administrative independence'. Ramadan as-Sueihli visited Tripoli. In Cyrenaica, Said Muhammad Idris as-Sanusi likewise attempted to come to terms. In 1921 at Sirte the Tripolitanian leaders agreed with him to join forces to obtain Libya's rights and to do homage to him as Amir of all Libya. Meanwhile the delegation to Rome had returned empty-handed and Ramadan as-Sueihli had been slain in a tribal fight.

ITALIAN COLONIZATION

The advent of the Fascists to power in Italy (1922) coincided with the appointment in Tripoli of a vigorous governor, Count Volpi. Thereafter, it took them until 1925 to occupy and pacify the province of Tripolitania and to disarm the population. In Cyrenaica, however, the famous Said Omar al-Mukhtar, representing the Amir Muhammad Idris, whose health had collapsed, maintained the struggle. The Italians realized that the only effective policy was to deprive the Sanusiya of their bases, the oases of the south. Jaghbub was occupied in 1925, Zella, Ojila and Jalo in 1927. In 1928 Marshal Badoglio was appointed Governor-General and in 1929 he occupied Mizda in the Fezzan. Omar Mukhtar still resisted. The Italians removed into concentration camps at al-Aqeila the tribes of the Jebel Akhdar. In 1930 Graziani was appointed to Cyrenaica, and the famous barbed-wire fence was erected along the frontier of Egypt. Finally, in 1931, isolated from all sup-

port, Omar Mukhtar, now an aged man, was surrounded, wounded, captured, and hanged.

Starting in the early 1920s, the Italians proceeded to colonize, in the sense of that word which is now in disrepute, those parts of Libya which they had occupied, and which geographical and ecological conditions rendered profitable for development. They enlarged and embellished the coastal towns. They extended throughout the cultivable areas an excellent network of roads. They bored wells, planted trees, and stabilized sand-dunes. But their civilizing policy was weighted heavily in favour of their own race. The object was clearly the settlement in Africa of as much as possible of Italy's surplus peasant population. These were encouraged to come in large numbers. Skilled cultivators of olives, vines, tobacco and barley, they needed the best lands and were provided with them. The priority given to the progress of the Libyans was a low one. Primary education for the Libyans was encouraged, and schools provided for them, but the main medium of instruction was Italian. Very few Libyans were accepted into Italian secondary schools.

INDEPENDENCE

There followed the Second World War, and the occupation in 1942 of Cyrenaica and Tripolitania by a British military administration and of the Fezzan by French forces. Thereafter, until 1950, the country was administered with the greatest economy on a care and maintenance basis. Its final fate was long in doubt, until the UN decreed its independence by 1952. On 24 December 1951 Libya was declared an independent united kingdom with a federal constitution under King Idris, the former Amir Muhammad Idris, hero of the resistance.

According to the Constitution promulgated in October 1951, the State of Libya was a federal monarchy ruled by King Muhammad Idris al-Mahdi as-Sanusi and his heirs, and divided into the three provinces of Tripolitania, Cyrenaica and the Fezzan. The federal Government consisted of a bicameral legislature, i.e. a Chamber of Deputies, to which was responsible a Council of Ministers appointed by the King, and a Senate of 24 members (eight for each province). The King had the right to nominate 12 of the senators, to introduce and to veto legislation, and to dissolve the Lower House at his discretion. The Constitution also provided that provincial legislatures should be created for the subordinate provinces of the new realm.

On the attainment of full independence serious political, financial and economic problems confronted Libya. Not the least of these was the task of fostering amongst the population a sense of national identity and unity. The loyalties of the people were still given to the village and the tribe, rather than to the new federal state.

These rivalries revealed themselves in the next two years. The Party of Independence, which supported the Constitution, won control in the February 1952 elections for the Federal Chamber of Deputies. The National Congress Party of Tripolitania, however, was opposed to the federal principle and advocated a unitary state, with elections based on proportional representation (which would have given Tripolitania the main voice). Disorders arising from this disagreement led to the outlawing of the Tripolitania party and the deportation of its leader, Bashir Bey as-Sa'adawi. A Legislative Council for Tripolitania was formed in 1952 but had to be dissolved in 1954 because of continued friction with the federal Government and the King.

Efforts were undertaken, with Western technical aid, to increase the economic resources of Libya, e.g. to improve irrigation and initiate schemes for water catchments, to extend reafforestation, to teach better methods of farming, and to explore the possibilities of extending industries which could process local products and raw materials such as edible oils, fruits, vegetables, fish, etc.

FOREIGN RELATIONS IN THE 1950s

The first important development in the sphere of foreign relations was the admission of Libya to the League of Arab States in March 1953. The second development reflected the economic difficulties of the new state and its close links with Western Europe. In July 1953 Libya concluded a 20-year treaty with the United Kingdom. In return for permission to maintain military bases in Libya, the United Kingdom undertook to grant the new state £1m. annually for economic development and a further annual sum of £2.75m. to offset budgetary deficits.

In September 1954 a similar agreement was signed with the USA. A number of air bases were granted to the USA in return for economic aid amounting to $40m. over 20 years, an amount which was later substantially increased. Libya also consolidated relations with France and Italy, signing a friendship pact with France in 1955 and a trade and financial agreement with Italy in 1957. In addition Libya was attempting to cement relations with its Arab neighbours. In May 1956 Libya concluded a trade and payments pact with Egypt, arranging the exchange of Libyan cattle for Egyptian foodstuffs.

The critical problem for Libya was to ensure that enough funds from abroad should be available to meet the normal expenses of the Government and to pay for much-needed improvements. At this time, its strategic position was all Libya had to sell, hence its involvement with the Western military alliance. The Libyan attitude to the communist world was much more reserved. Reliance on income from foreign military bases continued, therefore, to dominate foreign policy, and in the late 1950s and early 1960s Libya received subsidies and military assistance from both the United Kingdom and the USA in return for the use of military bases.

PETROLEUM DISCOVERIES

After 1955–56, when Libya granted concessions for petroleum exploration to several US companies, the search for petroleum resources became one of the main interests of the Libyan Government. By the end of 1959 some 15 companies held petroleum concessions in Libya. An oilfield at Zelten in Cyrenaica was discovered in June 1959. Before the year was out, six productive wells had been found in Tripolitania, four in Cyrenaica and one in the Fezzan. By the beginning of July 1960 there were 35 petroleum wells in production, yielding altogether a little less than 93,000 barrels of petroleum per day. (The development of the petroleum fields is dealt with in greater detail in the Economy section which follows this history.) Petroleum production showed a tremendous increase in the 1962–66 period, with exports rising from 8m. tons in 1962 to more than 70m. tons in 1966.

A UNITARY REALM

A general election was held in Libya on 17 January 1960. Most of the 55 seats were contested, but there was no party system in operation. The election was fought mainly on a personal basis. Secret balloting, limited in earlier elections to the urban areas, was now extended to the rural districts. The Prime Minister, Abd al-Majid Koubar, and the other members of his Cabinet retained their seats.

Libya's increasing wealth was making the business of government more complex and several changes of administration ensued between 1960 and 1963. Finally, in March 1963, a new Cabinet was appointed under the premiership of Dr Mohieddin Fekini.

Dr Fekini stated in April 1963 that his Government intended to introduce legislation designed to transform Libya from a federal into a unitary state—a change which would mean increased efficiency and considerable administrative economies. On 15 April the Prime Minister presented to the Chamber of Deputies a bill which contained a number of important reforms: (1) the franchise was to be granted to women; (2) Libya would have (as before) a bicameral parliamentary system, but henceforward the King was to nominate all the 24 members of the Senate (previously one-half were nominated and the other half were elected); (3) the Kingdom of Libya would cease to be a federal state comprising three provinces (Tripolitania, Cyrenaica and the Fezzan), becoming instead a unitary realm divided into 10 administrative areas; (4) the administrative councils established in each of the three provinces were to be abolished, the exercise of executive power residing now in the Council of Ministers. Libya became a unitary state by royal proclamation on 27 April 1963.

THE REALITY OF INDEPENDENCE

In the field of foreign relations, Libya was by now helped by the prospect of financial independence and was making its voice heard in international affairs, particularly in Africa. As a result of decisions taken at the Addis Ababa conference of African Heads of State in May 1963, Libya closed its air and sea ports to Portuguese and South African ships. The signing of pacts with Morocco (1962) and Algeria (1963) meant that Libya now had closer links with all the Maghreb countries. Libya was also showing signs of ending its dependence on the West. The 1955 agreement with France had allowed France to retain certain military facilities in Libya—notably in the field of communications—for the defence of French African territories, but Dr Fekini felt that, with the coming of independence to French African territories in the early 1960s, the matter should be reconsidered.

The question of foreign military bases in Libya now came to the fore. Dr Fekini resigned in January 1964 and the new Prime Minister was Mahmoud Muntasser, formerly Minister of Justice. The Government issued a statement on 23 February, stating that it did not propose to renew or extend its military agreements with the United Kingdom and the USA and that it supported the other Governments of the Arab world in the resistance to imperialism. Muntasser defined the aim of his Government as the termination of the existing agreements with the United Kingdom and the USA and the fixing of a date for the evacuation of the bases in Libya. The Chamber of Deputies then passed a resolution calling for the achievement of this aim and providing that, if negotiations were unsuccessful, the Chamber would pass legislation to abrogate the treaties and close the bases.

The Anglo-Libyan treaty of 1953 was due to expire in 1973. Under the treaty, the United Kingdom maintained a Royal Air Force staging post near Tobruk, an Air Force detachment at Idris airport in Tripoli and Army District Headquarters at Tripoli and Benghazi. The American-Libyan agreement of 1954 was to expire in 1971. Near Tripoli was situated the largest American air-base outside the USA. Under the treaties, Libya had received large amounts of financial, economic and military aid from the USA and from the United Kingdom. Petroleum revenues had greatly reduced Libyan dependence on such aid. The United Kingdom withdrew the bulk of its forces in February and March 1966.

At elections for the Libyan Parliament, held in October 1964, in which women voted for the first time, moderate candidates won most of the 103 seats. King Idris dissolved the Parliament, however, on 13 February 1965, because of complaints about irregularities in the election procedure. The Prime Minister resigned, to be succeeded by Hussain Maziq, Minister for Foreign Affairs. A new election for Parliament was held on 8 May 1965, over 200 candidates contesting the 91 seats, 16 members being returned unopposed.

The outbreak of the six-day Arab-Israeli war in June 1967 was followed by serious disturbances in Tripoli and Benghazi, in which port and oil workers and students, inflamed by Egyptian propaganda, played a prominent part. The British and US embassies were attacked and the Jewish minorities were subjected to violence and persecution which resulted in the emigration of most of them to Italy, Malta and elsewhere. The Prime Minister, Hussain Maziq, proved unable to control the situation and was dismissed by the King on 28 June. Firm measures by his successor, Abd al-Qadir Badri, brought a return to order but the antagonisms which he aroused forced him, in turn, to resign in October. He was succeeded as Prime Minister on 28 October by the Minister of Justice, Abd al-Hamid Bakkoush.

An immediate result of the June war was a fall of about 80% in the Libyan output of crude petroleum because of the boycott of oil supplies from Arab countries to the United Kingdom, the USA and Federal Germany. There was a gradual return to full production in the months following the conflict, however, and the ban on the export of petroleum was lifted in September. The closure of the Suez Canal brought about a considerable increase in Libya's petroleum exports and general prosperity, although the Libyan Government agreed to make annual aid payments totalling £30m. to the United Arab Republic (UAR) and Jordan to alleviate the consequences of the war. Libya's petroleum output increased by about 50% in 1968 and the country became, after only seven and a half years, the second largest producer in the Arab world, with the great advantage, as a supplier to Europe, of being on the right side of the Suez Canal.

The new Prime Minister, Abd al-Hamid Bakkoush, initiated a programme of progressive change, seeking to modernize Libya's administration, reform the civil service and improve the educational system. He also sought to provide the armed forces with modern equipment, and, under a contract announced in April 1968, the purchase from a British firm of a surface-to-air missile defence system, costing £100m., was arranged. An agreement to buy British heavy arms followed, but in September 1968 Bakkoush was replaced as premier by Wanis al-Qaddafi, since the pace of Bakkoush's reforms had apparently alienated some conservative elements. Both cabinets enjoyed close relationships with the Western countries but played little part in Arab politics.

THE 1969 COUP

On 1 September 1969 a military coup was staged in Tripoli while the King was in Turkey for medical treatment. Within a few days the new regime gained complete control of the entire country. The coup was remarkable for the absence of opposition, relatively few arrests, virtually no fighting and no deaths at all being reported. A Revolution Command Council (RCC) took power and proclaimed the Libyan Arab Republic. The RCC initially remained anonymous but was soon revealed as a group of young army officers, the leader, Col Muammar al-Qaddafi, being only 27. The aged King Idris refused to abdicate but accepted exile in Egypt when it became obvious that the revolution had been completely accepted by his people. He remained there until his death, aged 93, in May 1983.

A provisional Constitution, announced in November, stated that supreme power would remain in the hands of the RCC, which appointed the Cabinet; there was no mention of any future general election or of a national assembly, and the royal ban on political parties continued. A largely civilian Cabinet was appointed, under close military supervision. The Ministers of Defence and of the Interior were accused of organizing an abortive counter-revolution in December, and were tried and sentenced in 1970. In January Col Qaddafi himself became Prime Minister and several of his colleagues also joined the Cabinet.

The principal force underlying the regime's policies was undoubtedly the professed one of Arab nationalism. Internally, this led to the strict enforcement of the royal law requiring businesses operating in Libya to be controlled by Libyans—banks being particularly affected. The remaining British military establishment in Libya, requested to leave as soon as possible, was finally removed in March 1970, and the much larger US presence at Wheelus Field was removed in June. Most of the European and American specialists (managers, teachers, technicians and doctors), were replaced by Arabs, mainly from Egypt. English translations disappeared from street signs, official stationery and publications, and most hoardings, the use of Arabic alone being permitted; similarly, the Islamic prohibitions on alcoholic drinks and certain Western clothes were officially revived. In July 1970 the property of all Jews and Italians still living in Libya— some 25,000 people—was sequestered by the Government, and both communities were encouraged to leave without delay; some Jews were, however, offered compensation in government bonds. In the same month the three main petroleum marketing companies—Shell, Esso and an ENI subsidiary— had their distribution facilities nationalized.

Another anti-government plot was reported to have been crushed in July 1970. In the autumn two ministers resigned and there were signs of a power struggle developing within the RCC. The internal dissension apparently increased in the first part of 1970 over the proposed federation with the UAR, Syria and Sudan, and over Qaddafi's promises of a constitution and political institutions, including an elected President. A step towards introducing these was the announcement in June 1971 that an Arab Socialist Union (ASU) was to be created as the state's sole party.

FOREIGN POLICY AFTER THE COUP

The new regime almost immediately received enthusiastic recognition from the radical Arab countries and the USSR, and the rest of the world also granted recognition within a few days. As would be expected from the Arab nationalist inspiration behind the revolution, the monarchy's close ties with Western powers were abandoned in favour of close relations with the Arab world and Egypt in particular; this friendship became the basis of a triple alliance announced late in 1969, Sudan being the third member. The alliance was intended to develop both politically—as a strong bulwark against Israel and the West—and economically, in that the economies of the three countries complemented each other to a considerable extent. However, when a federation agreement was signed in April 1971, it was Syria which became the third member. Libya also adopted a militant position on the Palestine question, and this created some diplomatic problems regarding arms contracts, particularly with the United Kingdom.

Although in July 1970 the Libyan Government followed Egypt in accepting US proposals for a cease-fire with Israel, it continued its militant statements on the Middle East problem. Qaddafi stated that a peaceful solution was impossible and rejected the UN Security Council resolution on which the US initiative was based. During the fighting between Palestinian guerrillas and the Jordanian army in September 1970, Libya redirected its financial aid from the Jordan Government to the guerrillas and severed diplomatic relations with King Hussein's government.

The coup appeared to have reoriented Libya away from the Maghreb; in the summer of 1970 Libya withdrew from the Maghreb Permanent Consultative Committee. Relations with Tunisia improved in the latter half of 1970, after initial concern in Tunis in 1969 at the radical leanings of the new regime, and Qaddafi headed a delegation which visited Tunisia in February 1971. Relations with Morocco were severed in July 1971, after the Libyan Government prematurely gave its support to an attempt to overthrow King Hassan, which failed within 24 hours.

There was little evidence of any closer relationship with the communist powers, although the People's Republic of China was recognized in June 1971 and the USSR was given due credit for its Middle East policies. However, communism was regarded in Libya as a 'foreign' ideology, antipathetic to more 'progressive' Arab socialism (as in Sudan). Hence, in July 1971, Qaddafi was ready to help President Nimeri of Sudan to regain power after a coup, led by communists, had ousted him. A regular BOAC flight from London to Khartoum was forced down over Libya and two leaders of the Sudanese coup (one of whom, Col Babiker an-Nur, was travelling back to become Head of State), were taken from the plane and handed over to Sudan. They were almost immediately executed by the restored regime.

PETROLEUM POWER

In April 1971 the negotiations with the oil companies operating in Libya, which had begun soon after the 1969 coup, finally ended in a new five-year agreement raising the total posted price for Libyan crude petroleum to US $3.447 per barrel. In the last stage of the negotiations, conducted in Tripoli, the Libyan Government also represented the interests of the Algerian, Iraqi and Saudi Arabian Governments. Threats of an embargo on the export of crude petroleum were used as a lever in the negotiations.

In 10 years Libya's position had changed from one of penury and dependence to one of power, based entirely on the country's ability to cut off petroleum supplies. The pronouncements of Qaddafi were, therefore, by now of great moment to the West. In July 1971 the Deputy Prime Minister, Maj. Abd as-Salam Jalloud, visited the Federal Republic of Germany, France and the United Kingdom. Federal Germany, which bought a particularly large proportion of its crude petroleum from Libya, needed to maintain good relations. France was anxious over the use to which Libya would put the *Mirage* jet-engined fighter aircraft that were being supplied under the 1970 agreement. The same anxiety was revealed in the

United Kingdom over the supply of armaments, but none of these countries could afford to alienate Libya.

In December 1971, avowedly in retaliation for the United Kingdom's failure to prevent the Iranian occupation of the Tumb islands in the Gulf, Libya nationalized the assets of British Petroleum. This began the process of nationalizing the foreign oil companies (described in more detail in the Economy of Libya; see below).

Relations with the United Kingdom became very strained in the winter of 1971–72, not only because of the nationalization of BP but also because of Libyan intervention in the dispute with Malta over the British bases there. Libya had, for some time, been actively fostering relations with Malta, and talks on possible Libyan aid to Malta were held in August 1971. In January 1972 the British naval training mission was ordered to leave Libya, and in February the 1954 agreement with the USA was abrogated.

Libya's attitude towards the USSR had remained cool, and the Government was violently opposed to the Iraqi/Soviet treaty, signed in April 1972. Nevertheless, in February 1972, Maj. Jalloud visited Moscow and in March an agreement on petroleum co-operation was signed. It was also reported that the USSR might supply arms to Libya.

At home, Qaddafi continued his attempts to run the legislature and the Government entirely in accordance with Islamic principles. At the end of March 1972 the ASU held its first national congress. At subsequent sessions, the ASU adopted resolutions to clarify its position and policies, and to abolish censorship of the press, while, at the same time, maintaining financial control of newspapers.

In July 1972 disagreement within the RCC led to Qaddafi's replacement as Prime Minister by Maj. Jalloud, who formed a new Cabinet in which all but two of the ministers were civilians.

ARAB UNITY

A recurrent feature of Qaddafi's foreign policy has been the announcement of proposals for the union of Libya with neighbouring states, and the subsequent collapse of such planned mergers. The Tripoli Charter of December 1969, establishing a revolutionary alliance of Libya, Egypt (then the UAR) and Sudan, was followed by gradual moves towards federation and the adhesion of Syria. Sudan withdrew, but in September 1971 referenda in Libya, Egypt and Syria approved the constitution of the Federation of Arab Republics, which officially came into existence on 1 January 1972, but which had few practical consequences.

The Federation was not Qaddafi's only attempt to export his ideals by means of merger. At the time of Malta's dispute with the United Kingdom over the use of bases, in 1971, he proposed a union of Malta with Libya, but was rebuffed. In December 1972, in a speech in Tunis, he proposed the union of Libya and Tunisia, much to the surprise of his audience, not least President Bourguiba, who immediately rejected the idea, making some pointed remarks about Qaddafi's inexperience.

A merger of Libya and Egypt was agreed in principle in August 1972 but, as the date of implementation approached, certain difficulties became apparent. Qaddafi, who had recently launched his 'Cultural Revolution' of April 1973, was seen as a reactionary Muslim puritan in Egypt, and he was openly critical of Egyptian moral laxity. Egyptian suspicion of Libyan revolutionary enthusiasm, notwithstanding, the union came into effect on 1 September 1973, with the establishment, in theory, of unified political leadership and economic policy and a constituent assembly. The union soon fell apart, wrecked by Qaddafi's opposition to Egypt's conduct of the October 1973 Arab-Israeli war.

President Qaddafi's attitude towards the Palestine problem had long been a source of discord between Libya and other Arab states. He gave financial support to the Palestinian guerrillas, and a number of Libyan volunteers were sent to assist them, Qaddafi's objective being the complete destruction of Israel. He was extremely critical of what he saw as the lack of total commitment to the Palestinian cause on the part of Egypt and Syria, and frequently expressed the opinion that the Arab states could not, and did not deserve to, defeat Israel.

He accused Egypt and Syria of being more interested in the recovery of territory lost in the 1967 war than in aiding the Palestinian resistance movement, which was being 'destroyed by the Arabs in co-operation with Israel'. Qaddafi was not informed of the Egyptian and Syrian plan to attack Israel in October 1973, was strongly critical of their battle plan, and refused to attend the Algiers meeting of Arab Heads of State after the war, declaring that it would only ratify Arab capitulation. Libya was nevertheless an enthusiastic proponent of the use of the Arab petroleum embargo against countries which were considered to be pro-Israel. During the war, Libya's participation had been limited to the supply of arms and equipment, and its conclusion seemed only to complete Qaddafi's disillusionment concerning the union with Egypt.

Presidents Qaddafi and Bourguiba announced the union of Libya and Tunisia on 12 January 1974, following two days of talks. A referendum to approve the decision was to be held on 18 January, but was almost immediately postponed. The decision had been taken in the absence of the Tunisian Prime Minister, Hedi Nouira. When he returned to Tunisia, the pro-merger Minister of Foreign Affairs was dismissed, and Tunisia's attitude changed to one of indefinite deferment of the union. Qaddafi's impetuous action aimed to produce a unified state, but Tunisia now treated the agreement as merely a declaration of principle, without any practical effect.

Qaddafi's enthusiasm for Arab unity continued unabated, but the failure of political mergers led him to propound a new course. His speeches attacked the Arab leaders who blocked unity and failed to 'liberate' Palestine, and he spoke of Libyan aid for revolution and the achievement of Arab union by popular pressure on the Governments of Tunisia, Egypt, Algeria and Morocco. Libya had, for some time, been providing money, arms and training for subversive or 'liberation' organizations operating in Ireland, Eritrea, the Philippines, Rhodesia, Portuguese Guinea, Morocco and Chad, as well as providing aid for sympathetic countries such as Pakistan, Uganda, Zambia, Togo and, after May 1973, Chad. Now it appeared that Libya was supporting subversion in Egypt and Sudan. Attempted coups in Egypt in April and Sudan in May 1974 were believed to have had Libyan support, and relations between Libya and other Arab states became increasingly hostile. Qaddafi's failed mergers and his interference in the internal affairs of other countries were believed to have been major factors in his withdrawal from an active political role in April 1974, when it was seen that he had failed in his policy of exporting the ideals of the Libyan 'Cultural Revolution'.

THE CULTURAL REVOLUTION

President Qaddafi's somewhat idiosyncratic political and social philosophy first obtained full expression in a speech in April 1973, when he called for the immediate launching of a 'cultural revolution to destroy imported ideologies, whether they are eastern or western' and for the construction of a society based on the tenets of the Koran. The form which this revolution was to take was laid down in a five-point programme: 'people's committees' would be set up to carry out the revolution, the 'politically sick' would be purged, the revolutionary masses would be armed, a campaign would begin against bureaucracy and administrative abuses, and imported books which propagated communism, atheism or capitalism would be burned. The people's committees set about their task of supervising all aspects of social and economic life, criticizing and dismissing officials and business executives who failed to show the required revolutionary fervour, and destroying offensive books and magazines.

In May 1973 Qaddafi presented his 'third international theory', which was 'an alternative to capitalist materialism and communist atheism'. In effect, it appeared to be an appeal for a return to Islamic fundamentalism (an appeal which was subsequently echoed in other Middle Eastern countries), together with a rather confused combination of socialism and respect for private property, and much talk of tolerance and the rights of oppressed nationalities. While the 'Cultural Revolution' proceeded apace in Libya, Qaddafi seemed more concerned with foreign policy and his new-found role as a revolutionary philosopher, who had proposed a universally applicable theory which would replace existing ideologies.

Qaddafi concentrated on the formulation and propagation of his theory, and on his erratic, unsuccessful attempts to export the Libyan revolution by merger or by subversion, while the mundane details of administration were increasingly referred to Maj. Jalloud, the Prime Minister.

The return to the teachings of the Koran and the rejection of external influences took several forms, some of them petty, such as the insistence upon the use of Arabic in foreigners' passports, and some macabre, as in the revival of such features of Koranic law as the dismembering of thieves' hands. The theory was also invoked in the disputes with foreign oil companies in 1973 (dealt with in detail in the Economy section), presented as an expression of Libyan independence.

On 5 April 1974 it was announced that Qaddafi, while remaining Head of State and Commander-in-Chief, had been relieved of political, administrative and ceremonial duties, and was to devote himself to ideological and mass organization work. It appeared that, willingly or otherwise, Qaddafi had effectively been replaced by Prime Minister Jalloud. After a five-month withdrawal from active direction of the Government, Qaddafi re-emerged in the autumn of 1974 and it soon became apparent that he was more firmly in command than ever.

THE CREATION OF THE SOCIALIST PEOPLE'S LIBYAN ARAB JAMAHIRIYA

President Qaddafi's theories had, since 1973 (when he presented his third international theory), shown a strong desire to foster 'people's assemblies' at all levels of Libyan life. Under a decree promulgated by the ruling RCC in November 1975, provision was made for the creation of a 618-member general national congress of the Arab Socialist Union (ASU), the country's only permitted political party. The congress, which held its first session in January 1976, comprised members of the RCC, leaders of existing 'people's congresses' and 'popular committees', and trade unions and professional organizations. Subsequently the General National Congress of the ASU became the General People's Congress (GPC), which first met in November 1976. Qaddafi announced plans for radical constitutional changes and these were endorsed by the GPC in March 1977. The official name of the country was changed to The Socialist People's Libyan Arab Jamahiriya, and power was vested in the people through the GPC and the groups represented in it. The RCC disappeared and a General Secretariat of the GPC, with Qaddafi as Secretary-General, was established. The Council of Ministers was replaced by the General People's Committee, with 26 members, each a secretary of a department. People's committees were set up at local level, ostensibly to give citizens control over their own affairs. In reality, their creation enabled Qaddafi to dispose of governors, ministers and local officials, some of whom were beginning to resist his more radical reforms. In March 1979 Qaddafi resigned from the post of secretary-general of the General Secretariat of the GPC, so that he could devote more time to 'revolutionary work'. The General Secretariat was reorganized, as was the General People's Committee, which was reduced to 21 members.

In late 1979 Qaddafi urged Libyans living abroad to take over Libyan embassies; diplomats were ousted and 'people's bureaux' established in most Western countries. At the fifth meeting of the GPC, in January 1980, several government ministers were dismissed, notably the experienced Petroleum Secretary, Izzedin Mabrouk, who was accused of inefficiency in nationalizing the petroleum industry. The sixth meeting of the GPC, in January 1981, reshuffled several ministerial appointments, discussed the 1981–85 economic plan, and made further proposals for transforming Libyan society along the lines described in Qaddafi's 'Green Book' (published in three volumes over the period 1976–79). The Ministry of Foreign Affairs was abolished and replaced by a Bureau of Foreign Liaison.

QADDAFI'S EXTERNAL INVOLVEMENTS

Relations with Egypt deteriorated after Qaddafi boycotted the Rabat summit meeting of Arab Heads of State in October 1974. Qaddafi was unhappy about the decision to recognize the PLO,

under Yasser Arafat, as the sole legitimate representative of the Palestinians. He subsequently showed his support for the 'rejectionist front'—the wing of the Palestinian guerrilla movement which rejected the concept of a possible settlement of the Arab-Israeli conflict under terms which could be acceptable to Arafat, Jordan and Egypt.

The war of words with Egypt continued in 1975, with articles in the Libyan press containing bitter personal attacks on President Sadat and with the Egyptian press accusing Qaddafi of preparing to mount an invasion of Egypt. A delegation from the National Assembly of the Federation of Arab Republics, which visited Tripoli and Cairo in May, was able to bring about a temporary reconciliation but, at the end of May, relations deteriorated again after reports that Libya was to allow the establishment of Soviet military bases on its territory in return for huge supplies of Soviet weapons. It later appeared that the arms deal did not include the establishment of Soviet military bases in Libya, and was, in fact, smaller than at first reported. Libya, in turn, condemned Egypt for signing the second interim disengagement agreement between Egypt and Israel in September 1975. Relations with Egypt did not improve in 1976 or 1977, and in July 1977 for a while, frontier clashes had the appearance of open war.

Relations with Egypt were not improved when, in November 1977, President Sadat of Egypt launched his peace initiative by visiting Israel. Qaddafi condemned Sadat's move and was a leading instigator of the Tripoli summit of 'rejectionist' states which formed a 'front of steadfastness and confrontation' against Israel in December 1977. Qaddafi remained strongly opposed to Sadat's peace initiative throughout 1978 and following the signing of the Egyptian-Israeli treaty in March 1979, Qaddafi walked out of the Baghdad summit meeting of Arab states on the grounds that the sanctions which were being contemplated against Egypt were insufficiently far-reaching.

In early 1980 a serious rift developed between Qaddafi and Arafat, leader of the PLO, who was accused of having abandoned the armed struggle in favour of a strategy of diplomacy and moderation. In January relations were formally broken with al-Fatah, the largest component organization of the PLO, and all aid was suspended, although Libya continued to support other wings of the movement. The Libyan authorities began to organize Palestinians in the country into 'people's congresses' to pursue war against Israel independently, and by May about 27 such groups were reported to have been set up. However, a summit meeting of the 'steadfastness front' in Tripoli in April seemed to restore a measure of solidarity, and the PLO representative returned to Tripoli in May.

Relations with the USA were erratic throughout 1979 and the first half of 1980. In early 1979 Qaddafi threatened to cut off petroleum exports unless US President Jimmy Carter lifted a ban on sales to Libya of agricultural and electronic equipment and transport aircraft. The sacking of the US Embassy in Tripoli by mobs, protesting at the presence in the USA of the exiled Shah of Iran, led to the withdrawal of the US Ambassador in December 1979. In May 1980 Qaddafi announced that he was exacting compensation to the value of thousands of millions of dollars from the USA, the United Kingdom and Italy for damage which had been sustained by Libya during the North African campaigns of the Second World War. These countries were threatened with a petroleum embargo and the withdrawal of Libyan assets from their banking systems if the demands were not met. In mid-1979 Libyan petroleum accounted for an estimated 600,000 of the 8m. barrels per day which were being imported by the USA.

Although Qaddafi strenuously denied Libyan involvement, a guerrilla raid on the Tunisian mining town of Gafsa in January 1980, with the presumed intent to incite a popular rebellion, was attributed to Libya. France sent military aid to support the Tunisian Government against the potential Libyan threat, and in February the French Embassy in Tripoli and consulate in Benghazi were burned as a demonstration of Libya's anger at this action. The incident prompted Qaddafi to pledge publicly his determination to counter French intervention in Africa by any means. In February 1982, however, relations between Libya and Tunisia improved when Qaddafi visited Tunisia and a co-operation agreement between the two countries was signed.

In March and April 1979 a Libyan military presence in Uganda was unable to prevent the overthrow of Idi Amin, and heavy losses were incurred. Morocco severed diplomatic relations in April 1980, following the decision by Libya to recognize the independence of the Western Sahara.

During the early months of 1981 there was a build-up of Soviet and East European military advisers in Libya, and in March 1983 it was announced that Qaddafi was to sign a treaty of friendship and co-operation with the USSR. The treaty was not expected, however, to contain military clauses which would commit the USSR to supporting Libya in the event of armed clashes. This increasing interest in the USSR closely paralleled worsening relations with the USA. The US Embassy in Tripoli was closed down in May 1981 and relations deteriorated further in August, when US aircraft shot down two Libyan aircraft which had intercepted them over the Gulf of Sirte, claimed by Libya as its territorial waters. In November 1981 President Ronald Reagan alleged that a Libyan 'hit-squad' had been sent to assassinate him.

In February 1983 relations with the USA deteriorated further with the discovery of an alleged Libyan coup plot against the Sudanese Government. US naval vessels moved into Libyan waters and four US surveillance aircraft were spotted over the Libyan-Sudanese border. The US Administration, however, denied that these events were anything more than routine military movements, and said that US troops were merely training Egyptian forces.

LIBYA'S INVOLVEMENT IN CHAD: 1973–88

For many years Libya had been supporting the Front de libération nationale du Tchad (FROLINAT) in its rebellion against the Chad Government. In 1973 Libya occupied the Aozou strip, a region of 114,000 sq km (reputed to contain valuable deposits of minerals) in the north of Chad, basing its action on an unratified treaty of 1935, whereby Italy and France altered the frontiers between their two colonies and, according to Libya, sovereignty over the strip passed to Italy and subsequently to Libya, when it achieved independence in 1951. Chad raised this grievance at the OAU conference in Gabon in July 1977, and an *ad hoc* committee of reconciliation was established to regulate affairs in the disputed area, but Libya consistently refused to attend its sessions. In March 1978 the FROLINAT rebels were achieving such success against the Chad army that Gen. Félix Malloum (the President of Chad) was forced to appeal to Libya to arrest the progress of the rebels. A cease-fire was arranged at reconciliation meetings, held in the Libyan towns of Sebha and Benghazi, at the end of March. Sporadic fighting continued, however, amid allegations that certain factions of FROLINAT were still receiving substantial Libyan support.

A series of military reverses resulted in the downfall of the Malloum Government in March 1979 and, following an initiative by Nigeria, a cease-fire was signed at Kano by the four opposing Chadian factions. With the prospect of a share in the government of Chad at last, the mainstream of FROL-INAT and, earlier, certain splinter groups withdrew their support from Libya over its annexation of the Aozou strip. Although a signatory of the Kano agreement, Libya engaged in a series of retaliatory attacks deep inside the northern border in mid-April. In June a 2,500-strong Libyan army invaded northern Chad and was driven back after several days' fierce fighting by FROLINAT forces. Chad's new coalition Government, formed in late April, was dominated by former FROLINAT insurgents and excluded the extreme factions from the south. The secessionist movement which subsequently appeared in the south was soon known to be receiving considerable support from Libya, while Libyan military aid continued to be received by certain guerrilla groups in the north. Dissent by the south and external pressure led to the disintegration of the coalition Government, but a second attempt to implement a 'Government of National Unity' foundered as, parallel to the north-south conflict, the inter-Muslim conflict intensified between President Goukouni Oueddei and the Minister of Defence, Hissène Habré. By March 1980 the Chad capital, N'Djamena, was the site of a pitched battle

between the armies of the President and his allies and Habré's forces. In May Libya responded to an appeal from President Goukouni (some of whose Muslim rivals had received Libyan backing a year earlier) for reinforcements to help in stemming the rapid advance of Habré's forces in the capital.

During the latter half of 1980 an increasing number of Libyan troops were engaged in Chad, eventually helping President Goukouni to overcome the forces of Hissène Habré in December. In January 1981 it was announced that Libya and Chad had resolved to work for 'complete unity'. This could have been interpreted either as an agreed merger or as an occupation which was imposed on Chad by Libya. Some Libyan units withdrew from Chad in May 1981, but others remained because of a supposed threat from Sudan, which distrusted Qaddafi's African intentions. Some observers considered that Qaddafi had plans for the creation of a vast 'Saharan Republic', comprising Libya, Niger, Chad, Algeria, Tunisia and Mauritania, but, if so, this plan received a set-back in October 1981, when President Goukouni of Chad requested the removal of some 10,000 Libyan troops from his country. They were subsequently replaced by an OAU peace-keeping force, although Libya maintained troops in the Aozou strip. Despite Libyan support, Goukouni was unable to keep control of Chad, and the capital, N'Djamena, was captured by Habré's forces in June 1982.

Qaddafi persistently denied the charge of interfering in Chad's internal affairs, but in June 1983 Libyan aircraft supported troops of ex-President Goukouni Oueddei in capturing the city of Faya-Largeau, in northern Chad, from Chadian government forces. Government troops repossessed the town at the end of July but, after prolonged bombing by Libyan aircraft, it again fell to the rebel forces in August. France responded to a request for aid from President Habré by deploying 3,000 troops in Chad from August, ostensibly in the role of military instructors, although they had orders to retaliate if fired upon. A defensive line across Chad at latitude 15° N, secured by French troops, caused a military stalemate, and serious fighting did not resume until after the collapse of peace negotiations in January 1984, when French troops extended the defensive line 100 km northwards to latitude 16° N. By April 1984 Libya was reported to have annexed the northern desert area of Chad and to have 6,000–7,000 troops in the region. The French force remained to the south, in the hope of a political solution. Libya, having made the Aozou strip secure, seemed to have achieved its main objective and to have abandoned all pretence of simply supporting the rebels. In May Qaddafi offered to withdraw Libyan troops from Chad if France would, in turn, withdraw its forces. In September, without consulting the Government of Chad, France and Libya reached an agreement providing for the evacuation of both countries' forces. In November it was reported that the joint withdrawal had been completed, although US and Chadian intelligence reports maintained that some 4,000–5,000 Libyan troops remained in northern Chad. In December 1984 President Mitterrand of France declined to intervene to remove Libyan forces from Chad by force, except in the event of their moving south of latitude 16° N.

Libyan forces allegedly supported the rebel army of Goukouni Oueddei, when it ended a lull in the civil war in February 1986, by launching an offensive southwards, across latitude 16° N. France sent a small 'deterrent' force to support President Habré, and French fighter-bombers attacked the Libyan-built rebel airfield at Ouadi Doum. In October Libya transferred its support from the Chadian rebels who were led by Goukouni to those led by Acheikh Ibn Oumar, the leader of the Conseil Démocratique Révolutionnaire (CDR), one of the factions in the loose GUNT coalition of opposition groups. The latter replaced Goukouni as the leader of the GUNT in November. Goukouni had been pursuing a conciliatory policy towards President Habré, and at the end of October he was reportedly wounded while resisting arrest in Tripoli. Goukouni's Forces Armées Populaires (FAP) declared allegiance to Habré's Government, in opposition to the Libyan presence in Chad. The FAP lost control of the oasis town of Zouar, in north-western Chad, in December, but recaptured it in January 1987, with the assistance of government troops, who had earlier occupied the Libyan garrison town of Fada, near latitude 16°N. At the end of March Libyan forces abandoned their last important base in Chad, at Faya-Largeau (after it had been rendered indefensible by the government troops' capture of the airbase at Ouadi Doum, 150 km to the north-west), and retreated towards Aozou. An estimated 4,000 Libyan soldiers were killed between January and the end of March, and Libya was forced to abandon Soviet-made aircraft at Ouadi Doum, valued at $500m. Libyan troops in Chad (whose involvement in the fighting Col Qaddafi publicly continued to deny) were supported by the motley Islamic Pan-African Legion, a force consisting of mercenaries and volunteers from many African countries, which was formed in Libya.

President Habré's forces advanced into the Aozou strip and captured the town of Aozou in a new offensive on 8 August 1987. France, which maintained a force of 2,400 troops to the south of latitude 16° N, refused to provide protective fighter aircraft, or to deploy troops north of that latitude, in support of the Chadian Government offensive, which it had counselled against. Libya responded to the loss of Aozou by bombing towns in northern Chad, including Faya-Largeau, Ouadi Doum and Aozou itself. Libyan counter-attacks on Aozou on 14 and 20 August were both repulsed, but on 28 August Libyan forces recaptured the town, and advanced on Ounianga-Kebir, 100 km south of the disputed strip. Chadian forces responded by capturing and destroying an airbase at Maaten as-Sarra, 100 km inside Libya (claimed to be a base for Libyan raids on Chad), on 6 September. France criticized the Chadian incursion into Libya, reiterating its opinion that the question of sovereignty over the Aozou strip should be determined by international arbitration. On 11 September Chad and Libya agreed to observe a cease-fire proposed by the OAU. Later in the month Col Qaddafi refused to attend a session in Lusaka, Zambia, of the six-nation *ad hoc* committee established by the OAU to consider the conflict in Chad. However, President Habré was present, and Libya was represented by the Secretary for Foreign Liaison, Jadallah Azouz at-Tali.

In November 1987 the UN General Assembly refused to debate the Aozou issue, concluding that its resolution was the responsibility of the OAU. The OAU *ad hoc* committee accordingly proposed a summit meeting of the Libyan and Chadian Heads of State, which, after several postponements, was finally scheduled for 24 May 1988. However, on the eve of the summit, it was announced that Col Qaddafi would not be attending, in protest at Chad's treatment of prisoners of war. Qaddafi had continued to state his terms for a peaceful settlement of the dispute as: the recognition of Libyan sovereignty over the Aozou strip; the withdrawal of 'foreign troops' from Chad; the conclusion of an armistice between President Habré and the opposition forces led by Goukouni; and the release of prisoners of war. On 25 May, however, in a speech delivered in Tripoli to celebrate the 25th anniversary of the foundation of the OAU, Col Qaddafi announced his willingness to recognize the Government of Hissène Habré. He also invited Habré and Goukouni to hold reconciliation talks in Libya and offered to provide financial aid for the reconstruction of bombed towns in northern Chad. In June Habré said that he was ready to re-establish diplomatic relations with Libya, which had been severed in 1982. The Ministers of Foreign Affairs of Libya and Chad held further talks in Gabon in July but, apart from reaching agreement, in principle, to the restoration of diplomatic links, no progress was made on the crucial issues of sovereignty over the Aozou strip, the return of Libyan prisoners of war and the future security of common borders.

On 3 October 1988 Libya and Chad announced the resumption of diplomatic relations and an undertaking to settle their differences by peaceful means and to co-operate with the OAU committee appointed for that purpose.

SETTLEMENT OF CHAD CONFLICT

On 31 August 1989 a peace accord was signed in Algiers by the Libyan Secretary for Foreign Liaison, Jadallah Azouz at-Tali, and Chad's Minister of Foreign Affairs, Acheikh Ibn Oumar, envisaging an end to fighting over the disputed Aozou strip. The agreement, concluded with the help of Algerian mediation, envisaged that the parties would attempt to resolve their dispute through a political settlement within one year.

It further provided for the withdrawal of all forces from the disputed region, which was to be placed under the administration of a group of African observers, pending a settlement. All hostilities were to cease, and all prisoners being detained by both sides were to be released.

In October 1989 Chad claimed that its forces had killed 600 members of the Libyan-backed Islamic Pan-African Legion near its border with Sudan. Libya denied Chadian claims that it was involved in the activities of the Legion, including border violations contrary to the peace accord signed in Algiers. In November a joint commission, composed of delegations from Chad and Libya, held its first meeting to consider the provisions of the Algiers agreement.

In March 1990 Chad claimed that a further violation of its borders by mercenaries belonging to the Islamic Pan-African Legion had taken place with the support of the Sudanese Government, which was alleged to have allowed its territory to be used to launch the incursion. In April the Chadian Government claimed to have intercepted and destroyed forces belonging to the legion within Chadian territory, and accused Libya of reinforcing its military presence in the Aozou strip with Palestinian mercenaries. Libya again denied any involvement in the activities of the Legion. Following a meeting in August in the Moroccan capital, Rabat, between Col Qaddafi and President Habré, the Chadian Minister of Foreign Affairs announced that the dispute over the Aozou strip would be referred to the International Court of Justice and that both countries would continue to seek a political settlement to the conflict.

In December 1990 the Government of President Habré was overthrown, following a three-week campaign by the rebel Patriotic Salvation Movement, led by Col Idris Déby. Déby, who proclaimed himself President, had used Sudan as a base for his activities and had been supplied with weapons and other equipment by Libya. He received immediate congratulations from Col Qaddafi, who welcomed the new regime's decision to repatriate 2,000 Libyan prisoners of war, detained in Chad since the end of the 1986–87 war. However, some 700 Libyan prisoners of war who opposed Qaddafi and who had reportedly been training at a camp near Lake Chad that was operated by the US Government's Central Intelligence Agency (CIA), were evacuated by the USA, arousing protests from Tripoli. Despite President Déby's denials of involvement, the incident resulted in a sharp decline in relations between Chad and Libya. In May 1991 the USA was reported to have offered asylum to some 350 of the former Libyan soldiers.

QADDAFI'S ATTEMPTS TO QUELL OPPOSITION AT HOME AND ABROAD

In February 1980 the third meeting of the revolutionary committees, bodies dominated by students and young male adults, which are responsible for ensuring the progress of the revolution at popular level (and which, effectively, impose Qaddafi's will on the popular, or people's committees), called for the 'physical liquidation' of opponents of the revolution who were living abroad and of 'elements obstructing change' inside Libya. An extensive anti-corruption campaign was launched in the same month, ostensibly to eradicate 'economic' crime. Between February and April, more than 2,000 people were arrested, mainly on charges of bribery, to be tried by members of the revolutionary committees. However, the arrests of several senior military officers introduced political overtones. In April Qaddafi issued an ultimatum to Libyan exiles abroad to return to Libya by 10 June, beyond which date he could not undertake to protect them from the revenge of the revolutionary committees. Since February 1980 several Libyans who were known to be hostile to the regime have been killed in Western countries.

Of the two new ministerial posts created at the ninth meeting of the GPC in February 1984, one was that of secretary for external security (the other being secretary of universities), to which Col Younis Bilqassim Ali was appointed. Although the functions of the post were not officially described, its creation appeared to formalize the activities of the Libyan Government to protect its representatives abroad and to silence opponents of the regime inside Libya and elsewhere, which had already been pursued for some time. An office, attached to the Bureau of Foreign Liaison, to combat international terrorism was also established in early 1984. The chief of the People's Bureau in Rome had been assassinated in January, and generally the Libyan authorities seemed sensitive to the growth of opposition groups abroad. The National Front for the Salvation of Libya, which came to the fore in 1984, had been formed in 1981 and was based in Sudan under the leadership of Muhammad Yousuf Mugharief, a former Libyan Ambassador to India, but it was only one of several such groups opposed to Qaddafi, which he accused foreign governments of nurturing.

Early in March 1984, following a repetition of the official exhortation to Libyans, first made in 1980, to liquidate enemies of the revolution, seven bombs exploded in the United Kingdom, in Manchester and London. It was believed that these attacks were aimed at Libyan dissidents whom Qaddafi had recently accused the United Kingdom of harbouring. Then, on 17 April, during a demonstration outside the Libyan People's Bureau in London by Libyans opposed to Qaddafi's regime, a policewoman was killed and 11 people were injured by shots fired from inside the Bureau. A 10-day siege of the Bureau ensued, during which the United Kingdom broke off diplomatic relations with Libya and ordered its diplomats to leave the country—which they did on 27 April. Revolutionary students had taken over the Bureau in February with the tacit approval of the Libyan Government. Qaddafi denied responsibility for the murder of the policewoman but, after the United Kingdom broke off diplomatic relations, he was understood to have ordered so-called 'hit-squads' to suspend their activities in Europe for fear of economic or other sanctions.

Inside Libya, Qaddafi's opponents had been active already during 1984. In March an explosion at an ammunition dump in al-Abyar had killed or wounded several hundred Libyan soldiers, but the most serious incident took place on 17 May, when up to 20 commandos belonging to the National Front for the Salvation of Libya attacked Qaddafi's residence in a heavily fortified barracks in the suburbs of Tripoli. According to the Front, 15 of the commandos were killed but heavy casualties were inflicted on Libyan soldiers.

The actions of Qaddafi's opponents were the signal for a wave of arrests of suspected dissidents in the first half of 1984, and several students were hanged.

QADDAFI'S CONFUSED FOREIGN POLICY

With visits to Jordan, the Yemen Arab Republic, Saudi Arabia, Algeria and Morocco during the second half of 1983, Qaddafi seemed intent on ending Libya's diplomatic isolation, but there was no compromise on his support for Goukouni Oueddei in Chad and for the Polisario Front in the Western Sahara, issues on which he had ignominiously failed to win backing at the OAU summit in June. Libya, with Syria and the People's Democratic Republic of Yemen, again found itself in a minority by dissenting from the decision of the Organization of the Islamic Conference, taken in January 1984, to readmit Egypt to membership. Qaddafi was also open in his support of the revolt against Yasser Arafat's leadership of the Palestine National Liberation Movement (Fatah), and of Iran in the Iran–Iraq War. Iraq severed diplomatic relations with Libya in June 1985, after Qaddafi had signed a 'strategic alliance' with Iran.

After the attack on his Tripoli headquarters in May 1984, Qaddafi accused Tunisia of being involved with Sudan and the United Kingdom in the incident. Libyan agents had previously sabotaged an oil pipeline from Algeria to Tunisia. Tunisia withdrew its Ambassador to Tripoli for a time before relations were restored. In May 1984, in common with other Arab countries, Libya 'froze' diplomatic relations with Liberia and Zaire after they had restored their relations with Israel. Libya's support of the Fatah rebels and the secessionist movement in southern Sudan put it at variance with Jordan and Egypt, the leaders of an emergent moderate Arab tendency. The sacking of the Jordanian Embassy in Tripoli in February caused Jordan to break off diplomatic relations with Libya.

On 13 August 1984 Libya and Morocco unexpectedly signed a treaty of union in Oujda (Morocco). The proposed 'Arab-African Federation' was unanimously approved by the Libyan GPC on 31 August and endorsed by an overwhelming majority in a Moroccan referendum on the same day. From the outset, the incongruous partnership of King Hassan's moderate, pro-Western Morocco and Col Qaddafi's maverick Libya had an air of impermanence, particularly in the light of previous and, on the surface, more likely 'unions' of Arab states which had proved abortive. The union, which Qaddafi envisaged as the first step towards the creation of a politically united 'Greater Maghreb', soon demonstrated the weakness of its foundations. The first meeting of the joint parliamentary assembly of Libya and Morocco, which was due to take place in Rabat in July 1985, was cancelled by King Hassan in anger over Col Qaddafi's announcement of a treaty between Libya and Iran. King Hassan abrogated the treaty of union with Libya at the end of August 1986, following violent criticism by Qaddafi of his meeting in July with the Israeli Prime Minister, Shimon Peres.

A previous agreement establishing a confederation of Arab states involving Libya, which had been a dead letter for years, was effectively dissolved in October 1984, when Egypt unilaterally withdrew from the putative 'Union of Arab Republics' which it had entered into with Libya and Syria in 1971. Egypt had accused Libya and Iran of laying mines in the Red Sea and the Gulf of Suez, which had damaged 18 vessels in July and August 1984, and suspected it of other terrorist and espionage activities. Colonel Qaddafi caused Egypt further alarm when he visited Sudan in May 1985 to endorse the new regime of Lt-Gen. Abd ar-Rahman Swar ad-Dahab, who overthrew President Nimeri in a bloodless coup in April 1985. Nimeri had been one of the very few Arab leaders who had supported President Sadat of Egypt's peace initiative with Israel in 1978, which was anathema to Qaddafi, who was repeatedly accused of supporting plots to topple the Nimeri Government. Qaddafi urged the rebels in southern Sudan (the Sudanese People's Liberation Army), whom he had supported against Nimeri, to surrender their weapons and to begin negotiations with the new Government. He also advocated the overthrow of 'reactionary regimes' in the region, presumably a reference to Egypt and Jordan. Diplomatic relations between Libya and Sudan were restored in April, and a military protocol, whereby Libya was to aid Sudan in training its armed forces and supplying equipment, was signed in Tripoli in July. By 1988 Libya had emerged as Sudan's principal supplier of armaments. At the same time, Libyan troops and members of the Islamic Legion, recruited by Libya, were alleged to have crossed into Sudan, in the region of Northern Darfur which has borders with Libya and Chad, at will, while Chadian rebel forces, supported by Libya, launched raids into Chad from Southern Darfur. Following a military coup in Sudan in June 1989, the new regime announced its intention to negotiate a peace settlement with the rebels in southern Sudan. At a meeting in Libya in March 1990 the Sudanese military leader, Gen. Omar Hassan Ahmad al-Bashir, and Col Qaddafi discussed the framework for a possible union between their two countries. An agreement on integration, signed in Tripoli in August 1990, was intended to facilitate a full merger. Neighbouring countries reacted with concern at this development. A charter linking the Libyan province of Tahadi and the Darfur region of Sudan was scheduled to be considered at a meeting in October 1990. Little significant progress towards a merger has since been achieved, although 'minutes of integration' and an agreement on freedom of movement, residence, work and ownership were signed by Libya and Sudan in June 1991.

In December 1984 Libya and Malta signed a five-year security and economic co-operation treaty, whereby Libya was required to defend Malta if requested to do so by the Maltese Government. In June 1985 a ruling by the International Court of Justice in The Hague, on a maritime boundary dispute between Libya and Malta, extended Libya's territorial waters 18 nautical miles (33 km) northwards towards Malta.

In July 1985 Col Qaddafi barred Egyptians from working in Libya, in retaliation against a similar measure preventing Libyans from working in Egypt. In the following month, Tunisia expelled 283 Libyans (including 30 diplomats) for alleged spying. Earlier, Libya had begun to expel Tunisian workers from Libya. About 30,000 Tunisians were deported between

August and October, and thousands of others from Mali, Mauritania, Niger and Syria were also expelled, officially as part of a policy to achieve self-sufficiency in labour. Tunisian imports were halted, and Col Qaddafi urged the overthrow of Tunisia's President Bourguiba. On 26 September Tunisia severed its diplomatic relations with Libya.

CONFLICT WITH THE USA

Details of a plan by the CIA to undermine the Qaddafi regime in Libya were revealed in the American press in November 1985, and the growing US conviction that Libya was promoting international terrorism contributed to a serious worsening of relations between the two countries towards the end of 1985. Libya had already been accused by Egypt of co-ordinating the hijacking of an Egyptian airliner to Malta in November, as a result of which 60 people had died. The incident led to an increase of military tension along the Libyan-Egyptian border. On 27 December Palestinian terrorists killed 19 people in simultaneous attacks on passengers at the departure desks of the Israeli airline, El Al, in Rome and Vienna airports. The US Government accused Libya of harbouring and training the members of Abu Nidal's Fatah Revolutionary Council, who were believed to be responsible for the attacks, and of being a centre for international terrorism. On 7 January 1986 President Reagan ordered the severance of all economic and commercial relations with Libya, and, on the following day, 'froze' Libyan assets in the USA. However, he was unsuccessful in persuading the USA's European allies to impose economic sanctions against Libya. A meeting of the Ministers of Foreign Affairs of Arab countries belonging to the Organization of the Islamic Conference gave verbal support to Libya in January.

A dispute over navigational rights was the ostensible cause of the eventual clash between US and Libyan forces in 1986, though, as far as the USA was concerned, it had the appearance of a pretext for the clash itself, and the naval manoeuvres which led up to it, despite the fact that Libya was the first actually to use military force. Libya had maintained since 1973 that the entire Gulf of Sirte, and not merely the 12 nautical miles (22 km) off its coast that were recognized by international law, constituted Libyan territorial waters. In December 1985 Col Qaddafi drew a notional 'line of death' across the north of the Gulf of Sirte, along latitude 32° 30' N, which he warned US and other foreign shipping not to cross. At the end of January 1986, ostensibly in the exercise of its right to navigation in the area under international law, the US Navy's Sixth Fleet was deployed off the Libyan coast, though it appears that at no time did any US vessel cross the 'line of death'. On 24 March, the day after the Sixth Fleet had begun its fourth set of manoeuvres in the area since January (and the eighteenth since 1981), Libya fired Soviet SAM-5 missiles (which had been operational only since January) at US fighter aircraft flying over the Gulf of Sirte and inside the 'line of death'. In two retaliatory attacks on 24 and 25 March, US fighter aircraft destroyed missile and radar facilities in the coastal town of Sirte, and sank four Libyan patrol boats in the Gulf. A meeting of the League of Arab States criticized the US action, but rejected a Libyan appeal for Arab economic sanctions to be imposed against the USA.

On 5 April a bomb exploded in a discotheque in West Berlin, killing a US soldier and a Turkish woman. The USA gathered what it considered to be irrefutable evidence connecting Libya with this and a catalogue of other incidents and plots against US targets in Europe and the Middle East. On 15 April US military aircraft (including 18 F-111 fighter-bombers from bases in the United Kingdom and planes from the Sixth Fleet) bombed military installations, airports, government buildings (among them Col Qaddafi's own residential compound) and suspected terrorist training camps and communication centres in the Libyan cities of Tripoli and Benghazi. A total of 37 people were reported to have died in the raids, including many civilians, who were the inevitable victims of bombs and missiles which were directed against military or terrorist targets in largely civilian areas. On 16 April Libya fired two missiles at the Italian island of Lampedusa, the site of a US coastguard station.

The US raids were generally deplored as a new round in an escalation of violence in the Middle East, and an upsurge in

terrorist activity in Europe and the Middle East was feared. However, there was little sympathy for Libya. Most other Arab countries confined themselves to verbal condemnation of the USA, and Libya was disappointed by the Soviet reaction, which was purely rhetorical. A meeting of the League of Arab States failed to take place after a disagreement over the agenda, which Qaddafi demanded should only include discussion of the US raid. Libya expelled about 250 foreign journalists at the end of April 1986, and in May, after the EC had decided to limit the size of Libyan diplomatic and commercial delegations within the Community, to restrict the movement of Libyan diplomats, and to tighten immigration regulations against Libyans, Col Qaddafi ordered the expulsion from Libya of 36 diplomats representing seven West European countries.

In the weeks following the US raids, Col Qaddafi was only rarely seen in public. There were rumours that he had lost overall control of the Government to Maj. Abd as-Salam Jalloud, who, although he held no formal government post, was accepted to be Qaddafi's deputy and was head of Libya's revolutionary committees (popular organizations throughout the country, which exist independently of the government bureaucracy) and the revolutionary guard corps, which were entrusted with responsibility for preserving the integrity of the revolution. The US Government had hoped that the raids on Libya would destabilize the regime of Col Qaddafi and create the conditions in which opposition groups could stage a coup. However, as the year progressed, Qaddafi gradually emerged from his retreat and appeared to remain firmly in control of government. At the end of May 1986, the USSR promised to continue sales of military equipment to Libya, but urged the condemnation of terrorism.

Conflict with the USA erupted again in January 1989, when US aircraft shot down two Libyan fighter aircraft in 'self-defence' over international waters in the Mediterranean. The incident occurred at a time when the USA was becoming concerned that Libya was about to produce chemical weapons at a plant near Rabta, 60 km south of Tripoli. Qaddafi claimed that the plant was a pharmaceutical factory, being built with West German and Japanese help.

MAGHREB UNITY

In March and June 1986, in an attempt to consolidate its good relations with Algeria, Libya proposed a union of the two countries. The proposal was submitted to President Chadli of Algeria by Col Qaddafi's deputy, Maj. Jalloud, in June 1987. At the end of Jalloud's visit to Algiers, the parties issued a joint communiqué stating that President Chadli and Col Qaddafi would meet to discuss the proposal, although Algeria, reacting unenthusiastically, to Libya's approaches, emphasized the need for 'compatibilities' between the countries— apparently a reference to Algeria's concern over Libya's intervention in Chad and its policy towards Tunisia. Algeria subsequently suggested that a framework for a new Algerian-Libyan relationship (and, by definition, one not going as far as actual union) already existed in the Maghreb Fraternity and Co-operation Treaty of 1983, between Algeria, Mauritania and Tunisia. Later in June, at short notice, Col Qaddafi arrived in Algeria in an attempt to persuade President Chadli to accede to the union proposals. However, he succeeded only in achieving agreement on several minor co-operation issues.

Economic links between Libya and Algeria expanded, and in early October 1987 the two Governments agreed in principle on a treaty of political union. The accord was to be announced officially on 1 November, but, owing to political opposition in Algeria, the announcement was not made. Instead, the Algerian Government proposed that Libya should sign the Maghreb Fraternity and Co-operation Treaty. This eventuality was made more likely by the re-establishment of diplomatic relations (at consular level) between Libya and Tunisia at the end of December.

In February 1988 Col Qaddafi, President Chadli and President Ben Ali of Tunisia held discussions concerning a proposed regional political accord, following which the border between Libya and Tunisia was re-opened.

An expansion of economic co-operation was treated as the first stage towards regional integration in other fields. On 22

March 1988 Libya and Algeria signed two agreements relating to industrial development. The first was for a tripartite project to supply an estimated 90,000m. cu m of Algerian natural gas to Libya, via a trans-Tunisian pipeline. The second provided for the construction of a combined aluminium and petroleum coke complex in Zuwarah, Libya, to generate electricity for both countries, and the establishment of a joint company to undertake petrochemical projects. In April Libya and Tunisia signed a co-operation pact encompassing political, economic, cultural and foreign relations. Few details were released, but plans included the construction of an oil pipeline between Libya and Tunisia. Colonel Qaddafi announced that, from the date of the pact, Tunisians would be given priority among foreign nationals seeking employment in Libya, while the border posts on the frontier with Tunisia would be dismantled and Libyans and Tunisians would be guaranteed freedom of movement in both directions.

The leaders of the five countries of the Maghreb (Algeria, Morocco, Tunisia, Libya and Mauritania) held a meeting in Algiers (the first of its kind since they achieved independence), after the Arab summit there in June 1988, to discuss the prospects for 'a Maghreb without frontiers'. After the meeting, the participants issued a joint communiqué announcing the creation of a Maghreb commission, comprising a delegation from each of the five countries, to concentrate on the establishment of a semi-legislative, semi-consultative council which would co-ordinate legislation in the region and prepare joint economic projects. At the end of June, Algeria and Libya announced that they would each be holding a referendum on a proposed union of the two countries. The proposition to be considered by the peoples of Algeria and Libya, however, fell short of the total merger for which Col Qaddafi had hoped, and envisaged, instead, a federation of the two states, within a Great Arab Maghreb.

In July 1988 the Maghreb commission met for the first time, in Algiers, and announced the creation of five working parties to examine areas of regional integration (including education, finance, economy and regional security), which would report to the second meeting of the commission in October. In August President Ben Ali of Tunisia visited Libya, and he and Col Qaddafi signed a series of co-operation agreements and established a technical commission to examine means of accelerating co-operation and the merger process, as a prelude to the creation of the Great Arab Maghreb.

In February 1989, at a summit meeting in Morocco of North African Heads of State, the participants concluded a treaty proclaiming the formation of a 'Union of the Arab Maghreb' (UAM), comprising Algeria, Libya, Mauritania, Morocco and Tunisia. The treaty envisaged the establishment of a council of Heads of State, regular meetings of Ministers of Foreign Affairs, and the eventual free movement of goods, services and capital throughout the countries of the region. At the second summit meeting of the Union of the Arab Maghreb, held in Algiers in July 1990, it was decided that Libya would hold the annual presidency of the Union in 1991.

A third summit meeting of the UAM was held in Ras Lanuf, Libya, on 10 March 1991 and was opened by Col Qaddafi in his role as President of the organization for the first six months of that year. This was the first meeting of the UAM states since the invasion of Kuwait by Iraq in August 1990 and it reflected the difficulty they had encountered in maintaining a united response towards the conflict in the Gulf region. The final communiqué expressed 'deep pain over the tragic developments in the Gulf' and urged that the economic sanctions imposed on Iraq by the UN should be lifted. Agreement was reached on the establishment of a Maghreb Bank of Investment and Foreign Trade, and on co-operation in other fields. At a subsequent UAM summit meeting in Casablanca in September 1991 the forthcoming Middle East peace conference was discussed and the UN was urged to lift the economic sanctions that it had imposed on Libya.

GOVERNMENT CHANGES AND DOMESTIC REFORM

At its annual meeting in 1986, the GPC reduced the number of secretariats in the General People's Committee from 22 to 10. Several Committee posts were merged or abolished. Changes of personnel were also made in the composition of the General Secretariat of the GPC. The object of the changes was, apparently, greater administrative efficiency. The public service functions of the secretariats which were dismantled were, in future, to be handled by specially created national companies, such as already existed for the administration of the petroleum industry, the secretariat for which was among those to be abolished. The GPC also resolved to form 'suicide squads to strike at the enemy'. According to the human rights organization, Amnesty International, Libya assassinated at least 25 of its political opponents abroad between 1980 and 1987. In March 1987 the GPC elected a new General People's Committee. Only three Secretaries were re-elected from the previous Committee, and only two of these retained their former posts.

Increasing dissatisfaction at home with political repression, a deteriorating economy and shortages of basic commodities, combined with opposition to the military involvement in Chad, pressure from abroad to improve the image of his Government and ease his political isolation, caused Col Qaddafi to embark on a series of liberalizing economic and political reforms during 1988. In foreign policy, Qaddafi openly admitted the error of his involvement in Chad and adopted a more pragmatic approach to his ambition of union within the Maghreb and to his relations with other Arab and African countries, eliminating barriers to trade and tourism with neighbouring countries and declaring his opposition to terrorism. At home, he accused Libya's Revolutionary Committees of murdering political opponents of his regime. In early March Qaddafi began to encourage the reopening of private businesses, in recognition of the failure of the state-sponsored supermarkets to satisfy the demand for even the most basic commodities, which had caused a thriving 'black market' to emerge. At the same time, all prisoners (including foreigners), except those convicted of violent crimes or of conspiring with foreign powers, were released; Libyan citizens were guaranteed freedom of travel abroad; and the Revolutionary Committees were deprived of their powers of arrest and imprisonment, which had often been indiscriminately and arbitrarily used. A new secretariat (ministry) was formed in May for Jamahiri ('masses') Mobilization and Revolutionary Guidance, apparently to monitor and regulate the Revolutionary Committees. In June the General People's Congress (GPC) approved a charter of human rights, guaranteeing freedom of expression and condemning violence. In March the GPC had created a People's Court and a People's Prosecution Bureau to replace the 'revolutionary courts'.

At the end of August 1988, Col Qaddafi announced the abolition of the army and the police force. The army was to be replaced by a force of Jamahiri Guards, comprising conscripts and members of the existing army and police force, which would be supervised by 'people's defence committees' located in strategic areas. The most obvious sign of the practical implementation of a new policy of government decentralization was the decision in September to relocate all but two of the secretariats of the General People's Committee (ministries) away from the capital, Tripoli, mostly in Sirte, 400 km east of Tripoli. Further reform was promised when, in January 1989, Qaddafi announced that all state institutions, including the state intelligence service and the official Libyan news agency, were to be abolished.

There were reports, in November 1989, of a challenge to Col Qaddafi's leadership by Muslim fundamentalists. Armed clashes between them and the Libyan security forces were reported to have occurred, prompting Col Qaddafi to urge the GPC to consider legislation to suppress fundamentalist groups.

At the meeting of the 16th session of the GPC, held in Tripoli during 2–10 March 1990 to consider future government policy, Col Qaddafi strongly criticized corruption in government administration. The Secretary for Higher Education subsequently tendered his resignation, following criticism from delegates, and the Secretary for Transport also resigned, in protest at corruption and the exorbitant fares charged by the state-controlled Jerma Bus Company.

In October 1990 the GPC implemented the most extensive changes to the General People's Committee since March 1987. The appointment of the uncompromising Abu Zayd Umar Dourda as the new Secretary-General (Prime Minister) and of 11 new Secretaries was approved, increasing the number of secretariats in the GPC from 19 to 22. The opposition National Front for the Salvation of Libya claimed that several of those promoted had been involved in purges against dissidents and had been expelled from European countries. The former Secretary-General, the moderate Umar Mustafa al-Muntasser, was appointed Secretary of a new combined Economic and Planning Secretariat. The new Strategic Industries Secretariat was to be headed by another moderate, Jadallah Azouz, who was replaced as Secretary for Foreign Liaison by Ibrahim Mohammad Bashari. The Secretariats for Electricity, Social Security and Youth and Sports, which had been abolished in 1986, were revived. The Secretariat for Mass Mobilization and Revolutionary Guidance, formed in 1988, was abolished, and a new secretariat was created to promote co-operation with the Union of the Arab Maghreb. At the same time, three of the five-member General Secretariat of the GPC were replaced, Abd ar-Raziq Sawsa becoming Secretary-General of the GPC in place of Dr Muftah al-Usta Omar.

DEVELOPMENTS IN EXTERNAL RELATIONS

Following his reconciliation with Yasser Arafat's wing of the PLO in March 1987, Col Qaddafi sponsored efforts to reunite the divided Palestinian movement prior to the 18th session of the Palestine National Council in Algiers in April, although this strained relations with Syria, which had supported the revolt against Arafat's leadership of the PLO in 1983. It appeared that, after years of relative political isolation, Col Qaddafi found it expedient to realign Libyan policy with that of the majority of Arab states. After the Palestinian uprising (*intifada*) in the Israeli Occupied Territories began in December 1987, Col Qaddafi intensified his efforts to reconcile the opposing factions within the PLO, and in June 1988, at the request of Yasser Arafat, he sent Libyan representatives to Lebanon to mediate between Palestinian guerrillas loyal to Arafat and members of 'Abu Musa's' rebel Fatah, who were fighting for control of Beirut's Palestinian refugee camps. He subsequently intervened personally to persuade the Sunni Muslim militia in southern Lebanon to allow Arafat loyalists, who had been driven out of Beirut, to enter the Palestinian camp of Ain al-Hilweh, near Sidon. Yasser Arafat and representatives of the dissident, Syrian-backed PLO factions visited Tripoli in September 1988 to attend the anniversary celebrations of the Libyan revolution, and their presence gave rise to speculation of a reconciliation, engineered by Col Qaddafi. In June Col Qaddafi had attended an Arab summit meeting in Algiers (the first such summit that he had attended for 18 years), which had been arranged to discuss Arab support for the Palestinian uprising.

In May 1987 Australia ordered the closure of the Libyan People's Bureau in Canberra, accusing Libya of trying to destabilize the South Pacific region. Libya had been providing paramilitary training to dissident groups in the French territory of New Caledonia and the Indonesian provinces of Irian Jaya and East Timor, and, according to the Australian Government, had been involved in subversive activities in Australia.

In September 1987 Libya re-established 'fraternal' links with Iraq, modifying its support for Iran in the Iran–Iraq War and urging the observance of a cease-fire, according to the terms of UN Security Council Resolution 598. Later in the same month, Jordan restored its diplomatic relations with Libya. However, Libyan support for Iran had not completely ceased. Col Qaddafi refused to attend the extraordinary summit meeting of the League of Arab States which took place in Amman in November to discuss the war. His representative quickly dissociated Libya from an apparently unanimously supported resolution, which censured Iran for its occupation of Arab (i.e. Iraqi) territory and for failing to accept UN cease-fire proposals. Libya also dissented from the League's decision to remove the prohibition on diplomatic relations between member states and Egypt.

Libya attended an emergency summit meeting of the Arab League in Casablanca, Morocco, in May 1989, but not a meeting of the Ministers of Foreign Affairs of member states (held immediately prior to the summit meeting), at which Egypt was formally readmitted to the Arab League. Meetings between Col Qaddafi and President Mubarak of Egypt in October were thought to signal the countries' imminent reconciliation, but

by mid-1991 Libya remained the only Arab state not to have restored full diplomatic relations with Egypt following its diplomatic and economic isolation by Arab states in 1979. Meeting in Cairo in February 1990 for the fourth time since May 1989, Col Qaddafi and President Mubarak agreed to strengthen financial and economic ties between Egypt and Libya.

In March 1990 both the USA and the Federal Republic of Germany claimed that Libya had commenced production of mustard gas at a plant near Rabta, 60 km south of Tripoli (see above, 'Conflict with the USA'). When a fire broke out at the plant during the same month, Libya accused these countries, together with Israel, of involvement in sabotage. All three countries denied any involvement. The Federal German Government stated that it would take measures, in accordance with international law, to halt the production of chemical weapons at Rabta, while the US Government refused to discount future military action against the plant. In June the US Government alleged that the plant at Rabta had not been destroyed by fire, as Libya had claimed, and voiced suspicions that a second such plant, for the production of chemical weapons, was under construction. In July the US Government claimed that members of a Muslim movement, which was trying to overthrow the Government of Trinidad and Tobago, had received training in Libya.

Libya's relations with France improved in April 1990, after the release of three Europeans who had been held hostage in Lebanon. The French Government formally thanked the Libyan Government for its role in obtaining their release. In March France had returned to Libya three Mirage jet fighter aircraft which it had impounded in 1986 after their delivery to France for repairs. However, the French Government denied that the return of the aircraft had played any part in securing the release of the hostages. However, in September, following an official investigation, France alleged that Col Qaddafi, together with President Assad of Syria and the leader of the Popular Front for the Liberation of Palestine, Ahmad Jibril, had been responsible for planning the bombing of a French passenger aircraft over the Sahara in September 1989.

In June 1991, following a secret visit to Tripoli by a member of the United Kingdom Parliament, it was revealed that Col Qaddafi had offered £250,000 to a British police charity, together with a letter of regret for the killing of a policewoman outside the Libyan People's Bureau in London in 1984 (see Qaddafi's Attempts to Quell Opposition, above). The Member of Parliament was reported to have discussed with Col Qaddafi a series of proposals aimed at restoring diplomatic relations between the United Kingdom and Libya, which had been severed at the time of the incident. However, the proposal was rejected by the United Kingdom Foreign and Commonwealth Office (FCO), which said that there could be no possibility of a resumption of relations until there was convincing evidence that the Libyans had renounced their support for groups engaged in international terrorism, including the Irish Republican Army (IRA). In addition, the FCO emphasized that Libya should co-operate in bringing to justice those responsible for the murder.

Early in 1992 Col Qaddafi was reported to have given assurances, through intermediaries, that he would reveal to the United Kingdom Government information about his dealings with the IRA, in return for improved relations with the United Kingdom. However, in an interview with a British newspaper in May 1992 he appeared to renege on this promise, claiming that he feared that the revelation of such information might be used to 'trick' him. He admitted that Libya had supplied the IRA with arms and explosives, but denied that IRA members had trained in Libya. All links with the IRA had now been severed, he maintained.

THE GULF CONFLICT 1990–91

Col Qaddafi attended the emergency Arab League summit meeting, held in Cairo on 10 August 1990 to discuss the Arab response to the invasion of Kuwait by Iraq. Subsequently, 12 Arab nations voted in favour of a motion condemning the invasion and advocating the deployment of a pan-Arab force for the defence of Saudi Arabia and other states from possible Iraqi aggression. Libya voted against the measure, and in

September Libyan aircraft were reported to be transporting food supplies to Iraq in violation of UN Security Council Resolution 661 (of 6 August 1990) which imposed mandatory economic sanctions on Iraq. Libya also announced that its ports were at Iraq's disposal for the purpose of importing food supplies. Following the commencement, on 16 January 1991, by a multinational armed force, of 'Operation Desert Storm' to secure the liberation of Kuwait, anti-war demonstrations occurred in Libya. The Saudi Arabian Ambassador in Tripoli urged Col Qaddafi to support the concerted action, but during February the Libyan Government offered to supply food, medicine and blankets to Iraq.

President Mubarak of Egypt was thought to have persuaded Col Qaddafi to exercise restraint during the war between Iraq and the multinational force, and relations between Egypt and Libya continued to improve in its aftermath. Talks were held on moves towards greater economic integration, and in March 1991 Col Qaddafi abolished immigration and customs controls for Egyptians travelling to Libya. However, the subsequent flood of visitors resulted in the reimposition of checkpoints. Col Qaddafi visited Cairo in early July 1991 for the ratification of 10 integration agreements, and on 6 August the Egyptian Government announced the opening of Egypt's border with Libya, removing all obstacles to travel and trade. A security agreement on border movements was signed on 23 August.

INAUGURATION OF THE GREAT MAN-MADE RIVER

The first phase of Libya's 'Great Man-made River' project (GMR), begun in 1984 and designed to carry water from Saharan wells through 2,400 miles of 13ft-diameter pipes to the more populous coastal regions, and to provide irrigation for agriculture, was inaugurated by Col Qaddafi on 28 August 1991 in a ceremony near Benghazi, attended by several Arab and African leaders, PLO leader Yasser Arafat and the Secretary-General of the Arab League. Few Western leaders were present. The scheme, the largest irrigation project in the Middle East, will take 25 years to complete, at an estimated cost of $25,000m. During his visit for the ceremony, President Mubarak of Egypt held further talks with Col Qaddafi on economic co-operation. Libya had offered to resettle up to one million Egyptian farmers on lands to be irrigated by the GMR project.

THE LOCKERBIE AFFAIR AND THE IMPOSITION OF UN ECONOMIC SANCTIONS

In December 1988 all 259 people aboard Pan Am Flight 103 died when the aircraft exploded over Lockerbie, Scotland. Eleven people in the village also died. The plane had been flying from Frankfurt, Germany, where it was believed that a suitcase containing a bomb had been loaded on board. Investigations had revealed that this suitcase had arrived at Frankfurt on a flight from Malta, where an employee of Libyan Arab Airlines, Al-Amin Khalifa Fahima, was stationed. On 13 November 1991 Scotland's Lord Advocate and the acting US Attorney-General issued international warrants for the arrest of Fahima and the former security chief of the Libyan airline, Abdel Basset al-Megrahi, accusing them of responsibility for the bombing of the Pan Am aircraft. Two days later the Libyan Secretariat for Foreign Affairs issued a statement denying any Libyan involvement in the bombing, condemning all forms of terrorism and urging the investigation of the charges by a neutral international body or the International Court of Justice (ICJ). A British demand for the extradition of the two men, presented by the Italian ambassador in Tripoli on 18 November, was refused, as was a repeated demand by the British and US authorities on 27 November.

A campaign was mounted by Libya among its Arab neighbours to enlist their support in countering the allegations, and it continued to resist pressure for the extradition of the two Lockerbie suspects and also for the arrest of four other Libyans sought by France in connection with the bombing of a French DC-10 airliner over the Sahara (in Niger) in September 1989, in which 171 people had died. One of those accused over the latter incident, Abdallah Sannousi, was the brother-in-law of Col Qaddafi himself and deputy head of the Libyan intelligence services. On 5 December 1991, the Arab League Council, meeting in Cairo, expressed solidarity with Libya and urged the avoidance of sanctions. However, on 26 December President Bush extended economic sanctions, which the USA had imposed on Libya in January 1986, for a further year.

Meanwhile, Libya had announced that it would conduct its own inquiry into the Lockerbie allegations under the chairmanship of Judge Taher az-Zawi. He was reported to have stated, on 7 December 1991, that the two suspects had been detained and would stand trial in Libya. An offer by the Libyan Secretary for Foreign Liaison, Ibrahim al-Bishari, to send Libyan judges to London or Washington to discuss the case was rejected.

A unanimous resolution (No. 731) by the UN Security Council, adopted on 21 January 1992, demanded the extradition of the Lockerbie suspects to the USA or the United Kingdom as well as Libya's full co-operation with France's inquiry into the loss of its aircraft in Niger in 1989. Libya declined to extradite the men, but did offer to place them on trial in Libya. It also offered to allow French officials to interrogate the four men suspected of complicity in the Niger bombing. On 18 February al-Megrahi and Fahima appeared in court in Tripoli, where the judge refused to allow their extradition, claiming that there were no grounds for it in international or criminal law. The Libyan response to UN Security Council Resolution 731 was rejected by the USA, the United Kingdom and France, which urged the UN to impose sanctions on Libya.

On 23 March Libya applied to the ICJ for an order confirming its right to refuse the extradition of the Lockerbie suspects by applying the terms of the 1971 Montreal Convention on airline terrorism. It was claimed that the convention allowed Libya the option of trying the suspects in its own courts, a view opposed by lawyers acting for the United Kingdom and the USA, who claimed that Libya was 'wriggling, twisting and turning' in its attempts to evade the surrender of the suspects and the imposition of UN sanctions. Judgement was not expected for another two years but the ICJ nevertheless ruled, on 14 April, that it had no power to prevent the UN from enacting sanctions against Libya.

An offer in late March 1992 by Col Qaddafi to place the suspects under the jurisdiction of the Arab League was subsequently withdrawn. Intensive diplomacy by the League, spearheaded by President Mubarak of Egypt (who, at the request of the PLO, met Col Qaddafi in Tripoli on 12 April), came to nothing. On 31 March the UN Security Council adopted Resolution 748, imposing mandatory economic sanctions against Libya. Ten members voted in favour of the resolution, and five (China, Cape Verde, India, Morocco and Zimbabwe) abstained. From 15 April 1992 all civilian air links and arms trade with Libya were to be prohibited and its diplomatic representation reduced. An embargo on the sale of Libyan petroleum was not imposed. There was widespread hostility in the Arab world to the imposition of sanctions against a fellow Arab and Muslim state and deep concern about the repercussions of the sanctions on other Arab countries. The UN was accused of hypocrisy for not enforcing similar measures against Israel over its failure to comply with UN Security Council Resolution 242 (1967), which demands Israeli withdrawal from the Occupied Territories. It was also feared that Islamic fundamentalists in countries such as Egypt, Algeria, Tunisia and Morocco might exploit the ensuing economic hardships for their own political ends. President Mubarak and President Assad of Syria were adamant in their condemnation of sanctions when they spoke at a news conference in Cairo on 31 March.

In Libya itself demonstrators immediately took to the streets to condemn the West, and Col Qaddafi threatened to cut off oil supplies to, and withdraw all business from, those countries which complied with Resolution 748. On 2 April demonstrators besieged several Western embassies in Tripoli. The Embassy of Venezuela (which had held the presidency of the Security Council when Resolution 748 was passed) was ransacked and burned. It was reported that exit visas had been refused to a number of foreign nationals, despite earlier assurances, and fears were expressed that Col Qaddafi might seek to use some of them as hostages. On 1 April the UK Foreign and Commonwealth Office advised the 5,000 British nationals working in Libya to leave before the sanctions took effect, and other EC member states advised their citizens likewise. Speaking in Tripoli's Green Square on 4 April at a dawn rally to mark the end of the month of Ramadan, Col Qaddafi rejected Resolution 748 and sought to depict the situation as a new crusade against Islam by the Christian West. 'Muslims all over the world, the battle being waged by modern Western crusading forces, having ended against communism, is now being directed against Islam,' he declared.

UN sanctions took effect on 15 April 1992, the anniversary of the US air strikes against Tripoli and Benghazi in 1986 (see above). The previous day Col Qaddafi had severed all international communications and travel links in a day of self-imposed isolation to mark the anniversary. Prior to the imposition of sanctions, Libya was reported to have been stockpiling food and medicines and to have transferred liquid capital from Europe to banking centres in the Gulf region and the Far East. Arab neighbours rallied to find new land and sea routes to circumvent the air embargo, and it was announced that a hydrofoil service from Malta to Tripoli would operate five times a week instead of weekly. The immediate effect of the sanctions was thus primarily psychological and it was thought that this would cause little more than inconvenience, rather than actual hardship, in the foreseeable future. However, Arab diplomats feared an escalation of sanctions and further demands by the United Kingdom and the USA for an embargo on sales of petroleum if Libya continued to refuse to comply with Resolution 731.

In May 1992, at Col Qaddafi's instigation, 1,500 People's Congresses were convened in Libya and abroad, to enable ordinary citizens to debate the fate of the two Lockerbie suspects and their response to the UN sanctions. Arab diplomats and the more pragmatic member of Qaddafi's circle had begun to urge a compromise, fearing that the imposition of further UN sanctions, particularly an embargo on sales of petroleum (Libya earns 95% of its income from such sales), would be disastrous. Observers concluded that Qaddafi was seeking to resolve his dilemma and save face by using the People's Congresses as a means of distancing himself from any eventual 'surrender'. In late June the GPC announced its decision to allow the two Lockerbie suspects to stand trial abroad, provided the proceedings were 'fair and just'. It suggested that such a trial might take place under the auspices of either the Arab League or the UN. In August, at a meeting with Col Qaddafi, UN Under-Secretary-General Vladimir Petrovsky warned that, if Libya continued to refuse to comply with Resolution 731, the UN might strengthen the sanctions already in force against it. On 12 August, however, the UN Security Council merely renewed the sanctions for a further 120 days.

In early January 1993 Libya closed all of its land borders for three days in protest at the UN's decision, taken in early December 1992, to renew the sanctions in force against Libya. In mid-February an article appeared in the US press that alleged that Libya was constructing an underground factory for the manufacture of chemical weapons at Tarhounah, west of Tripoli. In January Libya refused to a sign a UN convention banning chemical weapons, on the grounds that not all Middle Eastern and North African states were party to the convention.

During the approach to the UN Security Council's sanctions review in April 1993, Libya attempted to rally Arab support and announced in late March that it was tabling new proposals to try and break the deadlock. In the USA a group of senators, led by Edward Kennedy, urged the US Senate Foreign Relations Committee to seek the expansion of UN sanctions against Libya. At the same time, there were new allegations in the American press that Libya was building a second chemical weapons plant. Despite the USA's efforts to secure a tightening of the economic embargo, at its April meeting the Security Council failed to modify the original sanctions which were retained for a further 120 days. Following the meeting, the USA stated that it would continue to consult its allies about tougher sanctions, including a possible ban on Libyan oil exports. However, the main European importers of Libyan crude petroleum, in particular Germany, Italy and Spain, remained firmly opposed to an oil embargo which would affect them badly. In July the French Minister of Foreign Affairs,

Alain Juppé, stated that France would demand tougher sanctions if Libya failed to comply with Resolution 731 before the next Security Council review in early August.

At its meeting on 13 August the Security Council decided to maintain existing sanctions. The USA, the United Kingdom and France, increasingly frustrated at Qaddafi's defiance, issued an ultimatum to Libya stating that if the two suspects were not surrendered for trial by 1 October 1993, they would propose a UN Security Council resolution imposing tougher sanctions, covering oil-related, financial and technical sectors. Libya rejected the deadline but repeated its offer to discuss holding the trial in a country other than the USA or the United Kingdom. In a television interview, Qaddafi claimed that 'all the sanctions in the world or even in the universe will never make Libya submit'. In September the Libyan Secretary for Foreign Liaison and International Co-operation, Omar al-Muntasser, submitted a memorandum to the UN Secretary-General in which Libya stated that it did not oppose handing over the two accused men to stand trial in Scotland and would try and persuade them to go voluntarily. The Western and Arab press interpreted this move as an indication that at long last Libya was about to capitulate. In the event, the memorandum turned out to be just another attempt by the Libyan regime to gain time and avoid the deadline. On 8 October the Libyan lawyer of the two accused men announced that he had advised them not to stand trial in Scotland and criticized the Libyan Government for urging them to surrender. It was widely assumed that his statement had been approved beforehand by the Libyan leader.

As the 1 October deadline approached, pressure on Libya had mounted. US President Bill Clinton, in his first speech to the UN General Assembly, vowed to bring the perpetrators of the Lockerbie bombing to justice. When Libya failed to comply with Western demands, on 1 October the USA, the United Kingdom and France introduced a draft resolution at the Security Council, seeking to impose tighter sanctions on Libya. After several weeks, when further negotiations failed to break the deadlock, the Security Council finally yielded to the demands of the USA, the United Kingdom and France. On 11 November UN Security Council Resolution 883 was adopted, imposing new sanctions against Libya. The resolution provided for the freezing of all Libyan assets abroad, with the exception of earnings from hydrocarbon exports, placed a ban on the sale to Libya of certain equipment for the downstream oil and gas sectors and placed further restrictions on Libyan civil aviation. All Libyan Arab Airlines offices abroad were to be closed immediately and the sale or lease of aircraft to Libya, the supply of spare parts and maintenance services and the training of pilots and engineers were also prohibited. The new measures came into force on 1 December 1993. Resolution 883 states that sanctions will be lifted as soon as the two Libyans accused of responsibility for the Lockerbie bombing are handed over for trial in the United Kingdom or the USA and Libya co-operates fully with the French authorities investigating the bombing of a UTA airliner over the Sahara in 1989. It also made provision for the reimposition of sanctions within 90 days if Libya failed to comply with all the demands set out in Resolutions 731 and 748. There seemed little doubt the real target of the sanctions was the Libyan leader himself. Russia had initially opposed the tightening of sanctions and Libya is reported to have offered to repay debts, estimated at between $1,800m. and $4,000m., in cash if Russia agreed to use its veto in the Security Council vote. Strong pressure was brought to bear on Russia by the USA, the United Kingdom and France and Russia voted for the resolution on 11 November.

In response to the resolution, Qaddafi declared that he was prepared to destroy Libya's oilfields and ports as a gesture of defiance to the West. In a series of public speeches he called on the Libyan people to make sacrifices in the cause of national dignity and rejected all further negotiations with the UN and the Western powers on the Lockerbie affair. Through the editorials in *Ash-Shams*, Qaddafi criticized his own foreign secretariat for urging the surrender of the two accused Libyans. This was interpreted as an attack on al-Muntasser. It appears that although al-Muntasser was against handing the two men over, he had advised Qaddafi to avoid direct confrontation with the West and to use diplomatic efforts in order to try to secure some relaxation of sanctions. Despite these criticisms al-Muntasser retained his post in the reshuffle of the General People's Committee at the end of January 1994. When the General People's Congress met in January 1994, the Lockerbie affair was high on the agenda but the statement issued at the end of the session contained no hint that a compromise was possible and instead accused the USA of using sanctions to continue its policy of oppressing Libya and causing suffering to the Libyan people. In a speech in Misurata in February 1994 Qaddafi declared that the Lockerbie affair was closed, but two weeks later he proposed that the two accused men be tried by an Islamic court either in the USA, the United Kingdom or any other country so long as the court officials were all Muslims. The proposal was rejected by the British Foreign Office. After the Secretary-General of the Arab League held talks in Tripoli at the end of February, JANA, the official Libyan press agency, accused the Arab League of giving in to US pressure over UN sanctions and declared that Libya wished to play no further part in the organization. Despite the stream of contradictory signals from Libya that have characterized this affair, it appeared that Qaddafi had more to fear from compliance with UN sanctions than from the threat posed by the sanctions themselves, so long as there was no embargo on the sale of Libyan crude petroleum. For the Libyan people, the new sanctions meant further hardship, uncertainty and isolation.

In December 1993 and the early months of 1994 press reports once again cast doubts on Libya's involvement in the bombing of Pan Am flight 103. One article based on intelligence reports stated that the Popular Front for the Liberation of Palestine—General Command (PFLP-GC), led by Ahmad Jibril from Syria, had planned the bombing. Another quoted CIA sources who argued that a group of Palestinian terrorists based in Syria had planned the operation, but had induced Libyan agents to carry it out when their own organization was infiltrated. At the same time the BBC World Service reported that the Swiss electronics firm which manufactured the detonators used to trigger the bomb planted on the Pan Am plane had supplied these devices to the former East Germany as well as to Libya. Shortly after, two employees of the Swiss company, MeBo Telecommunications, interviewed by the BBC, confirmed that detonators had been supplied to the East German security services and that this information had been given to the inquiry team in 1990. One of the key elements in the prosecution's case against Libya had been the fact that Libya alone had purchased detonators from the Swiss company. The PFLP-GC is reported to have enjoyed close links with the East German security forces. The head of US counter-terrorist operations told the BBC that Syria, Iran and the PFLP-GC were implicated in the bombing. According to this source, it was Iran that ordered the destruction of the Pan Am plane, in retaliation for the Iranian airliner shot down by the US navy over the Gulf in 1989, and that it was the PFLP-GC which actually planted the bomb. Despite calls for an international inquiry into the incident, the Scottish judiciary insisted that the evidence against the two Libyans was still sufficient to sustain the charges brought against them.

In February 1994 President Clinton renewed US sanctions against Libya, originally imposed in 1986, and reaffirmed his determination to see the two Libyans accused of the Lockerbie bombing extradited to face trial. He described Libya as an exceptional threat to US national security and interests.

RUMOURS OF AN ABORTIVE ARMY COUP

During the second week of October 1993 rumours began to circulate in the Western media that a revolt by a number of army units had been crushed by the Libyan air force which had remained loyal to Qaddafi. It was claimed that the most serious clashes had occurred around Misurata and Tobruk where there had been scores of casualties. There were unconfirmed reports that Libya had closed its borders and that after three days of unrest 2,000 people had been arrested and 12 officers executed. Qaddafi's Second-in-Command, Abd as-Salam Jalloud, was reported to have been placed under house arrest. There was speculation that the coup, described in the media as the most serious challenge to the Libyan leader since 1986, had arisen as a result of differences between Qaddafi

and Jalloud over the handling of the Lockerbie crisis and that the armed forces may have divided along tribal lines. Throughout the Lockerbie affair, Jalloud, who belongs to the Al-Megaha tribe, has been firmly opposed to surrendering the two suspects, both of whom are members of his tribe. The London-based daily *Al-Hayat* named Col Hassan al-Kabir and Col ar-Rifi Ali ash-Sharif as the leaders of the uprising and stated that al-Kabir had been arrested but ash-Sharif had fled to Switzerland. However, doubts have been expressed that a major uprising did in fact occur, although rumours circulating in Tripoli pointed to some kind of incident involving the military at this time. The main source of the rumours appears to have been one of the opposition groups in exile, the National Front for the Salvation of Libya (NFSL). Given the closed nature of Libyan society, little firm evidence has emerged to confirm or contradict the rumours. Qaddafi himself condemned the rumours of an army coup in a speech on 30 October describing them as a plot by British intelligence to humiliate the Libyan people. Nevertheless, it is perhaps significant that the government changes announced at the end of January 1994 placed men known for their personal loyalty to Qaddafi in key positions, suggesting that the Libyan leader felt the need to tighten his grip on power. Abu Zayd Umar Durdah, the Secretary-General of the General People's Committee and a close associate of Jalloud, was replaced by Abd al-Majid al-Qaoud. Ahmed Ibrahim was appointed Secretary for Information and Culture and Muhammad al-Hijazi Secretary for Justice and Public Security. Both are members of Qaddafi's personal entourage.

Libyan opposition groups in exile remain weak and divided and there is little evidence that they command significant support within the country. In October 1993 Muhammad Megarief, the leader of the NFSL, Maj. Abdel Moneim al-Houni of the Co-operation Bureau for Democratic and National Forces, and Mansour Kikhia of the National Libyan Alliance are reported to have met in either Algiers or Geneva to discuss forming a united front against the Qaddafi regime. Abdel Hamid al-Bakkush, the leader of the Libyan Liberation Organization, did not attend and the meeting appeared to have failed to resolve the differences between the various opposition groups. This was confirmed in February 1994 when some leading members of the NFSL announced that they had formed a breakaway movement and criticized the NFSL for failing to co-operate with other opposition groups in creating a united front against the Qaddafi regime.

Qaddafi has shown that he takes these opposition groups seriously and has regularly called for his opponents abroad to be hunted down and liquidated. Therefore in early December 1993, when Mansour Kikhia, a former Secretary for Foreign Liaison and since the early 1980s leader of the opposition Libyan National Alliance, disappeared while attending a meeting of the Alliance in Cairo, it was widely assumed that he had been abducted by Libyan security agents. The affair proved particularly embarrassing because Kikhia had been living in the USA, has an American wife and had only agreed to attend the meeting in Cairo after receiving personal assurances from senior Egyptian officials about his safety there. The Libyan Secretariat for Foreign Liaison and Libya's representative to the Arab League in Cairo, Ibrahim Beshari, denied Libyan involvement in the affair. Beshari stated that Kikhia presented no threat to the Libyan Government. Qaddafi himself told Egyptian journalists that Libya was co-operating with the Egyptian authorities to discover what had happened. Both President Clinton and Dr Boutros Boutros-Ghali, the UN Secretary-General, appealed to President Mubarak of Egypt to investigate Kikhia's disappearance. However, although Mubarak dispatched one of his advisors to Tripoli he failed to make any progress and the Egyptian police admitted at the end of January that they had no information about Kikhia's whereabouts.

In early March 1994 Libyan television broadcast interviews with four Libyans linked to the NFSL who were alleged to have carried out intelligence work for the CIA. Three of the men were army officers and all the accused were members of the Warfallah tribe which, according to some reports, was implicated in the alleged army coup in October 1993. The accused men stated that they had been briefed at meetings between exiled Libyan dissidents and US intelligence officers in Dallas, Texas and also in Zurich. A spokesman for the Libyan opposition in Cairo declared that the confessions were false and had been obtained under duress.

Qaddafi also attacked opponents of his regime within Libya, singling out a number of Islamist groups. In speeches in October 1993 and January 1994 he condemned the Islamists as 'spies' and 'heretics' and supported their instant liquidation without trial. Moves by the General People's Congress (GPC) to adopt laws based on the *Shari'a*, such as stiff penalties for the consumption of alcohol, may well represent part of the regime's campaign to try and undermine support in the country for the Islamists.

ICJ RULING ON AOUZOU STRIP

On 3 February 1994 the International Court of Justice (ICJ) ruled against Libya's claim to the Aouzou strip in northern Chad. Libya and Chad had agreed in 1989 to accept the ICJ's ruling over the disputed territory. Libya's border with its southern neighbour, Chad, had been defined in 1955 in an agreement between the newly-independent State of Libya and France, then the colonial power in Chad. However, in 1973 Libya unilaterally abrogated the treaty and annexed the Aouzou strip. Libya based its claim to northern Chad on the fact that the area had been part of the vast domain of the Sanusi order which had ruled much of Libya before the Italian colonial conquest in 1911. Most the disputed strip is desert and sparsely populated. Chad regained control of the area in 1987 with the exception of a large military base built by Libya at the oasis of Aouzou. After the court's ruling was announced, Libya appeared unwilling to relinquish its claim to the disputed territory and the Government of Chad reported that Libya had strengthened its military forces there. When negotiations between the two countries did begin in March, Libya demanded the release of some 500 prisoners of war captured in Chad in 1987. Then, Qaddafi suddenly announced that Libya was willing to abandon its claim to the disputed territory and a draft agreement on the withdrawal of Libyan forces was signed in Sirte on 5 April. Under the terms of the agreement the withdrawal was completed by the end of May 1994. In early June Libya signed a treaty of friendship and co-operation with Chad.

RELATIONS WITH EGYPT AND THE MAGHREB

Although President Mubarak has consistently resisted Qaddafi's plans for Arab unity, relations between Libya and Egypt have continued to improve in recent years. Egypt firmly opposed the UN sanctions imposed on Libya and has made strenuous diplomatic efforts to mediate between Libya and the West over the Lockerbie affair. In November 1993 President Mubarak told the newspaper *Al Ahram* that it was in Egypt's interest for 'stability' to prevail in Libya and that relations between the two countries should remain cordial. Qaddafi's regime is seen as a bulwark against the spread of militant Islamist movements in the region and offers the prospect of much needed economic opportunities for Egypt, especially the employment of Egyptian manpower. Libya has offered to resettle one million Egyptian farmers on lands to be irrigated by the Great Man-Made River scheme. For Libya, which has become increasingly isolated internationally through the efforts of the USA and the United Kingdom, Egypt serves as a valuable intermediary with the outside world. The close relationship between the two countries appeared to have survived the embarrassment resulting from the disappearance of Libyan opposition leader Mansour Kikhia in Cairo in December 1994 and Libya's strong condemnation of the Israel-PLO accord signed in September 1993. Early in 1994 the Libyan press agency, JANA, declared that Libya and Egypt were continuing to co-operate in many areas and acknowledged Egyptian efforts to persuade the West to ease sanctions against Libya. In February the Egyptian Minister of Foreign Affairs, Amr Musa, condemned the latest round of sanctions against Libya as 'unfair' and 'coercive' and reiterated his Government's commitment to seeking a peaceful solution to the Lockerbie affair.

Although Libya joined the UAM and Qaddafi assumed the presidency of the organization on 1 January 1991 for a period of six months, the Libyan leader appeared to show little interest in further integration with his country's western neighbours and preferred to look east to Egypt. However, since the imposition of UN sanctions against Libya, relations with Tunisia, often strained and sometimes hostile, have become friendly. Libya has come to depend increasingly on transit facilities through Tunisia as the air embargo on Libya has tightened. Tunisia has profited greatly from this transit traffic, and the remittances from the 20,000 Tunisians working in Libya represent another valuable source of foreign exchange. Despite misunderstandings with Algeria over Qaddafi's attitude towards the Front Islamique du Salut, the Islamist opposition in Algeria, Algeria has continued to support Libya in the UN and the Arab League. Morocco also supported Libya in the UN by abstaining during the vote in the Security Council in November 1993 to impose tougher sanctions on Libya. Although all of Libya's neighbours remain deeply suspicious of the Qaddafi regime, they have more to fear from its collapse, an event that could have serious consequences for the stability of the whole of North Africa.

Economy

Revised for this edition by ALAN J. DAY

Petroleum has transformed Libya. Before the discovery of oil in commercial quantities in the 1950s, agriculture was the basis of the economy and domestic revenue covered only about one-half of the Government's ordinary and development expenditure. Between 1962 and 1968, however, national income increased from LD 131m. to LD 798m. and gross national product (GNP) increased from LD 163m. to LD 909m. Exports of petroleum during the period increased by 835%, accounting for 51% of gross domestic product (GDP) in 1968. As a result of the dramatic rise in oil prices in the 1970s, the country's GNP, according to official estimates, rose to LD 3,534m. in 1974 before falling slightly to LD 3,497m. in 1975, when petroleum exports accounted for 46.3% of GDP. Oil revenues then rose steeply, reaching a peak of US $22,000m. in 1980, but fell equally sharply in the 1980s, as world oil prices declined rapidly. Estimated GNP fell from $25,984m. in 1985 to $22,300m. in 1987 and $18,400m. in 1988, while the country's population increased at an average annual rate of 4.1%

in 1980–90. During the greater part of the 1980s the petroleum sector accounted for 65% of GDP and 99% of export earnings, although it provided employment for less than 10% of the labour force. In 1989, according to estimates by the World Bank, Libya's GNP per head, measured at average 1986–88 prices, was $5,310. This was the highest level to be recorded among African countries, but represented an average annual decline, in real terms, of 3% over the period 1965–90. Libya's financial position deteriorated further in 1988–89, but then improved significantly following the Gulf crisis of 1990–91, when world oil prices rose sharply, albeit for a brief period, and generated an increase in Libyan oil revenues of nearly 25% in 1990, compared with 1989.

After the 1969 revolution, state intervention in the economy increased, in accordance with Col Qaddafi's ideas of 'Islamic socialism'. Apart, however, from the nationalization of distribution and marketing of petroleum in Libya in 1970, the Government refrained from directly taking over petroleum company assets until the dispute with BP in 1971. In September 1978 and the first two months of 1979, a large number of private companies were taken over by workers' committees. Similarly, in 1979, all direct importing business was transferred to 62 public corporations, and the issuing of licences was stopped. In March 1981, it was announced that all licences for shops selling clothes, electrical goods, shoes, household appliances and spare parts were to be cancelled, and that by the end of the year all retail shops would have to close. Retail activity became controlled by state-administered supermarkets. The whole private sector was to be completely abolished by the end of 1981, to be replaced by People's Economic Committees. These plans were never implemented according to schedule, and by the late 1980s Qaddafi was extolling the virtues of private enterprise.

Until the country's petroleum resources began to be exploited, not more than 25% of the population lived in the towns. This is no longer true: by 1990, according to the World Bank, the urban population comprised 70% of the total. Approximately one-half of the non-urban population is settled in rural communities, and the remainder are semi-nomads, who follow a pastoral mode of life. According to the results of the census carried out on 31 July 1984, Libya's population was 3.6m., compared with 2,249,237 at the census of July 1973; by mid-1990 the total was estimated by the World Bank to have risen to 4.5m. The country's labour force totalled an estimated 800,000 in 1981. By the end of 1982 it was estimated that there were 569,000 foreigners living in Libya, representing 18% of the total population. Egyptians accounted for 174,158 of these, while 73,582 were Tunisians and 44,546 were Turkish. In July 1985, however, Col Qaddafi barred Egyptians (whose numbers in Libya had fallen by 20,000 since January) from working in Libya, in retaliation against a similar measure preventing Libyans from working in Egypt. Tunisia ordered 283 Libyans (the majority of Libya's diplomats and more than 250 other Libyan nationals), accused of spying, to leave the country in August 1985, after Libya decided to expel some 30,000 Tunisian workers from Libya. It was estimated that Libya expelled or laid off more than 120,000 foreign workers during 1985 (including workers from Mali, Mauritania, Niger, and 10,000–20,000 Syrians, between August and October). Col Qaddafi maintained that the expulsions were part of a policy to achieve self-sufficiency in Libya's labour force, and not the result of economic stringency. However, remittances by foreign workers to their own countries were a substantial drain on Libya's reserves of foreign exchange, totalling some $2,000m. in 1983, when the number of expatriate workers was at its highest ever level. Libya began to reduce the number of these workers in 1984, and remittances in that year were estimated to have fallen to $1,500m. According to figures released by the International Labour Organization, there were 583,900 migrant workers in Libya in July 1985.

Since 1980 planned mergers with Syria, Morocco and Algeria, and the military adventure into Chad, have had adverse effects on the economy. The latter episode resulted in diplomatic relations being broken off with a number of West African countries. In the economic sphere, for example, Nigeria cut off uranium sales to Libya, which amounted to 500 tons in 1980. The purge on corruption in February 1980 increased payment delays and so deepened the reluctance of foreign companies to invest in Libya. In practical terms, little progress was made towards the 'merger' with Syria, although Libya paid off all Syria's debts to the USSR, and appeared to be moving closer to the USSR.

Relations with the USA worsened, and in March 1982 President Reagan banned imports of Libyan petroleum to the USA, and halted all exports to Libya other than food and medical supplies. Libya's perceived interference in the affairs of other nations (notably Chad) and its alleged association with international terrorism had further significant economic repercussions in January 1986, when President Reagan 'froze' Libyan assets in the USA and banned all trade between the USA and Libya. However, the effectiveness of this action was vitiated by the unwillingness of the USA's allies in Japan and Western Europe to institute a complementary economic boycott of Libya, and by the fact that assets worth some

$1,000m.–$2,000m. would have been surrendered to Libya by the US oil companies operating there if they had ceased operations immediately. These companies were given until 30 June 1986 to sell their assets to Libyan concerns, but only tenuous agreements had been reached by the time the deadline arrived. The assets were not nationalized and the companies signed agreements with Libya giving them the right to negotiate their return when circumstances allowed.

The US sanctions, rather than harming Libya, had their greatest impact on the departing oil companies, which estimated their annual losses from the oil operations that they had transferred to Libya at $2m.–$2.5m. The withdrawal of the US oil companies had a greater negative effect on Libya's ability to market its petroleum than on actual levels of production, which were lower than capacity, owing to weak world demand. Petroleum lifted by US companies was formerly guaranteed an outlet through their refineries, mainly in Europe. Following the US withdrawal, Libya had to compete with other countries for sales to refineries. In June 1986 the USA banned the export to third countries of goods and technology destined for use in the Libyan petroleum industry. A three-year 'standstill agreement' between the Libyan Government and the US oil companies officially expired at the end of June 1989, but continued to be observed by Libya, which confirmed in March 1991 that it had no plans to dispose of the US companies' Libyan areas to third parties. In January 1991 US sanctions were renewed for a further 12-month period, and in April the US Government published a list of 48 companies, based in various countries, which it believed to be acting as agents or 'fronts' for Libyan nationals and which were therefore to be subject to the US sanctions. A supplementary list published in August 1991 added 12 companies to the total. According to the US Treasury Department, the mid-1993 value of Libyan assets 'frozen' in the USA since 1986 was $903m.

In addition to Libya's increasingly isolated position among both African and Arab states, during the 1980s Libya's economy was severely restricted by the effect of the low prices for oil consequent on the global oil glut. Revenue from sales of petroleum declined from $22,000m. in 1980 to $5,000m. in 1988. Decreasing revenues caused serious cash-flow problems and necessitated a major revision of the 1981–85 Development Plan. Although in January 1986 the Central Bank claimed that 80% of projects under the Plan were either completed or under way, the slump in the price of oil in 1986 led to the suspension or cancellation of almost all new development projects (an outstanding exception being the 'Great Man-made River' scheme—see Agriculture, below). In the period 1980–89 GDP declined from $35,500m. to $23,000m. The crisis in the economy prompted Col Qaddafi to introduce a series of economic and political liberalization measures in March and April 1988. The state supermarket network, which was established in the early 1980s, was poorly organized and many basic commodities were usually unavailable, giving rise to a thriving black market. Subsequently, however, private shops were encouraged to reopen, and Col Qaddafi adopted measures to dismantle obstacles to trade and tourism with Libya's neighbours, closing customs and immigration posts along the borders with Egypt and Tunisia. Thousands of Tunisians entered Libya in 1988 to work on Libyan farms, while, along the border, a 'free zone' developed where Libyans could purchase items that were scarce in their own country. In September 1988 Qaddafi proposed an increase in 'privatization' and announced that Libyans would be able to import and export in complete freedom. In December the Government announced plans to reduce its budget deficit by removing subsidies on wheat, flour, sugar, tea and salt. However, controls on prices and on interest and exchange rates were maintained, and all important sectors of the economy remained under the effective control of the state (which in 1990 retained 70% of all Libyan salaried workers on its payroll).

At the second summit meeting of the Union of the Arab Maghreb (formed in February 1989 and comprising Algeria, Libya, Mauritania, Morocco and Tunisia), held in Algiers in July 1990, closer economic ties between the member states were proposed, including the establishment of a customs union before 1995. Moreover, a *rapprochement* with Egypt in October 1989 facilitated plans for wide-ranging economic integration and cross-border co-operation. This new relationship was one factor in Libya's decision ultimately to abide by the UN embargo that was imposed on Iraq in August 1990 because of its invasion of Kuwait (although Col Qaddafi opposed the US-led military action against Iraq). Another factor was Libya's need to take full advantage of the sudden rise in world oil prices, caused by the crisis. By increasing its output in the third and fourth quarters of the year, Libya recorded total oil revenues of $9,700m. in 1990 (compared with $7,846m. in 1989) and achieved a 9.4% increase in GDP, to LD 7,816m. ($27,370m.). It also converted the 1989 current account deficit estimated at US $940m. into an estimated surplus of $2,230m. in 1990. Libya thus emerged from the Gulf crisis of 1990–91 with its position enhanced both economically and diplomatically, notably in its relations with the EC, to which it was the second largest supplier of oil. The value of oil revenues in 1991 amounted to about $10,000m.

Libya's economic relations with the West nevertheless continued to be complicated by allegations of official Libyan involvement in international terrorism, including the 1988 Lockerbie airliner bombing and the destruction in 1989 of a French airliner over the Sahara (see History section, above). Under Resolution 748, adopted by the UN Security Council on 31 March 1992, Libya became subject to certain mandatory sanctions, in view of its failure to comply with Resolution 731 (of 12 January 1992) requiring Libyan co-operation in bringing those responsible for the terrorist actions to justice. As imposed from 15 April 1992, the sanctions included an arms embargo and the severance of air transport links with Libya, but did not, at least for the time being, encompass a general trade embargo or any moves against Libya's exports of petroleum. Prior to their imposition, the Libyan authorities took the precaution of transferring substantial Libyan assets from West European to Middle Eastern banks.

In response to Libya's continuing non-compliance with Resolution 731, the Security Council extended the existing provisions of Resolution 748 for successive 120-day periods. The extension agreed in August 1993 was accompanied by a warning from three Council members (the United Kingdom, France and the USA) that they would seek to extend the scope of the sanctions if the situation remained deadlocked at the end of September 1993. Libyan claims that the country had suffered direct and indirect revenue losses totalling $2,200m. during the first year of the sanctions regime were generally believed to be greatly exaggerated, the main reported trade effect of the sanctions being an increase in imports of priority items (including inputs for development projects) as a safeguard against a future UN decision to widen the scope of the sanctions.

A law promulgated by the General People's Congress in September 1992 formally authorized the privatization of Libyan industries and permitted 'individuals or groups to exercise the liberal professions and to invest freely in the private sectors'. In July 1993 the General People's Committee issued a decree ending state control of wholesale trade, which was opened up to partnerships and limited companies. In the previous month the Committee had banned state employees from concurrently engaging in private employment. The national debate on economic reform had, in 1992, been widened by Col Qaddafi to include the proposal that 50% of the state's oil revenues should be distributed directly to citizens, and that the 'very, very big octopus' of state administration should be cut back to a minimum by privatizing most educational and health-care facilities, shutting down unprofitable state economic enterprises and devolving many defence responsibilities to local administrative units. Other leading figures, including the Governor of the Central Bank, spoke out strongly in favour of a more orthodox transition to a mixed economy.

In May 1993 Col Qaddafi advocated the introduction of a law to guarantee foreign capital investment in Libya. In July 1993 representatives of some 250 Libyan and Tunisian companies met in Tripoli to discuss proposals for improving economic co-operation between the two countries, including the possible establishment of new joint ventures. Delegates

stressed the desirability of standardizing investment laws, pointing out that any Libyan move to introduce laws on the current Tunisian model would be consistent with the liberalization policies of the Libyan leadership.

Following the August 1993 extension of UN Security Council Resolution 748 and the subsequent circulation by the USA, France and the United Kingdom of draft proposals for stronger international action against Libya, the Libyan Government stepped up its efforts to minimize its exposure to harsher sanctions. Libya's liquid assets overseas (estimated to total up to $17,000m.), if not already located in financial 'safe havens', were constantly monitored to avoid unnecessary exposure to seizure. According to the Bank for International Settlements, Libya withdrew $2,800m. of its overseas deposits in the third quarter of 1993, including an estimated $430m. from OECD countries. The stockpiling of imported equipment for use in part-completed projects, and of spares for existing plant, was speeded up and carefully targeted on priority areas. The functions and ownership structures of Libya's fixed assets overseas (which had an estimated worth of up to $4,000m.) were analysed to assess their exposure to sanctions, and a number of deals were struck with foreign (predominantly Italian) equity partners whereby Libya relinquished control of high-profile companies.

In particular Oilinvest, the holding company through which Libya had controlled an extensive European oil refining and distribution network, was in September 1993 restructured with minority (45%) Libyan ownership, while Oilinvest's shareholding in its principal subsidiary company, Tamoil Italia, was in turn reduced to 45% and two Tamoil subsidiaries (Tamoil Transport and Chempetrol Overseas) were taken over by new owners.

The crucial Security Council vote on Libyan sanctions was delayed until 11 November 1993 because Russia (which was owed up to $3,000m. for Soviet arms and other supplies to Libya in the 1970s and 1980s) was reluctant to endorse any measure that might prompt Libya to default on agreed payment obligations. This objection was dropped after the draft resolution was expanded to include an explicit reference to Libya's 'duty scrupulously to adhere to all its obligations concerning the servicing of repayment of foreign debt'.

Security Council Resolution 882 called on UN member states to freeze all Libyan-controlled funds and financial resources abroad and to require the use of separate bank accounts for specified trade transactions; to prohibit the supply to Libya of specified items for use in the downstream oil and gas sector; to shut down overseas offices of Libyan Arab Airlines and to ban the supply of civil aviation equipment and services and the renewal of aircraft insurance; and to reduce staffing levels at Libyan diplomatic missions.

The freeze on Libyan funds prohibited withdrawals from, but not payments into, existing overseas bank accounts. The new 'external' bank accounts specified by the resolution were to be set up to handle payments to foreign contractors and suppliers to the Libyan market, using revenue derived from Libyan exports of hydrocarbons and agricultural products. All transactions through such accounts had to be supported by evidence of compliance with the sanctions regulations. The oil and gas equipment specified in a detailed annex to Resolution 883 included pumps, loading equipment and various essential items of oil refining equipment.

The resolution came into force on 1 December, but the complicated administrative arrangements meant that Libyan export revenues did not begin to reach the new 'external' accounts in overseas banks until mid-January 1994, delaying payments to many foreign contractors for some weeks beyond the due dates. Over-zealous actions by sanctions enforcers included the freezing of the US assets of a Bahrain-based financial services company with a Libyan minority shareholder. This decision was rescinded in early February 1994. The UN Security Council renewed the terms of Resolution 883 for a further 120 days on 8 April.

In mid-1994 the current sanctions appeared to have had no effect on the functioning of Libya's established oil and gas production facilities or the progress of development projects which had been under way when the sanctions were imposed. Many hydrocarbon facilities were not dependent on embargoed items, while others were fully supplied with stockpiled equipment. Some future projects had to be shelved for the duration of the current sanctions because they required embargoed items, but all were low-priority schemes for which no firm contracts had been awarded.

AGRICULTURE

Agriculture dominated the economy until the discovery of petroleum. Even now, the petroleum industry gives direct employment to less than 10% of the total labour-force (800,000 in 1981) and the present Government regards the agricultural sector as of primary importance, with Col Qaddafi himself regularly stating that more emphasis must be put on agriculture. Nevertheless, by 1982, the percentage of the population employed in agriculture had fallen to 16% from around 50% in the early 1970s. It is ironic that, despite having regularly received one-fifth of all state investment since 1970 (totalling an estimated $24,000m. in the period 1970–88), the contribution of the agricultural sector to GDP declined, in real terms, from 2.3% in 1975 to 1.9% in 1980, and Libya continued to be a major food importer. The appointment of the former Mayor of Tripoli, Abdul Majid al-Aoud, as Secretary of the GPC for Agriculture, in March 1989, indicated the Government's determination to give support to the agricultural sector. This objective was reaffirmed in Col Qaddafi's decision to make 1990 the 'year of agriculture', but the aim of achieving self-sufficiency in food remained a distant prospect.

About 95% of Libya's land area is desert. Of the remainder, a high percentage is used for grazing, only 1.4% is arable, and 0.1% is irrigated. In mid-1970 all Italian-owned land and property in Libya, including 37,000 ha of cultivated land, was confiscated and plans were made to distribute the expropriated lands to Libyan farmers, with government credits for seed, fertilizers and machinery. Several very large contracts were awarded for reclamation and irrigation work in various scheduled areas. The best-known schemes, dating from the 1970s, are the Kufra Oasis project to irrigate 10,000 ha; the Tawurgha project to reclaim 3,000 ha; the Sarir reclamation project; the Jebel al-Akhdar project; the Jefara plain project; and the Wadi Qatara reclamation project. The Wadi Jaref dam, one of the biggest in Libya, went into operation in 1976. All projects are meant to be fully integrated, providing for the establishment of farms, the building of rural roads, irrigation and drainage facilities and, in some cases, the introduction of agro-industries.

The Government invested a total of LD 700m. in agriculture over the 10-year period 1973–83. The Three-Year Plan, as revised in February 1975, provided LD 566.9m. for agricultural development and agrarian reform. The revised 1976–80 Development Plan provided LD 498m. plus LD 977m. for integral developments. Indeed, an important feature of Libya's economic planning in the 1970s was the high priority which was being given to agriculture. In 1975 agricultural development absorbed 21% of total budget expenditure whilst in 1976 it had risen to a corresponding 30%. In the 1978 financial year, the agricultural sector was allocated 18.9% of budgeted development expenditure and 14.6% of overall budget spending. In most other oil-rich countries, agriculture hardly received more than 10% of development funds. In 1979, however, investment in agriculture decreased, receiving only 6.4% of the general budget. In relative terms, the budget allocated to agriculture was expected to continue to decrease slightly during the 1980s, as the 1981–85 Five-Year Plan gave greater priority to industry. Nevertheless, the absolute level of expenditure on the agricultural sector was scheduled to increase. Thus, in the 1976–80 Development Plan LD 1,600m., or 21% of expenditure, were allocated to agriculture, whereas in the 1981–85 Plan the estimated expenditure on agriculture was LD 3,000m., representing about 20% of the total. This latest plan also envisaged that the proportion of the working population employed in agriculture would decline from 18.9% in 1980 to 16.8% in 1985. However, between 1983 and 1985, successive development budgets were underspent, and despite the official priority awarded to agricultural development, the agricultural sector was one of the most seriously affected, receiving 81.3% of budgeted investment in 1983, 86.9% in 1984, and only 66.7% in 1985.

In spite of the money invested in the sector, results in terms of production have been largely unsatisfactory. Climatic and soil factors will, it is hoped, cease to play such a large part in fluctuations of output, once irrigation schemes are operational and the distribution and use of fertilizers is well established. There have been signs in the production figures that this is indeed happening; according to the UN Food and Agriculture Organization (FAO), output of cereals increased from 62,000 metric tons in 1970 to 299,000 tons in 1988, while, over the same period, annual production of meat rose from 48,000 tons to 171,000 tons, root crops from 10,000 tons to 115,000 tons, oil crops from 20,000 tons to 31,000 tons and pulses from 2,000 tons to 12,000 tons. Nevertheless, in overall terms, the agricultural sector has not fulfilled expectations, and Libya continues to import around 80% of its food requirements, the value of which totalled US $1,117.3m. in 1987 (compared with $123.4m. in 1970). Problems, such as the lack of trained technicians and administrators and poor education among the farming communities, are not easily solved; Libya is obliged for the present to rely heavily on foreign expertise. The implementation of the various proposed agricultural projects has been particularly slow.

Libya's most ambitious project is the so-called 'Great Manmade River' project (GMR), first announced in November 1983. Under the first stage of the irrigation and water-supply project, the Dong Ah Construction Industrial Company, from the Republic of Korea, was contracted to build a man-made river, at a cost of $3,300m., to carry 2m. cu m of water per day along 2,000 km of pipeline from natural underground reservoirs at Tazerbo and Sarir, in the south-east Sahara desert, to Sirte and Benghazi and agricultural projects and towns on the Mediterranean coast, via Agedabia. A total of 270 wells are being drilled in the Tazerbo and Sarir areas, with the aim of irrigating approximately 280,000 ha, on which some 37,000 model farms are to be established. This is possibly the largest single contract ever awarded in the Middle East, and its cost had risen to $4,200m. by 1986. The $5,300m. second stage of the GMR will eventually pipe 2m. cu m of water per day from Sawknah to Tripoli, a distance of 600 km. Three additional stages are planned, including the extension of the first phase southwards to Kufra oasis (doubling its capacity to 4m. cu m per day) and the construction of pipelines to serve the north-eastern coastal town of Tobruk (from Agedabia) and to link the eastern and western systems of the first two stages along the coast (Tripoli–Sirte), thereby creating a national water grid. If all phases are completed, there will be a total of 4,040 km of pipeline, with a water-carrying capacity of 6m. cu m per day. The eventual cost of the GMR, including agricultural infrastructure, could be as high as $25,000m., and it is thought that Libya may have difficulties in paying for it, particularly following Saudi Arabia's refusal to contribute aid. In September 1989 the Dong Ah Construction Industrial Company was also awarded the main contract for the second stage of the GMR, on which it began preparatory road construction in mid-1990.

With 25% of the first phase still to be completed, the entire project came under review in March 1991, owing to various unforeseen problems, including the production of heavily contaminated water from some test pumping, as a result of collapsing well screens. Nevertheless, at a grand ceremony held near Benghazi on 28 August 1991 and attended by various Arab and African leaders, the first phase of the GMR was inaugurated by Col Qaddafi, who turned on a tap starting the flow of water into one of the project's reservoirs. The increase in Libya's oil revenues in 1990–91 had eased the burden of financing this priority project, which continued to be supported by a consortium of Arab banks. The Government also remained committed to the original objective that 80% of the water supplied by the GMR would be allocated to agriculture (which already accounted for 85% of total water consumption), despite evidence that, taking into account the real unit cost of irrigation water, the cost of using it to cultivate cereals was currently some six times the prevailing world market price. Another problem was shortage of labour for the newly-created agricultural land, in the light of which the Government hoped to attract large numbers of Egyptian and Moroccan nationals to work on GMR farms. Other uncertainties surrounded the post-inauguration cost and practicalities of maintaining the GMR, it being suggested in some quarters that the weaknesses of Libya's socio-political system would result in the project falling into disrepair. Among the special projects being assisted by the GMR Water Utilization Authority in mid-1991 were joint horticultural ventures with both private and state bodies from the Netherlands, in which particular emphasis was to be placed on the development of potato production for the lucrative north European market.

In mid-1993 the Dong Ah Construction Industrial Company, which had thus far completed 33% of the engineering and 20% of the construction work on its phase-two GMR contract, was instructed to modify certain pipeline routes and specifications in its future work schedule in ways which indicated a shift of priorities away from agricultural development in favour of accelerating the supply of water to coastal towns. The modifications effectively brought forward about half of the work originally included in phase three of the GMR plans, and would route an initial flow of 1.166m. cu m of water per day to the towns of Misurata and Khoms by 2000. Dong Ah, which currently employed 10,000 staff on GMR projects, expected the modifications (costing an estimated $760m.) to add substantially to its labour requirement. At the Banghazi end of the GMR system, Dong Ah expected to link the Benghazi reservoir to the city's supply system by the end of the third quarter of 1993. The depletion rate of local groundwater sources in the Libyan coastal region was reported to be alarmingly high in 1993.

Animal husbandry is the basis of farming in Libya and is likely to remain so until irrigation and reclamation measures really start to take effect. During the mid-1970s the breeding of cattle for dairy produce was expanded and milk production reached 62,000 tons in 1978, rising to an estimated 79,000 tons in 1990. The production of dairy produce rose from 6,000 tons in 1970, to 174,200 tons in 1986. Livestock is being imported on an increasing scale from a number of sources. Breeding cattle have been supplied by the United Kingdom, and stock-raising co-operation agreements signed with Argentina, Romania and Australia. In 1983 the Department of Agriculture reported that there were 109,000 camels in the country, compared with their figure of 71,000 for 1978. In 1990 the UN Food and Agriculture Organization (FAO) estimated the total number of camels at 193,000. There has also been a major increase in the numbers of poultry, from 5,099,000 in 1979 to 38,000,000 in 1990. In September 1990 the International Fund for Agricultural Development (IFAD) sponsored a conference on camel research in Tobruk.

In July 1990 the FAO held a special conference to raise funds to launch an emergency programme to eradicate from Libya the screw-worm fly, a parasitic insect which attacks livestock and wildlife. The fly was reported to have made its first appearance outside the western hemisphere in Libya some two years earlier, and the extent of its spread had raised fears that it would quickly infest the whole of the African continent. In January 1991 IFAD launched a $3m. pilot project as part of the programme, to which some $46m. had been pledged by February 1991. In October 1991 the FAO was able to report that the screw-worm eradication programme in Libya had been successful and that the forecast continental infestation had been averted.

Of the cereal crops, barley, which is the staple diet of most of the population, is the most important, although, despite wide fluctuations from year to year in the yields of both crops, production of wheat now equals barley output. Olives and citrus fruit are grown mainly in the west of the country, and other important food crops are tomatoes, almonds, castor beans, groundnuts and potatoes, also grown mainly in the west. Dates are produced in oases in the south and on the coastal belt. As part of the Jebel al-Gharbi project, 1.5m. fig, olive and apple trees are to be planted, thus expanding the country's fruit production capacity. Esparto grass, which grows wild in the Jebel, is used for the manufacture of high-quality paper and banknotes and was formerly Libya's most important article of export.

The 1976–80 Development Plan envisaged an annual growth of 15.8% in domestic production, so that Libya would be self-sufficient in vegetables and dairy products by 1980 and would also be able to produce 92% of its fruit requirements and 75% of its meat and wheat consumption. However, these targets were too optimistic and were not achieved. In September 1984 Col Qaddafi said that, for climatic reasons, Libya had achieved only 66% self-sufficiency in wheat and barley and that 60% of meat and 40% of milk requirements were produced locally.

The Government is continuing to further land development and reform. Polish assistance has been used to develop new farms in eastern Libya and in 1986 the Government claimed that during the preceding 17 years the ownership of 14,853 farms had been transferred to farmers. An interesting development in the 1970s, and one that is practicable only in an oil-rich economy, was the growth of hydroponic farming.

Although the Government has attempted some desert reclamation and afforestation projects, many have proved to be based on over-optimistic estimates of long-term environmental potential and economic return. Government-financed irrigation projects, for example, have resulted in serious groundwater depletion in north-western Libya.

The offshore waters abound in fish, especially tunny and sardines, but most of the fishing is done by Italians, Greeks or Maltese. Of special importance are the sponge-beds along the wide continental shelf. These are exploited by foreign fishermen and divers, mainly Greeks from the Dodecanese. As part of the expansion of Libya's fishing industry, the Zliten fishing port was opened in October 1983 at a cost of $16.8m. It is designed for use by 40 trawlers and provides storage for 200 tons of fish, together with refrigeration facilities for up to 20 tons of fish per day. In early 1990 the Arab Fund for Economic and Social Development agreed to lend Libya 11m. Kuwaiti dinars for the construction of two fish canning factories. An $18m. project to construct a fishing harbour at Susa was due to be undertaken by Greek contractors in 1993–94.

PETROLEUM

That petroleum was present in both Tripolitania and Cyrenaica had long been suspected and, for several years after Libya became independent, a large number of the bigger oil companies carried out geological surveys of the country. In 1955 a petroleum law came into force setting up a petroleum commission, which was empowered to grant concessions on a 50–50 profit-sharing basis, with parts of each concession being handed back to the Government after a given period. Under this law, concessions were granted to many US companies and to British, French and other foreign groups.

Important petroleum strikes first began to be made in 1957, and 10 years later Libya was already the fourth largest exporter in the world. The initial expansion of the Libyan petroleum industry was particularly rapid, owing to political stability, proximity to the Western European markets, and to the petroleum's lack of sulphur, which made it especially suitable for refining. The closing of the Suez Canal in 1967 was also an important factor in the growth of the industry. Production rose from 20,000 barrels per day (b/d) in 1962 to a peak of 3.3m. b/d in 1970, or 159.7m. metric tons in annual terms, equivalent to 13.6% of total output by OPEC members (then and future) and to 6.8% of world oil production. Output declined steadily to 71.3m. tons in 1975 (partly because of the reopening of the Suez Canal in 1974), rose again to 100.7m. tons in 1979, but then fell in the 1980s, reaching 47.9m. tons in 1987 (its lowest level since 1964), when Libya accounted for only 5% of OPEC production and 1.7% of world output. In 1988–89 a higher level of output was recorded, however. Production accelerated in 1990, as Libya took advantage of the rise in world oil prices caused by the 1990–91 Gulf crisis, and in mid-1993 the production level remained well above the depressed levels of the mid-1980s.

Oil is exported from five different sea terminals connected to the various fields by pipelines built by the five groups which have made the major finds. The pipeline system and the terminals are, however, available to other groups. The first of the five terminals to be opened was at Mersa Brega on the Gulf of Sirte, in 1961. The pipeline was built to Bir Zelten, in Cyrenaica, about 300 km south of Benghazi, where Esso Standard (Libya) had found oil in 1959. This group also operated a refinery at Mersa Brega and a gas liquefaction plant to prepare gas for shipment to Italy and Spain. The terminal for the Oasis group's Hofra field is at Ras as-Sidr, to the west of Mersa Brega. The Mobil/Gelsenberg group also found petroleum near Hofra, but built another pipeline to Ras Lanouf, just east of Ras as-Sidr. From a fourth terminal at Mersa al-Hariga, near Tobruk, a pipeline about 500 km long runs to Sarir, then the BP/Bunker Hunt concession. The terminal at Zuetina was opened in 1968 to serve the Augila and Idris fields. Here a US company, Occidental, which did not even obtain its concession until early in 1966, had found petroleum in large quantities. The Amoseas group, which produced petroleum from the Nafoora field, not far from Augila, had a pipeline connected to the Ras Lanouf terminal.

Libya has been a leader of those petroleum producers which demanded participation in petroleum activities, the National Oil Company (NOC) having been founded in 1968 for that express purpose. Extensive negotiations took place between the Libyan Government and the various petroleum producers in the early 1970s, with the result that, in 1973, the Libyan Government acquired a 51% share in the Libyan operations of Agip, Conoco/Marathon/Amerada Hess, Exxon, Mobil and Occidental, while it completely nationalized the holdings of Amoseas, BP/Bunker Hunt, Shell, Texaco, California Asiatic and Atlantic Richfield. Most outstanding claims by the companies were settled in 1977, following arbitration.

At the beginning of 1980, the experienced Secretary for Petroleum, Izzedin Mabrouk, was replaced by Abd as-Salam Muhammad Zagaar, for failing to speed up total Libyanization of the oil industry. In a restructuring of the management of state oil concerns during the previous year, the NOC's operational responsibilities had been devolved to specialist subsidiary companies, leaving the NOC as a holding company responsible for strategic planning and supervision of the state oil sector. By the end of 1982 the Libyan state had an 81% interest in the Libyan operations of Elf Aquitaine, 59.2% in Oasis, 51% in Occidental and 50% in Agip. All of Exxon's Libyan interests were taken over by the state when the company withdrew in 1981, and, after a year's prevarication, Mobil, which first began operating in Libya in 1955, announced its withdrawal from exploration and production activities at the end of 1982. In mid-1985 Occidental agreed to sell 25% of its oil production and exploration facilities in Libya to the Austrian state oil company ÖMV AG. These holdings provided about one-half of Occidental's net income in 1979 and 1980, but the proportion fell to less than 20% of the total in 1984. By 1988, following the withdrawal of US companies from their Libyan operations (see below), the overall state share in oil output was 82%, with Italian, German, Austrian and French operators producing the remaining 18%.

During 1979 Libya aligned itself with Iran as a 'hawk' in terms of the international oil market, and at the beginning of 1980 raised its oil price by 28% to $30 per barrel, only to raise it to $34.50 two weeks later. A further increase in May brought the price to $36.12 per barrel. This aggressive pricing policy continued throughout 1980, and in January 1981, the price of top-grade Zuetina was raised to $41 per barrel. In 1979 Libya's export revenue from petroleum and derivatives totalled $16,000m., and in 1980 it amounted to a record $21,919m., even though production declined to 88.4m. tons and exports were only 619m. barrels, compared with 718m. barrels in 1979. With the world oil glut persisting, the price of Zuetina and Brega crude was lowered to $39.9 per barrel in mid-1981, but this was still higher than most other world oil prices. In the summer of 1981 BP suspended liftings of Libyan oil, owing to its high price, and the 'spot' market price of Libyan oil then fell rapidly to $33 per barrel. Total Libyan output declined to 58.7m. tons in 1981 (equivalent to 1.22m. b/d), while oil revenues fell to $15,500m.

During 1982 OPEC set Libya's production 'ceiling' at 750,000 b/d but actual production averaged 1.135m. b/d (54.7m. tons in annual terms). At the end of 1982 'spot' prices for Libyan crude petroleum were as much as $4 per barrel below the official price. The March 1983 OPEC agreement gave Libya a quota of 1.1m. b/d, which represented some recognition of Libya's determination to continue with relatively high levels of production. The meeting set prices for Libyan oil at $30.5 per barrel for Brega 40° crude and $29.2 for Amna 36°. During most of 1983 Libya was producing only slightly more than the

set OPEC quota, and the Government's eventual petroleum revenues for the year were some $13,500m. The downward trend in oil prices on the 'spot' market continued in 1984, during which Libyan production continued at just more than 1.1m. b/d. In October OPEC decided to reduce its collective production to 16m. b/d, as a result of which Libya accepted one of the largest quota reductions, of 990,000 b/d. The country dissociated itself from the OPEC agreement on a new price structure, which was reached in January 1985, and the cost of Libya's Brega blend was held at $30.40 per barrel. However, as a large proportion of Libyan sales at the time were accounted for by barter deals involving discounts, the fact that its official price remained unchanged was of limited significance. During 1985 Libya consistently exceeded its OPEC production quota (average output during the year was 1.11m. b/d), but petroleum revenues continued to decline, falling to about $10,000m. in 1985, from $13,000m. in 1984. As market prices fell in 1986, Libya, Iran and Algeria opposed OPEC's majority policy of abandoning production restraint and seeking a 'fair' share of the world market as compensation for lower prices, advocating instead reductions in production as a means to revive prices. Accordingly, Libyan production was reduced in 1986 to an average of 1.01m. b/d (49.9m. tons), effectively anticipating the reintroduction of an OPEC production 'ceiling' in the last four months of the year, when Libya's quota averaged some 995,000 b/d. Nevertheless, a decline in 'spot' prices to under $10 per barrel in mid-1986 led to a severe fall in Libya's oil revenues for the year, to about $5,000m.

Another important development in 1986 was the enforced withdrawal of US oil companies from Libya. Having banned imports of Libyan petroleum in 1982, the US Government complemented this with a ban on imports of petroleum products in November 1985. Then, in January 1986, convinced of Libya's involvement in international terrorism, President Reagan 'froze' Libyan assets in the USA, and ordered all commercial transactions between US companies and Libya to cease by the beginning of February. The instruction was modified in February to allow about one dozen US companies in Libya (including five oil companies with equity holdings there) to continue their operations for a transitional period, while they terminated their activities. The oil companies (Occidental, Conoco, Marathon, Amerada Hess and W. R. Grace) ceased operations in Libya on 30 June, the new deadline that President Reagan had set in May. A three-year 'standstill period' officially expired at the end of June 1989, but has continued to be observed by Libya as a means of exerting pressure for the repeal of the US sanctions. Amid reports of renewed negotiations between Libya and the US companies, the Libyan Secretary for Petroleum confirmed, in March 1991, that the Government had no plans to sell the US companies' assets in Libya, adding that the companies were free to resume operations at any time.

In December 1986 OPEC imposed a 'ceiling' of 15.8m. b/d on collective production for the first half of 1987, incorporating a reduction of 7.25% in members' quotas, which, it was hoped, would support a fixed price for OPEC oil of $18 per barrel, which was applied from 1 February 1987. Libya's quota was reduced to 948,000 b/d. In June 1987 OPEC decided to retain the $18 reference price but to increase collective production by 800,000 b/d, to 16.6m. b/d, during the second half of the year, giving Libya a quota of 996,000 b/d. Although quota violations by some member states and the non-participation of Iraq made the 'ceiling' on output a purely notional one, Libya's production in 1987 was close to its quota, at about 975,000 b/d (47.9m. tons in the year, its lowest output since 1964), and revenues fell below $5,000m. At meetings of OPEC held in December 1987 and May 1988, it was agreed to retain the output 'ceiling' of 16.6m. b/d and the reference price of $18 per barrel for two further periods of six months, despite widespread quota violations, which had contributed to a renewed decline in the price of petroleum on the 'spot' market. The price of the Brent blend, a widely traded North Sea crude (to which the Libyan blends Zuetina, Brega, Sirtica, es-Sidr, Sarir and Amna were linked in July 1988), declined to $11.20 per barrel in early September 1988. Libya's production of crude petroleum during 1988 averaged 1.055m. b/d (50.6m.

tons), slightly above its OPEC quota, again yielding revenues of less than $5,000m. In November 1988 OPEC agreed to an output 'ceiling' of 18.5m. b/d, to be imposed from January 1989. Libya's share of the total was to be 1.037m. b/d. In June 1989 oil ministers from OPEC member states met and agreed a new production 'ceiling' of 19.5m. b/d, of which Libya was allocated a quota of 1.093m. b/d. Actual Libyan production in 1989 averaged 1.145m. b/d (54.8m. tons), yielding revenues of $7,846m., according to Libyan data. At the OPEC meeting of November 1989, quotas for the first half of 1990 were redistributed within a raised production 'ceiling' of 22m. b/d, Libya's share being set at 1.233m. b/d. Actual Libyan output was, however, raised to 1.65m. b/d in early 1990 (allegedly to test sustainable production capacity), before being reduced to 1.35m. b/d from mid-March. At the OPEC meeting of July 1990, Libya pressed for quota parity with Kuwait but was again allocated 1.233m. b/d within an overall production 'ceiling' of 22.5m. b/d, designed to underpin a minimum reference price of $21 per barrel.

However, the situation was then transformed by the onset of the Gulf crisis in August 1990 and by a rapid rise in world oil prices to more than $30 per barrel. Libya refused to attend an emergency OPEC meeting held in Vienna in late August, at which it was decided to suspend quotas to allow members to take advantage of the embargoes imposed on Iraqi and Kuwaiti oil production. While expressing opposition to this decision, Libya proceeded to raise its production as quickly as possible, to almost 1.5m. b/d by October, with the result that its total oil revenues in 1990 increased by 23%, compared with 1989, to $9,700m. The average production level for 1990 was 1.355m. b/d (the highest annual average since 1980). Following the end of the Gulf conflict in February 1991 and the stabilization of world oil prices at pre-crisis levels, OPEC reimposed quotas from the second quarter of 1991, Libya's allocation being 1.425m. b/d within an overall production 'ceiling' of 22.3m. b/d. For 1992 Libya's OPEC quota was set at 1.409m. b/d, later reduced to 1.35m. b/d from 1 April 1993 and adjusted to 1.39m. b/d from 1 October 1993. Actual Libyan output averaged 1.5m. b/d throughout 1991 and 1992 (producing revenue of at least $10,000m. per year). During 1993 Libyan oil production averaged just over 1.37m. b/d, a level that was steadily maintained in the first half of 1994. The monthly average 'spot' price of Brega crude, which had fallen from over $18 per barrel to under $14 per barrel during the course of 1993, had recovered to more than $16 per barrel by the second quarter of 1994.

In March 1989 the Petroleum Secretariat was revived, after a three-year period in which control of the oil industry had been in the hands of the national companies. The revived Petroleum Secretariat then drafted plans to reorganize and develop Libya's oil sector, which were implemented following the appointment as Secretary for Petroleum, in October 1990, of Abdullah al-Badri, hitherto chairman of the NOC. The changes involved a drastic reduction of the NOC's powers and the elevation to a dominant role of the Secretariat for Petroleum, to which all state oil companies were now required to report directly.

Libya's proven published reserves of crude petroleum at 1 January 1993 were 22,800m. barrels, sufficient to maintain output for 41.2 years at the level of production in 1991–92. Estimated probable reserves were 45,000m. barrels, which represented an 82:1 ratio of reserves to 1992 production. Nevertheless, some Western analysts believe that Libya will have difficulty in maintaining its current production level much beyond the end of the century unless new fields are discovered and known fields are developed rapidly. Although there was an increase in exploration activity in the early 1980s, sharp reductions in oil revenues from 1986 onwards resulted in a decline not only in exploration but also in development work on discovered fields. Moreover, the deficiencies in expertise and technology resulting from the withdrawal of US operators in 1986 (and compounded by the subsequent imposition of sanctions by the USA on Libya) have been only partially compensated by European, Canadian and Asian companies. Over the decade as a whole, only some 20% of current output was replaced by new proven reserves, while,

as a result of poor state management, several established fields fell substantially below their theoretical production capacity.

Against this background, the Libyan authorities have, in the light of the 1990–91 Gulf crisis, re-emphasized the need for an active exploration campaign, to which LD 200m. (US $700m.) were allocated in the NOC's 1991/92 budget.

In particular, the Government is keen to evaluate the oil potential of parts of the country outside the Sirte Basin in north-central Libya, where the commercial fields are currently grouped. There are two main areas of interest—western Libya (formerly Tripolitania) and offshore, with particular stress on the Tripolitanian offshore. Indeed, exploration interest in areas off the Tripolitanian coast has been stimulated in recent years by the discovery and successful development of the Bouri offshore oilfield, the largest so far discovered, in the Mediterranean, situated some 125 km north-west of Tripoli. Test production of 10,000 b/d at Bouri, Libya's first offshore oilfield, containing total reserves of up to 5,000m. barrels, began in August 1988. Output had risen to 75,000 b/d by mid-1990 and could rise to 150,000 b/d in the early 1990s if second-phase development work initiated in February 1991 is completed on schedule. In April 1989 Libya's NOC and the Tunisian state oil enterprise ETAP formed a Joint Oil Company (JOC) to exploit the '7 November' oilfield straddling the two countries' continental shelf boundary, but agreement on an initial drilling programme had yet to be finalized by mid-1993. New exploration concessions awarded to, or under negotiations with, Canadian, British, Austrian, Yugoslav, South Korean and other companies in late 1990 and early 1991 included substantial offshore areas north-west of Tripoli.

Exploration also continues in other parts of the country, with some work being undertaken in the largely unexplored south. New finds continue to be made in the Sirte Basin, despite the intensive exploration of previous years. In 1976, Occidental brought the new Almas field into production and the Libyan Umm al-Jawaby company also had two commercial finds, one on the eastern side of the Sirte Basin and one on the west. In 1984 an oilfield with reserves estimated at 624m. barrels was discovered north-west of the Abu at-Tifl field.

In the Murzuk basin, in south-western Libya, Rompetrol of Romania was the original foreign contractor for the development of a new field (NC-115) with estimated reserves of up to 2,000m. barrels, exploitation of which will involve the construction of extensive oilfield storage facilities, some 900,000 barrels of new coastal storage facilities at Zawia, a new refinery at Sebha and a pipeline network to connect the new facilities. By 1993 implementation of this $1,000m. project (originally approved in 1989) was seriously behind schedule because of financial constraints, prompting Rompetrol to sell its stake in the NC-115 field to Spain's Repsol Exploración, which subsequently opened negotiations with the NOC on the terms of a formal transfer of development rights. Also being given priority were water-injection projects to increase output from certain established fields. These included the giant Sarir field in the Sirte basin, where production has seldom exceeded one-half of its capacity since nationalization but which was scheduled to be raised from a current output of 200,000 b/d to 600,000 b/d by 1994; the field was also to supply associated gas to power stations driving the GMR irrigation project (see Agriculture, above). In June 1992 ÖMV of Austria announced a promising new oil discovery in a block some 350 km south of Benghazi.

Libya's reserves of natural gas at the beginning of 1993 were estimated at 1,300,000m. cu m. Marketed gas output (excluding gas flared or reinjected into the oilwells from which most Libyan gas is derived) totalled 6,780m. cu m in 1992—its highest level since 1979. Inaugurated in 1971, a liquefaction plant at Marsa Brega was the world's first scheme to convert flared gas into liquefied natural gas (LNG), annual exports of which, mainly to Italy and Spain, reached more than 4,000m. cu m in the mid-1970s, although they fell to under 1,500m. cu m in the 1980s, as Italy switched to cheaper Algerian supplies by gas pipeline. Further trade with Italy became impractical in 1990, when the Italian LNG import terminal was converted to accept normal-grade LNG. Spain, which still has import facilities for the high-calorie LNG currently exported by Libya, now takes the greater part of Libya's LNG exports; a new 20-year contract, for the supply of at least 1,000m. cu m per year, was signed with Enagás of Spain in March 1991. Exports to Spain totalled 1,580m. cu m in 1991, and 1,800m. cu m in 1992. A contract to supply Turkey with 1,500m. cu m of LNG over 25 years was signed in 1988, but implementation awaits the completion of a terminal at Marmara Ereglisi. Libya announced plans in 1993 to convert the Marsa Brega plant (which has a nominal daily capacity of 10.8m. cu m) to produce normal and low grades of LNG, rather than the high-calorie grade produced hitherto. However, when contractors who had submitted bids for this $200m.-project studied the latest UN sanctions on Libya, it was clear that it would be impossible to carry out the work without importing equipment included on the list of embargoed items. Eager to link its own gas network with that of Algeria, Libya, in 1990, initiated preparatory studies to extend its existing 670-km Mersa Brega–Homs coastal pipeline westward to the Tunisian border, with the eventual aim of linking up with the Algeria–Sicily pipeline running through Tunisia. The existing coastal pipeline had been completed by a Soviet company in 1988 and had opened in September 1989, with a capacity of 4m. cu m per year. At the same time, the concept of a direct pipeline linking Libya to Italy remained under consideration, despite previous assessments that its cost would be prohibitive. In December 1990 it was confirmed that AGIP of Italy and the NOC were engaged in feasibility studies for a direct pipeline, which could form part of a massive gas development programme in Libya, costing up to US $13,000m. Meanwhile, the NOC's priority plans included the development of the Kabir gas field close to the Tunisian border, at an estimated cost of $80m., and the use of gas output from other fields to fuel the GMR irrigation project. In mid-1992 the French company Total signed a contract to take 300,000 tons of liquefied petroleum gas from Libya starting in 1993 (the personal authorization of President Mitterrand was needed in view of the current UN sanctions against Libya).

On the marketing side, Libya has concluded various agreements involving the exchange of crude petroleum for specific goods or services. During recent years, France, Italy, Poland, the USSR, Yugoslavia and a number of other countries have concluded barter deals with Libya, involving purchases of petroleum. Libya also has special petroleum arrangements with Brazil and Greece, and, together with Algeria, Nigeria and Gabon, remains theoretically committed to reserve 4% of its output for delivery to African states. Libya's attempts to establish itself in the downstream marketing of oil products in developed countries have included the purchase, in 1986, of a 70% stake in the Italian Tamoil group, which subsequently provided an important overseas marketing outlet when the international oil glut developed in the late 1980s. Such overseas marketing investments are directed by the state-owned Oil Investments International Company (Oilinvest), established in 1988, while sales are effected through Chempetrol, a wholly-owned subsidiary, based in Malta.

In common with other large oil producers, Libya would much prefer to refine and process its own oil, rather than export it in the crude state. Owing to its freedom from sulphur, Libya's oil is particularly suited to refining. A report by the General People's Committee for Economies and Planning, published in June 1985, stated that, since 1970, 56 chemical projects and 21 oil refineries, capable of producing 5.7m. tons of petroleum products per year, had been completed. Zawia refinery was opened in 1974, enlarged in 1977, and has a capacity of 120,000 b/d. An upgrading programme was in preparation in 1993. The other main refinery locations are at Tobruk, where a refinery with a capacity of 20,000 b/d was opened in 1986, and Ras Lanouf. Previously supplied by tanker with crude petroleum shipped from Mersa Brega, the Zawia refinery will eventually draw all of its materials from fields near the Algerian frontier. The country's largest oil refinery, at Ras Lanouf, which was begun by Italian contractors in 1978, finally started production in February 1985 and had a capacity of 201,000 b/d at 1 January 1988, compared with planned capacity of 220,000 b/d. At the end of 1989 Libya had a total installed refinery capacity of 380,000 b/d, having achieved an output of refined products in 1988 of 255,600 b/d, of which 110,000 b/d were consumed domestically. Plans

were announced in 1991 to build a refinery at Hymed, to be supplied from the Bouri offshore field. In the following year plans were announced for a 20,000 b/d refinery at Sebha to process crude from oilfields under development in the Murzuk basin.

In the petrochemical sphere, NOC has built one ammonia plant and one ethanol plant, each with a capacity of 1,000 tons per day, at Mersa Brega. These came into production in September 1977. In 1978 NOC awarded a contract worth $150m. to an Italian company for the construction of a new ammonia plant, with a capacity of 1,000 tons per day, at Mersa Brega. A further $150m. contract has been granted at Mersa Brega for a urea plant with a capacity of 1,000 tons per day. (Most of the urea currently produced in Libya is exported to China, India, Turkey and Italy.) Sited near Exxon's LNG plant, the new units will process natural gas and are expected to make Mersa Brega the country's foremost centre for the production of petrochemicals. Local methanol production capacity, most of which is located at the Mersa Brega complex, was supplemented by the inauguration in September 1987 of a factory at al-Burayqah with a capacity of 2,000 tons per day. Libyan methanol production totalled 660,000 tons in 1987. In 1980 an Italian firm received a contract worth $60m. for the construction of an ethylene plant with a capacity of 330,000 tons per year at the Ras Lanouf refinery and petrochemical complex, and this, comprising, with the refinery, the first phase of the Ras Lanouf development, began production in 1987. A US company has signed a contract for a monoethylene glycol plant at the same refinery. In addition, the contract for a 1,750 tons-per-day urea plant has been won by a joint Federal German/Italian venture. The Abu Kammash chemical complex was opened in September 1980. Reductions in government revenues from petroleum in the 1980s necessitated some rationalization of the plans for the Ras Lanouf project, which is co-ordinated by the Ras Lanouf Oil and Gas Processing Company (Rasco). In early 1993 a $130m.-second-phase development contract, awarded in 1990 to a consortium from former Yugoslavia, was cancelled on grounds of non-performance and the work reopened to new tenders. The facilities concerned—an 86,000 tons-per-year benzene unit, a 58,600 tons-per-year butadiene unit, a 47,000 tons-per-year methyl-tertiary-butyl ether unit and an 18,300 tons-per-year butene-1 unit—were not now expected to be completed before 1997. Rasco's third-phase development project, involving the construction by South Korea's Hyudai Engineering and Construction Company of two 80,000 tons-per-year units to produce high-density and low-density polyethylene, was 20% complete by mid-1993. Plans were also in hand to build a 68,000 tons-per-year polypropylene plant.

INDUSTRY

Manufacturing in Libya has been largely confined to the processing of local agricultural products and such traditional crafts as carpet weaving, tanning and leather working and shoe making. Plans were made several years ago for a whole range of factories to make such diverse articles as prefabricated construction materials, cables, glass, pharmaceuticals, woollen and synthetic textiles, among others. Most of these factories did not get past the tendering stage, but efforts have been made, in successive development plans since the 1970s, to diversify the non-oil sector of industry and to increase its contribution to GNP.

Contracts for industrial plant have in the past been awarded mainly to Western European and US companies, but Japanese firms are becoming more active in Libya. Under the 1981–85 Development Plan, LD 1,200m. (of the total investment figure of $62,500m.) were allocated to light industry. Notwithstanding its support for smaller projects, the Government has given more attention, and resources, to a few major ventures in heavy industry and in infrastructure development. In January 1975 Col Qaddafi announced that Libya had plans for the establishment of a heavy industry sector involving vehicle and tractor assembly plants, shipbuilding and iron and steel works. In this context the master plan for the Misurata industrial city, due to house 180,000 people at a cost of $1,290m., was submitted in September 1979.

According to the OPEC news agency, some $62,500m. were spent by Libya between 1970 and 1983 to develop industry and reduce the country's dependence on the petroleum sector. The result has been that the value of non-oil production activities rose from $1,610m. in 1970 to $15,280m. in 1983, and their contribution to GDP from 37% to 50%, reducing the share of the petroleum sector from 63% to 50%. An economic report covering the years 1970–86, which was released by Jana, the Libyan news agency, in September 1986, claimed that investment in the industrial sector during the period totalled LD 3,959.8m., enabling 139 projects to reach the production stage (52 food industry projects; 23 chemical and petrochemical industry factories; 17 mineral and engineering industry factories; 16 textile, clothing and leather goods factories; 8 wood and paper industry factories). However, as oil revenues declined in the 1980s, the industrial sector, in common with other parts of the economy, suffered from under-spending compared with budgeted figures. Although heavy industry traditionally attracts the largest proportion of total development investment, actual spending in this sector in 1983, 1984 and 1985 was, respectively, 96.2%, 84.4% and 83.4% of the budgeted allocation. Light industry was even more seriously affected, with expenditure on the sector in the three years in question reaching only 74.6%, 76.5% and 75% of the budgeted level. (No official figures have been issued in recent years.)

Iron ore reserves, estimated at over 700m. metric tons, were discovered in 1974 at Wadi Shatti, in southern Libya, and plans for their exploitation are under way. Work was initially planned to begin in November 1979 on the construction of a steelworks at Misurata for completion in 1985 at a cost of some $1,000m. However, it was not until 1981 that Libya started awarding contracts for the Misurata steel works. Kobe Steel of Japan was awarded a contract worth $751m. for a section mill and a rod mill; a consortium of Korf Engineering of the Federal Republic of Germany and Voest Alpine of Austria won a $540m. contract for a steel production plant, while a $674m. contract for a second production plant was won by Friedrich Krupp of Federal Germany; and two consortia, both led by Voest Alpine, won contracts for hot and cold rolling mills. In 1982 the Hyundai Engineering and Construction Company of South Korea won a contract worth $520m. to build a 480-MW power station and a desalination plant, with a capacity of 31,500 cu m per day, to serve the steel complex. However, the repeated deferment of payments to contractors, caused by declining oil revenues, seriously delayed work on the project, which did not start full operations until September 1990. A 900-km railway is also to be built, linking the iron ore mines in the south to Misurata. The contract for a port to handle imports of iron ore was won by Sezai Turkes Feyzi of Turkey. It was originally planned that subsequent developments would increase production at Misurata to 5m. and 7m. tons per year (by 2005). However, in view of the shortage of revenue from petroleum to fund this expansion, these plans were deferred. The proposals to build a town to house 50,000 people at Misurata were scaled down, envisaging an initial phase to house 20,000 people, with possible later stages bringing the population to 40,000. In late 1990 all the production units at the Misurata steel plant were reported to be operating, employing 3,500 Libyan nationals and 1,000 expatriate workers.

In 1991 the Misurata complex operated at about two-thirds of design capacity, producing an estimated 800,000 tons of steel during that year. A $224m.-contract to add a 650,000 tons-per-year direct reduction plant, which would increase total capacity at Misurata to nearly 2m. tons per year, was awarded in January 1993 to a consortium led by Voest Alpine, which expected to complete the work within three years. Most of the new plant's output of hot briquetted iron was to be exported to Italy and Spain. In the first nine months of 1993 raw steel output at Misurata totalled 709,000 tons, nearly one-third more than in the corresponding period of 1992.

In October 1985 a Danish company, FLOTEC, was awarded a contract to build a gypsum plant. Italian contracts totalling $300m. have been granted for a water purification plant, workshops and electricity transformer stations. In 1983 plans were announced for the construction of a 120,000 tons-per-

year aluminium smelter complex at Zuwara, 120 km west of Tripoli, at a cost of $1,250m. to be run by a joint company, Libal, formed by Yugoslavia's Energoinvest and Libya's heavy industries Secretariat. Eventually it is hoped that a petroleum coke plant and an associated industrial port will be built at Zuwara. Under an agreement signed by Algeria and Libya in July 1987, Algeria was to have constructed a pipeline, via Tunisia, to supply an 800-MW power station forming part of the Zuwara smelting complex. However, the smelter project was postponed in 1987, pending a revival in Libya's revenues from sales of oil, on which it depends to finance industrial development. At the end of 1982 plans were revived to build a $1,000m. fertilizer complex at Sirte in two stages. Talks with the USSR on the construction of the delayed first stage began at the end of 1984, and it was hoped that it would come into production by the end of 1987. However, the second stage of the Sirte complex was postponed in April 1986, and the first stage was itself postponed in 1987, owing to the decline in oil revenues. The contractors (from the UK, Italy, Spain, the Federal Republic of Germany and the Republic of Korea) blamed the postponement on the abrupt fall in the price of oil, and the consequent shortage of funds. A second urea plant capable of producing 1,850 tons of fertilizer per day was opened at the new town of al-Brega in September 1984.

The construction work carried out under the development programme gave rise to a rapidly increasing demand for cement, which is imported in large quantities. The existing cement plant at Homs has been expanded and two more are being built at Souk al-Khemis and Darna, with others planned. A new Benghazi cement factory was opened in August 1978, and a new $150m. plant has been built at Homs by a French firm. In 1987 cement production rose by 30%, compared with 1986, to 2.7m. tons, some 2m. tons less than the domestic requirement and more than 3m. less than rated capacity. The Danish company FLOTEC was awarded a contract in October 1985 to build a gypsum factory. The gypsum, which is used in cement production, will be exported to Europe. The project includes the establishment of a natural gas energy plant at the factory and terminal facilities at the port of Tripoli. Other industrial diversification projects signed in 1991–92 included one with Candy Elettrodomestici of Italy for a refrigerator construction plant at Zuara with a projected capacity of 80,000 units a year, and another with Gold Star of South Korea for a video-cassette recorder factory at Benghazi with a capacity of 70,000 recorders a year.

Many of the contracts at the peak of the construction boom in the 1970s were awarded to Turkish firms. In 1981 there were 102 Turkish companies operating in Libya, with an estimated 80,000 Turkish workers. Falling oil revenues, though, forced Libya to inform Turkey early in 1982 that it wanted to deduct $70m. in oil debts from $100m. owed to various Turkish firms. By early 1991 debts owed to Turkish contractors had reached some $600m., adversely affecting Libyan–Turkish relations, which remained strained until the following year, when a schedule of oil deliveries in lieu of debt payments was agreed in bilateral talks. By March 1994 Libya's outstanding debts to Turkish contractors had been reduced to $250m., which it was hoped to clear by the end of 1994. South Korean companies, such as the Daewoo Corporation, have also been involved in the implementation of new contracts in Libya. In May 1981 100 South Korean dockers were used to clear severe congestion at Benghazi port. The Daewoo Corporation was awarded a $337m. contract in 1985 to build sewer and water facilities, roads, pumping stations and a telephone system in Benghazi.

Infrastructure expenditure has put great emphasis on power generation. Since 1974 the Government has awarded several large contracts for power stations, some in association with desalination plants. During the 1976–80 period $3,195m. were spent on power schemes. Installed generating capacity rose from 879 MW in 1975 to 1,700 MW in 1979. Under the 1980–85 plan, capacity was projected to increase from 1,950 MW to 3,878 MW. However, there have been delays in power station construction schemes, owing to lack of finance, and, according to the United Nations, installed capacity had declined to 1,460 MW in 1985. In 1982 an agreement was concluded with the USSR, designed to help to establish a national electricity grid by 1995. A 10-MW Soviet nuclear research reactor became operational at Tajura, near Tripoli, in 1982, but subsequent plans to develop a major nuclear generating plant were shelved in the mid-1980s. Work was expected to start in late 1993 on a three-year project to add more than 1,000 MW of new gas-turbine generating capacity at five Libyan power stations, several of them scheduled for expansion since the mid-1980s.

Scarcity of water is a continuing problem, and in 1982, in addition to the GMR project (see Agriculture, above), plans were announced for a 462,000 cu m-per-day desalination plant (Tripoli 1) to provide Tripoli with drinking water. Plans for a further 150,000 cu m-per-day desalination plant at Janzour, 20 km west of Tripoli, were also announced at the end of 1982. The site of Tripoli 1 was moved to Janzour in mid-1984. A water purification plant in Tobruk, with a daily capacity of 5,000 cu m for agricultural purposes (from 13,000 cu m of sewage), was inaugurated in April 1988. Plans for the power and water complex at Zuweitina (Zuetina), initially due to have been completed in 1987, have now been scaled down from a planned capacity of 40,000 cu m of water per day to 20,000 cu m, although still maintaining a power capacity of 720 MW. Bids for a further desalination plant, at the Zawia oil refinery, were submitted in October 1991 by Italian, Dutch and German companies. In 1993 the Hyundai Engineering and Construction Company signed a letter of intent to build Libya's largest power and desalination complex at Sirte. Costing an estimated $1,600m. and designed to provide 1,260 MW of generating capacity and 20,000m. cu m per day of desalination capacity, this project had formed part of Libya's development plans since the early 1980s, when its intended location was Mlita, west of Tripoli.

TRANSPORT AND COMMUNICATIONS

As might be expected, the large and increasing volume of imports has led to severe congestion at the main ports of Tripoli and Benghazi. Worsening port conditions have resulted in increases in surcharges. In addition, Darna and Misurata ports are being reconstructed. Tripoli, Mersa Brega and Benghazi are undergoing large-scale expansion. In 1986, according to the Libyan news agency, Jana, the handling capacity of the nation's ports was 9.5m. tons.

Port expansion is necessarily a long-term process and the development of rail, road and to some extent air freight is very important. There is an extensive road-building pro-gramme, and a number of large road-building contracts, such as the Sebha-Wadden road and the Mirzuk link, were awarded to Egyptian companies. In 1980 an Indian company won a $129m. contract for the construction of desert roads at a variety of locations throughout the country. The road from Tripoli to Sebha was opened at the end of 1983, providing 770 km of metalled surface. In September 1986 the Govern-ment claimed to have built 10,990 km of paved roads, and 6,250 km of rural roads during the preceding 17 years. There have been no railways in Libya since 1964, when the Benghazi-Barce line was abandoned, but during 1981 and 1982 plans were developed to link Tripoli with Tunisia, and to establish rail connections from Tripoli and Sebha to Misurata, and from Benghazi to Tobruk and Agedabia with a view eventually to the development of a national railway network of about 3,000 km in length. Following the *rapprochement* with Egypt in 1989, plans for bilateral co-operation included the construc-tion of a 180-km rail link between the Egyptian border town of Salloun and Tobruk. In October 1994 the Libyan news agency announced that construction of the Salloun-Tobruk line had begun and that the start of work was 'imminent' on a line from Tripoli to Ras Adjir on the Tunisian border. The UN ban on international flights to Libya, which in April 1992 effectively shut down the international operations of the national carrier, Libyan Arab Airlines, led to increased use of airports in neighbouring countries. There was particularly strong demand for flights from Tunis (now the nearest avail-able international airport to Tripoli) to the Tunisian island of Djerba, which is linked to Libya by a ferry service. Major users of this route included South Korean contractors working on large Libyan development projects, who were able to take advantage of regular Korean Airways flights into Tunis.

As part of Libya's aim to create a comprehensive telecom-munications network, in mid-1991 Swedish companies were awarded contracts for new installations in the south-west of the country; however, other parts of the programme, notably plans for 20 new exchanges and 182,000 extra lines in Tripoli and Benghazi, were not finalized until mid-1993. Provided that financing expectations were fulfilled, the work was expected to be completed by 1996.

EXTERNAL TRADE

Until production of oil began, Libya's exports consisted almost entirely of agricultural products, and its imports of manufac-tured goods. In 1960, for instance, imports were valued at LD 60.4m. and exports at LD 4.0m., leaving an adverse balance of LD 56.4m. (although LD 21m. of the total value of imports in 1960 was accounted for by goods imported for the account of the petroleum companies). Petroleum was first exported in the autumn of 1961, and by 1969, according to IMF data, imports totalled LD 241.3m. and exports LD 937.9m., of which LD 936.5m. was officially accounted for by crude petroleum. Although there were fluctuations within the overall trend, petroleum exports rose from LD 2,109.5m. in 1974 to LD 4,419.2m. in 1979, when they represented 99% of all Libyan exports by volume. The minute proportion of remaining exports were mainly hides and skins, groundnuts, almonds, metal scrap and re-exports.

Imports consist of a wide variety of manufactured goods, such as textiles, motor vehicles and luxury consumer goods. In the last few years imports of timber, chemicals and raw materials and, in particular, cement and building materials, have been stepped up. In addition, many foodstuffs have to be imported, for example tea, sugar, coffee and, in years of drought, wheat and flour. The value of imports increased by over 500% betweeen 1971 and 1979, from LD 250.4m. to LD 1,572m., whereas over the same period exports by value grew by 400%.

Since petroleum has been exported, Libya has experienced a considerable trade surplus. In 1971 exports f.o.b. (including re-exports) were valued at LD 962.5m., and imports c.i.f. at LD 250.4m., leaving a trade surplus of LD 712.1m. The general trend of increasing surpluses continued during the 1970s, and in 1980, when Libya's imports totalled LD 2,006.2m., and its exports LD 6,489.2m., a trade surplus of LD 4,483m., was recorded. Declining demand and lower prices for petroleum reduced the trade surplus to LD 2,129.8m. in 1981, and to LD 2,006.7m. in 1982. The value of exports fell to LD 3,283m. in 1983 (imports LD 1,989.5m.), and stabilized at LD 3,295.4m. in 1984 (imports LD 1,811.8m.), but fell to LD 3,235.2m. ($10,841m.) in 1985 (imports LD 1,444.7m.), of which exports of crude petroleum accounted for LD 3,234.2m. The value of imports declined to LD 1,279m. in 1986, rising slightly, to LD 1,293.2m., in 1987. Estimated exports in 1989 totalled US $7,320m., surpassing imports of $6,460m., a pattern which continued in 1990 (exports $11,530m., imports $7,250m.) and was forecast to be maintained in 1991 (projected exports $10,260m., projected imports $7,970m.).

In 1982 Italy (with 25.4% of total imports by value) was Libya's main supplier, followed by the Federal Republic of Germany (14.4%) and the UK (8%). In 1981 the USA (with 27.4% of Libyan exports by value), Italy (23.8%), the Federal Republic of Germany (10.3%) and Spain (6.7%) were the principal customers for Libyan exports (almost exclusively, crude petroleum). In 1977 the USA took 25% of Libya's oil exports. The USA and Western Europe together accounted for almost 90% of total oil exports from Libya. However, in 1982 all imports of Libyan petroleum to the USA were banned. Libyan imports from the USA fell by $500m. from the level of $831m. in 1981. In January 1986, convinced of Libya's involvement in promoting international terrorism, President Reagan banned all trade between the USA and Libya. The USA succeeded in persuading some of its allies to reduce sharply their purchases of Libyan oil after the bombing of Tripoli and Benghazi in April 1986, but Italy, by far the largest customer for Libyan oil, actually increased its imports. The US embargo on bilateral trade with Libya reduced Libyan imports from the USA to $46.2m. in 1986, while Libyan exports to the USA amounted to a mere $1.6m.

As Libyan debts (see below) have accumulated, imports from West European countries have also become much reduced. Italian companies claimed outstanding credits of about $500m. from Libya in 1984. An agreement between Libya and Italy in August 1984 failed to solve the credits issue, and a new agreement was signed in Rome in July 1985. Several countries, including India, Turkey and Uganda, have accepted oil as payment for goods or debts owed to them by Libya. In the late 1980s imports from Japan showed a rapid rise, from $296m. in 1987 to $602m. in 1988, while exports to Japan rose from virtually zero in 1987 to more than $600m. in 1989. Libya remained Italy's largest regional trading partner in 1990, supplying exports (mainly oil) of $4,700m. and taking Italian exports of $1,083m. Following the Gulf crisis of 1990–91, Libya's efforts to improve relations with Western Europe were encouraged by the visit of the Italian Prime Minister in June 1991 (the first by an EC Head of Government for more than 10 years), when an agreement was signed with the objective of increasing bilateral trade and Italian participation in Libyan development projects, such as the GMR irrigation scheme (see Agriculture, above). After Italy, Libya's most important trading partners are Germany (to which Libyan exports in 1990 increased to $2,186m., compared with imports of $1,622m.), Spain (Libyan exports in 1990 of $1,163m., imports of $776m.) and France (Libyan exports in 1990 of $762m., imports of $466m.).

FINANCE

Before the 1969 coup most Libyan banks were subsidiaries of foreign banks. However, among the first decrees issued by the Revolutionary Council was one which required 51% of the capital of all banks operating in Libya to be owned by Libyans; the majority of directors, including the chairman, of each bank had to be Libyan citizens. Under the monarchy the Government had followed a similar policy without compulsion, and a number of foreign banks had accordingly already 'Libyanized' themselves. In December 1970 all commercial banks were nationalized, with government participation set at 51%.

In March 1993 legislation was passed authorizing Libyan citizens and companies to establish privately owned commercial banks with a minimum capitalization of LD 10m. ($37m.). Under the same law, Libyan nationals were permitted to apply to the Central Bank of Libya for authorization to hold foreign currency in local bank accounts and to make unrestricted use of such holdings. The heavily overvalued Libyan dinar was currently being unofficially traded for convertible currencies at about one-sixth of its official exchange rate (which had been pegged to the IMF's special drawing rights since 1986). Speaking in May 1993, Col Qaddafi said that he favoured a move towards full convertibility of the Libyan dinar at such time as 'there was adequate production' in the Libyan economy to prevent 'catastrophic' consequences.

The growth in petroleum revenue in the 1970s allowed the Government to devote about one-half of its income to development expenditure, although this proportion declined in the 1980s, as oil revenues fell. Libya also gave generous aid abroad, in particular to the Yemen PDR, Egypt, Syria and Jordan, although the Government was somewhat capricious in implementing aid agreements. Aid was cut off from the Jordanian Government in September 1970 when it attacked the Palestinian guerillas. Egypt was criticized over its conduct of the war with Israel and in 1974 Libya demanded the return of a loan to Sudan. Aid to Egypt was suspended as a result of Egypt's signing the peace treaty with Israel in March 1979. There is no comparable organization in Libya to the Kuwait Fund for Arab Economic Development, but in 1974 Libya made a contribution to the Islamic Development Bank. In 1980 Libyan aid to developing countries was $281m., equivalent to 0.92% of GNP. This compares with the $261m. that was given in 1975, which then represented 2.3% of GNP.

Developments in the Libyan banking sector included the establishment of joint development banks with Algeria and Turkey and an agreement to establish a joint Libyan-Mali bank. In 1977 the Libyan Arab Foreign Bank (LAFB)—effectively the offshore arm of the Central Bank of Libya, and a key institution in Libyan trade finance—bought a 15.2% stake in the equity of Fiat, the Italian motor car company, for $400m. The deal was backed by a loan to Fiat from the LAFB of $105m. repayable over 10 years (with two years' grace). Until this purchase the LAFB had pursued a cautious and selective policy of putting Libyan capital into banking, hotel and tourism in many countries, as well as joint-stock ventures in agriculture, fishing and forestry projects in some African countries. Libya appeared to regard the Fiat purchase as the vanguard of its investment in industrial countries' manufacturing bases. Libya's holdings in Italy were enlarged at the end of 1981 when the LAFB bought the bankrupt Italian sugar and steel concern Malradi for $450m. In September 1986, however, Libya sold its shares in Fiat for $3,000m. The Libyan Ambassador to Rome denied that the sale had been prompted by the collapse of oil prices and the consequent shortage of foreign exchange. Other Libyan assets in Italy were 'frozen' in mid-1986 as 'guarantees' for Italian companies awaiting payment of millions of dollars from Libya in debt arrears. In December 1979 Kuwait and Libya signed a $1,000m. agreement to set up an Arab investment company, and in April 1980 Libya, together with Kuwait and the United Arab Emirates, decided to establish a new international insurance company. This was finally established with a capital of $3,000m. in October 1981. In September 1987 the Bankers' Trust Company of New York was ordered by a British High Court judge to release $292m. of Libyan assets placed with the bank's London branch, that were 'frozen' by order of President Reagan in January 1986.

The LAFB increased its paid-up capital to LD156m. in the 1991/92 fiscal year, during which it made a pre-tax profit of LD15m. Its paid-up shares in international affiliates (including 28 international banks outside Libya) totalled LD169.3m. In mid-1993 a proposal by the LAFB to increase its shareholding in the Athens-based Arab Hellenic Bank from 30% to 86% (thereby opening the way to the establishment of Libyan-controlled bank branches in other EC countries) was effectively halted by the Greek banking authorities. In 1992/93 the LAFB reported an increase in paid-up capital to LD 192m., an increase in net profits to LD 18.3m. and a 25% increase in total assets to LD 1,398m. The Bank's assets abroad were frozen in December 1993 under the terms of UN Security Council Resolution 883.

Although Libya enjoys a substantial trade surplus, it also experiences a considerable deficit on 'invisibles' (services and transfer payments). This 'invisible' deficit increased from $1,450m. in 1973 to $2,265m. in 1977. In the early 1970s this deficit partly offset the trade surplus, leaving a fluctuating surplus on current account, but in 1975 (when the trade surplus was reduced) the current account was pushed into deficit. Aid payments and purchases of military equipment (in 1986 Libya was estimated to owe the USSR $4,000m.–$5,000m. for sales of arms) tended to bring about a substantial outflow on capital account—so that Libya's basic balance of payments often yielded a deficit. Government debts were estimated at $7,000m. in 1989, and the practice of paying debts in petroleum has become more common. International reserves totalled $4,208m. at 31 December 1978, compared with $2,131m. at the end of 1973, and by the end of 1979 the figure had risen to $6,449m. At mid-1981 foreign exchange reserves amounted to $13,444m. They declined to $3,266m. at the end of 1984, recovered to $5,465m. at the end of 1985, but had fallen to an estimated $3,923m. by May 1990. By May 1991, however, reserves were estimated at $4,635m. In 1980 the current account showed a surplus of $8,240m. but this was followed by a deficit of $2,978m. in 1981, and further deficits in 1982, 1983 and 1984. However, Central Bank figures show that a surplus of $2,016m. was recorded in 1985, following a decline of 33% in the value of merchandise imports and substantial reductions in capital expenditure (see Development). The Central Bank reported a deficit of $252m. in 1986. A deficit of $800m. in 1987 was followed by further deficits of $1,260m. in 1988 and $940m. in 1989. In 1990, however, the increase in oil revenues, due to the Gulf crisis of 1990–91, produced a current account surplus of $2,200m., but in 1991 the current account was roughly in balance as world oil prices reverted to their pre-crisis level. According to World Bank figures, Libya had gross international reserves of $7,225m. at the end of 1990. Recent Libyan initiatives to increase non-oil foreign currency earnings have included the abandonment of ideological objections to the development of a mass tourism industry. However, by mid-1994 no practical steps had been taken to attract the necessary foreign investment, there being very little scope for forward planning in this area while Libya remained subject to UN sanctions.

The Central Bank reported in early 1994 that Libya's foreign exchange reserves totalled $5,972m. at 31 March 1993; that external earnings in the year ending 31 March 1993 had totalled about $7,000m. (some 13% less than forecast) and that public debt stood at an estimated $20,818m. on that date. The Bank for International Settlements said in early 1994 that Libyan funds in banks reporting to the BIS totalled $1,159m. on 30 September 1993.

DEVELOPMENT AND BUDGET

Libyan planning dates back to the 1960s, with the first Development Plan running from 1963/64 to 1967/68. The second Plan ran from 1969/70 to 1973/74, and the third Plan, with an investment of LD 2,200m. (of which 34% was for industry, petroleum and electricity), from 1973 to 1975. Development budgets in the 1970s favoured agriculture, and the 1976–80 Development Plan, known as the Economic and Social Transformation Plan, involved a total investment of LD 9.250m. with priority again given to agriculture. The Plan aimed at an annual increase of 10.5% in GNP and a 26% rise in industrial production. In 1978 GDP increased by 11%, which was above the planned rate of 10.7%, but the average growth for the period 1976–79 was only 9.5% a year. In 1978 the allocations of most sectors of the budget were increased, but it appears that by the end of the Plan only 80% of planned expenditure had been used. The overall aims of the Plan were to achieve diversity of production, thus reducing dependence on oil, to develop the economic and social infrastructure and to achieve a more equitable distribution of income and wealth.

The 1981–85 Five-Year Plan was seen as part of a major 20-year development programme, aiming at structural change in the economy to reduce its dependence on petroleum. Expenditure was initially set at LD 18,500m., more than double the allocation for the previous Plan, and it was forecast that by 1985 the non-oil sector would contribute 53% of national income, compared with 35% in 1980. Industry was to be allocated 23% of investment, and rapid growth was planned for electricity, transport, communications and housing. Agriculture was to receive 16%. The overall annual growth rate was intended to be 9.4%, compared with the last Plan's achieved rate of 7.6%, but industry's annual growth rate was projected at 21.6%. Agriculture's annual growth rate, on the other hand, was forecast at 7.4%. By 1983, owing to the abrupt reversal in Libya's petroleum revenues, the targets of the Five-Year Plan for 1981–85 were not being met and major reassessments, involving substantial reductions in expenditure, had to be undertaken. The building of roads and houses worth US $1,000m. was cancelled, and plans for a $4,200m. Soviet-made nuclear power plant were shelved.

The decline in government revenues curtailed budget expenditure throughout the 1980s. For 1982 the administrative budget was endorsed at LD 1,255m., and the development budget at LD 2,600m. (5% less than in 1981). The development budget for 1983, at LD 2,370m., was a further LD 230m. down on that of 1982. The 1984 budgets reflected this continuing trend. The administrative budget of LD 1,440.2m. represented a cut of 7.1% on the allocation for 1983, while development projects in 1984 were allocated LD 2,110m., a decrease of 11%.

Further reductions in projected spending were recorded in the budget allocations for 1985. The administrative budget totalled LD 1,200m. and the development budget LD 1,700m., representing reductions of 16.7% and 19.4%, respectively, compared with the previous year. In the event, actual capital expenditure on development has been well below the planned allocation. During 1985 actual spending on development was LD 1,211m., 28.8% less than the budgeted figure of LD 1,700m., continuing the trend established in 1983 (when actual spending was LD 2,096.3m., a shortfall of 11.5%, compared with planned spending of LD 2,370m.) and 1984 (actual spending: LD 1,824.8m.; planned spending: LD 2,110m.—a shortfall of 13.5%). Owing to the loss of revenue as a result of the decline in oil prices, the budget for 1986 was deferred. The development budget for 1987 represented a reduction of 14.7% compared with the allocation for 1985, to LD 1,450m.

The budget for 1988 projected total expenditure of LD 2,300m. (administrative budget LD 1,243.5m.; development budget LD 1,056.5m.), an increase of 6%, compared with 1987. For 1989 there was a draft operational budget of LD 1,174m., together with a draft changeover budget of LD 900 million. Few details of the 1990 budget were made available. It was reported that expenditure on defence and subsidies was to be reduced to LD 600m., compared with LD 750m. in 1989, in order to restrict the total budget deficit to LD 322m. With regard to expenditure on capital projects, LD 300m. was to be provided for the GMR project (see Agriculture, above). An estimated LD 380m. was to be allocated for the purchase of food imports and the hiring of foreign labour. As a result of the unexpected increase in income from oil exports in 1990, Libya's GDP increased by 9.4%, in comparison with 1989, to the equivalent of $27,370m., thereby enabling the Government to allocate additional funds for the development of the oil industry and other sectors during the 1990s.

The broad outlines of the Government's 1992/93 budget were revealed in February 1993 (the penultimate month of that fiscal year). Expenditure totalled LD 2,823m. ($9,700m.) and revenue LD 2,251m. ($7,735m.), leaving a deficit of LD 572m. ($1,965m.). Of the expected revenue, LD 1,284m. (57%) was derived from oil exports and the balance from taxes and duties. The total national oil revenue (including funds not earmarked for budgetary use) was expected to be about LD 3,000m. ($10,300m.). It was announced in January 1994 that Libya's budget year would henceforth coincide with the calendar year and that no budget had been in force in the nine months following the end of the last April–March budget year in 1993. No details of the 1994 budget were published, although the Government indicated that 'several billion dollars' of cutbacks had been made to take account of the impact of UN sanctions.

Statistical Survey

Source (unless otherwise stated): Census and Statistical Dept, Secretariat of Planning,
40 Sharia Damascus, 2nd Floor, Tripoli; tel. (21) 31731.

Area and Population

AREA, POPULATION AND DENSITY

Area (sq km)	1,775,500*
Population (census results)	
31 July 1973	2,249,237
31 July 1984 (provisional)	
Males	1,950,152
Females	1,687,336
Total	3,637,488
Population (official estimates at mid-year)†	
1992	4,509,000
1993	4,700,000
Density (per sq km) at mid-1993	2.6

* 685,524 sq miles.
† Figures refer to the *de jure* population. At the 1984 census the
de jure population was provisionally 3,237,160 (males 1,653,330;
females 1,583,830).

POPULATION BY BALADIYA (MUNICIPALITY)
(1984 census, provisional figures)

Tubruq (Tobruk).	94,006	Tarhuna . .	84,640
Darna . .	105,031	Tripoli . .	990,697
Jebel Akhdar .	120,662	Al-Azizia .	85,068
Al-Fatah . .	102,763	Az-Zawia (Azzawiya)	220,075
Benghazi. .	485,386	Nikat al-Khoms .	181,584
Agedabia. .	100,547	Gharian . .	117,073
Sirte . .	110,996	Yefren . .	73,420
Sofuljeen . .	45,195	Ghadames .	52,247
Al-Kufra . .	25,139	Sebha . .	76,171
Misurata. .	178,295	Ash-Shati .	46,749
Zeleitin (Zliten) .	101,107	Ubari . .	48,701
Al-Khoms . .	149,642	Murzuk . .	42,294

PRINCIPAL TOWNS (population at 1973 census)

Tripoli (capital) .	481,295	Darna . . .	30,241
Benghazi. .	219,317	Sebha . . .	28,714
Misurata. . .	42,815	Tubruq (Tobruk).	28,061
Az-Zawiya (Azzawiya)	39,382	Al-Marj . .	25,166
Al-Beida . .	31,796	Zeleiten (Zliten) .	21,340
Agedabia. .	31,047		

BIRTHS, MARRIAGES AND DEATHS

	Registered live births		Registered marriages		Registered deaths	
	Number	Rate (per 1,000)	Number	Rate (per 1,000)	Number	Rate (per 1,000)
1986 .	160,750	46.0	17,252	4.9	24,460	7.0
1987 .	167,020	46.0	17,862	4.9	25,420	7.0
1988 .	173,530	46.0	16,989	4.5	26,410	7.0

Expectation of life (UN estimates, years at birth, 1985–90): 60.6
(males 59.1; females 62.5) (Source: UN, *World Population Prospects: The 1992 Revision*).

EMPLOYMENT
(official estimates, '000 persons)

	1976	1977	1978
Agriculture, forestry and fishing	141.2	144.9	147.9
Mining and quarrying . .	18.5	19.2	20.4
Manufacturing . . .	37.4	41.7	47.4
Electricity, gas and water . .	13.9	14.7	15.8
Construction	167.8	171.4	164.3
Trade, restaurants and hotels .	52.0	52.3	47.5
Transport, storage and communications . . .	57.9	63.1	67.5
Financing, insurance, real estate and business services.	8.1	8.5	9.1
Community, social and personal services . .	175.8	185.9	191.2
Activities not adequately defined	60.1	63.3	62.1
Total	**732.7**	**765.0**	**773.2**

Mid-1992 (estimates in '000): Agriculture, etc. 159; Total labour
force 1,209 (Source: FAO, *Production Yearbook*).

Agriculture

PRINCIPAL CROPS ('000 metric tons)

	1990	1991*	1992*
Barley	141	145	145
Wheat	129	150	150
Olives	68	70	72
Oranges	91	95	98
Tangerines, mandarins, clementines and satsumas*	4	4	4
Lemons and limes . . .	3	4	4
Almonds	33.1	34.0	34.5
Tomatoes	150	170	175
Dates	74	75	76
Potatoes	145	148	150
Grapes.	37	38	40

* FAO estimates.
Source: FAO, *Production Yearbook*.

LIVESTOCK ('000 head, year ending September)

	1990	1991*	1992*
Cattle	120	125	135
Camels.	140	150	155
Sheep	5,200	5,500	5,600
Goats	1,100	1,200	1,250
Poultry	53,000*	55,000	58,000

* FAO estimate(s).
Source: FAO, *Production Yearbook*.

LIVESTOCK PRODUCTS
(FAO estimates unless otherwise indicated, '000 metric tons)

	1990	1991	1992
Beef and veal	19	23	24
Mutton and lamb . . .	51	60	62
Goats' meat	8	8	9
Poultry meat	68	70	74
Cows' milk. . . .	120	140	150
Sheep's milk	48	49	49
Goats' milk	20	21	21
Hen eggs	34.1*	34.7	35.8
Honey	1.2*	1.3	1.3
Wool:			
greasy	7.8	8.3	8.5
clean	2.3	2.4	2.4
Cattle and buffalo hides . .	2.6	3.2	3.3
Sheep skins . . .	11.0	12.7	13.0
Goat skins	1.3	1.4	1.4

* Official figure.

Source: FAO, *Production Yearbook*.

Forestry

ROUNDWOOD REMOVALS
(FAO estimates, '000 cubic metres, excl. bark)

	1990	1991	1992
Sawlogs, veneer logs and logs			
for sleepers* . . .	63	63	63
Other industrial wood . . .	44	46	47
Fuel wood*	536	536	536
Total	**643**	**645**	**646**

* Assumed to be unchanged since 1978.

Sawnwood production (1978–92): 31,000 cubic metres per year (FAO estimates).

Source: FAO, *Yearbook of Forest Products*.

Fishing

(FAO estimates, '000 metric tons, live weight)

	1989	1990	1991
Total catch	7.8	7.8	7.8

Source: FAO, *Yearbook of Fishery Statistics*.

Mining

	1989	1990	1991
Crude petroleum ('000 metric tons)	54,320	67,162	71,815
Natural gas ('000 terajoules) .	310	324	347

Source: UN, *Industrial Statistics Yearbook*.

Industry

SELECTED PRODUCTS
('000 metric tons, unless otherwise indicated)

	1989	1990	1991
Olive oil (crude)* . . .	10	10	10
Cigarettes (million) . . .	3,500	3,500	3,500
Jet fuels	1,400	1,460	1,535
Motor spirit (petrol) . .	1,675	1,743	1,800
Naphthas	1,812	2,080	2,220
Kerosene	200	240	242
Distillate fuel oils . . .	3,807	4,100	4,110
Residual fuel oils . . .	4,581	4,800	4,810
Liquefied petroleum gas:			
from natural gas plants . .	248	260†	300†
from petroleum refineries† .	150	160	170
Bitumen	80	90	90
Quicklime‡	263	263	263
Cement‡	2,700	2,700	2,722
Electric energy (million kWh) .	18,000	19,000	19,500

* FAO estimates.
† Provisional or estimated production.
‡ Estimates by the US Bureau of Mines.

Source: UN, *Industrial Statistics Yearbook*.

Finance

CURRENCY AND EXCHANGE RATES
Monetary Units
1,000 dirhams = 1 Libyan dinar (LD).

Sterling and Dollar Equivalents (31 May 1994)
£1 sterling = 476.18 dirhams;
US $1 = 314.98 dirhams;
100 Libyan dinars = £210.00 = $317.48.

Exchange Rate
Between February 1973 and March 1986 the value of the Libyan dinar was fixed at US $3.37778 ($1 = 296.053 dirhams). In March 1986 the link with the US dollar was ended, and the currency was pegged to the IMF's special drawing right (SDR), initially at a rate of LD 1 = SDR 2.800. In May 1986 the rate was adjusted to LD 1 = SDR 2.60465 (SDR 1 = 383.929 dirhams). This remained in force until March 1992, when a new rate of LD 1 = SDR 2.52252 (SDR 1 = 396.429 dirhams) was introduced. Further devaluations were implemented in 1992, with the Libyan dinar set at SDR 2.46696 (SDR 1 = 405.357 dirhams) in July, and at SDR 2.41379 (SDR 1 = 414.286 dirhams) in August. The currency was devalued to SDR 2.2400 (SDR 1 = 446.429 dirhams) in August 1993. For converting the value of external trade, the average exchange rate (US dollars per Libyan dinar) was: 3.5051 in 1988; 3.4229 in 1989; 3.7055 in 1990. In 1991 the conversion factor (dollars per dinar) for imports was 3.5587, while for exports it was 3.5551.

CENTRAL BANK RESERVES (US $ million at 31 December)

	1990	1991	1992
Gold	152	152	152
IMF special drawing rights .	409	461	383
Reserve position in IMF .	346	348	439
Foreign exchange* . . .	5,084	4,885	5,361
Total*	**5,991**	**5,846**	**6,335**

* Estimates.

1993 (US $ million at 31 December): IMF special drawing rights 417; Reserve position in IMF 438.

Source: IMF, *International Financial Statistics*.

MONEY SUPPLY (LD million at 31 December)

	1990	1991	1992
Currency outside banks . .	1,461.0	1,620.8	1,982.2
Private sector deposits at Central Bank	751.6	392.9	312.0
Demand deposits at commercial banks	2,239.6	2,279.1	2,693.0
Total money	4,452.2	4,292.8	4,987.2

Source: IMF, *International Financial Statistics*.

COST OF LIVING (Consumer Price Index, excluding rent, for Tripoli; base: 1979 = 100)

	1982	1983	1984
Food	134.9	152.9	169.5
Clothing	141.1	150.6	169.4
All items (incl. others) . .	137.6	152.2	165.8

Source: International Labour Office, *Year Book of Labour Statistics*.

NATIONAL ACCOUNTS (LD million at current prices)
National Income and Product

	1983	1984	1985
Compensation of employees .	2,763.1	2,865.8	2,996.2
Operating surplus . . .	5,282.7	4,357.8	4,572.4
Domestic factor incomes .	8,045.8	7,223.6	7,568.6
Consumption of fixed capital .	436.1	457.5	481.6
Gross domestic product (GDP) at factor cost . .	8,481.9	7,681.1	8,050.2
Indirect taxes	470.0	462.2	389.0
Less Subsidies	146.7	130.0	162.2
GDP in purchasers' values .	8,805.2	8,013.3	8,277.0
Factor income from abroad .	200.2	142.8	122.5
Less Factor income paid abroad	989.0	727.7	397.9
Gross national product . .	8,016.4	7,428.4	8,001.6
Less Consumption of fixed capital	436.1	457.5	481.6
National income in market prices	7,580.3	6,970.9	7,520.0
Other current transfers from abroad	8.6	2.3	2.6
Less Other current transfers paid abroad	25.2	27.9	16.0
National disposable income .	7,563.7	6,945.3	7,506.6

Source: UN, *National Accounts Statistics*.

Expenditure on the Gross Domestic Product
(estimates by the UN Economic Commission for Africa)

	1985	1986	1987
Government final consumption expenditure	3,010	2,133	2,251
Private final consumption expenditure	3,433	2,523	2,669
Increase in stocks	−41	—	—
Gross fixed capital formation .	2,399	1,573	1,660
Total domestic expenditure .	8,801	6,229	6,580
Exports of goods and services .	2,865	2,275	2,401
Less Imports of goods and services	2,736	2,031	2,144
GDP in purchasers' values .	8,930	6,473	6,837
GDP at constant 1980 prices	8,479	7,394	7,143

Source: UN Economic Commission for Africa, *African Statistical Yearbook*.

Gross Domestic Product by Economic Activity

	1988	1989	1990
Agriculture, hunting, forestry and fishing	367	396	643
Mining and quarrying . . .	1,775	2,008	2,276
Manufacturing	488	561	702
Electricity, gas and water . .	139	153	200
Construction	893*	920	1,083
Wholesale and retail trade, restaurants and hotels . .	440	491	752
Transport, storage and communications . . .	391	440	578
Finance, insurance, real estate and business services . .	591	621	1,039
Public administration and defence	920*	859	955
Other services	690*	774	644
GDP at factor cost . . .	6,694	7,224	8,872
Indirect taxes, *less* subsidies .	364	392	480
GDP in purchasers' values .	7,058	7,616	9,352

* Estimate.

Source: UN Economic Commission for Africa, *African Statistical Yearbook*

BALANCE OF PAYMENTS (US $ million)

	1988	1989	1990
Merchandise exports f.o.b. .	5,653	7,274	11,352
Merchandise imports f.o.b. .	−5,762	−6,509	−7,575
Trade balance	−109	765	3,777
Exports of services . . .	128	117	117
Imports of services . . .	−1,637	−1,481	−1,385
Other income received . . .	762	447	666
Other income paid	−437	−388	−493
Private unrequited transfers (net)	−497	−472	−446
Official unrequited transfers (net)	−37	−16	−35
Current balance	−1,826	−1,026	2,201
Direct investment (net) . .	42	90	54
Portfolio investment (net) . .	−222	−52	−115
Other capital (net) . . .	343	1,150	−945
Net errors and omissions . .	271	130	−37
Overall balance	−1,392	292	1,158

Source: IMF, *International Financial Statistics*.

External Trade

PRINCIPAL COMMODITIES (distribution by SITC, US $ '000)

Imports c.i.f.	1989	1990	1991
Food and live animals . . .	911,593	1,155,174	1,123,869
Beverages and tobacco . .	18,439	7,797	24,445
Crude materials (inedible) except fuels	91,770	118,242	134,282
Mineral fuels, lubricants, etc. .	16,651	16,049	20,641
Animal and vegetable oils, fats and waxes	89,797	106,554	172,132
Chemicals and related products	390,374	379,681	427,103
Basic manufactures . . .	1,238,154	1,331,192	1,270,811
Machinery and transport equipment	1,715,808	1,936,551	1,898,485
Miscellaneous manufactured articles	547,878	527,953	518,147
Total (incl. others) . .	5,048,725	5,598,631	5,609,024

Exports f.o.b.	1989	1990	1991
Mineral fuels, lubricants, etc. .	7,850,725	13,097,960	11,211,495
Crude petroleum oils, etc.	7,748,049	12,978,368	11,055,276
Chemicals and related products	387,985	524,710	393,892
Total (incl. others) . . .	8,240,262	13,876,843	11,750,156

Source: UN, *International Trade Statistics Yearbook*.
Total imports c.i.f. (LD million, derived from IMF, *Direction of Trade Statistics*): 1,469.8 in 1992; 1,622.3 in 1993 (Source: IMF, *International Financial Statistics*).

PRINCIPAL TRADING PARTNERS (US $ '000)*

Imports c.i.f.	1989	1990	1991
Austria	96,626	108,452	162,490
Belgium-Luxembourg . .	136,839	156,065	115,694
Brazil	44,447	95,403	78,503
Canada	56,374	56,239	66,070
China	34,241	49,491	121,614
France	344,532	412,513	348,824
Germany, Federal Republic .	745,055	819,436	733,878
Greece	53,285	81,209	68,219
Ireland	72,007	53,538	26,394
Italy	1,222,961	1,036,349	1,215,002
Japan	230,098	244,350	186,957
Korea, Republic . . .	171,273	115,413	178,350
Malta	45,672	60,913	72,314
Morocco	83,115	120,941	200,005
Netherlands . . .	167,215	313,237	216,756
Poland	68,772	36,913	21,107
Spain	62,047	53,751	50,194
Sweden	45,544	92,329	72,377
Switzerland . . .	98,645	195,143	132,262
Tunisia	42,943	122,544	120,008
Turkey	243,053	290,231	356,227
United Kingdom . . .	419,494	472,038	462,670
USA	76,932	69,962	72,910
Yugoslavia	74,163	74,724	n.a.
Total (incl. others) . . .	5,048,725	5,598,631	5,609,024

Exports f.o.b.	1989	1990	1991
Belgium-Luxembourg . .	186,646	305,618	323,120
Bulgaria	176,252	242,489	88,450
France	805,193	1,187,634	906,845
Germany, Federal Republic	442,146	900,789	1,958,202
Greece	479,718	611,748	609,899
Italy	4,000,668	6,642,085	4,784,464
Morocco	8,431	115,392	128,320
Netherlands . . .	454,529	387,915	203,939
Portugal	26,338	108,970	53,611
Romania	21,187	241,994	91,286
Spain	719,734	1,276,599	1,129,495
Sudan	68,143	150,732	160,317
Switzerland . . .	—	4,453	225,336
Tunisia	13,367	72,138	100,708
Turkey	264,612	506,589	258,056
USSR (former) . . .	129,808	203,502	n.a.
United Kingdom . . .	157,142	247,657	151,845
Yugoslavia	149,750	369,874	n.a.
Total (incl. others) . .	8,240,262	13,876,843	11,750,156

* Imports by country of origin; exports by country of destination.
Source: UN, *International Trade Statistics Yearbook*.

Transport

ROAD TRAFFIC (motor vehicles in use)

	1979	1980	1981
Private cars	308,746	415,531	473,383
Taxis	10,398	11,838	11,891
Lorries	167,748	208,464	271,815
Buses	2,835	2,658	3,990

INTERNATIONAL SEA-BORNE SHIPPING
(freight traffic, estimates, '000 metric tons)

	1989	1990	1991
Goods loaded	65,200	66,000	67,000
Goods unloaded	10,900	11,200	12,200

Source: UN Economic Commission for Africa, *African Statistical Yearbook*.

CIVIL AVIATION (traffic on scheduled services)

	1989	1990	1991
Kilometres flown (million) . .	17	19	19
Passengers carried ('000) . .	1,617	1,803	1,884
Passenger-km (million) . .	1,680	1,968	1,251
Freight ton-km (million) . .	5	10	9

Source: UN, *Statistical Yearbook*.

Communications Media

	1989	1990	1991
Radio receivers ('000 in use) .	980	1,020	1,060
Television receivers ('000 in use)	400	450	467
Telephones ('000 in use)* . .	83	84	85
Daily newspapers . . .	n.a.	3	n.a.

Source: UNESCO, *Statistical Yearbook*.
* Source of these estimates: UN Economic Commission for Africa, *African Statistical Yearbook*.

Education

	Teachers		Pupils/Students	
	1985	1991	1985	1991
Pre-primary	1,051	n.a.	15,028	n.a.
Primary	63,122	99,623	1,011,952	1,238,986
Secondary:				
General	5,977	11,429	81,864	138,860
Teacher training . .	2,639	4,113	34,746	39,491
Vocational . . .	2,149	2,959	26,503	37,157
Universities, etc. . . .	n.a.	n.a.	30,000	72,899

Schools: Pre-primary 78 in 1985; Primary 4,164 in 1985.
Source: UNESCO, *Statistical Yearbook*.

Directory

The Constitution

The Libyan Arab People, meeting in the General People's Congress in Sebha from 2–28 March 1977, proclaimed its adherence to freedom and its readiness to defend it on its own land and anywhere else in the world. It also announced its adherence to socialism and its commitment to achieving total Arab Unity; its adherence to the moral human values, and confirmed the march of the revolution led by Col Muammar al-Qaddafi, the revolutionary leader, towards complete People's Authority.

The Libyan Arab People announced the following:

(i) The official name of Libya is henceforth The Socialist People's Libyan Arab Jamahiriya.

(ii) The Holy Koran is the social code in The Socialist People's Libyan Arab Jamahiriya.

(iii) The Direct People's Authority is the basis for the political order in The Socialist People's Libyan Arab Jamahiriya. The People shall practise its authority through People's Congresses, Popular Committees, Trade Unions, Vocational Syndicates, and The General People's Congress, in the presence of the law.

(iv) The defence of our homeland is the responsibility of every citizen. The whole people shall be trained militarily and armed by general military training, the preparation of which shall be specified by the law.

The General People's Congress in its extraordinary session held in Sebha issued four decrees:

The first decree announced the establishment of The People's Authority in compliance with the resolutions and recommendations of the People's Congresses and Trade Unions.

The second decree stipulated the choice of Col Muammar al-Qaddafi, the Revolutionary Leader, as Secretary-General of the General People's Congress.

The third decree stipulated the formation of the General Secretariat of the General People's Congress (see The Government, below).

The fourth decree stipulated the formation of the General People's Committee to carry out the tasks of the various former ministries (see The Government, below).

In 1986 it was announced that the country's official name was to be The Great Socialist People's Libyan Arab Jamahiriya.

The Government

HEAD OF STATE

Revolutionary Leader: Col MUAMMAR AL-QADDAFI (took office as Chairman of the Revolution Command Council 8 September 1969; he himself rejects this nomenclature and all other titles).

Second-in-Command: Maj. ABD AS-SALAM JALLOUD.

GENERAL SECRETARIAT OF THE GENERAL PEOPLE'S CONGRESS

Secretary-General: ZENTANI MUHAMMAD ZENTANI.

Assistant Secretary-General: ABU ZAYD UMAR DURDAH.

Secretary for Women's Affairs: SALMA RASHID.

Secretary for Affairs of the People's Congresses: ALI MURSI ASH-SHAIRI.

Secretary for Foreign Affairs: SAAD MUJBIR.

Secretary for Affairs of the People's Committees: MAHMOUD AL-HITKI.

Secretary for Affairs of the Trade Unions, Syndicates and Professional Associations: ALI ASH-SHAMIKH.

GENERAL PEOPLE'S COMMITTEE
(September 1994)

Secretary-General of the General People's Committee: ABD AL-MAJID AL-QAOUD.

Secretary for Economic Planning and Finance: MUHAMMAD BAIT AL-MAL.

Secretary for Foreign Liaison and International Co-operation: OMAR AL-MUNTASSER.

Co-ordinators of the General Provisional Committee for Defence: ABU BAKR JABER YUNES, MUSTAFA KHARRUBI, KHOUELDI HAMIDI.

Secretary for Justice and Public Security: MUHAMMAD AL-HIJAZI.

Secretary for Energy: ABDULLAH SALIM AL-BADRI.

Secretary for the Economy and Trade: AT-TAHER AL-JEHIMI.

Secretary for Unity: JOMAA AL-FEZZANI.

Secretary for Industry: FATHI BIN SHATWAN.

Secretary for Education and Scientific Research: MAATOUQ MUHAMMAD MAATOUQ.

Secretary for Information and Culture: AHMED IBRAHIM.

Secretary for Marine Wealth: MUFTAH MUHAMMAD KUAIBAH.

Secretary for Agrarian Reform and Land Reclamation: ISA ABD AL-KAFI AS-SID.

Secretary for Transport and Communications: AZZ AD-DIN AL-HIN-SHIRI.

Secretary for Health and Social Security: BAGHDADI ALI AL-MAHMOUDI.

Secretary for Utilities and Housing: MUBARAK ABDULLAH ASH-SHAMIKH.

Secretary for the Great Man-made River: JADALLAH AZIZ AT-TALHI.

Secretary for the Supervision of Public Accounting and Control: MAHMOUD BADI.

As part of a radical decentralization programme undertaken in September 1988, all General People's Committee secretariats (ministries), except those responsible for foreign liaison (foreign affairs) and information, were relocated away from Tripoli. According to diplomatic sources, the former Secretariat for Economy and Trade was moved to Benghazi; the Secretariat for Health to Kufra; and the remainder, excepting one, to Sirte, Col Qaddafi's birthplace. In early 1993 it was announced that the Secretariat for Foreign Liaison and International Co-operation was to be moved to Ras Lanouf.

Legislature

GENERAL PEOPLE'S CONGRESS

The Senate and House of Representatives were dissolved after the *coup d'état* of September 1969, and the provisional Constitution issued in December 1969 made no mention of elections or a return to parliamentary procedure. However, in January 1971 Col Qaddafi announced that a new legislature would be appointed, not elected; no date was mentioned. All political parties other than the Arab Socialist Union were banned. In November 1975 provision was made for the creation of the 1,112-member General National Congress of the Arab Socialist Union, which met officially in January 1976. This later became the General People's Congress (GPC), which met for the first time in November 1976 and in March 1977 began introducing the wide-ranging changes outlined in 'The Constitution' (above). The most recent Ordinary Session of the GPC took place in January 1994.

Secretary-General: ABD AR-RAZIQ SAWSA.

Political Organizations

In June 1971 the Arab Socialist Union (ASU) was established as the country's sole authorized political party. The General National Congress of the ASU held its first session in January 1976 and later became the General People's Congress (see Legislature, above).

The following groups are in opposition to the Government:

Libyan Baathist Party.

Libyan Democratic Movement: f. 1977; external group.

Libyan National Alliance: f. 1980 in Cairo, Egypt; Leader: MANSOUR KIKHIA.

National Front for the Salvation of Libya (NFSL): f. 1981 in Khartoum, Sudan; aims to 'liberate Libya and save it from Qaddafi's rule', and to replace the existing regime by a democratically-elected government; Leader MUHAMMAD MEGARIEF.

Diplomatic Representation

EMBASSIES IN LIBYA

Afghanistan: POB 4245, Sharia Mozhar el-Aftes, Tripoli; tel. (21) 75192; Ambassador: (vacant).

Algeria: Sharia Kairauan 12, Tripoli; tel. (21) 40025; Ambassador: MOHAMMED SAIDI.

Argentina: POB 932, Sharia ibn Mufarrej al-Andaluz, Tripoli; tel. (21) 72160; telex 20190; Ambassador: ALFREDO CAMBACERES.

Austria: POB 3207, Sharia Khalid ibn al-Walid, Garden City, Tripoli; tel. (21) 43379; telex 20245; Ambassador: WILFRIED ALMOSLECHNER.

Bangladesh: POB 5086, Hadaba al-Khadra, Villa Omran al-Wershafani, Tripoli; tel. (21) 903807; telex 20970; Ambassador: M. AMINUL ISLAM.

Belgium: Tower 4, International Islamic Call Society Complex, Souk Ethulathah, Tripoli; tel. (21) 37797; telex 20564; fax (21) 75618; Ambassador: L. DOYEN.

Benin: Tripoli; tel. (21) 72914; Ambassador: El-Hadj ALASSANE ABOUDOU.

Brazil: POB 2270, Sharia ben Ashur, Tripoli; tel. (21) 607970; telex 20082; Chargé d'affaires: REGIS NOVAES.

Bulgaria: POB 2945, Sharia Talha ben Abdullah 5-7, Tripoli; tel. (21) 44260; Ambassador: VENTZISLAV KANEV.

Burundi: POB 2817, Sharia Ras Hassan, Tripoli; tel. (21) 608848; telex 20372; Ambassador: ZACHARIE BANYIYEZAKO.

Chad: POB 1078, Sharia Muhammad Mussadeq 25, Tripoli; tel. (21) 43955; Ambassador: IBRAHIM MAHAMAT TIDEI.

China, People's Republic: POB 5329, Gargaresh M 86, Tripoli; tel. (21) 830860; Ambassador: WANG HOULI.

Cuba: POB 83738, Al-Andaluz District, Gargarech, Tripoli; tel. (21) 71346; telex 20513; Ambassador: RAÚL RODRÍGUEZ RÁMOS.

Czech Republic: POB 1097, Sharia Ahmad Lotfi Sayed, Ben Ashour Area, Tripoli; tel. (21) 603444; fax (21) 609608; Ambassador: ALEXANDR KARYCH.

Egypt: The Grand Hotel, Tripoli; tel. (21) 605500; telex 20780; fax (21) 45959; Ambassador: EL-SHAZLY.

Ethiopia: POB 12899, Sharia Jamahiriya, Tripoli; tel. (21) 608185; telex 20572; Ambassador: ABDULMENAN SHEKA.

Finland: POB 2508, Tripoli; tel. (21) 38057; Ambassador: ANTTI LASSILA.

France: POB 312, Sharia Saïd, Loutfi ben Achour, Tripoli; tel. (21) 607861; fax (21) 607864; Ambassador: JACQUES ROUQUETTE.

Germany: POB 302, Sharia Hassan al-Mashai, Tripoli; tel. (21) 30554; telex 20298; fax (21) 48968; Ambassador: CARL-DIETER HACH.

Ghana: POB 4169, Sharia as-Sway Khetumi, Tripoli; tel. (21) 44256; Ambassador: (vacant).

Greece: POB 5147, Sharia Jalal Bayar 18, Tripoli; tel. (21) 36978; telex 20409; fax (21) 41907; Ambassador: ELIAS DIMITRAKOPOULOS.

Guinea: POB 10657, Andalous, Tripoli; tel. (21) 72793; Ambassador: BAH KABA.

Hungary: POB 4010, Sharia Talha ben Abdullah, Tripoli; tel. (21) 605799; telex 20055; Ambassador: LÁSZLÓ FEHERVARI.

India: POB 3150, 16–18 Sharia Mahmud Shaltut, Tripoli; tel. (21) 41835; telex 20115; fax (21) 37560; Chargé d'affaires a.i.: B. R. GHULIANI.

Iran: Sharia Gargaresh, Andalous, Tripoli; Ambassador: SEYYED MUHAMMAD QADEM KHUNSARI.

Iraq: Sharia ben Ashur, Tripoli.

Italy: POB 912, Sharia Uahran 1, Tripoli; tel. (21) 34131; telex 20602; Ambassador: GIORGIO REITANO; British interests section: POB 4206, Sharia Uahran, Tripoli; tel. (21) 31191; telex 20296; Consul: ALLEN BROWN.

Japan: Tower No. 5, That al-Imad Complex, Sharia Organization of African Unity, Tripoli; tel. (21) 607462; telex 20094; fax (21) 607462; Ambassador: AKIRA WATANABE.

Korea, Democratic People's Republic: Tripoli; Ambassador: LI WON-GUK.

Korea, Republic: POB 4781/5160, Gargaresh 6 km, Travito Project, Tripoli; tel. (21) 833484; fax (21) 833503; Ambassador: PHILIPS CHOI.

Kuwait: POB 2225, Sharia Omar bin Yasser 8, Garden City, Tripoli; tel. (21) 40281; telex 20328; fax (21) 607053; Chargé d'affaires: ABD AL-AZIZ AL-DUAIJ.

Lebanon: POB 927, Sharia Omar bin Yasser Hadaek 20, Tripoli; tel. (21) 33733; telex 20609; Ambassador: MOUNIR KHOREISH.

Malaysia: POB 6309, Andalous, Tripoli; tel. (21) 833693; telex 20387; Ambassador: AGAM HASMY.

Mali: Sharia Jaraba Saniet Zarrouk, Tripoli; tel. (21) 44924; Ambassador: EL BEKAYE SIDI MOCTAR KOUNTA.

Malta: POB 2534, Sharia Ubei ben Ka'ab, Tripoli; tel. (21) 38081; telex 20273; fax (21) 48401; Ambassador: GEORGE DOUBLESIN.

Mauritania: Sharia Eysa Wokwak, Tripoli; tel. (21) 43223; Ambassador: YAHIA MUHAMMAD EL-HADI.

Morocco: Sharia Bashir el-Ibrahim, Garden City, Tripoli; tel. (21) 34239; Chargé d'affaires: MEHDI MASDOUKI.

Netherlands: POB 3801, Sharia Jalal Bayar 20, Tripoli; tel. (21) 41549; telex 20279; fax 40386; Chargé d'affaires: B. F. TANGELDER.

Nicaragua: Beach Hotel, Andalous, Tripoli; tel. (21) 72641; Ambassador: GUILLERMO ESPINOSA.

Niger: POB 2251, Fachloun Area, Tripoli; tel. (21) 43104; Ambassador: KARIM ALIO.

Nigeria: POB 4417, Sharia Bashir el-Ibrahim, Tripoli; tel. (21) 43038; telex 20124; Ambassador: Prof. DANDATTI ABD AL-KADIR.

Pakistan: POB 2169, Sharia Abdul Karim al-Khattabi 16, Maidan Al-Qadasia, Tripoli; tel. (21) 40072; fax (21) 44698; Ambassador: KHAWAR RASHID PIRZADA.

Philippines: POB 12508, Sharia ed-Dul, Tripoli; tel. (21) 35607; telex 20304; Ambassador: ABDUL GHAFUUR MADKI ALONTO.

Poland: POB 519, Sharia ben Ashur, Tripoli; tel. (21) 607619; telex 20049; fax (21) 603641; Ambassador: STEFAN STANISZEWSKI.

Qatar: POB 3506, Sharia ben Ashur, Tripoli; tel. (21) 46660; Chargé d'affaires: HASAN AHMAD ABU HINDI.

Romania: POB 5085, Sharia Ahmad Lotfi Sayed, Tripoli; tel. (21) 45570; Ambassador: FLOREA RISTACHE.

Russia: POB 4792, Sharia Mustapha Kamel, Tripoli; tel. (21) 30545; telex 22029; Ambassador: VENYAMIN VIKTOROVICH POPOV.

Rwanda: POB 6677, Villa Ibrahim Musbah Missalati, Al-Andalous, Tripoli; tel. (21) 72864; telex 20236; fax (21) 70317; Chargé d'affaires: CHRISTOPHE HABIMANA.

Saudi Arabia: Sharia Kairauan 2, Tripoli; tel. (21) 30485; Chargé d'affaires: MUHAMMAD HASSAN BANDAH.

Senegal: Tripoli.

Spain: POB 2302, Sharia el-Amir Abd al-Kader el-Jazairi 36, Tripoli; tel. (21) 36797; telex 20184; fax (21) 43743; Ambassador: PABLO BENAVIDES ORGAZ.

Sudan: Tripoli; Ambassador: ABD AL-MAJID BASHIR AL-AHMADI.

Sweden: POB 437, 5th Floor, Tower No. 5, That al-Imad, Tripoli; tel. (21) 47583; telex 20154; fax (21) 70357; Ambassador: NILS-ERIK SCHYBERG.

Switzerland: POB 439, Sharia ben Ashur, Tripoli; tel. (21) 607365; telex 20382; fax (21) 607487; Chargé d'affaires: JOSEF BUCHER.

Syria: POB 4219, Sharia Muhammad Rashid Reda 4, Tripoli (Relations Office); tel. 31783; Head: MUNIR BORKHAN.

Togo: POB 3420, Sharia Khaled ibn al-Walid, Tripoli; tel. (21) 49565; telex 20373; Chargé d'affaires: OUYI KOFFI WOAKE.

Tunisia: POB 613, Sharia Bashir Ibrahimi, Tripoli; tel. (21) 31051; telex 20217; fax (21) 47600; High Representative: MANSOUR EZZEDDINE.

Turkey: POB 947, Sharia Jeraba, Tripoli; tel. (21) 37717; telex 20031; fax (21) 37686; Ambassador: ERDIM TÜZEL.

Uganda: POB 10978, Sharia Jeraba, Tripoli; tel. (21) 48006; Ambassador: WADADA MUSANI.

United Kingdom: (see Italy, above).

Venezuela: POB 2584, Sharia Abd ar-Rahman el-Kwakby, Tripoli; tel. (21) 36838; Ambassador: GONZALO SÁNCHEZ.

Viet Nam: POB 587, Sharia Talha ben Abdullah, Tripoli; tel. (21) 45753; Ambassador: DANG SAN.

Yemen: POB 4839, Sharia Ubei ben Ka'ab 36, Tripoli; tel. (21) 32323; Ambassador: ABD AL-WAHAB NASER JAHAF.

Yugoslavia: POB 1087, Sharia Turkia No. 14-16, Tripoli; tel. (21) 34114; Ambassador: DRAGO MIRŠIČ.

Zaire: POB 5066, Sharia Aziz al-Masri, Tripoli.

Judicial System

The judicial system is composed, in order of seniority, of the Supreme Court, Courts of Appeal, and Courts of First Instance and Summary Courts.

All courts convene in open session, unless public morals or public order require a closed session; all judgments, however, are delivered in open session. Cases are heard in Arabic, with interpreters provided for aliens.

The courts apply the Libyan codes which include all the traditional branches of law, such as civil, commercial and penal codes, etc. Committees were formed in 1971 to examine Libyan law and ensure that it coincides with the rules of Islamic Shari'a. The proclamation of People's Authority in the Jamahiriya provides that the Holy Koran is the law of society.

SUPREME COURT

The judgments of the Supreme Court are final. It is composed of the President and several Justices. Its judgments are issued by circuits of at least three Justices (the quorum is three). The Court hears appeals from the Courts of Appeal in civil, penal, administrative and civil status matters.

President: MUHAMMAD ALI AL-JADI.

COURTS OF APPEAL

These courts settle appeals from Courts of First Instance; the quorum is three Justices. Each court of appeal has a court of assize.

COURTS OF FIRST INSTANCE AND SUMMARY COURTS

These courts are first-stage courts in the Jamahiriya, and the cases heard in them are heard by one judge. Appeals against summary judgments are heard by the appellate court attached to the court of first instance, whose quorum is three judges.

PEOPLE'S COURT

Established by order of the General People's Congress in March 1988.

President: Dr KHALIFAH SAID AL-QADHI.

PEOPLE'S PROSECUTION BUREAU

Established by order of the General People's Congress in March 1988.

President: ABD AS-SALAM ALI AL-MIZIGHWI.

Religion

ISLAM

The Libyan Arabs, practically without exception, follow Sunni Muslim rites, although Col Qaddafi has rejected the Sunnah (i.e. the practice, course, way, manner or conduct of the Prophet Muhammad, as followed by Sunnis) as a basis for legislation.

Chief Mufti of Libya: Sheikh TAHER AHMAD AZ-ZAWI.

CHRISTIANITY

The Roman Catholic Church

Libya comprises three Apostolic Vicariates and one Apostolic Prefecture. At 31 December 1992 there were an estimated 40,000 adherents in the country.

Apostolic Vicariate of Benghazi: POB 248, Benghazi; tel. (61) 96563; Vicar Apostolic Mgr GIUSTINO GIULIO PASTORINO, Titular Bishop of Babra (absent).

Apostolic Vicariate of Darna: c/o POB 248, Benghazi; Vicar Apostolic (vacant).

Apostolic Vicariate of Tripoli: POB 365, Tripoli; tel. (21) 31863; fax (21) 34696; Vicar Apostolic Mgr GIOVANNI INNOCENZO MARTINELLI, Titular Bishop of Tabuda; also Apostolic Administrator of Benghazi.

The Anglican Communion

Within the Episcopal Church in Jerusalem and the Middle East, Libya forms part of the diocese of Egypt (q.v.).

Other Christian Churches

The Coptic Orthodox Church is represented in Libya.

The Press

Newspapers and periodicals are published either by the Jamahiriya News Agency (JANA), by government secretariats, by the Press Service or by trade unions.

DAILIES

Al-Fajr al-Jadid (The New Dawn): POB 2303, Tripoli; tel. (21) 33056; f. 1969; since January 1978 published by JANA; circ. 40,000.

PERIODICALS

Al-Amal (Hope): Tripoli; weekly; social, for children; published by the Press Service.

Ad-Daawa al-Islamia (Islamic Call): POB 2682, Tanta St, Tripoli; tel. (21) 32055; telex 20480; fax (21) 38125; f. 1980; weekly (Wednesdays); Arabic, English, French; cultural; published by the World Islamic Call Society.

Economic Bulletin: POB 2303, Tripoli; monthly; published by JANA.

Al-Jamahiriya: POB 4814, Tripoli; tel. (21) 49294; f. 1980; weekly; Arabic; political; published by the revolutionary committees.

Al-Jarida ar-Rasmiya (The Official Newspaper): Tripoli; irregular; official state gazette.

Libyan Arab Republic Gazette: Tripoli; weekly; English; published by the Secretariat of Justice.

Risalat al-Jihad (Holy War Letter): POB 2682, Tripoli; tel. (21) 31021; telex 20407; f. 1983; monthly; Arabic, English, French; published by the World Islamic Call Society.

Scientific Bulletin: POB 2303, Tripoli; monthly; published by JANA.

Ath-Thaqafa al-Arabiya (Arab Culture): POB 4587, Tripoli; f. 1973; weekly; cultural; circ. 25,000.

Al-Watan al-Arabi al-Kabir (The Greater Arab Homeland): Tripoli; f. 1987.

Az-Zahf al-Akhdar (The Green Army): Tripoli; weekly; ideological journal of the revolutionary committees.

NEWS AGENCIES

Jamahiriya News Agency (JANA): POB 2303, Sharia al-Fateh, Tripoli; tel. (21) 37106; telex 20841; branches and correspondents throughout Libya; main foreign bureaux: London, Paris, Rome, Beirut, Nairobi, Nouakchott and Kuwait; serves Libyan and foreign subscribers; Dir-Gen. IBRAHIM MUHAMMAD AL-BISHARI.

Foreign Bureaux

Informatsionnoye Telegrafnoye Agentstvo Rossii—Telegrafnoye Agentstvo Suverennykh Stran (ITAR—TASS) (Russia): Sharia Mustapha Kamel 10, Tripoli; Correspondent GEORG SHELENKOV.

ANSA (Italy) is also represented in Tripoli.

Publishers

Ad-Dar al-Arabia Lilkitab (Maison Arabe du Livre): POB 3185, Tripoli; tel. (21) 47287; telex 20003; f. 1973 by Libya and Tunisia.

Al-Fatah University, General Administration of Libraries, Printing and Publications: POB 13543, Tripoli; tel. (21) 621988; telex 20629; f. 1955; academic books.

General Co for Publishing, Advertising and Distribution: POB 959, Souf al-Mahmudi, Tripoli; tel. (21) 45773; telex 20235; general, educational and academic books.

Radio and Television

In 1991, according to UNESCO, there were an estimated 1,060,000 radio receivers and 467,000 television receivers in use.

Great Socialist People's Libyan Arab Jamahiriya Broadcasting Corporation: POB 3731, Tripoli; POB 119, el-Beida; tel. 32451; f. 1957 (TV 1968); broadcasts in Arabic and English from Tripoli and Benghazi; from September 1971 special daily broadcasts to Gaza and other Israeli-occupied territories were begun; External Service (Radio) and People's Revolution Broadcasting: POB 333, Tripoli; Dir-Gen. External Service ABDULLAH AL-MEGRI.

A national television service in Arabic was inaugurated in December 1968. Channels transmitting for limited hours in English, Italian and French have since been added.

Finance

(cap. = capital; p.u. = paid up; res = reserves; dep. = deposits; LD = Libyan dinars; m. = million; brs = branches)

BANKING

Central Bank

Central Bank of Libya: POB 1103, Sharia al-Malik Seoud, Tripoli; tel. (21) 33591; telex 20661; fax (21) 41488; f. 1955 as National Bank of Libya, name changed to Bank of Libya 1963, to Central Bank of Libya 1977; bank of issue and central bank carrying government accounts and operating exchange control; commercial operations transferred to National Commercial Bank 1970; cap. p.u. LD100m., res LD131m., dep. LD2,193m., total assets LD4,648m. (June 1984); Governor Dr ABD AL-HAFIDH AL-ZILITNI.

Other Banks

Agricultural Bank: POB 1100, 52 Sharia Omar Mukhtar, Tripoli; tel. (21) 38666; f. 1955; auth. cap. LD300m. (1981); Chair. AHMAD AL-AMIN AL-GADAMSI.

Jamahiriya Bank: POB 65155, Martyr St, Gharian; tel. (41) 31964; telex 20889; fax (41) 39402; f. 1969 as successor to Barclays Bank International in Libya; known as Masraf al-Jumhuriya until March 1977; wholly-owned subsidiary of the Central Bank; 42 brs throughout Libya; cap. p.u. LD25m., dep. LD946.8m., res LD22.1m., total assets LD1,446.6m. (Dec. 1987); Chair. MUSTAFA SALAH GEBRIL.

Libyan Arab Foreign Bank: POB 254, That al-Imad Administrative Complex, Tripoli; tel. (21) 41428; telex 20200; fax (21) 42970; f. 1972; offshore bank wholly owned by Central Bank of Libya; cap. and res LD199.1m., dep. LD682.1m., total assets LD1,111.8m. (Mar. 1992); Chair. and Gen. Man. REGED MISELLATI.

National Commercial Bank SAL: POB 4647, Shuhada Sq., Tripoli; tel. (21) 37191; telex 20169; f. 1970 to take over commercial banking division of Central Bank (then Bank of Libya) and brs of Aruba Bank and Istiklal Bank; 22 brs; cap. p.u. LD2.5m.; Chair. MUHAMMAD MUSTAFA GHADBAN.

Sahara Bank: POB 270, 10 Sharia 1 September, Tripoli; tel. (21) 32771; telex 20009; f. 1964 to take over br. of Banco di Sicilia; 20 brs; cap. p.u. LD525,000, res LD52.5m., dep. LD488.4m., total assets LD694m. (March 1988); Chair. and Gen. Man. OMAR ALI ASHABU.

Savings and Real Estate Investment Bank: POB 2297, Sharia Haite, Tripoli; tel. (21) 49306; telex 20309; f. 1975; 23 brs; cap. p.u. LD350m., dep. LD44m., res LD5m., total assets LD850m. (Dec. 1984); Chair. and Gen. Man. SAID LISHANI.

Umma Bank SAL: POB 685, 1 Giaddat Omar Mukhtar, Tripoli; tel. (21) 34031; telex 20256; fax (21) 32505; f. 1969 to take over brs of Banco di Roma; state-owned; 33 brs; cap. p.u. LD500,000, res LD96,712m., dep. LD556.2m. (Dec. 1982); Chair. and Gen. Man. SEDDIG OMAR EL-KABER.

Wahda Bank: POB 452, Fadiel Abu Omar Sq., El-Berkha, Benghazi; tel. (61) 24709; telex 40011; f. 1970 to take over Bank of North Africa, Commercial Bank, SAL, Nahda Arabia Bank, Société Africaine de Banque, Kafila al-Ahly Bank; state-owned; 49 brs; cap. LD36m., res LD77.1m., dep. LD935m., total assets LD1,463m. (March 1992); Chair. and Gen. Man. MUHAMMAD MUSTAFA GHADBAN.

INSURANCE

Libya Insurance Co: POB 2438, Osama Bldg, Sharia 1 September, Tripoli; tel. (21) 44151; telex 20071; fax (21) 44178; POB 643, Benghazi; tel. (61) 99517; f. 1964 (merged with Al-Mukhtar Insurance Co in 1981); cap. LD30m.; all classes of insurance; Gen. Commr and Chair. K. M. SHERLALA.

Petroleum

Until 1986 petroleum affairs in Libya were dealt with primarily by the Secretariat of the General People's Committee for Petroleum. This body was abolished in March 1986, and sole responsibility for the adminstration of the petroleum industry passed to the national companies which were already in existence. The Secretariat of the General People's Commitee for Petroleum was re-established in March 1989 and incorporated into the new Secretariat fo the General People's Committee for Energy in October 1992. Since 1973 the Libyan Government has been entering into participation agreements with some of the foreign oil companies (concession holders), and nationalizing others. It has concluded 85%–15% production-sharing agreements with various oil companies.

NATIONAL COMPANIES

National Oil Corporation (NOC): POB 2655, Tripoli; tel. (21) 46180; telex 61508; f. 1970 as successor to the Libyan General Petroleum Corporation, to undertake joint ventures with foreign companies; to build and operate refineries, storage tanks, petrochemical facilities, pipelines and tankers; to take part in arranging specifications for local and imported petroleum products; to participate in general planning of oil installations in Libya; to market crude oil and to establish and operate oil terminals; Chair. ABDALLAH AL-BADRI.

Agip (NAME) Ltd—Libyan Branch: POB 346, Tripoli; tel. (21) 35135; telex 20282; fax (21) 35153; Sec. of People's Cttee A. M. CREUI.

Arabian Gulf Oil Co: POB 263, Benghazi; telex 40033; Sec. of People's Cttee H. A. LAYASS.

Azzawiya Oil Refining Co: affiliated with NOC, POB 6451, Tripoli (tel. 021 605389; telex 30423), and POB 15715, Azzawiya (tel. 023-20125); fax 605948; f. 1973; Gen. Commr HAMMOUDA M. AL-ASWAD.

Brega Petroleum Marketing Co: POB 402, Sharia Bashir es-Saidawi, Tripoli; tel. (21) 40830; telex 20090; f. 1971; Sec. of People's Cttee Dr DOKALI B. AL-MEGHARIEF.

International Oil Investments Co: Tripoli; f. 1988 with initial capital of $500m. to acquire 'downstream' facilities abroad; Chair. MUHAMMAD AL-JAWAD.

National Drilling and Workover Co: POB 1454, 208 Sharia Omar Mukhtar, Tripoli; tel. (21) 32411; telex 20332; f. 1986; Chair. IBRAHIM BAHI.

Ras Lanouf Oil and Gas Processing Co: Ras Lanouf, POB 2323, Tripoli; tel. (21) 607924; telex 50613; fax (21) 607924; f. 1978; Chair. MUHMUD ABDALLAH NAAS.

Sirte Oil Co: POB 385, Tripoli; tel. (21) 602052; telex 30120; fax (21) 601487; f. 1955 as Esso Standard Libya, taken over by Sirte Oil Co 1982; absorbed the National Petrochemicals Co in October 1990; exploration, production of crude oil, gas, and petrochemicals, liquefaction of natural gas; Sec. of People's Cttee (vacant).

Umm al-Jawaby Petroleum Co: POB 693, Tripoli; Chair. and Gen. Man. MUHAMMAD TENTTOUSH.

Waha Oil Co: POB 395, Tripoli; tel (21) 31116; telex 20158; fax (21) 37169; Sec. of People's Cttee ABDULLAH S. AL-BADRI.

Zueitina Oil Co: POB 2134, Tripoli; tel. (21) 38011; telex 20130; fax (21) 39109; Chair. of People's Cttee Dr N. A. ARIFI.

FOREIGN COMPANIES

Aquitaine Libya: POB 282, Tripoli; tel. (21) 32411; telex 20148; Man. YVES PIROT.

Wintershall-Libya: POB 469 and 905, 9th Floor, Tower No. 4, That Al-Imad Complex, Tripoli; tel. and fax (21) 41493; telex 20103; Man. G. M. A. RENNER.

Trade and Industry

There are state trade and industrial organizations responsible for the running of industries at all levels, which supervise production, distribution and sales. There are also central bodies responsible for the power generation industry, agriculture, land reclamation and transport.

CHAMBERS OF COMMERCE

Chamber of Commerce, Trade, Industry and Agriculture for the Eastern Province: POB 208, Benghazi; tel. (61) 94526; telex 40077; f. 1953; Pres. Dr SADDEQ M. BUSNAINA; Gen. Man. YOUSUF AL-GIAMI; 5,400 mems.

Tripoli Chamber of Commerce, Industry and Agriculture: POB 2321, Sharia al-Fatah September, Tripoli; tel. (21) 33755; telex 20181; f. 1952; Pres. ABD AR-RAHMAN ABU SHOUASHI; Dir-Gen. MUHAMMAD SAAD KAYAT; 60,000 mems.

DEVELOPMENT

General National Organization for Industrialization: POB 4388, Sharia San'a, Tripoli; tel. (21) 34995; telex 200990; f. 1970; a public organization responsible for the development of industry.

Great Man-made River Authority (GMR): Tripoli; supervises construction of pipeline carrying water to the Libyan coast from beneath the Sahara desert, to provide irrigation for agricultural projects; Sec.-Gen. MUHAMMAD AL-MANQOUSH.

Kufra and Sarir Authority: Council of Agricultural Development, Benghazi; f. 1972 to develop the Kufra Oasis and Sarir area in south-east Libya.

TRADE UNIONS

General Federation of Producers' Trade Unions: POB 734, 2 Sharia Istanbul, Tripoli; tel. (21) 46011; telex 20229; f. 1952; affiliated to ICFTU; Sec.-Gen. BASHIR IHWIJ; 17 trade unions with 700,000 members.

General Union for Oil and Petrochemicals: Tripoli; Chair. MUHAMMAD MITHNANI.

Pan-African Federation of Petroleum Energy and Allied Workers: Tripoli; affiliated to the Organization of African Trade Union Unity.

Transport

Department of Road Transport and Railways: POB 14527, Sharia az-Zawia, Secretariat of Communications and Transport Bldg, Tripoli; tel. (21) 609011-30; telex 20533; fax (21) 605605; Secretary for Public Works, Utilities, Transport and Communications MUBARAK ASH-SHAMIKH; Dir.-Gen. Projects and Research MUHAMMAD ABU ZIAN.

RAILWAYS

There are, at present, no railways in Libya. An agreement was signed in 1983 with the People's Republic of China for the construction of a 170-km standard gauge line from Tripoli to Ras Jedir, on the Tunisian frontier. This was to be the first stage of a planned 364-km line along the coast from Ras Jedir to Tripoli and Misurata, and the first section in a proposed network totalling 3,000 km. Construction of a rapid transport system began in Tripoli in 1986. Owing to shortage of funds, neither of the above projects has been completed. In November 1990 Libya signed an agreement with Egypt to extend the Egyptian rail system westwards and link Benghazi to the Egyptian border. Work on the initial phase of the project—a rail link between As-Salum and Tubruq—commenced in October 1993.

ROADS

The most important road is the 1,822-km national coast road from the Tunisian to the Egyptian border, passing through Tripoli and Benghazi. It has a second link between Barce and Lamluda, 141 km long. Another national road runs from a point on the coastal road 120 km south of Misurata through Sebha to Ghat near the Algerian border (total length 1,250 km). There is a branch 247 km long running from Vaddan to Sirte. A 690-km road, connecting Tripoli and Sebha, and another 626 km long, from Agedabia in the north to Kufra in the south-east, were opened in 1983. The Tripoli-to-Ghat section (941 km) of the third, 1,352-km long national road was opened in September 1984. There is a road crossing the desert from Sebha to the frontiers of Chad and Niger.

In addition to the national highways, the west of Libya has about 1,200 km of paved and macadamized roads and the east about 500 km. All the towns and villages of Libya, including the desert oases, are accessible by motor vehicle. In 1984 Libya had 25,675 km of paved roads.

SHIPPING

The principal ports are Tripoli, Benghazi, Mersa Brega, Misurata and as-Sider. Zuetina, Ras Lanouf, Mersa Hariga, Mersa Brega and as-Sider are mainly oil ports. A 30-inch crude oil pipeline connects the Zelten oilfields with Mersa Brega. Another pipeline joins the Sarir oilfield with Mersa Hariga, the port of Tobruk, and a pipeline from the Sarir field to Zuetina was opened in 1968. A port is being developed at Darna. Libya also has the use of Tunisian port facilities at Sfax and Gabes, to alleviate congestion at Tripoli.

General National Maritime Transport Company: POB 80173, 2 Sharia Ahmad Sharif, Tripoli; tel. (21) 33155; telex 20208; f. 1970 to handle all projects dealing with maritime trade; in June 1994 Libya's merchant fleet consisted of 26 vessels (11 tankers, 1 chemical carrier and 14 general cargo and passenger vessels); Chair. SAID MILUD AL-AHRASH.

CIVIL AVIATION

There are four civil airports: Tripoli International Airport, situated at Ben Gashir, 34 km (21 miles) from Tripoli; Benina Airport 19 km (12 miles) from Benghazi; Sebha Airport; Misurata Airport (domestic flights only). In the late 1980s there were plans for a new international airport to be built at Ras Lanouf and for airports at Brak and al-Waigh. Since April 1992 international civilian air links with Libya have been suspended, in accordance with UN Security Council Resolution 748 of 31 March 1992.

Jamahiriya Libyan Arab Airlines: POB 2555, Haiti St, Tripoli; tel. (21) 602083; telex 21093; f. 1989 by merger of Jamahiriya Air Transport (which in 1983 took over operations of United African Airlines) and Libyan Arab Airlines (f. 1964 as Kingdom of Libya Airlines and renamed 1969); passenger and cargo services from Tripoli, Benghazi and Sebha to destinations in Europe, North Africa and the Middle East; domestic services throughout Libya; Public relations Man. MUSTAFA A. BELKHIR.

Tourism

The principal attractions for visitors to Libya are Tripoli, with its beaches and annual International Fair, the ancient Roman towns of Sabratha, Leptis Magna and Cyrene, and historic oases. Tourist arrivals totalled 120,000 in 1987.

Department of Tourism and Fairs: POB 891, Sharia Omar Mukhtar, Tripoli; tel. (21) 32255; telex 20179.

Defence

Commander-in-Chief of Armed Forces: Brig. ABU-BAKR YOUNIS JABER.

Chief of Staff of Armed Forces: Brig. MUSTAPHA KHARROUBI.

Commander of the Navy: ABD AL-LATIF AHMAD SHAKSHOUKI.

Estimated Defence Budget (1994): LD421m. (US $1,400m.).

Military Service: selective conscription; two years.

Total Armed Forces (June 1994): 70,000: army 40,000; navy 8,000; air force 22,000; Libya possesses 2,350 tanks.

People's Militia: 40,000.

Education

A steady increase in educational facilities has taken place since 1943. In 1991 the number of pupils attending primary and secondary schools was 1,454,464, compared with 1,042,917 (including kindergartens) in 1982/83. The number of teachers rose similarly, from 67,246 in 1982/83 to 118,124 in 1991. In 1985 there were 4,164 primary schools with 63,122 teachers and 1,011,952 pupils. By 1991 the total number of students at all educational establishments was 1,527,393. Education is officially compulsory for nine years between six and 15 years of age. Primary education begins at the age of six and lasts for nine years. Secondary education, beginning at 15 years of age, lasts for a further three years. The teaching of French was abolished in Libyan schools in 1983.

In 1958 the University of Libya opened in Benghazi with Faculties of Arts and Commerce, followed the next year by the Faculty of Science near Tripoli. Faculties of Law, Agriculture, Engineering, Teacher Training, and Arabic Language and Islamic Studies have since been added to the University. In 1973 the University was divided into two parts, to form the Universities of Tripoli and Benghazi, later renamed al-Fatah and Ghar Younis universities. The Faculty of Education at Al-Fatah University became Sebha University in 1983. There is a University of Technology (Bright Star) at Mersa Brega and the Al-Arab Medical University at Banghazi.

Bibliography

di Agostini, Col Enrico. *La popolazione della Tripolitania.* 2 vols; Tripoli, 1917.

La popolazione della Cirenaica. Benghazi, 1922–23.

Amministrazione Fiduciaria all'Italia in Africa. Florence, 1948.

Archivio bibliografico Coloniale. Florence, Libia, 1915–21.

Allan, J. A. *Libya: the Experience of Oil.* London, Croom Helm, 1981.

Ansell, Meredith O. and al-Arif, Ibrahim M. *The Libyan Revolution.* London, The Oleander Press, 1972.

Baruni, Omar. *Spaniards and Knights of St John of Jerusalem in Tripoli.* Tripoli, Arabic, 1952.

Berlardinalli, Arsenio. *La Ghibla.* Tripoli, 1935.

Blunsum, T. *Libya: the Country and its People.* London, Queen Anne Press, 1968.

Cachia, Anthony J. *Libya under the Second Ottoman Occupation, 1835–1911.* Tripoli, 1945.

Colucci Massimo. *Il Regime della Proprieta Fondiaria nell'Africa Italiana: Vol. I. Libia.* Bologna, 1942.

Cooley, John. *Libyan Sandstorm.* London, Sidgwick and Jackson, 1983.

Corò, Francesco. *Settantasei Anni di Dominazione Turca in Libia.* Tripoli, 1937.

Curotti, Torquato. *Gente di Libia.* Tripoli, 1928.

Davis, John. *Libyan Politics: Tribe and Revolution.* London, I. B. Tauris, 1987.

Deeb, Mary-Jane. *Libya's Foreign Policy in North Africa.* Boulder, CO, Westview Press, 1991.

Despois, Jean. *Géographie Humaine.* Paris, 1946.

Le Djebel Nefousa. Paris, 1935.

La Colonisation italienne en Libye; Problèmes et Méthodes. Paris, Larose-Editeurs, 1935.

Epton, Nina. *Oasis Kingdom: The Libyan Story.* New York, 1953.

Evans-Pritchard, E. E. *The Sanusi of Cyrenaica.* London, 1949.

Farley, Rawle. *Planning for Development in Libya.* London, Pall Mall, 1971.

First, Ruth. *Libya—the Elusive Revolution.* London, Penguin, 1974.

Franca, Pietro, and others. *L'Italia in Africa: Incivilimento e Sviluppo dell'Eritrea, della Somalia, e della Libia.* Rome, 1947.

Hajjaji, S. A. *The New Libya.* Tripoli, 1967.

Herrmann, Gerhard. *Italiens Weg zum Imperium.* Leipzig, Goldman, 1938.

Heseltine, Nigel. *From Libyan Sands to Chad.* London, Museum Press, 1960.

Hill, R. W. *A Bibliography of Libya.* University of Durham, 1959.

Khadduri, Majid. *Modern Libya, a Study in Political Development.* Johns Hopkins Press, 1963.

Khalidi, I. R. *Constitutional Developments in Libya.* Beirut, Khayat's Book Co-operative, 1956.

Kubbah, Abdul Amir Q. *Libya, Its Oil Industry and Economic System.* Baghdad, The Arab Petro-Economic Research Centre, 1964.

Legg, H. J. *Libya: Economic and General Conditions in Libya.* London, 1952.

Lethielleux, J. *Le Fezzan, ses Jardins, ses Palmiers: Notes d'Ethnographie et d'Histoire.* Tunis, 1948.

Lindberg, J. A. *General Economic Appraisal of Libya.* New York, 1952.

Martel, André. *La Libye 1835–1990: Essai de géopolitique historique.* Paris, Presses Universitaires de France, 1991.

Mattes, Hans-Peter. *Die innere und aussere islamische Mission Libyens.* Munich/Mainz, Kaiser-Gruenewald, 1987.

Micacchi, Rodolfo. *La Tripolitania sotto il dominio dei Caramanli.* Intra, 1936.

Murabet, Mohammed. *Tripolitania: the Country and its People.* Tripoli, 1952.

Norman, John. *Labour and Politics in Libya and Arab Africa.* New York, Bookman, 1965.

Owen, R. *Libya: a Brief Political and Economic Survey.* London, 1961.

Pelt, Adrian. *Libyan Independence and the United Nations.* Yale U.P., 1970.

Pichou, Jean. *La Question de Libye dans le règlement de la paix.* Paris, 1945.

Qaddafi, Col Muammar al-. *The Green Book.* 3 vols, Tripoli, 1976–79; Vol. I: The Solution of the Problem of Democracy, Vol. II: The Solution of the Economic Problem, Vol. III: The Social Basis of the Third Universal Theory.

Lord Rennell. *British Military Administration of Occupied Territories in Africa during the years 1941–47.* London, HMSO, 1948.

Rivlin, Benjamin. *The United Nations and the Italian Colonies.* New York, 1950.

Rossi, P. *Libya.* Lausanne, 1965.

Royal Institute of International Affairs. *The Italian Colonial Empire.* London, 1940.

Rushdi, Muhammad Rasim. *Trablus al Gharb.* Tripoli, Arabic, 1953.

Schlueter, Hans. *Index Libycus.* Boston, G. K. Hall, 1972.

Schmeider, Oskar and Wilhelmy, Herbert. *Die faschistische Kolonisation in Nordafrika.* Leipzig, Quelle and Meyer, 1939.

Steele-Greig, A. J. *History of Education in Tripolitania from the Time of the Ottoman Occupation to the Fifth Year under British Military Occupation.* Tripoli, 1948.

Villard, Henry S. *Libya: The New Arab Kingdom of North Africa.* Ithaca, 1956.

Waddams, Frank C. *The Libyan Oil Industry.* London, Croom Helm, 1980.

Ward, Philip. *Touring Libya.* 3 vols, 1967–69.

Tripoli: Portrait of a City. 1970.

Williams, G. *Green Mountain, an Informal Guide to Cyrenaica and its Jebel Akhdar.* London, 1963.

Willimott, S. G. and Clarke, J. I. *Field Studies in Libya.* Durham, 1960.

Wright, John. *Libya: a Modern History.* London, Croom Helm, 1982.

MOROCCO

Physical and Social Geography

The Kingdom of Morocco is the westernmost of the three North African countries known to the Arabs as Jeziret al-Maghreb or 'Island of the West'. It occupies an area of 458,730 sq km (177,117 sq miles), excluding Western (formerly Spanish) Sahara (252,120 sq km or 97,344 sq miles), a disputed territory under Moroccan occupation. Morocco has an extensive coastline on both the Atlantic Ocean and the Mediterranean Sea. However, owing to its position and intervening mountain ranges, Morocco remained relatively isolated from the rest of the Maghreb and served as a refuge for descendants of the native Berber-speaking inhabitants of north-west Africa.

According to official estimates, the population at mid-1993 was 26,069,000. About 35% of the total were Berber-speaking peoples, living mainly in mountain villages, while the Arabic-speaking majority was concentrated in towns in the lowlands, particularly in Casablanca (which was the largest city in the Maghreb, with a population of 3,406,000 at mid-1993), Marrakesh, the old southern capital (population 1,549,000), Fez (population 1,051,000), and Rabat (population 1,608,000, including Salé), the modern administrative capital.

PHYSICAL FEATURES

The physical geography of Morocco is dominated by the highest and most rugged ranges in the Atlas Mountain system of north-west Africa. They are the result of mountain-building in the Tertiary era, when sediments deposited beneath an ancestral Mediterranean Sea were uplifted, folded and fractured. The mountains remain geologically unstable and Morocco is liable to severe earthquakes, such as the one that took place at the port of Agadir in 1960, causing severe damage.

In Morocco the Atlas Mountains form four distinct massifs, which are surrounded and partially separated by lowland plains and plateaux. In the north, the Rif Atlas comprise a rugged arc of mountains that rise steeply from the Mediterranean coast to heights of more than 2,200 m above sea level. There, limestone and sandstone ranges form an effective barrier to east-west communications. They are inhabited by Berber farming families who live in isolated mountain villages and have little contact with the Arabs of Tétouan (estimated population, including Larache, 878,000 at mid-1993) and Tangier (579,000) at the north-western end of the Rif chain.

The Middle Atlas lie immediately south of the Rif, separated by the Col of Taza, a narrow gap which affords the only easy route between western Algeria and Atlantic Morocco. They rise to about 3,000 m and form a broad barrier between the two countries. They also function as a major drainage divide and are flanked by the basins of Morocco's two principal rivers, the Oum er-Rbia which flows west to the Atlantic and the Moulouya which flows north-east to the Mediterranean. Much of the Middle Atlas consists of a limestone plateau dissected by river gorges and capped here and there by volcanic craters and lava flows. The semi-nomadic Berber tribes spend the winter in villages in the valleys and move to the higher slopes in summer to pasture their flocks.

To the south the Middle Atlas chain merges into the High Atlas, the most formidable of the mountain massifs, which rises to about 4,000 m and is heavily snow-clad in winter. The mountains extend from south-west to north-east, and rise precipitously from both the Atlantic lowland to the north and the desert plain of Saharan Morocco to the south. There are no easily accessible routes across the High Atlas, but numerous mountain tracks allow the exchange of goods by pack animal between Atlantic and Saharan Morocco. A considerable Berber population lives in the mountain valleys in compact, fortified villages.

The Anti-Atlas is the lowest and most southerly of the mountain massifs. Structurally it forms an elevated edge of the Saharan platform which was uplifted when the High Atlas was formed. It consists largely of crystalline rocks and is joined to the southern margin of the High Atlas by a mass of volcanic lavas which separates the valley of the river Sous, draining west to the Atlantic at Agadir, from that of the upper Draa, draining south-east towards the Sahara. On the southern side of the chain, barren slopes are trenched by gorges from which cultivated palm groves protrude.

Stretching inland from the Atlantic coast is an extensive area of lowland, enclosed on the north, east and south by the Rif, Middle and High Atlas. It consists of the Gharb plain and the wide valley of the River Sebou in the north and of the plateaux and plains of the Meseta, the Tadla, the Rehamna, the Djebilet and the Haouz farther south. Most of the Arabic-speaking people of Morocco live in this region.

CLIMATE AND VEGETATION

Northern and central Morocco experience a 'Mediterranean' climate, with warm, wet winters and hot, dry summers, but to the south this gives way to semi-arid and eventually to desert conditions. In the Rif and the northern parts of the Middle Atlas mean annual rainfall exceeds 75 cm and the summer drought lasts only three months, but in the rest of the Middle Atlas, in the High Atlas and over the northern half of the Atlantic lowland rainfall is reduced to between 40 cm and 75 cm and the summer drought lasts for four months or more. During the summer intensely hot winds from the Sahara, known as the Sirocco or Chergui, occasionally cross the mountains and desiccate the lowland. Summer heat on the Atlantic coastal plain is tempered, however, by sea breezes.

Over the southern half of the Atlantic lowland and the Anti-Atlas semi-arid conditions prevail and rainfall decreases to between 20 and 40 cm per year, becoming very variable and generally insufficient for the regular cultivation of cereal crops without irrigation. East and south of the Atlas Mountains, which act as a barrier to rain-bearing winds from the Atlantic, rainfall is reduced still further and regular cultivation becomes entirely dependent on irrigation.

The chief contrast in the vegetation of Morocco is between the mountain massifs, which support forest or open woodland, and the surrounding lowlands, which tend to be covered only by scrub growth of low, drought-resistant bushes. The natural vegetation has, however, been depleted, and in many places actually destroyed, by excessive cutting, burning and grazing. The middle and upper slopes of the mountains are often quite well wooded, with evergreen oak dominant at the lower and cedar at the higher elevations. The lowlands to the east and south of the Atlas Mountains support distinctive species of steppe and desert vegetation, among which esparto grass and the argan tree (which is unique to south-western Morocco) are conspicuous.

NEWLY-ANNEXED TERRITORY

After independence the Moroccan Government claimed a right to administer a large area of the western Sahara, including territory in Algeria and Mauritania, and the whole of Spanish Sahara. The claim was based on the extent of Moroccan rule in medieval times. The existence of considerable deposits of phosphates in Spanish Sahara and of iron ore in the Algeria-Morocco border region further encouraged Moroccan interest in expansion. After Spanish withdrawal from the Sahara in 1976, Morocco and Mauritania divided the former Spanish Sahara (now known as Western Sahara) between them, with Morocco annexing the northern part of the territory, including the phosphate mines of Bou Craa. In August 1979 Mauritania renounced its share, which was immediately annexed by Morocco and incorporated as a new province, Oued ed-Dahab.

The current population of Western Sahara are of Moorish or mixed Arab-Berber descent with some negro admixture, who depend for their existence on herds of sheep, camels and goats which they move seasonally from one pasture to another. The main tribes are the R'gibat, Uld Delim, Izargien and Arosien. At the census of September 1982 the population of Western Sahara was estimated at 163,868, and by mid-1993 at 208,000. The principal towns in the area are el-Aaiún, es-Smara (formerly Smara) and Dakhla (Villa Cisneros).

The relief of most of the area is gentle. The coast is backed by a wide alluvial plain overlain in the south by extensive sand dunes aligned from south-west to north-east and extending inland over 250 km (155 miles). Behind the coastal plain the land rises gradually to a plateau surface broken by sandstone ridges that reach 300 m in height. In the north-east, close to the Mauritanian frontier, isolated mountain ranges, such as the Massif de la Guelta, rise to over 600 m. There are no permanent streams and the only considerable valley is that of the Sekia el-Hamra which crosses the northernmost part of the area to reach the coast at el-Aaiún north of Cape Bojador. The whole of the region experiences an extreme desert climate. Nowhere does mean annual rainfall exceed 100 mm and over most of the territory it is less than 50 mm. Vegetation is restricted to scattered desert shrubs and occasional patches of coarse grass in most depressions. Along the coast, summer heat is tempered by air moving inland after it has been cooled over the waters of the cold Canaries current which flows offshore from north to south.

History

Revised for this edition by RICHARD I. LAWLESS

EARLY HISTORY

The Phoenicians and Carthaginians established trading posts on Morocco's coasts, and later the Romans established the province of Mauritania Tingitana in the north of the country. Muslim warriors made raids in AD 684–85 and had conquered Morocco by the eighth century. The Berber tribes of Morocco rallied to Islam, but adopted Kharijite heresies, which, together with Berber particularism, led to a great rebellion in 739–40 and the subsequent fragmentation of Morocco into small Muslim principalities.

Idris, a descendant of the Prophet Muhammad, founded the first of the great ruling Muslim dynasties in Morocco. The regime lasted from 788–89 to 985–86 but, after the death of Idris' son (828–29), it fell into decline. There followed two centuries of internal conflict and tribal revolt, as well as pressures from the Umayyad Caliphate in Spain and from the Fatimid Caliphate in Ifriqiya (Tunisia and eastern Algeria) in 908–69. Subsequently, Morocco entered a glorious era, with the rise of the Almoravid religious movement among the nomadic Berbers of Sanhaja descent. The Almoravids declared Holy War (Jihad) and established control, under Yousuf ibn Tashufin (d. 1106), over all Morocco and much of Algeria, and also annexed Muslim lands in Spain. After the death of Tashufin's successor in 1142, however, Almoravid power declined rapidly.

A new religious force emerged after the death in 1130 of Muhammad ibn Tumart, a religious teacher who had gathered Berber adherents, called Almohads, around himself in the High Atlas. One of his disciples, Abd al-Mumin, led the Almohads in their conquest of the Maghreb as far east as Tripolitania and Cyrenaica in 1151–59. The Almohads prospered in the reign of al-Mansur (1184–98), who brought Muslim Spain under his control, but in 1212 they suffered a serious defeat at the hands of the Spanish Christians, and thereafter the Almohad empire began to decline. A new Berber house, the Merinids, became prominent, and by the mid-13th century they had eclipsed the Almohads. Their influence lasted for about 100 years but their attempts to reconstitute the Almohad empire were largely unsuccessful.

Nomadic tribes of Arab origin had penetrated the Maghreb in the 11th and 12th centuries, along with other Badawi elements during the later Almohad period. With the disintegration of the Merinid state, the Badawi tribes invaded, contributing greatly to the Arabization of the Maghreb. Until 1465 Morocco was prey to internal discords, which persisted until the emergence of the Wattasids, another Berber regime. Their pre-eminence was, however, short-lived, and they failed to halt the Portuguese and the Spaniards, who were establishing outposts along the Moroccan coasts.

A new movement of resistance to the Spaniards and Portuguese was born among the religious confraternities who now led the Jihad against the Christians. The Saadian regime arose, originating in a line of Sharifs from the Saharan side of the Atlas mountains. Ahmad al-Mansur (1578–1603) reorganized the Saadian regime under a new system which exempted various Arab tribes from taxation, in return for armed services to the State. Under this system, much depended on the character of the Sultan, as tribal rivalries broke out whenever the central government was weak or ill-directed. The period of Saadian rule, which ended in 1668, was, however, one of considerable prosperity.

Yet another wave of popular religious feeling brought to power the house of Alawi (Hasani or Filali), which originated among the Saharan Berbers and continues to reign in Morocco. Rashid II (1664–72) and Mulai Ismail (1672–1727) firmly established the regime, under which Morocco was more peaceful and united than it was ever to be again until French occupation. Mulai Ismail successfully repelled the Sanhaja Berbers, but a period of uncertainty followed his death, in the course of which one of his sons, Abdullah, was dethroned four times. His son, Sharif Muhammad ibn Abdallah (1757–90), and his immediate successors strove to maintain their power in the face of tribal dissidence and the threat of foreign intervention. However, the French conquest of Algiers in 1830 had repercussions in Morocco. Mulai Abd ar-Rahman, who was then Sultan of Morocco, gave military assistance to Abd al-Qadir, the Algerian Amir who led Muslim resistance to France, and Moroccan troops were later defeated by a French force at Wadi Isly in 1844.

A dispute over the limits of the Ceuta enclave, which had been under Spanish rule since 1580, led to a brief war between Morocco and Spain in 1860. Spanish troops defeated the Moroccans and, under the terms of the peace settlement, the Ceuta enclave was enlarged and Spain was given indemnities amounting to 100m. pesetas. Morocco also granted to Spain a territorial enclave on the Atlantic coast opposite the Canaries (Santa Cruz de Mar Pequeña, now Ifni). In 1884 Spain claimed a protectorate over the coastal zone to the south of Morocco, from Cape Bojador to Cape Blanco, the future Spanish Sahara. The borders between this territory, known as the Río de Oro, and the French possessions to the south and east were agreed between France and Spain in June 1900. A convention between France and Spain in October 1904 assigned to Spain two zones of influence, one in northern and the other in southern Morocco. The southern border of Morocco was set at 27° 40'N, beyond which were Spain's Saharan territories. The Germans now sought to intervene in Moroccan affairs and, at the conference of Algeciras in 1906, they secured the agreement of the Great Powers to the economic 'internationalization' of Morocco. A crisis in 1911, precipitated by the appearance of a German gun-boat off Agadir, ended in a Franco-German settlement whereby the Germans recognized Morocco as a

French sphere of influence. In March 1912 Morocco became a protectorate of France, with a French Resident-General empowered to direct foreign affairs, control defence and introduce domestic reforms.

FRENCH RULE

Under an agreement of 1912, Spain retained its zones of influence (somewhat reduced), but these were now granted by France as the protecting power rather than by the Sultan. The first French Resident-General in Morocco was Gen. Lyautey (1912–25). He established effective control, before 1914, over the plains and lower plateaux of Morocco from Fez to the Atlas mountains south of Marrakesh; then, before 1918, over the western Atlas, the Taza corridor as far as Algeria and some areas of the northern highlands. French troops helped Spain to subdue a formidable rebellion (1921–26) of the Rif tribe under Abd al-Krim. This success resulted in the subjugation of the northern mountains and allowed the French to concentrate on gaining control of the Middle Atlas and the Tafilalet—a task that was accomplished by 1934, when the pacification of Morocco could be regarded as complete.

From this time, nationalist sentiment began to make itself felt in Morocco. A 'Comité d'Action Marocaine' asked for a limitation of the protectorate. This 'Comité' was dissolved in 1937, but nationalist propaganda against the French regime continued. Morocco supported France in 1939 and the Free French movement in 1942. A Party of Independence (Istiqlal), formed in 1943, demanded independence for Morocco, with a constitutional government under Sultan Muhammad ibn Yousuf, who supported the nationalist movement. Although Istiqlal had a large following in the towns, the party had little support among the conservative tribes of Morocco, who supported Thami al-Glawi, the Pasha of Marrakesh. As a result, tension between the new and the old ideologies in Morocco increased in 1953. Sultan Muhammad ibn Yousuf had quarrelled with the French administration, and in May 1953 a number of Pashas and Cadis, led by al-Glawi, asked for his removal. The Berber tribes began to converge in force on the main urban centres in Morocco, and on 20 August 1953 the Sultan agreed to go into exile in Europe, but not to abdicate. Muhammad ibn Arafa, a prince of the Alawi house, was subsequently recognized as Sultan. The situation remained tense, with assassination attempts on the Sultan in 1953 and 1954, outbreaks of violence throughout Morocco in 1954–55 and intense nationalist fervour.

INDEPENDENCE—1956

Sultan Muhammad ibn Arafa renounced the throne and withdrew to Tangier in 1955. Muhammad ibn Yousuf, on 5 November that year, was recognized once more as the legitimate Sultan. A joint Franco-Moroccan declaration of 2 March 1956 stated that the protectorate agreement of 1912 was obsolete and that the French Government now recognized the independence of Morocco. A protocol of the same date covered the transitional phase before new agreements could come into effect. The Sultan would now have full legislative powers in Morocco. Henceforth a high commissioner was to represent France in the new State. France also undertook to assist Morocco in the organization of its armed forces and the reassertion of Moroccan control over the zones of Spanish influence. On 12 November 1956 Morocco became a member of the UN.

In August 1956 Istiqlal proclaimed the need to abrogate the Convention of Algeciras (1906), which had 'internationalized' the economic life of Morocco, and also to secure the withdrawal of all foreign troops from the land. Following an international conference in October 1956, Tangier was restored to Morocco. A royal charter of August 1957 preserved the former economic and financial system in force at Tangier, which included a free money market, quota-free trade with foreign countries and a low level of taxation. In 1959 Tangier lost its special status and was integrated financially and economically with Morocco, but a royal decree of January 1962 made it once more a free port. In 1956, prior to independence, Istiqlal had envisaged the creation of a 'Great Morocco' which would include certain areas in south-west Algeria, the Spanish territories in north-west Africa and also Mauritania, together with

the French Sudan (i.e. the Republic of Mali). These claims were to be reiterated by Morocco in the following years, beginning in 1960, with an intensive propaganda and diplomatic campaign against Mauritania.

The problem of the Spanish territories in north-west Africa also came to the fore at this time. Spain had recognized the independence of Morocco and had renounced the northern zone of the protectorate assigned to it in Morocco under the terms of the Franco-Spanish convention of 1912. No agreement was reached, however, on the enclaves of Ceuta and Melilla in the north, the enclave of Ifni in the south, or the Spanish territories to the south of Morocco. Since 1934 these territories had been divided in two parts—the northern Seguia el-Hamra and the southern Río de Oro—both administered jointly with Ifni, and separately from the contiguous southern zone of Spain's protectorate in Morocco. Raids on Ifni and the western Sahara by Moroccan irregular forces (the 'Armée de Libération du Grand Sahara') caused serious internal unrest between 1956 and 1958, although the Moroccan Government denied responsibility. Negotiations between Morocco and Spain, held at Cintra in Portugal, led in April 1958 to an agreement whereby Spain, in accordance with the settlement reached in April 1956, relinquished the southern zone of its former protectorate. Spain retained possession of the enclaves and of Seguia el-Hamra and Río de Oro, which were renamed Spanish Sahara and separated from Ifni.

KING HASSAN II AND ROYAL DOMINANCE OF GOVERNMENT

After independence, Istiqlal remained the dominant political force and obtained a majority in the Government. At the same time Sultan Muhammad strengthened the position of the monarchy. In July 1957 Prince Moulai Hassan was proclaimed heir to the throne and in August the Sultan assumed the title of king. Istiqlal's efforts to curb the power of the monarchy were hampered by internal division. Tension between the conservative and radical wings culminated in December 1958, when a Government was formed by Abdullah Ibrahim, a leader of the radical tendency. In the following months Ben Barka led a movement to establish a radical party organization independent of the conservative Istiqlal leadership of Allal al-Fassi. In September 1959 this new organization became an independent party, the Union Nationale des Forces Populaires (National Union of Popular Forces—UNFP). Although the UNFP supported Ibrahim's Government, it was subjected to repressive measures by the police and the army who were under the control of the King or of 'King's men' in the Cabinet. In May 1960 a new Government was formed with the King himself as Prime Minister and Prince Hassan as his deputy. Consequently the UNFP went into opposition. On the death of King Muhammad in February 1961 the Prince ascended the throne as King Hassan II, and also became Prime Minister. In December 1962 a new Constitution, which established a constitutional monarchy and guaranteed personal and political freedoms, was approved by referendum. In January 1963 a cabinet reshuffle deprived the Istiqlal leaders of their posts in the Government, and when elections for the House of Representatives were held in May, both Istiqlal and the UNFP appeared as opposition parties. The King was represented by the newly formed Front pour la Défense des Institutions Constitutionnelles (FDIC). The election, by universal direct suffrage, failed to produce the expected clear majority for the government party, the results being: FDIC 69 seats; Istiqlal 41 seats; UNFP 28 seats; Independents six seats. In the following months repressive action was taken against both opposition parties. Several Istiqlal deputies were arrested for protesting against corruption and mismanagement of the election, leading the party to boycott further elections later in the year. Almost all the leaders of the UNFP were arrested in July 1963 in connection with an alleged coup attempt. Many of them were held in solitary confinement, tortured and eventually sentenced to death. In November the King gave up the premiership and installed an FDIC Government to represent his interests.

RELATIONS IN THE MAGHREB

In July 1962 Moroccan troops entered the region south of Colomb-Béchar in Algeria—a region never officially demarcated. The Moroccan press also launched a strong campaign in support of the view that the Tindouf area in the extreme south-west of Algeria should belong to Morocco—a claim of some importance, since the area contained large deposits of high-grade iron ore and also considerable resources of oil and natural gas.

An arbitration commission was established by the OAU, and Algeria and Morocco submitted evidence in support of their respective territorial claims. On 20 February 1964 an agreement was reached to establish a demilitarized zone. Subsequently there was a swift improvement in relations between the two countries.

Relations between Morocco and Mauritania also became more amicable. The Ministers of Information of the two States met at Cairo in July 1964 during an African Summit Conference. An understanding was reached to bring an end to the 'war' of radio propaganda and criticism hitherto conducted between Morocco and Mauritania.

INTERNAL UNREST

In August 1964 the Moroccan Government was reorganized, although it remained composed largely of FDIC members. The reshuffle was part of an attempt to attract the opposition parties back into a coalition government, since the FDIC had an inadequate majority in the House of Representatives and was itself split into two factions, the Parti Socialiste Démocratique (PSD) and the mainly Berber Mouvement Populaire (MP). The weakness of the Government contributed to the tension which developed in the first half of 1965, as unemployment and rising prices generated discontent among the urban working class. In June King Hassan proclaimed a state of emergency, whereby he himself assumed full legislative and executive powers. Fresh elections, it was stated, would be held after the Constitution had been revised and submitted to a referendum. In October 1965 the UNFP leader, Ben Barka, disappeared in France, never to be seen again. At a subsequent French trial, Gen. Oufkir, one of the King's sturdiest supporters, was found guilty *in absentia* of complicity in Ben Barka's disappearance. Relations between Morocco and France became very strained and there were anti-government protest strikes in Morocco.

In July 1967 King Hassan relinquished the post of Prime Minister in favour of Dr Muhammad Benhima, and in 1967 and 1968 there were eight major Cabinet reshuffles. Considerable student and trade union unrest continued during this period, but the King won some approval for extensive nationalization measures and a degree of land redistribution.

There was a gradual return to normal political activity in 1969, albeit under royal direction. Communal elections were held in October, although these were boycotted by opposition parties, and the successful candidates were mostly independents. Following these elections, Benhima was replaced as Prime Minister by Dr Ahmad Laraki, formerly the Minister of Foreign Affairs. A national referendum on a new Constitution was eventually held in July 1970; official figures claimed that over 98% of the votes were affirmative, despite general opposition from the main political parties, trade unions and student organizations. Elections for a new unicameral legislature were held in August. Of the 240 members, 90 were elected by direct suffrage, 90 by local councils and 60 by an electoral college. The results were that 158 elected members were independents, 60 were MP members and 22 were from opposition parties.

In July 1971 there was an unsuccessful attempt, apparently engineered by right-wing army officers, to overthrow the King and establish a republic. In the following months, a series of talks took place between the Government and members of Istiqlal and the UNFP, who had united to form a National Front in July 1970, but the parties refused to compromise with government policies.

In March 1972 a new Constitution was promulgated, under which executive power was vested in the King. Legislative power was held by the Chamber of Representatives, with two-thirds of its members elected by universal suffrage, compared with one-half under the previous Constitution. On 30 April, however, King Hassan announced that the Chamber would remain dissolved, and that elections for a new Chamber were

being postponed until new electoral lists had been drawn up. In July a split occurred in the UNFP which separated the Rabat section from the rest of the party, effectively putting an end to the National Front.

In August 1972 King Hassan, after surviving another attempt on his life, assumed command of the armed forces and responsibility for defence. He approached the opposition parties again, asking for their co-operation in supervising general elections and collaboration with the Government. However, both Istiqlal and the UNFP demanded extensive reforms, which were unacceptable to the King, as they included curtailing his own powers and guaranteeing political freedom. The elections were postponed indefinitely, and a new Cabinet was formed in November without opposition participation.

FOREIGN RELATIONS 1967–72

Morocco continued to press its claim to Spanish-held territories in north-west Africa. In December 1967 the UN General Assembly adopted a resolution urging Spain to hold a referendum in Spanish Sahara to allow the population to determine its future. Spain accepted the principle of self-determination, but in June 1970 progress was halted, after the violent repression of riots in the Saharan town of el-Aaiún resulted in numerous deaths. Further UN resolutions in support of decolonization were adopted, and Morocco, Mauritania and Algeria each supported a rival Saharan liberation movement. In contrast, the question of Ifni was settled amicably in June 1969, when Spain ceded the small coastal enclave to Morocco.

Morocco abandoned its claim to Mauritania in 1969. Full diplomatic recognition and an exchange of ambassadors followed in 1970, and the two countries signed a treaty of solidarity and co-operation in June. Relations with France improved, and in December 1969 the diplomatic missions in Paris and Rabat were returned to full ambassadorial status for the first time since the Ben Barka affair in 1966.

In May 1970 a final agreement (ratified in May 1973) was reached in the frontier dispute with Algeria, and a joint commission agreed to maintain the boundaries of the colonial period. The disputed region of Gara-Djebilet, rich in iron ore deposits, thus became the property of Algeria, but Morocco was to be a partner in a joint company to be established to exploit these deposits.

HASSAN IN CONTROL

In March 1973 the King announced plans for the Moroccanization of sectors of the economy within two years. He also reinforced his traditional support in the rural areas by ordering the confiscation of foreign-owned lands and their redistribution among the peasantry. Since most of the landowners were French, relations between France and Morocco deteriorated again and French aid was suspended for a year, pending an agreement on compensation. In the same month relations with Spain became strained when Morocco announced the extension of its territorial waters from 12 to 70 nautical miles; in January 1974 the two Governments concluded an agreement allowing a limited number of Spanish vessels to fish in Moroccan waters. Hassan's new nationalist policy also led Morocco to take a more active part in the Arab-Israeli conflict. In February 1973 troops were despatched to the Syrian front, and during the October War further detachments were sent to Egypt; this resulted in a partial *rapprochement* between Morocco and the more extremist Arab states.

In the early months of 1974 political trials continued. A further series of arrests followed the discovery, in February, of a plot to free prisoners in Kénitra jail. The King, however, made some conciliatory gestures: in March he announced plans for university and judicial reforms, and in April several imprisoned UNFP leaders were released.

Meanwhile, Morocco pursued its claim to Spanish Sahara. The development of phosphate mining in the territory presented a threat to the Moroccan economy, which was itself dependent on revenue from phosphate exports. The opposition parties urged the Government to take action. In July 1974 the King held consultations with military leaders, ministers and leaders of all the political parties to prepare an international campaign for the annexation of the Sahara. Discussions with Spain in August were inconclusive, as the Spanish were pursuing their own plan for the decolonization of the Sahara, which involved the establishment of an independent state, closely allied to Spain. This project was opposed not only by Morocco but also by Mauritania, which reasserted its claim to the area. Both countries rejected Spain's plan to hold a referendum in the Sahara under UN supervision. In October the issue was debated in the UN General Assembly at the initiative of Morocco. Two months later the Assembly formally approved Morocco's suggestion that the matter be brought before the International Court of Justice (ICJ) in the Hague, and the UN Special Committee on Colonialism was instructed to send a mission to the territory. The referendum that Spain had proposed was to be postponed.

In the atmosphere of national unity produced by the Sahara issue in the second half of 1974 there was a revival of political activity. New parties were formed and existing parties reorganized. Most notably the split in the UNFP was confirmed, as the Rabat section of the party became the Union Socialiste des Forces Populaires (USFP). King Hassan again promised elections for the following year, and once more postponed them indefinitely, but even the opposition were content to give priority to the Sahara dispute. Although some political prisoners were released, harassment of opposition parties continued and they remained unrepresented in the Government.

SAHARAN TAKE-OVER

After Spain reiterated its readiness to withdraw from Spanish Sahara, it became clear that the chief conflict was between the rival North African countries and liberation movements. In October 1974 Morocco and Mauritania reached a secret agreement on the future division of the territory, which came to light in July 1975. Meanwhile, Algeria became the main target of Moroccan invective for its support of the Frente Popular para la Liberación de Saguia el-Hamra y Río de Oro (Popular Front for the Liberation of Saguia el-Hamra and Río de Oro—the Frente Polisario or Polisario Front), a Saharan liberation movement, founded in 1973, which aimed to establish an independent, non-aligned state in Spanish Sahara.

On 14 October 1975 a UN investigative mission reported that almost all the people whom it had consulted in the territory were 'categorically for independence and against the territorial claims of Morocco and Mauritania'. Two days later the ICJ ruled in favour of self-determination for the Sahrawi people. King Hassan immediately ordered a march of 350,000 unarmed civilians to take possession of Spanish Sahara. The Green March, as it was called, began on 6 November. The Spanish authorities allowed the marchers to progress a short distance across the border before halting their advance. On 9 November Hassan abandoned the march, and on 14 November a tripartite agreement was signed in Madrid, whereby Spain agreed to withdraw from Western Sahara (as the territory was redesignated) in 1976 and transfer the territory to a joint Morocco-Mauritanian administration. Algeria reacted angrily, increasing its support for the Polisario Front and making veiled threats of direct military intervention. Moroccan armed forces swiftly occupied the territory, and entered the capital, el-Aaiún, on 11 December. They encountered fierce resistance from Polisario guerrillas, and many Sahrawis fled to the Algerian border to avoid the Moroccan advance. The last Spanish troops left in January 1976, a month before they were due to depart under the terms of the tripartite agreement.

The Moroccan Prime Minister, Ahmad Osman, visited France in January 1976, and French deliveries of military equipment to Morocco were increased. On 27 January Algerian and Moroccan forces clashed at Amgalla, inside Western Sahara, and there was further fighting in February. On 27 February the Sahrawi Arab Democratic Republic (SADR) was proclaimed, a Saharan government-in-exile was formed in Algeria and on 7 March Morocco severed diplomatic relations with Algeria. The prospect of outright war between the two countries receded, however, as Algeria contented itself with arming and training Polisario guerrillas for raids into Western Sahara and providing camps for civilian refugees from the area, believed to number some 60,000.

In April 1976 Morocco and Mauritania reached agreement on the division of Western Sahara. The greater part of the territory, containing most of the known mineral wealth, was allotted to Morocco, which subsequently divided it into three new provinces and absorbed it into the Kingdom. By placing strong army garrisons in the territory's few scattered urban settlements, the Moroccans were able to secure them against guerrilla attacks, but incursions by forces of the Polisario Front into the surrounding desert areas could not be prevented. The conveyor belt from the important Bou Craa phosphate mines to the sea was sabotaged, and clashes between the Moroccan army and Polisario forces resulted in heavy casualties on both sides. Polisario units were too strong for Mauritania's very limited armed forces in the south, and Morocco took increasing responsibility for the defence of that region. The two countries formed a joint defence committee in May 1977, following a successful Polisario raid on the Mauritanian mining town of Zouérate, in which two French nationals were killed and six captured. In November King Hassan warned Algeria that Moroccan troops would pursue Polisario forces into Algerian territory if necessary; the Algerian Government retorted that any such incursion would result in war between the two countries.

Tension was increased when France, following the release of the French captives in December, launched three air attacks on the Polisario Front. Although the French Government maintained that its action was for the protection of French nationals working at the Saharan mines, and had been undertaken at the request of Mauritania, it was clear that France favoured the expansion of Moroccan interests in the area rather than those of Algeria, for both economic and strategic reasons. During 1978 intermittent fighting continued, and there was a further French air-raid in April. Proposed meetings of the OAU to discuss the issue were postponed on three occasions, revealing an apparent unwillingness on the part of many African leaders to commit themselves. The intransigence of both Morocco and Algeria was partly due to the fact that their Governments relied to a great extent on their respective Saharan policies for domestic popular support. In Morocco the various opposition parties remained united in support of the King in this respect, despite the enormous expense of the war, which accounted for at least a quarter of the 1979 budget, and the cost of confirming Morocco's control over the Saharan provinces by installing schools, hospitals and housing for those inhabitants remaining in the area. In January 1978 the Government had announced a Sahara Development Programme, involving proposed expenditure of US $292m. The programme envisaged the settlement of Saharan nomads and the creation of a sedentary economy.

The war was having an even more severe effect on the Mauritanian economy, and this was the chief reason for the coup which took place there in July 1978. The Polisario Front immediately announced a suspension of its hostilities against Mauritania; it was soon clear that the new President, Col Mustafa Ould Salek, would be willing to renounce the Saharan province altogether, were it not for the 10,000 Moroccan troops still stationed in Mauritania. Salek's coup was followed by renewed diplomatic activity, in which France played an important role. President Houphouët-Boigny of Côte d'Ivoire offered to act as mediator, proposing the creation of a Saharan Republic in the Mauritanian sector of Western Sahara alone, a suggestion which was rejected by all parties. In September King Hassan accepted the proposal by the President of the OAU, President Nimeri of Sudan, that the Heads of State of six African countries (Guinea, Côte d'Ivoire, Mali, Nigeria, Tanzania and Sudan) should form a committee of 'wise men' to mediate in the dispute. Spain also became increasingly involved, although it had to safeguard its fishing rights in Moroccan waters and, more importantly, its claim to the enclaves of Ceuta and Melilla. Nevertheless, in December 1980, following harassment of Spanish fishing boats by Polisario forces, the Spanish Government gave official recognition to the Polisario Front (though not to the SADR itself) and declared its support for Saharan self-determination.

Fighting continued, and in January 1979 Polisario forces attacked the town of Tan-Tan, some distance inside Morocco's pre-1975 borders. In March the Chamber of Representatives approved the formation of a National Defence Council to formulate defence policy. This council included members of all the main political groups: independents, Istiqlal, the MP, the USFP, the Mouvement Populaire Constitutionnel et Démocratique (MPCD), and the Parti du Progrès et du Socialisme (PPS). This suggested that the King was seeking to strengthen support for the war by enlarging the number and the variety of those responsible for its direction. At the same time, the Chamber of Representatives showed that its attitude was still belligerent by reaffirming Morocco's right to its Saharan territory, and recommended that the right of pursuit into foreign (i.e. Algerian) territory should be exercised.

In July 1979 Polisario forces broke their cease-fire agreement with Mauritania, and the OAU summit conference passed a resolution urging the holding of a referendum on self-determination in Western Sahara. Mauritania withdrew from the war, signing a peace treaty with the Polisario Front in August and renouncing its territorial ambitions in Western Sahara. King Hassan immediately claimed the former Mauritanian sector, and proclaimed it a Moroccan province, to be known as Oued ed-Dahab. In May 1981 elections were held for representatives from the province to the Moroccan Chamber of Representatives. Nevertheless, outside the towns, only a small area of this newly-annexed territory could strictly be said to be under Moroccan control, and, as a result, Morocco's military resources were considerably stretched. Polisario forces swiftly retaliated, and numerous battles took place during the next 18 months, often within Morocco's original borders and particularly around the garrison town of Zak. In 1980 Morocco resorted to defensive tactics, concentrating on the *triangle utile* between the towns of El-Aaiún, Bou Craa and Es-Smara. This area, containing most of the population and the chief phosphate mines, was to be protected by a line of defences about 600 km long, which was completed in May 1982, and the sand wall was further extended, from Zak to the Mauritanian frontier, in 1984.

Early in 1981 there were reports that Polisario, previously based only in Algeria, had set up bases in Mauritania, while in March the Mauritanians blamed Morocco for an attempted coup and suspended diplomatic relations. In April Col Qaddafi, the Libyan leader, proposed that Mauritania and Western Sahara should unite, and the two countries issued a joint condemnation of Morocco's occupation of the territory.

DIPLOMATIC INITIATIVES

During the early years of the Western Sahara conflict, the international community gradually recognized the SADR. In November 1979 the UN General Assembly adopted a resolution confirming the legitimacy of the Polisario Front's struggle for independence, and a year later it urged Morocco to end its occupation of Western Sahara. By February 1981, the fifth anniversary of the declaration of the republic, the SADR had been recognized by about 45 Governments. Earlier, at the OAU's annual summit meeting in July 1980, a majority (26 out of 50 countries) approved the admission of the SADR. Morocco, however, argued that a two-thirds majority was necessary, and threatened to leave the OAU if the SADR was admitted. The decision was referred to the committee of 'wise men', who recommended that a cease-fire be established by December, followed by a referendum, to be supervised jointly by the OAU and the UN. In June 1981, at the OAU summit conference, King Hassan agreed for the first time to a referendum, to be held according to OAU recommendations. However, Morocco still refused to negotiate directly with the Polisario Front, and insisted that the proposed referendum be based on the 1974 Spanish census of the area, which enumerated only 74,000 inhabitants. The Polisario Front stipulated that, before the poll could take place, Morocco must withdraw its troops and administration to a considerable distance inside its original borders, and allow refugees living in Algeria to return and participate in the referendum; and that an interim international administration be established. However, the conditions of the referendum were never finally agreed by all the parties concerned.

In October 1981 Moroccan aircraft were shot down near Guelta Zemmour by what Morocco claimed to be Soviet-built SAM-6 surface-to-air missiles. Mauritania was accused of allowing Polisario forces to establish bases on its soil, and of taking part in the attack itself. In response, King Hassan asked the USA for increased military assistance. Several visits by high-ranking US officials culminated in talks, in February 1982, between the Moroccan Government and Alexander Haig, then US Secretary of State, as a result of which US military aid to Morocco was tripled. In May the USA and Morocco signed a military co-operation accord providing for the establishment of US military aircraft bases on Moroccan territory in the event of crises in the Middle East or Africa. The accord, initially for six years, was to be automatically renewed unless either country gave two years' notice of cancellation.

The situation deteriorated further during that month, when the SADR delegation was admitted to a meeting of the OAU Council of Ministers in Addis Ababa. The Moroccan delegation withdrew in protest, and was followed by representatives of 18 other countries. Observers considered this to be the most serious crisis within the OAU since its inception, and it was feared that the organization's very future might be at risk. Subsequent OAU meetings often had to be postponed, since no quorum could be reached. However, in June 1983 the SADR delegation agreed not to attend an OAU summit meeting in Addis Ababa, thus ending the Moroccan boycott. The issue of the continuing conflict in Western Sahara was considered again at this summit, and the meeting adopted a resolution appealing for an immediate cease-fire; for direct negotiations to be held between the Polisario Front and the Moroccan Government; and for the proposed referendum on the issue of self-determination to be held in Western Sahara before the end of the year. Morocco still refused to hold talks with the Polisario Front, but once again agreed in principle to a referendum, although King Hassan stated that he would not necessarily consider Morocco to be bound by its result. However, Morocco and the Polisario Front still disputed who should be allowed to vote, and the referendum, scheduled for December 1983, did not take place.

PROGRESS TOWARDS DEMOCRACY

King Hassan won great domestic prestige and popularity from the Saharan take-over. The staging of the Green March had particularly captured the imagination of the Moroccan people. At last, Hassan felt himself secure enough to hold the long-awaited elections. With the exception of the UNFP, the opposition parties agreed to participate, despite the continuation of political trials arising from the March 1973 uprising, which resulted in heavy prison sentences for many of the accused in early 1977. Municipal elections were held in November 1976, followed by provincial elections in January 1977 and elections for professional and vocational chambers in March. At each election, independents, mostly pro-government and conservative, won more than 60% of the seats. Istiqlal and the USFP protested against electoral irregularities and administrative interference. On 1 March four party leaders, including Muhammad Boucetta of Istiqlal and Abd ar-Rahim Bouabid of the USFP, agreed to join the Government as Ministers of State without portfolio, in the hope of ensuring that the national elections would be fairly conducted. Before the national elections were held, press censorship was abolished. In June a new Chamber of Representatives was elected, signifying a return to parliamentary democracy after 12 years of direct rule. Of the 264 members in the new Chamber, 176 were directly elected on 3 June and 88 chosen by an electoral college on 21 June. Independents won 141 seats (including 60 by indirect election), while Istiqlal and the MP won 49 and 44 respectively, the USFP won 16 and other opposition parties 14. The new Government, announced in October, included former opposition members, notably Muhammad Boucetta as Minister of Foreign Affairs, with seven other members of Istiqlal, four members of the MP and Maati Bouabid of the UNFP, whose party, however, subsequently disowned him. Thus, the King gained the co-operation of the major part of the opposition, and appeared to have succeeded in his plan to combine democracy with strong royal authority.

Among the Moroccan people support for the war appeared solid, but there were signs of discontent which could be partly attributed to the heavy cost of the fighting. During the first few months of 1979 there were strikes by many different sections of the work-force, demanding higher wages. On 21 March the Prime Minister, Ahmad Osman, resigned, ostensibly to devote himself to the organization of the newly-formed Rassemblement National des Indépendants (RNI; in 1980 the rural branch of this party seceded to form the Parti des Indépendants Démocrates (PID), which included several Cabinet ministers). He was replaced by Maati Bouabid, the Minister of Justice and a former trade union leader. The new Prime Minister held talks with union leaders, after which wage rises were announced, including an increase of 40% in the minimum wage. Although this provided a temporary respite from social unrest, it could only add to the burden on the economy.

During 1980 attempts were made to cut spending on education, which accounted for nearly a quarter of the current budget. Student strikes ensued, supported by the USFP and PPS, and unrest continued between 1981 and 1983. In June 1981 at least 66 people were killed in Casablanca during a general strike against reductions in food subsidies. The USFP and the trade union organization, the Confédération Démocratique du Travail (CDT), were accused of fomenting this unrest. All CDT offices were closed, and union activists were arrested. Following USFP criticism of government Saharan policy in September, its leader Abd ar-Rahim Bouabid, and other senior officials were sentenced to terms of imprisonment, and the two USFP newspapers were suspended.

Further opposition was aroused in October by the implementation of the constitutional changes approved by referendum in May 1980, particularly the clause extending the maximum period between elections to the Chamber of Representatives from four to six years: the next parliamentary elections were thus postponed until 1983. The opposition parties were angered by the prolonged life of a body which, they maintained, had been irregularly elected in the first place, and in which the majority parties were guilty of absenteeism and passivity. Consequently, all 14 USFP deputies withdrew temporarily from the Chamber of Representatives, and in November all RNI ministers lost their portfolios in a Cabinet reshuffle.

Abd ar-Rahim Bouabid was pardoned in March 1982, and CDT and USFP offices were allowed to reopen in April. However, many CDT activists remained in prison and the ban on USFP newspapers was not withdrawn until 1983, when the USFP commenced publication of a new newspaper.

The result of the June 1983 municipal elections, decisively won by pro-government centre-right parties, was challenged by the opposition parties on the grounds of electoral irregularities. A general election for a new Chamber of Representatives was due to take place in September 1983 but was postponed until after the proposed referendum on Western Sahara. However, as the date of the referendum remained uncertain, legislative elections were eventually announced for 14 September 1984. The existing Government reached the end of its six-year mandate in November 1983 and was replaced by a caretaker 'Government of national unity', formed by King Hassan. The new Government was headed by Muhammad Karim Lamrani, an administrator chosen for his lack of party affiliation (who had also been Prime Minister in 1971–72), and included representatives of the six main political parties. It was to be responsible for organizing the general election and for drafting an economic programme for 1984.

In January 1984 the Government announced imminent increases in the prices of basic foodstuffs and in education fees. This provoked violent street riots in several northern towns. Troops were summoned to quell the disturbances and, in several instances, opened fire on demonstrators. Unofficial estimates of the number of civilians killed in the riots were as high as 110. The rioting eventually subsided after King Hassan announced the suspension of the planned price increases. An estimated 1,800 people were detained during the riots, many of whom subsequently received prison sentences of up to 10 years.

TEMPORARY IMPROVEMENTS IN REGIONAL RELATIONS

Relations between Morocco and Algeria improved considerably in the first half of 1983, following a summit meeting in February between King Hassan and President Chadli of Algeria. This meeting resulted in the opening in April of the Morocco-Algeria border to Moroccans resident in Algeria and Algerians resident in Morocco. The *rapprochement* continued in April with a meeting in Tangier of political parties from Morocco, Algeria and Tunisia, at which representatives called for the creation of a Great Arab Maghreb—a political and economic union in north-west Africa.

In August 1984 King Hassan and Col Qaddafi of Libya signed the Arab-African Federation Treaty at Oujda, Morocco, which established a 'union of states' between their countries as the first step towards the creation of a Great Arab Maghreb. The Oujda Treaty, as it became known, provided for close economic and political co-operation between Morocco and Libya, and for mutual defence in the event of attack. The treaty was to take effect only after approval by the peoples of each country. A referendum was therefore held in Morocco on 31 August, and the treaty was approved by 99.97% of voters. Libya's General People's Congress backed the agreement unanimously. Following the alliance of Algeria, Tunisia and Mauritania, through the Maghreb Fraternity and Co-operation Treaty, initiated in March 1983, and Mauritania's recognition of the SADR in February 1984, Morocco had found itself isolated in the Maghreb. By signing the treaty of union with Libya, Morocco not only gained an ally (though an unlikely one, considering the contrast between Morocco's pro-Western stance and Libya's radicalism under Qaddafi), but also persuaded Col Qaddafi to cut off Libyan aid to Polisario.

Polisario responded to the *rapprochement* with Libya by launching the 'Greater Maghreb Offensive', a major military initiative which resulted in widespread fighting in southern Morocco. At the same time, Muhammad Abd al-Aziz, President of the SADR, undertook an extensive African tour to gather support prior to the November summit of the OAU in Addis Ababa. As a result, the SADR delegation was seated at the summit with few objections from other states. However, Morocco resigned from the OAU in protest, thus becoming the first State to leave the organization.

Although Polisario claimed to have killed 5,673 Moroccan soldiers between 1982 and 1985, decisive victories proved elusive, owing to Morocco's defensive strategy of building a 2,500-km wall of sand, equipped with electronic detectors, to surround Western Sahara. At the UN General Assembly in October 1975, Morocco announced a unilateral cease-fire in Western Sahara on the condition that there was no aggression against territories under its jurisdiction, and that it would be ready to hold a referendum in the territory in January 1986. However, the latter offer was withdrawn in November, after the UN Decolonization Committee supported a settlement of the conflict through direct negotiations between Morocco and the Polisario Front. The Moroccan Minister of Foreign Affairs, Abd al-Latif Filali, announced that Morocco would boycott all UN discussions on Western Sahara, as the Government considered such discussions to be futile. In April and May 1986 a series of proximity talks between Morocco and Polisario took place through the UN and OAU, but failed to reach a resolution. By the end of 1985, Morocco appeared to be increasingly isolated, as 64 countries had officially recognized the SADR, and US-Moroccan relations remained uneasy, following Morocco's signature of the Oujda Treaty with Libya in 1984.

DOMESTIC AFFAIRS

About 67% of the electorate participated in elections to the Chamber of Representatives in September 1984. Despite widespread gains by the USFP (which won 36 seats), the legislature was again dominated by the centre-right parties, which together controlled 206 of the 306 seats. In October King Hassan invited the leaders of the six main parties to submit their planned programmes to enable him to choose a coalition Government. Meanwhile, the previous 'Government of national unity' remained in office. King Hassan finally named a new Government in April 1985. The Government, again led by Muhammad Karim Lamrani, was a coalition of four centre-right parties: the Union Constitutionnelle (UC), the RNI, the MP and the Parti National Démocrate (as the PID had been renamed). The new Government did not include any members of Istiqlal or the USFP, which had participated in the previous

Government. Lamrani presented the new Government's programme to the Chamber of Representatives on 22 April. Its policies included increased privatization, the decentralization of health and education, and reforms of the civil service and the education system. In September 1986 Lamrani resigned, owing to ill health, and was replaced by the Deputy Prime Minister and Minister of Education, Az ad-Dine Laraki.

Meanwhile, the Government mounted a campaign of repression against organizations which it deemed to pose a threat to internal security. In August 1985 26 members of a left-wing movement, Jeunesse Islamique (Islamic Youth), were charged with plotting to overthrow the monarchy and to establish an Islamic state; in September 14 were sentenced to death. A further 28 people were charged in October with membership of a clandestine fundamentalist group, the Moudjahedine Movement, and with subversive activities. In February 1986 27 left-wing activists were imprisoned for subversion. At their trial, the prosecuting counsel had claimed that the defendants were financed by the Polisario Front. Following Arab antipathy to the Morocco-Israeli initiative in July (see below), the Government introduced anti-terrorist measures in August, including entry restrictions for visitors from Arab countries. In the same month, four foreigners were arrested on charges of possessing explosives and plotting to bomb a synagogue in Casablanca. In November three people were imprisoned for membership of an illegal Marxist-Leninist organization, al-Kaaidiyine, and for disturbing public order.

In late 1986 and early 1987 King Hassan granted a series of pardons to both political and non-political detainees. In October 1987 the authorities announced that the family of Gen. Oufkir, who had staged an abortive coup attempt in 1972, would be allowed to emigrate, after 15 years in detention. However, the family were not released until March 1991, although Muhammad Ait Kaddour, who had been involved in one of the attempts to shoot down the King's aircraft, was pardoned after his return to Morocco.

In 1988 Morocco joined the UN Human Rights Commission and subsequently attempted to improve its reputation concerning human rights. For several years, political prisoners had held sporadic hunger strikes to focus attention on poor prison conditions, and in January 1988 the Paris-based Moroccan human rights group, the Association des Droits de l'Homme au Maroc (ADHM), organized demonstrations in France, Belgium, the Netherlands and the Federal Republic of Germany against alleged abuses of human rights in Morocco. The ADHM also drew attention to clashes between students and government forces in Fez earlier that month. The Moroccan authorities had claimed that one person died and 21 were wounded during the disturbances, but the ADHM alleged that casualties had been much more numerous, and that more than 400 subsequent arrests had been made. In May it was reported that about 12 suspected members of Ilal Amam, who had been arrested during the previous two months in a government campaign against Ilal Amam activists, had been released, along with Abdullah Zaidy, a lawyer whose arrest in December 1987 and sentence to three years' imprisonment for attacking 'sacred institutions' had attracted condemnation from the International Commission of Jurists. In the same month living conditions for political prisoners were reported to have been improved. However, the first meeting of the newly-formed human rights association, the Organisation Marocaine des Droits de l'Homme (OMDH), scheduled for late May, was postponed until the end of June, owing to government objections that some of its members were also members of 'banned extremist groups'. In August 1988 King Hassan ordered the release of 341 detainees to commemorate the 25th anniversary of the exile of Sultan Muhammad ibn Yousuf. The release of political prisoners continued, and about 2,000 were freed in the first six months of 1989. The most notable, freed at the end of the Islamic holy month of Ramadan, were 50 extremists, including 31 of those who had been imprisoned in February 1977 for complicity in the alleged scheme to establish a republic under the Jewish mining engineer, Abraham Serfaty. The others, some of whom were religious fundamentalists, had been arrested after the Marrakesh riots of 1984.

The question of political prisoners attracted more international attention to Morocco during 1989 and the first half of 1990 than any other issue. While the King tended to deny that there were any political prisoners, he did acknowledge their existence on one occasion when he remarked that they could be divided into three categories—those opposed to the Monarchy, Islam or the Saharan War. Large numbers continued to be released—200 in June 1989, 388 in July to commemorate the Islamic festival of Id al-Adha, 347 in August on the anniversary of the exile of Muhammad V, more than 200 in October for the Prophet's birthday, 288 in January 1990, 418 on Throne Day in March and 322 at the end of Ramadan in April. In June 1989 six of the Ilal Amam prisoners in Rabat jail went on hunger strike in an abortive attempt to gain the status of political prisoners. They were transferred to hospitals, where one of them died after 64 days but was immediately replaced by another.

The imprisonment of Islamic fundamentalists provoked condemnation from other quarters, including the Iranian Government, which had seemed unconcerned about the fate of left-wingers. As far back as 1974 Abd al-Salam Yassin had criticized the State for failing to observe Islamic precepts, and later he was imprisoned several times. It was not until 1989, however, that his followers, who had formed a group called Al Adl wa-'l Ihsan (Justice and Charity), seemed to alarm the Government, although the group had been refused official registration in 1982. In November 24 of its members were charged with belonging to an unauthorized organization, holding unauthorized meetings and possessing documents which threatened state security. The conviction of 17 of the accused and the placing of Sheikh Yassin under house arrest led to demonstrations by the organization's followers and further arrests. Although the King denounced the intolerance of 'non-progressive' fundamentalists and, in particular, their attitude to women, militant fundamentalists dominated the universities. In January 1990 the Government ordered the dissolution of Al Adl wa-'l Ihsan, arrested five of its members who were presumed to be its executive committee and sentenced them to terms of imprisonment ranging from nine months to two years. Four were released on appeal, while the fifth had his sentence commuted. On 10 May thousands of fundamentalists demonstrated in Rabat, bringing the capital to a halt; an estimated 2,000 were reportedly arrested, of whom many had also been beaten; all were subsequently released.

In April 1988, prompted in part by World Bank pressure, the King told Parliament that the state should retain sole control of strategic industries and sell off the remainder, including sugar refineries, bus services and possibly water and electricity. There was considerable debate over which industries should be retained in the public sector, while the trade unions were concerned about job losses resulting from privatization of state companies. It was not until October 1989, therefore, that real progress was made, following the appointments of a new Governor of the Central Bank and of a minister in charge of privatization. In December Parliament approved, by 78 votes to 45, a list of 113 enterprises to be privatized, including four leading banks, 37 hotels, the Nador steelworks and the tea and sugar monopolies. The legislation ensured that the monopolies would not fall under foreign control and that there would be opportunities for employees to buy shares in their firms; the process was expected to take six years. While foreign capital would be welcomed, the Government's priority was to create a larger national share-owning class. The moribund Bourse at Casablanca was revived. Morocco already had one of the most liberal economies in the developing world. There were emerging plans for free-trade zones and the King spoke of the country as a larger version of Hong Kong, ideally placed to trade with the European Community (EC).

At the end of 1988 the country suffered a period of industrial unrest, as strikes took place in mines, flour mills, the oil refinery at Mohamadiyyah and Air Maroc, until a series of pay settlements restored order. Mahjoub Ben Seddiq, who had led the largest trade union, the Union Marocaine du Travail (UMT), since its foundation in 1955, was re-elected Secretary-General. After the King's Throne Day speech in March 1990 (in which he appealed to the people to accept austerity because of the economic situation), demands for a general strike were ignored, following Government promises that food subsidies would be retained and that grievances would be discussed. On May Day the minimum wage was raised by 10%.

In December 1989 Hassan proposed a two-year postponement of the forthcoming general election, in order to accommodate the referendum to be held in Western Sahara. A referendum which showed that only 0.05% opposed the plan demonstrated the lack of popular interest in party politics at a time when no members of the Cabinet were party politicians. In late May 1990, for the first time in the 26-year history of the Chamber of Representatives, the opposition proposed a motion expressing 'no confidence' in the Government, criticizing its record on human rights and the revised budget. Although the motion was defeated by 200 votes to 82, it remained a significant precedent.

In December 1990 more than 20 people were alleged to have been killed in the city of Fez during a general strike, the first in Morocco since 1984. Demonstrators demanded a wage increase commensurate with rapidly rising prices; riots broke out, and government buildings and hotels were set on fire. Following two days of rioting, security was increased in Fez and Rabat, where tanks patrolled the streets and security forces guarded government buildings. The Government announced that a commission was to be established to ascertain the number of persons who had been killed and the circumstances of their deaths. In late December more than 100 people were accused of rioting, and received prison sentences. In March 1991 it was estimated by Amnesty International that more than 1,500 people had been detained in connection with the riots. It was widely accepted that rising frustration at the country's socio-economic problems had precipitated these events. This was confirmed when the commission published its report, which showed that the outbreak could not be attributed to organized subversion.

Industrial unrest continued throughout 1991 and into 1992. There were numerous strikes by government employees, health workers, teachers, the post office and nationalized industries. There was also violence as in June 1991, when 104 workers were injured in a clash with police at a textile factory. Despite the establishment of a National Council for Youth and the Future (which aimed to provide 300,000 new jobs), the problem of youth unemployment was highlighted in October, when 100,000 out-of-work graduates established a national association to present their case. Wage rises failed to keep pace with inflation, and a government announcement in early 1991 that the minimum wage would be raised by 15% was rejected by two of the trade unions, which demanded that it be doubled to 2,000 dirhams (about $250) per month. In January 1992 three trade union militants received prison sentences ranging from five to 10 months.

As in other Maghreb countries, many of the unemployed saw their salvation in Islamic fundamentalism. Some of the leaders of the banned group Al Adl wa-'l Ihsan, including Sheikh Yassin, remained in detention, and in April 1991 eight other members were arrested (although subsequently released). In May Adl and other opposition groups participated in a demonstration in Casablanca, in which an estimated 100,000 people demanded measures to enshrine the sovereignty of the people and reduce the powers of the King. At the same time, they denounced the proposed referendum in Western Sahara, asserting that the territory should simply be annexed to Morocco. The repression of the FIS in Algeria was welcomed by the Government, despite apprehension that local militants might conclude that their aims were not to be achieved by the democratic process. In September the Government approached the imprisoned Adl leaders, offering recognition as a legitimate party on certain conditions, including acceptance of the monarchy and a petition for pardon. However, the leaders made their release a pre-condition of any negotiations, and the initiative foundered.

Despite the creation (in May 1990) of the Consultative Council on Human Rights, humanitarian organizations continued to criticize the Government. In May 1991 the OMDH, headed by Khalid Nauri, held its inaugural conference, at which speakers denounced the arbitrary treatment, and even torture, of prisoners, and the lack of contact with their families. In July the Government refused to defend its record

before a UN panel in Geneva, because of the presence of French television cameras. In March 1991 Amnesty International claimed that 1,500 people had been detained in the previous few months, many for demonstrating against the despatch of troops to the Gulf War. In September Abraham Sertaty, the longest-serving political prisoner in Africa, was freed and expelled from the country. In the same month, in celebration of the Prophet's birthday, 119 prisoners were released, bringing the total for the year to more than 5,000, and the notorious Tazmamart jail, whose existence the government never admitted, was destroyed. During the winter of 1991–92 most of the remaining prisoners who had been condemned for the attempts on the King's life in 1971 and 1972 were freed. In December representatives of 23 political and humanitarian organizations, meeting in Casablanca, demanded the release of political prisoners and an amensty for exiles.

AN ACTIVE PERIOD IN FOREIGN AFFAIRS: 1986–92

In 1986 and 1987 Morocco made determined efforts to improve its relations with the USA and other Western nations, in order to increase military and diplomatic support for its policy in Western Sahara. In April 1986 King Hassan, as chairman of the Arab League, suspended a summit meeting, following Libya's insistence that the US raids on Libya on 15 April should be the sole topic on the agenda. In June King Hassan proposed the foundation of a 'Maghreb Community Consultative Committee', comprising Algeria, Morocco and Tunisia, thus isolating Libya.

In July 1986 King Hassan held two days of talks with Shimon Peres, the Israeli Prime Minister, at Ifrane, in Morocco, in an effort to salvage the peace initiative in the Middle East; he thus became the first Arab head of state to meet an Israeli leader since the late President Sadat of Egypt. However, the meeting merely highlighted the divisions between Israel and the moderate Arab states on means of resolving the conflict in the Middle East. Arab reaction was mixed: Syria immediately broke off diplomatic relations with Morocco; Libya condemned Morocco; while Egypt, Kuwait and Jordan supported the initiative. Following criticism of the meeting, King Hassan resigned as chairman of the Arab League. In August Libya attempted to improve relations with Morocco by reaffirming support for the Oujda Treaty, but this was abrogated by Hassan at the end of the month. The Moroccan-Israeli initiative and the abrogation of the Oujda Treaty resulted in a dramatic improvement in US-Moroccan relations by September 1986. The two countries held joint military exercises in November, and in July 1987 the US Defence Department approved the sale to Morocco of 100 M-48A5 tanks, suitable for use in desert terrain, along with other military equipment. Morocco re-emphasized its status as a moderate pro-Western Arab state by re-establishing diplomatic relations with Egypt in November, and in January 1988 the USA announced that Morocco was willing to allow US forces to resume 'partial activities' on Moroccan territory.

In the hope of gaining wider European support for its policy in Western Sahara and improved trading links, Morocco applied to join the EC in July 1987. In August an accord was reached with the EC, whereby Morocco extended, for a further five months, the 1983 fishing treaty with Spain, which was due to expire at the end of the month. During this period, negotiations on a new fishing agreement were held with the EC, as Spain had joined the Community in 1986. In October, however, the EC rejected Morocco's application for membership, on the grounds that Morocco was not a European country.

Hassan insisted that the movement towards a unified Maghreb did not preclude Morocco's ambition to join the EC. The European Parliament had on several occasions criticized Morocco for its policy in the Western Sahara and for repression at home, but in May 1988 the West German Minister of Foreign Affairs stated that the reforms which were to be implemented in 1992 would provide Morocco with great opportunities for trade and, consequently, aid from the Community was substantially increased to $392m. During a visit to Morocco in March 1989 the UK Prime Minister, Margaret Thatcher, said that there was no realistic possibility of Morocco's joining the EC, and in the following month, in Luxembourg at a meeting of the EC's Moroccan Co-operation Council, the Moroccan

Minister of Foreign Affairs, Abd al-Latif Filali, blamed Europe for protectionism which had damaged Moroccan exports.

In January 1987 King Hassan proposed the creation of a 'reflection cell' to consider the future of the Spanish African enclaves of Ceuta and Melilla, but Spain showed no willingness to discuss their sovereignty. In July, however, the Spanish Minister of Foreign Affairs visited Rabat and agreed to further discussions on the future of the enclaves. In June 1988 a bilateral trading agreement was signed; in July discussions were held over the installation of an electric cable under the Strait of Gibraltar, and in September an agreement was signed for the construction of a pipeline across Moroccan territory, connecting the oil fields of Algeria with consumers in Europe. In August Ahmad Alaoui, a Minister without portfolio, stated that the time was right to negotiate over the enclaves, a proposal for which Spain showed a predictable lack of enthusiasm. Although Spain refused to allow Polisario to reopen its office in Madrid, in October it voted against Morocco at the UN debate on the Western Sahara; in protest Hassan cancelled an official visit scheduled for November. Morocco could not, however, afford to pursue the quarrel, when Spain was about to assume the Presidency of the EC and a visit by Prime Minister González in May 1989 showed that amicable relations had been restored. In September King Hassan visited Spain and signed accords on defence, including joint military exercises, technology transfers and bilateral summits to be held annually.

Hassan has also played a prominent role in Arab relations. The Arab League summit meeting, held in Casablanca in May 1989, was a considerable triumph for Moroccan diplomacy since it brought Syria, with whom diplomatic relations had been restored through the mediation of the Saudi Arabian Crown Prince in January, together with Iraq, while Col Qaddafi of Libya consented to meet President Mubarak of Egypt. The meeting itself was less successful, for there was acrimonious disagreement over Lebanon. However, consensus was reached on the Palestinian *intifada,* which had evoked strong emotions in Morocco. The King was appointed, together with King Fahd of Saudi Arabia and President Chadli of Algeria, to head a Tripartite Arab Committee on Lebanon in order to seek a solution to the Lebanese conflict and to advocate the Palestinian case to the world. In practice the work was done by their respective Ministers of Foreign Affairs. In April 1990, following a meeting with the King, Yasser Arafat announced Hassan's intention to request the Heads of State Committee to work towards the convening of an international conference on the plight of Palestinians. He also stated that the King intended to visit the capitals of the five permanent members of the UN Security Council to draw their attention to the growing number of Soviet Jews settling in Israel. As Chairman of the OIC, Hassan was also expected to try to persuade the US Government not to recognize Jerusalem as the capital of Israel.

THE WESTERN SAHARA CONFLICT: 1986–87

During 1986 Polisario forces attacked several foreign fishing vessels in the Atlantic, off the Western Saharan coast, which the Polisario Front terms a 'war zone'. After a major outbreak of fighting between Moroccan troops and Polisario forces in February 1987, Morocco claimed to have repelled a major Polisario offensive near the Algerian border. In the same month the SADR representative in Algiers claimed that an attempted assassination of the SADR President, Muhammad Abd al-Aziz, had been foiled, and alleged that the Moroccan Minister of the Interior was implicated in the plot.

Tension in Western Sahara increased in April 1987, when Morocco completed the construction of its defensive wall on the southern border of the territory, parallel with the Mauritanian border. Mauritania protested that its neutrality was threatened, since Polisario troops might have to pass through Mauritanian territory to reach the Atlantic, and Algeria expressed its concern and confirmed its support for Mauritania. In April Hassan ordered a boycott by Morocco of all Palestinian events, after senior Polisario members attended a meeting of the Palestine National Council in Algiers.

A *rapprochement* between Morocco and Algeria was effected in May 1987, at a summit meeting attended by King

Hassan and the Algerian President, Ben Djedid Chadli, under the auspices of King Fahd of Saudi Arabia. The two leaders discussed the conflict in Western Sahara and issued a joint communiqué after the meeting, which stated that the two countries would remain in consultation. Before the meeting, Polisario urged a direct dialogue between Morocco and Polisario, and attacked King Fahd's role as mediator. Later in the month, 102 Algerian prisoners in Morocco were exchanged for 150 Moroccan prisoners in Algeria, and King Hassan sent an emissary to President Chadli with proposals to establish two joint commissions to settle various bilateral disputes. In July, after Col Qaddafi had proposed a union of Libya and Algeria, King Hassan met the Algerian Minister of Foreign Affairs, who delivered a message from President Chadli.

MOVES TOWARDS A SOLUTION IN WESTERN SAHARA

Meanwhile, the UN and the OAU made a concerted effort to settle the conflict in Western Sahara. In July 1987 UN missions visited Morocco, Algeria and the Congo to examine the possibility of organizing a UN-sponsored referendum on the question of self-determination in Western Sahara. In the same month there were signs of a *rapprochement* between Polisario and Morocco, following indirect talks in Geneva, under the auspices of the UN and the OAU. Afterwards, King Hassan announced that he would be willing to accept the results of the referendum, and Polisario issued a statement which welcomed some of Hassan's proposals. However, after the talks, further fighting broke out between Moroccan and Polisario forces near the Mauritanian border.

Polisario announced a three-week truce in November 1987 to coincide with a visit by a UN-OAU technical mission to Morocco, Western Sahara and Polisario refugee camps in Algeria, in order to assess conditions for holding a referendum. Although both Morocco and Polisario agreed on the need for a referendum, Morocco rejected Polisario's demand that the Moroccan armed forces and administration should withdraw from Western Sahara, and that the territory should be placed under an interim UN administration before the referendum. Morocco also refused to hold direct talks with Polisario representatives (a Polisario precondition of negotiations), as officially it continued to view Polisario as a front organization for Algerian mercenaries. In January 1988 Polisario renewed attacks on Moroccan positions in Western Sahara. Meanwhile, the UN announced that it was drafting detailed proposals for a cease-fire and a referendum. In April the President of the OAU, Dr Kenneth Kaunda of Zambia, visited Morocco, Western Sahara and Polisario refugee camps to discuss the conclusions of the UN technical mission. By mid-1988 a total of 71 countries had granted diplomatic recognition to the SADR.

RESTORATION OF DIPLOMATIC RELATIONS WITH ALGERIA AND MOVES TOWARDS MAGHREB UNITY

The conflict in Western Sahara was regarded by the other Maghreb nations as an obstacle to regional unity, and in late 1987 and 1988 they attempted to isolate Morocco, with the aim of forcing the kingdom to negotiate with the Polisario Front. Meanwhile, Morocco reiterated its commitment to Maghreb unity, at meetings with President Chadli of Algeria in November 1987 and with President Ben Ali of Tunisia in February 1988, and took no part in moves by Algeria, Libya, Mauritania and Tunisia to create a four-country Great Arab Maghreb. However, the emergence of such a power bloc was forestalled by Libya's refusal to sign the Maghreb Fraternity and Co-operation Treaty without the addition of several unacceptable conditions, and in early May King Hassan received the Algerian deputy leader with an invitation from President Chadli for Morocco to attend the Arab League summit in June. Hassan promptly despatched two of his senior advisers to Algiers to hold further discussions with Chadli, and on 16 May both countries announced the re-establishment of full diplomatic relations. In May 1989 a 1972 treaty with Algeria, on the demarcation of the joint border, was finally ratified by Morocco. These developments were considered to be a victory for Morocco and an apparent retreat by Algeria from its previous position that diplomatic relations could be resumed only if Morocco held direct talks with the Polisario Front. Following the *rapprochement* with Algeria, Morocco became fully involved in regional efforts to establish a Great Arab Maghreb, and attended the first Maghreb summit, held in June 1988.

Diplomatic relations improved further, as it became clear that Hassan and Chadli shared similar views on Maghreb unity. They rejected the Libyan concept of a vast 'superstate' but agreed on practical steps such as the abolition of visas, harmonization in economic, cultural and technical matters and joint ventures, which had been discussed at a bilateral meeting of Algeria and Morocco in October. In February 1989 at a meeting of North African Heads of State in Marrakesh, the Union of the Arab Maghreb (UAM), grouping Morocco with Algeria, Libya, Mauritania and Tunisia, was inaugurated. The new body aimed to promote unity by allowing free movement of goods, services and labour. King Hassan was appointed the first President of the UAM for the 1989/90 year. In October, at the first meeting of delegates from each national legislature, the former Prime Minister and brother-in-law of King Hassan, Ahmad Othman, was elected President of the UAM Assembly. In the same month the respective Ministers of Foreign Affairs met in Rabat and agreed to establish committees to discuss food, security, economic affairs, human resources and infrastructure. In January 1990 the national employers' organizations discussed closer co-operation, and in February a committee was created to co-ordinate petroleum policies. Plans were also drafted for the introduction of a common identity card which would serve as a travel document within the UAM. In February 1990 the Moroccan Chamber of Representatives endorsed two accords with Algeria; one for the establishment of joint ventures to consider proposals for the creation of a second gas pipeline to transport Algerian gas through Morocco to Europe; the other for closer economic and industrial relations. Morocco also increased its ties with Tunisia and Libya, which the King had visited for the first time in September 1989.

However, during late 1989 and early 1990 the renewal of the Polisario campaign provoked criticism of the Government within Morocco. Meanwhile, King Hassan continually stressed that the new alignment would not preclude Morocco's membership of the EC. Further divisions in the UAM surfaced in August 1990, following the invasion of Kuwait (see Kuwait and Iraq chapters). Whereas the other UAM members were slow to react, Morocco issued a vehement condemnation of the invasion, voted for the resolutions at the Arab summit condemning Iraq's action and agreed to contribute to the pan-Arab force defending Saudi Arabia. In mid-September 1990 King Hassan was host in Rabat to King Hussein of Jordan and President Chadli of Algeria in an attempt to launch a new peace initiative and avoid armed conflict. They failed, however, to persuade the Iraqi President, Saddam Hussain, to withdraw his troops from Kuwait. In October, however, the Iraqi President sent his Minister of Foreign Affairs, Tareq Aziz, and a Deputy Prime Minister, Taha Ramadan, to Rabat in an attempt to find a resolution. When these discussions failed, King Hassan attempted unsuccessfully to convene a summit meeting of the Arab League in November. By December some 1,500 Moroccan troops were stationed in Saudi Arabia, as part of the multinational alliance attempting to enforce Iraq's withdrawal from Kuwait.

However, in late January 1991, after pro-Iraqi demonstrations in Morocco, the Government gave implicit support to a one-day general strike, organized by the principal Moroccan trade unions to express solidarity with the Iraqi people. This action was reportedly taken by the Government in an attempt to ease internal political pressure, and to prevent any further disturbances, following the rioting of December 1990. Other members of the anti-Iraq alliance expressed concern that the Moroccan Government was not fully committed to the military campaign. In early February 1991 an estimated 300,000 people demonstrated in Rabat, where they denounced the war against Iraq and demanded that the Moroccan contingent withdraw from the multinational force. The Government, however, stressed that its troops were in the region to defend Saudi Arabia and not to force the withdrawal of Iraq from Kuwait. By late February the multinational force had liberated Kuwait from Iraqi occupation, and shortly afterwards Morocco, together with its fellow members of the UAM, demanded that the

sanctions which the UN had imposed on Iraq in August 1990 be immediately repealed.

UN PEACE PLAN FOR WESTERN SAHARA

In August 1988 the UN Secretary-General, Javier Pérez de Cuéllar, who had visited Morocco in May, announced that a detailed peace plan for Western Sahara had been drawn up and called for its approval by Morocco and Polisario by 1 September. The plan contained proposals for a cease-fire and a referendum to determine the status of Western Sahara. The implementation of the proposals was to be overseen by a UN representative with wide-ranging powers and a UN monitoring force comprising about 2,000 people. Prior to the referendum, Morocco was to reduce its presence in Western Sahara from 100,000 to 25,000 troops, who would then be confined to barracks, while Polisario forces (totalling an estimated 8,000) were to withdraw to their bases under UN supervision. Eligibility to vote in the referendum was to be decided by a UN team and was expected to be limited to those enumerated in the 1974 Spanish census of the then Spanish Sahara and to those born in Western Sahara. The referendum was to offer a choice between complete independence for the territory and its integration into Morocco; it was hoped that a further option would be added, offering a large measure of autonomy for the Sahrawi people under the Moroccan crown. On 30 August Morocco and the Polisario Front formally accepted the UN peace plan, although both sides expressed reservations.

However, the UN's expectation that a cease-fire could be secured within a month, and the referendum held within six months, seemed increasingly optimistic. Moreover, the belief that the UN proposals had been unconditionally accepted by both parties was undermined when the Polisario Front, at the beginning of September 1988, declared that the UN could arrange a cease-fire by the end of 1988 if Morocco was prepared to hold direct talks with its representatives. In mid-September Polisario forces attacked Moroccan troops at the Oum Dreiga section of the defensive wall, facing the Mauritanian border. Polisario was reported to have deployed 2,500 men, and there were more than 200 Moroccan casualties. There was increasing speculation that Polisario had mounted the offensive to demonstrate its ability to inflict substantial damage on Morocco without Algerian support, and to emphasize the need for Morocco to hold direct negotiations before a solution could be reached. Polisario representatives maintained that all Moroccan troops, administrators and colonists must be withdrawn before the proposed referendum, but two Cabinet reshuffles within a month suggested serious differences within their leadership. Meanwhile, the Moroccan Minister of Foreign Affairs, Abd al-Latif Filali, stated that, since both sides had accepted the UN proposal for a cease-fire, there was no need for direct talks. In October the UN General Assembly agreed, by 87 votes to nil with 58 abstentions (which included Morocco and the USA), that direct talks should be held, followed by a cease-fire and a referendum. The UN Secretary-General, Pérez de Cuéllar, appointed a personal representative, Héctor Gros de Espiel (a Uruguayan), to visit the area in November or December. Meanwhile, the Algerian Government pressed the Saharans to make concessions, and the SADR President, Muhammad Abd al-Aziz, hinted that there would be no objection if 10,000 Moroccan troops remained during the period of the referendum. This was later denied by the SADR Minister of Foreign Affairs, Mohammed Sidati.

In December 1988 there was a significant change in Morocco's stance on the Western Sahara, when King Hassan finally agreed to meet officials of Polisario and the SADR. The meeting took place in Marrakesh in the first week of January 1989. This was the first direct contact for 13 years and was reported to have been limited to exchanges of goodwill; no negotiations took place. In February Polisario announced a unilateral cease-fire. A second meeting, originally planned to take place in February, was postponed by King Hassan. Polisario put further pressure on Morocco for full negotiations by threatening to take fresh military action. By mid-March no more discussions had taken place, and Polisario resumed hostilities, bringing the six-week cease-fire to an end. In May 1989 the Politburo of Polisario, meeting in Tindouf, sent a message to the King complaining that the projected second round of talks had not been held and asking him to assist the peace process; at the same time it dismissed two of its members for 'infantile attitudes'. At the seventh Polisario Front Congress, held in May, frustration over Hassan's reluctance to resume talks was expressed; Polisario reiterated its own willingness to pursue direct dialogue, in the hope of achieving a peaceful settlement to the war and announced that, as a gesture of goodwill, 200 Moroccan soldiers would be released. Their release, however, was postponed 'for technical reasons'.

In June 1989 Pérez de Cuéllar, who had held talks with the King and the Polisario leadership in Tindouf, and visited Algeria and Mauritania, declared himself 'confident of progress in the near future.' The UN established a technical commission to expedite the peace plan which both sides had formally accepted in August 1988. The issue of entitlement to vote in any referendum on the future of Western Sahara remained unresolved, however, owing to the ambiguous status of the Moroccan settlers in the area, who now outnumbered the original inhabitants by three to two.

Hassan's vacillation was probably due, in part, to the defection, in August 1989, of Omar Hadhrami (one of the six founders of the Polisario Front), two leading guerrilla commanders and the chief propagandist in Algiers. This seemed to underline splits in the movement between authentic Sahrawis and new members from Algeria and Mauritania. In addition, mass arrests had taken place in the camps, aid from Eastern Europe had ceased, and assistance from other Maghreb States was diminishing, with the result that rationing had been introduced. The King welcomed these 'lost sheep' back into the fold, and other defections followed. The Moroccan Government let it be known that it was ready to consider any approach from oil companies seeking concessions to prospect for petroleum deposits in Western Sahara.

In October 1989 Polisario forces launched a series of major attacks, which continued unabated for more than a month. During the offensive, 15 km of the defensive wall facing the Mauritanian border was reportedly destroyed and hundreds of Moroccan soldiers were killed. The Government, however, claimed that only 45 soldiers had been killed. The extent of the onslaught suggested that it could not have been launched without Algerian support. During the campaign the Polisario Front demanded direct talks with the Government, but the King refused to 'negotiate with his own subjects', threatened to continue the conflict indefinitely and announced his readiness to order his troops across international borders in pursuit of Polisario forces. Despite Polisario assertions that its forces would intensify the conflict, no further fighting took place.

In March 1990 the UN Secretary-General said that he was pleased to find 'a more propitious atmosphere' than he had encountered during his June 1989 visit, but expressed caution over any practical outcome. Both the Moroccan Government and Polisario hoped that the referendum could take place within six months, but remained divided over the extent of the franchise, the maintenance of security during the voting process and the question of which Moroccan forces would withdraw. In July and August 1990 a special UN technical commission visited Western Sahara and the neighbouring states to investigate the practical difficulties of conducting a referendum on the territory's future. In April 1991 the UN Security Council approved a resolution (No. 690) which authorized the establishment of a UN Mission for the Referendum in Western Sahara (MINURSO, see p. 206), which was to implement the plan for a referendum on self-determination, proposed by the UN Secretary-General in 1988. A UN peace-keeping force, comprising contingents from 36 countries (including the five permanent members of the UN Security Council), was to supervise the operation. In May 1991 the UN Security Council approved plans for a referendum in the disputed territory. The plebiscite was to take place in January 1992, at a cost of approximately $200m., and an estimated 1,695 troops, 300 police and 800 civilians were to participate in the operation, headed by a representative of the Secretary-General. An additional $34m. was required to finance a proposed programme to resettle eligible Sahrawi voters. Spain was to contribute to the cost of this project.

In May 1991 King Hassan visited Western Sahara (his third visit to the region since 1976), where he was met by approxi-

mately 100,000 people. In recognition of the contribution of local tribes in the conflict between Moroccan forces and the Polisario Front, the King created a new province, Assa-Zag, on the Algerian border. The royal visit coincided with the preparations for the referendum. It was announced that a peace-keeping force of 200,000 Moroccan troops would be stationed in the area in the interim. In the same month, the UN Secretary-General, Javier Pérez de Cuéllar, met King Hassan to discuss the UN peace plan for Western Sahara.

In June 1991 the Polisario Front held its eighth congress to discuss the UN-supervised referendum and the future direction of the movement. After 15 years of armed struggle, Polisario would need to formulate new policies if it gained power, including the introduction of a multi-party political system and a mixed economy. Later in the month, King Hassan, in response to appeals from Saharan tribes, granted an amnesty to all Sahrawi opponents, including members of Polisario and refugees abroad. A further unspecified number of prisoners, including left-wing leader Abraham Serfaty, were released in the following months. It was believed that the King granted the amnesty to refugees abroad as part of a campaign to persuade Sahrawi who were disillusioned with the Polisario Front to vote for integration into Morocco instead of independence from the kingdom.

In July 1991 it was announced that a cease-fire in Western Sahara would come into effect on 6 September, from which date the UN special representative, Johannes Manz, would supervise the preparations for a referendum. The Moroccan presence would be reduced from about 190,000 to 65,000 troops, and MINURSO would commence operation. Morocco rejected any role for the OAU in the area, while Istiqlal and other political parties declared the referendum futile, as the return of the Saharan provinces was irreversible. The Polisario Front promised to abide by the result. Morocco, however, continued a building programme to develop the Saharan provinces—an autoroute from Tangier to Nouadhibou (in Mauritania), a university and housing at Smara.

In early August 1991 a significant increase in hostilities developed, with the Polisario Front denouncing Moroccan air strikes, while the Moroccan Government stated that it was engaged in clearing 'no man's land': each side was trying to intimidate rival elements into leaving the area before the cease-fire. On 10 August, after receiving a report from Manz, Pérez de Cuéllar expressed deep concern, but, after meeting Moroccan Foreign Minister Filali, he remained hopeful that the cease-fire would come into effect. One obstacle was the Polisario Front's demand for release of men allegedly held as prisoners of war: Morocco denied that there were any, but some 200 detainees were nevertheless released.

The main obstacle to holding the referendum was that Manz had prepared an electoral roll of about 74,000, based on the Spanish census of 1974. The Moroccans presented an alternative list of about 120,000 who, they claimed, were natives of the area or their children who had been omitted from the census because, at the time, they were refugees. The UN representatives ruled that, while applications from individuals could be considered, a block list could not. The Moroccans used this dispute as a pretext to prevent the deployment of MINURSO; the Polisario Front countered by repeating its former claim that the total population was 207,000, of whom 167,000 were in 'liberated areas' or in refugee camps in Algeria and Mauritania. The King then asked the UN for a postponement of the referendum, as preparations had fallen behind schedule, but, after meeting Polisario representatives, Pérez de Cuéllar insisted that it should go ahead.

The first 100 members of MINURSO, under Gen. Armand Roy of Canada, flew into El-Aaiún, and the cease-fire took effect, as planned, on 6 September. Within a fortnight, however, each side had accused the other of violating the cease-fire, while the Polisario Front alleged that the Moroccan Minister of the Interior, Driss Basri, was organizing a 'second Green March' of 170,000 people for whom temporary accommodation was being built. There were few signs that Moroccans were reducing their military presence. Algerian support for the Polisario Front effectively ceased, and there were important defections from its ranks: the editor of its newspaper and its best-known female leader. Both sides also complained of UN bias. By the end of November 1991 MINURSO had only 240 men in the territory. Manz resigned in December, and there was difficulty in finding a replacement. The Polisario front complained that Morocco was planting mines in 'no man's land' and arresting its supporters. Pérez de Cuéllar appeared to side with Morocco by recommending that a vote be given to anyone whose father had been born in the territory or who had had intermittent residence there for 12 years before 1974. This proposal was, however, delayed in the UN Security Council and on 1 January 1992 his successor, Dr Boutros Boutros-Ghali, was asked for a report within two months; it became clear that the vote could not take place before September. A US Senate report criticized the functioning of MINURSO, and noted that it had received little support from the UN and even less from Morocco, which had even threatened to fire upon its patrols.

In March 1992 Boutros-Ghali's report concluded that, unless there were progress by the end of May, the whole UN policy should be reconsidered. He also stated that, of the 77 violations of the cease-fire reported by MINURSO, Morocco had been responsible for 75. It was not until the end of the month that a veteran Pakistani diplomat, Yaqub Khan, was appointed as successor to Manz. He visited the area in April, and in May Boutros-Ghali announced that the two sides were to hold indirect talks under his auspices. These took place in Geneva, Switzerland, but proved inconclusive.

In June 1992 the Moroccan Interior Minister, Driss Basri, visited Western Sahara to encourage the population to enroll on the electoral register. This message was repeated by Ibrahim Hakim, who, as a former Minister of Foreign Affairs of the SADR and ambassador to Algeria, was a significant defector to Morocco in August. Hakim claimed that the Algerian Government was no longer committed to the foundation of an autonomous state in Western Sahara. He was subsequently appointed as the King's itinerant ambassador. Polisario threatened to resume hostilities if the Moroccan referendum on constitutional reform, in September, were extended to Western Sahara. In the event, however, the Ministry of the Interior announced a 100% participation of the electorate in the area, unanimously in favour of the amendments. King Hassan stated that Western Sahara would receive priority in the allocation of development funds and also that Morocco would abide by the result of the UN referendum. Polisario claimed that demonstrations in Western Sahara against the communal elections in October had been forcibly suppressed, but once more the Moroccan Ministry of the Interior announced an overwhelming rate of voter participation in the region.

Following the assassination of Muhammad Boudiaf, the Algerian Head of State, in June 1992, relations between Morocco and Algeria were strained, and the latter was reported to be increasing its aid to Polisario. At the beginning of December two groups of Sahrawi notables, composed of equal numbers of representatives from within the wall and from the camps at Tindouf in Algeria, travelled to Geneva, Switzerland, for a meeting under the chairmanship of Yaqub Khan. The Tindoufis, however, refused to negotiate, claiming that the other delegation had altered its composition. In January 1993 a *rapprochement* between Morocco and Algeria was reported.

The President of the SADR accused the UN Security Council of losing interest in the Western Sahara dispute, and in January Boutros-Ghali reported that there was little prospect of success from continuing talks on their present basis. At the beginning of March he suggested three alternatives to the Council: efforts to organize talks could continue; the UN could impose the Pérez de Cuéllar list; or there could be an entirely fresh initiative. Under Resolution 809, the Council decreed that the referendum should take place before the end of 1993, with or without Polisario co-operation, that further efforts should be made to compile a satisfactory electoral list, and that Boutros-Ghali should undertake a new round of negotiations. Morocco accepted the resolution at once and, after some delay, Polisario agreed to do likewise.

In April 1993 the UN special envoy for Western Sahara, Yaqub Khan, held talks in Algiers with senior Algerian officials before meeting King Hassan in Rabat in order to prepare a report on the situation in Western Sahara. In May

a senior UN diplomat, Erik Jensen, was appointed to begin work on registering voters prior to the referendum. Morocco nevertheless included its 'Saharan provinces' in the kingdom's general election, held in June. Talks which took place in July at El-Ayoun were the first to be held in the disputed territory itself, but proved inconclusive. Morocco had enjoyed a propaganda success on the eve of the talks when a notable Sahrawi chief defected.

According to a communiqué issued by Polisario in Algiers in September, the SADR president, Muhammad Abd al-Aziz, nominated a new government for the region in that month. Bouchraya Hammoudi Bayoun was appointed to lead the government, with the hardliner Grahim Ghali as his minister of defence. In the same month it was reported that, of 1,600 UN military personnel appointed to Western Sahara, only 360 were, in fact, stationed in the territory.

On 26 November 1993 Boutros-Ghali informed the UN Security Council that, because of unresolved differences as to voter eligibility, the referendum about the future of the disputed territory could not take place before the middle of 1994. In March 1994 he announced a new approach, involving three options: to proceed with the referendum by the end of 1994, even if one or both sides in the dispute disagreed; to cancel the referendum and withdraw most of the UN peace-keeping force; or to continue with talks between Morocco and the Polisario Front in order to compile acceptable voter lists. At the end of April Jensen stated that Polisario, after some initial misgivings, had accepted a voter registration plan proposed under Security Council Resolution 907, and that voter registration would begin in June.

FOREIGN POLICY IN THE 1990s

Morocco has determined to play a full part in world affairs in the 1990s, and in the first two years of the decade it established diplomatic relations with Namibia, South Africa (the first Arab country to do so), Viet Nam, Estonia, Ukraine and Kyrgyzstan. In August 1990 Foreign Minister Filali visited all five permanent members of the Security Council, and in the same month, at a meeting of the Ministers of Foreign Affairs of the Organization of the Islamic Conference, in Istanbul, Morocco presented proposals to increase the group's international scope. In September, following a visit by the Chinese Deputy Minister of Geology and Mineral Resources, Song Riuxiang, Morocco and China signed an agreement on co-operation in energy and mining. In the following year Crown Prince Sidi Mohammed became the most important Moroccan to visit Beijing since the establishment of diplomatic relations in 1958. The visit was returned by the Chinese President, Yang Shangkun. In October 1991 Morocco was elected to the UN Security Council for a two-year term beginning on 1 January 1992 (it had previously been a member in 1962–63). The King addressed the Council, and later agreed to send troops to help keep the peace in Somalia. Other prominent figures to visit the country were Nelson Mandela and Jonas Savimbi.

Morocco was quick to capitalize on the good will that it had generated in Washington by its strong support during the Gulf War. It benefited from both bilateral aid and credits from US-dominated agencies, receiving more from the World Bank than any other country in the Middle East or North Africa. Wheat and vegetable oil were provided on credit, and Morocco acquired 20 used F-16 military aircraft for $250m. In return, it supported the US peace initiative in the Middle East, and the King offered Morocco as a venue for the Arab-Israeli peace conference and expressed willingness to receive Prime Minister Shamir of Israel. In August 1991 the Chairman of the Palestine Liberation Organization (PLO), Yasser Arafat, and the US Secretary of State, James Baker, visited Morocco within a few days of each other. The King made a fruitful visit to Washington in September, establishing closer relations with President Bush, and apparently securing US support for Morocco's policy on Western Sahara. He announced that an American University, specializing in science, would be established in Ifrane, with financial support from the USA and Saudi Arabia. The former US President, Ronald Reagan, visited the King, to the outrage of Colonel Qaddafi, who was even more enraged when Morocco, as a member of the UN Security Council, did not veto the imposition of sanctions on Libya for its refusal to surrender the suspects wanted for trial in connection with the 1988 Lockerbie bombing. In August 1992, after Yasser Arafat had visited Rabat to discuss the forthcoming round of Middle East peace negotiations, the Moroccan Minister of Foreign Affairs, Abd al-Latif Filali, visited Washington, where he had talks with Baker. In December 1992 Morocco sent a contingent of 1,250 troops to support 'Operation Restore Hope' in Somalia. Five Moroccan soliders were killed during incidents in Mogadishu, Somalia, in June 1993. In April 1994 King Hassan held talks with the US Vice-President, Albert Gore, during meetings culminating in the signing of the Final Act of the Uruguay Round of the General Agreement on Tariffs and Trade (GATT), which took place in Marrakesh.

As expectations of the UAM diminished, Morocco intensified its efforts to become, if not a full member, at least a 'separate partner' of the EC. In February 1990 Amnesty International issued a list of 300 alleged prisoners of conscience in the Kingdom. Two of Amnesty's local representatives were subsequently expelled. In September 1991 a proposal of the European Parliament to send observers to monitor the cease-fire and referendum in Western Sahara was officially denounced in Rabat as 'shameful blackmail'. In January 1992 the European Parliament voted against a four-year programme of aid, worth $600m., for Morocco, in protest against alleged human rights abuses. In response to this decision, Morocco refused to renegotiate its fishing agreement with the EC, which was due to expire in February. There were separate visits to Rabat by the EC Commissioners for European Integration and for Mediterranean Policy, to discuss a new relationship based on a free trade zone. Filali visited Brussels in May, and a new fishing agreement, whereby Morocco would receive compensation of ECU 102m. per year, was signed. In December the European Commission approved loans worth $590m. to Morocco over four years, and the European Investment Bank made a loan to improve the telecommunications system. In March 1993 the EC announced that negotiations on a form of partnership, which would include permanent political dialogue, economic co-operation, financial aid and progressive moves towards a free trade zone, should start within a year. In December 1993 the EC Ministers of Foreign Affairs gave their approval for the European Union (EU), as the EC had become, to negotiate with Morocco on a new Europe-Maghreb association agreement.

Morocco continued to look to France for diplomatic support in the UN Security Council and within the EC. In August 1991 Filali visited Paris, and in November 1992 Pierre Bérégovoy became the first French Prime Minister to visit Morocco since 1986. He promised to support Moroccan interests in the EC as far as he could without prejudice to French farmers. His visit was followed by that of the Minister of Foreign Trade, who announced a 50% increase in French aid to 1,200m. francs. In July 1993 Edouard Balladur, the new French Prime Minister, made an official visit to Morocco, where he met King Hassan. Among the matters that they discussed were bilateral and EU relations, Western Sahara, security in the Middle East and the conflict in Bosnia and Herzegovina. In January 1994 the French Minister of the Interior, Charles Pasqua, visited Rabat for talks, which are believed to have covered the crisis in Algeria, Islamic terrorism, immigration and an offer by the French Government to mediate in the dispute between Morocco and the Polisario Front over Western Sahara.

Discussions continued with the Spanish Government on a proposed bridge or tunnel link across the Strait of Gibraltar, and official relations remained good. In July 1991, during a visit to Rabat by King Juan Carlos, the two countries signed a treaty of friendship. The sources of former conflict over fishing and immigration remained, but Spain seemed no longer to be concerned about its former colony of Western Sahara. Economic links between Morocco and Spain were strengthened, and Spain overtook France as the principal foreign investor in the Kingdom. In July 1992 the two countries signed a 25-year agreement to build and operate the second trans-Mediterranean gas pipeline, extending from Algeria to Spain, via Morocco. In March 1993 the Energy Ministers of Spain, Morocco and Algeria met in Rabat to discuss details, and a joint Moroccan-Spanish company, the Société pour le Pilotage

de la Construction du Gazoduc Maghreb-Europe (Metragaz), was founded, with its headquarters in Casablanca.

The UAM itself made halting progress towards its avowed goal of economic union. The Casablanca summit meeting of September 1991 was dominated by the need to agree a common policy for the forthcoming Madrid Peace Conference, to which it sent a joint delegation. The summit also advocated the creation of a charter of rights for UAM citizens working in Europe. Headquarters of the various UAM institutions were allocated, with Morocco hosting the General Secretariat, Algeria the Consultative Assembly, Mauritania the Supreme Court, Tunisia the Investment Bank, and Libya the Maghreb University and Academy of Science. In December 1991 the Ministers of Foreign Affairs, the Economy and Agriculture met to discuss the co-ordination of policies: there were agreements on the Maghreb Autoroute, and trade union representatives from the five countries presented a joint plea for a social charter. In February 1993, however, Filali announced that, at a recent meeting of the foreign ministers of the five UAM countries, it had been decided that there should be a 'pause' in the development of a closer union; it was noted that, of the 15 conventions signed since the inauguration of the UAM, none had as yet been fully applied.

Relations with Algeria improved in 1988, when diplomatic relations were restored between the two countries, and were particularly good in the first half of 1992, while Muhammad Boudiaf, who had lived in Morocco for more than 20 years, was Algerian Head of State. The two states collaborated on security matters, and the Algerian Government urged the Polisario Front to make peace. Following the assassination of Boudiaf, relations deteriorated again, the frontier was closed and Algerian supplies to Polisario were resumed. In January 1993, however, there was a reconciliation. Ambassadors were exchanged and the border was re-opened. By August 1994, however, relations had deteriorated once again, after Morocco imposed entry restrictions on Algerian citizens as a security measure against the threat of terrorism. In reprisal, the Algerian Government announced the complete closure of its frontier with Morocco.

In the Arab world as a whole Morocco benefited both from the personal prestige of its monarch as an experienced statesman and from its support for the liberation of Kuwait. In January 1992 Arab Ministers of Foreign Affairs met in Marrakesh to agree a common strategy for the Moscow session of the Middle East peace talks. In October, just before the seventh round of the talks (held in Washington), King Hassan made his most extensive tour of the Islamic world in 30 years, visiting Jordan (for the first time), Syria, Saudi Arabia, the Gulf states and Egypt. In September 1993, following the mutual recognition and signature of a peace accord between Israel and the PLO, the Israeli Prime Minister, Itzhak Rabin, and the Minister of Foreign Affairs, Shimon Peres, visited Rabat for talks with King Hassan. In October a group of Moroccan industrialists, including King Hassan's economic consultant, visited Israel to attend a business conference, the first official Moroccan delegation to visit the Jewish state.

THE 1993 GENERAL ELECTION

In October 1991 various opposition parties allied to form the Mouvement National, a new opposition grouping under a veteran Berber politician Mahjoubi Aherdane; the Minister of Finance had introduced budget proposals calculated to conciliate the urban poor, with projected increases of more than 20% in expenditure on education and health services, and over 180% on housing; in November Istiqlal and the USFP formed a united front, demanding a separation of powers, a reduction in the minimum voting age to 18 years, new electoral lists and constituency boundaries, and improvements in civil rights. The USFP was, however, weakened by the death of its veteran leader, Abd al-Rahim Bouabid. His successor, Abd al-Rahman Yousifi, did not have the same close links with the monarchy. In April a 16th political party, the Parti de l'Avant-garde Démocratique Socialiste (PADS, a breakaway from the USFP), was legalized. In March an apparent set-back for democracy had been the two-year sentence imposed on a trade union official and USFP Politburo member, Nubir Amaoui, who, in an interview with the Spanish newspaper *El País*, had said that the government were thieves acting out a parody of democracy. In late 1992 trade union activists demonstrating outside the prison at Salé to demand the release of Amaoui were forcibly dispersed. At around the same time a prominent member of the Association Marocaine des Droits de l'Homme (AMDH), Ahmed Belaichi, was sentenced to three years' imprisonment for making derogatory remarks about the armed forces. In January 1993 an appeal against Amaoui's sentence was rejected. In February the AMDH alleged that as many as 750 political prisoners were being detained in Morocco. However, on 12 July 1993, following the legislative elections, Amaoui was released, along with the leader of another, pro-Istiqlal, union, Driss Laghnimi.

In April 1992, in an address to a conference of local government bodies, the King declared that parliamentary elections would be preceded by those for regional and local councils. There was disagreement on the text of the electoral law, and the opposition parties (Istiqlal, the USFP, the PADS and the PPS) refused to enter discussions, complaining that their previous recommendations had always been ignored. Hassan, worried that these parties would boycott the poll (rendering it meaningless), asked them to negotiate with his close associate, Reda Guedira. It was agreed that a new Constitution should be submitted to a referendum. Declaring that his status as a religious, as well as a national, leader empowered him to arbitrate, King Hassan announced the establishment of two committees: one to draft the law and the other to monitor the electoral process. At the beginning of May he chaired a conference of three ministers and the leaders of five pro-government and four opposition parties, telling them that they had 10 days to agree on an electoral law. A law comprising 99 articles was approved, and the King reiterated his promise of 'transparency'. A commission, chaired by a judge and consisting of members of local authorities and party representatives, was established, with direct access to the King or to Guedira.

On 4 June 1992 the Chamber of Representatives adopted a new electoral law, in spite of a boycott by all opposition parties. The new law reduced the minimum voting age to 20 years and the minimum candidate age to 23 from 25. It also made provision for equal funding and media exposure for all parties, and was approved by 162 votes in favour, with two abstentions. The opposition parties had earlier formed the Bloc Démocratique, whose expressed aims were: a minimum voting age of 18 years; a minimum age of 21 for candidates; a two-tier voting system; and an independent chairman of a new body to supervise elections.

In July 1992 King Hassan announced preparations for elections to the Chamber of Representatives, and by the end of the month registration had taken place, increasing the electorate from 7m. to 11.7m. voters. In mid-August an interim Government was appointed to ensure the fairness of the political process. The new Prime Minister was Karim Lamrani, who had held the office on two previous occasions. Lamrani's Government contained just one member with party political affiliations, although the major portfolios were unchanged.

In an address to the nation on 20 August 1992 King Hassan stated that the revised Constitution would give more responsibilities to the legislature, but emphasized that this did not mean a reduction in the sovereign's prerogatives. Under the proposed changes, ministers would be chosen by the Prime Minister but appointed by the King. A new Constitutional Council of eight members, half of them appointed by the King, would be created to arbitrate at the request of one-quarter of the parliamentary deputies. The revised Constitution also reaffirmed the King's commitment to human rights.

On 4 September 1992 the revised Constitution, the fourth since independence, was endorsed by the Moroccan electorate. The Ministry of the Interior and Information announced that 99.96% had voted in favour (increasing to 100% in main cities, and three of the four 'Saharan provinces') and that 97.25% of the 11m. registered voters had participated. The opposition claimed that the results destroyed all credibility in the democratic process. However, the Minister of the Interior and Information, Driss Basri, dismissed accusations of irregularities. The revised Constitution requires the Government to reflect the composition of the Chamber of Representatives

and to submit its programme to a vote. New legislation will be automatically promulgated a month after approval by the Chamber.

In spite of protests over the result of the referendum, the opposition Bloc Démocratique contested the communal elections that took place on 16 October 1992. The RNI became the largest party in local government, winning 18.1% of the votes cast and 21.7% of the 22,282 seats contested. The independent list, Sans Appartenance Politique (SAP), which, despite its name, was loyal to the Government, obtained 13.8% of the votes, and the UC 13.4%. Istiqlal emerged as the largest opposition party (with 12.5% of the votes cast), followed by the USFP, which confirmed its strength in the two major cities, Casablanca and Rabat. The opposition parties, however, failed to improve on their performance in the previous communal elections, although they contested many more seats, and complained of widespread malpractices by local authorities in favour of 'loyalist' parties.

In December 1992 it was announced that the long-awaited national legislative election, the first since 1984, would not be held until 30 April 1993, to allow time for the compiling of new electoral registers. The opposition demanded that the lists should be radically revised, and the boundaries of constituencies redrawn. The Ministry of the Interior and Information stated that the new registers would include newly-eligible voters but rejected proposals for any other changes. In February 1993 the four leading opposition parties that formed the Bloc Démocratique—Istiqlal, the USFP and two smaller parties, the PPS and the Organisation de l'Action Démocratique et Populaire (OADP)—withdrew from the multi-party national commission responsible for overseeing the election, and threatened to boycott the election unless the Government agreed to changes in the electoral law and the electoral register, and responded to their demands for the release of all political prisoners. The threat of a boycott increased political tensions at a time when the Government was confronted with strikes by teachers and health workers and a week-long campaign of stoppages over unemployment, pay and living conditions, supported by the UMT. At the end of March King Hassan announced that the election would be postponed until 25 June, to allow more time to update electoral lists and to redefine electoral boundaries. The opposition parties welcomed the King's decision and agreed to participate in the election. Following boundary revisions (completed in late April), the Government announced that the number of seats in the Chamber of Representatives had been increased from 306 to 333. Of the total, 222 would be elected by universal adult suffrage, and the remainder by local councils and professional organizations.

At the general election, on 25 June 1993, the two main opposition parties, Istiqlal and the USFP, substantially increased the number of their seats in the Chamber (from 57 in 1984 to 91) to become the leading parties at the end of the first stage of the electoral process. The parties of the Bloc Démocratique won a total of 99 seats. Although the five loyalist parties won more seats overall, the UC and the RNI secured fewer seats than in 1984. The UC had been the largest single party at the 1984 election, with 55 seats, but won only 27 seats in 1993. The MP emerged with 33 seats, two more than in 1984. According to official figures, 62.75% of the electorate voted, but observers suggested that the level of participation may have been even lower. Despite reports of abuses by local officials, polling was judged to have been fairer than in previous elections. Nevertheless, the opposition parties demanded that the election of four cabinet ministers be annulled. In the second stage of the election, held on 17 September 1993, the loyalist parties made significant gains, winning 79 of the 111 seats contested. The UC alone won 27 seats, making it the second largest party in the new Chamber (after the USFP). The two main opposition parties, the USFP and Istiqlal, gained only 17 seats in the September election, and accused agents of the Ministry of the Interior of 'falsifying the popular will.' Abderrahmane Youssoufi, the USFP leader, resigned in protest at the attitude of the authorities during the election. At the end of the second stage the five loyalist parties had 195 seats in the new Chamber, while the opposition

Bloc Démocratique had 120 seats, with independents holding the remaining 18 seats.

After the election, it was reported that King Hassan had agreed that the USFP and Istiqlal grouping, known as the Koutla, could form a government on condition that he appointed three principal ministers. The two parties rejected the offer and announced that they would not participate in the new government. On 9 November 1993 the King therefore asked Karim Lamrani, who had led the interim Government appointed in August 1992 to oversee the election, to form a new government. This was the fourth occasion on which the 74-year-old Lamrani, one of the most trusted members of the King's inner circle, had been named Prime Minister. Two days later, Lamrani announced a Government largely composed of technocrats and independents. None of the ministers from the previous administration who had stood for election in June were included. Ten new ministers and five new junior ministers were appointed. Mohamed Saghou replaced Mohamed Berrada as Minister of Finance, a post that Berrada had held for eight years, and Serge Berdugo, appointed Minister of Tourism, became the first Jewish minister since 1957. Omar Azziman, a co-founder of the OMDH, was appointed to the new post of Minister Delegate responsible for Human Rights. The appointment was welcomed by the London-based Amnesty International, a persistent critic of Morocco's record in observing human rights. Amnesty appealed to the Government to release all prisoners of conscience, and presented a list of 80 Moroccans and 485 Sahrawis, whom it claimed to have 'disappeared.' At the end of November 1993 the Chamber of Representatives adopted the Government's new programme, promising economic reforms and greater social justice, by 202 votes to 118. The aim of the programme, which included further privatization and the encouragement of foreign investment, was to achieve growth and create employment.

In February 1994 there were clashes between radical Islamic and leftist students at Fez University, and courses were suspended indefinitely after the security forces intervened. At the end of the month the Lamrani Government banned a 24-hour general strike (planned for 25 February), called by the CDT to protest against declines in the standard of living. On 24 February, after 11 of its activists had been arrested in Casablanca, the CDT announced its decision to postpone the strike. The banning order was condemned by most opposition parties and by the three national trades unions. A number of parliamentary by-elections were held at the end of April, following a judicial decision to reorganize polling after complaints of irregularities during the 1993 legislative election. Of the 14 seats contested by 88 candidates in the by-elections, the USFP won two, and Istiqlal three. The RNI, which had won five of the seats in June 1993, retained only two. Nevertheless, the opposition parties again complained of irregularities during the voting.

FILALI BECOMES PRIME MINISTER

On 25 May 1994 Lamrani was replaced as Prime Minister by Abd al-Latif Filali, formerly the Minister of Foreign Affairs and Co-operation and another member of the King's inner circle. Filali, a former diplomat, had first held government office in 1968. The new Prime Minister was expected to promote economic liberalization more vigorously and, within a few days of his appointment, announced that he had begun consultations with all the political parties with members in the Chamber of Representatives about the political, economic and social situation of the country. After a week of consultation, however, Filali made no changes to the list of ministers presented to the King on 7 June. The Prime Minister retained control of the Ministry of Foreign Affairs and Co-operation. However, Ali Yata, the Secretary-General of the Parti du Renouveau et du Progrès (as the PPS had been renamed), stated that Filali had proposed the formation of a Government of national consensus within three or four months. On 21 July, as the result of a royal amnesty, 424 prisoners, the majority of whom were considered to be political, were released from detention in Morocco.

Economy

DR DAVID SEDDON

(Revised for this edition by RICHARD I. LAWLESS)

By the late 1970s, Morocco was seriously in debt and had a current account deficit on its balance of payments equivalent to nearly 17% of gross domestic product (GDP). In 1978 the Government introduced a three-year stabilization programme, but external factors (such as the oil price rise in 1979, increasing international interest rates, and a decline in revenues from phosphate exports and from migrant workers' remittances), combined with a continuing commitment to heavy expenditure on the war in Western Sahara and on subsidies for basic goods, ensured that the programme was largely ineffective. In early 1983 the Government imposed emergency import controls and reduced its expenditure. In September the IMF formally approved a new stabilization programme and issued a stand-by arrangement of SDR 300m., while Morocco's creditors agreed to reschedule US $13,800m. of debt. Inflation was high in the early 1980s, with increases in food prices and rising levels of unemployment particularly aggravating the living conditions of the urban poor. The 1982 census revealed a continuing drift to the towns, especially Casablanca, with more than two-thirds of the total population living in the major urban areas. Reductions in public expenditure exacerbated mounting discontent, and in 1981 and 1984 provoked major strikes and violent street demonstrations.

With the support of the World Bank and the IMF, the Government introduced policies of structural adjustment in 1984 and was able to reschedule its debts towards the end of 1985. Despite good harvests in 1985 and 1986, and the fall in oil prices, the trade balance deteriorated. At the beginning of 1986 the World Bank expressed its concern about the under-lying structural weakness of the Moroccan economy and argued that stronger corrective measures were needed, including reductions in public expenditure and food subsidies. The IMF was equally concerned by the Government's fiscal and economic performance, and subsequently cancelled its stand-by arrangement. Measures that were adopted during late 1986 and 1987 renewed confidence in Morocco's economic prospects. A firm commitment to a radical reform of the economy, involving a new emphasis on export production, trade liberalization, attraction of foreign investment and development of tourism, together with a domestic programme of privatization and encouragement of the private sector, was expressed in the 1988–92 Development Plan. In August 1988 the IMF approved a stand-by arrangement of SDR 210m., to be disbursed over the next 16 months, despite expressing some concern about the implementation of fiscal policy and the slow pace in the reduction of food subsidies. In October the 'Paris Club' of creditor Governments agreed to reschedule payments of principal and interest on external debt worth US $940m., and in December the World Bank approved another major structural adjustment loan, subject to further reforms. In May 1989 the text of the proposed law on privatization was published, committing the Government to the transfer of the majority of state enterprises to the private sector, and in October a Ministry of Privatization was created. The law came into effect in January 1990. Negotiations over the rescheduling of Morocco's commercial bank debt continued throughout 1989 and it was not until April 1990 that an agreement was reached with the 'London Club'. The IMF

16-month stand-by loan expired in December 1989, but was replaced in July 1990 by an eight-month stand-by arrangement authorizing purchases of up to SDR 100m. (then US $134m.).

In a speech on 5 November 1991, the Minister of Finance, Mohamed Berrada, stated that policies of structural adjustment, introduced since 1983, had produced a significant upturn in the economy. He forecast that the rescheduling cycle would end by 1993, by which date the dirham would be made convertible and Morocco would return to international capital markets. An important contributory factor in the improved economic climate was the cancelling of bilateral debt owed to Saudi Arabia and other Gulf states, estimated at around $3,600m. In February 1992 it was announced that the IMF had approved a stand-by credit of up to SDR 91.98m. ($129m.) to support the government's economic programme for the following year. According to the IMF, the economic programme for 1992 aimed at promoting investment and increasing productivity, and continued efforts to strengthen the budgetary position and the reorientation of credit towards the private sector. The programme aimed at an annual 4% growth in GDP, a decline in inflation to 5% per year and a reduction in the current account deficit. Measures were introduced to reduce the overall budget deficit from 3.1% of GDP in 1991 to 0.8% in 1992; this had been a major point of disagreement with the Fund in the past. The IMF states that, under the new programme, monetary policy will encourage the provision of private-sector credit, and trade barriers will be reduced by restructuring the tariff system. In February 1992 the 'Paris Club' welcomed the determination expressed by Morocco in not asking for any new reorganization of its external debt from 1993. Under the new 'Paris Club' agreement, official development assistance will be repaid over 20 years, and other credits over 15 years. The World Bank's vice-president for the Middle East and North Africa visited Rabat in April 1992 and stated that the Bank would give full support to the second phase of the country's adjustment programme. He emphasized that high priority should be given to the development of the capital and financial markets, and expressed concern about some social indicators, notably the high rates of infant mortality and illiteracy. To date Morocco has received $6,000m. from the Bank, and new commitments totalling $1,600m. were expected in 1992. In a statement in April 1992, the Minister in charge of Planning, Rachid al-Ghazouani, maintained that the number of poor people in Morocco had declined from 6.6m. to 3.9m. between 1985 and 1991, and that there had been a significant reduction in the gap between rich and poor. The opposition parties, however, dispute these claims, and argue that liberalization has widened the gap between rich and poor. In July 1992 the President of the World Bank, Lewis Preston, stated that Morocco had received more than $1,500m. in loans in the last decade and that lending worth a further $500m. was planned, with priority being given to housing, education and health projects. In his first statement on economic policy since his appointment as Prime Minister in May 1994, Abd al-Latif Filali pledged to expedite Morocco's programme of privatization. At the same time it was estimated that the debt owed by state enterprises was equivalent to about one-third of total public debt. Filali stated that privatization would be extended to public utilities, such as power generation, and might include other strategic companies, such as the Office Chérifien des Phosphates (OCP) and Royal Air Maroc. It was estimated that the Government would need to raise a further 2,700m. dirhams from privatization in the second half of 1994 in order to achieve a budget deficit less than 1.5% of GDP in that year, as stipulated by the King.

AGRICULTURE AND FISHERIES

About 55% of the Moroccan population live in the rural areas, and more than 40% of the working population are employed in agriculture, livestock-raising and fishing. In 1986 the agricultural sector (including forestry and fishing) accounted for 20.0% of GDP. However, changing climatic conditions cause substantial year-to-year variations in agricultural output. Severe drought in 1981—the worst for 35 years—caused cereal production to fall by 50% from 4.5m. metric tons in 1980. In 1985, when rainfall was good, cereal production increased by 41%, compared with the previous year, and in

1986 cereal production rose again by about 47% to a record 7.7m. tons. However, the 1987 harvest was very disappointing, with cereal production reaching only 4.2m. tons. 1988 was another record year, with a bumper harvest of nearly 8m. tons, and the 1989 harvest reached 7.3m. tons. In 1990 agriculture accounted for 16% of total GDP. In mid-1992 the Ministry of Agriculture and Agrarian Reform announced that it would cancel or reschedule debts owed by farmers affected by drought. Severe drought in 1992 and 1993 resulted in a decline in output by the agricultural sector. According to central bank figures, agricultural GDP decreased by 29% in 1992, a year when agriculture was the only sector of the economy to contract.

The principal crops are cereals (especially wheat, barley and maize), citrus fruit, as well as olives, beans, chick-peas, tomatoes and potatoes. Canary seed, cumin, coriander, linseed and almonds are also grown. Sugar beet and cane are cultivated on a large scale to substitute for imports; sugar is one of Morocco's principal food imports owing to the very high level of domestic consumption. In 1987 Morocco produced 2.75m. metric tons of beet and 848,000 tons of cane resulting in total sugar output of 412,000 tons. In 1988 sugar production rose to nearly 500,000 tons, which covered more than two-thirds of domestic requirements in 1989. Morocco produced 1.10m. metric tons of beet and an estimated 2.97m. metric tons of cane in 1990, rising to 1.15m. and 3.07m. metric tons, respectively, in 1991. Brazil and Thailand are the main suppliers of sugar imports.

Until the late 1950s, Morocco was a net cereal exporter, but particularly since the mid-1970s, food imports, especially cereals, sugar and dairy products, have become very substantial and now constitute a major element in Morocco's total import bill. In 1990 wheat output fell to 3.6m. tons from 3.9m. tons in the previous year. Coarse grains production also decreased, from an estimated 3.5m. tons in 1989 to approximately 2.6m. tons in 1990, and total cereal production declined from 7.4m. tons in 1989 to 6.3m. tons in the following year. After good rains in 1991, cereal production rose to 8.53m. tons (according to the Ministry of Agriculture and Agrarian Reform), of which 2.22m. tons was durum wheat, 2.73m. tons of soft bread wheat, 3.25m. tons barley and 335,000 tons maize. The cereal harvest decreased to 2.72m. tons in 1992, following a severe drought. It was estimated that as much as 4m. tons of wheat and barley needed to be imported as a result. In 1993 the cereal harvest was again depleted by drought, with rainfall 60% below average. In April 1993 the Ministry of Agriculture forecast that production of wheat, barley and maize would total approximately 2.5m. tons in that year. Initial estimates suggested that the 1994 cereal harvest could reach a record 8.5m. tons. In June 1994 it was reported that the Minister of Agriculture had obtained higher prices for wheat and subsidies for barley producers. But Morocco is also a major food exporter. Agricultural produce accounted for 59% of total export revenue in the period 1969–73, but its importance was later eclipsed by phosphate earnings. During the late 1980s agricultural products accounted for about 25% of total exports. The main agricultural exports are citrus fruit (mainly oranges), tomatoes, and fresh and processed vegetables. A fruit processing industry is being developed, and exports of preserved fruit, jam and fruit juice contribute to foreign exchange earnings. In 1984 there were about 700 firms which employed 40,000 people in the food processing sector. A growing proportion of processed food is based on fish and seafood products. In 1988 citrus production rose by 35% from 1987, reaching a total of around 1.2m. tons, about half of which was exported. Other crops, including legumes, vegetables, grapes and industrial crops (sugar beet, cane and cotton), all performed well in 1988. In 1989/90 citrus fruit production increased slightly, with exports totalling 436,500 tons. According to the Casablanca weekly *La Vie Economique*, 1990/91 produced record exports of citrus fruits and vegetables, with citrus sales rising to 648,500 tons. Maroc late oranges represented about one-half of the total citrus sales. Tomato exports increased from 91,400 tons in 1989/90 to 132,000 tons in 1990/91, potatoes from 60,500 tons to 110,000 tons, and vegetables from 9,400 tons to 9,500 tons. Morocco exports approximately 40% of its citrus products, of which about 70% goes to the European Union (EU), formerly the European Community (EC). In 1990/91 France was the largest importer, accounting for almost 250,000 tons. Morocco, however, is worried that its agricultural exports will be adversely affected by growing competition from other Mediterranean countries, in particular Spain and Portugal, in the EU. In March 1992 the EC formally offered to establish a free-trade agreement with Morocco. While Morocco expects to benefit from improved access to EU markets, an accord covering the free movement of agricultural products would be highly controversial, and it seems likely that only industrial goods will be included in the new agreement. Livestock numbers remained relatively static until the mid-1980s, but have begun to increase more recently, rising from around 24.2m. in 1986 to over 26m. in 1988 and to 28.6m. in 1989. Numbers of sheep—the most numerous species—rose in the same period from 14.6m. to 16.1m., and then to 17.5m. in 1989. Meat and dairy production have been increasing accordingly; meat production increased from 293,000 tons in 1987 to 302,000 tons in 1988, and to 310,000 tons in 1989. Morocco produces virtually all of its national meat requirements. Output of dairy products totalled 1,015,600 tons in 1987, increasing to 1,060,900 tons in the following year and then falling to 1,039,400 tons in 1989. In February 1992 the Ministry of Agriculture and Agrarian Reform announced a $50m. emergency programme to save some 22m. cattle, sheep and goats that were threatened by the severe drought. Some 60,000 tons of livestock feed had been distributed to those areas worst affected, and a further 100,000 tons would be distributed to farmers at half the price. The ministry would provide the necessary transport and would also distribute drinking water.

Financial assistance has been secured for the first phase of the Upper Abda-Doukkala irrigation scheme, south-west of Casablanca, from the African Development Bank ($181m.), the European Investment Bank ($74.8m.) and the Arab Fund for Economic and Social Development ($130m.). The new scheme aims eventually to irrigate some 64,000 ha in the Doukkala region, to increase food production for Casablanca and Rabat, and is scheduled to cost more than $1,000m. over the next 15–20 years. The first phase of the work involves building a main canal and pumping station to draw water from the Im Fout reservoir, on the Oued Oum er Riba, which will be carried some 60 km to irrigate an area of 16,000 ha. In July 1991 it was reported that work had started on the Wahada dam scheme, which will eventually irrigate 100,000 ha and involve the resettlement of some 20,000 farmers in the Sebou and Ouerrgh valleys. Financial support is provided by Italy, the Arab Fund for Economic and Social Development (AFESD) and the Kuwait Fund for Arab Economic Development (KFAED). The OPEC Fund for International Development agreed in February 1992 to provide a loan of $7.5m. for the Tassaouat project, which involves irrigating 44,000 ha with a new canal system and the rehabilitation of existing irrigation canals. Financial support is also provided by the AFESD, the Saudi Fund for Development and the EC. In January 1994 an accord was signed with the KFAED, which agreed to provide $60m. to finance part of the Tassaouat project. In December 1992 King Hassan inaugurated the $195m. Matmata gallery project, designed to channel 600m. cu m of water per year, to irrigate 25,000 ha of the Gharb valley. In August 1993 Japan agreed to provide a loan of $127m. to the Caisse Nationale de Crédit Agricole for agriculture and fisheries projects. In February 1994 the World Bank announced that it would lend $34.7m. to provide irrigation services to some 200,000 small farmers in order to raise production in irrigated areas. In May, in one of the last major allocations from the EU's fifth financial protocol, the European Investment Bank (EIB) agreed to provide $24.7m. for a five-year project to irrigate 23,000 hectares in the Haouz region. In July the World Bank provided a $121m. loan, repayable over 20 years, to support the government's agricultural investment programme (estimated at $993m. between 1994 and 1997) and to be used for projects in poorer regions of the country.

Fishing has become increasingly important. A separate Ministry of Fisheries, formerly the responsibility of the Ministry of Commerce, Industry and Tourism, was set up in April 1981. Special financial concessions were granted to the fishing industry in 1984 to improve its export potential; in addition, state control over exports was removed. Since 1984 annual landings have surpassed 400,000 metric tons; about half of the fish caught are sardines, which are mainly canned for export. In 1988 exports of fish and fish products totalled 179,000 tons and accounted for 50% of all food exports and 11% of total exports. In 1990 the volume of fish available for canning decreased by an estimated 8%, largely as a result of reductions in sardine catches landed at Agadir. Morocco's export of canned fish is mostly to the EC, although the export of sardines to the EC is limited to 17,500 tons per year, beyond which a 25% customs duty is levied. The Moroccan fishing fleet consists of nearly 2,000 boats, and the sector employs about 75,000 persons. In 1983 the Government signed a treaty with Spain, which gave Spanish vessels certain rights in Moroccan waters in exchange for finance for infrastructural development. Bilateral agreements with Spain were renegotiated in 1987 as accords with the EC, following Spanish accession to the Community in 1986. An agreement reached in February 1988 restricted EC vessels to a catch of 95,000 tons annually in Moroccan waters, in return for licence fees and compensation worth $48.3m. a year. Morocco also gained improved access to the European market for its canned sardine exports, the annual volume of which was to rise to 17,500 tons, compared with 14,000 tons in 1988. In February 1992, however, it was reported that the Moroccan Government had suspended talks with the EC about fishing rights for EC fleets, in retaliation for the EC's refusal to approve Morocco's fourth financial protocol in January. The 1988 agreement expired in March 1992. After lengthy negotiations, a new five-year accord came into force on 15 May 1992. It allows 650 Spanish, 50 Portuguese and 36 other trawlers into Moroccan waters, in return for increased compensation of 102m. ECUs ($131m.). The accord also envisages new conservation measures, the expansion of port facilities and the creation of joint marketing companies. In September 1992 it was reported that, in accordance with the EC agreement, an instalment of fishing rights payments worth $126m. had been paid to Morocco to cover the first year of the agreement. In June 1992 ONA, Morocco's largest private company, signed an agreement with the Union des Coopératives de Pêcheurs de France to establish a fish-canning and marketing enterprise to market canned sardines and mackerel. In January 1991 Morocco and the USSR signed an accord allowing Soviet vessels to catch, under direct licences, 750,000 tons of fish in the first year, with 100,000 tons to be caught by joint-venture companies, although Soviet boats would not be permitted to fish in traditional Moroccan sardine-fishing areas. It was agreed that, in return for these rights, the operators of the Soviet vessels would pay a sum in convertible currency, equivalent to 15% of the value of the catch, in addition to furnishing two science research boats to the Institut Scientifique des Pêches Maritimes and a training boat to facilitate Moroccan training in the fishing industry. Moroccan canned fish was to receive preferential treatment in the Soviet market.

MINING

The mining industry in Morocco employs about 65,000 persons and handles about 26m. metric tons of ores per year, of which 90% are phosphates, 3% metal-bearing ores and 7% other minerals (notably anthracite). The mining sector accounted for 2.6% of GDP in 1989 and almost one-third of Morocco's total exports, but there has been a progressive decline in the relative importance of the sector. Minerals accounted for 53.4% of all export earnings in 1984, but the proportion declined to 48.4% in 1985, to 39.7% in 1986 and 37.1% in 1987. There has also been a shift from the export of minerals to mineral derivatives. The sector is dominated by the production of phosphates, which totalled 25m. metric tons in 1988, of which 14.3m. tons were exported. In 1992 exports of phosphates earned less than a third of total exports by the OCP. Total exports by the OCP (including phosphates, phosphoric acid, fertilizers and chemicals) accounted for only 25% of the country's total exports. According to the Direction de la Statistique, mining production as a whole increased by 4.7% in 1992.

Morocco has about two-thirds of the world's known reserves of phosphate rock. Proven reserves are 10,600m. tons, and probable reserves 57,200m. tons. Major deposits are located at Khouribga, Youssoufia and Ben Guerir. Morocco now also controls production at Bou Craa in Western Sahara, which was reopened in July 1982. Morocco is the world's third largest producer of phosphate rock, after the USA and the former USSR. It produced 21.0m. tons in 1988, 18.1m. tons in 1989 and 21.4m. tons in 1990. With the opening of new mines at Ben Guerir in 1981 and at Sidi Hajjaj in 1984, annual output capacity has gradually increased and there are long-term plans to exploit large phosphate deposits at Meskala. Morocco is the world's largest exporter of phosphate rock, and its exports account for about one-third of world trade. As a result of high phosphate prices in the early to mid-1970s, there was a decline in demand, and the volume of Moroccan exports of phosphate fell by 22% between 1979 and 1982. In the early 1980s there was a slow recovery in world demand, but international phosphate prices fell from $49.50 per ton in 1980 to under $40 by 1983, to $34.80 in 1986 and to $31.95 in 1987, before rising in 1988 and 1989 to $40.50. Morocco is, as a result, investing heavily in the 'downstream' phosphate derivatives industry, to increase the value of its exports. Sales of phosphate rock for domestic processing into phosphate products increased to 30% of total output in 1984; of total sales of phosphate rock in 1988, domestic factories took nearly 44%. In 1987 the value of exports of phosphate derivatives (mainly phosphoric acid) surpassed that of phosphate rock for the first time, and in 1988 the combined value of phosphoric acid and fertilizers accounted for almost two-thirds of total exports of phosphates and phosphate derivatives. Exports by the OCP rose from 9,855m. dirhams in 1990 to 10,048m. dirhams in 1991. Phosphoric acid and phosphate fertilizers accounted for some 70% of sales. Exports by the OCP in 1992 declined to 8,491m. dirhams, but phosphoric acid and fertilizers continued to account for about 70% of sales revenue.

To increase 'downstream' capacity, contracts were awarded in early 1991 to develop the Sidi Chenane and Ben Guerir mines, as part of a $600m. development programme. The Sidi Chenane mine is being developed by a Spanish consortium, led by Industrias Mecanicas del Noroeste. In April 1991 three US companies were awarded contracts, totalling $28.7m., to supply phosphate mining equipment to the OCP. In November 1991 senior officials of the OCP announced that plans to build two major phosphate products plants had been postponed until 1992–93, and that priority was being given to development of the mining sector, to increase production.

As part of its drive to develop domestic sources of energy, the Government has increased coal production in recent years—by 61% between 1973 and 1981. Between 1982 and 1986 coal production ranged between 735,000 and 835,000 metric tons a year, but declined in 1988 and 1989 to 640,000 tons. Since 1983 the Jerrada anthracite mine in north-east Morocco has been expanded, with the aim of increasing total annual production from 400,000 tons to 1m. tons by 1992. Output, however, has failed to meet these targets and consequently coal and coke imports have grown dramatically, from 29,000 tons in 1980, to 218,000 tons in 1984, 817,000 tons in 1986 and an estimated 1.1m. tons in 1988. Diversification into coal represents an attempt to become less heavily reliant on oil imports. In 1990 coal imports decreased by 6%, to 1.2m. tons, compared with 1.3m. tons in the previous year. The USA provided 294,720 tons and replaced the UK as the second largest supplier.

Production of crude petroleum is negligible, reaching at most around 23,000 tons a year. Exploration for hydrocarbons intensified following the creation of the Office National de Recherches et d'Exploitations Pétrolières (ONAREP) in 1981, but there have been no significant finds. Extensive deposits of oil-bearing shale are known to exist, with a potential output of 100,000m. tons (15% of world reserves). By mid-1986 agreements had been reached with numerous foreign oil companies for exploration both onshore and offshore. However, the collapse in oil prices in 1986 prompted many of these companies to relinquish their interests; in any case, no major discovery had yet been made, apart from a gasfield owned by ONAREP in the Essaouira area. Even this, which was orig-

inally expected to satisfy 40% of Morocco's energy needs, proved, during 1985, to be more limited than anticipated. In 1991 incentives for international companies to explore for oil and gas were approved by the Chamber of Representatives, following the revision of laws which reduced the state's minimum share in agreements with international companies to 35% from 50%, reduced the minimum size of an exploration permit to 2,000 sq km from 5,000 sq km and reduced the minimum duration of an accord to eight years from 15. Two US oil companies, Ashland Exploration and Santa Fe Energy Co, were the first to sign an exploration and production-sharing agreement with ONAREP under the revised hydrocarbons code, which came into force in April 1992. The companies will explore in a 6,000 sq km area off shore of Essaouira and Agadir, with each company holding 50% in its part of the venture and with Ashland Exploration as operator. Gas production in the first half of the 1980s ranged between 78,800m. cu m in 1982 and 86,600m. cu m in 1985. Four major gasfields are in production, with two others, including the Meskala field in the Essaouira area, being developed. Gas treatment facilities have been developed at Meskala. In February 1993 Petro Canada International Management Services announced a major natural gas discovery in the Essaouria basin, where it had been working with ONAREP since 1990. In May 1993 it was reported that ONAREP had identified new gas deposits in the Gharb region.

In August 1991 Gaz de France (GdF) signed two agreements with Morocco's Ministry of Energy and Mines and the Société Nationale des Produits Pétroliers (SNPP), in preparation for the second trans-Mediterranean pipeline which will carry Algerian natural gas across Morocco to Europe. Morocco's SNPP, Algeria's state energy company SONATRACH, Spain's Enagaz, GdF, and Germany's Ruhrgas were each to have a 19% interest, while Gas de Portugal was allocated the remaining 5%. In March 1992 it was reported that a contract to conduct feasibility and initial engineering studies for the difficult Strait of Gibraltar section of the new gas pipeline had been awarded to Sofregaz of France. In July 1992 it was reported that Morocco and Spain had signed a 25-year agreement to build and exploit a second trans-Mediterranean gas pipeline from Hassi R'Mel in Algeria across Morocco and the Strait of Gibraltar to Spain. Spain's Enagas has established three companies to work on the project: Europe-Maghreb Pipeline (EMPL), Société Metragaz and Sodegas. The first phase of the project will supply 6,000m. cu m of natural gas to Spain, 1,300m. cu m to Morocco, with another 1,000m. cu m being used in Algeria. EMPL will handle the transit of gas from the border of Algeria to Spain. The Moroccan section will be 525 km long and will cost about $1,300m., with Enagas providing finance. The cost of the entire pipeline, which is owned by EMPL (a wholly-owned subsidiary of Enagas), was estimated at $2,500m. In January 1994 it was reported that the pipeline's capacity had been increased by 30% to 10,000 m. cu m per year because of a new contract to supply 2,400m. cu m per year to Portugal. By June 1994 work had still not begun on the Algerian section, and it seemed unlikely that the pipeline would be completed by the original deadline, set for October 1995.

Production of iron ore, mainly from mines in the north-east of Morocco, was as high as 1.5m. metric tons in 1958, but during the next 20 years annual output declined considerably. After 1982 there was an increase in production and in 1987 total output reached 280,000 tons, although it slumped in 1988 to 156,000 tons. Production in 1990 was 149,500 tons. The main hope for a revival is based on the construction of a steel and cold-rolling mill, with a projected annual capacity of 1m. tons, near Nador, the first stage of which began production in late 1984. There are also plans to open new mines in the Rif mountain area. Production of iron ore is currently undertaken by the Société d'Exploitation des Mines du Rif (SEFERIF).

Other minerals produced include barytes, lead, copper, zinc and manganese. Production of most other, non-ferrous ores had been falling, but there were signs of a recovery by the late 1980s. Apart from a sharp decline in estimated output in 1986, production of lead ore has generally increased, and the capacity of the lead smelter at Oued Heimer, operated by the

Société des Mines de Zellidja, was to be expanded, following studies which indicated a high lead content in nearby deposits. Zinc production has been increasing (although there was a fall in estimated output in 1986 and 1987). In 1991 Morocco's total output of zinc ore concentrate was 47,709 tons, with exports worth $13.3m. Production of fluorspar at el-Hammam, near Meknès, and of barytes and cobalt concentrate also increased. Another barytes mine was opened at Zelmou, with a production capacity of 100,000 metric tons a year. Production of barytes rose massively to 322,000 tons in 1988 from 127,000 tons in 1987. Output of lead has averaged, in the late 1980s, around 100,000 tons, and copper around 40,000 tons. Zinc production has risen to reach 40,000 tons in 1990. The production of silver rose from 76 tons in 1987 to 132 tons in 1988. In an attempt to increase copper production, which had fallen in the 1980s, a major mine was developed at Bleida. Interest has been shown in the possibility of recovering uranium from the phosphate rock reserves, and exploration by the Bureau de Recherches et de Participation Minières (BRPM) has revealed traces of uranium in the upper Moulouya valley, east of Zeida, in the High Atlas. At the end of 1987 the BRPM signed an agreement with its French counterpart for survey work on deposits of copper, zinc, and lead in the Anti Atlas region. As a result of a recent USAID project, US and Moroccan researchers have identified traces of nickel, cobalt and gold in the Foum Zguid region of the Anti Atlas. There were also reports from OPEC sources that deposits of up to 20m. tons of bauxite had been discovered in Morocco. The Guemassa polymetallic mine in the High Atlas was officially opened in December 1992. In July 1993 ONA (formerly Omnium Nord Africain), which owns and operates the mine, was seeking a $100m. loan to increase annual production to 130,000 tons of zinc, 32,000 tons of copper and 12,000 tons of lead. In May 1994 BRPM signed an agreement with Placer Outokumpu Exploration, a Canadian/Finnish company, which will invest $2m. in mineral exploration work and drilling in the Marrakesh region where the Guemassa mine is located.

INDUSTRY

In the 1980s the Government made particular efforts to promote industrial development, in order to reduce Morocco's dependence on agriculture and phosphate-mining, to create employment and to reduce imports. The manufacturing sector remains relatively small, accounting for about 20% of GDP, but it has expanded significantly since 1984. Official policy is to promote export-oriented industry and to encourage private-sector investment; this has been supported by the World Bank, which has provided two industrial and trade policy loans, worth $350.4m., since 1984. In 1987 investment in the industrial sector was increased by 32% (following an increase of 25% in 1986), and it was expected that this would generate an increase of 56% in the number of jobs available. Investment rose by 23% in 1988, by 39% in 1989 and by approximately 35% in 1990. Three-quarters of the invested funds were from private Moroccan investors; foreign investors accounted for 16% of the total in 1987 and 20% in 1988. Part of the Government's strategy has been to encourage the development of industry away from Casablanca, where it is most concentrated. In 1987 and in 1988 Casablanca received 43% of total investment in the industrial sector, and in 1987 55% of the total number of industrial projects were based in Casablanca. The main industry, in terms of investment and foreign exchange earnings, is the processing of phosphates, which continues to be undertaken by a state-controlled enterprise, the OCP, despite the Government's increasing commitment to privatization. Other industries, in order of importance, are petroleum refining, cement production, food processing, textiles and chemicals. Manufacturing remains a relatively small sector, and is primarily concerned with the processing of export commodities and the production of consumer goods. As a result of the investment code, promulgated in 1983 and amended in 1988, which provides attractive incentives for both national and foreign investors, investment has risen considerably. Industrial production increased by 4% between 1986 and 1987. Recent government policies have concentrated on encouraging export-oriented industry; consequently there has been a noticeable decline of interest in other sectors,

which rely almost exclusively on the domestic market. In 1990 industry accounted for 35% of Moroccan GDP. According to the Direction de la Statistique, industrial production increased in most sectors in 1992, but manufacturing registered a lower rate of growth than had been expected: output rose by only 1.7%, compared with 1991. Foreign investment decreased by 35% to $145m., mainly as a result of the recession in Europe. France was the principal foreign investor, followed by Spain and Italy, and the most attractive sectors for foreign investment were chemicals, agroindustry, textiles and leather. A number of state-owned industrial concerns were among the first to be offered for sale under the government's privatization programme. Among these were the Société des Dérivés du Sucre, in November 1992, and the Cimenterie de l'Oriental and the Société Nationale d'Electrolyse et de Petrochimie, in early 1993. In March 1994 it was announced that three sugar companies would be offered for privatization: Sucrerie de Beni Mellal, SUTA and Sucrerie du Tadla. The Minister of Privatization, Abderrahmane Saidi, announced that the state's remaining 22.2% share in the General Tire and Rubber Company would be sold off, along with the Société Nationale de Sidérurgie (SONASID), the Société Marocaine de Construction Automobiles (SOMACA) and the Société Marocaine des Fertilisants, a subsidiary of the OCP. The new Prime Minister, Filali, announced that the scope of privatization would be extended, and that private-sector participation in strategic industries was now a possibility. In August 1993 King Hassan had advocated the rationalization of the management of state companies.

While prices for phosphate rock have tended to decline until recently, superphosphate prices have been buoyant, rising from $21.17 per metric ton in 1986 to $138.25 per ton in 1987. Morocco has already invested heavily in the 'downstream' phosphates industry. In 1991 OCP awarded a contract worth $190m. to a Spanish company, Industrias Mecánicas del Novoeste (Imenosa), for the exploitation of phosphate deposits at Sidi Chennane. Imenosa will carry out infrastructural work and be responsible for electrical and computer equipment. Production is expected to begin in 1993, with projected annual output reaching 5m. tons. Four phosphate-processing plants are in operation at Safi: Maroc Chimie I, producing phosphoric acid and fertilizers; Maroc Chimie II, producing phosphoric acid; Maroc Phosphore I—a much larger plant, opened in 1976—producing phosphoric acid and mono-ammonium phosphate; and Maroc Phosphore II—opened in 1982, with three sulphuric acid lines and three phosphoric acid lines. The Safi complex has an annual capacity of 1.8m. tons of phosphoric acid and 790,000 tons of triple superphosphate. A second major fertilizer complex was being developed at the port of Jorf Lasfar, and the new phosphate mines at Sidi Hajjaj and Meskala were to come into production in 1990. The phosphoric acid treatment plant at Jorf Lasfar began production in 1986 and was expected to add 400,000 tons per year to Morocco's phosphoric acid production capacity. In 1987 the commissioning of two plants for phosphate calcination took place, as well as the entry into production of the fertilizer-manufacturing units of the Maroc Phosphore III and IV factories at Jorf Lasfar, which are producing a new type of fertilizer-diammonia. Maroc Phosphore III and IV were expected to add a further 784,000 tons of phosphoric acid per year to total production. In 1987 sales of phosphoric acid increased by 31.9%, to 1.4m. tons. In 1987 phosphoric acid was the leading earner of foreign exchange among Morocco's commodity exports (with shipments valued at 3,583m. dirhams or $429m.), outranking sales of phosphate rock, while fertilizers ranked eighth. In 1988 the value of phosphoric acid exports reached 4,672m. dirhams, exceeding sales of phosphate rock again. In 1990 exports of phosphoric acid increased by 116.8%, to 2m. tons. With this dramatic growth in phosphoric acid exports, Morocco has replaced the USA as the world's major exporter, accounting for about 42% of the world market in this product. In 1987 exports of phosphate derivatives as a whole increased by 19.4%, in volume terms, and generated revenues worth 4,483m. dirhams, an increase of 13.5% on the 1986 total. Revenues increased to 7,309m. dirhams in 1988. In 1990 export earnings from phosphates, phosphoric acid and fertilizers totalled 9,855m. dirhams. In 1991 the OCP announced a project to develop the Maroc Phosphore V and VI fertilizer and acid production units at Jorf Lasfar, with the aim of doubling annual capacity, estimated at 4.5m. tons of sulphuric acid, 1.4m. tons of phosphoric acid and 1.2m. tons of fertilizers. The Maroc Phosphore VI unit alone was to cost some $1,000m. However, in November 1991 it was announced that the project had been postponed until 1992–93 because priority was being given to 'upstream' investment in order to increase output. In July 1993 it was announced that a final decision on participation by French companies in the construction of Maroc Phosphore V and VI units had still not been made. The OCP is considering a number of options for the future, one of which involves the possible purchase of industrial units abroad to process output in third countries. In 1989 India's Minerals and Metals Trading Corporation (MMTC), the OCP's main client for phosphoric acid, reduced imports, causing serious balance-of-payments problems for Morocco. A new contract, worth $209.5m., was signed in April 1991 for 500,000 tons of phosphoric acid at $419 per ton. The OCP encountered strong international competition and accepted a lower price than originally tendered, to secure the order. In June 1991 MMTC placed a second order, for a further 200,000 tons of phosphoric acid, at $399.75 per ton for cash payment. The OCP expressed the hope that sales of phosphoric acid to India would reach $400m. in 1991, equal to the level prevailing before the 1989 dispute. A contract has also been signed to supply Saudi Basic Industries Corporation, and the OCP is exploring other new markets. According to the Direction de la Statistique, phosphate output increased in 1992 by 7% and phosphoric acid by 13.3%, but fertilizer production fell by 14.4%. In 1992 the value of phosphate exports was $283m., fertilizers and chemicals $264m., and phosphoric acid $369m.; together they accounted for 25% of the value of total exports. In September 1993 it was reported that exports by the OCP as a whole decreased by 17.6% in the first four months of 1993.

The largest industrial project in the 1980s, outside the phosphates industry, was the Nador steel rod and bar mill, with an annual capacity of 420,000 metric tons, built by a British company, Davy Loewy, with a £75m. contract agreed in 1980. The plant began production in 1984 with an output that included wire and reinforcing rods and bars. A steelworks producing 700,000 tons per year was planned at the site, but this project has been delayed, owing to a shortage of funds. The state-owned national steel company, SONASID, increased its overall production by 20% in 1988, continuing the growth trend established since 1984. In May 1992 it was reported that SONASID planned to build a steel mini-mill near Jorf Lasfor port. The operation will consist of a 258,000 tons-per-year continuous caster and a 250,000 tons-per-year bar mill, and is scheduled to commence in 1994. In May 1994 it was reported that SONASID was seeking foreign investors to finance its expansion. Investment funds were expected to be attracted through the privatization of the company in 1994.

Petroleum refining is another major industry, and the capacity of Morocco's biggest refinery, at Muhammadia, has increased to 6.75m. metric tons per year. There is another refinery, at Sidi Kacem, which has a capacity of 1m. metric tons per year.

One of Morocco's major import-substitution industries is cement production. The country's nine cement works produced a total of 3.9m. tons in 1987 (an increase of about 5.5% compared with 1986). Virtually all plants were working below capacity (average utilization of capacity was 70% in 1987), but there were indications of renewed growth in the construction industry and domestic production reached 4.6m. tons in 1988 and 5.4m. tons in 1990. In 1990 consumption of cement increased by 16.7%, compared with the previous year, and all the country's eight cement production units indicated consistent growth. Cement plants have attracted increased foreign investment in recent years, especially from France. Lafarge-Coppée of France now holds a 65% interest in Cementos Marroquies (Cemenmar), a 26.5% interest in the Cimenterie Nouvelle de Casablanca (Cinouca) and a 40% interest in Cimenterie de Meknès (Cadem). Annual capacity at the Cinouca plant in Casablanca has been increased to 1.9m. tons, following the opening of a new 700,000-ton production line. Production capacity at Cemenmar's Tétouan plant, cur-

rently 250,000 tons per year, may also be increased. Lafarge-Coppée has also taken an equity share in Readymix Maroc. Another French company Ciments Français, has a 51% share in Société des Ciments d'Agadir, which has a production capacity of 1m. tons per year, and controls 60% of Cimenterie de Safi, a new 600,000 tons-per-year plant to open in 1992. The IFC is providing financial assistance for the new Safi plant ($20.3m.) and for Cinouca's expansion programme ($17m.). In May 1994 the International Finance Corporation agreed to provide $10m. to modernize Ciment du Maroc's plant at Agadir. A further $4.2m. was to be provided by a syndicate led by Banque Indosuez of France. Among the largest privatizations to have been completed by mid-1994 were holdings of the Office pour le Développement Industriel, including Cimenterie de l'Oriental (Cior).

The food-processing industry remains of considerable importance. In 1981 the sector employed some 70,000 people and accounted for about 40% of the value of industrial production. It produces both for export and for domestic consumption. A large quantity of grain is processed into flour locally, but imported wheat is processed at a number of mills. There are currently 13 sugar beet factories with an annual processing capacity well in excess of 400,000 tons of raw sugar, as well as three cane works; annual capacity for raw sugar totals 534,000 tons, sufficient to meet 90% of local demand. In 1987 about 426,000 tons of raw sugar were produced, while the five sugar refineries produced nearly 686,000 tons of refined sugar for consumption. Sugar imports in 1986 reached nearly 300,000 tons and in 1987 declined by only 1.1%. Other food industries include fruit and vegetable processing and canning—mainly for export—and fish canning. Fruit and vegetable processing recorded low growth rates in the mid-1980s, despite the fact that manufacturers could market directly, rather than through the Office de Commercialisation et d'Exportation (OCE), which was dismantled as part of the Government's privatization programme. The major problem facing the sector lies in the restrictions imposed on exports by the EC, following its enlargement in 1986, with the inclusion of Spain and Portugal. In 1990 the agro-food sector comprised 69% of industrial investment.

The textile industry suffered from over-stocking in the mid-1960s, but in the 1970s its turnover grew at an annual rate of about 10%, and by 1981 it employed some 55,000 workers. Investment in textiles and leather increased from 361m. dirhams in 1982 to 717m. dirhams in 1984, and 966m. dirhams in 1986; in 1987 the level of investment nearly doubled, to 1,857m. dirhams. In 1988 textiles and leather accounted for 22% of total investment and 58% of projected employment, virtually all of this coming from textiles rather than leather. In 1990 investments in textiles and leathers increased by 45% (to 3,583m. dirhams, compared with 2,466m. dirhams in 1989). Textiles were at the forefront of export-led industrial growth, and export earnings increased significantly in the 1980s. Whereas in 1983 clothing exports were worth 683m. dirhams, by 1987 their value was 2,347m. dirhams (not far behind phosphates at 3,080m. dirhams). In 1988 Moroccan exports of textiles and leather goods together accounted for 38% of all manufactured exports. Owing to the Gulf crisis of 1990–91, Moroccan textile exports to Gulf markets were reported to have suffered. European markets for Moroccan products, however, had not been severely affected, although there has been a tendency for preference to be given to Portuguese and Eastern European goods. Spanish and Italian textiles firms have invested in Morocco in recent years, taking advantage of low labour costs. Tavex of Spain is majority shareholder in the Settavex textile scheme in Settat, which now employs 300 staff and produces 12m. sq m of denim cloth per year, with plans to double output. In January 1992 Carrera, the Italian textile firm, established a joint venture in Tangier with the local Nasco group to produce 2m. pairs of jeans per year.

In the engineering sector, there are four plants assembling cars and small utility vehicles: Renault Maroc, the Société de Promotion Industrielle et Automobile au Maroc (Peugeot-Talbot), SOMACA (Fiat), and the Société Méditerranéenne pour l'Industrie Automobile (Land Rover). Annual output has declined since the 1970s and now averages 10,000–13,000 vehicles. Heavy trucks (16.5 metric tons and over) are manufactured by Berliet Maroc and Saida; smaller capacity vehicles are assembled by Berliet, Auto-Hall and Siab. Berliet also assembles buses, and Somami-Rahali, a Casablanca-based firm, manufactures bus bodies for Daf chassis imported from the Netherlands. A limited range of motor vehicle components is made locally, as are tyres (847,000 units in 1984). Railway goods wagons, and mineral and tanker wagons are assembled by SCIF of Casablanca. In April 1994 the Ministry of Commerce, Industry and Privatization invited tenders to build and operate a plant producing an economy car for the local market and to develop the local components industry.

After severe droughts in 1992 and 1993 had exacerbated serious power shortages, the state power company, the Office National de l'Electricité (ONE), was forced to develop an emergency plan to increase generating capacity. Contracts for several new power stations were awarded in 1993 including the installation of 100MW new capacity at the CTZ-ZI power plant at Casablanca to be built by Technip of France at a cost of $88m. In October 1993 an agreement was signed between ONE and Tractabel of Belgium and AES of the USA to build and operate a 500MW oil-fired power station at Mohammadia. Output from the $600m. plant was to be sold exclusively to ONE under a long-term contract. An agreement for a second private power station was signed in November with Electricité de France and Endesa of Spain. The $400m. plant, to be built at Kenitra, was to have a capacity of 400MW and was to be supplied with natural gas from the Europe-Maghreb gas pipeline. By March 1994, however, little progress had been made on either project. After a number of senior management changes at ONE the state power corporation announced in April that the two private power projects would be put out to international tender. In June the Minister of Commerce, Industry and Privatization, Abderrahmane Saaidi, stated that the full or partial privatization of power distribution was under consideration. In July the EIB approved a loan of $96m. to ONE to help finance the interconnection of the Moroccan and Spanish power grids which will provide continuous capacity of 300MW, equivalent to 13% of the Kingdom's present power capacity. The $137m. contract to lay a 30km power cable under the Strait of Gibraltar was awarded to Pirelli of Italy and Alcatel Cable of France. The project represents the first power link between North Africa and Europe.

BALANCE OF PAYMENTS AND TRADE

Morocco's main sources of revenue are earnings from exports of phosphate rock and phosphate derivatives, agricultural products and manufactured goods, receipts from tourism and workers' remittances from abroad. The country's expenditure is mainly on imports of capital equipment, food and crude petroleum. After 1976 the deficit on the current account widened, as export earnings rose slowly while the cost of imports soared. In 1983 the government took strong measures to close the export/import gap by reducing budget expenditure and by restricting imports. This reduced the trade deficit from 13,552m. dirhams in 1982 to 11,218m. dirhams in 1983. However, the continuing decline in phosphate exports (by volume and value), and the high level of food and energy imports, resulted in further increases in the trade deficit, to 15,278m. dirhams in 1984 and to 16,938m. dirhams in 1985. Only the collapse of oil prices during 1986 enabled the trade deficit for that year to fall by 26%, to 12,505m. dirhams. In 1987 the trade deficit fell by a further 5%, to 11,881m. dirhams. Imports in 1987 rose by only 1.9%, to 35,271m. dirhams, while exports increased in value by 5.8%, to 23,390m. dirhams. However, the fact that total imports rose by over 14% in volume terms, compared with 1986, reflects Morocco's heavy reliance on a fall in international prices (particularly of oil and grain) for a reduced trade deficit. The trade deficit continued to fall in 1988, to 9,382m. dirhams, with imports of foodstuffs down by 3.9% and energy imports by 14.9%, while exports rose by 20%. The precarious nature of this improvement was revealed, however, by a sharp increase in the trade deficit in 1989, when exports declined by 5% and imports rose by 19%, compared with 1988. Even so, the improvements in the export performance of some sectors were encouraging, particularly the increase of more than 30% in export earnings from manufactured consumer goods in the first quarter of

1989. Results for the whole year, however, indicated that the trade deficit almost doubled, to 18,323.8m. dirhams. The decline in exports in 1989 was largely the result of a 75% drop in sales of phosphoric acid. In 1990 the trade deficit grew by 21% (despite an increase of 19% in exports), to 22,165m. dirhams. Imports increased by 22% in 1990, to 57,022m. dirhams. The 1990 trade deficit was equivalent to 10.5% of GDP. In 1991 the trade deficit rose to 22,437m. dirhams, despite a 7% increase in exports (from 34,858m. dirhams to 37,283m. dirhams and a decline in expenditure on energy imports. Imports rose from 57,023m. dirhams to 59,720m. dirhams, of which more than one-half were semi-finished products and industrial equipment. Food exports rose by 20.6% and there was a steady growth in sales of manufactured products. Exports of phosphates and derivatives accounted for 27% of total sales. The trade deficit increased in 1992 by almost 30%, to 28,846m. dirhams. Invisible earnings (remittances from migrant workers and tourist revenues) also increased, however, so that balance-of-payment problems were not anticipated. Sales of phosphates and products decreased from 10,047m. dirhams in 1991 to 8,491.7m. dirhams in 1992. Clothing sales remained constant at 4,137m. dirhams. Oil imports increased by almost 22%, and those of wheat nearly doubled as a result of the drought, totalling 2.42m. tons in 1992. Imports of industrial machinery rose from 2,460.7m. dirhams in 1991 to 2,711m. dirhams in 1992. In 1993 exports increased to 34,080.6m. dirhams and imports were reduced to 61,480.3m. dirhams, resulting in a reduction of the trade deficit to 27,400m. dirhams. Remittances from Moroccan migrants in Europe, the Kingdom's single largest source of hard currency, were projected to increase by 1% in 1993 from a total of $2,217m. in 1992.

Morocco's GDP is heavily dependent on agricultural performance. GDP grew at an average annual rate of 2.9%, in real terms, during 1978–84, although growth was depressed during several of those years, owing largely to poor harvests. Improved agricultural output in 1985 allowed GDP to rise by 6.3% in real terms, and an exceptional harvest in 1986 contributed substantially to the 8.4% growth in GDP for that year. In 1987 GDP declined by 2.6%, largely as a result of poor harvests, forcing agricultural output down by 13%, and stagnation in the phosphate sector, contributing to a 1.2% fall in output from the mining sector. A record harvest in 1988 boosted GDP growth to an estimated 10.4%. Other strong areas were manufacturing, energy production, commerce, transport and other services. In 1989, despite a good harvest, GDP grew by only 1.8%. GDP fell by approximately 3% in 1992, largely as a result of the drought, which reduced agriculture's share of GDP from 21% to 15%. At the end of September 1993 GDP was forecast to increase by as much as 3% in 1993 and to register a higher rate of increase in 1994.

France remains Morocco's largest trading partner, accounting for 24% of Moroccan imports and 29% of exports in 1989. In 1991 French exports to Morocco were worth 10,970m. francs, and imports from Morocco 10,849m. francs. Capital goods comprised about one-third of French exports, while consumer goods accounted for more than one-half of imports from Morocco. Its other major trading partners are Spain, Italy and Germany. Efforts have been made to diversify its trading partners, with some success: India became the fifth most important export market in 1987, Japan was the sixth largest importer in 1988, and there was likely to be growth in trade with Arab countries (which accounted for 7.3% of exports and 11% of imports in 1988). Iraq and the USA were major exporters to Morocco. US exports to Morocco increased from $398m. in 1989 to $497m. in 1990, the highest figure since 1984. Moroccan exports to the USA rose from $98m. in 1989 to $109m. in 1990. Trade with the other Maghreb countries remains limited but was expected to increase, following the creation in 1989 of the Union of the Arab Maghreb (UAM). Numerous initiatives have been taken to encourage closer economic collaboration and integration with other members of the UAM, including the lowering of customs and tariff barriers and promotion of trade and joint ventures. In the period January to November 1990 there was an increase in trade between Morocco and Algeria, although the total value of bilateral trade continued to remain lower than was previously forecast, reaching only 373.2m. dirhams for the period January to August. Morocco's surplus on its merchandise trade with Algeria increased from 1.5m. dirhams in 1988 to 35.8m. dirhams during the first eight months of 1990.

However, for the foreseeable future, Morocco's trade will be crucially dependent on Europe, as the EC takes more than 50% of exports and provides more than 40% of imports. In view of the importance of its trade relations with the EC, Morocco has continually sought more favourable trade agreements. A five-year agreement conferring 'partial association' on Morocco was negotiated in 1968 and came into force in 1969. A new agreement for an unlimited period was finalized in January 1976. Most Moroccan agricultural and industrial products are allowed free access to the EC, but restrictions remain on a few crucial items, such as olive oil, citrus fruit, wine, textiles and refined petroleum products. Most of these restrictions are being gradually reduced—the notable exception being textiles, where modified voluntary quotas came into operation in early 1987—and allowances are made for seasonal demand, in order to encourage Moroccan exports. In 1984 Morocco applied to join the EC, but, in the absence of European approval for its application, urged the Community to liberalize its trade policies; new quota agreements were signed in January 1985. The entry of Spain and Portugal into the EC in 1985 stimulated a whole series of discussions, in which Morocco, as one of the countries most affected, was deeply involved. It was later agreed that the voluntary quota system on manufactured goods should be abandoned, but no agreement was reached concerning agricultural exports. Proposals by the EC Commission covered the five-year transitional period up to 1990. However, ministers of foreign affairs from EC member states were unable to agree on the Commission's proposals, while Morocco also expressed serious concern at what it regards as the 'protectionism' of the EC and the inadequacy of the Community's arrangements for relations with Morocco. In July 1987 Morocco made a second application for full membership of the EC, which was rejected in October. In 1991 it was announced that the EC would provide a financial aid programme of $5,800m. for eight Mediterranean countries, of which Morocco was to be the largest benefactor (receiving $534m. in total funds). Concessionary loans would comprise 50%. In January 1992 the European Parliament decided to block $600m. of development aid, in protest at Morocco's record on human rights and in the disputed Western Sahara. Morocco then refused to agree a new fishing accord, and agreement was not reached until May. In April the EC Commission approved a policy document envisaging a new Euro-Maghreb partnership. In October the European Parliament eventually ratified a fourth financial protocol, according to which Morocco was to receive $580m. in new funding over four years. In September it was reported that the EC Commission was proceeding with plans to develop a free trade zone between the Community and the Maghreb states and that formal negotiations would begin in 1993. Negotiations would cover Moroccan demands for improved access to European markets for its agricultural products, and financial support for its industry during the transitional period. In March 1993 the President of the EC Commission, Jacques Delors, held talks with King Hassan during a visit to Morocco. In July 1993 it was reported that the EU had proposed an annual increase of 3% in quotas of citrus fruit, orange juice, fruit and vegetables from Morocco in 1997–2000. In December EU Ministers of Foreign Affairs gave their approval for negotiations to be opened with Morocco on the new Europe-Maghreb association agreement to be signed in 1996. The talks were expected to focus on means of improving terms for Moroccan agricultural exports, of compensating Morocco for the removal of its tariffs on industrial imports, and on Morocco's demands for substantial convergence funding.

In April 1994 Morocco hosted the signing of the General Agreement on Tariffs and Trade (GATT) Uruguay round trade pact in Marrakesh. Morocco had been one of the principal supporters of the GATT agenda in the Arab world. In July 1993 the maximum customs duty on imported goods was reduced from 40% to 35%, and, in line with the government's commitment to GATT, rates on some 2,300 products including textiles, fibres, paper and packaging, and foodstuffs, were reduced.

TOURISM

The tourist industry is an increasingly important source of foreign exchange. By 1987 the total revenue earned from tourism had reached 8,000m. dirhams, representing 23% of total exports of goods and services. Only phosphates and their derivatives, and workers' remittances, brought in more foreign exchange. Tourism is undoubtedly one of the growth areas of the Moroccan economy, and government incentives have played a significant part in its development. Special conditions drawn up in 1983 govern investment in tourism, including tax exemptions on capital goods imports, interest-free loans and, in certain circumstances, income tax exemptions for a ten-year period. Major tourist complexes were constructed at Casablanca, Agadir, Tangier and Restinga, near Tetouan. By the end of 1988 there were over 79,000 beds available in nearly 500 hotels, pensions and holiday villages. Most tourists stay on the southern, Atlantic coast. The total number of foreign tourist arrivals in 1987 was 1,566,254, an increase of 6.5% on the 1986 total. In 1989 the number of tourists visiting Morocco increased by 27% (to 2,515,251, compared with 1,978,420 in 1988). In 1990 3m. foreigners visited Morocco, increasing tourist remittances by 22%, to 10,500m. dirhams. This advance was due to a rise in the number of Algerian visitors, taking advantage of the 'open frontiers' that had been authorized by the UAM. In 1990 the number of visitors increased by 18%, although, owing to the Gulf crisis of 1990–91, tourist arrivals from Europe decreased by almost 7%, to 1.2m. As a result, the hotel occupancy rate in major tourist cities in 1991 was estimated at approximately 5%. In 1991 tourist receipts declined to 8,822.2m. dirhams, despite a 3.1% increase in arrivals, mainly accounted for by more visitors from other Maghreb countries. In January–May 1992 tourist receipts increased to 4,009m. dirhams, compared with 3,707m. dirhams for the same period in 1991. The number of visitors increased from 1.08m. to 1.28m. Tourist arrivals from Italy increased by 36%, and from Spain by 21.7%. There was also an increase in the number of tourists from Germany, the USA and Japan, although tourist arrivals from France decreased by 19%. France remains the principal source of tourists to Morocco. In September 1993 it was forecast that tourist revenues for that year would be 2% lower than expected as a result of the recession in Europe and Morocco's negative image in European countries.

In December 1992 the Ministry of Commerce, Industry and Privatization invited bids for five state-owned hotels in Tangier, Meknès and Casablanca, the first of 37 hotels owned by the Office National Marocain du Tourisme to be privatized. In March 1993 it was reported that all five hotels had been sold. A new approach to the privatization of state holdings in hotels was announced in April 1993. According to this, the Government will sell its holdings in four- and five-star hotels to international companies as a comprehensive transaction. The 1993 budget included a reduction in the allocation to the Office National Marocain du Tourisme to 90m. dirhams, indicating the government's commitment to disengage from the tourist industry. In May 1994 local investors purchased the Transatlantique hotel in Meknès, the sixth of 37 hotels to be privatized in accordance with the government programme.

TRANSPORT AND COMMUNICATIONS

There are 10 major ports: Casablanca, Safi, Muhammadia, Agadir, Kénitra, Jorf Lasfar, Tan Tan, Dakhla in the disputed territory of Western Sahara, along the Atlantic coast, and Nador in the north-east and Tangier in the north-west, both on the Mediterranean. Since the beginning of 1985 the major ports have been controlled by the Office d'Exploitation des Ports (ODEP). In 1985 ODEP began modernizing port equipment and facilities in a two-year development plan. In the period to 1990 ODEP planned to spend 1,350m. dirhams, more than half of which was to finance the development of ports. In 1991 several projects were announced, including a new container terminal at Casablanca, at a cost of 610m. dirhams, a 160m. dirham coal terminal at Jorf Lasfar and modernization of port equipment at ports controlled by ODEP. The World

Bank was to provide loans of $99m. to ODEP and $33m. to the central Government for the financing of these projects. The development at Casablanca involves building a 400-m quay, dredging, construction of a 'roll-on, roll-off' bridge, and associated infrastructure. The volume of traffic through all ports in 1988 reached a record 39.6m. tons, an increase of 12.7% over the 1987 total. In 1990 the volume of port traffic increased by almost 10%, compared with the previous year, to 37.9m. tons. In that year imports comprised 47% of the total volume and increased by 18.6%, compared with 1989. Exports increased by only 3% in the same year. The major goods handled include hydrocarbons and phosphates, sulphur and ammonia, triple superphosphate and phosphoric acid, citrus and other fruit, and vegetables. Of the total cargo handled in 1988, 42% went through Casablanca, 17% through Jorf Lasfar, 15% through Safi and 12% through Muhammadia. The volume of cargo traffic through Moroccan ports increased by 0.5%, to 40.5m. tons, in 1993; the 22.1m. tons of imports included 9.45m. tons of hydrocarbons and 3.87m. tons of cereals. In March 1994 work began on a new harbour at Dakhla in Western Sahara. When completed in 1996, it will become a centre for coastal and deep-sea fishing, and a 1,300-ha free-trade zone will also be established there.

The railways are operated by the Office National des Chemins de Fer Marocains (ONCFM). The national rail network covers around 2,000 km. There are two new extensions to the network, linking Nouasser to Jorf Lasfar, and Taourirt to the Nador port of Beni Enzar. In June 1988 Moroccan and Algerian officials met for discussions on a plan to re-establish an international rail link between the two countries. The ONCFM planned to invest 992m. dirhams in rail development in 1989. Projects included the doubling of the Rabat-to-Kénitra link, building a connection between Casablanca and the city's King Muhammad V airport, purchasing 21 locomotives and producing 80 passenger and 800 goods wagons. Also considered were an extension of the rapid transit system which runs between Casablanca and Rabat south to El Jadida, a rail link between Tourirt and Nador in the northeast, and a controversial plan to link Marrakesh and el-Aaiún, in Western Sahara. In mid-1992 it was announced that the African Development Bank had agreed to contribute $84m. towards an estimated $270m. programme to improve main railway routes, in particular the Casablanca-Fez line. Freight transport, of which 75% of the volume and 40% of the receipts are generated by the transport of phosphates, was 4.9m. metric ton-km in 1986. Passenger traffic increased steadily during the period 1984 to 1986 and reached 11.5m. in 1988. Receipts from passenger traffic amounted to 327m. dirhams in 1988.

The road network is well developed, comprising nearly 60,000 km of road, of which 47% is paved. Most of the roads are built to design standards appropriate for a volume of traffic substantially in advance of that which they are currently carrying. In 1990 there were 669,637 passenger cars and 215,323 commercial vehicles in use, as well as 19,409 motorcycles and scooters and 10,871 buses and coaches. Tonnage carried by public road freight transport under the auspices of the Office National des Transports (ONT) virtually doubled between 1976 and 1986, from 6.8m. tons to 13.4m. tons, and rose to an estimated 14.7m. tons in 1988. In 1991 the Government approved a decree permitting the Société Nationale des Autoroutes du Maroc to collect tolls on Moroccan motorways. The revenue received from the tolls on the Casablanca-Rabat motorway was to be used to finance the construction of the projected Tangier-Casablanca motorway. In April 1991 four international groups were invited to rebid for the construction of the central section of the Tangier-Casablanca motorway, between Rabat and Larache, and the contract was awarded to a group of Italian companies. The $220m. road project was to be funded by the AFESD and Italy. The first 40-km section north from Rabat via Kénitra was due to open in January 1995. The AFESD has agreed to a grant of $1.7m. for a study of the Maghreb Unity highway linking Nouadhibou, in Mauritania, with Benghazi, in Libya. Technical and economic feasibility studies are due for completion by the end of 1995. Sections of the highway are already complete or under construction. The state-owned road transport company, Compagnie de Transports du Maroc-Lignes Nationales (CTM-LN),

was privatized in 1993. The state retained 16% of CTM-LN equity for sale at a later date.

There are 10 major airports in Morocco, as well as about 50 landing strips for light aircraft. In addition, el-Aaiún in Western Sahara has an airport. In 1991 a four-year programme to expand and modernize Moroccan airports, at an estimated cost of 1,200m. dirhams, was announced. The Office National des Aéroports (ONDA) and the African Development Bank were each to provide a 25% loan to finance the project. The remaining 50% of the cost of the programme was to be negotiated. Marrakesh-Menara airport reopened in August 1991, after the extension of the runway and work on airport buildings at a cost of $8m. A new passenger terminal was opened in July 1992 at Casablanca's King Muhammad V airport. The airport handled 1.81m. passengers in 1991 and it was forecast that some 3.3m. passengers would pass through the airport in 1993. The ONDA plans the creation of a major industrial and commercial zone, occupying 200 ha, as the latest phase in the expansion of the airport. In 1993 a $36m. contract to build an aircraft maintenance centre at the airport was awarded to a group of US firms, led by Westinghouse Electric Corporation. In December 1992 the African Development Bank approved a loan of $102m. to support the ONDA's plans to upgrade the infrastructure of Morocco's airports. Royal Air Maroc (RAM), which was formed in 1953 and is 90% owned by the Government, is the national airline. It operates services to European and African countries, as well as to the USA. In 1988 RAM handled 1.7m. passengers, compared with 1.2m. in 1983. In 1989 the number of passengers travelling by RAM was 1.4m. Tourism accounts for a significant proportion of passengers carried, although flights for business-related purposes are increasingly important. Total freight carried by air has also continued to increase, reaching 47,700 tons in 1988. The RAM fleet consists of 24 aircraft. In 1985 RAM acquired the right to service its own aircraft. In a statement in January 1994 the Minister of Commerce, Industry and Privatization, Driss Jettou, stated that the privatization of RAM was under consideration.

Television and most radio services are controlled by the State, which runs a nationwide television network (Radiodiffusion Télévision Marocaine) and nine regional radio stations broadcasting in the Arabic, French and Berber languages. There is also a commercial radio network, which broadcasts from Tangier and Nador to North Africa (Radio Méditerranée Internationale). In 1990 there were 5.25m. radios and 1.85m. television sets in Morocco. A commercial television channel for subscribers opened in 1989. A $1,204m. plan by the Office National des Postes et Telecommunications (ONPT) to upgrade telecommunications received the support of local and international funds, including a loan of $125m. from the World Bank. In February 1994 the Minister of Post and Telecommunications stated that the government planned to increase the number of telephone subscribers from 830,000 to 1.56m.

BANKING AND FINANCE

Morocco's foreign debt rose sharply during the second half of the 1970s. In October 1980, in an attempt to control its escalating debt burden, Morocco negotiated a three-year loan from the IMF, totalling $1,000m., the largest loan ever granted to a developing country by the Fund at that time. The terms of the loan were modified in 1982, when the progress of the economy failed to meet the IMF conditions. By 1983 Morocco's debt had reached unmanageable proportions, and a new IMF agreement was negotiated as part of a debt-rescheduling arrangement with all of Morocco's creditors. Outstanding debt to the 'Paris Club' creditor countries and the Arab states was rescheduled in 1983, but negotiations with creditor banks continued until 1985. In 1985 Morocco negotiated a new arrangement with the IMF, but this encountered difficulties, as Morocco failed to achieve IMF targets in early 1986. Eventually, a new programme, with less stringent terms, was agreed in November 1986, to run until April 1988. The 'Paris Club' and the creditor banks agreed to reschedule debt repayments until the end of the IMF agreement. Meanwhile, between 1984 and 1987 the World Bank provided finance for several sectoral adjustment programmes within a general programme to restructure and reorient the Moroccan economy. The major elements of this restructuring programme included a shift to export-oriented production, privatization, a reduction in public expenditure, fiscal reform and tighter control over the economy as a whole. In September 1987 the World Bank declared that Morocco was 'well-poised' for economic success, as a result of its stabilization and structural adjustment programmes. The World Bank subsequently increased its lending, to make Morocco the Bank's third largest recipient after Turkey and Pakistan, during 1987. In mid-1988 the IMF approved in principle a new stand-by facility of SDR 220m. for the period from June 1988 to the end of 1989. The Fund generally approved of Morocco's macro-economic performance, but was somewhat critical of fiscal policy implementation. Debt owing to the 'Paris Club' of creditor countries was rescheduled in October 1988 and again in September 1990. In December 1988 the World Bank made further finances available as part of the structural adjustment support to assist Morocco with debt management. In early 1989 negotiations began for the rescheduling of $1,400m. owing to the commercial banks of the 'London Club' and continued until April 1990, when an agreement was reached. The new accord rescheduled about $3,200m. of medium-term debt over a period of up to 20 years and reduced the interest to be paid on the debt. The existing IMF stand-by agreement expired in December 1989 but was renewed for a further eight months in July 1990. In May 1991 Spain rescheduled official debt within Morocco's 'Paris Club' accords, which included credits provided by the concessionary lending agency Fondo de Ayuda al Desarrollo (FAD), repayable over 20 years. Total debt to Spain was estimated at 110,000m. pesetas ($1,012m.). In July the World Bank approved a $235m. loan to the financial sector, which would permit Morocco to develop domestic financial markets and to invest in private export-oriented industries. Morocco is also one of a small group of heavily indebted countries to benefit from a World Bank Export Credit Enhanced Leverage, which provides bank guarantees and some funds for private-sector projects already receiving support from credit agencies. According to the Ministry of Finance, Morocco's external debt at the end of 1991 totalled $21,000m., of which $10,600m. was outstanding to 'Paris Club' Governments, $3,600m. to the 'London Club' of commercial banks, $3,300m. to the World Bank, $1,600m. to the USA and $600m. to the IMF. In December 1988 the World Bank made further finances available to assist with debt management, and in 1991 the Bank announced that it would grant Morocco a loan of $300m. The money was to be disbursed later in the year and was to be used to restructure the mining sector and sugar industry. Morocco's economic prospects improved significantly at the end of 1991, when Saudi Arabia and other Gulf states agreed to cancel bilateral debts estimated at around $3,600m. In February 1992 the IMF approved a stand-by credit authorizing drawings of up to SDR 91.98m. ($129m.) to support the Government's economic programme from January 1992 to March 1993. At the end of this period the Government expected to be able to return to the international capital markets and to make no further demands on IMF resources. The 'Paris Club' Governments agreed to reschedule official debt worth $1,500m., and in March the World Bank approved a $275m. structural adjustment loan, the final loan in Morocco's economic rehabilitation, according to the country's official news agency. In August 1992, under the terms of the 'Paris Club' agreement signed in February, the USA announced that it would reschedule bilateral debt worth $101.1m. incurred up to 1983. Some $32.5m. in official development assistance is to be repaid over 20 years with a 10-year grace period. Some $68.6m. in consolidated debt and arrears is to be repaid over 15 years with an eight-year grace period. Figures released in May 1993 by the Ministry of Finance revealed that Morocco's external debt in 1993 was $21,305m. Paris Club member states accounted for $10,549m. (about half of the total debt), the London Club $3,525m. (17%) and international financial institutions $5,700m. (27%). Debt-service repayments in 1992 increased to $3,000m., but were projected to decrease from $2,848m. in 1993 to $2,126m. in the year 2000. In June 1993 the Ministry of Finance introduced new rules whereby Moroccan banks or private enterprises were allowed to raise credits with foreign financial institutions to finance imports of goods and services without prior authorization.

In November 1992 it was announced that France would increase the value of its 1992 financial protocol to 1,220m. francs from 800m. francs. In 1992 Morocco became the major recipient of concessionary financing from the Caisse Française de Développement, with loan commitments during the year totalling 274.5m. francs, compared with 160m. francs for Algeria and 110m. francs for Tunisia. In mid-1993, however, the French Ministry of Finance indicated that the level of support offered under the 1993 protocol would probably be less than that for 1992. In December Spain agreed to provide a new five-year credit programme worth $1,056m., renewing the credit line originally signed in 1988. The EU was to lend Morocco a total of ECU 438m. between 1992 and 1996, together with funds for structural adjustment and EIB loans for the Europe-Maghreb gas pipeline.

Continued pressure from the IMF to reduce the budget deficit proved effective in the short term. But windfall revenues earned from direct and indirect taxes in 1987 and 1988, as a result of a major overhaul of the fiscal system, gave scope for quite considerable increases in public expenditure in 1988 and 1989. A rise of 23% in VAT receipts (which had been introduced in 1986, despite considerable opposition as part of general reform of taxation), combined with an increase in direct tax revenues of 30% in 1989, was planned to contribute largely to the narrowing of the fiscal gap. In fact, the budget deficit continued to grow (see below).

Morocco's central bank, the Banque al-Maghrib, is the sole issuer of currency, holds and administers the State's foreign currency reserves, controls the commercial banking sector and advises the Government on its financial policies. Associated with the bank are six specialized credit institutions with specific sectoral responsibilities. There are 15 private commercial banks, of which the most important is the Banque Marocaine de Commerce Extérieur (BMCE), which has sole responsibility for arranging government export guarantees, all of which are at least 51% Moroccan-owned. In 1989 a new development bank, the Bank al-Amal, was established; three-quarters of its capital was to be made available in shares to Moroccans working abroad to encourage more investment from the expatriate community. The Crédit Populaire, which has specialized in handling the remittances of migrant workers for many years, was to be joined by the major Moroccan private bank, the Banque Commerciale du Maroc (BCM), which in 1989 acquired 10% of the capital of the Banque Méditer-ranéenne de Dépôts (BMD) in order to attract the savings of the 27,000 Moroccan workers in France who use the BMD. Several other Moroccan banks have heeded an appeal from the Minister of Finance and are extending their international activities. In February 1992 it was reported that the IFC had arranged a $110m. credit line for four commercial banks (Banque commerciale du Maroc, Banque Marocaine du Commerce Extérieur, Crédit du Maroc and Wafabank), the major source of term finance for the private sector. The credit lines will be used to make five 10-year loans to small and medium-sized private-sector firms. In December 1992 the Government approved a new banking law, which increased the scope for regulation in domestic banking. All local credit institutions are brought under the new legislation, which also gives greater protection for savers and borrowers. The law also codifies rules governing business banks and other credit institutions previously excluded from legislation. In the same month it was announced that Wafabank, one of Morocco's leading privately-owned banks, was increasing its capital through the issue of new shares on the Casablanca stock exchange. Other banks have been seeking foreign shareholders and increasing their capital to meet the growing demand for local banking services as the economy develops. In June 1993 the Banco Exterior de España became the first wholly-owned foreign company authorized to open a subsidiary in Morocco since the country won its independence. In August 1993 it was reported that the Banco Central Hispano-Americano (BCH) of Spain was to purchase a 15% interest in Morocco's largest bank, the BCM, subject to the approval of the Moroccan and Spanish monetary authorities, in an agreement valued at $48.8m. Preparations for the privatization of the BMCE were expected to begin in 1994. The state currently holds 50.39% of BMCE's capital.

By 1992 the volume of transactions on the Casablanca stock exchange had risen to 1,520m. dirhams, but this increased more than threefold in 1993 (to 4,870m. dirhams) as a result of the privatization of state companies, including CTM-LN and Ciments de l'Oriental. A major boost to stock exchange activity in 1994 was the issue of shares worth 1,500m. dirhams in Morocco's leading private company, ONA. The exchange traded 61 shares at mid-1994. In July 1993 it was reported that the government had approved a number of decrees to convert the Casablanca exchange into a private company with stock held by brokers, to create new stock-trading bodies, to channel small savers' funds into share issues and unit trusts, and to create a stock exchange commission.

In August 1991 Tangier became the kingdom's first 'offshore' banking zone. It is intended to attract major international banks, and their local operations must have a minimum capital of $500,000. Banks are offered exemption from corporation tax for 15 years, and during this period they pay a $25,000 annual licence fee. The new zone is intended to compete with other Mediterranean 'offshore' zones to attract capital into the kingdom. In April 1992 Crédit Lyonnais of France became the first bank to announce its participation in the new 'offshore' banking zone. Two local-French joint ventures, involving Crédit Lyonnais and Banque Nationale de Paris, were due to start operating in January 1993. In mid-1994 it was reported that the new Euratlas Capital Development Fund, and a new investment bank, the Maghreb International Bank, would be based in the Tangier 'offshore' zone.

DEVELOPMENT

The 1978 Five-Year Development Plan never came into effect, largely because of the disruption caused to the economy by the war in Western Sahara and the fall in phosphate revenues after 1975. Instead, a three-year transitional plan, which was to emphasize agriculture and industry, and attempt to reduce public expenditure, was introduced as part of the austerity measures adopted by the Government. The target for annual GDP growth was set at a modest 4.6%. Only 3% annual growth was, however, achieved in 1978 and 1979. In April 1981 a new Five-Year Development Plan came into operation, whose general aims were similar to that of its predecessor, but which envisaged a more rapid rate of GDP growth, at 6.5% a year. The level of investment was over-ambitious and, following the decision to reschedule the country's external debt in 1983, many of the Plan's targets were abandoned. The Government was obliged to make severe reductions in public expenditure in order to satisfy the terms of the IMF programme. Not only were the 1983 budget commitments for capital expenditure cut by over 20%, but even the revised targets for 1984 were reduced further. All major projects were postponed, except those already under way and likely to enhance export earnings or import savings.

The proposed 1986–88 Three-Year Plan, announced in April 1985, suggested further cuts in expenditure. Investment was to be reduced from the 1984 level of 20% of GDP to only 16.7%, while it was projected that GDP would rise by 2.9% per year. However, in late 1985 it was announced that this transitional plan was to be delayed, and a new set of proposals for a more expansionary programme was produced. These plans, however, were also deferred, largely as a result of IMF pressure, and a policy of bringing government spending more closely into balance with revenues was eventually pursued. Measures geared mainly towards tighter spending controls and the gradual reform of the fiscal system helped to reduce the treasury deficit in 1986. In 1990 the treasury deficit was reduced to approximately 3% of GDP. In October 1987 a new Five-Year Plan for 1988–92 was presented, in which 52% of funding was expected to come from the private sector. A large proportion of the investment funds was to be directed towards the newly-formed local authorities (collectivités locales), which were allocated 36,000m. dirhams. The Plan was expected to transform the current account deficit into a surplus, equivalent to 2.9% of GDP by 1992, and to enable exports to increase by 5.5% per annum. The Plan also aimed to mobilize

domestic savings for investment at a rate of 16.6% of GDP per year and to create jobs for the estimated 300,000 people entering the labour market every year. The Plan also included a reform of the public sector, envisaging the privatization of many state companies. Appropriate legislation for a privatization programme was approved by the Chamber of Representatives in April 1988 and came into force from January 1990. In early 1991 the Ministry of Economic Affairs and Privatization estimated the total cost of the Government's six-year privatization programme to amount to $10m. Later in the year, plans were announced to privatize state holdings in 112 enterprises, and two committees to monitor the transfer of shares until the end of 1995 were appointed. The first group of 10 companies selected for privatization, announced in March 1992, included the Cimenterie de l'Oriental, the Complexe Textile de Fès, Industrie Cotonnière d'Oued-Zem, the Compagnie de Transports au Maroc—Lignes Nationales, Chelco, the Société des Dérivés du Sucre, Iboval, Vetnord and the Hotel Mallabata. In April 1993 Moulay Zahidi, the Minister of Commerce, Industry and Privatization, stated that Morocco's privatization programme had started slowly but was now accelerating. In December 1993 it was announced that revenue from privatization in 1993 would probably total 2,500m. dirhams. In early 1994 plans were being finalized for the sale of SNI, which had holdings in 40 companies, and of Sofac-Credit. At the same time, the state began selling back to their original owners the petroleum products distributors nationalized in 1973. Royal Dutch Shell bought the state's holdings in Shell Maroc in January and Total and Mobil agreed to repurchase their local subsidiaries in May. In mid-1994 it was reported that nine privatizations in that year had yielded 775m. dirhams. In July 1994 the new Prime Minister, Abd al-Latif Filali, stated that the Government's privatization programme would be extended to include strategic sectors such as power generation.

The 1989 budget aimed to reduce further the budget deficit, mainly by increasing tax revenue, and to limit the increase in overall state expenditure to around 7%. In the event, however, revenues failed to increase as expected, and the budget deficit was greater than had been anticipated. The treasury deficit in 1989 was equivalent to 5.7% of GDP, rather than the projected 4.4%. The 1990 budget, which had been endorsed by the Chamber of Representatives at the end of 1989, was radically revised during the early part of 1990, while a variety of austerity measures were implemented to bring the situation under control, including a devaluation of the dirham in an attempt to improve the balance-of-payments deficit.

In accordance with the anticipated results of the 1988–92 Five-Year Plan, the main economic objectives for 1991 were to increase the rate of GDP growth to between 4% and 4.5%, a reduction in the annual rate of inflation to 5% (from a rate of 7%–8% in 1990) and a reduction of the budget deficit to 2% of GDP. The rise in investment in 1990 produced a more optimistic outlook for 1991. Foreign private investment increased to 2,582m. dirhams, compared with 1,230m. dirhams in 1989. This was equivalent to 23.7% of total investment of 10,888m. dirhams in 1990, compared with 15.3% of total investment of 8,046m. dirhams in the previous year. Consequently, 88,453 new jobs were created in 1990, compared with 66,271 in 1989. In November 1992 the government's Exchange Control Bureau reported that foreign investment rose by 70%, to 2,306m. dirhams in the first half of 1992, compared with the corresponding period of 1991. In October 1992 the head of the Office des Changes predicted that foreign investments during 1992 would exceed 5,000m. dirhams. Despite these positive indications, further economic reform is needed to improve Morocco's economic situation. In early 1991 the Government announced that domestic savings would be encouraged, that investment would be made more efficient and that concerted efforts would be made to reform foreign trade and the public and financial sectors, in an attempt to realize the year's economic objectives. The budget proposals for 1992, presented in November 1991, envisaged a substantial rise in social spending. Education was allocated 1,600m. dirhams (an increase of 21%), and health 552m. dirhams (an increase of more than 25%). Defence spending was to increase by 13.6%, to 10,000m. dirhams. Total spending was projected at 86,440m. dirhams, 5.5% higher than for 1991, and the deficit was to remain stable, at 1,450m. dirhams. To increase revenues, it was forecast that direct taxation would rise by 23.8%, and indirect taxes by 15.3%.

The budget proposals for 1993, presented in December 1992, envisaged a 6% increase in GDP during 1993. Overall revenue is expected to rise to 77,220m. dirhams, despite reductions in taxation. Expenditure was forecast at 80,000m. dirhams. Priority was to be given to education, public health, employment, irrigation and electric power generation. A reduction of the budget deficit was forecast, to 1% in 1993, compared with 2% in 1992 and 3% in 1991. Inflation was regarded as stable at 5.7% and foreign reserves had risen. Public investment was to increase by 11%. Under the 1993 budget, debts totalling 2,700m. dirhams owed by farmers will be rescheduled, and the Government was to pay off public-sector arrears worth 2,603m. dirhams to ease cash-flow problems besetting local suppliers. Some 800m. dirhams was allocated to increase youth employment, and more than 15,000 jobs were to be created in public administration. Under the 1994 budget proposals,

expenditure was projected to increase to 110,553m. dirhams. Of recurrent expenditure of 47,111m. dirhams, 12,900m. were allocated to education, and 9,400m. to defence. Revenues were projected at 105,352m. dirhams, including 23,719m. from indirect taxes, 17,098m. from direct taxes and 18,002m. from customs duties. The increase in recurrent expenditure was to be financed by an estimated 16% increase in tax revenues. The total projected deficit was 5,202m. dirhams. The Minister of Finance reported that debt-reservicing costs would increase by 17.3% in 1994, to 27,168m. dirhams. There was speculation that the Government's commitment to keep the budget deficit to 1.5% of GDP would be difficult to achieve because of pressure on state spending to maintain social stability.

In January 1993 the Government informed the IMF that the dirham was now convertible, except for capital transfers. The Minister of Finance stated that he was confident that the exchange rate would remain stable and forecast that hard currency reserves would increase again in 1993 from the current level of $3,400m. to $3,800m. Plans for convertibility have been the central pillar of the Finance Minister's policy.

Statistical Survey

Source (unless otherwise stated): Direction de la Statistique, Ministère du Plan, BP 178, Rabat; tel. 73606; telex 32714.

Note: Unless otherwise indicated, the data exclude Western (formerly Spanish) Sahara, a disputed territory under Moroccan occupation.

Area and Population

AREA, POPULATION AND DENSITY

Area (sq km)	710,850*
Population (census results)	
20 July 1971.	15,321,210
3 September 1982†	
Males	10,205,859
Females	10,182,358
Total	20,388,217
Population (official estimates at mid-year)†	
1992	25,547,000
1993	26,069,000
Density (per sq km) at mid-1993	36.7

* 274,461 sq miles. This area includes the disputed territory of Western Sahara, which covers 252,120 sq km (97,344 sq miles).
† Including Western Sahara, with a population of 163,868 (provisional) at the 1982 census.

PROVINCES AND PREFECTURES
(estimated population at mid-1993)

	Area (sq km)	Population ('000)*	Density (per sq km)
Agadir	5,910	831	140.6
al-Hocima	3,550	377	106.2
Azizal	10,050	421	41.9
Beni Mellal . . .	7,075	966	136.5
Ben Slimane . . .	2,760	206	74.6
Boujdour† . . .	100,120	10	0.1
Boulemane . . .	14,395	158	11.0
Chaouen . . .	4,350	369	84.8
el-Aaiún† . . .	39,360	144	3.7
el-Jadida . . .	6,000	944	157.3
el-Kellaa Srarhna . .	10,070	694	68.9
er-Rachidia . . .	59,585	511	8.6
es-Saouira . . .	6,335	431	68.0
es-Smara† . . .	61,760	26	0.4
Fès	5,400	1,051	194.6
Figuig	55,990	108	1.9
Guelmim . . .	28,750	171	5.9
Ifrane	3,310	118	35.6

	Area (sq km)	Population ('000)*	Density (per sq km)
Kénitra	4,745	940	198.1
Khemisset . . .	8,305	480	57.8
Khenifra . . .	12,320	450	36.5
Khouribga . . .	4,250	558	131.3
Marrakech . . .	14,755	1,549	105.0
Meknès . . .	3,995	765	191.5
Nador . . .	6,130	817	133.3
Ouarzazate . . .	41,550	661	15.9
Oued ed-Dahab† . .	50,880	28	0.6
Oujda . . .	20,700	992	47.9
Safi	7,285	862	118.3
Settat	9,750	799	81.9
Sidi Kacem . . .	4,060	610	150.2
Tanger . . .	1,195	579	484.5
Tan-Tan . . .	17,295	56	3.2
Taounate . . .	5,585	609	109.0
Taroudant . . .	16,460	668	40.6
Tata . . .	25,925	107	4.1
Taza . . .	15,020	724	48.2
Tétouan-Larache . .	6,025	878	145.7
Tiznit . . .	6,960	387	55.6
Casablanca . . . . Aïn Chok-Hay Hassani . Aïn Sebaa-H' Mohammadi . . Ben M'sick-S. Othmane . Mohammadia-Znata . .	1,615	3,406	2,109.0
Rabat-Salé . . . Skwrate-Temara . .	1,275	1,608	1,261.2
Total	**710,850**	**26,069**	**36.7**

* Figures are provisional.
† The provinces of Boujdour, el-Aaiún, es-Smara and Oued ed-Dahab form the disputed territory of Western Sahara.

PRINCIPAL TOWNS
(estimated population, incl. suburbs, '000 at mid-1993)

Casablanca . . .	3,406	Kénitra	.940
Rabat (capital)* . .	1,608	Tétouan†	.878
Marrakech		Safi	.862
(Marrakesh) . .	1,549	Agadir . . .	.831
Fès (Fez) . . .	1,051	Meknès . . .	.765
Oujda . . .	.992	Tanger (Tangier) .	.579

* Including Salé.   † Including Larache.

BIRTHS AND DEATHS (UN estimates, annual averages)

	1975–80	1980–85	1985–90
Birth rate (per 1,000) . .	39.4	37.3	35.6
Death rate (per 1,000). . .	13.0	11.4	9.8

Expectation of life (UN estimates, years at birth, 1985–90): 60.7 (males 55.5; females 61.5).

Source: UN, *World Population Prospects: The 1992 Revision*.

ECONOMICALLY ACTIVE POPULATION (1982 census)*

	Males	Females	Total
Agriculture, hunting, forestry and fishing	1,989,203	362,426	2,351,629
Mining and quarrying . . .	61,110	2,250	63,360
Manufacturing	593,738	336,877	930,615
Electricity, gas and water .	21,165	1,300	22,465
Construction	434,093	3,371	437,464
Trade, restaurants and hotels .	474,392	23,738	498,130
Transport, storage and communications . . .	136,853	4,128	140,981
Financing, insurance, real estate and business services.	} 725,938	280,974	1,006,912
Community, social and personal services . .			
Activities not adequately defined	381,488	166,216	547,704
Total	4,817,980	1,181,280	5,999,260

* Figures are based on a 5% sample tabulation of census returns. The data relate to employed persons aged 7 years and over and unemployed persons (excluding those seeking work for the first time) aged 15 years and over.

Mid-1992 (estimates in '000): Agriculture, etc. 2,853; Total 8,192 (Source: FAO, *Production Yearbook*).

Agriculture

PRINCIPAL CROPS ('000 metric tons)

	1990	1991	1992
Wheat	3,614	4,939	1,562
Rice (paddy)	3	25	22
Barley	2,138	3,253	1,081
Maize	436	335	216
Oats	47	77	30
Sorghum	16	15	18
Other cereals	22	24	25
Potatoes	882	1,074	900*
Sweet potatoes . . .	22	20	12
Dry broad beans . . .	134	204	68
Dry peas	63	68	10
Chick-peas. . . .	59	67	26
Lentils	33	51	19
Other pulses	56	67	40
Soybeans (Soya beans) . .	9	20	4
Groundnuts (in shell) . .	15	20	39
Sunflower seed . . .	159	87	187
Cottonseed. . . .	19	14	6
Olives	396	390†	500†
Artichokes. . . .	17	24	25*
Tomatoes	872	806	900*
Cauliflowers	37	20	21
Pumpkins, squash and gourds .	113	108	120
Cucumbers and gherkins . .	37	30	16
Aubergines (Eggplants) . .	42	32	30
Green chillies and peppers .	79	78	97
Onions (dry)	326	412	351
Green beans	33	23	25
Green peas	30	48	25
Carrots	180	187	161
Other vegetables . . .	510	565	463
Watermelons	394	367	238
Melons	371	308	313
Grapes	232	234†	294
Dates	120	107	82
Sugar cane	1,019	1,028	994

	1990	1991	1992
Sugar beets	2,984	3,036	2,754
Apples.	221	249	280
Pears	36	31	31
Peaches and nectarines . .	35	25	33
Plums	47	41	52
Oranges	781	1,097	784
Tangerines, mandarins, clementines and satsumas .	225	311	292
Lemons and limes . . .	18	20	20*
Apricots	74	92	66
Bananas	51	62	60*
Other fruits and berries . .	162	169	154
Almonds	58	67	55
Tobacco (leaves) . . .	7	7†	7*
Cotton (lint)†	10	7	3

* FAO estimate.   † Unofficial figure(s).

Source: FAO, *Production Yearbook*.

1993 ('000 metric tons): Wheat 1,573; Rice (paddy) 54; Barley 1,027; Maize 92; Oats 32; Sorghum 21; Pulses 77; Groundnuts (in shell) 34; Sunflower seed 45; Sugar cane 946; Sugar beet 3,162; Tangerines 300.

LIVESTOCK ('000 head, year ending September)

	1990	1991	1992
Cattle	3,346	3,438	3,300
Sheep	13,514	16,268	17,000
Goats	5,335	4,980	5,500
Camels.	34	33	33*
Horses	194	188	180
Mules	523	528	515
Asses	912	896	915

* FAO estimate.

Poultry (FAO estimates, million): 39 in 1990; 41 in 1991; 42 in 1992.

Source: FAO, *Production Yearbook*.

LIVESTOCK PRODUCTS ('000 metric tons)

	1990	1991	1992
Beef and veal	145	165	160
Mutton and lamb . . .	96	90	90
Goats' meat*	17	16	18
Poultry meat	147	143	152
Other meat	32	34	35
Cows' milk. . . .	974†	962	970*
Sheep's milk*	27	27	28
Goats' milk*	37	35	36
Butter*	15.3	15.2	15.3
Cheese*	7.5	7.3	7.5
Poultry eggs*	88.1	93.0	94.7
Honey*.	3.2	3.2	3.2
Wool (greasy)	35.0†	35.0†	36.0*
Wool (clean)	16.8†	16.8†	17.3*
Cattle hides (fresh)* . .	22.3	22.7	23.5
Sheep skins (fresh)* . .	11.2	12.0	12.0
Goat skins (fresh)* . .	2.5	2.4	2.7

* FAO estimate(s).   † Unofficial figure.

Source: FAO, *Production Yearbook*.

1993 ('000 metric tons): Beef and veal 142; Mutton and lamb 48; Goats' meat 10; Poultry meat 141; Poultry eggs (million) 1,600.

Forestry

ROUNDWOOD REMOVALS
('000 cubic metres, excluding bark)

	1990	1991	1992
Sawlogs, veneer logs and logs for sleepers	149	225	156
Pulpwood	158	597	472
Other industrial wood*	288	295	302
Fuel wood*	1,382	1,405	1,426
Total	**1,977**	**2,522**	**2,356**

* FAO estimates.

Source: FAO, *Yearbook of Forest Products*.

SAWNWOOD PRODUCTION
('000 cubic metres, including railway sleepers)

	1987*	1988	1989
Coniferous (soft wood)*	40	26	43
Broadleaved (hard wood)	40	27	40
Total	**80**	**53**	**83**

* FAO estimates.

1990–92: Annual production as in 1989 (FAO estimates).
Source: FAO, *Yearbook of Forest Products*.

Fishing

('000 metric tons, live weight)

	1989	1990	1991
Jack and horse mackerels	17.3	17.4	14.7
European pilchard (sardine)	330.1	345.9	370.6
European anchovy	8.0	10.5	19.6
Chub mackerel	35.6	27.7	11.2
Other fishes (incl. unspecified)	63.9	83.7	77.8
Total fish	**454.9**	**485.3**	**493.9**
Crustaceans	4.4	5.4	6.1
Cuttlefishes and bobtail squids	12.2	13.8	17.2
Octopuses	42.9	52.3	65.1
Other molluscs	6.1	8.6	10.6
Total catch	**520.4**	**565.5**	**592.9**
Inland waters	1.9	1.4	1.4
Atlantic Ocean	487.9	530.7	562.2
Mediterranean Sea	30.6	33.4	29.3

Source: FAO, *Yearbook of Fishery Statistics*.

1992 ('000 metric tons, live weight): Total catch 554.9.

Mining

('000 metric tons)

	1991	1992	1993
Hard coal	550.8	575.8	603.8
Crude petroleum	11.8	10.8	10.2
Iron ore*	98.7	84.7	66.3
Copper concentrates*	39.0	34.3	35.7
Lead concentrates*	103.4	105.0	111.9
Manganese ore*	59.3	49.1	42.6
Zinc concentrates*	51.5	42.4	125.7
Phosphate rock	17,900	19,145	18,305
Fluorspar (acid grade)	74.6	85.5	70.0
Barytes	434.7	401.6	349.6
Salt (unrefined)	143.9	164.5	147.0
Clay	37.6	38.1	8.7

* Figures refer to the gross weight of ores and concentrates. The estimated metal content (in '000 metric tons) was: Iron 58 in 1991; Copper 10.9 in 1991, 9.6 in 1992; Lead 70.6 in 1991, 72.4 in 1992; Manganese 30.4 in 1991; Zinc 26.8 in 1991 (Source: UN, *Industrial Statistics Yearbook* and *Monthly Bulletin of Statistics*).

Industry

SELECTED PRODUCTS*
('000 metric tons, unless otherwise indicated)

	1991	1992	1992
Cement	5,777	6,223	n.a.
Electric energy (million kWh)	9,205	9,720	9,895
Passenger motor cars ('000)†	23	17	n.a.
Phosphate fertilizers‡	1,180	1,070	n.a.
Carpets and rugs ('000 sq m)	1,156	879	900
Wine ('000 hl)	390	430	n.a.
Olive oil (crude)	40	55	n.a.
Motor spirit—petrol	352	403	397
Naphthas	465	542	301
Kerosene	47	45	43
Distillate fuel oils	1,797	2,080	1,919
Residual fuel oils	2,027	2,143	2,459
Jet fuel	183	206	223
Petroleum bitumen—asphalt	114	116	101
Liquefied petroleum gas	225	233	247

* Major industrial establishments only.
† Assembly only.
‡ Estimated production in terms of phosphoric acid (Source: FAO, *Quarterly Bulletin of Statistics*).

Finance

CURRENCY AND EXCHANGE RATES
Monetary Units
100 centimes (santimat) = 1 Moroccan dirham.

Sterling and Dollar Equivalents (31 May 1994)
£1 sterling = 14.02 dirhams;
US $1 = 9.27 dirhams;
1,000 Moroccan dirhams = £71.34 = $107.85.

Average Exchange Rate (dirhams per US $)
1991	8.707
1992	8.538
1993	9.299

BUDGET (estimates, million dirhams)

Revenue				1991	1992	1993
Direct taxes	.	.	.	13,505	16,694	15,342
Customs duties	.	.	.	12,908	14,470	14,743
Indirect taxes	.	.	.	17,328	19,336	20,359
Registration fees and stamp duties	.	.	.	2,591	2,650	2,567
Government property	.	.	.	118	152	117
State monopolies	.	.	.	2,668	2,811	2,980
Income carried in from adjusted expenditure	.	.	.	114	81	361
Gross borrowings	.	.	.	5,331	14,394	14,858
Nominal receipts	.	.	.	7	3	2
Total (incl. others)	.	.	.	57,562	73,465	75,919

Expenditure				1990	1991	1992
Current expenditure						
Administration	.	.	.	278	291	318
Personnel	.	.	.	21,873	22,754	25,430
Material and supplies	.	.		5,868	6,667	7,500
Common expenses	.	.		2,078	2,412	2,959
Debt servicing	.	.	.	22,433	24,604	22,437
Contingencies	.	.		250	996	1,081
Sub-total	.	.	.	52,780	57,724	59,725
Capital expenditure	.	.	.	12,675	12,900	13,592
Total	.	.	.	65,455	70,624	73,317

Source: Banque Al-Maghrib.

1993 (estimate, million dirhams): Expenditure 80,000.

CENTRAL BANK RESERVES (US $ million at 31 December)

				1991	1992	1993
Gold*	.	.	.	15	14	202
IMF special drawing rights	.			147	77	34
Reserve position in IMF	.	.		—	42	42
Foreign exchange	.	.	.	2,953	3,465	3,579
Total	.	.	.	3,115	3,598	3,857

* National valuation of gold reserves (704,000 troy ounces in each year).

Source: IMF, *International Financial Statistics*.

MONEY SUPPLY (million dirhams at 31 December)

	1991	1992	1993
Currency outside banks	34,269	35,745	37,202
Private sector deposits at Bank of Morocco	1,184	1,140	1,692
Demand deposits at deposit money banks	61,757	66,636	70,033
Checking deposits at post office	1,777	1,520	1,625
Private sector checking deposits at treasury	4,693	5,041	6,020
Total money	103,680	110,082	116,572

COST OF LIVING (Consumer Price Index; base: 1980 = 100)

				1990	1991	1992
Food	.	.	.	200.3	217.3	228.0
Clothing	.	.	.	176.9	189.5	198.6
All items (incl. others)	.	.		201.3	217.7	228.5

Source: ILO, *Year Book of Labour Statistics*.

1993 (base: 1989 = 100): Food 133.2; All items 128.5 (Source: UN, *Monthly Bulletin of Statistics*).

NATIONAL ACCOUNTS
Gross Domestic Product by Economic Activity
(million dirhams at current prices)

				1991	1992	1993*
Agriculture, forestry and fishing	.	.	.	48,010	36,031	35,419
Energy and water	.	.	.	15,515	17,795	18,994
Other mining and quarrying	.			5,313	5,054	4,872
Other manufacturing	.	.		41,739	43,699	44,637
Construction	.	.	.	12,060	12,040	11,641
Wholesale and retail trade†	.			49,445	51,310	51,659
Transport and communications				14,066	15,191	16,622
Government services	.	.		26,001	29,124	31,333
Other services‡	.	.	.	29,258	30,979	32,507
GDP in purchasers' values	.			241,407	241,224	247,683

* Estimates.
† Including import duties, less subsidies.
‡ After deducting imputed bank service charge.

BALANCE OF PAYMENTS (US $ million)

				1990	1991	1992
Merchandise exports f.o.b.	.			4,210	4,277	3,956
Merchandise imports f.o.b.	.			−6,282	−6,253	−6,692
Trade balance	.	.	.	−2,071	−1,976	−2,736
Exports of services	.	.		2,024	1,771	2,349
Imports of services	.	.		−1,441	−1,313	−1,457
Other income received	.	.		87	203	293
Other income paid	.	.		−1,130	−1,375	−1,416
Private unrequited transfers (net)	.	.	.	2,012	2,013	2,179
Official unrequited transfers (net)	.	.	.	320	280	360
Current balance	.	.	.	−200	−396	−427
Direct investment (net)	.	.		165	320	424
Other capital (net)	.	.		1,760	1,137	927
Net errors and omissions	.	.		9	88	2
Overall balance	.	.	.	1,734	1,149	926

Source: IMF, *International Financial Statistics*.

External Trade

PRINCIPAL COMMODITIES (million dirhams)

Imports c.i.f.				1991	1992	1993
Crude petroleum	.		.	6,580	8,007	6,693
Chemical products	.		.	2,529	2,393	2,718
Ships	.	.	.	945	274	644
Iron or steel sheets	.		.	1,016	1,100	828
Wood	.	.	.	1,343	1,666	1,400
Wheat	.	.	.	1,314	2,736	3,267
Sulphur	.	.	.	2,191	1,829	1,071
Fabrics	.	.	.	1,615	1,396	1,327
Synthetic plastics	.	.		1,433	1,459	1,484
Total (incl. others)	.	.	.	59,730	62,805	61,908

Exports f.o.b.				1991	1992	1993
Phosphates	.	.	.	3,016	2,621	2,416
Phosphoric acid	.	.		3,716	3,425	3,256
Fertilizers	.	.	.	3,316	2,446	2,895
Clothing	.	.	.	4,187	4,137	4,012
Crustaceans and molluscs	.		2,729	2,501	2,924
Citrus fruits	.	.	.	1,819	1,461	1,443
Hosiery	.	.	.	2,165	2,406	2,732
Canned fish	.	.	.	1,347	1,360	1,354
Fresh fish	.	.	.	1,205	871	738
Total (incl. others)	.	.	.	37,283	33,959	34,366

Source: Office des Changes, Rabat.

PRINCIPAL TRADING PARTNERS (US $ million)*

Imports c.i.f.	1990†	1991	1992
Belgium/Luxembourg . . .	182.9	197.7	199.5
Brazil	124.2	161.7	152.3
Canada	163.9	225.8	156.8
China, People's Republic . .	111.3	142.2	145.9
France	1,585.1	1,659.5	1,750.8
Germany	438.8	405.3	436.5
Iran	14.5	24.6	171.9
Italy	469.8	477.0	457.0
Japan	124.4	147.6	154.2
Libya	128.6	139.8	101.9
Netherlands	150.8	181.0	179.2
Saudi Arabia	185.0	336.2	405.1
Spain	579.6	567.4	627.9
Sweden	153.1	138.0	132.9
United Arab Emirates . .	367.3	260.7	259.8
United Kingdom . . .	243.1	237.2	201.5
USA	434.3	400.3	435.0
Total (incl. others) . .	6,922.0	6,858.8	7,355.9

Exports f.o.b.	1990†	1991	1992
Belgium/Luxembourg . . .	164.5	146.2	137.7
France	1,334.8	1,361.5	1,303.6
Germany	224.7	208.9	188.0
India	193.6	299.6	237.1
Italy	292.9	265.2	221.8
Japan	163.7	223.8	196.5
Libya	118.5	196.4	131.2
Netherlands	136.0	105.9	124.4
Saudi Arabia	95.3	114.2	65.4
Spain	388.0	377.1	359.1
United Kingdom . . .	137.7	117.4	133.2
USA	81.0	107.6	149.0
Total (incl. others) . .	4,231.4	4,282.0	3,977.4

* Imports by country of production; exports by country of last consignment.

† Source: UN, *International Trade Statistics Yearbook*.

Transport

RAILWAYS (traffic)*

	1991	1992	1993
Passenger-km (million) . .	2,345	2,233	1,904
Freight ton-km (million) . .	4,523	5,001	4,415

* Figures refer to principal railways only.

ROAD TRAFFIC (motor vehicles in use at 31 December)

	1991	1992	1993
Passenger cars	707,148	778,880	849,344
Buses and coaches . . .	11,292	11,660	11,967
Goods vehicles . . .	223,726	232,699	239,975
Motorcycles and scooters . .	19,487	19,592	19,689

SHIPPING
Merchant Fleet Displacement
(vessels registered at 30 June, '000 grt)

	1989	1990	1991
Total	454	488	483

International Sea-borne Freight Traffic
('000 metric tons)

	1988	1989	1990
Goods loaded . . .	23,900	21,450	20,257
Goods unloaded . . .	11,850	12,209	12,454

Source: UN, *Monthly Bulletin of Statistics*.

CIVIL AVIATION (traffic on scheduled services)

	1989	1990	1991
Kilometres flown (million) . .	27	30	27
Passengers carried ('000) . .	1,361	1,580	1,430
Passenger-km (million) . .	2,695	2,889	2,533
Freight ton-km (million) . .	34	32	56

Source: UN, *Statistical Yearbook*.

Tourism

FOREIGN TOURIST ARRIVALS

Country of Origin	1990	1991	1992
Algeria	1,452,645	2,048,616	1,659,634
France	451,817	290,630	428,983
Germany	161,186	108,462	184,645
Italy	80,372	67,505	113,348
Spain	210,802	193,207	276,988
United Kingdom . . .	89,467	58,473	95,267
USA	83,816	48,034	89,536
Total (incl. others) . . .	2,978,366	3,190,384	3,252,062

Source: Direction Générale de la Sûreté Nationale.

Communications Media

	1989	1990	1991
Radio receivers ('000 in use) .	5,100	5,250	5,385
Television receivers ('000 in use)	1,700	1,850	1,900
Telephones ('000 in use) . .	410	476	n.a.
Daily newspapers . . .	n.a.	13	n.a.

Sources: UNESCO, *Statistical Yearbook*; UN, *Statistical Yearbook*.

Education

(1989)

	Insti-tutions	Teach-ers	Pupils/Students		
			Males	Females	Total
Pre-primary . .	32,988	38,321	546,253	241,219	787,472
Primary . .	3,903	83,616	1,310,285	852,900	2,163,185
Secondary:					
General* . .	1,020	68,986	785,877	534,585	1,320,462
Vocational† . .	n.a.	n.a.	10,763	5,774	16,537
Higher:					
Universities, etc.	43	6,503	131,371	75,114	206,485
Other . . .	n.a.	n.a.	21,408	12,030	33,438

* State schools only.
† Data exclude professional schools.

Directory

The Constitution

The following is a summary of the main provisions of the Constitution, as approved in a national referendum on 4 September 1992.

PREAMBLE

The Kingdom of Morocco, a sovereign Islamic State, shall be a part of the Great Maghreb. As an African State, one of its aims shall be the realization of African unity. It will adhere to the principles, rights and obligations of those international organizations of which it is a member and will work for the preservation of peace and security in the world.

GENERAL PRINCIPLES

Morocco shall be a constitutional, democratic and social monarchy. Sovereignty shall pertain to the nation and be exercised directly by means of the referendum and indirectly by the constitutional institutions. All Moroccans shall be equal before the law, and all adults shall enjoy equal political rights including the franchise. Freedoms of movement, opinion and speech and the right of assembly shall be guaranteed. Islam shall be the state religion. All Moroccans shall have equal rights in seeking education and employment. The right to strike, and to private property, shall be guaranteed. All Moroccans shall contribute to the defence of the Kingdom and to public costs. Neither the state, system of monarchy nor the prescriptions related to the religion of Islam may be subject to a constitutional revision. There shall be no one-party system.

THE MONARCHY

The Crown of Morocco and its attendant constitutional rights shall be hereditary in the line of HM King Hassan II, and shall be transmitted to the oldest son, unless during his lifetime the King has appointed as his successor another of his sons. The King is the symbol of unity, guarantees the continuity of the state, and safeguards respect for Islam and the Constitution. The King shall have the power to appoint and dismiss the Prime Minister and other Cabinet Ministers (who are nominated by the Prime Minister), and shall preside over the Cabinet. He shall promulgate legislation that has been approved by the Chamber of Representatives within a 30-day period, and have the power to dissolve the Chamber; and is empowered to initiate revisions to the Constitution. The Sovereign is the Commander-in-Chief of the Armed Forces; makes appointments to civil and military posts; appoints Ambassadors; signs and ratifies treaties; presides over the Supreme Council of the Magistracy, the Supreme Council of Education and the Supreme Council for National Reconstruction; and exercises the right of pardon. In cases of threat to the national territory or to the action of constitutional institutions, the King, having consulted the President of the Chamber of Representatives and the Chairman of the Constitutional Council, and after addressing the nation, shall have the right to declare a State of Emergency by royal decree. The State of Emergency shall not entail the dissolution of the Chamber of Representatives and shall be terminated by the same procedure followed in its proclamation.

LEGISLATURE

This shall consist of a single assembly, the Chamber of Representatives, whose members are to be elected for a six-year term. Two-thirds of the members shall be elected by direct universal suffrage, and one-third by an electoral college composed of councillors in local government and employers' and employees' representatives. The Chamber shall adopt legislation, which may be initiated by its members or by the Prime Minister; authorize any declaration of war; initiate a revision of the Constitution; and approve any extension beyond 30 days of a state of emergency. The Chamber of Representatives shall hold its meetings during two sessions each year, which shall commence on the second Friday in April and the second Friday in October.

GOVERNMENT

The Government, composed of the Prime Minister and his Ministers, shall be responsible to the King and the Chamber of Representatives and shall ensure the execution of laws. The Prime Minister shall be empowered to initiate legislation and to exercise statutory powers except where these are reserved to the King. He shall present to the Chamber the Government's intended programme and shall be responsible for co-ordinating ministerial work.

RELATIONS BETWEEN THE AUTHORITIES

The King may request a second reading, by the Chamber of Representatives, of any draft bill or proposed law. In addition he may submit proposed legislation to a referendum by decree; and dissolve the Chamber if a proposal that has been rejected by it is approved by referendum. He may also dissolve the Chamber by decree after consulting the Chairman of the Constitutional Council, and addressing the nation, but the succeeding Chamber may not be dissolved within a year of its election. The Chamber of Representatives may force the collective resignation of the Government either by refusing a vote of confidence or by adopting a censure motion.

THE CONSTITUTIONAL COUNCIL

A Constitutional Council shall be established, consisting of a Chairman, four members appointed by the King for a period of six years, and four members appointed by the President of the Chamber of Representatives for the same period. Half of each category of the Council shall be renewed every three years. The Council shall be empowered to judge the validity of legislative elections and referendums, as well as that of organic laws and the Rules of Procedure of the Chamber of Representatives, submitted to it.

THE ECONOMIC AND SOCIAL COUNCIL

An Economic and Social Council shall be established to give its opinion on all matters of an economic or social nature. Its constitution, organization, prerogatives and rules of procedure shall be determined by an organic law.

JUDICIARY

The Judiciary shall be independent. Judges shall be appointed on the recommendation of the Supreme Council of the Judiciary presided over by the King.

The Government

HEAD OF STATE

HM King Hassan II (acceded 3 March 1961).

CABINET
(September 1994)

Prime Minister: Abd al-Latif Filali.

Minister of State: Moulay Ahmad Alaoui.

Minister of State for the Interior and Information: Driss Basri.

Minister of State for Foreign Affairs and Co-operation: Taieb el-Fassi Fihri.

Minister of Justice: Mohamed Idrissi Alami Machichi.

Minister of Public Health: Dr Abderrahim Harrouchi.

Minister of Finance: Mourad Cherif.

Minister of National Education: Mohamed Knidri.

Minister of Ocean Fisheries and the Merchant Navy: Mustapha Sahel.

Minister of Equipment, Cadres and Vocational Training: Mohamed Hassad.

Minister of Transport: Rachid al-Ghazouani.

Minister of Posts and Telecommunications: Abdesslam Ahizoun.

Minister of Agriculture and Agrarian Reform: Abd al-Aziz Meziane.

Minister of Youth and Sports: Moulay Driss Alaoui M'Daghri.

Minister of Commerce, Industry, Privatization, Foreign Trade and Handicrafts: Driss Jettou.

Minister of Religious Endowments (Awqaf) and Islamic Affairs: Abd al-Kaebir Alaoui M'Daghri.

Minister of Employment and Social Affairs: Rafiq Haddaoui.

Minister of Energy and Mines: Abd al-Latif Guerraoui.

Minister of Cultural Affairs: Mohamed Allal Sinaceur.

Minister of Housing: Driss Toulali.

Minister of Tourism: Serge Berdugo.

Secretary-General of the Government: Abdessadek Rabi.

Minister Delegate to the Prime Minister's Office in charge of Administrative Affairs: AZIZ HASBI.

Minister Delegate to the Prime Minister: ABDERRAHMANE SBAI.

Minister Delegate to the Prime Minister, in charge of the Moroccan Community Abroad: AHMED EL OUARDI.

Minister Delegate to the Prime Minister, in charge of Relations with Parliament: MOHAMED MOUTASSEM.

Minister Delegate to the Prime Minister: OMAR KABBAJ.

Minister Delegate to the Prime Minister, in charge of Human Rights: OMAR AZZIMAN.

Minister Delegate to the Prime Minister: ABDERRAHMANE SAIDI.

Deputy Secretary of State to the Interior Minister, in charge of the Protection of the Environment: CHAOUKI SARGHINI.

MINISTRIES

Ministry of Agriculture and Agrarian Reform: Quartier Administratif, Rabat; tel. (7) 60993; telex 31038.

Ministry of Commerce, Industry and Privatization: ave Tadla Aviation, Mabella, Rabat; tel. (7) 75-15-32; telex 32025; fax (7) 517-39.

Ministry of Cultural Affairs: rue Gandhi, Rabat; tel. (7) 66054.

Ministry of Employment and Social Affairs: Quartier Administratif, Rabat; tel. (7) 60521; telex 31057.

Ministry of Energy and Mines: ave Maa al-Ainane, Rabat; tel. (7) 77924; telex 32761.

Ministry of Equipment, Cadres and Vocational Training: Quartier Administratif, Rabat; tel. (7) 65473; telex 31613.

Ministry of Finance: ave Muhammad V, Quartier Administratif, Rabat; tel. (7) 62171; telex 31820.

Ministry of Foreign Affairs and Co-operation: ave Franklin Roosevelt, Rabat; tel. (7) 62841; telex 31007.

Ministry of Foreign Trade, Foreign Investments and Handicrafts: Quartier Administratif, Rabat; tel. (7) 61701; telex 36641.

Ministry of Housing: Quartier Administratif, Rabat; tel. (7) 60263; telex 32744.

Ministry of the Interior and Information: place de la Poste Centrale, Rabat; tel. (7) 66016; telex 31015.

Ministry of Justice: 485 blvd Muhammad V, Rabat; tel. (7) 60041; telex 31888.

Ministry of National Education: place de la Victoire, Rabat; tel. (7) 771822; telex 36016.

Ministry of Ocean Fisheries and the Merchant Navy: 63 blvd Moulay Youssef, Rabat; tel. (7) 63366; telex 32679.

Ministry of Posts and Telecommunications: ave Moulay Hassan, Rabat; tel. (7) 702091; telex 36043; fax (7) 705641.

Ministry of Public Health: 335 ave Muhammad V, Rabat; tel. (7) 61121; telex 31642.

Ministry of Religious Endowments (Awqaf) and Islamic Affairs: Enceinte du Palais Royal, Rabat; tel. (7) 62703; telex 31771.

Ministry of Tourism: Rabat.

Ministry of Transport: rue Maa al-Ainane, Casier Officiel, Rabat-Chellah; tel. (7) 73486; telex 31626.

Ministry of Youth and Sports: 485 blvd Muhammad V, Rabat; tel. (7) 60041; telex 32652.

Legislature

MAJLIS AN-NUWAB

(Chamber of Representatives)

President: AHMAD OSMAN.

1993 Elections
(direct voting on 25 June; electoral college voting took place on 17 September).

	Seats by Direct Election	Seats by Indirect Election	Total Seats
Union Socialiste des Forces Populaires	48	8	56
Union Constitutionnelle	27	27	54
Istiqlal	43	9	52
Mouvement Populaire	33	18	51
Rassemblement National des Indépendants	28	13	41
Mouvement National Populaire	14	11	25
Parti National Démocrate	14	10	24
Parti du Progrès et du Socialisme	6	4	10
Parti Démocratique pour l'Indépendance	3	6	9
Union Marocaine du Travail*	—	3	3
Organisation de l'Action Démocratique et Populaire	2	—	2
Parti de l'Action	2	—	2
Independents	2	2	4
Total	222	111	333

* A trade union federation.

Political Organizations

Bloc Démocratique (Koutla Dimocratya): f. 1992; opposition alliance comprising the USFP, Istiqlal, the OADP, the PPS and the UNFP; supported by trade unions and other groupings.

Entente Nationale: loyalist, centre-right coalition.

Istiqlal: 4 charia Ibnou Toumert, Rabat; tel. (7) 730951; fax (7) 725354; f. 1944; aims to raise living standards and to confer equal rights on all; stresses the Moroccan claim to Western Sahara; Sec.-Gen. MUHAMMAD BOUCETTA.

Mouvement National Populaire (MNP): f. 1991; Leader MAHJOUBI AHERDANE.

Mouvement Populaire (MP): 12 rue Marinin Hassan, Rabat; tel. (7) 730808; fax (7) 200165; f. 1959; conservative; Sec. Gen. MUHAMMAD LAENSER.

Mouvement Populaire Constitutionnel et Démocratique (MPCD): 352 blvd Muhammad V, Rabat; tel. (7) 702347; f. 1967; breakaway party from Mouvement Populaire; Leader Dr ABD AL-KARIM KHATIB.

Organisation de l'Action Démocratique et Populaire (OADP): BP 15797, Casablanca; tel. (2) 278442; f. 1983; Sec.-Gen. MUHAMMAD BEN SAÏD.

Parti de l'Action: 113 ave Allal ben Abdallah, Rabat; tel. (7) 24973; f. 1974; advocates democracy and progress; Sec.-Gen. ABDALLAH SENHAJI.

Parti de l'Avant-garde Démocratique Socialiste (PADS): an offshoot of the USFP; legalized in April 1992.

Parti du Centre Social: Centre socialist party.

Parti Démocratique pour l'Indépendance: Casablanca; tel. (2) 223359; f. 1946; Leader THAMI EL-OUAZZANI.

Parti Libéral Progressiste (PLP): Casablanca; f. 1974; advocates individual freedom and free enterprise; Leader AKHMOUCH AHMAD OULHAJ.

Parti National Démocrate (PND): 18 rue de Tunis, Rabat; tel. (7) 30754; f. 1981 from split within RNI; working within the framework of the constitutional monarchy, aims to support the democratic process, defend Morocco's territorial integrity and reduce social and economic disparities; Leader ARSALANE EL-JADIDI.

Parti National pour l'Unité et la Solidarité: Casablanca; tel. (2) 370501; f. 1982; Sec.-Gen. MUHAMMAD ASMAR.

Parti du Renouveau et du Progrès (PRP): 32 rue Lédru Rollin, BP 13152, Casablanca; tel. (2) 222238; f. 1974; successor to the Parti Communiste Marocain (banned in 1952), and the Parti de la Libération et du Socialisme (banned in 1969); name changed from Parti du Progrès et du Socialisme (PPS) in 1994; left-wing; advocates nationalization and democracy; 35,000 mems; Sec.-Gen. ALI YATA.

Rassemblement National des Indépendants (RNI): rue Erfour, Rabat; tel. (7) 65418; f. 1978 from the pro-government independents' group that formed the majority in the Chamber of Representatives; Leader MOULAY AHMAD ALAOUI.

Union Constitutionnelle (UC): 4 ave Bin El Ouidane, Rabat; tel. (7) 76935; telex 24645; f. 1983; 25-member Political Bureau; Leader MAATI BOUABID.

Union Nationale des Forces Populaires (UNFP): 28 rue Magellan, BP 747, Casablanca; tel. (2) 302023; f. 1959 by MEHDI BEN BARKA from a group within Istiqlal; left-wing; in 1972 a split occurred between the Casablanca and Rabat sections of the party; Leader MOULAY ABDALLAH IBRAHIM.

Union Socialiste des Forces Populaires (USFP): 17 rue Oued Souss, Agdal, Rabat; tel. (7) 73905; telex 31966; f. 1959 as UNFP, became USFP in 1974; left-wing progressive party, has consistently boycotted elections; 100,000 mems; First Sec. FATHALLAH OULAALOU.

The following group is active in the disputed territory of Western Sahara:

Frente Popular para la Liberación de Saguia el Hamra y Rio de Oro (Frente Polisario) (Polisario Front): BP 10, El-Mouradia, Algiers; f. 1973 to gain independence for Western Sahara, first from Spain and then from Morocco and Mauritania; signed peace treaty with Mauritanian Government in 1979; supported by the Algerian Government; in February 1976 proclaimed the Sahrawi Arab Democratic Republic (SADR), since recognized by 30 member-states of the OAU (to which it was admitted in February 1982 as the 51st member) and by more than 70 countries worldwide; its main organs are a seven-member executive committee, a 27-member Political Bureau and a 45-member Sahrawi National Council; Sec.-Gen. of the Polisario Front and Pres. of the SADR MUHAMMAD ABD AL-AZIZ; Prime Minister of the SADR BOUCHRAYA HAMMOUDI BAYOUNE.

Diplomatic Representation

EMBASSIES IN MOROCCO

Algeria: 46 blvd Tariq Ibn Ziad, Rabat; tel. (7) 65092; Ambassador: MOHAMED GHOUALMI.

Argentina: 12 rue Mekki Bitaouri Souissi, Rabat; tel. (7) 55120; telex 31017; Ambassador: MARCELO DELPECHE.

Austria: 2 Zankat Tiddas, BP 135, Rabat; tel. (7) 764003; telex 31623; fax (7) 765425; Ambassador: TASSILO OGRINZ.

Belgium: 6 ave de Marrakech, BP 163, Rabat; tel. (7) 64746; telex 31087; Ambassador: ANDRÉ FONTAINE.

Brazil: 1 charia Marrakech, Rabat; tel. (7) 765522; telex 31628; fax (7) 766705; Ambassador: ANTÔNIO S. CANTUARIA GUIMARÃES.

Bulgaria: 4 ave de Meknès, Rabat; tel. (7) 764082; telex 31761; fax (7) 763201; Ambassador: KOSSIO PROYKOV KITIPOV.

Cameroon: 20 rue du Rif, Souissi, Rabat; Ambassador: MAHAMAT PABA SALE.

Canada: 13 bis rue Jaafar as-Sadik, BP 709, Agdal, Rabat; tel. (7) 772880; telex 31964; fax (7) 772887; Ambassador: ROBERT KENNETH HIGHAM.

Central African Republic: Villa 42, ave Pasteur, Agdal, Rabat; tel. (7) 70203; telex 31920; Ambassador: JULES KOUALEYABORO.

China, People's Republic: 16 Charia al-Fahs, Rabat; tel. (7) 54056; telex 31023; Ambassador: AN GUOZHENG.

Côte d'Ivoire: 21 Zankat Tiddas, BP 192, Rabat; tel. (7) 63151; telex 31070; Ambassador: AMADOU THIAM.

Czech Republic: Zankat Ait Melloul, BP 410, Souissi, Rabat; tel. (7) 55421; telex 32941; fax (7) 55420; Chargé d'affaires a.i.: VIKTOR LORENC.

Denmark: 4 rue de Khémisset, BP 203, Rabat; tel. (7) 67986; telex 31077; fax (7) 69709; Ambassador: SVEN KUCHLER POULSEN.

Egypt: 31 Zankat Al Jazair, Rabat; tel. (7) 31833; Ambassador: MUHAMMAD BESHR.

Equatorial Guinea: 30 ave des Nations Unies, BP 723, Agdal, Rabat; tel. (7) 74205; telex 31796; Ambassador: RESURRECCIÓN BITA.

Finland: 18 rue de Khémisset, Rabat; tel. (7) 62352; Ambassador: HEIKKI KALHA.

France: 3 rue Sahnoun, Rabat; tel. (7) 777822; telex 31013; fax (7) 777752; Ambassador: HENRI DE COIGNAC.

Gabon: ave des Zaërs, Km 3.5, Rabat; tel. (7) 51968; telex 31999; Ambassador: CLAUDE ROGER OWANSANGO.

Germany: 7 Zankat Madnine, BP 235, Rabat; tel. (7) 709662; telex 36026; fax (7) 706851; Ambassador: Dr WILFRIED HOFMAN.

Greece: 23 rue d'Oujda, Rabat; tel. (7) 23839; telex 31953; Ambassador: DIMITRI SKOUROLIAKOS.

Guinea: 15 rue Hamzah, Rabat; tel. (7) 674148; telex 31796; fax (7) 672513; Ambassador: El-Haj GUIRANE NIDIAYE.

Holy See: rue Béni M'tir, BP 1303, Souissi, Rabat (Apostolic Nunciature); tel. (7) 772277; fax (7) 756213; Apostolic Nuncio: Most Rev. DOMENICO DE LUCA, Titular Archbishop of Teglata in Numidia.

Hungary: BP 5026, Souissi II, Rabat; tel. (7) 750757; telex 32718; fax (7) 775423; Ambassador: BÉLA BÉNYEI.

Indonesia: 63 rue Béni Boufrah, Rabat; tel. (7) 57860; telex 32783; fax (7) 57859; Ambassador: TAWFIQ RACHMAN SOEDARBO.

Iran: route de Zair, Kacem, Souissi, Rabat; tel. (7) 52167; fax (7) 50353; Ambassador: JA'FAR SHAMSIAN.

Iraq: 39 rue Béni Iznassen, Souissi, Rabat; tel. (7) 54466; telex 31663; Ambassador: FADHIL AL-SHAHIR.

Italy: 2 Zankat Idriss el-Azhar, BP 111, Rabat; tel. (7) 766597; telex 32731; fax (7) 766882; Ambassador: GIUSEPPE PANOCCHIA.

Japan: 70 ave des Nations Unies, Agdal, Rabat; tel. (7) 674163; telex 31901; fax 672274; Ambassador: KYOICHI OMURA.

Jordan: Villa al-Wafae, Lot 5, Souissi II, Rabat; tel. (7) 59270; telex 31085; fax (7) 58722; Ambassador: HUSSEIN HAMMAMI.

Korea, Republic: 41 ave Bani Iznassen, Souissi, Rabat; tel. (7) 751767; telex 31698; fax (7) 750189; Ambassador: KIM DONG-HO.

Kuwait: Rm 413, charia Iman Malik, Rabat; tel. (7) 56423; telex 31955; Ambassador: ABD AL-MUHSIN SALEM AL-HAROUN.

Lebanon: 19 ave de Fès, Rabat; tel. (7) 60728; telex 31060; Ambassador: SAMI OMAR KRONFOL.

Libya: 1 rue Chouaïb Doukkali, BP 225, Rabat; tel. (7) 68828; telex 31957; Chargé d'affaires a.i.: MUHAMMAD ZWAI.

Mauritania: 9 rue Taza, Souissi, Rabat; Ambassador: SIDNA OULD CHEIKH TALEB BOUYA.

Mexico: 10 ave de Marrakech, Rabat; tel. (7) 767956; telex 36248; fax (7) 758583; Ambassador: SALVADOR CAMPOS ICARDO.

Netherlands: 40 rue de Tunis, BP 329, Rabat; tel. (7) 733512; telex 31962; fax (7) 733333; Ambassador: Jonkheer D. M. SCHORER.

Nigeria: 70 ave Omar ibn al-Khattab, BP 347, Agdal, Rabat; tel. (7) 671857; telex 31976; fax 672739; Ambassador: Y. USMAN.

Oman: 21 rue Hamza, Agdal, Rabat; tel. (7) 71064; telex 31747; Ambassador: MUHAMMAD BIN SALIM AL-SHANFARI.

Pakistan: 2 blvd Soomat Hassan, Rabat; tel. (7) 31791; telex 31918; Ambassador: MUHAMMAD SAFDAR.

Peru: 16 rue d'Ifrane, Rabat; tel. (7) 723236; telex 32659; fax (7) 702803; Chargé d'affaires: ENRIQUE ZAÑARTU.

Poland: 23 Zankat Oqbah, Agdal, BP 425, Rabat; tel. (7) 71791; telex 31003; Ambassador: MIROSŁAW WOJCIECHOWSKI.

Portugal: 5 rue Thami Lamdouar, Souissi, Rabat; tel. (7) 56446; telex 31711; Ambassador: JORGE RITTO.

Qatar: 4 charia Tarik ibn Ziad, BP 1220, Rabat; tel. (7) 65681; telex 31624; Ambassador: ALI AHMED AS-SULAITI.

Romania: 10 rue d'Ouezzane, Rabat; tel. (7) 27899; Ambassador: Dr EMILIAN MANCIUR.

Russia: Km 4, route des Zaërs, Rabat; tel. (7) 53581; telex 31602; Ambassador: YURI M. RYBAKOV.

Saudi Arabia: 43 place de l'Unité Africaine, Rabat; tel. (7) 30171; telex 32875; Ambassador: ALI MAJED KABBANI.

Senegal: 17 rue Cadi ben Hamadi Senhaji, Souissi, Rabat; tel. (7) 54148; telex 31048; Ambassador: Gen. COUMBA DIOUF NIANG.

Spain: 3 Zankat Madnine, Rabat; tel. (7) 68638; telex 31073; Ambassador: JOAQUÍN ORTEGA SALINAS.

Sudan: 5 ave Ghomara, Souissi, Rabat; tel. (7) 52863; Ambassador: ABDALLA MAGHOUB.

Sweden: 159 ave John Kennedy, BP 428, Rabat; tel. (7) 759303; telex 36541; fax (7) 758048; Ambassador: MATHIAS MOSSBERG.

Switzerland: Sq de Berkane, BP 169, Rabat; tel. (7) 66974; telex 31996; fax (7) 05749; Ambassador: GÉRARD FRANEL.

Tunisia: 6 ave de Fès, Rabat; tel. (7) 30636; telex 31009; Ambassador: ABDERRAZAK KEFI.

Turkey: 7 ave de Fès, Rabat; tel. (7) 762605; telex 36164; fax (7) 704980; Ambassador: ONDER OZAR.

United Arab Emirates: 11 ave des Alaouines, Rabat; tel. (7) 30975; telex 31697; Ambassador: ISSAA HAMAD BUSHAHAB.

United Kingdom: 17 blvd de la Tour Hassan, BP 45, Rabat; tel. (7) 720905; telex 31022; fax (7) 704531; Ambassador: Sir ALLAN RAMSAY.

USA: 2 charia Marrakech, Rabat; tel. (7) 762265; telex 31005; fax (7) 765661; Ambassador: MARC CHARLES GINSBERG.

Yemen: 11 rue Abou-Hanifa, Agdal, Rabat; tel. (7) 74363; telex 32855; Ambassador: (vacant).

Yugoslavia: 23 ave Bni Znassen, Souissi, BP 5014, Rabat; tel. (7) 52201; telex 31760; Ambassador: DIMITRIJE BABIĆ.

Zaire: 34 ave de la Victoire, BP 537, Rabat-Chellah; tel. (7) 734862; telex 31954; Ambassador: TOMONA BATE TANGALE.

Judicial System

The **Supreme Court** (al-Majlis al-Aala) is responsible for the interpretation of the law and regulates the jurisprudence of the courts and tribunals of the Kingdom. The Supreme Court sits at Rabat and is divided into six Chambers.

First President: MUHAMMAD MIKOU.

Attorney-General: AHMAD ZEGHARI.

The 15 **Courts of Appeal** hear appeals from lower courts and also comprise a criminal division.

The **Courts of First Instance** pass judgment on offences punishable by up to five years' imprisonment. These courts also pass judgment, without possibility of appeal, in personal, civil and commercial cases involving up to 3,000 dirhams.

The **Regional Tribunals** pass judgment in the first and last resort in cases of personal property of 1,000 dirhams. The Regional Tribunals also pass judgment, subject to appeal before the Court of Appeal, in cases of minor offences in penal matters, punishable by a fine of 10 to 800 dirhams.

Labour Tribunals settle, by means of conciliation, disputes arising from rental contracts or services between employers and employees engaged in private industry. There are 14 labour tribunals in the Kingdom.

The **High Court of Justice**, comprising members elected from the Chamber of Representatives and a president appointed by royal decree, considers crimes and felonies allegedly committed by government members in the exercise of their functions.

Religion

ISLAM

About 99% of Moroccans are Muslims (of whom about 90% are of the Sunni sect), and Islam is the state religion.

CHRISTIANITY

There are about 69,000 Christians, mostly Roman Catholics.

The Roman Catholic Church

Morocco (excluding the disputed territory of Western Sahara) comprises two archdioceses, directly responsible to the Holy See. At 31 December 1992 there were an estimated 28,658 adherents in the country, representing 0.1% of the population. The Moroccan archbishops participate in the Conférence Episcopale Régionale du Nord de l'Afrique (f. 1985), based in Algiers (Algeria).

Archbishop of Rabat: Most Rev. HUBERT MICHON, Archevêché, 1 rue Henri Dunant, BP 258, Rabat; tel. (7) 709239; fax (7) 706282.

Archbishop of Tangier: Most Rev. JOSÉ ANTONIO PETEIRO FREIRE, Archevêché, 55 rue Sidi Bouabid, BP 2116, Tangier; tel. (9) 932762; fax (9) 949117.

Western Sahara comprises a single Apostolic Prefecture, with an estimated 150 Catholics (1992).

Prefect Apostolic of Western Sahara: Fr FÉLIX ERVITI BARCELONA, Misión Católica, BP 31, el-Aaiún; tel. 893270.

The Anglican Communion

Within the Church of England, Morocco forms part of the diocese of Gibraltar in Europe. There are Anglican churches in Casablanca and Tangier.

Protestant Church

Evangelical Church: 33 rue d'Azilal, Casablanca; tel. (7) 302151; f. 1920; established in 9 towns; Pres. Pastor ETIENNE QUINCHE; 1,000 mems.

JUDAISM

There are about 30,000 Jews.

Grand Rabbi of Casablanca: CHALOM MESSAS, President of the Rabbinical Court of Casablanca, Palais de Justice, place des Nations Unies.

The Press

DAILIES

Casablanca

Al-Bayane (The Manifesto): 62 blvd de la Gironde, BP 13152, Casablanca; tel. (2) 307666; Arabic and French; organ of the Parti du Progrès et du Socialisme; Dir ALI YATA; circ. 5,000.

Al-Ittihad al-Ichtiraki (Socialist Unity): 33 rue Emir Abdelkader, Casablanca 05; tel. (2) 241538; telex 24961; Arabic; organ of the Union Socialiste des Forces Populaires; Dir ABDALLAH BOUHLAL.

Maroc Soir: 34 rue Muhammad Smiha, Casablanca; tel. (2) 268860; telex 23845; fax (2) 262969; f. 1971; French; Dir DRISSI EL-ALAMI; circ. 50,000.

Le Matin du Sahara: 88 blvd Muhammad V, Casablanca; tel. (2) 268860; telex 23845; fax (2) 262969; f. 1971; French; Dir DRISSI EL-ALAMI; circ. 100,000.

Rissalat al-Oumma (The Message of the Nation): 158 ave des Forces Armées Royales, Casablanca; tel. (2) 310427; Arabic; weekly edition in French; organ of the Union Constitutionnelle; Dir MUHAMMAD ALAOUI MUHAMMADI.

Rabat

Al-Alam (The Flag): 11 ave Allal ben Abdallah, BP 141, Rabat; tel. (7) 32419; fax (7) 733896; f. 1946; organ of the Istiqlal party; Arabic; literary supplement on Fridays; weekly edition on Mondays; monthly edition on foreign policy; Dir ABD AL-KRIM GHALLAB; circ. 100,000.

Al-Anba'a (Information): 21 rue Patrice Lumumba, Rabat; tel. (7) 24644; f. 1970; Arabic; publ. by Ministry of Information; Dir AHMAD AL-YAAKOUBI; circ. 15,000.

Al-Maghrib: 6 rue Laos, Rabat; tel. (7) 22708; telex 31916; fax (7) 22765; f. 1977; French; organ of the Rassemblement National des Indépendants; Dir MUSTAPHA IZNASNI; circ. 15,000.

Al-Mithaq al-Watani (The National Charter): 6 rue Laos, Rabat; tel. (7) 22708; telex 31916; fax (7) 22765; f. 1977; Arabic; organ of the Rassemblement National des Indépendants; Dir MUSTAPHA IZNASNI; circ. 15,000.

An-Nidal Ad-Dimokrati (The Democratic Struggle): 18 rue Tunis, Rabat; tel. (7) 30754; Arabic; organ of the Parti National Démocrate; Dir MUHAMMAD ARSALANE AL-JADIDI.

L'Opinion: 11 ave Allal ben Abdallah, Rabat; tel. (7) 27812; fax (7) 32182; f. 1965; French; organ of the Istiqlal party; Dir MUHAMMAD IDRISSI KAÏTOUNI; circ. 60,000.

SELECTED PERIODICALS

Casablanca

Bulletin Mensuel de la Chambre de Commerce et d'Industrie de la Wilaya du Grand Casablanca: 98 blvd Muhammad V, BP 423, Casablanca; tel. (2) 264327; telex 24630; monthly; French; Pres. LAHCEN EL-WAFI.

Cedies Informations: 23 blvd Muhammad Abdouh, Casablanca; tel. (2) 252696; telex 23835; fax (2) 253839; weekly; French; Admin. A. OUALI.

Construire: 25 rue d'Azilal, Immeuble Ortiba, Casablanca; tel. (2) 305721; fax (2) 317577; f. 1940; weekly; French; Dir TALAL BOUCHAIB.

Les Echos Africains: Immeuble SONIR, angle blvd Smiha, rue d'Anjou, BP 13140, Casablanca; tel. (2) 307271; telex 27905; f. 1972; monthly; French; news, economics; Dir MUHAMMAD CHOUFFANI EL-FASSI; Editor Mme SOODIA FARIDI; circ. 5,000.

FLASH-économie: 28 ave des Forces Armées Royales, Casablanca; tel. (2) 203031; weekly; French; Dir KHODIJA IDRISSI.

Al-Ittihad al-Watani Lilkouate ach-Chaabia (National Union of Popular Forces): 28-30 rue Magellan, Casablanca; tel. (2) 302023; weekly; Arabic; organ of the Union Nationale des Forces Populaires; Dir MOULAY ABDALLAH IBRAHIM.

Lamalif: 6 bis rue Defly Dieude, Casablanca; tel. (2) 220032; f. 1966; monthly; French; economic, social and cultural magazine; Dir MUHAMMAD LOGHLAM.

Maroc Fruits: 22 rue Al-Messaoudi, Casablanca 02; tel. (2) 363946; telex 21666; f. 1958; fortnightly; Arabic, French; organ of the Association des Producteurs d'Agrumes du Maroc; Dir NEJJAI AHMED MANSOUR; circ. 6,000.

Matin Hebdo: 34 rue Muhammad Smiha, Casablanca; tel. (2) 301271; telex 27794; weekly; Dir AHMAD AL-ALAMI.

Matin Magazine: 88 blvd Muhammad V, Casablanca; tel. (2) 268860; telex 23845; fax (2) 268860; weekly; Dir DRISSI EL-ALAMI.

An-Nidal (The Struggle): 10 rue Cols Bleus, Sidi Bousmara, Médina Kédima, Casablanca; f. 1973; weekly; Dir IBRAHIMI AHMAD.

Al-Ousbouaa al-Maghribia: 158 ave des Forces Armées Royales, Casablanca; f. 1984; organ of the Union Constitutionnelle; Dir A. MUHAMMADI.

Panorama Interview: 17 rue Lapebie, Casablanca; tel. (2) 277396; monthly; French; Dir BOUJEMAÂ AMARA.

La Quinzaine du Maroc: 53 rue Dumont d'Urville, Casablanca; tel. (2) 302482; fax (2) 440426; monthly; English/French; Dir HUBERT MAURO.

Revue Douanes Marocaines: 69 rue Muhammad Smiha, Casablanca; tel. (2) 301613; f. 1959; monthly; French; general economic review; Dir MUHAMMAD KABOUS.

Revue Marocaine de Droit: 24 rue Nolly, Casablanca; tel. (2) 273673; telex 22644; quarterly; French and Arabic; Dirs J. P. RAZON, A. KETTANI.

La Vie Economique: 5 blvd ben Yacine, Casablanca; tel. (2) 443868; telex 28045; fax (2) 304542; f. 1921; weekly; French; Dir NAJIB SENHADJI.

La Vie Industrielle et Agricole: 142 blvd Muhammad V, Casablanca; tel. (2) 274407; 2 a month; French; Dir AHMAD ZAGHARI.

La Vie Touristique Africaine: 142 blvd Muhammad V, Casablanca; tel. (2) 274407; telex 21721; fortnightly; French; tourist information; Dir AHMAD ZAGHARI.

Rabat

Al-Aklam (The Pens): BP 2229, Rabat; monthly; Arabic; Dir ABD AR-RAHMAN BEN AMAR.

Anoual: 5 bis ave Hassan II, BP 1385, Rabat; tel. (7) 26733; fax (7) 738259; f. 1979; weekly; Arabic; organ of the Organisation de l'Action Démocratique et Populaire; Dir ABD AL-LATIF AOUAD.

Ach-Chorta (The Police): BP 437, Rabat; tel. (7) 23194; monthly; Arabic; Dir MUHAMMAD AD-DRIF.

Da'ouat Al-Haqq (Call of the Truth): al-Michwar as-Said, Rabat; publ. by Ministry of Religious Endowments (Awqaf) and Islamic Affairs; tel. (7) 60810; f. 1957; monthly; Arabic.

Al-Haraka: 8 Sahat al-Alaouiyine, Rabat; tel. (7) 64493; weekly; Arabic; organ of the Mouvement Populaire; Dir ALI ALAOUI.

Al-Imane: rue Akenssous, BP 356, Rabat; f. 1963; monthly; Arabic; Dir ABOU BAKER AL-KADIRI.

Al-Irchad (Spiritual Guidance): al-Michwar as-Said, Rabat; publ. by Ministry of Religious Endowments (Awqaf) and Islamic Affairs; tel. (7) 60810; f. 1967; monthly; Arabic.

Al-Khansa: 154 ave Souss Mohamedia, Rabat; monthly; Arabic; Dir ABOUZAL AICHA.

Al-Maghribi: 113 ave Allal ben Abdallah, Rabat; tel. (7) 68139; weekly; Arabic; organ of the Parti de l'Action; Dir ABDALLAH AL-HANANI.

At-Tadamoun: 23 ave Allal ben Abdallah, Rabat; monthly; Arabic; Dir ABD AL-MAJID SEMLALI EL-HASANI.

Tangier

Actualités Touristiques: 80 rue de la Liberté, Tangier; monthly; French; Dir TAYEB ALAMI.

Le Journal de Tanger: 11 ave Moulay Abd al-Aziz, BP 420, Tangier; tel. (9) 46051; fax (9) 45709; f. 1904; weekly; French, English, Spanish and Arabic; Dir BAKHAT ABD AL-HAQ; circ. 10,000.

NEWS AGENCIES

Wikalat al-Maghreb al-Arabi (WMA): 122 ave Allal ben Abdallah, BP 1049, Rabat; tel. (7) 764083; telex 36044; fax (7) 765005; f. 1959 as Maghreb Arabe Presse; Arabic, French, English and Spanish; government-owned; Man. Dir ABD AL-JALIL FENJIRO.

Foreign Bureaux

Agence France-Presse (AFP): 2 bis rue du Caire, BP 118, Rabat; tel. (7) 768943; telex 31903; fax (7) 700357; f. 1920; Dir IGNACE DALLE.

Agencia EFE (Spain): 14 ave du Kairouane, Rabat; tel. (7) 23218; telex 32806; fax (7) 32195; Bureau Chief MASEGOSA ALBERTO.

Agenzia Nazionale Stampa Associata (ANSA) (Italy): 10 rue el Yamana, Rabat; tel. (7) 311083; telex 31044; Dir RAFFA HOUCINE.

Austria Presse-Agentur (APA): 28 ave des Forces Armées Royales, BP 13906, Casablanca; tel. (2) 275762; telex 23959; Dir MUKAROVSKY GEZA.

Informatsionnoye Telegrafnoye Agentstvo Rossii—Telegrafnoye Agentstvo Suverennykh Stran (ITAR—TASS) (Russia): 11 rue Rif, Souissi, Route des Zaërs, Km 3.5, Rabat; tel. (7) 750315; telex 31018; Dir OLEG CHIROKOV.

Inter Press Service (IPS) (Italy): 46 rue Abou Derr, Rabat; tel. (7) 756869; fax (7) 727183; Dir BOULOUIZ BOUCHRA.

Reuters (United Kingdom): 509 Immeuble es-Saada, ave Hassan II, Rabat; tel. (7) 726518; fax (7) 722499; Correspondent STEPHEN HUGHES.

Rossiyskoye Informatsionnoye Agentstvo—Novosti (RIA—Novosti) (Russia): BP 281, Rabat; tel. (7) 69784; telex 31069; Dir BORIS BOUKAREV.

Xinhua (New China) News Agency (People's Republic of China): 4 rue Kadi Mekki el-Bitaouri, Rabat; tel. (7) 55320; telex 31674; Dir LIU ZUOWEN.

Publishers

Dar el-Kitab: place de la Mosquée, quartier des Habous, BP 4018, Casablanca; tel. (2) 246326; telex 26630; fax 244484; f. 1948; philosophy, history, Africana, general and social science; Arabic and French; Dir BOUTALEB ABDOU ABD AL-HAY; Gen. Man. SOAD KADIRI.

Editions La Porte: 281 ave Muhammad V, Rabat; tel. (7) 709958; fax (7) 706478; law, guides, economics, educational books; Man. Dir MUHAMMAD RAFII DOUKKALI.

Editions Maghrébines: 5–13 rue Soldat Roch, Casablanca; tel. (2) 245148; telex 22994; f. 1962; general non-fiction.

Government Publishing House

Imprimerie Officielle: ave Jean Mermoz, Rabat-Chellah; tel. (7) 65024.

Radio and Television

In 1991, according to UNESCO estimates, there were 5.4m. radio receivers and 1.9m. television receivers in use. Morocco can receive broadcasts from Spanish radio stations, and the main Spanish television channels can also be received in northern Morocco.

Radiodiffusion Télévision Marocaine: 1 Zenkat el-Brihi, BP 1042, Rabat; tel. (7) 64951; telex 31010; government station; *Radio:* Network A in Arabic, Network B in French, Network C in Berber, Spanish and English; Foreign Service in Arabic, French and English; *Television:* began 1962; 45 hours weekly; French and Arabic; carries commercial advertising; Dir-Gen. MUHAMMAD TRICHA; Dir Television MUHAMMAD LISSARI; Dir Radio ABD AR-RAHMAN ACHOUR; Dir Foreign Service AHMAD RAYANE.

2M International: Société d'études et de réalisations audiovisuelles, km 7, 3 route de Rabat, Ain-Sebaa, Casablanca; tel. (2) 354444; fax (2) 354071; f. 1988, transmission commenced 1989; private television channel, jointly owned by Moroccan interests (85%) and by foreign concerns; broadcasting in French and Arabic; Dir-Gen. TAWFIK BENNANI-SMIRES.

Radio Méditerranée Internationale: 3 et 5 rue Emsallah, BP 2055, Tangier; tel. (9) 936363; telex 33711; fax (9) 936363; Arabic and French; Man. Dir PIERRE CASALTA.

Voice of America Radio Station in Tangier: c/o US Consulate General, Chemin des Amoureux, Tangier.

Finance

(cap. = capital; dep. = deposits; m. = million; res = reserves; brs = branches; amounts in dirhams unless otherwise indicated)

BANKING

Central Bank

Bank Al-Maghrib: 277 ave Muhammad V, BP 445, Rabat; tel. (7) 702626; telex 31006; fax (7) 706677; f. 1959 as Banque du Maroc; bank of issue; cap. 500m., dep. 8,767.8m., res 3,605m., total assets 55,432m. (Dec. 1992); Gov. MUHAMMAD SEQAT.

Other Banks

Algemene Bank Marokko SA: Immeuble des Habous, place du 16 Novembre, BP 13478, Casablanca; tel. (2) 221275; telex 21709; fax (2) 204124; f. 1948; 50% owned by ABN AMRO Bank NV (Netherlands), 50% owned by Moroccan interests; cap. 155,000, dep. 1,496.5m., res 197.5m.; total assets 2,109.8m. (Dec. 1991); Pres. Hadj ABDERRAHMANE BOUFTAS; Gen. Man. AZZEDDINE MAÂCH; 17 brs.

Arab Bank Maroc: 174 blvd Muhammad V, BP 13810, Casablanca; tel. (2) 223152; telex 22942; fax (2) 200233; f. 1975; 50% owned by Arab Bank PLC, 50% by Banque Centrale Populaire; total assets 1,234m. (Dec. 1992); Pres. ABD AL-LATIF LARAKI; Gen. Man. SALAH HAROUN; 3 brs.

Banque Commerciale du Maroc SA: 2 blvd Moulay Youssef, BP 141, Casablanca; tel. (2) 224169; telex 22863; fax (2) 268829; f. 1911; 30.6% owned by Financière Diwan; cap. 937.2m., dep. 21,048m., res 1,251.1m., total assets 23,521m. (Dec. 1992); Pres. and Gen. Man. ABD AL-AZIZ ALAMI; 112 brs.

Banque Marocaine du Commerce Extérieur SA: 140 ave Hassan II, BP 13425, Casablanca 01; tel. (2) 200456; telex 21635; fax (2) 200490; f. 1959; partly state-owned; cap. 1,000m., dep. 23,657m., res 1,188.2m., total assets 26,030.7m. (Dec. 1992); Chair. and Chief Exec. ABD AL-LATIF JOUAHRI; Man. Dir DRISS GUEDDARI; 143 brs.

Banque Marocaine pour l'Afrique et l'Orient: 1 place Bandoeng, Casablanca; tel. (2) 307070; telex 26720; fax (2) 301673; f. 1975 to take over British Bank of the Middle East (Morocco); cap.

200m., dep. 1,589.0m., res 1.4m. (Dec. 1993); Chair. MUSTAPHA FARIS; Gen. Man. ABD AL-HAMID BENANI DAKHAMA; 32 brs.

Banque Marocaine pour le Commerce et l'Industrie SA: 26 place Muhammad V, BP 573, Casablanca; tel. (2) 224101; telex 21902; fax (2) 203096; f. 1964; cap. 145m., dep. 6,767.8m., res 283.1m., total assets 7,234.6m. (Dec. 1990); Chair. Hadj AHMAD BARGACH; Gen. Man. OMAR AKALAY; 77 brs.

Banque Nationale pour le Développement Economique: 12 place des Alaouites, BP 407, Rabat; tel. (7) 06040; telex 31942; fax (7) 03706; f. 1959; cap. 336m., dep. 6,542.4m., res 437m., total assets 7,357.7m. (1991); Gen. Man. FARID DELLERO; 4 brs.

Crédit Immobilier et Hôtelier: 187 ave Hassan II, Casablanca; tel. (2) 202480; telex 22839; fax (2) 266303; f. 1920; cap. 785m., dep. 15,064.9m., res 769.3m., total assets 16,729.7m. (Dec. 1991); Pres. and Chair. MOULAY ZAHIDI; Gen. Man. ABD AL-HAK BEN KIRANE; 18 brs.

Crédit du Maroc SA: 48–58 blvd Muhammad V, BP 13579, Casablanca; tel. (2) 224142; telex 21054; fax (2) 277127; f. 1963; cap. 833.8m., dep. 8,813m., total assets 10,271m. (Dec. 1993); Chair. JAWAD BEN BRAHIM; Gen. Man. MUHAMMAD TAZI MEZALEK; 105 brs.

Crédit Populaire du Maroc: 101 blvd Muhammad Zerktouni, BP 10622, Casablanca; tel. (2) 202533; telex 21723; fax (2) 267889; 51% state-owned, 49% privately-owned; cap. 286m., dep. 32,515.2m., res 2,174.4m., total assets 35,135.8m. (Dec. 1990); Chair. ABD AL-LATIF LARAKI; Gen. Man. ABD AL-HAK AL-ABDI.

Société de Banque et de Crédit SA: 26 ave de l'Armée Royale, BP 13972, Casablanca; tel. (2) 310330; telex 21848; f. 1951; affil. to Swiss Bank Corpn and Crédit Commercial de France; cap. 40m., dep. 1,435.8m., res 39m., total assets 1,556.2m. (Dec. 1990); Pres. FOUAD FILALI; Vice-Pres. ABD AL-LATIF GHISSASSI; 11 brs.

Société Générale Marocaine de Banques: 55 blvd Abd al-Moumen, Casablanca; tel. (2) 200972; telex 24076; fax (2) 200961; f. 1962; cap. 520m., dep. 7,341m. (Dec. 1993); Pres. MUHAMMAD BARGACH; Gen. Man. ABD AL-AZIZ TAZI; 94 brs.

Société Marocaine de Dépôt et Crédit: 79 ave Hassan II, BP 296, Casablanca; tel. (2) 224114; telex 21013; fax (2) 271590; f. 1974; cap. 101.25m., dep. 1,958.7m., res 64.6m. (Dec. 1989); Chair. ABD AL-KADER BEN SALAH; 21 brs.

Unión Bancaria Hispano Marroquí (UNIBAN): 69 rue du Prince Moulay Abdellah, Casablanca; tel. (2) 220230; telex 24997; fax (2) 207584; f. 1958; 50% participation of Banco Bilbao Vizcaya, Spain; cap. 246.4m., dep. 2,307m., res 175.5m., total assets 2,743.9m. (Dec. 1992); Chair. ENRIQUE MAS; Gen. Man. PEDRO GARCÍA; 20 brs.

Wafabank: 163 ave Hassan II, Casablanca 01; tel. (2) 224105; telex 21051; fax (2) 266202; f. 1964 as Compagnie Marocaine de Crédit et de Banque; cap. 425.5m., dep. 12,384.0m., res 734.8m., total assets 13,680.0m. (Dec. 1992); Pres. ABD AL-HAK BENNANI; 89 brs.

Bank Organizations

Association Professionnelle des Intermédiaires de Bourse du Maroc: 71 ave des l'Armées Royales, Casablanca; tel. (2) 314824; telex 22821; fax (2) 314903; f. 1967; groups all banks and brokers in the stock exchange of Casablanca, for studies, inquiries of general interest and contacts with official authorities; 11 mems; Pres. ABD AL-LATIF JOUAHRI.

Groupement Professionnel des Banques du Maroc: 71 ave des Forces Armées Royales, Casablanca; tel. (2) 314824; telex 22821; fax (2) 314903; f. 1967; groups all commercial banks for studies, inquiries of general interest, and contacts with official authorities; 18 mems; Pres. ABD AL-LATIF JOUAHRI.

STOCK EXCHANGE

Bourse des Valeurs de Casablanca: 98 blvd Muhammad V, Casablanca; tel. (2) 279354; telex 23698; fax (2) 200365; f. 1929; Pres. (vacant); Dir ABD AR-RAZAQ LARAKI.

INSURANCE

Al-Amane: 298 blvd Muhammad V, Casablanca; tel. (2) 304571; telex 27726; f. 1975; cap. 30m.; Vice Pres. and Dir-Gen. M. BOUGHALEB.

Al-Wataniya: 83 ave de l'Armée Royale, Casablanca; tel. (2) 314850; telex 21877; fax (2) 313043; Dir-Gen. M. ABD AL-JALIL CHRAIBI.

Alliance Africaine: 63 blvd Moulay Youssef, Casablanca; tel. (2) 200694; telex 45737; fax (2) 200694; f. 1975; cap. 8m.; Pres. ABD AR-RAHIM CHERKAOUI; Dir-Gen. KHALID CHEDDADI.

Atlanta: 49 angle rues Lafuente et Longwy, Casablanca; tel. (2) 260289; telex 21644; fax (2) 203011; f. 1947; cap. 12m.; Dir MOHAMED REYAD; Dir-Gen. OMAR BENNANI.

Cie Africaine d'Assurances: 120 ave Hassan II, Casablanca; tel. (2) 224185; telex 21661; fax (2) 260150; f. 1950; Pres. FOUAD FILALI; Dir-Gen. HAFID EL-ALAMY.

Cie Arabia: 123 rue Rahal El Meskini, Casablanca; tel. (2) 200766; Dir M. ABD AL-JALIL CHRAIBI.

Cie Atlantique d'Assurances (CADA): 3 rue des Hirondelles, Rond Point Racine, Casablanca; tel. (2) 390033; telex 22042; fax (2) 223664; f. 1931; cap. 2.8m.; Dir-Gen. AMAL KANOUNI.

Cie d'Assurances SANAD: 3 blvd Muhammad V, BP 13438, Casablanca; tel. (2) 260591; telex 21927; fax (2) 293813; f. 1975; Chair. MUHAMMAD AOUAD; Dir-Gen. ABDELTIF TAHIRI.

Cie Nordafricaine et Intercontinentale d'Assurances (CNIA): 157 ave Hassan II, Casablanca; tel. (2) 224118; telex 21096; fax (2) 267866; cap. 30m.; Man. Dir SAAD KANOUNI.

L'Entente: 122 ave Hassan II, Casablanca; tel. (2) 267272; telex 46480; fax (2) 267023; f. 1950; cap. 60m.; Pres. Dir-Gen. MUHAMMAD EL-MEHDI BOUGHALEB.

Garantie Générale Marocaine: 106 rue Abd ar-Rahman Sahraoui, Casablanca; tel. (2) 279015; telex 24885; Dir-Gen. HABIB BELRHITI.

La Marocaine Vie: 37 blvd Moulay Youssef, Casablanca; tel. (2) 206320; telex 46462; fax (2) 261971; f. 1978; cap. 12m.; Pres. and Dir-Gen. H. KETTANI.

Mutuelle Centrale Marocaine d'Assurances: 16 rue Abou Inane, BP 27, Rabat; tel. (7) 766960; telex 31739; Pres. ABD AS-SALAM CHERIF D'OUEZZANE; Dir-Gen. YACOUBI SOUSSANE.

Mutuelle d'Assurances des Transporteurs Unis (MATU): 40 blvd d'Anfa, Casablanca; tel. (2) 200028; Dir-Gen. M. BENYAMNA.

Remar: angle blvd Muhammad V, Casablanca; tel. (2) 305166; telex 45887; fax (2) 305305; f. 1970; cap. 6m.; Dir-Gen. MUHAMMAD CHERKAOUI.

La Renaissance: Siège Social, 197 ave Hassan II, Casablanca; tel. (2) 221613; telex 21680; fax (2) 276563; f. 1980; cap. 3m.; Dir-Gen. SELLAM SEKKAT.

La Royale Marocaine d'Assurances (RMA): 67–69 ave de l'Armée Royale, Casablanca; tel. (2) 312163; telex 21818; fax (2) 31-38-84; f. 1949; cap. 30m.; Chair. OTHMAN BEN JELLOUN; Dir SÉBASTIEN CASTRO.

Es-Saada, Cie d'Assurances et de Réassurances: 123 ave Hassan II, BP 13860, Casablanca; tel. (2) 224177; telex 22798; fax 262655; f. 1961; cap. 25m.; Pres. MEHDI OUAZZANI; Man. Dir SAÏD OUAZZANI.

Société Centrale de Réassurance: Tour Atlas, place Zallaqa, BP 13183, Casablanca; tel. (2) 308585; telex 28084; fax (2) 308672; f. 1960; cap. 30m.; Chair. FAROUK BENNIS; CEO YAHIA FILALI.

Société Marocaine d'Assurances à l'Exportation: 41–43 blvd d'Anfa, BP 15953, Casablanca; tel. (2) 294811; telex 45951; fax (2) 294816; f. 1988; insurance for exporters in the public and private sectors; assistance for export promotion; Pres., Dir-Gen. ABD AL-HAMID JOUAHRI; Asst. Dir-Gen. ABD EL-KADER DRIOUACHE.

Victoire: 50 ave Mers-Sultan, Casablanca; tel. (2) 297808; telex 23993; fax (2) 203076; f. 1982; Chair. ABAHMAOUI MUHAMMAD.

WAFA Assurance: 1–3 blvd Abd al-Moumen, Casablanca; tel. (2) 224575; telex 21867; fax (2) 209103; Dir-Gen. JAOUAD KETTANI.

INSURANCE ASSOCIATION

Fédération Marocaine des Sociétés d'Assurances et de Réassurances: 154 blvd d'Anfa, Casablanca; tel. (2) 391850; telex 45524; fax (2) 391854; f. 1958; 22 mem. companies; Pres. ABD AL-JALIL CHRAIBI; Dir ABD AL-FETTAH ALAMI.

Trade and Industry

CHAMBERS OF COMMERCE

La Fédération des Chambres de Commerce et d'Industrie du Maroc: 6 rue d'Erfoud, Rabat-Agdal; tel. (7) 767078; telex 36662; fax (7) 767076; f. 1962; groups the 25 Chambers of Commerce and Industry; Pres. MOULAY LAHCEN EL-IDRISSI; Dir-Gen. KAMAL BOUHAMDI.

Chambre de Commerce et d'Industrie de Rabat-Salé et de Skhirat-Temara: 1 rue Gandhi, BP 131, Rabat; tel. (7) 706444; telex 36898; fax (7) 706768; Pres. MOULAY LAHCEN EL-IDRISSI; Dir MUHAMMAD NAJIB AFFANE.

Chambre de Commerce et d'Industrie de la Wilaya du Grand Casablanca: 98 blvd Muhammad V, BP 423, Casablanca; tel. (2) 264327; telex 24630; Pres. LAHCEN EL-WAFI.

DEVELOPMENT ORGANIZATIONS

Bureau de Recherches et de Participations Minières (BRPM): 5 charia Moulay Hassan, BP 99, Rabat; tel. (7) 05005; telex 31066; fax (7) 09411; f. 1928; a state agency conducting exploration, valorization and exploitation of mineral resources; Gen. Man. Assou Lhatoute; Sec.-Gen. Ali Bennani.

Caisse de Dépôt et de Gestion: Sahat Moulay El-Hassan, BP 408, Rabat; tel. (7) 765520; telex 31072; fax (7) 763849; f. 1959; finances small-scale projects; Gen. Man. Muhammad Fadel Lahlou.

Caisse Marocaine des Marchés (Marketing Fund): Résidence El Manar, blvd Abd al-Moumen, Casablanca; tel. (2) 259118; telex 24740; fax (2) 259120; f. 1950; cap. 10m. dirhams; Man. Hassan Kissi.

Caisse Nationale de Crédit Agricole (Agricultural Credit Fund): 2 ave d'Alger, BP 49, Rabat; tel. (7) 725920; telex 31657; fax (7) 732580; f. 1961; cap. 1,575m. dirhams, dep. 2,710m. dirhams; Man. Dir Moulay Rachid Haddaoui.

Centre Marocain de Promotion des Exportations (CMPE): 23 blvd Hassan Majid el-Bahar, BP 10937, Casablanca; tel. (2) 302210; telex 27847; fax (2) 301793; f. 1980; state organization for promotion of exports; Dir-Gen. Mounir M. Bensaid.

Office National Interprofessionnel des Céréales et des Légumineuses: 25 ave Hassan I, BP 154, Rabat; tel. (7) 61735; telex 31930; f. 1937; Dir-Gen. Muhammad Guerraoui.

Office pour le Développement Industriel (ODI): 10 rue Gandhi, BP 211, Rabat; tel. (7) 708460; telex 31053; fax (7) 67695; f. 1973; a state agency to develop industry; Man. Dir Abd el-Hamid Belahsen.

Société de Développement Agricole (SODEA): ave Hadj Ahmed Cherkaoui, BP 6280, Rabat; tel. (7) 70813; telex 31675; fax (7) 74798; f. 1972; state agricultural development organization; Man. Dir M. Sabbari Hassani Larbi.

Société de Gestion des Terres Agricoles (SOGETA): 35 rue Daïet-Erroumi, BP 731, Agdal, Rabat; tel. (7) 72834; telex 31704; f. 1973; oversees use of agricultural land; Man. Dir Omar al-Hebil.

Société Nationale d'Investissement (SNI): 43 rue Aspirant Lafuenté, BP 38, Casablanca; tel. (2) 223081; telex 22736; f. 1966; cap. 150m. dirhams; Pres. Muhammad Bargach; Dir-Gen. Abdallah Belkziz.

PRINCIPAL STATE ENTERPRISES

Office Chérifien des Phosphates (OCP): blvd de la Grande Ceinture, route d'el Jadida, Casablanca; tel. (2) 360025; telex 21630; f. 1921; a state company to produce and market rock phosphates and derivatives; Dir-Gen. Muhammad Fettah.

Office National de l'Eau Potable (ONEP): 6 bis rue Patrice Lumumba, Rabat; tel. (7) 67243; telex 32075; fax (7) 31355; responsible for drinking-water supply; Dir Houcine Tijani.

Office National de l'Electricité (ONE): 65 rue Othman Ben Affan, BP 13498, Casablanca 20100; tel. (2) 224165; telex 22780; fax (2) 220038; f. 1963; state electricity authority; Dir-Gen. Aberrahmane Naji.

Office National des Pêches: 13/15 rue Chevalier Bayard, BP 21, Casablanca; tel. (2) 240551; telex 25708; f. 1969; state fishing organization; Man. Dir Abd al-Aziz el-Belgheti.

Société d'Exploitation des Mines du Rif (SEFERIF): 30 Abou-Faris el-Marini, BP 436, Rabat; tel. (7) 66350; telex 31708; nationalized 1967; open and underground mines produce iron ore for export and for the projected Nador iron and steel complex; Man. Dir Muhammad Harrak.

Société Nationale de Sidérurgie (SONASID): Route RP 18, Mont Arouit, BP 151, Nador; tel. (6) 609441; telex 65787; fax (6) 609442; f. 1974; iron and steel projects; cap. 390m. dirhams; Dir-Gen. Abdallah Souibri.

EMPLOYERS' ORGANIZATIONS

Association Marocaine des Industries Textiles et de l'Habillement (AMITH): 58 rue Lughérini, Casablanca; tel. (2) 300393; telex 45502; fax (2) 300442; f. 1958; mems 700 textile, knitwear and ready-made garment factories; Pres. Lahlou Muhammad; Sec.-Gen. Ali Berrada.

Association des Producteurs d'Agrumes du Maroc (ASPAM): 22 rue al-Messaoudi, Casablanca; tel. (2) 363946; telex 21666; f. 1958; links Moroccan citrus and vegetable growers; has its own processing plants; Chair. Ahmad Mansour Nejjai.

Association Professionnelle des Cimentiers: 239 blvd Moulay Ismail, BP 3096, Casablanca; cement manufacturers.

Confédération Générale Economique Marocaine (CGEM): 34 blvd Muhammad Abdou, Casablanca; tel. (2) 252696; telex 23835; fax (2) 253839; Pres. A. Bennani Smires; Sec.-Gen. Abd ar-Rahman Ouali.

Union Marocaine de l'Agriculture (UMA): 12 place des Alaouites, Rabat; Pres. M. Nejjai.

MAJOR INDUSTRIAL COMPANIES

Brasseries du Maroc: ave Pasteur, BP 87, Casablanca; tel. (2) 24-57-26; telex 25931; f. 1919; distillery, brewery and producer of soft drinks; Chair. Bachir Belabbes Taarji; Dir-Gen. Hamid ben Chekroun.

Charbonnages Nord Africains: 27 ave Moulay Hassan, BP 255, Rabat; tel. (7) 24147; telex 31923; f. 1946; coal mining; 5,000 employees.

Chérifienne de Travaux Africains: 1 blvd du Fouarat, Casablanca; tel. (2) 24-26-96; telex 25782; f. 1960; building and civil engineering contractors; cap. 10m. dirhams; Dir-Gen. Michel Delaporte; 2,000 employees.

Compagnie Marocaine des Hydrocarbures: 5 blvd Abdallah ben Yacine, BP 757, Casablanca; tel. (2) 30-82-45; telex 26091; marketing of petroleum and oil products; cap. 33m. dirhams; Dir-Gen. Hassan Agzenai.

Compagnie Sucrière Marocaine et de Raffinage SA (COSUMAR): 8 rue el Mouatamid ibnou Abbad, BP 3098, Casablanca; tel. (2) 24-73-45; telex 25032; fax (2) 241071; f. 1967; sugar refining and trading; cap. 60m. dirhams; Chair. Fouad Filali; Gen. Man. Muhammad al-Baz; 2,854 employees (April 1989).

Complexe Textile de Fès (COTEF): Quartier Sidi Brahim, route de Sefrou, BP 2267, Fez; tel. (6) 41309; telex 51606; f. 1967; production of yarns and textiles; Dir-Gen. Abd al-Hamid Seddiki.

Conserveries Chérifiennes: route du Djorf el-Youdi, BP 96, Safi; tel. 47-25-13; telex 71774; f. 1949; fish and food processing and canning; cap. 16.2m. dirhams; Gen. Man. Muhammad el-Jamali; 2,500 employees.

Manufacture Nationale de Textiles (MANATEX): 164 blvd de la Gironde, Casablanca; tel. (2) 24-65-65; telex 26734; f. 1957; manufacture of textiles and furnishings; Chair. Ali Kettani; Dirs Larbi as-Sakalli, Muhammad Lahlou, Muhammad Lazrak; 1,250 employees.

ONA: 52 ave Hassan II, BP 657, Casablanca; tel. (2) 22-41-02; telex 21859; fax (2) 261064; f. 1919; fmrly Omnium Nord Africain; largest private company in Morocco, owns subsidiaries in mining, printing and transport industries; cap. 954.2m. dirhams (1993); Pres. and Man. Dir Fouad Filali.

Phosphates de Boucraa SA (PHOSBOUCRAA): Immeuble OCP, angle route d'el Jadida et blvd de la Grande Ceinture, Casablanca; tel. (2) 36-00-25; telex 24033; f. 1962; production and processing of phosphate rock; cap. 328m. dirhams; Pres. Muhammad Karim Lamrani; Dirs Alfonso Alvarez Miranda, Muhammad ben Harouga; 1,146 employees.

SATFILAGE SA: route de l'Aviation, BP 1059, Tangier; tel. (9) 34049; telex 33047; f. 1962; production of synthetic fibres and textiles; 1,500 employees; Pres. Agha Adal Taleb.

Société Marocaine de Constructions Automobiles (SOMACA): km 12, autoroute de Rabat, BP 2628, Casablanca; tel. (2) 35-39-24; telex 25825; f. 1959; assembly of motor vehicles; owned by Moroccan Government, Fiat, Peugeot and SNI; Pres. Mehdi ben Bouchta; Dir-Gen. Muhammad A. Belarbi; 1,011 employees.

Société Nouvelle des Conduites d'Eau (SNCE): Résidence Kays Sahat Rabia, Al Adaouiya Agdal, Rabat; tel. (7) 723424; telex 31028; fax (7) 77-66-74; f. 1961; manufacture of steel and cast-iron pipes and materials; cap. 67.2m. dirhams; Chair. Omar Laraqui; Dir-Gen. Muhammad Abdellaoui; 2,600 employees.

TRADE UNIONS

Confédération Démocratique du Travail (CDT): 51 rue Abdallah Medyouni, BP 13576, Casablanca; tel. (2) 313432; telex 22662; fax (2) 310307; f. 1978; associated with USFP; 300,000 mems; Sec.-Gen. Noubir Amaoui.

Union Générale des Travailleurs Marocains (UGTM): 9 rue du Rif, angle Route de Médiouna, Casablanca; tel. (2) 282144; f. 1960; associated with Istiqlal; supported by unions not affiliated to UMT; 673,000 mems; Sec.-Gen. Abd ar-Razzaq Afilal.

Union Marocaine du Travail (UMT): Bourse du Travail, 232 ave des Forces Armées Royales, Casablanca; tel. (2) 302292; telex 27825; left-wing and associated with the Union Nationale des Forces Populaires; most unions are affiliated; 700,000 mems; Sec. Mahjoub ben Seddiq.

Union Syndicale Agricole (USA): agricultural section of UMT.

Union Marocaine du Travail Autonome: Rabat; breakaway union from UMT.

TRADE FAIR

Salon International du Matériel pour l'Industrie du Textile et du Cuir: 11 rue Boukraa, Casablanca; tel. (2) 222871; telex 22093; fax (2) 264949; f. 1991; textiles and leather; annually for three days in March.

Transport

Office National des Transports (ONT): rue al-Fadila, Quartier-Industriel, BP Rabat-Chellah; tel. (7) 797842; telex 36090; f. 1958; Man. Dir Mohamed el Yousfi Ahmed.

RAILWAYS

In 1992 there were 1,907 km of railways, of which 271 km were double track; 988 km of lines were electrified and diesel loco-motives were used on the rest. All services are nationalized.

Office National des Chemins de Fer du Maroc (ONCFM): rue Abderrahmane El Ghafiki, Rabat-Agdal; tel. (7) 774747; telex 31907; fax (7) 774480; f. 1963; administers all Morocco's railways; Pres. Minister of Transport; Dir-Gen. MOHAMED LAÂLEJ.

ROADS

In 1991 there were 59,474 km of classified roads, of which 49.5% were paved. There were 73 km of motorway, 10,906 km of main roads and 9,391 km of regional roads.

Compagnie de Transports au Maroc 'Lignes Nationales' (CTM—LN): 23 rue Léon l'Africain, Casablanca; tel. (2) 312061; telex 28962; agencies in Tangier, Rabat, Meknès, Oujda, Mar-rakesh, Agadir, el-Jadida, Safi, Casablanca, es-Saouira, Ksar es-Souk, Fez and Ouarzazate; privatized in mid-1993 with 40% of shares reserved for Moroccan citizens; Man. Dir MUHAMMAD AL-ALJ.

SHIPPING

Morocco's 21 ports handled 40.5m. tons of goods in 1993, an increase of 4.8% compared with the previous year's total. The most important ports, in terms of the volume of goods handled, are Casablanca, Muhammadia, Jorf Lasfar and Safi. Tangier is the principal port for passenger services. In 1992 ODEP announced a five-year investment programme (1993–97), costing a projected 1,595m. dirhams, that included plans for a container terminal at Casablanca (scheduled to be operational by the end of 1994).

Office d'Exploitation des Ports (ODEP): 175–177 blvd Zerk-touni, Casablanca; tel. (2) 232324; telex 46790; fax (2) 232335; f. 1985; Man. Dir MUHAMMAD HALAB.

Principal Shipping Companies

Agence Gibmar SA: 3 rue Henri Regnault, Tangier; tel. (9) 35875; telex 33091; fax (9) 33239; also at Casablanca; regular services from Tangier to Gibraltar; Chair. DRISS TAZI; Gen. Man. YOUSSEF BENY-AHIA.

Compagnie Chérifienne d'Armement: 5 blvd Abdallah ben Yacine, Casablanca 21700; tel. (2) 309455; telex 27030; fax (2) 301186; f. 1929; regular services to Europe; Chair. ABD AL-WAHAB LARAKI; Dir ABD AL-AZIZ MANTRACH.

Compagnie Marocaine d'Agences Maritimes (COMARINE): 45 ave des Forces Armées Royales, 21000, Casablanca; tel. (2) 311941; telex 21851; fax (2) 312570; f. 1969; Pres. AHMAD EL-OUALI EL-ALAMI; Dir-Gen. THIERRY LABAUE.

Compagnie Marocaine de Navigation (COMANAV): 7 blvd de la Résistance, BP 628, Casablanca; tel. (2) 303012; telex 26093; fax (2) 308455; f. 1946; regular services to Mediterranean, North-west European, Middle Eastern and West African ports; tramping; Pres. A. ALAOUI KACIMI; Dir-Gen. YAHIA SAOUDI.

Générale Maritime SA: 12 rue Foucauld, BP 746, Casablanca; tel. (2) 279590; telex 23802; f. 1974; chemicals; Dir-Gen. ABD AL-WAHAB BEN KIRANE.

Intercona SA (Transmediterránea and Isleña de Navegación): 31 ave de la Résistance, Tangier; tel. (9) 41101; telex 33005; fax (9) 43863; f. 1943; daily services from Algeciras (Spain) to Tangier and Ceuta (Spanish North Africa); Dir-Gen. ANTONIO FERRE CASALS.

Limadet-ferry: 3 rue Ibn Rochd, Tangier; tel. (9) 33639; telex 33013; fax (9) 37173; f. 1966; operates between Algeciras (Spain) and Tangier, six daily; Dir-Gen. RACHID BEN MANSOUR.

Messageries Marocaines: 65 ave des Forces Armées Royales, BP 69, Casablanca; telex 23762; Dir-Gen. MUHAMMAD EL-OUALI EL-ALAMI.

Société Marocaine de Navigation Atlas: 81 ave Houmane el-Fatouaki, 21000 Casablanca; tel. (2) 224190; telex 23067; fax (2) 274401; f. 1976; Chair. HASSAN CHAMI; Man. Dir M. SLAOUI.

Société Marocaine de Navigation Fruitière (SOFRUMA): 18 rue Colbert, Casablanca; tel. (2) 310003; telex 23097; fax (2) 310031; f. 1962; Dir-Gen. KHAMMAL ABD EL-HAMID.

Voyages Paquet: 65 ave des Forces Armées Royales, Casablanca; tel. (2) 311065; telex 24649; fax (2) 442108; f. 1970; Pres. MUHAMMAD EL-OUALI EL-ALAMI; Man. Dir BAKALI EL-OUALI EL-ALAMI.

CIVIL AVIATION

The main international airports are at Casablanca (King Muhammad V), Rabat, Tangier, Marrakesh, Agadir, Oujda, Al-Hocima and Fez.

Royal Air Maroc: Aéroport de Casablanca-Anfa; tel. (2) 912000; telex 21880; fax (2) 912397; f. 1953; 94% state-owned; domestic flights and services to 35 countries in Western Europe, Scandinavia, the Americas, North and West Africa, the Canary Islands and the Middle East; Chair. MUHAMMAD MEKOUAR; Dir-Gen. NOUREDDINE LAYT.

Tourism

Tourism is Morocco's second main source of convertible currency. The country's attractions for tourists include its sunny climate, ancient sites (notably the cities of Fez, Marrakesh, Meknès and Rabat) and spectacular scenery. There are popular holiday resorts on the Atlantic and Mediterranean coasts. In 1992 tourist arrivals increased by 1.9%, compared with the previous year, to 3,252,062.

Office National Marocain du Tourisme: 31 angle ave al-Abtal and rue Oved Fas, Agdal, Rabat; tel. (7) 775171; telex 31933; fax (7) 777437; f. 1918; Dir ABDERRAOUF LAHRESH.

Defence

Commander-in-Chief of the Armed Forces: HM King HASSAN II.

Estimated Defence Budget (1994): 9,700m. dirhams.

Military Service: 18 months.

Total Armed Forces (June 1994): 195,500 (army 175,000; navy 7,000; air force 13,500); royal guard 12,000. Paramilitary forces: 42,000. Reserves: 150,000.

Education

Since independence in 1956, Morocco has tried to solve a number of educational problems: a youthful and fast-growing population, an urgent need for skilled workers and executives, a great diver-sity of teaching methods between French, Spanish, Muslim and Moroccan government schools, and, above all, a high degree of adult illiteracy. Morocco spends about 25% of the national budget on education, of which a considerable proportion is devoted to constructing buildings for higher studies and technical education. Education for children of both sexes between seven and 15 years of age has been compulsory since 1985.

In 1989 there were 2,163,185 pupils in primary schools. At this level most instruction is given in government schools, where syllabuses have been standardized since 1967. Great progress was made in providing new schools between 1957 and 1964, but since then the increase in the number of places has slowed down. A decree of November 1963 made education compulsory for children between the ages of 7 and 13 years, and this has now been applied in most urban areas, but throughout the country only 72% of the age-group attended school in 1986. All primary teachers are Moroccan. Instruction is given in Arabic for the first two years and in Arabic and French for the next three years, with English as the first additional language.

Secondary education lasts for three or four years, depending on the type of course, and in 1989 provided for 1,320,462 pupils. Approximately a quarter of these pupils attended technical schools, where reforms have taken place since 1970 to attract more pupils and to provide relevant training to meet the country's need for technical manpower. In June 1987 it was announced that the sec-ondary school graduation examination, the *baccalauréat*, would be replaced by a system of continuous assessment from 1988. Most secondary teachers are Moroccan, but in 1986 there were 1,461 from abroad, chiefly from France. The Government aimed to have an entirely Moroccan teaching staff by 1988.

Higher education has a long history in Morocco. The Islamic Uni-versity of al-Quarawiyin at Fez celebrated its eleventh centenary in 1959-60. The Muhammad V University opened in Rabat in 1957 and had 28,689 students in seven faculties in 1991/92. In addition, there are five other universities, at Fez, Marrakesh, Oujda and Casa-blanca, and institutes of higher education in business studies, agric-ulture, mining, law, and statistics and advanced economics. In 1989 there was a total of 239,923 students engaged in higher education. In addition, there were 23,100 studying abroad and 48,241 at other institutions for higher education (1979/80). In 1987 the government announced plans to open 10 higher technical institutes per year before the year 2000, for students not wishing to attend normal institutions of higher education.

Adult education is being provided through the means of radio, simplified type, a special newspaper for the newly literate, and the co-operation of every teacher in the country. Another notable development in recent years has been the increasing attention given to education for girls. In 1989 40.4% of secondary school pupils were girls. There are now a number of mixed and girls' schools, and the proportion is growing every year, especially in urban areas.

Bibliography

Abu-Lughod, Janet L. *Rabat: Urban Apartheid in Morocco.* Guildford, England, Princeton University Press, 1981.

Amin, Samir. *The Maghreb in the Modern World.* Harmondsworth, Penguin, 1971.

Ashford, D. E. *Political Change in Morocco.* Princeton U.P., 1961.

    Perspectives of a Moroccan Nationalist. New York, 1964.

Ayache, A. *Le Maroc.* Paris, Editions Sociales, 1956.

Baduel, Pierre-Robert. *Enjeux Sahariens.* Paris, CNRS, 1984.

Barbier, Maurice. *Le Conflit du Sahara occidental.* Paris, L'Harmattan, 1982.

Barbour, Nevill. *Morocco.* London, Thames and Hudson, 1964.

Ben Barka, Mehdi. *Problèmes de l'édification du Maroc et du Maghreb.* Paris, Plon, 1959.

    Option Révolutionnaire en Maroc. Paris, Maspéro, 1966.

Bennett, Norman Robert. *A study guide for Morocco.* Boston, 1970.

Bernard, Stephane. *Le Conflit Franco-Marocain 1943–1956,* 3 vols. Brussels, 1963; English translation, Yale University Press, 1968.

Berque, Jaques. *Le Maghreb entre deux guerres.* Paris, Edns. du Seuil, 1962.

Brown, Kenneth. *People of Salé.* Manchester University Press, 1976.

Cohen, M. I., and Hahn, Lorna. *Morocco: Old Land. New Nation.* New York, Praeger, 1964.

Coulau, Julien. *La paysannerie marocaine.* Paris, 1968.

Eickelman, Dale F. *Moroccan Islam: Tradition and Society in a Pilgrimage Center.* Princeton University Press, 1986.

Hall, L. J. *The United States and Morocco, 1776–1956.* Metuchen, NJ, Scarecrow Press, 1971.

Halstead, John P. *Rebirth of a Nation: the Origins and Rise of Moroccan Nationalism.* Harvard University Press, 1967.

Hassan II, King of Morocco. *Le Défi.* Paris, Albin Michel, 1976.

Hodges, Tony. *Western Sahara: the Roots of a Desert War.* London, Croom Helm, 1983.

    Historical Dictionary of Western Sahara. London, Scarecrow Press, 1982.

Horton, Brendon. *Morocco: Analysis and Reform of Foreign Policy.* Economic Development Institute of the World Bank, 1990.

Julien, Charles-André. *Le Maroc face aux Impérialismes (1415–1956).* Paris, Editions Jeune Afrique, 1978.

Kay, Shirley. *Morocco.* London, Namara Publications, 1980.

Kininmonth, C. *The Travellers' Guide to Morocco.* London, Jonathan Cape, 1972.

Lacouture, J. and S. *Le Maroc à l'épreuve.* Paris, du Seuil, 1958.

Landau, Rom. *The Moroccan Drama 1900–1955.* London, Hale, 1956.

    Morocco Independent under Mohammed V. London, Allen and Unwin, 1961.

    Hassan II, King of Morocco. London, Allen and Unwin, 1962.

    The Moroccans—Yesterday and Today. London, 1963.

    Morocco. London, Allen & Unwin, 1967.

Landau, Rom and Swann, Wim. *Marokko.* Cologne, 1970.

Le Tourneau, Roger. *Evolution politique de l'Afrique du Nord musulmane.* Paris, Armand Colin, 1962.

Maxwell, Gavin. *Lords of the Atlas.* London, Longmans, 1966.

Metcalf, John. *Morocco—an Economic Study.* New York, First National City Bank, 1966.

Mumson, Henry Jr. *Religion and Power in Morocco.* London, Yale University Press, 1993.

Perrault, Gilles. *Notre Ami le Roi.* Paris, Editions Gallimard, 1991.

Perroux, F. and Barre, R. *Développement, croissance, progrès—Maroc-Tunisie.* Paris, 1961.

Robert, J. *La monarchie marocaine.* Paris, Librairie générale de droit et de jurisprudence, 1963.

Sutton, Michael. *Morocco to 1992 (Growth against the Odds).* London, Economist Intelligence Unit, 1987.

Terrasse, H. *Histoire du Maroc des origines à l'établissement du protectorat français,* 2 vols. Casablanca, 1949–50; English trans. by H. Tee, London, 1952.

Thompson, Virginia and Adloff, Richard. *The Western Saharans.* London, Croom Helm, Totowa, NJ, Barnes and Noble, 1980.

Tiano, André. *La politique économique et financière du Maroc indépendant.* Paris, Presses universitaires de France, 1963.

Trout, Frank E. *Morocco's Saharan Frontiers.* Geneva, 1969.

Waterson, Albert. *Planning in Morocco.* Baltimore, Johns Hopkins Press, 1963.

Waterbury, John. *The commander of the Faithful. The Moroccan political élite.* London, 1970.

World Bank. *The Economic Development of Morocco.* Baltimore, Johns Hopkins Press, 1966.

Zartman, I. W. *Morocco: Problems of New Power.* New York, Atherton Press, 1964.

OMAN

Geography

The Sultanate of Oman occupies the extreme east and south-east of the Arabian peninsula. It is bordered by the United Arab Emirates (UAE) to the north and west, by Saudi Arabia to the west and by Yemen to the south-west. A detached area of Oman, separated from the rest of the country by UAE territory, lies at the tip of the Musandam peninsula, on the southern shore of the Strait of Hormuz. Oman is separated from Iran by the Gulf of Oman, and it has a coastline of more than 1,600 km (1,000 miles) on the Indian Ocean. The total area of the country is about 300,000 sq km (120,000 sq miles). Oman's frontiers with its neighbours have never been clearly demarcated but agreement exists on their general course.

The first full census in Oman was held in 1993. Previous estimates of the country's population varied widely between the nation's own figures and those of independent international organizations. The UN Population Division, basing its assessment on a mid-1965 figure of 571,000, estimated totals of 654,000 for mid-1970, 766,000 for mid-1975, 984,000 for mid-1980 and 1,242,000 for mid-1985. The UN estimated Oman's mid-year population at 1,395,000 in 1988, at 1,447,000 in 1989, at 1,502,000 in 1990 and at 1,559,000 in 1991. It was also estimated that the population of the sultanate was increasing by 3.8% annually in the early 1990s. The first results of the population census were declared in December 1993. The population was estimated at 2.0m.; 74% Omani and 26% non-Omani. It was estimated that the population was increasing by 3.5% annually. The majority of the population are Ibadi Muslims, and about one-quarter are Hindus.

At Muscat the mean annual rainfall is 100 mm and the mean temperature varies between 20°C and 43°C (69°F and 110°F). Rainfall on the hills of the interior is somewhat heavier, and the south-western province of Dhofar is the only part of Arabia to benefit from the summer monsoon.

Oman may be divided into nine topographical areas. The largest urban area in the country is the capital region, around Muscat. Although most of the country is arid, the Batinah plain, which lies between the Gulf of Oman and the Hajar al-Gharbi range of mountains, comprises a fertile coastal region, and is among the most densely populated areas of the country. Another such plain is found between Raysut and Salalah, on the south-west coast in the Dhofar region, which in total occupies one-third of the country's area and extends north-wards into the Rub al-Khali, or 'empty quarter', on Oman's western border: a rainless, unrelieved wilderness of shifting sand, almost entirely without human habitation.

Irrigation has been developed in some parts of the country, including the Dhahira area, a semi-desert plain between the south-western Hajar mountains and the Rub al-Khali, which also provides clusters of cultivable land near the wadis Dank and Ain, and the Buraini oasis. From Jebel al-Akhdar, at the southern tip of the Hajar al-Gharbi range, towards the desert in the south, lies the Interior, the country's central hill region and the most densely populated zone. The area has four main valleys, two of which (Halafein and Samail) provide the traditional route to Muscat.

The less hospitable regions are sparsely populated by groups of tribal settlers. The Hajar al-Gharbi, running parallel to the coast southwards from Oman's border with the UAE, is the home of the Rostaq, Awabi and Nakhe tribes. To the east of the Hajar range, the Sharqiya area extends south towards the Arabian Sea. It is an area of sandy plains and the home of the various Bani tribes. Musandam, separated from Oman by the UAE, is a mountainous area inhabited by the ash-Shahouh tribes. Around the eastern coast of the Arabian Sea, the Barr al-Hekkman, a group of islands and salt-plains of 650 sq km (250 sq miles), is inhabited by fishermen.

For administrative purposes, the Sultanate is divided into 41 *wilayat* (provinces), each under the jurisdiction of a *wali*, or provincial governor.

History

Oman was probably the land of Magan (mentioned in Sumerian tablets) with which cities such as Ur of the Chaldees traded in the third millennium BC. The province of Dhofar also produced frankincense in vast quantities, which was shipped to markets in Iraq, Syria, Egypt and the West. Roman geographers mention the city of Omana, although its precise location has not been identified, and Portus Moschus, conceivably Muscat. Oman, at various times, came under the influence of the Himyaritic kingdoms of southern Arabia and of Iran, which are believed to have been responsible for the introduction of the *falaj* irrigation systems, although legend attributes them to Sulaiman ibn Daud (Solomon).

The people of Oman come from two main ethnic stocks, the Qahtan, who immigrated from southern Arabia, and the Nizar, who came in from the north. According to tradition, the first important invasion from southern Arabia was led by Malik ibn Faham, after the final collapse of the Marib dam in Yemen in the first or second century AD. Oman was one of the first countries to be converted to Islam by Amr ibn al-As, who later converted Egypt. Omanis of the tribe of al-Azd played an important part in the early days of Islam in Iraq. They subsequently embraced the Ibadi doctrine, which holds that the caliphate in Islam should not be hereditary or confined to any one family, and established their own independent Imamate in Oman in the eighth century AD. Subsequently, although subject to invasions by the Caliphate, Iranians, Moguls and others, Oman has largely maintained its independence.

During the 10th century Sohar was probably the largest and most important city in the Arab world, while Omani mariners, together with those from Basra and other Gulf ports, went as far afield as China. When the Portuguese arrived in 1507, on their way to India, Affonso d'Albuquerque and his forces found the Omani seaport under the suzerainty of the King of Hormuz, himself of Omani stock. The towns of Qalhat, Quryat, Muscat and Sohar were already prosperous.

However, the arrival of the Portuguese in the Indian Ocean radically altered the balance of power in the area. The Portuguese established themselves in the Omani ports, concentrating principally on Sohar and Muscat, where they built two great forts, Merani (1587) and Jalali (1588). British and Dutch traders followed in the wake of the Portuguese, though they did not establish themselves by force of arms in Oman. In 1650 the Imam Nasir ibn Murshid of the Yaariba dynasty, who was also credited with a period of Omani renaissance during which learning flourished, effectively expelled the Portuguese from Muscat and the rest of Oman. The Omanis then extended their power, and by 1730 had conquered the Portuguese settlements on the east coast of Africa, including Mogadishu (now in Somalia), Mombasa (Kenya) and Zanzibar (now part of Tanzania).

The country was, however, ravaged by civil war in the first half of the 18th century, when the authority of the Imam diminished. During this period the Iranians were called in to assist one of the contenders for the Imamate, but they were subsequently ousted by Ahmad ibn Said, who was elected Imam in 1749 and founded the al-Bu Said dynasty, one of the oldest dynasties in the Middle East, which still rules Oman. The country prospered under the new dynasty and its maritime influence revived. In about 1786 the capital of the country was transferred from Rostaq to Muscat, a move which led to a dichotomy between the coast and the interior, creating political problems between the two regions at various times.

The Imam, Said bin Sultan, ruled Oman from 1804 until 1856. He was a strong and popular ruler, who also gained the respect and friendship of European nations, in particular the British. Treaties providing for the establishment of consular relations were negotiated with the British in 1839 (there had been earlier treaties of friendship in 1798 and 1800), the USA in 1833, France in 1844 and the Netherlands in 1877. British relations with Oman were maintained almost uninterrupted from the early 18th century until the present day, while relations with the other states concerned were less continuous.

Said bin Sultan revived Omani interest in Zanzibar and, in the latter part of his reign, spent an increasing amount of his time there. He started the clove plantations which later brought great wealth to the islands of Zanzibar and Pemba, and he founded the dynasty which ruled there until the revolution in 1964. During Said's reign, Omani dominions expanded to their greatest extent. In 1829 Dhofar became one of the constituent parts of the Sultanate and has remained so ever since.

The latter half of the 19th century was a difficult period for Oman. Not only had it lost its East African possessions, but a series of treaties with Britain to curb the slave trade also brought about a decline in the local economy, as Muscat had been an important port for this lucrative traffic.

Although Britain's only formal links with the Sultanate have been a series of Treaties of Friendship, Commerce and Navigation signed in 1891, 1939 and 1951, it has given military assistance to Oman on a number of occasions and continues to do so.

Several insurrections took place towards the end of the 19th century, and in 1913 a new Imam was elected in the interior, in defiance of the Sultan who ruled from Muscat. This led to the expulsion of the Sultan's garrisons from Nizwa, Izki and Sumail. In the same year Sultan Faisal bin Turki, who had ruled since 1888, died, to be succeeded by his son Taimur. Efforts to come to terms with the rebels failed until 1920, when an agreement was reached between the Sultan and the principal dissidents, led by Isa bin Salih. It provided for peace, free movement of persons between the interior and the coast, limitation of customs duties and non-interference by the government of the Sultan in the internal affairs of the signatory tribes. A new Treaty of Friendship with Britain, signed on 20 December 1951, recognized the full independence of the sultanate, officially called Muscat and Oman. Relations between the Imam, Muhammad bin Abdullah al-Khalili, and the Sultan remained good until the Imam's death in 1954, when rebellion again broke out under the Imam's successor, Ghalib bin Ali, who sought external assistance to establish a separate principality. In December 1955 forces under the Sultan's control entered the main inhabited centres of Oman without resistance. The former Imam was allowed by the Sultan to retire to his village, but his brother, Talib, escaped to Saudi Arabia and thence to Cairo. An 'Oman Imamate' office was established there, and the Imam's cause was supported by Egyptian propaganda. In the summer of 1957 Talib returned and established himself, with followers, in the mountain areas north-west of Nizwa. The Sultan appealed for British help, and fighting continued until early 1959, when the Sultan's authority was fully re-established. In October 1960, despite British objections, 10 Arab countries succeeded in placing the 'question of Oman' on the agenda of the UN General Assembly. In 1961 a resolution in support of separate independence for Oman failed to secure the necessary majority, and in 1963 a UN Commission of Inquiry refuted the Imamate's charges of oppressive government and public hostility to the Sultan. Nevertheless, a committee was formed to study the problem and, after its report had been submitted to the General Assembly in 1965, a resolution was adopted which, among other things, demanded the elimination of British domination in any form. The question was debated on several further occasions until, more than a year after Sultan Qaboos's accession, Oman (as Muscat and Oman was renamed in 1970: see below) became a member of the UN in October 1971.

THE SULTANATE SINCE 1970

By 1970 Sultan Said's Government had come to be regarded as the most reactionary and isolationist in the area. Slavery was still common, and many medieval prohibitions were in force. The Sultan's insistence that petroleum revenues be used exclusively to fund defence was embarrassing for Britain, the oil companies and the neighbouring states, and provoked the rebellion that began in Dhofar province in 1964. On 23 July 1970 the Sultan was deposed (and later exiled) in a coup, led by his son, Qaboos bin Said, at the royal palace in Salalah. Qaboos, who was then 29 years of age and had trained at Britain's Royal Military Academy (Sandhurst), thus became Sultan amid general acclaim, both within the country and abroad. (The new Sultan's mother remained in residence in Oman until her death in August 1992.) The new Sultan intended to transform the country, using petroleum revenues for development, following the model of the Gulf sheikhdoms to the north. He asked the rebels for their co-operation, but only the Dhofar Liberation Front responded favourably. The Popular Front for the Liberation of the Occupied Arabian Gulf (reported to control much of Dhofar, and to be receiving aid, via Southern Yemen, from the People's Republic of China) and its ally, the National Democratic Front for the Liberation of the Occupied Arab Gulf, appeared to think that the palace coup changed little.

In August 1970 'Muscat' ceased to be part of the title of the country, which became simply the 'Sultanate of Oman'. Sultan Qaboos appointed his uncle, Tariq bin Taimur, as Prime Minister. Tariq resigned his office in December 1971, since when the Sultan has himself presided over Cabinet meetings and acted as his own Prime Minister, Minister of Defence and Minister of Foreign Affairs. Priority was given to providing the basic social and economic infrastructure which the former Sultan had rigidly opposed—housing, education, communications, health services, etc. In addition, restrictions on travel were abolished, many prisoners released, and many Omanis returned from abroad. None the less, a substantial proportion of the annual budget continued to be devoted to defence and to quelling the Dhofar insurgency.

Oman's admission to the UN in 1971 was achieved despite opposition from the People's Democratic Republic of Yemen (PDRY, formerly Southern Yemen), which supported the Popular Front for the Liberation of Oman and the Arab Gulf (PFLOAG), formed in 1972 by the unification of the two nationalist liberation fronts. The name of this organization was changed in July 1974 to the People's Front for the Liberation of Oman (PFLO). Oman's relationship with Britain also compromised Oman's candidature for UN membership. Britain continues to supply weapons, ammunition and military advisers to the Omani Government.

The progress which was achieved after the palace coup of 1970 did have some impact on the insurgents' following, with a number of defections to the Sultan's forces, but fighting continued until 1975. Omani forces attacked the border area of the PDRY for the first time in May 1972. In 1973 Iranian troops entered the conflict on the side of the Sultan, who also received assistance from Jordan, Saudi Arabia, the United Arab Emirates (UAE), Pakistan and India. Although the Sultan's forces gradually gained the upper hand, the war was prolonged, and during October 1975 the rebels used sophisticated weapons such as Soviet-made SAM-7 missiles. In December 1975, after an offensive, the Sultan claimed a complete victory over the insurgents. Saudi Arabia helped to negotiate a cease-fire in 1976, and an amnesty was granted to the Omanis who had been fighting for the PFLO.

Since then, only desultory conflicts have taken place and many rebels have returned to their homes in Oman. In January

1977 Iran withdrew the bulk of its forces from Dhofar, but a token force remained until the Iranian revolution in early 1979. A renewal of the insurrection against Sultan Qaboos occurred in June 1978, when a party of British engineers was attacked in the Salalah region of Dhofar. The PFLO has become largely an external force, however, and has had little success in attracting adherents within Oman, despite the assassination, in 1979, of the Governor of Dhofar, and reports of renewed insurgency. In January 1981 Oman closed its border with the PDRY, and more British officers were seconded to the Omani forces as the frontier defences were put on the alert. However, by October 1982, after talks at which Kuwait and the UAE mediated, Oman and the PDRY had re-established diplomatic relations, signing an agreement on 'normalization'. In late 1987 a series of minor clashes between border patrols of the PDRY and Oman took place in Dhofar Province.

Oman's relations with its other Arab neighbours have improved rapidly over the last few years. During the reign of Sultan Said, the Omani dependence on British military forces was viewed with disfavour by its neighbours, increasing Oman's isolation in the Arab world. However, since the accession of Sultan Qaboos, and more especially since the defeat of the Dhofar insurgents, relations have improved considerably. Both Kuwait and the UAE have supplied much-needed financial support to Oman, while Iraq, formerly a supporter of the PFLO, has established diplomatic relations. The establishment of economic and diplomatic links with Saudi Arabia was particularly significant. Oman's support for the Israeli-Egyptian peace treaty of 1979 threatened to damage relations with some of the Arab League's more uncompromising members, but promised closer ties with the USA and with Egypt, which has undertaken to respond to any request from Oman for military aid. Concern over regional security prompted Oman to join the Gulf Co-operation Council (GCC), founded in May 1981.

The strategic importance of military bases in Oman has long been recognized. The United Kingdom (UK) withdrew its forces from Masirah Island in 1977, and since then the USA has shown keen interest. In February 1980 Oman began negotiations with the USA concerning a defence alliance whereby, in exchange for US military and economic aid and a commitment to Oman's security, Oman would grant the USA use of port and air base facilities in the Gulf (including Masirah Island). Although direct alignment with a superpower is contrary to Oman's foreign policy, the agreement was finalized in June, and was bitterly condemned by the Arab People's Congress in Libya as a concession to 'US imperialism'. The outbreak of the Iran–Iraq War in September 1980 only served to underline Oman's strategic importance, particularly with regard to the Strait of Hormuz, a narrow waterway at the mouth of the Persian (Arabian) Gulf, between Oman and Iran, through which about two-thirds of the world's sea-borne trade in crude petroleum passes. The fact that Oman possesses export outlets other than the Strait brought some economic advantages to the country in May 1984, as its ports handled some trade which was destined for countries within the Gulf whose commerce was threatened by an escalation of the Iran-Iraq War.

A 45-member Consultative Assembly (consisting of 17 representatives of the Government, 17 representatives of the private sector and 11 regional representatives) was created in October 1981 in response to suggestions that Sultan Qaboos was not being made sufficiently aware of public opinion. In 1983 the Assembly's membership was expanded to 55, including 19 representatives of the Government. Its role, however, was confined to comment on economic and social development and recommendations on future policy. In November 1990 Sultan Qaboos announced that a new Consultative Council, comprising regional representatives, was to be established within one year, in order to allow 'wider participation' by Omani citizens in national 'responsibilities and tasks'. In March 1991 he announced that the Council would consist of 59 elected members. The President of the Council was to be appointed by the Government. In April 21 prominent figures met to nominate three candidates (of whom one was to be appointed to the Council) for each of the country's *wilayat* (provinces). On taking office, the members of the Council

were to appoint committees and executive officers. An annual meeting between the Council and members of the Government would also be held. Although the Council has no legislative power, ministers are obliged to present annual statements to it and to answer any questions addressed to them.

In 1981 the USA established a communications centre in Oman, and President Reagan pledged more than US $200m. in 1981–83 to develop port and airport facilities in return for the right to stockpile supplies in Oman for possible use by the US Rapid Deployment Force. By 1985 the total sum spent on the improvement of facilities in Oman had risen to $300m. United States forces were permitted to make landings in Oman during the massive 'Bright Star' military exercises, held in the region in December 1981. This aroused protest from the PDRY, as it contravened a clause of the 'normalization' agreement previously made. As a result, the other Gulf states, particularly Kuwait, attempted to discourage both countries' links with the superpowers by reportedly offering Oman $1,200m. to withdraw the US military facility. In a preliminary attempt to co-ordinate the Gulf's own independent defence system, the GCC focused its attention on Oman, awarding a five-year defence grant to the country in July 1983 and holding joint military exercises there in October.

Oman was keen to maintain relations with the GCC countries, and in November 1983 it joined with them in urging Iran to grant safe passage to traffic in the Strait of Hormuz. The Sultanate also continued to develop its own defences, with the support of the GCC, and by the end of 1984 had acquired two squadrons of Chieftain tanks and two squadrons of Jaguar aircraft.

In September 1985 Oman established diplomatic relations with the USSR. The move was encouraged by the peaceful relations which had been maintained between Oman and the PDRY since the resumption of diplomatic contact in 1982, and was interpreted as an indication of Oman's desire to preserve its political independence. However, an American presence was discreetly maintained, and US troops were allowed to use military bases in Oman only with the agreement of the Omani Government. The USA continued to make improvements to existing installations in the Sultanate, expanding fuel, ammunition, power and water facilities at Seeb airfield. In August 1985 Oman agreed to purchase a consignment of eight Tornado aircraft from the UK's British Aerospace. The contract was valued at more than $450m., and the first of these aircraft, which are designed for long-range interception, were delivered in 1992.

During 1987 attacks by Iran and Iraq on shipping in the Gulf increased, and in August, the UK and France, followed in September by the Netherlands, Belgium and Italy, sent minesweepers to clear mines, believed to have been laid by Iran, from the shipping lanes leading to Kuwait through the Strait of Hormuz. The escalation of tension in the Gulf, exacerbated by the presence of US and Soviet naval forces, resulted in the adoption of Resolution 598 by the UN Security Council on 20 July 1987, which urged an immediate cease-fire. Iraq agreed to observe a cease-fire if Iran would also, but Iran prevaricated, attaching conditions to its acceptance of the Resolution. In November, at an extraordinary meeting of the League of Arab States in Amman, Jordan, representatives of the member nations, including Oman, unanimously condemned Iran for prolonging the war against Iraq, deplored its occupation of Arab (i.e. Iraqi) territory, and urged it to accept Resolution 598 without preconditions. (For more detailed coverage of the Iran–Iraq War, see chapters on Iran and Iraq.)

In March 1988 the GCC and the Commission of the European Community concluded an agreement to promote economic co-operation. The agreement, which was signed by ministers of the EC in June, committed the Community to assisting the GCC states in the development and diversification of their energy, industrial and agricultural sectors. Further negotiations between the EC and the GCC, to discuss the liberalization and expansion of trade, began shortly afterwards. In October Oman and the PDRY signed an agreement to increase co-operation in the sectors of trade and communications. The signing took place during the first visit to the Sultanate by a President of the PDRY since the PDRY attained independence in 1967. In January 1989 the Omani Minister of Petroleum and Minerals, Said ash-Shanfari, became the first Omani minister to visit the USSR since the establishment of diplomatic relations between the two countries in 1985. The USSR's potential role in the stabilization of the global oil market was discussed. In early 1989 Oman adopted a more conciliatory policy towards Iran, and in March the two countries established an economic co-operation committee. However, Oman's support for Iran was conditional upon the latter's efforts to achieve political stability in the Gulf region.

After the invasion of Kuwait by Iraqi troops on 2 August 1990, many of the Gulf states suffered from shortages of food. Although Oman's food supplies were adequate, the Government banned the export of eight essential commodities, initially because traders were exporting these commodities to the UAE in order to profit from price increases there.

In response to the deepening crisis in the Gulf region, the Omani Government stated in September 1990 that the dispute between Iraq and Kuwait should be resolved without the use of force. When it became clear that Iraq was not going to withdraw from Kuwait, Oman, together with the other members of the GCC, gave its support to the deployment of a US-led defensive force in Saudi Arabia. The Omani Government expressed the view that the imposition of economic sanctions would force Iraq to withdraw from Kuwait. Oman was, however, prepared to tolerate the continuation in office of the Iraqi President, Saddam Hussain. In late November there was evidence that Oman had attempted to mediate in the crisis, when the Iraqi Minister of Foreign Affairs, Tareq Aziz, made the first official Iraqi visit to a GCC state, other than Kuwait, since August 1990.

In the aftermath of the Gulf crisis, Sultan Qaboos supported further integration among the GCC's members, and in December 1991, at the annual meeting of GCC Heads of State, he unsuccessfully proposed the creation of a 100,000-strong GCC army. Oman has expressed a particular desire to promote relations between the GCC states and Iran, and to support gradual political reform in the latter. In March 1991 Oman hosted a meeting at which diplomatic relations between Saudi Arabia and Iran were restored. In September 1992 the Governments of Oman and Iran signed an agreement to increase trade and economic co-operation, in particular in the sectors of transport and shipping.

In December 1991 a cabinet reshuffle produced wide-ranging ministerial changes and the amalgamation of several ministries. This was followed by a further reshuffle in May 1992.

On 5 January 1992 the inaugural session of the Consultative Council, created to replace the former State Consultative Assembly, was held. The new body's 59 members were appointed for a three-year term. Three new ministries were created in the cabinet reshuffle in January 1994, and in July it was announced that membership of the Consultative Council would be increased to 80 in 1995, allowing constituencies of 30,000 or more inhabitants to have two seats. Women would also be granted the right to vote and stand for election. Although the Council has no legislative power, ministers are obliged to present annual statements to it and to answer any questions addressed to them.

In January 1992 President Mitterrand of France arrived in Muscat for talks on increasing political ties and bilateral commerce, particularly in the defence, energy and banking sectors. In April Oman and the UAE agreed to relax travel regulations, to enable nationals to travel between the countries with identity cards, rather than passports. In May the President of the UAE, Sheikh Zayed an-Nahyan, visited the Sultan for talks, as a result of which diplomatic representation between the two countries was raised to ambassadorial level.

In October 1992 Oman signed an agreement with Yemen to establish the demarcation of their border. The agreement was officially ratified in December 1992, and in October 1993 Sultan Qaboos pledged US $21m. to finance the construction of a border road between the two countries. Normalization of relations were restored and in March 1994 Oman hosted talks with Yemen to discuss the furthering of bilateral co-operation. The efforts of Sultan Qaboos to mediate a settlement to the conflict in Yemen ended in disappointment when fighting broke out again between the two rival Yemeni factions in late April. However, the Sultanate was elected to be a member of the UN Security Council for 1994 in tribute to its mediatory role in the Middle East.

Diplomatic relations were established with the Czech Republic, Slovakia and Guatemala in 1993. In January 1994 bilateral talks were held with Egypt to promote the exchange of expertise between their respective armed forces. In March the Pakistani Prime Minister, Benazir Bhutto, made an official visit to Oman which resulted in an agreement to increase co-operation in various fields, especially in the sectors of economics and regional security. In the same month Oman welcomed King Hussein of Jordan on a private visit and played host to the first official visit by an Israeli minister to an Arab Gulf State since Israel's declaration of Independence in 1948.

Economy

Oman's economy is based largely on revenue from the petroleum sector. Petroleum was first produced commercially in 1967, but it was not until 1970, when Sultan Qaboos bin Said assumed power, that income from petroleum was invested in the country's economic development. Subsequently, Oman's economy expanded considerably under a prudent policy of avoiding external debt while developing both public and private sectors.

In 1992, according to estimates by the World Bank, Oman's gross national product (GNP), measured at average 1990-92 prices, was US $10,683m., equivalent to $6,490 per head. Between 1965 and 1990, it was estimated, GNP per head expanded, in real terms, at an average rate of 6.4% per year. Oman's economic growth since the mid-1960s has been rapid but uneven. Between 1965 and 1980, according to World Bank estimates, the country's gross domestic product (GDP) increased, in real terms, by 12.5% per year, one of the highest national growth rates in the world. The comparable increase between 1973 and 1984 was 6.1% per year, a rate that was maintained at 6% during 1985. Measured in current prices, Oman's annual GDP rose from an estimated mere $60m. in 1965 to $8,980m. in 1985. According to official estimates, the annual increase in GDP, measured in constant 1978 prices, was 11.5% in 1982, 16.7% in 1983, 16.6% in 1984 and 13.8%

in 1985. However, real GDP rose by only 3.3% in 1986 and it declined by 3.4% in 1987. During 1980–91 the average annual growth rate for GDP was 7.9%. In 1988, according to estimates by the World Bank, GDP (measured in current purchasers' prices) declined by 5.5%, to $7,700m., compared with $8,150m. in 1987. In 1990 GDP rose more rapidly than expected, as a result of the increased price of petroleum, to RO 4,051m. ($10,535m.), compared with RO 3,231m. ($8,402m.) in 1989. In 1991, however, current GDP decreased marginally, to RO 3,936m. ($10,236m.). In 1992 GDP increased by more than 11% to RO 4,417.4m. ($11,489m.).

Revenues from petroleum have been used to implement three development plans, covering 1976–80, 1981–85 and 1986–90. These plans aimed to provide the country with necessary social amenities while investing further in the petroleum sector, but in recent years there has been a strong emphasis on diversification within the economy. The delay in the implementation of these plans allowed Oman to plan development so as to ensure the minimum of competition with existing industries in the region. The third Five-Year Plan aimed to achieve greater industrial diversification and the construction of several major industrial estates. Agricultural development was also an important objective. However, the crisis in the oil industry led to some delays in the implementation of the third

Plan. In January 1991 the Government announced details of a fourth development plan, covering 1991–95. The plan imposed strict limits on projected external borrowing, and again emphasized the diversification of the economy, which was to be achieved through the expansion of the private sector, and renewed stress on industry, agriculture and fisheries, mining and services.

Oman is neither a member of the Organization of the Petroleum Exporting Countries (OPEC), nor of the Organization of Arab Petroleum Exporting Countries (OAPEC). However, its agreements on concessionary terms ensure that concession-holders are obliged to grant it the same privileges as those granted to members of OPEC. Oman is not, therefore, subject to controls on petroleum production and pricing, although it generally respects OPEC's policies. In the 1980s Oman benefited from its freedom to raise production levels to compensate for any loss of income resulting from the existence of large surplus stocks of petroleum during the first half of the decade. Owing to Oman's position on the southern shore of the Persian (Arabian) Gulf, the country was less vulnerable to the disruption of petroleum traffic caused by the 1980–88 war between Iran and Iraq. However, after the collapse in petroleum prices in 1986, Oman supported OPEC's decision to reduce output in September and October (in order to bring about an increase in prices) by announcing a reduction of 50,000 barrels per day (b/d) in its own production (see Petroleum and Natural Gas). Further reductions of 5% in production were introduced in February 1987 and February 1988, limiting output to 550,000 b/d, as its contribution to OPEC's attempt to support an international oil price of $18 per barrel. However, over-production depressed the price of oil on the 'spot' market in September 1988, and in January 1989 Oman announced that it would reduce production of crude petroleum by a further 5% from 1 April. In March it was estimated that Oman was producing 600,000 b/d. In June 1990 the level of oil production was 650,000 b/d and the Ministry of Petroleum and Minerals planned to raise it by an additional 50,000 b/d. However, in July 1990 the Omani Government suspended these plans in an attempt to co-operate with OPEC's efforts to raise international oil prices. In 1992 the price of Omani oil averaged $18 per barrel, but by the end of 1993 the price had sunk to less than $12 per barrel. In January 1994 Oman cut its output by 5% in the hope that other oil-producing countries would follow suit in order to raise the price of oil. By April, however, Oman abandoned its unilateral stance, resuming production to 800,000 b/d to average $14 per barrel by mid-1994. In 1993 Oman's petroleum reserves totalled 4,700m. barrels, sufficient to allow production, at present rates, to continue for a further 20 to 25 years.

Oman's development has been aided by grants from the Gulf Co-operation Council (GCC), an international organization that Oman joined at its inception in 1981. Among GCC regulations is an agreement to abolish tariffs on home-produced goods that are traded between member countries. Oman has retained these tariffs, however, in order to protect the country's developing industrial sector. In 1986 the Omani Government requested other members of the GCC to reveal the level of subsidy being applied to goods that they exported to Oman, in order to enable the tariff system to be updated.

In mid-1991 the annual rate of inflation was estimated at 3%, decreasing to 1.4% in 1992, and annual economic growth averaging 6% was forecast for the period 1991–95. An increase in regional expenditure and the encouragement of small-scale manufacturing, in addition to the growing confidence that Oman's stable economic situation has engendered, led to an economic growth rate of 9% in 1992. Oman suffered less than its GCC allies from the economic effects of the Gulf crisis. In 1991 the country registered exceptional growth, due mainly to a 40.5% increase in the petroleum sector, although there was also a 15.4% expansion in the non-oil sector.

AGRICULTURE AND FISHERIES

Since the development of the petroleum industry, the relative importance of agriculture has declined sharply. The Government estimated that 60% of arable land is under cultivation and, although nearly 40% of the working population were engaged in agriculture in 1992, agriculture (including forestry, hunting and fishing) contributed only 4% of Oman's GDP. Most agriculture currently takes the form of subsistence farming by traditional methods. The 1981–85 Development Plan allocated about RO 43m. for the development and modernization of farming methods, particularly irrigation. Total expenditure on agriculture and fisheries in the Plan was estimated at RO 110m. As a result, the sector's contribution to GDP in 1985 rose to RO 93.7m., an increase of 7.6% in comparison with 1984. In 1986 the sector contributed RO 95.9m. to GDP, representing an increase of 2.3% in comparison with the previous year. According to World Bank estimates, the average annual increase in agricultural output over the period 1980–89 was 5.1%. The 1986–90 Five-Year Plan emphasized the expansion of the fishing industry and the encouragement of production for export and the urban market. This was intended to reduce Oman's dependence on food imports, which cost RO 131m. (18.6% of Oman's total imports) in 1987 and RO 162.6m. in 1990. The Oman Bank for Agriculture and Fisheries provides loans to farmers, and there is a state marketing authority, the Public Authority for Marketing Produce, which aims to increase domestic consumption of local products. In 1987 Japan granted a concessionary loan of US $200m. to Oman for the development of agriculture and infrastructure. By the end of 1988, which was declared to be 'Agricultural Year' by the Sultan, about 2,500 government-owned research and experimental farms had been established. In January 1989 a 10-year plan was announced for the development of the agricultural and fishing industries. In March a loan of up to $186m. was secured from the Export-Import Bank of Japan for agricultural and infrastructural projects under the 1986–90 Plan. In 1989 government expenditure on agriculture, forestry and fishing was only RO 27.1m. (less than 2% of the total). In 1992 government expenditure on agriculture, forestry and fishing had increased marginally to RO 39.8m., just over 2% of the total.

Agriculture is heavily dependent on irrigation. In 1985 the Government announced that rural power and water networks were to be greatly expanded over the next five years, and in that year new dams at Khour ar-Rassagh and Wadi al-Koudh came into operation. In early 1988 a dam with a capacity of 3.6m. cu m was under construction at Wadi Jizzi in Sohar. In August 1989 three schemes to improve and expand the water distribution networks were announced: two in Nizwa and Sur, costing RO 2m. each, and one on Masirah island, at a cost of RO 500,000. In May 1990, contracts were awarded to improve water supply systems in Nizwa and Sur. The Nizwa project consisted of laying 45 km of pipeline, construction of a new section for the reservoir and the establishment of a telemetry system at a cost of RO 741,000. The Sur project involves a RO 688,000 contract to lay 10 km of transmission pipeline, 30 km of distribution pipeline and install a pumping station. In April 1991 the Ministry of Agriculture and Fisheries awarded a contract worth $8.3m. to build two recharge dams in the Batinah coastal region. Dams already constructed at Wadi Rubkah and Wadi Taww will eventually have respective capacities of 5m. cu m and 3.7m. cu m. The Ministry of Agriculture and Fisheries commissioned a recharge dam to be built at Wadi al-Fuleij, in Sur, at a cost of RO 1.2m. It was due to be completed in 1991 and will be 530 m long, enabling a saving of 2.2m. cu m of flood water which would normally flow from the wadi into the sea. In May 1990 the newly-created Ministry of Water Resources announced a programme for water rationalization which introduced new regulations for the registration of wells and a permit requirement for new wells.

About one-half of the area under cultivation is planted with dates. Other crops include lucerne (alfalfa), limes, mangoes, melons, bananas, papaya and coconuts. Oman is almost self-sufficient in tomatoes, cucumbers, onions and peppers. Imports of cereals increased from 52,000 metric tons in 1974 to 287,000 tons in 1987 and 332,000 tons in 1992. In 1988 405 ha of new land were brought under wheat cultivation. Livestock farming is practised in Dhofar, which benefits from monsoon rains between June and September. Cattle are raised in the hills north of Salalah, and goats in the Hajar mountains. The development of livestock was one of the principal aims of the 1981–85 Plan. In an effort to reduce the total cattle herd in Dhofar, and thereby protect the environment, the

Government announced in 1985 that, for every 20 sheep purchased from overseas, importers would have to buy one cow from Dhofar. In 1981, with the intention of curbing rural-to-urban migration, the Government established a bank for agriculture and fisheries, to provide loans to farmers and fishermen.

Fishing is a traditional industry in Oman, and during the 1970s it employed about 10% of the working population. In 1980 the Oman National Fisheries Company (ONFC) was formed to organize concession agreements, government trawlers and land facilities. By 1985 the ONFC was operating seven deep-sea trawlers and a processing and freezing plant at Mutrah. The inshore waters are rich in marine animals (mainly rock-cod, snapper and cuttlefish, together with some shellfish), which are the main source of protein in the diet of many Omanis, and provide some export revenue. In August 1991, however, new regulations to curb excess fishing of shellfish were introduced. The Government's Fishermen's Fund grants substantial subsidies to fishermen, while the Bank for Agriculture and Fisheries encourages small-scale fishermen, and had helped to provide about 500 boats and 2,000 outboard motors by early 1984. Most fishermen, however, were reluctant to change from subsistence to commercial fishing, despite the expansion of facilities for the storage and marketing of fish. During the late 1970s the annual catch was about 60,000 metric tons. Exports from the fishing industry in 1983 earned RO 4.4m. The value of fish exports rose to RO 6.3m. in 1984, and to RO 8.7m. in 1985. The total catch in 1985 was 101,180 tons; in 1986 it declined to 96,354 tons, but in 1987 it rose again, to 136,149 tons; and in 1988 it increased by 22%, to 165,576 tons. In 1989 fish exports were valued at RO 15m., although the total catch declined to 117,703 tons. The total catch in 1990 was 120,239 tons, declining to 117,780 tons in 1991. In March 1989 the Government held discussions with the US Agency for International Development (USAID) concerning the provision of finance for a project to develop and manage the local fishing industry. In July 1990 representatives of the USA and Oman concluded discussions concerning an agreement on the provision of aid. The USA pledged $75m. for a water programme already under way, and contributed approximately $40m. to a fisheries scheme. In November 1991 the newly-renamed Ministry of Agriculture and Fisheries Wealth announced the awarding of contracts for consultancy work on four fishing-harbour projects: at Qurayat, Bukha, Al-Lakbi and Mirbat. In 1992 electricity charges for the agriculture and fishery sectors were reduced as an incentive. In the fourth Five-Year Plan (1991–1996) RO 200m. was allocated to the fishing industry with the objective of raising its annual growth rate to account for 9.9% of GDP.

PETROLEUM AND NATURAL GAS

Since the early 1970s the economy of Oman has been dominated by the petroleum industry. In 1986 it was estimated that hydrocarbons provided 90% of government revenue, and, in 1991, that the extraction of crude petroleum and natural gas represented 42% of GDP. In 1937 Petroleum Concessions (Oman) Ltd, a subsidiary of the Iraq Petroleum Co, was granted a 75-year concession to explore for petroleum, extending over the whole area except for the district of Dhofar. A concession covering Dhofar was granted in 1953 to Dhofar Cities Service Petroleum Corporation. However, petroleum was not discovered until 1964, when deposits were found near Fahud. Commercial production began in 1967, and average output increased to around 300,000 barrels per day (b/d) in the 1970s. Production is managed by Petroleum Development Oman (PDO), in which the Government holds a 60% share, while Royal Dutch/Shell has 34%. PDO operates two main production areas: a group of central oilfields, south-west of Muscat, and a group of southern oilfields in Dhofar. The central area was the first to be developed, and four connected oilfields together produced crude petroleum at an average rate of 341,000 b/d in 1975. When production from the three Ghaba fields started in 1976, output from the total central area reached a peak level of 368,000 b/d. From then on, production declined, averaging about 250,000 b/d in early 1984. Development of the oilfields in the south has compensated for this fall. Production started at the Marmul field in

1980, and the Rima field came 'on stream' in 1982, producing 45,000 b/d in early 1984. Further fields, at Marmul, Nimr and Sayyala, were brought into production in late 1985. Output from the southern fields totalled some 150,000 b/d in early 1984. A north–south pipeline connects the oilfields to the port of Mina al-Fahal, near Muscat. Pipeline restoration and expansion, under way in 1985, was expected to provide the capacity to transport 650,000–670,000 b/d by 1988.

Apart from PDO, there are only two companies that produce petroleum in Oman. The most important of these is Elf Petroleum Oman. The company is 48% owned by Elf Aquitaine of France, which operates in partnership with Sumitomo and Wintershall. The other company is Occidental Oman, which began production in 1984. In June 1988 the Rajaa oilfield, situated in the Balija region of central Oman, commenced production. The new field, PDO's 50th to produce petroleum, was expected to increase daily output from the Balija field from 800 cu m to 3,000 cu m. Also in mid-1988 78 new wells were being drilled in the Yibal region of northern Oman, where 168 producing wells and 43 water-injection wells were already in operation.

The companies operating in Oman, with the dates of their agreements and the areas of their concessions, are as follows: PDO (1967, 129,000 sq km), Amoco (offshore, 1973, 21,246 sq km; onshore, 1981, 49,000 sq km), Elf Petroleum (Hormuz, 1973, 4,000 sq km; Butabul, 1975, 5,250 sq km; Saiwan, 1981, 27,000 sq km), Occidental/Gulf (Suneinah, 1975, 9,900 sq km), British Petroleum (1977, 48,000 sq km; 1984, 1,319 sq km), Japan Petroleum Exploration (1981, 3,713 sq km), Japan Petroleum Development (1981, 15,000 sq km), North-South Resources (1984, 60,000 sq km; 1985, 630 sq km) and Conquest Exploration Co (northern Oman, 1989, 1,390 sq km). All concessionnaires operate a production-sharing agreement with the Government.

Total Omani output of crude petroleum fell from 135m. barrels in 1976 to 103m. barrels in 1980, but the opening of new fields brought a recovery, and production reached 137m. barrels in 1983, at a rate of 375,000 b/d. The rate of production rose to 535,000 b/d in December 1985, giving an overall production figure for the year of 181.8m. barrels (an average level of 498,000 b/d), compared with 152.4m. barrels in 1984. In 1986 production averaged 560,000 b/d, despite a reduction of 50,000 b/d in September, after reaching a record level of 600,000 b/d in August. At the beginning of 1987 Oman reduced its level of production to 530,000 b/d, in solidarity with OPEC's attempts to stabilize the international price of crude petroleum at $18 per barrel. In 1990 the average rate of production was estimated at 660,000 b/d, compared with 640,000 b/d in 1989. The increase was attributed, in part, to the contribution of three new oilfields (Amin, Sadad and Wadi Haker), which raised the total number of Oman's oilfields to 64. In December 1993 Oman's proven published reserves of crude petroleum were estimated at 4,700m. barrels, which, at the rate of production in 1990, will not be exhausted until 2008. Oman's exports of petroleum were worth RO 1,409.6m. in 1982, RO 1,346.6m. in 1983, and RO 1,400.6m. in 1984. Revenue from the petroleum sector, in the form of sales and taxes, increased from RO 895.9m. in 1986 to RO 1,143.1m. in 1987 and was forecast at RO 1,065.3m. in 1988, and at RO 904.4m. in 1989. Exports of petroleum by volume in 1986 averaged 513,425 b/d, an increase of 13.7% compared with the previous year. In 1987 petroleum exports were estimated to be worth RO 1,194m., representing 82% of total revenue, and in 1988 they were worth RO 1,141.0m., according to estimates by the Central Bank. In 1989 Oman exported 215.9m. barrels of petroleum, valued at RO 1,344.4m. In 1990 229.3m. barrels of petroleum, valued at RO 1,828.8m., were exported from Oman. Japan is the principal recipient of Omani petroleum, taking 40.4% of the total in 1992, compared with 52.6% in 1986. Between January and November 1988, Japan imported oil to the value of $1,578m. from Oman. In 1989 sales to Japan represented 38.8% of total Omani petroleum exports. In 1990 exports of petroleum to Japan were worth RO 1,942.1m., an increase of 30.8% compared with the previous year. Following the rise in petroleum prices occasioned by the Gulf crisis, the Government's net oil revenues rose by almost 58%, to RO 1,538m., in 1990. In 1991 oil production increased by 3.4%, to 258.6m. barrels, an average of more than 708,000 b/d and to 270.8m. barrels in 1992. Oil exports rose to 252.5m. barrels in 1992 from 243.7m. in 1991. Net oil revenues fell to RO 1,241m. in 1991, rising slightly to RO 1,276m. in 1992, accounting for 79% and 77% of total revenue respectively. Oil production averaged 800,000 b/d in 1993. In January 1994 production was reduced to 720,000 b/d following an attempt by the Government to raise prices. The plan was abandoned when it became apparent that production quotas set by OPEC would not be reduced and the PDO announced that it aimed to produce an average of 800,000 b/d in 1994.

Oman's recoverable reserves of natural gas were estimated to total 263,500m. cu m (9,310,000m. cu ft) in 1987. By 1994, after further discoveries, known reserves had risen to 20,000,000m. cu ft (570,000m. cu m). The Yibal gas fields are thought to be capable of a daily yield of 4m. cu m (140m. cu ft). In September 1984 PDO embarked on a 10-year programme of exploration for unassociated gas, which, it was hoped, would enable more petroleum to be released for export. By September 1985 a total of 19 new discoveries of gas deposits had been reported. Gas production in 1985 reached 3,930m. cu m, of which 1,290m. cu m was reinjected, 900m. cu m was flared, 190m. cu m was lost and 1,550m. cu m was consumed. In 1985 PDO discovered gas reserves in Lekhwair, where it was planned, in 1989, to construct a gas injection plant in order to improve recovery levels, using surplus gas. The plant was part of a larger project to upgrade facilities at the Lekhwair field and its cost was estimated at $100m.–$130m. In June 1990 PDO announced that it was initiating several oil pipelines and gas lift projects. In August 1990 PDO awarded a contract to develop a water flood scheme at the Lekhwair oilfield. This project was allocated $500m. and will enable the scheme to have a daily capacity of 200,000 barrels of crude petroleum and 4m. cubic feet of gas. In June 1986 offshore gas was discovered in the Bukha field, in the Musandam Peninsula region. Its reserves were estimated at 31.2m. barrels of condensate, 500,000m. cu ft (14,000m. cu m) of dry gas and 7.3m. barrels of associated gas. A contract to develop the gas field was negotiated with a group led by a Canadian company, International Petroleum (IPL). At the end of 1987 natural gas was being extracted at the rate of 3.90m. cu m (140m. cu ft) per day, and by the end of the decade this was increased to between 14m. and 17m. cu m per day. A pipeline links Yibal to Muscat and Sohar, and in May 1989 the extension of the gas pipeline network from Yibal to Izki was nearing completion. The scheme is intended to provide sufficient supplies from Yibal to the coast until 2010. PDO has also initiated a programme to build a 10-in pipeline, 26 km in length, from Natih to Fahud. A further two pipelines, linking Qaharir to Marmul and Jalmu to Rima, were due to be completed in December 1991. Schemes are under way to convert domestic fuelling systems to natural gas in order to release more petroleum for export, and gas is also used to enhance the rate of petroleum recovery (by reinjection), and to power the country's copper smelter (see below). Gas liquefaction plants have been built at Yibal. In July 1989 a proposal to expand the plant producing natural gas liquids (NGL) at Yibal was announced. In 1987 output of liquefied petroleum gas (LPG) by the National Gas Company was 35,000 tons, and this was expected to increase to 37,000 tons in 1988. The Government has exclusive rights to revenue from gas, and in 1988 the National Gas Company's profits reached RO 649,000, 17.5% higher than in 1987. In April 1989 Oman agreed terms for a 10-year contract to supply natural gas for the world's first floating methanol plant, which was to begin production by 1991. The Government agreed to sell as much as 6,343m. cu m (224,000m. cu ft) of natural gas over the period of the agreement to the consortium owning the plant, which will have a capacity of 2,200 metric tons per day. In July 1989 PDO announced its largest gas discovery for 22 years, at the Saih Nihayda field in the central region. Recoverable reserves are estimated at 10,000m. cu m (350,000m. cu ft), making it Oman's fifth biggest gas field. A further large discovery of gas, at the Saih Rawl field, was announced in March 1991. In 1986 production of natural gas contributed 1.4% of GDP. In 1989 gas revenues increased to RO 56m. from RO 48.5m. in

1988. The contribution of natural gas receipts to total revenue has increased steadily in recent years. In 1990 gas revenues totalled RO 50.3m., equivalent to 2.7% of total revenue, rising to RO 63.1m. in 1992, accounting for 3.8% of total revenue. Receipts from natural gas were anticipated to rise by 15% to RO 69m. in 1994 from an estimated RO 60m. in 1993. In 1991 it was announced that more than RO 44m. had been allocated for exploration and exploitation of new gas discoveries. In February 1992 plans were announced for massive investment (estimated at $9,000m.) in a project to produce liquefied natural gas, to be implemented by the several partners in the PDO: the Government (51% share), Shell, Total, Partex and various Japanese companies. The Oman Liquefied Natural Gas Company (OLNGC) was established in 1992 to co-ordinate the project. Construction was scheduled to begin in 1996 at Bimmah and the plant was expected to be in operation in 1999. The Government aims to make natural gas the second most important source of revenue after oil by the end of the century.

Oman's first petroleum refinery came into production at Mina al-Fahal, near Muscat, in late 1982. As a result, the value of imports of refined products was reduced from RO 49.5m. in the first half of 1982 to RO 7m. in the comparable period of 1983. It was hoped that the new refinery would satisfy domestic demand for petrol. The refinery's average throughput was 38,000 b/d in 1983. In 1985 the throughput was reported to have risen to approximately 60,000 b/d. The refinery's capacity was increased to 77,000 b/d in 1987 and to 80,000 b/d in 1988. In July 1989 it was reported that the French oil group Total had begun refining 10,000 b/d of crude petroleum at Mina al-Fahal, utilizing the extra capacity. In June a syndicated loan of RO 6m. was signed by the Oman Refinery Company (ORC) to provide finance for a co-generation scheme at the refinery. In June 1992 Oman signed an agreement with Kazakhstan to explore for, develop and produce petroleum and gas in the republic. Later that year Oman agreed to collaborate with Kazakhstan, Azerbaijan and Russia in the 'Caspian Pipeline Consortium'. This project envisaged the construction, over three years, of a pipeline, costing about $1,000m., to transport about 1.5m. b/d of petroleum from the former Soviet republics. The feasibility study for the project was completed in 1994 and construction is due to commence in 1995. In 1993 the Governments of Oman and India signed a memorandum that envisaged the construction of a $4,000m. submarine pipeline, to transport Omani natural gas to the subcontinent. A further agreement was made to construct two refineries in India each with a capacity of 120,000 b/d. In the same year a preliminary accord was signed with Caltex of the USA to construct a $1,900m. refinery in Thailand which would have the capacity to refine 130,000 barrels of crude per day. Under the agreement Oman would reserve the right to export 80,000 b/d for refinement.

INDUSTRY AND MINERALS

Before 1964, industry in Oman was confined to small traditional handicrafts, such as silversmithing, weaving and boatbuilding. The development of petroleum generated activity in the construction sector, but it was not until the change of regime in 1970 that government investment in infrastructure projects and private spending on housing started a boom in construction. Some of the new projects were not well conceived, resulting in the drain of resources abroad to foreign contractors. By 1984, however, the construction industry in Oman was still healthy, at a time of relative inactivity in other Gulf states. This situation altered radically at the end of 1985, as major projects under the 1981–85 Plan, such as the Sultan Qaboos University, were completed. In early 1985 the Government began to impose selective import duties, in an effort to protect Oman's developing industrial sector. In 1986, however, petroleum prices declined sharply, and virtually all construction projects were brought to a halt. Manufacturing contributed 3.7% of GDP in 1987, 4.2% in 1988 and 1989, 3.7% in 1990 and 4.2% in 1991. In 1989 industrial exports were valued at RO 90.1m., compared with RO 71.4m. in 1987.

With smaller petroleum revenues than many other Middle Eastern states, Oman is not well placed to develop heavy industry or manufacturing on a large scale. The Government is, accordingly, concentrating more on the development of agriculture and fisheries, and encouraging construction in the rural areas, with the emphasis on social projects and roads. Small-scale industrial ventures in the private sector are also being promoted, and the Government offers incentives to private enterprise, such as cheap land and energy, exemption from duty on imports of raw materials and plant, and low-interest loans. The 1981–85 Development Plan aimed to quadruple industrial output, giving the industrial sector an average growth rate of 36.2% per year over the Plan's term. Between 1982 and early 1984, more than 640 small and medium-sized enterprises went into operation; and manufacturing's contribution to GDP increased from 1.1% in 1981 to 3.6% in 1986. A large proportion of Oman's labour force in construction and industry was provided by immigrant workers from India and Pakistan. During 1984, however, as the recession worsened and tenders for projects were fewer, many contractors reduced the numbers of their employees by between 20% and 50%. The 1986–90 Development Plan aimed to diversify Oman's economic base as a provision against an eventual exhaustion of hydrocarbon reserves. In March 1989 it was reported that the Ministry of Commerce and Industry had issued licences for six industrial projects, entailing investment totalling RO 122,000. In 1990 industry (including mining, manfacturing, construction and power) provided 56.5% of Oman's GDP, although the proportion was reduced to 51.7% in the following year. 1991 was designated the 'Year of Industry', and the Government allocated RO 24m. for industrial projects. These included a plant to manufacture 200m. glass bottles per year and another to produce 300,000 car batteries per year. The latter began production in 1992, which was also declared a 'Year of Industry' by the Sultan. In that year the Government adopted a 15-year industrial strategy, which included a liberalization of credit provision, regulations to simplify administrative procedures for business executives and development of the infrastructure. An industrial estate was established at Ruysal, near Muscat, and two new industrial estates were opened in November 1992 at Sohar and Raysut. Further industrial estates were planned, including one at Nizwa opened in late 1993.

Geological surveys are being undertaken to locate mineral deposits other than petroleum and natural gas. So far, sizeable reserves of copper and chromite (chromium ore) have been found. Chromite reserves, estimated at 2m. tons of medium-grade ore, exist on the coastal side of the Jebel Akhdar. The concession to develop the deposit is held by a Canadian-based company. The government-owned Oman Mining Company (OMC) began mining chromite in early 1984, and in 1986 about 5,000 tons of chromite were produced. In 1991 the new Oman Chromite Company, owned jointly by the Government (15%), private companies (45%) and public subscribers (40%), announced plans to exploit the country's chromite reserves at a rate of approximately 15,000 tons per year. The majority of its production will be sold to Japan. By 1992 it was estimated that Oman had reserves of about 200m. tons of chromite ore at as many as 600 sites. In 1989 OMC was ordered to suspend the mining and export of chromite while a joint committee of the Ministries of Commerce and Industry and Petroleum and Minerals established priorities for the sector. OMC was exploiting three copper mines, at Bayda, Avga and Lassail, near Sohar, north-west of Muscat, where drilling had indicated the presence of about 12m. tons of ore. In 1990 about 3,000 tons of copper ore per day was being handled from these pits. In its first full year OMC reported an operating profit of RO 1.7m. A complex for the smelting and refining of the copper ore, at Sohar, began operation in July 1983. The project cost more than US $200m., of which Saudi Arabia provided more than half. In 1989 Oman exported approximately 15,300 tons of refined copper cathodes, worth $40m. In 1994 bids were invited to expand the Wadi Jizzi copper smelter near Sohar at an estimated cost of RO 2m.–3.5m. In September 1988 a two-year study, costing an estimated RO 700,000, was begun in order to evaluate the viability of mining copper at Hail as-Safil and Rakah, near Sohar, where copper reserves, with a high gold and silver content, were estimated at 4m. tons. The Yibal–Ghubra gas pipeline has been extended to the Sohar region to provide fuel, both for the smelter and for cement

manufacturing. In 1990 a pre-feasibility study indicated adequate reserves to guarantee the short-term future of OMC's copper smelter. The survey revealed that the Yanqul region had an estimated 8m. tons of copper deposits. In July 1989 plans were announced for the construction of a plant to produce ferro-chrome near Sohar, on the Batinah coast, to begin after 1991. In August 1990, a French geological company won a RO 98,800 contract to explore for lead and zinc in the Saih Hatat and Jebel Akhdar regions. In 1991 the UN Development Programme agreed to co-operate with the Ministry of Petroleum and Minerals in a study of Oman's coal resources. The study, the cost of which was estimated at $1m., was to examine the possibility of using coal at Al-Kamil, near Sur, to generate electricity. Oman's recoverable coal reserves were estimated at 36m. tons, sufficient to satisfy the needs of domestic consumption but not enough to provide a surplus for export. In 1992 the Government investigated the feasibility of exploiting gold deposits at 15 sites in the Sultanate.

The economic and industrial changes which have taken place in the country since 1970 have led to a need for major increases in power and water supply. As a result, production of electricity in the capital area alone rose from 8m. kWh in 1970 to 642m. kWh in 1980, and in 1981 an extensive rural electrification scheme was completed. In 1985 there were plans for the extension of the Sohar power station, and by the end of the year about one-half of the country was connected to the National Grid. Net installed generating capacity in Oman rose from 479 MW in 1981 to 1,250 MW in 1993, while actual production rose from 1,148m. kWh in 1981 to 5,199m. kWh in 1992. In 1991 the Ministry of Electricity was preparing to evaluate bids for a number of major projects in the electricity sector, including a consultancy contract for the fourth-phase, 160 MW expansion of the Ghubrah power and desalination plant, scheduled for completion in 1995. The contract for a joint venture between Hitachi of Japan and ABB Kraftwerke of Germany was due to be signed in mid-1994 for the construction of a desalination plant at Ghubrah 5. The plant will have a desalination capacity of up to six million gallons per day, and a 30 MW back-pressure steam turbine will also be built. An agreement to construct a private power station at Manah, with a generating capacity of 90 MW and an estimated cost of $240m., was signed by the Government and United Power Group in June 1994. The United Power Company will operate the plant for 22 years and sell the power to Oman. The 1986–90 Development Plan, building on the work of its predecessors, aimed to connect 75% of the country to the National Grid by 1990.

FINANCE AND DEVELOPMENT

Expenditure on defence in Oman has increased rapidly in recent years, with the total doubling between 1979 and 1984. In 1979 the budget allocation for defence spending was RO 238m. By 1986 this figure had risen to RO 665m., representing 42% of total expenditure. Although the allocation for 1988 was reduced to RO 519m., it still places considerable strain on the country's finances. In 1989 defence expenditure was RO 597m. Defence expenditure increased to RO 777.8m. in 1992, however budget allocation for defence was reduced to RO 630m. in 1993 and 612m. in 1994. In view of Oman's strategic importance within the GCC, defence expenditure is supported by other Council countries, which, in July 1983, agreed to make a grant of $150m. per year to Oman for general military purposes, to be paid until 1995.

Infrastructural and communications projects are gradually being completed. Port facilities are being improved by the expansion of Mina Raysut and Salalah, and 12 new berths have been opened at Mina Qaboos. In June 1990 a contract was awarded for work on the third phase of a scheme to improve facilities at Nizwa. The project involved the construction of a 140-metre bridge and a 900-metre by-pass. Mina Qaboos handled 1.9m. tons of cargo in 1988. In April 1992 an RO 11.7m. contract for further development of Mina Qaboos was awarded to a British company, Wimpey Alan. In November 1993 it was announced that a new port would be built in the 1996–2000 plan. Roads link Seeb and Nizwa, and Salalah and Thumrait. New road construction under the 1986–90 Plan was expected to include the proposed coastal highway from

Qurayat to Sur. A $30m. project to build roads in the Sharqiya region is under way. In 1990 the Ministry of Communications proposed to build 140 km of roads and to upgrade a further 158 km, in addition to constructing 58 km of road in Al-Qabil, Ibra and Briddayah. The Dhofar Transport Company was awarded a contract in May 1990 to build a 13-km link road connecting Al-Ayjah and Sur, at a cost of RO 2.5m. Another planned project in 1990 was the construction of a 16-km road linking the Thumrait airforce base to the main Salalah-to-Thumrait highway, at a cost of RO 400,000. Between 1970 and 1985 an estimated 6,000 km of asphalt roads and 18,500 km of dirt roads were built in Oman. In 1989 243 km of roads were built, at a total cost of RO 36m. By 1994 a road linking Salalah with Sarfait, near the border with Yemen, had been completed. In late 1985 the World Bank announced a $30m. loan to Oman for further improvements to the road network. Air services to rural and outlying areas have been increased: by the end of 1984 there were rural air services to Khassab, Bayah, Buraimi, Sur and Masirah Island. A major expansion programme at Seeb International Airport was completed in 1985, and in the following year more than 1.4m. passengers passed through the airport. In 1993 five international airlines began operating regular flights to Oman.

The targets of the 1976–80 Development Plan were relatively modest, concentrating on establishing a workable basis for light industry and agriculture. The Omani Development Bank was established in December 1977 to encourage private sector investment. The 1981–85 Development Plan envisaged total expenditure of RO 7,400m., of which RO 3,300m. was to be allocated to development projects. The general aim was to reduce economic dependence on petroleum, in favour of private-sector industry. The Plan included development of tourism, education, health, welfare, housing and roads. In 1984 it was announced that total spending on projects undertaken during the 1981–85 Development Plan would probably total RO 1,800m., 28% more than was originally envisaged.

Despite the world oil surplus in the early 1980s, Oman raised its petroleum output during the 1981–85 Plan period, maintaining adequate revenues, but at a lower level than originally expected. Since 1982, falling oil prices have led to deficits in the annual budget. The budget for 1984 anticipated oil revenues of RO 1,100m., a fall of nearly 7% from the previous year's level, but the 1985 budget estimated oil revenues at RO 1,292m., an increase of 17.5% on the 1984 figure. The budget deficit declined slightly, to RO 199m., in 1985. In January 1986 the rial was devalued by 10.2%, to compensate for the reduction in petroleum revenues. By 1987 the effect of the decline in oil prices was evident, as expenditure fell to an estimated RO 1,551m. and estimated revenues rose to RO 1,468m. The actual budget deficit was RO 149m., and the development budget was estimated at RO 230m. Revenue from the petroleum sector, in the form of sales and taxes, increased from RO 895.9m. in 1986 to RO 1,143.1m. in 1987, and was forecast at RO 1,065.3m. in 1988 and at RO 904.4m. in 1989. In 1990 net petroleum revenue rose by almost 58%, to RO 1,538m. This resulted in a reduction in the budget deficit to RO 11m., compared with one of RO 296m. in 1989. In 1991 estimated oil revenue declined to RO 1,240m., and total revenue to RO 1,570m. Total expenditure was estimated at RO 1,853m. In 1992 total revenue was estimated at RO 1,661m., of which RO 1,276m. was oil revenue, and expenditure at RO 2,240m., resulting in a budget deficit of RO 579m. The budget for 1993 anticipated a decrease in total expenditure to RO 2,111m. and an increase in net oil revenues to RO 1,303m., resulting in a reduced deficit of RO 375m. An estimated 0.6% increase in net oil revenues to RO 1,311m., and a 15% rise in revenue from natural gas to RO 69m., coupled with a 5% reduction in total expenditure could result in a fiscal deficit of RO 301m. in 1994, 20% lower than 1993.

At the end of 1985 the 1986–90 Development Plan was approved, with proposed expenditure totalling RO 9,250m. ($26,780m.). Early in 1986, however, proposed spending was reduced to RO 8,830m. as a result of falling oil prices. The revised total was based on an estimated average petroleum price of $20 per barrel. The subsequent decline in oil prices, to less than $10 per barrel in July, necessitated further revision of proposed expenditure. Although oil prices rose above $17 per barrel by the end of 1986, the Plan was postponed for re-evaluation. In January 1991 the Government announced a fourth Development Plan, covering the period 1991–95. The plan envisaged total expenditure of RO 9,450m. The projected rate of annual GDP growth in the five years is about 6.3%. In April 1991 total development spending for the Plan period was reportedly budgeted at RO 2,107m. Of this, some RO 319m. was to be allocated to construction projects, including a hospital, housing and schools; to a $78m. extension of the airport at Seeb; to the $65m. development of the port of Mina Qaboos, gas fields and fishing ports; and to the upgrading of the Rusail-Nizwa highway and the renovation of the Muscat water networks.

Oman's trade pattern continues to reflect the dominance of petroleum in the economy. In 1987 the value of non-oil exports was RO 123.9m., equivalent to 8.6% of the value of total exports. In 1988 they rose to RO 155m., 12.4% of total exports. In 1989 the value of non-oil exports was RO 167.8m., representing 11% of the total exports of RO 1,512.2m. The value of non-oil exports in 1990 was $446.9m., representing just 8.6% of total exports. In 1991, however, the government's efforts at diversifying the economy began to show results and non-oil exports were valued at $613.1m., accounting for 13.4% of the total exports of $4,576.2m. The value of recorded imports in 1988 was RO 846.4m., compared with RO 700.7m. in 1987 (when unrecorded imports were estimated at RO 55m.). In 1989 the value of recorded imports was $2,257.3m., rising to $2,681.3m. in 1990. The value of recorded imports increased by 16% in 1991 to $3,194m. Oman's major trading partner is Japan, which in 1987 received 41.3% of exports of petroleum. The UAE was the principal supplier of imports in that year, providing 21% of the total, followed by Japan (15%) and the UK (14%). In 1989 Japan was the principal customer for Oman's exports (taking 34.6% of the total), followed by the Republic of Korea (28.8%) and Taiwan. In that year the UAE continued to be Oman's principal supplier of imports, providing 24% of imports, followed by Japan (15.7%) and the UK (11.7%). In 1990 Oman's balance of trade showed an improvement of 28.8% on the 1989 level, with recorded imports totalling RO 1,031m., compared with exports of RO 2,005m. The UAE remained the main source of imports, while Japan, followed by the Republic of Korea, was the main purchaser of Omani petroleum. In 1991 Oman recorded a trade surplus of $1,878m., with imports totalling $2,993m. and exports $4,871m. The trade surplus increased by 9% in 1992 to $2,047m. with total imports of $3,508m. and exports of $5,555m.

Between 1981 and 1982 Oman's balance-of-payments surplus fell by 39%, and in the following year it declined by a further 28%, to RO 209m., despite an economic growth rate of 5.5%. In 1986 a deficit of $1,017m. was recorded on the current account of the balance of payments, following a surplus of $265m. in 1985. In 1987 the deficit decreased slightly, to $851m. A major reason for the deficit on the current account, in addition to the decline in revenue from petroleum, was the level of remittances being transferred abroad by foreigners working in Oman. This increased by 52.5% between 1981 and 1982, to RO 236m., and reached RO 300m. in 1984. In 1990 Oman's balance of payments recorded a current account surplus of $1,166m., however a deficit of $138m. was recorded in 1991. In 1992 the current account deficit increased to $366m. In June 1990 the Government pledged that foreign workers would retain their tax-free status. The announcement was made after the Government had expressed its intention to impose a levy on foreign remittances, in an attempt to increase revenues. In October 1993 it was announced that income tax would be collected from all companies, whether Omani or foreign, from 1 January 1994 in order to increase government revenue. Despite its balance-of-payments surpluses, Oman has also received a substantial amount of foreign aid and loans, mainly in order to finance development projects. Oman's foreign debt declined from $1,931m. (with a debt-service ratio of 4.6%) in 1984 to $1,875m. at the end of 1985. Until 1986, Oman enjoyed an excellent credit rating, and in 1983 the country was able to raise a Eurodollar loan of $300m. with no difficulty. The sharp fall in petroleum prices altered this position, and an application for a Euroloan of $500m. in

1986 encountered difficulty in attracting a sufficient number of subscribers. According to World Bank data, Oman's total foreign debt increased to $2,959m. at the end of 1986, but declined to $2,848m. in 1987. However, petroleum prices revived in 1988, and the Government secured a syndicated loan of $500m. in June 1989, and another of $300m. in October 1991. The external debt stood at $2,468m. in May 1993 according to government sources. In January 1994 four international banks were awarded a mandate to raise a $300m. five-year syndicated sovereign loan. The loan, arranged to finance the fiscal deficit, was signed on 30 April.

In comparison with some other countries in the region, Oman has a small banking sector, with 22 banks holding licences to operate in the country at the end of 1991. Of these, 12 were foreign. There were also three development banks. At the end of 1990 the Central Bank of Oman's total assets stood at RO 889.4m. Between 1973 and 1986 the rial Omani was linked to the US dollar at a rate of $1 = RO 0.3454, but in January 1986 the rial was devalued by 10.1%, with the exchange rate adjusted to $1 = RO 0.3845. The Central Bank raised interest rates in April 1989, with the annual rate payable on non-government deposits increased by 1%, to 9.5%, and that on rial loans raised by 0.75%, to 11.25%. In mid-1983 only 40% of bank staff were Omani. Despite government efforts to reduce the number of foreign staff in the banking sector to 10%, by mid-1994 non-Omanis still constituted 30% of bank staff. By the end of 1995 banks will have to reduce their foreign staff to 10% of their work-force or face heavy penalties. In May 1992 the Government introduced a new law increasing the minimum requirement for a bank's paid-up capital to RO 10m., in order to encourage smaller banks to merge and thereby rationalize the banking system. By mid-1994 the number of commercial banks had been reduced to 18, of which 11 were foreign. In May 1990 Oman's first stock exchange was opened in Muscat, trading in shares in local companies with a potential total value of RO 250m. Oman's first investment fund open to non-GCC nationals was listed on the London and Muscat stock exchanges in March 1994. Subscriptions for the Oryx fund, launched to raise $52m., closed in June. A second investment fund set up in 1994 was the UAE-Omani Joint Holding Company with a capital of $78m. Both funds were fully subscribed. Plans were announced to establish a link between the stock exchanges in Muscat and Bahrain by the end of 1994. The latest five-year economic plan envisages receipts of RO 429m. from bonds by 1996.

The initial 10 days after the invasion of Kuwait by Iraq on 2 August 1990 caused panic withdrawals of deposits and increased demand for foreign currency. By late August 1990, however, the local banking system had stabilized, and by April 1991, encouraged by firm government action and by reports of high economic growth, deposits at local commercial banks had fully recovered from the impact of the Gulf crisis. Following the collapse of the Bank of Credit and Commerce International (BCCI) in July 1991, substantial support from the Omani Government enabled depositors and creditors in the country to be paid in full. On 15 February 1992 the Bank Dhofar al-Omani al-Fransi acquired the 12 BCCI branches in the Sultanate.

HEALTH

Oman has a free National Health Service, and in 1990 there were 48 hospitals, with a total of more than 3,578 beds. There were also 88 health centres, 96 preventive health centres, five mobile rural health centres and three maternity centres. The number of health centres was expected to increase to 120 by the end of 1995. Government expenditure on health in 1986 was RO 79.7m., representing 5% of total spending. In 1987 there were 1,240 physicians working in Oman. The Royal Hospital of Oman, with 629 beds, was completed in 1987. The hospital, situated in Muscat, became fully operational in 1988, with a staff of more than 2,000, including more than 220 doctors and 1,000 nurses, mainly recruited from overseas. The Ministry of Health has announced plans to construct a paediatric hospital, with 200 beds, in Muscat. In March 1989 it was announced that citizens of other GCC member-states would be eligible to the same health services as Omani citizens. Of total expenditure by the central Government in 1991, RO 85.3m. (5.4%) was for health services, and a further RO 53.0m. (3.4%) for social security and welfare. In June 1990 the Ministry of Health announced a programme to construct children's wards at four hospitals. The estimated cost is RO 800,000. In April 1992 Oman and the People's Republic of China signed an agreement for co-operation in the health sector. A 140-bed hospital in Buraimi and a 248-bed hospital at Rustaq were opened in May 1994. A regional hospital at Ibri was due for completion in 1994 and work had begun on a 248-bed hospital in Sohar, a 280-bed hospital at Nizwa, and an extension of Sultan Qatoos hospital.

Statistical Survey

Source (unless otherwise stated): Oman Directorate-General of National Statistics, Development Council, POB 881, Muscat; tel. 698900; telex 5384.

Area and Population

AREA, POPULATION AND DENSITY

Area (sq km)	212,457*
Population (census results) 30 November 1993	
Total	2,017,591†
Density (per sq km) at November 1993	9.5

* 82,030 sq miles. Other sources estimate the area at 300,000 sq km (about 120,000 sq miles).
† Comprising 1,480,531 Omani nationals (males 755,071; females 725,460) and 537,060 non-Omanis.

POPULATION BY GOVERNORATE (1993 census)

Al-Batinah	. .	538,763	Musandam	. . .	27,669
Al-Dakhiliya	. .	220,403	Muscat	. . . .	622,506
Al-Dhahira.	. .	169,710	Al-Sharqiya.	. .	247,551
Dhofar.	. . .	174,888	Al-Wosta	. .	16,101
			Total	. . .	. 2,017,591

BIRTHS AND DEATHS (UN estimates, annual averages)

	1975–80	1980–85	1985–90
Birth rate (per 1,000) . .	47.1	44.4	43.0
Death rate (per 1,000) . .	12.7	7.9	5.6

Expectation of life (UN estimates, years at birth, 1985–90): 67.9 (males 66.2; females 69.8).

Source: UN, *World Population Prospects: The 1992 Revision.*

ECONOMICALLY ACTIVE POPULATION
(ILO estimates, '000 persons at mid-1980)

	Males	Females	Total
Agriculture, etc.	135	4	140
Industry	55	7	61
Services	70	9	80
Total labour force . . .	260	20	280

Source: ILO, *Economically Active Population Estimates and Projections, 1950–2025.*

Mid-1992 (estimates in '000): Agriculture, etc. 169; Total 441 (Source: FAO, *Production Yearbook*).

Agriculture

PRINCIPAL CROPS ('000 metric tons)

	1990	1991*	1992
Cereals	5	5	2
Potatoes	5	5	5*
Tomatoes	29	30	32*
Onions (dry)	8	9	9*
Other vegetables	92	93	92*
Watermelons	26	27	30*
Dates	120	125	130*
Lemons and limes	26	27	28*
Mangoes	9	9	10*
Bananas	24	24	25*
Tobacco (leaves)	2	2	2*

* FAO estimate(s).

Source: FAO, *Production Yearbook*.

LIVESTOCK
(FAO estimates unless otherwise indicated, '000 head, year ending September)

	1990	1991	1992
Asses	25	26	26
Cattle	137*	138	140
Camels	87	90	92
Sheep	140	143	145
Goats	720*	725	730

* Official figure.

Poultry (million): 3 in 1990; 3 (FAO estimate) in 1991; 3 (FAO estimate) in 1992.

Source: FAO, *Production Yearbook*.

LIVESTOCK PRODUCTS (FAO estimates, '000 metric tons)

	1990	1991	1992
Beef and veal	3	3	3
Mutton and lamb	5	5	5
Goats' meat	4	5	5
Poultry meat	3	3	3
Cows' milk	18	18	18
Goats' milk	55	57	60
Hen eggs	6.0	6.1	6.1

Source: FAO, *Production Yearbook*.

Fishing

('000 metric tons, live weight)

	1989	1990	1991
Fishes	114.0	117.0	114.9
Crustaceans and molluscs . .	3.7	3.2	2.9
Total catch	117.7	120.2	117.8

Source: FAO, *Yearbook of Fishery Statistics.*

Mining

	1989	1990	1991
Crude petroleum ('000 metric tons)	31,803	34,018	35,128
Natural gas (petajoules) . .	91	106	104

Source: UN, *Industrial Statistics Yearbook.*

Industry

SELECTED PRODUCTS
('000 barrels, unless otherwise indicated)

	1988	1989	1990
Motor spirit (petrol) . .	3,431	3,592	4,056
Kerosene	947	1,115	2,255
Distillate fuel oils . . .	4,459	4,406	4,565
Bunker fuel	8,802	9,174	11,317
Refined copper (metric tons) .	16,267	14,963	12,015
Electric energy (million kWh) .	3,772.8	3,926.8	4,503.8

Finance

CURRENCY AND EXCHANGE RATES

Monetary Units
1,000 baiza = 1 rial Omani (RO).

Sterling and Dollar Equivalents (31 May 1994)
£1 sterling = 581.3 baiza;
US $1 = 384.5 baiza;
100 rials Omani = £172.03 = $260.08.

Exchange Rate
Between February 1973 and January 1986 the value of the rial Omani was fixed at US $2.8952 ($1 = 345.4 baiza). In January 1986 the currency was devalued by about 10.2%, with the exchange rate fixed at 1 rial = $2.6008 ($1 = 384.5 baiza).

INTERNATIONAL RESERVES (US $ million at 31 December)

	1991	1992	1993
Gold*	68.3	68.3	68.3
IMF special drawing rights .	22.2	4.7	6.8
Reserve position in IMF . .	32.5	54.1	52.0
Foreign exchange . . .	1,608.6	1,924.7	849.3
Total	1,731.6	2,051.8	976.4

* Valued at RO 90.8 per troy ounce.

Source: IMF, *International Financial Statistics.*

MONEY SUPPLY (RO million at 31 December)

	1991	1992	1993
Currency outside banks . .	215.9	226.7	232.9
Demand deposits at commercial banks	189.8	206.3	218.7
Total money	405.7	433.0	451.5

Source: IMF, *International Financial Statistics.*

BUDGET (RO million)*

Revenue†	1990	1991	1992
Taxation on income, profits, etc.	368.4	267.3	267.1
Oil companies . . .	352.1	246.4	244.3
Import duties . . .	32.6	38.9	47.8
Other tax revenue . . .	19.6	21.2	19.9
Entrepreneurial and property income	1,057.4	837.0	874.3
Petroleum	998.0	777.0	808.4
Fees, charges, etc. . .	13.9	15.3	19.7
Other current revenue . .	82.5	74.5	101.6
Capital revenue . . .	6.3	7.2	7.7
Total	1,580.7	1,261.4	1,338.1

Expenditure‡	1990	1991	1992
General public services . .	169.2	170.6	174.0
Defence	656.2	557.4	679.5
Public order and safety . .	103.5	106.8	120.5
Education	171.0	180.1	209.4
Health	74.3	85.3	108.5
Social security and welfare .	38.0	53.0	91.2
Housing and community amenities	107.2	153.7	156.3
Recreational, cultural and religious affairs . . .	34.5	36.8	51.5
Economic affairs and services	155.3	162.0	210.9
Fuel and energy . . .	74.1	77.6	117.6
Agriculture, forestry and fishing	31.6	38.3	39.8
Mining, manufacturing and construction . . .	2.2	1.0	2.7
Road transport . . .	17.9	20.7	23.0
Other transport and communications . .	8.9	6.9	7.0
Other economic affairs and services	20.6	17.5	20.8
Interest payments . . .	92.4	69.4	98.5
Total	1,601.6	1,575.1	1,900.3
Current	1,431.5	1,336.7	1,560.0
Capital	170.1	238.4	340.3

* The data refer to the consolidated accounts of the central Government, including ministries, regional government offices and municipalities.
† Excluding grants received from abroad (RO million): 6.6 in 1990; 23.0 in 1991; 0.9 in 1992.
‡ Excluding lending minus repayment (RO million): 18.5 in 1990; −6.4 in 1991; 23.2 in 1992.
Source: IMF, *Government Finance Statistics Yearbook.*
1993 (estimates, RO million): Total revenue 1,671.5; Total expenditure 2,111.5.
1994 (estimates, RO million): Total revenue 1,705.4; Total expenditure 2,006.3.
Source: Ministry of Financial and Economic Affairs.

NATIONAL ACCOUNTS
(RO million in current prices)
Expenditure on the Gross Domestic Product

	1990	1991	1992
Government final consumption expenditure	1,544.9	1,394.7	1,734.9
Private final consumption expenditure	1,080.6	1,485.3	1,476.6
Increase in stocks . .			
Gross fixed capital formation .	529.2	661.4	750.9
Total domestic expenditure .	3,154.7	3,541.4	3,962.4
Exports of goods and services	2,136.0	1,891.0	2,154.0
Less Imports of goods and services	1,240.0	1,515.0	1,699.0
GDP in purchasers' values .	4,050.7	3,917.4	4,417.4

Source: IMF, *International Financial Statistics.*

Gross Domestic Product by Economic Activity

	1989	1990	1991*
Agriculture and livestock† .	83.2	84.7	93.3
Fishing†	33.9	49.1	50.6
Mining and quarrying . . .	1,478.6	2,002.2	1,669.1
Crude petroleum . .	1,417.2	1,942.7	1,608.7
Natural gas	44.8	47.6	49.7
Manufacturing	137.1	152.4	168.3
Electricity and water . . .	48.2	59.7	62.7
Construction	106.0	123.3	164.1
Trade, restaurants and hotels .	393.6	468.5	540.6
Transport, storage and communications† . . .	112.3	129.3	146.8
Financing, insurance, real estate and business services‡	291.5	354.7	352.3
Government services . .	548.7	658.6	669.5
Public administration and defence	404.6	n.a.	n.a.
Other community, social and personal services . .	49.1	57.1	71.5
Sub-total	3,282.2	4,139.6	3,988.8
Import duties	29.4	32.9	39.5
Less Imputed bank service charge	81.0	121.8	92.5
GDP in purchasers' values .	3,230.6	4,050.7	3,935.8

* Provisional figures.
† Excluding activities of government enterprises.
‡ Including imputed rents of owner-occupied dwellings.

BALANCE OF PAYMENTS (US $ million)

	1990	1991	1992
Merchandise exports f.o.b. .	5,508	4,871	5,555
Merchandise imports f.o.b. .	−2,519	−2,993	−3,508
Trade balance . . .	2,990	1,878	2,047
Exports of services . .	68	61	13
Imports of services . .	−706	−947	−911
Other income received . .	320	333	273
Other income paid . . .	−631	−589	−660
Private unrequited transfers (net)	−817	−871	−1,118
Official unrequited transfers (net)	−57	−3	−10
Current balance . . .	1,166	−137	−366
Direct investment (net) . .	141	149	59
Other capital (net) . . .	−710	356	213
Net errors and omissions . .	−488	139	256
Overall balance	109	507	163

Source: IMF, *International Financial Statistics.*

External Trade

PRINCIPAL COMMODITIES
(distribution by SITC, US $ million)

Imports c.i.f.	1989	1990	1991
Food and live animals	383.2	421.1	439.2
Meat and meat preparations	58.1	56.0	64.9
Fresh, chilled or frozen meat and edible offals	57.1	55.0	62.8
Dairy products and birds' eggs	67.9	68.6	76.3
Cereals and cereal preparations	80.8	100.5	89.7
Vegetables and fruit	94.5	106.5	115.1
Beverages and tobacco	45.5	51.4	128.6
Tobacco and tobacco manufactures	24.5	21.7	94.4
Manufactured tobacco	24.3	21.6	94.2
Cigarettes	24.1	21.3	93.4
Mineral fuels, lubricants, etc.	47.8	109.9	59.0
Petroleum, petroleum products, etc.	44.9	107.8	57.6
Refined petroleum products	44.5	107.4	56.6
Motor spirit (gasoline) and other light oils	42.2	103.5	52.7
Chemicals and related products	139.3	167.7	189.7
Basic manufactures	410.1	434.7	558.0
Textile yarn, fabrics, etc.	80.5	94.2	112.4
Iron and steel	100.3	138.9	177.3
Tubes, pipes and fittings	65.0	93.5	114.1
Machinery and transport equipment	814.4	969.8	1,337.1
Power-generating machinery and equipment	30.8	43.8	133.2
Rotating electric plant and parts thereof	24.0	30.6	102.5
Machinery specialized for particular industries	175.3	164.0	243.0
Civil engineering and contractors' plant and equipment, etc.	150.7	138.6	206.0
General industrial machinery, equipment and parts	92.4	106.5	144.7
Telecommunications and sound equipment	48.2	56.0	85.6
Other electrical machinery, apparatus, etc.	94.4	106.6	120.5
Road vehicles and parts*	334.7	436.9	555.8
Passenger motor cars (excl. buses)	216.0	289.6	378.1
Parts and accessories for cars, buses, lorries, etc.*	83.3	95.4	111.7
Miscellaneous manufactured articles	222.8	235.7	249.5
Non-monetary gold (excl. ores and concentrates)	79.4	73.1	80.6
Total (incl. others)	2,257.3	2,681.3	3,194.0

* Excluding tyres, engines and electrical parts.

Exports f.o.b.	1989	1990	1991
Mineral fuels, lubricants, etc.	3,506.3	4,768.1	3,963.1
Petroleum, petroleum products, etc.	3,506.3	4,768.0	3,963.1
Crude petroleum oils, etc.	3,496.5	4,756.6	3,941.2
Machinery and transport equipment	181.6	189.9	307.6
Road vehicles and parts (excl. tyres, engines and electrical parts)	113.0	119.9	205.0
Passenger motor cars (excl. buses)	80.4	82.7	150.1
Total (incl. others)	3,932.8	5,215.0	4,576.2

Source: UN, *International Trade Statistics Yearbook*.
1992 (RO million): Imports c.i.f. 1,449; Exports f.o.b. 2,087.
1993 (RO million): Imports c.i.f. 1,582 (Source: IMF, *International Financial Statistics*).

PRINCIPAL TRADING PARTNERS (US $ '000)

Imports c.i.f.	1989	1990	1991
Australia	66,302	59,228	59,807
France	75,532	115,254	104,709
Germany	124,014	130,053	166,893
India	62,286	75,372	86,495
Italy	46,694	44,128	57,859
Japan	354,436	455,347	654,010
Korea, Republic	26,741	25,720	32,721
Malaysia	20,590	25,275	33,069
Netherlands	71,455	91,098	128,147
Saudi Arabia	45,479	58,153	83,770
Singapore	31,570	50,424	43,316
United Arab Emirates	502,020	580,291	732,114
United Kingdom	255,543	308,029	319,205
USA	190,832	247,657	243,865
Total (incl. others)	2,177,879	2,608,167	3,113,359

Exports f.o.b.	1987	1988	1989
France	2,182	40,925	30,551
India	132,765	36,921	5,267
Italy	137,690	5,527	5,147
Japan	1,440,378	1,445,166	1,361,257
Korea, Republic	560,611	671,817	1,132,410
Netherlands	66,657	17,161	10,363
Philippines	54,517	81,791	163
Saudi Arabia	18,547	18,805	39,751
Singapore	250,373	80,028	205,237
Thailand	124,485	54,395	45,579
United Arab Emirates	144,084	187,047	212,690
USA	207,891	51,035	109,449
Total (incl. others)	3,776,064	3,268,256	3,932,767

Source: UN, *International Trade Statistics Yearbook*.

Transport

ROAD TRAFFIC (vehicles in use at 31 December)

	1988	1989	1990
Private cars	87,909	96,559	109,968
Taxis	3,816	4,368	5,317
Commercial	66,860	70,231	74,958
Government	17,995	18,584	19,210
Motor-cycles	3,908	4,211	4,479
Private hire	454	234	918
Diplomatic	350	374	416
Total	181,292	194,561	215,266

INTERNATIONAL SEA-BORNE SHIPPING
(freight traffic, '000 metric tons)

	1988	1989	1990
Goods loaded	29,230	32,576	33,843
Goods unloaded	2,450	2,444	2,492

Source: UN, *Monthly Bulletin of Statistics*.

CIVIL AVIATION (traffic on scheduled services)

	1989	1990	1991
Kilometres flown (million)	12	13	12
Passengers carried ('000)	835	853	958
Passenger-km (million)	1,545	1,602	1,729
Freight ton-km (million)	40	44	51

Note: Figures include an apportionment (one-quarter) of the traffic of Gulf Air, a multinational airline with its headquarters in Bahrain.

Source: UN, *Statistical Yearbook*.

CIVIL AVIATION (traffic on scheduled services)

	1989	1990	1991
Kilometres flown (million). .	12	13	12
Passengers carried ('000) . .	835	853	958
Passenger-km (million) . .	1,545	1,602	1,729
Freight ton-km (million) . .	40	44	51

Note: Figures include an apportionment (one-quarter) of the traffic of Gulf Air, a multinational airline with its headquarters in Bahrain.

Source: UN, *Statistical Yearbook*.

Communications Media

	1989	1990	1991
Radio receivers ('000 in use) .	932	970	1,006
Television receivers ('000 in use)	1,100	1,150	1,150
Telephones ('000 in use) . .	88	93	104
Daily newspapers:			
Number	3	4	n.a.
Average circulation ('000 copies)	n.a.	62	n.a.

Sources: UNESCO, *Statistical Yearbook*; UN, *Statistical Yearbook*.

Education*

	1987/88	1988/89	1989/90
Government Schools			
Primary	367	370	388
Preparatory	249	267	283
Secondary	62	66	70
Pupils			
Boys	148,509	160,561	174,707
Girls	120,213	134,373	148,761
Teachers	11,990	12,860	13,695

* Figures cover general, not specialized, courses.

Directory

The Constitution

Oman has no written constitution. The Sultan has absolute power and legislates by decree. He rules with the assistance of an appointed Council of Ministers, which is permitted to take decisions in his absence. The country has no legislature, but there is a Consultative Council, the Majlis al-Shoura, established in November 1991, whose 59 members are chosen by the Government from lists of three candidates elected by each region and are empowered to discuss, and advise on, economic and social affairs.

The Government

HEAD OF STATE

Sultan: QABOOS BIN SAID (assumed power on 23 July 1970, after deposing his father).

COUNCIL OF MINISTERS
(October 1994)

Prime Minister and Minister of Foreign Affairs, Defence and Finance: Sultan QABOOS BIN SAID.

Deputy Prime Minister for Security and Defence: Sayed FAHAR BIN TAIMOUR AS-SAID.

Deputy Prime Minister for Cabinet Affairs: Sayed FAHD BIN MAHMOUD AS-SAID.

Deputy Prime Minister for Financial and Economic Affairs: QAIS BIN ABD AL-MUNIM AZ-ZAWAWI.

Special Representative of the Sultan: Sayed THUWAINI BIN SHIHAB AS-SAID.

Special Advisor to the Sultan: Sayed HAMAD BIN HAMOUD AL-BUSAIDI.

Minister of Legal Affairs: MUHAMMAD AL-ALAWI.

Minister of Petroleum and Minerals: SAID BIN AHMAD BIN SAID ASH-SHANFARI.

Minister of Justice and Awqaf (Religious Endowments) and Islamic Affairs: HAMOUD BIN ABDULLAH AL-HARTHI.

Minister of State for Foreign Affairs: YOUSUF BIN AL-ALAWI BIN ABDULLAH.

Minister of Information: ABD AL-AZIZ BIN MUHAMMAD AR-ROWAS.

Minister of Electricity and Water: Sheikh MUHAMMAD BIN ALI AL-QUTAIBI.

Minister of Posts, Telegraphs and Telephones: AHMAD BIN SOWAIDAN AL-BALUCHI.

Minister of Communications: SALIM BIN ABDULLAH AL-GHAZALI.

Minister of Education: SAUD AL-BUSAIDI.

Minister of Higher Education: YAHYA BIN MAHFOUZ AL-MANTHARI.

Minister of Social Affairs and Labour: AHMAD BIN SALIM AL-ISA'EE.

Minister of Housing: MALEK BIN SULAIMAN AL-MUAMMARI.

Minister of National Heritage and Culture: Sayed FAISAL BIN ALI AS-SAID.

Minister of the Interior: Sayed BADR BIN SAUD BIN HAREB AL-BUSAIDI.

Minister of Commerce and Industry: MAQBOOL BIN ALI BIN SULTAN.

Minister of Agriculture and Fisheries Wealth: Sheikh MUHAMMAD BIN ABDULLAH BIN ZAHIR AL-HINAI.

Minister of Water Resources: HAMID BIN SAID AL-AUFI.

Minister of Health: Dr ALI BIN MUHAMMAD BIN MOUSA.

Minister of Regional Municipalities and of the Environment: Sheikh AMIR BIN SHUWAIN AL-HOSNI.

Minister of the Civil Service: AHMAD BIN ABD AN-NABI MACKI.

Minister of State for Development Affairs: MUHAMMAD BIN MUSA AL-YUSUF.

Governor of Muscat and Minister of State: Sayed AL-MUTASSIM BIN HAMOUD AL-BUSAIDI.

Governor of Dhofar and Minister of State: Sayed MUSSALLAM BIN ALI AL-BOUSAIDI.

Minister of the Royal Court: Sayed SAIF BIN HAMAD BIN SAUD.

Minister of Palace Affairs: Gen. ALI BIN MAJID AL-MUAMARI.

Speaker of the Consultative Council: ABDULLAH BIN ALI AL-QATABI.

MINISTRIES

Diwan of the Royal Court: POB 632, Muscat; tel. 738711; telex 5016.

Ministry of Agriculture and Fisheries Wealth: POB 467, Ruwi; tel. 696300; telex 3503.

Ministry of the Civil Service: Muscat.

Ministry of Commerce and Industry: POB 550, Muscat; tel. 799500; telex 3665; fax 794238.

Ministry of Communications: POB 684, Muscat 113; tel. 702233; telex 3390; fax 701776.

Ministry of Defence: POB 113, Muscat; tel. 704096; telex 3228.

Ministry of Education: POB 3, Ruwi; tel. 775209; telex 3369.

Ministry of Electricity and Water: POB 4491, Ruwi; tel. 603800; telex 3358; fax 699180.

Ministry of Financial and Economic Affairs: POB 506, Muscat; tel. 738201.

Ministry of Foreign Affairs: POB 252, Muscat; tel. 699500; telex 3337.

Ministry of Health: POB 393, Muscat; tel. 602177; telex 5294.

Ministry of Housing: POB 173, Muscat; tel. 703366; telex 3694.

Ministry of Information: POB 600, Muscat; tel. 603222; telex 6265.

Ministry of the Interior: POB 3127, Ruwi; tel. 602244; telex 5650.

Ministry of Justice, Awqaf and Islamic Affairs: POB 3354, Ruwi; tel. 697699.

Ministry of National Heritage and Culture: POB 668, Muscat; tel. 602555; telex 5649.

Ministry of Petroleum and Minerals: POB 551, Muscat; tel. 603333; telex 5280.

Ministry of Posts, Telegraphs and Telephones: POB 3338, Ruwi; tel. 697888; telex 5625; fax 696817.

Ministry of Regional Municipalities and Environment: POB 323, Muscat; tel. 696444; telex 5404; fax 602320.

Ministry of Social Affairs and Labour: POB 560, Muscat; tel. 602444; telex 5002.

MAJLIS AL-SHOURA
(Consultative Council)

In November 1991 Sultan Qaboos issued a decree establishing a Consultative Council, the Majlis al-Shoura (in place of the Consultative Assembly). The Majlis comprises 59 nominated members (one for each of the country's regions), chosen by the Deputy Prime Minister for Legal Affairs from lists of three candidates submitted by each region, and a government-appointed Speaker. Regional representatives serve a three-year term of office. The Majlis is empowered to draft legislation on economic and social matters for acceptance by the appropriate ministry. The Majlis held its inaugural session in January 1992.

Speaker: ABDULLAH BIN ALI AL-QATABI.

There are no political parties, and no elections take place, in Oman.

Diplomatic Representation

EMBASSIES IN OMAN

Algeria: Al-Insharah St, POB 50216, Madinat Qaboos; tel. 601698; telex 5054; Ambassador: MUHAMMAD HANASH.

Austria: Moosa Complex Bldg, No 477, 2nd Floor, Way No. 3109, POB 5070, Ruwi; tel. 793135; telex 3042; fax 793669; Ambassador: Dr RUDOLF BOGNER.

Bahrain: POB 50066, Madinat Qaboos, Al-Khuwair; tel. 605074; Ambassador: KHALID AL-MUSALLAM.

Bangladesh: POB 3959, 112 Greater Muttrah; tel. 708756; telex 3800; Chargé d'affaires: AHMED SHARFUL AL-HUSSAIN.

Brunei: POB 91, Ruwi; tel. 605992; Chargé d'affaires: HAFI ABD MOKTI DAUD.

China, People's Republic: Madinat Al-Ilam, Way No. 1507, House No. 465, POB 3315, Ruwi; tel. 696782; telex 5114; Ambassador: ZANG SHIXIONG.

Egypt: Diplomatic City, Al-Khwair, POB 5252, Ruwi; tel. 600411; telex 5438; fax 603626; Ambassador: MUHAMMAD ABD AL-KHALIQ SHALABI.

France: Diplomatic City, Al-Khuwair, POB 50208, Muscat; tel. 604310; telex 5163; fax 604300; Ambassador: RÉGIS KOETSCHET.

Germany: POB 128, Ruwi 112; tel. 702482; telex 3440; fax 705690; Ambassador: KLAUS METSCHER.

India: POB 4727, Ruwi; tel. 702960; telex 3429; fax 797547; Ambassador: RANJIT GUPTA.

Iran: Madinat Qaboos East, Dal, POB 6155, Ruwi; tel. 696944; telex 5066; fax 696888; Ambassador: MUHAMMAD ARAB.

Iraq: Madinat Qaboos, Road D, Villa 2803, Way No. 1737, POB 4848, Ruwi; tel. 604178; telex 5110; Ambassador: KHALID ABDULLAH SALEH AS-SAMIRA'I.

Italy: Qurum Area, No. 5, Way No. 2411, House No. 842, POB 3727, Ruwi 112; tel. 560968; telex 5450; fax 564846; Ambassador: SERGIO EMINA.

Japan: Madinat Qaboos West, POB 6511, Ruwi; tel. 603464; telex 5087; fax 698720; Ambassador: HARUO HANAWA.

Jordan: Diplomatic City, Al-Khuwair, POB 5281, Ruwi; tel. 602561; telex 5518; Ambassador: SAMIR AR-RAFAI AL-HAMOUD.

Korea, Republic: POB 5220, Ruwi; tel. 702322; telex 3132; Ambassador: JUNG CHANG.

Kuwait: Diplomtic City, Al-Khuwair, Block No. 13, POB 4798, Ruwi; tel. 699626; telex 5746; Ambassador: ABD AL-MOHSIN SALIM AL-HAROON.

Malaysia: Madinat al-Ilam, Villa No. 1196, Way No. 1518, POB 3939, Ruwi 112; tel. 698329; telex 5565; fax 605031; Ambassador: ZULKIFLI IBRAHIM BIN ABDUL RAHMAN.

Morocco: Al-Ensharah Street, Villa No. 197, POB 6125, Ruwi; tel. 696152; telex 5560; Ambassador: MUSTAFA AL-ALAWI AL-MOHAMAIDI.

Netherlands: O.C. Centre, 7th Floor, POB 3302, Ruwi 112; tel. 705410; telex 3050; fax 799020; Ambassador: CHRISTIAAN C. SANDERS.

Pakistan: POB 4302, Ruwi; tel. 603439; telex 5451; Ambassador: SULTAN HAYAT KHAN.

Qatar: Al-Mamoura Road, POB 802, Muscat; tel. 701802; telex 3460; Ambassador: (vacant).

Russia: Shati al-Qurum Way 3032, Surfait Compound, POB 80, Muscat; tel. 602893; telex 5493; fax 602894; Ambassador: ALEKSANDR K. PATSEV.

Saudi Arabia: Al-Khuwair, Al-Alaam Area, POB 4411, Ruwi; tel. 601744; telex 5406; Ambassador: ABD AL-MOHSIN SALEH AL-BALLAA.

Somalia: Mumtaz Street, Villa Hassan Jumaa Baker, POB 1767, Ruwi; tel. 701355; telex 3253; Ambassador: MUHAMMAD SUBAN NUR.

Sri Lanka: POB 95, Madinat Qaboos; tel. 697841; telex 5158; fax 697336; Ambassador: M. M. AMANUL FAROUQUE.

Sudan: Diplomatic City, Al-Khuwair, POB 6791, Ruwi; tel. 697875; telex 5088; fax 699065; Ambassador: ABBAS AL-MAATASIM ASH-SHEIKH.

Syria: Madinat Qaboos, Al-Ensharah Street, Villa No. 201, POB 85, Muscat; tel. 697904; telex 5029; fax 603895; Ambassador: ABD AL-KARIM AS-SABBAGH.

Thailand: Villa No. 33–34, Madinat Qaboos East, POB 6367, Ruwi; tel. 602684; telex 5210; fax 605714; Ambassador: MANOP PARKSUWAN.

Tunisia: Building 183–185, Al-Ensharah Street, POB 220, Muscat; tel. 603486; telex 5252; Ambassador: YOUSEF AL-MOKADAM.

Turkey: Bldg. No. 3501, Street No. 3939, Al-Khuwair, South Boshar 239, POB 1511, Muttrah; tel. 697050; telex 5571; fax 697053; Ambassador: EMIN GÜNDÜZ.

United Arab Emirates: Diplomatic City, Al-Khuwair, POB 551, Muscat; tel. 600988; telex 5299; fax 602584; Ambassador: HAMAD HELAL THABIT AL-KUWAITI.

United Kingdom: POB 300, Muscat 113; tel. 738501; telex 5216; fax 736040; Ambassador: RICHARD JOHN SUTHERLAND MUIR.

USA: Diplomatic City, POB 202, Muscat; tel. 698989; telex 3785; fax 699771; Ambassador: DAVID DUNFORD.

Yemen: Shatia Ram Block 5, Area 258, Way No. 1840, POB 50105, Ruwi; tel. 604172; telex 5109; fax 605008; Ambassador: MUHAMMAD OMAR ABDULLAH BASSAD.

Judicial System

Jurisdiction is exercised by the Shari'a Courts, applying Islamic law. Local courts are presided over by Qadhis, officers appointed by the Minister of Justice, Awqaf and Islamic Affairs. The Chief Court is at Muscat. Appeals from local courts, including the court in the capital, go to the Court of Appeal at Muscat. In December 1987 a 'flying court' service was established to serve remote communities.

Religion

ISLAM

The majority of the population (75%) are Muslims, of whom approximately three-quarters are of the Ibadi sect and about one-quarter are Sunni Muslims.

HINDUISM

Approximately one-quarter of the population are Hindus.

CHRISTIANITY

The Anglican Communion

Within the Episcopal Church in Jerusalem and the Middle East, Oman forms part of the diocese of Cyprus and the Gulf. In Oman there are inter-denominational churches at Ruwi and Ghala, in Muscat, and at Salalah, and the congregations are entirely expatriate. The Bishop in Cyprus and the Gulf is resident in Cyprus, while the Archdeacon in the Gulf is resident in the United Arab Emirates.

Chaplaincy: POB 1982, Ruwi; tel. 561409; fax 799475; joint chaplaincy of the Anglican Church and the Reformed Church of America; Chaplain Rev. ROBERT FIELDSON.

The Press

NEWSPAPERS

Al-'Watan (The Nation): POB 463, Muscat; tel. 591919; telex 5643; f. 1971; daily; Arabic; Editor-in-Chief MUHAMMAD SULAIMAN AT-TAI; circ. 23,500.

Khaleej Times: POB 6305, Ruwi; tel. 700895; telex 3699.

Oman Daily Newspaper: POB 6002, Ruwi 112; tel. 701555; telex tel. 790524; 3638; daily; Arabic; Editor-in-Chief HABIB MUHAMMAD NASIB; circ. 15,560.

English Language

Oman Daily Observer: POB 3002, Ruwi 112; tel. 703055; telex 3638; fax 790524; f. 1981; daily; English; publ. by Oman Newspaper House; Editor SAID BIN KHALFAN AL-HARTHI; circ. 22,000.

Times of Oman: POB 3770, Ruwi; tel. 701953; telex 3352; fax 799153; f. 1975; daily; English; Founder, Propr and Editor-in-Chief MUHAMMAD AZ-ZEDJALI; Man. Dir ANIS BIN ESSA AZ-ZEDJALI; circ. 15,000.

PERIODICALS

Al-Adwaa' (Lights): POB 580, Muscat; tel. 704353; telex 3376; 2 a month; Arabic; economic, political and social; Editor-in-Chief HABIB MUHAMMAD NASIB; circ. 15,600.

Al-'Akidah (The Faith): Ruwi; tel. 701000; telex 3399; weekly illustrated magazine; Arabic; Editor SAID AS-SAMHAN AL-KATHIRI; circ. 5,000.

Al-Ghorfa (Oman Commerce): POB 1400, Ruwi; tel. 707674; telex 3389; fax 708497; six a year; English and Arabic; business; publ. by Oman Chamber of Commerce and Industry; Editor YAQOUB BIN HAMED AL-HARTHY.

Al-Markazi (The Central): Ruwi; tel. 702222; telex 3794; f. 1975; bi-monthly magazine; English and Arabic; publ. by Central Bank of Oman.

Al-Mawared at-Tabeey'iyah (Natural Resources): POB 551, Muscat; publ. by Ministries of Agriculture and Fisheries and of Petroleum and Minerals; monthly; English and Arabic; Editor KHALID AZ-ZUBAIDI.

Al-Mazari' (Farms): POB 467, Muscat; weekly journal of the Ministry of Agriculture and Fisheries; Editor KHALID AZ-ZUBAIDI.

An-Nahda (The Renaissance): POB 979, Muscat; tel. 563104; fax 563106; weekly; illustrated magazine; Arabic; Editor TALEB SAID AL-MEAWALY; circ. 10,000.

Oman Today: Apex Publishing, POB 2616, Ruwi 112; tel. 799388; fax 793316; f. 1981; quarterly; English; Editor BRENT MCCALLUM.

Al-Omaniya (Omani Woman): POB 3303, Ruwi 112; tel. 792700; telex 3758; fax 707765; monthly; Arabic; women's magazine; circ. 11,500.

Ash-Shurta (The Police): Muscat; tel. 569216; telex 5377; fax 562341; magazine of Royal Oman Police; Editor Director of Public Relations.

Al-Usra (The Family): POB 7440, Mutrah; tel. 794922; telex 3266; fax 795348; f. 1974; weekly; Arabic; socio-economic illustrated family magazine; Chief Editor SADEK ABDOWANI; circ. 12,585.

The Commercial: POB 2002, Muscat; tel. 704022; telex 3189; fax 795885; monthly; Arabic and English; advertising.

Jund Oman (Soldiers of Oman): POB 113, Muscat; tel. 613615; telex 5228; fax 613369; monthly; illustrated magazine of the Ministry of Defence; Supervisor: Deputy Prime Minister for Security and Defence.

Risalat al-Masjed (The Mosque Message): POB 6066, Muscat; tel. 561178; fax 560607; issued by Diwan of Royal Court Affairs Protocol Dept (Schools and Mosques Section); Editor JOUMA BIN MUHAMMAD BIN SALEM AL-WAHAIBI.

NEWS AGENCY

Oman News Agency: Ministry of Information, POB 6659, Ruwi; tel. 696970; telex 5256; Dir-Gen. MUHAMMAD BIN SALIM AL-MARHOON.

Publishers

Apex Publishing: POB 2616, Ruwi; tel. 799388; trade directory and maps, leisure and business magazines and guide books; Man. Dir SALEH M. TALIB.

Arabian Distribution and Publishing Enterprise: POB 7011, Muttrah; tel. 707079; telex 3085.

Dar al-Usra: POB 7440, Muttrah; tel. 712129; telex 5408.

National Publishing and Advertising LLC: POB 3112, Ruwi 112; tel. 795373; telex 3352; fax 796711; publishers and advertisers; Man. Dir ANEES ESSA AZ-ZEDJALI.

Oman Publishing House: POB 580, Muscat; tel. 704353.

Ash-Shahmi Publishers and Advertisers: POB 6112, Ruwi; tel. 703416; telex 3564; publishers and advertisers.

Radio and Television

In 1991, according to UNESCO estimates, there were 1,006,000 radio receivers and 1.15m. television receivers in use.

RADIO

Radio Sultanate of Oman: Ministry of Information, POB 600, Muscat 113; tel. 603222; telex 3265; fax 601393; f. 1970; transmits in Arabic 20 hours daily, English on FM 15 hours daily; Dir-Gen. ALI BIN ABDULLAH AL-MUJENI.

Radio Salalah: f. 1970; transmits daily programmes in Arabic and the Dhofari languages; Dir MUHAMMAD BIN AHMAD AR-ROWAS.

The British Broadcasting Corporation (BBC) has built a powerful medium-wave relay station on Masirah Island. It is used to expand and improve the reception of the BBC's Arabic, Farsi, Hindi, Pashtu and Urdu services.

TELEVISION

Oman Television: Ministry of Information, POB 600, Muscat; tel. 603222; telex 5454; fax 602381.

A colour television station, built at Qurm, outside Muscat, by the German company Siemens AG, was opened in 1974. A colour television system for Dhofar opened in 1975. Advertising was introduced on local television in August 1987.

Finance

(cap. = capital; p.u. = paid up; res = reserves; dep. = deposits; m. = million; brs = branches; amounts in rials Omani unless otherwise stated)

BANKING

At 31 October 1989 there were 24 licensed banks, with a network of 240 branch offices, operating throughout Oman. In 1993 the Central Bank of Oman issued instructions whereby the minimum capital for licensed banks was increased to RO 10m., and incentives were offered to encourage mergers, in an effort to rationalize the domestic banking system.

Central Bank

Central Bank of Oman: POB 1161, Ruwi 112; tel. 702222; telex 3794; fax 702253; f. 1974; cap. 175m., res 213.8m., dep. 308.7m., total assets 1,016.3m. (1992); 100% state-owned; Exec. Pres. HAMOUD SANGOUR HASIM; Deputy Chair. AHMAD BIN ABD AN-NABI MACKI; Pres. Dr ABD AL-WAHAB KHAYATA; 2 brs.

Commercial Banks

Bank Muscat Al-Ahli Al-Omani SAOG: POB 134, Ruwi 112; tel. 703044; telex 3450; fax 707806; f. 1993 by merger; wholly owned by Omani shareholders; cap. p.u. 15.0m., res 5.5m., dep. 249m., total assets 269.6m. (1993); Chair. Sheikh ZAHER BIN HAMAD AL-HARTHY; Gen. Man. YESHWANT C. DESAI; 14 brs.

Bank of Oman, Bahrain and Kuwait SAOG (BOBK): POB 1708, Ruwi 112; tel. 701528; telex 3290; fax 705607; f. 1973; 51% Omani-owned, 49% by Bank of Oman, Bahrain and Kuwait BSC; cap. p.u. 8.3m., res 3.9m., dep. 87.4m., total assets 99.7m. (1992); Chair. MOHSIN HAIDER DARWISH; Gen. Man. IAIN A. MARNOCH; 36 brs.

Commercial Bank of Oman Ltd SAOG: POB 4696, Ruwi; tel. 793226; telex 3275; fax 793229; f. 1976; 51% Omani-owned, 49% by United Bank Ltd (Pakistan); cap. 5.0m., res 1.4m., dep. 81.1m., total assets 87.8m. (Dec. 1992); Chair. AHMAD BIN ABDULLAH AL-GHAZALI; Dir and Gen. Man. SARFRAZ ALI PIRZADA; 23 brs.

National Bank of Oman Ltd SAOG (NBO): POB 3751, Ruwi; tel. 708894; telex 3281; fax 707781; f. 1973; 100% Omani-owned; cap. pu. 20m., res 2.5m., dep. 230.9m., total assets 270.5m. (1993); Chair. KHALFAN BIN NASSER AL-WOHAIBI; Gen. Man. AUBYN R. HILL; 50 brs.

Oman Arab Bank SAO: POB 2010, Ruwi 112; tel. 700161; telex 3285; fax 797736; f. 1984; purchased Omani European Bank SAOG in 1994; 51% Omani-owned, 49% by Arab Bank (Jordan) Ltd; cap.

10m., res 2.4m., dep. 111.0m., total assets 123.7m. (1993); Chair. AHMED BIN SWAIDAN AL-BALOUSHI; Gen. Man. ABD AL-QADER ASKALAN; 14 brs.

Oman Banking Corporation SAOG: POB 4175, Ruwi; tel. 702383; telex 3153; fax 702469; f. 1988; 60% owned by Gibcorp Oman LLC; cap. p.u. 6m., res 0.1m., dep. 2.0m., total assets 8.3m. (1991); Chair. SALIM BIN HASSAN MACKI; Gen. Man. PRADEEP SAXENA.

Oman International Bank SAOG: POB 1727, Muscat 111; tel. 682500; telex 5406; fax 682800; f. 1984; 100% Omani-owned; cap. 10m., res 2.7m., dep. 235.7m., total assets 256.4m. (1992); Chair. Dr OMAR BIN ABD MUNIEM AL-ZAWAWI; Dir and CEO JAMES T. M. MCNIE; Gen. Man. YAHYA SAID ABDULLA AL-JABRY; 54 brs.

Foreign Banks

ANZ Grindlays Bank PLC (UK): POB 550, Ruwi 112; tel. 703013; telex 3393; fax 706911; f. 1969; Man. IAIN B. MCDOUGALL; Dep. Man. MOHD ZAHRAN; 2 brs.

Bank of Baroda (India): POB 7231, Mutrah; tel. 714559; telex 5470; fax 714560; f. 1976; Man. C. B. CHAYYA; 3 brs.

Bank Dhofar al-Omani al-Fransi SAOC: POB 1507, Ruwi 112; tel. 790466; fax 797246; f. 1990; cap. 15m., res. 2m., dep. 78.6m., total assets 96.9m. (1992); acquired 12 branches of former Bank of Credit and Commerce International in 1992; Gen. Man. LUC ROUSSELET.

Bank Melli Iran: POB 2643, Ruwi; tel. 701579; telex 3295; fax 793017; f. 1974; Gen. Man. ALI JAFFARI LAFTI.

Bank Saderat Iran: POB 4269, Ruwi; tel. 793923; telex 3146; fax 796478; Man. M. SEFIDARI.

Banque de l'Orient Arabe et d'Outre Mer (BANORABE): POB 1608, Ruwi; tel. 703850; telex 3666; fax 707782; f. 1981; Man. WALID AZHARI.

British Bank of the Middle East (Channel Islands): POB 240, Ruwi 112; tel. 799920; telex 3110; fax 704241; f. 1948; CEO: KEITH HOLT; 4 brs.

Citibank NA (USA): POB 8994, Mutrah; tel. 795705; telex 3444; fax 795724; f. 1975; Vice-Pres. MUHAMMAD ZAHRAN.

Habib Bank AG-Zürich (Switzerland): POB 2717, Ruwi; tel. 799876; telex 3931; fax 703613; f. 1967; Exec. Vice-Pres. WAZIR MUMTAZ AHMAD; Asst Vice-Pres. MUHAMMAD IQBAL MUMAL; 5 brs.

Habib Bank Ltd (incorporated in Pakistan): POB 3538, Ruwi 112; tel. 705272; telex 3305; fax 795283; f. 1972; Sr Vice-Pres. and Gen. Man. S. FAZAL MABOOD; 12 brs.

National Bank of Abu Dhabi (UAE): POB 2293, Ruwi 112; tel. 798842; telex 3740; fax 794386; f. 1976; Man. DAVID J. RUNDLE.

Standard Chartered Bank (UK): POB 2353, Ruwi 112; tel. 703999; telex 3217; fax 796864; f. 1968; Man. A. J. PREBBLE; 4 brs.

Development Banks

Oman Bank for Agriculture and Fisheries SAOC: POB 3077, Ruwi 112; tel. 701761; telex 3046; fax 706473; f. 1981; short-, medium- and long-term finance for all activities in the public sector related to agriculture and fisheries; state-owned; total assets 19.6m. (1993); the total value of loans granted to mid-1989 was 26m.; Chair. Sheikh MUHAMMAD BIN ABDULLAH BIN ZAHER AL-HINAI; Gen. Man. TARIQ BIN ABDULREDHA BIN MUHAMMAD AL-JAMALI; 13 brs.

Oman Development Bank SAO: POB 309, Muscat; tel. 738021; telex 5179; fax 738026; f. 1977; short-, medium- and long-term finance for industrial development projects; 54.2% state-owned, 40% foreign-owned, 5.8% Omani citizens and companies; total assets 41.0m. (1991); Chair. MUHAMMAD BIN MUSA AL-YOUSUF; Gen. Man. MURTADHA BIN MUHAMMAD FADHIL.

Oman Housing Bank SAOC: POB 2555, Ruwi; tel. 704444; telex 3077; fax 704071; f. 1977; medium- and long-term finance for housing development; 100% state-owned; cap. 30m., total assets 121.3m. (1993); Chair. MALIK BIN SULAIMAN BIN SAID AL-MA'MARI; Gen. Man. MAHMOUD BIN MUHAMMAD OMAR BAHRAM; 9 brs.

STOCK EXCHANGE

Muscat Securities Market: Muscat; tel. 702607; telex 3220; fax 702691; f. 1990; Dir-Gen. MAHMOUD AL-JARWANI.

INSURANCE

Al-Ahlia Insurance Co SAO: POB 1463, Ruwi; tel. 709331; telex 3518; fax 797151; f. 1985; cap. p.u. 2m.; Chair. MOHSIN HAIDER DARWISH; Gen. Man. G. V. RAO.

Oman National Insurance Co SAOG (ONIC): POB 5254, Ruwi; tel. 795020; telex 3111; fax 702569; f. 1978; cap. p.u. 2m.; Chair. MUHAMMAD BIN MUSA AL-YUSEF; Gen. Man. MICHAEL J. ADAMS.

Oman United Insurance Co SAOG: POB 1522, Ruwi 112; tel. 703990; telex 3652; fax 796327; f. 1985; cap. pu. 2m.; Chair. SAID SALIM BIN NASSIR AL-BUSAIDI; Gen. Man. KHALID MANSOUR HAMED.

Trade and Industry

Oman Chamber of Commerce and Industry: POB 1400, Ruwi 112; tel. 707674; telex 3389; fax 708497; Pres. YAQOUB BIN HAMED AL-HARTHY; 55,000 mbr (1992).

STATE ENTERPRISES

Oman Cement Co SAO: POB 560, Ruwi; tel. 626626; telex 5139; fax 626414; f. 1977; development and production of cement; scheduled for partial privatization in early 1994; Chair. Dr ALYQDHAN AL-HINAI.

Oman Flour Mills Co Ltd SAO: POB 566, Ruwi; tel. 711155; telex 5422; fax 714711; f. 1976; sales US \$65m. (1992/93); cap. \$10m.; 60% state-owned; produces 6,000 tons per day (t/d) of various flours and 600 t/d of animal feedstuffs; Chair. RASHID BIN SALIM AL-MASROORY; 147 employees.

Oman Mining Co Ltd LLC: POB 758, Muscat; tel. 793925; telex 3041; fax 793865; f. 1978; cap. RO 25m.; state-owned; development of copper, gold and chromite mines; Chair. MOHSIN HAIDER DARWISH.

Oman National Electric Co SAO: POB 1393, Ruwi; tel. 796353; telex 3328; fax 704420; f. 1978; Chair. HAMOUD BIN SONGOR BIN HASHIM; Gen. Man. M. OSMAN BAIG.

PETROLEUM

Petroleum Development Oman LLC (PDO): POB 81, Muscat; tel. 678111; telex 5212; fax 677106; incorporated in Sultanate of Oman since 1980 by royal decree as limited liability company; 60% owned by Oman Govt, 34% by Shell, 4% by Total-CFP and 2% by Partex; production (1992) averaged 692,000 b/d from 69 fields, linked by a pipeline system to terminal at Mina al-Fahal, near Muscat; Man. Dir H. A. MERLE; 4,500 employees.

Amoco Oman Petroleum Co: POB 1690, Ruwi; tel. 698402; telex 5675; fax 698408; holds one concession area, totalling 15,000 sq km, in northern Oman. No production recorded to date; Man. A. E. ROBINSON.

BP Middle East: POB 92, 116 Mina al-Fahal; tel. 561801; telex 5419; fax 561283; Gen. Man. A. R. GRAHAM.

Elf Petroleum Oman: POB 353, Ruwi; tel. 694655; fax 694663; concession granted in 1975 for exploration in the onshore region of Butabul; area of 7,000 sq km; converted to a production sharing agreement in October 1976; 48% owned by Elf, 32% by Sumitomo and 20% by Wintershall; present concession area 4,033 sq km (1992) at Butabul; production 6,000 b/d.

Japex Oman: POB 543, Ruwi; tel. 602011; telex 5695; fax 602181; f. 1981; operates a concession at Wahibah; 49.6% owned by JNOC, 35.3% by JAPEX and 10.1% by CIECO; present concession area 1,856 sq km (1993) at Wadi Aswad; production, 8,000 b/d; Man. K. MAENAMI.

National Gas Co SAOG: POB 95, CPO Seeb Airport; tel. Rusail 626073; fax 626307; f. 1979; bottling of liquefied petroleum gas; Gen. Man. P. K. BAGCHI; 83 employees.

Occidental of Oman Inc.: POB 2271, Ruwi 112; tel. 603386; telex 5258; fax 603358; fmrly Occidental Petroleum Corpn (Occidental Oman); succeeded Gulf Oman Petroleum as majority shareholders in Suneinah concession in 1983; total area of 9,717 sq km; US \$11m. oil stabilization plant completed 1989.

Oman Liquefied Natural Gas Co (OLNGC): f. 1992; 51% state-owned; construction and management of 5,000 tons-per-year LNG plang at Bimma, shipping and marketing.

Oman Refinery Co LLC: POB 3568, Ruwi 112; tel. 561200; telex 5123; fax 561384; production of light petroleum products; Gen. Man. JAY RODNEY MCINTIRE; 286 employees.

The Government has granted exploration rights over a large area of western and south-western Dhofar to BP, Deminex, AGIP, Hispanoil, Elf/Aquitaine I, the Adolph Lundin Group, Quintana/Gulf and Cluff Oil.

MAJOR INDUSTRIAL COMPANIES

Al-Felaij Plastics: POB 5266, Ruwi; tel. 704481; telex 3448; fax 708352; f. 1978; sales RO 6.5m. (1991); cap. and res RO 8m.; manufacture of household and industrial plastic products; Gen. Man. SHAHID BASHIR; 120 employees.

Arabian Trade and Industry Est.: POB 437, Ruwi 112; tel. 626336; fax 626285; f. 1980; sales RO 1.5m. (1992); cap. and res RO 127,000; manufacture of tissue paper; Chief Exec. RAZAK MAHMOUD; 22 employees.

Construction Materials Industries SAOG: POB 1791, Ruwi 112; tel. 704603/4; fax 799203; f. 1977; sales RO 1.3m. (1993); cap. and res RO 6m.; manufacture and supply of calcium silicate bricks, paving and hydrated lime and limestone products; Gen. Man. P. NAMBIAR; 97 employees.

National Detergent Co Ltd SAOG: POB 6104, Ruwi; tel. 603824; telex 5635; fax 602145; f. 1980; cap. and res RO 1.7m.; manufacture and marketing of detergents; Chair. ABD AL-HUSSAIN BHACKER; Gen. Man. KISHORE ASTHANA; 210 employees.

Oman Fisheries Co SAOG: POB 5900, Ruwi; tel. 714129; telex 5092; fax 714765; f. 1980 as Oman National Fisheries Co; responsible for commercial development of fishing, processing and marketing of marine products; operates 4 deep-sea trawlers and a processing and freezing plant; Gen. Man. MUHAMMAD ALAWI (acting).

Oman Organic Fertilizer and Chemicals Industries SAO: POB 6781, Ruwi; tel. 591013; telex 5407; fax 590120; f. 1981; cap. RO 2m.; manufacture of organic fertilizers commenced 1986; Gen. Man. TEJ B. SARAF; 28 employees.

Oman Refreshment Co Ltd: POB 1030, Seeb Airport; tel. 591455; telex 5583; fax 591389; f. 1974; cap. RO 1.2m. (1984); bottling and distribution of soft drinks; Chair. ANWAR ALI SULTAN; Man. Dir. ABDULLAH MOOSA; 260 employees.

Poly Products LLC: POB 2561, Ruwi 112; tel. 626044; telex 5182; fax 626046; f. 1979; sales US $12m. (1992); cap. and res $4.5m.; manufacture of flexible and rigid polyurethane foam and spring mattresses, divan and upholstered beds; Man. Dir SAID AL-HINAI; Gen. Man. SAYED ANWAR AHSAN; 350–400 employees.

Yahya Costain LLC: POB 5282, Ruwi; tel. 591366; telex 5218; fax 591981; f. 1977; mechanical, electrical, civil and process engineering, building and geotechnical investigation, furniture manufacture and joinery; Gen. Man. N. F. SALE; 2,000 employees.

Transport

Directorate-General of Roads: POB 7027, Mutrah; tel. 701577; Dir-Gen. of Roads Sheikh MUHAMMAD BIN HILAL AL-KHALILI.

Directorate-General of Ports and Public Transport: POB 684, Muscat; tel. 702044; telex 7390; Dir-Gen. Eng. SALIM BIN HUMAID AL-GHASSANI.

ROADS

A network of adequate graded roads links all the main centres of population and only a few mountain villages are not accessible by Land Rover. In 1992 there were 4,948 km of asphalt road and 21,000 km of graded roads.

Oman National Transport Co SAOG: POB 620, Muscat; tel. 590046; telex 5018; fax 590152; operates local, regional and long-distance bus services from Muscat; Chair. TARIQ BIN MUHAMMAD AMIN AL-MANTHERI; Man. Dir SULEIMAN BIN MUHANA AL-ADAWI.

SHIPPING

Port Sultan Qaboos, at the entrance to the Persian (Arabian) Gulf, was built in 1974 to provide nine deep-water berths varying in length from 250 to 750 ft (76 to 228 m), with draughts of up to 43 ft (13 m), and three berths for shallow-draught vessels drawing 12 to 16 ft (3.7 to 4.9 m) of water. A total of 12 new berths have been opened and two of the existing berths have been upgraded to a container terminal capable of handling 60 containers per hour. The port also has a 3,000-ton-capacity cold store which belongs to the Oman Fisheries Company. In 1993 1,513 ships visited Port Sultan Qaboos, and 3.0m. tons of cargo were handled. In 1992 work commenced on the upgrading and expansion of Port Sultan Qaboos. The project was scheduled for completion in late 1994.

Port Services Corporation SAOG: POB 133, Muscat 113; tel. 714001; telex 5233; fax 714007; f. 1976; cap. p.u. RO 4.8m.; jointly owned by the Govt of Oman and private shareholders; Chair. SALIM BIN ABDULLAH AL-GHAZALI; Pres. AWAD BIN SALIM ASH-SHANFARI.

The oil terminal at Mina al-Fahal can also accommodate the largest super-tankers on offshore loading buoys. Similar facilities for the import of refined petroleum products exist at Mina al-Fahal. Mina Raysut, near Salalah, has been developed into an all-weather port, and, in addition to container facilities, has four deep-water berths and two shallow berths. During 1992 1,221 ships called at the port. Loading facilities for smaller craft exist at Sohar, Khaboura, Sur, Marbet, Ras al-Had, Kasab, Al-Biaa, Masirah and Salalah.

CIVIL AVIATION

Domestic and international flights operate from Seeb International Airport. Oman's second international airport, at Salalah, was completed in 1978. In 1986 more than 1.4m. passengers passed through Seeb International Airport, and approximately 73,000 passed through Salalah Airport. Most towns of any size have small air strips.

Directorate-General of Civil Aviation: POB 204, Muscat; tel. 519210; telex 5418; Dir-Gen. Eng. TARIQ BIN MUHAMMAD AL-MANTHERI.

Gulf Aviation Ltd (Gulf Air): POB 138, Bahrain; tel. 531166; telex 8255; fax 530385; f. 1950; jointly owned by the Govts of Bahrain, Oman, Qatar, and Abu Dhabi; international services to destinations in Europe, the USA, Africa, the Middle East and the Far East; Chair. YOUSUF AHMAD ASH-SHIRAWI; Pres. and Chief Exec. ALI IBRAHIM AL-MALKI.

Oman Aviation Services Co SAOG: POB 1058, Seeb International Airport; tel. 519223; telex 5424; fax 510805; f. 1981; cap. p.u. RO 7m.; 35% of shares owned by Government, 65% by Omani nationals; air-charter, maintenance, handling and catering; operators of Oman's domestic airline; Chair. SALIM BIN ABDULLAH AL-GHAZALI.

Tourism

Tourism, introduced in 1985, is strictly controlled. Attractions, apart from the capital itself, include Nizwa, ancient capital of the interior, Dhofar and the forts of Nakhl, Rustaq, and Al-Hazm. In 1990 there were 149,000 visitor arrivals in Oman and tourist receipts for that year totalled US $69m.

Director-General of Tourism: J. H. SAYYID FATIK.

Defence

Chief of Staff of the Sultan's Armed Forces: Lt-Gen. KHAMIS BIN SALIM AL-KABANI.

Defence Expenditure (1994 budget): 612m. Omani rials.

Military service: voluntary.

Total armed forces (June 1994): 42,900: army 25,000; navy 4,200; air force 3,500. There is a 4,500-strong Royal Guard.

Paramilitary forces: 3,500: tribal Home Guard (*Firqat*).

Education

Great advances have been made in education since 1970, when Sultan Qaboos came to power. Primary education begins at six years of age and lasts for six years. Secondary education also lasts for six years, divided into two equal stages: preparatory and secondary. In 1970 Oman had only 16 primary schools, with 6,941 pupils, and no secondary schools. As a proportion of the appropriate age-group, enrolment at primary schools was about 3%. Although education is still not compulsory, attendance has greatly increased. In 1986 the total attendance at primary and secondary schools was equivalent to 69% of all school-age children (boys 77%; girls 61%). Primary enrolment in that year included 80% of children in the relevant age-group (84% of boys; 76% of girls). In 1986/87 enrolment in general and technical institutes rose to a total of 247,546 students, of whom 56% were boys. By 1987/88 there were 367 primary schools, 249 preparatory schools and 62 secondary schools in Oman, and attendance figures had risen to 268,722, of whom 58% were boys. In that year there were 11,990 teachers. In 1988/89 there were 370 primary schools and 66 secondary schools. Enrolment increased to 294,934, of whom 54% were boys. More than 85% of the teachers were seconded from other countries, although by 1993 42% of teachers (including those in institutes and colleges) were Omani. In 1989/90 there were 388 primary schools, 283 preparatory schools and 70 secondary schools. The total number of students was 323,468, of whom 54% were males. The number of teachers rose by 6% in 1989/90, to 13,695, while in the same period, the number of pupils increased to 323,468, and the total of schools to 741. The number of schools increased to 857 in 1992/93, attended by 450,056 pupils, and the number of teachers increased to 18,325.

A Teacher Training Institute was opened in 1978, but, following changes in the education system in 1984, it became known as an Intermediate Teacher Training College, consisting of eight colleges by 1992. Special institutions have also been established to train students at the preparatory level in technical skills and in agriculture. In 1970 an estimated 80% of Oman's adult population were illiterate. In 1987/88 10,625 adults (2,086 males; 8,539 females) attended 248 government literacy centres, and 209 adult education centres served an additional 10,916 (4,611 males; 6,305 females). In 1992/93 8,906 adults attended literacy centres and 20,000 enrolled in adult education centres (10,347 males; 9,653 females). The first national university, named after Sultan Qaboos, was opened in September 1986. The university comprised five colleges: Education and Islamic Sciences, Agriculture, Engineering, Science and Medicine. An Arts college was opened in September 1987. The university originally had the capacity to enrol 3,000 students; in 1988/89 there were 1,140 and by 1990 there were over 3,600. In 1987/88 the university had a teaching staff of 203 rising to 515 in 1992. The first graduates of Sultan Qaboos University matriculated in 1990. Government spending on education in 1991 was RO 180.1m., representing 11.4% of total expenditure.

Bibliography

Aitchison, C. U. (Ed.) *Government of India Foreign Department—Collection of Treaties Relating to India and Neighbouring Countries. Volume XII*. Calcutta, 1932, reprint 1973.

Akehurst, John. *We Won a War: The Campaign in Oman 1965–75.* London, Michael Russell, 1982.

Allen, Calvin H. *Oman: the Modernization of the Sultanate.* London, Croom Helm, 1987.

Arkless, David C. *The Secret War: Dhofar 1971/72.* London, W. Kimber, 1988.

Badger, G. P. *The History of the Imams and Sayyids of Oman, by Salilbin-Razik, from AD 661 to 1856.* Hakluyt Society, 1871, reprint 1967.

Bhacker, M. *Trade and Empire in Muscat and Zanzibar.* London, Routledge, 1992.

Busch, B. C. *Great Britain and the Persian Gulf 1894–1914.* University of California Press, 1967.

Clements, F. A. *Oman: The Reborn Land.* London, Longman, 1980.

Düster, J., and Scholz, F. *Bibliographie über das Sultanat Oman.* All texts in both German and English. Hamburg, Deutsches Orient-Institut, 1980.

Eickelman, Christine. *Women and Community in Oman.* New York University Press, 1984.

Graz, Liesl. *The Omanis: Sentinels of the Gulf.* London, Longman, 1982.

Hill, Ann and Daryl. *The Sultanate of Oman: A Heritage.* London, Longman, 1977.

Kelly, J. B. *Great Britain and the Persian Gulf, 1793–1880.* London, 1968.

Eastern Arabia Frontiers. London, Faber and Faber, 1964.

Landen, R. G. *Oman Since 1856.* Princeton University Press, 1967.

Lorimer, J. C. *Gazetteer of the Persian Gulf, Oman and Central Arabia.* 2 vols. Calcutta, 1908 and 1915, reprint 1970 in 5 vols, and in 1986 in 9 vols.

Maurizi, Vincenzo. *History of Seyd Said.* Cambridge, Oleander Press, 1984.

Miles, S. B. *The Countries and Tribes of the Persian Gulf.* 3rd edition, London, Frank Cass, 1966.

Morris, James (now Jan). *Sultan in Oman.* London, Faber, 1957.

Oman Studies Bibliographic Info. Oman Studies Centre, Pforzheim, Germany.

Peterson, J. E. *Oman in the Twentieth Century.* London, Croom Helm, 1978.

Phillips, Wendell. *Unknown Oman.* London, Longman, 1966, reprint 1971.

Oman. A History. London, Longman, 1967, reprint 1971.

Pridham, Brian R. (Ed.). *Oman: Economic, Social and Strategic Developments.* London, Croom Helm, 1987.

Risso, Patricia. *Oman and Muscat: An Early Modern History.* London, Croom Helm, 1986.

St Albans, Duchess of. *Where Time Stood Still: A portrait of Oman.* London, Quartet, 1980.

Saleh, N. A. *The General Principles of Saudi Arabian and Omani Company Laws.* London, Namara Publications, 1981.

Shannon, M. O. *Oman and Southeastern Arabia: A Bibliographic Survey.* Boston, Hall, 1978.

Sirhan, Sirhan ibn Said ibn. *Annals of Oman.* Cambridge, Oleander Press, 1985.

Skeet, Ian. *Muscat and Oman: The End of an Era.* Faber and Faber, 1974.

Oman: Politics and Development. London, Macmillan, 1992.

Thesiger, Wilfred. *Arabian Sands.* London, Longman, 1959.

Townsend, John. *Oman: The Making of the Modern State.* London, Croom Helm, 1977.

Ward, Philip. *Travels in Oman: on the Track of the Early Explorers.* Cambridge, Oleander Press, 1986.

Wikan, U. *Behind the Veil in Arabia: Women in Oman.* London, Johns Hopkins Press, 1982.

Wilkinson, John C. *Water and Tribal Settlement in South-East Arabia.* Oxford University Press, 1977.

The Imamate Tradition of Oman. Cambridge University Press, 1987.

QATAR

Geography

The State of Qatar occupies a peninsula (roughly 160 km long, and between 55 km and 90 km wide), projecting northwards from the Arabian mainland, on the west coast of the Persian (Arabian) Gulf. Its western coastline joins onto the shores of Saudi Arabia, and to the east lie the United Arab Emirates (UAE) and Oman. The total area is 11,437 sq km (4,416 sq miles), and at the census of 16 March 1986 the population was 369,079, of whom fewer than one-third were native Qataris. About 60% of the total were concentrated in the town of Doha, on the east coast. Two other ports, Zakrit on the west coast and Umm Said on the east, were developed after the discovery of petroleum. Zakrit is a convenient, if shallow, harbour for the import of goods from Bahrain, while Umm Said affords anchorage to deep-sea tankers and freighters.

The climate of Qatar is hot and humid in summer, with temperatures reaching 44°C between July and September, and humidity exceeding 85%. There is some rain in winter, when temperatures range between 10°C and 20°C. Qatar is stony, sandy and barren; limited supplies of underground water are unsuitable for drinking or agriculture because of high mineral content. More than one-half of the water supply is now provided by sea-water distillation processes.

History

Qatar was formerly dominated by the Khalifa family of nearby Bahrain. The peninsula became part of Turkey's Ottoman Empire in 1872, but Turkish forces evacuated Qatar at the beginning of the First World War (1914–18). The United Kingdom (UK) recognized Sheikh Abdullah ath-Thani as Ruler of Qatar, and in 1916 made a treaty with him, in accordance with its policy in Bahrain, the Trucial States (now the United Arab Emirates) and Kuwait. The Ruler of Qatar undertook not to cede, mortgage or otherwise dispose of parts of his territories to anyone except the British Government, nor to enter into any relationship with a foreign government, other than the British, without British consent. In return, Britain undertook to protect Qatar from all aggression by sea, and to provide support in case of an overland attack. A further treaty, concluded in 1934, extended fuller British protection to Qatar.

The discovery of petroleum in 1939 promised greater prosperity for Qatar, but further development was delayed by the onset of the Second World War, and production did not begin on a commercial scale until 1949. The country used the revenues from the export of petroleum to finance an ambitious development programme. In January 1961 Qatar joined the Organization of the Petroleum Exporting Countries (OPEC), and in May 1970 it also became a member of the Organization of Arab Petroleum Exporting Countries (OAPEC). Qatar remains a developing country, although its relatively small reserves of petroleum and the recent fall in production, caused by OPEC embargoes and the world oil glut, have led to greater caution, and to attempts to develop sources of revenue which are independent of petroleum.

In October 1960 Sheikh Ali ath-Thani, who had been Ruler of Qatar since 1949, abdicated in favour of his son, Sheikh Ahmad ath-Thani. In 1968 the British Government announced its intention to withdraw British forces from the Persian (Arabian) Gulf area by 1971. As a result, Qatar attempted to associate itself with Bahrain and the Trucial States in a proposed federation. In April 1970 the Ruler, Sheikh Ahmad, announced a provisional constitution for Qatar, providing for a partially elected consultative assembly. Effective power remained, however, in the monarch's hands. In May 1970 the Deputy Ruler, Sheikh Khalifa ath-Thani (a cousin of Sheikh Ahmad), was appointed Prime Minister. After the failure of negotiations for union with neighbouring Gulf countries, Qatar became fully independent on 1 September 1971, when the Ruler took the title of Amir. The 1916 treaty was replaced by a new treaty of friendship with the UK. In February 1972 a bloodless coup, led by Sheikh Khalifa, the Crown Prince and Prime Minister, deposed the Amir during his absence abroad. Claiming support from the royal family and the armed forces, Sheikh Khalifa proclaimed himself Amir, while retaining the premiership.

Qatar has generally maintained close links with Saudi Arabia, with which it signed a bilateral defence agreement in 1982, and is usually considered to be one of the more moderate Arab states. It opposed the Camp David agreements between Egypt, Israel and the USA, and the subsequent Egyptian-Israeli treaty, signed in March 1979. In early 1981 Qatar joined the newly-established Gulf Co-operation Council (GCC). By May 1983 member countries were implementing new GCC regulations, including the abolition of import tariffs between member states, reduced restrictions on travel between GCC countries, and more favourable investment conditions for business. Co-operation on defence was also a priority, as was underlined by the threat to the security of GCC states of an escalation of the war between Iran and Iraq, which had begun in 1980. In October 1983 Qatari forces participated in the GCC's 'Peninsula Shield' joint military exercise in Oman, and in November Qatar was the venue for a three-day GCC summit meeting.

Since his accession in 1972, the Amir has pursued reform while preserving the Islamic pattern of life. In accordance with the 1970 Constitution, Sheikh Khalifa decreed the first Advisory Council, to complement the ministerial Government. Its 20 members, selected from representatives elected by limited suffrage, were increased to 30 in December 1975. The Advisory Council's term of office was extended by four years in May 1978 and by further terms of four years in 1982, 1986 and 1990. The Advisory Council's constitutional entitlements include power to debate legislation drafted by the Council of Ministers before ratification and promulgation. It also has power to request ministerial statements on matters of general and specific policy, including the draft budget.

Using the wealth that it acquired through petroleum sales, the Qatari Government made significant social and infrastructural improvements. By 1983 an estimated 6,000 families were housed by the state, a welfare and non-contributory pension scheme had been introduced, and a programme to construct schools and clinics was almost complete. In May 1989 the Supreme Council for Planning (SCP) was formed to co-ordinate plans for Qatar's social and economic development. Under the direction of the heir apparent (Sheikh Hamad bin Khalifa ath-Thani), the council promotes industrial diversification and agricultural development in order to reduce dependence on the petroleum sector.

In April 1986 Qatar raided the island of Fasht ad-Dibal, which had been artificially constructed on a coral reef in the Persian (Arabian) Gulf, and seized 29 foreign workers who were constructing a Bahraini coastguard station on the island. Officials of the GCC met representatives of both states in an attempt to reconcile them, and to avoid a division within the Council. In May the workers were released, and the two Governments agreed to destroy the island. In mid-1992 Qatar rejected Bahrain's demand to take the dispute to the International Court of Justice (ICJ) in The Hague. It was alleged that Bahrain had attempted to broaden the issue to include its claim to the potentially oil-rich Hawar islands and part of the Qatari mainland, around Zubara, while in April 1992 the Government of Qatar had issued a decree redefining its maritime borders to include territorial waters claimed by Bahrain. A hearing of the ICJ opened in The Hague in February 1994 with the aim of determining whether the court had jurisdiction to give a ruling on the dispute, and in March Bahrain began to give oral presentations to the court. In July the ICJ invited the two countries to resubmit their dispute by 30 November.

In November 1987 Qatar resumed full diplomatic relations with Egypt and in July 1988 diplomatic relations were established at ambassadorial level between Qatar and the People's Republic of China. In August 1988 Qatar established diplomatic relations with the USSR. This was followed, at the end of 1990, by an agreement on economic, commercial and technical co-operation with the USSR.

In May 1989 Iran's Minister of Oil, Gholamreza Aqazadeh, declared that one-third of the Qatari-controlled North Field, the world's largest natural gas field, was beneath Iranian waters. He provoked hostility from the Qatari Government by announcing that Iran planned to appropriate its share of the field and to pipe gas to an Iranian gas-processing plant.

In July 1989, in the first government reshuffle since 1978, seven ministers were replaced and 11 new members were appointed to a new 16-member Council of Ministers. Five new portfolios were created. The Ministry of the Economy and Commerce, which had been vacant, became the Ministry of Economy and Trade, and the Agriculture and Industry portfolio was divided. Agriculture was amalgamated with Municipal Affairs, while Industry was linked with Public Works under Ahmad Muhammad Ali as-Subay'i, the chairman of the Qatar Steel Company (QASCO). The Ministry of Industry and Public Works was expected to play a major role in the planning of industrial development, which will be stimulated by gas resources from the North Field. The Minister of Foreign Affairs, Abdullah bin Khalifa al-Attiyah, resigned in May 1990 and was replaced by Mubarak Ali al-Khatir, the former Minister of Electricity and Water.

In mid-January 1992 50 leading Qatari citizens petitioned the Amir to demand the establishment of a consultative assembly with legislative powers. They also expressed concern at abuse of power in the emirate and proposed reforms of the economy and the education system. In September there was another extensive reorganization of the Council of Ministers, expanding its membership from 14 to 17.

Qatar, as a member of the GCC, the Arab League and the UN, condemned Iraq's occupation of Kuwait in August 1990, although it had previously supported Iraq in its 1980–88 war with Iran. In late 1990 Qatar permitted the deployment of foreign forces on its territory, as part of the multinational attempt to force Iraq to withdraw from Kuwait. Units of the Qatari armed forces subsequently participated in the military operation to liberate Kuwait in January–February 1991. Qatar resumed tentative contact with Iraq in 1993. In February 1994

the Kuwaiti government recalled its ambassador from Qatar in protest at the *rapprochement* between Qatar and Iraq. In April Qatar stressed that co-operation with Iraq would depend on Iraq's implementation of the UN resolutions. In the same month an Iraqi cultural delegation was welcomed to Qatar for an Iraqi cultural week.

In May 1992 Qatar signed six agreements with Iran for co-operation in various sectors, including customs, air traffic and the exchange of news. In July 1993 the Deputy Amir, Sheikh Hamad, visited Teheran and in October an agreement was signed to establish a joint committee for co-operation in the oil and gas sector. In January 1994 Qatar hosted talks with Iran to discuss security issues and draw up plans to curb drug-trafficking in the Persian Gulf. Qatar chose to pursue good relations with Iran despite adverse reaction from its Arab neighbours and the USA. In April further discussions were held with regard to the proposed water pipeline from Iran to Qatar.

In June 1992 Qatar followed Kuwait and Bahrain in signing a defence pact with the USA. In mid-1993 Qatar and the UK signed a memorandum of understanding on defence. The Ministers of Foreign Affairs of Qatar and Tunisia signed an agreement in January 1994 to further political and economic relations. On 7 April Qatar became a contracting party to the General Agreement on Tariffs and Trade (GATT), and a week later the Qatari Minister of Foreign Affairs travelled to Bonn, Germany, for three days of talks on expanding mututal co-operation. The following month military co-operation was discussed with a Russian military official. Sheikh Hamad, the Deputy Amir, voiced Qatar's continuing support for the Palestinian reconstruction programme when a Palestinian delegation visited in June. In August Qatar and France signed a defence agreement which would entail Qatar receiving a number of Mirage 2000-5 aircraft. In the same month the Qatari Minister of Foreign Affairs met King Hussein of Jordan in London to discuss the Middle East peace process and ways of boosting bilateral relations.

At the end of September 1992 tension developed with Saudi Arabia when Qatar accused a Saudi force of attacking the al-Khofous border post, killing two soldiers and capturing another. As a result, Qatar announced the suspension of a 1965 agreement with Saudi Arabia on border demarcation (which had never been fully ratified) and withdrew its 200-strong contingent from the GCC 'Peninsula Shield' force in Kuwait. The Saudi Government denied the involvement of its armed forces. Qatar registered its disaffection by boycotting meetings of the GCC ministers in Abu Dhabi and Kuwait in November. However, on 20 December, following mediation by President Mubarak of Egypt, Sheikh Khalifa and King Fahd of Saudi Arabia signed an agreement whereby a committee was to be established formally to demarcate the border between the two states by the end of 1993. By mid-1994 the border had yet to be officially demarcated. On 21 December 1992 Sheikh Khalifa attended a GCC summit meeting in Abu Dhabi and good relations were restored between the two countries in 1993.

The foreign policy adopted by Qatar in 1994 differed from that of its GCC allies on a number of key issues. Qatar declined to support a final communiqué, issued by seven other Arab states, demanding an immediate cease-fire in Yemen, arguing that it was not their place to interfere in the domestic affairs of another country. Similarly, Qatar made contact with the Israeli government despite the Arab economic boycott: in January 1994 discussions took place with regard to the supply of natural gas to Israel. Following protests from its Arab neighbours, Qatar conceded that the agreement of sales would depend on a feasibility study and on Israel's withdrawal from all Arab territories occupied in 1967.

Economy

Dr P. T. H. UNWIN

(Revised for this edition by ALAN J. DAY)

Qatar is a largely barren peninsula, with stony and sandy soil which is generally unsuitable for arable farming. There are numerous coastal saline flats, known as *sabkha*, and the only agricultural soils are found in small depressions in the centre of the country and towards the north. Traditionally the Qatari economy was based on the nomadic farming of livestock, and on fishing and pearling. Since the discovery of significant reserves of petroleum in 1939, however, the exploitation of these deposits has transformed Qatar into one of the richest countries in the region, measured in terms of average income. In 1984, according to estimates by the World Bank, Qatar's gross national product (GNP), calculated on a 1982–84 base period (to adjust for fluctuations in prices and exchange rates), was US \$5,780m., equivalent to \$19,010 per head. As in 1983, Qatar's GNP per head in 1984 was the second highest national level in the world, being exceeded only by that of its neighbour, the United Arab Emirates (UAE). In 1985, however, Qatar's GNP per head (at average 1983–85 prices) declined to \$16,220, the sixth highest level in the world (exceeded by the UAE, Bermuda, Brunei, the USA and Switzerland). According to World Bank estimates, Qatar's GNP in constant prices, i.e. adjusted for inflation, actually diminished between 1973 and 1985, owing to declines in petroleum output and prices in the early 1980s. Over this period, real GNP per head declined by 8.5% per annum. Over the 12 years to 1985, it is estimated, the country's population increased at an average rate of 6.8% per year, mainly because of an influx of immigrant labour. In 1992 Qatar's GNP, measured at average 1990–92 prices, was \$8,511m., equivalent to \$16,240 per head. The World Bank estimated the average rate of decline in Qatar's real GNP per head as 11.2% per annum over the period 1980–92.

The economic changes that have taken place within Qatar in recent years have been made possible by the high level of labour immigration. In 1991 the number of indigenous Qataris was estimated at 350,000, while the World Bank estimated the total mid-year population at 506,000. The mid-year population in 1992 was estimated at 532,719. The first national census, which was held in March 1986, had recorded a total population of 369,079, of whom 60% resided in Doha. By the mid-1980s the economy still relied heavily on petroleum revenues, but a policy of diversification meant that between 1979 and 1983 the percentage of government revenues derived from crude oil fell from 93% to 80%. The collapse in world prices for crude petroleum during 1986 nevertheless placed an increased burden on an already stressed economy. Despite a recovery in the price of oil in the second half of the year, Qatar's total revenue from petroleum in 1986 was approximately \$1,720m., compared with \$3,068m. in 1985. Oil revenues remained at low levels during the second half of the 1980s. In 1984 the petroleum sector's contribution to GDP was 45%, but by 1988 the proportion had fallen to an estimated 27%. Qatar has a reputation for caution in its economic policy, but in the late 1980s moves towards economic restructuring were made, and reforms took place, in anticipation of a sharp reduction in Qatar's output of crude oil after 2010. As a result, in 1987 the Government introduced a programme of industrialization, centred on ambitious plans for the development of the North Field, the world's largest single natural gas deposit.

The ending of the Iran–Iraq War in August 1988 improved conditions of trade in the region, in particular by removing from neutral merchant shipping the threat of attack and by restoring confidence in local export industries, especially the petroleum industry. By 1990 the first phase of the North Field development programme was close to completion, but Iraq's invasion of Kuwait in August led to the suspension of major investment projects. Although the crisis raised oil revenues

to an estimated \$2,500m. in 1990, its overall impact was to depress economic activity. Since the liberation of Kuwait in February 1991, Qatar has revived its programme of industrial projects, the cost of which has been estimated at \$8,000m. Production from the North Field began on 3 September 1991, the 20th anniversary of Qatar's independence. In view of the huge capital cost of implementing the full industrialization programme, availability of financing is expected to be one of the major factors determining the pace of Qatar's economic development during the 1990s. In 1992 Qatar's estimated GDP at current prices was QR 27,202m., of which QR 9,750m. (35.8%) was contributed by the oil and gas sector and QR 3,450m. (12.7%) by non-oil manufacturing industries.

PETROLEUM AND NATURAL GAS

The first concession to explore for petroleum in Qatar was granted to the Anglo-Persian Oil Company in 1935, and was later transferred to Petroleum Development (Qatar) Ltd. Deposits of petroleum were first discovered in Qatar in 1939, although exploration and production was delayed during the Second World War. By 1949 a pipeline had been constructed from the Dukhan oilfield, on the west coast, to Umm Said in the east, where terminal facilities had also been built, and in December of that year the first shipment of Qatari petroleum was exported. In 1952 the Shell Company of Qatar acquired a concession to develop the entire continental shelf offshore area, and by 1960 petroleum had been discovered at Idd ash-Shargi, 100 km to the east of Qatar. Soon afterwards, a second offshore oilfield was discovered, to the north-east of the first, at Maydan Mahzam, and in 1970 a third offshore field, Bul Hanine, was discovered nearby. In 1953 Petroleum Development (Qatar) Ltd was renamed the Qatar Petroleum Company, and by 1960 Qatar's onshore production had reached 60,360,000 barrels, compared with 800,000 barrels in 1949. Qatar was admitted to membership of the Organization of the Petroleum Exporting Countries (OPEC) in 1961. In 1969 Qatar and Abu Dhabi agreed to a joint production scheme for the al-Bunduq field which straddles the border between Qatar and the UAE.

Following Qatar's attainment of full independence in 1971, the petroleum industry was reorganized, and in 1972 the Qatar National Petroleum Company was created to supervise the country's oil operations. In 1974 the Qatar General Petroleum Corporation (QGPC) was established, and new participation agreements were signed with the foreign oil companies operating in the country, to give the Government a 60% share in profits. In December 1974 the Government announced its intention to purchase the remaining 40% share in the ownership of QGPC and the Shell Company of Qatar. After lengthy negotiations, the state took over the assets and rights of QGPC in September 1976, and acquired those of the Shell Company of Qatar in February 1977.

Qatar's oil production varied considerably during the 1970s and the early 1980s, falling from 570,300 barrels per day (b/d) in 1973 to 437,600 b/d in 1975. By 1979 production had risen to 508,100 b/d, but it subsequently declined rapidly, and in 1982 output averaged only 332,000 b/d. However, even this reduced level of production was higher than Qatar's recommended OPEC quota of 300,000 b/d. In 1983 revenues from petroleum fell by 40%, as production levels fell to an average of 280,000 b/d, but in 1984 output again rose above the country's OPEC allocation, as production averaged 400,000 b/d. However, in October 1984 a meeting of OPEC members reduced the production quota for the country to 280,000 b/d. In spite of falling prices, OPEC effectively abandoned the October 1984 production 'ceiling' in December 1985, when it was decided to seek a larger share of the world market. Qatar's production rose in order to offset a fall in revenue, caused by the decline in petroleum prices, which fell below $10 per barrel in July 1986. Average production in July reached 450,000 b/d. In August OPEC decided to reduce its collective production in an attempt to stabilize prices, and a return to the production quotas which had been allocated in October 1984 was approved for two months beginning in September, permitting Qatar to produce at an average rate of 280,000 b/d. Oil prices rose in response to production restraint and, at a meeting held in October, OPEC's output 'ceiling' was raised, with Qatar's production quota increased to 300,000 b/d for November and December. Official figures indicated that Qatar's average production in 1986 was about 280,000 b/d, although for much of the year it was producing in excess of 300,000 b/d. The extent of its current budget deficit led to demands for Qatar's quota to be increased from the level of 285,000 b/d, which it was allocated by OPEC in December 1986, as part of a programme to support a fixed price for the organization's oil of $18 per barrel in the first half of 1987. Qatar's quota was duly increased to 299,000 b/d for the second half of 1987, and the 'ceiling' on OPEC production was raised by an overall 5%, reflecting the success of the organization's production programme in stabilizing prices. At the OPEC meetings in December 1987 and May 1988, the existing production quotas and the reference price for OPEC oil were retained for the following six months, although, owing to over-production, the price of oil on the 'spot' markets of the world had steadily declined and fell to more than $5 below the organization's target price of $18 per barrel in September 1988. In 1987 Qatar's production averaged 291,000 b/d, but in the first half of 1988 output rose to 330,000 b/d, above the revised quota of 312,000 b/d. Crude oil production stood at 330,000 b/d in May 1989, after fluctuating between 300,000 b/d and 375,000 b/d in early 1989. Crude oil production for the whole of 1989 averaged 395,000 b/d, of which 320,000 b/d were exported. By July 1990 Qatar's OPEC quota had been raised to 371,000 b/d. However, Iraq's invasion of Kuwait in August led to the suspension of quotas in order to allow OPEC member states to compensate for the loss of Iraqi and Kuwaiti production. Between August 1990 and February 1991 Qatari production averaged 420,000 b/d. After the liberation of Kuwait, Qatar's production quota was set by OPEC at 399,000 b/d, but the level was lowered to 377,000 b/d in February 1992 before being raised to 380,000 b/d for the first quarter of 1993 and further reduced to 364,000 b/d from the second quarter of 1993. From the fourth quarter of 1993 Qatar's OPEC production quota was 378,000 b/d. Qatar's actual production of crude oil averaged 385,700 b/d in 1991, 397,100 b/d in 1992 and 416,000 b/d in 1993, after which it fell to an estimated 403,000 b/d in the first five months of 1994.

Among the concessions that Qatar granted for petroleum exploitation in the 1980s was Amoco's 25-year production-sharing agreement for an 8,000-sq km area covering most of the country, except the Dukhan field and part of the north-east, which was concluded at the beginning of 1986. A six-year offshore exploration permit for 2,800 sq km was granted to Elf Aquitaine in 1988. An offshore concession agreement with the group of companies headed by Wintershall was terminated in June 1985, with the discovery of substantial quantities of gas in the area, but the consortium won a partial award against Qatar at the International Arbitration Tribunal at The Hague, after which a production-sharing agreement was concluded. The consortium announced plans in early 1994 for the development of facilities to produce gas and condensate for export before the end of the century.

Qatar's proven crude oil reserves at 1 January 1994 totalled 3,700m. barrels, sufficient for more than 20 years' production at 1993 levels. In mid-1993 QGPC was considering tenders from three oil companies—Elf Aquitaine, Atlantic Richfield and Occidental Petroleum—for a new 'development-cum-technical service agreement' to maximize the country's production of petroleum in return for a share of resultant incremental oil. A large new oilfield, called Diyab and located close to the existing Dukhan field, was expected to begin production in late 1992 or early 1993. Under QGPC's timetable for making available new exploration blocks to foreign oil companies, agreements were expected to be in force in respect of 90% of Qatar's territorial area by the end of 1994. Sustainable production capacity at existing oilfields totalled 450,000 b/d (two-fifths of this from offshore wells) at the end of 1992. A subsidiary of the US company Pennzoil signed a four-year offshore exploration agreement on production-sharing terms in July 1994, this being Qatar's first new exploration agreement for two years.

Qatar's first major refinery, at Umm Said, was commissioned in 1974 for the National Oil Distribution Company (NODCO), which had been founded in 1968 to manage the refining and distribution of oil products. Umm Said refinery had an initial capacity of 6,200 b/d, compared with an earlier refinery, built in 1953, which had a capacity of only 600 b/d. Expansion at Umm Said increased total capacity to 12,000 b/d in 1977. A second refinery, with a capacity of 50,000 b/d, was built by a French company, Technip, and commenced operations in 1984. It is situated close to the original Umm Said refinery and is linked to it. The new refinery was structured to allow for further expansion, to meet the expected increase in local consumption without any need for major modifications or additional equipment. In 1988 two new pipelines were constructed to carry light and heavy products from Umm Said to QGPC's export terminal. In April 1990 the two refineries at Umm Said were processing 62,000 b/d of crude petroleum and exporting 50,000 b/d of oil products. Modifications were being planned that would make it possible to include a proportion of North Field gas condensates in the refineries' mix of feed-stocks.

Qatar's proven reserves of natural gas at the start of 1993 totalled 6,400,000m. cu m, representing 4.6% of total world reserves at that date. The major part of Qatari reserves are in the offshore North Field (the world's largest single deposit of non-associated gas), which was discovered in the 1970s and subsequently assumed a central position in the Government's development plans. Prior to the inauguration of the North Field in 1991, Qatar's gas output was drawn from a relatively small onshore deposit of non-associated gas (used mainly for power generation) and from the onshore and offshore oilfields, whose output of associated gas is processed at two plants at Umm Said. Annual gas output averaged less than 10,000m. cu m during the 1980s, when low output of associated gas at periods of weak oil demand prevented some gas-dependent industries from achieving optimum production levels.

The first phase of Qatar's North Field Development Project (NFDP) is designed to produce a constant 22.6m. cu m per day of gas for domestic use, together with 1.65m. tons per year of liquefied petroleum gas and condensate for export. Having been completed at a cost close to the budgeted $1,300m., the first-phase facilities went into production in September 1991.

The second phase of the NFDP involves the construction of an integrated liquefied natural gas (LNG) complex and associated export facilities at Ras Laffan, at an estimated total cost of as much as $5,000m. The proposed liquefaction plant will have an annual capacity of up to 6m. tons of LNG, of which 4m. tons are to be shipped to Japan under a 25-year agreement with Chubu Electric Power Company. It was anticipated that Japan would play a major role in arranging financing, and that all financing arrangements would be finalized by the end of 1993. Contracts for most of the 'downstream' construction work were signed in July 1993, when the shareholders in the Qatargas company which would operate the LNG plant were QGPC (65%), Mobil (10%), Total (10%), Marubeni Corporation (7.5%) and Mitsui & Company (7.5%). Construction work on the liquefaction plant began in April 1994.

In a separate venture, QGPC (70%) and Mobil (30%) agreed in December 1992 to establish a new company, subsequently incorporated as the Ras Laffan Liquefied Natural Gas Company (RASGAS), with a view to developing another LNG export facility by the end of the decade, at a cost of up to $7,500m. Output of about 10m. tons per year was envisaged, and the most likely export markets were seen as Japan, the Republic of (South) Korea and Taiwan. Details of a project to export dry gas directly to Pakistan by pipeline were being finalized in 1994 by a consortium whose main sponsors were Crescent Petroleum (based in Sharjah, United Arab Emirates), Brown & Root (the US company which would handle the construction work) and TransCanada PipeLines. The consortium proposed to raise $3,200m. of private funding to finance the building of a 1,600-km pipeline with a capacity of 1,600 cu ft per day. The proposed pipeline route would cross about 100 km of land in the far north-east of the UAE (where a compressor station would be sited) but would otherwise run offshore. The proposed completion date was 1998.

INDUSTRY

Qatar's hydrocarbon-based industrialization strategy has centred on the development of 'downstream' processing facilities for oil and gas feedstocks, coupled with some diversification into heavy industry, using local gas as a low-cost fuel source. Three core schemes were initiated at Umm Said in the late 1970s and early 1980s. These are the Qatar Fertilizer Company (QAFCO), the Qatar Petrochemicals Company (QAPCO) and the Qatar Iron and Steel Company (QASCO).

The first of these projects was QAFCO, which was established in 1969 and which, since 1975, has been owned jointly by QGPC (75%) and Norsk Hydro of Norway (25%). Production of fertilizers began in 1973, with gas feedstocks being supplied from the Dukhan field. Work on a second plant, QAFCO II, began in 1976 and was completed in 1979. QAFCO made substantial profits in the first half of the 1980s, experienced a downturn in 1986 and 1987, as a result of difficult conditions in the world market, and made a steady recovery in succeeding years, after taking action to improve productivity. In 1990 production totalled 708,000 tons of ammonia and 761,000 tons of urea. Major export markets included India and China. In 1992 QAFCO's profits reached a record QR 172m. Plans are proceeding to increase QAFCO's production capacity by using gas from the North Field. A third QAFCO plant is to be built to produce 1,500 tons per day of ammonia and 2,000 tons per day of urea. It is expected to commence operations by late 1996, at an estimated cost of $520m.

The petrochemical facilities of QAPCO were commissioned at Umm Said during 1980 and 1981. The company was established in 1974. The plant has a potential capacity of 280,000 tons of ethylene per year, but in its first year of production it produced only 132,679 tons. The plant also produces low-density polyethylene and sulphur. Sales, particularly of ethylene, were substantially below production, and in 1983 plans were cancelled for a high-density polyethylene plant at the complex. In 1984, despite increases in production to 204,000 tons of ethylene, 150,000 tons of low-density polyethylene and 33,000 tons of sulphur, QAPCO operated at a loss of QR 69m. ($19m.). The company suffered from a shortage of ethane-rich gas, and therefore construction of an ethane recovery plant was completed in 1985. Nevertheless, QAPCO made a record loss of QR 156m. in 1985, as a result of the world-wide decline in prices of polyethylene, and a reduction in output of one-third. In early 1986 QAPCO's financial difficulties forced it to renegotiate a $100m. Euroloan which was signed in 1984. However, despite a loss of QR 57m. in 1986, QAPCO recorded a profit of QR 85m. in 1987. In 1988 production of ethylene declined by 2.3%, compared with the previous year, to 256,550 tons, sulphur production fell by 23%, to 36,900 tons, and production of linear low-density polyethylene (LLDPE) fell by 1.8%, to 170,700 tons. In early 1989 the rehabilitation of the value-control system at the ethylene plant was completed. QAPCO's performance in 1989 was much improved, with profits estimated at a record QR 420m., and production of ethylene increasing to 295,000 tons, LLDPE to 181,000 tons and sulphur to 52,000 tons. In September 1990 the French company Atochem, and in June 1991 the Italian company Enichem, each acquired a 10% interest in QAPCO. QGPC holds the remaining 80%. Another initiative in the field of petrochemicals was taken in 1991, when the QGPC and a Canadian company, International Octane, established the Qatar Fuel Additives Company (QAFAC), which was to build a plant to produce methyl tertiary butyl ether (MTBE) and methanol. In June 1992 QAPCO announced a programme of expansion, involving estimated expenditure of $385m., to increase capacity of the ethylene plant at Umm Said from 300,000 to 470,000 tons per year, and to raise the annual LLDPE capacity from 185,000 tons to 360,000 tons. Contracts worth $303m. were signed in March 1994 with a view to completion by early 1996.

The third major scheme, QASCO, was also established in 1974, and consists of a direct reduction plant, two electric-arc furnaces, two continuous casting machines and a rolling mill. The company began commercial production in 1978, and processes imported iron ore and local scrap for export, mainly to Saudi Arabia, Kuwait and the UAE. The Government owns 70% of the complex, and the remainder is held by the Kobe Steel Co of Japan (20%) and Tokyo Boeki (10%). Production levels have risen continuously, from 378,544 tons of steel bars in 1979 to 475,000 tons in 1984. In 1985, however, there was a growing stockpile, due to falling demand and lower world prices, and profits were smaller than anticipated. In an attempt to solve this problem, QASCO reduced its prices in 1985 and placed a 20% import duty on steel from non-GCC countries. In 1985 production reached 510,000 tons, exceeding consumption by 55%. QASCO made a loss of $13.7m. for the year, bringing the plant's accumulated loss since 1978 to about $109m. Following a decline in the level of production of steel bars to 493,000 tons in 1986, QASCO's production rose to 500,000 tons in 1987, and to 533,000 tons (53% above installed capacity) in 1988. The plant made a profit for the first time in 1988, despite a 12.14% increase in prices of raw materials. Production reached more than 550,000 tons in 1989, and a record 565,000 tons in 1990. QASCO assumed the management of the Umm Said steel mill in early 1989, although Japan's Kobe Steel Company, the former managers, maintained a consultancy at the plant. In June 1992 QASCO decided to commission a feasibility study with the aim of increasing capacity at the Umm Said plant by 140,000 tons per year, as the first stage of a plan to raise Qatari steel production to 1m. tons per year. QASCO's output in 1991 was 561,000 tons, yielding a profit of QR 127m. In 1992 production totalled 588,000 tons, yielding a profit of QR 155m., and in 1993 output reached 608,626 tons.

In addition to these major industrial schemes, many small enterprises have been established, mainly at Umm Said, now the industrial centre of the country. In 1973 the Industrial Development Technical Centre (IDTC) was founded to co-ordinate the development of non-oil related industry, and by 1983 it had reported the establishment of 72 industrial ventures. The Qatar Flour Mills Company began production at Umm Bab in 1969, and by 1985 output had reached a level of about 1,700 tons per day. Cement production began in Qatar at a rate of 330,000 tons per year, and was aimed solely at the domestic market. By the mid-1980s cheap imports, particularly from the UAE, had forced the Qatar National Cement Manufacturing Company (QNCMC) to reduce its prices by as much as 30%, but in 1984 production rose by 26%, to 313,000 tons, and profits for the year were QR 13.8m. In 1985 production increased further, to 319,740 tons, which was 1% above the capacity for which the plant was designed. In 1992 output of cement totalled 354,133 tons, output of clinker totalled 313,287 tons, and net profits were QR 25.8m. Other industries in the country include a ready-mix concrete factory, a plastics factory, a paint factory, a detergents company and several light industrial ventures.

Much of Qatar's initial industrial development depended on the operation of a power and desalination complex at Ras Abu Aboud, which can produce 11.5m. gallons of water per day and 210 MW of power. In 1983 a new power and desalination complex came into production at Ras Abu Fontas. Domestic demand for water in Qatar is among the highest per head in the world, and the Government has initiated several schemes to upgrade the water network. Qatar had an installed electricity generating capacity of 1,284 MW, and water desalination capacity of 68m. gallons per day, in mid-1993. The joint-stock Qatar Electricity and Water Company (QEWC) was founded in 1990 to manage the generating installations and associated facilities, leaving distribution under the control of the Ministry of Electricity and Water.

The joint-stock Qatar Industrial Manufacturing Company (QIMCO), established in 1990 to promote industrial joint ventures, made a net profit of QR 7m. in 1992, when it held investments of QR 64.5m. in eight industrial projects. In June 1993, in an attempt to attract foreign investment for industrial projects, the Government approved legislation to reduce the maximum rate of taxation on profits earned by foreign partners in joint ventures from 50% to 35%.

AGRICULTURE AND FISHING

Qatar's agricultural activity increased steadily during the 1970s, with the number of producing farms rising from 338 in 1975 to 406 in 1979. However, during the same period the number of non-producing farms also rose, owing to increased problems of water supply and water salinity. Agriculture (including forestry and fishing) provided less than 2% of Qatar's GDP in 1987. All agricultural land in the country is owned by the Government, and most farm owners participate only indirectly in the farming process, having permanent positions in other sectors of the economy. Consequently, most farms in Qatar are administered by immigrant managers employing Omani, Palestinian, Iranian and Egyptian labour. Vegetable production has been the most successful sector of the agrarian economy, and Qatar is now thought to be self-sufficient in winter vegetables, and nearly self-sufficient in summer vegetables, with some being exported to other Gulf countries. In 1987 vegetable production rose to 19,200 tons, cereal production rose to 3,000 tons, and fodder production to 70,000 tons. In 1985 date and other fruit trees accounted for 38% of cultivable land, vegetables for 37%, green fodder for 13% and cereals for 12%. In 1986 the value of agricultural production reached QR 318.1m. ($87.4m.), of which QR 87.3m. ($24m.) was accounted for by farm production; and cereal imports declined from 105,449 tons in 1985 to 95,936 tons in 1986, when 6% of Qatar's cereal requirements were met by local production. The Arab Investment and Agricultural Development Organization (AIADO) established the Arab-Qatari Company for Vegetable Production (AQCVP) in 1989. A dairy farm, completed in 1984, can satisfy about 60% of the local demand for dairy products. Egg production averaged about 1m. per year in 1985, which was sufficient to meet 80% of local demand. In 1988 the Arab-Qatari Dairy Company, in a joint venture with the Arab Company for Livestock Development, initiated a scheme to produce green fodder on 637 ha. In 1985 a study by the Arab Organization for the Development of Agriculture pointed out that the main problems facing the farming sector were lack of irrigation, soil infertility, harsh weather conditions, lack of pasture land and the unwillingness of Qataris to invest in agriculture. At the end of 1986, the Government announced a three-year programme to drill 77 wells, to a depth of 70 m, in order to increase the water resources available for agricultural purposes. At the end of 1991 Qatar and Iran announced plans for a $13,000m. pipeline to carry drinking water to Qatar from Iran's Karum river. In April 1992 the AQCVP signed a $5m. contract with Dace of the Netherlands for the supply of greenhouses, sufficient to treble the company's covered growing area.

Most of the country's fishing is undertaken by the Qatar National Fishing Company (QNFC), which was formed in 1966 and was nationalized in 1980. By 1985 the company had a refrigeration and processing plant near Doha, capable of handling 7 tons of shrimps per day. From the mid-1970s until 1980 the annual catch was estimated at about 2,000 tons. The total rose to 2,604 tons in 1981, but fell to 2,114 tons in 1983. In 1984 the QNFC achieved net profits of QR 1.9m., representing an increase of 24% compared with 1983's profits, and its total catch constituted 17% of local consumption. The catch in 1987 totalled 2,678 tons, increasing by 13.2% in 1988, to 3,086 tons.

In May 1992 the Government announced the provision of interest-free loans of up to QR 500,000 to farmers and fishermen, to encourage production by promoting modernization. The loans, repayable over 10 years, were to be administered by a special committee, established by the Ministry of Agriculture and Municipal Affairs. The value of agricultural and fisheries production totalled QR 487.8m. in 1992 (crops QR 241.3m., animal products QR 198.3m., fish QR 48.2m.), constituting 1.8% of GDP, while Qatar's 1992 spending on imports of foodstuffs and animals totalled QR 928.5m. Apart from forage (146,055 tons), the crops produced in 1992 were vegetables (40,691 tons), fruit and dates (10,499 tons) and cereals (3,872 tons). Some 26,659 tons of milk and dairy produce, 2,405 tons of bovine meat, 3,474 tons of eggs and 3,833 tons of poultry meat were produced in Qatar in 1992, while 7,845 tons of fish were marketed.

BUDGET AND FINANCE

The increases in petroleum revenue which occurred in the 1970s resulted in large budget surpluses, which enabled Qatar to embark on its impressive programme of industrial and infrastructural projects. However, after achieving a budget surplus of QR 7,993m. in 1980, the country recorded a deficit of QR 566m. in 1983. This was largely due to the fall in petroleum exports, and, in order to alleviate the problem, government current expenditure was reduced from QR 10,980m. in 1982 to QR 8,496m. in 1983. As a result of these cutbacks, less foreign investment was attracted to the country, and liquidity levels consequently suffered. In 1984/85, in an attempt to solve this problem, the government increased expenditure to QR 12,173m. As a result of the collapse of petroleum prices, no budget was announced for 1986/87, but it was understood that ministries were asked not to exceed the previous year's budget. In early 1986 the Government deferred $80m. worth of contracts. The 1987/88 budget envisaged total expenditure of QR 12,217m., 22% less than in the 1985/86 budget, and revenue of QR 6,745m., 30% less than in the previous budget. A deficit of QR 5,472m. was predicted, to be financed from foreign reserves and assets. The budget proposals contained no provisions for any substantial investment in the areas of gas, power or desalination, but placed more emphasis on social services, in an attempt to stimulate the depressed contracting sector. Expenditure on defence, however, continued to increase, and in 1986 France agreed to supply Qatar with four *Mirage* F-1 fighter aircraft, missiles and a radar system, at a cost of $243m. Nevertheless, the actual deficit for 1987, according to the Qatar Monetary Agency (QMA), was 34% below the predicted figure. The 1988/89 budget forecast total expenditure of QR 12,442.5m., revenue of QR 6,335.8m. and a budget deficit of QR 6,106.7m., the highest level yet projected. The 1989/90 budget, however, predicted a reduced deficit of QR 5,700m., with revenue falling to QR 5,800m., and expenditure (excluding military spending) falling to QR 11,480m.

From 1989 Qatar's financial year began on 1 April. The estimated budget deficit was QR 5,648m. in 1989/90, declining to QR 3,923m. in 1990/91, QR 3,268m. in 1991/92 and QR 2,792m. in 1992/93, when expenditure was projected at QR 12,399m., compared with revenue of QR 9,607m. The 1993/94 budget envisaged expenditure of QR 13,076.5m., of which QR 2,708.2m. was to be capital spending, and revenue of QR 10,373.2m., resulting in a deficit of QR 2,703.3m. Projected capital spending for 1993/94 included QR 994m. for public services and infrastructure; QR 1,059m. for economic services; QR 552m. for social and health services; and QR 103m. for education and youth welfare. The 1994/95 budget made provision for a 20% fall in revenue to QR 8,359m. (mainly because of low oil prices). Total expenditure was set to fall by 10% to QR 11,830m. (including a capital budget of QR 2,320m.), while the budget deficit was projected to rise by 28% to QR 3,471m. Cutbacks in expenditure were to include a halt to property loans for citizens, an accelerated shift from expatriate to local labour, and closures of some overseas information offices. The capital spending allocations for 1994/95 were public services and infrastructure projects QR 1,031m. (including QR 151m. for roads, QR 174m. for sewerage and QR 135m. for land purchases); economic services and industrial projects (including water and power supplies and airport expansion) QR 1,022m.; and health, social services, education and youth welfare QR 267m. Plans were being drawn up in 1994 to introduce treasury instruments to cover the budget deficit (hitherto financed by government borrowing from domestic banks).

In 1991 the QMA and 15 other banks were operating in Qatar. Three of these, the Qatar National Bank (QNB), the Commercial Bank of Qatar and the Doha Bank, are entirely locally owned, and there are 10 foreign banks. In 1992 the QNB had total assets of QR 14,830m. and made a net profit of QR 305.5m.; the Commercial Bank of Qatar recorded total assets of QR 1,721.3m. and made a net profit of QR 21.9m.; and the Doha Bank had total assets of QR 2,733.1m. and made a net profit of QR 38m. In October 1993 the QMA was superseded by the Qatar Central Bank, with paid-up capital of QR 50m. and overall capital and reserves totalling QR 156m. (unchanged at the start of 1994). The Central Bank's end-1993 assets totalled QR 2,875.1m. (including QR 2,599.2m. of foreign assets), while the principal liabilities on its end-1993 balance sheet were currency issued to the value of QR 1,517.7m. and local banks' deposits totalling QR 662.9m. The Central Bank has supervisory powers over all banks, foreign exchange houses, investment companies and finance houses operating in Qatar. Proposals to establish a local stock exchange were under consideration by the Government in 1994.

In addition to investment in industrial diversification at home, Qatar also allocated considerable sums of aid to poorer countries during the 1970s. In 1975 the level of aid was $339m., but in 1980 the total declined to $277m., representing 4.2% of GNP. In October 1990 the Government announced that the debts owing to it by 10 Arab and African countries (Cameroon, Egypt, Guinea, Mali, Mauritania, Morocco, Somalia, Syria, Tunisia and Uganda) were to be cancelled. The World Bank estimated that Qatar extended net aid of around $1m. (0.01% of GNP) in 1991 and that its cumulative net aid over the five years 1987–91 amounted to just $4m.

TRADE AND TRANSPORT

A primary objective in development has been to diversify Qatar's economic base away from dependence on petroleum. However, despite the decline in the price of oil during 1986 and its subsequent fragility, oil revenues continue to dominate the country's export earnings.

During the 1970s imports and exports grew quickly, but in the early 1980s there was a fall in Qatar's levels of trade. Imports were reduced over the period 1982–84, and in 1985 their value declined to QR 4,146.5m., the lowest annual total since 1976. The value of exports fell from QR 20,787m. in 1980 to QR 12,002m. in 1983, reflecting the reduction in petroleum exports. By 1985 the value of exports had declined to QR 11,277m. The value of imports fell to QR 3,999m. in 1986, and reached QR 4,128m. in 1987. Lower petroleum prices caused the value of exports to fall to QR 6,710m. in 1986, but it recovered to QR 7,224m. in 1987 and QR 8,045m. in 1988. The value of imports rose to QR 4,613m. in 1988, to QR 4,827m. in 1989, to QR 6,169m. in 1990 and to QR 6,261m. in 1991. Export earnings were QR 9,967m. in 1989 and QR 14,161m. in 1990, but fell to QR 11,684m. in 1991. In 1987 Japan provided 17% of Qatar's imports, followed by the UK (16.4%) and the Federal Republic of Germany (9.6%). Japan took 38.5% of Qatar's exports, followed by Singapore (13.1%). Japan remained Qatar's main trading partner in 1988, providing $172.5m. in imports and taking $1,139m. in exports. In 1989 Japan provided 19% of Qatar's imports, and the UK 12%. Japanese imports from Qatar rose to $1,546m. in 1989, to $2,153m. in 1990 and to $2,157m. in 1991. The principal suppliers of Qatar's imports in 1991 were Japan (accounting for 13.6% of the total), the UK (11.8%) and the USA (11.6%). According to analysts, Japan's imports of Qatari crude petroleum in 1988 accounted for more than one-half of the estimated value of Qatar's total oil exports. The principal commodities that Qatar imports are electrical items and machinery, and there is also considerable importation of food and live animals, textiles, clothing and chemicals. Apart from its exports of petroleum, most of Qatar's export trade is with its Arab neighbours. As a member of the GCC, Qatar brought its rates of customs duties into accordance with those of the other GCC member states in 1984, raising the duty for general goods from 2.5% to 4%.

In 1992 Qatar's exports were valued at QR 13,980m. (68% of this from petroleum) and its imports at QR 7,336m., leaving a visible trade surplus of QR 6,644m. Net outgoings of QR 6,703m. on the services account placed the current account in deficit by QR 59m., while net capital transfers of QR 400m. raised the overall balance-of-payments deficit to QR 459m. In early 1994 the Qatar Government was negotiating a $250m. sovereign loan for balance-of-payments support from a consortium of international banks.

The first contracts for a major port development project at Doha were awarded in mid-1993. Extensive dredging work on the 17-km port approach channel would serve the dual purpose of upgrading the maritime access facility and providing land-fill material to create 360,000 sq m of new quayside space at the port and to fill some 3.55m. sq m of reclaimed land, which was designated as the site of a new international airport. Also under development at Doha was a new container terminal with two berths and a roll-on, roll-off facility.

The Qatar Shipping Company, established in 1992, was scheduled to inaugurate a passenger and car ferry service between Doha and Bahrain in late 1994, while expanding its cargo-carrying capabilities to include the transport of crude oil, liquefied petroleum gas, petrochemicals and iron ore. The Qatar Government is a co-owner of the regional airline Gulf Air. Qatar Airways was established by Qatari business interests in 1993 and introduced its inaugural services (on routes to the United Arab Emirates and at fares which undercut Gulf Air) in January 1994. By July 1994 the new airline had added services to Colombo, Amman, Bombay, London, Kuwait and Cairo and expected to start flying to Damascus and Beirut in the near future as part of its plans to serve 12 international destinations by early 1995. The airline was wholly dependent on leased aircraft in mid-1994, but did not rule out the option of purchasing aircraft as it expanded its operations. Preliminary planning for Qatar's proposed new international airport envisaged a handling capacity of 3.5m. passengers per year and an opening date of 1998. The estimated cost exceeded $300m., and financing was to be sought from non-government sources.

SOCIAL SERVICES

In 1981 Qatar had four government hospitals, with a total of 733 beds, and there were 186 physicians working in official medical services. In 1988, according to the World Health Organization, there were 20 physicians, three dentists and 51 nurses for every 10,000 inhabitants in Qatar, the highest ratios for any Arab country. The Hamad General Hospital (opened in 1982) has 683 beds, and a 314-bed extension for women was due to be completed in 1987. In 1986 there were 21 local clinics and 22 school health clinics. A new hospital for women, offering 188 maternity beds, was due to open in September 1988. Social welfare developments within the country have been a high priority. Education has expanded, and by 1987 there were 172 schools in the country. The University of Qatar was established in 1977, and new campus buildings were completed in February 1985. In the 1991/92 fiscal year it was estimated that QR 282m. would be allocated to housing, education and health services.

Under the 1993/94 government budget, social services and health were allocated a total of QR 552m. plus an additional QR 235m. of capital funding from outside the budget. Major health facilities under development included a children's hospital and an outpatients' clinic, while there was a house-building target of more than 3,000 new dwellings in 1993/94. The 1994/95 capital budget for health and social services totalled QR 200.3m., to include broadcasting transmission stations as well as health centres and housing projects. A capital alllocation of QR 103m. for education and youth welfare in 1993/94 envisaged the construction of 13 schools and a new science faculty building at the University of Qatar. There was a continuing emphasis on school and university premises within the 1994/95 allocation of QR 66.7m.

Statistical Survey

Source (unless otherwise stated): Press and Publications Dept., Ministry of Information, POB 5147, Doha; telex 4552.

AREA AND POPULATION

Area: 11,437 sq km (4,416 sq miles).

Population: 369,079 (males 247,852; females 121,227) at census of 16 March 1986; 532,719 (official estimate) at mid-1992.

Density: 46.6 per sq km (mid-1992).

Principal Towns (population at March 1986): Doha (capital) 217,294; Rayyan 91,996; Wakrah 23,682; Umm Salal 11,161.

Births, Marriages and Deaths (1992): Registered live births 10,459 (birth rate 19.6 per 1,000); Registered marriages 1,578 (marriage rate 3.0 per 1,000); Registered deaths 944 (death rate 1.8 per 1,000).

Expectation of Life (UN estimates, years at birth, 1985–90): 68.6 (males 66.9; females 71.8). Source: UN, *World Population Prospects: The 1992 Revision.*

Economically Active Population (persons aged 15 years and over, March 1986): Agriculture and fishing 6,283; Mining and quarrying 4,807; Manufacturing 13,914; Electricity, gas and water 5,266; Building and construction 40,523; Trade, restaurants and hotels 21,964; Transport and communications 7,357; Finance, insurance and real estate 3,157; Social and community services 96,466; Activities not adequately defined 501; Total employed 200,238. **Mid-1992** (estimate): Total labour force 233,000 (Source: FAO, *Production Yearbook*).

AGRICULTURE, ETC.

Principal Crops ('000 metric tons, 1992): Cereals 3.87; Vegetables 40.7; Dates 9.5; Other fruit 0.9.

Livestock ('000 head, 1992): Horses 1; Cattle 11; Camels 29; Sheep 142; Goats 123; Deer 4, Chickens 3,517.

Livestock Products ('000 metric tons, 1992): Mutton and lamb 2.4; Poultry meat 3.8; milk and dairy products 26.7.

Fishing (metric tons, live weight, 1992): Total catch 7,845.

MINING

Production ('000 metric tons, unless otherwise indicated, 1991): Crude petroleum 18,831; Natural gas (petajoules) 339; Natural gasolene 180 (estimate). Source: UN, *Industrial Statistics Yearbook.*

INDUSTRY

Production ('000 metric tons, unless otherwise indicated, 1990): Wheat flour 112; Nitrogenous fertilizers (nitrogen content) 761 (official figure); Jet fuels 427 (1991); Motor spirit (petrol) 399 (1991); Distillate fuel oils 702 (1991); Residual fuel oils 943 (1991); Liquefied petroleum gas 1,360 (estimate 1991); Cement 336 (estimate 1991); Steel bars 588 (1992); Electric energy 4,716 million kWh (1991). Source: mainly UN, *Industrial Statistics Yearbook.*

FINANCE

Currency and Exchange Rates: 100 dirhams = 1 Qatar riyal (QR). *Sterling and Dollar Equivalents* (31 May 1994): £1 sterling = 5.503 riyals; US $1 = 3.640 riyals; 100 Qatar riyals = £18.17 = $27.47. *Exchange Rate:* Since June 1980 the rate has been fixed at US $1 = QR 3.64.

Budget (QR million, year ending 31 March): 1989/90: *Revenue:* 9,300; *Expenditure:* 10,525; 1990/91 (provisional): *Revenue:* 11,948; *Expenditure:* 11,388; 1991/92 (estimates): *Revenue:* 9,170; *Expenditure:* 10,600; 1992/93 (estimates): *Revenue* 9,607; *Expenditure* 12,399; 1993/94 (estimates): *Revenue* 10,373; *Expenditure* 13,077.

International Reserves (US $ million at 31 December 1993): Gold 41.5; IMF special drawing rights 25.6; Reserve position in IMF 46.4; Foreign exchange 621.7; Total 735.2. Source: IMF, *International Financial Statistics.*

Money Supply (QR million at 31 December 1992): Currency outside banks 1,311.5; Demand deposits at commercial banks 2,669.1; Total money 3,980.6.

Cost of Living (Consumer Price Index for Doha; base: 1988 = 100): 106.4 in 1990; 111.1 in 1991; 114.5 in 1992.

Expenditure on the Gross Domestic Product: (estimates, QR million at current prices, 1992): Government final consumption expenditure 8,990; Private final consumption expenditure 8,367;

Increase in stocks 275; Gross fixed capital formation 4,900; *Total domestic expenditure* 22,532; Exports of goods and services 13,920; *Less* Imports of goods and services 9,250; *GDP in purchasers' values* 27,202.

Gross Domestic Product by Economic Activity (preliminary estimates, QR million at current prices, 1992): Agriculture and fishing 242; Petroleum sector 9,750; Non-petroleum manufacturing 3,450; Electricity and water 309; Construction 1,110; Trade, restaurants and hotels 1,822; Transport and communications 798; Finance, insurance, real estate and business services 2,943; Other services 6,778; Total 27,202.

Balance of Payments (estimates, QR million, 1992): Exports f.o.b. 13,980; Imports c.i.f. –7,336; Trade balance 6,644; Services, private and official transfers (net) –6,703; Current balance –59; Capital (net) –400; Overall balance –459.

EXTERNAL TRADE

Imports c.i.f. (QR million): 6,169 in 1990; 6,261 in 1991; 7,336 in 1992.

Exports f.o.b. (QR million): 14,161 in 1990; 11,684 in 1991; 13,980 in 1992.

Principal Commodities (distribution by SITC, QR million, 1992): *Imports c.i.f.:* Food and live animals 928.5; Crude materials (inedible) except fuels 229.8; Chemicals and related products 462.5; Basic manufactures 1,333.7; Machinery and transport equipment 3,232.9; Miscellaneous manufactured articles 971.5; Total (incl. others) 7,336.0.

Principal Trading Partners (QR million): *Imports* (1992): Australia 162.1; France 404.7; Germany 532.2; Italy 481.5; Japan 1,144.9; Netherlands 203.3; Saudi Arabia 263.7; United Arab Emirates 270.3; United Kingdom 819.8; USA 838.6; Total (incl. others) 7,336.0. *Exports* (petroleum only, 1983): France 708.0; Federal Republic of Germany 403.0; Italy 806.0; Japan 5,119.7; Spain 620.9; Total (incl. others) 10,893.

TRANSPORT

Road Traffic (licensed vehicles, 1992): Government 5,169; Private 122,000; Public Transport 55,079; Heavy vehicles 3,847; Taxis 1,573; Motorcycles 2,798; Trailers 1,758; General transport 624; Total 192,848.

Shipping (international sea-borne freight traffic, '000 metric tons, 1990): *Goods loaded:* 18,145; *Goods unloaded:* 2,588. Source: UN, *Monthly Bulletin of Statistics*; (shipping fleet, '000 gross registered tons, mid-1991): 160. Source: UN, *Statistical Yearbook.*

Civil Aviation (scheduled services 1991): Kilometres flown 11 million; Passengers carried 876,000; Passenger-km 1,676 million; Freight ton-km 51 million. Figures include an apportionment (one-quarter) of the traffic of Gulf Air, a multinational airline with its headquarters in Bahrain. Source: UN, *Statistical Yearbook.*

TOURISM

Tourist arrivals (1990): 100,000. Source: UN, *Statistical Yearbook.*

Hotel beds (1992): 2,310.

COMMUNICATIONS MEDIA

Radio Receivers: 195,000 in use (1991).

Television Receivers: 198,000 in use (1991).

Telephones: 139,000 in use (1990).

Daily Newspapers: 5 in 1990.

Non-daily Newspapers: 1 in 1990.

Book Titles Published: 521 in 1990.

Sources: UNESCO, *Statistical Yearbook*; UN, *Statistical Yearbook.*

EDUCATION

Pre-primary (1991): 54 schools; 357 teachers; 5,684 pupils.

Primary: (1991): 157 schools; 4,598 teachers; 48,785 pupils.

Secondary (1991): 3,724 teachers (general 3,593, vocational 131); 31,120 pupils (general 30,277, vocational 843).

University (1992/93): 605 teaching staff; 6,666 students.

Directory

The Constitution

A provisional Constitution was adopted on 2 April 1970. Executive power is vested in the Amir, as Head of State, and exercised by the Council of Ministers, appointed by the Head of State, who is also Prime Minister. The Amir is assisted by the appointed Advisory Council of 20 members (increased to 30 in December 1975 and to 35 in November 1988), whose term was extended for six years in May 1975, for a further four years in May 1978, and for further terms of four years in 1982, 1986 and 1990. All fundamental democratic rights are guaranteed. In December 1975 the Advisory Council was granted power to summon individual ministers to answer questions on legislation before promulgation. Previously the Advisory Council was restricted to debating draft bills and regulations before framing recommendations to the Council of Ministers.

The Government

HEAD OF STATE

Amir: Sheikh KHALIFA BIN HAMAD ATH-THANI (assumed power 22 February 1972).

COUNCIL OF MINISTERS
(October 1994)

Prime Minister: Sheikh KHALIFA BIN HAMAD ATH-THANI.

Deputy Amir, Heir Apparent, Minister of Defence and Commander-in-Chief of the Armed Forces: Maj.-Gen. Sheikh HAMAD BIN KHALIFA ATH-THANI.

Minister of Finance, Economy and Trade: Sheikh MUHAMMAD BIN KHALIFA ATH-THANI.

Minister of Foreign Affairs: Sheikh HAMAD BIN JABER ATH-THANI.

Minister of Education: ABD AL-AZIZ ABDULLAH TURKI.

Minister of Health: Sheikh HAMAD BIN SUHAIM ATH-THANI.

Minister of Justice: Sheikh AHMAD BIN SAIF ATH-THANI.

Minister of the Interior: Sheikh ABDULLAH BIN KHALIFA ATH-THANI.

Minister of State for Defence Affairs and Deputy Commander-in-Chief of the Armed Forces: Sheikh HAMAD BIN ABDULLAH ATH-THANI.

Minister of Awqaf (Religious Endowments) and Islamic Affairs: Sheikh ABDULLAH BIN KHALID ATH-THANI.

Minister of Electricity and Water: AHMAD MUHAMMAD ALI AS-SUBAY'I.

Minister of Energy and Industry: ABDULLAH BIN HAMAD AL-ATTIYA.

Minister of Information and Culture: Dr ABD AL-AZIZ HAMAD AL-KUWARI.

Minister of Municipal Affairs and Agriculture: Sheikh AHMAD BIN HAMAD ATH-THANI.

Minister of Labour, Social Affairs and Housing: ABD AR-RAHMAN SAAD AD-DIRHAM.

Minister of Communication and Transport: ABDULLAH BIN SALEH AL-MANEI.

Minister of Amiri Diwan (Royal Court) Affairs: Dr ISSA GHANIM AL-KAWARI.

MINISTRIES

Ministry of Amiri Diwan Affairs: POB 923, Doha; tel. 468333; telex 4297; fax 412617.

Ministry of Awqaf (Religious Endowments) and Islamic Affairs: POB 232, Doha; tel. 466222; fax 327383.

Ministry of Communication and Transport: POB 3416, Doha; tel. 464000; telex 4800; fax 835888.

Ministry of Defence: Qatar Armed Forces, POB 37, Doha; tel. 404111; telex 4245.

Ministry of Education: POB 80, Doha; tel. 413444; telex 4316; fax 351780.

Ministry of Electricity and Water: POB 41, Doha; tel. 326622; telex 4478; fax 420048.

Ministry of Energy and Industry: POB 2599, Doha; tel. 832121; telex 4323.

Ministry of Finance, Economy and Trade: POB 83, Doha; tel. 434888; telex 4315; fax 413617.

Ministry of Foreign Affairs: POB 250, Doha; tel. 415000; telex 4577; fax 426279.

Ministry of Information and Culture: POB 1836, Doha; tel. 831333; telex 4229; fax 831518.

Ministry of the Interior: POB 920, Doha; tel. 330000; telex 4383.

Ministry of Justice: POB 917 (Dept of Legal Affairs), Doha; tel. 427444; telex 4238; fax 832868.

Ministry of Labour, Social Affairs and Housing: POB 201, Doha; tel. 321934; telex 4227; fax 432929.

Ministry of Municipal Affairs and Agriculture: POB 2727, Doha; tel. 413535; telex 4476; fax 413233.

Ministry of Public Health: POB 42, Doha; tel. 441555; telex 4261; fax 429565.

ADVISORY COUNCIL

The Advisory Council was established in April 1972, with 20 nominated members. It was expanded to 30 members in December 1975, and to 35 members in November 1988.

Speaker: ALI BIN KHALIFA AL-HITMI.

Diplomatic Representation

EMBASSIES IN QATAR

Algeria: POB 2494, Doha; tel. 662900; telex 4604; fax 663658; Ambassador: MUHAMMAD TALIB.

Bangladesh: POB 2080, Doha; tel. 671927; telex 5102; fax 671190; Ambassador: Kazi NASRUL ISLAM.

China, People's Republic: POB 17200, Doha; tel. 824200; telex 5120; fax 873959; Ambassador: TAN SHENGCHENG.

Egypt: POB 2899, Doha; tel. 832555; telex 4321; fax 832196; Ambassador: MOSTAFA MAHMOUD HUSSEIN.

France: POB 2669, Doha; tel. 832281; telex 4280; fax 832254; Ambassador: ANDRÉ JANIER.

Germany: POB 3064, Doha; tel. 671100; telex 4528; fax 670011; Ambassador: KLAUS SHRÖDER.

India: POB 2788, Doha; tel. 672067; telex 4646; fax 670448; Ambassador: K. P. FABIAN.

Iran: POB 1633, Doha; tel. 835300; telex 4251; fax 831665; Ambassador: SEYED BAGHER SAKHAIE.

Iraq: POB 1526, Doha; tel. 662244; telex 4296; Ambassador: ANWAR SABRI ADL AR-RAZZAQ.

Italy: POB 4188, Doha; tel. 436842; telex 5133; fax 446466; Ambassador: MARIO BONDIOLI-OSIO.

Japan: POB 2208, Doha; tel. 831224; telex 4339; fax 832178; Ambassador: MASAO KAWASE.

Jordan: POB 2366, Doha; tel. 832202; telex 4192; fax 832173; Ambassador: TRAD EL-FAYEZ.

Korea, Republic: POB 3727, Doha; tel. 832238; telex 4105; fax 833264; Ambassador: NAM JOON CHOI.

Kuwait: POB 1177, Doha; tel. 832111; telex 4113; fax 832042; Ambassador: M. AHMAD AR-ROUMI.

Lebanon: POB 2411, Doha; tel. 444468; telex 4404; fax 324817; Chargé d'affaires: ABDALLAH COMATY.

Mauritania: POB 3132, Doha; tel. 670458; telex 4379; fax 670455; Ambassador: OTHAMN AL-MALLI.

Morocco: POB 3242, Doha; tel. 831885; telex 4473; fax 833416; Ambassador: ABBES BERRADA SOUNNI.

Oman: POB 3766, Doha; tel. 670744; telex 4341; fax 670747; Ambassador: SAID BIN ALI BIN SALIM AL-KALBANI.

Pakistan: POB 334, Doha; tel. 832525; fax 832227; Ambassador: Mir MUHAMMED NASEER MENGAL.

Philippines: POB 24900, Doha; tel. 831585; fax 831595; Chargé d'Affaires: MARIANO DUMIA.

Romania: POB 22511, Doha; tel. 426740; fax 444348; Ambassador: AUREL TURBACEANU.

Russia: POB 15404, Doha; tel. 417417; Ambassador: MIKHAIL YOUDIN.

Saudi Arabia: POB 1255, Doha; tel. 427144; telex 4483; fax 883049; Ambassador: ABD AR-RAHMAN ASH-SHUBAILI.

Somalia: POB 1948, Doha; tel. 832200; telex 4275; Ambassador: SHARIF MUHAMMAD OMAR.

Sudan: POB 2999, Doha; tel. 423007; telex 4707; fax 351366; Ambassador: AWAD ELKARIM FADLALLA.

Syria: POB 1257, Doha; tel. 421873; telex 4447; fax 442167; Chargé d'Affaires: NIZAR AL-JOUNDI.

Tunisia: POB 2707, Doha; tel. 832645; telex 4422; fax 832649; Ambassador: M. HEDI DRISSI.

Turkey: POB 1977, Doha; tel. 865885; telex 4406; fax 864393; Ambassador: SELCUK TARLAN.

United Arab Emirates: POB 3099, Doha; tel. 822833; fax 822837; Ambassador: MUHAMMAD SULTAN EL-ZA'ABI.

United Kingdom: POB 3, Doha; tel. 421991; fax 438692; Ambassador: PATRICK FRANCIS MICHAEL WOGAN.

USA: POB 2399, Doha; tel. 864701; telex 4847; fax 861669; Ambassador: KENTON KEITH.

Yemen: POB 3318, Doha; tel. 432555; telex 5130; fax 429400; Ambassador: ABD AL-WAHAB NASSER JAHAF.

Judicial System

Justice is administered by five courts (Higher Criminal, Lower Criminal, Commercial and Civil, Labour and the Court of Appeal) on the basis of codified laws. In addition the *Shari'a* Court decides on all issues regarding the personal affairs of Muslims, specific offences where the defendant is Muslim, and civil disputes where the parties elect to have them adjudicated upon, by recourse to Islamic Law of the Holy Quran and the Prophet's Sunna or tradition. Non-Muslims are invariably tried by a court operating codified law. Independence of the judiciary is guaranteed by the provisional Constitution.

Presidency of Shari'a Courts and Islamic Affairs: POB 232, Doha; tel. 452222; telex 5115; Pres. Sheikh ABDUL BIN SAID AL-MAHMOUD.

Chief Justice: AL-FATEH AWOUDA.

Religion

The indigenous population are Muslims of the Sunni sect, most being of the strict Wahhabi persuasion.

The Press

Al-Ahd (The Pledge): POB 2531, Doha; tel. 601506; telex 4920; fax 671388; f. 1974; weekly magazine; Arabic; political; publ. by al-Ahd Est. for Journalism, Printing and Publications Ltd; Editor-in-Chief KHALIFA AL-HUSSAINI; circ. 15,000.

Akhbar al-Usbou' (News of the Week): POB 4896, Doha; tel. 445561; telex 4234; fax 433778; f. 1986; weekly magazine; Arabic; socio-political; publ. by Ali bin Ali Printing and Publishing Est.; Editor-in-Chief ADEL ALI BIN ALI; circ. 15,000.

Al-'Arab (The Arabs): POB 633, Doha; tel. 325874; telex 4497; fax 429424; f. 1972; daily; Arabic; publ. by Dar al-Ouroba Printing and Publishing; Editor-in-Chief KHALID NAAMA; circ. 20,000.

Aswaq al-Khaleej (Gulf Markets): POB 3344, Doha; tel. 436518; fax 439859; f. 1980; weekly; Arabic; economic; publ. by Dar Annabaa Press, Printing and Publishing; Editor-in-Chief M. SALIM AL-KUWARI; circ. 2,000.

Ad-Dawri (The Tournament): POB 310, Doha; tel. 447039; fax 447039; f. 1978; weekly; Arabic; sport; publ. by Abdullah Hamad al-Atiyah and Ptnrs; Editor-in-Chief Sheikh RASHID BIN OWAIDA ATH-THANI; circ. 2,000.

Gulf Times: POB 2888, Doha; tel. 350478; telex 4600; fax 350474; f. 1978; daily and weekly editions; English; political; publ. by Gulf Publishing and Printing Org.; Editor-in-Chief ABD AR-RAHMAN SAIF AL-MADHADI; circ. 15,000 (daily).

Al-Jawhara (The Jewel): POB 2531, Doha; tel. 423526; telex 4920; fax 671388; f. 1977; monthly; Arabic; women's magazine; publ. by al-Ahd Est. for Journalism, Printing and Publications Ltd; Editor-in-Chief ABDULLAH YOUSUF AL-HUSSAINI; circ. 5,000.

Al-Mash'al (The Torch): Qatar General Petroleum Corporation, POB 3212, Doha; tel. 491491; telex 4343; fax 831125; f. 1977; 2 a month; Arabic and English; Editor-in-Chief FAISAL A. AS-SUWAIDI; circ. 3,000.

Al-Masha'il (The Torches): POB 1838, Doha; tel. 448282; fax 446723; f. 1987; monthly; Arabic; children's magazine; publ. by Qatar Est. for Journalism, Printing and Publication; Editor-in-Chief HAMAD BIN ABD AR-RAHMAN ATH-THANI; circ. 16,000.

Al-Murshid (The Guide): POB 8545, Doha; tel. 429920; telex 4420; fax 447793; f. 1983; bi-monthly; Arabic and English; tourist and commercial information; publ. by Dallah Advertising Agency; Editor-in-Chief RASHID MUHAMMAD AN-NOAIMI; circ. 15,000.

Nada (A Gathering): POB 4896, Doha; tel. 445564; telex 4234; fax 433778; f. 1991; weekly; social and entertainment; published by Akhbar al-Usbou'; Editor-in-Chief ADEL ALI BIN ALI.

Al-Ouroba (Arabism): POB 633, Doha; tel. 325874; telex 4497; fax 429424; f. 1970; weekly; political; publ. by Dar al-Ouroba Press and Publishing; Editor-in-Chief ABDULLAH HUSSAIN NAAMA; circ. 12,000.

Qatar Lil Inshaa (Qatar Construction): POB 4500, Doha; tel. 417800; telex 4877; fax 437302; f. 1989; publ. Almaha Trade and Construction Co; Gen. Man. MUHAMMAD H. AL-MIJBER; circ. 10,000.

Ar-Rayah (The Banner): POB 3464, Doha; tel. 810536; telex 4600; fax 810456; f. 1979; daily and weekly editions; Arabic; political; publ. by Gulf Publishing and Printing Org.; Editor AHMAD ALI; circ. 25,000.

Ash-Sharq (The Orient): POB 3488, Doha; tel. 662444; telex 5103; fax 662450; f. 1985; daily; Arabic; political; publ. by Ash-Sharq Printing, Publishing and Distribution House; Gen. Supervisor NASSER AL-OTHMAN; circ. 40,000.

At-Tarbiya (Education): POB 9865, Doha; tel. 861412; telex 4672; fax 820911; f. 1971; quarterly; publ. by Qatar National Commission for Education, Culture and Science; Editor-in-Chief FAHD J. H. ATH-THANI; circ. 2,500.

This is Qatar and What's On: POB 3272, Doha; tel. 413813; telex 4787; fax 413814; f. 1978; bi-monthly; English; tourist and information; publ. by Oryx Publishing and Advertising Co (Qatar); Editor-in-Chief UUS ZWAANS; circ. 10,000.

NEWS AGENCY

Qatar News Agency (QNA): POB 3299, Doha; tel. 450450; telex 4394; fax 439362; f. 1975; Dir and Editor-in-Chief AHMAD JASSIM AL-HUMAR.

Publishers

There are more than 25 publishing houses in Qatar.

Qatar National Printing Press: POB 355, Doha; tel. 448452; telex 4072; Propr KHALED BIN NASSER AS-SUWAIDI; Dir ABD AL-KARIM DIB.

Radio and Television

In 1991, according to UNESCO, an estimated 195,000 radio receivers and 198,000 television receivers were in use.

RADIO

Qatar Broadcasting Service (QBS): POB 3939, Doha; tel. 894444; telex 4597; fax 822888; f. 1968; government service transmitting in Arabic, English, French and Urdu; Dir MUBARAK JAHAM AL-KUWARI.

TELEVISION

Qatar Television Service: POB 1944, Doha; tel. 894444; telex 4040; fax 874170; f. 1970; 200 kW transmitters began transmissions throughout the Gulf in 1972. Colour transmissions began in 1974. There are eight channels. Dir SA'AD MUHAMMAD AL-RUMAIHI; Asst. Dir ABD AL-WAHAB MUHAMMAD AL-MUTAWA'A.

Finance

(cap. = capital; p.u. = paid up; res = reserves; dep. = deposits; m. = million; brs = branches; amounts in Qatar riyals unless otherwise stated)

BANKING

Central Bank

Qatar Central Bank: POB 1234, Doha; tel. 456456; telex 4335; fax 413650; f. 1966 as Qatar and Dubai Currency Board; became Qatar Monetary Agency in 1973; renamed Qatar Central Bank in 1993; cap. 50m., res 20m., currency in circulation 1,515m. (1993); Gov. ABDULLAH BIN KHALID AL-ATTIYA; Dep. Gov. Sheikh ABDULLAH BIN SAID ABD AL-AZIZ ATH-THANI.

Commercial Banks

Al-Ahli Bank of Qatar QSC: POB 2309, Doha; tel. 326611; telex 4884; fax 444652; f. 1984; cap. 60m., res 37.1m., dep. 902.1m., total assets 1,015m. (1991); Chair. Sheikh MUHAMMAD BIN HAMAD ATH-THANI; Gen. Man. TAHA S. OMAR; 3 brs.

Commercial Bank of Qatar Ltd QSC: Grand Hamad Ave, POB 3232, Doha; tel. 490222; telex 4351; fax 438182; f. 1975; cap.

70.3m., res 105.2m., dep. 1,462.3m., total assets 1,920m. (1993); owned 20% by board of directors and 80% by Qatari citizens; Chair. Sheikh ALI BIN JABER ATH-THANI; Gen. Man. T. P. NUNAN; 7 brs.

Doha Bank Ltd: POB 3818, Doha; tel. 435444; telex 4534; fax 416631; f. 1979; cap. 78.7m., res 103.9m., dep. 2,333m., total assets 2,849m. (1993); Chair. JABER BIN MUHAMMAD ATH-THANI; Gen. Man. MAQBOOL H. KHALFAN; 11 brs.

Qatar Islamic Bank SAQ: POB 559, Doha; tel. 409409; telex 5177; fax 412700; f. 1983; cap. p.u. 100m., res 114.3m., dep. 1,988m., total assets 2,322m. (July 1991); Chair. Sheikh ABD AR-RAHMAN BIN ABDULLAH AL-MAHMOUD; Man. Dir KHALID BIN AHMAD AS-SUWAIDI; 4 brs.

Qatar National Bank SAQ: POB 1002, Doha; tel. 407407; telex 4212; fax 413753; f. 1965; owned 50% by Government of Qatar and 50% by Qatari nationals; equity 2,095m., total assets 15,268.5m. (1993); Chair. Sheikh MUHAMMAD BIN KHALIFA ATH-THANI (Minister of Finance, Economy and Trade); Man. Dir ABDALLA A. AL-KHATER; 18 brs in Qatar and 4 brs abroad.

Foreign Banks

ANZ Grindlays Bank PLC (UK): POB 2001, Rayyan Rd, Doha; tel. 327711; telex 4209; fax 428077; f. 1956; total assets 706.3m. (1989); Gen. Man. F. J. GAMBLE.

Arab Bank PLC (Jordan): POB 172, Doha; tel. 437979; telex 4202; fax 410774; f. 1957; total assets 958m. (31 Dec. 1989); Regional Man. GHASSAN BUNDAKJI; Dep. Man. SAAD AD-DIN ELAYAN; 2 brs.

Bank Saderat Iran: POB 2256, Doha; tel. 414646; telex 4225; fax 430121; f. 1970; Man. MANSOUR TAFAZZOLI.

Banque Paribas (France): POB 2636, Doha; tel. 433844; telex 4268; fax 410861; f. 1973; Gen. Man. CHRISTIAN MOUROT-BERGEON.

British Bank of the Middle East (Hong Kong): POB 57, Doha; tel. 423124; telex 4204; fax 416353; f. 1954; total assets 945m. (1989); Gen. Man. J. P. PASCOE; 2 brs.

Al-Fardan Exchange and Finance Co.: POB 339, Doha; tel. 426544; telex 4283; fax 417468.

Mashreq Bank PSC (UAE): POB 173, Doha; tel. 413213; telex 4235; fax 413880; f. 1971; Man. KHAWAJA ZAFARULLAH.

Standard Chartered Bank (UK): POB 29, Doha; tel. 414252; telex 4217; fax 413739; f. 1950; total assets 428.6m. (1991); Gen. Man. A. R. PARRY.

United Bank Ltd (Pakistan): POB 242, Doha; tel. 438666; telex 4222; fax 424600; f. 1970; Gen. Man. and Vice-Pres. RAI MANSOOR AHMAD KHAN.

INSURANCE

Al-Khaleej Insurance Co of Qatar (SAQ): POB 4555, Doha; tel. 414151; telex 4692; fax 430530; f. 1978; authorized and cap. p.u. 12m. (1994); all classes except life; Chair. ABDULLAH BIN MUHAMMAD JABER ATH-THANI; Gen. Man. MUHAMMAD NOOR AL-OBAIDLY.

Qatar General Insurance and Reinsurance Co SAQ: POB 4500, Doha; tel. 417800; telex 4742; fax 437302; f. 1979; cap. 15m.; all classes; Chair. Sheikh ALI BIN SAUD ATH-THANI; Gen. Man. GHAZI ABU NAHL.

Qatar Insurance Co SAQ: POB 666, Doha; tel. 831555; telex 4216; fax 831569; f. 1964; cap. 36m. (Jan. 1989); all classes; the Government has a majority share; Chair. Sheikh KHALID BIN MUHAMMAD ALI ATH-THANI; Gen. Man. KHALIFA A. AS-SUBAY'I; brs in Dubai and Riyadh.

Trade and Industry

CHAMBER OF COMMERCE

Qatar Chamber of Commerce and Industry: POB 402, Doha; tel. 425131; telex 4078; fax 447905; f. 1963; 17 mems appointed by decree; Pres. Sheikh HAMAD BIN JASSEM BIN MOHAMMED ATH-THANI; Dir-Gen. MUHAMMAD SELIM AL-MUSANNEF.

DEVELOPMENT ORGANIZATION

Department of Industrial Development: POB 2599, Doha; tel. 832121; telex 4323; fax 832024; government-owned; conducts research, development and supervision of new industrial projects; Dir-Gen. MAJID ABDULLAH AL-MALKI.

STATE ENTERPRISES

Qatar General Petroleum Corporation (QGPC): POB 3212, Doha; tel. 491491; telex 4343; fax 831125; f. 1974; cap. QR 5,000m.; the State of Qatar's interest in companies active in petroleum and related industries has passed to the Corporation. In line with OPEC policy, the Government agreed a participation agreement with the Qatar Petroleum Company and Shell Company of Qatar in 1974 to secure Qatar's interest and obtained a 60%

interest in both. In late 1976, under two separate agreements, the Government secured a 100% interest in both companies. The Qatar Petroleum Producing Authority (QPPA) was established in 1976 as a subsidiary, wholly owned by the Corporation, to undertake all operations previously conducted by the two companies. In February 1980 the QPPA was merged with the Corporation.

Qatar General Petroleum Corporation wholly or partly owns: National Oil Distribution Co (NODCO), Qatar Fertilizer Co Ltd (QAFCO), Qatar Liquefied Gas Co (QATARGAS), Qatar Petrochemical Co Ltd (QAPCO), Ras Laffan LNG Co, Compagnie Pétrochimique du Nord (COPENOR), Arab Maritime Petroleum Transport Co Ltd, Arab Petroleum Pipelines Co (SUMED), Arab Shipbuilding and Repair Yard Co (ASRY), Arab Petroleum Services Co and Arab Petroleum Investments Corpn (APICORP); Chair. ABDULLAH BIN HAMAD AL-ATTIYA (Minister of Energy and Industry); Dep. Chair. JABER ABD AL-HADI AL-MARRI.

National Oil Distribution Co (NODCO): POB 50033, Umm Said; tel. 776555; telex 4324; fax 771232; operates two refineries with a capacity of 62,000 b/d; responsible for the nationwide distribution of petroleum products; wholly owned by QGPC; Gen. Man. MAHMOUD H. AL-HIFNAWI.

Qatar Fertilizer Co (QAFCO) SAQ: POB 50001, Umm Said; tel. 779779; telex 4215; fax 770347; produced 763,000 tons of ammonia and 825,000 tons of urea in 1993; QGPC has a 75% share, Norsk Hydro holds the remaining 25%; Chair. ABDULLAH SALATT; Gen. Man. FAISAL M. AS-SUWAIDI.

Qatar Liquefied Gas Co (QATARGAS): POB 22666, Doha; tel. 327121; telex 4500; fax 327144; f. 1984 to develop North Dome field of unassociated gas; cap. QR 500m.; QGPC has a 65% share; Mobil and Total—Cie Française des Pétroles hold 10% each; the Marubeni Corpn and Mitsui and Co of Japan hold 7.5% each; Chair. ABDULLAH BIN HAMAD AL-ATTIYA (Minister of Energy and Industry).

QGPC (Onshore Operations): Doha; tel. 343287; telex 4253; fax 444554; produces and exports crude petroleum from the Dukhan oilfield and processes and exports natural gas liquids from the onshore and offshore oilfields in Qatar; also responsible for the internal distribution of fuel gas and support services; 182.6m. US barrels of condensate, 223,384 metric tons of butane and 362,180 tons of propane produced in 1987; Man. Dir JABER AL-MARRI; Dep. Exec. Man. AJLAN ALI AL-KUWARI.

QGPC (Offshore Operations): POB 47, Doha; tel. 402000; telex 4201; fax 402584; state-owned organization for offshore oil/gas exploration and production; (now merged with QGPC) average production in 1990 was 188,000 b/d, total approximately 68.7m. barrels; Man. Dir JABER A. AL-MARRI; Exec. Man. MUHAMMAD SAUD AD-DOLAIMI.

Qatar Petrochemicals Co (QAPCO) SAQ: POB 756, Doha; tel. 777111; telex 4871; fax 772674; f. 1974; QGPC has an 80% share; 10% is held by ELF-ATOCHEM (France); the remaining 10% is held by ENICHEM (Italy); total assets QR 2,600m.; operation of petrochemical plant at Umm Said (tel. 770111; telex 4871); produced 332,500 tons of ethylene, 184,000 tons of low-density polyethylene, and 63,000 tons of solid sulphur in 1992; Gen. Man. HAMAD AL-MOHANNADI.

Qatar Electricity and Water Co (QEWC): POB 22046, Doha; tel. 410161; fax 326176; f. 1990; manages state-owned utilities.

Qatar Flour Mills Co SAQ: POB 1444, Doha; tel. 770452; telex 4285; f. 1968; produced 26,200 metric tons of wheat flour in 1987; Chair. Sheikh AHMAD BIN ABDULLAH ATH-THANI; Gen. Man. GHAZI ABD AL-HALIM AS-SALIMI.

Qatar General Poultry Establishment: POB 3606, Doha; tel. 740042; telex 4348; produces between 1m. and 2.5m. broiler chickens, and between 10m. and 25m. eggs, per year; Dir ISMAIL FAITI AL-ISMAIL.

Qatar Steel Co (QASCO): POB 50090, Steel Mill, Umm Said; tel. 778778; telex 4606; fax 771424; the plant was completed in 1978, and produced 600,000 tons of concrete reinforcing steel bars in 1993; the Government owns a 70% share, with Kobe Steel (20%) and Tokyo Boeki (10%); Chair. AHMAD MUHAMMAD ALI AS-SUBAY'I; Man. Dir NASSER MUHAMMAD AL-MANSOURI.

Qatar National Cement Co SAQ: POB 1333, Doha; tel. 350805; telex 4337; fax 417846; f. 1965; produced 266,393 tons of ordinary Portland cement and 100,174 tons of sulphate-resisting cement in 1991; Chair. KHALIFA ABDULLAH AS-SUBAY'I; Gen. Man. SAEED M. AL-KUWARI.

MAJOR INDUSTRIAL COMPANIES

AKC Contracting: POB 1991, Doha; tel. 440474; telex 4138; fax 440497; f. 1975; building, plumbing, joinery, landscaping, etc.; sales QR 59m. (1992); Man. Dir Sheikh ABD AL-AZIZ BIN KHALIFA ATH-THANI; Gen. Man. MARK P. GOLDING; 700 employees.

Arab-Qatari Co for Dairy Production: POB 9310, Doha; tel. 601107; telex 4972; f. 1981; production of dairy products, ice creams and fruit juices; cap. p.u. QR 45m.; Gen. Man. (Commercial) KAMAL KANDALAFT.

Hempel's Marine Paints (Qatar) WLL: POB 3484, Salwa Industrial Estate, Doha; tel. 810881; telex 4864; f. 1981; manufacture of paint and of materials and tools for surface preparation; cap. p.u. QR 3.6m.; Chair. SALEH MUBARAK AL-KHULAIFI; Gen. Man. and CEO WILFRED THOMAS; 36 employees.

Kassem Darwish Fakhroo & Sons (KDS): POB 350, Doha; tel. 422781; telex 4298; fax 426378; f. 1911 (corporate group 1971); electrical, mechanical and civil contractors, general trading, manufacturers; Chair. KASSEM DARWISH FAKHROO; Man. Dir HASSAN K. DARWISH; 1,000 employees.

Mideast Constructors Ltd (MECON): POB 3325, Doha; tel. 415025; telex 4293; fax 415174; f. 1975; civil engineering and contracting; sales QR 173m. (1993); Chair. AHMAD AL-MANNAI; Gen. Man. IAN MATHESON; 550 employees.

National Industrial Gas Plants: POB 1391, Doha; tel. 422116; telex 4408; f. 1954; production of industrial gases (oxygen, carbon dioxide, nitrogen, argon and acetylene, liquid gases (oxygen, nitrogen and argon), and dry ice, hydrostatic pressure testing of high-pressure cylinders; Pres. M. H. ALMANA; 125 employees.

Qatar Dairy Company: POB 4770, Doha; tel. 689009; telex 4365; fax 689922; production of dairy products; Chair. MUHAMMAD BIN ABDULLAH AL-ATTIYA.

Qatar National Plastic Factory: POB 5615, Doha; tel. 689977; telex 4365; fax 689922; production of polyethylene bags, film and UPVC pipes; Chair. MUHAMMAD BIN ABDULLAH AL-ATTIYA.

Readymix (Qatar) Ltd: POB 5007, Doha; tel. 653070; telex 4668; fax 651534; f. 1978; production of ready-mixed concrete; Gen. Man. W. D. FORDE.

> **Qatar Quarry Co Ltd:** POB 5007, Doha; tel. 653070; telex 4668; fax 651534; f. 1983; production of aggregates, road materials and armour rock; Gen. Man. W. D. FORDE.

Transport

ROADS

In 1991 there were some 1,191 km (740 miles) of surfaced road linking Doha and the petroleum centres of Dukhan and Umm Said with the northern end of the peninsula. A 105-km (65-mile) road from Doha to Salwa was completed in 1970, and joins one leading from Al Hufuf in Saudi Arabia, giving Qatar land access to the Mediterranean. A 418-km (260-mile) highway, built in conjunction with Abu Dhabi, links both states with the Gulf network.

SHIPPING

Doha Port has four berths of 9.14 m depth and five berths of 7.5 m depth. Total length of berths is 1,699 m. At Umm Said Harbour the Northern Deep Water Wharves consist of a deep-water quay 730 m long with a dredged depth alongside of 15.5 m, and a quay 570 m long with a dredged depth alongside of 13.0 m. The General Cargo Wharves consist of a quay 400 m long with a dredged depth alongside of 10.0 m. The Southern Deep Water Wharves consist of a deep water quay 508 m long with a dredged depth alongside of 13.0 m. Cold storage facilities exist for cargo of up to 500 tons. The North Field gas project has increased the demand for shipping facilities. In 1991 QGPC invested US $800m. in a new industrial port at Ras Laffan. In mid-1993 a major upgrading and expansion of Doha port, at an estimated cost of $150m., was announced.

Department of Ports, Maritime Affairs and Land Transport: POB 313, Doha; tel. 457457; telex 4378; fax 413563; Dir of Ports G. A. GENKEER.

Qatar National Navigation and Transport Co Ltd (QNNTC): West Bay, Corniche St, POB 153, Doha; tel. 468666; telex 4206; fax 468777; f. 1957; 100%-owned by Qatari nationals; sole shipping agents, stevedoring, chandlers, forwarding, shipowning, repair, construction, etc.; Chief Exec. ABD AL-AZIZ H. SALATT.

CIVIL AVIATION

Doha International Airport is equipped to receive all types of aircraft. In 1993 the total number of passengers using the existing airport, excluding those in transit, was 1,715,000. In 1991 it was announced that a new international airport was to be built in Doha, at a cost of QR 1,000m. Construction of the airport was expected to commence in 1994, and completion was scheduled for 1997. The new airport would have the capacity to handle 2m. passengers per year.

Department of Civil Aviation: POB 3000, Doha; tel. 426262; telex 4306; fax 429070; Dir of Civil Aviation ABD AL-AZIZ AN-NOAIMI.

Doha International Airport: POB 3000, Doha; tel. 351550; telex 4306; fax 429070; Airport Man. MOHD AL-MUHANNADI.

Gulf Air Co Ltd: POB 3394, Doha; tel. 455455; telex 5150; jointly owned by the Governments of Bahrain, Oman, Qatar and Abu Dhabi (see Oman—Civil Aviation).

Gulf Helicopters: POB 811, Doha; tel. 433991; telex 4353; fax 411004; f. 1974; owned by Gulf Air Co GSC; Chair. ABDULLAH BIN HAMAD AL-ATTIYA.

Qatar Air: Doha; tel. 430707; telex 4444; fax 352433; services throughout the Middle East; CEO Sheikh HAMAD BIN JABER ATH-THANI.

Defence

Defence Budget (1994): QR 1,100m.

Total armed forces (June 1994): 10,100: army 8,500; navy 800; air force 800.

Education

All education within Qatar is provided free of charge, although it is not compulsory, and numerous scholarships are awarded for study overseas. In 1991 there were 5,684 children receiving pre-primary education. Primary schooling begins at six years of age and lasts for six years. In 1991/2 the 157 primary schools were attended by 48,785 pupils. The next level of education, beginning at 12 years of age, is divided between a three-year preparatory stage (with 18,703 pupils in 1991/2) and a further three-year secondary stage (11,564 pupils in 1991/2). General secondary education facilities are complemented by a technical school, a school of commerce and an institute of religious studies. An institute of administration and a language teaching institute help to raise the standard of government officials. In 1991 there were 3,724 teachers employed and 31,120 pupils enrolled at secondary level in Qatari schools. In 1991 an estimated 88% of all children in the relevant age-group were enrolled at primary schools, while the comparable ratio for secondary enrolment was 69% (68% males; 70% females). In 1992/93 some 1,164 Qataris were sent on scholarships to higher education institutions abroad, in other Arab countries, Britain, France or the USA. In October 1973 the first two Higher Teacher Training Colleges were opened, providing education to university level. In 1992/93 the University of Qatar comprised the faculties of education, science, social sciences, administration and economics, technology, engineering and religion. In the academic year 1992/93 there were 6,666 students and a teaching staff of 605 at the University of Qatar. Public expenditure on education in 1991 was QR 916m., equivalent to 3.7% of GDP. The average rate of adult illiteracy in 1986 was 24.3% (males 23.2%; females 27.5%).

Bibliography

Abu Nab, Ibrahim. *Qatar: A Story of State Building.* Ministry of Information, Qatar, 1977.

Al-Abdulla, Yousof Ibrahim. *A Study of Qatari-British Relations 1914–1945.* Orient Publishing and Translation, 1981.

Graham, Helga. *Arabian Time Machine: Self-Portrait of an Oil State.* Heinemann, 1978.

El-Mallakh, Ragaei. *Qatar, Energy and Development.* Croom Helm, 1985.

Nafi, Zuhair Ahmed. *Economic and Social Development in Qatar.* Frances Pinter, 1983.

Al-Othman, Nasser. *With Their Bare Hands: the Story of the Oil Industry in Qatar.* Longman, 1984.

For further titles, see Bibliography on Bahrain, p. 320, and the United Arab Emirates, p. 979.

SAUDI ARABIA

Physical and Social Geography of the Arabian Peninsula

The Arabian peninsula is a distinct geographical unit, delimited on three sides by sea—on the east by the Persian (Arabian) Gulf and the Gulf of Oman, on the south by the Indian Ocean, and on the west by the Red Sea—while its remaining (northern) side is occupied by the deserts of Jordan and Iraq. This isolated territory, extending over some 2.5m. sq km (about 1m. sq miles), is divided politically into several states. The largest of these is Saudi Arabia, which occupies 2,240,000 sq km (865,000 sq miles); to the east and south lie much smaller territories where suzerainty and even actual frontiers are disputed in some instances. Along the shores of the Persian Gulf and the Gulf of Oman there are, beginning in the north, the State of Kuwait, with two adjacent zones of 'neutral' territory; then, after a stretch of Saudi Arabian coast, the islands of Bahrain and the Qatar peninsula, followed by the United Arab Emirates and the much larger Sultanate of Oman. Yemen occupies most of the southern coastline of the peninsula, and its south-western corner.

PHYSICAL FEATURES

Structurally, the whole of Arabia is a vast platform of ancient rocks, once continuous with north-east Africa. Subsequently a series of great fissures opened, as the result of which a large trough, or rift valley, was formed and later occupied by the sea, to produce the Red Sea and Gulf of Aden. The Arabian platform is tilted, with its highest part in the extreme west, along the Red Sea, and it slopes gradually down from west to east. Thus the Red Sea coast is often bold and mountainous, whereas the Persian Gulf coast is flat, low-lying and fringed with extensive coral reefs which make it difficult to approach the shore in many places.

Dislocation of the rock strata in the west of Arabia has led to the upwelling of much lava, which has solidified into vast barren expanses, known as *harras*. Volcanic cones and flows are also prominent along the whole length of the western coast as far as Aden, where peaks rise to more than 3,000 m above sea-level. The mountains reach their highest in the south, in Yemen, with summits at 4,000 m, and the lowest part of this mountain wall occurs roughly halfway along its course, in the region of Jeddah, Mecca, and Medina. A principal reason for the location of these three Saudi Arabian towns is that they offer the easiest route inland from the coast, and one of the shortest routes across Arabia.

Further to the east the ancient platform is covered by relatively thin layers of younger rocks. Some of the strata have been eroded to form shallow depressions; others have proved more resistant, and now stand out as ridges. This central area, relieved by shallow vales and upstanding ridges and covered in many places by desert sand, is called the Najd, and is considered to be the homeland of the Wahhabi sect, which now rules the whole of Saudi Arabia. Farther east, practically all the land lies well below 300 m in altitude, and both to the north and to the south are desert areas. The Nefud in the north has some wells, and even a slight rainfall, and therefore supports a few oasis cultivators and pastoral nomads. South of the Najd, however, lies the Rub' al-Khali, or Empty Quarter, a rainless, unrelieved wilderness of shifting sand, too harsh for occupation even by nomads.

Most of the east coast of Arabia (al-Hasa) is low-lying, but an exception is the imposing ridge of the Jebel al-Akhdar ('Green Mountain') of Oman, which also produces a fjord-like coastline along the Gulf of Oman. Another feature is the large river valleys, or *wadis*, cut by river action during an earlier geological period, but in modern times almost, or entirely, dry and partially filled with sand. The largest is the Wadi Hadhramaut, which runs parallel to the southern coast for several hundred km; another is the Wadi Sirhan, which stretches north-westwards from the Nefud into Jordan.

CLIMATE

Because of its land-locked nature, the winds reaching Arabia are generally dry, and almost all the area is arid. In the north there is a rainfall of 100 mm to 200 mm annually; further south, except near the coast, even this fails. The higher parts of the west and south do, however, experience appreciable falls—rather sporadic in some parts, but copious and reliable in areas adjacent to the Red Sea.

Because of aridity, and hence relatively cloudless skies, there are great extremes of temperature. The summer is overwhelmingly hot, with maxima of over 50°C, which are intensified by the dark rocks, while in winter there can be general severe frost and even weeks of snow in the mountains. Another result of the wide variations in temperature is the prevalence of violent local winds. Also, near the coast, atmospheric humidity is unpleasantly high, and the coasts of both the Red Sea and the Persian Gulf are notorious for their humidity. Average summer temperatures in Saudi Arabia's coastal regions range from 38°C to 49°C (100°F–120°F), sometimes reaching 54°C (129°F) in the interior, or falling to a minimum of 24°C (75.2°F) in Jeddah. The winters are mild, except in the mountains. Winter temperatures range from 8°C (46.4°F) to 30°C (86°F) in Riyadh, and reach a maximum of 33°C (91.4°F) in Jeddah.

Owing to the tilt of the strata eastwards, and their great elevation in the west, rain falling in the hills near the Red Sea apparently percolates gradually eastwards, to emerge as springs along the Persian Gulf coast. This phenomenon, borne out by the fact that the flow of water in the springs greatly exceeds the total rainfall in the same district, suggests that water may be present underground over much of the interior. Irrigation schemes to exploit these supplies have been developed, notably in the Najd at al-Kharj, but results have been fairly limited.

ECONOMIC LIFE

Over much of Arabia, life is based around oases. Many wells are used solely by nomads for watering their animals, but in some parts, more especially the south, there is regular cultivation. Yemen, in particular, has a well-developed agriculture, showing a gradation of crops according to altitude, with cereals, fruit, coffee and qat (a narcotic) as the chief products. Other agricultural districts are in Oman and in the large oases of the Hedjaz (including Medina and Mecca). However, conditions in Arabia are harsh, and the population depends partly on resources brought in from outside, such as revenues from pilgrims. A major change in the economy of Saudi Arabia and the Gulf States resulted from the exploitation of petroleum, the revenues from which transformed those States.

RACE, LANGUAGE AND RELIGION

The inhabitants of the centre, north and west are of almost unmixed Mediterranean stock—lightly built, long-headed and dark. In coastal districts of the east, south and south-west, intermixture of broader-headed and slightly heavier peoples of Armenoid descent is a prominent feature; and there has been some exchange of racial type with the populations on the Iranian shores of the Persian Gulf and Gulf of Oman. Owing to the long-continued slave trade, negroid influences from Africa are also widespread. On this basis it is possible to delimit two ethnic zones within Arabia: a northern, central and western area, geographically arid and in isolation, with a relatively unmixed racial composition; and the coastlands of the south, south-west and east, showing a mixed population. A recent result of the rapid economic growth in the petroleum-producing countries has been the influx of large numbers of expatriates from the developed countries of the Western world, and labourers from developing countries further east. Arabic, however, is the sole language of Arabia. Unlike many other parts of the Middle East, European languages are not current.

As its borders enclose the holy cities of Mecca and Medina, Saudi Arabia is the centre of the Islamic faith. About 85% of Saudi Muslims belong to the Sunni sect of Islam, the remainder being Shi'ites. Except in the Eastern Province, Sunni rites prevail. The differences between the two branches of Islam have been the cause of some tension within Saudi Arabia, not least because the Shi'a Muslim minority considers itself to be oppressed. (See The Religions of the Middle East and North Africa, page 14.)

History

Revised for this edition by JON LUNN

ANCIENT AND MEDIEVAL HISTORY

For the most part, Arabian history has been the account of small pockets of settled civilization, subsisting mainly on trade, in the midst of nomadic tribes. The earliest urban settlements developed in the south-west, where the flourishing Minaean kingdom is believed to have been established in the 12th century BC. This was followed by the Sabaean and Himyarite kingdoms, which lasted until the sixth century AD. The term 'kingdom' in this connection implies rather a loose federation of city states than a centralized monarchy. As an important trading station between east and west, southern Arabia was brought into early contact with the Persian and Roman empires, and thereby with Judaism, Zoroastrianism, and later Christianity. Politically, however, the south Arabian principalities remained independent.

By the end of the sixth century the centre of power had shifted to the west coast, to the Hedjaz cities of at-Ta'if, Mecca and Medina. While the southern regions fell under the control of the Sasanid rulers of Persia, the independent Hedjaz grew in importance as a trade route between the Byzantine Empire, Egypt, and the East. From the fifth century, Mecca was dominated by the tribe of Quraish. Meanwhile, the central deserts remained nomadic, and the inhospitable east coast remained, for the most part, under Persian influence.

The flowering and development of Arabism from the 7th century AD, inspired by the prophet Muhammad (the founder of Islam) proceeded, for the most part, outside the Arabian peninsula itself. The Islamic unification of the Near and Middle East reduced the importance of the Hedjaz as a trade route. Mecca retained a unique status as a centre of pilgrimage for the whole Islamic world, but Arabia as a whole, temporarily united under Muhammad and his successors, soon drifted back into disunity. Yemen was the first to break away from the weakening Abbasid Caliphate in Baghdad, and from the ninth century onwards a variety of small dynasties established themselves in San'a, Zabid, and other towns. Mecca also had its semi-independent governors, though their proximity to Egypt made them more cautious in their attitude towards the Caliphs and the later rulers of that country, particularly the Fatimids of the 10th to 12th centuries. In Oman, in the south-east, a line of spiritual Imams arose who before long were exercising temporal power. To the north the Arabian shores of the Persian Gulf provided a home for the fanatical Carmathian sect, whose influence at times extended as far as Iraq, Syria, Mecca, and Yemen.

THE OTTOMAN PERIOD

Arabia remained unsettled until the beginning of the 16th century, when the whole peninsula came nominally under the suzerainty of the Ottoman Sultans in Istanbul. It was a hold that was never very strong, even in the Hedjaz, and in Oman and Yemen native lines of Imams were once again exercising unfettered authority before the end of the century. More important for the future of the peninsula was the appearance of European merchant adventurers in the Indian Ocean and the Persian/Arabian Gulf. The Portuguese were the first to arrive, in the 16th century, and they were followed in the 17th and 18th centuries by the British, Dutch and French. By

the beginning of the 19th century Britain had supplanted its European rivals and had established its influence firmly in the Gulf and, to a lesser extent, along the southern coast.

The political structure of Arabia was now beginning to develop along its modern lines. Yemen was already a virtually independent Imamate; Lahej broke away in the middle of the 18th century, only to lose Aden to Britain in 1839 and to become the nucleus of the Aden Protectorate. To the north of Yemen was the principality of the Asir, generally independent, though both countries were occupied by the Turks from 1850 until the outbreak of the First World War. The Hedjaz continued to be a province of the Ottoman Empire. In 1793 the Sultanate of Oman was established with its capital at Muscat, and during the 19th century all the rulers and chieftains along the Persian Gulf coast, including Oman, the sheikhdoms of the Trucial Coast, Bahrain and Kuwait, entered into 'exclusive' treaty relations with the British Government. Britain was principally concerned to prevent French, Russian and German penetration towards India, and to suppress trading in slaves and weapons.

Meanwhile, the Najd, in the centre of Arabia, was the scene of another upheaval with religious inspirations. The puritanical and reforming Wahhabi movement, launched in the middle of the 18th century, had by 1800 grown so powerful that its followers were able to capture Karbala and Najaf in Iraq, Damascus in Syria, and Mecca and Medina in the Hedjaz. They were defeated by Muhammad Ali of Egypt, acting in the name of the Ottoman Sultan, in 1811–18 and again in 1838, but the Wahhabi ruling house of Sa'ud continued to rule in the interior until 1890, when the rival Rashidi family, which had Turkish support, seized control of Riyadh.

In 1901 a member of the deposed Sa'udi family, Abd al-Aziz ibn Abd ar-Rahman, set out from Kuwait, where he had been living in exile, to regain the family's former domains. In 1902, with only about 200 followers, Abd al-Aziz captured Riyadh, expelled the Rashidi dynasty and proclaimed himself ruler of the Najd. Later he recovered and consolidated the outlying provinces of the kingdom, resisting Turkish attempts to subjugate him. Having restored the House of Sa'ud as a ruling dynasty, Abd al-Aziz became known as Ibn Sa'ud. To strengthen his position, Ibn Sa'ud instituted the formation of Wahhabi colonies, known as Ikhwan ('Brethren'), throughout the territory under his control. The first Ikhwan settlement was founded in 1912, and about 100 more were established, spreading Wahhabi doctrines to communities in remote desert areas, over the next 15 years. These colonies formed the basis of a centralized organization which was to prove a powerful instrument in later years. By the outbreak of the First World War (1914–18), Ibn Sa'ud was effectively the master of central Arabia, including the Hasa coast of the Persian Gulf.

EVENTS, 1914–26

When Turkey entered the war on the side of Germany in October 1914, Arabia inevitably became a centre of intrigue, if not necessarily of military action. British influence was paramount along the eastern and southern coasts, where the various sheikhs and tribal chiefs from Kuwait to the Hadhramaut lost no time in severing their remaining connections with the Ottoman Empire. On the other hand, the Turks had faithful allies in Ibn Rashid of the Shammar, to the north of the Najd, and in Imam Yahya of Yemen. The Turks also maintained garrisons along the west coast. In the centre, Ibn Sa'ud, who, in 1913, had accepted Turkish recognition of his occupation of the Hasa coast, enjoyed friendly relations with the British-controlled Government of India.

British military strategy developed, as the war dragged on, into a two-pronged thrust against the Turks from both Egypt and the Persian Gulf. In the implementation of this plan opinions were divided on the extent to which use could be made of the Arab population. The Indian Government on the eastern wing, while favouring the pretensions of Ibn Sa'ud, preferred to see the problem in purely military terms, and opposed any suggestion of an Arab revolt. This, however, was the scheme favoured by the Arab Bureau in Cairo, whose views eventually prevailed in London. They were alarmed at the Ottoman declaration of a *jihad* (holy war) and possible repercussions in Egypt and North Africa. Negotiations were started at a very early stage with Arab nationalist movements in Syria and Egypt, but these met with comparatively little success. More progress was made when the British negotiators turned their attentions to the Sharif of Mecca, Hussein, a member of the Hashimi family which had ruled in Mecca since the 11th century AD. The support of such a religious dignitary would be an effective counter to Turkish claims. Hussein was inclined to favour the Allied cause, but it was only after he had elicited from the British (in the MacMahon correspondence—see Documents on Palestine, p. 79) promises which he believed would meet Arab nationalist aspirations that he decided to move. On 5 June 1916 he proclaimed Arab independence and declared war on the Turks. By November things had gone so well that he felt able to claim the title of King of the Hedjaz. Military operations continued throughout the winter, and in July 1917 the port of Aqaba was captured and the Hedjaz cleared of Turkish troops except for a beleaguered garrison in Medina.

Arabia thereafter remained comparatively peaceful, and was not even greatly disturbed by the complicated post-war political manoeuvres in the Middle East. Hussein was a rather ineffectual spokesman for the Arab point of view at the peace conferences and over the allocation of mandates, and as a result forfeited the favour of the British Government. When, therefore, he was unwise enough to challenge the growing power of his former rival Ibn Sa'ud, he found himself entirely without support. Ibn Sa'ud's stature had been steadily growing since the end of the war. In November 1921 he had succeeded in supplanting the house of Ibn Rashid and annexing the Shammar, and a year later he was recognized by the Government of India as overlord of Hayil, Shammar and Jawf. On 5 March 1924 Hussein laid claim to the title of Caliph, made vacant by the deposition of the Ottoman Sultan. His claims were nowhere recognized, and Ibn Sa'ud overran the Hedjaz in a campaign of a few months, captured Mecca and forced Hussein's abdication. Hussein's eldest son, Ali, continued to hold Jeddah for another year, but was then ousted, and on 8 January 1926 Ibn Sa'ud proclaimed himself King of the Hedjaz. At first the Najd and the Hedjaz formed a dual kingdom, but on 23 September 1932 they were merged to form the Kingdom of Saudi Arabia.

THE KINGDOM OF SAUDI ARABIA*

Ibn Sa'ud's new status was recognized by Britain in the Treaty of Jeddah of 1927, while Ibn Sa'ud, in his turn, acknowledged his rival Hussein's sons, Abdullah and Faisal, as rulers of Transjordan and Iraq, and also the special status of the British-protected sheikhdoms along the Gulf coast. The northern frontier of his domains had previously been established by the Hadda and Bahra agreements of November 1925, which set the Mandate boundaries as the limit of his expansion. The border with Yemen was settled in 1934 after protracted negotiations and a brief war.

In the years that followed, the new king's priority remained the unification and development of his country. The colonization policy which he had begun in 1912 was pursued vigorously; land settlements were established and unruliness among the bedouin was suppressed. The modernization of communications was initiated, and the need for economic development emphasized. The main damage that Saudi Arabia suffered during the Second World War was economic. The pilgrimage traffic declined to almost nothing, and in April 1943 it was necessary to include Saudi Arabia as a beneficiary of Lend-Lease, the arrangement whereby the USA supplied equipment to allied countries.

Saudi Arabia's production of crude petroleum increased steadily as new oilfields were developed. In October 1945 a petroleum refinery opened at Ras Tanura, and two years later work started on the Trans-Arabian Pipeline (Tapline), to connect the Arabian oilfields with ports on the Mediterranean Sea in Lebanon. Petroleum first reached the Lebanese port of Sidon on 2 December 1950. In the same month the Saudi Arabian Government and the Arabian-American Oil Company (Aramco) signed a new agreement providing for equal shares of the proceeds of petroleum sales. In 1956 a government-owned National Oil Company was formed to exploit areas not covered by the Aramco concession (see Oil in the Middle East and North Africa, page 119).

Saudi Arabia was a founder member of the Arab League, formed in 1945, and initially played a loyal and comparatively inconspicuous part. Ibn Sa'ud sent a small force to join the fighting against Israel in the summer of 1948. When the solidarity of the League began to weaken, it was natural that he should side with Egypt and Syria rather than with his old dynastic enemies, the rulers of Iraq and Jordan. In the course of time, however, he began to turn once more to internal development, and to forget his political quarrel with the USA in his need for economic advice and aid. In August 1950 a US $15m. loan from the US Export-Import Bank was finally taken up. In January 1951 Saudi Arabia and the USA signed a four-point agreement, and in June the two countries reached agreement on a mutual assistance pact. However, the real basis of development was the revenue from the developing petroleum industry. This was sufficient to justify the announcement, in July 1949, of a $270m. Four-Year Plan, whose main feature was an ambitious programme of railway development. Apart from this, the King's policy was one of cautious modernization at home, and the enhancement of Saudi Arabian prestige and influence in the Middle East and in world affairs generally.

AFTER IBN SA'UD

On 9 November 1953 King Ibn Sa'ud died, at the age of 71, and was succeeded by one of his many sons, Sa'ud ibn Abd al-Aziz, hitherto the Crown Prince, who had been appointed Prime Minister in the previous month. Another of the late King's sons, Faisal ibn Abd al-Aziz, replaced Sa'ud as Crown Prince and Prime Minister. The policy of strengthening the governmental machine, and of relying less on one-man rule, was continued by the formation of new ministries and a regular Cabinet. In March 1958, bowing to pressure from the royal family, King Sa'ud conferred on Crown Prince Faisal full powers over foreign, internal and economic affairs, with the professed aim of strengthening the machinery of government and of centralizing responsibilities. In December 1960, however, the Crown Prince resigned as Prime Minister, and the King assumed the premiership himself. In the following month, a high planning council, with a team of international experts, was formed to survey the country's resources, and there followed steady progress in the modernization of the country.

Throughout his reign, King Sa'ud regarded his role as that of a mediator between the conflicting national and foreign interests in the Arab Middle East. He refused to join either the United Arab Republic (UAR) or the rival Arab Federation. Relations with Egypt ranged from the mutual defence pacts between Egypt, Syria and Saudi Arabia in October 1955 (which Yemen and Jordan also signed a year later) to the open quarrel in March 1958 over an alleged plot to assassinate President Nasser. Subsequently, relations improved. The Saudi Government also played a leading role in bringing the Arab Govern-

---

* For subsequent developments in the rest of the Arabian peninsula, see separate chapters on Bahrain, Kuwait, Oman, Qatar, the United Arab Emirates and Yemen.

ments together after Egypt's nationalization of the Suez Canal in July 1956 and the Israeli, British and French military action in the Sinai peninsula in November. In 1961 Saudi Arabia supported the Syrians in their break with the UAR, and in general relations with that country deteriorated. By 1964, however, in spite of the tensions over the revolution in Yemen, King Sa'ud attended the Cairo conference on the Jordan waters dispute in January, and in March, after a meeting in Riyadh, diplomatic relations with the UAR were resumed. In September Prince Faisal attended the Arab Summit Conference in Alexandria, and afterwards had talks with President Nasser on the situation in Yemen.

FAISAL IN POWER

In March 1964 King Sa'ud relinquished all real power over the affairs of the country to his brother, Crown Prince Faisal, who had again acted as Prime Minister intermittently during 1962, and continuously since mid-1963. The rule of Prince Faisal was expected to result in many concessions to 'Westernization', such as more cinemas and television, with more profound social and economic reforms to follow. The change of power, by which King Sa'ud retired as active monarch, was supported in a statement by the *ulema* council of religious leaders 'in the light of developments, the King's condition of health, and his inability to attend to state affairs'. In November 1964 Sa'ud was forced to abdicate in favour of Faisal. The new King retained the post of Prime Minister, and in March 1965 appointed his half-brother, Khalid ibn Abd al-Aziz, to be Crown Prince. On 24 August 1965 King Faisal confirmed his stature as an important Arab leader when he concluded an agreement at Jeddah with President Nasser of the UAR on a peace plan for Yemen.

Although the Yemen issue remained unresolved, there was evidence of Saudi Arabia's genuine anxiety that a solution should be found, even though in April 1966 the construction of a military airfield near the frontier brought protests from the Republican Government of Yemen and the UAR. Representatives of Saudi Arabia and the UAR met in Kuwait in August 1966 in an attempt to implement the Jeddah agreement, but relations with both the UAR and the Arab League continued to be tense.

In the June 1967 Arab-Israeli war, Saudi forces collaborated with Jordanian and Iraqi forces in action against Israel. At a summit conference of Arab leaders held in Khartoum at the end of August 1967 Saudi Arabia agreed to provide £50m. of a total £135m. fund to assist Jordan and the UAR in restoring their economic strength after the hostilities with Israel. An agreement was also concluded with President Nasser on the withdrawal of UAR and Saudi military support for the warring parties in Yemen. By way of recompense for these concessions, the Saudi Arabian Government persuaded other Arab states that it was in their best interests to resume shipments of petroleum to western countries—supplies had been suspended for political reasons after the war with Israel.

THE 1967 WAR AND AFTER

Although outwardly calm, the internal political situation was disturbed by abortive coups in June and September 1969. Plans for both seem to have been discovered in advance, the only visible evidence being the arrests of numbers of army and air force officers. A flight of private capital abroad was also reported. In Yemen the Royalist cause, which the Saudi Government had strongly supported, appeared to be within sight of victory early in 1968. By mid-1969, however, its remaining adherents had largely been driven into exile and the civil war seemed to have come to an end, although further hostilities were reported during the 1969–70 winter. Dissension amongst the Royalists, which led to the withdrawal of Saudi assistance, was a principal factor in this decline. Discussions between San'a representatives and Saudi officials took place in 1970, and the Yemen Arab Republic (YAR) was officially recognized in July. Relations with Southern Yemen (subsequently the People's Democratic Republic of Yemen—PDRY) deteriorated, however, and in December 1969 the two countries fought an extensive battle on the disputed frontier: Saudi Arabia won easily, owing mainly to its superior air power.

Relations with Sudan improved after the communist-inspired coup attempt there in July 1971. Saudi Arabia also played an important role in mediating between the Palestinian guerrillas and the Jordanian Government after the final confrontation between them in northern Jordan in July 1971.

The growing tension in the Gulf area generally was reflected in Saudi arms deals with the USA and the British Aircraft Corporation. Saudi Arabia, however, warned the USA that it might withhold petroleum supplies unless the US Government changed its attitude in the Arab–Israeli dispute.

When the Arab–Israeli war of October 1973 broke out and US aid to Israel continued, Saudi Arabia, despite its traditionally good relationship with the West, led a movement by all the Arab petroleum-producing countries to exert political pressure by cuts in petroleum production. Since there was no immediate response from the USA, OPEC members placed an embargo on petroleum supplies to that country and to several other developed Western countries as well. Supplies to the western world were not cut off entirely, but it was announced that production would be progressively reduced until attitudes towards support for Israel changed. Western nations attempted to repair their links with the petroleum-producing countries, who were debating among themselves how far they should wield the 'oil weapon' to achieve their ends.

As the possessor of 40% of the Middle East's petroleum reserves, and one-quarter of world reserves, Saudi Arabia, together with Egypt, was in the very forefront of negotiations. It soon became apparent, however, that the Saudis held different views from those of other producer nations (notably Libya, Algeria and Iran) on the extent to which their control of petroleum supplies could safely be used to put pressure on the West. It was feared in Riyadh that too much of this pressure would have unwanted economic repercussions. The more radical OPEC members wanted to retain the petroleum embargo until a satisfactory outcome to the October hostilities was reached. At a meeting in March 1974, however, Saudi Arabia pressed for a resumption of supplies to the USA and, when this was agreed, resisted any moves to increase prices for petroleum, which had risen to nearly four times the pre-hostilities level. It was reported that, in order to achieve their aim, the Saudis had threatened to leave OPEC and to lower prices unilaterally. Reluctantly, therefore, the more radical OPEC members agreed to a price freeze.

Meanwhile, in negotiations with consumer countries, the Saudis made it clear that the continued supply of petroleum was dependent not only on a change in attitudes towards Israel but on assistance to Saudi Arabia itself in industrializing and diversifying its economy, in preparation for the time when reserves of petroleum would be depleted. The USA, in particular, showed itself eager to satisfy these conditions, and an important economic and military co-operation agreement was signed in May 1974.

On 25 March 1975 King Faisal was assassinated by one of his nephews, Prince Faisal ibn Masaed ibn Abd al-Aziz. There were fears of a conspiracy but it soon became clear that the assassin had acted on his own initiative. King Faisal was succeeded by his half-brother, Khalid, hitherto Crown Prince. The new King Khalid also became Prime Minister, and appointed one of his brothers, Fahd ibn Abd al-Aziz (Minister of the Interior since 1962), to be Crown Prince and First Deputy Prime Minister.

No major change of policy followed Khalid's succession. He quickly announced that Saudi Arabia would follow the late King Faisal's policies of pursuing Islamic solidarity and the strengthening of Arab unity, and that Saudi Arabia's objectives remained 'the recovery of occupied Arab territories' and the 'liberation of the City of Jerusalem from the claws of Zionism'.

In March 1976 Saudi Arabia established diplomatic relations with the PDRY. Although the two countries had been ideological enemies since the PDRY achieved independence (as Southern Yemen) in 1967, they were both concerned about the presence of Iranian forces in Oman. A Saudi Arabian loan was made to the needy PDRY, and it was expected that, in return, the Yemenis would abandon their support for the People's Front for the Liberation of Oman.

An indication of the growth in stature of Saudi Arabia in Arab affairs in the late 1970s was the key role which the country played in October 1976 in bringing about the Riyadh summit—a meeting which was instrumental in ending the civil war in Lebanon and also brought about reconciliation between Egypt and Syria. Saudi Arabia also asserted itself at the OPEC summit in Doha in December 1976, when the country, along with the United Arab Emirates, showed itself firmly committed to a petroleum price rise of only 5%, while the other OPEC countries insisted on a 10% rise.

Saudi Arabia supported President Sadat of Egypt, fearing that his fall from power would result in Egypt's moving to the left. When Sadat visited Israel in November 1977, Saudi Arabia gave him discreet support in his peace initiative. This position, however, was abandoned following the signing of the Egyptian-Israeli treaty in the following spring. At the Arab summit meeting held in April 1979, Saudi Arabia aligned itself with the 'moderate' states in supporting the sanctions against Egypt which had been outlined at the Arab League meeting in the previous November. In July 1979 the Saudi Government withdrew from its arms manufacturing consortium with Egypt. Nevertheless, flights between Egypt and Saudi Arabia continued, and there was no ban on the employment of Egyptian workers in Saudi Arabia.

THE SIEGE OF THE MECCA MOSQUE

In domestic affairs, the Saudi Government was content to allow social change to unfold gradually, although the country's vast petroleum wealth and the development plans of 1975–80 and 1980–85 brought about a great improvement in communications, welfare services and the standard of living in general. The Saudi royal family received a severe shock in November 1979, when the Grand Mosque in Mecca was occupied by about 250 armed followers of Juhaiman ibn Seif al-Oteibi, a Sunni Muslim extremist who had come to proclaim a Mahdi on the first day of the Islamic year 1400. The siege continued for two weeks, until the extremists were defeated; 102 insurgents and 127 Saudi Arabian troops died.

SAUDI ARABIA IN THE 1980s

The siege of the Mecca Mosque revealed unease in Saudi Arabia. Although the royal family was firmly in control, the existing system entitled as many as 5,000 Saudi princes to royal privileges, and there were murmurings against the royal family's conspicuous consumption and privilege. An eight-man committee under the chairmanship of Prince Nayef, Minister of the Interior, was appointed in March 1980 to draft a 200-article 'system of rule' based on Islamic principles. Saudi Arabia's geo-political position, however, added to the unease. With the former PDRY already in the Soviet orbit, with the former YAR concluding an agreement to purchase armaments from the USSR in November 1979, and with the Soviet invasion of Afghanistan in December 1979, Saudi Arabia came to feel increasingly vulnerable. This feeling was intensified by the outbreak of war between Iran and Iraq in September 1980, which caused further instability in the region. Saudi Arabia initially supported Iraq, but later came to fear that Iranian retaliation might take the form of agitating Saudi Arabia's Shi'a minority. Saudi Arabia therefore concentrated on consolidating its position in the early 1980s. Defence spending became a major feature of Saudi Arabia's current expenditure, largely involving the purchase or loan of armaments and military equipment from the USA. In March 1981 President Ronald Reagan of the USA, in spite of congressional opposition, agreed to sell to Saudi Arabia five AWACS (airborne warning and control systems) aircraft in addition to the four that were supplied under US control after the outbreak of the Iran–Iraq War. Saudi Arabia has also purchased arms from the United Kingdom, France and the Federal Republic of Germany.

In May 1981 Saudi Arabia joined five other Gulf states in setting up the Gulf Co-operation Council (GCC), a pact for economic co-operation but also with some emphasis on the formation of a military alliance and a collective security agreement. The GCC made preliminary moves towards the co-ordination of its members' defences in November 1982, when it was agreed that its own Rapid Defence Force (RDF) would be formed. This decision was ratified in October 1983, when member countries participated in the 'Peninsula Shield' joint military exercises in Oman. Saudi Arabia's defence forces form a large part of the RDF's military strength.

Saudi Arabia was one of the leading mediators in the negotiations which ended the 1981 missile crisis in Lebanon, and has become increasingly involved in trying to find a solution to the whole Arab–Israeli question and the issue of Palestinian autonomy. The basis of Saudi Arabia's policy with regard to these questions was the eight-point 'Fahd Plan', first publicized by Prince Fahd in August 1981. The plan (reproduced on page 95) caused concern in the remainder of the Arab world because it recognized the legitimacy of Israel, by implication, although Saudi Arabia was reluctant to admit this. The plan was due to be discussed at an Arab summit meeting at Fez, in Morocco, in November, but there was disagreement over its implications and the summit quickly broke up in disarray.

King Khalid died suddenly on 13 June 1982 and was succeeded by his younger brother, Fahd, hitherto Crown Prince. Owing to Khalid's ill-health, Fahd had already exercised considerable power. The new King Fahd also became Prime Minister, and he appointed a half-brother, Abdullah ibn Abd al-Aziz (commander of the national guard since 1962), to be Crown Prince and first deputy prime minister. The previous Saudi policy of positively seeking a solution to the Palestine question, inflamed still further by the Israeli move into Lebanon in June, was continued. The Saudi Government was unwilling to exercise the political influence over Syria (particularly concerning Syrian involvement in Lebanon) which Western countries assume it to have, demonstrating clearly its priority of Arab unity. In February 1984 Crown Prince Abdullah expressed support for the Syrian position in Lebanon, demanding a withdrawal of US Marines from the area.

After 1982 there was a considerable slump in government revenues from petroleum (see Economy, below). Supportive loans to other Arab countries, including Syria and Iraq, proved to be a significant burden on the kingdom's finances. Donations to Iraq were widely thought to have totalled US $25,000m. by April 1984, and there seemed little likelihood that Saudi Arabia would abrogate the responsibility which it had assumed for supporting Iraq in its war with Iran. Under an agreement reached in the first year of the Iran–Iraq War, Saudi Arabia and Kuwait sold up to 310,000 b/d of oil (250,000 b/d from the Neutral/Partitioned Zone and the remainder from Saudi Arabia) through the Arabian Oil Company, the proceeds of which went to Iraq, to compensate it for lost export capacity. In mid-1987, however, Saudi Arabia assured Iran that it was selling only a negligible amount of oil on Iraq's behalf.

As the war between Iran and Iraq showed signs of escalating towards the end of 1983 and in early 1984, Saudi Arabia appeared to be in danger of becoming involved militarily in the conflict. In April 1984 a Saudi Arabian merchant ship, a tanker loading at Iran's Kharg Island oil terminal, was struck by missiles from Iraqi fighter aircraft. In retaliatory incidents in May, Iranian aircraft attacked two more tankers, one of which was travelling in Saudi Arabian waters. In response, Saudi Arabia approached the USA to request help in improving its defence systems, by extending its air defence zone (with the new 'Fahd Line'), and by mobilizing its defences to patrol the region. At a meeting of the UN's Security Council in May, the GCC countries tried unsuccessfully to secure a general condemnation of Iran's behaviour in the war. However, they were supported by Egypt, a move which heralded an improvement in relations between Egypt and the more moderate Arab countries. In an attempt to maintain tanker traffic which might be deterred both by the threat of attack and by the high premiums that are charged to insure chartered tankers, the GCC announced in 1984 that it would replace any petroleum that was lost as a result of attacks on shipping in the Gulf. There were also reports that Saudi Arabia had built up a stockpile of oil, stored in tankers outside the mouth of the Strait, apparently sufficient to continue exports for some days in the event of any closure of the waterway. The willingness of the USA to become involved in safeguarding the Strait presented problems for the Gulf countries, since GCC policy countenances the intervention of either superpower only in a case of urgent need, and the Gulf States retained certain reservations in their otherwise good relations with the USA concerning, for example, US policy in Lebanon. Therefore, Saudi Arabia refused to give the USA access to military facilities on its territory in the event of a major escalation of the war between Iran and Iraq.

Saudi Arabia's concern for the development of its own defences was apparent in 1985, and was reflected particularly in the announcement of the Peace Shield defence programme in February. The project, which was not expected to be complete before the mid-1990s, aimed to provide Saudi Arabia with a computerized command, control and communications system for all of its air defences, and also involved the establishment of factories producing avionics and telecommunications equipment. Other defence projects under way in 1985 included plans for the formation of a joint strike force involving Saudi Arabia and its allies in the Gulf region, and the construction of the King Khalid military city, which was eventually to accommodate 70,000 people. Arrangements were also being made in 1985 for the introduction of military conscription. This was one of the aims of the country's fourth Development Plan (1985–90), and reflected growing concern over the dependence of Saudi Arabian military forces upon foreign recruits.

In June 1986 a controversial sale of military equipment was agreed between Saudi Arabia and the USA. The deal, which was initially valued at $3,000m., was reduced to $265m. when plans to supply 800 *Stinger* anti-aircraft missiles and 60 advanced fighter aircraft were cancelled, owing to strong Congressional opposition. Also in June, another controversial agreement was signed between the two countries for the sale of five US-built AWACS aircraft, worth $8,600m. Saudi Arabia's co-operation became essential to the US naval convoys, which began to escort reflagged Kuwaiti tankers through the Persian Gulf in June, following an increase in attacks on shipping in the Gulf by Iran and Iraq during the year. Saudi minesweepers also helped to clear Iranian mines from the shipping lanes in the Gulf in June, when Saudi Arabia agreed to extend the area of operation of its AWACS aircraft, which had been carrying out surveillance operations in the region, monitoring Iranian and Iraqi military movements in the Iran–Iraq War. The escalation of tension in the Gulf, exacerbated by the presence of US and Soviet naval forces, resulted in the adoption of Resolution No. 598 by the UN Security Council on 20 July 1987, which urged an immediate ceasefire. Iraq agreed to observe a cease-fire if Iran would also, but Iran prevaricated, attaching conditions to its acceptance of the Resolution. In November, at an extraordinary meeting of the League of Arab States in Amman, Jordan, representatives of the member nations, including Saudi Arabia, unanimously condemned Iran for prolonging the war against Iraq, deplored its occupation of Arab (i.e. Iraqi) territory, and urged it to accept Resolution No. 598 without preconditions. (For more detailed coverage of the Iran–Iraq War and of the events that led to a cease-fire in August 1988, see chapters on Iran and Iraq.)

In early 1985, following a visit by the Saudi Minister of Foreign Affairs, Prince Sa'ud al-Faisal, to Teheran, Ali Akbar Velayati, his Iranian counterpart, visited Riyadh in an attempt to improve relations between the two countries. However, in May two bombs exploded in the Sulmaniya district of Riyadh, killing one person and injuring three others. The Iranian-based Islamic Jihad group claimed responsibility and threatened that this was the beginning of a major bombing campaign within the country. Relations between Saudi Arabia and Iran deteriorated further in 1987, following clashes on 31 July between Iranian pilgrims and Saudi security forces during the *Hajj* (the annual pilgrimage of Muslims to the Islamic holy city of Mecca). Saudi Arabia reported that 402 people, of whom 275 were Iranians, were killed in the disturbances. It is unclear exactly what took place in Mecca. Iran alleged that Saudi security forces opened fire on Iranian pilgrims, and accused Saudi Arabia and the USA of planning the incident. Mass demonstrations took place in Teheran, the Saudi Embassy was sacked and Iranian leaders vowed to avenge the pilgrims' deaths by overthrowing the Saudi ruling family. Saudi Arabia, on the other hand, denied that any shooting took place, and insisted that the deaths occurred during a stampede caused by Iranian pilgrims, following unlawful political demonstrations in support of Ayatollah Khomeini. The Mecca incident renewed fears in Saudi Arabia, which had first been aroused after the Islamic revolution in Shi'ite Iran in 1979, that the minority Saudi Shi'ite community would rebel against the Sunni majority, to which the Saudi royal family belongs. However, Khomeini's brand of Islam does not appear to be congenial to Saudi Shi'ites, who have been largely quiescent since 1979. A more pressing concern was that Saudi Arabia might become directly involved in the Gulf War between Iran and Iraq, if Iran carried out its threats of armed retaliation. In March 1988 the Saudi Arabian Government announced its intention of temporarily limiting the number of pilgrims to Mecca from abroad during the *Hajj* season, which was to begin in mid-July. National quotas would be allocated on the basis of 1,000 pilgrims for every million citizens. This formula gave Iran a quota of 45,000. Iran's religious leader, Ayatollah Khomeini, insisted that 150,000 Iranians, the same number as in 1987, would perform the *Hajj,* and that he would not prevent them from staging political protests at Mecca. In the event, Iran decided not to send pilgrims on the *Hajj,* and the pilgrimage passed without incident. Saudi Arabia severed its diplomatic relations with Iran in April 1988.

In October 1986 Sheikh Ahmad Zaki Yamani was dismissed from office by King Fahd, after serving for 24 years as Minister of Petroleum and Mineral Resources. His dismissal was interpreted as a sign of King Fahd's dissatisfaction with the OPEC 'fair share' policy, adopted at the end of 1985, whereby OPEC abandoned its system of official quotas for petroleum production in an attempt to regain its share of the world market. Sheikh Hisham Nazer, the Minister of Planning, was appointed to represent Saudi Arabia at the OPEC conference held in December 1986, when his proposals for a return to a fixed reference price for crude petroleum of $18 per barrel were endorsed. Sheikh Nazer was subsequently confirmed by King Fahd as the new Minister of Petroleum and Mineral Resources, and, in April 1988, he was appointed as the first Saudi Arabian chairman of Aramco, the largest oil company operating in Saudi Arabia.

In November 1987 Saudi Arabia resumed full diplomatic relations with Egypt, following a decision taken by the League of Arab States that permitted member states to restore relations with Egypt at their own discretion. Relations had been broken off in 1979, following the signing of a peace treaty between Egypt and Israel.

In March 1988 the disclosure that Saudi Arabia had taken delivery of an unspecified number of Chinese DF-3 (CSS-2) medium-range missiles provoked threats by Israel of a preemptive strike on the missiles' base at al-Kharj. The USA subsequently warned Israel against taking such action. In April, however, it was reported that King Fahd, in an unprecedented move, had requested the replacement of the US ambassador, following his delivery of an official complaint from the USA concerning Saudi Arabia's purchase of the missiles. In the same month Sino-Saudi relations were further strengthened when the Deputy Minister of Foreign Affairs of the People's Republic of China (PRC) became the first Chinese leader to undertake an official visit to the kingdom. In May 1988 the US Senate voted to ban sales of military equipment to Saudi Arabia (or to any other nation which had taken delivery of CSS-2 missiles), unless the President could certify that the country purchasing the missiles had no chemical, biological or nuclear warheads with which to equip them.

Following the refusal of the US Congress to sanction an arms agreement, valued at an estimated $1,000m., to supply military equipment to Saudi Arabia, the kingdom signed an agreement with the UK, valued at a record $20,000m., for the supply of 50 *Tornado* fighter-bomber aircraft, 60 *Hawker* trainer aircraft, 80 helicopters manufactured by Westland, minesweepers and two huge airbases to be built in collaboration with Ballast Nedam of the Netherlands. The contract involved the implementation of a wide-ranging offset programme, whereby bilateral investments will be made by Saudi and British companies. This latest agreement confirmed the UK in the position of Saudi Arabia's main supplier of military equipment, a position previously held by the USA. Following events in the Gulf in August 1990, however, the USA concluded arms sales agreements with Saudi Arabia, which restored it to the position of Saudi Arabia's main military supplier.

In October 1988 four Saudi Arabian Shi'a Muslims, convicted of sabotaging a petrochemical plant and collaborating with Iran, were executed. In an attempt to demonstrate Saudi Arabia's intention of improving relations with Iran, it was decreed that the Saudi official media would halt their campaign of attacks on that country. However, in late 1988 and early 1989 two senior Saudi Arabian intelligence officers, posing as diplomats in an attempt to trace members of the pro-Iranian Shi'a group believed to be responsible for the aforementioned sabotage, were assassinated in Turkey and in Thailand.

In December 1988 the Soviet Deputy Minister of Foreign Affairs visited Saudi Arabia to discuss the conflict in Afghanistan. Saudi Arabia, along with Sudan, recognized the Afghan Mujaheddin Government-in-exile, formed following the Soviet withdrawal, and, at a meeting of the Organization of the Islamic Conference (OIC) in March, it urged other countries to do likewise. However, the exclusion by the Government-in-exile of the eight Mujaheddin opposition groups based in Iran angered the Iranians. Relations between Saudi Arabia and Iran were further strained at the OIC meeting by King Fahd's tolerance on the controversial question of Salman Rushdie's novel, *The Satanic Verses*. Moreover, the issue of compensation for the families of the Iranian pilgrims who died in the July 1987 riots remains unresolved. Iran boycotted the pilgrimage for the second time in July 1989, owing to Saudi Arabia's refusal to abandon the quota system agreed in March 1988 by the OIC (see above). Two explosions, which killed one pilgrim and wounded 16 in Mecca during the *Hajj*, widened the rift between the two countries. Iran blamed the USA and Saudi Arabia for the bombings, while the Saudis accused Iran of promoting terrorism. Saudi Arabia neglected to send condolences upon the death of Ayatollah Khomeini, illustrating the deterioration in relations with Iran. Iranian pilgrims boycotted the *Hajj* for the third successive year in 1990, and Iran claimed that the Saudi Arabian Government opposed their participation. However, Saudi Arabian officials said that Iranian pilgrims were welcome on condition that Iran observed the allocated quota.

Relations between Saudi Arabia and other Gulf states improved in 1989. In March King Fahd signed a non-aggression pact with Iraq, a development apparently designed to ease concerns among conservative Arab Gulf states about Iraq's political ambitions following the war between Iran and Iraq. In April Saudi Arabia announced that it would help Iraq to rebuild the nuclear reactor that had been destroyed by Israel, if the installation were used for peaceful purposes. In August documents ratifying the November 1988 agreement concluded by Kuwait and Saudi Arabia, concerning the property of citizens of the two countries in the Neutral Zone, were signed and exchanged at the Kuwaiti Ministry of Foreign Affairs. King Fahd's visit to Egypt in March 1989 was viewed as signifying the end of Egypt's isolation from the Arab world. Saudi Arabia and Egypt agreed to increase co-operation in trade, transport, insurance and cultural relations, but no decision regarding economic aid to Egypt was announced by King Fahd. Both countries declared their support for efforts to create a Palestinian state and denounced Israeli repression of the Palestinians in the occupied West Bank and Gaza Strip.

Defence remained a major concern in Saudi Arabia. In February 1989 the US Department of State announced that the USA was considering the sale of a large volume of military equipment to the Middle East, of which Saudi Arabia would be the main recipient. In March British Aerospace revealed that the value of the defence agreements signed by Saudi Arabia and Britain in 1985 and 1988 (see above) could ultimately reach £150,000m., representing one of the biggest arms contracts in history. In the same month, allegations that bribery was used to secure the contract led to an official investigation in Britain. Saudi Arabia denied the allegations, stating that the sale was agreed by the two Governments without the use of intermediaries. In June the first two proposals for British-Saudi joint venture projects under the £1,000m. economic offset programme were presented to the Saudi Arabian offset committee. The first concerns the estab-

lishment of a missile engineering plant in the Kingdom, and the second a private-sector aluminium smelter.

OPERATION DESERT SHIELD AND ITS IMPLICATIONS

Saudi Arabia's concern about its capacity to defend itself and its fears of Iraqi expansionism were substantiated in August 1990, when Iraq invaded and annexed Kuwait and proceeded to deploy armed forces along the Kuwaiti-Saudi Arabian border. Following consultations with the US Secretary of Defense, Richard Cheney, King Fahd decided that he had no option but to invite—in accordance with Article 51 of the UN Charter—multinational armed forces to Saudi Arabia in order to deter an attack on the country by Iraq. Thus 'Operation Desert Shield' was launched (see chapters on Jordan, Kuwait and Iraq).

King Fahd condemned the Iraqi invasion of Kuwait and offered refuge to the Amir of Kuwait. Kuwait established a government-in-exile at Ta'if, Saudi Arabia. Meanwhile, Saudi Arabia stressed the role of Egyptian, Moroccan, Pakistani, Bangladeshi, Kuwaiti and Syrian contingents in the multinational force. By so doing, it sought to counter allegations— by President Saddam Hussain of Iraq principally, but also by the Palestine Liberation Organization (PLO) and all those opposed to the USA's policies in the Middle East—that, by allowing the deployment of US forces in its defence, it had allowed itself to become an instrument of US strategic interests in the Gulf. The perception, in the Arab world, of Saudi Arabia as such an instrument threatened the whole of its diplomacy, by which it set great store, and which was based not only on the country's wealth, its leading role in OPEC and its custodianship of the holy cities, but also on the standing of King Fahd. Saudi Arabia stressed that the presence of the multinational defensive force was temporary.

There was a shift in the pattern of Saudi Arabia's foreign relations after the onset of the Gulf crisis in August 1990. The co-operation of the USSR, within the structures of the UN, was regarded as vital to the defence of Saudi Arabia, and in September Saudi Arabia and the USSR re-established diplomatic relations after a rupture lasting 50 years. Syria, aware of the diplomatic benefits that it could gain, committed forces to the defence of Saudi Arabia.

Meanwhile, Saudi Arabia implemented retaliatory measures against Jordan and Yemen for the equivocal stance that they had adopted towards Iraq's invasion of Kuwait. In late September 1990 Saudi Arabia expelled some diplomats from Iraq, Jordan and Yemen, while emergency supplies of oil to Jordan were terminated. Privileges enjoyed by the estimated 1.5m. Yemeni expatriate workers in Saudi Arabia were withdrawn, which resulted in the return to Yemen of more than 300,000 of the expatriates. In early November discussions on the restoration of diplomatic relations were held between Saudi Arabia and Iran. In the same month President George Bush of the USA visited Saudi Arabia, where he conferred with King Fahd and the exiled Amir of Kuwait.

By early January 1991 some 30 countries had contributed ground troops, aircraft and warships to the multinational force based in Saudi Arabia and the Gulf region, although the USA played the principal logistical role in the operation. The entire Saudi Arabian armed forces (numbering about 67,500 men) were mobilized in defence of the country. Financial contributions to the cost of the multinational force included an estimated $6,000m. by Saudi Arabia itself, $3,000m. by Japan, $2,800m. by the EC and DM3,000m. by Germany.

In mid-January 1991, following the failure of international diplomatic efforts to effect Iraq's withdrawal from Kuwait, the US-led multinational force launched a military campaign (Operation Desert Storm) to liberate Kuwait, as authorized by the UN Security Council's Resolution 678, which had been adopted in late November 1990. As part of its response to the aerial bombardment which began the campaign, Iraq launched 35 *Scud* missiles (not carrying chemical warheads, as had been feared) against mainly urban targets in Saudi Arabia, and made similar attacks against Israel. Most of the missiles were intercepted by advanced air defence systems that had been installed by the USA, although one of those that struck Saudi Arabia demolished a US barracks near Dhahran, killing 28 soldiers, in February. A potentially more damaging retaliatory measure was taken by Iraq in late January, when it released an estimated 4m. barrels of petroleum from Kuwaiti storage tanks into the Gulf, thus causing what was believed to be the largest spillage ever to have occurred. Although the flow of petroleum was contained by US aerial action, the resultant slick caused extensive ecological damage and threatened many Saudi Arabian coastal installations, including desalination plants. However, the long-term effects of the spillage were eventually seen to be less devastating than had been feared. In late January Iraqi forces entered Saudi Arabia, briefly occupying the town of Ras al-Khafji, close to Saudi Arabia's border with Kuwait, before being repelled by US, Saudi Arabian and Qatari units. Other Iraqi incursions in the same region were likewise repelled, and there was no further fighting on Saudi Arabian territory. In early February Iraq formally severed diplomatic relations with Saudi Arabia. By the end of February, when hostilities were suspended, Saudi Arabian casualties included at least 26 men killed and 10 missing.

Following the liberation of Kuwait and the declaration of a cease-fire in late February 1991, the Kuwaiti Prime Minister and other members of his Government returned to Kuwait from Saudi Arabia in early March, followed subsequently by the Amir. Also in early March, Saudi Arabia and seven other Arab states in the anti-Iraq coalition (the remaining members of the GCC, Egypt and Syria) agreed to form an Arab peace-keeping force in the Gulf region, as part of a draft plan on security and economic co-operation. Later in the month the withdrawal of coalition forces from bases in Saudi Arabia began. The return to Iraq of an estimated 62,000 Iraqi prisoners of war, held in camps in Saudi Arabia, also began in March. In April Saudi Arabia announced its decision to give refuge to an estimated 50,000 Iraqis, many of whom had participated in an unsuccessful revolt against Saddam Hussain's regime in the previous month. (In mid-1992 the vast majority of these remained in temporary accommodation, isolated within Saudi Arabia.) In early May the GCC member states endorsed US proposals for an increased Western military presence in the Gulf region, as a deterrent to any future military aggression.

Diplomatic relations between Saudi Arabia and Iran were re-established in late March 1991. Futhermore, it was agreed that 115,000 Iranian pilgrims would be permitted to attend the *Hajj* later in 1991, in accordance with Saudi Arabia's quota system. However, in June, the month during which the *Hajj* took place, it was estimated that fewer than 100,000 Iranian pilgrims attended. In April the Iranian Minister of Foreign Affairs, Dr Ali Akbar Velayati, had visited Saudi Arabia, and in June his visit was reciprocated by the Saudi Arabian Minister of Foreign Affairs, Prince Sa'ud al-Faisal, when he visited Teheran. In the same month the Saudi authorities made a further concession to Iran, permitting an Iranian anti-US demonstration in Mecca, and the Iranian embassy in Riyadh was reopened. The 1992 *Hajj* proceeded peacefully, and more than 2m. Muslims, including pilgrims from Iraq, made the journey. King Fahd also paid the pilgrimage costs of more than 13,000 Muslims from the former USSR. In May 1994 an estimated 270 pilgrims were killed in a stampede at the *Hajj*.

In February and May 1991 two petitions, presented to King Fahd, appealed for more extensive Islamization in areas as diverse as the armed forces, the press and all administrative and educational systems. The first petition bore the signatures of as many as 100 senior Saudi religious dignitaries, including that of Sheikh Abd al-Aziz ibn Baz, the most influential Saudi theologian. Following the second petition, the Government immediately sent security force personnel to visit leading signatories, some of whom were forbidden to travel abroad. In June the Government's Higher Judicial Council issued a statement warning the signatories of the consequences of issuing any further criticism against the King. The creation of the Higher Judicial Council, within the Ministry of Justice, is considered to be an institutional challenge to the judicial powers of the *ulama* (religious scholars) in Saudi Arabia. Reform of the judicial system was one of the principal aims of the petition, as it stipulated the establishment of a supreme judiciary council with the authority to implement Islamic

laws, which would conflict with the powers of the existing Higher Judicial Council. The petitions illustrated the growing assertiveness and restlessness of Islamic conservatives in the domestic debate on the political future of the country, which intensified after the Gulf crisis of 1990–91. On the other hand, the growth of liberal opposition was illustrated in April, when 43 intellectuals and businessmen published an open letter requesting the King to establish national and municipal councils and to curb the excesses of the Islamic religious police the *mutaween*.

At the end of July 1991 the US Department of Defense agreed to sell military equipment (including laser-guided bombs), worth US $365m., to Saudi Arabia. This followed an agreement announced earlier in the month, to sell $473m. worth of army jeeps and aircraft support services to the Kingdom and brought the total value of US-Saudi Arabia arms agreements (signed or announced) in 1990/91 to US $17,865m.

In early September 1991 it was revealed that 37,000 of the 541,000 US troops who had been deployed in Saudi Arabia during the Gulf war remained, in a non-military capacity, in the country. However, resistance to closer military co-operation came from both Islamic fundamentalists within the kingdom, who opposed a formal defence accord with the USA and the forward deployment of US military equipment and logistical units, and from pro-Israeli elements in the US Congress. Nevertheless, in September President Bush announced that he was authorizing the sale of 72 F-15 aircraft to Saudi Arabia. In the same month Saudi Arabia was awarded the presidency of the 46th annual session of the United Nations General Assembly in New York, USA. In late September the US Administration ordered the rapid preparation of airfields in Saudi Arabia, in order to receive US combat and surveillance aircraft, armed helicopters, tankers and ground crews within the next few days, in the event of an Iraqi attack. Military manoeuvres were expected to be initiated, following the detention, for the second time, of a team of US inspectors who had found evidence in Baghdad of foreign involvement in Iraq's prohibited nuclear programme. Several days later, however, the team was released, and tension eased.

At the end of January 1992 there were widespread reports of repression of fundamentalist dissent in the previous two months. On 29 January it was reported that the Minister of Justice had ordered the deposition of Sheikh Abd al-Ubaykan, the president of Riyadh's main court, who had criticized government policies in his Friday sermons and opposed the deployment of US troops on Saudi Arabian soil and the Middle East peace conference, which had begun in October 1991. At the end of the month Agence-France Presse reported that 20 Muslim clerics had been arrested in recent weeks, and a preacher dismissed and condemned to 80 lashes for criticizing the Saudi women's association. Sheikh ibn Baz exhorted the people of Saudi Arabia to ignore the 'smear campaign' against the government and praised the implementation of *Shari'a* law in the kingdom. In February 15 Iraqi opposition leaders met in Riyadh in an attempt to form a united front to depose Saddam Hussain. The conference was held amid strict security and indicated that Saudi Arabia was prepared to be more forthright in its opposition to the Iraqi President. In March a royal decree announced the creation of a Consultative Council within six months. Its members were to be selected by the King every four years, but were not to have any legislative powers. Two further decrees provided the framework for the creation of regional authorities and for a 'basic law of government', equivalent to a written constitution. However, in an interview with the Kuwaiti newspaper *As-Seyassa*, King Fahd stated that the 'prevailing democratic system' in the world was unsuited to the Gulf region, and that Islam favoured 'the consultative system and openness between a ruler and his subjects', rather than free elections. In September Sheikh Muhammad al-Jubair, hitherto the Minister of Justice, was appointed Chairman of the Consultative Council.

In November 1992 a major reorganization of the 18-member Supreme Council of the Ulema was instigated by royal decree. Among 10 new members appointed by the King was the new Minister of Justice, Abdullah ibn Muhammad ash-Sheikh. In a speech in December King Fahd warned the religious community not to use public platforms to discuss secular matters.

He also denounced the spread of Islamic fundamentalism, and referred to attempts by 'foreign currents' to destabilize the kingdom. In May 1993 Saudi authorities disbanded a committee for the protection of human rights, established by a group of six prominent Islamic scholars and lawyers, less than two weeks after its formation. The six founders of the committee were also dismissed from their positions, and their spokesman arrested. In September 1993 the human rights organization, Amnesty International, expressed concern at the increasing incidence of public executions in the kingdom, which had totalled 70 in that year. In April 1994 it was reported that members of the committee for the protection of human rights (disbanded in May 1993) including its spokesman, had relocated their organization to London, United Kingdom. In August four royal decrees had defined the membership and administration of the new Consultative Council (*Majlis ash-Shoura*), and outlined new rules governing the composition and procedure of the Council of Ministers. The Consulative Council was to consist of 60 men selected by King Fahd from the educated and professional classes. It was to meet regularly in full session, and eight committees were to be established to review the activities of Government. The composition of the Council did not lead observers to expect many challenges from it to government policies. In relation to the Council of Ministers, King Fahd set fixed limits for the cabinet's term of office and that of each cabinet member. Many ministers have occupied the same portfolio since the mid-1970s.

In September 1993 a further decree concerned a provincial system of government, the last of the constitutional reforms promised in March 1992. The decree defined the nature of government for the 13 regions, as well as the rights and responsibilities of their governors, and created councils of officials and citizens for each province to monitor development and to advise the government. Each council was to meet four times a year under the chairmanship of its governor, who will be an emir with ministerial rank. By the end of 1993 both the Consultative Council and the provincial councils had been opened.

The limits of liberalization in Saudi Arabia were displayed in 1994 by the announcement of a ban on private satellite dishes in March. The Government intends to establish its own cable system for receiving satellite channels in order to ensure that its citizens receive only channels which respect Islamic religious and social values. In June 1994 owners were instructed to send their private satellite dishes outside the kingdom or risk their confiscation and fines.

In April 1992 Saudi Arabia paid the final instalment of US $16,839m. worth of repayments to the USA for costs incurred during the Gulf crisis. The greater part of the figure was paid in cash, with $4,000m. provided in services and fuels. At the beginning of June a meeting of Ministers of Foreign Affairs of GCC countries was held in Riyadh. In mid-1992 there were signs of a *rapprochement* between Saudi Arabia and Jordan, as well as the PLO; King Fahd sent best wishes to King Hussein for a speedy recovery from an operation in the USA, and the Saudi Arabian Minister of Foreign Affairs received the Palestinian envoy to Riyadh, the first indication of a reconciliation since the outbreak of the Gulf crisis. In January 1994 King Fahd met PLO leader Yasser Arafat for the first time since the Gulf crisis and pledged $100m. towards the reconstruction of the Gaza Strip and Jericho, the two sites for Palestinian interim self-rule agreed by Israel and the PLO in their 1993 peace agreement. In February 1994 Saudi Arabia pledged $53,000 to the families of each Palestinian victim of the Hebron massacre.

In August 1992 US, British and French pilots made Dhahran their main base from which to enforce the exclusion of Iraqi aircraft from the zone south of 32°N, in accordance with UN Security Council Resolution 688. The intimacy of relations between the USA and Saudi Arabia was further illustrated by the announcement in February 1994 that American companies were to be awarded the major part of the order of Saudi Arabia's civilian air carrier, Saudia, for new and replacement aircraft, worth a total of US $6,000m.

In September 1992 the Government sent a memorandum to the Government of Yemen in an attempt to expedite demarcation of the Saudi-Yemeni border. Sporadic negotiations, through the medium of a joint border commission, continued into 1993 but stalled in 1994 as a result of renewed civil war between north and south in Yemen. At the end of September 1992 trouble flared with Qatar, which accused a Saudi military force of attacking a border post at al-Khofous, killing two soldiers and capturing a third. On 1 October Qatar announced the suspension of the 1965 border agreement with Saudi Arabia, and in the same month it was reported that Qatar was to withdraw its contingent of 200 troops from the GCC 'peninsula shield' force, stationed in Kuwait. However, in late December 1992, following mediation by president Hosni Mubarak of Egypt, the Qatari Amir, Sheikh Khalifa signed an agreement in Medina with King Fahd to establish a committee which was to demarcate the border between the two states by 1994. In March 1993 the leaders of eight Afghan *mujahidin* factions travelled to Mecca, at the instigation of King Fahd, to discuss their differences. The leaders subsequently ratified the Islamabad-Afghanistan peace accord, which aimed at achieving a peaceful settlement in the region, and which was also signed by King Fahd and the Pakistani prime minister, Nawaz Sharif, as co-guarantors. However, with the resurgence of fighting soon after, Saudi Arabia appealed for a mediation effort by the OIC and a UN-sponsored cease-fire plan.

Economy

Revised for this edition by ALAN J. DAY

The economy of Saudi Arabia is dominated by petroleum, of which the country is by far the largest producer within the Organization of the Petroleum Exporting Countries (OPEC). Saudi Arabia has received massive revenues from petroleum exports (particularly since the dramatic increase in international petroleum prices in 1973–74), which it has used in part to finance an ambitious programme of infrastructural development and modernization, as well as far-reaching programmes for health, social and educational purposes. Substantial budgetary allocations have also been made to the country's armed forces and to the purchase of sophisticated weaponry from abroad. Conservative and strictly Islamic in orientation, the Saudi ruling family has consistently favoured a pro-Western, market-orientated economic strategy and has placed great reliance on Western and Japanese expertise for the development of the country's petroleum and other sectors.

There remains a substantial expatriate contribution to the management of various economic sectors, although Saudi nationals have come increasingly to the fore, especially in the petroleum and gas industries. Emphasis has been placed, under recent development plans, on the promotion of 'downstream' oil industries, such as refining and petroleum derivatives, and progress has also been made in developing the country's non-oil industries and in overcoming climatic obstacles to agricultural production.

Whereas in the 1970s and early 1980s Saudi Arabia's exports consisted almost entirely of petroleum, by the late 1980s non-oil exports represented more than 10% of total value. A similar pattern was apparent in the structure of gross domestic product (GDP), enhanced by a sharp fall in petroleum production in the mid-1980s. Having achieved an average annual growth rate of 10.6% in the period 1968–80, Saudi

Arabia's GDP declined, in real terms, at an average rate of 1.8% per year over the decade 1980–89, largely because petroleum output was reduced from a peak of almost 10m. barrels per day (b/d) in 1980 to 3.6m. b/d in 1985 (see Petroleum, below). Although production rose to more than 5m. b/d in 1988 and 1989, depressed international prices resulted in substantially reduced revenues, with adverse consequences for the current account and national budget, both of which moved into deficit. The situation was transformed by the Gulf crisis of 1990–91, as a result of which Saudi Arabia entered a new period of economic growth. The cost of the conflict to the Saudi Government was substantial, being estimated at between $50,000m. and $65,000m., with the result that the current account and budget deficits rose sharply in 1990–91. However, partly to compensate for the loss of Iraqi supplies, Saudi Arabia was able to increase its petroleum production to more than 8m. b/d, as international petroleum prices rose sharply because of the crisis. Overall GDP exceeded $100,000m. in 1990, for the first time since 1983, and stood at $108,640m. in 1991. The growth rate of GDP, in real terms, was estimated to be around 5% in 1992 and 1% in 1993, compared with 10.8% in 1990 and 9.8% in 1991. The Government reactivated a range of major projects under the 1990–95 Five-Year Plan, aiming, in particular, at industrial diversification and import substitution. In 1991, according to World Bank figures, Saudi Arabia's gross national product (GNP) per head was $7,820 (assuming a mid-year population of 15.4m.), having declined at an average annual rate of 3.4%, in real terms over the period 1980–91 (when the population increased by an estimated 4.6% per year).

AREA AND POPULATION

The area of Saudi Arabia has been estimated at 2,240,000 sq km (864,869 sq miles), but, since not all of the borders have been defined, it is not possible to arrive at a precise figure. The preliminary results of a census held in September and October 1992 recorded the total population as 16,929,294, of whom 12,304,835 (males 50.5%, females 49.5%) were Saudi Arabian citizens and 4,624,459 (males 70.4%, females 29.6%) were foreign nationals. The census results reflected the country's dependence on foreign contract labour in most areas of employment outside administration, banking and certain state enterprises. Total civilian employment in Saudi Arabia was estimated at 5,771,800 in 1991 and was expected to approach 6m. in 1995. It was estimated that more than three-quarters of Saudi Arabia's population resided in urban areas in 1990 (compared with less than one-half at the end of the 1960s).

A comprehensive socio-economic survey of the royal capital, Riyadh, published by the Ar-Riyadh Development Authority (ADA) in 1992, provided detailed examples of recent trends in the composition of the urban population and labour force in Saudi Arabia. Between 1986 and 1991, the survey showed, the area of land under development in Riyadh had almost doubled, while the population had likewise risen by 49%, to 2,073,800, comprising 1,334,800 Saudi nationals and 739,000 non-nationals. Net migration into the city accounted for more than one-third of the total population increase over this period. Some 153,000 Egyptians constituted the largest group of foreign nationals in Riyadh in 1991, a large number of Yemenis having been forced to leave the country after Iraq's invasion of Kuwait in 1990. The next largest group of non-nationals in 1991 comprised Syrians, Jordanians and Iraqis. The survey showed that 60% of Riyadh's 1991 population was aged less than 20 years, and just 2% aged more than 60, and that the average age of the Saudi nationals was 17.1 years. Total employment in the city was 584,779 in 1991, nearly 40% higher than in 1986, with Saudi nationals filling 254,182 jobs in 1991. The employment of women (severely restricted by Islamic law and custom) nearly doubled to 83,000 (of whom 72,000 were non-nationals) between 1986 and 1991, virtually all of the employed Saudi females in Riyadh being engaged in professional and technical positions. Riyadh's unskilled work-force (accounting for 28% of all jobs in the city) was almost entirely composed of foreign nationals in 1991, whereas Saudi citizens held nearly 50% of professional and technical jobs and about 73% of clerical jobs.

DEVELOPMENT PLANS

Since 1970 the development of the Saudi economy has been guided by a series of five-year plans. The first Plan (1970–75) was a relatively modest programme costing 56,223m. riyals, of which 32,762m. riyals was allotted to economic and social development. However, after the rise in petroleum revenues in 1973–74 (see Petroleum, below), the Government found itself in possession of vast financial resources and determined to embark on a massive programme of industrialization and modernization. Hence the second Five-Year Plan (1975–80) provided for expenditure of no less than 498,230m. riyals (about $142,000m.). It was described by the Saudi Minister of Planning, Hisham Nazer, as an 'experiment in social transformation'. The largest single investment item in the second Plan was defence, put at 78,157m. riyals, followed by education at 74,161m. riyals, urban development at 53,328m. riyals and industrial and mineral production at 45,058m. riyals.

A major feature of the second Plan was a project to increase industrial output, creating two new industrial cities, one at Jubail on the Gulf coast and the other at Yanbu on the Red Sea. Development of the two sites was to take 10 years and cost around $70,000m. Jubail was to have three petroleum refineries, six petrochemical plants, an aluminium smelter and a steel mill, as well as support industries, an industrial port and large-scale urban development. Yanbu was planned on a slightly smaller scale: two petroleum refineries, a natural gas processing plant, a petrochemical complex, other lighter industries, an industrial port and a new urban area. The Yanbu industries were to be supplied by an oil pipeline and a gas pipeline across the Arabian peninsula from the Eastern Province. There were also plans to expand existing industrial and commercial sites, at Dammam in particular.

Despite the pessimism of most foreign commentators, the Saudi Arabian Government pursued the goals of the second Plan with great determination, and the results were, on the whole, successful. Although the main industrial projects fell behind schedule, infrastructure grew apace, endowing the country with the basic transport and communications facilities which are required by a modern industrial state.

Consequently, the third Five-Year Plan (1980–85) was intended to shift the emphasis from infrastructure projects to the productive sectors, with particular importance accorded to agriculture and the aim of achieving 'food security' by being less dependent on imported foodstuffs. The Plan stressed the need for manpower training, to reduce reliance on foreign labour, and for Saudi private investors to be encouraged to play a more prominent role in the economy. Planned investment for the five-year period was set at 782,000m. riyals (about $235,000m.), but this total did not include defence spending, the largest item of expenditure under the previous Plan.

The fourth Five-Year Plan (1985–90), published in March 1984, envisaged a total expenditure of 1,000,000m. riyals at current prices, of which 500,000m. riyals were allocated to development projects in the civilian sector. Four essential policy themes underlay the Plan: greater operational efficiency; an emphasis on non-oil revenue-generating activities, particularly industry, agriculture and financial services; a campaign to develop private-sector involvement and initiatives; and the need for further economic and social integration among the countries of the Gulf Co-operation Council (GCC). Within the details of the Plan, considerable emphasis was also given to raising desalination capacity, the expansion of irrigation and power facilities, a review of subsidies, the reduction of expatriate labour, the development of new industrial estates, and the expansion of Saudi Arabia's health services.

By mid-1988, the fourth Development Plan was widely considered to have fallen short of its targets, mainly as a result of the steep decline in oil revenues following the collapse in oil prices in 1986. The implementation of many projects, in particular those involving public utilities, had been delayed.

Direct military spending was to receive 312,500m. riyals of the fourth Plan's allocation, sustaining the emphasis already given to defence by the Government. As a consequence of the Iran-Iraq war, large sums of money had already been spent on defence, in particular on the Peace Shield Defence System, which was announced in 1985. In the early part of that year the Boeing Aerospace Corporation of the USA was chosen to complete the project at a cost of $3,700m. The programme would provide a computerized command, control and communications system for Saudi Arabia's air defences. In July 1991 the Hughes Aircraft Company of the USA was awarded a contract to complete the Peace Shield air defence project, and so replaced the original contractor, Boeing. The scheme was estimated to cost $837m. Boeing was replaced because of substantial delays in implementing the programme. In early 1986 another major defence contract, worth about £7,500m., was signed with the British Government for the supply of 48 *Tornado* fighter-bomber aircraft from the European Panavia consortium, 30 *Hawk* trainer aircraft from British Aerospace and 30 *Pilatus* trainers. In July 1988 a new agreement, which more than doubled the value of the orginal contract, was signed. It included a revised £1,000m. offset programme which involved bilateral investments by Saudi and British companies. In addition to aircraft, the new agreement envisaged the supply of ships and the construction of two huge airbases. It is expected that the provisions of the agreement will not be fulfilled until the late 1990s.

The fifth Five-Year Development Plan (1990–95) envisaged a total expenditure of 753,000m. riyals. Owing to the crisis in the Gulf following the invasion of Kuwait by Iraq, Saudi Arabia increased military spending, and about 34% (255,000m. riyals) of total expenditure in the fifth Plan was to be allocated to defence, with education receiving 19% and health and social services 12%.

The six major themes of the 1990–95 Plan are: the expansion of government revenue, in particular from non-oil sources; increased reliance on the private sector; further job opportunities and training for the Saudi Arabian labour force; import substitution and the promotion of exports; the diversification of economic activities into non-oil areas; and a balanced development of the regions. Under the Plan, the encouragement of Saudi Arabian industry, notably in the construction sector, was to be reinforced by the '30% rule', according to which at least 30% of the value of government contracts has to be awarded to Saudi Arabian companies.

AGRICULTURE AND FISHING

Agriculture (including forestry and fishing), contributed only 8% of gross domestic product (GDP) in 1990, although the sector employed an estimated 39% of the labour force in that year. Its contribution to GDP increased from 3.3% in 1984, mainly as the result of the decline in revenue from petroleum that Saudi Arabia began to experience in the mid-1980s. In 1988 agricultural exports accounted for about 40% of non-oil exports. During the third Five-Year Plan (1980–85), the output of the agricultural sector expanded, in real terms, at an average of 8.7% per year, compared with its projected growth rate of 5.4%. Cultivation is confined to oases and to irrigated regions, which comprise only 2% of the total land area. About 39% of land is used for low-grade grazing. In 1988 the Ministry of Agriculture and Water reported that, over the previous 10 years, the area of cultivated land in Saudi Arabia had increased to approximately 2.5m. ha, at a time when the agricultural labour force was falling in numbers. A considerable area of this land lies fallow, however, and only about 600,000 ha are under regular cultivation. In mid-1988 a total of 776,111 ha of agricultural land was distributed amongst the Kingdom's farmers. The annual harvest of wheat increased from 142,000 metric tons in 1979/80 to a record level of 3.9m. tons in 1990/91, of which 1.7m. tons were exported. Local demand is estimated at about 1m. tons per year. In mid-1988 the Ministry of Agriculture and Water reduced its subsidy of 2,000 riyals per metric ton on wheat production, to 1,500 riyals for larger wheat producers only. The Grain Silos and Flour Mills Organization (GSFMO), the state-owned body responsible for overseeing the cereals sector, has storage capacity for about 2m. tons. These increases in production have been heavily subsidized by the Government, which, through the GSFMO, paid farmers about $1,000 per ton of wheat produced in the 1984 season; approximately six times the average world price. In 1985 a plan to reduce the volume

of wheat bought by the GSFMO to 60% received a hostile response and was abandoned. Levels of subsidy subsequently declined. In 1988/89 farmers were paid $533 per ton to produce wheat that was available on the world market for $120. However, government policy concerning the reduction of subsidies remained cautious, in order to maintain the stability of the agricultural sector and ensure its continued contribution to the diversification of the economy. Production of sorghum fell from 110,000 tons in 1979/80 to 63,000 tons in 1981/82, but recovered to an estimated 87,000 tons in each of the following two seasons. Levels of barley and millet production have remained low. Indeed, imports of barley have become a new problem, with record levels of barley being imported in 1986/87. A system of subsidies was introduced for domestic barley cultivation in 1986, in an attempt to reduce imports of barley, in particular from the USA and the UK, which reached 1,434,000 tons in the year to March 1987, compared with 506,000 tons in the year to March 1986. In early 1989 the remaining import subsidy of 100 riyals per ton was abolished, despite a barley harvest in 1988 estimated at only 187,000 tons. In an attempt to increase the barley harvest, the Government required the Kingdom's six large publicly-owned farms to cultivate one-third of their crop-land with barley. By 1990/91 the annual output of barley had risen to more than 400,000 tons. In 1987 Saudi Arabia became the world's sixth-largest exporter of cereals. By 1990 output from Saudi Arabia's flour mills had reached almost 1m. tons per year, compared with 748,000 tons in 1985. In 1993 a marked tightening of government agricultural policy—enforced partly through deliberate delays in payments to some cereal farmers—reduced the wheat harvest to 3.6m. tons (down from a record 4.07m. tons in 1992) while increasing the barley harvest to 1.1m. tons (up from 406,000 tons in 1992). The forecast harvests for 1994 were 1.8m. tons of wheat and 1.47m. tons of barley. In 1993 exports of wheat had totalled nearly 2.2m. tons, while imports of barley (mainly for livestock feed) totalled 3.7m. tons. The GSFMO had announced in August 1993 that it would buy no wheat in 1994 from the six main commercial producers while imposing quota restrictions on purchases from smaller commercial farmers, who would be entitled to an 'incentive' price of $400 per ton. The aggregate government subsidy to wheat farmers was estimated to have reached $1,300m. per year before the production cutbacks started. The GSFMO budget for 1994 was 2,697.8m. riyals, compared with 3,336.2m. riyals in 1993. In addition to grain production, the Kingdom has expanded its fresh food sector. By 1990/91 annual production of watermelons had increased to approximately 1m. tons, dates to 545,000 tons (Saudi Arabia is the world's leading producer of dates), tomatoes to 410,000 tons, and grapes to 110,000 tons. By 1986 Saudi Arabia was self-sufficient in eggs and broiler chickens. The annual output of eggs increased from 113,941 tons in 1987 to an estimated 170,000 tons in 1990/91.

The importance of developing the agricultural sector as a means of reducing imports has been emphasized by the Government. In 1987 an increase in local output reduced food imports to 65% of total food requirements, compared with 83% in 1980. The cost of imported food declined from $4,669m. in 1984 to $2,781m. in 1986, and stood at $2,799m. in 1987. It increased, in dollar terms, to $3,067m. in 1988, $4,438m. in 1989, $5,023m. in 1990 and $5,500m. in 1991.

Saudi Arabia is subject to important natural limitations on the development of agriculture, principally the scarcity of water. Agriculture accounts for 89% of water demand in the Kingdom. The Government has initiated an ambitious programme to improve the country's water supply, including surveys for underground water resources (20 main aquifers had been established by 1983, nine of which were being exploited), construction of dams, irrigation and drainage networks, combined with distribution of fallow land, settlement of bedouin and the introduction of mechanization. The eventual aim of the programme is to raise agricultural production to the level of near self-sufficiency in all foods. Consequently, budgetary allocations for the agricultural sector have increased considerably in recent years. The third Five-Year Plan (1980–85) projected spending on agriculture at 7,975m. riyals, and on water (mainly desalination plants) at no less than 52,979m. riyals, although much of this was to be used for developing urban water supplies. Surveys that were conducted in the 1960s indicated a potential for greatly increasing agricultural output by means of irrigation. Under the 1985–90 Plan, 50,000 ha of land were to be drained or irrigated, and 8,000 ha were to be converted into pasture land.

In 1981, according to FAO estimates, 395,000 ha of land were irrigated. Important projects which have been undertaken by the Government include the al-Hasa irrigation scheme, the Faisal Model Settlement scheme, the Wadi Gizan and Najran dam projects and the Abha dam. The al-Hasa irrigation and drainage scheme, inaugurated in December 1971, was completed over five years at a cost of 260m. riyals. It is the country's largest agricultural scheme and about 50,000 people benefit from it. The Faisal Model Settlement scheme, which cost 100m. riyals, has involved extensive land reclamation and irrigation, and provided permanent farmland and housing for 1,000 bedouin families. The Wadi Gizan dam, inaugurated in March 1971, has a reservoir with a capacity of 71m. cu m of water and was built at a cost of 42m. riyals. A second dam at Wadi Najran, completed in 1980, has added a further 68m. cu m to water storage capacity in the Gizan Najran area. The Abha dam, in the Asir region, was opened in April 1974, with a reservoir capacity of 2.4m. cu m. In all, the Kingdom operated a total of 104 dams in 1983.

Apart from lack of water, the major constraint on Saudi agriculture is shortage of labour, as the population is drawn away from rural areas by the attractions of urban development, and most farm workers are expatriates. The Government is countering the drift to the towns by improving rural facilities, but the future of Saudi agriculture must lie in capital-intensive, large-scale farming, highly mechanized and requiring only a small workforce. A major success has been achieved with dairy farming, using the most modern technical expertise from Sweden, Denmark and Ireland. In 1988 Masstock Saudia, a joint venture established by Ireland and Saudi Arabia in 1976, had 12 farms throughout the Kingdom, and a herd of 11,000 cows, yielding an average 7,900 litres of milk per year. The Saudi Arabian Agriculture and Dairy Company (SAADCO) was formed in 1980, and by the end of 1984 had 15,000 cows and a 60 sq km farm at al-Kharj. By 1991 Saudi Arabia was self-sufficient in fresh milk and *laban* (a yoghurt drink), milk production being 550m. litres in 1990/91. Subsidized milk powder from the EC constitutes the main competition to local production.

Government encouragement to farmers is substantial. Interest-free loans are available through the Agricultural Bank, set up in 1963, and a total of 9,209 loans, valued at 1,551m. riyals were disbursed by the bank in 1985/86. Chemical fertilizers, domestic or imported, are distributed at half-price. There are also large subsidies available to local farmers for the purchase of farm machinery (amounting to 45% of the total cost of the item), irrigation pumps and imported rearing stock. In response to these incentives, the agricultural sector has made rapid progress in recent years, and grew at over 6% per year in the early 1980s. As a result of declining revenue from petroleum in the early 1980s, expenditure on agriculture was reduced. In the 1985/86 financial year the total amount of loans by the Agricultural Bank was 33% lower than in the previous year, and less than one-half the level of four years earlier. Total planned lending under the fifth Development Plan is set at 14,411m. riyals, compared with 61,000m. riyals disbursed during the third Plan.

Criticism of Saudi Arabia's agricultural policy has concentrated on the high depletion rate of the non-renewable fossil aquifers from which farmers draw most of their water supply. It was estimated in 1992 that the water table in Qassim (the principal wheat-growing area) had fallen by 100 m in the previous decade. The export of subsidized wheat has also been criticized, and it has been calculated that dairy farming in Saudi Arabia uses 1,500 litres of water per litre of milk production.

The fishing industry has grown in recent years, and in 1988 Saudi Arabia's total catch was 46,773 tons, an amount which satisfied about one-half of total local demand. The Saudi Fisheries Company (SFC) recorded a net profit of 33.1m. riyals

in 1988. Sales increased in that year by 22%, in comparison with 1987, and included exports to seven countries. The company announced an increase in sales from 221m. riyals in 1989 to 235.5m. riyals in 1990. It recorded a minor decrease in net profit, to 30.2m. riyals, owing to the crisis in the Gulf region, which forced 3m. riyals of extra expenditure to be incurred on emergency measures. New projects launched by the company included a facility to convert fish to fodder, a processing factory and the purchase of shrimping vessels. The SFC reported in June 1992 that stocks of shrimps in the Gulf had been almost destroyed by pollution, caused by the Gulf hostilities. The SFC recorded losses of 18.4m. riyals in 1993 and a 22% fall in fish and shrimp catches compared with 1992.

PETROLEUM

The most important industry in Saudi Arabia is the production of crude petroleum and petroleum products. Saudi Arabia is the major petroleum-producer in OPEC, accounting for one-third of the organization's output in 1992/93, and is one of the three principal producers in the world, accounting for 13.5% of global oil output in 1992, slightly ahead of the USA (13.1%) and Russia (12.5%) in that year. Saudia Arabia's proven reserves of petroleum at the start of 1994 totalled 261,200m. barrels (25.9% of the world total and 33.8% of the OPEC total), sufficient to maintain production at 1993 levels for 84 years. Production is from 14 major oilfields, in particular Ghawar, Abqaiq, Safaniya and Berri. Ghawar is generally accepted as the world's largest oilfield, while Safaniya is the world's largest offshore field. The kingdom also enjoys equal rights with Kuwait to the petroleum reserves of the Saudi Arabia-Kuwait Neutral Zone, which totalled 5,000m. barrels at the start of 1993.

In 1933 a concession was granted to Standard Oil Company of California to explore for petroleum in Saudi Arabia. The operating company, the Arabian-American Oil Company (Aramco), began exploration in that year, and discovered petroleum in commercial quantities in 1938. By the end of the Second World War, four oilfields had been discovered, and the necessary facilities had been established to satisfy post-war demands for crude petroleum and refined products. Other US companies gradually acquired shares in Aramco, bringing the ownership structure in 1948 to: Standard Oil 30%, Texaco 30%, Exxon 30% and Mobil 10%.

In November 1962 the Government created the General Petroleum and Mineral Organization (PETROMIN) as the instrument for increasing state participation in the petroleum and gas industries. In accordance with the action of other Arab petroleum-producing states, the Saudi Government acquired a 25% share in Aramco in January 1973. A 100% takeover of the company was agreed in 1980 (for the subsequent creation of Saudi Aramco, see below).

The expansion of Saudi Arabia's petroleum output in the 1960s and 1970s was spectacular. Production increased from about 62m. metric tons (equivalent to 1.3m. b/d) in 1960 to 178m. tons (3.8m. b/d) in 1970, and to 412m. tons (8.5m. b/d) in 1974. This growth in output was accompanied by rising prices for petroleum, culminating in the huge increases of October and December 1973, which almost quadrupled the cost per barrel. The Saudi Government's petroleum revenues increased dramatically, from $1,214m. in 1970 to $22,573m. in 1974. The price rises reflected OPEC's collective will to exploit a favourable market situation. The industrialized countries' fear of a shortfall in petroleum supplies placed them completely at the mercy of OPEC.

After the events of 1973–74, however, Saudi Arabia emerged as a powerful conservative and pro-Western influence in OPEC, using its high potential output to hold down the price of petroleum. In the depressed market of 1975, the country's production of crude petroleum declined to 344m. tons (7.1m. b/d), but in 1977 it rose to a new peak of 455m. tons (9.2m. b/d), with government revenues at $36,540m. This increase in output resulted from a disagreement within OPEC over pricing. By raising output, Saudi Arabia put pressure on the market to depress prices, because countries charging higher prices would find it difficult to sell their petroleum. A compromise on OPEC pricing policy was reached in July 1977.

For most of 1978, the supply of petroleum was plentiful, prices remained steady, and Saudi Arabia kept its production below 8.5m. b/d. With the outbreak of the Iranian revolution in late 1978, however, the situation was transformed. To compensate for the Iranian shortfall, Saudi Arabia increased production to more than 10m. b/d. The country's total output for 1978 was 410m. tons (8.3m. b/d), with government revenue from petroleum reaching $32,234m., but 919m. barrels were produced in the last quarter alone. Output was maintained at around 9.5m. b/d for most of 1979, but prices increased sharply, as intense anxiety over petroleum supplies seized the industrialized West. Despite Saudi efforts, the price of the country's petroleum rose rapidly. The price of one grade, Saudi light crude, increased from $13.3 per barrel at the start of 1979 to $28 per barrel in May 1980, the most rapid rise since 1973–74. Since Saudi Arabia's total output for 1979 was 470m. tons (9.5m. b/d) and prices doubled in the course of the year, government revenues from petroleum reached a new peak of $48,435m.

The Saudi Government raised production in the last quarter of 1980 to 10.3m. b/d to compensate for output lost as a consequence of the Iran–Iraq war, giving a record total production for the year of 493m. tons (9.99m. b/d), which remains the peak output level for any one year. Prices continued to drift upwards, Saudi light crude reaching $32 per barrel by the end of 1980, and total government revenues from petroleum in that year were $84,466m., which represented an increase of 74% over the previous year's figure. During the first nine months of 1981, however, Saudi efforts to hold down prices finally began to have a real effect. Slack demand in the West, combined with the continued high level of Saudi output (maintained at more than 10m. b/d), made it difficult to sell petroleum at the official level and impossible for prices to rise any further. In October 1981, in an attempt to restore a unified price structure, Saudi Arabia induced OPEC to accept a package involving a $2 rise in the market price to $34 per barrel, accompanied by a cut in Saudi output to a ceiling of 8.5m. b/d. Total Saudi output for 1981 fell marginally, to 491m. tons (9.98m. b/d), but government revenues from petroleum reached a record level of about $102,000m.

During 1982 world demand for petroleum continued to fall and, after a further OPEC meeting in March, the Saudi Government declared a new upper limit of 7.5m. b/d for the country's production. In reality, output had already dropped below that figure. Total production for 1982 was 328m. tons, an average of only 6.6m. b/d, and the petroleum sector's output, as a proportion of real GDP, declined by 36.1% during the year 1982/83. Finally, in March 1983, OPEC bowed to market pressure. The member states agreed to reduce the market price by 15%, to $29 per barrel, and to limit total OPEC output to 17.5m. b/d. Total Saudi output for 1983 was 256m. tons (5.2m. b/d), and in 1984 production levels fell once again, to 233m. tons (4.8m. b/d), yielding revenues of $46,000m. Since 1984 Saudi Arabia has been involved in barter agreements, whereby petroleum is exchanged for other goods, particularly aircraft and military equipment.

Saudi Arabia's petroleum is mostly exported by tanker from terminals on the Gulf coast. In 1981 Petromin completed construction of a trans-Arabian pipeline to Yanbu on the Red Sea coast. The pipeline, designed to carry some 1.9m. b/d (mainly for export from a Red Sea tanker terminal), shortens the export route to Western Europe and North America by about 3,500 km. A new pipeline, linking the Iraqi oilfields to the Trans-Arabian pipeline, was completed in 1985, allowing Iraq and Saudi Arabia to share the pipeline until 1989, when a direct pipeline, with a capacity of 1.6m. b/d, was planned to link Iraqi oilfields to Yanbu. A former 1,200-km line from the Saudi oilfields to Lebanon and Jordan is no longer in use.

In the 1980s Saudi Arabia acted as a 'swing producer' within OPEC, adjusting its own production levels in order to keep overall production by OPEC member states within the organization's recommended limits. However, the lack of agreement among OPEC members on pricing and production, and the loss of revenue resulting from Saudi Arabia's much lower production levels, culminated in a major change of policy in late 1985. Saudi Arabia abandoned its former role and increased sales, with petroleum exports in the last quarter of

1985 at their highest since the end of 1983. Nevertheless, total production in 1985 was only 173m. tons (3.6m. b/d), yielding revenues of $27,000m. At the end of 1985 OPEC decided to end its official quota policy and to seek a greater share of the world market, to offset falling prices. As a result of a surge in production, international prices for crude petroleum fell precipitously in 1986, dipping below $10 per barrel in July. Accordingly, although Saudi Arabian output in 1986 rose to 251m. tons (5.2m. b/d), oil revenues fell to $20,000m.

In October 1986 the veteran Minister of Petroleum and Mineral Resources, Sheikh Ahmad Zaki Yamani, was dismissed by King Fahd. He was replaced by Sheikh Hisham Nazer, the former Minister of Planning, and a policy aimed at limiting production and increasing prices was implemented. The policy was proposed by Sheikh Nazer at an OPEC meeting held in December, whereby a target price for crude petroleum of $18 per barrel was to be supported by an arrangement ensuring strict output quotas, with a production ceiling for the first half of 1987 of 15.8m. b/d, a reduction of 7.25% in each country's quota compared with December. Saudi Arabia, which was allotted a nominal quota of 4,133,000 b/d, was again effectively the 'swing producer'. The new production agreement came into effect on 1 January 1987. In practice, however, production in the first half of 1987 was consistently below the ceiling and prices stabilized at slightly above the reference level of $18 per barrel.

In June 1987 OPEC members agreed to maintain the reference price of $18 per barrel in the second half of that year, but to increase their collective production by 800,000 b/d, to 16.6m. b/d. Under the revised arrangements, Saudi Arabia was allocated a quota of 4,343,000 b/d, its actual average output in 1987 being close to the quota, at 4.36m. b/d (annual production 212m. tons), yielding revenues of $25,000m. The agreement was extended for further six-month periods at OPEC meetings in December 1987 and May 1988. The ceiling for the other 12 members of OPEC was 15.06m. b/d. However, consistent over-production caused a renewed decline in the price of crude petroleum, which fell below $12 per barrel in September 1988. Total Saudi Arabian production in 1988 rose to 257m. tons (5.26m. b/d), but revenues fell to around $20,000m. In November 1988 OPEC agreed to form a committee, comprising representatives of eight member states, to monitor the production quotas of all members and to supervise adherence to the agreed production levels. At the same meeting OPEC agreed a collective production quota of 18.5m. b/d, of which Saudi Arabia's share was to be 4,524,000 b/d, to take effect from January 1989 and to operate for the first six months of the year. At the mid-1989 OPEC conference the production ceiling was raised to 19.5m. b/d, and in November quotas were redistributed within a new ceiling of 22m. b/d. Total Saudi Arabian output for the year was slightly reduced, at 256m. tons (5.2m. b/d), with revenues at $24,000m.

The OPEC meeting in Geneva in July 1990 was held in an atmosphere of increasing tension, caused by Iraq's threats of military action against those countries—principally the UAE and Kuwait—which it had accused of exceeding their production quotas. At the meeting Iraq sought to raise OPEC's minimum reference price for crude petroleum to $25 per barrel, but, in the event, OPEC's ministerial council adopted a price of $21 per barrel and fixed a new production ceiling of 22.5m. b/d for the remainder of 1990. Quotas for individual countries remained unchanged (Saudi Arabia's at 5.38m. b/d), except that of the UAE, which was raised to 1.5m. b/d.

Prior to the full OPEC meeting in July 1990, the five principal Gulf petroleum producers had met in Jeddah and agreed to curb over-production, thus facilitating the agreement that was reached in July. Prices had increased by about $2 per barrel as a result of the Jeddah meeting. Demand for OPEC crude petroleum was forecast at more than 22.5m. b/d for the second half of 1990, and it was hoped that restrained OPEC production would allow surplus supplies to be absorbed. However, by mid-August 1990 'panic buying' of crude petroleum, following Iraq's invasion of Kuwait at the beginning of the month, had caused 'spot' market prices to almost double. On 20 August Saudi Arabia announced that it would increase its production of crude petroleum by 2m. b/d unless OPEC agreed to hold an emergency meeting. Saudi Arabia claimed that the

Geneva agreement was now obsolete. Petroleum prices had risen to about $28 per barrel, and OPEC production—since Iraqi and Kuwaiti supplies could no longer be marketed—was some 4m. b/d below the ceiling agreed at the July meeting.

Saudi Arabia was initially concerned that soaring petroleum prices would damage the world economy and, in turn, weaken future demand. While stressing its willingness to achieve an agreement within the framework of OPEC, Saudi Arabia left no doubt that it would act unilaterally if an emergency meeting was not held, and also urged the major Western countries to draw upon their strategic reserves of petroleum in order to stabilize the market. An emergency meeting of OPEC was duly held in August 1990, at which it was agreed to allow members to increase production rates above the quotas fixed in July. Iraq and Libya were absent from the meeting, and Iran refused to endorse the agreement. By early September petroleum prices had risen above $30 per barrel in London and New York. Saudi Arabia was reported to have increased production to 7.4m. b/d, and to be exporting more than 7m. b/d. Despite OPEC's decision to increase production, the fear of hostilities in the Gulf caused prices to rise above $40 per barrel for the first time in almost a decade. Over 1990 as a whole, Saudi Arabian production averaged 6.4m. b/d (annual production 312m. tons), producing revenues of $31,500m.

OPEC quotas remained in effective suspension throughout 1991, and Saudi Arabia took advantage of the absence of Iraqi and Kuwaiti petroleum to increase its output to an average of 8.2m. b/d (annual production was almost 400m. tons, the highest level since 1981), of which only 1m. b/d was for domestic use. Although international petroleum prices eventually fell, they remained higher than the pre-crisis level, so that Saudi oil revenues rose to $43,450m. in 1991. In mid-February 1992 Saudi Arabia protested at an OPEC decision to allocate a ceiling of 7,887,000 b/d to the kingdom for the remainder of the year, demanding that it be allotted a minimum quota of 8m. b/d. In the event, Saudi crude oil production remained significantly above 8m. b/d throughout 1992, its final average for the year being 8,377,800 b/d. Saudi Arabia accepted an OPEC ceiling of 8,395,000 b/d for the first quarter of 1993, and 8m. b/d thereafter. Average oil export earnings were estimated at $3,568m. per month for the first half of 1993 and around $3,040m. per month for the remainder of the year, when prices weakened significantly. Saudi Arabia's 1993 crude oil production averaged 8,131,700 b/d, having been cut back to fractionally over 8m. b/d by the last quarter of the year. Output remained close to 8m. b/d during the first half of 1994.

Prior to the stimulus to its petroleum industry that the Gulf crisis provided, Saudi Arabia had undertaken a major reorganization of state structures responsible for the sector. This included the conversion of PETROMIN into a holding company and the creation of several affiliated operating companies with responsibilities for exploration, refining, marketing and shipping. The first of these, Petrolube, was established in February 1988, to operate the lubricating oil blending plants in Jeddah, Riyadh and Jubail. The most important of the successor companies was the Saudi Arabian Marketing and Refining Company (SAMAREC), formed in 1989 to manage petroleum refining and distribution for the Saudi domestic market and to handle state exports of refined products.

In April 1989 the Saudi Arabian Oil Company (Saudi Aramco) was formed to take control of the nationalized Aramco assets. It is an independent enterprise with the right to establish companies and initiate projects. In addition, a new Supreme Oil Council was formed to take responsibility for the country's petroleum industry. Chaired by King Fahd, the council's members include private businessmen as well as government ministers: an indication of the Government's determination to involve the private sector in the management of the economy. In June 1993 the Government effectively abolished SAMAREC, and placed its operations, together with other PETROMIN oil interests, under the management of Saudi Aramco.

In June 1989 Saudi Aramco announced that three major development projects would be proceeding as planned: the expansion of the east-west pipeline to carry crude petroleum

(Petroline); the upgrading of facilities at the Safaniya and Uthmaniya oilfields; and the development of two wet crude handling and gas-gathering facilities at the onshore Uthmaniya field. The expansion of Petroline's overall capacity from 3.6m. to 4.8m. b/d (completed in mid-1993) was the largest scheme to have been undertaken in the petroleum sector for several years. In the same month it was stated that new oilfields in the al-Hawtah region, south of Riyadh, were commercially viable, and that further exploration would be undertaken; subsequent evaluation indicated a production capacity of up to 170,000 b/d of high-quality crude. In June 1991 a US company, McDermott International, was awarded a contract for work on offshore pipelines at the Zuluf oilfield, as part of the kingdom's plan to raise petroleum production capacity to 10m. b/d by the mid-1990s. By mid-1994 sustainable production capacity had reduced the target level, representing a very substantial margin of excess capacity in current market conditions.

INDUSTRY, GAS AND MINING

Saudi Arabia is making determined efforts to achieve major industrial development, financed mainly by government revenues from petroleum, under the aegis of successive development plans (see Development Plans, above). The cornerstone of the industrialization programme is the construction of refineries and processing industries to exploit the country's huge reserves of petroleum and natural gas (Saudi Arabia had published proven gas reserves of 5,200,000m. cu m at the end of 1992). The major projects are being undertaken as joint ventures between the State and foreign companies.

Following its absorption of SAMAREC in mid-1993, Saudi Aramco took charge of the management of the entire range of state petroleum-refining and product-marketing interests. As well as handling the marketing of products from Saudi Aramco's Ras Tanura plant, SAMAREC had operated refineries at Jeddah, Riyadh and Yanbu and had been responsible for marketing the state share of output from export-oriented refineries at Jubail, Yanbu and Rabigh. Saudi Arabia's installed refinery capacity totalled 1,865,000 b/d in 1992, an increase of 1m. b/d since 1984. At the refineries' aggregate throughput level of about 1.5m. b/d of crude oil in 1992, the volume of refined products available for marketing through state channels was slightly more than 1m. b/d., of which about two-thirds was sold on the home market and the remainder exported.

One effect of the reorganization was the deferment of a proposed $4,000m. programme to upgrade the oil-refining facilities which had fallen within SAMAREC's sphere of influence for planning purposes. A separate $1,000m. upgrading programme for the Ras Tanura refinery received final approval in late 1993 and was under way by mid-1994. The LUBEREF company (owned 70% by Mobil and 30% by PETROMIN) announced in 1994 that it was to build a new lubricant basestock refinery at Yanbu. Scheduled for completion in 1997, the Yanbu plant would have an annual capacity of 2m. barrels, compared with 1.8m. barrels at LUBEREF's existing plant at Jeddah, and would aim primarily to supply the domestic market.

An important element of Saudi Arabia's overall product-marketing strategy for the 1990s is the acquisition by Saudi Aramco of refining interests in petroleum-importing countries. In November 1988 Saudi Aramco entered into a joint venture with Texaco, whereby it gained access to a refining and marketing network spanning 26 states in the southern and eastern USA. In 1991 Saudi Aramco acquired a 35% equity interest in South Korea's largest refining company, Ssangyong Oil, which had 265,000 b/d of installed capacity.

In 1993 Saudi Aramco was actively studying proposals for further joint ventures with established refiners in Asia, Europe and the USA, with a view to raising its effective overseas refining capacity to around 3m. b/d. There was also a complementary programme to acquire oil storage capacity in major overseas importing centres, in furtherance of which Saudi Aramco announced in mid-1993 that it was to buy a 34.35% interest in a 17m.-barrel import terminal at the Dutch port of Rotterdam. In February 1994 Saudi Aramco acquired a 40% shareholding in the Philippine company Petron, which through its 155,000 b/d Bataan refinery and its associated transportation and retailing network currently supplied 41% of the Philippine refined products market. In the following month a Saudi businessman acquired Sweden's largest oil firm, OK Petroleum, which had a refining capacity of 265,000 b/d and which obtained part of its current crude supply from Saudi Aramco.

The Saudi Basic Industries Corporation (SABIC), founded in 1976, is Saudi Arabia's main non-oil industrial enterprise, including among its holdings many major gas-utilization projects. Chief among them is the petrochemical development at Jubail, Jeddah and Yanbu. In 1983 the Saudi Methanol Company (ar-Razi) plant at Jubail, which cost 900m. riyals and has a capacity of 500,000 tons per year, became the first venture to begin production. It was followed by four new projects that began operations in 1984: the National Methanol Company (Ibn Sina) plant at Jubail, costing 1,468m. riyals; the Saudi Petrochemical Company (Sadaf) plant at Jubail, costing 8,596m. riyals and producing ethylene, ethylene dichloride, styrene, ethanol and caustic soda; the Al-Jubail Petrochemical Company (Kemya) plant, costing 4,480m. riyals, producing linear low-density polyethylene (LLDPE); and the Saudi Yanbu Petrochemical Company (Yanpet) plant, costing 7,876m. riyals, producing ethylene, ethylene glycol, LLDPE and high-density polyethylene. In 1985 two new plants also came into operation at Jubail: the Arabian Petrochemical Company (Petrokemya) plant, costing 3,055m. riyals, producing ethylene; and the Eastern Petrochemical Company (Sharq) plant, costing 4,936m. riyals, producing LLDPE and ethylene glycol. In March 1989 it was reported that the production of methyl-tertiary-butyl ether (MTBE), a lead substitute for petrol, had been initiated by one of SABIC's joint ventures, the Saudi-European Petrochemical Company (Ibn Zahr), at Jubail. In the same month Petrokemya began the production of plastic resin polystyrene, with the aim of producing 100,000 tons per year, while the annual output of ethylene was scheduled to reach 500,000 tons in 1993, increasing total ethylene capacity to 2.9m. tons per year. In July PVC production capacity at Ibn Hayyan was 100,000 tons per year. SABIC experienced severe problems in selling its products, as major market areas began to impose tariff restrictions in 1985. The company has, however, been able to sell a large volume of products in the Far East and in Europe, despite the tariffs. In 1988 SABIC's profits tripled to a record 3,553m. riyals. In 1989 SABIC's medium-term plans envisaged the expansion of existing ventures, rather than the creation of new affiliates.

In March 1991 SABIC expanded its marketing network when it opened a new ethylene glycol terminal in Livorno, Italy, to improve service to Italian and other southern European clients. In 1991 SABIC owned two European terminals for liquid products (in Italy and in the Netherlands), as well as three storage terminals for plastic resins, situated in Belgium, France and the UK. In June Ibn Zahr signed contracts for the construction of a polypropylene plant with a capacity of 200,000 tons per year and a new MTBE plant with a capacity of 700,000 tons per year. Ibn Zahr is Saudi Arabia's only producer of MTBE, pending construction of a new plant at Ibn Sina expected to commence production in July 1994. The Italian company Snamprogetti, which built the original plant at Jubail, was awarded part of the $250m. contract to build the MTBE plant, and the UK's John Brown Engineers and Constructors was to build the polypropylene plant.

In 1991 SABIC recorded profits of 2,300m. riyals, 24% less than in 1990, although total output of all SABIC affiliates and subsidiaries was only marginally reduced, from 13.1m. tons in 1990 to 13.0m. tons in 1991. SABIC claimed that the decline was largely due to the world recession. Features of SABIC operations in 1991 included the completion of expansion at the National Plastics Company (Ibn Hayyan), to a capacity of 300,000 tons per year, and of the Saudi Methanol Company (Ar-Razi), to a capacity of 1.2m. tons per year. Overall SABIC output of all products was projected to increase to 21m. tons per year by 1995. SABIC's net profit in 1992 was 1,964m. riyals (the fifth successive annual decline), while profit in the first half of 1993 was 860m. riyals. Total sales revenue in 1992 was 13,000m. riyals, about 3% less than in 1991, despite

a 19.3% rise in sales volume to 15.7m. tons in 1992 (a year of falling prices in most of SABIC's overseas markets). New companies established with SABIC participation in 1993 included the Arabian Industrial Fiber Company, which planned to establish the region's largest polyester fibre factory at Yanbu in 1995. In 1993 SABIC achieved a production volume of 17m. tons (including 13.6m. tons of exports to more than 75 countries), yielding a net profit of 2,117m. riyals (8% higher than in 1992). In the first half of 1994 output reached 10.15m. tons (40% higher than in the first half of 1993) following the completion of several expansion schemes, while net profit rose by 57% to 1,351m. riyals as demand strengthened in key markets. Following the start of polypropylene production at Jubail, SABIC was in 1994 manufacturing all five thermoplastics and was inviting joint-venture proposals to produce over 30 categories of finished product, ranging from cling film to footwear. Saudi Arabia's per caput consumption of plastic resins was forecast to approach European levels by the year 2000.

A joint venture with Taiwan Fertilizer Company, Saudi Fertilizer Company (Samad), has an annual capacity of 500,000 tons of urea. In August 1983 its production was 167,760 tons, but by the beginning of 1985 it had reached its full capacity. In early 1985 the Saudi Arabian Fertilizer Company (SAFCO) and SABIC formed a company to build a 1,500 ton-per-day ammonia plant at Jubail. In April 1989 SAFCO's annual output was 450,000 tons in Dammam. In 1988 SAFCO produced 176,591 tons of ammonia, 284,994 tons of urea, approximately 91,728 tons of sulphuric acid and 17,839 tons of melamine. In 1991 SAFCO had a net income of 167m. riyals and announced plans for the construction of a new fertilizer complex at Jubail, at an estimated cost of 1,400m. riyals. Saudi Arabia's third fertilizer manufacturer, the National Chemical Fertilizer Company, opened a factory at Jubail in 1987. The aggregate annual capacity of Saudi Arabian fertilizer plants exceeded 3m. tons in 1993 and was targeted to reach 4m. tons before the end of the decade. The producing companies (all affiliates of SABIC) signed a 'services agreement' in January 1994 to consolidate many of their operational and management functions.

In the iron and steel industry, the Saudi Iron and Steel Company (Hadeed), based in Jubail, is a joint venture with Germany's Korf-Stahl. In 1991 Hadeed began exporting iron products to Far East and South-East Asian countries. In July a shipment of about 10,000 tons of reinforcing bars and wire rod coils was exported to Japan, and further sales to Singapore, Taiwan and South Korea, in July and August, raised exports to more than 40,000 tons. The Jeddah Steel Rolling Mill (Sulb) has a capacity of 140,000 tons of steel rods and bars per year, and in 1984 sold 317,000 tons of steel billets. In 1985 production of steel was 1.18m. tons, and in 1986 output increased to 1.9m. tons. An expansion programme, for which a seven-year loan of 500m. riyals was signed in August 1991, was intended to increase steel capacity at Hadeed's Jubail plant to 2m. tons per year. In 1991, owing to Hadeed exports, self-sufficiency was achieved within the Saudi Arabian steel industry, which expanded to satisfy construction requirements within the Kingdom and other GCC countries. Steel output from the expanded Hadeed plant reached a record 2.3m. tons in 1993, when the company announced plans to build a flat-products plant with an annual capacity of 700,000 tons. In mid-1988 the National Industrialization Company (NIC) announced plans to construct a steel foundry at Dammam with a capacity of 10,000 tons per year, at an estimated cost of 117m. riyals. Construction work was expected to reach completion in 1991. NIC is also planning the construction of a steel wire plant at Jubail, with a provisional capacity of about 50,000 tons per year, to produce specialized steel wires and related wire products. In 1990 profits fell from 17m. riyals in 1989 to 14m. riyals. This decline was attributed to the failure of certain companies, in which NIC has shareholdings, to announce dividends. The reduction in profits continued to reflect NIC's poor performance in its delayed implementation of the many industrial projects that it had initiated. By 1992, however, NIC's net profits had recovered to total 36.5m. riyals.

One of the most interesting developments in SABIC's proposals for joint ventures was agreed in 1983 between SABIC and private Saudi Arabian investors. Called the National Gas Company (Gas), it was expected to produce 146,000 tons of nitrogen and 438,000 tons of oxygen per year by 1985. Further joint ventures, agreed in 1984, included a partnership with Italy and Finland to produce fractionated gases.

The success of these ventures depends, to a large extent, on effective marketing, and all partners are bound to market at least 40% of production in their own countries. The basis for such ambitious heavy industrial schemes is a gas-gathering project, Master Gas System (MGS), which is being implemented by Saudi Aramco. Natural gas will provide the raw material for the petrochemical industry and an energy source for the steel plant. The scheme was initiated in 1975, when it was expected to cost $5,000m. and to produce 156m. cu m per day (cm/d) (5,500m. cu ft per day—cf/d). By the time of its completion in 1982, however, the first phase of the scheme had cost an estimated $12,000m., with a capacity of 98m. cm/d (3,460m. cf/d). Three processing plants have been built (at Berri, Shedgum and Uthmaniyah) to separate out natural gas liquids (NGLs) from methane, and two fractionation plants, at Juaymeh on the Gulf coast and at Yanbu on the Red Sea, process the NGLs into ethane, liquefied petroleum gas (LPG) and condensate. Gas is carried to Yanbu through a 1,200-km trans-Arabian pipeline which came into operation in 1981. The Berri, Shedgum and Juaymeh plants had all started production by mid-1980, the Uthmaniyah plant began operating in 1981, and the Yanbu plant started in 1982. Apart from fuelling industrial development, the scheme should make Saudi Arabia one of the world's largest exporters of LPG, with shipments of about 650,000 b/d. In 1991, however, SAMAREC amended its LPG price-indexing mechanism, owing to the exceptional volatility of the LPG market. As a result, SAMAREC introduced an upper limit on the permitted volume of exported LPG, in order to compensate for any rapid change in prices. In June 1992 SAMAREC signed 15 five-year contracts for the supply of a total of 42m. tons of LPG to Japanese, South Korean, British and Saudi Arabian companies. There are also facilities for the recovery of sulphur: three plants, with a combined annual capacity of about 1.3m. barrels, came into operation in 1981, and total sales in 1982 reached 800,000 tons.

Most of the gas which is produced in Saudi Arabia is associated gas (i.e. it is found in conjunction with petroleum), so the decline in petroleum output in the mid-1980s led to shortfalls in the production of gas and its 'downstream' products. Work on the second phase of the MGS scheme is under way, aiming to exploit associated gas from offshore fields and to reduce the problem of gas shortages created by declines in production of petroleum. The installed processing capacity of the MGS in 1993 was estimated at 121.8m. cm/d, based on crude oil output of about 8.2m. b/d. During 1985 a major new gasfield was discovered in the onshore Farhah and Sabha area. Saudi Aramco's refinery at Ras Tanura has been producing NGLs since 1962, and production totalled 155m. barrels in 1982. Recovery of NGLs from associated gases rose by 27%, from 420,946 b/d in 1989, to 533,229 b/d in 1990. Similarly, production of refined products at Ras Tanura increased from 174m. barrels in 1989 to 192m. barrels in 1990, with significant increases in the output of jet fuel and fuel oil. There were plans to exploit unassociated gas, independent of petroleum extraction, by 1986. The Khuff reservoir of unassociated gas in the Ghawar oilfield, estimated to contain more than one-half of Saudi Arabia's natural gas reserves, was scheduled to yield 20m. cm/d (700m. cf/d).

The Government is encouraging Saudi private enterprise to develop smaller-scale industries. A total of eight industrial estates offer basic infrastructure and services at minimal charge, credit is available on favourable terms, and selected products are protected by duties on imports. The Saudi Industrial Development Fund (SIDF) was established in 1974 to provide concessionary loans to private investors, and the NIC was established in 1984, by private investors, to develop and control investment by private individuals. By 1991 the SIDF had an authorized capital of 8,000m. riyals and had granted 1,404 loans, amounting to 18,738m. riyals. The building mate-

rials sector, and in particular the cement industry, is flourishing, as are electrical equipment manufacturing, the production of chemical rubber and plastics, and food processing and soft drinks. National cement output of 14.1m. tons in 1992 covered only 98% of the rapidly rising domestic demand, prompting five of the kingdom's seven publicly-traded cement companies to announce expansion plans, which would increase total cement production capacity by almost one-third, to 18.5m. tons per year. Some 1m. tons of cement and 1.6m. tons of clinker were imported in 1993. Between 1975 and 1978 about 70% of the industrial projects which were authorized were wholly Saudi-owned, the rest being joint ventures, and during 1982 a total of 2,689 new licences for privately-owned enterprises were approved. In 1991 the Ministry of Industry and Electricity approved a licence for the newly-established Saudi Industrial Development Company (SIDC) to build a ceramics plant in the Western Province. The new scheme would involve a total investment of 311m. riyals. The output of the new plant and that of the Saudi Ceramics Company, based in Riyadh, was expected to satisfy 80% of the domestic market. As part of its policy to stimulate the Saudi private sector, the Government sold 30% of SABIC's capital in 1984, and aims ultimately to transfer 75% into private control. At the end of 1986 the Government reported that there were 3,345 licensed factories in the Kingdom, of which 2,022 were operating, with a total work-force of 130,494. In 1990 there were 2,255 factories in operation, of which the metal industry accounted for 28.1%, building materials 24.8% and drinks and food 16%. Total investment in factories for 1990 was 96,900m. riyals, of which the largest amount (52,900m. riyals) was invested in the chemicals industry. A public flotation of shares in the SIDC in mid-1992, intended to raise 250m. riyals, was oversubscribed by more than three times. The SIDC planned to invest in various industrial projects, including a $90m. ceramics plant and a $64m. pharmaceuticals factory. Government figures were published in June 1994 showing that new factories had recently been opened at an average rate of six per month, representing an average job creation rate of 395 per month and an average capital investment of 90m. riyals per month.

Other minerals being produced are limestone (for cement production), gypsum, marble, clay and salt. Substantial deposits of bauxite, iron ore and magnesite, as well as copper, gold, lead, zinc, silver and some uranium, are known to exist. A mine at Mahd adh-Dhahab, with 1.2m. tons of ore (including gold), was inaugurated in 1983. At the end of 1984 work started on the construction of a gold-mining town at Mahd adh-Dhahab, and annual output of gold from the mine reached 3.5 tons in 1991, with estimated reserves of 1,123,000 tons. In 1991 there were 495 known sites of gold deposits in Saudi Arabia (and 800 'indications' of gold occurrence), of which 31 were estimated to contain more than 1,000 kg each and a further 99 were estimated to contain at least 100 kg each. In 1986 large quantities of gold were discovered in the Sukhayrat area, and in 1991 the Saudi Company for Precious Metals (a joint venture between PETROMIN and a Swedish company, Boliden) began gold production, which reached 978 kg by the end of the year. Reserves at Sukhayrat were estimated at 8.4m. tons. The private-sector Arabian Shield Development Company was awarded a 30-year mining lease in 1993 for the Al-Masane area of south-western Saudi Arabia, where substantial copper, zinc, gold and silver deposits were known to exist. Feasibility studies were in progress in 1994 for a proposed $50m. mining project and associated plans to create zinc processing facilities at Yanbu. In 1994 the Government invited applications to develop a recently evaluated iron ore deposit at Wadi Sawawin in north-western Saudi Arabia. It was estimated that an investment of US $550m. would be needed to develop an open-pit mine and ore beneficiation facility for the production of pellets at an annual rate of 2.2m. tons for 25 years. During 1984 a large coal field was discovered in central Qassim Province. In early 1989 Compagnie Générale des Matières Nucléaires (COGEMA) of France secured mineral-prospecting rights in an area of 500,000 sq km from the Ministry of Petroleum and Mineral Resources. Outside the Kingdom, SABIC's interests include two ventures in Bahrain, with the Gulf Petrochemical Industries Company (GPIC) and

Aluminium Bahrain (ALBA). There are 213m. tons of proved phosphate-bearing ore (averaging 21% phosphoric anhydride content) at Al-Jalamid in the far north of Saudi Arabia. In May 1994 the Government invited proposals for the extraction from these reserves of 4.5m. tons of phosphate concentrate per year, to be transported by slurry pipeline to Jubail as feedstock for a proposed 2.9m. tons-per-year diammonium phosphate plant. A feasibility study was initiated in 1993 on proposals to establish a 150,000 tons-per-year copper smelter and refinery at Yanbu. Strategic control of the minerals sector is exercised by the Directorate-General of Mineral Resources (DGMR).

ELECTRICITY AND WATER

Saudi Arabia's electricity system has to satisfy rapidly growing urban and industrial demand, and also to supply power for small, widely-scattered rural settlements. Until the 1970s, generation was controlled by a large number of small companies: 26 of them were operating in the Eastern Province alone. The main aim was to create regional grids, each operated by a single company. In 1977 the companies operating in the Eastern Province merged into a single Saudi Consolidated Electric Company (SCECO-East), managed by Aramco. A unified company for the southern region (SCECO-South) was formed in 1979. The other unified regional companies are SCECO-West and SCECO-Central. Northern areas continued to be supplied by separately-run local plants in 1994. SCECO-Central imports about 40% of its supply from SCECO-East via the only connection between two regional grids. Total sales of electric power increased from 1,690m. kWh in 1970 to 55,201m. kWh in 1988/89, of which 15,524m. kWh were used by industry. Electricity generation capacity was 16,850 MW at the end of 1991, and there were 2.4m. subscribers. Industry accounts for 30% of total consumption. An increasing amount of electricity is now produced in association with sea-water desalination. By the end of 1992 the kingdom's installed electricity generating capacity totalled 17,049 MW, and the combined power capacity of water desalination projects was 2,825 MW. Peak load in 1992 was 14,389 MW. Industrial users accounted for 27% of total power consumption in 1992. By 1994 peak load was approaching 19,000 MW following steep rises in demand, attributable in part to low tariff levels which covered less than half the costs of production. A major capacity expansion programme was planned, coupled with a campaign to reduce wasteful consumption (accounting for an estimated 30% of current electricity usage).

The state body with overall responsibility for the Saudi electricity system is the General Electricity Corporation, founded in 1976. The Corporation has been especially active in establishing power networks in rural areas. These networks will, where possible, be integrated into one of the regional grids under the control of the appropriate unified company. By 1982 SCECO-South was implementing its own rural schemes, including the largest single rural project, Tihama rural electricity supply programme, costing an estimated 4,000m. riyals. By August 1984 the overall target of the 1980–85 Development Plan, which was to provide 80% of the population with electricity and water, had already been reached. Under the fifth Five-Year Plan, electricity generating capacity was to be increased by 3,500 MW between 1990/91 and 1994/95, and daily water production from desalination plants to 3m. cu m. By mid-1992 approval had been given for some 300 water projects across the kingdom, involving the drilling of 450 wells, the improvement of 100 others, the construction of 49 dams and the installation of 350 pumping units.

Urban water supply has been a major challenge. At one time, the exploitation of underground sources appeared to be the best solution, but this method has encountered technical difficulties. However, aquifers at depths as great as 1,700 m are to be tapped. The largest projects are at Riyadh: the Minjur aquifer began supplying the city in 1979, and the huge Wasia aquifer produced 200,000 cu m of water per day in 1983, while an additional 110,000 cu m per day were supplied by Salbakh and Buwaib. In June 1989 a drinking water project was inaugurated in Khamis Mushait, to be completed in three years, and a project to build reservoirs and a sanitary disposal network near Medina was being planned. The construction of dams throughout the kingdom, as a means of preserving rainwater, has also expanded in recent years. By 1986 a total of 169 dams had been built, and in 1987 work began on a project, costing an estimated 239.8m. riyals, to construct a dam at Bisha, with the capacity to store 325m. cu m of water. The dam is expected to be completed in 1992.

Desalination projects are in the hands of the Saline Water Conversion Corporation (SWCC), which is the world's largest producer of desalinated water. Jeddah already receives 350,000 cu m per day, or 91% of its water, from SWCC, and massive new plants at Jubail and al-Khobar will supply the Eastern Province. In 1991 the Western Province Water and Sanitary Disposal Department approved contracts worth 327m. riyals to undertake three maintenance programmes in Mecca and Jeddah. A pipeline carries water from the Jubail plant inland to Riyadh. The Shuaiba desalination plant now pumps 35m. gallons to Mecca and 15m. gallons to Ta'if daily. The 1985–90 Plan foresaw investment of 31,789m. riyals in water projects. The aim was to increase desalination capacity to 1.8m. cu m per day by 1990. Emphasis will be placed on developing reclaimed and surface water resources for direct use and for recharging aquifers. In 1991 a contract worth 31m. riyals was awarded to As-Saiqh Trading to implement an expansion project in Yanbu, and a contract worth 15m. riyals was awarded to Al-Fahd Corporation for Trading, Contracting and Industry to work on one of a series of projects to dispose of rising ground water in Riyadh. In 1994 the SWCC had 24 plants in 15 locations with a combined capacity of about 2m. cu m (450m. gallons) per day; was in the process of constructing 1m. cu m per day of additional capacity; and was considering plans for 15 new units with a combined capacity of 1.2m. cu m per day.

TRANSPORT AND COMMUNICATIONS

Until 1964 the only surfaced roads, besides those in the petroleum network, were in the Jeddah-Mecca-Medina area. Since then, roads have been given priority, and in 1990 there were about 100,000 km of roads, of which about 40% were paved. In early 1992 there were about 60 road-building projects in progress in the kingdom. During the third Plan period (1980–85), the length of paved roads increased at an annual average rate of 15.8%, a major project being the 317-km Riyadh-to-Qassim highway, which was completed in the late 1980s. In 1991 Kuwait was awarded a contract worth $25.8m. to implement part of a project which would link Mecca by road with the Riyadh-to-Ta'if expressway. Some 1,840 km of major roads were built in 1993. Saudi Arabia's national bus operator, the Saudi Public Transport Company (SAPTCO, whose 1,700 vehicles serve mainly inter-city routes), made a net profit of 82.6m. riyals in the first half of 1994.

The main sea ports are at Jeddah, Yanbu and Gizan on the Red Sea and at Dammam and Jubail on the Gulf. A programme of rapid expansion and modernization was undertaken by the Saudi Ports Authority in the late 1970s. With the completion of a 16-berth port at Jubail and an industrial port also at Jubail, Saudi Arabia had 170 berths in mid-1987. In the year ending mid-1987 these handled 6,886 vessels. At Yanbu the existing commercial port has grown, and a new industrial port was being built 20 km to the south. The port of Gizan has been extensively modernized. In 1988 the expansion of exports from the agricultural and industrial sectors led to a revival in cargo-handling, despite the continuing decline in the volume of imports. During 1988 the total cargo handled by the kingdom's ports was 68m. tons. The emergence of the industrial ports of Jubail and Dammam as important export centres has been prompted by the decision, in 1987, to reduce port tariffs for industrial and some agricultural goods produced locally by 50% and to extend the period of free storage from two to 10 days. Jeddah port, however, has continued to suffer from the decline in imported cargo, and therefore SEAPA agreed in late 1988 to revise the regulations to allow transhipment. In 1983 Saudi Arabia became the 40th member of the London-based International Maritime Satellite Organization (INMARSAT).

Saudi Arabia has installed one of the world's most advanced telecommunications systems, placing the kingdom at the hub of the Gulf communications network. In the late 1980s Saudi Arabia established satellite transmission and reception stations, facilitating direct telephone dialling to most of the rest of the world.

There is a total of 23 airports in the kingdom. The principal international airports are at Jeddah (King Abd al-Aziz), Dhahran (the Eastern Province International Airport) and Riyadh (King Khalid). In the late 1970s plans were announced for new airports in the three main regions. King Fahd International Airport in Dhahran came into operation in 1990. The new Riyadh airport, inaugurated in November 1983, cost about US $5,000m. to build and is the largest in the world. The Jeddah project cost about $4,400m. Dammam airport is also undergoing expansion, Medina and Bisha airports have been improved, and new airports have been built at Abha, Hayil, Badanah, Ta'if, Turayf, Najran, Tabouk, Gizan, Jouf, Rafah, Wajh, al-Qurayat and Jubail. In May 1989 it was announced that the expansion of Abha airport, abandoned in the early 1980s, was to proceed. The Government operates the national airline, Saudia, which links important Saudi cities and operates regular flights to many foreign countries. In 1993 the airline carried 11.86m. passengers, including 3.8m. on international services, and handled 195,833 tons of freight, 71% of it on international routes. It had a fleet of 108 aircraft, over half of which were earmarked for replacement under plans announced in 1994. Saudia's budget for 1994 was 8,350m. riyals, compared with 7,834m. riyals in 1993.

Saudi Arabia has the only rail system in the Arabian peninsula; in the year ending June 1994 it carried 402,570 passengers and 1.9m. tons of freight. Operating revenue in excess of 70m. riyals (28% from passengers and the balance from freight) was insufficient to cover costs, and the 1994 government subsidy totalled 192.4m. riyals. The principal lines are a 571-km single-track railway which connects the port of Dammam, on the Gulf, with Riyadh, and a 322-km line, linking Riyadh with Hufuf, which was inaugurated in May 1985. A 90-km single-track railway is planned between Dammam and Jubail, and the possibility of a rail link between Riyadh and Jeddah is also being considered. A detailed feasibility study for the proposed Damman-Jubail line, expected to cost 2,000m. riyals, was initiated in early 1993, after major Jubail-based industrial enterprises had indicated their willingness, in principle, to support the scheme. In 1991 it was announced that a driverless light railway service was to be built, to take pilgrims from parking areas to the Grand Mosque, as part of the project to develop the holy places in Mecca and Medina. The project was estimated to cost $100m.

A causeway linking Bahrain with the Saudi mainland was opened in late 1986. It is open for 24 hours per day, although trucks and lorries may only use it at off-peak times.

In June 1992 the Saudi Automotive Services Company (SASCO) approved plans to produce light and heavy trailers, refrigerated boxes, wagons and tankers. In the latter half of 1992 the company began manufacturing spares for the main makes of cars available in Saudi Arabia (i.e. for US, Japanese and German models).

FOREIGN TRADE

The total value of the country's exports, of which more than 90% was provided by petroleum before 1988, rose from 138,242m. riyals in 1978 to 362,885m. riyals in 1980, then to 405,481m. riyals in 1981, but fell to 271,090m. riyals in 1982, to 158,444m. riyals in 1983, and to 132,299m. riyals in 1984. In 1985 exports fell to 99,536m. riyals, and in 1986 they fell by a further 25%, to 74,377m. riyals. Total exports rose to 86,880m. riyals in 1987, to 91,288m. riyals in 1988 and to 106,241m. riyals in 1989. Excluding re-exports, sales of petroleum and petroleum products accounted for 86.9% of total export revenue of 103,892m. riyals in 1989. The principal customers for Saudi Arabia's exports in 1989 were the USA (taking 25.8% of the total), Japan (17.5%), Singapore (6.0%), France (5.2%), Bahrain (4.5%), the Netherlands (4.5%) and Italy (4.1%). Other important sources of foreign exchange are the local expenditure of foreign companies and the pilgrimage traffic.

The value of Saudi Arabia's imports increased from 69,180m. riyals in 1978 to 139,335m. riyals in 1982, but fell to 135,417m. riyals in 1983, and to 118,737m. riyals in 1984. The value of imports fell to 85,564m. riyals in 1985, and to

70,800m. riyals in 1986. The value of imports rose by 6.4%, to 75,313m. riyals, in 1987, and by 8.3%, to 81,582m. riyals, in 1988. In 1989, owing to a substantial increase in the local production of goods, the value of imports declined by 2.9%, to 79,219m. riyals. The main categories of imports are machinery and transport equipment, consumer goods, and food and beverages. In 1989 the kingdom's major suppliers were the USA (accounting for 18.2% of total imports), Japan (14.2%), the UK (10.2%), the Federal Republic of Germany (6.3%), Italy (5.7%), Switzerland (5.0%), France (4.3%) and the Republic of Korea (4.0%). The main items to be imported from Japan are cars, pick-up trucks and spare parts. Cars and machinery are the main imports from the USA, and from the UK military equipment is pre-eminent. In 1987 there was a large increase in the trade surplus, due to a rise in the value of oil exports. In 1988, however, oil sales declined, leading to slower growth in exports. Meanwhile, the value of imports increased, causing the trade surplus to fall by 16.1% in 1988, to 9,706m. riyals. In 1989, after substantial growth in the value of oil exports and a decline in imports, the trade surplus increased sharply, to 27,022m. riyals. There was a further significant increase in 1990, when the visible surplus in dollar terms was $22,806m. (exports $44,296m., imports $21,490m.). In 1991 there was a surplus of $21,648m. (exports $47,615m., imports $25,968m.). The surplus for 1992 was $12,991m. (exports $42,769m., imports $29,778m.) and the estimated surplus for 1993 was $15,000m. (exports $44,000m., imports $29,000m.).

Saudi Arabia's current-account surplus increased dramatically from 9,334m. riyals in 1973 to 81,990m. riyals in 1974, under the influence of the increases in the price of petroleum. A surplus was sustained until 1977, but in 1978 a small deficit was recorded. With the doubling of petroleum prices in 1979, a surplus of 37,321m. riyals was achieved in that year, followed by record surpluses of 137,746m. riyals in 1980 and 154,105m. riyals in 1981. The impact of the fall in petroleum output in 1982 was dramatic: the decline in export revenues was far greater than the drop in imports. In spite of cutbacks on services and transfers (which fell by 32%), a deficit of 4,000m. riyals was recorded for the year. By 1983 the deficit had increased to 53,772m. riyals, most of which was financed by drawing on the country's reserves. In 1984 a further increase, to US $18,401m., was recorded in the deficit. The deficit decreased to $12,932m. in 1985, to $11,795m. in 1986, to $9,773m. in 1987 and to $7,340m. in 1988. The current account deficit for 1989 widened to $9,172m., but in 1990 the deficit was reduced to $4,267m. Because of extraordinary payments and costs arising from the Gulf conflict, the current account deficit increased sharply in 1991, to $27,730m., and stood at $19,431m. in 1992. The estimated deficit in 1993 was $10,297m.

In June 1993 Saudi Arabia, which had held observer status in GATT since 1985, submitted an application for full GATT membership. No decision was expected before 1994.

FINANCE

Since mid-1977, and particularly since July 1978, the Saudi Arabian Monetary Agency (SAMA) has made a series of frequent small adjustments in the exchange rate of the Saudi riyal against the US dollar. At the end of June 1984 the rate was $1 = 3.505 riyals, and by the end of the year the riyal had been devalued seven times. Following three further adjustments in the first six months of 1985, the exchange rate stood at $1 = 3.645 riyals in June. This rate remained unchanged until June 1986, when a rate of $1 = 3.745 riyals was established. This remained in effect at mid-1993, after which the currency came under heavy pressure from speculators who maintained that it was overvalued at a time of weak oil prices. However, the Government ruled out any devaluation, accepting a rise in Saudi interest rates at the end of 1993 in order to defend the existing exchange rate. SAMA, established in 1952, is the central bank.

At the end of 1977 Saudi Arabia's international reserves totalled $30,034m. and were surpassed only by those of the Federal Republic of Germany. From April 1978 Saudi Arabia's reserves were redefined to exclude foreign exchange cover against the note issue, then about $5,300m. Under the new definition, reserves declined to $16,756m. in October 1979, but they then made a sharp recovery, rising to $32,422m. at the end of 1981. Another decline brought total reserves down to $25,201m. in July 1983. They recovered to $29,492m. in February 1984, but by the end of the year they had fallen to $24,906m. Reserves totalled $25,181m. in December 1985, but fell to $18,521m. at the end of 1986. At the end of 1987 they stood at $22,912m. Reserves declined to $20,768m. at the end of 1988, to $16,959m. at the end of 1989 and to $11,897m. (including gold valued at $229m.) in December 1990. By the end of May 1993 total reserves minus gold stood at only $5,646m., following heavy expenditure to finance the international action against Iraq in 1990–91 and to purchase new military equipment in the aftermath of the crisis.

There are 12 commercial banks in Saudi Arabia, of which three are wholly Saudi and nine joint ventures. The largest Saudi commercial bank is the National Commercial Bank (NCB). In 1988 the formalities were completed for the creation of the country's twelfth commercial bank, the Ar-Rajhi Banking and Investment Company (ARABIC), which had previously been the country's leading money-changing company, and had been endeavouring to become a commercial bank since 1984.

Specialized credit institutions provide project finance: the Saudi Industrial Development Fund (SIDF) is the major source, and was set up by the Government in 1974. It grants low-interest loans for up to 50% of the total cost of a project (up to 80% in the case of electricity projects). The SIDF is managed by Chase Manhattan Bank. The Public Investment Fund, established in 1972, finances large-scale commercial and industrial projects in the public sector. A new institution, the National Industrialization Company, was established in 1984 by private investors: its object is to encourage and plan development in the private sector.

Another major state financial institution which assists in the country's development is the Real Estate Development Fund (REDF), whose capital has been raised successively from 240m. riyals to 23,800m. riyals. The REDF provides a home-loan scheme under which purchasers are required to pay 80% of loan principal. The Saudi Agricultural Bank, set up in 1963, offers medium- and short-term loans for farmers. The Saudi Credit Bank was set up in 1973 to advance interest-free loans to low-income Saudis for purposes such as getting married or carrying out home repairs.

Saudi banks have become more outward-looking, and the most obvious example of this trend is the 55% Saudi-owned Saudi International Bank, which opened as a fully-fledged merchant bank in London in March 1976. SAMA holds 50% of the capital, while the NCB and Riyad Bank have 2.5% each. The principal non-Saudi partner in the enterprise is the Morgan Guaranty Trust Company, a US bank, which also provides management. The other shares are held by leading Western and Japanese banks. The first wholly private Saudi bank abroad—As-Saudi Banque—opened in Paris in the autumn of 1976. Riyad Bank has a share in the Paris-based Union de Banques Arabes et Françaises, and in the Gulf Riyad Bank in Bahrain. The NCB has small stakes in European-Arab Holding and the Compagnie Arabe et Internationale d'Investissement, both based in Luxembourg, and in the Amman-based Arab-Jordanian Investment Bank, which opened in the spring of 1978.

Total assets of Saudi banks grew by 12%, to 191,059m. riyals in 1987/88, and nearly one-half of these were held abroad. In 1988 the performance of the banking sector improved, although the recovery was not uniform among all the 12 commercial banks. The United Saudi Commercial Bank, Riyad Bank and the Arab National Bank increased their profits, but NCB recorded no profit and the Saudi Cairo Bank trebled its losses. The main reason for the poor performance of the banking sector in the mid-1980s was the domestic recession, but they also needed to make substantial provision against loan losses. In 1985 SAMA began requiring banks to report their non-performing loans. In March 1987 King Fahd ordered the central bank to establish a committee to arbitrate in bank loan disputes. By mid-1988 the outstanding loans and advances disbursed by the Saudi Agricultural Bank, the Saudi Credit Bank, the Public Investment Fund, SIDF and the Real Estate Development Fund totalled 166,600m. riyals. In 1992

the Saudi commercial banking sector experienced very strong growth. The audited accounts released by the 11 publicly-quoted banks showed aggregate assets of 234,233m. riyals, an increase of 13.4% on the 1991 total, and aggregate profits of 3,712m. riyals, a rise of nearly 29% on the previous year's level.

In May 1987 Saudi Arabia opened its first stock-exchange trading floor in Riyadh, under the jurisdiction of SAMA. However, the Central Trading Hall was closed indefinitely less than a month after it had opened, owing to technical problems and to disagreement about procedures between the Ministry of Finance, which is responsible for SAMA, and the Ministry of Commerce. Shares are traded by banks and independent brokers, and in 1990 SAMA introduced an electronic trading system. Although the market is limited, the value of traded shares rose by 80% in 1991, compared with 1990, to some 8,000m. riyals, and share prices increased overall by about 70%. The market capitalization of the Saudi stock market totalled 244,110m. riyals at the end of 1992. Saudi Arabia's insurance market, in which about 80 companies and agencies were active in 1992, was worth some 1,870.5m. riyals in gross written premiums in that year. The only locally registered insurer, the National Company for Co-operative Insurance, wrote 619m. riyals of insurance premiums in 1993, when it had gross claims of 228.4m. riyals and made a net surplus of 61.6m. riyals.

In July 1989 Saudi Arabia signed a syndicated loan for $660m., apparently the first international borrowing by the Saudi Government for a quarter of a century. There has been a reluctance to raise funds publicly over the last two decades, due to the memory of the 1950s, when an excess of borrowing led to economic crisis. Economists in Saudi Arabia have speculated that the loan, raised in the name of the Public Investment Fund (PIF), could be used to finance the budget deficit, while other observers claim that it will be used to refinance concessionary loans made by the Government to SABIC.

Owing to the Saudi Government's own budget deficit, in 1991 it was forced to sign a term-loan worth $4,500m. with international banks, in addition to borrowing $2,500m. in foreign currency from domestic banks. It was agreed that the larger Saudi banks would lend up to $400m. each to the Government and the smaller banks would lend $50m.–100m. each. The major part of the foreign borrowing was believed to be needed to defray costs incurred as a result of the multinational military assistance provided to Saudi Arabia during the Gulf crisis in 1990–91. In November 1991 SAMA announced the kingdom's first issue of Treasury bills, starting with issues of up to 2,000m. riyals per week, to finance the budget deficit. The Government's other main public financing instrument is medium-term development bonds, first introduced in 1988. The first repayment of $900m. to international banks under the terms of the 1991 loan was made on schedule in May 1994. In April 1994 a new loan had been signed under which a syndicate of local banks would lend the Finance Ministry $1,300m. over seven years, with two years' grace.

INVESTMENT

SAMA is also Saudi Arabia's investment authority, responsible for managing the country's vast foreign assets. Most of this money is held in the USA and Europe. Although SAMA has recently been making more long-term investments, the vast bulk of its assets are still thought to be liquid. Very little official Saudi money goes into equities and almost nothing into property. Major Western banks seem to be the main beneficiaries of the vast funds at SAMA's disposal, and SAMA's investment department is advised by a small team which has been seconded from Baring Brothers & Co., a London merchant bank, and White Weld, a US investment bank. IMF figures reveal that SAMA's foreign assets increased from about 16,940m. riyals in December 1973 to 472,930m. riyals in December 1982, but declined to 202,760m. riyals (US $54,140m.) in March 1991.

AID

Between 1973 and 1989, grants and concessional loans that Saudi Arabia made available to developing countries totalled $59,470m., representing 5.5% of GNP and placing the kingdom fourth in the world list of aid-donors. Among OPEC members, Saudi Arabia is by far the largest aid-donor, having contributed more than 80% of OPEC allocations in the period 1980–89. Between 1972 and 1983, aid totalling $25,568m. was provided to other Islamic states, where most aid is sent (in particular to the 'front-line' countries and Pakistan). Saudi contributions to the 'front-line' states after 1974 amounted to $1,000m. per year. The country has generally been the principal contributor to the various Arab funds that have been established to help poor Arab and poor African states, as well as to the IMF oil facilities. In April 1981 Saudi Arabia made a $10,000m. loan to the IMF for two years. Following further loans, the country was estimated to have advanced $15,000m. by 1984. It has also lent large sums to the World Bank at commercial rates. The Saudi Fund for Development (SFD), established in 1974, makes concessionary loans to Africa, Asia and Latin America, as well as to the Arab world. Financial support was given to Iraq during its war with Iran from 1980 to 1988, and in 1983 a substantial loan was granted to France. The SFD disbursed $610m. in 1982. In March 1989 Saudi Arabia donated $85.5m. to the PLO, the last tranche of a 10-year programme of payments to the organization. A further $6m. per month during 1989 was pledged for Palestinians in the Israeli-occupied territories. In the period 1975–91 the SFD granted 277 loans to 61 countries, totalling 18,727m. riyals.

In May 1991 Saudi Arabia gave US $3,650m. in cash payments towards the US military effort in the Gulf War in January–February 1991. The USA had so far received $8,186m. in cash for its military contribution. In July the Saudi Government approved a loan worth 64m. riyals to Egypt by the Saudi Fund for Development, to build an expressway from Asyut to Cairo. In the same month the US received a further $850m. for costs incurred during the Gulf crisis (1990–91). Saudi Arabia pledged to give $16,839m. in total, and as of August the outstanding balance was $4,110m. In August the Government announced its intention to give Turkey $1,000m. worth of free crude petroleum, in addition to supplies that Turkey had already received, worth $1,600m., to compensate for the adverse effects that the Gulf crisis had had on the Turkish economy. Bangladesh was to receive aid worth $100m. to help in the rebuilding of infrastructure which was destroyed during the flood disaster in May 1991. In mid-August Saudi Arabia paid $175m. of its $1,000m. pledge to the UK towards that country's military costs during the Gulf War. Aid allocations approved in 1993 included $100m. for reconstruction in Lebanon and $26m. for Bosnian refugee relief.

BUDGETS

Government revenues from petroleum traditionally provide more than 90% of the State's budget revenue. In 1974/75 petroleum revenues totalled 94,190m. riyals out of total revenue of 100,103m. riyals, while expenditure was only 32,038m. riyals. With the advent of the second Development Plan, expenditure began to catch up with income. A budget deficit was recorded in 1977/78, with expenditure of 138,027m. riyals and revenue of 130,659m. riyals. In 1978/79 expenditure increased, despite austerity measures, to 147,400m. riyals, with revenue at 132,871m. riyals. In 1979/80, owing to the unexpected sharp rise in petroleum prices, actual revenue rose far above the 160,000m. riyals that was forecast, to around 220,000m. riyals.

Budget estimates for 1980/81, 1981/82 and 1982/83 reflected this increase in revenue, with projected expenditure rising to 245,000m. riyals, 290,000m. riyals and 313,400m. riyals respectively. Actual expenditure for 1982/83 was much lower than projected, however, at 244,900m. riyals, while revenue totalled 246,200m. riyals. The 1983/84 budget reflected the sharp fall in petroleum revenues, with expenditure set at 260,000m. riyals and receipts at 225,000m. riyals. In reality, both revenue and expenditure were lower than expected, but, at 206,400m. riyals and 230,200m. riyals respectively, they resulted in a budget deficit. Another deficit was recorded in 1984/85, when expenditure totalled 212,900m. riyals and revenue 166,900m. riyals. The effect of the growing economic crisis was shown in the provisional budget figures for 1985/86, which suggest that revenue may

have been as low as 112,000m. riyals, and expenditure 180,900m. riyals. A deficit of 69,700m. riyals, to be financed from the kingdom's general reserve, was also recorded. Publication of the 1986/87 budget, due in March 1986, was postponed for 10 months, owing to uncertainty over the level of petroleum prices. The monthly government expenditure on essential items during the months continued at the same average monthly rate as in the 1985/86 financial year. Budget revenues from petroleum in the financial year 1986/87 were projected at 65,200m. riyals, representing 55.6% of total government revenues, and a 6.5% increase compared with the previous year. The budget for 1986/87 envisaged total expenditure of 170,000m. riyals, 6% less than in 1985/86, and a deficit of 52,720m. riyals was projected. Spending plans for 1988 were concentrated mainly in the defence sector, followed by education and public utilities. Total expenditure was set at 141,200m. riyals. The Government anticipated revenues, mainly from oil, of 105,300m. riyals, resulting in a deficit of 35,900m. riyals. The budget proposals for 1989 predicted total expenditure of 140,460m. riyals.

As originally presented in December 1989, the Government's budget proposals for 1990 envisaged expenditure of 143,000m. riyals, and a deficit of 25,000m. riyals. In view of the Gulf crisis, no separate 1991 budget was prepared, the 1990 provisions being extended through the year. In the event, official figures for 1990, published in April 1992, revealed that actual expenditure had reached 210,430m. riyals and revenue 154,721m. riyals, producing a deficit of 55,709m. riyals. Provisional figures for 1991 showed that expenditure increased to 261,570m. riyals, and the deficit to 77,000m. riyals. In 1992 expenditure totalled 204,900m. riyals and revenue 165,400m. riyals, leaving a deficit of 39,500m. riyals. The 1993 budget proposals forecast total expenditure of 196,950m. riyals and total revenue of 169,150m. riyals, producing a deficit of 27,800m. riyals. Itemized spending categories included defence and security (61,636m. riyals), education (34,094m. riyals), health and social development (14,087m. riyals), domestic subsidies (9,167m. riyals), transport and communications (9,078m. riyals), economic resource development (8,930m. riyals), municipal services and water authorities (6,980m. riyals) and infrastructure (2,095m. riyals). The budget statement made no distinction between capital and current spending, and categorized a total of 50,884m. riyals as 'residual allocations'. The budget announcement also reported that in 1992 Saudi Arabia recorded 6% private-sector growth, 6.4% industrial growth, 7.5% agricultural growth and a 0.5% decrease in the consumer price index. The 1994 budget provided for expenditure of 160,000m. riyals, about 19% below the previous year's budgeted spending, and for revenue of the same amount, this being the first balanced budget since 1982.

EDUCATION, HEALTH AND SOCIAL SECURITY

Within the Government's development policy, considerable emphasis has been placed on the improvement of education, health services and other aspects of social security. The number of schools and institutes of higher education increased from 3,107 in 1970 to 17,268 in 1991, with the number of students increasing from 547,000 to 3.1m. over the same period. There are plans to expand the universities at Umm al-Qura, Jeddah and Medina. The number of hospitals under the control of the Ministry of Health increased from 47 in 1970 to 253 in 1990, with medical and para-medical personnel increasing from 4,494 to 56,628, and the number of beds to 40,000. In early 1991 there were four hospital beds for every 1,000 inhabitants, a ratio similar to that in the USA, and 1,639 health centres. In 1988 a total of 18 hospitals, including the 1,400-bed King Fahd Medical City in Riyadh, were being constructed. In August 1994 the Ministry of Health announced that work would soon commence on the construction of 2,000 additional primary health care centres and that the possibility of setting up a comprehensive health insurance programme was being studied. Social security payments are made available by the Deputy Ministry of Social Care, and total disbursements increased from 41.7m. riyals (to 198,000 beneficiaries) in 1970 to 1,540m. riyals (to 903,000 beneficiaries) in 1984. A total of 1,537m. riyals was disbursed in the form of social security payments (to 314,117 beneficiaries) in 1985/86. The budget allocation for expenditure on health and social services was reduced from 11,094m. riyals in 1987 to 10,806m. riyals in 1988. In the 1989 budget, projected expenditure on health and social services was reduced further, to 10,634m. riyals, but in the budget for 1990 it was increased to 11,239m. riyals, the same allocation applying to 1991. In the 1992 budget the allocation for health and social development was 12,200m. riyals, and the 1993 budget proposals allocated 14,087m. riyals. Housing has also been an important part of government

policy, and since 1974 it is estimated that more than 500,000 housing units have been constructed throughout the kingdom: about half by the Government and half by the private sector. By late 1991 a total of 477,000 housing units had been wholly or partly funded by the REDF. All adult Saudi Arabians, if not independently wealthy, are entitled to a plot of land and a loan of $80,000 with which to build a home. In 1988 a total of 347,260 people received the loan.

Statistical Survey

Sources (unless otherwise indicated): Kingdom of Saudi Arabia, *Statistical Yearbook;* Saudi Arabian Monetary Agency, *Annual Report* and *Statistical Summary.*

Area and Population

AREA, POPULATION AND DENSITY

Area (sq km)	2,240,000*
Population (census results)	
9–14 September 1974	7,012,642
September–October 1992	16,929,294
Density (per sq km) at 1992 census . . .	7.6†

* 864,869 sq miles.
† Preliminary results.

SAUDI ARABIA-IRAQ NEUTRAL ZONE

The Najdi (Saudi Arabian) frontier with Iraq was defined in the Treaty of Mohammara in May 1922. Later a Neutral Zone of 7,044 sq km was established adjacent to the western tip of the Kuwait frontier. No military or permanent buildings were to be erected in the zone and the nomads of both countries were to have unimpeded access to its pastures and wells. A further agreement concerning the administration of this zone was signed between Iraq and Saudi Arabia in May 1938. In July 1975 Iraq and Saudi Arabia signed an agreement providing for an equal division of the diamond-shaped zone between the two countries, with the border following a straight line through the zone.

SAUDI ARABIA-KUWAIT NEUTRAL ZONE

A Convention signed at Uqair in December 1922 fixed the Najdi (Saudi Arabian) boundary with Kuwait. The Convention also established a Neutral Zone of 5,770 sq km immediately to the south of Kuwait in which Saudi Arabia and Kuwait held equal rights. The final agreement on this matter was signed in 1963. Since 1966 the Neutral Zone, or Partitioned Zone as it is sometimes known, has been divided between the two countries and each administers its own half, in practice as an integral part of the State. However, the petroleum deposits in the Zone remain undivided and production from the onshore oil concessions in the Zone is shared equally between the two states' concessionaires (Aminoil and Getty).

PRINCIPAL TOWNS (population at 1974 census)

Riyadh (royal		Hufuf . .	101,271
capital) . .	666,840	Tabouk . . .	74,825
Jeddah (adminis-		Buraidah . .	69,940
trative capital)	561,104	Al-Mobarraz . .	54,325
Makkah (Mecca) .	366,801	Khamis-Mushait . .	49,581
At-Ta'if . .	204,857	Al-Khobar . .	48,817
Al-Madinah (Medina)	198,186	Najran . . .	47,501
Dammam. .	127,844	Ha'il (Hayil) . .	40,502

BIRTHS AND DEATHS (UN estimates, annual averages)

	1975–80	1980–85	1985–90
Birth rate (per 1,000) . . .	45.9	43.2	42.1
Death rate (per 1,000) . .	10.7	9.0	7.6

Expectation of life (UN estimates years at birth, 1985–90): 60.7 (males 59.1; females 62.5).

Source: UN, *World Population Prospects: The 1992 Revision.*

ECONOMICALLY ACTIVE POPULATION
(ILO estimates, '000 persons at mid-1980)

	Males	Females	Total
Agriculture, etc.	1,289	43	1,333
Industry	387	9	395
Services	903	121	1,023
Total labour force . . .	2,579	172	2,751

Source: ILO, *Economically Active Population Estimates and Projections, 1950–2025.*

Mid-1992 (estimates in '000): Agriculture, etc. 1,860; Total 4,964 (Source: FAO, *Production Yearbook).*

Agriculture

PRINCIPAL CROPS ('000 metric tons)

	1990	1991	1992
Wheat	3,722	3,861†	4,100†
Barley	361	400†	410†
Millet	12	12†	12*
Sorghum	152	210*	220*
Potatoes	62	49*	50*
Pulses*	7	7	7
Sesame seed	4	4*	4*
Tomatoes	451	470*	480*
Pumpkins, squash and gourds .	62	78*	79*
Cucumbers and gherkins . .	90	91*	93*
Aubergines (Eggplants) . .	71	71*	72*
Onions (dry)	15	14*	15*
Carrots*	19	17*	19*
Other vegetables*	392	394	75
Watermelons	454	450*	450*
Melons	139	140*	140*
Grapes	102	105*	105*
Dates	537	540*	545*
Citrus fruit	29	29*	30*
Other fruits	32	32*	33*

* FAO estimate(s).   † Unofficial figure.

Source: FAO, *Production Yearbook.*

LIVESTOCK ('000 head, year ending September)

	1990	1991	1992
Cattle	192	213	216†
Sheep	6,067	6,067†	6,008†
Goats	3,262	3,300*	3,350*
Asses*	104	103	102
Camels.	413	417*	419*

* FAO estimates.   † Unofficial figure.

Poultry (FAO estimates, million): 76 in 1990; 80 in 1991; 83 in 1992.

Source: FAO, *Production Yearbook*.

LIVESTOCK PRODUCTS ('000 metric tons)

	1990	1991	1992
Beef and veal†	28	27	28
Mutton and lamb† . . .	77	78	80
Goats' meat†	19	19	20
Poultry meat†	265	285	303
Other meat	33	32	32
Cows' milk.	220†	225*	230*
Sheep's milk*	40	39	39
Goats' milk*	36	36	36
Hen eggs†	160	158	157

* FAO estimates.   † Unofficial figure.

Source: FAO, *Production Yearbook*.

Fishing

(metric tons, live weight)

	1989	1990	1991
Fishes	47,361*	41,189*	40,246
Crustaceans and molluscs . .	6,030*	5,238*	3,005
Total catch . . .	53,391*	46,427*	43,251
Inland waters	1,201	1,427	1,982
Indian Ocean and adjacent seas	52,190*	45,000*	41,269

* FAO estimate.

Source: FAO, *Yearbook of Fishery Statistics*.

Mining

('000 metric tons, unless otherwise indicated)

	1989	1990	1991
Crude petroleum* . . .	252,433	320,375	404,506
Natural gasoline* . . .	3,879	4,517	6,651
Natural gas ('000 terajoules)	1,042.2	1,101.3	1,452.3
Gypsum (crude) . . .	375†	375	375

* Including 50% of the total output of the Neutral or Partitioned Zone, shared with Kuwait.
† Estimated production.

Source: UN, *Industrial Statistics Yearbook* and *Monthly Bulletin of Statistics*.

Industry

SELECTED PRODUCTS
('000 metric tons, unless otherwise indicated)

	1988	1989	1990
Nitrogenous fertilizers* . .	417	428	584
Jet fuel	1,850	1,900	1,950
Motor spirit (petrol) . .	8,795	9,350	9,600
Naphtha	3,900	3,910	3,920
Kerosene	4,307	4,400	4,460
Distillate fuel oils . .	22,062	22,170	24,100
Residual fuel oils . . .	25,028	25,100	26,700
Lubricating oils . . .	310	410	400
Petroleum bitumen (asphalt) .	1,207	1,230	1,390
Liquefied petroleum gas:			
from natural gas plants . .	9,397	9,690	12,699
from petroleum refineries .	700	720	890
Cement	9,525	9,500	10,000
Crude steel†	1,614	1,810	1,833
Electric energy (million kWh)‡	42,201	46,300	47,400

* Production in terms of nitrogen.
† Data from the US Bureau of Mines (the 1989 figure is an estimate).
‡ Including 50% of the total output of the Neutral Zone.

Source: UN, *Industrial Statistics Yearbook*.

Finance

CURRENCY AND EXCHANGE RATES

Monetary Units
100 halalah = 20 qurush = 1 Saudi riyal (SR).

Sterling and Dollar Equivalents (31 May 1994)
£1 sterling = 5.662 riyals;
US $1 = 3.745 riyals;
100 Saudi riyals = £17.663 = $26.702.

Exchange Rate
Since June 1986 the official mid-point rate has been fixed at US $1 = 3.745 riyals.

BUDGET ALLOCATIONS (million riyals)

	1992	1993
Defence and security	54,300	61,636
Transport and communications . . .	8,300	9,078
Education	31,100	34,093
Municipal services.	6,300	6,980
Economic resources	8,000	8,930
Health and social services. . . .	12,200	14,087
Infrastructure	2,100	2,095
Local subsidies	7,100	9,167
Residual allocations	51,600	50,884
Total expenditure	181,000	196,950
Total revenue	151,000	169,150

Source: *Middle East Economic Digest*.

INTERNATIONAL RESERVES
(US $ million in December each year)

	1991	1992	1993
Gold*	230	221	221
IMF special drawing rights .	89	278	553
Reserve position in IMF . .	1,848	1,096	1,193
Foreign exchange . . .	9,737	4,561	5,682
Total	11,904	6,156	7,649

* Valued at 35 SDRs per troy ounce.

Source: IMF, *International Financial Statistics*.

MONEY SUPPLY (million riyals in December)

	1989	1990	1991
Currency outside banks . .	33,887.2	44,776.2	44,620.1
Demand deposits at commercial banks	57,874.5	57,488.4	75,850.3
Total money	91,751.7	102,264.6	120,470.5

COST OF LIVING (consumer price index for middle-income Saudi households; base: 1988 = 100)

	1989	1990	1991
Food, drink and tobacco . .	102.3	104.1	111.9
Housing	98.1	98.2	102.7
Textiles and clothing . .	98.9	99.0	99.6
House furnishing . . .	100.0	100.6	104.3
Medical care	102.7	101.3	100.5
Transport and communications	104.8	119.2	124.0
Entertainment and education .	100.3	100.8	104.3
All items (incl. others) .	101.1	103.2	108.2

NATIONAL ACCOUNTS
(million riyals at current prices)
Expenditure on the Gross Domestic Product*

	1990	1991	1992
Government final consumption expenditure	120,130	165,000	166,250
Private final consumption expenditure	155,870	168,750	173,780
Increase in stocks† . . .	2,750	5,220	8,660
Gross fixed capital formation .	73,800	78,510	102,240
Total domestic expenditure .	352,550	417,480	450,930
Exports of goods and services	181,130	197,280	178,980
Less Imports of goods and services	141,690	182,840	176,380
GDP in purchasers' values .	391,990	431,920	453,530

* Figures are rounded to the nearest 10 million riyals.
† Including errors and omissions.
Source: IMF, *International Financial Statistics*.

Gross Domestic Product by Economic Activity

	1989	1990*	1991†
Agriculture, forestry and fishing	22,650	25,143	26,902
Mining and quarrying:			
Crude petroleum and natural gas	83,847	139,277	149,575
Other	1,812	1,812	1,866
Manufacturing:			
Petroleum refining . .	9,405	9,902	10,655
Other	15,822	17,404	19,144
Electricity, gas and water . .	750	780	811
Construction	32,475	34,099	36,486
Trade, restaurants and hotels .	26,078	27,382	29,751
Transport, storage and communication	23,121	24,758	26,953
Finance, insurance, real estate and business services:			
Ownership of dwellings . .	6,071	6,314	6,692
Other	16,998	17,848	18,331
Community, social and personal services . . .	11,414	11,985	12,185
Less Imputed bank service charges	4,200	−4,326	−4,672
Sub-total	246,243	312,378	334,679
Producers of government services	57,840	72,616	90,240
GDP in producers' values .	304,083	384,994	424,919
Import duties	6,740	7,000	7,000
GDP in purchasers' values	310,823	391,994	431,919

* Revised estimates.   † Preliminary estimates.
Source: Central Department of Statistics, Ministry of Finance and National Economy.

BALANCE OF PAYMENTS (US $ million)

	1990	1991	1992
Merchandise exports f.o.b. .	44,296	47,615	42,769
Merchandise imports f.o.b. .	−21,490	−25,968	−29,778
Trade balance . . .	22,806	21,648	12,991
Exports of services . .	2,999	2,945	3,119
Imports of services . .	−22,414	−38,822	−28,339
Other income received . .	9,199	8,668	8,499
Other income paid . . .	−854	−1,562	−1,501
Private unrequited transfers (net)	−11,602	−14,117	−12,700
Official unrequited transfers (net)	−4,401	−6,489	−1,501
Current balance . . .	−4,267	−27,730	−19,431
Direct investment (net) . .	1,864	160 ⎫	
Portfolio investment (net) .	−3,340	470 ⎬	13,767
Other capital (net) . .	367	27,150 ⎭	
Overall balance . . .	−5,376	49	−5,664

Source: IMF, *International Financial Statistics*.

External Trade

PRINCIPAL COMMODITIES (million riyals)

Imports c.i.f.	1989	1990	1991
Live animals and animal products.	4,392	4,838	5,613
Vegetable products	4,499	3,737	3,610
Prepared foodstuffs, beverages, spirits, vinegar and tobacco	3,461	3,639	4,446
Products of chemical and allied industries	5,274	7,232	8,065
Artificial resins, plastic materials, rubber, etc.	2,943	3,518	4,213
Textiles and textile articles	7,754	7,947	9,169
Pearls, precious stones, etc.	3,848	6,213	5,531
Base metals and articles of base metal	6,476	7,830	9,931
Machinery (incl. electric) and parts	14,557	14,777	21,115
Transport equipment and parts thereof	14,640	18,471	22,868
Scientific instruments, photographic equipment, watches, musical instruments, recorders, etc.	2,927	2,836	3,072
Total (incl. others)	79,219	90,139	108,881

Exports (excl. re-exports)	1988	1989	1990*
Mineral products	75,987	90,840	150,873
Crude petroleum	55,055	70,624	123,281
Refined petroleum products	20,613	19,612	27,002
Products of chemical and allied industries	6,333	5,616	5,720
Artificial resins, plastic materials, rubber, etc.	3,813	4,160	3,819
Total (incl. others)	88,896	103,892	166,339

* Including re-exports, totalling 2,414 million riyals.

1991 (million riyals): Crude petroleum 139,830; Refined petroleum products 23,660; Total (incl. others) 178,974 (of which re-exports 2,297).

PRINCIPAL TRADING PARTNERS (million riyals)

Imports c.i.f.	1989	1990	1991
Belgium	1,115	1,558	2,044
Brazil	886	943	1,434
China, People's Republic	1,501	1,668	2,345
France	3,410	3,573	4,366
Germany, Fed. Republic	4,959	6,645	8,520
India	1,014	987	1,088
Indonesia	585	793	1,154
Italy	4,531	4,180	5,028
Japan	11,288	13,815	14,915
Korea, Republic	3,154	2,959	3,220
Netherlands	1,629	2,036	2,101
Spain	1,017	984	1,385
Sweden	1,001	1,169	1,433
Switzerland	3,964	5,929	5,282
Taiwan	2,270	1,969	2,128
Thailand	1,100	1,021	1,182
Turkey	1,427	1,116	1,316
United Kingdom	8,064	10,182	12,267
USA	14,392	15,062	22,003
Total (incl. others)	79,219	90,139	108,881

Exports (incl. re-exports)*	1989	1990	1991
Bahrain	4,777	6,564	5,836
Brazil	2,452	5,482	4,933
Egypt	528	2,423	3,048
France	5,549	7,917	8,203
India	2,571	4,115	4,103
Indonesia	439	621	2,301
Italy	4,305	5,978	7,675
Japan	18,545	31,559	28,689
Korea, Republic	2,100	6,254	9,938
Kuwait	1,096	746	2,501
Netherlands	4,746	7,857	10,802
Philippines	660	2,215	2,016
Singapore	6,352	8,917	9,094
Spain	1,827	2,181	3,563
Taiwan	4,069	5,634	4,968
Turkey	787	2,838	5,235
United Arab Emirates	1,868	3,010	3,193
United Kingdom	1,620	2,664	3,525
USA	27,437	39,890	40,969
Total (incl. others)	106,241	166,339	178,974

* Figures for individual countries exclude bunker fuel, totalling (in million riyals): 271 in 1989; 449 in 1990; 490 in 1991.

Transport

RAILWAYS (traffic)

	1989	1990	1991
Passenger-km (million)	156	151	139
Freight ton-km (million)	797	763	800

Source: *Railway Directory*, 1994.

ROAD TRAFFIC (motor vehicles in use at 31 December)

	1989	1990	1991
Passenger cars	2,550,465	2,664,028	2,762,132
Buses and coaches	50,856	52,136	54,089
Goods vehicles	2,153,297	2,220,658	2,286,541
Total	4,754,618	4,936,822	5,103,205

Source: IRF, *World Road Statistics*.

SHIPPING
Merchant Fleet
(displacement, '000 grt, vessels registered at 30 June)

	1989	1990	1991
Oil tankers	1,214	928	561
Total (incl. others)	2,119	1,683	1,321

Source: UN, *Statistical Yearbook*.

International Sea-borne Freight Traffic
('000 metric tons*)

	1988	1989	1990
Goods loaded	161,666	165,989	214,070
Goods unloaded	42,546	42,470	46,437

* Including Saudi Arabia's share of traffic in the Neutral or Partitioned Zone.

Source: UN, *Monthly Bulletin of Statistics*.

CIVIL AVIATION (traffic on scheduled services)

	1989	1990	1991
Kilometres flown ('000) . .	101,000	103,000	87,000
Passengers carried ('000) . .	9,988	10,311	9,409
Passenger-kilometres (million).	15,695	16,068	14,881
Freight ton-km ('000) . . .	605,000	610,000	487,000

Source: UN, *Statistical Yearbook*.

Tourism

PILGRIMS TO MECCA FROM ABROAD*

Country of Origin	1984/85	1985/86	1986/87
Egypt	130,872	98,606	97,216
India	33,691	39,344	40,854
Indonesia	41,965	59,172	57,519
Iran	152,227	152,149	157,395
Iraq	33,856	14,551	29,522
Pakistan	87,889	92,305	93,013
Turkey	41,693	54,624	96,711
Yemen Arab Republic . . .	41,121	43,512	61,416
Total (incl. others) . . .	851,761	856,718	960,386

Total pilgrims: 762,755 in 1987/88; 774,560 in 1988/89.

* Figures relate to Islamic lunar years. The equivalent dates in the Gregorian calendar are: 26 September 1984 to 14 September 1985; 15 September 1985 to 4 September 1986; 5 September 1986 to 24 August 1987; 25 August 1987 to 12 August 1988; 13 August 1988 to 1 August 1989.

1993/94: more than 2m. pilgrims.

Communications Media

	1989	1990	1991
Radio receivers ('000 in use) .	3,800	4,500	4,670
Television receivers ('000 in use)	3,750	4,000	4,100
Daily newspapers . . .	n.a.	12	n.a.
Non-daily newspapers . . .	n.a.	6	n.a.

Source: UNESCO, *Statistical Yearbook*.

Telephones ('000 main lines): 1,384 in 1990 (Source: UN, *Statistical Yearbook*).

Education*

(academic year 1990/91)

	Schools	Teachers	Pupils
Pre-primary	646	4,839	67,069
Primary	9,068	119,370	1,875,593
Intermediate	3,289	43,201	570,080
Secondary	1,354	20,195	289,562
Higher	78	12,863	131,811
Total	14,435	200,468	2,934,115

* Excluding vocational and technical education.

Source: Ministries of Education and of Higher Education, and the General Presidency of Girls' Education.

Directory

The Constitution

An eight-man committee under the Chairmanship of Prince Nayef, Minister of the Interior, was formed in March 1980 to prepare a 200-article basic 'system of rule', based entirely on Islamic principles. Plans, for which King Fahd pledged his support, were also to be made for the establishment of a consultative council. In March 1992 royal decrees were issued that provided for the introduction of a basic law of government and for the creation of a consultative council (comprising 60 members and a chairman), to be appointed by the King for a term of four years.

Meanwhile Saudi Arabia is an absolute monarchy, with no legislature or political parties. The King rules in accordance with the *Shari'a*, the sacred law of Islam. He appoints and leads the Council of Ministers, which serves as the instrument of royal authority in both legislative and executive matters. The term of office of the Council of Ministers, and that of each of its members, is fixed at four years. The King is also assisted by advisory councils, nominated or approved by him.

The organs of local government are the General Municipal Councils and the tribal and village councils. A General Municipal Council is established in the towns of Mecca, Medina and Jeddah. Its members are proposed by the inhabitants and must be approved by the King. Functioning concurrently with each General Municipal Council is a General Administration Committee, which investigates ways and means of executing resolutions passed by the Council. Every village and tribe has a council composed of the sheikh, who presides, his legal advisers and two other prominent personages. These councils have power to enforce regulations. A system of provincial government was announced in late 1993 by royal decree. The decree defined the nature of government for 13 newly-created regions, as well as the rights and responsibilities of their governors, and appointed councils of prominent citizens for each region to monitor development and advise the government. Each council is to meet four times a year under the chairmanship of a governor, who will be an emir with ministerial rank. A royal decree, issued in April 1994, further divided the 13 regions into 103 governorates.

The Government

HEAD OF STATE

King Fahd Ibn Abd al-Aziz as-Sa'ud (acceded to the throne 13 June 1982).

Crown Prince: Abdullah Ibn Abd al-Aziz as-Sa'ud.

COUNCIL OF MINISTERS
(October 1994)

Prime Minister: King Fahd Ibn Abd al-Aziz as-Sa'ud.

First Deputy Prime Minister and Commander of the National Guard: Crown Prince Abdullah Ibn Abd al-Aziz as-Sa'ud.

Second Deputy Prime Minister and Minister of Defence and Civil Aviation: Prince Sultan Ibn Abd al-Aziz as-Sa'ud.

Deputy Ministers of Defence and Civil Aviation (with ministerial rank): Gen. Othman al-Humaid, Prince Abd ar-Rahman Ibn Abd al-Aziz.

Minister of Public Works and Housing: Prince Mutaib Ibn Abd al-Aziz.

Minister of the Interior: Prince Nayef Ibn Abd al-Aziz as-Sa'ud.

Minister of Foreign Affairs: Prince Sa'ud al-Faisal.

Minister of Petroleum and Mineral Resources: Sheikh Hisham Mohi ad-Din Nazer.

Minister of Labour and Social Affairs: Muhammad al-Ali al-Fayez.

Minister of Education: Dr Abd al-Aziz al-Abdullah al-Khuwaiter.

Minister of Higher Education: Khalid Ibn Muhammad al-Angari.

Minister of Communications: Sheikh Hussein Ibrahim al-Mansouri.

Minister of Finance and National Economy: Sheikh Muhammad Ali Aba al-Khail.

Minister of Planning: ABD AL-WAHAB AS-SALIM AL-ATTAR.

Minister of Information: ALI HASSAN ASH-SHAER.

Minister of Industry and Electricity: ABD AL-AZIZ AZ-ZAMIL.

Minister of Commerce: Dr SULAIMAN ABD AL-AZIZ AS-SULAIM.

Minister of Justice: Dr ABDULLAH IBN MUHAMMAD ASH-SHEIKH.

Minister of Pilgrimage (Hajj) Affairs: MAHMOUD IBN MUHAMMAD SAFAR.

Minister of Municipal and Rural Affairs: MUHAMMAD IBN ABD AL-AZIZ IBN ABDULLAH IBN HASSAN ASH-SHEIKH.

Minister of Agriculture and Water: Dr ABD AR-RAHMAN IBN ABD AL-AZIZ IBN HASSAN ASH-SHEIKH.

Minister of Awqaf (Religious Endowments), Dawa, Mosques and Guidance Affairs: ABDULLAH IBN ABD AL-MOHSEN AT-TURKI.

Minister of Health: FAISAL IBN ABD AL-AZIZ AL-HEJAILAN.

Minister of Posts, Telegraphs and Telecommunications: Dr ALAWI DARWISH KAYYAL.

Ministers of State: Sheikh MUHAMMAD IBRAHIM MASOUD, OMAR ABD AL-QADER FAQIH, Dr FAYEZ BIN IBRAHIM BADR, ABD AL-WAHAB ABD AL-WASI, Sheikh ABD AL-AZIZ IBN BAZ (General Mufti).

MINISTRIES

Most ministries have regional offices in Jeddah.

Council of Ministers: Murabba, Riyadh 11121; tel. (1) 488-2444; telex 6655766.

Ministry of Agriculture and Water: Airport Rd, Riyadh 11195; tel. (1) 401-6666; telex 40690; fax (1) 404-4592.

Ministry of Commerce: POB 1774, Airport Rd, Riyadh 11162; tel. (1) 401-2222; telex 401057; fax (1) 403-8421.

Ministry of Communications: Airport Rd, Riyadh 11178; tel. (1) 404-3000; telex 4031401.

Ministry of Defence and Civil Aviation: POB 26731, Airport Rd, Riyadh 11496; tel. (1) 478-9000; telex 4055500.

Ministry of Education: POB 3734, Airport Rd, Riyadh 11481; tel. (1) 411-5777; telex 402650; fax (1) 411-2051.

Ministry of Finance and National Economy: Airport Rd, Riyadh 11177; tel. (1) 405-0000; telex 401021.

Ministry of Foreign Affairs: Nasseriya St, Riyadh 11124; tel. (1) 405-5000; telex 405000.

Ministry of Health: Airport Rd, Riyadh 11176; tel. (1) 401-5555; telex 404020; fax (1) 402-9876.

Ministry of Higher Education: King Faisal Hospital St, Riyadh 11153; tel. (1) 441-9849; telex 401481; fax (1) 441-9004.

Ministry of Industry and Electricity: POB 5729, Omar bin al-Khatab St, Riyadh 11432; tel. (1) 477-666; telex 401154.

Ministry of Information: POB 570, Nasseriya St, Riyadh 11161; tel. (1) 406-8888; telex 401461; fax (1) 404-4192.

Ministry of the Interior: POB 2833, Airport Rd, Riyadh 11134; tel. (1) 401-1111; telex 404416.

Ministry of Justice: Riyadh 11137; tel. (1) 405-7777; telex 405-9443.

Ministry of Labour and Social Affairs: Omar bin al-Khatab St, Riyadh 11157; tel. (1) 477-8888; telex 401043; fax (1) 478-9175.

Ministry of Municipal and Rural Affairs: Nasseriya St, Riyadh 11136; tel. (1) 441-8888; telex 404018; fax (1) 441-7368.

Ministry of Petroleum and Mineral Resources: POB 247, Airport Rd, Riyadh 11191; tel. (1) 478-1661; telex 400997.

Ministry of Pilgrimage (Hajj) Affairs: Omar bin al-Khatab St, Riyadh 11183; tel. (1) 404-3003; telex 400189.

Ministry of Planning: POB 358, University St, Riyadh 11182; tel. (1) 401-3333; telex 402851; fax (1) 404-9300.

Ministry of Posts, Telegraphs and Telecommunications: Sharia al-Ma'azer, Intercontinental Rd, Riyadh 11112; tel. (1) 463-4444; telex 400200.

Ministry of Public Works and Housing: POB 56095, Ma'ather St, Riyadh 11554; tel. (1) 407-3618; telex 400415.

MAJLIS ASH-SHOURA
(Consultative Council)

In March 1992 King Fahd issued a decree to establish a Consultative Council of 60 members, whose powers include the right to summon and question ministers. The composition of the Council was announced by King Fahd in August 1993, and it was officially inaugurated in December of that year. Each member is to serve for four years.

Chairman: Sheikh MUHAMMAD IBN IBRAHIM AL-JUBAIR.

Diplomatic Representation
EMBASSIES IN SAUDI ARABIA

Afghanistan: Tariq al-Madina, Kilo No. 3, Jeddah; tel. (2) 53142.

Algeria: POB 94388, Riyadh 11693; tel. (1) 488-7616; telex 402828; Ambassador: ABD AL-KARIM GHARIB.

Argentina: POB 94369, Riyadh 11693; tel. (1) 465-2600; telex 405988; Ambassador: MARIO A. PEPE.

Australia: POB 94400, Riyadh 11693; tel. (1) 488-7788; fax (1) 488-7973; Ambassador: WARWICK WEEMAES.

Austria: POB 94373, Riyadh 11693; tel. (1) 477-7445; telex 406333; fax (1) 476-6791; Ambassador: Dr MARIUS CALLIGARIS.

Bahrain: POB 94371, Riyadh 11693; tel. (1) 488-0044; telex 407055; Ambassador: ISSA MUHAMMAD AL-KHALIFA.

Bangladesh: POB 94395, Riyadh 11693; tel. (1) 465-5300; telex 406133; Ambassador: Maj.-Gen. QUAZI GOLAM DASTGIR.

Belgium: POB 94396, Riyadh 11693; tel. (1) 488-2888; telex 406344; fax (1) 488-2033; Ambassador: PIETER BERGHS.

Brazil: POB 94348, Riyadh 11693; tel. (1) 488-0018; telex 406711; Ambassador: LUIZ VILLARINHO PEDROSO.

Burkina Faso: POB 94300, Riyadh 11693; tel. (1) 454-6168; telex 403844; Ambassador: HAROUNA KOUFLA.

Burundi: POB 94355, Riyadh 11693; tel. (1) 464-1155; telex 406477; fax (1) 465-9997; Ambassador: JACQUES HAKIZIMANA.

Cameroon: POB 94336, Riyadh 11693; tel. (1) 488-0022; telex 408866; fax (1) 488-1463; Ambassador: MOHAMADOU LABARANG.

Canada: POB 94321, Riyadh 11693; tel. (1) 488-2288; telex 404893; fax (1) 488-0137; Ambassador: ALLAN N. LEAVER.

Chad: POB 94374, Riyadh 11693; tel. (1) 465-7702; telex 406366; Ambassador: al-Hajji DJIME TOUGOU.

China, People's Republic: Riyadh; Ambassador: SUN BIGAN.

Denmark: POB 94398, Riyadh 11693; tel. (1) 488-0101; telex 404672; fax (1) 660-7268; Ambassador: POUL HOINESS.

Djibouti: POB 94340, Riyadh 11693; tel. (1) 454-3182; telex 406544; Ambassador: IDRISS AHMAD CHIRWA.

Egypt: POB 94333, Riyadh 11693; tel. (1) 465-2800; Ambassador: FATHY AL-SHAZLY.

Ethiopia: POB 94341, Riyadh 11693; tel. (1) 479-0904; telex 406633; fax (1) 478-2461; Ambassador: MOGUES HABTEMARIAM.

Finland: POB 94363, Riyadh 11693; tel. (1) 488-1515; telex 406099; fax (1) 488-2520; Ambassador: ANTERO VIERTIÖ.

France: POB 94367, Riyadh 11693; tel. (1) 488-1255; telex 406966; fax (1) 488-2882; Ambassador: JEAN BRESSOT.

Gabon: POB 94325, Riyadh 11693; tel. (1) 456-3328; telex 406766; fax (1) 456-4068; Ambassador: MOHAMED MAURICE LEFLEM.

Gambia: POB 94322, Riyadh 11693; tel. (1) 454-9156; telex 406767; Ambassador: Dr OMAR JAH.

Germany: POB 94001, Riyadh 11693; tel. (1) 488-0700; telex 402297; fax (1) 488-0660; Ambassador: Dr RUDOLF RAPKE.

Ghana: POB 94339, Riyadh 11693; tel. (1) 464-1383; telex 406599; fax (1) 462-3089; Ambassador: Dr ALHASAN MUHAMMAD.

Greece: POB 94375, Riyadh 11693; tel. (1) 465-5026; telex 406322; Ambassador: PAUL APOSTOLIDES.

Guinea: POB 94326, Riyadh 11693; tel. (1) 231-0631; telex 404944; Ambassador: el-Hadj MAMADOU S. SYLLA.

India: POB 94387, Riyadh 11693; tel. (1) 477-7006; telex 406077; fax (1) 477-8627; Ambassador: ISHRAT AZIZ.

Indonesia: POB 94343, Riyadh 11693; tel. (1) 488-9127; telex 406577; Ambassador: H. A. KUNAEFI.

Iran: POB 94394, Riyadh 11693; tel. (1) 482-6111; telex 406066; Ambassador: ABD AL-LATIF AL-MEIMANI.

Ireland: POB 94349, Riyadh 11693; tel. (1) 488-2300; telex 406877; fax (1) 488-0927; Ambassador: BRENDAN J. LYONS.

Italy: POB 94389, Riyadh 11693; tel. (1) 4881212; telex 406188; fax 4880590; Ambassador: MARIO SCIALOJA.

Japan: POB 4095, Riyadh 11491; tel. (1) 488-1100; telex 405866; fax (1) 488-0189; Ambassador: HIROSHI OTA.

Jordan: POB 7455, Riyadh 11693; tel. (1) 454-3192; telex 406955; Ambassador: Maj.-Gen. MUHAMMAD RASOUL AL-KILANI.

Kenya: POB 94358, Riyadh 11693; tel. (1) 488-2484; telex 406055; Ambassador: ALI MUHAMMAD ABDI.

Korea, Republic: POB 94399, Riyadh 11693; tel. (1) 488-2211; telex 406922; fax (1) 488-1317; Ambassador: JOONG-BAE NA.

Kuwait: POB 2166, Riyadh 11451; tel. (1) 488-3401; telex 401301; Ambassador: ABD AR-RAHMAN AHMAD AL-BAKR.

Lebanon: POB 94350, Riyadh 11693; tel. (1) 465-1000; telex 406533; fax (1) 462-6774; Ambassador: ZOUHEIR HAMDAN.

Libya: POB 94365, Riyadh 11693; tel. (1) 454-4511; telex 406399; Ambassador: MILOUD RAMADAN ERIBI.

Malaysia: POB 94335, Riyadh 11693; tel. (1) 488-7100; telex 406822; Ambassador: Datuk Haji MOKHTAR BIN Haji AHMAD.

Mali: POB 94331, Riyadh 11693; tel. (1) 465-8900; telex 406733; Ambassador: SEICKO SOUMANO.

Mauritania: POB 94354, Riyadh 11693; tel. (1) 465-6313; telex 406466; Ambassador: BABA OULD MUHAMMAD ABDULLAH.

Mexico: POB 94391, Riyadh 11693; tel. (1) 476-1200; fax (1) 478-1900; Ambassador: RICARDO VILLANUEVA.

Morocco: POB 94392, Riyadh 11693; tel.(1) 465-4900; telex 406155; Ambassador: Dr AHMAD RAMYI.

Nepal: POB 94384, Riyadh 11693; tel. (1) 402-4758; telex 406288; Ambassador: Prof. SURENDA BAHADUR SHRESTHA.

Netherlands: POB 94307, Riyadh 11693; tel. (1) 488-0011; telex 403820; fax (1) 488-0544; Ambassador: H. PHILIPSE.

New Zealand: POB 94397, Riyadh 11693; tel. (1) 488-7988; telex 405878; fax (1) 488-7912; Ambassador: GORDON N. PARKINSON.

Niger: POB 94334, Riyadh 11693; tel. (1) 464-3116; telex 406722; Ambassador: ABDOULAYE MOUMOUNI DJERNAKOYE.

Nigeria: POB 94386, Riyadh 11693; tel. (1) 482-3024; telex 406177; fax (1) 482-4134; Ambassador: Prof. SHEHU AHMAD S. GALADANCI.

Norway: POB 94380, Riyadh 11693; tel. (1) 488-1904; telex 406311; fax (1) 488-0854; Ambassador: PAAL MOE.

Oman: POB 94381, Riyadh 11693; tel. (1) 465-0010; telex 206277; Ambassador: HAMAD H. AL-MO'AMARY.

Pakistan: POB 6891, Riyadh 11452; tel. (1) 476-7266; telex 406500; Ambassador: WALIULLA KHAN KHAISHGI.

Philippines: POB 94366, Riyadh 11693; tel. (1) 454-0777; telex 406377; Ambassador: Dr MAUYAG MUHAMMAD TAMANO.

Portugal: POB 94328, Riyadh 11693; tel. (1) 464-4853; telex 404477; Ambassador: JOSÉ MANUEL WADDINGTON MATOS PARREIRA.

Qatar: POB 94353, Riyadh 11461; tel. (1) 482-5544; telex 405755; Ambassador: M. ALI AL-ANSARI.

Russia: Riyadh; Ambassador: GENNADY TARASSOV.

Rwanda: POB 94383, Riyadh 11693; tel. (1) 454-0808; telex 406199; fax (1) 456-1769; Ambassador: SIMON INSONERE.

Senegal: POB 94352, Riyadh 11693; tel. (1) 454-2144; telex 406565; Ambassador: Alhaji AMADOU THIAM.

Sierra Leone: POB 94329, Riyadh 11693; tel. (1) 463-3149; telex 406744; fax (1) 464-3892; Ambassador: UMARU WURIE.

Singapore: POB 94378, Riyadh 11693; tel. (1) 465-7007; telex 406211; Chargé d'affaires a.i.: RAM CHANDRA NAIR.

Somalia: POB 94372, Riyadh 11693; tel. (1) 454-0111; Ambassador: ABD AR-RAHMAN A. HUSSEIN.

Spain: POB 94347, Riyadh 11693; tel. (1) 488-0606; telex 406788; Ambassador: JOSÉ LUIS XIFRA DE OCERIN.

Sri Lanka: POB 94360, Riyadh 11693; tel. (1) 463-4200; telex 405688; fax (1) 465-0897; Ambassador: ABD AL-CADER MARKAR.

Sudan: POB 94337, Riyadh 11693; tel. (1) 488-7728; Ambassador: OMER YOUSIF BIRIDO.

Sweden: POB 94382, Riyadh 11693; tel. (1) 488-3100; telex 406266; fax (1) 488-0604; Ambassador: STEEN HOWÜ-CHRISTENSEN.

Switzerland: POB 9265, Riyadh 11413; tel. (1) 488-1291; telex 406055; Ambassador: MAURICE JEAN RENAUD.

Syria: POB 94323, Riyadh 11693; tel. (1) 465-3800; telex 406677; Ambassador: MUHAMMAD KHALID AT-TALL.

Tanzania: POB 94320, Riyadh 11693; tel. 454-2839; telex 406811; fax (1) 454-9660; Ambassador: Prof. A. A. SHAREEF.

Thailand: POB 94359, Riyadh 11693; tel. (1) 482-6002; telex 406433; Ambassador: THONGTERM KOMOLSUK.

Tunisia: POB 94368, Riyadh 11693; tel. (1) 465-4585; telex 406464; Ambassador: KACEM BOUSNINA.

Turkey: POB 94390, Riyadh 11613; tel. (1) 464-8890; telex 406206; Ambassador: YASAR HYAKIS.

Uganda: POB 94344, Riyadh 11693; tel. (1) 454-4910; telex 406588; fax (1) 454-9260; Ambassador: al-Haj Prof. BADRU DDUNGU KATEREGGA.

United Arab Emirates: POB 94385, Riyadh 11693; tel. (1) 482-6803; telex 406222; Ambassador: ISSA K. AL-HURAIMIL.

United Kingdom: POB 94351, Riyadh 11693; tel. (1) 488-0077; telex 406488; fax (1) 488-2373; Ambassador: DAVID ALWYN GORE-BOOTH.

USA: POB 94309, Riyadh 11693; tel. (1) 488-3800; telex 406866; fax (1) 488-3278; Ambasdsador: RAYMOND MABUS.

Uruguay: POB 94346, Riyadh 11693; tel. (1) 462-0739; telex 406611; fax (1) 462-0638; Chargé d'affaires a.i.: FERNANDO ARROYO.

Venezuela: POB 94364, Riyadh 11693; tel. (1) 476-7867; telex 405599; fax (1) 476-8200; Ambassador: NORMAN PINO.

Yemen: POB 94356, Riyadh 11693; tel. (1) 488-1757; Ambassador: GHALIB JAMIL.

Judicial System

Judges are independent and governed by the rules of Islamic *Shari'a*. The following courts operate:

Supreme Council of Justice: consists of 11 members and supervises work of the courts; reviews legal questions referred to it by the Minister of Justice and expresses opinions on judicial questions; reviews sentences of death, cutting and stoning; Chair. Sheikh SALIH AL-LIHAYDAN.

Court of Cassation: consists of Chief Justice and an adequate number of judges; includes department for penal suits, department for personal status and department for other suits.

General (Public) Courts: consist of one or more judges; sentences are issued by a single judge, with the exception of death, stoning and cutting, which require the decision of three judges.

Summary Courts: consist of one or more judges; sentences are issued by a single judge.

Specialized Courts: Article 26 of the judicial system stipulates that the setting up of specialized courts is permissible by Royal Decree on a proposal from the Supreme Council of Justice.

Religion

ISLAM

Arabia is the centre of the Islamic faith, and Saudi Arabia includes the holy cities of Mecca and Medina. Except in the Eastern Province, where a large number of people follow Shi'a rites, the majority of the population are Sunni Muslims, and most of the indigenous inhabitants belong to the strictly orthodox Wahhabi sect. The Wahhabis originated in the 18th century but first became unified and influential under Abd al-Aziz (Ibn Sa'ud), who became the first King of Saudi Arabia. They are now the keepers of the holy places and control the pilgrimage to Mecca. In 1986 King Fahd adopted the title of Custodian of the Two Holy Mosques. The country's most senior Islamic authority is the Council of Ulema.

Mecca: Birthplace of the Prophet Muhammad, seat of the Great Mosque and Shrine of Ka'ba, visited by 993,000 Muslims in the Islamic year 1413 (1992/93).

Medina: Burial place of Muhammad, second sacred city of Islam.

CHRISTIANITY

The Roman Catholic Church

Apostolic Vicariate of Arabia: POB 54, Abu Dhabi, United Arab Emirates; responsible for a territory comprising most of the Arabian peninsula (including Saudi Arabia, the United Arab Emirates and Yemen), containing an estimated 750,000 Roman Catholics at 31 December 1992; Vicar Apostolic GIOVANNI BERNARDO GREMOLI, Titular Bishop of Masuccaba; Vicar Delegate for Saudi Arabia Fr NICHOLAS WIDHAMMER.

The Anglican Communion

Within the Episcopal Church in Jerusalem and the Middle East, Saudi Arabia forms part of the diocese of Cyprus and the Gulf. The Anglican congregations in the country are entirely expatriate. The Bishop in Cyprus and the Gulf is resident in Cyprus, while the Archdeacon in the Gulf is resident in the United Arab Emirates.

Other Denominations

The Greek Orthodox Church is also represented.

The Press

Since 1964 most newspapers and periodicals have been published by press organizations, administered by boards of directors with full autonomous powers, in accordance with the provisions of the Press Law. These organizations, which took over from small private firms, are privately owned by groups of individuals experienced in newspaper publishing and administration (see Publishers).

There are also a number of popular periodicals published by the government and by the Saudi Arabian Oil Co, and distributed free of charge. The press is subject to no legal restriction affecting freedom of expression or the coverage of news.

DAILIES

Arab News: POB 4556, Jeddah 21412; tel. (2) 669-1888; telex 604397; fax (2) 667-1650; f. 1975; English; publ. by Saudi Research and Marketing Co; Editor-in-Chief KHALED A. AL-MAEENA; circ. 110,000.

Al-Bilad (The Country): POB 6340, Jeddah 21442; f. 1934; Arabic; publ. by Al-Bilad Publishing Org.; Editor-in-Chief Dr ABD AL-MAJID ASH-SHUBUKSHI; circ. 30,000.

Al-Iktesadia: Jeddah; f. 1992; Arabic; economic and financial; Editor-in-Chief MOHAMMAD AT-TUNISI.

Al-Jazirah (The Peninsula): POB 354, Riyadh 11411; tel. (1) 402-5555; telex 401479; fax (1) 402-1795; Arabic; Dir-Gen. SALEH AL-AJROUSH; Editor-in-Chief MUHAMMAD IBN NASSIR IBN ABBAS; circ. 90,030.

Al-Madina al-Munawara (Medina—The Enlightened City): POB 807, Jeddah; tel. (2) 688-0344; telex 601356; f. 1937; Arabic; publ. by Al-Madina Press Est; Editor OSMAN HAFEZ; circ. 46,370.

An-Nadwah (The Council): Jarwal Sheikh Sayed Halabi Bldg, Mecca; tel. (2) 542-7868; telex 401205; f. 1958; Arabic; publ. by Mecca Printing and Information Establishment; Editors HAMED MUTAWI'E, SALEH MUHAMMAD JAMAL; circ. 35,000.

Okaz: POB 1508, Jeddah 21412; tel. (2) 672-2630; telex 401360; f. 1960; Arabic; Editor-in-Chief HASHIM ABDU HASHIM; circ. 75,000.

Ar-Riyadh: POB 851, Riyadh; tel. (1) 442-0000; telex 401664; fax (1) 441-7580; f. 1965; Arabic; publ. by Al-Yamama Press Establishment; Editor TURKI A. AS-SUDARI; circ. 150,000 (Sat.–Thurs.), 90,000 (Friday).

Saudi Gazette: POB 5576, Jeddah; tel. (2) 672-2630; telex 600920; f. 1975; English; economic and financial; publ. by Okaz Org.; Dir-Gen. IYAD A. MADANI; Editor RIDAH MUHAMMAD LARRY; circ. 17,900.

Al-Yaum (Today): POB 565, Dammam; tel. (3) 833-1906; telex 801109; f. 1965; Dir ABD AL-AZIZ AT-TURKI; circ. 25,000.

WEEKLIES

Arabian Sun: POB 5000, Dhahran 31311; tel. (3) 966-38743856; fax (3) 966-38738490; f. 1945; English; publ. by Saudi Aramco, Dhahran.

Ad-Da'wa (The Call): POB 626, Islamic University, Sharia Ibn Khaldun, Riyadh; f. 1965; Arabic.

Al-Mujtama' (Society): POB 354, Riyadh; f. 1964; Dir-Gen. SALEH SALEM.

Al-Muslimoon (The Muslims): POB 4556, Jeddah 21412; tel. (2) 669-1888; telex 604397; Arabic; cultural and religious affairs; publ. by Saudi Research and Marketing Co.

News from Saudi Arabia: Ministry of Information, Jeddah; f. 1961; English; domestic affairs; Editor IZZAT MUFTI.

Rabitat al-'Alam al-Islami (The Journal of the Muslim World League): POB 538, Mecca; tel. (2) 543-6530; telex 60009; fax (2) 543-1488; monthly in both Arabic and English; Editors ABDULLAH A. ADH-DHARI (Arabic), Sayyid HASAN MUTAHAR (English).

Saudi Arabia Business Week: POB 2894, Riyadh; English; trade and commerce.

Saudi Business: POB 4556, Jeddah 21412; tel. (2) 669-1888; telex 40570; f. 1975; English; publ. by Saudi Research and Marketing Co; Editor-in-Chief Dr TALAL K. HAFIZ; circ. 27,300.

Saudi Economic Survey: POB 1989, Jeddah 21441; tel. (2) 651-4952; fax (2) 651-4952; f. 1967; English; a weekly review of Saudi Arabian economic and business activity; Publr S. A. ASHOOR; Man. Editor ABD AL-HAKIM GHAITH; circ. 3,000.

Sayidati (My Lady): POB 5455, Jeddah; telex 401205; Arabic; women's magazine; publ. by Saudi Research and Marketing Co.

Al-Yamama: Al-Yamama Press Establishment, POB 851, Riyadh; telex 401664; f. 1952; Dir AHMAD AL-HOSHAM; circ. 35,000.

OTHER PERIODICALS

Ahlan Wasahlan (Welcome): POB 8013, Jeddah 21482; tel. (2) 686-2349; telex 601007; fax (2) 6862006; monthly; flight journal of Saudi Arabian Airlines; Gen. Man. and Editor-in-Chief YARUB A. BALKHAIR; circ. 150,000.

Arabia: POB 4288, Jeddah; telex 402687; publ. by Islamic Press Agency.

Al-'Arab (The Arabs): POB 137, Hamad al-Jasser St, Riyadh 11411; tel. (1) 462-1223; fax (1) 462-1223; f. 1967; every 2 months; history and geography of the Arabian Peninsula; Editor HAMAD AL-JASSER.

Al-Faysal: POB 3, Al-Orouba St, Solaymaniyah, Riyadh; tel. 4653027; telex 402600; f. 1976; Arabic; Editor-in-Chief ALAWY TAHA AS-SAFY.

Hajj: Ministry of Pilgrimage Affairs and Awqaf, Omar bin al-Khatab St, Riyadh 11183; tel. (1) 402-2200; telex 401603; f. 1947; Arabic and English; general interest; Editor MUHAMMAD SAID AL-AMONDI.

Al-Leqa' (The Meeting): POB 812, Riyadh; monthly; Editor IBRAHIM AL-ULAI AL-MAIMAN.

Al-Manhal (The Spring): POB 2925, Jeddah; tel. (2) 643-2124; fax (2) 642-8853; f. 1937; monthly; Arabic; cultural, literary, political and scientific; Editor NABIH ABD AL-QUDOUS ANSARI.

Majallat al-Iqtisad wal-Idara (Journal of Economics and Administration): Research and Development Center, King Abd al-Aziz University, POB 1540, Jeddah; monthly; Chief Editor Dr MUHAMMAD M. N. QUOTAH.

Saudi Review: POB 4288, Jeddah; tel. (2) 642-4043; telex 601845; fax (2) 643-2821; f. 1966; English; monthly; newsletter from Saudi newspapers and broadcasting service; Publr and Chief Editor MUHAMMAD SALAHUDDIN; Man. Dir SHAKER AS-SANTAWI; circ. 5,000.

Ash-Sharkiah-Elle (Oriental Elle): POB 6, Riyadh; telex 40112; monthly; Arabic; women's magazine; Editor SAMIRA M. KHASHAGGI.

As-Soqoor (Falcons): POB 2973, Riyadh 11461; tel. (1) 476-6566; f. 1978; 2 a year; air-force journal; cultural activities; Editor HAMAD A. AS-SALEH.

At-Tadhamon al-Islami (Islamic Solidarity): Ministry of Pilgrimage (Hajj) Affairs and Awqaf, Omar bin al-Khatab St, Riyadh 11183; monthly; Editor Dr MUSTAFA ABD AL-WAHID.

At-Tijarah (Commerce): POB 1264, Jeddah; f. 1960; monthly; for businessmen; publ. by Jeddah Chamber of Commerce and Industry; Chair. Sheikh ISMAIL ABU DAUD; Gen. Man. ABDULLAH S. DAHLAN; circ. 8,000.

At-Tijarah as-Sina'iya (Industrial Trade): POB 596, Riyadh; Arabic.

NEWS AGENCIES

Islamic Press Agency: POB 4288, Jeddah; telex 402687.

Saudi Press Agency: c/o Ministry of Information, POB 570, Nasseriya St, Riyadh 11161; tel. (1) 402-3065; telex 401074; f. 1970; Dir-Gen. ABDULLAH HILAIL.

Publishers

Al-Bilad Publishing Organization: POB 6340, As-Sahafa St, Jeddah 21442; tel. (2) 671-1000; telex 601205; publishes *Al-Bilad* and *Iqra'a*; Dir-Gen. AMIN ABDULLAH AL-QARQOURI.

Dar al-Yaum Press, Printing and Publishing Ltd: POB 565, Dammam; tel. (3) 833-1906; telex 801109; f. 1964; publishes *Al-Yaum*; Dir-Gen. MANSOUR M. AL-HASSAN.

Al-Jazirah Organization for Press, Printing and Publishing: POB 354, Riyadh 11411; tel. (1) 402-5555; telex 401479; fax (1) 402-1795; f. 1964; 27 mems; publishes *Al-Jazirah* and *Al-Masaeyah* (both dailies); Dir-Gen. SALEH AL-AJROUSH; Editor-in-Chief KHALID AL-MALEK.

Al-Madina Press Establishment: POB 807, Jeddah; tel. (2) 688-0344; telex 601356; f. 1937; publishes *Al-Madina al-Munawara*; Admin. Man. A. S. AL-GHAMDI; Gen. Man. AHMAD SALAH JAMJOOM.

International Publications Agency (IPA): POB 70, Dhahran Airport; tel. (3) 8954921; telex 671229; publishes material of local interest; Man. SAID SALAH.

Mecca Printing and Information Establishment: Jarwal Sheikh Sayed Halabi Bldg, Mecca; tel. (2) 574-8150; telex 640039; publishes *An-Nadwah* daily newspaper; Man. Dir ABBAS A. ZOWAWI.

Okaz Organization for Press and Publication: POB 5941, Jeddah; tel. (2) 660-0789; telex 402645; publishes *Okaz, Saudi Gazette* and *Child*; Man. Dir ALI H. SHOBOKSHI.

Saudi Publishing and Distributing House: Al-Jouhara Bldg, South Block, Bughdadia, Medina Road, POB 2043, Jeddah 21451; tel. (2) 642-4043; telex 601845; fax (2) 643-2821; publishers, importers and distributors of English and Arabic books; Chair. MUHAMMAD SALAHUDDIN.

Saudi Research and Publishing Co: POB 4556, Jeddah 21412; tel. (2) 669-1888; telex 604397; publishes *Arab News, Asharq al-Awsat, Al-Majalla, Al-Muslimoon* and *Sayidati*; Dirs-Gen. HISHAM ALI HAFEZ, MUHAMMAD ALI HAFEZ.

Al-Yamamah Press Establishment: POB 25848, Riyadh; tel. (1) 442-0000; telex 401664; fax (1) 441-7580; publishes *Ar-Riyadh* and *Al-Yamamah*; Dir-Gen. FAHED AL-ORAIFY.

Radio and Television

In 1991 there were an estimated 4.7m. radio receivers and 4.1m. television receivers in use.

RADIO

Saudi Arabian Broadcasting Service: c/o Ministry of Information, POB 570, Riyadh; tel. (1) 401-4440; telex 401040; fax (1) 402-5253; 43 medium-wave stations, including Jeddah, Riyadh, Dammam and Abha, broadcast programmes in Arabic and English; 23 FM stations; overseas service in Bengali, English, Farsi, French, Indonesian, Somali, Swahili, Turkestani, Turkish and Urdu; Dir-Gen. KHALID H. GHOUTH.

Saudi Aramco FM Radio: Bldg 3030 LIP, Dhahran; tel. (3) 876-2818; telex 801120; fax (3) 874-0238; f. 1957; private station broadcasting music and programmes in English for the entertainment of employees of Saudi Aramco; Man. A. A. AL-ARFAJ.

TELEVISION

Saudi Arabian Government Television Service: POB 570, Riyadh 11421; tel. (1) 401-4440; telex 401030; fax (1) 404-4192; began transmission 1965; 112 stations, incl. six main stations at Riyadh, Jeddah, Medina, Dammam, Qassim, Abha, transmit programmes in Arabic and English; Dir-Gen. A. RAHMAN YAHMOOR (Channel 1).

Saudi Arabian Government Television Service Channel 2: POB 7959, Riyadh 11472; tel. (1) 442-8400; telex 401030; fax (1) 403-3826; began transmission 1983; Dir-Gen. ABD AL-AZIZ S. ABU ANNAJA.

Dhahran HZ-22 TV, Channel 3 TV: Bldg 3030 LIP, Dhahran; tel. (3) 875-4634; telex 801120; fax (3) 874-0238; non-commercial private co; started 1957, since 1970 English language film-chain operation only; Man. (Media Productions and Operations) A. A. AL-ARFAJ.

Finance

(cap. = capital; p.u. = paid up; res = reserves; dep. = deposits; m. = million; brs = branches; amounts in Saudi riyals unless otherwise stated)

BANKING

In 1990 the Saudi Arabian banking system consisted of: the Saudi Arabian Monetary Agency, as central note-issuing and regulatory body; 12 commercial banks (three national and nine foreign banks); and five specialist banks. There is a policy of 'Saudiization' of the foreign banks.

Central Bank

Saudi Arabian Monetary Agency (SAMA): POB 2992, Riyadh 11169; tel. (1) 463-3000; telex 404400 (English), 401466 (Arabic); f. 1952; functions include stabilization of currency, administration of monetary reserves, regulation of banking and issue of notes and coins; cap. and res 24,457m., dep. 177,408m., total assets 275,192m. (Dec. 1992); Gov. Sheikh HAMAD SA'UD AS-SAYARI; 10 brs.

National Banks

National Commercial Bank (NCB): POB 3555, King Abd al-Aziz St, Jeddah 21481; tel. (2) 644-6644; telex 605571; f. 1954; cap. 6,000m., res 952.3m., dep. 51,274m. (Dec. 1993); Chair. and Gen. Man. Sheikh SALIM AHMAD IBN MAHFOUZ; 235 brs, incl. international representative offices.

Riyad Bank Ltd: POB 22622, Old Airport Rd, Riyadh 11416; tel. (1) 401-3030; telex 407490; fax (1) 404-1255; f. 1957; cap. 2,000m., res 4,000m., dep. 41,628m., total assets 50,022m. (Dec. 1992); Chair. Sheikh ISMAIL ABU DAUD; Gen. Man. Sheikh SULAIMAN AL-MANDEEL; 179 brs.

United Saudi Commercial Bank (USCB): POB 25895, Riyadh 11476; tel. (1) 478-4200; telex 405461; fax (1) 478-3197; f. 1983; jointly owned by Saudi nationals (70%), Saudi International Bank (10%), Bank Melli Iran (10%) and United Bank Ltd (10%); cap. p.u.500m., res 585m., dep. 9,113.8m., total assets 10,438.9m. (Dec. 1993); Gen. Man. and CEO MAHER G. AL-AUJAN; 15 brs.

Specialist Banks

Arab Investment Co SAA (TAIC): POB 4009, Riyadh 11491; tel. (1) 476-0601; telex 401011; fax (1) 476-0514; f. 1974 by 15 Arab countries for investment and banking; dep. US $252m. (1990); Chair. Dr AHMAD ABDULLAH AL-MALIK, Dir-Gen. Dr SALIH AL-HUMAIDAN; 4 brs throughout Middle East.

Ar-Rajhi Banking and Investment Corporation (ARABIC): POB 28, Riyadh 11411; tel. (1) 405-4244; fax (1) 403-2969; f. 1988; fmrly Ar-Rajhi Co for Currency Exchange and Commerce; operates according to Islamic financial principles; 44% owned by Ar-Rajhi family; cap. 1,500m., total assets 28,598m. (1993); Chair. Sheikh SALEH IBN ABD AL-AZIZ AR-RAJHI; Man. Dir Sheikh SULAIMAN IBN ABD AL-AZIZ AR-RAJHI; 316 brs.

Saudi Arabian Agricultural Bank (SAAB): POB 11126, Riyadh; tel. (1) 402-2361; telex 201184; f. 1963; cap. 10,000m. (1982); Controller-Gen. ABDULLAH SAAD AL-MENGASH; Gen. Man. ABD AL-AZIZ MUHAMMAD AL-MANQUR; 71 brs.

Saudi Credit Bank: POB 3401, Riyadh; tel. (1) 402-9128; f. 1973; provides interest-free loans for specific purposes to Saudi citizens of moderate means; Chair. OSAMA JAAFAR FAQITH.

Saudi Investment Bank (SAIB): POB 3533, Riyadh 11481; tel. (1) 477-8433; telex 401170; fax (1) 477-6781; f. 1976; provides a comprehensive range of traditional and specialized banking services to business and individuals; foreign shareholders, incl. Chase Manhattan Bank, Industrial Bank of Japan and J. Henry Schroder Wagg & Co. Ltd, have provided 25% of cap.; cap. p.u. 90m., res 271m., dep. 5,883.7m., total assets 6,245.1m. (Dec 1993); Chair. Dr ABD AL-AZIZ O'HALI; Gen. Man. JACK J. KNIPPENBERG; 7 brs.

Banks with Foreign Interests

Al-Bank as-Saudi al-Fransi (Saudi French Bank): POB 56006, Riyadh 11554; tel. (1) 404-2222; telex 407666; fax (1) 404-2311; f. 1977; Saudi Arabian nationals have 68.9% participation, Banque Indosuez has 31.1%; cap. 900m., res 1,430m., dep. 20,630.4m., total assets 22,960.8m. (Dec. 1992); Chair. IBRAHIM A. AL-TOUQ; Man. Dir GÉRARD DELAFORGE; 59 brs.

Arab National Bank (ANB): POB 56921, Riyadh 11564; tel. (1) 402-9000; telex 402660; fax (1) 402-7747; f. 1980; fmrly Arab Bank Ltd, Jordan, but Saudi public acquired 60% participation; cap. 1,200m., res 1,200m., dep. 18,946m., total assets 32,407m. (Dec. 1993); Chair. Sheikh RASHID AR-RASHID; Man. Dir ELIE EL-HADJ; 123 brs.

Bank al-Jazira: POB 6277, Jeddah 21442; tel. and fax (2) 651-8070; telex 601574; 91.5% Saudi-owned; cap. p.u. 400m., dep. 4,992.8m., total assets 5,661.9m. (Dec. 1992); Chair. Sheikh MUHAMMAD IBN SALEH IBN SULTAN; Gen. Man. MISHARI I. MISHARI; 23 brs.

Saudi American Bank (SAMBA): POB 833, Riyadh 11421; tel. (1) 477-4770; telex 400195; fax (1) 477-4770; 70% owned by Saudi nationals; cap. 1,200m., res 2,025m. dep. 35,908m., total assets 38,786m. (Dec. 1993); Chair. ABD AL-AZIZ IBN HAMAD AL-GOSAIBI; Man. Dir MEHLI MISTRI; 37 brs.

Saudi British Bank: POB 9084, Riyadh 11413; tel. (1) 405-0677; telex 402349; fax (1) 405-0660; a joint-stock co f. in 1978, when Saudi citizens acquired a 60% interest in the British Bank of the Middle East; cap. 1,000m., res 1,500.1m., dep. 16,748.9m., total assets 22,767.7m. (Dec. 1993); Chair. Sheikh ABDULLAH MUHAMMAD AL-HUGAIL; Man. Dir ANDREW DIXON; 58 brs.

Saudi Cairo Bank: POB 11222, Jeddah 21453; tel. and fax (2) 660-8820; telex 600205; f. 1979; fmrly Banque du Caire; Saudi shareholders have 55% participation; cap. 1,200m., res 300m, dep. 11,205m., total assets 13,443m. (Dec. 1992); Chair. Sheikh WAHIB IBN ZAGR; Gen. Man. EL-REFAI KAMAL EISA; 69 brs.

Saudi Hollandi Bank (Saudi Dutch Bank): POB 1467, Riyadh 11431; tel. (1) 401-0288; telex 401488; fax (1) 403-1104; a joint-stock co f. in 1977 to take over the activities of Algemene Bank Nederland NV in Saudi Arabia; ABN AMRO Bank (Netherlands) has 40%, Saudi citizens have 60% participation; cap. p.u. 210m., res 962m., dep. 13,928m., total assets 15,101m. (Dec. 1993); Chair. SULAIMAN A. R. AS-SUHAIMI; Man. Dir SHELDON E. BOEGE; 36 brs.

INSURANCE COMPANIES

In 1990 there were 38 insurance companies based in Saudi Arabia.

Al-Alamiya Insurance Co Ltd (E.C.): POB 2374, Jeddah 21451; tel. (2) 671-8851; telex 606456; fax (2) 671-1377; managed by Sun Alliance, London; total assets US $21.3m. (1993); Chair. Sheikh WAHIB S. IBN ZAGR; Man. Dir C. ROBERT BRADSHAW.

Arabia CIGNA Insurance Co Ltd (E.C.): POB 276, Dammam 31411; tel. (3) 832-4441; telex 801259; fax 834-9389; f. 1976 as Pan Arabian Insurance Co; cap. p.u. US $1m.; Chair. Sheikh ABD AL-KARIM AL-KHERELJI; Gen. Man. A. AHMAD.

Gulf Union Insurance Co: POB 5719, Damman 31432; tel. (3) 833-3802; telex 802458; fax 833-3517; f. 1982; primarily non-life insurance; cap. p.u. US $20m.; Chair. SAAD MUHAMMAD AL-MOAJIL; Gen. Man. PERCY A. SEQUEIRA.

Independent Insurance Co of Saudi Arabia Ltd: POB 1178, Jeddah 21431; tel. (2) 651-7732; telex 601580; fax (2) 6511968; f. 1977; all classes of insurance; cap. p.u. US $1m.; Pres. KHALID TAHER.

National Company for Co-operative Insurance (NCCI): POB 86959; Riyadh 11632; tel. (1) 482-6969; telex 406828; fax (1) 488-1719; f. 1985 by royal decree; owned by three government agencies; auth. cap. SR500m.; Chair. AHMED ABD AL-LATIF.

National Insurance Co SA: POB 5832, Jeddah 21432; tel. (2) 660-6200; telex 601791.

Red Sea Insurance (Saudi Arabia) E.C. Group: POB 5627, Jeddah 21432; tel. (2) 660–3538; telex 601228; fax (2) 665-5418; f. 1974; insurance, development, and reinsurance; cap. US $27.5m.; Chair. SALEH SALIM BIN MAHFOUZ; Man. Dir KHALDOUN B. BARAKAT.

Saudi Arabian Insurance Co Ltd: POB 58073, Riyadh 11594; tel. (1) 479-3311; telex 407017; fax (1) 477-2376; f. 1979; all classes of insurance; cap. p.u. 4m. Bahraini dinars; Chair. Prince FAHD IBN KHALID IBN ABDULLAH AS-SA'UD.

Saudi Continental Insurance Co: POB 2940, Riyadh; tel. (1) 476-6903; telex 406325; fax (1) 476-9310; f. 1983; all classes of insurance; cap. p.u. US $3m.; Chair. OMAR A. AGGAD; Gen. Man. J. A. MCROBBIE.

Saudi United Insurance Co Ltd: POB 933, Al-Khobar 31952; tel. (3) 894-9090; telex 871335; fax 894-9428; f. 1976; all classes of insurance and reinsurance except life; cap. p.u. US $5m.; majority shareholding held by Ahmad Hamad al-Gosaibi & Bros; Chair. and Man. Dir Sheikh ABD AL-AZIZ HAMAD AL-GOSAIBI; Dir and Gen. Man. AHMAD MUHAMMAD SABBAGH; 6 brs.

U.C.A. Insurance Co (E.C.): POB 5019, Jeddah 21422; tel. (2) 653-0068; telex 601906; fax (2) 651-1936; f. 1974 as United Commercial Agencies Ltd; all classes of insurance; cap. p.u. US $4m.; Chair. Dr GHAITH R. PHARAON; Exec. Vice-Pres. JACQUES G. SACY.

Al-Yamanah Insurance Co Ltd: POB 41522, Riyadh 11531; tel. (1) 477-4498; telex 400818; fax (1) 477-4497; f. 1979; all classes of insurance; cap. p.u. 15m.; Chair. ABDULLAH AHMAD AL-GOREER; Man. Dir FAYED MAHMOUD ASH-SHEHABI.

Trade and Industry

(cap. = capital; p.u. = paid up; m. = million; amounts in Saudi riyals)

DEVELOPMENT

Arab Petroleum Investments Corpn: POB 448, Dhahran Airport 31932; tel. (3) 864-7400; telex 870068; fax (3) 894-5076; f. 1975; affiliated to the Organization of Arab Petroleum Exporting Countries (see p. 237); specializes in financing petroleum and petrochemical projects and related industries in the Arab world and in other developing countries; shareholders: Kuwait, Saudi Arabia and the United Arab Emirates (17% each), Libya (15%), Iraq and Qatar (10% each), Algeria (5%), Bahrain, Egypt and Syria (3% each); cap. p.u. US $400m. (1992); Chair. ABDULLAH A. AZ-ZAID; Gen. Man. Dr NUREDDIN FARRAG.

General Investment Fund (Public Investment Fund): c/o Ministry of Finance and National Economy, Airport Rd, Riyadh 11177; tel. (1) 405-0000; telex 401021; f. 1970; provides government's share of capital to mixed capital cos; 100% state-owned; cap. p.u. 1,000m.; Chair. Sheikh MUHAMMAD ALI ABA AL-KHAIL (Minister of Finance and National Economy); Sec.-Gen. SULEIMAN MANDIL.

National Agricultural Development Co (NADEC): POB 2557, Riyadh 11461; tel. (1) 404-0000; telex 403681; fax (1) 405-5522; f. 1981; interests include a dairy farm, 39,760 ha for cultivation of wheat, barley, forage and vegetables and processing of dates; the government has a 20% share; chief agency for agricultural development; cap. 400m.; Chair. Dr ABD AR-RAHMAN IBN ABD AL-AZIZ IBN HASSAN ASH-SHEIKH (Minister of Agriculture and Water).

National Industrialization Co (NIC): f. 1984 to develop private investment in industry; cap. 600m.; 86% of cap. owned by Saudi nationals (1985); Chair. MAHSOUN BAHJAT JALAL.

Royal Commission for Jubail and Yanbu: POB 5964, Riyadh 11432; tel. (1) 479-4445; telex 401386 (English), 404560 (Arabic); f. 1975 to create the basic infrastructure for new industrial cities at Jubail and Yanbu; Chair. Prince ABDULLAH IBN FAISAL IBN TURKI AL-ABDULLAH AS-SA'UD; Dir-Gen. for Jubail AHMAD AL-MUBARAK, for Yanbu ABD AR-RAZAG A. ALGAIN.

Saudi Consulting House (SCH): POB 1267, Riyadh 11431; tel. (1) 448-4533; telex 401152; f. 1979; engineering, economic, industrial and management consultants; Chair. ABD AL-AZIZ AZ-ZAMIL (Minister of Industry and Electricity); Vice-Chair. and Man. Dir AHMAD SALEH AT-TWAIJRI.

Saudi Fund for Development (SFD): POB 1887, Riyadh 11441; tel. (1) 464-0292; telex 401145; fax (1) 464-7450; f. 1974 to help finance projects in developing countries; cap. p.u. 31,000m. (1991); had financed 320 projects by 1992; total commitments amounted to 25,814m.; Chair. Sheikh MUHAMMAD ALI ABA AL-KHAIL (Minister of Finance and National Economy); Vice-Chair. and Man. Dir MUHAMMAD A. AS-SUGAIR.

Saudi Industrial Development Fund (SIDF): POB 4143, Riyadh 11149; tel. (1) 477-4002; telex 401065; fax (1) 4790165; f. 1974; supports and promotes industrial and electrical development in the

private sector, providing long-term interest-free loans to industry; also offers marketing, technical, financial and administrative advice; cap. p.u. 7,000m. (1992); Chair. Dr AHMED AL-MALEK; Dir-Gen. SALEH ABDULLAH AN-NAIM.

CHAMBERS OF COMMERCE

Council of Saudi Arabian Chambers of Commerce and Industry: POB 16683, Riyadh 11474; tel. (1) 405-3200; telex 405808; fax (1) 402-4747; comprises one delegate from each of the 19 chambers of commerce in the Kingdom; Chair. Sheikh ABD AR-RAHMAN AL-JERAISY; Sec.-Gen. ABDALLAH T. DABBAGH.

Abha Chamber of Commerce and Industry: POB 722, Abha; tel. (7) 227-1818; telex 905001; fax 227-1919; Pres. ABDULLAH SAFEED ABU MELHA; Sec.-Gen. HAMDI ALI AL-MALKI.

Al-Ahsa Chamber of Commerce and Industry: POB 1519, Horuf 31982; tel. (3) 582-0458; telex 861230; fax 587-5274; Pres. ABD AL-AZIZ SULAIMAN AL-AFALIQ; Sec.-Gen. SAAD ABD AR-RAHMAN AL-IBRAHIM.

Ar'ar Chamber of Commerce and Industry: POB 440, Ar'ar; tel. (4) 662-6544; telex 812058; fax 662-4581; Pres. SALIH YAHYA AL-AS'AF; Sec.-Gen. MATAB MOZIL AS-SARRAH.

Al-Baha Chamber of Commerce and Industry: POB 311, al-Baha; tel. (7) 725-4116; telex 731048; fax 727-0308; ; Pres. AHMED WANNAN AL-GHAMDI; Sec.-Gen. YAHYA AZ-ZAHRANI.

Eastern Province Chamber of Commerce and Industry: POB 719, Dammam 31421; tel. (3) 857-1111; telex 801086; fax 857-0607; f. 1952; Chair. Sheikh SAAD MUHAMMAD AL-MOAJIL; Sec.-Gen. HAMDAN M. AS-SORAIHY.

Federation of Gulf Co-operation Council Chambers (FGCCC): POB 2198, Dammam 31451; tel. (3) 826-5943; telex 802176; fax 826-6794; Pres. Sheikh HAMAD IBN JASSEM IBN MUHAMMAD ATH-THANI; Sec.-Gen. MUHAMMAD A. AL-MULLA.

Ha'il Chamber of Commerce and Industry: POB 1291, Ha'il; tel. (6) 532-1060; telex (6) 311086; fax 533-1366; Pres. SAAD AD-DAKHIL ALLAH AS-SAID; Sec.-Gen. KHADDAM AS-SALIH AL-FAYEZ.

Islamic Chamber of Commerce and Industry: Riyadh; tel. (1) 532339; telex 25533; Chair. Sheikh ISMAIL ABU DAUD; Sec.-Gen. ELION WATT.

Jeddah Chamber of Commerce and Industry: POB 1264, Jeddah 21431; tel. (2) 651-5111; telex 601069; fax (2) 651-7373; f. 1950; Chair. Sheikh ISMAIL ABU DAUD; Sec.-Gen. Dr ABDULLAH SADIQ DHAHLAN.

Al-Jizan Chamber of Commerce and Industry: POB 201, al-Jizan; tel. (7) 322-3763; telex 911065; fax 322-3507; Pres. ABDO HASSAN HAKAMI; Sec.-Gen. YAHYA Y. ASH-SHARIF.

Al-Jouf Chamber of Commerce and Industry: POB 585, al-Jouf; tel. (4) 624-9060; telex 821065; fax 624-0108; Pres. MA'ASHI DUKAN AL-ATTIYEH; Sec.-Gen. AHMAD KHALIFA AL-MUSALLAM.

Al-Majma' Chamber of Commerce and Industry: POB 165, al-Majma' 11952; tel. (6) 432-0268; telex 447020; fax 432-2655; Pres. FAHD MUHAMMAD AR-RABIAH; Sec.-Gen. ABDULLAH IBRAHIM AL-JAAWAN.

Mecca Chamber of Commerce and Industry: POB 1086, Mecca; tel. (2) 5343838; telex 540011; fax 534-2904; f. 1945; Pres. ABD AR-RAHMAN A. FAKIEH; Sec.-Gen. NABIL M. S. QUTUB.

Medina Chamber of Commerce and Industry: POB 443, Airport Rd, Medina; tel. (4) 822-5190; telex 570009; fax 826-8965; Sec.-Gen. TARRIEF HUSSAINHASHIM.

Najran Chamber of Commerce and Industry: POB 1138, Najran; tel. (7) 522-2216; telex 921066; fax 522-3926; Pres. FAISAL HASSAN ABU SAAQ; Sec.-Gen. MAKHFOUR ABDULLAH AL-BISHER.

Qassim Chamber of Commerce and Industry: POB 444, Buraydah, Qassim; tel. (6) 381-4000; telex 301060; fax 381-4528; Pres. ABD AR-REHMAN AL-MUSHAIKEH; Sec.-Gen. ABDALLAH AL-YEHYA ASH-SHARIDA.

Al-Qurayat Chamber of Commerce and Industry: POB 416, Al-Qurayat; tel. (4) 642-3034; fax 642-3172; Pres. OTHMAN ABDULLAH AL-YOUSEF; Sec.-Gen. JAMAL ALI AL-GHAMDI.

Riyadh Chamber of Commerce and Industry: POB 596, Riyadh 11421; tel. (1) 404-0044; telex 401054; fax (1) 402-1103; f. 1961; acts as arbitrator in business disputes, information centre; Chair. ABD AR-RAHMAN AL-JERAISY; Sec.-Gen. Sheikh SALEH ABDULLAH AT-TOAIMI; 23,000 mems.

Tabouk Chamber of Commerce and Industry: POB 567, Tabouk; tel. (4) 422-2736; telex 681173; fax 422-7387; Pres. ABDULAZIZ M. OWADEH; Sec.-Gen. AWADH AL-BALAWI.

Ta'if Chamber of Commerce and Industry: POB 1005, Ta'if; tel. (2) 746-4624; telex 751009; fax 738-0040; Pres. IBRAHIM ABDULLAH KAMAL; Sec.-Gen. Eng. YOUSUF MUHAMMAD ASH-SHAFI.

Union of Arabian Chambers of Commerce and Industry: POB 112837, Riyadh; tel. (1) 814269; telex 20347; Chair. BADR ED-DIN SHALLAH; Sec.-Gen. BURHAN AD-DAJANI.

Yanbu Chamber of Commerce and Industry: POB 58, Yanbu; tel. (4) 322-4257; telex 661036; fax 322-6800; f. 1979; produces quarterly magazine; 2,500 members; Pres. Dr Talal Ali ash-Shair; Sec.-Gen. Muhammad Abdullah al-Omar.

PETROLEUM

Saudi Arabian Oil Co (Saudi Aramco): POB 5000, Dhahran 31311; tel. (3) 875-5110; telex 801220; fax (3) 873-8190; f. 1933; previously known as Arabian-American Oil Co (Aramco); in 1993 incorporated the Saudi Arabian Marketing and Refining Co (SAMAREC, f. 1988) by merger of operations; holds the principal working concessions in Saudi Arabia; Pres. and CEO Ali Naimi; Exec. Vice-Pres. S. Husseini.

Arabian Drilling Co: POB 708, Dammam 31421; tel. (3) 857-6060; telex 871212; fax 857-7114; f. 1964; PETROMIN shareholding 51%, remainder French private cap.; undertakes contract drilling for oil (on shore and off shore), minerals and water both inside and outside Saudi Arabia; Chair. Suleiman J. al-Herbish; Man. Dir Suleiman M. al-Amry.

Arabian Geophysical and Surveying Co (ARGAS): POB 2109, Jeddah 21451; tel. (2) 671-0087; telex 601786; fax (2) 6726352; f. 1966, with the General Petroleum and Mineral Organization (PETROMIN) having a shareholding of 51%; remainder provided by Cie Générale de Géophysique; geophysical exploration for petroleum, other minerals and ground water, as well as all types of land, airborne and marine surveys; Man. Dir Sultan J. Shawli; Tech. Dir Robert Galin.

Arabian Marine Petroleum Co (MARINCO): POB 50, Dhahran Airport 31932; tel. (3) 891-3831; telex 870047; f. 1968; SAMAREC shareholding 51%, remainder held by McDermott Co of New Orleans, USA; undertakes marine construction work (pipelines, rigs, sea terminals, etc.); Chair. Ali I. ar-Rubaishi.

Jeddah Oil Refinery Co (JORC): POB 1604, Jeddah 21441; tel. (2) 636-7411; telex 601150; f. 1967; SAMAREC shareholding 75%, remainder held by Saudi Arabian Refining Co (SARCO); the refinery at Jeddah, Japanese-built, has a capacity of 90,525 b/d; total production 30.7m. barrels (1990); responsible for distribution in the Western Province; Chair. Mansour A. as-Suhaimi; Man. Dir Matouq H. Jannah.

Petromin—Jet: POB 7550, Jeddah 21472; tel. (2) 685-7592; telex 603402; f. 1979 as a subsidiary of the General Petroleum and Mineral Organization (PETROMIN); became wholly-owned by SAMAREC; supplies petroleum products, in particular jet fuel, to King Abd al-Aziz International Airport; Chair. and Exec. Asst Abdullah O. Attas (acting).

Petromin Lube Oil Blending and Grease Manufacturing Plant (SAUDI LUBE): POB 10382, Jubail 31961; tel. (3) 341-1209; telex 832168; f. 1987; wholly-owned by PETROLUBE; production and marketing of lubricants and grease, capacity 1m. barrels lubricants and 4,000 tons grease per year; Man. Dirs Baddah S. as-Sebai'e (Finance and Trade), Abd ar-Rahman M. al-Cabbani.

Petromin Lubricating Oil Co (PETROLUBE): POB 1432, Jeddah 21431; tel. (2) 651-0909; telex 606175; f. 1968; PETROMIN took a 71% share, Mobil Oil Investment owns 29%; for the processing, manufacture, marketing and distribution of lubricating oils and other related products; production 199m. litres (1988); cap. 15.5m.; Chair., Pres. and CEO Ahmad al-Muhammad al-Khereiji.

Petromin Lubricating Oil Refining Co (LUBEREF): POB 5518, Jeddah 21432; tel. (2) 636-7411; telex 602781; fax (2) 636-6932; f. 1975; owned 70% by PETROMIN and 30% by Mobil; production 1,889,000 barrels (1992); Chair. and Exec. Man. Dir Bakr A. Khoja.

Petromin Marketing (PETMARK): POB 5250, Jeddah 21422; tel. (2) 667-6233; telex 870009; fax (2) 669-4081; f. 1967; wholly-owned by SAMAREC; operates the installations and facilities for the distribution of petroleum products in the Eastern, Central, Southern and Northern provinces of Saudi Arabia; Pres. and CEO Hussein A. Linjawi.

Petromin Mobil Yanbu Refinery: POB 30078, Yanbu; tel. (4) 396-4000; telex 662325; fax 396-0942; f. 1984; operated by SAMAREC and Mobil, capacity 300,000 b/d; Man. Dir Ali Taher ad-Dabbagh.

Petromin Riyadh Refinery (PRR): POB 3946, Riyadh 11199; tel. (1) 498-0995; telex 401015; f. 1974; wholly-owned by SAMAREC; production capacity 120,000 b/d; total production 43.6m. barrels (1990); Exec. Man. Dir Anwad A. al-Naqqar.

Petromin Services Department (PETROSERVE): POB 2329, Jeddah 21451; tel. (2) 636-6309; telex 601867; f. 1968; operates all types of services in medical care, social and sports activities, telecommunications, computers, housing, security and training; Pres. Hussain A. Linjawi.

Petromin-Shell Refinery Co: POB 10088, Jubail 31961; tel. (3) 357-2000; telex 832060; operated by SAMAREC and Shell;

capacity 250,000 b/d; exports began in 1985; Chair. Dr Faisal Bashir.

Petromin Yanbu Refinery: POB 30021, Yanbu; tel. (4) 321-8402; telex 662337; fax 396-2756; f. 1983, with an initial capacity of 170,000 b/d; production 60m. barrels (1990); Exec. Dir Yahya A. az-Zaid; Vice-Pres. Awdah A. al-Ahmadi.

Vela International Marine Ltd (VELA): T-1010, Tower Building, Dhahran; tel. (3) 875-3445; fax (3) 873-2039; Pres. D. A. F. al-Utaibi.

Saudi Basic Industries Corpn (SABIC): POB 5101, Riyadh 11422; tel. (1) 401-2033; telex 401177; fax (1) 401-3831; f. 1976; to foster the petrochemical industry and other hydrocarbon-based industries through joint ventures with foreign partners, and to market their products; cap. 10,000m.; 30% of shares sold to Saudi and other GCC nationals in 1984; production 13.0m. tons (1992); total assets 32,852m. (1990); Chair. Abd al-Aziz az-Zamil (Minister of Industry and Electricity); Vice-Chair. and Man. Dir Ibrahim bin Salamah.

Projects include:

Al-Jubail Fertilizer Co (Samad): POB 10046, Jubail 31961; tel. (3) 341-6488; telex 832024; fax (3) 341-7122; f. 1979; capacity of 620,000 tons per year of urea; jt venture with Taiwan Fertilizer Co; Pres. Ahmad A. al-Ahmad.

Al-Jubail Petrochemical Co (Kemya): POB 10084, Jubail 31961; tel. (3) 357-6000; telex 832058; f. 1980; began production of linear low-density polyethylene in 1984, of high-density polyethylene in 1985, and of high alfa olefins in 1986, capacity of 330,000 tons per year of polyethylene; jt venture with Exxon Corpn (USA) and SABIC; Pres. Khalil I. al-Gannas; Exec. Vice-Pres. Clay Lewis.

Arabian Petrochemical Co (Petrokemya): POB 10002, Jubail 31961; tel. (3) 358-7000; telex 832053; fax 358-4480; produced 1.2m. tons of ethylene, 135,000 tons of polystyrene and 50,000 tons of butene-1 in 1992; wholly-owned subsidiary of SABIC; owns 50% interest in ethylene glycol plant producing 203,000 tons per year of monoethylene glycol, 21,700 tons per year of diethylene glycol and 1,300 tons per year of triethylene glycol; Chair. Ibrahim A. ibn Salamah; Pres. Nabil A. Mansouri.

Eastern Petrochemical Co (Sharq): POB 10035, Jubail 31961; tel. (3) 357-5000; telex 832037; fax 358-0383; f. 1981 to produce linear low-density polyethylene, ethylene glycol; total capacity 330,000 tons of ethylene glycol and 140,000 tons of polyethylene per year; a SABIC joint venture; Pres. Ahmad M. an-Nekhilan.

Jeddah Steel Rolling Co (Sulb): POB 1826, Jeddah 21441; tel. (2) 636-7462; telex 602127; fax (2) 6368161; f. 1967; capacity of 150,000 tons per year of reinforcing steel bars; cap. 62.4m.; Chair. Youssef M. Alireza.

National Industrial Gases Co (Gas): POB 10110, Jubail; tel. (3) 341-1992; telex 832082; to produce oxygen and nitrogen, total capacity of 584,000 tons per year; jt venture with Saudi private sector; Dir-Gen. Saad H. al-Ghurairi.

National Methanol Co (Ibn Sina): POB 10003, Jubail 31961; tel. (3) 340-5500; telex 832033; fax 340-5506; began commercial production of chemical-grade methanol in November 1984; capacity 1m. tons per year; began commercial production of MTBE in May 1994; capacity 7m. tons per year; jt venture of SABIC, Hoechst-Celanese (Germany) and Panhandle Eastern Corpn (USA); Pres. K. S. Rawaf.

National Plastics Co (Ibn Hayyan): POB 10002, Jubail; tel. (3) 358-7000; telex 832053; fax 358-4480; produces 300,000 tons per year of vinylchloride monomer and 200,000 tons per year of polyvinylchloride; jt venture with Lucky Group (Republic of Korea), SABIC and three other cos; Pres. Ibrahim S. ash-Sheweir.

Saudi Arabian Fertilizer Co (SAFCO): POB 553, Dammam 31421; tel. (3) 857-5011; telex 807117; fax 857-4311; produced 353,744 tons of urea, 225,735 tons of ammonia, 98,535 tons of sulphuric acid and 20,240 tons of melamine in 1993; owned 41% by SABIC, 10% by its staff and 49% by private Saudi investors; Pres. Hussein Eid al-Jubeihi.

Saudi-European Petrochemical Co (Ibn Zahr): POB 10330, Jubail 31961; tel. (3) 341-5060; telex 832157; f. 1985; annual capacity 500,000 tons of methyl-tertiary-butyl ether (MTBE); SABIC has a 70% share, Ecofuel, Nesté Corpn and APICORP each have 10%; Pres. Abd ar-Rahman A. al-Garawi.

Saudi Iron and Steel Co (Hadeed): POB 10053, Madinat al-Jubail as-Sinaiyah 31961; tel. (3) 357-1100; telex 832022; fax (3) 358-7385; f. 1979; produced 1.8m. tons of steel reinforcing rods and bars in 1992; Pres. Sami A. as-Suwaigh.

Saudi Methanol Co (ar-Razi): POB 10065, Jubail Industrial City 31961; tel. (3) 357-7838; telex 832023; fax 358-5552; f. 1979; capacity of 1,280,000 tons per year of chemical-grade methanol; total methanol exports in 1992 were 1,338,000 tons;

jt venture with a consortium of Japanese cos; cap. 259m.; Pres. ABD AL-AZIZ I. ALAUDAH; Exec. Vice-Pres. T. SEKI.

Saudi Petrochemical Co (Sadaf): POB 10025, Jubail Industrial City 31961; tel. (3) 357-3000; telex 832032; fax 357-3142; f. 1980; to produce ethylene, ethylene dichloride, styrene, crude industrial ethanol and caustic soda; total capacity of 2,490,000 tons per year; Shell (Pecten) has a 50% share; Pres. A. A. AL-ASSAF.

Saudi Yanbu Petrochemical Co (Yanpet): POB 3033, Madinat Yanbu as-Sinaiyah; tel. (4) 396-5000; telex 662359; f. 1980; to produce ethylene, high-density polyethylene, ethylene glycol; total capacity 1,692,200 tons per year by 1990; Mobil and SABIC each have a 50% share; Pres. ALI AL-KHURAIMI; Exec. Vice-Pres. P. J. FOLEY.

Foreign Concessionaires

Arabian Oil Co Ltd (AOC): POB 50584, Riyadh 11533 (Head Office in Japan); f. 1958; holds concession (2,200 sq km at Dec. 1987) for offshore exploitation of Saudi Arabia's half-interest in the Kuwait-Saudi Arabia Neutral Zone; Chair. HIROMICHI EGUCHI; Pres. KEIICHI KONAGA.

Saudi Arabian Texaco Inc: POB 363, Riyadh; tel. (1) 462-7274; fax (1) 464-1992; also office in Kuwait; f. 1928; fmrly Getty Oil Co; holds concession (5,200 sq km at Dec. 1987) for exploitation of Saudi Arabia's half-interest in the Saudi Arabia-Kuwait Neutral Zone.

MAJOR INDUSTRIAL COMPANIES

Figures for sales and capital are in Saudi riyals.

Arabian Cement Co Ltd: POB 275, Jeddah; tel. (2) 682-8270; telex 600718; fax (2) 6829989; f. 1956; produces ordinary Portland cement and sulphate-resistant cement; subsidiary company Cement Product Industry Co Ltd; cap. 600m.; Chair. Prince TURKI IBN ABD AL-AZIZ AS-SAUD; Dir-Gen. Eng. MOHAMMED NAJIB KHEDER; 150 employees.

The Concrete Company LLP (CONCO): POB 5703, Jeddah 21432; tel. (2) 682-0305; telex 603023; f. 1977; manufacture and erection of pre-cast concrete; member of the Dallah Group; cap. p.u. 60m.; Chair. Sheikh SALEH ABDULLAH KAMEL; Gen. Man. MAGD H. TURKI; 450 employees.

Grain Silos and Flour Mills Organization: POB 3402, Airport Road, Riyadh 11471; tel. (1) 464-3500; telex 401052; autonomous body formally responsible to the Ministry of Commerce; production of flour and animal feeds for domestic consumption; grain capacity 585,999 tons (1988); Chair. Dr ABD AR-RAHMAN IBN ABD AL-AZIZ IBN HASSAN ASH-SHEIKH (Minister of Agriculture and Water); Dir-Gen. SALEH AS-SULEIMAN.

Hoshanco: POB 509, Riyadh 11421; tel. (1) 476-6800; telex 401436; f. 1965; construction and trading, agriculture and livestock investment and insurance co; cap. 160m.; Chair. AHMAD AL-HOSHAN; Gen. Man. AHMAD AL-HARAFI; 2,200 employees.

Manufacturing and Building Co Ltd (MABCO): POB 1549, Riyadh 11441; tel. (1) 477-8421; telex 401364; f. 1977; manufacture of pre-cast components for construction of buildings; also turnkey contractors for pre-cast construction; sales 830m. (1984); cap. p.u. 100m.; Chair. HASSAN MISHARI AL-HUSSEIN; Gen. Man. YOUSUF H. AL-HAMDAN; 2,800 employees.

National Fisheries Co: POB 19199, Jeddah 21435; tel. (2) 644-7246; telex 606288.

National Pipe Company Ltd: POB 1099, al-Khobar 31952; tel. (3) 857-7150; telex 870966; f. 1978; manufacture and marketing of spiral-welded steel pipes for oil and gas transmission; sales 56m. (1988); cap. 50m.; Chair. Prince SA'UD IBN NAYEF BIN ABD AL-AZIZ; Gen. Man. SHIGEHIRO MITSUNARI; 121 employees.

Qassim Cement Co: POB 345, Buraydah, Qassim; tel. (6) 381-1802; telex 301202; production of 2,000 tons per day; Hon. Chair. Prince ABDULLAH AL-FAISAL AS-SA'UD; Chair. Prince SULTAN AL-ABDULLAH AL-FAISAL AS-SA'UD.

Saline Water Conversion Corporation (SWCC): POB 4931, Jeddah 21221; tel. (2) 682-1343; telex 601473; fax 6820415; Dir-Gen. ABD AL-AZIZ OMAR NASSIEF.

Saudi Arabian Agriculture and Dairy Company (SAADCO): POB 10525, Riyadh 11443; tel. (1) 495-1400; telex 402356; f. 1976.

Saudi Arabian Fertilizer Co (SAFCO): POB 553, Dammam 31421; tel. (3) 857-5011; telex 870117; Gen. Man. HUSSEIN EID.

Saudi Cable Group of Companies: POB 4403, Jeddah 21491; tel. (2) 6694060; telex 607151; fax (2) 6693935; f. 1975; manufacture of building wires, power and telecommunication cables including fibre optic cables, copper aluminium rod, PVC compounds, information technology products, power transmission and distribution products, turnkey services; revenue 1,458m.; cap. 300m. (1993); revenue 1,380m.; cap. 300m. (1991); Chair. KHALID ALIREZA; 2,000 employees.

Saudi Cement Co: POB 306, Dammam 31411; tel. (3) 834-4500; telex 801068; fax 834-5460; f. 1955; cap. p.u. 420m.; Chair. SULEIMAN A. BALGHONEIM; Gen. Man. ABD AL-AZIZ M. SHOWAIL; 1,765 employees.

Saudi Fisheries Co (SFC): POB 6535, Dammam 31452; tel. (3) 857-3979; telex 802020; fax 8572493; total catch 16,615 metric tons (1988); Chair. Dr ABD AR-RAHMAN IBN ABD AL-AZIZ IBN HASSAN ASH-SHEIKH (Minister of Agriculture and Water); Gen. Man. Dr NASSER OTHMAN AS-SALEH.

Saudi Metal Industries Ltd: POB 6765, Dammam; tel. (3) 857-1692; telex 801526; f. 1978; manufacture of chain-link fencing systems, production of steel reinforcing fabric for concrete; cap. p.u. 16.5m.; Chair. Sheikh ABDULLAH AL-ANKARY; Gen. Man. P. J. GREY; 160 employees.

Saudi Plastic Products Co Ltd (SAPPCO): POB 2828, Riyadh 11461; tel. (1) 448-0448; telex 401025; fax (1) 4461392; f. 1969; manufacture and supply of UPVC pipes and fittings; cap. p.u. 50m.; total assets 194m.; Chair. Sheikh OMAR A. AGGAD; Gen. Man. ABBAS A. AGGAD; 155 employees.

Saudi United Fertilizer Co: POB 4811, Salaheldin Ayyoubi Rd, al-Malaz area, Riyadh 11412; tel. (1) 478-1304; telex 401865; fax (1) 4789581; import and export of agricultural fertilizers, pesticides, forage seeds, field sprayers and agricultural machinery; Man. Dir SAMIR ALI KABBANI.

Southern Province Cement Co: (Head Office) POB 548, Abha; tel. (7) 227-1500; telex 905010; fax (7) 227-1407; Chair. Prince KHALID IBN TURKI AT-TURKI; Gen. Man. Eng. AMER SAEED BARGAN.

Tamimi Co: POB 172, Dammam 31411; tel. (3) 857-4050; telex 801561; fax (3) 857-1592; f. 1964; pipeline construction, mechanical and civil construction, industrial catering, real estate; cap. 100m.; Chair. ALI A. TAMIMI.

Yanbu Cement Co: POB 5330, Jeddah; POB 467, Yanbu; tel. (4) 322-6652; fax (2) 6531420; Chair. Prince MESHAL IBN ABD AL-AZIZ; Dir-Gen. Dr SAUD SALEH ISLAM.

Az-Zamil Group: POB 9, al-Khobar; tel. (3) 864-2567; telex 670132; f. 1930; involved in real estate and land development as well as the marketing of products from numerous subsidiary companies, including Az-Zamil Aluminium Factory Ltd, Zamil Soule Steel Building Co Ltd, Yamama Factories, Arabian Gulf Construction Co Ltd, Bahrain Marble Factory, Az-Zamil Nails and Screws Factory, Saudi Plastics Factory; Pres. MUHAMMAD A. AZ-ZAMIL; 2,500 employees.

TRADE UNIONS

Trade unions are illegal in Saudi Arabia.

Transport

RAILWAYS

Saudi Arabia has the only rail system in the Arabian peninsula. The Saudi Government Railroad comprises 719 km of single and 157 km of double track. In addition, the total length of spur lines and sidings is 348 km. The main line, which was opened in 1951, is 578 km in length; it connects Dammam port, on the Gulf coast, with Riyadh, and passes Dhahran, Abqaiq, Hufuf, Harad and al-Kharj. A 310-km line, linking Hufuf and Riyadh, was inaugurated in May 1985. A total of 399,000 passengers travelled by rail in the Kingdom in 1991/92.

Saudi Railways Organization: POB 36, Dammam 31241; tel. (3) 871-3001; telex 801050; fax 871-2293; an independent entity with a Board of Dirs headed by the Minister of Communications; Pres. FAISAL M. ASH-SHEHAIL.

ROADS

Asphalted roads link Jeddah to Mecca, Jeddah to Medina, Medina to Yanbu, Ta'if to Mecca, Riyadh to al-Kharj, and Dammam to Hufuf as well as the principal communities and certain outlying points in Aramco's area of operations. During the 1980s the construction of other roads was undertaken, including one extending from Riyadh to Medina. The trans-Arabian highway, linking Dammam, Riyadh, Ta'if, Mecca and Jeddah, was completed in 1967. A causeway linking Saudi Arabia with Bahrain was opened in November 1986. A 317-km highway linking Riyadh to Qassim was completed in the late 1980s. During the 1980–85 Development Plan the length of paved roads expanded at an annual average rate of 15.8%. At the end of 1992 there were 151,532 km of roads, of which 21,746 km were main roads (including motorways) and 18,776 km were secondary roads. In 1992 there were about 60 road-building projects in progress in the Kingdom. Metalled roads link all the main population centres. At the end of 1991 there were 5.1m. road motor vehicles registered in Saudi Arabia.

Saudi Public Transport Co (SAPTCO): POB 10667, Riyadh; tel. (1) 454-5000; telex 402414; fax (1) 454-2100; f. 1979; operates a public bus service throughout the country and to neighbouring countries; the Government holds a 30% share; Chair. Dr NASIR AS-SALOOM; CEO Dr ABD AL-AZIZ AL-OHALY.

National Transport Company of Saudi Arabia: Queen's Bldg, POB 7280, Jeddah 21462; tel. (2) 643-4561; telex 401235; specializes in inward clearance, freight forwarding, general and heavy road haulage, re-export, charter air freight and exhibitions; Man. Dir A. D. BLACKSTOCK; Operations Man. I. CROXSON.

SHIPPING

The commercial ports of Jeddah, Dammam, Yanbu and Gizan, the King Fahd Industrial Ports of Jubail and Yanbu, and the oil port of Ras Tanura, as well as a number of minor ports, are under the exclusive management of the Ports Authority. In 1989 the total cargo handled by Saudi Arabian ports, excluding crude petroleum, was 63.8m. metric tons.

Jeddah is the principal commercial port and the main point of entry for pilgrims bound for Mecca. It has berths for general cargo, container traffic, 'roll on, roll off' (ro-ro) traffic, livestock and bulk grain shipments, with draughts ranging from 8 m to 14 m. The port also has a 200-ton floating crane, cold storage facilities and a fully-equipped ship-repair yard. In 1989 a total of 3,684 vessels called at Jeddah Islamic Port, and 12.76m. tons of cargo were handled.

Dammam is the second largest commercial port and has general cargo, container, ro-ro, dangerous cargo and bulk grain berths. Draughts at this port range from 9 m to 14 m. It has a 200-ton floating crane and a fully equipped ship repair yard. In 1989 a total of 1,394 vessels called at King Abd al-Aziz Port in Dammam, and 6.31m. tons of cargo were handled.

Yanbu, which comprises one commercial and one industrial port, is Saudi Arabia's nearest major port to Europe and North America, and is the focal point of the most rapidly growing area, in the west of Saudi Arabia. The commercial port has general cargo, ro-ro and bulk grain berths, with draughts ranging from 10 m to 12 m. It also has a floating crane, and is equipped to handle minor ship repairs. In 1989 a total of 28 vessels called at Yanbu Commercial Port, and 337,473 tons of cargo were handled. The industrial port has berths for general cargo, containers, 'roll on-roll off' traffic, bulk cargo, crude petroleum, refined and petrochemical products and natural gas liquids, and a tanker terminal on the open sea. In 1989 King Fahd Industrial Port in Yanbu handled 23.35m. tons of cargo, of which 23.26m. tons were exported.

Gizan is the main port for the southern part of the country. It has general cargo, ro-ro, bulk grain and container berths, with draughts ranging from 8 m to 12 m. It also has a 200-ton floating crane. In 1989 a total of 35 vessels called at Gizan Port, and 1.29m. tons of cargo were handled.

Jubail has one commercial and one industrial port. The commercial port has general cargo, bulk grain and container berths with ro-ro facilities, and a floating crane. Draughts at this port range from 12 m to 14 m. In 1989 a total of 112 vessels called at Jubail Commercial Port, and 1.21m. tons of cargo were handled. The industrial port has bulk cargo, refined and petrochemical and ro-ro berths, and an open sea tanker terminal suitable for vessels up to 300,000 dwt. Draughts range from 6 m to 30 m. In 1989 King Fahd Industrial Port in Jubail handled 19.70m. tons of cargo, of which 17.68m. tons were exported.

In addition to these major ports, there are a number of minor ports suitable only for small craft, including Khuraiba, Haql, Dhiba, al-Wajh, Umlujj, Rabigh, al-Lith, Qunfoudah, Farasan and al-Qahma on the Red Sea coast and al-Khobar, Qatif, Uqair, Darin and Ras al-Khafji on the Gulf coast. Ras Mishab, on the Gulf coast, is operated by the Ministry of Defence and Civil Aviation.

Arabian Marine Operating Co Ltd: POB 5449, Al-Jawhara Bldg, Bagh da Dieh, Jeddah 21422; tel. (2) 642-9408; telex 601083; Chair. Prince ABDULLAH AL-FAISAL AS-SA'UD; Gen. Man. C. HAKIM.

Arabian Petroleum Supply Co Ltd: POB 1408, Quarantina Rd, Jeddah 21431; tel. (2) 637-1120; telex 602613; fax (2) 636-2366; Gen. Man. V. C. CAMINITI.

Nashar Saudi Lines: POB 6697, Jeddah; tel. (2) 642-3600; telex 601156; owners of livestock carriers trading in Arabian Gulf, Red Sea, Mediterranean and Black Sea.

National Shipping Co of Saudi Arabia (NSCSA): POB 8931, Riyadh 11492; tel. (1) 478-5454; telex 405624; fax (1) 477-8036; f. 1979; regular container, ro-ro and general cargo service from USA to the Middle East, South East Asia and Far East; capacity 25,053 20-ft equivalent units; Chair. SALEH A. AL-NAIM; Chief Exec. MUHAMMAD SULAIMAN AL-JARBOU.

Saudi International Petroleum Carriers Ltd (SIPCA): POB 5572, Riyadh 11432; tel. (1) 465-9077; telex 401709; Chair. OMAR AGGAD.

Saudi Lines: POB 66, Jeddah; regular cargo and passenger services between Red Sea and Indian Ocean ports; Pres. M. A. BAKHASHAB PASHA; Man. Dir A. M. BAKHASHAB.

Saudi Shipping and Maritime Services Co Ltd: POB 7522, Jeddah 21472; tel. (2) 644-0577; telex 601845; fax (2) 644-0932; Chair. Prince SA'UD IBN NAYEF IBN ABD AL-AZIZ; Man. Dir Capt. MUSTAFA T. AWARA.

Seaports Authority (SEAPA): POB 5162, Riyadh 11188; tel. (1) 405-0005; telex 401783; fax (1) 402-7394; f. 1976; Pres. and Chair. Dr FAYEZ IBN IBRAHIM BADR; Vice-Chair. and Dir-Gen. MUHAMMAD IBN ABD AL-KARIM BAKR.

Shipping Corpn of Saudi Arabia Ltd: POB 1691, 2nd Floor, National Marketing Group Bldg, 8 Malik Khalid St, Jeddah 21441; tel. (2) 647-1137; telex 601078; fax (2) 647-8222; Pres. and Man. Dir ABD AL-AZIZ AHMAD ARAB.

CIVIL AVIATION

King Abdulaziz International Airport, which was opened in 1981, has three terminals, one of which is specifically designed to cope with the needs of the many thousands of pilgrims who visit Mecca and Medina each year. The King Khalid International Airport, at Riyadh, opened in 1983 with 4 terminals. It handled 7.9m. passengers in 1993. A third major airport, the King Fahd International Airport, with an initial handling capacity of 5.2m. passengers per year, opened in the Eastern Province in 1993. Expansion of 21 domestic airports began in 1984. Saudia, the Kingdom's national airline, carried 20.9m. passengers in 1993. There is a total of 25 commercial airports in the kingdom.

Presidency of Civil Aviation (PCA): POB 887, Jeddah 21421; tel. (2) 640-5000; telex 601093; fax (2) 640-1477; Pres. Dr ALI ABD AR-RAHMAN AL-KHALAF.

Saudia—Saudi Arabian Airlines: POB 620, Saudia Bldg, Jeddah 21231; tel. (2) 686-0000; telex 601007; fax (2) 686-4552; f. 1945 and began operations in 1947; in 1993 Saudia carried 12.3m. passengers, its fleet numbering 111 aircraft; regular services to 25 domestic and 54 international destinations; regular international services worldwide; Chair. Prince SULTAN IBN ABD AL-AZIZ; Dir-Gen. KHALID IBN ABDULLAH IBN BAKR; Exec. Vice-Pres. (operations) ADNAN AL DABBAGH.

Tourism

All devout Muslims try to make at least one visit to the holy cities of Medina, the burial place of Muhammad, and Mecca, his birthplace. In 1993/94 a total of more than 2m. pilgrims visited Saudi Arabia. In 1988 there were 246 hotels in the kingdom, with a total of 22,298 rooms.

Saudi Hotels and Resort Areas Co (SHARACO): POB 5500, Riyadh 11422; tel. (1) 465-7177; telex 400366; fax (1) 4657172; f. 1975; Saudi Government has 40% interest; cap. SR500m.; Chair. Dr SOLIMAN AL-HUMAYYED; Dir-Gen. ABD AL-AZIZ AL-AMBAR.

National Tourism Co: f. 1992.

Defence

Chief of the General Staff: Maj.-Gen. MUHAMMAD AS-SALAH AL-HAMMAD.

Director-General of Public Security Forces: Brig.-Gen. ABDULLAH IBN ASH-SHEIKH.

Commander of Land Forces: Maj.-Gen. ABD AL-MUHSIN ALI AL-AMRAN.

Commander of Air Force: Maj.-Gen. AHMAD IBRAHIM AL-BUHAYRI.

Estimated Defence Budget (1993): 61,636m. riyals.

Military Service: male conscription (18–35 years of age).

Total Armed Forces (June 1993): 101,000 (army 68,000; navy 11,000; air force 18,000); air defence forces 4,000; National Guard 57,000 active personnel.

Paramilitary Forces: 77,000 National Guard and 10,500 Frontier Force and Coastguard.

Education

The educational system in Saudi Arabia resembles that of other Arab countries. Educational institutions are administered mainly by the Government. The private sector plays a significant role at the first and second levels, but its total contribution is relatively small compared with that of the public sector.

Pre-elementary education is provided on a small scale (with 67,069 children enrolled in 1990/91), mainly in urban areas. Elementary or primary education is of six years' duration and the normal entrance age is 6+. The total number of pupils at this stage in 1990/91 was 1,875,593, with 119,370 teachers. Intermediate education begins at 12+ and lasts for three years. The total number of pupils at this stage in 1990/91 was 570,080, with teachers numbering 43,201. Secondary education begins at 15+ and extends for three years. After the first year, successful pupils branch into science or arts groups. The total number of pupils at this stage in 1990/91 was 289,562, with 20,195 teachers. In 1990/91 the total number of students enrolled at all levels of education was 2,934,115 (1,608,133 males, 1,325,982 females), in 14,435 schools, with 188,891 teachers.

Industrial and commercial schools can be entered after the completion of the intermediate stage. In 1990/91 there were eight industrial schools, 22 commercial schools and one agricultural school. In addition, there were seven higher technical and four higher commercial colleges offering two-year courses. Vocational craft-training institutes are maintained in 62 centres, providing courses in electrical, mechanical and allied trades. In 1990/91 a total of 9,253 students attended technical and vocational institutes.

There are seven universities, with a total of 78,713 students in 1992/93, and 66 colleges. There are also 10 colleges and one higher institute for girls. In 1990/91 there were 131,811 students (71,935 males, 59,876 females) and 12,863 teachers in higher education. Adult education continues for three years. In 1990/91 there were 103,111 students enrolled at adult education schools.

Bibliography

Abir, Mordechai. *Saudi Arabia: Society, Government and the Gulf Crisis*. London, Routledge, 1993.

Al-Farsy, Fouad. *Saudi Arabia. A Case Study in Development*. London, Kegan Paul International Ltd, 1981.

Anderson, Irvine H. *Aramco, the United States, and Saudi Arabia: a study in the dynamics of Foreign Oil Policy, 1935–50*. Princeton University Press, 1982.

Anderson, Prof. Sir Norman. *The Kingdom of Saudi Arabia*. London, Stacey International, 1977.

Assah, Ahmed. *Miracle of the Desert Kingdom*. London, Johnson, 1969.

Atlas of Saudi Arabia. London, Edward Stanford, 1978.

Benoit-Méchin, S. *Ibn Séoud ou la naissance d'un royaume*. Paris, Albin Michel, 1955.

Brown, E. Hoagland. *The Saudi-Arabia-Kuwait Neutral Zone*. Beirut, 1964.

De Gaury, Gerald. *Faisal*. London, Arthur Barker, 1969.

Dequin, Horst. *Saudi Arabia's Agriculture and its Development Possibilities*. Frankfurt, 1963.

Field, Michael. *The Merchants: The Big Business Families of Arabia*, London, John Murray, 1984.

Gharaybeh, A. *Saudi Arabia*. London, 1962.

Helms, Christine Moss. *The Cohesion of Saudi Arabia*. Croom Helm, 1981.

Hobday, Peter. *Saudi Arabia Today: An Introduction to the Richest Oil Power*. London, Macmillan, 1978.

Holden, David, Johns, Richard, and Buchan, James. *The House of Saud*. London, Sidgwick & Jackson, 1981.

Howarth, David. *The Desert King: Ibn Sa'ud*. New York, McGraw Hill, 1964.

Lees, Brian. *Handbook of the Sa'ud family of Saudi Arabia*. London, Royal Genealogies, 1980.

Lipsky, George A., and others. *Saudi Arabia: Its People, Its Society, Its Culture*. New Haven, 1959.

Mackey, Sandra. *The Saudis*. London, Harrap, 1987.

McLoughlin, Leslie. *Ibn Saud, Founder of a Kingdom*. London, Macmillan, 1993.

Montague, Carolyn. *Industrial Development in Saudi Arabia*. London, Committee for Middle East Trade, 1987.

Niblock, Tim. *State, Society and Economy in Saudi Arabia*. London, Croom Helm, 1981.

Philby, H. St. J. B. *Arabia and the Wahhabis*. London, 1928.

Arabia. London, Benn, 1930.

Arabian Jubilee. London, 1951.

The Empty Quarter. London, 1933.

The Land of Midian. London, 1957.

A Pilgrim in Arabia. London, 1946.

Saudi Arabia. London, 1955.

Quandt, Willam B. *Saudi Arabia in the 1980s: Foreign Policy, Security and Oil*. Oxford, Basil Blackwell, 1982.

Robinson, Jeffrey. *Yamani: The Inside Story*. London, Simon and Schuster, 1988.

Sarhan, Samir (Ed.). *Who's Who in Saudi Arabia*. Jeddah, Tihama, and London, Europa, 3rd edn, 1984.

Troeller, Gary. *The Birth of Saudi Arabia: Britain and the Rise of the House of Sa'ud*. London, Frank Cass, 1976.

Van der Meulen, D. *The Wells of Ibn Sa'ud*. John Murray, 1957.

Wilkinson, John. *Arabia's Frontiers*. London, I. B. Tauris, 1991.

Williams, K. *Ibn Sa'ud: the Puritan King of Arabia*. London, Cape, 1933.

Winder, R. Bayly. *Saudi Arabia in the Nineteenth Century*. London, Macmillan, 1965.

SPANISH NORTH AFRICA

Geography

Spanish North Africa comprises Ceuta and Melilla, two enclaves within Moroccan territory, and several rocky islets off the Moroccan coast. The average temperature is 17°C.

CEUTA

The ancient port and walled city of Ceuta is situated on a rocky promontory on the North African coast overlooking the Strait of Gibraltar, the Strait here being about 25 km wide. Ceuta was retained by Spain as a plaza de soberanía (a presidio, or fortified enclave, over which Spain has full sovereign rights) when Morocco became independent from France in 1956, and is administered as part of Cádiz Province. The Portuguese first established a fort at Ceuta in 1415, and it was subsequently ceded to Spain by Portugal. It developed as a military and administrative centre for the former Spanish Protectorate in Morocco, and now functions as a bunkering and fishing port. Ceuta occupies an area of 19.5 sq km. In March 1991 its *de facto* population was 73,208.

MELILLA

Melilla is situated north of the Moroccan town of Nador, on the eastern side of a small peninsula jutting out into the Mediterranean Sea. It was retained by Spain as a plaza de soberanía when Morocco became independent in 1956, and is administered as part of Málaga Province. The Spanish Crown assumed control in 1556, and the territory has served as a military stronghold ever since. Melilla is an active port. The territory's area totals 12.5 sq km. In March 1991 its *de facto* population was estimated to be 63,670 (including the islets separately mentioned below).

THE PEÑÓN DE VÉLEZ DE LA GOMERA, PEÑÓN DE ALHUCEMAS AND CHAFARINAS ISLANDS

These rocky islets are administered with Melilla. The Peñón de Vélez de la Gomera is situated 117 km south-east of Ceuta, lying less than 85 m from the Moroccan coast, to which it is connected by a narrow strip of sand. This rocky promontory, of 1 ha in area, rises to an altitude of 77 m above sea-level, an ancient fortress being situated at its summit. Spain maintains a small military base on the rock. The Peñón de Alhucemas lies 155 km south-east of Ceuta and 100 km west of Melilla, being 300 m from the Moroccan coast and the town of al-Hocima. A military garrision of fewer than 100 men is stationed on the islet, which occupies an area of 1.5 ha. The uninhabited rocks of Mar and Tierra lie immediately to the east of the Peñón de Alhucemas. The three Chafarinas Islands (from west to east: Isla del Congreso, Isla de Isabel II and Isla del Rey) are situated 48 km east of Melilla and about 3.5 km from the Moroccan fishing port of Ras el-Ma (Cabo de Agua). The islands are of volcanic origin, their combined area being 61 ha. A garrison of about 100 Spanish soldiers is maintained on Congreso.

History

CEUTA

Ceuta was conquered by Juan I of Portugal in 1415. Following the union of the crowns of Spain and Portugal in 1580, Ceuta passed under Spanish rule and in 1694, when Portugal was formally separated from Spain, the territory requested to remain under Spanish control. During the 16th, 17th and 18th centuries Ceuta had to endure a number of sieges by the Muslims. Ahmad Gailan, a chieftain in northern Morocco, blockaded the town in 1648–55. The Sultan of Morocco, Mulai Ismail (1672–1727), attacked Ceuta in 1674, 1680 and 1694, after which he maintained a blockade against the town until 1720. Ahmad Ali ar-Rifi, a chieftain from northern Morocco, made yet another unsuccessful assault in 1732. A pact of friendship and commerce was negotiated between Spain and Morocco at Aranjuez in 1780, a peaceful agreement following in the next year over the boundaries of the Ceuta enclave. In 1844–45 there was a sharp dispute once more about the precise limits of Ceuta. Further disagreement led to the war of 1859–60. Spanish forces, after an engagement at Los Castillejos, seized Tetuán from Morocco. After another battle at Wadi Ras in March 1860 the conflict came to an end. A settlement was then made, which enlarged the enclave of Ceuta and obliged Morocco to forfeit to Spain 100m. pesetas as war indemnities. In 1974 the town became the seat of the Capitanía General de Africa.

MELILLA

Spain secured control of Melilla in 1556, the town having been conquered in 1497 by the ducal house of Medina Sidonia, which had been empowered to appoint the governor and seneschal with the approval of the Spanish Crown. The Rif tribesmen attacked Melilla in 1562–64. Later still, the Sultan of Morocco, Mulai Ismail (1672–1727) assaulted the town in 1687, 1696 and 1697. Sultan Muhammad b. Abdallah (1757–90) besieged Melilla in 1771 and 1774. An agreement concluded between Spain and Morocco in 1780 at Aranjuez led, however, in the following year, to a peaceful delimitation of the Melilla enclave. There was a brief period of tension in 1844 and then, in 1861, under the terms of an agreement signed at Madrid, after Spain's Moroccan campaign of 1860, Melilla received an extension of its boundaries. Conflict with the Rif tribesmen gave rise in 1893–94 to the so-called 'War of Melilla', which ended with a settlement negotiated at Marrakesh. It was not until 1909 that Spanish forces, after a hard campaign, occupied the mountainous hinterland of Melilla between the Wadi Kert and and Wadi Muluya—a region in which, some 15 km behind Melilla, were situated the rich iron mines of Beni Bu Ifrur. In July 1921 the Rif tribes, under the command of Abd al-Krim, defeated a Spanish force near Annual and threatened Melilla itself. Only in 1926, with the final defeat of the Rif rebellion, was Spanish control restored over the Melilla region. Melilla was the first Spanish town to rise against the government of the Popular Front on 17 July 1936, at the beginning of the Spanish Civil War. Since 1939 both Ceuta and Melilla have been ruled as integral parts of Spain, though this arrangement is disputed in the territories.

OTHER POSSESSIONS

The Chafarinas Islands came under Spanish control in 1847. The Peñón de Alhucemas was occupied in 1673. The Peñón de Vélez de la Gomera, about 80 km farther west, came under Spanish rule in 1508, was then lost not long afterwards and reoccupied in 1564. All three possessions are, like Melilla, incorporated into the province of Málaga. Spanish sovereignty over the uninhabited island of Perejil, which lies north-west of Ceuta, is uncertain.

RECENT EVENTS

Those born in Ceuta, Melilla and the island dependencies, whether Christian or Muslim, are Spanish citizens and subjects. Both Ceuta and Melilla have municipal councils (ayuntamientos), and are administered as an integral part of Spain by an official (Delegado del Gobierno) directly responsible to the Ministry of the Interior in Madrid. This official is usually assisted by a government sub-delegate. There is also one delegate from each of the ministries in Madrid.

In October 1978 King Hassan of Morocco attempted to link the question of the sovereignty of Melilla to that of the return of the British dependent territory of Gibraltar to Spain. In November King Hassan stated his country's claim to Ceuta and Melilla. In October 1981 Spain declared before the UN that Ceuta and Melilla were integral parts of Spanish territory. In April 1982 the Istiqlal, a Moroccan political party, demanded action to recover the territories from Spain, and in March 1983 the Moroccan Government blocked the passage of goods across the frontiers of Ceuta and Melilla. In August the movement of Moroccan workers to Ceuta, Melilla and also Gibraltar was restricted.

From 1984 there was increasing unease over Spanish North Africa's future. The riots in Morocco in January 1984 and the signing of the treaty of union between Libya and Morocco in August gave rise to disquiet. Following the opening of the Spanish frontier with Gibraltar, in early 1985 Morocco reiterated its claim to Ceuta and Melilla. King Hassan indicated, however, that he desired a political solution to the problem. Spain rejects any comparison between the two enclaves and Gibraltar. In July 1985 the joint Libyan-Moroccan assembly passed a resolution calling for the 'liberation' of Ceuta and Melilla. In the same month the leaders of the nationalist parties of both Ceuta and Melilla visited Gibraltar for talks with the Chief Minister, in an effort to secure support for their cause.

Details of the enclaves' new draft statutes, envisaging the establishment of two local assemblies, with jurisdiction over such matters as public works, agriculture, tourism, culture and internal trade, were announced in August and approved by the central Government in December 1985. Unlike Spain's other regional assemblies, however, those of Ceuta and Melilla were not to be vested with legislative powers, and this denial of full autonomy was much criticized in the two enclaves. In March 1986 up to 20,000 people took to the streets of Ceuta in a demonstration to demand autonomy.

Meanwhile, the introduction of Madrid by a new aliens law in July 1985 required all foreigners resident in Spain to register with the authorities or risk expulsion. In Ceuta most Muslims possessed the necessary documentation. However, in Melilla (where the Muslim community was estimated to number 27,000, of whom only 7,000 held Spanish nationality) thousands of Muslims staged a protest against the new legislation in November 1985, as a result of which the central Government gave an assurance that it would assist the full integration into Spanish society of Muslims in Ceuta and Melilla, and promised to improve conditions in the territories. In December an inter-ministerial commission, headed by the Minister of the Interior, was created to formulate plans for investment in the enclaves' transport, health services (in 1982 Ceuta had 112 doctors and Melilla 110) and other public facilities.

Tension in Melilla was renewed in December 1985, when 40,000 members of the Spanish community attended a demonstration in support of the new aliens law. In January 1986 the brutality with which the police dispersed a peaceful rally by Muslim women provoked outrage in all quarters. In addition to the hunger strike already being undertaken by a number of Muslims, a two-day general strike was called. In February 1986, however, the Ministry of the Interior in Madrid and the leaders of the Muslim communities of Ceuta and Melilla reached agreement on the application of the aliens law. A joint commission to study the Muslims' problems was to be established, and a census to determine those eligible for Spanish citizenship was to be carried out. The agreement was denounced as unconstitutional by the Spanish populations of the enclaves. The Minister of the Interior visited the territories in April and reiterated that the implementation of the aliens law (the deadline for registration having been extended to 31 March 1986, following three postponements) would not entail mass expulsions of Muslim immigrants.

After negotiations with representatives of the Muslim community, in May the Government agreed to grant Spanish nationality to more than 2,400 Muslims resident in the enclaves. By mid-1986, however, the number of Muslims applying for Spanish nationality in Melilla alone had reached several thousand. As a result of the delays in the processing of the applications by the authorities, Aomar Muhammadi Dudú, the leader of the newly-founded Muslim party, Partido

de los Demócratas de Melilla (PDM), accused the Government of failing to fulfil its pledge to the Muslim residents.

At the general elections of June 1986 the ruling Partido Socialista Obrero Español (PSOE) was successful in Ceuta, but was defeated by the centre-right Coalición Popular (CP) in Melilla, the latter result indicating the strong opposition of local Spaniards to the Government's plan to integrate the Muslim population. Tight security surrounded the elections in Melilla, where 'parallel elections', resulting in a vote of confidence in the PDM leader, were held by the Muslim community. The elections were accompanied by several days of unrest, involving right-wing Christians and local Muslims, and there were further violent clashes between the police and Christian demonstrators demanding the resignation of the Government Delegate in Melilla, Andrés Moreno.

In August 1986 work began on the census of Muslim residents in Ceuta and Melilla. In the same month Juan Díez de la Cortina, Secretary-General of the extreme right-wing Partido Nacionalista (Español) de Melilla, was arrested on suspicion of planning a terrorist attack against the Government Delegate in Melilla. Following talks in Madrid between representatives of the main political parties in Melilla and the Ministry of the Interior, concessions to the enclave included the replacement of Andrés Moreno as Government Delegate by Manuel Céspedes. The Madrid negotiations were denounced by Aomar Muhammadi Dudú, the Muslim leader of Melilla, who nevertheless in September agreed to accept a senior post in the Ministry of the Interior in Madrid, with responsibility for relations with the Muslim communities of Spain.

In October 1986 it was reported tha Dudú had travelled to Rabat for secret discussions with the Moroccan Minister of the Interior. In November Muslim leaders in Melilla announced that they wished to establish their own administration in the enclave, in view of the Madrid Government's failure to fulfil its promise of Spanish citizenship for Muslim residents. The Spanish Minister of the Interior, however, reiterated an assurance of the Government's intention to carry out the process of integration of the Muslim community. Later in the month, Muslim traders staged a four-day closure of their businesses to draw attention to their plight, and thousands of Muslims took part in a peaceful demonstration, reaffirming support for Dudú, who had resigned from his Madrid post after only two months in office. (Dudú subsequently went into exile in Morocco and lost the support of Melilla's Muslim community.) A similar protest, to have taken place in Ceuta in December, was banned by the Spanish authorities.

In January 1987 the Spanish Minister of the Interior paid an official visit to Morocco. King Hassan proposed the establishment of a joint commission to seek a solution to the problem of the Spanish enclaves, but the proposal was rejected by Spain. There was a serious escalation of tension in Melilla in early February, when a member of the Muslim community died from gunshot wounds, following renewed racial clashes. Police reinforcements were flown in from Spain to deal with the crisis. Numerous demonstrators were detained. Several prominent Muslims were charged with sedition and transferred to a prison in Almería on the Spanish mainland, but were released shortly afterwards. The indictment of a total of 27 Muslims was completed in mid-1988.

In March 1987 King Hassan of Morocco reaffirmed his support for the Muslims of the Spanish enclaves, and later warned that a serious crisis in relations between Rabat and Madrid would arise if Spain were to grant autonomy to the territories. King Hassan renewed his proposal for dialogue, ruling out the possibility of a 'green march' similar to the campaign organized in 1975, when 300,000 unarmed Moroccan volunteers had attempted to occupy the Spanish Sahara, which Spain had subsequently agreed to relinquish. In April 1987 Spanish and Moroccan troops participated in joint manoeuvres on Moroccan territory adjacent to Melilla, as part of a programme of military co-operation.

In early May 1987 thousands of Melilla residents attended a demonstration in favour of autonomy for the enclave. During a visit to Melilla a senior official of the ruling PSOE emphasized the need for the integration of Christians and Muslims, while asserting that Spanish sovereignty would continue and would form the basis of the territory's future autonomy statute. In

July, following a visit to Rabat by the Spanish Minister of Foreign Affairs, King Hassan declared that agreement had been reached on the holding of talks on the question of Ceuta and Melilla. The Spanish Government, however, denied the existence of such an agreement, maintaining that the issue was not negotiable. At the end of July Spain was obliged to order its fishing fleet to withdraw from Moroccan waters, upon the expiry of an agreement signed with Morocco in 1983 (prior to Spain's accession to the European Community—EC, now European Union—EU), allowing Spain access to the rich fishing grounds off the Moroccan coast in exchange for financial aid of US $550m. Having previously appeared unwilling to extend the treaty, in an attempt to link the issue of fishing rights to that of Spanish North Africa, Morocco unexpectedly agreed to a provisional renewal of the accord, whereby Spanish vessels would be permitted to continue operating in Moroccan waters until December 1987, pending the negotiation of a new agreement between Morocco and the EC. At the end of 1987, when the temporary accord expired, Spanish fishing vessels were once again expelled from Moroccan waters and were unable to resume operations until March 1988, upon the entry into force of a new four-year agreement between the EC and Morocco. This agreement was renewed for a further four years in May 1992 (see Morocco, p. 741). In September 1994, however, Morocco demanded that the accord be renegotiated and that fishing quotas be drastically reduced.

In Ceuta, meanwhile, there was renewed unrest in August 1987, following the indiscriminate shooting dead of a Muslim by a member of the security forces. On a visit to that territory in September, the Spanish Minister of Justice emphasized the difficulty of elevating the status of the enclaves to that of an autonomous region. In February 1988 it was announced that, in accordance with EC regulations, Moroccan citizens would in due course require visas to enter Spain. Entry to Spanish North Africa, however, was to be exempt from the new ruling.

In March 1988 a group of seven Muslims began an indefinite occupation of the Melilla office responsible for the processing of applications for Spanish nationality, to protest against its alleged inefficiency. Of the 8,000 applications presented, it was claimed, fewer than one-half had been granted. After several months of negotiations, in March the central Government and main opposition parties in Madrid reached a broad consensus on the draft autonomy statutes for the Spanish External Territories.

Spain's relations with Morocco improved in June 1988, when the two countries signed an agreement on bilateral economic co-operation, whereby Spain was to grant credits totalling 125,000m. pesetas to Morocco. In the same month the Melilla representative to the Madrid Senate requested that the Government clarify all aspects of Spanish North Africa's security position, in view of the territories' exclusion from the NATO 'umbrella'.

In July 1988 a senior member of the ruling PSOE acknowledged that the party's Programme 2000 contained contradictory proposals regarding Ceuta and Melilla. Although it was envisaged that Spain would retain the territories, the possibility of a negotiated settlement with Morocco was not discounted. In late July, seven years after the enclaves' first official request for autonomy, the central Government announced that the implementation of the territories' autonomy statutes was to be accelerated. Revised draft statutes were submitted by the PSOE to the main opposition parties for consideration. The statutes declared Ceuta and Melilla to be integral parts of Spain and, for the first time, the Spanish Government undertook to guarantee financial support for the territories. A further innovation contained in the revised draft provided for the establishment of mixed commissions to oversee the movement of goods and services through the territories. As previously indicated by the Spanish Government, the two Spanish North African assemblies were to be granted 'normative' rather than legislative powers. Each new assembly would elect from among its members a city president.

It was subsequently revealed that the revised statutes encompassed only the enclaves of Ceuta and Melilla, thus excluding the associated Spanish North African islands (the Chafarinas Islands, the Peñón de Alhucemas, the Peñón de Vélez de la Gomera and the island of Perejil, Spanish sovereignty over the latter being uncertain), and that they had been erroneously incorporated in the preliminary statutes, approved by the Government in December 1985. Although remaining the responsibility of the Spanish Ministry of Defence, these islands were not, therefore, to become part of any Spanish autonomous region.

In August 1988 a Moroccan Minister of State asserted that Spain should negotiate a peaceful, political solution to the question of Ceuta and Melilla. In October the Moroccan Minister of Foreign Affairs formally presented his country's claim to Ceuta and Melilla to the UN General Assembly. An official visit by King Hassan to Spain, scheduled for November, was indefinitely postponed without explanation, and in Melilla a Muslim group acknowledged that it had been in receipt of financial assistance from the Moroccan Government. By December 1988 a total of 5,257 Muslims in Melilla had been granted Spanish citizenship since 1986, and a further 1,126 applications were pending. (By 1990 nearly all residents were in possession of an identity card.) On a visit to Ceuta in December 1988 a Spanish government official stated that the enclaves would be granted autonomy during the present Government's term of office.

In January 1989, however, King Hassan reiterated Morocco's claim to Ceuta and Melilla. A planned visit to Rabat by the Spanish Minister of Foreign Affairs was postponed, but in March Narcís Serra, the Spanish Minister of Defence, travelled to Morocco for consultations with King Hassan on security matters. In April the Spanish Government and the Partido Popular (PP), the main opposition party, reached agreement on the revised statutes for Ceuta and Melilla. In May the Spanish Prime Minister and King Hassan met in Casablanca for discussions on the situation in the Middle East. King Hassan paid an official visit to Spain in September 1989. The question of Spanish North Africa was not discussed, although the King of Morocco reiterated his country's claim to the territories, while discounting the use of force as a means of settling the dispute. Spain and Morocco agreed to hold annual summit meetings, in order to improve relations.

At the general election held in October 1989 the ruling PSOE retained its Ceuta seats, despite allegations by the opposition PP that many names on the electoral register were duplicated. In Melilla, however, the election results were declared invalid, following the discovery of serious irregularities. Melilla's one seat in the Congress of Deputies and one of its two seats in the Senate in Madrid had originally been allocated to the PSOE, the PP winning the second seat in the Senate. At the repeated ballot held in March 1990, however, at which 52% of the electorate voted, both Senate seats and the one Congress seat were won by the PP, the latter result stripping the PSOE of its overall majority in the Madrid lower chamber. The Government Delegate in Melilla claimed that voting irregularities had again occurred.

In January 1990, meanwhile, the Partido Comunista de España (PCE) and its Moroccan counterpart, the Parti du Progrès et du Socialisme (PPS), had issued a joint communiqué urging the Governments of Spain and Morocco to open dialogue and work towards a satisfactory solution to the question of Ceuta and Melilla. Relations between Spain and Morocco were strained in March, when Spanish fishermen blockaded Algeciras and other ports (thereby disrupting communications with Ceuta) in protest at the Moroccan authorities' imposition of greatly-increased penalties on Spanish fishing vessels found to be operating without a licence in Moroccan waters. Following negotiations between the EC and Morocco, Spain agreed to grant financial compensation to Morocco.

In a newspaper article in March 1990 a Moroccan government minister repeated his country's claim to Spanish North Africa, maintaining that, with the accession of Namibia to independence, Ceuta and Melilla were the last vestiges of colonialism in Africa. In April the Spanish Government decided to open negotiations with the political groupings of Ceuta and Melilla, the autonomy statutes being presented for discussion in the territories. It was confirmed that the enclaves were to remain an integral part of Spain, and that they were to be granted self-government at municipal, rather than regional, level. The Spanish Government's decision provoked a strong reaction from Moroccan political parties, which were united in their denunciation of the perceived attempt to legalize Spanish possession of the territories. In June a two-hour strike in Ceuta, in support of demands for full autonomy for the enclave, was widely observed.

In July 1990 the Istiqlal, the Moroccan opposition party, announced that it was initiating a new campaign to press for the 'liberation' of Ceuta and Melilla. In the following month the Istiqlal organized a protest march through the streets of Martil, a Moroccan town 40 km from Ceuta. The Muslim community of Ceuta, however, expressed its concern at these developments.

In mid-August 1990 Spain granted its Government Delegate in Melilla direct powers to expel illegal residents from the territory. In the same month King Hassan and the Spanish Prime Minister, met near Rabat for talks. Their discussions focused on the Gulf crisis, caused by Iraq's invasion of Kuwait, and on their bilateral relations, particularly increased co-operation and security. In December a Spanish delegation, led by Felipe González, travelled to Morocco, where the first of the planned regular summit meetings between the Spanish and Moroccan Prime Ministers took place. Among the topics discussed was the forthcoming implementation (in May 1991) of new visa requirements for North Africans entering Spain, which had caused dismay in the Muslim community. Special arrangements were to apply to Moroccan citizens who worked in, or travelled regularly to, Ceuta and Melilla. At the meeting a Spanish credit to Morocco of 25,000m. pesetas (in addition to that agreed in 1988) was also arranged.

The outbreak of the Gulf war in early 1991 gave rise to renewed disquiet in Spanish North Africa. In February 800 Muslims marched through the streets of Melilla to protest against the war, in which the US military bases in Spain were to play a crucial role. In the same month, as anti-Western sentiment in North Africa increased, the Spanish Minister of Foreign Affairs embarked on a tour of five Maghreb countries. Discussions with his Moroccan counterpart took place in Rabat.

Elections for the 25-member municipal councils of Ceuta and Melilla were held in May 1991, and in each territory the PSOE Mayor was replaced. In Ceuta Francisco Fraiz Armada of the Progreso y Futuro de Ceuta (PFC) became Mayor. In Melilla, where the PP had secured 12 of the 25 seats, Ignacio Velázquez Rivera of the right-wing Partido Nacionalista de Melilla (PNM) was elected Mayor of the enclave.

In July 1991, in Rabat, the Spanish and Moroccan heads of government signed a treaty of friendship. In addition to the promotion of co-operation in the fields of economy, finance, fisheries, culture and the judiciary, agreement was also reached on Spanish military aid to Morocco. Shortly afterwards the Moroccan Minister of the Interior, Driss Basri, and a cabinet colleague unexpectedly accepted an invitation from the Spanish Minister of the Interior to visit Ceuta, their brief trip being the first ever visit by members of the Government of King Hassan.

The draft autonomy statutes of Ceuta and Melilla were submitted to the Chamber of Deputies in Madrid for discussion in October 1991. During the debate the PP accused the PSOE of supporting Moroccan interests. In November thousands of demonstrators, many of whom had travelled from the enclaves, attended a protest march in Madrid (organized by the Governments of Ceuta and Melilla), in support of demands for autonomy for the territories. In early 1992, however, the central Government confirmed that the assemblies of Ceuta and Melilla were not to be granted full legislative powers. In May a general strike in Ceuta, to protest against this denial of full autonomy, was widely supported.

In mid-1992 relations between Spain and Morocco were dominated by the issue of illegal immigration. In addition to the problem of the large numbers of Moroccans trying to enter Spain (many drownings in the Strait of Gibraltar being reported), there had been a sharp increase in the numbers of those from other (mainly West African) countries attempting to gain entry to Europe via Morocco and the two Spanish enclaves. In July the Spanish Minister of Foreign Affairs flew to Rabat for discussions on the problem.

In March 1993 it was revealed that Spain would require the permission of NATO before employing its most modern military equipment in the defence of the enclaves. In the same month, in an attempt to bring about the transfer of powers to the territories, the PP submitted its own draft statute for Melilla to the central Government, which immediately condemned the document as unconstitutional. All political parties in Melilla, except the PSOE, demanded that a local referendum be held on the issue of autonomy. In September the Spanish Minister of Public Administration affirmed his commitment to the conclusion, within the next few months, of an agreement on the territories' statutes.

At the general election of June 1993, meanwhile, the PSOE of Ceuta lost its one seat in Congress and its two seats in the Senate to the PP. In Melilla the PSOE candidate defeated the incumbent PP Congress member; the PP also lost one of its two seats in the Senate.

In February 1994 the Mayor of Ceuta, Francisco Fraiz Armada, was obliged to resign, following the Supreme Court's ratification of a lower court ruling that barred him from holding public office for six years. His disqualification resulted from his involvement in irregularities in the housing sector in 1984, when unauthorized evictions had been carried out. He was replaced by Basilio Fernández, also of the PFC.

In March 1994 King Hassan declared his opposition to the forthcoming adoption of the autonomy statutes, repeating Morocco's claim to the territories. By May, however, the final statutes had still not been presented to the Cortes in Madrid. Representatives of Ceuta were particularly critical of the dilatory conduct of the Minister of Public Administration, and urged the central Government and the opposition PP to bring the matter to a speedy conclusion. In the same month King Juan Carlos of Spain received a delegation from Melilla, led by the Mayor, Ignacio Velázquez Rivera, who emphasized the necessity for a swift adoption of the enclave's autonomy statute and conveyed his citizens' concern at the Moroccan monarch's recent statement.

In September 1994 the final statutes of autonomy were approved by the Spanish Government, in preparation for their presentation to the Cortes. The statutes provided for 25-member local assemblies with powers similar to those of the municipal councils of mainland Spain. Following the statutes' approval, Morocco announced that it was initiating a new diplomatic campaign to reassert its claim over the territories.

These proposals for limited self-government were generally acceptable in Melilla but not in Ceuta, where, in October 1994, a general strike received widespread support. An estimated 20,000 residents of Ceuta participated in a demonstration to demand equality with other Spanish regions and full autonomy for the enclave. Earlier in the month, following expressions of concern regarding the territories' protection in the event of Moroccan aggression, the Minister of Defence confirmed that Spain would continue to maintain an appropriate military presence in Ceuta and Melilla.

Economy

CEUTA AND MELILLA

Ceuta and Melilla, both free ports, are in fact of little economic importance, while the other possessions, with a 1982 population of 312, mostly military personnel and fishermen, are of negligible significance. The basic reason for Spanish retention of these areas was their predominantly Spanish population. The registered populations of both Ceuta and Melilla have fallen since the 1960s, owing to the lack of economic opportunities in the towns, although the proportion of Arab residents has greatly increased, particularly in Melilla. There are large number of immigrants from Morocco.

In 1991 Ceuta's gross domestic product (GDP) was 33.6% below the average for the whole of Spain, while that of Melilla was 30.5% below. In the same year the average disposable family income of Ceuta was only 76.85% that of Spain, the figure in Melilla being 84.76%. Social security benefits accounted for 22.75% of the average family income in Ceuta and 24.25% in Melilla. In 1992 the GDP of the two territories totalled 133,767m. pesetas, equivalent to 1,072,607 pesetas per head.

The hinterland of the two cities is small. Development is restricted by the lack of suitable building land. Most of the population's food has to be imported, with the exception of fish, which is obtained locally. Sardines and anchovies are the most important items. Melilla's total catch in 1986 was 956 metric tons, worth 186.5m. pesetas. A large proportion of the tinned fish is sold outside Spain. More important to the economies of the cities is the port activity; most of their exports take the form of fuel supplied—at very competitive rates—to ships. Most of the fuel comes from the Spanish refinery in Tenerife. Ceuta's port is the busier, receiving a total of 8,387 ships in 1989. Apart from the ferries from Málaga and Almería in Spain, Melilla's port is not so frequented and its exports are correspondingly low. Ceuta's main exports are frozen and preserved fish, foodstuffs and beer. Industry is limited to meeting some of the everyday needs of the cities. There is a local brewery in Ceuta.

In both cities a negligible percentage of the working population is employed in agriculture. In 1989 the economically active population of the two enclaves totalled 49,400, of whom 15,200 were unemployed, 1,800 were employed in the construction sector, 1,400 in industry and 100 in agriculture; 30,800 were employed in the services sector. In late 1993 the territories' level of unemployment was estimated at 26.7% of the labour force. A total of 8,259 persons were registered as unemployed in August 1994. The average annual rate of inflation was 5.4% in 1992 and 5.8% in 1993. In the 12 months to September 1994 the rate of inflation was 4.5% in each of the enclaves.

In 1986 the Spanish Government announced that it was to grant 6,500m. pesetas to Ceuta and 8,500m. to Melilla for the purposes of infrastructural development. In 1989 a campaign to attract more investment to Ceuta began. Tax concessions and other incentives were offered. In the three years to 1990 the Spanish Government's investment in Melilla totalled 32,000m. pesetas. Ceuta received 9,000m. pesetas for the purposes of public works, and its health service was allocated 347m. pesetas. In early 1993 investment of a further 18,000m. pesetas for housing and transport projects in Melilla was announced. In Ceuta the apparent lack of banking controls and alleged corruption at senior levels drew criticism in April 1993, when evidence of the territory's use as a 'money-laundering' centre for the proceeds of drugs-trafficking was revealed. A sum of more than 25,000m. pesetas was believed to be involved. Furthermore, in December fraudulent operations, allegedly involving almost 100m. pesetas and in which two civil servants were implicated, were uncovered at the city hall of Ceuta.

Tourism makes a significant contribution to the territories' economies. Almost 1m. tourists visited Ceuta in 1986, attracted by duty-free goods. High ferry-boat fares and the opening of the Spanish border with Gibraltar, however, were expected to have an adverse effect on the enclaves' duty-free trade. Proposed defence cuts led not only to fears for Spanish North Africa's security but also to fears of losses in income from military personnel stationed in the territories.

Upon the accession of Spain to the European Community (EC, now European Union—EU) in January 1986, Ceuta and Melilla were considered as Spanish cities and European territory, and joined the Community as part of Spain. They retained their status as free ports. The statutes of autonomy, approved by the Spanish Government in September 1994, envisaged the continuation of the territories' fiscal benefits. In June 1994 the EU announced substantial regional aid: between 1995 and 1999 Ceuta and Melilla were to receive totals of ECU 28m. and ECU 45m., of which ECU 20m. and ECU 18m., respectively, were to be in the form of direct aid.

Statistical Survey

Ceuta

Area: 19.5 sq km.

Population (1 January 1990): 68,970 (34,136 males, 34,834 females); (1 March 1991): 73,208 (*de facto*) or 67,615 (*de jure*).

Density (*de facto*, 1991): 3,768 per sq km.

Births, Marriages and Deaths (1989): Live births 1,180; Marriages 360; Deaths 431.

Finance: Spanish currency: 100 céntimos = 1 peseta. *Sterling and Dollar Equivalents* (31 May 1994): £1 sterling = 204.96 pesetas; US $1 = 135.575 pesetas; 1,000 pesetas = £4.879 = $7.376. *Average exchange rate* (pesetas per US $): 103.91 in 1991; 102.38 in 1992; 127.26 in 1993.

External Trade: Ceuta is a duty-free port. Trade is chiefly with Spain, the Balearic and Canary Islands and Melilla. In 1988 Ceuta supplied 570,850 metric tons of fuel and 60,327 metric tons of water to ships entering the port. Other exports include frozen and preserved fish, beer and foodstuffs.

Transport: *Road Traffic* (vehicles registered, 1989, provisional): 2,991. *Shipping* (1989): Ships entered 8,387; (1992, provisional): Goods loaded and unloaded 4,441,000 metric tons (of which petroleum products 1,767,000 metric tons, fish 496 metric tons); Passenger departures and arrivals 2,397,000.

Education (1987/88): Pre-school 2,141 pupils, 67 centres; General basic 9,879 pupils, 306 schools; Secondary 2,068 pupils, 3 schools; Vocational 873 students, 3 centres.
1990/91 (incl. Melilla): 4,054 pre-school pupils, 17,933 general basic pupils, 3,820 secondary pupils, 1,682 vocational students.

Melilla

Area: 12.5 sq km.

Population: (March 1982) 54,741 (incl. Peñón de Alhucemas 61, Chafarinas 191, Peñón de Vélez de la Gomera 60); (1 January 1990): 62,569; (1 March 1991): 63,670 (*de facto*) or 56,600 (*de jure*).

Density (1991): 5,087 per sq km.

Births, Marriages and Deaths (1988, provisional): Live births 997; Marriages 332; Deaths 396.

Finance: Spanish currency (see Ceuta). 1985 budget: 2,700m. pesetas.

External Trade: Melilla is a duty-free port. Most imports are from Spain but over 90% of exports go to non-Spanish territories. The chief export is fish.

Transport: *Road Traffic* (vehicles registered, 1987, provisional): 1,498. *Shipping* (1989): Ships entered 819; (1992, provisional): Goods loaded and unloaded 639,000 metric tons; Passenger departures and arrivals 476,000. *Civil Aviation* (1989): Goods loaded and unloaded 560 metric tons; Passenger departures and arrivals 168,000.

Education (1987/88): Pre-school 1,961 pupils, 61 centres; General basic 8,256 pupils, 245 schools; Secondary 1,863 pupils, 4 schools; Vocational 927 students, 1 centre. (See Ceuta for 1990/91 pupil and student numbers.)

Directory

Ceuta

GOVERNMENT
(October 1994)

Delegación del Gobierno: Beatriz de Silva 4, 11701 Ceuta; tel. (56) 51-25-23; fax (56) 51-36-71; Government Delegate in Ceuta María del Carmen Cedeira.

Mayor of Ceuta Basilio Fernández López (PFC). Deputy elected to the Congress in Madrid Francisco Antonio González Pérez (PP). Representatives to the Senate in Madrid José Luis Morales Montero (PP), Francisco Olivencia Ruiz (PP). Commandant-General Carlos Gabari Lebrón (acting).

POLITICAL ORGANIZATIONS

Centro Democrático y Social (CDS): Ceuta; centre-left; Leader José Francisco Rios Claro.

Ceuta Unida (CEU): Ceuta; nationalist party; Sec.-Gen. José Antonio Querol.

Iniciativa por Ceuta (INCE): Plaza de Africa 10, 1°, 11701 Ceuta; fax (56) 516890; f. 1993; Muslim party; 380 mems; Pres. Ahmed Subaire; Sec. Abdelkader Maimon.

Partido Humanista: B. Príncipe Alfonso, Ceuta; Leader Mohamed Ali.

Partido Nacionalista Ceutí (PNC): Ceuta; nationalist party; Leader Francisco Alcántara Trujillo.

Partido Popular (PP): Ceuta; fmrly Alianza Popular; centre-right; Leader Francisco Antonio González Pérez.

Partido Socialista Obrero Español (PSOE): Ceuta; socialist workers' party; Leader Juan José León Molina.

Partido Socialista del Pueblo de Ceuta (PSPC): Carretera del Embalse 10, 11704 Ceuta; dissident group of PSOE; Leader Alejandro Curiel Cabezudo.

Partido Socialista de los Trabajadores (PST): B. Príncipe Alfonso, Ceuta; Leader Sr Abbas.

Progreso y Futuro de Ceuta (PFC): Marina de Ceuta, Ceuta; Leader Francisco Fraiz Armada.

There are branches of the major Spanish parties in Ceuta, and also various civic associations. The **Asociación Ceuta y Melilla (Acyme)** is based in Granada (Pres. Francisco Godino), and is opposed to the proposals for limited autonomy for the enclaves.

RELIGION

The majority of the European inhabitants are Christians, almost all being adherents of the Roman Catholic Church. Most Africans are Muslims, totalling about 13,000 in 1991. The Jewish community numbers several hundred.

Christianity
The Roman Catholic Church

Bishop of Cádiz and Ceuta: Antonio Ceballos Atienza (resident in Cádiz); Vicar-General: (vacant), Plaza de Nuestra Señora de Africa, 11701 Ceuta; tel. (56) 51-32-08.

THE PRESS

El Faro de Ceuta: Francisco Lería 1, Ceuta; tel. (56) 51-10-24; f. 1934; morning; Dir Elisa Beni Uzábal; Publr Joaquín Ferrer y Cía; circ. 5,000.

El Periódico de Ceuta: Ampliación Muelle de Poniente, P-104-10, Ceuta; tel. (56) 50-74-81; fax (56) 50-74-80; f. 1989; daily; Dir Luis Manuel Aznar Cabezón.

Semanal Ceuta: Ramón y Cajal 24, Ceuta; tel. (56) 51-17-62; weekly; Dir José-María Delgado Arnau.

RADIO

Radio Ceuta: Real 90, Ceuta; tel. (56) 51-18-20; f. 1934; commercial; owned by Sociedad Española de Radiodifusión (SER); Dir Elisa Beni Uzábal.

Radio Nacional de España: Beatriz de Silva 12, Ceuta; tel. (56) 52-22-03.

Radio Perla: Grupos Alfau, 4, 3° Izquierda, Ceuta; tel. (56) 51-78-87; Dir Antonio Rubín Luna.

Radio Popular de Ceuta: Sargento Mena 8, Ceuta; operated by Onda Cero; Dir Higinio Molina.

TELEVISION

Tele Ceuta: Calle Real 90, Ceuta; tel. (56) 52-31-13; Dir Manuel González Bolorino.

FINANCE

At the end of 1989 total deposits in the private banking sector stood at 42,500m. pesetas, deposits at savings banks totalling 18,600m. The main Spanish banks have branches in Ceuta.

Banco Bilbao Vizcaya (BBV): Serrano Orive 3, Ceuta; tel. (56) 51-84-44; 2 brs.

Banco Central Hispano Americano (BCH): Paseo del Revellín 23, Ceuta; tel. (56) 51-11-39.

Banco de España: Plaza de España, Ceuta; tel. (56) 51-32-53.

Banco Español de Crédito: Camoens 6, Ceuta; tel. (56) 51-30-09.

Banco Exterior de España: Paseo del Revellín 5, Ceuta; tel. (56) 51-21-56.

Banco Meridional: Jáudenes 30, Ceuta; tel. (56) 51-57-86.

Banco Popular Español: Paseo del Revellín 1, Ceuta; tel. (56) 51-53-40.

Banco Santander: Marina Española 10, Ceuta; tel. (56) 51-66-85; 2 brs.

Banco Urquijo: Antioco, Ceuta; tel. (56) 51-25-52.

TRADE AND INDUSTRY

Cámara Oficial de Comercio, Industria y Navegación: Muelle Cañonero Dato s/n, 11701 Ceuta; tel. (56) 50-95-90; fax (56) 50-95-89; Pres. José María Campos Martínez; Sec.-Gen. Francisco Olivencia Ruiz.

Confederación de Empresarios de Ceuta: Teniente Arrabal 2, 11701 Ceuta; tel. (56) 51-69-12; employers' confederation; Pres. José María Campos Martínez; Sec.-Gen. Evaristo Rivera Gómez.

TRANSPORT

Much of the traffic between Spain and Morocco passes through Ceuta; there are ferry services to Algeciras, Spain. Plans for an airport are under consideration.

TOURISM

Visitors are attracted by the historical monuments and museums, and by the availability of duty-free goods. In 1992 Ceuta had four hotels and 27 hostels and guest houses. Plans to build additional accommodation were under way.

Oficina de Información de Turismo: Muelle Cañonero Dato 1, Ceuta; tel. (56) 50-92-75.

DEFENCE

Military authority is vested in a commandant-general (see Government). The enclaves are attached to the military region of Sevilla. In June 1993 Spain had 10,000 troops deployed in Spanish North Africa, compared with 21,000 in mid-1987. Two-thirds of Ceuta's land area are used exclusively for military purposes.

EDUCATION

The conventional Spanish facilities are available. In higher education, links with the University of Granada are maintained.

Melilla

GOVERNMENT
(October 1994)

Delegación del Gobierno: Plaza de España s/n, 29871 Melilla; tel. (52) 67-58-40; fax (52) 67-26-57; Government Delegate in Melilla: Manuel Céspedes Céspedes.

Mayor of Melilla: Ignacio Velázquez Rivera (PP/PNM). Deputy elected to the Congress in Madrid: Julio Bassets Rutllant (PSOE), Representatives to the Senate in Madrid: Gonzalo Hernández Martínez (PSOE), Carlos A. Benet Cañete (PP). Commandant-General: Vicente Cervera García.

POLITICAL ORGANIZATIONS

Centro Democrático y Social (CDS): Edif. Monumental 3a, Teniente Aguilar de Mera 1, Melilla; centre-left.

Lucha por la Libertad de Melilla: Melilla; extreme right-wing; opposed to granting of Spanish citizenship to Muslims.

Movimiento para la Liberación de Melilla: Melilla; f. 1986; clandestine group; advocates use of violence.

Partido de Acción Social de Melilla: Melilla; favours full autonomy.

Partido de los Demócratas de Melilla (PDM): Melilla; f. 1985; Muslim party; Leader Abdelkáder Mohamed Alí.

Partido Independiente Hispano Bereber: Melilla; Pres. Laarbi Bumedien.

Partido Nacionalista de Melilla-Asociación Pro Melilla (PNM-Aprome): Miguel Zazo 30, 29804 Melilla; extreme-right-wing nationalist party; allied to PP; Pres. Amalio Jiménez; Sec.-Gen. Antonio Ciendones García.

Partido Popular (PP): Gral Marina 8, Melilla; tel. (52) 68-50-94; centre-right; absorbed Melilla branch of Democracia Cristiana (DC) in July 1988; Pres. Luis Fernández Muñoz.

Partido Progresista Liberal de Melilla (PPLM): Melilla; Leader Francisco Cintas García.

Partido Socialista de Melilla-Partido Socialista Obrero Español (PSME-PSOE): Cándido Lobera 7-1°, Melilla; tel. (52) 68-18-20; socialist workers' party; favours self-government but not full autonomy; Pres. José Torres Vega; Sec.-Gen. Julio Bassets Rutllant.

Unión de Melillenses Independientes (UMI): Melilla; advocates independence; Spokesman José Imbroda Domínguez.

Unión del Pueblo Melillense (UPM): Ejército Español 7, 1° al derecha, Apdo 775, 29801 Melilla; tel. (52) 681987; fax (52) 673545; f. 1985; right-wing; Pres. JUAN JOSÉ IMBRODA ORTIZ; Gen. Sec. DANIEL CONESA MÍNGUEZ.

There are branches of the major Spanish parties in Melilla, and also various civic associations.

RELIGION

As in Ceuta, most Europeans are Roman Catholics. The registered Muslim community numbered 20,800 in 1990. The Jewish community numbered 1,300.

THE PRESS

Diario Sur: Edif. Monumental 3a, Oficina 17, Melilla; tel. (52) 68-18-54; fax (52) 68-39-08; Perm. Rep. AVELINO GUTIÉRREZ PÉREZ.

Guía del Ocio: Melilla; tel. (52) 68-37-34; leisure guide; Dir JOSÉ LUIS CÉSPEDES MERCADO.

Melilla Costa del Sol: Melilla; tel. (52) 68-68-48; f. 1985; Rep. LAUREANO FOLGAR VILLASENÍN; circ. 2,500.

Melilla Hoy: Teniente Aguilar de Mera 1, Edif. Monumental 1a, 29801 Melilla; tel. (52) 68-40-24; fax (52) 68-48-44; f. 1985; Dir IRENE FLORES SAEZ; Editor-in-Chief ENRIQUE BOHÓRQUEZ LÓPEZ DORIGA.

RADIO

Antena 3: Edif. Melilla, Urbanización Rusadir, Melilla; tel. (52) 68-88-40; Dir TOÑI RAMOS PELÁEZ.

Cadena Rato: Melilla; tel. (52) 68-58-71; Dir ANGEL VALENCIA.

Radio Melilla Ser: Falda de Carmellos s/n, Melilla; tel. (52) 68-17-08; commercial; owned by Sociedad Española de Radiodifusión (SER); Administrator FRANCISCO RUIZ RIPOLL.

Radio Nacional de España (RNE): Mantelete 1, Apdo 222, Melilla; tel. (52) 68-19-07; fax (52) 68-31-08; state-controlled; Rep. PEDRO A. MEDINA BARRENECHEA.

TELEVISION

A fibre optic cable linking Melilla with Almería was laid in 1990. From March 1991 Melilla residents were able to receive three private TV channels from Spain: Antena 3, Canal+ and Tele 5.

FINANCE

At the end of 1989 total deposits in the private banking sector stood at 29,300m. pesetas, deposits at savings banks totalling 16,400m. The following banks have branches in Melilla: Banco Bilbao-Vizcaya (2 brs), Banco Central Hispano Americano, Banco Español de Crédito, Banco Meridional, Banco Popular Español and Banco de Santander (2 brs).

TRADE AND INDUSTRY

Cámara Oficial de Comercio, Industria y Navegación: Cervantes 7, 29801 Melilla; tel. (52) 68-48-40; fax (52) 68-31-19; f. 1906; Pres. FRANCISCO MARQUÉS VIVANCOS; Sec.-Gen. MARÍA JESÚS FERNÁNDEZ DE CASTRO Y PEDRAJAS.

Confederación de Empresarios de Melilla: Paseo Marítimo Mir Berlanga 26—Entreplanta, Apdo de Correos 445, 29806 Melilla; tel. (52) 67-82-95; telex 79407; fax (52) 67-61-75; f. 1979; employers' confederation; Pres. MARGARITA LÓPEZ ALMENDÁRIZ; Sec.-Gen. JERÓNIMO PÉREZ HERNÁNDEZ.

TRANSPORT

There is a daily ferry service to Málaga and a service to Almería. Melilla airport, situated 4 km from the town, is served by daily flights to Málaga and Almería, operated by Iberia. There are also services to Madrid and Granada. Plans to extend the runway were approved in early 1993.

TOURISM

There is much of historic interest to the visitor. Melilla had 19 hotels in the late 1980s. Further hotels, including a luxury development, were under construction in 1990.

DEFENCE

See Ceuta. More than one-half of Melilla's land area is used solely for military purposes.

EDUCATION

In addition to the conventional Spanish facilities, the Moroccan Government finances a school for 600 Muslim children in Melilla, the languages of instruction being Arabic and Spanish. The curriculum includes Koranic studies. In 1982 only 12% of Muslim children were attending school, but by 1990 the authorities had succeeded in achieving an attendance level of virtually 100%. The Spanish open university (UNED) maintains a branch in Melilla.

The Peñón de Vélez de la Gomera, Peñón de Alhucemas and Chafarinas Islands

These rocky islets, situated respectively just west and east of al-Hocima (Alhucemas) and east of Melilla off the north coast of Morocco, are administered with Melilla. The three Chafarinas Islands lie about 3.5 km off Ras el-Ma (Cabo de Agua). The Peñón de Alhucemas is situated about 300 m from the coast. The Peñón de Vélez de la Gomera is situated about 80 km further west, lying 85 m from the Moroccan shore, to which it is joined by a narrow strip of sand. Small military bases are maintained on the Peñón de Vélez, Peñón de Alhucemas and on the Isla del Congreso, the most westerly of the Chafarinas Islands. A supply ship calls at the various islands every two weeks. Prospective visitors must obtain the necessary military permit in Ceuta or Melilla.

Bibliography

Areilza, José María de, and Castiella y Maíz, Fernando María. *Revindicaciones de España.* Madrid, 1941.

Boucher, M. *Spain in Africa* (3 articles, *Africa Institute Bulletin,* May–July 1966).

Domínguez Sánchez, Constantino. *Melilla.* Madrid, Editorial Everest, 1978.

Habsbourg, Otto D. E. *Européens et Africains: L'Entente Nécessaire.* Paris, Hachette, 1963.

Mir Berlanga, Francisco. *Melilla en los Siglos Pasados y Otras Historias.* Madrid, Editora Nacional, 1977.

Resumen de la Historia de Melilla. Melilla, 1978.

Patronato Municipal de Turismo. *Ceuta—La España Inédita.* Madrid, 1988.

Pélissier, René. *Los Territorios Españoles de Africa.* Madrid, 1964.

SYRIA

Physical and Social Geography

W. B. FISHER

Before 1918 the term 'Syria' was rather loosely applied to the whole of the territory now forming the modern states of Syria, Lebanon, Israel and Jordan. To the Ottomans, as to the Romans, Syria stretched from the Euphrates to the Mediterranean, and from the Sinai to the hills of southern Turkey, with Palestine as a smaller province of this wider unit. Although the present Syrian Arab Republic has a much more limited extension, covering 185,180 sq km (71,498 sq miles), an echo of the past remains to colour the political thinking of some present-day Syrians and from time to time there are references to a 'Greater Syria' as a desirable but possibly remote aspiration. None the less, there is evidence of the attachment to the idea of a 'Greater Syria' in current Syrian policy towards Israel and, especially, Lebanon.

The frontiers of the present-day state are largely artificial, and reflect to a considerable extent the interests and prestige of outside powers—Britain, France and the USA—as these existed in 1918–20. The northern frontier with Turkey is defined by a single-track railway line running along the southern edge of the foothills—probably the only case of its kind in the world; whilst eastwards and southwards boundaries are highly arbitrary, being straight lines drawn for convenience between salient points. Westwards, the frontiers are again artificial, although less crudely drawn, leaving the headwaters of the Jordan river outside Syria and following the crest of the Anti-Lebanon hills, to reach the sea north of Tripoli.

PHYSICAL FEATURES

Geographically, Syria consists of two main zones: a fairly narrow western part, made up of a complex of mountain ranges and intervening valleys; and a much larger eastern zone that is essentially a broad and open platform dropping gently towards the east and crossed diagonally by the wide valley of the Euphrates river.

The western zone, which contains over 80% of the population of Syria, can be further subdivided as follows. In the extreme west, fronting the Mediterranean Sea, there lies an imposing ridge rising to 1,500 m above sea-level, and known as the Jebel Ansariyeh. Its western flank drops fairly gradually to the sea, giving a narrow coastal plain; but on the east it falls very sharply, almost as a wall, to a flat-bottomed valley occupied by the Orontes river, which meanders sluggishly over the flat floor, often flooding in winter, and leaving a formerly malarial marsh in summer. Farther east lie more hill ranges, opening out like a fan from the south-west, where the Anti-Lebanon range, with Mount Hermon (2,814 m), is the highest in Syria. Along the eastern flanks of the various ridges lie a number of shallow basins occupied by small streams that eventually dry up or form closed salt lakes. In one basin lies the city of Aleppo, once the second town of the Ottoman Empire and still close to being the largest city of Syria. In another is situated Damascus, larger, irrigated from five streams, and famous for its clear fountains and gardens—now the capital of the country. One remaining sub-region of western Syria is the Jebel Druse, which lies in the extreme south-west, and consists of a vast outpouring of lava, in the form of sheets and cones. Towards the west this region is fertile, and produces good cereal crops, but eastwards the soil cover disappears, leaving a barren countryside of twisted lava and caverns, for long the refuge of outlaws, bandits, and minority groups. Because of its difficulty and isolation, the Jebel Druse has tended socially and politically to go its own way, remaining aloof from the rest of the country.

The entire eastern zone is mainly steppe or open desert, except close to the banks of the Euphrates, the Tigris and their larger tributaries, where recent irrigation projects have allowed considerable cultivation on an increasing scale. The triangularly-shaped region between the Euphrates and Tigris rivers is spoken of as the Jezireh (Arabic *jazira* = island), but is in no way different from the remaining parts of the east.

The presence of ranks of relatively high hills aligned parallel to the coast has important climatic effects. Tempering and humid effects from the Mediterranean are restricted to a narrow western belt, and central and eastern Syria show marked continental tendencies: that is, a very hot summer with temperatures often above 100°F (38°C) or even 110°F (43°C), and a moderately cold winter, with frost on many nights. Very close to the Mediterranean, frost is unknown at any season, but on the hills altitude greatly reduces the average temperature, so that snow may lie on the heights from late December to April, or even May. Rainfall is fairly abundant in the west, where the height of the land tends to determine the amount received; but east of the Anti-Lebanon mountains the amount decreases considerably, producing a steppe region that quickly passes into true desert. On the extreme east, as the Zagros ranges of Persia are approached, there is once again a slight increase, but most of Syria has an annual rainfall of under 250 mm.

ECONOMIC LIFE

There is a close relationship between climate and economic activities. In the west, where up to 750 mm (30 in) or even 1,000 mm (40 in) of rainfall occur, settled farming is possible, and the main limitation is difficult terrain. From the Orontes Valley eastwards, however, natural rainfall is increasingly inadequate, and irrigation becomes necessary. The narrow band of territory where annual rainfall lies between 200 mm and 380 mm (8 in to 15 in) is sometimes spoken of as the 'Fertile Crescent', since it runs in an arc along the inner side of the hills from Jordan through western and northern Syria as far east as Iraq. In its normal state a steppeland covered with seasonal grass, the Fertile Crescent can often be converted by irrigation and efficient organization into a rich and productive territory. Such it was in the golden days of the Arab caliphate; now, after centuries of decline, it has been revived. From the 1950s onwards, a marked change was seen and, initially because of small-scale irrigation schemes and the installation of motor pumps to raise water from underground artesian sources, large areas of the former steppe began to produce cotton, cereals and fruit. Syria used to have a surplus of agricultural production, especially cereals, to export to Jordan and Lebanon, neither of which are self-sufficient in foodstuffs. It was expected that production would increase with the eventual doubling of Syria's irrigated area (by 640,000 ha) as the Euphrates Dam at Tabqa developed fully. However, only about 60,000 ha had been irrigated by 1988; difficulties have been experienced in irrigating part of the designated area and some experts believe that perhaps 300,000 ha may be impossible to develop according to the original plans. Over the last few years, production of cereals and cotton has declined, partly owing to lack of technical and management skills, and partly to drought. High military expenditure has also reduced available development funds.

Because of its relative openness and accessibility and its geographical situation as a 'waist' between the Mediterranean and the Persian Gulf, Syria has been a land of passage, and for centuries its role was that of an intermediary, both commercial and cultural, between the Mediterranean world and the Far East. From early times until the end of the Middle Ages there was a flow of traffic east and west that raised a number of Syrian cities and ports to the rank of international markets. Since the 1930s, following a long period of decline and eclipse resulting from the diversion of this trade to the sea, there has been a revival of activity, owing to the new elements of air transport and the construction of oil pipelines from Iraq.

In addition, Syria was able to develop its own deposits of petroleum and phosphate; and its greatly improved political standing (as, temporarily at least, the successor of Egypt as the leading politically activist Arab state) brought economic benefits. The Syrian economy became stronger, and the country was able to 'balance' between the Soviet and Western political groups, although the cost of wars and internal political uncertainties eroded some development gains. After 1981, however, Syria became more isolated from its Arab neighbours, and the policy of balance, both in external and internal affairs, was less successful. In response to the collapse of communism in eastern Europe and the diminution of Soviet influence, Syria's foreign policy has remained, above all, pragmatic. This was clearly illustrated by the country's allying itself with the Western powers and the 'moderate' Arab states against Iraq in 1990/91, in return for diplomatic and economic gains.

RACE AND LANGUAGE

Racially, many elements can be distinguished in the Syrian people. The nomads of the interior deserts are unusually pure specimens of the Mediterranean type, isolation having preserved them from intermixture. To the west and north there is a widely varying mosaic of other groups: the Kurds and Turkish-speaking communities of the north, and the Armenians, who form communities in the cities; groups such as the Druzes, who show some affinity to the tribes of the Persian Zagros, and many others.

As a result, there is a surprising variety of language and religion. Arabic is spoken over most of the country, but Kurdish is widely used along the northern frontier and Armenian in the cities. Aramaic, the language of Christ, survives in three villages.

History

ANCIENT HISTORY

From the earliest times, Syria has experienced successive waves of Semitic immigration—the Canaanites and Phoenicians in the third millennium BC, the Hebrews and Aramaeans in the second, and, unceasingly, the nomad tribes infiltrating from the Arabian peninsula. This process has enabled Syria to assimilate or reject, without losing its essentially Semitic character, the alien invaders who, time and again, in the course of a long history, have established their domination over the land. Before Rome assumed control of Syria in the first century BC, the Egyptians, the Assyrians and the Hittites, and, later, the Persians and the Macedonian Greeks had all left their mark to a greater or lesser degree. Damascus is claimed to be the oldest capital city in the world, having been continuously inhabited since about 2000 BC, and Aleppo may be even older. Under Roman rule the infiltration and settlement of nomad elements continued, almost unnoticed by historians, save when along the desert trade routes a Semitic vassal state attained a brief importance as, for example, the kingdom of Palmyra in the Syrian desert, which the Emperor Aurelian destroyed in AD 272 or, later still, when the Byzantines ruled in Syria, the Arab state of Ghassan, prominent throughout the sixth century AD as a bulwark of the Byzantine Empire against the desert tribes in the service of Sasanid Persia.

ARAB AND TURKISH RULE

When, after the death of the Prophet Muhammad in AD 632, the newly-created power of Islam began a career of conquest, the populations of Syria, Semitic in their language and culture and, as adherents of the Monophysite faith, ill-disposed towards the Greek-speaking Orthodox Byzantines, did little to oppose the Muslims, from whom they hoped to obtain a greater measure of freedom. The Muslims defeated the Byzantine forces at Ajnadain in July 634, seized Damascus in September 635, and, by their decisive victory on the River Yarmuk (August 636), virtually secured possession of all Syria. From 661 to 750 the Umayyad dynasty ruled in Syria, which, after the conquest, had been divided into four military districts or junds (Damascus, Homs, Urdun, i.e. Jordan, and Palestine). To these the Caliph Yazid I (680–83) added a fifth, Kinnasrin, for the defence of northern Syria, where in the late seventh century, the Mardaites, Christians from the Taurus, were making serious inroads under Byzantine leadership. Under Abd al-Malik (685–705), Arabic became the official language of the state, in whose administration, hitherto largely carried out by the old Byzantine bureaucracy, Syrians, Muslim as well as Christian, now had an increasing share. For Syria was now the heart of a great Empire, and the Arab army of Syria, well trained in the ceaseless frontier warfare with Byzantium, bore the main burden of imperial rule, taking a major part in the two great Arab assaults on Byzantium in 674–8 and in 717–18.

The new regime in Syria was pre-eminently military and fiscal in character, representing the domination of a military caste of Muslim Arab warriors, who governed on the basic assumption that a large subject population, non-Muslim and non-Arab in character, would continue indefinitely to pay tribute. But this assumption was falsified by the gradual spread of Islam, a process which meant the progressive diminution of the amount of tribute paid to the state, and the consequent undermining of the fiscal system as a whole. In theory, conversion meant for the non-Arab convert (*mawla*; in the plural, *mawali*) full social and economic equality with the ruling caste, but in practice it was not enough to be a Muslim, one had to be an Arab as well. The discontent of the *mawali* with their enforced inferiority expressed itself in an appeal to the universal character of Islam, an appeal which often took the form of religious heresies, and which, as it became more widespread, undermined the strength of the Arab regime.

To the ever present fiscal problems of the Arab state and the growing discontent of the *mawali* was added a third and fatal weakness: the hostility between those Arab tribes which had arrived in Syria with or since the conquest, and those which had infiltrated there at an earlier date. The Umayyad house strove to maintain a neutral position over and above the tribal feuds; but from the moment when, under the pressure of events, the Umayyads were compelled to side with one faction to oppose the other (Battle of Marj Rahit 684), their position was irretrievably compromised.

When in AD 750 with the accession of the Abbasid dynasty the centre of the empire was transferred to Iraq, Syria, jealously watched because of its association with the former ruling house, became a mere province, where in the course of the next hundred years, several abortive revolts, inspired in part by the traditional loyalty to the Umayyads, failed to shake off Abbasid control. During the ninth century Syria was the object of dispute between Egypt and Baghdad. In 878 Ahmad ibn Tulun, Governor of Egypt, occupied it and, subsequently, every independent ruler of Egypt sought to maintain a hold, partial or complete, over Syria. Local dynasties, however, achieved from time to time a transitory importance, as did the Hamdanids (a Bedouin family from northern Iraq) who, under Saif ad-Daula, ruler of Aleppo from 946–967, attained a brief ascendancy, marked internally by financial and administrative ineptitude, and externally by military campaigns against the Byzantines which did much to provoke the great Byzantine re-conquest of the late 10th century. By the treaty of 997, northern Syria became Byzantine, while the rest of the country remained in the hands of the Fatimid dynasty which ruled in Egypt from 969. Fatimid control remained insecure and from about 1027 a new Arab house ruled at Aleppo—the Mirdasids, who were soon to disappear before the formidable power of the Seljuq Turks. The Seljuqs, having conquered Persia, rapidly overran Syria (Damascus fell to them in 1075) but failed to establish there a united state. As a result of dynastic quarrels, the Seljuq domination disintegrated into a number of amirates: Seljuq princes ruled at Aleppo and Damascus, a local dynasty held Tripoli and, in the south, Egypt controlled most of the littoral.

This political fragmentation greatly favoured the success of the First Crusade which, taking Antioch in 1098 and Jerusalem in 1099, proceeded to organize four feudal states at Edessa, Antioch, Tripoli and Jerusalem, but did not succeed in conquering Aleppo, Homs, Hama, and Damascus. From the death of Baldwin II of Jerusalem in 1131, the essential weakness of the crusading states began to appear. Byzantium, the Christian state of Lesser Armenia, and the Latin principalities in Syria never united in a successful resistance to the Muslim counter-offensive which, initiated by the energetic Turkish general Zangi Atabeg of Mosul, developed rapidly in the third and fourth decades of the century. Zangi, who seized Aleppo in 1128, and the Latin state of Edessa in 1144, was succeeded in 1146 by his able son Nur ad-Din, who by his capture of Damascus in 1154 recreated in Syria a united Muslim power. On Nur ad-Din's death in 1174, the Kurd Saladin, already master of Egypt, assumed control of Damascus and, in 1183, seized Aleppo. His victory over the Crusaders at Hattin (July 1187) destroyed the kingdom of Jerusalem. Only the partial success of the Third Crusade (1189–92) and, after his death in 1193, the disintegration of Saladin's empire into a number of separate principalities, made it possible for the Crusaders to maintain an ever more precarious hold on the coastal area of Syria. The emergence in Egypt of the powerful Mamluk sultanate (1250) meant that the end was near. A series of military campaigns, led by the Sultan Baibars (1260–77) and his immediate successors, brought about the fall of Antioch (1268) and Tripoli (1289), and, with the fall of Acre in 1291, the disappearance of the crusading states in Syria.

Before the last crusading states had been reduced, the Mamluks had to encounter a determined assault by the Mongols until, in 1260, the Mongol army of invasion was crushed at the Battle of Ain-Jalut, near Nazareth. The Mongol Il-Khans of Persia made further efforts to conquer Syria in the late 13th century, negotiating for this purpose with the papacy, the remaining crusader states, and Lesser Armenia. In 1280 the Mamluks defeated a Mongol army at Homs; but in 1299 were themselves beaten near the same town, a defeat which enabled the Mongols to ravage northern Syria and to take Damascus in 1300. Only in 1303, at the Battle of Marj as-Suffar, south of Damascus, was this last Mongol offensive finally repelled.

The period of Mamluk rule in Syria, which endured until 1517, was on the whole one of slow decline. Warfare, periodical famine, and not least, the plague (there were four great outbreaks in the 14th century, and in the 15th century 14 more recorded attacks of some severity) produced a state of affairs which the financial rapacity and misrule of the Mamluk governors and the devastation of Aleppo and Damascus by Timur (1400–01) served only to aggravate.

The ill-defined protectorate which the Mamluks asserted over Cilicia and considerable areas of southern Anatolia occasioned, in the late 15th century, a growing tension with the power of the Ottoman Turks, which broke out into inconclusive warfare in the years 1485–91. When to this tension was added the possibility of an alliance between the Mamluks and the rising power of the Safavids in Persia, the Ottoman Sultan Selim I (1512–20) was compelled to seek a decisive solution to the problem. In August 1516 the battle of Marj Dabik, north of Aleppo, gave Syria to the Ottomans, who proceeded to ensure their continued hold on the land by conquering Egypt

(1517). Turkish rule, during the next three centuries, although unjustly accused of complete responsibility for a decay and stagnation which appear to have been well advanced before 1517, brought only a temporary improvement in the unhappy condition of Syria, now divided into the three provinces of Damascus, Tripoli, and Aleppo. In parts of Syria the Turkish pashas in reality administered directly only the important towns and their immediate neighbourhood; elsewhere, the older elements—Bedouin emirs, Turcoman chiefs, etc.—were left to act much as they pleased, provided the due tribute was paid. The pashas normally bought their appointment to high office and sought in their brief tenure of power to recover the money and bribes they had expended in securing it, knowing that they might, at any moment, be replaced by someone who could pay more for the post. Damascus alone had 133 pashas in 180 years. As the control of the Sultan at Constantinople became weaker, the pashas obtained greater freedom of action, until Ahmad Jazzar, Pasha of Acre, virtually ruled Syria as an independent prince (1785–1804).

The 19th century saw important changes. The Ottoman Sultan Mahmoud II (1808–39) had promised Syria to the Pasha of Egypt, Muhammad Ali, in return for the latter's services during the Greek War of Independence. When the Sultan declined to fulfil his promise, Egyptian troops overran Syria (1831–33). Ibrahim Pasha, son of Muhammad Ali, now gave to Syria, for the first time in centuries, a centralized government strong enough to hold separatist tendencies in check and to impose a system of taxation which, if burdensome, was at least regular in its functioning. But Ibrahim's rule was not popular, for the land-owners resented his efforts to limit their social and political dominance, while the peasantry disliked the conscription, the forced labour, and the heavy taxation which he found indispensable for the maintenance of his regime. In 1840 a revolt broke out in Syria, and when the Great Powers intervened on behalf of the Sultan (at war with Egypt since 1839), Muhammad Ali was compelled to renounce his claim to rule there.

Western influence, working through trade, through the protection of religious minorities, and through the cultural and educational efforts of missions and schools, had received encouragement from Ibrahim Pasha. The French Jesuits, returning to Syria in 1831, opened schools, and in 1875 founded their University at Beirut. The American Presbyterian Mission (established at Beirut in 1820) introduced a printing press in 1834, and in 1866 founded the Syrian Protestant College, later renamed the American University of Beirut. Syria also received some benefit from the reform movement within the Ottoman Empire, which, begun by Mahmoud II, and continued under his successors, took the form of a determined attempt to modernize the structure of the Empire. The semi-independent pashas of old disappeared, the administration being now entrusted to salaried officials of the central Government; some effort was made to create schools and colleges on Western lines, and much was done to deprive the landowning classes of their feudal privileges, although their social and economic predominance was left unchallenged. As a result of these improvements, there was, in the late 19th century, a revival of Arabic literature which did much to prepare the way for the growth of Arab nationalism in the 20th century.

MODERN HISTORY

By 1914 Arab nationalist sentiment had made some headway among the educated and professional classes, and especially among army officers. Nationalist societies like al-Fatat soon made contact with Arab nationalists outside Syria—with the army officers of Iraq, with influential Syrian colonies in Egypt and America, and with the Sharif Husain of Mecca. The Husain-McMahon Correspondence (July 1915–January 1916) encouraged the Arab nationalists to hope that the end of the First World War would mean the creation of a greater Arab kingdom. This expectation was disappointed, for as a result of the Sykes-Picot Agreement, negotiated in secret between England, France, and Russia in 1916 (see Documents on Palestine, p. 79), Syria was to become a French sphere of influence. At the end of the war, and in accordance with this agreement, a provisional French administration was established in the coastal districts of Syria, while in the interior an Arab government came into being under Amir Faisal, son of the Sharif Husain of Mecca. In March 1920 the Syrian nationalists proclaimed an independent kingdom of Greater Syria (including Lebanon and Palestine); but in April of the same year the San Remo Conference gave France a mandate for the whole of Syria, and in July, French troops occupied Damascus.

By 1925 the French, aware that the majority of the Muslim population resented their rule, and that only amongst the Christian Maronites of the Lebanon could they hope to find support, had carried into effect a policy based upon the religious divisions so strong in Syria. The area under mandate had been divided into four distinct units; a much enlarged Lebanon (including Beirut and Tripoli), a Syrian Republic, and the two districts of Latakia and Jebel Druse. Despite the fact that the French rule gave Syria a degree of law and order which might have rendered possible the transition from a medieval to a more modern form of society, nationalist sentiment opposed the mandate on principle, and deplored the failure to introduce full representative institutions and the tendency to encourage separatism amongst the religious minorities. This discontent, especially strong in the Syrian Republic, became open revolt in 1925–26, during the course of which the French twice bombarded Damascus (October 1925 and May 1926).

The next 10 years were marked by a hesitant and often interrupted progress towards self-government in Syria, and by French efforts to conclude a Franco-Syrian treaty. In April 1928 elections were held for a Constituent Assembly, and in August a draft constitution was completed; but the French High Commissioner refused to accept certain articles, especially Article 2, which, declaring the Syrian territories detached from the old Ottoman Empire to be an indivisible unity, constituted a denial of the separate existence of the Jebel Druse, Latakia, and the Lebanese Republic. After repeated attempts to reach a compromise, the High Commissioner dissolved the Assembly in May 1930 and, on his own authority, issued a new constitution for the State of Syria, much the same as that formerly proposed by the Assembly, but with those modifications which were considered indispensable to the maintenance of French control. After new elections (January 1932) negotiations were begun for a Franco-Syrian treaty, to be modelled on that concluded between the United Kingdom (UK) and Iraq in 1930, but no compromise could be found between the French demands and those of the nationalists who, although in a minority, wielded a dominant influence in the Chamber and whose aim was to limit both in time and in place the French military occupation, and to include in Syria the separate areas of Jebel Druse and Latakia. In 1934 the High Commissioner suspended the Chamber indefinitely. Disorders occurred early in 1936 which induced the French to send a Syrian delegation to Paris, where the new Popular Front Government showed itself more sympathetic towards Syrian aspirations than former French Governments had been. In September 1936 a Franco-Syrian treaty was signed which recognized the principle of Syrian independence and stipulated that, after ratification, there should be a period of three years during which the apparatus of a fully independent state should be created. The districts of Jebel Druse and Latakia would be annexed to Syria, but would retain special administrations. Other subsidiary agreements reserved to France important military and economic rights in Syria. It seemed that Syria might now enter a period of rapid political development; but the unrest caused by the situation in Palestine, the crisis with Turkey, and the failure of France to ratify the 1936 treaty were responsible, within two years, for the breakdown of these hopes.

In 1921 Turkey had consented to the inclusion of the Sanjak of Alexandretta in the French mandated territories, on condition that it should be governed under a special regime. The Turks, alarmed by the treaty of 1936, which envisaged the emergence of a unitary Syrian state including, to all appearance, Alexandretta, now pressed for a separate agreement concerning the status of the Sanjak. After long discussion the League of Nations decided in 1937 that the Sanjak should be fully autonomous, save for its foreign and financial policies which were to be under the control of the Syrian Government.

A treaty between France and Turkey guaranteed the integrity of the Sanjak, and also the Turco-Syrian frontier. Throughout 1937 there were conflicts between Turks and Arabs in the Sanjak, and in Syria a widespread and growing resentment, for it was clear that sooner or later Turkey would ask for the cession of Alexandretta. The problem came to be regarded in Syria as a test of Franco-Syrian co-operation, and when, in June 1939, under the pressure of international tension, Alexandretta was finally ceded to Turkey, the cession assumed in the eyes of Syrian nationalists the character of a betrayal by France. Meanwhile, in France itself, opposition to the treaty of 1936 had grown steadily; and in December 1938 the French Government, anxious not to weaken its military position in the Near East, declared that no ratification of the treaty was to be expected.

Unrest in Syria led to open riots in 1941, as a result of which the Vichy High Commissioner, Gen. Dentz, promised the restoration of partial self-government; while in June of the same year, when in order to combat Axis intrigues the Allies invaded Syria, Gen. Catroux, on behalf of the Free French Government, promised independence for Syria and the end of mandatory rule. Syrian independence was formally recognized in September 1941, but the reality of power was still withheld, with the effect that nationalist agitation, inflamed by French reluctance to restore constitutional rule and by economic difficulties owing to the war, became even more pronounced. When at last elections were held once more, a nationalist government was formed, with Shukri al-Kuwatli as President of the Syrian Republic (August 1943).

Gradually all important powers and public services were transferred from French to Syrian hands; but conflict again developed over the Troupes Spéciales, the local Syrian and Lebanese levies which had existed throughout the mandatory period as an integral part of the French military forces in the Levant, and which, transferred to the Syrian and Lebanese Governments, would enable them to form their own armies. Strongly supported by the newly-created Arab League, Syria refused the French demand for a Franco-Syrian Treaty as the condition for the final transfer of administrative and military services which had always been the main instruments of French policy. In May 1945 disturbances broke out which ended only with British armed intervention and the evacuation of French troops and administrative personnel. The Troupes Spéciales were now handed over to the Syrian Government, and with the departure of British forces in April 1946 the full independence of Syria was at last achieved.

UNSTABLE INDEPENDENCE

After the attainment of independence Syria passed through a long period of instability. It was involved in a complicated economic and financial dispute with the Lebanon (1948–50) and also in various schemes for union with Iraq—schemes which tended to divide political opinion inside Syria itself and, in addition, to disrupt the unity of the Arab League. Syria, in fact, found itself aligned at this time with Egypt and Saudi Arabia against the ambitions of the Hashemite rulers of Iraq and Jordan. These rivalries, together with the profound disappointment felt at Damascus over the Arab failures in the war of 1948–49 against Israel, were the prelude to three *coups d'état* in 1949. Dislike of continued financial dependence on France, aspirations towards a greater Syria, the resentments arising out of the unsuccessful war against the Israelis—all help to explain the unrest inside Syria.

The intervention of the army in politics was itself a cause of further tension. Opposition to the dominance of the army grew in the Syrian Chamber of Deputies to such an extent that yet another *coup d'état* was carried out in December 1951. Syria now came under the control of a military autocracy with Col Shishakli as Head of State. The Chamber of Deputies was dissolved in December 1951; a decree of April 1952 abolished all political parties in Syria. After the approval of a new constitution in July 1953 Shishakli became President of Syria in August of that year. The formation of political parties was now allowed once more. Members of the parties dissolved under the decree of April 1952 proceeded, however, to boycott the elections held in October 1953, at which President Shishakli's Movement of Arab Liberation obtained a large majority in the Chamber of Deputies. Politicians hostile to the regime of President Shishakli established in November 1953 a Front of National Opposition, refusing to accept as legal the results of the October elections and declaring as their avowed aim the end of military autocracy and the restoration of democratic rule. Demonstrations at Damascus and Aleppo in December 1953 led soon to the flight of Shishakli to France. The collapse of his regime early in 1954 meant for Syria a return to the Constitution of 1950. New elections held in September 1954 brought into being a Chamber of Deputies notable for the large number of its members (81 out of 142) who might be regarded as independents grouped around leading political figures.

INFLUENCE FROM ABROAD

There was still, however, much friction in Syria between those who favoured union or at least close co-operation with Iraq and those inclined towards an effective *entente* with Egypt. In August 1955 Shukri al-Kuwatli became President of the republic. His appointment was interpreted as an indication that pro-Egyptian influence had won the ascendancy in Syria. On 20 October 1955 Syria made with Egypt an agreement for the creation of a joint military command with its headquarters at Damascus.

The USSR, meanwhile, in answer to the developments in the Middle East associated with the Baghdad Pact, had begun an intensive diplomatic, propaganda and economic campaign of penetration into the Arab lands. In the years 1954–56 Syria, the only Arab state where the Communist Party was legal, made a number of barter agreements with the USSR and its associates in Eastern Europe. A report from Cairo intimated, in February 1956, that Syria had joined Egypt in accepting arms from the USSR.

At the end of October 1956 there occurred the Israeli campaign in the Sinai peninsula, an event followed, in the first days of November, by the armed intervention of Great Britain and France in the Suez Canal region. On 30 October the President of the Syrian Republic left Damascus on a visit to the USSR. A state of emergency was declared in Syria. Reports from Beirut revealed on 3 November that Syrian forces had put out of action the pipelines which carried Iraqi oil to the Mediterranean. The damage that Syrian elements had done to the pipelines earned the sharp disapproval of such Arab states as Iraq and Saudi Arabia, both of whom were now faced with a severe loss of oil revenues. The Syrian Government declared that it would not allow the repair of the pipelines until Israel had withdrawn its troops from Gaza and the Gulf of Aqaba. Not until March 1957 was it possible to restore the pipelines, Israel having in the mean time agreed to evacuate its forces from the areas in dispute.

UNION WITH EGYPT

The Syrian National Assembly, in November 1957, passed a resolution in favour of union with Egypt and the formal union of Egypt and Syria to constitute one state under the title of the United Arab Republic (UAR) received the final approval of the Syrian National Assembly on 5 February 1958. President Nasser of Egypt, on 21 February, became the first head of the combined state. A central Cabinet for the UAR was established in October 1958, also two regional executive councils, one for Syria and one for Egypt. A further move towards integration came in March 1960, when a single National Assembly for the whole of the UAR consisting of 400 deputies from Egypt and 200 from Syria, was instituted.

Syrian dissatisfaction with the union grew over the next three years, as administrators and officials of Egyptian origin came to hold influential positions in the Syrian Region, and on 28 September 1961 there occurred in Syria a military *coup d'état* which aimed—successfully—at the separation of Syria from Egypt and at the dissolution of the UAR. Political figures representing most of the parties which existed in Syria before the establishment of the UAR in 1958 met at Damascus and Aleppo on 3 October 1961, issuing a declaration of support for the new regime and calling for free elections to a new legislature. President Nasser recognized the *fait accompli*. Most foreign states made haste to grant formal recognition to the Government at Damascus. On 13 October 1961 Syria became once more a member of the United Nations (UN). A provisional constitution was promulgated in November and elections for a Constituent Assembly took place on 1 December 1961.

The regime thus established in Syria rested on no sure foundation. At the end of March 1962 the Syrian army intervened once more, bringing about the resignation of Dr Nazim Kudsi, the President of the republic, and also of the ministers who had taken office in December 1961. After demonstrations at Aleppo, Homs and Hama in April 1962, Dr Kudsi was reinstated as President, but further ministerial resignations in May of that year pointed to the existence of continuing tensions within the Government.

THE REVOLUTION OF 1963

A military junta, styled the National Council of the Revolutionary Command, seized control in Damascus on 8 March 1963. In May the Baathists (members of the Arab nationalist socialist party) took measures to purge the armed forces and the administration of personnel known to favour a close alignment with Egypt. A new government, formed on 13 May and strongly Baathist in character, carried out a further purge in June and at the same time created a National Guard recruited from members of the Baath movement. These measures led the pro-Egyptian elements to attempt a *coup d'état* at Damascus on 18 July 1963. The attempt failed, however, with a considerable loss of life. On 27 July Maj-Gen. Amin al-Hafiz, Deputy Prime Minister and Minister of the Interior, became president of the National Council of the Revolutionary Command, a position equivalent to Head of State.

BAATH SOCIALISM

The nationalization of all Arab-owned banks in 1963, and of various industrial enterprises, also the transfer of land to the peasants—all had contributed to bring about much dissatisfaction in the business world and amongst the influential landed elements. The Baath regime depended for its main support on the armed forces which, however, had been recruited in no small degree from the religious minorities in Syria, including adherents of the Alawi faith (a schism of the Shi'ite branch of Islam)—most Syrians being, in fact, of Sunni or orthodox Muslim allegiance. In general, conservative Muslims tended to oppose the Baath Government under guidance of the *ulema* (scholars/lawyers) and of the Muslim Brotherhood. The mass of the peasant population was thought to have some pro-Nasser sympathies; the working class (small in number) was divided between pro-Nasser and Baathist adherents; the middle and upper classes opposed the domination of al-Baath. The unease arising out of these frictions and antipathies took the form of disturbances and finally of open revolt—soon suppressed—at Hama (April 1964).

On 25 April 1964 a provisional constitution had been promulgated, describing Syria as a democratic socialist republic forming an integral part of the Arab nation. A Presidential Council was established on 14 May 1964, with Gen. Hafiz as Head of the State.

The, as yet, undeveloped petroleum and other mineral resources of Syria were nationalized in 1964, together with other industrial concerns. On 7 January 1965 a special military court was created with sweeping powers to deal with all offences, of word or deed, against the nationalization decrees and the socialist revolution. General Hafiz denounced the *ulema* and the Muslim Brotherhood as being involved in the resulting demonstrations. Further nationalization followed.

A National Council, almost 100 strong, was established in August 1965 with the task of preparing a new constitution which would be submitted to a public referendum. Meeting for the first time on 1 September 1965, it created a Presidential Council, of five members, which was to exercise the powers of a Head of State.

RADICAL REACTION

The tensions hitherto visible in al-Baath were, however, still active. Two groups stood ranged one against the other—on the one hand the older, more experienced politicians in al-Baath, less inclined than in former years to insist on the unrestrained pursuit of the main Baathist objectives, socialism and Pan-Arab union, and, on the other hand, the extreme left-wing elements, doctrinaire in their attitude and enjoying considerable support amongst the younger radical officers in the armed forces.

The tensions thus engendered found expression in a new *coup d'état* on 23 February 1966. A military junta representing the extreme radical elements in al-Baath seized power in Damascus and placed under arrest a number of personalities long identified with al-Baath and belonging to the international leadership controlling the organization throughout the Arab world—amongst them Michael Aflaq, the founder of al-Baath; Gen. Hafiz, the Chairman of the recently established Presidential Council; and Salah ad-Din Bitar, the Prime Minister of the displaced administration.

ARAB–ISRAELI WAR OF 1967

The friction ever present along the frontier between Syria and Israel had provoked violent conflict from time to time during recent years, particularly in the region of Lake Tiberias. Now, in the winter of 1966–67, the tension along the border began to assume more serious proportions. Israel, in October 1966, complained to the Security Council of the UN about guerrilla activities from Syria across the frontier into Israeli territory. In April 1967 mortars, cannon and air force units from Syria and Israel were involved in fighting south-east of Lake Tiberias.

The continuing tension on the Syrian-Israeli frontier was now to become a major influence leading to the war which broke out on 5 June 1967 between Israel and its Arab neighbours Egypt, Syria and Jordan. During the course of hostilities, which lasted six days, Israel defeated Egypt and Jordan and then, after some stubborn fighting, outflanked and overran the Syrian positions on the hills above Lake Tiberias. With the breakthrough accomplished, Israeli forces made a rapid advance and occupied the town of Quneitra about 65 km from Damascus. On 10 June Israel and Syria announced their formal acceptance of the UN proposal for a cease-fire, but Syria effectively boycotted the Arab summit conference held at Khartoum in August 1967 and in September the Baath Party of Syria rejected all idea of a compromise with Israel. The resolution adopted by the UN Security Council in November, urging the withdrawal of the Israelis from the lands occupied by them during the June war and the ending of the belligerency which the Arab Governments had until then maintained against Israel, was rejected by Syria, which alone maintained its commitment to a reunified Palestine.

STRUGGLE FOR POWER 1968–71

The ruling Baath Party had for some years been divided into two main factions. Until October 1968 the dominant faction had been the 'progressive' group led by Dr Atassi and Dr Makhous, the Premier and Foreign Minister respectively. This group was distinguished by its doctrinaire and Marxist-oriented public pronouncements and by the strong support it received from the USSR. It held that the creation of a strong one-party state and economy along neo-Marxist lines was of paramount importance, overriding even the need for a militant stand towards Israel and for Arab unity.

By October 1968 the Government felt particularly insecure, partly owing to a feud with the new Baath regime in Iraq, and at the end of the month a new cabinet was formed including several members of the opposing 'nationalist' faction. This group took less interest in ideological questions and favoured a pragmatic approach to the economy, improved relations with Syria's Arab neighbours and full participation in the campaign against Israel, including support for the *fedayeen* movement. Its leader was Lt-Gen. Hafiz al-Assad, who assumed control of the all-important Ministry of Defence. His critical attitude to the powerful Soviet influence on the Government, seen by some 'nationalists' as tantamount to colonialism in restricting Syria's freedom of action, led to a prolonged struggle with the 'progressive' leadership. Cabinet reshuffles took place in March and May, but both Dr Atassi and Gen. Assad retained their positions. During the spring of 1969 a number of communists were arrested or sent into exile,

and the leader of the Syrian Communist Party, still technically an illegal organization, flew to Moscow.

General Assad attempted to take over the government in February 1969 but was forestalled by Soviet threats that if he did so all military supplies (including spares), economic and technical aid, and trade agreements would end. This would have brought about a major disruption in the national economy and the armed forces, and the 'nationalists' were obliged to yield. In May Gen. Mustafa Tlass, the Army Chief of Staff and Gen. Assad's principal assistant, led a military delegation to Peking to negotiate for the purchase of military equipment. The incident indicated a new independence of Moscow. Some observers also saw this independence in the creation of a joint military command with Iraq (with whom relations improved during the spring) and Jordan. Relations with Lebanon worsened, owing to Syria's support of the Lebanese *fedayeen* movement, containing many Syrian members. In the 1968–70 period this appeared to direct much of its activity towards bringing down the precarious Lebanese Government, presumably in the hope that a more militantly anti-Israel ministry would take power.

In November 1970, following a reported coup attempt backed by Iraq in August, the struggle between the two factions of the Baath Party culminated in Gen. Assad's seizure of power. Dr Atassi, who was in hospital at the time, was placed under guard and a retired general, Salah Jadid, Assistant Secretary-General of the Baath Party and leader of the civilian faction, was arrested. Other members of the civilian wing were arrested or fled to Lebanon. The coup was precipitated by attempts of Jadid and his supporters to oust Assad and Tlass from their posts. This power struggle had become acute as a result of differences over support for the Palestine guerrillas during the fighting with the Jordanian army in September. Jadid and Yousuf Zeayen, a former Prime Minister, controlled the movement of tanks from Syria into Jordan to support the Palestinian guerrillas' efforts against the Jordanian army. This Assad and the military faction opposed. Their approach to the Palestinian problem was more akin to Nasser's and they wanted to avoid giving any provocation to Israel, because they considered the Syrian armed forces to be unready to offer adequate resistance.

ASSAD IN POWER

There was no obvious opposition to the military *coup d'état*. Ahmad Khatib became acting President and Gen. Assad Prime Minister and party secretary-general. A new Regional Command of the Baath Party was formed. The old leaders were removed from their posts in a purge which stretched into the new year. Following amendments to the 1969 provisional constitution in February 1971, Gen. Assad was elected President for a seven-year term in March. In the following month Maj.-Gen. Abd ar-Rahman Khlefawi became Premier and Mahmoud al-Ayoubi was appointed Vice-President. In February the first legislative body in Syria since 1966, the People's Council, was formed. Of its 173 members, 87 represented the Baath Party.

The Nasserite leanings of the new regime in foreign policy soon became apparent. Although Syria continued to reject the November 1967 UN Security Council resolution (No. 242), relations with the UAR and Jordan improved, and Syria's isolation in the Arab world was soon reduced. Syria's willingness to join a union with the UAR, Sudan and Libya almost immediately became apparent and agreement on federation with Libya and the UAR was reached in April 1971, but the Federation had little effect.

After coming to power, the Assad regime increased the Syrian army's control over the Palestinian guerrilla group, Saiqa (Vanguard of the Popular Liberation War). In April 1971 guerrilla operations against Israeli positions from the Syrian front were banned by the Government. Then, at the beginning of July, some guerrilla units were forced out of Syria into south Lebanon and arms destined for them and arriving from Algeria were seized by the Syrian authorities. Yet, after the Jordanian Government's final onslaught on the Palestinian guerrillas in north Jordan in July, Syria closed its border and in August severed diplomatic relations when the tension had become so great that tank and artillery clashes developed between the two armies. Egyptian mediation reduced the chances of any more serious conflict developing, but diplomatic links remained severed with Jordan until October 1973. Relations with the USSR improved during the last half of 1971 and in 1972, and in May Marshal Grechko, the Soviet Minister of Defence, visited Damascus. Syria was not prepared, however, at that time to sign a friendship treaty with the USSR, like Egypt and Iraq. On the other hand, the Syrian Government, which had been broadened in March 1972 to include representatives of parties other than the Baath, like the communists, did not follow Egypt's example in July and expel its Soviet advisers.

In December 1972 Maj.-Gen. Khlefawi resigned from the post of Prime Minister for health reasons, and a new government was formed by Mahmoud al-Ayoubi, the Vice-President, who allotted 16 out of 31 government portfolios to the Baath Party. A new Syrian Constitution, proclaiming socialist principles, was approved by the People's Council in January 1973 and confirmed by a referendum in March. The Sunni Muslims were dissatisfied that the Constitution did not recognize Islam as the state religion, and, as a result of their pressure, an amendment was passed, declaring that the President must be a Muslim. Under the Constitution, freedom of belief was guaranteed, with the state respecting all religions, although the Constitution recognized that Islamic jurisprudence was 'a principal source of legislation'. In 1972 a National Charter created a National Progressive Front, a grouping of the Baath Party and its allies. Elections were held in March 1973 for the new People's Council, under the aegis of the Front, and 140 out of the 186 seats were won by the Progressive Front, while 42 seats were won by independents and four by the opposition.

THE FOURTH ARAB–ISRAELI WAR AND ITS AFTERMATH

On the afternoon of 6 October 1973, Egyptian and Syrian forces launched a war against Israel in an effort to regain territories lost in 1967. On both the Egyptian and Syrian fronts, complete surprise was achieved, giving the Arabs a strong initial advantage, much of which they subsequently lost. (The course of the war is described in 'The Arab–Israeli Confrontation 1967–93', pp. 23–71.) Although Egypt signed a disengagement agreement with Israel on 18 January 1974, fighting continued on the Syrian front, in the Golan Heights area, until a disengagement agreement was signed on 31 May, after much diplomacy and travel by the US Secretary of State, Dr Henry Kissinger (see 'Documents on Palestine' p. 89).

Syria continued to maintain an uncompromising policy in the Middle East, especially regarding the Palestinian question, and after the 1973 war it received vast amounts of Soviet military aid in order to fully re-equip its forces. Contact with Moscow and Eastern European states remained close. Syria's strong support for the PLO was vindicated in October 1974 at the Arab summit meeting in Rabat, Morocco, where the PLO's claim to the West Bank was recognized. By June 1976, however, Syria was in the position of invading Lebanon to crush the Palestinians, and finding most of the remainder of the Arab world agreeing to send a peace-keeping force to the Lebanon to quell the conflict.

FOREIGN AFFAIRS 1975–78

This reversal for Syria arose out of a lengthy chain of events. An improvement in relations with Jordan took place in 1975, with King Hussein visiting Damascus in April and President Assad visiting Amman in June. A joint military and political command was set up between the two countries, and by the spring of 1977 their customs, electricity networks and education systems were unified. Plans were made for the eventual union of the two countries. Relations between Syria and Jordan deteriorated, however, after Jordan appeared to give guarded support to Sadat's peace initiative in November 1977.

The second Egyptian-Israeli disengagement agreement in Sinai, signed in September 1975, met with Syria's strong condemnation. Syria accused Egypt of acting without the agreement of other Arab states and, by agreeing to three years of peace with Israel, of weakening the general Arab position and betraying the Palestinians.

Syria had shown considerable interest in the Lebanese civil war since it began in April 1975. Initially, Syria wanted to protect the position of the Palestinians in Lebanon and perhaps also to further plans for a 'Greater Syria', sending in about 2,000 Saiqa troops in January 1976. After having secured a cease-fire, Assad pledged that he would control the Palestinians in Lebanon, and the core of the PLO, under Yasser Arafat, began to be apprehensive that they would be dominated by Syria. By early June 1976 the fighting in Lebanon was so fierce that Syria felt obliged to intervene militarily and overtly. This time, Syria's intervention was welcomed by the Christian right-wing parties and condemned by the Palestinians and the Muslim left (and also Egypt).

A meeting of the Arab League Ministers of Foreign Affairs on 8–9 June agreed that an Arab peace-keeping force should be sent to Lebanon to effect a cease-fire. After some delay, a peace-keeping force, consisting of Syrian and Libyan troops in equal proportions, did arrive in Lebanon, but the fighting continued unabated until October 1976, when Arab summit meetings, at Riyadh and Cairo, secured a more lasting cease-fire. A 30,000-strong Arab Deterrent Force, consisting largely of Syrian troops, was given authority at the Arab summit meetings to maintain the peace. President Assad's prestige, in Syria and the Arab world, was considerably strengthened by this success. Relations with Egypt improved after a tacit understanding that Syria would end its criticism of the September 1975 Egyptian-Israeli agreement on Sinai in return for Egypt's acceptance of Syria's intervention in Lebanon.

In August 1976 Syria's Prime Minister, Mahmoud al-Ayoubi, was replaced by his predecessor, Gen. Khlefawi. He held office until March 1978, when he was succeeded by Muhammad Ali al-Halabi, previously Speaker of the People's Council.

Relations with the USSR, which had been extremely poor during most of 1976, improved after the October 1976 summit meetings and were consolidated when Assad visited Moscow in April 1977. With Iraq, however, relations remained poor. Iraq shut off the flow of petroleum from its Kirkuk oilfield to the Syrian port of Banias in protest at Syria's intervention in Lebanon. Another Iraqi grievance was Syria's use of water from the Euphrates river for irrigation projects. When an attempt to assassinate the Syrian Vice-Premier and Minister of Foreign Affairs, Abd al-Halim Khaddam, was made in December 1976, voices in Syria were swift to blame terrorists trained in Iraq. Relations between Syria and Egypt deteriorated again as a result of President Sadat's peace initiative in November 1977. Syria's President Assad strongly criticized the move and diplomatic relations between the two countries were severed in December.

Syria's rift with Egypt grew even wider after Sadat and Prime Minister Begin of Israel signed the Camp David agreements (see p. 90 et seq.) in the USA in September 1978. The third summit meeting of the 'Steadfastness and Confrontation Front', comprising Arab countries strongly opposed to Egypt's attempt to make a separate peace with Israel, met in Damascus in late September 1978. When the Egyptian-Israeli peace treaty was finally signed in March 1979 (see p. 92), Syria joined most of the other Arab League member countries at a meeting in Baghdad which endorsed political and economic sanctions against Egypt.

Egypt's *rapprochement* with Israel led to a brief improvement in Syria's relations with Iraq. In October 1978 Syria and Iraq signed a 'national charter for joint action' in which the eventual intention was complete political and economic union between the two countries. Although the oil pipeline from Iraq to Banias was reopened, the scheme for union collapsed when an internal conspiracy in Iraq in July 1979 was attributed to Syrian intrigue.

DIFFICULTIES OF THE EARLY 1980s

Although President Assad was comfortably returned for a second seven-year term of office in February 1978, there was growing evidence of internal dissatisfaction in Syria. Important government posts were largely in the hands of Alawites, a minority Muslim sect to which Assad belongs, and after 1977 assassinations of Alawites became an increasing problem. Some dramatic killings took place in June 1979, when more than 60 army cadets, most of them thought to be Alawites, were massacred. The slaughter was officially attributed to the Muslim Brotherhood, who were also held responsible for subsequent killings.

President Assad's attempts to end this violence met with little lasting success. In January 1980 he appointed a new Council of Ministers with Dr Abd ar-Rauf Kassem as Prime Minister, and 23 of the 37 ministers had never before held ministerial posts. Militias of workers, peasants and students were set up, but were ineffective in helping the regular authorities to curb violence.

During the spring of 1980 the number of Soviet advisers in the country grew to more than 4,000, and in October 1980 Syria signed a 20-year treaty of friendship and co-operation with the USSR. By 1986 Syria had received $2,000m. from the USSR in military loans since 1982, and a total of between $12,000m. and $13,000m. since 1973. A proposed merger between Syria and Libya, announced in September 1980, has not been achieved.

On the outbreak of war between Iraq and Iran in September 1980, Syria supported Iran, on account of its own long-standing distrust of the rival Baath Party in Iraq. A crisis with Jordan soon developed, partly because of Syrian allegations that Muslim Brotherhood treachery was being planned from within Jordan and partly because of Jordan's support for Iraq in the Iran–Iraq War. Towards the end of 1980 Syrian and Jordanian troops faced each other across the frontier and conflict was finally averted by Saudi mediation.

Syria's biggest distraction, however, was its involvement in Lebanon. The 30,000 Syrian troops of the Arab Deterrent Force had been in Lebanon since 1976, and had been a severe drain on Syrian resources. In the summer of 1980 the Phalangist militia consolidated its position in Lebanon and came to occupy the town of Zahle in the Beka'a valley, east of Beirut. Clashes developed in the Zahle area between Syrian troops and the Phalangist militia, and the Christian forces found themselves under siege in Zahle in April 1981. Syria maintained that Zahle and the Beka'a valley were vital to its security against Israel. Israeli aircraft made repeated sorties into Lebanon, and at the end of April Syria moved surface-to-air (SAM) missiles into the Beka'a valley after two Syrian helicopters had been shot down by Israeli planes. A prolonged international crisis developed, with a serious threat of war between Israel and Syria. After Saudi and Kuwaiti mediation, however, the siege of Zahle was lifted at the end of June, and the Phalangist militia withdrew. The SAM missiles remained in the Beka'a valley, as the Syrians maintained that this was a separate issue.

In the following year, however, there were a number of reversals for President Assad. In December Israel formally annexed the Golan Heights, a development which prompted Syria to try to obtain more arms from the USSR. A huge car bomb explosion in Damascus in November was attributed to the Muslim Brotherhood, and this was followed by further indications of incipient unrest, culminating in February 1982 in an uprising in Hama which lasted for nearly three weeks. This was eventually suppressed by Assad's forces with brutal ferocity, and, although it was again attributed to the Muslim Brotherhood, other opposition elements were also involved. On 20 February an opposition group called the National Alliance of the Syrian People was formed, consisting of 19 factions drawn from, among others, Baathists, Nasserites, Christians, Alawites and the Muslim Brotherhood.

These problems were completely overshadowed, however, by the Israeli invasion of Lebanon in June 1982. Israeli forces quickly reached Beirut, trapping the PLO guerrillas there; the Syrian missiles in the Beka'a valley were destroyed; and the Syrian presence in northern Lebanon, in the guise of the Arab Deterrent Force, was rendered impotent.

In August agreement was reached on the evacuation of PLO and Syrian forces from Beirut, and their withdrawal, supervised by an international peace-keeping force, took place between 21 August and 1 September. The number of evacuees was estimated to be more than 14,500. No change occurred in the relative positions of Syrian and Israeli forces in Lebanon as a whole, however.

In January 1983, shortly after the start of negotiations between Lebanon and Israel for an agreement covering the withdrawal of foreign forces from Lebanon, Syria took delivery of a number of Soviet SAM-5 anti-aircraft missiles. Soviet *Scud* ground-to-ground rockets were already deployed with Syrian forces, but the SAM missiles, with a range of 240 km, posed a potential threat to aircraft over Lebanon, parts of Jordan and over Israel almost as far as Jerusalem. Two bases were built to accommodate the missiles: one at Dumeir, north of Damascus, and the other at Shinshar, near Homs. These missiles had never before been deployed outside the USSR and Eastern Europe, and the arrival of the technicians who were employed to operate the system was thought to have increased the number of Soviet military personnel in Syria to 6,000.

Syria opposed all US-sponsored diplomatic initiatives towards a peace agreement between Lebanon and Israel, and categorically rejected President Reagan's proposed settlement of the Palestinian question, based on an eventual Palestine-Jordan confederation, which he announced on 1 September 1982. Finally, on 17 May 1983, after almost six months of talks, an agreement was reached between Lebanon and Israel announcing the end of hostilities and imposing a time limit of three months for the withdrawal of foreign troops from Lebanon. The agreement, formulated by the US Secretary of State, George Shultz, was rejected outright by President Assad, who refused to withdraw Syrian forces from northern Lebanon—thus creating a stalemate with Israel, which refused to leave Lebanon unless the Syrians and the PLO did so first. President Assad insisted on Israel's unconditional withdrawal, declaring that the status of Syrian troops, who had been invited into Lebanon by the Lebanese Government in 1976, was not to be compared with that of the invading Israeli forces. He stated that the agreement between Israel and Lebanon placed unacceptable limitations on Lebanon's sovereignty and threatened Syrian security. Support for the Syrian position from the rest of the Arab world was less than unanimous, with only Libya, the People's Democratic Republic of Yemen (PDRY) and Kuwait expressing outright opposition to the agreement.

THE STRUGGLE FOR CONTROL OF THE PLO

By July 1983 the position was little changed. About 40,000 Syrian troops, camped in the Beka'a valley, and between 8,000 and 10,000 PLO guerrillas, entrenched in the eastern Beka'a and northern Lebanon, faced some 25,000 Israelis in the south of the country. Neither side seemed eager for war, but, equally, neither was prepared to withdraw. Syria, which continued to supply, and, effectively, to control the militias of the Lebanese Druze and Shi'ite factions in their struggle with the Lebanese Government and the Christian Phalangists in and around Beirut, began to address itself to destabilizing the regime of President Amin Gemayel of Lebanon by trying to unite Lebanese opposition groups in a pro-Syrian 'national front'. Syria was also supporting Palestinian rebels involved in the struggle for power within the PLO which erupted in the Beka'a valley in May, fundamentally over dissatisfaction with what radical Fatah members viewed as the compromise diplomacy of the PLO Chairman, Yasser Arafat, which, they believed, had been responsible for the Palestinians' humiliation in Beirut in 1982. Arafat accused Syria and Libya of inspiring the revolt in order to win control of the PLO, and at the end of June he travelled to Damascus to receive a personal letter of support from President Andropov of the USSR, only to be ordered out of the country by the Syrian authorities. Syrian forces now faced armed opposition in Lebanon, not only from the Israeli army, but also from Sunni Muslims in Tripoli, Maronite Christians in the centre of the country, and guerrillas loyal to Arafat in the Beka'a valley.

Syrian and rebel PLO forces, led by 'Abu Musa' and 'Abu Saleh', finally trapped Arafat in the Lebanese port of Tripoli in November 1983. After fierce fighting, a truce, arrived at through the mediation of Saudi Arabia, allowed Arafat and some 4,000 of his followers to leave Lebanon in December, in five Greek ships, under UN protection. Syria had failed to gain control of the Palestine Liberation Movement, though it had been instrumental in effecting a dilution of Arafat's authority within the PLO. This became apparent in a series of reconciliation talks held between several of the rival Palestinian factions (though not those which had sent troops against Arafat in Tripoli) in the first half of 1984. The agreements reached at these talks saw the PLO wishing to move towards a more collective style of leadership. Whether this style would give rise to policies deferential to Syria's preferred role as leader of the Arab world remained to be seen.

Syria's progress towards a position of pre-eminence in the Arab world was eroded during 1984, as the rehabilitation of Egypt continued. Syria dissented from the decision to readmit Egypt to membership of the Organization of the Islamic Conference in March 1984, and opposed Jordan's restoration of diplomatic relations with Egypt in September and King Hussein's alliance with Yasser Arafat. Syria's attempt to wrest control of the PLO from Yasser Arafat succeeded in splitting the movement. Arafat retained his leadership of the bulk of the organization and manoeuvred it towards an emergent moderate Arab alliance including Egypt, Jordan, Iraq and Saudi Arabia.

SYRIAN INFLUENCE IN LEBANON

Although Israel withdrew its forces from Beirut, redeploying them along the Awali river, south of the capital, in September 1983, Syria's army remained entrenched in northern Lebanon. There were occasional exchanges of fire between Syrian forces around Beirut and aircraft and naval guns of the US fleet standing off shore in support of the US contingent in the multinational peace-keeping force in Beirut. The state of civil war existing in and around Beirut eventually compelled the evacuation of the multinational force in the first three months of 1984.

In March President Gemayel of Lebanon was forced to succumb to the controlling influence of Syria in Lebanese affairs. He abrogated the 17 May agreement with Israel, as President Assad had always insisted that he should, and reconvened the National Reconciliation Conference of the rival Lebanese factions (which had first met in Geneva in November 1983) in Lausanne, Switzerland, under pressure from Syria to agree constitutional reforms which would give the majority Muslim community of Lebanon greater representation in government. In return, Gemayel received guarantees of internal security from Syria. These involved Syrian agreement to restrain the Druze and Shi'ite Amal militias (led by Walid Joumblatt and Nabih Berri, respectively) which relied on Syria to continue their armed struggle.

The National Reconciliation Conference failed to produce the results for which Syria had hoped and it marked the beginning of the rapid disintegration of the Lebanese National Salvation Front, comprising leading Lebanese opponents of President Amin Gemayel, which had been created, with Syrian backing, in July 1983. At the Conference, a member of the Front, the former Lebanese President, Sulaiman Franjiya, vetoed Syrian plans for constitutional changes in Lebanon involving the diminution of the powers of the President, traditionally a Maronite Christian. So, despite careful Syrian orchestration, the Conference broke up without having agreed any reforms of the Lebanese system of government.

The reversal was short-lived, for, in April, President Gemayel returned to Damascus to gain approval from President Assad for plans for a government of national unity in Lebanon, giving equal representation in the Cabinet to Muslims and Christians. Assad accepted the terms of composition of the government under the premiership of Rashid Karami (who had been Prime Minister of Lebanon on 10 previous occasions); Gemayel was to retain the presidency. Walid Joumblatt and Nabih Berri greeted their appointment to posts in the new Lebanese Cabinet on 30 April, and the very idea of a government of national unity under a Christian President, with scepticism. After consulting Syrian officials, however, both agreed to participate in the Government. Inter-factional fighting, which continued and intensified in Beirut despite the creation of the new Government, threatened its existence. It was only through the intercession of the Syrian Vice-President for Political Affairs (and former Minister of Foreign Affairs; see below), Abd al-Halim Khaddam, and the negotiation, with his help, of a comprehensive security agreement between the warring factions, that the Government survived, and some semblance of order was restored in Beirut. Although this

agreement, like many before it, and the political basis on which the new Lebanese Government was built, seemed fragile and prone to collapse, still, the fact that they existed at all was testimony to the extent of Syrian influence in the country's affairs.

INTERNAL TENSION

In November 1983 President Assad suffered what was thought to be a heart attack, though this was denied by the Syrian authorities. He recovered, but his evidently weakened condition aroused speculation regarding his eventual successor. During Assad's illness, potential rivals for the succession made displays of military force in and around Damascus, involving various units of the armed forces, to establish the strength of their claims to power. Prominent among these was Rifaat Assad, the President's brother and commander of the 20,000–30,000-strong Defence Brigades which, effectively, controlled Damascus and defended the regime's authority. The defence brigades and units of the regular army confronted each other in further, similar displays up to March 1984.

On 4 March the Council of Ministers under Prime Minister Abd ar-Rauf Kassem resigned. Kassem was then invited to form a new Council of Ministers to fill four vacancies left as a result of the deaths of ministers. It was the first ministerial reshuffle for four years. At the same time as a new Council of Ministers was being formed, President Assad appointed an unprecedented three Vice-Presidents. Rifaat Assad was made Vice-President for Military and National Security Affairs; Abd al-Halim Khaddam, the former Minister of Foreign Affairs, was made Vice-President for Political Affairs; and Zuheir Masharkah was promoted from his post as a regional secretary of the Baath Party to become Vice-President for Internal and Party Affairs. Ostensibly, President Assad's intention was to ease his workload after his debilitating illness, but another possible motive for the appointment of three Vice-Presidents was to distribute power evenly between his potential successors, giving none an overall advantage. Rifaat Assad thus gained some recognition of his claim to the succession and retained control of the defence brigades; but the regular army (Assad's power-base in what is, essentially, a military dictatorship) was still commanded by officers loyal to President Assad, including the Chief of Staff, Gen. Hikmat Shehabi, who was responsible for the appointment and dismissal of senior officers in the army, and a rival of Rifaat Assad.

In what was seen, in the event, as a disciplinary measure against those principally responsible for the confrontations between military units which took place in and around Damascus after President Assad's illness in November 1983, Rifaat Assad, Gen. Ali Haydar (commander of the Special Forces élite army unit), and Gen. Shafiq Fayyadh (commander of the Third Armoured Division) were sent as part of a delegation to Moscow in June. While the rest of the delegation returned to Syria within one week, these three were, apparently, not permitted to do so. Rifaat Assad was sent to Geneva, Switzerland, and Gens Haydar and Fayyadh to Sofia, Bulgaria, into what appeared to be temporary exile. While Rifaat Assad was abroad, the defence brigades were absorbed into the army, with the exception of a few units which were put under the command of Rifaat Assad's son-in-law. Rifaat Assad was finally permitted to return to Syria in November 1984 and was given responsibility for national security affairs. President Assad was re-elected for a third seven-year term of office in February 1985 and appeared to have regained much of his former authority. In January 1985 he declared an amnesty for some members of the Muslim Brotherhood who were imprisoned in Syria, and invited those in exile to return to the country. A ministerial reshuffle took place in April 1985.

THE IRAN-IRAQ WAR AND OIL SUPPLIES

Syria's reliance on Iran for supplies of crude oil for processing at its oil refineries (see Economy), which occurred as a direct result of its support for Iran in the Iran-Iraq War, was exposed as a serious weakness in 1984, as hostilities in the conflict began to affect the passage of oil tankers in the Gulf. Attacks on shipping were made by both sides in the first half of the year, threatening Syria's oil link with Iran. President Assad attempted to restrain Iran from widening the conflict and endangering vital oil supplies. An agreement on the continued delivery of Iranian oil to Syria was reached in May, but attacks on Gulf shipping by both Iran and Iraq continued. A Soviet attempt to bring about a reconciliation between the rival Baathist regimes in Syria and Iraq, involving the reopening of the oil pipeline between Kirkuk, in Iraq, and Banias, in Syria, made no progress.

ISRAEL'S WITHDRAWAL FROM LEBANON

By dint of Syrian mediation, a security plan for Beirut was agreed and put into operation at the beginning of July 1984. The plan met with only limited success, and the extent of Syria's influence with its Lebanese allies came into question when, in September, even the threat of force failed to win Walid Joumblatt's unequivocal approval of an extension of the security plan to allow the Lebanese army into the Druze stronghold of the Chouf mountains. In September Syria arranged a truce to end fighting in Tripoli between the pro-Syrian Arab Democratic Party and the Sunni Muslim Tawheed Islami (Islamic Unification Movement). This prepared the way for the Lebanese army to enter the city in November, under the terms of an extended security plan, backed by Syria, to assert the authority of the Lebanese Government in Beirut, Tripoli and south of the capital. On this occasion, Walid Joumblatt's opposition to the plan's provisions for the army to take control of the coastal road south of Beirut appeared to have tacit Syrian approval. However, the plan finally went ahead in January 1985.

Syria's rejection of Israel's demand that any withdrawal from Lebanon should be undertaken by both sides simultaneously was vindicated as it became clear, during the latter half of 1984, that Israel would be forced by domestic economic, political and social pressures to withdraw unilaterally. Syria approved Lebanese participation in talks with the Israelis to co-ordinate the departure of the Israeli Defence Force (IDF) from southern Lebanon with other security forces, in order to prevent an outbreak of civil violence. A series of talks began in Naqoura (Lebanon) in November and repeatedly foundered on the question of which forces should take the place of the IDF. Under Syrian influence, the Lebanese wanted the UN Interim Force in Lebanon (UNIFIL) to police the Israel–Lebanon border (as it had been mandated to do in 1978), and the Lebanese army to deploy north of the Litani river, between UNIFIL and the Syrians in the Beka'a valley. Israel was not convinced of the competence of the Lebanese army, and wanted UNIFIL to be deployed north of the Litani, while the Israeli-backed, so-called 'South Lebanon Army' (SLA) patrolled the southern Lebanese border. In the absence of an agreement, Israel withdrew from the talks, and on 14 January 1985 the Israeli Cabinet voted to take steps towards a three-phased unilateral withdrawal to the international border.

The first phase involved the evacuation of the IDF from the western sector of occupied southern Lebanon, covering about 500 sq km around Sidon, and this was carried out in February 1985. In the second phase the IDF left the occupied central and eastern sectors where it faced the Syrian army and its Palestinian allies in the Beka'a valley, completing the operation on 29 April. On 10 June Israel announced the accomplishment of the third and final phase of the withdrawal, taking its forces behind the southern Lebanese border and leaving a protective buffer zone inside Lebanon, policed by the SLA with IDF support. Although Syria was evidently determined to retain control of events in Lebanon, the Israeli withdrawal offered the opportunity of reducing its costly military presence in the north and east of the country. At the end of June and the beginning of July Syria withdrew an estimated 10,000 troops from the Beka'a valley, leaving some 25,000 in position.

SYRIA LOSES ITS GRIP ON LEBANON

In March 1985 Samir Geagea, a regional commander of the Christian Lebanese Forces (LF) militia, rebelled against the Phalange Party leadership and the extent to which it was prepared to accept the Syrian influence in Lebanese affairs, particularly as manifested in President Gemayel's apparent willingness to accommodate Syrian-backed plans for constitutional reform favouring the Muslim majority in Lebanon.

Geagea immediately secured the support of the greater part of the LF and threatened to set up an independent Christian administration. Syria, though unwilling to be drawn into the civil-military entanglement in Lebanon, feared the necessity of having to send troops into Christian east Beirut to quell the revolt, which threatened to precipitate the partition of Lebanon along sectarian lines, creating a number of unstable mini-states close to the Syrian border, in a condition of perhaps permanent conflict and vulnerable to exploitation by Syria's enemies. Indeed, Syria accused Israel of inciting the revolt. It ended, however, as suddenly as it had begun, in May, when the LF elected a new leader, Elie Hobeika, who announced his readiness to negotiate with Syria and its Druze allies.

The extent of Syria's diminishing influence over the actions of its allies in Lebanon was repeatedly demonstrated by its inability to prevent renewed inter-factional fighting in Beirut. If the members of the LF were alarmed by the prospect of constitutional reform, their Muslim counterparts were dissatisfied with the lack of progress towards it. This could account for continued fighting between Christians and Muslims, but other factors now led to conflict between rival Muslim factions. On 17 April Prime Minister Rashid Karami, a Sunni Muslim, tendered his resignation, partly over the failure of the Council of Ministers to agree to reinforce the army, which was engaged in heavy fighting against elements of Samir Geagea's rebel LF around Sidon, and partly over attacks on Sunni Muslims by the Shi'ite Amal militia. The Shi'ites had combined with the Druze in trying to eliminate the Sunni Murabitoun militia, which had joined forces with members of the PLO, whose numbers in Beirut were growing again. Amal hoped to prevent the re-emergence anywhere in Lebanon of a PLO power-base which might attract Israeli military retaliation. Karami withdrew his resignation later on 17 April and, on a subsequent visit to Damascus, was persuaded to remain as Prime Minister and ensure the survival of the Government of national unity.

In May and June, however, Syria itself backed Amal in attempting to suppress a resurgence of the PLO (in particular the pro-Arafat wing of the movement) in the Palestinian refugee camps of Sabra, Chatila and Bourj el-Barajneh in Beirut. Many of the estimated 5,000, mostly pro-Arafat, Palestinians who had infiltrated Lebanon since the Israeli withdrawal became inevitable, had made their way to Beirut. Walid Joumblatt's Druze militia refused to assist its former allies in imposing a siege on the camps, but Amal had the support of the predominantly Shi'ite sixth brigade of the Lebanese army. In the bloody battle for the camps, which spanned May and June, more than 600 people were killed, but Amal failed to take control of the camps. An unforeseen development was the extent to which pro- and anti-Arafat PLO factions united to resist the attack on the Palestinian community. On 17 June a fragile Syrian-sponsored cease-fire agreement was reached in Damascus between Amal and the Palestinian National Salvation Front (PNSF), representing the pro-Syrian, anti-Arafat element in the camps.

Weeks of fighting between Christians and Muslims along the 'Green Line' dividing east and west Beirut, and between Muslims and Druze in the west of the capital, preceded an attempt to enforce another Syrian-sponsored security plan for the city. The plan was introduced in July, after 13 Muslim and Druze leaders had met to discuss it in Damascus. Under the terms of the plan, Muslim west Beirut was to comprise five security zones; the militias were to leave the streets and close their offices, with the police taking their place, supported by a unit of the sixth army brigade. These measures were meant to lay the foundations for the extension of the plan to Christian east Beirut and the renewal of inter-sectarian dialogue on political and constitutional reform. However, more heavy fighting soon reduced the plan to utter ineffectiveness, like so many before it.

President Assad was able to demonstrate that he retained some command over events in Lebanon when his intercession was instrumental in securing the release of 39 American hostages from a hijacked TWA airliner, who had been detained at secret locations in Beirut since 17 June 1985 by members of the extremist Shi'ite group Hezbollah (the Party of God). Assad threatened to sever relations with Hezbollah and to provide no further aid if the hostages were not released. The hostages were freed and driven to Damascus on 30 June.

Four weeks of intensive fighting between rival militias in the Lebanese town of Tripoli in September and October were interpreted as part of Syria's campaign to prevent the re-emergence of the pro-Arafat wing of the PLO in Lebanon. The pro-Arafat, Sunni Muslim group, Tawheed Islami, and the pro-Syrian, Alawite Arab Democratic Party fought for control of the town and its port, which was allegedly being used to distribute weapons and supplies to Arafat loyalists in other parts of the country. A cease-fire was agreed in Damascus in November, and troops of the Syrian army moved into the town.

THE ABORTIVE NATIONAL AGREEMENT IN LEBANON

One month of negotiations, under Syrian auspices, between the three main Lebanese militias, the Druze forces, Amal and the LF, which began in October 1985, led to the preparation of a draft accord for a politico-military settlement of the civil war. The agreement was finally signed by the three militia leaders (Walid Joumblatt, Nabih Berri and Elie Hobeika) on 28 December, in Damascus. It provided for an immediate cease-fire and for an end to the state of civil war within one year; the militias would be disbanded, and the responsibility for security would pass to a reconstituted and religiously-integrated army, supported by Syrian forces. The accord sought the immediate establishment of a national coalition government which would preside over the abolition of the confessional system of power-sharing government and the creation of a secular administration. It also recognized Lebanon's community of interest with Syria and envisaged a 'strategic integration' of the two countries in the fields of military relations, foreign policy and security.

It was always doubtful that the Damascus accord could be implemented. The Shi'ite Hezbollah and the Sunni Murabitoun militias were not party to the agreement, the Christian community was divided over it, and it made no provision for dealing with the problem of Palestinian refugees or the PLO. Among the Muslim community, only Amal appeared to be wholly in favour of the accord. President Gemayel, who had not been consulted during the drafting of the agreement, refused to endorse it, and at the end of December 1985 clashes erupted in east Beirut between elements of the LF who supported the agreement and those loyal to President Gemayel, who resented the concessions that had been made on their behalf by Elie Hobeika. In January 1986 Hobeika was forced into exile, and Samir Geagea resumed command of the LF, urging the renegotiation of the Damascus agreement. The long round of inter-sectarian clashes in Beirut resumed in earnest on 22 January.

Fighting between Palestinian guerrillas and Shi'ite Amal militiamen for control of the refugee camps in the south of Beirut, which had continued sporadically ever since a cease-fire nominally took effect in June 1985, escalated into major exchanges on 19 May 1986. The Palestinian refugee camps of Sabra, Chatila and Bourj el-Barajneh were increasingly under the control of guerrillas loyal to Yasser Arafat, who were continuing to return to Labanon. Concentrations of PLO guerrillas were also identified in and around the refugee camps on the outskirts of Tyre and Sidon, while mobile PLO bases resumed rocket attacks on settlements in the north of Israel during 1986, drawing retaliatory attacks from the Israeli air force. Syria appeared to be powerless to prevent the resurgence of the PLO in Lebanon, despite the efforts of the Syrian-backed Amal militia to keep Palestinian and radical pro-Iranian Hezbollah guerrillas, who were growing in strength, away from the Israeli security zone inside the southern Lebanese border. The PLO claimed that the number of guerrillas in Lebanon in 1986 exceeded the 14,300 who, according to its own figures, had been evacuated from Beirut in 1982. Independent estimates assessed the number in Beirut at several thousands. Syria itself apparently ignored Israeli warnings not to fill the military vacuum which had been left by their withdrawal in 1985. In May 1986 it was reported that Syrian forces were constructing fortifications and tank and gun emplacements in the Lake Karoun area, in the southern Beka'a, immediately to the north of the SLA-patrolled security zone.

THE SYRIAN ARMY RETURNS TO BEIRUT

Leaders of the Muslim communities in Lebanon met Syrian Government officials in Damascus, and agreed to impose a cease-fire around the Palestinian refugee camps in Beirut on 14 June. The cease-fire, which reduced the fighting to exchanges of sniper fire, proved to be the first element in a Syrian-sponsored peace plan for Muslim west Beirut. About 1,000 Lebanese troops were deployed in west Beirut at the end of June. The Amal, Druze and Murabitoun militias were ordered to close their offices and to leave the streets. Crucial to their co-operation in the plan was the appearance in Beirut, for the first time since 1982, of uniformed Syrian soldiers (several hundred in number), supported by members of the Syrian security service, Muhabarat (literally, 'information'), under the command of Brig.-Gen. Ghazi Kena'an. The security plan was successful in its limited objective of curbing the activities of militias in west Beirut, but the plan (and Syria's visible involvement in it) was strongly opposed in Christian east Beirut, and the Syrians hesitated over extending the plan into the southern suburbs, which contained the majority of the city's Palestinian refugees and was controlled by the radical Shi'ite Hezbollah, who were backed by Iran, which Syria was concerned not to offend. (See Histories of Israel and Lebanon.)

RAPPROCHEMENT WITH JORDAN

Syria opposed the joint Jordanian-Palestinian agreement, which was signed by King Hussein and Yasser Arafat in Amman in February 1985, and its proposals for a Middle East peace settlement. In August, with Algeria, Lebanon, Libya and the PDRY, Syria boycotted the extraordinary meeting of the League of Arab States in Casablanca, which was convened partly to consider the Amman accord. The PLO's persistent refusal to acknowledge the UN Security Council resolutions (Nos 242 and 338) on the Palestinian issue, and a series of terrorist incidents in the second half of 1985 in which the PLO was implicated, reducing its credibility as a potential partner in peace negotiations, and reducing the prospects that the joint peace initiative would make progress, led King Hussein to seek a reconciliation with Syria. (It was suggested in some quarters that factions of the PLO, and other Palestinian groups supported by Syria, were involved in a campaign to discredit Yasser Arafat's wing of the movement.) Relations between Jordan and Syria had been poor since 1979, when Syria had accused Jordan of harbouring anti-Syrian groups. Apart from their different sympathies in the struggle for control of the PLO, a further cause of contention was Syria's support for Iran in the Iran-Iraq War, in which Jordan openly backed Iraq. In November 1985 King Hussein admitted that Jordan had, unwittingly, been a base for the Sunni fundamentalist Muslim Brotherhood in its attempts to overthrow President Assad, but he stated that members of the group would no longer receive shelter in Jordan. The Prime Ministers of the two countries met in Damascus in November, and agreed on the need for 'joint Arab action' to achieve peace in the Middle East. At subsequent talks in Riyadh (Saudi Arabia) in October, Jordan and Syria rejected 'partial and unilateral' solutions (ruling out separate negotiations with Israel) and affirmed their adherence to the Fez plan, omitting all reference to the Jordanian-Palestinian peace initiative. President Assad and King Hussein confirmed the improved state of Syrian-Jordanian relations when they met in Damascus in December. In February 1986 King Hussein withdrew from his political alliance with Yasser Arafat, and in April Jordan appointed its first ambassador to Syria since 1980.

King Hussein acted as a mediator between President Assad and President Saddam Hussain of Iraq during the first half of 1986. However, a meeting between the Syrian and Iraqi Ministers of Foreign Affairs, which was heralded as the beginning of a reconciliation between the two countries, was cancelled by President Assad, shortly before it was due to take place, in June 1986. Only days before, Syria had concluded an agreement with Iran to renew purchases of Iranian petroleum, while in southern Lebanon the guerrilla activities of pro-Iranian groups (in particular, Hezbollah) had been threatening Syria's already tenuous hold on the region through its proxy, Amal.

Syria broke off diplomatic relations with Morocco in July 1986, after King Hassan held talks with the Prime Minister of Israel, Shimon Peres.

BOMB ATTACKS IN SYRIA

On 13 March 1986 a bomb exploded in Damascus causing casualties which were estimated at 60 dead and 110 wounded. Syria blamed Iraqi agents for the attack. Then, on 15 April, bombs exploded, almost simultaneously, in five Syrian towns. Several more bomb attacks were made on buses and trains in towns, including Damascus, before the end of the month. In May the Government admitted that 144 people had been killed, and 149 injured, during the campaign of bombings in April. According to the Voice of Lebanon radio station, a hitherto unknown Syrian group (the '17 October Movement for the Liberation of the Syrian People') claimed responsibility for the campaign, and its message suggested that it was a pro-Iraqi, Islamic fundamentalist organization.

SYRIA AND INTERNATIONAL TERRORISM

Although it failed to provide conclusive proof of Syrian involvement, the USA claimed that there was evidence of a link between Syria and the Palestinian terrorists who carried out attacks on Rome and Vienna airports in December 1985, and on a discotheque in West Berlin in April 1986. The USA attacked the Libyan cities of Tripoli and Benghazi in April 1986, as punishment for alleged Libyan involvement in international terrorism, and reserved the right to use force against other countries which had proven links with terrorist operations. President Assad denied that Syria was sponsoring terrorism, and refused to restrict the activities of Palestinian groups (including the Abu Nidal faction, the Fatah Revolutionary Council) on Syrian territory, which, he claimed, were 'cultural and political'.

In October 1986 a Jordanian, Nezar Hindawi, was convicted in the UK of attempting to plant a bomb on an Israeli airliner at London's Heathrow airport in the previous April. The British Government claimed that it had proof of the complicity of Syrian diplomats in the affair, and, on 24 October, severed diplomatic relations with Syria. One month later, three Syrian diplomats were expelled from the Federal Republic of Germany (FRG), after a court in West Berlin ruled that the Syrian Embassy in East Berlin was implicated in the bombing of a discotheque in the West of the city in 1986. In November the UK and its partners in the EC (excluding Greece), and the USA and Canada, imposed limited diplomatic and economic sanctions against Syria (the US and Canadian ambassadors to Syria were both recalled). Syria persistently denied any involvement in international terrorism, and by April 1987 several EC countries had made tentative advances to Syria, seeking to upgrade diplomatic relations, and only the UK continued to insist on a ban on high-level (ministerial) contacts. It had always seemed unlikely that the isolation of Syria would last long. Several EC countries, in particular France, had been unenthusiastic supporters of the sanctions demanded by the UK, mindful of the crucial role that Syria had to play in the Middle East peace process, and of the need for its co-operation in securing the release of Western hostages being held by Islamic fundamentalist groups in Beirut. For its part, Syria appeared to be anxious to be seen to dissociate itself from terrorist groups and to use its influence in Lebanon to free Western hostages. In June 1987 it was reported that the offices of Abu Nidal's Fatah Revolutionary Council, near Damascus, had been closed, and many of its members expelled, by the Syrian authorities, and that Abu Nidal himself had moved to Libya. The EC, with the exception of the UK, lifted its ban on ministerial contacts with Syria in July, and financial aid was resumed in September, although a ban on the sale of arms to Syria remained in force. The UK, although it had withdrawn its opposition to its EC partners' restoration of contacts with Syria, remained sceptical as to the true extent of Syria's rejection of terrorism, and alleged that Abu Nidal's group was still active in Lebanon, in the Syrian-controlled Beka'a valley.

PAX SYRIANA IN LEBANON

In October 1986 the Syrian-backed resistance to the re-emergence of the pro-Arafat PLO in Lebanon spread from Beirut to the Palestinian refugee camps around Tyre and Sidon, which were besieged by the forces of Amal. In February 1987 Syria reportedly asked Amal to abandon the blockade of the camps, but the respite for the inhabitants of the camps of Bourj el-Barajneh, in Beirut, and Rashidiyah, near Tyre, where supplies were allowed in, proved to be brief, and the siege of the other camps remained in force.

In February 1987 fierce fighting took place in west Beirut between Amal forces and an alliance of Druze, Murabitoun and Communist Party militias. Muslim leaders appealed for Syria to intervene, to restore order, and about 4,000 Syrian troops were deployed in west Beirut on 22 February. The Syrian force (which was soon increased to some 7,500 troops) succeeded in enforcing a cease-fire in the central and northern districts of west Beirut, and moved into areas occupied by Hezbollah, killing 23 Hezbollahi and forcing others to return to their stronghold in the southern suburbs, into which the Syrians still declined to venture.

A Syrian-supervised cease-fire at the embattled Palestinian refugee camps in Beirut took effect on 6 April 1987. The cease-fire agreement was negotiated by representatives of Syria, Amal and the pro-Syrian PNSF, and brought an end to the worst fighting. Members of the PNSF and Arafat loyalists had made common cause in defence of the camps, and their alliance was a contributory factor in the re-unification of the PLO under Arafat's leadership, which took place at the 18th session of the Palestine National Council (PNC) in Algiers in April, turning the Syrian-backed PNSF into a rump, depriving it of the support of the largest and most influential groups that had rebelled against Arafat in 1983. The PNC adopted a resolution committing itself to improving PLO relations with Syria.

It was not until September 1987 that the Arafat wing of the PLO and Amal reached a comprehensive cease-fire agreement, which provided for the lifting of the siege of the Beirut, Tyre and Sidon camps, in return for a withdrawal by PLO forces from the positions around Ain al-Hilweh camp in Sidon, which they had captured from Amal in October and November 1986. However, neither measure was implemented, and differences concerning the withdrawal of Palestinian guerrillas led to renewed fighting around the disputed positions to the east of Sidon in mid-October. In January 1988, avowedly as a gesture of support for protests by Palestinians living in Israeli-occupied territories, Nabih Berri, the leader of Amal, announced the lifting of the siege of the Palestinian refugee camps in Beirut and southern Lebanon. On 21 January Syrian troops replaced Amal militiamen and soldiers of the Sixth Brigade of the Lebanese army in positions around the Beirut camps, and the 14-month siege of Rashidiyah camp, near Tyre, was lifted. However, PLO guerrillas loyal to Yasser Arafat refused to withdraw from their positions overlooking Ain al-Hilweh, interrupting the withdrawal of Amal from around Rashidiyah.

A new political crisis overtook Lebanon in mid-1987, which emphasized the division between the Muslim and Christian communities and the extent of the problem that Syria faced in its attempts to oversee a political settlement. The Lebanese Prime Minister, Rashid Karami, who had tendered his resignation on 4 May, as a result of the Cabinet's failure to agree on measures to alleviate the country's acute economic problems, was assassinated on 1 June. Although it was not clear who was responsible for Karami's death, the Muslim community strongly suspected the Christian section of the divided Lebanese army and the Christian LF militia. Karami, a Sunni Muslim, had been a firm ally of Syria and had been one of the leaders who invited Syrian troops into Beirut in February, in the face of Christian opposition. Syria had yet to confront the problem of Christian-controlled east Beirut, to which no attempt had been made to extend the security plan.

In July 1987 representatives of Walid Joumblatt's Druze Parti Socialiste Progressiste, Nabih Berri's Amal, the Communist, Baath and Arab Democratic parties, and the Popular Nasserite Organization formed a brittle-seeming Unification and Liberation Front (the third of its type to be formed under Syrian auspices since 1977). The stated aims of the new, largely Muslim, left-wing front were: the unification of Lebanon; the expulsion of Israeli forces from southern Lebanon: the abolition of the confessional system of government; and the reintegration of the army.

RELATIONS WITH IRAN AND IRAQ

A realignment of Syrian policy towards Iran, which became more apparent during 1987, led to an increasingly uneasy relationship between the two countries. As international opinion turned against Iran in the Iran-Iraq War and moves were made to engineer a diplomatic settlement of the conflict, Syria's support for Iran became more of a liability. The USSR was critical of Syria's stance (reportedly withholding sales of arms to Syria in July), and, as the only Arab country, apart from Libya, to support Iran, Syria attracted the displeasure of other Arab states. (Libya switched its allegiance to Iraq in September.) Syria, significantly, responded to Iranian threats of reprisals against Saudi Arabia and Kuwait, after the deaths on 31 July of 275 Iranian pilgrims in riots in Mecca, by stating that it would not stand by and allow a fellow Arab country to be attacked with impunity. Syria's concern to regain the favour of Western nations and to play a full role in proposed Middle East peace initiatives by distancing itself from Islamic fundamentalist and anti-Arafat terrorist groups, and by seeking the release of Western hostages in Lebanon, brought it into dispute with Iran. Syrian troops in Beirut did not venture into the southern suburbs where Hezbollah (a group inspired by the Islamic revolution and backed by Iran) was based, but, after their deployment in February and to Iran's obvious annoyance, they harassed Hezbollah members and limited their freedom of movement in the parts of Lebanon under the group's effective jurisdiction. Syria also controlled the entry of Iranians into the country, and in June sent tanks and 'special forces' to surround the camps of Hezbollah militiamen and several hundred Iranian Revolutionary Guards, who were stationed at Baalbek in the Beka'a valley. Syria was evidently concerned about the destabilizing influence of Hezbollah's brand of Islamic fundamentalism, which aimed to create in Lebanon an Islamic republic on the Iranian model.

Syria's relations with Iran were further strained by the kidnapping in June 1987 of Charles Glass, an American journalist, allegedly by Hezbollah. This was the first abduction of a Westerner in west Beirut since the Syrian army assumed responsibility for security there in February, and was the cause of annoyance and embarrassment to Syria, which was eager to improve its relations with the USA. When, four weeks later, Glass escaped from his captors, his freedom was attributed to Syrian mediation with Hezbollah. Syrian influence was also instrumental in securing the release in September of a West German hostage, one of 23 Western captives who were being held in south Beirut. At the beginning of September the US Ambassador to Damascus, who had been recalled to Washington in November 1986, returned to Syria, and the US Government withdrew its opposition, of the preceding 10 months, to operations by US oil companies in Syria.

Rumours of a *rapprochment* between Syria and Iraq were revived by reports that President Assad and President Hussain had met secretly in Jordan in April 1987, at the instigation of King Hussein of Jordan and Crown Prince Abdullah of Saudi Arabia. It was confirmed that this meeting had taken place when, in November, the two leaders held talks with King Hussein and other leaders at an extraordinary summit meeting of the League of Arab States in Amman, Jordan. The summit, which had been organized by King Hussein to discuss the Iran-Iraq war, produced a unanimous statement expressing solidarity with Iraq, condemning Iran for prolonging the war and for its occupation of Arab (i.e. Iraqi) territory, and urging it to observe the cease-fire proposals contained in UN Security Council Resolution 598. Syria's acquiescence in the statement appeared to represent a significant modification in its support for Iran. It was widely reported that Syria had been offered financial inducements by Saudi Arabia (which is Syria's principal source of aid), Kuwait and other Gulf states to realign its policy on the Iran-Iraq War with majority Arab opinion, and compensatory supplies of oil, should such a realignment result in Iran's withholding oil shipments. However, after the

summit meeting, Syria announced that it had succeeded in obstructing an Iraqi proposal that Arab states should sever diplomatic relations with Iran, that a reconciliation with Iraq had not taken place, and that Syrian relations with Iran remained fundamentally unchanged. Syria had used its veto to prevent the adoption of an Iraqi proposal to readmit Egypt to membership of the League of Arab States, but it could not prevent the inclusion in the final communiqué of a clause permitting individual member nations to re-establish diplomatic relations with Egypt. By mid-February 1988, 11 Arab countries, including Iraq, had resumed diplomatic links with Egypt.

In March 1988 the Minister of Information, Muhammad Salman, announced that two months of Syrian mediation between Iran and the Arab states of the Gulf (designed to prevent an escalation of the Iran–Iraq War), which had been fiercely criticized by Iraq, had produced an Iranian undertaking to desist from attacks on tankers belonging to the members of the Gulf Co-operation Council (GCC).

In July 1987 Syria and Turkey signed a security protocol in which both agreed to curb the activities on their soil of terrorist and separatist groups carrying out operations against the other. Turkey believed that guerrilla attacks in its southeastern provinces had been organized by Kurdish exiles in Damascus. Turkey also assured Syria that the series of dams that it was building on the Euphrates river would not be deliberately used in such a way as to deprive Syria of vital water supplies further downstream.

GOVERNMENT CHANGES

A major government reshuffle took place in November 1987, following the resignation of the Prime Minister, Abd ar-Rauf al-Kassem. His Government had been accused of corruption and inefficiency, and of failure to solve the country's severe economic problems. Earlier, four ministers (in June those of Agriculture and of Construction; and, in October, those of Industry and of Supply and Internal Trade) had been forced to resign, following accusations of mismanagement, which led to votes of 'no confidence' in the People's Assembly. Mahmoud az-Zoubi, the Speaker of the People's Assembly, was appointed Prime Minister on 1 November. His Council of Ministers contained 15 new members.

SYRIAN AND IRANIAN SURROGATES CLASH IN LEBANON

The Syrian-inspired lifting of the siege of the Palestinian refugee camps in January 1988, was a carefully calculated move. Cynically speaking, it was politically inexpedient for Syria to continue to employ its proxy, Amal, in its attempt to suppress the PLO in Lebanon, at a time when the Palestinian *intifada* (uprising) in the Israeli-occupied territories (see below) was attracting the sympathy of the world (in particular, the Arab world) to the plight of the Palestinians and increasing support for Arafat's mainstream PLO. By suspending Amal's campaign against the (pro-Arafat) PLO, Nabih Berri's Amal forces could be deployed against the Iranian-backed Hezbollah, whose strength was viewed by Syria as a threat to its own ambitions to control Lebanon.

Amal's attacks were initially directed against Hezbollah bases in southern Lebanon, and clashes (the first military confrontation between the two groups) occurred at the end of March in the Nabatiyah area. On 9 April Amal claimed to have captured Hezbollah's last stronghold in the south, at Siddiqin, while Iranian Revolutionary Guards stationed at Sharqiyah and Jibshit had been ordered to leave the area.

In Beirut, Syria had demonstrated its opposition to hostage-taking by preventing a Kuwaiti Boeing 747, which had been hijacked by Islamic fundamentalists (alleged to be Lebanese), from landing at the city's airport in early April 1988. On 5 May fighting broke out between the Amal and Hezbollah militias (the latter supported by Iranian Revolutionary Guards) in the southern suburbs of Beirut. Attempts to impose a cease-fire through Iranian and Syrian mediation failed, and Syrian troops became involved in the fighting on 13 May when Hezbollah guerrillas, who had wrested control of about 90% of the 36-sq-km southern suburbs from Amal, briefly advanced into a Syrian-controlled area of west Beirut. On 15 May 7,500

Syrian troops encircled the southern suburbs, ready to advance into the enclave to restore order, while intensive negotiations took place between Syria and Iran, neither of which, despite their divergent ambitions in Lebanon, was eager to alienate the other. On 27 May several hundred Syrian troops moved into the southern suburbs of Beirut to enforce a cease-fire agreement reached by Syria, Iran and their militia proxies on the previous day. When the Syrian deployment was complete, Amal and Hezbollah were to close down their military operations in all parts of the southern suburbs, except in areas adjoining the Green Line which separated west Beirut from the Christian-controlled east of the city, where they would continue to be allowed to post their men. On 3 June, in accordance with the agreement, Nabih Berri announced the disbandment of the Amal militia in Beirut and the Beka'a valley (areas under Syrian control) and all other areas of the country except the south (which was not controlled by Syrian troops).

ARAFAT LOYALISTS DRIVEN OUT OF BEIRUT

In April 1988 a reconciliation was reported to have taken place between President Assad and Yasser Arafat, though Assad continued to insist on the severance of all relations between Arafat's Fatah and Egypt. The two leaders held discussions (their first since Arafat's expulsion from Syria in 1983) when Arafat attended the funeral in Damascus of Khalil al-Wazir ('Abu Jihad'), the military commander of the Palestine Liberation Army. At the end of April, Arafat loyalists in the Palestinian refugee camps of Chatila and Bourj el-Barajneh in Beirut, possibly interpreting Syria's support for the Palestinian *intifada* and subsequent indications of a *rapprochement* between their leader and Assad as evidence of the Syrian President's waning commitment to the revolt within the PLO, attempted to drive out the fighters belonging to the Syrian-backed group, al-Fatah Intifada (Fatah Uprising), led by PLO dissident 'Abu Musa'. The Syrian troops who had surrounded the camps in April 1987, did not attempt to intervene in the fighting but, with Syria's other surrogate in Lebanon's factional conflict, the Amal militia, otherwise occupied, they allowed reinforcements to reach the rebel Fatah group. On 27 June the Arafat loyalists in the camp of Chatila were overrun and surrendered to the forces of 'Abu Musa'. On the following day, Syria granted 100 PLO guerrillas safe passage from Chatila to the Palestinian camp at Ain al-Hilweh, near Sidon. On 7 July Bourj el-Barajneh, Yasser Arafat's last stronghold in Beirut, fell to 'Abu Musa' and 120 Arafat loyalists were evacuated to Ain al-Hilweh.

LEBANON FAILS TO ELECT A NEW PRESIDENT

Amin Gemayel's term of office as President of Lebanon was due to expire on 22 September 1988 and the National Assembly was required to elect a new President prior to that date. Syria, naturally, was concerned that a candidate sympathetic to its views should be elected. Talks between Syria and the US Under-Secretary of State for Near Eastern and South Asian Affairs, Richard Murphy, during the summer, failed to produce agreement on a candidate who would be acceptable to both sides and who would be likely to gain the support of both Muslims and Christians in Lebanon.

Three main contenders for the presidency (traditionally a post occupied by a Maronite Christian) emerged: Gen. Michel Awn, the Commander-in-Chief of the Armed Forces; Raymond Eddé, the exiled leader of the Maronite Bloc National; and Sulayman Franjiya, who was President of Lebanon between 1970 and 1976. The latter did not announce his candidacy until 16 August, two days before the election was scheduled to take place, and the news immediately united President Gemayel and Samir Geagea, the commander of the Christian LF militia, in opposition to Franjiya's candidature, on the grounds that he represented Syrian interests. It was Franjiya who, as President, had invited Syria to intervene militarily in Lebanon to end the civil war in 1976.

On 18 August, only 38 of the 76 surviving members of the National Assembly attended the session at which the new President was to be elected. The Speaker declared the session inquorate and the election was postponed. It was strongly alleged that a number of Christian deputies had been intimi-dated, threatened or forcibly prevented from attending the election by the LF and soldiers under the command of Gen. Awn.

Consultations between Syria and the USA resumed during September to find a compromise candidate for the presidency. It was reported that they had agreed to support the candidacy of Mikhail ad-Daher, a deputy in the National Assembly, but Christian leaders in Lebanon repeated their rejection of any candidate imposed upon them by foreign powers.

A second attempt to stage the presidential election was made on 22 September, but, again, the session of the National Assembly failed to achieve a quorum.

Only minutes before his term of office was due to expire, President Gemayel appointed a six-member interim military government, composed of three Christian and three Muslim officers, led by Gen. Awn, to rule until a new President was elected. Muslim politicians had refused to participate in an interim civilian government headed, contrary to the Constitution, by a Maronite Prime Minister, Pierre Hélou, instead of a Sunni Muslim. The three Muslim officers named in the interim military Government refused to take up their posts, while the two Christian members of the existing civilian Government surrendered their posts in recognition of the authority of the interim military administration.

Lebanon was plunged into a constitutional crisis, with two Governments, one Christian, in east Beirut, and one predominantly Muslim, in west Beirut, claiming legitimacy. Syria refused to recognize the interim military Government and there were fears that, unless a new President could be elected, the fact of dual-authority would formalize what was already an effective partition of the country into Christian and Muslim cantons.

The new interim military Government was regarded with suspicion by the LF militia, which feared that it would seek an accommodation with Syria in order to further the presidential ambitions of Gen. Awn. In February 1989 there was a major confrontation between the LF and Lebanese army brigades (both Christian and Muslim) loyal to Gen. Awn. While neither side achieved a decisive victory, the authority of the Lebanese army (which had been steadily eroded) was restored as a result of the clashes. On 17 February, after having suffered heavy losses, the LF was ordered by its commander, Samir Geagea, to withdraw from many parts of east Beirut. In response to allegations by Gen. Awn that it was levying illegal taxes, the LF agreed to close its 'customs point' in east Beirut, and Geagea subsequently claimed that both the LF and the Lebanese army were united in the aim of expelling Syrian forces from Lebanon.

GEN. AWN'S 'WAR OF LIBERATION'

In March 1989 the most violent clashes for two years erupted in Beirut between Christian and Muslim brigades of the Lebanese army, loyal to Gen. Awn, and Syrian-backed Muslim militia, positioned on either side of the Green Line. While the immediate cause of the fighting was the blockade of illegal ports in west and south Beirut by Christian forces, Gen. Awn declared at a press conference on 14 March that his Government had decided to take all measures for the immediate withdrawal of Syrian forces from Lebanon.

During the ensuing six months, Gen. Awn's self-declared 'war of liberation' developed into one of the most violent confrontations of the Lebanese conflict, causing heavy casualties in both the Christian and Muslim communities. Syria's claim that its forces were not directly involved in the hostilities was regarded as disingenuous (to say the least), but most observers doubted whether Gen. Awn realistically expected to achieve the withdrawal of Syrian forces from Lebanon by military means. Rather, his aim was perceived to be the 'internationalization' of the Lebanese conflict in order to increase diplomatic pressure on Syria to effect such a withdrawal.

The ferocity of the fighting and the scale of the casualties prompted several diplomatic initiatives to secure a peace settlement (for a full account, see chapter on Lebanon). However, successive plans for peace foundered on the question of the withdrawal of Syria's estimated 35,000–40,000 troops in Lebanon, on which Gen. Awn insisted as an essential condition of any cease-fire agreement. At an emergency summit meeting of Arab leaders in Casablanca during 23 May–28 May, the proposal (supported by Egypt, Iraq, Jordan and the PLO) that Syria should immediately withdraw its troops from Lebanon was abandoned in response to Syrian opposition. Indeed, as the 'war of liberation' progressed, it became apparent that no agency was able or willing to exert sufficient diplomatic pressure on Syria to gain such a concession. While the Arab League was on one occasion officially to condemn Syria as the principal obstacle to peace in Lebanon, and while many Arab leaders were reportedly ready to admit, in private, that this was so, the Arab world feared that Syria's withdrawal from Lebanon would be perceived as a victory by Iraq (for Syrian–Iraqi rivalry in Lebanon, see below) and that it might lead to a direct confrontation between Iraq and Syria. While the USSR endorsed the proposals of the Tripartite Arab League Committee on Lebanon (formed at the Arab League summit meeting in May 1989), and urged Syria to accept them, the influence that it was able to exert as Syria's principal supplier of arms was limited.

By August 1989 it had become clear that Syria was prepared to disregard international censure of its role in Lebanon and to wage a war of attrition against the Lebanese army. Its refusal to consider any compromise with regard to the withdrawal of its forces stemmed from the longstanding strategic consideration of its need to control Lebanon in order to guard against any Israeli strike in the Beka'a valley. However, Syria was restrained from using its overwhelming military superiority to impose its authority on 'Christian Lebanon' by several factors. Initially, Syria feared that Israel might come to the defence of Lebanese Christians in the event of a full-scale military assault on the Christian enclave. Also, for economic reasons, it was anxious to avoid any further deterioration of its relations with Western countries, and with the USSR, which such an assault might have provoked.

In September 1989 the Tripartite Arab Committee on Lebanon announced details of a seven-point plan for peace in Lebanon which, unlike its previous diplomatic initiatives, did not demand the withdrawal of Syrian forces from Lebanon. Rather, in recognition of the futility of attempting to persuade Syria to withdraw its forces, diplomatic efforts in support of the new peace plan now concentrated on persuading Gen. Awn to accept its terms. The new plan for peace envisaged a cease-fire (to be supervised by a Lebanese security committee under the auspices of the Assistant Secretary-General of the Arab League, Lakhdar al-Ibrahimi); the ending of the Syrian naval blockade of the Christian enclave; and the convening of the Lebanese National Assembly to discuss a 'charter of national conciliation' drafted by the Tripartite Committee. The new plan presented Gen. Awn with a dilemma, since he had already, on previous occasions, rejected its principal proposals. At the same time, it had become clear that the 'war of liberation' was being fought in vain. The evacuation in early September of US diplomatic personnel and the closure of the US embassy in Beirut, in response to alleged threats of 'Christian terrorism', were widely regarded as signalling the end of Awn's hopes of achieving his aim though international intervention. Moreover, by September more than 800 people were reported to have been killed, and more than 2,000 injured, in the six months since the escalation of the hostilities. The Christian population (those who had not already fled Beirut), which had at first enthusiastically supported the 'war of liberation', was badly demoralized. On 22 September, following reports that the French Minister of Foreign Affairs had warned him that he could expect no international assistance if he refused to accept the Tripartite Arab Committee's latest proposals, Gen. Awn announced that he had abandoned the 'war of liberation' against Syria and agreed to the seven points of the Committee's peace plan for Lebanon. However, he subsequently vowed to continue the war by political means until the liberation was complete. For Syria, therefore, the problem remained of how to impose its authority on Christian Lebanese by means other than military force, since, ultimately, it had been international pressure which had forced Gen. Awn to abandon his campaign. On 25 September it was announced that the Lebanese National Assembly would convene in Saudi Arabia on 30 September to discuss political reforms aimed at

ending the Lebanese conflict. The proposed reforms envisaged, among other things the transfer of executive powers from the Christian Maronite president to the Sunni Muslim Prime Minister; the ending of sectarianism in the army and the civil service; and an increase in the number of seats in the National Assembly, from 99 to 108.

In October 1989 the Lebanese National Assembly endorsed a charter of national reconciliation (the Taif agreement—for full details, see chapter on Lebanon, p. 659), which envisaged a continuing role for the Syrian armed forces in Lebanon by stipulating that they should assist in the implementation of a security plan incorporated in the agreement. The endorsement of the charter by the National Assembly was denounced by Gen. Awn as a betrayal of Lebanese sovereignty, since Christian deputies to the Lebanese National Assembly had reportedly assured Gen. Awn that they would permit concessions on the question of political reform in Lebanon only in exchange for a full withdrawal of Syrian forces.

Following a meeting of the newly-formed Lebanese Cabinet on 28 November 1989, it was announced that Gen. Awn had again been dismissed as Commander-in-Chief of the Lebanese army, and that Gen. Emile Lahud had been appointed in his place. It was feared that Syrian forces would now launch an assault on Awn's stronghold in Baabda, east Beirut. Samir Geagea, the commander of the LF, announced that, in the event of such an assault, the LF would fight beside Gen. Awn, even though the Taif agreement had, to a large extent, been facilitated by the co-operation of Lebanon's Maronite leaders. Geagea's refusal to reject the Taif agreement led Gen. Awn to declare the LF to be an ally of Syria, and precipitated intense fighting between Awn's forces and the LF in early 1990 for control of the Christian enclave in Beirut.

In October 1990 thousands of Syrian troops were deployed to evict Gen. Awn from the presidential palace at Baabda, after President Hrawi of Lebanon had requested their assistance.

THE INTIFADA AND THE SHULTZ PLAN

In December 1987 a violent Palestinian uprising (*intifada*) against Israeli occupation of the West Bank and Gaza Strip, erupted in the Occupied Territories. At the end of February 1988, with the *intifada* showing no sign of moderating in intensity, the US Secretary of State, George Shultz, embarked on a tour of Middle Eastern capitals, including Damascus, in an attempt to solicit support for a new peace initiative. The Shultz Plan proposed an international peace conference and direct talks between Israel and each of its adversaries (excluding the PLO), and an interim period of limited autonomy for Palestinians in the Occupied Territories, pending a permanent negotiated settlement (for full details, see Documents on Palestine, p. 97). President Assad stopped short of rejecting the plan outright, but, in certain fundamental respects, it was impossible for any Arab leader to accept: it failed to recognize the right of the PLO to participate in peace negotiations or the right of the Palestinians to self-determination. Further talks between Shultz and Assad in April failed to reconcile the two sides.

At the beginning of June 1988 an extraordinary summit meeting of the Arab League was held in Algiers to discuss the *intifada* and the Arab–Israeli conflict in general. The final communiqué of the summit, endorsed by all 21 League members, including Syria, rendered the Shultz Plan effectively moribund by demanding the participation of the PLO in any future peace conference, endorsing the Palestinians' right to self-determination and urging the establishment of an independent Palestinian state in the West Bank.

Syria, alone of all the Arab states, refused to recognize the independent Palestinian State (proclaimed at the 19th session of the PNC in Algiers in November 1988), in accordance with its long-standing policy of preventing any other force in Lebanon from acquiring sufficient power to challenge Syrian interests there (for full details of the Declaration of Palestinian Independence, see Documents on Palestine, p. 97).

FOREIGN RELATIONS

The cease-fire in the Iran–Iraq War, which came into force on 20 August 1988, created a number of problems for Syria. As the sole Arab supporter of Iran, Syria was already isolated, and the cessation of hostilities presented Iraq with an opportunity to settle old scores with its Baath rival, initially by attempting to thwart Syrian plans for domination over Lebanon. In September, Iraq was reportedly supplying arms and money to the Christian LF in Lebanon and, following the failure of the Lebanese National Assembly to elect a new President, Iraq proclaimed its support for the interim military administration appointed by President Gemayel, which was opposed by Syria. After March 1989, when the 'war of liberation' waged by the Lebanese army against Syrian forces in Lebanon began, Iraq became the principal supplier of arms to the Lebanese army. The expression of Syrian–Iraqi rivalry by proxy in Lebanon also complicated attempts by the Arab League to achieve a cease-fire there following the escalation of hostilities in March 1989, since it was feared that the withdrawal of Syrian forces from Lebanon might provoke a direct confrontation between Iraq and Syria.

Syria found itself on the same side as Iraq in a dispute with Turkey over the diversion of water from the Euphrates river in order to fill the reservoir supplying Turkey's newly-constructed Atatürk dam. In January 1990 Syria lodged a formal complaint with Turkey over the effects of the diversion on Syria's water and electricity supplies. However, the Turkish Government rejected the complaint, claiming that it had increased the supply of water to Iraq and Syria by 50% between November 1989 and January 1990 in order to make good the loss of water caused by the diversion in early 1990. The Syrian and Turkish Ministers of Foreign Affairs met in Turkey in June 1990 to discuss relations, in particular the sharing of the Euphrates waters.

SYRIA AND THE 1990–91 GULF CRISIS

In April 1990 Syria expressed support for Iraq's right to defend itself in any conflict with Israel, the ideological differences between Syria and Iraq notwithstanding. In August 1990, however, Syria was eager to exploit the diplomatic opportunities arising from Iraq's invasion of Kuwait, and, in particular, to improve its relations with the USA and Egypt. In December 1989 Egypt and Syria had agreed to re-establish diplomatic relations after a rupture lasting almost 12 years, and in May 1990 President Mubarak of Egypt visited Syria, the first such visit by an Egyptian leader since 1977. The talks he held with President Assad reportedly concentrated on the faltering Middle East peace process and on means of achieving Arab unity to oppose the increased emigration of Soviet Jews to Israel, a process which had begun in 1989 and accelerated in early 1990.

Syria supported Egypt's efforts to co-ordinate Arab responses to Iraq's invasion of Kuwait, and agreed, at an emergency summit meeting of the Arab League, held in Cairo on 10 August 1990, to send troops to Saudi Arabia as part of a pan-Arab deterrent force supporting the US effort to deter an Iraqi invasion of Saudi Arabia. Despite widespread popular support among Syria's Palestinian population for the Iraqi President, Saddam Hussain, Syria committed itself to the demand for an unconditional Iraqi withdrawal from Kuwait, and later in August the first contingent of Syrian troops was deployed in Saudi Arabia, joining a multinational force that was predominantly composed of US military personnel. In September the US Secretary of State, James Baker, made a visit to Damascus, where he held talks with President Assad. The USA emphasized the importance of establishing a dialogue with Syria, in view of its opposition to Iraq's occupation of Kuwait. Syria, for its part, claimed that its troops were in Saudi Arabia purely for defensive purposes. In late September President Assad visited Iran, where he held discussions with President Rafsanjani. They reportedly agreed on the desirability of a regional security system, but were unable to elaborate a common position regarding the deployment of Western forces in the Gulf region, which Iran had strongly condemned.

In late October 1990 the objections of the United Kingdom prevented the EC from removing the economic sanctions which it had applied against Syria since 1986. In late November 1990, however, it became apparent that Syria's participation in the US-led multinational force was transforming its relations with the West, when diplomatic ties were restored between Syria and the United Kingdom. By the beginning of December it was estimated that some 20,000 Syrian troops had been deployed in Saudi Arabia.

In mid-January 1991 President Saddam Hussain of Iraq rejected a message from President Assad, who sought to persuade him that Iraq's occupation of Kuwait benefited Israel alone. Following attacks by Iraqi *Scud* missiles on Israel, Syria warned Israel not to become militarily involved in the crisis in the Gulf region, and implied that it might be obliged to withdraw from the multinational force in the event of an Israeli attack on an Arab state. Subsequent statements, however, indicated that Syria would tolerate limited Israeli retaliation against Iraq for the missile attacks.

In early 1991 the overwhelming military defeat of Iraq by the US-led multinational force placed Syria in a stronger position with regard to virtually all of its major regional concerns, thus vindicating the pragmatic stance adopted by the Government with regard to the crisis in the Gulf region. Syria consolidated the improvement in relations with Egypt which had begun in December 1989, and laid the foundation for increased co-operation with Egypt in matters of regional security. In early March 1991 the Ministers of Foreign Affairs of the members of the GCC (Saudi Arabia, Kuwait, Qatar, Bahrain, the UAE and Oman) met the Egyptian and Syrian Ministers of Foreign Affairs in Damascus to discuss regional security issues. The formation of an Arab peace-keeping force, comprising mainly Egyptian and Syrian troops, was subsequently announced. In early May, however, Egypt announced its decision to withdraw all of its forces from the Gulf region within three months, thus casting doubt on the future of joint Syrian-Egyptian security arrangements. These have remained in doubt, although in May 1992 the Secretary of the GCC stated the determination of its member states to create a regional security role for Egyptian and Syrian forces.

Syria's decision to ally itself, in opposition to Iraq, with the Western powers and the so-called 'moderate' Arab states led the USA to realize that it could no longer seek to exclude it from any role in the resolution of the Arab-Israeli conflict. After the conclusion of hostilities with Iraq, US diplomacy focused on seeking to initiate negotiations between Israel, the Arab states, including Syria, and Palestinian representatives. The loss of credibility which the PLO had suffered as a result of its support for Iraq in the Gulf War left all the Arab states in a stronger position to dictate the final terms of a peace settlement with Israel, and was especially gratifying to Syria, which had long opposed Yasser Arafat's leadership.

In March 1991 the Israeli Prime Minister, Itzhak Shamir, indicated that Israel was prepared to take steps to reduce tension in the Middle East, and reaffirmed his commitment to the peace initiative which he had proposed in May 1989 (see chapter on Israel). However, he was dismissive of the prospects for peace with Syria. In late April, immediately prior to a visit to Damascus by the US Secretary of State, James Baker, the official Syrian newspaper, *Tishrin*, listed a number of Syrian conditions for a peace settlement with Israel. These included the unconditional withdrawal of Israel from the Occupied Territories; the safeguarding of Palestinian national rights; and a prominent role for the UN in any future peace conference. The Israeli Government had already made it clear that it regarded these conditions as unacceptable.

Despite attempts in early May 1991 by both the USA and the USSR to create sufficient common ground between Israel and Syria for peace negotiations to begin, Baker stated that there were still 'significant' differences between Israel and Syria regarding the holding of a Middle East peace conference. Syria remained adamant that talks with Israel should take place within the framework of an international conference, with the full participation of the UN, and that afterwards such a conference should reconvene at regular intervals. Israel remained opposed both to the participation of the UN and to the reconvening of the conference after an initial session had been held. The USA, for its part, excluded the possibility of holding a peace conference without Syrian participation.

On 18 July 1991, in a remarkable *volte-face*, President Assad agreed for the first time, following a meeting with the US Secretary of State, to participate in direct negotiations with Israel at a regional peace conference, for which the terms of reference would be a comprehensive peace settlement based on UN Security Council Resolutions 242 and 338. By agreeing to participate in a peace conference on the terms proposed by the USA, Syria decisively increased the diplomatic pressure on Israel to do likewise. However, the publicly-stated positions of the Syrian and Israeli Governments remained as far apart as ever. Each claimed, towards the end of July 1991, to have received confidential (and incompatible) assurances from the USA: Israel with regard to the composition of a Jordanian-Palestinian delegation to the peace conference; and Syria with regard to the return of the Israeli-occupied Golan Heights. On 4 August the Israeli Cabinet formally agreed to attend a peace conference on the terms proposed by the USA and the USSR.

NEGOTIATIONS WITH ISRAEL

By late October 1993—following an initial, 'symbolic' session of the conference held in Madrid, Spain, in October 1991, and attended by Israeli, Syrian, Egyptian, Lebanese and Palestinian-Jordanian delegations—11 sessions of bilateral negotiations had been held between Israeli and Syrian delegations. In April 1992 they had proceeded to debate the precise meaning of UN Security Council Resolution 242, but the Israeli Government continued firmly to reject any exchange of occupied land—including the Golan Heights—in return for a peace settlement. In May, owing to the failure of bilateral negotiations to achieve any progress towards a peace settlement, Syria and Lebanon refused to attend multilateral negotiations, convened in Belgium, Austria, Canada and Japan, to discuss, among other issues, water resources and the question of Palestinian refugees. In the aftermath of the further disintegration of the USSR, which took place in December 1991, and the consequent erosion of its position as a potential counterfoil to the USA's Middle Eastern policies, Syria remained obliged actively to support and participate in the US peace initiative. With regard to other regional issues, however, the Syrian Government appeared determined not to simply acquiesce in the interests of the USA, announcing, in mid-April 1992, that it would continue to maintain air links with Libya, in defiance of the sanctions which the UN had imposed on that country (see chapter on Libya). In late April, in an attempt to allay suspicions of its Middle Eastern policies, the US Administration formally assured the Syrian Government that it had no hostile intentions towards it.

The formation, in mid-July 1992, of a new Israeli coalition government, in which the Labour Party was the dominant element, aroused fears in Syria that any improvement in such a government's relations with the USA might increase the pressure on Syria to make disadvantageous concessions in the ongoing Middle Eastern peace process. The sixth round of bilateral negotiations between Israeli and Syrian delegations, which commenced on 24 September in Washington, DC, and lasted for a month, seemed at times to be close to achieving real progress on the issue of the Israeli-occupied Golan Heights. The new Israeli Government was reported to have indicated its willingness to consider some form of compromise, although there was no sign that it was prepared to meet Syria's minimum demand: Israel's full and unconditional compliance with UN Security Council Resolution 242, which requires, among other things, the withdrawal of Israeli armed forces from territories occupied in 1967.

Initially, the Declaration of Principles on Palestinian Self-Rule in the Occupied Territories, signed by Israel and the PLO on 13 September 1993, drew a guarded response from Syria. Subsequently, however, President Assad indicated that he had serious reservations about the agreement, and that he regarded the secret negotiations between Israel and the PLO which had led to it as having weakened the united Arab position in the ongoing peace process with Israel. It appeared that Syria would not actively oppose the agreement, but there was no sign that it would cease to support those Palestinian factions, such as the Damascus-based Popular Front for the Liberation of Palestine—General Command (PFLP—GC), which had vowed to do so. Syria was reported to fear that Israel might now view the terms of the Declaration of Principles concluded with the PLO as a model for an agreement with Syria on the Golan Heights (i.e. the exchange of only a

partial withdrawal of Israeli armed forces from the Golan Heights for a comprehensive peace settlement).

In January 1994 Syria agreed to resume bilateral negotiations with Israel, claiming that it had secured a commitment from Jordan to delay the finalization of any agreement with Israel until Lebanon and Syria had negotiated their own agreements with Israel. On 16 January President Assad met with the US President Clinton for talks in Geneva aimed at giving fresh momentum to the negotiations. The Israeli Prime Minister, Itzhak Rabin, responded by announcing that a referendum would have to be held in Israel on the issue of the withdrawal from the Golan Heights; Syrian Minister of Foreign Affairs, Farouk ash-Shara', claimed that this would contravene international law. Talks between the two countries continued in Washington, DC, on 24 January, but were temporarily suspended on 27 February following the murder of some 30 Muslim worshippers at a mosque in Hebron on the West Bank by a right-wing Jewish extremist. Assad continued to reject proposals to hold secret talks with Israel and ignored Israeli demands to prevent attacks by Lebanese militia groups on the Israeli forces in south Lebanon. In late April Warren Christopher, the US Secretary of State, visited the Middle East in what was seen as an attempt to break the deadlock over the Golan Heights. Under the Israeli plan, which would be phased over a period of eight years, Syria would initially be granted control over the four Druze settlements in the Golan Heights, the next stage would involve the closure of Israeli settlements in the Golan, and the final phase would be a full-scale withdrawal. In May, when an agreement was signed between Israel and the PLO providing for Palestinian self-rule in the Gaza Strip and Jericho, Syrian officials remained sceptical, arguing in favour of a united Arab approach to the peace settlement. Syria similarly expressed dissatisfaction at the agreement reached between Israel and Jordan in early June, accusing the two sides of placing obstacles in the way of reaching a comprehensive peace settlement in the region.

In July and August 1994 Warren Christopher visited Damascus for further talks; following the August trip he acknowledged that major differences still remained between Israel and Syria, but claimed that a 'psychological barrier' had been broken through. The UN envoy, Dennis Ross, met with Israeli and Syrian leaders in September as speculation grew about possible secret talks between the two countries. In Israel Itzhak Rabin faced growing public discontent over the prospect of withdrawal from the Golan Heights, and in late September a group of Labour party members submitted a proposal to the Knesset to table a law requiring the Government to secure an absolute majority in order to withdraw from the Golan. The Middle East peace process was again curtailed in mid-October following the events in the Gulf (see Kuwait). On 18 October a group of 300 Syrian Jews were allowed to emigrate to Israel in what was seen as a gesture of goodwill on the part of the Syrian Government towards its Israeli neighbour. President Clinton attended the signing of the peace treaty between Israel and Jordan on 26 October and on the following day he visited Syria—the first visit to the country by a US President for 20 years. Pressure on President Assad to reach an agreement with Israel over the Golan Heights increased following the Israeli-Jordanian treaty and it was reported that Assad might be considering Israel's proposal for a phased withdrawal but over a shorter period of time.

SYRIAN DOMINANCE IN LEBANON

By aligning itself with the Western powers and the moderate Arab states against Iraq in August 1990, Syria had obtained a free rein to consolidate its interests in Lebanon. In October 1990 it had acted to suppress the revolt led by Gen. Michel Awn (see above) as the first step towards the implementation of the Taif agreement. The Taif agreement stipulated a formal role for Syrian forces in Lebanon, assigning to them the responsibility for maintaining security there until the various Lebanese militia had been disbanded and the Lebanese army could itself assume that role. The implementation of the Taif agreement accelerated in the aftermath of Iraq's military defeat by the US-led multinational force in February 1991, and it culminated in the signing, in May, of a treaty of 'fraternity, co-operation and co-ordination' between Syria and Lebanon.

In late May 1992 there was international concern at the escalating tension between Israel and Syria, as expressed in southern Lebanon. Syria feared that the USA might permit Israel to undermine, through military action, the implementation of the Taif agreement. The possibility of direct conflict between Syrian and Israeli armed forces arose from Syria's decision to allow Hezbollah fighters to continue to mount attacks on northern Israeli settlements, in the belief that only by continued coercion would Israel withdraw from occupied Arab territories. It is widely recognized that Syria has used its ability to control the supply of Iranian arms to Hezbollah in order to raise, or reduce, pressure on the Israeli Government in the context of the Middle East peace process. By the same token, the Israeli Government cited attacks by Hezbollah fighters in justification of its refusal to comply with UN Security Council Resolution 425 and withdraw its armed forces from the southern Lebanese 'buffer zone'. In July 1993 Israeli armed forces launched their most intense offensive against the positions of Hezbollah and other guerrilla factions in southern Lebanon since 'Operation Peace for Galilee' in 1982. Israeli aircraft were also reported to have attacked the positions of Syrian armed forces in the Beka'a valley. In February 1994 four Israeli soldiers were killed by Hezbollah fighters in the 'buffer zone'. In May the leader of an Islamic resistance group was abducted by Israeli forces and on 21 June, following an ambush by the Hezbollah in which three Israeli soldiers were killed, the Israeli forces conducted air raids over the 'buffer zone'.

In late March 1992 some Syrian armed forces began to withdraw from Beirut, in preparation for the withdrawal of all Syrian armed forces to eastern Lebanon by September 1992 (in accordance with the Taif agreement). However, Syrian influence on Lebanese internal affairs remained pervasive and was regarded by some observers as having contributed to the resignation of the Lebanese Government on 6 May. The former Lebanese Prime Minister, Omar Karami, alleged that, had it not been for Lebanon's close relations with Syria, Western economic aid to Lebanon would have been more substantial, and the economic crisis that had led to his Government's resignation less severe.

The decision of the new Lebanese Government to hold elections to the National Assembly in August and September 1992, before the redeployment of Syrian armed forces to eastern Lebanon had taken place, attracted strong criticism both in Lebanon and abroad. Lebanese Maronites and other Christian groups, and Western governments argued that the continued presence of the Syrian forces would prejudice the outcome of the elections. However, the Lebanese Government argued that its own army was still unable to guarantee the country's security in the absence of the Syrian armed forces, and that the timetable for elections, as stipulated by the Taif agreement, should be observed. Syria claimed that the continued presence of its forces did not contravene the Taif agreement, which allowed for them to remain to assist the Lebanese Government until constitutional reforms had been fully implemented. There was no doubt, however, that the electoral process had been severely compromised in the eyes of Christian, especially Maronite, Lebanese. In many Maronite constituencies the participation of the electorate was very low, although there was not—as some Maronite leaders urged—a total boycott. Other Maronite leaders adopted a more pragmatic approach, acknowledging Syria's domination of Lebanon as a *fait accompli*. In late 1993 some 35,000 Syrian troops were deployed throughout Lebanon.

POLICY IN THE 1990s

In May 1990 elections were held to the People's Assembly, in which the number of seats had been increased from 195 to 250. Candidates representing the Baath Party were elected to 134 seats, 54% of the total, compared with 66% of the total in elections held in 1986. Other parties which had joined the Baath Party in the National Progressive Front, an electoral coalition, were elected to 32 seats, while independent candidates were elected to 84 seats. Some 60% of the electorate were reported to have participated in the elections, which were contested by 9,765 candidates.

There was speculation in late 1991 that President Assad was preparing to introduce a degree of liberalization into Syria's political system, which is widely regarded as one of the most autocratic in the world. In December it was announced that 2,864 political prisoners were to be released. In March 1992, in a speech to the People's Assembly, Assad indicated that new political parties might in future be established in Syria. However, he rejected the adoption by Syria of foreign democratic frameworks as unsuited to the country's level of economic development. In late June a reshuffle of the Council of Ministers took place in which most senior ministers retained their portfolios.

In January 1994 the future stability of the regime appeared to be in jeopardy when Assad's eldest son, Basel, who had been expected to succeed his father as president, died in a motor accident. The President's second son, Bashar, was instructed to take up the role played by his brother in a move to avoid a power struggle. In June the Minister of Electricity, Kamal al-Baba, was dismissed following two years of electricity shortages and power cuts. In August 16 senior officials, including the Special Forces Commander, Ali Haidar, were removed from office in what considered to be an attempt by Assad to consolidate his position, weaken the influence of the old guard and improve the country's international stance. At the People's Assembly elections held on 24 August more than 7,000 candidates were presented, but turnout at the polls was recorded at just over 50% of the electorate. The coalition parties in the National Progressive Front maintained their dominant position, winning 167 seats; the remaining seats were won by independent candidates. Leading business people were reported to be among the 158 newly-elected members.

Syria remained on the US list of countries which sponsored the drugs trade and terrorism; however, US President Clinton visited Damascus in October 1994 (see above) and it was widely believed that Western aid and investment had in the past been offered to Syria in exchange for its disassociation with the PFLP-GC and other, similar groups. The Syrian Government indicated that it would not bow to pressure from the USA and in June a military co-operation agreement was signed with Russia securing new Russian military supplies. Agreements were also pursued with European nations and in March the Minister of Foreign Affairs, Farouk ash-Shara', visited Germany to strengthen bilateral economic ties. In September Farouk ash-Shara' travelled to London for talks with British Foreign Minister, Douglas Hurd, following the latter's visit to Damascus in October 1993. Hurd was reported to be in favour of ending the EU embargo on weapons supplies to Syria, although the lifting of the embargo would require EU and US approval.

The Prime Ministers of Egypt and Syria met on two occasions in 1993 to discuss issues concerning foreign policy, trade, industry, agriculture, water resources and energy. Agreements were signed with Lebanon on 20 September 1994 covering tax and customs exemptions, the allocation of water from the Orontes river, and plans for joint investment in a cement plant in Syria. Following a meeting of the Ministers of Foreign Affairs of Iran, Turkey and Syria in mid-August, a statement was issued reaffirming their commitment to the territorial integrity of Iraq and appealing to Saddam Hussain to increase co-operation with the UN and to lift the economic blockade against Iraq's Kurdish and Shi'a populations.

Economy

Revised for this edition by ALAN J. DAY

The Syrian economy must be viewed against a background of regional geopolitics and the internal political developments that have taken place since the Baath Party came to power in 1963. As a 'confrontation' state, a portion of whose land has been under Israeli occupation since 1967, Syria bears a heavy burden of defence expenditure, which consumes more than one-half of current spending under the annual budget. At the same time, its position as a regional power has encouraged Syria to intervene elsewhere in the area, notably in Lebanon, where it has had a costly military presence since 1976. The continuing involvement in Lebanon, combined with the threat of outright war with Israel and the history of bad relations with neighbouring Iraq (which have, in turn, influenced relations with the moderate Arab states of the Persian (Arabian) Gulf), all affect the Syrian economy. In 1976–77, for example, Iraq decided to stop pumping petroleum through Syria to the Mediterranean coast, thus depriving the Government in Damascus of valuable transit revenues and the benefits of easily accessible petroleum supplies at a favourable price. The pipeline was closed again in 1982, but Syria was subsequently able to buy oil from Iran at concessionary rates.

Syria has been heavily dependent on aid from other Arab petroleum-producing countries. However, there have been interruptions in this aid. At the Baghdad summit meeting of the Arab League in 1978, Arab states pledged $1,850m. per year, for 10 years, to Syria's military effort, but the recession in the oil industry and displeasure with Syria's regional policy, in particular its support for Iran in the Gulf War against Arab Iraq, reduced the amount of Arab aid from $1,600m. in 1981 to about $700m. in 1986, most of which was provided by Saudi Arabia.

The internal political upheavals of the past three decades have also profoundly affected the Syrian economy and disrupted attempts at sustained development. During the three-year union with Egypt (the United Arab Republic—UAR) from 1958 to 1961, agrarian reform and nationalization were introduced. The country's first Five-Year Plan was inaugurated during the union, and covered the period 1961–65. The nationalization programme was reversed after the dissolution of the union, and the land reform law was amended in favour of the landowners. However, in June 1963, following the Baath-dominated coup, all amendments to the agrarian reform law were abrogated, and the law itself was made even stricter. The banks were nationalized in that year, and a rigorous nationalization of industry and trade was begun in 1965. By the time that Hafiz al-Assad seized power in November 1970, there had been a radical transformation of the country's economic structure, with the economic power of the landowners, merchants and industrialists greatly weakened, and the public sector dominant.

President Assad relaxed the economy somewhat after coming to power, partly in an attempt to widen his power base: he introduced some liberalization of foreign trade early in his presidency; a foreign investment law was promulgated in 1971; and this was followed by several related articles of legislation.

The Arab–Israeli war of October 1973 caused damage to Syria estimated at $1,800m. Latakia port, the Banias and Tartous oil terminals and the huge Homs complex in central Syria, which then housed the country's only petroleum refinery and generated more than 40% of its power needs, were virtually destroyed. The reconstruction effort necessary to restore the Syrian economy was immense, but the Government acted swiftly, introducing measures of economic liberalization, to encourage investment, in early 1974. Business confidence gradually began to return, to the extent that the third Development Plan (1971–75) ended with a flourish of unprecedented growth. This, in turn, prompted the Government to reinforce investment incentives in certain sectors and to initiate an ambitious fourth Development Plan for the

period 1976–80, only to find itself confronted, once again, with the economic repercussions of regional political problems.

The fifth Development Plan (1981–85) and its successor (1986–90) concentrated on trying to finish projects already under way rather than launching ambitious new schemes. The growth targets set by the fifth Plan were noticeably more modest than those in the fourth, but even these were not achieved.

In the late 1980s, the economy was in a state of crisis, with the population suffering increasing hardship. According to the IMF, Syria's total reserves minus gold in mid-1986 stood at only $10m., although by the end of 1987 reserves had risen to $223m., the highest end-of-year total since 1984. At the end of 1988 reserves of foreign exchange amounted to $191m. The scarcity of foreign exchange caused a shortage of spare parts and raw materials for industry, and production was substantially below capacity, with some factories ceasing production altogether. Corruption and mismanagement in the state industrial and agricultural sectors also affected output. The economic crisis led to the imposition of strict curbs on the 'black market' and on the issuing of import licences, which created difficulties for the private sector.

Budget expenditure was reduced in real terms during the late 1980s, and zero or negative economic growth rates were recorded from 1986 to 1988. According to World Bank estimates, Syria's GNP per head in 1991, was $1,160, having declined in real terms at an average rate of 1.4% per year since 1980. Syria's GDP in 1991 was estimated to be $17,236m., having grown in real terms at an average rate of 2.6% per year since 1980 (compared with an average annual growth of 9.9% between 1970 and 1980).

In the absence of a Middle East peace settlement, Syria's best hope for economic progress lies in diversification of its sources of development finance and export revenues and in improved economic management to restore confidence in investment. The 1980 friendship treaty with the USSR and Syria's alleged links with international terrorism affected US aid to the country. In 1983 such aid was halted altogether. Syria's alleged involvement in international terrorism also affected the flow of aid from the EC and from individual European countries. Lending by multinational institutions, meanwhile, has been hampered by the slow rate of project implementation and, more recently, by Syria's debt arrears. Syria does, however, enjoy considerable support from the various Arab aid organizations.

Participation in the US-led multinational force against Iraq in 1990/91 was calculated to increase Syria's access to aid from the USA, the EC and the 'moderate' Arab states, among other diplomatic benefits. In the event, Syria was widely regarded as the main regional beneficiary of the war, particularly in the economic sphere. Bolstered by higher world oil prices, GDP grew by more than 5% in real terms in 1991 and the trade balance went into healthy surplus. At the same time there was a major influx of aid from Arab, Western and Japanese sources, while economic deregulation and new tax incentives helped to stimulate private investment by local and foreign businesses. On the negative side, the collapse of the USSR in 1991 presaged economic problems for Syria, to the extent that large sectors of its economy had been oriented towards exporting low-quality goods to the USSR.

Syria's leading exports remain petroleum, cotton and phosphates, which depend on the fickle world commodity markets and, in the case of cotton, on agricultural policies and the unreliable rainfall in much of the country. The services sector, dependent on tourism and transit trade, remains extremely vulnerable to the political situation in the region.

In 1992–93, the main constraints on Syria's economic development were the poor condition of much of the physical infrastructure and the inefficient administration within highly centralized public-sector organizations. The disbursal of available funding for important public-sector projects was frequently delayed for long periods by procedural obstacles, while the financing of some private-sector projects was greatly complicated by Syria's complex foreign-exchange rules and limited banking services. Despite these and other impediments, the rate of real economic growth was estimated to have exceeded 5% in 1992 and to have reached 10% in 1993 (when the annual inflation rate was 5.7%). The already positive outlook for the Syrian economy was further strengthened in 1994 as the regional peace process gathered momentum.

AREA AND POPULATION

Syria covers an area of 185,180 sq km (71,498 sq miles), of which about 45% is considered to be arable land. The remainder consists of bare mountain, desert and pastures capable of sustaining only nomadic populations. Of the total cultivable area of 8.7m. ha, little more than about 70% is under cultivation. Syria's estimated total population at mid-1993 was 13,400,000. The average annual increase between 1980 and 1990 was estimated to be 3.6%. Census totals in September 1970 and September 1981 were 6,304,685 and 9,052,628 respectively.

There has been a continuing movement from village to town. In 1965 about 40% of the population were classified as urban. By 1990 the proportion had risen to 50%. The urban population increased at an annual rate of 4.4% in 1980–90, almost identical to the 4.5% of 1965–80. The process of urbanization has put a strain on services in the cities. One of the achievements of President Assad's regime, however, has been to extend development projects to rural areas, notably through the ambitious rural electrification programme. The population of Damascus and its surrounding province approximately doubled between 1959 and 1973, from more than half a million to an estimated 1.46m. At the census of September 1981 the city itself had a population of 1,112,214, while the total for the city and its environs had risen to 2.5m. The population of Aleppo, estimated at 466,026 in 1959, rose to 985,413 by 1981, while Homs had a population of 346,871. The distribution of employment changed markedly between the mid-1960s and the late 1980s, reflecting industrial growth and the expansion of the service sector. In 1989, of a total economically active population of 2,951,100, 23% were employed in agriculture, forestry and fishing, compared with 52% in 1965, while manufacturing and construction employed 28.8% in 1989, compared with 20% in 1965. It was estimated in 1993 that the public sector (excluding the armed forces) employed about 31% of the Syrian labour force, and that the total number of Syrians supported by public-sector employment (including employees' dependants) was approaching 6m.

AGRICULTURE

Agriculture retains its position as a mainstay of the Syrian economy, despite the existence of a traditionally strong trading sector and partially successful attempts at industrialization. The agricultural sector employed about 24% of the labour force in 1991. The main areas of cultivation form a narrow strip of land along the coast, from the Lebanese to the Turkish frontiers, which enjoys a Mediterranean climate, is exceedingly fertile and produces fruit, olives, tobacco and cotton. East of this strip lies the northward continuation of the Lebanon range of mountains, which falls sharply on the east to the Orontes river valley, whose marshes have been reclaimed to form one of Syria's most fertile areas. In central Syria this valley joins the steppe-plain, about 150 km wide, which runs from the Jordanian borders north-eastward towards the Euphrates valley. The plain is traditionally Syria's major agricultural area, with cereals as the principal crops. Also in this region are the country's main cities, Damascus, Homs, Hama and Aleppo. The importance of this plain is now being rivalled by a fourth area, the Jezira, which lies between the Euphrates in Syria and the Tigris in Iraq. Although fertile lands along the banks of the Euphrates and its tributaries had previously been cultivated, the Jezira's value was recognized only in the early 1950s, when large-scale cotton cultivation was introduced in former pasture lands. It is now vastly increasing its output with the development of the Euphrates Dam, and the Government has made

efforts to promote the social and economic development of this previously neglected area.

One of the chief characteristics of Syria's agricultural performance, in the absence of any established large-scale irrigation system, has been an extreme fluctuation in annual output, owing to wide variations in rainfall. Dependence on rainfall for good harvests is illustrated by the Central Bureau of Statistics' general indices for agricultural production, which show fluctuations from 78 in 1979 to 109 in 1983, to 99 in 1984, to 104 in 1985 and to 110 in 1986 (1980 = 100). In 1989 agricultural output by value fell by nearly 20%. By the early 1990s, however, the implementation of irrigation schemes and investment in modern techniques had begun to yield results in the shape of higher and more consistent output, especially of cereal crops. In 1990 agricultural output by value rose by 11.5%.

Agriculture's share in Syria's GDP has fallen steadily since the early 1960s. It contributed 32.2% of GDP in 1962, falling to 27% in 1990. Initially, the decline was attributable to under-use of potential, caused by the discouraging effects of the 1958 agrarian reform law on investment and the removal of the large rural landowners and urban money-lenders who had formerly provided the traditional channels of credit. The area of unused cultivable land (excluding fallow) increased from 1,892,000 ha in 1963 to 2,825,000 ha by 1970. Suspicion of government intentions was gradually tempered, however, by the relaxation of the reform law and, under the post-1970 Assad administration, by a number of significant amendments. One reason for the continued decline in more recent years has been the growing comparative importance of the mining and manufacturing sectors. Agriculture, forestry and fishing contributed £S10,935m. to GDP in 1980 and the annual growth rate for this sector was projected at 7.8% under the fifth Five-Year Development Plan. The fifth Plan (1981–85) gave the agricultural sector a high priority, allocating £S17,200m. to its development. Agriculture's share of total investment in the sixth Plan (1986–90) was projected to rise to 18.9%, compared with 16.9% in the fifth Plan. Under the Government's 1992 budget, 26% of investment expenditure was allocated to agriculture and irrigation.

Extensive irrigation programmes, now under way, should eventually have the effect of steadying agricultural output as well as increasing it. It was with this in mind that, out of agricultural investments accounting for a sizeable 35% of total investment under the third Five-Year Plan (1971–75), the Government devoted the largest share to the Euphrates Dam project (see below under Economic Development). The main task for the fourth Development Plan, which ran from 1976 to 1980, was to put the dam's stored waters to work and to irrigate an additional 240,000 ha of land in the Euphrates basin by the end of the decade. However, statistics for 1984 showed that only some 60,000 ha had actually been irrigated, which means that it will be a very long time before the final Euphrates irrigation target of 640,000 ha (which, it was originally intended, would be achieved by the end of the century) is reached. In the mean time, emphasis has been placed not only on the Euphrates, but also on other irrigation schemes, including those on the Yarmouk river (on which three pumping stations and 400 km of canals are being constructed to irrigate about 300 ha of farmland) and in the Ghab, in order to increase the area available for the cultivation of cereals, sugar beet and cotton. In September 1987 Jordan and Syria signed an agreement on the use of the waters of the Yarmouk, whereby the countries undertook to share irrigation systems and the power from a hydroelectricity plant associated with the al-Wahdeh dam, which was to be built on the Yarmouk in Jordan.

With the Euphrates scheme having produced somewhat disappointing results, the Government gave increasing attention to the rain-fed areas, which account for 84% of the total cultivated area. In the southern provinces of Dera'a and Suweidiya a $76.3m. project began in the mid-1980s to increase food production and improve living standards on 25,400 ha of rain-fed land. The project was funded by the World Bank ($22m.), the International Fund for Agricultural Development (IFAD, $18m.), and the UN Development Programme ($2.2m.). Syria has benefited from the presence near Aleppo of the

International Centre for Agricultural Research in the Dry Areas (ICARDA), one of the 13 centres throughout the world of the Consultative Group on International Agricultural Research (CGIAR). ICARDA is attempting to improve yields and farming systems in areas of low and medium rainfall throughout the Middle East.

In January 1993 the European Investment Bank agreed to finance the construction of the 65m. cu m Ath-Thawra earth-fill dam on the Snobar river, designed to irrigate 10,500 ha of land in the Latakia area. Scheduled for completion in 1994, the project would stimulate cultivation of market-garden crops, mainly for local consumption, and would facilitate tree planting to combat soil erosion. Later in 1993, bids were invited from Western consultants for the redesign of unimplemented irrigation schemes originally drawn up by East European firms in the mid-1980s. The main redesign contract (to be funded by the Kuwait Fund for Arab Economic Development) related to a proposed 5-km dam on the Khabour river, which formed part of a scheme to irrigate 40,000 ha of farmland in north-eastern Syria. The unimplemented designs for this scheme had been prepared by a Bulgarian firm in 1985.

Although medium-staple cotton had been grown in Syria for many years, it was the high prices prevalent after the Second World War and during the Korean War that provided the greatest impetus to cotton production. In the early 1950s the previously neglected Jezira area was opened up for large-scale agriculture on a new capital-intensive basis, relatively free from traditional agricultural relations, still semi-feudal in the rest of the country. Syria's output of unginned cotton increased from 38,000 tons in 1949 to 220,800 tons in 1954. The area under cotton increased from 25,300 ha in 1949, to 78,000 ha in 1950 and to 250,000 ha in 1971/72. By 1987/88, this area had declined to 128,000 ha, but in the following year it increased to 165,000 ha, and the area designated for cotton in 1989/90 was 170,000 ha.

Petroleum overtook cotton as Syria's most valuable source of export earnings in 1974, as cotton exports (raw, yarn and textiles) declined, both in value and volume. Output of cotton lint was 200,000–250,000 metric tons per year in 1968–73, but by the 1980/81 season it had declined to 117,800 tons. Production subsequently recovered, and in 1983/84 a record cotton crop of 523,418 tons yielded 194,000 tons of cotton lint, although there was a decline in cotton output, to 125,931 tons of lint in 1986/87. Cotton export earnings rose from £S453m. in 1982 to £S1,076m. in 1984, but dropped to £S391m. in 1986. The 1987/88 crop was affected by bad winter weather, and this, combined with the decrease in area, yielded only 95,000 tons of lint. The 1988/89 crop yielded 116,000 tons of lint, and total cotton production rose to 441,000 tons in 1989/90 and to 555,000 tons in 1990/91. The official prices payable to Syrian farmers for their cotton have been progressively increased in recent years, but the sector has suffered to some extent from competition from other major crops. The local textile industry (historically one of the Syrian economy's leading sectors) uses an appreciable proportion of the cotton crop, averaging about 50,000 tons a year in the early 1990s. Syria's cotton crop reached a new record level of 622,000 tons in 1992 and was expected to reach 680,000 tons in 1994. Exports of ginned cotton totalled 158,000 tons in 1993.

One of the crops that has competed with cotton is sugar beet. The Government has been keen to foster a domestic sugar industry, and the area planted with beet rose from 22,000 ha in 1980 to 35,700 ha in 1984. However, the failure of the domestic refining industry to perform as planned has led to a drastic reduction in the beet area, to 13,200 ha in 1986. The harvest of sugar beet declined from 1.3m. tons in 1984 to 412,000 tons in 1985, rising to 440,000 tons the following year. Production rose again, to 457,000 tons, in 1987, but declined to 222,000 tons in 1988. It rose again to 412,000 tons in 1989, to 422,000 tons in 1990 and to 637,000 tons in 1991. Production of refined sugar by local factories reached a peak of 206,000 tons in 1983 but dropped to 54,000 tons in 1985, rising only marginally to 57,000 tons in the following year. The decline in the sugar industry was partly the result of the fall in the world price of sugar. In the mid-1970s, when Syria started to develop the industry, prices were high, while those of cotton were low. Imports of sugar

fluctuated during the 1980s. Those of raw sugar rose from 96,600 tons in 1985 to 261,200 tons in 1986, while those of refined sugar declined from 321,700 tons to 268,200 tons. In 1994 the state sugar refining company anticipated a local beet crop of 1.32m. tons, sufficient to cover 51% of its raw sugar requirement, and planned to import 128,000 tons of raw sugar in order to fulfil its 1994 production target of 260,000 tons of refined sugar (about 48% of current consumption). Construction of a new 129,000 tons-per-year sugar refinery was scheduled to begin in 1995.

Syria's cereal crop is also of prime importance, accounting in 1993 for nearly 80% of the £S45,000m. spent on crop purchases by the agricultural marketing authorities. Wheat and barley together occupied 2.65m. ha in 1985, two-thirds of the total cropped area. Output of both crops has varied considerably from year to year, depending on the rainfall. In 1987/88 the cereal harvest more than doubled, to almost 5m. tons, including more than 2m. tons of wheat. However, low rainfall in early 1989 adversely affected the harvest, leading to substantial decreases. Wheat production was 2m. tons in 1990, 2.1m. tons in 1991 and 3m. tons in 1992. Barley production was 1m. tons in 1990, after which efforts were made to stabilize yields in marginal growing areas. (During the 1980s the average annual barley yield had ranged from as little as 235 kg per ha to as much as 1,044 kg per ha.) The Government's 1994 barley production target of 1.5m. tons was underfulfilled by 50% because of weather-related crop damage. About 300,000 tons of corn (sufficient to supply 60% of the state fodder company's requirement) were produced in 1993.

In 1993 the wheat harvest reached 3.6m. tons, placing a severe strain on available storage space despite the construction of 15 additional grain silos over the past year. The state grain marketing authorities launched an emergency programme to build 13 more silos during 1994 and to expand local flour-milling capacity, which fell far short of current requirements. The main reasons for the strong upturn in wheat production in 1993 were favourable rainfall, improved cultivation techniques, and increases in areas planted (attributable partly to price liberalization to improve the financial returns to farmers). Syria's annual wheat consumption was around 2.2m. tons in the early 1990s, while national flour-milling capacity was around 1.35m. tons, necessitating a heavy reliance on Lebanese mills to process part of the Syrian wheat harvest. Weather damage limited the 1994 wheat harvest to 2.6m. tons.

There are several other actual and potential agricultural exports. Tobacco production averaged around 15,000 tons per year, and exports about 3,000 tons per year, in the early 1990s. There is also considerable scope for expansion in the production of fruit and vegetables. The fruit harvest in 1990 included 423,000 tons of grapes, 73,000 tons of apricots, 205,000 tons of apples and 43,000 tons of plums. Syria has embarked on a project to double production of citrus fruit. In 1990 it produced 171,000 tons of oranges. The production of tomatoes and onions in 1990 totalled 430,000 tons and 95,000 tons, respectively. Demand for fruit and vegetables is necessitating imports from other sources, including Lebanon. In recent years there have, at times, been shortages of fruit and vegetables, partly as a result of the official curbing of imports in general. Syria does export a certain amount of fruit and vegetables, and in 1986 such exports included 33,512 tons of potatoes, 415 tons of onions, 5,935 tons of lentils, 1,788 tons of dried figs and 4,183 tons of watermelons. Fruit growers who had expanded production for export to guaranteed markets in the former Soviet Union suffered some losses when trade was cut back after the late 1980s. Production of grape and apple juice is due to start in 1995 at a new processing plant near Damascus which aims to provide growers with an assured outlet for a proportion of these crops.

Stockraising is another important branch of agriculture. In 1990, there were 787,000 cattle, 1m. goats and 14.5m. sheep. Some 1m. tons of milk was produced in 1990.

PETROLEUM AND GAS

Syria was formerly thought to have no petroleum. The Iraq Petroleum Company group had rights throughout Syria but abandoned them in 1951 after failing to find petroleum in commercial quantities. Concessions were granted to an independent American operator in 1955 and to a West German-led consortium in 1956. These led to the discovery of petroleum, first of the Karatchouk field, in the north-eastern corner of the country, then of the Suweidiya field and finally of the field at nearby Rumelan. However, in addition to the cost of extraction being high, the petroleum from all three oilfields was of low quality. The petroleum which was found by the Americans at Karatchouk had a density of 19° API and a sulphur content of 4.5%, while that found by the German group at Suweidiya had a density of 25° API and a 3.5% sulphur content. By 1964, several years before any of the three fields had begun production on a commercial basis, Syria became one of the first Arab states to discard the notion of petroleum concessions and to nationalize its petroleum operations. Even at that early stage, Syria's industrial planners were anxious to use the country's petroleum not only for export in its crude state, but also as a raw material for domestic industry. For the next 10 years all exploration and exploitation was conducted solely by the state-owned General Petroleum Authority and its offshoot, the Syrian Petroleum Company (SPC), with Soviet assistance.

Output from Suweidiya started in July 1968 and totalled 1m. tons in the first year, of which 833,000 tons were exported. Output in 1969, when the Karatchouk field began to produce, failed to reach expectations, totalling only 3.2m. tons, of which 2.3m. tons were exported. The October war in 1973 reduced production from a level of 6.3m. tons in the previous year to just 5.4m. tons, recovering in 1974 to 6.2m. tons. Production remained at about that level in the late 1970s; by the early 1980s, with oil prices falling and its known petroleum reserves being exhausted, Syria was actually a net importer of petroleum. From the mid-1980s, however, the petroleum industry was transformed by the discovery of large reserves of high-quality crude oil near Deir ez-Zor by a consortium of foreign oil companies.

The new discoveries were the result of the reversal of the Government's 'no-concessions' policy in the mid-1970s. In May 1975 the first Syrian concession to be won by any Western company for over 15 years was awarded to a US group, on production-sharing terms heavily tilted in the Government's favour and stipulating that $20m. be invested in exploration off shore. In June 1975 the Government took its new policy one stage further by offering a dozen onshore oil concessions for international bidding. Altogether, 50,000 sq km were to be made available. The oil companies' response to the invitation was initially slow and, when the first US group, Tripco, relinquished its concession in March 1976, no other company had come forward to join the search. In July 1977, however, a US-Syrian consortium called Samoco took up a concession in the Deir ez-Zor area, and in December another concession, in Raqqa province, was taken by Shell subsidiaries, Syria Shell Petroleum Development and Pecten Syria Company. Both Shell and Samoco insisted on a larger share of eventual petroleum production than was agreed between the Government and Tripco. This softening of terms reawakened the interest of other firms, including Chevron of the USA.

By 1983, however, Samoco, Chevron and Rompetrol of Romania (which was exploring west of Hassakeh) had all followed Tripco in relinquishing their concessions, leaving Pecten and Marathon of the USA as the only foreign operators in the country. In early 1983 Pecten, together with Royal Dutch/Shell and Deminex of the Federal Republic of Germany, assumed control of Samoco's concession area. At the end of 1984 it was revealed that the consortium had discovered reserves of high-quality crude oil at ath-Thayyem, near Deir ez-Zor. In 1985 the three foreign partners and the SPC formed the Al-Furat Petroleum Company (AFPC) to develop the concession. Full commercial production began in September 1986, adding an initial 60,000 b/d (3m. tons per year) to Syria's total production capacity. Because the oil from the field is light crude (36° API), with a very low sulphur content, it has considerably reduced the need to import light crudes for blending with heavy Syrian ones at Syrian refineries. Previously Syria had imported between 5m. and 6.6m. tons of oil every year. Related to the main ath-Thayyem field are the

later discoveries of the al-Ward, al-Asharah, al-Shula and al-Kharata fields. In May 1989, it was reported that ath-Thayyem was producing 65,000 b/d, with output from the related fields bringing the total output of this system to 100,000 b/d out of total Syrian production in 1989 of 15.2m. tons (310,000 b/d).

Marathon had discovered gas reserves capable of producing 450m. cu m per day at a well named Cherrife 2 in 1982, and had made a further gas and condensate discovery in mid-1985, at ash-Shair. In December 1988, after a long period of resisting government pressure to develop gas reserves, Marathon agreed to a production-sharing scheme, with investment of up to $20m. in converting the oil-fired Muhardeh and Banias power stations to gas. The agreement was the first in Syria to include a gas sales clause. Turkey has expressed an interest in developing Syrian gas reserves (which were estimated to total 225,000m. cu m in 1992) with a view to possible export to Turkey.

Syria's crude oil production reached 21m. tons (400,000 b/d) in 1990, 24.5m. tons (465,000 b/d) in 1991 and 25.2m. tons (475,000 b/d) in 1992, about two-thirds of the latter total being light crude and the balance heavy crude. Syria's proven oil reserves totalled 1,700m. barrels at the end of 1993, sufficient to maintain the previous year's rate of production for a further 8.2 years. In mid-1993 production was reported to have increased to 565,500 b/d (including 400,000 b/d from fields operated by AFPC). The latest unofficial estimates put Syria's recoverable oil reserves at 3,000m. barrels.

While AFPC continued to widen the scope of its own development programme (which included increasing use of water-injection techniques to maintain production from 'mature' oilfields), Elf Aquitaine was preparing to increase or commence production from new wells in the Atallah North and Jafra areas of the Deir ez-Zor field in 1993, while the Shell, Tullow Oil, Unocal and Occidental companies were engaged in active oil exploration programmes in other parts of the country. During the third quarter of 1994 Syrian oil output reached 615,000 b/d following the completion of current oilfield development programmes. Oil exploration activity was very limited and was currently yielding disappointing results. Major gas development projects in progress or under active planning in 1993/94 included: the expansion of productive capacity in the Omar Field in the Deir ez-Zor region from 4.5m. cu m per day to about 7m. cu m per day, and the construction of pipelines to convey the Omar field's supplies to the 400-MW Tishrin power station in Damascus, the 650-MW Mhardeh power station near Homs and the 600-MW Jandar power station to be built also near Homs; a $300m.-programme for the Palmyra region fields designed to achieve production of 6m. cu m per day; and a $50m.-extension of the Jbeissa gas treatment plant, using gas from the SPC's Audeh field and aimed at increasing capacity from 1.7m. cu m per day to 2.8m. cu m per day; and a $200m.-programme to gather and treat gas from three fields in the Suweidiya region for use in a planned 150-MW power station in Suweidiya. By mid-1994 Syrian production of natural gas totalled 6.94m. cu m per day. It was scheduled to exceed 16.5m. cu m per day by the middle of 1995 on completion of current expansion projects.

The generally poor quality of Syrian petroleum until the late 1980s, together with opposition on the part of some of the major oil companies to Syria's nationalization experiment, combined, at the outset of the country's petroleum development, to cause considerable marketing difficulties. However, with increasing sales (particularly to Greece, France, Italy and the USSR), crude petroleum became Syria's most important export. The value of exports of petroleum and petroleum products soared from £S291.2m. in 1972 to £S1,607.5m. in 1974 and to £S6,253m. in 1980, but it fell subsequently as a result of the slump in world oil prices. In 1981 Syria became a net importer of petroleum by value for the first time since petroleum exports began in the mid-1970s, recording a deficit on its trade in petroleum of £S262m. There was a surplus of £S189m. in the petroleum account in 1982, although deficits of £S123m. and £S767m. were recorded in 1983 and 1984. In 1986 oil imports were halved, from 5.4m. tons in 1985, to 2.7m. tons, while exports fell from 7.4m. tons to 6.3m. tons—an oil trade surplus of 3.7m. tons, worth £S346m. (compared with a surplus of £S315m. in 1985). In 1986 sales of oil and oil products accounted for 42% of total exports by value, compared with 74% in 1985, the decline being caused by lower oil prices. By 1990 oil and other minerals accounted for 45% of Syria's merchandise exports by value, and in 1991 exports of oil were valued at £S17,218m. The volume of oil exports fluctuated within the range of 300,000 b/d to 360,000 b/d in early 1994, at which point the state marketing company had 21 term customers abroad and was seeking to conduct an increasing proportion of its business through term contracts rather than 'spot' sales.

The capacity of petroleum refineries in Syria totalled 11.4m. tons per year (228,000 b/d) at 1 January 1988, comprising 5.4m. tons per year (102,000 b/d) at the Homs refinery and 6m. tons per year (126,000 b/d) at the Romanian-built refinery at Banias, which came 'on stream' in 1980. For a long time, however, the Banias plant operated at considerably below capacity, owing to repeated shortfalls in deliveries of crude petroleum. It was this problem which delayed construction of the refinery, as its specifications had to be altered to enable it to process different grades of crude and thus reduce its dependence on uncertain Iraqi supplies, which were subsequently discontinued by Syria's closure of the Kirkuk–Banias pipeline, which had a capacity of 500,000 b/d. The sixth expansion of the Homs refinery was carried out by Technoexport of Czechoslovakia. The seventh expansion was to have entailed construction of a base lube oil complex with a capacity of 100,000 tons per year (t/y) but, owing to Syria's budgetary constraints, this project was replaced by one for a plant to process used lubricating oils, with a capacity of 30,000 t/y, to be increased to 40,000 t/y. In 1994 the Government accepted the recommendations of a 1992 study by a US consultancy which advocated a major restructuring of both existing refineries in order to boost their output of light products. About half of the current refining capacity was devoted to the production of heavy fuel oil, Syrian demand for which was due to fall substantially in coming years as new gas-fired power stations were constructed. Also in 1994, a private-sector business backed by Saudi Arabian and other Gulf region investors announced plans (approved in principle by the Government) to build a new oil refinery in Syria with a capacity of about 100,000 b/d.

Royalties for the transit of foreign crude petroleum through Syrian territory were, for many years, more valuable than indigenous production. Two pipelines carry petroleum from the Kirkuk oilfield, in Iraq, through Syria. One, built in 1934, leads on to a terminal at Tripoli in Lebanon. The second, completed in 1952, branches off at Homs to the Syrian terminal at Banias. A third pipeline, belonging to the Trans-Arabian Pipeline Company (Tapline) which used to carry 24m. tons of Saudi crude petroleum per year to a terminal near Sidon in Lebanon, crosses about 150 km of Syrian territory, much of which was occupied by Israel in 1967. After nationalizing the Iraq Petroleum Company in June 1972, the Iraqi Government took over payment of royalties to Syria and in January 1973, after lengthy negotiations, Syria and Iraq signed a transit agreement which provided both for transit dues and the supply of petroleum for Syria's own domestic use. However, the flow of petroleum through the Kirkuk–Banias pipeline has been interrupted more than once since then. Throughput was suspended in 1976, when negotiations between Iraq and Syria on renewing the financial clauses of the transit agreement broke down, with Iraq demanding higher prices for its petroleum (to match the 1973–74 increases) and Syria seeking a proportionate increase in transit fees. For more than two years, Iraq refused to use the pipeline, instead directing its petroleum southwards to the Gulf and also via Turkey, through a pipeline that came 'on stream' in 1977. The short-lived improvement in Iraqi-Syrian political relations in late 1978, combined with the world shortage of petroleum arising from the Iranian revolution, brought a resumption of pumping from Kirkuk to Banias in 1979, but this was halted yet again in September 1980 at the start of the Iran–Iraq War. When, despite the continuation of the war, Iraq recommenced exports of petroleum on a limited scale, the situation in the Gulf put Syria in a relatively stronger position and the Iraq–Syria pipeline came into use again in February 1981. However, Syria remained dissatisfied with the transit royalties, stating that

in 1981 the pipeline cost $31m. to operate but brought revenues of only $25.7m. In April 1982, having signed an agreement to buy 8.7m. tons of petroleum per year from Iran, Syria closed the Kirkuk–Banias pipeline to Iraqi petroleum. With the closure of the pipeline, concessional supplies from Iran played an important part in fulfilling Syria's oil import needs. From 1982 onwards, yearly agreements were negotiated with Iran for the supply of oil; typically, 1m. tons supplied free to the Syrian army and the rest at a discount. The oil agreements were, however, plagued by political disagreements between the two countries, and by Syria's mounting oil debt to Iran, which was reported in mid-1986 to be at least $1,500m. For some periods Iranian oil supplies were halted altogether. In April 1987, 12-month agreements were signed for the supply of 1m. tons of oil free of charge to the Syrian army, and 2m. tons at OPEC prices on a cash-payment basis. A new one-year agreement, allowing for the supply of 1m. tons of free oil was reached in April 1988. The smaller quantity of oil involved in the recent agreements reflected the impact that the Deir ez-Zor production has had on Syria's oil import needs. In mid-June 1989, the Syrian Minister of Petroleum stated that Iran had made no deliveries of 'free' oil since the end of 1988.

From the late 1980s the Government's desire to maximize oil output was apparent in the easing of state bureaucratic constraints on the sector. Nevertheless, foreign companies continued to be deterred by the difficulties they experienced in Syria, added to which the prospects of major new discoveries were seen as limited. Against this background, the appointment in June 1992 of the AFPC chairman, Nadir an-Nabulsi, as Minister of Petroleum and Mineral Wealth was seen as signalling a new commitment to commercial principles and to removing obstacles to oil development. An estimated 65% of Syria's geological structures remained unexplored in 1993, when the Government's policy on oil development terms was broadly based on prevailing Egyptian practices.

INDUSTRY

A remarkable industrial boom, mainly based on textiles, occurred in Syria shortly after independence and was the main cause of the dissolution of the customs union with Lebanon in 1959, since the protectionist policies which were adopted by the Syrian Government to safeguard this growth came into direct conflict with Lebanon's free-trade tradition. Since then the industrial (manufacturing and mining) sector has grown steadily. In 1971, for the first time, it replaced agriculture as the main generator of wealth, accounting for 19.5% of Syria's GDP, compared with 19.1% for agriculture. Manufacturing output expanded strongly in the early 1980s, with the index of production rising from 108 in 1982 to 167 in 1983 (1980 = 100). Until the early 1990s, however, production stagnated, with the industrial index standing at 163 in 1986. In some sectors, there was a marked decline in 1986: the wood and furniture index fell from 80 to 14; that for paper, printing and binding from 252 to 165; and that for the main mineral industries from 175 to 132. The target for average annual industrial growth under the 1976–80 Development Plan was an ambitious 15.4%, while the investment allocation for the industrial sector was £S11,289m., representing 20.8% of the total. There has been something of a change of heart since then, however, partly because of disappointing growth rates in this sector, and industry's allocation under the 1981–85 Plan fell to 16.6% of the total, or £S16,899m. In Syria's national accounts, the industrial sector comprises manufacturing, with mining, electricity, gas and water. In terms of GDP at constant 1980 prices, the value of mining, manufacturing and utilities fell by 17% in 1984, to £S7,622m. In 1985 it rose by 5%, to £S7,997m. Provisional figures show a further increase of 33% in 1986, to £S10,767m. However, this is likely to have been caused by increases in the output of oil and phosphates, rather than the result of an improvement in the performance of the manufacturing sector in general. According to the World Bank, in 1992 the industrial sector contributed 23% of GDP, compared with the agricultural sector's 30% and the service sector's 48%.

Production of phosphates started from mines in the Palmyra area in 1972. A sudden rise in world phosphate prices in 1974 took the price of Syrian rock up to $53 per metric ton, despite its high chlorine content and low quality. Prices and production subsequently fluctuated. Under the provisions of the 1981–85 Plan, phosphate production was expected to reach 5m. tons per year by 1985, but actual output was considerably less than this figure. Production declined from 1.46m. tons in 1982 to 1.23m. tons in 1983. It rose to 1.51m. tons in 1984 but fell to 1.2m. tons in 1985. In 1986 production rose to 1.6m. tons, and exports increased from 694,000 tons, worth £S75.6m., in 1985, to 1.3m. tons, worth £S150m. Production in 1987 amounted to almost 2m. tons. Official sources have claimed that, by the year 2000, production could equal that of Morocco. Syria's phosphate reserves have enabled the establishment of a phosphatic fertilizer industry. Production of a Romanian-built triple superphosphate (TSP) plant at Homs, costing $180m., began in 1981 with an annual capacity of 450,000 tons of TSP. Production of phosphatic fertilizers rose from 68,333 tons in 1981 to 192,720 tons in 1986. An ammonia urea plant was completed at Homs in 1979, with a daily capacity of 1,000 tons of ammonia, of which 600 tons was to be used to manufacture 1,050 tons of urea per day. Production of nitrogenous fertilizers increased from 59,607 tons in 1981 to 116,543 tons in 1982. In 1984 and 1985 production was 110,206 tons and 104,000 tons, respectively, rising to 109,919 tons in 1986. In December 1986 Syria and the USSR signed a protocol on co-operation in the phosphate industry, providing for the annual volume of Syrian phosphate exports to the USSR to rise to 6m. tons by the year 2000. (After the collapse of the USSR in 1991, Syria sought to renegotiate such contracts with the Russian Government and other successor republics.) In mid-1993 plans were being finalized for a new $500m.-fertilizer plant near Palmyra, to be partly financed by Saudi Arabian and other Gulf sources, with an annual capacity of 500,000 tons of TSP.

The iron and steel industry, centred on Hama, comprises a smelter (capacity 120,000 tons per year), a rolling mill and a steel pipe plant, built by firms from West Germany and Switzerland. The potential for developing Syria's own deposits of iron ore, estimated at about 530m. tons, has been studied by Indian consultants. After the 1990/91 Gulf crisis, Saudi Arabia pledged funding for a new $1,000m.-iron and steel complex at az-Zara (near Hama), which would have an annual capacity of 700,000 tons and specialize in coils, bars and industrial sections. Contract negotiations had not been concluded by the end of 1993. Syria's cement output (once targeted to reach 6m. tons by 1980) amounted to 2.85m. tons in 1982. However, completion of a big cement works at Tartous in 1983, together with other factories at Adra, Hama, Musulmiya and Aleppo, brought output to 4.3m. tons in 1985. In 1993 Syrian cement demand was expected to total 5m. tons, which was roughly in balance with the country's current production capacity. An import requirement emerged again in 1994, when Jordan was among the sources of supplies to meet the shortfall. The Government announced plans in March 1994 to double the capacity of the Adra cement plant to 6,000 tons per day, while private Gulf Arab investors received outline approval in August 1994 for a proposal to build a new cement plant with a capacity of 1m. tons per year, to be owned 75% by the private sector and 25% by the state. Syria's seven sugar refineries supplied nearly half of local demand of 550,000 tons in 1994, when plans were announced to build an eighth plant which would raise the country's total sugar refining capacity to 389,000 tons per year.

Other established industries include the manufacture of textiles, rubber, glass and paper, and the assembly of tractors, refrigerators and television receivers (including colour sets). Plans for a motor car assembly plant were postponed following the financial difficulties of 1976, and cars have since been imported in large numbers from Japan. However, a new private-sector scheme to assemble pick-up trucks, jeeps and small passenger vehicles was approved in principle by the Government in August 1994. To be based on the import of kits supplied by the US manufacturer General Motors, the proposed plant would begin production within two years of final approval for the project and would reach its full capacity of 30,000 vehicles per year within seven years. Food processing industries have also been developed. In April 1992 Alfamatex of Spain won a $125m.-contract to build a new textiles mill at

Idleb, with Kuwait and Islamic Development Bank financial aid. At the same time, bids were invited for a $150m.-textiles mill at Latakia, to be funded in part by the Abu Dhabi Fund for Arab Economic Development and with a projected output of 150,000 tons a year of cotton products.

Despite the dominance of large-scale state industries, the private sector has continued to play an important role in industrial manufacture. In 1986 the private sector accounted for 56% of the production of refrigerators, 62% of paints, 23% of biscuits, 100% of olive oil and 34% of detergents. Under Law 10 of May 1991, encouragement was given to Syrian and foreign investment in industrial ventures, particularly in the light industry sector. Syrian officials estimated in April 1993 that £S90,000m. (equivalent to about $1,700m. at the applicable currency exchange rate) had so far been invested in a total of about 700 projects under Law 10, creating employment for up to 55,000 people. About £S46,000m. ($1,000m.) had been invested in 204 manufacturing projects, mainly in the areas of food processing, textiles and chemicals. The remaining investments were mostly in transport projects (many of which were reportedly private car import schemes with little or no genuine economic significance). By May 1994 cumulative investment under Law 10 had reached £S174,000m., and the private sector's contribution to GDP was officially estimated as 64%. Infrastructural improvement to aid commercial activity included a plan to install 600,000 new telephone lines (double the existing number), for which a contract was awarded to Siemens of Germany in mid-1991.

Since its inauguration in 1978, the Euphrates Dam, with its eight 100-MW turbines, has made an important contribution to power generation in Syria. However, from an early stage extensive Turkish exploitation of the Euphrates waters often reduced the level of water in Lake Assad to such an extent that only three turbines could operate. In July 1987 Turkey undertook to use 500m. cu m of water from the Euphrates per year for irrigation until agreement was reached with Syria and Iraq on the use of the river's waters. Syria has considered various ways of overcoming its power shortage. There has long been talk of a nuclear power plant, possibly using uranium obtained from local phosphate deposits. Four Western companies were short-listed to carry out the pilot study for a 1,200-MW station in 1979/80, but none was ever given the go-ahead. In mid-1983 Syria and the USSR signed a protocol whereby both sides were to study the construction of Syria's first nuclear power station, but little progress appeared to have been made in this direction before the disintegration of the USSR in 1991.

In recent years Syria has suffered frequent interruptions in the supply of electric power. Electricity demand soared, owing to rapid industrialization in the 1970s, and the Euphrates Dam (see above) did not, as was hoped, meet Syria's growing needs, as shortfalls in its water supply due to erratic rainfall and Turkish offtake upstream were compounded by an almost total lack of maintenance of the dam and its generating plant. By early 1993 the generating capacity of the dam was thought to be barely 150 MW, while its actual output fell below 100 MW at some points, contributing to chronic power shortages which led to electricity supplies being cut off for seven or more hours per day. Many Syrian businesses relied on diesel generators to keep factories running. An ambitious programme of power station construction, launched in the 1980s, was increasingly geared to the exploitation of local natural gas resources as a fuel source, but failed to keep pace with the growth of demand because of chronic delays between the planning and construction stages. (Only three contracts were finalized between 1983 and 1992.) In 1993 Syria was estimated to have a total of 1,900 MW of operational generating capacity (10.5% hydro, 63% thermal and 26.5% gas-turbine) out of a theoretical installed capacity of 3,002 MW (30% hydro, 51% thermal and 19% gas-turbine), while the minimum operational capacity needed to meet current demand was estimated to be 2,500 MW. Demand was officially projected to rise to 3,284 MW in 1995 and 4,882 MW in 2000. In a bid to rectify the situation, the authorities approved contracts in the first half of 1993 for the construction of three new power stations with a combined capacity of 1,570 MW, and were expected to award contracts for another 600-MW plant before the end of the year. In

September 1983 President Assad affirmed that 'every citizen has the right to a steady supply of electricity', after which contracts were speedily awarded for the construction of eight 125-MW gas-fired plants, to be financed by Kuwait. The long-serving Minister of Electricity was subsequently dismissed from the Government in June 1994, shortly before the completion of the first of the new plants.

The regional political situation has not helped Syria in encouraging private investment or in developing its ports. Free zones which were set up in the 1970s in Damascus, Aleppo, Homs, Latakia and Tartous, with the aim of attracting foreign investment in light industries, assembly plants and warehouses, failed to have the desired effect. Jordan's support for Iraq in the Iran–Iraq War compounded the discord between Syria and Jordan, and although in 1985 there was a dramatic improvement in relations, plans for a joint industrial free zone south of Dera'a had been undermined. Operations at the ports of Latakia and Tartous (both equipped to handle transit traffic bound for the Gulf) were adversely affected by the closure of the border with Iraq in 1982. The volume of goods handled at the two ports declined markedly after 1981, when it totalled 7.63m. tons. In 1985 the total was 5.5m. tons, and in 1986 4.37m. tons.

TRADE AND TOURISM

Commerce has traditionally been a major occupation of Syria's towns, especially of Damascus and Aleppo which lie on the main east-west trade route. There have been, however, some radical changes in both the direction and the composition of Syria's trade over the years. During the mid-1960s Syria's principal suppliers were among the Eastern European bloc. In 1968 the USSR and Czechoslovakia together provided more than 20% of all imported goods. In 1974, although the value of their supplies had increased, those two countries accounted for just under 7.2% of the total. Meanwhile, the value of Syria's imports over the six-year period had risen nearly four-fold, reaching £S4,571m. in 1974, and the bulk of the increase had resulted from flourishing trade ties with Western Europe. In the 1980s, the pendulum swung back in favour of the Eastern bloc again. The trend towards the East was reinforced during this period by trade agreements with Eastern bloc countries and by the willingness of some of these to accept barter deals and thereby accommodate Syria's shortage of foreign exchange. Yugoslavia, for example, agreed in 1985 to take almost one-third of Syrian phosphate exports in return for construction machinery, iron and steel, timber, pharmaceuticals and medical equipment. Czechoslovakia also agreed to exchange engineering equipment for phosphates and farm produce, while Romania was a close trading partner for some years. The USSR, after signing a friendship treaty with Syria in 1980, followed this up with an agreement to boost bilateral trade to the equivalent of some $2,600m. in the five years up to 1985. This was renewed for a further five years in 1985. The fields in which Soviet companies were active in Syria included transport, the oil industry, the phosphate industry, agriculture, power generation, and the search for reserves of water. Another friendship and co-operation treaty, this time with Bulgaria, was signed in May 1985. In 1980 socialist countries took 16.1% of Syria's exports, and in 1986 the proportion rose to 46.4%. The proportion of Syria's imports supplied by socialist countries rose from 14.6% in 1985 to 20.2% in 1986. However, the EC's share also increased, from 29.9% to 34.8%, while that of Iran declined from 17.8% to 6.8%, as a result of the fall in Iranian oil imports. After the post-1989 changes in Eastern Europe and the disintegration of the USSR in 1991, the pendulum swung again towards trade with the West. Exports to the USA increased to $206.6m. in 1991 (from $150.4m. in 1990), while imports fell from $52.1m. to $27.1m.

Syria's exports increased dramatically during the 1970s, mainly owing to large increases in the value of petroleum sales. Largely as a result of the decline in oil prices and the volume of exports, Syria's export earnings declined every year between 1980 and 1986. From £S8,273m. in 1980, the value of exports fell to £S6,427m. in 1985 and £S5,199m. in 1986. Exports in 1987 nearly trebled, in terms of local currency, to £S15,200m., although these figures used an exchange

rate of US $1 = £S11.20, which did not replace the former rate of US $1 = £S4.05 until early 1988. In terms of US dollars, the value of exports in 1987 increased by only 6%, to $1,356m.

In view of the country's alarming shortage of foreign exchange, there have been strict curbs on imports (although large amounts of goods are smuggled into the country). In 1981 the value of imports totalled £S19,781m. In 1985 the figure was £S15,570m., and in 1986 there was a drop of 31.9%, to £S10,611m. The change in the exchange rate affected import figures, in local currency, with an almost three-fold increase in 1987 to £S27,900m. In terms of US dollars, however, there was a 6% drop, to $2,492m. The trade deficit declined from $1,360m. in 1986 to $1,136m. in 1987. The USSR was Syria's leading trade partner in 1986, taking 29.7% of Syria's exports, and providing 10.1% of its imports. Syria's second biggest customer was Italy (12.1%), followed by Romania (9.4%) and the Federal Republic of Germany (4.1%). Its second biggest supplier was the Federal Republic of Germany (9.1%), followed by France (8.7%) and Italy (7.5%). Iran, previously Syria's largest supplier, fell to fifth place, with a 6.8% share.

In March 1990 the Government announced a trade surplus of £S10,430m. for 1989. The value of exports was reported to have totalled £S33,740m., while that of imports amounted to £S23,310m. However, local analysts cast doubt upon the accuracy of these figures, observing that few of the goods smuggled into Syria from Lebanon were recorded in trade statistics. Furthermore, it was noted that at least three exchange rates applied to imports: the official fixed rate of US $1 = £S11.225; an 'incentive' rate of $1 = £S20.22; and a free market rate of $1 = £S45. Since it was unclear on which rate the calculation of the trade balance had been based, it was impossible to ascertain the accuracy of the Government's figures in hard currency terms. According to IMF estimates published in October 1993, Syria had visible trade surpluses of $2,094m. in 1990 (exports $4,156m., imports $2,062m.), of $1,084m. in 1991 (exports $3,438m., imports $2,354m.) and of $159m. in 1992 (exports $3,100m., imports $2,941.). In June 1992 the Minister of Economy and Foreign Trade stated that there was a need to set up a special Syrian export bank.

In May 1993 the Government launched an unprecedentedly thorough clampdown on smuggling across the Lebanese border, causing the black-market price of illegally imported American cigarettes (the main indicator of the level of smuggling activity) to triple within a month. The Government subsequently announced that a state trading organization would in future import foreign cigarettes for sale at the prices which smugglers had been charging before the clampdown (when the trade in illegal cigarette imports had been worth an estimated $1m. per day).

Syria's entire system of foreign trade, based on laws dating back to 1952, was under review in 1993 as the Government studied the extent to which current import and export controls were hampering the growth of private-sector enterprises.

In 1993 Syria was visited by 2.9m. tourists who generated $700m. of tourism revenue. A joint private and public sector consortium was in 1994 preparing to invite construction bids for a $70m. resort development near Tartous, to include hotel and bungalow accommodation, sports facilities, restaurants and shops.

FINANCE

The sudden increase in Syrian exports from 1972 onwards was one of the major results of a reform in the country's regulations on foreign exchange. The method of valuing exports, other than cotton and crude petroleum, was transferred from the official exchange rate (then US $1 = £S3.80) to the 'parallel' (free) market rate ($1 = £S4.30), which meant a *de facto* devaluation of Syrian currency in relation to most transactions. The 'parallel' market was discontinued in July 1973 and remained suspended for nearly eight years. In April 1981, in an attempt to mobilize remittances to finance imports by the private sector and thereby reduce pressure on the Syrian pound, the Government announced that remittances from abroad and other private sector 'invisible' earnings would be convertible into Syrian currency at a freely floating 'parallel' rate. At the same time, it imposed very tight restrictions on private businesses wishing to open letters of credit for imports. These were not eased until late 1984, and, even then, importers were advised that suppliers might have to wait nearly a year to receive payment. In late 1984 there was also an official reduction in the Syrian currency's value in terms of the tourist exchange rate, which was adjusted from $1 = £S7 to $1 = £S8. From September 1985, resident Syrians were permitted to open accounts in foreign currency at the Commercial Bank of Syria, to be used for imports. In the previous year this concession had been granted to foreigners and non-resident Syrians. In early 1986 there was a major currency crisis, with the value of the Syrian pound on the 'black' market dropping to $1 = £S17, or more. There were widespread arrests of currency dealers, and large quantities of gold and foreign currency were seized. The effect of these measures was to bring about a short-term appreciation in the value of the currency, but it soon began to depreciate once more, weakened by Syria's shortage of reserves of foreign exchange. Between October 1985 and October 1986 the Syrian pound lost 50% of its value against the US dollar. In August 1986 one of Syria's five exchange rates was devalued from $1 = £S11.75 to $1 = £S22, a level more comparable with the 'black' market rate, which fell to $1 = £S24–£S25 at the end of 1986, when the tourist exchange rate stood at $1 = £S9.75. The fixed official rate for government accounts and strategic imports remained at $1 = £S3.925, as it had been since April 1976. A decree of September 1986 rendered currency smugglers liable to prison terms of 15–25 years, and smugglers of precious metals to terms of three to 10 years. In September 1987 the Syrian pound, according to the official exchange rate, was devalued from $1 = £S3.925 (a level maintained since 1976) to $1 = £S11.20–£S11.25—a move that many observers considered to be long overdue.

Subsidies have been paid to Syria by other Arab countries since the Khartoum summit meeting of 1967. They were reinforced at the Rabat summit of 1974, which resulted in the promise of an annual $1,000m. to Syria in its capacity as a 'confrontation' state. The Baghdad summit of 1978 pledged to increase these subsidies to $1,800m. per year for a period of 10 years. The amount of Arab aid which Syria actually received reached $690m. in 1975 but dropped to only $355m. in 1976. The amounts received in 1979 and 1980 were estimated at $1,600m. and $1,400m., respectively, but donations were adversely affected by the Iran–Iraq war (in which Syria's former backers provided financial support to Iraq, while Syria sided with Iran) and by the erosion of the financial surpluses that OPEC countries accumulated before the decline in oil prices. Aid to Syria from the Gulf states was estimated to have dropped to $600m.–$700m. in 1986, although it has been difficult to gauge with any true accuracy the amount of aid from Gulf states under the Baghdad summit agreement. Saudi Arabia has been the most consistently conscientious of the Arab states in meeting its aid commitments to Syria.

Syrian political actions that have met with the approval of 'moderate' Arab states are often accompanied by reports of large sums being channelled from Saudi Arabia. Thus it was widely believed that Syria received a substantial 'reward' for attending the Arab summit held in Amman in November 1987, which was critical of Iran's actions in the Iran–Iraq War. Moreover, Syria's participation in the US-led multinational force which defeated Iraq in the Gulf War of 1991 led to further 'rewards' in the form of special aid totalling over $1,000m.

Syria also obtains considerable sums from multilateral and bilateral development aid sources, its receipts of official development aid (ODA) being in the $600m.–$700m. range in 1984–87, falling to $191m. in 1988 and to $127m. in 1989, rising to $650m. in 1990 (when ODA represented 4.4% of GNP) and falling to $373m. in 1991. Syria's debt arrears to funding institutions, particularly the World Bank, have, however, created problems. The arrears to the World Bank led to disbursements of new loans being 'frozen' in late 1986; in mid-1991 Syria's debt to the Bank was estimated at more than $400m. Political events have at times cast a shadow over Western governmental aid. In November 1983 the US Congress voted for US economic aid to Syria to be terminated; already in 1981 Congress had decided to 'freeze' $138.2m. in aid instalments totalling $227.8m. The Federal Republic of Germany cut off

aid in late 1986, after two Jordanians were sentenced for a bomb attack in Berlin in which Syria was implicated—a line of credit suspended since 1980 had only been restored in 1985. In 1987 aid was restored. The EC imposed a *de facto* 'freeze' on its aid to Syria in late 1986, but aid was resumed after the visit of the EC's North-South commissioner, Claude Cheysson, to Damascus in September 1987. In the third EC protocol, which came into effect at the start of 1993, Syria was allocated ECU 146m. A fourth EC protocol, providing for an allocation of ECU 158m., failed to gain the necessary support when it was submitted to the European Parliament for approval in March 1993. Syria's total external debt (including military debt to the former Soviet bloc countries of about $10,000m.) was estimated by the World Bank to have been $16,815m. at the end of 1991, compared with $3,549m. in the early 1980s. However, the debt-service ratio as a percentage of exports was reduced from 15.6% in 1986 to 3.9% in 1990.

In May 1994 the Minister of Economy and Foreign Trade said that Syria was currently making interest payments of $6m. per month on its World Bank debt of about $500m., and was seeking to negotiate arrangements whereby the Government would pay off one-third of the debt while a 'friends of Syria' donor group would pay off the remainder. He ruled out the option of a formal IMF/Paris Club arrangement as 'unacceptable in our political climate'. He said Syria was currently settling its outstanding debts to the export credit agencies of several West European states; that it had reduced its indebtedness to commercial banks to about $500m. through repayments and restructuring agreements; and that it regarded its military debt to the former Soviet Union as a matter for discussion 'in its proper context as a mutual obligation'. It had been reported in April 1994 that Syria had sought an 80% write-off of military debt during exploratory talks with Russian officials.

Syria's economic problems intensified during the 1980s. Import controls, restrictions on the availability of (and dealings in) foreign exchange and an anti-corruption programme hampered private business, and failed to attract the capital of wealthy Syrians resident abroad. The annual rate of inflation was officially acknowledged to be 60% in 1987, compared with 36% in 1986, but fell to 11.4% in 1989, before rising to an average of 20% from 1990 to 1993.

After the October 1973 war, state expenditure also clearly reflected the inflow of foreign funds. The general budget soared from a total of £S6,976m. in 1974 to £S16,564m. in 1976. The events of 1976, however, caused the authorities to reconsider and in 1977 and 1978 overall budget expenditure increased by only about 5% in absolute terms over each of the previous years. In 1979, as a result of the pledges made at the Baghdad summit, a big increase in defence spending raised total budget expenditure to £S22,600m. By 1985 the total had increased to £S42,984m. ($10,950m.), with defence, at £S13,000m., continuing to take a major share of current spending. The 4% nominal increase in total expenditure compared with an annual rate of inflation estimated at 10%. Investment expenditure under the 1985 budget was estimated at only £S19,436m., compared with £S17,886m. in 1984 and £S17,981m. in 1983. In the 1986 budget total spending amounted to £S37,091m., a substantial drop in real terms, taking inflation into account. In the 1987 budget, expenditure was cut by 4.4% to £S35,443m. Current expenditure was reduced by 14.1% to £S23,029m. Defence received the largest single allocation (£S14,327m., accounting for 62.2% of current expenditure), while agriculture was allocated about 20% (£S3,500m.) of total investment spending, compared with almost 25% in 1986. The 1988 draft budget was the first for a number of years to feature a substantial increase in spending. Total expenditure was raised by more than one-fifth to £S51,545m., compared with actual spending of £S35,443m. in 1987. Current expenditure rose from £S23,029m. to £S29,665m., and investment spending from £S12,414m. to £S21,880m. Of revenues of £S51,545m., taxes, aid and services were budgeted to provide £S34,848m. and the state sector surplus £S16,697m. The 1989 and 1990 budgets provided for expenditure of £S57,413m. and £S61,875m. respectively. The 1991 budget set expenditure at £S84,690m. and envisaged an effective deficit of £S13,676m., although this was treated as exceptional financing in order to achieve a technical balance. The 1992 budget was also technically balanced, providing for expenditure and revenue of £S93,043m.; this represented a nominal spending increase of almost 10% over 1991, although after allowing for inflation of 20% budgeted spending was lower in real terms. The 1992 expenditure total consisted of £S56,793m. in current spending and £S36,250m. in investment, with defence accounting for 26% of current spending (considerably less than in previous years), education 20% and health 5%. The largest allocation in the investment budget, some 26%, was for agriculture and irrigation. The effective deficit in the 1992 budget was equivalent to 20.9% of total revenue, to be funded by concessional loans totalling £S13,904m. and other foreign loans totalling £S5,607m.

The 1993 budget provided for total expenditure of £S123,018m., including £S27,869m. for defence (up 2.5% on 1992) and £S12,671m. for electricity, water and gas (up 157% on 1992). Overall, investment spending was nearly twice as high as in 1992, and represented about half of total budgeted spending for 1993. The effective deficit was equal to 34.9% of the total budget in Syrian pounds, the borrowing elements on the revenue side being concessional loans of £S9,000m., other foreign loans totalling £S22,868m. and domestic loans of £S11,026m. (compared with a zero requirement for domestic loans in the 1992 budget). The real increase in foreign borrowing between 1992 and 1993 was estimated to be around 6.5% in dollar terms after allowance was made for the Government's use of an exchange rate of $1 = £S43 (rather than the official accounting rate of $1 = £S11.2) to calculate this component of the 1993 budget. The overall size of the deficit was nevertheless criticized by several deputies during the budget debate in the Syrian legislature (which formally adopted the Government's proposals on 9 May 1993). The 1994 budget provided for total expenditure of £S144,162m. (17.2% higher than in 1993). Public-sector wages were raised by 30% in May 1994, while price increases were announced for electricity, petrol and many other items. In the same month the currency exchange rate used to levy customs duties on items other than basic commodities and most industrial raw materials was changed from $1 = £S11.2 to $1 = £S23. (The former rate continued to apply to the 'basic' import category.)

The current account of Syria's balance of payments was $959m. in surplus in 1979. In 1980 the surplus fell to $251m., and there was a deficit in every subsequent year until 1989. In that year a surplus of $1,222m. was recorded, followed by surpluses of $1,762m. in 1990, $699m. in 1991 and $55m. in 1992, when increased spending on imports coincided with reduced revenue from oil exports. Remittances from Syrians working abroad were estimated at $550m. in 1992, while capital inflows through government channels totalled $313m.

Total official reserves (excluding gold) fluctuated considerably in the 1980s. At the end of the first half of 1986 they declined to only $10m., but by the end of 1988 they had increased to $191m. Net foreign assets rose from $2,000m. at the end of 1989 to $3,700m. at the end of 1990.

The Government was in mid-1994 finalizing a draft law to establish a stock market in Syria in order to facilitate a structured transition to a market economy. The Government was also coming under increasing pressure from the private business sector to relax the state monopoly on banking. Savers had recently been depositing funds with unlicensed finance houses, several of which had collapsed in circumstances which prompted the passage of legislation to shut down the remaining such operations in June 1994.

ECONOMIC PLANNING

The most ambitious of the projects contained in the third Five-Year Plan (1971–75) was the Euphrates Dam project, on which construction work began in 1968. Most of the country's future industrial and agricultural development depends on this scheme, and nearly one-quarter of public investment over the Plan period was earmarked for its implementation, with £S950m. allocated for the dam itself and £S643m. for land reclamation and development in the Euphrates basin. The project involved the construction of a dam 4.6 km long and 60 m high, with a width of 500 m at the bottom. The reservoir thus created, Lake Assad, was designed to hold 12,000m. cu m

of water, operating eight turbines and enabling the long-term irrigation of 640,000 ha of land, including 550,000 ha by 1990. The scheme was undertaken with the help of 1,200 Soviet technicians and about £S600m. in Soviet financial assistance, under an agreement reached with the USSR in April 1966. By 1977, however, only 100 Soviet experts remained on the site. In the spring of 1978 the entire project was formally opened, although the dam's first turbines had started to operate, ahead of schedule, in early 1974. Despite its advantages, the dam has exacerbated friction between Syria and Iraq, which also relies on water from the Euphrates river. Disputes over water rights reached a crisis point in 1974–75, when Turkey started to fill the reservoir behind its Keban dam, also on the Euphrates, at the same time as Syria started to fill Lake Assad, leaving Iraq with much less water than usual. Tension over this issue subsided in 1977–78, but resurfaced in 1984 between Syria and Turkey after the latter had started work on its new Atatürk dam. It is thought that the Atatürk dam and the associated South East Anatolian project (GAP) could remove 5,000m. cu m of water per year, or more, from the Euphrates, once they are completed, in or around the year 2015.

The fourth Five-Year Plan started in 1976 but was interrupted by the events of that year and was reissued in 1977. It envisaged expenditure of nearly £S53,000m., comprising £S27,000m. for projects already under way, £S17,600m. for new projects and £S8,000m. to be held in reserve. Mining and manufacturing were to take 22% of the £S44,600m. allocated to specific projects, followed by energy and fuel development (17.8%) and Euphrates projects (16.6%). The target for the average annual growth of GDP during the Plan period was 12%, compared with 8.2% under the previous Plan. One important aspect of the Fourth Plan, in its original form, was its emphasis on tourism, which was expected to become the country's third main source of foreign currency, after petroleum and cotton, by 1980. This objective has not been achieved, however, partly because of political factors. Tourist traffic declined from 774,500 tourists in 1979 to 346,800 in 1982, though it rose to 565,000 in 1984, largely because of an arrangement whereby Iranians visited Syria in part-payment for Iranian oil supplies. The number of Iranian visitors dropped from 157,200 in 1984 to 132,600 in 1985, and there was a decline in the overall number of tourists to 486,700. In 1986, however, the number of Iranian tourists rose to a record 174,000 and the total number of tourists reached 567,700. The number of tourists from Western Europe is still modest—by far the largest number in 1986 came from West Germany (17,100) and France (14,800), followed by the UK and Italy, each with 5,600. Western tourists are doubtless deterred by the instability in the region and by fear of terrorist attacks. Since 1978, a number of joint public/private sector companies, in which the Government has a minority interest, have been set up.

Like its predecessor, the fifth Five-Year Plan (for 1981–85) started late, and details of its targets did not become available until 1982. Its main features included a decisive shift in investment from industry to agriculture, with the agricultural sector receiving a provisional allocation of £S17,200m., or 16.9% of the overall £S101,493m. spending target. The annual growth rate target for agriculture was set at 7.8%, compared with a projected 8% under the previous Plan and an average annual growth rate target of 7.7% for the economy as a whole.

The role that the private sector should play in the economy has been subject to debate. Private sector funding for the Fifth Plan was set at £S23,351m., compared with £S68,705m. from the public sector and £S59,437m. from foreign sources. However, the Baath Party Congress of January 1985 criticized public sector performance and specifically encouraged private sector investment. In 1986 the first joint public/private sector company in agriculture was established, 75% owned by the private sector and 25% by the state. Several other such ventures were subsequently created. Previously, these joint ventures had been found only in the tourist industry.

Few details on the Sixth Plan (1986–90) were released and, in view of Syria's economic constraints, five-year plans have tended to be a somewhat academic exercise anyway. Like its predecessor, the Plan concentrated on completing projects in hand and making those already complete operate efficiently, rather than embarking on a series of new projects. Syrian officials revealed that the share of agriculture in proposed investment was projected to increase from 16.9% to 18.9%, and that of industry from 12.2% to 13.7%. In real terms, spending under the Plan was to be only slightly more than under the fifth Plan.

Statistical Survey

Source (unless otherwise stated): Central Bureau of Statistics, rue Abd al-Malek bin Marwah, Malki Quarter, Damascus; tel. (11) 335830; telex 411099.

Area and Population

AREA, POPULATION AND DENSITY

Area (sq km)	
Land	184,050
Inland water	1,130
Total	185,180*
Population (census results)†	
23 September 1970	6,304,685
8 September 1981	
Males	4,624,761
Females	4,427,867
Total	9,052,628
Population (official estimates at mid-year)†	
1991	12,529,000
1992	12,958,000
1993	13,393,000
Density (per sq km) at mid-1993	72.3

* 71,498 sq miles.
† Including Palestinian refugees, numbering 193,000 at mid-1977.

PRINCIPAL TOWNS (estimated population at 30 June 1990)

Damascus (capital)	1,378,000	Hama . . .	237,000
Aleppo . . .	1,355,000	Al-Kamishli . .	132,000*
Homs . . .	481,000	Rakka . . .	122,000
Latakia . . .	267,000	Deir ez-Zor . .	118,000

* At 30 June 1989.
Source: UN, *Demographic Yearbook*.

REGISTERED BIRTHS, MARRIAGES AND DEATHS

	Births	Marriages	Deaths
1987	478,136	102,626	51,581
1988	435,795	99,323	44,899
1989	421,733	102,557	45,481
1990	385,316	91,705	39,897

Expectation of life (years at birth, 1981): males 64.42; females 68.05 (Source: UN, *Demographic Yearbook*).

ECONOMICALLY ACTIVE POPULATION
(sample survey, persons aged 10 years and over, April 1991)*

	Males	Females	Total
Agriculture, hunting, forestry and fishing	625,001	291,951	916,952
Mining and quarrying . . .	6,651	—	6,651
Manufacturing	421,523	34,639	456,162
Electricity, gas and water . .	7,866	556	8,422
Construction	334,343	6,436	340,779
Trade, restaurants and hotels .	368,955	9,295	378,250
Transport, storage and communications . . .	158,358	8,607	166,965
Financing, insurance, real estate and business services	20,176	4,475	24,651
Community, social and personal services . . .	767,428	183,676	951,104
Total employed	2,710,301	539,635	3,249,936
Unemployed	147,281	88,151	235,432
Total labour force . . .	2,857,582	627,786	3,485,368

* Figures refer to Syrians only, excluding armed forces.
Source: ILO, *Year Book of Labour Statistics*.

Agriculture

PRINCIPAL CROPS ('000 metric tons)

	1990	1991	1992
Wheat	2,070	2,140	3,046
Barley	846	917	1,092
Maize	180	224	216
Chick peas	36	28	74
Dry broad beans	10	9	10
Haricot beans	3	2	6
Lentils	110	75*	52
Seed cotton	441	555	689
Tobacco	13	16	24
Sesame seed	8	10	12
Grapes	423	487	533
Olives	461	226	491
Apricots	73	56	81
Apples	205	215*	248
Plums	43	35	46
Oranges	171	202	154
Almonds	13	25	54
Watermelons	250	270*	347
Melons	44	46	48*
Cucumbers	173	165*	152
Squash	104	124*	111
Sugar beet	422	653	1,272
Onions	95	80	108
Cabbages	52	46	36
Cauliflowers	40	35*	27
Aubergines (Egg-plants) . .	135	140*	127
Green peppers	40	45*	36
Tomatoes	430	428	448
Potatoes	398	452	420

* FAO estimate.
Source: FAO, *Production Yearbook*.

LIVESTOCK ('000 head, year ending September)

	1990	1991	1992
Cattle	787	771	762
Horses	41	39	42†
Camels	5	5	6†
Asses	168	161	165†
Mules	26	25	28†
Sheep	14,509	15,194	15,782
Goats	1,008	963	986

Chickens (million): 15 in 1990; 15 in 1991; 16* in 1992.
* Unofficial figure. † FAO estimate.
Source: FAO, *Production Yearbook*.

LIVESTOCK PRODUCTS ('000 metric tons)

	1990	1991	1992
Beef and veal	27†	24*	24*
Mutton and lamb . . .	90	91*	91*
Goats' meat	6	6*	6*
Poultry meat	57	59*	57
Cows' milk	771	780†	775*
Sheep's milk	497	500*	505*
Goats' milk	63	67*	68*
Butter and ghee . . .	12.4	13.1*	13.4*
Cheese	64.5	66.4*	67.6*
Hen eggs	76.0†	70.0*	65.3*
Wool:			
greasy	31.4	31.9*	32.6*
clean	15.7	18.5*	19.0*

* FAO estimate. † Unofficial figure.
Source: FAO, *Production Yearbook*.

Forestry

ROUNDWOOD REMOVALS ('000 cubic metres, excl. bark)

	1990	1991	1992
Sawlogs, veneer logs and logs for sleepers	22	44	51
Other industrial wood* . .	19	19	19
Fuel wood	13	23	25
Total	54	86	95

* FAO estimates.
Sawnwood production ('000 cubic metres): 9 in 1980; 9 per year (FAO estimates) in 1981–92.
Source: FAO, *Yearbook of Forest Products*.

Fishing

('000 metric tons, live weight)

	1989	1990	1991
Inland waters	3.5	4.2	4.0
Mediterranean sea . . .	1.5	1.6	1.5*
Total catch	5.1	5.8	5.5*

* FAO estimates.
Source: FAO, *Yearbook of Fishery Statistics*.

Mining

('000 metric tons, unless otherwise indicated)

	1990	1991	1992*
Crude petroleum ('000 cubic metres)	23,474	27,276	29,763
Phosphate rock . . .	1,633	1,469	1,265
Salt (unrefined) . . .	127	74	84
Natural asphalt . . .	71	67	72

* Figures are provisional.
Source: Central Bank of Syria, *Quarterly Bulletin*.

Industry

SELECTED PRODUCTS
('000 metric tons, unless otherwise indicated)

	1990	1991	1992*
Cotton yarn (pure) . . .	37.2	n.a.	n.a.
Silk and cotton textiles . .	27	28	26
Woollen cloth (metric tons) .	533	n.a.	498
Cement	3,049	2,843	3,246
Glass and pottery products .	38	54	50
Soap	15	16	17
Refined sugar	135	179	178
Margarine	6	n.a.	n.a.
Olive oil	86	39	103
Vegetable oil and fats . .	32	33	34
Cottonseed cake . . .	121	117	119
Manufactured tobacco . .	7	8	8
Electricity (million kWh) .	10,548	11,249	10,186
Refrigerators ('000) . .	39.9	84.7	68.0
Washing machines ('000) .	43.8	29.2	40.9
Beer ('000 hectolitres) . .	99	n.a.	n.a.
Wine ('000 hectolitres) . .	3	n.a.	n.a.
Arak ('000 hectolitres) . .	20	n.a.	n.a.

* Figures are provisional.
Source: Central Bank of Syria, *Quarterly Bulletin*.

Finance

CURRENCY AND EXCHANGE RATES

Monetary Units
100 piastres = 1 Syrian pound (£S).

Sterling and Dollar Equivalents (31 May 1994)
£1 sterling = £S16.970;
US $1 = £S11.225;
£S1,000 = £58.93 sterling = $89.09.

Exchange Rate
Between April 1976 and December 1987 the official mid-point rate was fixed at US $1 = £S3.925. On 1 January 1988 a new rate of $1 = £S11.225 was introduced. In addition to the official exchange rate, there is a promotion rate (applicable to most travel and tourism transactions) and a flexible rate.

BUDGET (estimates, £S million)

Revenue	1990	1991	1992
Taxes and duties	22,123.0	27,720.0	29,408.2
Services, commutations and revenues from state properties and their public investments	2,666.0	3,453.8	4,857.5
Various revenues . . .	18,464.3	26,762.0	36,815.9
Supply surplus . . .	13,064.6	13,078.1	16,126.8
Exceptional revenues . .	11,176.0	13,676.4	5,833.8
Total	67,493.9	84,690.3	93,042.2

Expenditure	1990	1991	1992
Community, social and personal services . . .	48,216.4	64,120.8	63,330.4
Agriculture, forestry and fishing	7,067.1	7,912.9	10,192.8
Mining and quarrying . .	2,525.1	1,697.9	2,683.5
Manufacturing. . . .	1,497.4	2,020.5	3,953.6
Electricity, gas and water . .	3,166.5	3,020.3	4,934.2
Building and construction . .	384.5	289.2	911.2
Trade	984.8	867.5	1,226.5
Transport, communications and storage	2,140.5	3,156.2	3,920.8
Finance, insurance and companies . . .	365.0	355.0	638.7
Non-distributed funds . . .	1,150.0	1,250.0	1,250.0
Total	67,497.3	84,690.3	93,042.2

CENTRAL BANK RESERVES (US $ million at 31 December)

	1986	1987	1988
Gold*	29	29	29
Foreign exchange . . .	144	223	193
Total	173	252	222

* Valued at $35 per troy ounce.
Source: IMF, *International Financial Statistics.*

MONEY SUPPLY (£S million at 31 December)

	1990	1991	1992
Currency outside banks . .	76,202.0	92,450.1	107,556.6
Demand deposits at Central Bank	6,627.0	11,840.5	21,227.2
Demand deposits at commercial banks	35,745.5	41,972.8	53,341.0
Total money	118,574.5	146,263.4	182,124.8

Source: Central Bank of Syria, *Quarterly Bulletin.*

COST OF LIVING
(Consumer Price Index for Damascus; base: 1980 = 100)

	1990	1991	1992
Food	795.5	823.9	851.6
Fuel and light	493.7	544.7	766.8
Clothing	769.9	906.5	952.9
Rent	281.8	282.3	282.3
All items (incl. others) . .	715.4	770.2	843.5

Source: ILO, *Year Book of Labour Statistics.*
1993: Food 962.9; All items 942.5 (Source: UN, *Monthly Bulletin of Statistics*).

NATIONAL ACCOUNTS (£S million at current prices)
Expenditure on the Gross Domestic Product

	1990	1991	1992*
Government final consumption expenditure	38,502	47,582	59,943
Private final consumption expenditure	187,433	236,523	265,696
Gross capital formation . .	41,351	55,992	87,624
Total domestic expenditure .	267,286	340,097	413,263
Exports of goods and services .	76,042	76,038	97,577
Less Imports of goods and services	75,000	99,931	139,850
GDP in purchasers' values .	268,328	316,204	370,990
GDP at constant 1985 prices	89,485	99,277	109,510

* Provisional figures.

Gross Domestic Product by Economic Activity

	1990	1991	1992*
Agriculture, hunting, forestry and fishing	76,514	94,367	110,587
Mining and quarrying . . .	40,154		
Manufacturing. . . .	14,111	63,144	61,498
Electricity, gas and water . .	−208		
Construction	10,128	12,163	14,132
Trade, restaurants and hotels .	60,875	66,251	87,846
Transport, storage and communications . . .	25,542	29,819	33,723
Finance, insurance, real estate and business services . .	9,996	10,984	12,308
Government services . .	26,127	33,334	43,788
Other community, social and personal services . .	4,986	6,024	6,973
Non-profit private services .	103	118	135
GDP in purchasers' values .	268,328	316,204	370,990

* Provisional figures.
Source: mainly Central Bank of Syria, *Quarterly Bulletin.*

BALANCE OF PAYMENTS (US $ million)

	1990	1991	1992
Merchandise exports f.o.b. .	4,156	3,438	3,100
Merchandise imports f.o.b. .	−2,062	−2,354	−2,941
Trade balance . . .	2,094	1,084	159
Exports of services . .	874	1,065	1,281
Imports of services . .	−892	−1,002	−1,102
Other income received . .	45	65	69
Other income paid . . .	−831	−1,096	−1,214
Private unrequited transfers (net) . . .	385	350	550
Official unrequited transfers (net) . . .	88	234	313
Current balance . . .	1,762	699	55
Capital (net)	−1,836	−515	−50
Net errors and omissions . .	110	−112	70
Overall balance . . .	36	72	76

Source: IMF, *International Financial Statistics.*

External Trade
PRINCIPAL COMMODITIES (£S million)

Imports c.i.f.	1990	1991	1992
Cotton textiles, other textile goods and silk . . .	1,913.4	2,421.2	2,941.6
Mineral fuels and oils . .	805.7	737.2	1,519.6
Live animals, meat and canned meat.	493.6	2,932.9	1,414.4
Vegetables and fruit . . .	98.9	766.4	291.6
Sugar	1,577.3	1,179.1	1,113.6
Other foodstuffs . . .	5,837.0	5,042.5	4,051.9
Machinery and apparatus . .	4,266.5	4,631.0	6,989.5
Base metals and manufactures	4,149.1	3,323.9	5,776.0
Chemicals and pharmaceutical products.	2,757.6	3,808.6	3,849.2
Transport equipment . . .	1,041.8	2,034.7	5,153.6
Paper and paper products . .	665.6	899.1	734.7
Wood and wood products . .	387.8	298.5	562.0
Resins, artificial rubber, etc. .	1,304.8	1,681.6	2,971.3
Total (incl. others) . . .	26,936.1	30,794.4	39,178.3

Exports f.o.b.		1990	1991	1992
Raw cotton		1,716.3	1,920.8	2,038.1
Textiles		10,030.3	8,985.7	2,616.5
Vegetables and fruit (fresh and prepared)		2,334.1	2,388.1	2,634.6
Live animals and meat. . .		2,588.7	1,391.6	1,303.7
Lentils.		272.6	134.2	113.8
Wool		23.6	43.9	28.7
Raw hides and leather. . .		120.5	109.4	194.2
Phosphates . . .		420.6	394.4	488.0
Crude petroleum . . .		16,498.7	17,217.8	20,773.5
Total (incl. others) . .		47,281.6	38,504.0	34,719.8

PRINCIPAL TRADING PARTNERS (£S million)

Imports c.i.f.		1990	1991	1992
Austria		454.9	495.3	482.3
Belgium		883.6	1,062.6	1,240.7
Bulgaria		437.4	866.5	1,677.4
China, People's Republic . .		463.3	632.3	1,045.7
Cuba		246.0	253.2	218.2
Czechoslovakia . . .		217.1	377.1	620.6
Denmark		127.2	259.1	140.7
Egypt		227.2	295.1	481.4
France.		3,425.2	2,090.5	2,479.4
Germany		2,509.5	3,130.0	4,006.1
Greece.		324.3	427.7	307.2
Hungary		253.2	286.4	357.3
India		129.2	208.8	295.8
Iran		365.7	16.9	135.4
Italy		1,714.9	2,257.1	3,208.4
Japan		890.8	1,403.8	3,899.6
Kuwait		275.7	2.6	38.0
Lebanon		188.3	330.4	519.4
Netherlands		638.6	793.3	1,137.2
Poland.		321.5	477.3	319.3
Romania		244.5	831.2	1,698.2
Russia		766.9	417.8	825.8
Saudi Arabia		368.6	411.6	465.1
Spain		482.5	552.3	443.3
Sri Lanka		310.7	276.6	246.7
Sweden		526.8	693.7	500.4
Switzerland		207.1	215.8	319.2
Turkey		2,073.1	2,851.7	2,431.8
United Kingdom . . .		711.7	810.8	1,154.8
USA		2,892.8	2,907.8	2,397.1
Yugoslavia. . . .		440.3	672.2	230.6
Total (incl. others) . .		26,936.1	30,794.4	39,178.3

Exports f.o.b.		1990	1991	1992
Bulgaria		391.6	892.6	829.2
Egypt		534.7	152.5	189.8
France.		6,039.4	6,811.3	6,446.0
Germany		1,110.2	1,135.1	853.2
Greece		410.9	233.2	139.5
Italy		9,845.9	8,622.6	12,163.7
Jordan.		275.0	768.4	581.7
Kuwait		138.9	188.3	692.1
Lebanon		2,988.0	3,695.2	4,516.3
Netherlands . . .		1,001.8	627.8	244.9
Poland.		44.8	221.1	138.9
Romania		77.2	677.3	378.0
Russia		15,445.8	7,259.6	534.0
Saudi Arabia . . .		3,035.4	2,238.4	1,498.1
Spain		321.8	264.2	1,232.1
Switzerland . . .		179.3	210.8	189.4
Turkey		1,274.6	1,036.4	482.0
United Kingdom . .		935.7	729.3	647.0
USA		405.3	208.5	273.6
Total (incl. others) . .		47,281.6	38,503.9	34,719.8

Source: Central Bank of Syria, *Quarterly Bulletin*.

Transport

RAILWAYS (traffic)

	1988	1989	1990
Passenger-km ('000) . .	1,132,804	1,112,657	1,139,926
Freight ('000 metric tons) .	5,992	5,341	5,236

ROAD TRAFFIC (motor vehicles in use)

	1988	1989	1990
Passenger cars. . . .	112,337	112,259	112,906
Buses and coaches. . .	12,004	12,477	13,127
Lorries, trucks, etc. . .	126,401	118,056	118,492
Motor cycles	75,464	78,141	79,406

SHIPPING

	1988	1989	1990
Vessels entered (number) . .	2,184	2,150	2,087
Cargo unloaded ('000 tons) .	3,497	4,303	4,588
Cargo loaded ('000 tons) .	9,059	12,087	1,743

CIVIL AVIATION (traffic on scheduled services)

	1989	1990	1991
Kilometres flown (million). .	9	10	11
Passengers carried ('000) .	456	613	661
Passenger-km (million) .	797	1,105	1,136
Freight ton-km (million) .	10	18	14

Source: UN, *Statistical Yearbook*.

Tourism

VISITOR ARRIVALS ('000 visitors)

	1990	1991	1992*
Jordanians, Lebanese and Iraqis	780	923	982
Other Arabs	194	210	255
Europeans	88	69	100
Asians	348	340	357
Others	32	28	45
Total visitors	1,442	1,570	1,739

* Preliminary figures.

Tourist Accommodation: 29,396 tourist hotel beds (1990).

Communications Media

	1989	1990	1991
Radio receivers ('000 in use) .	3,000	3,150	3,270
Television receivers ('000 in use)		710	740	770

Source: UNESCO, *Statistical Yearbook*.

Education

	Teachers			Pupils		
	1989/90	1990/91	1991/92	1989/90	1990/91	1991/92
Pre-primary	3,283	3,122	3,257	84,763	83,552	86,006
Primary . .	90,272	97,811	102,617	2,357,981	2,452,086	2,539,081
Secondary:						
General .	42,623	44,875	46,218	856,942	847,783	849,530
Vocational	8,379	9,240	8,811	66,590	66,467	53,289

Source: UNESCO, *Statistical Yearbook*.

Directory

The Constitution

A new and permanent constitution was endorsed by 97.6% of the voters in a national referendum on 12 March 1973. The 157-article Constitution defines Syria as a 'Socialist popular democracy' with a 'pre-planned Socialist economy'. Under the new Constitution, Lt-Gen. al-Assad remained President, with the power to appoint and dismiss his Vice-President, Premier and government ministers, and also became Commander-in-Chief of the armed forces, Secretary-General of the Baath Socialist Party and President of the National Progressive Front. Legislative power is vested in the People's Assembly, with 250 members elected by universal adult suffrage (84 seats are reserved for independent candidates).

The Government

HEAD OF STATE

President: Lt-Gen. HAFIZ AL-ASSAD (elected 12 March 1971 for a seven-year term; re-elected 8 February 1978, 10 February 1985 and 2 December 1991).

Vice-Presidents: ABD AL-HALIM KHADDAM (responsible for Political and Foreign Affairs), RIFAAT AL-ASSAD (responsible for Military and National Security Affairs*), ZUHEIR MASHARKAH (responsible for Internal and Party Affairs).

* Reportedly resigned from all official posts in April 1988.

COUNCIL OF MINISTERS
(October 1994)

Prime Minister: MAHMOUD AZ-ZOUBI.

Deputy Prime Minister and Minister of Defence: Gen. MUS-TAFA TLASS.

Deputy Prime Minister in charge of Public Services: RASHID AKH-TARINI.

Deputy Prime Minister in charge of Economic Affairs: SALIM YASSIN.

Minister of Foreign Affairs: FAROUK ASH-SHARA'.

Minister of Information: MUHAMMAD SALMAN.

Minister of the Interior: Dr MUHAMMAD HARBAH.

Minister of Supply and Internal Trade: NADIM AKKASH.

Minister of Local Government: YAHYA ABU ASALAH.

Minister of Education: GHASSAN HALABI.

Minister of Higher Education: Dr SALIHAH SANQAR.

Minister of Electricity: MUNIB ASAAD SAIM AL-DAHER.

Minister of Culture: Dr NAJAH AL-ATTAR.

Minister of Transport: Dr MUFID ABD AL-KARIM.

Minister of Economy and Foreign Trade: Dr MUHAMMAD AL-IMADI.

Minister of Petroleum and Mineral Wealth: Dr NADIR AN-NABULSI.

Minister of Industry: Dr AHMAD NIZAM AD-DIN.

Minister of Finance: KHALID AL-MAHAYNI.

Minister of Housing and Utilities: Eng. HUSAM AS-SAFADI.

Minister of Justice: Dr ABDULLAH TULBAH.

Minister of Agriculture and Agrarian Reform: ASSAD MUSTAFA.

Minister of Irrigation, Public Works and Water Resources: Eng. ABD AR-RAHMAN MADANI.

Minister of Communications: Eng. RADWAN MARTINI.

Minister of Health: Dr IYAD ASH-SHATTI.

Minister of Construction: MAJID IZZU RUHAYBANI.

Minister of Awqaf (Islamic Endowments): ABD AL-MAJID AT-TARAB-ULSI.

Minister of Tourism: AMIN ABU ASH-SHAMAT.

Minister of Labour and Social Affairs: ALI KHALIL.

Minister of State for Presidential Affairs: WAHIB FADEL.

Minister of State for Council of Ministers Affairs: DANHU DAOUD.

Minister of State for Planning Affairs: Dr ABD AR-RAHIM SUBAYI.

Minister of State for Environmental Affairs: ABD AL-HAMID AL-MOUNAJJID.

Minister of State for Foreign Affairs: NASIR QADDOUR.

Ministers of State: Eng. YOUSUF AL-AHMAD, HUSSEIN HASSUN, NABIL MALLAH, Eng. HANNA MURAD.

MINISTRIES

Office of the President: Damascus.

Office of the Prime Minister: Damascus.

Ministry of Agriculture and Agrarian Reform: 29 rue Ayar, Damascus; tel. (11) 113613.

Ministry of Communications: nr Majlis ash-Sha'ab, Damascus; telex 411993.

Ministry of Economy and Foreign Trade: Damascus; tel. (11) 113513; telex 411982.

Ministry of Electricity: BP 4900, 41 rue al-Jamhourieh, Damascus; tel. (11) 227981; telex 411256.

Ministry of Finance: POB 13136, Jule Jamal St, Damascus; tel. (11) 2239624; telex 411932; fax (11) 2224701.

Ministry of Foreign Affairs: Damascus; telex 411922.

Ministry of Industry: place Yousuf Ahmad, Damascus; tel. (11) 115647.

Ministry of Information: ave al-Mazzeh, Imm. Dar al-Baath, Damascus; tel. (11) 6664600.

Ministry of Petroleum and Mineral Wealth: rue Moutanabbi, Damascus; tel. (11) 116783; telex 411006.

Ministry of Public Works and Water Resources: rue Saadallah Jabri, Damascus.

Ministry of Supply and Internal Trade: opposite Majlis ash-Sha'ab, Damascus; tel. (11) 720604; telex 412908.

Ministry of Tourism: rue Victoria, Damascus; tel. (11) 2215916; telex 411672; fax (11) 2242636.

Ministry of Transport: BP 134, rue Abou Roumaneh, Damascus; tel. (11) 336801; telex 411994.

Legislature

MAJLIS ASH-SHA'AB

(People's Assembly)

Speaker: ABD AL-QADIR QADDURAH.

Election, 24 August 1994

Party	Seats
Baath Party	135
Arab Socialist Unionist Party	7
Syrian Arab Socialist Union Party	7
Arab Socialist Party	6
Socialist Unionist Democratic Party	4
Communist Party	8
Independents	83
Total	**250**

Political Organizations

The **National Progressive Front**, headed by President Assad, was formed in March 1972 by the grouping of the following five parties:

Arab Socialist Party: Damascus; a breakaway socialist party; contested the 1994 election to the People's Assembly as two factions; Leader ABD AL-GHANI KANNOUT.

Arab Socialist Unionist Party: Damascus; Leader SAMI SOUFAN; Sec.-Gen. FAYIZ ISMAIL.

Baath Arab Socialist Party: National Command, BP 849, Damascus; Arab nationalist socialist party; f. 1947; result of merger of the Arab Revival (Baath) Movement (f. 1940) and the Arab Socialist Party (f. 1940); brs in most Arab countries; in power since 1963; supports creation of a unified Arab socialist society; Sec.-Gen. Pres. HAFIZ AL-ASSAD; Asst Sec.-Gen. ABDULLAH AL-AHMAR; Regional Asst Sec.-Gen. Dr SULEIMAN QADDAH; more than 800,000 mems in Syria.

Communist Party of Syria: Damascus; tel. (11) 448243; f. 1924; until 1943 part of joint Communist Party of Syria and Lebanon; Sixth Party Congress January 1987; contested the 1994 election to the People's Assembly as two factions; Sec.-Gen. YOUSUF FAISAL.

Syrian Arab Socialist Union Party: Damascus; tel. (11) 239305; Nasserite; Leader Dr JAMAL ATASI; Sec.-Gen. SAFWAN KOUDSI.

A sixth party, the **Socialist Unionist Democratic Party**, contested the elections held to the People's Assembly in May 1990 and August 1994 as a member of the National Progressive Front. There is also a **Marxist-Leninist Communist Action Party**, which regards itself as independent of all Arab regimes.

Diplomatic Representation

EMBASSIES IN SYRIA

Afghanistan: Immeuble Muhammad Amin Abd ar-Rabou, 2nd Floor, rue al-Bizan, West Malki; tel. (11) 713103; Ambassador: ABDUL JALIL PORSHOR.

Algeria: Raouda, Immeuble Noss, Damascus; telex 411344; Ambassador: SALEM BOUJOUMAA.

Argentina: BP 116, Raouda, rue Ziad ben Abi Soufian, Damascus; telex 411058; Ambassador: ANDRÉS GABRIEL CEUSTERMANS.

Australia: 128A rue Farabi, East Villas, Immeuble Dakkak, Mezzeh, Damascus; tel. (11) 662603; telex 419132; Ambassador: VICTORIA OWEN.

Austria: BP 5634, Raouda, rue Chafik Mouayed, Immeuble Sabri Malki, Damascus; tel. (11) 3337528; telex 411389; fax (11) 3329232; Ambassador: Dr ROBERT KARAS.

Belgium: rue Ata Ayoubi, Immeuble Hachem, Damascus; tel. (11) 3332821; telex 411090; fax (11) 3330426; Ambassador: MICHEL LASTCHENKO.

Brazil: BP 2219, 76 rue Ata Ayoubi, Damascus; telex 411204; Ambassador: LUIZ CLAUDIO PEREIRA CARDOSA.

Bulgaria: 4 rue Chahbandar, Damascus; Ambassador: GEORGI YANKOV.

Canada: POB 3394, Damascus; tel. (11) 2236892; telex 412422; fax (11) 2236892; Ambassador: GARY R. HARMAN.

Chile: 43 rue ar-Rachid, Damascus; tel. (11) 3338443; telex 411392; fax (11) 3331563; Chargé d'affaires a.i.: ALFREDO LABBÉ.

China, People's Republic: 83 rue Ata Ayoubi, Damascus; Ambassador: LI QINGYU.

Cuba: 40 rue ar-Rachid, Immeuble Oustwani and Charabati, Damascus; tel. (11) 3339624; telex 419155; fax (11) 3333802; Ambassador: ERNESTO GÓMEZ ABASCAL.

Cyprus: BP 3853, Abd al-Malek al-Marouan, Jaded ar-Rais, Abou Roumaneh, Damascus; tel. (11) 332804; telex 411411; Ambassador: NICOLAS MACRIS.

Czech Republic: place Abou al-Ala'a al-Maari, Damascus.

Denmark: BP 2244, Immeuble Patriarcat Grec-Catholique, rue Chekib Arslan, Abou Roumaneh, Damascus; tel. (11) 3331008; telex 419125; fax (11) 3337928; Ambassador: CHRISTIAN OLDENBURG.

Egypt: Damascus; Ambassador: MOUSTAFA ABD AL-AZIZ.

Ethiopia: Damascus; Ambassador: ABD AL-MONEM AHMAD.

Finland: BP 3893, Hawakir, Immeuble Yacoubian, West Malki, Damascus; tel. (11) 3338809; telex 411491; fax (11) 718524; Ambassador: ARTO KURITTU.

France: BP 769, rue Ata Ayoubi, Damascus; tel. (11) 247992; telex 411013; Ambassador: JEAN-CLAUDE COUSSERAN.

Germany: BP 2237, 53 rue Ibrahim Hanano, Immeuble Kotob, Damascus; tel. (11) 3323800; telex 411065; fax (11) 3323812; Ambassador: THOMAS TRÖMEL.

Greece: 1 rue Farabi, Immeuble Tello, Mezzeh, Damascus; tel. (11) 244031; telex 411045; Ambassador: GEORGE CONSTANTIS.

Holy See: BP 2271, 82 rue Masr, Damascus (Apostolic Nunciature); tel. (11) 3332601; telex 412824; fax (11) 3327550; Apostolic Nuncio: Most Rev. PIER GIACOMO DE NICOLÒ, Titular Archbishop of Martana.

Hungary: 102 rue al-Fursan (Villas Eastern), al-Akvam, Damascus; tel. (11) 3337966; telex 419151; Ambassador: LÁSZLÓ KÁDÁR.

India: 40/46 ave Adnan al-Malki, Immeuble Noueilati, Damascus; tel. (11) 718203; telex 411377; fax (11) 713294; Ambassador: R. N. MULYE.

Indonesia: 19 rue al-Amir Ezz ed-Din, Damascus; tel. (11) 3331238; telex 419188; fax (11) 3331485; Ambassador: WIDODO ATMOSUTIRTO.

Iran: Mezzeh Outostrade, nr ar-Razi Hospital, Damascus; telex 411041; Ambassador: Hojatoleslam MUHAMMAD HASSAN AKHTARI.

Italy: 82 ave al-Mansour, Damascus; Ambassador: RAFFAELE BERLENGHI.

Japan: 15 ave al-Jala'a, Damascus; tel. (11) 339421; telex 411042; Ambassador: RYUJI ONODERA.

Jordan: rue Abou Roumaneh, Damascus; telex 419161; Ambassador: ALI KHURAIS.

Korea, Democratic People's Republic: rue Fares al-Khouri-Jisr Tora, Damascus; Ambassador: YI WON-KUK.

Kuwait: rue Ibrahim Hanano, Damascus; telex 419172; Ambassador: AHMAD ABD AL-AZIZ AL-JASSEM.

Libya: 36/37 Abou Roumaneh, Damascus; Head of People's Bureau: AHMAD ABD AS-SALAM BIN KHAYAL.

Mauritania: ave al-Jala'a, rue Karameh, Damascus; telex 411264; Ambassador: MUHAMMAD MAHMOUD OULD WEDDADY.

Morocco: Damascus; Ambassador: IDRIFF DHAHAQ.

Netherlands: POB 702, Immeuble Tello, rue al-Jalaa, Abou Roumaneh, Damascus; tel. (11) 3335119; telex 411032; fax (11) 3339369; Ambassador: R. H. MEYS.

Oman: Damascus.

Pakistan: BP 9284, rue al-Farabi, East Villat, Damascus; tel. (11) 662391; telex 412629; Ambassador: S. AZMAT HASSAN.

Panama: BP 2548, Malki, rue al-Bizm, Immeuble az-Zein, Apt 7, Damascus; tel. (11) 224743; telex 411918; Chargé d'affaires: CARLOS A. DE GRACIA.

Poland: BP 501, 21 rue Mehdi Ben Barakeh, Damascus; tel. (11) 333010; telex 412288; fax (11) 333010; Ambassador: KRZYSZTOF BALIŃSKI.

Qatar: BP 4188, Abou Roumaneh, place Madfa, Immeuble Allawi No. 20, Damascus; tel. (11) 336717; telex 411064; Ambassador: FAHD FAHD AL-KHATER.

Romania: rue Ibrahim Hanano No. 8, Damascus; telex 411305; Ambassador: PARASCHIV BENESCU.

Russia: Boustan al-Kouzbari, rue d'Alep, Damascus; telex 411221; Ambassador: ALEKSANDR IVANOVICH ZOTOV.

Saudi Arabia: ave al-Jala'a, Damascus; telex 411906; Ambassador: ABDULLAH BIN SALEH AL-FADL.

Slovakia: POB 33115, place Mezza, East Villas ash-Shafei St, Damascus; tel. (11) 6669043; telex 412054; fax (11) 6616714; Ambassador: BENEDIKT DURMEK.

Somalia: ave Ata Ayoubi, Damascus; telex 419194; Ambassador: (vacant).

Spain: 81 ave al-Jala'a, Immeuble Sawaf, Damascus; telex 411253; Ambassador: JESÚS RIOSALIDO.

Sudan: Damascus; telex 411266.

Sweden: BP 4266, rue Chakib Arslan, Abou Roumaneh, Damascus; tel. (11) 3327261; telex 411339; fax (11) 3327749; Ambassador: STIG ELVEMAR.

Switzerland: rue al-Mehdi ben Baraka, Immeuble Chora, Damascus; tel. (11) 715474; telex 411016; Ambassador: ERIC PFISTER.

Tunisia: BP 4114, Villa Ouest, Jaddat Chafei, No. 6 Mezzeh, Damascus; tel. (11) 660356; telex 431302; Ambassador: Muhammad Cherif.

Turkey: 56–58 ave Ziad bin Abou Soufian, Damascus; tel. (11) 331370; Ambassador: Erhan Tunçel.

United Arab Emirates: rue Raouda No. 62, Immeuble Housami, Damascus; telex 411213; Ambassador: Salim Rashid al-Aqroubi.

United Kingdom: POB 37, Damascus; tel. (11) 712561; telex 411049; fax (11) 713592; Ambassador: Adrian Sindall.

USA: BP 29, rue al-Mansour 2, Damascus; tel. (11) 333052; telex 411919; fax (11) 718687; Ambassador: Christopher W. S. Ross.

Venezuela: BP 2403, Abou Roumaneh, rue Nour Pacha, Immeuble Tabbah, Damascus; tel. (11) 335356; telex 411929; Ambassador: José Miguel Quintana Guevara.

Viet Nam: 9 ave Malki, Damascus; tel. (11) 333008; Ambassador: Le Thanh Tam.

Yemen: Abou Roumaneh, Charkassieh, Damascus; Ambassador: Abdullah Hussain Barakat.

Yugoslavia: POB 739, ave al-Jala'a, Damascus; tel. (11) 336222; telex 412646; fax (11) 333690; Ambassador: Radmilo Trojanović.

Judicial System

The Courts of Law in Syria are principally divided into two juridical court systems: Courts of General Jurisdiction and Administrative Courts. Since 1973 the Supreme Constitutional Court (Damascus; tel. (11) 3331902) has been established as the paramount body of the Syrian judicial structure.

THE SUPREME CONSTITUTIONAL COURT

This is the highest court in Syria. It has specific jurisdiction over: (i) judicial review of the constitutionality of laws and legislative decrees; (ii) investigation of charges relating to the legality of the election of members of the Majlis ash-Sha'ab (People's Assembly); (iii) trial of infractions committed by the President of the Republic in the exercise of his functions; (iv) resolution of positive and negative jurisdictional conflicts and determination of the competent court between the different juridical court systems, as well as other bodies exercising judicial competence. The Supreme Constitutional Court is composed of a Chief Justice and four Justices. They are appointed by decree of the President of the Republic for a renewable period of four years.

Chief Justice: Nasrat Mounla-Haydar.

COURTS OF GENERAL JURISDICTION

The Courts of General Jurisdiction in Syria are divided into six categories: (i) The Court of Cassation; (ii) The Courts of Appeal; (iii) The Tribunals of First Instance; (iv) The Tribunals of Peace; (v) The Personal Status Courts; (vi) The Courts for Minors. Each of the above categories (except the Personal Status Courts) is divided into Civil, Penal and Criminal Chambers.

(i) **The Court of Cassation:** This is the highest court of general jurisdiction. Final judgments rendered by Courts of Appeal in penal and civil litigations may be petitioned to the Court of Cassation by the Defendant or the Public Prosecutor in penal and criminal litigations, and by any of the parties in interest in civil litigations, on grounds of defective application or interpretation of the law as stated in the challenged judgment, on grounds of irregularity of form or procedure, or violation of due process, and on grounds of defective reasoning of judgment rendered. The Court of Cassation is composed of a President, seven Vice-Presidents and 31 other Justices (Councillors).

(ii) **The Courts of Appeal:** Each court has geographical jurisdiction over one governorate (Mouhafazat). Each court is divided into Penal and Civil Chambers. There are Criminal Chambers which try felonies only. The Civil Chambers hear appeals filed against judgments rendered by the Tribunals of First Instance and the Tribunals of Peace. Each Court of Appeal is composed of a President and sufficient numbers of Vice-Presidents (Presidents of Chambers) and Superior Judges (Councillors). There are 54 Courts of Appeal.

(iii) **The Tribunals of First Instance:** In each governorate there are one or more Tribunals of First Instance, each of which is divided into several Chambers for penal and civil litigations. Each Chamber is composed of one judge. There are 72 Tribunals of First Instance.

(iv) **The Tribunals of Peace:** In the administrative centre of each governorate, and in each district, there are one or more Tribunals of Peace, which have jurisdiction over minor civil and penal litigations. There are 227 Tribunals of Peace.

(v) **Personal Status Courts:** These courts deal with marriage, divorce, etc. For Muslims each court consists of one judge, the 'Qadi Shari'i'. For Druzes there is one court consisting of one judge, the 'Qadi Mazhabi'. For non-Muslim communities there are courts for Roman Catholics, Orthodox believers, Protestants and Jews.

(vi) **Courts for Minors:** The constitution, officers, sessions, jurisdiction and competence of these courts are determined by a special law.

PUBLIC PROSECUTION

Public prosecution is headed by the Attorney General, assisted by a number of Senior Deputy and Deputy Attorneys General, and a sufficient number of chief prosecutors, prosecutors and assistant prosecutors. Public prosecution is represented at all levels of the Courts of General Jurisdiction in all criminal and penal litigations and also in certain civil litigations as required by the law. Public prosecution controls and supervises enforcement of penal judgments.

ADMINISTRATIVE COURTS SYSTEM

The Administrative Courts have jurisdiction over litigations involving the state or any of its governmental agencies. The Administrative Courts system is divided into two courts: the Administrative Courts and the Judicial Administrative Courts, of which the paramount body is the High Administrative Court.

MILITARY COURTS

The Military Courts deal with criminal litigations against military personnel of all ranks and penal litigations against officers only. There are two military courts; one in Damascus, the other in Aleppo. Each court is composed of three military judges. There are other military courts, consisting of one judge, in every governorate, which deal with penal litigations against military personnel below the rank of officer. The different military judgments can be petitioned to the Court of Cassation.

Religion

In religion the majority of Syrians follow a form of Islamic Sunni orthodoxy. There is also a considerable number of religious minorities: Shi'a Muslims; Ismaili Muslims; the Ismaili of the Salamiya district, whose spiritual head is the Aga Khan; a large number of Druzes, the Nusairis or Alawites of the Jebel Ansariyeh (a schism of the Shi'ite branch of Islam, to which President Assad belongs, who comprise about 11% of the population) and the Yezidis of the Jebel Sinjar, and a minority of Christians.

The Constitution states only that 'Islam shall be the religion of the head of the state'. The original draft of the 1973 Constitution made no reference to Islam at all, and this clause was inserted only as a compromise after public protest. The Syrian Constitution is thus unique among the constitutions of Arab states (excluding Lebanon) with a clear Muslim majority in not enshrining Islam as the religion of the state itself.

ISLAM

Grand Mufti: Ahmad Kuftaro.

CHRISTIANITY

Orthodox Churches

Greek Orthodox Patriarchate: His Beatitude Ignatius Hazim, Patriarch of Antioch and all the Orient; BP 9, Damascus; has jurisdiction over Syria, Lebanon, Iran and Iraq.

Syrian Orthodox Patriarchate: BP 914, Bab Touma, Damascus; tel. (11) 447036; Syrian Orthodox Patriarch: His Holiness Ignatius Zakka I Iwas, Patriarch of Antioch and All the East; the Syrian Orthodox Church includes one Catholicose (of the East), 30 Metropolitans and one Bishop, and has an estimated 3m. adherents throughout the world.

The Armenian Apostolic Church is also represented in Syria.

The Roman Catholic Church

Armenian Rite

Patriarchal Exarchate of Syria: Exarcat Patriarcal Arménien Catholique, Bab Touma, Damascus; tel. (11) 5433438; represents the Patriarch of Cilicia (resident in Beirut, Lebanon); 4,000 adherents; Exarch Patriarchal Mgr Georges Tayroyan.

Archdiocese of Aleppo: Archevêché Arménien Catholique, BP 97, rue Tillel 121, Aleppo; tel. (21) 213946; 15,000 adherents (31 December 1992); Archbishop Mgr Boutros Marayati.

Diocese of Kamichlié: Evêché Arménien Catholique, BP 17, Al-Qamishli; tel. (531) 20211; 6,300 adherents (31 December 1992); Bishop (vacant).

Chaldean Rite

Diocese of Aleppo: Evêché Chaldéen Catholique Alep, Soulémaniya; tel. (21) 441660; 15,000 adherents (31 December 1992); Bishop ANTOINE AUDO.

Latin Rite

Apostolic Vicariate of Aleppo: BP 327, 19 rue Antaki, Aleppo; tel. and fax (21) 210204; f. 1644; 10,500 adherents (31 December 1993); Vicar Apostolic ARMANDO BORTOLASO, Titular Bishop of Raphanea.

Maronite Rite

Archdiocese of Aleppo: Archevêché Maronite, BP 203, Aleppo; tel. (21) 248048; 3,650 adherents (31 December 1992); Archbishop Mgr PIERRE CALLAOS.

Archdiocese of Damascus: Archevêché Maronite, Bab Touma, Damascus; tel. (11) 5430129; 8,000 adherents (31 December 1992); Archbishop HAMID ANTOINE MOURANY.

Diocese of Latakia: Evêché Maronite, BP 161, rue Hamrat, Tartous; tel. (431) 23433; 24,500 adherents (31 December 1992); Bishop Mgr ANTOINE TORBEY.

Melkite Rite

Melkite-Greek-Catholic Patriarchate: BP 22249, Damascus, or POB 50076, Beirut, Lebanon; tel. (11) 5433129; fax (11) 5431266 (Damascus), or 413111 (Beirut); jurisdiction over 1.5m. Melkites throughout the world (including 163,500 in Syria); Patriarch of Antioch and all the East, of Alexandria and Jerusalem MAXIMOS V HAKIM. The Melkite Rite includes the patriarchal sees of Damascus, Cairo and Jerusalem and four other archdioceses in Syria; seven archdioceses in Lebanon; one in Jordan; one in Israel; and five Eparchies (in the USA, Brazil, Canada, Australia and Mexico).

Archdiocese of Aleppo: Archevêché Grec-Catholique, BP 146, Aleppo; tel. (21) 213218; Archbishop Mgr NÉOPHYTOS EDELBY.

Archdiocese of Busra and Hauran: Archevêché Grec-Catholique, Khabab, Hauran; tel. 13; Archbishop Mgr BOULOS NASSIF BORKHOCHE.

Archdiocese of Homs: Archevêché Grec-Catholique, BP 1525, rue El-Bahri, Boustan ad-Diwan, Homs; tel. (31) 21587; Archbishop Mgr IBRAHIM NEHMÉ.

Archdiocese of Latakia: Archevêché Grec-Catholique, BP 151, Latakia; tel. 36077; Archbishop Mgr MICHEL YATIM.

Syrian Rite

Archdiocese of Aleppo: Archevêché Syrien Catholique, rue Salibé, Aleppo; tel. (21) 241200; Archbishop DENYS ANTOINE BEYLOUNI.

Archdiocese of Damascus: Archevêché Syrien Catholique, BP 2129, rue Bab Charki, Damascus; tel. (11) 5432311; telex 411778; Archbishop Mgr EUSTACHE JOSEPH MOUNAYER.

Archdiocese of Hassaké-Nisibi: Archevêché Syrien Catholique, BP 6, Hasakeh; tel. (521) 20052; Archbishop JACQUES GEORGES HABIB HAFOURI.

Archdiocese of Homs: Archevêché Syrien Catholique, BP 368, rue Hamidieh, Homs; tel. (31) 21575; Archbishop Mgr THÉOPHILE JEAN DAHI.

At 31 December 1992 the total number of adherents of the Syrian Rite within the jurisdiction of the four Syrian archbishops was 28,914.

The Anglican Communion

Within the Episcopal Church in Jerusalem and the Middle East, Syria forms part of the diocese of Jerusalem (see the chapter on Israel).

Protestant

National Evangelical Synod of Syria and Lebanon: POB 70890, Antelias, Lebanon; tel. 405490; f. 1920; 70,000 adherents (1993); Exec. Sec. Rev. Dr SALIM SAHIOUNY.

Union of the Armenian Evangelical Churches in the Near East: POB 110-377, Beirut, Lebanon; tel. 443547; fax 582191; f. 1846 in Turkey; comprises about 30 Armenian Evangelical Churches in Syria, Lebanon, Egypt, Cyprus, Greece, Iran and Turkey; 9,500 mems (1985); Moderator Rev. HOVHANNES KARJIAN; Sec. Rev. BARKEV APARTIAN.

The Press

Since the Baath Arab Socialist Party came to power, the structure of the press has been modified according to socialist patterns. Most publications are published by organizations such as political, religious, or professional associations, trade unions, etc. and several are published by government ministries. Anyone wishing to establish a new paper or periodical must apply for a licence.

The major dailies are *Al-Baath* (the organ of the party), *Tishrin* and *Ath-Thawra* in Damascus, *Al-Jamahir al-Arabia* in Aleppo, and *Al-Fida'* in Hama.

PRINCIPAL DAILIES

Al-Baath (Renaissance): BP 9389, Mezze Autostrade, Damascus; tel. (11) 664600; telex 419146; fax (11) 240099; f. 1946; morning; Arabic; organ of the Baath Arab Socialist Party; Gen. Dir and Chief Editor TURKI SAQR; circ. 65,000.

Barq ash-Shimal (The Syrian Telegraph): rue Aziziyah, Aleppo; morning; Arabic; Editor MAURICE DJANDJI; circ. 6,400.

Al-Fida' (Redemption): rue Kuwatly, Hama; morning; Arabic; political; publishing concession holder OSMAN ALOUINI; Editor A. AULWANI; circ. 4,000.

Al-Jamahir al-Arabia (The Arab People): Al-Wihdat Press, Printing and Publishing Organization, Aleppo; Arabic; political; Chief Editor MORTADA BAKACH; circ. 10,000.

Al-Oroubat: Al-Wihdat Press, Printing and Publishing Organization, Homs; morning; Arabic; published by Al-Wihdat Printing and Publishing Organization; circ. 5,000.

Ash-Shabab (Youth): rue at-Tawil, Aleppo; morning; Arabic; Editor MUHAMMAD TALAS; circ. 9,000.

Syria Times: Tishrin Foundation for Press and Publication, BP 5452, Corniche Meedan, Damascus; English; circ. 12,000.

Ath-Thawra (Revolution): Al-Wihdat Press, Printing and Publishing Organization, BP 2448, Damascus; morning; Arabic; political; circ. 55,000; Chief Editor M. KHAIR AL-WADI.

Tishrin (October): Tishrin Foundation for Press and Publication, BP 5452, Corniche Meedan, Damascus; tel. (11) 886900; telex 411916; Arabic; Chief Editor M. KHEIR WADI; circ. 70,000.

Al-Wihdat (Unity): Al-Wihdat Press, Printing and Publishing Organization, Latakia; Arabic; published by Al-Wihdat Press, Printing and Publishing Organization.

WEEKLIES AND FORTNIGHTLIES

Al-Ajoua' (The Air): Compagnie de l'Aviation Arabe Syrienne, BP 417, Damascus; fortnightly; Arabic; aviation; Editor AHMAD ALLOUCHE.

Al-Esbou ar-Riadi (The Sports Week): ave Fardoss, Imm. Tibi, Damascus; weekly; Arabic; sports; Asst Dir and Editor HASRAN AL-BOUNNI; circ. 14,000.

Al-Fursan (The Cavalry): Damascus; Arabic; political magazine; Editor Major RIFAAT AL-ASSAD.

Homs: Homs; weekly; Arabic; literary; Publisher and Dir ADIB KABA; Editor PHILIPPE KABA.

Jaysh ash-Sha'ab (The People's Army): BP 3320, blvd Palestine, Damascus; f. 1946; fortnightly; Arabic; army magazine; published by the Political Department of the Syrian Army.

Kifah al-Oummal al-Ishtiraki (The Socialist Workers' Struggle): Fédération Générale des Syndicats des Ouvriers, rue Qanawat, Damascus; weekly; Arabic; labour; published by General Federation of Labour Unions; Editor SAID AL-HAMAMI.

Al-Masirah (Progress): Damascus; weekly; Arabic; political; published by Federation of Youth Organizations.

Al-Maukef ar-Riadi: Al-Wihdat Press, Printing and Publishing Organization, BP 2448, Damascus; weekly; Arabic; sports; published by Al-Wihdat Press, Printing and Publishing Organization; circ. 50,000.

An-Nas (The People): BP 926, Aleppo; f. 1953; weekly; Arabic; Publisher VICTOR KALOUS.

Nidal al-Fellahin (The Struggle of the Fellahin): Fédération Générale des Laboureurs, BP 7152, Damascus; weekly; Arabic; peasant workers; Editor MANSOUR ABU AL-HOSN.

Nidal ash-Sha'ab (People's Struggle): Damascus; fortnightly; Arabic; published by the Communist Party of Syria.

Ar-Riada (Sport): BP 292, near Electricity Institute, Damascus; weekly; Arabic; sports; Dir NOUREDDINE RIAL; Publisher and Editor OURFANE UBARI.

As-Sakafat al-Usbouiya (Weekly Culture): BP 2570, Soukak as-Sakr, Damascus; weekly; Arabic; cultural; Publisher, Dir and Editor MADHAT AKKACHE.

Al-Yanbu al-Jadid (New Spring): Immeuble Al-Awkaf, Homs; weekly; Arabic; literary; Publisher, Dir and Editor MAMDOU AL-KOUSSEIR.

OTHER PERIODICALS

Ad-Dad: rue Tital, Wakf al-Moiriné Bldg, Aleppo; monthly; Arabic; literary; Dir RIAD HALLAK; Publisher and Editor ABDALLAH YARKI HALLAK.

Ecos: BP 3320, Damascus; monthly review; Spanish.

Al-Fikr al-Askari (The Military Idea): BP 4259, blvd Palestine, Damascus; f. 1950; 6 a year; Arabic; official military review published by the Political Dept of the Syrian Army; Editor NAKHLE KALLAS.

Flash: BP 3320, Damascus; monthly review; English and French.

Al-Irshad az-Zirai (Agricultural Information): Ministry of Agriculture and Agrarian Reform, 29 rue Ayar, Damascus; tel. (11) 113613; 6 a year; Arabic; agriculture.

Al-Jundi al-Arabi (The Arab Soldier): BP 3320, blvd Palestine, Damascus; telex 411500; monthly; published by the Political Department of the Syrian Army.

Al-Kalima (The Word): Al-Kalima Association, Aleppo; monthly; Arabic; religious; Publisher and Editor FATHALLA SAKAL.

Al-Kanoun (The Law): Ministry of Justice, Damascus; monthly; Arabic; juridical.

Al-Ma'arifa (Knowledge): Ministry of Culture, Damascus; tel. (11) 331556; telex 411944; f. 1962; monthly; Arabic; literary; Editor ABD AL-KARIM NASIF; circ. 7,500.

Al-Majalla al-Batriarquia (The Magazine of the Patriarchate): Syrian Orthodox Patriarchate, BP 914, Damascus; tel. (11) 447036; f. 1962; monthly; Arabic; religious; Editor SAMIR ABDOH; circ. 6,000.

Al-Majalla at-Tibbiya al-Arabiyya (Arab Medical Magazine): rue al-Jala'a, Damascus; monthly; Arabic; published by Arab Medical Commission; Dir Dr SHAMS AD-DIN AL-JUNDI; Editor Dr ADNAN TAKRITI.

Majallat Majma' al-Lughat al-Arabiyya bi-Dimashq (Magazine of the Arab Language Academy of Damascus): Arab Academy of Damascus, BP 327, Damascus; tel. (11) 713145; f. 1921; quarterly; Arabic; Islamic culture and Arabic literature, Arabic scientific and cultural terminology; Editor Dr SHAKER FAHAM; circ. 2,000.

Al-Mawkif al-Arabi (The Arab Situation): Ittihab al-Kuttab al-Arab, rue Murshid Khatir, Damascus; monthly; Arabic; literary.

Monthly Survey of Arab Economics: BP 2306, Damascus and POB 6068, Beirut; f. 1958; monthly; English and French editions; published by Centre d'Etudes et de Documentation Economiques, Financières et Sociales; Dir Dr CHAFIC AKHRAS.

Al-Mouallem al-Arabi (The Arab Teacher): Ministry of Education, Damascus; f. 1948; monthly; Arabic; educational and cultural.

Al-Mouhandis al-Arabi (The Arab Engineer): BP 2336, Immeuble Dar al-Mouhandisen, place Azme, Damascus; tel. (11) 214916; telex 411962; f. 1961; bi-monthly; Arabic; published by Inst. of Syrian Engineers; scientific and cultural; Dir Dr Eng. GHASSAN TAYARA; Editors Eng. ADNAN IBRAHIM and Dr Eng. AHMAD AL-GHAFARI; circ. 21,000.

Al-Munadel (The Fighter): c/o BP 11512, Damascus; fax (11) 246933; f. 1965; monthly; Arabic; magazine of Baath Arab Socialist Party; Dir Dr FAWWAZ SAYYAGH; circ. 10,000.

Revue de la Presse Arabe: 67 place Chahbandar, Damascus; f. 1948; French; 2 a week.

Risalat al-Kimia (Chemistry Report): BP 669, Immeuble al-Abid, Damascus; monthly; Arabic; scientific; Publisher, Dir and Editor HASSAN AS-SAKA.

Saut al-Forat: Deir ez-Zor; monthly; Arabic; literary; Publisher, Dir and Editor ABD AL-KADER AYACHE.

Ash-Shourta (The Police): Directorate of Public Affairs and Moral Guidance, Damascus; monthly; Arabic; juridical.

Souriya al-Arabiyya (Arab Syria): Ministry of Information, ave al-Mazzeh, Immeuble Dar al-Baath, Damascus; tel. (11) 660412; monthly; publicity; in four languages.

Syrie et Monde Arabe: BP 3550, place Chahbandar, Damascus; f. 1952; monthly; French and English; economic, statistical and political survey.

At-Tamaddon al-Islami (The Spreading of Islam): Darwichiyah, Damascus; tel. (11) 215120; telex 411258; f. 1932; monthly; Arabic; religious; published by At-Tamaddon al-Islami Association; Pres. of Asscn. MUHAMMAD ZAHIR KOUZBARI; Editor ADEL KOLTAKGY.

At-Taqa Wattanmiya (Energy and Expansion): BP 7748, rue al-Moutanabbi, Damascus; tel. (11) 233529; telex 411031; monthly; Arabic; published by the Syrian Petroleum Co.

Al-Yakza (The Awakening): Al-Yakza Association, BP 6677, rue Sisi, Aleppo; f. 1935; monthly; Arabic; literary social review of charitable institution; Dir HUSNI ABD AL-MASSIH; circ. 12,000.

Az-Zira'a 2000 (Agriculture 2000): Ministry of Agriculture and Agrarian Reform, 29 rue Ayar, Damascus; tel. (11) 213613; telex 411643; f. 1985; monthly; Arabic; agriculture; circ. 12,000.

PRESS AGENCIES

Agence Arabe Syrienne d'Information: Damascus; f. 1966; supplies bulletins on Syrian news to foreign news agencies; Dir-Gen. Dr SABIR FALHUT.

Foreign Bureaux

Agencia EFE (Spain): Damascus; Correspondent ZACHARIAS SARME.

Agence France—Presse (AFP): BP 2400, Immeuble Adel Charaj, place du 17 avril, Damascus; tel. (11) 428253; telex 419173; Correspondent JOSEPH GHASI.

Agenzia Nazionale Stampa Associata (ANSA) (Italy): Hotel Méridien, BP 2712, Damascus; tel. (11) 233116; telex 411098; f. 1962; Correspondent ABDULLAH SAADEL.

Allgemeiner Deutscher Nachrichtendienst (ADN) (Germany): BP 844, Damascus; tel. (11) 332093; telex 411010; Correspondent FRANK HERRMANN.

Associated Press (AP) (USA): c/o Hotel Méridien, BP 2712, Damascus; tel. (11) 233116; telex 411196.

Deutsche Presse-Agentur (dpa) (Germany): c/o Hotel Méridien, BP 2712, Damascus; tel. (11) 332924; telex 411098.

Informatsionnoye Telegrafnoye Agentstvo Rossii—Telegrafnoye Agentstvo Suverennykh Stran (ITAR—TASS) (Russia): POB 2507, Damascus; telex 411061; Correspondent BICHIR BASHA.

Publishers

Arab Advertising Organization: BP 2842-3034, 28 rue Moutanabbi, Damascus; tel. (11) 2225219; telex 411923; fax (11) 2220754; f. 1963; exclusive government establishment responsible for advertising; publishes *Directory of Commerce and Industry, Damascus International Fair Guide, Daily Bulletin of Official Tenders*; Dir-Gen. MUHAMMAD QATTAN.

Damascus University Press: Damascus; tel. (11) 2215100; telex 411971; fax (11) 2236010; arts, geography, education, history, engineering, medicine, law, sociology, economics, sciences, architecture, agriculture, school books.

Office Arabe de Presse et de Documentation (OFA-Edition): BP 3550, 67 place Chahbandar, Damascus; tel. (11) 459166; telex 411613; fax (11) 426021; f. 1964; numerous periodicals, monographs and surveys on political and economic affairs; Dir-Gen. SAMIR A. DARWICH. Has two affiliated branches, OFA-Business Consulting Centre (foreign company representation and services) and OFA-Renseignements Commerciaux (Commercial enquiries on firms and persons in Syria and Lebanon).

The Political Administration Press: BP 3320, blvd Palestine, Damascus; telex 411500; publishes *Al-Fikr al-Askari* (6 a year) and *Jaysh ash-Sha'ab* (fortnightly) and *Al-Jundi al-Arabi* (monthly).

Syrian Documentation Papers: BP 2712, Damascus; f. 1968; publishers of *Bibliography of the Middle East* (annual), *General Directory of the Press and Periodicals in the Arab World* (annual), and numerous publications on political, economic and social affairs and literature and legislative texts concerning Syria and the Arab world; Dir-Gen. LOUIS FARÉS.

Al-Wihdat Press, Printing and Publishing Organization (Institut al-Ouedha pour l'impression, édition et distribution): BP 2448, Dawar Kafr Soussat, Damascus; publishes *Al-Jamahir al-Arabia, Al-Ouroubat, Ath-Thawra, Al-Fida'* and *Al-Wihdat* (dailies), *al-Maukef ar-Riadi* (weekly) and other commercial publications.

Radio and Television

In 1991 there were an estimated 3.3m. radio receivers and 770,000 television receivers in use.

Directorate-General of Broadcasting and Television: place Omayyad, Damascus; tel. (11) 720700; telex 411138; f. 1945; Dir-Gen. KHUDR OMRAN.

RADIO

Broadcasts in Arabic, French, English, Russian, German, Spanish, Portuguese, Hebrew, Polish, Turkish, Bulgarian.

Director of Radio: SAFWAN GHANIM.

TELEVISION

Services started in 1960.

Director of Television: M. ABD AS-SALAM HIJAB.

Finance

(cap. = capital; res = reserves; p.u. = paid up; dep. = deposits;
m.= million; brs = branches; amounts in £S)

BANKING
Central Bank

Central Bank of Syria: POB 2254, Altajrida al-Mughrabia Sq., Damascus; tel. (11) 2224800; telex 411007; fax (11) 2227109; f. 1956; cap. p.u. 10m., dep. 22,689m., total assets 46,202m. (June 1987); 9 brs; Gov. Dr HISHAM MUTEWALLI.

Other Banks

Agricultural Bank: BP 5325, rue Euphrates, Damascus; f. 1924; Dir-Gen. MAEN RISLAN; 55 brs.

Commercial Bank of Syria: BP 933, place Yousuf al-Azmeh, Damascus; tel. (11) 218890; telex 411002; fax (11) 2216975; f. 1967; govt-owned bank; cap. p.u. 191.8m., res 5,881.1m., dep. 119,633m. (Dec. 1991); 37 brs; Chair. and Gen. Man. MUHAMMAD RIYADH HAKIM.

Industrial Bank: BP 7578, 29 rue May, Damascus; tel. (11) 228200; f. 1959; nationalized bank providing finance for industry; cap. 100m.; 13 brs; Chair. ABD AL-QADIR OBEIDO.

Popular Credit Bank: BP 2841, rue Fardoss, Dar al-Mohandessin Blvd, 6th Floor, Damascus; tel. (11) 114260; f. 1967; government bank; provides loans to the services sector and is sole authorized issuer of savings certificates; cap. 25m., dep. 2,313m., res 42,765m. (Dec. 1984); 43 brs; Chair. and Gen. Man. MUHAMMAD HASSAN AL-HOUJJEIRI.

Real Estate Bank: BP 2337, rue al-Furat, Damascus; tel. (11) 218602; telex 419171; f. 1966; provides loans and grants for housing, schools, hospitals and hotel construction; cap. 515m.; 13 brs; Chair. and Gen. Man. MUHAMMAD A. MAKHLOUF.

INSURANCE

Syrian General Organization for Insurance: BP 2279, rue Tajheez, Damascus; tel. (11) 2218430; telex 411003; fax (11) 2220494; f. 1953; authorized cap. 250m.; a nationalized company; operates throughout Syria; Chair. and Gen. Man. AMIN ABDULLAH.

Trade and Industry

CHAMBERS OF COMMERCE

Federation of Syrian Chambers of Commerce: POB 5909, Mousa Ben Nousair St, Damascus; tel. (11) 331127; telex 411194; fax (11) 335920; f. 1975; Chair. Dr RATEB ASH-SHALLAH.

Aleppo Chamber of Commerce: BP 1261, rue al-Moutanabbi, Aleppo; tel. (21) 38236; telex 331012; f. 1885; Pres. MUHAMMAD MAHROUSSEH; Sec. EUGENE GLORE; Dir ZEKI DAROUZI.

Alkalamoun Chamber of Commerce: POB 2507, Bucher A. Mawla St, Damascus; telex 411061; fax (11) 778394; Pres. M. SOUFAN.

Damascus Chamber of Commerce: BP 1040, rue Mou'awiah, Damascus; tel. (11) 211339; telex 411326; f. 1890; 8,000 mems.; Pres. BADR ED-DIN SHALLAH; Gen. Dir HISHAM AL-HAMWY.

Hama Chamber of Commerce and Industry: POB 147, rue al-Kouatly, Hama; tel. (11) 233304; telex 431046; fax (11) 223910; f. 1934; Pres. ABD AS-SALAM SABEH.

Homs Chamber of Commerce and Industry: BP 440, rue Abou al-Of, Homs; tel. 231000; telex 441025; fax (11) 224247; f. 1938; Pres. Eng. WALID TULIEMAT; Dir MUHAMMAD FARES AL-HUSAIMI.

Latakia Chamber of Commerce: rue al-Hurriyah, Latakia; Pres. JULE NASRI.

CHAMBERS OF INDUSTRY

Aleppo Chamber of Industry: BP 1859, rue al-Moutanabbi, Aleppo; tel. (21) 339812; telex 331090; f. 1935; Pres. MUHAMMAD M. OUBARI; 7,000 mems.

Damascus Chamber of Industry: BP 1305, rue Harika-Mou'awiah, Damascus; tel. (11) 2215042; telex 411289; fax (11) 2245981; Pres. Dr YEHYA AL-HINDI; Dir-Gen. Dr ABD AL-HAMID MALAKANI.

EMPLOYERS' ORGANIZATIONS

Fédération Générale à Damas: Damascus; f. 1951; Dir TALAT TAG-LUBI.

Fédération de Damas: Damascus; f. 1949.

Fédération des Patrons et Industriels à Lattaquié: Latakia; f. 1953.

TRADE UNIONS

Ittihad Naqabat al-'Ummal al-'Am fi Suriya (General Federation of Labour Unions): POB 2351, rue Qanawat, Damascus; f. 1948; Chair. IZZ AD-DIN NASIR; Sec. MAHMOUD FAHURI.

PETROLEUM

Syrian Petroleum Company (SPC): BP 2849, rue al-Moutanabbi, Damascus; tel. (11) 227007; telex 411031; f. 1958; state agency; holds the oil and gas concession for all Syria; exploits the Suwei-diya, Karatchouk, Rumelan and Jbeisseh oilfields; also organizes exploring, production and marketing of oil and gas nationally; Dir-Gen. Dr Eng. ALI JEBRAN.

Al-Furat Petroleum Company: f. 1985; owned 50% by SPC and 50% by a foreign consortium of Pecten International, Royal Dutch/Shell and Deminex; exploits the ath-Thayyem, al-Asharah and al-Ward oilfields.

STATE ENTERPRISES

Syrian industry is almost entirely controlled and run by the state. There are national organizations responsible to the appropriate ministry for the operation of all sectors of industry, of which the following are examples:

Cotton Marketing Organization: BP 729, rue Bab al-Faraj, Aleppo; tel. (21) 238486; telex 331210; fax (21) 218617; f. 1965; monopoly authority for purchase of seed cotton, ginning and sales of cotton lint; Pres. and Dir-Gen. ABD AS-SATTAR.

General Organization for Phosphate and Mines (GECOPHAM): BP 288, Homs; tel. 20405; telex 441000; production and export of phosphate rock.

General Organization for the Exploitation and Development of the Euphrates Basin (GOEDEB): Raqqa; telex 31004; Dir-Gen. Dr Eng. ABDO KASSEM.

General Organization for the Textile Industries: BP 620, rue Fardoss, Damascus; tel. (11) 116200; telex 411011; control and planning of the textile industry and supervision of textile manufacture; 13 subsidiary cos.

Transport

RAILWAYS

The present railway system totals 1,918 km of track (1990) and is composed of the following main lines:
Meydan Ekbez (Turkish frontier)–Aleppo–Ar-Rai (166 km); Cobanbey (Turkish frontier)–Aleppo; Nassibin (Turkish frontier)–Jaroubieh (Iraq frontier) (81 km); Aleppo–Homs–Damascus (422 km); Homs–Akkari (Lebanese frontier)–Tartous–Latakia (110 km); Hama–M'hardeh (24 km); there are 1,686 km of normal gauge track (1,435 mm) and 232 km of narrow gauge track (1,050 mm), including the Hedjaz railway. A line from Latakia to Qamish-liya, via Aleppo, (757 km) has been completed and is operating for passenger and goods traffic. Other new lines completed include an 180-km line from Homs to the phosphate mines at Khenefes and to Palmyra, a 19-km line from Hama to M'hardeh and a 42-km line from Tartous to Akkari. The line from Homs to Damascus (194 km) was opened in 1983, one from Damascus to Aleppo has also been completed, and an 80-km line from Tartous to Latakia is operating for passenger and goods traffic. A 170-km line from Deir ez-Zor to Abou Kemal, near the Iraqi border, is under construction.

Syrian Railways: BP 182, Aleppo; tel. (21) 213900; telex 331009; fax (21) 228480; f. 1897; Pres. of the Board of Administration and Dir-Gen. MUHAMMAD GHASSAN AL-KADDOUR.

General Organization of the Hedjaz-Syrian Railway: BP 134, place Hedjaz, Damascus; tel. (11) 215815; Gen. Man. Eng. A. ISMAIL; the Hedjaz Railway has 232 km of track (gauge 1,050 mm) in Syria; services operate between Damascus and Amman, and a branch line of 24 km from Damascus to Katana was opened in 1977; in 1987 a study into the feasibility of reconstructing the historic railway to Medina, in collaboration with Jordan and Saudi Arabia, concluded that such a project would be financially viable only if the line were to be connected with European railway systems.

ROADS

Arterial roads run across the country linking the north to the south and the Mediterranean to the eastern frontier. The main arterial networks are as follows: Sidon (Lebanon)–Quneitra–Suweidiya–Salkhad–Jordan border; Beirut (Lebanon)–Damascus–Khan Abu Chamat–Iraqi border–Baghdad; Tartous–Tell Kalakh–Homs–Palmyra; Banias–Hama–Salemie; Latakia–Aleppo–Rakka–Deir ez-Zor–Abou Kemal–Iraqi border; Tripoli (Lebanon)–Tartous–Banias–Latakia; Turkish border–Antakya;

Amman (Jordan)–Dera'a–Damascus–Homs–Hama–Aleppo–Azaz (Turkish border); Quneitra–Damascus–Palmyra–Deir ez-Zor–Hassetche–Qamishliya.

At 31 December 1991 there were 712 km of motorways, 5,052 km of main, or national roads and 18,374 km of secondary, or regional roads.

General Co for Roads: BP 3143, Aleppo; tel. (21) 555406; telex 331403; f. 1975; Gen. Man. Eng. M. WALID EL-AJLANI.

PIPELINES

The oil pipelines which cross Syrian territory are of great importance to the national economy, representing a considerable source of foreign exchange. Iraq halted the flow of oil through the pipeline between Kirkuk and Banias in April 1976, but it was resumed in February 1979. Syria closed the pipeline in April 1982, but it has since been used to pump output from the oilfield at ath-Thayyem, which came into operation in 1986, to the refinery at Homs, via a 92-km spur line. In May 1992 Syria was reported to be ready to enter into negotiations with Iraq and the UN regarding the use of the pipeline for exports of Iraqi petroleum.

Following the Iraqi Government's nationalization of the Iraq Petroleum Company, the Syrian Government nationalized the IPC's pipelines, pumping stations and other installations in Syria, setting up a new company to administer them:

Syrian Company for Oil Transport (SCOT): BP 13, Banias; tel. 22300; telex 441012; f. 1972; Dir-Gen. MUHAMMAD DOUBA.

SHIPPING

Latakia is the principal port; it handled 5.88m. tons of goods in 1984. The other major ports are at Banias and Tartous. The amount of phosphates handled at Tartous doubled to 2.6m. tons in 1986.

Syrian General Authority for Maritime Transport: BP 730, 2 rue Argentina, Damascus; tel. (11) 226350; telex 411012.

Ismail, A. M., Shipping Agency Ltd: BP 74, rue du Port, Tartous; tel. 20543; operates a fleet of 1 tanker and 9 general cargo vessels; Man. Dir MAHMOUD ISMAIL.

Sea Transport Agency: BP 78, Kamilieh Quarter, Harbour St, Latakia; tel. 33964; telex 510044; operates 3 general cargo vessels; Gen. Man. WADIH M. NSEIR.

Syrian Navigation Company: BP 314, rue Baghdad, Latakia; tel. 33778; telex 451028; f. 1975; state-owned company operating 4 general cargo ships; Chair. and Man. Dir AHMAD RIDA MOUSALAMANI.

Syro-Jordanian Shipping Co: BP 148, rue Port Said, Latakia; tel. 2316356; telex 451002; fax (11) 230250; f. 1976; operates 2 general cargo ships; transported 70,551 metric tons of goods in 1992; Chair. OSMAN LEBBADY.

Tabalo, Muhammad Abd ar-Rahman: BP 66, rue al-Mina, Tartous; tel. 20906; telex 470008; operates 4 general cargo vessels (1 refrigerated); Man. Dir ABDULLAH TABALO.

CIVIL AVIATION

There is an international airport at Damascus, and the upgrading of Aleppo airport, to enable it to handle international traffic, is planned.

Directorate-General of Civil Aviation: place Nejmeh, Damascus; tel. (11) 331306; telex 411928.

Syrian Arab Airlines (Syrianair): BP 417, 5th Floor, Social Insurance Bldg, Jabri St, Damascus; tel. 232154; telex 411593; f.

1946, refounded 1961 to succeed Syrian Airways, after revocation of merger with Misrair; domestic passenger and cargo services (from Damascus, Aleppo, Latakia and Deir ez-Zor) and routes to Europe, the Middle East, North Africa and the Indian sub-continent; Chair. OMAR ALI REDA.

Tourism

Syria's tourist attractions include a pleasant Mediterranean coastline, the mountains, the town bazaars and the antiquities of Damascus and Palmyra. A total of 1,739,884 foreigners visited Syria in 1992.

Ministry of Tourism: rue Victoria, Damascus; tel. (11) 215916; telex 411672; f. 1972; Minister of Tourism AMIN ABU ASH-SHAMAT; Dir of Tourist Relations and Ministerial Adviser Mrs SAWSAN JOUZY.

Middle East Tourism: BP 201, rue Fardoss, Damascus; tel. (11) 211876; telex 411726; f. 1966; Pres. MUHAMMAD DADOUCHE; 7 brs.

Defence

Commander-in-Chief of the Armed Forces: Lt-Gen. HAFIZ AL-ASSAD.

Minister of Defence and Deputy Commander-in-Chief of the Armed Forces: Maj.-Gen. MUSTAFA TLASS.

Chief of Staff of the Armed Forces: Maj.-Gen. HIKMAT ASH-SHEHABI.

Deputy Chiefs of Staff: Maj.-Gen. ALI ASLAN, Maj.-Gen. HASAN AT-TURKMANI.

Air Force Commander: Maj.-Gen. SUBHI HADDAD.

Special Forces Commander: Gen. ALI HABIB.

Estimated Defence Expenditure (1992): £S24,700m. (US $2,200m.).

Military Service: 30 months (Jewish population exempted).

Total Armed Forces (June 1994): 408,000 (army 300,000, air defence command (an army command) 60,000, navy (estimated) 8,000, air force 40,000); reserves 400,000.

Paramilitary Forces: 8,000 Gendarmerie (under control of Ministry of Interior).

Education

Primary education, which begins at six years of age and lasts for six years, is officially compulsory. Secondary education, beginning at 12 years of age, also lasts for six years. In 1990/91 there were 2,452,086 pupils in primary education in the public and private sectors, and 914,250 in preparatory and secondary education.

Agricultural schools prepare students mainly for work in agriculture and are open to the sons of peasants. Technical schools prepare students for work in all types of factories. Higher education is provided by the universities of Damascus, Aleppo, Tishrin (the October University, in Latakia) and Homs (the Baath University, formerly the Homs Institute of Petroleum). There were 169,759 students enrolled at the universities in 1992/93. The main language of instruction in schools is Arabic, but English and French are widely taught as second languages. The Government allocated £S3,921.9m., or 8.9% of the consolidated budget, to education in 1986.

Bibliography

Abd-Allah, Dr Umar. *The Islamic Struggle in Syria.* Berkeley, Mizan Press, 1984.

Abu Jaber, Kamal S. *The Arab Baath Socialist Party.* New York, Syracuse University Press, 1966.

Asfour, Edmund Y. *Syrian Development and Monetary Policy.* Harvard, 1959.

Degeorge, Gérard. *Syrie.* Paris, Editions Hermann.

Devlin, John F. *Syria: A Profile.* London, Croom Helm, 1982.

Drysdale, Alastair, and Hinnebusch, Raymond A. *Syria and the Middle East Peace Process.* New York, Council on Foreign Relations, 1992.

Fedden, Robin. *Syria: an Historical Appreciation.* London, 1946.

Syria and Lebanon. London, John Murray, 1966.

Glubb, J. B. *Syria, Lebanon, Jordan.* London, Thames and Hudson, 1967.

Haddad, J. *Fifty Years of Modern Syria and Lebanon.* Beirut, 1950.

Helbaoui, Youssef. *La Syrie.* Paris, 1956.

Hinnebusch, Raymond E. *Authoritarian Power and State Formation in Ba'thist Syria: army, party and peasant.* Oxford, Westview Press, 1990.

Hitti, Philip K. *History of Syria; including Lebanon and Palestine.* New York, 1951.

Homet, M. *L'Histoire secrète du traité franco-syrien.* New Ed., Paris, 1951.

Hopwood, Derek. *The Russian presence in Syria and Palestine 1843–1914.* Oxford, 1969.

Hourani, Albert H. *Syria and Lebanon: A Political Essay*. New York, 1946.

Hureau, Jean. *La Syrie aujourd'hui*. Paris, Editions Afrique.

Kienle, Eberhard (Ed.). *Contemporary Syria: Liberalization between Cold War and Cold Peace*. London, I. B. Tauris, 1994.

Lloyd-George, D. *The Truth about the Peace Treaties, Vol. II*. (London, 1938).

Longrigg, S. H. *Syria and Lebanon Under French Mandate*. Oxford University Press, 1958.

Petran, Tabitha. *Syria*. London, Benn, 1972.

Pipes, Daniel. *Greater Syria: the History of an Ambition*. New York, Oxford Unversity Press, 1990.

Rabbath, E. *Unité Syrienne et Devenir Arabe*. Paris, 1937.

Runciman, Steven. *A History of the Crusades*. London, Vol. I 1951, Vol. II 1952.

Seale, Patrick. *The Struggle for Syria*. London, 1965.

Springett, B. H. *Secret Sects of Syria and the Lebanon*. London 1922.

Stark, Freya. *Letters from Syria*. London, 1942.

Thubron, C. A. *Mirror to Damascus*. London, Heinemann, 1967.

Tibawi, A. L. *Syria*. London, 1962.

   American Interests in Syria 1800–1901. New York, Oxford University Press, 1966.

   A Modern History of Syria. London, Macmillan, 1969.

Torrey, Gordon H. *Syrian Politics and the Military*. Ohio, State University, 1964.

Tritton, A. S. *The Caliphs and their Non-Muslim Subjects*. London, 1930.

Van Dam, Nikolaos. *The Struggle for Power in Syria*. London, Croom Helm, 1979.

Weulersse, J. *Paysans de Syrie et du Proche Orient*. Paris, 1946.

Yamak, L. Z. *The Syrian Social Nationalist Party*. Cambridge, Mass., Harvard University Press, 1966.

Ziadeh, N. *Syria and Lebanon*. New York, Praeger, 1957.

TUNISIA

Physical and Social Geography

D. R. HARRIS

Tunisia is the smallest of the countries that comprise the 'Maghreb' of North Africa, but it is more cosmopolitan than Algeria or Morocco. It forms a wedge of territory, 163,610 sq km (63,170 sq miles) in extent, between Algeria and Libya. It includes the easternmost ridges of the Atlas Mountains but most of the country is low-lying and bordered by a long and sinuous Mediterranean coastline that faces both north and east. Ease of access by sea and by land from the east has favoured the penetration of foreign influences and Tunisia owes its distinct national identity and its varied cultural traditions to a succession of invading peoples: Phoenicians, Romans, Arabs, Turks and French. It was more effectively arabized than either Algeria or Morocco and remnants of the original Berber-speaking population of the Maghreb are confined, in Tunisia, to a few isolated localities in the south.

At the March 1984 census the population was 6,966,173 and the overall density was 42.6 per sq km. Most of the people live in the more humid, northern part of the country, and at the 1984 census about 8.6% (596,654) lived in Tunis. Situated where the Sicilian Channel links the western with the central Mediterranean and close to the site of ancient Carthage, Tunis combines the functions of capital and chief port. No other town approaches Tunis in importance, but on the east coast both Sousse (population 83,509 in 1984) and Sfax (population 231,911) provide modern port facilities, as does Bizerta (population 94,509) on the north coast, while some distance inland the old Arab capital and holy city of Qairawan, now known as Kairouan (population 72,254), serves as a regional centre. Other sizeable towns include Djerba (population 92,269), Ariana (98,655) and Gabès (92,258).

The principal contrasts in the physical geography of Tunisia are between a humid and relatively mountainous northern region, a semi-arid central region of low plateaux and plains, and a dry Saharan region in the south. The northern region is dominated by the easternmost folds of the Atlas mountain system which form two separate chains, the Northern and High Tell, separated by the valley of the River Medjerda, the only perennially flowing river in the country. The Northern Tell, which is a continuation of the Algerian Tell Atlas, extends along the north coast at heights of between 300 m and 600 m. South of the Medjerda valley lies the broader Tell Atlas, which is a continuation of the Saharan Atlas of Algeria, and is made up of a succession of rugged sandstone and limestone ridges. Near the Algerian frontier these reach a maximum height of 1,544 m at Djebel Chambi, the highest point in Tunisia, but die away eastward towards the Cap Bon peninsula which extends north-east to within 145 km of Sicily.

South of the High Tell or Dorsale ('backbone') central Tunisia consists of an extensive platform sloping gently towards the east coast. Its western half, known as the High Steppe, is made up of alluvial basins rimmed by low, barren mountains, but eastward the mountains give way first to the Low Steppe, a gravel-covered plateau, and ultimately to the flat coastal plain of the Sahel. Occasional watercourses cross the Steppes, but they flow only after heavy rain and usually fan out and evaporate in salt flats, or sebkhas, before reaching the sea.

The central Steppes give way southward to a broad depression occupied by two great seasonal salt lakes or shotts. The larger of these, the Shott Djerid, lies at 16 m below sea-level and is normally covered by a salt crust. It extends from close to the Mediterranean coast near Gabès almost to the Algerian frontier and is adjoined on the north-west by the Shott ar-Rharsa, which lies at 21 m below sea-level. South of the shotts Tunisia extends for over 320 km into the Sahara. Rocky, flat-topped mountains, the Monts des Ksour, separate a flat plain known as the Djeffara, which borders the coast south of Gabès, from a sandy lowland which is partly covered by the dunes of the Great Eastern Erg.

The climate of northern Tunisia is Mediterranean in type, with hot, dry summers followed by warm, wet winters. Average rainfall reaches 150 cm in the Kroumirie Mountains, the wettest area in north Africa, but over most of the northern region it varies from 40 cm to 100 cm. The wetter and least accessible mountains are covered with forests in which cork oak and evergreen oak predominate, but elsewhere lower rainfall and overgrazing combine to replace forest with meagre scrub growth. South of the High Tell rainfall is reduced to between 20 cm and 40 cm annually, which is insufficient for the regular cultivation of cereal crops without irrigation, and there is no continuous cover of vegetation. Large areas of the Steppes support only clumps of wiry esparto grass, which is collected and exported for paper manufacture. Southern Tunisia experiences full desert conditions. Rainfall is reduced to below 20 cm annually and occurs only at rare intervals. Extremes of temperature and wind are characteristic and vegetation is completely absent over extensive tracts. The country supports only a sparse nomadic population except where supplies of underground water make cultivation possible.

History

Revised for this edition by RICHARD I. LAWLESS

EARLY HISTORY

By 550 BC Carthage had achieved a position of commercial and naval supremacy in the Mediterranean. The empire reached its height in the course of the fourth century BC but was later challenged by the Roman Republic. The Punic Wars (264–241 BC, 218–201 BC and 149–146 BC) ended in the total destruction of the Carthaginian Empire and its incorporation within the empire of Rome. Carthage was rebuilt by the Emperor Augustus and intensive colonization brought a new prosperity. During the first two centuries AD Carthage was accounted the empire's second city but, with the decline of Rome's power, the city was lost to the Vandals (AD 439), to be recovered for the Byzantine Empire in 533–34. Byzantine rule was by no means secure: the tendency of the local governors to reject the control of Constantinople was compounded by religious dissent among the native Berber population, who adopted Christian heresies in opposition to imperial rule. It was, however, the rise of Islam in Arabia and its rapid expansion after the death of the Prophet (632) that led to the destruction of Byzantine power and to the Arab invasion of North Africa. Arab control was finally established there with the conquest of Carthage in 698 and the foundation of Tunis. Islam spread rapidly among the Berbers, but they adopted Kharijite heresies; the eighth century was dominated by Berber-supported risings, manifestations of militant Islam against the central Government, and constant revolts among the occupying Arab forces. In the last years of the Umayyad dynasty (overthrown 748–50) Tunisia escaped completely from imperial control: the new dynasty of the Abbasids, ruling from Iraq, retook Qairawan, the centre of Arab rule in the Maghreb, but lost it in 767, and a period of complete anarchy ensued. Tunisia was restored to Abbasid control in 800 and Ibrahim ibn Aghlab was appointed tributary ruler of Ifriqiya—corresponding roughly to present-day Tunisia.

For most of the ninth century the country was relatively prosperous, but the Aghlabid dynasty began to decline from 874 and was finally overthrown between 905 and 909 by the Fatimids, fanatical adherents of the heretical doctrines of Shi'ism, who pursued a vigorous policy of expansion and conquest; by 933 Fatimid rule was established throughout the Maghreb. Between 943 and 947 a Berber revolt took place, but it was effectively supressed, allowing Tunisia to enjoy a certain amount of prosperity for the subsequent 25 years. In 969–70 the Fatimids gained control of Egypt and Syria: three years later Mahdiya was abandoned for the new capital of Cairo, and the Government of Tunisia was handed over to the Berber Zirid family. The golden age of Zirid rule was brought to an end in 1050 when the dynasty transferred its allegiance to the orthodox caliph at Baghdad. The economy crumbled and the country lapsed into political fragmentation. In 1087 Italian forces from Pisa and Genoa took Mahdiya, allowing the Zirids to continue as its rulers. Early in the 12th century the Zirids renewed their loyalty to Cairo, but were driven out by the Normans in 1148. Norman rule in Tunisia was over by 1160, and for the next 50 years Tunisia formed part of the empire of the caliphs of Marrakesh (the Almohads). In the 13th century the authority of Baghdad was briefly restored over Tunisia: a strong provincial government was established in 1207 under the Berber family of the Hafsids, who had held the governorship of Tunis since 1184. For most of the 13th century they ruled over North Africa from Tripoli to central Algeria but, in the face of tribal and Arab unrest, the town of Jerba fell into Christian hands (1284–1337). In the reign of Abu'l-Abbas (1370–94) the fortunes of the dynasty revived, but by the end of the 15th century the Hafsid Empire was disintegrating and Tunisia had become involved in the struggle between the Spanish and Ottoman forces for control of the Mediterranean.

By 1520 Bougie, Tripoli and Jerba had fallen to Spain; then in 1534 Khair ed-Din (Barbarossa), high admiral of the Ottoman fleet, drove the Emir al-Hasan from Tunis. In 1535 a great Spanish naval expedition recaptured the town, and al-Hasan was returned as the Emperor's vassal. In 1542 he was deposed by his son Ahmad, who made a final attempt to reunite Tunisia against Spain. Ahmad finally fell at the siege of Malta (1565) which, together with the Spanish naval victory of Lepanto six years later, ended the struggle for maritime supremacy. The Pasha of Algiers stationed a garrison in Tunis in 1564, only to be driven out briefly (1572) in the aftermath of Lepanto; but in 1574 an Ottoman expedition put an end to Spanish power in Tunis and to the Hafsid dynasty itself.

Direct Ottoman rule was brief, a military revolt in Tunisia in 1591 reducing the power of the Pasha, the representative of the sultan, to a cypher. State affairs were taken over by one of the 40 deys, or high officers of the Ottoman army of occupation. By about 1600 the diwan, or governing council, had come to share a pre-eminent place with the taifa, or guild of corsair chiefs. By about 1606 the *de facto* independence of Tunisia had been recognized, although it was to remain nominally part of the Ottoman Empire for more than 250 years.

In the first half of the 17th century trade and commerce flourished, but from about 1650 the deys' power declined, authority passing to the beys, originally subordinate in rank. Hammuda, bey from 1659 to 1663, became master of the entire country, and his family—the Muradids—retained power until 1702. This was a period of decline, with tribal unrest and incursions from Algiers. With the accession of Hussain Ali Turki in 1705, a new line of beys brought some semblance of order. The remainder of the 18th century passed fairly uneventfully, with some prosperity, despite uncertain relations with Algeria and the growth of European naval power in the Mediterranean.

After the Napoleonic Wars the European powers forced the bey, Mahmud (1814–24), to suppress the activities of the corsairs, which had provided a considerable part of state revenues. The French occupied Algiers in 1830, and reduced Algeria to colonial status; for the next 50 years Tunisia desperately tried to avoid the same fate. Increasingly the influence of France and Britain, and later Italy, became apparent through the activities of their consuls. The beys Ahmad (1837–55) and Muhammad (1855–59) attempted reforms, but merely increased dependence on France. The next bey, Muhammad as-Sadiq (1859–82), promulgated a constitution (suspended 1864). Increased taxes, however, provoked tribal rebellion, and in 1869 the bey was obliged to accept financial control by France, Britain and Italy. Imminent financial collapse prompted France to intervene, and French forces invaded Tunisia in April 1881. They encountered little resistance and the Treaty of Kassar Said was signed, under which the bey remained the nominal ruler, while French officials took over military, financial and foreign affairs.

FRENCH PROTECTORATE

The Treaty of Mersa (1883) formally established a French protectorate over Tunisia and brought the actual Government of the country under French control, effective power passing to the French Resident-General. The international control commission was abolished in 1884, the currency was reformed along French lines in 1891, and the extra-territorial privileges of other Europeans were abrogated. Encouraged by large-scale grants of land, there was a considerable influx of settlers from France, and also from Italy, especially after 1900. Besides being confronted with the task of sustaining the economy, which they tackled by investment in the development of the country's resources, the French were faced with rivalry from Italy and with the rise of Tunisian nationalism.

Tunisian cultural and political life absorbed many French ideas, but was also influenced by movements in other parts of the Islamic world. An attempt to emulate the Young Turk reformers in the Ottoman Empire was the foundation, in 1908, of the Young Tunisian Movement, which called for the restoration of the authority of the bey together with democratic reforms. The achievement of independence in eastern Arab countries after the First World War, and the example of the nationalist movement in Egypt, inspired Tunisians with a greater national consciousness, and in 1920 the Destour (Constitution) movement was formed under the leadership of Sheikh ath-Tha'libi, one of the founders of the Young Tunisians.

The Destour called for a self-governing constitutional regime with a Legislative Assembly. French attempts to conciliate opinion by administrative reforms, dating from 1920 with the formation of economic councils on which Tunisians were represented, failed to satisfy the more radical elements, and, in the face of further nationalist activity, the French administration resorted to repressive measures. Sheikh ath-Tha'libi was exiled in 1923, and in 1925 the Destour movement was dissolved. It was revived in the early 1930s but soon split, the former leaders of the Destour being accused of collaboration with France by younger members eager for political action on a broad front. In 1934, led by Habib Bourguiba, a Tunisian lawyer, the latter formed the Néo-Destour (New Constitution) Party. The new party employed methods of widespread political agitation as a result of which Bourguiba was exiled. After the victory of the Popular Front in France in 1936 he returned to Tunisia, but little was achieved in direct negotiations with the new French Government. The Néo-Destour became a powerful organization, its influence extending to all parts of the country, and its strength was proved in a successful general strike in 1938. Widespread clashes with the police followed, martial law was proclaimed, some 200 nationalists were arrested, and both the Destour and Néo-Destour parties were dissolved.

At the outbreak of the Second World War Tunisian opinion rallied in favour of France, and when Italy entered the war some 23,000 Italians in Tunisia were interned. With the fall of France Tunisia came under Vichy rule, and Bizerta, Tunis and other ports were used by Germany and Italy to supply their armies in Libya until the defeat of the Axis forces by the Allies in 1943 restored French authority. The bey, Muhammad al-Monsif, was accused of collaboration with the Axis powers and deposed; he was replaced by his cousin, Muhammad al-Amin.

GROWING AUTONOMY

The virtual restoration of peace in 1944 brought a relaxation of political restrictions and during the following years there was renewed agitation for political change. As a result of subsequent French repression, Habib Bourguiba went into exile in Cairo in 1945 but his chief lieutenant, Salah ben Yousuf, remained in Tunisia. The French authorities turned their attention to political reforms, and by beylical decrees in 1945 the Council of Ministers and the Grand Council (an elected body with equal French and Tunisian representation) were reorganized, the authority of the latter being extended. These moves did not satisfy the nationalists, however, who demanded complete independence. Later in 1946 a government was formed under Muhammad Kaak, which included an increased number of Tunisians (moderate leaders being appointed after the Destour and Néo-Destour had refused to participate); the French, however, retained ultimate control. Bourguiba returned to Tunisia in 1949. In April 1950 the Néo-Destour proposed the transfer of sovereignty and executive control to Tunisian hands, under a responsible government with a Prime Minister appointed by the bey and an elected National Assembly which would draft a democratic constitution. Local French interests would be protected by representation on municipal councils, and Tunisia would co-operate with France on equal terms. These proposals received a reasonable response in France, and a new Tunisian Government was formed in August 1950, composed of an equal number of Tunisian and French ministers, with Muhammad Chenik as Prime Minister and Salah ben Yousuf as Minister of Justice. The object of the new Government was stated to be the gradual restoration of Tunisian sovereignty, in co-operation with France. Despite strong opposition to these developments from the European settlers (some 10% of the population), further reforms were effected in September 1950

and February 1951, when French advisers to the Tunisian ministers were removed and the Resident-General's control over the Council of Ministers was diminished.

Peaceful progress towards autonomy came to a halt, however, owing to growing settler opposition, procrastination on the part of the French Government and consequent alienation of the nationalists. Tunisian resentment erupted in strikes and demonstrations early in 1952. The Néo-Destour had formed an intimate alliance with the influential trade union movement, and many leaders held office in both organizations. In February 1952 Bourguiba and other Néo-Destour leaders were arrested on the order of the new Resident-General, Jean de Hauteclocque, and a wave of violence spread throughout the country, culminating in the arrest and removal from office of the Prime Minister, Chenik, and the imposition of French military control.

A new government was formed under Salaheddine Baccouche, and a French-inspired scheme designed to lead to eventual internal autonomy was announced in April 1952. Meanwhile, the now-proscribed Néo-Destour took its case to Cairo and the UN General Assembly. Against a background of increasing terrorism, countered by French repressive action, and in the face of opposition from both the Néo-Destour and the settlers, little in the way of reform could be achieved. The bey at first refused to sign French reform decrees, and when he yielded in December 1952 under the threat of deposition, the proposals were promptly repudiated by the Néo-Destour.

Terrorist activities continued and a settler counter-terrorist organization, the 'Red Hand', came to prominence. The situation approached civil war in 1953, with bands of fellagha active in the western highlands and around Bizerta and terrorism and counter-terrorism in the towns. In July 1954 the newly-formed French Government, led by Pierre Mendès France, offered internal autonomy for Tunisia, with France retaining responsibility only for defence and foreign affairs. The French proposals were accepted, and in August a new Tunisian Government was formed, headed by Tahar ben Ammar and containing three members of the Néo-Destour as well as moderate nationalists. Negotiations with the French Government opened in Carthage in September 1954. The talks had reached deadlock when the Mendès France Government fell in February 1955, but they resumed in March and a final agreement was signed in Paris on 2 June.

The accord granted internal autonomy to Tunisia while protecting French interests and preserving Tunisia's close links with France. France retained responsibility for foreign affairs, defence (including the control of frontiers) and internal security. Although the agreement was supported by a majority of the Néo-Destour, the extremist wing, headed by the exiled Salah ben Yousuf, and the old Destour and Communist elements, opposed it, as did the settlers' organizations. An all-Tunisian Cabinet was formed in September 1955 by Tahar ben Ammar, with members of the Néo-Destour holding six of the 12 posts.

Habib Bourguiba had returned from three years' exile in June 1955, to be followed by Salah ben Yousuf in September. In October Ben Yousuf was expelled from the Néo-Destour for opposition to the recent agreement and for 'splitting activities'. A Néo-Destour party congress at Sfax in November endorsed the agreement, but reaffirmed that the party would be satisfied only with independence and demanded the election of a constituent assembly. Clashes between 'Bourguibist' and 'Yousufist' factions followed, and in December a conspiracy to set up a terrorist organization to prevent the implementation of the agreement was discovered. Ben Yousuf fled to Tripoli in January 1956, and many suspected 'Yousufists' were placed in detention. At the same time fellagha activity revived, rebel bands became active in the remoter parts of the country and acts of terrorism were committed against both French settlers and members of the Néo-Destour.

INDEPENDENCE

Against the background of these events, a Tunisian delegation led by Bourguiba began independence negotiations with the French Government in Paris on 27 February 1956. In a protocol signed on 20 March, France formally recognized the independence of Tunisia and its right to exercise responsibility over foreign affairs, security and defence, and to raise a national army. A transitional period was envisaged during which French forces would gradually be withdrawn from Tunisia, including Bizerta.

Elections for the Constituent Assembly, held on 25 March 1956, resulted in all 98 seats being won by candidates of the National Front, all of whom acknowledged allegiance to the Néo-Destour. The elections were boycotted by the 'Yousufist' opposition. Habib Bourguiba became Prime Minister on 11 April, leading a government in which 16 of the 17 ministers belonged to the Néo-Destour.

In the early years of independence Tunisia's relations with France were dominated by the question of the evacuation of French forces. A Tunisian demand for their withdrawal was rejected in July 1956 by the French Government, which was preoccupied with the deteriorating situation in Algeria. Bourguiba visited Paris in September in an attempt to promote a mediated settlement in Algeria based on French recognition of Algeria's right to independence, but hopes of progress in this direction were shattered by the French kidnapping in October of five leading Algerian nationalists. Tunisia immediately severed diplomatic relations with France, anti-French riots broke out, and there were clashes between French troops and Tunisian demonstrators resulting in deaths on both sides.

Moves were made early in 1957 to strengthen Tunisia's relations with its neighbours. In January a treaty of good-neighbourliness was signed with Libya, as a step towards establishing a 'Great Arab Maghreb', and in March a 20-year treaty of friendship was concluded with Morocco.

The bey, Muhammad al-Amin, had been the object of constant criticism from Tunisian nationalist leaders, who accused him of reluctance to participate actively in the struggle for independence. After independence his remaining powers were eroded and on 25 July 1957 the Constituent Assembly voted to abolish the monarchy, proclaim Tunisia a republic and invest Bourguiba with the powers of Head of State.

RELATIONS WITH FRANCE

Although diplomatic relations with France had been resumed in January 1957, differences between the two Governments concerning the Algerian revolt persisted. The most serious Franco-Tunisian incident during the Algerian war occurred in February 1958, when French aircraft from Algeria attacked the Tunisian border village of Sakhiet Sidi Yousuf, the scene of several clashes the previous month. The Tunisian Government's reaction was to sever diplomatic relations with France, to forbid all French troop movements in Tunisia, to demand the immediate evacuation of all French bases, including Bizerta, and to take the matter before the UN Security Council. French troops were blockaded in their barracks, and the extra-territorial status of Bizerta, from which French warships were banned, was abolished. In addition some 600 French civilians were expelled from the frontier area and five of the seven French consulates were closed.

British and US mediation was accepted, and on 15 April it was agreed that all French troops would be evacuated and Tunisian sovereignty over Bizerta recognized; at the same time the French consulates would be reopened and the cases of the expelled French civilians examined. When further clashes between Tunisian and French forces occurred in May, a state of emergency covering the whole country was proclaimed and Tunisia again took the matter to the UN Security Council.

A new phase in Franco-Tunisian relations began with the accession to power of Gen. de Gaulle in June 1958. An agreement was concluded on 17 June under which French troops stationed outside Bizerta were to be withdrawn during the next four months, while negotiations for a provisional agreement on Bizerta were to follow. Restrictions on French troops were removed and diplomatic relations resumed. By October the only French troops remaining in Tunisia were in Bizerta.

The eradication of French interests had meanwhile commenced. In June the French-owned transport services and in August the electricity services of Tunis were nationalized. On 29 November President Bourguiba announced proposals for the purchase of all agricultural land in Tunisia owned by French citizens by 1960, and for its redistribution to landless Tunisians.

POLITICAL CONSOLIDATION

With the improvement of relations with France, the Tunisian Government was able to consolidate its internal position, by restructuring the Néo-Destour Party and by instituting court proceedings against members of the former regime and 'Yousufist' opponents. Prince Chadli, the eldest son of the bey, and former Prime Ministers Tahar ben Ammar and Salaheddine Baccouche were among those tried in late 1958 on charges that included the misuse of public funds and collaboration with the French authorities; sentences imposed ranged from heavy fines to imprisonment and loss of civic rights. Salah ben Yousuf (*in absentia*) and 54 of his supporters were charged with plotting to assassinate President Bourguiba, smuggling arms from Libya, and aiming to overthrow the Government. Ben Yousuf and eight others were sentenced to death, with most of the remainder receiving long prison sentences.

This trial widened the breach between Tunisia and the United Arab Republic (UAR—Egypt), from where Ben Yousuf had been conducting his activities. In October 1958 Tunisia had joined the Arab League, only to withdraw from a meeting of its council 10 days later, after accusing the UAR of attempting to dominate the organization. Diplomatic relations with the UAR were severed later in the month on the grounds of its alleged complicity in the 'Yousufist' attempt to assassinate President Bourguiba. On the eve of Ben Yousuf's trial, Bourguiba announced the capture of Egyptian officers who had secretly entered Tunisia to assist subversive elements to overthrow his Government.

A further step in the establishment of a presidential system of government was taken with the promulgation on 1 June 1959 of a new Constitution, which provided for the election of a President with a five-year mandate (renewable three times consecutively). The President was empowered to lay down the general policy of the state, choose the members of the Government, hold supreme command of the armed forces and make all appointments to civil and military posts. The Constitution also provided for the election of a national assembly for five years and required the approval of the assembly for the declaration of war, the conclusion of peace and the ratification of treaties. In elections which followed on 8 November President Bourguiba was elected unopposed, and all 90 seats in the new National Assembly were won by the Néo-Destour, their only opponents being the Communists.

THE BIZERTA CRISIS

The forging of cordial relations with France continued during 1959–60. A trade and tariff agreement was signed on 5 September 1959, and further agreements on technical co-operation and the transfer of property of the French State in Tunisia to the Tunisian Government were concluded. In October 1959 President Bourguiba announced his support for President de Gaulle's offer of self-determination for Algeria, and Tunisia subsequently acted as intermediary between France and the Algerian rebels in moves towards a negotiated settlement.

None the less, Tunisia continued to press for the return of the Bizerta base, and on 5 July 1961 President Bourguiba made a formal demand for its return and repeated the claim (first made in 1959) to Saharan territory in Algeria adjacent to the south-western part of Tunisia. Demonstrations ensued against the continued French occupation of Bizerta, and fighting between Tunisian and French troops began around the Bizerta base and in the disputed area of the Sahara. On 19 July diplomatic relations were again severed, and Tunisia called for a meeting of the UN Security Council. The fighting ended on 22 July with the French in firm control of the base and town of Bizerta, over 800 Tunisians having been killed. In the south a Tunisian attempt to seize the fort of Garat el-Hamel also failed. A subsequent visit to Bizerta by the UN Secretary-General, Dag Hammarskjöld, in an attempt to promote a settlement, was unsuccessful. According to a French statement released on 28 July, France wished to continue to use the base while a state of international tension persisted but was prepared to negotiate with Tunisia over its use during this period.

The immediate results of the Bizerta crisis were a *rapprochement* between Tunisia and other Arab states, a deterioration in relations with the West and an improvement of relations with the communist bloc. The final settlement of the dispute occupied the remainder of 1961 and much of 1962. The Algerian cease-fire in March 1962 benefited Franco-Tunisian relations, and the French installations at Menzel Bourguiba, near Bizerta, were handed over to Tunisia on 30 June. In March 1963 agreement was reached on the transfer of some 370,000 acres of French-owned agricultural land to the Tunisian Government. Other agreements, on trade and finance, were reached, in order to reduce Tunisia's balance-of-payments deficit with France.

Although Algerian independence had been warmly welcomed by Tunisia, the extremist doctrines of the new state conflicted with Tunisian moderation and relations quickly deteriorated. In January 1963 the Tunisian Ambassador was recalled from Algiers on the grounds of alleged Algerian complicity in a recent unsuccessful attempt on the life of President Bourguiba, in which 'Yousufists' in Algeria, as well as supporters of the old Destour and army elements, were implicated. Moroccan mediation facilitated a conference of the Maghreb states in Rabat in February, at which the Tunisians demanded the cessation of 'Yousufist' activities in Algeria. After further negotiations a frontier agreement between Tunisia and Algeria was signed in July.

EXPROPRIATION

On 11 May 1964 the Tunisian National Assembly enacted legislation which authorized the expropriation of all foreign-owned lands (some 300,000 ha). The French immediately suspended, then cancelled, all financial aid. This nationalization of foreign-owned land was a step towards the development of socialism in the agrarian sector of the economy. The Néo-Destour's commitment to 'Tunisian socialism' was emphasized in the change of the party's name to the Parti Socialiste Destourien (Destour Socialist Party—PSD) prior to the presidential and general elections in November 1964, in which President Bourguiba was again elected unopposed and the PSD, the only party to present candidates, filled all 90 seats in the National Assembly. Subsequent cabinet changes included the appointment of the President's son, Habib Bourguiba, Jr, as Minister of Foreign Affairs.

From 1964 onwards, domestic politics became more settled and the attention of the Government was turned to the task of economic development. The hold of the PSD on the country was strengthened and President Bourguiba's position was unchallenged.

FOREIGN POLICY

After 1964 Tunisia's relations with the world beyond the Arab states and Africa were influenced by the need for foreign aid, most of which was received from Western countries where the moderation of Tunisian policies inspired confidence. Tunisia also made cautious overtures towards the communist bloc. Some economic assistance was obtained from the USSR while Tunisia maintained its non-aligned position. Diplomatic relations with the People's Republic of China were established, following a visit to Tunisia by the Chinese Premier, Zhou Enlai, in January 1964. None the less, President Bourguiba publicly criticized Chinese policies, in particular the Chinese policy of encouraging revolution in Africa.

Relations with the rest of the Arab world continued to be the focus of President Bourguiba's attention and the source of bitter controversy. In April 1965 he openly attacked Arab League policy on Palestine and advocated a more flexible approach, including direct negotiations with Israel over the UN partition plan of 1948. This provoked severe criticism from the Arab states (excepting Morocco, Libya and Saudi Arabia). After violent demonstrations in Cairo and Tunis, the UAR and Tunisia withdrew their respective ambassadors. Tunisia's refusal at the end of April to follow the example of other Arab League states in severing relations with the Federal Republic of Germany, which had exchanged ambassadors with Israel, widened the rift. A conference of Arab Heads of State at Casablanca in May, at which Tunisia was not represented, categorically rejected President Bourguiba's proposal that Israel should be asked to cede territory to the Palestinian refugees in return for recognition by the Arab states, and

reaffirmed their determination to bring about the complete overthrow of Israel. In an open letter to those attending, President Bourguiba accused the Egyptian President, Gamel Abd an-Nasser, of attempting to use the Arab League as an instrument of UAR national policy and of interfering in the affairs of every Arab state; Tunisia was not prepared to take part in the debates of the Arab League under such circumstances. In October 1966 Tunisia announced the complete severance of diplomatic relations with the UAR.

The six-day war between Israel and the Arab states in June 1967 brought about immediate reconciliation in the Arab world. Tunisian troops were dispatched to the front, but the Israeli success was so swift and the cease-fire came so soon that they were recalled before they had reached the scene of the fighting. Diplomatic relations between Tunisia and the UAR were restored, and Tunisia was represented at the Arab summit meeting in Khartoum in September, when Arab nations agreed neither to recognize nor to negotiate with Israel.

In May 1968, however, following criticism of President Bourguiba by the Syrian Prime Minister, who charged him with having betrayed the Arab struggle in Palestine, the Syrian chargé d'affaires and his staff in Tunis were accused of inciting subversive activities and expelled. At a meeting in Cairo on 1 September, the Arab League refused to hear a statement from the Tunisian delegate criticizing the Arab attitude, particularly that of the UAR, towards Israel. On 26 September the Tunisian Government announced its intention to boycott future meetings of the League. Nevertheless, Tunisia reaffirmed its support for the Palestine Liberation Organization (PLO).

An exchange of visits by the Ministers of Foreign Affairs of Tunisia and Algeria in early 1969 brought about an improved climate for negotiation on the demarcation of their common frontier and on economic matters, especially those arising from the nationalization by each country of property owned by nationals of the other. On 6 January 1970 a treaty of co-operation and friendship was signed, which settled all outstanding issues between the two countries.

THE FALL OF AHMAD BEN SALAH

Between 1964 and 1969 the chief issue in internal affairs was the drive to collectivize agriculture, carried out under the leadership of Ahmad ben Salah, Minister of Finance and Planning. The programme was carried out in the face of massive opposition in affected areas and disagreement within the ruling party itself. In September 1969 the policy was abandoned; Ben Salah was stripped of all office, arrested, tried and sentenced to 10 years' hard labour. However, he escaped from prison in February 1973 and took refuge in Europe, from where he issued statements condemning President Bourguiba for acting against the people in the interests of a privileged class, and became the leader of the radical Mouvement de l'Unité Populaire (Popular Unity Movement—MUP), which was declared illegal in Tunisia.

Ben Salah was the first of several ministers to experience a sharp reversal of fortune. In November 1969 President Bourguiba appointed Bahi Ladgham to be Prime Minister, but in October 1970 replaced him by Hedi Nouira. A year later the President declared that Nouira would be his successor. In March 1973 Ladgham resigned from all his political posts. Mahmoud Mestiri was the next minister to fall into disgrace. As Minister of the Interior in 1970 and 1971, he demanded the liberalization of the Government. Consequently he was dismissed from the cabinet in September 1971, expelled from the party in 1972 and from the National Assembly in May 1973. When a revision of the Constitution was finally proposed in March 1973, it included almost none of the measures suggested by Mestiri to modify the presidential nature of the Government. Indeed, during the next two years President Bourguiba and Prime Minister Nouira consolidated their power. In September 1974 the ninth party congress of the PSD elected Bourguiba as President-for-life of the party and confirmed Nouira in the post of Secretary-General. Bourguiba appointed a new political bureau of 20 members, including 14 ministers, confirming a tendency to draw the PSD and the Government closer together. In November Bourguiba was re-elected unopposed as President of Tunisia, and in the National

Assembly elections all 112 PSD candidates were returned, also without opposition. The new Assembly voted amendments to the Constitution, designating the Prime Minister as the President's successor and allowing for the appointment of a President-for-life, a post to which the assembly elected Bourguiba in March 1975. Constitutional reforms in December 1975 increased presidential powers still further.

UNION WITH LIBYA

In June 1970 the President's son, Habib Bourguiba, Jr, was replaced as Minister of Foreign Affairs by Muhammad Masmoudi. From that date relations with the more radical Arab states and with radical powers outside the area improved. Normal relations were resumed with the UAR and Syria, and Tunisia rejoined the Arab League.

On 12 January 1974, after a meeting between President Bourguiba and Col Qaddafi, the Libyan leader, on the island of Djerba, it was announced that Tunisia and Libya had agreed to form a union. The Djerba Agreement was greeted with general surprise for, despite an improvement in relations between the two countries in previous years, President Bourguiba had always shown himself to be hostile to such a union. Bourguiba was to be president of the new state, with Qaddafi as his deputy. It would seem that the Djerba Agreement was managed by Muhammad Masmoudi, without the consent of the Prime Minister, Hedi Nouira, who was out of the country at the time. Nouira returned swiftly to Tunisia, and Masmoudi was dismissed from his post in the Government and the PSD.

In the aftermath of this confused affair, relations with Libya were tense. The Libyans continued to urge fulfilment of the Djerba Agreement, and in 1975 Bourguiba expressed concern at the increase in strength of the Libyan army. Another source of contention between the two countries was the delimitation of their respective sectors of the continental shelf, in which important deposits of petroleum were to be found. In June 1977 both sides agreed to submit to arbitration by the International Court of Justice and agreement was finally reached in February 1982. In October 1977 a joint statement was issued, saying that Tunisia and Libya had agreed to 'reactivate mutual co-operation' and set up a scheme to link the electricity networks of the two countries, while experts were to discuss the possibility of other joint ventures. Relations with Algeria also improved in 1977, after Tunisia had abandoned its attempts at conciliation in the Western Sahara dispute (in which it sided with Morocco): a co-operation agreement was signed in July by the respective Ministers of the Interior.

DOMESTIC UNREST

By 1977, with President Bourguiba in his seventies and in poor health, there was growing uncertainty over the future of the system of government which he had dominated for so long. Hedi Nouira, his designated successor, appeared to lack the powerful personality which had kept Bourguiba in command of the country, and there were signs of a succession struggle in the increasing demands for the free development of a pluralist democracy from, among others, former ministers Ahmad ben Salah, in exile, and Ahmad Mestiri, leader of the unofficial Mouvement des Démocrates Socialistes (Social Democrats—MDS). The arrest and trial (from June to August 1977) of 33 members of the MUP, on charges of threatening state security and defaming the President, indicated the continuing hostility of the Government to any form of organized opposition.

Meanwhile, however, a more effective political force was beginning to make itself felt. After a number of strikes by workers in 1976, a 'social contract' had been drawn up early in 1977 between the Government and the Union Générale des Travailleurs Tunisiens (General Union of Tunisian Workers—UGTT) under the leadership of Habib Achour, involving inflation-linked pay rises for the duration of the 1977–81 Development Plan. In spite of this agreement there were further strikes in various sectors of industry towards the end of 1977, demanding better pay and conditions, and backed by the UGTT, which was becoming (particularly through its weekly newspaper *Ach-Cha'ab*) an increasingly vocal critic of government policy and an outlet for political dissenters. In

December Muhammad Masmoudi, the former Minister of Foreign Affairs, returned from exile in Libya and declared his support for the UGTT, thereby underlining its potential as a political force. Tahar Belkhodja, the Minister of the Interior, was dismissed on 23 December 1977, after having suggested that the unrest should be attributed to social and economic problems, such as a rapidly increasing population and severe unemployment. Six other moderate members of the cabinet resigned in sympathy, but President Bourguiba reaffirmed his support for Nouira by forming a new government in which the dissidents were replaced mainly by civil servants and technocrats, all of whom could be expected to accept Nouira's tough policy; in addition, Bourguiba brought in his son, Habib Bourguiba, Jr, as special adviser.

On 10 January 1978 Achour resigned from the Political Bureau and Central Committee of the PSD after pressure from members of the UGTT who felt that his dual role had become unacceptable. The UGTT national council called for urgent changes in the method of government and an end to the use of 'intimidation' in suppressing strikes and demonstrations. On 26 January the union finally took the drastic step of calling a general strike as a warning to the Government and in retaliation for attacks on union offices. There was rioting in Tunis and several other cities, the army was called in and at least 51 people were killed, while hundreds more were injured; a state of emergency was declared and a curfew imposed. Hundreds of demonstrators were arrested, tried and imprisoned, and Achour and other members of the UGTT executive were also taken into custody and charged with subversion. The Government accused the UGTT of a long-standing conspiracy against the state and hinted at foreign backing, presumably from Libya.

There was considerable international criticism of the irregular conduct of the trial of Achour and 30 other union leaders, which began in August 1978. Nevertheless, Achour was sentenced to 10 years' hard labour, and prison sentences were also passed on all but six of the other defendants. Under a new Secretary-General, Tijani Abid, the UGTT expressed regret at the recent events and declared its willingness to cooperate with the Government. Although Achour was pardoned by President Bourguiba in August 1979, he remained under house arrest; 263 others serving prison terms for their involvement in the riots had been pardoned in May, but it was nevertheless clear that the power of the UGTT as a source of opposition had, for the moment, been crushed.

In July 1979 the National Assembly approved an amendment to the electoral code, allowing, for the first time, the number of candidates in legislative elections to be twice the number of seats although it remained unclear whether members of parties other than the PSD would be permitted to stand. At the PSD congress in September, the need to 'open up' the party to new adherents and new ideas was emphasized, but the Prime Minister rejected the idea of a multi-party system and a 'national pact' proposed two years previously by the MDS. The main opposition groups—MUP, MDS and the Parti Communiste Tunisien (PCT—the Communist Party)—declared that they would boycott the legislative elections in November, since participation would indicate support of the present system (and would presumably not have been permitted in any case, since none of the groups had official party status). At 81%, the turn-out in the elections was substantially lower than on previous occasions, when it had averaged 95%.

In January 1980 there was an attack on the town of Gafsa in western Tunisia by guerrillas, originally estimated to number 300, although only 60 were later brought to trial. The Tunisian armed forces quickly regained control of the town, but 41 deaths were reported. Responsibility for the attack was claimed by a hitherto unknown group, the Tunisian Armed Resistance, who declared that they aimed to free Tunisia from the 'dictatorship' of the PSD. The Tunisian Government claimed that the attackers were Tunisian migrant workers who had been trained in Libya and encouraged to make the attack in order to destabilize the Bourguiba administration: diplomatic relations with Libya were suspended. Libya expressed its incredulity at these allegations, and referred to the incident as a 'popular uprising'. Nevertheless, the attack caused international concern, particularly in France, which sent military transport aircraft to Gafsa and naval vessels to the Tunisian coast, while the USA also offered to speed up military supplies. The Gafsa attack was condemned by the more established opposition groups within Tunisia, bringing about a temporary national solidarity, although the same groups condemned the execution of 13 of the guerrillas which took place in April.

MOVES TOWARDS POLITICAL LIBERALIZATION

The sudden illness of Hedi Nouira in February 1980 renewed political uncertainty. The Minister of Education, Muhammad Mzali, was appointed as temporary government co-ordinator and in April as Prime Minister, thereby becoming Bourguiba's successor under the terms of the Constitution. The new Government headed by Mzali included three of the ministers who had resigned in 1977 in protest at the harsh measures taken against strikers, while a member of the MDS was also included as Minister of Transport. In December Tahar Belkhodja, the former Minister of the Interior who had been dismissed in 1977, was readmitted to the Government. Most political prisoners were released in the course of the year, and in January 1981 a pardon was granted to nearly 1,000 members of the UGTT who had been convicted of involvement in the 1978 riots. Greater tolerance was also shown towards opposition parties: in July 1980 permission was granted to the MDS to publish two weekly periodicals, and in the following February an amnesty was granted to all members of the proscribed MUP, except its leader-in-exile, Ahmad ben Salah. In April 1981 President Bourguiba declared that he saw no objection to the emergence of political parties provided that they rejected violence and religious fanaticism and were not dependent 'ideologically or materially' on any foreign group (which suggested that Islamic fundamentalists would not be welcome candidates). The congress elected a new PSD central committee of 80 representatives, some 75% of whom had not previously been members of the committee.

An extraordinary congress of the UGTT was also held in April 1981, the first since the riots of January 1978. Of the 13 members of the executive committee elected by the congress, 11 were former committee members who had been imprisoned in 1978. The new Secretary-General—Taieb Baccouche—was the first non-PSD member to be elected to this post. Habib Achour was finally released in December 1981, when he was allowed to resume his position as leader of the UGTT.

The process of installing a multi-party system continued with the announcement of legislative elections for November 1981; Bourguiba promised that any participating group which gained a minimum of 5% of the votes cast would be officially recognized as a political party. Several parties refused to take part in the elections under these conditions. In July the one-party system was brought to an end with the official recognition of the PCT. As a former officially recognized political party (banned since 1963), the PCT was not required to fulfil the 5% condition laid upon the other groups. In contrast to this apparent political liberalization, as many as 50 leading members of the Mouvement de la Tendance Islamique (Islamic Tendency Movement—MTI) were arrested and given prison sentences in September. The Government continued to regard the MTI, a relatively moderate Islamic group, as a dangerous influence.

Although the PCT, MUP and MDS presented candidates in the November legislative elections, the result was a landslide victory for the Front National, a joint electoral pact formed by the PSD and the UGTT, which gained 94.6% of votes cast and won all 136 seats in the new assembly. The other parties all failed to win 5% of the vote, and consequently none was given official recognition. Formal protests of electoral irregularities were made by the three opposition groups. The MDS and the MUP were finally accorded official status in November 1983.

FURTHER UNREST

In January 1984 widespread rioting and looting broke out. The immediate cause was a rise of 115% in the price of bread and the abolition of government subsidies on flour and other staple foods, but the disturbances were also linked to long-

standing grievances, including the high level of unemployment (particularly among the young), and to unrest amongst Islamic fundamentalist groups. Rioting started in the south of the country, but spread to the northern cities of Sfax, Gabès and Tunis. On 3 January the Government declared a state of emergency, and troops were called in to control street demonstrations. The resulting clashes between troops and demonstrators left 89 people dead and 938 injured, according to official figures, and more than 1,000 people were arrested. After a week of disturbances President Bourguiba personally intervened to reverse the price rises, and order was re-established.

An official inquiry into the cause of the riots accused the Minister of the Interior, Driss Guiga, of exploiting the violence for his own political ends and of failing to inform the President of the magnitude of the disturbances. Guiga had been dismissed by President Bourguiba in January and subsequently left the country. The vacant portfolio was granted to Prime Minister Mzali, whose position was considerably strengthened by the downfall of his former rival for the presidential succession. In June Guiga was tried *in absentia* for high treason and sentenced to 15 years' imprisonment.

Throughout 1984 and in early 1985 Tunisia was troubled by a series of strikes in the public sector. The strikers demanded increases in public-sector salaries, which had been frozen for two years. In April 1985 riot police surrounded the UGTT headquarters, after the union urged a general strike in support of the demands of public-sector strikers. The UGTT subsequently postponed the strike, pending talks with government negotiators. However, in early May, the UGTT announced that negotiations had collapsed and that it would refuse to participate in the municipal elections later that month. The MDS, the PCT and the MUP also boycotted the elections. Nevertheless, there was a turn-out of 92.8% (compared with only 66.8% for the equivalent elections in 1980), which the PSD interpreted as a vote of support for its policies. In late July the UGTT declared the start of a campaign of renewed strike action. In the same month the union's newspaper, *Ach-Cha'ab*, was suspended by the Government for six months, on the grounds that it had attributed untrue statements to informed political sources. In October the police occupied the UGTT headquarters and arrested union leaders. Local UGTT committees were dissolved and replaced by pro-government committees. By early November about 100 UGTT leaders had been arrested, including the UGTT Secretary-General, Habib Achour, but many were released later in the month. In December the executive committee of the UGTT agreed to replace Habib Achour with a provisional Secretary-General, on condition that the Government released the union members who were still in detention and reinstated workers who had been dismissed for taking industrial action. In January 1986 the UGTT's administrative commission, considering that these conditions had not been met, voted to reinstate Achour as Secretary-General. In the same month, however, Achour was imprisoned on a charge of theft, dating from 1982. (In April he was sentenced to a further two years' imprisonment for alleged mismanagement of union funds, and in December his sentence was extended by another four years.) In May the UGTT elected a 'moderate', Ismaïl Lajeri, as Secretary-General.

The Tunisian Government's refusal to condemn the US raid on Libya in April 1986 prompted considerable popular disquiet, and anti-US sentiment was suppressed by the authorities. Ahmad Mestiri, leader of the MDS, was jailed for organizing a demonstration, and *al-Moustaqbal* (the MDS weekly magazine), *Réalités*, *ar-Rai* and two PCT magazines were seized by the Government. The Government suspended publication of *al-Moustaqbal* and a PCT magazine, *Tarik al-Jadid* for six months from May, and *Réalités* from July. The appointment of Gen. Zine al-Abidine ben Ali, who was regarded as a hard-liner, as Minister of the Interior, in late April, was considered a significant change in domestic policy.

BOURGUIBA ATTEMPTS TO TIGHTEN HIS GRIP ON POWER

In early 1986 Habib Bourguiba, Jr, was suspended from his post of special adviser, owing to his opposition to the wave of arrests at the end of 1985. In the following months Bourguiba announced a series of ministerial reshuffles, which gradually weakened the position of Muhammad Mzali, the Prime Minister, who had been regarded as Bourguiba's potential successor. During the 12th congress of the PSD in June, Bourguiba apparently confirmed Mzali's position as secretary-general of the PSD, yet he dispensed with the ballot to elect the members of the PSD central committee, and personally appointed 90 members, none of whom was an associate of Mzali. In July Mzali was replaced in the premiership by Rachid Sfar (previously Minister of Finance), and was dismissed as secretary-general of the PSD. Mzali subsequently fled across the border to Algeria, and in subsequent months was sentenced *in absentia* to one year's imprisonment for crossing the border illegally, to a further three years' imprisonment for defamatory comments against Tunisian leaders, and to 15 years' hard labour for mismanagement of public funds.

A general election for a new National Assembly was held in November 1986 , but was boycotted by the opposition parties. The PSD won all 125 seats, opposed by only 15 independent candidates. There was a high level of participation (82.9% of the electorate), according to official figures, although these were disputed by the opposition.

By 1987 the Government had consolidated its control over the UGTT, and left-wing militancy was no longer perceived as a threat. In December 1986 the UGTT elected a new 18-member executive bureau, and a new, apparently moderate, secretary-general, Abd al-Aziz Bouraoui. In January 1987 Bourguiba presided over the opening of an extraordinary congress of the UGTT, during which the union confirmed its support of the PSD and approved a new union charter. Habib Achour was released on humanitarian grounds in May. In the same month, Bourguiba pardoned 13 members of the Rassemblement Socialiste Progressiste, who had been sentenced to six months' imprisonment for illegal assembly.

SUPPRESSION OF ISLAMIC FUNDAMENTALISTS

Meanwhile, President Bourguiba had become increasingly concerned that Islamic fundamentalism was a threat to his regime, and attempts were made to suppress fundamentalist activity. In July 1986 four Islamic fundamentalists were sentenced to death, and about 22 others were imprisoned, for a series of offences. Dozens of arrests were reported by human rights organizations, following clashes between Islamic fundamentalists and left-wing students at the University of Tunis in early 1987. In March 1987 the Secretary-General of the MTI, Rached Ghanouchi, was arrested on charges of violence and collusion with foreign powers to overthrow the Government. Later in the month, Tunisia severed diplomatic relations with Iran, after Tunisians, suspected of terrorist offences, were arrested in France and Djibouti. The Tunisian Government accused the Iranian Embassy in Tunis of subversive acts, including the recruitment of Tunisian Islamic fundamentalists to perpetrate terrorist acts abroad, and thus undermine Tunisia's relations with friendly states. The Government also claimed to have evidence of an Iranian plot to overthrow Bourguiba, and to establish a pro-Iranian fundamentalist administration in Tunisia. On this pretext, a wave of arrests of Islamic fundamentalists ensued. According to the authorities, 1,500 people were detained, although opposition parties estimated that the total reached over 3,000. The arrests were condemned by the Ligue Tunisienne des Droits de l'Homme (Tunisian League of Human Rights—LTDH), and in April the opposition parties issued a communiqué, warning against a return to repressive practices and demanding guarantees for the freedom of the trade unions and the universities. There were further arrests after clashes broke out between police units and Islamic fundamentalists during an anti-government demonstration in April. Later in the month, the Secretary-General of the LTDH, Khemais Chamari, was arrested and accused of disseminating false information and defaming the state. (Chamari was later released on parole, and was acquitted in January 1988.) In May the Government approved the creation of the Association for the Defence of Human Rights and Public Liberty, as a rival to the LTDH, which the Government accused of being pro-MTI. In June 37 Islamic fundamentalists, mostly students, were sentenced to terms of imprisonment of between two and

six years for taking part in illegal demonstrations in April and for defaming Bourguiba. In August 13 foreign tourists were injured by bomb explosions, and the Government promptly insisted that the MTI was responsible, despite the publication of a statement from the radical Islamic group, Islamic Jihad, claiming responsibility. Six young Tunisians later confessed on television to planting the bombs, and stated that they were members of the MTI. They alleged that the bombings were part of an operation to damage the tourist trade on which Tunisia depended. In September the trial opened of 90 Islamic fundamentalists, accused of threatening state security and of plotting against the Government. The conduct of the trial was criticized by opposition parties and human rights groups. Despite the prosecution's demand that all 90 defendants should receive the death penalty, only seven were sentenced to death, five of them *in absentia*. Fourteen defendants were acquitted, and 69 (including Rached Ghanouchi) received prison sentences.

FOREIGN RELATIONS IN THE 1980s

In the 1980s President Bourguiba continued to pursue a moderate, pro-Western foreign policy. After the attack on Gafsa in January 1980, Tunisia strengthened its links with the USA and the two countries established a joint US-Tunisian military commission in November 1981.

Tunisian relations with other Maghreb countries improved considerably in the early 1980s. In March 1983 a meeting was held in Tunisia between President Bourguiba and President Chadli of Algeria. Discussions on the normalization of relations between the two countries, the demarcation of the frontier and common industrial projects resulted in the drafting of the Maghreb Fraternity and Co-operation Treaty. At the subsequent ratification of the treaty by the Tunisian National Assembly, calls were made for closer relations between the Maghreb states of Algeria, Libya, Mauritania, Morocco and Tunisia, and the introduction of a common political structure. Mauritania signed the treaty in December 1983.

However, relations with Libya reached a dangerously low ebb in August 1985 after Tunisia expelled 283 Libyan nationals, including most of the Libyan diplomats in Tunis, on charges of spying, in retaliation against Col Qaddafi's decision to expel some 30,000 Tunisians working in Libya. Qaddafi threatened to use military force to resolve the dispute, and Tunisia's armed forces were placed on alert before Morocco offered to mediate between the two countries. In September 1985 Tunisia severed diplomatic relations with Libya, following the expulsion of four Libyan diplomats who had been accused of sending letter-bombs to Tunisian journalists.

In response to the Libyan military threat, Tunisia's links with the USA were strengthened. However, in October 1985 relations between the two countries were soured, following the bombing by Israeli aircraft of the headquarters of the PLO, near Tunis. At the UN Security Council, the USA abstained on a Tunisian resolution condemning the raid, but resisted Israeli pressure to veto the motion. By March 1986 relations between the USA and Tunisia had improved, following a visit by US Vice-President George Bush. However, the US raid on Libya in the following month proved to be a further source of embarrassment for Tunisia. The Tunisian Government refused to condemn or to approve the US action and thus angered members of opposition parties and Islamic fundamentalists. Demonstrations ensued and many opposition figures were arrested (see above).

Meanwhile, there was growing Tunisian ambivalence over the PLO presence in Tunis. Following the Israeli raid on the PLO headquarters, a group of Palestinians 'hijacked' an Italian cruise liner, the *Achille Lauro*, off the Egyptian coast. The USA made it clear that it would not allow the hijackers to return to the PLO headquarters in Tunis, and the Tunisian authorities refused to let the Egyptian aircraft carrying the hijackers and a PLO official land in Tunisia (see chapter on Egypt). After the *Achille Lauro* incident, Tunisian sources hinted that the Tunisian Government was considering asking the PLO to leave the country. There was renewed speculation in late 1986 that the PLO would move its headquarters out of Tunisia, as a result of increasing restrictions imposed on PLO activities by the Tunisian Government. In October the PLO decided to remain in Tunisia but its staff of 500 was reduced to a minimal diplomatic and administrative level.

Relations with Libya began to improve in March 1987, when Bourguiba met a representative of the Libyan Government to discuss the issue of compensation for Tunisian workers, and the restoration of capital to companies expelled from Libya in 1985. In early 1987 Libya produced a written undertaking not to interfere in Tunisia's internal affairs. In July flights were resumed by Tunisia's national airline, Tunisair, to Tripoli. Following Col Qaddafi's proposals to unify Libya and Algeria, President Bourguiba and President Chadli of Algeria issued a joint communiqué in July, announcing that discussions had taken place on how to develop the unity of the Maghreb region, although it seemed that Bourguiba had agreed to increased co-operation between the Maghreb states, rather than merger. In September Tunisia announced that the dispute with Libya over the expulsion of the Tunisian workers had been resolved, and consular ties were resumed in the following month, when the border between the two countries was reopened.

BOURGUIBA'S DECLINE

In the second half of 1987 President Bourguiba's behaviour became increasingly erratic. In September the appointments were announced of a new Minister of Cultural Affairs, Director of the PSD Political Bureau, Director-General of the Tunisian broadcasting company, and editor of the state-owned newspaper, *al-Amal*. A few days later, in early October, Bourguiba revoked the appointments and dismissed Rachid Sfar from the premiership. Ben Ali was appointed Prime Minister, with responsibility for internal affairs, and Secretary-General of the PSD. A few weeks later, a new director of the PSD was appointed. In late October Bourguiba carried out a minor cabinet reshuffle in which the Ministry of Finance was divided into two portfolios and a Ministry of the National Economy was created.

Meanwhile, ministers, concerned about Bourguiba's behaviour, began to examine provisions in the Constitution which would allow for the retirement of the President. Reports emerged that Bourguiba was demanding a retrial of the Islamic fundamentalists who had been sentenced in September (see above), with the aim of having the death sentence imposed on all 90 defendants. A disagreement about the fate of the Islamic fundamentalists allegedly ensued between Bourguiba and Ben Ali, and it was rumoured in early November that Bourguiba intended to dismiss Ben Ali. Meanwhile, a plot to overthrow Bourguiba was disclosed, allegedly involving about 150 people, both military and civilian.

BEN ALI TAKES OVER

On 7 November 1987 seven doctors declared that President Bourguiba was unfit to govern, owing to senility and ill health, and, in accordance with the Constitution, the Prime Minister, Zine al-Abidine Ben Ali, was sworn in as President. There was no apparent opposition to Ben Ali's take-over, which had been approved in advance by the majority of ministers and senior military officers. President Ben Ali declared that he would continue to implement existing foreign and economic policies, but announced plans to revise the Constitution and to permit greater political freedom. He appointed Hedi Baccouche as Prime Minister, and a new cabinet was announced, which omitted four ministers closely associated with Bourguiba. Later in November, Ben Ali announced the formation of a National Security Council (comprising himself, the Prime Minister, the Minister of State for Defence, the Minister of Foreign Affairs and the Minister of the Interior) to safeguard internal security. The Council subsequently announced that 76 people, including members of the army and national guard, police, customs officers and members of the MTI, had been arrested on suspicion of plotting against the state.

On assuming power, President Ben Ali immediately began to effect a policy of national reconciliation. The publication was permitted of opposition newspapers which had been suspended by the Bourguiba administration, although radio and television networks continued to be controlled. In late November the National Assembly approved legislation which limited to four days the length of time during which a person

could be held in police custody without the authority of the public prosecutor: the length of time during which a person could be held on remand was limited to six months for most offences. In December the State Security Court was abolished, along with the post of Prosecutor-General. In the same month, 2,487 political and non-political detainees were released, including 608 MTI members and Ahmad Mestiri, the leader of the MDS. In January 1988 405 political prisoners were released, and in March Ben Ali granted amnesty to a further 2,044 political and common-law detainees.

Ben Ali also initiated attempts to normalize relations between the Government and the UGTT, as a result of which the two rivals for the leadership of the UGTT, Habib Achour and Abd al-Aziz Bouraoui, agreed to renounce their union responsibilities as a first step towards the reconciliation of the 'radical' and 'moderate' factions of the union. In May 1988 Ben Ali ordered the release of Rached Ghanouchi, the leader of the MTI. Ahmad ben Salah, the exiled leader of the MUP, was also pardoned, and he returned to Tunisia in June.

Meanwhile, the new Government continued to consolidate its power. The size of the PSD Political Bureau was reduced from 20 to 13 members in December 1987. Nine new members were appointed, including seven members of the cabinet formed in November, all of whom were close associates of President Ben Ali. In January 1988 the PSD won all the seats at five by-elections to the National Assembly with a comfortable majority, although there were allegations of electoral malpractice from the PCT. In a government reorganization in the following month, President Ben Ali assumed the defence portfolio and appointed a Secretary of State for Security Affairs. He also took the opportunity to dismiss several associates of Bourguiba, to merge the two Ministries of Agriculture and of Agricultural and Food Production, and to divide the Ministry of National Education.

POLITICAL LIBERALIZATION

In accordance with his promises after assuming power, President Ben Ali introduced proposals to increase political freedom and to introduce a more democratic system of government. In February 1988 the central committee of the PSD announced that the party's name had been changed to the Rassemblement Constitutionnel Démocratique (Democratic Constitutional Assembly—RCD). In July the National Assembly approved a series of proposals to reform the Constitution. Under the amendments, the post of President-for-life was abolished, and the President was to be elected by universal suffrage every five years, and limited to two consecutive terms in office. A maximum age of 70 years was to be introduced for presidential candidates. If the presidency fell vacant before the end of the term of office, the President of the National Assembly, rather than the Prime Minister, was to assume presidential powers until elections were held, but was himself prohibited from becoming a candidate. The reforms also redefined the role of the Prime Minister as a co-ordinator of government activities rather than as leader of the government.

In April 1988 legislation was passed by the National Assembly instituting a multi-party system, although, in order to gain legal recognition, political parties had to uphold the aims of, and work within the Constitution, and were not to be permitted to pursue purely religious, racial, regional or linguistic objectives. Gifts and donations to political parties were to be supervised by the Minister of the Interior, in order to prevent foreign interference. In July the National Assembly modified the Press Code, relaxing its repressive tendencies. In the same month, Tunisia became the first Arab nation to ratify the UN convention against torture and other inhumane or degrading treatment. In late July, as part of an amnesty extended to 932 detainees, Tunisia's remaining 180 classified political prisoners were released, and a further 1,075 people charged with political crimes or under police surveillance had their civil liberties restored. The beneficiaries of this amnesty included 50 Islamic fundamentalists arrested in 1987; members of the UGTT; Tunisians involved in the attack on Gafsa in 1980; and supporters of Salah ben Yousuf, who had been arrested in 1963. (However, about 170 prisoners accused of terrorist acts remained in detention.) Meanwhile, national holidays associated with former President Bourguiba were removed from the calendar, the Tunisian national anthem was revised to omit any allusions to Bourguiba, statues of Bourguiba were quietly removed, and many streets and towns named after Bourguiba were renamed.

In a major cabinet reshuffle in July 1988, seven ministers who had served under Bourguiba were dismissed, leaving Hedi Baccouche, the Prime Minister, as the only prominent member of the Council of Ministers to have served under the two Presidents. In an apparent move to separate the RCD from the state apparatus, as a prelude to a multi-party system, the Director of the RCD Political Bureau lost his right to sit in the Cabinet and the public health portfolio was allocated to Saadadine Zmerli, the President of the LTDH, who was not a member of the RCD. Ben Ali also divided the Ministry of Economy into a Ministry of Trade and Industry and a Ministry of Energy and Mines.

At the first congress of the RCD in late July 1988, President Ben Ali pledged that he would establish a multi-party system with fair elections and freedom of expression. In accordance with Ben Ali's call for pluralism, Ahmad Mestiri, the leader of the MDS, and Muhammad bel Hadj Amor, the leader of the PUP, were invited to address the congress, and both endorsed the policies of the Ben Ali Government. Ben Ali was re-elected as president of the RCD, despite speculation, following the recent cabinet reshuffle, that he would relinquish his party post. The perpetuation of ties between the RCD and the Government was also reflected in the appointments of Hedi Baccouche, the Prime Minister, as Vice-President of the party, and of the Minister of Foreign Affairs, the Minister of the Interior and the Governor of the Central Bank (who held cabinet rank) as members of the new streamlined seven-member political bureau. There was also concern over the disclosure that Ben Ali had personally appointed 122 members of the RCD's enlarged 200-strong central committee.

Ben Ali restated his desire to 'open a new page of pluralism and democracy' at the beginning of consultations held in September 1988 on a Tunisian 'National Pact' to set out the aims and values of the administration. Participants in the consultations included representatives from national organizations (the UGTT, employers' organizations, youth and womens' groups, etc), the Secretary-Generals of the RCD, MDS, PCT and PUP, and the leaders of the unofficial political parties (the leftist Rassemblement Socialiste Progressiste—RSP, the liberal Parti Social pour le Progrès—PSP, the MUP and the MTI). Later that month, the RSP and the PSP were granted legal recognition. Earlier in August, Rached Ghanouchi had announced that the MTI accepted the law on political parties and respected the Constitution, especially the personal status code enshrining womens' rights.

Ben Ali was faced with the problem of integrating the Islamic fundamentalists within the political system without totally abandoning the secularism of the Bourguiba regime, and he succeeded in establishing good relations with their leader. Following the release of leading fundamentalists in September and November 1988, Ghanouchi stated that the era of injustice was over. Stress was laid upon the Arab and Islamic identity of Tunisia, the *Azzan* and prayers were broadcast on television, *Hijri* dates appeared on official documents, and the seventh-century religious college, the Zeitouna, was given the status of a university. The MTI, transformed into a political party (Hizb al-Nahdah or Parti de la Renaissance), was, none the less, denied official status.

On the first anniversary of his rise to power Ben Ali announced a National Pact, which was designed to show Tunisia as a country ready for democracy. Basic freedoms were guaranteed, although political parties could be formed only with the approval of the Minister of the Interior. Elections, not due until 1991, were brought forward to April 1989. On 26 November 1988 a new political party, the Union Démocratique Unioniste, was legalized, and began to develop Arab nationalist and unionist policies.

During this period old associates of Bourguiba were indicted for corruption and embezzlement of considerable sums: Mahmoud Skhiri was sentenced to five years' imprisonment, Tahar Belhodja (*in absentia*) to five years, Mahmoud Belhassine to 10 years and a heavy fine, while Mzali's request, from abroad, for rehabilitation was refused. Moreover, Ben Ali dismissed

Habib Ammar, one of his oldest and closest associates (whose son had been involved in a smuggling case), from the Ministry of the Interior.

THE APRIL 1989 ELECTIONS

In February 1989, in an attempt to establish national consensus and also to guarantee the election of some non-RCD candidates, Ben Ali invited the leaders of the six opposition parties to present themselves to the electorate as a coalition. This offer was rejected, although the parties had previously agreed to support Ben Ali as sole candidate for the presidency. In a drastic purge conducted at local level, the RCD readopted only 20 of its 125 retiring members. The Communists, fearing humiliation at the polls, declined to participate. Hizb al-Nahdah, forbidden from campaigning as a party, presented 'independent' candidates in 19 out of the 25 constituencies, in which a total of 480 candidates contested 141 seats. The National Assembly elections were the first multi-party elections in Tunisia since 1981; the level of participation was 76% of the 2,700,000 eligible voters. The RCD won all 141 seats, with 80% of the votes cast, while the Islamic independents replaced the MDS as the main opposition force, taking 13% of the total votes and 25% of votes in many constituencies. Opposition allegations of widespread electoral fraud were denied by the RCD. Ben Ali was confirmed as President by 99% of voters.

On 11 April 1989 a new cabinet of 32 members was announced. Although the leading members, headed by Baccouche, were retained, the cabinet represented a new political generation. With an average age of 48 years, most ministers were too young to have taken part in the struggle for independence, and 28 of them had not held any office under Bourguiba. In addition, they were drawn from the whole country (one-third from the deprived south) rather than predominantly from Bourguiba's own Sahel area. Technocrats were given portfolios to address what Ben Ali defined as the main problems: foreign debts, expensive subsidies, a cumbersome and expensive public sector, unemployment and regional policies. As a conciliatory gesture to the opposition, the liberal Mohammed Charfi, a leading member of the LTDH, was placed in charge of Education and Scientific Research, while Daly Jazi, a founding member of the MDS, was appointed as Minister of Public Health.

POLITICAL DEVELOPMENTS

However, the National Pact failed to curb political dissent in the country, and tensions were exacerbated by the imposition of essential economic reforms. In April 1989 Ben Ali announced a general amnesty, which restored civil and political rights to 5,416 people condemned by the former regime, many of whom were Islamic activists. The remaining 48 Islamic prisoners, sentenced in 1987 for plotting against Bourguiba, were released in May 1989. In September Ben Ali dismissed his Prime Minister, Hedi Baccouche, following a disagreement over economic policy; Baccouche was replaced by Hamed Karoui, hitherto Minister of Justice. In November a further 1,354 people, including Bourguiba's close associates Mahmoud Skhiri and Tahar Belkhodja, were granted amnesty. In one of the few political trials, the leader of a breakaway faction of the MUP was sentenced in August to one year's imprisonment for defamation of the President (but was released in November); six communists were later imprisoned for similar offences. In May 1990 an Islamic leader, Professor Moncef Ben Salem, was sentenced to three years' imprisonment for criticizing the Government in an Algerian fundamentalist newspaper.

In late 1989 taxes were lowered in an attempt to reduce evasion, and Ben Ali announced a 10% increase in wages. However, the President failed to gain popular support and appeared increasingly autocratic, declaring that he alone would decide the pace and course of reform. The conflict between the country's need for reform and modernization and the traditional Islamic values held by certain factions was seemingly insoluble. The Government was also concerned that Islamic fundamentalists were receiving financial aid from foreign sources. After the April 1989 elections, Rached Ghanouchi went into voluntary exile in Paris, and a lawyer, Abd al-Fatha Mourou, assumed the leadership of al-Nahdah within Tunisia. In June official recognition of al-Nahdah was refused, on the grounds that 15 of its leaders had not yet regained their civil rights. Ben Ali also demanded that al-Nahdah clarify its position on the rights of women, and reiterated his opposition to the concept of a religious political party. In December a second application for registration was refused, although al-Nahdah was permitted to publish a weekly journal, *al-Fajr*. (The al-Nahdah weekly, *al-Moustaqbal*, had been closed down in the previous year.)

Following their failure to secure legal recognition, the fundamentalists increased their political agitation and gained support among students. In December 1989 96 students began a hunger strike after the Government tried to divide its opponents by dissolving the Theological Faculty of the Zeitouna University. A campus police station in Kairouan was ransacked, and casualties were reported on the campus at Sfax. In February 1990 the protests culminated in clashes between police and students belonging to the Union Générale des Etudiants Tunisiens (UGET), an organization allied to al-Nahdah. About 600 student activists were detained, and some were briefly drafted into the army. The Government accused al-Nahdah of exploiting the students and of inciting unrest among the work-force, including a strike by 10,000 municipal workers. Political tension in the country increased following severe floods in late January 1990, which killed 30 people and caused damage to property totalling more than US \$400m. Eight hundred demonstrators, incited by fundamentalist leaders who condemned the Government's dilatory relief efforts, attacked government offices in Sidi Bou Zid, and 26 were arrested. Ben Ali subsequently pledged \$445m. towards relief work. (In April five men were sentenced to three months' imprisonment for leading the riots.) In a reshuffle of some key government posts in March, Abd al-Hamid Escheikh, hitherto Minister of Foreign Affairs, was appointed Minister of the Interior.

The Government was keen that municipal elections, due to be held in June 1990, should be viewed as a serious move towards multi-party democracy. In January Prime Minister Karoui invited opposition leaders for discussions on the amendment of the electoral code and access to the media. However, the discussions were boycotted by three of the recognized opposition parties and by al-Nahdah, and little progress was made. In May 1990 the electoral law was amended to introduce a form of proportional representation in the forthcoming municipal elections. The winning party was to gain only 50% of the seats, while the remaining seats were to be divided between all the parties, according to the number of votes received. However, the six legal opposition groups and al-Nahdah boycotted the elections, held on 10 June, on the grounds that they were neither free nor fair. The RCD won control of all but one of the 245 municipal councils, taking 3,750 council seats. The remaining 34 seats were won by independent candidates, many of whom were former members of the RCD. According to official sources, an estimated 79.3% of the electorate voted. In the same month publication of *al-Fajr* was suspended, following an article by exiled leader Rached Ghanouchi which strongly criticized the Tunisian Government.

Disagreement over government policy regarding the Gulf crisis, and in particular the stance adopted concerning Iraq, was the apparent cause of the replacement, in late August 1990, of the Minister of Foreign Affairs, Ismaïl Khelil, by Habib Boulares (a prominent journalist and a former Minister of Culture and Information under Bourguiba).

In October 1990 it was reported by the human rights organization, Amnesty International, that although more than 10,000 common-law and political prisoners had benefited from amnesty measures since Ben Ali's accession to the presidency, human rights abuses, of which members of unregistered political groups were often the victims, continued. In the following month Ben Ali pardoned 113 prisoners, and announced the formation of a national commission on human rights (to be known as the Comité Supérieur des Droits de l'Homme et des Libertés Fondamentales—CSDHLF). In March 1991 an amnesty was announced for a further 836 prisoners, to comme-

morate the 35th anniversary of independence. The human rights commission was inaugurated in the following month.

In November 1990 several members of al-Nahdah were arrested, following the discovery of explosives which were allegedly to have been used for terrorist activities. Al-Nahdah's senior officials denied that the movement was involved in terrorism. In the same month it was announced that the authorities had dismantled an 'Islamic network' that had allegedly been planning an Islamic revolution. In late December senior officials of al-Nahdah were arrested, together with more than 100 other people, and accused of attempting to establish an Islamic state. The arrests provoked demonstrations by Islamic militants in January 1991, and in the same month thousands of Tunisians took part in pro-Iraqi demonstrations, following the outbreak of war between Iraq and the US-led multinational force. In February further demonstrations by Islamic militants were violently suppressed. In the same month the co-ordinator of the MUP, Brahim Hayder, was sentenced to three months' imprisonment on a charge of attempting to disturb public order (after having condemned the Government's banning of a pro-Iraqi demonstration in January).

On 17 February 1991 the Minister of the Interior, Abd-al Hamid Escheikh, whose attitude towards recent fundamentalist manifestations of support for Iraq had apparently been regarded by his government colleagues as insufficiently uncompromising, was replaced by Abdallah Kallel, hitherto Minister of Defence. Kallel was succeeded at the Defence Ministry by Habib Boulares. Escheikh's dismissal was announced within hours of an armed attack, allegedly by al-Nahdah supporters, on RCD offices in central Tunis, as a result of which one person was said to have been burned to death. On 7 March Abd al-Fatha Mourou and the two other members of the al-Nahdah executive committee who were still at liberty in Tunis (four members were reported to be in detention at this time, two had fled the capital to evade arrest, while Rached Ghanouchi remained in exile) responded to government pressure, denouncing violent acts committed in the name of al-Nahdah and 'freezing' their activities within the movement. However, tensions persisted, and in May two students were killed in a clash with the police. The students' union, UGET, was disbanded by the authorities after the police claimed to have found weapons and subversive material linked to al-Nahdah, and riot police were posted outside centres where the annual baccalaureate examinations were being held. Also in May some 300 people, including about 100 members of the security forces, were arrested in connection with an alleged fundamentalist plot: the Government claimed that it had been planned to assassinate Ben Ali and other government members in October. In June five Islamic fundamentalists were sentenced to death (two *in absentia*) for their part in the attack on the RCD headquarters. The executions of the three who were in detention took place in October, this reportedly being only the second occasion on which death sentences had been implemented since Ben Ali's accession to power.

In July 1991 Amnesty International reported that it had received accounts of the systematic torture of more than 100 prisoners, most of whom were suspected members of al-Nahdah. The Government requested the newly-created CSDHLF to investigate, and its findings, published in October, showed that there had indeed been abuses, but concluded that these had not been officially sanctioned. About 140 prisoners, many of them political, were released in November (on the anniversary of the President's accession to power), and the sentences of more than 900 other detainees were reduced. In March 1992 a further report by Amnesty International, which detailed the arrests of some 8,000 people—mostly suspected members of al-Nahdah—over an 18-month period, and cited 200 cases of the torture and ill-treatment of detainees, as well as the deaths in custody of at least seven fundamentalists, was immediately condemned by the Tunisian authorities as 'baseless'. However, the Government, while denying that any detainee in Tunisia could be classified as a prisoner of conscience, later conceded that some violations of human rights had been committed, and announced that it would investigate allegations of the abuse of detainees. Meanwhile, new restrictions were imposed on oganizations such as the LTDH, which in July 1991 had criticized restrictions on press freedom. In mid-June 1992 the LTDH was dissolved by its leadership, following the introduction of legislation which, in establishing new distinctions between the competences of political parties and hitherto quasi-political associations such as the LTDH, effectively banned members of the latter from participation in political life.

In addition to an apparently unsuccessful attempt to persuade Abd al-Fatha Mourou and his supporters to form a 'moderate' Islamic party, Ben Ali began to court the legalized opposition. In March 1991 he received opposition leaders and ordered that they should receive funds for party expenses and propaganda and that the police should not harass their activities. Ben Ali also appeared anxious to end the RCD's monopoly of power in the National Assembly, and offered not to present RCD candidates for nine by-elections pending to the legislature. However, the opposition, demanding a wider reform of the electoral system, boycotted the elections, and the vacant seats were taken by RCD candidates. The relatively high level of participation by voters, ranging from 69.5% and 92.4%, was interpreted as an indication of popular support for the Government's uncompromising attitude towards al-Nahdah. In late December Ben Ali announced that changes to the electoral code, to be formulated in co-operation with opposition parties, would be implemented during 1992, with the aim of ensuring greater representation at the national level for parties other than the RCD. The opposition resumed a dialogue with the Government in January 1992, although its cohesion was undermined by a number of incidents: Ahmed ben Salah and Muhammad Mzali, both still in exile, were reported to have declared support for al-Nahdah, and Ahmad Mestiri resigned from the MDS in early 1992, apparently in response to internal party differences which resulted in the 'suspension' of the activities within the MDS of three members of the party's political bureau.

Government changes in October 1991 resulted in the promotion of Abdallah Kallel to the rank of Minister of State. At the same time Ben Ali appointed a close associate, Abd al-Aziz ben Dhia, to replace Habib Boulares at the Ministry of Defence. (Boulares was subsequently appointed President of the National Assembly.) A new Ministry of the Environment and Land Planning was also created at this time. In March 1992, at the beginning of the Islamic month of Ramadan, a new Ministry of Religious Affairs was created. Further government changes in June included the creation of a Ministry of International Co-operation and Foreign Investment, as well as the appointment of Ben Ali's adviser on human rights, Sadok Chaabane, as Minister of Justice. In the following month the composition of the Cabinet was again modified.

Suppression of the Islamist movement, al-Nahdah, continued, with widespread arrests and a large security presence on the streets. At the end of July 1992 more than 100 Tunisians, said to belong to the Islamist terrorist group 'Commandos du Sacrifice', were put on trial at the Tunis military tribunal. The accused, who included army, police and customs officials, were charged with conspiring to take power by force and plotting to assassinate the President. During the trial, al-Nahdah's official spokesman, Ali Laaridh, insisted that the Commandos du Sacrifice were not part of the al-Nahdah movement and denied the existence of any plot to overthrow the state. Habib Laasoued, alleged to be the leader of the Commandos, also denied any link with al-Nahdah, which he described as a rival movement. At the same time, almost 200 alleged al-Nahdah members were put on trial for plotting to take power by force. Throughout both trials there were allegations of irregularities in the conduct of the hearings and of human rights abuses. Many of the accused claimed that torture had been used to extract a confession. International human rights groups urged that the trials should be delayed until these allegations could be investigated thoroughly. At the end of August the courts announced long prison sentences for the defendants. Among those receiving life sentences were three exiled al-Nahdah leaders, Rached Ghanouchi, Salah Karkar and Habib Moknil. It was claimed that Ghanouchi had received funds from the Governments of Iran, Sudan and Saudi Arabia to overthrow the Tunisian regime and was organizing violent Islamist revolution. These mass trials were seen as the culmination of the Tunisian Government's long campaign against al-Nahdah, whose organizational structures within the country were largely destroyed and its leaders imprisoned or forced into exile. Abdallah Kallel claimed that 'a Tunisian terrorist network' had been completely dismantled. Some members of opposition parties accused President Ben Ali of using the threat of 'Islamic fundamentalism' as an excuse to delay long-promised democratic reforms.

FOREIGN POLICY UNDER BEN ALI

President Ben Ali continued to pursue a moderate, pro-Western foreign policy. Relations with the USA remained cordial, and, during discussions on political and economic issues in March 1988 with the Tunisian Government, the US Secretary of State, George Shultz, announced US support for Ben Ali's political reforms. In April the US Secretary of Defence, Frank Carlucci, visited Tunis to discuss Tunisia's military debt to the USA, which totalled $400m. In June the Tunisian Government authorized two US banks to refinance the debt. The Tunisian Government attempted to improve relations between the USA and Libya after the shooting down of two Libyan aircraft in January 1989. It was hampered by the strength of popular sentiment, with anti-American demonstrations occurring across the country. During an official visit to the USA in May 1990, President Ben Ali met the US President, George Bush, to discuss the issue of peace in the Middle East. He also urged continued economic support from Western nations and an increase in US investment.

However, the new Tunisian Government was also interested in extending its co-operation with other Western nations. A military co-operation accord was reached with Spain in December 1987 and adopted by the Tunisian National Assembly in May 1988. Under the terms of the accord, the two countries were to establish joint ventures for the research, development and production of military equipment, to exchange military personnel and to carry out joint military exercises on each other's territory. Earlier, in January the UK announced that it was willing to assist in the training and equipping of Tunisian security forces. In April the Tunisian Government received a military delegation from the Federal Republic of Germany, with the intention of gaining German military co-operation. In September Ben Ali discussed economic co-operation with President Mitterrand, during a state visit to France. Co-operation between France and Tunisia was strengthened following visits by Laurent Fabius, the President of the French National Assembly, in December, and by Roland Dumas, the Minister of Foreign Affairs, in May 1989. President Mitterrand made a two-day state visit to Tunisia in June. He promised greater investment in Tunisia, and in August four agreements concerning financial aid were reached. The Turkish Prime Minister, Turgut Özal, also visited Tunisia. Although the two countries reached some trade agreements, Tunisia refused a request to recognize the 'Turkish Republic of Northern Cyprus'. In March 1990 a military co-operation agreement was signed with Turkey.

Following Iraq's invasion of Kuwait in August 1990 (see chapter on Iraq), President Ben Ali condemned the deployment of a US-led multinational force in the Gulf region, arguing that it was neither in the interests of Arabs nor of world peace. He refused to attend an emergency summit meeting of the Arab League, held in Cairo, and, in an apparent attempt to undertake a central mediatory role, asked that the meeting be postponed while he visited Baghdad to persuade the Iraqi President, Saddam Hussain, of the need for a settlement. His official pronouncements against intervention by Western nations were apparently influenced by the growing Arab nationalist support for Iraq within Tunisia. This solidarity was reflected by the formation of a new political organization, the National Committee for Support to Iraq, which comprised most opposition parties and professional associations. The Committee demanded a suspension of diplomatic relations with countries, such as Egypt and Saudi Arabia, which supported intervention in the Gulf region, and the enlistment of Tunisian volunteers to be sent to Iraq. In late August Ben Ali sent a number of emissaries to Arab and Western nations, as part of a diplomatic initiative to prevent war in the Gulf. In late September Tunisia restored diplomatic relations with

Iran, which had been broken off in 1987 after Tunisia had accused Iran of supporting fundamentalist opponents of then President Bourguiba.

RELATIONS WITHIN THE MAGHREB

Under the Ben Ali administration, relations with Libya improved dramatically, with the result that Tunisia was able to play a more active role in the development of Maghrebin unity. In December 1987 full diplomatic relations were resumed with Libya, after Libya had agreed to pay $10m. in indemnities to the Tunisian workers expelled in 1985 and to reimburse Tunisian assets, which had been frozen in Libya. Subsequently the Ministers of Foreign Affairs of Tunisia, Algeria and Mauritania met to discuss the possibility of Libya becoming a signatory to the Maghreb Fraternity and Co-operation Treaty of 1983, as a prelude to the creation of a Great Arab Maghreb. In January 1988 President Chadli of Algeria visited Tunisia and held further discussions with Ben Ali on the issues of the Great Arab Maghreb, bilateral co-operation and a lasting settlement for the Moroccan-occupied Western Sahara. Ben Ali discussed these matters again with the Moroccan Prime Minister, Az ad-Dine Laraki, at the beginning of February.

In January 1988 Col Qaddafi postponed a scheduled visit to Tunisia to demonstrate his displeasure at the Tunisian Government receiving the commanders of the US and French navies. In early February, however, the visit went ahead, and, following talks, Ben Ali and Col Qaddafi stated that they had agreed to abolish entry visas for Tunisians and Libyans crossing the Tunisian–Libyan border, and to abide by the judgement of the International Court of Justice concerning the delineation of their respective sectors of the continental shelf in the Gulf of Gabès. Several days later, Ben Ali, Col Qaddafi and President Chadli of Algeria met and expressed their determination to encourage co-operation between the Maghreb countries. In June Ben Ali attended the first summit meeting of the five heads of the Maghrebin countries in Algiers (for further details, see Algeria, History). In May Ben Ali and Col Qaddafi had held an unscheduled summit on the island of Djerba. The two leaders signed an agreement providing for a social and economic union of the two countries, the free movement of people and goods across their common frontier, the establishment of a common identity card system and the freedom to live, work and own property in the respective countries. A number of joint industrial, economic and cultural projects were initiated immediately after the summit. In August Ben Ali visited Col Qaddafi in Libya and signed a series of co-operation agreements and an agreement concerning the settlement of the dispute over the continental shelf in the Gulf of Gabès. During the visit, a technical commission was established to examine means of accelerating co-operation and merger between Tunisia and Libya. In September an agreement was signed establishing a joint Tunisian-Libyan company, which would exploit the '7 November' oilfield on the continental shelf in the Gulf of Gabès. An agreement to link the two countries' electricity grids was signed.

Taking advantage of the open frontier, an estimated 1m. Libyan tourists visited Tunisia, spending so much money that shortages of goods in the shops were reported. A new motorway from the frontier to Sfax was constructed to facilitate their entry. At least 30,000 Tunisians found employment in Libya. Qaddafi, visiting Tunisia in December 1988, spent much of his time in the south; he was invited to address the Tunisian National Assembly, where he said that he favoured 'constitutional unity' between the two countries but was not going to try to impose it. He returned with President Chadli of Algeria in February 1989.

Despite Tunisia's policy of 'active neutrality' in the Western Saharan war, bilateral relations with Morocco were cordial. In May 1989 Prime Minister Laraki made a three-day official visit to Tunisia in connection with a meeting of the joint Moroccan-Tunisian Committee, and the Minister of Foreign Affairs, Filali, went to Tunis to co-ordinate action at the forthcoming summit meeting of Arab countries. There was no departure from the policy of close alliance with Algeria.

Ben Ali was influential in the movement towards Maghreb unity, by convincing Chadli that unity would be impossible without the participation of Morocco; he had no wish to continue in a subordinate role in the Maghreb Fraternity and Co-operation Treaty. Tunisia was put in charge of the working party dealing with human and social affairs and security, and played a significant role in all the meetings of ministers and Heads of State, arguing for gradual progress towards unity.

Tunisia initially seemed the most committed member of the newly-created Union of the Arab Maghreb (UAM), while Col Qaddafi appeared reluctant to implement agreements, such as the joint exploration of the Gulf of Gabès and the financing of infrastructure programmes in Tunisia. The Tunisian Prime Minister, Hedi Baccouche, visited Tripoli in July 1989, in an attempt to promote economic co-operation, although little practical progress was achieved. During a preliminary meeting of Ministers of Foreign Affairs in January 1990 the Tunisian Foreign Minister, Abd al-Hamid Escheikh, proposed a series of measures, all of which were approved, including the creation of a permanent secretariat (preferably based in Tunis), the expansion of the Consultative Council to 100 members, the establishment of commissions to examine joint projects in food production, economy and finance, infrastructure and human resources, and negotiations with other groups, particularly the EC.

In February 1990 the Minister of the Economy, Moncef Belaid, proposed a single energy market for North Africa, with free trade in electricity, petroleum and natural gas, the linkage of grids and extension of pipelines. In the same month the first meeting of the Human Resource Committee, attended by Ministers of Education, was held, and special passport controls were provided for North African visitors at Tunis airports. In March a TV service, broadcast throughout North Africa, was established in Tunis. Also in March the newly-appointed Tunisian Minister of Foreign Affairs, Ismaïl Khelil, proposed that the EC should reschedule debts to provide for training and the creation of jobs in North Africa, with the aim of reducing emigration to Europe. Official sources estimated that 1,800,000 Maghrebis worked in Europe (with a further 600,000 working illegally), while the number of unemployed within the UAM totalled at least two million. The UAM also raised the issue of racial attacks upon their citizens in the EC. In June 1990 President Ben Ali proposed an agreement between the EC and UAM, which would guarantee the rights of North Africans working in Europe.

RELATIONS WITH OTHER ARAB NATIONS

Tunisia's status as a moderate Arab state was maintained under Ben Ali. Following discussions with PLO representatives and members of the Egyptian Government, the Tunisian Government announced in January 1988 that it would be resuming diplomatic relations with Egypt. (Relations had been severed by Tunisia in 1979 after Egypt signed the Camp David Agreement with Israel.) Meanwhile, Hedi Baccouche, the Tunisian Prime Minister, toured the Arab Gulf states, which ranked among Tunisia's major sources of economic aid, to explain to Arab leaders the new Tunisian Government's domestic and foreign policies. Baccouche reaffirmed Tunisia's support for the Gulf states, who feared an extension of the Iran-Iraq War, thus seeming to rule out the possibility that the Ben Ali Government would restore diplomatic relations with Iran in the near future. In late April Baccouche visited Egypt and concluded several bilateral agreements with the Egyptian Government. In January 1989 Dr Boutros Boutros-Ghali, then Minister of State for Foreign Affairs, became the first Egyptian minister to visit Tunisia for ten years.

Meanwhile, Tunisia was the scene of another Israeli operation against the PLO. In April 1988 'Abu Jihad', the military commander of the PLO, was assassinated at his home near Tunis in a combined operation by the Israeli secret service, Mossad, and Israeli army and naval commando forces. The Israeli operation was a source of embarrassment for the Tunisian authorities, as it was revealed that Mossad operatives had been based in Tunisia for some time before the assassination was carried out. After discovering evidence that an Israeli military aircraft (apparently carrying sophisticated equipment with which to 'jam' telecommunications) had passed close to Tunisian airspace when 'Abu Jihad' was killed, the Tunisian Government lodged a complaint with the UN Security

Council. Later in April, the Council adopted a resolution condemning 'the Israeli aggression against Tunisian territory'.

In March 1990 Ben Ali made the first visit to Cairo by a Tunisian President since 1965, and signed several agreements on bilateral co-operation with Egypt. Relations between Tunisia and Saudi Arabia also remained cordial; in March the Saudi-Tunisian Joint Commission met to discuss eight projects, financed by Saudi Arabia, and in July the Saudi Arabian Minister of Defence, Prince Sultan ibn Abd al-Aziz, visited Tunis. Despite the high level of co-operation between the two countries, the Tunisian Government was concerned about the extent of Saudi support for Tunisian Islamic fundamentalists. In April the Iraqi Deputy Prime Minister, Taha Yassin Ramadan, visited Tunis, where he signed a bilateral trade agreement. In September a majority of members of the Arab League decided to move the League's headquarters from Tunis (where it had been 'temporarily' established in 1979) back to its original site in Cairo. The Tunisian Government protested at the decision and the League's Tunisian Secretary-General, Chedli Klibi, resigned.

RELATIONS WITH THE ARAB WORLD AFTER THE GULF WAR

After the cease-fire in the Gulf War in February 1991, Tunisia instituted attempts to restore links that had been strained by its support for Iraq (a policy which probably prompted the replacement of the pro-Baathist Habib Boulares as Minister of Foreign Affairs by the less abrasive Habib Ben Yahia). Although Kuwait had withdrawn its ambassador from Tunis, Ben Ali sent a cordial message to the Amir, congratulating him upon regaining his sovereignty. Ben Ali undertook a tour of the Gulf region in November. Soon after his appointment Ben Yahia went to Cairo in an attempt to re-establish cordial relations. The Egyptian and Tunisian Interior Ministers met twice to discuss the problems posed by Islamic fundamentalism, and made arrangements for the exchange of intelligence. A trade pact was signed with Syria in August 1991, following an earlier visit to Damascus by Ben Yahia. In February 1992 further bilateral agreements covered co-operation in education and other fields.

Conversely, when in April 1991 the Iraqi Deputy Prime Minister, Tareq Aziz, visited the Maghreb, Ben Ali, alone among the regional Heads of State, refused to receive him, claiming fatigue and the need to prepare for a visit to the People's Republic of China. The Iraqi aircraft that had taken refuge in Tunis during the crisis were not returned, but Tunisia did join the other UAM countries in appealing for the ending of sanctions against Baghdad. Sudan had co-operated closely with Tunisia in the attempt to prevent the outbreak of war in the Gulf region, and Lt-Gen. al-Bashir, the Sudanese Head of State, visited Tunis in March 1991. However, in October Tunisia withdrew its ambassador from Khartoum, alleging that Sudan had been supporting Islamic terrorists. In late July 1992 Sudan announced the closure of its embassy in Tunis, in protest against the Tunisian authorities' alleged suppression of fundamentalism. In December 1992 a series of agreements was signed with Oman and relations between the two countries were described as exemplary. In mid-1993 there were signs that relations with Kuwait, badly strained during the Gulf crisis, might improve. In June the Tunisian Minister of Foreign Affairs, Habib Ben Yahia, made his first visit to Kuwait since the crisis, and President Ben Ali, in a letter to the Amir of Kuwait, sought improved relations. After a hostile reception from Kuwaiti politicians and from the press, Ben Yahia was forced to cut short his visit. However, after a visit to Tunis in April 1994 by the Kuwaiti Minister of Foreign Affairs and First Deputy Prime Minister, Sheikh Sabah al-Ahmad al-Jaber as-Sabah, it was reported that normal diplomatic relations would be restored and that Kuwait was ready to make new investments in Tunisia.

Tunisia claimed to have played a leading role, together with Norway, in the secret talks between the PLO and Israel which led to the signing of the Declaration of Principles on Palestinian Self-Rule on 13 September 1993. The PLO headquarters were based near Tunis for more than ten years. Tunis welcomed the breakthrough in PLO-Israeli relations, and on 20 September an Israeli delegation arrived in Tunis for talks with Tunisian and PLO officials. Salah Masawi, the director-general of foreign relations, declared that there was no obstacle to Tunisia's establishing diplomatic relations with Israel, but that the Tunisian Government was waiting for another North African state to make the first move; it was assumed that he was referring to Morocco, which has maintained contacts with the Jewish state through the Moroccan Jewish community for some years (see chapter on Morocco). After meeting Ben Yahia in Tunis in Decembeer 1993, Warren Christopher, the US Secretary of State, announced that progress was being made in the normalization of relations between Tunisia and Israel. The Tunisian foreign ministry welcomed the PLO-Israeli Cairo agreement of May 1994 on implementing Palestinian self-rule in Gaza and Jericho; and in early October it was announced that Tunisia was taking preliminary steps to establish diplomatic ties with Israel.

Within the UAM, Tunisia was chosen as the site of the new Maghreb Investment and Foreign Trade Bank. A Tunisian diplomat, Mohammed Amamou, was appointed UAM Secretary-General and represented the UAM at the opening session of the Middle East peace conference in Madrid, Spain, in October 1991. Tunisia was the only UAM member to contribute personnel to the UN monitoring body, MINURSO, in Western Sahara (see chapter on Morocco). In January 1993 Tunisia assumed the annual presidency of the UAM. The Government made clear its determination to reactivate the process of Maghreb union, as well as dialogue with the EC. However, according to a statement made by the Moroccan Minister of Foreign Affairs, Abd al-Latif Filali, in February 1993, following a meeting of the five UAM member states in Tunis, it had been decided to allow a 'pause' for reflection in the process of developing Maghreb union. Tunisian officials were keen to emphasize that Ben Ali's presidency had been a success and that 11 co-operation agreements had been signed during his one-year term of office, including plans for a Maghreb free-trade zone. Yet, in reality, he failed to give new impetus to the organization, largely because two of its members, Algeria and Libya, remained preoccupied with their own problems: Algeria plunged into civil war by escalating Islamist violence, and Libya subjected to even tighter UN sanctions. The summit meeting that should have marked the end of Tunisia's presidency was delayed three times and did not take place until April 1994. At the meeting, Ben Ali handed over the presidency to Gen. Zérroual, the new Algerian Head of State. Neither King Hassan of Morocco nor Col Qaddafi of Libya attended the summit. Although at least 40 accords had been adopted by the UAM, only five had been ratified by all five member states, indicating that little progress had been made in translating rhetoric into reality in developing a unified Maghreb.

The decision by the UN Security Council in April 1992 to impose sanctions against Libya over the Lockerbie affair (see chapter on Libya) was reluctantly accepted by Tunisia. Although flights to and from Libya were suspended, Tunisia acknowledged popular feeling and the close economic ties between the two countries by insisting that land and sea links would remain open. The Libyan sanctions created a mini-boom in southern Tunisia, amid a sharp increase in cross-border trade and in transit traffic, but relations deteriorated sharply in September 1992, when the Libyan leader remarked that Tunisia had no future and was doomed to unite with either Libya or Algeria. This outburst provoked an indignant response from President Ben Ali, who drew attention to Tunisia's achievements and commented that the Libyan people were suffering from the consequences of a crisis for which they were not responsible. Despite these differences, the Tunisian Government made efforts to negotiate a solution to the Lockerbie affair. In April 1993 President Ben Ali visited Libya and consulted with President Mubarak of Egypt in a further attempt to resolve the deadlock between Libya and the West in the approach to the UN Security Council's sanctions review. Failure to resolve the Lockerbie affair also frustrated Ben Ali's efforts to forge closer relations between the UAM and the EU. On a visit to Tunis in December 1993, the French Minister of Defence, François Léotard, left the President in no doubt that Libya's membership of the UAM was a serious impediment to closer relations between the UAM and the EU. There were reports of a flourishing black market as Tunisian traders took advantage of the overvalued Libyan dinar and heavily subsidized prices to import cheap food into southern Tunisia. In July 1993 representatives of some 250 Libyan and Tunisian companies met in Tripoli to examine ways of strengthening business relations in the formal sector of the economy. As a result of UN sanction, Tunisia has become the main point of entry for international companies working in Libya—international flights to Tunis link with Djerba, from where there are ferry services to Libya.

Tunisia's relations with Algeria continued to be dominated by the fundamentalist issue. In December 1991 Rached Ghanouchi and other senior al-Nahdah members were reportedly expelled from Algeria to Sudan. Relations with Algeria improved appreciably after the second round of Algerian elections were suspended in January 1992, and Tunisia welcomed the appointment of Muhammad Boudiaf as Chairman of the High Council of State, as well as the suppression of Algeria's Islamic fundamentalist movement. In February 1993 Boudiaf's successor, Ali Kafi, visited Tunis. During his stay he exchanged letters with President Ben Ali to ratify the official demarcation of the 1,000-km border between Tunisia and Algeria, which extended from the extreme south of Tunisia to the Mediterranean coast. Ben Ali and Kafi also expressed their determination to work together to counter the threat of terrorism in the region. In December 1993 the Ministers of Foreign Affairs of Algeria and Tunisia met at Tabarka, Tunisia, to celebrate the final demarcation of the frontier between the two countries, the precise line of which had been disputed for some years after independence. The new Algerian Head of State, Gen. Zérroual, visited Tunis for the UAM summit in April 1994 and held further talks with President Ben Ali after the meeting ended. The two leaders issued a statement expressing their commitment to democracy, pluralism and the promotion of human rights; and condemning fanaticism and extremism. General Zérroual's appeals for dialogue with Algeria's banned Front Islamique du Salut seem certain to have alarmed Ben Ali, who had rejected any negotiations with the Tunisian Islamist opposition.

RELATIONS WITH THE NON-ARAB WORLD AFTER THE GULF WAR

For a brief period in the aftermath of the Gulf War, Tunisia's stance during the crisis was seen to have damaged relations with those countries that had participated in the effort to liberate Kuwait, while reports, most notably by Amnesty International, of abuses of human rights in Tunisia continued to cause international disquiet. In February 1991 the USA reduced the level of economic aid to Tunisia (see Economy), and military aid was entirely discontinued, although subsequent investment agreements with Washington indicated a rapid improvement in relations. A visit by François Mitterrand in July 1991 (the French President's first visit to an Arab country since the end of the Gulf War) was interpreted as a sign of French support for the Ben Ali administration's campaign against Islamic fundamentalism. In December 1992 considerable anger was provoked in Tunisia by the trial, in Paris, of a group of mainly Tunisian suspects. Among these was the brother of President Ben Ali, who was sentenced *in absentia* to 10 years' imprisonment for drug-trafficking offences. In February 1993 the Tunisian Interior Minister, Abdallah Kalel, on a visit to Paris, criticized the French authorities for providing asylum to Tunisian Islamic militants. The election of a new French Government in March 1993 was, however, well received in Tunisia.

President Scalfaro of Italy visited Tunis in November 1993 for a two-day visit to boost bilateral trade and to discuss Mediterranean security issues. Italy is Tunisia's second largest trading partner (after France) and the third biggest source of foreign investment. Italy was anxious to ensure the continued co-operation of the Tunisian authorities in trying to curb illegal immigration from Tunisia. President Kravchuk of Ukraine signed a treaty of friendship and co-operation with Tunisia during a visit in December. Ukraine plans to open an embassy in Tunis with responsibility for all the Maghreb states and the EU through the creation of a free-trade zone. In December the EU's Council of Ministers mandated the European Commission to begin talks with Tunisia on a new partnership agreement to replace the co-operation agreement signed in 1976. The Minister of International Co-operation and Foreign Investment, Muhammad Ghannouchi, said that he expected the new accord to be in place by 1996 and that it would attract foreign investment to Tunisia and boost exports. The Tunisian Ministry of Foreign Affairs welcomed the talks, which it described as 'a political signal' marking European approval of Tunisia's progress towards political pluralism and its respect for human rights. During talks with the EU which began in Brussels in March 1994, Tunisian negotiators expressed their support for free entry of European goods into Tunisia but wanted tariffs to be lowered gradually, additional financial assistance to make its industries more competitive with their European counterparts and higher guaranteed quotas for its olive oil exports to Europe. The European Commission is reported to have impressed on EU governments that a new partnership agreement with the Maghreb states was essential, since strengthening their economies would lessen Islamist violence and stem the flow of emigrants to Europe. However, Spain and Italy are believed to be against higher quotas for olive oil, and some other states to be less than enthusiastic about Tunisia's demands for higher levels of financial assistance.

In November 1993 Tunisia hosted a meeting of the Ministers of Foreign Affairs of the members of the Organization of African Unity (OAU). Shortly before the meeting, Tunisia invited the South African Minister of Foreign Affairs, Pik Botha, to make an official visit, at the end of which both countries agreed to establish diplomatic relations. In May 1994 Tunisia announced that diplomatic relations with South Africa would soon be established and ambassadors exchanged. In April President Ben Ali assumed the presidency of the OAU for 12 months. South Africa attended its first OAU summit, in Tunis, in June 1994.

THE ELECTIONS OF 1994

In December 1992 President Ben Ali announced that presidential and parliamentary elections would be held in March 1994. Promising a revised electoral law and an up-to-date voting register, the President predicted that political pluralism in Tunisia would be consolidated. The ruling Rassemblement Constitutionnel Démocratique (RCD) held its second congress at the end of July 1993 (the first was in 1988, following Ben Ali's take-over and the renaming of the party) and nominated President Ben Ali as its candidate for the forthcoming presidential election. The party was reported to have 1.6m. members, including 60,000 elected cadres, linked through 321 federations and 27 co-ordinating committees in Tunisia and one in Paris. Leaders of the legal opposition parties, of which the largest is the Mouvement des Démocrates Socialistes (MDS), were present at the congress, and Ben Ali used the opportunity to reiterate his commitment to bring the opposition into the new parliament. On 7 November 1993, the sixth anniversary of his take-over, President Ben Ali formally announced that he would stand for a second term as president. Once again he was the only candidate and was supported by all the legal opposition parties. The Union Générale Tunisienne du Travail (UGTT) endorsed the President's candidature at its December congress. Under the terms of the new electoral system, the number of seats to be contested in the National Assembly was increased to 163. Of these, 144 seats were to be contested according to the existing majority list or 'first past the post' system, which gave all 141 seats in the old chamber to the RCD, but the remaining 19 seats would be distributed at a national level among the parties according to their proportion of the total vote. Ben Ali commended the system as one that would 'achieve pluralism in the National Assembly through the representation of political parties according to their weight and influence in society'. Other reforms to the voting system brought to an end the controversial practice of sponsorship for candidates. The State also agreed to contribute to the election expenses of candidates. Some of the opposition parties felt that the long-awaited electoral reform did not go far enough and that the number of seats allocated on a proportional basis should have been larger. Nevertheless, all six legal parties, the MDS, the Mouvement de la Rénovation (MR, the former communist party),

Rassemblement Socialiste Progressiste (RSP), Parti de l'Unité Populaire (PUP), Union Démocratique Unioniste (UDU) and the Parti Social pour le Progrès (PSP), which had boycotted all elections since 1989 because they maintained that the results were rigged by the RCD, accepted the new formula and indicated that they would take part. There were appeals from the opposition for equal access to the state-controlled media during the election campaign and complete freedom to hold public meetings without interference by the authorities. Their acceptance of the extremely modest and largely cosmetic electoral reform measures were seen by many as a clear indication of the weakness of the legal and secular opposition parties, reduced to an obedient official opposition to the ruling party.

The President continued to reject any dialogue with al-Nahdah, referring to its members as 'enemies of democracy and apostles of sedition and terrorism'. In particular, he condemned those members of al-Nahdah who had obtained political asylum in Europe. In August 1993 it was reported that Rached Ghanouchi, the leader of al-Nahdah (sentenced to life imprisonment *in absentia* in 1992), had been granted political asylum in Britain despite the Tunisian Government's efforts to obtain his extradition. The British Foreign Office emphasized that the decision to grant Ghanouchi asylum was taken by the Home Office and was not a matter of foreign policy. In October Salah Karkar, one of the leaders of al-Nahdah who had lived in France since he was sentenced to death *in absentia* by a Tunisian court in 1987, was arrested by French police and served with an expulsion order for supporting a terrorist movement in France and in other European countries. In December, following a request from Tunis, French police raided the homes of several alleged Tunisian Islamist activists who were suspected of planning attacks on people or property in France.

Despite government claims that al-Nahdah's organization had been destroyed in Tunisia, a high level of security was maintained. Early in 1994 Noufal Ziadi, the Secretary-General of the Union Générale des Etudiants de Tunisie (UGET), condemned the permanent presence of police on university campuses and complained about restrictions placed on union activity. The Ligue Tunisienne des Droits de l'Homme (LTDH), the Arab world's oldest human rights group, which had been dissolved in June 1992, began rebuilding its regional networks in January 1994. In April, in an unusually outspoken declaration, some 200 intellectuals denounced the regime's paranoia about security and alleged a sharp decline in human rights and freedom of speech. In a report published in January 1994 Amnesty International claimed that the Government's prominent role in international human rights organizations served to mask its own serious and systematic violations of human rights. Amnesty reported that, over the previous three years, thousands of suspected political opponents had been subjected to arbitrary arrest, held illegally, incommunicado, in prolonged detention, tortured or ill-treated and imprisoned after unfair trials. The Tunisian Government rejected Amnesty's allegations and accused it of being 'manipulated by the fundamentalists'.

The presidential and legislative elections on 20 March brought few surprises. President Ben Ali was re-elected for a second term, winning a reassuring 99.91% of the vote, according to official sources, which also reported that 94.89% of eligible voters had participated in the election. Abderrahmane el-Hani, a lawyer and leader of a political party not recognized by the Government, and Moncef Marzouki, the former president of the LTDH and an obstinate critic of the regime's human rights record, had both been arrested after announcing their intention to stand for the presidency. The Minister of the Interior, Abdallah Kallel, explained that the resounding support for the President in the elections was due to the 'climate of security, stability, development and social and political harmony' created under Ben Ali's benevolent rule. In the parliamentary elections the RCD swept to victory,

winning 97.73% of the vote and taking all 144 seats allocated under the majority list system. The six legal opposition parties secured only 2.27% of the vote, but, under the new electoral formula, the MDS was given 10 of the 19 'guaranteed' seats reserved for parties which did not secure a majority in the constituencies, the MR four seats, the UDU three seats, and the PUP two seats. In his address to the new National Assembly on 9 April, President Ben Ali proclaimed that Tunisia had achieved political pluralism and declared its commitment to strengthen democracy and human rights.

In contrast to the 1989 election, there were few complaints from opposition parties about the conduct of the 1994 poll. However, the LTDH claimed that secrecy of voting had not always been assured and accused the authorities of interfering with a number of opposition campaign meetings. When Boujamaa Rmili, an official of the MR, condemned the election as 'a scandal', he was quickly arrested and detained for a week. There were few foreign observers because, in the approach to the elections, the regime had moved to control the foreign press and television. Several French and British newspapers were banned, the BBC's correspondent in Tunis was expelled and a French television team deported for their alleged hostile attitude and 'intolerable attacks on Tunisia's dignity'. Local journalists who expressed criticism of the regime suffered harassment, dismissal and even imprisonment. *Le Monde Diplomatique* described the Tunisia that overwhelmingy re-elcted Ben Ali as President in March 1994 as 'a society kept in fear and ignorance'.

The opposition parties drawn into the National Assembly by the offer of a handful of seats have little power and do not threaten the dominant position of the ruling party and the President. Supporters of the regime claimed that democracy had to be introduced gradually or Tunisia would suffer the instability and violence that has engulfed neighbouring Algeria. There were appeals for further electoral reform from the leader of the largest opposition party, the MDS, and from the LTDH. Given its overwhelming victory in the elections, there was considerable speculation about why the regime was so unwilling to tolerate any criticism or opposition. Critics pointed, in particular, to the apparently vindictive arrests of el-Hani, Marzouki and Rmili, to the harsh sentence imposed in April 1994 on Hamma Hammami (the secretary of the banned Parti Ouvrier Communiste Tunisien) for belonging to an illegal organization, to press censorship and to the continued repression of Islamist sympathizers. Some argued that the Government was afraid to relax its strict controls in case this resulted in a resurgence of the Islamist threat. Others accused the Government of merely using the threat from militant Islam as an excuse to crush all opposition movements. Some felt that the regime was able to act in an increasingly arrogant manner because it could rely on the support of key foreign investors and the majority of Tunisians who, it was argued, were willing to accept restrictions on political freedoms and human rights in return for stability and economic prosperity. In March 1,793 prisoners were pardoned to mark the anniversary of independence, and a further 762 were released in July.

In February 1994 the US State Department, reporting on human rights practices in Tunisia, referred to continuing widespread human rights abuses, including torture, and deplored the prosecution of critics of the regime and the restrictions imposed on press freedom. In April the LTDH renewed its call for greater freedom of opinion, expression and organization. The French Government protested against the ban on French newspapers, and the Fédération Internationale des Ligues des Droits de l'Homme, which has its headquarters in Paris, strongly denounced the regime's attacks on individual liberty and restrictions on freedom of expression. In reply, the authorities maintained that fundamental liberties were guaranteed in Tunisia, and human rights respected. Despite criticism, the regime could feel confident that, as an island of political stability in a volatile region, Tunisia could rely on international support, especially from the EU countries and the USA, and on continued foreign investment.

Economy

Revised for this edition by ALAN J. DAY

Tunisia covers an area of 163,610 sq km (63,170 sq miles). At the census of May 1975 the population was 5,572,193, of whom over one-half were less than 25 years old, and at the census of 30 March 1984 the population was 6,966,173. The annual rate of increase in the population between 1974 and 1984 averaged 2.5%. According to World Bank estimates, the population totalled 8,200,000 at mid-1991, and the average annual rate of population growth during 1980–92 was 2.3%. The projected growth rate for the period 1992 to 2000 was 2.2% per annum. The preliminary results of a census carried out in April 1994 put the population at 8,700,000. Most of the towns, and also the greater part of the rural population, are concentrated in the coastal areas. In the centre and the south, the land is infertile semi-desert, the population scattered, the standard of living very low, and the rate of growth of the population even higher than in the north.

The capital and main commercial centre is Tunis (estimated population 637,000 in 1992), which, together with the adjacent La Goulette, is also the chief port. There are about 50,000 Europeans in Tunis, mainly French and Italians, their numbers having decreased rapidly since independence. Other towns of importance include Sfax (estimated population 237,000 in 1992), which is the principal town in the south, the second port and the centre for exports of phosphates and olive oil, Ariana (146,000), Sousse (109,000), and Kairouan (103,000). Nearly 600,000 Tunisians were resident abroad in 1993, relieving the domestic employment situation and providing a source of foreign exchange earnings through workers' remittances from overseas. The Government is trying to encourage Tunisians to work in Saudi Arabia and in other countries bordering the Persian (Arabian) Gulf, in an attempt to offset the reduction in demand for Tunisian workers in traditional markets, especially France. Even greater efforts were needed to be made to accommodate the 30,000 Tunisian workers who were expelled from Libya in 1985. However, the *rapprochement* with Libya in 1987–88 alleviated this problem, and a new agreement, signed in May 1988, included provisions allowing Tunisians to work, live and own property freely in Libya (see History).

Tunisia's development record in the 1970s was fairly impressive, with gross domestic product (GDP), measured in current prices, increasing from US $4,339m. ($773 per head) in 1975 to $8,667m. ($1,356 per head) in 1980. In the early 1980s, however, the economy entered a period of turbulence. Output of petroleum reached a peak level in 1980, and the countryside was devastated by a series of droughts. Measured at constant 1980 prices, GDP (in purchasers' values) declined from TD 3,736m. in 1981 to TD 3,718m. in 1982, but growth averaged 5.3% per year in 1983–85. Meanwhile, the deficit on the current account of the balance of payments remained at an unacceptably high level, resulting in a worrying increase in external debt (totalling $4,880m. at the end of 1985). These problems culminated in 1986, when the sudden fall in the international price of petroleum resulted in a balance-of-payments crisis, which forced the Government to seek assistance from the IMF. As agricultural output declined, GDP fell by 1.4%, in real terms, in 1986. With the IMF's assistance, the Government adopted a radical economic programme for the 1987–91 period, designed to provide a secure basis for the economy until the next decade, by which time it was anticipated that Tunisia would have become a net energy importer. The strategy depended on an increase in exports of agricultural and manufactured goods, a rise in revenues from tourism, and severe reductions in the Government's investment budget. Meanwhile, trade was to be liberalized, and the Tunisian dinar was to be devalued, in an attempt to maintain export competitiveness. The economy recovered in 1987, as a result of an increase in the international price of petroleum, an abundant harvest and the success of government measures to control public spending and to encourage higher output, exports and foreign investment. Accordingly, GDP expanded

by 5.5%, in real terms, and the current account deficit fell to the equivalent of 0.6% of GDP. However, in 1988 the combined effects of severe drought and locust damage on the harvest, and a fall in the oil price, reduced GDP growth to 1.5%, although the current account of the balance of payments showed an annual surplus (of $216m.) for the first time since 1974. In 1989 GDP increased by 3.5%, with the help of a substantial expansion in the tourism sector and higher remittances from workers abroad, although the current account was in deficit by $160m. (1.6% of GDP). In 1990 an ample harvest of cereals and a rise in the petroleum price contributed to real GDP growth of 6%, but the current account deficit increased to $523m. (4.1% of GDP).

In 1988 the IMF and the World Bank provided financial support for a medium-term adjustment programme for 1988–91. The policies of the 1987–91 programme were continued under the new programme, with a new emphasis being placed on the acceleration of the process of trade liberalization, the strengthening of the financial sector, the restructuring of state enterprises and the introduction of tax reforms. By 1989 substantial progress had been made and the programme was viewed as highly successful. In March 1991, however, it was announced that austerity measures would have to be adopted in order to counter the effects of the Gulf War on exports, tourism revenues and external funding sources. In protest at Tunisia's ambivalence at the time of the crisis, Kuwait and Saudi Arabia withdrew planned investment and aid totalling $412m. and $200m. respectively, while the USA reduced aid from $59m. in 1990 to a projected $19m. in 1991. Against this background the Government obtained a one-year extension to its agreement with the IMF and also secured balance-of-payments support from the World Bank and other sources. By the end of 1991 mid-year forecasts of zero GDP growth that year had been revised to projected growth of 3.5%, reflecting a record harvest, a recovery in tourism and an upturn in the industrial sector. As a result, both the trade deficit ($874m.) and the current account deficit ($191m. or 1.5% of GDP) showed improvements in 1991, and GDP growth of 6.5% was forecast for 1992. In July 1992 a new Five-Year (1992–96) Plan was inaugurated, amid optimism that Tunisia was set to become North Africa's leading centre of venture capital and technology. At the same time it was announced that the Government would not be seeking an IMF facility to replace the extended Fund facility which had expired in mid-1992. GDP growth of 8.6% was recorded in 1992, whereas the Government's mid-year forecast for 1993 was only 3%, reflecting lower agricultural, mining and oil production. Data published in mid-1994 indicated an actual growth rate of 2.2% in 1993 and an expected growth rate of 5% in 1994. The country's 1993 GDP was estimated as $14,848m. ($1,700 per head of population).

AGRICULTURE

About two-thirds of the total area of Tunisia is suitable for farming. For agricultural purposes the country is composed of five different areas: the mountainous north, with its large fertile valleys; the north-east, including the Cap Bon, where the soil is especially suitable for the cultivation of oranges and other citrus fruit; the Sahel, where olives grow; the centre, with its high tablelands and pastures; and the south, with oases and gardens, where dates are prolific. Harvests vary considerably in size, determined by the uncertain rainfall, since cultivation is largely by dry farming and irrigation is, as yet, limited. The main cereal crops are wheat, barley, maize, oats and sorghum. Fruit is also important, with grapes, olives, dates, oranges and figs grown for export as well as for the local market.

In recent years Tunisia has been importing increasing amounts of cereals, as local production has failed to keep pace with population growth. During the 1960s the agricultural sector grew at only about 1.5% per year, but exceptional weather conditions and improved irrigation in 1971 and 1972 resulted in excellent agricultural yields, and during the fourth Plan period (1973–76) good weather, except in 1974, led to an average annual growth rate of 3%. The 1977–81 Plan envisaged annual growth of 3.5% and the 1982–86 Plan projected average annual growth at 5%, as a higher proportion of investment was allocated to the agricultural sector. However, these targets were not reached, owing to poor crop conditions in 1977, 1982 and 1986. The collapse in agricultural output was particularly severe in 1986. The 1987–91 Plan projected annual growth of 6% per year, and directed even more investment to agriculture. In 1988, however, agricultural output declined drastically as a result of drought and a plague of locusts. Agriculture's contribution to GDP declined from 22% in 1965 to 12% in 1990. However, a record cereal harvest reversed the trend in 1991, when agriculture's share of GDP increased to 19.6%. Owing to population increase, the average index of food production per caput fell to 87 in the period 1988–90 (1979–81 = 100). By 1990 the proportion of the labour force engaged in agriculture had fallen to 24%, from 49% in 1965. In 1993 agriculture's share of GDP was 18%, and the total value of exports from this sector (TD 437.2m.) was some TD 108m. less than spending on agricultural and food imports. The 1992 deficit in agricultural trade had amounted to TD 63.2m. (exports TD 367.5m., imports TD 430.7m.).

The means by which self-sufficiency should be achieved has been the cause of political debate since the early 1970s. From 1960 until 1969, at the instigation of the Minister of Planning, Ahmad ben Salah, the basis of the Government's agrarian reform programme lay in the formation of collective 'agricultural units'. These units, consisting of at least 500 ha, were to be operated as collectives in order to consolidate small peasant holdings and, later, to exploit land expropriated from French farmers or acquired from owners of large or medium-sized farms. The system was controlled through credits provided by the Agricultural Bank. By 1968 some 220 State co-operatives were in existence and several hundred more were being set up. However, opposition to the scheme was widespread, and there were revelations of unsatisfactory performance, heavy debts and misappropriation of state funds. These discoveries were instrumental in the downfall and disgrace of Ben Salah, whose position was already weakened by the displeasure of foreign aid donors with his agricultural policies.

Following Ben Salah's downfall, farmers were given a chance to opt out of the State co-operatives, which were later dismantled. Meanwhile, the National Assembly approved legislation allowing for the eventual break-up of large private estates, to be split among individual farmers or private co-operatives. The Government also introduced a number of measures to stimulate output, including the provision of funds for mechanization, a reduction in taxes, and the introduction of subsidies for purchases of fertilizers and seed. By 1975 about 50% of the total cultivated area of 9m. ha was privately owned, a further 2.1m. ha were worked by private co-operatives and the remainder was farmed by state or religious institutions. In April 1974 a 'supervised credits scheme' was announced, whereby small and medium-sized farms could be given supervised credits on a short-term basis to improve farming methods. It was hoped that this would encourage the cultivation of diversified crops rather than the traditional staple crops.

The Government's current agricultural policy reflects several concerns: one is to achieve self-sufficiency, thus saving on expensive food imports which the country can ill afford, and a second is to reduce regional imbalance by developing rural areas. By making funds available for agriculture, the authorities hope to stem rural depopulation. The 1982–86 Plan allocated about 16% of total investment to agriculture, compared with only 13% in the previous Plan. In the 1987–91 Plan, investment in agriculture increased further, to about 20% of total proposed investment, a particular aim being to increase the role of the private sector in the financing of agriculture.

In June 1989 the World Bank agreed to provide Tunisia with credit of $84m. to finance the second phase of a seven-year agricultural reform programme launched in 1986. During the second phase of the programme it was intended to increase the share of the private sector in agricultural production, fortify agricultural support services and reform pricing and marketing structures. The need to boost domestic production was regarded as increasingly urgent since, by the mid-1980s, the value of Tunisia's agricultural exports was less than half that of its agricultural imports. In June 1990 the Government introduced the first stage of a further reform programme, financed by the World Bank, to improve agricultural extension and research. Under the 1992–96 Plan emphasis was to be given to encouraging private investment in agro-industrial ventures, with a view to maximizing export and food-processing potential.

Meanwhile, a major programme of water development, which includes the construction of a number of dams for irrigation and flood prevention, is being implemented under the supervision of the World Bank. Dams constructed under the scheme include the Sidi Salem dam, with a capacity of 500m. cu m per year, opened in May 1982; and the Sidi Saad dam, near Kairouan, irrigating more than 4,000 ha and formally opened in June 1982. Germany is currently financing the construction of the Bou Heurtna dam in Jendouba, which will irrigate 20,000 ha. In 1988 construction was to begin of a pipeline linking the Sidi Salem dam and the partly-built Sejnane dam with the water plant at Mateur. The saline water from Sidi Salem was to be mixed with the water from Sejnane at the plant, and was to be used to supply Tunis and to irrigate the northern cereal- and citrus fruit-growing areas. In the mid-1980s Tunisia's national water storage capacity was 1,500m. cu m and some 80,000 ha of land were irrigated. In mid-1992 two major dam projects, at El-Houareb and Sejnane, were near completion. Plans were also announced to build a dam creating a reservoir with a capacity of 130m. cu m at Zouitine, in the Barbera complex, and one creating a reservoir of 250m. cu m at Sidi El-Barek. Zouitine and Sidi El-Barek and a number of small hill dams constitute the final phase of government plans to utilize all available water resources by the end of the century. Work on the TD 122m. Sidi El-Barek project began in 1994, with a scheduled completion date of 1998. The Ministry of Agriculture has stated that, by the year 2000, 2,600m. cu m of water will be impounded, mainly in the north-west. Large dams would account for almost 2,000m. cu m, of which about 1,200m. have already been mobilized. After the discovery of a huge underground lake in the Sahara, there were moves to encourage 'desert farming' by developing new land.

In March 1992 the European Community (EC) approved a grant of ECU 45m. for soil and water conservation projects, including the production of 243 hill reservoirs, 1,000 small-scale sewage recycling schemes and several dam improvements. Other EC-funded water and agriculture schemes included the rehabilitation of 13 irrigated zones in Kasserine governorate, the construction of a new barrage at Hasi el-Fred and the provision of an ECU 12m. 'credit-line' for small and medium-sized farming. Two earlier EC-funded schemes, for agricultural development in Kef governorate and in the Sejnane region, were nearing completion in mid-1992.

Grown in a belt across the northern part of the country, wheat is the most important cereal crop. The Government guarantees the price to the grower and, among other incentives, pays the transport costs of merchants. The Government has encouraged the spread of the Mexican dwarf wheat, and this variety now accounts for more than one-tenth of Tunisia's output. Production of wheat and barley totalled 606,000 metric tons during the disastrous 1985/86 season, but output increased to 1.9m. tons in 1986/87. In 1987/88, however, production fell sharply, to 292,000 tons, as a result of severe drought and the worst plague of locusts to affect the country for 30 years. Total cereal production reached 636,000 tons in 1989, but increased to 1.6m. tons in 1990, despite floods in January 1990, which necessitated the import of large amounts of grain. In 1991 there was a record cereal harvest of 2.56m. tons, falling in 1992 to 2.18m. tons. The 1993 cereal harvest totalled 1.9m. tons, but in 1994 a greatly reduced harvest of between 800,000 and 1m. tons was forecast after poor rainfall in the first quarter of the year. Spending on imports of cereals was TD 124.1m. in 1990, TD 65m. in 1991, TD 80.1m. in 1992 and TD 95.2m. in 1993.

Grapes are grown around Tunis and Bizerta. Wine production reached a peak of 1,986,000 hl in 1963. However, annual output had declined to one-third of this amount by the end of the 1970s. Production increased from 513,000 hl in 1982 to 680,000 hl in 1984, but fell to only 210,000 hl in 1988. By the early 1990s average annual output was around 340,000 hl, and there was some new investment in vineyards. Some 90,000 hl of wine, worth TD 12.5m., was exported in 1993.

The size of Tunisia's annual harvest of olives fluctuates considerably, owing partly to the two-year flowering cycle of the tree. Tunisia is usually the world's fourth largest producer of olive oil. Production reached a record 180,000 metric tons in 1975/76 but fell to only 80,000 tons in 1978/79. Output of olive oil declined from 145,000 tons in 1980/81 to 80,000 tons in 1981/82. There was another sharp fall in 1982/83, but production reached 150,000 tons in 1983/84, before declining to about 100,000 tons per year in 1984/85, 1985/86 and 1986/87. The value of Tunisia's exports of olive oil has fluctuated dramatically since the late 1960s, reaching a peak of TD 70m. in 1974, but falling steeply in the late 1970s. Exports recovered in the mid-1980s, totalling TD 54m. in 1986, TD 66m. in 1987 and TD 71m. in 1988. Output of olive oil in 1991/92 reached a record 280,000 tons, falling to less than half this tonnage in the following year. Exports of olive oil rose from 96,473 tons (worth TD 138.5m.) in 1992 to 122,630 tons (worth TD 177.3m.) in 1993. Radical reforms of the export marketing system for olive oil included the ending in 1994 of a requirement to negotiate all export contracts through the industry's national marketing board.

Citrus fruits are grown on the north-eastern coast. Production declined from 220,000 metric tons in 1980/81 to 165,000 tons in 1981/82. Output fell again in 1982/83, but the annual crop rose to around 250,000 tons in 1985/86 and 1986/87, declining slightly in 1987/88. In 1992/93 citrus production totalled 281,000 tons, and in 1993 exports totalled 23,640 tons worth TD 9.6m. Tunisia's production of dates totalled 81,200 tons in 1990, 74,700 tons in 1991 and 74,800 tons in 1992, with average annual exports of 18,200 tons over the same period. Date exports of 18,510 tons in 1993 were worth TD 47.7m. Production of sugar beet was 291,000 tons in 1992. A sugar refinery at Béja is able to process 1,850 tons per day. A second refinery, at Ben Bechir in Jendouba governorate, was commissioned in 1983, with an annual capacity of 40,000 tons of sugar. Spending on sugar imports totalled TD 61.7m. in 1993. Other crops include tomatoes, chillis and peppers, melons, water melons and almonds.

In 1992, according to FAO estimates, Tunisia's livestock included 1.3m. goats, 6.4m. sheep, 636,000 cattle and 41m. poultry (which produced 53,300 tons of eggs). During the drought in 1987–88 the Government introduced measures to protect livestock, including the distribution of state-subsidized fodder to farmers, a reduction of the price of animal feedstuffs, a programme to import lucerne and bran, and a vaccination campaign.

The fishing industry employs about 22,550 people. Sfax is the main centre of the industry, which is being expanded with government encouragement and some foreign aid. The total catch rose steadily from 31,686 metric tons in 1975 to 102,674 tons in 1988, but declined to 95,091 tons in 1989, 88,600 tons in 1990, and 87,600 tons in 1991. In 1992 production was just under 90,000 tons. Exports of molluscs crustaceans, seafood and fish totalled 15,653 tons, worth TD 89.2m., in 1993.

A $69m. forestry development loan was approved by the World Bank in 1993 to finance the planting of trees on 25,000 ha of land, together with related schemes to promote the growth of forestry in Tunisia.

Two institutions have been established to address the problem of Tunisia's insufficient agricultural output. The Agence de Promotion des Investissements Agricoles (APIA) was created in 1982 to channel funds into productive projects, notably the development of new cash crops. In early 1983 the Banque Nationale du Développement Agricole (BNDA) was set up to ease investment in the agricultural sector. Although fully Tunisian-owned, the BNDA's funds—initially TD 140m.—were subscribed equally by Kuwait and the EC. In

1990 the BNDA and the Banque Nationale de Tunisie (BNT) were merged to form a new commercial bank based in the agricultural sector, designated the Banque Nationale Agricole (BNA).

MINERALS

Petroleum, which until recently was Tunisia's principal source of export earnings, was overtaken as a source of revenue by textiles and agricultural exports in the late 1980s. The collapse of oil prices in the mid-1980s resulted in a fall in export earnings from a peak of TD 665m. in 1980 to TD 341m. in 1986, although in 1987 earnings recovered to TD 418m. By 1990 exports of hydrocarbons were worth TD 533.4m., but in 1991, despite a 15% increase in oil output, export revenues fell to TD 489.8m., against energy imports of TD 365.8m. (TD 429.4m. in 1990). In 1992 there was a surplus of TD 141.3m. in energy-sector trade (exports TD 538.4m., imports TD 397.1m.), but in 1993 export earnings fell by 19.4% to TD 434.2m., some TD 22.9m. below spending on imports (up 15.1% to TD 457.1m.).

Intensive exploration for petroleum has been carried out in Tunisia since the discovery of hydrocarbons in neighbouring Algeria. In May 1964 a subsidiary of Ente Nazionale Idrocarburi (ENI), the Italian state energy enterprise, discovered petroleum at al-Borma, in southern Tunisia, near the Algerian border. When the discovery was announced, the Tunisian Government took a 50% share in the al-Borma operating company. The crude petroleum extracted from the al-Borma oilfield is transported to the terminal at La Skhirra on the Gulf of Gabès via a 'spur' pipeline which links with the pipeline from the oilfields at Zarzaitine and Edjeleh, in Algeria. The crude petroleum is then transported from La Skhirra to the refinery at Bizerta.

In 1968 Tunisia's second oilfield came into operation at Douleb, 200 km north of al-Borma. This field is operated by a joint French-Tunisian company, the Société de Recherche et d'Exploitation des Pétroles en Tunisie (SEREPT), and by Elf Hydrocarbures Tunisie (EHT, a wholly owned subsidiary of the French company Société Nationale Elf Aquitaine). A pipeline was subsequently built, connecting the Douleb oilfield to the refinery at La Skhirra. Other oilfields include Tamesmida, on the Algerian border south-west of Douleb, which was joined to the Douleb-La Skhirra pipeline in 1969; and Bihrat and Sidi al-Itayem, both of which began producing in 1972. Important discoveries of petroleum were made off shore at Ashtart, east of Sfax in the Gulf of Gabès, and these deposits accounted for more than one-quarter of Tunisia's total output in the mid-1980s. The Ashtart oilfield is operated jointly by EHT and the Tunisian state oil company ETAP. Output from the field totalled 1.15m. tons in 1992, after which EHT and ETAP signed a $210m.-development programme to maintain production above 1m. tons per year until 2002.

Other new Tunisian oilfields include, in the south, Makhrouga, Larich and Debbech, which are being developed by the Société d'Exploitation des Permis du Sud (SODEPS), FINA of Belgium, and the Entreprise Tunisienne d'Activités Petrolières (ETAP); the Tazerka field in the Gulf of Hammamet, operated by Shell with AGIP Africa, a subsidiary of ENI, and ETAP; the Isis field in the Gulf of Gabès, for which the concession is held by Shell, Tunirex, Total-CFP and AGIP; the Ezzaouia offshore field, operated by Marathon Oil of the USA; the Rhemoura onshore field, in the Karkemna concession of British Gas (BG) Tunisie; and the Belli field, also operated by Marathon Oil.

A dispute with Libya over demarcation of territorial waters in the Gulf of Gabès, where promising discoveries of petroleum had been made, was settled in February 1982. A ruling by the International Court of Justice delimited the two countries' offshore territories around a boundary approximately 26° east from the land border to latitude 34°10′30″ north, where it deviates 52° east. (In December 1985 Tunisia's application to the International Court of Justice for a revision of its judgement was rejected.) In August 1989 a joint Tunisian-Libyan company was established to exploit the '7 November' oilfield in the Gulf of Gabès. After 1980, US oil companies began to obtain permits for drilling rights in Tunisia. Promising discoveries included the offshore Cosmos well, near Hammamet, located by EHT, gas and condensate discoveries in the Douz area, found by the US company Amoco, the el-Bibane well in the extreme south, discovered by Marathon Oil, and the two offshore Maamoura wells, near Hammamet, discovered by the Italian company AGIP. In mid-1991 Marathon Oil was given permission to explore for oil and gas in a new area of 1,760 sq km at Grombalia, which is situated close to the Abiod gas-production structure, south-east of Tunis; Marathon Petroleum Grombalia, a new subsidiary of Marathon Oil, will finance all exploration costs. In 1985 the Government improved the terms of its oil exploration law to encourage prospecting companies to develop new discoveries. In 1986, however, the collapse of energy prices prompted many oil companies to reduce the scale of their operations, and the Government was forced to introduce an even more favourable law in April 1987. In 1990 23 foreign companies held permits for drilling rights in Tunisia, attracted by the range of financial incentives offered by the Government to encourage exploration and development.

At 1 January 1994 Tunisia's reserves of petroleum were estimated at 1,700m. barrels, sufficient to maintain output for 43.5 years at the rate of extraction in 1993. Production has exceeded 4m. metric tons per year since 1970, and reached a peak level of 5,627,000 tons in 1980. Production fell to 5.4m. tons in 1981 and to 5.1m. tons in 1982, but rose again to 5.6m. tons in 1983 because of increased production from Ashtart. Production fell to about 5m. tons in 1987, and continued to decline at an annual average of 4%, while domestic consumption rose at an annual average of between 5% and 6%. In 1991 production from the Ezzaouia field reversed the downward trend of oil production, which by mid-1992 was running at 120,000 barrels per day (b/d), as against domestic consumption of 90,000 b/d. Further exploration, and the development of known deposits, suggested that Tunisia might be able to increase its output from the mid-1990s. Total output in 1992 was 5.35m. tons, and projected output in 1993 was 5.02m. tons. ETAP concluded oil exploration agreements with 10 companies (three of them locally owned) in 1993 and aimed to reach a similar number of agreements in 1994.

Tunisia's main petroleum refinery, at Bizerta, has a capacity of 1.7m. metric tons per year. Actual production has not approached rated capacity, however, and Tunisia has been forced to import around 50% of its needs, estimated to be about 1.9m. tons in 1986. Plans to double the capacity of the Bizerta refinery, suspended since 1989 because of financing difficulties, were once more under active discussion in mid-1993 (when the cost of the project was estimated at $77m.).

Tunisia became a member of the Organization of Arab Petroleum Exporting Countries (OAPEC) in March 1982. In 1986, however, Tunisia withdrew from the organization, owing to the decline in the country's oil output.

Tunisia's reserves of natural gas are estimated at about 100,000m. cu m. Almost all of the country's current gas production comes from the al-Borma field, but substantial new supplies are expected from recently-discovered deposits, notably BG Tunisie's offshore Miskar field, which is believed to contain reserves of 30,000m. cu m. In October 1993 the Miskar field was inaugurated and it was expected that its development would make Tunisia self-sufficient in natural gas. Output of natural and manufactured gas was 399m. cu m in 1986, compared with 403m. cu m in 1985. A major new source of natural gas are liftings by the Société Tunisienne d'Electricité et du Gaz (STEG) from the Transmed pipeline, constructed to supply Italy with Algerian natural gas. The 2,500-km pipeline, which crosses Tunisia, was completed in November 1981, but disputes between Italy and Algeria over pricing delayed its commissioning for more than 18 months, and it was eventually opened in May 1983. Plans to expand the domestic gas pipeline system were announced in June 1989, and by mid-1991 the expansion project was expected to proceed, following the signing of an agreement, in March, between the Tunisian Government and ENI. The accord details the construction of a new 370-km pipeline, with a diameter of 48 in, running parallel to the existing one between Feriana, on the Tunisian-Algerian border, and the Cap Bou peninsula, where it will join the Transmed pipeline. The new pipeline is expected to increase capacity from the current 12,500m. cu m

per year to 20,000m. cu m per year. Construction of the pipeline was estimated to cost $800m., and the project is due to be completed in 1994. Tunisia's royalty is equivalent to 5.25% of all gas transported in the Transmed pipeline. In January 1984 Tunisia agreed to buy extra quantities of Algerian gas to feed a new domestic and industrial gas network. In December 1991 the World Bank approved a $60m. loan to finance a STEG plan to construct a new gas pipeline between Msaken and Gabès and to upgrade the existing gas grid. By mid-1994 the $640m.-Miskar development programme was well into its main construction phase and the first Miskar gas was scheduled to flow into the domestic grid from 1996.

Tunisia is the world's fourth largest producer of calcium phosphates, which are chiefly mined from six large deposits in central Tunisia. Phosphates and phosphatic fertilizers have long been an important source of export revenue. After remaining fairly static at 3.0m.–3.8m. metric tons per year in 1970–78, production of natural phosphates increased steadily after 1979, when it exceeded 4.1m. tons. Annual phosphate output then reached a peak of 5.9m. tons in 1983, fell to 4.5m. tons in 1985, but recovered to 5.8m. tons in 1986 and to slightly more than 6m. tons annually in 1987–89. The phosphate sector was affected by low world prices in 1986, and a recovery plan was implemented, aiming to reduce production costs and to increase output to 6m. tons annually in 1986–88. Some 60% of Tunisian phosphate exports are for Western markets, particularly France, while the balance goes to Eastern European countries and China. Government policy is to develop new resources and to concentrate efforts on the local manufacture of highly profitable fertilizer and phosphoric acid. Only about 25% of phosphate output is exported as raw phosphate rock, and production of triple superphosphate (TSP) and phosphoric acid increased dramatically in the early 1980s. Output of TSP reached 956,800 tons in 1986, an increase of more than 400,000 tons in 10 years, and 985,800 tons in 1987, while production of phosphoric acid rose from 93,000 tons in 1973—the first year of production—to 593,300 tons in 1987, and to 856,100 tons in 1988. Because the phosphate rock is of low quality, the processing plants use special methods to produce phosphoric acid and phosphatic fertilizers. The Compagnie des Phosphates de Gafsa (CPG), which mines phosphate rock in the Gafsa area, plans to maintain annual production at less than 6m. tons, developing new mines as existing ones become exhausted. Most of the fertilizer plants are at Gabès, but in 1985 a new plant was opened at M'Dilla, near the Gafsa mines. A new plant to produce superphosphoric acid was due to open at La Skhirra in 1987. However, a project to exploit the phosphate reserves at Sra Ouertane, in the north-west has been postponed, owing to the Government's budgetary problems. In July 1989 Tunisia was granted a loan of $34m. by the Kuwait Fund for Arab Economic Development in order to finance the renovation of its phosphate fertilizer plants.

In 1991 production of raw phosphates fell by 30% compared with 1990, although export revenues fell by only 19%, to TD 14m. Exports of phosphatic fertilizers fell by 4% in 1991, to TD 241m., mainly owing to a 35% shortfall on sales of ammonium nitrate to the Iraqi market. The value of exports of phosphoric acid, however, increased by 27% to TD 156m. The 1991 results reflected continuing problems in the Tunisian phosphates industry, especially within the CPG, as well as the disappearance of traditional markets in Eastern Europe. In 1992 the CPG doubled the volume of its export sales from 425,888 tons to 956,109 tons, while its domestic sales (to the state processing company Groupe Chimique) totalled 5.09m. tons. In 1991 the two companies had recorded combined losses of TD 522m. A government restructuring programme, announced in 1993, envisaged plant closures among other rationalization measures, including an eventual merger of the two companies. The CPG's phosphate production totalled 6.05m. tons in 1992 and 6.4m. tons in 1993 (85% from underground mines and the balance from surface mines). Tunisia's exports of phosphate rock were worth TD 32.4m. in 1993, while exports of phosphoric acid totalled TD 120.8m. and exports of phosphatic fertilizers totalled TD 183.3m. Initiatives to gain new export outlets in 1994 included co-operation with Brazilian agricultural research with a view to increasing that country's imports of Tunisian phosphates from 90,000 tons to 170,000 tons per year.

Production of iron ore has steadily declined since independence, when it was more than 1m. metric tons per year. Output was 310,000 tons (gross weight) per year between 1984 and 1986, compared with 275,000 tons in 1982 and 400,000 tons in 1981. In 1993 output was estimated at 295,000 tons. The ore's iron content is approximately 53%.

Lead is mined in the northern coastal region, and zinc in the north-west. In 1980 the Société Tunisienne d'Expansion Minière announced a US $50m. investment programme to expand production. Output of zinc concentrates totalled 17,400 metric tons in 1989, but fell to 9,400 tons in 1991. Output of lead concentrates, which totalled 14,000 tons in 1980, has been falling steadily, and reached only 3,100 tons in 1986, increasing to 3,400 tons in 1987 before declining to 1,300 tons in 1991. In 1989 a joint venture was established between the Société Minière Bougrine, the West German Metallgesellschaft and the Tunisian Office National des Mines in order to develop the exploitation of zinc and lead deposits in Bougrine. Production began in May 1994 and in July 3,000 tons of zinc and lead concentrates were exported to Belgium. A joint Tunisian-Bulgarian mining company was formed in January 1990 to exploit lead and zinc mines in Lahdoum and Siliana. The Government has postponed plans to exploit the country's uranium deposits until the world market improves. A pilot production plant has been built at Gabès. About 90% of the salt that the Compagnie Générale des Salines de Tunisie (COTUSAL) produces (320,000–350,000 tons per year) is exported, chiefly to Japan.

INDUSTRY

Tunisia's industrial sector ranges from the traditional activities, such as textiles and leather, to 'downstream' industries based on the country's phosphate reserves. During the period of the 1973–76 Plan, the industrial sector grew by 7.4% instead of the 10.2% planned. In 1977 the sector grew by only 4.2%, mainly because of a sharp fall in agri-business and the food processing industries. Apart from a zero rate of growth in the textile industries, the sector's performance improved in 1978, with a 10.6% growth rate, mainly because of higher output in three sectors: construction materials, mechanical and electrical industries. The growth rate of manufacturing industries fell to only 3% in 1982, but rose to around 9% per year in 1983, 1984 and 1985, in accordance with the 1982–86 Development Plan. In the late 1980s private sector small and medium-sized businesses became increasingly prominent, and the Government made considerable progress in attracting foreign venture capital to the industrial sector, as well as in promoting Tunisia as a regional centre for high technology. Figures issued by the Société de Participation et de Promotion des Investissements (SPPI) early in 1992 showed that in 1990–91 the SPPI had supported 22 joint venture projects involving total investment of TD 34m. According to the Agence de Promotion des Investissements (API), declarations of investment intent by local and international companies were 2% higher in 1991 than in 1990, although the impact of the Gulf crisis had contributed to a 20% decline in foreign investment applications in 1991. In June 1992 the new post of Minister of International Co-operation and Foreign Investment was created to signal the Government's commitment to industrial expansion. In 1992 new foreign investment in Tunisian manufacturing industry was estimated at TD 52m., out of total foreign investment of TD 160m.

During the 1982–86 Development Plan, the Government concentrated on large investment projects, until it was forced by budgetary constraints to alter its strategy in 1986. The 1987–91 Plan reflected this change, with more investment in small projects and a greater emphasis on attracting private investment into industry. Exports of industrial goods (excluding energy) rose steadily in the period of the 1987–91 Plan, reaching TD 1,812.6m. in 1990. Textiles and leather contributed TD 1,325m. to this total, mechanical and electrical items TD 416.4m., and other industries TD 254.7m. Under the 1992–96 Plan, the 6% annual GDP growth target was to be achieved mainly by means of expansion in the manufacturing and services sector.

More than one-half of Tunisia's industry is located in Tunis. Other industrial centres are Sousse, Sfax, Gabès, Bizerta, Gafsa, Béja and Kasserine. Major new industrial estates were under development near Tunis and Sfax in 1994 as the first phase of a government programme to provide a full range of modern infrastructural facilities at 15 locations across the country. In the past, manufacturing tended to concentrate on processing raw materials, especially foodstuffs, and was aimed at meeting local demand. In an attempt to attract foreign investment and to promote exports, the Government ratified a new industrial investment code during 1987. This law simplified and extended the provisions in the legislation of 1973 and 1981. A new code, adopted in November 1989, laid down guidelines for the activities of service companies, the aim being to increase private-sector investment; by mid-1992 some 600 new companies had been set up in the services sector. Other government initiatives included the approval of special legislation early in 1992 for the creation of 'offshore' free-trade zones for new industries. Site preparation for the 46-ha Bizerta zone began in late 1993, with a view to completing the installation of infrastructure by 1996. The aim of the zone's shareholders (42% banks, 32% public-sector companies, 26% private-sector companies) was to attract TD 60m. of new investment from Europe, North America and South-East Asia and to generate TD 120m. of exports per year.

The textiles sector (including leather) contributed 21% of domestic manufacturing value in 1989 (compared with 18% in 1970) and accounted for 38.6% of total export value in 1991. In mid-1991 two Algerian companies, Entreprise Nationale de Production de Machines Cutils (PMO) and Entreprise Nationale de Développement des Industries Manufacturières (ENEDIM), announced plans to build a plant producing textile factory equipment. Of Tunisia's TD 1,776.9m. of textile and leather exports in 1993 (46.5% of the country's total export earnings in that year), garments and accessories contributed TD 1,239.4m., hosiery TD 270.7m., footwear TD 148.8m. and cotton fabrics TD 62.8m. An estimated 216,000 workers were employed by 1,585 textile companies (about 500 of which were wholly export-oriented businesses) in 1993. Another major sector of manufacturing industry is food, which usually accounts for about one-quarter of industrial production.

In order of importance, the other leading sectors are: construction materials, mechanical and electro-mechanical, chemicals, and paper and wood. Tunisia also manufactures glass, furniture, batteries, paint and varnish, leather goods and shoes, and rubber goods. Ceramics are made at Nabeul, while sugar is refined at Béja and carpets are hand-woven at Kairouan. A cellulose factory and paper pulp plant at Kasserine uses locally grown esparto grass. The metallurgical, mechanical and electrical industries are expanding steadily. The al-Fouladh steel complex at Menzel Bourguiba, near Bizerta, is supplied with iron ore from Tamera and Djerissa. It has an annual capacity of 175,000 tons of iron bars, wire and small sections. Plans are in hand to increase the complex's capacity to 400,000 tons per year. A further steel mill, with a capacity of 100,000 tons per year, is sited at Bizerta.

In 1983 a farm machinery complex, managed by the Complexe Mécanique de Tunisie, began production. Output will eventually total 2,200 tractors, 6,000 diesel engines, 100 combine harvesters and 700 small farm machines per year. A scheme to manufacture tyres for the local market and for export was commissioned in 1986, with the assistance of the Italian company, Pirelli, the Government having nationalized the largest US investment in Tunisia—the Firestone Tyre and Rubber Company's tyre factory at Menzel Bourguiba in 1980. In early 1988 production of diesel engines was scheduled to begin at a plant being constructed at Sakiet Sidi Youssef, on the Algerian-Tunisian border. The plant, managed by the Société Maghrebine de Fabrication de Moteurs Thermiques, has an annual capacity of 25,000 diesel engines. Later in 1988 it was announced that joint ventures with Mercedes and Volkswagen would be established to produce car components. In November 1991 General Motors (GM) of the USA announced the reopening of its joint venture vehicle assembly plant at Kairouan, which was to produce up to 4,000 light commercial vehicles per year for the North African market. Known as Industries Mécaniques Maghrébines (IMM), the joint venture had been launched in 1982 but suspended in 1988. Also active in vehicle assembly in Tunisia is Saab-Scania of Sweden. Local assembly of Mercedes-Benz buses, imported from Germany in kit form, began in 1994 at the rate of 60 vehicles per year.

In the high technology sector, several computer companies have located operations in Tunisia. Plans for a special 'offshore' high technology zone, to be located in Tunis, were under consideration in mid-1992. By 1993 a 40-ha site near Tunis-Carthage airport had been earmarked for development, and steps were being taken to attract financing of up to $100m. Citing successful Malaysian 'technology parks' as its model, the Government regarded the venture as a means of encouraging the transfer of technology, creating jobs for graduates and attracting foreign investment.

Tunisian cement production averaged 4.23m. tons per year from 1990 to 1992. Several new cement plants are planned or under construction, while existing ones are being expanded. A cement works at Oum al-Khelil, built by Fives-Cail Babcock of France, started production in 1980. A works at Enifida, constructed by Japan's Kawasaki Heavy Industries, Marubeni Corporation and C. Itoh, was commissioned in March 1983. In January 1988 a white cement works at Feriana entered production. The plant, established as a joint project with Algeria, has an annual capacity of 210,000 tons, enough to meet both domestic and Algerian needs.

The chemical industry is receiving special attention from the Government, its share of industrial output having fallen from 13% in 1970 to 9% in 1989. The principal activity within this sector is the processing of phosphate rock into phosphatic fertilizers and phosphoric acid by the State-owned Industries Chimiques Maghrébines at Gabès and by 'mixed' (partly State-owned) companies at Sfax. In 1988 reforms for the chemical sector were announced, including consolidation of companies' capital, long-term restructuring of their debts and, possibly, plant closures. Paint, glue and detergents are also manufactured. Two works, each producing 650 metric tons of wet lime per day, are to be built at Thala and Mezuna, in the south.

Production of electricity for public use was 4,536m. kWh in 1989, compared with 2,429m. kWh in 1980. Most of this was generated by thermal means; hydroelectric power is of lesser importance. Altogether there are 18 power stations, and the Government prepared ambitious plans for new generating units in the early 1980s. However, implementation of these plans was postponed, owing to budgetary constraints and a fall in demand, and funding was reallocated to development of the power distribution network. In the light of the economic upturn, which followed the Gulf crisis, the Government confirmed, in June 1992, that the UK/French GEC Alsthom group had been contracted to build a 300-MW combined-cycle power station at Sousse, at an estimated cost of $250m. Completion of this plant (scheduled for 1995) would raise Tunisia's total installed capacity to 1,762 MW. Contracts to build a further 340-MW power plant (Rades-B, near Tunis) were expected to be finalized in 1994. The national electricity grid served over 75% of the country in 1994, and was due to provide 90% coverage by 1996 if current planning targets for rural electrification were met.

Tunisia inherited a relatively modern system of road and rail communications from the period of colonial rule. Substantial work is being carried out to modernize and extend the existing highway and railway networks. In mid-1991 it was announced that construction work on the motorway from Hammamet to M'Saken was due for completion by the end of 1993. By mid-1993 some 31 km (out of 90 km) of the road remained to be completed. In 1980 work began on the 30-km first phase of the Tunis city railway. The project was postponed in the mid-1980s, owing to budgetary constraints, before being revived in 1987. There are five international airports: at Tunis (two), Djerba, Monastir and Tozeur. In July 1991 the first phase of the Tunis–Carthage airport expansion project was near completion. It was expected that the second phase of the project will increase passenger capacity from 3.5m. to 4.5m. per year. The project was estimated to cost between TD 15m. and 20m. Other projects expected to be implemented were the refurbishment of Sfax airport (estimated cost $10.4m.) and an expansion of the Monastir airport, in addition to the TD 12m. air traffic control system project. The 85% state

shareholding in the national airline, Tunis Air, was to be reduced to 75% by 1994 as part of the government's privatization programme. The Compagnie Tunisienne de Navigation began operating in 1971 and carried around 25% of total trade in 1985. In early 1984 a contract was awarded to a Turkish firm for the expansion of the port at Gabès. Work began in early 1985 on the construction of a new commercial port at Zarzis, near Djerba, which will serve a planned chemical complex to be built nearby. In May 1990 the World Bank agreed to provide a loan of $17m. towards rural road improvement, and $80m. towards the development of railways and ports. In March 1992 the Office des Ports Nationaux Tunisiens (OPNT) announced a project to upgrade facilities in the Tunis-Goulette-Radès area. Contracts were awarded in 1994 for a major expansion of Tunisia's telecommunications infrastructure. A total of 880,000 new telephone lines were to be installed by 1996, when Tunisia expected to achieve the highest level of telephone ownership in Africa on a per-caput basis.

FINANCE AND BUDGET

The Banque Centrale de Tunisie (BCT) is the sole bank of issue of Tunisia's national currency, the dinar, and it performs all the normal central banking functions. On 1 March 1994 a new foreign exchange market opened in Tunis, bringing to an end the BCT monopoly on quoting prices for the dinar against hard currencies. Apart from the commercial banks, the Government has established several development institutions to channel aid into the economy. The Banque de Développement Economique de Tunisie (BDET) is the largest development bank. There is also a specialist tourism bank, the Banque Nationale de Développement Touristique (BNDT), and an agricultural bank, the Banque Nationale Agricole (BNA), formed from a merger of the Banque Nationale du Développement Agricole and the Banque Nationale de Tunisie. Agricultural aid from the EC is channelled through the BNA. Other development institutions, such as the World Bank, have established credit programmes with the BDET and the BNDT. A major development since 1981 has been the creation of six joint-venture banks with other Arab countries. These are: Banque Tuniso-Koweitienne de Développement, Société Tuniso-Saoudienne d'Investissement et de Développement (STUSID), Banque de Coopération du Maghreb Arabe, Banque Tunisienne des Emirats et d'Investissement, Banque Tuniso-Qatarie d'Investissement (BATUQAFI) and the Banque Arabe Tuniso-Libyenne pour le Développement et le Commerce Extérieur. In October 1991 it was announced that Tunis was to be the headquarters of the Banque Maghrebine d'Investissement et de Commerce Extérieur (BMICE), a development bank established by the five members of the Union of the Arab Maghreb (UAM).

The 'offshore' banking sector was regulated by legislation, enacted in 1976, which placed strict limits on the banks' activities. Offshore banks include Citibank, Tunis International Bank, Union Tunisienne de Banques and Arab African International Bank. Complaints from the offshore banks about lack of business have led to reductions in staffing levels and to the withdrawal of National Bank of Abu Dhabi in 1984. These complaints have been heeded by the Central Bank and the Ministry of Finance, and in March 1985 they approved the text of a law that was to give offshore banks a greater freedom to do business in the local currency and to participate in dinar treasury operations. The law was approved by the National Assembly towards the end of 1985.

The availability of local savings for investment has meant, firstly, that the need for foreign borrowings to finance development projects has been greatly reduced; and, secondly, that the local financial markets have expanded and become more sophisticated to meet the demand for loans. To encourage domestic savings, interest rates on deposits and loans were raised in September 1977, and the official discount rate increased from 5% to 5.75%. Overall national savings accounted for about 80% of total investment in the fifth Plan (1977–81), compared with a projected 65%. Since the early 1980s, the Government has been studying various proposals for tax reform, and in July 1988 64 taxes on turnover, production and consumer goods were replaced by a new value-added tax, which by 1991 was yielding 30% of tax receipts. However, with total tax receipts still only equivalent to 2.4% of GDP, the Government, in late 1991, introduced new measures to increase the tax base, including a strengthened inspectorate. Other sources of government income include oil and gas revenues, profits from state monopolies and, increasingly, the proceeds from the privatization of state assets. In June 1994 the Government issued five- and 10-year treasury bonds which were open to the public for the first time.

Tunisia made use of the Eurocurrency market for the first time in 1977 and obtained a $125m. loan to finance industrial development. In early 1979 a $100m. loan was arranged, through a consortium of international banks, to finance the Tunisian section of the Algeria-Italy gas pipeline. At the beginning of 1981, the Compagnie Financière Immobilière et Touristique was able to raise $25m. for seven years at 0.5% above the London interbank offered rate—a very low spread for a developing country. During the period of the 1982–86 Plan, borrowing remained at a relatively high level, although the Government managed to attract concessionary loans for development projects, especially from France and the Federal Republic of Germany. In May 1986 the Government raised $120m. on the international markets, but this proved to be the last international loan before the balance-of-payments crisis in mid-1986.

Under a medium-term IMF-sponsored programme for 1988–91, the Government committed itself to the reduction of the central government deficit, which was to be achieved by liberalizing external trade and pricing mechanisms, and by restructuring and, in some cases, 'privatizing' state enterprises. In addition, as stated above, the Government attempted to enhance its revenue base by implementing various tax reforms. In 1989 the principal objectives of the IMF's three-year extended programme, including the reduction of the central government deficit, had been, in part, achieved. As a reflection of this success, Tunisia requested that the amount of credit available in the three-year extended Fund facility (EEF) be reduced from US $275m. to US $183m. However, the effects of the 1991 Gulf crisis undermined adjustment efforts, and in June 1991 Tunisia became only the second country ever to request an extension of, and restoration of full access to, the IMF's EEF. This was granted, effectively extending the reform programme for a further year. In mid-1992 it was reported that the Government would not be seeking an IMF facility to replace the EEF, which had recently expired.

Following this extension, in December 1991 the World Bank approved a three-year loan of $250m. in support of Tunisia's restructuring programme, the total cost of which was put at almost $400m. In March 1992 a structural adjustment loan of ECU 40m. was granted by the EC, while the balance of funds required was made available by Japan and the Arab Monetary Fund. In addition, in December 1991 the Tunisian Government took the unprecedented step of issuing treasury bills to finance its budget deficit, while in June 1992 Tunisia raised a syndicated loan of $110m. on the international market. In March 1994 a further loan of ECU 20m. was granted by the EU. World Bank lending to Tunisia during the period 1994 to 1998 was expected to average around $250m. per year, mainly for agricultural and rural development, water and sewerage projects, banking reforms and measures to develop private investment.

The Government's 1991 budget provided for a 10% rise in expenditure, to TD 4,080m., and a deficit of TD 410m., which, in the event, widened to over TD 500m. The 1992 budget envisaged an 11.4% increase in expenditure and a reduction in the deficit to TD 320m. The Five-Year Plan for 1992–96 set as a target the reduction of the budget deficit to 1.2% of GDP. The 1993 budget projected expenditure totalling TD 4,950m. Sources of revenue included TD 330m. ($352m.) in foreign credits, to be extended by the World Bank ($149m.), Japan ($59m.), the African Development Bank ($42.6m.), France ($42.6m.), the USA ($32m.) and Italy ($27m.). The average annual inflation rate in 1987–91 was about 7%, the aim being to reduce the rate to 5% over the period 1992–96. From 8.3% in 1991, the annual rise in the consumer price index fell to 5.8% in 1992 and to 4% in 1993. The 1994 budget provided for expenditure of TD 5,515m., of which 52% was current

spending and 19% was capital investment, the remaining 29% being the debt-servicing requirement. Revenue was budgeted as TD 4,312m., leaving a deficit of TD 1,203m. (equivalent to 1.9% of GDP) to be financed by government borrowing, 28% of which would come from foreign loans. Over 47% of expenditure was linked to social policy, and spending to alleviate the impact of structural economic reform on the poorer sections of society included TD 230m. in price subsidies for basic commodities. Sectoral spending allocations included TD 304m. for agricultural projects.

Tunisia's deficit on its balance of trade (see External Trade, below) has normally been offset by earnings from tourism and remittances sent home by Tunisians working abroad, so that the overall position on current payments was roughly in balance until 1975. In that year the fall in petroleum prices and the slump in demand for phosphates widened the visible trade gap so seriously, despite continuing good harvests, that the current balance showed a deficit of TD 227.2m., compared with TD 90.9m. in 1974. Over the next decade, the deficit rose steadily, reaching TD 1,076m. in 1984. A severe cutback on imports reduced the deficit to TD 844m. in 1985, TD 50m. in 1986 and TD 78m. in 1987. In 1988 the trade deficit increased substantially as a result of a poor harvest and a low oil price; but, partly owing to a large increase in receipts from tourism, the current account of the balance of payments recorded a surplus of TD 52m. However, in 1989 the current account registered a deficit of TD 312.5m., equivalent to 3.6% of GDP, as a result of an increase in food imports after severe drought, and in capital goods imports, owing to the recovery of foreign investment. In 1990 the current account deficit widened to TD 580m. because of the negative impact of the Gulf crisis, which also contributed to the further large deficit of TD 527.3m. in 1991. A deterioration in the country's terms of trade contributed to an increase in the current-account deficit to TD 662.3m. in 1992, while the 1993 deficit was expected to exceed TD 700m. The Government's aim in 1994 was to reduce the current year's deficit to no more than TD 537m. The Government launched a 30,000m.-yen ($295m.) placement on the Japanese bond market in early 1994 to help cover Tunisia's balance-of-payments deficit, having chosen to borrow in yen to obtain a favourable interest rate. Part of this yen borrowing was subsequently swapped into French francs. Almost 600,000 Tunisians were resident abroad (about 80% of them in Europe) in 1993, when remittances from migrant workers amounted to TD 600m. ($588m.), some 18% higher than in 1992. The annual inflow of foreign exchange from this source was expected to reach TD 650m. by 1995.

PLANNING

It was not until 1961, when the ten-year perspective plan was formulated, that the Government laid down comprehensive plans for development. The broad lines of policy which had been put forward in the perspective plan were embodied in the first Three-Year Plan (1962–64) and then successive Four-Year Plans (1965–68, 1969–72 and 1973–76). These were followed by successive Five-Year Plans covering 1977–81, 1982–86, 1987–91 and 1992–96.

Although Tunisia has relied to a considerable extent on petroleum to underpin economic growth, it has to plan for a future in which it is likely to be a net importer of fuel. Because of petroleum, the country's exports during the 1977–81 Development Plan grew faster, in constant prices, than imports did—by 14.6% per year, compared with import growth of 8.9%. The 1982–86 Plan was designed to introduce the economic adjustments necessary to prepare Tunisia for an era of reduced income from petroleum. Stringent controls were to be maintained on the external debt and the balance of payments, while non-oil exports were to be encouraged, and various incentives given to increase employment. However, most of the Plan's targets were not achieved. Growth in real GDP averaged about 3% per year, instead of the projected figure of 6% per year, and job creation totalled about 200,000, compared with the Plan's target of 270,000. Investment spending rose above the targeted level, helping to bring about a worrying rise in the current account deficit and the external debt. The need for revised measures became apparent in 1986, when the collapse of international petroleum prices coincided with a poor harvest and a bad tourist season. In this situation, the Government brought forward its 1987–91 Plan, which constituted a radical attempt to restructure the economy and to reduce dependence on oil exports. The objectives of the 1987–91 Plan were more modest than those of its predecessors, with annual GDP growth targeted at 4% and job creation at 240,000, compared with the total expected demand of about 345,000 jobs during the Plan period. The various structural reforms, to be implemented with the assistance of the World Bank, were intended to promote non-oil exports, which were expected to increase by 8% per year, compared with the 2% growth rate achieved during 1982–86. One of the major instruments of economic reform has been the devaluation of the dinar, which has been maintained at a rate which competes with the currencies of other Mediterranean exporters, such as Greece, Spain and Portugal. As well as stimulating exports, the depreciation of the currency assists the tourism industry, which has become a major source of foreign exchange.

Investment was estimated to total about TD 10,400m. during the 1987–91 Development Plan, representing a substantial reduction, in real terms, compared with the 1982–86 period. A higher proportion of investment was directed into agriculture (20%, compared with 16% in the 1982–86 Plan). To compensate for reduced state investment, the Government envisaged that 52% of total investment would come from the Tunisian private sector, and also sought to attract TD 6,000m. in external investment support. A new five-year Development Plan (1992–96) was announced in 1991 and introduced in July 1992. It envisages total investment of TD 17,400m., of which 52.3% will be generated by the private sector, and the creation of 320,000 new jobs. Public expenditure will be focused on health, education, housing and services, with priority for investment in transport and communications, and emphasis will also be placed on regional development, particularly in western Tunisia. Also planned are further reductions in subsidies on consumer and other products (which, the Government has estimated, could cost TD 2,300m. per year by 1996); the disposal of all state assets except in strategic sectors such as electricity generation; the elimination of price controls on manufactured goods; and the introduction for the first time, of selective charges for health, education and other services. Assuming the implementation of fundamental reforms (the introduction of free trade zones and a relaxation of exchange controls, leading to full convertibility of the Tunisian dinar), it is projected that an average GDP growth rate of 6% per year can be attained in the period 1992–96.

There has been a notable change in Tunisian policy regarding foreign private investment since the fall of Ben Salah and Ladgham, who were widely reputed to favour economic policies tending towards socialism. The law of April 1972 provided a package of incentives to attract foreign and also domestic capital to set up manufacturing industries producing solely for export. By 1980 a total of about 250 export-oriented projects had been set up under the 1972 decree, employing some 25,000 people. Companies from Germany, France, Belgium and the Netherlands predominate, and about 65% are in the textile sector. In 1973 a special organization, the Agence de Promotion des Investissements (API), was established to centralize investment activities. Legislation was introduced in 1974 to promote investment in domestic-oriented manufacturing. In 1985 the API approved schemes with a total value of TD 504m., compared with a total of TD 583m. in 1984. Of the 1985 total, the largest single allocation was for the manufacture of construction materials, ceramics and glass, which took TD 142m. Mechanical and electrical industries received TD 123m. during the year, and food industries TD 100m. Investments receiving the API's approval created a total of 27,000 jobs in 1985, compared with nearly 30,000 in 1984. The private sector provided nearly two-thirds of the 1985 investment, and created nearly 90% of the jobs. In August 1987 the API was merged with the Centre Nationale d'Etudes and the Agence Foncière Industrielle. The newly-formed API was to carry out feasibility studies, to organize industrial training schemes and to set up industrial zones. In 1988/89 investment in the industrial sector totalled TD 774m., of which TD 250.4m. was allocated to the manufacture of textiles. In September 1990 Tunisia created an Employment and Training Bank, financed by the World Bank, to help the country's labour force to adapt to changing patterns in employment.

A revised foreign investment law which took effect in January 1994 was designed to unify existing sectoral codes, to update legislation relating to investment and to stimulate investment in priority areas, including high-technology and export-oriented industries. Emphasis was placed on the fulfilment of broad policy objectives such as job creation, decentralization and technology transfer. Drafting of the new law had begun in February 1992 as a condition of Tunisia's structural adjustment loan from the World Bank.

EXTERNAL TRADE

Tunisia's trade deficit grew steadily during the 1960s and 1970s. The deficit in 1987 totalled TD 738m., compared with TD 892m. in 1986 and TD 844m. in 1985. In 1988, as a result of severe drought and a plague of locusts, the cost of imports rose by 26.2% (with food imports up by 53% on those of 1987) and the trade deficit increased to TD 1,112m. (imports TD 3,167m., exports TD 2,055m.), despite a 16% rise in export revenues. The trade deficit for 1990 was TD 1,800m., which represented a 29% increase over the 1989 level, but in 1991 it narrowed to TD 1,372m., although rising in 1992 to TD 2,121.8m., due mainly to a rise in imports. According to World Bank estimates, the average annual growth rate of exports by value fell from 10.8% in 1965–80 to 4.8% in 1980–90, while the growth of imports showed a sharper decline, from 10.4% in 1965–80 to 1.1% in 1980–90. Exports in 1990 covered only 64% of imports, compared with 67% in 1989. The ratio of exports to imports has remained close to 60% for most of the period since 1960.

Petroleum and its derivatives were the main source of export earnings from the mid-1970s to the mid-1980s. However, the slump in oil prices in 1986 caused export earnings from petroleum to fall from TD 604m. in 1985 to TD 340m. in 1986. Oil was overtaken as the largest export, in terms of value, by textiles, worth TD 389m. in 1986, compared with TD 283m. in 1985. In 1987 oil prices recovered and Tunisian export earnings from petroleum accordingly increased to TD 418m., although declining to TD 331m. in 1988. Exports of crude petroleum were worth a total of TD 506m. in 1989, TD 451m. in 1990, and TD 411m. in 1991. Meanwhile, exports of textiles continued to grow, earning TD 511m. in 1987, rising to TD 1,325m. in 1991. Other major exports include agricultural products (such as seafood, olive oil, dates, citrus fruits and vegetables), leather goods and phosphates.

Tunisia's main imports are machinery, crude petroleum (grades not produced locally) and petroleum products, iron and steel, sugar (raw and refined), wheat, vegetable oils and fats, electrical machinery, vehicles, timber, raw cotton and cotton yarn. In 1986 imports of capital goods were worth TD 505m., a slight increase from the 1985 figure of TD 503m. Food imports cost TD 288m. in 1986, compared with TD 278m. in 1985. Semi-finished products cost TD 557m. in 1986, and energy imports TD 199m., a substantial reduction from TD 308m. in 1985. In 1987 total imports rose slightly to TD 2,509m., compared with TD 2,308m. in 1986. The value of total imports increased to TD 3,167m. in 1988, to TD 4,151m. in 1989, to TD 4,852m. in 1990 and to TD 4,789m. in 1991.

The main purchasers of Tunisia's goods in 1991 were France (which imported TD 862.7m. worth of products), followed by Italy (TD 674.4m.) and Germany (TD 561.1m.). Tunisia's trade deficit with the EC as a whole was TD 821.4m. in 1991, when exports to the other UAM countries rose sharply, to TD 298.1m. France remained the principal exporter to Tunisia in 1991 (supplying goods valued at TD 1,247.5m.), followed by Italy (TD 835.6m.) and Germany (TD 682.4m.). EC member countries account for around 60% of Tunisia's imports and 60% of its exports.

Under an agreement reached with the EC in January 1976, the import levy on Tunisian olive oil was abolished and tariffs on all other Tunisian agricultural products imported into EC countries were lowered. Nevertheless, Tunisia was disappointed with the way in which the agreement was implemented, and particularly with the delays in lifting the restrictions on imports of olive oil. In June 1977 the EC quota of textiles and clothing imports was reduced. This measure severely affected the Tunisian textile and clothing industries although Tunisia did not, in fact, fulfil its EC quotas in 1978, as a result of a two-month strike in the industry early in 1978. Nevertheless, negotiations on this issue continued into 1979, and in March Tunisia signed an agreement, under pressure from the EC, to limit its textile exports to EC countries in 1979 and 1980. In return, Tunisia sought a five-year freeze on its obligations to eliminate tariff barriers relating to goods imported from the EC. Tunisia registered its anxiety about the possible consequences of the entry of Spain and Portugal into the EC in January 1986, as the two countries are Tunisia's main agricultural competitors. In mid-1985 the Commission of the European Communities announced a plan to guarantee Tunisian exports to the EC at levels prevailing in the early 1980s. In December 1990 Tunisia was one of the states to benefit from a new 'horizontal' trade and co-operation agreement between the EC and Mediterranean non-Community countries. In September 1990 Tunisia had become a contracting party to the General Agreement on Tariffs and Trade (GATT), in a move designed to increase exports to foreign markets. Formal negotiations on a free-trade agreement with the EC were scheduled to begin in September 1993, with a view to concluding an agreement by 1996.

In 1993 Tunisia exported goods to the value of TD 3,818m. (7.6% up on the 1992 total of TD 3,549.7m.) and imported goods to the value of TD 6,236.1m. (9.6% more than in 1992), leaving a visible trade deficit of TD 2,418m. (13% higher than in 1992). The 1993 import total was boosted both by increased imports of foodstuffs and by substantial equipment purchases in the energy and transport sectors. The 1993 export total was affected by lower earnings from the energy sector (down 19.4% on 1992) and the phosphates sector (down 11% on 1992) at a time of strong export growth in other sectors. The sectoral shares of 1993 export earnings were textiles and leather 46.5%; products of mechanical and electrical industries 13.5%; agriculture and food products 11.5%; energy 11.4%; phosphates and by-products 9.4%; and products of other industries (including building materials, chemical products and paper and pulp) 7.7%. Of Tunisia's three largest trading partners, France had a surplus of TD 523.4m. in 1993 (exports to Tunisia TD 1,674.2m., imports from Tunisia TD 1,150.8m.); Italy had a surplus of TD 489.6m. (exports TD 1,133.8m., imports TD 644.2m.); and Germany had a surplus of TD 148.9m. (exports TD 812.3m., imports TD 663.4m.). Overall, the European Union supplied 71.6.% of Tunisian imports and bought 79.8% of Tunisian exports in 1993. In the first half of 1994 Tunisia's export earnings totalled TD 2,193.3m. (18.8% higher than in the corresponding period of 1993), while spending on imports increased by 8.9% to TD 3,328.1m. and the first-half trade deficit narrowed by 6.3% to TD 1,134.8m.

TOURISM

Between 1961 and 1972, total tourist arrivals grew at a rate of 30% annually. Tourism was the nation's principal source of foreign currency from 1968 to 1976 (when it was overtaken by petroleum). In the 1980s the number of annual tourist arrivals fluctuated wildly, owing to the effects of recession in Western European countries on the whole Mediterranean tourist industry. Tunisia has experienced difficulties in competing with other holiday destinations, such as Greece, Spain and Morocco, and foreign tourists have been deterred from visiting Tunisia by terrorist incidents and the bombing of Libya by the USA in 1986. The number of foreign visitors totalled 3,258,000 in 1989 and 3,204,000 in 1990. In 1991 the number of tourist arrivals increased marginally to reach 3,224,000. Libya is the main country of origin of tourists, followed by Algeria, Germany and France. There are four main centres for tourists: Hammamet, Sousse, Djerba and Tunis. A major scheme under way is the Sousse-Nord tourism project, which is being financed by the Tunisian Government, the IFC and various Arab Governments, and which will provide a total of 15,000 tourist beds in a development along 3 km of coast. Another major complex is being built at Mahdia

(Tunis-Nord). The Banque Nationale de Développement Touristique (BNDT) promotes and finances three types of ventures: construction of new hotels; modernization of existing hotels; and other activities related to tourism, such as transport, housing and real estate. The substantial devaluation of the dinar in mid-1986 has enabled the Tunisian tourist industry to compete with Mediterranean rivals. In November 1987 the Government announced a series of incentives to encourage the development of tourism in the Sahara, with the aim of attracting tourists, who generally arrive in the summer to stay at the seaside resorts, to Tunisia throughout the year. The 1987–91 Development Plan, envisaged that tourism would overtake petroleum as the principal source of foreign exchange, providing Tunisia with an average of TD 600m. per year. In 1988 receipts from tourism amounted to about $1,300m. In 1989 the number of tourist arrivals totalled 3,222,236, and receipts from tourism amounted to $951m. (a slight decrease compared with the previous year); arrivals in 1990 declined slightly, to 3,203,787, and tourist receipts in that year totalled $900m. Receipts from tourism were estimated at TD 950m. ($1,037m.) in 1992, up from $770m. in the previous year, and reached TD 1,114m. ($1,092m.) in 1993.

The tourism industry's long-term future appears promising, with the announcement by a group of investors from an Italian bank, the Istituto Bancario San Paolo di Torino, of plans to invest $120m.–$150m. in Tunisia, of which the majority will be in the tourism industry. Another Italian company, Trussardi, was in the process of signing a contract which will provide 5,000 beds in a development scheme at Kebilia, in addition to hotel constructions, villas, apartments, a shopping centre, sports and other facilities.

FOREIGN AID

The principal sources of economic aid for Tunisia continue to be Western countries and international institutions. The World Bank Group (IBRD, IDA and IFC) has been the most important multilateral donor, providing loans and credits for investment in a variety of projects—including participation in the BDET and the BNDT. The African Development Bank is another large multilateral donor. Tunisia's largest bilateral donor is France, which provides annual packages of mixed credits. In August 1989 an agreement was signed, under the terms of which France agreed to extend to Tunisia three new credit lines and a grant totalling 1,060m. French francs. In August 1990 Tunisia and France renewed the financial agreement, which comprised a loan of 1,000m. French francs. Protocols signed with France in late 1993 granted Tunisia a total of more than 900m. French francs. One of the agreements, signed in November 1993, granted 277m. French francs for exceptional balance of payments aid. Other important bilateral donors are the USA and the Gulf Arab states, although these countries have reduced lending, owing to recent budgetary constraints. In February 1991 the US Government announced its decision to reduce sharply its aid to Tunisia, owing to the country's muted support for Iraq during the Gulf crisis (1990–91). In recent years Japan has extended substantial credit to Tunisia for the purchase of Japanese goods and services. Tunisia's receipts of official development aid (ODA) rose from $178m. in 1984 to $316m. in 1988, $283m. in 1989, $393m. in 1990 and $322m. (2.5% of GNP) in 1991. Germany agreed to provide Tunisia with $33.4m. of development aid in 1994.

Tunisia's total foreign debt increased from $3,526m. in 1980 to $8,475m. in 1992. As a proportion of total exports of goods and services, the cost of debt-servicing rose correspondingly, from 14.8% to 20.6%. During the period of the 1982–86 Development Plan, Tunisia's total debt increased rapidly, owing partly to the appreciation of the US dollar in the early 1980s. As a proportion of Tunisia's GNP, the country's total external debt increased from 41.6% in 1980 to 73.9% in 1987. In 1991 the ratio stood at 66.2%. In 1993 the cost of debt-servicing was equal to 18.8% of current receipts from exports of goods and services.

Statistical Survey

Area and Population

AREA, POPULATION AND DENSITY

Area (sq km)	
Land	154,530
Inland waters	9,080
Total	163,610*
Population (census results)	
8 May 1975	5,572,193
30 March 1984	
Males	3,547,315
Females	3,418,858
Total	6,966,173
Population (official estimates at mid-year)	
1989	7,909,600
1990	8,073,900
1991	8,222,000
Density (per sq km) at mid-1991	50.3

* 63,170 sq miles.

PRINCIPAL COMMUNES (population at 1984 census)

Tunis (capital) .	596,654	Gabès . . .	92,258
Sfax (Safaqis) .	231,911	Sousse . . .	83,509
Ariana . . .	98,655	Kairouan (Qairawan)	72,254
Bizerta (Bizerte) .	94,509	Bardo . . .	65,669
Djerba . . .	92,269	La Goulette . .	61,609

BIRTHS, MARRIAGES AND DEATHS*

	Registered live births		Registered marriages		Registered deaths	
	Number	Rate (per '000)	Number	Rate (per '000)	Number	Rate (per '000)
1984 .	226,288	32.2	53,484	7.6	45,601	6.5
1985 .	227,465	31.3	50,025	6.9	48,730	6.7
1986 .	234,733	31.0	47,619	6.4	47,900	6.4
1987 .	224,169	29.3	49,452	6.5	47,400	6.2
1988 .	215,079	27.7	50,026	6.4	47,800	6.0
1989 .	199,459	25.2	55,163	7.0	47,800	6.0
1990 .	205,345	25.4	55,612	6.9	51,400	6.4
1991 .	207,455	25.2	59,010	7.2	51,400	6.2

* Birth registration is reported to be 100% complete. Death registration is estimated to be about 73% complete. UN estimates for average annual death rates are: 8.4 per 1,000 in 1980–85, 7.3 per 1,000 in 1985–90. UN estimates for average annual birth rates are: 33.7 per 1,000 in 1980–85, 31.1 per 1,000 in 1985–90.

Source: Institut National de la Statistique.

Expectation of life (UN estimates, years at birth, 1985–90): 65.6 (males 64.9; females 66.4) (Source: UN, *World Population Prospects: The 1992 Revision*).

ECONOMICALLY ACTIVE POPULATION
('000 persons aged 15 years and over, May–August 1989)

	Males	Females	Total
Agriculture, forestry and fishing	422.2	87.5	509.7
Manufacturing . . .	217.0	165.7	382.7
Electricity, gas and water* .	33.5	1.7	35.2
Construction	244.8	2.8	247.6
Trade, restaurants and hotels†	301.9	26.7	328.6
Community, social and personal services‡ . .	347.2	97.1	444.3
Activities not adequately defined	26.2	4.5	30.7
Total employed . . .	1,592.8	386.0	1,978.8
Unemployed	273.5	108.3	381.8
Total labour force . . .	1,866.3	494.3	2,360.6

* Including mining and quarrying.
† Including financing, insurance, real estate and business services.
‡ Including transport, storage and communications.

Source: International Labour Office, *Year Book of Labour Statistics*.

Mid-1992 (estimates in '000): Agriculture, etc. 635; Total 2,837 (Source: FAO, *Production Yearbook*).

Agriculture

PRINCIPAL CROPS ('000 metric tons)

	1990	1991	1992
Wheat	1,122	1,786	1,584
Barley	478	721	570
Other cereals	39	49	45
Potatoes	217	220	218
Broad beans (dry) . . .	23	44	40
Chick-peas	19	23	32
Olives	825	1,325	630*
Tomatoes	530	580	550
Chillies and peppers . .	175	180	190
Dry onions	45	47*	50*
Watermelons	353	275	298
Melons	97	76	82
Grapes	77	95	113*
Dates	81	75	82
Sugar beet	282	210	291
Apples	42	44	61
Peaches and nectarines . .	25	35	36†
Oranges	123	117	98
Tangerines, mandarins, clementines and satsumas .	45	41	28
Lemons and limes . . .	17	14	18
Grapefruit and pomelo . .	51	53	41
Apricots	17	20	20
Almonds	52	40	45
Tobacco (leaves) . . .	7	6	6

* Unofficial figure.   † FAO estimate.

Source: FAO, *Production Yearbook*.

LIVESTOCK ('000 head, year ending September)

	1990	1991	1992
Horses*	55	56	56
Mules*	78	79	80
Asses*	226	229	231
Cattle	622	631	636†
Camels*	230	230	230
Sheep	5,966	6,290	6,400*
Goats	1,279	1,313	1,300*

Poultry (million): 41 in 1990; 41 in 1991; 41* in 1992.

* FAO estimate(s).   † Unofficial figure.

Source: FAO, *Production Yearbook.*

LIVESTOCK PRODUCTS ('000 metric tons)

	1990	1991	1992
Beef and veal	34	36	37
Mutton and lamb . . .	34	35	35
Poultry meat	47	47	50
Other meat	15	16	18
Cows' milk.	401	396	418
Sheep's milk	14	14	15
Goats' milk	10	12	12
Poultry eggs	50.0	55.3	53.3
Wool:			
greasy*	12.0	12.3	12.4
clean	5.5	5.4	5.7
Cattle hides*	3.7	3.8	4.0
Sheep skins*	6.3	6.4	6.6

* FAO estimates.

Source: FAO, *Production Yearbook.*

Forestry

ROUNDWOOD REMOVALS ('000 cu m, excluding bark)

	1990	1991	1992
Sawlogs, veneer logs and logs for sleepers	15	17	6
Pulpwood	53	81	39
Other industrial wood . .	97	95	90
Fuel wood*	3,036	3,102	3,168
Total	3,201	3,295	3,303

* FAO estimates.

Source: FAO, *Yearbook of Forest Products.*

SAWNWOOD PRODUCTION ('000 cu m, including sleepers)

	1990	1991	1992
Coniferous.	16	5	2
Non-coniferous . . .	1	12	4
Total	16	17	6

Source: FAO, *Yearbook of Forest Products.*

Fishing

('000 metric tons, live weight)

	1989	1990	1991
Total catch	95.1	88.6	87.6

Source: Commissariat Général à la Pêche.

Mining

('000 metric tons, unless otherwise indicated)

	1989	1990	1991
Iron ore*	280	291	295
Lead concentrates* . . .	2.7	3.0	1.3
Calcium phosphate . .	6,610	6,259	6,352
Zinc concentrates* . . .	17.4	13.4	9.4
Crude petroleum . . .	4,916	4,502	5,195
Natural gas (petajoules) . .	15.5	14.0	12.5
Salt (unrefined)	480	402	431

* Figures refer to the gross weight of ores and concentrates. The metal content (in '000 metric tons) was: Iron 146 (provisional) in 1989, 153 (provisional) in 1990, 153 in 1991; Lead 1.7 in 1989, 1.8 in 1990, 3.0 in 1991; Zinc 9.5 in 1989, 7.3 in 1990, 8.0 in 1991.

Source: Institut National de la Statistique.

1992 ('000 metric tons): Iron ore (gross weight) 300; Lead ore (metal content) 1.2; Zinc ore (metal content) 2.2 (Source: UN, *Monthly Bulletin of Statistics*).

Industry

SELECTED PRODUCTS
('000 metric tons, unless otherwise indicated)

	1989	1990	1991
Superphosphates (16%) . .	30.2	26.3	25.5
Superphosphates (45%) . .	901.6	792.0	713.6
Phosphoric acid	834.5	777.3	806.4
Cement	3,777	4,140	3,942
Electric power—production by Société Tunisienne d'Electricité et de Gaz (million kWh)	4,485.2	4,897.2	5,095.8
Electric power—other producers (million kWh) .	612.1	637.1	646.7
Town gas ('000 cu m) . . .	1,800	n.a.	n.a.
Beer ('000 hl)	394	426	407
Cigarettes (million) . . .	6,571	6,852	7,790
Wine ('000 hl)	233	267	425
Olive oil	130	165	265
Semolina	491.7	466.1	468.9
Flour	540.5	563.9	566.4
Refined sugar	56.3	49.4	60.8
Crude steel	188	176	193
Lime	471	587	578
Petrol	250.8	258.9	269.9
Kerosene	152.0	142.2	149.9
Diesel oil	432.6	534.9	517.0
Fuel oil	609.3	566.9	506.4

Source: Institut National de la Statistique.

1992 ('000 metric tons): Cement 3,911 (Source: UN, *Monthly Bulletin of Statistics*); Olive oil 123 (Source: FAO, *Quarterly Bulletin of Statistics*).

Finance

CURRENCY AND EXCHANGE RATES

Monetary Units
  1,000 millimes = 1 Tunisian dinar (TD).

Sterling and Dollar Equivalents (31 May 1994)
  £1 sterling = 1.548 dinars;
  US $1 = 1.024 dinars;
  100 Tunisian dinars = £64.58 = $97.64.

Average Exchange Rate (dinars per US $)
  1991   0.9246
  1992   0.8844
  1993   1.0037

BUDGET (million dinars)*

Revenue†	1990	1991‡	1992§
Taxation	2,597.3	2,874.7	3,225.5
Taxes on income, profits, etc.	416.3	503.7	499.2
Social security contributions	439.2	426.3	488.9
Taxes on property . . .	64.9	69.1	64.8
Domestic taxes on goods and services . . .	646.3	786.7	935.5
Sales taxes . . .	256.6	361.2	354.5
Excises	290.8	324.2	469.4
Taxes on international trade	931.7	986.9	1,123.9
Import duties . . .	911.1	967.8	1,100.0
Other current revenue . .	723.7	604.9	721.7
Property income . . .	630.9	482.6	603.2
Capital revenue . . .	4.8	12.0	9.2
Total	3,325.8	3,491.6	3,956.4

Expenditure‖	1990	1991‡	1992§
General public services . .	694.6	736.7	852.0
Defence	217.7	224.2	236.7
Public order and safety . .	210.6	238.4	290.3
Education	637.4	702.3	770.7
Health	229.1	254.1	290.9
Social security and welfare .	531.0	558.3	627.2
Housing and community amenities	71.0	176.4	191.7
Recreational, cultural and religious affairs and services	88.9	92.3	114.6
Economic affairs and services	1,039.1	980.9	989.1
Agriculture, forestry and fishing	299.4	363.8	348.2
Mining (excl. fuel), manufacturing and construction . . .	120.3	97.7	46.3
Transport and communications . .	103.0	92.1	103.6
Other purposes . . .	358.8	416.0	451.0
Sub-total	4,078.2	4,379.7	4,814.2
Adjustment to cash basis . .	−335.6	−362.5	−422.5
Total	3,742.6	4,017.2	4,391.7
Current¶	2,923.4	3,176.0	3,478.7
Capital	819.2	841.2	913.0

* Figures refer to the consolidated accounts of the central Government, including administrative agencies and social security funds. The data exclude the operations of economic and social agencies with their own budgets.
† Excluding grants from abroad (million dinars): 70.5 in 1990; 32.5 in 1991; 72.0 in 1992.
‡ Provisional figures.
§ Estimates.
‖ Excluding net lending (million dinars): 239.2 in 1990; 3.9 in 1991; −14.3 in 1992.
¶ Including interest payments (million dinars): 358.8 in 1990; 416.1 in 1991; 451.0 in 1992.
Source: IMF, *Government Finance Statistics Yearbook*.

CENTRAL BANK RESERVES
(US $ million at 31 December)

	1991	1992	1993
Gold*	5.0	4.6	4.2
IMF special drawing rights .	32.9	12.1	1.8
Foreign exchange . . .	757.0	839.9	852.0
Total	794.9	856.6	858.0

* National valuation.
Source: IMF, *International Financial Statistics*.

MONEY SUPPLY (million dinars at 31 December)

	1991	1992	1993
Currency outside banks . .	1,104	1,156	1,179
Demand deposits at commercial banks	1,437	1,555	1,676
Total money (incl. others) .	2,697	2,894	3,093

Source: IMF, *International Financial Statistics*.

COST OF LIVING
(Consumer Price Index; base: 1980 = 100)

	1990	1991	1992
Food	225.4	244.6	255.0
Fuel, light and water . . .	191.2	207.3	223.7
Clothing	229.8	249.5	268.3
Rent	161.4	163.2	176.7
All items (incl. others) . .	218.4	236.5	249.3

Source: ILO, *Year Book of Labour Statistics*.
1993: Food 261.9; All items 259.3 (Source: UN, *Monthly Bulletin of Statistics*).

NATIONAL ACCOUNTS (million dinars at current prices)
Expenditure on the Gross Domestic Product

	1991	1992	1993
Government final consumption expenditure	1,974	2,168	2,380
Private final consumption expenditure	7,459	8,354	9,018
Increase in stocks . . .	170	473	203
Gross fixed capital formation	2,948	3,597	4,182
Total domestic expenditure	12,551	14,592	15,783
Exports of goods and services	4,806	5,379	6,095
Less Imports of goods and services	5,382	6,239	7,031
GDP in purchasers' values .	11,975	13,732	14,848
GDP at constant 1990 prices	11,212	12,123	12,433

Source: IMF, *International Financial Statistics*.

Gross Domestic Product by Economic Activity

	1989	1990	1991
Agriculture	1,261.3	1,757.4	2,135.2
Mining and quarrying . . .	760.7	730.9	765.8
Manufacturing	1,655.4	1,829.4	2,049.4
Electricity and water . . .	221.2	223.2	237.2
Construction	359.0	422.2	459.8
Wholesale and retail trade . .	1,927.2	2,215.2	2,411.7
Transport, storage and communications . . .	694.1	762.0	832.2
Hotels, cafés and restaurants	526.9	557.4	428.6
Government services . .	1,260.1	1,360.6	1,532.0
Other services	48.2	52.7	59.4
Sub-total	8,714.1	9,911.0	10,911.3
Less Imputed bank service charge	263.0	326.3	357.9
GDP at factor cost . .	8,451.1	9,584.7	10,553.4
Indirect taxes, *less* subsidies .	1,079.9	1,229.2	1,416.0
GDP in purchasers' values .	9,531.0	10,813.9	11,969.4

Source: Institut National de la Statistique.

BALANCE OF PAYMENTS (million dinars)

	1990	1991	1992
Merchandise exports f.o.b. .	3,087	3,417	3,567
Merchandise imports f.o.b. .	−4,561	−4,526	−5,376
Trade balance . . .	**−1,474**	**−1,109**	**−1,809**
Exports of services . .	1,478	1,309	1,759
Imports of services . .	−740	−776	−882
Other income received . .	611	578	591
Other income paid . . .	−491	−570	−582
Private unrequited transfers (net)	17	25	16
Official unrequited transfers (net)	1	−2	−1
Current balance . . .	**−598**	**−545**	**−908**
Grants	184	113	70
Direct investment (net) . .	68	112	331
Portfolio investment (net) . .	2	18	41
Other capital (net) . .	266	180	498
Net errors and omissions . .	16	27	41
Overall balance . . .	**−62**	**−95**	**73**

Source: Central Bank of Tunisia.

External Trade

PRINCIPAL COMMODITIES
(distribution by SITC, US $ million)

Imports c.i.f.	1990	1991	1992
Food and live animals . .	473.5	304.8	404.7
Cereals and cereal preparations	220.4	107.9	145.4
Wheat and meslin (unmilled)	140.8	69.4	90.6
Crude materials (inedible) except fuels	420.8	358.5	380.9
Crude fertilizers and crude minerals	167.6	154.1	131.9
Sulphur (excl. sublimed, precipitated or colloidal) .	137.1	126.2	101.4
Mineral fuels, lubricants, etc.	494.4	428.2	486.1
Petroleum, petroleum products, etc. . . .	354.7	303.9	316.3
Refined petroleum products .	290.0	280.5	271.1
Motor spirit (gasoline) and other light oils . .	288.3	278.5	268.7
Gas (natural and manufactured)	120.4	112.2	156.7
Petroleum gases, etc., in the gaseous state . . .	90.8	31.8	125.3
Chemicals and related products	475.8	484.8	523.0
Medicinal and pharmaceutical products	124.5	136.4	149.5
Medicaments (incl. veterinary) . . .	111.0	123.0	130.7
Artificial resins, plastic materials, etc. . . .	114.9	116.9	123.4
Basic manufactures . . .	1,494.6	1,456.0	1,961.3
Textile yarn, fabrics, etc. . .	789.2	824.8	998.5
Textile yarn	120.2	111.7	118.0
Woven cotton fabrics* . .	328.7	341.1	420.3
Bleached and mercerized fabrics*	309.3	316.2	390.5
Woven fabrics of man-made fibres*	186.9	208.1	265.9
Iron and steel	241.8	221.3	434.3
Tubes, pipes and fittings .	39.3	58.3	236.0
Machinery and transport equipment	1,551.0	1,575.7	1,951.1
Power-generating machinery and equipment . . .	109.9	121.9	134.4
Machinery specialized for particular industries . .	336.9	397.2	429.2
Textile and leather machinery	140.6	142.2	132.7
General industrial machinery, equipment and parts . .	294.3	297.3	325.5
Telecommunications and sound equipment	63.5	95.1	129.1
Other electrical machinery, apparatus, etc. . . .	265.4	279.8	357.9
Road vehicles and parts† . .	303.8	211.2	287.9
Other transport equipment† .	86.8	80.2	184.9
Miscellaneous manufactured articles	453.3	468.9	589.3
Clothing and accessories (excl. footwear)	190.7	208.2	250.6
Total (incl. others) . . .	5,476.0	5,189.1	6,432.0

* Excluding narrow or special fabrics.
† Excluding tyres, engines and electrical parts.

Exports f.o.b.	1990	1991	1992
Food and live animals . .	234.4	216.1	213.8
Fish, crustaceans and molluscs	108.3	82.0	72.9
Vegetables and fruit . . .	76.4	87.8	83.9
Crude materials (inedible)			
except fuels . . .	82.5	63.2	73.3
Mineral fuels, lubricants, etc.	604.4	529.8	610.1
Petroleum, petroleum			
products, etc. . . .	597.5	522.7	604.4
Crude petroleum oils, etc. .	521.4	441.6	511.6
Refined petroleum products	76.1	81.1	92.8
Motor spirit (gasoline)			
and other light oils . .	76.1	81.1	92.8
Animal and vegetable oils,			
fats and waxes . . .	121.2	290.9	158.5
Fixed vegetable oils and fats .	121.2	290.7	158.4
Olive oil	121.2	290.7	158.4
Chemicals and related			
products	506.8	516.4	517.7
Inorganic chemicals . .	210.7	230.1	230.1
Inorganic chemical			
elements, oxides and			
halogen salts . . .	140.5	170.8	164.2
Inorganic acids and			
oxygen compounds of			
non-metals	139.8	169.3	163.9
Phosphorus pentoxide			
and phosphoric acids	139.5	168.9	163.6
Manufactured fertilizers . .	259.4	239.6	236.4
Phosphatic fertilizers . .	245.5	230.8	225.2
Superphosphates . .	108.0	103.6	104.6
Basic manufactures . .	406.7	388.8	461.4
Leather, leather manufactures			
and dressed furskins . .	55.2	61.7	93.7
Manufactures of leather, etc. .	50.2	59.1	91.3
Parts of footwear (except			
metal and asbestos). .	49.6	58.3	90.7
Textile yarn, fabrics, etc. . .	111.7	100.9	121.3
Non-metallic mineral			
manufactures . . .	118.3	83.8	101.8
Machinery and transport			
equipment	272.7	298.8	351.8
Electrical machinery,			
apparatus, etc. . . .	189.9	219.4	275.7
Equipment for distributing			
electricity	58.6	65.3	117.4
Insulated electric wire,			
cable, etc. . . .	58.6	65.2	117.3
Miscellaneous manufactured			
articles	1,240.0	1,347.2	1,616.4
Clothing and accessories (excl.			
footwear)	1,126.0	1,221.3	1,477.5
Men's and boys' outer			
garments of non-knitted			
textile fabrics . . .	516.5	584.6	706.0
Women's, girls' and infants'			
outer garments of non-			
knitted textile fabrics . .	250.8	270.1	352.0
Undergarments (excl.			
foundation garments) of			
non-knitted textile fabrics	85.2	96.6	105.9
Knitted or crocheted outer			
garments and accessories			
(excl. gloves, stockings,			
etc.), non-elastic . .	144.7	133.6	146.5
Knitted or crocheted			
undergarments (incl.			
foundation garments of			
non-knitted fabrics) . .	100.4	102.9	129.3
Total (incl. others) . . .	3,498.4	3,699.6	4,039.9

Source: UN, *International Trade Statistics Yearbook.*

PRINCIPAL TRADING PARTNERS (US $ '000)*

Imports c.i.f.	1990	1991	1992
Algeria	111,794	99,994	151,994
Belgium/Luxembourg . . .	261,623	278,116	302,637
Canada	48,690	81,244	62,503
France.	1,526,400	1,351,676	1,637,792
Germany	683,015	741,795	901,235
Italy	871,149	905,398	1,168,202
Japan	99,515	121,121	147,313
Morocco	47,798	67,400	74.370
Netherlands	143,473	112,108	142,316
Poland.	54,466	46,839	67,824
Russia.	n.a.	n.a.	82,847
Spain	169,551	160,057	213,548
Sweden	55,510	67,722	70,202
Switzerland	61,048	70,993	69,786
USSR	95,671	70,696	—
United Kingdom . . .	92,329	92,176	113,840
USA	285,830	248,895	320,086
Total (incl. others) . . .	5,471,095	5,184,856	6,425,382

Exports f.o.b.	1990	1991	1992
Algeria	81,080	78,683	97,800
Belgium/Luxembourg . . .	244,707	231,190	278,905
France	931,685	933,943	1,093,979
Germany	528,227	607,527	685,971
Greece	15,211	23,235	84,199
India	43,288	68,098	75,508
Iraq	50,652	68	342
Italy	740,391	730,133	689,577
Libya	160,780	201,727	176,050
Morocco	23,561	26,777	46,059
Netherlands	89,012	99,618	103,418
Spain	91,922	135,718	110,816
USSR	43,701	41,199	—
United Kingdom . . .	57,297	47,481	72,759
Total (incl. others) . . .	3,498,273	3,699,503	4,039,731

* Imports by country of production; exports by country of last destination.

Source: UN, *Internatinal Trade Statistics Yearbook.*

Transport

RAILWAYS (traffic)

	1989	1990	1991
Passenger-km (million) . .	1,039	1,019	1,020
Freight ton-km (million) . .	2,064	1,834	1,813

Source: Ministère du Transport.

ROAD TRAFFIC (motor vehicles in use at 31 December)

	1987	1988	1989
Private cars	281,201	292,673	320,101
Buses	8,446	8,986	9,453
Commercial vehicles . .	147,697	151,826	157,689
Motor cycles . . .	12,247	12,290	12,472

Source: International Road Federation, *World Road Statistics.*

SHIPPING

Merchant Fleet (vessels registered at 30 June)

	Displacement ('000 gross reg. tons)		
	1989	1990	1991
Total	282	278	276

Source: UN, *Statistical Yearbook.*

International Sea-borne Freight Traffic
('000 metric tons)

	1990	1991	1992
Goods loaded*	5,916	6,384	6,653
Goods unloaded	10,056	9,732	9,612

* Excluding Algerian crude petroleum loaded at La Skhirra.
Source: UN, *Monthly Bulletin of Statistics.*

CIVIL AVIATION (traffic on scheduled services)

	1989	1990	1991
Km flown (million) . .	15	15	14
Passengers carried ('000) . .	1,315	1,313	1,201
Passenger-km (million) .	1,571	1,502	1,407
Freight ton-km (million) .	19	19	18
Mail ton-km (million) . .	1	1	1

Source: UN, *Statistical Yearbook.*

Tourism

FOREIGN TOURIST ARRIVALS BY NATIONALITY ('000)

	1989	1990	1991
Algeria	378.8	435.2	744.3
Austria	36.0	38.6	27.8
Belgium	78.2	74.4	39.1
France	467.7	458.1	210.9
Germany, Federal Republic .	461.4	479.4	393.4
Italy	169.0	189.5	152.5
Libya	957.0	795.8	1,154.4
Netherlands	102.2	96.7	46.9
Scandinavia	80.3	59.8	13.0
Switzerland	45.3	48.2	27.5
United Kingdom . . .	221.6	191.4	120.3
USA	9.6	8.9	5.6
Total (incl. others) . . .	3,258.4	3,203.8	3,224.0

Source: Ministère de l'Intérieur.

Communications Media

	1989	1990	1991
Radio receivers ('000 in use) .	1,500	1,600	1,640
Television receivers ('000 in use)	600	650	650
Daily newspapers (number) .	6	6	n.a.
Book production (titles)* . .	293†	n.a.	n.a.

* Excluding pamphlets.
† Excluding school textbooks, government publications and university theses.
Non-daily newspapers (1988): 9 (estimated circulation of 244,000 copies).
Source: UNESCO, *Statistical Yearbook.*

Education

	1990/91	1991/92	1992/93
Institutions			
Primary	3,841	3,940	4,044
Secondary	585	599	624
Teachers			
Primary	50,280	53,652	54,560
Secondary	24,474	25,445	26,097
Pupils			
Primary	1,398,119	1,417,803	1,432,112
Secondary	496,840	518,522	567,381

Source: Ministère de l'Education et des Sciences.

Directory

The Constitution

A new Constitution for the Republic of Tunisia was promulgated on 1 June 1959 and amended on 12 July 1988. Its main provisions are summarized below:

NATIONAL ASSEMBLY

Legislative power is exercised by the National Assembly, which is elected (at the same time as the President) every five years by direct universal suffrage. Every citizen who has had Tunisian nationality for at least five years and who has attained 20 years of age has the right to vote. The National Assembly shall hold two sessions every year, each session lasting not more than three months. Additional meetings may be held at the demand of the President or of a majority of the deputies.

HEAD OF STATE

The President of the Republic is both Head of State and Head of the Executive. He must be not less than 40 years of age and not more than 70. The President is elected by universal suffrage for a five-year term which is renewable twice, consecutively. The President is also the Commander-in-Chief of the army and makes both civil and military appointments. The Government may be censured by the National Assembly, in which case the President may dismiss the Assembly and hold fresh elections. If censured by the new Assembly thus elected, the Government must resign. Should the presidency fall vacant for any reason before the end of a President's term of office, the President of the National Assembly shall take charge of affairs of the state for a period of 45 to 60 days. At the end of this period, a presidential election shall be organized. The President of the National Assembly shall not be eligible as a presidential candidate.

COUNCIL OF STATE

Comprises two judicial bodies: an administrative body dealing with legal disputes between individuals and state or public bodies, and an audit office to verify the accounts of the state and submit reports.

ECONOMIC AND SOCIAL COUNCIL

Deals with economic and social planning and studies projects submitted by the National Assembly. Members are grouped in seven categories representing various sections of the community.

The Government

HEAD OF STATE

President: ZINE AL-ABIDINE BEN ALI (took office on 7 November 1987; re-elected 2 April 1989 and 20 March 1994).

THE CABINET
(October 1994)

Prime Minister: HAMED KAROUI.

Minister of State and of the Interior: ABDALLAH KALLEL.

Minister, Director of the Presidential Office: MUHAMMAD JERI.

Minister of Justice: SADOK CHAABANE.

Minister of Foreign Affairs: HABIB BEN YAHIA.

Minister of National Defence: ABD AL-AZIZ BEN DHIA.

Minister of Religious Affairs: ALI CHEBBI.

Minister of International Co-operation and Foreign Investment: MUHAMMAD GHANNOUCHI.

Minister of Finance: NOURI ZORGATI.

Minister of National Economy: SADOK RABAH.

Minister of Planning and Regional Development: MUSTAPHA NABLI.

Minister of Agriculture: MUHAMMAD BEN REJEB.

Minister of State Domains: MUSTAPHA BOUAZIZ.

Minister of Equipment and Housing: ALI CHAOUCH.

Minister of the Environment and Land Planning: MEHDI MELIKA.

Minister of Transport: MONDHER ZENAIDI.

Minister of Tourism and Handicrafts: MUHAMMAD JEGHAM.

Minister of Communications: HABIB LAZRAG.

Minister of Education and Science: AHMED FRIAA.

Minister of Culture: MONGI BOUSNINA.

Minister of Public Health: HEDI M'HENNI.

Minister of Social Affairs: FADHEL KHELIL.

Minister of Professional Training and Employment: MONCER ROUISSI.

Minister of Children and Youth: ABD AR-RAHIM ZOUARI.

MINISTRIES

Ministry of Agriculture: 30 rue Alain Savery, Tunis; tel. 660-088; telex 13378.

Ministry of Children and Youth: 89 ave Hédi Chaker, Tunis; tel. 788-473; telex 14246.

Ministry of Communications: Tunis.

Ministry of Culture: place du Gouvernement, la Kasbah, 1008 Tunis; tel. 661-000; telex 12032; fax 567-019.

Ministry of Education and Science: place de la Kasbah, Tunis; tel. 660-088; telex 13004.

Ministry of the Environment and Land Planning: Tunis.

Ministry of Equipment and Housing: Cité Jardin, Tunis; tel. 680-088; telex 13565.

Ministry of Finance: place Alizouaui, Tunis; tel. 650-621; telex 51922.

Ministry of Foreign Affairs: place du Gouvernement, la Kasbah, Tunis; tel. 660-088; telex 13470.

Ministry of the Interior: ave Habib Bourguiba, Tunis; tel. 333-000; telex 13994.

Ministry of International Co-operation and Foreign Investment: Tunis.

Ministry of Justice: ave Bab Benat, Tunis; tel. 660-088.

Ministry of National Defence: blvd Bab Menara, Tunis; tel. 260-244; telex 12580.

Ministry of National Economy: 7 rue du Royaume d'Arabie Saoudite, 1035 Tunis; tel. 285-134; telex 14341.

Ministry of Planning and Regional Development: place Ali Zouaoui, 1000 Tunis; tel. 354-222; telex 15177; fax 351-666.

Ministry of Public Health: Bab Saadoun, 1030 Tunis; tel. 662-040; telex 15235; fax 567-100.

Ministry of Religious Affairs: Tunis.

Ministry of Social Affairs: blvd Farhat Hached, Tunis; tel. 660-088; telex 13711.

Ministry of Tourism and Handicrafts: ave Muhammad V, Tunis.

Ministry of Transport: 3 rue d'Angleterre, Tunis; tel. 660-088; telex 13040.

President and Legislature

PRESIDENT

At the presidential election, which took place on 20 March 1994, the sole candidate, Zine al-Abidine Ben Ali, was re-elected to the presidency with 2,987,375 votes, 99.92% of the votes cast.

ASSEMBLÉE NATIONALE

President: HABIB BOULARES.

Election, 20 March 1994

Party	Votes	%	Seats
Rassemblement Constitutionnel Démocratique	2,768,667	97.73	144
Mouvement des Démocrates Socialistes	30,660	1.08	10
Mouvement de la Rénovation. . .	11,299	0.39	4
Union Démocratique Unioniste . .	9,152	0.32	3
Parti de l'Unité Populaire . . .	8,391	0.30	2
Parti Social pour le Progrès . . .	1,892	0.07	0
Rassemblement Socialiste Progressiste	1,749	0.06	0
Independents.	1,061	0.04	0
Total	2,832,871*	100.00	163†

* Excluding 8,686 spoilt ballot papers.

† Under the terms of an amendment to the electoral code adopted by the National Assembly in January 1994, 19 of the 163 seats in the National Assembly were reserved for candidates of opposition parties. These were allotted according to the proportion of votes received nationally by each party.

Political Organizations

Mouvement de l'Unité Populaire (MUP): Tunis; supports radical reform; split into two factions, one led by AHMAD BEN SALAH, living in exile until 1988; the other became the Parti de l'Unité Populaire (see below). Co-ordinator BRAHIM HAYDER.

Mouvement des Démocrates Socialistes (MDS): Tunis; in favour of a pluralist political system; participated in 1981 election and was officially recognized in November 1983; Political Bureau of 14 mems, National Council of 60 mems, normally elected by the party Congress; Sec.-Gen. MUHAMMAD MOUADA.

Mouvement de la Rénovation (MR): Tunis; f. 1939; fmrly Parti Communiste Tunisien, name changed 1993; Sec.-Gen. MUHAMMAD HARMEL.

Parti de la Renaissance—Hizb an-Nahdah: Tunis; formerly Mouvement de la Tendance Islamique (banned in 1981); Leader RACHED GHANOUCHI; Sec.-Gen. Sheikh ABD AL-FATHA MOUROU.

Parti des Ouvriers Communistes Tunisiens (POCT): Tunis; illegal; Leader HAMMA HAMMANI.

Parti Social pour le Progrès (PSP): 3B rue Gandhi, Tunis; tel. 341-023; f. 1988; officially recognized September 1988; liberal; Sec.-Gen. MOUNIR BEJI.

Parti de l'Unité Populaire (PUP): 7 rue d'Autriche, 1002 Tunis; tel. 289678; fax 796031; broke away from MUP (see above); officially recognized November 1983; Leader MUHAMMAD BELHADJ AMOR.

Rassemblement Constitutionnel Démocratique—RCD: blvd 9 avril 1938, Tunis; f. 1934 as the Néo-Destour Party, following a split in the Destour (Constitution) Party; renamed Parti Socialiste Destourien in 1964; adopted present name in February 1988; moderate left-wing republican party, which achieved Tunisian independence; Political Bureau of 13 mems, and a Cen. Cttee of 200, elected by the party Congress; Chair. ZINE AL-ABIDINE BEN ALI; Vice-Chair. HAMED KAROUI; Sec.-Gen. CHEDLI NEFFATI.

Rassemblement National Arabe: Tunis; banned in 1981; Leader BASHIR ASSAD.

Rassemblement Socialiste Progressiste (RSP): Tunis; f. 1983, officially recognized September 1988; leftist; Sec.-Gen. NEJIB CHEBBI.

Union Démocratique Unioniste (UDU): Tunis; officially recognized November 1988; supports Arab unity; Sec.-Gen. ABDERRAHMANE TLILI.

Diplomatic Representation

EMBASSIES IN TUNISIA

Algeria: 18 rue de Niger, Tunis; tel. 283-166; telex 13081; Ambassador: Dr MESSAOUD AIT CHAALAL.

Argentina: 10 rue al-Hassan et Houssaine, al-Menzah IV, 1004, Tunis; tel. 237-313; telex 13053; fax 750-058; Ambassador: MARIO EDUARDO CORCUERA IBÁÑEZ.

Austria: 16 rue ibn Hamdiss, BP 23, al-Menzah, 1004 Tunis; tel. 238-696; telex 14586; Ambassador: Dr JOHANN PASCH.

Bahrain: 72 rue Mouaouia ibn Abi Soufiane, al-Menzah 6, Tunis; tel. 231-811; telex 13733; Ambassador: JASSIM BUALLAY.

Belgium: 47 rue du 1er juin, BP 24, 1002, Tunis; tel. 781-655; telex 14342; fax 792-797; Ambassador: GUIDO COURTOIS.

Brazil: 37 ave d'Afrique, BP 64, al-Menzah V, 1004 Tunis; tel. 232-538; telex 14560; fax 750-367; Ambassador: LINDOLFO L. COLLOR.

Bulgaria: 5 rue Ryhane, Cité Mahragène, Tunis; tel. 796-182; telex 17289; fax 791-667; Ambassador: TCHAVDAR TCHERVENKOV.

Canada: 3 rue du Sénégal, Place Palestine, BP 31, Belvédère, Tunis; tel. 286-557; telex 25324; fax 792-371; Ambassador: MARIUS BUJOLD.

China, People's Republic: 41 ave Jugurtha, Mutuellevilk, Tunis; tel. 282-090; telex 12221; Ambassador: WU CHUANFU.

Côte d'Ivoire: 84 ave Hédi Chaker, Tunis; tel. 283-878; telex 14353; Ambassador: COLLET PHILIPPE VIEIRA.

Cuba: 20 ave du Golfe Arabe, 1004 al-Menzah VIII, Tunis; tel. 712-844; telex 14080; fax 714-198; Ambassador: JORGE MANFUGAS-LAVIGNE.

Czech Republic: 98 rue de Palestine, BP 53, Belvédère, 1002 Tunis; tel. 280-486; telex 14466; fax 793228.

Denmark: 5 rue de Mauritanie, BP 254, Belvédère, 1002 Tunis; tel. 792-600; telex 14352; fax 790-797; Ambassador: HERLUF HANSEN.

Djibouti: 5 rue Fatma al-Fahria, BP 71, Mutuelleville, Tunis; tel. 890-589; telex 13148; Ambassador: ALI ABDOU MUHAMMAD.

Egypt: Quartier Montplaisir, Routhi 6, Med V, Tunis; tel. 792-233; telex 13992; fax 794-389; Ambassador: ALI MAHER AS-SAYED.

France: place de l'Indépendance, Tunis; tel. 347-555; telex 15468; fax 354-388; Ambassador: JEAN-NOËL DE LACOSTE.

Germany: 1 rue al-Hamra, Mutuelleville, Tunis; tel. 786-455; telex 15463; fax 788-242; Ambassador: Dr KARL HEINZ KUNZMANN.

Greece: 9 impasse Antelas, Nord Hilton, BP 151, Mahrajane, 1002, Tunis; tel. 288-411; telex 13742; fax 789-518; Ambassador: CONSTANTIN PREVEDOURAKIS.

Hungary: 8 rue al-Jahedh, al-Menzah I, Tunis; tel. 751-987; fax 750-620; Ambassador: LÁSZLÓ NIKICSER.

India: 4 place Didon, Notre Dame, Tunis; tel. 891-006; telex 18072; fax 783-394; Ambassador: NIGAM PRAKASH.

Indonesia: BP 63, al-Menzah, 1004 Tunis; tel. 797188; telex 18173; fax 791303; Ambassador: AMBIAR TAMALA.

Iran: 10 rue de Docteur Burnet, Belvédère, Tunis; tel. 285-305; telex 15138.

Iraq: ave Tahar B. Achour, route X2 m 10, Mutuelleville, Tunis; tel. 890-633; telex 12245; Ambassador: NOURI ISMAIL TOHA AL-WAYES.

Italy: 37 rue Gamal Abd an-Nasser, Tunis; tel. 341-811; telex 13501; fax 354-155; Ambassador: FRANCESCO CARUSO.

Japan: 10 rue Mahmoud al-Matri, BP 95, Belvédère, Tunis; tel. 285-937; telex 15456; Ambassador: YOSHIKAZU SUGITANI.

Jordan: 87 ave Jugurtha, Mutuelleville, Tunis; tel. 288-401; telex 13745; Ambassador: NABIH AN-NIMR.

Korea, Democratic People's Republic: 10 rue Holima Saodia, al-Menzah, Tunis; tel. 231-715; Ambassador: YI CHIN KYO.

Korea, Republic: 16 rue Caracalla, Notre Dame, 1002 Tunis; tel. 894-357; telex 15157; Ambassador: CHOI BONG-RHEUM.

Kuwait: 40 route Ariane, al-Menzah, Tunis; tel. 236-811; telex 12332; Ambassador: MEJREN AHMAD AL-HAMAD.

Libya: 48 bis rue du 1er juin, Tunis; tel. 236-666; telex 12275; Ambassador: ABD AL-ATTI OBEIDI.

Mauritania: 17 rue Fatma Ennechi, BP 62, al-Menzah, Tunis; tel. 234-935; telex 12234; Ambassador: MOHAMED LAMINE OULD YAHYA.

Morocco: 39 ave du 1er juin, Tunis; tel. 782-775; telex 14460; fax 787-103; Ambassador: ABD AL-HAKIM IRAQUI.

Netherlands: 6–8 rue Meycen, Belvédère, BP 47, 1082 Tunis; tel. 799-442; telex 15260; fax 785-557; Ambassador: R. J. MULDER.

Norway: 20 rue de la Kahéna, BP 9, 1082 Tunis; tel. 802-158; Ambassador: KJELL ØSTREM.

Pakistan: 7 rue Ali ibn Abi Talib, BP 42, al-Menzah, Tunis; tel. 234-366; telex 14027; Ambassador: TARIQ KHAN.

Poland: 4 rue Sophonisbe, Notre Dame, Tunis; tel. 286-237; telex 14024; fax 795-118; Ambassador: JANUSZ FEKECZ.

Portugal: 2 rue Sufétula, Belvédère, 1002 Tunis; tel. 893-981; telex 18235; fax 791-008; Ambassador: CARLOS MILHEIRÃO.

Qatar: 2 Nahj al-Hakim Bourni, Belvédère, Tunis; tel. 285-600; telex 14131; Chargé d'affaires: MAJID AL-ALI.

Romania: 18 ave d'Afrique, al-Menzah V, Tunis; tel. 766-926; telex 15223; fax 767-695; Ambassador: GELU VOICAN VOICULESCU.

Russia: 1 el Manar, BP 48, Tunis; tel. 882-446; Ambassador: BORIS ALEKSEYEVICH SHCHIBORIN.

Saudi Arabia: 16 rue d'Autriche, Belvédère, Tunis; tel. 281-295; telex 13562; Ambassador: Sheikh ABBAS FAIK GHAZZAOUI.

Senegal: 122 ave de la Liberté, Tunis; tel. 282-544; telex 12477; Ambassador: IBRA DEGUENE KA.

Somalia: 6 rue Hadramout, Mutuelleville, Tunis; tel. 289-505; telex 13480; Ambassador: AHMAD ABDALLAH MUHAMMAD.

Spain: 22 ave Dr Ernest Conseil, Cité Jardin, Tunis; tel. 280-613; telex 13330; Ambassador: FERNANDO ARIAS SALGADO.

Sweden: 87 ave Taieb Mhiri, 1002 Tunis; tel. 795-433; telex 15258; fax 788-894; Ambassador: JOHN HAGARD.

Switzerland: 10 rue ach-Chenkiti, BP 501, Mutuelleville, 1025 Tunis; tel. 281-917; telex 14922; fax 788-796; Ambassador: Dr LUCIANO MORDASINI.

Syria: Cité al-Manor III, No. 119, Tunis; tel. 235-577; telex 13890; Ambassador: OMAR AS-SAID.

Turkey: 30 ave d'Afrique, BP 134, al-Menzah 5, Tunis; tel. 750-668; fax 767-045; Ambassador: ALTAN GUVEN.

United Arab Emirates: 15 rue du 1er juin, Mutuelleville, Tunis; tel. 783-522; telex 12168; Ambassador: HAMAD SALEM AL-MAQAMI.

United Kingdom: 5 place de la Victoire, Tunis; tel. 341-444; telex 14007; fax 354-877; Ambassador: MICHAEL L. TAIT.

USA: 144 ave de la Liberté, Tunis; tel. 782-566; telex 13379; fax 789-719; Ambassador: MARY ANN CASEY.

Venezuela: 30 rue de Niger, 1002 Tunis; tel. 285-075; telex 15091; Ambassador: JOSÉ ANTONIO QUIJADA SÁNCHEZ.

Yemen: rue Mouaouia ibn Soufiane, al-Menzah 6, Tunis; tel. 237-933; telex 13045; Ambassador: SALAH ALI AL-ACHOUAL.

Yugoslavia: 4 rue de Libéria, Tunis; tel. 281-032; telex 18399; Ambassador: NERKEZ ARIFHODZIĆ.

Zaire: 11 rue Tertullien, Notre Dame, Tunis; tel. 281-833; telex 12429; Ambassador: MBOLADINGA KATAKO.

Judicial System

The **Cour de Cassation** in Tunis has three civil and one criminal sections. There are three **Cours d'Appel** at Tunis, Sousse and Sfax, and 13 **Cours de Première Instance**, each having three chambers, except the **Cour de Première Instance** at Tunis which has eight chambers. **Justices Cantonales** exist in 51 areas.

Religion

The Constitution of 1956 recognizes Islam as the state religion, with the introduction of certain reforms, such as the abolition of polygamy. An estimated 7m., or 99% of the population, are Muslims. Minority religions include Jews (an estimated 2,000 adherents in 1993) and Christians. The Christian population comprises Roman Catholics, Greek Orthodox and French and English Protestants.

ISLAM

Grand Mufti of Tunisia: Sheikh MUHAMMAD HABIR BELKHODJA.

CHRISTIANITY

Reformed Church of Tunisia: 36 rue Charles de Gaulle, 1,000 Tunis; f. 1880; c. 40 mems; Pastor LEE DEHOOG.

Roman Catholic Prelature: 4 rue d'Alger, 1000 Tunis; tel. 335-225; fax 335-832; f. 1964; Prelate of Tunis Mgr FOUAD TWAL; 15,000 adherents (1994).

The Press

DAILIES

L'Action: 15 rue 2 Mars 1934, Tunis; tel. 264-899; telex 12163; f. 1932; French; organ of the Rassemblement Constitutionnel Démocratique (RCD); Dir MUSTAPHA MASMOUDI; circ. 50,000.

Al-Amal (Action): 15 rue 2 Mars 1934, Tunis; tel. 264-899; telex 12163; f. 1934; Arabic; organ of the RCD; Dir HUCINE MAGHREBI; circ. 50,000.

La Presse de Tunisie: 6 rue Ali Bach-Hamba, Tunis; tel. 341-066; telex 13880; fax 349-720; f. 1936; French; Dr MAHFOUZ MUHAMMAD; circ. 40,000.

As-Sabah (The Morning): 4 rue Ali Bach-Hamba, Tunis; tel. 340-222; f. 1951; Arabic; Dir HABIB CHEIKHROUHOU; circ. 50,000.

PERIODICALS

Al-Akhbar (The News): 1 passage d'al-Houdaybiyah, Tunis; tel. 344-100; f. 1984; weekly; general; Dir MUHAMMAD BEN YOUSUF; circ. 50,000.

Les Annonces: 6 rue de Sparte, BP 1343, Tunis; tel. 243-377; telex 13206; 2 a week; French/Arabic; Dir MUHAMMAD NEJIB AZOUZ.

Al-Anouar at-Tounissia (Tunisian Lights): 10 rue ach-Cham, 1002 Tunis; tel. 289-000; fax 289-357; f. 1981; weekly; general; Dir SLAHEDDINE AL-AMRI; circ. 165,000.

L'Avenir: 26 rue Gamal Abd an-Nasser, BP 1200, Tunis; tel. 258-941; f. 1980; weekly; organ of Mouvement des Démocrates Socialistes.

Al-Bayan (The Manifesto): 103 ave de la Liberté, Tunis; tel. 780-366; telex 13982; weekly; general; Dir HÉDI JILANI.

Al-Biladi (My Country): 15 rue 2 Mars 1934, Tunis; telex 12163; f. 1974; Arabic; political and general weekly for Tunisian workers abroad; Dir HÉDI AL-GHALI; circ. 90,000.

Bulletin Mensuel de Statistique: Institut National de la Statistique, BP 65, 70 rue ach-Cham, 1002 Tunis-Belvédère; monthly.

Ach-Chourouk (Sunrise): 10 rue ach-Cham, Tunis; tel 289-000; weekly; general; Dir SLAHEDDINE AL-AMRI; circ. 110,000.

Conjoncture: 37 ave Khereddine Pacha, 1002 Tunis; tel. 784-223; fax 782-742; f. 1974; monthly; economic and financial surveys; Dir HOSNI TOUMI; circ. 5,000.

Démocratie: 118 rue de Yougoslavie, Tunis; f. 1978; monthly; French; organ of the Mouvement des Démocrates Socialistes; Dir HASSIB BEN AMMAR; circ. 5,000.

Dialogue: Maison du RCD, blvd 9 Avril 1938, Tunis; telex 12163; f. 1974; weekly; French; cultural and political organ of the RCD; Dir NACEUR BECHEKH; circ. 30,000.

Etudiant Tunisien: 11 rue d'Espagne, BP 286, Tunis; f. 1953; French and Arabic; Chief Editor FAOUZI AOUAM.

Al-Fajr (Dawn): Tunis; f. 1990; weekly; to become daily; Arabic; publ. of the Hizb an-Nahdah movement; Dir HAMADI JEBALI (imprisoned Jan. 1991).

Al-Fikr (Thought): 13 rue Dar al-Jel, BP 556, Tunis; tel. 260-237; f. 1955; monthly; Arabic; cultural review.

Gazette Touristique: rue 8601, 40, Zone Industrielle, La Charguia 2, 2035 Tunis; tel. 786-866; fax 794-891; f. 1971; monthly; French; tourism; Dir TIJANI HADDAD; circ. 5,000.

L'Hebdo Touristique: rue 8601, 40, Zone Industrielle, La Charguia 2, 2035 Tunis; tel. 786-866; fax 794-891; f. 1971; weekly; French; tourism; Dir TIJANI HADDAD; circ. 5,000.

IBLA: Institut des Belles Lettres Arabes, 12 rue Jemaa el-Haoua, 1008 Tunis Bab Menara, Tunis; tel. 560-133; f. 1937; 2 a year; French; social and cultural review on Maghreb and Muslim-Arab affairs; Dir J. FONTAINE.

Al-Idhaa wa Talvaza (Radio and Television): 71 ave de la Liberté, Tunis; tel. 287-300; fax 781-058; f. 1956; fortnightly; Arabic language; broadcasting magazine; Dir Gen. ABD AL-HAFIDH HERGUEM; Editor WAHID BRAHAM; circ. 10,000.

Information Economique Africaine: 16 rue de Rome, BP 61, 1015 Tunis; tel. 245-318; telex 14459; fax 353172; f. 1970; monthly; Dir MUHAMMAD ZERZERI.

Irfane (Children): 6 rue Mohammed Ali, Tunis; tel. 256-877; telex 12163; f. 1966; monthly; Arabic; publ. of the Tunisian Union of Youth Organizations; Dir-Gen. KHALID ABASSI; circ. 100,000.

Jeunesse Magazine: 6 rue Mohammed Ali, Tunis; tel. 256-877; telex 12163; monthly; Arabic/French; Dir-Gen. KHALID ABASSI; circ. 50,000.

Journal Officiel de la République Tunisienne: ave Farhat Hached, 2040 Radès; tel. 299-914; telex 14939; fax 297-234; f. 1860; the official gazette; French and Arabic editions published twice weekly by the Imprimerie Officielle (The State Press); Pres. and Dir-Gen. ROMDHANE BEN MIRMOUNE; circ. 20,000.

Al-Maoukif: 6 rue de la Commission, Tunis; tel. 346-077; weekly; organ of the Rassemblement Socialiste Progressiste; Dir AHMAD NEJIB CHABI.

Al-Maraa (The Woman): 56 blvd Bab Benat, Tunis; tel. 260-178; fax 567-131; f. 1961; monthly; Arabic/French; political, economic and social affairs; issued by the Union Nationale de la Femme Tunisienne; Dir FAIZA KEFI; circ. 10,000.

Le Mensuel: 9 rue de Bassorah, 1002 Tunis; f. 1984; monthly; economic, social and cultural affairs.

Al-Moussawar: 10 rue ach-Cham, Tunis; tel. 289-000; fax 289-357; weekly; circ. 75,000.

Al-Omma: 6 rue Habib Thameur, Tunis; tel. 246-306; weekly; political; Dir MUHAMMAD MHADHBI.

Outrouhat: BP 492, 1049 Tunis; tel. 230-092; monthly; scientific; Dir LOTFI BEN AISSA.

Ar-Rai (Opinion): 118 rue de Yougoslavie, Tunis; tel. 242-251; f. 1977 by Mouvement des Démocrates Socialistes; weekly; opposition newspaper; Dir HASSIB BEN AMAR; circ. 20,000.

Réalités: 85 rue de Palestine, Belvédère, BP 227, 1002 Tunis; tel. 788-313; fax 283-659; f. 1979; weekly; French; Dir MONCEF BEN M'RAD; circ. 25,000.

At-Tariq al-Jadid (New Road): 23 ave de Zanche, 1000 Tunis; tel. 246-400; fax 350-748; f. 1981; organ of the Mouvement de la Rénovation; Man. Editor BOUJEMAA REMILI.

Le Temps: 4 rue Ali Bach-Hamba, Tunis; tel. 340-222; f. 1975; weekly; general news; French; Dir HABIB CHEIKHROUHOU; circ. 42,000.

Tounes al-Khadra: 6 ave Habib Thameur, Tunis; tel. 245-095; f. 1976; bi-monthly; agriculture; Dir ESSID TAOUFIK; Editor GHARBI HAMOUDA; circ. 5,000.

Tunis Hebdo: 1 passage d'al-Houdaybiyah, Tunis; tel. 344-100; f. 1973; weekly; French; general and sport; Dir MUHAMMAD BEN YOUSUF; circ. 40,000.

NEWS AGENCIES

Tunis Afrique Presse (TAP): 25 ave du 7 novembre, Tunis; telex 13400; f. 1961; Arab, French and English; Offices in Algiers, Rabat, Kuwait, Rome, Bonn, Paris and New York; weekly and monthly bulletins; Chair. and Gen. Man. RIDHA HAJRI.

Foreign Bureaux

Agence France-Presse (AFP): 45 ave Habib Bourguiba, Tunis; tel. 337-896; telex 14628; fax 352-414; Chief MARC HUTTEN.

Agencia EFE (Spain): 126 rue de Yougoslavie, 1000 Tunis; tel. 331-497; fax 345-976; Chief MANUEL OSTOS.

Agenzia Nazionale Stampa Associata (ANSA) (Italy): 1 impasse des Vagues, Tunis; tel. 733993; telex 12110; fax 733888; Chief MANUELA FONTANA.

Informatsionnoye Telegrafnoye Agentstvo Rossii—Telegrafnoye Agentstvo Suverennykh Stran (ITAR—TASS) (Russia): 2 rue de Damas, Tunis; tel. 282-794; telex 12544; Chief VIKTOR LEBEDEV.

Inter Press Service (IPS) (Italy): 6 rue de Nablouss, 1001 Tunis; tel. 880-182; fax 337-809; f. 1976; Chief ABD AL-MAJID BEJAR.

Reuters (United Kingdom): BP 369, Belvédère, 1002 Tunis; tel. 787-711; telex 13933; fax 787-454; Chief (vacant).

Rossiyskoye Informatsionnoye Agentstvo—Novosti (RIA—Novosti) (Russia): 102 ave de la Liberté, Tunis; tel. 283-781; telex 15448; Chief NICOLAS SOLOGUBOVSKI.

Tanjug (Yugoslavia): 4 rue du Libéria, Tunis; Rep. SIME VUCKOVIĆ.

United Press International (UPI) (USA): 28 rue Gamal Abd an-Nasser, Tunis; tel. 352-135; Chief MICHEL DEURÉ.

Xinhua (New China) News Agency (People's Republic of China): 6 rue Smyrne, Notre Dame, Tunis; tel. 281-308; telex 12127; Dir XIE BINYU.

Publishers

Addar al-Arabia Lil Kitab: 4 rue Mohieddine El Klibi, al-Manar 2, BP 32, 2092 al-Manar 2, Tunis; tel. 236-025; telex 14966; f. 1975; general literature, children's books, non-fiction; Dir-Gen. DEKHILI REBAH.

Agence de Promotion de l'Industrie (API): 63 rue de Syrie, Belvédère, 1002 Tunis; tel. 287-600; telex 14166; f. 1973; industrial investment; Man. Dir PACHA SLAHEDDINE.

Bouslama Editions: 15 ave de France, 1000 Tunis; tel. 243-745; telex 14230; fax 381100; f. 1960; history, children's books; Man. Dir ALI BOUSLAMA.

Ceres Productions: 6 ave Abd ar-Rahman Azzam, BP 56, 1002 Tunis; tel. 282-033; fax 787-516; f. 1964; art books, literature, novels; Dir MUHAMMAD BEN SMAIL.

Dar al-Amal: rue 2 Mars 1934, Tunis; tel. 264-899; telex 12163; f. 1976; economics, sociology, politics; Man. Dir S. ZOGHLAMI.

Dar al-Kitab: 5 ave Bourguiba, 4000 Sousse; tel. 25097; f. 1950; literature, children's books, legal studies, foreign books; Pres. TAIEB KACEM; Dir FAYÇAL KACEM.

Dar Arabia: Lil Kitab, 4 rue 7101 Al Manar 2, 1004 El Menzah Tunis; tel. 236-600; general literature; Man. Dir MAHDI YOUSSEF.

Dar as-Sabah: 4 rue Ali Bach-Hamba, Tunis; tel. 340-222; f. 1951; 200 mems; publishes daily and weekly papers which circulate throughout Tunisia, North Africa, France, Belgium, Luxembourg and Germany; Pres., Dir-Gen. HABIB CHEIKHROUHOU.

Imprimerie al-Manar: 12 rue du Tribunal, BP 121, Tunis; tel. 260-641; telex 14894; fax 560-641; f. 1938; general, educational, Islam; Man. Dir HABIB M'HAMDI.

Institut National de la Statistique: 70 rue ach-Cham, BP 260, 1080 Tunis; publishes a variety of annuals, periodicals and papers concerned with the economic policy and development of Tunisia.

Maison Tunisienne d'Edition: rue de l'Oasis, El Menzah, Tunis; tel. 235873; telex 12032; fax 353-992; f. 1966; all kinds of books, magazines, etc.; Dir ABDELAZIZ ACHOURI.

An-Najah—Editions Hedi Ben Abd al-Gheni: 11 ave de France, Tunis; tel. 246-886; Arab and French books, Koranic texts.

Société d'Arts Graphiques, d'Edition et de Presse: 15 rue 2 mars 1934, La Kasbah, Tunis; tel. 264-988; telex 13411; fax 569-736; f. 1974; prints and publishes daily papers, magazines, books, etc.; Chair. and Man. Dir HASSEN FERJANI.

Société Tunisienne de Diffusion (STD): 5 ave de Carthage, BP 440, Tunis; tel. 255-000; telex 12521; general and educational books, office supplies; Man. Dir SLAHEDDINE BEN HAMIDA.

Sud Editions: 3 ave Louis Braille, 1002 Tunis; tel. 785-179; telex 12363; fax 792-905; f. 1976; Arab literature, art and art history; Man. Dir M. MASMOUDI.

Government Publishing House

Imprimerie Officielle de la République Tunisienne: ave Farhat Hached, 2040 Radès; tel. 434211; telex 14939; fax 434234; f. 1860; Man. Dir ROMDHANE BEN MIMOUN.

Radio and Television

RADIO

In 1991, according to UNESCO estimates, there were 1.64m. radio receivers and 650,000 television receivers in use.

Radiodiffusion Télévision Tunisienne: 71 ave de la Liberté, Tunis; tel. 287-300; telex 14365; government service; broadcasts in Arabic, French and Italian; stations at Gafsa, El-Kef, Monastir, Sfax and Tunis (two); Dir-Gen. ABDELHAFIDH HARGUEM.

TELEVISION

Television was introduced in northern and central Tunisia in January 1966, and by 1972 transmission reached all the country. A relay station to link up with European transmissions was built at al-Haouaria in 1967, and a second channel was introduced in 1983. In 1988 it was announced that the two channels would accept advertising.

Finance

(cap. = capital; p.u. = paid up; dep. = deposits; res = reserves; m. = million; brs = branches; amounts in dinars unless otherwise stated)

BANKING

Central Bank

Banque Centrale de Tunisie: 7 rue de la Monnaie, BP 369, Tunis; tel. 340588; telex 15375; fax 340-615; f. 1958; cap. 6.0m., dep. 1,085.4m., res 42.6m., total assets 2,277.6m. (1990); Gov. ISMAIL KHELIL.

Commercial Banks

Alubaf International Bank: 90–92 ave Hédi Chaker, BP 51, Belvédère, 1002 Tunis; tel. 783-500; telex 14971; fax 784-343; f. 1985; cap. p.u. US $10m., dep. $69.9m., res $2.6m., total assets 82.6m. (1992); Chair. MUHAMMAD ABDULJAWAD; Man. Dir PATRICK J. MASON.

Arab Tunisian Bank: 9 rue de la Monnaie, 1001 Tunis; tel. 351-155; telex 14205; fax 247-820; f. 1982; cap. 10m., dep. 287.6m., res 10m., total assets 400.5m. (1990); Pres., Dir-Gen. HAMMOUDA BELKHADJE; 14 brs.

Banque Internationale Arabe de Tunisie: 70–72 ave Habib Bourguiba, BP 520, 1080 Tunis; tel. 340-733; telex 15396; fax 340-680; f. 1976; cap. 20m., dep. 1,121.7m., res 19.95m., total assets 1,168.4m. (1991); Pres. MOKHTAR FAKHFAKH; Dir-Gen. HABIB FOURATI; 65 brs.

Banque Nationale Agricole: rue de la Monnaie, 1001 Tunis; tel. 791000; telex 15436; fax 791765; f. 1990 by merger of the Banque Nationale du Développement Agricole and the Banque Nationale de Tunisie; cap. 33m. p.u., dep. 2,044.2m., res 49.9m., total assets 2,551.7m. (1991); Pres. HABIB NIFAR; 71 brs.

Banque du Sud: 95 ave de la Liberté, Tunis; tel. 289-400; telex 13855; f. 1968; cap. p.u. 15m. (1990), dep. 396.1m., res 6m. (1989); Pres. MONCEF KAOUECH; Man. Dir ALLOUCH MILED; 65 brs.

Banque de Tunisie: 3 ave de France, BP 289, 1015 Tunis; tel. 259-999; telex 14070; fax 352-321; f. 1884; cap. 15m., dep. 704.4m., res 18.3m., total assets 738.6m. (1992); Pres. BOUBAKER MABROUK; 5 brs.

Citibank N.A.: 3 ave Jugurtha, BP 72, Belvédère, 1002 Tunis; tel. 790-066; telex 15139; fax 785-556; Gen. Man. BRADLEY LALONDE.

Crédit Foncier et Commercial de Tunisie: 13 ave de France, BP 52, 1080 Tunis; tel. 340-511; telex 14079; f. 1967; cap. 17m., dep. 503.9m., res 7.7m., total assets 533.6m. (1990); Chair. and Pres. RACHID BEN YEDDER; Gen. Man. MAHMOUD BABBOU; 21 brs.

Société Tunisienne de Banque; rue de la Monnaie, 1001 Tunis; tel. 340-477; telex 14135; fax 340009; f. 1957; 29.5% govt-owned; cap. p.u. 50m., dep. 1,705m., res 34.4m., total assets 1,802.4m. (1992); Chair. and Gen. Man. ABDELLATIF JERIJINI; 108 brs.

Union Bancaire pour le Commerce et l'Industrie: 7–9 rue Gamal Abd an-Nasser, BP 829, 1000 Tunis; tel. 245-877; telex 14992; fax 346737; f. 1961; cap. p.u. 15m., total assets 687m. (1992); affiliated to Banque Nationale de Paris Intercontinentale; Chair. ABD AS-SALAM BEN AYED; 28 brs and agencies.

Union Internationale de Banques: 65 ave Habib Bourguiba, BP 109, Tunis; tel. 347-000; telex 13700; fax 340-763; f. 1963 as a merging of Tunisian interests by the Société Tunisienne de Banque with Crédit Lyonnais (France) and other foreign banks, including Banca Commerciale Italiana; cap. p.u. 10m., dep. 503.9m., res 4.6m. (1988); Pres. and Dir-Gen. NEJI SKHIRI; 43 brs.

Development Banks

Banque Arabe Tuniso-Libyenne pour le Développement et le Commerce Extérieur: 25 rue Kheireddine Pacha, BP 102, Belvédère, 1002 Tunis; tel. 781-500; telex 14938; fax 782818; f. 1983; promotes trade and development projects between Tunisia and Libya, and provides funds for investment in poorer areas; cap. 100m., dep. 15.9m. (1991); Chair. and Gen. Man. TAHAR BOURKHIS.

Banque de Coopération du Maghreb Arabe: 70 ave de la Liberté, BP 46, Belvédère, 1012, Tunis; tel. 780-311; telex 13404; f. 1981, began operations 1982; finances joint development projects between Tunisia and Algeria; cap. p.u. US $30m. (1988), res $1.8m. (1983); Chair. MAHFOUD ZEROUTA; Dir-Gen. AÏSSA HIDOUSSI.

Banque de Développement Economique de Tunisie (BDET): 34 rue Hédi El Karray, El Menzah 1004, BP 48, 1080 Tunis; tel. 718-000; telex 14133; fax 713-740; f. 1959; main source of long term and equity finance for industrial and tourist enterprises; cap. 35m., dep. 516.1m., res 44m., total assets 602,554m. (1992); Pres. and Gen. Man. TIJANI CHELLI.

Banque Tuniso-Koweïtienne de Développement: ave Muhammad V, BP 49, 1002 Tunis; tel. 340-000; telex 14834; fax 346-100; f. 1981; provides long-term finance for development projects; cap. 100m. (1990); res 103.8m. (1985); Dir-Gen. ABD AL-GHAFFAR EZZED-DINE.

Société Tuniso-Séoudienne d'Investissement et de Développement (STUSID): 32 rue Hedi Kharray, BP 20, 1002 Tunis; tel. 718-233; telex 13594; fax 719-233; f. 1981; provides long-term finance for development projects; cap. 100m.; Chair. Dr MAHSOUN BAHJET JALAL; Pres. ABD AL-MAJID FRAJ.

INSURANCE

Caisse Tunisienne d'Assurances Mutuelles Agricoles: 6 ave Habib Thameur, Tunis 1000; tel. 340-933; telex 12451; f. 1912; Pres. MOKTAR BELLAGHA; Dir-Gen. SLAHEDDINE FERCHIOU.

Compagnie d'Assurances Tous Risques et de Réassurance (ASTREE): 45 ave Kheireddine Pacha, BP 780, 1002 Tunis; tel. 792-211; telex 15149; fax 794-723; f. 1950; cap. 3m. dinars; Pres. and Dir-Gen. MUHAMMAD HACHICHA.

Compagnie Tunisienne pour l'Assurance du Commerce Extérieur (COTUNACE): ave Muhammad V/Montplaisir I, 8006 Tunis; tel. 783-000; telex 17373; fax 782-539; f. 1984; cap. 5m. dinars; 41 mem. cos; Pres. and Dir-Gen. AHMAD TRIKI.

Lloyd Tunisien: 7 ave de Carthage, 1000 Tunis; tel. 340-911; telex 13293; fax 340-909; f. 1945; fire, accident, liability, marine, life; cap. 1m. dinars; Chair. and Man. Dir M. ELTAIEF.

Société Tunisienne de Réassurance (Tunis-Ré): ave Muhammad V, 1002 Tunis; tel. 891-011; telex 18767; fax 789-656; f. 1981; all kinds of insurance and reinsurance; Pres., Dir-Gen. MUHAMMAD EL-HEDI DARGHOUTH.

Trade and Industry

CHAMBERS OF COMMERCE AND INDUSTRY

Chambre de Commerce et d'Industrie de Tunis: 1 rue des Entrepreneurs, 1000 Tunis; tel. 242-872; telex 14718; fax 354-744; f. 1888; 25 mems; Pres. YOUNES EL MENNAI.

Chambre de Commerce et d'Industrie du Centre: rue Chadli Khaznadar, Sousse; tel. (03) 25044; fax 24227; f. 1895; 23 mems; Pres. KABOUDI MONCEF; Dir-Gen. SASSI FETHI.

Chambre de Commerce et d'Industrie du Nord: 46 rue ibn Khaldoun, 7000 Bizerte; tel. 431-044; telex 21086; fax 439-033; f. 1903; 5 mems; Pres. MOKHTAI NAAMAR; Sec.-Gen. MUHAMMAD LARBI ALMIA.

Chambre de Commerce et d'Industrie du Sud: 127 rue Haffouz, BP 794, 3018 Sfax; tel. 04-296120; telex 40767; fax 04-296121; f. 1895; 45,000 mems.

STATE ENTERPRISES

Compagnie des Phosphates de Gafsa (CPG): Cité Bayech, Gafsa; tel. 22022; telex 60007; f. 1897; production and marketing of phosphates; Pres. MUHAMMAD AL-FADHEL KHELIL.

Office des Céréales: Ministry of Agriculture, 30 rue Alain Savery, Tunis; tel. 790-351; telex 14709; fax 789-573; f. 1962; responsible for the cereals industry; Chair. and Dir-Gen. A. SADDEM.

Office National des Mines: 24 rue 8601, Tunis; tel. 788-842; telex 15004; fax 794-016; f. 1962; mining of iron ores; research and study of mineral wealth; Pres. and Dir-Gen. ABD AR-RAHMAN TOUHAMI.

Office National des Pêches (ONP): Le Port, La Goulette, Tunis; tel. 275-093; telex 12388; marine and fishing authority; Dir-Gen. L. HALAB.

Office des Terres Domaniales (OTD): 43 rue d'Iran, Tunis; tel. 280-322; telex 13566; f. 1961; responsible for agricultural production and the management of state-owned lands; Dir BECHIR BEN SMAIL.

Société Générale des Industries Textiles (SOGITEX): Bir Kassaa, Ben Arous, Tunis; tel. 297-100; telex 12444; responsible for the textile industry; Chair. BECHIR SAIDANE.

Société Tunisienne de l'Electricité et du Gaz (STEG): 38 rue Kemal Atatürk, BP 190, 1080 Tunis; tel. 341-311; telex 14020; fax 349-981; f. 1962; responsible for generation of electricity and for production of natural gas; Pres. and Gen. Man. MONCEF BEN ABDALLAH; 36 branches.

ECONOMIC AND COMMERCIAL ORGANIZATIONS

Agence de Promotion de l'Industrie (API): 63 rue de Syrie, 1002 Tunis; tel. 792-144; telex 14166; fax 792-144; f. 1987 by merger; co-ordinates industrial policy, undertakes feasibility studies, organizes industrial training and establishes industrial zones; overseas offices in Belgium, France, Germany, Italy, the United Kingdom, Sweden and the USA; Pres. and Dir-Gen. MUHAMMAD BEN KHALIFA.

Centre de Promotion des Exportations (CEPEX): 28 rue Ghandi, 1001 Tunis; tel. 350-344; telex 14716; fax 353-683; f. 1973; state export promotion organization; Pres. and Dir-Gen. HABIB DALDOUR.

Office du Commerce de Tunisie (OCT): 1 rue de Syrie, 1060 Tunis; tel. 682-901; telex 14177; Dir-Gen. MUHAMMAD AMOR.

Union Nationale des Agriculteurs (UNA): 6 ave Habib Thameur, 1000 Tunis; tel. 246-920; fax 349-843; f. 1955; Pres. BACHA ABD AL-BAKI.

Union Tunisienne de l'Industrie, du Commerce et de l'Artisanat (UTICA): 103 ave de la Liberté, Belvédère, 1002 Tunis; tel. 780-366; telex 18982 TN; fax 782-143; f. 1946; mems: 12 national federations and 150 syndical chambers at national levels; Pres. HEDI JILANI; First Sec.-Gen. ABDALLAH BEN MBAREK.

MAJOR INDUSTRIAL COMPANIES

Entreprises Ali Mheni (EAM): 12 bis rue de Russie, BP 609, Tunis; tel. 252-433; telex 12562; f. 1934; construction and civil engineering, public works, building; Chair. ALI MHENI; 3,500 employees.

Bata Tunisienne SA: route de Mornag, Km 7, Ben Arous, Tunis; tel. 380-485; telex 12041; f. 1934; manufacture of shoes and sandals; Dir-Gen. ROGER SICCO.

Compagnie Générale des Salines de Tunisie (COTUSAL): 19 rue de Turquie, Tunis; tel. 347666; telex 15354; fax 246163; f. 1949; production of edible and industrial sea salt; Man. Dir NORBERT DE GUILLEBON.

Grands Ateliers du Nord SA: route de Mornag, GP 1 Km 12, az-Zahra Hammam-Lif, Tunis; tel. 482-422; telex 13254; f. 1975; manufacture of agricultural and building equipment; sales TD 10m., cap. p.u. TD 1.4m. (1991); Pres. ABDELAZIZ GUIDARA; 1,000 employees.

Groupe Chimique Tunisien: 7 rue Royaume d'Arabie Saoudite, 1002 Tunis; tel. 784488; telex 14705; f. 1952; production of Phosphoric acid and fertilizers; Chair. MUHAMMAD CHARFEDDINE GUELLOUZ.

Industries Maghrébines de l'Aluminium (IMAL): 2035 Tunis; tel. 795-979; telex 15376; fax 782-074; f. 1965; manufacture and distribution of aluminium products; cap. p.u. TD 57,000; Chair. T. OUNAIS; 50 employees.

Industries Mecaniques Maghrebines (IMM): Kairouan; tel. 722-028; fax 722-685; f. 1982; ownership 20% General Motors, 10% Isuzu Motors, 70% local investors; production of light commercial vehicles; Man. Dir TAHAR LATROUS.

Skanes Meubles: route de Sousse, 5000 Monastir; tel. 61390; telex 30734; manufacture of furniture and hotel equipment, toys; Pres. AHMAD TRIMECH.

Société Industrielle de Pêches et de Conserves Alimentaires SA: ave Habib Bourguiba, Megrine-Riadh; tel. 295-500; telex 12240; fish, fruit and vegetable processing and canning; Dir-Gen. ALI MABROUK.

Société Tunisienne Automobile, Financière, Immobilière et Maritime (STAFIM): 85 ave Louis Braille, 1003 Tunis; tel. 785055; telex 14581; f. 1932; manufacture of cars, spare parts, engines and mechanical machinery; Dir-Gen. GAEL DE GOUVION SAINT-CYR.

Tunisienne de Conserves Alimentaires (TUCAL): 15 rue Sidi Bou Mendil, Tunis; tel. 241-617; manufacture and distribution of canned food products; Pres. and Gen. Man. AMOR BEN SEDRINE.

TRADE AND OTHER UNIONS

Union Générale des Etudiants de Tunisie (UGET): 11 rue d'Espagne, Tunis; f. 1953; 600 mems; Pres. MEKKI FITOURI.

Union Générale Tunisienne du Travail (UGTT): 29 place Muhammad Ali, Tunis; f. 1946 by FARHAT HACHED; affiliated to ICFTU; mems 330,000 in 23 affiliated unions; 18-member executive bureau; Chair. HABIB TLIBA; Sec.-Gen. ISMAIL SAHBANI.

Union Nationale de la Femme Tunisienne (UNFT): 56 blvd Bab-Benat, Tunis; tel. 260-181; fax 567-131; f. 1956; 100,000 mems; Pres. FAIZA KEFI; Vice-Pres. RADHIA RIZA.

TRADE FAIR

Société Foire Internationale de Tunis SA: BP 1, 2015 Le Kram Tunis; tel. 730-111; telex 15189; fax 730-666; f. 1990; Gen. Man. NEJIB BEN MILED.

Transport

RAILWAYS

In 1993 the total length of railways was 2,260 km. A total of 30.6m. passengers travelled by rail in Tunisia in 1992.

Société du Métro Léger de Tunis (SMLT): 6 rue Khartoum, BP 4, 1002 Tunis; tel. 780-100; telex 14072; fax 780-371; f. 1981; operates light railway system in and around Tunis (total length 31 km); Dir-Gen. HABIB ALLEGUE.

Société Nationale des Chemins de Fer Tunisiens (SNCFT): 67 ave Farhat Hached, Tunis; tel. 249-999; telex 14019; fax 344-045; f. 1956; state organization controlling all Tunisian railways; Pres. and Dir-Gen. MAHMOUD BEN FADHL.

Société Nationale des Transports (SNT): 1 ave Habib Bourguiba, BP 660, 1001 Tunis; tel. 259-421; telex 15196; fax 342-727; f. 1963; operates 164 local bus routes with 817 buses; Chair. and Man. Dir MONCEF KAFSI; Gen. Man. HASSINE HASSANI.

Société Nationale de Transport Interurbain (SNTRI): ave Muhammad V, BP 40, Belvédère, 1012 Tunis; tel. 784-433; telex 18335; fax 786-605; f. 1981; Dir-Gen. ALI KHALBOUS.

ROADS

In 1989 there were 29,183 km of roads. Of these, 52 km were motorways, 10,758 km main roads and 6,163 km secondary roads.

Hammamet and M'Saken each have two **Sociétés Régionales des Transports**, responsible for road transport (one for passengers and one for freight).

SHIPPING

Tunisia has seven major ports: Tunis-La Goulette, Radès, Bizerta, Sousse, Sfax, Gabès and Zarzis. There is a special petroleum port at La Skhirra.

Office des Ports Nationaux Tunisiens: Bâtiment Administratif, Port de la Goulette, La Goulette, Tunis; tel. 735-300; telex 15386; fax 735812; maritime port administration; Pres. and Dir-Gen. HASSINE HASSANI.

Compagnie Tunisienne de Navigation SA: 5 ave Dag Hammarskjoeld, BP 40, Tunis; tel. 333-925; telex 12475; fax 350-976; brs at Bizerta, Gabès, La Skhirra, La Goulette, Radès, Sfax and Sousse; Chair. C. HAJRI.

Gabès Chimie Transport: 3 rue de Kenya, Belvédère, 1002 Tunis; tel. 283-174; telex 13323; fax 787-821; transportation of chemicals; fleet of 3 chemical tankers; Chair. BOUNATIROU TAOUFIK.

Société Nationale Maritime Corse-Méditerranée: 47 ave Farhat Hached, 1001 Tunis; tel. 338-222; telex 13078; fax 330-636.

CIVIL AVIATION

There are international airports at Tunis-Carthage, Sfax, Djerba, Monastir, Tabarka and Tozeur.

Office des Ports Aériens: BP 60, Aérodrome de Tunis, Carthage, Tunis; tel. 236-000; telex 13809; fax 781-460; air traffic control and airport administration; Chair. HOUCINE CHOUK.

Air Liberté Tunisie: Monastir; f. 1990; subsidiary of French airline Air Liberté; flights from Tunis, Djerba and Monastir airports to African countries, Scandinavia and other European countries; Chair. AZIZ MILED; Man. Dir SLAHEDDINE KASTALLI.

Tunis Air (Société Tunisienne de l'Air): blvd 7, novembre, 1060 Tunis; tel. 700-100; telex 15283; fax 700-754; f. 1948; 45.2% government-owned; flights to Africa, Europe and the Middle East; Pres. and Gen. Man. ABD AL-HAMID EL FEHRI.

Tunisavia (Société de Transports, Services et Travaux Aériens): Immeuble Saadi Spric, Tour CD, 2080 L'Ariana, Tunis; tel. 717-793; telex 13121; fax 718-100; f. 1974; helicopter and charter operator.

Tourism

The main tourist attractions are the magnificent sandy beaches, Moorish architecture and remains of the Roman Empire. Tunisia contains the site of the ancient Phoenician city of Carthage. Tourism, a principal source of foreign exchange, has expanded rapidly, following extensive government investment in hotels, improved roads and other facilities. The number of hotel beds increased from 71,529 in 1980 to 145,000 in 1993. In 1993 foreign tourist arrivals totalled 3.6m. (of whom some 2.2m. were European), while earnings from tourism in the same year increased to an estimated 1,100m. dinars.

Office National du Tourisme Tunisien: 1 ave Muhammad V, Tunis; tel. 341-077; telex 14381; fax 350997; f. 1958; Dir-Gen. WAHID IBRAHIM.

Defence

Chief of Staff of the Army: Gen. MUHAMMAD SAID AL-KATEB.

Chief of Staff of the Navy: Adm. HABIB FEDHILA.

Chief of Staff of the Air Force: Gen. RIDHA ATTAR.

Estimated Defence Expenditure (1994): 563.2m. dinars.

Military Service: 1 year (selective).

Total Armed Forces (June 1994): 35,500 (army 27,000; navy 5,000; air force 3,500).

Paramilitary Forces (June 1994): 23,000 (13,000 National Police, 10,000 National Guard).

Education

Education is compulsory in Tunisia. Approximately 80% of children of school age receive an education. In 1992/93 there were 1,432,112 pupils in 4,044 primary schools and 567,381 pupils in 624 secondary schools. In 1990 administrative expenditure by the central Government on education was projected at 642m. dinars (22% of total current expenditure in that year). Public expenditure on education was 725m. dinars in 1991, representing 14.2% of total government spending.

Since the 1970s Arabic only has been used in the first three years of primary school, but, with effect from the 1986/87 academic year, French was to be taught from the second year. In the higher grades French becomes progressively more important and is used almost exclusively in higher education. The University of Tunis was opened in 1959/60. In 1988 the university was divided into separate institutions: one for science, the other for arts. It has 54 faculties and institutes. In 1986 two new universities were opened, at Monastir and Sfax.

Bibliography

Anthony, John. *About Tunisia*. London, 1961.

Ardant, Gavriel. *La Tunisie d'Aujourd'hui et Demain*. Paris, 1961.

Ashford, Douglas E. *Morocco-Tunisia: Politics and Planning*. Syracuse University Press, 1965.

Basset, André. *Initiation à la Tunisie*. Paris, 1950.

Ben Salem, Mohamed. *L'Antichambre de l'Indépendance*. Tunis, CERES Productions, 1988.

Bessis, Sophie, and Belhassen, Souhayr. *Bourguiba Tome 1: A la conquête d'un destin (1901–1957)*. Paris, Jeune Afrique Livres, 1988.

Bourguiba, Habib. *La Tunisie et la France*. Paris, 1954.

   Hadith al-Jamaa. (Collected Broadcasts) Tunis, 1957.

Brunschvig, Robert. *La Tunisie au haut Moyen Age*. Cairo, 1948.

Camau, Michel. *Tunisie au présent. Une modernité au-dessus de tout soupçon?* Paris, Centre National de la Recherche, 1987.

Cambon, Henri. *Histoire de la régence de Tunisie*. Paris, 1948.

Depois, Jean. *La Tunisie, ses Régions*. Paris, 1959.

Duvignaud, Jean. *Tunisie*. Lausanne, Editions Rencontre, 1965.

Duwaji, Ghazi. *Economic Development in Tunisia*. New York, Praeger, 1967.

Garas, Felix. *Bourguiba et la Naissance d'une Nation*. Paris, 1956.

Guen, Moncef. *La Tunisie indépendante face à son économie*. Paris, 1961.

Joffe, E. G. H. Editor. *North Africa: Nation, State and Region*. London, Routledge, 1993.

Knapp, W. *Tunisia*. London, Thames and Hudson, 1972.

Laitman, Leon. *Tunisia Today: Crisis in North Africa*. New York, 1954.

Ling, Dwight D. *Tunisia, from Protectorate to Republic*. Indiana University Press, 1967.

Memmi, Albert. *Le Pharaon*. Paris, Julliard, 1988.

Micaud, C. A. *Tunisia, the Politics of Moderation*. New York, 1964.

Moore, C. H. *Tunisia since Independence*. Berkeley, University of California Press, 1965.

Nerfin, M. *Entretiens avec Ahmed Ben Salah*. Paris, F. Maspero, 1974.

Perkins, Kenneth J. *Historical Dictionary of Tunisia* (African Historical Dictionaries, No. 45). Metuchen, NJ, and London, The Scarecrow Press, 1989.

Raymond, André. *La Tunisie*. Series *Que sais-je*, No. 318, Paris, 1961.

Rudebeck, Lars. *Party and People: A Study of Political Change in Tunisia*. London, C. Hurst, 1969.

Salem, Norma. *Habib Bourguiba, Islam and the Creation of Tunisia*. London, Croom Helm, 1984.

Sylvester, Anthony. *Tunisia*. London, Bodley Head, 1969.

Tlatli, Salah-Eddine. *Tunisie nouvelle*. Tunis, 1957.

Ziadeh, Nicola, A. *The Origins of Tunisian Nationalism*. Beirut, 1962.

TURKEY

Physical and Social Geography

W. B. FISHER

Turkey is, in a remarkable sense, passage land between Europe and Asia, boasting land frontiers with Greece, Bulgaria, Armenia, Georgia, the Nakhichevan Autonomous Republic (part of Azerbaijan), Iran, Iraq and Syria. The west, the richest and most densely populated part of Turkey, looks towards the Aegean and Mediterranean seas and is very conscious of its links with Europe. However, in culture, racial origins and ways of life, there are frequent reminders of Turkey's geographical situation primarily as a part of Asia.

Turkey consists essentially of the large peninsula of Asia Minor, which has strongly defined natural limits; sea on three sides (the Black Sea to the north, the Aegean to the west, and the Mediterranean to the south), and high mountain ranges on the fourth (eastern) side. The small region of European Turkey, containing the cities of İstanbul (Constantinople) and Edirne (Adrianople), is, on the other hand, defined by a purely artificial frontier, the exact position of which has varied considerably since the 19th century, according to the fluctuating fortunes and prestige of Turkey itself. Another small territory, the Hatay, centred on İskenderun (Alexandretta) and lying as an enclave in Syrian territory, was acquired as part of a diplomatic bargain in 1939.

PHYSICAL FEATURES

The geological structure of Turkey is extremely complicated, and rocks of almost all ages occur, from the most ancient to most recent. Broadly speaking, Turkey consists of a number of old plateau blocks, against which masses of younger rock series have been squeezed to form fold mountain ranges of varying size. As there were several of these plateau blocks, and not just one, the fold mountains run in many different directions, with considerable irregularity, and hence no simple pattern can be discerned—instead, one mountain range gives place to another abruptly, and we can pass suddenly from highland to plain or plateau.

In general outline Turkey consists of a ring of mountains enclosing a series of inland plateaux, with the highest mountains to the east, close to Armenia and Iran. Mount Ararat is the highest peak in Turkey, reaching 5,165 m, and there are neighbouring peaks almost as high. In the west the average altitude of the hills is distinctly lower, though the highest peak (Mount Erciyas or Argaeus) is over 3,900 m. The irregular topography of Turkey has given rise to many lakes, some salt and some fresh, and generally more numerous than elsewhere in the Middle East. The largest, Lake Van, covers nearly 4,000 sq km (1,100 sq miles).

Two other features may be mentioned. Large areas of the east and some parts of the centre of Asia Minor have been covered in sheets of lava which are often of such recent occurrence that soil has not yet been formed—consequently wide expanses are sterile and uninhabited. Secondly, in the north and west, cracking and disturbance of the rocks has taken place on an enormous scale. The long, indented coast of the Aegean Sea, with its numerous oddly shaped islands and estuaries, is due to cracking in two directions, which has split the land into detached blocks of roughly rectangular shape. Often the lower parts have sunk and been drowned by the sea. The Bosphorus and Dardanelles owe their origin to this faulting action, and the whole of the Black Sea coast is due to subsidence along a great series of fissures. Movement and adjustment along these cracks has by no means ceased, so that at the present day earthquakes are frequent in the north and west of Turkey.

Because of the presence of mountain ranges close to the coast, and the great height of the interior plateaux (varying from 800 m to 2,000 m), Turkey has special climatic conditions, characterized by great extremes of temperature and rainfall, with wide variation from one district to another. In winter conditions are severe in most areas, except for those lying close to sea-level. Temperatures of minus 30° to minus 40°C can occur in the east, and snow lies there for as many as 120 days each year. The west has frost on most nights of December and January, and (again apart from the coastal zone) has an average winter temperature below 1°C. In summer, however, temperatures over most of Turkey exceed 30°C, with 43°C in the south-east. There can hence be enormous seasonal variations of temperature—sometimes over 50°C, among the widest in the world.

Rainfall, too, is remarkably variable. Along the eastern Black Sea coast, towards the Georgian frontier, over 2,500 mm (100 in) fall annually; but elsewhere, amounts are very much smaller. Parts of the central plateau, being shut off by mountains from the influence of sea winds, are arid, with annual totals of under 250 mm, and expanses of salt steppe and desert are frequent. Like Iran, Turkey also has a 'dead heart', and the main towns of Anatolia, including Ankara, the capital, are placed away from the centre and close to the hills, where rainfall tends to be greater and water supplies better.

It is necessary to emphasize the contrast that exists between the Aegean coastlands, which, climatically, are by far the most favoured regions of Turkey, and the rest of the country. Round the Aegean, winters are mild and fairly rainy, and the summers hot, but tempered by a persistent northerly wind, the Meltemi, or Etesian wind, which is of great value in ripening fruit, especially figs and sultana grapes.

ECONOMIC LIFE

The variety of geographical conditions within Turkey has led to uneven development, and this unevenness has been intensified by poor communications, due to the broken nature of the topography. Roads are relatively few, railways slow and often round about, and whole districts—sometimes even considerable towns—are accessible only by unsurfaced track. Many rivers flow in deep gorges near their sources and either meander or are broken by cascades in their lower reaches, so that none are navigable.

Thus, we find that the west of Turkey, situated close to the Aegean Sea, is by far the most densely peopled and the most intensively developed. Since 1923, however, attempts have been made to develop the Anatolian plateau and the districts in the extreme east, which, following the expulsion and massacre of the Armenians in 1914–18, for a time supported only a very scanty population. Development in the central plateau has been aided by the exploitation of several small but on the whole valuable mineral deposits, and by irrigation schemes to improve agriculture. A certain degree of industrialization (mainly undertaken by State-sponsored and -owned organizations) has also grown up, based on Turkish-produced raw materials—cotton, wool, mohair, beet-sugar, olive oil and tobacco. The eastern districts present a more intractable problem, and development so far has been slower.

The considerable increase of population in recent years (averaging 2.2% annually between 1985 and 1990) has led to intensification of settlement and to an increase in the use of available land for cultivation. Henceforth an important task for Turkey must be to improve yields from agriculture and industry. Because of the strategic importance of the country, there has been a considerable programme of road building, largely financed by the USA. Until recently, the absorption of Turkish labour in Western Europe (chiefly Germany) provided useful extra revenue from remittances. With the repatriation of many of these *gastarbeiter* during the recession of the last few years, however, there have been problems of reabsorption (the returning workers have higher expectations), together with the need to find other sources of revenue.

Latterly, Turkey has experienced severe economic crises, compounded by political uncertainty and social instability. In 1980 there were severe shortages, due to rampant inflation and the inability to finance necessary imports. Inflation, however, has fluctuated since 1981, while 'black market' activities have reduced, confidence has increased, export performance has improved and, most importantly, the country has returned to civilian rule. This has allowed the start of reform of the tax system, and a limited plan for land reform. Nevertheless, social problems (in part due to widespread unemployment, low credit-worthiness and the effects of military government) remain considerable handicaps, and doubts persist as to the real extent of civilian control and the ability of the Government to free itself from the legacy of the military regime. Corruption and bureaucratic inefficiency remain perennial problems.

RACE AND LANGUAGE

Racially, the bulk of the Turkish people show an inter-mixture of Mediterranean and Armenoid strains. In the western half of the country Mediterraneans and Armenoids are more or less equally represented; but further east the proportion of Armenoids steadily increases until, towards the former Soviet and Iranian borders, they become almost universal. Much of south-eastern Turkey is inhabited by Kurds, a people of Indo-European descent; estimates of their number range from 3m. to more than 8m. Turkey also has less important racial elements; there would seem to be small numbers of proto-Nordics in the north and west, and some authorities suggest a racial relationship between Galatia (the modern district of Ankara) and ancient Gaul. The Ottoman Turks were, in the main, of Turki (western Mongoloid) ancestry but, in the view of some authorities, their contribution to the ethnic stocks of Turkey was small, since they were really an invading tribal group that became an aristocracy and soon intermarried with other peoples. There are also numbers of Caucasians—particularly Circassians and Georgians—who have contributed to the racial structure of Turkey; and during 1951 a further element was added by the arrival of many thousands of Bulgarian Muslims who had been deported from their own country.

The Turkish language, which is of central Asiatic origin, is spoken over most, but by no means all, of the country. This was introduced into Turkey in Seljuq times, and was written in Arabic characters, but, as these are not really well adapted to the sound of Turkish, Roman (i.e. European) script has been compulsory since 1928. As well, there are a number of non-Turkish languages. Kurdish is widely spoken in the south-east, along the Syrian and Iraqi frontiers; and Caucasian dialects, quite different from either Turkish or Kurdish, occur in the north-east. Greek and Armenian were once widespread but, following the deportations which began in the 1920s, both forms of speech are now current only in the city of İstanbul, where considerable numbers of Greeks and Armenians still live.

History

ANCIENT HISTORY

The most ancient written records so far found in Asia Minor date from the beginning of the second millennium BC. They are in Assyrian, and reveal the existence of Assyrian trading colonies in Cappadocia. These documents, together with a growing amount of archaeological evidence, show an important Copper Age culture in Central Anatolia in the third and early second millennia. Later in the second millennium the greater part of Asia Minor fell under the rule of the Hittites, whose empire flourished from about 1600 BC to about 1200 BC, and reached its apogee in the 14th and 13th centuries, when it became one of the dominant states of the eastern Mediterranean. After the break-up of the Hittite Empire, Asia Minor was split up among a number of dynasties and peoples—Phrygians, Cimmerians, Lydians and others—about whom not very much is known. Towards the end of the Hittite period the Greeks began to invade the Aegean coast, and entered on a long struggle with the native states that is reflected in the story of the Trojan War. Greek culture spread in western Anatolia, which was gradually incorporated into the Hellenic world. A series of political changes, of which the most important are the Persian conquest in 546 BC, the conquest of Alexander in 334 BC, and the constitution of the Roman province of Asia in 133 BC, did not impede the steady spread of Greek language and culture in the cities.

In AD 330, the Emperor Constantine inaugurated the new city of Constantinople, on the site of the old Greek trading settlement of Byzantium. This city at once became the capital of the East Roman and then of the Christian Byzantine Empire. Asia Minor was now the metropolitan province of a great empire, and grew in wealth, prosperity and importance. Under Byzantine rule Greek Christianity, already firmly established in Roman times, spread over most of the peninsula.

SELJUQS AND OTTOMANS

At the beginning of the 11th century a new conquest of Anatolia began—that of the Turks. The early history of the Turkish peoples is still obscure. Some references in the ancient biography of Alexander show them to have been established in Central Asia at the time of his conquests, and Turkish tribal confederacies played an important part in the invasions of Europe from late Roman times onwards. The name 'Turk' first appears in historical records in the sixth century AD, when Chinese annals speak of a powerful empire in Central Asia, founded by a steppe people called Tu-Kiu. It is from this state that the oldest surviving Turkish inscriptions have come. From the seventh century onwards the Central Asian Turks came into ever closer contact with the Islamic peoples of the Near East, from whom they adopted the Islamic faith and the Arabic script, and with them much of the complex civilization of Islam. From the ninth century Turks entered the service of the Caliphate in increasing numbers, and soon came to provide the bulk of its armies, its generals and, eventually, its rulers.

From the 10th century whole tribes of Turks began to migrate into Persia and Iraq, and in the 11th century, under the leadership of the family of Seljuq, the Turks were able to set up a great empire comprising most of the eastern lands of the Caliphate. The Muslim armies on the Byzantine frontier had long been predominantly Turkish, and in the course of the 11th century they began a great movement into Anatolia which resulted in the termination of Byzantine rule in most of the country and its incorporation in the Muslim Seljuq Sultanate. A Seljuq prince, Süleyman ibn Kutlumush, was sent to organize the new province, and by the end of the 12th century his successors had built up a strong Turkish monarchy in Anatolia, with its capital in Konya (the ancient Iconium). Under the rule of the Anatolian Seljuqs, which in various forms lasted until the 14th century, Anatolia gradually became a Turkish land. Masses of Turkish immigrants from further east entered the country, and a Turkish, Muslim civilization replaced Greek Christianity.

In the late 13th century the Sultanate of Konya fell into decay, and gradually gave way to a number of smaller principalities. One of these, in north-western Anatolia, was ruled by a certain Osman, or Othman, from whom the name Ottoman is derived. The Ottoman state soon embarked on a great movement of expansion, on the one hand in Anatolia, at the expense of its Turkish neighbours, on the other in the Balkans. Ottoman armies first crossed to Europe in the mid-14th century, and by 1400 they were masters of much of the Balkan peninsula as well as almost all of Anatolia. The capital was moved first from Bursa to Edirne and then, in 1453, to Constantinople, the final conquest of which from the last Byzantine emperor completed the process that had transformed a principality of frontier-warriors into a new great empire. Constantinople, called İstanbul by the Turks, remained the capital of the Ottoman Empire until 1922. The wave of conquest was by no means spent. For more than a century Ottoman arms continued to advance into Central Europe, while in 1516–17 Sultan Selim I destroyed the Mamluk Sultanate and incorporated Syria and Egypt into the Empire. During the reign of Sultan Süleyman I (1520–66), called the Magnificent in Europe, the Ottoman Empire was at the height of its power. In three continents the Sultan held unchallenged sway over vast territories. A skilled and highly-organized bureaucracy secured for the peoples of the Empire peace, justice and prosperity; literature, scholarship and the arts flourished; and the Ottoman armies and fleets seemed to threaten the very existence of Western Christendom.

The decay of the Empire is usually dated from after the death of Süleyman. In the West great changes were taking place. The Renaissance and the Reformation, the rapid development of science and technology, the emergence of strong, centralized nation states with constantly improving military techniques, the deflection of the main routes of international trade from the Mediterranean to the open seas, all combined to strengthen Turkey's Western adversaries while leaving her own resources unchanged or even diminished, and helped to relegate her into a backwater of cultural and economic stagnation. An imposing military façade for a while masked the internal decay that was rotting the Empire, but by the end of the 17th century the weakness of the Ottoman state was manifest. Then began the struggle of the powers for pickings of Turkish territory and for positions of influence in the Empire. During the 18th century it was Austria and Russia that made the main territorial advances in the Balkans and in the Black Sea area, while Britain and France were content with commercial and diplomatic privileges. In a succession of wars one province after another was lost, while internal conditions went from bad to worse. During the 19th century Britain and France began to play a more active role. British policy was generally to support the Turks against their impatient heirs. In 1854 Britain and France went to war at the side of Turkey in order to check Russian ambitions and in 1877–78 British diplomatic intervention was effective to the same end. Meanwhile the ferment of nationalist ideas had spread from the West to the subject peoples of the Empire, and one by one the Serbs, Greeks, Romanians and Bulgarians succeeded in throwing off Ottoman rule and attaining independent statehood.

The first stirrings of a new spirit among the Turks themselves, and the first serious attempts at reform, occurred during the reign of Selim III (1789–1807), and during the 19th century a series of reforming sultans and ministers worked on a programme of reform and modernization which, though it fell short of its avowed objectives, nevertheless transformed the face of the Ottoman Empire and began a process of change, the effects of which are still visible. In 1878 the reforming movement came to an abrupt end, and from that year until 1908 the Empire was subjected to the iron despotism of Abd al-Hamid II, who ruthlessly repressed every attempt at liberal thought and reform. In 1908 the secret opposition group known as the Young Turks seized power, and in a wave of revolutionary enthusiasm inaugurated a constitution, parliamentary government, and a whole series of liberal reforms. Unfortunately the Young Turks had little opportunity to follow up their promising start. First internal dissension, then foreign wars, combined to turn the Young Turk regime into a military dictatorship. In 1911 the Italians suddenly started a war against Turkey which ended with their gaining Libya and the Dodecanese Islands; in 1912–13 a Balkan alliance succeeded in wresting from the Empire most of its remaining possessions on the continent of Europe. Finally, in October 1914, Turkey entered the war on the side of the Central powers. During the reign of Abd al-Hamid German influence had been steadily increasing in Turkey, and the process continued under the Young Turks. It was certainly helped by the growing friendship between the Western powers and Russia, which threw the Turks into the arms of the only power that seemed ready to support them against Russian designs. German officers reorganized the Turkish army; German businessmen and technicians extended their hold on the economic resources of the country, and German engineers and financiers began the construction of the famous Baghdad railway which was to provide direct rail communication between Germany and the Middle East.

The Turkish alliance was of immense military value to the Central powers. The Turkish armies, still established in Syria and Palestine, were able to offer an immediate and serious threat to the Suez Canal and to the British position in Egypt. By their dogged and successful defence of the Dardanelles they prevented effective co-operation between Russia and the Western powers. Their position as the greatest independent Muslim state and their prestige among Muslims elsewhere created a series of problems in the British and French Empires.

Despite their weakness and exhaustion after two previous wars, the Turks were able to wage a bitter defensive war against the Allies. At last, after two unsuccessful attempts, one on the Dardanelles and the other in Mesopotamia, a new British attack from Egypt and from India succeeded in expelling the Turks from Palestine, Syria, and most of Iraq. Defeated on all sides, cut off from their allies by the Salonika expedition, the Turks decided to abandon the struggle, and signed an armistice at Mudros on 30 October 1918. French, Italian and British occupation forces moved into Turkey.

For some time the victorious powers were too busy elsewhere to attend to the affairs of Turkey, and it was not until the San Remo Conference of April 1920 that the first serious attempt was made to settle the Turkish question. Meanwhile the victors were busy quarrelling among themselves. Partly, no doubt, with the idea of forestalling Italian ambitions, the British, French, and American Governments agreed to a Greek proposal for a Greek occupation of İzmir (Smyrna) and the surrounding country, and on 15 May 1919 a Greek army, under cover of Allied warships, landed there. The integrity of this move later became a cause for concern within the Allied camp, and in October 1919 the Inter-Allied Commission in İstanbul condemned it as 'unjustifiable' and as 'a violation of the terms of the Armistice'. The consequences of the invasion for Turkey were momentous. Now, it was no longer the non-Turkish subject provinces and the Ottoman superstructure of the Turkish nation that were threatened, but the Turkish homeland itself. Moreover, the Greeks, unlike the Western Allies, showed that they intended to stay, and that they were aiming at nothing less than the incorporation of the territories they occupied into the Greek kingdom. The Turkish reaction to this danger was vigorous and immediate. The Nationalist movement, hitherto limited to a small class of intellectuals, became the mass instrument of Turkish determination to preserve the integrity and independence of the homeland. A new leader appeared to organize their victory.

THE RISE OF ATATÜRK

Mustafa Kemal, later surnamed Atatürk, was born in Salonika, then an Ottoman city, in 1880. After a promising career as a regular army officer, he achieved his first active command in Libya in 1911, and thereafter fought with distinction in the successive wars in which his country was involved. After his brilliant conduct of the defence of Gallipoli, he fought on various fronts against the Allies, and at the time of the Armistice held a command on the Syrian front. A month later he returned to İstanbul, and at once began to seek ways and means of getting to Anatolia to organize national resistance. At length he was successful, and on 19 May 1919—four days after the Greek landing in İzmir—he arrived at Samsun, on the Black Sea coast, ostensibly in order to supervise the disbanding of the remaining Turkish forces. Instead he set to work at once on the double task of organizing a national movement and raising a national army.

Meanwhile the Allied powers were at last completing their arrangements for the obsequies of the Turkish Empire, which had long been known as 'the Sick Man of Europe'. After a series of conferences, a treaty was drawn up and signed by the Allied representatives and those of the Sultan's Government at Sèvres, on 10 August 1920. The Treaty of Sèvres was very harsh—far harsher than that imposed on Germany. The Arab provinces were to be placed under British and French Mandates, to prepare them for eventual independence. In Anatolia, Armenian and Kurdish states were to be set up in the east, the south was to be divided between France and Italy, and a truncated Turkish Sultanate confined to the interior. The Straits were to be demilitarized and placed under Allied administration, with a Turkish İstanbul surrounded by Allied forces. The rest of European Turkey was to be ceded to Greece, while the İzmir district was to be under 'Ottoman sovereignty and Greek administration'.

This treaty was, however, never implemented. While the Allies were imposing their terms on the Sultan and his Government in İstanbul, a new Turkish state was rising in the interior of Anatolia, based on the rejection of the treaty and the principles on which it was founded. On 23 July 1919, Mustafa Kemal and his associates convened the first Nationalist congress in Erzurum, and drew up a national programme. A second congress was held in September in the same year, and attended by delegates from all over the country. An Executive Committee, presided over by Mustafa Kemal, was formed, and chose Ankara, then a minor provincial town, as its headquarters. Frequent meetings were held in Ankara, which soon became the effective capital of the Nationalist movement and forces. It was there that they issued the famous National Pact, the declaration that laid down the basic programme of the Kemalist movement, renouncing the Empire and the domination of the non-Turkish provinces, but demanding the total and unconditional independence of all areas inhabited by Turks. This declaration won immediate support, and on 28 January 1920 was approved even by the legal Ottoman Parliament sitting in İstanbul. The growth of the Nationalist movement in İstanbul alarmed the Allies, and on 16 March British forces entered the Turkish part of the city and arrested and deported many Nationalist leaders. Despite this setback, followed by a new anti-Nationalist campaign on the part of the Sultan and his political and religious advisers, the Kemalists continued to advance. On 19 March 1920 Mustafa Kemal ordered general elections, and at the end of April a National Assembly of 350 deputies met in Ankara and voted the National Pact. The Sultan and his Government were declared deposed, a provisional constitution promulgated, and a government set up with Mustafa Kemal as President.

There remained the military task of expelling the invaders. The Greco-Turkish war falls into three stages, covering roughly the campaigns of 1920, 1921 and 1922. In the first campaign the Nationalists, hopelessly outmatched in numbers and material, were badly defeated, and the Greeks advanced far into Anatolia. Turkish resistance was, however, strong enough to impress the Allies, who, for the first time, accorded a certain limited recognition to the Nationalist Government and proclaimed their neutrality in the Greco-Turkish war. The second campaign began with Greek successes, but the Turks rallied and defeated the invaders first at İnönü—from which İsmet Pasha, who commanded the Turkish forces there, later took his surname—and then, on 24 August 1921, in a major battle on the Sakarya River, where the Turkish forces were under the personal command of Mustafa Kemal. This victory considerably strengthened the Nationalists, who were now generally realized to be the effective Government of Turkey. The French and Italians withdrew from the areas of Anatolia assigned to them, and made terms with the new Government. The Soviets, now established on Turkey's eastern frontier, had already done so at the beginning of the year.

A period of waiting and reorganization followed, during which the morale of the Greek armies was adversely affected by political changes in Greece. In August 1922 the third and final phase of the war of independence began. The Turkish Army drove the Greeks back to the Aegean, and on 9 September reoccupied İzmir. Mustafa Kemal now prepared to cross to Thrace. To do so he had to cross the Straits, still under Allied occupation. The French and Italian contingents withdrew, and, after a menacing pause, the British followed. On 11 October an armistice was signed at Mudanya, whereby the Allied Governments agreed to the restoration of Turkish sovereignty in Eastern Thrace. In November the Sultan's Cabinet resigned, and the Sultan himself went into exile. Turkey once more had only one Government, and İstanbul, the ancient seat of empire, became a provincial city, ruled by a governor appointed from Ankara.

The peace conference opened in November 1922. After many months of argument the treaty was finally signed on 24 July 1923. It recognized complete and undivided Turkish sovereignty and the abolition of the last vestiges of foreign privilege. The only reservation related to the demilitarization of the Straits, which were not to be fortified without the consent of the powers. This consent was given at the Montreux Conference in 1936.

THE TURKISH REPUBLIC

The military task was completed, and the demands formulated in the National Pact had been embodied in an international treaty. There remained the greater task of rebuilding the ruins of long years of war and revolution—and of remedying those elements of weakness in the Turkish state and society that had brought Turkey to the verge of extinction. Mustafa Kemal saw the solution of Turkey's problems in a process of Westernization—in the integration of Turkey, on a basis of equality, in the modern Western world. To do this it was not sufficient to borrow, as other reformers had done, the outward forms and trappings of Western civilization. It was necessary to change the very basis of society in Turkey, and to suppress, ruthlessly if need be, the opposition that was bound to come from the entrenched forces of the old order. Between 1922 and 1938, the year of his death, Kemal carried through a series of far-reaching reforms in Turkey.

The first changes were political. After the deposition of Sultan Vahdeddin in November 1922, a brief experiment was made with a purely religious sovereignty, and Abd al-Mejid was proclaimed as Caliph but not Sultan. The experiment was not successful. Abd al-Mejid followed his predecessor into exile, and on 29 October 1923, Turkey was declared a Republic, with Kemal as President. The regime of Kemal Atatürk was effectively a dictatorship—though without the violence and oppression normally associated with that word in Europe. A single party—the Cumhuriyet Halk Partisi (CHP) (Republican People's Party)—formed the main instrument for the enforcement of government policy. The Constitution of 20 April 1924 provided for an elected Parliament which was the repository of sovereign power. Executive power was to be exercised by the President and a cabinet chosen by him.

The next object of attack was the religious hierarchy already weakened by the removal of the Sultan-Caliph. In a series of edicts the Ministry of Religious Affairs was abolished, the religious orders disbanded, religious property sequestrated, religious instruction forbidden. With the religious leaders in retreat, the attack on the old social order began. Certainly the most striking reforms were the abolition of the fez and the Arabic alphabet, and their replacement by the hat and the Latin alphabet. But these were probably less important in the long run than the abrogation of the old legal system and the introduction of new civil and criminal codes of law adapted from Europe. In 1928 Islam itself was disestablished, and the Constitution amended to make Turkey a secular state.

Not the least of the problems that faced Mustafa Kemal was the economic one. Turkey needed capital. Rather than risk the independence of Turkey by inviting foreign capital in at a time of weakness, Kemal adopted the principle of *étatisme*, and made it one of the cardinal doctrines of his regime. From 1923 to 1933 the State made its main effort in railway construction, nearly doubling the length of line in that period. At the same time a start was made in establishing other industries. While often wasteful and inefficient, State-sponsored industry was probably the only form of development possible at the time without recourse to foreign aid. The progress achieved stood Turkey in good stead in the critical years that were to follow.

The foreign policy of the Republic was for long one of strict non-involvement in foreign disputes, and the maintenance of friendly relations with as many powers as possible. In 1935–36, however, Turkey co-operated loyally in sanctions against Italy, and thereafter the growing threat of German, and more especially Italian, aggression led to closer links with the West. In 1938 steps were taken to strengthen economic links between Turkey and the United Kingdom. A British credit of £16m. was granted to Turkey, and a number of contracts given to British firms by Turkey.

The establishment of the Republic also put an end to the prospect of Kurdish independence offered by the Treaty of Sèvres. The Kurds were opposed to Atatürk's secularist and nationalist policies and in 1925 rose up in revolt after the abolition of the Caliphate. They were ruthlessly crushed. A more nationalist uprising in 1930 and a further revolt against the repressive actions taken by the Government were also suppressed. The Kurdish provinces remained rigorously policed, garrisons were established in larger towns and Kurdish leaders were exiled. The Kurdish language was made illegal and the Government refused to recognize any aspect of the Kurds' separate ethnic identity, calling them 'mountain Turks'.

The death of Kemal Atatürk in November 1938 was a great shock to Turkey. He was succeeded as President by İsmet İnönü, who announced his intention of maintaining and carrying on the work of his predecessor. The new President was soon called upon to guide his country through a very difficult time. As early as 12 May 1939 a joint Anglo-Turkish declaration was issued, stating that 'the British and Turkish Governments, in the event of an act of aggression leading to war in the Mediterranean area, would co-operate effectively and lend each other all the aid and assistance in their power'. This prepared the way for the formal Anglo-French-Turkish Treaty of Alliance signed 19 October 1939. It had been hoped that this Treaty would be complemented by a parallel treaty with the USSR, but the equivocal attitude of the Soviet Government, followed by the Stalin-Hitler Agreement of August 1939, made this impossible, and the Turks proceeded with the Western alliance in the face of clearly expressed Soviet disapproval. They protected themselves, however, by Protocol II of the treaty, stipulating that nothing in the treaty should bind them to any action likely to involve them in war with the USSR.

TURKEY DURING THE SECOND WORLD WAR

The fall of France, the hostile attitude of the Soviet Government, and the extension of German power over most of Europe, led the Turkish Government to the conclusion that nothing would be gained by provoking an almost certain German conquest. While continuing to recognize the Alliance, therefore, they invoked Protocol II as a reason for remaining neutral, and in June 1941, when German expansion in the Balkans had brought the German armies within 100 miles of İstanbul, the Turks further protected themselves by signing a friendship and trade agreement with Germany, in which, however, they stipulated that Turkey would maintain her treaty obligations to Britain.

The German attack on the USSR, and the consequent entry of that country into the Grand Alliance, brought an important change to the situation, and the Western powers increased their pressure on Turkey to enter the war. The main consideration holding Turkey back from active participation in the war was mistrust of the USSR, and the widespread feeling that Nazi conquest and Soviet 'liberation' were equally to be feared. While stopping short of actual belligerency, however, the Turks, especially after 1942, entered into closer economic and military relations with the West and aided the Allied cause in a number of ways. In August 1944 they broke off diplomatic relations with Germany, and on 23 February 1945 declared war on Germany in order to comply with the formalities of entry to the United Nations (UN) Conference in San Francisco.

The war years subjected Turkey to severe economic strains. These, and the dangers of armed neutrality in a world at war, resulted in the imposition of martial law, of closer police surveillance, and of a generally more authoritarian form of government. And then, between 1945 and 1950, came a further

series of changes, no less remarkable than the great reforms of Atatürk. When the Charter of the UN was introduced for ratification in the Turkish Parliament in 1945, a group of members, led by Celâl Bayar, Adnan Menderes, Fuad Köprülü and Refik Koraltan, tabled a motion suggesting a series of reforms in the law and the Constitution which would effectively ensure inside Turkey those liberties to which the Turkish Government was giving its theoretical approval in the Charter. The motion was rejected by the Government, and its sponsors were forced to leave the party. In November 1945, however, under pressure of a by now active and informed public opinion, President İnönü announced the end of the single-party system, and in January 1946 the opposition leaders registered the new Democratic Party.

TURKEY UNDER THE DEMOCRATIC PARTY

In July 1946 new elections gave the Democrat opposition 70 out of 416 seats and there can be little doubt that completely free elections would have given them many more. During the years that followed, the breach in the dictatorship grew ever wider, and a series of changes in both law and practice ensured the growth of democratic liberties. Freedom of the press and of association were extended, martial law was ended, and on 15 February 1950 a new electoral law was approved, guaranteeing free and fair elections. In May 1950 a new general election was held, in which the Democrats won an overwhelming victory. Celâl Bayar became President, and a new Cabinet was formed, with Adnan Menderes as Prime Minister and Fuad Köprülü as Foreign Minister. The new regime adopted a more liberal economic policy, involving the partial abandonment of *étatisme* and the encouragement of private enterprise, both Turkish and foreign. For a while, the stability and progress of the Republic seemed to be threatened by the growing activities of groups of religious fanatics, whose programme appeared to require little less than the abrogation of all the reforms achieved by the Turkish revolution. After the attempt on the life of the liberal journalist Ahmet Emin Yalman in November 1952, the Government took more vigorous action against what were called the 'forces of clericalism and reaction'. Many arrests were made, and in the summer of 1953 the National Party, accused of complicity in reactionary plots, was for a time outlawed and legislation was passed prohibiting the exploitation of religion for political purposes. The relations between the two main parties, after a temporary improvement in the face of the common danger of reaction, deteriorated again in the course of 1953–54, though not to such an extent as to imperil national unity. On 2 May 1954, in Turkey's third general election since the war, the Democrats won a resounding victory.

In view of the smallness and weakness of the opposition parties, and the immense parliamentary majority of the Democratic Party, it was inevitable that sooner or later splits would appear within it. In October 1955 a serious crisis culminated in the dismissal or resignation from the party of 19 deputies. These were later joined by some others and formed a new party, the Freedom Party.

Meanwhile, in September 1955, severe anti-Greek outbreaks led to the imposition of martial law in İstanbul, İzmir and Ankara, the dismissal of several senior officers and several Cabinet changes. A new Cabinet, the fourth since the Democrat victory in 1950, was presented to the Assembly on 9 December.

Conflict between the Government and opposition was sharpened by the decision taken to advance the date of the general elections by more than eight months, to 27 October 1957. The three opposition parties—Republicans, Freedom and National Parties—first intended to present a united front, but the electoral law was changed to make this impossible. They were therefore obliged to present separate lists in each constituency, and so, although the combined votes won by opposition candidates were slightly more than 50% of the total, the Democrats again emerged triumphant, though with a diminished majority.

In the new Assembly the themes of debate continued to centre on the economic condition of the country and what the opposition considered inroads on liberty. A bill was passed in December 1957 amending the rules of the Assembly, and laying down a new scale of penalties for their infraction. At the same time a proposal to channel all newspaper advertisements through a single organization was interpreted as another device for ensuring government control over the press. There is no doubt that its running fight with the press contributed much to the downfall of the Menderes regime. The new regime, while not immediately sweeping away the old bans, encouraged newspaper owners and editors to draw up a 'code of self-control'.

FOREIGN AFFAIRS 1945–60

In foreign affairs, both the CHP and the Democrat Governments followed a firm policy of unreserved identification with the West in the Cold War. From May 1947 the USA extended economic and military aid to Turkey on an increasing scale, and in 1950 a first indication of both the seriousness and the effectiveness of Turkish policy was given with the dispatch of Turkish troops to Korea, where they fought with distinction. In August 1949 Turkey became a member of the Council of Europe, and early in 1952 acceded to full membership of the North Atlantic Treaty Organization, in which it began to play an increasingly important part. Thereafter other arrangements were made by which Turkey accepted a role in both Balkan and Middle Eastern defence. This culminated in November 1955 in Turkey's joining the Baghdad Pact, in which the country thereafter played a major role.

In January 1957 the President of the USA announced a new programme of economic and military assistance for those countries of the area which were willing to accept it. At a further meeting held in Ankara the Muslim states belonging to the Baghdad Pact expressed their approval of this 'Eisenhower Doctrine'. The USA in March 1957 made known its decision to join the military committee of the Baghdad Pact, and later in March Turkey promised to co-operate with the USA against all subversive activities in the Middle East. It was announced that financial aid would be forthcoming from Washington for the economic projects previously discussed between the members of the Baghdad Pact.

From 1958 Turkey was actively involved in settling terms for the constitution of an independent Cyprus. These were eventually agreed between Turkey, Greece, the UK and the Greek and Turkish Cypriots. Cyprus achieved independence in August 1960.

Fidelity to NATO and the Central Treaty Organization (CENTO) remained the basis of Turkey's foreign policy during the late 1950s. By the beginning of 1960, however, Turkey's relations with the USSR were becoming less frigid.

THE 1960 REVOLUTION

Economic difficulties continued to be one of the main preoccupations of the Turkish Government. The development plans envisaged since 1950 had been carried forward with financial aid from the USA and from such bodies as the World Bank. These policies had been accompanied by inflationary pressures, an unfavourable trade balance, decreased imports, a shortage of foreign exchange and, since the agricultural population was in receipt of subsidies from the Government, a higher demand for consumer goods which aggravated the prevalent inflation. Social and economic unease tended to reveal itself in a drift of people from the villages to the towns, the population of centres like Ankara, İstanbul, İzmir, Bursa and Adana being considerably increased during recent decades.

The influences which now led to a revolution had long been at work. Hostility between the Democrats in power and the CHP in opposition grew steadily more marked, and was sharpened towards the end of 1959 by suspicions that the Democrats were planning to hold fresh elections in the near future ahead of time. It was feared that these would, if necessary, be rigged to keep the Democrats in power indefinitely.

In May 1959, political tension between the two main parties had already broken into violence during a political tour of Anatolia conducted by the opposition leader İsmet İnönü. The Government banned all political meetings. Blows were struck in the Grand National Assembly, and the opposition walked out.

Much the same pattern of events ushered in the final breakdown a year later. At the beginning of April 1960, İsmet İnönü

undertook another political tour of Anatolia. At one point troops were called on to block his progress. The opposition tried, but failed, to force a debate in the Assembly. On their side the Democrats set up a commission of enquiry, composed entirely of their own supporters, to investigate 'the destructive and illegal activities of the CHP'. Again the Grand National Assembly was the scene of violence, and all political activity was suspended for three months.

At the end of April, student unrest led to the imposition of martial law. As administrator of martial law, the Turkish army found itself, contrary to its traditions, involved in politics. A group of officers decided that their intervention must be complete if Turkey was to return to Kemalist principles. In the early hours of 27 May they struck. President Bayar, Prime Minister Menderes, most Democratic deputies and a number of officials and senior officers were arrested. The Government was replaced by a Committee of National Unity headed by Gen. Cemal Gürsel, a much respected senior officer who had fought with Atatürk at Gallipoli.

The coup was immediately successful and almost bloodless. The accusation against the Menderes regime was that it had broken the Constitution and was moving towards dictatorship. The officers insisted that they were temporary custodians of authority and would hand over to the duly constituted civilian authorities. A temporary Constitution was quickly agreed, pending the drafting of a final new one. During this interval legislative power was vested in the Committee of National Unity, and executive power in a Council of Ministers, composed of civilians as well as soldiers. On 25 August, however, 10 of the 18 ministers were dismissed, leaving only three civilians in the Government. Gen. Gürsel was President of the Republic, Prime Minister and Minister of Defence. The courts were declared independent. Commissions were set up to inquire into the alleged misdeeds of the Menderes regime.

Although the new regime did not fail to meet political opposition, particularly among the peasants and around İzmir, a stronghold of Menderes, the main problems facing it were economic. The former regime had been heavily in debt. Austerity measures, including restrictions on credit, had to be put into operation and an economic planning board was set up to work out a long-term investment plan with the aid of foreign experts.

THE COMMITTEE OF NATIONAL UNITY

The Committee of National Unity, which originally consisted of 37 members, was reduced to 23 on 13 November 1960. The 14 officers dismissed represented a group led by Col Alparslan Turkeş, who had been pressing for the army to retain its postrevolutionary powers and to introduce radical social reforms.

This purge completed, preparations for a return to political democracy continued. A new Assembly, to act as a temporary parliament, was convened at the beginning of January 1961. It consisted of the National Unity Committee of 23, acting jointly with a House of Representatives of 271 members, both elected and nominated. In this the CHP predominated. At the same time party politics were again legalized and a number of new parties emerged. Some of them proved short-lived, but one, the Adalet Partisi (AP) (Justice Party), founded by Gen. Ragip Gümüşpala, who had been Commander of the Third Army at the time of the *coup d'état*, attracted the support of many former adherents of the Democratic Party, which had been declared illegal.

A special committee of the Assembly framed a new Constitution which had some significant changes from the 1924 version. It provided for a court to determine the constitutionality of laws, for a bicameral legislature, and it included a reference to 'social justice' as one of the aims of the State.

THE YASSIADA TRIALS

These constitutional developments took place against the background of the trial of the accused members of the Menderes regime. The trial was held on the little island of Yassiada in the Bosphorus, where the accused had been confined after arrest, and lasted from October 1960 to August 1961. The sentence of the court was pronounced on 15 September. There were 15 death sentences, 12 of which, including that on Bayar, were commuted to life imprisonment. Adnan Menderes, Fatin

Zorlu, the former Foreign Minister, and Hasan Polatkan, the former Minister of Finance, were duly hanged. In September 1990, following a prolonged campaign by right-wing factions (including the ruling Anavatan Partisi: (ANAP)—Motherland Party), the bodies were exhumed and buried in İstanbul with state honours.

The trial, in 1960, inevitably absorbed the attention of the country, and there were many reminders that sympathy for the former regime and its leaders was far from dead. The most serious setback for the authorities, however, appeared in the results of the referendum on the new Constitution. This was approved by 6,348,191 votes against 3,934,370, and the large minority was taken as an indication of continuing loyalty to the Democrats.

The campaign preceding elections in October 1961, perhaps because Yassiada was ruled out as a subject for discussion, proved unexpectedly quiet. On 15 October the elections gave the CHP 173 seats and the AP 158 seats in the National Assembly, and 36 and 70 respectively in the Senate.

These figures were a blow to the hopes of the CHP that they would achieve an overall working majority. A coalition became necessary. The election results were also further evidence of latent support for the Democrats.

THE NEW GOVERNMENT

On 25 October 1961, Parliament opened and the transfer of power from military to civilians was made. The revolutionaries had kept their word and a new epoch began. The next day Gen. Gürsel, the only candidate, was elected President. But forming a government proved a much harder process. On 10 November İsmet İnönü, leader of the CHP, was asked to form a government, and after much hesitation and strong pressure from the army, the AP agreed to join forces with its rival. A new Cabinet was formed with İnönü as Prime Minister, Akıf İyidoğan, of the AP, as Deputy Prime Minister, and ten more ministers from each of the two coalition parties.

The Government remained, as İnönü said, exposed to a double fire—from those who thought the army did too much (i.e. that civil liberties were still circumscribed) and those who thought it did too little (i.e. that it did not crush all signs of counter-revolution). The resignation of İnönü at the end of May weakened the extremists in the AP, who had wanted to grant an amnesty to former supporters of Menderes. They were now face to face with the army, the original movers of the 1960 revolution, and many of them felt it wise to moderate their demands.

By the end of June İnönü had formed a new coalition Government composed of 12 ministers from the CHP, six from the New Turkey Party, four from the Republican Peasants' Nation Party, and one independent minister.

The new Government's programme expressed attachment to the principles of Western democracy and to the NATO alliance. It covered almost every sphere of the national life, including education, taxation, employment and the problems of a rapidly rising birth-rate and an adverse balance of trade.

POLITICAL UNREST

The political climate during 1963 remained unsettled. In February the leading radical of the original Committee of National Unity, Col Türkeş, who had been in unofficial exile abroad, returned with plans to set up a new political organization. More immediately threatening to the regime were the enthusiastic crowds which greeted the temporary release of the former President, Celâl Bayar, from the prison in Kayseri where he had been since his sentence. The reception appeared as a direct challenge to the revolution and was countered by violent protests, in which students and members of the armed forces participated, denouncing Bayar and his supposed supporters in the AP.

In the early hours of 21 May 1963, Ankara was the scene of yet another abortive *coup d'état*. The coup was quickly suppressed, but martial law was repeatedly prolonged in Ankara, İstanbul and İzmir.

Although the Bayar incident and coup attempt produced divisions inside the ranks of the AP, it showed considerable successes at the local elections in November, the first to be held since 1954. These successes were mainly at the expense

of the New Turkey Party and the Republican Peasants' Nation Party, İnönü's two junior partners in the coalition. They resigned from the Government, and after Gen. Gümüşpala, the leader of the AP, had tried and failed to form a ministry, the President called again on İnönü, who on 23 December formed a minority government drawn from members of his own CHP and some independents. It received a vote of confidence in the Assembly.

The first months of 1964 were overshadowed by an attempt on the life of İnönü in February, and by the situation in Cyprus, where the fate of the Turkish minority created strong feeling on the mainland. İnönü's critics claimed that he had displayed a considerable lack of foresight by failing to intervene on the island with force when the trouble started.

RAPPROCHEMENT WITH THE USSR

This, and other diplomatic efforts towards a solution, failed, and public disaffection grew, not only with Greece, but also with Turkey's western allies, in particular the USA and the UK, who were accused of being lukewarm in their support of Turkey's case. In August this disaffection exploded in İzmir, when rioters wrecked the US and British pavilions at the trade fair. İnönü, though moving with characteristic caution, gave a warning that the alliance with the West, the basis of Turkey's foreign policy since the war, was in danger. To reinforce his warning, several steps were taken to improve relations with the USSR. Initially, the Soviet Government had appeared to side with Greece on the question of Cyprus, and the Soviet trade pavilion had also been a target for the İzmir hooligans. Diplomatic approaches were made in both Moscow and Ankara, however, and at the end of October 1964 Erkin visited the USSR—the first Turkish Foreign Minister to make this journey for 25 years. Before leaving he invoked the memory of the early days of friendship between Atatürk and Lenin, and the same precedent was made much of by his hosts, who tactfully refrained from pressing Turkey into premature neutralism, as they had done in the past. On Cyprus, the USSR appeared to have moved closer to the Turkish point of view, the communiqué which ended Erkin's talks speaking favourably of a solution 'by peaceful means on the basis of respect for the territorial integrity of Cyprus, and for the legal rights of the two national communities'. Erkin's journey was followed up in January 1965 by the visit to Ankara of a Soviet parliamentary delegation. A trade pact between the two countries followed in March.

FALL OF İNÖNÜ

For all this, Cyprus continued to give the opposition ammunition with which to harass the İnönü Government. At the Senate elections in June 1964, the AP won 31 out of the 51 seats contested, thus increasing its already large majority in this house. Its success was clouded by the death of the party's leader, Gen. Gümüşpala. In November Süleyman Demirel, a trained engineer and a former Director-General of the State Water Organization, was elected leader in his place, though he was without a seat in Parliament. İnönü survived more than one narrow vote of confidence, but was finally defeated on 13 February 1965, during voting in the Assembly on the budget—the first time that the term of a Turkish Government had been ended in this way. After a short delay, a coalition Government was formed from the four opposition parties—the AP, the New Turkish Party, the Republican Peasants' Party, and the Millet Partisi (MP) (National Party). An independent senator and former diplomat, Suat Ürgüplü, became Prime Minister.

Turkey suffered a bitter blow when, in December, the General Assembly of the UN approved a resolution urging all states to refrain from intervention in Cyprus. This was widely interpreted as a measure designed to discourage Turkish aid for the Turkish minority there. The Government in Ankara denounced the resolution as being unjust, unlawful and in contravention of international agreements.

DEMIREL CABINET

At the general election of 11 October 1965, the AP under Süleyman Demirel won an overall majority. On introducing his AP Government to the Assembly, Demirel declared that the most important task would be to withstand communism 'by the realization of social justice and measures of social security'. Emphasis was to be put on industrialization. In spite of its working majority, the Demirel Government proved only marginally more successful than its predecessors in getting things done. However, elections in June 1966 for a third of the seats in the Senate showed that the AP was not losing popularity.

To some extent this success was attributed to the innate conservatism of the Turkish peasantry, who may have been alarmed by İnönü's statement that the CHP was left of centre. This position was not approved by all the party—some thought that it went too far, others not far enough. A convention of the party in October showed a victory for the left-wingers. Bülent Ecevit, Minister of Labour in 1961–65, was elected General Secretary of the party, with the declared intention of turning it into a party of democratic socialism. Six months later 48 senators and congressmen, led by Turhan Feyzioğlu, a former minister, resigned from the party on the grounds that it was falling into a 'dangerous leftist adventure'. This was denied by Ecevit and İnönü, who supported him. They claimed that, on the contrary, their progressive policies would pre-empt the policies of and undermine support for other left-wing parties and therefore represented the best barrier against communism.

In May 1967 a majority of dissidents came together to form the new Reliance Party, which proclaimed its opposition to socialism and its belief in the 'spiritual values of the Turkish nation'. In June Ecevit forced a fresh election of the CHP executive, and by securing the elimination of two left-wing representatives on it he was able to emphasize that his party remained left of centre rather than left wing.

In March 1968 a new electoral law was approved, in spite of the protests of a united opposition, that abolished the so-called 'national remainder system'—a change which threatened the electoral chances of all the smaller parties but was thought to be particularly aimed at the Türkiye İşçi Partisi (TIP) (Turkish Workers' Party), which was accused by the Government of using communist tactics.

In March 1966 President Gursel was succeeded by Senator Cevdet Sunay.

FOREIGN POLICY 1966–69

Turkey's relations with her allies in 1966 deteriorated. The Turkish press's campaign against US bases in Turkey led to a riot in Adana in March 1966. Together with these manifestations against Turkey's formerly most stalwart ally, an effort by the Demirel Government to make its whole foreign policy more flexible was undertaken. This flexibility was symbolized by many official visits, given and received, between Turkey on the one hand, and the UK, Romania, Bulgaria, Egypt, Yugoslavia and Morocco on the other. One outcome of the exchanges with Arab leaders was that at the time of the June war with Israel the Turkish Government expressed its sympathy with the Arab cause.

The touchstone of Turkey's foreign relations continued to be Cyprus. In 1967 this perennial problem oscillated between near settlement and near war. Later in the year the situation suddenly deteriorated as a result of attacks by Greek Cypriots on the Turkish enclaves on the island on 15 November. Two days later the National Assembly voted by 432 votes to 1 to authorize the Government to send troops to foreign countries—in other words, to fight in Cyprus. There were daily Turkish flights over the island and the likelihood of war increased. As a result of strong intervention by US and UN intermediaries, however, a more serious conflict was avoided. On 3 December the Greeks undertook to withdraw their troops from the island and the Turks to take the necessary measures to ease tension. By February 1968 the situation had been so far restored that direct efforts to agree on a negotiated settlement for Cyprus were once again under way.

MILITARY INTERVENTION

Süleyman Demirel's AP Government was faced with the growing problem of political violence from early 1968 onward. Disorders in the universities, springing from non-political edu-

cational grievances and from clashes between political extremists of the right and the left, took an increasingly violent form. Students staged anti-American riots, and in June 1969 troops had to be summoned to prevent extremists disrupting examinations. The fighting between right and left factions became more serious in 1970, firearms and petrol bombs being used, and a number of political murders taking place.

Parliamentary politics also became rather confused. Elections in October 1969 produced an enlarged majority for the AP, but the party soon split, a number of Demirel's right-wing opponents forming the Demokratik Parti (DP) (Democratic Party). Party strengths became almost impossible to calculate, as factions and alliances formed and dissolved, and on crucial votes the support of Government and the combined opposition parties was almost equally balanced. A new party, the Milli Nizam Partisi (MNP) (National Order Party), with right-wing policies and theocratic tendencies, was formed in January 1970 by Prof. Necmettin Erbakan.

Throughout 1970 and the early part of 1971, political and social unrest continued, with outbreaks of violence among students, in the trade unions and by Kurdish separatist groups. Factional bickering prevented the Government from taking effective action and on 12 March 1971, the Chief of the General Staff and the army, navy and air force commanders delivered a memorandum to the President. They accused the Government of allowing the country to slip into anarchy and of deviating from Atatürk's principles. They threatened that, unless 'a strong and credible government' were formed at once, the armed forces would take over the administration of the State. Later that day the Demirel Cabinet resigned.

MILITARY DOMINATION OF POLITICS

A new Government was formed by Dr Nihat Erim, with the support of both the AP and the CHP. Bülent Ecevit, the CHP Secretary-General, resigned from office and refused to collaborate. Dr Erim's programme promised sweeping reforms in taxation, land ownership, education, power and industry, but the Government's attention was first directed to the suppression of political violence. The military ultimatum was followed by further bombings, kidnappings and clashes between right and left-wing students and between students and police. On 28 April 1971, martial law was proclaimed, initially for one month, in 11 provinces, including Ankara and İstanbul.

Newspapers were suppressed, strikes were banned and large numbers of left-wing supporters were arrested. The MNP was dissolved in May 1971 and the Turkish Labour Party in July. The murder of the Israeli Consul-General in İstanbul by the Turkish People's Liberation Army provided the military authorities with an opportunity to round up nearly 1,000 suspects in İstanbul alone, including many journalists, writers and intellectuals. In September 1971, Dr Erim introduced a number of amendments to the Constitution, limiting individual civil rights and the autonomy of universities and radio and television stations as well as placing restrictions on the press and trade unions and giving the Government powers to legislate by decree. Dr Erim's proposal to use the new powers to introduce sweeping social and economic reforms, supported by the armed forces, was opposed by the AP. Cabinet crises in October and December 1971 led to the formation of a new coalition Cabinet, again headed by Dr Erim, but his proposals for taking further executive powers were opposed by the four major parliamentary parties, and in April 1972 he resigned. A Cabinet formed by Suat Ürgüplü was rejected by President Sunay, and in May a Government drawn from the AP, National Reliance Party and CHP, headed by Ferit Melen, was approved. There was a swing to the left within the CHP in May; the veteran party leader İsmet İnönü resigned after 34 years as Chairman, and was replaced by Bülent Ecevit. Meanwhile, the terrorist activities of the Turkish People's Liberation Army continued, and martial law was prolonged at two-month intervals.

In July 1972, dissident CHP members, opposing the dominance of the left wing led by Ecevit, formed the Republican Party. In November the CHP withdrew its support from the Melen coalition Government, but its five ministers preferred to leave the party and stay in the Cabinet. This caused further resignations from the CHP, including that of İsmet İnönü and 25 other deputies and senators. A number of these dissidents, together with the National Reliance Party and the Republican Party joined to form the Cumhuriyetci Güven Partisi (CGP) (Republican Reliance Party) in February 1973. The CHP, without its right wing, began actively to oppose the Melen Government, which it considered to be dominated by the armed forces, and martial law, under which, it was alleged with increasing frequency, arbitrary arrest and torture were practised. In March 1973, for the first time, the CHP voted against the prolongation of martial law, following a heated debate in which the Minister of the Interior disclosed that in two years of martial law 1,383 persons had been sentenced by military courts, 553 acquitted, and that 179 trials were then taking place and 2,991 were in preparation.

President Sunay's term of office expired in March 1973, and the Grand National Assembly began the process of electing a new President. Gen. Gürler resigned his post as Chief of Staff in order to stand for election, his candidature receiving the strong support of the armed forces. He was opposed by members of the Justice and Democratic parties while the CHP decided to abstain from voting as a protest against military interference in the election and the censorship of electoral news in Ankara. Despite obvious military support for Gen. Gürler, 14 ballots failed to produce a result, and eventually the AP, CHP and CGP agreed on a compromise candidate, Senator Fahri Korutürk, former Commander-in-Chief of the Navy, who had not belonged to any political party. He was elected President on 6 April 1973. The following day Melen resigned, and was succeeded as Prime Minister by Naim Talû, an independent senator, who formed a Cabinet with AP and CGP participation.

The Talû Government, although considered to be merely a caretaker administration to last until the general election, scheduled for October 1973, brought about a number of reforms, and during its term of office the armed forces gradually withdrew from political affairs. A Land Reform Law, distributing some 8m. acres to 500,000 peasants, was passed in June 1973, and measures were taken to prevent foreign domination of the mining and petroleum industries. A strong element within the armed forces felt that the time had come to return to a strictly military role, and that martial law had achieved its objective by duly eradicating extremism. Gen. Sancar, who became Chief of Staff when Gen. Gürler resigned to make his unsuccessful attempt to become President, was opposed to military intervention in politics, and retired 196 senior officers. Many close associates of Gen. Gürler were transferred to politically insignificant posts, and the retirement of Gen. Batur, the air force commander, removed the last of the officers who had signed the armed forces' memorandum of March 1971. Martial law was gradually lifted from the affected provinces, and came to an end in September 1973.

FOREIGN POLICY DEVELOPMENTS

The traditional hostility between Turkey and Greece revived following the Greek announcement in February 1974 that oil had been found in Greek territorial waters in the Aegean. This led to a dispute over the extent of national jurisdiction over the continental shelf and territorial waters, with both sides making warlike moves in Thrace and the Aegean area. Turkey began a hydrographical survey of the continental shelf in this area, claiming oil exploration rights in the eastern Aegean. The Aegean issue contributed to making a preoccupation with the possibility of a confrontation with Greece rather than the USSR the dominating issue of Turkish foreign policy during the late 1970s. The potentially tense situation in the Aegean was overshadowed by the coup in Cyprus in July.

This coup was carried out by the Cypriot National Guard, led by officers from Greece, apparently with the support of the Greek military regime. Declaring its intention of protecting the Turkish community in Cyprus and preventing the union of Cyprus with mainland Greece, the Turkish Government proclaimed a right to intervene as a guarantor state under the Zürich agreement of 1959. On 20 July Turkish troops landed in Cyprus, and rapidly won control of the area around Kyrenia on the northern coast. The Turkish intervention in Cyprus was followed by negotiations in Geneva between Turkey,

Greece and the UK. Turkey pressed for the creation of an independent federal Cypriot state, with population movements to give the Turkish community their own sector in the north. The intransigence of both Greeks and Turks, and Greece's rejection of a possible cantonal solution put forward by Turkey, led to a further successful advance by the Turkish forces in Cyprus. When a second cease-fire was called on 16 August, Turkey controlled about one-third of the total area of Cyprus.

The sector under Turkish control, all of Cyprus north of a line running from Morphou through Nicosia to Famagusta, contained more than half the livestock, citrus plantations and mineral reserves of Cyprus, with access to two major seaports. The flight of Greek Cypriot refugees from the north left the Turks a free hand to take over the administration and economy, and establish an effective partition of the island. Ecevit claimed that the Turkish military success had laid the foundation of a federal state with two autonomous administrations, allowing the Turkish Cypriot community to concentrate in the conquered area and establish their own government. On 13 February 1975, the Turkish Cypriots unilaterally declared a 'Turkish Federated State' in northern Cyprus and continued pressing for the establishment of a bi-regional federal state system in Cyprus. Greek and Turkish Foreign Ministers held talks in Rome in May 1975 on outstanding disputes between the two countries, with the future of Cyprus among the main topics. The Greek-Turkish Aegean dispute was also discussed, including the issue of who held the rights over oil exploration in the area, the equitable division of the Aegean continental shelf and the question of air space control in the area. The dispute was submitted to the International Court of Justice. In April 1978 Turkey refused to recognize the jurisdiction of the Court on this question, preferring to try to negotiate a political settlement, and in October the Court ruled that it was not competent to try the issue.

The USA imposed an embargo on military aid and the supply of arms to Turkey in February 1975 on the grounds that American military equipment had been used in the Turkish invasion of Cyprus in July 1974 and that Turkey had failed to make substantial progress towards resolving the Cyprus crisis. In July Turkey implemented counter-measures, including the take-over of US bases in Turkey. After lengthy negotiations a new bilateral defence agreement was reached between the two countries in March 1976, but the agreement was not ratified in 1976 or 1977 due to the strength of the Greek lobby in the US Congress.

In January 1978, at the beginning of his term of office, Bülent Ecevit stated that his foreign policy would be aimed at the exploration at the highest level of possible compromises between Greece and Turkey. A summit meeting took place at Montreux, Switzerland, on 9 March and the progress made in personal relations between Ecevit and the Greek Prime Minister, Constantine Karamanlis, contributed to a general lessening of tension in the Aegean.

In response to a US statement about the linkage of the arms embargo relaxation and US arms aid, Ecevit turned to the USSR to demonstrate that Turkey had alternatives for her national defence. In April 1978 a trade pact was agreed between the two countries and in June a friendship document was signed, which Ecevit claimed not to be in conflict with Turkey's NATO responsibilities. In response to this *rapprochement* with the USSR, the US Congress lifted the arms embargo in October and four key US bases in Turkey were reopened. Finally, after lengthy negotiations, a five-year defence and economic co-operation agreement was signed on 29 March 1980. In return for economic aid to help Turkey modernize her army and fulfil her NATO obligations, the US was to obtain access to over 25 military establishments, allowing expanded surveillance of the USSR. The eagerness of the USA to come to an agreement grew after the Soviet invasion of Afghanistan in December 1979, which increased Turkey's strategic importance.

Some progress was achieved in the Greek-Turkish Aegean dispute in February 1980. On 22 February Turkey revoked Notam 714 which claimed Turkish control of all air traffic over the eastern half of the Aegean. In response, Greece revoked its civil aviation notice of 1974 which declared the

Aegean unsafe and banned all flights except its own. However, the dispute flared up again in June when Turkey held its annual NATO Sea Wolf air and naval manoeuvres in the Aegean, with Greece demanding flight plans for areas which Turkey does not regard as being within Greek airspace. On 14 July Turkish Airlines resumed flights to Athens from İstanbul and Ankara.

Intercommunal talks on Cyprus, sponsored by the UN, were resumed in June 1979 but were adjourned after a week with no agreement reached. Since then little progress has been made, in spite of efforts to resume talks by the UN, and the issues appear as intractable as ever. Turkey continues to maintain an estimated 30,000 troops in Cyprus.

ECEVIT GOVERNMENT

General elections for the National Assembly and for 52 Senate seats were held on 14 October 1973. In the National Assembly the CHP, with 185 seats, replaced the AP as the largest party, but failed to win an overall majority. The CHP was believed to have won many votes from former supporters of the banned TIP, while the AP lost support to the DP and a new organization, the Milli Selamet Partisi (MSP) (National Salvation Party). The latter, led by Prof. Necmettin Erbakan, was founded in 1972 to replace his banned MNP, and shared its traditionalist, Islamic policies, and became the third largest party in the new National Assembly. Prime Minister Talû resigned, but then remained in office for a further three months while negotiations on the formation of a coalition government continued. Despite this parliamentary crisis, the armed forces remained aloof from politics. Eventually, on 25 January 1974, a Government was formed by the CHP and MSP, with Bülent Ecevit as Prime Minister and Necmettin Erbakan as his deputy. The Cabinet was composed of 18 CHP members and 7 from the MSP.

The new Government, an apparently unlikely coalition of the left-of-centre CHP and the reactionary MSP, proclaimed its reforming intentions, but made concessions to the demands of its Muslim supporters which tended to deviate from Atatürk's strictly secular principles. In March 1974, Turkey was for the first time represented at an Islamic Summit Conference. The appointment of an MSP deputy as Minister of the Interior brought about a number of petty manifestations of Islamic puritanism, but the main lines of the Ecevit Government's policy seemed to be of a reforming, liberal nature, intended to remove the more excessive aspects of the police state created during the period of military intervention. In May 1972, to mark the 50th anniversary of the founding of the Republic, the Government gave amnesty to 50,000 prisoners.

The land reform passed by the Talû administration came into operation in a pilot project in Urfa province, and in July the ban on opium production introduced under American pressure in 1972 was rescinded, a move which, together with the successful handling of the Cyprus question, increased Ecevit's popularity. The differences between the MSP and the CHP had been submerged during the Cyprus crisis, but once more became apparent in September. On 16 September 1974, Ecevit announced that he had decided to resign, as the coalition was no longer viable, and to seek a stronger mandate in new elections. New elections, however, were not held immediately and President Korutürk sought to find a coalition government.

Following the resignation of the Cabinet of Bülent Ecevit on 18 September 1974, Turkey remained for over six months without a parliamentarily approved government. Prof. Sadi Irmak attempted unsuccessfully to form an interim coalition in November to prepare for new elections in 1975, but remained in office in a caretaker capacity whilst efforts were made to form a new government. Internal unrest increased during the lengthy government crisis with serious clashes between opposing political factions and between students.

DEMIREL RETURNS TO POWER

In March 1975 Süleyman Demirel returned to power, leading a right-wing coalition, the Nationalist Front, consisting of four parties: Demirel's AP, the MSP, the CGP and the neo-fascist Milliyetçi Hareket Partisi (MHP) (National Action Party) founded by Col Alparslan Türkeş, who became a Deputy Prime

Minister. Of the Cabinet of 30 the AP occupied 16 of the seats, the MSP eight, the CGP four, and the MHP two. However, the precarious nature of this coalition meant that the Government had to avoid taking radical measures which would upset the co-operation between the four parties. This prevented Demirel's Cabinet from tackling the pressing problems of a deteriorating economy and increasing political violence, for Erbakan refused to countenance the austerity measures demanded by the IMF while Türkeş stood in the way of a crackdown on political violence, most of which the 'Grey Wolves' of the MHP were thought to have instigated. The weakness of the coalition also hampered progress towards a settlement of the Cyprus question, with Demirel having to make concessions to the militant views of the extreme right wing represented by Necmettin Erbakan's MSP. Between 1974 and 1977 the fortunes of the MSP changed drastically and their representation in the National Assembly was reduced from 48 to 24. Erbakan became increasingly discredited, although his deputy and chief rival, Korbut Özal, grew in influence. At the same time support for the MHP increased substantially. It combined anti-communism, Islamic values and a desire for centrally-directed free enterprise with a nationalism that would dispense with democracy. During Demirel's administration, the MHP was able to build up a system of militant cadres by placing its supporters in the police and civil service.

In spite of its difficulties, the Demirel Government continued in power in 1976 and 1977 by suspending all action over controversial issues, such as the economy, Cyprus and Greece and relations with the EC and NATO, pending the general election scheduled for October 1977. Increasing political violence throughout Turkey and especially in the universities, between left- and right-wing groups, persuaded the authorities to bring forward the general elections to June. The political inactivity was matched by economic paralysis as it became clear that the economy was overloaded with short-term debt and banks struggled to pay foreign currency bills of payment.

Amid this financial uncertainty the election of June 1977 failed to produce the hoped-for decisive majority. While the CHP increased its share of seats in the National Assembly to 213 out of 450, the AP also increased its share from 149 to 189 seats. Bülent Ecevit, the leader of the CHP, formed a Council of Ministers but failed to agree a coalition with the smaller parties, and a week later was defeated in a vote of confidence in the Grand National Assembly. Süleyman Demirel, the leader of the AP, was subsequently invited to form a new Government and on 1 August a coalition came to power which gave key ministerial posts to members of the MSP and the MHP. As a result there was penetration of the university and college administrations by extreme right-wing factions and a consequent flare-up of violence on campuses. By mid-December one-third of the universities were shut and 250 people had died in political violence.

The MSP contributed to the financial crisis by blocking attempts to follow IMF prescriptions for the economy, insisting on the maintenance of a 5.5% growth rate and refusing to implement monetarist curbs to reduce inflation. Failure to agree on economic remedies led to the withdrawal of an IMF team on 19 December 1977, without agreeing the necessary restructuring for the foreign debt position.

Frustration at the coalition's powerlessness led to the progressive diminution of the AP's support in the Assembly between October and December 1977 as members resigned. By 27 December the coalition could muster only 214 votes and Bülent Ecevit was preparing a new coalition. Following a vote of 'no confidence' in the Grand National Assembly, the Demirel Government resigned on 31 December and formed a caretaker administration. On 2 January 1978 Bülent Ecevit formed a new Government.

ECEVIT RETURNS TO POWER

After the chaos of Demirel's administration, the appointment of Ecevit as Prime Minister was greeted with great popular enthusiasm and high hopes were entertained of his promise to deal with the economic crisis and the political violence. In the economic field there was an urgent need to restore confidence by rescheduling Turkish debts, devaluing the lira and obtaining foreign finance for necessary arms modernization for NATO commitments. By appointing a former general, İrfan Özaydinli, to the interior ministry, and a former police chief and Interior Minister, Necdet Uğur, to the education ministry, Ecevit hoped to curb the political violence that had racked the universities. Ecevit's popular support, however, was not reflected in the National Assembly. His majority was dependent upon the support of defectors from the AP, to 10 of whom he gave places in the Cabinet, while the number of deputies who had 'crossed the floor' had resulted in a pool of about 20 independents with no set allegiances. Radical reforms were urged on Ecevit, but the insecure parliamentary majority, the country's economic weakness and the unwanted reputation of the CHP in the conservative rural areas as a radical party enjoined on him the necessity for caution. He began a painstaking, relentless purge of right-wing elements in the public administration in response to the cramming of their ministries by Demirel, Erbakan and Türkeş in 1975–77. He adopted an economic stabilization programme, signed a stand-by arrangement with the IMF (providing for a total of US $450m. over two years) and began work on restructuring the severe short-term debt burden. He was, however, unable to secure the huge amounts of international financial assistance necessary to make the stabilization programme work and few of the targets aimed at were reached. Inflation continued at about 60%–70%, unemployment reached 20% and, for lack of raw materials, industry was working half-time. Nevertheless, Ecevit was unwilling to take further austerity measures demanded by the IMF as a condition for further aid. Moreover, political violence continued to escalate. Although the universities returned to normal, elsewhere more and more people were killed in acts of terrorism. Both the police force and the internal security forces (MIT) were riven by factions of left and right which made them unable to intervene. Here, too, the process of purging extremists was begun and in September Ecevit replaced the Chief of Security but, while the civilian tools of authority remained weak and unreformed, the maintenance of law and order depended on the armed forces and Ecevit was forced to ask the *gendarmerie* to undertake policing duties in urban areas. By December 1978 over 800 people had been killed, particularly in the eastern provinces. These new areas of violence reflected a change of tactics by the MHP, which during 1978 campaigned in central and eastern Anatolia, where the traditional elements of society had been least affected by modernization and which were most threatened by its arrival. Türkeş' appeal to nationalism gained him supporters, particularly in areas where Turks lived with other ethnic groups, notably the Kurds. The violence culminated in December at the south-eastern town of Karamanmaraş in the most serious outbreak of ethnic fighting since the 1920s. There the historic enmity between the orthodox Sunni majority and the Alevi (Shi'a) minority had been exacerbated by the activities of right- and left-wing agitators. On 21 December the funeral of two members of the left-wing teachers' association, murdered the day before, was turned into a large-scale demonstration by the Alevis. The mourners were fired on by Sunni supporters of Türkeş and indiscriminate rioting erupted. After three days, over 100 people had been killed, over 1,000 injured and large parts of the Alevi quarters reduced to ruins. The MIT had failed to alert the Government to the incidents leading up to the massacre and order was not restored until the intervention of the army on 24 December.

MARTIAL LAW

The violence led to the imposition of martial law on 26 December 1978. Although he had long been urged to take this step by Demirel, Ecevit had refused in view of Turkey's previous experiences of martial law. Martial law was imposed for two months (renewed subsequently at two-monthly intervals) in 13 provinces, all, excepting İstanbul and Ankara, in the east, although the mainly Kurdish areas of the south-east were excluded to prevent friction. Ecevit announced it was to be 'martial law with a human face' and instituted a co-ordination committee for its implementation comprising himself, Gen. Kenan Evren, the Chief of the General Staff, and Lt-Gen. Sahap Yardimoğlu, the Chief Martial Law Administrator. Special military courts were established to hear cases of those

arrested for martial law violations. However, even these new measures proved insufficient to curb the violence, which was now endemic.

In April 1979 a crisis developed on the political front when six ministers, members of the group of defectors from the AP, issued a public memorandum criticizing Ecevit for taking insufficient account of their views and demanding tougher measures to combat political violence, particularly by left-wing groups, and Kurdish separatism. They also demanded a redirection of economic policies to allow more Western investment and greater freedom for private enterprise. The gulf between these views and those of Ecevit's left-wing supporters in the CHP became more and more pronounced and the impossibility of reconciling the left- and right-wing elements in the coalition became clear. In response to the growth of Kurdish separatism, and alarmed by Kurdish violence in Iran, Ecevit agreed to extend martial law into six more provinces, all in the Kurdish south-east. Three CHP deputies promptly resigned, reducing the party's minority representation in the National Assembly to 211 out of 450.

As violence continued, the authorities imposed an all-day curfew in İstanbul and Ankara on May Day to prevent riots at the traditional parades. A march planned by the more radical of the union confederations, Devrimci İşçi Sendikaları Konfederasyonu (DİSK), was banned and the army ordered the arrest of its entire leadership, a severe blow to Ecevit's reputation as a champion of workers' rights and an indication of the army's increasing involvement in politics. At the general convention of the CHP, Ecevit was re-elected Chairman unopposed, in spite of fierce criticism from right and left. By June 1979, however, the crisis in the National Assembly was serious. During the next few months Ecevit's majority gradually dwindled after a series of resignations by CHP deputies, and in the October by-elections the AP achieved substantial gains. Ecevit's Government resigned on 16 October.

On 24 October 1979 Demirel formed a new Government with the backing of the rightist MHP and the MSP, affording the Government a majority of four. His Cabinet was entirely made up of moderate and uncontroversial AP deputies in an effort to avoid antagonizing the left-wing faction in the National Assembly and jeopardizing his slender majority. Demirel promised a tough policy on terrorism and proposed new legislation to accelerate court procedure and give wider powers to regional governors for dealing with terrorist incidents. However, the elections gave rise to a wave of left-wing protest and the proposed measures gained little headway due to obstruction by the CHP, who objected to what they saw as fascist measures.

With no reduction in the level of violence by the beginning of 1980, the armed forces again intervened. On 2 January the Turkish generals issued a public warning to all political parties, criticizing them for arguing and urging them to reach a consensus of opinion on anti-terrorist measures. Under threat of greater military intervention, the National Assembly immediately began to debate the package of anti-terrorist legislation proposed by the Government. In spite of this threat, the bill was defeated on 15 January, when the MSP voted against it, and sectarian and political killings continued at an average rate of 10 per day. A State factory in İzmir was the scene of fighting between left-wing strikers and the army for several weeks, leading to the imposition of martial law in İzmir and Hatay on 20 February. Twenty provinces were now under martial law. At this time a number of left-wing papers were shut down, including *Politika*, and in May the Türkiye Emekçi Partisi (TEP) (Workers' Party of Turkey) was dissolved by the Constitutional Court. Once again May Day processions were banned and violence broke out.

The instability of the Government was illustrated by the Grand National Assembly's inability to choose a new President after Korutürk's term expired in April 1980. This again provoked criticism from Gen. Kenan Evren, Chief of the General Staff. Neither the right nor the left was prepared to compromise on the choice of candidate and after much indecision, Ihsan Sabri Çağlayangil took office as acting President. In June the CHP tabled a censure motion intended to force the resignation of the Government before the summer recess. It accused Demirel of allowing prices to rise and violence to continue. However, the 22 MSP deputies voted against the motion, in spite of their opposition to Demirel's pro-Western, pro-NATO stance, and the Government survived the motion by one vote. By August political violence had almost reached the proportions of civil war. Although martial law continued to be extended every two months in 20 out of the 67 provinces, clashes between right and left had caused some 2,000 deaths since the beginning of the year. Meanwhile, inflation and foreign debts continued to escalate, food and power shortages and unemployment were widespread and the political bickering continued. At the beginning of September Demirel attempted to bring forward the elections (scheduled for June 1981), which he hoped would give his party a majority and the power to deal with the country's crisis. However, this move was defeated by the opposition and the Government remained paralysed, unable to make important decisions or implement vital measures.

THE 1980 COUP AND ITS AFTERMATH

On 11 September 1980 the armed forces, led by Gen. Evren, seized power in a bloodless coup, the third in 20 years. There appeared to be three main reasons for their intervention: the failure of the Government to deal with the country's political and economic chaos, the ineffectiveness of the police force, and, more immediately, the sudden resurgence of Islamic fundamentalism. This latter cause for alarm was precipitated by a rally at Konya in August, during which Necmettin Erbakan and the MSP staged a march calling for restoration of the *Shari'a*, Islamic Holy Law. The leaders of the coup formed a five-man National Security Council (NSC), sworn in on 18 September. The Chairman of the NSC, Gen. Evren, became head of state. Martial law was extended to the whole country and the Grand National Assembly was dissolved. On 21 September the NSC appointed a mainly civilian Council of Ministers, with a retired naval commander, Bülent Ulusu, as Prime Minister and Turgut Özal as Deputy Prime Minister and Minister for Economic Affairs. The new Government's main aims were 'to eradicate all seeds of terrorism' and to reduce the power of political extremists, to uphold Kemalist principles, to honour all foreign debts and existing agreements, and to return the country to democratic rule after the establishment of law and order. The generals immediately began putting their aims into practice. Former political leaders, suspected terrorists and political extremists were detained. All political activity was banned and trade union activities were restricted. At the same time, a severe programme of austerity was introduced by Turgut Özal. In October the NSC drafted a seven-point provisional Constitution which provided the generals with unlimited powers for an indefinite period. In January 1981 the military junta announced its decision to establish a Consultative Assembly between 30 August and 29 October 1981, as the first stage in the promised return to parliamentary rule.

Since the coup of September 1980, the military leaders had been systematically implementing a campaign to eradicate all possible sources of political violence. By February 1981 the new Government claimed to have eliminated the main left-wing terrorist groups, including the powerful guerrilla organization Dev Yol. By May 1982, according to varying reports, between 43,000 and 100,000 suspected left- and right-wing activists had been detained. The authorities also imposed harsh measures on Kurdish nationalist organizations, believing them to be supported by forces in the Eastern bloc. By May 1982 there had been a number of mass trials of Kurdish activists, especially members of the PKK, the left-wing separatist Kurdish Workers' Party. In December 1980 proceedings began against 2,000 members of the left-wing DİSK. In November 1981 a law was passed depriving the universities of their traditional administrative autonomy, and banning academics and students from political parties. In February 1982 there were 44 arrests in the biggest crackdown on left-wing intellectuals since the coup. Censorship of the press was not officially imposed but extremist publications were banned and the press and other media placed under strict self-censorship. By October more than 66,000 suspects were said to have been arrested, including the leaders of the MHP and the MSP, together with a large number of trade

unionists and the editors of some leading newspapers. The new Government succeeded in reducing the level of political violence in Turkey and in establishing law and order. However, the likelihood that this had been achieved only at the expense of human rights caused concern among the Western Governments: Turkey was banned from the Council of Europe, EC aid was suspended, and fellow-members of NATO urged Turkey to return to democratic rule as soon as possible.

On 15 October 1981 a Consultative Assembly was formed to draft a new Constitution and to prepare the way for a return to parliamentary rule. It comprised five members of the NSC and 160 others, of whom 40 were appointed directly by the NSC, while the remaining 120 were chosen by the NSC from candidates put forward by the governors of the 67 provinces. All former politicians (who had been banned from political activity in April 1981) were excluded and on 16 October all political parties were disbanded and their assets confiscated. The Assembly began work on 23 October 1981, and the new Constitution was approved by referendum on 7 November 1982, with a 91% majority—despite widely-expressed objections that excessive powers were to be granted to the President, while judicial powers and the rights of trade unions and the press were to be curtailed. An appended 'temporary article' automatically installed Gen. Evren as President for a seven-year term. The opposition was not allowed to canvass openly against the new Constitution. Under the Constitution, power was vested in the President, enabling him to dissolve the National Assembly, delay laws, call elections and make all key public appointments.

Following the referendum, the military regime dismissed left-wing university professors, closed newspapers, tightened press censorship and held mass trials of labour leaders and prominent Turks. In May the President lifted a 30-month ban on political activity and allowed political parties to be formed under strict rules. All the former political parties, which had been dissolved in October 1981, were to remain proscribed, along with 723 former members of the Grand National Assembly and leading party officials who were banned from active politics for 10 years. By the end of May it was clear to President Evren that proscribed political parties were resurfacing under new names and with new titular leaders. The first new political party to be banned, on 31 May, was the Great Turkey Party, whose leader was Husamettin Cindoruk. This party was the reconstructed AP, with discreet support from Süleyman Demirel. In response, Demirel's supporters formed the True Path Party (Dogru Yol Partisi—DYP). The President gave support to the Milliyetçi Demokrasi Partisi (MDP) (Nationalist Democracy Party), led by Gen. Turgut Sunalp, in the hope that it would become the main centre-right party in the new Parliament. On the centre-left the Sosyal Demokrasi Partisi (SDP) (Social Democratic Party) was formed, under the leadership of Prof. Erdal İnönü, and won support from the former CHP, although the leader, Bülent Ecevit, recommended boycotting the new political system. The SDP was banned on 24 June. The Halkçi Parti (HP) (Populist Party), led by Necdet Calp, had military approval as a centre-left party.

CIVILIAN RULE RETURNS UNDER ÖZAL

A general election was held on 6 November 1983, and parliamentary rule was restored, with a 400-seat National Assembly. Election was on the basis of proportional representation (with a minimum requirement of 10% of the total votes, to discourage small parties), voting was compulsory and every candidate had to be approved by the military council.

The President banned a total of 11 parties from participating in the general election. In a surprise result, ANAP, led by Turgut Özal, won 211 of the 400 seats in the unicameral National Assembly. The party had been allowed to participate only because the President felt that it would be no threat to the two parties that the military leadership favoured. However, the armed forces' preferred party, the centre-right MDP, was beaten into third place, with the centre-left HP coming second. The result reflected the great popularity of Turgut Özal, stemming from his performance while head of the State Trading Organization and later as Deputy Prime Minister and Minister for Economic Affairs. He was appointed Prime Minister and named his Cabinet in December.

The result of the election suggested a decisive rejection of military rule, and this view was strengthened when local elections were held on 25 March 1984. Three parties which had been banned from the general election (the SDP, the DYP and the Refah Partisi (RP) (Welfare Party)) were allowed to contest the local elections. ANAP received about 40% of the total votes (almost identical to the November general election result), with the moderate left-wing SDP obtaining 23.3% of the votes. Thus, the main opposition in the country to ANAP was a party not represented in Parliament, a fact which gave rise to further speculation about the undemocratic nature of the general election. The HP and the MDP (the official parliamentary opposition) fared badly in the elections, winning less than 10% of the votes each. In November 1985 the HP and the SDP, the main opposition parties within and outside the National Assembly respectively, merged to form a single party, known as the Sosyal Demokrat Halkçı Parti (SHP) (Social Democratic Populist Party). However, the left-wing opposition was split as a result of the formation, a few days later, of the Demokratik Sol Parti (DSP) (Democratic Left Party), led by Rahsan Ecevit (wife of the former Prime Minister, Bülent Ecevit) and drawing support from the former CHP.

The civilian Government's main priorities were economic: to cut the inflation rate, which was around 40% at mid-1984; to lower taxes; drastically to reduce the cumbersome bureaucracy; to boost exports and to liberalize imports; to encourage private enterprise; to relax foreign exchange controls; and to slim down the State-owned industries. Inflation was still running at an annual rate of around 55% in July 1985, and remained a major worry. Corruption continued to be a problem, and in October 1984 the Minister of Finance and Customs, Vural Arikan, was dismissed by President Evren after accusing the Minister of the Interior (who had resigned shortly before) of allowing the police to torture customs officials who had been accused of corruption. The press and labour unions were put under strict control, despite a few civilian appointments to important posts formerly held by the military. The police were given further widespread powers, in a new Police Act, to maintain law and order and to ensure that there was no return to the political violence which was prevalent in Turkey during the late 1970s.

Widespread concern continued throughout the 1980s and the early 1990s regarding the persistent and widespread use of torture of political prisoners. In May 1984, 1,256 academics and leading figures petitioned the Prime Minister for the eradication of torture and the restoration of full democratic rights. In December 1985 a case brought before the Human Rights Commission of the Council of Europe by five European countries, alleging that Turkey had violated the European Convention for the Protection of Human Rights, was settled out of court when Turkey agreed to rescind all martial law decrees within 18 months, to introduce an amnesty for political prisoners, and to allow independent observers from the Council of Europe to monitor progress. In February 1986 a group of leading intellectuals, members of a peace movement, were acquitted by a military court of violating the Constitution. In July 1987 all martial law decrees in Turkey were repealed when martial law was replaced with a state of emergency in the provinces of Diyarbakir, Mardin, Siirt and Hakkâri (making a total of nine provinces under an official state of emergency). The Government's signing, in January 1988, of the UN's and Council of Europe's agreements denouncing torture, however, received a cynical response from both the local and the international media. In November 1988 the eight-year state of emergency in İstanbul was revoked.

In November 1987 Dr Nihat Sargin and Haydar Kutlu, the respective leaders of the banned Workers' Party of Turkey and the Turkish Communist Party, returned to Turkey after seven years of self-imposed exile, with the intention of merging their two parties to form a new Turkish United Communist Party. They were both arrested at the airport and were charged with offences under the Turkish penal code, which specifically outlaws Communist organizations and the dissemination of Marxist-Leninist ideas. At their trial, which

began in June 1988, both men alleged that they had been tortured by the Turkish police. In April 1990 they undertook a 21-day hunger strike in protest at the Government's failure to implement planned reforms in the field of human rights. In May they were released from detention for the remainder of the trial, in anticipation of significant changes to the articles of legislation that had declared communist parties illegal. In June 1990 it was reported that an application for legal status for the Turkish United Communist Party put forward by the two men, had been rejected. In July 1989, at the end of a seven-year trial of members of the banned Dev Yol, a military court sentenced seven left-wing extremists to death, 39 to life imprisonment and more than 300 to jail terms of up to 21 years for activities dating back to the time of the 1980 military coup. In August 1989 two Kurdish prisoners died, following a two-month hunger strike by more than 1,000 prisoners, in protest at poor prison conditions. A report issued by Amnesty International in November 1989 claimed that more than 500 political prisoners had been tortured in the first 10 months of 1989. In April 1990 it was estimated that 25,000 had been detained for political reasons since 1980.

A sharp increase in outbreaks of urban terrorism in early 1990 coupled with a perceived increase in the influence of fundamentalist thought, led to widespread fears of a return to the extremist violence of the late 1970s. In October 1990 an unknown terrorist group, the Islamic Movement, claimed responsibility for a bomb attack which killed Dr Bahriye Ucok, an outspoken critic of the 'fundamentalist perversion' of Islam and a staunch defender of the secular rights of women. The increase in terrorist attacks by Islamic groups and left-wing groups was exacerbated by the Government's stance in the conflict in the Persian (Arabian) Gulf. A series of attacks against Western targets in Turkey were unleashed, including US civilians, diplomatic missions and offices of several national airlines and banks in İstanbul and Ankara.

In early April 1991 a draft anti-terrorism bill was approved by the National Assembly. Presented as a move towards greater liberalization and democratization, the bill contained provisions for the abolition of controversial articles 141, 142 and 163 of the penal code (which had proscribed the formation of religious or communist political parties), for the early release of as many as 35,000 prisoners, for the commuting of the death sentence for more than 250 prisoners and for a relaxation of the ban on the use of minority languages. The extent to which the bill would provide for greater democracy, however, was largely confused by the continued existence of separate laws reinforcing many of the articles abolished by the new legislation. By mid-April it was reported that some 5,000 political prisoners had already been released as a result of the new bill. In July 1991 Turkey's Constitutional Court again refused to afford legal status to the Turkish Communist Party.

The MDP voted to disband itself in May 1986. Many of its members joined the new right-wing Hür Demokrat Partisi (HDP) (Free Democratic Party), which was formed by Mehmet Yazar, the former President of the Union of Chambers of Commerce and Industry. In December there was much political manoeuvring when the HDP merged with ANAP, and the right-wing Vatandas Partisi (VP) (Citizen Party, formed earlier in the year) merged with the DYP (although the VP's leader, Vural Arikan, became an independent); the DSP became a legitimate parliamentary group (i.e. it had more than 20 deputies in the National Assembly) when several deputies from the SHP defected and joined its ranks. By the end of 1986, therefore, the number of recognized parliamentary groups in the National Assembly stood at four—ANAP, the SHP, the DSP and the DYP.

In May 1987 it became apparent that there were rifts within ANAP when its Secretary-General, Mustafa Tasar, resigned after criticizing the party's increasingly powerful Islamic fundamentalist wing. ANAP fared well, however, in the mayoral elections in June, winning 55 of the 84 seats contested. The DYP also proved its continuing popularity by winning 17 seats, whilst the SHP won only six seats and the DSP a mere three. Serious internal divisions within the DSP emerged in the same month, when a group of more than 100 of its founders convened and elected a new Chairman. The official leader, Rahsan Ecevit, anticipating the revolt, had already expelled the rebels from the party before the meeting and gained a legal injunction from the state prosecutor, declaring the meeting illegal.

FURTHER STEPS TOWARDS DEMOCRACY

In a national referendum, which was held in September 1987, a narrow majority (11,723,309 votes in favour and 11,641,961 votes against) approved the repeal of the 10-year ban imposed on over 200 politicians in 1981, which prohibited them from taking an active part in public life. This result enabled Bülent Ecevit to assume the leadership of the DSP, while Süleyman Demirel was elected as leader of the DYP. As the polls for the referendum closed, the Prime Minister, who had campaigned against the repeal of the ban, immediately announced that a general election would be held on 1 November (a year earlier than required). A few days later, the National Assembly approved legislation enabling a general election to be held at such short notice, by eliminating the procedure of primary elections within each party. After protests and threats of an electoral boycott by the opposition parties, however, the Government postponed the general election until 29 November, thus enabling primary elections to be held. Seven parties contested the general election, which was the first free election in Turkey since the 1980 military coup. ANAP obtained 36.3% of the votes cast (which, because of the 'weighted' electoral system, meant that it was allotted 292 of the seats in the National Assembly, now enlarged from 400 to 450 seats), while the SHP (24.7% of the votes) won 99 seats and the DYP (19.1% of the votes) won 59 seats. Because of the country's proportional representation system, which requires a party to obtain at least 10% of the national vote in order to be represented in the National Assembly, none of the four other parties contesting the election (including the DSP, with 8.5% of the votes, and the RP, with 7.2%) won seats. Özal formed a new expanded Cabinet in December. In February 1988 the Sosyalist Parti (SP) (Socialist Party), the first overtly socialist political party in Turkey since the 1980 coup, was formally established. In March Bülent Ecevit resigned from his post as leader of the DSP and a new Chairman, Necdet Karababa, was elected. The most serious political violence since 1980 occurred in İstanbul on 1 May, when violent skirmishes took place between the police and a group of about 800 trade unionists, led by seven SHP deputies, who were protesting against the ban on May Day rallies, the restrictions imposed on trade unions, and high inflation.

Shortly after his return from Athens (see below) in June 1988, an unsuccessful assassination attempt was made on Özal, as he addressed an ANAP meeting in Ankara. This incident raised fears of a right-wing conspiracy against the Prime Minister, since the would-be assassin had been a senior member of the neo-fascist 'Grey Wolves' group in the 1970s. The Prime Minister, who was wounded slightly in the hand in this attack, suffered a further set-back in the same month at ANAP's annual congress in Ankara. In the voting for the new party executive, a group of right-wing nationalists, who had supported the ultra-right MHP in the 1970s, allied themselves with the party's Deputy Chairman, Mehmet Kececiler, and the other Islamic conservatives against the Özal-backed liberals. This alliance surprisingly won 30 seats out of a total of 50 on the executive.

In August Özal made an unsuccessful attempt to pass a new piece of legislation through the Constitutional Court, which would, through an amendment to the Constitution, enable the holding of early local elections (held every five years) up to one year in advance. In the following month a national referendum was held to decide whether to adopt this amendment and to bring forward the holding of local elections (scheduled for March 1989) by five months to November. It was suggested by some sources that Özal wanted to hold early elections in order to gain a period free from electoral pressures, in which to impose unpopular austerity measures aimed at lowering the country's high rate of inflation. The political situation became more tense when opposition parties insisted that the result of the referendum should be interpreted as reflecting the extent of confidence in the Prime Minister and ANAP. The widespread public dissatisfaction with the Government and its policies was reflected in the fact that only 35% of the total votes cast were in favour of Özal's proposed amendment, which was, consequently, not adopted. The Government suffered a further set-back in January 1989, when the Deputy Prime Minister, Kaya Erdem, resigned, following alleged 'differences' with Özal. In the same month, Bülent Ecevit was re-elected Chairman of the DSP.

At the local elections, which were held, as scheduled, throughout Turkey in late March 1989, ANAP obtained only 22% of the total votes, while the SHP and the DYP won 28% and 26%, respectively. The ruling party's defeat included the loss of control of the local councils in the country's three largest cities (Ankara, İstanbul and İzmir) to the SHP. A few days after these elections, Özal implemented an extensive Cabinet reshuffle, which was aimed at restoring public confidence in the Government. In the following month, the Prime Minister requested and won a vote of confidence in the National Assembly. However, in May the Government was confronted with further problems when the steelworkers' union declared a strike to protest against low incomes and the continuing high rate of inflation.

ÖZAL BECOMES PRESIDENT

In mid-October Özal declared his candidacy for the presidential election to be held by members of the National Assembly on 31 October. Despite a boycott of the election by SHP and DYP deputies, who claimed that Özal no longer had a popular mandate, and attempts by a second ANAP candidate to divide support, Özal received the simple majority required in the third round of voting (having failed to secure the two-thirds majority of the 450 Assembly Deputies necessary for victory in the first two rounds), polling 263 of the votes. On 9 November Özal succeeded Gen. Kenan Evren as President and unexpectedly appointed Yıldırım Akbulut, the Speaker of the National Assembly and a former Minister of the Interior, as his successor to the premiership. Although Akbulut was considered by many ANAP supporters as likely to be an ineffectual leader, chosen to allow Özal a greater degree of control as President, a motion of confidence in the new Prime Minister was approved by the National Assembly, and Akbulut was later elected as party leader. Towards the end of 1989 the parliamentary position of the SHP was seriously undermined when a number of SHP deputies resigned in protest at the expulsion of six Kurdish deputies who had attended a Kurdish conference in Paris earlier in the year. Rumours of division within ANAP were confirmed in early 1990, when the Ministers of Foreign Affairs and of Finance and Customs both resigned, expressing disenchantment with party policy and leadership. In March Bedrettin Dalan, a former Mayor of İstanbul and an ANAP party member, announced his intention of forming a new Demokratik Merkez Partisi (DMP) (Democratic Centre Party) which was expected to attract many disaffected ANAP supporters.

At local elections held in June and August 1990, ANAP did surprisingly well. Despite allegations from opposition sources that voters had been bribed with false promises of massive municipal budgets, there were demands from within the SHP for administrative changes within the party following its election failures. In September Secretary-General Deniz Baykal, together with the party's Central Executive Committee, resigned pending new elections to be held during an extraordinary party congress scheduled for the end of September. Following the forcible annexation of Kuwait by Iraq in August 1990 the Government was afforded the *de facto* power to declare war at an emergency session of parliament where, despite strong opposition, a proposal allowing the Government to accept foreign troops in Turkey and deploy Turkish troops abroad in retaliation for acts of aggression against Turkey, was approved by 216 votes to 151.

In October 1990 the resignations of the Minister of Foreign Affairs, Ali Bozer, and the Minister of National Defence, Safa Giray (who were both members of a liberal movement within the ruling party), provided further evidence of factional disaffection within ANAP. Internal divisions continued to threaten to undermine the strength of the Government in early 1991, when the political ambitions of the President's wife, Semra, were supposedly linked to the dismissal of the Minister of National Defence, Hüsnü Doğan, in February and the resignation of the Minister of Energy and Natural Resources in April. In December 1990 the Chief of Staff of the Armed Forces had also resigned, suggesting (as had Bozer) that President Özal's exclusive and self-promoting handling of the crisis in the Persian (Arabian) Gulf had prompted his decision to resign. Later in December widespread concern was expressed by political opponents and by the Turkish media when it was revealed that procedural expedients, such as the completion of papers pre-signed by absent ministers, had been employed by the President and by the Government in recent crucial decision-making regarding the conflict in the Persian (Arabian) Gulf, and, moreover, that such practices had been used frequently during ANAP's six-year administration.

Although Özal's visible and vociferous support for the UN's sanctions against Iraq (and for US initiatives in particular) did much to enhance Turkey's international standing, political opponents accused the President of jeopardizing Turkey's position in the conflict unnecessarily. In mid-January 1991 a resolution expanding existing war powers, which had been granted to the Government in September 1990, was approved by the National Assembly, despite strong opposition from the SHP and the DYP. The new resolution effectively sanctioned the unrestricted use of NATO air bases in Turkey by coalition forces. However, President Özal stressed that Iraq's 'territorial integrity' would be violated by Turkish forces only in the event of direct military aggression against Turkey or of territorial incursions into Iraq by Iran or Syria.

An increase in industrial unrest towards the end of 1990 culminated in a general strike in early January 1991, organized by Turkey's two largest union federations and supported by the SHP and the DYP. Although in December 1990 the Government had declared the proposed action to be illegal, some 1.5m. workers supported the strike, joining 150,000 workers in the coal, steel and vehicle sectors who had already undertaken industrial action in protest at low levels of pay, poor working conditions and restrictive labour legislation. At the end of January (in a move interpreted as an attempt to prepare the country for the possibility of war) the Government imposed a 60-day ban on strike action, hoping to curtail disruption in crucial industrial sectors.

At an ANAP party congress convened on 15 June 1991 Prime Minister Yıldırım Akbulut was defeated by former Minister of Foreign Affairs Mesut Yılmaz in a contest for the party leadership. The following day Akbulut resigned as Prime Minister, and on 17 June, in accordance with the Constitution, President Özal invited Yılmaz to head a new administration. On 23 June Yılmaz announced the composition of a new, radically-altered Cabinet and the next day he assumed the premiership. The appointment of Yılmaz (the leader of the liberal faction within ANAP) and the composition of the Cabinet was widely interpreted as an attempt to balance the influence of the liberal and Islamic fundamentalist movements within the Government. In early July the economic programme of the new administration (reaffirming ANAP's commitment to free-market policies and deregulation) was approved by the ANAP majority in the National Assembly.

In August 1991 the Government announced that general elections (not legally required until November 1992) would be conducted in October 1991. Within five days of the announcement the justice, interior and transport portfolios were reallocated to independent deputies, as stipulated in the Constitution. In return for what the Government considered to be a concession to the opposition SHP and DYP (who had demanded that early general elections should be held on the grounds that ANAP no longer commanded sufficient popular support to govern effectively) Yılmaz hoped to secure opposition support for proposed constitutional changes including the lowering of the minimum voting age from 21 to 18, the expansion of the National Assembly from 450 to 600 seats, and provisions whereby future general and local elections would be conducted simultaneously.

THE 1991 GENERAL ELECTION

A general election was held on 20 October 1991. The DYP, under the leadership of Süleyman Demirel, received an estimated 27.3% of the votes cast, narrowly defeating ANAP (with 23.9%) and the SHP (with 20.6%). Although the DYP failed to attract the level of support necessary for the formation of a single-party government, it was expected that Demirel would assume the premiership at the head of a coalition government. Following the election, the incumbent Cabinet tendered its resignation. In accordance with the Constitution, Demirel was afforded a 45-day post-election period in which to finalize the composition of a new government. A new coalition government comprising members of the DYP and the SHP, who had negotiated a protocol for coalition in late November (and who together accounted for 266 of the 450 newly-elected deputies in the National Assembly), was approved by the Assembly later in the month. The new Cabinet, to be headed by Demirel, was to include 12 SHP ministers (with the deputy premiership assigned to SHP party leader Erdal İnönü). The remaining 20 cabinet positions were to be occupied by DYP members. On 25 November the coalition partners had announced a programme for political and economic reform that included the drafting of a new constitution, improvements in anti-terrorist legislation and matters of human rights, and increased levels of cultural recognition and of autonomy in local government for Kurds in Turkey. While international observers were impressed by Demirel's apparent commitment to human rights (the establishment of a separate ministry of human rights, to be headed by an ethnic Kurd, was promptly announced), the formal adoption of amendments to the criminal procedure code, designed to discourage torture (including a proposed reduction in the length of periods of legitimate police detention), were impeded by a lack of consensus within the coalition Government, and the situation was exacerbated during 1992 by a succession of political defections from the SHP, which had reduced the representation of the coalition parties in the 450-seat National Assembly to 231 by September. Although the DYP and the SHP had performed well at municipal elections conducted in early June (increasing their combined share of national support to 58%, compared with 48% in the October 1991 general election), the reactivation of the CHP in September 1992 (as a result of the adoption of more lenient guidelines for the formation of political parties, proposed by the Government) threatened to undermine left-wing support for the Government.

At a special ANAP party conference, convened in early December, concern was expressed that right-wing extremism had become the dominant force behind the party leadership, prompting the emergence of a dissident, more conservative faction of the party. Some 70 deputies subsequently announced their intention to leave ANAP in order to form a new party, to be headed by president Özal. However, in April 1993, Özal died as a result of heart failure.

FOREIGN AFFAIRS, 1980–93

Turkey is recognized as a key member of NATO, both on account of its strategic position in Europe and because it is the only NATO member of the Islamic Conference. In 1984 President Reagan of the USA announced plans to provide Turkey with almost twice as much aid as Greece: US $934m. compared with $501m.—a dramatic illustration of Turkey's importance to NATO. In the year to September 1985 the USA pledged a record $785m. in military aid. In December 1981 the NATO countries were divided over support for the Turkish Government: while the USA promised to speed up aid to Turkey, EC countries were considering the suspension of aid. In January 1982 the European Parliament voted to suspend relations with Turkey, while, at the same time, the Council of Europe condemned military rule, in protest against human rights abuses and other repressive measures, the imprisonment of the former Prime Minister, Bülent Ecevit, and the delay in returning to democratic rule. In March 1982 the EC decided to 'freeze' aid to Turkey. In January 1983 the EC agreed that Turkey could remain a member of the Council of Europe, but with its voting rights suspended until democracy was restored. The voting rights were restored in May 1984. However, in November 1984 Turkey was asked to forfeit its turn as President because of continued concern over human rights in the country.

Two outstanding problems between Turkey and the EC are the number of Turkish workers within EC member-states, and the quantity of textiles exported from Turkey to the

Community. According to the existing agreement, from December 1986, Turkish workers were to have the right of free circulation within the EC; it was feared that this would exacerbate the problem of unemployment, and the Federal Republic of Germany, which had more than 550,000 Turkish workers in 1985, was particularly strongly opposed to the plan. In September 1985, following a sharp increase in imports of low-priced textiles and clothing from Turkey, the EC imposed strict quotas on such imports. Full resumption of EC aid to Turkey (whose allocation of 600m. ECUs for the period 1981–86 had been suspended following the military coup) was expected to depend on improved observance of human rights in Turkey. Greece has also demanded, as a further condition to its agreement to the release of the EC aid to Turkey, the complete withdrawal of Turkish troops from Cyprus. In September 1986 Turkey was readmitted to associate membership of the EC, when the Turkish-EC Association Council (which was established in 1963, but had been suspended since the army coup in 1980) met for talks in Brussels. Turkey, however, failed to gain access to the suspended EC aid, and to extend the rights of Turkish workers in Europe. In October Turkey took over the presidency of the Council of Europe for six months. In the following month the Turkish Government expressed anger when the EC Ministers of Foreign Affairs declared that they did not intend to honour the agreement concerning the right of free circulation within the EC for Turkish workers, but that they were willing to negotiate certain economic and social improvements for workers resident in the Community. In April 1987 Turkey made a formal application to become a full member of the EC. Overruling Greek objections, the EC Council of Ministers agreed to submit the application to the Commission of the European Communities to formulate its opinion on the merits of the case. In April 1988 a meeting of the Turkish-EC Association Council in Luxembourg was postponed indefinitely after objections by the Turkish delegation to a reference to Cyprus, which was inserted at the request of the Greek delegates, in the EC's opening statement. President Evren's state visit to Britain in July (his first visit to Western Europe as President) was aimed principally at boosting his country's international image as a fully-fledged democracy and promoting its efforts to join the EC.

In December 1989 Turkey's application was effectively rejected, at least until 1993, by the Commission of the European Communities. The Commission emphasized that the completion of a single European market was necessary before any enlargement could take place, and cited factors including Turkey's unsatisfactory human rights record, high rate of inflation, dependence upon the rural population and inadequate social security provisions as falling short of EC expectations.

Following negotiations lasting more than a year, an addendum to the 1980 US-Turkish defence and economic agreement extending it until December 1990 was signed in March 1987 by the US Secretary of State, George Shultz, and the Turkish Minister of Foreign Affairs, Vahit Halefoğlu. Turkey gained few concessions on the relaxation of the quotas on US imports of Turkish textiles and steel, and, despite Turkish requests for military aid of at least US $1,000m. annually, the USA's military aid to Turkey totalled only $490m. in 1986/87. The Turkish Government refused, however, to ratify this extension, in protest against what was perceived to be insufficient US military and economic aid, until February 1988, by which time Turkey had benefited significantly from supplies of arms from US surplus stocks. Total aid from the USA to Turkey for 1987/88 was set at $525.3m. (compared with $593m. in 1986/87), of which $490m. was for military purposes.

Widespread concern that the US Government's increase in financial aid to Eastern Europe in 1990 had been achieved at Turkey's expense, threatened to undermine relations between the two countries. The Turkish Government, however, responded positively to requests from the USA for logistical aid following the forcible annexation of Kuwait by Iraq in August 1990, and in September the defence and economic co-operation agreement (which provides for the US military presence in Turkey) was extended. In January 1991 it was reported that the Turkish Government had requested that the USA should increase the number of US aircraft based in Turkey to 96, which (together with German, Italian and Belgian aircraft from NATO's Allied Command Europe (ACE) mobile force, which had been requested by the Government in December 1990) would constitute an effective deterrent to any possible Iraqi aggression while emphasizing NATO solidarity in the region. It was initially stipulated that the increased number of US aircraft would be used exclusively for humane and logistical support for US troops. Two US-supplied Patriot air defence missile systems were also to be deployed at bases in southern Turkey. In mid-January a resolution to extend the war powers of the Government and effectively endorse the unrestricted use of Turkish air bases by coalition forces was agreed by the National Assembly (see above). On the following day US aircraft embarked upon bombing missions into north-east Iraq from NATO bases inside south-east Turkey. In February and March 1991 the US Government announced substantial increases in military and economic aid to Turkey for 1991 and 1992. In September 1991 the 1980 defence and economic co-operation agreement was extended for a further year. In June 1992 it was anounced that all US military personnel were to be withdrawn from the jointly-administered base at Sinop, near the Black Sea, by the end of 1993.

Although Greece and Turkey agreed to relax tension in April 1982, relations were further strained when the Turkish-backed 'Turkish Federated State of Cyprus' made a unilateral declaration of independence in November 1983. Turkey is the only country to have recognized this state, the 'Turkish Republic of Northern Cyprus' ('TRNC'), and to have exchanged ambassadors with it (in May 1984). In July 1986 Turgut Özal became the first Turkish Prime Minister to make an official visit to the 'TRNC'. Tension between Greece and Turkey came to a head in March 1987 when a disagreement between the two countries over petroleum-prospecting rights in disputed areas of the Aegean Sea almost resulted in the outbreak of military conflict. Relations between Turkey and Greece improved considerably, however, in 1988: in February the Turkish Government officially annulled a decree, issued in 1964, which curbed the property rights of Greek nationals living in Turkey. In return, Papandreou officially accepted Turkey's status as an associate member of the EC by signing the Protocol of Adaptation (consequent on Greece's accession to the EC) to the EC–Turkey Association Agreement in April, which the Greek Government had, hitherto, refused to do. The situation deteriorated somewhat, however, later in the same month, when Greece insisted on linking the possibility of Turkey's entry into the EC with the ending of the Turkish presence in Cyprus. In May Melina Mercouri, the Greek Minister of Culture, became the first Greek minister to visit Turkey since 1974, and in the following month Özal became the first Turkish Premier to visit the Greek Prime Minister in Athens for 36 years. As regards Cyprus, Greece wanted the complete de-militarization of the island, on the basis of a set timetable, and the establishment of a joint Greek-Cypriot and Turkish-Cypriot police force under UN auspices. Özal insisted, however, that Turkey would remove its troops only after an overall peace settlement was reached (see chapter on Cyprus). In September 1988 the Turkish and Greek Ministers of Foreign Affairs chaired a session of a joint political committee, which had been proposed in January, in Ankara, while a joint economic committee was convened concurrently in Athens. In June 1989 Özal became the first Turkish premier to visit the Greek Prime Minister in Athens for 36 years. The discussions that took place there between Özal and Papandreou, however, ended without any significant progress towards a resolution of major differences. In February 1990 relations deteriorated again, following violent clashes between Christians and the Muslim minority in western Thrace, in Greece. In October 1990 it was reported that Turkey was seeking to strengthen links with the 'TRNC' by abolishing passport controls between the two territories, by offering increased financial aid and by strengthening military guarantees.

Other aspects of Turkey's foreign policy included neutrality in the Iran-Iraq war and commitment to full rights for the Palestinians. The assassinations of Turkish diplomats by

Armenian terrorists have soured Turkey's relations with France and Greece in particular. The guerrilla groups responsible for the attacks claim to be seeking revenge for the Turkish massacre of an estimated 1.5m. Armenians in 1915 and for the subsequent expulsion of Armenian survivors from their traditional territories in north-eastern Turkey, where a short-lived independent Armenian republic was violently suppressed by Turkish forces in 1920–21. In the autumn of 1984 tension arose between the USA and Turkey over a congressional resolution condemning alleged massacres of Armenians by Turks during the First World War. The resolution eventually lapsed, and the USA granted military aid, but the tension remained. The Turkish Government was angered once again in February 1987 when the European Parliament adopted a report 'deploring' the alleged massacres. The controversial 'Ottoman Archives', which may help to clarify the circumstances surrounding the alleged killings, were officially opened to scholars for the first time in İstanbul in May 1989.

POLITICAL DEVELOPMENTS AFTER ÖZAL

In August 1988 the Iraqi armed forces launched a major offensive against Kurdish separatists in northern Iraq. Thousands of Kurdish refugees (an estimated 100,000–150,000 by early September) fled to the Turkish border, where, after initial hesitation, the Turkish Government admitted them on 'humanitarian grounds' and provided asylum in makeshift camps. In addition, the Turkish Government refused a request by Iraq to allow Iraqi forces to pursue Kurdish guerrillas in Turkish territory. Although Turkey seeks to promote its international and national image as a democracy respecting fugitives' rights, the Government made it clear that the refuge being given to the Iraqi Kurds was only temporary. The situation became more serious when many of the refugees claimed that the Iraqi armed forces had launched numerous chemical bomb attacks against them. Despite strenuous denials by Iraqi officials, the physical evidence clearly indicated the use of chemical warfare. The Turkish Government, however, claimed that no traces of the use of chemical weapons had been found, and it would not permit a proposed visit by UN medical experts to investigate the allegations. According to some sources, this refusal on the part of the Turkish Government was due to the fact that it did not wish relations with Iraq to deteriorate further. In September 1988 Iraq was indebted to Turkey to the sum of US $2,400m., and, following the signing of the cease-fire between Iran and Iraq in August, Turkey hoped to be awarded a substantial number of Iraqi post-war reconstruction contracts. Iraq offered an amnesty to the Iraqi Kurds in Turkey in September, but very few returned. In the following month, Turkey evacuated about 20,000 Iraqi Kurds from Turkey to Iran. By August 1989 there were still about 36,000 Iraqi Kurds living in three camps in eastern Turkey, yet the Turkish authorities continued to refuse to recognize them officially as political refugees.

In January and February 1990 a 30-day diversion of water from the Euphrates river to the giant Atatürk dam, as part of an ambitious project to provide hydroelectricity and irrigation, encountered opposition from both Syria and Iraq, who were not satisfied that measures adopted by the Turkish Government since November 1989 to increase water supplies to both countries were sufficient to compensate for the diversion.

Following the Iraqi invasion of Kuwait in August 1990, the Turkish Government swiftly complied with UN proposals for economic sanctions against Iraq. The passage of Iraqi oil through pipelines (which had not been suspended by the Iraqis themselves) across the Turkish mainland to Mediterranean outlets was curtailed, all Iraqi assets in Turkey were 'frozen' and Turkey's border with Iraq was closed to the passage of all but essential supplies (and to all traffic in January 1991). Turkish nationals were swiftly evacuated from Iraq and Kuwait, and as many as 130,000 troops were redeployed along Turkey's border with Iraq. Despite the increase in the number of Turkish troops in the border region and the deployment of additional US and NATO aircraft in south-east Turkey in early 1991, President Özal continued to stress that Turkey had no intention of opening a second military front against Iraq

and that Turkish forces would continue to guarantee Iraq's 'territorial integrity'. In January 1991, following the Government's decision to allow US aircraft to conduct bombing missions into north-east Iraq from NATO bases in Turkey, the Iraqi Minister of Foreign Affairs accused the Turkish Government of committing 'unjustified aggression' against Iraq.

In early March 1991 President Özal revealed that high-level talks had been conducted in Turkey between senior Turkish foreign ministry officials and the leaders of Kurdish groups within Iraq, during which Turkey had endorsed the notion of some form of autonomy for Iraqi Kurds within Iraqi territory. The Turkish Government had also agreed to open its border for humanitarian aid to areas of northern Iraq which had been reportedly liberated by Kurdish rebels in the aftermath of the conflict in the Persian (Arabian) Gulf. By the beginning of April, however, having suffered serious reversals at the hands of the Iraqi armed forces, more than 500,000 Iraqi refugees (mainly Kurds) were reported to be fleeing to the Turkish border. Although the Turkish Government formally announced the closure of the border, claiming that it was unable to accommodate such a large-scale exodus (some 10,000 refugees, many of them ethnic Turks, had already been recently received by Turkish authorities), and appealed to the UN Security Council to consider the plight of the refugees and to take immediate action to ensure their safety, by mid-April it was estimated that some 600,000 refugees (including 400,000 within Turkish borders) were encamped in the mountainous border region. While reports of the appalling conditions confronting the refugees gave rise to grave international concern and the initiation of an ambitious humanitarian aid programme (with US Air Force transport planes from the İncirlik air base distributing supplies to the refugees), the Turkish minister of state in charge of the relief effort criticized Western governments for their slow response to the crisis. Following intense international pressure, the Turkish authorities (who had contained the refugees in the border region in the hope that a protected buffer zone would be created to accommodate the Kurds on flatlands just inside the Iraqi border rather than on equivalent land at a much greater distance inside Turkey) began to make provision for the removal of up to 20,000 of those refugees in greatest need of medical attention to better conditions at an existing camp at Silopi, inside Turkey. Prime Minister Yıldırım Akbulut insisted that such initiatives were merely temporary measures and that the ultimate aim of the relief effort must be the complete repatriation of the Kurds. In mid-April, in accordance with a UN-approved proposal to establish temporary 'safe havens' for the refugees in northern Iraq, Turkey agreed to allow coalition forces to use Turkish facilities to help the refugees, under UN auspices. By mid-May 1991 it was estimated that some 200,000 refugees had returned to Iraq, while 89,000 remained in Turkey (65,000 at Hakkâri and 24,000 at Sirnak) and a further 162,000 were still encamped on the Iraqi side of the border with Turkey.

Offers of financial and economic assistance from the USA, Japan, Kuwait and the EC, as well as concessionary oil prices offered by Saudi Arabia and the United Arab Emirates, were unlikely to be realized in time to offset the adverse economic effects of an estimated US $6,000m. loss in revenues from trade, transit and tourism as a result of the conflict, together with the cost of providing temporary shelter and relief for thousands of refugees.

Following the completion of the first phase of the international relief effort for the Kurdish refugees and the subsequent withdrawal of coalition forces, the Turkish Government agreed to the deployment in south-east Turkey of a 3,000-strong multinational 'rapid reaction force' which would respond to any further act of aggression by Iraq against the Kurds in the newly-created 'safe havens'. The force, to be jointly commanded by the USA and Turkey (the latter would reserve the right to veto attacks against Iraq launched from Turkish territory or airspace) and would include a 1,000-strong Turkish battalion. In September 1991 the Government approved a 90-day extension for the presence, in south-east Turkey, of a small allied air-strike force, and subsequently its mandate was granted six-month extensions. All allied ground forces, however, were withdrawn in October 1991.

Relations with Bulgaria deteriorated in 1985: Turkey protested vehemently against the campaign of forced assimilation, launched by the Bulgarian authorities in late 1984, in which ethnic Turks living in Bulgaria (estimated to number about 1.5m.) were forced to adopt Slavonic names and were banned from practising Muslim religious rites. In February 1988 Turkey took part in a six-nation Balkan conference in Belgrade. During this conference, the Ministers of Foreign Affairs of Turkey and Bulgaria signed a protocol to improve relations between the two countries. In May 1989, however, there were reports that ethnic Turks had been killed in Bulgaria during demonstrations against the continuing assimilation campaign, and the Bulgarian authorities began to deport hundreds of Turks to Turkey. The Bulgarian Government, however, continued to deny the existence of a resident Turkish minority in their country, and the official explanation was that the ethnic Turks were merely Slavs whose ancestors had been forcibly converted to Islam. In late May the Bulgarian authorities altered their policy and issued passports and exit visas to at least 150,000 Turks who wished to enter Turkey. In response, the Turkish Government opened the border and publicly stated its commitment to accepting all the ethnic Turks as refugees from Bulgaria. In late June a mass demonstration of about 100,000 people took place in İstanbul to protest against Bulgaria's treatment of its ethnic Turkish population. In late August the Turkish Government decided to demand visas from entrants from Bulgaria, but instructed the Turkish consulate in Bulgaria to give priority to the reunification of families when issuing visas. Many of them were placed in temporary settlement camps near the border, while others sought refuge with friends and relatives in Turkey. By mid-August an estimated 310,000 had crossed into Turkey, but more than one-third of that number had returned to Bulgaria by February 1990, as a result of disillusionment with conditions in Turkey and the proposed abolition of the assimilation campaign by a new Bulgarian administration.

Following the formal dissolution of the USSR in December 1991, the Turkish Government sought to further its political, economic and cultural influence in the central Asian region, and to forge strong links with the six Muslim states of the former Soviet Union in particular. In April 1992 Prime Minister Demirel undertook an official visit to several of the former Soviet republics, pledging aid of more than US $1,000m. in the form of credits for the purchase of Turkish goods and contracts. At the same time, programmes broadcast by the Turkish national television company were relayed, by satellite, to the region for the first time. In June 1992 leaders of 11 nations, including Turkey, Greece, Albania and six former Soviet republics, established a Black Sea economic alliance, and expressed their commitment to promoting greater co-operation with regard to transport, energy, information, communications and ecology. In December 1993 the group agreed to establish a joint investment bank, the Black Sea Trade and Development Bank, which was to be based in Greece, with a Turkish presidency.

POLICY TOWARDS THE TURKISH KURDS, 1980–94

In the 1980s the potential threat of separatism among the Kurds in the south-east of the country was a continuing problem. Despite the fact that there are an estimated 3m.–10m. Kurds in Turkey, they are not officially recognized as a separate ethnic group and it is illegal to speak Kurdish. In 1984 the outlawed Marxist Kurdish Workers' Party (PKK), which supports the creation of a Kurdish national homeland in Turkey and which is led by Abdullah Ocalan, launched a violent guerrilla campaign against the Turkish authorities in the south-eastern provinces. The Government responded by arresting suspected Kurdish leaders, dispatching more security forces to the region, establishing local militia groups, and imposing martial law in nine troubled provinces. By July 1987, however, martial law had been replaced by a state of emergency under a district governor in all of these provinces. In spite of this concession, the violence continued and the PKK began to concentrate their attacks on the local militia and civilians. By 1988 more than 1,000 people had been killed as a result of the Kurdish problem. In June 1988 the Government made no response to Abdullah Ocalan's offer of

a cease-fire and prisoner exchange and his demand for the legalization of the PKK. He threatened to spread the conflict to the cities and to attack Turkish politicians and diplomats if the Government continued to insist on a military solution. In April 1990 the Government introduced severe measures to combat ethnic unrest, including harsh restrictions on the media and an increase in the powers of local officials to outlaw strikes and impose internal banishment. Violence continued to escalate, however, and in April and May clashes between rebel Kurds, security forces and civilians left 140 dead, marking the bloodiest period of the conflict since August 1984.

In early 1991, in the context of the Kurdish uprising in Iraq, President Özal sought to alleviate mounting tension among Turkish Kurds by announcing the Government's decision to review existing legislation proscribing the use of languages other than Turkish and by allowing Kurds to celebrate openly the Kurdish new year for the first time. In April, as part of a draft anti-terrorism bill, the Government proposed the relaxation of restrictions on the use of Kurdish by the national media. By mid-1991, however, a new wave of violence between the PKK guerrillas and the security forces had erupted in the south-eastern provinces. In July three people were killed and more than 100 wounded when security forces clashed with some 20,000 mourners attending the funeral of a murdered Kurdish rights activist in Diyarbakir. The conflict entered a new phase when, in late 1991 and early 1992 (in retaliation for continuing cross-border attacks on Turkish troops), government fighter aircraft conducted numerous sorties into northern Iraq in order to attack suspected PKK bases there. In the course of these raids many civilians and refugees (mainly Iraqi Kurds) were reportedly killed, prompting international observers and relief workers publicly to call into question the integrity of the exercises. In October 1991 the Iraqi Government had lodged formal complaints with the UN, denouncing Turkish violations of Iraq's territorial integrity. In March 1992, in response to revelations that German-supplied armoured personnel vehicles had been used by Turkish security forces in attempts to suppress Kurdish insurgents, the German Government suspended all trade in armaments with Turkey. A deterioration in relations between the two countries was exacerbated in April by the insistence of the German Government that a formal EC protest deploring Turkish anti-insurgency operations should be drafted and delivered to Ankara. In April 1992 negotiations with Syria resulted in the reactivation of a 1987 security agreement designed to curb the activities of the PKK in the border region.

Violence in the south-eastern provinces, resulting from ethnic tension, persisted into 1992 and, despite the stated commitment of the new Demirel Government to foster new initiatives for improved relations with ethnic minorities, attempts to amend existing legislation so as to restrict the powers of the security forces were frustrated by lack of consensus within the ruling coalition. The armed response of the security forces to an escalation in violence in mid-1992 (together with the National Security Council's recommendation for a renewal of the state of emergency dating from 1987, in several southern provinces) demonstrated no significant departure from anti-insurgency measures employed by the previous administration.

In late 1992 Turkish air and ground forces (in excess of 20,000 troops), conducted further attacks upon PKK bases inside northern Iraq, hoping to take advantage of losses inflicted upon the Kurdish rebels by a simultaneous offensive, initiated by Iraqi Kurdish *peshmerga* forces in October, with the aim of forcing the PKK from Iraq. By mid-December most Turkish ground forces had been withdrawn from Iraqi territory, and in January 1993, the Turkish military offensive was redirected against PKK strongholds in south-eastern Turkey.

On 16 May Süleyman Demirel was successfully elected to the presidency, with a simple majority in a third round of voting by the National Assembly. In early June Minister of State Tansu Çiller was elected to the DYP party leadership, and subsequently assumed the premiership as Turkey's first woman Prime Minister. Çiller announced the composition of her Cabinet in late June. While all 12 SHP ministers retained their portfolios, the replacement of several prominent DYP ministers was interpreted as an attempt by the Prime Minister to consolidate support for her election to office.

On taking office as Prime Minister, Çiller was immediately confronted with a dramatic increase in separatist violence which escalated into a major domestic and international crisis. The PKK ended its unilateral ceasefire, which had been announced in March, by declaring 'war' on all Turkish targets. There followed a wave of bomb explosions in Turkish tourist resorts and abductions of foreign nationals by the PKK. There were also a series of attacks upon Turkish diplomatic missions and business interests in Europe. The Çiller Government responded by postponing measures to allow the use of the Kurdish language in schools and the media, and by withdrawing plans to give a degree of local autonomy to the southeastern provinces, in response to opposition from President Demirel, right-wing members of the DYP and military leaders. At the same time the armed forces, which numbered 150,000-200,000 in the south-east of the country, were given a virtual free hand against the PKK.

The pro-Kurdish Halkın Emek Partisi (HEP) (People's Labour Party) was outlawed in July 1993. In September Mehmet Sincar, a deputy of the Demokrasi Partisi (DEP) (Democratic Party), the successor to HEP, was assassinated. The PKK and the authorities each blamed the other for the assassination. In October the PKK issued a prohibition against press reporters and representatives of mainstream political parties from operating in the south-east of the country, in response to continuing repression of the separatist movement. (By November it was reported that the PKK controlled most of the region by night). The Government subsequently cancelled all public investment in the region. It was estimated that there had been 2,000 deaths in the region as a result of the conflict between June 1993 and the end of the year; in October, official reports estimated a total of 10,000 civilian, military and PKK deaths since 1984.

In early 1994 an intensified conflict between security forces and the PKK commenced with an extensive air bombing raid on a PKK camp in northern Iraq. Amidst this background, mainstream parliamentarians voted in March to strip seven members of the DEP (and one independent Kurdish deputy) of their parliamentary immunity from prosecution, and six deputies were subsequently detained on charges of separatism. On 16 June Turkey's Constitutional Court banned the DEP and ruled that its 13 deputies should be expelled from Parliament, owing to associations with the PKK. In August the six deputies, detained since March, went on trial on charges of treason. In early September the trial was adjourned for one month. As the tourist season in Turkey got underway the PKK resumed bomb attacks in Istanbul and popular coastal resorts.

Even as Çiller struggled to contain and defeat the PKK she was confronted by strains within her governing coalition. Her minority coalition partner, the SHP, was suspicious of her plans for privatization. In September 1993 the SHP elected a new leader, Marat Karayalcin. In October the Constitutional Court rejected a government decree on the privatization of the state telecommunications company after the case had been brought by 92 deputies of the SHP. It was widely expected that the Government would suffer heavy electoral losses in the local elections of March 1994; however, at the elections, the beneficiary was not the main opposition party, ANAP, but the Islamic conservative Refah Partisi (RP) (Welfare Party). The RP, which had campaigned against inflation and high interest rates and against Turkey's ties to NATO and the European Union (EU), won 19% of the votes and took control of both Ankara and İstanbul.

In May 1994 Çiller sought to consolidate relations with the SHP, and simultaneously to deflect international criticism of Turkey's human rights record in the south-eastern provinces, by unveiling plans to open up the political arena to groups that had been barred since the 1980 military coup. All restrictions on political activity by academics, students, labour unions and associations were to be lifted, the voting age was to be reduced to 18 from 21, and deputies were to be allowed to switch parties.

In foreign affairs Çiller has sought the creation of a UN peace-keeping force in Azerbaijan and a role for Turkey in the UN effort in the former Yugoslavia. In July 1994 around 1,455 Turkish troops were deployed in Bosnia and Herzegovina, but well away from Serb lines. Turkey has expressed concern that many of its neighbours have failed to take effective action against PKK bases on their territory. In October 1993 Turkey reluctantly agreed to the extension of UN sanctions against Iraq, but continued to advocate a removal of the embargo.

Economy

Dr DAVID SEDDON

Revised for this edition by Ergin Yıldızoglu and Ronnie Margulies

Turkey is about 1,450 km (900 miles) long and some 500 km (300 miles) wide, covering an area of 779,452 sq km (300,948 sq miles). The October 1985 census recorded a population of 50,664,458, and that of October 1990 showed the population to be 56,473,035. These totals exclude Turks working abroad, the largest number of whom are in Germany. The census results imply an average annual population increase between 1985 and 1990 of 2.2%, compared with 2.6% between 1980 and 1985. Turkey's population density was 65.0 per sq km in October 1985, and had increased to 73.5 per sq km by mid-1991. Turkey's largest cities are the former capital, İstanbul (population 6,620,241 within municipal boundaries in 1990), the capital, Ankara (2,559,471), and the port of İzmir (1,757,414). In 1991 an estimated 36.9% of the total population resided in rural areas.

The country possesses great natural advantages: the land yields good grain and a wide variety of fruit and other products; it is rich in minerals; and it has a number of natural ports. The climate is varied and, on the whole, favourable, but communications are hindered by the mountain ranges that ring the Anatolian plateau to the north, east and south.

Gross national product (GNP) expanded, in real terms, by an average of 7% annually between 1970 and 1978. However, in the severe economic and social crisis of the late 1970s, growth slowed to the extent that an actual decline of 1.1% was recorded in 1980. Following a structural adjustment programme introduced in January 1980, growth recovered to a rate of about 4.4% annually in 1981 and 1982, but fell to 3.3% in 1983. However, growth rates of 5.7% and 5.5%, respectively, were recorded in 1984 and 1985. In 1986, on the strength of capital goods imports, demand for consumer durables and a good harvest, GNP expanded by a record 8.1%, leading to IMF admonitions that the economy was dangerously overheated. In 1987 this rapid industry-led growth continued at 7.4%, and GNP, at current prices, reached US \$68,442m. The government set a target of 5% for the growth rate in 1988. However, partly owing to the Government's attempts to decrease domestic demand in order to try to curb the high rate of inflation, GNP grew by only 2.5% in 1988. With policies designed to squeeze inflation out of the system remaining in place in 1989, growth was restricted to 1.1%. Towards the end of 1989, however, these policies were relaxed and a growth rate of 9.2%, the highest for more than a decade, was achieved in 1990. In 1991 the adverse effects of the Gulf War contributed to growth of just 0.9%, with GNP amounting to US \$109,078m. The economy recovered in 1992, with GNP growth of 5.9%. This impressive growth performance continued in 1993, with a rate of 7.3%, owing essentially to a consumption boom fed by foreign borrowing. Per capita GNP stood at US $1,990 in 1993, having increased by about 4.5% in real terms. An official target growth rate of 4.5% was announced for 1994, but after a severe financial crisis early in the year and an austerity programme in April, it is estimated that growth may in fact fall to −1.6%.

AGRICULTURE

Turkey relies substantially on agriculture, although the sector's overall role is shrinking rapidly. However, it is believed that almost one-half of the labour force still works on the land. Agriculture provided 59.4% of total export revenue in 1979, but the proportion declined to around 20% in the late 1980s and stood at 15.2% in 1993. The agricultural sector, including forestry and fishing, contributed 14.9% of GNP in 1992 and 13.1% in 1993. Nearly 25m. ha, or about one-third of total land area, are under cultivation. Most of the farms are small and the average size of a family farm is only 8 ha. The country is basically self-sufficient in foodstuffs. The principal agricultural exports are cotton, tobacco, wheat, fruit and nuts. Other important crops are barley, sunflower and other oilseeds, maize, sugar beet, potatoes, tea and olives.

During the period 1963–70 Turkey's agricultural output rose by only 2.5% per annum, mainly because insufficient emphasis had been placed on agriculture in both the first and second economic development plans. However, with the introduction of land reforms and the improved utilization of land, machinery and farmer education resources, agricultural production in 1971 increased by some 30%. In 1975 real expansion in agriculture was 10.9%, but such good results were infrequent. In 1978 the rise in output was only 2.7%, while in 1981 it was just 0.3%. The rate of increase has fluctuated considerably in recent years. Inadequate rainfall in 1989 caused agricultural output to contract by 10.8%. In 1990, however, output increased by an impressive 11.6%, only to decline again by 1.5% in 1991. A modest increase of 3.7% was achieved in 1992, and official forecasts for 1993 failed to be met. A growth rate of 3.0% has been officially targeted for 1994.

Government policy is to increase agricultural productivity, but budget constraints restrict project financing. The funds that are available come mainly from international sources, notably the World Bank. However, there is increasing foreign commercial interest in developing Turkish agro-industry, particularly for Middle Eastern export markets. In an attempt to alleviate the poverty of the south-eastern provinces of Turkey, the government drew up a south-east Anatolia programme (GAP) in the early 1980s, covering a total area of 74,000 sq km. The estimated total cost of GAP is about US $11,000m. and it includes the construction of seven dams on the Euphrates and Tigris rivers. The dams will generate a total 7,513 MW of electricity and will irrigate large areas of land, thus doubling the region's agricultural output (notably cotton).

The Land and Agrarian Reform Bill of 1973 aimed at distributing 3.2m. ha to 500,000 peasants over a 15-year period. Many Turkish peasants own very little land and about one-tenth of all farming families have no land at all. The area covered by the Bill included 1.4m. ha of State-owned arable land, 1.0m. ha of uncultivated State-owned land and about 800,000 ha of private land, which was to be nationalized. However, in the political and economic uncertainty of the late 1970s, little was done about the land reform programme.

About one-half of the cultivated area is devoted to cereals, of which the most important is wheat. The principal wheat-growing area is the central Anatolian plateau but the uncertain climate causes wide fluctuations in production. Barley, rye and oats are other important crops grown on the central plateau. Maize is grown along the Black Sea coastal regions, and leguminous crops in the İzmir hinterland. Rice, normally sufficient for domestic needs, is grown in various parts of the country. Since 1977 the annual wheat harvest has usually stayed above the high level of 16m. metric tons, owing to good weather, improved cultivation methods and increased levels of irrigation. In 1993 there was a particularly good harvest of 21m. tons, although export earnings remained at a relatively low level of about US $70m.

Cotton has traditionally been Turkey's main export earner, grown mainly in the İzmir region and in the district round Adana, in southern Turkey. In recent years, however, it has lost some of its traditional importance. Production stood at 558,000 tons in 1993 when exports of cotton were valued at US $123m.

Turkey produces a particularly fine type of tobacco. The three principal producing regions are the Aegean district, the Black Sea coast and the Marmara-Thrace region. The bulk of the crop is produced in the Aegean region, where the tobacco is notable for its light golden colour and mild taste. The finest tobacco is grown on the Black Sea coast, around Samsun. Although a traditional Turkish export, its relative position as an export has been declining in recent years. Most of Turkey's tobacco exports go to buyers in the USA and East European countries. The size of the crop fluctuates considerably: in 1976 it reached a record level of 324,000 metric tons but by 1987 it had fallen to 175,000 tons. By 1993 output had reached 330,000 tons, with exports valued at US $348.3m. In 1984 the Government permitted the first legal imports of foreign cigarettes in more than forty years, breaking the monopoly over sales and distribution held by the State tobacco and beverages agency Tekel. Several international tobacco companies have started negotiations to manufacture cigarettes locally, and one joint-venture operation has been established at Bitlis in the south-east of the country to produce cigarettes for export. In mid-1992 construction work began on a new cigarette factory in İzmir, as part of a joint venture between the US tobacco company, Philip Morris, and the local Sabanci group. Tekel, however, has responded by raising capacity and output and improving the quality of its brands.

The coastal area of the Aegean, with mild winters and hot, dry summers, produces grapes, figs and olives. Exports of dried figs were valued at US $53m. in 1993. France is the main customer for figs. The outstanding product, however, is the sultana type of raisin, which is also grown in California and elsewhere. Turkey normally ranks second in the world as a sultana producer, but in good years becomes the largest producer in the world. Sultana harvests varied from 85,000 metric tons in 1976 to 138,000 tons in 1989, when exports were worth US $72m. In 1993 exports were valued at US $124.5m.

The Black Sea area, notably around the Giresun and Trabzon, produces the greatest quantity of hazel-nuts (filberts) of any region in the world; a harvest of 380,000 tons was recorded in 1993, with exports valued at US $341.6m. Substantial amounts of walnuts and almonds are also grown.

Tea is grown at the eastern end of the Black Sea, around Rize, and in other areas. Production of fresh leaves from State tea plantations has steadily increased since the early 1980s to total 731,000 tons in 1992.

Turkey is also an important producer of oilseeds, principally sunflower, cotton, sesame and linseed. It also produces olive oil, some of which is exported. Production fluctuates, partly because of the two-year flowering cycle of olive trees.

Turkey was, until 1972, one of the seven countries with the right to export opium under the UN Commission on Narcotic Drugs. Much opium was, however, exported illegally, particularly to the USA and Iran; partly as a result of pressure from the US Government, the Turkish Government made the cultivation of opium poppies illegal in 1972, but the ban was ended in July 1974 and the flowers are grown in certain provinces under strict controls. Opium gum is no longer tapped from the living plant. The poppy pods (opium straw) are sold to the government, which processes them into concentrate for export as the basis for morphine and other drugs.

Sheep and cattle are raised on the grazing lands of the Anatolian plateau. Stock-raising forms an important branch of the economy. The sheep population (an estimated 40.4m. in 1992) is mainly of the Karaman type and is used primarily as a source of meat and milk. The bulk of the clip comprises coarse wool suitable only for carpets, blankets and poorer grades of clothing fabric. However, efforts have been made in recent years to encourage breeding for wool, and there are some 200,000 Merino sheep in the Bursa region.

The Angora goat produces the fine, soft wool known as mohair. Turkey is one of the world's largest producers of mohair, with an average output of about 9,000 tons per annum.

MINERALS

Turkey has a diversity of rich mineral resources, including large quantities of bauxite, borax, chromium, copper, iron ore, manganese and sulphur. The mining and quarrying sector employs more than 200,000 workers. The share of minerals in total export earnings decreased gradually from 3.6% in 1989 to 1.6% in 1993. About 60% of all mineral output, and all coal production, derives from State enterprises. The most important State enterprise in the mining sector is Etibank, which works through its subsidiaries, Eregli Coal Mines, East Chromium Mines, Turkish Copper, Keban Lead Mines and Keçiborlu Sulphur Mines. During the early 1960s the State enterprises increased their predominance over the private sector, with an investment programme that was supported by the Mining Investment Bank, established in 1962. The policy of encouraging the private sector to play a greater part in the mining industry, through the establishment of the Turkish Mining Bank Corporation (TMBC) in 1968, has failed to overcome the general reluctance of private investors to view mining as a worthwhile area for long-term investment, with the result that the private sector is under-capitalized. An additional factor militating against the development of mining has been the long-held suspicion of foreign investment in mining. A law enacted in 1973 restricted foreign participation in mining development projects. However, this restriction was relaxed in January 1980, allowing up to 49% foreign participation in mining ventures. Since then, negotiations have proceeded slowly between Etibank and potential foreign partners for copper, lead and other mineral mining. In 1983, Etibank entered into a joint venture agreement with the US company, Phelps Dodge, for copper mining. Etibank is currently scheduled for privatization, and in 1993 its banking and mining operations were separated in the initial phase of this process.

Bituminous coal is found at and around Zonguldak, on the Black Sea coast. The seams are steeply inclined, much folded and strongly faulted. The coal is generally mined by the longwall system or a variation of it. These mines constitute Etibank's largest operation, and the coalfield is the largest in this part of the world, including the Balkans. Most of the seams are of good coking quality, the coke being used in the steel mills at nearby Karabük. Production amounted to 2.7m. tons in 1993. Many of the mines and the Karabük plant have been listed by the Government as loss-making enterprises that were to be closed down. Lignite is found in many parts of central and western Anatolia, and total reserves are estimated at 5,000m. tons. In 1989 Turkey's total production of lignite stood at 50.9m. tons, decreasing to 46m. tons in 1993. Seams located in western Turkey are operated by the West Lignite Mines. The other main mines are at Soma, Degirmisaz and Tunçbilek. The recently-discovered lignite deposits at Afsin Elbistan are being developed, with extensive German and international financial assistance, as part of an ambitious integrated energy project designed to increase capacity by 1360 MW.

Practically all of Turkish iron ore comes from the Divrigi mine, situated between Sivas and Erzurum, in the north-east of the country, and operated by the Turkish Iron and Steel Corporation. The average grade of ore is from 60% to 66%; reserves have been estimated at 28m. metric tons. Output of iron ore increased from 1.7m. tons in 1979 to 5.5m. tons in 1992. Production fell to 4.4m. tons in 1993.

Turkey is one of the world's largest producers of chromite (chromium ore). The richest deposits are in Güleman, south-eastern Turkey, in the vicinity of İskenderun; in the area around Eskişehir, north-west Anatolia; and between Fethiye and Antalya on the Mediterranean coast. The Güleman mines, producing 25% of the country's total, are operated by East Chromium Mines under Etibank. This agency is currently studying plans to increase annual chrome production at its plant at Elâziğ from 100,000 tons to 150,000 tons. Other mines are owned and worked by private enterprise. Little chromium is used domestically and the mineral is the principal earner of foreign exchange among Turkey's mining exports. Output of chromite fell from a peak of 800,000 tons of ore, mined in 1977, to less than 500,000 tons per year in the early 1980s, but recovered to reach 1.5m. tons in 1989. However, production decreased again to around 600,000 tons in 1992 with exports

valued at US $32m. In 1993 output decreased further, and export earnings fell to $18m.

Copper has been mined in Turkey since ancient times. Current production, conducted entirely by Etibank, comes from the Ergani Mines, at Maden in Elâziğ, and the Morgul Copper Mine, at Borçka in Çoruh province. Production of blister copper has tended to fluctuate, decreasing from 36,000 tons in 1986 to 21,300 tons in 1989 and reaching 31,293 tons in 1993. Most of the output is exported to Germany, the United Kingdom and the USA. Known reserves of copper ore are estimated at 90m. tons.

Eskişehir, in north-west Anatolia, is the world's leading centre for meerschaum mining. Meerschaum, a soft white mineral which hardens on exposure to the sun and looks like ivory, has long been used by Turkish craftsmen for pipes and cigarette holders.

Manganese, magnesite, lead, sulphur, salt, asbestos, antimony, zinc and mercury are important mineral resources. Of these, manganese ranks first in importance. Deposits, worked by private enterprise, are found in many parts of the country, but principally near Eskişehir and in the Eregli district. In 1981 Turkey announced the discovery of an estimated 400,000-ton deposit of manganese at Ulukent, near Denizli. Lead is mined at Keban, west of Elâziğ. Production of sulphur (public sector only), mainly from the Keciborlu mine, in Isparta province, totalled 39,000 tons in 1987. Antimony is mined in small quantities near Balikesir and Nigde. An important new find of mercury deposits, which may amount to 440,000 tons, has been made at Sizma, in Konya province. Large uranium deposits have been discovered in the Black Sea, between 1 km and 2 km below sea-level. Turkey's first commercially viable silver mine was opened in January 1988.

The Uludağ (Bursa) tungsten deposits, carrying an average grade of 0.43% WO_3, are among the richest in the world. Etibank and the German firm of Krupp are jointly working these deposits. Output of tungsten ore reached 3,400 tons in 1979. Other minerals are barytes, perlite, phosphate rock, boron minerals, cinnabar and emery (Turkey supplies more than 80% of the world market for emery).

Turkey's bauxite deposits are now supplying the aluminium complex which was built, with Soviet aid, at Seydişehir. The plant's initial annual capacity was 60,000 tons of aluminium but this is to be expanded to 120,000 tons. Output of alumina stood at 141,550 tons in 1993. The plant will also produce alumina for export, and semi-finished products. The reserves at Seydişehir are estimated at more than 30m. tons.

Petroleum was first discovered in Turkey in 1950, and all subsequent discoveries have been in the same area, in the south-east of the country. It is mostly heavy-grade petroleum with a fairly high sulphur content. Production of crude petroleum has fluctuated since it reached a peak of 3.5m. tons in 1973. Because of the small size of Turkey's main oilfields in the fractured terrain of the south-east, it declined steadily between 1980 and 1985. Production in 1992 and 1993 totalled 4.3m. tons and 3.5m. tons respectively. Total domestic output of crude petroleum of about 49,000 barrels per day (b/d), in addition to about 1,500 m. cu m of natural gas, accounts for roughly 12% of the country's hydrocarbon requirements. In 1993 21.9m. tons of petroleum was imported at a cost of US $2,550m. Saudi Arabia is Turkey's main supplier, with substantial volumes also imported from Iran and Libya. Prior to a UN embargo on trade with Iraq, that country was a major supplier of petroleum.

Three main companies produce petroleum: the Turkish Petroleum Corporation (TPAO), a 99% State-owned Turkish company, with an output of 26,000 b/d. Subsidiaries of the Royal Dutch/Shell Group and the US Mobil group produce 18,000 b/d and 5,000 b/d respectively. Proven reserves are expected to be exhausted by the mid-1990s. Ultimate reserves are put by TPAO at 10,000m. barrels. Exploration is continuing in the south-east and in the Aegean. Since 1980 there have been few indications that production will be able to rise significantly from its current low level. In 1983 the Government passed a new law which was intended to liberalize conditions for foreign companies, enabling them to export up to 35% of any onshore petroleum which they discovered, and up to 45% of any offshore output. At first, major foreign oil companies were dubious about Turkey as a viable political and economic base, but in 1984 quickening interest resulted in the signing of several joint-venture exploration agreements by new foreign major oil companies with TPAO.

Turkey has four petroleum refineries: at Mersin (annual capacity 4.4m. tons), at İzmit (where capacity is being raised to 12m. tons), at Batman (800,000 tons) and at Aliaga (now being increased to some 5m.–10m. tons).

TPAO operates a 500-km pipeline, with a diameter of 45 cm (18 in), which runs from the oilfields around Batman to Dörtyol on the Gulf of İskenderun. A 986-km pipeline from Kirkuk, in northern Iraq, to Turkey has a capacity of around 100,000 metric tons per day. A contract to expand the pipeline to a capacity of 1.5m. b/d was completed in mid-1984. Completion and full commissioning of a second pipeline, alongside the first, took place in July 1987. Agreement on the construction of a third pipeline originating in Iraq was reached in April 1987. Work on the line, which is to run 240 km from Ain Zalah in Iraq, to the Batman oil refinery in Turkey, with a capacity of 70,000 b/d, has been delayed by Turkish dissatisfaction with Iraq's failure to reduce its debt to Turkey. The pipeline from Kirkuk has been closed since August 1990, when economic sanctions were imposed upon Iraq by the UN, and this is estimated to have cost the Turkish pipeline authority, Botas, more than US $400m. per year in lost revenues. An estimated 3.2m. barrels of Turkish crude petroleum remain within the pipeline. Turkey is advocating that the pipeline be emptied and repaired as a first stage towards removing the UN embargo.

Several major schemes for further petroleum and gas export pipelines from the Gulf area have been proposed, but are still at pre-feasibility or feasibility study stage. Iran and Qatar have discussed constructing gas pipelines through Turkey to Europe, both of which would be massive projects in pipeline terms. A pipeline under construction for imported Soviet natural gas running from the Bulgarian border to Ankara has been completed. Purchases of gas produced in the countries of the former USSR, according to a countertrade agreement originally negotiated with the USSR, will continue to rise from the 1991 level of 4,000m. cu m and will be paid for with Turkish exports and construction work to be undertaken by Turkish contractors. Algeria is also negotiating the sale of gas to Turkey. This gas would enter the import pipeline via a terminal in the Sea of Marmara, and be used to supplement supplies from the successor states of the USSR. Should there be an interruption of the latter, Algerian gas would compensate for the shortage. In March 1993 agreement was reached between the Governments of Turkey and Azerbaijan, Botas and Western oil companies for a pipeline to run from Azerbaijani oilfields near Baku to Turkey's oil export terminal in Ceyhan, on the Mediterranean coast. It is proposed that the pipeline will run through Iranian territory for 60 km before entering the Nakhichevan Autonomous Republic (part of Azerbaijan), and finally Turkey, near Doğubeyazıt. Alternative proposals to extend the pipeline to a Russian terminal at Novorossisk on the Black Sea were opposed by Turkey. The prospect of this latter route being constructed became less likely since the imposition by Turkey of stricter controls for ships transporting hazardous goods through the Bosphorus, effective 1 July following a collision in March. Russia, which exports some 70% of its oil exports by means of the Bosphorus protested at the measure. In mid-1994 discussions were continuing between the Governments of Turkey and Turkmenistan on the construction of a gas pipeline that was to terminate in Turkey and become operational within two years. In addition, in May, Turkey signed a protocol agreement with Ukraine for the construction of a pipeline that was to supply Ukraine with petroleum from the Middle East via Turkey.

INDUSTRY

The leading role in the process of inaugurating industrialization was played by the State economic enterprises (SEEs). However, by the beginning of the 1970s the private sector accounted for nearly one-half of industrial output and its rate of capital investment had become almost equal to public sector investment. The Government announced its long-awaited plans for privatization of the SEEs in May 1987. Initially, the Government's stake in 22 private companies would be sold,

followed by the denationalization of the more efficient and profitable SEEs. As a first step, one-half of the Government's shareholding of 40% in Teletas, a telecommunications company, was sold to the private sector in early 1988. A sharp fall in share prices on the İstanbul stock exchange then slowed the privatization programme. Five State-owned cement works were sold directly to a French company (although the completion of this sale was suspended in 1991), and USAS, an aircraft services firm was sold directly to a Scandinavian airline in early 1989. The fact that these were sold directly to foreign companies, rather than to the public on the stock exchange, attracted widespread criticism. As the stock exchange recovered at the end of 1989, the Government proceeded with the sale of its minority shareholdings in private sector companies. Such holdings in six companies were sold in the spring of 1990 with great success. Subsequent privatizations have enjoyed varying degrees of success. Small portions of State-owned shareholdings have been sold in a number of major companies such as Petkim, the petrochemicals giant, and Erdemir, the iron and steel complex. In the first half of 1992 the Demirel Government undertook five such sales, with estimated total revenue of TL 552,000m. The Demirel administration demonstrated its own commitment to further extensive privatization with the announcement of an economic programme for 1992 which envisaged total revenues from divestments of TL 5,500,000m. In early July 1992 the Government announced the sale of 11 state cement companies which together accounted for 18% of total cement production in Turkey. In late 1992 and early 1993 the privatization programme continued at a steady rate. While the Çiller Government has made privatization a key aspect of its economic policy, the programme is being implemented at a slower rate than anticipated. In mid-1994 the programme was hindered when legislation to accelerate the privatization process was declared to be unconstitutional by the Constitutional Court. Subsequently, it was unlikely that revenue from privatization would reach its target total of US $2,500m. in 1994.

Turkey's recent high growth rates have been industry-led. The share of industry in the economy increased from 12% of GDP in 1952 to 31.5% in 1990, and 32.4% in 1993. Growth in the manufacturing sector has been the most noticeable, under the stimulus of the Government's export incentive scheme, although, latterly, domestic demand has equalled the demand made on manufacturing for exports. In 1986 the manufacturing sector expanded by a record 10.5%, followed by growth of 10.1% in 1987. In 1989 the growth rate decreased to 4.2%, but in 1990 it recovered to 9.7%, only to decrease again, to 6.7%, in 1993.

Production of such goods as paper, cotton and woollen yarn, cotton and woollen fabrics, refined fuels and petroleum products, steel products and glassware began a significant recovery in the early 1980s. Overall, the average annual rate of growth of industrial production was 7.1% in 1981–90.

The textile and clothing industry is Turkey's largest, accounting for about one-third of manufacturing employment and being responsible, in 1993, for 38.8% of the country's total export earnings. Clothing and leatherwear are the leading exports in this sector, and EC and US import quotas have long been an important factor in relations between these countries.

The iron and steel industry in Turkey is one of the fastest-growing in the world and prospects are good, compared with its difficulties in the early 1980s. However, following the liberalization of imports in 1989, the sector suffered a trade deficit of US $895m., although this was reduced to $312m. in 1990, only to increase again, to US $972m., in 1993. Both private and public manufacturers complain of dumping by European and Asian companies. Public sector capacity is 4.6m. tons per year and private sector capacity 2.7m. tons per year. Total output of crude steel reached 8.0m. tons in 1988 and rose to 10.3m. tons in 1993, when the value of exports of iron and steel totalled more than US $1,800m.

Cement production, on the strength of the expansion in the construction industry (due largely to the Government's mass housing programme), rose to a record 20m. tons in 1986. Production has continued to increase, in spite of occasional declines in years when the economy as a whole has done badly, and output stood at 31.3m. tons in 1993. The industry is now almost totally privately-owned as a result of the privatization programme. The private sector was responsible for 92.6% of total output in 1993.

Among food industries, the State-controlled sugar industry is the most important. In 1993 total production of raw sugar was 1.7m. tons, with the private sector accounting for only slightly over 25% of this total.

The paper and board industry is dominated by the government-owned SEKA corporation (scheduled for privatization), which has one old-established mill at İzmir, with an annual capacity of 126,000 metric tons of paper and board, plus six mills which have been opened since 1971. Total output of paper and board is relatively stable at around 400,000 tons annually.

The motor vehicle industry was established after 1956, and by 1971 had become the largest industrial employer after the textile sector, accounting for about 5% of total industrial output. Output, some of which is exported, is fragmented between 15 enterprises, with a resulting loss of the economies of scale. The process of merging of firms (there were 22 in 1967) is expected to continue under the impact of heavier taxation. After several years of suppressed demand and low capacity utilization in the early 1980s, the outlook began to improve in 1983. In 1988 output of cars (local versions of certain Fiat, Ford and Renault models) increased by 12.7%, to 120,800. By 1993 output had nearly trebled to just under 345,000. New models had been introduced and a number of foreign manufacturers expressed interest in local production. (Toyota entered into a joint venture with the local Sabanci Group; the joint car plant at Adapazari was scheduled to start operations in September 1994, with a potential capacity of producing 100,000 cars per year.)

In 1970 Turkey's first petrochemicals complex, situated at Izmit, began production of ethylene, polythene, polyvinyl chloride (PVC), chlorine and caustic soda. There is another petrochemicals plant at Aliaga, while a third is planned at Yumurtalık. They are operated by the State-owned firm Petkim. In 1992 the output of artificial fertilizers totalled 7.9m. tons, although this declined in 1993 to 5.5m. tons. The State-owned Turkish Nitrates Corporation (TNC) has a nitrate plant at Kutahya, a triple superphosphate plant at Samsun and a superphosphate plant at Elâziğ. There are several privately-owned fertilizer plants, including triple superphosphate plants at İskenderun and Yarimca. Turkey produces 75% of its requirements of fertilizers and, when new plants are completed, it will be self-sufficient.

Other manufacturing industries include tobacco, chemicals, pharmaceuticals, metal working, engineering, leather goods, glassware and ferrochrome.

The power sector, along with the transport, communications and tourism sector, has continued to hold priority in the Government's development programmes for every year since 1989. Nevertheless, together with other infrastructural projects, the power sector suffered from the attempt to cut back Government spending and progress was slow on power plant projects. In spite of the progress made in power plant construction in recent years, many more units will have to be built to meet an expected increase in demand to 170,000m. kWh annually by the end of the century, compared with 33,000m. kWh in 1986. Thermal sources accounted for about 70% of the 1986 total power generation and hydroelectricity the remainder. Output from stations operated by the Turkish Electricity Board (TEK) accounted for 62% of all electricity generated, while chartered companies and private generators provided the remainder. Total output stood at 66,983m. kWh in 1992 and rose to 73,734m. kWh in 1993.

Joint-venture defence manufacturing with foreign partners is the next major development for foreign investment in Turkish industry (a development that began with the US $4,000m. agreement concluded in 1983 with the US Government and the US company, General Dynamics, to assemble and, eventually, manufacture F-16 fighter aircraft at Murted outside Ankara). The Defence Industry and Support Administration (DIDA), established in 1985, will co-ordinate Turkey's 10-year, $15,000m. programme to modernize the armed forces. The modernization will involve, to a large extent, locally manufactured equipment and weapons. In July 1988 a joint-venture manufacturing agreement for multi-launch rocket systems was signed by a US company and a State-owned munitions company. According to the agreement, 180 rocket launchers were to be produced at a plant near Burda. Some of the launchers were to be bought by DIDA and the remainder were to be exported. Several other major deals with Western defence manufacturers are under serious negotiation, including projects for communications and transport aircraft. At the end of 1988, a consortium (including a US company and the Turkish company, Nurol) was awarded a contract to manufacture armoured personnel carriers in Turkey.

Tourism is one of Turkey's fastest growing industries and is an important source of foreign currency. In the 1990s, revenues from tourism have totalled around US $3,000-$3,500m. annually, with about 5.5m. foreign visitors each year. In 1993 tourist revenues totalled $3,959m. While these figures represent a substantial improvement on the previous decade, a huge potential still remains unrealized. One problem over the past few years has been the escalation of Kurdish nationalist activity which frequently spills over into the tourist resorts of the West, severely damaging the prospects of the tourism industry.

FINANCE

The Central Bank (Merkez Bankası), the sole bank of issue, started its operations on 3 October 1931. It controls exchange operations and ensures the monetary requirements of certain State enterprises by the discounting of bonds which are issued by these institutions and guaranteed by the treasury. However, legislation that was adopted in 1987 awarded the Government wide-ranging powers over the Central Bank, that could, if they were applied, theoretically reduce the bank to the level of an ordinary State bank. Other banks are described in the Finance section on pages 934–936.

The monetary unit is the kuruş (piastre) by the law of April 1916. The Turkish lira (pound), which is, in practice, employed as the monetary unit, is equal to 100 kuruş.

The principal sources of budgetary revenue are income tax, import taxes and duties, taxes and fees on services and revenues from State monopolies. Late in 1984, the Government introduced value-added tax (VAT) to replace the previous unwieldy system of production taxes.

In 1992 the budget deficit totalled some TL 43,606,000m., or 5.5% of GNP. It was planned that this would be reduced to TL 53,200,000m., or 4.3% of GNP, in 1993. In fact, the deficit nearly tripled to reach TL 122,000,000m., or 9.2% of GNP. The rising budget deficit continued to exert serious inflationary pressure on the economy and to attract much domestic and international criticism. The Government continued to borrow heavily in 1993, and the domestic debt stood at TL 356,555,000m. at the end of that year (compared with TL 181,101,000m. at the end of 1992). At the same time Turkey's foreign debt increased by 22.5% to US $67,000m. The pressure of servicing both the domestic and external debt indirectly fuels the rate of inflation. In 1993 the annual rate of inflation was 71.1%, up from 70.1% in 1992.

Under these inflationary pressures, in early 1994 two US credit rating agencies downgraded Turkey's credit rating, which resulted in a 'run' on foreign currencies. The value of the lira was officially devalued by 12% against the dollar; however the currency continued to plummet. Interest rates rose to 150%-200% as the Government and the Central Bank desperately tried to bring the financial markets under control. In early April the Government announced a programme of austerity measures to reduce the budget deficit, lower inflation and restore domestic and international confidence in the economy. The programme included a 'freezing' of wages, price increases of up to 100% on state monopoly goods, as well as longer-term restructuring measures such as the closure of loss-making state enterprises and an accelerated privatization process. By May the lira stabilized at around TL 30,000 to the dollar, having stood at some TL 16,000 at the beginning of the year. However, in late August the value of the lira fell once more but was steadied at a rate of TL 34,000 per dollar, following an increase in interest rates from 70% to 240%.

A heavy burden of foreign debt, contracted in the late 1970s and extended through reschedulings in 1978, 1980 and 1981, has severely hampered the Government's structural adjustment programme. In 1978, following a serious political and economic crisis which rendered the country virtually bankrupt, Turkey and the IMF reached agreement on a programme of restraints, while the Fund agreed to grant a US $450m. credit over two years. Following the IMF's lead, foreign banks and Governments agreed to reschedule about $2,500m. of Turkey's external debts. Further loans and credits were extended in 1979, and in January 1980 the Government introduced a further austerity package which set the economy on a more open footing, in contrast to its previously insular, State-dominated growth; for example, a ban on foreign investment in mining (including petroleum) exploration was lifted.

Turkey's foreign creditors responded with yet more large infusions of aid; the IMF pledged US $1,650m. over three years. In both 1980 and 1981, successful debt rescheduling operations were carried out, which left Turkey with a manageable short-term debt load by converting much of Turkey's debt into medium- and long-term credits. Turkey's international credit rating steadily improved in the second half of 1985 (after a setback earlier in the year, with the slow syndication of a $500m. Eurodollar loan). However, the Government has not managed to control external borrowing, which had reached more than $67,000m. by the end of 1993. In 1987 the short-term debt increased by 20.1% to $7,623m. Since then, however, efforts to reduce short-term debt have met with some success, and the total was reduced by 16% in 1988 and 10% in 1989. In 1990, however, short-term debt increased by some 65%, only to decrease by 4%, to $9,117m., in 1992.

Perennial balance-of-payments difficulties, compounded by the pressure of external debt servicing, have forced the Government to revise its debt-servicing schedule. It is estimated that foreign debt servicing will total US $28,300m. for the period 1990–95.

The World Bank has consistently provided strong support for what it regards as a model developing country coping with high external debt servicing by means of internal structural reform and rising inflows from increased exports. Although direct balance-of-payments support from the World Bank to Turkey was discontinued in 1985, it has continued to help Turkey through sector loans and 'B-loan' co-financings with commercial banks. Total World Bank lending to Turkey in its fiscal year ending 30 June 1987 totalled US $1,069.4m., which was only slightly less than in 1985/86. The World Bank was expected to extend a structural adjustment credit to Turkey in October 1994. However, by the end of August the Government had failed to respond to the Bank's policy recommendations.

Turkey's persistent trade deficit has been partly offset, for some time, by a net surplus on invisible earnings (services and transfers), particularly helped by expatriate workers' remittances. A major contributor to the invisibles balance since the early 1980s has been the contribution from Turkish contractors, who, although arriving late for the growth in the Middle East construction industry, quickly made their mark. Like other foreign firms, however, their fortunes have suffered as a result of the fall in the price of petroleum and the subsequent decrease in development revenues. In 1986 Turkish contractors won US $1,430m. worth of new work in the Middle East, 82% more than in 1985. Most of this total, however, was accounted for by a single order—the $775m. Turkish share in the Bekme dam scheme in Iraq. However, in the context of economic sanctions imposed upon Iraq by the UN in August 1990, work on the scheme has been suspended indefinitely at enormous cost to the Turkish contractors. Saudi Arabia, the source of most new work in 1985, registered only $5m. worth in 1986. Turkish contractors have found the Middle East market much less lucrative since then, and delays in payments by Libya and Iraq have become a constant source of worry for both the contractors and the Government.

Workers' remittances have long been an important source of foreign exchange. These totalled US $3,074m. in 1992 and $3,200m. in 1993. Receipts from tourism, also an important source of foreign exchange, totalled $3,639m. in 1992 and $3,959m. in 1993. The current account surplus of $272m. in 1991 was followed by a deficit of $943m. in 1992 and one of $5,010m. in 1993.

EXTERNAL TRADE

Since 1947, Turkey has had a persistent foreign trade deficit. But, following the economic reforms of 1980 and the introduction of free-market, export-led policies, the deficit decreased for a few years in the early 1980s. After 1985, however, the trade deficit increased every year until 1988, when it declined by about 33%, from US $3,968m. in 1987 to $2,673m. In 1989 there was a sharp increase again, to $4,136m., while in 1990 the deficit more than doubled to $9,343m., when imports increased significantly to $22,302m. and exports only slightly to $12,959. The expansion of the deficit was due to the overvalued TL, the continuing liberalization of the import regime and the phasing out of direct subsidies to exporters. In 1991 exports increased slightly to $13,593m., while imports decreased to $21,047m., resulting in a trade deficit of $7,454m. In 1992 both imports and exports were sluggish, rising to $22,872m. and $14,715m. respectively, resulting in a deficit of $8,157m. Favourable exchange rates resulted in a dramatic increase in imports to $29,429m. in 1993, while exports rose only slightly to $15,349m., thus yielding a record trade deficit of $14,080m. Principal imports were crude petroleum, non-electrical machinery, electrical machinery, chemical products, rubber and plastics, iron and steel, petroleum products, non-ferrous metals and fertilizers. The principal exports were textiles, iron and steel, tobacco, hazelnuts, leather goods, carpets, livestock and tinned foods. In 1993 Germany maintained its position both as Turkey's largest export market, taking 23.8% of all Turkish exports, and the main supplier, accounting for 15.4% of all Turkish imports. The fundamental shift in trade direction, which took place in 1986 as a result of the fall in petroleum prices, with exporters striving to compensate for lost Middle East markets by developing new export markets in Europe and the Americas, has persisted. The proportion of Turkish exports sold to Islamic countries declined from 25.2% of the total in 1987 to around 16.9% in early 1993. In contrast, the share of Turkish exports to other OECD countries increased from 61.7% in 1989 to 64.6% in 1992, although this fell to 59.8% in 1993.

In 1963 the Government signed an association agreement with the EC, under which Turkey was granted financial aid and preferential tariff quotas. A package of minor improvements was introduced at the end of 1976 and the association agreement was revised in July 1980, offering Turkey a five-year financial aid package. Since the military coup of September 1980, aid from EC countries has become increasingly dependent upon the restoration of democracy and human rights in Turkey. NATO countries have been divided on support for the Ankara regime: in December 1981 the USA promised to accelerate aid to Turkey, but in March 1982 EC aid worth $586m. was 'frozen'. This aid still remains blocked and differences with the EC persist, despite the reconvening of the Turkey-EC Association Council in September 1986. In 1987 Turkey submitted an application for full EC membership in March, followed by a concerted diplomatic effort to win support for its application in Europe. The 'frozen' aid was partly released in early 1988. Later in the year, the Turkish Prime Minister, Turgut Özal, met the Greek Prime Minister, Andreas Papandreou, in Athens for talks aimed at cultivating closer relations. This process of *détente* has a long way to go, however, before the Greek Government agrees not to veto Turkish membership of the EC. At the end of 1989 the European Commission published its report in response to Turkey's application for full membership. The report drew attention to both economic and political problems in Turkey, as well as the country's unsatisfactory human rights record, and proposed that negotiations should not start until after 1992. It is unlikely that Turkey will be admitted as a full member before the end of the decade. Discussions between the two sides in 1993 secured an agreement to construct a customs union, which was scheduled to be effective on 1 January 1995.

In recent years, the US Government's intended military and economic aid to Turkey has been affected by the determination of Congress to institute severe cuts in retaliation for the Turkish Government's refusal to modify its support for the

'Turkish Republic of Northern Cyprus' ('TRNC'). Turkish military leaders have said that they require much more support to modernize the armed forces, whose equipment, in some cases, dates back to the Korean War (1950–53). Differences within the US and Turkish Governments, as regards the level of military aid required by Turkey in the next five-year defence and economic co-operation agreement between Turkey and the USA to replace the one that expired in December 1985, impeded its ratification until February 1988. Relations between Turkey and the USA deteriorated to such an extent in 1987, that President Evren postponed a state visit to the USA in May. In June 1988, however, Özal made an official visit to the USA and relations appeared to have improved. The Turkish Government's unequivocal support for the actions of the multi-national alliance against Iraq at the time of the crisis in the Persian (Arabian) Gulf in 1990 and 1991, together with a visit to Turkey, undertaken by President Bush following the resolution of the conflict in early 1991, appeared to further cement this improvement in relations. The defence and economic co-operation agreement, which expired in December 1990, was extended for a further year in September 1991.

PLANNING

Successive Five-Year Economic Development Plans have aimed at the long-term target of self-sustained economic growth (independent of foreign loans), devoting a large proportion of investment to mining and manufacturing industry. During the years of the first Five-Year Plan (1962–67) a real growth rate of 6.6% per annum was achieved. The second Five-Year Plan, covering the years 1968 to 1972, envisaged an annual growth rate of 7%, which was almost exactly achieved. An annual growth rate of 7.9% in GNP was aimed at in the third Five-Year Plan (1973–77) but many targets were only 60% achieved and, in real terms, the overall growth rate was below target. The start of the fourth Plan (1978–82) was delayed by the economic crisis of 1978, and later shelved. The Evren Government drew up a fifth Five-Year Development Plan, but in June 1983 decided to leave its formal introduction to the new civilian Government after the transition to civilian rule in the November general elections. In the event, Prime Minister Özal's Government unveiled its own modified fifth Five-Year Plan in mid-1984.

In May 1989 the Government published the sixth Plan (1990–94). The Plan envisages an average annual growth rate of 7%, reaching 8.3% in 1994. Private sector investments are targeted to grow at an annual average rate of 11%, with growth reaching 15% by the end of the Plan period. The surplus on the current account of the balance of payments is expected to increase throughout the period, to reach $2,500m. in 1994. Exports are projected to grow at an average rate of 15% per year, and to exceed $22,000m. by 1994. Inflation is expected to have fallen to 10% per year by the end of the Plan period. In September 1994 the preparation for the seventh Plan was postponed by one year; an intermediary target plan was to be prepared for 1995.

PROSPECTS

After two years of severe economic crisis, an economic recovery plan, initiated under IMF pressure, led to a steadily increasing improvement in the economy, with GNP rising by 4.4% in both 1981 and 1982. However, in 1983 there were signs of trouble under the economic direction of Adnan Baser Kafaoğlu, who had replaced Turgut Özal as Finance Minister in July 1982. The loosening of monetary controls led to increasing inflation, and a number of companies were rescued expensively by the Government. Özal returned in the November general elections in 1983 with renewed determination to push through his export-led IMF-style recovery programme and also moved quickly to lay the foundation of what, if fully implemented, would be a transformation of Turkey's previously insular and State-dominated economy into one more similar to Western models. In particular, Özal and his advisers sought to emulate the economic models of Japan and South Korea, and the growth that was achieved in those countries through flourishing exports and the encouragement of large trading houses.

His sweeping measures included legislation paving the way for a partial privatization of the ponderous and inefficient State economic enterprise (SEE) system, encouraging the price competitiveness of Turkish exports abroad by the fine tuning of exchange rates and the complete revision and overhaul of foreign investment legislation. Along with this, the whole foreign exchange regime has been liberalized, and previously protectionist import duties greatly reduced, while, at the same time, the government has knocked away export incentives that acted as a prop to the export drive. Impressive statistical gains in exports, and the condition of the balance of payments in 1984 and 1985 appeared to vindicate the Government's policies. However, their vulnerability to adverse external factors, over which the Government has little control, was demonstrated in 1986 by the effects of the petroleum price crisis. The gains made through the decrease in Turkey's petroleum import bill were outweighed by the losses incurred through the decline in the Middle East's purchasing power for Turkish exports. As regards the invisible account in 1986, expatriate remittances continued to fall and receipts from tourism unexpectedly declined. At the same time, there was an appreciable increase in foreign borrowing, partly to cover the deterioration in the balance of payments.

Unfortunately for the Government, the benefits of its structural adjustment programme coincided with an increase in domestic demand in 1986. A large increase in the demand for consumer durables has been sustained by the continuing expansion in the construction industry. Mindful of the inflationary dangers of an excessively rapid economic expansion, the Government set a conservative growth target of 5% for 1987. In early 1987 the Government introduced extensive cuts in public expenditure and extended import curbs in an attempt to slow down the rate of economic expansion. All this, however, was negated by the complete subjection of economic policy-making to political expediency. In 1987 there were local elections in June, a referendum in September and a general election in November. All caution was abandoned as the Government attempted, successfully, to gain electoral support. As a result, estimates indicate that actual growth was 7.4%. The annual rate of inflation had increased to 60% by January 1988 and rose to 67.7% in the twelve months to the end of June, finally reaching 75.4%.

In February 1988, under pressure from the burden of foreign debt-servicing and rising inflation, the Government announced new austerity measures, introduced steep price increases and allowed interest rates to rise to 65%. The attempt to reduce effective demand had considerable success and the GNP growth rate was down to 2.5% in 1988. However, the rate of inflation continued to climb, reaching 75.4%. Businessmen and particularly industrialists affected by the problems of falling demand and the high cost of borrowing complained bitterly of a stagflationary situation. These problems continued unchanged through much of 1989 until, in the second half of the year, the Government began to allow a faster expansion of the economy. Although fears of a large increase in the rate of inflation had been voiced with growing frequency, the annual rate of inflation decreased in 1989 and 1990 to 63.3% and 60.3% respectively, only to increase to 66.0% in 1991, to 70.1% in 1992 and to 71.1% in 1993.

While revenue from exports and tourism has increased, and the current account of the balance of payments has improved, the economy's underlying structural problems remain as severe as ever—a large current account deficit, high external debt servicing, and high internal inflation spurred by an expanding budget deficit. The success of Turkey's exporters in Middle Eastern markets in the early 1980s will not be repeated in Europe and the Americas, where market saturation will quickly be compounded by rising protectionism. To meet Turkey's external debt-servicing, it has been calculated that exports would need to increase in value by around 10% per year. With the decline in Middle Eastern markets, this level of expansion cannot be guaranteed.

In mid-1989 the economy became a factor of secondary importance, as political instability threatened the country. Having performed very badly in local elections in March, Prime Minister Özal came under great pressure to call an early general election. Not only did Özal ignore this pressure, but he had himself elected President in November. This went against the tradition of a neutral, non-party President, and the fact that he was elected with the votes of a party which appeared no longer to enjoy majority support also cast a shadow over his Presidency. Özal attempted to run the Government indirectly, by installing a weak Prime Minister, Yıldırım Akbulut, in his place, a move which weakened the Government's cohesion and effectiveness. It was hoped that the installation of Mesut Yılmaz as Prime Minister in June 1991 would stabilize the party's diminishing popularity before the October 1991 general elections. In fact, the election results were inconclusive, with Özal's Motherland Party beaten into second place by Süleyman Demirel's conservative True Path Party (DYP). After lengthy negotiations, Demirel formed a coalition government with Erdal İnönü's social democratic SHP. While the economic programme of the new Government proved popular with the business community, it seemed unlikely that any signficant change would be made to the general economic orientation established by the Özal governments. The death of President Özal, in April 1993, resulted in a period of renewed political confusion, following which Süleyman Demirel was elected to the presidency and Tansu Çiller to the party leadership and, consequently, the premier-

ship. Çiller's economic experience (having served as a minister with responsibility for the economy for 18 months in Demirel's cabinet) made her a popular choice as premier with the business community. The new Prime Minister promptly identified the budget deficit and the drain on public resources represented by loss-making public sector enterprises as crucial economic problems to be immediately addressed. After a year and a half under Çiller's leadership, the coalition Government appeared weak and constantly beset by internal problems in mid-1994. The financial crisis in early 1994 severely affected domestic and international confidence in the economy. Local elections in March had already seen a surge in the Islamic fundamentalist Welfare Party's vote, indicating that large numbers of people were looking for a more radical alternative. The business community, however, continued to support Çiller, if only because there appeared to be no viable alternative. Çiller's austerity programme, that was announced in April, appeared to have stabilized the economy, with an initial reduction in the budget deficit (although at the expense of a large number of jobs), and had secured the support of the IMF, which in July approved a stand-by credit of US $742m. for the Government's economic reform programme for 1994–95.

Statistical Survey

Source (unless otherwise stated): Türkiye İş Bankası AS, Economic Research Dept, Atatürk Bul. 191, 06684 Kavaklıdere, Ankara; tel. (312) 4188096; telex 42082; fax (312) 4250750.

Area and Population

AREA, POPULATION AND DENSITY

Area (sq km)	779,452*
Population (census results)	
20 October 1985	
Males	25,671,975
Females	24,992,483
Total	50,664,458
21 October 1990	56,473,035†
Population (official estimates at mid-year)	
1989	54,890,000
1990	56,098,000
1991	57,326,000
Density (per sq km) at mid-1991	73.5

* 300,948 sq miles. The total comprises Anatolia (Turkey in Asia or Asia Minor), with an area of 755,688 sq km (291,773 sq miles), and Thrace (Turkey in Europe), with an area of 23,764 sq km (9,175 sq miles).
† Comprising 50,497,586 in Anatolia and 5,975,449 in Thrace.

PRINCIPAL TOWNS (population at 1990 census)

Ankara (capital)*	2,559,471	Diyarbakir . .	381,144
İstanbul* . .	6,620,241	Antalya . . .	378,208
İzmir (Smyrna)* .	1,757,414	Samsun . . .	303,979
Adana* . . .	916,150	Malatya . . .	281,776
Bursa . . .	834,576	Şanlıurfa. . .	276,528
Gaziantep . .	603,434	İzmit (Kocaeli) .	256,882
Konya . . .	513,346	Erzurum . . .	242,391
Mersin (İçel) . .	422,357	Kahramanmaraş .	228,129
Kayseri . . .	421,362	Sivas. . . .	221,512
Eskişehir. . .	413,082		

* Within municipal boundaries.

BIRTHS AND DEATHS (UN estimates, annual averages)

	1975–80	1980–85	1985–90
Birth rate (per 1,000) . . .	32.0	31.2	29.7
Death rate (per 1,000) . .	10.2	9.4	7.9

Expectation of life (UN estimates, years at birth, 1985–90): 65.3 (males 62.8; females 68.0).

Source: UN, *World Population Prospects: The 1992 Revision.*

ECONOMICALLY ACTIVE POPULATION
(sample survey, persons aged 12 years and over, 1991)

	Males	Females	Total
Agriculture, hunting, forestry and fishing	4,262,817	4,797,159	9,059,976
Mining and quarrying . .	201,750	2,950	204,700
Manufacturing. . . .	2,206,592	441,562	2,648,154
Electricity, gas and water . .	29,008	—	29,008
Construction	953,066	8,005	961,071
Trade, restaurants and hotels .	2,042,499	151,333	2,193,832
Transport, storage and communications . . .	733,319	39,844	773,163
Financing, insurance, real estate and business services.	332,832	105,810	438,642
Community, social and personal services . . .	2,206,248	501,576	2,707,824
Total employed . . .	12,968,131	6,048,239	19,016,370
Unemployed*	1,252,998	461,348	1,714,346
Total labour force . . .	14,221,129	6,509,587	20,730,716

* Including unemployed persons not previously employed.

Source: ILO, *Year Book of Labour Statistics.*

WORKERS ABROAD ('000)

	1990	1991	1992
Australia	29	29	29
Austria	58	56	62
Belgium	35	23	23
France	91	98	112
Germany	650	696	740
Libya	18	10	10
Netherlands	82	89	89
Saudi Arabia	75	130	130
Switzerland	39	35	36
Total (incl. others) . . .	1,115	1,235	1,300

WORKERS' REMITTANCES FROM ABROAD (US $ million)

	1990	1991	1992
Total	3,325	2,901	3,074

Agriculture

PRINCIPAL CROPS (provisional figures, '000 metric tons)

	1991	1992	1993
Wheat	20,400	19,300	21,000
Spelt	19	18	16
Rye	256	230	235
Barley	7,800	6,900	7,500
Oats	255	240	245
Maize	2,180	2,225	2,500
Millet	5	4	4
Rice (milled)	200	225	225
Dry beans	214	200	200
Chick peas	855	770	740
Lentils	640	600	735
Vetch	172	174	195
Broad beans (dry) . . .	70	68	65
Potatoes	4,600	4,600	4,650
Onions (dry)	1,600	1,700	1,650
Garlic (dry)	70	68	65
Tomatoes	6,200	6,400	6,150
Cabbages (incl. black) . .	684	698	697
Melons and watermelons .	5,700	5,480	4,900
Aubergines (Eggplants) .	750	740	750
Apples	1,900	2,100	2,080
Grapes	3,600	3,600	3,700
Pears	403	410	420
Hazel-nuts (Filberts) . .	380	520	305
Sultanas	130	120	180
Figs (dried)	45	35	45
Walnuts	122	120	115
Pistachios (in shell) . .	64	29	50
Almonds	46	47	48
Chestnuts	81	85	80
Oranges	830	820	840
Lemons	429	420	440
Mandarins	390	390	405
Peaches	350	370	370
Plums	186	190	200
Apricots (incl. wild) . .	276	320	230
Cherries (incl. sour) . .	150	155	155
Cotton (lint)	561	654	556
Cotton seed	n.a.	n.a.	n.a.
Tobacco (leaves) . . .	228	334	324
Sugar beet	15,474	15,126	15,563
Sesame seed	43	34	30
Sunflower seed . . .	800	950	815
Olives	640	750	550
Olive oil	60	100	n.a.
Tea (fresh leaves) . . .	683	731	579

LIVESTOCK ('000 head, year ending September)

	1990	1991	1992
Cattle	12,173	11,377	11,973
Buffaloes	429	371	336
Camels	2	2	2*
Pigs	8	12	10
Sheep	43,647	40,553	40,433
Goats	11,942	10,977	10,764
Horses	545	513	496
Mules	210	202	188
Asses	1,084	985	980*

Chickens (million): 64 in 1990; 97 in 1991; 139 in 1992.
Turkeys (million): 3 in 1990; 3 in 1991; 3 in 1992.

* FAO estimate.

Source: FAO, *Production Yearbook.*

LIVESTOCK PRODUCTS ('000 metric tons)

	1990	1991	1992
Beef and veal*	285	290	295
Buffalo meat	11	9	11†
Mutton and lamb* . . .	304	303	302
Goats' meat*	66	64	63
Horse meat†	3	3	3
Poultry meat	274	289	334
Edible offals†	118	115	116
Cows' milk	7,961	6,367*	6,106*
Buffalo milk	174	161	160†
Sheep milk	1,145	1,127	1,126†
Goats' milk	338	335	328‡
Butter and ghee . . .	115.0	115.4	111.8
Cheese	139.0†	140.8†	141.2
Hen eggs	384.9	384.1	390.0*
Honey	51.3	54.7	55.0†
Wool:			
greasy	45.2	44.7	42.0†
clean	24.9	24.6	23.1
Cattle and buffalo hides† . .	78.2	74.3	76.0
Sheep skins†	65.5	65.2	65.0
Goat skins†	9.8	9.8	9.8

* Unofficial figure(s).   † FAO estimate(s).

Source: FAO, mainly *Production Yearbook.*

Forestry

ROUNDWOOD REMOVALS ('000 cu m, excluding bark)

	1990	1991	1992
Sawlogs, veneer logs and logs			
for sleepers	3,625	3,197	3,197
Pulpwood*	705	705	705
Other industrial wood . .	1,630*	1,600	1,600*
Fuel wood	9,796*	9,750*	9,750*
Total	15,756	15,252	15,252

* FAO estimate(s). Annual output of pulpwood is assumed to be unchanged since 1987.

Source: FAO, *Yearbook of Forest Products.*

SAWNWOOD PRODUCTION ('000 cu m, incl. railway sleepers)

	1990	1991	1992
Coniferous (soft wood)* . .	3,354	3,354	3,354
Broadleaved (hard wood) . .	1,569*	1,574	1,574*
Total	4,923*	4,928	4,928*

* FAO estimate(s). Annual output of coniferous sawnwood is assumed to be unchanged since 1984.

Source: FAO, *Yearbook of Forest Products.*

Fishing

('000 metric tons, live weight)

	1989	1990	1991
Common carp	17.2	17.0	17.1
Whiting	20.5	19.0	22.7
Mullets	21.3	22.4	28.3
Bluefish	11.1	9.5	12.3
Atlantic horse mackerel . .	13.1	14.2	9.3
Mediterranean horse mackerel	99.8	71.9	24.5
European pilchard (sardine) .	25.9	18.8	30.3
European anchovy. . . .	98.6	74.0	90.6
Atlantic bonito . . .	5.0	14.7	19.6
Chub mackerel . . .	26.3	19.2	14.7
Other fishes (incl. unspecified)	66.8	56.4	66.2
Total fish	405.6	337.1	335.7
Crustaceans	10.2	7.7	2.1
Molluscs	40.1	38.9	26.9
Jellyfishes.	1.2	1.1	n.a.
Total catch	457.1	384.8	364.6
Inland waters	46.3	41.7	47.2
Mediterranean and Black Sea .	410.8	343.1	317.4

Source: FAO, *Yearbook of Fishery Statistics.*

Mining

('000 metric tons)

	1990	1991	1992
Crude petroleum	3,624	4,444	4,296
Iron ore*	5,220	5,358	5,450
Chromium ore*	1,011	1,015	613
Lignite†	36,968	43,997	49,847
Coal†	5,604	5,213	4,918
Copper (blister)† . . .	18	28	26

* Figures refer to the gross weight of ores.
† Production in the public sector only.

Industry

SELECTED PRODUCTS
('000 metric tons, unless otherwise indicated)

	1991	1992	1993
Paper*	403	466	370
Cotton yarn*	47	47	44
Woollen yarn*	4	3.7	5.4
Cotton fabrics (million metres)*	178	177	147
Woollen fabrics (million metres)*	6.3	4	5.3
Raki ('000 litres)* . . .	61,634	58,743	67,330
Beer ('000 litres) . . .	418,719	484,348	552,406
Cigarettes*	72	70	75
Pig iron	4,594	4,508	4,355
Cement	26,261	28,607	31,311
Sugar	1,824	1,593	1,743
Commercial fertilizers‡ . .	6,321	7,710	7,108
Electrolytic copper† . . .	21	7	n.a.
Polyethylene*	256	261	271
Coke	3,381	3,250	3,141
Motor spirit (petrol) . . .	2,568	2,727	3,215
Kerosene	147	145	165
Fuel oils	8,697	8,664	8,705
Hydroelectricity (million kWh)	22,680	26,531	33,963
Thermal electricity (million kWh)	37,540	40,659	39,764

* Public sector only.   † Private sector only.
‡ Excluding potassic fertilizers.

Finance

CURRENCY AND EXCHANGE RATES
Monetary Units
  100 kuruş = 1 Turkish lira (TL) or pound.

Sterling and Dollar Equivalents (31 May 1994)
  £1 sterling = 48,018 liras;
  US $1 = 31,762 liras;
  100,000 Turkish liras = £2.083 = $3.148.

Average Exchange Rate (liras per US $)
  1991   4,171.8
  1992   6,872.4
  1993   10,984.6

MONEY SUPPLY
(TL '000 million at 31 December)

	1991	1992	1993
Currency outside banks .	17,449	30,656	52,517
Demand deposits at deposit money banks . . .	29,325	50,686	79,484

GENERAL BUDGET (TL '000 million)*

Revenue†	1990	1991	1992
Taxation	45,431	78,734	141,797
Taxes on income, profits, etc. . . .	23,246	40,419	70,134
Taxes on property . .	101	144	259
Sales taxes . . .	12,371	22,832	42,088
Excises	957	3,357	9,147
Other domestic taxes on goods and services . .	3,924	4,952	8,203
Import duties . . .	3,336	4,574	7,813
Stamp taxes . . .	1,497	2,457	4,153
Property income . . .	658	881	1,502
Other current revenue . .	7,586	10,488	32,268
Capital revenue . . .	1,262	547	803
Total	54,937	90,650	176,370

Expenditure‡	1990	1991	1992
General public services . .	17,215	34,192	65,563
Defence	7,966	13,783	25,558
Education	13,088	23,294	45,114
Health	2,437	3,934	7,870
Social security and welfare .	1,445	2,661	4,782
Housing and community amenities	1,018	1,716	3,900
Other community and social services	507	787	1,554
Economic services . . .	12,155	33,385	43,909
Fuel and energy . .	3,824	7,148	11,724
Agriculture, forestry, fishing and hunting .	1,363	2,632	4,102
Mining, manufacturing and construction . .	607	1,503	1,437
Transport and communications . .	5,012	10,930	17,433
Other purposes . . .	12,487	18,598	27,006
Total	68,318	132,350	225,256
Current	59,207	110,875	198,455
Capital	9,110	21,475	26,801

* Figures exclude the operations of central government units with their own budgets.
† Excluding grants received (TL '000 million): 1,636 in 1990; 8,434 in 1991; 1,700 in 1992.
‡ Excluding net lending (TL '000 million): 38 in 1990; 51 in 1991; 142 in 1992.

Source: IMF, *Government Finance Statistics Yearbook.*

INTERNATIONAL RESERVES
(US $ million at 31 December)

	1991	1992	1993
Central bank:			
Gold holding. . . .	1,493	1,494	1,488
Foreign exchange . .	4,918	6,116	6,277
Reserve holdings of other			
banks	5,842	7,644	10,642
Total reserves . . .	12,253	15,254	18,407

COST OF LIVING
(Consumer Price Index for urban areas; base: 1987 = 100)

	1991	1992	1993
Food	851.7	1,459.2	2,385.9
Clothing	939.9	1,505.1	2,504.7
Household expenditures . .	678.6	1,097.3	1,830.4
Medical and personal care . .	897.6	1,530.0	2,575.8
Transport	866.1	1,511.7	2,371.0
Cultural and recreational			
expenditures . . .	721.5	1,272.3	2,207.2
Dwelling expenditures* . .	527.0	932.5	1,602.2
All items	754.5	1,283.1	2,131.2

* Rent is assumed to be fixed.

NATIONAL ACCOUNTS (TL '000 million at current prices)
Gross Domestic Product by Economic Activity

	1991	1992	1993
Agriculture and livestock . .	84,442	139,712	229,151
Forestry and logging . .	3,403	9,270	11,685
Fishing	2,943	4,363	7,520
Mining and quarrying . .	8,747	13,219	19,264
Manufacturing. . . .	111,350	188,751	326,642
Electricity, gas and water . .	13,288	27,616	49,575
Construction	41,649	69,679	122,261
Wholesale and retail trade. .	91,372	160,574	263,251
Transport, storage and			
communications . . .	74,058	132,282	225,267
Financial institutions . .	23,127	38,560	67,938
Ownership of dwellings . .	20,127	35,775	56,880
Other private services . .	38,670	67,763	117,053
Government services . .	61,051	111,841	203,922
Gross domestic product at			
factor cost	574,227	999,405	1,700,409
Indirect taxes	66,183	118,486	221,551
Less Subsidies	10,293	24,523	29,354
GDP in purchasers' values	630,117	1,093,368	1,892,606
Net factor income from abroad	4,314	10,475	16,099
Gross national product . .	634,431	1,103,843	1,908,705

BALANCE OF PAYMENTS (US $ million)

	1990	1991	1992
Merchandise exports f.o.b. .	13,026	13,672	14,891
Merchandise imports f.o.b. .	−22,581	−20,998	−23,082
Trade balance . . .	−9,555	−7,326	−8,191
Exports of services . .	7,275	7,659	8,452
Imports of services . .	−3,071	−3,218	−3,625
Other income received . .	1,658	1,656	1,999
Other income paid . . .	−3,425	−3,598	−3,637
Private unrequited transfers			
(net).	3,349	2,854	3,147
Official unrequited transfers			
(net).	1,144	2,245	912
Current balance	−2,625	272	−943
Direct capital investment (net)			
. . . . . .	700	783	779
Portfolio investment (net) . .	547	648	2,411
Other capital (net). . .	2,790	−3,828	458
Net errors and omissions . .	−469	926	−1,221
Overall balance	943	−1,199	1,484

Source: IMF, *International Financial Statistics.*

External Trade

PRINCIPAL COMMODITIES (US $ million)

Imports (excl. grants)	1991	1992	1993
Crude petroleum . . .	2,456	2,632	2,550
Iron and steel	1,993	2,100	3,057
Machinery	5,140	5,886	7,236
Transport vehicles . . .	1,540	2,222	4,012
Chemical products . . .	1,221	n.a.	n.a.
Plastic materials, natural and			
synthetic rubber . .	848	986	1,161
Total (incl. others) . . .	20,961	22,872	29,428

Exports	1991	1992	1993
Fruits (dried)	901	826	916
Iron and steel	1,445	1,549	1,991
Leather garments . . .	515	454	441
Cotton yarn and fabric,			
artificial and synthetic			
fibres, carpets, textile			
clothing and other textile			
goods	4,265	5,156	5,452
Tobacco (unprocessed leaves) .	563	309	396
Total (incl. others) . . .	13,593	14,715	15,344

PRINCIPAL TRADING PARTNERS (US $ million)

Imports (excl. grants)	1991	1992	1993
Belgium/Luxembourg . .	557	551	683
France	1,227	1,351	1,952
Germany	3,232	3,755	4,533
Iran	91	365	667
Italy	1,845	1,919	2,558
Japan	1,092	1,113	1,621
Libya	281	445	131
Netherlands	642	698	870
Saudi Arabia	1,829	1,665	1,500
Switzerland	489	688	651
USSR	1,097	1,244	2,285
United Kingdom . . .	1,166	1,187	1,546
USA	2,255	2,600	3,351
Total (incl. others) . . .	21,047	22,872	29,428

Exports			1991	1992	1993
Belgium/Luxembourg	.	.	288	291	294
France	.	.	689	809	771
Germany	.	.	3,413	3,661	3,654
Iran	.	.	487	455	290
Iraq	.	.	122	212	160
Italy	.	.	972	943	750
Japan	.	.	226	162	158
Libya	.	.	237	247	246
Netherlands	.	.	475	500	517
Saudi Arabia	.	.	485	486	652
Spain	.	.	238	298	195
Switzerland	.	.	246	223	216
USSR	.	.	611	686	1,047
United Kingdom	.	.	676	796	835
USA	.	.	913	865	986
Total (incl. others)	.	.	13,593	14,715	15,344

Transport

RAILWAYS (traffic)

	1990	1991	1992
Passenger journeys (million) .	139	133	131
Freight (million metric tons) .	14	15	16

* Source: Ministry of Transport and Communications.

ROAD TRAFFIC (motor vehicles at 31 December)

	1990	1991	1992
Passenger cars . . .	1,857,889	2,116,313	2,496,177
Goods vehicles . . .	414,026	431,046	458,632
Buses and coaches .	224,524	242,853	271,158
Vans . . .	262,298	278,459	313,092
Tractors etc. . .	770,220	794,651	826,308
Motorcycles and mopeds .	536,221	596,552	601,884

Source: IRF, *World Road Statistics*.

INTERNATIONAL SEA-BORNE SHIPPING*
(freight traffic, metric tons)

	1989	1990	1991
Goods loaded . . .	115,965,257	118,176,339	134,422,786
Goods unloaded . .	62,936,036	65,503,301	69,194,966

* Excluding livestock.
Source: Turkish State Railways (TCDD).

CIVIL AVIATION (Turkish Airlines)

	1990	1991	1992
Number of passengers ('000) .	4,574	3,307	4,700
Freight handled (metric tons)* .	56,662	35,000	51,494

* Cargo and mail.
Source: Turkish Airlines Annual Reports.

Tourism

	1991	1992	1993
Number of foreign arrivals ('000) . .	5,518	7,076	6,501
Receipts from foreign travel (million US $) . . .	2,654	3,639	3,959
Expenditures for foreign travel (million US $) . .	592	776	934

Source: Ministry of Tourism.

TOURISTS BY COUNTRY OF ORIGIN ('000)

Country	1991	1992	1993
France	117	248	301
Germany	780	1,165	1,119
Greece	139	147	148
Iran	253	150	120
Italy	64	158	135
Syria	120	123	121
United Kingdom . . .	201	315	442
USA	79	182	255
Yugoslavia (former) . .	159	156	170
Total (incl. others) . .	5,518	7,076	6,500

TOURIST ACCOMMODATION (Dec. 1993)
235,238 beds (registered by the Ministry of Tourism).

Communications Media

	1989	1990	1991
Telephones in use ('000) . .	7,467	8,517	n.a.
Radio receivers ('000) . .	8,800	9,000	9,200
Television receivers ('000) .	9,500	9,750	10,000

Book production: 6,291 titles in 1990; 6,365 in 1991.
Source: mainly UNESCO, *Statistical Yearbook*.

Education

(1991/92)

	Institutions	Teachers ('000)	Pupils ('000)
Primary	50,701	235	6,879
Secondary:			
General	8,064	118	3,011
Technical and vocational . .	2,971	57	977
Higher (incl. academies, teacher training and other higher technical and vocational schools, universities) . .	424	35	759

Directory

The Constitution

In October 1981 the National Security Council (NSC), which took power in September 1980, announced the formation of a Consultative Assembly to draft a new constitution, replacing that of 1961. The Assembly consisted of 40 members appointed directly by the NSC and 120 members chosen by the NSC from candidates put forward by the governors of the 74 provinces; all former politicians were excluded. The draft Constitution was approved by the Assembly in September 1982 and by a national referendum in November. Its main provisions are summarized below:

Legislative power is vested in the unicameral National Assembly, with 400 deputies, who are elected by universal adult suffrage for a five-year term. Executive power is vested in the President, to be elected by the National Assembly for a seven-year term and empowered to appoint a Prime Minister and senior members of the judiciary, the Central Bank and broadcasting organizations; to dissolve the National Assembly; and to declare a state of emergency entailing rule by decree. Strict controls on the powers of trades unions, the press and political parties were also included. An appended 'temporary article' automatically installed the incumbent President of the NSC as Head of State for a seven-year term, assisted by a Presidential Council comprising members of the NSC.

An amendment, adopted in June 1987, increased the number of deputies in the National Assembly from 400 to 450.

The Government

HEAD OF STATE

President: SÜLEYMAN DEMİREL (took office 16 May 1993).

CABINET
(September 1994)

A coalition of the True Path Party (DYP) and the Social Democratic Populist Party (SHP).

Prime Minister: TANSU ÇİLLER (DYP).

Deputy Prime Minister and Minister of State: MURAT KARAYALÇIN (SHP).

Minister of Justice: MEHMET MOĞULTAY (SHP).

Minister of National Defence: MEHMET GÖLHAN (DYP).

Minister of the Interior: NAHİT MENTEŞE (DYP).

Minister of Foreign Affairs: MUMTAZ SOYSAL (SHP).

Minister of Finance: İSMET ATİLLA (DYP).

Minister of National Education: NEVZAT AYAZ (DYP).

Minister of Public Works and Housing: (vacant).

Minister of Health: DOGAN BARAN (DYP).

Minister of Transport and Communications: MEHMET KÖSTEPEN (DYP).

Minister of Agriculture and Rural Affairs: REFAİDDİN ŞAHİN (DYP).

Minister of Forestry: HASAN EKİNCİ (DYP).

Minister of Labour and Social Security: NIHAT MATKAP (SHP).

Minister of Trade and Industry: MEHMET DONEN (SHP).

Minister of Energy and Natural Resources: VEYSEL ATASOY (DYP).

Minister of Culture: TIMURCIN SAVAS (SHP).

Minister of Tourism: HALIL CULHAOĞLU (SHP).

Minister of the Environment: RIZA AKÇALI (DYP).

Ministers of State: NECMETTİN CEVEHERI (DYP), YILDIRIM AKTUNA (DYP), ALİ SEVKİ EREK (DYP), İBRAHIM TEZ (SHP), BEKİR SAMİ DACE (DYP), TÜRKAN AKYOL (SHP), ESAT KIRATLIOGLU (DYP), NAFIZ KURT (DYP), MEHMET KAHRAMAN (SHP), AYKON DOĞAN (DYP), ABDÜLKABİ ATAÇ (DYP), ERMAN ŞAHIN (SHP), AYVAZ GOKDEMIR (DYP), ŞÜKRÜ ERDEM (DYP).

MINISTRIES

President's Office: Cumhurbaşkanlığı Köşkü, Çankaya, Ankara; tel. (312) 4407212.

Prime Minister's Office: Başbakanlık, Bakanlıklar, Ankara; tel. (312) 4189056; fax (312) 4180476.

Deputy Prime Minister's Office: Başbakan yard. ve Devlet Bakanı, Bakanlıklar, Ankara; tel. (312) 4191621; fax (312) 4191547.

Ministry of Agriculture and Rural Affairs: Tarım ve Köy İsleri Bakanlığı, Bakanlıklar, Ankara; tel. (312) 4191677; fax (312) 4177168.

Ministry of Culture: Kültür Bakanlığı, Opera, Ankara; tel. (312) 3240322; fax (312) 3111431.

Ministry of Energy and Natural Resources: Enerji ve Tabii Kaynaklar Bakanlığı, Konya Yolu, Beştepe, Ankara; tel. (312) 2231109; fax (312) 2229405.

Ministry of the Environment: İstanbul Cad. 88, İskitler, Ankara; tel. (312) 3423900.

Ministry of Finance: Maliye Bakanlığı, Dikmen Cad., Ankara; tel. (312) 4250018; fax (312) 4250058.

Ministry of Foreign Affairs: Dişişleri Bakanlığı, Yeni Hizmet Binası, 06520 Balgat, Ankara; tel. (312) 2871665; fax (312) 2873869.

Ministry of Forestry: Orman Bakanlığı, Atatürk Bul., Bakanlıklar, Ankara; tel. (312) 4176000.

Ministry of Health: Sağlik Bakanlığı, Yenişehir, Ankara; tel. (312) 4312486; telex 42770; fax (312) 4339885.

Ministry of the Interior: İçişleri Bakanlığı, Bakanlıklar, Ankara; tel. (312) 4254080; fax (312) 4181795.

Ministry of Justice: Adalet Bakanlığı, 06100 Bakanlıklar, Ankara; tel. (312) 4191331; fax (312) 4173954.

Ministry of Labour and Social Security: Çalişma ve Sosyal Güvenlik Bakanlığı, Eskişehir Yolu 42, Emek, Ankara; tel. (312) 4170727; fax (312) 4179765.

Ministry of National Defence: Milli Savunma Bakanlığı, 06100 Ankara; tel. (312) 4254596; fax (312) 4184737.

Ministry of National Education: Milli Eğitim Bakanlığı, Ankara; tel. (312) 4255330; fax (312) 4177027.

Ministry of Public Works and Housing: Bayındırlık ve İskan Bakanlığı, Vekaletler Cad. 1, 06100 Ankara; tel. (312) 4255711; fax (312) 4180406.

Ministry of Tourism: Turizm Bakanlığı, İsmet İnönü Bul. 5, Bahçelievler, Ankara; tel. (312) 2128300; fax (312) 2136887.

Ministry of Trade and Industry: Sanayi ve Ticaret Bakanlığı, Tandoğan, Ankara; tel. (312) 4314866; fax (312) 2304251.

Ministry of Transport and Communications: Ulaştırma Bakanlığı, Sok. 5, Emek, Ankara; tel. (312) 2124416; fax (312) 2124930.

Legislature

NATIONAL ASSEMBLY

Speaker: HÜSAMETTİN CİNDORUK.

General Election, 20 October 1991

Party	Seats
True Path Party (DYP)	178
Motherland Party (ANAP)	115
Social Democratic Populist Party (SHP)	88*
Welfare Party (RP)	62†
Democratic Left Party (DSP)	7
Total	450

* Including 22 seats for the Kurdish nationalist People's Labour Party (HEP).

† Including 19 seats for the Nationalist Labour Party (MÇP). Following the election the MÇP's alliance with the RP was dissolved and the MÇP deputies announced their intention to serve as independents.

The emergence of several new political parties since 1992 has resulted in a redistribution of allegiances within the National Assembly. At mid-August 1994 the distribution of seats was the following: True Path Party (DYP)—177; Motherland Party (ANAP)—96; Social Democratic People's Party (SHP)—54; Welfare Party (RP)—39; Republican People's Party (CHP)—18; Nationalist Party (MÇP)—14; Grand Union Party (BBP)—7; Democratic Left Party (DSP)—3; New Party (YP)—3; Nation Party (MP)—2; Independents—16; Vacant seats—21.

Political Organizations

All activities by political parties were banned by the National Security Council (NSC) on 12 September 1980, and all political parties were dissolved on 16 October 1981, prior to the formation of a Consultative Assembly. The most important parties which existed before that date were the Justice Party (Adalet Partisi), led by Süleyman Demirel, and the Republican People's Party (Cumhuriyet Halk Partisi—CHP), led by Bülent Ecevit.

From May 1983 new political parties were allowed to form, but their participation in the November general election was subject to strict rules: each had to have 30 party founders approved by the NSC and party organizations in at least 34 of the provinces, while candidates for the election were also subject to veto by the military rulers. Legislation enacted in March 1986 stipulated that a party must have organizations in at least 45 provinces, and in two-thirds of the districts in each of these provinces, in order to take part in an election. A political party is recognized by the Government as a legitimate parliamentary group only if it has at least 20 deputies in the National Assembly.

In mid-1992, following the adoption of more lenient guidelines for the formation of political parties (proposed by the new Demirel administration), several new parties were established, and the left-wing CHP, dissolved in 1981, was reactivated.

Anavatan Partisi (ANAP) (Motherland Party): 13 Cad. 3, Balgat, Ankara; tel. (312) 4468500; fax (312) 2865019; f. 1983; supports free-market economic system, moderate nationalist and conservative policies, rational social justice system, integration with the EEC, and closer ties with the Islamic world; merged with the Free Democratic Party (f. 1986) in December 1986; Chair. MESUT YILMAZ; Deputy Chair. EKREM PAKDEMİRLİ.

Büyük Birlik Partisi (BBP) (Grand Union Party): Tuna Cad. 28, Yenişehir, Ankara; tel. (312) 4413648; fax (312) 4355818; f. 1993; Chair. MUHSİN YAZICIOĞLU.

Cumhuriyet Halk Partisi (CHP) (Republican People's Party): Çevre Sok. 28, Ankara; tel. and fax (312) 4685969; f. 1923 by Kemal Atatürk, dissolved in 1981 and reactivated in 1992; left-wing; Leader DENİZ BAYKAL.

Demokrasi Partisi (DEP) (Democracy Party): Necatibey Cad. 40, Sihhiye, Ankara; tel. (312) 2318941; f. 1993; pro-Kurd; proscribed by the Constitutional Court in June 1994; Pres. HATİP DİCLE.

Demokratik Sol Parti (DSP) (Democratic Left Party): Fevzi Çakmak Cad. 17, Ankara; tel. (312) 2124950; fax (312) 2124188; f. 1985; centre-left; drawing support from members of the fmr Republican People's Party; Chair. BÜLENT ECEVİT.

Doğru Yol Partisi (DYP) (True Path Party): Akay Cad. 16, Ankara; tel. (312) 4172239; fax (312) 4185657; f. 1983; centre-right; replaced the Justice Party (f. 1961 and banned in 1981); Chair. TANSU ÇİLLER; Sec.-Gen. GÖKBERK ERGENEKON.

Halkın Emek Partisi (HEP) (People's Labour Party): Ankara; f. 1990; Kurdish nationalist, established by dissident members of the SHP; banned by the Government in July 1993; Chair. AHMET TÜRK.

Millet Partisi (MP) (Nation Party): İstanbul Cad., Rizgarlı Mah. Gayret Sok. 2, Ankara; tel. (312) 3127626; fax (312) 3127651; f. 1992; Chair. AYKUT EDİPALİ.

Milliyetçi Hareket Partisi (MÇP) (Nationalist Movement Party): Strazburg Cad. 36, Sihhiye, Ankara; tel. (312) 3218700; fax (312) 2311424; f. 1983; fmrly the Conservative Party; Leader ALPASLAN TÜRKEŞ.

OZEP (Freedom and Labour Party): Ankara; f. 1992 by disaffected Kurdish deputies from SHP; expected to absorb HEP (see above); Leader MAHMUT ALINAK.

Refah Partisi (RP) (Welfare Party): Ziyabey Cad. 11, Sok. 24, Balgat, Ankara; tel. (312) 2873056; fax (312) 2877465; f. 1983; Islamic fundamentalist; opposes integration with the EU; supports closer ties with neighbouring Islamic states; Chair. Prof. NECMETTİN ERBAKAN.

Sosyal Demokrat Halkçı Parti (SHP) (Social Democratic Populist Party): Cinnah Cad. Alabaş 5, Çankaya, Ankara; tel. (312) 2319432; f. 1985; formed by the merger of Halkçı Partisi (Populist Party) and the Sosyal Demokrasi Partisi (Social Democratic Party); centre-left; Chair. MURAT KARAYALÇIN; Sec.-Gen. HİKMET ÇETİN.

Yeni Parti (YP) (New Party): Rabat Sok. 27, Gaziosmanpaşa, Ankara; tel. (312) 4469254; fax (312) 4469579; f. 1993; Chair. YUSUF BOZKURT ÖZAL.

The Workers' Party of Turkey and the Turkish Communist Party, both illegal, merged in 1988 to form the Türkiye Birleşik Komünist Partisi (Turkish United Communist Party).

Diplomatic Representation

EMBASSIES IN TURKEY

Afghanistan: Cinnah Cad. 88, 06551 Çankaya, Ankara; tel. (312) 4381121; telex 46769; fax (312) 4387745; Chargé d'affaires: MUHAMMAD SARWAR.

Albania: Nenehatun Cad. 89, 06700 Gaziosmanpaşa, Ankara; tel. (312) 4466527; fax (312) 4466528; Ambassador: SKENDER DRINI.

Algeria: Şehit Ersan Cad. 42, 06680 Çankaya, Ankara; tel. (312) 4278700; telex 42053; fax (312) 4268959; Ambassador: CHERIF DERBAL.

Argentina: Uğar Mumcu Cad. 60/3, 06700 Gaziosmanpaşa, Ankara; tel. (312) 4462061; telex 42373; fax (312) 4462063; Ambassador: ADOLFO OCTAVIANO SARACHO.

Australia: Nenehatun Cad. 83, 06680 Gaziosmanpaşa, Ankara; tel. (312) 4461180; telex 44284; fax (312) 4461188; Ambassador: DAVID WYKE EVANS.

Austria: Atatürk Bul. 189, Kavaklıdere, Ankara; tel. (312) 4342172; telex 42429; fax (312) 4189454; Ambassador: Dr JOHANN PLUTNER.

Azerbaijan: Cemal Nadir Sok. 20, Çelikler Apt, Çankaya, Ankara; tel. (312) 4412621; telex 46404; fax (312) 4412600; Ambassador: MEHMET ALIEV.

Bangladesh: Karyağdı Sok. 18, 06690 Aşağı Ayrancı, Ankara; tel. (312) 4392750; telex 46068; fax (312) 4392408; Ambassador: MAHMUDUL HASSAN.

Belgium: Nenehatun Cad. 109, Gaziosmanpaşa, Ankara; tel. (312) 4468247; telex 42258; fax (312) 4468251; Ambassador: ERIC KOBIA.

Bosnia and Herzegovina: Hafta Sok. 20, Ankara; tel. (312) 4464090; fax (312) 4466228; Ambassador: HAYRUDIN SOMUM.

Brazil: İran Cad. 47/1, Gaziosmanpaşa, Ankara; tel. (312) 4685320; telex 42657; fax (312) 4685324; Ambassador: ERNESTO ALBERTO FERREIRA DE CARVALHO.

Bulgaria: Atatürk Bul. 124, 06680 Kavaklıdere, Ankara; tel. (312) 4267455; fax (312) 4273178; Ambassador: BRANIMIR PETROV.

Canada: Nenehatun Cad. 75, 06700 Gaziosmanpaşa, Ankara; tel. (312) 4361275; telex 42369; fax (312) 4464437; Ambassador: PETER HANCOCK.

Chile: Cinnah Cad. 78/1, 06690 Çankaya, Ankara; tel. (312) 4389444; telex 42755; fax (312) 4386145; Chargé d'affaires: CÉSAR EUGENIO DEL SOLAR.

China, People's Republic: Gölgeli Sok. 34, 06700 Gaziosmanpaşa, Ankara; tel. (312) 4361453; telex 44532; fax (312) 4464248; Ambassador: HU CHANGLIN.

Croatia: Kelebek Sok. 15/A, Gaziosmanpaşa, Ankara; tel. (312) 4469460; fax (312) 4366212; Ambassador: H. BIŠĆEVIĆ.

Cuba: Kuşkondu Sok. 7/1, Çankaya, Ankara; tel. and fax (312) 4394110; Ambassador: JORGE CASTRO BENÍTEZ.

Czech Republic: Uğur Mumcu Cad. 100/3, 06770 Gaziosmanpaşa, Ankara; tel. (312) 4461244; telex 42380; fax (312) 4461245; Chargé d'affaires a.i.: JAROMÍR JOHANES.

Denmark: Kırlangıç Sok. 42, 06700 Gaziosmanpaşa, Ankara; tel. (312) 4275258; telex 42377; fax (312) 4684559; Ambassador: NIELS HELSKOV.

Egypt: Atatürk Bul. 126, 06680 Kavaklıdere, Ankara; tel. (312) 4261026; fax (312) 4270099; Ambassador: MOHAMMED ELDIWANY.

Finland: Galip Dede Sok. 1/19, Farabi, 06680 Çankaya, Ankara; tel. (312) 4255921; telex 42856; fax (312) 4680072; Ambassador: RISTO KAUPPI.

France: Paris Cad. 70, 06540 Kavaklıdere, Ankara; tel. (312) 4681154; telex 42385; fax (312) 4679434; Ambassador: FRANÇOIS DOPFFER.

Germany: Atatürk Bul. 114, 06680 Kavaklıdere, Ankara; tel. (312) 4265465; telex 44394; fax (312) 4266959; Ambassador: Dr JÜRGEN OESTERHELT.

Greece: Ziya ül-Rahman 9–11, 06610 Gaziosmanpaşa, Ankara; tel. (312) 4368860; telex 42146; fax (312) 4463191; Ambassador: ALEXANDER PHILON.

Holy See: Çukurça Mah. 2, Sok. 55, PK 33, 06552 Çankaya, Ankara (Apostolic Nunciature); tel. (4) 4390041; fax (312) 4402900; Apostolic Pro-Nuncio: Most Rev. SERGIO SEBASTIANI, Titular Archbishop of Caesarea in Mauretania.

Hungary: Gazi Mustafa Kemal Bul. 10, 06440 Kızılay, Ankara; tel. (312) 4258528; fax (312) 4188322; Ambassador: Dr ISTVÁN VÁSÁRY.

India: Cinnah Cad. 77/A, 06680 Çankaya, Ankara; tel. (312) 4382195; telex 42561; fax (312) 4403429; Ambassador: K. GAJENDRA SINGH.

Indonesia: Abdullah Cevdet Sok. 10, 06552 Çankaya, Ankara; tel. (312) 4382190; telex 43250; fax (312) 4382193; Ambassador: SUKARNO ABDULRACHMAN.

Iran: Tahran Cad. 10, Kavaklıdere, Ankara; tel. (312) 4274320; Ambassador: MOHAMMAD REZA BAGHERI.

Iraq: Turan Emeksiz Sok. 11, 06692 Gaziosmanpaşa, Ankara; tel. (312) 4266118; telex 42577; fax (312) 4684832; Ambassador: DANHAM MEJWEL EL-TIKRITI.

Israel: Mahatma Gandhi Cad. 85, Gaziosmanpaşa, Ankara; tel. (312) 4463605; telex 42560; Chargé d'affaires: URI GORDON.

Italy: Atatürk Bul. 118, Kavaklıdere, Ankara; tel. (312) 4265460; telex 42624; fax (312) 4265800; Ambassador: Dr GIORGIO FRANCHETTI PARDO.

Japan: Reşit Galip Cad. 81, 06692 Gaziomanpaşa, Ankara; tel. (312) 4460500; telex 42435; fax (312) 4371812; Ambassador: YOICHI YAMAGUSHI.

Jordan: Cinnah Cad. 54/10, 06690 Çankaya, Ankara; tel. (312) 4402054; telex 43637; fax (312) 4404327; Ambassador: SALEH KABARITI.

Kazakhstan: Ebuzziya Tevfik Sok. 6, Çankaya, Ankara; tel. (312) 4412301; telex 46193; fax (312) 4412303; Ambassador: KANAT B. SAUDABAEV.

Korea, Republic: Cinnah Cad., Alaçam Sok. 5, 06690 Çankaya, Ankara; tel. (312) 4684822; telex 42680; fax (312) 4682279; Ambassador: DONG-SUK MOON.

Kuwait: Reşit Galip Cad. 110, Gaziosmanpaşa, Ankara; tel. (312) 4450576; telex 43238; fax (312) 4466839; Chargé d'affaires: ABDULLATEEF ALI AL-MAWNASH.

Kyrgyzstan: Boyabat Sok. 11, Eren Apt, Gaziosmanpaşa, Ankara; tel. (312) 4468408; fax (312) 4468413.

Lebanon: Kızkulesi Sok. 44, Gaziosmanpaşa, Ankara; tel. (312) 4667487; telex 46063; fax (312) 4461023; Ambassador: KHALIL AL-KHALIL.

Libya: Cinnah Cad. 60, 06690 Çankaya, Ankara; tel. (312) 4381110; telex 43270; fax (312) 4403862; Secretary of the People's Committee: AHMED ABDULHAMID EL-ATRASH.

Macedonia, former Yugoslav republic: Filistin Sok. 30/2, Gaziosmanpaşa, Ankara; tel. (312) 4469204; fax (312) 4469206.

Malaysia: Uğur Mumcu Cad. 6, 06700 Gaziosmanpaşa, Ankara; tel. (312) 4463547; telex 43616; fax (312) 4464130; Ambassador: H. A. ZAIBEDAH.

Mexico: Çankaya Cad. 20/2, Çankaya, Ankara; tel. (312) 4413204; telex 42278; fax (312) 4413203; Ambassador: RAFAEL STEGER CATAÑO.

Morocco: Reşit Galip Cad., Rabat Sok. 11, Gaziosmanpaşa, Ankara; tel. (312) 4376020; telex 42869; fax (312) 4468430; Ambassador: MOHAMED GUEDIRA.

Netherlands: Uğur Mumcu Cad. 16, 06700 Gaziosmanpaşa, Ankara; tel. (312) 4460470; telex 42612; fax (312) 4463358; Ambassador: Dr J. N. J. B. HORAK.

New Zealand: İran Cad. 13/4, 06700 Kavaklıdere, Ankara; tel. (312) 4679054; fax (312) 4469740; Ambassador: CLIVE PEARSON.

Norway: Kelebek Sok. 18, 06692 Gaziosmanpaşa, Ankara; tel. (312) 4379950; telex 42244; fax (312) 4376430; Ambassador: NILS BØLSET.

Oman: Mahatma Gandhi Cad. 63, 06700 Gaziosmanpaşa, Ankara; tel. (312) 4369691; telex 46507; fax (312) 4374445; Ambassador: FAKIR BIN SALIM BIN FARAKH.

Pakistan: İran Cad. 37, 06700 Gaziosmanpaşa, Ankara; tel. (312) 4271410; fax (312) 4671023; Ambassador: INAM-UL HAQUE.

Philippines: Cayhane Sok. 24, Gaziosmanpaşa, Ankara; tel. (312) 4465831; fax (312) 4465733; Ambassador: BONIFACIO ARRIBAS.

Poland: Atatürk Bul. 241, 06650 Ankara; tel. (312) 4261694; fax (312) 4273987; Ambassador: WOJCIECH HENSEL.

Portugal: Kuleli Sok. 26, 06700 Gaziosmanpaşa, Ankara; tel. (312) 4461890; telex 42771; fax (312) 4461892; Ambassador: DUANTE VAZ PINTO.

Qatar: Karaca Sok. 19, Gaziosmanpaşa, Ankara; tel. (312) 4411364; telex 46209; fax (312) 4411544; Ambassador: SAAD MOHAMED AL-KUBAIS.

Romania: Bükreş Sok. 4, 06680 Çankaya, Ankara; tel. (312) 4271243; telex 42760; fax (312) 4271530; Ambassador: ALEXANDRE MARGARITESCU.

Russia: Karyağdı Sok. 5, 06692 Çankaya, Ankara; tel. (312) 4392122; telex 46151; fax (312) 4383952; Ambassador: ALBERT SERGEYEVICH CHERNYSHEV.

Saudi Arabia: Turan Emeksiz Sok. 6, Gaziosmanpaşa, Ankara; tel. (312) 4681540; telex 42456; fax (312) 4274886; Ambassador: NAJI MUFTI.

Slovakia: Atatürk Bul. 245, 06692 Kavaklıdere, Ankara; tel. (312) 4265887; fax (312) 4682689; Ambassador: JÁN SZELEPCSÉNYI.

South Africa: Filistin Cad. 27, Gaziosmanpaşa, Ankara; tel. (312) 4464056; fax (312) 4466434; Ambassador: C. F. JACOBS.

Spain: Vali Dr. Reşit Sok. 6, 06680 Çankaya, Ankara; tel. (312) 4380392; telex 42551; fax (312) 4395170; Ambassador: JAVIER VILLACIEROS.

Sudan: Zia Ül-Rahman Cad. 3/1, 06690 Çankaya, Ankara; tel. (312) 4461200; telex 46719; fax (312) 4467516; Ambassador: OMER MOHAMED SHOUNA.

Sweden: Katip Çelebi Sok. 7, 06692 Kavaklıdere, Ankara; tel. (312) 4286735; telex 42230; fax (312) 4685020; Ambassador: ERIK CORNELL.

Switzerland: Atatürk Bul. 247, 06692 Kavaklıdere, Ankara; tel. (312) 4675555; telex 44161; fax (312) 4671199; Ambassador: (vacant).

Syria: Abdullah Cevdet Sok. 7, 06680 Çankaya, Ankara; tel. (312) 4409657; telex 46688; fax (312) 4385609; Ambassador: ABDULAZIZ AL-RIFA.

Thailand: Çankaya Cad. Kader Sok. 45/3, 06700 Gaziosmanpaşa, Ankara; tel. (312) 4673409; telex 46096; fax (312) 4386474; Ambassador: SANTAD KIARTITAT.

Tunisia: Kuleli Sok. 12, 06700 Gaziosmanpaşa, Ankara; tel. (312) 4377720; telex 42215; fax (312) 4377100; Ambassador: MOHAMED MEGDICHE.

'Turkish Republic of Northern Cyprus': Rabat Sok. 20, 06700 Gaziosmanpaşa, Ankara; tel. (312) 4376030; telex 42575; fax (312) 4465238; Ambassador NAZIF BORMAN.

Turkmenistan: Rabat Sok. 22, Gaziosmanpaşa, Ankara; tel. (312) 4468563; telex 46085; fax (312) 4468378.

Ukraine: Cemal Nadir Sok. 9, Çankara, Ankara; tel. (312) 4399973; fax (312) 4406815; Ambassador: IGOR M. TURYANSKIY.

United Arab Emirates: Mahmut Yesari Sok. 10, 06680 Çankaya, Ankara; tel. (312) 4408410; telex 46044; fax (312) 4389854; Ambassador: YOUSSEF ABDUL KHALIK MOHAMED AL-ANSARI.

United Kingdom: Şehit Ersan Cad. 46/A, Çankaya, Ankara; tel. (312) 4274310; telex 42320; fax (312) 4683214; Ambassador: JOHN GOULDEN.

USA: Atatürk Bul. 110, Kavaklıdere, Ankara; tel. (312) 4686110; fax (312) 4670019; Ambassador: RICHARD C. BARKLEY.

Uzbekistan: Ahmet Rasim Sok. 14, Çankaya, Ankara; tel. (312) 4392740; telex 46028; Ambassador: UBAYDULLA ABDURAZAKOV.

Venezuela: Cinnah Cad. 78/2, Çankaya, Ankara; tel. (312) 4387135; telex 42453; fax (312) 4406619; Ambassador: RAMÓN DELGADO.

Yemen: İlkadim Sok. 15, 06700 Gaziosmanpaşa, Ankara; tel. (312) 4379920; fax (312) 4461778; Ambassador: (vacant).

Judicial System

Until the foundation of the Turkish Republic, a large part of the Turkish civil law—the laws affecting the family, inheritance, property, obligations, etc.—was based on the Koran, and this holy law was administered by special religious (Shari'a) courts. The legal reform of 1926 was not only a process of secularization, but also a radical change of the legal system. The Swiss Civil Code and the Code of Obligation, the Italian Penal Code and the Neuchâtel (Cantonal) Code of Civil Procedure were adopted and modified to fit Turkish customs and traditions.

According to current Turkish law, the power of the judiciary is exercised by judicial (criminal), military and administrative courts. These courts render their verdicts in the first instance, while superior courts examine the verdict for subsequent rulings.

SUPERIOR COURTS

Constitutional Court: Consists of 11 regular and four substitute members, appointed by the President. Reviews the constitutionality of laws, at the request of the President of the Republic, parliamentary groups of the governing party or of the main opposition party, or of one-fifth of the members of the National Assembly, and sits as a high council empowered to try senior members of state. The rulings of the Constitutional Court are final. Decisions of the Court are published immediately in the Official Gazette, and shall be binding on the legislative, executive, and judicial organs of the state.

Court of Appeals: The court of the last instance for reviewing the decisions and verdicts rendered by judicial courts. It has original and final jurisdiction in specific cases defined by law. Members are elected by the Supreme Council of Judges and Prosecutors.

Council of State: An administrative court of the first and last instance in matters not referred by law to other administrative courts, and an administrative court of the last instance in general. Hears and settles administrative disputes and expresses opinions on draft laws submitted by the Council of Ministers. Three-quarters of the members are appointed by the Supreme Council of Judges and Public Prosecutors, the remaining quarter is selected by the President of the Republic.

Military Court of Appeals: A court of the last instance to review decisions and verdicts rendered by military courts, and a court of first and last instance with jurisdiction over certain military persons, stipulated by law, with responsibility for the specific trials of these persons. Members are selected by the President of the Republic from nominations made by the Military Court of Appeals.

Supreme Military Administrative Court: A military court for the judicial control of administrative acts concerning military personnel. Members are selected by the President of the Republic from nominations made by the Court.

Court of Jurisdictional Disputes: Settles disputes among judicial, administrative and military courts arising from disagreements on jurisdictional matters and verdicts.

The Court of Accounts: A court charged with the auditing of all accounts of revenue, expenditure and government property, which renders rulings related to transactions and accounts of authorized bodies on behalf of the National Assembly.

Supreme Council of Judges and Public Prosecutors: The President of the Council shall be the Minister of Justice, and the Under-Secretary to the Minister of Justice shall serve as an *ex-officio* member of the Council. Three regular and three substitute members from the Court of Appeals, together with two regular and two substitute members of the Council of State, shall be appointed to the Supreme Council by the President of the Republic for a four-year term. Decides all personnel matters relating to judges and public prosecutors.

Public Prosecutor: The law shall make provision for the tenure of public prosecutors and attorneys of the Council of State and their functions. The Chief Prosecutor of the Republic, the Chief Attorney of the Council of State and the Chief Prosecutor of the Military Court of Appeals are subject to the provisions applicable to judges of higher courts.

Military Trial: Military trials are conducted by military and disciplinary courts. These courts are entitled to try the military offences of military personnel and those offences committed against military personnel or in military areas, or offences connected with military service and duties. Military courts may try non-military persons only for military offences prescribed by special laws.

Religion

ISLAM

More than 99% of the Turkish people are Muslims. However, Turkey is a secular state. Although Islam was stated to be the official religion in the Constitution of 1924, an amendment in 1928 removed this privilege. After 1950 subsequent governments have tried to re-establish links between religion and state affairs, but secularity was protected by the revolution of 1960, the 1980 coup and the 1982 Constitution.

Diyanet İşleri Reisi (Head of Religious Affairs in Turkey): Prof. Mustafa Sait Yazicioğlu.

CHRISTIANITY

The town of Antioch (now Antakya) was one of the earliest strongholds of Christianity, and by the the 4th century had become a patriarchal see. Formerly in Syria, the town was incorporated in Turkey in 1939. Constantinople (now İstanbul) was also a patriarchal see, and by the 6th century the Patriarch of Constantinople was recognized as the Ecumenical Patriarch in the East. Gradual estrangement from Rome developed, leading to the final breach between the Catholic West and the Orthodox East, usually assigned to the year 1054.

In 1986 it was estimated that there were about 100,000 Christians in Turkey.

The Orthodox Churches

Armenian Patriarchate: Ermeni Patrikliği, Şarapnel Sok. 20–22; 34480 Kumkapı, İstanbul; tel. (212) 5170970; fax (212) 5164833; f. 1461; 45,000 adherents (1989); Patriarch Karekin Bedros Kazandjian.

Bulgarian Orthodox Church: Bulgar Ortodoks Kilisesi, Halâskâr Gazi Cad. 319, Şişli, İstanbul; Rev. Archimandrite Ganco Çobanof.

Greek Orthodox Church: Rum Ortodoks Patrikhanesi, 34220 Fener-Haliç, İstanbul; tel. (212) 5319670; fax (212) 5349037; Archbishop of Constantinople (New Rome) and Ecumenical Patriarch Bartholomeo I.

The Roman Catholic Church

At 31 December 1992 there were an estimated 25,111 adherents in the country.

Bishops' Conference: Conferenza Episcopale di Turchia, Ölçek Sok. 87, Harbiye, 80230 İstanbul; tel. (212) 2414552; fax (212) 2408801; f. 1978; Pres. Mgr Hovhannes Tcholakian (Archbishop of İstanbul).

Armenian Rite

Patriarchate of Cilicia: f. 1742; Patriarch Jean-Pierre XVIII Kasparian (resident in Beirut, Lebanon).

Archbishopric of İstanbul: Sakızağacı Cad. 31, PK 183, 80072 Beyoğlu, İstanbul; tel. (212) 2441258; f. 1830; two secular priests; 3,620 Catholics (1992); Archbishop Hovhannes Tcholakian.

Byzantine Rite

Apostolic Exarchate of İstanbul: Hamalbaşı Cad. 44, 80070 Beyoğlu, İstanbul; tel. (212) 2497104; f. 1861; one secular priest; 50 Catholics (1992); Vicar Delegate Rev. Archimandrite Thomas Varsamis.

Bulgarian Catholic Church: Bulgar Katolik Kilisesi, Eski Parmakkapı Sok. 15, Galata, İstanbul.

Chaldean Rite

Archbishopric of Diyarbakır: Hamalbaşı Cad. 48, PK 259, 80070 Beyoğlu, İstanbul; tel. (212) 2932713; six secular priests; 3,300 Catholics (1992); Archbishop Paul Karatas.

Latin Rite

Metropolitan See of İzmir: Church of St Polycarpe, Necatibey Cad. 2, PK 267, 35212 İzmir; tel. (232) 4848436; fax (232) 4845358; seven priests; 1,141 Catholics (1992); Archbishop of İzmir Giuseppe Germano Bernardini.

Apostolic Vicariate of Anatolia: PK 35, 33001 Mersin; tel. (74) 313227; fax (74) 376574; f. 1990; three secular priests, eight religious priests; 1,125 Catholics (1992); Vicar Apostolic Ruggero Franceschini, Titular Bishop of Sicilibba.

Apostolic Vicariate of İstanbul: Ölçek Sok. 83, 80230 Harbiye, İstanbul; tel. (212) 2480775; fax (212) 2408801; f. 1742; six secular priests, 28 religious priests; 15,000 Catholics (1992); Vicar Apostolic Louis Pelâtre, Titular Bishop of Sasima.

Maronite Rite

The Maronite Patriarch of Antioch is resident in Lebanon.

Melkite Rite

The Greek Melkite Patriarch of Antioch is resident in Damascus, Syria.

Syrian Rite

The Syrian Catholic Patriarch of Antioch is resident in Beirut, Lebanon.

Patriarchal Vicariate of Turkey: Türkiye Temsilcisi Yusuf Sağ, Ayazpaşa, Sarayarkası Sok. 15, PK 84, 80090 Ayazpaşa, İstanbul; tel. (212) 2432521; one secular priest, one religious priest; 2,000 Catholics (1992); Vicar Patriarchal Rev. Yusuf Sağ.

The Anglican Communion

Within the Church of England, Turkey forms part of the diocese of Gibraltar in Europe. The Bishop is resident in London, England.

Archdeacon of the Aegean and the Danube: Ven. Geoffrey Evans, (resident in Rome, Italy).

JUDAISM

Jewish Community of Turkey: Türkiye Hahambaşılığı, Yemenici Sok. 23, Beyoğlu, 80050 Tünel, İstanbul; tel. (212) 2435166; fax (212) 2441980; Chief Rabbi David Asseo.

The Press

Almost all İstanbul papers are also printed in Ankara and İzmir on the same day, and some in Adana. Among the more serious and influential papers are the dailies *Milliyet* and *Cumhuriyet*. The weekly *Gırgır* is noted for its political satire. The most popular dailies are the İstanbul papers *Sabah*, *Hürriyet*, *Milliyet*, *Yeni Günaydın* and *Zaman*; *Yeni Asır*, published in İzmir, is the best-selling quality daily of the Aegean region. There are numerous provincial newspapers with limited circulation.

PRINCIPAL DAILIES

Adana

Yeni Adana: Abidinpaşa Cad. 56, Adana; tel. (322) 3511891; fax (322) 3593655; f. 1918; political; Propr Çetin Remzi Yüreğir; Chief Editor Ayten Sensaliver; circ. 1,600.

Ankara

Ankara Ticaret: Rüzgârlı Sok. O. V. Han 2/6, Ankara; tel. (312) 4182832; telex 42308; f. 1954; commercial; Man. Editor Nuray Tüzmen; Chief Editor Muammer Solmaz; circ. 1,351.

Ankara Ulus: Rüzgarlı Gayret Sok. 1, Ulus, Ankara; tel. (312) 3091774; f. 1983; Propr AsıL NADİR.

Belde: Rüzgarlı GAyret Sok. 7/1, Ulus, Ankara; tel. (312) 3106820; f. 1968; Propr İLHAN IşBİLEN; circ. 3,399.

Tasvir: Ulus Meydanı, Ulus İş Hanı, Kat 4, Ankara; tel. (312) 4111241; f. 1960; conservative; Editor ENDER YOKDAR; circ. 3,055.

Turkish Daily News: Tunus Cad. 50/A-7, 06680 Kavaklıdere, Ankara; tel. (312) 4282957; fax 4278890; f. 1961; English language; Publisher İLHAN ÇEVİK; Editor-in-Chief İLNUR ÇEVİK; circ. 38,000.

Türkiye Ticaret Sicili: Karanfıl Sok. 56, Bakanlıklar, Ankara; f. 1957; commercial; Editor YALÇIN KAYA AYDOS.

Vakit: Konya Yolu 8km, 68 Balgat, Ankara; tel. (312) 2877906; f. 1978; Man. Editor NALİ ALAN; circ. 3,384.

Yeni Tanin: Rüzgârlı, Agâh Efendi Sok. Uçar Han, Kat 8/3, Ankara; f. 1964; political; Propr BURHANETTİN GÖĞEN; Man. Editor AHMET TEKEŞ; circ. 3,123.

Yirmidört Saat: Gazeteciler Cemiyeti Çevre Sok. 35, Çankaya, Ankara; tel. (312) 1682384; f. 1978; Propr BEYHAN CENKÇİ.

Bursa

Bursa Hakimiyet: Ünlü Cad. Çamlıbel İş Hanı 34/36, Bursa; tel. (224) 223982; f. 1973; political; Propr ARMAĞAN GERÇEKSİ; Chief Editor ENGİN ÖZPINAR; circ. 5,164.

Eskişehir

Milli İrade: Siurihisar Cad. 31, Ekişehir; f. 1967; political; Propr ETEM KARACA; Editor ERKUT ÖZGENCİL.

İstanbul

Apoyevmatini: İstiklâl Cad., Suriye Pasajı 348, Beyoğlu, İstanbul; tel. (212) 2437635; f. 1925; Greek language; Publr Dr Y. A. ADA-ŞOĞLU; Editor İSTEFAN PAPADOPOULOS; circ. 1,200.

Bugün: Medya Plaza Basın Ekspres Yolu, 34540 Güneşli, İstanbul; tel. (212) 5504850; f. 1989; Propr ÖNAY BİLGİN; circ. 184,884.

Cumhuriyet (Republic): Türkocağı Cad. 39, 34334 Cağaloğlu, İstanbul; tel. (212) 5120505; telex 22246; fax (212) 5138595; f. 1924; morning; liberal; Editor-in-Chief ÖZGEN ACAR; Man. Editor İBRAHİM YILDIZ; circ. 72,000.

Dünya (World): Narlıbahçe Sok. 15, 34440 Cağaloğlu, İstanbul; tel. (212) 5120190; telex 23822; fax (212) 5206457; f. 1952; morning; economic; Exec. Editor MUSTAFA MUTLU; circ. 50,000.

Fotomaç: Medya Plaza Basın Ekspres Yolu, 34540 Güneşli, İstanbul; tel. (212) 5504890; f. 1991; Propr SABAH YAYINCILIK.

Günlük Ticaret: Çemberlitaş Palas, Çemberlitaş, İstanbul; f. 1946; political; Editor SELİM BİLMEN; circ. 1,054.

Hürriyet: Babıali Cad. 15–17, 34360 Cağaloğlu, İstanbul; tel. (212) 5120000; telex 22249; fax (212) 5120026; f. 1948; morning; independent political; Propr EROL SİMAVİ; Chief Editor ERTUĞRUL ÖZKÖK; circ. 542,797.

Jamanak: İstiklâl Cad., Narmallı Yurdu, Beyoğlu, İstanbul; tel. (212) 2435639; f. 1908; Armenian; Editor HAGOP SİVASLIYAN; circ. 1,000.

Meydan: Prof. Kazım İsmail Gürkan Cad. 10, 34410 Cağaloğlu, İstanbul; tel. (212) 5194370; f. 1990; Propr REFİK ARAS.

Milli Gazete: Çayhane Sok. 1, 34040 Topkapı, İstanbul; tel. (212) 5674775; telex 23373; f. 1973; pro-Islamic; right-wing; Propr. HAZIM OKTAY BASER; Chief Editor HASAN KARAKAYA; circ. 24,496.

Milliyet: Nuruosmaniye Cad. 65, İstanbul; tel. (212) 5114410; telex 22884; fax (212) 5138742; f. 1950; morning; political; merged with *Hürriyet* in June 1994; Publr AYDIN DOĞAN; Editor-in-Chief UMUR TALU; monthly circ. 334,878.

Nor Marmara: İstiklâl Cad., Solakzade Sok. 5, PK 507, İstanbul; tel. (212) 2444736; f. 1940; Armenian language; Propr and Editor-in-Chief ROBER HADDELER; Gen. Man. ARİ HADDELER; circ. 2,200.

Sabah (Morning): Atakan Sok. 14, Mecideköy, İstanbul; tel. (212) 2752200; telex 26924; fax (212) 2752200; Propr DİNÇ BİLGİN; Editor ZAFER MUTLU; circ. 506,671.

Tercüman: Tercüman Tesisleri, Davutpaşa Cad. 115, Topkapı, İstanbul; tel. (212) 5779191; telex 22253; fax (212) 5671578; f. 1961; right-wing; Propr KEMAL ILICAK; Chief Editor ALTEMUR KİLİÇ; circ. 32,869.

Yeni Günaydın: Alayköşkü Cad., Eryılmaz Sok. 13, Cağaloğlu, İstanbul; tel. (212) 5285000; telex 22284; f. 1968; political; Propr HALDUN SİMAVİ; Chief Editor RAHMİ TURAN; circ. 300,000.

Yeni Nesil (New Generation): Sanayi Cad., Selvi Sok. 5, Yenibosna, Bakırköy, İstanbul; tel. (212) 5846261; telex 28620; fax (212) 5567289; f. 1970 as *Yeni Asya;* political; Propr MEHMET EMİN BİRİNCİ; Editor İHSAN ATASOY; monthly circ. 5,614.

Zaman: Cobancesme, Kalendar Sok. 21, Yenibosna, İstanbul; tel. (212) 5511477; fax (212) 5512822; f. 1962; morning; political, independent; Man. Editor ADEM KALAC; Chief Editor HALİT ESENDIR; circ. 210,000.

İzmir

Rapor: Gazi Osman Paşa Bul. 5, İzmir; tel. (232) 4254400; f. 1949; Owner DİNÇ BİLGİN; Man. Editor TANJU ATEŞER; circ. 9,000.

Ticaret Gazetesi: 1571 Sok. 16, 35110 Çınarlı, İzmir; tel. (232) 4619642; telex 52586; fax (232) 4619646; f. 1942; commercial news; Editor-in-Chief AHMET SUKÛTİ TÜKEL; Man. Editor CEMAL M. TÜKEL; circ. 5,009.

Yeni Asır (New Century): Gazi Osman Paşa Bul. 5, İzmir; tel. (232) 4252200; telex 53312; f. 1895; political; Propr DİNÇ BİLGİN; Editor-in-Chief CEMİL DEVRİM; monthly circ. 42,571.

Konya

Yeni Konya: Mevlâna Cad. 4, Konya; tel. (332) 2112594; f. 1945; political; Man. Editor M. NACİ GÜCÜYENER; Chief Editor ADİL GÜCÜYENER; monthly circ. 1,657.

Yeni Meram: Mevlâna Cad. 13, Sağlık Pasajı, Konya; tel. (332) 2112699; telex 48215; f. 1949; political; Propr M. YALÇIN BAHÇIVAN; Chief Editor YURDANUR ALPAY; monthly circ. 1,218.

WEEKLIES

Ankara

Bilim ve Teknik: Bilim ve Teknik Dergisi Yazı İşleri Müdürlüğü, İstanbul, Cad. 88, İskitler, Ankara; tel. (312) 3419251; f. 1967; Propr Dr MEHMET ERGİN; Man. Editor FEYZULLAH AKBEN.

Ekonomi ve Politika: Atatürk Bul. 199/A-45, Kavaklıdere, Ankara; f. 1966; economic and political; Publisher ZİYA TANSU.

Türkiye İktisat Gazetesi: Karanfil Sok. 56, 06582 Bakanlıklar, Ankara; tel. (312) 4184321; fax (312) 4183268; f. 1953; commercial; Chief Editor MEHMET SAĞLAM; circ. 11,500.

Turkish Economic Gazette: Atatürk Bul. 149, Bakanlıklar, Ankara; tel. (312) 4177700; telex 42343; publ. by UCCET.

Turkish Probe: Tunus Cad. 50/A-7, 06680 Kavaklıdere, Ankara; tel. (312) 4282956; fax (312) 4278890; English language; Publr A. ILHAN ÇEVİK; Editor-in-Chief İLNUR ÇEVİK; circ. 2,000.

İstanbul

Aktüel: Medya Plaza Basın Ekspres Yolu, 34540 Güneşli, İstanbul; tel. (212) 5504870; f. 1991; Gen. Man. GÜLAY GÖKTÜRK; Man. Editor ALEV ER.

Bayrak: Çatalçeşme Sok. 50/5, 34410 Cağaloğlu, İstanbul; tel. (212) 5275575; fax (212) 5268363; f. 1970; political; Editor MEHMET GÜNGÖR; circ. 10,000.

Doğan Kardeş: Türbedar Sok. 22, Cağaloğlu, İstanbul; f. 1945; illustrated children's magazine; Editor ŞEVKET RADO; circ. 40,000.

Ekonomik Panaroma: Büyükdere Cad. Ali Kaya Sok. 8, 80720 Levent, İstanbul; tel. (212) 2696680; f. 1988; Gen. Man. AYDIN DEMİRER.

Ekonomist: Hürgüç Gazetecilik AŞ Hurriyet Tesisleri, Kireçocağı Mevkii, Evren Mah., Güneşli Köy, İstanbul; tel. (212) 5500050; f. 1991; Gen. Man. ADİL ÖZKOL.

Gırgır: Alayköşkü Cad., Çağaloğlu, İstanbul; tel. (212) 2285000; satirical; Propr and Editor OĞUZ ARAL; circ. 500,000.

Hıbır: İstanbul; satirical; circ. 250,000.

İkibine Doğru: Nuruosmaniye Cad. 19/2 Cağaloğlu, İstanbul; f. 1987; Propr MEHMET SABUNCU; Man. Editor FERİT İLSEVER.

İstanbul Ticaret: İstanbul Chamber of Commerce, Gümüşpala Cad., PK 377, Eminönü, İstanbul; tel. (212) 5114150; telex 22682; f. 1958; commercial news; Publr YALIM EREZ.

Nokta: İstanbul; Editor ARDA USKAN; circ. 60,000.

Tempo: Hürgüç Gazetecilik AŞ Hürriyet Tesisleri, Güneşli, İstanbul; tel. (212) 5500081; f. 1987; Dir SEDAT SİMAVİ; Gen. Man. MEHMET Y. YILMAZ.

Türk Dünyasi Araştırmalar Dergisi: Hürgüç Gazetecilik AŞ Hurriyet Tesisleri, Güneşli, İstanbul; tel. (212) 5500081; Dir SEDAT SİMAVİ; Gen. Man. MEHMET Y. YILMAZ.

İzmir

Merhaba: Cumhuriyet Bul. 238/3, İzmir; f. 1979; magazine; Editor ÜMIT ÇELIKER; circ. 90,000.

PERIODICALS

Ankara

Adalet Dergisi: Adalet Bakanlığı, Ankara; tel. (312) 4192199; f. 1909; legal journal publ. by the Ministry of Justice; Editor HÜSEYİN ERGÜL; circ. 3,500.

Azerbaycan Türk Kültür Dergisi: Vakıf İş Hani 324, Anafartalar, Ankara; f. 1949; literary and cultural periodical of Azerbaizhanian Turks; Editor Dr AHMET YAŞAT.

Bayrak Dergisi: Bestekar Sok. 44/5, Kavaklidere, Ankara; f. 1964; Publr and Editor Hami Kartay.

Devlet Opera ve Balesi Genel Müdürlügü: Ankara; tel. (312) 3241476; telex 44401; fax (312) 3107248; f. 1949; state opera and ballet; Gen. Dir. Rengim Gokmen.

Devlet Tiyatrosu: Devlet Tiyatrosu Um. Md., Ankara; f. 1952; art, theatre.

EBA Briefing: Bestekar Sok. 59/3, Kavaklidere, Ankara; tel. (312) 4685376; telex 43204; fax (312) 4684114; f. 1975; publ. by Ekonomik Basın Ajansı (Economic Press Agency); quarterly; international business; Publrs Yavuz Tolun, Melek Tolun.

Eğitim ve Bilim: Ziya Gökalp Cad. 48, Yenişehir, Ankara; tel. (312) 4313488; f. 1928; quarterly; education and science; publ. by the Turkish Educational Asscn (TED); Editor Refik Çölaşan; circ. 500.

Elektrik Mühendisliği Mecmuası: Gülden Sok. 2/A Güvenevler, Kavaklıdere, Ankara; f. 1954; publ. by the Chamber of Turkish Electrical Engineers; Pres. Sefa Gömdeniz.

Halk Eğitimi: Millî Eğitim Bakanlığı, Halk Eğitimi Genel Müdürlüğü, Ankara; f. 1966; publ. by the Ministry of Education.

Karınca: Türk Kooperatifçilik Kurumu, Mithatpaşa Cad. 38/A, 06420 Kızılay, Ankara; tel. (312) 4316125; fax (312) 4340646; f. 1934; monthly review publ. by the Turkish Co-operative Asscn; Editor Prof. Dr Celâl Er; circ. 5,000.

Maden Tetkik Arama Enstitüsü Dergisi: İnönü Bul., Ankara; f. 1935; 2 a year; publ. by Mineral Research and Exploration Institute of Turkey; English Edition *Bulletin of the Mineral Research and Exploration Institute* (2 a year).

Mimarlık (Architecture): Konur Sok. 4, Kızılay, Ankara; tel. (312) 4173727; fax (312) 4180361; f. 1963; every 2 months; publ. by the Chamber of Architects of Turkey; Editor Aslı Özbay; circ. 11,000.

Mühendis ve Makina: Sümer Sok. 36/7, 06640 Demirtepe, Ankara; tel. (312) 2301166; fax (312) 2313165; f. 1957; engineering; monthly; Publr Chamber of Mechanical Engineers; Propr İsmet Rıza Çebi; Editor Tülay Akarsoy; circ. 30,000.

Nûr (the Light): Nuruosmaniye Cad., Sorkun Han 28/2, 34410, Cağaloğlu, İstanbul; tel. (212) 5277607; fax (212) 5208231; f. 1986; religion; Editor Cemal Uşak; circ. 10,000.

Ozgür Gündem (Free Agenda): İstanbul; f. 1992; pro-Kurdish nationalists; Editor Gultan Kısanak; Gen. Man. Gurbetelli Ersoz; circ. 30,000.

Resmi Kararlar Dergisi: Adalet Bakanlığı Eğitim Dairesi Başkanlığı, 06659 Bakanlıklar, Ankara; tel. (312) 4192199; fax (312) 4173954; f. 1966; legal; Editor Avni Özenç; circ. 3,500.

Teknik ve Uygulama: Konur Sok. 4/4, 06442 Kızılay, Ankara; tel. (312) 4182374; f. 1986; engineering; every 2 months; publ. by the Chamber of Mechanical Engineers; Propr İsmet Rıza Çebi; Editor Uğur Doğan; circ. 3,000.

Türk Arkeoloji Dergisi (General Directorate of Monuments and Museums): Kültür Bakanlığı, Anıtlar ve Müzeler Genel Müdürlüğü-II. Meclis Binası Ulus, Ankara; tel. (312) 3105363; fax (312) 3111417; archaeological.

Türk Dili: Türk Dil Kurumu, Atatürk Bul. 217, 06680 Kavaklıdere, Ankara; tel. (312) 4286100; fax (312) 4285288; f. 1951; monthly; Turkish literature and language; Editor Prof. Dr Hasan Eren.

Turkey—Economic News Digest: Karanfil Sok. 56, Ankara; f. 1960; Editor-in-Chief Behzat Tanir; Man. Editor Sadik Balkan.

Turkish Review: Atatürk Bul. 203, 06688 Kavaklıdere, Ankara; tel. (312) 4671180; telex 42384; fax (312) 4682100; f. 1985; 4 a year; cultural, social and economic; English; publ. by the Directorate General of Press and Information; Chief Officers M. Ömer Tarkan, Osman Üntürk, Kadir A. Parla.

Turkiye: Çatalçeşme Sok. 17, Cağaloğlu, İstanbul; tel. (212) 5261800; telex 22000; fax (212) 5209362; f. 1970; monthly; Man. Editor Dr Enver Ören; circ. 191,000.

Türkiye Bankacılık: PK 121, Ankara; f. 1955; commercial; Publisher Mustafa Atalay.

Türkiye Bibliyografyası: Milli Kütüphane Başkanlığı, 06490 Bahçelievler, Ankara; tel. (312) 2126200; fax (312) 2230451; f. 1934; monthly; Turkish national bibliography; publ. by the Bibliographical Centre of the Turkish National Library; Dir Orhan Doğan.

Türkiye Makaleler Bibliyografyası: Milli Kütüphane Başkanlığı, 06490 Bahçelievler, Ankara; tel. (312) 2126200; fax (312) 2230451; f. 1952; monthly; Turkish articles, bibliography; publ. by the Bibliographical Centre of the Turkish National Library; Dir Sema Akıncı.

Bursa

Tekstil ve Mühendis: Elmasbahçeler Mah. Sabunevi Sok., Mühendisler İş Hanı 19, Kat. 2, 16230 Bursa; tel. (24) 538018; fax (24) 525514; textile engineering; every 2 months; publ. by the Chamber of Textile Engineers; Propr Güngör Başer; Editor Zıya Özek; circ. 4,000.

İstanbul

Archaeology and Art Magazine: Hayriye Cad. 3/5 Çorlu Apt., Beyoğlu 80060, İstanbul; tel. (212) 2456838; fax (212) 2456877; f. 1978; quarterly; publ. by Archaeology and Art Publications; Publr and Editor Nezih Başgelen.

İstanbul Key: Halaskargazi Cad. 364, Şişli Meydanı, İstanbul; tel. (212) 2314631; telex 27800; f. 1989; publ. by Türk Turing, official travel agency of the Touring and Automobile Club of Turkey; Publr Prof. Kemal Kutlu; Editor-in-Chief Çelik Gülersoy.

İstanbul Ticaret Odası Mecmuası: Gümüşpala Cad., PK 377, Eminönü, İstanbul; tel. (212) 5114150; telex 22682; f. 1884; quarterly; journal of the İstanbul Chamber of Commerce (ICOC); English; Editor-in-Chief Cengiz Ersun.

Kulis: Cağaloğlu Yokuşu 10/A, İstanbul; f. 1947; fortnightly arts magazine; Armenian; Publr Hagop Ayvaz.

Musiki Mecmuası: PK 666, İstanbul; tel. (216) 3306299; fax (216) 3475273; f. 1948; monthly; music and musicology; Editor Etem Ruhi Üngör.

Pirelli Mecmuası: Büyükdere Cad. 117, Gayrettepe, İstanbul; tel. (212) 2663200; telex 26337; fax (212) 2726077; f. 1964; monthly; Publr Türk-Pirelli Lâstikleri AS; Editor Uğur Canal; circ. 24,500.

Présence (Aylık Dergi): Ölçek Sok. 82, 80230 Harbiye, İstanbul; tel. and fax (212) 2408801; f. 1986; 10 a year; publ. by the Apostolic Vicariate of İstanbul; Gen. Man. Fuat Çöllü.

Ruh ve Madde Dergisi (Spirit and Matter): Ruh ve Madde Dergisi, Yayınlari, PK 9, 80072 Beyoğlu, İstanbul; tel. (212) 2431814; fax (212) 2526125; f. 1959; organ of the Metapsychic Investigations and Scientific Research Society of Turkey; Publr Ergün Arıkdal.

Sevgi Dünyası (World of Respect): Aydede Cad. 4/5, 80090 Taksim, İstanbul; tel. (212) 2504242; f. 1963; monthly; social, psychological and spiritual; Publr and Editor Dr Refet Kayserili oğlu.

Tıp Dünyası: Ankara Cad. 31/51, Vakıf İş Hanı, Cağaloğlu, İstanbul; tel. (212) 5279611; f. 1927; monthly; organ of the Turkish Mental Health and Social Psychiatry Soc.; Editor Ord. Prof. Dr Fahreddin Kerim Gökay.

Turkey: Catalcesme Sok. 17, 34410 Cağaloğlu, İstanbul; tel. (212) 5110028; telex 22000; fax (212) 5135195; f. 1982; monthly; English language, economics; Editor Mehmet Soztutan; circ. 80,000.

Türkiye Turing ve Otomobil Kurumu Belleteni: Halaskargazi Cad. 364, Şişli Meydanı, İstanbul; tel. (212) 2314631; f. 1930; quarterly; publ. by the Touring and Automobile Club of Turkey; Publr Prof. Kemal Kutlu: Editor Çelik Gülersoy.

Varlık: Cağaloğlu Yokuşu 40/2, İstanbul; tel. (212) 5226924; fax (212) 5129528; f. 1933; monthly; literary; Editor Fíliz Nayır Deniztekin.

İzmir

İzmir Ticaret Odası Dergisi: Atatürk Cad. 126, İzmir; tel. (232) 4417777; telex 52331; fax (232) 4837853; f. 1927; every 2 months; publ. by Chamber of Commerce of İzmir; Sec.-Gen. Ertan Sakızlı; Man. Güler Özkan.

Konya

Çağrı Dergisi: PK 99, Konya; f. 1957; monthly; literary; Editor Feyzi Halıcı.

NEWS AGENCIES

Akajans: Tunus Cad. 28, Kat. 4, Bakanlıklar, Ankara; tel. (312) 4139720; Dir Yaşar Güngör.

Anatolian News Agency: Hanımeli Sok. 7, Sihhıye, Ankara; tel. (312) 2317000; telex 42088; fax (312) 2312174; f. 1920; Chair. Ali Aydın Dundar; Gen. Dir Behiç Ekşi.

ANKA Ajansı: Selanık Cad. 417/8, Kızılay, Ankara; tel. (312) 4172500; telex 42809; fax (312) 4180254; Dir-Gen. Müşerref Hekimoğlu.

EBA Ekonomik Basın Ajansı (Economic Press Agency): Bestekar Sok. 59/3, Kavaklıdere, 06680 Ankara; tel. (312) 4685376; telex 43204; fax (312) 4684114; f. 1969; private economic news service; Propr Mele Tolun.

Hürriyet Haber Ajansı: Babıali Cad. 15–17 Kat. 3, 34360 Cağaloğlu, İstanbul; tel. (212) 5120000; telex 22249; fax (212) 5223155; f. 1963; Dir-Gen. Hasan Yılmaer.

İKA Haber Ajansı (Economic and Commercial News Agency): Atatürk Bul. 199/A-45, Kavaklıdere, Ankara; tel. (312) 4267327; telex 42569; f. 1954; Dir Zíya Tansu.

Milha News Agency: Nuruosmaniye Cad. 65, Cağaloğlu, İstanbul; tel. (212) 5114410; telex 22251; fax (212) 5283018.

Ulusal Basın Ajansı (UBA): Meşrutiyet Cad. 5/10, Ankara; Man. Editor Oğuz Seren.

Foreign Bureaux

Agence France-Presse (AFP): Ahmet Rasik Sok. 10/1, 06550 Çankaya, Ankara; tel. (312) 4393550; telex 42399; fax (312) 4407815; Correspondent Hervé Couturier.

Agenzia Nazionale Stampa Associata (ANSA) (Italy): Sedat Simavı Sok. 30/5, Ankara; tel. (312) 4406084; telex 44337; fax (312) 4405029; Correspondent Romano Damiani.

Associated Press (AP) (USA): Tunus Cad. 87/3, Kavaklıdere, Ankara; tel. (312) 4282709; telex 42340; Correspondent Mrs Emel Anıl.

Bulgarska Telegrafna Agentsia (BTA) (Bulgaria): Hatır Sok. 25/6, Gaziosmanpaşa, Ankara; tel. (312) 4273899; Correspondent Lubomir Gabrovski.

Deutsche Presse-Agentur (dpa) (Germany): Yesil Yali Sok., Liman Apt 6/6 Yesilköy, İstanbul; tel. (212) 5738607; telex 44356; Correspondent Bahadettin Güngör.

Informatsionnoye Telegrafnoye Agentstvo Rossii—Telegrafnoye Agentstvo Suverennykh Stran (ITAR—TASS) (Russia): Kuloğlu Sok. 22/12 Çankaya, Ankara; tel. (312) 4391955; telex 42160; Correspondent Vladimir Zharov.

Reuters (United Kingdom): Umurbey Sok. 6, 06700 Gaziosmanpaşa, Ankara; tel. (312) 4462940; telex 42590; fax (312) 4464813; Chief Correspondent Alistair Lyon.

United Press International (UPI) (USA): Yerebatan Cad. 33, Cağaloğlu, İstanbul; tel. (212) 2285238; telex 22350; Correspondent İsmet İmset.

Xinhua (New China) News Agency (People's Republic of China): Horasan Sok. 16/4, Gaziosmanpaşa, Ankara; tel. (312) 4361456; telex 46138; fax (312) 4465229; Correspondent Wang Qiang.

Zhongguo Xinwen She (China News Agency) (People's Republic of China): Nenehatun Cad. 88-2, Ata Apartmani, Gaziosmanpaşa, Ankara; tel. (312) 4362261; Correspondent Chang Chiliang.

AFP also has representatives in İstanbul and İzmir. AP and Reuters are also represented in İstanbul.

JOURNALISTS' ASSOCIATION

Gazeteciler Cemiyeti: Cağaloğlu, İstanbul; tel. (212) 5138300; telex 23508; fax (212) 5268046; f. 1946; Pres. Necmi Tanyolaç; Sec. Rıdvan Yele.

Publishers

Altın Kitaplar Yayınevi Anonim ŞTİ: Celal Ferdi Gökçay Sok., Nebioğlu Han, Kat. 1, Cağaloğlu, İstanbul; tel. (212) 5268012; telex 22627; fax (212) 5268011; f. 1959; fiction, non-fiction, biography, children's books, encyclopaedias, dictionaries; Publr Fethi Ul-Turhan Bozkurt; Chief Editor Hüsnü Terek.

Archaeology and Art Publs: Hariye Cad. 3/5 Gorlu Apt., Beyoğlu, 80060 Istanbul; tel. (212) 2456838; fax (212) 2456877; classical, Byzantine and Turkish studies, art and archaeology, numismatics and ethnography books; Publr Nezih Basgelen.

Ark Ticaret Ltd ŞTI: PK 137-35220, Merkez, İzmir; tel. (232) 2469550; f. 1962; import-export representation; imports technical books and exports all kinds of Turkish books, periodicals and newspapers; Gen. Man. Atilan Tümer.

Cem Yayınevi: Nuruosmaniye Cad., Kardeşler Han 1/3, Cağaloğlu, İstanbul; tel. (212) 5271741; fax (212) 5269742; f. 1964; novels, poetry, modern classics, cultural and historical books, children's books.

Elif Kitabevi: Sahaflar Çarşısı 4, Beyazıt, İstanbul; tel. (212) 5222096; f. 1956; all types of publications, especially historical, literary; political, drama and reference; old Ottoman and Turkish books and periodicals; Publr Arslan Kaynardağ.

Gelişim Yayınları AŞ: Büyükdere Cad., Ali Kaya Sok., 80720 Levent, İstanbul; tel. (212) 2696680; telex 26510; f. 1974; encyclopaedias, magazines, reference and non-fiction; Man. Ercan Arıklı.

Hürriyet Yayınları: Cemal Nadir Sok. 7, Cağaloğlu, İstanbul; tel. (212) 2222038; telex 22276; fiction, history, classics, poetry, general reference books; Dir Çetin Emeç.

Kanaat Kitabevi: İlyas Bayar Halefi, Yakup Bayar, Ankara Cad. 133, İstanbul; f. 1896; textbooks, novels, dictionaries, posters, maps and atlases.

Karacan Yayınları: Köyaltı Mevki Oruç Reis Sok. 10, Yenibosna, Bakırköy, İstanbul; tel. (212) 5513038; f. 1980; literary books and magazines; Gen. Man. Ali Naci Karacan.

Öğretim Yayınevi: Ankara Cad. 62/2, Sirkeci, İstanbul; f. 1959; English, French, German, Italian, Spanish and Dutch language

courses, guides and dictionaries, phrase books for tourists; Dir İzidor Kant.

Remzi Kitabevi AŞ: Selvili Mescit Sok. 3, 34440 Cağaloğlu, İstanbul; tel. (212) 5220583; fax (212) 5229055; f. 1929; general and educational; Dirs Erol Erduran, Ömer Erduran, Ahmet Erduran.

Türk Dil Kurumu (Turkish Language Institute): Atatürk Bul. 217, 06680 Kavaklıdere, Ankara; tel. (312) 4268124; fax (312) 4285288; f. 1932; non-fiction, research, language; Pres. Prof. Dr Hasan Eren.

Varlık Yayınları: Cağaloğlu Yokuşu 40/42, İstanbul; tel. (212) 5226924; fax (212) 5129528; f. 1946; fiction and non-fiction books; Dir Filiz Nayir Deniztekin.

PUBLISHERS' ASSOCIATION

Türkiye Yayıncılar Birliği Derneği (The Publishers' Association of Turkey): Cağaloğlu Yokuşu, Edes Han 40/3, İstanbul; tel. 5125602; f. 1985; Pres. Aygören Dirim; Sec. ˇ

Radio and Television

In July 1993 the Turkish National Assembly voted to abolish the state monopoly of radio and television services. In 1991, according to UNESCO, an estimated 9.2m. radio receivers and 10m. television receivers were in use.

Türkiye Radyo Televizyon Kurumu (TRT) (Turkish Radio-Television Corpn): Merkez Kutuphane, Oran, Ankara; tel. (312) 4900379; telex 43164; fax (312) 4901109; f. 1964; controls Turkish radio and television services; Dir-Gen. Tayfun Akguner.

RADIO

Home Services: There are four national radio-broadcasting networks and more than 50 local radio stations in Turkey. Head of Radio İsmail H. Külahli.

Foreign Service (Voice of Turkey); PK 333, 06443 Yenişehir, Ankara; tel. (312) 4353816; telex 42832; fax (312) 4353816; Man. Dir Savaş Miratli.

Ankara: SW 250 kW (3), SW 500 kW (2). Fifteen daily shortwave transmissions in the following languages: Albanian, Arabic, Azerbaijanian Turkish, Bulgarian, Chinese, English, French, German, Greek, Hungarian, Persian, Romanian, Russian, Serbo-Croat, Turkish; Dir İsmail Hakki Toran.

There is also an educational radio service for schools and a station run by the Turkish State Meteorological Service. The American Forces have their own radio and television service.

TELEVISION

A limited television service was set up in 1965, and regular broadcasts for Ankara began in 1968. In 1986 there were two national channels transmitting programmes every day, averaging 90 hours per week. A third national channel began broadcasting in 1989 and a fourth and fifth channel were providing reduced services by 1991. Head of Television Bulent Varol; Dir. Ankara TV Atilla Oray.

Finance

(cap. = capital; p.u. = paid up; auth. = authorized; dep. = deposits; res = reserves; m. = million; brs = branches; amounts in Turkish liras unless otherwise stated)

The Central Bank of the Republic of Turkey was originally founded in 1930, and constituted in its present form in 1970. The central bank is the bank of issue and is also responsible for the execution of monetary and credit policies, the regulation of the foreign and domestic value of the Turkish lira jointly with the government, and the supervision of the credit system. In 1987 a decree was issued to bring the governorship of the Central Bank under direct government control.

There are 71 other banks operating in Turkey. Several banks were created by special laws to fulfil specialized services for particular industries. The Sümerbank directs the operation of a number of state-owned factories; Etibank operates primarily in the extractive industries and electric power industries; the Ziraat Bankası makes loans for agriculture; the Emlâk Bankası participates in industrial undertakings and the construction of all types of building.

The largest of the private sector Turkish banks is the Türkiye İş Bankası, which operates 808 branches.

There are several credit institutions in Turkey, including the Sınai Kalınma Bankası (Industrial Development Bank), which was founded in 1950, with the assistance of the World Bank, to encourage private investment in industry by acting as underwriter in the issue of share capital.

There are numerous co-operative organizations, including agricultural co-operatives in rural areas. There are also a number of savings institutions.

In 1990 the Turkish Government announced plans to establish a structure for offshore banking. A decree issued in October 1990 exempted foreign banks, operating in six designated free zones, from local banking obligations.

BANKING

Central Bank

Türkiye Cumhuriyet Merkez Bankası AŞ (Central Bank of the Republic of Turkey): Head Office, İstiklal Cad. 10, 06100 Ulus, Ankara; tel. (312) 3103646; telex 44033; fax (312) 3107434; f. 1931; bank of issue; cap. p.u. 25,000.0m., res 1,731,288.8m., dep. 138,882,663.7m. (Dec. 1992); Gov. YAMAN TÖRÜNER; 22 brs.

State Banks

Etibank: Tunus Cad. 33, 06680 Kavakhdere, Ankara; tel. (312) 4176230; telex 46626; fax (312) 4194576; f. 1935; cap. p.u. 36,750m., dep. 2,968,023m. (Dec. 1991); Gen. Man. REFIK ÇULPHAN; 140 brs.

İller Bankası (Municipalities Bank): Atatürk Bul. 21, 06040 Ulus, Ankara; tel. (312) 3103141; telex 42724; fax (312) 3107459; f. 1933; cap. p.u. 530,999m.; res 23,207m., total assets 5,204,351m. (Dec. 1991); Gen. Man. SAYHAN BAYOĞLU; 1 br.

Sümerbank AŞ: Atatürk Bul. 70, 06440 Kızılay, Ankara; tel. (312) 4178545; telex 44098; fax (312) 4178379; f. 1933; cap. p.u. 21,125m., dep. 3,744,396m., total assets 5,919,060m. (Dec. 1991); Pres. RECEP ÖNAL; 48 brs.

Türkiye Cumhuriyeti Ziraat Bankası (Agricultural Bank of the Republic of Turkey): Atatürk Bul. 42, 06107 Ulus, Ankara; tel. (312) 3103750; telex 44004; fax (312) 3101135; f. 1863; cap. p.u. 3,462,209.0m., res 2,543,332.7m., dep. 88,990,955.7m. (Dec. 1992); in November 1983 took over three commercial banks (Hisarbank AŞ, İstanbul Bankası TAŞ and Ortadoğu İktisat Bankası TAŞ) following their liquidation; Chair. Dr ŞERİF COŞKUN ULUSOY; 1,279 brs.

Türkiye Emlâk Bankası AŞ (Real Estate Bank of Turkey): Büyükdere Cad., Maslak Meydanı 43/45, 80670 Levent, İstanbul; tel. (212) 2761610; telex 27780; fax (212) 2761659; f. 1988 as a merger of Anadolu Bankası AŞ and Türkiye Emlâk Kredi Bankası; absorbed Denizcilik Bankası TAŞ in 1992; cap. p.u. 1,368,307m., res 1,333,409m., dep. 31,158,160m. (Dec. 1992); Chair. ŞÜKRÜ KARAHASANOĞLU; 429 brs.

Türkiye Halk Bankası AŞ: İlkiz Sok. 1, Sıhhiye, Ankara; tel. (312) 2317500; telex 44587; fax (312) 2295857; f. 1938; absorbed Türkiye Öğretmenler Bankası TAŞ in May 1992; cap. p.u. 923,314m., res 1,063,672m., dep. 19,362,744m. (Dec. 1992); Gen. Man. CIHAN PACACI; 782 brs.

Türkiye İhracat Kredi Bankası AŞ (Türk Eximbank) (Export Credit Bank of Turkey): Milli Müdafa Cad. 20, 06581 Bakanlıklar, Ankara; tel. (312) 4171300; telex 46106; fax (312) 4257896; f. 1964; fmrly Devlet Yatırım Bankası AŞ; cap. 575,510m., res 271,792m., total assets 12,551,254m. (Dec. 1992); extends credit to exporters, insures and guarantees export transactions; Pres. Dr AHMET ERTUĞRUL.

Türkiye Kalkınma Bankası AŞ (Development Bank of Turkey): İzmir Cad. 35, 06570 Kızılay, Ankara; tel. (312) 4179200; telex 43206; fax (312) 4183967; f. 1976, renamed in 1988 and in 1989 merged with Türkiye Cumhuriyeti Turizm Bankası AŞ; cap. p.u. 944,432m., res 59,140m., total assets 8,775,458m. (Dec. 1992); Chair. and Gen. Man. ÖZAL BAYSAL; 7 brs.

Türkiye Vakıflar Bankası TAO (Foundation Bank of Turkey): Atatürk Bul. 207, 06691 Kavaklıdere, Ankara; tel. (312) 4681160; telex 44428; fax (312) 4684541; f. 1954; cap. 1,000,000m., res 1,312,248m., dep. 44,046,492m. (Dec. 1993); Chair. FADİL ÜNVER; Gen. Man. YAŞAR YILMAZ ÖZEN; 326 brs.

Commercial Banks

Akbank TAŞ: Sabancı Center 4, 80745 Levent, İstanbul; tel. (212) 2699041; telex 24134; fax (212) 2818188; f. 1948; cap. p.u. 2,500,000m., res 2,553,000m., dep. 32,170,000m. (Dec. 1993); Chair. NAİM TALU; Gen. Man. ÖZEN GÖKSEL; 560 brs.

Demirbank TAŞ: Büyükdere Cad. 122, Blok B, 80280 Esentepe, İstanbul; tel. (212) 2751900; telex 27368; fax (212) 2731988; f. 1953; cap. p.u. 500,000m., res 27,168m., dep. 6,714,000m. (Dec. 1993); Chair. NURİ CINGILLIOGLU; Gen. Man. SELAHATTIN SERBEST; 14 brs.

Derbank: Abide-i Hürriyet Cad. 125, 80220 Şişli, İstanbul; tel. (212) 2249494; telex 27920; fax (212) 2314759; f. 1958; cap. p.u. 52,625m., res 9,773m., dep. 171,841m. (Dec. 1993); Gen. Man. TURGUT R. ERDEN; 2 brs.

Egebank AŞ: Büyükdere Cad. 106, 80280 Esentepe, İstanbul; tel. (212) 2887400; telex 39491; fax (212) 2887316; f. 1928; cap. 500,000m., res 321,707m., dep. 4,349,631m. (Dec. 1993); Gen. Man. NACİ AYHAN; 33 brs.

Eskişehir Bankası TAŞ (Esbank): Meşrutiyet Cad. 141, 80050 Tepebaşı, İstanbul; tel. (212) 2517270; telex 24535; fax (212) 2434118; f. 1927; cap. p.u. 1,300,000m., res 56,752m., dep. 6,704,682m. (Dec. 1993); Chair. MESUT EREZ; Gen. Man. ÖZER GÜNEY; 40 brs.

Finansbank AŞ: Büyükdere Cad. 123, 80300 Mecidiyeköy, İstanbul; tel. (212) 2752450; telex 39280; fax (212) 2752496; f. 1987; cap. p.u. 400,000m., res 107,343m., dep. 1,038,545m. (Dec. 1993); Gen. Man. Dr ÖMER ARAS; 4 brs.

Garanti Investment and Commerce Bank: Büyukdere Cad. Stan Had 85, Mecidiyeköy, Istanbul; tel. (212) 2751040; telex 27545; fax (212) 2758908; f. 1985, as Bank of Bahrain and Kuwait; purchased by Doğus Group in 1992; cap. 100,000m., res 3,760m., dep. 802,894m. (Dec. 1993); Chair. ZEKERIYA YILDIRIM.

İktisat Bankası TAŞ: Büyükdere Cad. 165, 80504 Esentepe, İstanbul; tel. (212) 2747111; telex 27685; fax (212) 2747028; f. 1927; cap. p.u. 800,000m.; res 628,186m., dep. 10,897,974m. (Dec. 1993); Gen. Man. ALİ AYANLAR; 13 brs.

Interbank (Uluslararası Endüstri ve Ticaret Bankası AŞ): Büyükdere Cad. 108/C, 80496 Esentepe, İstanbul; tel. (212) 2742000; telex 26098; fax (212) 2721622; f. 1888; cap. 1,200,000m., res 167,919m., dep. 2,033,987m. (Dec. 1993); specializes in import and export financing; Chair. YILDIRIM AKTÜRK; CEO MELİH E. ARAZ; 8 brs.

Kentbank AŞ: Tevfik Erdönmez Sok. 18, 80280 Esentepe, İstanbul; tel. (212) 2748900; telex 27247; fax (212) 2634610; f. 1992, as Türkiye Konut, Endüstri ve Ticaret Bankası; cap. 200,000m.; res 141,722m.; dep. 2,584,426m.; (Dec. 1993) Gen. Man. SAMİ ÇAKIR; 5 brs.

Koçbank AŞ: Barbaros Bul. Mörbasan Sok. Koza İş Merkezi, Blok C, 80700 Beşiktaş, İstanbul; tel. (212) 2747777; telex 39069; fax (212) 2672987; f. 1986; cap. 1,000,000m., res 116,932m., dep. 2,472,521m. (Dec. 1993); Gen. Man. ENGİN AKÇAKOCA; 7 brs.

Körfezbank AŞ (United Turkish Gulf Bank): Büyükdere Cad., Doğus Han 42–44, Kat 3–4, 80290 Mecidiyeköy, İstanbul; tel. (212) 2882000; telex 39714; fax (212) 2881217; f. 1988; cap. 250,000m., res 76,008m., dep. 4,291,074m. (Dec. 1993); Gen. Man. HALUK DAYIGİL; 4 brs.

Milli Aydın Bankası TAŞ (Tarişbank): Şair Eşref Bul. 3/1, 35214 Çankaya, İzmir; tel. (232) 4414304; telex 52433; fax (232) 4257390; f. 1913; cap. and res 115,016.5m., dep. 1,786,161.9m. (Dec. 1993); Chair. OĞUZ OYAN; Gen. Man. NAZIM DÖRTBUDAK; 42 brs.

Pamukbank TAŞ: Büyükdere Cad. 82, 80450 Gayrettepe, İstanbul; tel. (212) 2723484; telex 26959; fax (212) 2758217; f. 1955; cap. p.u. 1,500,000m., dep. 25,547,183m. (March 1994); Pres. CEMİL KÖKSAL; 151 brs.

Şekerbank TAŞ: Atatürk Bul. 171, 06442 Bakanlıklar, Ankara; tel. (312) 4179120; telex 42679; fax (312) 4254919; f. 1953; cap. p.u. 163,212.8m.; res 215,503.0m., dep. 3,483,613.8m. (Dec. 1992); Gen. Man. HASAN BASRİ GÖKTAN; 183 brs.

Toprakbank AŞ: Büyükdere Cad. Nilüfer Han 103/1-5, 80300 Gayrettepe, İstanbul; tel. (212) 2884120; telex 27046; fax (212) 2882447; f. 1992; cap. p.u. 500,000m., dep. 1,508,890m., total assets 3,287,833m. (Dec. 1993); Gen. Man. MEVLÜT ASLANOĞLU; 58 brs.

Türk Dış Ticaret Bankası AŞ (Turkish Foreign Trade Bank): Yıldız Posta Cad. 54, 80280 Gayrettepe, İstanbul; tel. (212) 2744280; telex 27992; fax (212) 2725278; f. 1964; cap. p.u. 200,000m., res 124,872m., dep. 3,403,741m. (Dec. 1992); Chair. ATILLA TAŞDEMİR; 21 brs.

Türk Ekonomi Bankası AŞ: Meclisi Mebusan Cad. 35, 80040 Fındıklı, İstanbul; tel. (212) 2512121; telex 25358; fax (212) 2496568; f. 1927; fmrly Kocaeli Bankası TAŞ; cap. p.u. 700,000m.; res 59,793m.; dep. 2,244,610m. (Dec. 1993); Chair ŞAHABETTİN BİLGİSU; Gen. Man. Dr AKIN AKBAYGİL; 10 brs.

Türk Ticaret Bankası AŞ (Türkbank): Yıldız Posta Cad. 2, 80280 Gayrettepe, İstanbul; tel. (212) 2885900; telex 22224; fax (212) 2886113; f. 1913; cap. 500,000m., res 1,065,538m., dep. 27,707,315m. (Dec. 1993); Chair. and Gen. Man. BEHZAT TUNCER; 345 brs.

Türkiye Garanti Bankası AŞ: Büyükdere Cad. 63, 80670 Maslak, İstanbul; tel. (212) 2855040; telex 27635; fax (212) 2854040; f. 1946; cap. p.u. 2,000,000m., res 318,220m., dep. 17,902,891m. (Dec. 1993); Chair. AYHAN ŞAHENK; Gen. Man. Y. AKIN ÖNGÖR; 238 brs.

Türkiye İmar Bankası TAŞ: Büyükdere Cad. Doğus Han. 42-46, 80290 Mecidiyeköy, İstanbul; tel. (212) 2751190; telex 26592; fax (212) 2724720; f. 1928; cap. p.u. 107,500m., res 4,678m., dep. 2,783,382m. (Dec. 1991); Chair. KEMAL UZAN; Gen. Man. HİLMİ BAŞARAN; 4 brs.

Türkiye İs Bankası AŞ (İşbank): Atatürk Bul. 191, 06684 Kavaklıdere, Ankara; tel. (312) 4281140; telex 42082; fax (312) 4250750;
f. 1924; cap. p.u. 1,936,326m., dep. 50,554,084m. (Dec. 1993);
Chair. İLHAN EVLİYAOĞLU; CEO ÜNAL KORUKÇU; 808 brs.

Türkiye Tütüncüler Bankası AŞ (Tütünbank): Yıldız Posta Cad.
21, 80280 Esentepe, İstanbul; tel. (212) 2758400; telex 27130;
fax (212) 2728314; f. 1924; cap. 300,000m., res 178,603m., dep.
5,701,020m. (Dec. 1992); Chair. SELÇUK YAŞAR; Gen. Man. M. SAMİ
ERDEM; 60 brs.

Yapı ve Kredi Bankası AŞ: Yapı Kredi Plaza, Blok A, Büyükdere
Cad., 80620 Levent, İstanbul; tel. (212) 2801111; telex 24718; fax
(212) 2801670; f. 1944; cap. p.u. 1,000,000m., dep. 19,737,604m.
(Dec. 1992); Chair. RONA YIRCALI; CEO BURHAN KARAÇAM; 361 brs.

Development and Investment Banks

Avrupa Türk Yatırım Bankası AŞ: Yapı Kredi Plaza, Büyükdere
Cad., Blok C, 22–23, Kat. 8, 80620 Levent, İstanbul; tel. (212)
2797070; telex 39460; fax (212) 2805376; f. 1990; cap. p.u.
20,000m., total assets 85,906m. (Dec. 1991); Gen. Man. STANISLAS
DE HAUSS; 1 br.

Birleşik Yatırım Bankası AŞ: Cumhuriyet Cad. 16, Kat. 3, 80200
Elmadağ, İstanbul; tel. (212) 2316666; telex 39338; fax (212)
2321866; f. 1989; cap. p.u. 87,500m., res 30,299m., total assets
866,245m. (Dec. 1993); Gen. Man. HİKMET KOSELİ; 1 br.

Park Yatırım Bankası AŞ: Büyükdere Cad., Meşeli Sok. 9, Kat 4,
80620 Levent, İstanbul; tel. (212) 2814820; telex 27117; fax (212)
2780445; f. 1992; Chair. HASAN KARAMEHMET; Gen. Man. RIZA SUAT
GÖKDEL.

Sınai Yatırım ve Kredi Bankası AO (Industrial Investment Credit
Bank of Turkey): Barbaros Bul. Akdoğan Sok. 41-43, 80690
Beşiktaş, İstanbul; tel. (212) 2597414; telex 26263; fax (212)
2580405; f. 1963; cap. p.u. 63,300m., res 74,026m., total assets
1,437,027m. (Dec. 1992); Chair. CAHİT KOCAÖMER; Gen. Man. Dr
ORHAN ALTAN; 1 br.

Türkiye Sınai Kalkınma Bankası AŞ (Industrial Development
Bank of Turkey): Meclisi Mebusan Cad. 137, PK 17, 80040 Fındıklı,
İstanbul; tel. (212) 2512792; telex 24344; fax (212) 2432975;
f. 1950; cap. 420,000m.; res 165,203m.; dep. 11,372,200m. (Dec.
1993); Chair. Prof. MEMDUH YAŞA; Gen. Man. B. SAFA OCAK; 3 brs.

Foreign Banks

Arap Türk Bankası AŞ (Arab Turkish Bank): Vali Konağı Cad.
10, PK 380-8223, 80220 Nişantaşı, İstanbul; tel. (212) 2250500;
telex 26830; fax (212) 2250526; f. 1977; cap. p.u. 150,000m., res
1,351m., dep. 740,380m. (Dec. 1993); 48% owned by Libyan Arab
Foreign Bank; Chair. YENAL CEVHERİOĞLU; Gen. Man. AYAD S. DAHAIM;
4 brs.

Banca di Roma (Italy): Tünel Cad. 18, 80000 Karaköy, İstanbul;
tel. (212) 2510917; telex 25440; fax (212) 2496289; f. 1911; cap.
p.u. 26,777m., res 5,868m. (Dec. 1992); Gen. Man. STEFANO GERMINI;
2 brs.

Bank Mellat (Iran): Büyükdere Cad. Binbirçiçek Sok. 1, PK 67,
80620 Levent, İstanbul; tel. (212) 2695820; telex 26502; fax (212)
2642895; f. 1982; cap. p.u. 29,602m., res 1,749m., dep. 72,550m.
(Dec. 1992); Chair. and Gen. Man. AZIZ AKHOUNDI ASL; 2 brs.

Banque Indosuez Türk AŞ (France): Yapı Kredi Plaza, Büyükdere
Cad. 20–21, Blok C, Kat. 7, 80620 Levent, İstanbul; tel. (212)
2797070; telex 25117; fax (212) 2691414; f. 1986; cap. p.u.
38,400m., res 9,420m., dep. 109,893m. (Dec. 1992); Pres. PIERRE
STRUB; 1 br.

Chase Manhattan Bank, NA (USA): Yıldız Posta Cad. 52/11,
80700 Esentepe, İstanbul; tel. (212) 2751280; telex 26625; fax
(212) 2759932; f. 1984; cap. p.u. 30,000m., res 1,458m., dep.
72,340m. (Dec. 1991); Gen. Man. İSAK ANTİKA; 1 br.

Chemical Bank AŞ (USA): Abdi İpekçi Cad. 63, 80200 Maçka,
İstanbul; tel. (212) 2314010; telex 39081; fax (212) 2483791;
f. 1991; cap. p.u. 35,034m., res 28,190m., dep. 33,359m. (Dec.
1991); Gen. Man. KEVIN KEHOE; 1 br.

Citibank (USA): Büyükdere Cad. 101, 80280 Esentepe, İstanbul;
tel. (212) 2887700; telex 26277; fax (212) 2887760; f. 1981; cap.
p.u. 207,537m., res 22,032m., dep. 302,100m. (March 1994); Gen.
Man. ANJUM Z. IQBAL; 3 brs.

Crédit Lyonnais (France): Setüstü Haktan Han 45, Kat. 4, 80040
Kabataş, İstanbul; tel. (212) 2516300; telex 26836; fax (212)
2517724; f. 1988; cap. p.u. 45,663m., res 1,948m., dep. 6,646m.
(Dec. 1992); Gen. Man. MICHEL MARTINOVITCH; 2 brs.

Habib Bank Ltd (Pakistan): Abide-i Hürriyet Cad. 11, PK 8, 80260
Şişli, İstanbul; tel. (212) 2460220; telex 27849; fax (212) 2340807;
f. 1983; cap. p.u. 22,337m., res 696m., dep. 6,467m. (Dec. 1992);
Gen. Man. TANVEER A. KHAWAJA; 2 brs.

Holantse Bank Uni NV (Netherlands): İnönü Cad. 15/17, 80090
Gümüşsuyu, İstanbul; tel. (212) 2938802; telex 24677; fax (212)

2492008; f. 1921; cap. p.u. 20,000m., res 1,359m., dep. 54,950m.
(Dec. 1991); Gen. Man. ABRAM RUTGERS; 1 br.

Manufacturers' Hanover Trust Co (USA): Abdi İpekçi Cad. 63,
80200 Maçka, İstanbul; tel. (212) 2484112; telex 31096; fax (212)
2483791; f. 1984; cap. p.u. 35,025m., res 1,975m., dep. 65,185m.
(Dec. 1990); Gen. Man. ATİLLA URAS; 1 br.

Midland Bank AŞ (England) (UK): Cumhuriyet Cad. Elmadağ
Han 8, 80200 Elmadağ, İstanbul; tel. (212) 2315560; telex 38385;
fax (212) 2305300; f. 1990; cap. p.u. 30,000m., res 49m., dep.
1,101m. (Dec. 1991); Gen. Man. CHRISTOPHER C. ELLIS; 1 br.

Osmanlı Bankası AŞ (Compagnie Financière Ottomane SA) (Luxembourg): Voyroda Cad. 35/37, PK 297, 80000 Karaköy, İstanbul;
tel. (212) 2523000; telex 24193; fax (212) 2446471; f. 1893; cap.
450,000m., dep. 2,788,709m. (May 1993); Gen. Man. JEAN DE BOIS-
GROLLIER; 66 brs.

Saudi American Bank (SAMBA) (Saudi Arabia): Cumhuriyet
Cad. 233, PK 49, 80230 Harbiye, İstanbul; tel. (212) 2300284;
telex 27224; fax (212) 2330201; f. 1985; cap. p.u. 10,000m., res
2,277m., dep. 73,079m. (Dec. 1991); Gen. Man. ZUBYR SOOMRO; 1 br.

Société Générale SA (France): Yapı Kredi Plaza, Büyükdere Cad.,
Blok B, Kat. 12, 80620 Levent, İstanbul; tel. (212) 2797051; telex
39454; fax (212) 2694574; f. 1990; cap. p.u. 31,340m., res 433m.,
dep. 44,447m. (Dec. 1991); Gen. Man. JEAN-PIERRE DUCROQUET; 1 br.

Türk Boston Bank AŞ: Yıldız Posta Cad. 17, 80280 Esentepe,
İstanbul; tel. (212) 2745222; telex 26537; fax (212) 2723348; f.
1990 as affiliate of Bank of Boston (USA); cap. p.u. 57,070m., res
7,823m. (Dec. 1992); Gen. Man. IAN LEVACK; Asst Gen. Man. MARK
FOLEY; 2 brs.

Türk Sakura Bank AŞ: Büyükdere Cad. 108/A, 80280 Esentepe,
İstanbul; tel. (212) 2752930; telex 27718; fax (212) 2724270; f.
1985 as Türk Mitsui Bank, adopted current name in 1992; cap.
29,100m., res 2,623m., dep. 160,608m. (Dec. 1991); Chair. ŞARIK
TARA; Gen. Man. HIROYUKI FUNATSU; 2 brs.

Turkish Bank AŞ ('TRNC'): Valikonağı Cad. 7, 80200 Nişantaşı,
İstanbul; tel. (212) 2250330; telex 27359; fax (212) 2250355; f.
1982; cap. p.u. 145,880m., res 11,916m., dep. 400,213m. (March
1994); Chair. TANJU ÖZYOL; 6 brs.

WestLB (Europa) AG (Westdeutsche Landesbank) (Germany):
Nispetiye Cad. 38, 80630 Levent, İstanbul; tel. (212) 2792537;
telex 26862; fax (212) 2802941; f. 1990; cap. p.u. 23,500m., res
1,512m., dep. 23,017m. (Dec. 1991); Gen. Man. GILLES LÉRAILLÉ;
2 brs.

Banking Organization

Banks' Association of Turkey: Mithatpaşa Cad. 12, 06410 Yenişehir, Ankara; tel. (312) 4340160; telex 46771; fax (312) 4316679;
f. 1958; Chair. Prof. Dr AYDIN AYAYDIN (acting); Sec.-Gen. ERHAN
YAŞAR.

STOCK EXCHANGE

İstanbul Menkul Kıymetler Borsası (İMKB): Rıhtım Cad. 245,
Eren Han, 80030 Tophane, Karaköy, İstanbul; tel. (212) 2524800;
telex 22748; fax (212) 2524915; f. 1866; revived in 1986 after
being dormant for about 60 years; 176 mems; Pres. TUNCAY ARTUN;
Vice-Chairs ARIL SEREN, ALİ İPEK, EMİN ALİ GÜNDEZ, ABDULLAH AKYÜZ.

INSURANCE

Anadolu Sigorta TAŞ (Anatolia Turkish Insurance Co): Rıhtım
Cad. 57, PK 1845, 80330 Karaköy, İstanbul; tel. (212) 2516540;
tel. (212) 2516540; telex 25407; fax (212) 242690; f. 1925; Chair.
BURHAN KARAGÖZ; Gen. Man. AHMET YAVUZ.

Ankara Sigorta TAŞ (Ankara Insurance Co): Bankalar Cad. 80,
80020 Karaköy, İstanbul; tel. (212) 2521010; telex 24394; fax
(212) 2524744; f. 1936; Chair. and Gen. Man. Dr SEBAHATTİN BEYAZ.

Cigna-Sabancı Sigorta AŞ: Barbaros Bul. 19, 80690 Beşiktaş,
İstanbul; tel. (212) 2932963; telex 26085; fax (212) 2494790;
f. 1964; fire, engineering, marine, accident; Chair. T. GÜNGÖR URAS.

Destek Reasürans TAŞ: Abdi İpekçi Cad. 75, 80200 Maçka, İs-
tanbul; tel. (212) 2312832; telex 27748; fax (212) 2415704; f. 1945;
reinsurance; Pres. SÜLEYMAN KAYA; Gen. Man. İBRAHİM YAYCIOĞLU.

Doğan Sigorta AŞ: Serdarı Ekrem Sok. 48, 80020 Kuledibi, İs-
tanbul; tel. (212) 2516374; telex 25854; fax (212) 2516379; f. 1942;
fire, marine, accident; Chair. T. GÜNGÖR URAS.

Güven Sigorta TAŞ: Bankalar Cad. 122–124, 80000 Karaköy,
İstanbul; tel. (212) 2547900; telex 24336; fax (212) 2555888;
f. 1924; Chair. ENVER AKOVA; Gen. Man. ENVER YALÇINKAYA.

Halk Sigorta TAŞ: Büyükdere Cad. 161, 80506 Zincirlikuyu, İs-
tanbul; tel. (212) 2743940; telex 26438; fax (212) 2751668; f. 1944;
Chair. HALUK CİLLOV; Gen. Man. ERHAN DUMANLI.

Hür Sigorta AŞ: Büyükdere Cad., Hür Han 15/A, 80260 Şişli,
İstanbul; tel. (212) 2322010; telex 27501; fax (212) 2463673;
Chair. BÜLENT SEMİLER; Gen. Man. GÜNER YALÇINER.

İMTAŞ İttihadı Milli Sigorta TAŞ: Büyükdere Cad. 116, 80300 Zincirlikuyu, İstanbul; tel. (212) 2747000; telex 26404; fax (212) 2720837; f. 1918; Chair. Prof. Dr ASAF SAVAŞ AKAT; Gen. Man. MUSTAFA AKAN.

İstanbul Reasürans AŞ: Halaskargazi Cad. 309, Kat. 4, 80260 Şişli, İstanbul; tel. (212) 2408070; telex 39014; fax (212) 2300464; f. 1979; Chair. CEMAL ZAGRA; Gen. Man. GÜLGÜN ÜNLÜOGLU.

Milli Reasürans TAŞ: Teşvikiye Cad. 43–57, 80200 Teşvikiye, İstanbul; tel. (212) 2314730; telex 26472; fax (212) 2308608; f. 1929; Chair. AHMET AYAYDIN; Gen. Man. CAHİT NOMER.

Şark Sigorta TAŞ: Bağlarbaşı, Kısıklı Cad. 9, 81180 Altunizade, İstanbul; tel. (212) 3101250; telex 29739; fax (212) 3101349; f. 1923; Chair. M. RAHMİ KOÇ; Gen. Man. CEMAL ZAĞRA.

Şeker Sigorta AŞ: Meclisi Mebusan Cad. 87, Şeker Sigorta Hanı, PK 519, 80040 Fındıklı, İstanbul; tel. (212) 2514035; telex 24252; fax (212) 2491046; f. 1954; Chair. MEHMET SERT; Gen. Man. YURDAL SERT.

Tam Sigorta AŞ: Prof. Dr Nurettin Öktem Sok. 20/2, Şişli, İstanbul; tel. (212) 2258350; fax (212) 2342948; f. 1964; all types of insurance except life; Chair. TURAN ÜLKER; Gen. Man. MEHMET NEZIR UCA.

Türkiye Genel Sigorta AŞ: Meclisi Mebusan Cad. 91, 80040 Sahpazarı, İstanbul; tel. (212) 2520010; telex 24453; fax (212) 2499651; f. 1948; Chair. MEHMET E. KARAMEHMET; Gen. Man. HULUSİ TAŞKIRAN.

Trade and Industry

DEVELOPMENT ORGANIZATIONS

Turkish Atomic Energy Authority: Cinnah Cad., Alaçum Sok. 9, 06540 Çankaya, Ankara; tel. (312) 4273071; telex 46459; fax (312) 4272834; f. 1956; controls the development of peaceful uses of atomic energy; 11 mems; Pres. Prof. YALÇIN SANALAN; Sec.-Gen. EROL BARUTÇUGİL.

Turkish Electricity Authority (Nuclear Power Plants Division): İnönü Bul. 27, Bahçelievler, Ankara; tel. (312) 2229855; telex 42245; fax (312) 2138870; state enterprise to supervise the building and operation of nuclear power stations; attached to the Ministry of Energy and Natural Resources; Dir Dr AHMET KÜTÜKÇÜOĞLU.

CHAMBERS OF COMMERCE AND INDUSTRY

Union of Chambers of Commerce, Industry, Maritime Commerce and Commodity Exchanges of Turkey (UCCET): 149 Atatürk Bul. 149, Bakanlıklar, Ankara; tel. (312) 4177700; telex 42343; fax (212) 4181002; f. 1952; represents 313 chambers and commodity exchanges; Pres. YALIM EREZ; Sec.-Gen. ŞEFİK TOKAT.

İstanbul Chamber of Commerce (ICOC): Ragip Gümüşpala Cad. 84, 34378 Eminönü, İstanbul; tel (1) 5114150; telex 22682; fax (212) 5262197; f. 1882; more than 130,000 mems; Pres. ATALAY ŞAHİNOĞLU.

İzmir Chamber of Commerce: Atatürk Cad. 126, Alsancak, İzmir; tel. (232) 4417777; telex 52331; fax (232) 4837853; f. 1885; Pres. HALİT ŞARLAK.

EMPLOYERS' ASSOCIATIONS

Türk Sanayicileri ve İşadamları Derneği (TÜSİAD) (Turkish Industrialists' and Businessmen's Association): Meşrutiyet Cad. 74, 80050 Tepebaşı, İstanbul; tel. (212) 2491131; telex 22318; fax (212) 2490913 f. 1971; 338 mems; Pres. HALİS KOMİLİ; Sec.-Gen. E. İHSAN ÖZOL.

Türkiye İşveren Sendikaları Konfederasyonu (TİSK) (Turkish Confederation of Employers' Associations): Meşrutiyet Cad. 1/4-5, 06650 Kızılay, Ankara; tel. (312) 4183217; telex 42122; fax (312) 4184473; f. 1962; represents (on national level) 18 employers' associations with 2,000 affiliated member employers or companies; official representative in labour relations; Pres. REFİK BAYDUR; Sec.-Gen. KUBİLAY ATASAYAR.

MAJOR INDUSTRIAL COMPANIES

Aksa (Akrilik Kimya San. AŞ): Miralay Şekipbey Sok. Ak Han 15–17, Kat. 5/6, Gumuşsuyu, İstanbul; tel. (212) 2514500; telex 25801; fax (212) 2514507; produces acrylic fibres and general chemical products; Pres. ALİ DINÇKÖK; 850 employees.

Alpet (Aliaga Petrokimya San. ve Tic. AŞ): PK 12, Aliaga, İzmir; tel. (232) 6161240; telex 51706; fax (232) 6161248; manufacture and distribution of petrochemicals; Pres. SEYFETTİN BİÇİCİ; 3,694 employees.

Arçelik AŞ: 41460 Çayırova, İstanbul; tel. (212) 3954515; telex 34138; fax (212) 3952727; turnover TL 2,375,133m. (1990); produces domestic appliances; Pres. SUNA KIRAÇ; 3,434 employees.

Bağfaş (Bandırma Gübre Fabrikaları AŞ): Susam Sok. 26, 80060 Cihangir, İstanbul; tel. (212) 2930885; telex 26185; fax (212) 2499744; produces fertilizers and acids; Pres. RECEP DİNÇER; 590 employees.

Beko Teknik Sanayi AŞ: Büyükçekmece Beylik Düzü Mevkii, İstanbul; tel. (212) 8721313; telex 23506; fax (212) 8721270; produces electronic consumer goods; Pres. A. İ. ÇUBUKÇU; 2,000 employees.

Boru Hatları ile Petrol Taşıma AŞ (BOTAŞ): Güneş Sok. 11, 06690 Güvenevler, Ankara; tel. (312) 4670150; telex 42898; fax (312) 4282646; operates petroleum and gas pipelines.

Brisa—Bridgestone Sabanci Tire Manufacturing and Trading Co Inc: Sabanci Centre Kule 2, Kat. 7-9, 80745 4 Levent, İstanbul; tel. (212) 2780021; telex 26145; fax (212) 2811681; manufactures tyres; Pres. SAKIP SABANCI; 1,628 employees.

Çolakoğlu Metalurji AŞ: Kemeraltı Cad. Karaköy Ticaret Merkezi 24, Kat. 6, Karaköy, İstanbul; tel. (212) 2520000; telex 25739; fax (212) 2495588; manufactures steel wire; Pres. MEHMET ÇOLAKOĞLU; 950 employees.

Çukurova Çelik Endüstrisi AŞ: Meclisi Mebusan Cad. Salıpazarı Yokuşu 1, 80040 Salıpazarı, İstanbul; tel. (212) 2513737; telex 25065; fax (212) 2511286; manufactures steel bloom; Gen. Man. MEHMET KUZEYLİ; 796 employees.

Çukurova Elektrik AŞ: PK 239, Adana; tel. (322) 2350681; telex 62735; fax (322) 2350256; manufactures electrical appliances; Pres. KEMAL UZAN; 1,382 employees.

Enka Holding Investment Co Inc: Balmumcu Mahallesi, Bestekar Şevki Bey Cad., ENKA II Binası, Beşiktaş, İstanbul; tel. (212) 2740970; telex 27035; fax (212) 2728869; f. 1957; contracting, industry, trading, tourism, banking and engineering with 44 specialized subsidiaries; Co-founder and Chair. ŞARIK TARA; Man. Dir VAHİTTİN GÜLERYÜZ; 18,000 employees.

Ereğli Demir ve Çelik Fabrikalari TAŞ: Zübeyde Hanım Bul. 7, Karadeniz, 67330 Ereğli; tel. (372) 3232500; telex 48523; fax (372) 3163969; manufactures steel and iron products; Chair. Prof. Dr MEHMET KAYTAZ; Pres. YALÇIN AMANVERMEZ; 7,612 employees.

Goodyear Lastikleri TAŞ: Büyükdere Cad. Maslak Meydanı 41, Alarko İş Merkezi, Levent, İstanbul; tel. (212) 2764693; telex 26491; fax (212) 2764751; manufactures tyres; Pres. J. KAPLAN; 2,000 employees.

İzmir Pamuk Mensucatı TAŞ: 1201 Sok. 11, PK 106, Halkapınar, İzmir; tel. (232) 4339810; telex 53220; fax (232) 4339782; f. 1914; manufacturers and exporters of cotton goods; Chief Exec. ÇETİN OKTAY.

Koç Holding AŞ: Nakkaştepe Aziz Bey Sok. 1, 80207 Kuzguncuk, İstanbul; tel. (216) 3414650; telex 24218; fax (216) 3431944; f. 1926; construction and engineering with 116 specialized subsidiaries; manufacturers of consumer durables; Chair. RAHMİ KOÇ; Vice-Pres. NECATI ARIKAN; 35,530 employees.

Kordsa (Kord Bezi San. ve Tic. AŞ): Sabancı Centre Kule 2, Kat. 5, 80745 4 Levent, İstanbul; tel. (212) 2810012; telex 26181; fax (212) 2810027; manufactures cord fabric; Pres. SAKIP SABANCI; 1,200 employees.

Kutlutaş Holding Co: İnönü Cad. 28/5, Taksim, İstanbul; tel. (212) 2512823; telex 24304; fax (212) 2434511; f. 1970; controlling interests in 18 cos engaged in manufacture of cranes, scaffolding elements, chemicals, electrical appliances, large-scale construction, as well as contracting and tourism.

Mensucat Santral TAŞ: Demirhane Cad. 90, 34770 Kazlıçeşme, İstanbul; tel. (212) 5823390; telex 22364; fax (212) 5582343; f. 1929; manufactures and exports domestic textile products; net sales US $98m. (1987); CEO HALİL BEZMEN.

Mercedes-Benz Türk AŞ: Burmalı Çeşme Sok. Askeri Fırın Yolu 2, 34022 Davutpaşa, İstanbul; tel. (212) 5670409; telex 22374; fax (212) 5770402; manufactures civil and military vehicles; Pres. EIKE LIPPOLD; 2,300 employees.

Metaş (İzmir Metalurji Fabrikası TAŞ): Kemalpaşa Cad. Işıkkent Girişi, 35070 İzmir; f. 1958; tel. (232) 4334010; telex 53384; fax (232) 4334041; steel producers and exporters; Gen. Man. NIYAZI ALTAN.

Naşas Alüminyum Sanayi ve Ticaret AŞ: Diliskelesi, Gebze, 41810 Kocaeli; tel. (199) 16550; telex 34128; fax (199) 17995; producers of aluminium sheet, foil and packaging materials.

Otosan (Otomobil San AŞ): Ankara Asfaltı 4 KM, Uzunçayır Mevkii, 81302 Kadıköy, İstanbul; tel. (216) 3267060; telex 29470; fax (216) 3390861; manufactures passenger cars, trucks and engines; 1,800 employees.

Oyak—Renault Otomobil Fab. AŞ: Emirhan Cad. Barbaros Plaza Blok C 145, Kat. 6, 80700 Dikilitaş, İstanbul; tel. (212) 2270000; telex 27774; fax (212) 2594545; manufactures automobiles; Pres. ALI BOZER; 4,500 employees.

Peg (Profilo Elektrikli Gereçler San. AŞ): İkinci Tasocaği Sok. 26/28, Mecidiyeköy, İstanbul; tel. (212) 2743300; telex 26171; fax (212) 2116512; manufactures electrical appliances; Pres. JAK KAMHİ; 4,600 employees.

Sasa Sun'i ve Sentetik Elyaf San. AŞ: Sabancı Centre Kule 2, 80745 4 Levent, İstanbul; tel. (212) 2785088; fax (212) 2786201; manufactures synthetic yarns and fibres; Pres. ÖZDEMİR SABANCI; 4,000 employees.

Sevil Giyim İhracat İthalat Sanayi ve Ticaret AŞ: Sanayi Cad. 49, Bornova, İzmir; tel. (232) 4350050; telex 53046; fax (232) 4350633; manufactures and exports ready-made garments.

Söktaş: Cumhuriyet Mah. Karasuluk Mevkii, PK 32, 09201 Söke; tel. (256) 5182255; telex 58505; manufacturers and exporters of cotton yarns and thread; Gen. Man. MUHARREM KAYHAN.

TDÇ Isl. Genel Müd. Karabük D.C. Mües. Müd.: Karabük; tel. (372) 4182001; telex 48522; fax (372) 4182110; manufactures iron, steel, coke and napthalene; Vice-Pres. COŞKUN AKTEM; 9,000 employees.

TDÇ İşl. İskenderun Demir ve Çelik Fabrikalari Mües. Müd.: Isdemir, Hatay; tel. (326) 7556260; telex 68696; fax (326) 6173895; manufactures steel and iron; Pres. SENCER İMER; 14,158 employees.

Tofaş (Türk Otomobil Fab. AŞ): Büyükdere Cad. 145/5, 80300 Zincirlikuyu, İstanbul; tel. (212) 2753390; telex 26451; fax (212) 2753988; manufactures automobiles and automobile parts; Pres. CAN KIRAÇ; 5,263 employees.

Türk Pirellı Lastikleri AŞ: Büyükdere Cad. 117, Gayrettepe, İstanbul; tel. (212) 2752280; telex 26337; fax (212) 2726077; manufactures and distributes tyres; Pres. BÜLENT ECZACIBASI; 850 employees.

Turkish Petroleum Corpn (TPAO): Mustafa Kemal Mah. II Cad. 86, 06520 Bakanlıklar, Ankara; tel. (312) 2869100; telex 42624; fax (312) 2869000; Turkey's largest State Economic Enterprise; explores for, drills and produces crude petroleum; 35 rigs and 474 oil wells; 5,113 employees.

Türkiye Elektrik Kurumu: İnönü Bulvarı 27, Bahçelievler, Ankara; tel. (312) 2126915; fax (312) 2138870; electrical goods; Pres. MUHİTTİN BABALIOĞLU; 69,801 employees.

Türkiye Petrol Rafinerileri AŞ (TÜPRAŞ): Körfez, İzmit; tel. (262) 5270600; telex 33152; fax (262) 2170658; refining of crude oil; Pres. Dr MEHMET SAVRAN; 5,000 employees.

Türkiye Şeker Fabrikaları AŞ: Mithatpaşa Cad. 14, 06100 Yenişehir, Ankara; tel. (312) 4359815; telex 42422; fax (312) 4317225; produces sugar and manufactures machinery used in sugar production; Gen. Dir ERDOĞAN ERTEKIN; 22,074 employees.

Türkiye Şişe ve Cam Fabrikaları AŞ: Ankara Asfalti İçmeler Mevkii 81700 İstanbul; tel. (216) 3955473; telex 36024; fax (216) 3954128; f. 1934; glass manufacturers and exporters; Gen. Man. ADNAN ÇAĞLAYAN; 15,000 employees.

Turyağ AS: PK 171, İzmir; tel. (232) 4845320; telex 53448; fax (232) 4844832; f. 1916; manufacturers of detergents and edible oils.

Tütün, Tütün Mamülleri, Tuz ve Alkol İşletmeleri Genel Müdürlüğü (TEKEL): Hisralti Cad., 34230 Cibali, İstanbul; tel. (212) 5339622; telex 23159; fax (212) 6311245; production and distribution of tobacco products, alcohol and salt; Pres. MEHMET AKBAY; 48,568 employees.

Unilever—İş Ticaret ve San. Türk Ltd Şti: Yıldız Posta Cad. Yener Sok. 3, Beşiktas, İstanbul; tel. (212) 2754545; telex 28548; fax (212) 2754579; produces edible fats; Pres. DEMİR TİRYAKIOĞLU; 1,050 employees.

Uzel Makine Sanayi AŞ: Topçular, Kışla Cad. 5, 34147 Rami, İstanbul; tel. (212) 5670841; telex 23416; fax (212) 5764595; manufactures tractors, wheels, brakes and automobile springs; Pres. AHMET UZEL; 1,767 employees.

Yarpet (Yarımca Petrokimya San. ve Tic. AŞ): 41744 Körfez, İzmit; tel. (262) 5281450; telex 33109; fax (262) 5281400; produces petrochemicals; Pres. MEHMET YILMAZ; 3,886 employees.

Yaşar Holding Corpn: Gaziosmanpaşa Bul. Bat, İşhanı Kat. 3-4-7, İzmir; tel. (232) 4890121; telex 53407; fax (232) 4256667; f. 1954; 40 member companies with interests in processed food, tourism, paints, chemicals, paper, banking, insurance, commerce and beer; Chair. SELÇUK YAŞAR; Vice-Chair. SELMAN YAŞAR; 7,000 employees.

Zihni Group: Rıhtım Cad. Zihni Han 28/30, 80030 Tophane, İstanbul; tel. (212) 2511515; telex 25227; fax (212) 2435325; f. 1930; integrated sea and land transport company specializing in imports and exports.

TRADE UNIONS
Confederations

DİSK (Türkiye Devrimci İşçi Sendikaları Konfederasyonu) (Confederation of Progressive Trade Unions of Turkey): Merter Sitesi, Ahmet Kutsi Tecer Cad. Sendikalar Binası 12, Kat. 5, 34010 Merter, İstanbul; tel. (212) 5048083; fax (212) 5061079; member of ICFTU and ETUC; 30 affiliated unions; Pres. KEMAL NEBİOĞLU; Sec.-Gen. SÜLEYMAN ÇELEBİ.

Türk-İş (Türkiye İşçi Sendikaları Konfederasyonu Genel Başkanlığı) (Confederation of Turkish Trade Unions): Bayındır Sok. 10, Yenişehir, Ankara; tel. (312) 4333125; fax (312) 4336809; f. 1952; member of ICFTU, ETUC, ICFTU-APRO and OECD/TUAC; 32 national unions and federations with 1.7m. mems; Pres. BAYRAM MERAL; Gen. Sec. ŞEMSİ DENİZER.

Principal DISK Trade Unions

Bank-Sen (Türkiye Devrimci Banka ve Sigorta İşçileri Sendikası): Nakiye Elgun Sok. 117, Şişli, İstanbul; tel. (212) 2321000; fax (212) 2464112; Pres. HULUSİ KARLI; 11,800 mems.

Basın-İş (Türkiye Basın İşçileri Sendikası) (Press Workers' Union): Nesihpaşa Mah. Azimkar Sok. Neşe Apt. 27/29, Kat. 4, Laleli, İstanbul; tel. (212) 5180492; fax (212) 5169525; f. 1964; Pres. YILMAZ ÖZDEMİR; Gen. Sec. DERVİŞ BOYOĞLU; 5,000 mems.

Birlesik Metal-İş (Birlesik Metal İşçileri Sendikası): Kirtasiyeci Sok. 21, 81300 Kadıköy, İstanbul; tel. (216) 3454703; fax (216) 3474598; Pres. ALİ RIZA İKİSİVRİ; 58,800 mems.

Demiryol-İş (Türkiye Demiryolu İşçileri Sendikası) (Railway Workers): Necatibey Cad., Sezenler Sok. 5, 06430 Yenişehir, Ankara; tel. (312) 2318029; fax (312) 2318032; f. 1952; Pres. ENVER TOÇOĞLU; Gen. Sec. NURETTİN GİRGİNER; 25,000 mems.

Deri-İş (Türkiye Deri İşçileri Sendikası) (Leather Industry): Ahmet Kutsi Tecer Cad. 12/6, Merter, İstanbul; tel. (212) 5048083; fax (212) 5061079; f. 1948; Pres. NUSRETTİN YILMAZ; Gen. Sec. ALİ SEL; 11,000 mems.

Dev. Sağlık-İş (Türkiye Devrimci Sağlık İşçileri Sendikası) (Health Employees): Oğuzhan Cad., Ahenk Apt. 39/8, Kat. 2, 34270 Fındıkzade, İstanbul; tel. (212) 5236190; fax (212) 5237647; f. 1961; Pres. DOĞAN HALİS; Gen. Sec. SABRİ TANYERİ; 15,000 mems.

Genel-İş (Türkiye Genel Hizmet İşçileri Sendikası) (Municipal Workers): Çankırı Cad. 28, Kat 5-9, Ulus, Ankara; tel. (312) 3091547; fax (312) 3091046; f. 1983; Pres. İSMAİL HAKKI ÖNAL; Gen. Sec. ATILA ÖNGEL; 50,000 mems.

Gıda-İş (Türkiye Gida Sanayii İşçileri Sendikası): Ahmet Kutsi Tecer Cad. 12/3, Merter, İstanbul; tel. (212) 5757229; fax (212) 5753099; Pres. KEMAL NEBİOĞLU; 31,000 mems.

Koop-İş (Türkiye Kooperatif ve Büro İşçileri Sendikası) (Cooperative and Office Workers): İzmir Cad. Fevzi Çadmak Sok. 15/11–12, Yenişehir, Ankara; tel. (312) 4300855; f. 1964; Pres. AHMET BALAMAN; Gen. Sec. AHMET GÜVEN; 29,000 mems.

Limter-İş (Liman, Tersane Gemi Yapım Onarım İşçileri Sendikası) (Harbour, Shipyard, Ship Building and Repairs): İcmeler Tren İstasyonu Yaru 12/1, Tuzla, İstanbul; tel. (216) 3955271; f. 1947; Pres. EMİR BABAKUŞ; Gen. Sec. ASKER ŞİT; 7,000 mems.

Nakliyat-İş (Nakliye İşçileri Sendikası) (Transportation Workers): Guraba Hüseyin Ağa Mah. Kakmaci Sok 10, Daire 11 Vatan Cad. Tranvay, Durağı Karşısı, Aksaray, İstanbul; tel. (212) 5332069; Pres. ŞEMSİ ERCAN; Gen. Sec. NEDİM FIRAT.

OLEYİS (Türkiye Otel, Lokanta ve Eğlence Yerleri İşçileri Sendikası) (Hotel, Restaurant and Places of Entertainment): Atatürk Bul. 57, Kızılay, Ankara; tel. (312) 4359680; fax (312) 4358654; f. 1947; Pres. ENVER ÖKTEM; Gen. Sec. MAHMUT AYDIN; 15,000 mems.

Petkim-İş (Türkiye Petrol, Kimya ve Lastik Sanayii İşçileri Sendikası): İzmir Cad., Fevzi Çakmak Sok. 7/13, Ankara; tel. (312) 2300861; fax (312) 2299429; Pres. MUSTAFA KARADAYI; 18,000 mems.

Sosyal-İş (Türkiye Sosyal Sigortalar, Eğitim, Büro, Ticaret Kooperatif Banka ve Güzet Sanatlar İşçileri Sendikası) (Banking, Insurance and Trading): Necatibey Cad. Sezenler Sok. Lozan Apt. 2/14, Yenişehir, Ankara; tel. (312) 2318178; fax (312) 2294638; Pres. ÖZCAN KESGEÇ; Gen. Sec. H. BEDRİ DOĞANAY; 31,000 mems.

Tekstil İşçileri Sendikası: Ahmet Kutsi Tecer Cad. 12/1, Merter, İstanbul; tel. (212) 6429742; fax (212) 5044887; Pres. RIDVAN BUDAK; 45,000 mems.

Tümka-İş (Türkiye Tüm Kağit Selüloz Sanayii İşçileri Sendikası): Gündoğdu Sok. 19/3, Merter, İstanbul; tel. (212) 5750843; Pres. SABRİ KAPLAN; 3,000 mems.

Other Principal Trade Unions

Denizciler (Türkiye Denizciler Sendikası (Seamen): Rıhtım Cad., Denizciler Sok. 7, Tophane, İstanbul; tel. (212) 2444838; f. 1959; Pres. EMİN KUL; Gen. Sec. MUSTAFA YÖNDEM; 12,000 mems.

Findik-Is (Fiskobirlik İşçileri Sendikası) (Hazelnut producers): Gazi Cad., Guven Pasajı 65/4, Giresun; tel. (51) 61950; fax (51) 62104; Pres. AKÇIN KOÇ; Gen. Sec. ERSAİT ŞEN.

Hava-İş (Türkiye Sivil Havacılık Sendikası) (Civil Aviation): İncirli Cad., Volkan Apt., 68/1 Bakırköy, İstanbul; tel. (212) 6601495; fax (212) 5719051; Pres. ATİLAY AYÇİN; Gen. Sec. ŞAFAK KURNAZ; 10,500 mems.

Likat-İş (Türkiye Liman ve Nakil Tahliye İşçileri Sendikası) (Longshoremen): Necatibey Cad., Sezenler Sok. 4, Kat. 5, Yenişehir, Ankara; tel. (312) 2317418; f. 1963; Pres. AHMET KURT; Gen. Sec. NEŞET MAZMANCI; 8,800 mems.

Şeker-İş (Türkiye Şeker Sanayii İşçileri Sendikası) (Sugar Industry): Karanfil Sok. 59, Bakanlıklar, Ankara; tel. (312) 4184273; f. 1952; Pres. HİKMET ALCAN; Gen. Sec. ÖMER ÇELİK; 35,000 mems.

Tarım-İş (Türkiye Orman, Topraksu, Tarım ve Tarım Sanayii İşçileri Sendikası) (Agricultural Irrigation and Forestry Workers): Necatibey Cad. 22/9-12, Ankara Apt., Yenişehir, Ankara; tel. (312) 2317856; fax (312) 2298592; f. 1961; Pres. SABRİ ÖZDEŞ; Gen. Sec. ZEKİ KARA; 43,500 mems.

Tekgıda-İş (Türkiye Tütün, Müskirat Gıda ve Yardımcı İşçileri Sendikası) (Tobacco, Drink, Food and Allied Workers' Union of Turkey): 4 Levent Konaklar Sok., İstanbul; tel. (212) 2644996; fax (212) 2789534; f. 1952; Pres. ORHAN BALTA; Gen. Sec. HÜSEYİN KARAKOÇ; 176,000 mems.

Teksif (Türkiye Tekstil, Örme ve Giyim Sanayii İşçileri Sendikası) (Textile, Knitting and Clothing): Ziya Gökalp Cad. Aydoğmuş Sok. 1, Kurtuluş, Ankara; tel. (312) 4312170; fax (312) 4357826; f. 1951; Pres. ŞEVKET YILMAZ; Gen. Sec. ZEKİ POLAT; 120,000 mems.

Tez-Koop-İş (Türkiye, Ticaret, Kooperatif, Eğitim, Büro ve Güzel Sanatlar İşçileri Sendikası) (Commercial and Clerical Employees): Üç Yıldız Cad. 29, Subayevleri, Ayınlikevler, Ankara; tel. (312) 3183979; fax (312) 3183988; f. 1962; Pres. AHMET TAMER; Gen. Sec. ERTUĞRUL KAKMACI; 30,000 mems.

Türk Harb-İş (Türkiye Harb Sanayii ve Yardımcı İşkolları İşçileri Sendikası) (Defence Industry and Allied Workers): İnkılap Sok. 20, Kızılay, Ankara; tel. (312) 4175097; fax (312) 4171364; f. 1956; Pres. İZZET CETİN; Gen. Sec. NURI AYCICER; 35,000 mems.

Türk-Metal (Türkiye Metal, Çelik, Mühimmat, Makina ve Metalden Mamul, Eşya ve Oto, Montaj ve Yardımcı İşçileri Sendikası) (Auto, Metal and Allied Workers): Gazi Mustafa Kemal Bul., Akıncılar Sok. 14, Maltepe, Ankara; tel. (312) 2317940; fax (312) 2297714; f. 1963; Pres. MUSTAFA ÖZBEK; Gen. Sec. ÖZBEK KARAKUS; 123,000 mems.

Yol-İş (Türkiye Yol, Yapı ve İnşaat İşçileri Sendikası) (Road Construction and Building Workers' Unions): İstanbul Cad. 58, İskitler, Ankara; tel. (312) 3422240; fax (312) 3412705; f. 1963; Pres. BAYRAM MERAL; Gen. Sec. TEVFİK ÖZÇELİK; 170,000 mems.

TRADE FAIR

İzmir Enternasyonal Fuarı (Izmir International Fair): Şair Eşref Bul. 50, 35230 Kültürpark, İzmir; tel. (232) 4821270; telex 53295; fax (232) 4254342; f. 1929; Pres. MUSTAFA H. BOYACIOĞLU; Dir-Gen. DOĞON İŞLEYEN.

Transport

RAILWAYS

The total length of the railways operated within the national frontiers is 10,413 km (1993), of which 8,430 km are main lines, 1,033 km are electrified, and 1,359 km are signalled. A new direct rail link between Ankara and İstanbul, cutting the distance from 577 km to 416 km, is expected to be completed by the year 2000. There are direct rail links with Bulgaria to Iran and Syria. A light railway system for İstanbul, expected to total 109 km in length upon its completion, is currently under construction. In April 1990 work started on the construction of a new 14.6 km 'metro' transport system in Ankara, to be completed by 1994. An 8.5 km light rail route for the city is also under construction.

Türkiye Cumhuriyeti Devlet Demiryolları İşletmesi Genel Müdürlüğü (TCDD) (Turkish Republic State Railways): Genel Müdürlük, Talatpaşa Bul., 06330 Gar, Ankara; tel. (312) 3090515; telex 42571; fax (312) 3123215; f. 1924; operates all railways and connecting ports (see below) of the State Railway Administration, which acquired the status of a state economic enterprise in 1953, and a state economic establishment in 1984; 556 main-line diesel locomotives, 1,515 passenger coaches and 19,513 freight wagons; Chair. of Board and Gen. Dir TALAT GÜNSOY.

ROADS

At 1 January 1994, 1,070 km of motorways were open to traffic and nearly 594 km of motorways were under construction; the total length of the highway network was 59,770 km and the total length of village roads was 308,000 km. In 1994 there were 56,466 km of roads in the maintenance programme with 48,149 km open all year and 8,327 km open, when possible, in winter.

Bayındırlık ve İskan Bakanlığı Karayolları Genel Müdürlüğü (General Directorate of Highways): KGM Sitesi, Yücetepe, 06100 Ankara; tel. (312) 4252343; fax (312) 4186996; f. 1950; Dir-Gen. DİNÇER YİĞİT.

SHIPPING

At mid-1992 Turkey's merchant fleet comprised 920 vessels and had an aggregate displacement of 3.8m. gross tons.

General-purpose public ports are operated by two state economic enterprises. The ports of Bandırma, Derince, Haydarpaşa (İstanbul), İskenderun, İzmir, Mersin and Samsun, all of which are connected to the railway network, are operated by Turkish State Railways (TCDD) (see above), while the smaller ports of Antalya, Giresun, Hopa, Tekirdağ and Trabzon are operated by the Turkish Maritime Organization (TDI).

Turkish Maritime Organization (TDI): Genel Müdürlüğü, Karaköy, İstanbul; tel. (212) 2515000; telex 24895; fax (212) 2495391.

Port of Bandırma: TCDD Liman İşletme Müdürlüğü, Bandırma; tel. (266) 2234966; fax (266) 2236011; Port Man. HASAN KARAKUŞ; Harbour Master IBRAHİM YALKIRI.

Port of Derince: TCDD Liman İşletme Müdürlüğü, Derince; Port Man. ALİ ARİF AYTAÇ; Harbour Master HAYDAR DOĞAN.

Port of Haydarpaşa (İstanbul): TCDD Liman İşletme Müdürlüğü Haydarpaşa, İstanbul; tel. (212) 3379988; telex 29705; fax (212) 3451705; Port Man. LAMİ TEKSÖZ; Harbour Master İSMAİL SAFAER.

Port of İskenderun: TCDD Liman İşletme Müdürlüğü, İskenderun; tel. (326) 6640047; telex 68109; fax (326) 6632424; Port Man. ABDULMUSA APAYDIN; Harbour Master CEVAT ÇOLAK.

Port of İzmir: TCDD Liman İşletme Müdürlüğü, İzmir; tel. (232) 4632252; fax (232) 4632248; Port Man. GÜNGÖR ERKAYA; Harbour Master MEHMET ONGEL.

Port of Mersin: TCDD Liman İşletme Müdürlüğü, Mersin; tel. (324) 2330687; telex 67279; fax (324) 2311350; Port Man. FAHRI SAYILI; Harbour Master H. TAŞKIN.

Port of Samsun: TCDD Liman İşletme Müdürlüğü, Samsun; tel. (362) 4357616; telex 82172; fax (362) 4317849; Port Man. SAFFET YAMAK; Harbour Master Capt. ARIF H. UZUNOĞLU.

DB Deniz Nakliyatı TAŞ (DB Turkish Cargo Lines): Meclisi Mebusan Cad. 151, 80104 Fındıklı, İstanbul; tel. (212) 2512696; telex 24125; fax (212) 2512696; f. 1955; regular liner services between Turkey and Mediterranean, Adriatic, Red Sea, Persian Gulf, Europe, Black Sea, US Atlantic, and Indian and Far East ports; Pres. TAHİR İLKER GÜLFİDAN; Chair. MUZAFFER AKKAYER; 31 general cargo ships, 4 roll-on, roll-off, 13 bulk/ore carriers, 6 tankers.

Private Companies

Cerrahgil Denizcilik, Nakliyat ve Ticaret AŞ: Abdi İpekçi Cad. 33, PK 108, 80200 Teşvikiye, İstanbul; tel. (212) 2324700; telex 39091; fax (212) 2310035; f. 1974; shipowners, bunker and paint suppliers, agents, charterers, brokers, traders; Gen. Man. HOSROF KOLETAVITOGLU; 5 vessels; 244,806 dwt (1993).

Cerrahoğulları Umumi Nakliyat, Vapurculuk ve Ticaret AŞ: Yıldız Posta Cad. 17, Kat. 4/5, 80280 Esentepe, İstanbul; tel. (212) 2749800; telex 26593; fax (212) 2668039; f. 1954; Pres. and Gen. Man. SAEED RABB CERRAHOĞLU; 2 vessels; 198,916 dwt.

Genel Denizcilik Nakliyati AŞ (Geden Line): Meclisi Mebusan Cad. 91, Kat. 2/3, 80040 Salıpazarı, İstanbul; tel. (212) 2516700; telex 24248; fax (212) 2490479; f. 1975; shipowners, agents, brokers; Man. Dir ALTAN NADIMLI; 4 vessels; 122,786 dwt (1993).

İstanbul Ship Management SA: Rıhtım Cad. Zihni Han 28–30 Kat. 2, PK 390, 80030 Tophane, İstanbul; tel. (212) 2931950; telex 25805; fax (212) 2458024; f. 1993; Chair. AHMET ŞAHAP ÜNLÜ; Man. GÖKALP TUNCER; 3 vessels; 326,604 dwt.

Kalkavan Denizcilik ve Ticaret AŞ: Rıhtım Cad. Fatih İş Hanı 135, Kat. 4-5, 80030 Karaköy, İstanbul; tel. (212) 2525880; telex 25779; fax (212) 2445659; Pres. SEFER KALKAVAN; 10 vessels; 72,665 dwt.

Koçtuğ Gemi İşletmeciliği ve Ticaret AŞ: Bankalar Cad., Bozkurt Han Kat. 3, PK 884, 80000 Karaköy, İstanbul; tel. (212) 2513380; telex 24512; fax (212) 2515256; f. 1956; cargo services to and from Europe, North Africa and the USA; Pres. A. KOÇMAN; Gen. Man. M. LEBLEBİCİOĞLU; 4 general cargo vessels; 25,961 dwt.

Marti Shipping and Trading Co: Mechisi Mebusan Cad. 85, Orya Ishani Kat. 6, 80040 Salipazari, İstanbul; tel. (212) 2515500; telex 24051; fax (212) 2432567; Gen. Man. NECMETTIN OZGELIK; 9 bulk carriers; 896,658 dwt.

Türkiye Denizcilik İşletmeleri Denizyolları İşletmesi Mudurlugu (TDI): Meclisi Mebusan Cad. 68, 80040 Salıpazarı, İstanbul;

tel. (212) 2521700; telex 25962; fax (212) 2515767; ferry company; Chair. KENAN ÖNER; Man. Dir BURHAN KÜLÜNK; 13 vessels; 14,218 dwt.

Shipping Associations

SS Gemi Armatörleri Motorlu Taşıyıcılar Kooperatifi (Turkish Shipowners' Asscn): Meclisı Mebusan Cad., Dursun Han, Kat. 7, No 89, Salıpazarı İstanbul; tel. (212) 2510945; telex 25553; fax (212) 2492786; f. 1960; Pres. GÜNDÜZ KAPTANOĞLU; Man. Dir A. GÖKSU; 699 vessels; 5,509,112 dwt (1993).

Türk Armatörler Birliği (Turkish Shipowners' Union): Meclisı Mebusan Cad. Dursun Han, Kat. 7 No. 89, Salıpazarı, İstanbul; tel. (212) 2453022; telex 25552; fax (212) 2492786; f. 1972; 460 mems; Pres. ŞADAN KALKAVAN; Co-ordinator ENVER ÖZYAZICI; 5,509,112 dwt (1993).

Vapur Donatanları ve Acenteleri Derneği (Turkish Shipowners' and Shipping Agents' Asscn): Mumhane Cad. Emek İş Hanı Kat. 3 No. 31, Karaköy, İstanbul; tel. (212) 2443294; f. 1902; worldwide agency service; Pres. Capt. M. LEBLEBİCİOĞLU; Man. Dir C. KAPLAN.

CIVIL AVIATION

There are airports for scheduled international and internal flights at Atatürk (İstanbul), Esenboğa (Ankara), Adnan Menderes (Izmir and Trabzon), while international charter flights are handled by Adana, Dalaman and Antalya. Fifteen other airports handle internal flights only.

Akendiz Hava Yollari: Atakan Sok, Berhan Ishani, K-2 Mesidi-yakby, İstanbul.

Birgenair: Cumhuriyet Cad., Efser Han 301/9, 80230 İstanbul; tel. (212) 2401150; telex 27988; fax (212) 2465711; f. 1989; scheduled and charter services; Chair. MUHİP İŞMEN; Gen. Man. ÇETİN BİRGEN.

İstanbul Hava Yolları AŞ: Firuzköy Yolu, Bağlar İçi Mevzii 26, 34850 Avcılar, İstanbul; tel. (212) 5092100; telex 21022; fax (212) 5936035; f. 1985; operates scheduled and charter services from major Turkish cities to European destinations; Gen. Man. SAFİ ERGİN.

Onur Air: Şenlikköy Catal Sok. 3, Florya, İstanbul; tel. (212) 6632300; fax (212) 6632314; f. 1992; scheduled and charter services; Gen. Man. SEVİNÇ PINAR.

Pegasus Hava Taşımacılığı AŞ: İstasyon Cad. 24, Kat. 1, Yeşilyurt, İstanbul; tel. (212) 6632934; telex 21117; fax (212) 5739627; f. 1990; charter services; Gen. Man. L. J. LOWTH.

Sun Express AŞ: Fener Mah. Sinanoğlu Cad. Oktay Apt., PK 28, Antalya; tel. (242) 3234047; telex 56139; fax (242) 3234057; f. 1990; scheduled and charter services; Gen. Man. GERHARDT DİNTER.

TUR European Airways: Rıhtım Cad., Nesli Han 207/5, 80300 Karaköy, İstanbul; tel. (212) 2525497; telex 38365; fax (212) 2498335; f. 1988; scheduled and charter services throughout Europe; Pres. ÖMER TÜRKKAN; Asst Gen. Man. Capt. YILMAZ TEMEL.

Türk Hava Yolları AŞ (THY): (Turkish Airlines Inc.): Atatürk Hava Limanı, Yeşilköy, İstanbul; tel. (212) 6636300; telex 21198; fax (212) 6634744; f. 1933; majority state-owned; extensive internal network and flights to the Middle East, North Africa, the Far East, Central Asia, the USA and Europe; Chair. ERMAN YERDELEN; Pres. YUSUF BOLAYIRLI.

Tourism

Visitors to Turkey are attracted by the climate, fine beaches and ancient monuments. Tourism is being stimulated by the Government, and the industry is expanding rapidly. In 1993 receipts from tourism reached a record US $3,959m., compared with $3,639m. in 1992, although the number of tourists decreased from 7.1m. in 1992 to 6.5m. in 1993.

Ministry of Tourism: İsmet İnönü Bul. 5, Bahçelievler, Ankara; tel. (312) 2128300; telex 42448; fax (312) 2128391; f. 1963; Dir-Gen. of Establishments MEVHİBE CAN; Dir-Gen. of Information FER-MANİ UYGUN; Dir-Gen. SEYHUN ÖRS.

Defence

Chief of General Staff: Gen. ISMAIL HAKKI KARADAYI.

Ground Forces Commander: Gen. HİKMET BAYAR.

Navy Commander: Adm. VURAL BAYAZIT.

Air Force Commander: Gen. HALIS BURHAN.

Defence Budget (1994): estimated at TL 93,453,000m.

Military Service: 15 months.

Total Armed Forces (June 1994): 503,800 (including 410,200 conscripts): army 393,000 men, navy 54,000 men, air force 65,000 men.

Paramilitary Forces: 120,000 gendarmerie.

Gendarmerie Commander: Gen. BURHANETTİN BIGALI.

Education

When the Turkish Republic was formed, the Ministry of Education became the sole authority in educational matters, replacing the dual system of religious schools and other schools. One of the main obstacles to literacy was the Arabic script, which required years of study before proficiency could be attained. In 1928, therefore, a Turkish alphabet was introduced, using Latin characters. At the same time the literary language was simplified, and purged of some of its foreign elements. By 1992 the Government's expenditure on education was more than 20% of the State budget.

PEOPLE'S SCHOOLS

This change of script created a need for schools in which reading and writing in the new alphabet could be taught to adults. Temporary institutions, known as 'people's schools' or 'national schools', were established throughout Turkey. During the winter months these schools gave instruction in reading and writing and other basic subjects to men and women beyond the normal school age. Between 1928 and 1935 about 2m. people received certificates of proficiency. Since then, education in Turkey has made significant advances, and the rate of adult literacy was estimated at 81% in 1990.

PRIMARY EDUCATION

Primary education may be preceded by an optional pre-school establishment which serves 3–6 year old children.

According to the 'Basic Law of National Education', the education of children between the ages of six and 14 is compulsory. Basic Education Institutes are organized to provide eight years of education and are essentially a combination of primary school and middle school. Basic Education, therefore, comprises two cycles, the first consisting of the primary school and the second of the middle school.

At the present time the transition from a system of primary and middle schools to that of a single eight-year basic education school is being experimented in about 634 pilot schools.

Primary education is now entirely free, and co-education is the accepted basis for universal education. The number of schools has risen from 12,511 in 1950 to 50,701 in 1991/92, and the number of teachers from 27,144 to some 235,000. In the same academic year, around 6.9m. children were enrolled at primary schools. In 1991 an estimated 100% of children in the relevant age-group were enrolled in primary schools.

SECONDARY EDUCATION

The reorganization of the system of secondary education began in the early 1920s. This period of education now lasts six years, and is free. The secondary schools are divided into two stages: middle schools and lycées, and students who intend to proceed to higher educational institutions must pass through both stages, spending three years in the middle school and three in the lycée.

The middle school, although complementary to the lycée, is a separate unit, designed to give a definite and complete education to those students who at the end of the course will proceed directly to work. The State examination is taken by all students at the end of the third year. Graduates of a middle school are qualified either to take up an unskilled occupation or to enter upon a vocational course at a school of a higher grade.

The lycée takes the student up to the age of 17 or 18 years, and those who wish to proceed to an institute of higher education must pass the state matriculation examination. The study of a modern language (English, French or German) is compulsory in middle schools and lycées. In addition, Latin and Greek have been taught in some lycées since 1940. There were 1,385 lycées in Turkey in 1988. In 1991/92 there were around 157,000 staff teaching at the secondary level and some 3,988,000 pupils were enrolled at an estimated total of 11,035 secondary schools. In 1991 the total enrolment at primary and secondary schools was equivalent to 78% of the school-age population (boys 84%; girls 71%).

ADULT EDUCATION

Since 1932, reading-rooms have been established in every town and many villages. They are centres of social and cultural life and provide evening classes. Their libraries, meeting-halls and recreational facilities are open to all. In the towns there are also evening trade schools which provide technical training for adults, and travelling courses are sent out to the villages.

HIGHER EDUCATION

Higher educational institutions in Turkey were founded, and are administered, by the State. These institutions include the universities and the higher professional schools. In 1988 there were 29 universities, and in 1991/92 there were an estimated 424 other institutes of higher education (including teacher training colleges and other technical and vocational institutions). The number of students enrolled at universities and equivalent institutes of higher education was about 759,000 in that academic year.

TECHNICAL EDUCATION

The problem of technical education began to be seriously considered first in 1926; specialists were invited from Europe and America, and a plan was drawn up for perfecting the existing vocational schools and for founding new ones to meet the economic needs of each region. In 1989/90 there were 2,542 technical and vocational lycées, giving training to some 772,000 students. In addition, plans were made for evening schools to train craftsmen and for the founding of teachers' technical training colleges. There are two such colleges in Ankara, one for men and one for women.

TEACHERS' TRAINING

In Turkey teachers' training colleges are divided into three basic categories: two-year teacher-training institutes which train teachers for primary schools, three-year teacher-training institutes which train teachers for middle schools and higher teacher-training schools offering a four-year course qualifying teachers for the lycées. Students of the higher teacher-training schools take specialist subject courses in the relevant university faculty and their pedagogy courses in the higher teacher-training schools.

Bibliography

GENERAL

Allen, H. E. *The Turkish Transformation*. Chicago, 1935.

Armstrong, H. C. *Grey Wolf: Mustafa Kemal: an Intimate Study of a Dictator*. London, 1937.

Auboyneau & Fevret. *Essai de bibliographie pour l'Empire Ottomane.*.Paris, 1911.

Bahrampour, Firouz. *Turkey, Political and Social Transformation*. New York, Gaus, 1967.

Bean, G. E. *Aegean Turkey*. London, Benn, 1966.

Turkey's Southern Shore. London, Benn, 1968.

Berkes, Niyazi. *The Development of Secularism in Turkey*. Montreal, McGill University Press, 1964.

Bisbee, Eleanor. *The New Turks*. Philadelphia, 1951.

The People of Turkey. New York, 1946.

Cohn, Edwin J. *Turkish Economic, Social and Political Change*. New York, Praeger, 1970.

Cooke, Hedley V. *Challenge and Response in the Middle East: The Quest for Prosperity, 1919–1951*. New York, 1952.

Dodd, C. H. *Politics and Government in Turkey*. Manchester University Press, 1969.

Edgecumbe, Sir, C. N. E. *Turkey in Europe*. New York, Barnes and Noble, 1965.

Eren, Nuri. *Turkey Today and Tomorrow*. New York, 1964.

Frey, F. W. *The Turkish Political Elite*. Cambridge, Mass., MIT Press, 1965.

Gökalp, Ziya. *Turkish Nationalism and Western Civilisation*. London, 1960.

Güntekin, Reşat Nuri (trans. Sir Wyndham Deedes). *Afternoon Sun*. London, 1950.

The Autobiography of a Turkish Girl. London, 1949.

Hale, William. *Aspects of Modern Turkey*. Epping, Bowker Publishing, 1977.

Harris, George S. *The Origins of Communism in Turkey*. Stanford, Calif., Hoover Institution, 1967.

Heyd, Uriel. *Foundations of Turkish Nationalism: the Life and Teachings of Ziya Gökalp*. London, Luzac and Harvill Press, 1950.

Language Reform in Modern Turkey. Jerusalem, 1954.

Hotham, David. *The Turks*. London, John Murray, 1972.

Jackh, Ernest. *The Rising Crescent*. New York, 1950.

Karpat, Kemal. *Turkey's Politics, The Transition to a Multi-Party System*. Princeton, 1959.

Kazamias, A. M. *Education and the Quest for Modernity in Turkey*. London, Allen and Unwin, 1967.

Keyder, Caglar. *State and Class in Turkey*. London, Verso, 1987.

Kinnane, Dirk. *The Kurds and Kurdistan*. Oxford, 1965.

Kinross, Lord. *Within the Taurus*. London, 1954.

Europa Minor: Journeys in Coastal Turkey. London, 1956.

Turkey. London, 1960.

Atatürk. London, Weidenfeld & Nicolson, 1964.

Kişlali, Ahmet Taner. *Forces politiques dans la Turquie moderne*. Ankara, 1967.

Koray, Enver. *Türkiye Tarih Yaynları Bibliografyası 1729–1950; A Bibliography of Historical Works on Turkey*. Ankara, 1952.

Kürger, K. *Die Türkei*. Berlin, 1951.

Lamb, Harold. *Suleiman the Magnificent: Sultan of the East*. New York, 1951.

Lewis, Bernard. *Turkey Today*. London, 1940.

The Emergence of Modern Turkey. London and New York, Oxford University Press, revised edn 1970.

Lewis, G. L. *Turkey* ('Nations of the Modern World' series). London, 1955; 3rd edn, New York, Praeger, 1965.

Linke, L. *Allah Dethroned*. London, 1937.

Lukach (Luke), Sir Harry Charles. *The Old Turkey and the New*. London, Geoffrey Bles, 1955.

Mellaart, James. *Earliest Civilizations of the Near East*. London, Thames and Hudson, 1965.

Çatal Hüyük. London, Thames and Hudson, 1967.

Moorehead, A. *Gallipoli*. New York, Harper, 1956.

Newman, Bernard. *Turkish Crossroads*. London, 1951.

Turkey and the Turks. London, Herbert Jenkins, 1968.

Orga, Irfan and Margarete. *Atatürk*. London, 1962.

Plate, Herbert. *Das Land der Türken*. Graz, Wien, Köln, Verlag Styria, 1957.

Robinson, Richard D. *The First Turkish Republic*. Harvard University Press, 1963.

Salter, Cedric. *Introducing Turkey*. London, Methuen, 1961.

Stark, Freya. *Ionia*. London, 1954.

Lycian Shore. London, 1951.

Riding to the Tigris. London, 1956.

Steinhaus, Kurt. *Soziologie der turkischen Revolution*. Frankfurt, 1969.

Szyliowicz, Joseph S. *Political Change in Rural Turkey: Erdemli*. The Hague, Mouton, 1966.

Toynbee, A. J. *The Western Question in Greece and Turkey*. London, Constable, 1923.

Toynbee, A. J., and Kirkwood, D. P. *Turkey*. London, 1926.

Lycian Shore. London, 1956.

Tunaya, T. Z. *Atatürk, the Revolutionary Movement and Atatürkism*. Istanbul, Baha, 1964.

Vali, Ferenc A. *Bridge across the Bosphorus: the Foreign Policy of Turkey*. Johns Hopkins Press, 1970.

Ward, Barbara. *Turkey*. Oxford, 1942.

Ward, Robert E., and Rustow, Oankwart A. (Eds). *Political Modernizations in Japan and Turkey*. Princeton University Press, 1964.

Webster, D. E. *The Turkey of Atatürk: Social Progress in the Turkish Reformation*. Philadelphia, 1939.

Yalman, A. E. *Turkey in my Time*. University of Oklahoma Press, 1956.

HISTORY

Ahmad, Feroz. *The Young Turks*. Oxford University Press, 1969.

The Turkish Experiment in Democracy 1950–1975. London, Hurst, for Royal Institute of International Affairs, 1977.

Alderson, A. D. *The Structure of the Ottoman Dynasty*. Oxford, 1956.

Allen, W. E. D., and Muratoff, P. *Caucasian Battlefields: A History of the Wars on the Turco-Caucasian Border, 1828–1921*. Cambridge, 1953.

Barchard, David. *Turkey and the West*. London, Routledge and Kegan Paul, 1985.

Birand, Mehmet Ali. *The Generals' Coup in Turkey: An Inside Story of September 12, 1980*. Oxford, Brassey's, 1987.

Boghossian, Roupen. *Le Conflit Turco-Arménien*. Beirut, Altapress, 1987.

Cahen, Claude. *Pre-Ottoman Turkey*. London, Sidgwick & Jackson, 1968.

Cassels, Lavender. *The Struggle for the Ottoman Empire, 1717–1740*. London, John Murray, 1967.

Coles, Paul. *The Ottoman Impact on Europe*. London, Thames and Hudson, 1968; New York, Brace and World, 1968.

Davidson, Roderic H. *Turkey*. New York, Prentice-Hall, 1968.

Geyikdagi, Mehmet Yaşar. *Political Parties in Turkey: The Role of Islam*. New York, Praeger, 1986.

Gurney, O. R. *The Hittites*. London, 1952.

Hale, William. *The Political and Economic Development of Modern Turkey*. London, Croom Helm, 1981.

Kazancigil, Ali, and Ozbudun, Ergun (Eds). *Atatürk: Founder of a Modern State*. London, Hurst, 1981.

Kedourie, Elie. *England and the Middle East: The Destruction of the Ottoman Empire, 1914–1921*. Cambridge, 1956.

Kushner, David. *The Rise of Turkish Nationalism*. London, Frank Cass, 1980.

Landau, Jacob M. *Pan-Turkism: A Study in Irredentism*. London, Hurst, 1981.

Lewis, Bernard. *Istanbul and the Civilization of the Ottoman Empire*. University of Oklahoma Press, 1963.

Lewis, Geoffrey. *La Turquie, le déclin de l'Empire, les réformes d'Ataturk, la République moderne*. Belgium, Verviers, 1968.

Liddell, Robert. *Byzantium and Istanbul*. London, 1956.

Lloyd, Seton. *Early Anatolia*. London, 1956.

Mantran, Robert. *Histoire de la Turquie*. Paris, 1952.

Miller, William. *The Ottoman Empire and its Successors, 1801–1927*. Cambridge, 1934.

Ostrogorsky, G. *History of the Byzantine State*. Oxford, 1956.

Pfeffermann, Hans. *Die Zusammenarbeit der Renaissance Päpste mit den Türken*. Winterthur, 1946.

Price, M. Philips. *A History of Turkey: From Empire to Republic*. London, 1956.

Ramsaur, E. E. *The Young Turks and the Revolution of 1908*. Princeton University Press, 1957.

Rice, David Talbot. *Art of the Byzantine Era*. New York, Praeger, 1963.

Byzantine Art. London, Penguin, 1962.

Rice, Tamara Talbot. *The Seljuks*. London, 1962.

Runciman, Sir Steven. *The Fall of Constantinople, 1453*. Cambridge University Press, 1965.

Shaw, Stanford. *History of the Ottoman Empire*. Cambridge University Press, 1976.

Sumner, B. H. *Peter the Great and the Ottoman Empire*. Oxford, 1949.

Vaughan, Dorothy. *Europe and the Turk: A Pattern of Alliances, 1350–1700*. Liverpool, 1954.

Vere-Hodge, Edward Reginald. *Turkish Foreign Policy, 1918–1948*. London, 2nd revised edition, 1950.

Walder, David. *The Chanak Affair*. London, Hutchinson, 1968.

ECONOMY

Hershlag, Z. Y. *Turkey: the Challenge of Growth*. Leiden, 1968.

Insel, Ahmet. *La Turquie entre l'Ordre et le Développement*. Paris, l'Harmattan, 1984.

Issawi, Charles. *The Economic History of Turkey*. University of Chicago Press, 1980.

Shorter, Frederic C. (Ed.). *Four Studies on the Economic Development of Turkey*. London, Cass, 1967; New York, Kelley, 1968.

THE UNITED ARAB EMIRATES

ABU DHABI　DUBAI　SHARJAH　RAS AL-KHAIMAH
UMM AL-QAIWAIN　AJMAN　FUJAIRAH

Geography

The coastline of the seven United Arab Emirates (UAE) extends for nearly 650 km (400 miles) from the frontier of the Sultanate of Oman to Khor al-Odaid, on the Qatari peninsula, in the Persian (Arabian) Gulf, interrupted only by an isolated outcrop of the Sultanate of Oman which lies on the coast of the Persian Gulf to the west and the Gulf of Oman to the east at the Strait of Hormuz. Six of the emirates lie on the coast of the Persian Gulf, while the seventh, Fujairah, is situated on the eastern coast of the peninsula, and has direct access to the Gulf of Oman. The area is one of extremely shallow seas, with offshore islands and coral reefs, and often an intricate pattern of sand-banks and small gulfs as a coastline. There is a considerable tide. The waters of the Gulf contain abundant quantities of fish, hence the role of fishing in local life.

The climate is arid, with very high summer temperatures; and, except for a few weeks in winter, air humidity is also very high. The total area of the UAE has been estimated at 30,000 sq miles (77,700 sq km), relatively small compared with neighbouring Oman and Saudi Arabia, and it has a rapidly growing population, totalling 1,622,464 at the census of December 1985 and reaching 1,909,000 (of whom only 20% were UAE nationals) by 1991, according to the Ministry of Planning. The population is concentrated in the emirates of Abu Dhabi and Dubai, the principal commercial regions of the country. Abu Dhabi is the largest emirate, with an area of about 26,000 sq miles (67,350 sq km), and a population of 798,000 in 1991. The town of Abu Dhabi is also the capital of the UAE. The most important port is Dubai, the capital of the UAE's second largest state. Its significance derives from its position on one of the rare deep creeks of the area, and it now has a very large transit trade.

Many inhabitants are still nomadic Arabs, and the official language is Arabic, which is spoken by most of the native inhabitants. Arabs are outnumbered, however, by non-Arab immigrant workers. In the coastal towns there are many Iranians, Indians, Pakistanis and Africans. Most of the native inhabitants are Muslims, mainly of the Sunni sect.

History

Revised for this edition by JON LUNN

In the early 16th century the Portuguese commercial monopoly of the Gulf area was challenged by other European traders. The Portuguese ascendency in the East gradually declined, and in 1650 they evacuated Oman, losing their entire hold on the Arabian shore. There followed a period of commercial and political rivalry between the Dutch and the British. The initial Dutch predominance weakened and in 1766 came practically to an end, while the British were consolidating their position in India.

Both European and Arab pirates were very active in the Gulf during the 17th, 18th and early 19th centuries. Attacks on British-flag vessels led to British expeditions against the pirates and eventually, in 1818, against the pirate head-quarters at Ras al-Khaimah and other harbours along the 240 km of 'Pirate Coast'. In 1820 a general treaty of peace, for suppressing piracy and slave traffic, was concluded between Great Britain and the Arab tribes of the Gulf. It was signed by the principal sheikhs of the Pirate Coast and Bahrain. A strong British squadron was stationed at Ras al-Khaimah to enforce the treaty.

Piracy persisted and accordingly, in 1835, the sheikhs agreed, in a 'maritime truce', not to engage, under any circumstances, in hostilities by sea during the pearl-diving season. The advantages of this were so noticeable that the sheikhs willingly renewed the truce for increasing periods until, in May 1853, a 'treaty of maritime peace in perpetuity' was concluded, establishing a 'perpetual maritime truce' on the newly-named 'Trucial Coast' (also called Trucial Oman). It was supervised by the British Government, to whom the signatories would refer any breach. The British did not interfere in wars between the sheikhs on land.

Britain's concern to stop the slave trade also led to contacts with the Trucial Coast, where the sheikhs had been engaged in carrying slaves from Africa to India and Arabia. In 1838–39 and 1847 the sheikhs undertook to prohibit the carriage of slaves on board vessels for which they were responsible, consenting to the detention and search of such vessels and to their confiscation in case of guilt.

Towards the end of the 19th century, France, Germany and Russia showed increasing interest in the Gulf area, and in 1892 Britain entered into separate but identical 'exclusive' treaties with the Trucial rulers, whereby the sheikhs undertook not to cede, mortgage or otherwise dispose of parts of their territories to anyone except the British Government, nor to enter into any relationship with a foreign government, other than the British, without British consent. Britain had already undertaken to protect the states from outside attack in the perpetual maritime treaty of 1853.

In 1820, when the general treaty was signed, there were only five Trucial states. In 1866, on the death of the Chief Sheikh of Sharjah, his domains were divided among his four sons, the separate branches of the family being established at Sharjah, Ras al-Khaimah, Dibba and Kalba.

Kalba was incorporated into Sharjah in 1952, when its ruler agreed to accept all existing treaties between the United Kingdom (UK) and the Trucial States, as did the ruler of Fujairah. This involved recognising the UK Government's right to define state boundaries, to settle disputes between the Trucial sheikhdoms and to render assistance to the Trucial Oman Scouts, a British-officered Arab force which was set up in 1952.

In 1952, on British advice, a trucial council was established, at which all seven rulers met at least twice a year, under the chairmanship of the political agent in Dubai. Its object was to encourage the pursuit of a common policy in administrative matters, possibly leading to a federation of the states.

The advent of the commercial production of petroleum in mid-1962 gave Abu Dhabi a great opportunity for development. A major obstacle to this development was removed in August 1966, when Sheikh Shakhbut bin Sultan an-Nahyan,

952

the ruler of Abu Dhabi since 1928, was deposed. The ruling family replaced Shakhbut by his younger brother, Sheikh Zayed bin Sultan. The subsequent history of Abu Dhabi has been a classic example of a society suddenly transformed by the acquisition of immense wealth. Petroleum was discovered in neighbouring Dubai in 1966, and that sheikhdom also benefited greatly from the petroleum boom.

In June 1965 Sheikh Saqr bin Sultan of Sharjah was deposed. In spite of an appeal to the UN Secretary-General, supported by Iraq and the United Arab Republic (now Egypt), the accession of his cousin, Sheikh Khalid bin Muhammad, proceeded without incident. There was an unsuccessful attempt on the Sheikh's life in July 1970.

Intending to relocate its major military base in the Middle East, Britain started work in 1966 on a base in Sharjah, which by 1968 had become the principal base in the Gulf. However, British forces had been withdrawn from the area by the end of 1971. The Trucial Oman Scouts, a force of some 1,600 men officered and paid for by Britain and based in Sharjah, were proposed as the nucleus of a federal security force after British withdrawal in 1971, but some states, notably Abu Dhabi, were already creating their own defence forces.

In order to avoid disputes over the ill-defined state borders, those between Qatar, Abu Dhabi and Dubai were settled early in 1970—although not without objection from Saudi Arabia, whose claimed territory overlapped that of Abu Dhabi to a considerable extent. In late 1974 a border agreement was signed with Saudi Arabia on the Liwa oases, whereupon Saudi Arabia recognized the UAE and ambassadors were exchanged.

The original proposals for the formation of a federation (after the British had withdrawn) included Bahrain and Qatar, as well as the seven Trucial States, but these larger and more developed states eventually opted for separate independence. On 1 December 1971 Britain terminated all existing treaties with the Trucial States. On the following day Abu Dhabi, Dubai, Sharjah, Umm al-Qaiwain, Ajman and Fujairah formed the United Arab Emirates (UAE), and a treaty of friendship was made with Britain. The federation approved a provisional constitution, which was to expire after five years, when a formal constitution would be drafted. This has not yet happened, however, and the provisional constitution has been repeatedly renewed. In practice this has lent a flexibility to the developing emirates, allowing the process of centralization to follow a gradual course and averting any serious dispute which could arise from an emirate's contravention of formal constitutional decrees. At independence, Sheikh Zayed, the ruler of Abu Dhabi, took office as the first President of the UAE. Sheikh Rashid bin Said al-Maktoum, the ruler of Dubai since 1958, became Vice-President, while his eldest son, Sheikh Maktoum bin Rashid (Crown Prince of Dubai), became Prime Minister. In December 1991 the UAE became a member of both the Arab League and the United Nations. In February 1972 Ras al-Khaimah became the seventh member of the federation.

In January 1972 the Ruler of Sharjah, Sheikh Khalid, was killed by rebels under the leadership of his cousin, Sheikh Saqr, who had been deposed in 1965. The rebels were captured, and Sheikh Sultan bin Muhammad succeeded his brother as ruler, confirming a continuation of the late Khalid's relatively liberal principles of government, and Sharjah's membership of the UAE.

Although the UAE remained one of the most conservative Arab states, it gave considerable support to the Arab cause in the October War of 1973 and participated in the associated petroleum cut-backs and boycotts. It was the first state to impose a total ban on exports of petroleum to the USA, and subsequently supported the Arab ostracism of Egypt, which followed the signature of the Camp David agreements between Egypt and Israel in 1978.

TOWARDS GREATER CENTRALIZATION

In December 1973 the separate Abu Dhabi Government was disbanded and, in a ministerial reshuffle, some of its members became federal ministers. Most notably, the Abu Dhabi minister responsible for petroleum, Dr Mana bin Said al-Oteiba, became the first federal Minister of Petroleum and Mineral Resources. The government reorganization involved a considerable extension of central authority and was a further

step towards the integration of the seven sheikhdoms. In May 1975, at a session of the Supreme Council, the seven emirs gave their consent, in principle, to further steps towards centralization. In November 1975 Sharjah merged the Sharjah National Guard with the Union Defence Force, and also granted control of its broadcasting station to the Federal Ministry of Communications, its police to the Ministry of the Interior and its courts to the Ministry of Justice. The Sharjah flag was abolished in favour of the federal tricolour. Fujairah and Abu Dhabi both discontinued the use of their flags.

The merger of the main defence forces (the Union Defence Force, the Abu Dhabi Defence Force and the Dubai Defence Force) was finally agreed in early May 1976, when Gen. Sheikh Khalifa bin Zayed an-Nahyan, the Crown Prince of Abu Dhabi, was made deputy supreme commander (Sheikh Zayed became supreme commander). In November 1976 the provisional constitution was amended so that the right to levy armed forces and acquire weapons was placed exclusively in the hands of the federal Government.

During 1976 Sheikh Zayed, impatient with the slow rate at which the emirates were achieving centralization, threatened not to stand for a second term as President of the UAE in November 1976. In the event, he was re-elected unanimously after the Supreme Council had granted the federal Government greater control over defence, intelligence services, immigration, public security and border control. A reshuffle of the Council of Ministers followed in January 1977, with ministers chosen on the principle of individual merit rather than equitable representation of the seven emirates. The new 40-member Federal National Council, which was inaugurated on 1 March 1977, showed the same spirit of reinvigoration, as only seven members of the first five-year session (1971–76) were included.

During 1978, however, the unity of the Federal Defence Force was under strain. A dispute arose in February, when Sheikh Zayed appointed his second son, Sheikh Sultan, as commander-in-chief of the armed forces. Sheikh Rashid of Dubai claimed that he had not been consulted. Thereafter the forces of Dubai and Ras al-Khaimah refused to accept orders from the federal commander, and Dubai independently ordered a number of British tanks.

Mounting pressure from within the emirates for a more united federation led, in 1978, to the setting up of a joint Cabinet-Federal National Council committee to discuss methods of achieving this. Events in Iran in 1979 and the resultant security threat prompted a full meeting of the Council of Ministers and the Federal National Council in February. The outcome of this was a 10-point memorandum advocating the abolition of all internal borders, the unification of defence forces and the merging of revenues in a federal budget. This plan was subsequently submitted to the Supreme Council.

Despite their widespread support in the emirates, these proposals aggravated the long-standing rivalry between Abu Dhabi, the financial mainstay of the federation, and Dubai, which had become increasingly critical of the centralized federal Government. Dubai rejected the memorandum completely and, together with Ras al-Khaimah, boycotted a Supreme Council meeting in March.

It was thought that the deadlock had been broken, at least temporarily, when Sheikh Rashid, ruler of Dubai, replaced his son as Prime Minister of the federal Government (while retaining the vice-presidency) in July 1979. A new Council of Ministers was formed, preserving a similar balance of power between the emirates as before. Ras al-Khaimah integrated its defence force with the federal force, and both Abu Dhabi and Dubai pledged to contribute 50% of their revenues from petroleum to the federal budget. Dubai's forces, however, remained, in practice, a separate entity. Further attempts at integration included the construction of national roads, the installation of telecommunications, and the central planning and financing of health, education and agriculture. In November 1981 Sheikh Rashid was re-elected Prime Minister by the Supreme Council, and Sheikh Zayed was re-elected President.

FOREIGN POLICY AND THE IRAN–IRAQ WAR

With the outbreak of war between Iran and Iraq in 1980, the UAE became vulnerable to external forces over which it had no control. Iran's repeated threats to close the Strait of Hormuz to traffic carrying exports of petroleum from Gulf countries represented a grave potential danger to states such as the UAE, which depend on revenues from petroleum. Partly in response to Iranian threats, the UAE joined with six other Gulf states to form the Gulf Co-operation Council (GCC) in March 1981 (see p. 231), to work towards economic, political and social integration in the Gulf. The GCC's primary concern initially was to develop greater economic co-operation, but this gave way to concern over the region's ability to defend itself. A bilateral defence agreement was signed with Saudi Arabia in 1982, and, in accordance with GCC policy, the UAE has substantially increased its defence expenditure. The largest share of the 1987 budget (Dh 5,826m.) was allotted to defence.

The foreign policy of the UAE is motivated chiefly by its support for Arab unity, especially in the Palestinian cause. In March 1985 President Zayed pledged his country's support for Lebanon in its fight against Israeli occupation forces. In the Iran–Iraq War, it made substantial donations to Iraq, but in 1984 these were reported to have been discontinued, owing to the UAE's financial difficulties. Whether or not this was the case, the report indicated the UAE's desire to maintain some neutrality in the conflict, an attitude which was less clearly perceptible in other GCC states. A substantial proportion of the UAE's population has some contact with Iran: either being immigrants, or natives of the UAE who have lived in Iran. There are also commercial ties, and, following the loss of the Iranian refinery at Abadan, Dubai was able to profit from the re-exportation of petroleum to Iran. Similarly, Sharjah depends on Iranian co-operation for its oil wealth. In March 1984, when fighting spread to include attacks on shipping, however, the UAE joined the Security Council of the GCC in requesting that the UN make attempts to mediate between the countries, and in seeking a condemnation of Iran's behaviour. As a response to the threat posed by the Iran–Iraq War, the UAE considerably increased its defence spending.

In November 1984 the UAE Government held further talks with leaders of other Arab states, in an effort to find a solution to the Iran–Iraq War. During the sixth regional summit meeting of the GCC, which was held in Oman in November 1985, the member states decided to adopt a more neutral stance in the Iran–Iraq War, and to improve relations with Iran. At the seventh GCC summit meeting, held in Abu Dhabi in November 1986, the member states expressed concern over the escalation of the Iran–Iraq War, and discussed the protection of petroleum installations and shipping in the area.

On 11 August 1987 a Panamanian-registered supertanker, the *Texaco Caribbean*, struck a mine 13 km off the coast of the UAE, near the port of Fujairah. This was the first incident of its kind during the Iran-Iraq War involving mines (presumed to be Iranian) laid outside the Persian Gulf. On 13 August the Government of the UAE declared Fujairah port a danger zone and banned all commercial shipping from a surrounding area of 100 sq km, while minesweeping operations were carried out. At the end of August the UAE gave provisional permission for the use of its ports as a base for British minesweeping operations. In April 1988 the Mubarak oilfield, which belongs to the emirate of Sharjah and is located 30 km off the coast of the UAE, was closed for two months, following an attack on its installations by forces involved in the Iran–Iraq War.

The decline in revenues from petroleum in the mid-1980s had little effect on the comfortable lifestyle of the UAE, although certain development plans were postponed or rescheduled. One effect of decreased revenue, and increased disruption in the area, was a greater commitment to local co-operation both within the UAE and among Gulf countries in general. Thus, bilateral agreements with Oman, Qatar, the People's Democratic Republic of Yemen and Iraq were made for the purpose of mutual aid in educational, scientific and cultural development. In November 1985 diplomatic relations were established between the UAE and the USSR. This was expected to lead to increased bilateral trade between the countries.

In November 1987 the UAE resumed diplomatic relations with Egypt, following the adoption of a resolution at a summit meeting of the League of Arab States, which permitted member states to resume relations with Egypt at their own discretion. The UAE subsequently ordered 50 armoured personnel carriers from Egypt; and in March 1988 the President of the UAE, Sheikh Zayed bin Sultan an-Nahyan, made an official visit to Egypt, during which the two countries signed a trade agreement.

The escalation of tension in the Gulf, exacerbated by the presence of US and Soviet naval forces, had resulted in the adoption of Resolution 598 by the UN Security Council on 20 July 1987, which urged an immediate cease-fire. In November, at an extraordinary meeting of the League of Arab States in Amman, Jordan, representatives of the member states, including the UAE, unanimously condemned Iran for prolonging the war against Iraq, deplored its occupation of Arab (i.e. Iraqi) territory, and urged it to accept Resolution 598 without preconditions. (For more detailed coverage of the war between Iran and Iraq and of the events that led to a cease-fire in August 1988, see chapters on Iran and Iraq.)

DEVELOPMENTS IN DOMESTIC POLITICS

In October 1986 the provisional federal constitution was renewed for a further five years, and Sheikh Zayed and Sheikh Rashid were unanimously re-elected to the posts of President, and Vice-President and Prime Minister, respectively.

An attempted coup took place in Sharjah in June 1987, when Sheikh Abd al-Aziz, a brother of the ruler (Sheikh Sultan bin Muhammad al-Qasimi), issued a statement, in his brother's absence which announced the abdication of Sheikh Sultan, on the grounds that he had mismanaged the economy. Since Sheikh Sultan assumed power in 1972, Sharjah had incurred debts estimated at US $920m. in mid-1987, as the result of an extravagant programme of construction ordered by the ruler. However, Dubai intervened and convened a meeting of the Supreme Council of Rulers, which endorsed Sheikh Sultan's claim to be the legitimate ruler of Sharjah, and restored him to power. As a result of the attempted coup, Sheikh Abd al-Aziz was given the title of Crown Prince and granted a seat on the Supreme Council. In July Sheikh Sultan formed an executive council in Sharjah, comprising the heads of local government departments and other individuals selected by him, to assist in the administration of the public affairs of the emirate. Sheikh Sultan also signed an agreement with bank creditors, whereby Sharjah's loan repayments would be rescheduled until 1993. In February 1990, however, Sheikh Sultan removed his brother from the post of Crown Prince and revoked his right to succeed him. In July 1990 Sheikh Sultan appointed Sheikh Ahmad bin Mohammed al-Qasimi, the head of Sharjah's petroleum and mineral affairs office, as Deputy Ruler of Sharjah. He was not given the title of Crown Prince. On 7 October 1990 the Ruler of Dubai, Prime Minister and Vice-President of the UAE, Sheikh Rashid bin Said al-Maktoum, died. He was succeeded in all of his offices by his eldest son, Sheikh Maktoum bin Rashid al-Maktoum.

In November 1990, a reorganization of ministerial portfolios took place. The Minister of Petroleum and Mineral Resources, Dr Mana bin Said al-Oteiba, was replaced by Yousuf bin Omeir bin Yousuf, a former executive at the Abu Dhabi Investment Authority. The post of Minister of Foreign Affairs, vacant since 1982, was filled by the Minister of State for Foreign Affairs, Rashid Abdullah an-Nuaimi. One of the President's sons, Sheikh Hamdan bin Zayed an-Nahyan, replaced an-Nuaimi as Minister of State for Foreign Affairs, while another, Sheikh Sultan bin Zayed an-Nahyan, was appointed Deputy Prime Minister. In October 1991 the Supreme Council confirmed Sheikh Zayed and Sheikh Maktoum as, respectively, President and Vice-President, each for a further five-year term. The provisional federal constitution was also renewed for a further period of five years. In February 1994 the Minister of Petroleum and Mineral Resources, Yousuf bin Omeir bin Yousuf, resigned, citing personal reasons. This was the first resignation from the federal cabinet since the creation of the UAE. In the same month Sheikh Zayed issued a decree whereby a wide range of crimes, including murder, theft, adultery and drug offences, would be tried in *Sharia* (Islamic religious law) courts rather than in civil courts.

THE GULF CONFLICT AND BEYOND

Iraq's occupation of Kuwait, in August 1990, caused political and economic crisis throughout the Gulf region. The UAE responded by supporting, with most other Arab states, resistance to Iraqi aggression, and on 20 August the UAE ordered all nationals to join the armed forces for six weeks' military training. At the same time it was announced that armed forces opposing Iraq's aggression would be granted military facilities in the UAE. Units from the British and French air forces were among those which were subsequently stationed there. In February 1991, after the outbreak of hostilities between Iraq and a US-led multinational force, the UAE air force conducted four raids against Iraqi targets. In March representatives from GCC Chambers of Commerce met in Dubai in order to discuss the role of GCC companies in the reconstruction of Kuwait.

In the aftermath of the war between Iraq and the US-led multinational force, the Ministers of Foreign Affairs of Egypt, Syria and the six GCC states met in Damascus, Syria, in order to discuss regional security arrangements. The meeting resulted in the signing, by all the participants, of the 'Damascus declaration' which envisaged, among other things, the formation of an Arab peace-keeping force comprising mainly Egyptian and Syrian troops. At the beginning of May 1991 the Ministers of Foreign Affairs of the GCC states held an emergency meeting in Kuwait to discuss further regional security measures. In early May Egypt announced that it would withdraw all of its armed forces from Saudi Arabia and Kuwait within three months: an apparent failure to honour its commitment, under the 'Damascus declaration', to participate in the Arab peace-keeping force. Egypt was reported to oppose the possible participation of non-Arab (i.e. Iranian and Turkish) troops in the force. At the beginning of April the President of the UAE had discounted the possibility of Iraq's participation in a Gulf security system while Saddam Hussain remained in power there; but he had indicated that the UAE would be prepared, in concert with the other GCC member states, to consider Iranian security proposals. In September 1992 a meeting attended by Egypt, Syria and the GCC states was presented with an Egyptian proposal to create a series of rapid deployment forces. However, the consideration of military co-operation was discontinued, in favour of discussion of political and economic co-ordination. In December 1993 discussions about military co-operation resumed. Amongst the proposals was one for the development of an enhanced Peninsula Shield Joint Force; another proposal was for the creation of a joint early warning system. But there remained few signs that these proposals were likely to be acted upon.

Tension between the UAE and Iran was not confined to matters relating to the GCC; there was also a territorial dimension. Rival claims to the island of Abu Musa had been made by Sharjah and Iran in 1970, when petroleum exploration began. In 1971 agreement was reached to divide any oil revenues. In August 1992, however, it was reported that Iran had, in effect, annexed Abu Musa after 20 years of joint control. It was claimed that Iranian authorities had denied landing permission to more than 100 residents of the island who were returning from Sharjah, and that Iran was refusing a compromise agreement. Iran subsequently claimed sovereignty over Abu Musa, together with the Great Tumb and Lesser Tumb Islands, thereby provoking the condemnation of the six members of the GCC. Discussions between representatives of the countries' Ministers of Foreign Affairs were convened in Abu Dhabi at the end of September, but collapsed almost immediately, with Iran refusing to discuss ownership of two of the three islands. At a GCC summit meeting in Abu Dhabi in December 1992 it was demanded that Iran reverse the 'virtual annexation' of the islands. In April 1993 a GCC statement expressed satisfaction at recent developments and support for bilateral negotiations. In the same month it was reported that all persons who had been expelled from (or refused entry to) Abu Musa in 1992 had been permitted to return. Both the UAE and Iran periodically proclaimed their commitment to direct talks throughout 1993 and early 1994, but none materialized.

In September 1993 the UAE welcomed the conclusion of the Israeli-Palestinian peace accord, and pledged financial support to the Palestinians. The UAE also continued to build up its defence capability, signing a defence agreement with the USA in July 1994 which extended the agreement signed in 1991 in the aftermath of the Gulf conflict. In September the British Prime Minister, John Major, visited the UAE and held talks with Sheikh Zayed in order to discuss regional issues, Gulf security, the Middle East peace process, and the furtherance of bilateral relations.

Economy

Dr P. T. H. UNWIN

(Revised for this edition by ALAN J. DAY)

INTRODUCTION

Prior to the discovery of petroleum, the economy of the seven sheikhdoms, or emirates, that comprised the Trucial States was based on pearling, fishing, trade and a limited amount of agriculture. In the 19th century, piracy, as defined by the Western powers that became dominant in the area, also formed an important source of income for the coastal tribes. Since 1958, when petroleum was first discovered off Abu Dhabi, and in particular since June 1962, when it was first exported, the economy of the area has undergone dramatic change. The pace of this change increased appreciably following independence in 1971, leading to the creation of the federal state of the United Arab Emirates (UAE), and the increases in the price of oil dictated by the Organization of the Petroleum Exporting Countries (OPEC), of which the UAE is a member. In 1992, according to estimates by the World Bank, the UAE's gross national product (GNP) per head was $22,020 (at average 1990–92 prices), slightly below the 1992 average for the industrialized OECD countries.

The UAE covers approximately 77,700 sq km, most of which is either sand desert or *sibakh* (salt flats). At the March 1968 census its population was 179,126. The pace of the UAE's rapid economic change can be seen in the dramatic increase in population during succeeding years: it reached 1,042,099 by the December 1980 census, and results from the December 1985 census indicated that the population had grown by 55.7% in the intervening five years, to 1,622,464, of whom about 670,000 were inhabitants of Abu Dhabi. According to the Ministry of Planning, the population had reached 1.9m. by 1991, although only 20% of the total were UAE nationals, while most of the remaining 80% were originally from the Indian sub-continent. The largest relative increases in population have been in the smallest emirates, reflecting their policy of economic expansion. The unequal distribution of the sexes (with males accounting for 65% of the total population in 1985) indicates the large amount of immigration that has been necessary to sustain the country's economic growth. There have been strong demands for the redeployment of labour from non-Arab Asians to Arabs. Immigrant labour has also been blamed for the increase in crime, which grew by 18% between 1980 and 1981. In 1989 the total number of people in employment was about 654,500, of whom 6% were engaged in agriculture and fishing (compared with 21% in 1965), 42% in industry (32% in 1965) and 52% in services

(47% in 1965). Between 1983 and 1984 the work-force in the UAE declined by 1.9%, and by 1986 the Government had begun to encourage foreign workers to bring their families with them, in order to increase the level of demand in the economy. In 1993 the UAE's total population was officially estimated as 2,083,100 and its total work-force as 794,400.

Despite progress in the UAE towards political integration, co-ordination in economic policies has proved to be difficult to accomplish. Abu Dhabi's wealth tends to overshadow the other emirates but, at the same time, it is the main factor which holds the seven emirates together. Apart from the difference between Abu Dhabi and Dubai over participation in the petroleum industry, the two main emirates have tended to pursue independent strategies in developing their various industries. An important instrument of development policy is the federal budget, which is essentially concerned with the implementation of federal infrastructure policy. Individual emirates also draw up separate budgets for municipal expenditure and local projects. The Constitution provides for social services, such as health and education, to come under federal control. In the 1970s Abu Dhabi contributed more than 90% of the federal budget revenue, but by 1990 its share had fallen to about 80%, with Dubai contributing about 16%. In terms of gross domestic product (GDP), Abu Dhabi continues to dominate the UAE, but its share of total GDP declined from 70% in 1980 to 61% in 1984. Dubai contributed 25% of total GDP, and Sharjah 8%, in 1984. Although no more recent analysis is available, approximately the same proportions applied into the early 1990s, when Dubai's growth as a commercial and trading centre was balanced by Abu Dhabi's continued dominance of petroleum exports and increased earnings therefrom. As a result of depressed petroleum prices from 1983, overall GDP declined in some subsequent years, but in 1989 the economic recovery which followed the cease-fire in the Iran–Iraq War enabled a number of industrial projects, postponed in the mid-1980s, to be revived. GDP in that year increased by 15.9%, to Dh 100,976m. ($27,506m.), and in 1990 the combination of increased oil production and higher prices produced a massive increase in GDP, to Dh 125,266m. ($34,110m.).

Iraq's invasion of Kuwait in August 1990 initially had a destabilizing effect upon the UAE economy. Work on development projects was suspended and banks lost between 15% and 30% of their deposits in August and September. More than 8,000 Kuwaitis fled to the UAE. Higher shipping insurance premiums acted as a restraint on trade. By the end of 1990, however, work on development projects had resumed, and confidence in the economy had revived as a result of the 54% increase in the revenue which the UAE had earned from its sales of petroleum in the course of the year. At $21,100m., the value of these sales was more than sufficient to meet the additional expenses which the UAE incurred as a result of the crisis in the Gulf. A large part of these expenses arose from the financial support it gave to the military operations of the anti-Iraq coalition; and from aid granted to those countries for which the economic effects of the crisis were most severe. (The UAE donated £275m. towards the cost of UK and $4,067m. towards the cost of US military operations. It also made a contribution of $1,469m. to the Gulf Financial Crisis Co-ordination Group.) After the liberation of Kuwait in February 1991 the UAE announced ambitious expenditure plans in both the petroleum and non-petroleum sectors. The UAE also benefited from participation in Kuwait's reconstruction programme, in the aftermath of its liberation, and from a revival of regional trade after the war. Economic confidence was disturbed in July 1991, however, owing to the collapse of the Bank of Credit and Commerce International (BCCI), in which the largest emirate, Abu Dhabi, had a 77% interest (see Finance and Banking below).

The federation's GDP totalled Dh 126,264m. in 1991 and Dh 130,163m. in 1992, and was provisionally estimated as Dh 131,660m. ($35,850m.) in 1993. The non-oil sectors of the economy accounted for 61% of GDP in 1993. Steady revenues from petroleum exports and rapidly growing non-oil trade provided a strong financial base to support the Government's ambitious plans for industrial expansion and diversification through the 1990s.

PETROLEUM AND GAS

The economy of the UAE is dominated by petroleum. At 1 January 1994 the UAE's proven oil reserves totalled 99,600m. barrels (9.9% of world reserves and 12.9% of OPEC reserves), of which 92,200m. barrels (92.6%) were in Abu Dhabi and the remainder in Dubai and the northern emirates. At 1 January 1993 the UAE's proven reserves of natural gas totalled 5,800,000m. cu m (4.2% of world reserves and 10.4% of OPEC reserves), of which 5,300,000m. cu m (91.4%) were in Abu Dhabi. Between 1971 and 1980 the UAE's revenue from petroleum increased about 25-fold, and, particularly between 1973 and 1976, the economy expanded very rapidly. In this period, public-sector spending increased at an annual rate of 72%. The second half of the 1970s, however, was a period of retrenchment, and there was a major recession in the mid-1980s. Owing to the surplus of petroleum supplies in the 1980s, government revenue from exports of petroleum was greatly reduced. Japan, which is the largest customer for crude petroleum from the UAE, imported 26.6% of its total crude oil requirements from the UAE in 1986. The petroleum sector's contribution to GDP declined from 63% in 1980 to 39% in 1993.

In 1983 Abu Dhabi produced 69.9% of the UAE's petroleum output, Dubai 29.5% and Sharjah 0.5%. Output rose rapidly, from an average of 14,200 b/d in 1962 (the first year of production) to 1,059,000 b/d in 1971. Output nearly doubled to 1,998,700 b/d in 1977 before falling gradually to 1,133,743 b/d in 1981—lower than in any year since 1971. Under the terms of an OPEC agreement in March 1983, the UAE was accorded a production quota of 1.1m. b/d. Average production from Abu Dhabi in 1983 was about 850,000 b/d; an average 330,000 b/d–360,000 b/d came from Dubai; and Sharjah produced over 50,000 b/d. At the end of 1984, Abu Dhabi's production level was reported to be running at 620,000 b/d. In October 1984 the Geneva meeting of OPEC lowered the UAE's production quota to 950,000 b/d, and Abu Dhabi was the most severely affected of the emirates. Crude petroleum production fell from 668.3m. barrels in 1979 to 417.6m. barrels in 1984, and to 416.7m. barrels in 1985.

Towards the end of 1985 it was evident that Abu Dhabi was exceeding its production quota. After the abandonment of oil-pricing agreements at an OPEC meeting held in Vienna in October 1985, the UAE's production rose appreciably. In December OPEC decided to abandon production restraint and to seek a larger share of the market. By March 1986 it was apparent that Abu Dhabi had raised production levels by almost 30%, while, at the same time, halving prices, in an attempt to maintain its revenue. The UAE's total production rose from 805,000 b/d at the end of 1985 to 1.7m. b/d in July 1986. The OPEC decision to seek a larger market share exacerbated the oil glut and precipitated the collapse in prices during 1986. In July the price of petroleum on the 'spot' market fell below $10 per barrel, and at the beginning of August OPEC agreed to reduce its members' overall production by about 4m. b/d for two months from 1 September, effectively reimposing the output quotas which were first allocated in October 1984, in an effort to stabilize prices. This had the effect of setting the UAE's quota at 950,000 b/d, and this level was reaffirmed at an OPEC meeting held in October 1986, when marginally higher collective production levels were established for November and December. Production of petroleum in the UAE in 1986 averaged 1.37m. b/d. In December, when prices had risen to about $17 per barrel on the 'spot' market, OPEC members agreed to reduce collective production by 700,000 b/d to 15.8m. b/d (in support of a fixed price for OPEC petroleum of $18 per barrel)—a notional 'ceiling', owing to Iraq's persistent refusal to participate in production programmes. The UAE's production quota for the first six months of 1987 was set at 902,000 b/d, with Abu Dhabi assuming 682,000 b/d to be its share of the quota, and Dubai taking 220,000 b/d. In February 1987, however, Abu Dhabi was producing approximately 780,000 b/d, and Dubai about 380,000 b/d, thereby continuing the trend of over-production that has been characteristic of the UAE in recent years. In June, petroleum prices having stabilized at around $18 per barrel, OPEC introduced new production quotas for the second half of 1987, raising collective production to a notional 16.6m. b/d. The UAE was allocated a quota of 948,000 b/d, but in July it was producing at an average rate of 1.35m. b/d. Over-production resulted in a decline in prices; the price of Dubai's Fateh crude fell from $17.55 per barrel in mid-August to $15.10 per barrel in mid-December. In mid-November the UAE's petroleum production was reported to be about 1.8m. b/d, well above its quota level. These high levels of production meant that in 1987 the UAE's exports of petroleum were worth approximately $7,900m., in comparison with $7,100m. in 1986, leading to the commencement of an economic revival by the beginning of 1988. In December 1987 OPEC members unofficially agreed to maintain the production quotas allocated in June for the first six months of 1988, in an attempt to stabilize petroleum prices at around $18 per barrel. In May 1988 this unofficial agreement was upheld for the remainder of the year. Despite this, the UAE's production increased to about 2m. b/d in September 1988, and general over-production within OPEC caused the price of oil on the 'spot' market to fall to $10.69 per barrel in October 1988. At the November 1988 meeting, OPEC members agreed to form a committee, consisting of representatives of eight member states, to monitor the production quotas of all members and to supervise adherence to the levels allocated. The UAE was widely acknowledged to be the most flagrant over-producer in OPEC and repeatedly rejected the quotas that it had been allocated, claiming that they were inconsistent with the country's large reserves and disproportionate to the quotas allotted to other OPEC member states. The UAE's quota was raised from 948,000 b/d to 988,000 b/d in January 1989 and to 1.041m. b/d in June, in accordance with increases in OPEC's overall quota to 18.5m. b/d and to 19.5m. b/d respectively. It was estimated in April that the OPEC quota was being exceeded by about 2m. b/d, but the increased demand for petroleum products during the first half of the year enabled this excess production to be absorbed without causing a reduction in the price of oil. The price of crude petroleum increased from $10.69 per barrel in October 1988 to more than $15 in July 1989. In March 1990 the UAE was producing 2.01m. b/d, against its OPEC quota (which it did not recognise) of 1.095m. b/d. By July 1990 the price of oil had fallen to $14 per barrel. The UAE agreed to a compromise proposal that its OPEC quota should be revised to 1.5m. b/d. Iraq's invasion of Kuwait in August 1990, however, led to the suspension of OPEC quotas as member states agreed to compensate for the loss of Iraqi and Kuwaiti production of petroleum due to the UN's mandatory trade embargo. The UAE's average output during the 1990/91 Gulf crisis was 2.4m. b/d, 63% more than its quota figure of July 1990. Increased production was accompanied until January 1991 by higher 'spot' prices. UAE oil revenues for 1990 were $15,700m., 54% more than in 1989. With the outbreak of hostilities between the US-led multinational force and Iraq, prices began to decline to pre-conflict levels. Having reached a maximum price of $32 per barrel in October 1990, by February 1991 the 'spot' price of Dubai crude petroleum had fallen to less than $15 per barrel. In March 1991 OPEC agreed to lower production levels by 5% in the second quarter of the year. The UAE agreed to reduce its level of production to 2.320m. b/d. The OPEC reference price was set at $21 per barrel. In June 1991, with the prospect of Iraqi or Kuwaiti petroleum's return to the world market still distant, the March agreement was extended. The UAE made it clear that it was reluctant to return to its 1.5m. b/d quota of July 1990 as part of a stabilization of the world petroleum market. Actual UAE output in 1991 averaged 2.39m. b/d, yielding earnings of some $14,000m., a fall of 11% from the 1990 level. From March 1992 the UAE's OPEC quota was set at 2.244m. b/d, which the UAE appeared to be observing, notwithstanding Abu Dhabi's decision to proceed with a $5,000m. development programme designed to develop an extra 600,000 b/d of oil production capacity by 1996. In 1992 crude oil production averaged 2,283,200 b/d. In the first quarter of 1993 the UAE accepted an OPEC production quota of 2.26m. b/d, which was subsequently reduced to 2.161m. b/d from April 1993. Actual UAE production averaged 2,191,700 b/d in 1993 and 2,169,550 b/d in the first half of 1994.

In June 1988 the Supreme Petroleum Council was formed, following the issuing of a presidential decree which proposed the abolition of the Department of Petroleum and the dissolution of the board of directors of the Abu Dhabi National Oil Company (ADNOC), in an attempt to unify the Government's petroleum policy and planning activities. The 11-member Council, headed by Sheikh Khalifah bin Zayed an-Nahayan, assumed the former responsibilities of ADNOC's directors and of the Department of Petroleum, namely the administration and supervision of all the country's petroleum affairs.

Abu Dhabi

The first company to obtain a concession to explore for petroleum in Abu Dhabi was the Trucial Coast Development Oil Company, which was granted a concession over the entire territory in 1939. In 1962 the consortium was renamed the Abu Dhabi Petroleum Company (ADPC), and during the 1960s it gradually relinquished much of its concession. Agreements made in the early 1970s gave ADNOC, founded in 1971, an eventual 60% share, back-dated to 1 January 1974. ADNOC has a monopoly over distribution and is responsible for all petroleum installations and oil-based industries in the emirate. The second largest oil company in Abu Dhabi was founded in 1954 as Abu Dhabi Marine Areas Ltd (ADMA), which in 1971 was a consortium of British Petroleum (BP) and Compagnie Française des Pétroles (CFP). In 1972 BP sold 45% of its shares to the Japan Oil Development Company (JODCO) and by 1974 the Abu Dhabi Government, in the form of ADNOC, had acquired a 60% share. In 1977 ADNOC and ADMA agreed to establish a new company, ADMA–OPCO (with the same shareholders as ADMA), for offshore work, and in 1978 the Abu Dhabi Company for Onshore Oil Operations (ADCO) was formed from ADPC for onshore work. These two companies produced 93% of Abu Dhabi's petroleum in 1979, and the remaining four companies in the emirate, the Abu Dhabi Oil Company Ltd, the Total Abu al-Bukhoosh Company, the Al-Bunduq Company Ltd and Amerada Hess, produced about 7%. The main onshore oilfields are the Murban, Bu Hasa and Asab fields, while the main offshore ones are Umm Shaif (which produced an average 133,599 b/d in 1983) and Lower Zakum (average 71,912 b/d in 1983). This level was broadly maintained into the 1990s. With the onset of the Gulf crisis in August 1990 and the suspension of OPEC quotas, Abu Dhabi provided 75% of the UAE's expanded production, at levels of up to 1.8m. b/d.

In 1981 a Federal German company, Deminex, was granted a 35-year offshore concession. Also in that year, the Umm ad-Dalkh Development Company, founded in 1978 by ADNOC and JODCO, began work on the offshore fields of Delma, Satah and Jamain. In October 1981 a new 1,561 sq km offshore concession was granted to Attock Oil for 35 years. Two new discoveries of petroleum were reported in 1982, and during 1983 ADNOC drilled a total of 16 exploration wells. In 1985 two further offshore oilfields came into operation, with the Sateh field producing at 10,000 b/d and the Umm ad-Dalkh field producing at 25,000 b/d. However, the oil glut and reductions in OPEC production quotas for the UAE led to a fall in output prior to the last quarter of 1985. Abu Dhabi had previously predicted a production rate of 2.2m. b/d by the mid-1980s, but the level at the end of 1984 stood at only 620,000 b/d. In line with this new, more conservative policy, ADCO decided in 1983 to reduce the number of its operating rigs, from 26 to 18. During the last quarter of 1985, however, Abu Dhabi raised production considerably in order to offset declines in prices, and the unfavourable prospects for the oil industry in the short term also led to the postponement of two schemes to increase the rate of recovery from the Sahil and Bab fields. The decline in oil prices during 1986 led ADCO to reduce its budget for 1987 by more than 37%, to $284m., compared with $455m. in 1986. During 1986, however, ADNOC produced 931,000 b/d, compared with 743,000 b/d in 1985. In August 1986 Abu Dhabi was producing approximately 1.3m. b/d, but during 1987 some rationalization of ADNOC's activities took place. ZADCO and UDECO were merged, and by 1988 ADCO was operating only four rigs, compared with 15 in mid-1986, but exploration drilling increased in 1989. In late 1987 Abu Dhabi's oil production was reduced to less than 500,000 b/d, in an attempt to maintain prices at $18 per barrel, but by May 1988 production had increased to more than 1m. b/d. Between September and November 1988 it attained a maximum level of 1.6m. b/d. In early 1989 there was an official decrease in production of 20%, but published figures for 1989 revealed that Abu Dhabi's production over the whole of 1989 remained at 1.6m. b/d. In March 1991 Abu Dhabi announced that, as part of a $7,000m. development plan (1991–95), $2,800m. was to be spent on doubling exports of liquefied natural gas (LNG), increasing long-term production capacity from 2m. b/d to 2.6m. b/d and doubling refining capacity to more than 250,000 b/d. Formal approval had been obtained for the release of the estimated $500m. that was needed to expand capacity at the onshore Bab field and the offshore Upper Zakum field. At the Bab field ADCO aimed to increase capacity from 60,000 b/d to 350,000 b/d. The capacity at the Upper Zakum field was to be increased by 200,000 b/d. Small discoveries that had been ignored over the past decade were also to be reappraised. In late 1994 the broad division of crude oil production within Abu Dhabi was 425,000 b/d from ADMA-OPCO offshore fields, 470,000 b/d from the Upper Zakum offshore field and 920,000 b/d from ADCO'S onshore fields.

The Government has consistently sought to develop its 'downstream' production, and its first refinery, at Umm an-Nar, came 'on stream' in 1976 with a capacity of 15,000 b/d. A second refinery, at Ruwais, went into operation in June 1981. The Ruwais refinery, which after expansion was originally planned to achieve an output of 300,000 b/d, was producing to a capacity of only 71,000 b/d in 1985 and 1986, after declines in demand had led to cutbacks in the scale of expansion. By 1991 its capacity had fallen to 50,000 b/d. As part of the 1991–95 development plan, the intention to increase the capacity of the Ruwais refinery to the long-held target of 300,000 b/d was reaffirmed. The capacity of the refinery's hydro-cracker was to be doubled to 55,000 b/d, at an estimated cost of $1,200m. Work on a 60,000 b/d extension of the Umm an-Nar refinery was completed in 1984, and further expansion and improvement of the complex was under consideration in mid-1992. In March 1991 Abu Dhabi had a total refining capacity of 185,000 b/d, of which 100,000 b/d was available for export. In 1993 the capacity of the Umm an-Nar refinery was raised to 85,000 b/d, bringing total refining capacity in Abu Dhabi to 215,500 b/d. Plans for a major increase in the capacity of the Ruwais refinery remained under active consideration in 1994. In early 1988 the Abu Dhabi-based International Petroleum Investment Company began to develop its refinery interests elsewhere, by purchasing a 10% interest in a Madrid-based refinery, Compañía Española de Petróleos, for $123m. This ensured a secure outlet for 60,000 b/d of Abu Dhabi's crude petroleum. The interest was doubled in early 1989. The International Petroleum Investment Company (which is jointly owned by ADNOC and the Abu Dhabi Investment Authority) announced plans in May 1994 to acquire a 20% interest in the Austrian energy and chemicals group OMV. During the 1970s there were several plans for the development of petrochemical industries in the emirate, but one of the few to come to fruition was the fertilizer complex at Ruwais, Ruwais Fertilizer Industries (FERTIL), of which two-thirds is owned by ADNOC and one-third by Total-CFP.

During the early 1970s much of the gas produced in association with petroleum was flared off, but in 1977 an LNG plant at Das Island started recovering offshore associated gas, and in 1981 the GASCO plant began onshore gas collection. In 1981 a new gasfield was found underlying the offshore Zakum oilfield, and in 1984 exploration began in Abu Dhabi's share of the Khuff formation, thought to be one of the largest offshore gasfields in the world.

In 1983 the Abu Dhabi Gas Liquefaction Company (ADGAS) borrowed $500m. to upgrade its Das Island complex by building three new LNG storage tanks and four for LPG, together with vapour recovery units. The Thamama C Gas project came on stream in 1984, processing gas from the Thamama C foundation of the Bab field. In 1988 Das Island produced 2.48m. tons of LNG, 7.8% above design capacity, for export to ADGAS's sole contract customer for LNG, Japan's Tokyo Electric Power Company. A third LNG production train and 34m. cu m per day of additional gas-gathering facilities

were completed in 1994, raising the plant's capacity to 5m. tons per year.

GASCO intended to expand its associated gas recovery capacity as it increased production of petroleum at the Bab field. ADNOC has stated that it aims to double onshore gas production by 1994.

Abu Dhabi's exports of petroleum are transported through two main terminals. The Jebel Dhanna terminal was completed in 1963. Additional installations, finished in 1974, increased the export capacity of ADPC's Murban petroleum to 1,280,000 b/d. ADMA-OPCO's Umm Shaif and Zakum petroleum is exported through the Das terminal. Two smaller terminals exist at Abu al-Bukhoosh and Mubarraz. At the beginning of 1980 ADNOC and JODCO began work on a new terminal, costing $750m., on Delma Island. As a result of the onshore petroleum expansion plans announced in March 1991, Jebel Dhanna was also to be expanded. Three new tanks were to be ready for commissioning in late 1992.

Dubai

Dubai is the second largest producer of petroleum in the UAE, producing approximately 420,000 b/d during 1991 and 380,000 b/d in 1992. By early 1994 output was down to an estimated 275,000 b/d, and steps were being taken to slow the rate of decline through increased use of enhanced recovery techniques. Output had risen to an estimated 320,000 b/d by mid-1994 following the drilling of new wells. In 1963 Conoco acquired the earlier petroleum concession, held from 1937 to 1961 by Iraq Petroleum Company, and formed the Dubai Petroleum Company (DPC), concentrating on offshore production. In 1954 CFP and Hispanoil had obtained an onshore concession, and formed Dubai Marine Areas Ltd (DUMA). In 1963 DPC acquired a 50% share in DUMA's concession and then released some of its shares to other companies, so that by the late 1960s CFP, Hispanoil, Continental Oil, Texaco, Sun Oil and Wintershall all had shares in DUMA–DPC's concession. By 1974 the Government of Dubai had acquired a 60% share in participation in DUMA–DPC. Nevertheless, the former concessionaire companies continued to operate under the same conditions until, in 1979, the Government decided to buy back 50% of the production to market it directly.

Although petroleum was first discovered in Dubai in 1966, production did not begin until 1969. Output averaged 34,236 b/d in 1970, rising to 362,346 b/d in 1978. This level fell slightly to 354,293 b/d in 1979, a similar figure was maintained in 1980 and 1981, but in 1982 it had risen again, to 358,000 b/d. In 1983 Dubai's production averaged 327,000 b/d, and production averaged about 350,000 b/d in 1984–86. Despite the OPEC quota, which should have restricted Dubai's production in the first half of 1987 to approximately 220,000 b/d, it is estimated that actual levels of production for the first quarter of the year were almost 380,000 b/d. Output is mainly from the two offshore oilfields of Fateh and South West Fateh, but some petroleum is also lifted from the Rashid and Falah offshore fields. In May 1982 a major new onshore discovery was made in the Margham field, and by 1988 production reached 40,000 b/d of condensate from 15 wells. In April 1989 a 59-km pipeline, linking the Margham field with the gas-processing plant at Jebel Ali, was brought into operation. The pipeline has a maximum capacity of 13.5m. cu ft per day. By the end of 1990 Dubai had a total of 341 oil wells. Exploration was not interrupted by the Gulf crisis, and development work at 21 wells was completed in 1990. DPC also installed a $200m. platform to increase capacity at the Fateh field in 1990. DPC's storage capacity stood at 2.3m. barrels at the end of 1990.

During 1982 Sheikh Rashid announced plans to grant concessions over the remainder of Dubai's territory, and by 1984 its total on- and offshore area was under exploration. Seven new concessions were granted in 1982 and 1983. These involved British Petroleum (BP), and a consortium of Taylor Woodrow Energy, Cliff Oil and Saxon Oil. KCA took over an area relinquished by Sedco and Houston Oil, Mapco took one concession and the Adolf Lundin Group took two. The final award went to DPC.

During the 1970s Dubai's natural gas was flared off, but in 1980 a gas treatment plant, owned by the Dubai Natural Gas

Company (DUGAS), began operations. Dubai's gas reserves are estimated at 125,000m. cu m, and the DUGAS plant, at Jebel Ali, began operations with a treatment capacity of 3m. cu m per day. In 1985 the plant had a production capacity of between 825 and 850 metric tons per day (t/d) of propane, 600 t/d of butane and 850 t/d–900 t/d of condensate. Most of the production from the plant is shipped to Japan. In 1988 DUGAS and two foreign companies, ASCO (of the USA) and British Petroleum (BP), signed an agreement to process associated gas from the Margham field at Jebel Ali. Previously this gas had been flared. Construction of a new DUGAS plant to produce methyl-tertiary-butyl ether, a lead substitute in petrol, was scheduled for completion in 1994. In 1992 the Dubai Government announced plans to build a major new refinery at Jebel Ali—the UAE's third—with a capacity of 150,000 b/d, at an estimated cost of $2,000m. No timetable was put forward for implementation of this proposal.

Sharjah

Production of petroleum began in Sharjah in 1974, with the Mubarak field producing at the rate of 60,000 b/d. The field lies in a 'protocol area', which is occupied by Iran, and in the north it lies in Iranian territorial concessions for hydrocarbons exploration. Sharjah has production and drilling rights, but shares production and revenue with Iran. This situation caused considerable difficulties following the onset of hostilities between Iran and Iraq, and in 1984 oil exploration was interrupted when Iranian patrol boats arrived near Abu Musa island. The security problems facing Sharjah became more apparent when Iranian naval forces attacked the Mubarak oilfield in April 1988, thereby causing its closure for a period of two months. Of the remaining revenue 20% is shared with Umm al-Qaiwain, and 10% with Ajman. The field has brought Sharjah revenues of around Dh 20m. per year since then, apart from in 1975 and 1976, when the value of exports was about Dh 30m. each year. Four consortia were responsible for exploration and production in the 1970s: Crescent Petroleum Company, Foreman Exploration, Reserve Oil and Gas and Amoco, which took over its concession in 1976. At the end of 1980, however, Amoco announced a major new onshore discovery of petroleum and natural gas. Exports of crude petroleum from this Sajaa field started in mid-1982 at a rate of 25,000 b/d. The emirate's total production in 1983 exceeded 50,000 b/d. It is estimated that Sharjah maintained production levels at an average of 65,000 b/d during 1987–90, although in 1991 output was about 25% lower, owing to problems at the Mubarak field. By 1992 output from the Mubarak field had fallen to 8,000 b/d.

Export revenues from Sharjah's two gasfields, Sajaa 1 and Sajaa 2, were expected to reduce substantially to reduce Sharjah's international debt, which was estimated at between $600m. and $700m. in 1986, and average production from the Sajaa fields in 1986 reached 16.98m. cu m per day. However, the collapse of the price of petroleum weakened Sharjah's ability to repay its international debt. A pipeline costing $190m. was completed in 1984, to carry gas from the Sajaa fields to power stations in Ras al-Khaimah, Fujairah, Ajman and Umm al-Qaiwain, and in 1985 this pipeline had a capacity of 60,000 b/d of condensate and 1.1m. cu m per day of gas. Following the settlement of the border dispute between Sharjah and Dubai in 1985, a 24-in (60-cm) gas pipeline was built to supply gas from the Sajaa field to the Dubai Electrical Company's power and desalination plant at Jebel Ali. An agreement was also reached in 1983 for Amoco to drill six wells over the ensuing 15 months, to bring the capacity of the Sajaa field to 14.2m. cu m per day. An LPG plant began production in July 1986, with a capacity of 13,000 b/d of mixed LPGs, 7,500 b/d of propane, 6,000 b/d of butane and 6,000 b/d of condensate. In June 1987 the plant was processing 11.32m. cu m of 'wet' gas per day, to produce the equivalent of 7,000 b/d of propane, 5,000 b/d of butane and more than 4,000 b/d of light oil. Many projects were postponed during the recession of the mid-1980s, but the economic revival following the 1990–91 Gulf crisis enabled the Government to revive development plans. In July 1992 the Amoco Sharjah Oil Company (owned 60% by the Sharjah Government and 40% by Amoco Corporation) announced significant new gas discoveries, and in 1993 plans

were announced to expand Sharjah's gas-processing capacity by 60% in 1994. A new contract to supply gas to power stations in the northern emirates was awarded by the UAE federal authorities in June 1994.

Ajman, Fujairah, Ras al-Khaimah and Umm al-Qaiwain

Of the remaining emirates, Ras al-Khaimah appears to have the largest reserves of petroleum and natural gas. Offshore discoveries, made in 1976 and 1977, proved not to be commercially exploitable, but Gulf Oil made new discoveries off the west coast in 1981. In the same year, an onshore concession was granted to a consortium of Amoco and Gulf Oil, and, following seismic tests, Gulf Oil announced significant discoveries of petroleum and gas in the second offshore test well, Saleh One X, in February 1983. The well started production in February 1984, at 5,000 b/d, followed in April by Saleh Two X at 3,500 b/d, and production there has since increased. At the beginning of 1985, however, Ras al-Khaimah was producing oil at a rate of only between 8,000 b/d and 10,000 b/d. A new well, Saleh Four X, began operating in February 1985, with a production rate of between 7,000 b/d and 8,000 b/d of oil, and a further well, Saleh Five X, was 'spudded' in April. Ras al-Khaimah's overall production has not, however, been as high as was anticipated, and in 1987 production was only 11,000 b/d, most of the revenue from which was used to finance exploration and development. By the end of 1987 a seventh well had been 'spudded' in the Saleh field, and production was reported to be about 12,000 b/d. By mid-1986 the four-stage programme to establish a 'downstream' oil industry in Ras al-Khaimah, at a cost of $45m.–$50m., had been completed. This consists of pipelines from the Saleh field to the mainland, separation and stabilization facilities, onshore storage facilities for 500,000 barrels, and an LPG plant. During 1986, uncertainty over the future of its petroleum industry led the Government of Ras al-Khaimah to relinquish its 50% share in the Saleh field, and in 1987 Chevron sold its 50.5% interest in Ras al-Khaimah's offshore concession. In 1991 the Omani Government agreed to allow gas from its Bukha offshore field to be processed at Ras al-Khaimah. Output was expected to be limited to around 5,000 b/d of condensate, 800 b/d of LPG and 40 cu feet of 'dry' gas per day. The emirate has been processing gas at Khor Khuwair since 1985, but utilization has been minimal.

Umm al-Qaiwain's first well was 'spudded' in 1981, and a Canadian concession in the emirate was due to start production in 1985. Exploration continues in Umm al-Qaiwain, as it does in Ajman, where drilling for petroleum finally began in 1982. In July 1983 Ajman formed the Ajman National Oil Company (AJNOC), with a capital of $37m. The GCC has discussed the construction of an oil export terminal and pipeline in Fujairah as a means of reducing threats to exports of petroleum from the Gulf in the event of future conflicts in the region.

The Federal Government supported exploration in the northern emirates during the 1980s, and in 1981 a plan for a 100,000 b/d refinery was announced for Fujairah. In February 1984 it was announced that two Canadian oil companies had been granted offshore concessions in Fujairah, and in 1988 Broken Hill Petroleum of Australia conducted a seismic survey off shore from the emirate. Further exploration of the northern emirates featured prominently in the UAE's 1991–95 development plan.

INDUSTRY

Since the UAE was formed in 1971, the diversification of the economy away from petroleum has been a clearly stated government policy. The development of an integrated infrastructure and extensive construction work took place in the 1970s, and this early industrial development was manned largely by immigrant labour. It is estimated that by 1982 the labour force of the UAE was 559,960, of whom a large majority—in some sectors over 90%—were non-nationals. In the early 1980s, anxiety over the large number of Asian workers and unemployment led to the enforcement of a restrictive labour-law and stricter visa regulations, making it increasingly difficult for overseas casual labourers to settle in the UAE. However, by 1986, when the expatriate work-force in

Dubai totalled only 75,070, the decline of the economy had led to a reversal of this policy, and the Government had begun to encourage immigrant labourers earning incomes above a certain level to bring their families with them. In September 1994 the federal authorities increased the qualifying income level from Dh 3,000 per month to Dh 5,000 per month (or Dh 4,000 in the case of an employee living in accommodation provided by the employer). A survey conducted by the UAE Ministry of Economy and Industry in 1988 indicated the poor productivity of capital invested in manufacturing industry in the UAE, a lack of new technology and the low level of wages paid to the mainly Asian work-force. The amount of value added in most enterprises was revealed to be very small. In 1987 non-oil manufacturing industry contributed 11% of GDP (compared with 4% in 1980), but in 1990 the proportion declined to 7.3%, its value being Dh 9,300m. In 1993 this sector contributed 8.3% of GDP, with a value of Dh 10,891m.

The industrial structure of the individual emirates varies largely according to the size of government revenues from petroleum. Thus Dubai, with its long tradition of entrepôt trading (which was valued at Dh 10,295m. in 1993) and its relatively small petroleum reserves, has developed non-oil industry to the greatest extent, whereas Abu Dhabi has tended to expand its 'downstream' hydrocarbon production.

The Ministry of Electricity and Water is responsible for 11 power stations: at Umm al-Qaiwain, Falaj al-Mualla, Dhaid, Masfut, Manama, Uzun, Masafi, Fujairah, Qidfa and Dibba. On the east coast a 33-kV overhead transmission system has been installed, and a number of small contracts were issued in 1980 to link the remainder of the power supply system in this area. In Dubai power is generated by the locally-owned Dubai Electricity Company, and in 1980 a steam power station at Jebel Ali was inaugurated with 60 MW generators. Ras al-Khaimah, Sharjah and Abu Dhabi are also responsible for their own power. In addition to the old diesel, gas and steam stations, Abu Dhabi's power is provided by the Umm an-Nar East and West stations, Units 9 and 10, a new 600-MW station at Bani Yas, and stations at Sadiyat and al-Ain. The UAE's installed generating capacity rose from 1,723.9 MW in 1979 to 3,933 MW in 1986. The UAE's output of electric energy increased from 4,991m. kWh in 1979 to 15,419m. kWh in 1989, with energy consumption per caput increasing from 126 kg of oil equivalent in 1965 to 10,874 kg in 1990.

In 1982 the power stations at Qidfa and Ghalilah began operations, resulting in a 97% rise in power output in the northern emirates during the first nine months of the year. In April 1989 it was announced that the Taweela A power station, under construction since 1984, would begin operation in August, supplying Abu Dhabi with 250 MW of power and 20m. gallons of water per day (g/d). The second phase, originally approved in January 1987, will entail the construction of a power station (Taweela B) with a capacity of 750 MW, and a desalination unit with a capacity of 75m. g/d. Work on the Taweela project was interrupted by the Gulf crisis of 1990–91. Further delays were caused by the decision, in March 1991, to invite retenders for construction of Taweela B, with a view to securing a bid closer to the sum allocated for the project. In the event, the 'turnkey' contract that was awarded for the Taweela B project in July 1992, to a Zürich-based consortium, envisaged an overall cost of $1,700m., compared with the Government's most recent allocation of $1,600m. Plans have also been announced for the expansion, by 1994, of Taweela A's capacity of 200 MW, for the expansion of the Jebel Ali E station by 232 MW to 472 MW, and for the construction of a new power station, Jebel Ali G, with a capacity of 440 MW. There are also plans to build a major station between Mirfa and Ruwais, to supply power and water to a large number of villages and islands in Abu Dhabi. Expenditure on power has often been subject to budgetary constraints, but, with demand rising by about 10% per year, the Government has decided to press rapidly ahead with expansion projects. By 1994 the total installed capacity of the UAE's power stations was 5,000 MW, while the anticipated demand in the year 2000 was 7,500 MW. Electricity prices are very heavily subsidized in the UAE.

The lack of water resources has led to much investment in the provision of fresh water, and by 1985 there were 22 desalination plants in the UAE. In 1982 annual water demand was estimated at 565m. cu m, of which agriculture used 410m. cu m. Examples of projects which have been completed are: a 3.3m. g/d desalination plant associated with the power station at Qidfa, in Fujairah, and a reverse osmosis desalination plant, with a capacity of 3.6m. g/d, at Ajman. Four 50 MW steam turbines, and two 18,000-cu m-per-day multi-stage flash desalination units were built at Raafah, in Umm al-Qaiwain. A project to divert water from two Turkish rivers, the Ceyhan and the Seyhan, to the Gulf along two pipelines, totalling 5,000 km in length, has been discussed, but has never come close to implementation. Total UAE water production in 1989 was 85,000m. gallons, compared with 81,000m. in 1987. The range of projects that the Government announced for expanding the UAE's electric power capacity after the end of the Gulf War in February 1991 all envisaged increases in desalination capacity. The proposed Jebel Ali G power station will incorporate a 60m. g/d desalination plant.

Abu Dhabi

Most of Abu Dhabi's heavy industry is centred on the Jebel Dhanna-Ruwais industrial zone, 250 km west of Abu Dhabi city, which was officially opened by Sheikh Zayed in March 1982. This is mostly oil-related, with a petroleum refinery capable of processing 120,000 b/d at Ruwais and a fertilizer plant forming the central projects (see Petroleum and Gas).

In 1979 the General Industries Corporation (GIC) was set up to co-ordinate non-petroleum development, and by early 1981 it was involved in a paper bag factory, a brick works, a concrete block factory, a steel-rolling mill, and an animal feed plant, all of which had begun production in the preceding two years. An industrial bank, the Emirates Industrial Bank, was founded in 1983 to fund new industrial projects. Light industry is concentrated in the al-Musalah area, just over the bridges joining Abu Dhabi island to the mainland. In 1985 there was a total of 221 industrial units in Abu Dhabi. A bottling plant for Coca-Cola opened in 1989, and the construction of a plant to manufacture 6,000 tons of polyurethane blocks per year has been announced.

Dubai

Dubai has taken the lead in developing non-petroleum industry (which could explain how in 1983, when the UAE witnessed a narrowing of its trade surplus, Dubai's increased by 30%, despite a 14% decline in petroleum revenues). This has been centred on the Jebel Ali port and industrial area, 30 km west of Dubai city. The decision to build a new deep-sea port was taken in August 1976, and there were 15 km of quays by mid-1981. A dry dock was developed in the early 1980s, and in 1985 a total of 111 ships, with a combined capacity of 10m. dwt, were repaired. The dock benefited greatly from the Iran–Iraq War, and was fully occupied by damaged vessels in 1988. The port possessed 67 berths by 1988, and is the largest man-made harbour in the world. In 1989 Jebel Ali Port handled 9.97m. tons of cargo. The older Port Rashid had 35 berths by mid-1984. By 1985 there was a total of 305 industrial units in Dubai. Despite a reduction in trade through Dubai's ports in the immediate aftermath of Iraq's invasion of Kuwait in August 1990, owing to raised war risk insurance premiums, shipping container tonnage in 1990 rose by 79% and general cargo tonnage by 61% compared with 1989. In May 1991 a new company, the Dubai Ports Authority (DPA), was established to take over the running of Port Rashid and Jebel Ali. Dubai's ports are playing an important role as transhipment points for Kuwait's reconstruction programme.

The first major plant to begin production was an aluminium smelter, owned by the Dubai Aluminium Company (DUBAL), which commenced operations at the end of 1979. It was built at a cost of $800m., and initially had an installed capacity of 135,000 metric tons of aluminium ingots per year. Production reached 151,170 tons in 1983 and 154,000 tons in the following year. In 1985 DUBAL's actual sales rose by 2%, compared with 1984, to 150,677 tons, of which Japan took 42,000 tons and the USA 34,314 tons. Nevertheless, the recession in the primary aluminium market forced DUBAL to reduce the work-force in 1986 in order to cut costs. In 1986, however, DUBAL achieved record sales of 155,605 tons of aluminium, while production of hot metal increased to 154,838 tons. In 1987 sales totalled 155,026 tons, of which Japan bought 70,000 tons. Production increased in 1988 to 163,445 tons, of which Japan purchased 64%. Output reached 168,000 tons in 1989, and about 170,000 tons in 1990. In May 1989 work began on the expansion of the plant by more than 40%, to a capacity of 240,000 tons per year. It was completed in early 1991. In 1992 DUBAL's production of hot metal totalled 244,605 tons, and a total of 250,000 tons of finished metals were sold to 21 countries, the main export markets being Japan (42.5% of sales), Taiwan, South Korea and Thailand. Sales comprised 50% billets, 36% foundry alloys and 14% high-purity ingots. DUBAL's output and sales volumes fell slightly in 1993 because of a temporary production problem, but were targeted to rise in 1994 to meet strong export demand. DUBAL is powered by five 100-MW gas turbines, driven by fuel from the neighbouring gas treatment plant, operated by DUGAS. Its associated desalination plant produces 15.6m. gallons (71m. litres) of water per day, supplying about 40% of Dubai's water requirements. In 1991 it was announced that DUBAL was to supply technology for a planned aluminium smelter complex in Bandar Abbas, Iran, a joint venture of the International Development Corporation of Dubai and Iranian enterprises under the control of Iran's Ministry of Mines and Metals. In 1979 another industrial plant, DUCAB (a cable manufacturer owned by the Dubai Government and BICC of Britain), came into production. Its sales of cables were worth a record Dh 212m. ($57.7m.) in 1993, when it won major new export orders in Asian markets. In May 1980, in an effort to promote Dubai's industrial development, Sheikh Rashid decreed that Jebel Ali should be a free-trade zone. The Jebel Ali Free Zone Authority, which offers the advantages of duty-free trade, was finally inaugurated, under full foreign ownership, in early 1985 (see Trade and Transport). Work on an $85m. plant to produce phosphoric acid, with a capacity of 500 metric tons per day, was due to be completed in 1991. By mid-1994 around 630 companies had set up businesses in the Jebel Ali Free Zone, and new companies were arriving there at an average rate of 15 per month. Major foreign companies locating there included Xerox, Union Carbide, 3M, Black and Decker, Mitsubishi, York International, BP Arabian Agencies and Shell Markets. Local firms at Jebel Ali include Dubai's National Cement Company and the National Flour Mills, which began production in 1987. A new sugar refinery with a daily capacity of 2,400 tons was due to go into production in late 1994. In 1990 a warehouse and distribution facility for the Sony Corporation and a $3m. manufacturing plant for the Kavoos Company of Iran, to make raw materials for paint production, were opened. Jebel Ali Free Zone has become an important distribution point for Kuwait's reconstruction programme. In 1990 investments in the zone reached Dh 1,500m., a 50% increase on 1989 levels. A second area for light industry has also been developed around the extended port area of Mina Rashid in Dubai itself. The garment-manufacturing sector has expanded dramatically, with the value of exports rising from an insignificant level in 1985 to Dh 9.37m. in 1987, and to Dh 17.0m. in the first half of 1988 alone. The industry is concentrated in Jebel Ali, where 25 factories were established by mid-1988, mostly by Indian businessmen. However, punitive quotas, introduced by the USA, have caused some units to close. The economic importance of this sector to the UAE is diminished by the fact that all raw materials and labour are imported, mainly from India.

In April 1993 the authorities introduced a new law that explicitly excluded licensed national firms from the 'offshore' provisions of the original free-zone legislation (see Trade and Transport, below), confirmed their liability to the provisions of Dubai's standard company laws, and made the granting of a licence subject to proof of at least 51% UAE or GCC ownership of the company concerned and at least 40% locally added value in its products. It was hoped that the removal of former ambiguities would encourage more local companies to take advantage of the infrastructure benefits of manufacturing within the zone. Industrial investment in Dubai in 1993 totalled Dh 10,500m. (8% up on 1992), while investment by foreign companies totalled Dh 1,800m. (23% up on 1992). Industrial production in 1993 was valued at Dh 9,600m. (an increase of 24.8%), including exports worth Dh 4,500m. (39.2% more than in 1992).

The Northern Emirates

Industrial development in the remaining emirates has been based largely on the construction industry and port expansion. Two container ports have been developed in Sharjah, where there is also a lubricating oil plant, a rope factory, the Sharjah Oxygen Company, a factory making plastic pipes and a cement plant producing 700 tons per day. The Gulf Industries Complex in Sharjah's industrial zone was opened in 1981, producing furniture and household utensils. In April 1982 a fodder factory at Mina Khaled, operated by the Gulf Company for Agricultural Development, was opened. An LPG plant came into operation on the site in July 1986. According to a study by the Emirates Industrial Bank, Sharjah was the focus of 35% of the UAE's industrial installations in 1987. However, many of these are small-scale enterprises, now threatened by rent increases which may force them to leave the complex. Total capital investment in Sharjah increased from Dh 461m. in 1977 to Dh 997m. in 1987, while the number of employees doubled, from 3,173 to 6,840, over the same period. Sharjah's industrial sector registered 48% growth in 1988.

Ras al-Khaimah has developed a valuable export business in aggregate (stones used in making concrete) from the Hajar Mountains. The first explosives factory in the Gulf was opened there in 1980, and a pharmaceutical factory was opened in 1981. The emirate has a cement factory, an asphalt company and a lime kiln, and in 1981 the Ras al-Khaimah Company for White Cement was established to build the Gulf's first white cement factory at Khor Khuwair. This joint Kuwaiti-UAE venture was due to commence operations in March 1986, producing 300,000 tons of white cement per year.

At the end of 1980 the Government of Fujairah established a department of industry and economy to organize industrial development. Fujairah has factories producing marble, tiles, rockwool (asbestos) insulation, concrete blocks, tyres and shoes, and many of these industries use materials from the Hajar mountains, where surveys have indicated significant quantities of copper, chromite, talc and magnesium. Commercial production of 1,600 tons per day began at a new cement plant in Dibba in 1982, when Fujairah's $4.9m. rockwool factory also started operations, with an annual capacity of 5,000 tons. Cement production capacity was due to rise to 2,500 tons per day during 1996. A new port with 11 berths was opened in Fujairah in the same year. Traffic at the port increased after Iraq's invasion of Kuwait in August 1990 as shippers attempted to avoid the war risk insurance premiums levied on the Gulf ports of Abu Dhabi and Dubai. Plans have been revealed to expand Fujairah's dry docking and ship repair facilities. In 1990 traffic at the port of Fujairah increased by 50% compared with 1989. A crushing plant, designed to produce 3m. tons per year of aggregate for cement production, went into production in May 1985. In 1988 plans were revived for the construction of a ferro-silicon plant to supply steel producers in the Gulf. The lack of an indigenous power source will, however, hamper the project. A five-year Development Plan, announced in 1988, included proposals for a $100m. industrial suburb and a $140m. break-shipment warehouse project. Fujairah outlined ambitious development plans in 1991, based on significant investment by the GCC member states. These include a Gulf railway, with the spur of the line connecting with the port of Fujairah, and a petrochemical complex.

Umm al-Qaiwain has concentrated on construction, and the newly-formed Umm al-Qaiwain Cement Industries Company plans to build a cement works producing 1m. tons per year to add to the one already in existence. Currently, however, the UAE's annual cement capacity is 8.4m. tons, which is four times the level of local demand of 2m. tons, and consequently the UAE's eight cement works are seeking to implement a production quota system. Cement production and related activities are likely to remain the dominant sector of the economy of Umm al-Qaiwain. Plans, announced in 1986, for the construction of an aluminium smelter, at a cost of $1,200m., were abandoned in 1988, and the smelter will now be built in Qatar. Umm al-Qaiwain has also followed Dubai's example by establishing a free zone by Amiri Decree in 1987. Ajman, the smallest emirate, has a cement factory, a dry dock and a ship repair yard. There is a pressing need for improved infrastructure in Ajman. In 1991 the Federal Government announced plans for a 240-MW increase in the electricity production capacity of the northern emirates.

AGRICULTURE

Since the establishment by the FAO of an agricultural experimental station at Digdagga (Ras al-Khaimah) in 1955, agriculture in the UAE has undergone a major transformation. Traditionally, agriculture was based on nomadic pastoralism, in association with some oasis cultivation on the east coast and at Liwa, Dhaid, al-Ain and Falaj al-Mualla. This cultivation was totally dominated by dates. Although dates are still the major crop in terms of area cultivated, the production of vegetables has increased dramatically. The UAE continues to import more than 70% of its food requirements, but it is now largely self-sufficient in salad vegetables, eggs and poultry. In April 1984 a ban was announced on imports of those foods in which the UAE is self-sufficient, during growing seasons. One sign of the UAE's increased confidence in its ability to grow its own food was the announcement, in 1984, that the Government would assume responsibility for managing the Digdagga experimental station. In 1987 the UAE imported 381,600 tons of vegetables and 325,000 tons of fruit, representing increases of 10% and 13%, respectively, in comparison with 1986. The World Bank estimated cereal imports in 1992 at 524,000 metric tons.

It is estimated that the total area under agricultural holdings doubled, to 320,000 dunums, in the decade after 1973/74. In 1982 the value of vegetable production was Dh 773m., of a total GNP of Dh 119,700m. Most agriculture takes place on the gravel plains on either side of the Hajar Mountains, at al-Ain or at Liwa. This expansion has been implemented through the creation of a widespread government extension service. In general, agricultural inputs are provided to farmers at about one-half of their real cost, with the Government subsidizing fertilizers, seeds and pesticides at 50% of cost. A central laboratory for the Ministry of Agriculture and Fisheries was officially opened near al-Ain in April 1982. In 1982 official figures stated that total production of fruit and vegetables reached 343,500 tons. Some of this has, in the past, gone to waste, and in 1983 the Government established the Public Corporation for Agricultural Produce to ensure that surplus vegetables are shared between the emirates, and to package and store produce. Agricultural production increased from 39,000 tons in 1972 to more than 600,000 tons per year in the late 1980s, while the area of cultivable land increased from about 48,000 ha to more than 280,000 ha during the same period. Date production rose from 62,000 tons in 1986 to an estimated 175,000 tons in 1992, while tomato production increased from 42,000 tons in 1990 to an estimated 85,000 tons in 1992. Government figures indicate that in al-Ain the number of farms increased from 980 in 1979 to 1,939 in 1983, with an increase in farm area over the same period from 43,000 dunums to 82,668 dunums. The area of forest in the al-Ain region also increased, from 10,617 ha in 1978 to 13,433 ha in 1983. In 1988, as a result of government incentives, there was a total of 18,265 farmers in the UAE, compared with 4,000 at the beginning of the decade.

There are a number of large-scale agricultural enterprises in the UAE. By 1981 there were three private dairy farms, four poultry farms, a French-sponsored fresh vegetable concern at al-Ain, and a government wheat project on 600 ha at al-Oha, near al-Ain. During 1984 the Arab Company for Animal Production's farm in Ras al-Khaimah was reported to be producing 16,000 cartons of milk and yoghurt daily from its 600 cows. A $26m. poultry farm has been built at Fujairah. This will produce 3.5m. birds and 11m. eggs per year. Experiments in hydroponics are being undertaken on Sadiyat Island. The Arab Company for Livestock Development, based in Damascus, Syria, plans to establish a 200-ha dairy farm, at a cost of Dh 13m., in Fujairah, where it also operates the poultry farm. In 1989 the UAE produced about 13,000 tons of poultry, making the country 45% self-sufficient. Output of eggs reached

170m. in 1989, satisfying 70% of domestic requirement. A vegetable-canning factory was opened at al-Ain in 1986.

The increased cultivation of vegetables and, in particular, the extensive forestry programme have led to severe problems with the water tables. Between 1976 and 1980, 1,545 new wells were dug by government teams, and it seems that at least this number were also dug privately. The consequent fall in the water table has been dramatic, especially near the coast. In 1980 the water table in Ras al-Khaimah fell by 3.37m. In places this has led to increased salinity of soil and water. Encroachment of seawater was also reported in 1982, when it apparently penetrated as far as 20 km inland in the northern emirates. As a result, several farms are now going out of production. The Government has attempted to alleviate the problem through the construction of desalination plants (see Industry) and catchment dams, such as those opened in 1982 at Wadi Ham and Wadi Bih. At the end of 1982 the Government barred the drilling of new wells in parts of the northern emirates. In November 1982 the Tebodin Company of the Netherlands began a comprehensive study of the fresh water needs of the four smallest emirates until the year 2011, to enable the Ministry of Electricity and Water to formulate policies for those emirates. In 1983 a new dam was opened in Fujairah, with a capacity of 10m. cu m of rain-water, and plans were laid for the construction of a 17,000 cu m-per-day desalination plant at Ajman. Despite the problems facing the UAE concerning its water supply, plans were shelved in 1984 for the construction of eight recharge dams. During 1987 Abu Dhabi's Executive Council announced plans to drill a further 200 artesian wells in three parts of the emirate to supply farmers with yet more water for irrigation purposes. Further plans for the western region in 1988 included the construction of small desalination plants to treat brackish water pumped by free pumps, and the cultivation of 600 ha, using sprinklers and drip irrigation. In 1990 Abu Dhabi announced its intention to cultivate 1,300 ha in Abu Dhabi, the western region and Al-Khaten. In order to irrigate this land 100 wells were to be sunk and two reservoirs were to be built.

Total subsidies for farming in the 1983 budget were estimated at Dh 35m., and the Ministry of Agriculture and Fisheries projected investments of Dh 1,172m. in farm development between 1983 and 1993. The food sector's contribution to GDP increased sixfold, to Dh 106.5m., in the nine years to 1984. In 1993 agriculture, livestock and fisheries contributed Dh 2,838m. (2.2%) to the UAE's total GDP at factor cost. By the year 2000, the UAE is expected to reach 100% self-sufficiency in wheat, and 95% self-sufficiency in fish, although in 1985 it was reported that over-fishing in breeding areas was beginning to have adverse effects on the fishing industry. The total catch was 95,129 tons in 1990, when there were 10,611 full-time fishermen, compared with about 4,000 in 1980. It was estimated in 1993 that the current annual catch of 97,200 tons exceeded local demand for fish by about 27,200 tons. Part of this surplus was exported and part was returned to the sea (there being no fish-processing industry in the UAE to provide a market for it).

TRADE AND TRANSPORT

During the 1970s the UAE's earnings from exports of petroleum enabled the country to retain a healthy overall balance of trade. In the early 1980s decreases in the levels of the UAE's petroleum production resulted in a relative decline in the country's trade surplus. The Iran–Iraq War brought considerable problems for the economies of other countries in the region, but Dubai continued to benefit from its trade links with Iran, and in 1987 its exports and re-exports to Iran reached Dh 1,300m. An upturn in economic activity, following the end of the Iran–Iraq War in August 1988, was partly responsible for an increase of 20% in imports, which contributed to a 28% reduction in the trade surplus, from Dh 19,000m. in 1987 to Dh 13,700m. in 1988. The trade surplus recovered to Dh 20,387m. in 1989, and rose to Dh 37,000m. in 1990, as a result of increased oil export volume and firmer oil prices, occasioned by the Gulf crisis. In 1991 the visible trade surplus fell to Dh 30,200m., and in 1992 it declined further, to Dh 21,800m., as in each year imports rose faster than exports. In 1992 exports and re-exports were provisionally valued at

Dh 85,800m. (of which petroleum contributed Dh 51,600m. and gas Dh 4,200m.), while imports were provisionally valued at Dh 64,000m. In 1993 exports and re-exports totalled Dh 86,500m. (including petroleum worth Dh 44,500m.), while imports totalled Dh 72,000m. (including Dh 25,500m. spent on items for re-export). The resulting visible trade surplus was Dh 14,500m. Overall, the current account of the balance of payments was in surplus by just Dh 670m. in 1993, compared with Dh 11,170m. in 1992.

The principal commodity groups in the UAE's imports are basic manufactures, machinery and transport equipment, and food and live animals. The leading purchasers of crude petroleum from Abu Dhabi are Japan, Western Europe and the Far East. All of Sharjah's petroleum exports go to the USA. In 1992 the leading suppliers of imports into the UAE were Japan, China, the USA, Germany and the United Kingdom. The UAE was admitted to GATT membership in March 1994.

One way in which trade has been allocated is through the designation of free trade zones, such as Jebel Ali and Port Zayed. From April 1982 customs duty in Dubai and Sharjah was lowered from 3% to 1%, to bring it in line with Abu Dhabi. In 1983 all the emirates introduced a 4% unified import tariff, following a GCC unified economic agreement, although this tariff was not uniformly applied throughout the federation until August 1994 (when individual emirates formally abandoned inconsistent customs practices). Imports from within the GCC area were exempt from the 4% tariff, as were many industrial raw materials, agricultural inputs, medicines and certain food items. Since the cease-fire in the Gulf War, several lines which had operated to the east coast during the conflict have returned to the Gulf, and investment in the free-trade zones has risen. The Jebel Ali Free Zone offers various incentives to investors, including: the right to 100% foreign ownership; the absence of taxes, import or export duties; and the right to full repatriation of profits and capital, as well as an ample supply of cheap labour. Similar free zones are planned to attract investment to Sharjah and Fujairah.

The modern internal transport system of the UAE was largely developed in the late 1960s and the 1970s, when main roads were constructed to link all the major cities. One of the characteristics of the country's economy over recent years has been the expansion in the number of major airports. Abu Dhabi's international airport was opened in 1968 and expanded during the 1970s. Because of congestion, a New Abu Dhabi International Airport (NADIA) opened in 1982 at an estimated cost of Dh 1,500m. In 1992 it was reported that $111m. was to be spent on an expansion of this airport, including construction of a new runway and enlargement of the main terminal. The airport handled 1,879,000 passengers in the first half of 1994, an increase of 27.6% compared with the first half of 1993. Dubai's international airport is the busiest in the region, and by 1984 the number of passengers using Dubai's international airport had reached 3.6m., and plans were announced for a new terminal which would allow the airport to handle up to 5.2m. passengers per year. In 1988 a record 4,347,402 passengers used the airport and 122,512 tons of cargo passed through the airport, representing a rise of nearly 70% compared with 1982. In 1990 it handled a record 144,282 tons of cargo, a 10% increase compared with 1989. A new air cargo terminal became operational in April 1991. In 1993 Dubai airport handled 5.67m. passengers and 218,264 tons of cargo, and was considering plans to increase its annual cargo-handling capacity from 250,000 to 350,000 tons. The third international airport in the country is at Sharjah, which experiences difficulties in attracting traffic, owing to the proximity of Dubai. In June 1989 28 airlines were operating an average of 150 flights per week through Sharjah airport. Flights from the airport increased from 4,225 in 1979 to 13,437 in 1988. Ras al-Khaimah has the fourth international airport but it, too, has had problems in attracting traffic. Abu Dhabi's second international airport, at al-Ain, was expected to be completed in 1993. The completion of work on an international airport in Fujairah was delayed by the lengthening of the runway by 700 m, to 3,750 m, to enable the airport to accommodate wide-bodied jet-engined aircraft, and it was eventually opened in October 1987. In 1985 Dubai founded its own airline, Emirates Airlines, which by mid-1993 was flying to 31 destinations. It is expected that the airline's development will lead to an expansion of the country's tourist industry. In its first two years of operation Emirates Airlines carried 700,000 passengers and 23,000 tons of freight. In 1989 some 9m. passengers passed through UAE airports. In 1992 Emirates Airlines announced a $1,000m. investment plan to purchase new aircraft over a 10-year period. There is strong competition from Gulf Air, which enjoys considerable regional superiority.

Port facilities have also been greatly expanded over recent years. The UAE's latest port, at Fujairah, was constructed at a cost of Dh 175m. and opened in 1982. The country's six other ports, already established, are Mina Zayed in Abu Dhabi, Mina Rashid and Mina Jebel Ali in Dubai, Mina Khalid in Sharjah, Mina Saqr in Ras al-Khaimah, and at Khor Fakkan. The crisis in world shipping has affected the Gulf. While the Jebel Ali container port exported 10,030 units in 1983, representing a 34% increase compared with 1982, and Mina Saqr handled a record 3,957,869 metric tons of cargo in 1983, Khor Fakkan suffered in competition with Fujairah and made a loss on trade. The high insurance premiums elsewhere in the region during the Iran–Iraq War enabled Fujairah to secure some contracts. In spite of doubts, the Abu Dhabi National Tankers Company proceeded with plans to expand its fleet, and by the end of 1983 the UAE's total fleet included 48 ships, with a combined displacement of 646,971 grt. Traffic at the UAE's ports increased in 1988 with the end of the Iran–Iraq War. Fujairah port's container throughput rose to a record 202,827 20-foot-equivalent units (TEUs) from 188,129 TEUs in 1987. Container traffic at Mina Rashid was 557,521 TEUs in 1988, while at Mina Jebel Ali the total freight handled was 4,475,175 metric tons. In 1992 the Dubai Ports Authority's area of operations (taking in Mina Rashid and Mina Jebel Ali) was ranked as the world's sixteenth busiest container port, with combined traffic of 1.48m. TEUs, shared almost equally between the two locations. The number of vessels calling at the Dubai ports in 1992 was 8,253, and the amount of general cargo handled, excluding petroleum, totalled 2.8m. tons. Sea-air cargo in 1992 totalled 9.1m. tons. The Dubai Ports Authority reported a 13% increase in container traffic and a 12% increase in overall tonnage handled in 1993. In the first six months of 1994 container traffic was 18% greater than in the same period of 1993, and seemed likely to reach an annual level of 2m. TEUs in 1995.

BANKING AND FINANCE

The unit of currency in the UAE is the dirham (Dh), which was created in 1973 to replace the Bahraini dinar and the Qatar/Dubai riyal, formerly used in the emirates. The dirham is linked officially to the IMF's Special Drawing Right but in practice to the US dollar. In 1979 and 1980 the Currency Board revalued the dirham by small amounts (up to 1%) against the dollar in order to try to curb capital outflows from the country (there are no exchange controls), which were attracted by generally higher interest rates elsewhere. The revaluations were also designed to ease the tightness of liquidity in the domestic money market which had been caused by the capital outflows. As a result of maintaining a fixed exchange rate of US $1 = Dh 3.671, the dirham lost more than 40% of its value in relation to the major European currencies between February 1985 and February 1987. During 1987 the dirham depreciated by a further 11.3% against an international 'basket' of currencies, as a result of the decline of the dollar.

During 1980 financial links with other countries in the Gulf were strengthened through the agreement between the UAE, Kuwait, Qatar and Libya to establish a new international insurance company. The UAE was also one of a number of Arab states which agreed to contribute to a fund whose purpose was to reduce economic and social disparities between Arab countries.

A central monetary institution, the UAE Currency Board, was established in 1973, but inter-emirate rivalry prevented it from being given full central banking powers. This has led to a rapid multiplication of banks in the country. The Currency Board, managed mainly by expatriates, was able to bring only a little order to the banking free-for-all. A moratorium on the opening of new banks was imposed in 1975, lifted temporarily and then re-imposed with a let-out for international banks of restricted licences (which allow all operations except domestic retail banking), only five of which have opened. In December 1980 the UAE Central Bank replaced the old Currency Board, and the rulers of Abu Dhabi and Dubai agreed to place one-half of their national revenues with the new institution. In April 1981 the moratorium on new banks was lifted again but in May the governor of the Central Bank announced that no foreign banks would be granted new branch licences. In July 1981 the Central Bank became more aggressive and told all foreign banks that they had until 1984 to reduce their operations to eight branches each. One way in which some banks tried to minimize the impact of this legislation was by becoming locally incorporated, with a 60% UAE shareholding. By the end of 1983, however, all foreign banks had complied with the legislation and reduced their number of branches to eight. Early in 1982 the Central Bank again intervened to keep a high level of liquidity in the country by imposing a 30% interest-free reserve requirement on dirham loans placed outside the UAE for less than one year, replacing the former 15% charge, imposed in May 1981, for loans up to three months.

Other disruptions to the banking sector were announced in early 1983. The ruler of Abu Dhabi decided that foreign banks should pay a tax of 20% on profits; and the Central Bank, implementing certain clauses of the 1980 bank law, established an upper limit on borrowing by individual bank directors and boards of directors. Despite this, many banks continued to do well in the early 1980s. In 1982 Umm al-Qaiwain opened its first locally incorporated bank, the National Bank of Umm al-Qaiwain. However, the general 'ceiling' of 5% on loans to individual directors led to the collapse, in 1983, of the Union Bank of the Middle East, which had loaned its Chairman, Abd al-Wahab Galadari, monies representing 25%–30% of the bank's total lending. The Central Bank forced his resignation in November 1983, and established a committee of bankers and businessmen to take over the management of the bank. By mid-1986, Abd al-Wahab Galadari's creditors had received a payment of 75% from the official receivers, which amounted to $321m. Other banks seem to have adopted policies in accordance with the Central Bank's requirements. It was not until the end of 1987, however, that final agreement was reached on loans valued at $68.6m. which were owed by A. R. E. Galadari Brothers to the nine-bank consortium headed by Citibank.

A further development in the banking sector was the establishment, in 1983, of the Emirates Industrial Bank, with an authorized capital of Dh 500m., to provide loans to new industries. Towards the end of 1984, in an attempt to discourage capital outflow, the Central Bank announced increases in the percentage of demand deposits accepted by local banks which would have to be placed with the Central Bank. In addition, since October 1984 all banks have had to maintain an interest-free balance with the Central Bank, equal to 30% of any dirham lendings or placements to non-resident banks with a remaining life of less than one year. The Central Bank's concern over the liquidity of many of the country's smaller banks has continued, and in 1985 a Central Bank circular obliged each of the UAE's banks to provide a detailed account of its financial operations, thus proving the existence of its inner reserves. This move was followed by a series of mergers involving the country's smaller banks. By 1988 the various reorganizations had reduced the total number of banks in the UAE to 17. In 1985 'bad debts' (i.e. debts unlikely to be repaid) increased by 15%–20%. During 1986 the problem of 'bad debts' increased considerably, and many borrowers had recourse to the courts in an attempt to reduce their debts, by arguing that compound interest was illegal. If interest payments were recalculated on the basis of simple interest, the banks would be obliged, in some cases, to return 80% of the total interest that they had received.

The collapse of the price of petroleum in 1986, and the deepening recession of the mid-1980s, caused an increasing number of problems for the majority of the banks in the UAE. In mid-1986 the Central Bank announced several measures that were aimed at imposing restraint in financial matters. The new measures, in particular, prohibited banks operating in the UAE from making unsecured loans. Net overall profits of the country's commercial banks declined from Dh 668m. in 1986 to Dh 592m. in 1987, although the two largest banks in the UAE, the National Bank of Abu Dhabi (with total assets of Dh 19,917m.) and the National Bank of Dubai (with assets of Dh 21,021m.), performed well. At the end of 1987 total assets of the country's commercial banks were Dh 107,700m. In 1987 provision for loan losses was reduced, and in 1988 the Central Bank announced that UAE banks were in a position to withstand bad debts. In 1989 the National Bank of Abu Dhabi recorded profits of Dh 107.2m., although total assets declined to Dh 20,977.8m. from Dh. 24,605m. in 1988. In 1990 it recorded a 15.8% decrease in net profits to Dh 90.2m. Its assets, however, increased by 12.5% to Dh 23,000m. The National Bank of Dubai recorded profits of Dh 466.2m. in 1990 and total assets reached Dh 24,144m. During 1987 a presidential decree specified that, in future, all debt cases would be considered by the civil court rather than the Shari'ah court, and a further decree spread considerable confusion by announcing that in all cases interest should not exceed the amount of the principal debt. Initially Iraq's invasion of Kuwait in August 1990 severely affected confidence in the banking sector. In August and September between 15% and 30% of total customer deposits were estimated to have been transferred out of the UAE. The continuous withdrawal of deposits forced the Central Bank to inject government money into at least two local banks. The bulk of these deposits have not returned to the UAE, although confidence has gradually returned to the banking sector. The outbreak of hostilities between the US-led multinational force and Iraq in January 1991 did not lead to further transfers of deposits out of the UAE banking sector.

According to UAE spokesmen, the banking sector overcame the negative effects of the Gulf crisis by virtue of speedy action by the Central Bank to ensure liquidity and confidence in the 47 existing commercial banks, whose consolidated balance sheet total increased by 9.5%, to $35,300m., in the second half of 1990. However, the effective failure of the National Investments and Security Corporation (NISCORP) in September 1991, after recording losses of $35m., impelled the federal authorities to seek to restore confidence by appointing a new Governor of the Central Bank. Total bank assets rose by 10% in 1991, to Dh 142,000m. In 1994, when 19 local and 28 foreign banks were active in the UAE, aggregate bank assets totalled Dh 155,000m. (the highest such figure in any Arab state except Saudi Arabia).

Inflation and the growth of bank credit have both been reduced since 1980. By 1984 the annual rate of inflation had fallen to around 4% from 25% in the mid-1970s; according to World Bank figures, it averaged only 1.1% per year in the period 1980–90, but official UAE sources indicate that the rate rose to 8%–10% in 1991 and was expected to reach 10%–12% in 1992. In mid-1994 the inflation rate was estimated to be around 7% per annum. Over the period 1986–88 the money supply expanded by 4%–6% per year, as increases in the banking system's net foreign assets and in credit to the private sector were largely offset by reductions in net credit to the Government and the increased retention of profits and provision for loan losses by the banks. The UAE has been considering the establishment of a stock exchange since 1985. Limited trading in shares is currently conducted by a group of five financial institutions. Companies whose shares are being traded include the 10 leading UAE banks, four local insurance companies, the state telecommunications company (Etislat) and some smaller industrial groups. Under existing rules, only UAE nationals are permitted to buy or sell shares. Several banks have diversified their operations in recent years, notably the Abu Dhabi Commercial Bank, which has introduced Islamic banking, and the British Bank of the Middle East, which has established a regional treasury centre.

In many economic matters, the individual emirates tend to pursue their own separate policies, although they rarely publish detailed budgets. Until recently, Abu Dhabi and, to a lesser extent, Dubai were the only two contributors to the federal budget, but by the beginning of 1986 Sharjah was also publicly committed to contributing to the budget. Nevertheless, by mid-1987, following the attempted coup in Sharjah, it became clear that the country's finances were in difficulties, as its total debt burden was in the order of $920m. By the beginning of July, however, loans valued at $130m. had been re-scheduled by a group of 17 foreign banks. Federal expenditure is divided into current expenditure, development and expenditure for investment.

The Government's budget proposals for 1988 envisaged revenue of Dh 12,426m. ($3,380m.) and expenditure of Dh 14,255m. ($3,880m.), resulting in a deficit of Dh 1,829m. ($500m.). The 1989 budget projections envisaged revenue of Dh 12,480m. ($3,400m.) and expenditure of Dh 14,650m. ($3,991m.), resulting in a deficit of Dh 2,170m. ($591.1m.). The budget for 1990 was finalized in December. The increase in oil prices after Iraq's invasion of Kuwait caused revenues from petroleum sales to increase to Dh 14,980m. Expenditure also increased, but less dramatically, enabling the UAE to reduce its budget deficit to Dh 660m. The 1991 budget envisaged reduced revenues of Dh 13,700m. and an increase in expenditure to Dh 19,700m., implying a deficit of Dh 6,000m. The 1992 federal budget, approved in March 1992, projected total expenditure of Dh 17,300m. and total revenue of Dh 15,900m., resulting in a deficit of Dh 1,400m. The proposed increase in the deficit in 1991 reflected the UAE's determination to advance major development projects, especially in the non-petroleum sector. It should be noted, however, that the federal budget reflects only about one-half of the country's total expenditure, as the individual emirates also have their own budgets. Figures for these are not always available, but in Abu Dhabi total budget expenditure declined from a record level of Dh 7,000m. in 1982 to Dh 6,525.4m. in 1983, when there was a deficit of Dh 2,900m. In 1984 a deficit of approximately Dh 1,487m. was recorded. Abu Dhabi has not published its budgets since 1984, although in 1988 total expenditure of Dh 3,600m. was announced.

The 1993 federal budget proposals envisaged expenditure of Dh 17,630m. and revenue of Dh 15,911m., leaving a deficit of Dh 1,719m., which was effectively increased to Dh 2,169m. after taking account of a remaining deficit of Dh 900m. from the previous fiscal year. The deficit was to be financed by contributions from Abu Dhabi and Dubai and by borrowing from the UAE Central Bank. New projects accounted for Dh 1,180m. of the budgeted expenditure for 1993. In July 1993 the federal authorities advised ministries not to propose new projects for inclusion in the 1994 budget until they had completed at least 80% of their current projects. Any increase in federal revenue in 1994 would, it was stated, be used to reduce the size of the budget deficit. In the event, expenditure was marginally trimmed to Dh 17,610m. in the 1994 federal budget, leaving a budget deficit of Dh 1,410m. after allowing for a 1.8% increase in revenue to Dh 16,200m. (80% of which was to come from the oil and gas sector). Spending allocations included Dh 5,340m. for federal civil service salaries, Dh 2,770m. for education, Dh 2,250m. for health services, Dh 1,120m. for water and electricity supply and Dh 1,200 for development projects.

In May 1991 the Federal Government announced that a study to assess the feasibility of establishing the UAE, and in particular Dubai, as a centre for 'offshore' banking was to be undertaken. On 5 July 1991, however, such considerations were overtaken by the effects of the closure of operations of the Bank of Credit and Commerce International (BCCI) by the regulatory authorities of seven countries in which it had operated. Within days BCCI operations had been suspended in most of the 69 countries in which it had operated.

Sheikh Zayed bin Sultan an-Nahyan, the ruler of Abu Dhabi and President of the UAE, was a founding shareholder of BCCI. In 1988 BCCI became involved in a scandal when two of its US subsidiaries were accused of 'laundering' profits from trade in illegal drugs. With the bank's problems mounting, Sheikh Zayed and Abu Dhabi agencies purchased a 77% stake in BCCI in mid-1990 and sought to formulate a plan for reconstructing BCCI. In September 1990 the headquarters of BCCI were moved from London to Abu Dhabi. The reconstruction plan was thought to involve dividing BCCI into three separately capitalized entities registered in London, Hong Kong and Abu Dhabi, respectively, and with the holding company based in Abu Dhabi. Abu Dhabi invested as much as $1,000m. in BCCI. These plans, however, were pre-empted

when BCCI was closed on 5 July 1991 in seven countries after a report by its auditors, Price Waterhouse, commissioned by the Bank of England, alleged major and systematic fraud by the bank. The UAE protested at the lack of prior consultation before BCCI's closure. The bank has contested moves by the UK authorities to terminate its operations and on 29 July received permission to attempt to formulate a viable reconstruction plan by the end of 1991.

The closure of BCCI caused hardship amongst traders, businessmen and shippers in the UAE. Agencies in Abu Dhabi are owed $1,400m. and 35,000 private depositors are owed $600m. The UAE Government has stated that it will compensate these private depositors. Abu Dhabi's intention appeared to be to reconstruct the bank as a Middle East and Asian bank. On 3 August 1991 the Bank of Credit and Commerce (Emirates) changed its name to the Union National Bank. It was intended that BCCI's 40% shareholding should be purchased in order to sever all ties with the parent bank. In mid-1992 the Abu Dhabi-based majority shareholders in the former BCCI warned creditors that their offer of 30% compensation payment was final. Creditors, however, appeared unwilling to accept this and ready to risk litigation. In July Abu Dhabi was criticized, in a draft of the official British report of the BCCI collapse, for withholding information as to the scale of the fraud from the Bank of England. In October it was reported that 90% of BCCI's creditors had voted to accept the joint liquidators' plan, but in mid-1993 the objections of a minority of creditors (who were pursuing their case in the Luxembourg courts) continued to delay acceptance of the plan. The Ministry of Justice in Abu Dhabi stated in July 1993 that 13 senior managers of BCCI would go on trial in October on charges including forgery of documents, concealment of banking losses, and making false loans. All but one of the 13 defendants were convicted at the conclusion of the trials in May 1994.

With effect from July 1993, the UAE Central Bank introduced new banking regulations whereby the minimum ratio for capital adequacy was raised to 10% (2% higher than the internationally recommended minimum). Moreover, the legal definition of a bank's 'core' capital and its 'supplementary' capital was respecified in accordance with current international standards. All on- and off-balance-sheet items were required to be ranked according to a schedule of risk. Banks were required to maintain a minimum level of 10% of total risk-weighted assets relative to their capital base, in which 'core capital' must reach a minimum of 6% of total risk-weighted assets, while 'supplementary capital' would be considered only up to a maximum of 67% of core capital. Banks would henceforth be required to report to the Central Bank every three months.

In October 1993 the Central Bank issued a circular tightening the banking regulations still further from the beginning of 1994 (with provision for deferral on a case-by-case basis until the end of 1995). This circular limited any bank's exposure to the following proportion of its capital base: 25% if the exposure was to a government-owned commercial entity; 5% to a director or board member, and no more than 25% in aggregate to the bank's whole board; 6% in aggregate to bank employees; 7% to one of its shareholders, or a single borrower, or a group of related borrowers; 20% to a subsidiary or affiliate. There were also ceilings on funded inter-bank exposures, letters of credit and guarantee, and other contingent liabilities. Banks were required to report large exposures (including those of subsidiaries) to the Central Bank on a quarterly basis, a large exposure being defined in the circular as all exposures to a single borrower or a group of related borrowers that total 7% or more of a bank's capital base. The Central Bank later agreed to exclude contingent liabilities from its definition of a large exposure, which was to be calculated after deductions for provisions, cash collateral and deposits under lien. The Central Bank also agreed to draw up a list of acceptable securities against which banks would be permitted to lend without reference to the 'large exposure' limits.

DEVELOPMENT PLANNING

Until 1981, development expenditure in the UAE came from the annual federal budget, and there was no attempt at detailed long-term integrated economic planning, although Abu Dhabi did have a loose development plan for 1977–79. The end of the 1970s saw a great increase in health facilities in the country, with the number of hospital beds available rising from 1,750 in 1979 to 3,500 in April 1981. This increase was partly brought about through the completion of two major new hospitals at al-Ain. In 1986 the UAE had 28 hospitals and 119 clinics. In 1989 a total of 10 new primary health care centres were planned, at a cost of Dh 10m.–12m. each.

The first Five-Year Plan was intended to have been implemented in 1981, to run until 1985, but the fall in revenues from petroleum severely restricted initial proposals. Overall expenditure was estimated to be Dh 16,000m. for the five years, with Abu Dhabi receiving 21%, Fujairah 12.5%, Sharjah 10.8%, Ras al-Khaimah 9.4%, Umm al-Qaiwain 7.7%, Dubai 5.3%, and Ajman 4.4%. The Plan initially predicted an overall increase of 20% in the country's GDP up to 1985. However, in 1983 alone GDP fell by 13.5%. According to provisional data, GDP at current prices was Dh 99,416m. in 1985 (a real decline of 2.4%) and Dh 78,344m. in 1986 (a real fall of 22.1%). The Plan also allocated Dh 3,800m. to the agricultural sector, which was expected to expand at an annual rate of 10.3%. It was hoped, in particular, to improve productivity and marketing services, and to aim for the best possible use of water resources. Of the Dh 16,000m. which was to be spent in the Plan, Dh 3,500m. was for investment projects and Dh 8,400m. for schemes already under construction. The experience of the first five-year plan for the UAE meant that there was little enthusiasm for a second and the emirates of the UAE returned to a more flexible approach to defining and planning development priorities. In early 1989 Abu Dhabi announced that the emirate planned to spend about Dh 14,800m. in the next decade on infrastructure and development. A total of Dh 875m. was allocated to the construction of 85 schools (as part of the fifth education plan), of which 41 were scheduled to be completed by the beginning of the 1990/91 academic year.

The creation of an agency law in 1982 brought increased government intervention in the economy, requiring all agencies to be held by UAE nationals. Amendments were also approved to the Commercial Companies Law, ensuring that only one of the four types of partnership which were permitted could involve any degree of foreign involvement. The enactment in mid-1984 of a law whereby only companies which are 100% UAE-owned were permitted to conduct insurance business was a further move clearly designed to restrict participation in the UAE's economic changes. A Companies Law, designed to bring UAE company practice into conformity with legislation elsewhere in the Gulf, was effected in February 1989. The law was first introduced in 1985, but was suspended a year later. It was announced that a law allowing full foreign ownership of businesses in Sharjah would come into effect by April 1989.

The UAE, however, has not only been concerned with its own development. Abu Dhabi, through its Fund for Arab Economic Development (ADFAED), has been a major source of international aid. External assistance in the form of grants, 'soft' loans and participations averaged $1,100m. per year in the period 1974–78, and in 1979 it was almost $1,500m. ADFAED was set up in 1971 with a capital of $120m.; its commitments up to the end of 1980 totalled $800m. However, in 1982, as a result of declining revenues from petroleum, the UAE reduced its foreign aid budget from Dh 9,400m. in 1981 to Dh 6,500m. in 1982. In 1984 Abu Dhabi further reduced its foreign aid, to Dh 2,443m. from the 1983 figure of Dh 3,800m. Some projects did, nevertheless, continue to receive funding. In February 1987 ADFAED offered Tunisia a loan valued at Dh 36.6m. to finance a major rural development project, and in June 1988 a loan of $600m. towards a land reclamation project in Egypt was announced. In 1989 ADFAED's committed capital was about $2,200m. ADFAED signed loans totalling Dh 151m. ($41.1m.) in 1988, compared with Dh 15.6m. ($4.2m.) in 1987. The ADFAED was renamed the Abu Dhabi Development Fund at the end of 1993 (reflecting its involvement in projects in some non-Arab countries).

The UAE made substantial contributions to the Gulf Financial Crisis Co-ordination Group (GFCCG), established to assist those states which had suffered the worst financial losses as a result of the UN trade embargo that had been imposed in response to Iraq's invasion of Kuwait in August 1990. The UAE disbursed $1,469m. through the GFCCG, $850m. of which was donated to Egypt, Jordan and Turkey. The UAE also made contributions towards the costs of the military operations of the anti-Iraqi coalition, in particular those of the USA, to which it gave $4,067m., and those of the UK, which received £275m. The total value of 'official grants' of all kinds was estimated in the UAE Central Bank's balance-of-payments data as Dh 10,800m. in 1990, Dh 17,000m. in 1991 and Dh 2,700m. in 1992.

On 22 April 1991 the UAE agreed, as part of the GCC, to establish a Gulf Development Fund, with a capital of $10,000m. for an initial 10-year period. The fund was to provide new finance for those Middle East countries whose economies are relatively weak. Finance will be aimed at the private sector and will be incorporated into World Bank and IMF programmes.

Statistical Survey

Source (unless otherwise indicated): Central Statistical Department, Ministry of Planning, POB 1134, Sharjah; tel. 22704.

Area and Population

AREA, POPULATION AND DENSITY

Area (sq km)	77,700*
Population (census results)	
15 December 1980	1,042,099
December 1985	
Males	1,052,577
Females	569,887
Total	1,622,464
Population (official estimates)†	
1991	1,908,800
1992	2,011,400
1993	2,083,100
Density (per sq km) in 1993	26.8

* 30,000 sq miles.
† Source: Central Bank of the United Arab Emirates.

POPULATION BY EMIRATE (1991, official estimates)

	Area (sq km)	Population	Density (per sq km)
Abu Dhabi	67,350	798,000	11.8
Dubai	3,900	501,000	128.5
Sharjah	2,600	314,000	120.8
Ras al-Khaimah . . .	1,700	130,000	76.5
Ajman	250	76,000	304.0
Fujairah	1,150	63,000	54.8
Umm al-Qaiwain . . .	750	27,000	36.0
Total	77,700	1,909,000	24.6

PRINCIPAL TOWNS (population at 1980 census)

Dubai . .	265,702	Sharjah . . .	.125,149
Abu Dhabi (capital)	242,975	Al-Ain . . .	.101,663

Source: UN, *Demographic Yearbook*.

BIRTHS, MARRIAGES AND DEATHS

	Registered live births		Registered marriages		Registered deaths	
	Number	Rate (per 1,000)	Number	Rate (per 1,000)	Number	Rate (per 1,000)
1988 . .	50,836	n.a.	9,282	n.a.	3,447	n.a.
1989 . .	51,903	29.8	7,734	4.4	3,640	2.1
1990 . .	52,264	28.3	7,357	4.0	3,938	2.1

Expectation of life (UN estimates, years at birth, 1985–90): 69.9 (males 68.6; females 72.9) (Source: UN, *World Population Prospects: The 1992 Revision*).

EMPLOYMENT ('000 persons)

	1988	1989	1990*
Agriculture, hunting, forestry and fishing	39.5	42.6	43.1
Mining and quarrying . . .	9.1	9.5	10.0
Manufacturing	61.1	61.8	63.4
Electricity, gas and water . .	19.8	20.2	20.6
Construction	110.0	114.2	119.2
Trade, restaurants and hotels .	96.2	99.1	101.4
Transport, storage and communications . .	68.0	70.4	71.7
Financing, insurance, real estate and business services	17.5	18.4	18.8
Community, social and personal services . .	222.5	230.9	241.3
Total	643.7	667.1	689.5

* Estimates.

Total employed: 737,700 in 1991; 769,300 in 1992; 794,400 in 1993 (Source: Central Bank of the United Arab Emirates).

Agriculture

PRINCIPAL CROPS ('000 metric tons)

	1990	1991	1992*
Cereals	8	8	8
Tomatoes	41	82	85
Cucumbers and gherkins . .	7	10	12
Aubergines	39	56	60
Chillies and peppers (green) .	10	12	13
Watermelons	4	4	5
Melons	1	3	3
Dates	141	173	175
Tobacco (leaves) . . .	1	1	1

* FAO estimates.
Source: FAO, *Production Yearbook*.

LIVESTOCK ('000 head, year ending September)

	1990	1991	1992*
Cattle	49	53	55
Camels	113	121	122
Sheep	254	272	275
Goats	657	703	720

* FAO estimates.
Poultry (FAO estimates, million): 7 in 1990; 7 in 1991; 7 in 1992.
Source: FAO, *Production Yearbook*.

LIVESTOCK PRODUCTS ('000 metric tons)

	1990	1991	1992
Beef and veal*	2	2	2
Mutton and lamb* . . .	20	21	21
Goats' meat*	3	3	3
Poultry meat*	15	14	15
Cows' milk	5	5	6*
Sheep's milk	5	5	6*
Goats' milk	15	16	17*
Hen eggs	10.2†	10.5†	10.8*

* FAO estimate(s).   † Unofficial figure.
Source: FAO, *Production Yearbook*.

Fishing

('000 metric tons, live weight)

	1989	1990	1991
Fishes	91.1	95.1	92.2
Crustaceans and molluscs . .	0.1	0.1	0.1
Total catch	91.2	95.1	92.3

Source: FAO, *Yearbook of Fishery Statistics*.

Mining

('000 metric tons, unless otherwise indicated)

	1989	1990	1991
Crude petroleum . . .	89,265	101,959	114,769
Natural gasoline* . . .	970	1,030	1,100
Natural gas (petajoules) . .	783	788	932

* Provisional or estimated figures.
Source: UN, *Industrial Statistics Yearbook*.

Industry

PETROLEUM PRODUCTS ('000 metric tons)

	1989	1990	1991
Jet fuels	1,090	1,100	1,110
Motor spirit (petrol) . . .	1,300	1,250	1,300
Naphthas	810	900	920
Kerosene	60	80	85
Distillate fuel oils . . .	2,510	2,700	2,750
Residual fuel oils . . .	2,620	2,800	2,900
Liquefied petroleum gas:			
from natural gas plants* .	2,360	2,470	2,500
from petroleum refineries* .	200	240	256

* Provisional or estimated figures.
Source: UN, *Industrial Statistics Yearbook*.

ELECTRIC ENERGY (million kWh)

	1989	1990	1991
Production.	13,270	13,590	13,790

Source: UN, *Industrial Statistics Yearbook*.

Finance

CURRENCY AND EXCHANGE RATES

Monetary Units
100 fils = 1 UAE dirham (Dh).

Sterling and Dollar Equivalents (31 May 1994)
£1 sterling = 5.550 dirhams;
US $1 = 3.671 dirhams;
100 UAE dirhams = £18.02 = $27.24.

Exchange Rate
The Central Bank's official rate has been fixed at US $1 = 3.671 dirhams since November 1980.

GENERAL BUDGET (million UAE dirhams)*

Revenue	1987	1988	1989†
Taxation	473	479	573
Social security contributions	38	41	42
Domestic taxes on goods and services	435	438	531
Other current revenue. .	2,288	1,438	766
Capital revenue . . .	8	4	9
Grants from other levels of government	9,865	10,950	11,298
Total	12,634	12,871	12,646

Expenditure	1987	1988	1989†
General public services . .	786	739	613
Defence	5,827	5,827	5,827
Public order and safety . .	1,713	1,697	1,789
Education	1,773	1,882	1,985
Health	912	919	916
Social security and welfare .	423	420	420
Housing and community amenities . . .	86	58	54
Recreational, cultural and religious affairs and services	352	353	357
Economic affairs and services .	670	582	572
Fuel and energy . . .	401	324	329
Agriculture, forestry, fishing and hunting . .	106	105	96
Other purposes . . .	716	708	731
Total	13,258	13,185	13,264
Current	13,031	13,038	13,131
Capital	227	147	133

* Excluding the operations of the seven Emirate Governments.
† Provisional.

Source: IMF, *Government Finance Statistics Yearbook*.

1990 (million dirhams): Revenue 15,251 (incl. grants 12,909); Expenditure 14,394.
1991 (provisional, million dirhams): Revenue 14,621 (incl. grants 12,997); Expenditure 15,220.
1992 (provisional, million dirhams): Revenue 16,717 (incl. grants 12,511); Expenditure 15,538.
1993 (estimates, million dirhams): Revenue 15,900; Expenditure 17,630.
1994 (estimates, million dirhams): Revenue 16,200; Expenditure 17,610 (Education 2,770, Health 2,250, Water and electricity 1,120).

CENTRAL BANK RESERVES (US $ million at 31 December)

	1991	1992	1993
Gold*	181.7	182.0	182.5
IMF special drawing rights .	136.6	72.1	74.4
Reserve position in IMF . .	180.4	217.6	223.6
Foreign exchange† . . .	5,048.4	5,422.1	5,805.7
Total	5,547.1	5,893.8	6,286.2

* Valued at US $228 per troy ounce.
† Figures exclude the Central Bank's foreign assets and accrued interest attributable to the governments of individual emirates.

Source: IMF, *International Financial Statistics*.

MONEY SUPPLY (million UAE dirhams at 31 December)

	1991	1992	1993
Currency outside banks . .	4,676	5,108	5,667
Demand deposits at commercial banks	8,336	9,873	12,507
Total money	13,012	14,981	18,174

Source: IMF, *International Financial Statistics*.

NATIONAL ACCOUNTS (million UAE dirhams at current prices)
National Income and Product

	1988	1989	1990
Compensation of employees .	25,226	26,769	27,996
Operating surplus . . .	49,193	60,848	81,633
Domestic factor incomes .	74,419	87,617	109,629
Consumption of fixed capital .	14,382	15,127	16,078
Gross domestic product (GDP) at factor cost . .	88,801	102,744	125,707
Indirect taxes, *less* subsidies .	−1,695	−1,768	−1,699
GDP in purchasers' values .	87,106	100,976	124,008
Factor income from abroad .	9,940	10,600	10,900
Less Factor income paid abroad	9,690	10,178	12,200
Gross national product . .	87,356	101,398	122,708
Less Consumption of fixed capital	14,382	15,127	16,078
National income in market prices	72,974	86,271	106,630
Other current transfers from abroad (net)	−1,040	−744	−11,000
National disposable income .	71,934	85,527	95,630

Source: UN, *National Accounts Statistics*.

Expenditure on the Gross Domestic Product

	1990*	1991†	1992†
Government final consumption expenditure	20,100	21,350	23,380
Private final consumption expenditure	46,700	51,520	58,660
Increase in stocks	1,200	1,320	1,630
Gross fixed capital formation	24,100	25,200	27,250
Total domestic expenditure	92,100	99,390	110,920
Exports of goods and services	82,000	84,240	89,110
Less Imports of goods and services	50,600	59,440	72,700
GDP in purchasers' values	123,500	124,190	127,330

* Source: IMF, *International Financial Statistics*.
† Source: Ministry of Planning.

Gross Domestic Product by Economic Activity
(at factor cost)

	1991	1992	1993*
Agriculture, livestock and fishing	2,563	2,730	2,838
Mining and quarrying	54,592	53,471	51,719
Manufacturing	9,770	9,942	10,891
Electricity and water	2,700	2,869	2,961
Construction	10,365	11,125	11,582
Trade, restaurants and hotels	11,943	13,020	13,382
Transport, storage and communications	6,711	7,167	7,390
Finance, insurance and real estate	12,928	14,611	15,139
Government services	13,634	14,376	14,881
Other community, social and personal services	2,689	2,931	3,107
Domestic services of households	551	605	638
Sub-total	128,446	132,847	134,528
Less Imputed bank service charge	2,182	2,684	2,868
Total	126,264	130,163	131,660

* Provisional figures.
Source: Central Bank of the United Arab Emirates.

BALANCE OF PAYMENTS
(estimates, million UAE dirhams)

	1990	1991	1992
Merchandise exports f.o.b.	79,500	81,300	85,800
Merchandise imports c.i.f.	42,500	51,100	64,000
Trade balance	37,000	30,200	21,800
Services and private transfers (net)	−7,000	−7,200	−9,400
Official transfers (net)	−10,800	−17,400	−2,700
Current balance	19,200	5,600	9,700
Capital (net)	−14,600	−8,000	−8,000
Net errors and omissions	−5,600	7,580	−2,390
Overall balance	−1,000	5,180	−690

Source: Central Bank of the United Arab Emirates.

External Trade

COMMODITY GROUPS (million UAE dirhams; Abu Dhabi, Dubai and Sharjah)*

	Imports c.i.f.†		National Exports‡		Re-exports§	
	1990	1991	1987	1988	1990	1991
Food and live animals	1,919	1,664	86.7	70.1	467.0	605.8
Beverages and tobacco	131	131	27.5	50.3	10.4	31.8
Crude materials (inedible) except fuels	154	160	101.1	139.7	39.7	22.5
Mineral fuels, lubricants, etc.	119	138	138.2	120.2	10.0	10.9
Animal and vegetable oils and fats	35	81	1.6	2.6	4.3	5.3
Chemicals	1,027	1,088	81.1	92.7	82.9	110.5
Basic manufactures	2,091	2,642	978.6	1,251.0	374.7	581.5
Machinery and transport equipment	4,493	5,233	27.6	57.3	957.5	2,292.5
Miscellaneous manufactured articles	874	1,039	68.0	121.1	660.2	1,276.8
Other commodities and transactions	228	173	0.0	0.0	23.3	9.2
Total	11,071	12,349	1,510.3	1,905.1	2,629.9	4,946.9

* Figures exclude inter-emirate trade. Also excluded is trade in gold and silver.
† Excluding transit trade, and not including Dubai (total imports 31,041.5m. dirhams in 1990, 38,111.3m. dirhams in 1991).
‡ Excluding crude petroleum, petroleum products and fertilizers.
§ Excluding Dubai (total re-exports 7,602.7m. dirhams in 1990, 7,525.5m. dirhams in 1991).
Total Imports c.i.f. (million dirhams): 42,500 in 1990; 51,100 in 1991; 64,000 in 1992.
Petroleum Exports (million dirhams): 54,500 in 1990; 52,700 in 1991; 51,600 in 1992.
Total Exports and Re-exports f.o.b. (million dirhams): 79,500 in 1990; 81,300 in 1991; 85,800 in 1992.
Source: Central Bank of the United Arab Emirates.

PRINCIPAL TRADING PARTNERS

Imports (million UAE dirhams)*	1990	1991
Australia	809	944
Bahrain	487	416
France	1,507	2,249
Germany, Fed. Rep.	3,148	3,359
Hong Kong	438	473
India	1,696	2,310
Indonesia	525	953
Iran	620	804
Italy	1,916	2,032
Japan	5,988	7,863
Korea, Republic	1,852	2,325
Malaysia	675	930
Netherlands	926	1,055
Pakistan	494	526
Qatar	475	453
Saudi Arabia	1,525	1,328
Singapore	785	857
Switzerland	678	891
Taiwan	1,073	1,526
Thailand	1,152	1,318
United Kingdom	4,198	4,145
USA	3,851	4,984
Total (incl. others)	42,115	50,461

* Figures refer to Abu Dhabi, Dubai and Sharjah.

Source: Central Bank of the United Arab Emirates, *Bulletin*.

Exports (US $ million)†	1980	1981	1982
Australia	201	240	292
Brazil	243	303	370
France	2,152	2,140	793
Germany, Fed. Rep.	1,120	774	227
India	420	607	384
Italy	575	728	470
Japan	7,697	7,631	5,858
Netherlands Antilles	944	698	315
Pakistan	286	394	373
Saudi Arabia	232	290	320
United Kingdom	712	388	355
USA	1,804	1,458	667
Total (incl. others)	21,618	21,238	16,837

† Figures refer to Abu Dhabi and Dubai.

Source: UN, *International Trade Statistics Yearbook*.

Transport

INTERNATIONAL SEA-BORNE SHIPPING
(estimated freight traffic, '000 metric tons)

	1988	1989	1990
Goods loaded	63,380	72,896	88,153
Crude petroleum	54,159	63,387	78,927
Other cargo	9,221	9,509	9,226
Goods unloaded	8,973	8,960	9,595

Source: UN, *Monthly Bulletin of Statistics*.

CIVIL AVIATION (traffic on scheduled services)*

	1989	1990	1991
Kilometres flown (million)	26	31	34
Passengers carried ('000)	1,482	1,686	2,042
Passenger-km (million)	3,351	3,876	4,861
Freight ton-km (million)	118	145	184

* Figures include an apportionment (one-quarter) of the traffic of Gulf Air, a multinational airline with its headquarters in Bahrain.

Source: UN, *Statistical Yearbook*.

Communications Media

	1989	1990	1991
Radio receivers ('000 in use)	490	515	530
Television receivers ('000 in use)	165	175	175
Book production:			
Titles*	152	281	n.a.
Copies ('000)*	2,815	4,423	n.a.

* Data refer only to school textbooks.

Daily newspapers: 10 (combined circulation 300,000 copies) in 1988; 8 in 1989; 8 (250,000 copies) in 1990.

Source: UNESCO, *Statistical Yearbook*.

Telephones ('000 in use): 655 in 1990. Source: UN, *Statistical Yearbook*.

Education

(1991/92)

		Students		
	Teachers	Males	Females	Total
Pre-primary	2,374	25,585	23,479	49,064
Primary	13,139	120,362	111,312	231,674
Secondary				
General	}9,430 {	57,364	59,754	117,118
Vocational		893	—	893
University	728	1,947	6,721	8,668
Other higher	354	627	1,110	1,737

Source: UNESCO, *Statistical Yearbook*.

Directory

The Constitution

A provisional Constitution for the UAE took effect in December 1971. This laid the foundation for the federal structure of the Union of the seven emirates, previously known as the Trucial States.

The highest federal authority is the Supreme Council of Rulers, which comprises the rulers of the seven emirates. It elects the President and Vice-President from among its members. The President appoints a Prime Minister and a Council of Ministers. Proposals submitted to the Council require the approval of at least five of the Rulers, including those of Abu Dhabi and Dubai. The legislature is the Federal National Council, a consultative assembly comprising 40 members appointed by the emirates for a two-year term.

In July 1975 a committee was appointed to draft a permanent federal constitution, but the National Council decided in 1976 to extend the provisional document for five years. The provisional Constitution was extended for another five years in December 1981, and for further periods of five years in 1986 and 1991. In November 1976, however, the Supreme Council amended Article 142 of the provisional Constitution so that the authority to levy armed forces was placed exclusively under the control of the Federal Government.

The Government

HEAD OF STATE

President: Sheikh ZAYED BIN SULTAN AN-NAHYAN, Ruler of Abu Dhabi (took office as President of the UAE on 2 December 1971; re-elected 1976, 1981 and 1991).

Vice-President: Sheikh MAKTOUM BIN RASHID AL-MAKTOUM, Ruler of Dubai.

SUPREME COUNCIL OF RULERS
(with each Ruler's date of accession)

Ruler of Abu Dhabi: Sheikh ZAYED BIN SULTAN AN-NAHYAN (1966).

Ruler of Dubai: Sheikh MAKTOUM BIN RASHID AL-MAKTOUM (1990).

Ruler of Sharjah: Sheikh SULTAN BIN MUHAMMAD AL-QASIMI (1972).

Ruler of Ras al-Khaimah: Sheikh SAQR BIN MUHAMMAD AL-QASIMI (1948).

Ruler of Umm al-Qaiwain: Sheikh RASHID BIN AHMAD AL-MU'ALLA (1981).

Ruler of Ajman: Sheikh HUMAID BIN RASHID AN-NUAIMI (1981).

Ruler of Fujairah: Sheikh HAMAD BIN MUHAMMAD ASH-SHARQI (1974).

COUNCIL OF MINISTERS
(October 1994)

Prime Minister: Sheikh MAKTOUM BIN RASHID AL-MAKTOUM.

Deputy Prime Minister: Sheikh SULTAN BIN ZAYED AN-NAHYAN.

Minister of the Interior: Lt-Gen. MUHAMMAD SAID AL-BADI.

Minister of Foreign Affairs: RASHID ABDULLAH AN-NUAIMI.

Minister of Finance and Industry: Sheikh HAMDAN BIN RASHID AL-MAKTOUM.

Minister of Defence: Sheikh MUHAMMAD BIN RASHID AL-MAKTOUM.

Minister of Economy and Commerce: SAID GHOBASH.

Minister of Information and Culture: KHALFAN BIN MUHAMMAD AR-ROUMI.

Minister of Communications: MUHAMMAD SAID AL-MU'ALLA.

Minister of Public Works and Housing: RAKAD BIN SALEM BIN RAKAD.

Minister of Higher Education: Sheikh NAHYAN BIN MUBARAK AN-NAHYAN.

Minister of Education: HAMAD ABD AR-RAHMAN AL-MADFA.

Minister of Electricity and Water: HUMAID NASSER AL-OWAIS.

Minister of Health and Acting Minister of Petroleum and Mineral Resources: AHMAD BIN SAID AL-BADI.

Minister of Labour and Social Affairs: SAIF AL-JARWAN.

Minister of Planning: Sheikh HUMAID BIN AHMAD AL-MU'ALLA.

Minister of Agriculture and Fisheries: SAID MUHAMMAD AR-RAQABANI.

Minister of Youth and Sports: Sheikh FAISAL BIN KHALED BIN MUHAMMAD AL-QASIMI.

Minister of Justice: Dr ABDULLAH BIN OMRAN TARYAM.

Minister of Islamic Affairs and Awqaf (Religious Endowments): Sheikh MUHAMMAD BIN HASSAN AL-KHAZRAJI.

Minister of State for Affairs of the Council of Ministers: SAID AL-GHAITH.

Minister of State for Supreme Council Affairs: Sheikh MUHAMMAD BIN SAQR BIN MUHAMMAD AL-QASIMI.

FEDERAL MINISTRIES

Office of the Prime Minister: POB 899, Abu Dhabi; tel. (2) 361555; telex 23245.

Office of the Deputy Prime Minister: POB 831, Abu Dhabi; tel. (2) 651881.

Ministry of Agriculture and Fisheries: POB 213, Abu Dhabi; tel. (2) 662781.

Ministry of Communications: POB 900, Abu Dhabi; tel. (2) 651900; telex 22668; fax (2) 668675.

Ministry of Defence: POB 2838, Dubai; tel. (4) 532330; telex 45554; fax (4) 531406.

Ministry of Economy and Commerce: POB 901, Abu Dhabi; tel. (2) 215455; telex 22897; fax (2) 215339.

Ministry of Education: POB 295, Abu Dhabi; tel. (2) 213800; telex 22581.

Ministry of Electricity and Water: POB 629, Abu Dhabi; tel. (2) 344030; telex 46453; fax (2) 213738.

Ministry of Finance and Industry: POB 433, Abu Dhabi; tel. (2) 726000; telex 22937; fax (2) 773301.

Ministry of Foreign Affairs: POB 1, Abu Dhabi; tel. (2) 652200; telex 22217; fax (2) 668015.

Ministry of Health: POB 848, Abu Dhabi; tel. (2) 214100; telex 22678; fax (2) 215422.

Ministry of Information and Culture: POB 17, Abu Dhabi; tel. (2) 453000; fax (2) 451155.

Ministry of the Interior: POB 398, Abu Dhabi; tel. (2) 447666; telex 22398; fax (2) 461621.

Ministry of Islamic Affairs and Awqaf (Religious Endowments): POB 2272, Abu Dhabi; tel. (2) 212300; fax (2) 316003.

Ministry of Justice: POB 753, Abu Dhabi; tel. (2) 652224.

Ministry of Labour and Social Affairs: POB 809, Abu Dhabi; tel. (2) 651890; fax (2) 665889.

Ministry of Petroleum and Mineral Resources: POB 59, Abu Dhabi; tel. (2) 651810; telex 22544; fax (2) 663414.

Ministry of Planning: POB 904, Abu Dhabi; tel. (2) 211699; telex 22920.

Ministry of Public Works and Housing: POB 878, Abu Dhabi; tel. (2) 651778; telex 23833.

Ministry of State for Affairs of the Council of Ministers: POB 899, Abu Dhabi; tel. (2) 651113; telex 23245.

Ministry of State for Supreme Council Affairs: POB 545, Abu Dhabi; tel. (2) 343921.

Legislature

FEDERAL NATIONAL COUNCIL

Formed under the provisional Constitution, the Council is composed of 40 members from the various emirates (8 each from Abu Dhabi and Dubai, 6 each from Sharjah and Ras al-Khaimah, and 4 each from Ajman, Fujairah and Umm al-Qaiwain). Each emirate appoints its own representatives separately. The Council studies laws proposed by the Council of Ministers and can reject them or suggest amendments.

Speaker: HILAL BIN AHMAD LOOTAH.

Diplomatic Representation

EMBASSIES IN THE UNITED ARAB EMIRATES

Algeria: POB 3070, Abu Dhabi; tel. (2) 448943; telex 23414; Ambassador: MUHAMMAD MELLOUH.

Argentina: POB 3325, Abu Dhabi; tel. (2) 216838; telex 23998; Ambassador: ALBERTO ADEN.

Austria: POB 3095, Abu Dhabi; tel. (2) 324103; telex 22675; Ambassador: MARIUS CALLIGARIS.

Bangladesh: POB 2504, Abu Dhabi; tel. (2) 668375; telex 22201; Ambassador: ZIA-US-SHAMS CHOWDHURY.

Belgium: POB 3686, Abu Dhabi; tel. (2) 319449; telex 22860; fax (2) 319353; Ambassador: CLAUDE MISSON.

Brazil: POB 3027, Abu Dhabi; tel. (2) 665352; fax (2) 654559; Ambassador: JOSÉ FERREIRA-LOPES.

China, People's Republic: POB 2741, Abu Dhabi; tel. (2) 211174; telex 23928; Ambassador: LIU BAOLAI.

Croatia: POB 41227, Abu Dhabi; tel. (2) 311700; fax (2) 338366; Ambassador: VANJA KALOGJERA.

Czech Republic: POB 27009, Abu Dhabi; tel. (2) 312800; fax (2) 316567; Chargé d'affaires: JOSEF BUZALKA.

Denmark: POB 46666, Abu Dhabi; tel. (2) 325900; telex 23677; fax (2) 351690; Ambassador: BENT KIILERICH.

Egypt: POB 4026, Abu Dhabi; tel. (2) 445566; telex 22258; Ambassador: BAHAA ELDIN MOSTAFA REDA.

Eritrea: POB 2597, Abu Dhabi; tel. (2) 318388; fax (2) 346451; Ambassador: MOHAMED OMAR MAHMOUD.

Finland: POB 3634, Abu Dhabi; tel. (2) 328927; telex 23161; fax (2) 325063; Chargé d'affaires: CAJ SÖDERLUND.

France: POB 4014, Abu Dhabi; tel. (2) 435100; telex 22325; fax (2) 434158; Ambassador: JEAN-PAUL BARRE.

Germany: POB 2591, Abu Dhabi; tel. (2) 331630; telex 22202; fax (2) 323625; Ambassador: UWE SCHRAMM.

Greece: POB 5483, Abu Dhabi; tel. (2) 316818; telex 24383; fax (2) 316815; Ambassador: SPYRIDON MORMORIS.

Hungary: POB 44450, Abu Dhabi; tel. (2) 660107; telex 22322; fax (2) 667877; Chargé d'affaires a.i.: CSABA KORÖSI.

India: POB 4090, Abu Dhabi; tel. (2) 337700; telex 22620; fax (2) 322403; Ambassador: MUTHAL MENON.

Indonesia: POB 7256, Abu Dhabi; tel. (2) 669233; telex 22253; fax (2) 653932; Chargé d'affaires: ABD FUAD RACHMAN.

Iran: POB 4080, Abu Dhabi; tel. (2) 447618; telex 22344; Ambassador: HASSAN AMINIAN.

Iraq: POB 4030, Abu Dhabi; tel. (2) 669900; telex 22367; Ambassador: TAHA RAJAB URIEM.

Italy: POB 46752, Abu Dhabi; tel. (2) 215622; telex 23861; Ambassador: GIOVANNI FERRERO.

Japan: POB 2430, Abu Dhabi; tel. (2) 344696; telex 22270; Ambassador: SHIN WATANABE.

Jordan: POB 4024, Abu Dhabi; tel. (2) 447100; telex 24411; Ambassador: AWADH M. ABU OBEID.

Kenya: POB 3854, Abu Dhabi; tel. (2) 666300; telex 24244; Ambassador: MUDE DAE MUDE.

Korea: POB 3270, Abu Dhabi; tel. (2) 435337; telex 24237; fax (2) 435348; Ambassador: JUNG HO-KEUM.

Kuwait: POB 926, Abu Dhabi; tel. (2) 446888; telex 22804; fax (2) 444990; Ambassador: IBRAHIM AL-MANSOUR.

Lebanon: POB 4023, Abu Dhabi; tel. (2) 323863; telex 22206; Ambassador: GEORGE SIAM.

Libya: POB 2091, Abu Dhabi; tel. (2) 342749; Ambassador: MOHAMED FETORI.

Malaysia: POB 3887, Abu Dhabi; tel. (2) 656698; telex 22630; fax (2) 656697; Chargé d'affaires: SYED SULTAN IDRIS.

Mauritania: POB 2714, Abu Dhabi; tel. (2) 462724; telex 22512; fax (2) 465772; Ambassador: TELMIDI OULD MOHAMED AMMAR.

Morocco: POB 4066, Abu Dhabi; tel. (2) 345863; telex 22549; fax (2) 313158; Ambassador: ABD EL-MANSOUR.

Netherlands: POB 46560, Abu Dhabi; tel. (2) 321920; telex 23610; Ambassador: RONALD MOLLINGER.

Oman: Al-Muharba Al-Jadid Al-Khaleej St, Villa 674, Abu Dhabi; tel. (2) 463333; fax (2) 464633; Ambassador: SULTAN AL-BUSAIDI.

Pakistan: POB 846, Abu Dhabi; tel. (2) 447800; telex 23003; Chargé d'affaires: ABDUL SOOMRO.

Philippines: POB 3215, Abu Dhabi; tel. (2) 345664; telex 23995; Ambassador: FORTUNATO OBLENA.

Poland: Room 202, Khalidia Palace Hotel, Abu Dhabi; tel. 663470; Chargé d'affaires: ANDRZEJ KAPISZEWSKI.

Qatar: Sudan St, Al-Minaseer, POB 3503, Abu Dhabi; tel. (2) 338900; telex 22664; Ambassador: ABDULLAH FAKHROO.

Romania: POB 70416, Abu Dhabi; tel. (2) 666346; telex 23546; Ambassador: NICOLAE VIRGIL IRIMIE.

Russia: POB 8211, Abu Dhabi; tel. (2) 721797; Ambassador: OLEG DERKOVSKY.

Saudi Arabia: POB 4057, Abu Dhabi; tel. (2) 665700; telex 22670; Ambassador: SALEH MOHAMMED AL-GHUFAILI

Slovakia: POB 3383, Abu Dhabi; tel. (2) 321674; fax (2) 315839; Chargé d'affaires: DUSAN HORNIAK.

Somalia: POB 4155, Abu Dhabi; tel. (2) 323800; telex 22624; Ambassador: HUSSEIN MOHAMMED BULLALEH.

Spain: POB 46474, Abu Dhabi; tel. (2) 213544; telex 23340; Ambassador: JAVIER NAVARRO.

Sri Lanka: POB 46534, Abu Dhabi; tel. (2) 666688; telex 23333; fax (2) 667921; Ambassador: MUHAMMAD JAMEEL.

Sudan: POB 4027, Abu Dhabi; tel. (2) 772750; telex 22706; Chargé d'affaires: MOHIEDDIN SLAIM AHMED.

Switzerland: POB 46116, Abu Dhabi; tel. (2) 343636; telex 22824; fax (2) 216127; Chargé d'affaires: EMANUEL DUBS.

Syria: POB 4011, Abu Dhabi; tel. (2) 448768; telex 22729; fax (2) 449387; Ambassador: MUSTAFA OMRAN.

Tunisia: POB 4166, Abu Dhabi; tel. (2) 661331; telex 22370; Ambassador: ABDELKRIM MOUSSA.

Turkey: POB 3204, Abu Dhabi; tel. (2) 463372; telex 23037; Ambassador: ALI ARSIN.

Ukraine: POB 45714; Abu Dhabi; tel. (2) 327585; fax (2) 327506; Chargé d'affaires: OLEH SEMENETS.

United Kingdom: POB 248, Abu Dhabi; tel. (2) 326600; telex 22234; fax (2) 341744; Ambassador: ANTHONY DAVID HARRIS.

USA: POB 4009, Abu Dhabi; tel. (2) 436691; fax (2) 435441; Ambassador: WILLIAM A. RUGH.

Yemen: POB 2095, Abu Dhabi; tel. (2) 448454; telex 23600; Ambassador: MUHAMMAD HATEM AL-KHAWI.

Judicial System

The 95th article of the provisional Constitution of 1971 provided for the establishment of the Union Supreme Court and Union Primary Tribunals as the judicial organs of State.

The Union has exclusive legislative and executive jurisdiction over all matters that are concerned with the strengthening of the federation such as foreign affairs, defence and Union armed forces, security, finance, communications, traffic control, education, currency, measures, standards and weights, matters relating to nationality and emigration, Union information, etc.

President Sheikh Zayed signed the law establishing the new federal courts on 9 June 1978. The new law effectively transferred local judicial authorities into the jurisdiction of the federal system.

Primary tribunals in Abu Dhabi, Sharjah, Ajman and Fujairah are now primary federal tribunals, and primary tribunals in other towns in those emirates have become circuits of the primary federal tribunals.

The primary federal tribunal may sit in any of the capitals of the four emirates and have jurisdiction on all administrative disputes between the Union and individuals, whether the Union is plaintiff or defendant. Civil disputes between Union and individuals will be heard by primary federal tribunals in the defendant's place of normal residence.

The law requires that all judges take a constitutional oath before the Minister of Justice and that the courts apply the rules of *Shari'a* (Islamic religious law) and that no judgment contradicts the *Shari'a*. All employees of the old judiciaries will be transferred to the federal authority without loss of salary or seniority.

In February 1994 President Sheikh Zayed ordered that an extensive range of crimes, including murder, theft and adultery, be tried in *Shari'a* courts rather than in civil courts.

Chief Shari'a Justice: AHMAD ABD AL-AZIZ AL-MUBARAK.

Religion

ISLAM

Most of the inhabitants are Muslims of the Sunni sect. About 16% of the Muslims are Shi'ites.

CHRISTIANITY

Roman Catholic Church

Apostolic Vicariate of Arabia: POB 54, Abu Dhabi; tel. (2) 461895; fax (2) 465177; responsible for a territory covering most of the Arabian peninsula (including Saudi Arabia, the UAE and Yemen), containing an estimated 750,000 Catholics (31 December 1992); Vicar Apostolic Fr GIOVANNI BERNARDO GREMOLI, Titular Bishop of Masuccaba.

The Anglican Communion

Within the Episcopal Church in Jerusalem and the Middle East, the UAE forms part of the diocese of Cyprus and the Gulf. The

Anglican congregations in the UAE are entirely expatriate. The Bishop in Cyprus and the Gulf resides in Cyprus.

Archdeacon in the Gulf: Ven. MICHAEL MANSBRIDGE, St Andrew's Church, POB 262, Abu Dhabi; tel. (2) 461631; fax (2) 465869.

The Press

The Ministry of Information and Culture has placed a moratorium on new titles.

Abu Dhabi

Abu Dhabi Chamber of Commerce Review: POB 662, Abu Dhabi; tel. (2) 214000; telex 22449; f. 1969; Arabic, some articles in English; monthly; circ. 16,500.

Adh-Dhafra: POB 4288, Abu Dhabi; tel. (2) 328103; Arabic; weekly; independent; publ. by Dar al-Wahdah.

Emirates News: POB 791, Abu Dhabi; tel. (2) 451446; telex 22763; fax (2) 453662; f. 1975; English; daily; publ. by Al-Ittihad Press, Publishing and Distribution Corpn; Chair. KHALFAN BIN MUHAMMAD AR-ROUMI; Man. Editor PETER HELLYER; circ. 15,000.

Al-Fajr (The Dawn): POB 505, Abu Dhabi; tel. (2) 478300; telex 22834; fax (2) 478436; Arabic; daily; circ. 23,800.

Hiya (She): POB 2488, Abu Dhabi; tel. (2) 478400; Arabic weekly for women; publ. by Dar al-Wahdah.

Al-Ittihad (Unity): POB 17, Abu Dhabi; tel. (2) 461600; telex 22984; f. 1972; Arabic; daily and weekly; publ. by Al-Ittihad Press, Publishing and Distribution Corpn; Editor-in-Chief ABDULLAH AN-NOWAIS; circ. 58,000 daily, 60,000 weekly.

Khaleej Times: POB 3082, Abu Dhabi; tel. 336000; telex 23872; fax 336424; daily; circ 60,000.

Majed: POB 3558, Abu Dhabi; tel. (2) 451804; telex 22984; fax (2) 451455; Arabic; weekly; children's magazine; Man. Editor AHMAD OMAR; circ. 160,000.

Ar-Riyada wa-Shabab (Sport and Youth): POB 4230, Abu Dhabi; Arabic; weekly; general interest.

UAE and Abu Dhabi Official Gazette: POB 899, Abu Dhabi; Arabic; official reports and papers.

UAE Press Service Daily News: POB 2035, Abu Dhabi; tel. (2) 44292; f. 1973; English; daily; Editor RASHID AL-MAZROUI.

Al-Wahdah (Unity): POB 2488, Abu Dhabi; tel. (2) 478400; f. 1973; daily; independent; Man. Editor RASHID AWEIDHA; Gen. Man. KHALIFA AL-MASHWI; circ. 10,000.

Zahrat al-Khaleej (Splendour of the Gulf): POB 3342, Abu Dhabi; tel. (2) 455555; fax (2) 451481; f. 1979; Arabic; weekly; women's magazine; circ. 100,000.

Dubai

Akhbar Dubai (Dubai News): Department of Information, Dubai Municipality, POB 1420, Dubai; f. 1965; Arabic; weekly.

Al-Bayan (The Official Report): POB 2710, Dubai; tel. (4) 444400; telex 47707; fax (4) 445973; f. 1980; owned by Dubai authorities; Arabic; daily; Editor-in-Chief Sheikh HASHER MAKTOUM; circ. 44,950.

Dubai Annual Trade Review: POB 516, Dubai; tel. (4) 531076; telex 47470; fax (4) 531959; English.

Gulf News: POB 6519, Dubai; tel. (4) 447100; telex 47030; fax (4) 441627; f. 1978; An-Nisr Publishing; English; daily; two weekly supplements, *Junior News* (Wednesday), *Gulf Weekly* (Thursday); Editor-in-Chief OBAID HUMAID AT-TAYER; circ. 79,250.

Al-Jundi (The Soldier): POB 2838, Dubai; tel. (4) 451516; telex 4554; fax (4) 455033; f. 1973; Arabic; monthly; military and cultural; Editor ISMAIL KHAMIS MUBARAK.

Khaleej Times: POB 11243; Dubai; tel. (4) 382400; telex 48620; fax (4) 383676; f. 1978; a Galadari enterprise; English; daily; free weekly supplement, *Weekend* (Friday); Exec. Editor KHALID A. H. ANSARI; Editor S. NIHAL SINGH; circ. 70,000.

Trade and Industry: POB 1457, Dubai; tel. (4) 221181; telex 45997; fax (4) 211646; f. 1975; Arabic and English; monthly; publ. by Dubai Chamber of Commerce and Industry; circ. 17,500.

What's On: POB 2331; tel. (4) 246060; telex 48366; fax (4) 245270; Motivate Publishing; English; monthly; circ. 22,000.

Ras al-Khaimah

Akhbar Ras al-Khaimah (Ras al-Khaimah News): POB 87, Ras al-Khaimah; Arabic; monthly; general interest.

Ras al-Khaimah Chamber of Commerce Magazine: POB 87, Ras al-Khaimah; f. 1970; Arabic and English; free monthly; Editor ZAKI H. SAQR.

Ras al-Khaimah Magazine: POB 200, Ras al-Khaimah; Arabic; monthly; commerce and trade; Chief Editor AHMAD AT-TADMORI.

Sharjah

Al-Azman al-Arabia (Times of Arabia): POB 5823, Sharjah; tel. 356034; telex 68674.

Al-Khaleej (The Gulf): POB 30, Sharjah; tel. (6) 598777; telex 68055; fax (6) 598547; f. 1970; Arabic; daily; political, independent; Dir-Gen. and Editor-in-Chief RASHID OMRAN TARYAM; circ. 60,000.

Sawt al-Khaleej (Voice of the Gulf): POB 1385, Sharjah; tel. 358003; telex 68551.

Ash-Sharooq (Sunrise): POB 30, Sharjah; f. 1970; Arabic; monthly; general interest; Editor YOUSUF AL-HASSAN.

At-Tijarah (Commerce): Sharjah Chamber of Commerce and Industry, POB 580, Sharjah; tel. (6) 541444; telex 68205; fax (6) 541119; f. 1970; Arabic/English; monthly magazine; circ. 50,000; annual trade directory; circ. 100,000.

UAE Digest: POB 6872, Sharjah; tel. (6) 354633; telex 68715; fax (6) 354627; English; monthly; publ. by Universal Publishing; commerce and finance; Man. Dir FARAJ YASSINE; circ. 10,000.

NEWS AGENCIES

Emirates News Agency (WAM): POB 3790, Abu Dhabi; tel. (2) 464600; telex 22979; f. 1977; operated by the Ministry of Information and Culture; Dir IBRAHIM AL-ABED.

United Arab Emirates Press Service: POB 2035, Abu Dhabi; tel. (2) 820424; telex 22353.

Foreign Bureaux

Agenzia Nazionale Stampa Associata (ANSA) (Italy): POB 44106, Abu Dhabi; tel. (2) 454545; telex 23823; Correspondent MUHAMMAD WADHA.

Inter Press Service (IPS) (Italy): Airport Rd, near the Radio and Television Bldg., Abu Dhabi; tel. (2) 464200; telex 23823; fax (2) 454846; Correspondent (vacant).

Reuters (UK): POB 7872, Abu Dhabi; tel. (2) 328000; telex 24145; fax (2) 333380; Man. JEREMY HARRIS.

Publishers

Al-Ittihad Press, Publishing and Distribution Corpn: POB 791, New Airport Rd, Abu Dhabi; tel. (2) 455555; telex 22984; fax (2) 454885; Chair. KHALFAN BIN MUHAMMAD AR-ROUMI.

All Prints: POB 857, Abu Dhabi; tel. (2) 338235; telex 22844; publishing and distribution; Partners BUSHRA KHAYAT, TAHSEEN S. KHAYAT.

Motivate Publishing: POB 2331, Dubai; tel. (4) 824060; telex 48366; fax (2) 824436; f. 1979; books and eight magazines; Dirs OBAID HUMAID AT-TAYER, IAN FAIRSERVICE.

Radio and Television

In 1991, according to estimates by UNESCO, there were 530,000 radio receivers and 175,000 television receivers in use. Television stations take advertisements, as do Capital Radio (Abu Dhabi) and Dubai Radio.

Abu Dhabi Radio: POB 63, Abu Dhabi; tel. (2) 451000; telex 22557; fax (2) 451155; f. 1968; stations in Abu Dhabi, Dubai, Umm al-Qaiwain and Ras al-Khaimah, all broadcasting in Arabic over a wide area; Abu Dhabi also broadcasts in English, French, Bengali, Filipino and Urdu, Dubai in English and Ras al-Khaimah in Urdu; Dir-Gen. ABD AL-WAHAB RADWAN.

Capital Radio: POB 63, Abu Dhabi; tel. (2) 451000; telex 22557; fax (2) 451155; English-language FM music and news station, operated by the Ministry of Information and Culture; Station Manager AHMAD A. SHOULY.

Dubai Radio and Colour Television: POB 1695, Dubai; tel. (4) 370255; telex 45605; broadcasts domestic Arabic and European programmes; Chair. Sheikh HASHER MAKTOUM; Dir-Gen. ABD AL-GHAFOOR SAID IBRAHIM.

Ras al-Khaimah Broadcasting Station: POB 141, Ras al-Khaimah; tel. (7) 51151; two transmitters broadcast in Arabic and Urdu; Dir Sheikh ABD AL-AZIZ BIN HUMAID.

Sharjah Broadcasting Station: POB 155, Sharjah; broadcasts in Arabic and French.

Umm al-Qaiwain Broadcasting Station: POB 444, Umm al-Qaiwain; tel. (6) 666044; fax (6) 666055; f. 1978; broadcasts music and news in Arabic, Sinhala and Urdu; Gen. Man. ALI JASSEM.

UAE Radio and Television—Dubai: POB 1695, Dubai; tel. (4) 370255; telex 45605; fax (4) 371079; broadcasts in Arabic and English to the USA, India and Pakistan, the Far East, Australia and New Zealand, Europe and North and East Africa; Chair. Sheikh HASHEM MAKTOUM; Dir-Gen. ABD AL-GHAFFOUR AS-SAID IBRAHIM.

UAE TV—Abu Dhabi: POB 637, Abu Dhabi; tel. (2) 452000; telex 22557; fax (2) 451470; f. 1968; broadcasts programmes incorporating information, entertainment, religion, culture, news and politics; Dir-Gen. ALI OBAID.

UAE Television—Sharjah: POB 111, Sharjah; tel. (6) 361111; telex 68599; fax (6) 541755; f. 1989; broadcasts in Arabic and Urdu in the northern emirates; Executive Dir MUHAMMAD DIAB AL-MUSA.

Finance

(cap. = capital; p.u. = paid up; dep. = deposits; res = reserves; m. = million; brs = branches; amounts in dirhams)

BANKING

In early 1994 the UAE's 19 domestic and 28 foreign banks had a combined local network of 326 branches, and Dh 155,000m. in assets.

Central Bank

Central Bank of the United Arab Emirates: POB 854, Abu Dhabi; tel. (2) 652220; telex 22330; fax (2) 668483; f. 1973; acts as issuing authority for local currency; superseded UAE Currency Board December 1980; authorized cap. 300m.; total assets 21,073.1m. (1992); Chair. MUHAMMAD EID AL-MURAIKHI; Gov. SULTAN NASSER AS-SUWAIDI.

Principal Banks

Abu Dhabi Commercial Bank (ADCB): POB 939, Abu Dhabi; tel. (2) 720000; telex 22244; fax (2) 776499; f. 1985 by merger; cap. p.u. 1,250m., dep. 11,527m., res 148m., total assets 13,033m. (Dec. 1993); 64% government-owned, 36% owned by private investors; Chair. Sheikh SUROOR BIN SULTAN ADH-DHAHERI; CEO and Man. Dir KHALIFA HASSAN; 29 brs in UAE, 1 br. overseas.

Arab Bank for Investment and Foreign Trade: POB 46733, Abu Dhabi; tel. (2) 721900; telex 22455; fax (2) 777550; f. 1976; jointly owned by the UAE Govt, the Libyan Arab Foreign Bank and the Banque Extérieure d'Algérie; cap. 570m., dep. 1,947.3m., res 79.6m., total assets 2,627.0m. (Dec. 1993); Chair. ABD AL-HAFID ZLITNI; Gen. Man. HADI M. GITELI; 2 brs in Abu Dhabi, and one each in Dubai and al-Ain.

Bank of the Arab Coast Ltd (BOAC): POB 5536, Maktoum St, Deira, Dubai; tel. (4) 223101; telex 46177; f. 1975; cap. 40m. (Dec. 1986); Chair. Sheikh SALEH AHMAD ASH-SHAL; Gen. Man. and Chief Exec. Officer HENRI P. DERKX; br. in Ras al-Khaimah.

Bank of Sharjah Ltd: POB 1394, Sharjah; tel. (6) 352111; telex 68039; fax (6) 350323; f. 1973; cap. 84.0m., dep. 666.6m., res 75.0m., total assets 845.7m. (1993); Chair. AHMAD AN-NOMAN; Gen. Man. VAROUJ NERGUIZIAN; br. in Abu Dhabi.

Commercial Bank of Dubai Ltd: POB 2668, Deira, Dubai; tel. (4) 523355; telex 49600; fax (4) 520444; f. 1969; cap. 220m., dep. 1,947.4m., res 157.9m., total assets 2,380.4m. (Dec. 1993); Chair. AHMAD HUMAID AT-TAYER; Sr Chief Exec. and Gen. Man. OMAR ABD AR-RAHIM LEYAS; 9 brs.

Dubai Islamic Bank PLC: POB 1080, Deira, Dubai; tel. (4) 214888; telex 45889; fax (4) 237243; f. 1975; cap. 200m., dep. 4,174.4m., res 63.8m., total assets 4,878.9m. (1992); Chair. and Man. Dir SAID AHMAD LOOTAH; 2 brs.

Emirates Bank International Ltd (EBI): POB 2923, Dubai; tel. (4) 256256; telex 46426; fax (4) 268005; f. 1977 by merger; the Govt of Dubai has an 80% share; cap. 450.2m., dep. 10,526.7m., res 934.6m., total assets 11,911.5m. (Dec. 1993); Chair. AHMAD HUMAID AT-TAYER; Gen. Man. DAVID BERRY; 9 brs in the UAE, 11 brs overseas.

First Gulf Bank: Al-Ittihad St, POB 414, Ajman; tel. (6) 423450; telex 69510; fax (6) 446503; f. 1979; cap. 120.0m., dep. 313.1m., res 88.2m., total assets 521.3m. (Dec. 1990); Chair. RASHID OWEIDAH; brs in Abu Dhabi and Sharjah.

Investment Bank for Trade and Finance PLC (INVESTBANK): Al-Borj Ave, POB 1885, Sharjah; tel. (6) 355391; telex 68083; fax (6) 546683; f. 1975; cap. 135.5m., dep. 1,426.1m., res 26.6m., total assets 1,588.2m. (Dec. 1993); Chair. Sheikh SAQR BIN MUHAMMAD AL-QASIMI; Gen. Man. AFIF N. SHEHADEH; brs in Abu Dhabi, Dubai and al-Ain.

Mashreq Bank Ltd: POB 1250, Deira, Dubai; tel. (4) 229131; telex 45429; fax (4) 226061; f. 1967 as Bank of Oman; cap. 516.5m., dep. 9,196.4m., res 620.9m., total assets 11,035.4m. (1993); Chair. SAIF AHMAD AL-GHURAIR; Pres. ABDULLAH AHMAD AL-GHURAIR; 25 brs in UAE; 13 brs overseas.

Middle East Bank Ltd: POB 5547, Deira, Dubai; tel. (4) 256256; telex 46074; fax (4) 255322; f. 1976; controlling interest held by EBI; cap. and res 258.0m., total assets 3,820.9m. (1989); Chair. AHMAD HUMAID AT-TAYER; Chief Gen. Man. IBRAHIM TAHLAK; 10 brs in UAE, 4 brs overseas.

National Bank of Abu Dhabi (NBAD): POB 4, Abu Dhabi; tel. (2) 335262; telex 22266/7; fax (2) 336078; f. 1968; owned jointly by Abu Dhabi Investment Authority and UAE citizens; cap. 941.6m., dep. 20,690.8m., res. 893.0m., total assets 23,016.8m. (Dec. 1993); Chair. Sheikh MUHAMMAD HABROUSH AS-SUWAIDI; CEO JOHN S. W. COOMBS; 37 brs in UAE, 10 brs overseas.

National Bank of Dubai Ltd: POB 777, Dubai; tel. (4) 267000; telex 45421; fax (4) 268939; f. 1963; cap. 861.8m., dep. 19,638.6m., res 2,630.9m., total assets 23,176.9m. (Dec. 1993); Chair. SULTAN ALI AL-OWAIS; Gen. Man. D. F. MCKENZIE; 17 brs, 3 overseas.

National Bank of Fujairah: POB 887, Fujairah; tel. (9) 224518; telex 89050; fax (9) 224516; f. 1982; cap. and res 183.5m., dep. 667.5m., total assets 936.4m. (1993); owned jointly by Govt of Fujairah (43.4%), Govt of Dubai (19.56%), and UAE citizens and cos (37.04%); Chair. Sheikh SALEH BIN MUHAMMAD ASH-SHARQI; Gen. Man. MICHAEL J. CONNOR; brs in Abu Dhabi, Dubai, Fujairah and Dibba.

National Bank of Ras al-Khaimah PSC: POB 5300, Ras al-Khaimah; tel. (7) 221127; telex 99109; fax (7) 223238; f. 1976; cap. 129.8m., dep. 956.9m., res 67.9., total assets 1,200.2m. (Dec. 1993); Chair. Sheikh KHALID BIN SAQR AL-QASIMI; Gen. Man. J. R. G. PARSONS; 7 brs.

National Bank of Sharjah: POB 4, Sharjah; tel. (6) 547745; telex 68085; fax (6) 543483; f. 1976; commercial bank; cap. p.u. 260m., dep. 2,297.3m., res 142.5m., total assets 4,538.5m. (1988); Chair. AHMAD AN-NOMAN; CEO and Gen. Man. GORDON D. ABERNETHY; 8 brs.

National Bank of Umm al-Qaiwain Ltd: POB 800, Umm al-Qaiwain; tel. (6) 655225; telex 69733; fax (6) 655440; f. 1982; cap. 250.0m., dep. 617.9m., res 74.8m., total assets 1,011.9m. (1993); Chair. Sheikh SAUD BIN RASHID AL-MU'ALLA; Man. Dir and CEO Sheikh NASSER BIN RASHID AL-MU'ALLA; 8 brs.

Union National Bank: POB 3865, Abu Dhabi; tel. (2) 321600; telex 23693; fax (2) 320986; f. 1982; formerly Bank of Credit and Commerce (Emirates); cap. p.u. 352m., total assets 6,222.7m. (1989); Chair. Sheikh NAHYAN BIN MUBARAK AN-NAHYAN; CEO and Man. Dir ZAFAR IQBAL; Gen. Man. BASHIR TAHIR; 7 brs in Abu Dhabi, 4 brs in Dubai, and one each in al-Ain, Sharjah, Ras al-Khaimah and Fujairah.

United Arab Bank: POB 3562, Abu Dhabi; tel. (2) 325000; telex 22759; fax (2) 338361; f. 1975; cap. 90.0m., dep. 937.5m., res 46.1m., total assets 1,094.8m. (1992); affiliated to Société Générale, France; Chair. Sheikh FAISAL BIN SULTAN AL-QASIMI; Gen. Man. J. P. NEDELEC; 7 brs.

Foreign Banks

ABN AMRO Bank NV (Netherlands): Faraj Bin Hamoodah Bldg, Sheikh Hamdan St, POB 2720, Abu Dhabi; tel. (2) 335400; telex 22401; fax (2) 330182; f. 1974; POB 2567, Deira, Dubai; tel. (4) 512200; POB 1971, Sharjah; tel. (6) 355021; Man. (Abu Dhabi) M.P.T. KLEIN.

ANZ Grindlays Bank PLC (UK): POB 241, Abu Dhabi; tel. (2) 330876; telex 22252; fax (2) 331767; POB 357, Sharjah; tel. (6) 359998; telex 68011; fax (6) 357046; telex 45618; fax 222018; POB 1100, al-Ain; tel. (3) 643400; telex 33531; fax (3) 645121; Gen. Man. ALAN COOPER.

Arab Bank Ltd (Jordan): POB 875, Abu Dhabi; tel. (2) 334111; telex 24195; fax (2) 336433; f. 1970; POB 1650, Dubai; POB 130, Sharjah; POB 4971, Ras al-Khaimah; POB 300, Fujairah; POB 17, Ajman; Man. FATHI M. SKAIK; 8 local brs.

Arab-African International Bank (Egypt): POB 1049, Dubai; tel. (4) 223131; telex 45503; fax (4) 222257; f. 1970; POB 928, Abu Dhabi; tel. (2) 323400; telex 22587; fax 216009; f. 1976; Chair. Dr FAHD AR-RASHID; Deputy Chair. and Man. Dir MUHAMMAD FARID.

Bank of Baroda (India): POB 2303, Abu Dhabi; tel. (2) 330244; telex 22391; fax (2) 335293; f. 1974; Sr Vice-Pres. J.K. SHAH; also brs in Deira (Dubai), Sharjah and Ras al-Khaimah.

Bank Melli Iran: Regional Office and Main Branch, POB 1894, Dubai; tel. (4) 268207; telex 46404; fax (4) 269157; f. 1969; Regional Dir AZIZ AZIMINOBAR; brs in Dubai, Abu Dhabi, al-Ain, Sharjah, Fujairah and Ras al-Khaimah.

Bank Saderat Iran: POB 700, Abu Dhabi; tel. (2) 335155; telex 45456; fax (2) 325062; POB 4182, Dubai; also Sharjah, Ajman, Ras al-Khaimah, Fujairah and al-Ain; Man. NASER RAFAATI.

Banque Banorabe (France): POB 4370, Dubai; tel. (4) 284655; telex 45801; fax (4) 236260; f. 1974; fmrly Banque de l'Orient Arabe et d'Outre Mer; Chair. and Gen. Man. Dr NAAMAN AZHARI; UAE Regional Man. BASSEM M. AL-ARISS.

Banque du Caire (Egypt): POB 533, Abu Dhabi; tel. (2) 328700; telex 22304; fax (2) 323881; POB 1502, Dubai; POB 254, Sharjah; POB 618, Ras al-Khaimah; Gulf Regional Man. FOUAD ABD AL-KHALEK TAHOON.

Banque Indosuez (France): POB 9256, Dubai; tel. (4) 314211; telex 45860; fax (4) 313201; f. 1975; POB 46786, Abu Dhabi; tel. (2) 338400; telex 22464; fax 338581; f. 1981; UAE Regional Man. ALAIN DE TRUCHIS.

Banque Libanaise pour le Commerce SA (France): POB 4207, Dubai; tel. (4) 222291; telex 45671; fax (4) 279861; POB 854, Sharjah; POB 3771, Abu Dhabi; tel. (2) 320920; telex 22862; fax (2) 213851; POB 771, Ras al-Khaimah; UEA Regional Man. JEAN MAHER.
ANTOINE B. DIAB.

Banque Paribas (France): POB 2742, Abu Dhabi; tel. (2) 335560; telex 22331; fax (2) 215138; POB 7233, Dubai; tel. (4) 525929; telex 45755; fax (4) 521341; Gen. Man. (Abu Dhabi) PIERRE IMHOF; Gen. Man. (Dubai) GEORGES TABET.

Barclays Bank PLC (UK): POB 2734, Abu Dhabi; tel. (2) 335313; telex 22456; fax (2) 345815; POB 1891, Deira, Dubai; tel. (4) 226158; telex 45829; fax (4) 282788; POB 1953, Sharjah; tel. (6) 355288; telex 68100; fax (6) 543498; Man. M.J.McQAID (Dubai).

British Bank of the Middle East (BBME) (Hong Kong): POB 242, Abu Dhabi; tel. (2) 332200; telex 22231; fax (2) 331564; f. 1946; total assets 5,800.6m. (1991); CEO DAVID HOWELLS; Deputy CEO ABD AL-JALIL YOUSUF; 8 brs throughout UAE.

Citibank NA (USA): POB 749, Dubai; tel. (4) 522100; telex 45422; fax (4) 524942; f. 1963; POB 346, Sharjah; POB 999, Abu Dhabi; POB 294, Ras al-Khaimah; POB 1430, al-Ain; total assets 1,372.1m. (1988); Man. S. CRABTREE.

First Interstate Bank of California (USA): POB 46643, Abu Dhabi; tel. (2) 321897; telex 23496; fax 330209; Vice-Pres. OSMAN MORAD.

First National Bank of Chicago (USA): POB 1655, Dubai; tel. (4) 226161; telex 45633; Vice-Pres. and Gen. Man. RICHARD L. KOLEHMAINEN.

Habib Bank AG Zürich (Switzerland): POB 2681, Abu Dhabi; tel. (2) 329157; telex 22205; fax (2) 351822; f. 1974; POB 1166, Sharjah; POB 3306, Dubai; POB 168, Ajman; POB 181, Umm al-Qaiwain; POB 767, Ras al-Khaimah; Joint Pres. H. M. HABIB; Vice-Pres. HATIM HUSAIN.

Habib Bank Ltd (Pakistan): POB 888, Dubai; tel. (4) 268514; telex 45430; fax (4) 267493; f. 1967; POB 897, Abu Dhabi; tel. (2) 325665; telex 22332; f. 1975; Vice-Pres. and Chief Man. (Dubai) MOHAMMAD A. BAQAR; Vice-Pres. and Chief Man. (Abu Dhabi) IZHAR JUNEJO; 6 other brs in UAE.

Janata Bank (Bangladesh): POB 2630, Abu Dhabi; tel. (2) 331400; telex 22402; POB 3342, Dubai; CEO and Gen. Man. MUHAMMAD RUHUL AMIN; Man. K. M. SHAFIQUR RAHMAN; brs in al-Ain, Dubai and Sharjah.

Lloyds Bank PLC (UK): POB 3766, Dubai; tel. (4) 313005; telex 46450; fax (4) 375026; f. 1977; dep. 284.5m., total assets 895.7m. (1988); Regional Man. CHARLES J. NEIL.

National Bank of Oman SAOG: POB 3822, Abu Dhabi; tel. (2) 339543; telex 22866; fax (2) 216153; Man. MIRAJUDDIN AZIZ.

Nilein Industrial Development Bank (Sudan): POB 6013, Abu Dhabi; telex 22884; Man. ABDULLAH MAHMOUD AWAD.

Rafidain Bank (Iraq): POB 2727, Abu Dhabi; telex 22522; f. 1978; Man. ADNAN R. KASAB BASHI.

Royal Bank of Canada: POB 3614, Dubai; tel. (4) 225226; telex 45926; fax 215687; f. 1976; Man. GLENN S. KLEIN.

Standard Chartered PLC (UK): POB 240, Abu Dhabi; tel. (2) 330077; telex 22274; fax (2) 341511; POB 999, Dubai; tel. (4) 520455; telex 45431; fax (4) 526679; POB 5, Sharjah; tel. (6) 357788; telex 68245; fax (6) 546676; POB 1240, al-Ain; tel. (3) 641253; telex 34082; fax (3) 654824; Gen. Man. JAMES ALLHUSEN.

United Bank Ltd (Pakistan): POB 1000, Dubai; tel. (4) 223191; telex 45433; POB 237, Abu Dhabi; tel. (2) 338240; telex 22272; fax (2) 344090; f. 1959; Sr Vice-Pres. and Zonal Chief S. M. ASGHAR; 7 other brs in UAE.

Bankers' Association

United Arab Emirates Bankers' Association: POB 44307, Abu Dhabi; tel. (2) 322541; telex 22781; fax (2) 324158; f. 1983.

INSURANCE

Abu Dhabi National Insurance Co (Adnic): POB 839, Abu Dhabi; tel. (2) 343171; telex 22340; fax (2) 211358; f. 1972; subscribed 25% by the Government of Abu Dhabi and 75% by UAE nationals; all classes of insurance; Chair. and Gen. Man. KHALAF A. AL-OTAIBA.

Al-Ahlia Insurance Co: POB 128, Ras al-Khaimah; tel. (77) 21749; telex 47677; f. 1977; Gen. Man. T. A. SAID; 3 brs.

Al-Ain Ahlia Insurance Co: POB 3077, Abu Dhabi; tel. (2) 323551; telex 22352; fax (2) 323550; f. 1975; Chair. HAMIL AL-GAITH; Gen. Man. WISAM AL-HAIMUS; brs in Dubai and al-Ain.

Dubai Insurance Co (S.A.D.): POB 3027, Dubai; tel. (4) 693030; telex 45685; fax (4) 693727; f. 1970; Chair. MAJID AL-FUTTAIM; Gen. Man. FAROUK HUWAIDI.

Sharjah Insurance and Reinsurance Co: POB 792, Sharjah; tel. (6) 355090; telex 68060; fax (6) 352545; f. 1970; Gen. Man. ADIB S. ABED.

Union Insurance Co: Head Office: POB 460, Umm al-Qaiwain; tel. (6) 666223; POB 4623, Dubai; POB 3196, Abu Dhabi; Gen. Man. L. F. DOKOV.

Trade and Industry

CHAMBERS OF COMMERCE

Federation of UAE Chambers of Commerce and Industry: POB 3014, Abu Dhabi; tel. (2) 214144; telex 23883; fax (2) 339210; POB 8886, Dubai; tel. (4) 212977; telex 48752; fax (4) 235498; Pres. HASSAN ABDULLAH AN-NOMAN; Sec.-Gen. KHALIFA AL-JALLAFF.

Abu Dhabi Chamber of Commerce and Industry: POB 662, Abu Dhabi; tel. (2) 214000; telex 22499; fax (2) 215867; f. 1977; 7,000 mems; Pres. RAHMAN MUHAMMAD AL-MASOUD; Dir-Gen. TAHER MUSBEH AL-KINDI.

Ajman Chamber of Commerce and Industry: POB 662, Ajman; tel. (6) 422177; telex 69523; fax (6) 427591; f. 1977; Pres. HAMAD MUHAMMAD ABU SHIHAB; Dir-Gen. MUHAMMAD BIN ABDULLAH AL-HUMRANI.

Dubai Chamber of Commerce and Industry: POB 1457, Deira, Dubai; tel. (4) 221181; telex 45997; fax (4) 211646; f. 1965; 29,031 mems; Pres. SAID JUMA AN-NABOODAH; Dir-Gen. ABD AR-RAHMAN GHANEM AL-MUTAIWEE.

Fujairah Chamber of Commerce, Industry and Agriculture: POB 738, Fujairah; tel. (9) 222400; telex 89088; fax (9) 221464; Pres. SAIF SULTAN SAID; Dir-Gen. SHAHEEN ALI SHAHEEN.

Ras al-Khaimah Chamber of Commerce, Industry and Agriculture: POB 78, Ras al-Khaimah; tel. (7) 333511; telex 99140; fax (7) 330233; f. 1967; 5,220 mems; Pres. ALI ABDULLAH MUSABEH; Dir MUHAMMAD ALI AL-HARANKI.

Sharjah Chamber of Commerce and Industry: POB 580, Sharjah; tel. (6) 541444; telex 68205; fax (6) 541119; f. 1970; 23,000 mems; Chair. HASSAN ABDULLAH AN-NOMAN; Dir-Gen. SAID OBEID AL-JARWAN.

Umm al-Qaiwain Chamber of Commerce and Industry: POB 436, Umm al-Qaiwain; tel. (6) 656915; telex 69714; fax (6) 657056; Pres. ABDULLAH RASHID AL-KHARJI; Man. Dir SHAKIR AZ-ZAYANI.

DEVELOPMENT ORGANIZATIONS

Abu Dhabi Development Finance Corpn: POB 30, Abu Dhabi; tel. (2) 22656; telex 820431; fax (2) 728890; purpose is to provide finance to the private sector; Deputy Man. Dir SAID MUHAMMAD.

Abu Dhabi Fund for Development (ADFD): POB 814; tel. (2) 725800; telex 22287; fax (2) 728890; f. 1971; purpose is to offer economic aid to other Arab states and other developing countries in support of their development; cap. 4,000m.; Chair. Sheikh KHALIFA BIN ZAYED AN-NAHYAN; Dir-Gen. KHALIFA MUHAMMAD AL-MUHAIRI.

Abu Dhabi Investment Authority (ADIA): POB 3600, Abu Dhabi; tel. (2) 213100; telex 22674; f. 1976; responsible for co-ordinating Abu Dhabi's investment policy; Chair. Sheikh KHALIFA BIN ZAYED AN-NAHYAN; Pres. Sheikh MUHAMMAD HABROUSH AS-SUWAIDI; 1 br. overseas.

Abu Dhabi Investment Company (ADIC): POB 46309, Abu Dhabi; tel. (2) 328200; telex 22968; fax (2) 212903; f. 1977; investment and merchant banking activities in the UAE and abroad; 90% owned by ADIA and 10% by National Bank of Abu Dhabi; total assets Dh 3,845m. (1991); Chair. HAREB MASOOD AD-DARMAKI; Gen. Man. HUMAID DARWISH AL-KATBI.

Abu Dhabi Planning Department: POB 12, Abu Dhabi; tel. (2) 727200; telex 23194; fax (2) 727749; f. 1974; supervises Abu Dhabi's Development Programme; Chair. MUSALLAM SAEED ABDULLAH AL-QUBAISI; Under-Sec. AHMED M. HILAL AL-MAZRUI.

Emirates Industrial Bank: POB 2722, Abu Dhabi; tel. (2) 339700; telex 23324; fax (2) 326397; f. 1982; offers low-cost loans to enterprises with at least 51% local ownership; 51% state-owned; cap. p.u. Dh 200m.; Chair. MUHAMMAD KHALFAN KHIRBASH; Gen. Man. MUHAMMAD ABD AL-BAKI MUHAMMAD.

General Industry Corpn (GIC): POB 4499, Abu Dhabi; tel. (2) 214900; telex 22938; fax (2) 325034; f. 1979; responsible for the promotion of non-oil-related industry.

International Petroleum Investment Company (IPIC): POB 7528, Abu Dhabi; tel. (2) 336200; telex 22520; fax (2) 216045; f. 1984; cap. p.u. $200m.; state-owned venture to develop overseas investments in energy and energy-related projects; Chair. JOUAN SALEM ADH-DHAHIRI; Man. Dir KHALIFA MUHAMMAD ASH-SHAMSI.

Sharjah Economic Development Corpn (SHEDCO): POB 3458, Sharjah; tel. (6) 371212; telex 68789; industrial investment co; joint venture between Sharjah authorities and private sector; authorized cap. Dh 1,000m.; Gen. Man. J. T. PICKLES.

United Arab Emirates Development Bank: Abu Dhabi; tel. (2) 344986; telex 22427; f. 1974; participates in development of real estate, agriculture, fishery, livestock and light industries; cap. p.u. Dh 500m.; Gen. Man. MUHAMMAD SALEM AL-MELEHY.

PRINCIPAL PETROLEUM CONCESSIONS

Supreme Petroleum Council: POB 26555, Abu Dhabi; tel. (2) 666000; telex 23300; fax (2) 661469; f. 1988; assumed authority and responsibility for the administration and supervision of all petroleum affairs in Abu Dhabi; Chair. Sheikh KHALIFA BIN ZAYED AN-NAHYAN; Sec.-Gen. SOHAIL FARES AL-MAZRUI.

Abu Dhabi

Abu Dhabi National Oil Co (ADNOC): POB 898, Abu Dhabi; tel. (2) 666000; telex 22215; fax (2) 722244; f. 1971; cap. p.u. Dh7,500m.; state company; deals in all phases of oil industry; owns two refineries: one on Umm an-Nar island and one at Ruwais; Habshan Gas Treatment Plant; a salt and chlorine plant; holds 60% participation in operations of ADMA-OPCO and ADCO, 88% of ZADCO and 88% of UDECO; has 100% control of Abu Dhabi National Oil Company for Oil Distribution (ADNOC-FOD), Abu Dhabi National Tanker Company (ADNATCO), National Drilling Co (NDC) and interests in numerous other companies, both in the UAE and overseas; ADNOC is operated by Supreme Petroleum Council, Chair. Sheikh KHALIFA BIN ZAYED AN-NAHYAN; Gen. Man. SOHAIL FARES AL-MAZRUI.

Abu Dhabi Co for Onshore Oil Operations (ADCO): POB 270, Abu Dhabi; tel. (2) 666100; telex 22222; fax (2) 669785; name changed from Abu Dhabi Petroleum Co Ltd (ADPC) in February 1979; shareholders are ADNOC (60%), British Petroleum, Shell and Total (9.5% each), Exxon and Mobil (4.75% each) and Partex (2%); average production (1990): 1.2m. b/d; Chair. SOHAIL FARES AL-MAZRUI; Gen. Man. DAVID WOODWARD.

Abu Dhabi Drilling Chemicals and Products Ltd (ADDCAP): POB 46121, Abu Dhabi; tel. (2) 730400; telex 23267; fax (2) 730725; f. 1975; manufacture and marketing of drilling chemicals and operation of an offshore supply marine base; ADNOC has a 75% share and NL Industries 25%; Chair. SOHAIL FARES AL-MAZRUI; Gen. Man. R. GONINON.

Abu Dhabi Gas Industries Co (GASCO): POB 665, Abu Dhabi; tel. (2) 651100; telex 22365; fax (2) 6047414; started production in 1981; recovers condensate and LPG from Asab, Bab and Bu Hasa fields for delivery to Ruwais natural gas liquids fractionation plant; cap. $2,100m., of which ADNOC has a 68% share; Total, Shell Gas and Partex have a minority interest; Chair. SOHAIL FARES AL-MAZRUI; Gen. Man. ANDREW B. PIRRIE.

Abu Dhabi Gas Liquefaction Co (ADGAS): POB 3500, Abu Dhabi; tel. (2) 333888; telex 22698; fax (2) 6065456; f. 1973; owned by ADNOC, 51%; the British Petroleum Co, 16⅓%; Total, 8⅙%; Mitsui and Co, 22$\frac{9}{20}$%; Mitsui Liquefied Gas Co, 2$\frac{1}{20}$%; operates LGSC and the LNG plant on Das Island, which was commissioned in 1977. The plant uses natural gas produced in association with oil from offshore fields and has a design capacity of approx. 2.3m. tons of LNG per year and 1.29m. tons of LPG per year. The liquefied gas is sold to the Tokyo Electric Power Co, Japan. Chair. ABDULLAH NASSER AS-SUWAIDI; Gen. Man. PETER CARR.

Abu Dhabi Marine Operating Co (ADMA-OPCO): POB 303, Abu Dhabi; tel. (2) 776600; telex 22284; fax (2) 720099; operates a concession 60% owned by the Abu Dhabi National Oil Co, POB 898, Abu Dhabi and 40% by Abu Dhabi Marine Areas Ltd, Britannic House, Moor Lane, London, EC2Y 9BU, England (BP-Japan Oil Development Co Ltd 26.67%; Total 13.33%). The concession lies in the Abu Dhabi offshore area and currently produces oil from Lower Zakum and Umm Shaif fields. ADMA-OPCO was created in 1977 as an operator for the concession. Production (1984): 67,884,769 barrels (8,955,721 metric tons); Chair. SOHAIL FARES AL-MAZRUI; Gen. Man. M. VIALLARD.

Abu Dhabi National Oil Company for Distribution (ADNOC-FOD): POB 4188, Abu Dhabi; tel. (2) 771300; telex 22358; fax (2) 722322; 100% owned by ADNOC; distributes petroleum products in Abu Dhabi; Chair. SOHAIL FARES AL-MAZRUI; Dir-Gen. ABDULLAH SAID AL-BADI.

Abu Dhabi National Tanker Co (ADNATCO): (see Shipping).

Abu Dhabi Petroleum Ports Operating Co (ADPPOC): POB 61, Abu Dhabi; tel. (2) 336700; telex 22209; fax (2) 216002; f. 1979; manages Jebel Dhanna, Ruwais, Das Island, Umm an-Nar and Zirku Island SPM terminal, Mubarraz; cap. p.u. Dh50m.; of which ADNOC has a 60% share and LAMNALCO Kuwait 40%; Chair. SOHAIL FARES AL-MAZRUI; Gen. Man. T. E. DENNIS.

Ruwais Fertilizers Industries Ltd (FERTIL): POB 2288, Abu Dhabi; tel. (2) 727100; telex 24205; fax (2) 728084; 66⅔% owned by ADNOC and 33⅓% by Total—CFP; began production of ammonia and urea in 1984; Chair. SOHAIL FARES AL-MAZRUI; Gen. Man. YOUSUF AN-NOWAIS.

The Liquefied Gas Shipping Co Ltd (LGSC): POB 3500, Abu Dhabi; tel. (2) 333888; telex 22698; f. 1972; cap. $1m.; ADNOC holds 51% share, Mitsui 24.5%, Shell 16.3%, BP 8.2%; Gen. Man. Dr D. BROOKS.

National Drilling Company (NDC): POB 4017, Abu Dhabi; tel. (2) 316600; telex 22553; fax (2) 317045; drilling operations; Chair. RASHID SAIF AS-SUWAIDI; Gen. Man. MICHAEL MURPHY.

National Marine Services Co (NMS): (see Shipping).

National Petroleum Construction Co Ltd (NPCC): POB 2058, Abu Dhabi; tel. (2) 774100; telex 22638; fax (2) 727763; f. 1973; 'turnkey' construction and maintenance of offshore facilities for the petroleum and gas industries; cap. p.u. Dh 100m.; Chair. MUHAMMAD KHALIFA AL-KINDI; Gen. Man. FARID B. ASFOUR.

Abu Dhabi Oil Co Ltd (Japan) (ADOC): POB 630, Abu Dhabi; tel. (2) 661100; telex 22260; fax (2) 665965; consortium of Japanese oil companies, including Cosmo Oil, JNOC and Nippon Mining Co; holds offshore concession, extended by 1,582.5 sq km in 1979; export of oil from Mubarraz Island terminal began in June 1973, production 6,332,897 barrels (1985); Gen. Man. TOSHIO KUWAHARA.

Amerada Hess Oil Corpn of Abu Dhabi (AHOC): POB 2046, Abu Dhabi; tel. (2) 779500; telex 22275; fax (2) 779500; operates the Arzanah field; owned 41.25% by AHOC, 31.5% Pan Ocean, Bow Valley 2.5%, Syracuse Oil 7.5%, Wington Enterprises 4.75%, Neste Oy 10%, Sunningdale 2.5%; Gen. Man. M. MURPHY.

Bunduq Oil Co: POB 46015, Abu Dhabi; tel. (2) 213380; telex 23872; fax (2) 321794; f. 1975; production in al-Bunduq oilfield; Gen. Man. T. FUJIMURA.

Neyrfor UAE: POB 46135; Abu Dhabi; tel. (6) 371805.

Total Abu al-Bukhoosh Oil Co Ltd: POB 4058, Abu Dhabi; tel. (2) 785000; telex 22347; fax (2) 788477; owned by Total, operator of Abu al-Bukhoosh field; began production from the Abu al-Bukhoosh offshore field in July 1974; average production of 40,000 b/d in 1991; partners in the field are Sunningdale Oil Ltd (Abu Dhabi) and Kerr McGee Corpn.

Zakum Development Co (ZADCO): POB 6808, Abu Dhabi; tel. (2) 661700; telex 22948; fax (2) 669448; joint venture between ADNOC (88%) and JODCO (12%); develop and produce from Upper Zakum, Umm ad-Dalkh and Satah fields on behalf of its owners; manages UDECO; Chair. SOHAIL FARES AL-MAZRUI; Gen. Man. I. NAHARA.

Ajman

Ajman National Oil Co (AJNOC): POB 410, Ajman; tel. (6) 421218; f. 1983; 50% government-owned, 50% held by Canadian and private Arab interests.

Dubai

DUGAS (Dubai Natural Gas Company Ltd): POB 4311, Dubai (Location: Jebel Ali); tel. (4) 46234; telex 45741; fax (4) 46118; wholly owned by Dubai authorities; Dep. Chair. and Dir MIRZA H. AS-SAYEGH.

Dubai Petroleum Co (DPC): POB 2222, Dubai; tel. (4) 442990; telex 45423; fax (4) 462200; holds offshore concession which began production in 1969; wholly owned by Dubai authorities; Pres. JOHN I. HORNING.

Emirates General Petroleum Corpn (EGPC): POB 9400, Dubai; tel. (4) 373300; telex 47980; fax (4) 373200; f. 1981; wholly owned by Ministry of Finance and Industry; distribution of petroleum.

Emirates National Oil Co (ENOC): Dubai; f. 1993; responsible for management of Dubai-owned companies in petroleum-marketing sector; Chair. Sheikh HAMDAN BIN RASHID AL-MAKTOUM.

Emirates Petroleum Products Co (Pvt.) Ltd: POB 5589, Dubai; tel. (4) 372131; telex 48342; fax (4) 375990; f. 1980; joint venture between Govt. of Dubai and Caltex Alkhaleej Marketing; sales of petroleum products, bunkering fuel and bitumen; Chair. Sheikh HAMDAN BIN RASHID AL-MAKTOUM.

Sedco-Houston Oil Group: POB 702, Dubai; tel. (4) 224141; telex 45469; holds onshore concession of over 400,000 ha as well as the offshore concession formerly held by Texas Pacific Oil; Pres. CARL F. THORNE.

Sharjah

Amoco Sharjah Oil Co: POB 1191, Sharjah; telex 68685; holds two offshore concession areas, of 1,018 sq km and 2,428 sq km.

Crescent Petroleum Co Internation: POB 2222, Sharjah; tel. (6) 543000; telex 68015; fax (6) 542000; subsidiary of BGOI INc; Chair. and CEO H. D. JAFAR.

Meridian Oil N.L. Co: POB 3943, Sharjah; tel. (6) 331388; telex 68577.

Petroleum and Minaral Affairs Department: POB 188, Sharjah; tel. (6) 541888; telex 68708; Dir ISMAIL A. WAHID.

Sharjah Liquefied Petroleum Gas Co (SHALCO): POB 787, Sharjah; tel. (6) 543666; telex 68799; fax (6) 548799; f. 1984; gas processing; 60% owned by Sharjah authorities, 25% Sharjah Amoco-Oil Co, 7.5% each Itochu Corp. and Tokyo Boeki of Japan; Gen. Man. SALEH ALI.

Umm al-Qaiwain

Petroleum and Mineral Affairs Department: POB 9, Umm al-Qaiwain; tel. (6) 666034; Chair. Sheikh SULTAN BIN AHMAD AL-MU'ALLA.

MAJOR INDUSTRIAL COMPANIES

Abu Dhabi

Admak General Contracting Co: POB 650, Abu Dhabi; tel. (2) 322237; telex 22320; f. 1968 as M. A. Kharafi, in 1981 adopted present name; general civil engineering and road contractors; part of the M. A. Kharafi Group of Kuwait; Man. Dir IBRAHIM SWEIDAN; Exec. Dir MUNIR MUSTAFA; 1,200 employees.

Arabconstruct International Ltd: POB 238, Abu Dhabi; tel. (2) 322668; telex 22558; f. 1967; general civil works, construction, engineering and contracting; cap. p.u. Dh12m.; Chair. and Propr ADNAN M. DERBAS; 1,500 employees.

International Aluminium: POB 2329, Abu Dhabi; tel. (2) 325326; telex 22949; specialist contractors, design, manufacture and erection of high-rise applications; Propr HUSSAIN GHULAM HAJIPOUR.

Mechanical and Civil Engineering Contractors (MACE) Ltd: POB 2307, Abu Dhabi; tel. (2) 330144; telex 22816; fax (2) 335659; Chair. and Man. Dir WILLIAM A. T. HADDAD; 500 employees.

Nitco Concrete Products: POB 654, Abu Dhabi; tel. (2) 344255; telex 22407; f. 1980; production and supply of ready-mix concrete, concrete fences and paving stones; sales Dh 15m. (1981/82); cap. p.u. Dh 8m.; Chair. FARAH ABD AR-RAHMAN HAMED; Man. Dir ABDULLAHI FARAH.

Pilco (Pipeline Construction Co): POB 2021, Abu Dhabi; tel. (2) 554500; telex 23210; fax (2) 559053; f. 1968; fabrication of steel, piping, tanks, pressure vessels and machine components; general services to the oil industry; Gen. Man. E. N. HAWA; 200 employees.

Ash-Shaheen Gypsum Products Est: POB 2618, Abu Dhabi; tel. (2) 361240; telex 22926; f. 1978; fabrication of gypsum blocks for use in dry wall partitioning; Dirs OBAID AL-MANSOURI, FRANÇOIS LAMA.

Ajman

Ajman Mosaic Company: POB 406, Ajman; tel. (6) 422104; production of marble and terrazzo; Chair. Sheikh HUMAID.

Dubai

Al-Ahmadia Contracting and Trading: POB 2596, Dubai; tel. (4) 450900; telex 45703; f. 1970; building and civil engineering contractors; Pres. and Propr Sheikh HASHER MAKTOUM JUMA AL-MAKTOUMI; Exec. Vice-Pres. S. K. JOSHI; 1,500 employees.

Dubai Aluminium Company (DUBAL): POB 3627, Dubai; tel. (84) 46666; telex 47240; fax (84) 46919; f. 1979; production of primary aluminium; supply of fresh water to Dubai City; produces about 250,000 tons of cast metal per annum; Chair. Sheikh HAMDAN BIN RASHID AL-MAKTOUM.

Fibroplast Industries Co (PVT) Ltd: POB 10192, Dubai; tel. (4) 257575; telex 46912; f. 1977; manufacture of glass fibre-reinforced polyester pipes, tanks, fittings; sales Dh 49.8m. (1982); cap. Dh 8m.; Chair. ABD AL-GHAFFAR HUSSAIN; Man. Dir W. NAJARIAN; 187 employees.

Al-Futtaim Tower Scaffolding (PVT) Ltd: POB 5502, Dubai; tel. (4) 257726; telex 46086; f. 1975; manufacture of scaffolding and steel products; general fabrication; Chair. MAJID MUHAMMAD AL-FUTTAIM; Gen. Man. V. M. G. RAMAN; 150 employees.

Al-Ghurair Group of Companies: POB 727, Abu Dhabi; tel. (2) 820176; telex 24373; f. 1960/61; general contracting, banking, import and export, aluminium extrusion and manufacture of aluminium doors, windows, etc., PVC pipes, tiles and marbles, cement and mineral waters; gold and exchange dealers, owners of grain silos and flour mills, printing press, packaging factory, real estate dealers; cap. Dh 1,000m.; Chair. SAIF AHMAD MAJED AL-GHURAIR; Vice-Chair. ABDULLAH AHMAD MAJED AL-GHURAIR; 1,600 employees.

Gulf Eternit Industries S.A.: POB 1371, Dubai; tel. (4) 857256; telex 47040; fax (4) 851935; manufacture of Fibrecement and glass reinforced plastic pipes; Pres. FOUAD MAKHZOUMI.

Al-Habtor Engineering Enterprises Co (PVT) Ltd: POB 320, Dubai; tel. (4) 257215; telex 45603; f. 1971; civil and building contracting; Dirs KHALAF A. AL-HABTOOR; RIAD T. SADIK; about 2,000 employees.

Bin Hussain Aluminium Factories: POB 1535, Dubai; tel. (4) 660643; telex 45947; process and fabrication of aluminium doors, windows, shop fronts, balustrades, rolling shutters, etc.; Chair. HUSSAIN MUHAMMAD BIN HUSSAIN.

Bin Ladin Organization for Construction and General Trading: POB 1555, Dubai; tel. (4) 691500; tel. 45991; fax (4) 691350; f. 1967 in UAE; civil engineering, roadworks, piling, ground services and building, electrical contracting; Chair. and Man. Dir ABU BAKR SALIM AL-HAMID; 4,000 employees.

National Cement Co Ltd: POB 4041, Dubai; tel. (4) 480671; telex 47202; production and sale of cement; Chair. SAIF AHMAD AL-GHURAIR.

Shirawi Contracting and Trading Co: POB 2032, Dubai; tel. (4) 220251; telex 45483; f. 1971; building and civil engineering contractors, supply of building materials; sales Dh 290m.; cap. Dh 50m; Chair. ABDULLAH ASH-SHIRAWI; 2,000 employees.

United Foods Ltd: POB 5836, Dubai; tel. (4) 382688; telex 46689; fax (4) 381987; f. 1976; manufacture and trading of hydrogenated vegetable oil and cooking oil; Chair. ABD AL-AZIZ AL-OWAIS; Gen. Man. M. TAWFIQ BAIG; 130 employees.

Fujairah

Fujairah Cement: POB 600, Fujairah; tel. (70) 223111; telex 89047; fax (2) 227718.

Ras al-Khaimah

Alltek Emirates Ltd: POB 1569, Ras al-Khaimah; tel. (07) 668865; telex 99117; fax (07) 668977; manufacture and marketing of spray plasters, decorative paints and limestone powder.

Raknor (PVT) Ltd: POB 883, Ras al-Khaimah; tel. (07) 66351; telex 99251; fax (07) 66910; f. 1976; manufacture of concrete blocks.

Union Contracting Co (UNCO): POB 162, Ras al-Khaimah; tel. (07) 445627; telex 99253; fax (07) 445474; f. 1972; building and civil works contracting; Chair. SAMIR HAKOURA; 1,200 employees.

Sharjah

CME Contracting Marine Engineering: POB 1859, Sharjah; tel. (6) 354511; telex 68069; turnkey industrial projects, water and electricity plants, construction, building, marine works; joint venture between Chair. and German cos Klaus Stuff, Helma Greuel-Mainz; Chair. Dr F. AL-GAWLY; 323 employees.

Conforce Gulf Ltd Co: POB 289, Sharjah; tel. (6) 591433; telex 68082; f. 1979; building contractor, exporter of building and electrical materials; Man. ABDULLAH MUHAMMAD BUKHATIR.

Dafco General Constructing and Trade: POB 515, Sharjah; tel. (6) 593333; telex 68106; f. 1980; general contracting trading company; operates factories producing bricks and concrete; Man. M. AL-FARHAN.

General Enterprises Co: POB 1150, Sharjah; tel. (6) 591727; telex 68020; general trading and contracting; Gen. Man. Sheikh AHMAD BIN MUHAMMAD SULTAN AL-QASIMI.

Gulf Building Materials Co Ltd (GBM): POB 1612, Sharjah; tel. (6) 354683; telex 68089; production and supply of building materials: cement, marble and aluminium.

Hempel's Marine Paints (UAE) Ltd: POB 2000, Sharjah; tel. (06) 283307; telex 68197; f. 1977; manufacture and sale of paints for offshore marine, domestic and industrial use; cap. Dh 500,000; Chair. SA'UD ABD AL-AZIZ AR-RASHID; CEO and Gen. Man. GARY BALL.

Sharjah Electrodes: POB 2019, Sharjah; tel. (6) 593888; f. 1976; manufacture and distribution of arc welding electrodes and wire nails; Chair. MUHAMMAD SHARIF ZAMAN; 37 employees.

Umm al-Qaiwain

Umm al-Qaiwain Aluminium Co (UMALCO): Umm al-Qaiwain.

Umm al-Qaiwain Asbestos and Cement Industries Co: POB 547, Umm al-Qaiwain; tel. (6) 666641; telex 69711; Chair. Sheikh SA'UD BIN RASHID AL-MU'ALLA.

Transport

ROADS

Roads are rapidly being developed in the United Arab Emirates, and Abu Dhabi and Dubai are linked by a good road which is dual carriageway for most of its length. This road forms part of a west coast route from Shaam, at the UAE border with the northern enclave of Oman, through Dubai and Abu Dhabi to Tarif. An east coast route links Dibba with Muscat. Other roads include the Abu Dhabi–al-Ain highway and roads linking Sharjah and Ras al-

Khaimah, and Sharjah and Dhaid. An underwater tunnel links Dubai Town and Deira by dual carriageway and pedestrian subway. In 1993 there were more than 3,000 km of paved highways in the UAE.

SHIPPING

Dubai has been the main commercial centre in the Gulf for many years. Abu Dhabi has also become an important port since the opening of the first section of its artificial harbour, Port Zayed. There are smaller ports in Sharjah, Fujairah, Ras al-Khaimah and Umm al-Qaiwain. Work on a dry-dock scheme for Dubai was completed in 1979. It possesses two docks capable of handling 500,000-ton tankers, seven repair berths and a third dock able to accommodate 1,000,000-ton tankers. In 1988 the Dubai port of Mina Jebel Ali, which has the largest man-made harbour in the world, contained 67 berths. Current modernization of Port Khalid in Sharjah was to double its berth capacity, and the two-berth port of Fujairah was opened in 1983.

Abu Dhabi National Tanker Company (ADNATCO): POB 2977, Abu Dhabi; tel. (2) 331800; telex 22747; fax (2) 322940; subsidiary company of ADNOC, operating owned and chartered tankships, and transporting crude petroleum, refined products and sulphur; Chair. KHALAF RASHID AL-OTEIBA; Gen. Man. BADER M. AS-SUWAIDI.

Ahmad bin Rashid Port and Free Trade Zone: POB 279, Umm al-Qaiwain; tel. (6) 655882; telex 69717; fax (6) 651552.

Dubai Drydocks: POB 8988, Dubai; tel. (4) 450626; telex 48838; fax (4) 450116; state-owned dry-docks with cleaning facilities, galvanizing plant, transport systems and facilities for maintenance and repair of ships of any size; Chief Exec. E. S. WARE.

Dubai Ports Authority (DPA): POB 17000, Dubai; tel. (4) 815000; telex 47398; fax (4) 816093; offers duty-free storage areas and facilities for loading and discharge of vessels; supervises ports of Mina Jebel Ali and Mina Rashid; handled more than 1.7m. containers in 1993; Chair. SULTAN AHMAD BIN SULAYEM; Exec. Dirs EDWARD BILKEY, DAVID GIBBONS.

Fujairah Port: POB 787, Fujairah; tel. (9) 228800; telex 89085; fax (9) 228811; f. 1982; offers facilities for handling full container, general cargo and 'roll on, roll off' traffic; Chair. Sheikh SALEH BIN MUHAMMAD ASH-SHARQI; Gen. Man. Capt. ROGER M. SAUNDERS.

Jebel Ali Free Zone Authority (JAFZA): POB 17000, Dubai; tel. (4) 815000; telex 47398; fax (4) 815001; the authority administers a 100 sq km zone, created by the Government of Dubai in 1985, which includes the 7,500-acre Jebel Ali port and industrial area offering 67 berths; offers facilities for handling container, bulk, general and liquid traffic; 'roll on, roll off' berths; 42,000 cu m capacity cold store; aluminium smelter; desalinization and power generating plants; by December 1990 300 companies had established business in the Free Zone; Jebel Ali port handled 24m. metric tons of cargo in 1993; Chair. SULTAN AHMAD BIN SULAYEM.

Jebel Dhanna/Ruwais Petroleum Port: c/o ADCO, POB 898, Abu Dhabi; tel. (2) 666100; telex 22222; fax (2) 669785; facilities include 5 tanker berths, export of crude petroleum, refined products, fertilizers, ammonia and sulphur; Terminal Superintendent J. B. SHEEHAN.

Mina Zayed Port: POB 422, Abu Dhabi; tel. (2) 730600; telex 22731; fax (2) 731023; facilities include 21 deep-water berths of up to 13 metres draft; 3 container gantry cranes of 40 tons capacity; specializes in container traffic, general and reefer cargoes; in 1993 Port Zayed handled 1.412m. metric tons of cargo; Chair. Sheikh SAID BIN ZAYED AN-NAHYAN; Dir MUBARAK AL-BU AINAIN.

National Marine Services Co (NMS): POB 7202, Abu Dhabi; tel. (2) 339800; telex 22965; fax (2) 211239; operate, charter and lease specialized offshore support vessels; cap. p.u. Dh 25m.; owned 60% by ADNOC and 40% by Jackson Marine Corporation USA; Chair. SOHAIL FARES AL-MAZRUI; Gen. Man. Capt. HASSAN A. SHAREEF.

Ras al-Khaimah Port Services: POB 5130, Ras al-Khaimah; tel. (7) 668444; telex 99280; fax (7) 668533; operate Mina Saqr port; govt-owned; Chair. Sheikh MUHAMMAD BIN SAQR AL-QASIMI; Man. Capt. HAZEM RAOUF ASSAD.

Sharjah Ports and Customs Department: POB 510, Sharjah; tel. (6) 281666; telex 68138; fax (6) 281425; the authority administers Port Khalid and Port Khor Fakkan and offers specialized facilities for container and 'roll on, roll off' traffic, reefer cargo and project and general cargo; in 1992 Port Khalid handled 37,400 20-ft equivalent units of containerized shipping, and Port Khor Fakkan 358,000 20-ft equivalent units; total cargo handled: 2.4m. metric tons; Chair. (Ports and Customs) Sheikh SAUD BIN KHALID AL-QASIMI; Dir-Gen. ABD AL-AZIZ SULAIMAN AS-SARKAL.

Umm al-Qaiwain Port: POB 225, Umm al-Qaiwain; tel. (6) 666126; telex 69611.

CIVIL AVIATION

There are five international airports at Abu Dhabi, Dubai, Fujairah and Ras al-Khaimah, and a smaller one at Sharjah, which forms part of Sharjah port, linking air, sea and overland transportation services. A sixth airport, at al-Ain (Abu Dhabi), was due to be opened in 1994. In 1988 900,000 passengers used Sharjah international airport. In 1992 5.44m. passengers used Dubai international airport, and 2.4m. passed through Abu Dhabi airport.

Civil Aviation Department: POB 20, Abu Dhabi; tel. (2) 757500; telex 24406; responsible for all aspects of civil aviation; Chair. HAMDAN BIN MUBARAK AN-NAHYAN.

Abu Dhabi Aviation: POB 2723, Abu Dhabi; tel. (2) 722733; telex 23409; Chair. ALI BIN KHALFAN ADH-DHAHRI; Gen. Man. ALI SAID ASH-SHAMSI.

Emirates Air Service: POB 322, Abu Dhabi; tel. (2) 778222; telex 23056; fax (2) 770451; f. 1976 as Abu Dhabi Air Services; operates passenger and cargo charter flights within the UAE and to other destinations within the Gulf region; also operates contract flights for oil cos; wholly owned by Muhammad bin Masaood and Sons of Abu Dhabi; Pres. ABDULLAH MASAOOD; Man. Dir. C. O. MILLER.

Emirates (EK) Dubai: POB 686, Dubai; tel. (4) 223698; telex 48085; fax (4) 214560; f. 1985; services to the Middle East, Europe and the Far East; owned by the Dubai authorities; in 1991 the airline carried 1.2m. passengers, an increase of 26% on the previous year's total, and 37,615 tons of freight, an increase of 25%; Chair. Sheikh AHMAD BIN SAID AL-MAKTOUM; Man. Dir. MAURICE FLANAGAN.

Gulf Air Dubai: Al Naboodah Bldg, al-Maktoum St, POB 4410, Dubai; tel. (4) 231700; f. 1950; serves 51 destinations world-wide.

Gulf Air Co GSC (Gulf Air): POB 5015, Sharjah; tel. (6) 356356; fax (6) 354354; f. 1950; jointly owned by Governments of Bahrain, Oman, Qatar and Abu Dhabi since 1974; flights world-wide; Pres. and Chief Exec. SALIM BIN ALI BIN NASSER.

Tourism

Tourism is an established industry in Sharjah, and plans are being implemented to foster tourism in other emirates, notably in Abu Dhabi (where a 'themed', 10 sq-km leisure complex, Lulu Island, is planned, at a cost of some US $2,500m.) and Dubai. In 1990 foreign visitors to the UAE totalled approximately 616,000.

Dubai Information Department: POB 1420, Dubai; Dir OMAR DEESI.

Ras al-Khaimah Information and Tourism Department: POB 141, Ras al-Khaimah; tel. (77) 51151; Chair. Sheikh ABD AL-AZIZ BIN HUMAID AL-QASSIMI.

Sharjah Department of Tourism: POB 8, Sharjah; tel. (6) 581111; telex 68185; fax (6) 581167; f. 1980; Dir. MUHAMMAD SAIF AL-HAJRI.

Defence

The Union Defence Force and the armed forces of the various emirates were formally merged in May 1976, although difficulties have since been experienced (see History). Abu Dhabi and Dubai retain a degree of independence. Military service is voluntary.

Chief of Staff of Federal Armed Forces: Brig.-Gen. MUHAMMAD SA'ID AL-BADI.

Total armed forces (June 1994): 61,500 (army 57,000; navy 2,000; air force 2,500).

Estimated defence expenditure (1992): 7,700m. dirhams (US $2,100m.); federal expenditure on defence has been substantially reduced since the early 1980s, but procurement and project costs are not affected, as individual emirates finance these separately. In 1992 a scheme was announced to draft thousands of local men and women into the army, and to replace the estimated 30% expatriate section of the army with nationals.

Education

The UAE is engaged in expanding education, which is regarded as a unifying force for the future of the federation. As a result, major accomplishments in the provision of education have been achieved within the emirates. By 1985/86 there were an estimated 255,000 students at all stages of education in the country as a whole, compared with 141,424 in 1980/81 and about 109,000 in 1978/79. In 1991/92 a total of 49,064 children attended government kindergartens, and 231,674 attended primary schools in the UAE. At the same time, secondary enrolment totalled 118,011. There are primary and secondary schools in all the emirates, and further education in technical fields is available in the more advanced areas. Teachers from other Arab countries, most notably Kuwait, Egypt and Jordan, supplement the UAE's inadequate native teaching staff; of a total of 8,859 teachers in 1983, only 646 were UAE nationals. Many students receive higher education abroad. The UAE has one university, at al-Ain in Abu Dhabi, where 9,394 students were enrolled in 1992/93. The four higher colleges of technology (two for male and two for female students) in Abu Dhabi admitted a total of 1,150 students in 1992/93, all of whom were citizens of the UAE.

Bibliography

Abdullah, M. Morsy. *The Modern History of the United Arab Emirates*. London, Croom Helm, 1978.

Albaharna, H. M. *The Legal Status of the Arabian Gulf States*. Manchester University Press, 1969.

Amni, Sayed Hassan. *International and Legal Problems of the Gulf*. Menas Press, 1981.

Bulloch, John. *The Gulf*. London, Century Publishing.

Busch, B. C. *Britain and the Persian Gulf 1894–1914*. University of California Press, 1967.

Cordesman, Anthony H. *The Gulf and the Search for Strategic Stability*. Mansell, 1984.

Daniels, John. *Abu Dhabi: A Portrait*. London, Longman, 1974.

Fenelon, K. G. *The United Arab Emirates: an Economic and Social Survey*. London, Longman, 1973.

Gabriel, Erhard F. (Ed.). *The Dubai Handbook*. Ahrensburg, Germany, Institute for Applied Economic Geography, 1989.

Hawley, Donald Frederick. *Courtesies in the Trucial States*. 1965.

The Trucial States. London, George Allen and Unwin, 1971.

Hay, Sir Rupert. *The Persian Gulf States*. Washington, DC, Middle East Institute, 1959.

Heard-Bey, Dr Frauke. *From Trucial States to United Arab Emirates*. London, Longman, 1982.

The Arabian Gulf States and the Islamic Revolution. Bonn, German Institute for Foreign Policy Research.

Khalifa, Ali Mohammad. *The United Arab Emirates: Unity in Fragmentation*. London, Croom Helm, 1980.

McLachlan, Keith, and Joffé, George. *The Gulf War—A Survey of Political Issues and Economic Consequences*. London, Economist Intelligence Unit, 1984.

Mann, Clarence. *Abu Dhabi: Birth of an Oil Sheikhdom*. Beirut, Khayats, 1964.

Marlowe, John. *The Persian Gulf in the 20th Century*. London, Cresset Press, 1962.

Miles, S. B. *The Countries and Tribes of the Persian Gulf*. 3rd edn, London, Cass, 1966.

Ministry of Information and Culture. *United Arab Emirates: A Record of Achievement, 1979–81*. Abu Dhabi, 1981.

Oteiba, Mani Said al-. *Petroleum and the Economy of the United Arab Emirates*. London, Croom Helm, 1977.

Essays on Petroleum. London, Croom Helm, 1982.

Peck, M. C. *The UAE—A Venture in Unity*. London, Croom Helm.

Qasimi, Sultan bin. *Myth of Arab Policy in the Gulf*. London, Croom Helm, 1986.

Sadiq, Muhammad T., and Snavely, William P. *Bahrain, Qatar and the United Arab Emirates: Colonial Past, Present Problems, and Future Prospects*. Lexington, Mass., Heath, 1972.

Sakr, Nadwi. *The UAE to 1990–One market or Seven?* (Special Report No. 238). London, Economist Intelligence Unit, 1986.

Taryam, A. O. *The Establishment of the UAE*. London, Croom Helm.

Yorke, V., and Turner, L. *European Interests and Gulf Oil*. Royal Institute of International Affairs/Gower, 1986.

Zahlan, Rosemarie Said. *The Origins of the United Arab Emirates*. London, Macmillan, 1978.

YEMEN

Geography

On 22 May 1990 the Yemen Arab Republic (YAR) and the People's Democratic Republic of Yemen (PDRY) merged to form the Republic of Yemen. Yemen consists of the south-west corner of the Arabian peninsula—the highlands inland, and the coastal strip along the Red Sea; and the former British colony of Aden (195 sq km or 75.3 sq miles) and the Protectorate of South Arabia (about 333,000 sq km or 128,570 sq miles), together with the islands of Perim (13 sq. km or 5 sq miles) and Kamaran (57 sq km or 22 sq miles). The Republic of Yemen lies at the southern end of the Arabian peninsula, approximately between longitude 43°E and 56°E, with Perim Island a few km due west, in the strait marking the southern extremity of the Red Sea; and Socotra in the extreme east. Yemen has frontiers with Saudi Arabia and Oman but these have not been adequately delimited and atlases still show considerable variation in the precise boundaries of the three countries, or sometimes do not indicate them at all. The capital of the Republic of Yemen is San'a, which lies on the al-Jehal plateau (2,175 m above sea-level).

Physically Yemen comprises the dislocated southern edge of the great plateau of Arabia. This is an immense mass of ancient granites, once forming part of Africa, and covered in many places by shallow, mainly horizontal layers of younger sedimentary rocks. The whole plateau has undergone down-warping in the east and elevation in the west, so that the highest land (over 3,000 m) occurs in the extreme west, near the Red Sea, with a gradual decline to the lowest parts (under 300 m) in the extreme east. The whole of the southern and western coasts of Yemen were formed by a series of enormous fractures, which produced a flat but very narrow coastal plain, rising steeply to the hill country a short distance inland. Percolation of molten magma along the fracture-lines gave rise to a number of volcanic craters, now extinct, and one of these, partly eroded and occupied by the sea, forms the site of Aden port.

An important topographic feature is the Wadi Hadramawt, an imposing valley running parallel to the coast at 160 km–240 km distance inland. In its upper and middle parts, this valley is broad, and occupied by a seasonal torrent; in its lower (eastern) part it narrows considerably, making a sudden turn south-eastwards and reaching the sea. This lower part is largely uninhabited, but the upper parts, where alluvial soil and intermittent flood water are available, support a farming population.

Rainfall is generally scarce, but relatively more abundant on the highlands and in the west. The climate of the highlands is considered to be the best in all Arabia since it experiences a regime rather like that of East Africa: a warm, temperate and rainy summer, and a cool, moderately dry winter with occasional frost and some snow. Aden receives 125 mm of rain annually, all of it during winter (December–March), whilst in the lowlands of the extreme east, it may rain only once in five or 10 years. In the highlands a few miles north of Aden, falls of up to 760 mm occur, for the most part during summer, and this rainfall also gradually declines eastwards, giving 380 mm–500 mm in the highlands of Dhofar. As much as 890 mm of rain may fall annually on the higher parts of the interior, off the Red Sea coast, with 400 mm–500 mm over much of the plateau; but the coast receives less than 130 mm generally, often in the form of irregular downpours. There is, therefore, the phenomenon of streams and even rivers flowing perennially in the western highlands but failing to reach the coast.

Ultimately, to the north and east, rainfall diminishes to almost nil, as the edges of the Arabian Desert are reached. This unusual situation of a reversal in climatic conditions over a few miles is thought to be the result of two streams of air; an upper one, damp and unstable in summer, and originating in the equatorial regions of East Africa; and a lower current, generally drier and related to conditions prevailing over the rest of the Middle East. In this way the low-lying coastal areas have a maximum of rainfall in winter, and the hills of Yemen a maximum in summer. Temperatures are everywhere high, particularly on the coastal plain, which has a southern aspect: mean figures of 25°C (January) to 32°C (June) occur at Aden town, but maxima of over 38°C are common. Owing to this climate gradation from desert temperate conditions, Yemen has a similar gradation of crops and vegetation. In the interior, off the Red Sea coast, the highest parts appear as 'African', with scattered trees and grassland. Crops of coffee, qat, cereals and vegetables are grown, while, lower down, 'Mediterranean' fruits appear, with millet and, where irrigation water is available, bananas. The date palm is the only tree to grow successfully in the coastal region.

To the east, except on the higher parts, which have a light covering of thorn scrub (including dwarf trees which exude a sap from which incense and myrrh are derived), and the restricted patches of cultivated land, the territory is devoid of vegetation. Cultivation is limited to small level patches of good soil on flat terraces alongside the river beds, on the floor and sides of the Wadi Hadramawt, or where irrigation from wells and occasionally from cisterns can be practised. The most productive areas are: Lahej, close to Aden town; two districts near Mukalla (about 480 km east of Aden), and parts of the middle Hadramawt. Irrigation from cisterns hollowed out of the rock has long been practised, and Aden town has a famous system of this kind, dating back many centuries. Today, however, the main system of irrigation is provided by floodwater.

The area of Yemen is approximately 536,869 sq km (207,286 sq miles) and its population was 12.5m. at mid-1991, according to World Bank estimates.

History

ROBIN BIDWELL

Revised for this edition by RICHARD I. LAWLESS

PRE-ISLAMIC YEMEN

In the millenium before Christ there were three centres of civilization in the Arabian Peninsula; one in the northwest around Madain Salih, the second based in Bahrain and in what is now the UAE; and the third, the most advanced, in the Yemen. Traditional Arab genealogists assign to the Yemenis a different ancestor (*Qahtan*) from that of the northern tribes (*Adnan*). Yemen was unique amongst ancient civilizations in that it was not dependent on a great river, but relied upon rainfall to irrigate terraced fields, controlling the waters by a sophisticated system of dams, of which the one at Marib was famous throughout Arabia. In addition to flourishing agriculture, the incense trade and the use of its ports as a link between India, China, Africa and the Mediterranean made it one of the richest regions of the ancient world. References in the Bible and Classical authors and archeology indicate that it had a social structure that has endured even into this century: towns with an hereditary literate class, trades divided into noble and ignoble, settled agriculturalists and, separate from these, tribesmen who were sometimes soldiers and sometimes predators. The chronology is uncertain, but it is clear that about 110 BC the whole area including what are now parts of Saudi Arabia and Oman came under the domination of the Himyarites whose rule continued almost until the rise of Islam at which time, after half a century of Abyssinian rule, Yemen had recently been conquered by the Persians.

EARLY ISLAMIC YEMEN

The Persian *satrap* appears to have accepted an invitation from the Prophet to adopt Islam and, according to tradition, the whole of the great tribe of Hamdan, the ancestors of the Hashid and Bakil tribes, were converted in a single day by Muhammad's son-in-law Ali; this forged a link between them and the Hashemites which lasted until the Revolution of 1962. Although huge numbers of Yemenis served in the Islamic armies (which conquered territories from the Atlantic to the borders of China), for a while it seemed that Yemeni particularism might prove too strong to accept a religion of foreign origin, and a series of revolts occurred. The Caliphs of Baghdad took little interest in such a remote area and in 822 their local Governor, Ibn Ziyad, revolted and reunited most of the old Himyarite state under his own rule from the city of Zabid. Although short-lived, this had the effect of splitting the Yemen away from the main Arab Empire and reasserted its individuality.

The second half of the ninth century was a period of religious strife as the Ismailis attempted to seize control of the Yemen. In 1037, while the Ismailis were ruling in Cairo, a local chieftain conquered most of the old Himyaritic area and ruled it from San'a in their name. The Sulayhid dynasty survived in great prosperity for almost a century, but as it declined local governors asserted their independence. In 1174, the great Saladin (Salah ad-Din al-Ayyubi), who had overthrown the Ismailis in Egypt, sent his brother to destroy their adherents in Yemen and once again most of South West Arabia was governed by a single ruler. The Ayyubids remained for half a century and left affairs in the hands of an official, ar-Rasul, who later assumed an independent sovereignty.

The Rasulids, from their capital at Taiz, had diplomatic relations with Persia, India and China and were so effective that they were able to organize a trilateral campaign by land and sea against a rebellious vassal in Dhofar. Their state, in turn, disintegrated and the area was totally fragmented when the Portuguese attacked Aden in 1513.

FROM THE SIXTEENTH TO THE EARLY NINETEENTH CENTURY

The fear that the Portuguese might establish a presence in South Arabia which could serve as a base to attack the Holy Places led to the intervention of the Ottoman Sultan. An army, using firearms for the first time in the area, succeeded in installing a Pasha in San'a who ruled almost all of the historic Yemen. The Zaidis in the mountains remained detached and in the east the Kathiri family established a semi-independent state in Hadramawt, although they acknowledged Ottoman sovereignty. The discovery of the route to India round the Cape practically destroyed the importance of Aden as an entrepôt, but, from c. 1600, British and Dutch traders travelled to Mocha to buy coffee and sell textiles.

At about the same time a new Zaidi Imam launched a guerrilla war against the Turks who, after nine years' fighting, agreed to leave him in control of the area north of San'a. His son launched a religious and national war which, in 1636, led to their departure. He and succeeding Imams brought the whole of South Arabia, including Dhofar and Asir under their rule.

Once more central authority declined and in 1728 the Governor of Lahej and Aden proclaimed himself an independent Sultan and his example was followed in Asir and most of the South. By the time the explorer Niebuhr visited San'a in 1763 the writ of the Imam was only valid in San'a, Taiz and the Tihamah.

In 1804 the Wahhabis occupied Mecca and Medina and also penetrated into the Tihamah. Some years later the Ottoman Sultan, as Protector of the Holy Places, requested his vassal Muhammad Ali, Pasha of Egypt, to expel them. This he did and went on to take over the Tihamah and monopolize the coffee trade; in 1837 he bought control of Taiz.

In 1834, taking advantage of the plundering of an Indian vessel flying the British flag, the Bombay Government sent Captain Haines of the Indian navy to exact restitution and at the same time to negotiate for the purchase of Aden (a valuable fuelling station between the UK and India). The Sultan of Lahej, fearing that it might be seized by the Egyptians, agreed to sell but then reneged on the deal. His son then tried to kidnap Haines in order to repossess the document and this provided a pretext for an attack in which Aden was stormed on 19 January 1839.

In 1841 as part of a general peace settlement Muhammad Ali Pasha evacuated his troops from Yemen. A period of lawlessness ensued, during which the Imam requested a treaty of protection with the British. Haines, who was at that time Political Agent in Aden, was ordered to refuse. The Turks decided to reassert control and in 1849 they occupied Hodeidah.

THE BRITISH IN ADEN 1839–1918

At the time of the conquest, Aden was in a state of dilapidation with about 600 inhabitants, but Haines had the vision to realize that it could be built into a great port to serve the Hinterland and resume its historic role as an entrepôt. In seven years the population rose to 25,000. After repelling two attempts by the Sultan of Lahej to recapture the town, Haines sought the friendship of the local tribes by giving small subsidies to their leaders, often through the Sultan of Lahej, and by abstaining from interference in their internal affairs. Aden became a free port in 1850 and from 1869 benefited from the substantial increase in shipping that resulted from the opening of the Suez Canal, although until 1881 it was not master of its own water supply. Aden was a military base, secured by the acquisition of Perim Island and Little Aden, which had been sought by the French, and occupation of part of the Somali coast which ensured that no hostile power could dominate the entrance to the Red Sea. The Kuria Muria Islands were a gift to Queen Victoria from Saiyid Said of Oman.

In the early 1870s the Turks in San'a established contact with some of the tribes, including those of Hadramawt, that had been at least nominally subject to the Ottoman Sultan during the first occupation. This alarmed the British who presented Constantinople with a list of nine tribes that they regarded as under their sphere of influence and in which they would oppose Turkish interference. The Turks occupied part of the Sultanate of Lahej, but withdrew in December 1873 after strong diplomatic action in Constantinople. The British then consolidated their position with a series of treaties, similar to the Exclusive Treaties with the Gulf Sheikhdoms, signed with the tribes, who, in return for protection against outside attack and regular subsidies, undertook to refrain from correspondence with foreign powers to whom they were not to cede any territory without approval. These events were significant in Yemeni history because for the first time south Arabia was formally divided into two distinct territories separated by a boundary which was apparent to the tribes and recognized by international agreement.

Despite proposals by the Foreign Office that Aden should be taken over by the Colonial Office, it continued to be administered as part of the Bombay presidency. Consequently, Aden began to adopt a distinctly Indian style of government and trade. Despite the emergence of small numbers of educated local Arabs, the increasing use of English and Urdu words and expressions made its colloquial language difficult for outsiders to understand and it took on a cultural identity of its own which was quite different from the traditional Arab background of San'a.

THE TURKS IN YEMEN AND THE FIRST WORLD WAR

The Turks had occupied Hodeida in 1849 and, after concluding a treaty with the Imam, proceeded to settle in San'a but were expelled with heavy casualties by its inhabitants. There followed twenty years of near anarchy until the opening of the Suez Canal enabled Constantinople to send large reinforcements by sea as part of its general policy of reasserting its position in Arabia. San'a was occupied again in 1871 and while the Zaidis were left alone, the rest of the country was virtually controlled by occupying forces despite frequent skirmishes with the tribes. Yemen was regarded as a place of exile for Ottoman officials whose financial dishonesty and lax morals caused great resentment.

In 1891 Muhammad Hamid ad-Din was elected Imam and, taking the regnal name assumed by the leader of the seventeenth century revolt, he issued a proclamation denouncing the religious unworthiness of the Turks to rule the country, once again showing the symbiosis of Zaidi doctrine and Yemeni nationalism. Soon all the highlands rallied to him but Constantinople retaliated by sending a notoriously ruthless Pasha who crushed the rebellion. The Turks then attempted to modernize their administration, but the secular nature of many of their reforms alienated the Shafai inhabitants of the Tihamah and Hujariyah.

In 1904 Muhammad's son, Yahya, succeeded him as Imam and called for a new uprising. In addition to their immorality and secularization, he was particularly incensed by the Turkish agreement with the British to delimit a frontier which he regarded as recognizing the separation of territory he considered as part of historic Yemen. Despite the deployment of almost 100,000 troops, the Turks were unable to destroy Yahya's tribal levies and in 1911, anxious to redeploy their troops to confront the Italian invasion of Tripoli and imminent war in the Balkans, they concluded with him the treaty of Da'an. Yahya conceded that the Ottoman Sultan was responsible for the defence and foreign affairs of the Islamic community as a whole, including Yemen, in return for non-interference in the religious and legal affairs of the Zaidis: in effect he was left in control of the Highlands while the Turks ruled the Tihamah where unrest continued.

Despite several British efforts to buy his support after the outbreak of war in 1914, Yahya remained loyal to the treaty. The Turks, by exploiting British military incompetence, occupied Lahej and besieged Aden for over three years. Having failed to win over Yahya, the British sought to undermine

his position by providing the intensely ambitious *de facto* independent ruler of Asir, Said Muhammad Ali al-Idrisi, with the financial means to subvert the Hashid and Bakil tribes and encouraged plots to overthrow the Imam. Yahya also resented apparent British support for the pretensions of Sharif Hussain of Mecca to be King of the Arabs and the seizure of Kamaran, just off the Yemeni coast. The Turks occupied the north-western part of the Protectorate, tried unsuccessfully to incite the tribes east of Aden and only withdrew after their Government, defeated elsewhere, sought an armistice.

BRITISH RELATIONS WITH THE IMAM YAHYA

After the war, relations between Yahya and the British Government were extremely uncordial. They deteriorated further when, upon the withdrawal of the Turks from territories within the recognized area of the Aden Protectorate, Yahya sent his troops to replace the Turkish contingent while the British seized Hodeida and encouraged Idrisi to extend his influence in the Tihamah where, as a Shafai, he was preferred to the Zaidi Imam. When Hodeida was evacuated, Idrisi was allowed to occupy it. The British then attempted to conciliate Yahya in the same way as had been the strategy with other Peninsular rulers, most of whom received subsidies from Britain in return for accepting direction in their foreign affairs. A mission sent for the purpose was detained in Tihamah by Shafai tribesmen opposed to the Imam. Negotiations lingered on because the British wished to discuss details of a frontier which Yahya, claiming by right of inheritance all that had once been ruled by his Himyaritic ancestors, declared had no legal existence. He also denied the right of the authorities in Aden to have relations with the Protectorate chiefs whom he regarded as Yemeni subjects. After a serious incident in 1928 the British bombed Taiz and other cities and Yahya agreed to withdraw his troops.

In 1933 Yahya, aware of the probability of war with Ibn Sa'ud on his northern frontier, settled his dispute with the British. In the Treaty of San'a, signed in February 1934, he tacitly accepted the boundaries agreed between Britain and the Turks, although he considered this as merely permitting Aden to administer part of his territory. In deference to his claims, no further boundary pillars were erected and no further survey carried out. It was agreed that no changes would be made in the boundaries for forty years after which the matter would be discussed again. The British elevated Yahya's status by recognizing him as king. The treaty ushered in a period of generally peaceful coexistance which lasted for the rest of the reign of Imam Yahya. He resented the toleration of his political opponents in Aden while the British were concerned about his apparent friendship with Fascist Italy although during the Second World War he remained strictly neutral.

POST-WAR ADEN AND THE HINTERLAND

In 1937, in addition to the Hinterland, the Colonial Office had taken control of Aden itself. In 1947 a nominated Legislative Council for Aden was established and in 1949 the first elections, for a township authority, were held. Meanwhile, the town was transformed by the construction of a refinery, and the efficient bunkering service that followed ensured that Aden, still a free port, was by 1957 fourth after London, Liverpool and New York in the amount of shipping that it handled. Local industries were created to satisfy the needs of a population which trebled within a few years and increased still further after the British Government's Defence White Paper of 1957 made the Colony the largest British military base outside Europe. The increase in prosperity enabled the Government in Aden to establish what were, at the time, the best social services in the Arab world. Most who came to work in Aden were from the North, and locally-born Arabs were outnumbered by Yemeni immigrants.

There was no evidence of discontent with colonial rule before December 1947, when there was a general strike, followed by riots in which over 100 people were killed, as a protest against British policy in Palestine. Subsequently three nationalist groups emerged—the Aden Association, which aimed at eventual independence within the Commonwealth, to be achieved by co-operation; the South Arabian League, seeking independence for a united Colony and Protectorate under the Sultan of Lahej; and a radical United National Front, demanding union with Yemen and Muscat as a republic.

These movements were supported by the freest press in the Arab world, but it was the rise of a trade union movement that strengthened their position. At a time when the voice of Nasser could be heard through the newly-invented transistor radios, the Imam's union with Egypt led to the first talk of 'the occupied South', and, when a reform gave the elected members a majority on the Legislative Council, the question arose of votes for immigrants from North Yemen, who constituted the majority of trade unionists. When, in January 1959, voting was held for 12 seats, there was a boycott by many Arabs: nine Arabs, two Somalis and an Indian were elected.

After the Treaty of San'a, the administration in Aden believed that more should be done for the Protectorate, and the first measure was to appoint a Political Officer and to enlist local tribesmen to police their own areas. There was a considerable increase in security, and progress was made in educational, health and agricultural matters. In 1937 the Qu'aiti Sultan of Mukalla had become the first ruler to bind himself to accept a resident adviser and 'for the welfare of his state to accept his advice in all matters except those concerning Muhammadan religion and custom'. Within five years the area had an effective, locally-run administration, directed by a State Council.

The Hinterland was divided into the Eastern and Western Aden Protectorates. The EAP comprised the Hadramawt, the coastal strip of Mahra and the associated island of Socotra, and two minor Wahidi sultanates to the west of Mukalla with a total population estimated at 326,000. The WAP consisted of 17 states and various territories where there was no administration of any sort and which were never even visited by government officials, Arab or English.

Advisory treaties were later signed with the other states of the EAP and with many of those of the WAP. Their effect depended upon the working relationship that the adviser could establish with his local ruler for he had no executive powers. A Sultan who rejected 'advice' tendered through the Governor could be deposed, but this needed the approval of the Secretary of State for the Colonies, who, wrestling with problems of communism in Malaya or the Mau-Mau in Kenya, would have little time for the misconduct of a minor sheikh. An Arab chief who was knowledgeable about the area and who was liked or feared by the people, could normally impose his views upon a transitory British official. In practice the Sultanates were not colonies because they enjoyed a large degree of independence, albeit hampered by financial dependence on the British.

During the Second World War British intervention increased because of the need to maximize local production of food. By 1954 the number of chiefs in relation with Aden had grown to more than 50 and this incensed the Imam who imposed his own interpretation of the Treaty of San'a, which he declared to have been violated. He therefore initiated a determined effort to incite the tribes to revolt against Christian encroachments. This caused the Governor, Sir Tom Hickinbotham, to reverse the old policy of relying on tribal particularism in order to prevent union against the British and to attempt to form a federal union which would create a distinct South Arabian nation. He attempted, but failed, to impose a ready-made formula, which made no mention of eventual independence and was unsuited to local conditons.

The idea of federation, despite its failure, provoked the Imam into intensifying his efforts to arouse subversion. He was assisted by Egyptian and Russian advisers and technicians. Violent incidents culminated in the spring of 1958, when an estimated 1,000 dissidents besieged a British Political Officer in a fort near the frontier while, at the same time, bombs were being thrown in Aden Colony. The idea of federation also encouraged the Sultan of Lahej to attempt to unite South Arabia under his own rule and consequently began to recruit adherents in other states while at the same time he talked of joining the Arab League and of employing Egyptian advisers. He was deposed.

The double threat from Lahej and Yemen, which would become more dangerous when Badr, known to be pro-Nasser, succeeded his father; the fact that the increase in economic

activity made the existence of customs posts every few miles an absurd inconvenience; and the possibility that oil would be discovered in Hadramawt which would be unlikely to share its benefits unless there was some form of unity, revived the idea of federation. The British authorities primed the most trusted Amirs with financial rewards and promises and feigned surprise when the rulers of six WAP states, Beihan, Audhali, Fadhli, Dhala, Lower Yafa and the Upper Aulaqi Sheikhdom travelled to Britain to request assistance in forming a federation.

THE MUTAWAKILITE KINGS (1919–1962)

During the war in 1914 Yahya had only exerted authority in the Zaidi areas and after the departure of the Turks, Idrisi made a determined effort to assume control of the Shafai areas. In 1920, however, the British discontinued his subsidy and his supporters decreased. He died in 1923, leaving feuding successors and a situation in which both Yahya and Ibn Sa'ud could intervene. Although a certain amount of fighting was involved, Yahya managed to bring both Zaidi and Shafai areas under either his own control or that of friendly chiefs. British officials travelling to San'a to negotiate the treaty of 1934 were astonished at the tranquillity of the country, which contrasted strongly with the insecurity prevailing in the Aden Protectorate.

Yahya managed to retain some Turkish soldiers and officials to form a backbone for his administration but otherwise he relied upon the traditional allies of the Imamate—the Saiyids and the traditional literate class of Qadis and upon the Hashid and the Bakil to comprise an armed force.

Yemen, before the discovery of oil in the Peninsula, was practically the only state that was self-supporting and Yahya saw no need for foreigners who might interfere with his independence and corrupt his people. Not even Arab states were permitted to establish embassies in San'a, foreign newspapers were forbidden, prospecting for oil or minerals was prohibited and though some weapons were obtained from Italy, Yahya ensured that it exercised no political influence. His determination to reconstitute the Himyarite 'empire' led to maladroit encroachments in Asir and Najran which culminated in a war with Saudi Arabia. An army under the future King Faisal advanced through the Tihamah, capturing Hodeida, but Ibn Saud, unwilling to commit his troops to fighting in the mountains and to risk European intervention, made peace on generous terms, although Yahya had to withdraw his claims to Asir and Najran. Towards the end of his reign, Yahya joined the Arab League and the UN, uniting with other Arabs in opposition to Zionism.

Yahya had allowed young men to study abroad and had even sent some to Baghdad for military training. They returned convinced of the backwardness of Yemen and formed an opposition group, the *Ahrar*, the Free Yemenis, based in Aden where they received support in the local press. They were financed by merchants who wished to end royal monopolies. Yahya had provoked some of the religious leaders by breaking Zaidi tradition in requiring oaths of allegiance to his son Ahmad as Crown Prince. This particularly affronted the influential Saiyid Abd Allah al-Wazir who considered his right to the throne at least equal to that of Ahmad. These dissidents coalesced in a 'Sacred National Pact' which would establish a constitutional Imamate under al-Wazir, and enlisted tribal outlaws who in February 1948 assassinated Yahya in the first post-war coup in the Arab world.

Ahmad, though personally unpopular, managed to rally the tribes because of the shock of the murder, the failure of the new regime to attract support at home or abroad, and a promise that his tribal followers might sack San'a. He moved the capital to Taiz and ruled as autocratically as his father had done, showing the same immense knowledge of the country and intuitive understanding of the causes of local events. He survived a failed military coup and several assassination attempts.

He ended the country's isolation, admitting resident ambassadors, giving concessions to oil prospectors, accepting Soviet aid to develop Hodeida harbour and a Chinese-built road up to San'a. He maintained the claim to rule the whole of South Arabia and his dislike of the British, intensified by suspicions that they had connived at the murder of his father and by their adoption of a forward policy in the Aden Protectorate at a time when imperialism was in retreat elsewhere. In 1953, with the support of other Arab states, he raised the issue with the UN. He feared that the British might formally annex Shabwa, where there was believed to be oil. His officials fomented trouble across the frontier, attracting malcontents with arms and money. In order to acquire arms he signed a treaty in 1955 with Saudi Arabia and Egypt and later made agreements with several Eastern Bloc countries. Criticism grew of his reactionary and arbitrary policies, but he disconcerted his opponents by joining with Egypt and Syria in the United Arab States, which implied the backing of Nasser, the champion of radical Arab nationalism. In April 1959 Ahmad was the first Imam ever to leave the country, travelling to Rome, Italy, for treatment for morphine addiction. The unnatural union did not survive Egyptian intervention during his absence and he denounced it. Consequently, hostility to Nasser led to a *rapprochement* with the British. He reverted to morphine addicton after another assassination attempt and gradually allowed Badr to assume power before his death in September 1962.

THE FEDERATION OF SOUTH ARABIA

After a Treaty in which the British extended to the new entity, as a whole, the Protectorate Treaties previously concluded with its individual members, the Federation came into existence in February 1959. The British would continue to meet the cost of its defence. Its ultimate aim, for which the Colonial Secretary pledged help to prepare, was independence. A new capital, al-Ittihad, was built and Sultans, sitting as the Supreme Council, constituted its only political and legislative organ. The ruler of each state, eventually numbering seventeen, had to be given a cabinet portfolio. The Federation, dependent on British officials and British finances, initially appeared to be an instrument for British foreign policy and was never recognized by Arab Governments, many of which worked to destroy it. Nevertheless, considerable economic and some social progress was made, and in 1961 the Federation acquired its own armed forces, consisting of five infantry battalions, an armoured car regiment with signals and administrative units.

In 1961 the British Government, believing that the security of the base in Aden was threatened by the turbulence engendered by Trade Union activists, now calling themselves the People's Socialist Party, decided to overwhelm the nationalists there by merging the Colony into the new Federation. Britain would retain sovereignty over the Colony. Many Aden politicians were strongly opposed, but enough were coerced or bribed and some genuinely supported it. A motion to unite was forced through the Legislative Council in September 1962 and took effect from January 1963, but many, particularly the intellectuals, never ceased to resent the way in which merger was brought about. All those with grievances found a ready hearing amongst those in the British Labour Party who were ideologically opposed to a government of Sultans.

Mutual jealousies amongst the rulers meant that the federation had neither a president nor a prime minister and its titular head was the Chairman of the Supreme Council—an office which rotated monthly. The important states of the EAP refused to join and the British declined to coerce them although federal leaders saw their membership as vital. A constitutional conference arranged for December 1963 had to be postponed when a grenade was thrown amongst the rulers assembled at Aden airport, and it did not take place until June 1964. The leaders assembled in London, England, were relentlessly intimidated by the Colonial Secretary, Duncan Sandys, to the extent that one of the founding Sultans defected, joining the nationalist opposition in Cairo, Egypt. It was announced, however, that independence would come in 1968 and that in the interim there would be a President and a Prime Minister, an elected assembly and complete arabization of the civil service. These reforms were not implemented, for there was no agreement as to who should occupy the principal offices and outside Aden there was still no real administrative structure and no political organization to mobilize the people in support of the Federation. The rulers, in

offices in the capital, started to lose touch with what was occurring in their home states. Aden remained under a state of emergency imposed after the grenade attack and there was an increasing tendency amongst British officials to see its population as 'disloyal' in comparison with the 'trustworthy' Sultans.

The Yemeni Revolution had brought bribed Egyptian officers to the frontier to incite subversion. With their encouragement, young men from the Protectorates, inspired by the ideals of Arab nationalism, formed the National Liberation Front (which was allegedly entirely financed by Egypt) announcing in a declaration of 14 October 1963 that they intended not merely to expel the British from South Arabia, but to make a socialist revolution. Their first triumph was to provoke a tribal revolt in Radfan which was suppressed by the use of British troops, helicopters and even heavy bombers. The campaign attracted wide publicity and led to criticism by left-wingers in Britain and the Arab world which seriously damaged the image of the Federation, in whose name it was undertaken. Further denunciation followed the destruction of a Yemeni fort after Egyptian aircraft had dropped bombs on the territory of the Federal Government which then invoked the Defence Treaty with Britain. The anti-colonial group at the UN became increasingly interested in the area, passing, in 1963, Resolution 1949 which called for self-determination for South Arabia, elections under UN supervision and the removal of the British base. Doubts about the future of the Federation increased after the election of Harold Wilson as the Prime Minister of the British Government in October 1964.

In April 1964, visiting San'a, Nasser had sworn 'by Allah, to expel the British from all parts of the Arabian peninsula' and a campaign of urban terror was launched to make Aden ungovernable. It was estimated that between December 1963 and May 1966, 60 people were killed and 350 injured in Aden alone, one-third of the casualties being British. On joining the Federation Aden had been given a Chief Minister and Abd al-Qawi Makkawi, appointed to that post in March 1965, appeared more anxious to appease the terrorists than to collaborate with the British. He denounced the state of emergency and the banning of the NLF. After Makkawi had refused publicly to condemn the murder of a respected official, he was dismissed by the Governor, Sir Richard Turnbull, who suspended the Constitution and imposed direct colonial rule in September 1965. He went into exile, joined soon afterwards by Asnaj and they and the NLF amalgamated, as a result of Egyptian pressure, to form the Front for the Liberation of Occupied South Yemen (FLOSY).

Financial difficulties and the need to conciliate internal party opposition led the Wilson Government, in February 1966, to announce that there was no further need for the Aden base—the defence of which had been the paramount reason for creating the Federation. Moreover, there would be no further British military presence in South Arabia after independence in 1968. The Federal leaders, realizing that they had isolated themselves from much of the Arab world by supporting the British, felt betrayed and defenceless. Around the same time militants of the NLF became more radical, finding the ideas of Mao and Guevara more to their liking than those of the bourgeois Nasser and of the FLOSY leaders and, by bank robberies and extortion, they freed themselves from financial dependence on Egypt. Assisted by fellow tribesmen in the police force and the Federal Armed Forces, they fought the British and at the same time wrested control of the Aden streets from FLOSY. Aden was still formally a Colony and the British refused to allow the Federal Government to use its own forces to improve security there and its members started to lose confidence in their own future and attempted to negotiate on a basis of Resolution 1949. In December 1966 the NLF declared itself the sole representative of the people of South Arabia.

The British Government was now preoccupied with withdrawing from South Arabia with the minimum cost in British lives and with the lesser objective of leaving a stable government behind. Various expedients were tried, including inviting help from Nasser and from the UN, promising a short-term security cover and working for an alliance between the Federal Government and the NLF, with which secret contacts were established. It was even hoped that Saudi Arabia might take over responsibility for the area. There was also a desperate attempt to organize a new administration under an Adeni Prime Minister, after a brief but bloody military mutiny in June 1967 but this failed owing to the jealousies of the tribal ministers.

The NLF started to take control of state after state in the hinterland and on 4 September 1967 the High Commissioner stated that the Federal Government had ceased to exist. Although the NLF was known to have extreme left-wing views, the British preferred it to the pro-Nasser FLOSY and assisted its assumption of power. FLOSY, deprived of external support as a result of the Egyptian withdrawal from Yemen, was defeated with heavy losses after the Federal Army declared support for the NLF. The handover to the NLF was formalized by a meeting at Geneva, after which force and threats were used by the British to prevent any of the Federal rulers from returning home.

One of the main causes of the failure of the Federation was the fact that it had been created when there was a need for a base and abandoned when there was not. It had an abnormal status, completely dependent on the UK for military and financial support, and unable to negotiate on its own behalf with other Arab states. Nevertheless, it was not a colony in which the British could force the rulers to establish a reasonable form of government or come to terms with moderate nationalists like Asnaj and Makkawi when this would have been possible. Its problems might have been overcome if it had had more time and not been plagued almost from the beginning with armed opposition. It made no serious attempt to win acceptance, apart from distributing money obtained from the British tax-payer; it never attracted any ideological support and it had no organization throughout the country. The brief period of the Federation, was, however, an essential bridge between the local particularism of the past and the centralized state of the future.

REVOLUTION AND EGYPTIAN INTERVENTION IN THE NORTH

The Imam Ahmad died on 19 September 1962 and Badr assumed the throne. Nasser welcomed this development as it seems likely that he had sanctioned a coup against Ahmad but ordered its postponement on his death as he regarded Badr as an ally who would support his version of Arab nationalism. His instructions were, however, disregarded by the Commander-in-Chief, Field Marshal Abd al-Hakim Amer, who was anxious to find an independent and profitable source of revenue for the Egyptian army. With the help of Egyptian officers, Yemeni officers on the night of 26/27 September bombarded the palace of Badr and announced that he had been assassinated. A senior officer, Col Abd Allah Sallal, who does not seem to have been involved in the coup, was proclaimed President in the expectation that he would later be replaced. Within days, in order to 'oppose any foreign intervention', Egyptian troops arrived with such speed that they had clearly been deployed beforehand, in anticipation of the coup.

The Royalists rallied under Badr's uncle, Hassan, who was proclaimed Imam and called for the tribes to rally to him. Although many supported the new Imam, the traditional allies of the Imamate, the Hashid and Bakil, whose chiefs had suffered at the hands of Ahmad, did not. Hassan set up a government in Saudi Arabia and also received help from the federal rulers of the south, with the connivance of the British. In October the Royalists captured Marib in the east but were repelled at Sada in the north. The Egyptians, knowing that this could not have been achieved without Saudi help, bombed Saudi towns and the two countries appeared on the brink of open war. Sallal called for all-out war, proclaimed a republic of the Arabian peninsula and demanded the return of Najran and Asir.

In November 1962 Badr reappeared, gave a press conference, and resumed the Imamate. The Americans, believing that the Republic controlled the whole country and anxious to conciliate Nasser, recognized the new regime but the British who were better informed, did not and their legation was closed. The Yemen Arab Republic was admitted to the UN.

Sallal promoted himself Field Marshal and was determined to rule. However, despite several attempts to secure constitutional legitimacy, he was never able to do so. Practically without local adherents, he had to rely on the Egyptians, who, though they often treated him with contempt, were unable to find a more convincing representative. The Egyptian forces were increased, in 1963 numbering about 28,000, and in April the UN attempted to bring about the disengagement of Egyptian and Saudi forces by providing an Observer Mission (UNYOM) but as it was not forbidden to contact the Royalists, it proved totally futile and was withdrawn in September 1964.

Many Yemenis came to realise that their country was merely providing a battlefield on which Nasser and King Faisal were contesting the leadership of the Arab world. Moderate republicans and moderate royalists therefore attempted to make a peace between Yemenis at a conference at Erkowit in Sudan in October 1964. They agreed that both Badr and Sallal should relinquish power and that Egyptian forces should be asked to leave, but the initiative failed owing to the intransigence of the Egyptians and of Sallal. A cease-fire was proclaimed, but it lasted only a few days and was followed by a series of Royalist successes, which left them in control of one-third of the country. The Republicans split and the moderates, led by the Prime Minister, Ahmad Nu'man, tried to make peace but were again frustrated by Sallal's belligerence.

Nasser, realizing that he could not win a war which was becoming extremely unpopular at home, tried to end it by negotiating with King Faisal on the basis that he would withdraw his forces, now estimated at 50,000 provided the Saudis stopped supplying the Royalists. Negotiations continued until the publication of the British White Paper on Defence of February 1966 with the statement of the intended departure from Aden by 1968.

For the next year there was a stalemate—which the armed forces, subsidized by at least one side and with unusual opportunities to loot—were in no hurry to end. Egyptian military activity was confined to bombing and poison gas attacks, while the Royalists were divided by internal feuds in the absence of Badr through ill-health.

The situation was transformed by the Egyptian defeat in the June War of 1967. At the Khartoum Summit, Nasser, now dependent upon Saudi Arabian financial assistance, agreed to withdraw his troops from Yemen. This was opposed by Sallal who feared for his own position but the withdrawal of Egyptian troops was nevertheless completed by the end of November, by which time he was out of the country on his way to seek alternative support from the Eastern Bloc. No one rallied to his support, there was no bloodshed and he was succeeded by a three-man Council headed by Qadi Abd ar-Rahman al-Iryani who had been one of the old *Ahrar* but had also been an adviser to the Imam Ahmad.

The Royalists launched a major offensive and in December they began a three-month siege of San'a. The Republicans, led by General Hassan al-Amri, conducted a vigorous defence in which they were supported firstly by Russian aircraft and secondly by the NLF which had by then taken power in Aden and which sent volunteers who succeeded in opening the road from Hodeida. Amri, without the Egyptian forces previously thought indispensable, succeeded in reconquering much of the country, helped by intensified Royalist feuding which led to the brief deposition of Badr by his cousin Muhammad bin Hussain. Many tribal chiefs defected.

By February 1970 King Faisal had decided that he could tolerate the moderate Republic of Iryani, a pious Muslim, and indeed use it as an ally against the communist South. He therefore terminated all aid to the Royalists and 'ordered' them to cease fighting. Nearly all except members of the ruling family returned and were integrated in the new regime which was then recognized by Saudi Arabia and the UK. It was estimated that during the war 200,000 Yemenis, 4% of the population, had been killed. Although the Egyptians had done some good work in improving education and other social services, they had also installed a ponderous bureaucracy, modelled on the one in Cairo, which was quite unsuitable for Yemeni needs.

THE SOUTH GOES LEFT (1967–1978)

Qahtan ash-Shaabi, the only one amongst the chiefs of the NLF with sufficient seniority to be credible as a statesman, had emerged as their leader at their first Congress at Taiz in 1965. He led the delegation to the Geneva talks and upon the formal take-over of sovereignty on 30 November 1967 he proclaimed himself President, Prime Minister and Commander in Chief. He at once declared South Yemen a unitary state, abolished the old sheikhdoms and demanded the abandonment of all tribal bloodfeuds. Other parties were banned, the press was controlled, a State Security Supreme Court was created and quickly established firm control throughout the country by means of a police force trained by East Germans. A rising amongst the Aulaqis, who had been the greatest beneficiaries of the Federation but who also had preferred FLOSY to the NLF, was crushed with such savagery that henceforth they played little part in affairs and an attempt by the Sharif of Beihan, with Saudi backing, to regain his state was defeated.

Relations with the UK deteriorated rapidly as advisers who had remained to assist in the build-up of new armed forces were expelled and replaced by Russians who also provided arms. The handing over to Muscat by the British of the Kuria Muria islands caused bitterness in Aden. Although it was believed that the USA had given covert help to the NLF when it was a clandestine anti-British movement, their military attaché was given 24 hours' notice to leave, and the controlled press made much of their connections with Israel and with Saudi Arabia which had emerged as the principal enemy of the new state.

On the day he assumed office Shaabi declared that 'the aim of our Revolution has been since the beginning to unite both parts of Yemen. We are all one people'. He appointed one of the most influential NLF leaders, Abd al-Fattah Ismail, as Minister of Yemeni Unity Affairs; a similar Ministry was set up in San'a. No Ambassadors were appointed between the two Governments, whose relations were handled by these Ministries. North and South helped each other against local opponents and there was talk of a Greater Yemen embracing Asir, Najran and even Muscat.

The country was in a desperate financial plight as a result of the ending of British subsidies and the departure of the large, free-spending expatriate community which coincided with the closure of the Suez Canal which had been Aden's only other source of income. Faced with the problem of actually running the country, Shaabi showed a definite pragmatism by refusing to dismantle working institutions. Although he had been imprisoned by Nasser, Shaabi believed, like the Egyptian leader, in egalitarianism, imposed by firm authority, and was in no way a communist. Opposing him was an extreme left group, under the leadership of Ismail and Ali Salim al-Baid which called for a complete new beginning with 'scientific socialism' based on rural soviets, collectivization of land, a People's Militia, nationalization of banks and foreign trade and the export of revolution throughout the Peninsula. These policies divided the party at the Zinjibar Congress of March 1968 and the leftist view prevailed. Shaabi, however, persuaded the army that its status would be theatened by the proposed Militia and, on his behalf, it arrested his leading opponents.

Shaabi had, however, been alarmed by the strength of the extremists and he moved to the left. He spoke of the socialist path and the redistribution of land. He took control of imports although he was still anxious to encourage the investment of foreign capital. He called on the Saudi people to overthrow their monarch and provided bases for the Dhofari rebels. His numerous visits abroad included Moscow and Pyongyang (North Korea) among the destinations. These moves, at a time when the YAR was moving into the Saudi orbit, led to verbal hostilities between San'a and Aden.

Shaabi had released his left-wing opponents and even included some of them in his Government. In June 1969 he quarrelled over the posting of an officer with the Minister of the Interior, Muhammad Ali Haitham, a man with very similar political views, and dismissed him. Haitham, who had considerable influence with the army and with the tribes, thereupon joined forces with the left, and later that month, in a bloodless coup, Shaabi and his cousin, Prime Minister Faisal

Abd al-Latif, were deposed. He was replaced by a five-man Presidency Council, chaired by Salim Rubai Ali and including Ismail and Haitham, who was appointed Prime Minister. The shift to the left was signalled immediately by the recognition of East Germany by the new Minister of Foreign Affairs, Ali Salim al-Baid. In October, having called on all Arab countries to follow his lead, he broke off diplomatic relations with the USA.

There followed a period of harsh repression with constant speeches about conspiracies, mass arrests with special courts untrammelled by ordinary law 'to review anti-state activity'. Large numbers of citizens, some estimated up to a quarter of the population, fled abroad. The army, whose commander escaped to Taiz, and the police, were subjugated through purges and indoctrination. Military training started in schools. Ismail encouraged the spread of party branches throughout the country.

The Government called for revolution in 'the Occupied Gulf' and refused to recognize the independence of Bahrain, Qatar and the UAE. There was a frontier clash with Saudi Arabia at al-Wadiah in November 1969. Such stong support was given to the rebels in Dhofar that they also succeeded in capturing Salala. Haitham, however, worked to improve relations with the YAR and in November 1970 was the first South Yemeni Prime Minister to visit Taiz where he urged unification. A new Constitution, with its adoption of the name People's Democratic Republic of Yemen was announced. Drawn up by an East German and an Egyptian, its commitment to socialism, tolerance of Islam, stress on the rights of women, and vesting of all power in the party differed greatly from the constitution adopted shortly afterwards in the YAR. This, drawn up after intensive local consultations, was, more than any other recent Arab Constitution, based on Islamic principles, with a constitutional court of *ulama*, empowered to ensure that laws were based on Islamic principles.

Abd al-Fattah Ismail, as Secretary-General, was immersed in party and doctrinal affairs, building a following amongst the urban proletariat. Ali, the Chairman, visited the People's Republic of China, returning inspired by Maoist ideas of spreading the revolution in the countryside by encouraging the seizure of land by the peasants and in 1970 he signed a series of decrees nationalizing businesses and concentrating most economic activities in the hands of the state. In the same year Aden ceased to be a free port. Aid from the USSR alone kept the country afloat. Facing the problem of actually administering a country in a perpetual economic crisis, Haitham tried to moderate foreign and domestic policies to encourage foreign and local investment. His colleagues, Ali and Ismail, both adopted a more dogmatic approach and conspired against him. He was replaced in August 1971 by Ali Nasir Muhammad, the Minister of Defence. There followed a new wave of purges and arrests.

The Constitutions of 1970 had shown that there was no common ideological grounds between North and South Yemen and the financial dependence of one on Saudi Arabia and the other on the USSR prevented any move towards unity: indeed neither the Cabinet of the PDRY nor that of the YAR contained a Minister of Unity Affairs. The situation was intensified by the presence on Northern territory of thousands of exiles from the South, armed and funded by Saudi Arabia. Border incidents followed their incursions and a leading Northern tribal sheikh was lured across the frontier and murdered with 60 of his followers. In San'a, army officers, who were partly funded by Saudi Arabia, called for war to end communism in the South. Each side accused the other of increasingly grave acts of aggression and in September there was widespread fighting which continued for several days, in the course of which the North captured Kamaran. An Arab League mission mediated a cease-fire and then, on 28 October 1972, to general amazement, an agreement was reached in Cairo, Egypt which provided for a single unified state, with one flag, one capital, one leadership, with single legislative, executive and judicial organs. A formal Treaty of Union was signed between the two Presidents in Tripoli, Libya in November.

Eight committees were set up to discuss the details of unification with instructions to finalize proceedings within a year, after which a new Constitution would be put to a referendum. Saudi Arabia and the USSR both publicly welcomed the union but each feared that its own protégé would be the weaker partner and become submerged beneath the predominance of the opposing camp. Conservatives in San'a, who had contacts with Saudi Arabia, put obstacles in the way of progress and when in May 1973 a leading opponent of unification was murdered, it was generally believed that Aden had been responsible. President Iryani personally favoured unification but admitted that little progress had been made by the committees. After his removal from office, prospects for unity seemed to increase, for his successor, Lt-Col Ibrahim al-Hamadi, established cordial personal relations with Ali; each felt the support of the other would be beneficial in internal politics in which each was under threat, and in foreign affairs in weakening dependence on their respective patrons. They agreed on a gradual approach to unity through economic co-operation and in February 1977 they constituted a council of themselves and senior ministers to meet every six months. A joint diplomatic mission toured the oil states. There was speculation that there would be an important announcement concerning unification when Hamadi visited Aden in October 1974 but, two days before he was due to arrive, he was murdered. After his death Lt-Col Ahmad ibn Hussein al-Ghashmi, his successor, established closer contacts with the Saudis and relations with Aden deteriorated.

The death of King Faisal enabled the establishment of diplomatic relations with Saudi Arabia and in August 1977 Ali visited Riyadh. A cease-fire was announced with Oman. Kuwait and Abu Dhabi provided aid. Relations with Britain improved and the Aden refinery was taken over by agreement. In October 1977 at the UN Ali made preliminary overtures to the USA. He tried to maintain equal loyalty to the USSR and the People's Republic of China. All these moves angered Ismail who wanted friendship exclusively with the USSR and with Cuba which provided instructors. The foreign policy of the PDRY followed an erratic course as the two leaders struggled for control. Ismail managed to send troops to assist the new revolution in Ethiopia, the success of which was vitally important to the USSR. Ali, meanwhile, had arranged to receive an envoy from the USA.

It seems that at this juncture Ali attempted to establish with Ghashmi the same close ties that he had had with Hamadi. He sent a special messenger in whose briefcase a bomb, possibly placed by an agent of Ismail, exploded, killing both the YAR President and the envoy. Fighting immediately broke out in Aden, either because Ali attempted to arrest his opponents or Ismail ordered an attack, in which it is said Soviet and Cuban elements took part, on the Presidential Palace. Ali was captured, found guilty of numerous crimes and shot.

THE NORTH GOES RIGHT (1970–1978)

Abd ar-Rahman al-Iryani, who had succeeded Sallal, played an indispensable role in national reconciliation after eight years of war. An obviously pious Muslim with a liberal background, he had to take account of a central government weakened by the war, conservative tribal sheikhs and the *ulama*, and young modernisers and townsfolk anxious for reform against a background of financial crisis with an army demanding expensive new equipment. He played a major part in drafting a Constitution which was a real attempt to find a political system suitable to the country. Consequently, the first (indirect) elections in Yemeni history took place in April 1971.

In foreign affairs he succeeded in creating good relations with all the Arab states and with the West without alienating the USSR. The YAR could reasonably be described as a neutral country, despite its government's dependence on Saudi Arabia for financial aid. This largesse was also extended to influential individuals, especially the tribal chiefs whose domination of the Consultative Council hampered moves towards the unity with the South agreed in 1972.

Within a month of its signature, its principal architect, the Prime Minister Mohsin al-Aini, a man of leftist tendencies but influential tribal background, resigned. Iryani appointed a deeply religious conservative, Qadi Abdullah al-Hajari to succeed al-Aini. Al-Hajari immediately went to Riyadh to reassure the Saudis and received financial aid in return for renouncing

the Yemeni claim to Asir and Najran. Hajari made no attempt at administrative reform in a period of inefficiency and corruption and executed several supporters of unification. In August 1973, Iryani went into exile to show his discontent but returned to build up support against his Prime Minister whom, in February 1974, he felt strong enough to replace by the more competent and progressive Dr Hassan Makki. In June a plot backed by Iraq to overthrow the regime was discovered and Iryani opposed any strong action. When the army and tribal leaders threatened a coup, he resigned and went to live in Syria.

His successor was Colonel Ibrahim al-Hamadi, not a tribesman but a member of the Qadi class, who appointed al-Aini as his Prime Minister. He suspended the Constitution and the Consultative Council. Hamadi gradually became immensely popular, with inspiring oratory, evident honesty and sincerity and his youth, (he was about 30). He seemed to represent a new generation and engendered new hope after decades of harsh rule and civil war. He and al-Aini made a determined effort to eradicate corruption but in January 1975, feeling the need of a technocrat with financial expertise, Hamadi appointed Abd al-Aziz Abd al-Ghani as Prime Minister.

During 1975 Hamadi travelled widely, visiting nearly every Arab country, Iran and Europe. He returned with financial aid which would enable him to launch new projects and reduce dependence on Saudi Arabia, thus realizing one of his main objectives. He was concerned to develop rural areas on which he concentrated the ambitious development plan of 1977. He paid special attention to the Shafais and enlisted their help in making the army less a monopoly of Zaidi tribal notables. He aimed at a strong centralized state with wide political participation and he encouraged the emergence of the leftist National Democratic Front. These moves offended the practically independent northern chiefs, some of whom rebelled and were consequently bombed by the airforce. On the night of 11/12 October 1977 Hamadi and his brother were murdered. The assassins were never caught nor were the motives for the crime established. He was succeeded by the Chief of Staff, Ahmad al-Ghashmi, a tribesman of the Hashid confederation. A Shafai officer attempted to incite an uprising in Taiz but Ghashmi, with the help of the Zaidi tribes, crushed it and the rebels with other members of the NDF sought refuge in Aden where Ismail hoped to use them to bring about unity by overthrowing the Government in San'a. Ghashmi therefore loosened ties with Aden and strengthened relations with Saudi Arabia. He spoke of democracy and nominated a 99-man Constitutional Assembly which was to prepare the way for eventual elections. Preoccupied with day-to-day affairs, he had neither the ability nor the time to make a mark on Yemeni history before his murder on 24 June 1978.

ABD AL-FATTAH ISMAIL AND ALI NASIR MUHAMMAD (1979–1986)

After the execution of Ali in July 1978 several days of heavy fighting ensued with a new flood of refugees to the North. Ali Nasir Muhammad became Chairman of the Presidency Council to which were added the Communist, Ali Badeeb and the former guerrilla, Ali Antar. Ismail succeeded in his ambition of changing the NLF into a 'Vanguard Party'—the Yemen Socialist Party—with stringent rules for admission and discipline and which contained all his close collaborators, including al-Baid. In December Ismail became Head of State.

The YAR, now led by Colonel Ali Abdullah Saleh, blamed Aden for the murder of Ghashmi and prevailed upon the other Arab states to suspend relations with the PDRY. In February 1979, while the world was preoccupied with the fall of the Shah of Iran and a war between China and Viet Nam, the PDRY seized the opportunity to attack the North, to bring about unity by force. In well-planned attacks the main frontier towns were captured and the YAR army appeared to be on the verge of disintegration. Other Arab states intervened and on 30 March in Kuwait the two Presidents signed an agreement to unite, almost identical with that signed nearly seven years before.

In January 1980 it was stated that 134 articles of a constitution had been agreed. Previously, Ismail had visited the USSR where he signed a Treaty of Friendship which appeared more intimate than those with other Arab states. The PDRY endorsed the Soviet invasion of Afghanistan. As an administrator Ismail was incompetent and in domestic policies he was so extreme that it was reported that even Brezhnev, the Soviet Head of State, had urged him to restrain his enthusiasm. There was general surprise when on 20 April 1980 he resigned on grounds of ill health, was given an honorary title and went into exile in the USSR.

Ali Nasser Muhammad resumed the Presidency and although he still maintained the Soviet alliance he showed that it was not exclusive by visiting Saudi Arabia, where he established his Muslim credentials by performing *umrah*. He also attended the Islamic Summit in Ta'if. Saudi Arabia gave generous help after floods in March 1982 in which it was estimated that 500 people had perished and 64,000 were made homeless. The hostility to Oman which had existed since independence and continued despite the defeat of the Dhofari rebels nearly a decade before finally ended with an agreement to exchange ambassadors, although this did not happen for several years.

The departure of Ismail did not end Aden's support for the NDF which was extremely active in 1980 and 1981. The two Yemens also adopted different stances in the Iran–Iraq War. San'a was, however, angered by not being allowed to join the Gulf Co-operation Council and drew nearer to Aden. After a visit by Saleh, in December 1981, Muhammad agreed to reduce help to the NDF and the two Presidents laid down common foreign policy goals in which Saleh appeared to make concessions. They constituted themselves the Supreme Yemeni Council, which would hold regular meetings to discuss the practical details of unification. They also set up Joint Ministerial Committees. Sessions in San'a in August 1983 and in Aden in March 1984 showed some co-ordination of foreign policy. In January 1985 the PDRY and the YAR agreed to co-operate in joint exploitation of natural resources.

Local elections were held in 1981 in which the YSP announced that it had received 94.6% support. Despite nearly twenty years of official condemnation of tribalism, it was noticeable that the President entrusted more and more posts to people from his native Dathina and Abyan. However, when in March 1985 Muhammad decided to divest himself of the Premiership, a Saiyid from Hadramawt, Haidar Abu Bakr al-Attas, succeeded him.

In February 1985 Ismail returned from exile and was later given a place on the Politburo. He was clearly worried that Muhammad regarded the purity of Marxist-Leninist dogma as secondary to the practical needs of the country. In January 1986 Muhammad determined to arrest or kill his opponents at a meeting of the Politburo, was only partially successful and set off a brief but intensive civil war in which at least 2,000, including 55 senior party figures, were killed. The tribes of Dathina rallied to his side while those of the north-west fought to avenge Ali Antar, who had been killed in the Politburo fighting. Ismail disappeared and his body was never found: al-Baid, of whom Muhammad had hoped to rid himself, escaped. Some 6,000 foreigners were evacuated to Djibouti. Muhammad fled to Ethiopia where he was joined by the navy which had remained loyal to him. During the battle Saleh closed the frontier to prevent YAR tribesmen from joining either side.

ALI ABDULLAH SALEH AS PRESIDENT OF THE YAR (1978–1990)

Evidence that the assassination of Ghashmi in October 1974, was plotted from outside the YAR is provided by the fact that no group in San'a was prepared to take advantage of the incident. There was no obvious successor so a temporary Presidential Council was formed in 1978, under the chairmanship of the politically neutral Speaker of the Constitutional Assembly, Qadi Abd al-Karim al-Arshi. Nearly a month later the Assembly, by a large majority, elected as President, Lieutenant-Colonel Ali Abdullah Saleh, commander of the Taiz military area, who was, like his predecessor, a tribesman of the Hashid. He appointed al-Arshi Vice-President and Abd al-Ghani retained his portfolio as Prime Minister. At first his position was extremely precarious and he was fortunate to escape assassination in September and to survive what appeared to be an attempted military coup, with backing from

Aden, in October. The Shafai South, restless since the murder of Hamadi, was stirrred up by the NDF, based on Aden. There were also reports of fighting in the regions of Sada, Marib and Jawf and the YAR appeared on the point of collapse as Saleh was forced to revert back to the old Imamate policy of relying on the Hashid and Bakil to deal with internal threats. Only the intervention of other Arab states saved the country from complete disaster during the war with the South in September 1979.

Over the next few years Saleh acquired the skills, shown by the old Imams, required to rule an unusually difficult country. He also made a persistent effort to win support by increasing public participation in government. One of his first speeches promised 'real democracy', starting with municipal elections which took place in 1979. Later that year he appointed a 15-man Consultative Council and expanded the membership of the Constituent Assembly. In February 1980 he announced that there would be a general election and in May he set up a 'committee for national dialogue' to prepare for it. He also launched a new party called 'the Unified Yemeni Organisation' with a charter that comprised both the principles of the Revolution and the 'sublime principles of Islam'. In October he called into being a national Assembly of 1,000 representatives, 700 of whom were elected through elections in co-operatives which met in August 1982.

Progress towards elections was disrupted by increased activity by the NDF, whose leader, Sultan Ahmad Omar, stated that he would only participate if the Government committed itself to a series of measures which included land reform, nationalization of industry and less dependence on Saudi Arabia. The NDF overran considerable areas during 1981 but then Aden decreased its support and the Zaidi tribes, worried about the advance of the 'godless', rallied to the support of Saleh. Early in 1982 Saleh ordered a full-scale offensive, defeated the NDF and allowed the survivors to be reintegrated in the North.

In October 1980 there had been a change of Prime Minister when Abd al-Ghani, the Shafai economist, was replaced by another technocrat, an agricultural economist, Dr Abd al-Karim al-Iryani, a member of the Qadi class. In general Saleh's policy was to choose competent officials and not to interfere in administrative matters.

In foreign policy Saleh avoided total commitment either to the East or the West. The Saudis provided enough aid to keep his Government solvent but not enough to permit total economic independence. At the UN, the YAR abstained from voting on the Afghanistan question. Saleh's Ministers sought aid and investment from the West but Saleh also needed to obtain Soviet arms and exert pressure on Aden to reduce its backing for the NDF. As a result relations between the YAR and Saudi Arabia were downgraded. Saleh refused to endorse the American Rapid Deployment Force but did not join the Tripartite Pact of Libya, Ethiopia and the PDRY formed to denounce it. The Republic did not join the Gulf Co-operation Council but sent volunteers to fight for Iraq against Iran. In December 1982 the YAR provided a base for 2,000 PLO guerrillas after their expulsion from Beirut.

In 1984 Saleh revisited Moscow and signed a treaty of friendship similar to those concluded by the USSR with Syria and the PDRY, but refused to Libya. About the same time it was announced that although the Russians had failed to find oil in the YAR, the Americans had succeeded in doing so. Western help was essential for its exploitation and also in the development of agriculture to which the government attached almost equal importance. Also, in the same year, the YAR signed a five-year trade and aid agreement with the EC.

In November 1982 an earthquake devastated central Yemen, resulting in the deaths of more than 3,000 people and causing damage worth an estimated $3,000m. In December Dr Iryani was put in charge of reconstruction and Abd al-Ghani replaced him as Prime Minister. In 1985 Iryani was given the newly-created post of Chairman of the Supreme Council for Oil and Mineral Resources and another well-known economist, Dr Muhammad Said al-Attar was appointed Deputy Prime Minister and Minister of Development. Much of the attention of the Government had to be devoted to economic matters as the country exported less than 1% of the value of its imports.

Until its oil could be fully exploited, the YAR was dependent upon aid and remittances from citizens working abroad and had to observe the utmost austerity in restricting imports. There was, however, a great improvement in the infrastructure with the spread of roads and electricity. A particularly striking feature of the 1980s was the emergence of educated women, holding responsible posts in business and administration. Central Government control was loose in the tribal areas with the mountain tribes benefiting both from Saudi subsidies and from smuggling goods across its border.

In May 1983 Saleh unexpectedly resigned, annoucing that he would not stand for re-election. The Assembly, however, unanimously re-elected him for a further five years. In July 1985 the YAR held its first free elections when 17,500 representatives were elected to local councils working for co-operative development. About one half of the electorate voted and the polls were seen as a significant development which would eventually bring into political life educated young Yemenis and weaken the powers of the tribal sheikhs. On 5 July 1988 the long-postponed general election took place for 128 seats in the new 159-member Consultative Council which replaced the old Constituent Assembly. The remaining 31 members were appointed by the President. More than a million registered to vote, including 60,000 women, and more than 1,200 candidates stood for election. None of the fifteen women candidates was successful. Approximately one-sixth of the elective seats, including all six constituencies in San'a were won by candidates sympathetic to the Muslim Brotherhood and many others to tribesmen of conservative background. The Consultative Council was to have a life of five years and was empowered to legislate, to ratify treaties and supervise the work of government, in which it could pass a vote of no confidence. Its first action was to re-elect Saleh for another five years by 152 votes to none with 2 abstentions and five absentees. The post was strengthened by no longer having to share power with the Military Command Council. Saleh announced his aim to achieve democracy without repression, claimed that there were no political prisoners and stated that he would give priority to agriculture and industry making use of local materials. Abd al-Ghani was reappointed as Prime Minister. Subsequent events showed that the Parliament operated more freely than almost any other in the Arab world, criticizing government policies despite the intensification of a personality cult of the President.

In foreign policy Saleh aimed at being on good terms with as many states as possible by avoiding involvement in other people's quarrels. The exploitation of oil, which was first exported in December 1987, required investment and technology from most major states. In Arab matters the YAR tried to work through bilateral agreements through which Joint Committees arranged co-operation over a wide range of activities. In November 1987, following an Arab League decision that members might resume diplomatic relations with Egypt, the YAR did so and in mid-1988 President Mubarak visited San'a. The Government tried to maintain good relations with both Iraq and Syria and the Prime Minister negotiated aid agreements with both countries for the development of the oil industry. In October 1988 the Organization of the Islamic Council met in Sana'a, the first time that the city had hosted an international gathering on such a large scale. Saleh visited Pakistan and China, where he obtained aid worth $42m. In January 1989 President Saddam Hussain of Iraq visited San'a in order to thank Yemeni troops for their participation in the war with Iran. In the same year the YAR became a founder-member of the Arab Co-operation Council, with Jordan, Iraq and Egypt. The ACC was formed with the object of creating an Arab Common Market of those states that were ineligible to join the GCC, allowing free movement of labour and capital within the bloc and hoping to double trade between its members in the next few years.

Despite occasional frontier incidents, the outcome of local rivalries rather than government policies, with Saudi Arabia, relations were generally good. The Saudi-Yemeni Co-ordinating Committee, formed in 1975, continued to meet to distribute aid. In May 1989 Saudi Arabia lifted almost all restrictions imposed on Yemeni emigrant workers, giving them almost equal rights with Saudi citizens. At various stages of

the process towards unity with the South, Saleh travelled to Saudi Arabia to reassure King Fahd.

The USSR continued to provide training and technical personnel and in January 1990 Saleh visited the USA for the first time and was saluted by President Bush as 'a pillar of stability'. Saleh took every opportunity to put forward the case for the Palestinians and returned with increased aid.

Following a bomb explosion in the Grand Mosque in San'a in March 1989, three alleged members of the Muslim Brotherhood were summarily executed. In August twelve people were killed in the Marib area when tribesmen opposed the introduction of vehicle registration (which made smuggling more difficult). Following reports of unrest amongst Zaidi tribesmen who realised that the Shafais would be a majority in a united Yemen, their leader, the Paramount Sheikh of the Hashid who had been one of the most influential figures in the country for nearly 30 years, claimed that tribesmen should retain their right to bear arms. Religious leaders, too, continued to regard the Southerners as atheistic communists and to oppose unification.

THE PDRY 1986–1990

When Ali Nasir Muhammad attempted his coup in January 1986, the Prime Minister, Haidar Abu Bakr al-Attas, was on a mission to India, which he interrupted by visiting Moscow, USSR, hoping for some intervention to achieve a peace settlement. Upon his return, he assumed Muhammad's posts as President and Secretary-General of the YSP and appointed as Prime Minister the Deputy Prime Minister and Minister of Fisheries, Dr Yasin Said Numan. As a result of casualties and mass arrests of Muhammad's supporters, the Cabinet, the Politburo and the Central Committee underwent drastic changes. The first problem of the new regime was to restore a situation of normality. There were reports of three assassination attempts aimed at Attas. Muhammad had taken refuge in the North, where he was allegedly joined by numerous armed supporters. It was uncertain whether Saleh would be willing or able to prevent Muhammad and his supporters launching an invasion but, with assistance from the USSR, he managed to counteract any such action. Most of Muhammad's supporters who had been detained were gradually released and Attas succeeded, by a series of amnesties, in persuading most of those who had fled to return, including the entire navy which had sailed to Ethiopia. By October it was felt safe to hold the delayed general election in which 176 candidates contested the 111 seats in the Supreme People's Council. Attas was elected President for five years but it became apparent that al-Baid, Secretary-General of the YSP, held an equally important post.

In December 1986 the Supreme Court began the public trial of Muhammad and 93 others (48 of whom, including the ex-President, *in absentia*) on charges of treason and terrorist activities. After a year death sentences were passed on 35 of the defendants (19, including Muhammad still *in absentia*). There were international appeals for clemency and Attas commuted 24 of the death sentences to life imprisonment. Only five were actually executed and in May 1988 Muhammad was offered a retrial if he returned voluntarily. Later that year 35 of the remaining 59 prisoners, including three former ministers, were released. In January 1990, prior to unification, there was a general amnesty for all political offenders.

At a time when it was imperative to neutralize Muhammad and his followers, much power appeared to rest with the military, particularly in the hands of his tribal opponents from the north west, to the extent that the fourth Congress of the YSP in June 1987 expressed concern about 'opportunist rightists' in the armed forces. Despite the glorification of Ismail, Ali Antar and other 'martyrs' of January 1986 there appeared to be little change in either the internal affairs or foreign policy of the new regime. In the same year Attas stated that the relationship with Russia was the 'corner-stone' of government policy and there was close co-operation in trade, oil and economic matters. The USSR replaced the weapons destroyed in January 1986 and agreed to continue aid until 2005.

Nevertheless one of the first visits that Attas made as President of the PDRY was to assure King Fahd of Saudi

Arabia that there would be no further encouragement to incite revolutionary activities against the Saudi Government. It was noticeable that King Fahd did not, unlike his brother Faisal, finance or arm exiled opponents of the Aden regime. A Joint Ministerial Commission was established, several projects were financed, and the Saudis were the first to give aid after disastrous floods in March 1989. The reconciliation with Oman continued and in October 1988 Attas became the first PDRY Head of State to visit Muscat. Amidst references to "brother-hood", several agreements were signed including one to delimit the frontier. Other Gulf states provided aid. Relations with Ethiopia, a supporter of Muhammad during the fighting of January 1986, were restored as were those with Somalia which had been strained since Ismail had sent troops to oppose the advance into the Ogaden in the war of 1977. As part of the PDRY's attempt to present a more moderate image abroad, diplomatic relations were restored with Morocco, and with Egypt as soon the Arab League lifted its veto. Attas visited Baghdad, Iraq in July 1988, and later there was an agreement to increase the processing of Iraqi oil at Aden refinery with Iraqi crude piped across Saudi Arabia to Yanbu. Abd al-Aziz al-Dhali in 1989 became the first PDRY Foreign Minister to visit an EC capital and also in 1989 William Waldegrave of the UK Foreign Office was the first British Minister to visit Aden since independence. Attas stated that the USA had been approached for the resumption of relations which were in fact restored just before unification. The PDRY therefore ended its separate existence with no outstanding feuds and indeed had achieved international recognition by election to the UN Security Council. In January 1990 Attas opened a regional peace conference called by the Organisation for Afro-Asian Solidarity, attended by 45 states with a call for withdrawal of all fleets from the Red Sea, the Gulf and the Indian Ocean: Western nations, Iran and Israel were not invited.

Meanwhile, the domestic economy had collapsed after two decades of ideologically-led mismanagement and people were on the verge of starvation. Despite some pressure from military leaders, the USSR under the leadership of Gorbachev stated that there was no need for the Aden base after the end of the cold war and Soviet aid declined from $400m. in 1988 to $50m. in 1989. In 1989 the communist regimes of Eastern Europe started to collapse. There changes were set in motion by a popular revolt but in the PDRY they were introduced by the Government. In early July the YSP set up six working parties to study a comprehensive list of changes, including that of its own role and relationship with the state, and concerning economic, administrative and cultural affairs. There had long been a chronic shortage of housing and it was announced that private individuals might build for sale or rent; then private ownership of hotels and factories was permitted. Adenis were encouraged to invest their capital locally with exemptions from taxes and tariffs. Foreign investors might transfer profits abroad. In particular investment was sought in oil, tourism and the port of Aden. In December the Government promised to compensate owners of shares in the banks nationalized in 1969. Just before unification the Government announced that the properties of exiles would be restored. The ponderous communist bureaucracy was dismantled and government monopolies, such as that of supplying ships, were ended. In February 1990 plans were published to re-establish Aden as a free zone.

Al-Baid put forward a programme for political *perestroika*, including a rotating presidency, civil rights and correction of 'wrong stands on Arab and Islamic culture and religion'. In October Numan stated that a multi-party system was 'very necessary for democracy' and that the private sector should 'play its true role in economic developments'. Al-Baid said that things had gone wrong because of the 'leftist adventurist tendency rather than right-wing deviationism'. Pluralism and democracy were more important than ideology. The Institute of Scientific Socialism was renamed the Institute of Social Sciences while the two al-Shaabis and Salim Rubai Ali were rehabilitated as they had been condemned in the 'absence of democratic thought'. Citizens were given the right to travel abroad. There were local elections, the fifth since independence but the first with any real choice of candidates.

In December 1989 the YSP ended its monopoly and the formerly outlawed Nasserist Unionist Organisation applied for recognition and was quickly followed by the Yemeni Unity Party, the first to have members both South and North of the frontier. Even the partisans of former President Muhammad were able to form the Unionist Democratic Party. In January 1990 the ban on foreign publications was lifted and later permits were issued for a range of independent newspapers and journals.

The relaxation of controls set off a wave of inflation which, in turn, provoked an unprecedented series of strikes for higher pay. The first, on 13 January 1990, was at the oil refinery and was followed by strikes in the electricity, banking, textile and fishing industries. Workers claimed that the cost of living had risen by 30% and wages had not kept pace. The Government made concessions and the strikes were usually of short duration.

THE ROAD TO UNIFICATION

Presidents Saleh and Ali Nasir Muhammad had established a good working relationship but during the fighting in Aden in January 1986, San'a remained neutral and abstained from commenting upon events in Aden. The new regime of President Attas quickly declared its commitment to unity but the situation was complicated by the presence of Muhammad and his followers in camps just north of the frontier. Gradually the conciliatory policy of the Aden Government led many of them to go home and those that remained refrained from provoking any confrontational incidents between the two states.

In July 1986 both Heads of State met for the first time as participants in a summit in Tripoli, Libya. Although an agreement was not reached they consulted again in September and Saleh stated that he would give prioriy to unity. Although the exiles were inactive, their presence still caused difficulties and after a death sentence had been passed on Muhammad, Aden demanded his extradition which San'a refused. Kuwait tried to mediate a settlement of the refugee problem but it was still a high priority when al-Baid went to San'a in July 1987 in the hope of co-ordinating economic and social policies. Meanwhile, there had been disputes concerning the exact location of the frontier which had never been delimited and was particularly vague in the area of Shabwa where it was anticipated that oil would be found. In December 1987 Iryani denied that there had been armed clashes but in the following April there were reports that both sides were reinforcing their border troops. Saleh declared that the long-standing dispute could only be resolved through unification and in May al-Baid travelled to San'a and negotiated a series of agreements. The Higher Yemeni Council, the Joint Ministerial Committee and other joint committees were reconstituted. There was a declaration that there should be no recognition of frontiers drawn up during foreign occupation or during the reign of the Imamate, existing border posts would be replaced by new ones, jointly manned, movement between the two states should be unrestricted, troops should be withdrawn from frontier areas and there should be joint exploitation of a zone of 2,200 sq km in the Marib/Shabwa area which would be demilitarized. Saleh travelled to Riyadh, Saudi Arabia, to reassure King Fahd that this *rapprochement* was not directed against Saudi Arabia, while Muhammad declared that he welcomed the agreement. The first practical results were the abolition of the need for passports for travel between North and South and a meeting of the Ministers of Oil who agreed on the establishment of the Yemeni Company for Investment in Oil and Mineral Resources for joint exploitation of Marib/Shabwa. The HQ was in San'a, its capital was $10m. and it was soon able to announce that it had received 45 bids from international oil companies. The Southern Oil Minister said that neither North nor South could develop properly unless they were united while al-Baid spoke of 'creating unified economic interests that would be a material basis for the political success of unity'. A major objective was to revive the port of Aden as a free zone and to provide it with a larger and more prosperous hinterland. It was clear that neither state could finance its own development unilaterally or attract enough outside help but through unification this would be possible. The AFESD agreed to provide $18m. and subsequently $63m. to link the two electricity systems. It appeared that the two Yemens were now set upon at least economic integration.

However a financial crisis, leading to *perestroika* started in Aden shortly afterwards and in the general ferment, the stability of the YAR became more attractive. In November 1989 Iryani and the assistant Secretary-General of the YSP, Salim Salih Muhammad spent three days in San'a discussing a 136-article Constitution, based on agreements reached by the constitutional committee established following the war in 1979. It was published while Saleh was in Aden and he proposed that it should be referred to both Legislatures and then be put to a referendum; this set a target date for unification of November 1990. Al-Baid emphasized that unity in the Yemen should be seen as a step towards full Arab unity. Delegations were sent to all the Arab countries to inform them of the Yemen's intention to form a single state. The PDRY removed obstacles to a joint foreign policy by ending its last diplomatic dispute, including the restoration of relations with the USA and an invitation to Sultan Qaboos of Oman to visit Aden. The ACC had no objection to the adherence of the PDRY. It was agreed that the YSP and the General People's Congress, which was regarded as its northern equivalent, should preserve their independence and that there should be room for political parties; the Yemen Unity Party, set up in January 1990, was the first to recruit from both North and South. In the same month Iryani travelled to Aden to discuss preparations for elections and for merging the Ministries of the Interior. Plans were announced for a merger of the state airlines. A new press law was introduced in both states. A few days later the two Cabinets held a joint meeting in San'a. All political prisoners were released and a joint committee set up to negotiate with other political parties. This led to an agreement concluded in April that there should be no foreign funding nor campaigning in mosques or barracks and Saleh welcomed 'a multi-party system provided that it is of Yemeni origin'. In February there was a second joint Cabinet meeting, in Aden, at which 46 laws were approved on such matters as customs procedures, taxation, trade unions and education. Plans were drawn up for a single currency from a unified central bank and later Aden promised pay rises to ensure parity with wages in the North. After a brief summit in Mukayras, south of the frontier, Saleh visited Riyadh, Saudi Arabia, and announced that King Fahd supported unity 'totally and without limit', although many doubted that he would really welcome a united democratic Yemen on his southern flank. The USSR, USA and the People's Republic of China welcomed the prospect of unity.

In early March 1990 there was a prolonged summit in Taiz, Aden and again in Taiz, which ended without a communiqué suggesting that problems had arisen. There still appeared to be opposition amongst hard-line communists in Aden while in the North dissatisfaction amongst religious and tribal leaders was more public. There were reports of fighting in the Saada and of tribesmen receiving Saudi arms and money. A leading Muslim Brother attacked 40 articles of the proposed Constitution as unislamic and demanded that the Shari'a should be the only source of law. There was concern over Aden's tolerance of alcohol and freedom given to women. In a four-day meeting in San'a in April Saleh and al-Baid decided to pre-empt the opposition by bringing forward the date of unification to 22 May. On 4 May both currencies were declared legal tender. On 21 May the agreement to unite was passed unanimously in Aden but in San'a three Islamic fundamentalist members walked out and five abstained amidst demonstrations by their supporters. The following day a joint session of the two Assemblies elected a five-man Presidential Council, headed by Saleh (promoted to the rank of General), al-Baid (Vice-President), Salim Salih Muhammad, Abd al-Ghani and the former Speaker al-Arshi.

The priorities of the Government of the Republic of Yemen, which were announced in late May 1990, were to develop the country's economic infrastructure and to improve relations with other Arab states. In particular, the Government was committed to resolving long-standing border disputes with neighbouring Saudi Arabia and Oman. In July 1990 both President Mubarak of Egypt and the chairman of the PLO, Yasser Arafat, visited Yemen and were reported to have discussed regional issues with President Saleh.

Following the amalgamation of the two Yemeni economies, the high level of indebtedness of the former PDRY was identified as one potential source of economic difficulties. There were also some signs of social unrest in parts of Yemen which formerly belonged to the PDRY. Rising prices there led to industrial action and demands for a general strike.

In September 1990 it was reported that more than 30 new political parties had been formed in Yemen since unification. The Yemeni Islah Party (YIP), an Islamic party with widespread support in the new House of Representatives, was regarded as the most important of the new parties.

In November 1990 the Government established a supreme council for national defence which would be responsible for military mobilization and wartime civil defence. The council would be authorized to declare war and states of emergency. It was to be chaired by the President and would comprise the Vice-President and various members of the Council of Ministers.

In mid-May 1991 the people of Yemen voted in a referendum on the constitution for the unified state. A few days earlier religious fundamentalists and sympathizers, among whom were members of the YIP, demonstrated about the role of Islam under the proposed Constitution, and urged a boycott of the referendum: a clause in the Constitution stated that *Shari'a* law would be the main source of legislation, but the Islamists stipulated that *Shari'a* law should be the only source of legislation. Those who participated in the referendum approved the new Constitution by a large majority, although fewer than 50% of the electorate registered to vote. Members of the YIP and other opposition groups claimed that irregularities in the voting procedure had rendered the result null and void.

YEMEN'S RESPONSE TO THE GULF CRISIS

In August 1990 Iraq's invasion and annexation of Kuwait placed the Government of Yemen in an especially difficult position. The economy of Yemen was heavily dependent on trade with, and aid from, Iraq, and also on aid from Saudi Arabia, which normally hosts very large numbers of Yemeni expatriate workers. Moreover, there was evidence of widespread popular support in Yemen for President Saddam Hussain of Iraq. These factors explained the Government's equivocal response to the Iraqi invasion of Kuwait and to subsequent developments in the Gulf region. In the immediate aftermath of the invasion the Government condemned Iraq, but also criticized the arrival of US and other western military forces to defend Saudi Arabia. At the summit meeting of leaders of Arab League member states, held in Cairo on 10 August 1990, Yemen voted against the proposal to send Arab forces to Saudi Arabia as part of a multinational force to deter aggression by Iraq. Yemen also abstained in the UN Security Council vote to impose economic sanctions on Iraq. By late August, however, the Government appeared to implementing the UN sanctions against Iraq, albeit reluctantly. In October the Yemeni Minister of Foreign Affairs, Abd al-Karim al-Iryani, announced that Yemen would support any measures taken to achieve a peaceful withdrawal of Iraqi troops from Kuwait, but that this should result in the withdrawal of all foreign forces from the area.

Yemen's relations with Saudi Arabia deteriorated as a result of Yemen's initial strong opposition to the presence of foreign armed forces in the Gulf and to the ambiguous stance it subsequently adopted in this respect. On 15 September 1990, in what was regarded as a retaliatory action, Saudi Arabia announced that it had withdrawn the privileges which Yemeni workers in Saudi Arabia had previously enjoyed. This resulted in an exodus from Saudi Arabia of an estimated 500,000–800,000 Yemeni workers during October and November, which caused widespread economic and social disruption. The expulsion and return of the Yemeni workers not only caused a reduction in the country's income from remittances sent home by the expatriates, but also led to a serious increase in unemployment.

In November 1990 the Yemeni Government voted against the UN Security Council resolution to authorize the multinational contingent stationed in the Gulf to use 'all necessary means' against Iraq in order to remove its forces from Kuwait if they had not withdrawn by 15 January 1991. This prompted a visit to Yemen by the US Secretary of State, James Baker, in an attempt to persuade Yemen to modify its position concerning the UN resolution. In late November the Minister of Foreign Affairs, Abd al-Karim al-Iryani, visited France, Germany and Algeria in the hope of gathering support to prevent the UN Security Council resolution from being passed. In December Yemen assumed the chair of the UN Security Council (which rotates on a monthly basis) and the Government increased its efforts to mediate in the Gulf crisis: the Vice-President of Yemen, Ali Salim al-Baid, met King Hussein of Jordan, in Amman, and the Iraqi President, Saddam Hussain, in Baghdad, for talks concerning the crisis. In January 1991 Yemen presented a peace plan in an attempt to prevent war in the Gulf; the plan included an Iraqi withdrawal from Kuwait, the withdrawal of the multinational military force, and the holding of an international conference on the Arab-Israeli conflict. Despite numerous diplomatic initiatives undertaken by the Yemeni Government, prior to the UN deadline of 15 January, the peace plan failed to prevent the outbreak of war in the Gulf on 16–17 January. Following the US-led military offensive against Iraq, Yemen issued a statement in which it condemned the action, and hundreds of thousands of Yemenis demonstrated in support of Iraq. Later in January it was confirmed that US aid to Yemen was to be severely reduced, apparently as a result of Yemen's policy towards Iraq.

POLITICAL AFFAIRS AFTER REUNIFICATION

The two government parties, the Northern GPC and the Southern YSP, had agreed to share power equally until elections were held in November 1992 but within months of the referendum there were reports that extreme members of each were building up stocks of weapons for use against the other. Due to the disparity in the population—10m. in the North and two million in the South—posts had to be found in the North for southerners, who were regarded as secularists, indeed as former communists, and whose presence was resented. Northerners were shocked by the un-Islamic lifestyle of many in Aden and by the enhanced role of women. The deaths and injuries in both cities that attended an Aden-San'a football match were indicative of the mutual animosity.

In September 1991 a YSP official was murdered; in December two more were killed at a party meeting in Ibb, where a fourth was killed in February. Two were later wounded in Sa'ada and another killed in Taiz. In April 1992, the Justice Minister Abd al-Wasi Salam, a YSP leader, survived after gunmen opened fire on his car; there was suspicion that the attempt was connected with his imminent departure for Muscat for frontier negotiations. In May the house of Salem Salih Muhammad, a YSP representative on the Presidential Council, was attacked. Only three days later there was a bomb at the house of the Prime Minister who denied that it had any connection with the Oman dispute. In June the YSP claimed, but the government denied, that there had been an attack on the home of the editor of their newspaper and the brother of the Prime Minister was murdered in the southern port of Shihr: this was seen as an attempt to disrupt the unification process as he had played no part in politics. In July, in circumstances that are disputed, a colonel, a member of the YSP central committee, 'killed himself' after a shootout in which two policemen were also killed: his car which had failed to stop at a road block was found to be full of weapons. A former Deputy Prime Minister of the PDRY, Anis Hassan Yahya, escaped assassination in Aden and at the beginning of August security forces defused a mine outside the house in San'a of the former Prime Minister Muhammad Ali Haitham. The YSP also claimed that several of their local officials had been shot dead in provincial towns, mainly in the North of the country. However, in September there were reports of bomb attacks on the homes of leading GPC members.

These incidents were only part of the general breakdown of law and order. In August 1991 the Secretary-General of the GPC, Ahmad al-Asbahi was seriously wounded in his office by an employee whom he had refused to promote. In September a senior civil servant was killed in an ambush which, it was believed, had been intended for Umar al-Jawi, leader of the National Grouping Party and editor of a strongly anti-Iraqi newspaper which also attacked tribal leaders and Islamic fundamentalists. Shortly afterwards an MP, the son of the paramount chief of the Hashid tribe, survived an ambush which his party blamed on the YSP. In October there were riots in San'a in which public buildings were set on fire, in protest at an incident in which a colonel shot a policeman who had stopped him for driving through a red light; officials stated that two people were killed, while unofficial reports estimated the toll as nine. In December two groups of heavily-armed saboteurs were arrested in Hadramawt. In March 1992 there was a gun-battle in the presidential office when a senior officer killed two guards before being himself killed in a dispute over forged papers. In May the government outlawed the carrying of firearms in the cities, and there was a possibility that even the *jambiah*, the curved dagger which is the traditional badge of a tribesman, might be banned.

One of the ways in which the YSP could assert its strength was through its control of the trade unions, particularly in Aden. President Saleh declared industrial unrest unpatriotic but in March 1992 100,000 workers in Aden brought everything from the airport to government services and the university to a halt. They threatened a three-day stoppage unless wages were raised by 40%, a job creation scheme for people expelled from Saudi Arabia and a price freeze were implemented but later they settled for 25% backdated to January and a barely credible promise to keep prices at 1991 levels. Different labour grievances then emerged as the staff of the government newspaper in Aden went on strike for parity of wages with their colleagues in the San'a press.

Amnesty International said that all political prisoners in the South had been released before reunification, although there were possibly 25 in the North. No executions had taken place although there had been five amputations of hands. Much forcibly nationalized property in the South was restored to its former owners and journalists sacked under Ismail were reinstated. In May 1992 an amnesty was extended to former President Ali Nasir Muhammad and five of his associates.

The government estimated that the Gulf crisis had cost the Yemeni economy $3,000m., and although some of this was recouped by the sale of oil concessions, the economic situation remained serious. Only 20% of debt repayments were met. In March 1992 the budget envisaged a deficit of $1,000m. Hundreds of thousands, who had worked in the Gulf and Saudi Arabia, no longer sent home remittances but squatted unemployed in shanty towns. The general economic conditions and social unrest proved fertile soil for Islamic fundamentalists, who provided education and other services which the state could not. The question of the place of the *Shari'a* in the legal system continued to provoke controversy. The YIP became, after the two government parties, the next strongest and probably displaced the YSP in the North. It seemed, however, likely to split between its religious and its tribal leadership and even within its tribal element. It was also attacked by some religious leaders, such as Shaykh Ahmad al-Shami, Secretary-General of the *al-Haq* party as an instrument of Saudi Arabia and in thrall to old-fashioned tribal sheikhs. President Saleh was said to have guaranteed Vice-President al-Baid that his position would not be affected whatever the result of the elections but that other parties would join the government. Meanwhile political parties, the estimated number of which varied between 30 and 40, were encouraged to merge in order to reduce electoral confusion.

FOREIGN AFFAIRS AFTER THE GULF WAR

Yemen's stance during the Gulf War was not forgotten in the Arabian Peninsula and, a year later, relations with some of its states were still, as Foreign Minister Iryani said in February 1992, 'cool'. In the same month the Secretary-General of the Arab League, Dr Esmat Abd al-Meguid, on his first visit to San'a, agreed that it would take time for rifts to be healed. On the first anniversary of reunification the only Arab Head of State to attend was Yasser Arafat, although Yemen had tried to establish its Arab credentials, by raising the question of Israeli settlements at the UN Security Council and denying that it had approved an Israeli plan to resettle the remaining

1,500 Yemeni Jews. In mid-1992 French, UK and American Jewish groups mounted a diplomatic campaign in order to organize the discreet departure from Yemen of the small remaining Jewish community. The Yemeni response was that, whereas emigration was open to all its citizens, emigration to Israel was forbidden by the Constitution. Israel claimed in July 1993 to have secretly airlifted about 250 Yemeni Jews into the country, although the Yemeni Government denied all knowledge of the affair.

In addition to its resentment at Yemen's attitude to the Gulf crisis, Saudi Arabia, which had ceased its financial support of some $600m. per year and had expelled immigrant workers constituting about 8% of the total population of Yemen, disliked Yemen's new political pluralism and free press, and, in any case, can scarcely have been enthusiastic about reunification. Saudi Arabia delayed the sale of its 49% share-holding in the San'a-based airline Yemenia, thus preventing the company's merger with the AHeni airline Alyemda. Contrary to previous practice, Saudi visas were required from Yemeni Hajjis. More seriously, in April 1992, Saudi Arabia warned the four oil companies, including BP, that were prospecting in the eastern desert in an area where the frontier had not been precisely delimited that they were trespassing on Saudi territory, and, to the great indignation of the Yemenis, the companies ceased work. A similar threat to the American Hunt Oil Company was said to have been withdrawn after an intercession by President Bush. The frontier dispute continued, with the Saudis claiming that the Yemenis were not serious about wanting a settlement while the Yemenis felt that the dispute was being prolonged to sabotage their development. In September 1992, however, a committee of experts assembled in Riyadh to discuss the border dispute. No apparent progress was made, either on this occasion, or at further meetings in October and November. The process was subsequently suspended during Ramadan and the Yemeni elections, but in August 1993, against a background of improved relations between Yemen and Saudi Arabia, the committee assembled for a fifth round of talks aimed at solving the dispute. Little progress had been made by January 1994 when the talks entered their seventh round. Nevertheless, the Foreign Minister, Muhammad Salim Basindwa, appointed because of his good relations with the Gulf states, declared that improving relations with Saudi Arabia was his top priority and the eighth round of talks concerning demarcation took place in April.

The Saudis also disapproved of Yemen's increasing friendship with Iran. Both Foreign Minister Velayati and Speaker Mahdi Karrubi visited San'a, and agreements were signed for co-operation in a whole range of fields. There were proposals for a joint fishing company and for processing Iranian oil at Aden refinery. The GCC stopped funding the expansion of Aden port and Kuwait instructed its airline not to sell tickets to Yemenis. In mid-1993 it was reported that the Ministers of Foreign Affairs of Kuwait and Yemen were to meet in Vienna, Austria, reflecting a gradual improvement in relations between the two states. The meeting was subsequently cancelled, however, following opposition from the Speaker of the Kuwaiti National Assembly. Yemen's one ally in the Arabian peninsula was Oman, with frequent high-level visitors exchanging messages between Sultan and President. In December 1991 President Saleh said that the agreement upon frontier delimitation, provided for in the Oman-PDRY reconciliation of 1988, would be concluded within two weeks. However, opposition arose, as it was believed that Yemen would sign away nearly 6,000 square miles of territory, and the Yemeni Unionist Party and the local Mahra authorities challenged the government's right to do so. On 1 October 1992 a treaty, described as a comprehensive border settlement, was eventually signed, and co-operation between Yemen and Oman in the areas of construction, transport and commerce was subsequently envisaged. The frontier was officially opened in May 1993.

Relations with the three remaining GCC member states also showed signs of gradual improvement. In February 1993 Sheikh Muhammad al-Maktoum, the UAE Minister of Defence, visited Yemen, and in the following month his visit was returned by the Yemeni Minister of Planning and Development. In June 1993 the Yemeni Minister of Foreign Affairs, Muhammad Basindwa, declared that improving relations with the Gulf states was his highest priority, and in the following month he visited Bahrain.

In August 1991 Iryani flew to Egypt and relations were repaired, although Cairo later rejected Yemen's proposal for a revival of the Arab Co-operation Council (ACC), initially without Iraqi participation. In late 1992 a senior official of the Egyptian Ministry of Foreign Affairs visited San'a, and it was reported that Egypt had offered to mediate in the dispute between Yemen and Saudi Arabia. Yemen's relations with the other ACC member, Jordan, were cordial, and in September 1991, during a visit to Amman, Prime Minister Attas signed a series of agreements for co-operation in trade, agriculture, educational exchanges and tourism. In the same month, Yemen and Iraq signed a cultural agreement, and in May 1992 Iraq undertook to provide teachers to support Yemen's campaign to develop education. Yemen continued to oppose sanctions against Iraq, but in March 1993 Saddam Hussain sent his half-brother to San'a to protest at Yemeni attempts to improve its relations with the Gulf states.

Reconciliation with the Western powers was smoother. The USA, unwilling to offend its more important GCC allies, let it be known that its attitude would depend upon Yemen's actions in the Security Council and over human rights, but in August 1991 it agreed to sell Yemen 300,000 tons of subsidized wheat, more than ever before. Yemen fully supported the American Middle-East peace initiative. American firms were chosen to draw up the master plan for Aden free port and a feasibility study for a gas-fired power station in Marib. In January 1992 the Deputy Secretary of State for Energy, Hanson Moore, visited the country.

The British had been less upset than their allies over Yemen's attitude to the Gulf War, and relations were fully restored in time for a successful visit by Iryani to London in February 1992. Al-Baid had already visited Britain in August 1991, followed by a financial team to seek investment in the free port. British firms won various contracts such as to prospect for gold in the Hadramawt and to print new currency. The cordiality of relations between Britain and Yemen was confirmed by a successful visit of the Yemeni Minister of Planning and Development to London.

In the West there was a growing belief that Yemen had developed into the most genuine democracy in the Arab world—a sentiment articulated by the French foreign minister on a visit in October 1991. The EC sent a parliamentary delegation to San'a in June 1992 and in the same month the German President, Richard von Weizsacker, made a state visit during which he promised aid. The Yemeni Chief of Staff, General Busheiry, also visited Paris. The problems of investment were discussed in July at a conference in Geneva at which the presence of Qatar gratified the Yemenis. The need for aid and also the broad range of the participants in the development of its oil industry—including Japan, Indonesia, Norway and Canada—kept Yemen active diplomatically, although financial difficulties forced the closure of 16 Yemeni embassies at the end of 1992.

Yemen had increasingly been drawn into the affairs of its neighbours across the Red Sea. In July 1991 the Minister of State for Foreign Affairs, Abd al-Aziz ad-Dhali, collaborated with French diplomats to settle disputes in Djibouti. After the fall of Colonel Mengistu, ships of the Ethiopian navy took refuge in Aden: Zimbabwe's Minister of Foreign Affairs helped to mediate and the fleet returned home. More serious was the crisis that arose from the civil war in Somalia, which obliged Yemen to give refuge to more than 60,000 Somali refugees during 1992 and 1993. The Yemeni Government had great problems in accommodating and feeding them. Finally an agreement was reached whereby Yemen would accept further refugees on the understanding that the UN should take responsibility for their welfare.

THE 1993 ELECTIONS AND THE ENSUING POLITICAL CRISIS

In spite of the climate of unrest, voter registration for the legislative elections, scheduled for 27 April 1993, took place between 15 January and 16 February. An outbreak of attacks on expatriate workers prompted a warning, in February, that the Government could not guarantee the safety of expatriate residents owing to the threat of certain hostile Yemeni tribes. There were 3,400 candidates for the 301 seats in the House of Representatives, many standing as independents. Of the major political parties presenting candidates, the General People's Congress (GPC), led by the President, Ali Abdullah Saleh, and the Yemeni Socialist Party (YSP), led by the Vice-President, Ali Salim al-Baid, were the largest. The two other major parties were the Yemeni Islah Party (YIP), widely reported to have received substantial financial assistance from Saudi Arabia, led by Sheikh Abdullah bin Hussain al-Ahmar, and the Baath (Renaissance) party, led by Mujahid Abu Shuarib. There were also over 40 smaller parties, but most of them were in alliance with one of the four major parties.

After lively campaigning in the run-up to the elections, the turnout on election day was very high. International observers expressed broad satisfaction with the conduct of the elections, the first nationwide, multi-party elections based on universal suffrage in the Arabian peninsula. Inevitably there were reports of disturbances in several towns and accusations of fraudulent practices by both of the leading parties. When the results were announced the GPC had, not surprisingly, won the majority of the vote and gained 123 of the 301 seats, most of them in the former YAR. The YIP took second place with 62 seats, again mainly in the former YAR, with the YSP relegated to third place with 56 seats, most of them in the former PDRY. The Baath party took seven seats, minor parties five seats and independents 47 seats. Of the 50 women candidates who stood for election, two won seats.

After the election the YIP is reported to have threatened to boycott the new House of Representatives unless it was admitted to government. The three main parties eventually agreed to form a coalition with the GPC and YSP each taking two seats on the Presidential Council and the YIP the one remaining seat. The YIP was also allocated six cabinet posts but these did not include the portfolios of education and finance which the party had demanded. However, the leader of the YIP, Sheikh Abdullah bin Hussain al-Ahmar, became speaker of the House of Representatives. The YSP leadership was disappointed by the election results and became increasingly apprehensive and resentful about the emerging alliance between the GPC and the YIP. The GPC found it easier to co-operate with the YIP on a number of important political issues, especially proposed constitutional changes, than with the YSP; this co-operation was assisted by the fact that the GPC leader's tribe, the Sanhan, belonged to the Hashed tribal federation, of which the YIP leader was the paramount Sheikh. In August 1993 the Vice-President refused to take part in the Government and decided to return to Aden. His departure from San'a marked the official beginning of a political crisis that was to lead to civil war. This crisis intensified following a series of assassinations of YSP officials including the Vice-President's nephew who was shot in Aden on 29 October. It was widely rumoured in San'a that these assassinations were ordered by the President's 'entourage', notably his brother and three half-brothers who commanded key military units and the security services.

In an attempt to put pressure on President Ali Abdullah Saleh to make concessions that would restore southern influence, the Vice-President had issued an 18-point list of demands in September. They included security and military reforms and decentralization to allow each governorate more freedom in administrative and financial affairs. In November al-Baid declared that the north was attempting to annex the south rather than unifying with it. Efforts to mediate between the two factions by Oman, Jordan, PLO Chairman Arafat, the USA and the *ulema* (religious scholars) failed to resolve the crisis, while the departure of the Vice-President and other southern officials including the Prime Minister, Haidar al-Attas, brought the business of government to a standstill, aggravating already chronic economic problems. Riots in San'a and Taiz in early January 1994 reflected popular discontent at rising prices and the falling value of the Yemeni riyal. Meanwhile the security situation in the country continued to deteriorate. There were more political killings—al-Baid

claimed that over 150 YSP members had been killed since May 1990—and further kidnappings of foreign nationals.

Amidst the deepening political crisis a National Dialogue Committee was formed with representatives from across the political spectrum, to try to work out a formula acceptable to both factions. After months of discussions and deliberations, the committee drew up a 'Document of Pledge and Agreement' on 18 January 1994 which incorporated many of the demands made by al-Baid in his 18-point list. The document proposed major constitutional reform that would clearly define the powers of the Presidential Council, the President and the Vice-President, devolution of power from central government to local and regional assemblies, the restructuring of the armed forces and the arrest and trial of those responsible for the wave of assassinations largely directed at YSP officials. On 20 February the President and Vice-President signed the document at a public ceremony in Amman, Jordan, attended by representatives from Oman, the USA, France, the PLO and the Arab League. There was no reconciliation between the two Yemeni leaders however; they refused to shake hands after signing the document and al-Baid demanded that Ali Abdullah Saleh order the immediate arrest of his brothers. Al-Baid and his principal lieutenants walked out on follow-up talks and further strained relations with the President by visiting Saudi Arabia and the Gulf states to seek support for their cause. Some analysts argued that President Saleh had no intention of honouring the concessions made in Amman, but only wanted to gain time, having already chosen the military option. The real intentions of the southern leadership were also unclear. Several observers maintained that while some of the YSP leaders wanted secession, the majority had sought to escalate the political crisis in order to topple the President and take over a united Yemen.

The day after the ceremony there were clashes between rival military units in the southern province of Abyan and in other parts of the country. After unification the armed forces of the former YAR and PDRY had not been integrated; the GPC continued to control the northern forces and the YSP those of the south. The fighting that continued sporadically for some months involved not only forces under the command of the GPC and the YSP but also YSP forces loyal to the former South Yemen President, Ali Nasir Muhammad, as well as tribal militias which used the opportunity to promote their own interests. The GPC was reported to have mobilized the powerful Hashed tribal federation, while the YSP called on the support of their traditional rivals, the Bakil tribes. At the beginning of March a joint military committee of northern and southern officers, Jordanian and Omani officers and the US and French military attachés, attempted to disengage the widely dispersed and intermixed rival military units. Jordan, Oman, Egypt and the UAE all made diplomatic efforts to mediate between the two main rival factions but made no progress. In April both Oman and Jordan withdrew from the joint military committee.

THE CIVIL WAR

On 27 April 1994, the anniversary of the general elections, a major tank battle took place between rival army units at Amran, some 60 km to the north of San'a. It was the biggest clash between the opposing forces since the crisis began. Some 200 tanks were involved in the fighting; 85 tanks were reported to have been destroyed and over 400 soldiers killed or wounded. Both sides claimed that the other attacked first. The YSP claimed that the attack was tantamount to a declaration of war, while the President accused al-Baid of secessionism and pledged to fight to defend the unity of the country. During the night of 4 May fighter aircraft under the command of the YSP attacked northern airports at San'a, Taiz and Hodeida, the presidential palace in San'a, the country's two main power stations, Hodeida port, and oil storage and pipeline facilities at Marib. Northern aircraft retaliated on 5 May, badly damaging the airport at Aden. The northern military command reported pitched battled in several areas along the old frontier between the YAR and PDRY and claimed that southern forces had suffered heavy losses in seven of the country's 17 provinces. The civil war had begun in earnest. The President declared a 30-day state of emergency and dismissed the Vice-President. France announced that it was evacuating its nationals and the USA advised its citizens to leave. On 10 May Prime Minister al-Attas, a southerner, was dismissed after he appealed for outside forces to help end the civil war. The Minister of Petroleum and Minerals, Hussainoun, was among other YSP members dismissed from their cabinet posts. On 21 May al-Baid proclaimed the breakaway 'Democratic Republic of Yemen' (DRY) and began diplomatic efforts to secure recognition of the old frontier. Al-Attas, the former Prime Minister of Yemen, who had joined the secessionist government in Aden, travelled to Egypt to seek the backing of Arab moderates and called on the West for support and recognition for the southern government. President Saleh denounced the secession, offering an amnesty to all those in the former PDRY who rejected it, with the exception of al-Baid and 15 other YSP leaders.

As northern forces advanced on Aden, Saudi Arabia together with Bahrain, Oman, the UAE and Egypt requested a meeting of the UN Security Council to discuss the Yemeni conflict. San'a's UN representative strongly objected to what it considered interference in its internal affairs. Nevertheless, on 1 June the Security Council unanimously adopted Resolution No. 924 calling for an immediate cease-fire and requesting the dispatch of a UN commission of inquiry to assess prospects for a renewed dialogue between the belligerants. It also urged an immediate cessation of the supply of arms and other materials that might contribute to the conflict. The resolution, which Prince Bandar bin Sultan, the Saudi Arabian ambassador to Washington, was reported to have played an important role in drafting, deliberately omitted any direct endorsement of Yemeni unity. Two days later the UN Secretary-General, Boutros Boutros-Ghali, appointed the much respected former Algerian Foreign Minister, Lakhdar Brahimi, as his special envoy and head of the fact-finding mission. Spokesmen for the north and south welcomed Brahimi's appointment and promised their full co-operation. However, before the commission of inquiry began, the Foreign Ministers of the Gulf Co-operation Council meeting on 4–5 June, issued a statement effectively blaming the north for the conflict and implicitly recognizing the Democratic Republic of Yemen. The Ministers warned that continued hostilities would have repercussions for the GCC states, forcing them to adopt appropriate measures against 'the party that does not abide by the cease-fire'. Only Qatar dissented. While Saudi Arabia maintained that its only concern was to prevent the destabilization of the region, many observers argued that the YSP leadership, given the smaller military forces under its command, would not have declared independence unless it had the support of its powerful neighbour. The Government in San'a condemned the GCC statement and Abd al-Karim al-Iryani, the Minister of Planning and principal political councillor to President Saleh, maintained that they had clear evidence that arms purchased with Saudi funds were being supplied to the south. The north accused Saudi Arabia of encouraging the secessionists in order to create a new oil emirate in the Hadramawt under Saudi influence and providing it with an outlet to the Indian Ocean. One of the principal oil concessions in Hadramawt is held by the Nimir company, owned by the Saudi Arabian Bin Mahfouz family, who were originally from the Hadramawt. Saudi Arabia had not forgiven Yemen for its support for Iraq during the Gulf crisis and feared that a united and democratic Yemen would threaten its supremacy in the Arabian peninsula. Despite official statements of strict neutrality in the conflict, it was widely believed that Egypt was hostile to the north because the GPC leadership had allowed Egyptian Islamist militants to train in camps set up in Yemen under the protection of Sheikh Abdel Majid Zindani, the leading ideologue of the YIP and a member of Yemen's Presidential Council. Sheikh Zindani is reported to have raised 63m. riyals for the northern war effort through collections from mosques and religious associations. Support for the North came from Iraq, Iran and Sudan. The south accused both Iraq and Sudan of providing military assistance to the North, accusations which Iraq and Sudan denied.

By the first week in June northern forces were besieging the southern capital of Aden and there were reports of air attacks on strategic installations and heavy shelling and artillery fire from northern forces. On 6 June, shortly after the arrival of the UN Commission of Inquiry, San'a agreed to observe a cease-fire, as did the South. Brahimi managed to secure the agreement of both factions to the formation of a monitoring body to police the truce, but when San'a suggested that the joint military committee should be revived, Aden objected and demanded a full UN multinational peace-keeping force and the withdrawal of northern forces to behind the old frontier between the YAR and the PDRY. The cease-fire lasted only six hours. Talks arranged in Cairo by Brahimi also broke down because San'a insisted that it would only negotiate with the YSP in the context of a united Yemen, whereas the South demanded that negotiations should be between two independent states. The southern negotiating team, led by Muhsin bin Farid, the 'Deputy Prime Minister' of the self-proclaimed DRY, walked out of the talks and called for UN intervention to enforce a truce and punish the North for continuing its assault on Aden. Southern officials admitted publicly in mid-June that they were being supplied with arms by 'friendly Arab countries'. On 17 June it was reported that military equipment, including 30–40 tanks and more than 100 missiles, had been unloaded at the port of Mukalla in the south over the past two weeks. Later in June there were reports that the South had acquired new MiG-29 fighter planes from Eastern Europe, with Gulf funding, and was using its air power to bomb the Marib oilfields.

At the end of June the UN Secretary-General reported that UN efforts to mediate between the two rival factions had made no progress. He expressed concern that the fighting had not stopped and drew attention to the deteriorating humanitarian situation. The Security Council, meeting on 29 June, adopted Resolution No. 931 which requested that the Secretary-General continue to mediate between the two factions in order to secure a durable cease-fire and called for a monitoring force to supervise the truce. The resolution was seen as a setback for supporters of the self-proclaimed DRY who had urged the UN to condemn the North for the continued fighting and to initiate moves that might extend to the official recognition of the DRY. Several observers pointed to the critical role of the USA which finally decided to support a unified Yemen and warned Saudi Arabia against interfering. Despite talks in Moscow on 30 June and again in New York on 2 July on implementing and supervising a cease-fire, northern forces continued their advance and by 4 July had entered northern districts of Aden which was without water or electricity. On 7 July Aden surrendered to northern forces; the self-proclaimed DRY collapsed and its leaders fled into exile.

THE AFTERMATH OF THE CIVIL WAR

President Saleh reported that 931 civilians and soldiers had been killed in the civil war and 5,000 had been wounded, although others claimed that the death toll was much higher. Saleh estimated that it would cost $7,500m. in post-war reconstruction. Following the announcement of a general amnesty and the termination of the state of emergency, southern Yemeni soldiers began returning to the country, although al-Baid remained in Oman. Despite the election of a new YSP leadership in September, it was announced that the YSP would be excluded from Saleh's new government as it would need to 'reorganize its position' as a civilian party. On 1 October Saleh was re-elected President and constitutional amendments were announced which abolished the Presidential Council and specified that the Islamic *Shari'a* was the 'source of all laws'. Abd Rabbuh Mansur Hadi was appointed Vice-President and Abd al-Aziz Abd al-Ghani became Prime Minister. The new cabinet was reduced from 30 to 26 ministers and included no members of the YSP. Saleh declared that the priorities of the new Government would be to stabilize the currency, halt inflation and reduce the level of unemployment; emphasis would also be placed on administrative, economic and financial reform and on rooting out corruption in government institutions.

Economy

Revised for this edition by Alan J. Day

INTRODUCTION

On the unification of North and South Yemen in May 1990, the principal economic aim of the new Government was stated as being to expand the country's industrial base by developing its infrastructure. Central to the Government's economic plans is the creation of a free trade zone at the port of Aden which, it is hoped, will attract a high level of new investment. The new Government has stated that it will allow freedom of economic activity and encourage the private sector. The development of the country's mineral resources, especially of hydrocarbons and of potential gold reserves, is a priority task, as is the maximization of the unified country's considerable agricultural and fisheries potential. However, plans for economic development and integration were quickly disrupted by the Gulf crisis of 1990–91, particularly by the UN trade embargo on Iraq, which Yemen applied with some reluctance in view of its close economic links with that country. Also damaging was the enforced return of up to 1m. Yemeni workers from Saudi Arabia and other Gulf States and the consequential loss of crucial remittance income. Financial difficulties associated with the crisis obliged the Government to adjust economic policy, notably by reducing expenditure and food subsidies, with the result that social unrest increased in 1992. During the following year the Government appeared to be moving towards the introduction of fundamental structural reforms, but in 1994 normal economic planning was again disrupted by a political crisis, associated on this occasion with the onset of civil war.

Unification created a country of 536,869 sq km with a population estimated at 11,282,000 in mid-1990, excluding some 2.5m. Yemenis working abroad, mainly in Saudi Arabia. Of the two components, North Yemen, officially the Yemen Arab Republic (YAR), had a population of 9,274,173 (including nationals abroad) according to the provisional results of its February 1986 census, while South Yemen, officially the People's Democratic Republic of Yemen (PDRY), had a population of 2,345,266 at the census of 29 March 1988. The combined population is thought to be at least equal to the total native population of the whole of the rest of the Arabian peninsula and to represent about one-half of the actual population of the region (i.e. including expatriates). Possessing much fertile land receiving relatively high rainfall, North Yemen had fared better economically, achieving a GNP per caput of $640 by 1988 (according to the World Bank), whereas South Yemen's equivalent statistic was $430. On an aggregate basis for Yemen as a whole, GNP per caput rose to $650 in 1989, according to the World Bank, which published no figures for 1990. The World Bank estimated unified Yemen's mid-1992 population as 13.0m. In the 1980s the economic prospects of both countries were improved dramatically by the discovery of oil reserves in commercial quantities, although North Yemen made speedier progress in exploiting its fields than did South Yemen, whose Marxist orientation was a deterrent to Western investment. Indeed, the perceived need for rapid joint development of their oil and gas sectors was a major factor in the two countries' decision to unite. Prior to unification, both countries had sought to promote development by means of three- or five-year plans, but both had usually failed to achieve their targets.

North Yemen's development effort was channelled into a Three-Year Plan (1974–76) and three Five-Year Plans (1977–81, 1982–86 and 1987–92). Planned allocations were 936m. Yemeni riyals under the first Plan, and those of the three subsequent Five-Year Plans were 16,500m. riyals, 28,100m. riyals and 37,000m. riyals, respectively. There was no possibility that the YAR could generate capital sums of this size domestically, so massive foreign investment was called for, calculated at 75% of financing for the Three-Year Plan and 42% and 45%, respectively, for the first two Five-Year Plans. A large proportion of this was expected to come from foreign aid, in particular from Saudi Arabia and Kuwait.

However, by 1985, the amount of foreign aid for the Plan was only between $250m. and $300m. per year, doubtless reflecting the depressed condition of the economies of Gulf States, which were adversely affected by the world oil glut and, consequently, lower revenues from sales of oil. Therefore, about 60% of the 37,000m. riyals allocated to the 1987–92 Development Plan was to be generated locally, mainly in the agricultural sector. Japan was expected to be the only country to increase its contributions to the YAR during the period of the third Plan. The YAR's gross domestic product (GDP) was projected to expand, in real terms, by 7.0% annually under the second Five-Year Plan, but this target was not achieved. Between 1980 and 1987 the average annual growth rate of GDP was 5.6%. Between 1980 and 1987, it was estimated, GNP per caput increased, in real terms, at an average rate of 4.7% per year. Government figures showed that GDP had risen by 10.8% (measured at current prices) in 1988, and that the rate of inflation fell from 22% in 1987 to 16.4% in 1988 (compared with an annual average of 11.6% in the period 1980–88). By 1988, according to the World Bank, industrial output accounted for 26% of GDP (of $5,900m.), having grown by an average of 11.5% per year since 1980; agriculture for 23%, having grown by 2.9% per year since 1980; and services for 50%. North Yemen's urban population was still only 23% of the total in 1988 (compared with 5% in 1965), while the agricultural sector accounted for more than two-thirds of the working population. The unemployment rate in 1986 was 13%.

The second Five-Year Plan had been disrupted when, in December 1982, a major earthquake in Dhamar province caused the deaths of about 3,000 people and widespread damage which, it was estimated, would cost $650m. to repair. The Supreme Council for the Reconstruction of Areas Affected by Earthquakes was established in 1983 to co-ordinate the process of reconstruction, and loans were sought from oil-rich states with which to implement reconstruction schemes. In 1983, moreover, there was a slump in earnings from the remittances of North Yemenis working abroad, caused by cutbacks in petroleum production, reduced revenues and, hence, less profitable employment in the petroleum industries of Saudi Arabia and the Gulf States. These factors caused a crisis in the economy of the YAR, leading to the introduction of austerity measures. However, in 1984 the country's prospects improved, following increases in aid for the relief of the earthquake region.

In July 1984 it was announced that petroleum had been discovered in promising quantities in the Marib/al-Jawf basin by Hunt Oil of the USA, which began commercial production in 1985 and subsequently spearheaded further discoveries which established North Yemen as a potential exporter of significant quantities of oil and gas. The third Development Plan allocated 5,000m. riyals to both the gas and petroleum sectors, with the result that production had risen to a rate of about 180,000 barrels per day (b/d) by the time of unification in May 1990.

Under British rule, South Yemen was sustained by Aden's position as an entrepôt on the main shipping route to Europe from the Far East, India and East Africa via Suez. The British Petroleum refinery, completed in 1954, was the focus of industry and trade. However, the closure of the Suez Canal in 1967, and the withdrawal of British troops in the same year, put an end to Aden's commercial prosperity, making it impossible for the post-independence Government to cover the budget deficit. In such a situation, South Yemen had no choice but to turn to other countries for sources of finance and technical aid to assist it in the transition from a service economy to one based on agriculture and manufacturing. The favourable terms that were offered by the communist countries, coupled with a seeming lack of interest on the part of the West, made it inevitable that the Aden Government should turn to the Eastern bloc. In November 1969 the Government decreed the nationalization of all important foreign assets in the republic, with the exception of the BP refinery, which was not taken over until 1977. Meanwhile, the reopening of the Suez Canal in 1975 had not produced the anticipated revival in Aden's economy.

The South Yemeni Three-Year Development Plan (1971–74), although limited by shortage of funds, aimed for the creation of a communications network, the expansion of agricultural production and the establishment of small-scale light industries, based on locally produced raw materials. Some progress was made, notably in telecommunications, and it was estimated that about 80% of the total allocation was invested. The first Five-Year Plan (1974–79) began in April 1974. Total capital investment in the Plan was set at 92m. dinars, but this figure was later reduced to 75m. dinars. In the event, however, actual investment over the Plan period was estimated by the IMF at 39m. dinars per year. The second Five-Year Plan (1979–83) was allocated 370m. dinars. The priority was increased productivity in manufacturing, fisheries and agriculture. In 1980, however, this Plan was abandoned and a revised Plan (1981–1985) was introduced. It had become clear that the targets set for increased productivity were unrealistic. The Plan gave priority to making the best use of existing industries—the Aden oil refinery, the cement and salt industries and fisheries. Projected investment under the revised Plan was 558.8m. dinars, of which the industrial sector received the largest single allocation, taking 25% of the total, followed by housing, with 15%, and agriculture, with 11%. A new Plan, to run from 1986–90, was scheduled prior to the fighting between rival factions of the Yemen Socialist Party in January 1986, and was later subject to some revision, rescheduling and the reallocation of funds to reconstruction. The Plan allocated approximately 60% of projected spending to the construction sector, and envisaged further agricultural developments. Projected investment in the draft third Five-Year Plan (1988–92) was set at 582.9m. dinars, of which 348.1m. dinars was to be allocated to the manufacturing sector, 136.7m. dinars to the services sector, and 98.1m. dinars to the social services sector. It was, however, overtaken by new requirements arising from unification with North Yemen in May 1990 and the effects of the 1990–91 Gulf crisis.

In 1980 the PDRY Government introduced measures of liberalization, aimed mainly at helping farmers, fishermen and merchants. These measures were reinforced by the Law to Encourage Investment, introduced in February 1982. This law sought to induce Yemenis working abroad to invest their money in productive enterprises in the PDRY, by offering extensive tax concessions and guarantees against nationalization. The political turmoil of January 1986, when the regime of Ali Nasser Muhammad was overthrown by an uncompromising Marxist faction, caused considerable economic disruption in the country. The new Government called for international aid to rebuild the city of Aden, large areas of which had been destroyed, and promised to honour its contacts with foreign companies. The discovery of petroleum in commercial quantities in 1983 in Shabwah governorate improved the PDRY's economic prospects, although development of production (by Soviet companies) made only slow progress, to an output level of 10,000 b/d, by early 1990. While few reliable statistics were available on the PDRY's performance in the 1980s, its GNP and GDP in 1987 were estimated at $1,000m. and $840m. respectively. According to the World Bank, industry accounted for 23% of GDP in 1988, the country's urban population having risen to 42% of the total, from 30% in 1965. In early 1989 the PDRY and the YAR established a joint-venture company for the exploration and development of the oilfields along their common border.

Less than three months after the unification of North and South Yemen (May 1990), the onset of the Gulf crisis in August 1990 seriously disrupted Yemen's economy, especially when the Government, after some hesitation, decided to adhere to UN sanctions against Iraq and Iraqi-occupied Kuwait. Prior to the crisis Yemen had been dependent on trade with, and aid from, both Iraq and, to a lesser extent, Kuwait. It had also relied heavily, for balance-of-payments purposes, on hard currency remittances from Yemeni workers in Saudi Arabia and the Gulf States, who returned home in large numbers, especially from Saudi Arabia, which in late September 1990 terminated Yemeni workers' privileges in retaliation for Yemen's opposition to the US-led military build-up in the Gulf. In October 1990 the Government, in support of a request for special aid from the international community, calculated its actual and prospective losses in 1990–91 at $1,686m., made up of $400m. in lost remittances, $397m. in undisbursed Kuwaiti development aid, $259m. in lost Iraqi and Kuwaiti oil supplies at preferential prices to the Aden refinery, $157m. in lost exports to Iraq and Kuwait, $145m. in lost budget and project support from Iraq, $28m. in lost budget and project support from Kuwait, and $300m. in indirect costs (including balance-of-payments effects and increased unemployment). A further setback was the suspension of most US aid allocations to Yemen for fiscals 1990/91 and 1991/92 (totalling some $45m.) in retaliation for the Government's stance on the Gulf crisis. Later Yemeni estimates of the overall cost of the crisis included one by President Saleh in May 1991 which put Yemen's total prospective losses, including 1992, at over $3,000m. Moreover, in April 1991 the Government valued property and assets lost by Yemeni nationals forced to leave Saudi Arabia at $7,900m., and stated its determination to obtain compensation under international law. By then the total number of returnees from Saudi Arabia was estimated by Yemeni officials at up to 1m., representing a 10% increase in the country's population and giving rise to serious social problems and pressure on scarce resources. Against this background, the World Bank co-ordinated international moves to provide emergency aid and credits for Yemen totalling $245m. Aggravating Yemen's problem was a foreign debt which was disclosed in July 1991 as totalling more than $7,000m., nearly 50% higher than previous Western estimates (see Finance and Foreign Aid, below).

In November 1991 President Saleh conceded that Yemen was experiencing an economic crisis, with unemployment between 25% and 30%, and lost aid and other negative effects producing a 50% shortfall in government receipts compared with the original 1991 budget. In response, the Government implemented austerity measures, including cuts in food subsidies and defence expenditure, and co-operated informally with the IMF and other international agencies in adjusting short-term economic policy. On the positive side, activity in the oil and gas sectors accelerated sharply in 1991–92, on the strength of discoveries of significant new reserves, although output from existing oilfields declined in 1992, when government oil revenues remained modest in relation to the country's current financial needs. By mid-1993 there were signs that relations with Saudi Arabia and other GCC states were beginning to improve, and in August 1993 oil production started to rise when the first shipments were made from a newly-developed field.

In 1994 political events led once more to deep economic crisis as the armed conflict of May–July further destabilized the deficit-ridden public finances and burdened the country with a costly agenda of post-war repair work to be undertaken before the normal development programme could resume. An initial assessment of civil war damage by the UN Development Programme put the cost of essential repairs to basic infrastructure and services in the Aden area at between $100m. and $200m., and in mid-August the UN launched an appeal for $22m. of emergency aid to cover the immediate needs of the population of the southern war zone for the next six months. The Yemen Government estimated the overall cost of the war at $4,000m., and anticipated a $3,500m. spending requirement for reconstruction work. Widespread shortages of food, water and electricity continued to be reported in many parts of the country in September 1994, when a particular cause of popular discontent was the fivefold rise in prices of some basic foodstuffs since early July.

Prior to the outbreak of civil war, the Yemen Government had discussed the prospects for structural economic reform in some detail with experts from the World Bank, whose primary recommendation was that the Government should curb the fiscal deficit, adjust the currency exchange rate and adopt a disciplined monetary policy as first steps in any reform programme.

AGRICULTURE

Unified Yemen is predominantly agricultural, in that 62.5% of its labour force is engaged in the agricultural sector, as against 11% in industry and 26.4% in services. What was the Yemen Arab Republic (YAR), i.e. North Yemen, until unification contains some of the most fertile land in the Arabian peninsula, both in the highlands, where agriculture has always been extensively practised, and in the dry coastal plain of the Tihama. The total area cultivated, according to estimates made in 1987, amounts to 1,500,000 ha, equivalent to 8% of total area. Of this cultivated land, 85% is irrigated solely by rain-water. Four-fifths of all holdings are estimated to be smaller than 5 ha in area, and two-thirds are smaller than 1 ha. However, although a mainstay of the YAR economy, the agricultural sector achieved only slow growth. It grew by only 1% per year during the first Five-Year Plan (1977–81), instead of the projected 5%. The second Five-Year Plan (1982–86) allocated 4,430m. riyals to agriculture and envisaged growth of 4.8% per year in this sector. The third Five-Year Plan (1987–92) allocated 3,800m. riyals to the agricultural sector. According to the World Bank, agricultural output grew by an annual average of 2.9% in the period 1980–88 and accounted for 23% of GDP in 1988, although more than two-thirds of the working population were engaged in the sector.

North Yemen's best-known crop was traditionally coffee, grown mainly in the hills behind the Tihama, although it was cultivated in various degrees all over the country. It was once the largest foreign exchange earner, but the amount of land devoted to it has decreased, partly because of fluctuation in demand on the world market and partly because the farmers found the stimulant, qat (the consumption of which is a social ritual in both North and South Yemen), to be a more profitable crop. Although the Government announced measures to limit the cultivation and consumption of qat in 1972, production of the stimulant recovered from this setback. The increase in consumer spending in the second half of the 1970s especially favoured qat production for the local market as against coffee production for export. In 1985 an estimated 47,000 ha, including some of the best ground for cultivation in the country, was given over to the qat crop, which is valued at $1,200m. per year. Qat farmers do not receive any of the concessionary loans and other benefits offered by the state-owned agricultural bank.

The major cereal crop in the North is sorghum (durra), grown at any altitude up to 3,000m. Other cereals are wheat, barley and maize. Total cereal production in 1988 was 775,000 tons, compared with 675,000 tons in 1984 and 812,000 tons in 1981. In the past the YAR exported grain to Ethiopia and Saudi Arabia but, although a comparatively large area is allocated to cereals, the yield is poor and Yemen has increasingly come to rely on imports of staple foods. Floods, as well as drought, can cause loss of output, and the Yemen General Grain Corporation was set up in 1976 to encourage farmers to increase production and to supervise imports and distribution. A grain distribution system, involving the building of silos at Hodeida and the establishment of flour mills and bakeries, was also instituted. In 1988, however, the YAR imported a record level of cereals of 1.06m. tons, compared with 954,000 tons in 1987. Imports of wheat and wheat flour accounted for 84% of total cereal imports in 1988: Australia maintained its position as the leading supplier.

The highland areas also produce many fruits and vegetables. Citrus fruits, apricots, peaches, grapes, tomatoes and potatoes are the main crops; but others, such as cauliflowers, lettuces, peas, cucumbers and water melons are being introduced at the instigation of the Ministry of Agriculture. A nine-year agricultural development programme for the central highlands, costing $20m., was instituted in 1984 with a loan of $8m. from the International Development Association (IDA)—the largest of several international loans. Production of fruit and vegetables increased from 479,000 tons in 1979/80 to about 740,000 tons in 1988.

The hot Tihama plain produces dates, and tobacco and cotton plantations have been established there to form the basis for local industries. Cotton assumed some importance as a cash crop; in 1973/74 total cotton and cottonseed exports were worth 35.2m. riyals. However, after 1974/75 cotton production fell sharply, and by 1981 annual production was only 5,000 tons. Exports have virtually ceased. This decline appears to have been due to the low level of prices maintained by the Government, shortage of agricultural credit facilities, lack of improved seeds and adverse weather conditions. Imports of fruit and vegetables were banned in 1984, in an effort to stimulate local production. This resulted in a surplus in 1986, and in the following year a small quantity of bran and watermelons were exported for the first time. The number of livestock increased slightly between 1985 and 1988. According to FAO estimates, in 1989 there were 1.08m. cattle, 2.75m. sheep and 1.73m. goats.

Because droughts are so frequent, one of the YAR's major concerns was to achieve efficient irrigation systems and water storage schemes and to utilize the ground water which exists in the Tihama. Development of the Tihama region is the pivot of Yemen's agricultural policy. A Tihama Development Authority (TDA) has been set up and finance is being provided by the UN, the IDA, the International Fund for Agricultural Development (IFAD) and other sources. Development of the Tihama plain remained a priority following unification in May 1990, with emphasis being placed on providing loans to individuals and groups once a basic infrastructure was in place. Such loans were to be channelled through the state-owned Co-operative and Agricultural Credit Bank (CACB). In September 1991 the TDA invited bids for the construction of a canal network in Tihama, as part of the $47m. Wadi Sihan project, designed to provide irrigation for an additional 5,700 ha and to improve the local infrastructure. A European Union grant of 7.5m. ECUs ($9.2m.) was approved in 1994 for dam-building work at Barquqa.

Another major project in the North is the Marib dam and irrigation scheme, of which the Abu Dhabi Fund for Arab Economic Development (ADFAED) financed $100m.–$200m. The scheme provides perennial irrigation for 6,000 ha of sorghum and wheat, and 5,000 ha of intermittent irrigation. The new Marib dam, built across Wadi Abida, 5 km upstream from the site of the old dam (constructed in 500 BC), is 40 m high and 763 m long, and capable of retaining 390m. cu m of water. The first stage of the project was completed in mid-1986, and irrigation channels were built in December 1986. In August 1990 plans were confirmed for a 65-km secondary network from the Marib dam, to irrigate a further 7,000 ha at an estimated cost of $22.4m. During 1983 work finally began on three other agricultural projects: the Wadi Mawr integrated agricultural development scheme, costing $76m., to improve 25,000 ha of farm land; the second phase of the Wadi Rima project; and the $28.7m. agricultural research centre at Rasaba/Jahran. During 1984 it was announced that two other agricultural research stations were to be built, at Wadi Surdud and Dhamar, at a cost of $2.4m. Apart from the major schemes itemized above, other, recent, smaller projects include the construction of the Sar an-Nu'man dam (150 km west of San'a), the Shahek dam (100 km south-east of San'a) and the Amaqia dam in Sa'ada province, in the north of the country. Another important agricultural scheme involves the development of the Wadi al-Jawf area, north-east of San'a, at a cost of $38m.

Yemen is also receiving agricultural aid from the Netherlands, the United Kingdom, the People's Republic of China (PRC), Japan and Arab states. In 1986 the US Agency for International Development allocated the following funds for agricultural development: $29m. to establish an agricultural faculty at San'a University (which was expanded in 1988); $21m. for the Ministry of Agriculture to develop its own schemes; $11m. for agricultural schools; and $6m. to expand poultry farming. The EC funded a seed improvement centre and an agricultural centre at Yarim, which were opened in March 1989. The Livestock Development Corporation (LDC), was formed in 1976 with the aim of establishing eight 50-cow dairy farms, a livestock-fattening farm, a poultry unit and a feedmill, to construct three urban slaughterhouses and about 154 municipal retail market stalls, to improve production of hides and skins, to aid animal health services and to ensure supervised credit to some 900 traditional sector landowners, smallholder livestock and poultry owners and irrigated fodder-crop producers. In 1984 work also began on a 4.3m.-riyal ($796,000) fruit-farming scheme, 100 km to the west of San'a.

Early in 1985 work began on the 50m.-riyal ($9.2m.) grain, livestock and fruit farm to be operated by the Yemen Company for Agricultural Development at Jarabeh in Wadi Surdud. Most farmers receive concessionary loans and assistance with the purchase of inputs such as fertilizers, the poor use of which has contributed, to a large extent, to low farm output in both the YAR and the PDRY. In 1986 only 20,000 tons of fertilizers were used in the YAR, one-fifth of the amount necessary, although by 1989/90 consumption of fertilizer in Yemen as a whole had risen to 1,100 g per ha of arable land, compared with just 100 g in 1970/71. In 1987 a private-sector agricultural company was established, which planned to institute a national network for the purchase of agricultural produce. Local agricultural development authorities were also established.

What was South Yemen is much less favoured than the North in terms of agricultural potential. The area of cultivable land in the former PDRY is estimated at 320,000 ha, only 1% of the total land area, and a mere 100,000 ha is actually under cultivation. The agricultural sector, although the principal source of employment, provided only about 16% of GDP in 1988. The most intensively cultivated areas are Abyan, east of Aden, and Lahej, north of Aden. The river valleys of the Hadramawt area are also fertile and relatively well-developed. The Kuwait Fund for Arab Economic Development (KFAED) financed a pre-investment study of the Abyan delta and in May 1974 agreed to lend 4.2m. Kuwaiti dinars to help finance land reclamation and irrigation in the area. Bulgaria also backed the project. The Abyan dam project began in 1974 and is now completed. The major scheme in the 1980s was the Hadramawt agricultural development project, designed to raise production on 3,225 ha of agricultural land. It was reported in August 1989 that the third phase of the Wadi Hadramawt project, costing $41.8m. and due for completion in 1996, would be extended to include flood control, in response to the considerable flood damage sustained in March 1989. The project, concentrating on the provision of irrigation water and development training, is being financed by the IDA, KFAED and the Arab Fund for Economic and Social Development (AFESD). The IDA has also loaned $8m. for development work in the Wadi Baihan, which began in early 1982. Plans were also finalized at the end of 1983 for the construction, with World Bank and AFESD support, of wells and a reservoir in Saiwun, with a water distribution network to serve the villages of the Wadi Hadramawt. Other foreign assistance (mainly from the Eastern bloc, Arab and UN sources) was given to the PDRY in the form of finance and technical aid projects, such as irrigation and safe water development and the introduction of new farming methods and equipment. In April 1989 an agricultural co-operation agreement was concluded with Egypt.

Cotton, the PDRY's principal export crop, is produced mainly in Lahej and Abyan. The government-controlled Abyan Board supervises the whole process of growing and marketing and has its own ginnery at al-Kad. Cotton is also produced in other areas and the Cotton Producers' Associations were the most flourishing co-operatives in the country. The area under cotton has been declining, however, in spite of cash incentives offered to growers, with an estimated 12,000 ha devoted to cotton in 1981, as against 14,000 ha in 1971. Two more ginneries are planned, as well as a cottonseed oil factory at Ma'alla. In December 1987 the Council of Ministers approved proposed increases in the prices of long- and medium-staple cotton fibre in an effort to increase the annual yield and to develop the area under cotton cultivation.

The PDRY was able, on the whole, to meet local demand for most vegetables but imported onions, potatoes and fruit. The main fruits and vegetables grown in the South are tomatoes, carrots, salad vegetables, bananas and melons. In 1984 the PDRY produced 50,000 tons of vegetables, an increase of 14% compared with 1983. Bananas in particular are produced in quantity and the FAO has recommended an expansion of banana growing, provided export markets can be found. In 1981 the banana crop was estimated at 22,000 metric tons. In 1992 unified Yemen began exporting bananas to the United Kingdom.

Wheat is grown mainly in the Hadramawt and Beihan but was insufficient to satisfy domestic requirements in the PDRY. The balance was imported mainly from Australia. In 1993 Oman agreed to finance the construction of a 30,000-metric ton grain silo in Aden, at a location accessible to sea-going vessels. Implementation of this project was, however, deferred in the aftermath of the 1994 civil war. Other cereals produced include barley, millet and sorghum. Cereal production was estimated at 102,000 metric tons in 1981, a slight fall from previous years. Tobacco is grown in the coastal areas, mainly in the Ghail Ba Wazir area, and efforts have been made to introduce coffee cultivation in the eastern region. The production of the stimulant, qat, was brought under strict government control, and its use restricted to weekends and holidays in Aden and most other areas. Livestock production in the PDRY remained fairly static in the 1980s, and considerable numbers of sheep and goats had to be imported to satisfy local meat demand. In 1989 the FAO estimated that the PDRY's livestock included 96,000 cattle, 935,000 sheep, 1.4m. goats, 170,000 asses and 81,000 camels.

Agricultural production in the PDRY was periodically disrupted by weather conditions. Because of drought in 1976 and 1977, recourse to food aid was necessary and the UN World Food Programme alone supplied $9.5m. in aid for drought victims. In 1982, by contrast, the country experienced severe floods, which damaged agricultural land, rural housing and communications. In early 1989 torrential rain and floods devastated the Hadramawt region, resulting in the destruction of the homes of tens of thousands of people and causing extensive damage to the country's agricultural sector. Economic reforms, introduced after the 1986 coup, allowed farmers and fishermen to sell more of their produce in the free market and agricultural taxes were reduced. It was reported that, following these developments, more vegetables and fish became available to the consumer.

Following unification in May 1990, the lifting of restrictions on chewing the stimulant, qat, in what was the PDRY led to an increase in its production and consumption. The agricultural sector was adversely affected by the loss of markets for local produce in Iraq and Kuwait as a result of the Gulf crisis, although agriculture was estimated to have contributed 22% of Yemen's GDP in 1991. Post-crisis recovery plans, tabled by the Government, included the allocation of substantial resources to the agricultural sector. The Government's priority aim was to increase food production in view of the population increase caused by returning Yemeni nationals. In June 1992 the World Food Programme approved the allocation of $13.4m. in food aid to Yemen to support the Government's development of rural areas in six governorates in the South (Aden, Hadramawt, Lahej, Abyan, Shabwah and al-Mahra); currently costed at $76.8m., the mainly state-financed programme was expected to take four years to complete. Other recent international funding related to the agricultural sector has included a World Bank loan of $33m., approved in July 1992, to help finance a $47.6m. programme to strengthen sustainable agriculture and to improve water resources management. Rural areas were also given priority in infrastructural development initiated in 1991–92 (see Infrastructure, below), while the Netherlands remained an important source of technical assistance and aid, especially in the sphere of water resources development. Floods caused extensive damage in early 1993, reportedly destroying all the dams in Anyan and Lahej governorates. The estimated cost of repairing the damage was between 2,000m. riyals and 3,000m. riyals. In late May 1993 Shabwah was declared a disaster area, after crops had been extensively damaged by locusts. In August 1994 the Government banned the importation of fruit and vegetables 'in order to protect local producers'.

FISHERIES

The fishing grounds of the Arabian Sea are one of Yemen's greatest potential sources of wealth after oil. Most productive grounds are located off the former PDRY, whose exports of fish and fish products were estimated to be worth about 20m. dinars per year in the late 1980s. Most of the 10,000 fishermen in the South work only in territorial waters, while their equipment is often poor, and efficient marketing of the catch is impossible with the present state of communications. In 1979, however, co-operatives were permitted to sell 40% of their catch direct to the market at a significantly higher price than that paid by the National Fish Marketing Corporation. Cuttlefishes are important to the export market, while there is much potential for increased sales of mackerels and tuna to the domestic market. The PDRY's total catch declined between 1980 and 1982, but subsequently increased, to 51,778 tons in 1985. The total catch declined to 47,706 tons in 1986, but increased to 48,492 tons in 1987.

The importance of the PDRY's fisheries sector was reflected in the level of investment allocated to it in successive development plans. The first (three-year) Plan for 1971–74, allocated 7% of total investment to the fishing industry, and the first Five-Year Plan (1974–79) 13.7%. The investment in fishing fell to 5% of total expenditure in the 1980–85 Plan, but, in absolute terms, the amount rose from 2.3m. dinars in the 1971–74 Plan to 26.8m. dinars in the first Five-Year Plan, and to 38.2m. dinars in the second.

The PDRY's fishing fleet had 17 deep-sea fishing boats provided by the USSR, Japan and the PRC. Local fishermen, who are organized into 13 co-operatives, operate smaller coastal vessels while independent fishermen fish in one-man boats. A Russian-Yemeni company and two Japanese companies are currently fishing in Yemeni waters. On the processing side there are two fish-canning factories, at Mukalla and Shukra, a fishmeal factory (with another due to go into production) and a fish-freezing plant at Mukalla. Soviet contractors have worked on the development of Hedjuff fishing port. A project, financed by Libya, to develop a two-berth general cargo and fishing harbour at Mukalla is now under way. Danish firms have constructed a fishing port at Nishtun, costing $50m., which was opened in 1984, and the USSR was committed to building a fishing port and refrigeration facilities at Aden. In December 1987 an economic and technical co-operation agreement was signed between the PDRY and the USSR, whereby the fishing port of Aden was to be developed and a fisheries complex was to be set up on Socotra Island, in the Indian Ocean. In December 1988 the USSR undertook to maintain aid to the programme until 2005. In May 1989 the Government approved the establishment of a Yemeni-Soviet Joint Fishing Company, with initial capital of $17m.

Efforts were also made by North Yemen to exploit its fish resources, although its output remained well below that of South Yemen. The YAR's catch increased from 18,170 tons in 1984 to 22,241 tons in 1986, to 22,254 tons in 1987, and to about 21,700 tons in 1988, while exports of fish averaged 50m. riyals per year in the 1980s. Danish firms were contracted to develop fishing ports and related shore facilities at Hodeida and three other sites. Another private-sector company was also established in 1987 to develop commercial fishing potential in the Red Sea. In early 1989 the Council of Ministers approved the establishment of the Yemen Fisheries Company.

Following unification in May 1990, integration of the PDRY and YAR fisheries sectors was initiated. The emphasis was on further development of the industry in the South, where the $22m. 'Fisheries 3' expansion project, initiated in 1988 with external support, had made substantial progress. In June 1991 it was announced that the IDA would lend $12.8m. for 'Fisheries 4', which was designed to benefit some 3,500 artisanal fishermen in the Mukalla and Sayhut areas in the South. Other external funding was negotiated in 1992 with the EC and IFAD. The importance of the sector was illustrated by the creation of two new companies early in 1992: the Red Sea Company for Fisheries and Shrimps (in which the Government took a 60% stake) and the Socotra Fisheries Company.

PETROLEUM AND NATURAL GAS

From the early 1970s both the YAR (North Yemen) and the PDRY (South Yemen) gave priority to the search for hydrocarbon reserves, which were eventually found in commercial quantities in both countries in the early 1980s in the region of their common border. Exploitation of the discoveries proved to be a slow process in South Yemen, where the Marxist Government relied mainly on Soviet operating companies, which experienced technical difficulties and shortage of

investment finance. In North Yemen, where US companies assumed the dominant role, development of oil resources was speedier, resulting in the growth of oil output to significant, albeit relatively small, levels in the late 1980s.

Development of North Yemen's oil resources was the responsibility of the Yemen Petroleum Company (YPC), a joint venture between the Government and the Yemen Bank for Reconstruction and Development. In 1970 a joint company, the Yemen Oil and Mineral Industrial Company (YEMINCO), was formed by the YPC with the Algerian state-owned oil concern, SONATRACH. It was claimed in 1972 that petroleum had been found in the Tihama but in the same year the company had to be dissolved because of lack of capital. The Government made it known that it would welcome other foreign firms who wished to prospect for petroleum, and exploration/production sharing agreements were signed with US, Federal German, British, Japanese and Brazilian companies covering both onshore and offshore areas. In July 1984 the US Hunt Oil Company announced that it had found oil in the Alif field in the Marib/al-Jawf basin, with a production capacity of about 7,800 barrels per day (b/d). Later in the year this figure was revised upwards to 10,000 b/d, and in December the Yemen Hunt Oil Company, the local subsidiary of Hunt Oil of the USA, confirmed that its 19,600-sq km Marib concession could eventually produce a yield of between 75,000 b/d and 400,000 b/d. A Ministry of Petroleum and Mineral Wealth was created in July 1985. At the end of 1985 the Alif field was producing at a rate of 10,000 b/d, and total reserves in the Marib/al-Jawf basin were then estimated at 300m.–500m. barrels. Yemen Hunt Oil embarked on a $50m. programme to establish five wells, a petroleum-gathering network and a refinery. The refinery has been built by the US company, Petrofac, at a cost of $18m., at Marib, near the site of Alif 1, the first well in the Alif field. It was opened in April 1986, with an initial output capacity of 10,000 b/d. A 440-km pipeline was completed in 1987 to link the Alif field with loading terminals at the port of Salif, on the Red Sea. Export capacity through the pipeline, from Marib to a new offshore terminal at Ras Isa, is 225,000 b/d. Also in 1987 further oil strikes were made by Hunt Oil in the Marib/al-Jawf basin, establishing the Azal, Raydan, Kamran and Bilqis fields as commercial propositions. Exports of crude from the Alif field began in December 1987, and in 1988 $432m. was received in oil revenues, representing 89% of total export value although well below original expectations because of the slump in world oil prices. The Azal field was declared commercial in August 1989 and its output of 25,000 b/d was pumped through the pipeline from Marib to the coast. By August 1989 YAR production had reached about 180,000 b/d (compared with 150,000 b/d in mid-1988), representing about 10% of non-OPEC Arab output. In 1989 exports of petroleum accounted for 90% of the YAR's total export earnings.

Other companies active in North Yemen included British Petroleum (BP), which in early 1984 signed a production-sharing agreement with the YPC, under which BP was to conduct seismic surveys within a 22,000-sq km area in the northern part of the Tihama plain. In June 1985 the US Exxon Corporation was granted a 22,000-sq km concession in the area between Yarim (230 km south of San'a) and Saada (250 km north of San'a) in which to explore for oil, and in August Total-CFP of France was granted a 9,047-sq km concession, 100 km west of Taiz, in the southern Tihama. Exxon, of the USA, which already held a 20,000-sq km concession in the central highlands, bought a 49% share in Hunt Oil's Marib/al-Jawf concession at the end of 1985. Exxon commenced drilling in 1988 in a 20,000-sq-m field near Dhamar province, the scene of an earthquake in 1982; and Total-CFP announced plans to commence drilling near Modra in the south. In May 1988 the International Petroleum Corporation (IPC), a Swedish-owned, Bermuda-registered company, signed an oil concession agreement with the YAR covering 4,300 sq km in the Marib/al-Jawf basin.

In South Yemen exploration agreements were first signed with companies from the German Democratic Republic and the USSR, and Western participation was also welcomed; a Canadian firm was awarded a concession in 1975. A joint Yemeni/Algerian company did some prospecting in the Hadramawt but went into liquidation in 1976. In 1977 Agip, the refining and distribution subsidiary of the Italian state agency ENI, signed an offshore petroleum exploration agreement, and Siebens Oil and Gas of West Germany began drilling in the Samaha offshore concession. In June 1979 ENI signed a long-term agreement for the exploration and production of petroleum and natural gas in two more zones, one onshore and one offshore, covering 15,000 sq km. Hunt Oil of the USA was also interested in exploration, and the Brazilian company Braspetro was awarded an offshore concession in 1982. Having struck oil offshore in 1982, the following year Agip was the first company to locate petroleum in potentially commercial quantities onshore. In April 1987 the first oil well in the country was inaugurated at Shabwah. Production from Shabwah was being transported by road to the Aden refinery at the rate of 5,000 b/d–10,000 b/d in 1987. In 1983 the private Kuwaiti Independent Petroleum Group signed a production-sharing agreement to search for oil in Shabwah governorate. During 1983 alone, the Government planned to spend $40m. on oil exploration, and total investment in the petroleum industry between 1980 and 1983 was reported to have been $86.9m.

Further attempts to attract foreign oil companies were made during 1984, and five new concession areas for exploration were announced: at Aden, Abyan, Balhaf, North Hadramawt/Rub al-Khali (all coastal offshore areas), and Socotra offshore. To take account of the country's new petroleum interests, a Ministry of Energy and Minerals was formed in February 1985. In the same year Braspetro drilled the first exploratory well in its 42,000-sq-km Hawarim Ghaydah onshore concession, and Elf Aquitaine purchased a 35% share in the 18,500-sq-km offshore and onshore concession east of Aden held by the Independent Petroleum Group in the Balhaf block. In early 1987 the PDRY signed a six-year production-sharing agreement with Elf Aquitaine of France to boost exploration in the Aden-Abyan region. Another six-year production-sharing agreement was signed between the PDRY, Canadian Occidental Petroleum (CanOxy) and the International Contractors' Federation for exploration in the Masilah region. In April 1987 an agreement was signed between the PDRY's Ministry of Energy and Minerals and the French company Total-CFP, for exploration work to be carried out in the East Shabwah area. The USSR undertook the construction of a 230-km pipeline, with an initial capacity of 100,000 b/d, to transport crude petroleum from the newly-discovered oilfields in Shabwah to Bir Ali, on the Gulf of Aden. The pipeline, built at an estimated cost of $473m., was eventually completed in late 1990 and opened in May 1991 at an initial flow of 35,000 b/d. Prior to its opening, production from Shabwah had been suspended, because of technical problems, since July 1990, when ouput had been running at only 10,000 b/d.

In June 1988, following a meeting held in Taiz between the YAR and the PDRY, an agreement was signed to establish a joint oil company for the exploration and development of a 2,200-sq km area along the common border, where the Marib al-Jawf and Shabwah fields are located. The company, the Yemeni Company for Investment in Oil and Mineral Resources (YCIOMR), was established in January 1989, and by July about 45 oil companies had offered bids for exploration in the zone. Following unification in May 1990, an exploration agreement was finalized with a foreign consortium (consisting of Hunt Oil and Exxon, Total/CFP, the Kuwait Foreign Petroleum Exploration Company and two Soviet companies) under which seismic surveying of the joint development area began in late 1990. Intensive exploratory drillings from early 1991 resulted in a series of new discoveries of commercial potential, particularly in CanOxy's Masilah concession, which was established as Yemen's largest oilfield, with reserves of around 460m. barrels. Other companies subsequently applied for adjacent exploration blocks, including Lasmo and Clyde Petroleum (both British), which planned to start drilling in late 1993. At the end of 1993 unified Yemen's proven oil reserves totalled 4,000m. barrels sufficient to maintain the previous year's rate of production for a further 55.7 years. Overall responsibility for oil development in the unified country was held by the General Corporation for Oil and Mineral Resources (GCOMR), which in 1991–92 signed a new round of exploration/production-sharing agreements with various foreign companies covering unallocated blocks in the Shabwah area as well as areas in the south and off-shore in the Red Sea. In the new licensing round, the Yemeni Government was able to insist on much more favourable terms, notably as regards the level of expenditure pledged by the exploring companies and the proportion of eventual oil output which would accrue to the Government. By 1993, however, the Government was under pressure to moderate its terms in order to attract new investment from larger oil companies.

Yemen's decision to abide by the UN embargo on Iraq and Iraqi-occupied Kuwait, imposed in August 1990, obliged the Government to suspend Yemeni oil exports in September, on grounds of *force majeure*, in order to divert domestic production to the Aden oil refinery. The refinery had hitherto received most of its crude supplies from Iraq (30,000 b/d) and Kuwait (20,000 b/d) at a preferential price. In the fourth 1990 quarter Yemen's exports accordingly fell to about 40,000 b/d, compared with 85,000 b/d in the third quarter, with consequential loss of foreign earnings despite the increase in world oil prices. Oil exports in 1990 were worth 6,188m. riyals (88% of total export value), compared with 5,802m. riyals in 1989. Because of the suspension of supplies from Shabwah (see above), Yemen managed only a small increase in oil production during the Gulf crisis, its 1991 average output being officially assessed at 197,400 b/d, compared with an original target of 235,000 b/d. The Government's share of 1991 output was 111,600 b/d, of which 48,900 b/d went to the Aden refinery and 62,700 b/d to export. In the first half of 1992 production continued at below 200,000 b/d, and in July it declined to 160,000 b/d because of various technical problems, the full-year average for 1992 being 185,000 b/d. However, Yemeni spokesmen confidently predicted that, on the basis of development work in progress, output would reach 750,000 b/d by 1996, placing Yemen on a par with the smaller OPEC producers.

A complication arose in April 1992, when Saudi Arabia officially objected to exploration work in a border area which, it claimed, was Saudi Arabian territory. Notified of the Saudi position, several oil companies suspended their drilling operations pending resolution of the dispute, on which preliminary talks opened between the two sides in July 1992. The talks entered their fifth round in August 1993 against a background of generally improved relations between the two countries.

In August 1993 the first 550,000-barrel consignment of crude oil from CanOxy's Masilah field was shipped from a coastal terminal at Al Shihr. The field was due to be brought up to its full production rate of 120,000 b/d in late September, at which time Yemen's overall oil output was expected to exceed 300,000 b/d. In the same month Total-CFP announced a commercial discovery in its East Shabwah exploration block. The expiry date of Total-CFP's permit to conduct further exploration work in East Shabwah was extended by two years to October 1995.

Of CanOxy's expected output of 120,000 b/d in the last quarter of 1993, the state share would amount to 51,000 b/d, all of which was destined for export sale to major oil companies. In the first half of 1993 the demands of Yemen's domestic oil market had helped to restrict state oil revenues to an average of $52.5m. per month. According to official estimates, the state's cumulative oil revenues during the first three years of unified government amounted to about $2,000m. (an average of $55.5m. per month). Apart from a five-day suspension of exports from Hunt Oil's Marib/al-Jawf fields while a pumping station was repaired, Yemen's crude oil production was not subject to any significant interruption during the 1994 civil war, and the few attacks made on oil installations produced little or no damage. At the end of the war production was running at around 350,000 b/d, including about 160,000 b/d from CanOxy's Masilah field.

Gas and condensate have been found in Yemen, usually in association with oil, but exploitation of reserves has taken a lower priority than oil development and exploration. In early 1988 condensate and gas were discovered in the Asad al-Kamil field (15 km east of the Azal field), where eight hydrocarbon wells were subsequently drilled. In 1987 reserves of natural gas, discovered in the Alif field, were estimated at more than

140,000m. cu m. In August 1989 the Ministry of Petroleum and Mineral Wealth announced that proven reserves of natural gas in the Marib/al-Jawf region were 198,240m. cu m. Three further gas/condensate discoveries by Hunt Oil in the Marib/al-Jawf basin were declared commercial in May 1991, when it was stated that production would begin in mid-1994, on completion of a gas processing plant currently under construction in the nearby Asad al-Kamil field by a Greek company. Named Al-Raja, Dostour al-Wihdah and Al-Saidah, the three new fields were estimated to contain reserves of up to 170,000m. cu m, bringing total probable reserves in the Hunt Oil concession area to 400,000m. cu m. At mid-1992 Yemen's total proven gas reserves were given as between 356,800m. cu m and 424,800m. cu m, output in 1991 having averaged 17.4m. cu m per day. In November 1993 Yemen's General Gas Corporation reached an outline agreement with the US company Enron Corporation for a major gas development project using reserves from the Marib/al-Jawf area. Enron proposed to invest an estimated $2,500m. to pipe gas to a liquefaction plant and export terminal, to be sited either at Aden or at Hodeida, and to handle the export marketing of up to 5m. tons of LNG per year, with India (where Enron was building a gas-fired power plant) as a probable principal market. The scheme would also provide supplies of piped gas to power stations and industries within Yemen. Hunt Oil, which had earlier put forward an alternative proposal (co-sponsored by Exxon Corporation and the South Korean company Yukong), continued to urge acceptance of its own scheme. Negotiations to secure the gas development rights were expected to resume in the latter part of 1994.

INDUSTRY AND MINING

The future state of unified Yemen's industrial sector depends on the pace at which oil and gas reserves are developed and the extent to which prospective oil revenues are used to diversify the economy. As separate countries, both the YAR (North Yemen) and the PDRY (South Yemen) had allocated considerable resources to industrial development, but with only limited results in terms of transforming their essentially undeveloped and agriculture-based economies. Following unification in May 1990, most government hopes for more rapid industrialization centred on the industrial free-trade zone at Aden, the former PDRY capital which was now recognized as the country's economic capital.

During the early 1980s, it was calculated that industry accounted for about 16% of North Yemen's GDP and that it employed about 5% of the country's labour force. Between 1980 and 1988, the average annual growth rate of the manufacturing sector was 12.8%, illustrating the recent expansion in the industrial sector, which contributed only 12% of GDP in the early 1970s. According to the World Bank, the industrial sector (broadly defined) contributed 26% of GDP in 1991, about one-third of this being provided by manufacturing. With a few exceptions, the existing and projected new industries were mainly based on traditional occupations such as textiles, leather work, basketry, jewellery and glass-making, and, where possible, using local raw materials. The Government's aim was to become self-sufficient in food-processing, clothing and construction industries. A state-owned spinning and weaving factory at San'a, established under an agreement of 1958 with the PRC, was completed in 1967. China continued to make aid available for the textile industry, financing a cotton gin at Hodeida which started production in 1982 with a capacity of 4,100 tons per year. There are also two privately-owned cotton-cleaning plants in Hodeida, and one in Zabid, and a cottonseed oil and cake plant in Hodeida. The Yemen General Cotton Company, owned 51% by the Government, 30% by the Yemen Bank for Reconstruction and Development and 19% by private interests, provides plants with raw cotton, over which it has monopoly rights.

Other industries in what was North Yemen include soft drinks factories, a cigarette plant at Hodeida, built with Italian aid, an oxygen plant, originally set up by the USSR and now state-operated, and a plant making aluminium products. A plastics plant outside Taiz, built in 1973, produces mattresses, plastic tubes and plasticized paper. The Yemeni Company for Industrial Development was formed to develop light industry,

particularly in San'a, Taiz and Hodeida. However, industrialization progressed very slowly, even with the increased aid which became available, and skilled industrial labour remained scarce, owing to insufficient training facilities. During 1985 the Industrial Bank of Yemen identified the following six sectors for special attention in future development and investment plans: food processing; construction materials; light and household chemicals and plastics; light engineering; woodworking; and electrical and mechanical services. The emphasis on the food industry was reflected in figures for 1984, which indicated that one-third of the loans made by the Industrial Bank of Yemen were used for food and drink projects.

The Soviet-built cement factory at Bajil, which uses local limestone deposits, has proved one of the more successful ventures. The USSR financed an expansion of the factory which was completed in 1983, bringing capacity up to 250,000 tons per year. By 1985 capacity had reached 350,000 tons per year and a further expansion of production facilities to 500,000 tons was being discussed with the USSR. A Japanese-built cement works at Amran, completed in 1982, has a capacity of 500,000 tons per year. In January 1989 it was announced that the Al-Ghannami Industrial Group was to establish a joint venture with Exide International of Britain to produce automotive batteries at a plant at Al-Burh, near Taiz, although subsequent delays meant that construction had still not been completed in mid-1991.

The state-run rock salt factory at Salif utilizes local salt deposits, estimated to contain at least 25m. tons. Until 1975 the salt, which is of high quality, was nearly all exported to Japan. The Salt Company had invested about $400,000 to raise production to 500,000 tons per year and Kuwait provided loans to extend bulk-loading facilities at Salif port. A further Kuwaiti loan of KD1.2m. was given to exploit the deposits further and to raise production to 1m. tons per year by 1974. In 1975, however, Japanese customers ceased imports of salt, claiming that it contained impurities. The Government was understandably concerned in view of the large investments in the industry and the amount of goods imported from Japan. During 1977 the planned expansion of salt mining facilities which commenced under the Three-Year Plan was completed. With design capacity of 1m. tons per year, Salif is likely to be profitable in the long term due to fairly high salt purity, proximity to deep water and low-cost open pit mining. The Yemen Salt Mining Corporation is now seeking new market outlets. The USSR, Bangladesh and North Korea are among the countries to have accepted shipments, but full capacity working at Salif may have to await the completion of new chloralkali plants in other Middle East countries. The Yemen Company for Salt Refining and Packing, which was set up at the beginning of 1984, plans to build a 45m.-riyal ($8.3m.) table salt plant at Hodeida, with an annual capacity of 20,000 tons, using salt from the Salif mine.

Studies have been conducted into the possibility of exploiting copper and nickel deposits at Hamoura, near Taiz, and commercial quantities of zinc and lead have been located in the Nihm area, as well as copper in the Beida area. In 1982 the two Yemens set up a joint organization to co-ordinate mineral exploration. Deposits of coal, iron, sulphur, silver, gold and uranium are also known to exist. In 1982 a marble quarry started production, and during 1983 work began on the construction of three new factories: an $8.7m. marble factory; a $6m. gypsum plant; and a $6m. butane gas filling plant.

In South Yemen the State's dominance of the economy (it accounted for 64% of industrial, and 56% of total output) resulted partly from its control of the Aden petroleum refinery, the country's only large industrial complex. Nationalized in 1977 and placed under the Aden Refinery Company, the refinery became of paramount importance to the country's economic development, although its poor performance through most of the 1970s was shown in the figures for refined petroleum exports. Between 1970 and 1973 the export of petroleum products in value terms fell from 45m. dinars to 28.4m. dinars. With the large increase in petroleum prices, exports of petroleum products appeared to soar—but only by value—in 1974, rising to 78.7m. dinars, but there was an obvious fall, by any criteria, to 59.2m. dinars in 1978. In the following years, exports from the refinery staged a recovery, to 152.8m. dinars in 1979 and to 255.4m. dinars in 1980. Although much of this rise was attributable directly to an increase in prices, it gave the Government grounds for hope. Experts from BP were brought back to manage a set of improvements to the refinery, equipping it to produce light-grade products. In 1982 the PDRY signed a valuable agreement to refine Iranian crude petroleum and to provide bunker fuel, and in 1983 the PDRY and Algeria signed an agreement whereby 280,000 tons of Algerian crude petroleum would be refined at Aden, although in recent years the bulk of the refinery's external supplies have come from Iraq and Kuwait (see Oil and Gas, above), with the USSR providing smaller quantities of bunkering oil.

Only about one-third of the Aden refinery's nominal capacity of 170,000 b/d was in use in the early 1990s, when the Government of unified Yemen was seeking financing for a two-phase modernization programme to raise that capacity by 80,000 b/d (the first 30,000 b/d at an estimated cost of $150m., and the final 50,000 b/d at an estimated cost of $200m.). The Yemeni Government also had plans to build a new 100,000 b/d refinery at Mukalla, at a cost of $300m. Exploratory talks were held in 1993 with a number of potential partners, including Oman's state refining company. The Aden refinery was shut down for some weeks during and immediately following the 1994 civil war after several of its storage tanks were destroyed in the fighting. There was no major damage to the distillation facilities, and the plant was operating at its normal pre-war production volume by early August 1994.

A plant for blending lubricating oils was due to be established at Taiz in 1994, as a joint venture between Royal Dutch Shell and a Yemeni firm which had previously distributed imported lubricants. In 1993 unified Yemen achieved self-sufficiency in bottle liquefied petroleum gas (LPG, for which there had previously been a $40m. annual import requirement), following the opening of a bottling plant at San'a.

Under a co-operation agreement with the PDRY, the PRC built a cigarette factory, which went into operation in 1973, and a textile mill, which opened in 1975 with a capacity of 7.2m. metres of cloth per year. Other industries established in the Aden area included the manufacture of cement blocks, tiles and bricks; salt production; soft drinks bottling; and dairy plants. The Arabian peninsula's only brewery, in the Aden suburb of Mansura, became a focus of political controversy in the 1994 civil war and was destroyed by northern troops when they gained control of the city. In the western governorates there are also cotton ginneries, flour mills and seed-crushing plants. The German Democratic Republic helped with the establishment of factories making flour, biscuits, vegetable oil and animal fodder. A tomato purée factory, capable of producing 1,500 tons per year, started operating in 1976. An agricultural implements factory set up in 1976 was later expanded. There is a plastics factory, an aluminium goods plant, and a paint factory with an output of 431,000 gallons in 1982. The country's liquid batteries factory underwent expansion in the mid-1980s, at a cost of $2.3m., to increase production to 25,000 batteries per year. Overall, the value of industrial output was reported to have risen from 10.3m. dinars in 1973 to 20m. dinars in 1980, at 1977 market prices. In 1987 industrial production accounted for 23% of GDP.

Development of minerals became a priority of the post-unification Government, which obtained financial assistance from the World Bank, the UN Development Programme (UNDP) and the IDA for a series of projects to map and evaluate the whole country's natural resources. Preliminary findings indicated that considerable potential existed for commercial production of gold, lead-zinc and industrial minerals such as marble, granite and limestone (for use in local construction). Most government interest centres on the possibility of Yemen's becoming a significant producer of gold, which Soviet surveyors had first discovered at Wadi Madam (in the southern Hadramawt governorate) in the early 1980s. Gold-prospecting licences were held by Irish, Dutch and British companies in 1992, and in 1993 prospecting rights in a further 30,000 sq km were granted to a Yemeni company. Increased

cement production also featured in government plans, the aim being to expand capacity at the Bajil plant (in the former YAR) to 1m. tons per year and to implement long-postponed projects in the former PDRY, including the development of cement works in the Abyan valley.

The centre-piece of unified Yemen's industrial strategy is the free industrial and commercial zone at Aden, modelled on similar initiatives in other developing countries. Inaugurated in May 1991, the zone is expected to be extended in stages to cover the whole of Aden, as the necessary legislative and infrastructural measures are implemented. At the inauguration the Government stated that some 50 industrial projects had been approved for the zone and was confident that financial support for the $60m. anticipated cost of creating the zone would be forthcoming from Arab and other foreign donors. In late 1991 the Government commissioned a US consultancy firm to produce a master-plan for the zone. Submitted in May 1993, the plan recommended total investment of $5,600m. in four phases over a period of 25 years, centred on the development of port infrastructure to take full advantage of Aden's potential as a transhipment centre. The plan included proposals for new harbour facilities, an airport extension, a new 300-MW gas-turbine power station and new manufacturing infrastructure, and recommended that development be on a fully-privatized basis. The Yemen Free Zones Public Authority subsequently announced its intention to seek full privatization of all administrative operations at the port and airport, to countenance full private ownership of the proposed extensions, and to open up Aden's existing port and airport facilities to some form of joint-venture participation by private interests. The full privatization of existing facilities was not, however, an option. A French company signed an agreement in October 1993 whereby the Authority authorized it to seek private-sector financing for free-zone development projects and to act as an agent for the Authority in promoting investment projects in the zone.

Following the reimposition of central authority on the South in July 1994, the Government reaffirmed its intention to treat Aden as a major development centre, describing the city as Yemen's 'economic capital'. Moreover, it was now intended that Yemen's government institutions should be based in Aden during the winter months in future years.

INFRASTRUCTURE

It was only after the revolution in 1962 that the former YAR established regular communications with the outside world, and that good roads connecting the main towns were built. Road construction was later given high priority in development plans. Reasonable tarred roads connect San'a with Hodeida, San'a with Mocha via Taiz, and Hodeida with Taiz. The San'a-Hodeida road, completed in 1962, was built by Chinese engineers and was a spectacular achievement. The San'a-Taiz-Mocha road was built with US aid. A road north through Sa'ada to the Saudi border and a Chinese-built road from Amran to Hajjah were completed in 1982. The 172-km road from San'a to Marib, financed by the United Arab Emirates (UAE), was completed in May 1984 at a cost of 250m. riyals ($54.4m.), and work is continuing on a road from Dhamar to Raada and Baida (on the former border with the PDRY) across difficult mountain terrain. The repair and maintenance of existing roads has proved to be a problem, since neither the equipment nor the personnel is available locally. At the end of 1987 there was estimated to be a total of 37,285 km of roads in the YAR, of which 2,359 km were main (asphalted) roads, 1,537 km were secondary roads, and 33,389 km were other roads, including gravel feeder roads. These are of great importance for the transport of agricultural produce which otherwise cannot reach centres of distribution. More asphalting is being done, especially around San'a. Improvement in the road system is reflected in the increasing imports of motor vehicles, both commercial and private. In October 1988 the OPEC Fund for International Development agreed to finance part of the upgrading of a road from Hodeida to Salif, where the new Ras Isa oil terminal is located. In December 1988 China approved a loan of $40.32m. for the construction of a 127-km road from Highana to Marib, and the Government has initiated a project to improve road access to San'a, at an estimated cost of 128.6m. riyals.

There are three ports in the former YAR: Hodeida, Mocha and Salif, of which the most important is Hodeida, where a large harbour was completed in 1962 by the USSR. Mocha, the oldest, cannot be used by large ships at present. With the expansion of salt mining at Salif and of oil production inland, Salif harbour has been deepened to enable it to take ships of up to 5,000 tons and a bulk petrol plant is also planned. The Yemen Port Corporation obtained finance totalling $6m. in 1977 from the IDA to develop the port of Hodeida, which suffers badly from silting. The project involved construction of a deep-sea berth, restoration of existing berth facilities, dredging and the installation of new equipment. The project also involved the improvement of existing port facilities at Mocha, which was to be provided with 10 more berths. In 1981 Hodeida port handled a total of 1,123 ships, and all the ports in the YAR together handled a total of approximately 2m. tons of cargo.

There are three international airports in the former YAR, at San'a, Hodeida and Taiz, and small airstrips in other towns. San'a airport was built by the USSR and equipped by the Federal Republic of Germany. A project for its expansion and modernization was begun in 1983 with finance of $34m. from the Saudi Fund for Development. In May 1977 a YAR-Saudi Arabian airline company was established to take over the national airline, Yemenia. Work on strengthening and widening the runway at San'a airport began in late 1988, and plans for the construction of a new airport at Taiz and improvements at San'a airport have been announced. Air traffic increased considerably in the YAR in the 1980s, owing to the expansion of foreign investment and the development of tourism (see below).

Much work was undertaken to provide the YAR with a satisfactory telecommunications system, one of the Development Plan priorities. The three main towns, San'a, Taiz and Hodeida, are linked by a 600-km telephone line, built by the German Democratic Republic (GDR), and there are also connections to a number of other towns where telephone exchanges are in operation: Bajil, Ibb, Dhamar, Yarim, Manakha, Zabid, Bait al-Faqih and Hais. The GDR also helped to found a Communications College at San'a. In 1980 work was started on a network to connect remote villages with the main system, and by 1981 the number of telephones had almost doubled from 14,000 in 1976 to 27,000. A six-channel microwave scanner system linking San'a and Taiz is being implemented by the UN and San'a is linked internationally via Aden. There are radio transmitters at San'a and Taiz and various small wireless communications posts throughout the country. The first television station was opened in 1975 and a national TV network achieved in 1980. An earth satellite station was completed in October 1976 by Cable and Wireless (UK) and Nippon Electric of Japan. Sited at Ghuraf, near San'a, and costing close to $1m., it is linked to the INTELSAT (International Telecommunications Satellite Organization) system and can provide over 100 channels. As a further development, Cable and Wireless has proposed an internal microwave system. In June 1989 the YAR and Japan signed a memorandum for the expansion of the rural communication network, at a cost of $3.7m.

Overseen by the Yemeni Electricity Corporation, the expansion of electricity supply was a major development priority in the YAR. Installed capacity rose from 103 MW in 1978 to 213 MW in 1981. In October 1988 the AFESD agreed to provide a loan of KD 18m. to finance an ambitious plan to link the YAR's national power grid to that of the PDRY. The project involves the construction of an overhead line from Taiz to Aden, including spurs to nearby towns and villages. An agreement was signed in March 1989 by the YAR's electricity authority and the Jordan Electricity Authority (JEA) to co-operate in a project to supply electricity to 800 villages and settlements in the YAR, funded by a loan from the AFESD. In August 1989 Eleject of Egypt signed a contract to extend electricity to 300 villages in the Dhamar region, financed by the KFAED and the Japanese Government.

In the former PDRY the drive for industrial development also necessitated major infrastructural improvements, par-

ticularly in the fields of energy and transport facilities. A new 500-kW power station at Shukra, in Abyan governorate, was inaugurated in April 1986. In May 1989 the third turbo-generator at the Adenskaya thermoelectric power station came into operation, bringing the generating capacity of the power station to 75 MW, about half of total capacity in the PDRY. The complex includes a power station with an overall capacity of 125 MW (five turbogenerators each with a capacity of 25 MW) and a desalination complex with a productivity of 42,000 tons of distillate per day.

Soviet assistance was also provided for the development and improvement of the PDRY's air communications and infrastructure. A new international terminal, capable of handling 250,000 passengers per year, was undertaken at Aden airport, at a cost of $191m. In August 1989 it was announced that the national airline, Alyemdag, was to acquire a Soviet-made Tu-154 airliner, and in October it was reported that it would begin scheduled weekly flights to Muscat, Oman, in the near future. The PDRY also had airports at Khormaksar (formerly a British air base) and at Riyan.

Aden port handles nearly all the international trade of the former PDRY, as well as some of the former YAR's trade, although the development of the port of Hodeida (in the former YAR) has provided increasing competition. In the past, the free port of Aden attracted a large volume of traffic, and all the commercial activities associated with a large port flourished, providing comfortable livings for Adeni merchants but contributing little to the development of the other sectors of the economy. The closure of the Suez Canal and the British withdrawal, both in 1967, affected Aden severely.

In view of the disastrous effect of Aden's stagnation on a precarious economy, the Government viewed the reopening of the Suez Canal in June 1975 with a satisfaction verging on jubilation. Optimistic forecasts that up to 500 ships per month would use the port once the Suez Canal link was reopened were not realized, and the increase in traffic fell far short of expectations, mainly because the port lacked container-handling facilities. Through the 1980s the port was handling about 200 ships per month, less than one-third of its capacity, in part because cargo ships using the canal had increased their range and thereby reduced their dependence on refuelling ports such as Aden. An agreement to expand Aden port was made by the Yemen Ports Authority and a Panamanian company in September 1987, and congestion was further relieved by the completion of deep-water facilities at Mukalla and Nishtun. The nascent petroleum industry was expected to lead to increased activity at the ports, while the new Aden free industrial and commercial area, inaugurated in May 1991, was expected to reverse the decline of Yemen's principal trading outlet.

The port expansion was partly associated with a drive by the PDRY to promote tourism. In 1982 there were 5,200 tourist visits by cruise passengers from the USSR and Eastern Europe. An international hotel opened in Aden in 1983, and, under the 1981–85 Plan, the Government invested 20m. dinars ($58.5m.) in expanding tourism. In 1982 the PDRY and YAR Governments established the Yemen Tourism Company to promote 'package' tours to both countries. Adversely affected by the political unrest in early 1986, tourism increased thereafter. In 1987 about 28,000 tourists visited the PDRY, 5% more than in 1986.

Aden is an important cable communications centre. The Soviets have built a radio station in Aden, and the Greeks another station in Mukalla. In March 1978 the local operations of Cable and Wireless, a British company, were nationalized by the Yemen Telecommunications Corporation (YTC). A satellite telephone link was installed in February 1989, and Aden opened its first international direct-dial telephone link in June. The national network is now connected to the YAR, Saudi Arabia and Djibouti, and the six former PDRY governorates are linked.

There are good roads round Aden and motorable tracks throughout the western area. A new road has been built, with massive Chinese aid, between Aden and Mukalla. A 92-km road from Naqubah to Nisab is being built with finance from the IDA, KFAED and the OPEC Fund for International Development. The Chinese are also constructing a road from Shihr to Sayhut. The Yemen Company for Land Transport, set up jointly by the two Yemens in 1982, provides regular road transport behind Aden and Taiz. In 1981 about 37,200 vehicles were in use in the PDRY, of which 17,800 were passenger cars. In addition to congestion at its ports, Aden also suffers from considerable traffic congestion on its roads, and at the beginning of 1985 it was reported that the German Democratic Republic was to finance the construction of three road bridges and a tunnel to alleviate this problem.

The post-unification Government has sought finance from the World Bank for the construction and rehabilitation of roads, and to support the Civil Aviation Authority and the Ports and Marine Affairs Corpn. The development of transport infrastructure, particularly North-South links, is a priority, and loans for road construction have also been sought from the PRC. In mid-1993 approval had still to be obtained from the World Bank for the main road-upgrading schemes. In early 1993 the Omani Government expressed its willingness to finance the construction of a highway across its newly-opened border with Yemen. Plans have been announced to merge the airlines of the former YAR and the PDRY—Yemenia and Alyemda—to form a new national carrier, Yemen Airways. However, by mid-1993 no real progress had been made towards merging the two airlines and promised Saudi Arabian participation in the new airline remained unconfirmed. Alyemda had, in 1992, initiated a unilateral expansion programme, which was regarded as adding to the complications of a merger. Further development plans in air transport include the lengthening of the runway at San'a airport from 750 m to 4,000 m in order to accommodate the largest Boeing aircraft. In August 1994 the deputy head of Alyemda was quoted as saying that the civil war had 'removed obstacles' to his airline's proposed merger with Yemenia. He estimated Alyemda's war-related revenue loss as $37m.

In July 1990 France granted Yemen's Ministry of Planning and Development a concessionary loan of $21m., part of which is to finance a communications project to improve telephone links between northern and southern Yemen. The linking of the electricity grids of the two former Yemeni states is the Government's priority project in the power sector, OPEC financial assistance having been promised in January 1989. According to World Bank figures, Yemen's domestic energy consumption grew by 23.8% per year in the period 1980–90, as against 21% per year in the period 1965–80; over the same period (1965 to 1990), energy consumption per caput increased from six kg of oil equivalent per year to 234 kg. Inadequate electricity-generating capacity led to severe power shortages in San'a in 1993. As a result, the Government announced emergency plans to install 60 MW of temporary LPG-fuelled generating plant in 1994, pending completion of a permanent 180-MW gas-turbine power station at Marib.

Prior to the outbreak of civil war in May 1994, Yemen had an aggregate generating capacity of 700 MW and was experiencing an estimated supply shortfall of about 200 MW. The 160-MW Mocha power station (the largest plant supplying the northern electricity grid) was forced to shut down from mid-June after southern aircraft attacked its fuel storage tanks, destroying half of them and seriously damaging the remainder. In September 1994 the Government was finalizing plans to bring the Mocha plant back into production as soon as possible, subject to securing financial backing for the estimated repair costs of up to $3m. In the south, war damage to Aden's main power station was limited to auxiliary facilities and caused a relatively brief disruption of output, which was restored to its pre-war level by early August 1994. However, the distribution of electricity to customers of the southern grid remained erratic in the following month.

It is also planned to develop the tourism sector through the construction of a chain of hotels throughout the country. The EC has pledged $500,000 to support this project, although the Gulf crisis delayed the completion of the necessary studies. A new Ministry of Tourism has been created, and this will assume the functions of the General Corpn for Tourism which was established by the Governments of the YAR and the PDRY. In 1989 tourist arrivals in the YAR rose by 11%, to 55,088, compared with 1988, while tourist spending rose by 27%, to $22m. In 1992 there were 83,000 tourist arrivals in

unified Yemen, over half of them from European countries, generating an estimated revenue of $47m.

After the Gulf crisis, the Government relaunched plans to develop the country's water resources, notably through the Laboos water project, which aimed to bring drinking water to 45,000 people in over 100 villages on the Laboos plateau north of Aden. The $37m. first phase of this project, involving the drilling of wells in the coastal Wadi Bani and the construction of the means of raising the water 1,500m. to the Laboos plateau, was under way in late 1991. The Radaa water supply and sanitation project, involving the supply of drinking water to some 30,000 people, was also under way. Aden's water supply system and sewerage facilities were severely disrupted during the civil war in 1994, and serious water shortages continued to be reported three months after the end of the fighting in the city. United Nations agencies identified an emergency requirement for up to $5m.-worth of essential repairs to water and sewerage infrastructure.

FOREIGN TRADE

As separate States until May 1990, both the YAR (North Yemen) and the PDRY (South Yemen) experienced perennial foreign trade deficits, although in the case of the YAR the development of oil exports in the late 1980s helped to reduce the gap somewhat. With the PDRY also having discovered oil in commercial quantities, unified Yemen seemed likely to move to a healthier balance-of-trade position in the 1990s, albeit entirely dependent on one export commodity.

Until the late 1980s, the YAR's merchandise exports covered less than 3% of the value of imports. World Bank statistics showed that in the period 1965–80 exports grew at an annual average rate of only 2.8%, whereas imports grew by 23.3% per year. In the period 1980–88, however, the average annual growth in exports was 35.6%, while imports actually fell by 10% a year. This transformation in export performance was entirely due to the start of oil exports at the end of 1987: in 1987 exports were worth only $19m., against imports of $1,311m.; in 1988 exports rose sharply to $485m., against imports of $1,310m. In the early 1980s the YAR's official annual trade deficit ran at around $1,500m., falling to around $1,200m. per year in 1986 and 1987 and to $835m. in 1988. The official estimates of imports are almost certainly much less than the real figures, however, since large quantities of goods are smuggled into the country to avoid the high import duties. The value of smuggled imports is believed to have increased by nearly 50%, to $1,000m., in 1983. In the recent past, the YAR relied almost entirely on the twin props of foreign currency from workers' remittances and foreign aid to offset its huge trade deficits.

Until 1977 the YAR's major exports were coffee and cotton. In 1976/77 cotton accounted for 24.9m. riyals and coffee for 10.2m. riyals out of total exports of 51.3m. riyals. By 1979/80, however, there were no recorded cotton exports and coffee exports were worth only 4.4m. riyals out of a total 91.7m. riyals. The largest single export item in that year was biscuits (12.7m. riyals). Other exports include hides and skins, salt, confectionery and artisanal products. According to the World Bank, exports of oil and other minerals accounted for 88% of total export value in 1988 (compared with 9% in 1965), manufactured goods for 11% (0% in 1965) and other primary commodities for 1% (91% in 1965).

Officially recorded imports more than doubled between 1976/77, when they totalled 3,035.3m. riyals, and 1980 when the total was 8,454.3m. riyals. The failure of Yemen's agriculture led to a rise in imports of food and live animals from 868.4m. riyals in 1976/77 to 2,212.6m. riyals in 1979/80, while the influx of capital goods for development projects under the first Five-Year Plan pushed up imports of machinery and transport equipment from 965.7m. riyals to 2,348.0m. riyals over the same period. However, the largest percentage increase between 1976/77 and 1980 was in imports of basic manufactured goods (668.2m to 2,140.1m. riyals), as money which had been earned in Saudi Arabia was spent on a flood of foreign consumer goods. In 1983 registered imports decreased by about 8%, to $1,800m., and the deficit on the current account of the balance of payments fell by 8%, compared with 1982, to 2,556.5m. riyals. In 1986 a deficit of

149.1m. riyals was recorded in the current account. In 1987 the Government imposed stricter import procedures, in order further to restrict the outflow of foreign exchange, in an attempt to reduce the volume of imports. Among the measures that the Government introduced was the application of import licences to all categories of imports. In January 1988 the Government announced its intention of easing import restrictions by easing credit restrictions and by reducing cash deposits covering letters of credit. World Bank figures showed that food imports accounted for 28% of total import value in 1988 (compared with 41% in 1965), manufactured goods for 55% (47% in 1965), fuels for 8% (6% in 1965) and other primary commodities for 6% (6% in 1965).

Until 1988, Japan was the YAR's major supplier, providing 18.5% of all imports (with sales worth $295.4m.) in 1983, a proportion which would be considerably higher if smuggled items could be taken into account. In 1988 the USA became the major supplier. Other important suppliers are Saudi Arabia ($174m. in 1983), France, Germany, Italy, the United Kingdom and the Netherlands.

Before 1982, almost all of the YAR's wheat imports were obtained from Australia. In 1983, however, the USA supplied all of the country's wheat imports, which were financed by a blended credit programme. Australia subsequently regained its position as the YAR's main supplier of wheat.

During the 1960s the PDRY's trade deficit grew, and in 1970 the Government introduced austerity measures to reduce imports by over £7m. In 1971 and 1972 both imports and exports declined but the value of imports, particularly of petroleum products, rose steeply after 1973 as a result of increased petroleum prices and general inflation. The Government was forced to call on the IMF petroleum facility. The trade balance continued to deteriorate, with the rate of increase in the value of imports outpacing that in exports. The rise in exports was almost entirely due to an increase in the value of petroleum products exported: from 59.1m. dinars in 1978 to 266.8m. dinars in 1982. According to IMF figures the trade deficit rose to 319.1m. dinars ($897.5m.) in 1984, with exports reaching 222.9m. dinars (petroleum products contributing 213.8m.) and imports rising to 532.9m. dinars. According to the World Bank, exports declined in value in the period 1965–80 by an annual average of 13.7%, while imports fell by 7.5% per year. In the period 1980–88, however, exports increased by an average of 1.9% per year and imports by 4.4% per year. In 1988 exports were worth $80m., while imports reached $598m. The non-oil trade deficit fell from 253.3m. dinars in 1982 to 251.1m. dinars ($726.9m.) in 1983, when exports were valued at 10.1m. dinars and imports at 261.2m. dinars. In 1988 the IDB approved a $15m. loan to finance foreign trade, covering purchases of crude petroleum, petroleum products and refined petroleum products. World Bank figures showed that fuels accounted for 40% of import value in 1988 (the same proportion as in 1965), manufactures for 40% (36% in 1965), food for 16% (19% in 1965) and other primary commodities for 2% (5% in 1965).

The main commodities exported (excluding petroleum products) are cotton, hides and skins, fish, rice and coffee. The chief imports (excluding petroleum) are manufactured goods for development projects, clothing, foodstuffs and livestock. Petroleum products are now chiefly exported to markets in Africa and Asia rather than Europe. The share of the PDRY's non-oil trade taken by communist countries rose from 16.8% in 1982 to 24.5% in 1983. According to the World Bank, exports of fuels and minerals accounted for 90% of export value in 1988 (against 80% in 1965), other primary commodities for 9% (14% in 1965) and manufactured goods for 1% (8% in 1965).

Following unification, Yemen's external trade experienced serious distortion as a result of the 1990–91 Gulf crisis. Under the UN embargo, Yemen was obliged to halt trade with Iraq and Kuwait, both important trading partners, and to replace crude oil supplies from those countries with domestic output which would have gone for export (see Petroleum and Natural Gas, above). Since the cost of Iraqi and Kuwaiti oil had been significantly below world price levels (which increased sharply as a result of the crisis), reductions in export revenue were substantially greater than savings on import costs.

Official balance-of-payments figures, published in July 1992, showed that Yemen's merchandise exports in 1990 totalled 7,066m. riyals (including 6,188m. riyals from oil), whereas merchandise imports totalled 20,863m. riyals, so that the 1990 trade deficit was 13,795m. riyals, compared with a combined deficit for the YAR and PDRY in 1989 of 11,533m. riyals (exports 6,765m. riyals, imports 18,298m. riyals). United Yemen's main trading partners in 1991 were, for imports, Australia, Thailand, the USA, France, the United Kingdom and Argentina; for non-oil exports they were Saudi Arabia, Jordan and the United Arab Emirates.

On the current account, the July 1992 figures showed a deficit of 1,711m. riyals in 1990, compared with 9,853m. riyals in 1989. In both years the deficit on the trade account was partly offset by a surplus on the services account, which showed receipts of 17,518m. riyals in 1990 (5,519m riyals in 1989) exceeding payments of 5,432m. riyals (3,839m. riyals in 1989). A feature of the 1990 current account figures was the beneficial effect of a surge of private transfer remittances attributable to Yemeni nationals returning from Saudi Arabia because of the Gulf crisis. Conversely, the 1991 current account was expected to show a massive decline in private transfers, because Yemeni workers had not gone abroad again in the same numbers as before. World Bank estimates, published in mid-1993, assessed Yemen's net remittance income at $800m. in 1991, and suggested that the current account was $20m. in surplus in that year. Prior to the 1990 Gulf crisis, remittance income had averaged around $2,000m. per year. In mid-1994 the Arab Monetary Fund extended a $47m. loan to Yemen to support the financing of the country's 1993 balance-of-payments deficit.

FINANCE AND FOREIGN AID

Prior to unification (May 1990), both Yemeni States ran constant budget deficits and were able to maintain precarious financial viability only on the strength of remittances from nationals working abroad and inflows of foreign aid. In the case of the YAR (North Yemen), the start of oil export revenues in 1988 provided a measure of relief from perennial balance-of-payments problems.

For 1985/86 the YAR's budget expenditure was forecast at 8,895m. riyals ($1,513m.) and revenue at 6,228m. riyals ($1,059.6m.), giving a projected deficit of 2,667m. riyals ($453m.). Under the 1986/87 budget, expenditure was set at 9,944m. riyals ($1,170m.) (a rise of 12% compared with 1985/86) and revenue at 7,179m. riyals, giving a projected deficit of 2,765m. riyals. In 1987/88 the projected budget deficit rose to 3,523m. riyals, with revenue estimated at 8,310m. riyals and expenditure at 11,833m. riyals. In 1989 the budget deficit was estimated at 2,204m. riyals, with revenue at 17,050m. riyals and expenditure at 19,254m. riyals.

Much practical aid in the fields of health, education and social welfare flowed into the YAR, particularly from oil-rich Arab countries and organizations, the PRC, the USSR, the World Health Organization and UNICEF. Kuwait, Saudi Arabia and, more recently, the UAE, provided schools, hospitals and clinics, and many other Arab countries sent teachers to the YAR. Qatar provided aid for schools, hospitals and roads, and staff training for radio and television productions. Arab aid supported major infrastructural projects, such as the San'a sewerage scheme, the modernization of San'a International Airport and road building schemes. During the first half of the 1980s the USSR spent about $1,000m. to arm and train the army of the YAR. Thereafter, however, military equipment was purchased increasingly from the USA, with finance provided by Saudi Arabia, which had a vested interest in minimizing Soviet influence in the YAR. Although the USSR remained a major aid donor, increasing amounts of aid were provided in the 1980s by Western sources, including the Netherlands, the Federal Republic of Germany, the USA and Britain, and also by Japan. The World Bank was also an important source of loans through the IDA, and UN agencies provide much technical assistance, especially the UNDP. According to the World Bank, the YAR's receipts of official development aid (ODA) from all sources totalled $412m. in 1982, $328m. in 1983, $326m. in 1984, $283m. in 1985, $275m. in 1986, $348m. in 1987 and $223m. in 1988. Between 1962 and 1982, it is estimated, the YAR borrowed some $2,325m., of which the USSR lent $819m., and other Arab countries $744m. In September 1987, according to Central Bank figures, the debt to the Soviet Union was $1,064m., almost half of the country's total external debt of $2,136m. During 1984 two interesting examples of the YAR's search for economic aid were the 20-year friendship treaty signed with the USSR and the five-year co-operation agreement with the EC.

Increased aid was an important factor in the YAR's economic planning and played a part in keeping the country financially viable. Still more important was the flow of remittances from Yemenis working abroad. In 1981 the value of remittances from North Yemenis abroad was $971m., increasing to $1,080m. in 1983. However, the surplus of petroleum on world markets from the mid-1980s and the consequent decline in oil prices in 1986–88 caused a slump in the petroleum industries of the Gulf States. The effect of this was to reduce both the level of remittances from Yemenis employed in the Gulf oil industry, and the amount of aid received by the YAR from Arab nations. Arab aid fell from $440m. in 1982 to $160m. in 1983. Saudi Arabia, however, did renew its pledge of several hundred million dollars per year in budgetary aid. Workers' remittances declined to $800m. in 1988.

The YAR's international reserves (excluding gold) rose from $126.9m. at the end of 1973 to $1,459.4m. at the end of 1978, but they then fell with increasing rapidity. By the end of 1981 reserves had declined to $961.6m., and by 31 December 1985 they had dropped to only $297m. They rose, however, to $432m. by the end of December 1986, and to $540m. in 1987. Reserves declined again in 1988, to $285.6m., and to $279.6m. in 1989.

The economic effects of the reduction in industrial activity elsewhere in the Arabian peninsula, and of the aftermath of the earthquake in Dhamar province in 1982, began to be felt sharply in 1983. In June 1983 there was a small surplus on the current balance of payments, but by July this had given way to a deficit of 221m. riyals. The principal cause of this reverse was the increase in the cost of imports and a dramatic slump in the value of remittances from expatriate workers. The Government accordingly introduced austerity measures to restrict the purchase of convertible currency by the private sector. The banks were told to trade at the official exchange rate of $1 = 4.775 Yemeni riyals, with a discretionary margin of 1%, whereas the free market rate had been $1 = 4.8 Yemeni riyals. The gradual devaluation of the riyal was official policy from 1984, when the link with the US dollar was broken, in order to restrict the use of foreign exchange.

Despite the Government's efforts, reserves fell to $352m. by September 1983, and legislation was introduced to reduce 'non-essential' imports. Partly as a result of the austerity measures introduced at mid-year, the current account deficit was reduced to 2,556.5m. riyals ($550m.) in 1983, a fall of 8% compared with 1982. In 1981 the current account deficit had been as high as 2,989.4m. riyals. There were significant falls in expenditure on both visible and invisible imports, which outweighed a 14% decline in invisible earnings. The economic situation affected the 1982–86 Development Plan, under the original provisions of which spending on development was to total $650m. per year. In 1984, however, the annual rate of expenditure was only an estimated $400m. The current account deficit, after official transfers, was $607m. in 1987 and $695m. in 1988, according to World Bank statistics. A 23% devaluation of the YAR riyal, announced in February 1990, was reportedly intended to provide a preferential rate for remittances from nationals abroad; however, the resultant parity of US $1 = 12 riyals quickly became the effective official rate for all transactions.

The PDRY also had difficulty in maintaining financial stability after independence. In December 1966 international reserves amounted to $62.4m. By the end of 1970 they were $59.3m. In the same period, the budget deficit grew from 100,000 dinars to over 4m. dinars. This deficit was substantially cut in 1971, mainly because more foreign grants were obtained, but expenditure still had to be held down with adverse effects on development. The situation was considered to be so serious in 1972 that the salaries of many government employees were cut by anything from 15% to 50% and restric-

tions were placed on foreign travel. By the end of 1973 the situation was a little better and international reserves were $76.0m. In 1975 the IMF agreed to the purchase of SDR 7.25m. to help with balance-of-payments problems and general inflation. The overall payments deficit in 1974 was $24m. but the Government's measures, combined with the IMF aid, were having their effect by 1976 and the economy was being brought under control. At the end of 1975 reserves (excluding gold) had fallen to $54.0m., including drawings of $27.7m. on IMF facilities, but by the end of 1976 reserves had recovered to $81.5m., with IMF drawings having increased to $42.8m. The situation continued to improve in subsequent years. At the end of 1982 reserves were $286.9m., although by the end of 1988 reserves (excluding gold) had fallen to $79.93m.

It must be assumed that the increase in net reserves in the early 1980s reflected inflows of foreign aid, resulting in part from the general *détente* with neighbouring Middle Eastern countries. A study team, sent by the IMF in 1978/79, recommended a move away from strict leftist policies towards a restimulation of the private sector. In 1980, in response to this pressure, the Government introduced measures to stimulate private enterprise and the free market economy. Remittances from expatriate workers became such an important factor in the economy that in 1982 the Government offered expatriates tax concessions and guarantees against nationalization if they would invest in the PDRY. Remittances reached a peak annual total of nearly $500m. in 1984, but declined to about $300m. in 1986 and reached $404m. in 1987, according to World Bank estimates.

The abrupt cessation of British aid, after the withdrawal of troops in November 1967, caused a crisis which enabled the communist bloc to step into the breach. The USSR, under an agreement of February 1969 (which included aid specifically for fisheries), undertook to provide technical aid and experts for a number of development projects. A separate agreement, signed in August 1969, covered aid for agriculture and irrigation. The first agreement was extended in February 1970 to include aid in kind and, most important of all, a low-interest loan, repayable over 12 years. This loan was significant in that actual financial aid was offered rather than aid in the form of goods or technical assistance. Thenceforward, the USSR remained the PDRY's main development partner under a series of economic agreements. Soviet aid financed several major projects under the second Five-Year Plan (1981–85): notably the Aden port and airport developments, the exploitation of fishery resources, and mineral surveys. The PDRY also benefited from infrastructural work carried out by the USSR in connection with its military facilities in the country. In late 1988 the USSR undertook to provide aid for oil exploration and the development of water resources, energy, fisheries, building materials, communications and training until 2005.

Most of the communist bloc countries offered aid to the PDRY, particularly for communications projects (such as the Aden television station, built with Czechoslovak aid). Large development loans were obtained in 1979 from Bulgaria and Czechoslovakia, while China lent a further $12.5m. for the purchase of industrial goods. In the 1980s Czechoslovakia and the GDR were involved in mineral survey work, Bulgaria undertook to help in the development of tourist facilities, and China continued to finance and to execute road-building schemes. The richer Arab states were also a major source of aid. In the early 1970s their contribution was on a fairly small scale, but in 1975 the Government launched a diplomatic offensive to improve relations with the rich Gulf States. Aid from Arab countries subsequently increased sharply, despite occasional contretemps, especially with Saudi Arabia. Official grants from Arab states reached a record $126m. in 1982, but declined to an annual average of $40m. in subsequent years. The main sources of aid, other than the socialist countries and the Arab States, were the UN and the World Bank. World Bank figures showed that the PDRY's receipts of ODA from all sources totalled $143m. in 1982, $106m. in 1983, $103m. in 1984, $113m. in 1985, $71m. in 1986, $74m. in 1987 and $76m. in 1988.

The deficit on the current account of the PDRY's balance of payments was estimated at $250m. in 1986, compared with

$310m. in the previous year. The reduced deficit followed the introduction of import restrictions. In September 1988 the AMF agreed to provide the PDRY with a loan of $25m. to improve the balance of payments and the budget deficit. (It was the second AMF loan awarded to the PDRY in 1988, and brought the total value of the Fund's loans to the PDRY during the year to $93m.) After official transfers, the current account deficit in 1988 was estimated at $383m., some $253m. having been received in net remittances in that year. In late 1989 and early 1990 the PDRY Government announced various economic liberalization measures under which foreigners were to be allowed to own local enterprises and to remit profits abroad, and also to be accorded tax and tariff exemptions for up to six years.

After reunification, respective currencies of the two former Yemeni States are legal tender in the Republic of Yemen and can be used at a rate of 1 (South) Yemeni dinar = 26 (North) Yemeni riyals. A single unit of currency was to be agreed during the 30-month transitional period following unification in May 1990. At that point the exchange rate against the US dollar was fixed at US $1 = 0.462 (South) Yemeni dinar. The San'a-based Central Bank has clarified regulations regarding foreign exchange. No more than $3,000 (or its equivalent) may be imported or exported without the permission of the Central Bank. Up to $1,500 (or its equivalent) may be remitted abroad from local foreign currency accounts, up to a maximum of $4,500 per year. Nevertheless, research published in August 1991 showed that 38% of foreign currency deposits had been transferred out of the country. In June 1990 the World Bank confirmed that Yemen would be entitled to concessionary finance and that loan programmes and development projects under way in the YAR and the PDRY would continue in the new State.

In mid-1993, when the standard official exchange rate was $1 = 12.01 riyals (as it had been since February 1990), the black-market value of the Yemeni currency was approximately $1 = 46 riyals (reflecting, in part, the country's current inflation rate of about 200% per year). In 1992 the Government had introduced a 'customs rate' of $1 = 18 riyals for all non-essential imports, and in May 1993 it had introduced an 'incentive rate' of 25 riyals to the US dollar for oil companies and tourists.

Iraq agreed to grant Yemen a $50m. loan for balance-of-payments support and for 'general and strategic' projects. However, only half of this had been disbursed before the UN imposed economic sanctions on Iraq in August 1990. In July 1990 Saudi Arabia agreed to provide Yemen $75m. of aid, but future grants are in doubt as a result of the Yemeni Government's equivocal attitude towards Iraq's invasion of Kuwait. Because of this, most US aid for fiscals 1990/91 and 1991/92—totalling some $45m.—was suspended in late 1990, a decision which added to the financial problems arising from the crisis (see Introduction, above). Yemen's aggregate annual receipts of official development aid (ODA) rose from $326m. in 1984 to $422m. in 1987, fell to $303m. in 1988, and then increased to $370m. in 1989 and to $405m. in 1990, before falling to $313m. in 1991 (which year ODA represented 3.9% of GNP).

Figures disclosed in July 1990 showed unified Yemen's total foreign debt as standing at $7,256m. as of March 1990, equivalent to about 110% of current GNP and some 50% higher than the previous Western estimate of about $5,000m. Of the total, $4,366m. was debt attributable to the former PDRY (owed mainly to the USSR, China and East European countries) and $2,890m. to the former YAR. In September 1990 France agreed to cancel all of Yemen's outstanding debt to it—some $55m.—and Japan also granted debt-relief aid. According to the World Bank, Yemen's external debt totalled $6,598m. at the end of 1992.

In the unified State's first budget, for 1991, expenditure was projected at 50,980m. riyals (compared with an aggregate figure of 46,256m. riyals in 1990) and revenue at 35,218m. riyals (24,704m. in 1990). The resultant forecast deficit of 15,762m. riyals represented a 27% reduction against the 1990 combined deficit of 21,552m. riyals. The biggest allocation in the 1991 budget was for defence (12,700m. riyals), followed by investment and development (11,000m. riyals) and education (8,300m. riyals). The investment and development allocation did not include loans and grants from external sources, which were seen as crucial for offsetting losses attributable to the Gulf crisis.

The 1992 budget provided for estimated revenue of 45,778m. riyals and expenditure of 58,114m. riyals, and thus for a deficit of 12,336m. riyals. The Government's financial projections for the year envisaged: that its foreign exchange resources would total $2,185m. to meet anticipated commitments of $2,349m. (as against resources of $1,836m. and outgoings of $2,212m. in 1991); that imports of wheat, flour, rice and essential drugs would cost $368m.; that all foreign debt obligations would be met in 1992; and that defence spending would be reduced by 12% compared with 1991. The Government did not publish 1993 budget proposals, and was assumed to be organizing its finances on a month-to-month basis, using its 1992 spending as a guideline for the current year. According to press reports (said to be based on internal Finance Ministry records), actual spending in 1992 had totalled 58,060m. riyals (of which 53,637m. riyals was current spending), while actual revenue had amounted to only 32,008m. riyals (about one-third of estimated GNP). The largest single component of expenditure in 1992 was the public-sector salary bill, reported to total 32,735m. riyals. In 1994 the Government again failed to reach any agreement on a national budget, and was assumed to be maintaining a form of month-to-month accounting system until May, when established procedures were disrupted by the onset of civil war. According to estimates published by independent Yemeni economists in January 1994, the Government spent 74,000m. riyals in 1993 and collected revenue of 32,000m. riyals, leaving a deficit of 42,000m. riyals, equivalent to more than one-third of the current GDP (which was estimated to be between 110,000m. and 120,000m. riyals). It was not known how the budget deficit had been financed. Following the end of the civil war in July 1994, the Government said that it planned to issue bonds to raise funds for post-war reconstruction work. The Yemeni currency's unofficial exchange rate against the US dollar, which had declined to 80 riyals before the outbreak of hostilities, fell below 100 riyals for the first time during June 1994.

Statistical Survey

Source (unless otherwise indicated): Republic of Yemen Central Statistical Organization, POB 13434, San'a; tel. (1) 250619; telex 2266; fax (1) 250664.

Area and Population

AREA, POPULATION AND DENSITY

Area (sq km)	536,869*
Population (official estimates at mid-year)	
1992	11,952,000
1993	12,302,000
Density (per sq km) at mid-1993	22.9

* 207,286 sq miles.

Capital: San'a (capital of the former YAR), population 427,185 at 1 February 1986.

ECONOMICALLY ACTIVE POPULATION

Mid-1992 (estimates in '000): Agriculture 1,635; Total 3,007.
Source: FAO, *Production Yearbook*.

Agriculture

PRINCIPAL CROPS ('000 metric tons)

	1990	1991	1992
Wheat	155	100	152
Barley	55	29	63
Maize	66	46	70
Millet	50	25	66
Sorghum	441	247	459
Potatoes	157	157	165
Pulses	76	43	75
Sesame seed . . .	9	10†	12†
Cottonseed	14*	14*	14†
Cotton (lint) . . .	7*	7*	7†
Tomatoes	168	172	172†
Onions (dry) . . .	70	59	70†
Other vegetables . .	79	92	92†
Watermelons . . .	174	126	170†
Melons	44	36	48†
Grapes	142	145†	145†
Dates	21	18†	16†
Bananas	50	52†	55†
Papayas	51	50†	50†
Other fruit	50	52†	53†
Coffee (green) . . .	7	8†	8†
Tobacco (leaves) . .	7	7†	8†

* Unofficial figure.   † FAO estimate.

Source: FAO, *Production Yearbook*.

LIVESTOCK ('000 head, year ending September)

	1990	1991	1992
Horses*	3	3	3
Asses*	690	690	690
Cattle	1,175	1,180*	1,190*
Camels	175	180*	185*
Sheep	3,756	3,800*	3,850*
Goats	3,333	3,400*	3,470*

Poultry (million): 25* in 1990; 24* in 1991; 24* in 1992.

* FAO estimate(s).

Source: FAO, *Production Yearbook*.

LIVESTOCK PRODUCTS ('000 metric tons)

	1990	1991	1992
Beef and veal*	28	29	29
Mutton and lamb* . . .	38	38	39
Goats' meat*	30	31	32
Poultry meat	57	55*	55*
Cows' milk*	97	98	99
Sheep's milk*	62	63	64
Goats' milk*	156	156	156
Cheese*	22.7	22.9	23.0
Butter*	4.5	4.6	4.6
Hen eggs*	17.5	17.5	17.7
Wool:			
greasy*	4.1	4.1	4.2
clean*	2.2	2.3	2.3
Cattle hides*	2.8	2.9	3.0

* FAO estimate(s).
Source: FAO, *Production Yearbook*.

Fishing

('000 metric tons, live weight)

	1989*	1990	1991
Freshwater fishes	n.a.	0.4	0.9
Marine fishes	69.2	71.9*	79.9*
Other marine animals . .	3.6	5.5*	4.5*
Total catch	72.9	77.9	85.3

* FAO estimate(s).
Source: FAO, *Yearbook of Fishery Statistics*.

Mining

('000 metric tons)

	1991
Crude petroleum	9,345*

* Provisional.
Source: UN, *Industrial Statistics Yearbook*.

Industry

SELECTED PRODUCTS
('000 metric tons, unless otherwise indicated)

	1991
Motor spirit (petrol)	322
Distillate fuel oils	1,281
Residual fuel oils	1,946
Electricity (million kWh)	1,750

Source: UN, *Industrial Statistics Yearbook*.

Finance

CURRENCY AND EXCHANGE RATES

Monetary Units
100 fils = 1 Yemeni riyal.

Sterling and Dollar Equivalents (31 May 1994)
£1 sterling = 18.157 Yemeni riyals;
US $1 = 12.010 Yemeni riyals;
1,000 Yemeni riyals = £55.08 = $83.26.

Average Exchange Rate (Yemeni riyals per US $)
1987   10.3417
1988   9.7717
1989   9.7600

Note: The exchange rate of US $1 = 9.76 Yemeni riyals, established in the YAR in 1988, remained in force until February 1990, when a new rate of $1 = 12.01 riyals was introduced. Following the merger of the two Yemens in May 1990, the YAR's currency was adopted as the currency of the unified country.

BUDGET (million riyals)

Revenue*	1990	1991	1992†
Taxation	13,733	20,077	27,109
Taxes on income, profits, etc.	4,882	8,164	7,941
Excises	2,283	2,746	8,192
Import duties . .	4,012	6,013	7,900
Other current revenue. .	10,173	17,672	n.a.
Property income. . .	8,367	15,489	n.a.
Capital revenue . . .	35	233	338
Total	23,941	37,982	n.a.

Expenditure‡	1990	1991	1992†
General public services . .	4,913	4,644	n.a.
Defence	10,382	13,227	11,220
Public order and safety . .	3,248	4,110	4,431
Education	6,120	8,461	11,615
Health	1,439	1,954	2,540
Housing and community amenities	427	1,116	n.a.
Recreational, cultural and religious affairs and services	730	1,242	1,686
Economic affairs and services .	3,643	2,579	8,061
Other purposes . . .	2,957	4,279	n.a.
Unallocable capital expenditure	5,758	2,050	—
Unallocable capital transfers .	—	390	n.a.
Total	39,617	44,052	54,545
Current§	27,877	36,728	44,237
Capital	11,740	7,324	10,309

* Excluding grants received from abroad (million riyals): 1,397 in 1990; 300 in 1991.
† Projected figures.
‡ Excluding lending minus repayment (million riyals): 1,312 in 1990; 1,335 in 1991; 2,717 in 1992.
§ Including interest payments (million riyals): 2,956 in 1990; 4,279 in 1991; 5,182 in 1992.

Source: IMF, *Government Finance Statistics Yearbook*.

Note: The Government did not publish budget proposals for 1993, when it continued to operate according to its 1992 proposals. The Government had not published budget proposals for 1994 by June of that year.

NATIONAL ACCOUNTS (million riyals at current prices)
National Income and Product

	1989	1990
Domestic factor incomes*	52,098	66,010
Consumption of fixed capital . . .	2,499	4,202
Gross domestic product (GDP) at factor cost	54,597	70,212
Indirect taxes, *less* subsidies . . .	6,809	6,947
GDP in purchasers' values . . .	61,406	77,159
Net factor income from abroad . . .	1,454	1,658
Gross national product (GNP) . . .	62,860	78,817
Less Consumption of fixed capital . .	2,499	4,202
National income in market prices . .	60,361	74,615
Other current transfers from abroad (net)	3,706	10,875
National disposable income . . .	64,067	85,490

* Compensation of employees and the operating surplus of enterprises.

Expenditure on the Gross Domestic Product

	1989	1990
Government final consumption expenditure	16,470	21,154
Private final consumption expenditure .	48,322	58,030
Increase in stocks	134	700
Gross fixed capital formation . . .	11,356	11,970
Total domestic expenditure . . .	76,282	91,854
Exports of goods and services . .	10,205	10,471
Less Imports of goods and services . .	25,081	25,166
GDP in purchasers' values . . .	61,406	77,159

Gross Domestic Product by Economic Activity

	1989	1990
Agriculture, hunting, forestry and fishing	14,682	16,101
Mining and quarrying	3,912	7,030
Manufacturing	5,861	6,586
Electricity, gas and water . . .	1,191	1,400
Construction	2,838	3,394
Trade, restaurants and hotels . .	7,784	9,590
Transport, storage and communications .	5,202	6,015
Finance, insurance, real estate and business services	4,154	4,929
Government services	10,875	18,201
Other community, social and personal services	483	572
Private non-profit services to households	79	95
Sub-total	57,061	73,913
Import duties	5,000	3,996
Less Imputed bank service charge . .	655	750
GDP in purchasers' values . . .	61,406	77,159

Transport

ROAD TRAFFIC (vehicles in use at 31 December)

	1990	1991	1992
Passenger cars . . .	162,961	165,438	186,172
Buses and coaches . .	1,986	2,223	2,576
Goods vehicles . . .	235,042	235,734	251,779

Source: IRF, *World Road Statistics*.

INTERNATIONAL SEA-BORNE SHIPPING
(freight traffic, '000 metric tons)

	1988	1989	1990
Goods loaded	1,836	1,883	1,936
Goods unloaded . . .	7,189	7,151	7,829

Source: UN, *Monthly Bulletin of Statistics*.

Communications Media

	1991
Radio receivers ('000 in use)	325
Television receivers ('000 in use)	330

Source: UNESCO, *Statistical Yearbook*.

Statistical Survey of the former Yemen Arab Republic

Source (except where otherwise stated): Yemen Arab Republic Central Planning Organization, Data Processing Centre, POB 175, San'a; tel. 3506; telex 2266.

Area and Population

AREA, POPULATION AND DENSITY

Area (sq km)	200,000*
Population (census results)†	
February 1981	8,556,974‡
1 February 1986§	
Males	4,647,310
Females	4,626,863
Total	9,274,173
Density (per sq km) at February 1986	46.4

* 77,220 sq miles.
† The totals include Yemeni nationals abroad, numbering 1,395,123 (males 1,177,562; females 217,561) in 1981.
‡ Including an adjustment for underenumeration, estimated at 705,662.
§ Provisional.

PRINCIPAL PROVINCES (population; census results)

	1981	1986
San'a*	1,740,744	1,429,651
Taiz	1,053,520	1,643,901
Hodeida	1,085,376	1,294,359
Hajja	880,619	897,814
Baida	327,539	381,249

* Excluding San'a City, population: 277,818 in 1981; 427,185 in 1986.

PRINCIPAL TOWNS
(population, including suburbs, at 1986 census)
San'a (capital) 427,185; Taiz 178,043; Hodeida 155,110.

BIRTHS AND DEATHS (UN estimates, annual averages)

	1975–80	1980–85	1985–90
Birth rate (per 1,000) . . .	55.6	54.4	53.6
Death rate (per 1,000). . .	20.7	18.3	16.1

Source: UN, *World Population Prospects 1990*.

ECONOMICALLY ACTIVE POPULATION
(persons aged 10 years and over at census of 1 February 1975, excluding underenumeration)

Agriculture	830,340
Mining	576
Manufacturing	33,920
Electricity	1,511
Construction.	52,640
Trade	68,979
Transport	24,709
Finance	1,976
Social services	85,775
Unstated activities	27,326
Total labour force	1,127,572*

* Of whom 1,057,566 (males 932,440; females 125,126) were employed and 70,006 (males 63,120; females 6,886) were unemployed.

Mining

('000 metric tons)

	1988*	1989	1990
Crude petroleum*	7,070	8,982	8,468
Salt (unrefined)	163	222	220
Gypsum (crude)	60	66	66

* Provisional.
Source: UN, *Industrial Statistics Yearbook*.

Industry

SELECTED PRODUCTS
('000 metric tons, unless otherwise indicated)

	1988	1989	1990
Motor spirit (petrol) . . .	100	100	110
Distillate fuel oils	124	125	130
Residual fuel oils	130	135	136
Cement*	646	700	700
Electricity (million kWh) . .	820	830	830

* Provisional.

Source: UN, *Industrial Statistics Yearbook.*

Finance

CENTRAL BANK RESERVES
(US $ million at 31 December)

	1987	1988	1989
Gold*	0.5	0.5	0.5
IMF special drawing rights .	26.9	32.2	20.8
Foreign exchange . . .	512.6	252.9	258.3
Total	540.0	285.6	279.6

* Valued at 35 SDRs per troy ounce.

Source: IMF, *International Financial Statistics.*

MONEY SUPPLY (million riyals at 31 December)

	1987	1988	1989
Currency outside banks .	20,159	20,166	21,206
Demand deposits at commercial banks	4,646	4,714	5,135

Source: IMF, *International Financial Statistics.*

NATIONAL ACCOUNTS
(million riyals at current prices)

Expenditure on the Gross Domestic Product

	1985	1986	1987
Government final consumption expenditure	5,520	6,086	7,778
Private final consumption expenditure	29,457	35,728	40,115
Increase in stocks . . .	−75	50	150
Gross fixed capital formation .	4,547	4,938	6,200
Total domestic expenditure .	39,449	46,802	54,243
Exports of goods and services	1,164	1,155	1,616
Less Imports of goods and services	−9,644	−9,568	−12,300
GDP in purchasers' values .	30,969	38,389	43,559
GDP at constant 1985 prices	30,969	33,880	35,507

Source: IMF, *International Financial Statistics.*

BALANCE OF PAYMENTS (US $ million)

	1987	1988	1989
Merchandise exports f.o.b. .	48.2	447.0	606.0
Merchandise imports f.o.b. .	−1,189.4	−1,309.4	−1,282.7
Trade balance . . .	−1,141.2	−862.4	−676.6
Exports of services . .	128.0	170.9	204.9
Imports of services . .	−271.0	−346.9	−407.2
Other income received . .	44.1	29.4	42.7
Other income paid . .	−61.0	−89.2	−81.4
Private unrequited transfers (net)	707.7	313.7	242.3
Official unrequited transfers (net)	141.2	90.4	96.2
Current balance . . .	−452.2	−694.3	−579.0
Direct investment (net) .	1.1	—	—
Portfolio investment (net) .	1.1	—	—
Other capital (net) . .	481.3	476.1	510.9
Net errors and omissions . .	36.6	−58.8	57.9
Overall balance . . .	67.7	−277.0	−10.3

Source: IMF, *International Financial Statistics.*

External Trade

PRINCIPAL COMMODITIES
(distribution by SITC, million riyals)

Imports c.i.f.	1988	1989	1990
Food and live animals . .	3,901.9	4,387.8	5,522.6
Live animals chiefly for food .	414.9	456.2	700.1
Dairy products and birds' eggs	595.7	496.1	574.4
Cereals and cereal preparations	1,069.6	1,709.5	2,548.9
Sugar, sugar preparations and honey	704.7	746.6	1,034.0
Beverages and tobacco . .	308.0	242.6	290.6
Tobacco and tobacco manufactures . . .	301.7	237.8	286.5
Crude materials (inedible) except fuels . . .	343.0	389.5	388.5
Cork and wood . . .	266.3	331.6	307.3
Mineral fuels, lubricants, etc.	1,927.9	2,172.6	796.9
Petroleum, petroleum products, etc. . .	1,777.6	1,957.4	720.5
Animal and vegetable oils, fats and waxes . . .	189.5	257.9	303.6
Fixed vegetable oils and fats .	187.4	254.6	303.6
Chemicals and related products	1,348.2	874.6	1,114.1
Medicinal and pharmaceutical products	623.5	438.2	386.6
Artificial resins, plastic materials, etc. . . .	358.1	204.3	337.7
Basic manufactures . . .	2,920.6	2,215.3	2,803.2
Paper, paperboard and manufactures . . .	348.9	221.4	360.0
Non-metallic mineral manufactures . . .	398.1	351.2	274.5
Iron and steel	809.7	639.0	961.2
Machinery and transport equipment	1,848.5	2,462.5	2,102.2
Machinery specialized for particular industries . .	346.6	459.5	356.1
General industrial machinery, equipment and parts . .	355.1	451.3	239.9
Electrical machinery, apparatus, etc. . . .	397.3	520.2	701.0
Road vehicles and parts (excl. tyres, engines and electrical parts)	503.9	780.4	542.3
Miscellaneous manufactured articles	705.6	696.1	626.1
Total (incl. others) . . .	13,523.6	13,669.8	13,954.0

Exports f.o.b.	1988	1989	1990
Food and live animals . .	485.9	519.4	215.3
Crude materials (inedible) except fuels	119.8	223.5	221.0
Hides, skins and furskins (raw)	73.9	135.0	169.7
Mineral fuels, lubricants, etc.	3,887.7	5,462.3	5,790.5
Petroleum, petroleum products, etc.	3,887.7	5,462.3	5,789.8
Total (incl. others) . . .	4,607.3	6,345.2	6,352.9

PRINCIPAL TRADING PARTNERS (million riyals)

Imports c.i.f.	1988	1989	1990
Australia	479.9	459.0	853.3
Belgium	311.4	275.0	483.6
China, People's Republic . .	285.0	420.0	563.5
Djibouti	122.4	207.8	296.7
France	700.7	1,409.3	1,094.1
Germany, Federal Republic .	872.4	580.1	869.5
Italy	522.1	453.5	390.8
Japan	847.5	1,135.4	589.5
Jordan	58.5	52.8	192.9
Korea, Republic . . .	497.4	375.5	444.1
Kuwait	209.1	89.7	294.7
Malaysia	316.4	469.7	448.4
Netherlands	1,182.7	567.8	604.3
Saudi Arabia	2,294.9	2,329.7	1,280.4
Singapore	392.0	315.8	338.3
Somalia	185.4	221.0	391.4
Sweden	171.0	99.2	164.5
Thailand	123.8	178.9	318.4
United Arab Emirates . .	164.3	112.9	360.5
United Kingdom . . .	1,079.5	781.6	896.6
USA	746.9	1,118.2	1,026.0
Total (incl. others) . . .	13,523.6	13,669.8*	13,954.0*

* Including imports from unspecified EC countries (million riyals): 177.0 in 1989; 188.2 in 1990.

Exports f.o.b.	1988	1989	1990
Cuba	—	—	263.6
Djibouti	5.9	53.5	65.4
Italy	779.9	1,129.5	1,894.4
Japan	181.2	152.9	55.2
Kenya	—	91.6	—
Saudi Arabia	526.1	516.5	223.5
Singapore	165.9	17.7	45.9
United Kingdom . . .	516.5	0.0	686.3
USA	1,330.1	1,320.6	2,979.1
Yemen, People's Democratic Republic	82.3	104.6	—
Total (incl. others) . . .	4,607.3	6,345.2*	6,352.9

* Including exports for which the destination was not stated (2,838.3 million riyals).

Transport

CIVIL AVIATION (traffic on scheduled services)

	1989	1990	1991
Kilometres flown (million) . .	9	13	7
Passengers carried ('000) . .	426	671	413
Passenger-km (million) . .	665	929	421
Freight ton-km (million) . .	8	12	6

Source: UN, *Statistical Yearbook*.

Education

	Teachers		Pupils	
	1988	1990*	1988	1990*
Primary . . .	27,732	35,350	1,250,599	1,291,372
Secondary:				
General . . .	10,841	12,106	289,615	394,578
Teacher training .	716‡	783	12,806‡	21,051
Vocational . .	279†	464	3,269§	5,068

Higher education: 454 teachers, 17,417 students in 1987; 470 teachers, 23,457 students in 1988.

* Figures for 1989 are not available.
† 1985.   ‡ 1986.   § 1987.

Source: UNESCO, *Statistical Yearbook*.

Statistical Survey of the former People's Democratic Republic of Yemen

Source (unless otherwise stated): Central Statistical Organization, Steamer Point, POB 1193, Aden; tel. 22235.

Area and Population

AREA, POPULATION AND DENSITY

Area (sq km)	336,869*
Population (census results)	
14 May 1973.	1,590,275
29 March 1988†	
Males	1,184,359
Females	1,160,907
Total	2,345,266
Population (official estimates at mid-year)	
1988	2,337,000
1989	2,398,000
1990	2,460,000
Density (per sq km) at mid-1990	7.3

* 130,066 sq miles.   † Preliminary figures.

GOVERNORATES (estimated population, mid-1986)

	Area (sq km)	Population ('000)	Density
Aden	6,980	407	58.3
Lahej	12,766	382	29.9
Abyan	21,489	434	20.2
Shabwah	73,908	226	3.1
Hadhramaut	155,376	686	4.4
Al-Mahra	66,350	85	1.3
Total	336,869	2,220	6.6

Capital: Aden (estimated population 271,590 at mid-1977).

BIRTHS AND DEATHS (UN estimates, annual averages)

	1975–80	1980–85	1985–90
Birth rate (per 1,000) . .	47.6	47.0	47.3
Death rate (per 1,000). . .	20.9	17.4	15.8

Source: UN, *World Population Prospects 1990*.

EMPLOYMENT (estimates, 1986)

Agriculture and fishing	216,000
Industry	57,000
Construction	49,000
Transport	34,000
Commerce	52,000
Services	107,000
Total	515,000

Forestry

ROUNDWOOD REMOVALS
(FAO estimates, '000 cubic metres, excl. bark)

	1987	1988	1989
Total (all fuel wood) . . .	306	312	324

1990–91: Annual output as in 1989 (FAO estimates).
Source: FAO, *Yearbook of Forest Products*.

Mining

('000 metric tons)

	1986	1987	1988*
Crude petroleum . . .	n.a.	n.a.	200
Salt (unrefined)	40	56	72

1989 ('000 metric tons): Crude petroleum 750*.
1990 ('000 metric tons): Crude petroleum 800*.
* Provisional.
Source: UN *Industrial Statistics Yearbook*.

Industry

SELECTED PRODUCTS
('000 metric tons, unless otherwise indicated)

	1988	1989	1990
Frozen fish	3.3	3.0*	n.a.
Salted, dried or smoked fish .	6.1	6.1*	6.3*
Motor spirit (petrol) . . .	200	210	220
Kerosene	170	165	170
Jet fuels	260	260	260
Distillate fuel oils . . .	1,130	1,140	1,150
Residual fuel oils . . .	1,360	1,370	1,800
Liquefied petroleum gas . .	45†	46†	50†
Electric energy (million kWh) .	845	850	910

* FAO figure.   † Estimate.
Source: UN, *Industrial Statistics Yearbook*.

Finance

CURRENCY AND EXCHANGE RATES
Monetary Units
   1,000 fils = 1 Yemeni dinar (YD).

Sterling and Dollar Equivalents (31 May 1990)
   £1 sterling = 774.6 fils;
   US $1 = 461.9 fils;
   100 Yemeni dinars = £129.09 = $216.49.

Exchange Rate
   Between February 1973 and May 1990 the Yemeni dinar's value was fixed at US $2.8952 ($1 = 345.4 fils).

CENTRAL BANK RESERVES (US $ million at 31 December)

	1987	1988	1989
Gold*	1.77	1.77	1.77
IMF special drawing rights .	2.96	20.00	2.39
Foreign exchange . . .	94.14	59.93	74.46
Total	98.87	81.70	78.62

* Valued at $42.22 per troy ounce.
Source: IMF, *International Financial Statistics*.

MONEY SUPPLY (million dinars at 31 December)

	1987	1988	1989
Currency outside banks .	299.65	315.79	322.87
Demand deposits at commercial banks .	152.60	156.12	268.38
Total money . . .	452.25	471.91	591.25

Source: IMF, *International Financial Statistics*.

COST OF LIVING
(Consumer Price Index for Aden; base: 1980 = 100)

	1986	1987	1988
Food	121.2	125.5	125.1
Fuel, light and water . .	120.6	121.2	121.2
Clothing	127.4	127.4	127.4
Rent	100.0	100.0	100.0
All items (incl. others) . .	135.4	139.2	139.2

Source: ILO, *Year Book of Labour Statistics*.

BALANCE OF PAYMENTS (US $ million)*

	1987	1988	1989
Merchandise exports f.o.b. .	70.9	82.2	113.8
Merchandise imports f.o.b. .	−456.9	−596.1	−553.9
Trade balance . . .	−385.9	−513.9	−440.1
Exports of services . .	102.8	135.2	134.9
Imports of services . .	−203.2	−313.3	−339.3
Other income received . .	15.9	15.1	14.2
Other income paid . .	−13.6	−16.5	−13.3
Private unrequited transfers (net)	302.6	252.8	171.7
Official unrequited transfers (net)	51.8	36.2	55.3
Current balance . . .	−129.7	−404.5	−416.6
Capital (net) . . .	−70.3	315.6	403.0
Net errors and omissions . .	11.4	62.9	−2.3
Overall balance . . .	−48.0	−26.0	−15.9

* Imports and exports of petroleum by the Aden refinery are not included in merchandise trade. Such transactions are reflected in a processing fee appropriate to exports of services, on the assumption that no change of ownership has taken place.
Source: IMF, *International Financial Statistics*.

External Trade

PRINCIPAL COMMODITIES ('000 dinars)

Imports c.i.f.*	1980	1985	1986
Food and live animals . . .	66,117	70,819	49,292
Wheat and wheat flour . .	18,907	19,238	10,471
Rice	4,043	8,316	4,982
Refined sugar . . .	10,862	3,838	3,311
Crude materials (inedible) except fuels	9,537	5,771	2,648
Petroleum products . . .	51,920	36,551	23,581
Animal and vegetable oils and fats	5,497	9,222	6,374
Chemicals	8,103	10,938	9,520
Basic manufactures . . .	30,098	39,574	24,740
Machinery and transport equipment	50,847	52,948	31,591
Miscellaneous manufactured articles	8,802	12,341	5,388
Total (incl. others) . . .	236,259	241,115	154,357

Exports f.o.b.*	1980	1985	1986
Food and live animals . . .	7,645	6,695	7,033
Fresh fish	6,386	5,167	4,665
Beverages and tobacco . .	958	1,265	618
Crude materials (inedible) except fuels	4,321	1,625	853
Petroleum products . . .	875	3,356	1,212
Basic manufactures . . .	422	78	117
Miscellaneous manufactured articles	220	248	123
Total (incl. others) . . .	14,547	13,852	10,021

* Excluding imports and exports of foreign-owned companies. In 1980 total imports were 527.4 million dinars, and total exports 268.5 million dinars.

Detailed trade figures for 1981–84 are not available. Total imports (in million dinars) were: 490.1 in 1981; 552.4 in 1982; 512.3 in 1983; 532.9 in 1984. Total exports (in million dinars) were: 209.8 in 1981; 274.6 in 1982; 232.7 in 1983; 222.9 in 1984.

1987 (million dinars, excl. trade of foreign-owned companies): Imports c.i.f. 170; Exports f.o.b. 24.
1988 (million dinars, excl. trade of foreign-owned companies): Imports c.i.f. 226; Exports f.o.b. 28.

PRINCIPAL TRADING PARTNERS ('000 dinars)*

Imports	1980	1985	1986
China, People's Republic . .	7,927	11,422	8,547
Denmark	5,002	7,528	8,476
France	13,435	11,634	4,398
Germany, Fed. Republic . .	4,660	7,857	5,457
Iran	n.a.	2,358	4,546
Japan	24,075	15,678	8,637
Netherlands	9,561	13,168	7,432
Saudi Arabia	6,692	3,712	5,761
Singapore	3,329	9,991	7,605
USSR	18,103	34,327	25,247
United Arab Emirates . .	292	1,534	5,042
United Kingdom . . .	18,713	17,070	11,349
Total (incl. others) . .	213,171	212,993	142,937

Exports				1980	1985	1986
Djibouti	.	.	.	169	196	126
Ethiopia	.	.	.	261	99	47
France .	.	.	.	9	517	2,321
Italy	.	.	.	1,352	416	432
Japan	.	.	.	5,991	3,981	2,731
Saudi Arabia	.	.	.	736	739	1,293
Singapore	.	.	.	1,102	1,005	163
USSR	.	.	.	n.a.	583	102
United Arab Emirates	.	.		55	135	1,127
Yemen Arab Republic	.	.		1,741	2,639	1,022
Total (incl. others)	.	.		13,938	11,125	9,826

* Excluding imports and exports of foreign-owned companies. Also excluded is trade with North and South America.

Figures are not available for 1981–84.

Education

	Teachers		Pupils/Students	
	1989	1990	1989	1990
Pre-primary	475	n.a.	11,500	n.a.
Primary*	13,744	13,240	331,042	379,908
Secondary				
General	1,915	n.a.	34,179	n.a.
Teacher training . .	128	126	2,410	2,752
Vocational	n.a.	532	n.a.	6,351
Higher	643†	n.a.	3,999†	n.a.

* Excluding schools for nomads.   † 1987.

Source: UNESCO, *Statistical Yearbook.*

Directory

The Constitution*

A draft constitution for the united Republic of Yemen (based on that endorsed by the Yemen Arab Republic (YAR) and the People's Democratic Republic of Yemen (PDRY) in December 1981) was published in December 1989, and was approved by a popular referendum on 15–16 May 1991. The general principles of the draft constitution were as follows:

Article 1: The Republic of Yemen is an independent, indivisible state enjoying full sovereignty. The Yemeni people are part of the Arab nation and the Islamic world.

Article 2: Islam is the state religion and Arabic the official state language.

Article 3: The Islamic Shari'a is the principal source of legislation.

Article 4: The people are the source of all authority, which is exercised directly, through referenda and general elections, and indirectly, through the legislative and executive bodies, through the judiciary and through elected local councils.

Article 6: The economy of the Republic of Yemen is based on Islamic social justice and the protection of private ownership. It aims to develop a public sector capable of possessing the principal means of production.

Article 10: The State guarantees equal political, social, economic and educational opportunities to all citizens.

Article 26: Every citizen has the right to participate in political, economic, social and cultural life, and the State guarantees freedom of thought and freedom of expression within the limitations of the law.

Article 27: All citizens are equal before the law and all have equal rights and duties.

Article 32: The State guarantees the personal freedom of all citizens and protects their dignity and security.

* On 28 September 1994 52 articles were amended, 29 added and one cancelled, leaving a total of 159 articles in the constitution. The five-member Presidential Council was abolished and in future the President would be elected by direct universal suffrage for a five-year term, renewable once. Amendments included articles 1 and 3 as follows:

Article 1: The Yemeni Republic is an independent and sovereign Arab and Islamic country. It is an indivisible whole, and it is impermissible to concede any part of it. The Yemeni people are part of the Arab and Islamic nation.

Article 3: The Islamic Shari'a is the source of all laws.

The Government

HEAD OF STATE

President: Gen. ALI ABDULLAH SALEH (took office 24 May 1990, re-elected 1 October 1994).

Vice-President: ABD AR-RABBUH MANSUR HADI.

PRESIDENTIAL ADVISERS

Dr HASAN MUHAMMAD MAKKI
Brig.-Gen. MUJAHID ABU SHAWARIB

HASAN AL-SALAMI

COUNCIL OF MINISTERS
(October 1994)

A coalition mainly of the General People's Congress (GPC) and the Yemeni Islah Party (YIP).

Prime Minister: ABD AL-AZIZ ABD AL-GHANI (GPC).

Deputy Prime Minister and Minister of Industry: Dr MUHAMMAD SAID AL-ATTAR (GPC).

Deputy Prime Minister and Foreign Minister: Dr ABD AL-KARIM AL-IRYANI (GPC).

Deputy Prime Minister: ABD AL-WAHAB ALI AL-ANISI (YIP).

Deputy Prime Minister and Minister of Planning and Development: ABD AL-QADIR BAJAMMAL (GPC).

Minister of Petroleum and Minerals: FAISAL UTHMAN BIN SHAMLAN (Independent).

Minister of Supply and Trade: MUHAMMAD ABD AL-WAHAB ZUBARI (YIP).

Minister of Local Administration: MUHAMMAD HASSAN DAMAJ (YIP).

Minister of the Interior: YAHYA MUHAMMAD AL-MUTAWAKKIL (GPC).

Minister of Finance: Eng. MUHAMMAD AHMAD AL-JUNAYD (GPC).

Minister of Justice: ABD AL-WAHAB LUTFI AL-DAYLAMI (YIP).

Minister of Religious Endowments and Guidance: GHALIB ABD AL-KAFI AL-QURSHI (YIP).

Minister of Information: MUHAMMAD SALIM BASINDWAH (GPC).

Minister of Culture and Tourism: YAHYA HUSSAIN AL-ARASHI (GPC).

Minister of Transport: AHMAD MUSAID HUSSAIN (GPC).

Minister of Construction, Housing and Urban Planning: ALI HAMID SHARAF (GPC).

Minister of Health: Dr NAJIB GHANIM (YIP).

Minister of Agriculture and Water Resources: AHMAD SALIM AL-JABALI (GPC).

Minister of Fisheries: Dr ABD AL-RAHMAN BAFADL (YIP).

Minister of Defence: ABD AL-MALIK ALI AS-SAYYANI (Independent).

Minister of Social Security and Labour: MUHAMMAD ABDULLAH AL-BATTANI (GPC).

Minister of Electricity and Water: ABDULLAH MUHSIN AL-AKWA (YSP).

Minister for Parliamentary and Legal Affairs: ABDULLAH AHMAD GHANIM (GPC).

Minister for the Civil Service and Administrative Reform: SADIQ AMIN ABU RAS (GPC).

Minister of Communications: Eng. AHMAD MUHAMMAD AL-ANISI (GPC).

Minister of Youth and Sport: Dr ABD AL-WAHAB RAWIH (GPC).
Minister of Education: ABD ALI AL-QUDATI (YIP).

MINISTRIES

All ministries are in San'a.

Legislature

THE HOUSE OF REPRESENTATIVES

The House of Representatives has 301 members. It originally comprised the 159 members of the Consultative Council (*Majlis ash-Shura*) of the former YAR; the 111 members of the Supreme People's Council of the former PDRY; and 31 new members nominated by President Saleh. A general election for a new House of Representatives was held on 27 April 1993.

Speaker: Sheikh ABDULLAH BIN HUSSAIN AL-AHMAR.

General Election, 27 April 1993

Party	Seats
General People's Congress (GPC)	123
Yemeni Islah Party (YIP)	62
Yemen Socialist Party (YSP)	56
Independents	47
Baathist parties	7
Nasserite parties	3
Al-Haq	2
Void	1
Total	**301**

Political Organizations

In the PDRY the YSP was the only legal political party until December 1989, when the formation of opposition parties was legalized. There were no political parties in the former YAR. The two leading parties that emerged in the unified Yemen were the GPC and the YSP. During 1990 an estimated 30 to 40 further political parties were reported to have been formed. Following the civil war from May to July 1994, President Saleh declared that the YSP would be excluded from the new government formed in October 1994.

Al-Haq: San'a; conservative Islamic party; Sec.-Gen. Sheikh AHMAD ASH-SHAMI.

General People's Congress (GPC): San'a; a broad grouping of supporters of President Saleh; Leader Gen. ALI ABDULLAH SALEH; Sec.-Gen. AHMAD AL-ASBAHI.

League of the Sons of Yemen (LSY): Aden; represents interests of southern tribes; Leader ABD AR-RAHMAN AL-JIFRI; Sec.-Gen. MOHSEN FARID.

Nasserite Unionist Organization: Aden; f. 1989 as a legal party.

Yemen Socialist Party (YSP): San'a; f. 1978 as successor to United Political Organization—National Front (UPO—NF); fmrly Marxist-Leninist 'vanguard' party based on 'scientific socialism'; has Political Bureau, Central Committee; Sec.-Gen. ALI SALEH OBAD.

Yemeni Islah Party (YIP): POB 23090, San'a; tel. 213281; fax 213311; f. 1990 by members of the legislature and other political figures, and tribal leaders; seeks constitutional reform based on Islamic law; Leader Sheikh ABDULLAH BIN HUSSAIN AL-AHMAR; Sec. Gen. Sheikh MUHAMMAD ABDULLAH AL-WAJIH.

Yemen Unionist Rally Party: Aden; f. 1990 by intellectuals and politicians from the former YAR and PDRY to protect human rights; Leader OMAR AL-JAWI.

Diplomatic Representation

EMBASSIES IN YEMEN

Albania: San'a; Ambassador: ALKYZ CERGA.

Algeria: POB 509, 67 Amman St, San'a; tel. (1) 209689; fax (1) 209688; Ambassador: BEN HADID CHADLY.

China, People's Republic: Az-Zubairy St, San'a; tel. (1) 275337; Ambassador: LI LIUGEN.

Czech Republic: POB 2501, Safiya Janoobia, San'a; tel. (1) 247946; fax (1) 244418; Ambassador: KAROL FISHER.

Egypt: POB 1134, Gamal Abd al-Nasser St, San'a; tel. (1) 275948; fax (1) 274196; Ambassador: ATA'A M. HARDUN.

Ethiopia: POB 234, Haddah Rd, San'a; tel. (1) 208833; Ambassador: YOUSUF H. NASSER.

France: POB 1286, al-Baonia, San'a; tel. (1) 275995; telex 2248; fax (1) 275996; Ambassador: MARCEL LAUGEL.

Germany: POB 2561, Outer Ring Rd, West Hadaa, San'a; tel. (1) 216756; telex 2245; fax (1) 216758; Ambassador: Dr KURT MESSER.

Hungary: POB 11558, As-Safiya Al-Gharbiyya, St No. 6B, San'a; tel. (1) 216250; fax (1) 216-251; Ambassador: MIHÁLY BAYER.

India: POB 1154, San'a; tel. (1) 241980; fax (1) 263062; Ambassador: M. VENKATARAMAN.

Iran: POB 1437, Haddah St, San'a; tel. (1) 206945; telex 2241; Chargé d'affaires: WAHID FARMENO.

Iraq: POB 498, South Airport Rd, San'a; tel. (1) 244153; telex 2237; Ambassador: MUHSIN KHALIL.

Italy: POB 1152, No. 5 Bldg, St No. 29, San'a; tel. (1) 78846; telex 2560; Ambassador: Dr PIETRO CORDONE.

Japan: POB 817, San'a; tel. (1) 207356; telex 2345; fax (1) 209531; Ambassador: KAZUO WANIBUCHI.

Jordan: POB 2152, San'a; tel. (1) 216701; telex 2703; Ambassador: AHMAD AL-ADIALEH.

Korea, Democratic People's Republic: POB 1209, al-Hasaba, Mazda Rd, San'a; tel. (1) 232340; telex 2603; Ambassador: CHU WANG CHOL.

Kuwait: POB 17036, near Ring Rd 60, San'a; tel. (1) 216317; telex 2481; Ambassador: MANSOUR AL-AWADI.

Lebanon: POB 2283, Haddah St, San'a; tel. (1) 203459; telex 2438; Ambassador: ABD AL-LATIF MAMLOUK.

Libya: POB 1506, Ring Rd, St No. 8, House No. 145, San'a; telex 2219; Secretary of Libyan Brotherhood Office: MILAD AL-FEQHI.

Morocco: POB 10236, West Safiya, San'a; tel. (1) 247964; telex 2299; Ambassador: AHMED DRISSI.

Netherlands: POB 463, Hadda Rd, San'a; tel. (1) 215626; telex 2429; Ambassador: G. BOZ.

Oman: POB 105, Aser area, Az-Zubairy St, San'a; tel. (1) 208933; telex 2253; Ambassador: AWAD M. BAKTHEER.

Pakistan: POB 2848, Ring Rd, San'a; tel. (1) 248812; Ambassador: FAIZUR ARIF.

Romania: POB 2169, Hadda Rd, San'a; tel. (1) 215579; telex 2361; Chargé d'affaires: VALENTIN MORARU.

Russia: POB 1087, 26 September St, San'a; tel. (1) 278719; telex 2952; fax (1) 203142; Ambassador: IGOR G. IVASHENKO.

Saudi Arabia: POB 1184, Zuhara House, Hadda Rd, San'a; tel. (1) 240429; telex 2420; Ambassador: ALI AL-QUFAIDI.

Somalia: POB 12277, Hadda Rd, San'a; tel. (1) 208864; telex 2610; Ambassador: ABD AS-SALLAM MU'ALLIM ADAM.

Sudan: POB 2561, 82 Abou al-Hassan al-Hamadani St, San'a; tel. (1) 265231; fax (1) 265233; Ambassador: OMAR AS-SAID TAHA.

Syria: POB 494, Hadda Rd, St No. 1, San'a; tel. (1) 247750; telex 2335; Chargé d'affaires: AHMAD WALID RAJAB.

Tunisia: POB 2561, Diplomatic area, St No. 22, San'a; tel. (1) 240457; telex 2451; Ambassador: ABBÈS MOHSEN.

Turkey: POB 12450, As-Safiya, San'a; tel. and fax (1) 241395; telex 3159; Ambassador: VOLKAN COTUR.

United Arab Emirates: POB 2250, Ring Rd, San'a; tel. (1) 248777; telex 2225; Ambassador: SAIF BIN MAKTOOM AL-MANSOORY.

United Kingdom: POB 1287, 129 Haddah Rd, San'a; tel. (1) 215630; telex 2251; fax (1) 263059; Ambassador: DOUGLAS GORDON.

USA: POB 1088, Sa'awan St, San'a; tel. (1) 238842; telex 2697; fax (1) 251563; Ambassador: ARTHUR H. HUGHES.

Religion

ISLAM

The majority of the population are Muslims. Most are Sunni Muslims of the Shafi'a sect, except in the north-west of the country, where Zaidism (a moderate sect of the Shi'a order) is the dominant persuasion.

CHRISTIANITY

The Roman Catholic Church

Apostolic Vicariate of Arabia: POB 54, Abu Dhabi, United Arab Emirates; tel. (2) 461895; fax (2) 465177; responsible for a territory comprising most of the Arabian peninsula (including Saudi Arabia, the UAE and Yemen), containing an estimated 750,000 Catholics (31 December 1992); Vicar Apostolic GIOVANNI BERNARDO GREMOLI, Titular Bishop of Masuccaba (resident in the UAE); Vicar Delegate for Yemen Rev. MATHEW VADACHERRY.

The Anglican Communion

Within the Episcopal Church in Jerusalem and the Middle East, Yemen forms part of the diocese of Cyprus and the Gulf. The

Anglican congregations in San'a and Aden are entirely expatriate; Bishop in Cyprus and the Gulf: Rt Rev. JOHN BROWN (resident in Cyprus); Archdeacon in the Gulf: Ven. MICHAEL MANSBRIDGE (resident in the UAE).

HINDUISM
There is a small Hindu community.

Judicial System

In the former YAR:

President of the State Security Court: GHALEB MUTAHIR AL-QANISH.

Public Prosecutor: ABD AR-RIZAQ AR-ROQAIHI.

Attorney General: MUHAMMAD AL-BADRI.

Shari'a Court: San'a; deals with cases related to Islamic law.

Central Organization for Supervision and Accountancy: replaces old Disciplinary Court; presides over cases of misappropriation of public funds; Chair. IZZ AD-DIN AL-MOAZEN.

In the former PDRY:

The administration of justice in the PDRY was entrusted to the Supreme Court and Magistrates' Courts. In the former Protectorate states, Islamic (Shari'a) law and local common law (Urfi) were also applied.

President of the Supreme Court: Dr MUSTAFA ABD AL-KHALIQ.

The Press

Legislation embodying the freedom of the press in the unified Republic of Yemen was enacted in May 1990. The lists below include publications which appeared in the YAR and the PDRY prior to their unification in May 1990.

DAILIES

Ar-Rabi' 'Ashar Min Uktubar (14 October): POB 4227, Crater, Aden; f. 1968; not published on Saturdays; Arabic; Editorial Dir FAROUQ MUSTAFA RIFAT; Chief Editor ABDULLAH SHARIF SAID; circ. 20,000.

Ash-Sharara (The Spark): 14 October Corporation for Printing, Publishing, Distribution and Advertising, POB 4227, Crater, Aden; Arabic; circ. 6,000.

Ath-Thawra (The Revolution): Ministry of Information, San'a; Arabic; government-owned.

WEEKLIES AND OTHERS

Attijarah (Trade): POB 3370, Hodeida; telex 5610; monthly, Arabic; commercial.

Al-Bilad (The Country): POB 1438, San'a; weekly; Arabic; inclined to right.

Al-Fanoon: POB 1187, Tawahi 102, Aden; tel. 23831; f. 1980; Arabic; monthly arts review; Editor FAISAL SOFY; circ. 15,500.

Al-Gundi (The Soldier): Ministry of Defence, Madinat ash-Sha'ab; fortnightly; Arabic; circ. 8,500.

Al-Hikma (Wisdom): POB 4227, Crater, Aden; monthly; Arabic; publ. by the Writers' Union; circ. 5,000.

Al-Hares: Aden; fortnightly; Arabic; circ. 8,000.

Al-Ma'in (Spring): Ministry of Information, San'a; monthly; general interest.

Majallat al-Jaish (Army Magazine): POB 17, San'a; monthly; publ. by Ministry of Defence.

Al-Maseerah (Journey): Ministry of Information, San'a; monthly; general interest.

Al-Mithaq (The Charter): San'a; weekly; organ of the General People's Congress.

Qadiyat al-Asr (Issues of the Age): Aden; f. 1981; weekly; Arabic; publ. by Central Committee of Yemen Socialist Party.

Ar-Ra'i al-'Am (Public Opinion): San'a; weekly; independent; Editor ALI MUHAMMAD AL-OLAFI.

Ar-Risalah (The Message): 26 September St, San'a; weekly; Arabic.

As-Sahwa (Awakening): San'a; weekly; Islamic fundamentalist; Editor MUHAMMAD AL-YADDOUMI.

As-Salam (Peace): POB 181, San'a; f. 1948; weekly; Arabic; political, economic and general essays; circ. 7,000; Editor ABDULLAH ASSAKAL.

San'a: POB 193, San'a; monthly; Arabic; inclined to left.

Sawt al-'Ummal (The Workers' Voice): POB 4227, Crater, Aden; weekly; Arabic.

Sawt al-Yemen (Voice of Yemen): POB 302, San'a; weekly; Arabic.

At-Ta'awun (Co-operation): At-Ta'awun Bldg, Az-Zubairy St, San'a; weekly; Arabic; supports co-operative societies.

Ath-Thaqafat al-Jadida (New Culture): POB 1187, Tawahi 102, Aden; tel. 23831; f. 1970; a cultural monthly review; Arabic; circ. 3,000.

Ath-Thawri (The Revolutionary): POB 4227, Crater, Aden; weekly; published on Saturday; Arabic; organ of Central Committee of the Yemen Socialist Party; Editor Dr AHMAD ABDULLAH SALIH.

26 September: POB 17, San'a; tel. (1) 274240; telex 2557; armed forces weekly; circ. 25,000.

Al-Wahda al-Watani (National Unity): Al-Baath Printing House, POB 193, San'a; tel. (1) 77511; f. 1982; fmrly *Al-Omal*; weekly; Editor MUHAMMAD SALEM ALI; circ. 40,000.

Al-Yemen: POB 1081, San'a; tel. (1) 72376; f. 1971; fortnightly; Arabic; inclined to right; Editor MUHAMMAD AHMAD AS-SABAGH.

The Yemen Times: San'a; independent weekly; Editor ABDULAZIZ AL-SAQQAF.

Yemeni Women: POB 4227, Crater, Aden; monthly; circ. 5,000.

NEWS AGENCIES

Aden News Agency (ANA): Ministry of Culture and Information, POB 1187, Tawahi 102, Aden; tel. 24874; telex 2286; f. 1970; government-owned; Dir-Gen. AHMAD MUHAMMAD IBRAHIM.

Saba News Agency: POB 1475, San'a; tel. (1) 233228; telex 2568; f. 1970; Dir HASSAN AL-ULUFI.

Foreign Bureaux
In the former YAR:

Informatsionnoye Telegrafnoye Agentstvo Rossii—Telegrafnoye Agentstvo Suverennykh Stran (ITAR—TASS) (Russia): San'a; Correspondent VIKTOR LYSSECHKO.

Xinhua (New China) News Agency (People's Republic of China): POB 482, Az-Zubairy St, San'a; tel. (1) 72073; Correspondent CHEN WENRU.

In the former PDRY:

Informatsionnoye Telegrafnoye Agentstvo Rossii—Telegrafnoye Agentstvo Suverennykh Stran (ITAR—TASS) (Russia): POB 1087, Aden; Correspondent VLADIMIR GAVRILOV.

Xinhua (New China) News Agency (People's Republic of China): POB 5213, Aden; tel. 42710; Correspondent FENG ZHERU.

Publishers

Armed Forces Printing Press: POB 17, San'a; tel. (1) 274240; telex 2557.

14 October Corporation for Printing, Publishing, Distribution and Advertising: POB 4227, Crater, Aden; under control of the Ministry of Information; Chair. and Gen. Man. SALIH AHMAD SALAH.

Yemen Printing and Publishing Co: POB 1081, San'a; telex 2363; Chair. AHMAD MUHAMMAD HADI.

Radio and Television

In 1991 there were an estimated 325,000 radio receivers and 330,000 television receivers in use in the unified Republic of Yemen. The radio and television stations of the YAR were merged with their PDRY counterparts following unification to form the Yemen Radio and Television General Corporation.

Finance

(cap. = capital; auth. = authorized; p.u. = paid up; dep. = deposits; res = reserves; m. = million; brs = branches; amounts in Yemeni riyals, unless otherwise indicated)

BANKING
Central Bank
Central Bank of Yemen: POB 59, Ali Abd al-Mughni St, San'a; tel. (1) 274371; telex 2280; fax (1) 274131; f. 1971; united with Bank of Yemen in May 1990; Gov. ALAWI SALIH AS-SALAMI; Dep. Gov. SALEM AL-ASHWALI; 7 brs.

Principal Banks
Arab Bank Ltd (Jordan): POB 475, Az-Zubairy St, San'a; tel. (1) 240922; telex 2239; fax (1) 263187; f. 1972; Man. GHASSAN BUNDAHJI; brs in Aden, Hodeida and Taiz.

Banque Indosuez (France): POB 651, Al-Qasr al-Jumhuriya St, San'a; tel. (1) 272801; telex 2412; fax (1) 274161; Gen. Man. MANUEL GARCIA-LIGERO; brs in Hodeida, Aden, and Taiz.

Co-operative and Agricultural Credit Bank: POB 2015, Banks Complex, Az-Zubairy St, San'a; tel. (1) 207327; telex 2544; fax 203714; f. 1976; cap. p.u. 280m., dep. 470m.; Chair. ABDALLAH AL-BARAKANI; Dir-Gen. HUSSAIN QASSIM AMER; 27 brs.

Housing Credit Bank: POB 638, Az-Zubairy Bldg, San'a; tel. (1) 77126; f. 1977; dep. 8.7m. (June 1987); Chair. ALI ABD AR-RAHMAN AL-BAHR.

Industrial Bank of Yemen: POB 323, Banks Complex, Az-Zubairy St, San'a; tel. (1) 207381; telex 2580; f. 1976; industrial investment; cap. 100m., total assets 269.8m. (1987); Chair. and Man. Dir ABBAS ABDU MUHAMMAD AL-KIRSHY; Gen. Man. ABD AL-KARIM ISMAIL AL-ARHABI.

International Bank of Yemen YSC: POB 2847, 106 Az-Zubairy St, San'a; tel. (1) 272920; telex 2523; fax (1) 274127; f. 1980; commercial bank; cap. 96.3m., res 123.1m., dep. 2,698.5m., total assets 3,092.0m. (1992); Chair. ALI LUTF ATH-THOUR; Gen. Man. MOHAMMEDMIAN SOOMRO; 3 brs.

National Bank of Yemen: POB 5, Arwa Rd, Crater, Aden; tel. 253484; telex 2224; fax 255004; f. 1970 as National Bank of Southern Yemen; adopted current name 1971; cap. 5m., res 8.1m. Yemeni dinars, total assets 554.4m. Yemeni dinars (1991); Chair. SALEM AL-ASHWALI; Gen. Man. MUHAMMAD ALI OMAYA; 30 brs.

United Bank Ltd (Pakistan): POB 1295, Ali Abd al-Mughni St, San'a; tel. (1) 272424; telex 2228; fax (1) 274168; Vice-Pres. and Gen. Man. INAYATULLAH BUTT; br. in Hodeida.

Yemen Bank for Reconstruction and Development (YBRD): POB 541, 26 September St, San'a; tel. (1) 271621; telex 2291; fax (1) 271684; f. 1962; cap. 100m., dep. 17,663.2m., total assets 17,950m. (1990); consolidated bank; Chair. YAHIA AD-DAILAMI; Gen. Man. AHMAD MUHAMMAD ALI; 38 brs.

Yemen Commercial Bank: POB 19845, Az-Zubairy St, San'a; tel. (1) 213662; telex 3373; fax (1) 209566; f. 1993; Chair. MUHAMMAD AR-ROWAISHAN; Gen. Man. MEHDI NAQVI; br. in Hodeida.

Yemen-Kuwait Bank for Trade and Investment YSC: POB 987, Az-Zubairy St, San'a; tel. (1) 240783; telex 2478; f. 1977; total assets 549m. (1988); Chair. and Man. Dir BADER N. AL-BISHER.

INSURANCE

Marib Yemen Insurance Co: POB 2284, Az-Zubairy St, San'a; tel. (1) 206114; telex 2279; fax (1) 206118; f. 1974; all classes of insurance; cap. 40m.; Chair. KASSIM M. AL-SABRI; Man. Dir ABDULLATIF AL-QUBATI.

National Insurance and Re-insurance Co: POB 456, Aden; tel. 51464; telex 2245; f. 1970; Lloyd's Agents; cap. 5m. Yemeni dinars; Chair. and Gen. Man. FAROUQ NASSER ALI.

United Insurance Co (YSC): POB 1983, Al-Qasr al-Jumhuriya St, San'a; tel. (1) 272891; telex 2366; fax (1) 272080; f. 1981; all classes of general insurance and life; cap. 20m.; brs in Taiz and Hodeidah; Gen. Man. SARGON D. LAZAR.

Yemen General Insurance Co (SYC): POB 2709, YGI Bldg, 25 Al Giers St, San'a; tel. (1) 265191; telex 2451; fax (1) 263109; f. 1977; all classes of insurance; cap. 20m.; brs in Aden, Taiz and Hodeida; Chair. ABD AL-GABBAR THABET; Gen. Man. WAMIDH AL-JARRAH.

Trade and Industry

CHAMBERS OF COMMERCE

Federation of Chambers of Commerce: POB 16992, San'a; tel. (1) 224262; telex 2229; Dir MUHAMMAD ABDULLAH SABRAH.

Hodeidah Chamber of Commerce: POB 3370, Az-Zubairy St, Hodeida; tel. (3) 217401; telex 5610; fax (3) 211528; f. 1960; over 1,000 mems; cap. 1m. riyals; Dir ABD AL-HAMEED ADH-DHUFAJRI.

National Chamber of Commerce and Industry: POB 473, 14th October Street, Crater 101, Aden; tel. 51104; telex 2233; f. 1886; 4,000 mems; Pres. ALI ABD AL-KARIM MUHAMMAD; Gen. Man. ABDULLAH SALEM AL-KHADER.

San'a Chamber of Commerce and Industry: Airport Rd, Al-Hasabah St, POB 195, San'a; tel. (1) 232361; telex 2629; fax (1) 232412; f. 1963; Pres. Al-Haj HUSSAIN AL-WATARI; Dir-Gen. ABDULLAH H. AR-RUBAIDI.

Taiz Chamber of Commerce: POB 5029, 26 September St, Taiz; tel. (4) 210580; telex 8960; fax (4) 212335; Dir ABD AL-HADI.

Ibb also has a Chamber of Commerce.

PRINCIPAL PUBLIC CORPORATIONS

Public Corporation for Maritime Affairs (PCMA): POB 19395, San'a; tel. (1) 414412; telex 4025; fax (1) 414645; f. 1990; Chair. SAEED YAFAI.

Public Electricity Corporation (PEC): San'a; telex 2850; fax (1) 263115; Man. Dir AHMAD AL-AINI.

Yemen Free Zone Public Authority: Aden; tel. 241210; fax 221237; f. 1990; supervises creation of a free zone for industrial investment; Chair. ABD AL-QADIR BA-JAMMAL.

In the former YAR:

General Corporation for Foreign Trade: POB 77, 163 Al-Matar St, San'a; tel. (1) 223858; telex 2348; Dir ALI A. HAJAR.

General Corporation for Foreign Trade and Grain: POB 710, San'a; tel. (1) 207571; telex 2349; formerly Yemen General Grain Corporation; present name adopted 1987; cap. and dep. 270m. riyals; Chair. ABDULLAH AL-BARAKANI; Gen. Man. KASSIM M. AS-SABRI.

General Corporation for Oil and Mineral Resources: San'a; f. 1990; state petroleum company; Pres. AHMAD BARAKAT.

General Corporation for Tourism: San'a; telex 2592.

General Corporation for Transport: POB 1827, San'a; tel. (1) 77711; telex 2400.

General Cotton Co: Hodeida; tel. (3) 238390; telex 5562.

Government Consumption Assembly for Public and Semi-Public Sector Employees: POB 833, San'a.

Military Economical Corporation: POB 1207, San'a; tel. (1) 262501; telex 2244; fax (1) 262508; Commercial Man. A. KARIM SAYAGHI.

National Company for Construction & Industrial Materials (YEMROCK): POB 2564, San'a; tel. (1) 208016; telex 2472; Gen. Man. HASIM BAKR.

Yemen Agricultural Evolution Office: Taiz; telex 8837.

Yemen Agricultural Marketing Corporation: POB 10159, San'a; tel. (1) 202467; telex 2767.

Yemen Cement Industry Corporation: POB 3393, Hodeida; tel. (3) 72952; telex 5594; Chair. AMIN ABD AL-WAHID AHMAD.

Yemen Company for Industry and Commerce Ltd: POB 5302, Taiz; tel. (4) 215171; telex 8804; Chair. ALI MUHAMMAD SAID.

Yemen Company for Investment and Finance Ltd: POB 2789, San'a; tel. (1) 274102; telex 2564; fax (1) 274178; f. 1981; cap. 100m.; Chair. ABDULLAH ISHAQ; Chair. and Gen. Man. ABDULLAH ISHAQ.

Yemen Construction Company: San'a; f. 1984; initial cap. 100m. riyals.

Yemen Drug Company for Industry and Commerce: POB 40, San'a; tel. (1) 234250; telex 2289; fax (1) 251595; Chair. HAZIM BAKER; Gen. Man. Dr ALI SALEH AL-HAMDANI.

Yemen Land Transport Corporation: POB 279, Taiz St, San'a; tel. (1) 262108; telex 2400; f. 1961; Chair. Col ALI AHMAD AL-WASI; Gen. Man. HAMID MUKRID.

Yemen Oil and Mineral Industrial Company (YEMINCO): San'a; f. 1970; Chair. ALI ABD AR-RAHMAN AL-BAHR.

Yemen Petroleum Company: POB 81, San'a; tel. (1) 70432; telex 2257; Chair. HUSSAIN ABDULLAH AL-MAKDANI; Gen. Man. YEHIA ABDULLAH AD-DAILAMI.

Yemen Telecommunication Corporation: POB 17045, San'a; tel. (1) 251140; telex 2617; fax (1) 251150; f. 1981; operates public telecommunication network.

Yemen Textile and Weaving Corporation: POB 214, San'a; tel. (1) 202460; telex 2249.

State organizations in the former PDRY:

Cottonseed Oil Factory: Main Pass Roundabout, Maalla, Aden; manufacture and export of cottonseed oil.

Ministry of Energy and Minerals: POB 5176, Maalla, Aden; tel. 24542; telex 2215; f. 1969; responsible for the refining and marketing of petroleum products, and for prospecting and exploitation of indigenous hydrocarbons and other minerals; subsidiaries include:

    Aden Refinery Company: POB 3003, Aden 110; tel. 76234; telex 2213; fax 76600; f. 1952; operates petroleum refinery; capacity 8.6m. tons per year; output 4.2m. tons (1990); operates 1 oil tanker; Exec. Dir MUHAMMAD HUSSEIN AL-HAJ; Refinery Man. AHMAD HASSAN AL-GIFRI.

    Yemen National Oil Company: POB 5050, Maalla, Aden; sole petroleum concessionaire, importer and distributor of petroleum products; Gen. Man. MUHAMMAD ABD HUSSEIN.

National Corporation for Bottling Soft Drinks: POB 352, Crater, Aden; tel. 82237; telex 2500; f. 1972; manufacturer and distributor of soft drinks, distilled water, ice and carbon dioxide; Gen. Man. ABD AL-HAFEZ MUQBIL.

National Company for Foreign Trade: POB 90, Crater, Aden; tel. 42793; telex 2211; fax 42631; f. 1969; incorporates main foreign trading businesses (nationalized in 1970) and arranges their supply to the National Co for Home Trade; Gen. Man. AHMAD MUHAMMAD SALEH (acting).

National Company for Home Trade: POB 90, Crater, Aden; tel. 41483; telex 2211; fax 41226; f. 1969; marketing of general consumer goods, building materials, electrical goods, motor cars and spare parts, agricultural machinery etc.; Man. Dir ABD AR-RAHMAN AS-SAILANI.

National Corporation for Marketing Fish: POB 1139, Tawahi, Aden; tel. 24275; telex 2244; operates 18 deep-sea fishing vessels; Gen. Man. ABD AL-MAJEED MURSHED.

National Dockyards Company: POB 1244, Tawahi, Aden; tel. 23837; telex 2217; Man. Dir SALEH AL-MUNTASIR MEHDI.

National Drug Corporation: POB 192, Crater, Aden; tel. 204912; telex 2293; fax 221242; f. 1972; import of pharmaceutical products, chemicals, medical supplies, baby foods and scientific instruments; Chair. and Gen. Man. Dr AWADH SALAM ISSA BAMATRAF.

National Tanning Factory: POB 4073, Sheikh Othman, Aden; tel. 81449; f. 1972; Gen. Man. MANSOUR A. MANSOOR.

National Yemeni Petroleum Co: f. 1988 to exploit and market petroleum produced in the PDRY.

Public Building Corporation: POB 7022, al-Mansoura, Aden; tel. 342296; telex 2373; fax 345726; f. 1973; government contractors and contractors of private housing projects; Dir-Gen. HUSSAIN MOHAMMED ALWALI.

Public Corporation for Fish Wealth: POB 2242, Pier Rd, Tawahi, Aden; telex 2244; operates 1 fishing vessel.

Public Corporation for Manufacturing Textiles: POB 2063, Sheikh Othman, Aden; tel. 82364; telex 2273; Gen. Man. SAEED SHARAF.

Public Corporation for Poultry Development: POB 4145, Crater, Aden; tel. 82201; f. 1984 to replace General Corpn for Poultry Devt; cap. 5m. riyals ($14.5m.).

Public Organization for Carpentry: POB 5034, Maalla, Aden; tel. 23619; telex 2273.

Public Organization for Dairy Products: POB 1416, Crater, Aden; tel. 31257; telex 2273.

Public Organization for Salt: POB 1169, Tawahi, Aden; tel. 202048; telex 2250; f. 1970.

Public Trading Corporation for Textiles and Electrical Goods: POB 4490, Crater, Aden; tel. 42242; telex 2223; marketing of all kinds of textiles, ready-made garments and electrical goods; Man. Dir SALEM ABD AS-SALEM.

Yemen Company for Perfumes and Cosmetics Ltd: POB 5042, Maalla, Aden; tel. 23830; telex 2273.

TRADE UNIONS

General Confederation of Workers: POB 1162, Maalla, Aden; f. 1956; affiliated to WFTU and ICFTU; 35,000 mems; Pres. RAJEH SALEH NAJI; Gen. Sec. ABD AR-RAZAK SHAIF.

Trade Union Federation: San'a; Pres. ALI SAIF MUQBIL.

Transport

RAILWAYS

There are no railways in Yemen.

ROADS

At 31 December 1991 the Republic of Yemen had 51,467 km (31,980 miles) of roads, including 4,754 km of main roads, 2,384 km of secondary roads and 44,329 km of other roads.

Yemen Land Transport Co: Aden; telex 2307; f. 1980; incorporates former Yemen Bus Company and all other public transport of the former PDRY; Chair. ABD AL-JALIL TAHIR BADR; Gen. Man. SALIH AWAD AL-AMUDI.

SHIPPING

Aden is the main port. In 1986 the port handled vessels with a combined displacement of 8.3m. net registered tons. Aden Main Harbour has 28 first-class berths. In addition there is ample room to accommodate vessels of light draught at anchor in the 18-foot dredged area. There is also 800 feet of cargo wharf accommodating vessels of 300 feet length and 18 feet draught. Aden Oil Harbour accommodates four tankers of 57,000 tons and up to 40 feet draught. A new port at Nishtun was opened in 1984 to assist in the exploitation of the rich fishing grounds nearby. A multi-purpose terminal at Maalla, part of a programme to expand facilities at Aden port, was opened in September 1993.

There were three ports in the former YAR: Hodeida, Mocha and Salif. Hodeida is a Red Sea port of some importance, which has been considerably extended with Soviet aid. The Yemen Navi-gation Line, which is based in Aden, operates passenger and cargo services to many parts of the Middle East and Africa.

Aden Refinery Co: POB 3003, Aden 110; tel. (1) 76234; telex 2213; Exec.-Dir M. H. AL-HAJ.

Elkirshi Shipping and Stevedoring Co: POB 3813, Al-Hamdi St, Hodeida; tel. (3) 224263; telex 5569; operates at ports of Hodeida, Mocha and Salif.

General Ports and Marine Affairs Corporation: POB 3183, Hodeida; tel. (3) 79034; telex 5565.

Hodeida Shipping and Transport Co Ltd: POB 3337, Hodeida; tel. (3) 238130; telex 5510; fax (3) 211533; cargo, container and ro-ro handling.

Middle East Shipping Co Ltd: POB 3700, Hodeida; tel. (3) 217276; telex 5505; fax (3) 211529; f. 1962; Chair. ABD AL-WASA HAYEL SAEED; Gen. Man. ABD AR-RAHIM ABD AL-GHAFUR; brs in Mocha, Aden, Taiz and Salif.

National Shipping Co: POB 1228, Steamer Point, Aden; tel. 24861; telex 2216; fax 22664; shipping, bunkering, clearing and forwarding, and travel agents; Gen. Man. MUHAMMAD BIN MUHAMMAD SHAKER.

Yemen Navigation Line: POB 4190, Aden; tel. 24861; telex 295; fleet of 3 general cargo vessels.

Yemen Ports Authority: POB 1316, Steamer Point, Aden; tel. 22666; telex 2278; fax 43805; f. 1888; state administrative body; Dir-Gen. MUHAMMAD AHMED ALI.

Yemen Shipping Development Co Ltd: POB 3686, Hodeida; tel. (3) 239252; telex 5530; fleet of 4 general cargo vessels.

CIVIL AVIATION

There are six international airports—San'a International (13 km from the city), Aden Civil Airport (at Khormaksar, 11 km from the port of Aden), al-Ganad (at Taiz), Mukalla (Riyan), Seyoun and Hodeida Airport. In 1989 a total of 426,000 passengers travelled on scheduled services in the former YAR.

It was announced in June 1990 that the former national carriers of the YAR and the PDRY (see below) would begin to operate as one airline (Yemen Airways) from 28 October 1990. The merger of the airlines was delayed by a disagreement between the Governments of Saudi Arabia (a 49% shareholder in Yemenia) and Yemen, caused by the Gulf War. Despite the Saudi Arabian Government's decision, in March 1992, to relinquish its shareholding in Yemenia, the merger of the two airlines had not been accomplished by May 1994.

Yemen Airways (Yemenia): POB 1183, Airport Rd, San'a; tel. (1) 232389; telex 2204; originally formed in 1963 as Yemen Airlines; reorganized as Yemen Airways Corpn 1972 following nationalization; present name adopted 1978, following establishment of new airline, owned 51% by Government of former YAR and 49% by Government of Saudi Arabia; internal services and external services (all carriers) to destinations in the Middle East, Asia, Africa and Europe; supervised by a ministerial committee headed by the Minister of Communications; Chair. MUHAMMAD AHMAD AL-HAIMI; Man. Dir RIDA T. HAKIM.

Alyemda (Democratic Yemen Airlines): POB 6006, Alyemda Bldg, Khormaksar, Aden; tel. 52267; telex 2269; f. 1961 as wholly owned corporation by the Government of the former PDRY; internal flights and passenger and cargo services to destinations in the Middle East, Asia, Africa and Europe; Chair. and Gen. Man. ABDULLAH ALI ABDULLAH.

Tourism

The former YAR formed a joint tourism company with the PDRY in 1980. In 1992 a total of 72,164 tourists visited the unified Yemen, and tourists receipts for that year were estimated at US $47m.

Yemen Tourist Co: POB 1526, San'a; Chair. ABD AL-HADI AL-HAMDANI.

Defence

The armed forces of the former YAR and the PDRY were officially merged in May 1990, but by early 1994 the process had not been completed and in May civil war broke out between the forces of the two former states, culminating in victory for the North. In October President Saleh announced plans for the modernization of the armed forces, which would include the banning of party affiliation in the security services and armed forces.

Commander-in-Chief of the Armed Forces: Gen. ALI ABDULLAH SALEH.

Chief of Staff of the Armed Forces: (vacant).

Chief of the General Staff: Brig.-Gen. ABDULLAH ALI ULAYWAH.

Defence Budget (1993): 6,200m. riyals ($375.0m.).

Military Service: conscription, 2 years.

Total Armed Forces (1994): 66,000: army 61,000; navy 1,500; air force 3,500. Reserves 85,000 (army).

Paramilitary Forces: 75,000 (10,000 Ministry of National Security Force, at least 20,000 tribal levies, 15,000 People's Militia, 30,000 Public Security Force).

Education

Following the unification of the YAR and the PDRY in May 1990, the educational systems of the two countries were to be merged.

In the former YAR, primary education began at seven years of age and lasted for six years. Secondary education, beginning at the age of 13, lasted for a further six years, comprising two cycles of three years each. As a proportion of the school-age population, the total enrolment at primary and secondary schools (according to UNESCO estimates) was 56% (males 85%; females 25%) in 1990, compared with only 7% in 1970. Enrolment at primary schools in 1990 was equivalent to 76% of children in the relevant age-group, while the comparable ratio for secondary enrolment was 31%. In 1988 23,457 students were enrolled in higher education. There is a university in San'a. Of total estimated expenditure by the central Government in 1990, 4,486.4m. riyals (19.0%) was allocated to education. A major project to improve teacher training and to reduce costs in the sector of primary education was commenced in mid-1987. The scheme was expected to result in the replacement by Yemeni teachers of all but 1,000 of the 12,900 expatriate primary school teachers working in the YAR, and to encourage more women to join the teaching profession. According to estim-ates by UNESCO, the average rate of adult illiteracy in the former YAR in 1990 was 61.5% (males 46.7%; females 73.7%).

In addition to military colleges, more specific institutions were being established under the Educational Development Project, especially in the field of vocational training.

Primary education in the former PDRY, which was officially compulsory, began at seven years of age and lasted for eight years. Secondary education, beginning at the age of 15, lasted for a further four years. As a proportion of the school-age population, the total enrolment at primary and secondary schools was 62% (males 81%; females 42%) in 1989, compared with 36% in 1970. Enrolment at primary schools in 1989 was equivalent to 80% of children in the relevant age-group, while the comparable ratio for secondary enrolment was 21% (boys 30%; girls 12%).

In the 1986/87 academic year there were 29 kindergartens, 969 primary schools, 63 secondary schools, 20 technical and vocational institutes, including 1 university in Aden (founded in 1975), and 9 teacher training colleges. Other higher education was received abroad. The total school population rose from 65,000 in 1967 to 336,332 in the 1986/87 academic year. Of the total, 11,587 were accounted for by kindergartens, 290,082 by primary schools, 32,796 by secondary schools and 1,867 by teacher training colleges. In the same year, there were 2,745 students attending technical and vocational colleges and 4,386 at the national university. By 1986/87 24 specialized institutes with capacity for 6,695 students had been established in all the PDRY's main towns, offering training in a wide range of subjects. According to estim-ates by UNESCO, the average rate of adult illiteracy in the former PDRY in 1990 was 60.9% (males 47.2%; females 73.9%).

In 1991 the International Development Association (IDA) approved a $19.4m. loan to Yemen for the $35.6m. secondary teacher training project. In 1992 the IDA agreed to finance most of a basic educational project aimed at classroom construction and education for girls in rural areas.

Bibliography

Amin, Dr S. H. *Law and Justice in Contemporary Yemen.* Glasgow, Royston, 1987.

Ansaldi, C. *Il Yemen nella storia e nella leggenda.* Rome, 1933.

Attar, Mohamed Said El-. *Le sous-développement economique et social du Yémen.* Algiers, Editions Tiers-Monde, 1966.

Badeeb, Said M. *The Saudi–Egyptian Conflict over North Yemen 1962–70.* Colorado, Westview Press, 1986.

Balsan, François. *Inquiétant Yémen.* Paris, 1961.

Behbehari, Hashim, S. H. *China and the People's Democratic Republic of Yemen,* London, KP1, 1985.

Bethmann, E. W. *Yemen on the Threshold.* American Friends of the Middle East, Washington, 1960.

Bidwell, Robin. *The Two Yemens.* London, Longman, 1983.

Brinton, J. Y. *Aden and the Federation of South Arabia.* Washington, DC, American Society of International Law, 1964.

Burrowes, Robert D. *The Yemen Arab Republic: The Politics of Development 1962–1986.* London, Croom Helm, 1987.

Central Office of Information. *Aden and South Arabia.* London, HMSO, 1965.

Chelhod, Joseph. *L'Arabie du Sud. Histoire et civilisation.* 3 vols, Editions Maisonneuve et Larose; Vol. I: *Le peuple yéménite et ses racines;* Vol. II: *La société yéménite de l'hégire aux idéologies modernes;* Vol. III: *Culture et institutions du Yémen* (1985).

Colonial Office. *Accession of Aden to the Federation of South Arabia.* London, HMSO, 1962.

    Aden and the Yemen. London, HMSO, 1960.

    Treaty of Friendship and Protection between the United Kingdom and the Federation of South Arabia. London, HMSO, 1964.

Deutsch, Robert. *Der Yemen.* Vienna, 1914.

Doe, Brian. *Southern Arabia.* London, Thames and Hudson, 1972.

Federation of South Arabia. *Conference on Constitutional Problems of South Arabia.* HMSO, 1964.

Gavin, R. J. *Aden 1839–1967.* London, Hurst, 1973.

Gehrke, Dr Ulrich. *Südarabien, Südarabische Föderation oder Süd-Jemen?* Hamburg, Orient Magazine, German Near and Middle East Association, 1967.

Helfritz, H. *The Yemen: A Secret Journey.* London, Allen and Unwin, 1958.

Heyworth-Dunne, G. E. *Al-Yemen: Social, Political and Economic Survey.* Cairo, 1952.

Hickinbotham, Sir Tom. *Aden.* London, Constable, 1959.

Ingrams, Doreen. *A Survey of the Social and Economic Conditions of the Aden Protectorate.* London.

Ingrams, W. H. *A Report on the Social, Economic and Political Conditions of the Hadhramaut, Aden Protectorate.* London, 1936.

    Arabia and the Isles. London, Murray, 1947.

Ingrams, Harold. *The Yemen; Imams, Rulers and Revolutions.* London, 1963.

Ismail, Tareq Y. and Jacqueline S. *The People's Democratic Republic of Yemen.* Politics, Economics and Society. London, Pinter, 1986.

Jacob, Harold F. *Kings of Arabia.* London, 1923.

Jenner, Michael. *Yemen Rediscovered.* London, Longman, 1983.

Johnston, Charles. *The View from Steamer Point.* London, Collins, 1964.

King, Gillian. *Imperial Outpost—Aden.* New York, Oxford University Press, 1964.

Knox-Mawer, June. *The Sultans Came to Tea.* London, Murray, 1961.

Kour, Z. H. *The History of Aden, 1839–1972.* London, Frank Cass, 1980.

Lackner, Helen. *The People's Democratic Republic of Yemen: Outpost of Socialist Development in Arabia.* London, Ithaca Press, 1985.

Ledger, David. *Shifting Sands: the British in South Arabia.* London, Peninsula Publishing, 1983.

Little, Tom. *South Arabia.* London, Pall Mall Press, 1968.

Macro, Eric. *Bibliography of the Yemen, with Notes on Mocha.* University of Miami Press, 1959.

    Yemen and the Western World since 1571. London, C. Hurst, and New York, Praeger, 1968.

Mallakh, Ragaie El-. *The Economic Development of the Yemen Arab Republic.* London, Croom Helm, 1986.

Naval Intelligence Division. *Western Arabia and the Red Sea.* (Admiralty Handbook) 1946.

O'Ballance, Edgar. *The War in the Yemen.* London, Faber, 1971.

Page, Stephen. *The Soviet Union and the Yemens: Influence in Assymetrical Relationships.* New York, Praeger, 1985.

Paget, Julian. *Last Post: Aden 1964–67.* London, Faber and Faber, 1969.

Pawelke, Gunther. *Der Yemen: Das Verbotene Land.* Düsseldorf, Econ. Verlag., 1959.

Peterson, J. E. *Yemen, the Search for a Modern State.* London, Croom Helm, 1981.

Pieragostini, Karl. *Britain, Aden and South Arabia.* London, Macmillan, 1992.

Pridham, B. R. (Ed.) *Contemporary Yemen: Politics and Historical Background.* London, Croom Helm, 1984.

　Economy and Society and Culture in Contemporary Yemen. London, Croom Helm, 1985.

Qat Commission of Inquiry. *Report.* Aden, 1958.

Rouaud, Alain. *Le Yémen.* Brussels, Editions Complexe, 1979.

Schmidt, Dana Adams. *Yemen, the Unknown War.* London, Bodley Head, 1968.

Scott, H. *In the High Yemen.* London, Murray, 1942.

Serjeant, R. B. *The Portuguese off the South Arabian Coast.* Oxford, Clarendon, 1963; reprinted Beirut, 1974.

Serjeant, R. B., and Lwecokc, Ronald. *San‘a: an Arabian Islamic City.* London, 1983.

Smith, G. Rex. *The Yemens.* Oxford, World Bibliographical Series, Clio Press, 1984.

Stookey, Robert W. *Yemen: The Politics of the Yemen Arab Republic.* Westview Press, 1978.

Trevaskis, Sir Kennedy. *Shades of Amber, A South Arabian Episode.* London, Hutchinson, 1967.

Van der Meulen, Daniel. *Hadhramaut: Some of Its Mysteries Unveiled.* Leiden, 1932, reprinted 1964.

Waterfield, Gordon. *Sultans of Aden.* London, Murray, 1968.

Wenner, Manfred W. *Yemen: a selected Bibliography of Literature since 1960.* Washington, DC, Library of Congress Legislative Reference Service, 1965.

　Modern Yemen, 1918–1966. Baltimore, Johns Hopkins Press, 1967.